DOMI MINA NVS TIO ILLV MEA

THE OXFORD ENGLISH DICTIONARY

SECOND EDITION

THE OXFORD ENGLISH DICTIONARY

First Edited by

JAMES A. H. MURRAY, HENRY BRADLEY, W. A. CRAIGIE
and C. T. ONIONS

COMBINED WITH

A SUPPLEMENT TO THE OXFORD ENGLISH DICTIONARY

Edited by

R. W. BURCHFIELD

AND RESET WITH CORRECTIONS, REVISIONS
AND ADDITIONAL VOCABULARY

THE OXFORD ENGLISH DICTIONARY

SECOND EDITION

Prepared by

J. A. SIMPSON *and* E. S. C. WEINER

VOLUME XIII

Quemadero–Roaver

CLARENDON PRESS · OXFORD

Oxford University Press, Great Clarendon Street, Oxford OX2 6DP
Oxford New York
Athens Auckland Bangkok Bogotá Buenos Aires Calcutta
Cape Town Chennai Dar es Salaam Delhi Florence Hong Kong Istanbul
Karachi Kuala Lumpur Madrid Melbourne Mexico City Mumbai
Nairobi Paris São Paulo Singapore Taipei Tokyo Toronto Warsaw
and associated companies in
Berlin Ibadan

Oxford is a registered trade mark of Oxford University Press

First published 1989
Reprinted 1991 (with corrections), 1998

British Library Cataloguing in Publication Data
Oxford English dictionary.—2nd ed.
1. English language—Dictionaries
I. Simpson, J. A. (John Andrew), 1953-
II. Weiner, Edmund S. C., 1950-
423
ISBN 0-19-861225-7 (vol. XIII)
ISBN 0-19-861186-2 (set)

Library of Congress Cataloging-in-Publication Data
The Oxford English dictionary.—2nd ed.
prepared by J. A. Simpson and E. S. C. Weiner
Bibliography: p.
ISBN 0-19-861225-7 (vol. XIII)
ISBN 0-19-861186-2 (set)
1. English language—Dictionaries. I. Simpson, J. A.
II. Weiner, E. S. C. III. Oxford University Press.
PE1625.087 1989
423—dc19 88-5330

Data capture by ICC, Fort Washington, Pa.
Text-processing by Oxford University Press
Typesetting by Pindar Graphics Origination, Scarborough, N. Yorks.
Manufactured in the United States of America by
World Color Book Services, Taunton, Mass.

KEY TO THE PRONUNCIATION

THE pronunciations given are those in use in the educated speech of southern England (the so-called 'Received Standard'), and the keywords given are to be understood as pronounced in such speech.

I. *Consonants*

b, d, f, k, l, m, n, p, t, v, z *have their usual English values*

g as in *go* (gəʊ)
h ... *ho!* (həʊ)
r ... *run* (rʌn), *terrier* ('tɛrɪə(r))
(r) ... *her* (hɜː(r))
s ... *see* (siː), *success* (sək'sɛs)
w ... *wear* (wɛə(r))
hw ... *when* (hwɛn)
j ... *yes* (jɛs)

θ as in *thin* (θɪn), *bath* (bɑːθ)
ð ... *then* (ðɛn), *bathe* (beɪð)
ʃ ... *shop* (ʃɒp), *dish* (dɪʃ)
tʃ ... *chop* (tʃɒp), *ditch* (dɪtʃ)
ʒ ... *vision* ('vɪʒən), *déjeuner* (deʒøne)
dʒ ... *judge* (dʒʌdʒ)
ŋ ... *singing* ('sɪŋɪŋ), *think* (θiŋk)
ŋg ... *finger* ('fɪŋgə(r))

(FOREIGN AND NON-SOUTHERN)
ʎ as in It. *serraglio* (ser'raʎo)
ɲ ... Fr. *cognac* (kɔɲak)
x ... Ger. *ach* (ax), Sc. *loch* (lɒx), Sp. *frijoles* (fri'xoles)
ç ... Ger. *ich* (ɪç), Sc. *nicht* (nɪçt)
ɣ ... North Ger. *sagen* ('zaːɣən)
c ... Afrikaans *baardmannetjie* ('baːrtmanəci)
ɥ ... Fr. *cuisine* (kɥizin)

Symbols in parentheses are used to denote elements that may be omitted either by individual speakers or in particular phonetic contexts: e.g. *bottle* ('bɒt(ə)l), *Mercian* ('mɜːʃ(ɪ)ən), *suit* (s(j)uːt), *impromptu* (ɪm'prɒm(p)tjuː), *father* ('fɑːðə(r)).

II. *Vowels and Diphthongs*

SHORT
ɪ as in *pit* (pɪt), *-ness*, (-nɪs)
ɛ ... *pet* (pɛt), Fr. *sept* (sɛt)
æ ... *pat* (pæt)
ʌ ... *putt* (pʌt)
ɒ ... *pot* (pɒt)
ʊ ... *put* (pʊt)
ə ... *another* (ə'nʌðə(r))
(ə) ... *beaten* ('biːt(ə)n)
i ... Fr. *si* (si)
e ... Fr. *bébé* (bebe)
a ... Fr. *mari* (mari)
ɑ ... Fr. *bâtiment* (bɑtimɑ̃)
ɔ ... Fr. *homme* (ɔm)
o ... Fr. *eau* (o)
ø ... Fr. *peu* (pø)
œ ... Fr. *boeuf* (bœf) *coeur* (kœr)
u ... Fr. *douce* (dus)
ʏ ... Ger. *Müller* ('mʏlər)
y ... Fr. *du* (dy)

LONG
iː as in *bean* (biːn)
ɑː ... *barn* (bɑːn)
ɔː ... *born* (bɔːn)
uː ... *boon* (buːn)
ɜː ... *burn* (bɜːn)
eː ... Ger. *Schnee* (ʃneː)
ɛː ... Ger. *Fähre* ('fɛːrə)
aː ... Ger. *Tag* (taːk)
oː ... Ger. *Sohn* (zoːn)
øː ... Ger. *Goethe* ('gøːtə)
yː ... Ger. *grün* (gryːn)

NASAL
ɛ̃, æ̃ as in Fr. *fin* (fɛ̃, fæ̃)
ɑ̃ ... Fr. *franc* (frɑ̃)
ɔ̃ ... Fr. *bon* (bɔ̃)
œ̃ ... Fr. *un* (œ̃)

DIPHTHONGS, etc.
eɪ as in *bay* (beɪ)
aɪ ... *buy* (baɪ)
ɔɪ ... *boy* (bɔɪ)
əʊ ... *no* (nəʊ)
aʊ ... *now* (naʊ)
ɪə ... *peer* (pɪə(r))
ɛə ... *pair* (pɛə(r))
ʊə ... *tour* (tʊə(r))
ɔə ... *boar* (bɔə(r))

aɪə as in *fiery* ('faɪərɪ)
aʊə ... *sour* (saʊə(r))

The incidence of main stress is shown by a superior stress mark (') preceding the stressed syllable, and a secondary stress by an inferior stress mark (ˌ), e.g. *pronunciation* (prəˌnʌnsɪ'eɪʃ(ə)n).

For further explanation of the transcription used, see *General Explanations*, Volume I.

LIST OF ABBREVIATIONS, SIGNS, ETC.

Some abbreviations listed here in italics are also in certain cases printed in roman type, and vice versa.

a. (in Etym.)	adoption of, adopted from
a (as *a* 1850)	*ante*, 'before', 'not later than'
a.	adjective
abbrev.	abbreviation (of)
abl.	ablative
absol.	absolute, -ly
Abstr.	(in titles) *Abstract, -s*
acc.	accusative
Acct.	(in titles) *Account*
A.D.	*Anno Domini*
ad. (in Etym.)	adaptation of
Add.	Addenda
adj.	adjective
Adv.	(in titles) *Advance, -d, -s*
adv.	adverb
advb.	adverbial, -ly
Advt.	advertisement
Aeronaut.	(as label) in Aeronautics; (in titles) *Aeronautic, -al, -s*
AF., AFr.	Anglo-French
Afr.	Africa, -n
Agric.	(as label) in Agriculture; (in titles) *Agriculture, -al*
Alb.	Albanian
Amer.	American
Amer. Ind.	American Indian
Anat.	(as label) in Anatomy; (in titles) *Anatomy, -ical*
Anc.	(in titles) *Ancient*
Anglo-Ind.	Anglo-Indian
Anglo-Ir.	Anglo-Irish
Ann.	Annals
Anthrop., *Anthropol.*	(as label) in Anthropology; (in titles) *Anthropology, -ical*
Antiq.	(as label) in Antiquities; (in titles) *Antiquity*
aphet.	aphetic, aphetized
app.	apparently
Appl.	(in titles) *Applied*
Applic.	(in titles) *Application, -s*
appos.	appositive, -ly
Arab.	Arabic
Aram.	Aramaic
Arch.	in Architecture
arch.	archaic
Archæol.	in Archæology
Archit.	(as label) in Architecture; (in titles) *Architecture, -al*
Arm.	Armenian
assoc.	association
Astr.	in Astronomy
Astrol.	in Astrology
Astron.	(in titles) *Astronomy, -ical*
Astronaut.	(in titles) *Astronautic, -s*
attrib.	attributive, -ly
Austral.	Australian
Autobiogr.	(in titles) *Autobiography, -ical*
A.V.	Authorized Version
B.C.	Before Christ
B.C.	(in titles) British Columbia
bef.	before
Bibliogr.	(as label) in Bibliography; (in titles) *Bibliography, -ical*
Biochem.	(as label) in Biochemistry; (in titles) *Biochemistry, -ical*
Biol.	(as label) in Biology; (in titles) *Biology, -ical*
Bk.	*Book*
Bot.	(as label) in Botany; (in titles) *Botany, -ical*
Bp.	Bishop
Brit.	(in titles) *Britain, British*
Bulg.	Bulgarian
Bull.	(in titles) *Bulletin*
c (as *c* 1700)	*circa*, 'about'
c. (as 19th c.)	century
Cal.	(in titles) *Calendar*
Cambr.	(in titles) *Cambridge*
Canad.	Canadian
Cat.	Catalan
catachr.	catachrestically
Catal.	(in titles) *Catalogue*
Celt.	Celtic
Cent.	(in titles) *Century, Central*
Cent. Dict.	*Century Dictionary*
Cf., cf.	*confer*, 'compare'
Ch.	Church
Chem.	(as label) in Chemistry; (in titles) *Chemistry, -ical*
Chr.	(in titles) *Christian*
Chron.	(in titles) *Chronicle*
Chronol.	(in titles) *Chronology, -ical*
Cinemat., *Cinematogr.*	in Cinematography
Clin.	(in titles) *Clinical*
cl. L.	classical Latin
cogn. w.	cognate with
Col.	(in titles) *Colonel, Colony*
Coll.	(in titles) *Collection*
collect.	collective, -ly
colloq.	colloquial, -ly
comb.	combined, -ing
Comb.	Combinations
Comm.	in Commercial usage
Communic.	in Communications
comp.	compound, composition
Compan.	(in titles) *Companion*
compar.	comparative
compl.	complement
Compl.	(in titles) *Complete*
Conc.	(in titles) *Concise*
Conch.	in Conchology
concr.	concrete, -ly
Conf.	(in titles) *Conference*
Congr.	(in titles) *Congress*
conj.	conjunction
cons.	consonant
const.	construction, construed with
contr.	contrast (with)
Contrib.	(in titles) *Contribution*
Corr.	(in titles) *Correspondence*
corresp.	corresponding (to)
Cotgr.	R. Cotgrave, *Dictionarie of the French and English Tongues*
cpd.	compound
Crit.	(in titles) *Criticism, Critical*
Cryst.	in Crystallography
Cycl.	(in titles) *Cyclopædia, -ic*
Cytol.	(in titles) *Cytology, -ical*
Da.	Danish
D.A.	*Dictionary of Americanisms*
D.A.E.	*Dictionary of American English*
dat.	dative
D.C.	District of Columbia
Deb.	(in titles) *Debate, -s*
def.	definite, -ition
dem.	demonstrative
deriv.	derivative, -ation
derog.	derogatory
Descr.	(in titles) *Description, -tive*
Devel.	(in titles) *Development, -al*
Diagn.	(in titles) *Diagnosis, Diagnostic*
dial.	dialect, -al
Dict.	Dictionary; *spec.*, the *Oxford English Dictionary*
dim.	diminutive
Dis.	(in titles) *Disease*
Diss.	(in titles) *Dissertation*
D.O.S.T.	*Dictionary of the Older Scottish Tongue*
Du.	Dutch
E.	East
Eccl.	(as label) in Ecclesiastical usage; (in titles) *Ecclesiastical*
Ecol.	in Ecology
Econ.	(as label) in Economics; (in titles) *Economy, -ics*
ed.	edition
E.D.D.	*English Dialect Dictionary*
Edin.	(in titles) *Edinburgh*
Educ.	(as label) in Education; (in titles) *Education, -al*
EE.	Early English
e.g.	*exempli gratia*, 'for example'
Electr.	(as label) in Electricity; (in titles) *Electricity, -ical*
Electron.	(in titles) *Electronic, -s*
Elem.	(in titles) *Element, -ary*
ellipt.	elliptical, -ly
Embryol.	in Embryology
e.midl.	east midland (dialect)
Encycl.	(in titles) *Encyclopædia, -ic*
Eng.	England, English
Engin.	in Engineering
Ent.	in Entomology
Entomol.	(in titles) *Entomology, -logical*
erron.	erroneous, -ly
esp.	especially
Ess.	(in titles) *Essay, -s*
et al.	*et alii*, 'and others'
etc.	et cetera
Ethnol.	in Ethnology
etym.	etymology
euphem.	euphemistically
Exam.	(in titles) *Examination*
exc.	except
Exerc.	(in titles) *Exercise, -s*
Exper.	(in titles) *Experiment, -al*
Explor.	(in titles) *Exploration, -s*
f.	feminine
f. (in Etym.)	formed on
f. (in subordinate entries)	form of
F.	French
fem. (*rarely* f.)	feminine
fig.	figurative, -ly
Finn.	Finnish
fl.	*floruit*, 'flourished'
Found.	(in titles) *Foundation, -s*
Fr.	French
freq.	frequent, -ly
Fris.	Frisian
Fund.	(in titles) *Fundamental, -s*
Funk or *Funk's Stand. Dict.*	*Funk and Wagnalls Standard Dictionary*
G.	German
Gael.	Gaelic
Gaz.	(in titles) *Gazette*
gen.	genitive
gen.	general, -ly
Geogr.	(as label) in Geography; (in titles) *Geography, -ical*

Geol.	(as label) in Geology; (in titles) *Geology, -ical*
Geom.	in Geometry
Geomorphol.	in Geomorphology
Ger.	German
Gloss.	Glossary
Gmc.	Germanic
Godef.	F. Godefroy, *Dictionnaire de l'ancienne langue française*
Goth.	Gothic
Govt.	(in titles) *Government*
Gr.	Greek
Gram.	(as label) in Grammar; (in titles) *Grammar, -tical*
Gt.	Great
Heb.	Hebrew
Her.	in Heraldry
Herb.	among herbalists
Hind.	Hindustani
Hist.	(as label) in History; (in titles) *History, -ical*
hist.	historical
Histol.	(in titles) *Histology, -ical*
Hort.	in Horticulture
Househ.	(in titles) *Household*
Housek.	(in titles) *Housekeeping*
Ibid.	*Ibidem*, 'in the same book or passage'
Icel.	Icelandic
Ichthyol.	in Ichthyology
id.	*idem*, 'the same'
i.e.	*id est*, 'that is'
IE.	Indo-European
Illustr.	(in titles) *Illustration, -ted*
imit.	imitative
Immunol.	in Immunology
imp.	imperative
impers.	impersonal
impf.	imperfect
ind.	indicative
indef.	indefinite
Industr.	(in titles) *Industry, -ial*
inf.	infinitive
infl.	influenced
Inorg.	(in titles) *Inorganic*
Ins.	(in titles) *Insurance*
Inst.	(in titles) *Institute, -tion*
int.	interjection
intr.	intransitive
Introd.	(in titles) *Introduction*
Ir.	Irish
irreg.	irregular, -ly
It.	Italian
J., (J.)	(quoted from) Johnson's *Dictionary*
(Jam.)	Jamieson, *Scottish Dict.*
Jap.	Japanese
joc.	jocular, -ly
Jrnl.	(in titles) *Journal*
Jun.	(in titles) *Junior*
Knowl.	(in titles) *Knowledge*
l.	line
L.	Latin
lang.	language
Lect.	(in titles) *Lecture, -s*
Less.	(in titles) *Lesson, -s*
Let., Lett.	letter, letters
LG.	Low German
lit.	literal, -ly
Lit.	Literary
Lith.	Lithuanian
LXX	Septuagint
m.	masculine
Mag.	(in titles) *Magazine*
Magn.	(in titles) *Magnetic, -ism*
Mal.	Malay, Malayan
Man.	(in titles) *Manual*
Managem.	(in titles) *Management*
Manch.	(in titles) *Manchester*
Manuf.	in Manufacture, -ing
Mar.	(in titles) *Marine*
masc. (*rarely* m.)	masculine
Math.	(as label) in Mathematics; (in titles) *Mathematics, -al*
MDu.	Middle Dutch
ME.	Middle English
Mech.	(as label) in Mechanics; (in titles) *Mechanics, -al*
Med.	(as label) in Medicine; (in titles) *Medicine, -ical*
med.L.	medieval Latin
Mem.	(in titles) *Memoir, -s*
Metaph.	in Metaphysics
Meteorol.	(as label) in Meteorology; (in titles) *Meteorology, -ical*
MHG.	Middle High German
midl.	midland (dialect)
Mil.	in military usage
Min.	(as label) in Mineralogy; (in titles) *Ministry*
Mineral.	(in titles) *Mineralogy, -ical*
MLG.	Middle Low German
Misc.	(in titles) *Miscellany, -eous*
mod.	modern
mod.L	modern Latin
(Morris),	(quoted from) E. E. Morris's *Austral English*
Mus.	(as label) in Music; (in titles) *Music, -al; Museum*
Myst.	(in titles) *Mystery*
Mythol.	in Mythology
N.	North
n.	neuter
N. Amer.	North America, -n
N. & Q.	*Notes and Queries*
Narr.	(in titles) *Narrative*
Nat.	(in titles) *Natural*
Nat. Hist.	in Natural History
Naut.	in nautical language
N.E.	North East
N.E.D.	*New English Dictionary*, original title of the *Oxford English Dictionary* (first edition)
Neurol.	in Neurology
neut. (*rarely* n.)	neuter
NF., NFr.	Northern French
No.	Number
nom.	nominative
north.	northern (dialect)
Norw.	Norwegian
n.q.	no quotations
N.T.	New Testament
Nucl.	Nuclear
Numism.	in Numismatics
N.W.	North West
N.Z.	New Zealand
obj.	object
obl.	oblique
Obs., obs.	obsolete
Obstetr.	(in titles) *Obstetrics*
occas.	occasionally
OE.	Old English (= Anglo-Saxon)
OF., OFr.	Old French
OFris.	Old Frisian
OHG.	Old High German
OIr.	Old Irish
ON.	Old Norse
ONF.	Old Northern French
Ophthalm.	in Ophthalmology
opp.	opposed (to), the opposite (of)
Opt.	in Optics
Org.	(in titles) *Organic*
orig.	origin, -al, -ally
Ornith.	(as label) in Ornithology; (in titles) *Ornithology, -ical*
OS.	Old Saxon
OSl.	Old (Church) Slavonic
O.T.	Old Testament
Outl.	(in titles) *Outline*
Oxf.	(in titles) *Oxford*
p.	page
Palæogr.	in Palæography
Palæont.	(as label) in Palæontology; (in titles) *Palæontology, -ical*
pa. pple.	passive participle, past participle
(Partridge),	(quoted from) E. Partridge's *Dictionary of Slang and Unconventional English*
pass.	passive, -ly
pa.t.	past tense
Path.	(as label) in Pathology; (in titles) *Pathology, -ical*
perh.	perhaps
Pers.	Persian
pers.	person, -al
Petrogr.	in Petrography
Petrol.	(as label) in Petrology; (in titles) *Petrology, -ical*
(Pettman),	(quoted from) C. Pettman's *Africanderisms*
pf.	perfect
Pg.	Portuguese
Pharm.	in Pharmacology
Philol.	(as label) in Philology; (in titles) *Philology, -ical*
Philos.	(as label) in Philosophy; (in titles) *Philosophy, -ic*
phonet.	phonetic, -ally
Photogr.	(as label) in Photography; (in titles) *Photography, -ical*
phr.	phrase
Phys.	physical; (*rarely*) in Physiology
Physiol.	(as label) in Physiology; (in titles) *Physiology, -ical*
Pict.	(in titles) *Picture, Pictorial*
pl., plur.	plural
poet.	poetic, -al
Pol.	Polish
Pol.	(as label) in Politics; (in titles) *Politics, -al*
Pol. Econ.	in Political Economy
Polit.	(in titles) *Politics, -al*
pop.	popular, -ly
Porc.	(in titles) *Porcelain*
poss.	possessive
Pott.	(in titles) *Pottery*
ppl. a., pple. adj.	participial adjective
pple.	participle
Pr.	Provençal
pr.	present
Pract.	(in titles) *Practice, -al*
prec.	preceding (word or article)
pred.	predicative
pref.	prefix
pref., Pref.	preface
prep.	preposition
pres.	present
Princ.	(in titles) *Principle, -s*
priv.	privative
prob.	probably
Probl.	(in titles) *Problem*
Proc.	(in titles) *Proceedings*
pron.	pronoun
pronunc.	pronunciation
prop.	properly
Pros.	in Prosody
Prov.	Provençal
pr. pple.	present participle
Psych.	in Psychology
Psychol.	(as label) in Psychology; (in titles) *Psychology, -ical*
Publ.	(in titles) *Publications*
Q.	(in titles) *Quarterly*
quot(s).	quotation(s)
q.v.	*quod vide*, 'which see'
R.	(in titles) *Royal*
Radiol.	in Radiology
R.C.Ch.	Roman Catholic Church
Rec.	(in titles) *Record*
redupl.	reduplicating
Ref.	(in titles) *Reference*
refash.	refashioned, -ing
refl.	reflexive
Reg.	(in titles) *Register*

reg.	regular
rel.	related to
Reminisc.	(in titles) *Reminiscence, -s*
Rep.	(in titles) *Report, -s*
repr.	representative, representing
Res.	(in titles) *Research*
Rev.	(in titles) *Review*
rev.	revised
Rhet.	in Rhetoric
Rom.	Roman, -ce, -ic
Rum.	Rumanian
Russ.	Russian
S.	South
S.Afr.	South Africa, -n
sb.	substantive
sc.	*scilicet*, 'understand' or 'supply'
Sc., Scot.	Scottish
Scand.	(in titles) *Scandinavia, -n*
Sch.	(in titles) *School*
Sc. Nat. Dict.	*Scottish National Dictionary*
Scotl.	(in titles) *Scotland*
Sel.	(in titles) *Selection, -s*
Ser.	Series
sing.	singular
Sk.	(in titles) *Sketch*
Skr.	Sanskrit
Slav.	Slavonic
S.N.D.	*Scottish National Dictionary*
Soc.	(in titles) *Society*
Sociol.	(as label) in Sociology; (in titles) *Sociology, -ical*
Sp.	Spanish
Sp.	(in titles) *Speech, -es*
sp.	spelling
spec.	specifically
Spec.	(in titles) *Specimen*
St.	Saint
Stand.	(in titles) *Standard*
Stanf.	(quoted from) *Stanford Dictionary of Anglicised Words & Phrases*
str.	strong
Struct.	(in titles) *Structure, -al*
Stud.	(in titles) *Studies*
subj.	subject
subord. cl.	subordinate clause
subseq.	subsequent, -ly
subst.	substantively
suff.	suffix
superl.	superlative
Suppl.	Supplement
Surg.	(as label) in Surgery; (in titles) *Surgery, Surgical*
s.v.	*sub voce*, 'under the word'
Sw.	Swedish
s.w.	south-western (dialect)
Syd. Soc. Lex.	Sydenham Society, *Lexicon of Medicine & Allied Sciences*
syll.	syllable
Syr.	Syrian
Syst.	(in titles) *System, -atic*
Taxon.	(in titles) *Taxonomy, -ical*
techn.	technical, -ly
Technol.	(in titles) *Technology, -ical*
Telegr.	in Telegraphy
Teleph.	in Telephony
(Th.),	(quoted from) Thornton's *American Glossary*
Theatr.	in the Theatre, theatrical
Theol.	(as label) in Theology; (in titles) *Theology, -ical*
Theoret.	(in titles) *Theoretical*
Tokh.	Tokharian
tr., transl.	translated, translation
Trans.	(in titles) *Transactions*
trans.	transitive
transf.	transferred sense
Trav.	(in titles) *Travel(s)*
Treas.	(in titles) *Treasury*
Treat.	(in titles) *Treatise*
Treatm.	(in titles) *Treatment*
Trig.	in Trigonometry
Trop.	(in titles) *Tropical*
Turk.	Turkish
Typog., Typogr.	in Typography
ult.	ultimately
Univ.	(in titles) *University*
unkn.	unknown
U.S.	United States
U.S.S.R.	Union of Soviet Socialist Republics
usu.	usually
v., vb.	verb
var(r)., vars.	variant(s) of
vbl. sb.	verbal substantive
Vertebr.	(in titles) *Vertebrate, -s*
Vet.	(as label) in Veterinary Science; (in titles) *Veterinary*
Vet. Sci.	in Veterinary Science
viz.	*videlicet*, 'namely'
Voy.	(in titles) *Voyage, -s*
v.str.	strong verb
vulg.	vulgar
v.w.	weak verb
W.	Welsh; West
wd.	word
Webster	*Webster's* (*New International*) *Dictionary*
Westm.	(in titles) *Westminster*
WGmc.	West Germanic
Wks.	(in titles) *Works*
w.midl.	west midland (dialect)
WS.	West Saxon
(Y.),	(quoted from) Yule & Burnell's *Hobson-Jobson*
Yrs.	(in titles) *Years*
Zoogeogr.	in Zoogeography
Zool.	(as label) in Zoology; (in titles) *Zoology, -ical*

Signs and Other Conventions

Before a word or sense

† = obsolete
‖ = not naturalized, alien
¶ = catachrestic and erroneous uses

In the listing of Forms

1 = before 1100
2 = 12th c. (1100 to 1200)
3 = 13th c. (1200 to 1300), etc.
5-7 = 15th to 17th century
20 = 20th century

In the etymologies

* indicates a word or form not actually found, but of which the existence is inferred
:— = normal development of

The printing of a word in SMALL CAPITALS indicates that further information will be found under the word so referred to.

. . indicates an omitted part of a quotation.

- (in a quotation) indicates a hyphen doubtfully present in the original; (in other text) indicates a hyphen inserted only for the sake of a line-break.

PROPRIETARY NAMES

THIS Dictionary includes some words which are or are asserted to be proprietary names or trade marks. Their inclusion does not imply that they have acquired for legal purposes a non-proprietary or general significance nor any other judgement concerning their legal status. In cases where the editorial staff have established in the records of the Patent Offices of the United Kingdom and of the United States that a word is registered as a proprietary name or trade mark this is indicated, but no judgement concerning the legal status of such words is made or implied thereby.

‖**quemadero** (kema'ðero). [Sp., f. *quemar* to burn.] In Spain and former Spanish territories, a place where convicted heretics were executed by burning. Also *transf.*

1855 W. H. PRESCOTT *Hist. Reign Philip II* I. II. iii. 353 The place of execution—the *quemadero*, the burning-place, as it was called—was a spot selected for the purpose without the walls of the city. **1874** W. H. RULE *Hist. Inquisition* I. xiv. 208 Outside the city..was a hearth, or place of burning. As our own language is too poor to provide a name for such a thing, we consent to borrow from Spanish its peculiar and exclusive designation, and call it the *quemadero*. The quemadero was a piece of pavement devoted to the single use of burning human bodies. **1908** H. C. LEA *Inquisition in Spanish Dependencies* vi. 206 It was not until 1596 that the municipality [*sc.* Mexico], at a cost of four hundred pesos, constructed a *quemadero* or burning place, where concremation could be performed decently and in order. **1932** C. ROTH *Hist. Marranos* ii. 43 A *quemadero*, or burning place, was constructed in the Campo de Tablada. **1934** A. HUXLEY *Beyond Mexique Bay* 189 On each mound were.. hearths of broken potsherds, blackened with smoke—the *quemaderos*, or burning places of the Indians. **1960** S. BECKER tr. *Schwarz-Bart's Last of Just* (1961) I. 11 He died very old..on the vast white slab of the *Quemadero* in Seville. Around him, scattered among the fagots, was the daily ovenful of three hundred Jews.

†**queme**, *sb. Obs.* Also 2–3 **cweme**, 5 **wheme.** [App. subst. use of next.] Pleasure, satisfaction. Chiefly in phr. ***to queme***, so as to please or satisfy; also, ***to take to queme***, to accept.

c **1175** *Lamb. Hom.* 23 Ne þu ne miȝt beon wel iscrifen god almihti to cweme. *a* **1300** *Cursor M.* 1064 (Gött.) Godd toke to queme his sacrefis. *c* **1330** R. BRUNNE *Chron. Wace* (Rolls) 2018 Of alle scheo was most til his queme. *a* **1400** *Minor Poems fr. Vernon MS.* 624/444, I was cros to monnes quemus. *c* **1460** *Towneley Myst.* vii. 62 Thou shall..serue to wheme God with all thi hart.

queme, *a. Obs.* exc. *north. dial.* Forms: α. 3 **cweme**, 3–5 **queme**, 4–5 **quem**, 5 **qwem(e**, 6 **queeme**, 7–8 *Sc.* **quim**, 9 *Sc.* **queem**. β. *north.* 5 **wheme**, 7 **wheeme**, 7–9 **wheam**, **wheem**, 8–9 **whim**, 9 **weam**, **weme**. [ME. *cweme*, *queme*, repr. OE. **cwéme* (cf. *cwéman*, *cwémnes*), or *ȝecwéme* I-QUEME = ON. *kvæm-r* (MSw. *qväm*): cf. OHG. *piquâmi* (MHG. *bequæme*, G. *bequem* = MDu. *bequame*, Du. *bekwaam*). The stem *kwǣmi-* belongs to the ablaut-series of the vb. COME: for the sense cf. Goth. *gaqimiþ* it is fitting, Eng. BECOME *v.* 7 ff., and L. *convenīre*.]

†**1.** Pleasing, agreeable, acceptable *to* a person. (In early use with dat. of person.) *Obs.*

c **1200** ORMIN 466 He wass..god prest & Godd full cweme. *c* **1200** *Trin. Coll. Hom.* 63 Þat me is quemere þat unbindeð þe bendes of wiðerfulnesse. *c* **1250** *Gen. & Ex.* 3764 Ðan sulde we..sen Quilc gure sal god quemest ben. *a* **1300** *Cursor M.* 26559 To deme quic and ded als him es queme. *c* **1375** *Sc. Leg. Saints* l. (*Katharine*) 29 Quha sacrifice mad till hym quem. *c* **1460** *Towneley Myst.* i. 42 This warke to me is queme.

b. Of pleasing appearance; specious; beautiful, fair; neat, tidy.

a **1300** *Cursor M.* 28128, I..sayd my scryft wit wordes queme þat my syn þe lesse suld seme. **13..** *E.E. Allit. P.* B. 1178 Me payed ful ille to be outfleme..Fro alle þo syȝtez so quykez & queme. *c* **1400** *Destr. Troy* 6203 The whelis full wheme, all of white aumber. *c* **1450** *Mirour Saluacioun* 2892 A newe grave fulle qweme. **1883** *Almondb. & Huddersf. Gloss.*, *Weam, weme*,..tidy..'A nice little weme packet'.

c. *dial.* Closed against or protected from the wind, snug; unruffled, smooth.

1674–91 RAY *N.-C. Words, Wheam, wheem*, near, close, so as no wind can enter it. **1820** *Marmaiden o' Clyde* in Whitelaw *Bk. Sc. Ballads* (1874) 93/2 Whan the year grown auld brings winter cauld We flee til our ha's sae queem. **1824** MACTAGGART *Gallovid. Encycl.* (1876) 391 Dream that the ocean's queem.

2. Fit, fitting, suitable; convenient, handy; near at hand, close. Const. *to* or dative.

a **1300** *Cursor M.* 8734 Sai me nu quat yow thinc queme. *Ibid.* 8809 Þe tre was als mete and quem, Als animan þar-to cuth deme. *a* **1400–50** *Alexander* 5078 [A way] þat to þe marche of Messedone was him mast qweme. **1570** LEVINS *Manip.* 60/15 Queeme, *æquus, compar.* **1674–91** RAY *N.-C. Words, Wheam, wheem*,..very handsome and convenient for one. **1812** T. WILKINSON *Death of Roger* in Gilpin *Poetry Cumberl.* 206 How wheem to Matty's elbow draws his chair. **1882** *Lancash. Gloss.*, *Wheem*, handy, convenient.

3. Of persons: †**a.** Friendly or well-disposed (*to*), intimate (*with*). *Obs.*

c **1325** *Metr. Hom.* 20 That he be til us quem that day. *c* **1400** *Destr. Troy* 1763 To qwit claym all querels, & be qweme fryndes. *c* **1440** *Bone Flor.* 145 They lefte a burges feyre and wheme, All ther schyppys for to yeme. *a* **1687** McWARD *Contend.* 262 (Jam.) They shall fall..into an intimacy with the malignant enemies to the work of God, and grow quim and cosh with them. **1731** *Plain Reasons Presbyt. Dissent.* 53 Quim and cosh with them.

b. Quiet, still, etc.

c **1375** *Sc. Leg. Saints* v. (*John*) 324 Sa þu wil þis folk mak quem..I sal sone consent þar-to. **1873** *Swaledale Gloss.*, *Wheem*, smooth, demure, still, slyly quiet, mock-modest. **1883** *Almondb. & Huddersf. Gloss.*, *Weam* or *Weme*, quiet ..'A weme woman in a house is a jewel'.

†**c.** Skilled, clever; smart, active. *Obs. rare.*

c **1400** *Destr. Troy* 4202 Who is now so qweme or qwaint of his wit, That couthe mesure our might. **1611** COTGR., *Adroit*,..Handsome, nimble, wheeme, readie or quicke [etc.].

†**4.** As *adv.* = QUEMELY. *Obs. rare.*

c **1375** *Sc. Leg. Saints* vi. (*Thomas*) 180 And ȝe þe bidding ȝeme of þe apostil wel & queme. **1513** DOUGLAS *Æneis* IX. xii. 6 He thristis to the levys of the ȝet, And closit queym the entre.

†**queme**, *v. Obs.* Forms: 1 **cwéman**, 3 **cweme(n**, **-enn**; 2–3 **quemen**, (4–5 **-yn**), 3–6, 8 **queme**, (4 **quem**, **quime**, **kueme**), 5–6 **queeme**, (5 **qw-**); 3–5 **qweme**, (5 **qwh-**, **wh-**). *Pa. t.* 1 **quemde**, 1–3 **cwemde**, 3 **cwemmde**, **quem-**, **quamede**, 4 **quemed**, (5 **-et**, 6 *Sc.* **-it**). *Pa. pple.* 3 **cwemedd**, **cwemmd**, 3–5 **quemed**, (5 **-yd**). [OE. *cwéman* (= *ȝecwéman* I-QUEME *v.*) f. (*ȝe*)*cwéme* adj.; see prec. and cf. MSw. *qvämma*, *qvemma*, G. *bequemen* (f. *bequem* adj.).]

1. Of persons: To please, gratify (another, esp. a superior); to act so as to please (one). Orig. const. with dat. or *to*, later with objective case.

a **750** *Blickl. Glosses* 13 in *O.E. Texts* 123 *Conplacebam*, quemde. *c* **897** K. ÆLFRED *Gregory's Past.* xix. 146 Ðæt ic monnum cweme & liciȝe. *c* **1175** *Lamb. Hom.* 67 Ȝef þu þus dost..þu quemest god. *c* **1250** *Gen. & Ex.* 1380 Him..Wið watres drinc ghe quemede wel. **1340** *Ayenb.* 26 To..do þet kuead, uor to kueme kuead-liche to þe wordle. *c* **1374** CHAUCER *Troylus* v. 695 My fader nyl..do me grace..for ought I kan hym queme. **1496** *Dives & Paup.* (W. de W.) VIII. xiv. 342/1 We haue not gyuen hym ne wherwith to queme hym but that we take of hym. [**1530** PALSGR. 676/2, *I queme*,..This worde is nowe out of use.]

absol. *c* **1275** *Moral Ode* 96 in *O.E. Misc.*, Hwat schulle we beren vs bi-voren; Mid hwan schulle we queme. *a* **1300** *E.E. Psalter* lii. 6 God skatered banes of þa Unto men þat qwemes swa.

2. Of things: **a.** To please, to be acceptable or agreeable to (a person). Const. as prec.

a **1000** *Sal. & Sat.* (Gr.) 165 Næniȝ man scile oft orðances ut abredan wæpnes ecȝȝe, ðeah ðe him se wlite cweme. *a* **1225** *Ancr. R.* 338 Seruises inedde ne cwemeð nout ure Louerde. *c* **1330** R. BRUNNE *Chron. Wace* (Rolls) 578 Þy dom vs alle quemes. **1390** GOWER *Conf.* II. 273 Every newe love quemeth To him which newefongel is. **1447** BOKENHAM *Seyntys* (Roxb.) 196 Tyl it hym queme To returnyn ageyn. *a* **1500** *How the good wife* etc. in Hazlitt *E.P.P.* I. 188 A dede wele done herte it whemyth. **1579** SPENSER *Sheph. Cal.* May 15 Such merimake holy Saints doth queme [*gloss.* please]. **1602** DAVISON *Rhapsody* (1611) 53 Like peerlesse pleasures wont us for to queeme.

b. To be suitable or fitting *for*. *rare*$^{-1}$.

c **1400** *Destr. Troy* 3404 Paris..Worshippit þat worthy in wedys full riche As qwemet for a qwene.

3. *trans.* To satisfy, appease, mitigate. *rare.*

c **1250** *Gen. & Ex.* 408 Swilc tiding ðhugte adam god, And sumdel quemeð it his seri mod. *Ibid.* 978 At a welle quemede hire list. **1430–40** LYDG. *Bochas* (1494) I. xxiii. 125 All the worlde outcrieth of vs tweyn Whos hatful ire by vs may nat be quemyd.

4. To join or fit closely. *Sc. rare.*

1501 DOUGLAS *Pal. Hon.* III. lxvii, And thame [the stones] coniunctlie jonit fast and quemit. **1808–80** JAMIESON, *To Queem*, to fit exactly; as, to *queem the mortice*, or joint in wood. Upp. Lanarks.

5. To slip in. *rare*$^{-0}$.

1727 BAILEY vol. II, *To Queme*, as to queme a Thing into one's Hand, to put it in privately.

Hence †**quemed** *ppl. a.*; †'**queming** *vbl. sb.*

c **1250** *Gen. & Ex.* 86 Til ihesus crist fro helle nam His quemed wid eue and adam. *a* **1300** *E.E. Psalter* cxlvi. 10 Noght..in schines of man queming bes him tille. **1340** *Ayenb.* 26 Þe ilke ssame comþ of kueade kuemynge. *c* **1440** *Promp. Parv.* 420/1 Qwemynge, or peesynge, *pacificacio*.

†'**quemeful**, *a. Obs.* Also **quemful(l**, **qwem-**, **queemeful**. [f. QUEME *sb.* + -FUL.] Pleasing, pleasant, agreeable; kind, gracious.

a **1340** HAMPOLE *Psalter, Cant.* 499 Dwelland out tharof, psalme is noght quemeful til ihū crist. **1388** WYCLIF *Job* xxxiii. 26 God..schal be quemeful to hym.

Hence †'**quemefully** *adv. Obs. rare*$^{-1}$.

c **1375** *Sc. Leg. Saints* i. (*Katharine*) 1204 To leyd oure lyff sa quemfully till hyme, þat we ma cum..to þat Ioy.

'**quemely**, *adv.* ? *Obs.* Also 5 **qwem-**, 8 **wheem-**, **whim-**, 9 **queem-**. [f. QUEME *a.* + -LY^{2}. Cf. MSw. *qvämelika*.] In a pleasing, agreeable, or becoming manner; neatly, gently, smoothly, etc.

c **1380** WYCLIF *Serm.* Sel. Wks. II. 361 No þing is more resonable þan to quemely serve God. *c* **1400** *Destr. Troy* 11783 The golde was all gotyn, & the grete sommes.. qwemly to-gedur. *c* **1475** *Rauf Coilȝear* 684 The flure.. couerit full clene, Cumand fra the Cornellis closand quemely. **1703** THORESBY *Let. to Ray* (E.D.S.), *Wheemly*, neatly. **1788** W. MARSHALL *Yorksh.* Gloss. (E.D.S.), *Whimly*, softly, silently, or with little noise. **1824** MACTAGGART *Gallovid. Encycl.* s.v. *Queem*, 'The gled glides queemly along'; the kite glides smoothly along.

So †'**quemeness**, pleasure, satisfaction. *Obs. rare.*

c **900** tr. *Bæda's Hist.* I. xvi. [xxvii.] (1890) 82 Cwemnis uncysta. *c* **1200** *Trin. Coll. Hom.* 55 Ne muge we noht singe þe blissfulle songes..gode to quemnesse.

quen, obs. form of QUEEN, WHEN.

quence, obs. form of QUENCH, QUINCE.

quench, *sb.* [f. the vb.] **1.** The act of quenching; the state or fact of being quenched.

1529 MORE *Dyaloge* II. Wks. 184/1 [To] lye and smolder as coles doth in quenche. **1546** J. HEYWOOD *Prov.* (1867) 9 A whyle kepe we in quenche All this Case. *c* **1611** CHAPMAN *Iliad* XIX. 365 A harmfull fire let runne..none came To giue it quench. **1818** T. BROWN in Welsh *Life* vi. (1825) 389 The quench Of hope..Made even the ghastly change..Seem ghastlier. **1972** A. D. FRANKLIN in Crawford & Slifkin *Point Defects in Solids* I. i. 33 The special property of ductility possessed by many metals allows thin wires to be drawn, which may be very rapidly quenched, at maximum cooling rates of 10^5 deg/sec or higher. With such rapid quenches, one may hope to retain the equilibrium defects present at the high quench temperature.

2. *Electronics.* The process of stopping an oscillation, esp. in a superregenerative receiver; a signal used for this. Freq. *attrib.*, as **quench frequency**, the frequency with which oscillations are stopped.

1938 *Proc. IRE* XXVI. 94 The use of a rectangular wave quench voltage would not be practicable in most applications of superregenerative receivers. *Ibid.* 96 In a given design of a separately quenched superregenerative receiver there is a particular quench frequency which gives maximum sensitivity. **1948** *Electronics* Sept. 98/3 This action..is eliminated by restricting the frequency content of the quench. **1950** J. R. WHITEHEAD *Super-Regenerative Receivers* vii. 125 A super-regenerative receiver with grid quench and a.g.s. controlling the oscillator grid bias. **1959** G. TROUP *Masers* vii. 118 A 600 c/s quench frequency was used. **1965** *Wireless World* July 336/2 Quench oscillators in super-regenerative receivers..have..set their own problems. **1975** D. G. FINK *Electronics Engineers' Handbk.* IX. 56 Electron current flow is initiated by an rf input signal and is terminated at the end of the rf input signal either by a voltage pulse or a dc bias voltage applied to a quench electrode.

quench (kwɛnʃ), *v.* Forms: 3 *Orm.* **cwennkenn**, 3–5 **quenchen**, 3–6 **quenche**, 4– **quench**, (also 4–5 **qwench**, **whench**, 5 **quynche**, 6 **quence**, **-she**, 7 **quensh**). *Pa. t.* 3 **cwen(ch)te**, **quein(c)te**, 5 **queynte**, 6 **qwent**; 4– **quenched** (4–5 **-id**, **-yd**). *Pa. pple.* 3 *Orm.* **cwennkedd**, (**-enn**), 4 **ykuenct** (**-ȝt**), **-quenct**, 4–5 **(i)queynt**, (5 **yqueynte**), 4–6 **queint**, **quaynt**, 6 **quent**; 4– **quenched** (4–5 **-id**, 5 **-yd**). [Early ME. *cwenken*, *quenchen*:—OE. **cwęncan* (cf. *ácwęncan* AQUENCH):—**cwancjan*, causative form corresponding to the strong vb. *cwincan* (*ácwincan*) to go out, be extinguished = Fris. *kwinka* (see QUINKLE): cf. *drench*, *drink*.]

I. *trans.* **1. a.** To put out, extinguish (fire, flame, or light, *lit.* or *fig.*). †Also with *out*. Now *rhet.*

a **1200** *Moral Ode* 249 Þet fur..ne mei nawiht hit quenchen. *c* **1200** ORMIN 10126 Waterr hafeþþ mahht To sleckenn fir & cwennkenn. *c* **1320** *Cast. Love* 1708 Fyre that may not be queynte. **1340** *Ayenb.* 186 Huanne hit faileþ, þet uer is y-kuenct. **1387** TREVISA *Higden* (Rolls) I. 119 Ȝif þe liȝt is i-queynt, it duppeþ doun and dryncheþ. **1481** CAXTON *Myrr.* III. xiii. 161 In one day alle the fyre thurgh out Rome faylled and was quenchid. **1581** RICH *Farew.*, I..will not.. extinguishe or quence the flames of so fervent and constaunte a love. **1604** E. G[RIMSTONE] *D' Acosta's Hist. Indies* III. viii. 142 Greene wood..smoakes most when the flame is quenched. **1622** MASSINGER & DEKKER *Virg. Mart.* II. iii, O! my admired mistress, quench not out The holy fires within you. **1713** BERKELEY *Guardian* No. 35 ¶5 He had almost quenched that light which his Creator had set up in his soul. **1810** SCOTT *Lady of L.* III. xi, Quench thou his light, Destruction dark! **1863** E. WETHERELL *Old Helmet* (1864) I. xi. 230 In Africa they sit in the darkness of centuries, till almost the spark of humanity is quenched out. **1880** MRS. FORRESTER *Roy & V.* I. 49 A tear comes into either eye and quenches the fire there.

b. To put out, extinguish, the fire or flame of (something that burns or gives light, *lit.* or *fig.*). †Also with *away*, *out*. Now only *rhet.*

1382 WYCLIF *2 Chron.* xxix. 7 Thei..quencheden the lanterns. **1382** —— *Isa.* xlii. 3 Flax smokende he shal not quenchen. **1382** —— *Eph.* vi. 16 Ȝe mown quenche alle the firy dartis of the werste enmye. **1413** *Pilgr. Sowle* II. lxi. (1859) 58 Wax smelleth wors after it is quenchid, than doth any talowe. **1513** DOUGLAS *Æneis* IV. ii. 60 The lycht of day Ay mair and mair the mone quenchit away. **1548** UDALL, etc. *Erasm. Par. Matt.* xii. 71 He wyll not quenche out the smokyng flaxe. **1604** SHAKS. *Oth.* II. i. 15 The winde-shak'd-Surge..Seemes to..quench the Guards of th'euer-fixed Pole. [**1667** MILTON *P.L.* XII. 492 Able to resist Satans assaults, and quench his fierie darts.] **1810** SCOTT *Lady of L.* III. xi, The..points of Sparkling Wood He quenched among the bubbling blood. **1853** C. BRONTE *Villette* xxii, There stood the candle quenched on the drawers. **1870** MORRIS *Earthly Par.* I. I. 392 As she turned..To quench the lamp.

c. To destroy the sight or light of (the eye).

1667 MILTON *P.L.* III. 25 These eyes, that rowle in vain.. So thick a drop serene hath quencht thir Orbs. **1792** S. ROGERS *Pleas. Mem.* II. 137 When age has quenched the eye and closed the ear. **1850** MRS. BROWNING *Lam. for Adonis* ii, His eyeballs lie quenched.

d. *Radio.* To cause (the spark in a spark transmitter) to cease by mechanical means, so that the secondary (aerial) circuit is no longer coupled to the primary; hence, to stop (oscillation).

1910 G. W. PIERCE *Princ. Wireless Telegr.* xxiii. 267 The spark is quenched when the energy in the primary attains its first minimum. **1913** *Chambers's Jrnl.* Mar. 232/2 The oscillatory current in the aerial, and therefore the wave-train radiated, continue long after the spark has been quenched. **1927** O. F. BROWN *Elements of Radio Communication* iv. 53 The spark is produced between projecting studs on a rapidly revolving metal disc and two fixed electrodes... The rotation of the disc will rapidly increase the distance between the studs and the electrodes, so that the spark is quenched and the oscillation in the primary circuit ceases. **1938** *Proc. IRE* XXVI. 76 In a typical superregenerative receiver the regenerative coupling between the plate and grid circuits of the detector tube is great enough so that self-sustained oscillations are produced, and these oscillations are periodically quenched, by applying..an alternating voltage having a frequency much lower than that of the oscillations. **1959** G. Troup *Masers* vii. 117 These authors measured the noise figure of an ammonia maser amplifier operated superregeneratively: that is, oscillations were allowed to build up and then quenched. **1966** *McGraw-Hill Encycl. Sci. & Technol.* I. 362/1 A regenerative detector in which the oscillations are periodically stopped or quenched is called a superregenerative detector.

2. a. To extinguish (heat or warmth, *lit.* or *fig.*) by cooling. †Also with *out*.

1406 Hoccleve *La Male Regle* 135 Heuy purs, with herte liberal, Qwenchith the thirsty hete of hertes drie. *c* **1410** —— *Mother of God* 28 That al the hete of brennyng Leccherie He qwenche in me. **1513** Douglas *Æneis* iv. Prol. 119 Heit..in to agit failȝeis, and is out quent. **1604** E. G[rimstone] *D'Acosta's Hist. Indies* iii. ix. 150 A kinde of cold so piercing, that it quencheth the vitall heate. **1884** Tennyson *Becket* ii. ii, Pity, my lord, that you have quenched the warmth of France toward you.

b. To cool (a heated object) by means of cold water or other liquid.

1398 Trevisa *Barth. De P.R.* vii. xxxv. (1495) 250 Gotes mylke in the whyche stones of ryuers ben quenchyd. **1460–70** *Bk. Quintessence* 7 þanne quenche ȝoure floreyn in þe beste whiȝt wiyn. **1584** Cogan *Haven Health* x. (1636) 34 [Rice]..boyled in Milke wherein hot stones have beene quenched. **1612** Woodall *Surg. Mate* Wks. (1653) 358 Hot Bricks, somewhat quenched with water. **1747** Wesley *Prim. Physic* (1762) 61 Quench it in half a Pint of French white Wine. **1826** Scott *Woodst.* i, Was the steel quenched with water from Rosamond's well.

fig. **1719** Young *Paraphr. Job* Wks. 1757 I. 208 Who can refresh the burning sandy plain, And quench the summer with a waste of rain?

†**c.** To slake (lime). *Obs. rare.*

1577 Harrison *England* ii. xii. (1877) i. 234 The white lime..being quenched. **1643** J. Steer tr. *Exp. Chyrurg.* i. 3 When Lyme is quenched..it is..heated.

3. *transf.* **a.** To put an end to, stifle, suppress (a feeling, act, condition, quality, or other non-material thing, in early use chiefly something bad).

c **1200** Ormin 4911 All idell ȝellp & idell ros þu cwennkesst. *c* **1325** *Songs of Mercy* in *E.E.P.* (1862) 120, I whenched al þi care. *c* **1330** R. Brunne *Chron. Wace* (Rolls) 16357 Louerd! þou quenche his wykkednesse. **1494** Fabyan *Chron.* v. xci. 67 In thyse Prouynces the faythe of Criste was all quenchyd. **1545** Brinklow *Compl.* iii. (1874) 16 How mercifully dyd God quench the fury of the peple. **1632** Lithgow *Trav.* iii. 84 Quenching the least suspition he might conceiue. **1742** Young *Nt. Th.* ii. 340 All god-like passion for eternals quencht. **1833** Ht. Martineau *Loom & Lugger* ii. v. 81 The observance of this rule would soon quench the desire for protection. **1876** Tait *Rec. Adv. Phys. Sc.* vii. (ed. 2) 172 The final effect of the tides in stopping or quenching the earth's rotation.

b. To slake (thirst) completely; †rarely, to satisfy or dispel (hunger).

1390 Gower *Conf.* II. 201 Thus the thurst of gold was queynt. *a* **1533** Ld. Berners *Gold. Bk. M. Aurel.* (1546) D ij b, His hunger is not thereby quenched. **1535** Coverdale *Ps.* ciii[i]. 11 That the wylde asses maye quench their thyrste. **1661** Lovell *Hist. Anim. & Min.* 235 Stickle-backs..serve better to quench hunger, than to nourish. **1752** Young *Brothers* iv. i, Friends, sworn to..quench infernal thirst in kindred blood. **1841** Elphinstone *Hist. Ind.* I. 489 Where they could quench their thirst at a well of brackish water.

†**c.** With personal object. *Obs. rare.*

1611 Shaks. *Cymb.* v. v. 195 Being thus quench'd Of hope, not longing [etc.]. **1614** B. Jonson *Barth. Fair* ii. ii, A botle of Ale, to quench mee, Rascal.

d. *Physics.* To suppress (luminescence); hence, to de-excite (an atom that would otherwise give rise to this effect).

1928 *Proc. Nat. Acad. Sci.* XIV. 851 The results show that hydrogen quenches the resonance radiation of cadmium as effectively as it does that of mercury. **1932** *Jrnl. Amer. Chem. Soc.* LIV. 572 The apparent decrease in quenching at high pressures or temperatures does not at all preclude the possibility that some fraction of the mercury atoms are being quenched to the normal state. **1954** C. Zwikker *Physical Properties of Solid Materials* xiii. 230 Fluorescence may be quenched by radiation, *e.g.* infra-red of too long a wavelength to excite fluorescence. The quenching photons raise electrons from the crystal lattice..to the copper ions..and thus inhibit the recombination effect. **1976** *Sci. Amer.* June 47/2 (Advt.), While the list of molecules which will react with $^1O_2$ is growing rapidly, the list of molecules which will quench $^1O_2$ back to O_2 is much smaller.

e. *Physics* and *Chem.* To suppress (the orbital angular momentum of an electron and the associated magnetic moment).

1932 J. H. Van Vleck *Theory of Electric & Magn. Susceptibilities* xi. 282 Solids or solutions in which inter-atomic forces quench the orbital angular momentum but leave the spin free. **1955** Townes & Schawlow *Microwave Spectrosc.* vii. 175 In nonlinear molecules, the orbital motion of electrons is almost completely 'quenched' or suppressed, and a spin momentum is the only angular momentum in the molecule of distinctly electronic origin. **1962** Cotton & Wilkinson *Adv. Inorg. Chem.* xxiv. 508 The electric fields of other atoms, ions, and molecules surrounding the metal ion in its compounds interfere with the orbital motion of the electrons so that the orbital angular momentum and hence the orbital moment are wholly or partially 'quenched'. **1971** J. D. Patterson *Introd. Theory of Solid State Physics* iv. 240 The cubic field acts to 'quench' the orbital angular momentum.

f. To prevent (the discharge in a Geiger counter) from continuing too long and reducing the possible counting rate; also with the counter as obj.

1940 *Physical Rev.* LVII. 1036/1 If we merely assure ourselves that the counter wire is falling somewhat below the starting potential with each discharge, then we can be sure that the discharge is quenched after the first stage and we will have a clean, fast pulse. **1942** Pollard & Davidson *Applied Nucl. Physics* iii. 30 A very common device to quench a counter is to employ a vacuum tube. **1958** O. R. Frisch *Nucl. Handbk.* xv. 14 The discriminator circuit used with Geiger counters..should provide facilities for quenching the counter for a period of several hundred microseconds after each pulse. **1963** W. E. Burcham *Nuclear Physics* vi. 218 It is the function of the alcohol in the gas filling to 'quench' the discharge. **1975** K. H. Goulding in Williams & Wilson *Biologist's Guide to Princ. & Techniques Pract. Biochem.* vi. 178 To overcome this, the tube is quenched by the addition of a suitable gas, which reduces the energy of the ions.

4. a. To destroy, kill (a person); to oppress or crush. †Also with *out*. Now *rare.*

c **1200** Ormin 19632 þeȝȝ wolldenn himm forrfarenn all & cwennkenn. *c* **1380** Wyclif *Sel. Wks.* III. 363 He wiþ his part þat loveþ þe world quenchen men þat speken þis. **1399** Langl. *Rich. Redeles* iii. 327 They constrewed quarellis to quenche the peple. **1567** *Triall Treas.* (1850) 44, I, Tyme,..quenche out the ungodly, their memory and fame. **1850** Dobell *Roman* iv. Poet. Wks. (1875) 54 Oh sea, if thou hast waves, Quench him! **1859** Tennyson *Vivien* 216 (67) His greatness whom she quench'd.

absol. *c* **1200** Ormin 15213 Swillc iss winess kinde, ȝiff..mann drinnkeþþ itt att oferrdon, itt cwennkeþþ.

b. To put down (in a dispute), to squash.

1840 Dickens *Barn. Rudge* ix, I knew I should quench her, said Tim. **1868** Miss Alcott *Little Women* (1869) I. vi. 94 Jo quenched her by slamming down the window.

†**5.** To destroy some quality of (a thing). *Obs.*

1398 Trevisa *Barth. De P.R.* xvi. vii. (1495) 556 Quycke syluer..is quenchyd wyth spotyll whanne it is frotyd therwyth.

II. *intr.* †**6. a.** Of fire, a burning thing, etc.: To be extinguished, to go out, to cease to burn or shine. *Obs.*

c **1290** *S. Eng. Leg.* I. 19/6 Heore liȝt queincte ouer-al. *c* **1386** Chaucer *Knt.'s T.* 1479 Right anon on of the fires queinte..And as it queinte, it made a whisteling. **1460** *Lybeaus Disc.* 1805 The torches that brende bryght Quenched anon ryght. **1513** Douglas *Æneis* iv. xii. 121 Thair with all the naturall heit out quent. *c* **1586** C'tess Pembroke *Ps.* cxx. iv, Coales..which quickly fired, Flame very hott, very hardly quenching. **1623** Fletcher *Bloody Brother* iv. iii, Like a false star that quenches as it glides.

†**b.** *transf.* Of non-material things: To come to an end, perish, disappear. *Obs.*

c **1305** *St. Edmund* 111 in *E.E.P.* (1862) 74 Quenche miȝte hire fole þoȝt mid blod þat heo schadde. *c* **1400** *Rom. Rose* 5324 This love..wole faile, and quenche anoon. **1641** Milton *Reform.* Wks. 1738 I. 16 The Spirit daily quenching and dying in them.

†**c.** Of a person: To cool down. *Obs. rare*$^{-1}$.

1611 Shaks. *Cymb.* i. v. 47 Dost thou thinke in time She will not quench, and let instructions enter Where Folly now possesses.

7. *Physics.* To change from the superconducting state to the non-superconducting state.

1969 *Sci. Jrnl.* Apr. 42/2 Increasing current is passed through the superconductor until the material 'quenches' (goes normal). **1975** *Physics Bull.* May 214/1 The normal metal (copper or combinations of copper and cupro-nickel) is still required to protect the conductor when it reaches the limit of its current carrying capacity and 'quenches' (ie undergoes a transition to the normal state).

III. 8. Combs. (from sense 2 b): **quench-ageing**, changes in the properties of steel, notably hardening, which occur after the metal has been quenched from a high temperature (see quot. 1968); **quench-cracking**, fracture of a metal caused by thermal stresses during rapid cooling; **quench-hardening**, hardening of steel by heating it above a critical temperature for some time, quenching rapidly, and then allowing further slow cooling; also = *quench-ageing* above; so **quench-harden** *v. trans.*

1935 *Trans. Amer. Soc. Metals* XXIII. 1049 To one of the three most important examples of aging, found in practically all soft steels, the designation 'Carbonizing' has been given for purposes of this discussion. It has also been called 'sub-critical quench-aging'. **1938** *Jrnl. Iron & Steel Inst.* CXXXVIII. 247P The usual theory put forward to explain the process of quench-ageing, whether in steel or in any other age-hardening alloy, is that it is caused by the precipitation from super-saturated solid solution of particles of the solute in a highly dispersed form on the lattice of the solvent,..preliminary to precipitation. **1961** G. E. Dieter *Mech. Metallurgy* v. 137 Quench aging is a type of true precipitation hardening that occurs on quenching from the temperature of maximum solubility of carbon and nitrogen in ferrite. **1968** E. R. Petty *Physical Metall. of Engin. Materials* v. 92 These changes involve an increase in hardness, elastic limit and tensile strength, accompanied by a fall in ductility and impact resistance, and may occur in low carbon steels finished by rapid cooling from a softening temperature above 600°C or by cold working. In the former case the phenomenon is referred to as quench ageing while the latter is known as strain ageing. **1971** *Engineering* Apr. 20/1 The absence of the defects of material or liquation on the surface of the pins and journals is of particular importance..where these areas are to be hardened by flame or induction, as the risk of quench cracking is almost entirely eliminated. **1973** J. G. Tweeddale *Materials Technol.* I. vi. 172 There is usually a limiting rate of cooling from the outside for any given steel, beyond which it is impractical to go because too-rapid contraction from the outside may cause quench-cracking. **1934** H. O'Neill *Hardness of Metals & its Measurement* vi. 201 Mehl..has reported that quench-hardening a pearlitic steel does not alter its compressibility. *Ibid.* 202 Ordinary quench-hardening practice by continuous rapid cooling to room temperatures will produce martensite if the rate is sufficient to preserve austenite down to Ar''. **1961** G. E. Dieter *Mech. Metallurgy* v. 146 Quench hardening results in an increase in yield stress and a decrease in the rate of strain hardening. **1969** D. K. Allen *Metallurgy Theory & Pract.* vii. 194/2 Most all carbon steels can be quench-hardened but the hardness does not become appreciable until the carbon content..reaches about 0·35 percent. *Ibid.* 196/2 The second requirement for quench hardening is that the steel be heated to the recommended hardening temperature and held for a sufficient length of time to allow the steel to become fully austenitized.

quench, obs. variant of quince.

quenchable ('kwɛnʃəb(ə)l), *a.* [f. prec. + -able.] That may be quenched.

1611 Cotgr., *Amortissable*, quenchable, stintable, dissolueable. *a* **1620** J. Dyke *Sel. Serm.* (1640) 8 If..it be a quenchable fire. **1818** Scott *Br. Lamm.* v, Had we thought that your..drought was quenchable. **1837** Carlyle *Fr. Rev.* II. iv. ix, Fire itself is quenchable, yet only quenchable at first.

Hence '**quenchableness** (Bailey vol. II. 1727).

†'**quench-coal.** *Obs.* [f. as prec. + coal.] Something which extinguishes burning coal. In quots. *fig.*: An extinguisher.

1615 S. Ward *Coal fr. Altar* Serm., etc. (1862) 71 Zeal hath in this our earthly mould little fuel, much quench-coal. **1641** Symonds *Serm. bef. Ho. Comm.* ¶iii b, Opinions should not be quench-coales of love. **1742** J. Willison *Balm of Gilead* ii. (1800) 25 Carnal company oft proves a dangerous quench-coal to zeal.

quenche, obs. form of quince.

quenched (kwɛnʃt), *ppl. a.* [f. quench *v.* + -ed^1.] **a.** That has been quenched. Also with *out*.

1814 Byron *Lara* i. xxix, Quench'd existence crouches in a grave. **1825** J. Neal *Bro. Jonathan* III. 412 He could not bear the look of the quenched eyes. **1868** Browning *Ring & Bk.* vi. 148 To relume the quenched flax. **1881** O. Wilde *Poems* 211 The quenched-out torch, the lonely cypress-gloom. **1938** [see quench *sb.* 2]. **1946** [see *quenching rate* s.v. quenching *vbl. sb.* 2]. **1958** [see aggregate *sb.* 6]. **1963** B. Fozard *Instrumentation & Control Nucl. Reactors* v. 50 Organically quenched counters are characterised by high starting and operating voltages.

b. Radio. ***quenched spark***, a spark in a spark transmitter that is extinguished mechanically soon after it begins (see quench *v.* 1 d); so ***quenched gap***, a spark-gap designed to bring this about.

1910 G. W. Pierce *Princ. Wireless Telegr.* xxiii. 269 The quenched spark is..economical in transmitting energy, and is favorable to sharp tuning. **1927** O. F. Brown *Elements of Radio Communication* iv. 53 The two methods most frequently employed for quenching are either the use of a rotating spark gap or a specially designed spark gap known as the 'quenched gap'. **1962** J. H. & P. J. Reyner *Radio Communication* vii. 294 Owing to the rapid cooling a very high spark frequency may be used, and quenched spark sets operated with a spark frequency of 1,500 per second or more.

quencher ('kwɛnʃə(r)). [f. as quench + -er^1.] **a.** One who, or that which, quenches.

c **1440** Capgrave *Life St. Kath.* i. 820 Norysshere of vertu and quenchere of vice. **1561** Preston *King Cambyses* 904 Of the same [heat] the quencher you must be. *a* **1665** J. Goodwin *Filled w. the Spirit* (1867) 353 Those quenchers of the Spirit in themselves. **1704** F. Fuller *Med. Gymn.* (1711) 86 Liquorice..was ever reputed by the Ancients, for the greatest quencher of Thirst in Nature. **1848** Dickens *Dombey* viii, Mrs. Pipchin's presence was a quencher to any number of candles. **1879** H. N. Hudson *Hamlet* Pref. 4 A feast so overlaid with quenchers of the appetite. **1950** H. W. Leverenz *Introd. Luminescence of Solids* iv. 132 A phosphor center may function as..a poison (or killer, or quencher), by having the excited-state equilibrium level sufficiently near or above *f* so that radiationless transitions predominate. **1961** G. R. Choppin *Exper. Nuclear Chem.* v. 61 The effect of multiple discharges due to failure of the quencher is included..but will be negligible for a good tube operating at the proper plateau voltage. **1971** *Nature* 13 Aug. 444/3 It is well known that paramagnetic ions are efficient quenchers of electronically excited states. **1976** *Sci. Amer.* June 47/2 (Advt.), This is because the excitation energy of $^1O_2$ is unusually low; a quencher molecule to relieve $^1O_2$ of this energy must have an even lower excited state.

b. *colloq.* Something to quench thirst; a drink.

1840 Dickens *Old C. Shop* xxxv, Mr. Swiveller replied..that he was still open to a 'modest quencher'. **1856** T. Hughes *Tom Brown* i. i, A pleasant public, whereat we must really take a modest quencher. **1857** Kingsley *Two Y. Ago* xviii, Trebooze..now offers Tom a 'quencher', as he calls it.

†'**quench-fire.** *Obs. rare*$^{-1}$. An apparatus, or substance, for extinguishing fires.

1667 Evelyn *Diary* 10 July, I went to see Sir Sam. Morland's inventions and machines, arithmetical wheeles, quench-fires, and new harp.

quenching ('kwɛnʃɪŋ), *vbl. sb.* [f. quench *v.* + -ing^1.]

1. a. The action of the vb. in various senses.

c **1220** *Bestiary* 207 Ðat is soule drink, sinnes quenching. *c* **1290** *S. Eng. Leg.* I. 315/556 þer is þanne selde wete to maken quenchingue of fuyre. **1398** Trevisa *Barth. De P.R.* v. xxx. (1495) 141 Quenchyng and deynge of the herte is in the nayles moste openly schewed. **1544** Phaer *Regim. Life* (1553) I ij, Stinking thinges, as assa fetida..and the quenchyng out of candels. **1664** Marvell *Corr.* Wks. 1872–5 II. 176 Engins, such as are used frequently in the quenching of great fires. **1730** Savery in *Phil. Trans.* XXXVI. 307 Steel hardened by quenching. *a* **1864** Hawthorne *Amer. Note-bks.* (1879) I. 222 A quenching of the sunshine. **1908** J. A. Fleming *Elem. Man. Radiotelegr.*

& Radioteleph. 338 (Index), Quenching noise of an electric spark. **1928** *Proc. Nat. Acad. Sci.* XIV. 849 (*heading*) The quenching of cadmium resonance radiation. **1943** B. F. WELLER *Radio-Technol.* iv. 114 Quenching may be effected by a separate valve,..or the reacting detector valve may be arranged to oscillate at the quenching frequency, as well as the radio-frequency. **1963** B. FOZARD *Instrumentation Nucl. Reactors* ii. 25 Because of the need for 'quenching' in a Geiger-Mueller counter for example, its detailed design may be quite different from that of an ionisation chamber. **1972** DE PUY & CHAPMAN *Molec. Reactions & Photochem.* iii. 37 Sensitization and quenching are important methods for determining the spin multiplicity of excited states responsible for photochemical reactions.

b. *spec.* The process of throwing water upon the molten metal in a refining-hearth or crucible, so that it may be removed in disks or 'rosettes'.

1875 KNIGHT *Dict. Mech.* 1847/2, 1984/1.

2. *attrib.* and *Comb.* as ***quenching crack, medium, rate, -test, trough, -tub.***

1926 A. SAUVEUR *Metallogr. & Heat Treatment of Iron & Steel* (ed. 3) xv. 220 Water quenching is to be preferred to oil quenching if it can be performed without producing quenching cracks. **1966** C. R. TOTTLE *Sci. Engin. Materials* x. 224 The strain in the transformed martensite is tensile, in the circumferential direction, and so radial cracks form in the martensite to relieve the stress; these are known as quenching cracks. **1932** E. GREGORY *Metallurgy* iv. 112 Water is obviously the cheapest quenching medium, and is invaluable for tools and purposes where an extremely hard surface is desired. **1946** *Nature* 31 Aug. 308/1 Experiments with various iron-carbon alloys quenched in various ways tend to show that the amounts of ferrite, martensite and retained austenite obtained in the quenched specimen are independent of the quenching-rate so long as a certain critical rate..is not exceeded. **1879** *Cassell's Tech. Educ.* IV. 373/1 These conditions provide for the so called 'quenching' and bending tests being applied to a piece cut from each plate and bar. **1875** KNIGHT *Dict. Mech.* 1847/2 Quenching-tub. **1896** F. S. MEYER *Handbk. Art Smithing* ii. 19 In the front part of the forge are found, as a rule, a quenching trough, hollows and receivers for fuel and slack. **1973** *Canad. Antiques Collector* May–June 7 (*caption*) The stone quenching trough from the oldest smithy in eastern Ontario.

So **'quenching** *ppl. a.*, that quenches.

1382 WYCLIF *Wisd.* xix. 19 Water forȝat his quenchende kinde. **1398** TREVISA *Barth. De P.R.* x. ix. (1495) 379 Cinis is lytyll asshes lefte of quenchynge and sparklynge matere. **1559** *Mirr. Mag., George Plantag.* fiv, Like quenching blastes, which oft reuive the flame. **1611** BIBLE *Wisd.* xix. 20 The water forgat his owne quenching nature. **1954** [see QUENCH *v.* 3 d]. **1958** W. K. MANSFIELD *Elem. Nucl. Physics* vi. 50 Positive ions arriving at the cathode are sometimes able to eject an electron. If this were to occur..a continuous series of pulses might be observed. This is prevented in a Geiger counter by the inclusion of a quenching agent. **1966** D. G. BRANDON *Mod. Techniques Metallogr.* iii. 154 The addition of a small amount of a second, 'quenching', gas.. serves to prevent secondary electron emission by the positive ion bombardment of the cathode.

quenchless ('kwɛnʃlɪs), *a.* [f. as QUENCHING *vbl. sb.* + -LESS.] That cannot be quenched; unquenchable, inextinguishable.

1557 *Tottell's Misc.* (Arb.) 137 These hellish houndes, with paines of quenchlesse fyre. *c* **1632** COWLEY *Elegy Ld. Carleton*, An angry Fever, Whose quenchless Thirst, by Blood was sated never. **1742** YOUNG *Nt. Th.* VI. 473 In faculties of endless growth, In quenchless passions. **1816** BYRON *Ch. Har.* III. xlii, Fire.., but once kindled, quenchless evermore. **1838** W. HOWITT *Rural Life Eng.* II. I. ii. 35 The Romances of Scott..have..piled quenchless fuel on this social flame. **1877** C. GEIKIE *Christ* lvii. (1879) 691 A last sad look of quenchless pity. **1895** YEATS *Poems* 12 And with quenchless eyes and fluttering hair A beautiful young man followed behind. **1952** C. DAY LEWIS tr. *Virgil's Aeneid* IV. 78 And consecrated their quenchless flames. **1976** *New Yorker* 15 Nov. 59/1 Vaccaro and Jack Smith, the underground filmmaker, shared a quenchless passion for 'Siren of Atlantis', 'White Savage', 'Cobra Woman', and other nineteen-forties epics starring Miss Montez.

Hence **'quenchlessly** *adv.*; **'quenchlessness.**

1594 KYD *Cornelia* V. 403 Sacred Temples quenchlessly enflam'd. **1848** CRAIG, *Quenchlessness.*

† **'quenchour.** *Obs. rare*⁻¹. Quenching.

1460–70 *Bk. Quintessence* 6 Loke þat ȝe haue a sotilte and a sleiȝþe to quenche sodeynly þe fier..and whanne ȝe haue do ȝoure quenchour, putte alle þe watris togidere.

quency, obs. form of QUINSY.

† **quene,** obs. form of COIN *sb.*

1505 *Will of Leek* (Somerset Ho.), Exspencis bielding of the church and makyng of my tombe wᵗ such Quene as I shall leve in their hande.

quene, obs. form of QUEEN, WHEN.

‖ **quenelle** (kə'nɛl). [F., of uncertain origin.] In *Cookery*, a seasoned ball, of which the chief ingredient, commonly meat or fish, has been reduced to a paste. Also **quenelle de volaille,** a ball made with chicken or other fowl meat.

1845 E. ACTON *Mod. Cookery* vi. 180 *French Forcemeat called Quenelles.* This is a peculiarly light and delicate kind of forcemeat. **1846** [see CROÛTON]. **1861** MRS. BEETON *Bk. Househ. Managem.* 202 *Veal Quenelles...* If the quenelles are not firm enough, add the yolk of another egg. **1883** V. STUART *Egypt* 296 Savoury quenelles of mutton enveloped in fennel leaves. **1888** *Queen* 15 Dec. 786/2 The insipid sweetbread..the pasty quenelle, the sticky jelly. **1889** J. WHITEHEAD *Steward's Handbk.* IV. 420/1 *Richelieu garnish*, quenelles of chicken, cockscombs and slices of fat livers in brown onion sauce. **1936** LUCAS & HUME *Au Petit Cordon Bleu* 53 Decorate the tops of each *paupiette* with small fillets of anchovy and the *quenelles* with strips of anchovy. **1976** *Punch* 27 Oct. 737/1 Is it also prejudice..to prefer *quenelles* to fish cakes, to hate Coca-Cola and adore wine? **1977** C. MCFADDEN *Serial* (1978) vi. 18/1 She could really dig *quenelles* about now.

† **quengeoun,** var. CONGEON. *Obs.*

c **1430** *Syr Gener.* (Roxb.) 1339 Thou mysproude quengeovn, Whi answerst thou not to my reason.

† **quenger,** obs. var. CONJURE.

1567 *Tales & Quicke Answ.* (Berthelet) *Contents* lxxx, Of the olde man that quengered the boy oute of the apletre with stones.

† **quenqueste,** obs. form of CONQUEST.

1422 tr. *Secreta Secret., Priv. Priv.* 171 Ihon de curcy, and many otheres of the quenqueste of Irland.

quenselite ('kwɛnsəlaɪt). *Min.* [ad. G. *quenselit* (G. Flink 1925, in *Geol. Föreningens i Stockholm Förhandl.* XLVII. 377), f. the name of P. D. *Quensel* (b. 1881), Swedish mineralogist: see -ITE¹.] An oxide of lead and manganese, $PbMnO_2(OH)$, found as black, tabular, monoclinic crystals.

1926 *Mineral. Abstr.* III. 110 Quenselite, another new mineral from Långban, Sweden, occurs as small (1 mm.) pitch-black crystals with calcite and baryte in crevices of the granular haematite ore. **1958** *Proc. Nat. Inst. Sci. India* A. XXIV. 95 This is probably the first reported occurrence of quenselite in manganese ores of metamorphic origin. **1971** *Zeitschr. für Kryst.* CXXXIV. 331 The significance of the quenselite structure lies in its role as a connecting link between certain of the Pb oxides and the lithiophorite-chalcophanite group... In addition to red and yellow PbO, quenselite has structural similarities to Pb_2O_3.

quenstedtite ('kwɛnstɛtaɪt). *Min.* [Named in 1888 after Prof. F. A. von *Quenstedt*: see -ITE¹.] Hydrous sulphate of iron found in Chile.

1888 *Amer. Jrnl. Sc.* XXXVI. 156 The name quenstedtite is given to a salt occurring in reddish-violet, tabular crystals.

† **quent,** *sb. Obs. rare.* [ad. Sp. *quento, cuento* = It. *conto*, OF. *conte*, COUNT *sb.*] A million (of maravedis).

1555 EDEN *Decades* 314 Luys of S. Angell..sente theym syxe quentes of marauedes. **1577** HELLOWES *Gueuara's Fam. Ep.* 68 A..gentleman of more than a Quent of rent.

† **quent,** *v. Obs. rare.* Also 6 **queint.** [erron. f. *queint*, obs. pa. pple. of QUENCH *v.*] *trans.* and *intr.* To quench.

1557 *Tottell's Misc.* (Arb.) 262 Set about my hersse, Two lampes to burne and not to queint [*rime* spent]. **1567** TURBERV. *Epit.*, etc., *Myrr. Fall of Pride*, He thought forth-with his thirst to quent..But there he found or ere he went a greater drougth.

† **quent,** Sc. f. *a(c)quent*, ACQUAINT *ppl. a.*

1536 BELLENDEN *Cron. Scot.* (1821) I. 149 New servandis ar in derisioun amang the quent servitouris.

quent, obs. f. QUAINT *a.*; obs. pa. pple. of QUENCH *v.*

quentance, -ise, var. QUAINTANCE, -ISE.

quenthing, erron. f. QUETHING.

† **'quentin.** *Obs. rare*⁻⁰. [a. F. *quentin* 'French Laune' (Cotgr.). Cf. QUINTIN.] 'A sort of French Linnen-cloth that comes from S. Quentin in Picardy' (Miége 1687; also in Phillips 1706, Bailey 1721).

queor, obs. form of CHOIR.

quep, erron. archaism for *guep*: see GUP.

1822 SCOTT *Nigel* iv, Marry quep of your advice. **1825** —— *Betrothed* ix, Marry quep, my cousin the weaver.

† **quequer,** late var. COCKER, a quiver. *Obs.*

c **1500** *Robin Hood & Potter* 51 in Child *Ballads* III. 112 To a quequer Roben went, A god bolt owthe he toke.

quer, obs. form of CHOIR, WHERE.

† **queral,** obs. form of CORAL.

1533 GAU *Richt Vay* 85 Mony prayis ye psalter of our ladie ..vith queral bedis.

† **querant.** *Obs. rare*⁻¹. [a. F. *querant*, pple. of *querir* to inquire (cf. QUERE *v.*).] = QUERENT *sb.*¹

1591 SPARRY tr. *Cattan's Geomancie* 81 The questions.. touching the siluer of the brother or sister of the querant.

† **querbole,** obs. form of CUIR-BOUILLI.

1453 *Test. Ebor.* (Surtees, 1855) II. 190, j par of tables.. case of querbole.

quercetin ('kwɜːsɪtɪn). *Chem.* [Arbitrarily f. L. *querc-us* oak + -IN¹. (Cf. L. *quercētum* an oak-wood.)] A yellow crystalline substance widely distributed in the vegetable kingdom, but usually obtained by decomposition of quercitrin; 3, 3′, 4′, 5, 7-Pentahydroxyflavone, $C_{15}H_{10}O_7$.

1857 MILLER *Elem. Chem.* III. 512 When quercitrin is boiled with dilute sulphuric or hydrochloric acid, it is decomposed into glucose and quercetin. **1872** WATTS *Dict. Chem.* 1st Suppl. 982 Gintl..has found quercetin in the leaves of the ash-tree. **1949** *Thorpe's Dict. Appl. Chem.* (ed. 4) IX. 300/2 Quercetin gives red-brown, brown-orange, bright orange and olive-black shades on wool mordanted with chromium, aluminium, tin, and iron, respectively. **1962** T. R. SESHADRI in T. A. Geissman *Chem. Flavonoid Compounds* ii. 9 Quercetin and its glycosides can be conveniently extracted by borax and can be liberated by acidification.

Hence **quer'cetamide,** an amide obtained from quercetin in the form of an amorphous orange-yellow powder. **quercetic** (kwɜː'sɛtɪk) *a.*, derived from quercetin, as in ***quercetic acid.***

1868 WATTS *Dict. Chem.* V. 3 On adding ammonia to the acid filtrate, quercetamide is obtained. *Ibid.* 5 Quercetin heated with potash yields quercetic acid and other products. **1893** T. E. THORPE *Dict. Chem.* III. 324 If the melting is continued longer than necessary to obtain quercetic acid, then quercimeric acid is obtained.

† **querch(e,** obs. forms of CURCH, kerchief.

c **1375** *Sc. Leg. Saints* ii. (*Paul*) 265 With þe querch [he] hid his face. *Ibid.* 295 Paule myn querche gaf to me.

quercimeric (kwɜːrsɪ'mɛrɪk), *a. Chem.* [f. *querci-*, comb. form of L. *quercus* oak + Gr. *μέρος* part + -IC.] ***quercimeric acid,*** an acid derived from quercetin or quercetic acid.

1868 WATTS *Dict. Chem.* V. 5 Quercimeric acid.. Produced by the action of melting potash on quercetic acid. **1893** T. E. THORPE *Dict. Chem.* III. 324 Quercimeric acid.. is isolated in the same manner as quercetic acid, from which it differs by being much more soluble in water. [See also QUERCETIC.]

quercin ('kwɜːsɪn). *Chem.* [f. L. *quercus* oak + -IN¹.] (See quots.)

1845 *Penny Cycl.* Suppl. I. 349/2 *Quercin*, a neutral crystalline substance procured from the bark of the oak. **1894** *Watts' Dict. Chem.*, Quercin..occurs in oakbark, being obtained from the mother-liquors in the preparation of quercite.

quercine ('kwɜːsaɪn), *a.* [ad. L. *quercin-us*, f. *quercus* oak: see -INE².] Of or pertaining to the oak; made of oak, oaken.

1656 BLOUNT *Glossogr.*, *Quercine*, oken, make of Okes. **1658** PHILLIPS *Quercine*, belonging to an oak. **1854** B. TAYLOR *Lands Saracen* xxxvii. (1855) 440 The mast..was as sweet and palatable as chestnuts, with very little of the bitter quercine flavour.

quercitannin (kwɜːsɪ'tænɪn). *Chem.* [f. L. *querci-* oak- + TANNIN.] A form of tannin obtained from oak-bark. So **querci'tannic** *a.*, in ***quercitannic acid*** = quercitannin.

1845 W. GREGORY *Outl. Org. Chem.* 416 Tannic Acid.. Syn. Quercitannic Acid, Tannine. This acid occurs chiefly in oak-bark and in nut-galls. **1852** MORFIT *Tanning and Currying* (1853) 78 The tannin of tea is similar in properties to quercitannin. **1895** *Naturalist* 25 A tannin, which is probably quercitannin.

quercite ('kwɜːsaɪt). *Chem.* [f. L. *quercus* oak + -ITE¹ 4.] A sweet crystalline alcohol obtained from acorns.

1857 MILLER *Elem. Chem.* III. 72 Quercite..from acorns. .. Transparent prisms. **1863** FOWNES *Chem.* 434 The juice of the acorn is submitted to fermentation. The fermented liquor, on evaporation, yields small prisms of quercite.

Hence **quercitin(e)** = QUERCETIN (Webster 1864, citing Gregory). **'quercitol** = QUERCITE (Watts *Dict. Chem.* 3rd Suppl. 1881).

quercitron ('kwɜːsɪtrən). [Abbreviated for *querci-citron*, f. L. *quercus* oak + CITRON. Named by Dr. Bancroft about 1784.]

1. a. The black or dyer's oak of N. America (*Quercus tinctoria*): also called ***quercitron oak.*** **b.** The inner bark of this, used as a yellow dye and in tanning: also ***quercitron bark.***

1794 BANCROFT *Philos. Perman. Colours* xii, The Quercitron bark..is one of the objects of a discovery, of which the use and application for dying, calico-printing, &c. are exclusively vested in me..by an act of parliament passed in the 25th year of his present Majesty's reign. **1852** MORFIT *Tanning & Currying* (1853) 100 The black, or quercitron oak, is a large tree found throughout the United States. *Ibid.* 101 The quercitron, so much used in dyeing, is obtained from the cellular integument.

attrib. **1823** URE *Dict. Chem.* (ed. 2) 398/1 Cloth.. subjected to the quercitron bath.

2. Special Combs. **quercitron lake, yellow,** the yellow pigment obtained from quercitron bark, yielding quercetin and rhamnose on hydrolysis; quercetrin.

1886 H. C. STANDAGE *Artists' Man. Pigments* iv. 43 Yellow Lakes (Madder Yellow,..Quercitron Yellow or Lake). **1918** PERKIN & EVEREST *Natural Org. Colouring Matters* xix. 628 Quercitron-yellow lake, Flavin-lake, or Dutch pink can be made..by precipitating a decoction of quercitron bark containing alum with chalk. **1934** Quercitron lake [see *Italian pink*]. **1947** L. S. PRATT *Chem. & Physics Org. Pigments* vii. 65 Quercitron lake is a yellow coloring matter made from the inner bark of a species of oak, *Quercus tinctoria*, that is indigenous to North America.

Hence **quer'citrein,** a product of quercitrin. ? *Obs.* **quer'citric** *a.*, derived from quercitrin, as in ***quercitric acid*** (Watts *Dict. Chem.* 1868). **'quercitrin,** the yellow crystalline colouring matter of quercitron bark.

1833 *Encycl. Brit.* (ed. 7) VIII. 320/2 To this colouring matter Chevreul has given the name of *quercitrin. Ibid.* 321/1 Yellow crystals possessing the characters of quercitrin. **1841** *Penny Cycl.* XIX. 211/1 The tannin which quercitrin contains..gives a green colour with peroxide of iron. **1845** *Ibid.* Suppl. I. 349/2 On boiling a solution of quercitrin, it becomes turbid, and deposits a quantity of small acicular crystals of quercitrein.

quercivorous (kwɜːˈsɪvərəs), *a.* [f. L. *quercus* oak + *-vorus* devouring.] Feeding on oak-leaves.
1858 *Zoologist* XVI. 6154 An individual [caterpillar] which had already become quercivorous.

querck, obs. form of QUIRK *sb.*[1]

†**querculane**, *a. Obs. rare*$^{-0}$. [ad. mod.L. *quercul̄an-us*, f. *quercus* oak.] = QUERCINE *a.*
1656 BLOUNT *Glossogr.* [Hence in some later dicts.]

querdlynge: see CODLING[2].

†**quere**, *v. Obs. rare.* Also 5 quire. [a. OF. *quer-re* (in conj. *quier*, *quer-*; mod.F. *querir*):—L. *quærĕre*: see INQUIRE.] To ask, inquire.
13.. *Propr. Sanct.* (Vernon MS.) in *Archiv neu. Spr.* LXXXI. 319/7 He wolde wite and quere What-maner mon þat he were. *a* **1400-50** *Alexander* 1703 His qualite, his quantite, he quirys [*Dubl. MS.* enquirez] all-to-gedire. *a* **1425** *Cursor M.* 19611 (Trin.) As he þus went to quere [*Cott.* sek] & aske..þe fuyr of helle him smot. *c* **1425** *Seven Sag.* (P.) 691 Alas! that thow grevest the so sore, Or thow haddyst queryd more. [*c* **1810** *Merry-Cock Land* vii. in Child *Ballads* (1888) III. v. clv. 250 And if my play-fellows come to quere for me, Tell them I am asleep.]

quere, obs. form of CHOIR, QUÆRE, QUEER.

quereboly, obs. form of CUIR-BOUILLI.

†**querelatory**, *a. Obs. rare*$^{-1}$. [f. ppl. stem of med.L. *querēlāre* to complain (see QUERELE) + -ORY.] Of the nature of a complaint.
1553 in Strype *Eccl. Mem.* (1721) III. I. ii. 23 [Bonner did present his libel called in the instrument] a certain appellatory and querelatory Libel.

†**querele**, *sb. Obs.* [Orig. form of QUARREL *sb.*[3] (q.v.), occasionally employed (prob. under influence of L. *querēla*) after *quar(r)el* had become the usual form.]
1. A complaint; an action. = QUARREL 1.
1494 FABYAN *Chron.* an. 1123 To go before the king with a lamentable querele expressing how with true despites he was deformed. **1542** UDALL *Erasm. Apoph.* 146 Such persones, as dooe by a wrongfull querele obiecte vnto me, that [etc.]. **1628** COKE *On Litt.* 292 If a man release all Quereles..all actions reall and personall are released. **1726** AYLIFFE *Parerg.* [189] Not in Causes of Appeal, but in Causes of first Instance and simple Querele only.
2. A cause, affair, etc. = QUARREL 2.
1552 *Order St. Bartholomew's* Av, So sufficiently..set forth this enormitie of the Citezeins, as semed behouefull for the querele of charitie. **1566** GRINDAL *Lett. to Sir W. Cecil* Wks. (Parker Soc.) 289 All ministers, now to be deprived in this querele of rites.
So †**querele** *v.* = QUARREL *v.* Hence †**quereler**, quarreller, objector. *Obs.*
1542 UDALL *Erasm. Apoph.* 306 The faulte fynder or quereler. **1548** —— *Par. Luke* xv. 133 The elder sonne.. proudely quereled and reasoned the mattier with his father.

querele, -ell, obs. forms of QUARREL *sb.*[3]

†**querelous**, *a. Obs. rare.* [ad. late L. *querēlōs-us*, f. *querēla* QUERELE.] = QUERULOUS (q.v.).
For earlier examples of the form see QUARRELLOUS.
1581 J. HAMILTON in *Cath. Tract.* (S.T.S.) 84 Thir ar murmurers, querelus [L. *querulosi*]. **1614** BP. HALL *No Peace with Rome* §2 That querelous libell of the Macedonians. *a* **1661** FULLER *Worthies, Kent* II. (1662) 74 Though generally the Irish are querelous of their Deputies ..yet Sir Henry left a good memory. **1751** *Affecting Narr. of Wager* 32 A Midshipman..of an insolent querelous Temper.
Hence †**querelousness**. *Obs. rare*$^{-1}$.
1643 PRYNNE *Open. Gt. Seal* Ep., The querelousnesse of the clamorous Opposites.

‖**querencia** (keˈrenθja). [a. Sp. *querencia* lair, haunt, home ground, f. *querer* to seek, desire, f. L. *quærere* to seek.] **1.** *Bullfighting.* The part of the arena where the bull takes his stand; stamping ground.
1932 E. HEMINGWAY *Death in Afternoon* xiii. 150 A querencia is a place the bull naturally wants to go to in the ring; a preferred locality. That is a natural querencia and such are well known and fixed, but an accidental querencia is more than that. It is a place which develops in the course of the fight where the bull makes his home. **1957** R. CAMPBELL *Portugal* vi. 115 He [*sc.* the bull] may choose his *querencia* for some strategical advantage—near the body of a dead horse, for instance. **1964** *Listener* 27 Aug. 317/1 It is when the bull leaves his *querencia*—the place where he feels safe—that he falls a victim to delusion. **1974** F. NOLAN *Oshawa Project* i. 3 Some taunted fighting bull seeking its *querencia*.
2. *fig.* A (person's) favourite place; home ground, refuge.
1952 R. CAMPBELL *Lorca* i. 8 Andalusia is Lorca's *querencia*. **1977** A. SCHOLEFIELD *Venom* III. 98 Returning always to the centre of the gold carpet for there, like a bull in a ring, he had instinctively made his *querencia*, his territory.

querent (ˈkwɪərənt), *sb.*[1] Also 7 quær-. [ad. L. *quærent-em*, pres. pple. of *quærĕre* to inquire: cf. QUERANT, QUERIST.] One who asks or inquires; *spec.* one who consults, or seeks to learn something by means of, an astrologer.
1598 F. WITHER tr. *Dariot Astrol. Judg.* O 3, By this meanes the Querent shall not haue his desyre. **1647** LILLY *Chr. Astrol.* vi. 49 [see QUESITED]. **1653** SIR G. WHARTON *Comets* Wks. (1683) 141 Many Queries..which I have answered..to my own and the Querents admiration. **1696** AUBREY *Misc.* (1784) 129 The Magicians now use a crystal-sphere,..which is inspected..sometimes by the Querent himself. **1705** BOSMAN *Guinea* 152 If the Priest is enclined to oblige the Querent, the Questions are put. **1845** *Whitehall* xxi. 151 The astrologer, fixing his keen, cunning eyes on the querent. **1881** [see QUESITED].

ˈ**querent**, *sb.*[2] and *a. rare.* [ad. L. *querent-em*, pres. pple. of *querī* to complain.]
a. *sb.* 'A complainant, plaintiff' (J.). **b.** *adj.* Complaining.
1727 in BAILEY, vol. II. **1845** *Whitehall* li. 363 A process in which Joyce assisted with manifest sulkiness, and many a querent glance at his young commander.

quereour, queresoeuer, querester(e, querf, querfore, obs. ff. QUARRIER[1], WHERESOEVER, CHORISTER, WHARF, WHEREFORE.

Queres, var. KERES.

‖**Querflöte** (ˈkveːrfløːtə). *Mus.* [a. G. *querflöte* cross-flute, f. *quer* transverse + *flöte* flute.]
1. A transverse flute, blown through an opening at the side; = *cross-flute* s.v. CROSS B.
1876 STAINER & BARRETT *Dict. Mus. Terms* 373/1 *Querflöte* (*Ger.*),..The flute played sideways, as opposed to the flute which was blown at one end, and held straight in front of the performer. **1914** H. M. FITZGIBBON *Story of Flute* iii. 30 (*caption*) Prætorius' Bass Querflote, 1620. **1959** WESTRUP & HARRISON *Collins Mus. Encycl.* 525/1 *Querflöte*, ..'Cross' or 'transverse flute', i.e. the modern flute as distinct from the recorder or *Blockflöte*. **1976** D. MUNROW *Instruments Middle Ages & Renaissance* 53/3 Back in medieval times the different playing positions of the two instruments had provided a means of distinction..: hence the use of..*Querflöte*, or *Querpfeife* (German, cross flute) for the transverse flute.
2. An organ stop that emits a sound resembling that of a flute.
1921 G. A. AUDSLEY *Organ-Stops* 217 *Querflöte*... The name..has been frequently used by German organ-builders to designate the stop which, in its voice, imitates, as closely as practicable in organ-pipes, the tone of the Flute of the orchestra. **1966** P. WILLIAMS *European Organ 1450–1850* 286 *Querflöte* (Ger. 'cross flute'), properly, an open cylindrical metal or wood flue stop (usually 4'), over-blowing to the first or second overtone due to the pipe's narrow scale, large foot-holes and fairly low cut-up.

†ˈ**querical**, *a.* and *sb. Obs. rare.* [f. *quere* QUÆRE *sb.*, or QUERY *sb.* + -ICAL.] **a.** *adj.* Of the nature of a query or queries. **b.** *sb.* A query.
1699 (*title*), Querical Demonstrations writ by Prince Butler Author of the Eleven Queries [etc.]. *Ibid.* 24 Don't disdain, My Querical Strain, And I..have yet in store, Of such Quericals more, At least a whole Score.

‖**querida** (keˈriða). [Sp. *querida*, pa. pple. *querer* to seek, desire, f. L. *quærĕre* to seek.] A sweetheart, darling: freq. used as a term of address. Also **querido** (-ðo), the male equivalent.
1846 R. FORD *Gatherings from Spain* xx. 274 His short-petticoated *querida*. **1926** W. N. BURNS *Saga of Billy the Kid* xiv. 185 In every *placeta* in the Pecos some little señorita was proud to be known as his *querida*. **1963** E. LININGTON *Death of Busybody* i. 9 Be careful now, *querida*. Lock both doors on your way home. **1970** KOENIG & DIXON *Children are Watching* iii. 23 Did her *querido* have to go back to work at the restaurant? **1976** 'S. WOODS' *My Life is Done* 40 Everything will be well, *querido*.

querie, obs. var. EQUERRY (q.v.).

ˈ**queried**, *ppl. a.* [f. QUERY *v.* + -ED[1].] Called in question; marked with a query.
1772 *Ann. Reg.* 241/2 You have insisted..that you should not have rejected the queried votes, if you had not been convinced..that they were all corrupted.

querier (ˈkwɪərɪə(r)). [f. QUERY *v.* + -ER[1].] One who queries; also *slang*, a chimney-sweep who asks for work.
1672 PENN *Spir. Truth Vind.* 93 That would have been no Answer to their weighty Question, nor any allay to that earnest Enquiry..the Queriers were under. **1861** MAYHEW *Lond. Labour* II. 377 The knuller is also styled a 'querier', a name derived from his making inquiries at the doors of the houses as to whether his services are required.

querimonious (kwerɪˈməʊnɪəs), *a.* Also 7 quere-. [ad. late L. *querimōniōs-us*: see next and -OUS. Cf. obs. F. *querimonieux* (Godef.).] Full of, addicted to, complaining.
1604 in R. CAWDREY *Table Alph.* **1630** J. TAYLOR (Water P.) *Epigr.* xxxvi. Wks. II. 266/1 Querimonious paines Doe pulverise the concaue of my braines. **1658** OSBORN *Adv. Son* (1673) 206 Querimonious accusations of his best Servants. **1791** COLLINSON *Hist. Somerset* 608 It was on this solitary island that Gildas..composed his querimonious treatise. **1848** MOZLEY *Ess., Luther* (1878) I. 354 That passionate and querimonious temper.
Hence queriˈ**moniously** *adv.*; queriˈ**moniousness** (Bailey vol. II. 1727).
a **1668** DENHAM *A Dialogue*, Most queremoniously confessing That I of late have been compressing.

querimony (ˈkwerɪmənɪ). [ad. L. *querimōnia*, f. *querī* to complain: cf. F. *quérimonie* (16th c.).] Complaint, complaining.
1529 in Froude *Hist. Eng.* (1856) I. 217 By way of querimony and complaint. *a* **1548** HALL *Chron., Edw. IV* 239b, The king..troubled with hys brothers dayly querimonye. **1610** BP. HALL *Apol. Brownists* 39 *marg.*, To which vniust and triuiall querimony, our most iust defence hath beene [etc.]. **1887** BLACKMORE *Springhaven* (ed. 4) I. viii. 61 The scholars of the Virgil class..had recovered from the querimonies of those two sons of Ovid.

†ˈ**querism**. *Obs. rare*$^{-1}$. [f. as next + -ISM.] The practice of inquiring or asking.
1648 JENKYN *Blind Guide* iv. 88 Your engagement against querism or seeking..will come to nothing.

querist (ˈkwɪərɪst). [f. L. *quær-ĕre* to ask + -IST: cf. QUERENT, QUERY.] One who asks or inquires; a questioner, interrogator.
1633 EARL MANCH. *Al Mondo* (1636) 147 Those Querists who must haue a reason for every thing in Religion. **1713** STEELE *Englishm.* No. 5. 31 This Querist thinks himself.. very seasonable in the Questions. *a* **1774** GOLDSM. *Surv. Exp. Philos.* (1776) II. 2 Were we asked..what is air, we should refer the querist to his experience alone. **1875** JOWETT *Plato* (ed. 2) III. 92 A troublesome querist comes and asks, 'What is the just and good?'

querister, variant of CHORISTER.

querity, querk, obs. ff. QUEERITY, QUIRK *sb.*[1]

querken (ˈkwɜːk(ə)n), *v. Obs.* exc. *dial.* Forms: 5 querkyn, qwerken, -yn, 6 quarken, 7 quirk-, whirken, 8 *dial.* quacken, 9 *dial.* wirken, quocken, 5–6 (8–9 *dial.*) querken. [= OFris. *querka* (mod. *kværen*, *quirke*), ON. *kvirkja*, *kyrkja* (Da. *kværke*, *kyrke*), f. OFris. *querk*, ON. *kverk* (MSw. *qvärk*), OHG. *querca* throat.] *trans.* To choke, suffocate, stifle. Hence ˈ**querkening** *vbl. sb.*
c **1440** *Promp. Parv.* 420/2 Querkenyd, *suffocatus*. Querkenynge, *suffocacio*. Querkyn, *idem quod* quellyn. **1450–1530** *Myrr. our Ladye* 249 The bytternesse of sorowe querkynde & stopped..the virgins harte. **1540** PALSGR. *Acolastus* Hij, I haue a throte bolle almoste strangled, snarled, or quarkennyd with extreme hunger. **1541** R. COPLAND *Guydon's Quest. Chirug.*, *Maner exam. lazares*, Qiv, Yf there apere any straytnes of breth as yf wolde querken [*sic*]. **1607** WALKINGTON *Opt. Glass* 124 It wil.. send up such an ascending fome that it will been ready to quirken and stifle vs. **1611** COTGR., *Noyer*, to drowne, to whirken, or stifle with water, etc. *Ibid.*, *Suffocation*, a suffocation,..whirkening. **1783** LEMON *Eng. Etym.*, *Querkened*, sometimes written, and pronounced quackned. **1828** *Craven Gloss.*, *Querkened*, suffocated. **1848** A. B. EVANS *Leicestersh. Words* s.v., The wind was so high..that I was welly quockened. **1880** in *Cheshire Gloss.* (1886), *Wirken.*

querl (kwɜːl), *sb. U.S.* Also quirl. [? var. of CURL, or a. G. *querl*, *quirl* from MHG. *twirl* TWIRL.] A curl, twist, twirl.
1854 B. F. TAYLOR *Jan. & June* 23 [The grape vine's] aspirations were manifested in the display of divers mermaidish-looking ringlets, with two or three dainty 'quirls' therein. **1871** L. M. ALCOTT *Little Men* v. 78 Sally, loading her pie with quirls and flourishes. **1880** in WEBSTER *Suppl.* **1883** *Cent. Mag.* Dec. 201/1 The forms are grotesque beyond comparison: twists, querls, contortions. **1885** *Harper's Mag.* LXX. 219 The crooks and querls of the branches on the floor. **1889** R. T. COOKE *Steadfast* xv. 162 A hundred resolute little quirls above the low forehead. **1950** *Publ. Amer. Dial. Soc.* XIV. 55 *Quirl*, a curl, as on a watermelon vine. A melon is supposed to be nice when the quirl is dead.
So **querl, quirl** *v.*, to twirl, coil, etc. (Knowles, 1835); **querled** *ppl. a.*, ˈ**querling** *vbl. sb.* and *ppl. a.*
1787 *Amer. Museum* II. 571/1 She thought there was something alive in her side, for, to use her own expression, she plainly perceived a tickling and quirling in it. *Ibid.* 574/1 She next complained of a quirling pain, that would last three or four hours with the utmost violence. **1830** *Northern Watchman* (Troy, N.Y.) 30 Nov. 3/5 We..come out of the plagid lock, wrong eend foremost, all quirled up in a h——l of a twist. **1840** J. F. COOPER *Pathfinder* I. xiii. 206 One of his hands coiled a rope against the Sun, and he called it *querling* a rope, too, when I asked him what he was about. **1890** *Dialect Notes* I. 75 'Quirled way up'... 'Quirl, both noun and verb, is familiar to me.' **1893** H. A. SHANDS *Some Peculiarities of Speech in Mississippi* 52 *Quirl*,..this word is largely used by negroes, and to some extent by white people, for *curl*. It is also thus used in New England. In Mississippi a snake is nearly always said to be *quirled* or *quoiled up*, instead of *curled* or *coiled up*. **1944** *Publ. Amer. Dial. Soc.* II. 30 *Quirl*, to curl. 'Does hit *quirl* like a pig's tail?'... Common.

quern[1] (kwɜːn). Forms: 1 cweorn, cwyrn, (cœrn, cern), cweorne, cwearne, 4 queern(e, quyerne, qwhern, 4–7 querne, 5 queren, 5–6 qwern, 6 quearn, (wherne, wyrne), *Sc.* queirn, 7 quarn, 8 *Sc.* quirn, 7– quern. [OE. *cweorn*, *cwiern* str. fem., *cweorne* wk. fem. = OFris. *quern*, OS. *quern* (or *querna*, MDu. *queren-e*, Du. *kweern*), OHG. *quirn*, *churn* and *chuirna* (MHG. *kurn*, *kürne*), ON. *kvern* (Icel. *kvörn*, Sw. *qvarn*, Da. *kværn*), Goth. *-qairnus*, from a pre-Teut. stem *g^{w}*ern-*, variations of which appear in synonymous forms in other Aryan languages, as Lith. *girnos*, OSl. *žrŭny* and *žrŭnŭvŭ*, Russ. *zhernov*, Pol. *žarna*, OIr. *bró* (gen. *broon*), W.

breuan, etc.] A simple apparatus for grinding corn, usually consisting of two circular stones, the upper of which is turned by hand; also, a small hand-mill for grinding pepper, mustard, or similar substances (see *pepper-*, *mustard-quern*).

c **950** *Lindisf. Gosp.* Matt. xxiv. 41 Tuu wif ʒegrundon on coernae [*Rushw.* æt cweorne]. *c* **1000** ÆLFRIC *Exod.* xi. 5 þære wylne..þæt sitt æt þære cweornan. *c* **1305** *Pilate* in *E.E.P.* (1862) 111 Bi a melewardes douȝter he lai..And biȝat on hire vnder þe querne þe liþere bern. **1340** *Ayenb.* 181 Samson..uil into þe honden of his yuo, þet him deden grinde ate querne. *c* **1374** CHAUCER *Former Age* 6 Onknowyn was þᵉ quyerne and ek the melle. *c* **1420** *Pallad. on Husb.* I. 831 Eek as for hail a russet weede is To kest vpon the querne. **1513** DOUGLAS *Æneis* I. iv. 39 For skant of victuall the cornes in quernis of stane Thai grand. **1577** B. GOOGE *Heresbach's Husb.* (1586) 10 A Querne or a hand Mill doth but a little good. **1647** LILLY *Chr. Astrol.* l. 354 Some necessary thing ..to use in his house, as a Furnace or Quern, or such like. **1699** EVELYN *Acetaria* (1729) 148 The seeds are pounded in a Mortar, or..ground in a Quern contriv'd for this Purpose. **1771** PENNANT *Tour in Scotl.* (1794) 232 Saw here a Quern, a sort of portable mill made of two stones. **1841** S. C. HALE *Ireland* III. 296 Two women generally worked the Quern, one sitting facing the other, the quern between them. **1884** J. COLBORNE *Hicks Pasha* 60 The circular querns of Lower Egypt, which are turned by means of a wooden handle.

b. *attrib.* and *Comb.*, as ***quern-chant***, ***-house***, ***-mill***, ***-picker***, ***-song***, ***-staff***; ***quern-like*** adv. See also QUERN-STONE.

1898 *Edinb. Rev.* Apr. 440 In the North, where he often heard the rhythmical *quern-chant. **1525** in *Southwell Visit.* (1891) 123, ij leads that standes in *wherne-house. **1591** SYLVESTER *Du Bartas* I. vi. 595 Two equall ranks of Orient Pearls..(*Quern-like) grinding small Th' imperfect food. **1600** HOLLAND *Livy* XXXIII. xlv. 706 Troughs and *querne mils. **1441** in *Bury Wills* (Camden) 256 [The will of William Toly], '*quernepykker', [1441, is in Lib. Osbern, f. 247]. **1816** W. TAYLOR in *Monthly Rev.* LXXXI. 73 We will now subjoin the Grotta-Saungr or *quern-song. **1483** *Cath. Angl.* 297/1 A *Querne-staffe, *molucrum*.

†**quern²**. *Obs. rare*⁻¹. In 5 qwerne, qweryn. App., a large piece of ice.

a **1400-50** *Alexander* 3003 Alexander..rydis To þe grete flode of Granton & it on a glace fyndis. Or he was soȝt to þe side ȝit sondird þe qweryns [*Dubl. MS.* qwernes].

quern, obs. variant of KERN *v.*¹

'quernal, *a. rare.* [f. L. *quern-us*, f. *quercus* oak + -AL¹.]

†**1.** Made of oak-leaves; oaken. *Obs. rare*⁻¹.

1599 THYNNE *Animadv.* (1875) 49 The Quernall crowne gyven to those whiche had saued a cytyzen.

2. *Bot.* ***quernal alliance***, Lindley's name for his 'alliance' of diclinous exogens, containing the orders *Corylaceæ* and *Juglandaceæ*.

1846 LINDLEY *Veget. Kingd.* 289 If it were not for the minute embryo..it might take its place in the Quernal Alliance.

†**querne**. *Obs. rare*⁻¹. [a. OF. *querne* (Godef.) for *quaterne*, after *terne*.] A quatre or four in dice-playing (in quot. *fig.*).

13.. *Coer de L.* 2009 Richard..gave him a stroke on the molde..Ternes and quernes he gave him there.

quernell, square: see QUARNELL.

querner, obs. form of CORNER *sb.*¹

'quern-stone. [Cf. ON. *kvernsteinn*.] One of the two stones forming a quern; a millstone.

c **950** *Lindisf. Gosp.* Matt. xviii. 6 Behofas him þæt he ʒehongiʒa coern-stan..in suire his [*c* 1000 *Ags. Gosp.* cwyrn-, cweorn-stan]. **1388** WYCLIF *Num.* xi. 8 And the puple ȝede aboute, and gaderide it, and brak with a queerne stoon. **14..** *Nom.* in Wr.-Wülcker 725/24 *Hec mola*, a qwernston. **1582** STANYHURST *Æneis* I. (Arb.) 23 Theyre corne in quernstoans they doe grind. **1610** HOLLAND *Camden's Brit.* I. 760 Round stones as much as milstones or quernstones. **1662** *Ireland, Stat. at Large* (1765) II. 416 Quern-stones, large, the last, £13. 10*s.* **1812** J. SMYTH *Pract. of Customs* (1821) 242 Quern Stones under three feet in diameter, and not exceeding six inches in thickness. **1875** W. MCILWRAITH *Guide Wigtownshire* 43 Opposite the east gable of the Church a quern-stone..has been stuck up.

querof, obs. form of WHEREOF.

†**queror**. *Obs. rare*⁻⁰. [a. OF. *quereor*, *-eur*, agent-n. f. *querre*, *querir* QUERE *v.*] An inquirer.

14.. *Voc.* in Wr.-Wülcker 610/18 *Scitor*, a querour.

querpo, variant of CUERPO *Obs.*

querquedule ('kwɜːkwɪdjuːl). *Ornith.* [ad. L. *querquedula* a species of duck.] **a.** 'A genus of ducks, one species of which..is the common teal' (Worcester, 1860). **b.** 'The pin-tail duck' (Webster, 1864, citing *Eng. Cyc.*).

querre, var. QUAR *v.*; obs. f. QUARRY *sb.*¹

querrell, querrister, querrour, querry, obs. ff. QUARREL *sb.*³ and *v.*, CHORISTER, QUARRIER¹, EQUERRY.

quert: see QUART *a.* and *sb.*¹

†**querulation**. *Obs. rare*⁻¹. [n. of action f. med.L. *querulāri* to complain, f. *querul-us*: see QUERULOUS *a.*] Complaint, complaining. So also (from stem *querul-*) **queru'lental**, **-'lential** *a.*, querulous. **'queruling** *vbl. sb.*, complaining. **'querulist** one who complains. **que'rulity**, **queru'losity** (cf. QUERULOUS *a.*), habit or spirit of complaining.

1614 T. ADAMS *Sinners Passing Bell* Wks. (1629) 264 Will not these mournings, menaces, *querulations, stirre your hearts? **1785** R. CUMBERLAND *Observer* No. 103 ⁋3 A lady.. rather captious and *querulental. **1806** —— *Mem.* 17 Walpole had..a plea for being captious and *querulential, for he was a martyr to the gout. **1838** S. BELLAMY *Betrayal* 94 The Devil give thee heed! Haply he'll better care thy *querulling Than He I follow mine. **1788** T. TOUCHSTONE *Trifler* 431, I have carefully examined the various subjects of complaint..If my third fair *querulist would [etc.]. **1922** C. E. MONTAGUE *Disenchantment* iv. 52 The querulist of the book took it hard..that more kind words did not come to the men. **1866** *Pall Mall G.* 27 June 1 The Premier had..very insufficient grounds for his *querulity. **1882** F. T. PALGRAVE in Grosart *Spenser's Wks.* IV. p. lxiv, Unreasonable *querulosity.

querulous ('kwɛrʊləs), *a.* Also 6 -ose, 7 querr-. [ad. late L. *querulōs-us*, f. *querulus*, f. *querī* to complain: cf. QUERELOUS, QUARRELLOUS.]

1. Of persons: Complaining, given to complaining, full of complaints, peevish.

In first quot. possibly for *querelous* QUARRELLOUS; a certain confusion between the words is also suggested by some 17th c. quots., which at least do not imply peevish or whining complaint.

? *a* **1500** *Mankind* (Brandl 1896) 46/200 My body wyth my soull ys euer querulose [*rime* house]. **1594** HOOKER *Eccl. Pol.* III. xi. §9 A people..by nature hard-hearted, querulous, wrathfull. *a* **1610** HEALEY *Theophrastus* (1636) 63 These are the maners of a querrulous waiward man. **1651** BAXTER *Inf. Bapt.* 242, I would have no godly man be over querulous, when God hath done so much for us. **1750** JOHNSON *Rambler* No. 73 ⁋1 The querulous are seldom received with great ardour of kindness. **1837** WHEWELL *Hist. Induct. Sc.* (1857) II. 149 He was naturally querulous and jaundiced in his views. **1879** FROUDE *Cæsar* xxvi. 445 His sons and nephews were equally querulous and dissatisfied.

b. Of animals or things: Uttering or producing sounds expressive or suggestive of complaint.

1635 SWAN *Spec. M.* viii. §2 (1643) 409 The Lapwing..is a querulous bird. *a* **1643** W. CARTWRIGHT *Poems, Corinna's Tomb* 18 Hither sad Lutes they nightly bring, And gently touch each querulous string. **1699** POMFRET *Pastoral Ess.* 174 Ye purling quer'llous Brooks! o'ercharged with grief. **1847** DICKENS *Haunted M.* (C. D. ed.) 205 One querulous rook, unable to sleep, protested now and then.

2. Of the nature of, characterized by, complaining.

c **1540** tr. *Pol. Verg. Eng. Hist.* (Camden) 100 Querulous repetition, as well of late as of almost forgotten faultes. **1642** HOWELL *For. Trav.* (Arb.) 19 French..hath a whining kind of querulous tone. **1714** *Spect.* No. 618 ⁋2 His Versification ..should be soft, and all his Numbers flowing and querulous. **1783** JOHNSON *Let. to Mrs. Thrale* 19 June, I am almost ashamed of this querulous letter. **1848** DICKENS *Dombey* xxxiv, She uttered a querulous cry of disappointment and misery. **1874** L. STEPHEN *Hours in Library* (1892) II. vii. 225 The querulous comments of old ladies.

'querulously, *adv.* [f. prec. + -LY².] In a querulous manner.

1652 GAULE *Magastrom.* 147 Querulously accusing her for playing with her own gifts. **1728** YOUNG *Love Fame* VI. 138 His wounded ears complaints eternal fill, As unoil'd hinges, querulously shrill. **1812** H. & J. SMITH *Rej. Addr.* x, Objections..captiously urged and querulously maintained. **1883** SIR T. MARTIN *Ld. Lyndhurst* xiv. 366 [They] complained almost querulously of the bitterness of Lord Lyndhurst's invectives.

'querulousness. [f. as prec. + -NESS.] The state or condition of being querulous.

1652 J. AUDLEY *Engl. Commonw.* Ded., To answer the querulousnesse of some persons. **1750** JOHNSON *Rambler* No. 50 ⁋7 The querulousness and indignation which is observed so often [etc.]. **1828** D'ISRAELI *Chas. I*, I. ii. 23 That impatient querulousness, which betrays its moments of weakness. **1884** *Expositor* Feb. 87 Querulousness and the captiousness of despair took possession of them.

query ('kwɪərɪ), *sb.*¹ Also 7 queree, quæree, 7-8 quæry. [Anglicizing of *quere*, QUÆRE.]

1. Introducing a question: = QUÆRE 1.

Now rarely written in full, being usually expressed by the abbreviation *qy.* (*qr.*, *qu.*) or the sign ?.

1667 PEPYS *Diary* 23 Aug., Query, whether a glass-coach would have permitted us to have made the escape? **1732** SWIFT *Corr.* (1766) II. 690 That..the subscription be.. paid into the hands of (query, Mr. Thorn,..a very proper person?). **1763** HOYLE *Back-gammon* 200 Query, Whether the Probability is for his gammoning me, or not? **1888** *N. & Q.* 7th Ser. V. 185/2 It was afterwards repurchased by that monarch (but query if purchase money was ever paid).

2. a. A question: = QUÆRE 2.

a. **1645** R. SYMONDS *Diary* (Camden) 270 The cowardly commissioners..put queries. Where shall wee have winter quarters? **1658** J. DURHAM *Exp. Revelation* (1680) VII. 342 This is the scope of the Queree. **1692** BENTLEY *Boyle Lect.* vi. (1735) 203 We are now enabled to give Answers to some bold Queries and Objections of Atheists. **1767** A. YOUNG *Farmer's Lett. to People* 270 It may..admit of a query, Whether the above expences are not too great for the crops to repay? **1813** SCOTT *Rokeby* I. x, [He] forced the embarrass'd host to buy, By query close, direct reply. **1866** GEO. ELIOT *F. Holt* (1868) 22 She had prepared herself..to suppress all..queries which her son might resent.

β. *a* **1635** CORBET *Poems* (1807) 63 He that is guilty of no quaery here, Out-lasts his epitaph. **1648** JENKYN *Blind Guide* iv. 96 My first quæree, is whether grace be an adjutory. **1684** T. BURNET *Th. Earth* II. 218 A great many quæries and difficulties might be proposed relating to the millennium. **1719** D'URFEY *Pills* (1872) II. 99 What News, is the Quæry.

b. *spec.* in the Society of Friends, an item in a formal list of questions issued for the guidance of Friends; now freq. in phr. ***Advices and Queries*** (see quot. 1954).

1654 BURROUGH & HOWGILL (*title*) Answers to severall queries put forth to the despised people called Quakers. **1701** G. KEITH *Answer to 17 Queries Quarterly Meeting Quakers, Oxford* 3 Those seventeen Queries ye sent me being only Queries, contain little or nothing Affirmatively or Negatively, by way of position. **1768** in *Extracts Minutes Yearly Meeting Friends, London* (1783) 269 This meeting directs, that the 11th query remain as it now stands. **1797** *Encycl. Brit.* XV. 737/2 At the quarterly-meeting are produced written answers from the monthly-meetings, to certain queries respecting the conduct of their members, and the meeting's care over them. **1898** *Friends' Q. Examiner* 483 For about a century it was uncertain whether the interrogations addressed to the meetings of Friends should be termed 'questions' or 'queries'. The former term was chiefly employed up to 1762, but 'queries' has held the field since 1783. **1921** R. M. JONES *Later Periods of Quakerism* I. iv. 134 At first the Queries were formal questions asked for the sake of securing information in reference to the number of members suffering under persecution. *Ibid.* 135 As fresh moral issues arose,..the list of Queries enlarged. They grew in number and in importance until they embodied almost all the essential aspects of the Quaker moral ideal, and they furnished a kind of silent confessional for each individual member, as well as a moral measuring rule to guide the Overseers in their work of looking after the flock. **1928** *Advices & Queries* (Society of Friends) 5 The Queries being directed in recent years to arouse the thought and conscience..rather than to obtain specific information. **1954** H. LOUKES *Friends face Reality* viii. 107 Quakers have performed this process of moral illumination of each other, while at the same time guarding against the danger of setting up an external moral code, by a system of 'Advices and Queries', moral and spiritual reflections couched in the form most calculated to set the individual searching his own heart.

3. A mark of interrogation (?), used to indicate a doubt as to the correctness of the statement, phrase, letter, etc. to which it is appended or refers; the abbreviation *qy.* etc. used for the same purpose. Also written out as a quasi-*adj.* or *-adv.*, preceding the word(s) to which it refers.

1836 in SMART. **1882-** in OGILVIE, etc. **1942** *Jrnl. R. Naval Med. Service* XXVIII. 21 Admitted with a diagnosis of 'query' septicæmia. **1953** R. LEHMANN *Echoing Grove* 61 'You reminded me of someone I once knew...' (Query her sister?) **1967** G. F. FIENNES *I tried to run Railway* iii. 21 It would have had to be an unwary Hun that let me get near him with my pike—design Circa 1500; origin query Birmingham Small Arms Company. **1977** J. MCCLURE *Sunday Hangman* x. 109 '*Murders*...,' snapped Colonel Muller. 'Query murders,' corrected Kramer, recognising an urgent need..to treat the situation as routinely as possible.

†**query**, *sb.*² *Obs. rare*⁻¹. [App. f. L. *querī* to complain.] ? Complaint.

13.. *E.E. Allit. P.* A. 802 As a schep to þe slaȝt þer lad was he, & as lombe..So closed he hys mouth fro vch query.

query ('kwɪərɪ), *v.* Also 7 quæry. [f. QUERY *sb.*¹ Cf. QUÆRE *v.*]

1. a. *trans.* To put as a question. ? *Obs.*

1657 *Narr. late Parlt.* in *Select. fr. Harl. Misc.* (1793) 409 The like may be queried concerning the swordsmen's capacity to sit. **1661** GLANVILL *Van. Dogm.* 188 It's queried whether there be any Science in the sense of the Dogmatists. **1726** BERKELEY *Let.* 12 Oct., in Fraser *Life* iv. (1871) 136, I do..entreat you to answer all that I have queried on that head. **1755** B. MARTIN *Mag. Arts & Sc.* 130, I..shall suspend what I have further to query 'till To-morrow.

b. With interrogative clause or direct speech as obj.: To ask, inquire, put a question (*whether*, *if*, *what*, etc.).

1657 S. PURCHAS *Theat. Pol. Flying-Ins.* 15 Some query whether a living creature can subsist without the head. **1658** SIR T. BROWNE *Pseud. Ep.* v. xxii. (ed. 3) 328 We shall not proceed to querie, What truth there is in Palmistrie. **1681** E. MURPHY *State Ireland* §40 The Deponent..queried if Captain Butler was come thither. **1756** H. WALPOLE *Lett. to Mann* 17 Oct. (1846) III. 245 Should not one query whether he had not those proofs in his hands antecedent to the cabinet? **1818** SCOTT *Hrt. Midl.* xiii, 'Shall we remove Mr. Butler?', queried the assistant. **1866** WHITTIER *Marg. Smith's Jrnl.* Pr. Wks. 1889 I. 64 On my querying whether any did find treasures hereabout, my aunt laughed. **1905** *Smart Set* Sept. 119/2 'Been here long?' I queried. **1976** B. FREEMANTLE *November Man* iii. 38 'The elections?' queried Hollis.

c. *absol.* To ask a question or questions.

1681 T. FLATMAN *Heraclitus Ridens* No. 4 (1713) I. 23 Nay, if you be for that Sport, e'en Query by your self. **1720** S. PARKER *Bibliotheca Biblica* I. 394 He queried, and reason'd thus with himself. **1728** POPE *Dunc.* II. 349 Each prompt to query, answer, and debate. **1814** BYRON *Lara* I. 1 *note*, A passenger queried as to the author.

2. To question, interrogate (a person). Now chiefly *U.S.*

1654 GAYTON *Pleas. Notes* 97 The Don..assaults the first pittifull Scout..whom he should have quæried in this manner. **1690** CHILD *Disc. Trade* (1698) 47 So I have been assured by many antient men whom I have queried particularly as to this matter. *c* **1890** A. MURDOCH *Yoshiwara Episode* in *Fr. Austr. to Japan* (1892) 49 He.. began to query her about the financial part of the business. **1943** *Sun* (Baltimore) 30 Nov. 10/7 He queries me concerning the passage. **1952** *Time* 14 Apr. 17/1 Before an issue of *Time* goes to press..a twin-bed position may be dummied, a stringer queried for a checking point. **1974** *Spartanburg* (S. Carolina) *Herald* 18 Apr. A6/2 College

Students..who were queried at Iowa State University, have some curious ideas about what 'academic freedom' means. 1977 *Daily Times* (Lagos) 11 Jan. 20/2 When these officers were queried, they felt unhappy.

3. a. To call (a thing) in question; to mark as doubtful.

1772 *Ann. Reg.* 54/2 The returning officer..had queried 76 [votes]. 1839 D'ISRAELI *Curios. Lit.* (1849) II. 224 Sir John..afterwards came to doubt it with a '*sed de hoc quære*' query this! 1961 [see EAR *sb.*[1] 5].

b. To question, doubt, *if*, etc.

1815 W. H. IRELAND *Scribbleomania* 140, I very much query if two, and sometimes three of Sonini's Alpine pictures were not condensed into one by the author.

Hence **'querying** *vbl. sb.* and *ppl. a.*; **'queryingly** *adv.*; **'queryist** = QUERIST.

1669 W. SIMPSON *Hydrol. Chym.* 107 One able physitian being asked... The querying person returned, that [etc.]. 1706 W. JONES *Synop. Palmar. Matheseos* 140 The Querying Term in the 3d. Place. 1863 *Reader* 19 Dec. 729 A queryist in the American Publishers' Circular. 1865 E. BURRITT *Walk to Land's End* 286 A pair of baby eyes, peering upward with querying wonder. 1890 *Harper's Mag.* July 272/1 The queryings of philosophy. 1890 JEAN MIDDLEMASS *Two False Moves* I. xv. 226 He looked at her queryingly.

queryster, obs. form of CHORISTER.

‖**quesadilla** (kesa'diʎa). [Sp.] A variety of turnover, usu. with a cheese filling.

1944 E. ZELAYETA *Elena's Famous Mexican & Sp. Recipes* iv. 35 Quesadilla. Tortilla Stuffed with Cheese. Take fresh tortillas..place generous piece of Monterey cream cheese.. in the center, and fold it over as you would a turnover... Cook lightly, turning often until cheese is melted. 1957 *House Beautiful* Sept. 176/4 Quesadillas. Small-size tortillas made into turnovers and filled with cheese or squash flowers or sometimes chicken *molé*. They are baked or deep-fat fried. 1963 *Sunset* Jan. 70/1 Quesadillas (Fruit and Cheese Turnovers). 1965 *House & Garden* Sept. 223/3 Quesadillas. These turnovers are made with unbaked tortillas stuffed with a variety of fillings. 1978 *Chicago* June 249/1 Start with nachos..and quesadillas (miniature tortillas filled with guacamole or thick white cheese and onions—60c).

quesal, variant of QUETZAL.

quesing, quesion, obs. ff. COUSIN, CUSHION.

quesited (kwɪ'saɪtɪd), *a.* and *sb.* [f. med.L. *quēsīt-*, L. *quæsīt-*, ppl. stem of *quærĕre* to seek + -ED[1]. Cf. QUÆSITUM.]

†**1.** *adj.* Sought for, asked about, etc. *Obs. rare.*

1647 LILLY *Chr. Astrol.* vi. 49 Significator of the Querent or thing quesited. 1674 JEAKE *Arith.* (1696) 20 The remains are the Numbers quesited.

2. *sb. Astrol.* The thing or person inquired about.

1647 LILLY *Chr. Astrol.* xx. 123 The Quesited is he or she, or the thing sought and enquired after. 1881 SHORTHOUSE *J. Inglesant* I. xv. 282 A very good argument that the querent should see the quesited speedily.

So †**quesi'titious** *a.* = QUESITED *a. Obs. rare.* **'quesitive** *a.*, interrogative. '*Quesitive quantity*, quantity expressed by an interrogative numeral' (*Cent. Dict.* 1891).

1674 JEAKE *Arith.* (1696) 334 As in Extraction of Roots and Equations, A..is called the Supposititious or Quesit[it]ious Root. 1690 LEYBOURN *Curs. Math.* 341 Multiplying the assumed Root $b + c$ in the place of the Quesititious Root *a*.

quesomen: see QUEASOM.

quest (kwɛst), *sb.*[1] Also 4 quiste, 4–6 queste, 5–6 whest, (qw-), 6 queast. [a. OF. *queste* (F. *quête*) = Prov. *questa, quista*, Sp. *cuesta*, It. *chiesta*:—pop. L. **questa*, pa. pple. of *quærĕre*, L. *quærĕre* to seek, inquire: cf. INQUEST *sb.*]

I. 1. An official or judicial inquiry. = INQUEST *sb.* 1. *Obs.* exc. *dial.* (cf. CROWNER[2]).

1303 R. BRUNNE *Handl. Synne* 5508 Þerof shal Gode take a quest. c1330 —— *Chron.* (1810) 238 Of clippers, of roungers, of suilk takes he questis. 1377 LANGL. *P. Pl.* B. xx. 161 Her syre was a sysour..ateynte at vch a queste. c1440 *Gesta Rom.* I. lxx. 387 (Addit. MS.) When the Iustice was comyn, he ordeyned a false queste. 1545 BRINKLOW *Lament.* (1874) 91 There is a custome in the Cytie, ones a yeare to haue a quest called the warnmall queste, to redresse vices. a1577 SIR T. SMITH *Commw. Eng.* (1609) 73 Enquest or quest is called this lawfull kinde of triall by twelue men. 1694 LUTTRELL *Brief Rel.* (1857) III. 417 The lord mayor and aldermen of London have forbid feasting at the quests. 1876– In dial. glossaries (Yks., Chesh., Som., etc.).

2. The body of persons appointed to hold an inquiry. = INQUEST *sb.* 2. Now *rare.*

13.. *Evang. Nicod.* 243 in *Archiv neu. Spr.* LIII. 396 He chesed a quest, on him to pas. c1440 *Jacob's Well* 257 Þou schalt..aftyrward be pourgyd out wyth a quest of clerkys. 1470–85 MALORY *Arthur* III. viii, By ordenaunce of the quene ther was set a quest of ladyes on syr gauayn. 1549 LATIMER *5th Serm. bef. Edw. VI* (Arb.) 153 The quest commes in and sayes not guilty. 1579 FULKE *Heskins' Parl.* 499 He shoulde haue twelue which make a quest, to giue verdict in this matter. 1612 T. TAYLOR *Comm. Titus* iii. 1 Which is as if a theife should be tried by a quest of cut-purses. a1661 FULLER *Worthies* (1840) II. 483 One quest of gentlemen, another of yeomen passed upon him. 1706 [see QUESTMAN 1]. a1845 HOOD *To Tom Woodgate* vi, Twelve brave mermen for a 'quest. 1884 *St. James's Gaz.* 4 Jan. 3/2 The coroner's quest pronounces 'in accordance with the evidence'.

fig. c1600 SHAKS. *Sonn.* xlvi, To side this title is impannelled A quest of thoughts, all tennant to the heart.

†**b.** *transf.* A dozen (cf. quot. 1579 above). *Obs.*

1589 *Almond for Parrat* 14 Ile haue a spare fellowe shall make mee a whole quest of faces for three farthinges.

3. Any inquiry or investigation made in order to discover some fact; also, the object of such inquiry.

1598 FLORIO *Dict.* Ep. Ded. 3, I in this search or quest of inquirie haue spent most of my studies. 1627 *Lisander & Cal.* III. 39 The quest ended with no more knowledge than it began. 1727 SWIFT *To Earl of Oxford*, In quest, who might this parson be. 1831 CARLYLE *Sart. Res.* II. viii, Let us not forget the great generality, which is our chief quest here. 1878 *Masque Poets* 101 The guest Half paused to ask in idle quest.

II. 4. Search or pursuit, made in order to find or obtain something. Const. *of, for.*

13.. *E.E. Allit. P.* B. 39 Hit arn fettled in on forme..& by quest of her quoyntyse enquylen on mede. 1526 *Pilgr. Perf.* (W. de W. 1531) 96b, Peace & brotherly concorde dissolueth this quest & assaute of enuy. 1605 SHAKS. *Lear* I. i. 196 What..Will you require in present Dower with her, Or cease your quest of Loue? 1655 H. VAUGHAN *Silex Scint.* I. *Search* (1858) 34 My Quest is vaine, Hee'll not be found where he was slaine. 1704 F. FULLER *Med. Gymn.* (1711) 138 To rouse People into a Quest of Health. 1816 BYRON *Ch. Har.* III. lxxvi, Whose desire Was to be glorious; 'twas a foolish quest. 1874 GREEN *Short Hist.* viii. §4. 491 Luckily the quest of gold proved a vain one.

b. Freq. in phr. ***in quest of*** (†***after***, or inf.).

1575 CHURCHYARD *Chippes* (1817) 24 In quest of solace, he retired to Bath. c1600 SHAKS. *Sonn.* cxxix, Had, hauing, and in quest to haue. 1663 BUTLER *Hud.* I. iii. 233 He went in quest of Hudibras. 1705 HEARNE *Collect.* 6 Oct. (O.H.S.) I. 52 He is in quest after other Pieces. 1820 W. IRVING *Sketch Bk.* II. 349 The ghost rides forth to the scene of battle in nightly quest of his head. 1862 GOULBURN *Pers. Relig.* IV. i. (1873) 256 Eager running to and fro in quest of worldly wealth.

†**c.** A person (or set of persons) employed in searching. *Obs. rare*[−1].

1604 SHAKS. *Oth.* I. ii. 46 The Senate hath sent about three seuerall Quests, To search you out.

5. In mediæval romance: An expedition or adventure undertaken by a knight to procure some thing or achieve some exploit; the knights engaged in such an enterprise. Also *transf.*

c1384 CHAUCER *H. Fame* III. 648 They that have do noble jestes And acheved all hir questes. c1450 *Merlin* 503 Thei entered in to many questes forto knowe which was the beste knyght. 1470–85 MALORY *Arthur* XVI. xii, They supposed he was one of the quest of the Sancgreal. 1590 SPENSER *F.Q.* III. viii. 53 Her well beseemes that Quest. 1813 SCOTT *Triermain* I. xi, Rather he chose, that Monarch bold, On vent'rous quest to ride. 1850 KINGSLEY *Alt. Locke* xl, You are my servant now, by the laws of chivalry, and you must fulfil my quest. 1876 GREEN *Stray Stud.* 262 The Quest of Æneas is no self-sought quest.

6. a. The search for game made by hounds. **b.** The baying of hounds in pursuit of game; a peculiar barking uttered by dogs when in sight of game. *Obs.* exc. *dial.*

13.. *Gaw. & Gr. Knt.* 1150 At þe fyrst quethe of þe quest quaked þe wylde. c1420 *Anturs of Arth.* 49 Withe gret questes and quelles Bothe in frethes and felles. 1513 DOUGLAS *Æneis* V. v. 26 For hundis quest it semyt the lift rife wald. 1589 R. ROBINSON *Gold. Mirr.* (Chetham Soc.) 12 Thus as I stood to heare this merry quest I heard the names of houndes that hunted best. 1649 G. DANIEL *Trinarch., Hen. IV*, lxxiv, 'Twas soe resolu'd; vpon the doubtfull Quest The Game gets to safe Covert. 1688 HOLME *Armoury* III. 188/2 Quest,..the first opening, or cry, of the Dogs when they have found the scent. 1876 SWINBURNE *Erechtheus* 1306 Lo, night is arisen on the noon, and her hounds are in quest by day. 1878 *Cumbld. Gloss.*, *Quest*, the early morning search for a hare by the scent of the hounds. 1886 ELWORTHY *W. Somerset Word-bk.* s.v., He don't never give no quest 'thout he's right 'pon it.

transf. 13.. *S. Erkenwolde* 133 in Horstmann *Altengl. Leg.* (1881) 269 Þe masse he begynnes..With queme questis of þe quere with ful quaynt notes. a1633 G. HERBERT *Temple, Content* ii, Gad not abroad at ev'ry quest and call Of an untrained hope or passion.

7. *R.C.Ch.* The collection of alms or donations for religious purposes.

1528 ROY *Rede me* (Arb.) 76 The observauntis no people do spare, Makynge their quest every wheare With most importunate cravynge. 1691 tr. *D'Emilliane's Frauds Romish Monks* 262 The Farmer [of Purgatory money] sends some of his Emissaries into the Fields, to carry on the Quest there for the said Souls. 1748 *Earthquake Peru* i. 85 If we consider the extraordinary Product of the Quest [of the Franciscans]. 1873 BROWNING *Red Cott. Nt.-cap* 971 When Marquise jokes 'My quest, forsooth? Each doit I scrape together goes for Peter-pence.'

8. *Comb.*, as †**quest-ale**, prob. ale of special quality (cf. *audit-ale*); †**quest-diter, -ganger**, = QUEST-MONGER. Also QUEST-HOUSE, -MAN.

c1460 *Towneley Myst.* xxii. 24 All fals endytars, Quest-gangars, and Iurars,..Ar welcome to me. *Ibid.* xxx. 185 Thise rolles Ar of bakbytars And fals quest-dytars. a1704 T. BROWN *Pleas. Epistle* Wks. 1730 I. 110 Private deliberations over brawn and quest-ale.

†**quest**, *sb.*[2] *Obs.* [Related to QUETHE *v.*, as *bequest* (q.v.) to *bequeath*.] A bequest.

c1300 *Havelok* 219 He made his quiste swithe wel. c1400 *Gamelyn* 64, I byseke yow..For Gamelynes love, that my queste stonde. 1418 *E.E. Wills* (1882) 35 After my dettis payde and my questes fulfilled. 1478 *Croscombe Church-w. Acc.* (Som. Rec. Soc.) 8 And bryngs in of the quest of Water Bigge xij*d.*

So †**questword**. *Obs. rare*[−1].

1792 *Archaeologia* X. 197 The legacies or questword of the deceased supplied the rest.

quest (kwɛst), *v.*[1] [a. OF. *quester* (F. *quêter*), f. *queste* QUEST *sb.*[1]]

1. a. *intr.* Of hunting dogs, etc.: To search for game. Also with *about.*

c1350 *Ipomadon* (Kölbing) 619 A brachet of thee beste, That euer wold trewly queste And securly pursewe. c1420 *Anturs of Arth.* 49 Þay questede and quellys By frythis and fellis. 1523 SKELTON *Garl. Laurell* 1409 The howndes began to yerne and to quest. 1607 TOPSELL *Four-f. Beasts* (1658) 133 Such [Dogs] as delight on the land, play their parts, either by swiftness of foot, or by often questing, to search out and to spring the bird. a1680 BUTLER *Rem.* (1759) II. 88 If they prosper they..give the Jackal some small Snip for his Pains in questing. 1826 SCOTT *Woodst.* xxxi, Bevis, questing about, found the body. 1954 J. I. LLOYD *Beagling* 142 *Quest*, draw for a hare. 1969 M. PUGH *Last Place Left* x. 60 We heard the shot then saw the spaniel questing. 1976 *Shooting Times & Country Mag.* 16–22 Dec. 25/2 Two short toots on the horn..had hounds questing among the tufts of coarse grass and gorse bushes.

fig. 1590 SOUTHWELL *M. Magd. Funerall Teares* 113 Why doth thy sorrow quest so much upon the place where he is? 1668 DRYDEN *Even.'s Love* II. i, Cast about quickly,.. Range, quest, and spring a lie immediately.

b. Of animals: To search *about* for food.

1796 PEGGE *Anonym.* (1809) 137 It would be natural for them [the whales] to quest about for that jelly they live upon. 1879 JEFFERIES *Amateur Poacher* xii. 236 There was the pheasant not fifteen yards away, quietly questing about.

2. a. Of hunting dogs: To break out into a peculiar bark at the sight of game; to give tongue; to bark or yelp. *Obs.* exc. *dial.*

c1420 in *Rel. Ant.* II. 7 Kenettes questede to quelle, Al so breme so any belle. 1470–85 MALORY *Arthur* IX. xxi, This lytel brachet..lepte vpon hym and..whyned and quested. 1577 STANYHURST *Descr. Irel.* in *Holinshed* VI. 41 The hunter may perceive the beast resting on the one banke, the dogs questing on the other brim. 1616 SURFL. & MARKH. *Country Farme* 681 You shall then take care, that not at any time,..he dare to quest or open his mouth, but that he hunt so silent and mute as is possible. 1681 OTWAY *Soldier's Fort.* IV. (1735) 84 Lie still, you knave, close, close,..you had best quest, and spoil the Sport, you had. 1831 MISS MITFORD in L'Estrange *Life* (1870) II. xiv. 328 Just before the coursing season began, he [a dog] began to dream of going out and 'quested' in his sleep. 1886 in ELWORTHY *W. Somerset Word-bk.*

†**b.** *transf.* Of frogs: To croak. *Obs. rare*[−1].

1607 TOPSELL *Serpents* (1658) 725, I mean the little Frog questing hoarse voyce amain.

3. a. Of persons: To go about in search of something; to search or seek. Also with *about*, and constr. *after, for.* (Chiefly *transf.* from sense 1.)

1624 HEYWOOD *Captives* I. i. in Bullen *O. Pl.* IV, This too yeares I have quested to his howse. 1686 F. SPENCE tr. *Varilla's Ho. Medicis* 281 This young Lord had won the prize of a Turnament, and lay questing after a panegyrick. 1701 COLLIER *M. Aurel.* (1726) 89 They went questing with flambeaux. 1864 MISS YONGE *Trial* I. v. 91 One of the bridal pairs..was seen questing about as if disposed to invade our premises. 1882 STEVENSON *Mem. & Portraits* xxi. (1887) 288 Neither Mr. James nor the author..has ever gone questing after gold.

b. *R. C. Ch.* To ask for alms or donations.

1748 *Earthquake Peru* iii. 303 If the Friars go into the Country, a questing for their Monastery. 1867 R. PALMER *Life Philip Howard* 104 There were not to be more than thirteen religious, who were never to quest or beg alms.

4. *trans.* **a.** To search for, pursue, seek *out.*

1751 BYROM *Enthusiasm* in *Poems* 1773 II. 34 Averse to Heav'n,..They quest Annihilation's monst'rous Theme. 1842 MISS MITFORD in *Friendsh. Miss Mitford* (1882) II. v. 77 Flush found a hare, and quested it for two miles. 1855 SINGLETON *Virgil* I. 164 In noontide heats Quest out a shady dell. 1882 SIR E. ARNOLD *Pearls of Faith* xxviii. (1883) 99 A wild bee questing honey-buds.

b. To question, request, demand. *rare.*

1897 F. THOMPSON *New Poems* 35, [I] quested its secret of the sun.

†**quest**, *v.*[2] *Obs. rare.* [? cf. LG. *questen*, var. *quessen, quetsen* (G. *quetschen*, Du. *kwetsen*) to press, squeeze.] *trans.* To crush.

1647 HARVEY *Schola Cordis* xv. 8 If Thy presse stand, Mine heart may chance slip out. O quest it into nothing. 1674–91 RAY *N.C. Words* s.v., Pies are said to be quested, whose sides have been crushed by each other.

quest, variant of QUEEST, ring-dove.

questane, obs. form of WHETSTONE.

†**'questant.** *Obs. rare*[−1]. = QUESTER.

1601 SHAKS. *All's Well* II. i. 16 You come Not to wooe honour, but to wed it, when The bravest questant shrinkes.

quest-dove: see QUEEST.

quester ('kwɛstə(r)). [f. QUEST *v.*[1] + -ER[1].] One who quests, in senses of the vb.

a1550 *Image Hypocr.* iv. in *Skelton's Wks.* (1843) II. 440 Redy regesters, Pardoners and questers. 1707 J. STEVENS tr. *Quevedo's Com. Wks.* (1709) 208 The wicked Quester tuck'd up his..Robe. 1718 ROWE tr. *Lucan* IV. (R.), The quester.. to the wood they loose, Who silently the tainted track pursues. 1875 DOWDEN *Shakspere* 10 It is the ascetic quester, Galahad..who beholds the mystical Grail.

questeroun, variant of CUSTRON. *Obs.*

'questful, *a. rare*[−1]. [f. QUEST *sb.*[1] + -FUL.] Full of questing or searching.

1869 LOWELL *Invita Minerva* 246 The summer day he spent in questful round.

†**quest-house.** *Obs.* The house at which the inquests in a ward or parish were commonly held.

1571 *Acc. St. Giles, Cripplegate* in *MS. Addit.* 12222 [cited by Halliwell, s.v.]. 1607 DEKKER & WEBSTER *Northw. Hoe* I. D.'s Wks. 1873 III. 12 Are all the Quest-houses broken vp? 1668 PEPYS *Diary* 24 Jan., At the Quest House, where the company meets to the burial of my cozen Joyce. 1696 *Lond. Gaz.* No. 3239/4 At the Quest-house on Little-Tower-Hill is a Grammar-School. 1828 NARES *Let. to A. Dyce*, A Quest-house was the chief Watch-house in a parish. .. Some parishes in London still have them, e.g. St. Giles's Cripplegate.

fig. 1635 QUARLES *Embl.* 102 It is a world, whose Work.. Is vanity, and vexation;..A Quest-house of complaint.

attrib. 1628 SPELMAN *De Sepult.* (1641) 22 A Parish Audit, or a Quest-House dinner.

questing ('kwɛstɪŋ), *vbl. sb.* [f. QUEST *v.*[1] + -ING[1].] The action of the vb. in various senses.

1470–85 MALORY *Arthur* I. xix, The noyse was..lyke vnto the questyng of xxx coupyl houndes. 1540–1 ELYOT *Image Gov.* Pref. (1556) 10 After two or three questynges, he lept to the great Olyphante. 1603 FLORIO *Montaigne* II. xi. (1632) 238 A long questing and beating for some game. 1700 JER. COLLIER *2nd Def. Short View* 118 All this Questing has sprung but very little Game. 1824 MISS MITFORD *Village* Ser. I. (1863) 109 Nothing is more certain than Dash's questing,..for a better spaniel never went into the field. 1839 BAILEY *Festus* vi. (1848) 63 Must thou still Revel in bootless questings? 1923 M. SADLEIR *Desolate Splendour* iv. 72 From externals only need the weary questing of a stranger mind seek teaching or enlightenment.

questing ('kwɛstɪŋ), *ppl. a.* [f. as prec. + -ING[2].] That quests, in senses of the vb.

1513 DOUGLAS *Æneis* XIII. iii. 25 Than the remanent of that questing sort,..Wythdrawis. c1600 DRAYTON *Miseries Q. Margaret* cxlvi, When they heare the questing Spaniels gone. 1714 *Earthquake Peru* i. 80 Even the Questing-brothers presume to interrupt People at their Prayers. 1810 SCOTT *Lady of L.* III. xiii, Thread the brake like questing hound. 1888 P. FITZGERALD *Fatal Zero* xxvii. 168 That questing, roving eye..that looks out of the corners sharply.

'**questingly**, *adv.* [-LY[2].] In a questing manner.

1926 R. CLEMENTS *Stately Southerner* 89, I..looked questingly right and left.

question ('kwɛstjən), *sb.* Also 4 questiun, 4–6 -oun, questyon, (4 qw-, 5 -one, -oun), 5 whestion. [a. AF. *questiun*, OF. *question* (Godef.), ad. L. *quæstiōn-em*, n. of action from *quærĕre* to ask, inquire: cf. QUÆRE, QUERY.]

I. The action of inquiring or asking.

1. a. The stating or investigation of a problem; inquiry into a matter; discussion of some doubtful point. †*to make question*, to raise discussion or talk, to express or entertain doubt (*whether*, *of*, *about*). *Obs.*

1375 BARBOUR *Bruce* I. 249 Than mayss clerkis questioun ..Quhethir he his lordis neid suld let. c1386 CHAUCER *Knt.'s T.* 1656 Peples..holdynge hir question Dyuynynge of thise Thebane knyghtes two. 1447 BOKENHAM *Seyntys* (Roxb.) 2 If be what or why Be questyoun maad of thys tretyhs [etc.]. 1523 LD. BERNERS *Froiss.* I. 592 Qvestyon was made therof before the marshalles. 1599 SHAKS. *Hen. V*, I. i. 5 The..vnquiet time Did push it out of farther question. 1638 R. BAKER tr. *Balzac's Lett.* II. 102 Let us..never make question whether we ought to call them infirmities of age, or fruits of reason. 1778 F. BURNEY *Evelina* xxxiv, As to consulting you..it was out of all question. 1824 J. MARSHALL *Const. Opin.* (1839) 311 We cannot perceive how the occupation of these vessels can be drawn into question. 1886 RUSKIN *Præterita* I. vi. 185 [My father] allowed it without question.

b. In adverbial phrases, as ***beyond*** (***all***) ***question***, ***out of***, ***past***, ***without question***: Unquestionably.

1586 T. B. *La Primaud. Fr. Acad.* 189 Out of question we will judge those men verie blinde. 1601 SHAKS. *Twel. N.* I. iii. 104 *And.* Why, would that haue mended my haire? *To.* Past question. 1680–90 TEMPLE *Ess., Heroic Virtue* Wks. 1731 I. 212 He was without Question, a Great and Heroick Genius. 1756 BURKE *Vind. Nat. Soc.* Wks. 1842 I. 5 In the state of nature, without question, mankind was subjected to many and great inconveniences. 1818 JAS. MILL *Brit. India* II. v. viii. 684 He is beyond all question the most eminent of the chief rulers. 1880 L. STEPHEN *Pope* v. 118 The Dunciad ..is beyond all question full of coarse abuse.

c. †***in question***, in dispute, in controversy; in a doubtful or undecided state. *Obs.* So also with ***into*** and ***in*** = into; chiefly, and now only, in phr. ***to call in question***: see CALL *v.* 18.

1390 in *Rec. Coldingham Priory* (Surtees) 65 That yhour richte be na mare putt in questioun. 1494 FABYAN *Chron.* (1533) VII. ccxxxii. 158 b, A longe whyle thys fyghte stode in questyon, whyther partye shulde obteyne vyctorye. 1513 MORE in Grafton *Chron.* (1568) II. 769 If it fortune the Crowne to come in question. 1529 —— *Dyaloge* I. Wks. 123/2 The thynge standinge in debate and question. 1565 JEWEL *Def. Apol.* (1611) 324 How could these so doubtfull matters euer haue fallen in question amongst your fellowes. 1620 J. WILKINSON *Coroners & Sherifes* 13 It hath beene in question and ambiguity. 1683 DRYDEN *Life Plutarch* in *P.'s Lives* (1700) I. 18 The Pyrrhonians..who bring all certainty in Question. 1720 WATERLAND *Eight Serm.* 138 Which is supposing the Thing in Question. 1768 T. POWNALL *Admin. Brit. Col.* (1774) I. 5 A right to call into question some..exertions of power.

d. ***in question***, under consideration, forming the subject of discourse. ***to come into question***, to be thought of as possible.

1611 SHAKS. *Cymb.* I. i. 34 His Father..had (besides the Gentleman in question) Two other Sonnes. 1653 DOROTHY OSBORNE *Lett. to Sir W. Temple* (1888) 100 After dinner we sit and talk till Mr. B. comes in question, and then I am gone. 1775 SHERIDAN *Rivals* II. i, He does not think his friend..ever saw the lady in question. 1831 MACKINTOSH *Hist. Eng.* II. 96 The very ill-fated man in question was John de la Pole. 1874 STUBBS *Const. Hist.* I. i. 7 The succession of masters was too rapid to allow a change of language to come into question among the greater..part of the people. 1893 TRAILL *Soc. Eng.* Introd. p. xxxvi, Discoveries of a far-reaching..character, have during the period in question been made.

2. a. The action of questioning, interrogating, or examining a person, or the fact of being questioned, etc.; †hence, talk, discourse.

1390 GOWER *Conf.* I. 1013 Ferst he let the Prestes take,.. He put hem into questioun. 1456 SIR G. HAYE *Law Arms* (S.T.S.) 185 He aw nocht to be stoppit, bot frely to have passage throu all realmes but questioun. 1596 SHAKS. *Merch. V.* IV. i. 346 Ile stay no longer question. 1605 —— *Macb.* III. iv. 118 *Ross.* What sights, my Lord? *La.* I pray you speake not..Question enrages him. 1690 LOCKE *Govt.* II. ii. §13 One Man..may do..whatever he pleases, without the least question or controll. 1849 M. ARNOLD *Sonnets, Shaksp.*, Others abide our question. Thou art free. 1869 TENNYSON *Coming Arthur* 311 Fixing full eyes of question on her face.

b. *spec.* The application of torture as part of a judicial examination.

1583 *Exec. for Treason* (1675) 12 No one was called to any capital or bloody question upon matters of Religion. 1651 EVELYN *Mem.* (1857) I. 275 A malefactor was to have the question, or torture, given to him. 1689 BURNET *Tracts* I. 80 The common Question that they give..is, that they tye the Hands of the suspected Person behind his back [etc.]. 1761 HUME *Hist. Eng.* III. li. 110 He urged too, that Felton should be put to the question in order to extort from him a discovery of his accomplices. 1871 H. AINSWORTH *Tower Hill* III. xix, Let him be submitted to the question, ordinary and extraordinary.

†**c.** ***in question***: Under judicial examination; on trial. *Obs. rare.*

1589 HORSEY *Trav.* (Hakluyt Soc.) App. 330 John Chapele..was..ymprisoned almost a yeare, in question to have bene executed. 1597 SHAKS. *2 Hen. IV*, I. ii. 68 He that was in question for the robbery.

d. ***to call in*** (†***or into***) ***question***: To examine judicially, bring to trial; to take to task, call to account.

1611 BIBLE *Acts* xix. 40 We are in danger to be called in question for this dayes vprore. a1641 BP. MOUNTAGU *Acts & Mon.* (1642) 59 Socrates..was called into question, and had sentence of death pronounced against him. 1647 J. CARTER *Nail & Wheel* 78 Presently he was..called in question as a delinquent.

II. What is asked or inquired (about).

3. a. The interrogative statement of some point to be investigated or discussed; a problem; hence, a matter forming, or capable of forming, the basis of a problem; a subject involving more or less difficulty or uncertainty. ***the question***: the precise matter receiving or requiring deliberation or discussion. ***to beg the question***: see BEG *v.* 6.

a1300 *Cursor M.* 26104 þar-wit-al sum questiones we sal vndo þe merk resons. 1387 TREVISA *Higden* (Rolls) I. 15 Wel nyh al problemys and questiouns of the wiseste men. 1467 in Rymer *Foedera* (1710) XI. 579 If..any Difficultie or Question in the Lawe happen to ryse. c1510 MORE *Picus* Wks. 3/2 Some good simple folk, that should of zele to the faith..impugne those questions, as new thinges. 1598 SHAKS. *Merry W.* I. i. 227 But that is not the question: the question is concerning your marriage. 1663 BUTLER *Hud.* I. ii. 465 It was a Question, whether he Or's Horse were of a Family More worshipful. 1768 T. POWNALL *Admin. Brit. Col.* (1774) I. 7 This American question..must now come forward. 1854 KINGSLEY *Lett.* (1878) I. 416 This is a question involving the lives of thousands and tens of thousands of human beings. 1879 MCCARTHY *Own Time* II. xxv. 219 The Eastern Question it was that disturbed the dream of peace.

b. *spec.* A subject for discussion, a proposal to be debated or voted on, in a meeting or deliberative assembly, esp. in Parliament; †the putting of this proposal to the vote. From the 18th cent., *spec.* a question put in Parliament by a Member to the Government or to a Minister. ***question!***, used (*a*) to recall a speaker to the subject under discussion, †(*b*) to demand that the vote be taken (quot. 1817). ***previous question***: see PREVIOUS.

1549 *House of Commons Jrnl.* 28 Mar. 21/1 In the Question, it is agreed, That the Number, which said No to the Bill, be the greater Number by One Person. 1559 *Ibid.* 17 Apr. 60/1 Carnesew declared to the House, that Thrower, Servant to the Master of the Rolls, did say against the State of the House, that if a Bill were brought in for Womens Wyers in their Pastes, they would dispute it, and go to the Question. 1614 *Ibid.* 13 Apr. 464/1 Mr. Hackwill:—That nothing to pass, by Order of the House, without a Question; and that no Order, without a Question Affirmative and Negative: And that ordered to be, upon the Question. 1658–9 *Burton's Diary* (1828) IV. 37 The persons concerned must withdraw when any question is. 1678 MARVELL *Growth Popery* 24 Whereupon the greater number called for the Question, and had it in the Affirmative, that the Debate should be laid aside. 1778 *Parl. Reg.* 16 Dec. 181 Lord Newhaven put a variety of questions to the gentlemen belonging to the board of ordnance. 1791 *Debate Abolit. Slave-Trade* 119 A loud cry [being] kept up a considerable time for the question. 1817 *Hansard's Parl. Debates* XXXV. 758/2 Lord Cochrane rose, amidst reiterated cries of question, to state [etc.]. 1844 T. E. MAY *Treat. Law, Privileges, Proceedings & Usage of Parl.* viii. 166 Any member may propose a question, which is called 'moving the house', or, more commonly, 'making a motion'. *Ibid.* 171 In the commons, when the motion has been seconded, it merges in the question, which is then proposed by the speaker to the house, and read by him. 1863 H. COX *Instit.* I. ix. 139 The Speaker,..when it has been seconded, proposes it to the House, and then the House are said to be in possession of the question. *Ibid.* 140 If it be wished to avoid a question, it is usual to move that the chairman do leave the chair. 1908 A. E. STEINTHAL tr. *Redlich's Procedures House of Commons* II. VII. vi. 241 Requests for information, 'Questions' are regularly addressed by members of the House to the Government, and at times to the Speaker or to private members. 1929 G. F. M. CAMPION *Introd. Procedures House of Commons* iv. 124 Oral Questions are by far the most numerous. To them is allotted the whole of 'Question time' proper, *i.e.* from not later than three o'clock to not later than a quarter to four. 1956 P. HOWARTH *Questions in House* i. 17 Apart from the procedural reasons, there were also reasons of a political or a constitutional nature why the custom of asking parliamentary questions developed slowly. 1958 S. HYLAND *Who goes Hang?* xvi. 72 As the only office-holder present, he knew about the Colonial Secretary's statement due at the end of Questions. 1971 P. D. G. THOMAS *House of Commons in 18th Cent.* ii. 30 The eighteenth century saw the evolution of the Parliamentary question. *Ibid.* 32 Questions in the House proper may well have been established practice long before the first instance found of a question put to and answered by a minister. 1976 *Ann. Rep., Howard League for Penal Reform 1975/76* 6 On the Bail Bill..the two organizations suggested a number of amendments... We are grateful to several MP's ..who asked Questions, some at our suggestion.

c. Const. *of* (the subject-matter or sphere). Now freq. in phr. ***it is a question of*** = what is required or involved is, etc.

1382 WYCLIF *Acts* xviii. 15 If questiouns ben of the word, and names of the lawe. 1526 TINDALE *Acts* xviii. 15 Yf it be a question off wordes or off names or of youre lawe. 1812 H. & J. SMITH *Rej. Addr., Living Lustres* ii, The question of Houses I leave to the jury. 1836 J. GILBERT *Chr. Atonem.* ix. (1852) 275 The recovery of transgressors is not a question of mere power. 1867 FREEMAN *Norm. Conq.* (1876) I. iv. 223 It was a question of time.

d. Phr. ***out of the question***, foreign to the subject; hence, not to be considered or thought of.

1700 COLLIER *2nd Def. Short View* 122 His Objection..is out of the Question. 1815 B'NESS BUNSEN in Hare *Life* (1879) I. iii. 88 To go on describing the different effects..is out of the question. 1878 BOSW. SMITH *Carthage* 210 The third alternative was no longer open..for retreat was out of the question. 1930 G. B. SHAW *Apple Cart* I. 17 You cant. You mustnt. Of course not. Out of the question. 1977 A. ECCLESTONE *Staircase for Silence* iv. 76 Anything like an attempt to impose a parochial structure, new or old, was out of the question.

4. A subject of discussion, debate, or strife *between* parties, or of one party *with* another.

OF. *question* occurs freq. in the sense of 'difference', 'dispute', 'quarrel'.

1382 WYCLIF *John* iii. 25 A questioun is maad of Johnis disciplis with the Jewis, of the purificacioun. 1390 GOWER *Conf.* VII. 4148 A question betwen the tuo Thus writen in a bok I fond. 1456 SIR G. HAY *Law Arms* (S.T.S.) 115 It efferis to the constable to here all questiounis, querelis and complayntis of his menȝe. 1484 CAXTON *Fables of Æsop* v. x, Telle me your resons and caas..that the better I may gyue the sentence of your dyferent and question. 1533 BELLENDEN *Livy* III. xxv, þe samyn place & land, of quhilk now þe questioun occurris [*cf. infra* for quhilk þe debate occurris]. 1606 SHAKS. *Tr. & Cr.* II. ii. 18 Since the first sworde was drawne about this question. 1818 CRUISE *Digest* (ed. 2) VI. 249 A question arose between the heir at law and the younger children, whether it passed by the will.

5. a. In negative expressions. ***it is no*** (or ***not a***) ***question***, ***there is no question***, †or simply ***no question***: There is no room for dispute or doubt (*but*, *that*). ***to make no question***: To raise or entertain no doubt (*of* or *about* a thing, *but* or inf.).

1583 W. FULKE *Def. Tr. Script.* Pref. 5 We make no question but that it is Apostolical. 1593 SHAKS. *2 Hen. VI*, IV. ii. 61, I am able to endure much. No question of that. 1596 —— *Merch. V.* I. i. 184, I no question make To haue it. 1605 VERSTEGAN *Dec. Intell.* ii. (1628) 25 That our Saxon ancestors came out of Germanie..is no question. 1625 BURGES *Pers. Tithes* 2 My Purpose is not here to fall vpon that Question, (for I make no Question of it) Whether [etc.]. 1711 ADDISON *Spect.* No. 59 ¶3, I make no Question but it would have been looked upon as one of the most valuable Treasuries of the Greek Tongue. 1815 JANE AUSTEN *Emma* I. ix, I cannot make a question..about that; it is a certainty. 1845 MCCULLOCH *Taxation* Introd. (1852) 21/2 It is no longer a question that the disgust occasioned by this inequality..mainly contributed to throw France into a flame.

†**b.** ***no question*** (used parenthetically): No doubt, without question. *Obs.*

1594 O. B. *Quest. Profit. Concern.* 27 We haue set at naught..the poore..whose accusations, no question, are gone vp into heauen. 1621 BP. MOUNTAGU *Diatribæ* 273 Alluding, no question, vnto that of the Psalme. a1674 CLARENDON *Surv. Leviath.* (1676) 260 This no question is his meaning. 1722 DE FOE *Plague* (1884) 125 There were, no Question, Accounts kept of their Charity.

c. ***no questions asked***: with no need to give an account of oneself or one's conduct.

1948 M. LASKI *Tory Heaven* ix. 121 Under the old system, I could have had the pair of them and no questions asked. 1962 WODEHOUSE *Service with Smile* x. 160 Give him a skipper and a little daughter..and he could have made straight for the reef of Norman's Woe, and no questions asked. 1968 *Listener* 4 July 30/2 They can..sign a contract with a sports or tobacco firm and will then be..able to play lawn tennis for profit 365 days in the year—and no questions asked.

6. a. A sentence of interrogative form, addressed by one person to another in order to elicit information; an interrogation, query, inquiry. ***a good question***: see GOOD *a.* 14 c.

a **1300** *Cursor M.* 22891 (Cott.) An crafti clerc.. asked him a questiun of a wolf and a leon. **1340** HAMPOLE *Pr. Consc.* 8288 Now may þou ask me.. A questyon, and say.. Salle þai [etc.]? *a* **1400–50** *Alexander* 1110 Inquire me noght þis question, I queth it þe neuer. *c* **1485** *Digby Myst.* IV. 1311 Ye askit hym.. a whestion. *c* **1580** SIDNEY *Ps.* XLII. ii, Their daily questions.. Where is now thy God soe good? **1665** BOYLE *Occas. Refl.* IV. xvii, Before we could answer that Question, we must ask one of him, which was, what he had been doing. **1773** GOLDSM. *Stoops to Conq.* III. 111 Ask me no questions and I'll tell you no fibs. **1776** *Trial of Nundocomar* 73/2 If you do not give a plain answer to a plain question, you will be committed. **1869** *Q. Rev.* July 211 Go and put that question to the great armies of Austria.

†**b.** ***questions and commands***, the name of a game in which one person addressed ludicrous questions and commands to each member of the company. *Obs.*

1673 WYCHERLEY *Gentl. Dancing-Master* II. ii, He is as dull as a country-squire at questions and commands. **1709** STEELE *Tatler* No. 144 ¶1 Just as one is chosen King at the game of Questions and Commands. **1731** FIELDING *Grub St. Opera* III. vii, Unless when we have [kissed] at questions and commands.

c. *Sc.* in *pl.* The catechism (cf. *question-book* in 7). Also *transf.*

1795 BURNS *Election* v, The billie is gettin' his questions, To say in St. Stephen's the morn. **1893** STEVENSON *Catriona* 31, I judged.. he would think the better of me if I knew the questions.

d. In various proverbial phrases and expressions, as ***ask me no questions and I'll tell you no lies*** and varr.; ***a civil question deserves a civil answer*** and varr. Also ***ask a silly question and you get a silly answer***: see SILLY *a.*

1773 GOLDSMITH *She stoops to Conq.* III. 51 Ask me no questions and I'll tell you no fibs. **1818** SCOTT *Ht. Midl.* I. ix. 247 If ye'll ask nae questions, I'll tell ye nae lees. **1844** T. C. HALIBURTON *Attaché* 2nd Ser. II. iv. 62 Let me give you a piece of advice;—Ax me no questions, and I'll tell you no lies. **1853** —— *Sam Slick's Wise Saws* II. ii. 48 Give a civil answer to a civil question. **1858** S. A. HAMMETT *Piney Woods Tavern* xxvii. 285 The Squire there asked me a civil question, and that desarves a civil answer,—at least that's manners where I come from. **1900** H. LAWSON *Over Sliprails* 135 'Where did you buy the steer, father?' she asked. 'Ask no questions and hear no lies.' **1955** W. C. MACDONALD *Destination Danger* xii. 140 Quist smiled. 'Ask me no questions, I'll tell you no lies.' **1970** V. CANNING *Great Affair* xii. 221 'What has happened to Sarah?'.. 'Ask no questions hear no lies.'

III. 7. *attrib.* and *Comb.* **a.** attrib., as ***question-box, -hour***; **b.** objective and objective gen., as ***question-answerer, -answering, -asking, -beggar, -begging*** (see BEG *v.* 6), ***-putting, raising***, sbs. or adjs.; **c.** phrasal: see QUESTION AND ANSWER; **d. question-book** *Sc.*, a catechism (formerly often containing also the alphabet or a spelling-book); **question-master**, the chairman of a discussion panel (PANEL *sb.*[1] 5 b), by whom the questions are put; **question pitch**, the rising intonation of an interrogative sentence; †**question-sick**, having a mania for questioning; **question-stop**, = QUESTION MARK; **question time**; *spec.* a time set apart in Parliament for Members to question Ministers; †**question-wise** *adv.*, as a question; **question word**, an interrogative pronoun, etc., used to introduce a question.

1900 *Westm. Gaz.* 20 Jan. 9/2 (Advt.), It is also a great question-answerer, or work of reference. **1972** *Computers & Humanities* VII. 9 Simmons is particularly good in describing the extensive progress made in second-generation question-answering systems. **1977** *Dædalus* Fall 123 The various attempts to process natural language by machine—analysis and synthesis of speech, automatic translation, question-answering,.. and the like. **1884** E. YATES *Recoll.* (ed. Tauchn.) II. vii. 259 Much is said of.. their constant question-asking. **1938** *Ann. Reg. 1937* CLXXIX. 303 To the same medley of generations in England belong Mr. Richard Aldington's *The Crystal World*.. and Mr. W. H. Auden's question-asking *Spain*. **1972** *Jrnl. Social Psychol.* LXXXVII. 9 English praise delivered to small groups of these children by a familiar Anglo adult exerted some degree of reinforcing effects on their question-asking behavior. **1935** A. P. HERBERT *What a Word!* viii. 229 The chief kind is the Question-beggar, the epithet or phrase which assumes or imputes that the question under discussion has been conclusively answered already. **1824** J. BENTHAM *Book of Fallacies* IV. i. 213 (*heading*) Fallacies of Confusion, the object of which is, to perplex, when Discussion can no longer be avoided... Question-begging appellatives. *c* **1860** WHATELY *Comm-pl. Bk.* (1864) 263 What Jeremy Bentham calls 'question-begging appellatives'. **1863** GEO. ELIOT *Romola* III. xiii. 130 There was no argument more widely convincing than question-begging phrases in large type. **1910** A. SIDGWICK *Application of Logic* vii. 217 Question-begging in the extended sense.. occurs just so far as any attempt is made on the part of either disputant to prevent question-*raising*. **1911** H. G. WELLS *New Machiavelli* I. iv. 113, I scoffed at that pompous question-begging word 'Evolution'. **1957** *Times Lit. Suppl.* 27 Dec. 782/2 He is not above question-begging in the most ingenuous way. **1979** C. MOULE in M. Goulder *Incarnation & Myth* v. 138 Evidence of this kind in no way depends.. upon question-begging theories of scriptural authority. *c* **1700** in Wodrow's *Hist. Ch. Scot.* (1828) II. 54 Having a mind to learn to read, I bought a Question Book. **1946** L. MACNEICE *Dark Tower* (1947) 165 Listeners will have the privilege of hearing a number of experts on Truth, all of them equally infallible; our question-master is the March Hare. **1952** *Gloucestershire Echo* 3 Oct. 6/2 It has become traditional for the Festival to end.. with a Brains Trust. With Gilbert Harding as question-master and.. a varied team. **1977** 'E. CRISPIN' *Glimpses of Moon* ii. 36 The bright, uncommitted fashion of a television question-master.. in a quiz. **1933** L. BLOOMFIELD in Saporta & Bastian *Psycholinguistics* (1961) 244/2 *Yeah?* and *Is that so?* with a peculiar modification of the question-pitch, have been used as facetious vulgarisms expressing disbelief. **1964** C. C. FRIES in D. Abercrombie et al. *Daniel Jones* 244 Formal yes-or-no questions, along with question-pitch. **1884** E. W. HAMILTON *Diary* 30 July (1972) II. 663 My main points are:.. 2. Confinement of question-putting to Private Members' nights [etc.]. **1910** Question-raising [see *question-begging* above]. **1959** *Times* 25 Sept. 8/4 Curious and question-raising as they are, the megapodes are worth a more serious.. programme of research. **1647** TRAPP *Comm. Acts* viii. 24 All Christ's scholars are questionists, though not question-sick. **1862** T. A. TROLLOPE *Marietta* I. xi. 200 Looking at her like a question stop. **1852** MRS. GASKELL *Let.* 4 Sept. (1966) 197 (*heading*) Saty schoolroom, Question-time. **1885** *Manch. Exam.* 28 Feb. 6/1 Sitting apathetically through a rather lively question time. **1891** W. FRASER *Disraeli & his Day* 381 Colonel Makins, the.. Member for Essex.. said, 'They have got it hot this afternoon about a Dissolution.' I replied, 'Oh, nonsense!' This was during 'Question-time'. **1936** H. NICOLSON *Diary* 3 Dec. (1966) 281 Members crowd in as question-time draws to its end. **1976** H. WILSON *Governance of Britain* vii. 132 Harold Macmillan, a highly successful performer at Question time. **1642** R. HARRIS *Sermon* 29 If wee follow Chrysostom's sense.. and read the words Questionwise, *Will hee suffer long?* **1924** H. E. PALMER *Gram. Spoken Eng.* 263 In Direct Questions, the question-words are said to be interrogative; in Indirect Questions, they are said to be conjunctive. **1964** E. ULDALL in D. Abercrombie et al. *Daniel Jones* 274 Question-word question: 'What did he think they were doing?' **1978** *Language* LIV. 86 In English, questions are typically initiated by question words or verbs, so as to distinguish them from declarative sentences.

question ('kwɛstjən), *v.* Also 5–6 **-yon**, (5 **-one**). [a. OF. *questionner* (13th c.), f. *question* QUESTION *sb.*]

1. a. *trans.* To ask a question or questions of (a person or *fig.* a thing); to interrogate. †Also with double object (quot. 1604).

1490 CAXTON *Eneydos* xv. 58 Fame.. sette herself.. with the porters and mynystres for to questyone theym. **1600** SHAKS. *A. Y. L.* II. iv. 64 One of you question yon'd man, If he for gold will giue vs any foode. **1604** —— *Oth.* I. iii. 129 Her Father.. Still question'd me the Storie of my life. **1714** SWIFT *Imit. Hor.* II. vi, And question me of this and that. **1814** CARY *Dante, Paradise* III. 133, I to question her became less prompt. **1863** GEO. ELIOT *Romola* Introd., The night-student, who had been questioning the stars or the sages.. for that hidden knowledge.

b. To examine judicially; hence, to call to account, challenge, accuse (*of*). Now *rare.*

1637 HEYLIN *Answ. Burton* 60 When you were questioned publickely for your misdemeanours. *a* **1641** BP. MOUNTAGU *Acts & Mon.* (1642) 240 Socrates was questioned and condemned at Athens. **1656** BRAMHALL *Replic.* ii. 96 He had rather his own Church should be questioned of Idolatry. **1789** *Constitution U.S.* Art. i. §6 For any speech or debate in either house [members of Congress] shall not be questioned in any other place. **1839** MACAULAY *Ess.* (1843) II. 458 [He] cannot be questioned before any tribunal for his baseness and ingratitude.

†**c.** To challenge, defy (one) *to* do something. *Obs. rare*$^{-1}$.

1643 SIR T. BROWNE *Relig. Med.* I. §27, I cannot see why the Angel of God should question Esdras to recall the time past, if it were beyond his owne power.

†**2.** *intr.* ***to question with***: To ask questions of; to hold discourse or conversation with; to dispute with. *Obs.*

1470–85 MALORY *Arthur* x. iv, These two knyghtes mette with syre Tristram and questyoned with hym. **1555** EDEN *Decades* 10, I questioned with hym as concernynge the eleuation of the pole. **1614** JACKSON *Creed* III. i. §5 Little would it boote vs to question with them about their meaning. **1760–72** H. BROOKE *Fool of Qual.* (1809) II. 97, I was not far from murmuring and questioning with my God.

3. a. *intr.* To ask or put questions.

1584 LYLY *Campaspe* v. ii, Thy sighs when he questioned, may breed in him a jealousy. **1593** SHAKS. *3 Hen. VI*, III. ii. 122 Goe wee.. to the man that tooke him To question of his apprehension. **1626** D'EWES in Ellis *Orig. Lett.* Ser. I. III. 217 Others hearing not well what he saied hindred those by questioning which might have heard. **1725** POPE *Odyss.* XXIII. 110, I scarce uplift my eyes, Nor dare to question. **1858** LONGF. *M. Standish* IX. 53 Questioning, answering,.. and each interrupting the other.

b. *trans.* with clause stating the question. ?*Obs.*

1592 GREENE *Upst. Courtier* in *Harl. Misc.* (Malh.) II. 237, I.. was so bould as to question what they were, and of their businesse. **1611** SHAKS. *Wint. T.* I. ii. 433 'Tis safer to Auoid what's growne, then question how 'tis borne. **1651** HOBBES *Leviath.* II. xxi. 110 They never questioned what crime he had done.

†**c.** *intr.* To inquire or seek *after*. *Obs. rare*$^{-1}$.

1606 G. W[OODCOCKE] *Hist. Iustine* XXXI. 105 Which flattery.. so much delighted him that them which before his affection hated, now his desire earnestly questioned after.

4. a. *trans.* To make a question of, to raise the question (*whether, if*, etc.); hence, to doubt, hold as uncertain.

1533 FRITH *Answ. More* Wks. (1573) 33 Whether it be so or not it may be questioned. **1659** SLINGSBY *Diary* (1836) 356, I sent you a leter.. but I question whether you received it. **1745** P. THOMAS *Jrnl. Anson's Voy.* 286, I much question if those who left them had once fired them. **1758** JOHNSON *Idler* No. 4 ¶9 No man can question whether wounds and sickness are not really painful. **1883** *Law Times* 20 Oct. 408/1 Whether the request.. can be complied with.. may be questioned.

b. In negative expressions, as ***I do not question*** (***but***, etc.) = I have no doubt, I am sure (that); also pass. (cf. 5) ***it cannot be questioned*** = it is certain; etc.

1613 SHAKS. *Hen. VIII*, II. iv. 50 It is not to be question'd, That they had gather'd a wise Councell. **1687** T. BROWN *Saints in Uproar* Wks. 1730 I. 82, I.. question not but you'll do me and these two martyrs justice. *a* **1720** SEWEL *Hist. Quakers* (1795) I. Pref. 23 Some cases which I did not question to be true. **1749** FIELDING *Tom Jones* XVIII. ii, He did not in the least question succeeding with his daughter. **1869** HUXLEY in *Sci. Opin.* 21 Apr. 464/3 Nor can it be questioned that [etc.]. **1878** SIMPSON *Sch. Shaks.* I. 120 He did not question but the native Irish would join him.

5. a. To call in question, dispute, oppose.

1632 *Galway Arch.* in *10th Rep. Hist. MSS. Comm.* App. V. 478 Wee question the truth of your informacion. **1647** N. BACON *Disc. Govt. Eng.* I. lix. (1739) 112 This the wilful Archbishop never questioned, till he questioned all Authority. **1781** GIBBON *Decl. & F.* xxvii. III. 3 The worthless delegates of his power, whose merit it was made sacrilege to question. **1832** HT. MARTINEAU *Life in Wilds* vii. 96 There would be no true humility in questioning your decision. **1883** FROUDE *Short Stud.* IV. II. i. 164 Any one who openly questioned the truth of Christianity was treated as a public offender.

b. To bring into question, make doubtful or insecure. *rare.*

1637 HEYWOOD *Royall King* III. Wks. 1874 VI. 43 This emulation Begets our hate, and questions him of life. *a* **1643** SUCKLING *Goblins* v. (1646) 58 Behold (grave Lords) the man Whose death questioned the life of these. **1879** G. MEREDITH *Egoist* III. xiv. 291 At the game of Chess it is the dishonour of our adversary when we are stale-mated: but in life.. such a winning of the game questions our sentiments.

†**c.** To state as a question. *Obs. rare*$^{-1}$.

1643 SIR T. BROWNE *Relig. Med.* I. §21 Myself could shew a Catalogue of doubts, never yet imagined nor questioned.

†**6.** To ask or inquire about, to investigate (a thing). *Obs. rare.*

1599 SHAKS. *Hen. V*, II. iv. 142 Dispatch vs with all speed, least that our King Come here himselfe to question our delay. *a* **1633** AUSTIN *Medit.* (1635) 133 When they Question such things, as the Holy-ghost is silent in. **1655** STANLEY *Hist. Philos.* III. (1701) 87/1 Socrates asked them if.. he might be permitted to question what he understood not.

questiona'bility, = QUESTIONABLENESS.

1845 CARLYLE *Cromwell* (1871) V. 125 Widening into new dreariness, new questionability. **1966** *Listener* 1 Sept. 317/3 It is in the fact that only *one* of this grossly neglected composer's works has appeared that the questionability lies. **1969** R. HARPER *World of Thriller* ii. 51 Only occasionally for most men is life reduced to total questionability by any particular situation.

questionable ('kwɛstjənəb(ə)l), *a.* [f. QUESTION *v.* + -ABLE.]

†**1. a.** Of a person: That may be interrogated; of whom questions may be asked. **b.** Of a question: That may be asked or put. **c.** Of a place: Where questions may easily be asked. *Obs. rare.*

1590 C. S. *Right Relig.* 1 It is a question, scarse questionable. **1602** SHAKS. *Ham.* I. iv. 43 Thou com'st in such a questionable shape, That I will speake to thee. **1607** MIDDLETON *Five Gallants* II. iii, In such public as a tavern, such a questionable place. [**1878** SIMPSON *Sch. Shaks.* II. 119 (tr. *Prodigal Son*) Hollah! boy.. Stay still and be questionable. Tell me [etc.].]

†**2.** Of persons or acts: Liable to be called to account or dealt with judicially. *Obs.*

1639 GENTILIS *Servita's Inquis.* (1676) 833 The delinquent shall be sent to the place where he is questionable for spiritual Matters. **1660** *Trial Regic.* 51 Whatever was done by their Commands, or their Authority, is not questionable by your Lordships. **1685** COTTON tr. *Montaigne* (1877) I. 60 Many have thought we are not fairly questionable for anything but what we commit against our conscience.

3. Of things, facts, etc.: That may be questioned or called in question (rarely const. *by*); open to question or dispute; doubtful, uncertain. Freq. in phr. ***it is questionable*** (***whether, if***, etc.).

1607 TOPSELL *Four-f. Beasts* (1658) 96 It is questionable, whether they have any Hindes or females. **1643** PRYNNE *Treach. & Disloyalty* III. 127 (R.) Making it a thing not questionable by our Prelates and Clergie. **1685** LADY RUSSELL in *Buccleuch MSS.* (Hist. MSS. Comm.) I. 341 The Queen, is not at all well;.. 'tis questionable if she can endure the ceremony of the Coronation. **1772** *Junius Lett.* Ded. 6 The right of juries to return a general verdict, in all cases whatsoever is.. not.. in any shape questionable by the legislature. **1790** BURKE *Fr. Rev.* 63 Whatever rendered property questionable, ambiguous, and insecure. **1818** CRUISE *Digest* (ed. 2) IV. 147 This doctrine is very questionable. **1882** SPURGEON *Treas. Dav.* Ps. cxxiv. Introd., They have ventured upon so many other questionable statements that we are not bound to receive this dictum. **1883** SIR J. C. MATHEW in *Law Rep. 11 Queen's Bench Div.* 592 It was very questionable whether the words used were defamatory per se.

b. Of doubtful or obscure meaning. *rare.*

1742 RICHARDSON *Pamela* III. 408 When I cannot answer for myself, to render anything dark or questionable in it. **1835** I. TAYLOR *Spir. Despot.* IV. 119 In the lapse of ages, the phraseology of law may become first obsolete, and then questionable.

c. of qualities, properties, etc.: About the existence or presence of which there may be question.

1796 MORSE *Amer. Geog.* I. vii, The propriety of importing any of our school books from Great Britain..is very questionable. **1856** KANE *Arct. Expl.* I. xii. 123 The questionable privilege of having as many wives as he could support. **1885** *Manch. Exam.* 20 Feb. 5/1 Either its object is of questionable expediency, or its work is imperfectly done.

d. Of doubtful nature, character, or quality; dubious in respect of goodness, respectability, etc.

1806 SURR *Winter in Lond.* II. 261 There are a thousand questionable thoughts rushing at once upon my mind. *a* **1822** SHELLEY *Chas. I*, II. 203 Stick not even at questionable means. **1880** L. STEPHEN *Pope* iii. 79 A coolness ensued between the principal and his partners in consequence of these questionable dealings.

'questionableness. [f. prec. + -NESS.] The state of being questionable; doubtfulness, etc.

1668 H. MORE *Div. Dial.* II. xxii. (1713) 158 *marg.*, From the Questionableness whether..there does not as much good redound to the Universe. **1857** DE QUINCEY *Keats* Wks. 1862 V. 270 The questionableness of its particular statements. **1867** C. J. SMITH *Syn. & Antonyms* s.v. *Apparent*, The adverb apparently admits the sense of questionableness still more strongly.

'questionably, *adv.* [f. as prec. + -LY^{2}.] In a questionable manner.

1859 WILSON & GEIKIE *Mem. E. Forbes* i. 8 This dim prehistoric dawn, through which the shadowy figures of.. Druids questionably hover. **1885** *Mag. of Art* Sept. 443/1 An eccentric and questionably drawn performance.

† **'questional,** *a. Obs. rare*$^{-1}$. [f. QUESTION *sb.* + -AL^{1}.] Relating to questions.

1607 R. C. tr. *Estienne's World Wond.* xxxix. 327 The Decretals haue had their part,..the Questionall, Distinctionall, Quodlibeticall bookes..theirs.

question and answer. A dialogue consisting of alternate question and answer. Also (with hyphens) *attrib.*; occas. also **question-answer**.

1817 KEATS *Let.* 10 Sept. (1931) 39 My dear Fanny, Let us now begin a regular question and answer—a little pro and con. **1839** *Lett. fr. Madras* (1843) 255 The question-and-answer lessons on Scripture History. **1908** MRS. H. WARD *Diana Mallory* II. xii. 237 The trivial question-and-answer of the tea-making. **1940** N. MARSH *Surfeit of Lampreys* (1941) xiii. 187 She maintained a question-and-answer attitude, replying in the most meagre phrases. **1941** L. MACNEICE *Poetry of W. B. Yeats* i. 14 He may be answering quite different questions from mine but the question-answers which he evolves are the same kind of organism, and result from the same kind of activity as my own question-answers. **1945** C. S. LEWIS *Great Divorce* 41 That question-and-answer conception of thought only applies to matter of fact. **1957** E. BOTT *Family & Social Network* ii. 42 The question-and-answer pattern of fact-collecting. **1960** *Guardian* 9 June 9/1 Police interrogators..now hold a daily ..question-and-answer session with the former Nazi. **1965** *Language* XLI. 387 The question-answer pair *What does he do? He draws cartoons* can be analyzed in the same way. **1977** *Oxford Diocesan Mag.* Oct. 20/2 It was decided to organise ..a question-and-answer programme on an electronic screen. **1980** *English World-Wide* I. I. 28 It is not easy to elicit syntactic information by using the short direct question-answer technique.

† **'questionary,** *sb.*^{1} *Obs. rare.* Also 9 quæst-. [ad. med.L. *questiōnāri-us*: see QUESTION and -ARY^{1}.] **1.** = QUESTIONIST.

1435 MISYN *Fire of Love* 3, I trowe þies þinges here contenyd, of þies questionaries..may noȝt be vnderstandyd. **1563** FOX *A. & M.* 589/2 Then did he rede openly..Paules Epistles, and put by Douns and Dorbel, & yet he was a questionary him selfe. **1787** *Minor* II. xx. 141 Are you become a questionary at this time of day?

2. = QUESTOR I.

1820 SCOTT *Abbot* xxvii, A quæstionary or pardoner, one of those itinerants who hawked about..reliques.

'questionary, *sb.*^{2} [ad. med.L. *questiōnārium*; or, in mod. use, ad. F. *questionnaire*: see -ARY^{1}.] A list of questions; †a treatise in the form of questions, a catechism. Also *attrib.*

Now largely superseded by QUESTIONNAIRE, exc. in *Med.* use.

1541 R. COPLAND *Guydon's Quest. Chirurg.* Pref., This lytell questyonary & formulary..haue ben often requyred and soughte for. **1887** *Athenæum* 10 Sept. 345/3 Answers to the society's questionary of sociology and ethnography. **1951** *Lancet* 7 July 23/1 The questionary method used in this particular study has certain limitations. **1957** *Brit. Med. Jrnl.* 7 Sept. 550/2 The clinical concept of the disappointed undergraduate is therefore given some support by the answers to a general questionary. **1959** *Times* 5 Sept. 10/2 The proposed Welsh dialect atlas, information for which was gathered by means of a questionary of about 1,000 items. **1970** *Jrnl. Gen. Psychol.* Jan. 97 How did you answer when the item was difficult? And why did you answer in such a manner? (verbalization questionary). **1977** *Lancet* 27 Aug. 417/2 After 21 days, the patient was interviewed by one of us..using a standard questionary.

questionary ('kwɛstjənərɪ), *a.* [ad. late L. *quæst-*, *questiōnāri-us* (Boethius): see QUESTION and -ARY^{1}.]

1. Having the form of a question; consisting of questions; conducted by means of questioning.

1653 MANTON *Exp. James* iii. 13 The questionary proposal intimateth the rare contemporation of these two qualities. *a* **1715** BURNET *Own Time* (1724) I. 35 The questionary trial came last, Every Minister asking such questions as he pleased. **1775** ADAIR *Amer. Ind.* 60 The reply confirms the meaning of the questionary salute. **1838** CHALMERS *Wks.* XIII. 75 Let us institute a questionary process upon the doings.

2. That asks questions. *rare*$^{-1}$.

1711 STEELE *Spect.* No. 80 ¶6 Let those two questionary Petitioners try to do thus with their Who's and their Whiches.

† **'questionatively,** *adv. Obs. rare*$^{-1}$. [Perh. on anal. of *interrogatively*, *imperatively*, etc.] As a question.

1657 REEVE *God's Plea* 7 These words are put questionatively.

questioned ('kwɛstjənd), *ppl. a.* [f. QUESTION *v.* + -ED^{1}.] That is questioned, in senses of the vb. Also *absol.* as *sb.*

1680 BAXTER *Answ. Stillingfl.* xxxiv. 58 The little differences of our questioned Assemblies. **1753** H. JONES *Earl of Essex* (1756) 26 Clear Your question'd conduct from disloyal guilt. **1881** *Times* 18 May 11/5 At other times questioner and questioned agree in seeking an occasion to state a fact.

questio'nee. One who is questioned.

1838 CARLYLE *Lett. to Mill &c.* (1923) lix. 164 Your answer is according to your question, and your questionee, —'as the fool thinks the bell clinks'. **1866** *Sat. Rev.* 12 May 564 Questioner and questionee will soon lose each other in the wilderness of words. **1905** *Grand Mag.* Feb. 131 The.. questionee does not overlook the fact that [etc.]. **1953** *Rep. Sel. Comm. Delegated Legislation* 27/2 in *Parl. Papers 1952–3* IV. 115, I am not sure that the questioner could not answer that rather better than the questionee. **1971** J. WAINWRIGHT *Last Buccaneer* II. 183 He..murmured his questions in a very low voice. This forced the questionee consciously to *listen*.

questioner ('kwɛstjənə(r)). [f. QUESTION *v.* + -ER^{1}.] One who questions; an interrogator, inquirer; †an interrogative form of speech; erotema.

1551 CRANMER *Answ. Gardiner* 73 The curious questioner, the foolishe answerer. **1589** PUTTENHAM *Eng. Poesie* III. xix. (Arb.) 220 This figure I call the Questioner or inquisitiue. **1645** MILTON *Tetrach.* Wks. (1851) 228 (Matt. xix. 7–8) God..was making hel for curious questioners. **1709** STEELE *Tatler* No. 41 ¶6 He was a Questioner, who.. is one who asks Questions, not with a Design to receive Information, but an Affectation to show his Uneasiness for Want of it. **1801** SOUTHEY *Thalaba* v. xvi, Stranger, in thy turn,..who art thou, the questioner? **1890** H. S. SALT *Thoreau* 20 He was..a fearless thinker and questioner on.. matters social and religious.

† **'questionful.** *nonce-wd.* [f. QUESTION *sb.* + -FUL.] A full reply to a question.

1647 WARD *Simp. Cobler* 30 If any body comes to me for a question-full or two about fashions, they never complain of me for giving them hard measure, or under-weight.

questioning ('kwɛstjənɪŋ), *vbl. sb.* [f. QUESTION *v.* + -ING^{1}.]

1. The action of the vb., in various senses.

a **1635** SIBBES *Confer. Christ & Mary* (1656) 94 The ministeriall questioning of sinners. **1646** SIR T. BROWNE *Pseud. Ep.* 208 The questioning of their true endowments. **1776** JOHNSON in *Boswell* Mar. (at Lichfield), Questioning is not the mode of conversation among gentlemen. **1861** GEO. ELIOT *Silas M.* 48 Silas now told his story under frequent questioning.

attrib. **1837** WHEWELL *Hist. Induct. Sc.* I. 25 The vigour and confidence of the questioning spirit.

2. With *a* and *pl.*: An instance of this.

1607 HIERON *Wks.* I. 266 An aduised questioning with himselfe, touching the value of this offered treasure. **1677** GILPIN *Demonol.* (1867) 303 Unseemly questionings of his goodness and compassion. **1803–6** WORDSW. *Ode Intim. Immort.* 142 Those obstinate questionings Of sense and outward things. **1885** SIR R. BAGGALLAY in *Law Rep. 15 Queen's Bench Div.* 59 There are four species of questionings to which the debtor is to be subject.

questioning ('kwɛstjənɪŋ), *ppl. a.* [f. as prec. + -ING^{2}.] That questions, in senses of the vb.

1801 CHARLOTTE SMITH *Lett. Solit. Wand.* I. 234 Under ..the questioning eye of his father. **1818** SHELLEY *Rev. Islam* v. xii, Earnest countenances on me shed The light of questioning looks. **1858** LONGF. *M. Standish* VI. 31 Like a ghost that is speechless, Till some questioning voice dissolves the spell of its silence.

Hence **'questioningly** *adv.*, in a questioning manner; inquiringly.

1863 B. TAYLOR *H. Thurston* I. 87 As he looked keenly and questioningly at the little figure.

questionist ('kwɛstjənɪst). Also 7 **-est.** [f. QUESTION *v.* + -IST.]

1. A habitual or professed questioner, *spec.* in theological matters. (In early use applied to certain of the schoolmen, as Aquinas and Duns Scotus.)

1523 [COVERDALE] *Old God & New* (1534) R ij, Opiniators & questionistes braulynge and striuyng among them selues. **1528** ROY *Rede Me* (Arb.) 43 They sent thether Thomas and Scote With wother questionistes. *a* **1568** ASCHAM *Scholem.* (Arb.) 137 The worst of all, as Questionistes, and all the barbarous nation of scholemen. **1660** INGELO *Bentiv. & Ur.* I. (1682) 142 They let alone the trifling niceties of Questionists. **1762** *Gentl. Mag.* 84 Your respectable rendezvous of curious questionists. **1812** COLERIDGE *Lett., to his Wife* (1895) 581 He is a fearful questionist, whenever he thinks he can pick up any information. **1874** SYLVESTER in *Proc. Roy. Instit.* VII. 184 *note*, A questionist in the 'Educational Times'.

2. Formerly, at Cambridge and Harvard: An undergraduate in his last term before proceeding to the degree of B.A.

1574 M. STOKYS in Peacock *Stat. Cambridge* (1841) App. A. p. iv, The Questionists shall gyue the Bedels warnynge.. that they may proclayme..thentrynge of their Questions. **1650** [see INCEPTOR I]. **1661** K. W. *Conf. Charac.* (1860) 95 A Petition of Questionests to Mr. Frost for their degrees. **1772** JEBB *Remarks* 20 The Examination of the Questionists; this being the appellation of the Students during the last six weeks of their preparation. **1887** *Cambridge Univ. Cal.* 64 If any Questionist have been prevented by illness from keeping all his terms, a Certificate must be delivered.

questionless ('kwɛstjənlɪs), *a.* and *adv.* [f. QUESTION *sb.* + -LESS.]

A. *adj.* **1.** Not admitting of question; unquestionable, indubitable.

1532 MORE *Confut. Tindale* Wks. 814/2 Thys questionlesse and cleare vndowted churche. *c* **1611** CHAPMAN *Iliad* IV. 17 The conquest yet is questionless. **1642** J. EATON *Honey-c. Free Justif.* 81 It is questionlesse that all our sins are in Gods sight. **1862** LYTTON *Str. Story* II. 37 Reft from my senses are the laws which gave order and place to their old questionless realm. **1870** LOWELL *Among my Bks.* Ser. I. (1873) 226 He..remained always its born and questionless master.

2. That asks no questions; unquestioning.

1880 L. WALLACE *Ben Hur* 498 With the same clear mind and questionless faith.

B. *adv.* Without question, beyond all question; unquestionably; undoubtedly.

In common use from about 1550 to 1750; since then somewhat rare.

1412–20 LYDG. *Chron. Troy* II. xix, And questionles reporte this of me That [etc.]. **1550** BALE *Eng. Votaries* Q iv, Questionlesse theyr brutishe heades are to blockish. **1624** CAPT. SMITH *Virginia* 107 If they..had not so soone returned, questionlesse the Indians would haue destroied the Fort. **1676** HALE *Contempl.* I. 83 Each did questionless make a deep impression upon our Saviour. **1760–72** H. BROOKE *Fool of Qual.* (1809) IV. 23 The first man who came into the world was, questionless, the most perfect. **1809** MALKIN *Gil Blas* VII. xiii. ¶6 Questionless, said I, talents like yours are convertible to every purpose. **1866** GEO. ELIOT *F. Holt* v, A young man..who can questionless write a good hand and keep books.

Hence **'questionlessly** *adv.* (*a*) = QUESTIONLESS B. (*b*) Without asking questions.

1658 EARL MONM. tr. *Paruta's Wars Cyprus* 169 The advantage of the League, which was questionlesly known, would be very great. **1865** MRS. WHITNEY *Gayworthys* II. 175 To-day, still calmly, questionlessly, he did more. **1877** RUSKIN *Fors Clav.* lxxx. 225 Being simply and questionlessly father-laws from the beginning.

question mark. **1.** A mark of interrogation, represented by the sign ?

1905 T. F. & M. F. A. HUSBAND *Punctuation* II. vi. 74 A question-mark is sometimes placed in the middle of a sentence. In such a position it concentrates attention on certain elements of the thought. **1930** M. A. PINK *Dict. Correct Eng.* 147 To complete the list of stops we may mention here that the Question Mark (?) is used at the end of direct questions. **1960** KIERZEK & GIBSON *Macmillan Handbk. Eng.* II. 278 A question mark is used after a direct question but not after an indirect question. **1971** N. STACEY *Who Cares?* xii. 207 We agreed that the article should be called 'A Mission's Failure'. But I thought it ought to have a question mark after it.

2. *fig.* A point about which there is uncertainty or doubt; an unresolved problem, an enigma. Also, a person whose character is unknown or unfathomable (usu. in some particular respect). Freq. in phr. ***a question mark hangs*** (etc.) ***over*** (something), there is doubt about (that thing).

1869 LOWELL *Cathedr.*, This age, that blots out life with question-marks. **1924** R. MACAULAY *Orphan Island* xxv. 322 Across the future of Orphan Island..is scrawled a question mark. **1945** A. HUXLEY *Time must have Stop* xxx. 286 Contemporary science..is engaged in destroying, not only things and lives, but entire patterns of civilization. So we find ourselves faced with yet another set of question marks. **1952** M. ALLINGHAM *Tiger in Smoke* xv. 215 Luke was destined to become one of the great policemen... The man was a living question-mark. **1957** J. S. HUXLEY *Relig. without Revelation* (rev. ed.) iii. 62 The great question-mark of our continuance after death. **1958** *Daily Express* 23 July 4/3 It is a question mark which has been ringing in my mind. **1960** *Economist* 15 Oct. 215/2 Question marks now loom hugely over the future of the white-dominated states of southern Africa. **1963** *Listener* 24 Jan. 152/1 His death will take its place as one of the great question marks in English political history. **1971** A. PRICE *Alamut Ambush* viii. 95 Razzak, the unknown quantity,..wasn't quite such a question mark since he'd turned up at the Ryle reception. **1973** *Times* 15 Oct. 22/1 The project..is near to completion of its first stage. But a question mark hangs over the second stage. **1974** *Plain Dealer* (Cleveland, Ohio) 19 Oct. 6-D/2 Caffery..could become a question mark if his knee does not respond to a couple of operations. **1978** G. GREENE *Human Factor* II. iii. 85 A question mark kept him awake for a long while: had there always been a taxi rank so close to Davis's flat? **1979** *Nature* 15 Feb. 506/1 The question mark hanging over the whole meeting was precisely what principle was at stake.

3. (With hyphens). *attrib.*

1962 *Listener* 15 Nov. 835/2 The effect of changing Byron's tragic question-mark ending to a kind of 'redemption'..is quite unconvincing. **1966** J. S. COX *Illustr. Dict. Hairdressing* 124/1 *Question-mark curl*, a stand up curl with a very long stem, like a quaver in music. **1973** M. AMIS *Rachel Papers* 130 Shaving-cream bubbled inside the nearer of his question-mark ears.

Hence **'question-marked** *a.*, accompanied by a question mark.

1950 G. Barker *True Confession* vi. 33, I will not care who Or what you are, save palliation Of the question marked heart. **1975** C. Weston *Susannah Screaming* (1976) x. 52 The guff was already sorted, checked where possible, question-marked where not.

questionnaire (kwɛstjəˈnɛə(r), ‖kɛstjɔnɛr). [a. F. *questionnaire*, f. *questionner* to ask questions.]

a. A list of questions by which information is sought from a selected group, usu. for statistical analysis; a questionary.

The word was resisted by purists (see Fowler *Mod. Eng. Usage* (1926) 479/1) for many years after its first use in English. Some retained a Fr. pronunc. (kɛstjɔnɛr), whilst others preferred the Eng. word questionary *sb.*² The anglicized pronunc. is now dominant.

1901 E. B. Titchener *Exper. Psychol.* I. i. xii. 197 The questionary or 'questionnaire' is a series of questions bearing upon the matter to be investigated, and submitted to a large number of persons for introspective answer. **1920** *Glasgow Herald* 20 Aug. 7/1 Valuable information, never previously collected, is being obtained through a questionnaire by the Federation of British Industries concerning the fuel requirements of the great industrial centres. **1924** W. B. Selbie *Psychol. Relig.* i. 4 A careful study of the phenomena of religious experience derived mainly from biographies, introspection, and a systematic use of the questionnaire. **1931** *Times Lit. Suppl.* 19 Feb. 126/2 There was issued recently the report of a study (by *questionnaire*) of two hundred marriages. **1952** *Shell Aviation News* June 9/2 The moment for the distribution of a printed questionnaire is obviously in flight, when passengers are frequently bored and glad of any distraction. **1975** *New Yorker* 21 Apr. 45/2 The reports involve the verification of routine information that has already been supplied by citizens in response to questionnaires included in application forms for insurance, for employment, for mortgages or apartment leases. **1978** S. Brill *Teamsters* viii. 312 Drivers..responded to questionnaires placed as advertisements in trucking magazines.

b. *attrib.*

1924 R. M. Ogden tr. *Koffka's Growth of Mind* ii. 45 With the aid of Hall's questionnaire-method, one of his students has collected a large mass of material concerning children's play. **1941** J. S. Huxley *Uniqueness of Man* xi. 231 The questionnaire method is widely used. **1949** M. Mead *Male & Female* 457, I have had access to enormous varieties of.. original questionnaire blanks. **1964** I. L. Horowitz *New Sociology* 6 Specialized techniques of questionnaire design [etc.]..make the interviewing process into the end of research rather than merely its instrument. **1978** *Regional Lang. Stud.—Newfoundland* viii. 31 The purpose of the project was..to give experience in questionnaire design and administration.

questionous (ˈkwɛstjənəs), *a. rare.* [f. question *sb.* + -ous.] Given to asking questions; inquisitive.

1893 R. Bridges *Humours of Court* ii. i. 914 Of late you are grown questionous and prying.

ˈquestman. [f. quest *sb.*¹ + man.]

1. A member of a 'quest'; one appointed to make official inquiry into any matter; *spec.* †**a.** a parish or ward official elected annually (see quot. 1706). *Obs.*

1548 Geste *Serm.* in H. G. Dugdale *Life* (1840) 188 All judges, all officers, all quest men which have sworne to speake the truthe. **1599** Nashe *Lenten Stuffe* Wks. 1883–4 V. 239 They..come to bear office of Questman and Scauinger in the Parish where they dwell. **1631** Brathwait *Whimzies, Questman* 125 This Questman..becomes frequently versed in sundry ancient Presidents. **1706** Phillips (ed. Kersey), *Quest* or *Quest-Men*, Persons who are chosen yearly in every Ward, and meet about Christmas, to enquire into Abuses and Misdemeanours committed therein, especially such as relate to Weights and Measures. **1761** *London & Environs* IV. 23 [The mob of 1381] levelled to the ground the houses of all lawyers and questmen.

b. *Eccl.* A churchwarden's assistant; a sidesman. Now only *Hist.*

1454 in T. Gardner *Hist. Dunwich* (1754) 149 To the Quest Men for the Ton 12*d.* **1555** Bp. Hoplin in Ellis *Orig. Lett.* Ser. i. II. 189, I dyd sende ymedyatlie for the sayd Curate, the Churche wardeyns, and the questmen. **1624** Bp. Hall *True Peace Maker* in *Var. Treat.* (1627) 543 Who troubles the house?.. In the Church..not the carelesse questman, not the corrupt officiall; but the clamorous preacher. *a* **1656** —— *Rem. Wks.* (1660) 342 We have in every Parish..Churchwardens, Questmen, or Sidemen, and Overseers for the Poor. [**1732** Neal *Hist. Purit.* I. 307 To give it in charge to their Quest-men to present the names of all Non-conformists. **1895** J. Brown *Pilgrim Fathers* I. 35 He swore in six questmen to bring presentments against such as come not to church.]

†**2.** = questor 1. *Obs. rare*⁻¹.

1691 tr. *Emilianne's Frauds Rom. Monks* (ed. 3) 262 One of the Quest-men told her, That they would take care to make a little shift of it, for some small Soul in Purgatory.

†**ˈquestmonger.** *Obs.* Also 4–6 -mongere, 5 -manger, 6- -moonger. [f. quest *sb.*¹ + monger.] One who made a business of conducting inquests.

1377 Langl. *P. Pl.* B. xix. 367 Lyeres and questmongeres that were forsworen ofte. *c* **1449** Pecock *Repr.* v. vi. 516 Vnpiteful questmongers and forsworen iuerers. **1494** Fabyan *Chron.* iii. 530 They..slewe as many men of lawe and questmongers as they myght fynde. **1553** Latimer *Serm. Lord's Prayer* iv. 28 Aboue all thynges, these questmongers had neede to take heede. **1622** Bacon *Hen. VII*, 211 Hauing euer a Rabble of Promoters, Questmongers and Leading Iurors at their Command. [**1776** Entick *London* I. 293 Lawyers, jurors, and questmongers.]

questor (ˈkwɛstə(r)). Also 6, 9 quæstor. [a. med.L. *questor* agent-n. f. *quērĕre* = *quærĕre* to ask (cf. quæstor): hence also It. *questore*, F. *questeur*.]

1. *R.C.Ch.* An official appointed by the Pope or by a bishop to grant indulgences on the gift of alms to the Church; a pardoner.

1387 Trevisa *Higden* (Rolls) IV. 49 Now cherles and pardoneres beeþ i-cleped questores. **1415** *York Myst.* Introd. 26 Escriueners, Lum[i]ners, Questors [Pardoners *written above*], Dubbers. **1502** *Ord. Crysten Men* (W. de W. 1506) iv. xxi. 239 Yf he hath suffred wyttyngly questours to renne thrughe his dyocese in prechynge false indulgences. **1580** Fulke *Agst. Allen* 168 Men pay monie to the Pope or his pardoning quæstors, for leaden bulls. **1748** *Earthquake Peru* i. 85 The great Monastery alone has twenty-four Questors. **1823** Lingard *Hist. Eng.* VI. 125 Ninety-five short theses on the nature of indulgences and the errors of the questors. **1895** *Month* July 447 The malpractices of the Questors.

2. a. In France: One of the treasurers of the National Assembly.

1848 W. H. Kelly tr. *L. Blanc's Hist. Ten Y.* I. 413 He arrived at the Palais Bourbon..went straight to the questors [etc.]. **1896** *Daily News* 28 Mar. 5/5 There seemed a danger yesterday..that the Questors would be obliged to call in the police.

b. In Italy: A commissary of police.

1865 Maffei *Brigand Life* II. 169 The indefatigable questor of Naples..says [etc.].

3. [? f. quest *v.*] One who seeks or searches.

1887 Miss Betham-Edwards *Next of Kin Wanted* II. x. 117 Unhappy questors after something to their advantage. **1977** *Times Lit. Suppl.* 23 Dec. 1498/5 The prosing of that coruscating bore Dr Emily Brightman, a notator and questor of the first water.

questor, obs. variant of quæstor.

‖**Questore** (kwesˈtore). [It. *questore*, f. L. *quæstor*, contraction of *quæsitor* investigator, f. *quærere* to seek, enquire.] = questor 2 b.

1943 I. Origo *Diary* 10 Dec. in *War in Val d'Orcia* (1947) 120 His family succeeded in speaking to the Questore, and inquired what charge there was against him. **1969** G. Greene *Travels with my Aunt* ii. vii. 296 If the *Questore* had described me as a rat, I would have had no objection. **1972** K. Benton *Spy in Chancery* v. 36 The Questore of Rome had done his polished best to make the luncheon for the Interpol delegates a success.

questorian, -ie: see quæstorian, -y.

†**questrel**, variant of custrel, groom. *Obs.*

1551 Edw. VI *Lett.* in *Lit. Rem.* (Roxb.) 72 They had noe pages, questrells, nor demilaunces, but al wel armed.

†**ˈquestrist.** *Obs. rare*⁻¹. [f. quester + -ist.] One who goes in quest of another.

1605 Shaks. *Lear* iii. vii. 17 Thirty of his Knights Hot Questrists after him, met him at gate.

quest rope: see guest rope.

†**ˈquestry.** *Obs. rare*⁻¹. [f. quest *sb.*, prob. after *jury, vestry*.] Only in **questrymen**, jurymen.

c **1690** *Sir Hugh of the Græme* in *Roxb. Ball.* (1888) VI. 596 The Quest of Jury-men was call'd..Then other Questrymen was call'd.

questuary, obs. form of quæstuary.

‖**Questura** (kwesˈtura). [It. *questura*, f. L. *quæstura* the office of a quæstor: see Questore] In Italy: the police station or headquarters; the police.

1907 *Daily Chron.* 22 Aug. 4/4 He had been kicked out of the Central Questura, whither he had gone to give information, because the Neapolitan city police were in the pay of Camorrist assassins. **1950** E. Hemingway *Across River & into Trees* viii. 65, I fill out a slip there for the Questura. **1965** 'W. Haggard' *Hard Sell* ii. 15 Charles Russell took a taxi from the *questura* back to his hotel. **1975** 'D. Rutherford' *Mystery Tour* vii. 149 No one leaves before the inspector from the Questura in Varese gets here.

questure: see quæsture.

questword: see quest *sb.*²

quet, variant of qued(e, bad. *Obs.*

quetans, obs. form of quittance.

quetch, quitch, *v. Obs.* exc. *dial.* Forms: *α.* 1 cweccan, (cu-), 3 quecchen, queche, 6 queech, queatche, 6–7 que(t)ch; *β.* (? 3 cwich, quic), 5 qvycch-, qvyhch-, qvytchyn, quycche, 6 quytch(e, quyche, quich, 6–7 quitch, 9 *dial.* quitchy; *γ.* 6 (9 *dial.*) quatch. *Pa. t.* 1 cwæhte, 1, 3 cwehte, 3 quehte, qu-, cuahte, 4 quei(ȝ) te, quaȝte; also 6 quitched, 6–7 quetched, 7 quatched, quitcht. [OE. *cweccan*:—**cwacjan*, causative from the root **cwac-*: see quake, and cf. OS. *quekilik* glossing L. *versatilem* or *vibrabilem* (*gladium*). See also aquetch.]

†**1.** *trans.* To shake; to brandish; to drive, chase. *Obs.* (OE. and early ME.)

c **825** *Vesp. Psalter* vii. 13 Nemne ʒe sien ʒecerde, sweord his [he] cweceð. *c* **1000** *Ags. Gosp.* Matt. xxvii. 39 þa weʒferenden..cwehton [*v.r.* cwæhton] heora heafod. *c* **1205** Lay. 23907 Heo quehten [*c* **1275** cwehten] heore scaftes. *Ibid.* 31475 Hiȝendliche he heom quehte ouer þere Humbre.

†**2.** *intr.* Of things: To shake, tremble. *Obs.*

c **1205** Lay. 20141 þa eorðe aȝæn quehte [*c* **1275** cwehte]. *Ibid.* 26919 Quahten on hafden helmes heȝen. *c* **1380** *Sir Ferumb.* 607 So sterne strokes þay arauȝte..þat al þe erthe þer-of quaȝte a myle & more on lenghþe.

†**3.** *intr.* To stir or move from one place to another; to go, run, hasten. *Obs.*

c **1205** Lay. 826 Ne lete ȝe nenne quick quecchen to holte [*c* 1275 scapie to felde]. *Ibid.* 7271 þa heo weoren ouercumen þæ quahten [*c* 1275 wenden] heo wide. *c* **1350** *Will. Palerne* 4344 þat werwolf..queite toward þe quene.

4. *intr.* Of persons (or animals): **a.** To move the body or any part of it; to stir; in later use *esp.* to shrink, wince, twitch (with pain), and usually in negative clauses. *Obs.* exc. *dial.*

The phr. *cwich ne cweð* in *Leg. St. Kath.* 1261, *quic ne queð* in *Ancr. R.* 122 (two MSS.), app. belongs here, meaning 'stirred nor spoke', though the form is difficult to account for.

c **1205** Lay. 25844 þa fond he þer ane quene quecchen mid hafde. *c* **1330** *Arth. & Merl.* 9051 (Kölbing) þe stede he smot, þat it queiȝte. *c* **1440** *Promp. Parv.* 421/1 Qvycchyn, or mevyn. **1530** Palsgr. 677/2, I quytche, I styrre or move with my bodye. **1579–80** North *Plutarch* (1676) 587 He.. never stirred hand nor foot, nor quitched when the fire took him. **1596** Spenser *F.Q.* v. ix. 33 With a strong yron chaine and coller bound, That once he could not move, nor quich at all. **1609** Holland *Amm. Marcell.* xxix. i. 357 Simonides ..endured the flames, and never quetched [L. *immobilis*]. **1636** Featly *Clavis Myst.* iii. 33 He who suffereth all this, quatcheth not, stirreth not. *a* **1664** Frank *Sermons* (1672) 147 To..look up stedfastly still, not quich aside. **1685** Cotton tr. *Montaigne* I. 253, I have seen men..that would neither cry out, wince nor quitch, for a good swinging beating. **1886** Elworthy *W. Somerset Word-bk.*, *Quitchy*, to twitch; to make sudden, involuntary movements.

b. *intr.* To utter a sound. (Usually in negative clauses). Also with *against, at. Obs.* exc. *dial.*

1530 Palsgr. 601 She layde upon him lyke a mantle sacke and the poore boye durste nat ones quytche [F. *nosa pas tynter*]. **1531** Tindale *Exp. 1 John* (1538) 23 b, Thys doth Paule..so confirme, that all the worlde can not quytch against it. **1657** W. Morice *Coena quasi Κοινὴ* Def. xvi. 256 To snatch their mouths full of earth, that they might not be heard to quetch or groan. **1672** Marvell *Reh. Transp.* I. 159, I will speak alwayes with so Magisterial a confidence, that no modest man..shall so much as quetch at me. **1847–78** Halliwell, *Quatch*, to betray, tell... *Oxf.* **1888** *Berksh. Gloss.*, [? *Not to*] *Quatch*, to keep absolute silence as regards a certain subject.

†**c.** Freq. in phr. ***one dare*** (or ***durst***) ***not quetch***, implying fear or absolute submission. Also const. *against, at. Obs.*

13.. *K. Alis.* 4747 Dar no man agein hym queche. **1496** *Dives & Paup.* (W. de W.) ix. viii. 358/1 Be he so solempne & so myghty, that no man dare quycche ayenst hym. **1528** in Furnivall's *Ballads from MSS.* I. 359 Thow knowyste how..mortimer, in þis lande dyd Rule & Rayne, For whom no man durste quyche. **1565** Golding *Ovid's Met.* v. (1593) 124 The seelie lamb that dares not stirre nor quetch, when he heares the howling of the woolfe. **1587** Fleming *Contn. Holinshed* III. 975/1 They durst not queech in his presence, but were like a sort of timorous cattell. **1638** Featly *Strict. Lyndom.* i. 110 A most learned worke, against which never a Papist yet durst quatch. **1653** H. Cogan tr. *Pinto's Trav.* xix. 67 Which put them in such a fear as they durst not so much as quetch.

Hence †**ˈquetching, ˈquitching** *vbl. sb. Obs.*

1676 H. More *Rem. Disc. Hale* 94 The quitching of the skin.

‖**quête** (kɛt). [Fr., quest.] The traditional act of begging for food or alms to the accompaniment of folk-song; *spec.* as part of a folk-play. Also *attrib.*, as **quête song**. Cf. quest *sb.*¹ 7.

1903 E. K. Chambers *Mediaeval Stage* I. vi. 119 Hardly a rural merry-making..is without its procession; if it is only in the simple form of the *quête* which the children consider themselves entitled to make. *Ibid.* viii. 168 The rest..have either become..mere *quête* songs, or..have taken on a Christian colouring. **1933** —— *Eng. Folk-Play* 13 Structurally, the piece falls into three parts: the Presentation .., the Drama.., the *Quête*. *Ibid.* 21 To his normal lines Father Christmas may add others which..are also found as independent *quête*-songs of the Christmas season. **1967** A. L. Lloyd *Folk Song in England* ii. 102 Here is another set of wassailing verses... The begging motive..is important... We call such pieces *quête* songs. **1979** R. Palmer *Eng. Country Songs* 15 A number of such songs..provided the opportunity for a *quête*.

quete, obs. form of wheat.

quetenite (ˈkwɛtənaɪt). [Named 1890 (*Quetenit*) from *Quetena*, in Chile, its locality: see -ite¹.] 'Hydrous sulphate of iron and magnesium, found in reddish-brown masses' (Chester).

1890 *Amer. Jrnl. Sc.* Ser. iii. XL. 259 Quetenite occurs at the Salvador Mine in Quetena.

queter, obs. form of quitter *sb.*¹

†**quethe**, *sb. Obs. rare.* Also 6 *Sc.* queith. [f. the vb.] Speech, address; sound, cry.

13.. *Gaw. & Gr. Knt.* 1150 At þe fyrst quethe of þe quest quaked þe wylde. **1513** Douglas *Æneis* v. ii. 102 Quairfor Enee begouth again renew His faderis hie saull queith.

†**quethe**, *v. Obs.* (exc. in pa. t. quoth). Forms: *Inf.* 1 cweðan, (cwæðan, cwiðan, cuoeða, etc.), 2 cweþen, 2–3 queðen, 5 queth(yn, (qv-, qw-). *Pres. t.* (1 *sg.*) 1 cweðe, (cweoðu, cueðo, etc.), 4 queþe, 4–5 queth(e, 5 qwethe, 6 queythe. *Pa. t.* 1 cwæð, etc., 1–2 cwed, 1–3 cweð, 2 cwet, quað, 3 cwaþþ, qu(u)ad, queð, 4 quaþe, quath, (queþed, 5 ?

qwithit): see also QUOTH. *Pa. pple.* 1 cweden, 2 i-cweðe(n, 2–3 i-queðen, 3 i-cwede, i-queðe, queðen, 6 queythed. [OE. *cweðan* (*cwæð, cwǣdon, cweden*) = OFris. *quetha, queda, quan,* OS. *queđan* (*quađ, quath, quad; quâdun, quâdun*), OHG. *quedan, chweden* (*quad, quat; quâdun, quâtun*: MHG. *queden, keden*), ON. *kveđa* (*kvađ, kvâđum, kveđinn*: Da. *kvæde*, Sw. *qväda* to sing), Goth. *qiþan* (*qaþ, qêþum, qiþan*):—OTeut. **kweþan, kwaþ, kwǣđum, kweđono-*.]

1. *trans.* To speak, say, tell, declare, call.

c **825** *Vesp. Psalter* ii. 7 Dryhten cwæð to me, 'sunu min ðu earð'. *Ibid.* xli. 4 Ðonne bið cweden to me..'hwer is god ðin'. **971** *Blickl. Hom.* 183 Þa cwæþ Neron to Petre, 'gehyrstu, Petrus, hwæt Simon cwiþ'? c **1175** *Lamb. Hom.* 37 Do summe of þisse þinge þe ic wulle nu cweþen. c **1250** *Gen. & Ex.* 1496 Sel me ðo wunes, ðe queðen ben ðe firme sunes. a **1300** *Cursor M.* 22973 Mani man..Wat noght þis word i for-wit quath. c **1330** R. BRUNNE *Chron. Wace* (Rolls) 1224 Sertes, þys were our most profit, Wiþ loue & leue he queþe [*v.r.* quede] vs quyt. a **1400–50** *Alexander* 4325, I sall quethe þe forqui & quat is þ e cause.

b. *intr.* in phr. ***quick and quething***: Alive and able to speak.

1529 MORE *Dyaloge* I. Wks. 131/2 A man and a woman whyche are yet quicke and quething. **1546** GARDINER *Declar. Joye* 39b, I meruayle where he had lerned that lesson being yet quicke and quethynge.

2. To promise. *rare.*

c **1250** *Gen. & Ex.* 64 God hem quuad ðor seli suriurn. *Ibid.* 2788 Nu am ic ligt to fren hem ðeðen And milche and hunige lond hem queðen.

3. To assign by will, to bequeath.

1303 R. BRUNNE *Handl. Synne* 6294 Hous, and rente, and ouþer þyng, Mow þey queþe at here endyng. c **1330** —— *Chron.* (1810) 135 To temples in Acres he quath fiue þousand marke. **1387** TREVISA *Higden* (Rolls) V. 321, I queþe me to þe trone of þat Iuge þat neuere haþ ende. **1426** LYDG. *De Guil. Pilgr.* 4794 My body, I quethe also To the sepulkre, for dayes thre. **1463** *Bury Wills* (Camden) 16 Item I geue and quethe to William Hussher iijs. iiijd. **1530** PALSGR. 676/2 Hath he queythed you any thyng in his testament?

b. ? To bestow, deliver. *rare*⁻¹.

c **1400** *Destr. Troy* 6973 To Qwintilion the quem he qwithit a dynt, Woundit hym wickidly.

Hence †**'quething** *vbl. sb.*, bequeathing; **quething word**, last farewell. Also †**'quethe-word**, a legacy, bequest.

c **1380** WYCLIF *Sel. Wks.* III. 373 By beggynge, by queethyng [*v.r.* queþinge]..and oþer fals meenes [they] cryen evere after worldly godis. **1481** in T. Gardner *Hist. Dunwich* (1754) 148 Of Cutberd Eyer, for the Queth Word of Tym Chawmbyr 40s. c **1490** *Promp. Parv.* 420/2 (MS. K) Qvethe worde..*legatum.* **1513** DOUGLAS *Æneis* IX. viii. 62 Thi last regrait and quething wordis to say. **1532** *Churchw. Acc. Wigtoft, Lincs.* in Nichols *Illustr. Anc. Mann.* (1797), Item, receyvyd of Margaret Brygg for yᵉ quethword of Robᵗ Brygg hir husband 1/-.

quethe, var. QUED(E, bad.

queðen, var. QUETHE *v.*, WHETHEN *adv.*

quethen, -un, varr. WHETHEN, whence.

queðer, quedir, -ur, obs. ff. WHETHER, WHITHER.

quether, -ur, obs. ff. WHETHER.

quetor, -our, -ure, obs. ff. QUITTER *sb.*¹

quetsch (kvɛtʃ, kwɛtʃ), *sb.* Also **quetsche**, †**quitch**. [a. G. *quetsche*, dial. form of *zwetsche* plum.] A variety of plum with oval, dark-skinned fruit; also, the liqueur made from plums of this kind. Also *attrib.*

1839 C. MCINTOSH *Orchard & Fruit Garden* 327 The German Quitch Plum is dried and preserved in immense quantities. **1842** J. C. LOUDON *Suburban Horticulturist* III. iv. 559 Quetsche... A good bearer, and well adapted for drying. **1860** R. HOGG *Fruit Man.* 251 Quetsche... Fruit medium sized, oval... Skin dark purple... A culinary plum. **1936** BENTLEY & ALLEN *Trent's Last Case* xi. 130 His wife was a Lorrainer and responsible for the Quetsch, the liqueur made from her father's plums. **1940** [see MIRABELLE]. **1961** *Sunday Times* 16 July 36/6 Of plums and damsons there will not be a single one, and worst of all there will be no quetsch for jam making. Quetsch jam is one of the very best. **1966** P. V. PRICE *France: Food & Wine Guide* 51 Two [plums] that may be met with in open tarts are *mirabelles*..and *quetsches*. **1969** *Listener* 2 Jan. 31/1 The [Romanian] national drink..is a plum brandy like quetsch or slivovitch. **1975** WOOD & CROSBY *Grow it & cook It* vi. 234 Quetsche. .. October. Long oval, black. When stewed has the flavour of Carlsbad plums. **1977** M. JANCATH *Seatag* II. v. 99 A heavy lunch of Quenelles with sauerkraut and..a Quetsch tart.

quetstone, obs. f. WHETSTONE.

quetzal ('kɛtsəl). Also **quezal, quesal**. [a. Sp. *quetzal*, older *quetzale*, a. Aztec *quetzalli* a tail-feather of the bird called *quetzaltototl* (f. the comb. form of *quetzalli* + *tototl* bird).] **1.** An extremely beautiful bird (*Pharomachrus mocino*) of Central America (esp. Guatemala), belonging to the Trogon family; the cock is remarkable for its long tail-coverts, of a resplendent golden-green colour.

1827 J. WILSON *Let.* in *Mem.* iv. (1859) 124 That long-tailed fellow, the quezal from Vera Paz. **1838** J. GOULD *Trogonidæ* Plate 21, *Trogon resplendens*..Habitat Guatimala in Mexico, where it is called *Quesal.* **1864** G. R. MATHEW *Let.* in Ld. Malmesbury *Mem. Ex-Minister* (1885) 586 One of the famed 'quezals', whose plumage under the Aztec Emperor was reserved for imperial wear. **1887** W. T. BRIGHAM (*title*) Guatemala, the Land of the Quetzal. **1930** R. MACAULAY *Staying with Relations* ii. 26 Above their heads a quetzal, bright emblem of his country, his lovely tail caught in a liquorice vine. **1950** *Caribbean Q.* II. II. 24 The gorgeous plumage of the Macaw, the Quetzal and the Wild Turkey were sewn or gummed, feather by feather, onto cotton cloth to form resplendent cloaks. **1961** *Guardian* 22 May 5/4 The quetzal is a bird of rainbow plumage which symbolises Central America. **1978** *Washington Post* 7 July B2/3 The normal heart rejoices to think of wolves and quetzals flourishing in the great world.

2. (Pl. **quetzales.**) The name of a silver Guatemalan coin, initially equivalent to one U.S. dollar, and comprising 100 centavos.

1928 *Whitaker's Almanack* 778 Revenue (Budget, 1927–28) *Quetzals* 11,031,102. **1962** R. A. G. CARSON *Coins* 433 The coinage reform [in Guatemala] of 1924 created a new unit the quetzal in silver with subdivisions and with multiples in gold..on obverse the quetzal, a Central American bird of the parrot family. **1974** *Nat. Geographic* Nov. 673 For five quetzals (five dollars, U.S.) I savored a grilled filet mignon, [etc.]. **1977** *Westworld* (Vancouver, B.C.) May–June 20/2 The average income of a [Guatemalan peasant] family ranges from 200 to 300 quetzales a year (a quetzal equals one American dollar).

Quetzalcoatl (ˌkɛtsælkəʊ'ɑ:t(ə)l). Forms: 6 **Quecalcouatl**, 7 **Quetzaalcoalt, Quezalcouatl**, 8 **Quatzalcoatl, Quezalcoatl**, 8– **Quetzalcoatl.** [a. Nahuatl *quetzalli* (see QUETZAL) + *coatl* snake.] The Plumed Serpent of the Toltec and Aztec civilizations, traditionally known as the god of the morning and evening star, later as the patron of priests, inventor of books and of the calendar, and as the symbol of death and resurrection. Hence **ˌQuetzalco'atlian** *a.* and **ˌQuetzal-co'atlism.**

1578 T. NICHOLAS tr. *L. de Gomara's Pleasant Hist. Conqu. Weast India* 203 There was one rounde temple dedicated to the God of the ayre called Quecalcouatl. **1604** E. GRIMSTONE tr. *Acosta's Naturall & Morall Hist. E. & W. Indies* v. ix. 354 In *Cholula* which is a common-wealth of *Mexico*, they worship a famous idoll which was the god of marchandise, being to this day greatly given to trafficke. They called it *Quetzaalcoalt.* **1613** PURCHAS *Pilgrimage* I. VIII. ix. 656 They had sacrificed ten children..to *Quezalcouatl* their god. *Ibid.* 657 Their chiefe god was *Quezalcouatl*, god of the Aire. **1725** J. STEVENS tr. *de Herrera's Gen. Hist. Amer.* II. II. v. vi. 375 There were forty or more great or small, and other lesser Temples..which being all of different Sizes, and each of them dedicated to a several God, there was one among them round, consecrated to the God of the Air, call'd Quezalcoatl. **1726** —— *Ibid.* III. II. x. iii. 206 At Chulula, a City near Mexico, they ador'd a famous Idol that was the God of Commerce... His Name was Quatzalcoatl, he stood in a very lofty Temple, in a spacious Square, with Gold, Silver, Feathers, and costly Cloaths about him, bearing the Figure of a Man, his Face like a Bird... His name signify'd Snake of rich Feathers. **1787** C. CULLEN tr. *Clavigero's Hist. Mexico* I. II. 88 The Toltecas..built in honour of their beloved god Quetzalcoatl, the highest pyramid of Cholula. **1843** W. H. PRESCOTT *Hist. Conqu. Mexico* I. I. iii. 53 A far more interesting personage in their mythology was Quetzalcoatl, god of the air, a divinity who, during his residence on earth, instructed the natives in the use of metals, in agriculture, and in the arts of government. **1907** L. SPENCE *Mythol. Anc. Mexico & Peru* ii. 20 The worship of Quetzalcoatl was antipathetic if not directly opposed to that of the other deities of Anahuac. **1924** D. H. LAWRENCE *Let.* 15 Nov. (1962) 820 Well, I shall try and finish my *Quetzalcoatl* novel [sc. *The Plumed Serpent*] this winter. **1926** —— *Plumed Serpent* xxvii. 459 If you want to be so—so abstract and Quetzalcoatlian, then bury your head sometimes, like an ostrich in the sand, and forget. **1934** A. HUXLEY *Beyond Mexique Bay* 300 The Indians..can..practise whatever queer blend of catholicism and Quetzalcoatlism pleases them best. **1955** W. GADDIS *Recognitions* I. i. 56 True, many stirred with indignant discomfort..to find they had been attending, not Christ, but..Balder, Attis, Amphion, or Quetzalcoatl. **1973** *Guardian* 23 Mar. 12/4 Quetzalcoatl, the ancient god of the Toltecs.

queue (kju:), *sb.* Also 9 **queu.** [a. F. *queue*, OF. *coue, cue, coe*:—L. *cauda* tail: see CUE *sb.*³]

1. *Her.* The tail of a beast.

queue fourché*(e*, having a forked or double tail.

1592 WYRLEY *Armorie* 41 Gold ramping Lion queue doth forked hold. **1864** BOUTELL *Her. Hist. & Pop.* xiv. (ed. 3) 164 The lion of Gueldres is also queue fourchée. **1868** CUSSANS *Her.* (1893) 86 A Lion, with its tail between its legs, is said to be *Coward*; when furnished with two tails, *Queue fourché*, or *Double queued.*

2. A long plait of hair worn hanging down behind, from the head or from a wig; a pig-tail.

1748 SMOLLETT *Rod. Rand.* (1760) II. xlix. 116 A..coat over which his own hair descended in a leathern queue. **1774** GOLDSM. *Nat. Hist.* II. v. 100 The largeness of the doctor's wig arises from the same pride with the smallness of the beau's queue. **1802** JAMES *Milit. Dict.*, *Queue*..an appendage that every British soldier is directed to wear in lieu of a club. **1843** LE FEVRE *Life Trav. Phys.* I. I. viii. 183 Old cocked-hats, and tied queues, still stalk about the town. **1888** W. R. CARLES *Life in Corea* iii. 40 These boys were all bachelors, and wore their hair in a queue down their backs. **1904** L. HEARN *Japan: an Attempt at Interpretation* xii. 257 All classes excepting the nobility, samurai, Shinto priests, and doctors, shaved the greater part of the head, and wore queues. **1947** R. BENEDICT *Chrysanthemum & Sword* iv. 77 Insignia and distinctive dress of caste were outlawed—even queues had to be cut. **1959** E. TUNIS *Indians* 117/1 The Hopi had brown skins and straight black hair. Men wore it either in a queue bound up in the back or in the long bob they inherited from the Basket-makers. **1976** 'D. FLETCHER' *Don't whistle 'Macbeth'* 22 One of her habitual wigs..that.. ended in a pert *queue* at the back.

3. A number of persons ranged in a line, awaiting their turn to proceed, as at a ticket-office; also, a line of carriages, etc. Also *transf.* and *fig.* ***to jump the queue***: see JUMP *v.* 10c.

1837 CARLYLE *Fr. Rev.* I. VII. iv, That talent..of spontaneously standing in queue, distinguishes..the French People. **1862** THACKERAY *Philip* II. viii. 177 A half-mile *queue* of carriages was formed along the street. **1876** C. M. DAVIES *Unorth. Lond.* (ed. 2) 120 A long queue, like that outside a Parisian theatre. **1903** E. CHILDERS *Riddle of Sands* xxvi. 298, I joined a *queue* of three or four persons who were waiting their turn, flattened myself between them and the partition till I heard him walk out. **1943** E. M. ALMEDINGEN *Frossia* ii. 64 Paulina had a mind above bread queues and unlit streets. **1951** *Jrnl. R. Statistical Soc.* B. XIII. 152 My own interest in the subject arose from a correspondence.. about queues of taxis in station yards and of customers in retail shops. **1953** *Times* 5 Nov. 4/2 It would be for the Commons to discuss whether the claim of the judges on salaries in the queue of claims should be met before others. **1956** *Newsweek* 9 Jan. 43/1 In Leningrad, Gershwin's music and Heyward's 'Porgy' were anticipated by a two-day queue for tickets priced up to $15 apiece in rubles. **1958** *Listener* 20 Nov. 839/3 After the war the railways had to take their place in the queue after housing and housing repairs. **1966** *Rep. Comm. Inquiry Univ. Oxf.* II. 279 In arts and social studies, most of those with a college post before a university post were tutorial fellows in the 'queue' for a CUF lectureship. **1968** *Sci. Amer.* Aug. 96/1 Airplanes stacked over an airport, shoppers,..freight cars lined up for unloading at a railroad terminal and messages seeking a free path through a telegraph network all have one thing in common: they are members of a queue, or a line waiting for a service. **1969** *Listener* 28 Aug. 267/3 Are we going to wait until Marxism and socialism have conquered the world, and then stand there last in the queue, waiting for its return to us? **1977** *Spare Rib* May 19/4 Women in poor areas are always at the end of the queue for anything.

4. A support for the butt of a lance.

1855 in OGILVIE *Suppl.* **1860** HEWITT *Ancient Armour* Suppl. 647 The butt of the lance..is supported by the piece called the queue: this was of iron, and made fast to the body-armour by screws.

5. a. 'The tail-piece of a violin or other instrument.' **b.** 'The tail of a note' (Stainer & Barrett *Dict. Mus. Terms* 1876).

6. (Perh. a different word.) A barrel or cask capable of holding approximately one and a half hogsheads of liquid, usu. wine.

1777 P. THICKNESSE *Year's Journey* I. vi. 47 The carriage of a queue of wine from Dijon to Dunkirk..costs an hundred livres..but if sent in the bottle, the carriage will be just double. **1851** C. REDDING *Hist. & Descr. Mod. Wines* v. 91 The names applied in various wine districts of France to the casks which they use, differ without reference to the measure; in the department of the Marne, the *tonneau* is called the *queue.* **1931** W. E. MEAD *Eng. Medieval Feast* iii. 81 In 1385–6 Jean de Neele declared that his household used in one year between six and seven 'queues' of verjuice or between 2,346 and 2,737 litres. **1956** *Atlantic Monthly* June 94/2 In Burgundy the barrel is called *pièce* and contains from 226 to 228 liters, in the Mâconnais 215 liters, in the Beaujolais 216 liters, in Alsace 114 liters. In the Champagne it's called a *queue* and contains 216 liters.

7. *attrib.* and *Comb.*, as ***queue day, discipline, driving, form, number, system, theory*** (hence ***queue-theoretic*** adj.); **queue-barging** *vbl. sb.*, = QUEUE-JUMPING.

1977 *Time Out* 30 Sept.–6 Oct. 15/1 The elaborate queue system is an attempt to eliminate queue barging. **1908** *Daily Chron.* 4 Aug. 3/4 It was queue day at the Franco-British Exhibition yesterday. At 6 o'clock..a line of people a quarter of a mile long extended on either side of the Flip Flap. **1951** *Jrnl. R. Statistical Soc.* B. XIII. 152 The queue-discipline is the rule or moral code determining the manner in which the customers form up into a queue and the manner in which they behave while waiting. **1972** *Guardian* 29 Aug. 2/1 The high standard of British queue discipline. **1970** *Sunday Tel.* 20 Dec. 7/5 Yet another factor contributing to fast 'queue' driving in fog on motorways..is that drivers with their families as passengers tend to drive quickly for fear that a car behind might ram them. **1902** *Westm. Gaz.* 14 Nov. 10/1 From the pens to the steps of the car the intending passengers will go in queue form, as now adopted with so much success at most of the theatres. **1956** R. BRADDON *Nancy Wake* I. i. 9 Each day they received queue numbers so that they could take up their correct positions next morning. **1941** *New Statesman* 27 Dec. 523/2 The argument that the queue system is fair to everybody. **1966** S. BEER *Decision & Control* ix. 176 This thoroughly basic situation is so important in operational research as applied to dynamic systems that a whole branch of mathematical statistics, known as queue theory, has been developed round it. *Ibid.* 178 Some of the earliest queue-theoretic notions were developed around the problem of the doctor's waiting room.

queue (kju:), *v.* [f. prec. sb.]

1. *trans.* To put up (the hair) in a queue. Also with personal obj.

1777 W. DALRYMPLE *Trav. Sp. & Port.* lxvi, They came not out..in the morning till their hair was queued. **1820** W. IRVING *Sketch Bk.* II. 385 Their hair generally queued in the fashion of the times. **1858** CARLYLE *Fredk. Gt.* (1872) II. IV. viii. 19 While they are combing and queuing him. **1885** *Century Mag.* XXIX. 891/2 Some of them clubbed and some of them queued their hair.

2. a. *intr.* To move *in*, in a line of people.

1893 *Westm. Gaz.* 31 Jan. 6/3 You queue in, hand your card to somebody, pass on.

b. *trans.* To cause to form a queue; to arrange (persons or things) in or as in a queue or queues.

1928 *Daily Express* 8 Oct. 1/1 The foot and mounted police..had queued the concourse into twisting lines of people. **1973** P. C. SANDERSON *Interactive Computing in*

BASIC ii. 23 Multiplexors..checking for transmission errors, and storing and queuing the messages received.

c. *intr.* To stand in a queue; to form *up* in a queue; to take one's place at the end of a queue; also *fig.*

1933 *Observer* 5 Mar. 23/4 There were stuffs at the White City which made French buyers queue up. **1938** E. BOWEN *Death of Heart* I. iv. 71 They hung their hats and coats in the annexe cloakroom, and queued up for the mirror. **1945** 'TACKLINE' *Holiday Sailor* i. 9 Whilst we queued-up before him to have our cap-tallies—*not* cap-ribbons, we now discovered—secured. **1949** E. TAYLOR *Wreath of Roses* i. 11 They have to do all the wretched jobs not even a paid servant will do—queue for tomatoes, etc. **1955** *Times* 1 Aug. 8/7 Everywhere people are queueing—even at the bureau de change and of course at the cafeteria. **1964** L. DEIGHTON *Funeral in Berlin* xxiii. 128 Do you think that the whole of Germany was queueing up to fight Bolshevism? **1976** C. DEXTER *Last seen Wearing* xx. 155 The suspects are beginning to queue up, aren't they, Lewis? **1978** D. FRANCIS *Trial Run* i. 17 We are damned lucky to have been given the few weeks' option. They've got other buyers practically queueing for it.

3. *trans.* To follow or track (a person's steps, etc.).

1906 HARDY *Dynasts* II. v. i. 254 Perhaps within this very house and hour, Under an innocent mask of Love or Hope, Some enemy queues my ways to coffin me.

Hence **'queueing** *ppl. a.*

1949 N. MITFORD *Love in Cold Climate* I. ix. 91 The large crowd in Park Lane was rewarded by good long stares into the queuing motor cars. **1976** M. RUSSELL *Double Deal* xi. 88, I don't happen to be the queueing type.

†queué *a. Her. Obs. rare*⁻¹. [a. OF. *queué, coé*:—L. *caudāt-um*, f. *cauda* tail, QUEUE] = next.

1613 PEACHAM *Painting* 170 The King of Bohemia beares Gules, a Lion double Queue.

queued (kjuːd), *a. Her.* Also 7 queved. [f. QUEUE *sb.* + -ED².] Furnished with a tail; in comb. ***double-queued***.

1688 HOLME *Armoury* II. 459/2 A Lion double queved and crowned. **1727–41** CHAMBERS *Cycl.* s.v. *Queue*, If a lion have a forked tail, he is blazoned by double-queued. **1868** [see QUEUE *sb.* 1].

queueing, queuing ('kjuːɪŋ), *vbl. sb.* [f. QUEUE *v.*]

a. The action of waiting in a queue. Also const. *up*.

1927 *Brit. Weekly* 21 Apr. 55/3 When the public-houses opened their doors in the evening there was no queuing-up. **1946** G. MIKES *How to be an Alien* I. 44 Queueing is the national pastime of an otherwise dispassionate race. The English are rather shy about it, and deny that they adore it. **1948** M. LASKI *Tory Heaven* ii. 28 James was delighted to see a row of taxis... There was none of that queuing he had been led to expect. **1951** *Jrnl. R. Statist. Soc.* B. XIII. 180, I assumed that a newly arriving vehicle could always find somewhere in the station yard to unload, so that the problem was in effect not one of queueing. **1956** L. H. C. TIPPETT *Statistics* (ed. 2) vii. 125 This is typical of a number of congestion problems that arise in telephony, in road and rail traffic, in the queuing of patients at a hospital, and so on. **1958** *Manch. Guardian Weekly* 22 May 15/4 Even with a Ponselle a day or two of queueing was all you needed. **1967** *Times Rev. Industry* Aug. 28/2 These techniques include stock control, linear programming and queueing. **1979** *Bookseller* 23 June 2816/3 To avoid queueing..we did not ask visitors to register attendance.

b. *attrib.*, as **queueing theory**, the mathematical study of the structure and behaviour of queues of people or articles.

1951 *Jrnl. R. Statist. Soc.* B. XIII. 168 The different people associated with a queueing system will assess its merits and demerits in different ways. *Ibid.* 181 The congestion should be measured at the peak, but this would need the non-steady solution of a complex queueing problem with non-steady traffic conditions. **1954** *Science News* XXXIV. 112 One particular application [of operational research] is that of queueing theory. This was employed during the design of London Airport and has also been used for such diverse subjects as omnibus routing, toll gate staffing, and determining the number of grinding wheels required by a toolroom. **1966** *Listener* 3 Feb. 162/2 Queueing theory has in fact been used in this calculation in an attempt to relate the time on the waiting list to the number of beds made available, and the demand for these beds. **1974** GROSS & HARRIS *Fundamentals Queueing Theory* i. 1 'How long must a customer wait?' and 'How many people will form in the line?' Queueing theory attempts (and in many cases succeeds) to answer these questions through detailed mathematical analysis.

'queue-jumping. [f. QUEUE *sb.* + JUMPING *vbl. sb.*] Pushing forward out of one's turn in a queue; also *fig.* Cf. JUMP *v.* 10c. Hence (as a back-formation) **'queue-jump** *v.*; also **'queue-jumper**, one who jumps a queue.

1959 *Guardian* 22 Oct. 1/1 Mrs. Braddock..complained of Tory queue-jumping. **1960** *Ibid.* 17 June 2/3 There are three types [of private patients]—the snobs..the queue-jumpers..and the business executive. **1965** M. DRABBLE *Millstone* 67 Afraid that I would be accused of queue-jumping, I rose to my feet and went in search of authority. **1968** *Daily Tel.* 13 Nov. 14/7 A major hindrance to smooth traffic-flow is the queue-jumper, who invariably gets stuck. **1972** *Ibid.* 30 Mar. 16 Private patients in National Health hospitals..are widely regarded as rich queue-jumpers. **1973** *Listener* 6 Sept. 298/3 News reports of Asians who were trying to 'queue-jump' into Britain. **1975** J. PIDGEON *Flame* i. 7 Daniels, having queue-jumped up the crowded stairs.. gazed out above the lowered, pebbled window. **1976** *Daily Tel.* 20 Dec. 3/8 The row started when shop stewards complained that the women had queue jumped a union waiting list of people wanting to become ferry drivers.

queuer ('kjuːə(r)). [f. QUEUE *v.* + -ER¹.] One who waits in a queue.

1948 'J. TEY' *Franchise Affair* xxii. 260 This was fare that not even the most optimistic queuer outside the court had anticipated. **1952** *Time* 6 Oct. 64/1 The queuers were hoping for standing room. Reserved seats had been gone since July. **1958** *Times Lit. Suppl.* 21 Nov. 669/4 They become refugees somewhere across the border, queuers for charitable soup, squatters on alien school-room floors. **1960** V. JENKINS *Lions down Under* xv. 230 Some queuers who had been waiting from 3.30 a.m. **1976** *Times* 10 June 10/3 He watched a senior army officer walk straight to the head of a long taxi queue. The tired queuers grumbled curses.

Queuetopia (kjuː'təʊpɪə). [Blend of QUEUE *sb.* + UTOPIA; cf. SUBTOPIA.] A humorous designation of Great Britain under Labour or Socialist rule, supposedly characterized by universal queueing. Also *transf.*

Said to have been coined by Winston Churchill.

1950 *Manch. Guardian Weekly* 2 Mar. 9/1 (*heading*) 'Queuetopia'. Few of our national disorders have made better campaign material than..the continual queues, the swelling bureaucracy.., and the general mechanisation of the British Way of Life. **1975** S. POTTER *Changing Eng.* 82 London..has far too many *queuetopias* at its bus stops and supermarket checkouts.

†queve, for *queue*, obs. var. CUE *sb.*²

1659 H. L'ESTRANGE *Alliance Div. Off.* 317 They had no other queve to direct them, then the loud pronunciation [etc.].

‖quevée, *a. Her.* [For *queuée* = QUEUÉ *a.*] Tailed, in comb. ***double quevée*** (cf. QUEUED).

1761 *Brit. Mag.* II. 532 Supporters. Two lions double quevée. **1840** H. AINSWORTH *Tower of London* 1 A lion rampant, or, double quevée, vert.

†queven, *v. Obs. rare*⁻¹. [? Related to ON. *kvefja* (*kefja*) to put under water.] ? To plunge.

c **1325** *Metr. Hom.* 128 Quen Satenas sal Jowes queuen [*printed* quenen; *rime* heuin] In ouer mirkenes.

quever, quew, obs. forms of QUIVER *a.*, CUE.

‖que voulez-vous (kə vule vu). [Fr., lit. 'what do you want?'] An expression denoting mild exasperation or resignation; 'what do you expect?', 'what can one expect?'.

[**1830** C. CLAIRMONT *Let.* 28 Mar. in J. Marshall *Life & Lett. Mary Shelley* (1889) II. xxi. 202 He [*sc.* Trelawny] receives all his impressions through his heart, I through my head. *Que voulez vous? Le moyen de se recontrer* when one is bound for the North Pole and the other for the South?] **1841** W. M. THACKERAY in *Britannia* 5 June 363/2 No doubt she was dancing away last night..and finished the morning at the Courtille. *Que voulez vous?* it is her nature. **1878** H. JAMES *Europeans* I. vi. 239 The Baroness gave a little philosophic shrug. 'Que voulez-vous? They are princes.' **1880** G. GISSING *Let.* 21 Dec. in J. Korg *George Gissing* (1965) iii. 90, I fear they put me down for a prig, an upstart, an abominable aristocrat, but *que voulez-vous?* **1923** W. J. LOCKE *Moordius & Co.* xxi. 288 *Que voulez-vous*, mademoiselle? A train-omnibus stopping at every station is bound to be late. **1935** LADY FORTESCUE *Perfume from Provence* 35 Are there not floods..all over the world? *Que voulez-vous?* **1945** 'O. MALET' *My Bird Sings* I. v. 37 The poor Comte is hopelessly in love..but *que voulez-vous?* She will not have him.

quey (kweɪ). *Sc.* and *north. dial.* Forms: α. 4 **qwy**, 5 **qui**, 5–6 **qwye**, 6 **quy**, 6–7 **quye**; 5 **que**, 5–9 **quee**; 8– **quey**; 6 **koy**, 6–9 **quoy**, 9 **coy**. β. *north.* 5–9 **why(e**, 6 **qwhy**, 7–8 **whee**, **whie**, 7–9 **whey**, 9 **wy(e**, etc. [a. ON. *kvíga* (Sw. *qviga*, Da. *kvie*), app. f. *kú* cow.] A young cow before it has had a calf; a heifer.

α. **1374** *Durh. Halm. Rolls* (Surtees) 124, xij stots et qwyis. *c* **1425** *Voc.* in Wr.-Wülcker 669/10 *Hec juuenca*, quee. **1485** *Will* in *Ripon Ch. Acts* (Surtees) 277 That Elyne Peke have a quye. **1508** DUNBAR *Flyting* 142 Beggand koy and ox. **1513** DOUGLAS *Æneis* IV. ii. 19 Ane vntamyt ȝoung quoy. **1673** *Depos. Cast. York* (Surtees) 196 A quye..which now pines away. **1725** RAMSAY *Gentle Sheph.* II. i, Ye..sauld your crummock, and her bassand quey. **1768** A. ROSS *Fort. Shepherdess* III. 112 The beef of the new slaughter'd quoy. **1818** SCOTT *Hrt. Midl.* xxxix, If Gowans, the brockit cow, has a quey. **1884** STREATFEILD *Lincoln & Danes* 263 The garthman..will be proud to show you..the stots and quees.

β. **1483** *Cath. Angl.* 416/1 A Why, *bucula, juuenca.* **1565** *Wills & Inv. N.C.* (Surtees 1835) 230, vj oxen iiij^or kye or qwhyes. **1614** *Inv.* in *Trans. Cumbld. & Westmld. Arch. Soc.* III. 113, 20 stotts, 5 whies, 14 younger neats. **1726** *Dict. Rust.* (ed. 3), *Whee* or *Whey*, a Word us'd in Yorkshire, for an Heifer. **1802** in Anderson *Cumbld. Ball.* 23, I carried our whye to the bull.

b. *Comb.* **quey-calf** [= ON. *kvígukalfr*, Sw. *qvigkalf*, Da. *kviekalv*], a female calf.

1568 *Wills & Inv. N.C.* (Surtees 1835) 293, I gyue vnto.. my dowghter one quye calfe. **1575** in R. Welford *Hist. Newcastle* (1885) II. 465 The first whey calf that God sends him. **1725** RAMSAY *Gentle Sheph.* III. ii, Twa quey cawfs I'll yearly to them give. **1855** STEPHENS *Bk. of Farm* (ed. 2) I. 506/2 The quey-calf occupies the near, and the bull-calf the off-side horn.

Hence **'queyock** (also 6 **quiok**, 7 **quoy-**, **quyach**, 9 **queyoch**, etc.); = QUEY.

1513 DOUGLAS *Æneis* VIII. iv. 76 In the cave..a quyok lowis. **1536** BELLENDEN *Cron. Scot.* (1821) I. p. iv, The quiokis war nevir slane quhill they wer with calfe. **1609** SKENE *Reg. Maj.* 2 b, Item for the Serjant, ane colpindach (ane quyach, ane ȝoung kow).

queyd, var. QUED(E, bad.

queyere, obs. f. CHOIR.

queynose, obs. f. QUINSY.

queynt: see QUAINT *a.*, QUENCH *v.*

queynt-a(u)nce, -ise, varr. QUAINTANCE, -ISE.

queyr, obs. f. CHOIR *sb.*, QUEER *a.*

queyse, var. QUEASE *v.*

queysie, obs. f. QUEASY *a.*

queythe, var. QUETHE *v.*

‖queyu ('kweɪuː). Also **keweyu**, **kuyu**, **kway**, **queyou**, etc. [Guyana Creole, app. from a Cariban language.] In Guyana and neighbouring regions, a small apron-like garment worn by the women of certain Amerindian peoples, consisting of a panel of coloured beads set in intricate geometrical patterns and surrounded by a fringe of cotton.

1796 J. G. STEDMAN *Narr. Five Years' Exped.* I. xv. 386 The women wear an apron of cotton, with party-coloured glass beads strung upon it, which they call *queiou*. This covering is no great size, being only one foot in breadth by eight inches in length..but being heavy..it answers all the purposes for which it was intended. **1806** G. PINCKARD *Notes on West Indies* II. 444 Sometimes, instead of the band, the women use a small apron about three or four inches square, which being tied around the waste [*sic*], and left to hang loose before, serves by way of a fig-leaf. These aprons they call *kways*. **1866** R. DUFF *Brit. Guiana* xi. 261 The only covering which the females wore was the quieyoo, an article of dress, worked out of seeds of trees, about ten inches long, and six or eight broad, hung in front of the person by a string fastened round the loins. **1867** W. T. VENESS *El Dorado* 141 '*Cuyus*', or '*Queyus*', the entire dress of Indian women, of the Accawai tribe. **1895** *Timehri* June 144 The queyus too were remarkable owing to their small bead surface, the greater extent being taken up by wide cotton fringes. **1904** W. H. HUDSON *Green Mansions* v. 71 Oalava herself would be ready to bestow her person—queyou, worn fig-leaf-wise, necklace of accouri teeth, and all—on so worthy a suitor as myself. **1912** J. RODWAY *Guiana* 216 Geometrical patterns of most intricate lines are found on basket-work, old pottery, *queyus* or aprons, and on their [*sc.* the Indians'] painted faces. **1923** W. E. ROTH tr. *R. Schomburgk's Trav. Brit. Guiana, 1840–1844* II. xii. 379 The queyu of the woman was made out of seed pips. **1924** *38th Ann. Rep. U.S. Bureau Amer. Ethnol.* xxi. 446 The Creole terms kway.., queyu, kuyu, etc., applied to the glass-bead apron, is [*sic*] apparently identical with that of the original cotton loin-cloth guayuco of the Orinoco Indians. **1964** V. G. C. NORWOOD *Jungle Life in Guiana* v. 99 The commonest form of covering adopted by Indian women generally is a small apron made from..coloured glass beads strung on cotton strands, this latter form originally Acawoian, called a 'quayo'. **1965** J. YDE *Material Culture of Waiwái* 199 The bead apron, *keweyu*.., is as indispensable a garment to the women as is the *kamisa* to the men.

quezal, var. QUETZAL.

queziness, obs. f. QUEASINESS.

quezzen, dial. var. QUEASOM.

quh-, an obs., chiefly Scottish, variant of the initial combination *wh-* (OE. *hw-*), as in *quhan, quhat, quhele, quhete* = when, what, wheel, wheat. (Also *quhou, quhow, quhu* = how.) The use of *quh-* for original *qu-* is much rarer, in most cases perhaps accidental. See the introductory note on the letter Q.

qui, obs. form of QUEY, WHY.

‖quia timet ('kwiːə 'tɪmɛt). *Law.* [L., lit. 'because he fears'.] An action brought to prevent a possible future injury. Also as *attrib.* or *advb. phr.*

1628 E. COKE *First Part of Institutes of Lawes of Eng.* II. vi. 100 There be 6. Writs in Law that may be maintained quia timet, before any molestation, distresse, or impleading. **1697** *Cases Argued & Decreed in High Court of Chancery* 223 It was objected, that the Daughter is not of Age, and so this Bill is *quia timet* only;..and the Court would be vexed with vain Suits if any one might be admitted to sue only *quia timet*, to prevent a remote Possibility. But the Court answered, that Suits *quia timet* only were proper in Law and Equity. **1815** H. MADDOCK *Treat. on Princ. & Pract. High Court of Chancery* I. ii. 178 The denomination of Bills *Quia Timet* was borrowed, probably, from the Title of some ancient Writs at the Common Law. **1860** J. J. S. WHARTON *Law-Lexicon* (ed. 2) 619/1 *Quia Timet Bill*, it is filed for the purpose of quieting a present apprehension of a probable or possible future injury to property. **1927** P. G. OSBORN *Conc. Law Dict.* 41 *Bill Quia Timet*, a proceeding in the old Court of Chancery for providing against an apprehended injury. Now replaced by the injunction. **1961** *Times* 14 Feb. 5/1 Dismissing with costs their *quia timet* claim for an injunction. **1971** [see LIE *v.*¹ 12].

†quib, *sb. Obs.* Also 6 -be, 7 -bbe. [App. ad. (orig. in pl.) L. *quibus*, dat. or abl. pl. of *qui* 'who, which', as a word of frequent occurrence in legal documents and hence associated with the 'quirks and quillets' of the law.

For other allusive uses of the L. word, cf. F. *quibus* money, cash; Du. *kwibus* fool, weathercock.]

1. = QUIBBLE *sb.* 2.

a **1550** *Image Hypocr.* in *Skelton's Wks.* (1843) II. 427 His tottes and quottes Be full of blottes: With quibes and quaryes Of inventataries. **1592** GREENE *Upst. Courtier* in *Harl. Misc.* (Malh.) II. 232 These lawiers haue..such quibs and quiddits, that beggering their clients they purchase to themselues whole lordships. **1608** HIERON *Defence* II. 221 M. H. answereth by an unsound reason, two quibbes & two authors onely produced.

2. A gibe, gird, QUIP. *rare*$^{-1}$.

1656 BRADFORD *Plymouth Plant.* 151 Mr. Weston..gave them this quib (behind their baks)..That though they were but yonge justices, yet they wear good beggers. [**1736** in AINSWORTH; hence in JOHNSON and later dicts.]

† **quib**, *v. Obs. rare.* [f. prec. sb.] *trans.* and *intr.* To taunt, gibe (at), QUIP.

1592 KYD *Murther. I. Brewen* Wks. (1901) 291 When he quibd her with vnkindnes..she asked him if he would haue her forsworne. **1608** HIERON *Defence* II. 223 He goeth on & saith..thus quibbing at the Ministers.

† **quib**, *adv. Obs. rare*$^{-1}$. [Cf. prec. sb. and vb.] In an affected or punning style.

1614 B. JONSON *Barth. Fair* I. i, When a quirk, or a quiblin do's scape thee, and thou dost not watch, and apprehend it, and bring it afore the Constable of conceit (there now, I speake quib too).

quibble ('kwɪb(ə)l), *sb.* [? dim. of QUIB.]

1. A play upon words, a pun.

1611 L. BARRY *Ram Alley* III. i, We old men have our crotchets, our conundrums, Our figaries, quirks and quibbles, As well as youth. **1711** SHAFTESB. *Charac.* I. §2 (1737) I. 64 All Humour had something of the Quibble. The very Language of the Court was Punning. **1779–81** JOHNSON *L.P., Pope* Wks. IV. 156 The opposition of *Immortalis* and *Mortalis*, is a mere sound, or a mere quibble. **1858** O. W. HOLMES *Aut. Breakf.-t.* xi. 100 Several questions, involving a quibble or play upon words.

2. An equivocation, evasion of the point at issue; an argument depending on some likeness or difference between words or their meanings, or on some circumstance of no real importance.

1670 *Moral State Eng.* 23 An unnatural Antithesis, a forced quibble. **1675** BAXTER *Cath. Theol.* I. III. 41 To answer all these fallacies and quibbles, founded in some false supposition or ambiguous word. **1768** H. WALPOLE *Hist. Doubts* 100 *note*, Henry was so reduced to making out any title to the crown, that he catched even at a quibble. **1855** MACAULAY *Hist. Eng.* xiv. III. 471 To a plain understanding his objections seem to be mere quibbles. **1878** LECKY *Eng. in 18th C.* I. ii. 280 Those advocates of persecution, who would stoop to any quibble in their cause.

fig. **1796** MRS. M. ROBINSON *Angelina* II. 184 His features were all quibbles; for it was impossible to guess what they meant for two minutes together.

b. The use of quibbles, quibbling.

1710 PALMER *Proverbs* 100 A liar is upon the reserve, and wou'd throw off the odium by quibble and equivocation. **1771** *Junius Lett.* lxi. 319 You attribute it to an honest zeal in behalf of innocence, oppressed by quibble and chicane.

3. *attrib.* and *Comb.*, as ***quibble-catching***, ***-loving*** adj., ***-sanctioning*** adj., ***-springe***.

1678 RYMER *Trag. last Age* 4 Much less have I cast about for Jests, and gone a quibble-catching. **1802–12** BENTHAM *Ration. Judic. Evid.* (1827) V. 234 A quibble-loving lawyer. **1829** —— *Justice & Cod. Petit.* 115 The quibble-sanctioning judge. **1830** MORIARTY *Husband Hunter* III. 202 Law pun-traps and quibble-springes.

quibble ('kwɪb(ə)l), *v.*[1] Also 7 quible. [f. prec. sb.]

†**1.** *intr.* To pun, to play on words. *Obs.*

a **1629** T. GOFFE *Careless Sheph.* Præl. 129 His part has all the wit, For none speaks, carps and Quibbles besides him. **1670** EACHARD *Cont. Clergy* 130 How the ministers themselves do jingle, quibble, and play the fools with their texts. **1711** ADDISON *Spect.* No. 61 ¶2 Nothing is more usual than to see a Hero weeping and quibbling for a dozen Lines together. **1751** CHESTERF. *Lett.* (1792) III. 121 Were I inclined to quibble I would say [etc.; a pun on *air*].

2. *intr.* To argue in a purely verbal way; to evade the real point by a quibble.

1656 CROMWELL *Sp.* 17 Sept. in *Carlyle*, Needlessly to mind things that are not essential; to be quibbling about words. **1839** JAMES *Louis XIV*, II. 83 Mazarin proceeded to irritate De Retz..by quibbling upon the words of his bargain. **1854** tr. *Lamartine's Celebr. Char.* II. 26, I shall not quibble between the titles of King or Protector. **1864** BOWEN *Logic* ix. 293 A satirical disputant quibbling about the meaning of words.

b. To wriggle *out of*, to trifle or deal unfairly *with*, by quibbling. *rare.*

1842 DICKENS *Amer. Notes* (1850) 99/1 The simple warriors..who only learned..from white men how to break their faith, and quibble out of forms and bonds. **1859** G. MEREDITH *R. Feverel* xxxiv, Sensible that she had been quibbled with.

3. *trans.* with advbs.: To cheat or bring *out of*, waste or explain *away*, by quibbling.

1713 BIRCH *Guard.* No. 36 ¶4 Who ever lost his estate in Westminster Hall, but complained that he was quibbled out of his right? **1768** BOYER *Dict. Royal* II. s.v., He endeavoured to quibble away, (to elude,) the sanctity of an oath. **1857** TOULMIN SMITH *Parish* 101 This Act has also, in many cases, been quibbled away.

'**quibble**, *v.*[2] *Obs.* exc. *dial.* [? Onomatopœic: cf. QUIVER.] *intr.* To quiver; to shake.

1726 BAILEY, *Quibble*, to move as the Guts do. **1886** ELWORTHY *W. Som. Word-bk.* s.v., I be afeard I've a catcht a chill, I do quibbly all over.

'**quibbleism.** *rare*$^{-1}$. [f. QUIBBLE *sb.* + -ISM[1].] The practice of quibbling.

1836 *New Monthly Mag.* XLVII. 417 The use he may make of the most ordinary words for the purposes of quibbleism.

quibbler ('kwɪblə(r)). [f. QUIBBLE *v.*[1] + -ER[1].] One who quibbles, in senses of the verb.

a **1680** BUTLER *Rem.* (1759) II. 206 A Quibbler is a Jugler of Words, that shows Tricks with them, to make them..serve two Senses at once. **1737** LAW *Demonstr. gross Err. of late Bk.* (1769) 227 If your heart is shut up in death and dryness, your reason will be a poor quibbler in words and dead images. **1807** *Med. Jrnl.* XVII. 42 M. C.,..as all Quibblers do, works in words which are not mine. **1883** *Law Times* 27 Oct. 231/2 A race of astute quibblers, and not a body of scientific lawyers.

quibbling ('kwɪblɪŋ), *vbl. sb.* [-ING[1].] The action of the verb QUIBBLE. Also with *a* and *pl.*, an instance or specimen of this.

1628 SHIRLEY *Witty Fair One* III. ii, I have made a quibbling in praise of her. **1658–9** *Burton's Diary* (1828) IV. 36 You say you will bound, and you will not bound. It looks like quibbling. **1681** W. ROBERTSON *Phraseol. Gen.* (1693) 487 There's nothing which these disputants will not oppose by their niceties and quibblings. **1831** BLAKEY *Free-will* 172 The various quibblings, shufflings, reservations, and qualifications..must be abundantly evident to every one. **1855** MACAULAY *Hist. Eng.* xv. III. 514 In spite of this quibbling, he was pronounced guilty.

quibbling ('kwɪblɪŋ), *ppl. a.* [-ING[2].] That quibbles; characterized by quibbles.

1657 J. JORDAN *Walks Islington* II. ii, Pox on your Cobling jeasts, you quibling Coxcombe. **1675** BAXTER *Cath. Theol.* II. II. 250, I have detected the fraud of their quibling distinction. **1772** *Junius Lett.* lxviii. 353 A cunning quibbling attorney might..discover a flaw. **1875** JOWETT *Plato* (ed. 2) I. 266 The quibbling follies of the Sophists.

Hence '**quibblingly** *adv.*

1657 J. SERGEANT *Schism Dispach't* Post-scr., Their old method of talking preachingly, quotingly, and quibblingly. **1901** W. J. CRAIG *King Lear* 117 *note*, Perhaps 'roarer' in *Tempest* I. i. 18, quibblingly applied to the raging waters.

'**quibbly**, *a. rare*$^{-1}$. Of the nature of a quibble.

1895 *Cath. News* 28 Dec. 4/3 The arguments—small, quibbly and lacking in elemental foundation.

quibe, variant of QUIB *sb.*

quibib(e, -bibbe, obs. forms of CUBEB.

† **quibibble**, obs. var. QUIBBLE *sb.* (Cf. next.)

1606 *Choice, Chance*, etc. (1881) 40 You are so full of quibibbles, that I feare you meane knauery.

† **qui'bibe.** *Obs. rare*$^{-1}$. [? A fanciful extension of *quibe* QUIB; cf. prec.] = QUIBBLE *sb.* 2.

a **1550** *Image Hypocr.* in *Skelton's Wks.* (1843) II. 440 Lawyers and scribes With many quibibes.

† **qui'bible.** *Obs.* Also 6 -byble. [Of obscure origin.] ? A pipe or whistle. Also *fig.*

a **1529** SKELTON *Dk. Albany* 389 Your braynes are ydell It is time for you to brydell, And pype in a quibyble. **1642** SHIRLEY *Sisters* II. i, *Morulla*. I'll try what I can do! [*Draws her knife.*] *Piperollo.* Oh! my quibibles!

quible, -ler, obs. forms of QUIBBLE, -LER.

quiblet ('kwɪblɪt), *Obs.* exc. *U.S.* [f. QUIB or QUIBBLE: see -LET.] = QUIBBLE *sb.*

1630 J. TAYLOR (Water P.) *Wit & Mirth* Wks. 181/2 A quiblet..Nay, then I cannot blame you to be angry. **1636** ABP. WILLIAMS *Holy Table* (1637) 128 This Quiblet is grounded upon a mere Errour of the Printer. **1681** T. FLATMAN *Heraclitus Ridens* No. 46 (1713) II. 43, I cannot admire the Quiblet of the Influences of a Half-moon. **1890** BARRÈRE & LELAND *Slang Dict.*, *Quiblets* (American), a kind of witticism much in vogue in negro minstrelsy.

† '**quiblin.** *Obs.* [f. QUIB or QUIBBLE; cf. QUIBBLING.] A pun or quibble; a trick.

1605 CHAPMAN, etc. *Eastw. Hoe* III. i, 'Tis a trick rampant; 'tis a very quiblin. **1610** B. JONSON *Alch.* IV. vii, This is some trick; Come, leave your quiblins, Dorothee. **1614** —— *Barth. Fair* I. i, When a quirk, or a quiblin do's scape thee.

quibling, obs. form of QUIBBLING *ppl. a.*

quibyb(e, -byble: see CUBEB, QUIBIBLE.

quic, obs. f. QUICK *a.*; see also QUETCH *v.*

† **quice.** *Obs. rare.* In 5 qwyce. [Of obscure origin.] Only in ***quice-tree*** = gorse, whin.

c **1440** *Promp. Parv.* 162/1 Fyrrys, or qwyce tre, or gorstys tre, *ruscus*. *Ibid.* 204/1, 421/1.

quice, quich, variants of QUEEST, QUETCH.

quich(e, obs. forms of WHICH.

quiche[1] (kiːʃ). [Fr., ad. Alsatian *küchen* (G. *kuchen*).] An open flan or tart with a savoury filling. Also *attrib.* ***quiche Lorraine***: properly, a quiche containing a savoury custard with bacon or ham; also used of other types of quiche.

1949 A. L. SIMON *Dict. Gastron.* 199/1 *Quiche*, a savoury custard in an open tart, a Lorraine *spécialité*. **1951** E. DAVID *French Country Cookery* 92 *Quiche Lorraine*..Make a pastry... Onto the pastry spread the bacon..beat the 2 eggs into the cream..pour on to the pastry..bake for about 30 minutes. **1960** —— *French Provincial Cooking* 206 There have been various evolutions in the composition of a *quiche*...A *quiche* is a flat open tart... The fillings, of course, vary enormously. **1966** *Daily Tel.* 18 Oct. 13/5 After a soup..we had a smoked salmon *quiche*. **1967** *Woman's Day* (Austral.) 5 June 55 Most widely known is Quiche Lorraine, which traditionally contains only eggs, cream or milk, and bacon or ham. **1969** S. BURNFORD *Without Reserve* v. 180 So we sat in the sun on the dock, eating the quiche Lorraine that Mary had providently packed for just such an occasion. **1970** *Islander* (Victoria, B.C.) 16 Aug. 8/1 Some writers tell us this savory custard tart belongs to German cookery... Designed as a main dish, the quiche originally was baked in a pie pan..and was basically a custard, sometimes flavored with bacon. **1972** K. STEWART *Times Cookery Bk.* viii. 107 Roll the pastry out..slightly larger all round than an 8-inch flan or quiche tin. **1979** P. SIMMONDS *Mrs Weber's Diary* 27 Quiches are marvellous! They're all out of my freezer. Now, the vegetarian ones are at the front.

Quiché[2] (kiː'tʃeɪ), *sb.* and *a.* [Native name.]

A. *sb.* **a.** Name of a people inhabiting the western highlands of Guatemala; a member of this people. **b.** One of the principal languages of the Mayan family, spoken by this people. **B.** *adj.* Of or pertaining to this people.

1823 J. BAILY tr. *Juarros' Statistical & Commercial Hist. Guatemala* II. ii. 168 In all these places the Quiché language is spoken. *Ibid.*, It may be inferred..that the greater part of the province of Sapatitlan,..was a colony of the Quichées. **1823** [see KEKCHI *sb.* and *a.*]. **1883** *Encycl. Brit.* XVI. 208/1 The *Popol-Vuh* or national book of the Quiché kingdom of Guatemala. *Ibid.*, After this comes the creation of the four men and their wives who are the ancestors of the Quichés. **1933** A. HUXLEY *Let.* 24 Mar. (1969) 368 From there to Chichicastenango, which is the centre of the native life of the Quiché Indians, who thickly inhabit the plateaus. **1934** [see LADINO[1] 2]. **1948** A. L. KROEBER *Anthropol.* (rev. ed.) xviii. 794 Highland Maya, of upland Guatemala, speaking languages like Quiché, Cakchiquel, and Mam. **1950** I. VELIKOVSKY *Worlds in Collision* vi. 131 In the years of this gloom, when the world was covered with clouds and shrouded in mist, the Quiché tribe migrated to Mexico. **1963** *Times* 7 May 14/6 Judas is dressed in the costume of a Solola tribe—it is told that they were jealous of the Quiche and appealed for help to the Spaniards, who sent de Alvarado to liquidate them. **1968** *Language* XLIV. 191 It is in Quiché that the fascinating legends and history of the *Popol vuh*, 'the sacred book of the ancient Quichés', were recorded. It is also in Quiché and its near relatives of the 'Quichean' group that we have the largest accumulation of other written documents. **1974** *Encycl. Brit. Micropædia* VIII. 353/1 The Quiché Maya had an advanced civilization in pre-Columbian times. *Ibid.*, Written records of Quiché history and mythology are preserved in the *Popol Vuh*, written down in the Quiché language..shortly after conquest by the Spaniards in 1524. **1977** *Language* LIII. 261/2 In a final appendix, a 100-word vocabulary list is given in..Quiché (also Mayan), and in Proto-Mayan as reconstructed by Kaufman.

Hence **Qui'chean** *a.*, applied to the subgroup of the Mayan family of languages to which Quiché belongs.

1956 N. A. MCQUOWN in *Internat. Jrnl. Amer. Linguistics* XXII. 195/2 It differs from Kroeber..in suggesting a closer link between Quichean and Kekchian than between Quichean and Mamean. **1968** [see above]. **1978** *Language* LIV. 496 Kaufman's paper, 'New Mayan languages in Guatemala', summarizes identifications of 'new languages' made since 1969: Sacapultec and Sipacapa in the Quichean subgroup; [etc.].

Quichua, Quichuan: see QUECHUA *sb.* and *a.*, QUECHUAN *a.*

quick (kwɪk), *a.*, *sb.*[1], and *adv.* Forms: α. 1 cwic(u), c(w)ucu, cuc-, cwyc, 1–2 cwuc, (2 cwuce), 1–3 cwic, 3 cwicc, cwi(c)k-, 4 kuic, kuik; 3–4 quic, 3–5 quick-, 4 quyc, 5 quyck, 5–6 quycke, (5 qw-), 5–7 quicke, (5 qw-), 5- quick; 3–6 quik, quyk, (5–6 qw-), 4 quiyk-, 4–5 quikke, quyk(k)e, (5 qw-), 5 quike, quikk, (qw-); 4–5 quek, 5 qu-, qweke. *β. Sc.* and *north.* 5 quhyk, qwhick, -ikke, -yke, 5 whik, whicke, whyk, 6–9 whick, 9 wick. *γ.* 5 whyt, 7 whitt. [Comm. Teut.: OE. *cwicu*, *c(w)ucu* and *cwic*, *c(w)uc-*, = OFris. *quik*, *quek* (mod.Fris. *quick*, *queck*), OS. *quik* (MDu. *quic*, Du. *kwik*), OHG. *quec*, *quecch-* and *chec*, *checch-* (MHG. *quec*, *queck-* and *kec*, *keck-*, G. *keck* lively, pert, bold; also dial. *queck*, *quick*), ON. *kvik-r*, *kvikv-* and *kyk-r*, *kykv-* (MSw. *qvik*, *qvek*, Sw. *qvick*; Da. *kvik*, also *kvæg* sb., 'cattle', and *kvæg-*, *kvik-* in combs. as *kvæg-* or *kviksand*):—OTeut. **kwikwo-z*. The origin of the second *k* is obscure; it is absent in the Gothic **qius* (in pl. *qiwai*):—**kwiwo-z*, from the common Aryan **gʷīwo-* which appears in Skr. *jīvá*, L. *vīvus* (for **gvīvus*), Lith. *gývas*, OSlav. *živŭ*, OIr. *biu*, *beo* alive, living, Gr. *βίος* life. An ablaut-variant of the Teut. stem is found in ON. *kveikja* to kindle.]

A. *adj.*

I. Characterized by the presence of life.

1. a. Living, endowed with life, in contrast to what is naturally inanimate. Now *dial.* or *arch.*

c **888** K. ÆLFRED *Boeth.* xxxix. §3 Þætte men & ealle cwuca wuhta habbað..andan betwuh him. *c* **1200** ORMIN 3691 He þatt fedeþþ ennglelþeod & alle cwike shaffte. *c* **1300** *St. Brandan* 163 As a quic thing hupte up and down. **1387** TREVISA *Higden* (Rolls) I. 383 Goddes heste, þat heet þe erþe brynge forþ gras and quyk bestes. **1422** tr. *Secreta Secret.* 208 Sowne of thynges that bene not quycke as the Sowne of watyr, & brekynge of trees, thundyr [etc.]. **1523** FITZHERB. *Husb.* §102 The bottes..be quycke, and stycke faste in the mawe-syde. **1611** Speed *Hist. Gt. Brit.* ix. xiii. (1623) 741 They could see no quicke things left but onely Owles. **1820** Shelley *Witch Atl.* ix, Where the quick heart of the great world doth pant. **1857** E. Waugh *Lanc. Life* 29 There isn't a wick thing i' this world can wortch as it should do, if it doesn't heyt [= eat] as it should do.

†**b.** Of possessions or property: Consisting of animals; live (stock). Freq. in phrases ***quick cattle, good(s, stock***, etc., and hence, by analogy, ***quick beast***. *Obs.* Cf. also OE. *cwicæht, -feoh.*

871–89 *Charter* 45 in Sweet *O.E. Texts* 451 Ic..sello werburge..þas lond mid cwice erfe & mid earðe. **971** *Blickl. Hom.* 39 þone teoþan dæl on urum wæstmum & on cwicum ceape. **1297** R. Glouc. (Rolls) 11108 Sir Ion giffard nom to him is quic eiȝte echon. **1433** *E.E. Wills* 95 Alle my goodes & catelles, bothe quike & dede. **1523** Fitzherb. *Surv.* xii. (1539) 29 He that hath no quycke good, shall giue his beste deed good. **1526** *Lanc. Wills* I. 15, I bequeth ffor my mortuarye my best qwyk beast. **1592** West *1st Pt. Symbol.* §25 Houses and landes and quicke beastes, as sheepe and oxen. **1649** Bp. Hall *Cases Consc.* ix. (1654) 62 If they be quick commodities, as horses, sheep, kine and the like. **1686** R. P. in *Phil. Trans.* XX. 383 Houshold-goods.. lost; besides many quick Goods. **1745** W. Stout *Autobiog.* (1851) *ad fin.*, A public sale of all his quick goods and cattle.

c. Applied to things properly inanimate in various *transf.* or *fig.* uses (cf. II).

c **900** tr. *Bæda's Hist.* iv. xx. [xviii.] (1890) 314 He..þeaw þæs songes cwicre stæfne..sangeras lærde. *c* **950** *Lindisf. Gosp.* John iv. 11 [He] ualde ȝesealla ðe uæter cuic. *a* **1175** *Cott. Hom.* 241 Ic am cwuce bread. **1382** Wyclif *Heb.* iv. 12 Forsoth the word of God is quyk. [Also in later versions.] —— *1 Pet.* ii. 5 ȝoure silf as quike stoones be aboue bildid spiritual housis. **1502** Atkinson tr. *De Imitatione* iii. x. 205 Of me..pore & ryche, drawe quycke water as of the well of lyfe. **1586** J. Hooker *Hist. Irel.* in *Holinshed* II. 101/2 To rush through such quicke iron walles [armed Galloglasses]. **1732** Pope *Ess. Man.* i. 234 See thro'..this earth All matter quick, and bursting into birth. **1894** Crockett *Raiders* 13 Young green leaves breaking from the quick and breathing earth.

2. a. Of persons and animals: In a live state, living, alive. Now *dial.* or *arch.*

c **888** K. Ælfred *Boeth.* xxxvi. §7 [Ne] ma ðe we maȝon.. habban deadne mon for cwucone. *c* **1000** *Sax. Leechd.* I. 362 Wið miltwræce, cwices hundes milte abred of. *a* **1225** *Leg. St. Kath.* 63 þe riche reoðeren & schep..brohten to lake, þe poure cwike briddes. *a* **1300** *Cursor M.* 8645 Mi quik child has þou stoln..And has þi ded barn laid bi me. **1326** Langl. *P. Pl.* A. ii. 14 Ther nis no qweene qweyntore that quik is alyue. *c* **1450** *Two Cookery-bks.* ii. 99 Take a quyk lamprey, And lete him blode at þe nauell. *a* **1529** Skelton *Elynour Rummyng* 431 A cantell of Essex chese..well a fote thycke, Full of maggottes quycke. **1584** R. Scot *Discov. Witchcr.* v. vi. (1886) 81 *marg.*, To hold a quick eele by the taile. *a* **1661** Fuller *Worthies* (1840) I. v. 212 Not the quick but dead worthies properly pertain to my pen. **1790** Mrs. Wheeler *Westmld. Dial.* (1821) 98 Wor thor giants alive? *Mary.* Nay, nay,..they er net whick I racken. **1873** *Spectator* 23 Aug. 1069/1 'Quick' animals, to use a Yorkshire phrase, are sold here. **1875** *Sussex Gloss.*, s.v., I thought at first that sheep was dead, but I found it was quick still.

b. Freq. as complement to the subject of intr. and pass. verbs, or to the object (rarely subj.) of trans. verbs; sometimes with intensive *all* prefixed.

c **825** *Vesp. Psalter* cxxiii. 3 Cwice forswelȝað usic. **971** *Blickl. Hom.* 191 He woldan..þone casere cwicne forbærnan. *c* **1122** *O.E. Chron.* (Laud MS.) an. 1009 þæt he Wulfnoð cuconne oððe deadne beȝytan sceolde. *c* **1200** Ormin 1364 An bucc rann þær aweȝȝ all cwicc. **1297** R. Glouc. (Rolls) 4166 Some he mid strencþe nom & al quic hom vret. **13..** *Evang. Nicod.* 1082 in Herrig *Archiv* LIII. 411 Ely þe prophete..whik to heuen yhede. *c* **1400** *Rom. Rose* 4070 Al quik I wolde de dolven depe. *c* **1450** *Mirour Saluacioun* 737 But offred hire vnto godde to serue hym qwhikke swetlye. *a* **1533** Ld. Berners *Huon* xlvii. 159 Yᵉ lechour..shalbe flayne all quycke. **1632** Lithgow *Trav.* i. 37 There was a gray Frier burning quicke at S. Markes pillar. **1678** R. L'Estrange *Seneca's Mor.* (1702) 246 Privacy, without Letters, is but the Burying of a Man Quick. **1708** J. Philips *Cyder* i. 12 Ingulft By the wide yawning Earth, to Stygian Shades Went quick.

c. Of the flesh or parts of the body; *spec.* ***quick flesh***; now also ***quickflesh***.

a **1225** *Ancr. R.* 112 So þet flesch is cwikure, so þe pine þerof & þet hurt is more & sarre. *Ibid.*, His fleschs were tendrust & cwickest of alle vlesches. **1382** Wyclif *Lev.* xiii. 15 If the quyk flesh is spreynt with lepre, it is vnclene. *c* **1420** *Chron. Vilod.* 2624 A lyuyng mone, þᵗ hadde be lette blode in a quyke veyne. **1513** Douglas *Æneis* viii. viii. 69 Quhill quyk mouthis dyd deyd mouthis kys. **1527** L. Andrew tr. *J. Brunswyke's Distyl. Waters* C ii, The lame lymmes and membres..become quycke agayne. **1603** Florio tr. *Montaigne* ii. iii. (1897) III. 51 To cut and slice great mammocks of their quicke flesh. **1649** Drumm. of Hawth. *Poems* Wks. (1711) 1/2 My wasted heart, Made quick by death, more lively still remains. **1926** T. E. Lawrence *Seven Pillars* (1935) xliii. 251 If such animals [*sc.* camels] were taken suddenly inland for long marches over flints or other heat-retaining ground, their soles would burn, and at last crack in a blister; leaving quick flesh..in the centre of the pad. **1928** H. A. Manhood *Nightseed* 56 Men worn away to quickflesh, their eyes staring, reddened at the rims, men who coughed and coughed with a dry, torn-paper sound, mud to the waist. **1956** D. Lessing in *New Statesman* 30 June 768/3 With quickflesh contest if you need: There is no argument with bone.

d. *transf.* and *fig.*, chiefly of qualities, feelings, etc. (cf. II).

c **1200** *Trin. Coll. Hom.* 171 þo unbileffule men þe bi here quica liue here sunnes ne forleten. *c* **1380** Wyclif *Wks.* (1880) 369 þai suffre not criste to be alyue in þe sowlis of his peple bi qwike faythe. **1547** *Homilies* i. *Faith* i. (1640) 22 As the other vaine faith is called a dead faith, so may this be called a quicke or lively fayth. **1599** Shaks. *Hen. V*, ii. ii. 79 The mercy that was quicke in vs..is suppresst and kill'd. **1631** Chapman *Cæsar & Pompey* Plays 1873 III. 132 Strike dead our feare..Rather then keepe it quick. **1728** Pope *Dunc.* i. 59 Hints, like spawn, scarce quick in embryo lie. **1895** I. Zangwill *The Master* ii. vii. 213 Not only..the glamour of the dead past, but the poetry of the quick.

3. a. Of plants or their parts: Alive, growing. See also quickwood.

c **1000** *Ags. Ps.* (Th.) ciii. 16 Cwice cederbeamas. *c* **1200** Ormin 10002 þeȝȝ wærenn o þe treo All cwike & grene boȝhess. **1552** Huloet, Arboure or place made with quicke springes. **1577** *Nottingham Rec.* IV. 168 Dressyng of the hedge of quycke grose. **1626** Bacon *Sylva* §514 Dividing a Quick-Tree downe to the Ground. **1647–8** Cotterell *Davila's Hist. Fr.* (1678) 27 If there be any quick roots left, which may send forth new sprouts. **1802** W. Forsyth *Fruit Trees* (1824) 214 If any of the old dead snags remain they should be cut off close to the quick wood.

b. Composed of living plants, esp. hawthorn, as ***quick fence***, †***frith, hedge*** (cf. Du. *kwikhaag*), ***mound***. Cf. quickset.

1467 *Bury Wills* (Camden) 45 The qwyk heige set frome the gate on to the hall doore. **1563** Hyll *Art Garden.* (1593) 7 A quick hedge, which we cal a quickset hedge. **1564** *MS. Acc. St. John's Hosp., Canterb.*, To enclose the vij acres of land..wyth a quyk fryth. **1627** F. Little *Man. Chr. Munif.* (1871) 93 They fenced it with a quick mound. **1669** Worlidge *Syst. Agric.* (1681) 15 A thousand Acres of Land divided with good Quick-fences. **1719** De Foe *Crusoe* i. viii, A quick or living hedge. **1894** J. T. Fowler *Adamnan* Introd. 38 On top a palisade and quick hedge.

4. Constr. *with*.

a. ***quick with child***, said of a female in the stage of pregnancy at which the motion of the fœtus is felt. Now *rare* or *Obs.*

(This use has app. arisen by the inversion of the phr. ***with quick child*** exemplified in the following quots. *c* **1450** *Merlin* 12 She was grete with quyk childe. **1752** J. Louthian *Form of Process* (ed. 2) 217 You of the Jury of Matrons..say, that E. L. is not pregnant with quick Child.)

c **1450** Lonelich *Merlin* 826 (Kölbing) This good man sawh, that sche Qwyk with childe was. **1493** *Festivall* (W. de W. 1515) 106 Thenne conceyued Elyzabeth and whan she was quycke wᵗ chylde [etc.]. **1616** R. C. *Times' Whistle* iii. 1163 His vnckles wife surviues, purchance Left quick with childe. **1678** Lady Chaworth in *12th Rep. Hist. MSS. Comm.* App. V. 51 Sister Salisbery and sister Ansley [are] both quicke with child. **1774** Goldsm. *Nat. Hist.* (1776) II. 43 Women..quick with child, as their expression is, at the end of two months.

fig. **1870** Lowell *Among my Bks.* Ser. i. 238 Puritanism, believing itself quick with the seed of religious liberty, laid, without knowing it, the egg of democracy.

†**b.** *absol.* in same sense. *Obs.*

1588 Shaks. *L.L.L.* v. ii. 687 Then shall Hector be whipt for Iaquenetta that is quicke by him. **1647** Trapp *Comm. Rom.* ix. 11 Acknowledging..her issue for their Prince, before she as yet had felt her self quick.

c. Alive, instinct *with* (life, soul, feeling, etc.).

In some cases prob. associated with sense 19.

1837 Disraeli *Venetia* iv. iv, That languid form quick with excitement. **1839** Bailey *Festus* xxiii. (1852) 416 Thy palpitating piles of ruin..quick With soul immortal. **1873** Dixon *Two Queens* i. i. ix. 63 In Barcelona everyone was quick with rage. **1883** A. E. Hake *Story Chinese Gordon* xii. (1884) 294 To give peace to a country quick with war.

II. Of things: Having some specific quality characteristic or suggestive of a living thing.

* *In a sound or natural condition; fresh; productive.*

†**5.** Of the complexion: Having the freshness of life. *Obs. rare.*

a **1225** *Ancr. R.* 332 þe cwike rude of þe nebbe makeð to understonden þet te soule þet..nefde bute dead heou, haueð ikeiht cwic heou. **1422** tr. *Secreta Secret.* 223 The [fifth token] Is that a man haue quyke coloure. **1656** [see quickness 2]. *a* **1693** Aubrey *Lives* (1898) I. 60 (*W. Aubrey*) He had a delicate, quick, lively..complexion.

†**6.** Of things seen: Lifelike, vivid. *Obs. rare.*

13.. *E.E. Allit. P.* A. 1179 Fro alle þo syȝtez so quykez [? *read* quyke] & queme. *c* **1450** tr. *De Imitatione* i. xviii. 19 Beholde þe quicke ensamples of olde fadres. **1533** Bellenden *Livy* Prol. (1901) 4 Of awfull batallis,..ȝe may fynd here,..Als quyk as þai war led afore ȝour Ee.

†**7. a.** Of rock: Natural, 'living'. **b.** Of earth: (see quot. 1620). *Obs.*

a **1475** *Partenay* 1125 Vppon the quicke Roche thay it sett tho. *Ibid.* 4352 A caue..Within the quike roche. **1620** Markham *Farew. Husb.* ii. ii. (1668) 7 You shall be sure to raise up the quick earth which had not been stirred up with the Plough before.

8. a. *Mining.* Of veins, etc.: Containing ore, productive. (Cf. dead *a.* 10.)

1676 J. Beaumont in *Phil. Trans.* XI. 735 Subterraneous Vaults or Grotto's, whereof some..are said by our Miners to be quick, having often oar in them. **1747** Hooson *Miner's Dict.* Q ij b, Veins, Scrins, Pipes, &c. if they bear any Ore, are called Quick; and such as have no Ore, go by the Names of Dead Veins. **1881** in Raymond *Mining Gloss.*

b. Of stock, capital, etc.: Productive of interest or profit.

1701 Luttrell *Brief Rel.* (1857) V. 1 The quick stock of both companies shal be paid for discharge of their debts. *a* **1711** Ken *Christophil* Poet. Wks. 1721 I. 423, I..spent on the Quick-stock which I could never drain. **1818** Jas. Mill *Brit. India* I. i. v. 81 The estimate which was formed of their quick and dead stock. **1891** *Pall Mall G.* 19 Nov. 7/1 The quick assets [of the American Cotton Oil Trust]..amounted on August 31 last to 5,928,338 dols.

** *Possessed of motion.*

9. Of wells, springs, streams, or water: Running, flowing. (Cf. OE. *cwicwelle* adj.) Now *rare.* Also *transf.*

c **1000** *Ags. Ps.* (Th.) cxiii. 8 He..clifu cyrreð on cwicu.. wæteres wellan. *c* **1220** *Bestiary* 341 Bihoueð us to rennen to cristes quike welle. **1340** *Ayenb.* 98 To lhade of þe zeue streames þe quikke weteres. *c* **1375** *Sc. Leg. Saints* xxxiii. (*George*) 319 In þe mydis þe altere a quyk wel sprang. *c* **1430** Lydg. *Compl. Bl. Knt.* xi, A litel welle, That had his cours ..with quikke stremes colde. **1600** Holland *Livy* xlii. liv. 1147 The place is..watered also with many quicke and running springs. **1677** Evelyn *Diary* (1827) II. 425 Whose house stands inviron'd with very sweete and quick streams. *c* **1710** Celia Fiennes *Diary* (1888) 289 Its not a quick spring and very often is dranke drye. **1816** Byron *Parisina* xx, The living stream lies quick below, And flows, and cannot cease to flow. **1857** Thoreau *Jrnl.* 30 July in *Maine Woods* (1864) 276 The Indian navigator naturally distinguishes by a name those parts of a stream where he has encountered quick water and forks. **1889** Pater *G. de Latour* 75 Gently winding valleys, with clear, quick water. **1894** *Harper's Mag.* Apr. 782/1 That quick water's the Mahkin Rapids. **1905** L. Mott *Jules of Great Heart* xxi. 260 Nearer and nearer sounded the quick water of the thoroughfare between Lac des Rochers and the dead-water of Rivière du Renard. **1951** H. E. Giles *Harbin's Ridge* xxiii. 201, I couldn't say a word for the knot in my throat, and my eyes stung with quick water. **1958** *Montreal Star* 22 Oct. 14/3 On the subject of water also there is the definition of quickwater... It used to be used in the Maritimes, a term designating water running rapidly but not broken by rapids.

10. Of soil, etc.: Mobile, shifting, readily yielding to pressure. Cf. *quick-clay* in sense D, quicksand.

a **1340** Hampole *Psalter* i. 1 As he þᵗ gas on qwik grauel, þat gers him synk þᵗ standis þar on. **1552** Huloet, Quycke sandes or shelues, *syrtes.* **1602** Carew *Cornwall* 8 b, The quicke ground (as they call it) that mooued with the floud. **1696** *Phil. Trans.* XIX. 352 Great Freshes..make the Sands Shift, and consequently Quick. **1771** Smollett *Humph. Cl.* 12 Sept., The Solway sands,..as the tide makes,..become quick in different places. **1890** Emerson *Wild Life* 58, I pulled my legs out of the soft ooze, and was soon across the patch of quick ground. **1895** *Trans. Australasian Inst. Mining Engin.* III. 141 *Quick.* Veins are said to be quick when productive, and dead when non-productive. *Quick-ground*, ground in a loose incoherent state; soft watery strata, e.g., running sand. **1901** *Norges Geol. Undersøgelse* No. 32. 221 All kinds of soft clay are often called 'quick' clay; in a more restricted sense it means clay which has the property of being comparatively stiff when it lies in its original bed, but becomes fluid when it is set in motion. **1963** Means & Parcher *Physical Prop. Soils* xi. 333 The velocity of the upward flowing water required to cause the soil to become quick. **1967** A. R. Jumikis *Introd. Soil. Mech.* iv. 32 Quicksand is not a special type of soil, but a condition. Any granular material through which an upward flow of water takes place may become 'quick' under proper hydraulic conditions. **1978** *Sci. Amer.* Nov. 143/2 Sand does not become quick without an influx of water, because any extra water separates out on top of a bed of closely packed sand, creating a situation similar to the ones encountered on the beach and in the demonstration with a bottle.

*** *Having some form of activity or energy.*

11. †**a.** Of coals: Live, burning. *Obs.*

c **1000** *Sax. Leechd.* II. 224 Do to fyre on croccan, ofer wylle on godum gledum clænum & cwicum. **1340** *Ayenb.* 205 A quic col berninde ope an hyeape of dyade coles. *c* **1400** Maundev. (Roxb.) xxxi. 142 If a man..couer þe coles þeroff with aschez, þai will hald in quikk a twelfmonth. **1413** *Pilgr. Sowle* (Caxton 1483) iii. ix. 55 Quyck coles whiche brente them full bytterly. **1581** T. Howell *Deuises* (1879) 200 Kindled coales close kept, continue longest quick. **1657** Trapp *Comm. Ps.* cxx. 4 Juniper..maketh a very scorching fire, and quick coals, such as last long. **1764** Harmer *Observ.* iii. 118 They..put it into an oven upon the quick coals.

b. Of fires or flames: Burning strongly or briskly. Also of an oven: Exposed to a brisk fire.

c **1374** Chaucer *Boeth.* iv. pr. vi. 104 (Camb. MS.) A ryht lyfly and quyk fyre of thowht. **1604** E. G[rimstone] *D'Acosta's Hist. Indies* ii. vii. 96 If it [the fire] bee quicke and violent, it doth greatly evaporate the quick-silver. **1624** Quarles *Sion's Sonn.* xx. 19 Thy breath..incends quicke flames, where Ember'd sparkes but shine. **1708** J. C. *Compl. Collier* (1845) 16 It makes a hot quick Fire. **1769** Mrs. Raffald *Eng. Housekpr.* (1778) 4 Bake it in a quick oven three hours. **1821** Shelley *Prometh. Unb.* iii. i. 38 God! Spare me! I sustain not the quick flames. **1863** Reade *Hard Cash* xiv, You will cook your own goose—by a quick fire.

†**12.** Of speech, writings, etc.: Lively, full of vigour or acute reasoning; smart, sprightly. *Obs.*

a **1225** *Ancr. R.* 170 Ye eihtuðe reisun is uorte habben cwike bone. **1340** *Ayenb.* 134 þet is to zigge: oþer þane quicke scele oþer aperte miracle. *c* **1386** Chaucer *Prol.* 306 That [speech] was..short and quyk, and ful of hy sentence. *c* **1400** *Apol. Loll.* 8 Aȝen swilk feynid..indulgens, howiþ a feiþful prest to multiply quek resouns. **1531** Elyot *Gov.* i. x, Some quicke and mery dialoges elect out of Luciane. **1589** Puttenham *Eng. Poesie* i. xxviii. (Arb.) 70 An inscription.. in few verses, pithie, quicke and sententious. **1625** Gill *Sacr. Philos.* Pref., Though his writings be easie and quicke, yet his matiers are scattered.

†**13.** Of places or times: Full of activity or business; busy. Of trade: Brisk. *Obs.*

c **1386** Chaucer *Frankl. T.* 774 Amyd the toun, right in the quyke strete. **1538** Leland *Itin.* I. 8 A good quik Market Toune. **1641** Best *Farm. Bks.* (Surtees) 102 The kinge beinge there, the markets were very quicke. *a* **1661** Fuller *Worthies* (1840) II. 190 He called Manchester the fairest and quickest town in this county. *a* **1687** Petty *Pol. Arith.* (1690) 18 Some where or other in the World, Trade is always quick enough. **1726–46** Thomson *Winter* 779 Pure, quick, and sportful is the wholesome day.

†**14.** Of sulphur: Readily inflammable, fiery. *Obs.*

c **1530** *Hickscorner* in Hazl. *Dodsley* I. 179 He asked for a mouthful of quick brimstone. **1559** Morwyng *Evonym.* 323, ij unces of bothe kindes of Sulphur or brimstone, that is of the quik and dead. **1590** Spenser *F.Q.* i. vii. 13 That divelish yron Engin,..With windy Nitre and quick Sulphur fraught. **1661** Lovell *Hist. Anim. & Min.* 107 Honey, nitre, ..and quick brimstone, reduced unto the consistence of honey.

†**15.** Of wine and other liquors: Brisk, effervescent. *Obs.*

1620 VENNER *Via Recta* ii. 25 A pure and quicke wine. **1677** YARRANTON *Eng. Improv.* 122 As the different heat of the Climate is, so the Liquor shall ripen and grow quick and fit to drink. **1730–46** THOMSON *Autumn* 706 The mellow-tasted burgundy; and, quick As is the wit it gives, the gay champagne.

**** *Producing a strong effect on the senses or mind.*

16. †**a.** Of the voice: Loud, clear. *Obs. rare*⁻¹.

c **1205** LAY. 12306 Heo..him to cleopeden quickere stæuene [*c* 1275 mid swiþe loude stemne].

b. Of colour: Vivid, bright, dazzling. *rare.*

1664 POWER *Exp. Philos.* I. 13 Eyes..of a very quick and lively transparency or fulgour. **1851** G. MEREDITH *Love in the Valley* xx, Slain are the poppies that shot their random scarlet Quick amid the wheatears.

17. Of feelings: Lively, vivid, keen, strongly felt.

c **1449** PECOCK *Repr.* II. viii. 183 Quyk and feruent and.. deuout remembraunce. **1551** ROBINSON tr. *More's Utop.* II. ix. (1895) 284 Onles they, by quycke repentaunce approue the amendement of their lyffes. **1665** GLANVILL *Def. Vain Dogm.* 75, I have still a quick resentment of the Vanity of Confiding in Opinions. **1710** STEELE *Tatler* No. 196 ¶5 These have in their several Stations a quick Relish of the exquisite Pleasure of doing Good. **1752** CHESTERF. *Lett.* (1792) III. 254 The scene of quick and lively pleasures. **1839** BAILEY *Festus* viii. (1848) 87 Firestranded, rolling in quick agony.

18. †**a.** Of a taste or smell: Sharp, pungent; brisk. Also of things in respect of taste or smell (cf. 15). *Obs.*

1573 *Treas. Hid. Secrets* xliii, If white Saunders..be old, and have no pleasant and quicke odour, they are nothing worth. **1578** LYTE *Dodoens* v. xx. 574 These two Purcelaynes are..of a sharpe or quicke taste. **1641** FRENCH *Distill.* v. (1651) 126 It will tast as quick as bottle beer that is a fortnight old. **1670** NARBOROUGH *Jrnl.* in *Acc. Sev. Late Voy.* (1694) I. 68 This Rind..is hotter than Pepper and more quicker. **1758** REID tr. *Macquer's Chym.* I. 33 Its smell is..extremely quick and suffocating when it smokes. **1797** *Encycl. Brit.* (ed. 3) I. 625/2 Their smell is quick and penetrating, their taste pungent.

†**b.** Of speech or writing: Sharp, caustic. *Obs.*

1580 LYLY *Euphues* (Arb.) 280 A quicke aunswere that might cut him. **1589** NASHE *Pref. Greene's Menaphon* (Arb.) 9 In Scholler-like matters of controuersie, a quicker stile may pass as commendable. **1616** BULLOKAR *Eng. Expos.*, *Quippe*, a quicke checke, a pretty taunt. **1685** *Roxb. Ball.* IV. 284 These quirks are too quick, you do put on me. **1748** JOHNSON *Van. Hum. Wishes* 62 How wouldst thou..Dart the quick taunt, and edge the piercing gibe?

c. Of air or light: Sharp, piercing. *rare.*

1608 SHAKS. *Per.* IV. i. 28 The air is quick there, And it pierces and sharpens the stomach. **1818** KEATS *Endym.* II. 918 Other light, Though it be quick and sharp enough to blight The Olympian eagle's vision, is dark.

†**d.** Of what causes pain. *Obs. rare*⁻¹.

a **1716** SOUTH *Serm.* (1744) II. 27 The punishment of the Cross is..the quickest and the most acute.

III. Having in a high degree the vigour or energy characteristic of life, and hence distinguished by, or capable of, prompt or rapid action or movement.

19. a. Of persons (or animals): Full of vigour, energy, or activity (now *rare*); prompt or ready to act; acting, or able to act, with speed or rapidity (freq. with suggestion or implication of sense 23).

13.. *E.E. Allit. P.* B. 624 He..Comaunded hir to be cof and quyk at þis oneȝ. *c* **1330** R. BRUNNE *Chron. Wace* (Rolls) 16372 Þey smette to-gedere so bitterlyke, þat eyþer side fond oþer quyke. **1434** MISYN *Mending Life* 118 So þat qwen þa rise to pray, þa be qwhickar þen þai before were. *c* **1440** *Promp. Parv.* 421/1 Quyk, or lyvely, or delyvyr, *vivax.* **1535** COVERDALE *Ezra* vii. 6 Ezdras..was a quycke scrybe in the lawe of Moses. *a* **1548** HALL *Chron., Hen. IV* 32 b, This king was..formally compact, quicke and deliver and of a stout courage. **1611** BIBLE *Ecclus.* xxxi. 22 In all thy workes bee quicke. *a* **1715** BURNET *Own Time* III. (1724) I. 382 Seimour ..was a graceful man, bold and quick. **1816** BYRON *Ch. Har.* III. xlii, Quiet to quick bosoms is a hell. **1833** TENNYSON *Rosalind* ii, The quick lark's closest-caroll'd strains.

b. Of qualities in a person (or animal).

c **1380** WYCLIF *Serm.* Sel. Wks. I. 109 Crist fastide fourty daies.. he was in quyke age, and listide wel to ete. **1535** STEWART *Chron. Scot.* I. 12 Thair curage..that tyme wes so quik. *c* **1580** SIDNEY *Ps.* XXXIII. xi, Of quick strength is an horse. *a* **1661** FULLER *Worthies* (1840) II. 536 He was a good patriot, of a quick and clear spirit. **1732** NEAL *Hist. Purit.* I. 342 He was a little man, of a quick spirit. **1819** SHELLEY *Cenci* I. iii. 173 The resolution of quick youth Within my veins.

c. Of things (material and immaterial).

1545 ASCHAM *Toxoph.* II. (Arb.) 117 So that he [a bow] be ..quycke and spedye ynoughe for farre castynge. **1551** ROBINSON tr. *More's Utop.* II. iv. (1895) 149 They..finde spedy and quicke remedies for present fautes. **1592** SHAKS. *Rom. & Jul.* v. iii. 120 O true Apothecary: Thy drugs are quicke. **1699** *Pennsylvania Arch.* I. 127, I am obliged for thy quick Care about ye Wine. **1820** SHELLEY *Vision of Sea* 50 A lead-coloured fog..Whose breath was quick pestilence. **1883** GRESLEY *Gloss. Coal-mining* s.v., Blasting powder is said to be quick when it burns or goes off very rapidly.

d. *Cricket.* Of a bowler.

1967 [private letter from Mr. R. Bowen]. **1976** J. SNOW *Cricket Rebel* 36, I was not fast enough to be classed as a genuine quick bowler.

20. a. Of the eye, ear, etc.: Keen or rapid in its function; capable of ready or swift perception.

c **1420** *Pallad. on Husb.* VIII. 126 Digestioun hit macth and eyon quyk. *a* **1450** *Knt. de la Tour* (1868) 18 She..hadd a quicke yee, and a light. **1590** SPENSER *F.Q.* I. ii. 26 Busying his quicke eies her face to view. *a* **1661** FULLER *Worthies* (1840) III. 104 They have a quicker palate than I, who can make any such discovery. **1778** JOHNSON *L.P., Milton* Wks. I. 140 His eyes..must have been once quick. **1818** SHELLEY *Rosal. & Helen* 1212 The same lady..With silver locks and quick brown eyes. **1864** *Cornh. Mag.* Dec. 655 The quick ear of Midwinter detected something wrong in the tone of Mr. Brock's voice.

b. So of the senses, perception, feeling, etc.

a **1548** HALL *Chron., Hen. VI* 130 The kynges counsaill, whiche did not with quicke sight, forese..thynges for to come. **1604** E. G[RIMSTONE] *D'Acosta's Hist. Indies* IV. xxxvii. 309 Those [birds]..have a very quicke sight. **1849** MACAULAY *Hist. Eng.* v. I. 618 Several dogs of quick scent were turned out. **1870** ROCK *Text. Fabr.* Introd. 87 Women being gifted with such quick feeling of finger.

21. a. Mentally active or vigorous; of ready apprehension or wit; prompt to learn, think, invent, etc.

1484 CAXTON *Fables of Poge* xii, Two prestes..of whome that one was quyck and coude putte hym self forth. **1551** ROBINSON tr. *More's Utop.* II. vi. (1895) 212 The people be gentle, merye, quycke, and fyne wytted. **1606** SHAKS. *Ant. & Cl.* v. ii. 216 The quicke Comedians Extemporally will stage vs. **1640** BP. REYNOLDS *Passions* xiii. 121 Another by nature quicke and of noble intellectuals wholly applyeth himselfe unto it [learning]. **1792** *Ld. Auckland's Corr.* (1861) II. 410 He is a quick, sensible man. **1847** TENNYSON *Princ.* Prol. 137, I would teach them all that men are taught; We are twice as quick.

b. So of mind, wit, etc., and of qualities or operations (cf. 25) of the mind.

c **900** tr. *Bæda's Hist.* v. xvii. [xix.] (1890) 452 He þa cwices modes ȝeornlice leornade þa þing. **1526** *Pilgr. Perf.* (W. de W. 1531) 8 In theyr owne pregnaunt and quycke wytte and reason. **1589** PUTTENHAM *Eng. Poesie* III. xvii. (Arb.) 196 *Synecdoche*,..because it seemeth to aske a good, quick, and pregnant capacitie,..I chose to call him the figure..of quick conceite. **1651** HOBBES *Leviath.* I. xiii. 60 One man..of quicker mind then another. *a* **1715** BURNET *Own Time* III. (1724) I. 354 Lord Sunderland was a man of..a quick decision in business. **1785** PALEY *Mor. Philos.* (1818) I. 361 At our public schools..quick parts are cultivated, slow ones are neglected. **1804** *Ann. Rev.* II. 79/1 The author is evidently a man of quick observation and lively fancy. **1855** MACAULAY *Hist. Eng.* xix. IV. 310 Queen Mary..had naturally a quick perception of what was excellent in art.

22. a. Hasty, impatient, hot-tempered. ? *Obs.*

1549 LATIMER *6th Serm. bef. Edw. VI* (Arb.) 172 The Byshop was some what quicke wyth theym, and signified that he was muche offended. **1588** SHAKS. *L.L.L.* II. i. 118 You must not be so quicke. **1628** FORD *Lover's Mel.* II. i, Are you so quick? Well, I may chance to cross Your peevishness.

b. So of temper, disposition, etc.

1837 DISRAELI *Venetia* I. viii, The expressions of a quick and offended temper. *c* **1850** *Arab. Nts.* (Rtldg.) 89 The quick and violent disposition of his master.

23. Moving, or able to move, with speed.

c **1450** *Cov. Myst.* xxx. (Shaks. Soc.) 298, I am as whyt [= whyk] as thought. *a* **1529** SKELTON *Elynour Rummyng* 337 Her tonge was verye quycke, But she spake somwhat thycke. **1599** SHAKS. *Hen. V*, v. i. 91 Ile..something leane to Cutpurse of quicke hand. **1605** —— *Lear* IV. vii. 35 The most terrible and nimble stroke Of quick, cross lightning. **1730–46** THOMSON *Autumn* 526 The quick dice..leaping from the box. **1821** SHELLEY *Epipsych.* 532 The young stars glance Between the quick bats in their twilight dance. **1861** THORNBURY *Brit. Artists* I. 247 The quick lizard is already out.

24. Of movement or succession: Rapid, swift.

1297 R. GLOUC. (Rolls) 4544 He sywede after þe traytour mid wel quic pas. **1602** T. MIDDLETON in *Shaks. Cent. of Praise* (1879) 51 To keep quick time unto the owl. **1610** SHAKS. *Temp.* IV. i. 39 Incite them to quicke motion. **1632** LITHGOW *Trav.* VI. 298 The Dromidory hath a quicke and hard-reaching trot. **1655** STANLEY *Hist. Philos.* I. (1701) 63/2 The Body, which is continually in quick motion, is.. called æther. **1759** JOHNSON *Rasselas* vi, There may be danger of too quick descent. **1771** *Junius Lett.* lix. 310 There is a quick succession of subjects. **1860** TYNDALL *Glac.* II. xxvii. 384 The quicker flow of the centre causes this structure to bend.

25. a. Of an action, occurrence, process, etc.: That is done, happens, or takes place, rapidly or with speed; *esp.* that is over within a short space of time; that is soon finished or completed.

a **1548** HALL *Chron., Hen. VI* 169 And therfore willed her in so quicke a mischief, to provide a hasty remedy. **1591** SHAKS. *1 Hen. VI*, v. iii. 8 This speedy and quicke appearance argues proofe Of your accustom'd diligence. **1607** —— *Timon* I. i. 91 Morall Paintings..That shall demonstrate these quicke blowes of Fortune. **1634** MILTON *Comus* 284 They..purpos'd quick return. *Ibid.* 841 She.. underwent a quick immortal change. **1664** MARVELL *Corr.* Wks. 1872–5 II. 151 Give me a quick dispatch one way or other. *a* **1756** MRS. HEYWOOD *New Present* (1771) 263 A quick Way to take Grease out of Woollen Cloth. **1819** SHELLEY *Mask of Anarchy* lxxv, With a quick and startling sound. **1820** —— *Prometh. Unb.* III. iii. 135 It feeds the quick growth of the serpent vine. **1821** —— *Epipsych.* 547 The pebble-paven shore, Under the quick, faint kisses of the sea Trembles. **1854** RONALDS & RICHARDSON *Chem. Technol.* (ed. 2) I. 343 A quick process of distillation.

b. ***quick one***: an alcoholic drink intended to be taken rapidly. *colloq.*

1928 D. L. SAYERS *Unpleasantness at Bellona Club* ix. 105 They had a quick one together. **1936** A. HUXLEY *Eyeless in Gaza* xlii. 503 After the second 'quick one' in the bar of the theatre. **1948** R. A. KNOX *Mass in Slow Motion* viii. 80 The conductor slipping in to the Corner house to have a quick one. **1959** B. COBB *Don't lie to Police* (1960) xii. 194 We go in a bunch at half-past eleven and have a quick one, or rather one or two quick ones. **1968** *Listener* 19 Dec. 811/3 We've time for a quick one and then we'll go and do our bit of business. **1976** G. MOFFAT *Over Sea to Death* vii. 79 Ken Maynard came into the cocktail lounge... 'Just in time for a quick one... Two lagers, please.'

†**26.** Of steel: Breaking readily; brittle. *Obs.*

1677 MOXON *Mech. Exerc.* 55 The Spanish Steel..is too quick (as Workmen call it) that is, too brittle for Springs or Punches.

27. Of a curve, turn, etc.: Sharp.

1725 W. HALFPENNY *Sound Building* 9 If the Arch is required to be quicker or flatter on the Hanse. **1793** SMEATON *Edystone L.* §81 A much quicker curve, or sweep of a less Radius. **1858** *Skyring's Builders' Prices* (ed. 48) 57 Mouldings..circular on plan..quick sweep.

fig. **1732** POPE *Ep. Cobham* 64 Tho' strong the bent, yet quick the turns of mind. **1781** COWPER *Charity* 544 The turns are quick, the polished points surprise.

28. With constructions:

a. with *to* and infin.

1297 R. GLOUC. (Rolls) 9327 Slou to fiȝte & quic to fle & þat nis no manhede. **1584** LYLY *Campaspe* II. ii, A wit apt to conceive, and quick to answer. **1593** SHAKS. *Rich. II*, II. i. 234 Quicke is mine eare to heare of good towards him. **1808** SCOTT *Marm.* II. Introd. 95 The widow's deafen'd ear Grows quick that lady's step to hear. **1879** CHURCH *Spenser* 139 Those who..are quick to respond to English manliness and tenderness.

b. with *in.*

c **1449** PECOCK *Repr.* II. xvi. 243 Summe othere..weren quycker in natural witt and waxiden better philsophiris. **1551** ROBINSON tr. *More's Utop.* II. vi. (1895) 218 The wyttes therefore of the Vtopians..be maruelous quycke in the inuentyon of feates. **1588** SHAKS. *L.L.L.* I. ii. 31, I do say thou art quick in answers. **1642** FULLER *Holy & Prof. St.* II. i. 51 Others that are so quick in searching, seldome search to the quick. **1837** MARRYAT *Percival Keene* xii, He's not very quick in temper. **1882** J. H. BLUNT *Ref. Ch. Eng.* II. 190 So quick was justice in overtaking the rebels.

c. with *of, about.*

1560 ROLLAND *Crt. Venus* Prol. 27 Quik of Ingyne, of Lordschip couetous. **1573** TUSSER *Husb.* (1878) 173 Launders and millers be quick of their toll. **1607–12** BACON *Ess., Death* (Arb.) 384 The most vitall partes are not the quickest of sence. *a* **1626** BP. ANDREWES *Serm.* (1841) IV. 43 More quick of touch than the rest. **1840** DICKENS *Barn. Rudge* x, He is quick of foot. **1859** TENNYSON *Elaine* 1198 It may be, I am quicker of belief. **1937** W. H. SAUMAREZ SMITH *Let.* 29 July in *Young Man's Country* (1977) ii. 85, I shall have to be very quick about writing this letter as the Air Mail goes from the Club in half an hour.

d. with *at, for, unto.*

1590 SHAKS. *Mids. N.* III. ii. 342 Your hands then mine, are quicker for a fray. **1640** A. MELVILLE *Commonpl. Bk.* (1899) 18 Quhick at meitt, quhick at work. **1850** TENNYSON *In Mem.* xxxiii, Her hands are quicker unto good.

IV. 29. Combs., chiefly parasynthetic adjs., as ***quick-answered, -born, -chapt, -eared, -footed, -handed, -hearted, -nosed, -paced, -scented, (-sensedness), -shod, -spirited,*** (†***-sprighted***), ***-tempered, -thoughted, -voiced, -winged, -worded.*** Also QUICK-EYED, -SIGHTED, WITTED.

1611 SHAKS. *Cymb.* III. iv. 161 Ready in gybes, *quicke-answer'd, sawcie. *a* **1300** *Cursor M.* 28547 Þat *quikborne child i haue fordon. **1824** BYRON *Def. Transf.* I. ii. 81 His own twin, quickborn of the same womb. **1598** E. GILPIN *Skial.* (1878) 59 Here his wife's bated by some *quick-chapt youth. **1771** MRS. GRIFFITH *Hist. Lady Barton* I. 118 They are..*quick-eared as the mole. **1920** D. H. LAWRENCE *Lost Girl* viii. 182 He turned like a quick-eared animal. **1839** W. C. BRYANT in *U.S. Democratic Rev.* Apr. 406 Here the *quick-footed wolf..crushed the flower Of Sanguinaria. **1938** *Times Lit. Suppl.* 5 Mar. 158/1 A very quick-footed batsman. **1847** JAMES *J. Marston Hall* vii, You are a good, *quick-handed boy. **1820** L. HUNT *Indicator* No. 29 (1822) I. 231 Ending with that simple, *quick-hearted line. **1561** T. NORTON *Calvin's Inst.* I. 40 Many *quicknosed men do laugh at this. **1607** TOPSELL *Four-f. Beasts* (1658) 111 Dogs ..are called sharp..and quick-nosed. **1590** R. HARVEY *Pl. Perc.* A ij b, Being *quicksented [I] thrust forward on the trale. **1647** SANDERSON *Serm.* II. 216 So quick-scented where there is a likelihood of gain. **1656** W. D. tr. *Comenius' Gate Lat. Unl.* 149 The sagacitie or *quick-sensedness of reason. **1645** *City Alarum* 23 If the Souldier be *quickshod with this mettall [etc.]. **1552** HULOET, *Quycke spirited, and quycke of spirite. *a* **1653** GOUGE *Comm. Heb.* iv. 12 That is said to be 'quick'..which is active..as..quick-spirited. **1598** E. GILPIN *Skial.* (1878) 27 My quick-sprighted lasse can speake. **1830** MISS MITFORD *Village* Ser. IV. (1863) 149 She used to be a little *quick-tempered! **1782** COWPER *Expostulation* 316 Laborious and *quick-thoughted man. **1820** KEATS *Hyperion* I. 149 Thus she *quick-voiced spake. **1833** MRS. BROWNING *Prometh. Bound* Wks. 1850 I. 152 On the back of the *quick-winged bird I glode. **1954** J. R. R. TOLKIEN *Two Towers* III. iv. 81 It [*sc.* a song] is..*quick-worded, and soon over.

B. Elliptical or absolute uses passing into sb.

1. a. *pl.* (Without article or *-s.*) Living persons. (Chiefly in echoes of Acts x. 42 or the Apostles' Creed, in phr. ***quick and dead.***)

c **897** K. ÆLFRED *Gregory's Past.* xv. 96 Se þe demende is cwicum & deadum. *a* **900** CYNEWULF *Christ* 997 Ðær bið cirm ond cearu ond cwicra ȝewin. **1067** *Charter of Eadweard* in Kemble *Cod. Dipl.* IV. 220 For alle quiken and for alle dede to helpe. *c* **1200** ORMIN 10557 To demenn cwike & dæde. *c* **1380** WYCLIF *Serm.* Sel. Wks. II. 213 His preier.. doiþ more harm to quike and dede. *c* **1440** *Jacob's Well* 65 Paye..to qwyke & to dede, þat þou owyst. **1562** COOPER *Answ. Priv. Masse* (1850) 56 For then ye applied it to high, to low,..to quick, to dead. **1667** MILTON *P.L.* XII. 460 To judge both quick & dead. **1732** LAW *Serious C.* ii. (ed. 2) 22 The Judge of quick and dead.

b. ***the quick***, the living. Usu. *pl.*, and in conjunction with *the dead* (cf. 1 a).

c **888** K. ÆLFRED *Boeth.* xxxvi §7 Ne bið se cwuca ðonne nyttra ðe se deada. *c* **900** tr. *Bæda's Hist.* I. xi. [xiv.] (1890) 50 Ða cwican no ȝenihtsumedon þæt hi ða deadan bebyriȝdan. *a* **1200** *Moral Ode* 190 Þet he scal deme þa quike and þa dede. **1297** R. GLOUC. (Rolls) 5877 Me halt euere mid þe quike; þe dede was sone stille. *c* **1330** R. BRUNNE *Chron. Wace* (Rolls) 4388 þe quyke vpon þe dede ȝede. *c* **1400** *Apol. Loll.* 49 What riȝtfulnes is þis to ȝef ȝeftis to þe dead, &

spoyle þe quek? **1567** *Gude & Godlie B.* (S.T.S.) 41 Gif ony to the quick ȝeid from the deide, Trewlie they suld repent. **1654** FULLER *Two Serm.* 55 Such Volumes as concern the Quick at that Day. **1727** DE FOE *Hist. Appar.* vii. 99 The dead could never come to the quick. **1800–24** CAMPBELL *Death-Boat of Heligoland* 2 The quick have their sleep-walkers, so have the dead. **1850** BLACKIE *Æschylus* I. 156 He, who was dead, has slain the quick.

†**c.** That which is alive. (OE. and early ME. in gen. sing.) *Obs.*

Beowulf (Z.) 2314 No ðær aht cwices lað lyft floga læfan wolde. *c* **1000** ÆLFRIC *Gen.* viii. 21 Ne ofslea ic.. mid wætere ælc þing cuces. *c* **1205** LAY. 25758 Na whit heo ne funden quikes uppen wolden. *a* **1225** *Ancr. R.* 334 Þe reade [deade C.] see, þet nowiht cwices [nis] inne.

†**d.** Live stock, cattle. (So OFris. *quek*, *quik*, LG. *queck*, *quick*, Da. *kvæg*.) *Obs. rare*$^{-1}$.

a **1400–50** *Alexander* 4469 Of any gud at ȝe geet a gift ye þam offirre, A quantite of all-quat, of quike & of ellis.

2. With *a* and *pl.* A living thing. *rare* (now only *dial.*).

c **1000** *Ags. Ps.* (Th.) ciii. 24 His is mycel sæ.. þær is unrim on ealra cwicra. **13..** *E.E. Allit. P.* B. 567 As to quelle alle quykez for qued þat myȝt falle. **1579** SPENSER *Sheph. Cal.* Mar. 74, [I] Might see the moving of some quicke Whose shape appeared not. **1664** POWER *Exp. Philos.* I. 34 You shall see these little Quicks.. grow feebler in their motion. **1899** *Cumbld. Gloss.*, *Whicks*,.. maggots.

3. a. *coll.* Living plants, *spec.* of white hawthorn, set to form a hedge. = QUICKSET 1 a.

1456–7 *Durham Acc. Rolls* (Surtees) 241 Pro factura unius fosse et insercione de lez Whyke. **1484–5** *Ibid.* 98 Pro CC[ma] qweke et plantacione ejusdem. **1641** EVELYN *Diary* (1871) 33 The workes.. are curiously hedg'd with quick. **1725** BRADLEY *Fam. Dict.* s.v. *Quickset*, The same Method is used in planting all Sorts of Quick.. except the Alder, Elder, Furz, and Holly. **1764** *Museum Rusticum* III. lxiii. 285, I keep the quick regularly clipped, which, in a few years, renders the fence impenetrable. **1818** *Relig. Clerici* 405 Hedges of living quick, a yew alcove. **1881** *Gard. Chron.* 26 Mar. 409 Planting two hollies and six quick in every yard.

b. With *a* and *pl.* A single plant of this description. = QUICKSET 1 b.

1507–8 *Durham Acc. Rolls* (Surtees) 660 Et sol... sepientibus cum lez Wykkes.. querend. le Whikkes. **1671** *Vestry Bks.* (Surtees) 202 For quickes, 5*s.* 8*d.* **1765** EARL HADDINGTON *Forest trees* 40 Upon this I laid another turf.. and a row of thorns, or quicks. **1792** *Trans. Soc. Arts* (ed. 2) III. 173 Quicks thus planted will at an early age, form a fence. **1850** TENNYSON *In Mem.* lxxxviii, Wild bird, whose warble,.. Rings Eden thro' the budded quicks.

†**c.** (See quot.) *Obs. rare*$^{-0}$.

1753 CHAMBERS *Cycl. Supp.* App., *Quick*, the name by which some call a species of *Mespilus*, or medlar.

4. a. ***the quick***: The tender or sensitive flesh in any part of the body, as that under the nails or beneath callous parts; the sensitive part of a horse's foot, above the hoof; also, the tender part of a sore or wound. Usu. in phr. ***to the quick***. †Also without article (quot. 1562). Also *attrib.*

1523 FITZHERB. *Husb.* §115 An hurte, that commeth of yll shoynge, whan a smyth dryueth a nayle in to the quycke. **1562** J. HEYWOOD *Prov. & Epigr.* (1867) 178 Itching and smartyng, both touch vs at quicke. **1571** *Satir. Poems Reform.* xxvi. 168 Fra tyme ye spur and hit him on the quik. **1602** SHAKS. *Ham.* IV. vii. 124 But, to the quick o' the ulcer:—Hamlet comes back. **1697** DRYDEN *Virg. Georg.* III. 673 The raw Rain has pierc'd them to the quick. **1726** SWIFT *Gulliver* II. iii, They would fix upon my nose or forehead, where they stung me to the quick. **1767** WESLEY *Jrnl.* 1 Nov. (1827) III. 293 Five nails were driven into the quick. **1825** KNAPP & BALDW. *Newgate Cal.* IV. 350/2 Picking his fingers until he brought blood thro' the quick. **1862** SALA *Seven Sons* I. x. 243 He was in the habit of biting his nails to the quick. **1925** W. G. L. TAYLOR *Saddle Horse* i. 81 The hoof is pared down to the quick in streaks, leaving only enough for the animal to stand on. **1940** W. FAULKNER *Hamlet* iii. 60 The newcomer darting between Houston and the raised hoof and clapping the shoe onto it and touching the animal's quick with the second blow of the hammer. **1949** D. F. MONTGOMERY *Essentials of Horsemanship* iv. 37 The sensitive sole or 'quick' inside the foot follows the shape of the hoof. **1954** W. FAULKNER *Fable* 196 They was trying.. to pull the quick shoe. **1963** M. C. SELF *Compl. Bk. Horses & Ponies* iii. 56 As with your finger nail, we must be careful not to trim too close to the 'quick', or sensitive part of the horse's foot.

b. *fig.* with ref. to persons, chiefly in phrases denoting acute mental pain or irritation, as ***touched, galled, stung,*** etc. ***to the quick***.

1526 SKELTON *Magnyf.* 1630 Yf a man fortune to touche you on the quyke, Then feyne yourselfe dyseased. **1551** ROBINSON tr. *More's Utop.* I. (1895) 46 Their tenauntes,.. whom they polle and shaue to the quycke, by reysing their rentes. **1579–80** NORTH *Plutarch* (1676) 433 Tigranes.. was galled to the quick, and hit at the heart. **1628** WITHER *Brit. Rememb.* II. 933, I confesse that on the quick they grated, Who in this manner have expostulated. **1647** TRAPP *Comm. Rom.* ii. 3 This is preaching to the conscience, to the quick. **1722** DE FOE *Moll Flanders* (1840) 44 This stung the elder brother to the quick. **1793** MAD. D'ARBLAY *Lett.* 21 Oct., I could not deeply consider the situation of these venerable men, without feeling for them to the quick. **1842** TENNYSON *Walk. to the Mail* 73 A Tory to the quick. **1883** FROUDE *Short Stud.* IV. I. iv. 45 His proud temper was chafed to the quick, and he turned sick with anger.

c. *transf.* of things (esp. immaterial things): The central, vital, or most important part.

1567 R. EDWARDS *Damon & Pithias* in Hazl. *Dodsley* IV. 12 In comedies the greatest skill is this, rightly to touch All things to the quick. **1600** SURFLET *Countrie Farme* III. xlvi. 516 There is neede to digge trees at the foote in winter vnto the very quick of the earth. **1643** BURROUGHES *Exp. Hosea* ix. (1652) 314 If things were examined to the quick in our receiving the Sacrament. **1693** EVELYN tr. *De la Quint. Compl. Gard.* II. 19 The Tree.. must be refresh'd as far as the quick. **1837** HOWITT *Rur. Life* VI. i. (1862) 404 It is existence shorn of all its spreading and flowering branches, but not pared to the quick. **1876** GEO. ELIOT *Dan. Der.* VII. li, The point touched the quick of his experience.

d. With *a* and *pl.*: A tender, sensitive, or vital part. *rare.*

c **1550** BALE *K. Johan* (Camden) 77 To drive hym to holde and searche hym in the quyckes. **1705** WROE in *Phil. Trans.* XXV. 1900 There appearing great quicks (as they call them) or Roots under the Nails. **1892** J. LUCAS tr. *Kalm's England* 69 They have ready to hand a multitude of the quicks [Sw. *qwickan*] or inner parts of Ox-horns.

5. ***the quick***: The life (see LIFE *sb.* 7). Chiefly in phr. ***to the quick***.

1563 MAN tr. *Musculus' Commonpl.* 43 Images.. with maruelouse deuice set forth to the quicke. **1727** BOYER *Dict. Royal* II, To draw to the quick (or to the life). **1858** J. BROWN *Horæ Subs.* (1863) 3, I think I have only to sit down and write it [my father's life] off, and do it to the quick. **1880** G. MEREDITH *Trag. Com.* (1881) 96 Our blood runs through it, our history in the quick.

†**6.** = *quick-mire* (See D.). *Obs. rare*$^{-1}$.

1648 SANCROFT in H. Cary *Mem. Gt. Civ. War* (1842) II. 40, I am here in Sloughland, in the midst of quicks and quagmires.

7. *U.S. Mining.* Abbrev. of QUICKSILVER. (So G. *quick*.)

1882 *Rep. to Ho. Repr., Prec. Met. U.S.* 651 From this groove the amalgam and quicksilver run in gas-pipes to the securely-locked 'amalgam safes', in which the surplus 'quick' is strained off.

8. *Cricket.* A fast bowler.

1960 I. PEEBLES *Bowler's Turn* 63 He was a fine player of every type of bowling, fast of foot against spin, and strong and resolute against the quicks. **1977** *World of Cricket Monthly* June 66/3 He.. still considers Lindwall the greatest of quicks he faced.

C. *adv.* **1. a.** = QUICKLY.

This use is now usually avoided in educated speech and writing, though found in some standard colloq. constructions.

c **1290** *Michael* 502 in *S. Eng. Leg.* 314 Heo.. mai beo nouþe here and þer ase quik ase mannes muynde. *c* **1330** R. BRUNNE *Chron.* (1810) 79 Bot comen is William quik, and sekes þam fulle streit. **1377** LANGL. *P. Pl.* B. XIV. 189 He shulde take the acquitance as quik. *a* **1529** SKELTON *Elynour Rummyng* 206 This ale shal be thycker, And flowre the more quicker. **1610** SHAKS. *Temp.* V. i. 304 Such discourse, as.. shall make it [the night] Goe quicke away. **1667** MILTON *P.L.* IV. 1004 The latter quick up flew, and kickt the beam. **1692** LOCKE *Educ.* §160 Any.. Person who writes well, and quick. **1748** CHESTERF. *Lett.* (1792) II. 25, I am told that you speak very quick. **1788** CHARLOTTE SMITH *Emmeline* (1816) IV. 55, I am going.. to Havre, whence I shall get the quickest to Southampton. **1840** DICKENS *Barn. Rudge* x, The person who'd go quickest, is a sort of natural. **1865** TENNYSON *On a Mourner* iii, Nature.. on thy heart a finger lays, Saying 'Beat quicker'. **1874** GREEN *Short Hist.* ii. 88 A peaceful invasion.. followed quick on the conquest of the Norman soldiery. **1901** M. FRANKLIN *My Brilliant Career* xxxii. 272 Lizer, shut the winder quick. **1922** JOYCE *Ulysses* 47 He [*sc.* a dog].. pissed quick short at an unsmelt rock. **1936** C. SANDBURG *People, Yes* 83 Some men dress quick, others take as much time as a woman. **1968** *Listener* 11 July 38/3 I've never known a journey go so quick. **1979** *Times* 23 Nov. 5/4 The brash and selfish values of a 'get rich quick' society.

b. Phr., (*as*) ***quick as lightning, thought, wink***, etc. (cf. A. 23, quot. *c* 1450).

1813 SCOTT *Rokeby* I. xix, Thoughts.. Glance quick as lightning through the heart. **1825** *Brother Jonathan* I. 111 Fire away as quick as wink. **1871** B. TAYLOR *Faust* (1875) II. I. ii. 8 As quick as thought.. Him to replace there came another. **1881** *Scribner's Mag.* XXII. 108/2 Quick as thought, Roger slipped his hands from their.. noose. **1893** FORBES MITCHELL *Remin. Gt. Mutiny* 88 Quick as thought I.. clasped it.

2. Used imperatively. (In some cases perh. representing the adj. in the phr. ***be quick!***) See also QUICK MARCH 2.

1596 SHAKS. *Merch. V.* II. ix. 1 Quick, quick I pray thee, draw the curtain strait. **1604** —— *Oth.* V. i. 3 Quicke, quicke, feare nothing; Ile be at thy Elbow. **1822** SHELLEY tr. *Calderon* III. 176 Livia, quick, bring my cloak. **1852** MRS. STOWE *Uncle Tom's C.* v. 31 Get on your clothes, old man, quick! **1872** TENNYSON *Gareth & Lynette* 147 Nay—quick! the proof to prove me.

3. *Combs.* **a.** With present participles, as ***quick-acting, -burning, -coming, -conceiving, -decaying, -designing, -devouring, -drying, -fading*** (see quot.), ***-falling, -firing, -flowing, -glancing, -growing, -guiding, -gushing, -labouring, -loading, -moving, -piercing, -relishing, -returning, -rolling, -running, -scenting, -seeing, -self-lessening, -setting, -shifting, -shutting, -speeding, -spouting, -springing, -stepping, -surprising, -talking, -thriving***, (chiefly adjs.).

1878 ABNEY *Photogr.* (1881) 222 Those *quick-acting lenses.. for taking instantaneous pictures. **1931** A. HUXLEY *Music at Night* I. 12 Chemically pure pornography.. is a quick-acting emotional drug. **1960** *Farmer & Stockbreeder* 8 Mar. 88 'Nitro-Chalk' 21, a granular fertilizer containing 21%N, is free-flowing, quick-acting. **1799** G. SMITH *Laboratory* I. 43 Prime it with a *quick-burning charge. **1870** MORRIS *Earthly Par.* Apol. 3, I cannot.. make *quick-coming death a little thing. **1596** SHAKS. *1 Hen. IV*, I. iii. 189 To your *quicke conceyuing Discontents, Ile reade you Matter, deepe and dangerous. **1708** J. PHILIPS *Cyder* II. 64 Freezing Nose, and *quick-decaying feet. **1676** D'URFEY *Mad. Fickle* IV. ii, I'll.. bring it off with *quick designing Wit. **1621** QUARLES *Div. Poems, Hadassa* (1638) 91 The *quick-devouring fire of heaven. **1869** *Bradshaw's Railway Man.* XXI. 460/3 (Advt.), Varnishes.. *Qck. Dryg. Copal.. Qck. Drying Oak. **1913** V. B. LEWES *Oil Fuel* 91 Explosions.. from leakages of volatile spirit used in making up anti-fouling and quick-drying paint.. led to extended investigations being made. **1969** *R. & E. Coordinator* Apr. 8/1 A meter and a modified IGT Printability Tester are used to measure the drying time and penetration of quick drying inks into paper. **1597** GERARDE *Herbal* II. cxxvii. §2. 395 *Ephemerum Mathioli*, *Quicke fading flower. **1661** LOVELL *Hist. Anim. & Min.* 57 The quick fading flower, drunk with the grapes of wild vine. **1832** TENNYSON *Œnone* 200 *Quick-falling dew Of fruitful kisses. **1887** *Pall Mall G.* 17 Dec. 6/2 *Quick-firing gun ammunition. **1890** G. S. CLARKE *Fortification* xiv. 207 Quick-firing guns require only two or three men.. to work them. **1940** *Chambers's Techn. Dict.* 691/1 *Q.F. guns*, quick-firing guns. These may be guns, or howitzers, that are loaded with ammunition having brass cartridge cases, either attached to the shell or separate. **1979** A. FOX *Threat Warning Red* i. 3 That twin 4.5" turret-radar-controlled, quick-firing automatic. **1632** W. LYNNESAY in *Lithgow's Trav.* B iij, Thou hast sweetly sung.. in our *quick-flowing tongue. **1751** GRAY *Spring* 30 The insect youth.. show their gayly-gilded trim *Quick-glancing to the sun. **1879** MRS. A. E. JAMES *Ind. Househ. Managem.* 62 Planting a *quick-growing shrub to form a hedge. **1941** J. S. HUXLEY *Uniqueness of Man* III. vi. 100 The quick-growing beast.. suffers. **1968** *Trees* Spring 15 The algaroba.. is a quick-growing tree. **1793** HOLCROFT tr. *Lavater's Physiog.* xxvii. 129 The work of the *quick-guiding Providence. **1845** MRS. NORTON *Child of the Islands* (1846) 135 The shy, *quick-gushing blood. **1535** COVERDALE *Prov.* x. 4 A *quycke laboringe hande maketh riche. **1874** J. W. LONG *Wild-Fowl Shooting* 37 A *quick-loading [powder] flask, i.e., one having a large feed-hole to the charger, should also be used. **1793** HOLCROFT tr. *Lavater's Physiog.* xxxv. 180 The cheerful, open, free, *quick-moving mouth. **1633** FORD *Broken Heart* I. iii, Their *quick-piercing eyes, which dive.. Down to thy thoughts. **1708** J. PHILIPS *Cyder* I. 29 That from Harvey nam'd, *Quick-relishing. **1728–46** THOMSON *Spring* 999 A *quick-returning pang Shoots thro' the conscious heart. **1584** *Three Ladies Lond.* I. in Hazl. *Dodsley* VI. 338 *Quick-rolling eyes, her temples high. **1742** FIELDING *J. Andrews* III. vi, The *quick-scenting dogs attacked him. **1925** J. GREGORY *Maid of Mountain* xxxvi. 327 Very keen, *quick-seeing eyes withal. **1962** H. C. WESTON *Sight, Light & Work* (ed. 2) viii. 229 It is desirable to select workers who are quick-seeing for objects of the apparent size with which they will have to deal. **1613–6** W. BROWNE *Brit. Past.* II. i, Braue birds they were, whose *quick-selfe-less'ning kin Still wonne the girlonds from the Peregrin. **1837** SMITH tr. *Vicat's Mortars* 22 The Harwich.. is a *quicker-setting cement. **1887** J. NEWMAN *Notes on Concrete* iv. 25 The hardening of slow-setting cements is generally considered more trustworthy than that of quick setting cements. **1963** C. R. COWELL et al. *Inlays, Crowns, & Bridges* ii. 7 Very deep parts of a cavity.. should have a sedative sub-lining of quick-setting zinc oxide and eugenol. **1973** J. WAINRIGHT *Touch of Malice* 188 She stiffened—as if quick-setting concrete was suddenly working in her veins. **1593** SHAKS. *Lucr.* 459 There appears *Quick-shifting antics, ugly in her eyes. **1876** T. HARDY *Ethelberta* (1890) 142 Faith's soft, *quick-shutting eyes looked unutterable things. **1919** V. WOOLF *Night & Day* xxviii. 416 The *quick-speeding silver moon. **1663** R. HEAD *Hic et Ubique* sig. A2v, Your sublime dignity, *quick-springing wit. **1911** E. M. CLOWES *On Wallaby* xi. 308 To grapple with all the quick-springing mass of undergrowth which leaps to life, almost in a night. **1813** T. BUSBY *Lucretius* I. III. 731 *Quick-spouting blood.. And fierce convulsions. **1884** *Times* 27 Feb. 7/6 The high-standing, *quick-stepping Clydesdales. **1937** BLUNDEN *Elegy* 42 And though you marked my last arising, My next shall be as *quick-surprising. **1963** *Punch* 4 Sept. 358/2 Gerry is a show-off, a *quick-talking egotist. **1980** P. LIVELY *Judgement Day* v. 51 Those long-haired quick-talking women. **1669** WORLIDGE *Syst. Agric.* (1681) 93 The Ash is a gallant *quick-thriving wood.

b. With pa. pples., as ***quick-compounded, -drawn, -gone, -raised, -spread, -wrought*** adjs.

1730–46 THOMSON *Autumn* 1363 The mind, The varied scene of *quick-compounded thought. **1882** J. HAWTHORNE *Fort. Fool* I. xii, A *quick-drawn, panting sigh. **1887** BOWEN *Virg. Æneid* v. 202 The limb and the feverish lip Quiver with quick-drawn breath. **1818** KEATS *Endym.* I. 375 He could not miss His *quick gone love. **1596** SHAKS. *1 Hen. IV*, IV. iv. 12 The King, with mightie and *quick-raysed Power. **1895** KIPLING *Second Jungle Book* 8 The *quick-spread ears of the deer caught the last sentence. **1898** *Q. Rev.* Apr. 435 He wove for Theseus a snare *quick-wrought.

D. Special combs. or phrases (chiefly the adj. in close connexion with a sb., sometimes written as a single word, or hyphened): **quick-action**, *attrib.* of apparatus having a quick action; †**quick anatomy** (see ANATOMY 1 b); **quick-and-dirty** orig. *U.S.*, (*a*) *sb.* (*slang*), a cheap café; = *greasy spoon* s.v. GREASY *a.* 9 (*rare*); (*b*) *adj. phr.* (*colloq.*), that will produce the desired effect rapidly but by irregular methods; of a solution, etc.: makeshift, instant; hastily-compiled, produced, or erected; **quick bread**, a bread or cake that can be prepared quickly, usu. one made with a leavening agent that permits immediate baking; **quick-break** *a. Electr. Engin.*, applied to (the action of) a switch designed to break a circuit and stop a current quickly regardless of the speed with which it is operated; **quick buck** chiefly *U.S.* [BUCK *sb.*[8]] = *fast buck* s.v. FAST *a.* 11; **quick-cake**, a cake that can be prepared and baked in a short time; **quick-change**, *attrib.* as epithet of an actor or other performer who quickly changes costume or appearance in order to play a different part; *v. intr.*, to perform a 'quick change'; *trans.*, to change (clothes) quickly; also *transf.* and *ellipt.*; **quick-clay** [tr. Norw. *kvikkleire*, formerly *kvikler*], clay that is quick (sense 10); **quick**

death *U.S.* = *sudden death* s.v. SUDDEN *a.* 3 b; **Quick Dick** *Mil. slang*, a quick-firing gun; **quick-disconnect**, *attrib.* of couplings and the like that can be quickly disconnected; †**quick dissection**, vivisection; **quick-fire**, *attrib.* of a type of gun which can fire shots in rapid succession; also *fig.*; **quick-firer**, a quick-firing gun; also *fig.*; **quick-fix** *a.*, that can be quickly fixed into place; also *fig.*; **quick-foot** *adv.*, in haste, swiftly; †**quickfrith**, plants to form a quick hedge; **quickgold** *fig.* [prob. modelled on QUICKSILVER *sb.*], living or liquid gold; **quick-heel** *v. intr.*, in Rugby Football, to heel rapidly from a scrum; **quick-in-the-hand**, a popular name of the yellow balsam; †**quick-iron**, the load-stone, magnet; **quick kill**, a sudden or rapid victory (cf. KILL *sb.*[1] 2); also *attrib.*; **quick-knit** *a.*, used (*a*) of very thick wool with which a garment can be knitted in a short time; (*b*) of a garment made with such wool; also *ellipt.*; †**quick-line**, asbestos; **quick-loader**, a device to enable a gun to be loaded quickly; **quick-look** *Astronautics*, used *attrib.* with reference to the rapid provision of information; **quick-lunch(eon**, *attrib.* of a person or establishment selling lunches that can be served and eaten quickly; also *fig.*; **quick-minded** *a.*, having a quick or ready mind; quick-witted; †**quick-mire**, a quagmire; **quick reference** *attrib.*, giving quick and easy access to information; **quick-release**, *attrib.* of any device designed for rapid release; also *ellipt.*; **quick relief**, *Naut.*, 'one who turns out speedily to relieve the watch' (Smyth *Sailor's Word-bk.* 1867); **quick-return**, *attrib.* of gearing in a cutting machine which brings the bed quickly back after each cut of the tool (Knight *Dict. Mech.* 1875); more widely, applied to any reciprocating motion or mechanism in which the speed in one direction is greater than the speed in the other; also *ellipt.*; **quick saver**, *Naut.*, 'a span formerly used to prevent the courses from bellying too much when off the wind' (Smyth); †**quick-scab**, a form of scab in horses; **quick-seller**, an article, esp. a book, that sells quickly; **quick-service** *attrib.*, that is characterized by quick service; †**quick shot**, *fig.*, small drinking-vessels that are quickly emptied; **quick-side**, *Naut.*, = FREE-BOARD; **quick-spot** (see quot.); †**quick-spring**, a running spring; †**quick-spur**, one who rides quickly (in quot. *fig.*); **quick-start** *a.*, pertaining to or characterized by rapid starting; **quick-stick(s)**, quickly, without delay (also *in quick sticks*); also as *v. intr.* (see quot. 1935); **quick succession**, a change in ownership of property twice within a limited period; used *attrib.* of remission of part of capital transfer tax (formerly estate duty) in such an eventuality; **quickthorn**, thorn used for hedging, esp. a hawthorn; †**quickthorned** *a.*, resembling hedge-thorn; **quick trick**, in Bridge, a card or combination of cards which should furnish a trick in the first or second round of the suit; a trick won 'on top'; *attrib.*, of a system valuing the hand according to the holding of such cards; **quick turnover**, *attrib.* of a person concerned with selling goods as rapidly as possible after they have been bought or produced; **quick-water** [= G. *quick-wasser*], a solution of nitrate of mercury and gold used in water-gilding (Knight); **quick worker** *colloq.*, one who rapidly achieves intimacy with persons of the opposite sex. See also QUICKBEAM, -LIME, MARCH, -MATCH, -SAND, -SET, -SILVER, STEP, TIME, -WOOD, -WORK.

1909 *Cent. Dict.* Suppl. *Quick-action *a.* **1960** *Farmer & Stockbreeder* 1 Mar. 72/1 Four quick-action jacks adjust the tilt to vary the throughput. **1968** *Harper's Mag.* Jan. 14/2 The office of the Massachusetts Electric Company was temporarily converted into a mock-up of a *quick-and-dirty and its sign replaced with one that read *Al's bean pot.* **1977** *Sci. News* 24 Dec. 438/3 A study by Oak Ridge National Laboratory concluded that any country with access to spent fuel could build a 'quick and dirty' reprocessing plant to produce bomb-grade plutonium. **1978** *Washington Post Mag.* 26 Feb. 4/2 It became clear that Jerry would be able to finesse the whole thing with very little substantive input—what he and his adviser Tom Quinn call the quick and dirty approach. **1981** T. KIDDER *Soul of New Machine* (1982) vi. 110 If you can do a quick-and-dirty job and it works, do it. **1986** *Amer. Banker* 5 May 10 The market could be plundered and go as low as 92. Ms. Mullins says the move down could be as 'quick and dirty' as the move up. **1920** M. WILSON *Cook Book* 36 *Quick breads include griddle cakes, waffles, muffins, Sally Lunn's, shortcakes and biscuits. **1940** *Quantity Food Service Recipes* 20 (*heading*) Quick breads. Baking powder biscuits... muffins... griddle cakes. **1960** A. E. BENDER *Dict. Nutrition* 106/1 *Quick breads* include biscuits, muffins, popovers, waffles and griddle cakes. **1970** *Islander* (Victoria, B.C.) 29 Nov. 8/2 Use it [*sc.* cranberry sauce] as an ingredient in pies, quick bread and basting sauce. **1891** J. B. VERITY *Electr. up to Date* v. 62 (*caption*) 'Quick-make and *quick-break' switch. **1900** *Electrician* 21 Dec. 325/2 Mr. Duddell..pointed out a danger with concentric cables and metal break, quick-break switches. **1930** MOYER & WOSTREL *Industr. Electr. & Wiring* xvii. 382 Circuits carrying large currents..should be provided with either a quick-break switch or a circuit breaker. **1962** *Newnes Conc. Encycl. Electr. Engin.* 728/1 Shunt limit switches range from the very simple, in which speed of break is entirely dependent on the speed of operation, to considerably more elaborate designs in which some form of quick-break action is incorporated. **1960** *Christian Herald* July 12/2 This is most discouraging to those who stoop to make a '*quick buck' through propagating immorality. **1972** *National Observer* (U.S.) 27 May 20/2 Richard Chamberlain is no dripping-behind-the-ears graduate of the school of 'charm acting' (his phrase) out for a quick buck at the expense of the classics. **1980** R. BARNARD *Death in Cold Climate* xvii. 193 Dreaming of luxury, of the quick buck dubiously acquired. **1925** J. GREGORY *Maid of Mountain* ii. 15 I'll stir up a *quick-cake for him. **1889** *Pall Mall G.* 3 Apr. 6/1 The celebrated *quick-change artist. **1896** Quick change [see *trick-change* s.v. TRICK *sb.* 14]. **1905** *Daily Chron.* 13 Mar. 5/7 Mr. Balfour's first..Ministry may reasonably be dubbed the 'Quick-change Ministry'. **1906** *Ibid.* 12 Nov. 6/4 He quick-changed with the deftness and speed of a Fregoli. **1928** *Collier's* 18 Aug. 18/3 We had to quick-change our hats, put on badges [etc.]. **1939** T. S. ELIOT *Old Possum's Bk. Pract. Cats* 22 As knockabout clowns, quick-change Comedians.. They had an extensive reputation. **1973** C. EGLETON *Seven Days to Killing* i. 14 They stripped off their uniforms and changed into civilian clothes..in a time which would have been a credit to a troupe of quick-change artists. **1901** *Quick clay [see sense A. 10 above]. **1950** *Geotechnique* II. 58 A very soft and extremely sensitive clay, known in Norway as *kvikkleire* (quick-clay). **1968** R. W. FAIRBRIDGE *Encycl. Geomorphol.* 640/2 A special class of mudflows are those developing in quick clays which spontaneously liquefy and may flow readily on very gentle slopes, rafting houses, roads and trees appreciable distances. **1972** Quickclay [see ILLITE]. **1942** Z. N. HURSTON in A. Dundes *Mother Wit* (1973) 225/1 I'm *quick death and easy judgment. **1958** *Washington Post* 20 June A 16/4 Miss McKeever advanced to the final..by beating medalist Mrs. Thomas Konopa..on the 19th green with a birdie in a quick death playoff. **1918** *Sat. Even. Post* 31 Aug. 34 A fifty-millimeter gun which they dubbed *Quick Dick played on them with direct fire. **1936** J. G. HARBORD *Amer. Army in France 1917–1919* xvii. 283 The time of warning usually varied from practically nothing with the 'Quick Dicks' as the boys called the Austrian 88's..to as many as five seconds with the heavier calibers. **1962** F. I. ORDWAY et al. *Basic Astronautics* xii. 468 *Quick-disconnect pins allow the astronaut to detach himself from a conventional aircraft type seat..once the period of acceleration is over. **1969** *Jane's Freight Containers 1968–69* 577/3 Two hydraulic pressure lines to trailer, with quick-disconnect couplings. **1578** BANISTER *Hist. Man* IV. 54 This is the notable vtilitie of Diaphragma, as the same Author reporteth to haue beholden in *quicke dissections. **1891** *Times* 7 Oct. 4/6 A Gruson *quick-fire howitzer, which is intended to discharge shells in rapid succession. **1954** *Encounter* Mar. 70/2 Such chiefly subjective variables are difficult to elicit in fairly short, single, quick-fire interviews. **1960** I. PEEBLES *Bowler's Turn* 44 He was an even timer with a beautiful economical action, and a sure quick-fire return. **1977** *Cleethorpes News* 27 May 5/5 They have a polished act which includes skilful harmony, impressions and quickfire jokes. **1891** MARQUIS OF SALISBURY *Let.* 20 Sept. in G. Cecil *Life Salisbury* (1932) IV. 314 They must carry Maxims and *quickfirers. **1894** *Pall Mall G.* 23 Oct. 2/1 They..carry in their huge fighting masts an arsenal of quick-firers. **1901** *Spectator* 12 Oct. 524/1 The newest 6 in. quick-firers are not officially known as quick-firers, because they have not a metal cartridge-case. **1933** F. RICHARDS *Old Soldiers never Die* xii. 162 When we had no time to write letters we sent field-service post cards which we called 'quick-firers'. We simply wrote the address on them and signed our names and dates of sending on the backs. **1956** Quick-firer [see MORALE 3]. **1959** *Archit. Rev.* CXXV. p. xcv (Advt.), *Quick-fix reflectors and diffusers, heavy duty bi-pin lampholders. **1972** *Times* 30 Nov. 18/5 Quick-fix, switch-operated adaptor fittings. **1976** *National Observer* (U.S.) 25 Dec. 5/4 On the one hand, he is urged to make quick-fix tax cuts and get the economy moving. **1891** ATKINSON *Last of Giant-killers* 52 Willy..was sent off *quick-foot. **1536** *MS. Acc. St. John's Hosp., Canterb.*, Payd for gatheryng *quykfryth.. iiijd. **1877** G. M. HOPKINS *Poems* (1967) 66 The grey lawns cold where gold, where *quickgold lies! **1954** I. MURDOCH *Under Net* xx. 276, I took two gulps of the whiskey; it ran through me like quickgold. **1936** *Times* 30 Nov. 5/4 A pack who shoved to the last man and *quick-heeled from the tight and loose. **1785** MARTYN *Rousseau's Bot.* xxvi. (1794) 407 We have also a wild species called Yellow Balsam, and also by the familiar names of *Quick-in-hand and Touch-me-not. **1864** PRIOR *Plant-n.*, Quick-in-the-hand, that is 'alive in the hand', the Touch-me-not, from the sudden bursting and contortion of its seed pods upon being pressed. **1398** TREVISA *Barth. De P.R.* XVI. lxii. (1495) 573 The stone magnes drawyth to itself yron, therfore in the comyn speche this yren is callyd *quycke yren. **1601** HOLLAND *Pliny* II. 515 The ignorant people seeing these rings thus rubbed with the load-stone,..call it quick-yron. **1969** *Listener* 14 Aug. 221/3 Wilson..lost interest in the '*quick kill' approach and tried to make a deal with Smith. *a* **1974** R. CROSSMAN *Diaries* (1975) I. 382 James Callaghan, for example, said he thought that..we should try to get a quick kill.. In that case the preparations for the quick kill should have taken place *before* U.D.I. **1935** *Home Notes 2nd Knitting Bk.* p. iii (Advt.), W. B. *Kwiknit The original quick-to-knit wool. *Ibid.*, W. B. Kwiknit is a thick 2 ply, ideal for outdoor sportswear. **1957** *Vogue Knitting Bk.* 16 (Advt.), Two such outstanding wools as Patons Quickerknit Botany and Quickerknit Baby Wool. **1960** *Ibid.* 9 Lister Lavenda *quick-knits are the.. chunkiest, quickest-to-knit-with wools in knitting today! **1962** J. WADE *Running Sand* vi. 64 Some Tyrolean quick-knit jumper. **1966** G. N. LEECH *Eng. in Advertising* xv. 141 More or less common types of compound structure: 'quick-knits'; 'speedy-knit'; 'flip-tops'. **1972** C. FREMLIN *Appointment with Yesterday* xi. 84 Milly turned down the third remnant of tattered quick-knit cardigan. **1601** HOLLAND *Pliny* II. 4 There is a kind of Line found out which will not consume in the fire: this in Italy they call *Quick-line. **1884** *Sat. Rev.* 16 Feb. 209/2 A contrivance called a '*quick-loader' has been issued for simultaneous trial with the Martini-Enfield. **1964** *Proc. Joint Computer Conf.* (*Spring*) 125/1 The requirement of the programming system for OGO was to provide *quick-look analysis and control of the status of the spacecraft and selective experiments on board the satellite. **1966** *Electronics* 3 Oct. 134 Displaying quick-look performance data for evaluation by the astronaut. **1975** *Geos* (Dept. Energy, Mines, & Resources, Canada) Spring 8/1 A 'Quick Look' facility attached to the satellite station at Prince Albert, Sask., provides black and white photography of Arctic sea-ice within 20 minutes of the satellites pass over Canada. **1979** *Nature* 3 May 47/1 We concluded that to within the accuracy of the SAS 3 quick-look data timing (± 1 s), the onset of the optical burst was coincident with that in X rays. **1903** *Everybody's Mag.* Aug. 191/1 He figured them out with the stub of a blue pencil..sometimes on the slippery edge of reeking *quick-lunch counters. **1903** *N.Y. Even. Post* 24 Sept. 8 The quick lunch man a few blocks away from the grocery store. **1909** CHESTERTON *Tremendous Trifles* 242 One of those quick-lunch restaurants in the City. **1911** E. M. CLOWES *On Wallaby* iii. 51 The haste of the Fisher Government to do things lately moved Alfred Deakin to describe its proceedings as 'quick-lunch legislation'. **1930** [see DRIVE-IN]. **1975** *New Yorker* 22 Sept. 96/3 Men whose money derives from, and whose deepest loyalties adhere to, insurance companies,..quick-lunch chains, and the like. **1928** J. BUCHAN *Runagates Club* viii. 220 At a *quick-luncheon counter he got into talk with a man. **1852** W. BAGEHOT *Coll. Works* (1965) I. 346 But he was a *quick-minded..man of the world. **1908** *Daily Chron.* 24 Aug. 1/3 They say they never met such a quick-minded man. *c* **1394** *P. Pl. Crede* 226 Wiþ a face as fat as a full bledder..þat all wagged his fleche as a *quyk myre. **1577** DEE *Relat. Spir.* I. (1659) 12 A place, where Springs, Quick-mires, and Bogs are. **1938** L. M. HARROD *Librarian's Gloss.* 124 **Quick-reference books*, Books which are essentially of a reference character, such as directories, dictionaries, and gazetteers. **1978** *Early Music* Oct. 599/2 Part II is a quick-reference chart summarizing the advice given on French in Part I. **1905** *Internat. Libr. Technol.* LXII. XLI. 48 Instead of moving the valve handle to this [slow-release] position..it is moved to the extreme left to *quick-release position... The brake-cylinder air rushes out, allowing the release springs to release the brakes suddenly. **1916** G. FRANKAU *Guns* 11 Now the foul clay cakes on britching strap and clogs the quick-release. **1933** *Gloss. Aeronaut. Terms* (*B.S.I.*) 73 *Quick release*, a device enabling the user to clear himself from the parachute and/or the harness. **1942** *Tee Emm* (Air Ministry) Sept. 135/2 Immediately you are grounded, turn on your back and unlock the quick release mechanism. **1961** *AWA Techn. Rev.* XI. Fig. 8 (*caption*) The sub-chassis can be removed by means of quick-release fasteners. **1972** [see HARNESS *sb.* 4 c]. **1976** J. WAINWRIGHT *Walther P.38* 58, I saw him bend to work the quick-release mechanism. The car gave a gentle heave as the weight of the caravan left its rear bumper. **1864** *Quick return [see RAM *sb.*[1] 5 e]. **1894** W. J. LINEHAM *Text-Bk. Mech. Engin.* v. 169 The tool cuts in one direction only, and the back stroke is wasted. To minimise this loss, and at the same time reverse the stroke without changing the continuous rotation of main shaft, ingenious motions called quick returns have been devised. **1915** [see KINEMATICALLY *adv.*]. **1930** *Engineering* 14 Mar. 341/3 Starting, stopping and the quick-return motion are all effected through a plate clutch. **1964** S. CRAWFORD *Basic Engin. Processes* viii. 218 Shaping machines are fitted with a quick-return mechanism. **1639** DE GRAY *Expert Ferrier* II. xvii. 297 This malady, which we call the *Quick-scab,.. runneth from one member of the horse to the other. **1926** *Ironmonger* Suppl. 16 Jan. 50 (Advt.), Dealers who stocked early are now enjoying the profits from this *quick-seller. **1934** *Archit. Rev.* LXXV. 11 True, academicians like Herkomer..deigned to use photographic labour-saving devices for *quick-service portraiture. **1976** H. MACINNES *Agent in Place* vii. 63 A hamburger at a Madison Avenue quick-service counter. **1624** *Skelton's Ghost* 20 in *S.'s Wks.* (1843) II. 155 With froth-canne and nickpot, and such nimble *quick shot. **1627** CAPT. SMITH *Seaman's Gram.* ix. 39 Lest they..if her *quicke side lie in the water, ouerset the ship. **1694** MOTTEUX *Rabelais* v. xvii. (1737) 76 Lest the Ship's Quick-Side should lye in the Water. **1873–4** G. M. HOPKINS *Note-Books & Papers* (1937) 223 Every visible palpable body has..a centre of illumination or *highspot* or **quickspot*. **1622** A. COURT *Constancie* I. 33 Hence as from a *quick-spring did flow that Constancie. **1660** SHARROCK *Vegetables* 89 You need but open that very place to your quick-spring, and give it a clear vent, and certainly your bog would decay. **1600** SURFLET *Countrie Farme* III. xxi. 473 As concerning the grafting of it, you must take the time of autumne, for..this tree is a *quickespur and forerider. **1950** *Archit. Rev.* CVIII. 424 *Quickstart or starter switch control gear can be supplied and the four-lamp fittings can be arranged for two-circuit control. **1962** A. NISBETT *Technique Sound Studio* viii. 147 Quick-start techniques fall into two categories, depending on the type of drive employed by the turntable. **1977** *Gramophone* Oct. 716/2 Technics have applied the quartz control direct-drive principle of their high-torque (quick-start) SP10 Mk. 2 turntable..to a lower priced deck. **1835** *Dublin Univ. Mag.* Apr. 391/2 'All's right,' said Denis, putting the musket to his shoulder; 'I see them. Now stand clear, boy, and hand along fresh cartridges cleverly. I'll give them a blaze in *quick sticks—nothing like a long range; stand clear!' **1860** HOTTEN *Dict. Slang* (ed. 2) 196 *Quick sticks*, in a hurry, rapidly; 'to cut *quick sticks*', to be in a great hurry. **1877** BLACKMORE *Erema* lvi. (1880) 424 Die he must, and quick stick. **1890** R. BOLDREWOOD *Squatter's Dream* xvi. 204 We should have a note to settle our little account in quick sticks. **1935** A. J. POLLOCK *Underworld Speaks* 94/1 *Quicksticks*, to escape from the law. **1936** J. B. PRIESTLEY *They walk in City* xvi. 483 She can pop into that kitchen an' dish yer up something nice in quicksticks. **1966** *Listener* 29 Sept. 461/1 Then, with Mr Buchanan safely making up, it was quick-sticks for the Hippodrome and a performance of *Mercenary Mary*. **1914** *Act 4 & 5 Geo. V.* c. 10 §15 Relief in respect of *quick succession where property consists of land or a business. **1936** G. M. GREEN *Death Duties* v. 123 If any such other allowance is available on the second death, the 'quick succession' allowance is computed first and the other allowance is made against the reduced duty. **1967** E.

RUDINGER *Wills & Probate* 14 Estate duty might have to be paid twice on the same property... There is a reduction in duty, known as quick succession relief, which helps a bit in this situation. **1973** *Times* 6 Oct. 19/2 Quick succession relief will reduce the double burden to some extent. **1611** A. STANDISH *Commons Complaint* 44 Have a good ditch double or treble set with *quicke Thornes,.. which hedge will last well three yeares. **1785** COWPER in *Life* (1836) V. 166 The people of Turvey have burnt him.. in effigy, with a bundle of quickthorn under his arm. **1838** J. C. LOUDON *Arboretum et Fruticetum Britannicum* II. 836 Three rows of quick-thorns shall be set in each ridge. **1971** *Country Life* 21 Oct. 1066/1 A variety of hedge plants—elm, ash, quick-thorn, dogwood—.. show the boundary hedge line is of great age. **1567** MAPLET *Gr. Forest* 89 The Hedgehog hath a sharp and *quickthorned garment. **1927** M. C. WORK *Contract Bridge* iii. 58 Two *quick tricks.. is the minimum strength with which a Contract denial should be made. **1955** I. FLEMING *Moonraker* viii. 81 Its a famous Culbertson hand... He used it to spoof his own quick-trick conventions. **1958** *Listener* 23 Oct. 669/2 East's King might fill West's club suit to produce nine quick tricks at No Trumps. **1977** *Homes & Gardens* Feb. 17 Your five quick tricks ought to be enough to see him [*sc.* your partner] home in Five Diamonds. **1951** M. MCLUHAN *Mech. Bride* (1967) 129/2 If there's anything this type of *quick-turnover gent can't see.. its cold facts. **1956** Quick-turnover [see EASY *a.* 13]. **1938** E. WAUGH *Scoop* II. ii. 157, I will say you're a *quick worker. Sorry to barge in on the tender scene. **1969** O. HESKY *Sequin Syndicate* v. 48 'But there's something going on.' 'Well,' the old man said cheerfully, 'that's all right, isn't it? I didn't think Tarni was such a quick worker, though.'

quick, *sb.*^{2} Also 4 quike, 5 quyke, quikk, 9 *north.* w(h)ick. [Northern form of QUITCH *sb.*^{1}] *coll.* or *pl.* Couch-grass, and other field-grasses and weeds, or their underground stems. = QUICKEN *sb.*^{2} Cf. QUICK-GRASS.

a **1387** *Sinon. Barthol.* (Anecd. Oxon.) 23 *Gramen*,.. specialiter accipitur in medicina pro quadam herba.. an^{ce} quikes. **1483** *Cath. Angl.* 297/1 Quikk (*A.* Quyke), *eruus.* **1764** *Museum Rusticum* III. 296 A machine, that would clear.. land from quicks, or other weeds. **1800** TUKE *Agric.* 85 Heavier harrows.. are used to clean the land from quicks. **1876-** In northern dial. glossaries, in form *which* or *wick*.

quick (kwɪk), *v.*^{1} *arch.* Forms: 1 cwic-, cwyc-, cucian, 3 quikie, 5 quykee (?); 2 quiken, 4 quik(e, quyk(ke, 4–5 quyke, 5 qwyk, queke, quek-, qvyk-, whykyn, 5–6 quycke, 6 quicke, 4, 7- quick. [OE. *cwician*:—**cwicōjan*, f. *cwic* QUICK *a.*, = OS. *quikôn*; properly intransitive, but even in OE. also used transitively, there being no causative form corresponding to OHG. *quichan, quicken*. In common use from *c* 1300–1450, after which examples are very rare.]

†**1.** *intr.* Of persons, animals, and plants, or their parts: To come to life; to revive. *Obs.* = QUICKEN *v.* 6.

c **1000** *Sax. Leechd.* II. 338 Smire mid þa saran limu; hie cwiciaþ sona. *c* **1200** *Trin. Coll. Hom.* 177 To-ȝenes sumere alle moren quiken, and eorðe and trewes growen. *c* **1290** *S. Eng. Leg.* I. 476/485 Miȝhte þis wumman quikie a-ȝein; and liuen and hire sturie? *c* **1425** *Cursor M.* 20883 (Trin.) A ded mon quyked bi his shade. *c* **1520** L. ANDREWE *Noble Lyfe* in *Babees Bk.* (1868) 234 Whan she feleth her yonges quycke, or stere in her body.

fig. c **1000** ÆLFRIC *Hom.* I. 494 Se synfulla mid godcundre onbryrdnysse cucaþ.

†**b.** Of a firebrand or fire: To kindle, begin to burn. *Obs. rare.*

c **1175** *Lamb. Hom.* 81 þe brond þe is al aquenched.. ne quikeð he neure. *c* **1384** CHAUCER *H. Fame* III. 988 As fire ys wont to quyk and goo. *c* **1386** —— *Knt.'s T.* 1477 Oon of the fyres queynte And quyked agayn.

†**c.** Of a rumour: To arise, spread. *Obs. rare*$^{-1}$.

c **1425** *Cursor M.* 17476 (Trin.) Wo was hem.. whenne þis tiþing bigon to quyk.

2. †**a.** *trans.* To give or restore life to. *Obs.* = QUICKEN *v.* 1.

c **950** *Lindisf. Gosp.* John v. 21 Suæ se fæder a-uæcceð ða deado & cuicað, suæ æc ðe sunu ðaðe [he] wil cwicað. *c* **1300** *Cursor M.* 8622 þe barn to fir in barm sco bar, And wel sco wend to quik it þar. **1377** LANGL. *P. Pl.* B. xv. 23 'The whiles I quykke the corps', quod he, 'called am I Anima'. *c* **1440** CAPGRAVE *Life St. Kath.* IV. 1801 Whan to the body he cam it for to queke. **1447** BOKENHAM *Seyntys* (Roxb.) 85, I.. beseeche for thi dede man Qwyk hym ageyne lord.

fig. c **1000** *Ags. Ps.* (Th.) cxviii. 50 Me þin spræc spedum cwycade. *c* **1430** LYDG. *Min. Poems* (Percy Soc.) 177 Pray we to Crist.. To quyke a figure in oure conscience.

b. To give or restore vigour to; to stir up, inspire, etc. Now *rare.* = QUICKEN *v.* 2.

a **1300** *Cursor M.* 25581 þou.. quiked vr hertes, suete iesu. *c* **1330** R. BRUNNE *Chron. Wace* (Rolls) 13247 þe ton quiked þe toþer to lyue, þe Romayns to greue, fast gon þey stryue. *c* **1386** CHAUCER *Pars. T.* ¶ 462 Ire.. is the feruent blood of man yquyked in his herte. *c* **1449** PECOCK *Repr.* II. xv. 237 Forto quykee [*sic*] in hem the mynde.. of the bifore seid thingis. **1567** DRANT *Horace, Ep.* II. i. G vij, That poet.. That can stere vp my passions, or quicke my sprytes at all. **1615** *Albumazar* I. ii. in Hazl. *Dodsley* XI. 308 Your lovesome sir, like strong water.. quicks your feeble limbs. **1898** T. HARDY *Wessex Poems* 188 That swift sympathy With living love Which quicks the world.

†**c.** To kindle (a fire). *Obs. rare.* = QUICKEN 3.

c **1374** CHAUCER *Troylus* III. 484 (435) Pandarus to quyke alwey þe fyr Was euere y-lyk prest and dyligent. *c* **1386** —— *Frankl. T.* 322 Hire [the moon's] desire Is to be quiked and lighted of your [the sun's] fire.

quick (kwɪk), *v.*^{2} [f. QUICK *a.* B. 3.] **1.** *trans.* To furnish with a quickset hedge. *rare.*

1801 *Trans. Soc. Enc. Arts* XIX. 73 A ditch.. quicked with a double row of fine plants. **1819** T. THOMAS *Acc. Fencing.* For quicking and ditching Leasehold.

2. *trans.* To coat with mercury by immersion. Cf. QUICKEN *v.* 4 b, QUICKING *vbl. sb.*^{2} 2.

1873 E. SPON *Workshop Receipts* I. 308/1 A little of this solution is poured into a basin, and with a brush dipped therein they stroke over the surface of the metal to be gilt, which immediately becomes quicked. **1891** G. E. BONNEY *Electro-Platers' Handbk.* v. 112 Brass and silver are best quicked in a solution of the double cyanide of mercury and potassium. **1923** W. R. COOPER *W. G. McMillan's Treat. Electro-Metallurgy* (ed. 4) vi. 116 Many articles are 'quicked' before being subjected to the operation of depositing other metals, especially silver and gold, upon their surfaces.

quick (kwɪk), *v.*^{3} Also *dial.* w(h)ick. [f. QUICK *sb.*^{2}] To pull up 'quicks' or couch-grass. Hence ***quicking-drag*** (see quot. 1800), ***-rake.***

1800 TUKE *Agric.* 85 Quicking-drag. In the northern part of the vale of York, a drag on an excellent construction is used, for cleaning the land from quicks. **1874** E. PEACOCK *J. Markenfield* III. 113 Their boys and girls released.. from 'wicking' and 'singling' turnips.

'quickbeam. *Obs.* exc. *dial.* [App. f. QUICK *a.* + BEAM, but the precise force of the adj. is not clear: cf. G. *queck-* and *quickenbaum* (also *quitz-, quitzen-, quitschenbaum*) service-tree. The name belongs to the south of England.] = QUICKEN *sb.*^{1}

In OE. glosses, *cwicbeam* usually renders L. *cariscus*, which seems to be otherwise unknown, and is perh. an error for *tamariscus* (cf. quot. 1587 below).

a **700** *Epinal Gloss.* 238 *Cariscus*, cuicbeam. *c* **1000** *Sax. Leechd.* II. 66 þorn, æsc, cwicbeam. *c* **1050** *Ags. Voc.* in Wr.-Wülcker 423/23 *Iuniperum*, quicbeam. **1533** ELYOT *Cast. Helthe* (1541) 59 Purgers of melancolye.. Bourage: Hartis tongue: Quickbeme. **1562** [see QUICKEN *sb.*^{1}]. **1578** LYTE *Dodoens* VI. lii. 727 The barke of one kinde of Sorbus (whiche is our Quickbeme). **1579** LANGHAM *Gard. Health* (1633) 628 The barke of the roots of heath may be vsed in stead of the barke of the root of Tamariske, rather then the barke of quickebeame. **1731** MILLER *Gard. Dict., Sorbus*, The wild Service or Quickbeam. **1836** BRAY *Descr. Tamar & Tavy* vii. 122 Oaks.. interspersed with what is called in Devonshire the quick-beam, or mountain-ash. **1873** O'CURRY *Lect. Ancient Irish* II. 213 Let them cut down and carry out loads of the quickbeam. **1884** JEFFERIES *Red Deer* xii. 112 In the Exmoor country the mountain-ash is called the quick-beam.

attrib. c **1000** *Sax. Leechd.* II. 78 Wyl on wætere æscrinde, cwicbeam rinde. **1562** TURNER *Herbal* II. (1568) 59 b, The quikbem tre which is a kynde of sorbus. **1587** MASCALL *Govt. Cattle, Hogges* (1627) 263 Tamarix, which as I thinke, is called in the English quick-beame wood. **1760** J. LEE *Introd. Bot.* App. 324 Quickbeam-tree, *Sorbus.*

quick-chaws, obs. variant of KICKSHAW.

quicken ('kwɪk(ə)n), *sb.*^{1} Also 4 quiken, 6 quickene; 6- whicken, 7 whighen, 9 wicken, wiggin. [The northern equivalent of QUICKBEAM, and presumably from QUICK *a.*, but the exact nature of the ending is not clear: in early use always in comb. with *tree.* Cf. QUICK TREE.

An OE. *cwictreow* is found in glosses, rendering an obscure L. *cresis* or *gnesis*.]

1. a. The mountain-ash, or rowan-tree (*Pyrus aucuparia*). **b.** The service-tree (*Sorbus domestica*). †**c.** The juniper. (*Obs.*)

Comb. with *tree. a* **1387** *Sinon. Barthol.* (Anecd. Oxon.) 26 *Juniperus*, quikentre. **1548** TURNER *Names Herbes* (E.D.S.) 75 The seconde kynde [of sorbus] is called.. in Englishe a rountree or a Quicken tree. **1562** —— *Herbal* II. (1568) 71 The tre whiche we call in the North countre a quicken tre or a rown tre, & in the South countre a quikbeme. **1686** PLOT *Staffordsh.* 223 The *Fraxinus sylvestris* or Quicken-tree, which they firmly believe will certainly preserve them from all fascinations, and evill spirits. **1756** SIR J. HILL *Brit. Herbal* 514 We have two other species. 1. The common Service... 2. The Quicken-tree. **1844** M. A. RICHARDSON *Borderer's Table-bk.* VII. 182 Witchwood, the mountain ash.. called in divers parts of Northumberland the whicken-tree. **1857** O'GRADY *Pursuit Diarmuid* 143 He.. followed Diarmuid's track to the foot of the quicken tree.

absol. **1674** in *Depos. Cast. York* 209 They tye soe much whighen about him, I cannot come to my purpose, else I could have worn him away once in two yeares. **1756** POCOCKE *Trav.* (1889) II. 217 The quicken and yew grow here. **1769** R. FRENCH in A. Young *Tour Irel.* (1780) I. 380 Two small groves.. consisting of quicken or mountain ash. **1857** O'GRADY *Pursuit Diarmuid* 143, I know that Diarmuid is in the top of the quicken.

2. *attrib.*, as ***quicken-berry, -bough, -branch.***

1579 LANGHAM *Gard. Health* (1633) 88 Mulberies, Quicken-berries, greene Grapes. **1671** SIR W. BOREMAN in F. P. Verney *Mem. Verney Fam.* (1892) I. 15 The king's.. thanks for the Quickenberry tree y^{u} sent his ma^{ty}. **1879** HENDERSON *Folk-lore* vi. 184 Twigs of mountain-ash or quicken-berry. **1894** YEATS *Celtic Twilight* 86 One of these bands carried quicken boughs in their hands.

quicken ('kwɪk(ə)n), *sb.*^{2} *Sc.* and *north. dial.* Also *north.* whick-, wicken. [f. QUICK *sb.*^{2}, the northern form of QUITCH.] Couch-grass; also *pl.* the underground stems of this and other grasses.

1684 MERITON *Yorksh. Dial.* 41 Our Land is tewgh, and full of strang whickens. **1816** SCOTT *Antiq.* xxxv, The plant Quicken, by which, *Scottice*, we understand couch-grass, dog-grass, or the *Triticum repens* of Linnæus. **1842** J. AITON *Domest. Econ.* (1857) 173 Quickens, docks, thistles,.. furze, broom. **1898** J. R. CAMPBELL in *Trans. Highl. & Agric. Soc.* 85 Quickens are in reality underground stems. Unlike roots they are jointed... Quickens are not confined to one species of grass.

b. *attrib.* and *Comb.*, as ***quicken-grass, -producer, quickens-scutch.***

1843 HARDY in *Proc. Berw. Nat. Club* II. No. 11. 63 *note*, Loosening and breaking the roots of the quicken-grass. **1858** R. S. SURTEES *Ask Mamma* lxv. 295 The rushes of one field and the whicken grass of the other. **1898** J. R. CAMPBELL in *Trans. Highl. & Agric. Soc.* 85 The grass that is best known to farmers as a quicken-producer is couch-grass. *Ibid.* 88 It is a common belief that fibrous root-scutch belongs to Agrostis, and that quickens-scutch belongs to couch-grass.

†**'quicken**, *sb.*^{3} *Obs. rare*$^{-1}$. In 6 quiken. [f. QUICK *a.* Cf. B. 2.] A living creature.

1523 FITZHERB. *Husb.* §55 If thou cut the lyuer, therin wyll be lyttell quikens lyke flokes.

quicken ('kwɪk(ə)n), *v.* Forms: *α.* 4 quicken, -in, quikken, -in, quiken, -yn, queken, qui-, quykne, quicn-, quykene(n, qwi-, qwycken, (-kk-), qwi-, qwykyn, qwykn-, 4–5 qwyken, 5 quyknyn, 4–6 quyken, 5–6 quikin, 5–8 quickn-, 6 quycken, -yn, quyckn-, *Sc.* quyckyn, -kkin, quikkine, quikn-, 6– quicken. *β.* 4 quhykine, whiken, 5 qwhykkyn. [f. QUICK *a.* + -EN^{5}. Cf. ON. *kvikna, kykna* to come to life, come into being, Sw. *qvickna*; Da. dial. *kvægne* to refresh. In Eng. the trans. sense is more usual than the intr.]

I. Transitive senses.

1. a. To give or restore life to; to make alive; to vivify or revive; to animate (as the soul the body).

a **1300** *Cursor M.* 20883 Petre.. a ded he quickend wit his schade. *c* **1380** WYCLIF *Wks.* (1880) 344 Whenne he had qwickened lazar, he brouȝt him out of his sepulcre. *c* **1440** *Promp. Parv.* 421/1 Quyknyn [*K., P.* quykyn], *vegeto, vivifico.* **1535** COVERDALE *2 Kings* v. 7 Am I God then, that I can kyll and quycken agayne. **1601** SHAKS. *All's Well* II. i. 77 A medicine.. able to breath life into a stone, Quicken a rocke. **1674** N. FAIRFAX *Bulk & Selv.* 28 The soul that I was quickned with at birth day, is the same that I am quickned with at this day. **1730–46** THOMSON *Autumn* 664 Still the fresh Spring finds New plants to quicken. **1819** SHELLEY *Cenci* IV. i. 189 Ill things Shall, with a spirit of unnatural life, Stir and be quickened. **1876** MORRIS *Sigurd* II. 84 How many things shalt thou quicken, how many shalt thou slay!

b. *fig.* in renderings of Biblical passages, or echoes of these, occas. with ref. to spiritual life.

a **1300** *E.E. Psalter* lxxxiv. 6 God, þou turned qwycken vs sal. **1357** *Lay Folks Catech.* 150 [Crist] whikend [*Lamb. MS.* qwyknyd] us un-to lyf thurgh his risyng. **1382** WYCLIF *John* vi. 64 It is the spirit that quykeneth, the fleysch profiteth nothing. **1513** DOUGLAS *Æneis* x. Prol. 128 To quykkin thy sclavys tholit schamful deid maiste fell. **1563** WINȜET tr. *Vincent. Lirin.* Wks. 1890 II. 23 He wald.. quikin his spiritual peple efoir slane. *a* **1653** BINNING *Serm.* (1845) 9 The second Adam aspired to quicken what Adam killed.

†**c.** *to be quickened* = 6 b. *Obs.*

1599 NASHE *Lenten Stuffe* Wks. 1883–4 V. 268 She was now quicknd, and cast away by the cruelty of Æolus. **1607** MARKHAM *Caval.* I. (1617) 50 Let their Mares after they are quickned, be moderately travelled or wrought.

2. To give, add, or restore vigour to (a person or thing); to stimulate, stir up, rouse, excite, inspire.

a. a person.

1523 LD. BERNERS *Froiss.* I. lxxxix. 111 Loue quickened hym day and night. **1525** *Ibid.* II. cx. [cvi.] 317, I am quickened so to do. **1542** N. UDALL in *Lett. Lit. Men* (Camden) 7 A contynuall spurre.. to pricke and to quicken me to goodnes. *a* **1632** T. TAYLOR *God's Judgem.* I. II. lii. (1642) 413 You.. he now quickened and stirred up to his love. **1703** PENN in *Pa. Hist. Soc. Mem.* IX. 271, I hope.. you will be quickened to show yourselves men in that affair. **1856** KANE *Arct. Expl.* I. xxvii. 352 We were like men driven to the wall, quickened, not depressed. **1874** GREEN *Short Hist.* viii. §5. 519 He rode through England to quicken the electors to a sense of the crisis.

b. a feeling, faculty, action, course of things, etc. †Also with *up.*

1423 JAS. I *Kingis Q.* clxxxi, To quikin treuly day by day my lore. **1450–1530** *Myrr. our Ladye* 68 Other bokes ther be that ar made to quyken, & to sturre vp the affecцyons of the soule. **1579–80** NORTH *Plutarch* (1595) 236 The first honour that valliant mindes do come vnto, doth quicken vp their appetite. **1659** RUSHW. *Hist. Coll.* I. 538 Sir Dudley Diggs quickned his motion and spoke roundly. **1723** DE FOE *Col. Jack* (1840) 89 This quickened my resolution. **1781** COWPER *Charity* 522 The frequent interjected dash Quickens a market, and helps off the trash. **1853** MAURICE *Proph. & Kings* ix. 150 The savage impulses of the soldier became quickened. **1883** FROUDE *Short Stud.* IV. II. iii. 194 Other conventional beliefs, too, were quickened into startling realities.

c. *absol.*

1581 MULCASTER *Positions* xxxix. (1887) 215 To consider of education and learning, what is good and quickneth. **1637** HEYWOOD *Royall King* II. Wks. 1874 VI. 33 The King.. quickens most where he would most destroy. *a* **1859** DE QUINCEY in 'Page' *Life* (1877) I. ii. 20 Pillar of fire, that didst go before me to guide and to quicken.

3. To kindle (a fire); to cause or help to burn up.

a **1340** HAMPOLE *Psalter* xvii. 10 Coles þat before ware ded.. ere kyndild and qwikynd agayn. *c* **1386** CHAUCER *Frankl. T.* 322 Her desir Is to be qwykkened and liȝtned of ȝour fire. **1556** J. HEYWOOD *Spider & F.* xiv. 59, I will yet once againe, quicken this cole. **1751** *Affect. Narr. of Wager* 105 The Fire they dress'd by was.. quickned by the Timber of one of the Casks. **1870** MORRIS *Earthly Par.* III. IV. 75 While she Quickened the fire. **1887** BROWNING *Parleyings, F. Furini* xi, Let my spark Quicken your tinder.

4. a. To make (liquor or medicine) more sharp or stimulant. ? *Obs.*

1591 SPENSER *Muiopotm.* 196 Dull Poppie, and drink-quickning Setuale. **1713** STEELE *Guard.* No. 143 ¶8 Rack-punch, quickned with brandy and gun-powder. **1733** CHEYNE *Eng. Malady* II. xi. §3 (1734) 232 Diaphoreticks.. quickened with volatill Spirits. **1799** M. UNDERWOOD *Diseases Children* (ed. 4) I. 55 A few grains of magnesia.. forms a much neater medicine (which may be quickened and warmed by the addition of a few drops of tincture of senna).

b. To imbue (tin) with quicksilver. *rare.*

1799 [see QUICKENING *vbl. sb.* and *ppl. a.*]. **1825** J. NICHOLSON *Operat. Mechanic* 728 Mercury.. soon unites itself with the tin, which then becomes very splendid, or, as the workmen say, is quickened.

c. *dial.* To work with yeast. (Halliwell.)

5. a. To hasten, accelerate, give speed to.

1626 BACON *Sylva* §990 You may sooner by Imagination quicken or slacke a Motion, than raise or cease it. **1691** T. H[ALE] *Acc. New Invent.* 127 In what proportion Smoothness, Sope and Tallow doth quicken [a ship's way]. **1776** ADAM SMITH *W.N.* (1869) I. I. i. 11 To facilitate and quicken their own particular part of the work. **1786** MAD. D'ARBLAY *Diary* 17 July, I was only quickening my pace, when I was again stopped. **1838** THIRLWALL *Greece* IV. 381 It had induced him to quicken his departure. **1855** BAIN *Senses & Int.* II. iv. §11 (1864) 275 In rapid walking, the very thoughts are quickened.

b. To make (a curve) sharper or (a slope) steeper.

1711 W. SUTHERLAND *Shipbuild. Assist.* 162 To Quicken the Sheer; to shorten the Radius that strikes out the Curve. **1838** *Civil Engin. & Archit. Jrnl.* I. 376/2 Retaining walls, or quickening the slopes, might perhaps get over the difficulty. *c* **1850** *Rudim. Navig.* (Weale) 139 *To quicken*, to give anything a greater curve.

II. Intransitive senses.

6. a. To receive life, to become living; †also, to recover life, to revive.

1382 WYCLIF *1 Kings* xvii. 22 The soule of the child is turned aȝen with ynne hym, and he aȝen quikenyde. **1530** PALSGR. 677/1, I quycken, I revyve, as a thyng dothe that fyrst doth begyn to styrre, or that was wyddered, or almoste deed. **1553** T. WILSON *Rhet.* 29 Hym that killeth the child so sone as it beginneth to quicken. **1604** SHAKS. *Oth.* IV. ii. 67 As Sommer Flyes.. That quicken euen with blowing. **1691** RAY *Creation* (1692) 74 Their Spawn would be lost in those Seas, the bottom being too cold for it to quicken there. **1823** SCOTT *Peveril* xiii, The seed which is sown shall one day sprout and quicken. **1842** TENNYSON *Vision of Sin* 210 Below were men and horses pierced with worms, And slowly quickening into lower forms.

fig. **1851** DIXON *W. Penn* xv. (1872) 132 The germ of Pennsylvania was quickening into life.

b. Of a female: To reach the stage of pregnancy at which the child shows signs of life. Cf. 1 c.

1530 PALSGR. 677/1 She quyckynned on al hallon day. **1662–3** PEPYS *Diary* 1 Jan., She quickened at my Lord Gerard's at dinner. **1748** [see QUICKENING *vbl. sb.*]. **1822–34** *Good's Study Med.* (ed. 4) IV. 183 A woman.. became pregnant, quickened and had a flow of milk in the breasts.

fig. **1695** BLACKMORE *Pr. Arth.* II. 26 Barren Night did pregnant grow, And quicken'd with the World in Embrio.

7. *fig.* **a.** To come into a state of existence or activity comparable to life. Const. *to*, *into*.

a **1300** *Cursor M.* 26482 All quickens [a]gain his first penance þat tint was. **13..** *E.E. Allit. P.* C. 471 þat þer quikken no cloude bifore þe cler sunne. *c* **1386** CHAUCER *Pars. T.* ¶474 Looke how that fir of smale gleedes that been almoost dede vnder asshen wollen quike agayn. **1435** MISYN *Fire of Love* 81 þe self sawle.. qwhykkynand to heuenly likyng. **1470** *Paston Lett.* No. 648 II. 406 The mater qwykennythe bothe ffor yowe and yowres. **1568** GRAFTON *Chron.* II. 203 At this time also, the warre began to quicken in Guyan. **1821** SHELLEY *False Laurels & True* 11 The hopes that quicken.. Are flowers that wither. **1829** I. TAYLOR *Enthus.* vi. 177 Countries that were quickening into freedom. *a* **1881** ROSSETTI *House of Life* ii, At her heart Love lay Quickening in darkness.

b. To grow bright.

1712–4 POPE *Rape Lock* I. 144 Sees.. keener lightnings quicken in her eyes. **1859** TENNYSON *Geraint & Enid* 535 The pale and bloodless east began To quicken to the sun. **1885** BRET HARTE *Maruja* i, Meanwhile the light [of day] quickened.

8. To become faster, to be accelerated.

1805 [see QUICKENING *ppl. a.*]. **1857** W. SMITH *Thorndale* III. iv. 226 His step quickened, his countenance lighted up with joy. **1891** T. HARDY *Tess* xxx, Tess's breath quickened.

†'quickenance. *Obs. rare.* Also 7 quicknance. [f. prec. + -ANCE.] = QUICKENING *vbl. sb.*

a **1617** BAYNE *On Eph.* (1643) 396 Could he not.. swallow up death, create life and quicknance in us. **1656** JEANES *Fuln. Christ* 21 A living member of her, which hath.. quickenance from the head of the Church.

'quickened, *ppl. a.* [f. QUICKEN *v.* + -ED¹.] Made living or quick; animated, stimulated; hastened, accelerated; etc.

1612 DRAYTON *Poly-olb.* iii. 208 Not from the quick'ned mine. **1660** *Charac. Italy* to Rdr. A iv, Some Squeamish Zealot, who.. is become a meer lump of quickened Care. **1805** SOUTHEY *Madoc in Aztlan* i, His blood Flow'd from its quicken'd spring. **1894** H. DRUMMOND *Ascent Man* 389 Courtship, with its vivid perceptions and quickened emotions.

quickener ('kwɪk(ə)nə(r)). [f. QUICKEN *v.* + -ER¹.] One who or that which quickens, in various senses of the verb.

1513 DOUGLAS *Æneis* XII. Prol. 254 Welcum quyknar of florist flowris schene. **1581** MULCASTER *Positions* vi. (1887) 40 The soule,.. the quickner of the body. **1653** H. MORE *Antid. Ath.* II. xii. §12 Notable whetters and quickners of the spirit of life. **1767** S. PATERSON *Another Trav.* I. 425 Re-edifiers of fallen temples, and quickeners of dead laurels. **1820** W. IRVING *Sketch Bk.* (1859) 137 These tokens of regard, and quickeners of kind feelings. **1879** M. D. CONWAY *Demonol.* I. I. ii. 9 Baal.. represents the Sun in his glory as quickener of Nature.

'quickening, *sb. rare*⁻¹. = QUICKEN *sb.*² So also **'quickening-grass.**

1765 *Museum Rusticum* IV. 454 Stones, quickenings, and every other thing that may hinder the growth of the flax, should be removed. *Ibid.* 456 Quickening grass should not be taken up. **1765** A. DICKSON *Treat. Agric.* (ed. 2) 106 Of the first sort is the quickening-grass, or couch-grass.

quickening ('kwɪk(ə)nɪŋ), *vbl. sb.* [f. QUICKEN *v.* + -ING¹.] **a.** The action of the vb. QUICKEN, in various senses.

c **1430** *Pilgr. Lyf Manhode* II. cviii. (1869) 116 He hadde with inne gret quiknyng of cole. **1526** *Pilgr. Perf.* (W. de W. 1531) 11 b, For the.. quyckenynge of theyr reason. **1577** tr. *Bullinger's Decades* (1592) 45 Justification of life therefore is .. a quickening or translating from death to life. **1626** *Naworth Househ. Bks.* (Surtees Soc.) 237 To Eyst for iij quickinings,.. xviijᵈ. **1655** H. VAUGHAN *Silex Scint.*, *Holy Commun.* i, Nothing that is, or lives, But hath his Quicknings, and reprieves. **1748** *Phil. Trans.* XLV. 132 After Quickening her Health became better. **1799** G. SMITH *Laboratory* I. Pref. 6 Quickening is a singular expression to be employed in gilding. **1874** GREEN *Short Hist.* vii. §7. 419 The intellectual quickening of the age had now reached the mass of the people. **1890** BILLINGS *Med. Dict.* II. 424/2 *Quickening*.., first sensation of movement of the foetus in a pregnant woman, occurring generally in the first or second week of the fifth month. **1922** JOYCE *Ulysses* 377 Send us, bright one, light one, Horhorn, quickening and wombfruit. **1975** *Church Times* 27 June 20/5 A foetus that had not reached the time of quickening (twelve to fourteen weeks old).

b. *concr.* That which quickens; hence, yeast, a quantity of yeast. *dial.*

1598 FLORIO, *Cremóre*, yeast, barme, quickning. **1790** MRS. WHEELER *Westmld. Dial.* (1821) 81 Me mudder lent her a whicknin, an we wor bawn at brew.

quickening ('kwɪk(ə)nɪŋ), *ppl. a.* [f. QUICKEN *v.* + -ING².] That quickens, in senses of the vb.

1382 WYCLIF *1 Cor.* xv. 45 The laste Adam [is made] in to a spirit quykenynge. **1531** FRITH *Judgm. Tracy* (1573) 80 Fayth is.. the quickning power out of which all good fruites spring. **1590** SPENSER *F.Q.* I. v. 12 Quickning faith.. The creeping deadly cold away did shake. **1674** J. B[RIAN] *Harv. Home* Postscr. 53, I finisht have The first part of this quickning Text. **1799** G. SMITH *Laboratory* I. 89 A quickening water. Take one ounce of quicksilver, and as much aqua fortis [etc.]. **1805** WORDSW. *Prelude* IV. 1 When quickening steps Followed each other. **1870** H. MACMILLAN *Bible Teach.* Pref. 15 Bursting buds and quickening roots.

quickening-grass: see QUICKENING *sb.*

quicken-tree: see QUICKEN *sb.*¹

quick-eyed, *a.* Having a quick eye (see QUICK *a.* 20). Also *fig.*

a **1616** BEAUM. & FL. *Bonduca* IV. iii, Care, counsel, Quick-eyed experience, and victory. **1647** H. MORE *Song of Soul* II. iii. III. xli, The cheerfull children of the quick-ey'd Morn. **1727–46** THOMSON *Summer* 253 The quick-eyed trout Or darting salmon. **1809–10** COLERIDGE *Friend* (1865) 214 Brissot.. was rather a sublime visionary than a quick-eyed politician. **1876** T. HARDY *Ethelberta* (1890) 215 A quick-eyed, light-haired, slight-built woman.

quick-freeze ('kwɪkfriːz), *v.* Also written as one word. [f. QUICK *adv.* + FREEZE *v.*] *trans.* To freeze (perishable material) rapidly so that it can be stored at a low temperature for a long time. Also *absol.*

1930 *Popular Science* Sept. 27/2 Obviously, it would take longer to quick-freeze a six-pound cut of beef than a half-pound fillet. **1940** *Daily Progress* (Charlottesville, Va.) 20 Mar. 1/5 The range of food which can be quick-frozen has .. brought a variety of business combinations into the field. **1957** *Daily Mail* 5 Sept. 11/5 In Florida.. they are quick-freezing water-melon concentrate.. and making it available to any hospital anywhere in the country. **1959** *Times* 4 Nov. 23/11 (*heading*) Crosse & Blackwell to quick-freeze. **1967** *Heretaunga Plains* (School Publications Branch, N.Z.) 48/1 Fifteen tons of raspberries were quickfrozen and two more tons processed.

Hence **'quick-freeze** *attrib.*, that consists of or is used for quick-freezing; also *absol.*; **'quick-freezing** *vbl. sb.* and *ppl. a.*; **'quick-frozen** *ppl. a.*

1930 *Popular Science* Sept. 26/1 Clarence B. Birdseye.. succeeded in placing quick-frozen fish on the market. *Ibid.* (*caption*) Oysters, sealed in a package, are turned solid by quick-freeze process. **1932** *Sun* (Baltimore) 26 May 29/2 The comparatively new process known as quick-freezing. **1940** *Daily Progress* (Charlottesville, Va.) 20 Mar. 1/5 Quick-frozen foods.. are rapidly becoming an important part of the American food production and distribution scene. **1943** J. S. HUXLEY *TVA* 103 TVA research has also led to the marketing of new types of quick-freezing machinery. **1945** NELSON & WRIGHT *Tomorrow's House* vi. 74/2 A kitchen.. will almost inevitably have a quick-freeze unit. **1950** *Times* 27 Feb. 4/5 No points are now needed for canned pork and some other imported ready-cooked and quick-frozen meats. **1951** *Good Housek. Home Encycl.* 514/2 Set the dial at 'maximum' or 'quick freeze' about an hour before the mixture is ready. **1959** *Times* 4 Nov. 23/11 The plant.. would provide some quick freezing facilities.. to enable the company to enter the quick freezing field on a limited scale. **1965** *Supermarket & Self-Service* (Johannesburg) June/July 13/3 Quick-frozen polywrapped broilers. **1973** *Press & Jrnl.* (Aberdeen) 3 Aug. 3/2 The processing and quick-freezing of prawns. **1976** *Woman's Day* (U.S.) Nov. 95/1 Another argument against performing a biopsy.. is that it depends on quick-frozen sections of the suspicious tissue.

quick-grass ('kwɪgrɑːs, -æ-). [f. QUICK *sb.*² + GRASS *sb.*¹ Cf. Da. *qvik-*, *qvækgræs*.]

1. = QUICK *sb.*²

1617 MINSHEU *Ductor*, Quickgrasse,.. *Gramen caninum*. **1712** tr. *Pomet's Hist. Drugs* I. 52 There are several other Roots sold in the Shops.. as the Dog grass, or Quick grass. **1765** *Museum Rusticum* IV. xxi. 94 It takes fresh root at its joints, like quick-grass. **1770–4** A. HUNTER *Georg. Ess.* (1804) II. 213 Turned over when the least particle of quick-grass appears. **1878** *Golden Hours* X. 200/2 She tripped lightly past a knot of Quick Grasses.

2. *S. Afr.* = KWEEK.

1931 E. P. PHILLIPS *Introd. Study S. Afr. Grasses* vi. 79 Quick grass. *Cynodon Dactylon*; *C. incompletus*; *Stenotaphrum secundatum*. **1972** *Stand. Encycl. S. Afr.* V. 320/2 The quick-grasses (*Cynodon* spp.).. are amongst those grasses that are commonly planted as lawns.

quickhatch ('kwɪkhætʃ). Also 8 queeque-, 9 quicke-. [An adaptation of the Cree (Indian) name, given by Richardson as *okeecoohagees* or *-gew*, by Watkins (1865) as *kwekwukao*; from other Algonquin dialects come the forms CARCAJOU and KINKAJOU.] The wolverine.

1743 M. CATESBY *Nat. Hist.* I. xxx, The quickhatch.. has not been observed by any author, or known in Europe, till the year 1737, one was sent to Sir Hans Sloane. **1744** A. DOBBS *Countries Adjacent to Hudson's Bay* 40 The beavers have three enemies, man, otters, and the carcajou or queequehatch. **1829** J. RICHARDSON *Fauna Boreali-Americana* I. 42 The European labourers in the service of the Hudson's Bay Company term it Quickehatch.

quick hedge: see QUICK *a.* 3 b.

quickie ('kwɪkɪ). *colloq.* Also **quickey, quicky.** [f. QUICK *a.* + -Y⁶, -IE.] **1. a.** A cinematographic film that is made quickly and cheaply. See also *quota quickie* s.v. QUOTA *sb.* 4.

1926 *Amer. Mercury* Dec. 465/1 Motion pictures which are ground out wholesale by the studios at the rate of one a week are called *quickies*. **1937** *Times* 13 Nov. 8/1 It is not handicapped, as the quickie is, by the expenditure of £1 a foot. **1946** *Sun* (Baltimore) 4 Oct. 12/1 The possibilities of the subject are barely touched on in 'Down Missouri Way', for this is a quickie, made.. on a limited budget. **1958** *Observer* 16 Mar. 15/2 Those early wartime quickies. **1961** *John o' London's* 14 Sept. 307/4 An equally pleasant semi-amateur quicky, *One More River*. **1977** *Time* 22 Aug. 43/3 Producer Charles Band plans to return by Christmas with another quickie titled *Laser Blast*.

b. In various extended and *transf.* senses: anything produced or carried out quickly.

1940 *Washington Post* 6 July 5/7 The publishers have their firecrackers, too. They call them 'quickies'. They are books pushed through the presses to meet the headlines of the day, to go off with a bang, even if they are but rubbish in the grass when the holiday is over. **1941** B. SCHULBERG *What makes Sammy Run?* x. 187, I may not have time to see you again. This trip is one of those quickies. **1942** *Gen* 1 Sept. 14/1 Then he [*sc.* a fighter pilot] 'screams downhill' and sends the German into the 'drink' with a 'quickie'. **1943** *Newsweek* 8 Feb. 56/1 Some observers interpreted the growing trend toward 'quickies'—undeclared strikes in the form of work stoppages for a few hours or a day or two—as the rank and file's way of spurring their leaders to a crackdown on the WLB for more money. **1944** *Sun* (Baltimore) 19 July 22/8 It [*sc.* a meeting] looked like 'one of those quickies which the Mayor held in his office'. **1948** *Variety* 25 Aug. 54/1 Deitz, due back by air from a quickie to Paris last week. **1950** W. HAMMOND *Cricketers' School* xvi. 151 Close was bowling right-arm off-spinners, and 'quickies' with the new ball. **1952** *Word Study* Feb. 8/1 In a publicity release Alfred A. Knopf, Inc., describes one of its Fall books, Richard G. Baumhoff's *That Dammed Missouri*, as follows: 'Though the appearance of this book could not be better timed, it is not what in publishing circles is called a 'quicky' (or, 'quickie') —that is, a book written and rolled off the presses hot on the heels of a national news event.' **1957** *Spectator* 15 Mar. 341/1, I think we've just got time for a quickie, and it's a real tickler from Mr. Bumple, of Bedford. **1958** [see LIBRARY¹ 3]. **1969** A. GLYN *Dragon Variation* v. 142 Debbie had been keen on a Mexican divorce, a quickie in Mexico City followed by a honeymoon in Acapulco. **1970** *Times* 13 Jan. 8/3 The usual mishmash of buzzers, bonus points and quickies to confuse the looker-on. **1971** *Petticoat* 17 July 38/3 Here's a quicky for you when you get a blank spot about what to make for that summertime snack or light supper. **1975** R. H. RIMMER *Premar Experiments* II. 210 Yesterday they were asking some of the girls if they were hookers or 'hos'. Kathy told Mohammed that a tough Irish kid offered her ten dollars for a 'quickie'.

c. A rapidly-taken alcoholic drink; a short drink.

1941 BAKER *Dict. Austral. Slang* 58 *Quickie*, a drink taken quickly. **1942** BERRY & VAN DEN BARK *Amer. Thes. Slang* §101/4 Cocktail names of slang and facetious origin.. quickie. **1943** S. LEWIS *Gideon Planish* xv. 143, I guess that calls for a drink. Let's make it a quickie, because I got to go out shopping with George. **1947** B. MARSHALL *Red Danube* iii. 25 'I could do with a quicky'... Lined along the bar the other high ups.. were having quickies too. **1959** H. HOBSON *Mission Ho. Murder* iii. 21 Have you finished with the bottle?.. Give it to the musicians, there's just about three quickies. **1970** H. MCLEAVE *Question of Negligence* xxiv. 220 'Drink?' Conway-Smith asked. 'Just a quickie,' she replied. **1974** P. HAINES *Tea at Gunter's* xv. 156 Are you in the bar, dear?.. Ronald and I just dropped in for a quickie—we're on our way back from a party.

2. *Cricket.* A fast bowler.

1934 *Evening News* 21 June 1/1 Whatever chance England may or may not have, it will be a better one if there are two or three 'quickeys' in the side in any of the remaining Tests. **1963** R. GILCHRIST *Hit me for Six* i. 15 It just happened that the first team wanted a 'quickie'. **1966** B. JOHNSTON

Armchair Cricket 1966 108 *Quickie*, a slang term for a fast bowler. **1977** *News of World* 17 Apr. 20/8 Their other unknown quickie, Len Pascoe.., isn't as fast as Lillee or Thomson.

3. *attrib.* or as *adj.*

1927 *Daily Express* 12 Dec. 13 The most eminent 'quickie' producer is Phil Goldstone, who can make a full-length film ..in eight days. **1936** *Sun* (Baltimore) 21 Dec. 8/2 In recent months there have been scores of 'sit-down' or 'quickie' strikes in the automobile factories. **1940** *Common Sense* Mar. 20/1 [Cordell Hull] found his way to a quicky law school in the county. **1944** *Sun* (Baltimore) 15 Nov. 11/2 Another quickie bridge and the town was ours. **1959** M. DOLINSKY *There is no Silence* iv. 57 Virtually every model in the country lived on these quickie love affairs. **1960** *Guardian* 27 Oct. 9/6 He made as many as eight 'quickie' Westerns..a year. **1969** A. GLYN *Dragon Variation* v. 142 Joann's rumour that there now were quickie divorces in Nevada too was apparently unfounded. **1976** H. NIELSEN *Brink of Murder* ii. 19 He's kept a packed travel-bag in his office for these quickie trips. **1979** *Yale Alumni Mag.* Apr. (Suppl.) cn14/3 The deadline conflicts with a planned quickie vacation in Puerto Rico.

'quicking, *vbl. sb.*[1] *rare.* [f. QUICK *v.*[1] + -ING[1].] = QUICKENING *vbl. sb.*

c **1400** *Apol. Loll.* 54 þe principale and þe finale wark of Crist..is þe quiking of soulis. *a* **1666** BROME *On Death K. Charles* 18 He did fall, Whose influence gave quicking to us all. **1825** J. NICHOLSON *Operat. Mechanic* 719 Sometimes the amalgam is applied to the surface to be gilt, without any quicking, by spreading it with aqua-fortis.

'quicking, *vbl. sb.*[2] [f. QUICK *v.*[2] + -ING[1].]

1. *rare.* **a.** The action of planting with 'quick'. **b.** *concr.* The quicksets for a hedge.

1469–70 *Durham Acc. Rolls* (Surtees) 244 Et sol .ijs. pro le qwyking sepium unius clausuræ. **1485–6** *Ibid.* 649 Pro le qwhykkyng circa clausur... vijs. **1664** EVELYN *Sylva* (1776) 402, I find most do greatly affect the vulgar way of Quicking.

2. Coating with mercury by immersion; also *concr.*

1863 *Brit. Patent 1512* 1 This Invention consists in preserving the silvering or quicking applied on glass and objects made of silvered or quicked glass. **1873** E. SPON *Workshop Receipts* (Ser. 1) 307/2 When a sufficient quantity of mercury is dissolved, the articles to be gilt are put into the solution, and stirred about with a brush till they become white. This is called quicking. **1923** W. R. COOPER *W. G. McMillan's Treat. Electrometallurgy* (ed. 4) vi. 116 Quicking is..often resorted to in order to increase the adhesiveness of deposited metals on objects which would have no action on the bath; for the mercury..retains a bright surface when exposed to the air for a period which would suffice to provide a film of oxide upon an unquicked surface. *Ibid.* 117 The quicking-solutions more commonly used are: the per-nitrate or proto-nitrate of mercury..or the cyanide of mercury. **1930** FIELD & WEILL *Electro-Plating* 104 A thin, bright film of mercury is applied by simple immersion in a suitable solution. This process is called quicking. **1952** H. SILMAN *Chem. & Electro-Plated Finishes* (ed. 2) 478/2 (Index), 'Quicking' solutions.

quicking-drag: see QUICK *v.*[3]

'quickish, *a.* [f. QUICK *a.* + -ISH[1].] Somewhat quick; in *Cricket*, of a bowler, fast-medium.

1900 O. AGNUS *Jan Oxber* iii. 194 Be quickish downstairs, mind 'ee. **1955** *Times* 9 July 4/7 Neame and Parker, for Harrow, made steady progress against Sinclair and Douglas Pennant, a quickish left-hander. **1963** *Times* 4 June 3/6 He is tall, well built, and quickish, and Hampshire think that they may have a real find in him. **1977** *Sunday Times* 3 July 28/6 Nottinghamshire's quick and quickish bowlers had two wickets..in the first four overs. **1978** *Gramophone* Apr. 1713/1 The quickish pulse, less accommodatingly shaped than Karajan's.., does occasionally suggest a nature ramble being hastened along by a warden who senses rain in the offing.

quicklike, *adv.* Chiefly *U.S.* [f. QUICK *a.* + -LIKE.] In a quick manner; quickly.

1913 G. STRATTON-PORTER *Laddie* viii. 235 He..looked down the hole I showed him and he cried out quicklike. **1951** H. E. GILES *Harbin's Ridge* xxi. 186 He slewed his eyes at me quick-like. **1978** A. PRICE *'44 Vintage* vi. 70 We've to nip in quick-like.

'quicklime. [f. QUICK *a.* + LIME, after L. *calx viva* (Vitruvius), F. *chaux vive*, etc.] Lime which has been burned and not yet slaked with water; calcium oxide, CaO.

c **1400** *Rom. Rose* 4179 The mortere..Of quykke lyme persant and egre. **1489** CAXTON *Faytes of A.* II. xxxix. 163 To be cast to the shyp of the enemies pottes full of quyk lyme made in to pouldre. *a* **1533** LD. BERNERS *Huon* cxii. 389 They cast vpon them hote lede and boylynge oyle and quycke Lyme. **1590** WEBBE *Trav.* (Arb.) 31 Constrained to drinke salte water and quicklime. **1685** BOYLE *Salubr. Air* 61 Such a thick smoke as good quicklime is wont to doe, whilst men slake it with water. **1703** MOXON *Mech. Exerc.* 242 Quick Lime..consumes dead Bodies put therein. **1813** SIR H. DAVY *Agric. Chem.* vii. (1814) 317 Quicklime in its pure state..is injurious to plants. **1873** B. STEWART *Conserv. Force* iii. 58 Limestone..is decomposed when subjected to the heat of a lime-kiln, carbonic acid being given off, while quick-lime remains behind.

attrib. **1684** BOYLE *Porousn. Anim. & Solid Bod.* vi. 55 Dip a very large Sponge in good Quick-lime-water. **1861** FLOR. NIGHTINGALE *Nursing* ii. 23 Washing the walls and ceilings with quick-lime wash.

†**'quickly**, *a. Obs. rare*⁻¹. In 5 qwhikly. [f. QUICK *a.* + -LY[1]. Cf. ON. *kvikligr.*] Lively.

1435 MISYN *Fire of Love* 96 If þou lufe in þis maner..to þat qwhikly syght þou salt be nere full glorius.

quickly ('kwɪklɪ), *adv.* Forms: see QUICK *a.* (Also *comp.* 3 cwicluker, 5 qwyklyar, qwhykliar; *sup.* qwhikestly, 6 quyklyst.) [f. QUICK *a.* + -LY[2]. Cf. ON. *kvikliga.*]

†**1.** In a living or lively manner; with animation or vigour; also, with strong feeling, sensitively. *Obs.*

c **1000** *Ags. Ps.* (Th.) cxviii. 37 Me on soðne weȝ þinne.. læde cwiculice. *c* **1330** R. BRUNNE *Chron. Wace* (Rolls) 6722 Be ȝe doughty, & lereþ of armes, & quykly defende ȝow fro harmes. *c* **1380** WYCLIF *Serm.* Sel. Wks. II. 251 Men shulden..do quycly wiþ þer lippis bi resoun of Goddis cause. **1435** MISYN *Fire of Love* 77, I suld more Ioy or ellis qwyklyar synge. *c* **1440** HYLTON *Scala Perf.* (W. de W. 1494) II. xxviii, Suche a man..is soo quyckely and soo felyngly inspired. *c* **1449** PECOCK *Repr.* I. ix. 47 It is quikli and smertli spoken. **1596** DALRYMPLE tr. *Leslie's Hist. Scot.* IX. 153 Al his speiking euer taisted of heavinlines..to..steir thame up quiklier, quha war in the gud way. **1738** WARBURTON *Div. Legat.* II. iv. (R.), It was proper to represent a perfect lawgiver as quickly touched with all the affections of humanity. **1800** in *Spirit Pub. Jrnls.* IV. 340 Ministers of state have a right to feel rather quickly upon the subject of character.

†**b.** With quickness of perception. *Obs.*

c **1330** R. BRUNNE *Chron. Wace* (Rolls) 7782 By alle þe costes quykly to wake þat no Saxoyn on ȝow aryue. **1486** *Bk. St. Albans* C viij b, Of sharpenesse of hir corage and of hir lokyng quicly. **1587** GOLDING *De Mornay* xiv. 217 There are beasts which do heere, see, smel, taste, and feele much better and quicklier than man doth.

†**c.** In a life-like manner; to the life. *Obs.*

c **1477** CAXTON *Jason* 84 An ymage of fyn golde so quickly made after the facon of appollo that it semed proprely his persone. *c* **1525** SKELTON *Garl. Laurel* 592 A lybbard,..As quikly towchyd as it were flesshe and bones. *a* **1529** —— *P. Sparowe* 1121 Handes soft as sylke..That are so quyckely vayned. *a* **1605** *Bankis Helicon* 41 in Montgomerie's *Poems* (1887) 274 Not abill, in tabill, With colours competent, So quiklie or liklie A form to represent.

2. Rapidly, with haste or speed.

a. Describing the rate of progress in a motion, action, or process, without consideration of the time at which it begins and ends.

1297 R. GLOUC. (Rolls) 7455 His folc quicliche to þe bataile sscet. *a* **1400–50** *Alexander* 1414 Sum braidis to þar bowis..Quethirs out quarels quikly betwene. **1526** *Pilgr. Perf.* (W. de W. 1531) 119 We may fele our pulses bete quikly and continually. *a* **1548** HALL *Chron., Hen. V* 50 He ..folowed so quickely that the Frenchmen turnyng to flyght, ranne [etc.]. **1829** LANDOR *Imag. Conv., Marvel & Bp. Parker* Wks. 1853 II. 111/1 We..throw them down in the dirt to make them follow us the quicklier. **1860** TYNDALL *Glac.* II. ii. 226 The wings of the small insect vibrate more quickly than those of the larger one.

b. Denoting that the whole action or process is begun and ended within a comparatively short space of time.

a **1225** *Ancr. R.* 270 Ich chulle gon nu slepen & arisen nunon, & don cwicluker þen nu þet ich schulde don nu. *c* **1420** *Pallad. on Husb.* VI. 122 So smyte hem of, quycly that hit be do. **1435** MISYN *Fire of Love* 81 Now qwhykliar, now slawlyer, it warmes. **1544** PHAER *Regim. Lyfe* (1553) E iij, A little good wine..is the chiefe thing that quickliest restoreth him. **1596** DALRYMPLE tr. *Leslie's Hist. Scot.* I. 95 Breid wil thay make quiklier..[in this way] nor vthirwyse. **1629** EARLE *Microcosm., High-spirited Man* (Arb.) 92 A man quickly fired, and quickly laid downe with satisfaction. **1677** JOHNSON in *Ray's Corr.* (1848) 128 Possibly their stomach may digest very quickly. **1747** WESLEY *Prim. Physic.* (1762) 117 This quickly heals even cut Veins and Sinews. **1811** A. T. THOMSON *Lond. Disp.* (1818) 607 On this account decoctions should be quickly made. **1861** FLOR. NIGHTINGALE *Nursing* 41 Leave the sick room quickly and come into it quickly, not suddenly, nor with a rush.

c. Denoting that there is little or no interval between a given point in time and the doing of an act or happening of an event (freq. also implying a or b); without delay; very soon, shortly.

c **1205** LAY. 4697 He..bad hine quicliche aȝeuen him his quene. *c* **1330** *Arth. & Merl.* 7809 (Kölbing) Soriandes.. oȝain ferd For to taken quiclike þe children. **1393** LANGL. *P. Pl.* C. XXI. 76 Quikliche cam a cacchepol, and craked a-two here legges. **1490** CAXTON *Eneydos* xxvi. 94 Aryse vp quykly without taryenge. **1539** TAVERNER *Erasm. Prov.* (1545) 25 He gyueth twyse, yᵗ gyueth quyckelye. **1593** SHAKS. *3 Hen. VI*, IV. i. 132 They are alreadie, or quickly will be landed. **1605** —— *Macb.* IV. iii. 200 If it be mine Keepe it not from me, quickly let me haue it. **1666** BUNYAN *Grace Abound.* §29 But quickly after this, I fell in company with one poor man. **1779–81** JOHNSON *L.P., Mallet* Wks. 1787 IV. 282 The series of great men, quickly to be exhibited. **1847** MRS. A. KERR *Hist. Servia* 308 Retaliation and vengeance quickly followed. **1888** *Pall Mall G.* 12 Dec. 12/1 Quickly afterwards a Conservative member..carried it off.

3. Used with ppl. adjs., as ***quickly-aging***, ***gone***, ***-growing***, ***-speaking***, ***working***.

1597 GERARDE *Herbal* Table Eng. Names, Quickly gone flower, that is Uenice Mallow. **1866** ODLING *Anim. Chem.* 50 A quickly-growing leafy plant. **1870** W. D. CHRISTIE in *Dryden's Wks.* (Globe) p. xv, An active and quickly working brain. **1874** LISLE CARR *Jud. Gwynne* I. i. 44 The quickly-speaking eyes of the dashing warrior.

quick march. *Mil.* [In 1, f. QUICK *a.* + MARCH *sb.* In 2, f. (or altered to) QUICK *adv.* 2 + MARCH *v.*]

1. A march in QUICK TIME. Also *fig.*

1752 HUME *Ess. & Treat.* (1777) I. 287 That quick march of the spirits..does in the end exhaust the mind. **1796** *Instr. & Reg. Cavalry* (1813) 247 The Quick March, 108 steps in a minute. **1867** SMYTH *Sailor's Word-bk.*, *Quick march*,.. the ordinary pace is 3½ miles to the hour, or 110 paces (275 feet) to the minute.

attrib. **1852** DICKENS *Bleak Ho.* II. iii. 32 Softly whistling, in quick-march time.

2. Used as a command to soldiers to march in quick time (see quots. 1802 and 1833).

1802 JAMES *Milit. Dict.*, *Quick*..forms the cautionary part of a word of command when troops are ordered to move in quick time; as Quick—March. **1833** *Regul. Instr. Cavalry* I. 18 *Quick March.*—The command *Quick, March*, is to be given with a pause between the words, the word *Quick* being considered as a caution. **1887** *Times* (weekly ed.) 18 Nov. 2/4 The words of command were..'Eyes front, by your right, quick march'.

quick-match. A quick-burning match used for firing cannon, igniting fire-works, shells, etc., consisting of cotton-wick soaked in a composition of gum, spirits, water, and gunpowder.

1765 R. JONES *Fireworks* ii. 66 Quick-match is generally made of such cotton as is put in candles. **1803** WELLINGTON *Let. to Col. Stevenson* in Gurw. *Desp.* (1837) II. 418 A shell or two..having in them a bit of quick match, besides the fuse. **1847** ALB. SMITH *Chr. Tadpole* xxxviii. (1879) 324 Any family wrong acted like a quick-match amongst them all.

attrib. **1802** JAMES *Milit. Dict.* s.v. *Laboratory*, Stores for a Fire-ship of 100 tons..Quick-match barrels 1.

quickness ('kwɪknɪs). [f. QUICK *a.* + -NESS.]

1. Life, vitality, vital principle. Now *rare.*

a **1225** *Ancr. R.* 150 þe rinde..is þe treouwes warde, & wit [= keeps] hit ine strencðe & ine cwicnesse. *c* **1440** *Promp. Parv.* 421/1 Quyknesse, of lyve, *vita.* **1538** STARKEY *Dialogue* 87 In a goute the handys and fete..be as dede, wythout lyfe and quyknes to procure thyngys necessary for the body. **1545** RAYNOLD *Byrth Mankynde* 139 The lyfe and quycknesse of the grayne is vtterly destroyed. **1613** M. RIDLEY *Magn. Bodies* 63 As though they had a new life of quicknesse infused into them. **1655** H. VAUGHAN *Silex Scintill.* II. *Quickness* v, Life is..A quickness, which my God hath kist. **1883** *Pop. Sci. Monthly* XXII. 168 All the energies seen in nature are..but manifestations of the essential life or quickness of matter.

†**2.** Animation, liveliness, briskness, vigour, freshness, etc. *Obs.*

1369 CHAUCER *Dethe Blaunche* 26 Defaulte of slepe, and hevynesse Hath sleyne my spirite of quyknesse. *c* **1430** *Pol. Rel. & L. Poems* (1866) 28 To grant it [a statue] lyfe and qwiknesse of langage. **1529** MORE *Dyaloge* II. Wks. 1557 1183/1 Make hym do al hys good workes wearyly, and withoute consolacion or quyckenes. **1589** PUTTENHAM *Eng. Poesie* I. xxvii. (Arb.) 69 That disticke of Virgil..I will recite for the breifnes and quicknes of it. **1656** *Artif. Handsom.* 162 Adding a quicknesse of complexion to the face.

3. Liveliness, readiness, rapidity, or acuteness of feeling, perception or apprehension.

a. Physical; esp. *of* the eyes or sight.

1398 TREVISA *Barth. De P.R.* v. xxix. (1495) 140 For quyknes and lyfnes of the synewes..in the ouermest partyes of the fyngres. **1623** COCKERAM II, Quicknesse of sight, *perspicacitie.* **1695** LD. PRESTON *Boeth.* I. 3 A Woman..with sparkling Eyes, which were of an extraordinary Force and Quickness. **1841** LANE *Arab. Nts.* I. 127 The astonishing quickness of sight of one of the hawks.

b. Mental; *of* the mind, etc.

1526 *Pilgr. Perf.* (W. de W. 1531) 216b, He hath this viuacite or quycknes of wytte. **1596** DALRYMPLE tr. *Leslie's Hist. Scot.* I. 118 Our elderis, throuch quiknes of thair ingine perceiued perfytlie..the dissolute maneris of thair people. *a* **1661** FULLER *Worthies* (1840) II. 382 Whom he much resembled in quickness of parts. **1735** POPE *Ep. Lady* 97 With too much Quickness ever to be taught. **1798** EDGEWORTH *Pract. Educ.* (1822) I. 115 Attentive patience can do as much as quickness of intellect. **1884** L. J. JENNINGS *Croker Papers* I. viii. 233 A man of great quickness of spirit and acuteness.

4. a. Speed, rapidity (of action, motion, etc.); sharpness (of a curve); hastiness (of temper).

a **1548** HALL *Chron., Hen. V* 60 Their quicknes and swiftnes did more preiudice to theyr enemyes. **1597** HOOKER *Eccl. Pol.* v. xxxiii, As if they were darts thrown out with a kind of sudden quickness. **1698** G. THOMAS *Pensilvania* 41 The Water-Mills far exceed those in England..for quickness. **1729** *Col. Rec. Pennsylv.* III. 366 His Horse was hurt through the quickness of the Journey. **1796** MORSE *Amer. Geog.* I. 62 The quickness of vegetation..proceeds from the duration of the sun above the horizon. **1858** *Skyring's Builder's Prices* (ed. 48) 57 The quickness of the curve and depth of the quirks make them difficult of access to work. **1863** A. BLOMFIELD *Mem. Bp. Blomfield* II. ix. 180 A quickness of temper which..marred the perfection of his character.

b. With *a* and *pl.*: A case or instance of this.

1656 tr. *Hobbes' Elem. Philos.* (1839) 218 The sum of all the several quicknesses or impetus. **1883** BESANT *All in a Garden Fair* (1886) 78 Little quicknesses of gesture.

†**5.** Sharpness, keenness; pungency or acidity of taste; sharpness of speech. *Obs.*

1611 BEAUM. & FL. *Maid's Trag.* I. i, To see my sword, and feel The quickness of the edge. **1647** CLARENDON *Hist. Reb.* I. §83 Her Majesty answering with some quickness. **1652–62** HEYLIN *Cosmogr.* III. (1682) 29 Lemmons, Pomegranats, Citrons..much praised for their quickness of taste. **1741** *Compl. Fam.-Piece* I. i. 52 The Quickness of the Liquor, which may make him weep. **1748** RICHARDSON *Clarissa* I. xvii. (1811) 117 This quickness upon me..is not to be borne.

6. Mobility or plasticity (of soil).

1969 *Engin. Geol.* III. 135 A series of experiments..was carried out with the purpose to investigate if quickness could be produced by leaching of a clay deposited in salt water. **1972** *Nature* 28 Jan. 220/2 It may be the hitherto neglected non-clay mineral fraction which is responsible for quickness.

quicksand ('kwɪksænd). [ME. (f. QUICK *a.* 10), = Du. *kwikzand*, G. *quick-*, Da. *kvik-*, Sw. *qvicksand*, Icel. *kviksandr*; but it is doubtful whether all of these are independent formations.]

1. A bed of extremely loose wet sand, easily yielding to pressure and thus readily swallowing up any heavy object resting on it. Quicksands are frequent on some coasts, and are very dangerous to travellers, stranded ships, etc.

14.. *Burlesque* in *Reliq. Antiq.* (1841) I. 82, .vij. acurs of londe betwyxe Dover and Qwykkesand. **1480** CAXTON *Chron. Eng.* ccxliv. (1482) 304 He brought hem thurgh a quyke sand and so in to an Ile. **1523** FITZHERB. *Husb.* § 128 It is in manner of a quycke sande that harde it is for any thynge to goe ouer. **1610** HOLLAND *Camden's Brit.* I. 753 Uncertaine sands..ready to catch and swallow, they call them Quick-sands. *c* **1700** PRIOR *The Ladle* 26 Amphitrite clears his way From rocks and quicksands in the sea. **1784** COWPER *Tiroc.* 870 Conscious that there lay..quicksands in his way. **1851** MAYNE REID *Scalp Hunt.* v. 39, I was sinking in a quicksand.

b. *fig.* Applied to things (more rarely to persons) having the absorbent, yielding, or treacherous character of a quicksand.

1593 SHAKS. *3 Hen. VI*, v. iv. 26 What [is] Clarence, but a Quick-sand of Deceit? **1602** MARSTON *Antonio's Rev.* IV. iv, I am a poore, poore orphant..the very ouze, The quick-sand that devours all miserie. **1608** MIDDLETON *Trick to Catch Old One* I. i, Swallowed in the quicksands of law-quillets. **1697** JOS. WOODWARD *Relig. Soc.* x. (1704) 157 Self-conceit..is a quicksand in which thousands have been swallowed up. **1781** COWPER *Progr. Err.* 552 Sinking in the quicksand he defends, He dies disputing. **1879** CHURCH *Spenser* 161 He once more tried the quicksands of the Court.

attrib. *a* **1616** BEAUM. & FL. *Bonduca* II. i, Fling their fame and fortunes Into this Britain gulf, this quicksand ruin.

2. Without article: Loose yielding sand.

1838 *Civil Eng. & Arch. Jrnl.* I. 151/1 It passes through quicksand, clay [etc.]. **1859** MARCY *Prairie Trav.* iii. 75 A man incurs no danger in walking over quicksand provided he step rapidly. **1881** RAYMOND *Mining Gloss.*, *Quicksand*, sand which is..shifting, easily movable or semi-liquid.

Hence **ˈquicksand** *v.* in *pass.*, to be stuck in a quicksand. **ˈquicksanded** *a.*, full of quicksands. *fig.* **ˈquicksandy** *a.*, of the nature of a quicksand.

1614 T. ADAMS *Phys. from Heaven* Wks. 1861 I. 358 The rotten, moorish, quicksandy grounds, that some have set their edifices on. **1618** MYNSHUL *Ess. Prison, Jaylors* 30 Many men..forsake the calmes of their owne happy fortunes, to arriue on these quicksanded Shores. **1899** *Westm. Gaz.* 20 May 5/2 The animal and the cart became quicksanded.

quickset (ˈkwɪksɛt), *sb.*[1] and *a.*[1] Also 5–6 **quyk-**, 6 **quyck-**, **quyke-**, 7 **quic-**, etc. [f. QUICK *a.* 3 + SET *ppl. a.* and *sb.*]

A. *sb.* **1. a.** *collect.* Live slips or cuttings of plants, set in the ground to grow, *esp.* those of whitethorn or other shrub of which hedges are made.

1484 *Rent roll St. Wolstan's Hosp., Worcester* (Bodleian Rolls, Worc. No. 1), Et soluti pro fodicione..cum Quyksette hoc anno—ijs. *jd.* **1573** TUSSER *Husb.* (1878) 51 Where speedy quickset for a fence ye wil drawe. **1607** J. NORDEN *Surv. Dial.* v. 237 They plant them in hedges, and the quickset of them make a strong fence. **1727** BRADLEY *Fam. Dict.* s.v. *Agriculture*, To make a Hedge and lay the Quickset, is three Pence a Pole. **1816** SOUTHEY *Ess.* (1832) I. 206 He..inclosed the ground with a single row of quickset. **1837** DICKENS *Pickw.* v, To extricate their unfortunate companions from their bed of quickset.

fig. **1847–9** HELPS *Friends in C.* Ser. I. (1851) II. 4 Men would have one sturdy quickset of the same height and colour—both in their fellow-men and their hedges.

b. With *a* and *pl.* A single slip or cutting of this kind.

1523 FITZHERB. *Husb.* §124 Get thy quyckesettes in the wode-contrey and let them be of whyte thorne and crabtre for they be beste; holy and hasell be good. **1601** HOLLAND *Pliny* I. 530 When a quick-set of a vine is planted in a vineyard. **1669** WORLIDGE *Syst. Agric.* (1681) 266 Plant Timber-trees, or any Coppice-wood, or Hedge-wood; and also Quick-sets. **1794** *Act for inclosing South Kelsey* 13 For preserving the young Quicksets to be planted in the Fences. **1866** ROGERS *Agric. & Prices* I. xviii. 428 Quicksets are also purchased, for the same purposes as those which are familiar to the modern agriculturist. **1938** M. HADFIELD *Everyman's Wild Flowers & Trees* 63 Common Hawthorn... A valuable hedge plant, as such, called quick-set.

2. A quickset hedge or thicket.

1573 TUSSER *Husb.* (1878) 45 Learne soone to get A good quickset. **1634** HEYWOOD & BROME *Lancash. Witches* IV. H.'s Wks. 1874 IV. 219 Theres a deepe ditch, and a hye quick-set about mee. **1680** OTWAY *Caius Marius* IV. i, A new Quick-set, which I had just made to keep the Swine from the Beans. **1768** PENNANT *Brit. Zool.* II. 338 They generally chuse a quickset to make their nest in. **1896** *Cornh. Mag.* Dec. 799 We strode with difficulty..through this great dark quickset of nature. **1973** R. ADAMS *Watership Down* xlv. 375 Hazel halted among the quickset on top of the nearer bank.

transf. **1605** BACON *Adv. Learn.* II. vii. §7 The haires of the Eye-liddes are for a quic-sette and fence about the Sight. **1650** FULLER *Pisgah* IV. ii. §34 Esau, who Satyr-like had a quickset of hair on his body.

B. *adj.* **a.** (or *attrib.*) Of a hedge: Formed of living plants. So also with *fence*, *rank*, *row*, *screen*, etc. Cf. QUICK *a.* 3 b.

1535 *Nottingham Rec.* III. 374 For cuttyng up the quyke set hege. **1597–8** BP. HALL *Sat.* v. i, As thicke as wealthy Scrobioes quicke-set rowes. *Ibid.* iii, Beset around with treble quickset ranks. **1644** in Rushw. *Hist. Coll.* III. II. 743 Between the Pallisado's and the quick-set Hedge. **1774** GOLDSM. *Nat. Hist.* (1776) IV. 10 An hare, sorely hunted, has got upon the top of a cut quick-set hedge. **1819** SHELLEY *Peter Bell the Third* v. xi, Many a ditch and quickset fence. **1875** W. S. HAYWARD *Love agst. World* 11 They approached the first hedge, a pretty stiff quickset one.

transf. and *fig.* **1632** HEYWOOD *2nd Pt. Iron Age* II. Wks. 1874 III. 382 Are we not rounded with a quick-set hedge Of pointed steele? **1652** STERRY *Eng. Deliv. North. Presb.* 7 Enclosed with the Quick-set hedge of his Divine Wisdome. **1816** COLERIDGE *Statesm. Man.* (1817) 356 Aristotle's works a quickset hedge of fruitless and thorny distinctions!

b. *transf.* Of a beard: Rough, bristling. Also *fig.*

1599 B. JONSON *Ev. Man out of Hum.* v. viii, Hang him rascall..with his wilde quickset beard there. **1938** L. MACNEICE *Earth Compels* 56 Columns of ads, the quickset road to riches. **1948** [see HAIR-TRIGGER b].

quick-set, *sb.*[2] (See quot.)

1852 *P. Parley's Ann.* 174 What are technically called quick-sets, which consist of a screw and a nut, provided with a large hook at the top, and a small pointed hook at the bottom.

†**quickset**, *v. Obs.* [f. QUICKSET *sb.*[1]] *trans.* To furnish (plant, enclose, etc.) with a quickset hedge. Also *absol.*

1508 in *Cal. Doc. Scotl.* (1888) 351 [To] diche, quyk set, enclose, and dyvyde into clausures the boundes of Berwyk. **1523** FITZHERB. *Husb.* §123 It is lesse cost for hym..to quyck set dyche and hedge. **1573** TUSSER *Husb.* (1878) 113 Bankes newly quicksetted, some weeding doo craue. **1632** EARL OF CORK *Diary* in *Lismore Papers* Ser. I. (1886) III. 166 Enclosing and quicksetting the lands. **1672** PETTY *Pol. Anat.* (1691) 14 Gardens..ditch'd and quicksetted.

Hence †**quicksetting** *vbl. sb. Obs.*

1523 FITZHERB. *Husb.* §124 If thou haue pastures, thou muste nedes haue quyckesettynge, dychynge and plasshynge. **1541** *Nottingham Rec.* III. 390 Dykyng and quycksettyng of the Long Hedge.

quick-set (ˈkwɪksɛt), *a.*[2] [f. QUICK *adv.* + SET *v.*]

1. Also **quickset**. Applied to a type of surveyor's level in which the foot-screws in the levelling head are replaced by a ball and socket joint to facilitate quick setting.

1930 S. W. PERROTT *Surveying for Schools* xiv. 114 In the case of the Quickset level, there are no foot-screws, the telescope and bubble being set approximately level by a ball and socket joint. **1948** B. G. MANTON *Highway Surveying & Setting Out* iii. 58 Many instruments of the 'quick-set' type are fitted with a prismatic device which enables the bubble position to be seen from the eye-piece end of the telescope. **1971** R. J. P. WILSON *Land Surveying* x. 215 The essential difference between the quickset level and other types is that it is a tilting level without footscrews in the levelling head.

2. That hardens or dries quickly.

1967 KARCH & BUBER *Offset Processes* vii. 266 Quick-set inks are also used when printing on coated paper stock. **1970** R. JOHNSTON *Black Camels of Qashran* xi. 178 The quickset cement was dry and hard.

†**quickshaw**, obs. variant of KICKSHAW.

1655 tr. *Com. Hist. Francion* III. 73 Tarts, Custards, Fruit, and such like quickshawes.

†**quickship.** *Obs. rare*$^{-1}$. = QUICKNESS.

a **1225** *Ancr. R.* 150 Ine strencðe & ine cwicnesse [*MS. C.* quicshipe].

quick-sighted. (Stress variable.) [f. *quick sight* + -ED[2]: see QUICK *a.* 20 b.] Having quick sight. (*lit.* and *fig.*)

1552 HULOET, Quycke syghted, *oculatus.* **1571** GOLDING *Calvin on Ps.* lxiii. 17 They doo nought else but dote, that wil bee wel eyed and quicksighted of themselves. **1610** HOLLAND *Camden's Brit.* I. 348 A man right skilfull and deeply quick-sighted. **1677** HORNECK *Gt. Law Consid.* v. (1704) 253 Such writings, as acute and quick-sighted men had dispersed throughout the world. **1755** SMOLLETT *Quix.* (1803) IV. 296 The boys, who are quick-sighted as lynxes. **1772** PRIESTLEY *Inst. Relig.* (1782) I. 400 They are quick-sighted to foresee. **1837** W. IRVING *Capt. Bonneville* II. 93 It was dangerous to..light a fire..where such..quick-sighted enemies were at hand. **1870** MISS BRIDGMAN *R. Lynne* I. xi. 165 Rose was quicker-sighted.

Hence **quickˈsightedness.**

1652 J. WRIGHT tr. *Camus' Nat. Paradox* IV. 84 The Symptomes, whereby his quick-sightedness read her Disease. **1749** FIELDING *Tom Jones* XI. x, Quick-sightedness into evil. **1869** J. MARTINEAU *Ess.* II. 400 The mere quicksightedness of a pilot in a strange sea.

quicksilver (ˈkwɪkˌsɪlvə(r)), *sb.* [OE. *cwic seolfor* = OHG. *quecsilbar*, *-silper* (MHG. *quec-*, *kecsilber*, G. *quecksilber*), Du. *kwikzilver*, ON. *kviksilfr* (Sw. *qvicksilfver*, Da. *kvæg-*, *kviksölv*), after L. *argentum vivum* (Pliny): see QUICK *a.* and SILVER.]

1. The metal mercury, so called from its liquid mobile form at ordinary temperatures.

c **1000** *Sax. Leechd.* II. 356 Wiþ maᵹan wærce rudan sæd & cwic seolfor. *c* **1386** CHAUCER *Can. Yeom. Prol. & T.* 269 The firste spirit quyksiluer called is. **1436** *Pol. Poems* (Rolls) II. 160 Commodytes..commynge out of Spayne,..Bene fygues..Saffron, quicksilver. **1555** EDEN *Decades* 335 By the helpe of quickesyluer it is drawen owt. **1625** N. CARPENTER *Geog. Del.* II. v. (1635) 71 Quick-siluer..will gather it selfe to a round body. **1669** WORLIDGE *Syst. Agric.* (1681) 309 This Column of Quick-silver in the Tube, is supported by the weight of the Air Ambient. **1782** COWPER *Progr. Err.* 21 Like quicksilver, the rhetoric they display Shines as it runs, but grasped at slips away. **1825** J. NEAL *Bro. Jonathan* I. 326 A profusion of little rain-drops; like spattered quicksilver. **1870** YEATS *Nat. Hist. Comm.* 360 Quicksilver is met with pure in minute globules, but for the purposes of commerce it is obtained from one of its ores,—cinnabar, a red sulphide of mercury.

2. Used allusively. **a.** with reference to the quick motion of which the metal is capable.

1562 J. HEYWOOD *Prov. & Epigr.* (1867) 165 She is quycke syluer. **1622** BACON *Hen. VII* 192 Perkin (who was made of Quick-silver, which is hard to hold or imprison) began to stirre. **1820** SCOTT *Abbot* xix, Thou hast quicksilver in the veins of thee to a certainty. **1889** *Boy's Own Paper* 17 Aug. 730/3, I..had come off the journey with my veins full of quicksilver.

b. with ref. to its use in mirrors (see the vb.).

1851 ROBERTSON *Serm.* Ser. II. xii. (1864) 166 The dull quicksilver of their own selfishness behind the glass.

3. *attrib.* and *Comb.* **a.** attributive, in senses 'consisting of, containing, pertaining to, etc. quicksilver', as ***quicksilver bath***, ***battery***, ***earth***, ***field***, ***globe***, ***mine***, ***ore***, ***plaster***, ***ship***, ***tank***, ***valve***, ***water***, etc.

1552 HULOET, Quyckesyluer earth, *antrax.* *a* **1631** DONNE *Poems, Apparition*, In a cold Quicksilver bath. **1685** *Lond. Gaz.* No. 1996/1 The Quick-Silver Ships may be expected this month at Cadiz. **1751** MRS. DELANY *Autobiog.* (1861) III. 53 Quick-silver-water is the most effectual remedy for worms. **1756–7** tr. *Keysler's Trav.* (1760) IV. 152 Cinnabar or quicksilver ore. **1839** MARRYAT *Phant. Ship* iii. (1874) 25 In the centre of the ceiling hung a quicksilver globe, a common ornament in those days. **1877** RAYMOND *Statist. Mines & Mining* 19 A very important quicksilver-field is about to be opened in the far north. *Ibid.* 260 A..clever arrangement of quicksilver-tanks.

b. attrib. in sense 'resembling quicksilver (in quickness of movement)', as ***quicksilver mind***, ***rebel***, ***rogue***, ***temper***.

1655 GURNALL *Chr. in Arm.* V. §4 (1669) 94/1 Labour therefore in hearing the Word to fix thy quick-silver mind. **1676** W. HUBBARD *Happiness of People* 29 These are *Inquieta ingenia* of Quick-silver tempers. **1796** EARL BALCARRES in Bryan Edwards *Proc. Maroon Negroes* (1796) 35 Until such time as these quick-silver rebels are under lock and key. **1863** COWDEN CLARKE *Shaks. Char.* xiv. 360 That prince of quicksilver rogues—Master Autolycus.

c. objective, and obj. genitive, as ***quicksilver-feeder***, ***-fixation***, ***-producing*** adj., ***-reduction***, etc.

1834 MACAULAY *Ess., Pitt* (1887) 306 The periwig company, and the Spanish-jack-ass-company, and the quicksilver-fixation-company. **1877** RAYMOND *Statist. Mines & Mining* 19 Coming south from Trinity, the next quicksilver-producing locality..is in the Coast Range. **1882** *Rep. Ho. Repr. Prec. Met. U.S.* 507 A quicksilver feeder has been devised for feeding mercury to gold mills.

Hence **ˈquickˌsilverish** *a.*, somewhat quicksilvery (hence **ˈquickˌsilverishness**); **ˈquickˌsilvery** *a.*, of the nature of, resembling, quicksilver.

1611 COTGR., *Vif-Argentin*, quicke-siluerie. **1829** *Anniversary, Honeycomb & Bitter Gourd* 118 The flighty and quicksilvery youth of the parish. **1852** MRS. CRAIK *Agatha's Husband* II. i. 17 She had..a certain quicksilverishness of manner, jumping here there everywhere like mercury on a plate. **1891** T. HARDY *Tess* (1900) 70/2 The quicksilvery glaze on the rivers and pools.

quicksilver (ˈkwɪkˌsɪlvə(r)), *v.* [f. prec. sb.] To treat, imbue, or mix with quicksilver; *esp.* to coat (the back of glass) with an amalgam of tin in order to give a reflecting power.

1704 NEWTON *Optics* (1721) 94 Metal..reflects not so much Light as Glass quick-silver'd over does. **1799** G. SMITH *Laboratory* I. 178 How to Quicksilver the inside of Glass Globes, so as to make them look like Looking-glass. **1831** BREWSTER *Optics* i. 4 The glass is always quicksilvered on the back, to make it reflect more light.

Hence **ˈquickˌsilvered** *ppl. a.* (in early quots. *fig.*). **ˈquickˌsilvering** *vbl. sb.*, the action or process of coating, etc., with quicksilver; also *concr.* a coating of quicksilver or amalgam.

1599 E. SANDYS *Europæ Spec.* (1632) 80 Those nimble and quicksilverd braines which itch after change. *c* **1645** HOWELL *Lett.* (1650) I. iv. 21 The Leaden-heeld pace of the one, and the Quick-silver'd motions of the other. **1753** PARSONS in *Phil. Trans.* XLVIII. 380, I took a quicksilver'd glass. **1825** J. NICHOLSON *Operat. Mechanic* 728 The quicksilvered tin-foil adheres..firmly to the glass.

quick step, **ˈquickstep** *sb.*

1. *Mil.* The step used in marching in quick time. Also quasi-*adv.*, at a quick step.

1802, etc. [see QUICK TIME]. **1864** *Sunset Stories No. 1* 10 Stir round, can't you, Jem? take your fingers out of your mouth, and get some kindlins, quick step. **1875** W. MCILWRAITH *Guide Wigtownshire* 51 We now move, quick-step, over the pasture-fields.

transf. **1877** TALMAGE *50 Serm.* 26 Nearly all the verses of the Bible have a quick-step.

2. *Mus.* A march in military quick time.

1811 BUSBY *Dict. Mus.*, *Quick-step*, a species of march generally written in two crotchets in a bar. **1885** *Harper's Mag.* Feb. 384/1 The drum..beats a..quickstep. **1897** H. PORTER *Campaigning with Grant* in *Century Mag.* Apr. 826 Bands were playing stirring quicksteps.

3. A quick dance; *spec.* a fast modern ballroom dance in 4/4 time.

1880 [see LASSU]. **1927** V. SILVESTER *Mod. Ballroom Dancing* 25 For Charleston, Quickstep, and Tango the right hand should be held further round. *Ibid.* 64 Owing to the speed at which foxtrots are played, it is not possible to do the slow foxtrot unless the orchestra plays slowly, hence the evolution of the Quickstep. This dance is now done mixed in with the Charleston. **1937** E. PORTER *Music through Dance* viii. 142 The dances of the post-war period were still the Quickstep, and the Foxtrot in its quick and slow variations. **1955** *Radio Times* 22 Apr. 7/2 The Gold Star Trophy..will be awarded for the best all-round performance in the four basic ballroom dances—the waltz, foxtrot, tango, and quickstep. **1976** *Times* 11 June 14/6 The bandleader..

changed the tempo to what the programme said was a foxtrot but which.. was more of a quickstep.

'quick-step, *v.* [f. the *sb.*] **1.** *intr.* To march in quick time; also quasi-*trans.* and *fig.*

1906 *Daily Chron.* 27 Aug. 4/4 They quick-step it up and down the asphalted front at Hythe. **1961** *Time* 28 Apr. 22/2 The G.O.P. majority quick-stepped behind his program. **1964** G. McDonald *Running Scared* vi. 78 The streets were filled with people.. all slim and quick-stepping. **1975** *New Yorker* 17 Feb. 101/1 Lightning Mandate, who won a division of the recent Malibu, was right behind him, and these two probably quickstepped themselves out of the money.

2. To dance the quick-step.

1935 C. Day Lewis *Time to Dance* 32 For no silver posh plane was their pigeon, no dandy dancer quick-stepping through heaven.

Hence **'quick-stepping** *ppl. a.*

1908 *Daily Chron.* 1 Oct. 7/3 The quick-stepping figure in white flannels glanced around at the click of the latch. **1936** C. Day Lewis *Friendly Tree* i. 14 Her gait was delicate, quick-stepping.

quick-stick(s: see QUICK *a.* D.

quick time. *Mil.* **a.** A brisk rate of marching consisting of about 120 paces of at least 30 inches each in a minute (cf. DOUBLE-QUICK).

In the British army the rate has been raised during the past two centuries (see quots.); in 1988 the rate for the light infantry was 142 paces of 33 inches each per minute.

1802 James *Milit. Dict.*, *Quick Step*, or *Quick Time*, is 108 steps of 30 inches each, or 270 feet in a minute, and is the step used in all filings of divisions. *Quickest Step*, or *Quickest Time* is 120 steps of 30 inches each, or 300 feet in a minute. **1833** *Regul. Instr. Cavalry* I. 18 *The Quick Step.* The cadence of the slow pace having become.. habitual to the recruits, they are.. to be taught to march in 'quick time', which is 108 steps in a minute, each of 30 inches. **1876** Voyle & Stevenson *Milit. Dict.*, *Quick-time*, a pace soldiers ordinarily march at, viz. 3·3 miles an hour. *Ibid.* s.v. *Step*, *Quick step*, a military step of 30 inches, with a cadence.. of 116 per minute, in the British army. It constitutes what is technically called *quick time* in marching.

b. quasi-*adv.* In quick time.

1816 Scott *Old Mort.* x, Come, come, Mrs. Janet—march, troop—quick time. **1956** in Cassidy & Le Page *Dict. Jamaican Eng.* (1967) 372/1 You better come here quick time!.. Him run quick-time an' tell him mumma. **1971** *Jamaican Weekly Gleaner* 3 Nov. 5/1 The real tourist types ..did not miss the chance to dress quick time in tee-shirt and so forth emblazoned with 'Miami, Florida'.

†**quick tree.** *Obs. rare*⁻¹. = QUICKEN *sb.*¹

1548 Turner *Names Herbes* (E.D.S.) 54 Myrica, otherwyse named tamarix.. The Poticaries of London vse nowe for thys quik tree.

quick-witted, *a.* (Stress variable.) [f. *quick wit* + -ED².] Having a quick or ready wit; mentally acute, sharp, clever.

1530 Tindal *Pent.*, *Lev.* Prol. (1884) 297 Allegoryes make a man qwick witted. **1596** Shaks. *Tam. Shr.* v. ii. 38 How likes Gremio these quicke-witted folkes? **1693** Dryden *Juvenal* iii. (1697) 50 Quick-Witted, Brazen-fac'd, with fluent Tongues. **1702** Mead *Mech. Acc. Poisons* Wks. (1775) 50 Impatient, ready to action, quickwitted. **1824** Miss Mitford *Village* Ser. I. (1863) 133 There is always great freshness and originality in an uneducated and quick-witted person. **1870** Lowell *Among my Bks.* Ser. I. (1873) 189 The cultivated and quick-witted men in whose familiar society he lived.

Hence **quick'wittedness.**

1863 Cowden Clarke *Shaks. Char.* x. 257 He has French quick-wittedness, French good temper. **1883** P. Schaff *Hist. Church* Per. I. II. lxxxiii. 712 The curiosity and quickwittedness of the Samaritan Magdalene.

'quickwood. [f. QUICK *a.* 3.] = QUICK *sb.* 3, QUICKSET. (Chiefly *attrib.*)

1473–4 *Durham Acc. Rolls* (Surtees) 645 Pro.. plantacione de le Whikwod. **1696** Aubrey *Misc.* (1721) 104 A Pond.. adjoyning to a Quick-wood-hedge. **1769** *Adome Inclos. Act* 10 All the new quick-wood fences. **1800** Tuke *Agric.* 91 White thorn (provincially quickwood) constitutes the most common fence throughout the Riding. **1892** J. D. Hood *Waterspouts Yorksh. Wolds* 25 Rooting up a strong quickwood fence.

'quick-work. *Naut.* (See quots.)

1711 W. Sutherland *Shipbuild. Assist.* 162 Quick-work; that part of a Ship's Sides both within and without Board, above the Channel-wales and Decks. **1730** Capt. W. Wriglesworth *MS. Log-bk. of the 'Lyell'* 21 Sept., This morning begun to Caulk the Quick Work on the Quarter deck. **1776** Falconer *Dict. Marine* (ed. 2), *Quick-Work*,.. a general name given to all that part of a ship which is under the surface of the water when she is laden. **1780** *Ibid.* (ed. 3), *Vibord*, the quick-work, or that part of a ship's side.. comprehended between the drift-rails and the waist-rail. *c* **1850** *Rudim. Navig.* (Weale) 139 *Quickwork.* A denomination given to the strakes which shut in between the spirketing and clamps. **1867** Smyth *Sailor's Word-bk.*, *Quick-Work*, is also applied to that part of the inner upperworks of a ship above the covering board. Also, the short planks worked inside between the ports... In general parlance quick-work is synonymous with spirketting.

†**quic'quidlibet.** *Obs. rare*⁻¹. [L., f. *quicquid* whatever + *libet* it pleases.] Whatever one pleases, anything whatsoever.

1647 Ward *Simp. Cobler* 22 A multimonstrous maufrey of heteroclytes and quicquidlibets.

‖**Quicunque vult** (kwiː'kʊŋkweɪ vʊlt). Also Quicumque vult. [L.] The Athanasian Creed, so called from its opening words *quicumque vult* (*salvus esse*) 'whosoever will (be saved)'. Also *ellipt.*, as *Quicunque*, and *fig.*

c **1400** *Mandeville's Travels* (1967) xvi. 106 Seynt Athanasie, that was bisshopp of Alisandre, that made the psalm *Quicumque vult.* *a* **1530** *Myroure of oure Ladye* (1873) II. 139 This psalme *Quicumque vult*, enformeth vs fyrste in faythe of the godhed and after in faythe of the manhode of cryste. *Ibid.* III. 312 And the thyrde crede that ys. *Quicunque vult*, was made by a holy bysshop. called Athanasius. **1567** J. Jewel *Def. Apol. Ch. Eng.* II. 83 The Creede called, *Quicunque vult*, written, as some thinke, by Athanasius. **1724** D. Waterland *Crit. Hist. Athanasian Creed* ii. 25 Robertus Paululus, Presbyter of Amiens, in the Diocess of Rheims, speaking of the Offices recited at the Prime, observes that the Piety of good Christians had thereunto added the *Quicunque vult*, that the Articles necessary to salvation might never be forgotten any hour of the Day. **1855** F. Procter *Hist. Book Common Prayer* II. i. 214 Another title of this Creed was 'Psalmus *Quicunque vult*': hence the custom of reciting it antiphonally. **1877** *Encycl. Brit.* VI. 562/2 Nothing definite as to the authorship of the Quicunque can be rested on such resemblances. **1910** *Jrnl. Theol. Studies* XI. 401 (*heading*) A critical text of the *Quicumque Vult.* *Ibid.* 402 The first three are the earliest known MSS of the *Quicumque.* **1921** G. Sampson *English for the English* ii. 32 Let *Quicunque vult* and threatened excommunications of all kinds remain in the realm of theology and outside the realm of education. **1963** Auden *Dyer's Hand* 54 Herewith, then, what I might describe as.. a kind of private *Quicunque vult.* **1964** J. Kelly *Athanasian Creed* vii. 126 For these reasons the Quicunque deserves to retain its place among the normative formularies of Christendom. **1967** H. Chadwick *Early Church* xv. 235 It was a theologian living in Southern Gaul, or perhaps in Spain, who produced the catechetical compendium ..*Quicunque Vult*, which soon (if not from the start) passed under the august title of the Creed of St. Athanasius. **1980** *Times* 20 Nov. 17/7 The very bases of belief.. the Catechism, the Quicunque Vult, the Thirty-nine Articles.

‖**quid** (kwɪd), *sb.*¹ [L. *quid* what, anything, something, neut. sing. of *quis* who, any one, etc.]

1. That which a thing is. Cf. QUIDDITY 1.

1606 Marston *Parasitaster* I. ii, My age Hath seene the beings and the quide [*sic*] of things. **1611** L. Barry *Ram Alley* in Dodsley (1874) X. 363 A widow that has known the quid of things. **1675** [Bp. Croft] *Naked Truth* 25 The quid, the quale, the quantum, and such-like quack-salving forms. **1727–41** Chambers *Cycl.* s.v., Hence we have two kinds of *quids*, nominal.. and real. **1875** Jowett *Plato* (ed. 2) I. 270 When I do not know the 'quid' of anything how can I know the 'quale'?

†**2.** = QUIDDIT, QUIDDITY 2. *Obs. rare*⁻¹.

1576 Gascoigne *Steele Gl.* (Arb.) 77 That Logicke leape not ouer euery stile.. With curious quids to maintaine argument.

3. *U.S.* (abbrev. of *tertium quid.*) A name given to a section of the Republican party in 1805–11.

1805 Jefferson *Writ.* (1830) IV. 45 Those called the third party, or Quids. **1882** H. Adams *J. Randolph* (1884) 182 He belonged to the third party, the quiddists or quids, being that tertium quid.. which had no name, but was really an anti-Madison movement.

quid, *sb.*² *slang.* [Of obscure origin.]

1. a. A sovereign; one pound sterling; †a guinea. *slang.*

(Pl. usually without *-s*, as *two quid, a few quid*, etc.).

1688 Shadwell *Sqr. Alsatia* III. i, Let me equip thee with a Quid. **1791–3** in *Spirit Pub. Jrnls.* (1799) I. 244 The man ..rarely has more than from thirty to fifty quids a year. **1796** *Mod. Gulliver* 165 The twenty last are worth full forty quid. **1834** H. Ainsworth *Rookwood* III. III. xiii. 166 One quid, two coach wheels. **1883** Besant *All in Garden Fair* II. x, It isn't two quid a week that will keep a young gentleman of your powers. **1907** G. B. Shaw *Major Barbara* II. 241, I ad two quid saved agen the frost; an Ive a pahnd of it left. **1917** A. G. Empey *Over Top* 304 *Quid*, Tommy's term for a pound or twenty shillings... He is not on very good terms with this amount as you never see the two together. **1929** W. P. Ridge *Affectionate Regards* 71 Milton received only ten quid for the first edition of 'Paradise Lost'. **1951** *People* 3 June 2/2 It took less than a couple of quid on the down trip. **1959** I. Jefferies *Thirteen Days* xi. 183 You buy a car, it costs you a thousand quid; but you get a girl like that free. **1968** K. Weatherly *Roo Shooter* 74, I was thinking of moving on a bit but there are still enough here to make a few quid. **1971** *Venerabile* XXV. III. 191 It is surprising what difficulties the good old English quid can cause. **1977** C. McCullough *Thorn Birds* vii. 160 Do you want to go after Auntie Mary's thirteen million quid?

b. Phr. *quids in*: in luck or profit; well off for money. *slang.*

1919 *Athenæum* 1 Aug. 695/2 *Quid's in*, for a stroke of good fortune. **1939** W. Allen *Blind Man's Ditch* 236 We'll be quids in to-morrow. **1960** O. Manning *Great Fortune* xix. 226 Anyone who financed the trip would be quids in. **1969** J. N. Chance *Abel Coincidence* x. 187 If you know about people and they know nothing about you, you're quids in at the starting grid. **1976** *News of World* 14 Mar. 19/4 And to make sure you are quids in anyway, we'll give you as well the starting price odds to £10 each way on whichever horse does win.

c. Phr. *the full quid*: (see quot. 1959). *Austral.* and *N.Z. slang.*

1946 *Coast to Coast 1945* 106 'There's some say Lizzie's not the full quid either,' he said. **1959** Baker *Drum* II. 111 *Full quid*, in full possession of one's faculties. A person who is said to be *ten bob in the quid* or any smaller sum down to *tuppence in the quid*, is held to be stupid. **1960** N. Hilliard *Maori Girl* III. vi. 213 Not that she was simple in the sense that she was short of the full quid. **1972** I. Moffitt *U-Jack Society* xiv. 227 We avoid individuality as firmly as we suspect joy ('You're not the full quid!'). **1975** *Sydney Morning Herald* 5 July 9 It's perfectly clear that not all members of our community are the full quid.

†**2.** *pl.* (with *-s*.) Money, cash. *Obs. rare.*

a **1700** B. E. *Dict. Cant. Crew.*

quid (kwɪd), *sb.*³ [var. of CUD *sb.* q.v.] **1.** A piece of something (usu. of tobacco), suitable to be held in the mouth and chewed.

1727 in Bailey vol. II. **1731** *Gentl. Mag.* I. 349 Spitting about the church.. As if he'd got a quid in's mouth. **1789** G. Keate *Pelew Isl.* 27 Beetle-nut and Chinam, of which they had always a quid in their mouths. **1833** Marryat *P. Simple* (1863) 89 The first lieutenant.. perceived that he had a quid of tobacco in his cheek. **1883** Stevenson *Silverado Sq.* (1886) 68 His mind was.. revolving the problem of existence like a quid of gum.

fig. **1805** W. Hunter in *Naval Chron.* XIII. 35, I chewed my Quid of bitterness.

2. = CAST *sb.* 19 and PELLET *sb.*¹ 2 c.

1834 [see PELLET *sb.*¹ 2 c]. **1879–81** G. F. Jackson *Shropshire Word-bk.* 315 Them owls.. sin a mouze.. an' ketchen 'im.. an' chawen 'im.. 'an crushen 'im, an' sooken 'im till theer inna nuthin' left on 'im, an' then they droppen the quid.

†**quid,** *v.*¹ *Obs.* Forms: 1 cwyddian, 2–3 cwidden, quidd(i)en. [OE. *cwiddian*, f. **cwidi-* QUIDE (q.v.).] *trans.* and *intr.* To say, speak.

c **1000** Ælfric *Hom.* II. 388 Crist hi befran hu men cwyddodon be him. *c* **1200** Ormin 3048 þatt illke word wass cwiddedd ær. *c* **1205** Lay. 9825 Bi-þenc þu a þine quides þe þu sulf quiddest. *c* **1275** *Woman Samaria* 55 in *O.E. Misc.* 85 Nv quiddeþ men, þat cumen is Messyas.

quid, *v.*² [f. QUID *sb.*³]

1. *intr.* To chew tobacco; to chew the cud.

1775 in Ash. **1778** *Gentl. Mag.* July 311/1 The cow chews her cud, and the man, when he chews tobacco, calls it quidding. **1893** *Surrey Gloss.*, *Quidding*, chewing the cud. 'The heifer's getting better, she's quidding all right'. **1902** J. Masefield *Salt-Water Ballads* 66 Quiddin' bonded Jacky out a-lee.

2. *trans.* Of horses: To let (food) drop from the mouth when half chewed.

1831 Youatt *Horse* (1847) 258 The Horse quids his hay, and gulps his water. **1888** W. Williams *Princ. Vet. Med.* (ed. 5) 376 Soreness of the throat is indicated by 'quidding of the food'.

Hence **'quidder,** a horse which 'quids' (*Cassell's Encycl. Dict.* 1886).

‖**quidam** ('kwaɪdəm). *rare.* [L., f. *quī* who: cf. QUÆDAM.] Somebody; a certain person.

1579 E. K. *Ded. Spenser's Sheph. Cal.* Post-scr., So many vnworthy Quidams, which catch at the garlond which to you alone is dewe. **1624** Bedell *Lett.* xi. 143 Who were these quidams that laid hands on Scory? *a* **1641** Bp. Mountagu *Acts & Mon.* (1642) 48 Some *Individuum vagum*, a certaine *Quidam* in the Clouds.

Hence **qui'damity,** an allusion to 'somebody'.

1892 *Athenæum* 9 July 65/1 A retort lay ready to his hand more effective than any indulgence in *quidam*-ities.

†**'quiddany,** *sb.* *Obs.* Also 7 quiddanet, -onie, quidenie, 7–8 quiddeny, -ony, 8 quidony. [ad. obs. F. *codignat, condoignac*, etc. (mod.F. *cotignac*, It. *cotognato*) = med.L. *codōniātum*, var. of *cydōniātum*, f. L. *cydōnia*: see QUINCE, and cf. CODINIAC, COTINIATE, QUINDINIAC.] A thick fruit-syrup or jelly; orig. and properly, one made from quinces.

1616 Bullokar *Eng. Expos.*, *Quiddanet*, a sweete mixture thicker than a sirupe, and not so thicke nor stiffe as marmalet. **1638** tr. *Bacon's Life & Death* (1651) 42 That which they call Quiddeny of Quinces. *a* **1655** Sir T. Mayerne *Archimag. Anglo-Gall.* No. 150 (1658) 101 Boyle the Syrrup, untill it be as thick as for quiddonie. **1695** Westmacott *Script. Herb.* 203 Sloes in the form of a Quiddeny, or Marmalade. **1712** tr. *Pomet's Hist. Drugs* I. 133 It is us'd in Rob or Quiddony, made with Damask-Rose-Water. **1736** Bailey *Househ. Dict.* 494 Quiddany of Quinces.

Hence †**'quiddany** *v. trans.*, to make into a quiddany. (In quot. *fig.*)

1647 Ward *Simp. Cobler* 18 He will.. Quidanye Christ with Sugar and Rats-bane.

'quiddative, *a.* *rare.* [For *quidditative*; cf. *qualitive, quantitive.*] = QUIDDITATIVE.

1642 J. Jackson *Bk. Conscience* 18 Find out the very quiddative nature and being of Conscience. **1727–41** Chambers *Cycl.* s.v. *Quiddity*, What is essential to a thing is said to be quiddative—as quiddative knowledge. **1898** *Dublin Rev.* Oct. 299 The quiddative unity of things.

quiddenie, -eny, varr. QUIDDANY.

'quidder, (? *a.* and) *adv.* *Sc. rare.* [Cf. Norw. dial. *kvidra* to dart about.] Only in phr. *quick and quidder*, quickly, forthwith.

In first quot. perh. as adj. = 'alive and lively'.

1633 *Fife Witch-Trial* in *Statist. Acc. Scotl.* XVIII. 658 He gave her, soul and body, quick and quidder full to the devil. **1866** Edmondston *Gloss. Shetl. & Orkn.*, *Quick-and-Quidder*, swiftly, quickly.

quiddist: see QUID *sb.*¹ 3, quot. 1882.

quiddit ('kwɪdɪt). Now *arch.* = QUIDDITY 2.

1592 Greene *Upst. Courtier* in *Harl. Misc.* (Malh.) II. 232 These lawiers haue.. such quibs & quiddits. *a* **1613** Overbury *A Wife*, etc. (1638) 188 He makes his Will in forme of a Law-case, full of quiddits. **1635** Heywood *Hierarch.* IV. 202 He.. Stretches each Quiddit of the Law to finde Him culpable. **1838** Hor. Smith *Tor Hill* II. 221 Rhyming couplets, quirks, quiddits and riddles. **1855** Browning *Old Pict. Florence* xx, The first of the new.. Beats the last of the old; 'tis no idle quiddit.

‖**quidditas** (ˈkwɪdɪtɑːs, -æ-). [L.: see QUIDDITY.] = QUIDDITY 1.
1878 *Encycl. Brit.* VIII. 758/1 This matter is differentiated into particular things.. through the addition of an individualizing principle (*hæcceitas*) to the universal (*quidditas*). **1911** *Ibid.* XXIV. 354/2 The additional determinations are as truly 'form' as the universal essence. If the latter be spoken of as *quidditas*, the former may be called *haecceitas*. **1934** 'H. MACDIARMID' *Stony Limits* 16 Lyin' in wait in vain for a single grey drop To quicken into a perfect quidditas. **1976** 'M. INNES' *Gay Phoenix* iii. 41 A man's identity—his *quidditas*, as the learned might say.

†ˈ**quidditative**, *a.* *Obs.* [f. QUIDDIT-Y + -ATIVE. See also QUIDDATIVE.]
1. Pertaining to the quiddity or essence of a thing.
1650 CHARLETON *Paradoxes* 9 The quidditative and peculiarly expresse causes of all those admirable effects of the Loadstone. **1656** [? J. SERGEANT] tr. *T. White's Peripat. Inst.* 220 The quidditative notion of an Element.
2. Full of equivocations, quirky.
1611 COTGR., *Quidditatif*, quidditatiue, doubtfull, obscure, full of quirkes, fraught with quiddities. **1637** GILLESPIE *Eng. Pop. Cerem.* I. ix. 31 A weak and easily penetrable hedge of some quidditative Cautions.
Hence †ˈ**quidditatively** *adv.*
c **1600** *Timon* IV. iii. (1842) 66 The moone may bee taken .. either specificatiuely, or quidditatiuely, or superficially, or catapodially.

quiddity (ˈkwɪdɪtɪ). [ad. schol. L. *quidditas*: see QUID *sb.*[1] and -ITY; so F. *quiddité* (14th c.).]
1. The real nature or essence of a thing; that which makes a thing what it is.
1569 J. SANFORD tr. *Agrippa's Van. Artes* 21 The true demonstration .. is that whiche is made (as the Logitioners speake) by Quiddites, and by the proper difference of things. **1628** T. SPENCER *Logick* 75 Dissent is in the qualitie not the quidditie, or being of the subject. **1670** MAYNWARING *Vita Sana* x. 106 These notions being too .. remote from the quiddity, essence and spring of the Disease. **1710** BERKELEY *Princ. Hum. Knowl.* §81 The positive abstract idea of quiddity, entity, or existence. **1828** DE QUINCEY *Rhetoric* Wks. 1862 X. 76 The quiddity, or characteristic difference, of poetry as distinguished from prose. **1897** S. S. SPRIGGE *Life of T. Wakley* xiii. 125 The quiddity of each attitude was the desire to curtail the privileges of the hospital surgeons.
b. Something intangible. *rare*$^{-1}$.
1774 BURKE *Sp. Amer. Tax.* Wks. 1842 I. 158 Fighting for a phantom; a quiddity; a thing that wants, not only a substance, but even a name.
2. A subtlety or captious nicety in argument; a quirk, quibble. (Alluding to scholastic arguments on the 'quiddity' of things.)
1539 TAVERNER *Gard. Wysed.* I. 18 b, [He] must nat playe with hys sophemes and quyddities. **1579** FULKE *Heskins' Parl.* 475 Hee saith hee will not vse the quiddities of the schooles, but plaine examples. **1678** R. BARCLAY *Apol. Quakers* § 12. 371 To find out and invent subtile Distinctions and Quiddities. **1731** *Plain Reas. for Presbyt. Dissent.* 138 The most honest cause is often run down with the torrent and speat of law-quirks and quiddities. **1807** W. IRVING *Salmag.* (1824) 33, I humbly solicit .. A quiddity, quirk, or remonstrance to send. **1877** C. GEIKIE *Christ* xxv. (1879) 281 Their .. quiddities and quillets, and casuistical cases.
Comb. **1863** DE MORGAN *Pref.* in *From Matter to Spirit* 40, I went back to the old quiddity-mongers.
b. Subtlety (of wit); ability or tendency to employ quiddities.
1600 W. WATSON *Decacordon* (1602) 140 How shall euer those come in heauen, that haue neither qualitie of body to get it .. nor quidditie of wit to keepe it? **1881** W. S. GILBERT *Patience*, To stuff his conversation full of quibble and of quiddity. **1884** R. BUCHANNAN in *Pall Mall G.* 16 Apr., With the intellectual strength and bodily height of an Anak, he possessed the quiddity and animal spirits of Tom Thumb.

quiddle (ˈkwɪd(ə)l), *sb.* *dial.* and *U.S.* [f. QUIDDLE *v.*] A fastidious person.
1856 EMERSON *Eng. Traits* vi. 108 The Englishman is very petulant and precise about his accommodation .. a quiddle about his toast and his chop [etc.].

quiddle (ˈkwɪd(ə)l), *v.* Now chiefly *dial.* and *U.S.* [Of obscure origin: cf. *twiddle, fiddle*.]
1. *intr.* **a.** To discourse in a trifling way.
1567 EDWARDS *Damon & Pithias* in Hazl. *Dodsley* IV. 81 Set out your bussing base, and we will quiddle upon it. **1587** FLEMING *Contn. Holinshed* III. 1275/2 Which name of the Marishes, Marshes, or Moores, if it like them to expound it, as I doubt not but manie will quiddle therevpon. **1863–70** [see QUIDDLING].
b. To trifle, waste time (*with*).
1832 in WEBSTER. *a* **1877** in J. Cook *Orthodoxy* iv. (1882) 81 Don't quiddle with the goody little notes to Gibbon by Milman and others.
†**2.** *trans.* To trifle or play with. *Obs.*
a **1652** BROME *City Wit* III. i. Wks. 1873 I. 311 *Cras.* How does she feel your hand? *Lin.* O, she does so quiddle it, shake it, and gripe it!
Hence ˈ**quiddling** *vbl. sb.* and *ppl. a.* Also ˈ**quiddler**, a trifler.
1832 in WEBSTER. **1860** EMERSON *Cond. Life* iv. (1861) 92 Neither will we be driven into a quiddling abstemiousness. 'Tis a superstition to insist on a special diet. **1863** W. PHILLIPS *Speeches* vii. 181 Lawyers, bound by quiddling technicalities. **1870** H. STEVENS *Bibl. Histor.* Introd. 14 He indulged in .. bibliographical quiddling about the mechanical and manufacturing points of the books.

quiddonie, -y, variants of QUIDDANY.

†**quide.** *Obs.* Forms: 1 cwyde, 1–2 cwide, 3 quede, queðe, 3–4 quide, 4 qwede. [OE. *cwide* (*cwyde*) = OS. *quidi*, OHG. *quidi, chwiti*, etc., ON. *kviðr* verdict:—OTeut. **kwiði-z*, f. the root **kweþ-* to say, QUETHE.]
1. A saying, speech, statement.
c **888** K. ÆLFRED *Boeth.* III. §4 Is þis nu se cwide þe þu me ȝeo sædest? *c* **1080** *O.E. Chron.* (Parker MS.) an. 1070 Se ar'b .. mid strangan cwydan þæt ylce ȝefæstnode. *c* **1205** LAY. 9141 Hit wes ȝare iqueðen, þa quides beoð nu soðe. *a* **1250** *Owl & Night.* 685 Alvered seide of olde quide [etc.].
b. A promise. *rare*$^{-1}$.
c **1250** *Gen. & Exod.* 1463 He bad god .. ðat he sulde fillen ðat quede, ðe he abraham quilum dede.
2. A will, legacy, bequest.
950 in Thorpe *Diplom.* 500/1 Ðis is Byrhtrices & Ælfswyðe his wifes nihsta cwide. Þe hi cwædon .. on heora maȝa ȝewitnesse. *a* **1050** *Liber Scintill.* xliv. (1889) 146 On cwyde þinum læf þearfum. *c* **1205** LAY. 14857 Ich forȝiue ælchere widewe hire lauerdes quide. **13..** *K. Alis.* 8020 To have theo kyngis qwede, Muche bataile was heom myde.

quidenie, variant of QUIDDANY.

quider, obs. form of WHITHER.

†**quiˈdifical**, *a.* *Obs.* *rare*$^{-1}$. [f. QUID *sb.*[1] + -(I)FIC + -AL[1].] Quibbling, captious.
1542 UDALL *Erasm. Apoph.* 124 Diogenes mockyng suche quidificall trifles saied [etc.].

quidighe, var. CUDDY[1]. (See QUIDRATHE.)

quidlet (ˈkwɪdlɪt). *slang.* [f. QUID *sb.*[2] + -LET.] A sovereign; one pound sterling; (see also quot. 1912).
1911 L. TRACY *Sylvia's Chauffeur* v. 96 [He] handed Dale a fiver—five golden quidlets, if you please! **1912** J. W. HORSLEY *I Remember* xi. 254 'Quidlet', for half a sovereign, has recently been coined from the older 'quid'. **1940** A. W. UPFIELD *Bushranger of Skies* xvi. 183 It cost four thousand quidlets—Australian.

†**quidlit**, obs. var. of (or misprint for) QUIDDIT or QUILLET. (In quot. *attrib.*)
1598 GILPIN *Skial.*, *Satyr* II. 43 Then whats a wench but a quirke, quidlit case, Which makes a Painters pallat of her face?

quidnunc (ˈkwɪdnʌŋk). [f. L. *quid* what + *nunc* now.] One who is constantly asking: 'What now?' 'What's the news?'; hence, an inquisitive person; a gossip; a newsmonger.
1709 STEELE *Tatler* No. 10 ¶2 The Insignificancy of my Manners .. makes the Laughers called me a Quid Nunc. **1782** COWPER *Wks.* (1837) XV. 126 Acknowledge, now .. that I should make no small figure among the quidnuncs of Olney. **1832** W. IRVING *Alhambra* II. 95 He was a sort of scandalous chronicle for the quid-nuncs of Granada. **1874** L. STEPHEN *Hours in Library* (1892) I. x. 352 Some wretched intrigue which had puzzled two generations of quidnuncs.
attrib. **1880** *19th Cent.* VII. 191 Not for the mere gratification of quidnunc curiosity.
Hence **quid-nunc-ism, quidnunckery**, curiosity, love of news or gossip. *nonce-wds.*
1804 in *Spirit Pub. Jrnls.* VIII. 93 His attachment to quidnunckery is as constant as ever. **1847** J. CAIRNS *Let.* in *Life* xi. (1895) 281 The ne plus ultra of disappointed religious quid-nunc-ism.

quidony, variant of QUIDDANY.

‖**quid pro quo** (kwɪd prəʊ kwəʊ), *sb.* [L. *quid* something, *pro* for, *quo* (abl. of *quid*) something.]
1. a. One thing in place of another; *orig.* and *esp.* one medicinal substance used for another, either intentionally, fraudulently, or by mistake.
1565 CALFHILL *Answ. Martiall* 32 b, A leude Apoticarie, that vnderstandeth not his bil, but giueth *Quid pro Quo*. **1601** HOLLAND *Pliny* II. A vj b, *Succedan*, that drug which may be used for default of another. The Apothecaries call such *Quid pro quo*. **1654** R. WHITLOCK *Zootomia* 60 The Apothecaries themselves, both take, and receive (from Herbe-women) *Quid pro Quo*, one thing for another, many, many Times. **1738** STEWARD in *Phil. Trans.* XL. 449 A Mistake .. and a putting of *quid pro quo* (as 'tis commonly express'd). **1804** *Edinb. Rev.* III. 416 Referring the proximate cause of this disease to a deficiency of azote is only substituting *quid pro quo*.
b. The action or fact of using or putting one thing for another; the result of this; a mistake or blunder consisting in such a substitution.
1679 EVERARD *Discourses* 35 A Capital *quid pro quo* of Estate of the most part of the Potentates of Europe. **1687** MIEGE *Grt. Fr. Dict.*, *Quid-pro-quo* or mistake, *un Qui pro quo*. **1727–41** CHAMBERS *Cycl.* s.v. *Quid*. A northern physician, in a printed thesis on *quid pro quo's*, owns ingenuously, that they are very frequent. **1824** LADY MORGAN *Salvator Rosa* I. v. 263 He .. produces the most ludicrous *quid pro quo's* by misapplied erudition, witty absurdities, and naïve questions. **1843** THACKERAY *Misc. Essays* (1885) 44 A laughable *quid pro quo* .. occurred to him in a conversation.
†**c.** One who assumes a false character. *Obs.*
1689 HICKERINGILL *Modest Inquiries* II. 10 Have we not still .. some (*Quid pro quo's*, amongst us) Papists in Masquerade?
2. One thing (or action) in return or exchange for another; tit for tat.
1591 SHAKS. *1 Hen. VI*, v. iii. 109, I cry you mercy, 'tis but *Quid* for *Quo*. **1608** MIDDLETON *Mad World* II. iv. 44 Let him trap me in gold, and I'll lap him in lead; *quid pro quo*. **1705** HICKERINGILL *Priest-cr.* IV. (1721) 206 Every Church is the Old-Exchange, Spiritual Things in exchange for Carnal Things; Heaven for Earth; *Quid pro Quo*. **1727** BOYER *Dict. Royal* II. s.v. *Quid*. To give one *Quid-pro-quo* (or tit for tat). **1820** COMBE *Dr. Syntax* II. xxix. (1869) 167, I shall be able .. to bestow What you will find a *quid pro quo*. **1871** M. COLLINS *Mrq. & Merch.* II. ix. 276 The tradesman gets his *quid pro quo*.
attrib. **1838** J. S. MILL in *Westm. Rev.* Aug. 489 We did not expect that the *petite morale* almost alone would have been treated, and that with the most pedantic minuteness, and upon the *quid pro quo* principles which regulate *trade*. **1861** T. A. TROLLOPE *La Beata* II. xvii. 187 A system of conduct based on the theory of a quid-pro-quo purchase.
3. With substantial elements considered discretely.
1939 S. DE MADARIAGA *Christopher Columbus* xii. 136 The contractual sense, that attitude which sees every event of life as a transaction and expects and demands a definite *quid* for every *quo*. **1961** *Daily Tel.* 1 Sept. 12 She could well take all and give nothing in return, pocket the quos as well as the quids. **1979** M. MCCARTHY *Cannibals & Missionaries* xi. 304 Conditions for the committee's release .. had never been 'aired'... Not a *quid* or a *quo* vouchsafed.

†**quidrathe.** *Obs.* *rare.* Also -raighe. [Ir. *cuid* part, portion + *ráithe* quarter of a year.] A quarterly tax, payment, or entertainment.
1570 in *11th Rep. Dep. Kpr. Irel.* 235 An Irish custom of £10 sterling called quidrathe. **1592** in *Acts Privy Council* N.S. XXII. 564 Unlawfull taxacions of Iryshe customes as Quony, Quoshirs, Nightsupers called Quidighe, Quartersupers called Quidraighe, Hueryе for their horses or anie other like taxes.

quidsworth (ˈkwɪdzwɜːθ). *slang.* [f. QUID *sb.*[2] + WORTH *sb.*[1]] The amount of anything which may be bought for one pound.
1966 P. O'DONNELL *Sabre-Tooth* v. 83 Modesty was after that ten million quidsworth of diamonds. **1968** 'O. MILLS' *Sundry Fell Designs* xix. 192 There's thousands of quidsworth of equipment in there. **1977** F. BRANSTON *Up & Coming Man* v. 51, I went to a Chinese takeaway and bought a couple of quidsworth of indigestion.

quie, obs. form of QUEY.

†**quiell**, obs. var. KEEL *sb.*[1] (after F. *quille* or Pg. *quilha*).
1582 N. LICHEFILD tr. *Castanheda's Conq. E. Ind.* 336 They have no quiell, but are flat-bottomed.

†**quiennal.** *Obs.* *rare.* In 4 qui-, quyenal. [For *quinquennal*, on anal. of BI-, TRIENNAL, q.v.] A dispensation or indulgence for five years.
c **1380** WYCLIF *Sel. Wks.* III. 398 Freris .. mony times bringen veyne pardouns, quienals, and oþer veyne privilegies. —— *Wks.* (1880) 66 To paie .. for pardons, quyenals, priuylegies, for assoilyngis of wowes, & many feyned iapis.

‖**quien sabe** (ˌkjen ˈsabe). [Sp.] 'Who knows?', 'who can tell?' Also *attrib.*
1836 in *Papers of M. Buonaparte Lamar* (1921) I. 436 Austin .. will be elected and will do well provided he selects a *good* Cabinet—and an honest one—quen Sabe—. **1846** J. W. ABERT *Jrnl.* 17 Oct. in *Rep. Exam. of New Mexico* (1848) 51 To all our other questions with regard to this ancient town, we received the usual Mexican reply of 'quien sabe'. **1849** T. ARNOLD *Let.* 7 July (1966) 124, I wonder what you are doing now. Whether the 'daily possibility of falling in love' .. has ripened into a certainty .. ? Quien sabe? as Matt used to say. **1864** *Weekly New Mexican* 23 Dec. 2/4 We cannot trust an answer in the common vernacular to which we are accustomed, and must reply in all the Spanish we are master of, *quien sabe*. **1925** D. H. LAWRENCE *Reflections on Death of Porcupine* 110 What makes the difference? *Quien sabe!* **1933** A. HUXLEY *Let.* 13 Aug. (1969) 372 Do you think I am kind and unpossessive? Quien sabe? **1947** M. LOWRY *Under Volcano* i. 38 But why had all this happened? he asked himself now. Quién sabe? **1949** *Southwestern Rev.* Summer 235/1 One yarn thrown in as a sort of *quien sabe?* item suggests an even more unpalatable morsel. **1965** L. MEYNELL *Double Fault* I. i. 14 'Does this mean that he is .. too wealthy to work, or what?' '*Quien sabe?* Maybe he's just on holiday.' **1976** A. WHITE *Long Silence* iii. 28 It's one thing for us all to make our decision here .. but there—quien sabe?

quier, obs. form of QUEER *a.*[2]

quier(e, obs. forms of CHOIR, QUIRE *sb.*[1]

quierie, obs. variant of *querry* EQUERRY.

quiesce (kwaɪˈɛs, kwɪ-), *v.* [ad. L. *quiēscĕre* to be quiet, f. *quiēs* QUIET *sb.*]
1. *intr.* To become quiescent; to subside *into*.
1833 *Wild Sports of West* I. 27 Did tired nature quiesce for a moment, I was .. roused with a tornado of .. sounds. **1888** HOWELLS *Annie Kilburn* xxx. 330 The village, after a season of acute conjecture, quiesced into .. sufferance of the anomaly.
2. *intr.* Of a letter: To become silent; said of the feeble consonants in Hebrew when their sound is absorbed in that of a preceding vowel.
1828 STUART *Elem. Heb. Lang.* (1831) 25 A moveable consonant is one which is sounded, and does not quiesce or coalesce. **1853** J. R. WOLF *Practical Heb. Gr.* 8 The letters אהוי are said to quiesce in the vowels after which they are placed.

quiescence (kwaɪˈɛsəns, kwɪ-). [ad. late L. *quiēscentia*: see QUIESCENT and -ENCE.] **a.** The state of being quiescent; quietness; an instance of this. Also, the action of making quiet or calm.

a **1631** DONNE *Lett.* lxxx. Wks. (ed. Alford) VI. 397 Bless them with a satisfaction and Quiescence. **1664** POWER *Exp. Philos.* Pref. 11 That there is no such thing in the World as an absolute quiescence. **1751** JOHNSON *Rambler* No. 137 ⁋2 To sleep in the gloomy quiescence of astonishment. **1812** WOODHOUSE *Astron.* xxiii. 239 The anomalous retrogradations and quiescences of the planets. **1830** LYELL *Princ. of Geol.* (1875) II. II. xxx. 177 The local quiescence or dormant condition of the subterranean igneous causes. **1859** TROLLOPE *Bertrams* viii. 71 He had been useful as a great oil-jar, from whence oil for the quiescence of troubled waters might ever and anon be forthcoming. **1879** PROCTOR *Pleas. Ways Sc.* ii. 29 The usual condition of the air..is one of motion, not of quiescence.

b. *spec.* in Hebrew grammar: see QUIESCE *v.* 2.

1828 STUART *Elem. Heb. Lang.* (1831) 54 Quiescence sometimes happens when the *Evi* would (by analogy) have a vowel. **1853** J. R. WOLF *Practical Heb. Gram.* 112 This quiescence consists in such letters losing their consonantal power when preceded by certain vowels.

quiescency (kwaɪˈɛsənsɪ, kwɪ-). [See prec. and -ENCY.] = QUIESCENCE.

1649 BULWER *Pathomyot.* II. i. 82 To find a quiescency many Muscles working. **1664** POWER *Exp. Philos.* I. 70 When the Animal Spirits are in Quiescency. **1824** LANDOR *Imag. Conv., Southey & Porson* Wks. 1853 I. 79/2 Much of this quiescency induces debility. **1882–3** SCHAFF *Encycl. Relig. Knowl.* I. 465 His Godhead..was in a state of quiescency during his humiliation.

quiescent (kwaɪˈɛsənt, kwɪ-), *a.* and *sb.* [a. ppl. stem of L. *quiēscĕre* to QUIESCE. So mod.F. *quiescent*.]

A. *adj.*

1. a. Motionless, inactive, at rest.

1646 SIR T. BROWNE *Pseud. Ep.* 190 The active or moving side..the weaker or more quiescent part. **1710** BERKELEY *Princ. Hum. Knowl.* §114 A man in a ship may be said to be quiescent with relation to the sides of the vessel. **1753** CHAMBERS *Cycl.* Suppl. *App.* s.v. *Force*, The pressure of the quiescent body against the obstacle that hinders it to move. **1812** WOODHOUSE *Astron.* i. 3 The pole, which is the place of a quiescent star. **1874** LUBBOCK *Orig. & Met. Ins.* iv. 63 The quiescent and death-like condition of the pupa.

†**b.** *quiescent reason*, the fallacy of sorites.

1656 STANLEY *Hist. Philos.* VIII. (I.) xxxii, Sorites..is called also ἡσυχάζων λογὸς, the quiescent reason, because the way to withstand it, is by stopping, and withholding the assent.

2. a. Of a letter: Not sounded, silent; *spec.* in Hebrew grammar (see QUIESCE *v.* 2). *quiescent verb*: (see quot. 1853).

1609 C. BUTLER *Fem. Mon.* (1634) p. iv, The E silent or quiescent, which yieldeth no sound. **1711** J. GREENWOOD *Eng. Gram.* 301 Other Letters..are quiescent or silent. **1807** G. CHALMERS *Caledonia* I. I. iv. 160 The Irish Raths have the same origin, the [th] being quiescent. **1807** HURWITZ *Elem. Heb. Lang.* 101 According to the system of reading by points, the letters אהוי are in many instances quiescent. **1853** J. R. WOLF *Practical Heb. Gram.* 111 Quiescent verbs are those in which one of the feeble letters אהוי occurs as a radical letter.

b. Of a person: Silent, not speaking. *rare.*

1791 BOSWELL *Johnson* an. 1784. 17 May, Johnson was very quiescent to-day.

3. *Electronics.* Corresponding to or characterized by an absence of an input to a device ready to receive one.

1923 E. W. MARCHANT *Radio Telegr. & Teleph.* vi. 84 Attempts have been made to arrange the transmitter in such a way that the speech-current will act as a switch for starting up the continuous waves at the transmitting end. This arrangement of circuit has been called the 'Quiescent aerial' system. **1952** E. ARMITAGE *Wireless Fund.* ix. 167 The advantage of Class B amplification is that the steady anode current flowing through the circuit when the valve is quiescent is very much smaller than under Class A conditions. **1965** *Wireless World* July 325/2 This imposes a problem on the restricted signal handling capacity of Tr1 due to its very low quiescent current. **1975** D. G. FINK *Electronics Engineer's Handbk.* IX. 56 In the absence of an rf input signal, these amplifiers remain quiescent even with full operational voltage applied.

B. *sb.* **1.** A quiescent letter.

1727 in BAILEY, vol. II. **1807** HURWITZ *Elem. Heb. Lang.* 134 Whenever a letter is written and not pronounced, it is called by Hebrew Grammarians..an invisible quiescent, or a mute. **1831** LEE *Hebr. Gram.* (1832) 36 The..letters, considered either as consonants or quiescents, will occasionally be changed for one another. **1882–3** F. BROWN in Schaff *Encycl. Relig. Knowl.* I. 583/1 The weaker Shemitic gutturals and the quiescents.

2. A quiescent verb (see 2 above).

1831 LEE *Hebr. Gram.* (1832) 222 We do not think it necessary here to divide these verbs into Defectives and Quiescents as has usually been done.

qui'escently, *adv.* [f. prec. + -LY².] In a quiescent manner; at rest; in repose.

1805 FOSTER *Ess.* II. iii. 146 Quiescently regarding the conclusions. **1887** *Twin Soul* I. xiii. 131 They float quiescently upon the fleecy clouds.

†**qui'esceous**, *a. Obs. rare*⁻¹. [irreg. f. QUIESCE *v.* + -OUS.] Belonging to quiescence.

1688 R. HOLME *Armoury* II. 388/2 The Sense of Ease and Rest..it shall be termed The Quiesceous sense.

quiese, obs. form of QUEEST, wood-pigeon.

quies kiteer, quiess kateer, varr. QUAISS KITIR *int.*

quiet (ˈkwaɪət), *sb.* Also 4–6 quyet(e, quiete, 7 quiett. [ad. L. *quiēt-*, stem of *quiēs* rest, repose, quiet. An AF. *quiete* may have existed beside *quieté* QUIETY.]

1. Absence of disturbance or tumult; peaceful condition of affairs in social or political life.

13.. *Cursor M.* 29341 (Cott. Galba), [Cursed] er þai þat..robbes or reues on ani side, Whare pese and quiet suld bityde. *c* **1375** *Sc. Leg. Saints* iii. (*Andrew*) 519 Þe quyet of our lord Ihesu, luk in vnreste ȝe turne nocht now. **1470–85** MALORY *Arthur* XX. xvii, In this realme wyll be now no quyete but euer stryf and debate. **1542–3** *Act 34 & 35 Hen. VIII*, c. 27 §119 Lawes and ordinaunces for the..good quiet of his saide dominion of Wales. **1651** HOBBES *Leviath.* IV. xlvi. 380 To whom the care of the Publique quiet is committed. **1763** BURKE *Corr.* (1844) I. 43 Why is not the nation's quiet secured, and its independance asserted? **1874** BANCROFT *Footpr. Time* i. 104 A long period of almost absolute quiet followed the establishment of the empire.

personified. **1590** SPENSER *F.Q.* I. i. 41 Carelesse Quiet lyes, Wrapt in eternall silence farre from enimyes. **1632** MILTON *Penseroso* 45 Join with thee calm Peace, and Quiet, Spare Fast, that oft with gods doth diet. **1754** GRAY *Pleasure* 53 Humble quiet builds her cell.

b. Absence of noise or (rapid) motion; calmness, stillness.

a **1400** *Stockh. Medical MS.* ii. 382 in *Anglia* XVIII. 316 Ageyn cowrs of watyr wyll he flete, ȝif þe water renne in good quiete. **1602** MARSTON *Antonio's Rev.* I. i. Wks. 1856 I. 73 No breath disturbs the quiet of the ayre. **1816** SHELLEY *Alastor* 393 A smooth spot Of glassy quiet mid those battling tides Is left. **1867** SMILES *Huguenots Eng.* iii. (1880) 51 It was only the quiet that preceded the outbreak of another storm.

2. Freedom from external disturbance, molestation, interruption, or noise; †freedom from work or occupation; rest, repose.

1340 HAMPOLE *Pr. Consc.* 9128 Whare alle ryghtwyse men salle won at ees, In ioyfulle quyete, and rest, and pese. *c* **1430** LYDG. *Min. Poems* (Percy Soc.) 249 Lat me nat reste nor have no quyete, Occupye my soule with spiritual travayl. **1494** FABYAN *Chron.* VII. ccxxx. 156 This foresayd countesse ..with her sonne..was in quyete of theyr countrey and castell. **1592** GREENE *Conny catching* III. 12 She seeing him laid in bed..commits him to his quiet. **1638** R. BAKER tr. *Balzac's Lett.* (vol. II) 26, I have too much care of my own quiet, to goe about to trouble his. **1749** FIELDING *Tom Jones* VIII. xi, An arrant vixen of a wife soured his domestic quiet. **1865** HOOK *Lives Abps.* III. 301 It often happens that a man, turbulent in his youth, will make great sacrifices to procure peace and quiet in his old age.

pl. **1650** WELDON *Crt. Jas. I*, 185 More beneficiall to the Subjects in respect of their quiets.

b. Freedom from mental agitation or excitement; calm or peace of mind.

a **1628** PRESTON *New Covt.* (1634) 421 As wondrous quiet and peaceableness, and calmness in the heart. **1688** LADY R. RUSSELL *Lett.* I. lxxi. 156 Such letters as yours, Sir, do not disturb my quiet. **1726** SWIFT *Corr.* Wks. 1841 II. 586 An accident that must be so fatal to my quiet. **1840** LADY C. BURY *Hist. of Flirt* vi, A matter that concerns my quiet.

3. The condition of remaining quiet, of refraining from disturbance, hurry, exertion, etc.

1559 *Mirr. Mag.*, *Henry VI*, vii, My mynde to quyet bent, had not bene tossed so. *c* **1586** C'TESS PEMBROKE *Ps.* CXXXI, None more [than me] for quiet might compare Ev'n with the babe. **1604** E. G[RIMSTONE] *D'Acosta's Hist. Indies* V. v. 343 That God was a great Lord, who with great quiet and leasure performeth his workes. **1750** JOHNSON *Rambler* No. 74 ⁋12 Knowledge and genius are often enemies to quiet, by suggesting ideas of excellence. **1889** PATER *G. de Latour* (1896) 41 How becomingly..that self-respecting quiet sat upon their high-bred figures.

4. Freq. in phrases *at*, †*in*, and †*out of quiet*, with vbs. of being, remaining, maintaining, etc.

1377 LANGL. *P. Pl.* B. I. 121 God..garte the heuene to stekye and stonden in quiete. *c* **1450** tr. *De Imitatione* II. vi. 46 An evel conscience is euer dredful and oute of quiete. **1533** FRITH *Another Bk. agst. Rastell* Prol. (1573) 61 They could neuer be at quiet..untill they had dronken his bloud. **1577** *Test. XII Patriarchs* (1604) 101 Bear your losses willingly, and be not out of quiet for it. **1699** BURNET *39 Art.* i. (1700) 21 Every part of it is at quiet till it is put in motion. **1771** JEFFERSON *Writ.* (ed. Ford) II. 129 Matters..are too much in quiet to send you news from hence. **1830** SCOTT *Demonol.* viii. 266 The country remained at quiet. **1886** STEVENSON *Dr. Jekyll* 54 Mr. Utterson began..to grow more at quiet with himself.

†**b.** With adjs., esp. *at (a) good* (or *better*) *quiet*.

c **1470** HENRY *Wallace* VIII. 587 The ost he maid in gud quyet to be. **1603** KNOLLES *Hist. Turks* (1638) 62 The other Christian Princes also being at no better quiet. **1652** COTTERELL *Cassandra* IV. (1676) 68 He began to be at a little better quiet. **1663** PEPYS *Diary* 30 June, My differences with my uncle Thomas at a good quiett, blessed be God!

quiet (ˈkwaɪət), *a.* Forms: 4–7 quyet, (4–6 -te, 6 -tt), 5 quiete, 6 quyat, quyit, queat, 8 *Sc.* quait, 6– quiet. [a. OF. *quiete* or ad. L. *quiētus*, pa. pple. to *quiēscĕre* to come to rest, f. root of *quiēs* rest, QUIET *sb.* The popular Fr. form *coi* is represented by COY *a.*]

I. 1. a. Of persons (or animals): Making no stir, commotion, or noise; causing no trouble or disturbance; remaining at rest; not moving or acting.

1382 WYCLIF *1 Thess.* iv. 11 We preyen ȝou..that ȝe be quyet, and do ȝoure nede. **1560** DAUS tr. *Sleidane's Comm.* 277 b, Obteyne of the Clergie, that they wyll be quiet, tyll suche tyme as the other States may declare [etc.]. **1586** WARNER *Alb. Eng.* I. vi. (1612) 24 Lycus..did cast his haughtie armes abroad, as who would say, be queat. **1715** RAMSAY *Christ's Kirk Gr.* II. vi, Let gae my hands, I say, be quait. **1738** SWIFT *Polite Conv.* Wks. 1883 IX. 403, I wish you would be quiet, you have more tricks than a dancing bear. **1837** MRS. SHERWOOD *Henry Milner* III. iii. 44 The young men began to call to them crying, 'Whisht, whisht, what ails the curs?—quiet there, Viper'. **1843** MIALL in *Nonconf.* III. 635 Rebecca's rights once obtained we will be as quiet as mice.

b. (Also of nature or disposition.) Habitually or naturally peaceful or averse to making stir, noise, etc. Of an animal: Gentle. Also phr. *quiet American*: freq. used ironically, as of an undercover agent or spy.

1432–50 tr. *Higden* (Rolls) II. 167 The peple of the sowthe is meke and quiete. **1535** COVERDALE *1 Chron.* xxii[i]. 9 The sonne which shal be borne vnto the, shal be a quyete man. **1609** BIBLE (Douay) *Mic.* iv. *comm.*, Quiet patient people.. suffering persecution with alacritie of minde. **1669** CLARENDON *Ess.* Tracts (1727) 148 Quiet and easy natures are like fair weather. *a* **1720** SEWEL *Hist. Quakers* (1795) I. Pref. 18 They always were quiet and never made any resistance. **1811** *Sporting Mag.* XXXVIII. 212 The defendant did not put the question..whether it were a quiet horse? **1840** DICKENS *Barn. Rudge* vi, Barnaby is not in his quietest humour to-night. **1863** *Q. Rev.* July 262 It is a great relief to quiet people when the Easter ceremonies are wound up. **1955** G. GREENE (*title*) The quiet American. **1963** *Listener* 10 Jan. 96/3 She has much data on these delightful grasshopper people, though a certain 'Quiet American' ingenuousness is difficult to digest. **1963** *Times* 23 Feb. 4/5 Mr. H. F. Johnson..is a model quiet American. **1973** *Times* 11 Jan 10/6 There never was much 'reality' about Washington's presence in Vietnam from the moment when the first quiet Americans moved in. **1980** J. MCNEIL *Spy Game* ix. 99 I've heard of you..The Quiet American, no less.

†**c.** *Sc.* in specific senses: Acting or living quietly; remaining hid or secret; fast asleep. *Obs.*

1533 GAU *Richt Vay* 17 Thay that ar quiet and fals flatterers. **1536** BELLENDEN *Cron. Scot.* x. vii, Traistyng.. sum quiet personis liand ay in wait to inuaid hym. **1632** LITHGOW *Trav.* x. 444, I could not beleeue, that the Patrone of so great a Monarchy, could be so quiet; yea, as quiet as a Countrey Baron is with vs. **1651** WELDON *Crt. Jas. I*, 107 Loveston replies, He is quiet (which in the Scotish dialect is fast asleep).

2. a. Of things: Not active; not moving or stirring; also, making no noise; still.

quiet disease, latent hip-joint disease in children (*Syd. Soc. Lex.* 1897). †*quiet letter*, a quiescent letter.

1599 SHAKS. *Hen. V*, III. ii. 36 For Pistoll, hee hath a killing Tongue, and a quiet Sword. **1658** P. GOODWIN *Myst. Dreams* in Spurgeon *Treas. Dav.* Ps. cxxvii. 2 The Hebrew word..being with *aleph*, a quiet or resting letter. **1798** WORDSW. *Tintern Abbey* 47 An eye made quiet by the power Of harmony. **1816** SCOTT *Antiq.* iii, The dust was very ancient, peaceful, quiet dust about an hour ago. *a* **1889** ELIZA COOK *Poems* (Rtldg.) 51, I prize the soul That slumbers in a quiet eye. **1898** J. HUTCHINSON in *Arch. Surg.* IX. 330 Doubts might have been felt as to whether the induration was really malignant. It was quite quiet.

b. Free from excess; not going to extremes; moderate, gentle; *esp.* of colour, dress, style, etc.: Not obtrusive, glaring or showy.

1560 DAUS tr. *Sleidane's Comm.* 261 b, That for the appeasing of religion, they would use lawfull and quiet remedies. **1634** SIR T. HERBERT *Trav.* 5 Now you shall have a quiet breath and gale, and suddenly an unexpected violent gust. **1685** DRYDEN *Horace*, *Odes* III. xxix. 54 The tide of bus'ness..Is sometimes high, and sometimes low, A quiet ebb, or a tempestuous flow. **1768** STERNE *Sent. Journ.* (1778) I. 63 (*Remise Door*), I made them a quiet bow, and wished them a good passage to Dover. **1838** LYTTON *Alice* 21 A woman of quiet and pleasing exterior. **1853** C. BRONTË *Villette* I. xiv. 257 Her dress was almost as quiet as mine. **1856** RUSKIN *Mod. Paint.* III. IV. App. 346 The beautiful quiet English of Helps. **1885** R. L. & F. STEVENSON *Dynamiter* 185 He was conscious of a certain regular and quiet sound. **1889** *Catholic News* 15 June 8/6 There was a quiet trade in pigs. **1895** G. B. SHAW in *Sat. Rev.* 28 Sept. 409/1 He associates low tones ('quiet colors' they call them in Marshall & Snellgrove's) with dignity and decency. **1957** *Observer* 28 July 5/6 Both Hardy Amies and Victor Stiebel are masters of the art of inserting contrasting lines which define the figure in the quietest way. **1977** *Spare Rib* May 15/1 Quiet shades of blue, brown and grey were almost *de rigueur*.

c. Avoiding or escaping notice; private, secret, underhand. (In older use only *Sc.*)

a **1578** LINDESAY (Pitscottie) *Chron. Scot.* (S.T.S.) I. 87 He..send quyit messagis to his freindis. *a* **1600** MONTGOMERIE *Misc. Poems* xviii. 65 Thair companie [it] wes not quyet, Bot or they wist they wer beuryde. **1609** SKENE *Reg. Maj.* 52 (*Acts Robt. III*, c. 2) The kings lieges, are trubled in their lands, be volunter and quyet recognitions, made be the overlords. **1899** *Westm. Gaz.* 29 Dec. 8/2 'Quiet cases' meaning the insurance of lives without the knowledge of the persons so insured.

d. Of the sun: marked by an absence of all transient and localized emission of radio waves such as accompanies sunspots. Of other celestial objects: = *radio-quiet* adj. s.v. RADIO *sb.* 7. Also, in *Geophysics*, marked by no local fluctuations of magnetism.

1946 *Nature* 2 Nov. 632/2 Edlén's recent work..shows that the coronal matter is normally at a temperature approaching 10^6 degrees. We should therefore expect to find black-body radiation of about 1 metre wave-length having a normal (quiet sun) intensity corresponding nearly to $T = 10^6$. **1961** *I.U.G.G. Chron.* No. 34. 6 To December 1963 (i.e. approximately up to the commencement of the proposed International Year of the Quiet Sun). **1962** *Nature* 24 Mar. 1145/1 During magnetically quiet days. **1963** *Daily Tel.* 18 Mar. 19 (*heading*) 60 nations will seek 'quiet sun' secrets. **1966** *Sci. Amer.* Nov. 54/1 At the beginning of each [sunspot] cycle the surface of the sun is quiet, disturbed only by the 'granulation' effect. **1974** *Nature* 13 Sept. 129/1 The seamount possesses a strong magnetic signature..in marked contrast to the main part of the Rockall Trough which is magnetically quiet. **1977** *Sci. Amer.* Aug. 32/1 A number of giant elliptical galaxies radiate prodigiously at radio wavelengths, where stars and normal galaxies are quiet.

II. 3. Free from disturbance, molestation, or annoyance; not interfered or meddled with; left in peace. **a.** of a state, condition, procedure, etc. Phr. ***anything for a quiet life***: see LIFE *sb.* 3 c.

1382 WYCLIF *1 Tim.* ii. 2 That we lede quyet and pesyble lyf. *c* **1450** *St. Cuthbert* (Surtees) 3720 In quiete prayers he contenued. *c* **1532** DU WES *Introd. Fr.* in Palsgr. 921 A quyete slepe is right necessary and delycious. **1560** DAUS tr. *Sleidane's Comm.* 94 b, If they maye have their Religion quiet untill the counsell, they are also contented to become contributaries. **1601** R. JOHNSON *Kingd. & Commw.* (1603) 96 They sent..to Cæsar, to intreat a quiet passage through the Romana province. **1642** FULLER *Holy & Prof. St.* (1648) 18 Though prayer purchaseth blessings, giving praise doth keep quiet possession of them. **1766** BLACKSTONE *Comm.* II. 304 The grantor may covenant..for the grantee's quiet enjoyment.

†**b.** of a person, people, or country. Also const. *from*. *Obs.*

1558 GOODMAN *How to Obey* 175 Hauing your Realme free from strangers, and quiete from all enimies. **1599** SHAKS. *Much Ado* II. i. 266 While she is heere, a man may liue as quiet in hell, as in a sanctuary. **1611** BIBLE *Job* iii. 26, I was not in safetie, neither had I rest, neither was I quiet. **1655** FULLER *Ch. Hist.* II. iii. §26 That the abbot should be quiet from the bishop's right. **1671** MILTON *P.R.* III. 360 Long to enjoy it quiet and secure.

†**c.** Quit, clear. *Obs. rare*$^{-1}$.

1473–4 in Swayne *Sarum Church-w. Acc.* (1896) 16, Iiijs. vijd. the which ben forgeven them..and so they ben quyete.

d. ***quiet number***, an easy job (cf. NUMBER *sb.* 6 f (iii)). *Naut. slang.*

1948 PARTRIDGE *Dict. Forces' Slang 1939–1945* 129 *Number, quiet,* an easy job at sea or ashore. **1977** *Navy News* July 18 (*caption*) 'Got a nice quiet number for you after the Review,' he says... 'Just scoop up any odd little bit of gash,' he says.

4. a. Characterized by the absence of all strife, bustle, stir, or commotion; also, free from noise or uproar, silent, still. ***quiet-room***, (*a*) a room set aside for quiet activities; (*b*) a room especially designed so as not to transmit any noise made within it, usu. in a mental institution.

1514 BARCLAY *Cyt. & Uplondyshm.* (Percy Soc.) 11 Than ..Wedlocke was quyet & pleasaunt without stryfe. **1596** SHAKS. *1 Hen. IV*, v. i. 25, I could be well content To entertaine the Lagge-end of my life With quiet houres. **1611** BIBLE *Wisd.* xviii. 14 While all things were in quiet silence. **1655** FULLER *Ch. Hist.* III. xii. §27 He chose a quiet county before a cumbersome kingdom. **1791** MRS. RADCLIFFE *Rom. Forest* x, In the second chamber all was quiet and in order. **1831–3** E. BURTON *Eccl. Hist.* i. (1845) 9 If the state of things might be described as at all quiet. **1856** KANE *Arctic Explor.* II. xxiv. 204 We gave two quiet hours to the memory of our dead brother. **1872** RUSKIN *Eagle's N.* §179 My hope..that the streams of the Isis and Cherwell will be kept pure and quiet. **1938** [see PAD *sb.*[3] 1 c]. **1968** M. TORRIE *Your Secret Friend* i. 15 The Sixth have the boudoir as their 'quiet' room and the bedroom is now the staff common-room. **1976** [see PADDED *ppl. a.*[2]]. **1977** C. H. JAQUES *Dragon Century 1877–1977* xxi. 241 A complete re-organisation..with..the Doctor's surgery and consulting room taking over the Quiet Room, while the old Dining area is divided up into new Quiet Room, Headmaster's study and Secretary's office. **1977** *Spare Rib* Jan. 15/2 The second half of the day passes so quickly and imperceptibly that at first I don't grasp why it's suddenly got so noisy in our 'quiet' room.

b. Remote from scenes of activity; retired.

1500–20 DUNBAR *Poems* (S.T.S.) xliii. 33 In quyet place, ..They can, percaice, Purchess some grace. *a* **1578** LINDESAY (Pitscottie) *Chron. Scot.* (S.T.S.) I. 187 They.. past to the wall heid at ane quyit place quhair the watches might haue no sight of them. **1738** GRAY *Propertius* iii. 105 Then to my quiet Urn awhile draw near. **1861** H. KINGSLEY *Ravenshoe* xxxvii, As soon as he and Lady Ascot were seated on a quiet sofa.

c. Partaken of, or enjoyed, in quiet.

1837 DICKENS *Pickw.* xxvi, To have a quiet cup of tea. **1891** [see THINK *sb.* 1]. **1892** ANSTEY *Voces Pop.* Ser. II. 85 A cup of coffee, and a quiet cigar. **1905** CHESTERTON *Heretics* xiv. 181 A place where a man can have what is somewhat fantastically called a quiet chop. **1953** R. USBORNE *Clubland Heroes* II. 99 An off-day for a good Buchan type was: a cold bath or plunge, a big breakfast, a quiet pipe, and then off to the hills in filthy tweeds. **1963** E. SUMMERS *Where No Roads Go* v. 72 I'll go out on the verandah for a quiet smoke. **1977** *Private Eye* 1 Apr. 23/3 (Advt.), A quiet word about hair transplants. **1977** *Zigzag* Apr. 28/1, I can just see the nice young couples out for a quiet Sunday drink.

d. Of a period of time: spent in seclusion for the purposes of prayer, meditation, etc.; ***quiet time***: a daily session of private Bible study or prayer.

1884 *Lichfield Diocesan Mag.* Jan. 10 A *Quiet* day, to which all the clergy and lay readers of the archdeaconry were invited, was held at Stoke, on Tuesday Dec. 18th. **1896** C. T. STUDD *Let.* in N. P. Grubb *C. T. Studd* (1933) xi. 106, I have had such a good day to-day, early up and a quiet time for most of the day and the Lord has been opening up the Word. **1934** R. MACAULAY *Going Abroad* xxx. 263 That must have been about the same time I was having *my* quiet time. **1935** *Methodist Recorder* 1 Aug. 5/4 A large number of ministers assembled..for the 'Quiet Day'. **1945** [see SHARING *vbl. sb.*[2] 2]. **1957** J. R. W. STOTT *Being a Christian* 23 What many people call the daily 'quiet times', first thing in the morning and last thing at night. **1960** I. KUHN *In Arena* iii. 35 Some students were trying to let classwork reading [of the Bible] do for personal quiet time. *Ibid.* 36 Letting the day's business occupy the central place and trying to fix a quiet time with the Lord somewhere shoved into the odd corner. **1967** M. GRIFFITHS *Take my Life* iii. 61 Maintaining a regular 'Quiet Time' unhurriedly in the Lord's presence, reading the Bible, hearing His word and responding in prayer from the heart, becomes harder. **1973** *Franciscan* XV. 169 A quiet afternoon during the Pentecost season was conducted by the Dean of Worcester.

5. Of the mind, conscience, etc.: Not troubled or distressed; free from agitation or excitement. So also of persons in respect of the mind, etc.

1535 COVERDALE *Prov.* xv. 15 A quyete herte is as a contynuall feast. **1552** *Bk. Com. Prayer* Commun., With a quiet conscience. **1558** GOODMAN *How to Obey* 230 That you cannot be quiete in conscience. **1593** SHAKS. *Rich. II*, I. iii. 96 Truth hath a quiet breast. **1631** GOUGE *God's Arrows* I. §5. 8 The bond of a Creditor, so lies on the debter, that he is not quiet till it be discharged.

†**6.** Sheltered from the wind. *Obs. rare.*

1596 DALRYMPLE tr. *Leslie's Hist. Scot.* I. 30 In the scoug of the craig and castell is a verie quyet hauining place. **1697** DRYDEN *Virg. Georg.* IV. 10 For thy Bees a quiet Station find, And lodge 'em under Covert of the Wind.

III. †**7.** Used as *adv.* = QUIETLY. *Obs. rare*$^{-1}$.

1573 TUSSER *Husb.* (1878) 63 More profit is quieter found (where pastures in several bee).

8. Quasi-*sb.*, in phr. ***on the quiet***, privately, in secret. (Abbrev. *q.t.*: see Q II. 2.) *slang* or *colloq.*

1862 *Otago: Goldfields & Resources* 35 Unless men can work [the gold] on 'the quiet', they are not likely to make 'piles' so rapidly as Messrs. Hartley and Riley. **1863** HOTTEN *Dict. Slang* (ed. 2) s.v., 'On the quiet', clandestinely, so as to avoid observation, 'under the rose'. **1873** 'MARK TWAIN' *Gilded Age* xi. 112 The other day he let me into a little secret, strictly on the quiet. **1881** *Punch* 8 Jan. 4/1 I'd just like to have a bit of chinwag with you on the quiet about the..troubles of a Cabby. **1889** H. O'REILLY *50 Yrs. on Trail* 7 Having on the quiet found out a passenger steamboat. **1903** A. H. LEWIS *Boss* 59 They've put out a lot of money on the quiet among my own people. **1967** N. FREELING *Strike out where not Applicable* 36 She has a good act of letting Francis rule the roost, but on the quiet I think she makes the decisions.

9. *Comb.*, as ***quiet-eyed***, ***-footed***, ***-mannered***, ***-minded***, ***-spoken***, ***-tempered***, ***-tinted***, ***-toned***, ***-voiced***, ***-walled***; ***quiet-going***, ***-living***, ***-looking***, ***-moving***, ***-seeming***, ***-smiling***, adjs.

1895 W. B. YEATS *Poems* 197 The Druid, gray, woodnurtured, quiet-eyed. **1956** R. FINLAYSON in *Landfall* (N.Z.) X. 12 A handsome..Jersey, sleek and quiet eyed. **1954** J. R. R. TOLKIEN *Fellowship of Ring* I. ii. 62 Long after, but still very long ago, there lived by the banks of the Great River on the edge of Wilderland a clever-handed and quiet-footed little people. **1886** H. F. LESTER *Under two Fig Trees* 59 The exciting incidents which now and then ruffle the life of even the most quiet-going family. **1888** BRYCE *Amer. Commw.* II. II. xlii. 119 A larger sum than a quiet-living man can need. **1825** J. NEAL *Jonathan* II. 194 An old, stately, quiet-looking negro. **1780** S. J. PRATT *Emma Corbett* (ed. 4) I. 107, I can..impress the quiet-seeming sentiment. **1952** R. CAMPBELL tr. *Baudelaire's Poems* 84 An huntress born, sure-eyed, and quiet-smiling. **1848** DICKENS *Dombey* iv, He was a slow, quiet-spoken..old fellow. *Ibid.* iii, She was a quiet-tempered lady. **1909** *Westm. Gaz.* 14 Sept. 1/2 It included the following: Shirts, 72;..socks of quiet-tinted silk, 2 dozen; hats, evening suits, smoking coats. **1965** *Times Lit. Suppl.* 25 Nov. 1049/4 A quiet-toned, carefully tender book. **1940** T. S. ELIOT *East Coker* ii. 9 Had they deceived us Or deceived themselves, the quiet-voiced elders. **1974** P. GORE-BOOTH *With Great Truth & Respect* 394 What disturbed me immensely was their quiet-voiced extremism. **1865** G. M. HOPKINS *Poems* (1967) 34 Those charms accepted of my inmost thought The towers musical, quiet-walled grove.

quiet ('kwaɪət), *v.* Also 6 quyet. [ad. med.L. *quiētāre*, f. L. *quiētus* QUIET *a.*]

†**1.** *trans.* To quit, acquit (oneself or another).

c **1440** *Generydes* 2861 Eche of hem iij so wele quiete them ther. **1472–3** *Rolls Parlt.* VI. 50/1 That your said suppliaunt .. be discharged, relesed and quieted, of almaner..fynes, paynes [etc.].

2. To make quiet (in various senses); to reduce to quietness:

a. a person or people, a material thing, etc.

1550 CROWLEY *Way to Wealth* 269 Quiet thy selfe therfore, and striue not againste the streame. **1599** SHAKS. *Hen. V*, v. i. 54 Quiet thy Cudgell, thou dost see I eate. **1609** HOLLAND *Amm. Marcell.* 109 Those savage nations whom he had quieted. **1665** MANLEY *Grotius' Low-C. Warres* 520 A very difficult piece of Work..to quiet all the right side of the Rhine. **1786** MAD. D'ARBLAY *Diary* 8 Nov., I did what was possible to quiet her, but to no purpose. **1855** MACAULAY *Hist. Eng.* xii. III. 211 In trying to quiet one set of malecontents, he had created another. **1866** G. MACDONALD *Ann. Q. Neighb.* vi. (1878) 73 She knew she had no chance of quieting the girl.

b. a feeling or emotion, *esp.* of fear.

1526 *Pilgr. Perf.* (W. de W. 1531) 2 b, His naturall inclinacyon and appetyte can neuer be sacyate, contented and quieted. **1552** *Bk. Com. Prayer* Commun., If there be any of you which..cannot quiet his own conscience. **1748** *Anson's Voy.* II. xi. 253 This quieted our apprehensions for some days. **1855** MACAULAY *Hist. Eng.* xi. III. 32 The event quieted the fears of one party. **1888** BRYCE *Amer. Commw.* III. lxxxviii. 190 In order to quiet these suspicions the comptroller played a very bold game.

c. a disturbance, dissension, etc.

1560 DAUS tr. *Sleidane's Comm.* 174 The byshop wyl sende thether..to quiet the controversy. **1601** J. WHEELER *Treat. Comm.* 33 Till the said King Edward had quieted the troubles with his subiects at home. **1674** *Essex Papers* (Camden) I. 193 Some companys of yᵉ Guard being comanded together to quiet yᵉ Tumult. **1792** BURKE *Let. to R. Burke* Corr. IV. 4 Measures which may quiet the unhappy divisions of the country. **1846** TRENCH *Mirac.* iv. (1862) 147 Quieting with a word the tempest in their bosoms. **1875** JOWETT *Plato* (ed. 2) V. 360 The motion.. quiets the restless palpitation of the heart.

d. *Electronics.* To reduce automatically the gain of (a radio receiver) in the absence of a usable signal; = SQUELCH *v.*

1950 J. K. HENNEY *Radio Engin. Handbk.* (ed. 4) xvii. 821 The purpose of these circuits is to squelch or quiet the receiver when sufficient signal for satisfactory reception is not present. **1960** COOKE & MARKUS *Electronics & Nucleonics Dict.* 453/2 *Squelch,* to quiet a receiver automatically by reducing its gain in response to a specified characteristic of the input.

3. To settle or establish in quiet. Chiefly *Law.*

c **1586** C'TESS PEMBROKE *Ps.* LXXXII. iii, You should unto the weake extend Your hand, to loose and quiet his estate. **1654** G. GODDARD *Introd. Burton's Diary* (1828) I. 190 A Bill for quieting the possession of the government. **1668** *Ormonde MSS.* in *10th Rep. Hist. MSS. Comm.* App. V. 69 Your petitioner..made surrender of his estate unto the Crowne so soone as he was quieted in the possession thereof. **1884** SIR J. BACON in *Law Rep.* 27 *Chanc. Div.* 47 The Plaintiffs are entitled..to be quieted in the possession they have had for so many years.

4. *intr.* To become quiet. Also ***to quiet down***. Now chiefly *N. Amer.*

1791 PAINE *Rights of Man* (ed. 4) 27 The mind can hardly ..conceive the possibility of its quieting so soon. **1851** MAYNE REID *Scalp Hunt.* xxxii. 247, I have never seen buffaloes 'quieting' down before. **1865** MRS. WHITNEY *Gayworthys* II. 237 By and by she quieted, and, from pure exhaustion, fell asleep. **1897** A. BEARDSLEY *Let.* 17 Mar. (1970) 279 There has been no return of haemorrhage. The lung too is quieting down. **1914** G. B. SHAW *Misalliance* 85 You would then be charged and imprisoned until things quieted down. *Ibid.* 93 Let us postpone the discussion. Wait until Monday: we shall have Sunday to quiet down in. **1916** *Daily Colonist* (Victoria, B.C.) 30 July 7/4 The trade had quieted down somewhat lately and some mills have lacked an adequate supply of logs. **1944** *New Yorker* 25 Mar. 84/2 Moved back into London when things quieted down. **1974** *Sci. Amer.* July 47/2 The effect of the drugs is often dramatic, with the children quieting down, paying attention to their schoolwork and in some cases doing better in school.

Hence **'quieted** *ppl. a.*

1894 E. F. BENSON *Dodo* 185 The darkened house, the quieted movements.

†**quietance.** *Obs.* [ad. med.L. *quiētāncia*, f. *quiētāre* to QUIET: see -ANCE.] = QUITTANCE 2.

1451 *Rolls Parlt.* V. 224/1 Libertees, Fraunchises and Quietaunces conteyned in the same. **1571** *Act 13 Eliz.* c. 29 All manner of Liberties, Franchises, Immunities, Quietances and Privileges.

‖**quieta non movere** (kwiːˈeɪtə nəʊn məʊˈvɛəriː). [L., lit. 'not to move settled things'.] A maxim expressing preference for the *status quo*; 'let sleeping dogs lie'.

1771 H. WALPOLE *Let.* 26 Mar. in *Corr.* (1937) VII. 289 My father's maxim, *Quieta non movere*, was very well in those ignorant days. **1854** W. BAGEHOT in *Prospective Review* X. 526 It lived on the fat of the land; *quieta non movere*, was its motto. **1887** *Athenæum* 27 Aug. 276/2 But was the book quite worth publishing? 'Quieta non movere' holds good even of dormant articles. **1905** D. M. WALLACE *Russia* I. xix. 373 *Quieta non movere* is her [*sc.* the Russian Church's] fundamental principle of conduct. **1960** *Encounter* XIV. III. 88 *Quieta non movere* is the motto of many once aggressive..radicals.

quietant ('kwaɪətənt). [f. QUIET *v.* + -ANT[1].] Anything that makes quiet or soothes.

1875 H. C. WOOD *Therap.* (1879) 340 As a nocturnal quietant and hypnotic, it would appear to offer very great advantages.

†**quie'tation.** *Obs.* Also 6 quietacion, -cyon, quyat-, quyetacyon, -cion. [ad. med.L. *quiētātiōn-em*, n. of action f. *quiētāre* to QUIET. Cf. obs. F. *quietacion* (Godef.).] The action of quieting; the state of being quieted or quiet.

1502 W. ATKYNSON tr. *De Imitatione* III. xl. 229 If thou seke here rest, how shalt thou come to euerlastyng rest & quietacion in heuen? **1526–9** LD. DUDLEY in Ellis *Orig. Lett.* Ser. III. II. 84 For the quyatacion of the Kyngs subgetts. **1640** J. STOUGHTON *Def. & Distrib. Divinity* iii. 90 Such a fruition of all good..as brings with it a perfect quietation of the natural appetite. *a* **1711** KEN *Anodynes* Poet. Wks. 1721 III. 427 From God I ease or succour find, And Quietation to my Mind.

quiete, variant of QUIETY *Obs.*

quieten ('kwaɪət(ə)n), *v.* [f. QUIET *a.* + -EN[5].]

1. *trans.* To make quiet. Also const. *down*.

1828 in *Craven Gloss.* **1844** *N. Brit. Rev.* I. 182 To 'quieten' the children..is not English. **1853** MRS. GASKELL *Ruth* III. x. 280, I will stay,..partly to quieten the fears of this poor, faithful fellow. **1888** *Chamb. Jrnl.* 7 Apr. 223 The incident did not quieten the audience. **1902** C. HYNE *Mr. Horrocks, Purser* 37 Mr Horrocks had given the wink to the chief steward to go and quieten down the Second-Class passengers. **1908** G. A. BIRMINGHAM *Spanish Gold* xxi. 296 We got them quietened down after a bit.

2. *intr.* To become quiet. Commonly with *down*.

1890 C. DIXON *Stray Feathers* v. 67 They soon quieten down. **1897** *Westm. Gaz.* 21 Aug. 5/1 Towards the close the market quietened. **1897** *Daily Tel.* 28 Aug. 6/4 It [*sc.* Afghanistan] is beginning to quieten down now, in my opinion.

Hence **'quietener** (also 9 **quietner**) = QUIETER. (Cf. QUIETANT.)

1856 *Punch* 19 July 22/1 The conjugal powders are called in the town of Bolton 'Quietners'... These quietners are sold at one penny each. **1882** *Fraser's Mag.* XXV. 35 The poisonous method of giving soothing or narcotic quieteners to children.

ˈquietening, *ppl. a.* [-ING².] That quietens or becomes quiet.

1905 *Daily Chron.* 25 Mar. 7/3 The presence of a large addition of police has had a quietening effect on the.. operatives on strike. **1907** *Smart Set* Mar. 26/1 She lay there on her pillow, grateful.. for the sheltering, homely realities, that enmuffled her and gave tangibility to her quietening thoughts.

quieter (ˈkwaɪətə(r)). [f. QUIET *v.* + -ER¹.] One who or that which makes quiet.

a **1541** WYATT in *Tottel's Misc.* (Arb.) 45 The bodyes ease, and troubler of my heart: Quieter of minde. **1547–64** BAULDWIN *Mor. Philos.* (Palfr.) 140 It is also a satisfier or ioyfull quieter of the minde. **1832** SOUTHEY *Lett.* (1856) IV. 261 Half an hour of some goodly grave old book.. as a quieter for the night.

†**ˈquietful**, *a. Obs. rare*⁻¹. [f. QUIET *sb.* + -FUL.] Full of quiet; calm.

c **1440** HYLTON *Scala Perf.* (W. de W. 1494) III. xv, A quyetful langynge with a trusty desyrynge to heuenly Joye.

quietie, variant of QUIETY *Obs.*

ˈquieting, *vbl. sb.* [f. QUIET *v.* + -ING¹.] **1.** The action of the vb.

a **1548** HALL *Chron., Hen. VIII*, 179 He.. for quietyng of his conscience called together the best lerned of the realme. *a* **1652** J. SMITH *Sel. Disc.* x. 511 A pacifying and quieting of all those riots and tumults. **1783** MAD. D'ARBLAY *Diary* 18 Jan., I felt so fagged.. that I really wanted quieting and refitting. **1861** GOLDW. SMITH *Irish Hist.* 105 To withhold the capital 'grace' concerning the quieting of titles to land.

2. *Radio.* **a.** The automatic reduction of the gain and therefore the noise of a receiver when there is no usable signal.

1937 F. E. TERMAN *Radio Engin.* (ed. 2) xiii. 561 In tuning a sensitive receiver provided with automatic volume control, the noise output between stations is high because, when no signal is being received, the A.V.C. system increases the sensitivity of the receiver to the maximum possible value. Arrangements for eliminating this interstation noise are variously known as *Q* circuits, quieting systems, squelch circuits, etc. **1959** R. L. SHRADER *Electronic Communication* xvii. 554 (*caption*) A squelch interstation quieting, or Q, circuit.

b. The reduction of the noise level in a receiver caused by the presence of an input at the frequency to which it is tuned.

1949 *Proc. IRE* XXXVII. 1373/2 The quieting-signal-sensitivity test input is the least unmodulated signal input which, when applied to the receiver through the standard dummy antenna, reduces the receiver noise by a factor of 20 decibels. **1960** *IRE Trans. Vehicular Communications* Dec. 32/2 Two methods of measuring sensitivity are recognized. .. The oldest and probably the most used is the quieting method. This procedure measures the on-frequency signal level required to reduce the noise output of a receiver by 20 db. **1974** HARVEY & BOHLMAN *Stereo F.M. Radio Handbk.* iii. 41 Receiver sensitivity must be quoted together with the corresponding noise figure; a typical figure for a good circuit is 2μV for 30 dB quieting.

ˈquieting, *ppl. a.* [-ING².] That quiets.

1659 A. HAY *Diary* (S.H.S.) 80 There is a quieting rest under Christ's wings. **1759** H. WALPOLE *Lett. to Mann* 9 Feb. (1846) III. 432 The Parliament has taken a quieting-draught. **1839** I. TAYLOR *Anc. Chr.* I. 22 The quieting recollection that they themselves are members of a series. **1846** TRENCH *Mirac.* xxxii. (1862) 450 The Lord spoke these quieting words to his disciples.

quietish (ˈkwaɪətɪʃ), *a.* [f. QUIET *a.* + -ISH¹.] Somewhat quiet.

1913 R. BROOKE *Let.* May (1968) 464, I wasn't *sick*: just quietish, and I had a bleedin' headache. **1925** G. S. GORDON *Let.* 13 May (1943) 177 The house seems quietish without you! **1939** N. MARSH *Overture to Death* xiii. 125 Though lately it's been quietish—hasn't it, Mr. Alleyn? **1977** *Hot Car* Oct. 49/1 It's obviously got to be neat, safe and quietish.

Quietism (ˈkwaɪətɪz(ə)m). [ad. It. *quietismo* (whence also F. *quiétisme*, mod.L. *quiētismus*, etc.): see QUIET *a.* and -ISM.]

1. A form of religious mysticism (originated prior to 1675 by Molinos, a Spanish priest), consisting in passive devotional contemplation, with extinction of the will and withdrawal from all things of the senses; hence, any form of mysticism in which such principles are enjoined.

The *Guida spirituale* in which Molinos expounded his views was published at Rome in 1675, and condemned by the Inquisition in 1685.

1687 in Burnet *Lett.* (1688) Suppl. 46, I will here digress a little from the business of Quietism. **1698** tr. *Fenelon's Maxims of Saints* Introd., There are but a few people that have not heard of Molinos, and his Doctrine of Quietism. **1773** WESLEY *Wks.* (1872) XIII. 25 Her [Madame Guion's] writings will lead any one who is fond of them, into unscriptural Quietism. **1838** SIR J. STEPHEN *Eccl. Biog.* (1850) II. 70 Quietism, indigenous in the East, is an exotic in this cold and busy land of ours. **1873** C. M. DAVIES *Unorth. Lond.* 200 To avoid the Charybdis of carnalism, there is no need to seek the Scylla of Quietism.

2. With lower-case initial. A state of calmness and passivity of mind or body; repose, quietness, tranquillity.

1772 *Town & Country Mag.* 86 This discovery deprived him of all his quietism. **1795** JEFFERSON *Writ.* (1859) IV. 122 That quietism into which people naturally fall after first sensations are over. **1836** *Fraser's Mag.* XIII. 526 They could.. disturb his quietism by acrimonious attacks. **1976** *Gramophone* Aug. 266/1 In its place there is.. almost a sense of quietism.

Quietist (ˈkwaɪətɪst). [ad. It. *quietista* (F. *quiétiste*): cf. prec. and -IST.]

1. One who believes in or practises Quietism, or any form of mysticism resembling it. Also *fig.*

1685 BURNET *Letter from Rome* (1689) 205 A state of inward quietness, from which the name of Quietists was given to all his followers. **1687** *Lond. Gaz.* No. 2269/3 They write from Rome that the Pope had assisted a third time at a Congregation held concerning the Quietists. **1732** BERKELEY *Alciphr.* III. § 14 The disinterested Stoics (therein not unlike our modern Quietists). **1840** THIRLWALL *Greece* VII. liii. 14 He conceived a like admiration for the Indian quietists. **1893** C. G. LELAND *Memoirs* I. 23 Reading works by Mystics, Quietists, and the like. **1923** W. DEEPING *Secret Sanctuary* xxiii. 241 In love he had become a Quietist. **1924** —— *Three Rooms* xxix. 268 She sat like a quietist, hands folded, her brown eyes benignly equivocal.

2. With lower-case initial. One whose attitude towards political or social movements is analogous to Quietism in religion.

1798 CHARLOTTE SMITH *Yng. Philos.* IV. 393, I will not talk to you about politics because you are among the moderates and quietists. **1834** SOUTHEY *Doctor* cii. (1862) 232 He was not like him a political quietist from indifference. **1871** R. H. HUTTON *Ess.* II. 442 He was, in political and social conviction, a democratic quietist; one might almost say a fatalist.

3. *attrib.* or as *adj.*

1856 R. A. VAUGHAN *Mystics* (1860) II. XI. ii. 224 The Quietist doctrine of unconsciousness. **1860** O. W. HOLMES *Elsie V.* xxviii. (1891) 413 Hymns.. of the Methodist and Quietist character. **1873** MORLEY *Rousseau* II. x. 29 Rousseau raised feeling, now passionate, now quietist.

quietistic (kwaɪəˈtɪstɪk), *a.* [f. QUIETIST: see -ISTIC.] Belonging to, or characteristic of, quietists. Also *transf.*

1850 H. BUSHNELL *God in Christ* 321 They make a study of the mystic and quietistic writers. **1876** *Macm. Mag.* XXXIV. 194 He displays.. the most tender love and quietistic resignation. **1909** *Quarterly Rev.* July 117 Altogether, quietistic analysis breaks down while leaving the reality and value of the experience untouched. **1973** B. R. WILSON *Magic & Millennium* xii. 387 Among less-developed peoples the autonomous introversionist movement would appear to rely on the quietistic prophet. **1978** *Gramophone* July 231/1 He does not overpoint the ostinato of No. 4, which remains essentially quietistic.

quietive (ˈkwaɪətɪv). [f. QUIET *v.* + -IVE.] That which tends to produce quiet; a sedative.

1894 BRUCE *Paul's Concept. Chr.* xx. 365 It is his quietive amid disgusts.

ˈquietize, *v. rare*⁻¹. [f. QUIET *a.* + -IZE.] *trans.* To make quiet.

1791 MAD. D'ARBLAY *Diary* (1842–6) V. VI. 271 Solitude, and patience, and religion, have now quietized both father and daughter into tolerable contentment.

ˈquietless, *a. rare*⁻¹. [f. QUIET *sb.* + -LESS.] Devoid of quiet.

1839 BAILEY *Festus* (1852) 376 The moon.. comes haunting the cold earth.. quietless.

quietlike, *a.* and *adv.* orig. *Sc.* [See -LIKE 2 b.] Apparently quiet; quietly.

In some or all of the modern examples the formation may have been influenced by the parenthetic use of *like* (see LIKE *adv.* 7).

c **1470** HENRY *Wallace* v. 577 All his four men bar thaim quietlik. *a* **1902** *Mod. Sc.* Your horse is a quietlike beast. **1909** J. MASEFIELD *Tragedy of Nan* II. 31 He was fiddlin' quiet-like, all the time 'e were a-singing. **1913** W. DE LA MARE *Peacock Pie* 98 Calling me, 'Sam!'—quietlike. **1976** *New Yorker* 8 Mar. 102/2 Someone said, 'It wasn't no mortar round,' real quietlike. **1977** I. SHAW *Beggarman, Thief* I. iv. 49 Wesley turned to him and said, quiet-like, 'Shut your big trap about Americans, limey.'

quietly (ˈkwaɪətlɪ), *adv.* Forms: 5–6 **quyetly, -lie,** 6 **quietlie, -ely,** 6– **quietly,** (9 *dial.* **whietly**). [f. QUIET *a.* + -LY².] **a.** In a quiet manner; without molestation, peacefully; without excitement, tumult, or noise; without moving or stirring, etc. Also, surreptitiously, without attracting public notice.

1494 FABYAN *Chron.* I. iv. 11 He was stablysshed in his Realme quyetly. **1535** COVERDALE *1 Sam.* xxiv. 4 Dauid stode vp and cut of the typpe of Sauls garment quyetly. **1568** GRAFTON *Chron.* II. 378 They entred into the Citie, and there abode quietly. **1611** TOURNEUR *Ath. Trag.* I. ii. Wks. 1878 I. 35 That he may sleepe the quietlier. **1729** BUTLER *Serm. Hum. Nat.* ii. Wks. 1874 II. 20 Let every one then quietly follow his nature. **1793** SMEATON *Edystone L.* § 227 A weight of lead.. which, in all such trials as had hitherto been made thereof, had lain quietly. **1878** HUXLEY *Physiogr.* xvii. 281 When the river.. quietly deposited mud and sand. **1961** *Minnesota Rev.* I. III. 349 In the prison camp's Black Market civilian clothes were quietly bought.. for him. **1976** *N.Y. Rev. Bks.* 15 Apr. 22/4 When the recent coal rush got underway, companies would quietly obtain mineral leases for as little as twenty-five cents an acre from the Interior Department.

b. *just quietly* advb. phr., confidentially, between ourselves. *Austral.* and *N.Z. colloq.*

1937 PARTRIDGE *Dict. Slang* 448/2 *Just quietly* was, in the G[reat] W[ar], a tag-c[atch] p[hrase] among New Zealanders. It had virtually no meaning. **1941** BAKER *Dict. Austral. Slang* 40 *Just quietly*, between you and I. **1952** E. LAMBERT *Twenty Thousand Thieves* II. 123 'That Chips Prentice is a soldier and a half. Just quietly, he's up for a decoration.' Dick found no cause for surprise at this. Chips with a decoration seemed natural. **1966** G. W. TURNER *Eng. Lang. in Austral. & N.Z.* viii. 177 Much New Zealand colloquialism is shared with Australia, e.g. *just quietly* 'between you and me', [etc.].

quietness (ˈkwaɪətnɪs). Forms: 5–7 **quietnes(se,** 6 **quyetnes(se,** 7 **quiett-, quyettnes,** 6– **quietness.** [f. as prec. + -NESS.] The condition of being quiet or undisturbed; absence of noise, motion, or excitement; calmness, tranquillity.

c **1450** tr. *De Imitatione* I. ix. 10 þou shalt neure finde quietnes but in meke subieccion under a prelate. **1526** *Pilgr. Perf.* (W. de W. 1531) 142 It is lesse labour and more quietnes. *a* **1578** LINDESAY (Pitscottie) *Chron. Scot.* (S.T.S.) I. 185 Althocht the conspiratouris thocht to have this matter .. in quyetnes, yet.. the king of France gat wit of the samin. **1682** NORRIS *Hierocles* 71 The knowing man.. will learn quietness and sedateness. **1730** EARL OF OXFORD in *Swift's Lett.* (1768) IV. 25 Enjoying the fruit of his victory, peace and quietness. **1807** WORDSW. *White Doe* I. 294 Happy in the shy recess Of Barden's lowly quietness. **1874** GLADSTONE in *Contemp. Rev.* Oct. 664 A word spoken in quietness.. can rarely fail to be in season.

†**b.** With *a* (not followed by *that*). *Obs.*

a **1548** HALL *Chron., Hen. V* 75 b, To set all thynges in a quietnes. **1549** LATIMER *2nd Serm. bef. Edw. VI* (Arb.) 73 That she wold let the great man haue a quietnes in hyr Lande. **1596** SHAKS. *Merch. V.* IV. i. 12, I.. am arm'd To suffer, with a quietnesse of spirit [etc.].

†**ˈquietous**, *a. Obs. rare.* [f. QUIET *sb.* + -OUS.] Quiet, peaceful. Hence †**ˈquietously** *adv.*

1550 BALE *Image Both Ch.* 84 b, Quietously to rest for a season. *Ibid.* 93 b, Bringing men to a quietous holde and sure stay in the Lord.

ˈquietsome, *a. Obs.* exc. *dial.* [f. QUIET *a.* + -SOME.] Quiet.

1595 SPENSER *Epithal.* 326 Let the night be calme and quietsome. **1876** *Whitby Gloss., Quietsome*, retired; silent.

quietude (ˈkwaɪətjuːd). [a. F. *quiétude* (*c* 1500) or ad. late L. *quiētūdo*, f. *quiēt-us* QUIET *a.*] = QUIETNESS; rest, calm, tranquillity.

1597 A. M. tr. *Guillemeau's Fr. Chirurg.* 46 b/2 That parte requireth nothinge els then quietude. **1675** OTWAY *Alcibiades* III. i, How sweet a Quietude's in Fetters found. **1755** J. SHEBBEARE *Lydia* (1769) II. 3 Love,.. urged his bosom too vehemently, to suffer a moment's quietude or delay. **1832** LYTTON *Eugene A.* I. v. 28 Philosophy has become another name for mental quietude. **1877** 'H. A. PAGE' *De Quincey* II. xvi. 29 The quietude of the Meadows .. made them his favourite resorts.

‖**quietus** (kwaɪˈiːtəs). [Short for next.]

1. A discharge or acquittance given on payment of sums due, or clearing of accounts; a receipt.

1540 *Act 32 Hen. VIII* (Pardon), Such issues fines or amerciaments.. and haue his or their Quietus for the same. **1623** WEBSTER *Duch. Malfi* III. ii, You had the tricke in Audit time to be sicke, Till I had sign'd your Quietus. **1688** EVELYN *Diary* 15 Mar., I gave in my account about the Sick and Wounded, in order to have my quietus. **1780** BURKE *Sp. Econ. Reform* Wks. 1826 III. 297 A final acquittance, (or a *quietus*, as they term it) is scarcely ever to be obtained [from the exchequer]. **1887** *48th Dep. Keeper's Rep.* 628 The several Books.. being preserved, and.. the satisfaction or *quietus* being therein entered.

†**2.** A discharge from office or duty. *Obs.*

c **1670** WOOD *Life* an. 1650–1, 16 Jan. (O.H.S.) I. 166 Had A. W. continued postmaster a little longer, he had, without doubt, received his quietus. **1687** LUTTRELL *Brief Rel.* (1857) I. 401 Sir Francis Withens, a judge of the Kings bench, hath his quietus. *a* **1711** KEN *Hymnotheo* Poet. Wks. 1721 III. 155 The Guardian to relieve, Who his Quietus shall in Heav'n receive. **1788** WALPOLE *Letters* (1902) 104 A Veteran Author ought to take out his quietus as much as the Superannuated of any other Profession.

3. Discharge or release from life; death, or that which brings death.

1602 SHAKS. *Ham.* III. i. 75 When he himselfe might his quietus make With a bare bodkin. **1768–74** TUCKER *Lt. Nat.* (1834) II. 639 Some obtain their quietus without any signs of pain at all. **1775** SHERIDAN *Rivals* v. iii, If an unlucky bullet should carry a quietus with it. *a* **1839** PRAED *Poems* (1864) II. 65 Sought his quietus in a duel. **1872** BAKER *Nile Tribut.* v. 65 This shot, far from producing a quietus, gave rise to a series of convulsive struggles.

b. Final settlement or extinction.

1806–7 BERESFORD *Miseries Hum. Life* (ed. 5) I. 233 We have now, I think, given a quietus to the parlour. **1885** CLODD *Myths & Dr.* I. iv. 73 This law gave the quietus to theories of common origin.

4. (By assoc. with *quiet.*) Something which quiets or represses.

1824 MISS FERRIER *Inher.* xxxii, This disaster.. had the effect of a quietus upon Miss P. for some time. **1855** THACKERAY *Newcomes* II. 304 The nurse ran to give its accustomed quietus to the little screaming infant.

Hence †**quietus** *v. trans.*, to discharge. *Obs.*

1688 in Ellis *Corr.* II. 22 The other Powell and Holloway, who are quietus'd.

‖**quietus est.** *Obs.* [(med.)L. = 'he is quit'.] = QUIETUS.

1427–8 *Rolls Parlt.* V. 409/2 That thei haue not theire Quietus est out of the Eschequier. **1530** LATIMER *Rem.* (Parker Soc.) 309 To have.. your quietus est sealed with the blood of our Saviour Christ. **1594** CAREW *Huarte's Exam. Wits* (1616) 217 That Steward.. salued vp all his reckonings, and got his quietus est. **1681** LUTTRELL *Brief Rel.* (1857) I. 74 On Monday the 11th of Aprill the lord cheif justice Scroggs received his quietus est. **1706** PHILLIPS (ed. Kersey), *Quietus est*.. a Phrase us'd by the Clerk of the Pipe and Auditors in the Exchequer, in their Acquittances and Discharges given to Accountants: A *Quietus est* granted to the Sheriff likewise discharges him of all Accounts due to the Queen.

†'quiety. *Sc. Obs. rare.* In 6 quiete, -tie, 7 quyetie. [a. OF. *quieté, quité* (Godef.):—L. type **quiētāt-em*, f. *quiēt-us* QUIET *a.*] Quietness.

c **1470** HENRYSON *Mor. Fab.* II. (*Town & C. Mouse*) xxxi, Blissit be sober feist in quiete [*ed.* 1621 quyetie]. **1528** LYNDESAY *Dreme* 283 Secreit synnis done in quietie.

quife, quig, quight, obs. ff. COIF, WHIG, QUITE.

quiff (kwɪf), *sb.*[1] *U.S.* and *dial.* Also quift. [Var. of WHIFF *sb.*[1]] **1.** A puff or whiff of tobacco smoke. Also *fig.*

1831 J. M. GALLOWAY *Poems* 27 Thou'st warm'd my nose at mony a speil; Ae quiff o' thee [*sc.* a pipe] Has made me play wi' care and skill. **1840** *Southern Lit. Messenger* VI. 447/2 A quiff would now and again ascend and hang like a tropical cloud over the hemisphere of his cranium. **1866** J. E. BROGDEN *Provincial Words* 159 *Quiff*, a puff. *Ex.* Should you like a quiff? **1876** F. K. ROBINSON *Gloss. Whitby* 149/2 *Quiff*, a whiff, a puff of smoke, an exhalation. 'I got a *quiff* on 't,' caught the scent. **1889** *Brighouse News* 14 Sept. 3/7 Hah nivver heeard a quift on't.

2. A puff or blast of wind.

1912 J. MASEFIELD *Dauber* v. 268 She came within two shakes of turning top, Or stripping all her shroud-screws, that first quiff.

quiff, *sb.*[2] *dial.* and *slang* (esp. naut.). [Origin unknown.] A clever trick or dodge; a hint.

1881 *Advertiser Notes & Queries* I. 77/2 *Quiff*. What is the origin of this word, so often used in the sentence, 'I'll teach thee a quiff', meaning something clever. It is often heard in Cheshire. **1890** BARRÈRE & LELAND *Dict. Slang* II. 164 *Quiff*..(Tailors), a word used in expressing an idea that a satisfactory result may be obtained by other than strictly recognised rules or principles. **1925** FRASER & GIBBONS *Soldier & Sailor Words* 223 *Quiff, a*, any specially ingenious smart, tricky, or novel or improvised way of doing anything. (Navy). In the Army used of any drill method peculiar to a battalion, and not usually done in others. Where the wording of the Drill Book is vague, units often read different meanings into the phraseology and invent their own 'Quiffs'. **1925** N. LUCAS *Autobiogr. of Crook* v. 72 I'll give you one quiff, right now, because I like your face and your nerve. Never touch the dope, it's hell—and worse than that. **1928** *Weekly Dispatch* 13 May 10/4 Suddenly a faint grey blur on the horizon in the expected direction. The seaman blinks his eyes—an old quiff which prevents many a false alarm—and then makes his report. **1933** J. MASEFIELD *Bird of Dawning* 107 It was young Mr. Abbott worked that quiff on you, sir. **1961** F. H. BURGESS *Dict. Sailing* 166 *Quiff*, a trick or artifice that makes a job easier.

quiff, *sb.*[3] Also quif. [Origin obscure: cf. QUIFF *sb.*[1]] A curl or lock of hair plastered down on the forehead, worn orig. by soldiers; more recently, a tuft of hair brushed upwards over the forehead. Also *attrib.*

1890 BARRÈRE & LELAND *Dict. Slang* II. 164 *Quiff* (military), the small curl on a soldier's temple just showing under his glengarry or forage cap. **1908** *Daily Chron.* 19 Mar. 4/4 He wears a quif of hair soaped down on his forehead in a slimy arc that nearly touches his eyebrows. **1919** H. G. JENKINS *John Dene of Toronto* XVI. 255 He's quite a nice youth, with black hair greased into what I think he would call a 'quiff'. **1925** H. G. WELLS *Christina Alberta's Father* II. iii. 224 He had..highly oiled and entirely subjugated sandy hair with an army 'quif' on the forehead. **1929** P. GIBBS *Hidden City* xlii. 206 Revealing his well-plastered hair curled into a quiff over his forehead. **1953** N. JACOB *Morning will Come* iv. 72 A man with a short clipped beard and his hair parted in what was called a 'militiaman's quiff'. **1965** M. BRADBURY *Stepping Westward* ii. 108 He could see the quiffs of his three cabin-mates as they moved round getting dressed. **1968** J. IRONSIDE *Fashion Alphabet* 197 *Quiff*, where the hair falls forward over the forehead before being brushed back. Made fashionable by Elvis Presley and Cliff Richard, so adapted for girls. **1969** H. E. BATES *Vanished World* iii. 38 There were..plenty of men who were great dandies in that generation [his grandfather's]— the moustache-waxers, the quiff-plasterers, [etc.]. **1976** *Times* 8 Mar. 6/3 Mr Reagan..is certainly the best turned out candidate. The 1950s quiff is immaculate.

quiff, *sb.*[4] *dial.* and *slang.* [Origin obscure: cf. QUIFF *v.*[1]] A young woman; *spec.* a prostitute, a 'tart'.

1923 G. WATSON *Roxburghshire Word-bk.* 244 *Queef*,..an engaging girl. **1931** *Amer. Speech* VI. 440 *Quiff*, a cheap prostitute. **1966** R. H. RIMMER *Harrad Experiment* 107 'This looks like a rich quiff,' King Arthur said. 'I think we'll look into her suitcase.' **1973** L. SNELLING *Heresy* I. i. 6 If only there was some other quiff about I might be able to deal with her indifference.

†quiff, *v.*[1] *Obs. coarse slang.* [Origin obscure.] *intr.* To copulate *with.* As **'quiffing** *vbl. sb.* in quots.

1719 T. DURFEY *Wit & Mirth* V. 243 By quiffing with Cullies three Pound she had got. **1796** GROSE *Dict. Vulgar T.* (rev. ed.), *Quiffing*, rogering.

quiff, *v.*[2] [f. QUIFF *sb.*[3]] *trans.* To arrange hair into a quiff. Also with *up.*

1940 R. LEHMANN in *Folios of New Writing* Spring 101 There was one [sailor] in particular, large, with a genial, knobby raw-beef face and a flaxen curl quiffed up in the forefront of his sailor cap. **1972** *Daily Tel.* 24 Jan. 11/5 Fringes can be quiffed up too. **1977** *West Briton* 25 Aug. 5/8 They turned up in three-quarter length jackets, drainpipe trousers and shoelace ties. Their hair was quiffed and oiled.

‖**qui-hy** (kwaɪhaɪ). Also 9 qui-hi, qui-hye; quoi hai, quai hai, etc.; koi hai. [Urdū (Hindī) *koī hai* 'is (*hai*) any one (*koī*) there?' a call used in India to summon a servant.] An Anglo-Indian, esp. one belonging to the Bengal Presidency.

1816 'QUIZ' (*title*), The Grand Master, or Adventures of Qui Hi in Hindostan. **1822** *Blackwood's Mag.* Aug. 133 So if you are neither a qu, hy [sic] nor a politician [etc.]. **1834** MEDWIN *Angler in Wales* I. 7 An apparition..not unusual at that refuge for Indians, a 'qui hi'. **1848** J. H. STOCQUELER *Oriental Interpreter* 195/1 *Qui-hye! qui-hi!* or *koee-hye!* 'Who is there?' or 'Who waits?' In domestic establishments in Bengal..a servant..is summoned to the presence by the foregoing exclamations. Hence, the Europeans who reside in Bengal are called *Qui-hyes*, to distinguish them from the residents of Bombay, Madras, or Ceylon. **1858** G. F. ATKINSON *Curry & Rice* Pref., The 'Qui Hye' of Bengal, the 'Mull' of Madras, and the 'Duck' of Bombay. **1864** TREVELYAN *Compet. Wallah* (1866) 170 Old Quihyes, with clogged livers and shattered nerves. **1939** 'E. BELL' *Memory be Good* i. 15, I must have been a bit of a nuisance to the old *quoi hais* who wanted to read quietly in their deck-chairs [on an India-bound Anchor Line boat]. **1960** M. MALGONKAR *Distant Drum* II. xxiii. 162 The very senior officers, right close to the top and steeped in the tradition of the old *koi-hais*. **1962** *Listener* 8 Nov. 776/1 There was dry knowing laughter among the *Koi Hais* in the shuttered clubs. **1965** B. SWEET-ESCOTT *Baker Street Irregular* viii. 240 Most of Gavin's principal assistants were drawn from British business houses operating in the Far East... There was an inevitable tendency for some of them to regard themselves as old qua'hais. **1967** *Listener* 11 May 610/1 It is..almost a generation since the last of the *koi hais* packed up..and the ghosts of Poona are now faint indeed. **1973** *Times* 19 Feb. (India Suppl.) p. ix/2 The *Koi Hais* and 'bottoms up, old boy', are confined, in Britain, to the personal column of *The Times*, and in India, to a brittle crust of individuals who seem to prefer the caricature to the real thing. **1977** *Times* 25 June 15/4 An Old Quai Hai, as the diminishing band of servants of the Raj still living in this country [*sc.* India] are affectionately known.

attrib. **1840** E. E. NAPIER *Scenes & Sports For. Lands* II. iv. 91, I sent to my Qui Hi friend an Arab pony. **1971** *Illustr. Weekly India* 4 Apr. 22/3 On the boat, coming out to rejoin Maurice, I had learnt quite a lot of Hindustani, unfortunately from a very charming British army officer who had an atrociously *koi hai* accent which I never quite managed to shed.

quik(e, quikk(e, etc., obs. ff. QUICK *a.* and *v.*

quil, obs. form of WHILE, WHICH.

†quilate. *Obs.* Also 6 quillat(e. [a. Sp. or Pg. *quilate*: cf. KILLAT.] = CARAT, q.v.

1577 FRAMPTON *Joyfull Newes* II. 55 They shall put the water lower, in Quillats. **1622** MABBE tr. *Aleman's Guzman d'Alf.* I. 27 Shee would rather die..then..faile one quilate in the touch and finenesse of her punctualitie. **1622** *Ibid.* II. 320 Hee teacheth vs the quilates and aloy of that gold.

quilc, obs. f. WHICH.

quile, var. COIL *sb.*[5] haycock, WHILE.

quiler, var. QUOILER.

†quilicom. *Obs. rare*$^{-1}$. [Of obscure formation.] App., an idle fancy, conceit, or quibble.

1644 QUARLES *Barnabas & B.* (1651) 43 It is enough for me to know, that God is a good man..and for all other Quilicoms, they shall never trouble my braines.

quilis, -ist, obs. forms of WHILES, WHILST.

quilk, obs. form of WHICH.

quill (kwɪl), *sb.*[1] Forms: 4–7 quil, 5 quyl, qwil, qvylle, 6 quyll, 6– quill. [Of obscure etym.: cf. LG. *quiele*, G. *kiel*, dial. *keil* (MHG. *kîl*), quill (of a feather).]

1. † **a.** A hollow stem or stalk, as that of a reed; a smooth piece of stem between two joints. *Obs.*

1412–20 LYDG. *Chron. Troy* I. vi, They take a quil..or a large can, And in the ende this stone they set. c **1440** *Promp. Parv.* 421/1 Qvylle, stalke, *calamus.* **1688** R. HOLME *Armoury* II. 84/2 Of a Tree..the Quill, is the Cane, or space between two such joints.

b. A piece of reed or other hollow stem on which yarn is wound; hence, a bobbin, spool, or pirn of any material.

14.. *Voc.* in Wr.-Wülcker 613/1 *Spola*, a Quyl, or a Spole. **1547** SALESBURY *Welsh Dict.*, *Prikied edafedd*, a quyll of yorne. **1610** GUILLIM *Heraldry* IV. vii. (1611) 204 Hee beareth Argent three Weauer's Shuttles Sable tipped and furnished with Quils of Yarne. **1635** *Roxb. Ball.* (1890) VII. 142 If I should a Weaver have,..Either wind silk, or fill his quills, 'tis either I can fit. **1771** MRS. DELANY *Lett.* Ser. II. I. 382 Neither by force or art can I get the present quill off the spindle. **1831** G. R. PORTER *Silk Manuf.* 221 The quantity of silk wound upon each of these quills is necessarily but small. **1886** ELWORTHY *W. Som. Word-bk.*, *Quill*, to wind the yarn from the hank or skein on to a bobbin, called a quill, for the weaver's shuttle.

c. A musical pipe, made of a hollow stem. In pl. *spec.* = PAN-PIPE (*U.S.*).

1567 TURBERV. *Epit.*, etc. 56 Assist mee with your skilfull Quilles and listen when I call. **1633** P. FLETCHER *Purple Isl.* XI. ii, Who now shall teach to change my oaten quill For trumpet 'larms. **1710** PHILIPS *Pastorals* iv. 28 Yet Colinet.. My fingers guided on the tuneful Quill. **1749** COLLINS *Superstit. Highlands* ii, There, must thou wake perforce thy Doric quill. **1878** BROWNING *Poets Croisic* xlviii, Joining the Delphic quill and Getic trump. **1883** J. C. HARRIS *Nights with Uncle Remus* xiii. 69 Uncle Remus declared that Brother Rabbit could perform upon the quills, an accomplishment to which none of the other animals could lay claim. **1886** *Century Mag.* Feb. 521/2 But to show how far the art of playing the 'quills' could be carried..see this 'quill tune'..from a gentleman who heard it in Alabama. **1952** B. ULANOV *Hist. Jazz in Amer.* (1958) iii. 20 The homemade instruments of the Negro are described in some detail, the tambo, bones, quills, fife, triangle. **1970** *Western Folklore* XXIX. 231 Blues singer Big Joe Williams..recalls ..a two-stringed cigar box guitar, a cane fife, a set of pan pipes or 'quills', and an upturned bucket, which served as a drum.

d. A piece of cinnamon or cinchona bark curled up in the form of a tube. Also, the extent to which such bark curls up in drying.

1797 *Encycl. Brit.* (ed. 3) V. 12/2 The bark which is rolled up into short thick quills..was esteemed the best. **1811** A. T. THOMSON *Lond. Disp.* (1818) 116 The secondary [characteristics]..are exterior coat, fracture, weight, thickness, and quill. **1852** MORFIT *Tanning & Currying* (1853) 86 It is known to commerce as cassia, and comes in single quills. **1880** C. R. MARKHAM *Peruv. Bark* 71 The bark which comes from Loxa is in the minutest quills.

e. The whistle of a steam locomotive. *U.S.*

1945 F. H. HUBBARD *Railroad Avenue* ii. 9 With its interpretive tone the ballast scorcher could make that quill say its prayers or scream like a banshee. **1961** *Listener* 24 Aug. 270/2 The fabled Casey Jones..was a 'quill artist' of note, who always carried with him his own quill (that is what they used to call a chime in the deep South).

f. An improvised straw or channel through which narcotics may be sniffed or smoked; the narcotic itself. *U.S.*

1935 A. J. POLLOCK *Underworld Speaks* 94/2 *Quill*, choicest grade opium. **1970** C. MAJOR *Dict. Afro-Amer. Slang* 95 *Quill*, folded matchbook cover in which a narcotic is held and smoked or sniffed. **1971** *Black Scholar* Sept. 36/1 He..rolled a ten dollar bill up into a quill and gave the coke and quill to Christine, who snorted up half of the line on the card.

2. † **a.** A small pipe or tube; *esp.* a small water-pipe. *Obs.*

c **1433** in Willis & Clark *Cambridge* (1886) II. 429 That thei mowe take oonly to their vse a qwil out of the pipe of the conduyt. **1579–80** NORTH *Plutarch* (1676) 297 He cut off the pipes and quils private men had made to convey Water into their Houses and Gardens. **1660** BOYLE *New Exp. Phys. Mech.* vi. 57 We took a slender Quill of Glass which happen'd to be at hand. **1712** J. JAMES tr. *Le Blond's Gardening* 197 The Bore of the Quill ought to be four Times less than the Bore..of the Conduit-Pipe.

† **b.** A tap or faucet. *Obs.*

1611 SPEED *Hist. Gt. Brit.* IX. xv. (1623) 811 With what quill these wines were vented from the setled Lees. **1611** COTGR., *Guille*, the quill, or faucet of a wine vessel. **1727** BOYER *Dict. Royal* II, The Quill (or Tap) of a Barrel.

c. The hollow steel mandrel of a seal-engraver's lathe, into which the engraving tools are fitted.

1875 KNIGHT *Dict. Mech.* 2081/2 The quill is of steel, about 2 inches long and ½ inch in diameter.

d. A hollow sleeve rotating in bearings which is used to transmit the drive from a motor to a concentrically-mounted axle.

1910 *Engineering* 12 Aug. 246/3 A gearless concentric motor for each driving-axle is mounted on a quill flexibly connected to the driving-wheels. **1930** *Ibid.* 6 June 722/1 Two new types of drive had been developed... The first consisted of a geared quill surrounding the driving axle and carrying two crankpins, the latter being connected by a flexible linkage to two crankpins on the driving wheels. **1968** D. W. & M. HINDE *Electr. Traction Systems & Equipment* ii. 32/2 A certain amount of experimental work has been carried out with the motor armature shaft of the hollow or quill pattern. **1975** BRAM & DOWNS *Manuf. Technol.* vii. 208 The spindle rotates in the quill to provide the rotary motion for cutting tools.

3. a. The tube or barrel of a feather, the part by which it is attached to the skin. Sometimes extended to include the shaft, or used loosely in the sense of 'feather' (*esp.* one of the strong wing- or tail-feathers) and *poet.* for 'wing'.

1555 EDEN *Decades* 163 Suche thinges as they make of fethers and quilles impaled with golde. **1575** TURBERV. *Faulconrie* 331 The seconde kinde of Teynte which fretteth the principals of a Hawke to the verie Quill. **1593** Q. ELIZABETH *Boeth.* IV. met. i. 76 Spedy quilles haue I That fur aboue the Pole do reache. a **1682** SIR T. BROWNE *Tracts* 83 A hard reed about the compass of a Goose or Swans quill. **1713** C'TESS WINCHELSEA *Misc. Poems* 216 No Quill, thence pull'd, was shap'd into a pen. **1774** GOLDSM. *Nat. Hist.* (1776) V. 102 One of the quills was two feet four inches long; and the barrel, or hollow part, was six inches and three quarters. **1834** MCMURTRIE *Cuvier's Anim. Kingd.* 114 The bony tail..has a range of large quills, which..assist in supporting the bird.

b. The feather of a large bird (usually a goose) formed into a pen by pointing and slitting the lower end of the barrel.

brother, knight of the quill: see BROTHER, KNIGHT. ***to draw the quill***: see DRAW.

1552 [see GOOSE-QUILL]. **1581** DERRICKE *Image Irel.* (1883) 19 Lorde guide my quiuryng quill. **1591** FLORIO *2nd Fruites* 97 A serpents tooth bites not so ill, As dooth a schollers angrie quill. **1663** BOYLE *Usef. Exp. Nat. Philos.* I. iv. 87 The quill that a philosopher writes with, being dipt in ink [etc.]. **1704** SWIFT *T. Tub* i. (1709) 32 A quill worn to the pith in the service of the State. **1771** SMOLLETT *Humph. Cl.* 10 June, Let. i, His house is open to all unfortunate brothers of the quill. **1871** B. TAYLOR *Faust* (1875) II. II. i. 84 The quill ..Wherewith his compact with the devil he signed.

c. A plectrum formed of the quill of a feather, used for plucking the strings of a musical instrument; in instruments of the harpsichord type, a piece of crow-quill, fixed on a jack and set in motion by the keys.

1552 HULOET, Quyll, with whiche a musician vseth to play to saue his fingers, or any lyke thinge, *plectrum.* **1647** WARD

Simp. Cobler 84 The world's a well strung fidle, mans tongue the quill. **1697** DRYDEN *Æneid* VI. 879 His flying fingers, and harmonious quill, Strike sev'n distinguish'd notes. **1776** BURNEY *Hist. Mus.* (1789) I. ix. 150 To produce a clear tone ..by the common means of quills or hammers.

d. The float of a fishing-line, made of a quill.

a **1639** SIR H. WOOTTON *On a Bank* 8 (Percy Soc.) VI. 17 There stood my friend, with patient skill Attending of his trembling quill. **1650** E. POWEL in Walton *Angler* (1875) 13 This Fisherman..sits by a brook, watching a quill. *a* **1678** MARVELL *Upon Appleton House* 649 But now away my Hooks, my Quills, And Angles, idle Utensils.

e. A toothpick made of a quill.

1784 COWPER *Task* II. 628 He picks clean teeth, and, busy as he seems With an old tavern quill, is hungry yet.

f. *Mining.* A blasting-fuse, consisting of a quill filled with powder (*Cent. Dict.* 1891).

g. Phr. ***the pure quill***: see PURE *a.* 8 d.

4. One of the hollow sharp spines forming part of the covering of a porcupine.

1602 SHAKS. *Ham.* I. v. 20 Make..each particular haire to stand an end, Like Quilles vpon the fretfull Porpentine. **1675** GREW *Disc. Tastes Plants* vi. §9 As the Quills in the Skin of a Porcupine. **1774** GOLDSM. *Nat. Hist.* (1776) IV. 108 All these quills..incline backwards, like the bristles of an hog. **1855** LONGF. *Hiaw.* IV. 41 Leggings, Richly wrought with quills and wampum.

†**5.** One of the cylindrical plaits or folds of a ruff (Nares); ? a quilled ruff. *Obs.*

a **1828** *The Gardener* xi. in Child *Ballads* IV. 213 The lily white to be your smock..And the jelly-flower to be your quill.

6. A quill-gnat (see 8 b).

1899 *Westm. Gaz.* 2 June 3/2 They prefer to kill their.. fish with smaller patterns—a red quill, or a Wickham's Fancy.

7. (In full ***quill-stroke***.) A particular stroke in the game of billiards.

1896 R. D. WALKER in W. Broadfoot *Billiards* 370 The so-called quill or feather stroke, which was tabooed years and years ago. **1901** *Q. Rev.* Apr. 483 What was known as the feather stroke or the 'quill' Mardon considered extremely serviceable.

8. *attrib.* and *Comb.* **a.** General combs., as (sense 1 b) ***quill-boy, -machine, -winder***; (sense 3 or 3 b) ***quill-barrel, -case, -cleaner, -dealer, -dresser, -employment, -end, -gun, -man, -merchant, -nib, -pen, -shaped*** adj., ***-timber, -vendor***; (sense 4) ***quill-darting, -like*** adjs.

1770 KUCKHAN in *Phil. Trans.* LX. 314 An incision just big enough to introduce the end of a *quill-barrel. **1812** SOUTHEY in *Q. Rev.* VIII. 351 What quantity of quill-barrel ought to be allowed for a clerk's daily consumption. **1727** BOYER *Dict. Royal* II, *Quill-Boy, *Epeulier*. **1795** J. WOODFORDE *Diary* 28 Mar. (1929) IV. 186 Mr. Thorne.. applied a Caustic to it just touching the part with it with a small kind of very fine hair pencil in a *Quill-Case. **1968** *Canadian Antiques Collector* Nov. 25/2 It would seem that the ink bottle was usually on the right of the inkstand, the pounce on the left, with the quill standing in the central bottle, which was the *quill cleaner. **1971** *Country Life* 1 July 23/1 This shelf carried writing equipment: inkpot, quill cleaner and sand box. **1670** S. CLARKE *4 Plant. Amer.* 32 *Quil-darting Porcupines and Rackcoones. *a* **1735** ARBUTHNOT & POPE *Mem. M. Scriblerus* xiv, The quill-darting Porcupine. **1885** *Census Instruct.*, *Quill Dresser, Dealer. **1764** *Antiq.* in *Ann. Reg.* 171/2 The most ancient grant of nobility in France to a *quill employment was to the King's secretaries. **1797** *Encycl. Brit.* (ed. 3) XVII. 692/2 The small *quill ends which touch the strings. **1839** URE *Dict. Arts* 454 Into this the quill end of the feather must be plunged. **1617** LANE *Contn. Sqr.'s T.* (1887) 37 What *quill-gon bownces dares shee not fall flye? **1856** KANE *Arct. Expl.* I. xxx. 408 The cheeks and lips are completely masked by the heavy *quill-like bristles. **1846** G. DODD *Textile Manuf. Gt. Brit.* VI. 182 Sail-making. The *quill machines..have a considerable number of quills arranged in a row, and made to rotate rapidly. **1709** STEELE *Tatler* No. 19 ¶2 Small *Quill-men and Transcribing Clerks. **1830** SCOTT *Ayrsh. Trag.* I. i, Quintin the quillman, Quintin the comptroller. **1813** *Examiner* 8 Feb. 86/1 J. Jones,..*quill merchant. **1853** SIMMONDS *Dict. Trade* 310 *Quill-nibs. **1875** KNIGHT *Dict. Mech.* 1848/2 Bramah probably first suggested quill-nibs. **1862** MRS. CARLYLE *Lett.* III. 109 A couple of good *quill-pens of your own making. **1852** MORFIT *Tanning & Currying* (1853) 86 Cinnamon of Ceylon..is found in commerce in thin *quill-shaped pieces. **1650** FULLER *Pisgah* III. v. 419 They conceive this third..Temple never had other then paper-wals, inke-mortar, and *quil-timber. **1833** J. HOLLAND *Manuf. Metal* II. 324 The *quill-venders have found their occupation to fall off. **1885** *Census Instruct.*, *Quill Winder.

b. Special combs.; **quill-back**, an American fish of the genus *Carpiodes*; the spearfish (*Cent. Dict.* 1891); **quill-bark**, cinchona bark in the form of quills; **quill-bit**, a boring-tool for a brace, having a hollow barrel (Simmonds *Dict. Trade* 1853); **quill-coverts**, the feathers which cover the base of the quill-feathers; **quill drive**, (the apparatus for) the transmission of power from a motor by means of a quill (sense 2 d); **quill-feather**, one of the stiff, comparatively large, feathers arranged in two rows along the edge of a bird's wing; also, one of the similar feathers of the tail; **quill-gnat**, a species of gnat, or an imitation of it used in angling; **quill-jack**, a jack fitted with a quill (see 3 c); **quill shaft** = sense 2 d above; **quill-stroke** (see 7); **quill-tail (coot)** *U.S.*, the spiny-tailed duck (*Cent. Dict.*); **quill-tool, -tube** (see quots.); **quill-turn, -wheel**, a wheel for winding spools; **quillwork**, a type of embroidery, using the quills of a porcupine, done by North American Indians; hence **quillworker**; **quill-wort**, an aquatic plant of the genus *Isoetes*, esp. *I. lacustris*, Merlin's grass, having quill-like leaves.

1785 *Gentl. Mag.* LV. 61 The red-bark is in much less esteem abroad than the *quill-bark. **1880** C. R. MARKHAM *Peruv. Bark* 72 The root-shoots had scarcely grown to a sufficient size to yield anything but quill bark. **1912** SHELDON & HAUSMANN *Electr. Traction* 306/1 (Index), *Quill drive. **1927** R. E. DICKINSON *Electr. Trains* vi. 111 There are several other forms of suspension; e.g. the quill drive in which the motor-armature is on a hollow 'quill' inside which is the axle of the wheel. **1970** LIGHTBAND & BICKNELL *Direct Current Traction Motor* iii. 47 The great majority of direct-current traction motors in service are either axle-suspended or fitted with some form of quill drive. **1766** PENNANT *Zool.* (1768) I. 156 The *quil feathers are dusky, barred with red. **1854** OWEN *Skel. & Teeth* in *Circ. Sc., Organ. Nat.* I. 223 The ulna is often impressed by the insertions of the great quill-feathers of the wing. **1867** F. FRANCIS *Bk. Angling* 189 The *Quill gnat..makes its appearance late in April. **1891** *Field* 7 Mar. 342/2 In a disused fly-book..reposes a small collection of quill gnats. **1875** KNIGHT *Dict. Mech.* 1691/1 The substitution of *quill-jacks for the hammer. **1934** *Jrnl. R. Aeronaut. Soc.* XXXVIII. 738 The turbine itself is mounted on a *quill shaft which telescopes the pinion shaft, the latter being attached to the quill shaft at the low pressure end of the turbine. **1949** *Ibid.* LIII. 143/1 As originally designed the gear was a compound epicyclic gear, the sun gear of which was driven by a quill shaft from the front end of the compressor. **1859** SALA *Gas-light & D.* ii. 23 Another is fluting columns with a thin brush called a '*quill tool'. **1867** SMYTH *Sailor's Word-bk.*, *Quill-tubes, those in use with port-fires for firing guns before the introduction of detonating and friction tubes. **1617** MINSHEU *Ductor*, A *Quil-turne, that turnes the quilles, or spoyling Wheele. **1886** ELWORTHY *W. Som. Word-bk.*, *Quill-turn*, the hand-wheel and spindle upon which the bobbin or quill is wound for the weaver's use. **1825** KNAPP & BALDW. *Newgate Cal.* III. 379/1 The block of the *quill-wheel. **1843** *Knickerbocker* XXII. 164 The Indians prepare it in bark, curiously ornamented with *quill work and beads. **1908** *Encycl. Relig. & Ethics* I. 827/2 Closely akin to beadwork is quillwork, especially among the Plains Indians (now done in its purity by few except the Eskimos, the tribes of the north-west coast, and the northern Athapascans). **1966** L. COHEN *Beautiful Losers* I. 97 With a bowed head she received the compliments which the quillwork on her deerskin gown evoked. **1976** *San Antonio* (Texas) *Express* 8 Dec. 5-B/2 *Quillworkers' tools have not changed. Today they still consist of some awls, strands of sinew and a knife. **1787** tr. *Linnæus' Fam. Plants* II. 832 *Quillwort. **1796** WITHERING *Brit. Plants* (ed. 3) III. 300 Quillwort. At the bottom of lakes. **1864** T. MOORE *Brit. Ferns* 103 The European Quillwort, or Merlin's Grass.

Hence **'quilldom**, the province of literature. **'quill-less** *a.*, not provided with quills.

1888 *Century Mag.* XXXVI. 611/1 [A porcupine's] quilless and vulnerable under side. **1891** I. ZANGWILL *Bachelors' Club* 69, I was recognised in quilldom as.. brilliant.

†**quill**, *sb.*[2] *Obs. rare.* Also 6 quille. [? a. OF. **quille* = F. *cueille* gathering, harvest, sb. f. *cueillir* (OF. *quillir*, etc.) to gather, CULL *v.*[1]]

1. = COIL *sb.*[3]

1588 *Book of Charges* July (Dom. St. Papers, P.R.O. CCXV. 88) A Quille of ropes wayeing xxv[li].

2. ***in the*** (or ***a***) ***quill***: In a body; in combination or concert. ***to jump in quill***, to act simultaneously or in harmony.

1593 SHAKS. *2 Hen. VI*, I. iii. 4 Let's stand close..and then wee may deliuer our Supplications in the Quill. **1687** *Hist. Sir J. Hawkwood* x. 18 Nor..did they less jump in quill; for just as he was debating this matter with himself, they came down to him, and besought him that he would dismiss them. *c* **1690** *Roxb. Ball.* II. 136 Thus those Females were all in a Quill, and following on their Pastime still.

quill (kwɪl), *v.* [f. QUILL *sb.*[1]]

1. *trans.* To form into small cylindrical plaits or folds resembling a quill; to goffer.

1712 STEELE *Spect.* No. 478 ¶12 It might have been as expensive in Queen Elisabeth's time only to wash and quill a ruff. **1758–65** GOLDSM. *Ess.* v. Wks. (Globe) 296/1 His cravat seemed quilled into a ruff. **1865** *Art Jrnl.* No. 321 91/2 'Quilled' her frills as usual. **1869** MRS. WHITNEY *We Girls* v. (1873) 82 Ribbon that she was quilling up.

2. To cut the quills off (a wing). *rare*[−1].

1710–11 SWIFT *Lett.* (1767) III. 115 As for Patrick's bird ..His wings have been quilled thrice, and are now up again.

3. a. To cover with, or as with, quills.

1783 WOLCOTT (P. Pindar) *Ode to R.A.'s* Wks. 1812 I. 64 Thou'rt like a hedgehog quill'd By the dire shafts of merciless Ridicule. **1814** SOUTHEY *Roderick* XVII, His whole body had been gored with wounds, And quill'd with spears.

b. To fit (a harpsichord) with quills.

1785 [see QUILLING *vbl. sb.*].

4. *intr.* To wind thread or yarn on a quill; to fill spools.

c **1640** [see QUILLING *vbl. sb.*]. **1825** KNAPP & BALDW. *Newgate Cal.* III. 377/1 Quilling, i.e. putting silk on a shuttle. **1851** S. JUDD *Margaret* ii. (1871) 5 The child Margaret sits..with a small wheel, winding spools, in our vernacular 'quilling'. **1886** [see QUILL *sb.*[1] 1 b].

5. *trans.* To write (with a quill), to pen.

1890 J. COGHILL *Poems, Songs, & Sonnets* 67 This screed whilk he's juist new dune quillin'. **1945** J. DICKSON in *Sc. Nat. Dict.* (1968) VII. 309/3 For each and a' the cheque's been quilled Wi' nae successors. **1977** *Even. Standard* 18 July 13/2 In 1677..Henry Vaughan quilled the immortal lines [etc.].

quill, obs. form of WHILE.

‖**quillai** (kɪ'laɪ). Also cullay. [Chilean (Araucanian) *quillai*, *quillay*, f. *quillcan* to wash.] The soap-bark tree of Chile (*Quillaia saponaria*): see next. Also *attrib.*, as ***quillai-bark, -tree***.

1866 *Treas. Bot.* 952/2 *Q. Saponaria*, the Quillai or Cullay of the Chilians, is a tree from fifty to sixty feet high.

‖**quillaia** (kwɪ'leɪjə). Also **quillaja**. [mod.L., f. prec.] **a.** A genus of S. American rosaceous trees, the bark of which possesses soap-like properties. **b.** The quillai-tree (see prec.) or its bark (also ***quillaia-bark***).

1848 in CRAIG. **1866** *Treas. Bot.* 952/2 Quillaja differs..in the ten stamens being in two instead of one row. **1886** *Pall Mall G.* 13 Sept. 10/2 Ginger-beer..the head or foam is produced either by white of egg or by quillaia bark.

Hence **quillaic** (kwɪ'leɪɪk) *a.* in ***quillaic acid***, an acid of quillaia-bark; **qui'llain**, an extract of quillaia-bark (*Syd. Soc. Lex.* 1897).

1891 W. MARTINDALE *Extra Pharmacop.* (ed. 6) 386 The bark..contains quillaic acid and sapotoxin.

quillat(e, variants of QUILATE, carat.

'quill-driver. [QUILL *sb.*[1] 3 b.] One who works with a quill or pen; a clerk or author. (Chiefly with contemptuous force.)

1760 *Voy. W. O. G. Vaughan* I. 129 As good as any of the Grub-street Quill-drivers cou'd write. **1846** THACKERAY *Crit. Rev.* Wks. 1886 XXIII. 96 The quill-driver of the present day, with his doubtful position and small gains. **1887** T. A. TROLLOPE *What I remember* II. xix. 379, I used ..to do all my writing standing; and I strongly recommend the practice to brother quill-drivers.

So **'quill-driving** *vbl. sb.* and *ppl. a.* (*pres. pple.*).

1719 D'URFEY *Pills* (1872) IV. 319 Quill-driving Prigs, Flocked to St. James's. **1756** TOLDERVY *Hist. 2 Orphans* I. 181 Richmond..went to quill-driving till ten. **1829** SCOTT *Jrnl.* 13 Jan., At such times I have wished myself a clerk, quill-driving for twopence per page. **1877** O. WILDE *Let.* Aug. (1962) 47, I had two jolly letters yesterday, one from Bouncer who is quill-driving or going to. **1880** BROWNING *Clive* 39 That greenhorn, that quill-driving clerk.

quille, variant of QUILL *sb.*[2]

quilled (kwɪld), *a.* and *ppl. a.* [f. QUILL *sb.*[1] and *v.* + -ED.]

1. Having the form of a quill or quills.

a. of cinchona bark: see QUILL *sb.*[1] 1 d.

1727–41 CHAMBERS *Cycl.* s.v. *Cortex*, The small, fine, quilled barks..are the most esteemed. **1786** T. SKEETES *(title)* Experiments and Observations on Quilled and Red Peruvian Bark. **1822–34** *Good's Stud. Med.* (ed. 4) I. 630 The lance-leaved, pale, or quilled bark. **1895** *Chambers' Encycl.* s.v. *Cinchona*, The quilled form of the thinner bark is acquired in drying.

b. of cloth: see QUILL *v.* 1. Also (of persons) ***quilled up***: wearing a quilled ruff.

1783 COLMAN *Prose Sev. Occas.* (1787) III. 237 (The Maidens of Queen Bess's reign) Quill'd up like Porcupines, they shot their darts. **1804** COLLINS *Scripscrap* 32 A close quill'd-up coif, their noddles just did fit. **1858–61** J. BROWN *Horæ Subs., Jacob. Fam.* (1882) 110 A close cap with a quilled border. **1886** *St. Stephen's Rev.* 13 Mar. 14/1 The border..was entirely composed of fully quilled black lace.

c. of glass: (see quot. 1854).

1800 HENRY *Epit. Chem.* (1808) 8 It is expedient to have the quilled part accurately ground to the neck of the bottle. **1854** J. SCOFFERN in *Orr's Circ. Sc., Chem.* 301 Every portion of the glass tube is of the kind known as quilled glass, not much larger..than the stem of a clay tobacco-pipe.

d. *Bot.* of florets: Tubular, instead of normally ligulate. Hence of flowers: Having tubular florets.

1825 *Greenhouse Comp.* I. 126 The varieties of the Chrysanthemum..are, the..Quilled white,.. Quilled yellow [etc.]. **1849** *Florist* 233 The quilled form is an instance of it. **1876** *Encycl. Brit.* IV. 129 In the Dahlia the florets are rendered quilled [by cultivation].

2. Having, or fitted with, a quill or quills.

a. of a receiver: Ending in a narrow tube.

1767 WOULFE in *Phil. Trans.* LVII. 411 The retort was set in a reverberatory furnace, and an adopter and quilled receiver luted to it. **1800** HENRY *Epit. Chem.* (1815) I. 7 To some receivers a pipe is added..which may enter partly into a bottle beneath. This vessel..is termed a quilled receiver.

b. of a suture: Having the thread secured to pieces of quill on each side of the wound.

1768 tr. *Heister's Surg.* I. I. vi. 74 A large crooked needle, for stitching large Wounds, with a double Thread, to make the quilled Suture.

c. of a jack in a harpsichord: Tipped with a piece of crow-quill.

1842 *Penny Cycl.* XXII. 349/1 The Spinet had but one string to each note, which was struck by a quilled jack.

d. *Her.* of a feather: Having a quill (of a specified tincture).

1864 in BOUTELL *Her. Hist. & Pop.* (ed. 3) 86.

†**'quiller**, *sb.*[1] *Obs. rare*[−1]. [f. QUILL *sb.*[1] 2 + -ER.] A bird not fully fledged. In quot. *fig.*

1591 LYLY *Endym.* v. ii, O sir, your chinne is but a quyller yet, you will be most majesticall when it is full fledge.

quiller ('kwɪlə(r)), *sb.*[2] [f. QUILL *v.* + -ER[1].] One who quills material, esp. into the form of a ruff.

1853 MRS. GASKELL *Ruth* II. vii. 172, I shall quill up a ruff for you. You know I am a famous quiller of net.

quillet ('kwɪlɪt), *sb.*[1] Also 6 **coylett, quyllett**, 6–7 **quillett**. [Of obscure origin.]

1. A small plot or narrow strip of land. Now only *local* or *Antiq.*

1533–4 *Act 25 Hen. VIII*, c. 13 §10 No maner person.. shall take in ferme..any quillettes of landes or pastures. **1538** LELAND *Itin.* IV. 82 §2 Impropriating Benefices unto them and giving them Coyletts of Land. *c* **1640** J. SMYTH *Lives Berkeleys* (1883) I. 151 Reducinge his scattered quillets of ground togeather into entire enclosures. **1774** T. WEST *Antiq. Furness* p. xlv, The abbots of Furness permitted the inhabitants to enclose quillets to their houses. **1824** HEBER *Jrnl.* 9 Aug., Each quillet..had its little stage and shed for the watchman. **1888** *Archæolog. Rev.* Mar. 17 The fields..in North Wales are still, in many cases, divided into..'quillets', that is to say, into open strips marked off from each other merely by boundary stones.

†**2.** A hamlet. *Obs. rare*[−1].

1597–8 *Act 39 Eliz.* c. 25 The sayde Hundred doth consiste onely of five small villages and thre small Quyllettes or Hamlettes.

quillet ('kwɪlɪt), *sb.*[2] Also 7 **quilit**, 7–9 **quillit**. [? Abbrev. of QUILLITY; cf. *quip, quippy* and *quiddit, quiddity*.] A verbal nicety or subtle distinction; a quirk, quibble.

1588 SHAKS. *L.L.L.* IV. iii. 288 Some tricks, some quillets, how to cheat the diuell. **1609** HOLLAND *Amm. Marcell.* xxx. iv. 386 Linking and entangling causes with insoluble quirkes and quilits. **1674** MARVELL *Gen. Councils* Wks. 1875 IV. 117 [Thou] didst ask them concerning a frivolous quillet of a question. **1708** *Brit. Apollo* No. 69. 3/2 Like Ignoramus, For Quillets most famous. **1818** SCOTT *Hrt. Midl.* x, Sharp-eyed as a lynx..in the nice sharp quillits of legal discussion. **1890** J. H. STIRLING *Gifford Lect.* viii. 153 The word is too unequivocal for any quillet to be hung upon it.

Hence †'**quillet** *v. intr.*, to quibble. *Obs.*

1653 HOLCROFT *Procopius* I. xx. 25 It is inconvenient for men in hazard for the main, to quillet about the rest.

quillet ('kwɪlɪt), *sb.*[3] [app. f. QUILL *sb.*[1] + -ET[1].] A small quill, or tube, etc., resembling this.

1872 C. M. YONGE *P's & Q's* ix. 95 Rolling up her papers into little quillets. **1876** BLACKMORE *Cripps* II. xiv. 211 Sprays, that..held in every downy quillet liquid, rather than solid, gem. **1879** *Daily Tel.* 29 May, As many codicils as there are paper quillets to a schoolboy's kite.

quilleted ('kwɪlɪtɪd), *a.* [f. QUILLET *sb.*[1] + -ED.] Divided into quillets.

1888 *Archæolog. Rev.* Mar. 21 The whole of this quilleted tract is grouped about the ancient site of the parish church. **1893** A. N. PALMER *Hist. Wrexham* IV. 102 The quilleted close nearest the town.

quillety, variant of QUILLITY.

quilling ('kwɪlɪŋ), *vbl. sb.* [f. QUILL *v.*]

1. The action of the vb. QUILL; *esp.* filling a quill with thread or yarn.

c **1640** J. SMYTH *Lives Berkeleys* (1883) I. 167 The charges in..quillinge, weavinge..and the like. **1780** A. YOUNG *Tour Irel.* I. 315 Quilling, warping, and winding; the quilling by children. **1785** JEFFERSON *Writ.* (1859) I. 440, I do not altogether despair of making something of your method of quilling [a harpsichord]. **1856** WHITTIER *Ranger* vii, Leave your quilling, leave your spinning.

2. A ribbon, strip of lace or other material gathered into small cylindrical folds resembling a row of quills.

1790 A. M. WOODFORDE *Let.* 3 Sept. in *Parson Woodforde Soc. Jrnl.* (1972) V. iii. 56 Lady Bacon was dress'd in a striped muslin Gown and Coat..and a quilling of Black Lace at the edge. **1813** LADY BURGHERSH *Lett.* (1893) 61 An immense quilling of lace or ribbon round the poke. **1829** *Glover's Hist. Derby* I. 247 Quillings or narrow edgings of lace. **1882** *Standard* 11 Sept. 6/6 Quillings and ruchings continue dull.

3. *U.S.* The art of blowing distinctive sounds on the whistle of a steam locomotive. Cf. QUILL *sb.*[1] 1 e.

1945 F. H. HUBBARD *Railroad Avenue* ii. 8 The engineman put on a whistle of his own with a tone that suited him and then practised a technique of blowing it that would be distinctive. This was called 'quilling' and was a highly developed art. **1947** *Richmond* (Va.) *News Leader* 13 May 13/5 But the art of '*quilling*', or 'making her talk', went out with electric and diesel locomotives, with their shrill horns and pneumatic whistles. **1966** *Listener* 14 Apr. 542/1 The variety of weird sounds he was able to extract from the six-tone engine whistle of his own property—an art known in railroad vernacular as 'quilling'.

†'**quillity**. *Obs. rare.* Also 7 **quillety**. [? An alteration of QUIDDITY 2.] A quillet, a quibble.

1573 G. HARVEY *Letter-bk.* (Camden) 135 In nise poyntes and quillityes none more præcise. **1616** ABP. MATTHEWS in *Usher's Lett.* (1686) 36 Our adversaries do not..intangle others..in any one Quillity, or Cavil, more than in that particular.

transf. **1653** URQUHART *Rabelais* I. xi. (1900) 56 One of them would call it..her staffe of love, her quillety. [**1678** MRS. BEHN *Sir P. Fancy* v. i, We shall soon rectifie the quiblets and quillities of his blood, if he observes our directions and diet.]

‖**quillon** (kijɔ̃). [Fr. (1611 in Cotgr.), app. f. *quille* ninepin: see KAYLES.] **1.** One or other of the two arms forming the cross-guard of a sword.

1884 R. F. BURTON *Book of Sword* 125 The quillons may be either straight—that is disposed at right angles—or curved. **1888** *Archæologia* LI. I. 513 The quillons, which start from a rectangular block through which the blade passes. **1894** R. S. FERGUSON *Charters of Carlisle* 292 His sword which has plain straight quillons, hangs at his left side. **1978** N. K. SANDARS *Sea Peoples* 158 The sword has a tapered blade, flanged tang and quillons.

2. *Comb.*, as **quillon-dagger** (see quot. 1960).

1950 *Proc. Prehist. Soc.* XVI. 24 The 'short iron sword' from Woodcuts, Dorset,..is actually a quillon-dagger of the 13th or 14th century A.D. **1960** H. HAYWARD *Antique Coll.* 232/1 *Quillon dagger*, a type of dagger with a simple cross-guard.

quilly ('kwɪlɪ), *a.* [f. QUILL *sb.*[1] + -Y[1].]

1. Resembling a quill; pertaining to quills.

1565 J. HALLE *Hist. Expost.* 90 The circulare or quilly hardnes of fistules. **1886** *Sat. Rev.* 19 June 844/2 Being men rather of horny hands than of quilly pens.

2. Consisting of or covered by quills.

1935 E. R. EDDISON *Mistress of Mistresses* xviii. 355 A porcupine's quilly rump. **1938** T. H. WHITE *Sword in Stone* xx. 294 Archimedes [*sc.* a hedgehog] got married, and brought up several handsome families of quilly youngsters.

quilome, quilpe, quils, obs. ff. WHILOME, WHELP, WHILES.

quilt (kwɪlt), *sb.*[1] Forms: α. 3 **cowlte**, *pl.* **quoiltene**, 4 **qwylte**, 4–5 **quilte**, 5 **qu-, qvylte, (coylte)**, 5–6 **quylt**, 5– **quilt**. β. *north.* 5 **qwhilte, wilt, wylt**, 5–6 **whilt(e**. γ. 5–6 **twilt, twylt**. [a. OF. *cuilte* (12th c.), *coilte* (later *coite, coete, couete,* mod. *couette*):—**colcta*, **culcta*:—L. *culcita* a stuffed sack, mattress, cushion, etc., whence also Sp. and Pg. *colcha*. Also OF. *coute* (later written *couste, coulte*):—**colta*, **culta*. The L. variant *culcitra* is represented by It. *coltrice*, OSp. *colcedra*, and its shortened form **cultra* by It. *coltre*, Genevan *coitre, couatre*, OF. *cotre*.]

1. a. An article of bed-furniture, consisting essentially of two large pieces of woven material having a layer of some soft substance (such as wool, flock, or down) placed between them; originally, an article of this kind for lying on (now *obs.*); in later use, a coverlet of similar make, *esp.* one in which the lining is kept in place by stitches or lines of stitching passing through the whole (the mediæval *quiltpoint* or *counterpoint*, q.v.); hence, any thick outer bed-covering, a counterpane.

c **1290** *S. Eng. Leg.* 188/125 Maketh a bed..Of quoiltene and of materasz. *a* **1300** *Body & Soul* in *Map's Poems* 334 Ȝwere beon..Thine cowltes and thi covertoures? *c* **1320** *Sir Beues* (MS. A.) 3996 Foure hondred beddes of selk echon, Quiltes of gold þar vpon. *c* **1450** *Merlin* 539 Thei lay down to slepe vpon the grasse for other quyltes ne pilowes hadde thei noon. **1454** *Durham Acc. Rolls* (Surtees) 148, ij qwhiltez ..j whilte. **1477** in *Ripon Ch. Acts* (Surtees) 179 Unum twylt. **1489** CAXTON *Faytes of A.* II. xxxvi. 154 Coyltes or matrases or sacques. **1544** PHAER *Regim. Lyfe* (1553) A viij b, A coife, made of double linnen clothe, and sowed like a cotten quilt. **1626** MIDDLETON *Women Beware Women* III. i. 27 Never a green silk quilt is there..To cast upon my bed? **1692** LOCKE *Educ.* 23 Let his Bed be hard, and rather Quilts than Feathers. **1725** DE FOE *Voy. round World* (1840) 237 The way of lodging upon quilts, and in beds..I need not describe. **1758** JOHNSON *Idler* No. 13 ⁋8 We have..three flourished quilts for every bed. **1852** MRS. SMYTHIES *Bride Elect* xxv, She threw herself on her knees by her bed side, and hid her face in the quilt.

b. *transf.* A thick covering (†or soft bed). †Also humorously applied to a fat person.

1596 SHAKS. *1 Hen. IV*, IV. ii. 54 How now blowne Jack? how now Quilt? **1693** EVELYN *De la Quint. Compl. Gard.* II. 92 You must lay a finger thick of Moss upon those Shelves, which may serve, as it were for a kind of Quilt. **1801** WOLCOTT (P. Pindar) *Tears & Smiles* Wks. 1812 V. 58 To hide their slumbering heads beneath Those downy quilts, their wings. **1863** BARING-GOULD *Iceland* 115 The dull quilt of cloud obscuring the sun.

c. The material of or for a quilt; quilting.

1766 W. GORDON *Gen. Counting-ho.* 427, 1 piece yard-wide quilt.

d. A layer of warm, thick material placed over the frames of a bee-hive to prevent draughts and contain the bees.

1870 *Amer. Bee Jrnl.* June 258/2 We finally had some little quilts (or whatever you choose to call them) made, and they answer admirably. **1873** *Brit. Bee Jrnl.* Nov. 100/1 His quilts, for so they are called by him, are laid close to the tops of the frames; they are not sufficiently heavy to crush the bees, even if laid directly on them, and they mould themselves to any possible condition. **1904** J. R. G. DIGGES *Irish Bee Guide* 50 Sheets and Quilts are required upon the frames or supers to preserve heat; to prevent draught; and to keep the bees from ascending into the roof... The quilts should be of felt, carpet, or other warm material. **1927** *Chambers's Jrnl.* XVII. 91/2 Place between the tops of the frames containing the combs and the bottom 'quilt' or cover two strips of wood an inch or two apart. **1952** H. MACE *Bee-Keeper's Handbk.* i. 15 Although many bee-keepers still use quilts, an increasing number have returned to an improved form of Crown board. **1962** A. S. C. DEANS *Bees & Beekeeping* x. 66 November. Carry out a periodic inspection of all hives to make sure that mice have not settled under the roofs and on top of the quilts if crown boards are not in use.

2. A piece of padded material used to defend the body, as a substitute or lining for armour.

1592 WYRLEY *Armorie, Capitall de Buz* 127 No hardned steele, no quilt, no warped meale Could make resist. **1625** K. LONG tr. *Barclay's Argenis* II. vii. 84 The inside of the Bracelet..being lined with a silken quilt, next to his arme. **1791** COWPER *Iliad* IV. 219 The hauberk, and the tough interior quilt..its force repress'd. **1870** BRYANT *Homer* I. IV. 111 The plated quilt which next his skin The hero wore.

†**3.** A pad smeared or stuffed with a medicinal substance, and applied to some part of the body.

1601 HOLLAND *Pliny* II. 339 The same rennet applied as a cataplasme vpon a quilt of wooll. **1626** BACON *Sylva* §56 The Quilts of Roses, Spices,..&c. are nothing so helpfull as to take a Cake of New bread. **1684** tr. *Bonet's Merc. Compit.* III. 68 Concerning Quilts and Caps..such as are made of very strong scented things do affect the Head.

4. The interior of a cricket ball (see quot. 1921).

1882 *Baily's Mag.* Nov. 391, I took up the inside of a [cricket] ball just newly finished..and laid it on a bench, and hammered it with a wooden mallet, which rebounded without making the slightest impression on the substance which is called 'the quilt'. **1921** *Dict. Occup. Terms* (1927) §688 *Quilter*.., wraps worsted thread, by hand, round a cork to make quilt, or core, of cricket ball.

5. *attrib.* and *Comb.* **a.** objective gen., as ***quilt-maker, -manufacturer***; †**b.** = quilted, as ***quilt-cap, -nightgown, -work***.

c **1515** *Cocke Lorell's B.* 9 Quylte makers, shermen, and armorers. **1623** T. GOAD *Dolef. Euen. Song* 7 Hee..put vpon his head a red quilt cap, hauing a linnen white one vnder it. **1676** *Lond. Gaz.* No. 1081/4 Also Six Holland Shifts..one Quilt Night Gown. **1709** *Ibid.* No. 4559/4 Michael Scott of Fetter-lane,..Quilt-maker.

quilt, *sb.*[2] *dial.* ? *Obs.* [Related to QUILT *v.*[2]] The swallowing-point of the throat.

a **1722** LISLE *Husb.* (1757) 347 (E.D.S.) He puts them down the calf's throat beyond the quilt.

quilt (kwɪlt), *v.*[1] Also 6 **quilte**, 6 (9 *dial.*) **twilt(e**. [f. QUILT *sb.*[1]]

1. a. *trans.* To pad, line, or cover (a thing) with some material, after the method employed in making a quilt, or in some similar way.

1555 J. PROCTOR *Hist. Wyat's Rebellion* 35 A priuie cote that he had quilted with angels. **1577** HARRISON *England* II. xvi. (1877) I. 279 Jackes quilted and couered ouer with leather. **1626** BACON *Sylva* §56 A Bagge quilted with Bran, is likewise very good. **1682** WHELER *Journ. Greece* I. 16 Course Ticking-Cloth, well quilted with Wool. **1712** ARBUTHNOT *John Bull* (1727) 82 Mayn't I quilt my rope? It galls my neck strangely. **1828** SCOTT *F.M. Perth* iv, His black velvet bonnet was lined with steel, quilted between the metal and his head. **1869** TROLLOPE *He knew*, etc. xxxvi. (1878) 205, I am quilting your cap.

transf. and *fig.* **1630** DEKKER *2nd Pt. Honest Wh.* Wks. 1873 II. 149 Ile so quilt your cap with old Iron, that your coxcombe shall ake the worse these seuen yeeres for 't. **1650** FULLER *Pisgah* v. xxi. 184 Long standing tents were quilted with timber, for their stronger support. *a* **1678** MARVELL *Upon Appleton House* 422 The plain Lyes quilted ore with bodies slain. **1808** SCOTT *Marm.* v. iii, His steel-jack, a swarthy vest, With iron quilted well. **1924** R. CAMPBELL *Flaming Terrapin* v. 75 The lilies..quilted the land with snow. **1930** —— *Adamastor* 79 The gorgeous Ram..whose great pelt is rolled To quilt a thousand hills with fire.

b. To cover with interlaced cord; *spec.* with a ball as object.

c **1611** CHAPMAN *Iliad* x. 230 His helmit fashion'd of a hide; the workman did bestow Much labour in it, quilting it with bowstrings. **1776** [see QUILTING *vbl. sb.* 1]. **1802** JAMES *Milit. Dict.* s.v. *Laboratory*, With a strong pack-thread the whole is quilted to keep the shot from moving. **1838** DICKENS *Old C. Shop* (C.D. ed.) 197 A short pipe quilted over with string. **1886** W. H. LONG *Dict. Isle of Wight Dial.* 53 *Quilt*,..to cover a ball with a network of twine.

2. a. To fasten together (two pieces or thicknesses of woven material) by stitches or lines of stitching, so as to hold in position a layer of some soft substance placed between them. Also, to sew (several thicknesses) together, usually by stitches arranged in some regular or decorative pattern.

1555 EDEN *Decades* 79 The mens [apparell] is double and quilted. **1599** A. M. tr. *Gabelhouer's Bk. Physicke* 96/1 Quilte the bagge least the herbes sacke the one vpon the other. **1615** MARKHAM *Eng. Housew.* II. i. (1668) 12 Quilt it in a manner of a course imbroydery. **1727** SWIFT *Gulliver* I. viii, By quilting thirteen fold of their strongest linnen together. **1794** W. FELTON *Carriages* (1801) II. 16 Quilting the lining [of a Coach] with small tufts. **1870** ROCK *Text. Fabr.* I. 14 Skirt of a Lady's Dress..quilted round the lower border with a scroll.

transf. **1593** NASHE *4 Lett. Confut.* 63 Thy Father..had neuer the art to twilt vp such a grim triangle of hair as that.

b. *intr.* To admit of being sewn as a quilt.

1622 MARKHAM *5 Decades War* x. 38 Buckram..is too stiffe and unplyable, by which means it will not quilt like the other.

c. *fig.* To compile (a literary work) by putting together scraps from various sources; to join *together* (extracts) as in a quilt.

In some cases the reference is to a patchwork quilt: cf. QUILTED 2.

1605 CAMDEN *Rem.* (1636) 14 It's quilted as it were out of shreds of divers Poets. **1649** MILTON *Eikon.* i. Wks. (1851) 344 Manuals, and Handmaids of Devotion,..clapt together and quilted out of Scripture phrases. **1891** *Rev. of Rev.* 510/2 Mrs. Ross quilts together numerous extracts.

d. To mark or seam with points or lines resembling the stitching in a quilt.

1760 GOLDSM. *Cit. W.* xlvi, A hateful phiz, quilted into a thousand seams by the hand of deformity. **1808** *Sketches of Character* (1813) I. 164 'Poor Amelia!' cried Mrs. Pytt, 'she's terribly quilted' [with smallpox].

3. To sew up (some object or material) between two pieces of stuff, as in making a quilt.

1562 BULLEYN *Bk. Simples* (1579) 65 The Nutmegge..is holsome in plasters for the stomacke, quilted in Leather and Sylke. **1634** T. JOHNSON *Parey's Chirurg.* XXVI. xxxix. (1678) 656 The powders..must be sewed up or quilted in a bag of Linnen or Taffaty. **1695** BLACKMORE *Pr. Arth.* IX. 361 Those that.. were found too light Quilt Lead into their Belts to give them weight. **1745** BYROM *Rem.* (1857) 410 He had three guineas quilted in the flap of his waistcoat. **1891** W. D. HAMILTON *Pref. St. Papers, Dom. Ser.* 1645–47 p. ix, These secret despatches.. were carried by a woman quilted up in a truss of linen.

fig. **1642** SIR E. DERING *Sp. on Relig.* 54 Some of the Protestant [Bishops] doe quilt a gentler sence into these words.

4. *intr.* To make a quilt or quilts. *U.S.*

1861 MRS. STOWE *Pearl Orr's Isl.* 21 Miss Roxy and Miss Ruey.. could upholster and quilt. **1882** C. D. WARNER *Washington Irving* iii. 32 A number of girls were quilting.

quilt (kwɪlt), *v.*² *dial.* Also quilty. [Of unknown origin: current in most S. and S.W. dialects.] *trans.* and *intr.* To swallow.

a **1658** CLEVELAND *Obsequies* 52 With as intens'd a Zeal, As Saints upon a fast Night quilt a Meal. **1864** BLACKMORE *Clara Vaughan* (1872) 49, I learned that to 'quilty' is the proper English for to 'swallow'. **1893** *Wiltsh. Gloss., Quilt,* to swallow.. used of swallowing in the natural way, while *glutch* is to swallow with difficulty.

quilt (kwɪlt), *v.*³ *dial.* and *U.S.* Also **twilt.** [Perh. a transf. use of QUILT *v.*¹, originating in the common phr. *to quilt one's jacket* (cf. QUILT *v.*¹ 1, quot. 1630 *fig.*).] **a.** *trans.* To beat, thrash, flog. *dial., U.S.,* and *Austral.*

1836 HALIBURTON *Clockm.* Ser. I. xix. (1837) 195 Your Cumberland critters,.. the more you quilt them, the more they wont go. **1852** R. S. SURTEES *Sponge's Sp. Tour* iii. 10 [He] quilted the old crocodile of a horse all the way. **1945** BAKER *Austral. Lang.* 120 One of the inevitable consequences.. has been the development of an extensive vocabulary of fighting terms. Here are some of the best ..*roll into, vacuum, quilt* and *stoush* a person. **1973** D. STUART *Morning Star Evening Star* 111 More than one bloke I've seen Joe quilt good and proper for trying to make a joke of it.

b. *Cricket.* To hit (the ball, bowling, etc.) about the field with great force, usu. for a sustained period of time.

1866 *Baily's Mag.* Feb. 92 Mr Lyttleton had an early taste of the lobs; these he quilted awfully. **1867** *J. Lillywhite's Cricketers' Compan.* 69 That punishing bats-man, Mr. Lucas, 'quilted' the Colts' bowling tremendously. **1897** K. S. RANJITSINHJI *Jubilee Bk. Cricket* ii. 56 A batsman may get bowled first ball, a bowler may be quilted all over the field without getting a wicket, but both can redeem themselves by good fielding.

quilted ('kwɪltɪd), *ppl. a.* [f. QUILT *v.*¹ + -ED¹.]

1. a. Of cloth, a garment, etc.: Padded with some soft substance held in position by being sewn as in a quilt; composed of several layers sewn together.

1533 ELYOT *Cast. Helthe* (1541) 79, I dyd throwe away my quylted cappe, and my other close bonettes. **1594** NASHE *Unfort. Trav.* 20 A round twilted Taylors cushion, for a target. **1682** *Lond. Gaz.* No. 1739/4 A quilted Petticoat of Lead-colour'd Sattin. **1768** STERNE *Sent. Journ.* (1778) II. 97 (*Temptation*), Lined with a little bit of white quilted sattin. **1865** LIVINGSTONE *Zambesi* xx. 405 A present of a quilted coverlet.

†**b.** ? Stuffed. *Obs. rare*⁻¹.

1668 PEPYS *Diary* 26 Sept., I had two quilted pigeons, very handsome and good meat.

2. Pieced or joined together, as in a quilt. †Also *transf.* of a person.

1617 COLLINS *Def. Bp. Ely* II. ix. 371 So cult you are, or so quilted in your tearmes. **1624** QUARLES *Div. Poems, Samson* (1717) 331 The quilted Quarters of the Earth's great Ball. **1877** LONGF. *Keramos* 11 O'er his features, like a mask, The quilted sunshine and leaf-shade Moved. **1885** *Pall Mall G.* 1 Jan. 2/1 That is a modest programme of quilted shreds and patches. **1925** E. SITWELL *Troy Park* 50 One candle spills out thick gold coins Where quilted dark with tree shade joins. **1968** *National Observer* (U.S.) 3 June 15/1 This quilted personality has regenerated a sorrowful team. **1971** A. SAMPSON *New Anat. Brit.* xxxi. 561 The English pattern of hedgerows and quilted landscape.

3. Covered with, or as with, a quilt or quilted garments. *quilted grape*: (see quot.).

1843 CARLYLE *Past & Pres.* I. ii, All manner of quilted trumpeters. **1845** —— *Cromwell* Introd. (1861) I. 78 Lord Clarendon.. speaks always in official language; a clothed, nay sometimes even quilted dialect. **1876** VOYLE & STEVENSON *Milit. Dict.* 321/1 *Quilted Grape,* the old pattern grape shot.. quilted with canvas, and tied so as to appear.. something like a bunch of grapes.

4. Tossed in a quilt.

1881 DUFFIELD *Don Quixote* I. 210 The cries which the hapless quilted one gave forth.

Hence †'**quiltedly** *adv. Obs. rare*⁻⁰.

1659 TORRIANO, *Borrevolménte,* stuffingly, gulchingly, quiltedly.

quilter ('kwɪltə(r)). [f. QUILT *v.*¹ + -ER¹.] A person who quilts; an apparatus for quilting.

1563 T. NEWBERY *Dives Pragmaticus* Prol. 67 in Huth *Fugitive Tracts* Ser. I, Al Broyderers, Taylers, Quylters and Limners. **1723** *Lond. Gaz.* No. 6191/4 Jane Clubb,.. Quilter. **1765** *Chron.* in *Ann. Reg.* 67/1 This.. will only be ..taking the bread from the poor quilters. **1879** *Daily Chron.* 30 Apr., Quilters.. wanted for infants' cloaks. **1895** *Montgomery Ward Catal.* Spring & Summer 264 Each.. Sewing Machine will be supplied.. with.. 1 braider, 1 binder, 1 quilter, 4 hemmers. **1908** *Sears, Roebuck Catal.* 41/2 We furnish with every [sewing] machine a complete set of accessories, consisting of one quilter, six bobbins.. and one instruction book. **1964** *McCall's Sewing* v. 74/2 The quilter has a short open foot and an adjustable or removable space guide that may be used to the right or left of the needle.

quilting ('kwɪltɪŋ), *vbl. sb.*¹ [f. QUILT *v.*¹]

1. The action of padding, sewing together, etc.

1611 FLORIO, *Abborracciaménto,* a stuffing, or quilting. **1776** FALCONER *Dict. Marine, Quilting,*.. the operation of weaving a sort of coat, or texture, formed of the strands of rope, about the outside of any vessel, to contain water.

2. a. Quilted material; quilted work. **b.** Material for making a quilt. **c.** A kind of cloth with a diagonal pattern suggestive of the appearance of an ordinary quilt.

c **1710** CELIA FIENNES *Diary* (1888) 236 The next room has such a bed but that is fine Indian quilting. **1718** LADY M. W. MONTAGU *Lett. to C'tess Mar* 10 Mar., Fine Indian quilting, embroidered with gold. *a* **1850** ROSSETTI *Dante & Circ.* I. (1874) 244 Quilting from Cortona warm and tough. **1867** SMYTH *Sailor's Word-bk., Quilting,* a kind of coating formed of sinnet, strands of rope, &c., outside any vessel containing water.

3. *dial.* and *N. Amer.* A quilting-party.

1768 in *Essex Inst. Hist. Coll.* (1879) XVI. 260 Quilting at my house. **1770** J. PARKER *Diary* 22 Feb. in *New-England Hist. & Geneal. Reg.* (1915) LXIX. 10 Naby went to Mr Wildes to Quilting. **1819** ANDERSON *Cumbld. Ball.* 108 Now, lasses: aw thrang at our quiltin. **1825** J. NEAL *Bro. Jonathan* I. 58 She returned however to the quilting and Peters.. to the study of Mr. Harwood. **1890** HOSMER *Anglo-Sax. Freed.* 279 Zekle squired Huldy.. to the singing-school or apple-paring, to quilting or sugaring off. **1913** *Atlantic Monthly* Dec. 826/2 Zobbie often met Pauline at the quiltings and other gatherings at the homes of non-partisans. **1939** L. M. MONTGOMERY *Anne of Ingleside* xxxii. 228 The Ladies' Aid is going to have their quilting at Ingleside. **1975** *Budget* (Sugarcreek, Ohio) 20 Mar. 15/6 Mrs. Eli Y. Byler had 2 quiltings last week and will have another one this week.

4. *attrib.* as ***quilting-needle, -seam***; **quilting-bee, -feast, -frolic, -party,** (chiefly *N. Amer.*) a gathering of women held for the purpose of making a quilt, and serving as an occasion for enjoyment; **quilting-cotton,** raw cotton prepared for stuffing quilts; **quilting day** *N. Amer.,* a day devoted to a quilting-party; **quilting frame,** a frame on which a counterpane is stretched during the process of quilting; **quilting match** *U.S.* = *quilting-party.*

1832 S. G. GOODRICH *System of Univ. Geogr.* vii. 167 The females also have similar meetings called 'quilting bees', when many assemble to work for one, in padding or *quilting* bed coverings or *comforters.* *a* **1859** W. IRVING *Knickerb.* VII. ii. (1900) 255 Now.. were instituted 'quilting bees',.. and other rural assemblages. **1921** *Daily Colonist* (Victoria, B.C.) 5 Oct. 6/5 It was decided to hold a quilting bee at the home of Mrs. Scott. **1976** 'D. HALLIDAY' *Dolly & Nanny Bird* x. 126 He looked.. like a lush from a quilting bee. **1939** L. M. MONTGOMERY *Anne of Ingleside* xxxii. 230 The quilting day was more like June than October. **1968** Quilting feast [see *quilting-party* below]. **1739** *Pennsylvania Gaz.* 15 Nov. 4/1 Just imported and to be sold by John Brientnall, in Chestnut-street Tenterhooks of several sizes, fit for Butchers, Skinners, Fullers, and for Quilting-Frames. **1854** M. J. HOLMES *Tempest & Sunshine* xx. 274 Said she, 'Mighty good opinion Mr. Quilting-frames has of me (alluding to Mr. Miller's height); glad I know his mind.' **1908** L. M. MONTGOMERY *Anne of Green Gables* xxi. 235 If Marilla.. was actuated by any motive save her avowed one of returning the quilting-frames. **1825** J. NEAL *Bro. Jonathan* I. 54 She gives what is there called a quilting frolick. **1813** M. L. WEEMS *Drunkard's Looking Glass* (ed. 2) 5 He does not trouble his head about asking the Fool where he has been, whether at a Funeral or a Wedding.. or a Quilting-match. **1881** A. B. ALCOTT *New Connecticut* 108 The Wolcott Dialect.. Quilting match. **1833** S. SMITH *Life & Writings J. Downing* 139 A few others.. wouldn't invite poor Mrs. No-tea to their husking and quilting parties. **1835** *Knickerbocker* VI. 180 It so happened that there was a great quilting-party invited to Tecumseh-Place, which assembled all the principal young people of the county. **1879** H. GEORGE *Progr. & Pov.* IV. ii. (1881) 214 Husking bees, and apple parings, and quilting parties. **1907** *St. Nicholas* (N.Y.) 1044/2 She has gone, with her grandmother whom she was visiting, to a quilting-party. **1948** *Minneapolis Star* 17 Sept. 31/1 Nobody sees Nellie home when the women of Halvarson Bowers post 187, VFW auxiliary, have a quilting party. **1968** J. ARNOLD *Shell Bk. Country Crafts* xxix. 310 It was.. possible for as many as six people.. to be sewing at the same time. Such gatherings became known as quilting parties or feasts.

quilting ('kwɪltɪŋ), *vbl. sb.*² [f. QUILT *v.*³] A flogging.

1829 P. EGAN *Boxiana* 2nd Ser. II. 242 The *quilting* Bob had previously received, rendered him in a great measure incapable of taking advantage of his adversary's distress. **1836** HALIBURTON *Clockm.* Ser. I. xix. (1837) 191, I'll give you such a quiltin as you never had. **1885** *Sat. Rev.* 20 June 809/2, I will give him such a quilting as will cause him bitterly to remember the consequences.

†'**quiltpoint.** *Obs. rare.* Also 4 **queldepoynte.** [a. OF. *cuilte pointe*:—L. *culcita puncta* pierced quilt: see QUILT and POINT, and cf. COUNTERPOINT *sb.*²] A counterpane.

13.. *Gaw. & Gr. Knt.* 877 Whyssynes vpon queldepoyntes, þat koynt wer boþe. **1386** *Will* in T. Madox *Formul. Anglic.* 428 Item lego.. i. lectum rubeum quiltpoint cum i. testro de eâdem settâ.

quilum, obs. form of WHILOM.

quim (kwɪm). *coarse slang.* [Origin obscure: perh. rel. to QUEME *a.* or *v.*; cf. QUAINT *sb.*]

1. The female external genital organs; the vagina.

An example of 1613 cited in Farmer & Henley's *Dict. Slang* has not been traced.

c **1735** *Harlot Un-mask'd* (Ballad), Tho' her Hands they are red, and her Bubbies are coarse, Her Quim, for all that, may be never the worse. **1796** GROSE *Dict. Vulgar Tongue* (rev. ed.), *Quim,* the private parts of a woman: perhaps from the Spanish *quemar,* to burn. **1846** *Swell's Night Guide* (rev. ed.) 57 Vell, rattle my dice box for a musty quim, but that Sall is a splitter! *c* **1863** 'PHILO CUNNUS' *Festival of Passions* II. 7 Gently pulling up my shift his hand touched my thigh, and instantly I sighed as it was laid on my quim. **1882** in 'P. Fraxi' *Catena Librorum Tacendorum* (1885) 267 My imagination fills the empty galligaskins with cosy bottoms and hirsute quims. **1922** JOYCE *Ulysses* 550 Were you brushing the cobwebs off a few quims? **1936** H. MILLER *Black Spring* 253 'Now,' he says, 'I'm going to pay you as usual,' and taking a bill out of his pocket he crumples it and then shoves it up her quim. **1951** N. COGHILL tr. *Chaucer's Cant. Tales* 113 He made a grab and caught her by the quim And said, 'O God, I love you!' **1966** P. WILLMOTT *Adolescent Boys* iii. 50, I got my hand on her tit and I thought well, that's all right. So I thought I'd try for her quim. **1974** H. R. F. KEATING *Underside* ii. 25 Is it worse to have it on me belly than to have it in me quim?

2. A woman; women collectively. *N. Amer. slang.*

1935 A. J. POLLOCK *Underworld Speaks* 94/2 *Quim,* a female. **1974** *Saturday Night* (Toronto) Jan. 35/2 The key to success in this contest is a flashy car; and if the car is both expensive and impressive 'you have to beat the quim off with a hockey stick'.

quim, late Sc. variant of QUEME *a.*

quin (kwɪn), *sb.*¹ [Of obscure etym.: cf. QUEEN 10a, and SQUIN.] A variety of pecten (*P. opercularis*).

1840 *Penny Cycl.* XVII. 358/1 Pectens.. make a rich and sapid dish, as might be expected from the name of them when so prepared, 'Quins'. **1851–6** WOODWARD *Mollusca* 257 The Scallop (*P. maximus*) and 'quin' (*P. opercularis*) are esteemed delicacies; the latter covers extensive banks, especially on the N. and W. of Ireland.

quin, *sb.*² [Shortened f. QUINTUPLET.] One of five children born at one birth; such a child in later life. Also *attrib.*

1935 *Dionne Quintuplets growing Up* (*caption*), My, what big girls the 'Quins' are getting to be. **1936** W. THORNTON *Country Doctor* 127 In Portugal in 1866, one quin baby attained an age of 50 days. **1937** R. MACAULAY *I would be Private* I. i. 16 Another little boy! Win's got quins! Can you beat it?... It took me and her poor father ten years to get five, and here's you and Win done it in a year. **1951** L. BARKER *Truth about Dionne Quins* i. 11 Dr. Dafoe.. held Press conferences.. in addition to his quin column, a newspaper feature, written by various ghost writers. *Ibid.* xxiii. 178 Emilie, the happy-go-lucky tomboyish quin,.. was not inclined to worry. **1968** *Economist* 15 June 49/1 Despite the title [of the book], Dr Scheinfeld is less good on supertwins, on triplets, quads and quins. **1976** *Liverpool Echo* 6 Dec. 1/1 The condition of Fiona, the fourth quin, has deteriorated and she has had difficulty in breathing since birth.

†**quin,** Sc. var. of *cun* CON *v.*¹ 3. *Obs.*

c **1560** *Sat. Toun Ladyes* 83 in *Maitland Poems* (1830) 30 My counseill I geve generallie To all women.. This lessoun for to quin perqueir.

quina ('kiːnə, 'kwaɪnə). [Sp. spelling of Quichua *kina* bark: see QUINQUINA.]

a. The bark of several species of *Cinchona* that yield quinine. **b.** *Chem.* = QUINIA, QUININE *sb.*

1830 LINDLEY *Nat. Syst. Bot.* 205 The febrifugal properties.. of Cincona are known to depend upon the presence of two alkalies, called cinchonia and Quina. **1841** *Penny Cycl.* XIX. 221/1 The salts of quina are in general distinguished by their strong taste of Cinchona, and by their pearly lustre.

attrib. **1880** C. R. MARKHAM *Peruv. Bark* 432 *note, Quinetum,*.. a collection of quina alkaloids.

quinacridone (kwɪ'nækrɪdəʊn). *Chem.* [f. QUIN(OLINE + ACRID(INE + -ONE.] Any of four synthetic isomeric compounds, $C_{20}H_{12}N_2O_2$, or their substituted derivatives, which have a heteroaromatic structure consisting of a string of five fused rings (three benzene and two 4-pyridone arranged alternately) and which include a class of usu. red or violet pigments. Also *attrib.* and in *Comb.*, as ***quinacridone red, violet,*** etc.

[**1896** *Jrnl. Chem. Soc.* LXX. I. 261 Hydroxy-quinacridone.] **1906** *Ibid.* XC. I. 459 Quinacridone,.. crystallises in yellow needles.. and dissolves in concentrated sulphuric acid to a yellow solution with a greenish-blue fluorescence. **1958** *Chem. Abstr.* LII. 10215 Dihydroquinacridones.. can be oxidized to quinacridones, pigments of good light fastness. **1963** *Jrnl. Oil & Colour Chemists' Assoc.* XLVI. 29 Quinacridone red yellowish, quinacridone red bluish and quinacridone violet which were issued by Du Pont in 1958,.. were the first of the quinacridones. Chemically, all three pigments are one and the same unsubstituted linear *trans*-quinacridone. **1969** R. MAYER *Dict. Art Terms & Techniques* 321/2 Besides this relatively yellowish or scarlet shade, bluish, magenta, and violet shades are also made from the same dyestuff (linear quinacridone) that yields quinacridone red. **1972** *Materials & Technol.* V. xi. 358 Quinacridone reds, maroons and violets are a comparatively recent introduction. These very expensive pigments have excellent light-fastness in full colours and in pastel shades. **1973** TILAK & AYYANGAR in R. M. Acheson *Acridines* (ed. 2) viii. 603 Diketoquinolinoacridines are designated by the trivial name 'quinacridones'. They can be linear *trans* (71) and *cis*.. or angular... The compound 71, which is usually referred to as quinacridone, and its derivatives are.. valuable as high quality pigments.

quinacrine (ˈkwɪnəkriːn). *Pharm.* [f. QUIN(INE + ACR(ID)INE.] A name for mepacrine (hydrochloride). Also *attrib.* and in *Comb.*, esp. with reference to the use of quinacrine or quinacrine mustard to stain chromosomes.

Formerly a proprietary term in the U.S.

1934 *Official Gaz.* (U.S. Patent Office) 23 Oct. 771/1 Société des Usines Chimiques Rhone-Poulenc, Paris... *Quinacrine*... Pharmaceutical product to be used in the treatment of malaria. Claims use since Feb. 20, 1933. **1934** *Chem. Abstr.* XXVIII. 3792 Quinacrine is chloro-2-diethylaminopentylamino-5-methoxy-7-acridine dihydrochloride. **1936** *Trade Marks Jrnl.* 4 Mar. 267/1 *Quinacrine*... Chemical substances used in medicine and pharmacy. Société des Usines Chimiques Rhone-Poulenc, ..Paris..; manufacturers. **1960** C. ACHEBE *No Longer at Ease* xi. 105 He said the poor man must be suffering from malaria, and the next day he bought him a tube of quinacrine. **1970** *Nature* 6 June 897/1 The quinacrine staining test shows up the number of *Y* chromosomes in a human interphase (non-dividing) cell. *Ibid.* 961/2 (*caption*) A group of quinacrine-stained spermatozoa showing fluorescence. **1971** *Oxford Times* 26 Mar. 2/5 Samples of fluid surrounding the foetus were treated with quinacrine dihydrochloride, an anti-malaria drug. The effect was to make the 'Y' chromosomes..take on a fluorescent glow when viewed through an ultra-violet microscope. **1975** FRASER & NORA *Genetics of Man* ii. 10/1 Quinacrine binds preferentially to certain regions of metaphase chromosomes to produce characteristic banding patterns ('Q-bands').

2. Special Comb.: **quinacrine mustard**, a nitrogen mustard derived from quinacrine and used as a fluorescent stain for chromosomes.

1957 R. JONES et al. in *Jrnl. Org. Chem.* XXII. 783/2 We here wish to report on the conversion..of 2-methoxy-6,9-dichloroacridine to 2-methoxy-6-chloro-9-[4-bis(β-chloroethyl)-amino-1-methylbutylamino]acridine (quinacrine mustard). **1970** [see MUSTARD *sb.* 3 b]. **1970** *Nature* 4 July 101/1 The trivial name 'quinacrine mustard' has been used..to describe at least two chemical species. *Ibid.* 101/2 May I..suggest that if authors wish to continue to use the expression 'quinacrine mustard' this be restricted to the true quinacrine derivative [*sc.* 2-methoxy - 6 - chloro - 9 - [4 - *bis*(2 - chloroethyl)amino - 1 - methyl-butylamino] acridine]. **1971** *New Scientist* 18 Mar. 606/1 When hamster and bean chromosomes were stained with..quinacrine mustard, and viewed with long wave-length ultraviolet light, the chromosomes fluoresced differently along their length.

† **qui'nade.** *Obs. rare*⁻¹. [a. OF. **quinade*, f. **quin*, *coin* COYN + -ADE.] A conserve of quinces.

c **1430** *Two Cookery-bks.* 27 Quynade. Take Quynces, & pare hem clene [etc.].

quinalbarbitone (ˌkwɪnælˈbɑːbɪtəʊn). *Pharm.* [f. L. *quin-que* five + AL(LYL + BARBITONE.] The compound 5-allyl-5-(1-methylbutyl)-barbituric acid, which is used as a sedative-hypnotic, esp. for pre-operative sedation, usu. in the form of its sodium salt, $C_{12}H_{17}N_2O_3Na$, a white powder often known by the proprietary name SECONAL. Cf. SECOBARBITAL.

1951 *Addendum to Brit. Pharmacopœia 1948* 46 Quinalbarbitone Sodium should be kept in a well-closed container. **1960** *Brit. Med. Jrnl.* 19 Mar. 872/2 For older children quinalbarbitone ('seconal') may be given. **1971** 'D. HALLIDAY' *Dolly & Doctor Bird* xiv. 199, I..stayed behind to administer a mild dose of quinalbarbitone. **1977** *Proc. R. Soc. Med.* LXX. 773/2 Barbiturates took pride of place as the commonest lethal drug, and quinalbarbitone sodium (Tuinal) headed the list.

quinamine (ˈkwɪnəmaɪn). *Chem.* [f. QUIN-A + AMINE.] A natural crystallizable alkaloid found in the bark of *Cinchona succirubra* by Dr. Hesse in 1872. Also called **quina'mina** and **qui'namia.**

Hence **qui'namicine, qui'namidine**, artificial isomeric alkaloids obtained from quinamine.

1875 WATTS *Dict. Chem.* 2 Suppl. 346 Quinamine crystallises in delicate, asbestiform anhydrous prisms. **1880** C. R. MARKHAM *Peruv. Bark* 430 He also detected, in all of them, the presence of a new alkaloid called quinamine. **1889** *Watt's Dict. Chem.* II. 180 Quinamicine..Formed by heating quinamine with dilute acids at 130°. *Ibid.*, Quinamidine..Formed by the action of acids upon quinamine.

quinancy, obs. form of QUINSY.

† **quina'quina.** *Obs. Med.* Also **china-china, kina-kina.** = QUINQUINA, q.v.

1707 *Phil. Trans.* XXV. 2446 The Skin or Bark of that Tree, which is called China China. **1727–41** CHAMBERS *Cycl.* s.v. *Quinquina*, The tree that produces the *quina-quina* is tall. **1797** *Encycl. Brit.* (ed. 3) V. 12/1 The bark..called..Kinakina or..Quinaquina.

† **qui'nare.** *Obs. rare*⁻¹. [ad. L. *quīnārius*: cf. DENARE.] = QUINARY B. 2 a.

1601 HOLLAND *Pliny* (1634) II. 463 That the siluer denier, which went beforetime for ten Asses, should be worth sixteene; the halfe Denier or Quinare, eight.

quinarian (kwɪˈnɛərɪən), *a.* and *sb.* [See QUINARY and -IAN.]

A. *adj.* Pertaining to, characterized by, a quinary division.

1845 CHAMBERS *Vestiges Nat. Hist. Creation, Classif. Organisms*, The quinarian part of the theory. **1865** *Athenæum* No. 1953. 460/2 The circular quinarian system of nature.

B. *sb.* One who advocates or adopts the quinary system in zoology.

1851–6 WOODWARD *Mollusca* 58 The Quinarians make out five molluscous classes by excluding the Tunicata. **1885** NEWTON in *Encycl. Brit.* XVIII. 16/1 Whose common sense refused to accept..the mystical jargon of the Quinarians.

† **qui'narity.** *Obs. rare*⁻¹. [f. QUINARY *a.* + -ITY.] ? The nature of a quintessence.

1471 RIPLEY *Comp. Alch.* x. xi. in Ashm. (1652) 181 Of thy Medcyn..trew graduacyon; Tyll hyt be brought to a quynaryte temperat.

quinarius (kwɪˈnɑːrɪəs). Pl. quinarii (-ɪiː). [L.: see QUINARY *a.* and *sb.*] = QUINARY *sb.* 2 a.

1601 P. HOLLAND tr. *Pliny's Nat. Hist.* II. XXXIII. iii. 463 At what time ordained it was, that the Denarius or Denier should go for tenne Asses or pounds of brasse money; the halfe Denier, Quinarius, should be currant for five; and the Sesterce reckoned worth two and a halfe. *a* **1666** EVELYN *Diary* an. 1645 (1955) II. 398 Now other observations I made in Rome are these amongst other, As to Coynes & Medails, that 10 Asses make the Roman Denarius, 5 the quinarius. **1708** KERSEY *Dict. Anglo-Britannicum*, *Quinarius*.., a Roman Coin of the Value of Five Asses, equal to 3 Pence 3 Farthings English. **1771** [see SESTERCE]. **1840** [see DENARIUS 1]. **1962** R. A. G. CARSON *Coins* 110 The new system comprised three denominations in silver—the denarius worth ten asses, the quinarius of five asses and the sestertius of two and a half.

quinary (ˈkwaɪnərɪ), *a.* and *sb.* [ad. L. *quīnāri-us*, f. *quīnī* distrib. to *quinque* five: cf. F. *quinaire.*]

A. *adj.* **1.** Pertaining to, characterized by, the number five; consisting of five (things or parts). ***quinary system***, a principle of division in zoology, introduced by Macleay in 1819, but now discarded.

1603 HOLLAND *Plutarch's Mor.* 1342 Plato hath reduced the number of five worldes to the five primitive figures of regular bodies, saying, that God in ordaining and describing the whole world used the Quinarie construction. **1682** H. MORE *Annot. Glanvil's Lux Orient* 180 Every number, suppose, Binary, Quinary, Ternary, is such a setled number and no other. **1788** T. TAYLOR *Proclus* I. xcvi. (Disser.), The quinary, and septenary numbers are especially attributed to the soul. **1826** KIRBY & SPENCE *Entomol. Let.* xlvii. IV. 399 Though Mr. MacLeay regards this quinary arrangement of natural objects as very general, it does not appear that he looks upon it as absolutely universal. **1837** WHEWELL *Hist. Induct. Sc.* (1857) I. 93 Designating the successive numbers ..by means of names, framed according to the decimal, quinary or vigenary scale. **1843** *Penny Cycl.* XXVII. 810/1 On the Continent the Quinary System has never found favour, and it has now few if any followers in this country.

2. Of or belonging to the fifth order or rank; fifth in a series.

1924 [see QUATERNARY *a.* 3]. **1953** *Amer. Econ. Rev.* May *Papers & Proceedings* 365 Logically and empirically, quinary industries as we shall define them are not once more a residual category. These industries comprise medical care, education, research, and recreation... The principle that guides this grouping is that they all have to do with the refinement and extension of human capacities. **1973** *New Society* 15 Nov. 386/3 The 'tertiary' sector contains at least three divisions—'tertiary' proper (pure service provision ..); 'quarternary' [*sic*] (information exchange and decision-making); and 'quinary' (research, development and education).

B. *sb.* **1.** A set of five; a compound consisting of five things. Now *rare*.

1651 J. F[REAKE] *Agrippa's Occ. Philos.* 391 Angels, who might rule the signs, triplicities, decans, quinaries, degrees and stars. **1678** CUDWORTH *Intellect. Syst.* I. iv. § 36. 625 The juniour Platonists..did..no longer acknowledge a Trinity, but either a quaternity, or a quinary, or more, of Divine Hypostases. **1889** *Pop. Sci. Monthly* XXXIV. 740 Quaternaries,..quinaries, sextaries, etc., according as the number of the constituent elements increases.

† **2. a.** A Roman silver coin, of the value of half a denarius. **b.** A small Roman medal. *Obs. rare.*

1727–41 CHAMBERS *Cycl.* s.v., The gold quinary is the half of a gold medal. *Ibid.*, The quinaries were of a finer and more finished coin than the other medals.

3. Something that belongs to the fifth order or rank.

1937, 1946 [see QUATERNARY *sb.* 2].

quinate (ˈkwɪn-, ˈkwaɪnət), *sb. Chem.* Also **kinate.** [f. QUIN-A + -ATE 1 c.] A salt of quinic acid.

1836 J. M. GULLY *Magendie's Formul.* 56 The quinia and cinchonia of the quinates are precipitated and collected; the quinate of lime remains in solution. **1841** *Penny Cycl.* XIX. 221/1 Kinate, or rather Superkinate of Quina, is the salt which exists naturally in the bark. **1857** MILLER *Elem. Chem.* III. 352 Adding a solution of subacetate of lead to a neutral kinate [**1862** quinate].

quinate (ˈkwaɪnət), *a. Bot.* [f. L. *quīnī* (see QUINARY), after *binate.*] Of a leaf: Composed of five leaflets; quinquefoliolate.

1806 GALPINE *Brit. Bot.* 233 L[eaf] pinnate, quinate & ternate. **1861** MISS PRATT *Flower. Pl.* I. 4 A quinate leaf consists of five leaflets, as in Marsh Cinquefoil.

Comb. **1825** *Greenhouse Comp.* II. 42 Quinate-leaved.

quinazoline (kwɪˈnæzəliːn). *Chem.* [ad. G. *chinazolin* (A. Weddige 1887, in *Jrnl. f. prakt. Chem.* XXXVI. 142), f. *chinolin* QUINOLINE with inserted *az-* (see AZO-).] A yellow, basic, crystalline solid, $C_8H_6N_2$, which has a bicyclic structure formed from fused benzene and pyrimidine rings; any substituted derivative of this.

1887 *Jrnl. Chem. Soc.* LII. II. 1044 Anhydroacetyl-orthamidobenzamide is regarded as a derivative of a hypothetical base, quinazoline,..isomeric with cinnoline and quinoxaline. **1903** *Ibid.* LXXXIV. I. 446 By oxidising this base with potassium ferricyanide, quinazoline..was at last successfully prepared; it..crystallises from light petroleum in glistening flakes resembling naphthalene, has a bitter, burning taste, and..is odourless at the ordinary temperature. **1926** H. G. RULE tr. *J. Schmidt's Text-bk. Org. Chem.* 700 Quinazolines..are strong bases, which are readily reduced to their dihydro-compounds. **1950** *Thorpe's Dict. Appl. Chem.* (ed. 4) X. 346/2 A variety of substituted quinazolines have been prepared recently as part of the search for effective antimalarials. **1968** L. A. PAQUETTE *Princ. Mod. Heterocyclic Chem.* ix. 326 Quinazoline 3-oxide ..shows the same reactivity as quinazoline toward nucleophilic reagents, but the addition products frequently eliminate water with the net effect that 4-substituted quinazoline results.

‖ **quincaillerie** (kɛ̃kajəri). [Fr.] **a.** (See quot. 1883). **b.** A hardware or ironmonger's shop. Also *attrib.*

1883 J. W. MOLLETT *Illustr. Dict. Art & Archæol.* 272 *Quincaillerie*, a general term for all kinds of metallurgical work in copper, brass, iron, etc. **1951** W. SANSOM *Face of Innocence* xi. 164 Past the paper shop... Past the dark leathern hole of the shoe-menders, past the sharp quincaillerie. **1966** P. V. PRICE *France: Food & Wine Guide* 83 Spend an hour in the hardware department of a good store or a *quincaillerie*. **1968** *Guardian* 3 May 9/1 Red-faced *quincaillerie* reps sit in the dark brown bar totting up their accounts over a Ricard.

quince (kwɪns). Forms: α. (4 wince), 5 **qwince, quence,** 5–6 **quynce, quynse,** (5 **qw-**), 7– **quince.** β. 6 **quench,** 6–7 **quinch.** [Prop. pl. of *quine, quyne* COYN (q.v.), used first as a collective and then as a sing.]

1. a. The hard, acid, yellowish, pear-shaped fruit of a small tree (*Pyrus Cydonia*) belonging to the pear-family, used in cookery as a preserve or to flavour dishes of other fruits; the seeds are also employed in medicine and the arts. Also, the tree bearing this fruit.

Several varieties are named after their localities, as the ***Barbary, Chinese, Japanese, Lyons, Portugal***, etc., ***quince***.

α. *c* **1325** [see *quince-tree* in 3]. *a* **1400** *Pistill Susan* (Phillips MS.) 102 Ouere her hedis gan hyng The qwince [*Vernon MS.* wince] and þe qwerdlyng. *c* **1420** *Pallad. on Husb.* II. 249 Ek graffe hem.. In whit thorn in hem silf, in quynce also. *c* **1430** *Two Cookery-bks.* 51 Take fayre raw Quynces, & pare hem with a knyf. **1533** ELYOT *Cast. Helthe* (1539) 20 b, Quynces be colde and drye. **1604** E. G[RIMSTONE] *D'Acosta's Hist. Indies* IV. xxxvii. 311 The quinces, poungranets, and other fruites there. **1731** FIELDING *Grub St. Opera* III. iii, An apple-pye with quinces—why quinces, when you know quinces are so dear? **1875** H. C. WOOD *Therap.* (1879) 579 The seeds of the quince contain a large quantity of mucilage.

β. **1501** HOLLYBUSH *Hom. Apoth.* 14 The karnels of quinches. *Ibid.* 27 b, As yelowe as a quenche. **1615** W. LAWSON *Country Housew. Gard.* (1626) 3 We meddle not with Apricocks nor Peaches, nor scarcely with Quinches.

b. Phr. ***to get on (a person's) quince***, to irritate or exasperate. *Austral. slang.*

1941 BAKER *Dict. Austral. Slang* 58 *Get on one's quince*, to annoy or aggravate deeply. **1948** *Sydney Morning Herald* 3 July 9/1 Aw, can it boss! You're gettin' on me quince. **1963** A. E. FARRELL *Vengeance* ii. 19 These bloody trees are getting on me quince! **1974** D. O'GRADY *Deschooling Kevin Carew* 95 In an unguarded moment, he told Bill Moynihan 'This joint is getting on my quince.'

2. Applied to other fruits or trees resembling the quince.

Bengal quince: see BENGAL 2. **native quince**, the Australian bitter-bark, emu-apple, or quinine-tree. **wild quince**, the Australian black ash (Morris *Austral Engl.*).

1876 HARLEY *Mat. Med.* (ed. 6) 696 Indian Bael or Bengal Quince is common in India. **1882** *Garden* 27 May 358/2 What Mr. Ross calls..'the wild Quince' is a handsome large flowered tree.

3. *attrib.* and *Comb.*, as ***quince-apple, -cake, -cheese, -cream, -gum, jam, jelly, -marmalade, -mucilage, -peach, -pear, -pie, pudding, -stock, -tinct, -tree, -wine, -wood; quince-coloured, -flavoured*** adjs.

1600 SURFLET *Countrie Farme* III. xxv. 480 The male..is called the *quince apple. **1664** EVELYN *Kal. Hort.* (1729) 216 Lording-Apple, Pear-Apple, Quince-Apple. **1616** SURFLET & MARKH. *Country Farm* III. l. 423 To make *Quince-cakes thin [etc.]. **1625** MASSINGER *New Way* II. ii, Put these few quince-cakes into your pocket. **1884** *Leisure Hour* June 375/1 Apple syrup, *quince cheese, candied fruits, were among the delicacies of the age. **1907** *Quince-coloured [see *low-sized* s.v. LOW *a.* 21]. **1723** J. NOTT *Cook's & Confectioner's Dict.* sig. Ee 4 (*heading*) To make *quince cream. **1974** J. GRIGSON *Eng. Food* 216 (*heading*) Gooseberry, pear, apple or quince cream. **1950** D. GASCOYNE *Vagrant* 55 And whilom most becomingly strums On his poignantly *Quince-flavoured lute! **1936** *Farmhouse Fare* 113 *Quince jam... Put the pulp through a sieve, or mash very finely with wooden spoon. **1978** R. V. JONES *Most Secret War* xxxvii. 330 My moment came when I asked him one day whether he had ever made quince jam. **1861** MRS. BEETON *Bk. Househ. Managem.* 795 **Quince jelly*. .. To every pint of juice allow 1 lb. of loaf sugar. **1971** M. MCCARTHY *Birds Amer.* 35 They stole quinces..and she put up quince jelly. **1636** P. MASSINGER *Great Duke of Florence* IV. ii. sig. H3, This *Quince-Marmalade Was of my owne making. **1663** BOYLE *Usef. Exp. Nat. Philos.* II. i, A kind of jelly, in colour and consistence not unlike quince marmalade. **1728** E. SMITH *Compleat Housewife* (ed. 2) 190 (*heading*) To make white Quince Marmalade. **1832** L. M. CHILD *Amer. Frugal Housewife* 118 Quince Marmalade.—To two pounds of quince put three quarters of a pound of nice sugar. **1963** A. L. SIMON *Guide Good Food & Wines* (rev. ed.) IV. 292/1 Its name in Portuguese—*Marmelo*—is the origin of the name *Marmalade*, which was at first applied to no other but *Quince Marmalade*. **1664** EVELYN *Kal. Hort.* (1729) 213 Roman Peach, Man Peach, *Quince Peach. **1552** HULOET, *Quince peare, *cidonium*. **1596** BARROUGH *Math. Physick* (ed. 3) 436 The iuice of quince peares and pomegranates. **1620** VENNER *Via Recta* vii. 111 Quince-Peares are of a very hard and wooddish substance. **1608** ARMIN *Nest Ninn.* (1842) 13 Hee tolde them it was a *quince pie. **1723** J. NOTT *Cook's & Confectioner's Dict.* sig. Ee 6 (*heading*) To make a *quince pudding. **1706** LONDON & WISE *Retir'd Gard'ner* I. II. xii. 160 You would graft a Pear-tree upon a *Quince-stock. **1845** BROWNING *Flight of Duchess* xi, Her cheek.. whitened thro' all its *quince-tinct. *c* **1325** *Gloss. W. de Bibbesw.* in Wright *Voc.* 163 A coyn-tre (*quince-tre), *coigner*. **1398** TREVISA *Barth. De P.R.* XVII. cxlviii. (MS. e Museo 16), Storax.. is a tre of Arabia liche to a quynce tree. *c* **1440** *Promp. Parv.* 420/1 Quencetree, *coctonus*. **1707** *Curios. in H. & Gard.* 197 Vines, Fig-trees, Quince-Trees. **1837** BROWNING *Strafford* v. ii, Under a quince-tree by a fishpond side. **1706** BAYNARD in Sir J. Floyer *Hot & Cold Bath.* II. 239 Hey! for Lime-water, *Quince-wine. **1885** LADY BRASSEY *The Trades* 201 The principal exports.. are logwood.. and *quince wood.

quince, variant of QUINCH *v.*

quincentenary (kwɪn'sɛntɪnərɪ, -sɛn'tiːnərɪ), *a.* and *sb.* [Irregularly f. L. *quin(que)* five + CENTENARY, q.v. Cf. QUINGENTENARY.] **a.** *adj.* Pertaining to, connected with, a five-hundredth year. **b.** *sb.* A five-hundredth anniversary, or the celebration of this.

1879 *Sat. Rev.* 4 Oct. 412 Duocentenaries, tercentenaries, and quin-centenaries have all lately taken place. **1884** *Manch. Exam.* 22 May 5/1 The quin-centenary celebration of the death of Wickliffe.

So **quincen'tennial**.

1884 J. L. WILSON *Life Wyclif̄fe* i. 12 To aid in giving to the revival, in this quincentennial year, somewhat of meaning and force.

† **'quincess.** *Obs. rare.* The 'female' quince.

1600 SURFLET *Countrie Farme* III. xxv. 480 The male is lesse, more writhled and wrinkled, dryer, of a sweeter smell and of a more golden colour than the quincesse.

† **quinch**, *sb.* *Obs. rare*$^{-1}$. [f. next.] ***not a quinch*** = 'not a start', not the least.

1571 R. EDWARDS *Damon & Pithias* in Dodsley (1780) I. 182, I wyll change my coppy, how be it I care not a quinche, I know the galde horse will soonest winche.

† **quinch**, *v.* *Obs.* Also 7 quince. [? var. of *quitch* QUETCH, by assoc. with *winch* WINCE; or related to *winch* as *quag* to *wag*.] *intr.* To move, stir, make a slight noise; to start, flinch.

1530 PALSGR. 677/1, I Quynche, I styrre, *je mouue*. *Ibid.*, I quynche, I make a noyse, *je tynte*. **1576** HOLINSHED *Chron.* (1586) III. 583/2 (He was) so manfull of mind as neuer seene to quinch at a wound. **1607** R. C[AREW] tr. *Estienne's World of Wonders* 49 None durst once quince or speake a word against him. **1627** F. E. *Edward II* (1680) 81 Which single durst not quinch, much less encounter.

quinch, quincie, obs. ff. QUINCE, QUINSY.

quincite ('kwɪnsaɪt). *Min.* Also -yte, -eite. [Named (*Quincyte*) by Berthier in 1825, from its locality, *Quincy* in France.] Hydrous silicate of magnesium and iron, found in limestone in carmine-red particles.

1835 SHEPARD *Min.* II. 151 Quincyte. Massive, composition granular. **1837** DANA *Min.* 257 Quincite of Berthier, is a red colored substance, which is disseminated through a limestone deposit.. in France.

quinck, variant of QUINK.

Quincke ('kvɪŋkə). *Med.* The name of Heinrich I. *Quincke* (1842–1922), German physician, used in the possessive and with *of* to designate an acute form of urticaria, described by him in 1882 (*Monatshefte für prakt. Dermatol.* I. 129–31).

1894 *Jrnl. Nerv. & Mental Dis.* XXI. 627 The recognition of angioneurotic œdema as a special form of disease is generally credited to Quincke who described it.. as acute circumscribed œdema, and it has by some authors been designated as Quincke's disease. **1933** E. A. COCKAYNE *Inherited Abnormalitites of Skin* xiv. 370 (*heading*) Angioneurotic oedema. Acute circumscribed oedema. Quincke's oedema. **1934** DORE & FRANKLIN *Dis. of Skin* iv. 46 Giant urticaria sometimes called acute circumscribed œdema of Quincke.., is characterized by the rapid development on the cutaneous or mucous surfaces of large patches of localized œdema, varying in size from a hazel-nut to an ordinary orange. **1974** WARIN & CHAMPION *Urticaria* i. 5 Bannister.. protested at the use of the term Quincke's disease.

† **quincunce**, obs. var. QUINCUNX *sb.*

1686 GOAD *Celest. Bodies* i. ii. 39 The new Aspects.. are not much to be regarded, unless perhaps the Quincunce and Semisextile. **1712** J. JAMES tr. *Le Blond's Gardening* 3 Quincunce in its original Signification, was a Plantation of Trees, like the Cinque Points of a Die repeated.

quincuncial (kwɪn'kʌnʃəl), *a.* Also 7 -untial. [ad. L. *quincunciāl-is*: see QUINCUNX *sb.* and cf. F. *quinconcial*.] Arranged in the form of a quincunx or quincunxes; involving or characterized by this arrangement.

1601 HOLLAND *Pliny* I. 512 For the order of setting trees.. wee ought to follow the vsuall maner of checquer row, called Quincuntiall. **1658** SIR T. BROWNE *Gard. Cyrus* i. 89 The Quincunciall, Lozenge or Net-work Plantations of the Ancients. **1705** T. GREENHILL in *Phil. Trans.* XXV. 2011 They were in number 22, some triangular, quadrangular, quincuncial, etc. **1870** GILLMORE tr. *Figuier's Reptiles & Birds* iii. 102 Scales on the back rounded, quincuncial, imbricate. **1885** *Macm. Mag.* Nov. 75/2 Cocoa-nut palms, planted in quincuncial fashion.

b. *Bot.* Of æstivation: Having five leaves so disposed that two are exterior and two interior, while the fifth is partly exterior and partly interior.

1830 LINDLEY *Nat. Syst. Bot.* 63 Petals equal in number to the segments of the calyx, with a quincuncial æstivation. **1887** *Jrnl. Educ.* Dec. 520 The quincuncial or tristichous arrangement [of leaves].

Hence **quin'cuncially** *adv.*, in a quincuncial manner; in the form of a quincunx.

1658 SIR T. BROWNE *Gard. Cyrus* 153 The legges alone do move Quincuncially by single angles. **1842** JOHNSTON in *Proc. Berw. Nat. Club* II. No. 10. 34 The tongue is very long.. with the spinous teeth arranged quincuncially in five series.

quincunx ('kwɪnkʌŋks), *sb.* [a. L. *quincunx* (*quincunc-em*) five-twelfths, f. *quinque* five + *uncia* a twelfth, OUNCE. Hence also F. *quinconce* (†*-cunce, -cunx*): cf. QUINCUNCE.]

1. *Astrol.* An aspect of planets in which these are at a distance of 5 signs or 150 degrees from each other. *rare.*

1647 LILLY *Chr. Astrol.* iii. 32 One Kepler, a learned man, hath added some new ones, as follow, viz.: A Quincunx Vc consisting of 150 degrees. **1686** GOAD *Celest. Bodies* II. iv. 199 Whereas if ♂ be about the Quincunx of Sol, a Sign distant from the Oppositional Line, he is in a chill posture.

2. An arrangement or disposition of five objects so placed that four occupy the corners, and the fifth the centre, of a square or other rectangle; a set of five things arranged in this manner.

This sense, which also existed in L., is app. due to the use of five dots or dashes, thus arranged, to denote five-twelfths of an as.

1658 SIR T. BROWNE *Gard. Cyrus* iii. 122 The single Quincunx of the Hyades upon the neck of Taurus. **1750** *Phil. Trans.* XLVII. 107 These cellules are.. disposed in the manner of a quincunx. **1785** MARTYN *Rousseau's Bot.* vi. (1794) 68 The florets.. are placed very thick.. in form of a quincunx, or the checks upon a chess-board. **1858** W. CLARK tr. *Van der Hoeven's Zool.* (1866) II. 64 Teeth crowded, arranged in a quincunx.

b. *spec.* as a basis of arrangement in planting trees, either in a single set of five or in combinations of this; a group of five trees so planted.

1664 EVELYN *Pomona* 15 [The orchard] may assume the Ornament of Cyrus, and flourish in the Quincunx. **1731** POPE *Ep. Burlington* 80 His Quincunx darkens, his Espaliers meet. **1782** V. KNOX *Ess.* clviii. (1819) III. 189 Plantations perfectly regular, and laid out in quincunxes. **1880** C. R. MARKHAM *Peruv. Bark* 20 For every tree felled, the bark collector should plant a quincunx.

c. *Bot.* Quincuncial æstivation.

1832 LINDLEY *Introd. Bot.* 411.

d. *attrib.* In the form, on the principle of, a quincunx, as ***quincunx arrangement, fashion, form, order.***

1707 WOODWARD *Acct. Roman Urns* (1713) §19 In some the squares were.. ranged in a quincunx order. **1759** tr. *Duhamel's Husb.* I. vii. (1762) 17 These heaps are disposed in a quincunx form. **1802** W. FORSYTH *Fruit Trees* xxiii. (1824) 345 If trees are planted in the quincunx order. **1883** *19th Cent.* Nov. 871 Where trees are planted in straight lines, on the quincunx arrangement, that is every four trees forming not a square but a diamond.

3. A cruciform reliquary having five equal parts, which can be closed up by folding the outer parts over the central one. (Fallows *Suppl. Dict.* 1886.)

Hence **quin'cunxial** *a.* = QUINCUNCIAL. *rare.*

1676 WORLIDGE *Cyder* (1691) 100 That the one may stand against the space last preceding in a quincunxial order. **1835** J. S. HENSLOW *Descr. Phys. Bot.* 130 The 'quincunxial' arrangement, where the appendages [on the stem] range in five ranks.

'quincunx, *v. rare.* [f. the sb.] *trans.* To put in quincunx arrangement.

1847 *Simmonds' Colonial Mag.* June 165 Some [say] that the bushes are not near enough together, and that I ought to quincunx them.

† **quin'cupedal**, *sb.* and *a.* *Obs. rare*$^{-0}$. [a. L. *quincupedal* var. *quinquepedal*: see QUINQUE- and PEDAL.] (See quots.)

1656 BLOUNT *Glossogr.*, *Quincupedal*, a measure or rule of five foot long. **1658** PHILLIPS, *Quincupedal*, having five feet, or of the measure of five feet.

† **'quincuple**, *a.* *Obs. rare*$^{-1}$. [ad. L. *quincuplex*, f. *quinque* five + *plic-* fold.] = QUINTUPLE.

1774 MITFORD *Ess. Harmony Lang.* 276 The sescuplex, which we should, by analogy, perhaps rather call quincuple time, as it would make a bar of five equal notes.

† **quin'curion.** *Obs. rare*$^{-1}$. [f. L. *quinque* five, after *decurion*.] A leader of five men. So † **quincury**, a body of five men. *Obs. rare*$^{-1}$.

1632 HOLLAND *Cyrupædia* 38 The best Decurions should be advanced to the rowme of Caporals: and the Quincurions likewise to the leading of Decuries. *Ibid.*, That the Quincury under his charge may be like unto himselfe.

quincy, obs. form of QUINSY.

'quindecad. *rare*$^{-1}$. [f. L. *quindec-im* after *decad*.] A set of fifteen.

1855 W. H. MILL *Applic. Panth. Princ.* (1861) 154 The first quindecad is accurate according to the Old Testament genealogies.

quindecagon (kwɪn'dɛkəgən). *Geom.* Also 7 -gone, 8 -deka-. [irreg. f. L. *quindecim*, after *decagon*, *dodecagon*: see -GON. So F. *quindécagone*.] A plane figure having fifteen angles.

1570 BILLINGSLEY *Euclid* IV. xvi. 124 In a circle geuen to describe a quindecagon or figure of fiftene angles. **1651** T. RUDD *Euclide* 179 In a given Circle to inscribe a Quindecagon. *a* **1696** SCARBURGH *Euclid* (1705) 174 The Quindecagon is the only derivative Polygon that Euclide thought necessary to be consider'd. **1778** *Learning at a Loss* II. 88 A Fellow.. who.. crams you with Pentagons, Hexagons and Quindekagons. **1886** NIXON *Euclid Revised* IV. xvi. 202 A regular.. quindecagon can be circumscribed about a circle.

quindecangle. *rare*$^{-1}$. [f. as prec. + *-angle* as in *quadrangle*, *quinquangle*, etc.] = prec.

1788 T. TAYLOR *Proclus* II. 69 Those who describe in a circle a quindecangle passing through the poles [etc.].

quindecasy'llabic, *a. rare.* [f. as prec., after *decasyllabic*.] Consisting of fifteen syllables.

1880 *Athenæum* 6 Nov. 602/1 A fair specimen of the quindecasyllabic verse in which many of the popular Byzantine songs are composed.

quindecemvir (kwɪndɪ'sɛmvə(r)). *Rom. Antiq.* [L., f. *quindecim* fifteen + *vir* man.] A member of a body, commission, etc., of fifteen men; *esp.* one of the priests who had charge of the Sibylline books.

1601 HOLLAND *Pliny* I. 177 One of the fifteen Quindecemvirs deputed for diuision of lands among the souldiers. **1781** GIBBON *Decl. & F.* xxviii. III. 70 Fifteen keepers of the Sybilline books (their name of Quindecemvirs was derived from their number).

Hence **quinde'cemvirate**, 'the body of fifteen priests and their office' (Craig 1848).

† **'quindecil(e**, *a.* *Astrol.* *Obs.* [ad. med. or mod.L. *quindecilis*, f. *quindecim* fifteen: cf. *quartile*, *quintile*, etc.] Of a planetary aspect: Containing one-fifteenth of a circle, or 24°.

1674 JEAKE *Arith.* (1696) 10 Astronomicks.. Aspects.. *Quindecilis*, Quindecil. **1686** GOAD *Celest. Bodies* I. ii. 39 Then the Vigintile, and Quindecile, and Decile, &c. will also look to be counted; while we hope.. we shall never be forced to own such Driblets of Aspects.

quindecim ('kwɪndɪsɪm), † **-disme.** Forms: 5 **quyndesyn, quindecym(e**, 5 **-dezim**, 6 **quyndezim, -dsime**, 6–7 **quindecim, -disme**, 7 **-desme, -dizm(e.** [Alteration of AF. *quinzisme* QUINZIÈME, after L. *quindecim* and Eng. *disme* DIME.]

† **1.** A tax or duty of a fifteenth part. *Obs.*

a **1467** GREGORY *Chron.* (Camden) 142 In the whyche Parlyment was grauntyd a quyndesyn and a dyme to the kynge. *c* **1470** HARDING *Chron.* CL. iii, For which yᵉ Church a disme Hym graunted, so dyd the Commons a quindecyme. **1512** *Act 4 Hen. VIII*, c. 8 The two quyndezims graunted.. in this present Parliament. **1611** SPEED *Hist. Gt. Brit.* IX. xxi. (1623) 1033 A taxe or quindecim, granted vnto you by Act of Parliament. **1647** N. BACON *Disc. Govt. Eng.* I. lxvi. (1739) 140 Some extraordinary exaction.. Quindizms, Benevolences, or other such like.

2. *Eccl. Antiq.* = QUINDENE.

1472–3 *Rolls Parlt.* VI. 44/2 The other Fyne was levied in the Quindezim of Seint John Baptist. **1511–2** *Act 3 Hen. VIII*, c. 19 Preamble, The monday nexte after the quindecim of Seynt John Baptyst. **1629** in Picton *L'pool Munic. Rec.* (1883) I. 126 Die Mercurii next after Quindecim Pasche next. **1802–12** BENTHAM *Ration. Judic. Evid.* (1827) IV. 296 Octaves, quindecims, and morrows of All Souls.

quindekagon, obs. form of QUINDECAGON.

† **quin'denary.** *Obs. rare.* [ad. late L. *quindēnāri-us*, f. *quindēnī*, distrib. to *quindecim* fifteen.] A set of fifteen.

1681 H. MORE *Exp. Dan.* 237 Both the Numbers consisting.. of Quindenaries or Indictions. *Ibid.* 238 This happened in the last Quindenarie of the first Number.

quindene ('kwɪndiːn). *Eccl. Antiq.* [ad. med.L. *quindēna*, f. L. *quindēnī*, distrib. of *quindecim* fifteen.] The fifteenth (in mod. reckoning, fourteenth) day after a church-festival. Cf. QUINZIÈME.

1494 FABYAN *Chron.* II. 460 He toke his leue of seynt Denys about yᵉ quyndene of Pasche. **1605** STOW *Ann.* 487 On the eleuenth of March, the Parliament was prorogued vnto the quinden of Pasch. **1610** HOLLAND *Camden's Brit.* II. *Ireland* 177 In the Quindene of Easter, news out of England arrived in Ireland. **1700** TYRRELL *Hist. Eng.* II. 873 The Quindene, or Fifteenth day after Easter was appointed.

1758 Bp. Lowth *Life William of Wykeham* 157 In the Parliament holden at Westminster, on the Quindene of St. Hilary last past. 1875 Stubbs *Const. Hist.* II. xiv. 65 *note*, The second parliament was held at Oxford in the quindene of Easter.

†**quinderkyn**, obs. form of KILDERKIN.
1439 *Litt. Red Bk. Bristol* (1900) II. 165, j quinderkyn [shall contain] xv. galons, litell more or litell lasse.

quindesme, -dezim: see QUINDECIM.

†**quin'diniac.** *Obs. rare*⁻¹. [ad. obs. F. *condoignac*, var. *codignac* CODINIAC.] = QUIDDANY.
a 1655 Sir T. Mayerne *Archimag. Anglo-Gall.* No. 148 (1658) 100 To make Quindiniackes of an Apricocke Colour.

quindisme, -izm(e, -dsime: see QUINDECIM.

†**quine**, *a. Bot. Obs. rare*⁻¹. [f. L. *quīnī* five by five.] Arranged in fives.
1760 [see QUATERN *a.*].

quine, obs. f. COIN *sb.* and *v.*; COYN, quince; QUOIN; WHINE, whence; also Sc. f. QUEAN.

Quinean ('kwaɪnɪən), *a.* [f. the name of the U.S. logician Willard Van Orman *Quine* (b. 1908) + -AN.] Of, pertaining to, or characteristic of Quine or his theories.
1966 S. Beer *Decision & Control* viii. 170 For the record, this is what the three propositions look like in formal Quinean terms. 1972 J. J. Katz *Semantic Theory* vi. 243 Quinean arguments do not apply to the analytic-synthetic distinction..such as the one developed here. 1978 C. Hookway in Hookway & Pettit *Action & Interpretation* 31 Once we recognise that relativism of this kind is at least an option in translation theory, we can see how to construct a Quinean response to the charge that the argument involves arbitrary discrimination in favour of the theory of nature and against translation theory.

quinella (kwɪ'nɛlə). orig. *U.S.* Also **quinela**, quiniela. [ad. Amer. Sp. *quiniela* in same sense.] A form of (usu. totalizator) betting in which the punter is required to select the first two place-getters in a race or other contest, not necessarily in the correct order.
1942 Berrey & Van den Bark *Amer. Thes. Slang* §734/6 *Quinella*, a separate betting pool in which the bettor attempts to pick the first and second horses of a given race. 1944 *Amer. Speech* XIX. 231/2 *Quinella*, Saturday and Sunday off together. The term is used in dog races where the better must pick two winners on a single ticket. 1949 *Rocky Mountain News* 2 July 9/1 A parlay or quiniela is a combination wager coupling the first two animals to finish in one race... Odds on parlay and quiniela are heavy and, when hit, the return is great. 1956 *Sun* (Baltimore) 6 Oct. (B. ed.) 9/1 A petition for quinella wagering at Maryland thoroughbred tracks. 1964 A. Wykes *Gambling* viii. 193 Or there is the 'quiniela', in which the bettor tries to pick the first and second horse of a race. 1967 *Punch* 5 July 20/2 Incomprehensible to the non-punter are notices which attest the management's determination to accept, or not to accept, Castellas, Couplets, Duellas, Eliminators, Jackpots, Plums, Quinellas and Yankees. 1969 *Australian* 7 June 36/1 She picked..first and second in two races—including the final quinella which paid $7.60. 1971 [see NAP *sb.*⁵ 2 c]. 1974 *Dominion* (Wellington, N.Z.) 11 July 9/9 Two relative outsiders..returned a quinella of $473.60 when they were first and second in the Seatoun Handicap. 1977 *Listener* 30 June 847/3 Didn't put number five in the Quinela.

quinesye, obs. form of QUINSY.

quinet, variant of QUINNET.

quinetum (kwɪ'ni:təm). *Med.* [f. QUINA + L. term. *-ētum* taken as = 'a collection': named by Dr. De Vrij.] A mixture of febrifugal alkaloids obtained from red cinchona bark, used in India as a cheap substitute for quinine; cinchona febrifuge.
1880 C. R. Markham *Peruv. Bark* 432 About 10,000 lbs. of cinchona febrifuge or quinetum can be annually issued. 1891 W. Martindale *Extra Pharmacop.* 326 Quinetum.. consists principally of cinchonidine.

†**quinfoil** (in 5 quynfole, qwynfoile), obs. var. CINQUEFOIL (q.v.).
1448 [see CINQUEFOIL 2]. 1486 *Bk. St. Albans, Her.* B iij b, Gerattyng haue .ix. bagges of cootarmuris... The fifthe baage is quynfolis.

†**quinge'narious**, *a. Obs. rare*⁻⁰. [ad. L. *quingēnāri-us*, f. *quingēnī*, distrib. of *quingentī* five hundred.] 'Of five hundred, or weighing five hundred pound' (Blount *Glossogr.* 1656).

quingenary (kwɪn'dʒi:nərɪ), *sb.* and *a.* [ad. L. *quingēnārius*, f. *quingēnī*, distrib. of *quingentī* five hundred.] **A.** *sb.* A five-hundredth anniversary or the celebration of this; = QUINCENTENARY *sb.*
1926 Fowler *Mod. Eng. Usage* 72/2 Quingē'nary, sescē'nary, septingē'nary. 1965 E. Gowers *Fowler's Mod. Eng. Usage* (ed. 2) 83/1 *Quatercentenary* and *quincentenary*.. are unlikely to be ousted by *quadringenary* and *quingenary*.
B. *adj.* Of an ancient Roman military unit: consisting of five hundred men.
1969 G. Webster *Roman Imperial Army* iii. 148 There are examples of the six barrack blocks of a quingenary fort at the Welsh fort of Gellygaer. *Ibid.* 149 According to Hyginus, the quingenary unit was composed of 380 infantry and 120 cavalry. 1976 E. N. Luttwak *Grand Strategy of Roman Empire* ii. 122 The new formations were clearly useful in bridging the gap between the legions and the quingenary *auxilia*.

quingentenary (kwɪn'dʒɛntɪnərɪ, -dʒɛn'ti:nərɪ), *a.* and *sb.* [f. L. *quingentī* five hundred, after *centenary*, etc.] = QUINCENTENARY.
1884 *Guardian* 758/1 The quingentenary festival is a commemoration of his death. 1892 *Sat. Rev.* 26 Nov. 609/2 The quingentenary of Winchester.

†**quingen'tumvirate.** *Obs. rare*⁻¹. [f. L. *quingentī* (see prec.), after *triumvirate*, etc.] A government consisting of five hundred men.
1642 Howell *True Informer* (1661) 29 England is turned hereby from a Monarchy to a Democracy, to a perpetual kind of Quingentumvirat.

quinhydrone (kwɪn'haɪdrəʊn). *Chem.* [f. QUIN-A + HYDRONE.] **1.** A brown crystalline substance with a green lustre formed by direct union of quinol and quinone. Also, any analogous molecular compound formed by a quinone and another aromatic compound.
1857 H. Watts tr. *Gmelin's Hand-bk. Chem.* XI. 164 Quinhydrone. [*Ibid.*, When kinhydrone is heated, it sublimes partly undecomposed, partly converted into yellow kinone.] 1865–72 [see HYDROQUINONE]. 1893 T. E. Thorpe *Dict. Applied Chem.* III. 340 Quinhydrones..the composition of which has not been established with certainty. 1908 *Chem. Abstr.* II. 104 In the reaction of α-hydronaphthoquinone with quinone, the former is oxidized to α-naphthoquinone and the latter reduced to hydroquinone, and these react to give the mixed quinhydrone. 1963 I. L. Finar *Org. Chem.* (ed. 4) I. xxvii. 670 Quinhydrones are a group of coloured substances formed from quinones and other aromatic compounds. Some are believed to be charge-transfer complexes. *Ibid.* 671 Another type of quinhydrone is the one formed between one molecule of benzoquinone and one molecule of quinol. .. It is believed that the rings of the two molecules are parallel and held together by hydrogen bonds at both ends.
2. *attrib.* **quinhydrone electrode**, an electrode (usu. of platinum) immersed in a test solution to which quinhydrone has been added, which has a potential dependent upon the pH of the solution and can thus be used to measure the pH potentiometrically.
1921 E. Biilmann in *Jrnl. Soc. Leather Trades' Chemists* V. 27 In the quinhydrone electrode two hydrions disappear, and at the same time a mol. of quinone is hydrogenated to one of hydroquinone. 1930 G. D. Elsdon in C. A. Mitchell *Recent Advances in Analytical Chem.* I. vii. 250 Certain difficulties are encountered in the determination of the *p*H value of milk. These have been overcome to a considerable extent..by the use of the quinhydrone electrode. 1969 H. Rossotti *Chem. Applications Potentiometry* viii. 92 The quinhydrone electrode can..be used as a probe for hydrogen ions in the acidity range $1 \leqslant pH \leqslant 8$.

quinia ('kwɪnɪə). *Chem.* (*Med.*) [mod.L., f. QUINA: see -IA¹.] = QUININE *sb.*
1826 Henry *Elem. Chem.* (ed. 9) II. 311 Quinia was discovered by Pelletier and Caventou in the yellow bark of the *Cinchona Cordifolia.* 1832 Babbage *Econ. Manuf.* xxxv, The greatest part of the sulphate of quinia now used in this country is imported from France. 1876 Gross *Dis. Bladder*, etc. 32 When hectic irritation is present, the best remedies are quinia and elixir of vitriol.

†**qui'nible**, *a.* and *sb. Obs. rare.* Also 5 quynnyble. [Irreg. f. L. *quin(que)* five, on anal. of *trible*, TREBLE, *quatrible*, QUATREBLE.]
A. *adj.* Fivefold; quintuple.
1398 Trevisa *Barth. De P.R.* v. xxxix. (MS. e Museo 16), In some treble and in some quatreble, in some quynyble.
B. *sb.* **1.** A fivefold amount.
14.. [see QUATREBLE B. 1].
2. A part in music, one octave above the treble. (Cf. QUATREBLE B. 2.)
c 1386 Chaucer *Miller's T.* 146 Ther to he song som tyme a loud quynyble. *a* 1550 *Image Ipocr.* III. 78 in *Skelton's Wks.* II. 434/1 They finger ther fidles And cry in quinibles.

quinic ('kwɪnɪk), **kinic** ('kɪnɪk), *a. Chem.* [f. QUIN-A + -IC. Cf. F. *quinique.*] Derived from quina. ***quinic acid***: a vegetable acid found chiefly in cinchona barks. ***quinic fever***: a fever which sometimes attacks persons engaged in the manufacture of quinine (*Syd. Soc. Lex.* 1897).
1814 Sir H. Davy *Agric. Chem.* 108 The Kinic Acid in a Salt afforded by Peruvian bark. 1857 Miller *Elem. Chem.* III. 352 Kinic [1862 quinic] acid crystallizes in colourless, oblique rhombic prisms, which have a strongly acid taste. 1860 *New Sydenham Soc. Year-bk.* (1861) 413 Quinic ether inhalations in ague. 1880 C. R. Markham *Peruv. Bark* 31 In 1803 another chemist found a crystalline substance in the bark which..was nothing more than the combination of lime with an acid which was named quinic acid.

quinicine ('kwɪnɪsaɪn). *Chem.* [f. prec. + -INE⁵.] An alkaloid, isomeric with quinine and quinidine, from which it is obtained by heating with glycerol.
1853 L. Pasteur in *Pharmac. Jrnl.* XIII. 374 When any salt of this base [quinine] is heated, a new alkaloid is formed, isomeric with it... To this new base I give the name of quinicine. 1857 Miller *Elem. Chem.* III. 275 Quinicine is freely soluble in alcohol.

qui'nidamine. *Chem.* [Cf. next and AMINE.] A natural alkaloid of red cinchona bark.
1890 J. S. Billings *National Med. Dict.* I. 281.

quinide ('kwɪnaɪd). *Chem.* [f. QUIN-A + -IDE.] A crystalline anhydride formed by heating quinic acid.
1894 *Watts' Dict. Chem.* IV. 374 Quinide is acid in reaction, and is reconverted by bases into quinic acid.

qui'nidia. *Chem.* [-IA¹.] = next.
1856 G. B. Wood *Therap. & Pharmacol.* I. 281 Sulphate of quinidia..is obtained for use from the barks which most abound in quinidia. 1876 Harley *Mat. Med.* (ed. 6) 559 Quinidia is isomeric with quinia.

quinidine ('kwɪnɪdaɪn). *Chem.* Also quino-. [f. QUIN-A + *-id-* + -INE⁵.] An alkaloid found in some cinchona barks along with quinine, with which it is isomeric.
1836 J. Gully *Mag.'s Formul.* 68 There remains another alkaloid substance, found in 1833, in the yellow cinchona, by MM. Henry and Delondre... This is quinodine. 1853 L. Pasteur in *Pharmac. Jrnl.* XIII. 375 When subjected to the action of a moderate heat,..quinidine, like quinine, is converted into quinicine. 1857 Miller *Elem. Chem.* III. 275. 1880 C. R. Markham *Peruv. Bark* 324 Their bark was found to produce the more efficacious alkaloid quinidine, instead of..chinchonine.

qui'niferous, *a. Chem.* [f. QUIN-A + -(I)FEROUS.] Yielding quinine.
1854 J. Scoffern in *Orr's Circ. Sc., Chem.* 94 A quiniferous solution. *Ibid.*, A quiniferous liquid.

qui'nimetry. *Chem.* [f. as prec. + -METRY.] The measuring of the amount of quinine and other alkaloids in cinchona bark (*Sid. Soc. Lex.* 1897).

‖**qui'nina.** *Chem.* (*Med.*) [mod.L.: see next.] = QUININE *sb.*
1838 T. Thomson *Chem. Org. Bodies* 230 Sulphate of quinina has come into general use as a medicine, and has almost superseded the administration of bark. 1839 Ure *Dict. Arts* 1054 Quinina and cinchonina are two vegetable alkalis, which exist in Peruvian bark.

quinine (kwɪ'ni:n, -'aɪn, *U.S.* 'kwaɪnaɪn), *sb.* Also **quinin.** [f. QUIN-A + -INE⁵.] An important alkaloid ($C_{20}H_{24}N_2O_2$) found in the bark of various species of cinchona and remigia, used largely in medicine as a febrifuge, tonic, and antiperiodic, chiefly in the form of the salt, sulphate of quinine, which is popularly termed quinine.
'Quinine was introduced into medical practice in 1820' (*Syd. Soc. Lex.* 1897).
1826 S. Cooper *First Lines Surg.* (ed. 5) 36 A still better preparation, now much used, is the sulphate of quinine. 1834 [see CINCHONINE]. 1859 Wilson & Geikie *Mem. E. Forbes* iv. 127 A few grains of silky white crystals of quinine were found sufficient to dispel the fever. 1887 *Athenæum* 19 Feb. 260/1 Antifebrin is stated to be more effective than quinine in reducing fever.
b. *attrib.* and *Comb.*, as ***quinine-bark***, ***-compound***, ***-purifier***, ***-test***; ***quinine-producing***, ***-yielding*** adjs.; **quinine-flower** *U.S.*, a plant of the gentian family, used locally as a febrifuge; **quinine-tree** *Austral.*, (*a*) the horse-radish tree; (*b*) the native quince.
1880 C. R. Markham *Peruv. Bark* 216 The richest of quinine yielding trees. *Ibid.* 249 The tree has peculiarities not possessed by any other quinine-producing species. 1884 Bower & Scott *De Bary's Phaner.* 537 Examples are afforded..by the Quinine barks. 1898 P. Manson *Trop. Diseases* vi. 105 The quinine test is generally conclusive in intermittents.
Hence **qui'ninic** *a.*, pertaining to, derived from, quinine. **qui'ninism** = QUINISM (Mayne *Expos. Lex.* 1858). **qui'ninize** *v.* = QUINIZE. **quini'nometry** = QUINIMETRY.

'**quinine**, *v.* [f. the sb.] *trans.* To dose or treat with quinine.
1927 *Bulletin* (Glasgow) 18 Mar. 5/5 The 'choleric colonel from India'..is apparently more sinned against than sinning. His medical man has 'quinined' him.

†**quinio**, variant of COYNYE, billeting, etc.
1577 Campion *Hist. Irel.* in *Holinshed* II. 74/2 The Irish impositions of Quinio and Liuery.

quinion ('kwɪnɪən), abbrev. of QUINTERNION.
1897 R. Garnett in *Bibliographica* III. 37 Their [*sc.* Sweynheym and Pannartz's] spacious premises are choked with unbound sheets in quinions. 1927 E. K. Rand in W. M. Lindsay *Palaeographia Latina* v. 53 A quinion may consist of a quaternion ruled four leaves at a time plus an extra leaf. 1959 P. H. Blair in *Moore Bede* 11/2 It contains thirteen gatherings of which II, IV, V and VIII–XII inclusive are regular quinions, that is, each of five bifolia making ten leaves after folding.

quiniretin (kwɪnɪ'rɛtɪn). *Chem.* [f. QUINI-A + RETIN.] A yellowish-brown precipitate formed in quinine solutions when exposed to sunlight, isomeric with quinine, but without alkaline reaction.
1881 Watts *Dict. Chem.* 3rd Suppl. 1736.

Quinisext ('kwɪnɪsɛkst), *a. Eccl. Hist.* [ad. med.L. *quinisexta* (tr. G. πενθέκτη sc. σύνοδος), f. *quīnī* five each, five + *sext-us* sixth.] ***Quinisext Council***: The Council in Trullo, convoked by Justinian II at Constantinople in 692, so called because it was regarded as supplementary to the fifth and sixth œcumenical councils.

1657 J. COSIN *Canon Script.* ix. 143 Towards the end of this Century the Sixt General Council was held at Constantinople, and the Quini-sext there in Trullo. **1890** T. W. ALLIES *Peter's Rock* 263 Justinian II summoned a Greek Council to meet in the same hall of his palace, called the Dome.. It called itself the Quinisext.

So **Quini'sextine** *a.*

1868 LIGHTFOOT *Philip.* 186 *note*, He quotes..Can. 10 of the Quinisextine Council..as favouring his view.

quinism ('kwaɪnɪzm). *Path.* [f. QUIN-A + -ISM.] The abnormal physical state (giddiness, deafness, loss of sight, etc.) produced by the excessive use of quinine; cinchonism.

1897 *Allbutt's Syst. Med.* II. 375 [Quinine] may be given ..until symptoms of quinism shew themselves.

qui'nizarin. *Chem.* [f. QUIN-A + (AL)IZARIN.] A crystalline compound obtained from quinol, isomeric with alizarin.

1881 WATTS *Dict. Chem.* 3rd Suppl. 1736.

quinize ('kwaɪnaɪz), *v.* [f. QUIN-A + -IZE.] To dose or impregnate with quinine; to cinchonize. Hence **'quinized** *ppl. a.*

1875 H. C. WOOD *Therap.* (1879) 64 In the quinized animal neither galvanization of a sensitive nerve nor asphyxia was able to produce vascular contraction.

quink. *Sc.* [? Imitative of the cry.]

†**1.** A variety of goose, variously identified with the grey-legged goose (*Anser ferus*) and the brent-goose (*Bernicla brenta*). *Obs.*

1551 *Sc. Acts Mary* c. 11 (1814) II. 484 The claik quink and rute the price of the peece xviijd. **1578** LESLEY *De Orig. Scot.* 37 Alia sex Anserum genera apud nos inueniuntur. *Margin.* Vulgus his uocibus eos distinguit: Quinck [etc.].

2. The golden-eyed duck.

1808 in JAM. **1866** EDMONSTON *Orkney Vocab.* 88.

†**quinkle,** *v.* *Sc. Obs. rare*[−1]. In 6 quynkill. [App. freq. f. **quink* = OE. *cwincan*: see QUENCH *v.*] Of a light: To go *out*.

1513 DOUGLAS *Æneis* XIII. Prol. 29 The lycht begouth to quynkill owt and faill.

quinnat ('kwɪnət). [N. Amer. Indian: Clatsop *ikwínna*, *ikwúnna*, Chinook *ikwána* (Gibbs *Chinook Vocab.* 1863).] The king-salmon; the Californian, Columbian, or Chinook salmon (*Oncorhynchus tschawytscha*) of the N. Pacific coast. Also *attrib.*

1829 SIR J. RICHARDSON *Fauna Bor. Amer.* 219 This salmon..is known by the name of quinnat. **1859** COOPER & SUCKLEY *Nat. Hist.* 322 The quinnat..is by far the most valuable salmon of any species found in Oregon. **1874** J. S. HITTELL *Resources Calif.* 407 The most important fish of California is the quinnat salmon. **1881** [see *king salmon* s.v. KING *sb.* 13 a]. **1907** T. W. LAMBERT *Fishing in Brit. Columbia* 73 They are the king salmon or quinnat, a large fish running up to over 80 lb. **1925** J. T. JENKINS *Fishes Brit. Isles* 216 The Chinook, Quinnat or King Salmon.., the most valuable species [of Pacific salmon], attaining a length of 4 to 5 feet. **1948** *Pacific Discovery* July 26/2 When referring to 'salmon' we will mean the true salmon (also known as quinnat, chinook or king) which invariably dies after spawning. **1962** L. WEDLICK *Fishing in Austral.* III. 87 It is unfortunate that the king or chinook salmon—known as quinnat salmon in Australia—has never been successfully acclimatized in our streams, for this fish is the largest of all the Pacific salmon.

quinnet ('kwɪnət). *dial.* Also 9 quinet. [a. OF. *quignet*, var. *coignet*, dim. of *coign*, *coin* a wedge, QUOIN.] A wedge (see quots.).

1684 J. BEAUMONT in *Phil. Trans.* XV. 854 A little Iron wedge 4 inches in length, by the Miners call'd a Quinnet. **1847–78** HALLIWELL, *Quinet*, a wedge. *Glouc.* [**1890** in *Glouc. Gloss.*] **1893** *Wiltsh. Gloss.*, *Quinnet*, a wedge, as the iron wedge fastening the ring of the scythe nibs in place, or the wooden wedge or cleat which secures the head of an axe or hammer.

quino, var. KENO

quinoa ('kiːnəʊə, kwɪ'nəʊə). Also quinua. [Sp. spelling of Peruvian (Quichuan) *kinua*, *kinoa*.] An annual plant (*Chenopodium Quinoa*, N.O. *Chenopodiaceæ*) found on the Pacific slopes of the Andes, cultivated in Chile and Peru for its edible farinaceous seeds. Also *attrib.*

1625 PURCHAS *Pilgrims* IV. VII. xiii. 1465 They had Maiz, Quinua, Pulse. **1760–72** tr. *Juan & Ulloa's Voy.* (ed. 3) I. 289 This useful species of grain, here called *quinoa*, resembles a lentil in shape, but much less, and very white. **1880** C. R. MARKHAM *Peruv. Bark* 484 The earliest mention of the quinua grain of Peru occurs in the 'Cronica' of Pedro de Cieza de Leon. *Ibid.* 485 The Indians also make a beverage of the quinua. **1886** A. H. CHURCH *Food Grains Ind.* 110 Quinoa seeds are extremely small.

quinodine, obs. form of QUINIDINE.

'quinogen. *Chem.* [f. QUIN-A + -O- + -GEN.] 'A hypothetical radical of the alkaloids of cinchona' (Webster *Suppl.* 1880).

quinoid ('kwɪnɔɪd), *a.* and *sb.* *Chem.* [f. QUIN(ONE + -OID.]

A. *adj.* = QUINONOID *a.* **B.** *sb.* A quinonoid compound.

1900 E. F. SMITH tr. *V. von Richter's Org. Chem.* (ed. 3) II. 364 The colored alkali salts are quinoïd derivatives of phenolphthaleïn. **1907** *Chem. Abstr.* I. 300 (*heading*) Oxidation of benzidine. (VIII Communication on quinoids.) **1908** *Ibid.* II. 827 The quinoid theory of colour. **1938** G. H. RICHTER *Textbk. Org. Chem.* xxx. 627 The *ortho* and *para* quinoid structures show strong chromophoric properties. **1949** ENGLISH & CASSIDY *Princ. Org. Chem.* xx. 396 It is thought that some metabolic processes involve a reduction-oxidation system involving quinoid and hydroquinoid molecules. **1961** B. J. STOKES *Org. Chem.* xxiv. 437 Addition of alkali to phenolphthalein causes a change in structure and a molecule containing a quinoid ring is made. **1975** LEWIS & PETERS *Facts & Theories Aromaticity* v. 76 The quinones and quinoids generally are usually thought to be non-aromatic yet they apparently contain the magic 6π-electrons in a ring, an electron arrangement which is often regarded as characteristic of aromaticity.

Hence **qui'noidal** *a.*

1907 *Chem. Abstr.* I. 302 The presence of methylene destroys the ability of the two phenyl groups to assume the quinoidal state. **1975** *Nature* 20 Feb. 625/1 Its infrared spectrum in $CHCl_3$ further substantiates a quinoidal structure, showing a strong carbonyl absorption at 1,654 cm^{-1} and an olefinic absorption at 1,584 cm^{-1}.

quinoidine (kwɪ'nɔɪdaɪn). *Chem.* Also -ina. [f. QUIN-A + -OID + -INE[5].] A brownish-black, resinous substance, consisting of amorphous alkaloids, obtained as a by-product in preparing salts of quinia. **b.** *animal quinoidine*, an alkaloid substance resembling quinine found in animal tissues.

1845 *Penny Cycl.* Suppl. I. 350/1 *Quinoidina*, the name given by Sertuerner to a third alkali, contained in yellow and red bark. **1853** L. PASTEUR in *Pharmac. Jrnl.* XIII. 375 *Quinoidine*..is always a product of transformation of the cinchona alkalies. **1857** MILLER *Elem. Chem.* III. 273. **1867** *Proc. Royal Soc.* XV. 92 This fluorescent substance..has a very close optical and chemical resemblance to quinine..we have therefore called it 'animal quinoidine'.

quinoil: see QUINOYL.

quinol ('kwɪnɒl). *Chem.* [f. QUIN-A + -OL.] = HYDROQUINONE. Also *attrib.*

1879 *Jrnl. Chem. Soc.* XXXVI. 464 (*heading*) Derivatives of quinol (hydroquinone). **1881** WATTS *Dict. Chem.* 3rd Suppl. 1742. **1886** ROSCOE & SCHORLEMMER *Treat. Chem.* III. III. §995 Quinol is.. found in the distillation products of the salts of succinic acid. **1889** *Anthony's Photogr. Bull.* II. 365 Quinol ammonia, quinol soda, and quinol potash. **1964** [see CATECHOL]. **1976** *Nature* 17 June 621/3 The central biological roles of quinones, quinols and chromanols had become as acceptable as they were surprising.

Hence **qui'nolic** *a.*, derived from quinol; **'quinolene**, a hydrocarbon obtained from quinol.

1881 WATTS *Dict. Chem.* 3rd Suppl. 1742 Quinolic Ether. **1894** *Ibid.* IV. 379 Quinolic acid. **1896** *Naturalist* 91 The.. quinolene series of hydrocarbons.

quinoline ('kwɪnəlaɪn). *Chem.* Also -olein(e. [f. as prec. + -INE[5].] = CHINOLINE.

1845 W. GREGORY *Outl. Org. Chem.* 481 Quinoline..is formed artificially, by distilling quinine, cinchonine, or strychnine, along with caustic potash. **1845** *Penny Cycl.* Suppl. I. 350/1 The taste of quinolein is very acrid and bitter. **1881** *Athenæum* 12 Mar. 370/2 Heating quinoline and benzoyl chloride in sealed tubes.

quinologist (kwɪ'nɒlədʒɪst). [f. QUIN-A + -(O)LOGIST.] One who makes a special study of, or is an authority on, quinine.

1869–76 J. E. HOWARD *Quinology E. Indian Plant.* 13 The Quinologist appointed by Government. **1890** *Times* 5 Feb. 9/5 [The] late quinologist to the Bengal Government.

So **qui'nology**, the scientific study of quinine; cinchonology. (Cf. Sp. *quinologia*, F. *quinologie*.)

1862 J. E. HOWARD *Illustr. Nueva Quinologia* 2 Much valuable assistance..in the pursuit of Quinology. **1869–76** —— (*title*) The Quinology of East Indian Plantations.

†**quinombrom,** obs. variant of CONUNDRUM.

1659 HOWELL *Lexicon Tetragl.* Let. French Prov., You will judge perhaps, that the Author hath some strange freaks, or quinombroms in his noddle.

quinone ('kwɪnəʊn, kwɪ'nəʊn). *Chem.* Also 9 kinone. [f. QUIN-A + -ONE.] **a.** *spec.* A crystalline compound (benzoquinone, $C_6H_4O_2$), the simplest type of the class of quinones. **b.** Any one of a series of aromatic compounds derived from the benzene series of hydrocarbons when two hydrogen atoms are replaced by two of oxygen.

'Quinone was first obtained, in 1838, by Woskresensky' (Thorpe *Dict. Appl. Chem.* III. 338); see QUINOYL.

1853 STENHOUSE in *Pharmac. Jrnl.* XIII. 384 The kinone was..obtained in crystals from the coffee-bean. **1857** MILLER *Elem. Chem.* III. 353 When kinone [**1862** quinone] is treated with reducing agents. **1885** REMZEN *Org. Chem.* 306 The quinones are peculiar bodies which in some ways are allied to the ketones.

Comb. **1886** ROSCOE & SCHORLEMMER *Treat. Chem.* III. III. §1006 A sharp taste and a weak quinone-like odour.

quinonoid ('kwɪnəʊnɔɪd), *a.* *Chem.* [f. QUINON(E + -OID.] Being, resembling, or characteristic of a quinone; being or exhibiting a molecular structure typified by that of quinone, viz. a doubly unsaturated ring with double bonds to two substituents (usu. in *para* positions).

1878 *Chem. News* 5 July 9/1 (*heading*) Quinonoid body found in a species of agaric. **1892** *Proc. Chem. Soc.* VIII. 101 It was maintained that in the case of azo-dyes, the rosanilines, methylene-blue, &c., colour was conditioned by a quinonoid structure. **1908** *Jrnl. Chem. Soc.* XCIV. I. 806 The meaning of the term quinonoid must be widened to include substances..in which the quinonoid oxygen atom is displaced by a bivalent imine or hydrocarbon group. **1951** I. L. FINAR *Org. Chem.* I. xxvii. 545 The yellow colour of *p*-benzoquinone is due to the presence of the quinonoid structure = ⟨=⟩ =. **1956** *Nature* 14 Jan. 79/2 The quinonoid product of the catecholase reaction..is an active oxidase in the cresolase reaction. **1974** *Ibid.* 20 Dec. 710/2 The sclerotisation and tanning of insect cuticles is generally thought to result from a crosslinking of the cuticular proteins by quinonoid derivatives of tyrosine.

quino'tannic, *a.* *Chem.* [f. QUIN-A + -O- + TANNIC.] *quinotannic acid*, a form of tannic acid found in cinchona bark. Hence **quino'tannate**.

1868 WATTS *Dict. Chem.* V. 30 Quinotannic acid is a light-yellow, friable, very hygroscopic mass, which becomes electric by friction. *Ibid.*, The quinotannate of lead.

quinova- (kwɪ'nəʊvə), an arbitrary comb. form of mod.L. *quina nova* false cinchona bark, as in **quinova-bitter** = quinovin; **quinova-red**, a resinous substance obtained from quinovatannic acid; **quinova-sugar**, a saccharine substance obtained from quinovin; **quinova-'tannic** (*acid*) *a.*, derived from *quina nova*.

1868 WATTS *Dict. Chem.* V. 31 The alcoholic solution.. leaves the quinova-sugar, on evaporation, as an uncrystallisable hygroscopic mass. *Ibid.* 32 Quinova-bitter [see QUINOVIN]. **1894** *Ibid.* IV. 392 Quinova red is a nearly black resin. *Ibid.*, Quinovatannic acid.

quinovic (kwɪ'nəʊvɪk), **ki'novic,** *a.* *Chem.* [See prec. and -IC.] *quinovic acid*, an acid found in false cinchona bark (see quot. 1868).

1838 T. THOMSON *Chem. Org. Bodies* 805 The kinovic acid of Pelletier and Caventou has considerable analogy with the oily acids. **1868** WATTS *Dict. Chem.* V. 31 Quinovic Acid ..was originally used as a synonym for quinovin or quinova-bitter, but is now applied..to an acid produced, together with quinova-sugar, by the decomposition of quinovin.

So **qui'novate, ki'novate** [-ATE 1 c], a salt of quinovic acid (Mayne *Expos. Lex.* 1855). **qui'novin, ki'novin** [-IN[1]], an amorphous bitter compound found in (false and other) cinchona-barks. **qui'novite**, a product of the resolution of quinovin.

1868 WATTS *Dict. Chem.* V. 32 Quinovin... Quinova-bitter; formerly also called Quinovic, Quinovatic or Chiococcic acid. **1894** *Ibid.* IV. 392 Quinovin..occurs also in true cinchona bark..and in tormentilla root. *Ibid.*, Resolved by acids into quinovic acid and quinovite.

quinoxaline (kwɪ'nɒksəliːn). *Chem.* [ad. G. *chinoxalin* (O. Hinsberg 1884, in *Ber. d. Deut. Chem. Ges.* XVII. 319), f. *chin-olin* QUINOLINE + *-oxal* (f. *glyoxal* GLYOXAL) + *-in* -INE[5]. So named on account of its structural similarity to quinoline and its preparation from glyoxal.] A weakly basic colourless crystalline solid, $C_8H_6N_2$, which was first prepared by reaction of glyoxal and *o*-phenylenediamine, and has a bycyclic structure formed from fused benzene and pyrazine rings; any substituted derivative of this compound.

1884 *Jrnl. Chem. Soc.* XLVI. 1052 He [*sc.* Hinsberg].. proposes to call this series of compounds quinoxalines. The formula of quinoxaline (the lowest homologue) is undoubtedly $C_6H_4\langle{N:CH \atop N:CH}\rangle$. **1887** [see AZINE]. **1926** H. G. RULE tr. *J. Schmidt's Text-bk. Org. Chem.* 700 Quinoxalines..are weakly basic compounds, which may be reduced to hydro-quinoxalines, but are stable towards oxidising agents. **1951** I. L. FINAR *Org. Chem.* x. 189 It [*sc.* glyoxal]..combines with *o*-phenylenediamines to form quinoxalines..; *e.g.*, with *o*-phenylenediamine it forms quinoxaline itself. **1974** *Nature* 20 Dec. 654/1 The quinoxaline chromophores of echinomycin are similar in size to the quinoline chromophore of chloroquine, which is known to bind to DNA by intercalation.

quinoyl ('kwɪnəʊɪl). *Chem.* Also kinoyle, quinoïl. [f. QUIN-A + -O- + -YL.] **a.** = QUINONE. **b.** (See quot. 1868.)

Woskresensky, the discoverer of quinone, named it *chinoyl*, for which Berzelius substituted *chinon*.

1845 *Penny Cycl.* Suppl. I. 350/1 *Quinoïl*, a neutral substance obtained when kinic acid is decomposed by heat. .. It is of a golden yellow colour. **1848** CRAIG, *Kinoyle*, a sublimate obtained in golden yellow needles when a kinate is distilled. **1868** WATTS *Dict. Chem.* V. 32 *Quinoyl*, a diatomic radicle, which may be supposed to exist in quinone and its derivatives, quinone itself being regarded as the hydride.

†**quin'quadrate.** *Math. Obs. rare*[−1]. [f. L. *quin(que)* + QUADRATE.] A thirty-second power.

1674 JEAKE *Arith.* (1696) 273 [see QUAQUADRATE].

quinquagenarian (ˌkwɪnkwədʒɪ'nɛərɪən), *sb.* and *a.* [f. as next + -AN.]

A. *sb.* †**1.** A captain of fifty men. *Obs. rare.*

1569 J. SANFORD tr. *Agrippa's Van. Artes* 130 Moses did then appoint them.. Centurians, Quinquagenarians, and Decans. **1609** BIBLE (Douay) *Exod.* xviii. 21 Centurions, and quinquagenarians, and deanes.

2. A person aged fifty; or between fifty and sixty.

1843 *New Mirror* (cited in *Cent. Dict.*).

B. *adj.* †**1.** Commanding fifty men. *Obs. rare.*

1600 W. WATSON *Decacordon* (1602) 356 Two Quinquagenarian Captains. **1629** MABBE tr. *Fonseca's Dev. Contemp.* 592 One Elias consumed with fire Ahabs Quinquagenarian Captaines and their souldiers.

2. Of fifty years of age; characteristic of one who is fifty years old.

1822 *New Monthly Mag.* V. 46 The quinquagenarian bachelor. **1848** CLOUGH *Amours de Voy.* II. 141 The trembling Quinquagenarian fears of two lone British spinsters.

quinquagenary (kwɪnˈkwædʒɪnərɪ), *sb.* and *a.* [ad. L. *quinquāgēnāri-us* consisting of fifty, fifty years old, captain of fifty, f. *quinquāgēnī*, distrib. of *quinquāgintā* fifty: cf. F. *quinquagénaire*.]

A. *sb.* †**1.** = QUINQUAGENARIAN *sb.* 1. *Obs. rare.*

1382 WYCLIF *Deut.* i. 15, I haue ordeynd hem.. tribunes, and centuriouns, and quynquagenaryes. **1483** CAXTON *Gold. Leg.* 59/2 Moyses.. ordeyned them.. tribunes Centuriones quinquagenaries.

2. A fiftieth year or anniversary.

1588 J. HARVEY *Disc. Probl.* 25 The Quinquagenarie, or 50 yeere,.. termed the yeere of Iubilee. **1894** *Westm. Gaz.* 28 June 2/2 Rossall, which has been celebrating its jubilee—not a quingentenary like Winchester, but a modest quinquagenary.

B. *adj.* = QUINQUAGENARIAN *a.* 2.

1715 tr. *Pancirollus' Rerum Mem.* I. IV. viii. 171 The Servant of Claudius, had in his Time a Quinquagenary Charger, which was valu'd at 5000 Crowns. **1829** BENTHAM *Let. to O'Connell* 10 Nov., Wks. 1843 XI. 28 My dear quinquagenary child shall never more be thus tormented by.. his octogenary.. guardian.

†**ˈquinquagene.** *Obs. rare.* [ad. L. *quinquāgēnī*, distrib. of *quinquāgintā* fifty.] A set of fifty.

1560 ABP. PARKER *Ps.* II. (*title*), The Seconde Quinquagene of Dauids Psalter translated into Englishe Metre.

‖**Quinquagesima** (kwɪnkwəˈdʒɛsɪmə). [med.L., fem. (sc. *dies*) of L. *quinquāgēsimus* fiftieth.

It is not certain whether the name is due to the fact that the Sunday in question is the fiftieth day before Easter (reckoning inclusively), or was simply formed on anal. of QUADRAGESIMA (cf. *sex-*, *septuagesima*).]

†**a.** The period beginning with the Sunday immediately preceding Lent and ending on Easter Sunday. *Obs.* †**b.** The first week of this period. *Obs.* **c.** (Also *Quinquagesima Sunday*.) The Sunday before Lent; Shrove Sunday.

1387 TREVISA *Higden* (Rolls) VIII. 297 He.. was i-crowned.. þe Sonday in Quinquagesima, þat is þat day a fourtenyȝt after Alleluya is i-closed. **1398** —— *Barth. De P.R.* IX. xxix. (1495) 364 Quinquagesima begynnyth the thyrd Sondaye after Septuagesima and endyth in the sonday of the Resurreccion. **1432–50** tr. *Higden* (Rolls) VII. 143 This emperoure goynge to here masse.. in the Sonneday of Quinquagesima. **1612** SELDEN *Illustr. Drayton's Polyolb.* xi. 185 The foure last daies of the Quinquagesima, that is Ash wednesday, Thursday, Friday, and Saturday. **1656** BLOUNT *Glossogr.*, Quinquagesima Sunday is always that which we vulgarly call Shrove Sunday. **1710** WHEATLY *Bk. Com. Prayer* iv. §8. 78 The Tuesday after Quinquagesima Sunday is generally call'd Shrove Tuesday. **1885** *Catholic Dict.* (1897) 559/2 St. Ambrose.. censures those who began Lent with Sexagesima or Quinquagesima.

attrib. **1885** *Catholic Dict.* (1897) 559/1 On the Monday in Quinquagesima week. **1901** PROCTOR & FRERE *Bk. Com. Prayer* 533 The Quinquagesima Collect.

quinquaˈgesimal, *a.* [f. as prec. + -AL[1].] Belonging to a set of fifty; containing fifty days.

1844 LINGARD *Anglo-Sax. Ch.* (1858) II. xi. 179 *note*, The quinquagesimal days were the fifty days between Easter and Whitsunday. **1884** SCHAFF *Encycl. Relig. Knowl.* III. 1801/2 As designating the last day of this quinquagesimal period, the word 'Pentecost' is first found in.. 305.

†**Quinquagesime, -gesme.** *Obs.* Also 5 quynquegesym, qwynquasim (?), 6 -gissime. [a. OF. *quinquagésime* (14th c.) or ad. med.L. *quinquagesima*: see above.] = QUINQUAGESIMA.

c **1380** WYCLIF *Sel. Wks.* II. 40 þe Gospel on þursdai in Quinquagesme. *Ibid.* 265 On Quinquagesme Sondai Pistle. **1387** TREVISA *Higden* (Rolls) VII. 143 þe emperour comynge ones on þe Sonday of Quynquagesme to a chapel. **1483** *Cath. Angl.* 297/2 Quynquegesym (*A.* Qwynquasim), *quinquagesima.* **1533** MORE *Debell. Salem* Wks. 1030/2 The priestes should eate no flesh fro quinquagissime to Easter. *c* **1535** FISHER *Wks.* (E.E.T.S.) 434 Y[e] gospell, redde in the church this quinquagesime sondaye. **1658** in PHILLIPS.

quinquagint (ˈkwɪnkwədʒɪnt). *nonce-wd.* [ad. L. *quinquāgintā* fifty.] A set of fifty persons or things.

1843 THACKERAY *Irish Sk.-Bk.* II. xiv. 264 There are 220 voters, it appears;.. but as parties are pretty equally balanced, the votes of the quinquagint.. carry an immense weight.

†**ˈquinquangle,** *a.* and *sb.* *Obs. rare.* [ad. late L. *quinquangulus, -um* (Priscian, Boeth.), f. *quinque* five + *angulus* ANGLE. Cf. obs. F. *quinquangle* (Godef.).]

A. *adj.* 'Having five angles or corners' (Blount *Glossogr.* 1656).

B. *sb.* A pentagon.

1668 H. MORE *Div. Dial.* I. 29 To inscribe a Quinquangle into a Circle. **1677** PLOT *Oxfordsh.* 334 Rather a quinquangle than a square. **1788** T. TAYLOR *Proclus* I. 178 A triangle.. will in this case have all its angles acute, and a quinquangle all its angles obtuse.

quinquangular (kwɪnˈkwæŋgjʊlə(r)), *a.* [f. as prec. + -AR: cf. F. *quinquangulaire*.] Having five angles or corners; pentagonal.

1653 H. MORE *Antid. Ath.* II. vi. (1712) 54 If it [a stone] be but exactly round.. or ordinately Quinquangular. **1657** TOMLINSON *Renou's Disp.* 258 The leaves of Briony are broad, and quinquangular. **1704** *Collect. Voy.* (Churchill) III. 701/1 The.. Fortress.. was of a Quinquangular Figure. **1826** in KIRBY & SP. *Entomol.* IV. 262. **1872** E. TROLLOPE *Sleaford* 430 Its east end terminates in a quinquangular apse.

So **quinˈquangulate, -ous** *adjs.* (Lee *Introd. Bot.* 1788; Mayne *Expos. Lex.* 1858).

quinquarticular (kwɪnkwɑːˈtɪkjʊlə(r)), *a.* [ad. mod.L. *quinquarticulār-is*, f. *quinque* five + *articulus* ARTICLE.] Relating to the five articles or points of Arminian doctrine condemned by the Calvinists at the Synod of Dort in 1618.

1661 GLANVILL *Van. Dogm.* 102 That darkness and confusion that is upon the face of the quinquarticular debates. **1674** HICKMAN *Hist. Quinquart.* (ed. 2) 2 Our Subject must be the unhappy Quinquarticular Controversie. **1755** CARTE *Hist. Eng.* IV. 53 The troubles complained of by the Dutch deputies related to what was called the quinquarticular controversy. **1834** FABER *Lett.* (1869) 17 The quinquarticular doctrines of the Synod of Dort. **1861** W. S. PERRY *Hist. Ch. Eng.* I. x. 348 One long versed in the intricacies of these quinquarticular disputes.

Quinˈquatric, *a. rare.* [f. L. *quinquātrūs* f. pl. or *quinquātria* n. pl. + -IC.] *Rom. Antiq.* Pertaining to the festival of Minerva (March 19–23).

1839 J. TAYLOR *Poems & Transl.* 210 The name of the Quinquatric Festival is derivable from the 5¼ days by which the year exceeds twelve months of thirty days each.

quinque- (ˈkwɪnkwɪ), a first element (a. L. *quinque-* five-) employed in combs. with the sense 'having, consisting of, etc. five (things specified)'. Examples of such formations in classical L. are the sbs. *quinquefolium, quinquennium, quinquerēmis, quinquevir(ī)*, the adjs. *quinquefolius, -mestris, quinquennālis*, and the ppl. form *quinquepartītus*; others appear in the later language. Those adopted or formed in English are chiefly terms of *Bot.* or *Zool.*, and correspond to similar formations in F., as *quinquédenté, -digité, -lobé, -loculaire, -nervé, valve*, etc. For the meaning of the second element in the following compare the corresponding forms under BI-, QUADRI-.

†**quinque-ˈangle, -ˈangled, -ˈangular** *adjs.*, quinquangular, pentagonal; **quinque-ˈannulate, -arˈticulate, -ˈcapsular, -ˈcostate, -ˈdentate,** †**-dentated, -ˈdigitate(d), -ˈfarious** *adjs.*; **ˈquinquefid** *a.* (see QUINQUIFID); †**quinquefoil,** cinquefoil; **quinqueˈfoliate,** †**-foliated, -ˈfoliolate, -ˈjugous, -ˈlateral, -ˈlibral** *adjs.*; **quinqueˈliteral** *a.* and *sb.*; **quinqueˈlobate, -lobed, -ˈlocular,** †**-mestrial** *adjs.*; †**-metre; -ˈnerval, -nerved, -pedal, -peˈdalian, -ˈpetaloid, -ˈpunctal, -ˈpunctate, -ˈradiate, -ˈseptate, -ˈserial, -ˈseriate, -syˈllabic** *adjs.*; **quinqueˈsyllable; quinque-tuˈbercular, -tuˈberculate** *adjs.*; **quinquevalent** *a.* = QUINQUIVALENT; **ˈquinquevalve** *a.* and *sb.*, †**-ˈvalvous, -ˈvalvular,** †**-ˈverbal, -ˈverbial** *adjs.*

1590 MARLOWE *2nd Pt. Tamburl.* III. iii, In champion grounds what figure serves you best, For which the *quinque-angle form is meet. **1679** MOXON *Math. Dict.* 125 **Quinque-Angled.* **1760** P. MILLER *Introd. Bot.* 21 A *quinqueangular or five cornered leaf. **1856–8** W. CLARK *Van der Hoeven's Zool.* I. 318 Abdomen *quinqueannulate. *Ibid.* 300 Antennæ filiform, *quinquearticulate. **1870** ROLLESTON *Anim. Life* 74 A pair of quinquearticulate legs. **1760** J. LEE *Introd. Bot.* II. xxix. (1765) 145 In *Aconitum* some are tricapsular, and others *quinquecapsular. **1861** BENTLEY *Man. Bot.* 152 It is said to be.. five-ribbed or *quinquecostate. **1760** J. LEE *Introd. Bot.* II. xx. (1765) 116 The Brim *quinque-dentate. **1870** BENTLEY *Man. Bot.* (ed. 2) 217, 5-toothed or quinquedentate. **1777** PENNANT *British Zool.* (ed. 2) IV. 4 Smooth body, *quinque-dentated front. **1858** MAYNE *Expos. Lex.*, *Quinquedigitatus*, .. *quinquedigitated. **1828** WEBSTER, **Quinquefarious.* **1617** MINSHEU *Ductor*, *Quinquefoile, or Cinquefoile. **1693** *Phil. Trans.* XVII. 620 It is a *Quinquefoliate and Siligniferous Tree, with winged Seed. **1861** BENTLEY *Man. Bot.* 170 It is quinate or quinquefoliate, if there are five [leaflets]. **1727** BAILEY vol. II, **Quinquefoliated Leaf.* **1832** LINDLEY *Introd. Bot.* (1839) 463 We say.. *quinquefoliolate or quinate, if there are five [leaflets] from the same point. **1819** *Pantologia* X. **Quinquejugous leaf*,.. a pinnate leaf, with five pairs of leaflets. **1856–8** W. CLARK *Van der Hoeven's Zool.* I. 157 Body cylindrical or *quinquelateral. **1656** BLOUNT *Glossogr.*, **Quinque-libral*,.. of five pound weight. **1674** JEAKE *Arith.* (1696) 91 Some mention a Triple Choenix, as Bilibral, Quadrilibral, and Quinquelibral. **1793** BEDDOES *Math. Evid.* 133 They assume triliteral and quadriliteral.. roots, and are doubtful whether there are not *quinqueliteral. **1846–52** B. DAVIES tr. *Gesenius' Heb. Gram.* II. §30 Combining into one word two triliteral stems, by which process even quinqueliterals are formed. **1819** *Pantologia* X. **Quinquelobate leaf.* **1849–52** TODD *Cycl. Anat.* IV. 875/1 Sometimes it [the tooth] is made quinquelobate by a double notch. **1775** J. JENKINSON tr. *Linnæus' Brit. Pl.* Gloss. 255 *Quinquelobed. **1760** J. LEE *Introd. Bot.* II. xxxii. (1765) 157 *Campanula*, with Fruit *quinquelocular. **1870** BENTLEY *Man. Bot.* (ed. 2) 290 The ovary is quinquelocular. **1611** CORYAT *Crudities* Char. Authour, Author of these *Quinque-mestriale Crudities. *c* **1560** ABP. PARKER *Psalter* Bj, Dauid Metres made; *Quinquemetres: some trimetres. **1671** GREW *Anat. Pl.* vii. §4. 45 Some just *Quinquenerval, as in *Anisum.* **1856** HENSLOW *Dict. Bot. Terms* 151 **Quinquenerved.* **1855** *Fraser's Mag.* LI. 63 A series of tripedal, quadrupedal, and *quinquepedal cocks. **1841** HODGSON *Life Napoleon* in R. Oastler *Fleet Papers* (1842) II. 397 Its lengthened *quinquepedalian notes. **1678** PHILLIPS (ed. 4) *List Barbarous Words*, **Quinquipunctal*, having five points. **1858** MAYNE *Expos. Lex.*, *Quinquepunctatus*, .. *quinquepunctate. **1886** *Athenæum* 12 June 782/3 There are four, six and seven rayed forms as well as the more ordinary *quinquiradiate specimens. **1858** MAYNE *Expos. Lex.*, *Quinqueseriatus*,.. *quinqueseriate. **1888** *Amer. Naturalist* XXII. 663 In the Mixodectidæ the crowns of the lower molars are *quinquetubercular. **1856–8** W. CLARK *Van der Hoeven's Zool.* II. 753 Last molar tooth of lower jaw *quinquetuberculate. **1776** DA COSTA *Elem. Conchol.* xiv. 279 Anatiferæ or Barnacles. These shells are *quinque-valves. **1777** PENNANT *Brit. Zool.* (ed. 2) IV. 5 Mouth quinquevalve, placed beneath. **1681** GREW *Catal. Rarities Gresham Coll.* Tab. 14 Indian Plum-stones.. *Quinquevalvous, Oval. **1828** WEBSTER, **Quinquevalvular.* **1664** H. MORE *Synopsis Proph.* 332 The papal transubstantiation.. by virtue of their *quinqueverbal charm. —— *Antid. Idolatry* x. 128 No more.. then their *Quinqueverbiall Charm can transubstantiate the Bread and Wine into the Body and Bloud of Christ.

quinquenary, *a. rare.* [For *quinary*, after L. *quinque*.] = QUINARY.

1690 LEYBOURN *Curs. Math.* 339 All Squares.. are to be marked with Points.. over every Binary or second Figure... Sursolids over every Quinquenary Figure. **1825** T. THOMSON *1st Princ. Chem.* I. 37 Nitrous acid is a quinquenary compound, composed of 1 atom sulphur and 3 atoms oxygen.

†**quinˈquennal,** *a.* and *sb.* *Obs.* Also 6 quinquinall. [ad. L. *quinquennāl-is*: cf. F. *quinquennal*.] **a.** *adj.* = QUINQUENNIAL. **b.** *sb.* = QUINQUENNIUM.

1532 [see QUINQUENNIAL *a.* 1]. **1601** HOLLAND *Pliny* I. 543 At what time as.. the two Censors held their Quinquennall solemne sacrifices. **1618** BOLTON *Florus* (1636) 114 At the Quinquennal, or Five-yeerely playes. *a* **1646** J. GREGORY *Posthuma, De Æris et Epochis* (1649) 140 Allowing for each of those a Lustrum or Quinquennal.

†**quinqueˈnnalian,** *a.* *Obs.* *rare*[−1]. [f. QUINQUENNAL + -IAN.] = QUINQUENNIAL *a.* 2.

1692 O. WALKER *Gr. & Rom. Hist. Illustr.* II. 224 Certain Quinquennalian Games celebrated at Actium.

quinqueˈnnarian. *rare*[−1]. [f. L. *quinquenn-is* quinquennial.] One who is five years old.

1821 *Blackw. Mag.* X. 118 Teaching scholars.. mostly quinquennarians, or at most sexennarians.

quinquenniad (kwɪnˈkwɛnɪæd). [f. as next + -AD, after *decad*.] = QUINQUENNIUM.

1842 TENNYSON *Day-Dream* L'Envoi ii, Thro' sunny decads.. Or gay quinquenniads. **1878** DOWDEN *Stud. Lit.* 202 Prolonged through many decades and quinquenniads. **1897** *Allbutt's Syst. Med.* II. 185 At all ages.. except in the quinquenniad ten to fourteen.

quinquennial (kwɪnˈkwɛnɪəl), *a.* and *sb.* Also 5 quinqueniale. [f. L. *quinquennis* + -AL[1], or ad. L. *quinquennālis*: cf. *biennial, centennial*, etc.]

A. *adj.* **1. a.** Lasting, continuing, holding office, etc., for five years.

c **1460** FORTESCUE *Abs. & Lim. Mon.* xii. (1885) 140 When the reaume gaff to thair kyng a quinsime and a desime quinqueniale [**1532** *MS. Digby* quinquinall]. **1601** BP. W. BARLOW *Defence* 30 So splendently appearing these 60 yeares together (onely a quinquennial Eclyps.. excepted). *a* **1648** LD. HERBERT *Hen. VIII* (1683) 79 To procure a general League among Christian Princes (or at least a quinquennial Truce). **1711** STEELE *Spect.* No. 32 ¶2, I find by my quinquennial Observations that we shall never get Ladies enough to make a Party. **1822** T. TAYLOR *Apuleius* 290 [He] placed me among the quinquennial Decurions. **1876** BANCROFT *Hist. U.S.* V. xv. 507 The fifteen 'gentlemen' thus chosen constituted the quinquennial senate of Maryland, and themselves filled up any vacancy that might occur in their number during their term of five years.

b. Consisting of five years.

1847 J. S. MILL *Let.* 19 Nov. in *Wks.* (1963) XIII. 725 The number of deaths.. is *less* in each quinquennial period. **1884** *Law Reports* 12 Queen's Bench Div. 393 The business profits made.. during the quinquennial period.

2. Occurring every fifth year.

1610 HOLLAND *Camden's Brit.* I. 105 The Quinquennial feasts and solemnities of the.. Cæsars. **1687** in *Magd. Coll. & Jas. II* (O.H.S.) 112 His visitations are.. limited to quinquennial. **1749** G. WEST tr. *Pindar, Nemean Odes* xi, The great Quinquennial Festival of Jove. **1848** MILL *Pol. Econ.* I. x. §3 The population.. in every quinquennial census. **1871** ALABASTER *Wheel of Law* p. xxxiv, He orders his subjects to hold quinquennial assemblies. **1903** *Westm. Gaz.* 14 Jan. 5/2 The Board of the London Hospital.. has been impelled to issue its quinquennial appeal two or three weeks in advance of the appointed time. **1955** *Times* 3 May

15/2 A quinquennial valuation of the 'Royal' life and annuity business was made at December 31.

3. Five years old (Blount *Glossogr.* 1656).

B. *sb.* **1.** A period of five years.

2. A magistrate holding office for five years.

1895 *Oracle Encycl.* II. 118 They had duumvirs, quinquennials, and decurions, in imitation of the consuls, censors, and praetors of Rome.

3. A fifth anniversary.

1903 *Westm. Gaz.* 14 Jan. 5/2 The hospital only begs widely every five years, and this year is our quinquennial.

Hence **quin'quennially** *adv.*, every five years. Also **quin'quennialist**, one who advocates a (legislative) period of five years.

1727 in BAILEY vol. II. **1816** G. S. FABER *Orig. Pagan Idol.* II. 478 In one region annually, and in another quinquennially. **1868** GLADSTONE *Juventus Mundi* i. (1870) 21 To provide..for the recitation of his songs.. quinquennially at the Panathenaia. **1888** *Times* (weekly ed.) 3 Feb. 16/3 On behalf of the quinquennialists, it was argued that the change was one of mere expediency. **1972** *Nature* 4 Feb. 246/3 Is this fraction to be reviewed annually or quinquennially, and, if so, by whom? **1979** *Daily Tel.* 3 Jan. 2/1 There is no excuse for the use of phrases like reversionary bonus compounded quinquennially, when what is meant is a five-yearly pay-out with interest added.

† **quin'quennie**, anglicized f. next. *Obs. rare*$^{-1}$.

1606 *True & Perfect Relat.* H 3 In the Quinquennie, the five yeeres of Queene Mary, there were cruelly put to death, about 300 persons for Religion.

‖ **quinquennium** (kwɪn'kwɛnɪəm). Pl. **-ennia.** [L., f. *quinque* five + *annus* year.] A period of five years; †*spec.* in *Law* (see quot. 1823).

1621 B. JONSON *Gipsies Metam.* Wks. (Rtldg.) 619/1 He.. looks as if he never saw his *quinquennium.* **1654** tr. *Scudery's Curia Pol.* 77, I am but young, and have not seen more then a Quinquennium of my reign. **1771–2** *Ess. fr. Batchelor* (1773) II. 204 In the quinquenium (*sic*) of Lord Townshend's administrations. **1823** CRABB, *Quinquennium*, a respite of five years, which insolvent debtors formerly obtained, by virtue of the King's letter, to have time for the payment of their debts. **1879** GLADSTONE in *19th Cent.* Sept. 580 The last quinquennium of trade does not exhibit an increase.

quinquepartite (kwɪnkwɪ'pɑːtaɪt), *a.* [ad. L. *quinquepartītus*, f. *quinque* five + *partītus* pa. pple. of *partīrī* to divide: cf. F. *quinquépartite.*] Divided into, consisting of, five parts.

1592 WEST *1st Pt. Symbol.* §47 These deedes indented are not only bypartite..but also may be made tripartite,.. quinquepartite [etc.]. **1677** PLOT *Oxfordsh.* 107 A sort of quinquepartite or stellated eggs. **1725** *Lond. Gaz.* No. 6377/1 The Quinquepartite Indenture. **1760** P. MILLER *Introd. Bot.* 24 A quinquepartite leaf. **1879** SIR G. SCOTT *Lect. Archit.* II. 197 It may be adopted on one side only, and so be quinquepartite [vaulting].

quinquereme ('kwɪnkwɪriːm), *a.* and *sb.* [ad. L. *quinquerēmis*, f. *quinque* five + *rēmus* oar: cf. F. *quinquérème* (1530).]

A. *adj.* Of ancient ships: Having five banks of oars.

1654–66 EARL ORRERY *Parthen.* (1676) 716 Hardly any one had escaped, but a few Quinquereme Galleys. **1697** [see QUADRIREME A]. **1852** GROTE *Greece* II. lxxxii. X. 669 One among his newly-invented quinquereme vessels.

B. *sb.* A ship having five banks of oars.

1553 BRENDE *Q. Curtius* IV. 41 b, The firste Galley of the Macedons that came nere them was a quinquereme. **1600** HOLLAND *Livy* XLII. xlvii. 1143 Himselfe was sent back againe with certaine Quinqueremes. **1734** tr. *Rollin's Anc. Hist.* (1827) I. II. 376 Quinqueremes, or galleys with five benches of oars. **1799** [see QUADRIREME B]. **1840** ARNOLD *Hist. Rome* II. 566 They had not a single quinquereme, the class of ships which may be called the line of battle ships of that period. **1865** *Athenæum* No. 1949. 307/3 A Carthaginian quinquereme.

† **quin'quertian**, *a.* *Obs. rare*$^{-1}$. [f. L. *quinquerti-um*, f. *quinque* + *ars* ART.] = PENTATHLIC.

1623 BINGHAM *Xenophon* 80 Other wrestled, and fought with fists, and vsed the Quinquertian exercise.

quinquesect ('kwɪnkwɪsɛkt), *v.* Also 7–9 quinqui-. [f. L. *quinque* five + *sect-* ppl. stem of *secāre* to cut, after *bi-*, *trisect.*] To cut into five (equal) parts. Hence **'quinquesecting** *vbl. sb.*

1697 G. K. *Disc. Geom. Problems* 7 By quinquisection of the Cord of an Angle it [the angle] is quinquisected. **1786** *Phil. Trans.* LXXVI. 16 Mr. Graham..perceived..how very much more easy a given line was to bisect than to trisect or quinquesect. **1809** CAVENDISH *ibid.* XCIX. 225 Let *a a* be the arch to be quinquesected. *Ibid.* 227 In quinquesecting the error of the two middle points is 2.4 times greater than in bisecting. **1853** SIR W. R. HAMILTON in R. P. Graves *Life* (1889) III. 453 The Royal Commissioners..have precisely quinquisected the diligence.

So **quinque'section**, section into five parts.

1684 [see QUINTUPLATION]. **1697** [see above]. **1786** *Phil. Trans.* LXXVI. 16 The division of the arc of 90..required trisections and quinquesections. **1825** J. NICHOLSON *Operat. Mechanic* 320, I was apprehensive some error might arise from quinquesection and trisection.

quinquevirate (kwɪn'kwɛvɪrət). Also 8 quinquin- (?). [ad. L. *quinquevirātus*, f. *quinqueviri* five men.] An association, board, etc., consisting of five men. Also *attrib.*

1710 HARLEY *Secr. Hist. Arlus & Odolphus* 20 Odolphus ..went himself Express with the news of his Defeat to the Quinquinvirate. **1762** tr. *Busching's Syst. Geog.* V. 513 The quinquevirate-court for the reparation of injuries. **1885** *Sat. Rev.* 3 Jan. 1/1 When the Quinquevirate sat round that famous table.

quinquifid ('kwɪnkwɪfɪd), *a.* *Bot.* Also 8–9 quinque-. [ad. L. *quinquifid-us*, f. *quinque* + *fid-*: see QUADRIFID.] Cleft in five.

1703 J. PETIVER in *Phil. Trans.* XXIII. 1425 The calyx is quinquifid and hoary. **1785** MARTYN *Rousseau's Bot.* xxi. (1794) 291 Their common characters are a quinquefid calyx. **1876** HARLEY *Mat. Med.* (ed. 6) 711 The..true calyx is one-leafed..with an obtusely quinquifid Margin.

† **quinquin, -quene**, varr. KINKIN, kilderkin.

a **1600** *Aberd. Reg.* (Jam.), A quinquin of oynyeonis. *Ibid.*, Ane quinquene of peares.

quinquina (kɪn'kiːnə, kwɪn'kwaɪnə). *Med.* Also 7 **kinkina**, 8 **kinquina**. See also QUINAQUINA. [Sp. spelling of Peruvian (Quichuan) *kin-kina* or *kina-kina*, redupl. of *kina* bark, QUINA.

'In Quichua, when the name of a plant is reduplicated, it almost invariably implies that it possesses some medicinal qualities'. C. R. Markham *Peruv. Bark* (1880) 5.]

a. Peruvian or Jesuits' bark; the bark of several species of cinchona, yielding quinine and other febrifugal alkaloids. **b.** One or other of the trees producing cinchona-bark.

1656 SIR K. DIGBY *Let.* in *Winthrop Papers* (1849) 15, I haue made knowne..in these partes, a barke of a tree that infallibly cureth all intermittent feauours. It cometh from Peru; and is the barke of a tree called by the Spaniardes Kinkina. **1681** (*title*) tr. Bellon's New Mystery in Physick discovered by curing of fevers and agues by quinquina or Jesuites' Powder. **1755** *Gentl. Mag.* XXV. 406 Physicians, who..prescribe the bark of the Quinquina. **1852** THACKERAY *Esmond* I. v, He cured him of an ague with quinquina. **1871** W. H. G. KINGSTON *On the banks of the Amazon* (1876) 101 Since its use became general in Europe, the export trade of the quinquina has been very considerable.

attrib. **1727–41** CHAMBERS *Cycl.* s.v., The corregidor of Loxa sent to the viceroy a quantity of the quinquina bark. **1880** C. R. MARKHAM *Peruv. Bark* 17 The first description of the quinquina-tree is due to that memorable French expedition to South America.

quinquinvirate: see QUINQUEVIRATE.

† **quin'quiplicate**, *v.* *Obs. rare*$^{-0}$. [f. ppl. stem of L. *quinquiplicāre*: cf. QUADRUPLICATE *v.*] 'To multiply by fives, to double five times' (Blount *Glossogr.* 1656). So † **quinquipli'cation**, 'a making four times double' (Phillips, 1678).

quinquisect, variant of QUINQUESECT.

'quinquity. *rare*$^{-1}$. [f. L. *quinque* + -ITY: cf. F. *quinquinitie* (Littré).] A set of five things.

1849 tr. *Hamilton's Fairy Tales* (Bohn) 129 She..was composed of nothing but quinquities; for she had five arms, five legs [etc.].

quinquivalent (kwɪn'kwɪvələnt), *a.* *Chem.* [f. L. *quinqui-* five- + *valent* as in *equivalent*, *quadrivalent.*] Capable of combining with five univalent atoms; pentavalent.

1877 WATTS *Fownes' Chem.* I. 256 Quinquivalent elements, or Pentads. **1880** CLEMINSHAW *Wurtz' Atom. Th.* 229 It is quinquivalent in chloric acid. **1885** REMSEN *Org. Chem.* (1888) 209 In contact with certain substances it [the nitrogen] becomes quinquivalent.

† **quinse**, *v.* *Obs. rare.* Also 6 **cuinse**, **kinse.** [Origin obscure. The form *cuinse*, cited by Halliwell from the *Bk. of Hunting* 1586, may be a misprint: the *Bk. St. Albans* gives 'A Plouer Mynsed' as the proper term.] To cut, carve.

1598 [see KINSING]. **1598** BP. HALL *Sat.* IV. xi. 44 Good man! him list not spend his idle meales In quinsing plouers, or in wining Quailes. [**1863** SALA *Capt. Dangerous* III. i. 6, I..succeeded in Quincing his face as neatly as a housewife would slice Fruit for a Devonshire Squab Pie.]

† **quinsell.** *Obs. rare*$^{-0}$. Also 6 -zell. [ad. obs. F. *guinsal* (Godef.), or It. *guinzaglio* rein, leash.] A horse-rein.

1598 FLORIO, *Guinzaglio*,..among riders a long rayne of leather called a quinzell. **1611** COTGR., *Dillon*, a Quinsell, for a horse.

quinsie(s)m, -sime, obs. forms of QUINZIÈME.

quinsy ('kwɪnzɪ). Forms: *α.* 4 **qwinaci**, **quinesye**, 5 **queynose**. *β.* 5 **quynsy**, **qwynse**, 5–6 **quynce**, 6 **quency**, 6 **quinsye**, 7 **-se**, **-cy**, 8 **-sie**, 6–9 **quinsey**, (8 **-zey**), 6– **quinsy**. *γ.* 6 **quynnancy**, **quinancie**, 6, 9 **-cy**. [ad. med.L. *quinancia*, f. Gr. κυνάγχη CYNANCHE, perh. as a refashioning of the commoner *squinancia*, whence the current Romanic forms, and Engl. *squinacy* (13th c.), *-ancy*, SQUINSY.] Inflammation of the throat or parts of the throat; suppuration of the tonsils; tonsillitis. Also, a form or attack of this.

α. **13..** *Minor Poems fr. Vernon MS.* 164 Men called þat vuel Comuynli, þat he hedde the Qwinaci. **14..** *Voc.* in Wr.-Wülcker 791/9 *Hec squ[in]acia*, a queynose. *a* **1450** *ME. Med. Bk.* (Heinrich) 215 Ferst lete hym blod..to rype þe quinesye.

β. **14..** *Voc.* in Wr.-Wülcker 587/32 *Gutturna*, Quynsy. **14..** *Nominale* ibid. 709/1 The qwynse. **1493** *Festivall* (W. de W. 1515) 95 b, On a tyme he was nere deed of the quency. **1534** MORE *Comf. agst. Trib.* III. Wks. 1246/1 He collereth them by the neck with a quinsye. **1570** B. GOOGE *Pop. Kingd.* III. 38 b, Blase driues away the quinsey quight, with water sanctifide. **1646** SIR T. BROWNE *Pseud. Ep.* 102 A famous medicine in Quinses, sore throats, and strangulations. **1753** RICHARDSON *Grandison* (1781) II. xvi. 167 She tried to swallow, as one in a quinsey. **1841** CATLIN *N. Amer. Ind.* (1844) II. lvii. 221 An alarming attack of the quinsey or putrid sore throat. **1892** *Daily News* 6 Oct. 5/3 Since the gout left his throat the patient has had three quinsies.

γ. **1530** PALSGR. 182 *Les escrovelles*, a disease called the quynnancy or the kynges yvell. **1587** MASCALL *Govt. Cattle, Horses* (1627) 125 The quinancy is an ill sorenesse..in the throat of the horse.

b. *Comb.*, as **quinsy-berry**, the black currant *Ribes nigrum* (*Treas. Bot.* 1866); **quinsy-wort**, the small woodruff (*Asperula cynanchica*).

1846 SOWERBY *Brit. Bot.* (ed. 3), Quinsey wort. **1861** MISS PRATT *Flower. Pl.* III. 159 Its specific name..as well as its English name of Quinsey-wort or Quinancy-wort, refer to its ancient uses in disorders of the throat.

Hence **'quinsied** *a.*, afflicted with quinsy.

1855 SINGLETON *Virgil* I. 178 Drips from their nostrils sable blood, And presses quinsied jaws a furry tongue.

quinszisme, obs. form of QUINZIÈME.

quint (kwɪnt), *sb.*[1] Also 6 quinte. [a. F. *quint* m. (sense 1), or *quinte* f. (senses 2 and 3):—L. *quint-us*, *-a*, *-um*, ordinal to *quinque* five.]

1. A tax of one-fifth.

1526 in Dillon *Customs of Pale* (1892) 83 He must paye to the kinge the vth pennie of his goods for the quinte. **1852** TH. ROSS tr. *Humboldt's Trav.* I. v. 176 The payment of the quint to the officers of the crown.

2. *Mus.* **a.** An interval of a fifth.

1865 tr. *Spohr's Autobiog.* II. 14 Three ugly quints follow each other. **1887** A. RILEY *Athos* 406 It is not founded upon the modern system of octaves, but is a succession of similar quints.

b. (In full *quint-stop.*) An organ-stop which gives a tone a fifth higher than the normal.

1855 E. J. HOPKINS *Organ* xxi. 110 Some [stops] sound g on the C key..Those are called 'fifth-sounding' or Quint Stops. *Ibid.* 117 The Quint on the Pedal is almost invariably composed of stopped pipes.

quint (kɪnt, kwɪnt), *sb.*[2] [a. F. *quinte* f.: see prec. Formerly pronounced (kɛnt) or (kæ̃t).]

1. In piquet: A sequence of five cards of the same suit, counting as fifteen.

1680 COTTON *Compl. Gamester* 59 A Quart is a sequence of four Cards, a Quint of five. *Ibid.* 60 You must reckon for every..Quart four, but for a Quint fifteen. **1719** R. SEYMOUR *Court Gamester* 76 Quint or Quinze, fifteen, though by a Corruption of Pronunciation we call it Kent. **1826** MISS MITFORD *Village* Ser. II. (1863) 342 Never dealt the right number of cards..did not know a quart from a quint. **1877** SIR S. NORTHCOTE in *Life* (1890) I. i. 3 *note*, He got the point and also two quints, and thus a repique.

b. *quint major*, the ace, king, queen, knave and ten of a suit. *quint minor*, the five cards from the knave to the seven.

1659 *Shuffling, Cutting & Deal.* 3 Two Quint Minors will win the game. **1663** DRYDEN *Wild Gallant* IV. i. Wks. 1882 II. 84 Zounds, the rogue has a quint-major. **1720** R. SEYMOUR *Compl. Gamester* I. 93 He who..has a Quint-Major in his Hand..cuts the other off from counting any inferior Quint, Quart or Tierce. **1860** *Bohn's Hand-bk. Games* II. 44 Suppose you have ace..with a quint-major of another suit. **1873** 'CAVENDISH' *Piquet* 34 The elder hand, when calling his sequence, names it thus: 'A quint minor' [etc.].

† **2.** *transf.* A set of five persons. *Obs. rare*$^{-1}$.

1678 BUTLER *Hud.* III. ii. 1541 Since the State has made a Quint Of Generals, he's listed in't.

quint, *sb.*[3], abbrev. of QUINTET 3.

1897 *Daily News* 8 June 9/4 Betts was obliged to stop, the chain of his pacing quint having given way.

quint, *a.* *rare*$^{-1}$. [ad. L. *quint-us*: see QUINT *sb.*[1]] Quinary.

1881 A. H. KEANE in *Nature* XXIII. 220 They often still retain the old quint system..in the Oceanic area now mostly replaced by the decimal.

quint-, erroneously used in combs. in place of QUINQU(E)-, as *quintangular*, *quintennial*, † *quintpartite*. (Cf. QUINTI-.)

1687 *Good Advice* 52 The Indenture will at least be, quint-pertite, and Parties are not so mortal as Men. **1787** M. CUTLER in *Life, Jrnls. & Corr.* (1888) I. 206 Large timbers, laid..so as to make the form of the wells quintangular. **1871** *Daily News* 14 Aug., A system of annual, triennial, or quintennial Parliaments. **1894** *Westm. Gaz.* 5 Apr. 2/1 The Quintangular Tournament which followed this event.

‖ **quinta** ('kinta). [Sp. and Pg., orig. denoting a house and farm let at a rent of one-fifth (*quinta parte*) of the produce of the latter.] A country-house or villa in Spain or Portugal. Also, a country estate; in Portugal, a wine-growing estate; in S. America, a house or estate on the outskirts of a town. Also *attrib.*

1754 FIELDING *Let.* Aug.-Sept. in A. Dobson *At Prior Park* (1912) 143 He hath a little Kintor..or Villa at a Place called Jonkera. *a* **1770** A. HERVEY *Jrnl.* an. 1748 (1953) 75, I used, too, to go out to my friend Mr. Mayne and Barn's quinta, where I was very much at ease. **1777** W. DALRYMPLE *Trav. Sp. & Port.* cxxix, Passed several quintas or country houses. **1811** WELLINGTON *Let. to Hill* in Gurw. *Desp.* (1838) VIII. 167 My head quarters are in a quinta near Portalegre. **1818** C. A. RODNEY *Let.* in *Amer. State Papers: Foreign Relations* (1834) IV. 219 The small farms, or quintas, in the neighborhood of cities, are in fine order. Those around Buenos Ayres..are, by irrigation, in the highest state of culture. **1870** *Weekly Standard* (Buenos Aires) 7 Sept. 2/5 The people in the quintas and suburbs were all flocking into Montevideo. **1878** E. CLARK *Visit S. Amer.* x. 128 The elegant quintas and country houses that surround the city. **1893** T. B. FOREMAN *Trip to Spain* 27 We pass some charming quintas, surrounded by gardens ablaze with flowers. **1931** *Discovery* Oct. 310/2 The dipleidoscope and the gravity escapement are both due to a gifted inventor who worked at my Quinta [in Madeira]. **1960** *Spectator* 15 Jan. 91/3 'Noval' is the name of the *quinta*, or estate, from which the port comes. **1969** J. MANDER *Static Soc.* v. 132 Bolivar's *quinta*, a modest eighteenth-century lodge on the slopes overlooking the city, may still be inspected. **1976** F. GREENLAND *Misericordia Drop* I. i. 14 The property.. belonged to..the venerable hospital that employed him... Periodic inspection of this *quinta* was one..of Dr Sá's duties. **1976** *Times* 6 Nov. 13/2 Quinta wines—ports from one particular vineyard.

quintage'narian, erron. f. QUINQUAGENARIAN.
1844 W. H. MAXWELL *Sport & Adv. Scot.* ix. (1855) 88 A literary quintagenarian at your elbow.

quintain[1] ('kwɪntɪn). *Obs.* exc. *Hist.* Forms: α. 5–6 quyn-, 6 quintayne, 6–7 -aine, 6– quintain; 5 qwaintan, 7 quintan(e, whinta(i)ne; 7 quinten. β. 5 quyntyne, 6 -ine, 6–8 quintine, 7, 9 -in. γ. 7 quintel(l, -al, -il. [a. OF. *quintaine, -tene, -tine*, etc. (see Godef.) = Prov., It. *quintana*, med.L. *quintana, -tena*; usually regarded as identical with L. *quintāna* the market and business-place of a camp (f. *quintus* fifth, sc. maniple), on the supposition that military exercises may have been practised there.] A stout post or plank, or some object mounted on such a support, set up as a mark to be tilted at with lances or poles, or thrown at with darts, as an exercise of skill for horsemen or footmen; also, the exercise or sport of tilting, etc. at such a mark.

The actual form of the quintain, and the object of the sport, varied considerably. In some cases the post or block had to be struck so as to break the lance; in others the quintain consisted of a revolving figure, or a bar weighted with a sand-bag, which swung round and struck the unskilful tilter. In the middle ages tilting at the quintain was a common knightly exercise; in the 17–18th c. it is mentioned as a favourite country sport at weddings.

[*a* **1259** MATTH. PARIS *Cron. Maj.* (Rolls) V. 367 Eodem tempore (an. 1253) juvenes Londinenses, statuto pavone pro bravio, ad stadium quod quintena vulgariter dicitur, vires proprias et equorum cursus sunt experti.]

α. *c* **1400** *Destr. Troy* 1627 Somur qwenes and qwaintans, & oþer qwaint gamnes. *c* **1450** *Merlin* 133 After mete was the quyntayne reysed. *c* **1530** LD. BERNERS *Arth. Lyt. Bryt.* (1814) 530 Than Hector caused a faire quintayne to be pyght vp in the myddes of the cyte: and therat ran these yonge knyghtes, brekynge and sheueringe of theyr speres. **1611** COTGR., *Quintaine*, a Quintane (or Whintane) for countrey youthes to runne at. **1621** BURTON *Anat. Mel.* II. ii. IV, Keelpins,..quintans,..which are the common recreations of country folkes. **1693** *Lond. Gaz.* No. 2845/2 This day there is to be a Carousel, *viz.* Running at the Quintain and the Ring. **1727–41** CHAMBERS *Cycl.* s.v., The custom is still retained in Shropshire, and some other counties, among the nuptial solemnities.—He that breaks most poles against the quintain, has the prize. **1814** SCOTT *Chivalry* (1874) 26 Making him ride a career against a wooden figure holding a buckler called a quintaine. **1898** *Westm. Gaz.* 26 July 10/1 This quintain [at Offham, Kent] (said to be the only surviving specimen in England).

β. *c* **1440** *Promp. Parv.* 421/1 Quyntyne, *quirinarium.* **1530** PALSGR. 178 *Bersault*, a quyntine. **1575** LANEHAM *Let.* (1871) 21 Before the Castl..whear az waz pight a cumly quintine for featz at armz. **1656** BLOUNT *Glossogr.* s.v., A Quintin..is set fast in the ground in the Highway, where the Bride and Bridegroom are to pass. **1707** HEARNE *Collect.* (O.H.S.) I. 334 Sports on the Sabbath amongst which the Quintine. **1885** J. PAYN *Talk of Town* I. 137 That ancient game the quintin.

γ. **1617** MINSHEU *Ductor*, A Quintaine, or Quintell, a game in request at marriages, when Jac and Tom, Dic, Hob, and Will, striue for the gay garland. **1644** QUARLES *Sheph. Orac.* vi, Harmless sports..And ceremonious Quintils, that belongs To Shepheard's rural mirth. **1677** PLOT *Oxfordsh.* 200 Running at the Quinten,..or Quintel.

b. *transf.* or *fig.*

1598 BP. HALL *Sat.* IV. iv. 32 Paune thou no gloue..Nor make thy Quintaine others armed head. **1600** SHAKS. *A.Y.L.* I. ii. 263 That which here stands vp Is but a quintine, a meere liuelesse blocke. **1641** EARL MONM. tr. *Biondi's Civil Warres* I. 20 Imagining himself to bee..the only quintan those lances addressed themselves against. **1694** S. JOHNSON *Notes Past. Let. Bp. Burnet* I. 98 [It] was afterwards set up by it self for a Countrey Quintin, to be thrown at by all the Loyal Sparks of the Nation.

c. *attrib.*, as ***quintain-knight, -post.***

1575 LANEHAM *Let.* (1871) 46 Her quintine knights, & proper bickerings of the Couentree men. **1857** TROLLOPE *Barchester T.* III. 31 The quintain post stood..before him.

Hence †**'quintaining**, riding at the quintain.

1575 LANEHAM *Let.* (1871) 24 Theez ryderz..leaft thear quintining, and ran one at another.

†**quintain**[2]. *Obs. rare*$^{-1}$. [f. L. *quint-* fifth, after *quatrain.*] A stanza of five lines; a cinquain.

1589 PUTTENHAM *Eng. Poesie* II. x[i]. (Arb.) 102 This is in a staffe of..ten verses: whereas without a band in the middle, it would seeme..two quintaines.

quintain[3]: see QUINTIN.

quintal ('kwɪntəl), **'kintal, 'kentle.** Forms: α. 6 quintale, 6–7 quintall, 7 -tell, 5– quintal. β. 5 *pl.* kyntawes, 5–6 kyntal(l, 6 -tayl, 6–7 kintall, 6 kintal; 6–7 kentall, 7 -tal, 9 kentle. [a. OF. *quintal* (13th c.), pl. *quintaus*, Sp. and Pg. *quintal*, It. *quintale*, med.L. *quintale (-allus), quintile*, ad. Arab. *qinṭār*: see KANTAR.]

a. A weight of one hundred pounds; a hundred-weight (112 lbs.). **b.** In the metric system: A weight of 100 kilograms.

α. *c* **1470** in *Bl. Bk. Excheq.* (Rolls) II. 193 Of eche quintal of balayn, iiij *d.* **1555** EDEN *Decades* 213 Two or more quintales of powder. **1580** HOLLYBAND *Treas. Fr. Tong*, Betweene the quintall..of Englande to that of Fraunce, there is foure poundes lost. **1613** PURCHAS *Pilgrimage* VIII. i. 608 They draw yearely eight thousand quintals of Quicksilver. **1692** LUTTRELL *Brief Rel.* (1857) II. 627 Some French privateers have taken 3 or 4 English ships, with 15,000 quintals of fish. **1712** N. TREVANION in D. W. Prowse *Hist. Newfoundland* (1895) x. 272/2 And planters very backward in paying, he got only one hundred quintals of fish this season. **1732** LEDIARD *Sethos* II. VII. 26 Elephants teeth so large that those of one elephant weigh two quintals. **1825** J. NICHOLSON *Operat. Mechanic* 761 A quintal of the ore is put into a retort. **1873** RUSKIN *Fors Clav.* xxx. (1896) II. 135 The Easter ox..weighed well its twenty-five quintals. **1897** KIPLING *Captains Courageous* vii. 144 Then pray back my son to me! Pray back a nine-thousand-dollar boat an' a thousand quintal of fish. **1912** N. DUNCAN *Best of Bad Job* xxv. 169 A quintal here an' a quintal there. **1918** A. HUXLEY *Let.* 12 Aug. (1969) 160 He drains..twelve hogsheads of rich milk, to say nothing of the nineteen Imperial Kilderkins of cream and the thirty two quintals of sugar. **1964** *Newfoundland Q.* Spring 27/1 A prior pre-quintal charge is reserved from the entire voyage's value for this labour called 'fish-making'. **1967** *Times* 23 Nov. 5/7 An agreement for the sale of 200 tons of Sudan cotton c.i.f. Bombay, at a price of Rs. 393.68 per quintal. **1974** D. AVERY *Not on Queen Victoria's Birthday* vi. 102 By February 1815 the price of imported south American copper had risen to 20 dollars a *quintal* (£8 per 100 lb).

β. **1477** EARL RIVERS (Caxton) *Dictes* 16 b, He wolde yeue him C Kyntawes of golde. **1502** ARNOLDE *Chron.* (1811) 190, xv. kyntayls yron of the weyght of Este Spayne. **1539** T. PERY in Ellis *Orig. Lett.* Ser. II. II. 140 He sawe a brassyne bell, whiche bell myght waye ij kyntalles. **1593** NASHE *Christ's T.* 39 b, Nothing he talks on but Kentalls of Pearle. **1623** WHITBOURNE *Newfoundland* 79 It will then make at Marseiles aboue two and twenty hundred Kentalls of that weight. **1645** in *Deeds Suffolk Co., Mass.* (1880) I. 65 One thousand Kintall of dry Cod fish. **1678** WANLEY *Wond. Lit. World* I. xxiv. §16. 38/2 An Ass with his load which commonly weighed three Kintals. **1842** BISCHOFF *Woollen Manuf.* II. 17 Wool [from Smyrna]..2,000 Kintals. **1861** L. L. NOBLE *Icebergs* 282 Kentles of white-fleshed cod.

quintal, obs. variant of QUINTAIN[1].

quintan ('kwɪntən), *a.* and *sb.* [ad. L. *quintāna* (sc. *febris*), fem. of *quintānus* f. *quintus* fifth: cf. F. *quintane*, †*quintaine* (Paré, 16th c.). See QUARTAN.] **a.** *adj.* Of a fever or ague: Having a paroxysm every fifth (= fourth) day. **b.** *sb.* A fever or ague of this kind.

1747 tr. *Astruc's Fevers* 63 What is called a quintan, is in fact a tertian, whose third accession is either suppressed or imperceptible. **1803** *Med. Jrnl.* IX. 216 A type more resembling a quartan and quintan than any other. **1897** *Allbutt's Syst. Med.* II. 317 Further modifications have been recognized by nosologists as quintan, sextan, octan.

quintan(e, -ayne, obs. forms of QUINTAIN[1].

†**'quintant.** *Obs. rare*$^{-1}$. [f. L. *quint-us* fifth, after QUADRANT *sb.*[1]] The fifth part of a circle.

1684 J. WALLIS *Angular Sections* iv. 31 The same Chord subtends on the one side to one Quintant, and on the other side to four such.

†**'quintary.** *Obs. rare*$^{-1}$. [f. L. *quint-us* fifth: cf. QUINARY.] A multiple of five.

1729 SHELVOCKE *Artillery* IV. 230 Every Number between the Quintaries of this table.

‖**quinte** (kæ̃t). [F.: see QUINT *sb.*[1] and *sb.*[2]]

1. The fifth thrust or parry of the eight taught in fencing-schools. Also *attrib.*

1707 SIR W. HOPE *New Method Fencing* iv. 58 There is also a Quinte, or fifth Position, as they pretend, of the Sword-Hand. **1765** ANGELO *School Fencing* 20 The thrust in quinte is made by making a feint on the half-circle parade, having your wrist in carte. *Ibid.*, The outside Thrust under the wrist, called Quinte Thrust. *Ibid.* 21 With the quinte parade, you parry seconde and flanconade. **1889** POLLOCK *Fencing* 44 *Quinte.*—The hand to the left in pronation, at the height of the belt; the point well beyond the inside line.

†**2.** = QUINT *sb.*[2] I. *Obs. rare*$^{-1}$.

1720 A. SEYMOUR *Compl. Gamester* I. 93 Cards..which are Sequents..are called, either Tierces, Quartes, Quintes ..according to their Number and Value.

quintel(l, -en, obs. forms of QUINTAIN[1].

quintennial: see QUINT-.

quinternion (kwɪn'tɜːnɪən). [f. L. *quinque* five, or *quintus* fifth, after *quaternion.*] A set or 'gathering' of five sheets of paper.

1652 URQUHART *Jewel* Wks. (1834) 189 The quinternion consisting of five sheets, and the quire of five and twenty. **1883** AXON *Introd. Caxton's Chesse* p. xi, The book.. consists of eight quaternions..and one quinternion or section of five sheets folded together.

quinteron, -oon, variants of QUINTROON.

quintessence (kwɪn'tɛsəns), *sb.* Also 5 -essencie, quyntencense, 6 quintaessence; *Sc.* quintessance, -iscence, quentassens, 7 -escense. [a. F. *quintessence*, †*quinte essence* (14th c.), or ad. med.L. *quinta essentia* 'fifth essence'.

Metrical quots. show that during the 16–18th c. the stress was usually on the first and third syllables (hence the abbrev. *quint'ssence* in Quarles), but *quin'tessence* is found as early as 1597; both stressings occur in Milton's *Par. Lost* (III. 716 and VII. 244).]

1. The 'fifth essence' of ancient and mediæval philosophy, supposed to be the substance of which the heavenly bodies were composed, and to be actually latent in all things, the extraction of it by distillation or other methods being one of the great objects of alchemy.

c **1430** LYDG. *Min. Poems* (Percy Soc.) 51 Aurum potabile ..In quyntencense, best restauracioun. **1460–70** *Bk. Quintessence* 14 If ȝe putte seedis or flouris..into oure 5 essencie forsoþe sich 5 essence ȝe schulen haue þerfore. **1500–20** DUNBAR *Poems* xxxiii. 58 Me thocht sair fassonis he assailȝeit, To mak the quintessance, and failȝeit. **1561** EDEN *Arte Nauig.* I. iv, The quint essence or fyfte substaunce, is a body of it selfe. **1622** MALYNES *Anc. Law-Merch.* 256 This cannot bee done without proiection of the Elixar or Quintescense vpon mettalls. **1660** tr. *Paracelsus' Archidoxis* I. IV. 35 The Quintessence therefore, is a certain matter Corporally extracted out of all things, which Nature hath produced. **1702** tr. *Le Clerc's Prim. Fathers* 309 That the Soul was of the same Nature with Heaven or of the Quint-Essence which Heaven is made of. **1847** EMERSON *Poems, Uriel*, The young deities discussed..Orb, quintessence, and sunbeams. **1879** *Cassell's Techn. Educ.* IV. 330/2 The vivifying quintessence of the elements of Raymond Lully.

2. The most essential part of any substance, extracted by natural or artificial processes; a highly refined essence or extract; *spec.* in older chemistry, an alcoholic tincture obtained by digestion at a gentle heat.

1576 BAKER (*title*) tr. Gesner's New Jewell of Health,.. treating very amplye of all Dystillations of Waters, of Oyles, Balmes, Quintessences, etc. **1582** HESTER *Secr. Phiorav.* I. xvii. 18 Then vse our Quintaessence of Wine. **1671** SALMON *Syn. Med.* III. lxxv. 671 Quintessence of Vipers..is of wonderful virtue for purifying the blood, &c. **1709** ADDISON *Tatler* No. 131 ¶9, I looked upon that sooty Drug..as the Quintessence of English Bourdeaux. **1850** ROBERTSON *Serm.* Ser. III. i. (1872) 3 In the drop of venom..there is concentrated the quintessence of a poison.

b. The most essential part or feature of some non-material thing; *esp.* the purest or most perfect form or manifestation of some quality.

1570 R. HICHCOCK *Quintess. Wit* A ij, A naturall quintessence of knowledge. **1611** CORYAT *Crudities* 29 Certayne artificiall rocks, most curiously contriued by the very quintessence of art. **1649** MILTON *Eikon.* vi. 53 The Law of England, which Lawyers say is the quintessence of reason. **1759** FRANKLIN *Ess.* Wks. 1840 III. 408 The last period of the governor's message was the very quintessence of invective. **1879** FARRAR *St. Paul* II. 181 *note*, This passage contains the very quintessence of Pauline theology.

c. The most perfect embodiment of the typical qualities of a certain class of persons, etc.

1590 R. HARVEY *Pl. Perc.* 8 A Quintessence of all the picked yoouth. **1610** *Histrio-m.* II. 161 Heere's the very quintessence of Duckes. **1823** SCOTT *Fam. Lett.* (1894) II. xix. 176 You have escaped the quintessence of bores. **1845** JAMES *Arrah Neil* ii, He was the quintessence of an ordinary-minded man.

quintessence, *v.* Now *rare.* [f. prec. sb. Cf. F. *quintessencier* (1611 in Cotgr.).] *trans.* **a.** To extract the quintessence of. **b.** To take *out of* (something) as a quintessence.

1585 JAS. I *Ess. Poesie* (Arb.) 25, I quint-essence the Poets soule. **1593** NASHE *Christ's T.* (1613) 154 It is a kind of Alchimical quintessensing a heauen out of earth. **1638** DRUMM. OF HAWTH. *Irene* Wks. (1711) 170 For quintessencing and alembicking thee, and using thee, as alchymists do gold. **1844** *For. Q. Rev.* XXXIII. 186 The science of the cook consists..in quintessencing (so to speak) the viands.

quin'tessenced, *ppl. a. rare.* [f. QUINTESSENCE *v.* + -ED[1].] Reduced to its quintessence; quintessential.

1898 G. E. B. SAINTSBURY *Short Hist. Eng. Lit.* VII. vii. 467 Its charms..consist in extreme strangeness, in quintessenced or preternatural art.

quintessential (kwɪntɪ'sɛnʃəl), *a.* and *sb.* [f. as QUINTESSENCE *sb.* + -IAL: cf. *essential* and F. *quintessenciel* (16th c., Paré).] **A.** *adj.* Of the nature of a quintessence; the purest or most refined of its kind.

1605 TIMME *Quersit.* Pref. 6 The æthereal and quintessential physick. **1681** H. MORE *Exp. Dan.* v. Notes 157 Mere Quintessential Devils, such as consist onely of envy, pride and malice. *a* **1711** KEN *Hymns Evang.* Poet. Wks. 1721 I. 32 The..Flow'rs..all strove their quintessential Sweets to drain, Perfuming Earth. **1823** BYRON *Juan* IX. lxvii, A quintessential laudanum. **1887** T. A. TROLLOPE *What I remember* I. ii. 48 Eldon's quintessential Toryism.

B. *sb.* The most essential part of a thing; a quintessential element.

1899 'MARK TWAIN' in *Harper's Mag.* Sept. 529/1 These are the very quintessentials of good citizenship. **1916** J. G. HUNEKER *Ivory, Apes, & Peacocks* 37 He, too, dreamed of quintessentials, of the sheer power of golden vocables and the secret alchemy of art.

Hence **quintessenti'ality; quinte'ssentially.**

1838 *New Monthly Mag.* LIII. 304 A concentrated quintessentiality of them all. **1887** T. A. TROLLOPE *What I remember* I. xv. 315 Quintessentially German in manner. **1936** *Delineator* CXXIX. 49/2 All of those early musicians in New Orleans were quintessentially swing players. **1958** [see

BALDING *a.*]. **1971** *Country Life* 24 June 1584/3 Montgeoffroy is everything that is quintessentially French. **1978** *Language* LIV. 275 That master negotiator and persuader, the quintessentially pragmatic Odysseus.

quinte'ssentialize, *v.* [f. prec. + -IZE.] *trans.* To make quintessential; to refine or purify in the highest degree.

1829 *Examiner* 7/1 Congreve in his discourses has so distilled, re-distilled, and quintessentialized each individual period. **1880** SWINBURNE in *Fortn. Rev.* XXVII. 766 As he advances in age the poet quintessentializes..his thought.

Hence **quinte'ssentialized** *ppl. a.*

1847 MRS. C. CLARKE *Shaks. Prov.* 7 Such quintessentialised drops of wisdom are surely not ill stored up.

quinte'ssentiate, *v. rare.* [f. as QUINTESSENCE *sb.* + -ATE: cf. *essentiate.*] = QUINTESSENCE *v.* Hence **quinte'ssentiated** *ppl. a.*

1606 BRETON *Sidney's Ourania* 3 He kens no Crotchets of contentious breed Nor has that Quintessentiated skill. **1894** *Daily Chron.* 10 Jan. 3 Was there ever a talent so hard to formulate, to quintessentiate, as that of Goethe?

quintet, quintette (kwɪn'tɛt). Also 9 -tett. [a. F. *quintette*, ad. It. *quintetto*: see next.]

1. *Mus.* A composition for five voices or instruments. Also *attrib.*

1811 L. M. HAWKINS *C'tess & Gertr.* II. 67 One of the quartet and quintet gentlemen. **1864** *Home News* 19 Dec. 21/1 The quintette..which forms the first finale. **1880** *Academy* 13 Nov. 356 Arranged..as a quintet for strings.

2. a. *Mus.* A set of five singers or players. **b.** A set of five persons or things.

1882 *Daily News* 8 June 2/6 The Ascot Derby Stakes, for which a quintette came to the post. **1893** *Chicago Advance* 7 Sept., A remarkable quintet surely, to have lived in the same generation.

3. A cycle for five riders; a quintuplet. (Cf. QUINT[3].) Also *attrib.*

1896 *Westm. Gaz.* 28 Oct. 7/2 We are threatened with a 'quintet' match,..but we would rather be spared the sight of two quintets racing neck and neck round a bend! **1898** *Daily News* 30 June 4/5 During a cycle race..one of the handle bars of a quintette ridden by pacers broke.

‖**quintetto** (kwɪn'tɛtəʊ). ? *Obs.* [It., f. *quinto* fifth: cf. *quartetto.*] **1.** = QUINTET 1.

1792 A. YOUNG *Trav. France* 201 It was the *Impresario in Augusta*, by..Cimarosa; there is a quintetto in it. **1795** MASON *Ch. Mus.* i. 77 The finest Quintetto of Haydn.

2. = QUINTET 2 b.

1779 SHERIDAN *Critic* II. ii, A very orthodox quintetto! **1816** T. L. PEACOCK *Headlong Hall* vi, This amiable..quintetto were busily employed in flattering one another.

†**quintfoil,** obs. variant of QUINFOIL (q.v.).

1595 *Bk. of Armorie* 53 Flower de luce, & Quint foiles.

quinti-, properly a comb. form of L. *quint-us* fifth, but sometimes incorrectly employed in place of QUINQUE-, as in ***quintiliteral, -partition, -ped.*** (Cf. QUINT-, and F. *quintiforme, -section.*)

1674 JEAKE *Arith.* (1696) 33 Quintipartition, or to divide by 5 may likewise be effected thus. **1839** PAULI *Analecta Hebraica* xxviii. 205 The so-called Quadri- and Quintiliterals are compounds. **1889** H. MACCOLL *Mr. Strange's Sealed Packet* v. 50 All the creatures..were quadrupeds; there were no quintipeds, sexipeds, or anything of that sort.

quintic ('kwɪntɪk), *a.* and *sb. Math.* [f. L. *quint-us* fifth + -IC.]

A. *adj.* Of the fifth order or degree.

1853 SYLVESTER in *Philos. Mag.* May, To express the number of distinct Quintic and Sextic invariants. **1876** CAYLEY *Math. Papers* (1896) X. 11 A general quintic equation is not solvable by radicals.

B. *sb.* A quantic or surface of the fifth degree.

1856 A. CAYLEY *Wks.* (1889) II. 253 In the case of a quantic of the fifth order or quintic. **1884** W. R. W. ROBERTS in *Hermathena* X. 183 Covariants of binary quintics.

quintil, obs. variant of QUINTAIN[1].

quintile ('kwɪntɪl, -aɪl), *a.* and *sb.*[1] Also 7 -il(l. [f. L. *quint-us* fifth + -ILE, after *quartile.*] **1.** *Astrol.* ***quintile (aspect)***: A planetary aspect, introduced by Kepler, in which the planets are one-fifth of a circle, or 72 degrees, distant from each other.

c **1610** SIR C. HEYDON *Astrol. Disc.* (1650) 95 In these our days our late Artists..have added unto these former Aspects three others, viz. the Quintile [etc.]. **1647** LILLY *Chr. Astrol.* iii. 32 A Quintill consists of two Signes twelve degrees. **1686** GOAD *Celest. Bodies* I. ii. 39 This Notable Effect may be accounted for without these Quintiles.

2. *Statistics.* Any of the four values of a variate which divide a frequency distribution into five groups, each containing one fifth of the total population; also, any of the five groups so produced.

1951 *Brit. Jrnl. Nutrition* V. 199 For the purposes of classification of the subjects into categories of fatness, we have used the twentieth, fortieth, sixtieth and eightieth percentile. These limit values are sometimes called 'quintiles'. **1973** *Jrnl. Genetic Psychol.* CXXIII. 79 Each class's ranked students were divided into quintiles: high, medium-high, middle, medium-low, and low status. **1974** *Nature* 22 Nov. 294/2 These are quintiles for temperature and terciles for rainfall. **1976** *Lancet* 6 Nov. 979/2 Apart from smoking, where no such division into quintiles is practicable, the five measures used are systolic and diastolic blood-pressure, overweight, [etc.].

†**quintile,** *sb.*[2] *Obs. rare*$^{-0}$. [ad. L. *quintīlis*: cf. prec.] July. (Blount *Glossogr.* 1656.) Hence †**quintilian** *a. Obs. rare*$^{-0}$.

1623 COCKERAM, *Quintilian moneth*, the moneth of July.

†**quin'tille.** *Obs. rare*$^{-1}$. [a. F. *quintille*, ad. Sp. *quintillo* f. *quinto* fifth: cf. QUADRILLE *sb.*[1]] A form of ombre, played by five persons.

1734 R. SEYMOUR *Compl. Gamester* (ed. 3) i. 46 Quintille, or Ombre by Five, from whence Quadrille has its Original.

quintillion (kwɪn'tɪljən). [f. L. *quint-us* fifth + *(m)illion*: see BILLION.] **a.** In Great Britain: The fifth power of a million, expressed by 1 followed by thirty ciphers. **b.** In U.S. (as in France): The cube of a million, or 1 followed by eighteen ciphers.

1674 JEAKE *Arith.* (1696) 14 Others..call..the Thirty first place Quintillion, &c. **1841** TUPPER *Twins* xxii, A thousand men in all earth's huge quintillion. **1862** SIR H. HOLLAND *Ess., Life & Organization* 66 A quintillion of living beings.

Hence **quin'tillionth** *a.*

a **1845** HOOD *To Hahnemann* v, Would a quintillionth dose of the New Drop Restore him?

†**quintin.** *Obs. rare.* Also 9 quintain. [a. F. *quintin*, †*quintain*, f. *Quintin*, a town in Brittany. Cf. QUENTIN.] A kind of lawn.

1721 C. KING *Brit. Merch.* II. 348, 809 pieces of Quintins at 10s. [**1869** MRS. PALLISER *Lace* ii. 15 Beneath this network was gummed a piece of fine cloth, called quintain.]

quintin, variant of QUINTAIN[1].

quintine ('kwɪntaɪn). [f. L. *quint-us* fifth.]

1. *Bot.* Mirbel's name for a supposed fifth integument of an ovule (cf. QUARTINE).

1832 LINDLEY *Introd. Bot.* 159 It is apparently this quintine that Mr. Brown describes, in the ovulum of the Orchis tribe.

2. *Chem.* (See quot.)

1873 RALFE *Phys. Chem.* p. xviii, Triads, Glycerin Series, Quintine or Valerylene C_5H_8.

quintine, variant of QUINTAIN[1].

quintis, variant of QUAINTISE.

quintole ('kwɪntəʊl). *Mus.* [Obscurely f. It. *quinto* or L. *quint-us* fifth.] A group of five notes to be played in the time of four. (Stainer & Barrett 1876). So **'quintolet.**

1884 GROVE *Dict. Mus.* IV. 173 These groups, which are sometimes called *quintolets, sextolets*, etc...always have their numbers written above them.

‖**quinton** (kɛ̃tɔ̃). [Fr.] A musical instrument of the viol or violin families, having five strings (see also quots. 1941, 1954).

[**1870** C. ENGEL *Descr. Catal. Mus. Instr. in S. Kensington Mus.* 77 Five-stringed viol. Called by the French *Quinton.*] **1889** [see PARDESSUS 2]. **1916** STANFORD & FORSYTH *Hist. Mus.* ix. 195 True viols have no fewer than six strings apiece. .. But the makers are beginning to see the necessity of reducing the number... They are just introducing a modified type of instrument with five strings. They call these the *quintons*. **1941** [see PARDESSUS 2]. **1954** *Grove's Dict. Mus.* (ed. 5) VI. 1037/1 The rather ugly word quinton seems to have originated as a 19th-century dealers' name to decribe a curious hybrid sort of viol-violin... The instruments appear to belong to the late 18th century... The name drifted into reference books where it was misapplied to the perfectly normal treble and *par-dessus* French viols of the mid-16th century, which often have only five strings. **1961** T. DART in A. Baines *Mus. Instr. through Ages* 189 During the eighteenth century certain hybrids between the two families of viols and violins made a brief appearance on the musical scene—for instance, the quinton, the baryton, and the arpeggione—but few musicians regretted their equally abrupt departure. **1976** *Early Music* July 361/2 The quinton is built basically like a violin, with arched back, shallow ribs and pointed bouts, but with sloping viol shoulders.

quint-pertite: see QUINTI-.

quintroon ('kwɪntruːn). *rare.* Also quinteron, -oon. [ad. Sp. *quinteron*, f. *quinto* fifth.] One who is fifth in descent from a Negro (cf. QUADROON 1 b), and has one-sixteenth of Negro blood.

1797 *Encycl. Brit.* (ed. 3) XII. 796 *note*, The children of a white and quinteroon consider themselves as free from all taint of the negro race. **1835** D. BOOTH *Anal. Dict.* 324 'The child of a Quintroon by a white father is free by law.' Such was recently the West-Indian slave-code. **1878** BARTLEY tr. *Topinard's Anthrop.* II. vii. 374 The first are called mulattoes,..the fourth, quintroons.

†**quintu'plation.** *Obs. rare*$^{-1}$. [f. QUINTUPLE *v.* + -ATION.] = QUINTUPLICATION.

1684 J. WALLIS *Angular Sections* iv, Of the Quintuplation and Quinquisection of an Arch or Angle.

quintuple ('kwɪntjuːp(ə)l), *a.* and *sb.* [a. F. *quintuple* (1484), f. L. *quint-us* fifth, after *quadruple.*]

A. *adj.* **a.** Fivefold; multiplied by five; consisting of five things or parts.

quintuple power, proportion, ratio, the ratio of five to one. ***quintuple time*** in *Mus.* (see quot. 1806).

1570 BILLINGSLEY *Euclid* XIII. ii. 391 If a right line be in power quintuple to a segment of the same line. **1605** BACON *Adv. Learn.* II. xvi. §6 A proportion quintuple at most of the writing infolding to the writing infolded. **1633** HEYWOOD *Eng. Trav.* I. i. Wks. 1874 IV. 7 Bring backe His ship and charge, with profits quintuple. **1672** PETTY *Pol. Anat.* (1691) 24 The number and natural force of the Irish [was] quintuple to that of the English. **1711** WYLDE *Eng. Master Defence* 26 A Falsify is made single,..quadruple, quintuple, or as oft as your Fancy directs. **1806** CALLCOTT *Mus. Gram.* iii. 40 A species of Time called Quintuple, which contains five Crotchets in a Bar. **1875** BLAKE *Zool.* 335 In the Sea-urchins..the body has a quintuple arrangement.

b. *Comb.*, as ***quintuple-nerved, -ribbed.***

1832 LINDLEY *Introd. Bot.* (1839) 129 A leaf..is called triple, quintuple, &c. nerved, if the nerves all proceed from the midrib towards the margin. **1861** BENTLEY *Man. Bot.* 153 If two such ribs arise on each side of the midrib, it is termed quintuple-ribbed or quintuplicostate.

B. *sb.* A fivefold amount; a group of five.

1684 J. WALLIS *Angular Sections* iv. 27 The Quintuple of the Subtense of an Arch. *Ibid.* The Quintuple of the Cube of the same Subtense. **1784** HERSCHEL in *Phil. Trans.* LXXV. 91 Five more [stars] in view, differently dispersed about the quintuple. **1975** N. CHOMSKY *Logical Struct. Linguistic Theory* ix. 327 A set of ordered quintuples $\{(Z, K, Z^1, Pr^{(1)}, Pr^{(2)})\}$.

quintuple ('kwɪntjuːp(ə)l), *v.* [f. prec. Cf. F. *quintupler.*]

1. *trans.* To multiply by five; to make five times as much or as great.

1639 SHIRLEY *Ball* II. i, In three months your estate Will be five times as much, or quintupled. **1674** JEAKE *Arith.* (1696) 200 Quintuple it, and the Product shall be the Divisor. **1796** BURNEY *Mem. Metastasio* III. 101, I beg of you to quintuple,..the embraces, which I consign to you for her use. *a* **1852** MACGILLIVRAY *Nat. Hist. Dee Side* (1855) 21 Who has by his various improvements quintupled his rental. **1889** *Spectator* 13 Apr., The endless difficulty of communication..quintuples all other difficulties.

b. To produce five times as much as.

1824 LANDOR *Imag. Conv., Pallavinchi & Landor* Wks. 1853 I. 42/2 This, and the celebrated vine at Hampton Court..have quintupled the most prolific.

2. *intr.* To increase fivefold; to become five times as many or as great.

1816 SOUTHEY in *Q. Rev.* XV. 538 The population of London must at least have quintupled since that time. **1872** BUCKLE *Misc. Wks.* I. 468 It is stated that within sixty years rents had quintupled.

quintuplet ('kwɪntjuːplɪt, kwɪn'tjuːplɪt). [f. QUINTUPLE *a.*]

1. A set of five things; in *Mus.* = QUINTOLE.

1873 H. C. BANISTER *Music* 13 Other irregularities..such as four notes for three, termed a Quadruplet; five for four, a Quintuplet. **1884** KNIGHT *Dict. Mech. Suppl.* 733/2 *Quintuplet*, said of springs when five of similar type are associated in a group. **1885** *Archæologia* L. 77 These rays are arranged in quintuplets.

2. *pl.* Five children born at a birth.

1889 *Lancet* No. 3417. 392/1 Five years subsequently she gave birth to quintuplets. **1895** *Aberdeen Free Press* 25 Oct. 4 This is the first case of quintuplets in England.

3. A cycle for five riders; a quintet.

1895 *Westm. Gaz.* 17 Oct. 7/2 The latest cycling machine is a quintuplet. **1896** *Daily News* 17 July 7/1 Five spun along at a terrific pace on a quintuplet.

quintupli-, comb. form of QUINTUPLE *a.*, employed in a few terms of *Bot.*, as **,quintupli'costate, -nerved, -ribbed, -veined.**

1861 [see QUINTUPLE 1 b]. **1880** GRAY *Struct. Bot.* 93 The appearance of a second pair of such strengthened veins makes the venation quintupli-ribbed or quintupli-nerved.

quintuplicate (kwɪn'tjuːplɪkət), *a.* and *sb.* [f. QUINTUPLE, after *duplicate, quadruplicate.*]

A. *adj.* Five times repeated; consisting of five things, similar parts, etc. ***quintuplicate proportion***: cf. QUADRUPLICATE *a.* 1.

1656 tr. *Hobbes' Elem. Philos.* (1839) 240 The lengths transmitted shall be to the times in which they are transmitted, in proportion quadruplicate, quintuplicate [etc.].

B. *sb.* **a.** A set of five. Also, ***in quintuplicate.*** **b.** One of a set of five similar things. *rare.*

1851 TRENCH *Stud. Words* vi. (1869) 229 We possess in English a great many duplicates, not to speak of triplicates or of such a quintuplicate as that which I adduced just now. **1941** F. SCOTT FITZGERALD *Last Tycoon* iii. 41 Miss Doolan's notes would be typed in quintuplicate. **1968** H. EDWARDS *Thirty Years Spiritual Healer* v. 51 In Holland, no one can be admitted to a healing meeting unless he becomes a member of the society, and even then records in quintuplicate have to be made for each person attending. **1978** B. NORMAN *To nick a Good Body* vii. 55 Statements..typed out in quintuplicate.

quintupli'cation. *rare.* [noun of action to **quintuplicate* vb.: cf. prec.]

1. The action of multiplying by five.

1674 JEAKE *Arith.* (1696) 24 To multiply by 5, called Quintuplication, adjoyn a Cypher..and take the half thereof. **1888** *Encycl. Brit.* XXIV. 119 The perceptible are evolved out of the imperceptible elements by the process of quintuplication.

2. *Civil* and *Canon Law.* A reply on behalf of the pursuer to the defendant's quadruplication.

1860 MOTLEY *Netherl.* xviii. II. (1869) 376 Lord Henry's harmless thunder was answered..by a 'Quintuplication'.

quin'tupling, *vbl. sb.* [f. QUINTUPL(E *v.* + -ING[1].] Fivefold increase, multiplication by five.

1975 *N.Y. Times* 25 Sept. 65/7 The quintupling of oil prices in the last two years, most economists agree, has accelerated world inflation and intensified the recent slump in world business. **1976** *Times Lit. Suppl.* 20 Feb. 193/3 The burden on the British balance of payments of a quintupling of the price of oil.

† **quintuply**, *sb. Sc. Law. Obs.* [f. QUINTUPLE, after *duply*, *quadruply*.] = QUINTUPLICATION 2.
1663 *Proc. Justiciary Court* (MS.) 85 Quintuplyes. Maxwell for the Pursuer. The Testificate forsaid proceeds [etc.]. **1674** *Ibid.* 654 Quintuplys. Sir Andrew Birnie. That the Defender Robert Steuart cannot pretend ignorance [etc.].

'**quintuply**, *adv. rare.* [f. QUINTUPLE *a.* + -LY².] In a fivefold manner.
1870 H. SPENCER *Princ. Psychol.* (ed. 2) I. v. §239. 548 We may say that they [sensations] are thus characterized by being quintuply-clustered.

‖ **quintus.** *Mus.* [a. L. *quintus* fifth.] (See quot. 1883.)
1883 GROVE *Dict. Mus.* III. 61/1 *Quintus*.., the Fifth Part in a composition for five Voices: called also Pars quinta and Quincuplum. **1954** *Ibid.* (ed. 5) VI. 570/1 When a *quintus* is needed half of it is written on the left-hand page below the *tenor* and the remainder (*reliquium*) below the *bassus*, on the right-hand page. **1977** *Early Music* July 419/3 Those intending to sing through the motet volume should note that the quintus is not in the same vocal range throughout and six voices are needed.

quinua, variant of QUINOA.

† '**quinyie.** *Sc. Obs.* Also 6 quinȝe, -ȝie, 7 -ȝee, 8 quine, qunie. [var. CUNYE, Sc. f. COIN *sb.*]
1. A coin. ***quinyie-house***, the mint. *rare.*
1596 DALRYMPLE tr. *Leslie's Hist. Scot.* VIII. 97 To lat stryk a brassin quinȝie. *Ibid.* x. 350 Onything that in his tyme he had spendet in the Quinȝehous.
2. A corner. ***quinyie-stane***, corner-stone.
1588 in McCrie *Life A. Melville* I. 440 That the bell and clock be transported to the high steeple, and that the kirk have a quinȝee left at the steeple foresaid for the relief thereof. **1734** *Jrnl. fr. London to Scarborough* 1–2 A whittle that lies i' the quinyie o' the maun [= basket]. *a* **1800** in Child *Ballads* V. 248 Ye [have] tane out the quinë-stane. *Ibid.* 11 The qunie-stane.

quinzaine ('kwɪnzeɪn, F. kɛ̃zɛn). *rare.* [a. F. *quinzaine*, a set of fifteen things, a period of fifteen days, f. *quinze*: see next.
Blount *Glossogr.* (1656) has '*Quinzain* (Fr.) a term or delay of fifteen days; also a staff of fifteen verses'. Through Phillips, Bailey, &c., the latter sense has passed into mod. Dicts., but there is no evidence that it has ever been in actual Eng. use. In sense 2 *quinzaine* represents AF. *quinzein*, for *quinzime* QUINZIÈME.]
1. A fortnightly event, meeting, etc. *rare*⁻¹.
1856 MRS. HAWTHORNE in *N. Hawthorne & Wife* (1885) II. 85 Aunt Sue intended to have Quinzaines (fortnightly soirées) this winter.
2. *Hist.* = QUINDENE, QUINZIÈME 2.
1863 J. R. WALBRAN *Mem. Fountains Abbey* (Surtees Soc.) 143 The military levies granted in the Parliament at Lincoln in the Quinzaine of St. Hiliary 9 Edw. II. **1899** R. SHARPE *Cal. Let. Bk.* A. 16, £12 10s. for wine, to be paid in the quinzaine of St. Michael [1277]. *Ibid.* 17, £9 for leather; .. to be paid in the quinzaine of Easter.

quinze (kwɪnz, F. kɛ̃z). [a. F. *quinze*:—L. *quindecim* fifteen.] A card-game depending on chance, in which the winner is that player who obtains fifteen points, or comes nearest to that number without exceeding it.
1716 LADY M. W. MONTAGU *Let. to C'tess Mar* 14 Sept., When the ladies were come in, she sat down to quinze. **1778** SHERIDAN *Camp* II. iii, I daresay you would have thought of proper marquees for hazard and quinze. **1811** LADY GRANVILLE *Lett.* (1894) I. 22 They play at quinze half the night.
Comb. **1762** in Cunningham *Handbk. London* (1850) 546/2 The Quinze players shall pay for their own cards. **1782** J. HARE *Let.* 11 Feb. in *15th Rep. R. Comm. Hist. Manuscripts* App. VI. 576 in *Parl. Papers 1897* (C. 8551) LI. 1 A deep Quinze Table has taken away from Richard and Charles almost the whole profits of the Bank. **1803** *Lett. Miss Riversdale* II. 190 'I never before knew Mrs. Blandford guilty of affectation,' said Lord Lessingham, from the quinz-table.

quinzell, variant of QUINSELL.

quinzième (F. kɛ̃zjɛm). Forms: 5 quynz(i)eme, -zyeme, -sym(e, quinzeme, -zi(s)me, -zyme, 5–6 quinsime, 6 -siem, -ziesme, 7 -siesme, 8 -zieme, 9 -zième. [a. AF. *quinzisme*, *-zime*, *-zieme* (mod.F. *quinzième*), ordinal f. *quinze* fifteen: cf. QUINDECIM. In sense 3 substituted for *quinseine* QUINZAINE.]
1. A tax or duty of a fifteenth. Now only *Hist.*
1429 *Rolls Parlt.* IV. 336/2 Graunt to you our.. Lord the Kyng..an hole Quinszisme, and an hole Disme. *c* **1460** FORTESCUE *Abs. & Lim. Mon.* xii. (1885) 140 When the reaume gaff to thair kyng a quinsime and a desime quinqueniale. **1480** CAXTON *Chron. Eng.* clviii. 140 A quinzeme of goodes were graunted for the newe chartres. **1559** in Strype *Ann. Ref.* (1824) I. II. App. viii. 427 The clergie chardged with quinsiems and other payements. *a* **1577** SIR T. SMITH *Commw. Eng.* (1633) 145 Incident acquisitions, bee they rents customes tenths quinziesmes taxes [etc.]. **1777** *Ann. Reg.* II. 41 The clergy had compounded for a tax called the quinzieme or fifteenth penny. **1891** *Q. Rev.* Oct. 111 It paid the highest quinzième of any port except London.
† **2.** The fifteenth (= fourteenth) day after a church festival; = QUINDENE. *Obs.*
1433 *Rolls Parlt.* IV. 420/2 Bytwix this and the Quinszisme of Seint Michell next. *c* **1450** *Merlin* 374 This was the quynsyme after Pentecoste. **1480** CAXTON *Chron. Eng.* ccxxvi. 232 At his parlement holden at Westmynstre the quynzeme of Paske.
† **3.** A period of fifteen days; *spec.* the day of a church festival and the two weeks following. *Obs.*
c **1430** *Pilgr. Lyf Manhode* III. x. (1869) 146, I selle it bi dayes and bi wookes, bi vtases and bi quinzimes, bi monethes, and bi yeeres al hol. **1480** CAXTON *Chron. Eng.* lxiii. 47 Tho two bretheren of Constance shall come byfore a quynzieme passed.

† **quinzine.** *Obs. rare.* In 5 quynsine, -syn(n)e, 6 -zysne. [Alteration of prec.]
1. = QUINZIÈME 1.
1502 ARNOLDE *Chron.* 179 The quynzysne by your saide commons afore this tyme so often graunted.
2. The fifteenth (= fourteenth) day after a specified day; *spec.* = QUINZIÈME 2.
c **1450** *Merlin* 62 Thus suffred Merlyn to the quynsyne of Pentecoste. *Ibid.* 65 That ye somownera grete courte.. and that ye make hem all to wite that it shall holde to the quynsine, and that eche come araide to a-bide xv dayes.

quiok, obs. variant of QUEYOCK, heifer.

quip (kwɪp), *sb.* Also 6 quyppe, 6–7 quipp(e. [var. of QUIPPY (q.v.), perh. associated with words of similar ending (as *clip*, *nip*, *snip*, *whip*) which contain the idea of something sharp or cutting.]
1. A sharp or sarcastic remark directed against a person; a clever gird or hit. In later use also without implication of sharpness: A clever, smart, or witty saying; a verbal conceit. Freq. in phr. ***quips and cranks*** (after quot. 1632).
In common use down to *c* 1650, after which literary examples are rare till after 1800.
1532 MORE *Confut. Tindale* Wks. 709/2 With this goodly quyppe agaynste me. **1584** LYLY *Alex. & Camp.* III. ii, What's a quip? *Man.* Wee great girders call it a short saying of a sharpe wit, with a bitter sense in a sweet word. **1632** MILTON *L'Allegro* 27 Quips and Cranks, and wanton Wiles. **1665** MANLEY *Grotius' Low C. Warres* 351 This by a military jest, and facetious quip, they called the Commonwealth. **1784** COWPER *Task* II. 472 Direct me to a quip Or merry turn in all he [Paul] ever wrote. **1843** LEVER *J. Hinton* xliv, The whole conversation is..a hailstorm of short stories, quips, and retorts. **1855** A. MANNING *O. Chelsea Bun-ho.* xvi. 274 She..gave him back quip for crank.
b. A verbal equivocation; a quibble.
c **1590** GREENE *Fr. Bacon* ix. 225 These Schollers know.. How to vse quips and sleights of Sophistrie. **1812** KNOX & JEBB *Corr.* II. 95 The practical goodness may be readily overlooked, whilst theological quips and quiddities may be fastened on. **1850** KINGSLEY *Alt. Locke* xxxvii, I will not.. entrap you by quips and special pleading. **1875** JOWETT *Plato* (ed. 2) III. 73 Tricks of controversy and quips of law.
2. a. A curious, odd, or fantastic action or feature.
1820 SHELLEY *Witch Atlas* li, Many quips and cranks She played upon the water. *a* **1864** HAWTHORNE *Amer. Note-bks.* (1879) I. 136 His manner was full of quirks and quips. **1878** MRS. STOWE *Poganuc P.* ix. 75 All the quips and turns and oddities of human nature.
b. An odd and whimsical trifle; a knick-knack.
1820 SHELLEY *Let. to Maria Gisborne* 55 Upon the table More knacks and quips there be than I am able To catalogize. **1824** MISS MITFORD *Village* Ser. I. (1863) 216 The quips and quiddities of these degenerate days, little bits of riband, and pasteboard, and gilt paper.
Hence '**quipful**, '**quippish** (also **-ly**, **-ness**), '**quippy**, '**quipsome** *adjs.*, given to or characterized by quips; so '**quipsomeness**; '**quipster**, one given to quips.
a **1834** S. T. COLERIDGE in *N. & Q.* (1888) 7th Ser. VI. 501/2, I prefer Fuller's [version] as more quippish and adagy. **1859** W. CHADWICK *Life De Foe* vii. 372 As a writer, he was a quippy slack-wire performer. **1876** J. WEISS *Wit, Hum. & Shaks.* vi. 198 There never was such a jaunty and irrepressible quipster. **1881** *Sat. Rev.* 23 Apr. 528 His very style is young, and not without a certain quipsomeness. **1884** MISS YONGE in *Eng. Illustr. Mag.* I. 462 Is it only that the lad is thy very marrow, quipsome one? **1909** A. BENNETT *Literary Taste* vi. 31 Charles Lamb's essay on *Dream Children*..enlivened by a certain quippishness concerning the children. **1962** *Punch* 15 Aug. 224/2 The one who provides the old Russian sayings is his nearest equivalent to [Bob] Hope's tarmac quipster. **1976** *New Scientist* 22 July 190/3 Another speaker quippishly suggested that we should treat them [*sc.* 'core' journals] like apples. **1976** *National Observer* (U.S.) 14 Aug. 16/2 He doesn't mind being called Gooey Lombardo or Guy Lumbago; he smiles when quipsters dub him the Pied Piper of the geriatric set. **1977** *Time* 6 June 39/2 A quipster with no audience for his one-liners?

quip (kwɪp), *v.* [f. prec. sb.]
1. a. *trans.* To assail with a quip or quips.
1584 LYLY *Alex. & Camp.* III. ii, Didst thou not finde I did quip thee? **1625** W. B. *True School War* 56 Hee spake these expresse words to some that quipped him for this. *a* **1670** HACKET *Cent. Serm.* (1675) 791 The Heathen quipt them that they had no Images nor Altars. **1841** D'ISRAELI *Amen. Lit.* (1859) I. 286 If any one quipped the profession of another.
b. With speech as direct object: to say or reply as a quip.
1950 *New Yorker* 25 Mar. 26/3 'Looks like somebody lost their head!' quipped Detective Garnet P. Quail. **1965** D. LODGE *Brit. Mus. is falling Down* viii. 132 'Someone taking my name in vain?'.. 'In bane,' Adam quipped, and laughed immoderately. **1974** *Times* 11 Oct. 10/1 'I became a tremendous bargain. I went from a million to nothing,' she quipped to reporters. **1978** *Woman's Own* 16 Sept. 12/1 My daughter was rather amused and quipped: 'Most parents have problem teenagers but we have a problem mother.'
2. *intr.* To use a quip or quips; to be wittily sarcastic. Const. *at*, *with*.
1579 LYLY *Euphues* (Arb.) 206 Ye malitious haue more minde to quip, then might to cut. **1603** FLORIO *Montaigne* II. ix. (1897) III. 129 Tacitus doth pleasantly quip and jest at the men of war of our ancient Gaules. **1633** PRYNNE *1st Pt. Histrio-m.* VIII. vi. 796 If you will learne..to deride, quippe, scorne,..you neede not goe to any other schooles. **1908** *Smart Set* June 50 Audrey in her blithesome way Would quip and jest with roguish glee. **1942** Z. N. HURSTON *Dust Tracks on Road* xii. 225 The educated Negro..is fighting entirely out of his class when he tries to quip with the underprivileged.
Hence '**quipper**, one who quips.
1589 NASHE *Introd. Greene's Menaphon* (Arb.) 14 Here, peraduenture, some desperate quipper will canuaze my proposed comparison. *a* **1603** in Nichols *Progr.* III. 143 What meane you, a starmonger, the quipper of the firmament. **1611** COTGR., *Lardonneur*, a quipper, girder, flowter. **1951** O. NASH *Family Reunion* 36 She'll nogg his eggs and she'll toast his kippers, And disparage the quips of the current quippers. **1960** *Guardian* 19 Nov. 3/6 His intervention has at least provided the quippers with a not very good quip.

quip(pe, obs. forms of WHIP.

quippery ('kwɪpərɪ). *rare.* [f. QUIP *sb.* or *v.* + -ERY.] The uttering or bandying of quips; quips collectively.
1960 *Guardian* 22 July 10/6 This is campaign quippery, and we shall have a bellyful of it before the winter.

quipping ('kwɪpɪŋ), *vbl. sb.* [f. QUIP *v.* + -ING¹.] The action of the vb.
1579 G. HARVEY *Letter-bk.* (Camden) 61 Whisperings open or close, quippinge notorious or auricular iybinge. **1603** FLORIO *Montaigne* II. xi. (1632) 233 The nimble saying or wittie quipping of Arcesilaus. **1658** ROWLAND *Moufet's Theat. Ins.* 1007 Terambus a Satyrist, did not abstain from quipping of the Muses. **1887** SAINTSBURY *Elizab. Lit.* xii. (1890) 437 In contradistinction to this perpetual quipping.. the general style of Fuller is..rather more modern.

quipping ('kwɪpɪŋ), *ppl. a.* [f. as prec. + -ING².] That quips; of the nature of a quip.
1577–87 HOLINSHED *Chron.* I. 34/1 In frumping of his adversaries with quipping taunts. **1603** KNOLLES *Hist. Turks* (1621) 703 The bishop..after his quipping manner requested [etc.]. **1605** CAMDEN *Rem.* 195 His salt and sharpe quipping speeches. **1660** *Charac. Italy* 54 A Conceit no less facetious than quipping.

† '**quippy.** *Obs. rare.* Also 6 quipp-, quyppie. [Of obscure origin; perh. a. L. *quippe* indeed, forsooth (with sarcastic force).] = QUIP *sb.*
1519 HORMAN *Vulg.* 61 §3 To rayle and rage vpon hym in rymes and quyppies. **1549** CHALONER *Erasm. on Folly* Sj, Which quippie in waie of reproche is used against blockheades. **1569** J. SANFORD tr. *Agrippa's Van. Artes* 116 Sometimes they mainetaine talke with fond quippies.

‖ **quipu** ('kiːpuː, 'kwɪpuː). Also quipo, quippu, -o. [Quichuan *quipu* knot.] A device of the ancient Peruvians and others for recording events, keeping accounts, sending messages, etc., consisting of cords or threads of various colours, knotted in various ways.
1704 tr. *Ovalle's Kingd. Chile* in *Churchill's Voy.* III. 74 They have their quipoes, which is a sort of strings of different bigness in which they make knots of several colours, by which they remember... When they go to confession these quipoes serve them to remember their sins. **1777** ROBERTSON *Hist. Amer.* II. VII. 304 The quipos seem to have been a device for rendering calculation more expeditious and accurate. **1853** TH. ROSS *Humboldt's Trav.* III. xxvi. 88 These quipos or knotted cords are found in Canada, in Mexico, in Peru, in the plains of Guiana, in Central Asia, in China, and in India. **1870** LUBBOCK *Orig. Civiliz.* ii. (1875) 43 Even the Peruvians had no better means of recording events than the Quippu or Quipu.
attrib. **1830** CARLYLE *Misc.* (1857) II. 168 History has been written with quipo-threads, with feather pictures, with wampum-belts. **1845** —— *Cromwell* (1871) I. Introd. 4 Monumental stoneheaps and Quipo thrums to keep record by.
b. *transf.* and *fig.*
1781 *Mrs. Delany's Corr.* Ser. II. II. 64, I believe you would contrive to knot them some quipos of kind remembrance. **1885** MRS. LYNN LINTON *Chr. Kirkland* III. iii. 83 Marian Evans, whose first knot in the quipos of her fame was made by this work.

quir, obs. form of *quire* CHOIR.

† **quirace**, obs. f. CUIRASS. (Also pl. *quiracies*.)
1584 HUDSON *Du Bartas' Judith* v. 365 All their bucklers, Morions, and Quiraces Were of no proofe against their peisant maces. **1596** DANETT tr. *Comines* (1614) 12 There were not foure hundred of them armed with quiracies.

quirboil(l)y, obs. form of CUIR-BOUILLI.

quire (kwaɪə(r)), *sb.*¹ Forms: *α.* 3 cwaer, quaer, 4–5 quayer, (5 -ere, qwayer, quaier), 4–6 quayre, (5 qwayre, qvayr), 5–6 qv-, quare, quair, 5–7 quaire, (6 qw-). *β.* 6 quear(e, quere, 6–7 queere, 6–7 (9 *dial.*) queer. *γ.* 6 quier, quyer, 5– quire. [a. OF. *quaer*, *quaier* (later *caier*, mod. *cahier* a quire of six sheets, a copy-book, writing-book, etc.) = Prov. *cazern*, It. *quaderno*:—pop.L. **quaternum* (med.L. *quaternus*, *-um*), f. L. *quaterni* a set of four, f. *quattuor* four: see QUATERNION. The loss of the final *-n* in F. *quaer* for **quaern* is normal; cf. *chair*, *enfer*, etc. Icel. *kver* a quire, little book, is from F. or Eng.

There are three main forms of the word in Eng., *quair*, *quear* (*quere*), *quire*. The second of these arises from a narrowing of the vowel after the *k-* sound (cf. *quail* and *queal*, *quaisy* and *queasy*, *kay* and *key*, *kayles* and *keals*, *kaiser* and *keasar*), and the further change to *quier*, *quire* is similar to that of *brere*, *frere* to *briar*, *friar*.]

1. a. A set of four sheets of parchment or paper doubled so as to form eight leaves, a common unit in mediæval manuscripts; hence, any collection or gathering of leaves, one within the other, in a manuscript or printed book. Also, twenty-four (formerly sometimes twenty-five) sheets of writing-paper.

α. *c* **1450** *St. Cuthbert* (Surtees) 1549–50 Of quayers seuen I haue a boke We may ilk a day a quayer loke. **1469** *Paston Lett.* II. 335, I did write to quairs of papir of witnessis, every quair conteynyng xiiij leves. **1531** Elyot *Gov.* 172 Muche more he wrote, as it seemed, for diuers quaires lacked in the boke. **1613** *Mem. St. Giles's, Durham* (Surtees) 42 A quaire of paper for the use of the parishe.

β. **1530** Palsgr. 164 *Mayn*, bothe for a hande and for a queare of paper. **1575** Churchyard *Chippes* (1817) 106 If heere I should all skirmishes expresse..Of paper sure, a quere would not suffice. **1597** Bp. Hall *Sat.* II. i. 10 Lo what it is that makes white rags so deare, That men must giue a teston for a queare. **1696** in *Pall Mall G.* (1889) 8 Jan. 7/2 A Queer of paper..A Coppy Booke. **1825** Brockett *N.C. Gloss.*, *Queer*, a quire of paper.

γ. **1497** *Naval Acc. Hen. VII* (1896) 128, j reame & vij quires of small paper. **1560** *Ludlow Churchw. Acc.* (Camden) 96 A quyer of paper..iiij *d.* **1589** *Pappe w. Hatchet* B, Hee'le spend all he hath in a quire of paper. **1646** J. Hall *Poems* I How better were it for you to remain (Poore Quires) in ancient raggs. **1688** R. Holme *Armoury* III. 120/1 Cassie Quires, are the two outside Quires in a Ream, called also Cording Quires. **1772** *Junius Lett.* lxviii. 354 He was charged..for feloniously stealing eleven quires of writing paper. **1879** *Print. Trades Jrnl.* No. 26. 20 The cost of paper from one quire to one ream.

b. *in quires*: Unbound, in sheets.

c **1480** *Paston Lett.* III. 301 Item, in quayers, Tully *de Senectute*. *Ibid.*, Item, in qwayers, a Boke *de Sapiencia*. **1549** *Bk. Com. Prayer* (Grafton) colophon, The Imprinter to sell this Booke in Queres for two shillynges and sixe pence. **1679** Wood *Life* 10 Feb. (O.H.S.) II. 439, I gave my book..to the Heralds Office in quires. **1733** Swift *On Poetry* 144 Your poem sunk, And sent in quires to line a trunk. **1885** *Bookseller* 5 Mar. 313 *Advt.*, The valuable publication stock, in Cloth and Quires.

fig. **1682** Grew *Anat. Plants* Ep. Ded., So that a Plant is, as it were, an Animal in Quires.

†**2.** A small pamphlet or book, consisting of a single quire; a short poem, treatise, etc., which is or might be contained in a quire. *Obs.*

a **1225** *Ancr. R.* 248 þeo ancre þet wernde an oðer a cwaer uorto lenen. *Ibid.* 282 ȝif þu hauest knif oðer cloð..scrowe oðer quaer. *c* **1430** Lydg. *Compl. Bl. Knt.* xcvii, Go litel quayre, go unto my lyves queene. *c* **1430** *Life St. Kath.* (1884) 1 Ther was take to me a quayere. Where yn was drawe in to englesshe..hire martirdom. *c* **1500** *MS. Selden* B. 24 lf. 191 Heirefter followis the quair maid be King James of Scotland the first, callit the kingis quair. *a* **1529** Skelton *Sp. Parrot* 280 Go litell quayre, namyd the Popagay. *c* **1535** Fisher *Wks.* (E.E.T.S.) 429 Who so euer ye be, yᵗ shall fortune to rede this queare. **1570** Foxe *A. & M.* 1393/2 The bishop of Salis. drewe out a quire of the Concordance, and layd it before the bishop of Harford.

3. *Comb.*, as *quire signature* [signature *sb.* 6 a], *-work*; *quire-folded* adj.; **quire stock**, books in quires; **quire-wise** *adv.*, on double leaves, which can be formed into quires to be sewed.

1688 R. Holme *Armoury* III. 124/1 When quire work is Printed. **1882** J. Southward *Pract. Printing* xiii. 117 Folio sheets are sometimes required to be..folded within each other, or *quirewise*. **1885** *Bookseller* 5 Mar. *Advt.*, Bookselling Business for Sale..including..bound and quire Stock. **1888** C. T. Jacobi *Printers' Vocab.* 108 *Quire folded*.., folded in quires—not sent in 'flat'. *Ibid.* 109 *Quirewise*, jobs of single leaves printed on both sides of the paper. **1922** Joyce *Ulysses* 120 The nethermost deck of the first machine jogged forward its flyboard with sllt [*sic*] the first batch of quirefolded papers. **1957** N. R. Ker *Catal. MSS. containing Anglo-Saxon* p. xl (*heading*) Quire-Signatures and Leaf-Numbers. **1978** *Anglo-Saxon England* VII. 232 It may have its own series of quire signatures.

quire, *sb.*²: see choir.

quire (kwaɪə(r)), *v.*¹ [f. quire *sb.*¹] *trans.* To arrange in quires. Hence **quired** *ppl. a.*

1683 Moxon *Mech. Exerc., Printing* xxii. ¶4 If they be Quir'd Sheets, that is, two, three, or four Sheets Quir'd together. *Ibid.* xxv. ¶4 The Backs of the Quired Books. **1688** R. Holme *Armoury* III. 124/1 The number of Sheets Quired one in the other. **1875** Southward *Dict. Typogr.* 117 *Quired.* Two sheets so imposed as when folded and made up will lie one within the other.

quire, *v.*², to sing: see choir *v.*

quire, obs. f. quarry *sb.*¹, queer *a.*²; var. quere *v.* to inquire.

†**quirer.** *Obs.*⁻¹ [f. quire *v.*²] A chorister.

1624 Heywood *Gunaik.* VII. 335 Neere to the chamber doore the Quirers thus sing.

quirester, obs. form of chorister.

quirie, obs. variant of *querry* equerry, q.v.

†**'quirily**, *adv. Obs. rare*⁻¹. ? Quiveringly.

1582 Stanyhurst *Æneis* I. (Arb.) 24 Some doe slise owt collops on spits yeet quirilye trembling.

Quirinal ('kwɪrɪnəl). [ad. It. *Quirinale* (also used), f. L. *collis Quirīnālis*.] The name of the royal (now presidential) palace on the Quirinal hill in Rome, and hence used to designate the Italian monarchy or government, *esp.* as distinct from the Vatican. Also *attrib.*

1851 W. E. Gladstone tr. *Farini's Roman State* II. i. 3 The Civic Guards and the commonalty gave the wonted expression of their thanks in the Piazza of the Quirinal. **1881** E. W. Hamilton *Diary* 7 Dec. (1972) I. 195 Errington.. whom suspicious people regard as a probable diplomatic agent at the Quirinal, seems..to be going rather too fast ahead. **1905** J. Webster *Wheat Princess* vii. 78 Being interested in the domestic arrangements of kings, she was insistent that they visit the Quirinal. **1917** N. Douglas *South Wind* xxxiv. 408 A feeling of joyous elation at the prospect..of a battle between the Vatican and the Quirinal. **1922** *Contemp. Rev.* Nov. 583 The complete accord which exists in practice between the Vatican and the Quirinal. **1927** E. M. Forster *Aspects of Novel* viii. 193 He..sets him out to explore [Roman] society..café, studio, Vatican and Quirinal purlieus are all reached. **1949** N. Mitford *Love in Cold Climate* I. x. 107 Friendship with royal personages only ever began for her when their days of glory were finished. Tsarkoe-Selo, Schönbrunn, the Quirinal,..and the island of Corfu had never known her, unless among an enormous crowd in the state apartments. **1979** N. Slater *Falcon* v. 91 He looked more like a country squire than Her Majesty's Ambassador to the Quirinale.

quiring ('kwaɪərɪŋ), *vbl. sb.* [f. quire *v.*¹ + -ing¹.] **a.** A series of signatures indicating the order of quires. **b.** The arrangement of a series of quires.

1922 *J. & J. Leighton's Catal. Old & Interesting Bks.* N.S. III. 209 Without printed quiring, &c., but original MS. signatures remain. **1957** N. R. Ker *Catal. MSS. containing Anglo-Saxon* p. xxv, A book in which the sheets are arranged like this shows two hair sides where one quire ends and the next begins... The collation of such books is simple and the original quiring can be made out even if the leaves have been mounted separately. **1968** G. Pollard in *Bodl. Libr. Rec.* VIII. 82 Having thus established the arrangement of the first twenty-eight leaves, we must now consider the quiring at the opposite end of the book. **1975** N. Barker in R. W. Hunt et al. *Studies in Bk. Trade in Honour of G. Pollard* 11 The quiring may have been put in and later trimmed away.

quiring: see choiring *vbl. sb.* and *ppl. a.*

quirister, obs. or arch. form of chorister.

quiritarian (kwɪrɪ'tɛərɪən), *a. Rom. Law.* [f. as next + -an.] = quiritary.

1842–3 *W. Smith's Dict. Gr. & Rom. Antiq.* s.v. *Legatum*, The legatee had the quiritarian..ownership of the legacy. **1861** [see bonitarian]. **1871** Poste *Gaius* III. §80 Quiritarian ownership is only acquired by usucapion.

quiritary ('kwɪrɪtərɪ), *a.* [ad. late L. *quirītāri-us*, f. *Quirītēs* Roman citizens.] That is in accordance with Roman civil law; legal, as opposed to equitable (see bonitarian). Also of property: Held by legal right or under Roman law.

1865 Merivale *Rom. Emp.* VIII. lxvii. 285 Every citizen ..so far as he was the occupier of Roman or Quiritary soil, ..enjoyed exemption from the tribute or rent-charge due to the state. **1871** Poste *Gaius* III. 285 A quaestor..who sold under the spear, the symbol of quiritary dominion. **1880** Muirhead *Gaius* I. 119, I say that this slave is mine in quiritary right.

†**quiri'tation.** *Obs. rare.* [ad. L. *quirītātio* (Livy), n. of action f. *quirītāre* to cry, lament.] A complaint, lament.

1634 Bp. Hall *Contempl., N.T.* IV. *Crucifixion*, How is it then, with thee, O Saviour, that thou thus astonishest men and Angels with so woful a quiritation. **1656** in Blount *Glossogr.*

quiritian (kwɪ'rɪʃən). *rare.* [f. L. *Quirīt-ēs* (see quiritary) + -ian.] A Roman citizen.

1880 Muirhead *Gaius* II. §40 A man was either owner according to the law of the Quiritians, or he was not held to be owner at all.

quirk (kwɜːk), *sb.*¹ Also 6 **quircke**, **queerk**, 6–7 **quirke**, 6–9 **querk**, 7 **quirck**, **quer(c)ke**, **quirt**, (**qirk**). [Of obscure origin and history; app. native in western dialects.

The original sense was prob. as in 6, whence on the one hand the techn. and dial. uses in 7, in which the 'quirk' is in some material thing, and on the other hand the literary uses in 1–5, referring to mental operations, modes of action, etc. The earliest trace of the word appears in Salesbury's Welsh Dict. (1547), where *Kwyrk-hosan* is given as the W. equivalent of Eng. *clock* (see 7 a); the term is still current in Wales, but its form proves it to be from Eng.]

1. a. A verbal trick, subtlety, shift or evasion; a quibble, quibbling argument.

1565 T. Stapleton *Fortr. Faith* 100* Not vpon quirkes and suttelties in matters indifferent. **1566** Drant *Horace, Sat.* I. v. C iij b, The quiddityes and queerks of logique darke. **1583** Stubbes *Anat. Abus.* II. (1882) 46 They inuente quirckes and quiddities, shiftes, and put-offes ynough to blinde the eies of the magistrates. **1625** W. Pemble *Justification* (1629) 190 The shifting quercke of a schoolemans braine. **1678** R. L'Estrange *Seneca's Mor.* (1702) 131 Not with Syllogisms or Quirks of Wit; but with plain and weighty Reason. **1711** E. Ward *Vulgus Brit.* II. 132 Perverting solid Sense, With artful Querks and Impudence. **1782** Cowper *Progr. Err.* 550 His still refuted quirks he still repeats. **1814** D'Israeli *Quarrels Auth.* (1867) 251 A true feeling of religion does not depend on the quirks and quibbles of human reasonings. **1878** Browning *Poets Croisic* cxxx, In vain the Chevalier beat brain for quirk To help in this conjuncture.

Comb. **1802–12** Bentham *Ration. Judic. Evid.* (1827) IV. 386 The quirk-abjuring ejaculation..of lord Hale.

b. The employment of quirks; quibbling.

1674 N. Fairfax *Bulk & Selv.* 173 This indeed smells pretty strong of quirk, but relishes as faintly as may be of reason. **1796** Charlotte Smith *Marchmont* IV. 221 His fears lest chicane and quirk..should deprive Althea..of the two thousand pounds. **1839** Carlyle *Chartism* v. (1858) 25 Shiftiness, quirk, attorney-cunning..fancies itself..to be talent.

2. A clever or witty turn or conceit; a quip.

1599 Shaks. *Much Ado* II. i. 245, I may chance haue some odde quirkes and remnants of witte broken on mee. **1633** T. Adams *Exp. 2 Peter* i. 4 It is not enough to have quirks of wit, but soundness of doctrine. **1699** Bentley *Phal.* iii. 145 His Quirks and Witticisms upon Me are all grafted upon his own mistakes. **1794** Godwin *Cal. Williams* 28 Your rhymes and your rebusses, your quirks and your conundrums. **1835** Marryat *Jac. Faithf.* xxvii, He had a quiz and a quirk for everybody that passed. **1882** L. Campbell *Life Clerk Maxwell* ii. 31 He must..enliven it with some quirk of fancy.

3. *Mus.* A sudden turn; a fantastic phrase. *rare.*

1579 Gosson *Sch. Abuse* (Arb.) 28 How many noates, how many restes, how many querks. **1731** Pope *Ep. Burlington* 143 Light quirks of Music, broken and uneven. **1883** Lathrop *Span. Vistas* 126 The quirks of the melody are not unlike those of very old English ballads.

4. a. A trick or peculiarity in action or behaviour; †a knack, a fad.

1601 Shaks. *Twel. N.* III. iv. 268, I have heard of some kinde of men that put quarreles purposely on others, to taste their valour; belike this is a man of that quirke. *a* **1635** Corbet *Poems* (1807) 100 He hath besides a pretty quirk.. how to work In iron with much ease. **1656** Earl Monm. tr. *Boccalini's Advts. fr. Parnass.* I. xli. (1674) 54 Having their heads full of querks and new inventions. **1791** Learmont *Poems* 42 He is..markin' out some dyke, or drainin' Wi' mony a quirk. *a* **1864** Hawthorne *Amer. Note-bks.* (1879) I. 136 His manner was full of quirks. **1868** Miss Alcott *Lit. Women* (1869) I. iii. 44 How do you learn all the proper quirks?

b. A peculiar feature or result (*of* an event); a peculiarity, an anomaly, a freak.

1961 *Yale Rev.* LI. 190 It is one of the ironic quirks of history that the viability and usefulness of nationalism and the territorial state are rapidly dissipating at precisely the time that the nation-state attained its highest number. **1973** A. H. Sommerstein *Sound Pattern Anc. Gr.* ii. 74 The other two rules..are mere quirks, survivals that play no active role in the system of the language, but merely go on existing. **1976** *Scotsman* 20 Nov. (Weekend Suppl.), In the San Blas Islands, off the coast of Panama, they found that through a quirk of history they had come a step closer to home. **1976** *Star* (Sheffield) 29 Nov. 12/7 Perhaps..it was something of an unfortunate quirk of the draw that they had to meet in the first round of the Roebuck Cup.

5. A fit, start, sudden stroke.

1601 Shaks. *All's Well* III. ii. 51, I haue felt so many quirkes of ioy and greefe. **1928** Galsworthy *Swan Song* II. x. 188 That indefinable look of a damned soul..awakened within Soames..the queerest little quirk of sympathy.

6. A sudden twist, turn, or curve; *esp.* in drawing or writing: A flourish.

1605 B. Jonson *Volpone* III. vii, Some yong Frenchman.. That..Knew euery quirke within lusts laborinth. **1840** Thackeray *George Cruikshank* Wks. 1900 XIII. 309 These little dots and specks, and fantastical quirks of the pencil. **1860** Bushnell in *Life* xx. (1880) 437 Write a large, full, regular, and free hand. Bring in no quirks and flourishes.

7. *techn.* or *dial.*

a. In a stocking = clock *sb.*²

1547 [see etym. note]. **1583** Stubbes *Anat. Abus.* I. E iij b, Then haue they nether-stocks to these gay hosen..with quirks and clocks about the ancles. [**1834** Planché *Brit. Costume* 260 Hose..with quirks, clocks, open seams.] **1879–** In dial. glossaries (Chesh., Shropsh., Som., etc.).

b. A diamond-shaped piece of leather inserted at the junction of the fingers with the palm in some makes of gloves.

1688 R. Holme *Armoury* III. 18/1 Of a Glove..the Querks, the little square peeces at the bottom of the Fingers. **1881** *Oxfordshire Gloss.* Suppl., *Quirks*, the bits between the fingers of leather gloves, where they open.

c. A piece added to, or taken from, a regular figure, or cut out of a certain surface (see quots.).

1679 Moxon *Mech. Exerc.* I. 130 If either a Quirk or any Addition be added to the Building, on any side of your Ground-plot, you must describe it also proportionably. **1688** R. Holme *Armoury* III. 110/2 A square being struck into four parts, one of those parts in Carpentry Terms is called a Quirk. **1842** Francis *Dict. Arts* s.v., The irregular garden beds, cut out of grass lawns, are..as truly quirks as any other example that can be adduced.

d. An irregular pane of glass (see quots.).

1688 R. Holme *Armoury* III. 385/2 Querke, is a nook shoten Pane, or any Pane whose sides and top run out of a square form. **1847–78** Halliwell, *Quirk*,..a pane of glass cut at the sides and top in the form of a rhomb.

e. *Arch.* An acute hollow between the convex part of certain mouldings and the soffit or fillet. Also *attrib.* or as *adj.*

1799 A. Young *View Agric. Lincoln* 29 Window shutters quirk, ogee and astragal with ¼ and 2 heights and 4 panels, at 12 d. **1816** J. Smith *Panorama Sc. & Art* I. 173 The Grecian mouldings are often..worked with a small return, technically called a quirk. **1836** Parker *Gloss. Archit.* (1850) I. 379 In Gothic architecture quirks are abundantly used between mouldings. **1842** Gwilt *Encycl. Archit.* §2367 A two-panel door, square on one side, with quirk ovolo and bead upon the other. **1876** T. Hardy *Ethelberta* v, Along fillet, quirk, arris, and moulding. **1882** Nodal & Milner

Gloss. Lancs. Dial. 220 *Querk, sb.*, a moulding in joinery. **1966** J. FLEMING et al. *Penguin Dict. Archit.* 181/2 *Quirk*, a sharp v-shaped incision in a moulding and between mouldings.

8. *Comb.* **quirk-float**, a plasterer's float used for angles; **quirk-moulding**, a moulding with a quirk or sharp return (Crabb, 1823); hence ***quirk-moulded*** ppl. adj.

1833 LOUDON *Encycl. Archit.* 1129/2 *Quirk moulding*, a quirk in a moulding signifies a sharp turn. **1842** GWILT *Encycl. Archit.* §2368 Shutters... Add ·016 to the rate for every extra panel, and ·012 for any extra height, and ·008 if they are quirk moulded. **1842–59** *Ibid.* §2242 Floats are of three sorts: the hand float..; the quirk float, which is used on or in angles; and the Derby.

† **quirk** (kwɜːk), *sb.*[2] *R.A.F. slang. Obs.* [Perh. f. prec.: cf. ERK.] **a.** An inexperienced airman.

1916 *Daily Chron.* 13 Oct. 4/5 The quirk becomes used to the handling of the craft.. until.. the instructor allows him to fly the machine himself. **1917** *Sunday Times* 20 May 8/4 'Quirks', it may be explained, are young enemy aviators in an embryonic stage. **1918** E. C. MIDDLETON *Glorious Exploits Air* ii. 33 Once he has his air-legs there is little the 'hun' or 'quirk'—Service terms for beginners—does not feel himself capable of tackling. **1919** *Glasgow Herald* 19 Dec. 14/2 The.. airman.. uses the word 'quirk' in two senses, first to denote the learner's aeroplane, the clanging, clattering 'rumpty' of his youth, or, secondly to denote the learner himself. **1928** C. F. S. GAMBLE *Story N. Sea Air Station* ix. 133 The pilot, a very harmless, innocent 'quirk', hardly fledged, straight from Chingford. **1931** [see KIWI 3].

b. (See quot. 1925.)

1917 'CONTACT' *Airman's Outings* 128 The ferry-pilot who had brought me left for Rafborough almost immediately on a much-flown 'quirk'. **1917** *Let.* Apr. in A. J. L. Scott *60 Squad* (1920) iii. 49 One place was pointed out to us where there was an old 'quirk'. [*Note*] A pet name used for artillery machines of the B.E. type. **1919** [see prec. sense]. **1925** FRASER & GIBBONS *Soldier & Sailor Words* 234 *Quirk*,.. a name for a 'B.E.' type of aeroplane; very stable, but very slow. Also any freak type, or unusually designed aeroplane.

quirk (kwɜːk), *v.*[1] [f. QUIRK *sb.*[1]]

1. a. *trans.* To assail with quirks or quips. **b.** *intr.* To use quirks or quips. Also with *it.*

1596 NASHE *Saffron Walden* 41 Not so much to quirke or crosse me thereby, as to blesse himselfe. **1599** —— *Lenten Stuffe* Wks. 1883–4 V. 307 Wee shall haue some spawne of a goose-quill.. quirking and girding. **1823** *Blackw. Mag.* XIII. 673 Merely quirking it upon the strength of a dozen or two hard words.

2. *trans.* To form or furnish with a quirk; to groove. Usually in *pa. pple.*

1842–59 GWILT *Archit.* §2106 When a bead is stuck so that it does not on the section merely fall in with its square returns, but leaves a space.. between the junctions at the sides, it is said to be quirked. **1886** ELWORTHY *W. Somerset Word-bk.*, *Quirk*,.. used by carpenters and stonemasons. To form a narrow groove, usually in a moulding.

3. a. To move in a sudden and jerky manner. [Perh. an independent formation.]

1821 CLARE *Vill. Minstr.* II. 33 We saw many a mouse Quirking round for the kernels. [See also QUIRKING *ppl. a.*] **1876** G. MEREDITH *Beauch. Career* xiv, That is the thing to set an audience bounding and quirking. **1948** G. H. JOHNSTON *Death takes Small Bites* i. 8 Her mouth quirked with tiny crinkles of amusement. **1958** S. ELLIN *Eighth Circle* II. xx. 159 'I really am better. Just a little weak in the knees, that's all.' Her lips quirked in a pale smile. 'You must think I'm pretty much of a mess, don't you?' **1975** L. GILLEN *Return to Deepwater* ii. 28 His wide mouth quirked briefly into an answering smile.

b. *trans.* To move (something) jerkily.

1978 J. KRANTZ *Scruples* viii. 222 He quirked one eyebrow at Billy.

quirk (kwɜːk), *v.*[2] *dial.* Also **querk.** [Imitative.] To grunt, groan, croak, etc.; to grumble. So **quirking** *ppl. a.*

1746 *Exmoor Scolding* (E.D.S.) 43 Thee art a crewnting, querking,.. chockling Baggage. **1787** GROSE *Prov. Gloss.*, *Quirking*, Complaining. Wilts. **1830** MISS MITFORD *Village* Ser. IV. (1863) 195 The poor little lass.. sighed, and quirked, and fidgeted, and seemed ready to cry. **1886–** In dial. glossaries (Surrey, Berks, Wilts, Som., etc.). **1894** E. H. BARKER *Two Summers in Guyenne* 289 Green frogs.. quirked defiance from the banks. **1946** J. W. DAY *Harvest Adventure* vii. 94 Mallard and querking teal.

quirk, var. QUIRT *sb.*

quirked (kwɜːkt), *ppl. a.* [f. QUIRK *v.*[1] or *sb.* + -ED.] **1.** *Arch.* Furnished with a quirk.

1823 P. NICHOLSON *Pract. Build.* 162 A moulding denominated a Quirked Ovolo. **1836** PARKER *Gloss. Archit.* (1850) I. 379 The quirked ogee from the arch of Constantine. **1842–59** GWILT *Archit.* §2126 The cylindrical part is called a bead, and the sinking a quirk; the whole combination being called a quirked bead.

2. Of the mouth, eyebrow, etc.: set in an attitude by quirking. Also with *down.*

1951 H. GILES *Harbin's Ridge* iv. 28 Lucibel's mouth was quirked down at the corners. **1955** W. GADDIS *Recognitions* II. vii. 619 Her eyes searched his face, to find no betrayal but a quirked eyebrow which started to rise, and did not.

quirken, variant of QUERKEN, to choke.

quirkily (ˈkwɜːkɪlɪ), *adv.* [f. QUIRKY *a.* + -LY[2].] In a manner which displays a randomness or quaintness of choice or performance.

1957 *New Yorker* 2 Nov. 166/3 All the way from the primarily non-objective.. to the quirkily archaic. **1965** *Times Lit. Suppl.* 25 Nov. 1068/3 In a much more quirkily disorganized way, a poem like John Berryman's *Homage to Mistress Bradstreet* (1959) makes a similar effort of disenchanted excavation. **1969** *Daily Tel.* (Colour Suppl.) 1 Aug. 8/3 Miss Norway likes to read poetry. Miss Ireland likes the Moderns. Miss Sweden, quirkily, likes Science Fiction. **1975** J. BUTCHER *Copy-Editing* xiii. 221 Scientists and mathematicians often use terms which have not yet become absorbed into general scientific language and may be quirkily hyphenated and capitalized.

ˈquirkiness. [f. QUIRKY *a.* + -NESS.] The quality of being quirky.

1879 SIR G. SCOTT *Lect. Archit.* I. 355 All the.. pieces of quirkiness which one sees, are things which I have rarely if ever found in old work. **1971** *Record* (Oxford Univ. Press) Dec. 1/2 He enjoyed anecdotes of human quirkiness and folly. **1977** *Times Lit. Suppl.* 15 July 846/1 It is an example of the 'quirkiness' which makes Powell such a difficult colleague.

quirking (ˈkwɜːkɪŋ), *vbl. sb.* [f. QUIRK *v.*[1] + -ING[1].] The action of the vb. in its various senses, or the result of this.

a **1688** BUNYAN *Mr. Badman* (1767) I. 735 Forbear quirking and mocking. **1820** SHELLEY *Œd. Tyr.* I. 254 If you had hung her With canting and quirking. **1892** *Harper's Mag.* Feb. 411/1 *Ed.* In all uncomely? *Ath.* Ay, to the very quirking of her eyebrows.

quirking (ˈkwɜːkɪŋ), *ppl. a.*[1] [f. as prec. + -ING[2].] That quirks.

1605 F. MASON *Serm.* (1607) 25 Surely.. quirking braines may haue their conceits. **1679** C. NESSE *Antid. agst. Popery* 65 This quirking fryar. **1821** CLARE *Vill. Minstr.* II. 23 The quirking rabbit scarcely leaves her hole.

quirkish (ˈkwɜːkɪʃ), *a.* [f. QUIRK *sb.* + -ISH.]

1. Of the nature of a quirk.

a **1677** BARROW *Serm.* (1687) I. xiv. 195 A smart answer, .. a quirkish reason. **1882** E. P. HOOD in *Leisure Hour* Apr. 227 He sets forth a number of quirkish reasons.

2. Eccentric, idiosyncratic; erratic, random; = QUIRKY *a.* 1 b.

1969 A. STEVENSON *Reversals* 23 The wall's approach, the quirkish ambivalence of photographs, today in daylight, were pieces of balance. **1972** *Daily Tel.* 16 Nov. 14/7 Is this because their leader.. succumbed less frequently to his quirkish approach to notes by deviously subtle routes that so often misfire? **1975** *Ibid.* 24 June 11 Quirkish and baffling to the last, *Churchill's People* (BBC 1) ended last night with a protracted scene showing five men.. being hanged after failing to assassinate the Cabinet. **1977** *Times* 31 Oct. 5/4 The selection of Caribbean territories visited has been a trifle quirkish. **1978** *Gramophone* Feb. 1439/2 There are other small details of phrasing in this performance more quirkish than gracious, though certainly the music flows with a will.

Hence **ˈquirkishly** *adv.*

1963 *Times* 15 Jan. 11/4 Two of L. S. Lowry's quirkishly lively figure-subjects catch the eye.

ˈquirksome, *a. rare.* [f. as prec. + -SOME.] Quirky.

1896 CROCKETT *Grey Man* xlvi. 310 For all his quirksome guile, he had gotten on the wrong side.

quirky (ˈkwɜːkɪ), *a.* [f. as prec. + -Y[1].]

1. a. Full of quirks or shifts; tricky.

1806 R. JAMIESON *Pop. Ballads* I. 297 Tam Tod was an ald-farran birkie,.. Slee, snackie, and wilie, and quirkie. **1823** GALT *Entail* II. xviii. 164 A quirkie bodie, capable o' making law no law at a'. **1898** A. BALFOUR *To Arms* xiv. 153 Out upon you for a quack—a quirky quibbling quack, Sir.

b. Characterized by certain unexpected and often unspecified traits; idiosyncratic; peculiar. Also as *sb.*, an eccentric or peculiar person.

1960 *Guardian* 8 July 4/2 There is.. quirky colloquialism, idiomatic punning, play with unusual words. **1966** *New Statesman* 8 July 62/3 It was perhaps unduly testing to place two substantial new works in the same programme; it was certainly quirky to preface them with Poulenc's Organ Concerto. **1972** *Times Lit. Suppl.* 5 May 520/2 The best of it is individual, quirky, and moving. **1975** *Publishers Weekly* 21 July 62/1 Capricorn of Scotland Yard.. investigates Smoky's suspect connections. He encounters quirkies aplenty. **1976** *National Observer* (U.S.) 31 July 6/4 (Advt.), We're fascinated by strange, quirky questions that can lead us into corners of reality most people never even think about. **1978** *Amer. Poetry Rev.* July/Aug. 36/3 Schwartz was also a fine (if uneven) writer of fiction whose best prose is characterized by a cynical urban realism that foreshadows Bellow's quirky, densely textured work.

2. Full of twists, turns, or flourishes.

1885 in *Cent. Dict.* **1896** N. MUNRO *Lost Pibroch* (1902) 80 [The] quirky lanes and closes were as black as the pit.

quirl, variant of QUERL.

quirl, *sb.* and *v.*: see QUERL *sb.* and *v.*

quirlewind, obs. form of WHIRLWIND.

quirley (ˈkwɜːlɪ). *U.S.* and *Austral. slang.* Also **quirly.** [f. *quirl*, var. QUERL *v.* + -Y[6].] A (usu. hand-rolled) cigarette.

1932 'SPINDRIFT' *Yankee Slang* 30 *Quirly, quirley*,.. cigarette. **1940** *Amer. Speech* XV. 335/2 A cigarette is a ..*lung-duster*, or a *quirley* (or *spill-quirley*). (*Note*) Dr. R. D. Scott reports the use of *quirley*.. among the cowpunchers of Arizona and New Mexico. **1945** R. F. ADAMS *Western Words* 122/1 *Quirly*, the cowboy's name for his cigarette. **1953** BAKER *Austral. Speaks* iv. 106 To return to the field of popular Australianisms, here are some more items worthy of record.. *quirley*, a cigarette; [etc.]. **1955** W. FOSTER-HARRIS *Look of Old West* iv. 113 The cowboy's hand-built smoke was, as he called it, a quirly.

quirlicue, variant of CURLICUE *sb.*

1885 *Home Missionary* (N.Y.) Apr. 459 The Rocky Mountains,.. like little feather quirlicues on a map.

quirn, dial. variant of QUERN.

quirpo, variant of CUERPO *Obs.*

† **quirré.** *Obs. rare*[−1]. In 5 quyrre. [a. OF. *quiree, quirie*, var. *cuirie*: see CUIRASS.] A leathern habergeon or cuirass.

c **1400** tr. *Secreta Secret., Gov. Lordsh.* 110 Wende noght in host with oute haberion or quyrre.

quirrester, -ister, obs. forms of CHORISTER.

quirry, obs. variant of *querry* EQUERRY.

quirt (kwɜːt), *sb. U.S.* Also **quirk.** [ad. Mexican Sp. *cuarta* whip.] A kind of riding-whip used in the western United States and Spanish America, having a short handle and a braided leather lash about two feet long.

1845 *Amer. Rev.* Feb. 127/2 The 'quirt', with its long heavy lash of knotted raw-hide. **1851** MAYNE REID *Scalp Hunt.* xxxi. 240 The young hunter laid his quirt to the flanks of the mustang. **1870** DE. B. R. KEIM *Sheridan's Troopers* xx. 139 While belaboring the poor brute with the heavy end of a quirk. **1888** [see QUIRT *v.*[2]]. **1894** *Outing* (U.S.) XXIV. 215/2 The spectators even went so far as to strike the bare backs of their favorites with quirts, or whips, to urge them on. **1910** C. E. MULFORD *Hopalong Cassidy* v. 61 Hopalong cut him short by hitting him across the face with his quirt. **1929** *Amer. Speech* V. 62 When the 'rider' is 'saddled' on the 'pony', he may hold in one hand a 'quirk' ('quirt') or 'lasher', a short whip, having a small lead-filled handle and rawhide lashes two feet or more long. **1934** *Amer. Ballads & Folk Songs* 377 My quirt in my hand, my slicker on my saddle. **1955** W. FOSTER-HARRIS *Look of Old West* vii. 218 The cowboy's quirt was ordinarily about 2 or 3 feet long, of plaited leather, though sometimes of stitched buckskin or woven horsehair. **1972** K. BONFIGLIOLI *Don't point that Thing at Me* xiii. 101 She.. flicked the thong of her quirt under the stallion's belly and was away. **1980** *Daily Tel.* 18 July 1/3 Police in South Africa have unveiled their latest riot control weapon, which they call a quirt, a whip made of flexible plastic about three to four feet long.

† **quirt**, *v.*[1] *Obs. rare.* Also 7 quurt. [Of obscure origin.]

1. *trans.* To block, fill, or stop up (an opening).

1587 FLEMING *Contn. Holinshed* III. 1009/1 The said earle ..did leuie and build a new weere in the said aperture.. stopping, filling, and quirting the same, with great trees, timber, and stones. **1602** CAREW *Cornwall* 105 b, To let.. three or foure shouels full of earth fall softly downe by the inner side of the floodgate, which will quirt vp his chinkes.

2. *intr.* Of a river: To be dammed *back.*

1602 CAREW *Cornwall* 152 Under it runneth the river Lo, ..thwarted by a sandy banke, which forceth the same to quurt back a great way.

quirt (kwɜːt), *v.*[2] *U.S.* [f. QUIRT *sb.*] *trans.* To strike with a quirt. Hence **ˈquirting** *vbl. sb.*

1888 TH. ROOSEVELT in *Century Mag.* Apr. 854 A first-class rider will sit throughout it all.. quirting his horse all the time... Quirt is the name of the short flexible riding-whip used throughout cowboy land. The term is a Spanish one. **1897** *Westm. Gaz.* 8 Oct. 2/1 One [horse].. was 'quirted', 'raked', and nearly killed. **1910** C. E. MULFORD *Hopalong Cassidy* vii. 76 He says you did—an' somebody quirted him. **1918** W. M. RAINE in *Popular Mag.* 20 June 23/1 Quirt him on the shoulders and rake him down the hip. **1932** H. W. BENTLEY *Dict. Spanish Terms in Eng.* 131 From the noun has come the verb to *quirt* and the Anglicized *quirting* used in such a phrase as 'He gave the animal a sound quirting'. **1973** R. D. SYMONS *Where Wagon Led.* I. iv. 49 So I quirted that pony a couple of times.

quirtayn, obs. f. CURTAIN.

quiry, var. *querry*, EQUERRY.

quis (kwɪs, kwɪz), *pron.* *School slang.* [L. interrog. pron., = who.] 'Who (wants this)?', asked by the possessor of a specified object which he no longer requires, to a group of his fellows.

The first person to reply 'ego' (EGO 2) receives the object.

1913 [see EGO 2]. **1916** E. F. BENSON *David Blaize* vi. 111 '*Quis* for a catapult?' he said heroically, and a chorus of 'Ego' answered him. **1927** W. E. COLLINSON *Contemp. Eng.* 22 While at the Prep. I fell into the way of using pater for *father* and came to know the schoolboy question quis for *who wants?* with the answer ego. **1945** E. WAUGH *Brideshead Revisited* II. v. 281 Who wants it? Quis? Would you like it, Cara? No, of course you would not. Cordelia? **1959** [see EGO 2]. *a* **1966** 'M. NA GOPALEEN' *Best of Myles* (1968) 217 'Quis?' 'Ego.' 'See, man, you meant him.'

quis, obs. f. QUIZ.

quisby (ˈkwɪzbɪ), *sb.* *slang.* [Of obscure formation.] An idler. ***doing quisby***, not working.

1837 *Fraser's Mag.* XVI. 155 He eyes the twaddler who'd enjoin a halt,.. Hating.. a stop by such a quisby. **1851** MAYHEW *Lond. Labour* III. 219 One morning, when we had been doing 'quisby', that is, stopping idle.

quisby (ˈkwɪzbɪ), *a. slang.* Also **quizby.** [cf. prec.] Queer, not quite right; bankrupt.

1807 H. TUFTS *Narrative* III. iv. 316 *Quisby cove*, a mean fellow. **1846** *Swell's Night Guide* 129/1 *Quisby*, bad. **1848** *Ladies' Repository* (U.S.) Oct. 316/2 *Quisby*, ragged; dirty; suspicious. **1853** *Household Wds.* VIII. 75/2 To say that a man is without money, or in poverty, some persons remark that he is.. quisby, done up. **1854** *Tait's Mag.* XXI. 532 Larson is not so well as he should be—rather quisby about the throat. **1892** *Punch* 12 Mar. 123/1 He's a-looking queer and quisby. **1897** A. ST. J. ADCOCK *East End Idylls* iv. 69 'Ow's the missus?.. An' the kid? Bin quisby, ain't 'e?

quischen, -on, etc., obs. forms of CUSHION.

quiscos(kos): see QUISQUOSE.

† **quish**, obs. form of CUISSE.
a **1548** HALL *Chron., Hen. IV* an. 1 (R.) One sort had the quishes, the greues, the surlettes, yᵉ sockettes on the ryght side and on the left side sylver. **1557** GRIMALD *Death Zoroas* in *Tottell's Misc.* (Arb.) 122 Aboue the greaue, At th' opening of his quishes.

quishan, -en, etc., obs. forms of CUSHION.

quisle, obs. form of WHISTLE *v.*

Quisling (ˈkwɪzlɪŋ). Also with lower-case initial. [The name of Major Vidkun *Quisling* (1887–1945), Norwegian officer and diplomatist, who collaborated with the Germans during their occupation of Norway from 1940 to 1945.]

1. A traitor to one's country, a collaborationist, esp. during the war of 1939–45. Also *transf.* and *fig.*
1940 *Times* 15 Apr. 5/3 Comment in the Press urges that there should be unremitting vigilance also against possible 'Quislings' inside the country [*sc.* Sweden]. **1940** H. NICOLSON *Diary* 10 May (1967) II. 81 He is hurrying back to Holland to fight. He says..they will fight to the last man, but that they are worried about their Quislings. **1941** *Sun* (Baltimore) 7 Mar. 1/6 No report of the size of the attacking fleet..was given, but small craft actually allowed British and Norwegian troops to take 215 Germans and ten 'Quislings' as prisoners. **1943** C. S. LEWIS *Christian Behaviour* i. 9 The results of bad morality..press on us every day: war and poverty and graft and quislings and shoddy work. **1946** *Downside Rev.* 51 In our striving after this way of love, we are confronted by a threefold enemy, the devil, the world, both external to us, and the quisling within us, called 'Self', the most dangerous of all the foes. **1950** *N.Y. Times* 1 July 16/5 The attempts that the Communist-dominated governments are making to create 'national' Catholic Churches through the appointment of religious 'Quislings'. **1958** P. KEMP *No Colours or Crest* vii. 125 Isa Toska, a notorious Albanian quisling..was a brigand who with Italian help had equipped a strong band of mercenaries. **1961** B. FERGUSSON *Watery Maze* iii. 78 They brought back 225 prisoners (including a dozen quislings), 314 Norwegian volunteers, [etc.]. **1966** 'H. MACDIARMID' *Company I've Kept* xiii. 260 A Scot far more typical in his attitude than the English care to recognise, or Anglo-Scottish quislings dare admit. **1974** *Globe & Mail* (Toronto) 22 Apr. 3/2 But a spokesman..denounced the appointment, dismissing Mr. Marouf as a 'quisling' who did not represent the Kurdish liberation movement. **1976** *Economist* 16 Oct. 74/2 But for years the government has used them [*sc.* moderate leaders of South African blacks] only to put on a front of 'consultation', while paying scant regard to their views. It is this which has left them feeling like quislings whose only purpose is to give the system a look of respectability.

2. a. *Comb.*, as ***Quisling-hearted***, ***-minded*** adjs.
1940 *Times* 4 Oct. 9/6 Its organizers had assembled.. sympathizers and other potentially Quisling-minded adults from neutral countries. **1946** P. BOTTOME *Lifeline* xxi. 176 The boastful triumph of the quisling-hearted.

b. *attrib.* passing into *adj.*
1941 *Times* 11 Mar. 4/7 The quisling newspapers not only endorse this but accuse the British of plundering Lofoten shops. **1942** 'G. ORWELL' in *Partisan Rev.* Mar.–Apr. 159 The quisling intellectual is a phenomenon of the last two years. **1943** S. G. EVANS *Christians in World Struggle* 2 The normal service of the cathedral..had been replaced by a pagan 'Quisling' ceremony. **1945** H. G. WELLS *Happy Turning* v. 13 He [*sc.* Jesus] began his career as a good illiterate patriotic Jew in indignant revolt against the Roman rule and the Quisling priests who cringed to it. **1947** *Times* 28 Apr. 8/3 Certainly the story itself shows no lingering trace of quisling quality: it is conventional to the very last joint. **1959** *Listener* 30 Apr. 765/1 *Brand* was written in anger against Ibsen's smug, quisling and bourgeois Norway of the nineteenth century. **1973** *Ibid.* 16 Aug. 226/3 Television..cast a regretful backward glance at Czechoslovakia under the heel of its wretched Quisling government.

Hence (as a back-formation) **ˈquisle** *v.* (*joc.*), to betray one's country, in the manner of a Quisling; **ˈquisler**, one who 'quisles'; **ˈquislingism**, a political doctrine based on the collaborationist principles of Quisling; **ˈquislingist**, a Quisling; also *attrib.*; **ˈquislingite**, a Quisling; **ˈquislingize** *v.*, to cause to act as a Quisling; **ˈquislingized** *ppl. a.*; also *transf.*
1940 *Times* 22 Apr. 8/2 There seem to have been no Quislings, partly because it was unnecessary to 'quisle' in a country which, as the Nazis have always said 'could be taken by telephone'. *Ibid.* 4 Oct. 5/2 The Quislingists have begun Jew-baiting in Norway. *Ibid.* 15 Oct. 3/5 Lunde, the Quislingist Minister of Propaganda—the Norwegian Goebbels—has announced his intention to 'Quislingize' all newspapers. **1940** *Amer. Speech* XV. 261/1 '*Quislings* everywhere', 'Nazi sympathisers who might *quisle*', 'Other potential *quislers* are now at large'. **1940** *Manch. Guardian* 19 Oct. 6/3 So far the most significant and valuable addition in this war is 'Quisling'. Will there be a verb, 'to quisle'? **1941** *Times* 6 Feb. 3/5 The new secret police..have arrested many hundreds of persons who were known to be hostile to Quislingism. **1942** *Ann. Reg. 1941* 239 But for the protection of the German troops..the Quislingites would.. undoubtedly have been wiped out. *Ibid.* 240 After the British raid..the Reichs-kommissar..ordered them to pay the maintenance of the Germans and Quislingites taken to England. **1942** *Times* 28 Feb. 3/5 Over 1,000 teachers stuck to their resignations from the quislingized teachers' association even after the Church Department had decreed that such resignations were tantamount to resignation of office. **1944** 'G. ORWELL' in *Horizon* X. 244 The modern political scene, in which..bribery and quislingism are normal. **1945** *Sun* (Baltimore) 28 Sept. 11/2 They bear the label of Quislingism, but they also carry the cross of illegitimacy. **1946** 'G. ORWELL' in *Tribune* 26 Apr. 7/2 All that is left of him [*sc.* the Vicar of Bray] is a comic song and a beautiful tree, which..must surely have outweighed any bad effects which he produced by his political quislingism.

† **quiˈsquilian**, *a.* *Obs. rare*⁻¹. [f. as next + -AN.] Quisquilious. So **quiˈsquiliary** *a.*
1716 M. DAVIES *Athen. Brit.* II. 394 Miscreant quisquilian Scraps and Fragments. **1817** *Blackw. Mag.* I. 470 Those shallow and fidimplicitary coxcombs, who fill our too credulous ears with their quisquiliary deblaterations.

quisquilious (kwɪˈskwɪlɪəs), *a. rare.* [f. L. *quisquiliæ* f. pl., waste matter, refuse, rubbish, etc.] Of the nature of rubbish or refuse.
1802–12 BENTHAM *Ration. Judic. Evid.* (1827) IV. 412 The science is overloaded by the quisquilious matter they rake together. *a* **1832** —— *Deontol.* (1834) I. 295 Dr. Priestley..expunged what, in the quaint phraseology once in vogue, was called the 'quisquilious matter'. **1857** *Fraser's Mag.* LVI. 460 Besides garden fruit insects and worms, the Jay's diet is sufficiently quisquilious.

quisquose, -quous, *a. Sc.* Also 9 quiscos(kos); quisquis. [Of obscure origin.] Difficult to deal with or settle, ticklish, 'kittle'.
1720 *Wodrow Corr.* (1843) II. 485 Being biassed with his opinion in quisquose and difficult matters. **1721** WODROW *Hist. Suffer. Ch. Scot.* (1829) II. II. xiii. 499 The truths delivered by ministers..on quisquous subjects. **1830** GALT *Lawrie T.* IV. ix. (1849) 175 Your conduct this day has been very quiscos. **1836** —— in *Tait's Mag.* III. 33 The ladies maybe a wee quiscoskos in character. **1856** J. STRANG *Glasgow & its Clubs* 61 Mr. G. M——, a very unpopular and *quis-quis* character. **1899** J. B. MONTGOMERIE-FLEMING *Desultory Notes on Jamieson's Scott. Dict.* 122 Strangers arriving in a place and being considered of doubtful character are spoken of as 'Very quisquis sort of people'.

† **quissers**. *Obs. rare*⁻¹. [a. OF. *cuissere*, *-iere*, f. *cuisse* thigh.] = CUISSE.
c **1330** *Arth. & Merl.* 2976 (Kölbing) Helme & brini & hauberioun, Saumbers, quissers & aketoun.

quisshen, -in(g, quissin(g, -ion, -yn, obs. ff. CUSHION.

quissonday, obs. f. WHITSUNDAY.

† **quist**, obs. variant of WHIST, silent.
1598 R. BERNARD tr. *Terence* 289 Quist, quist, what man art thou well in thy witts? *Ibid.* 310 He is quist.

quister, variant of WHITSTER *Obs.*

quisteroun, obs. form of CUSTRON.

† **quistounes, -sumnes**. [Form and meaning uncertain; the ref. is to the wheel of Fortune.]
a **1400–50** *Alexander* 3303 Lo! so þe quele of qwistsumnes my qualite has changid. *Ibid.* 4660 For so þe quele of qwistounes ȝoure qualite encreses.

quistrel, variant of COISTREL or CUSTREL.

quistron, variant of CUSTRON.

quit (kwɪt), *sb.*¹ [Perh. imitative; but Gosse suggests that it may be African.] The popular name of many small Jamaican birds.
1847 GOSSE *Birds Jamaica* 254 The name of *Quit* is applied without much discrimination by the negroes of Jamaica, to several small birds, such as the Banana Quit, which is a Creeper, and the Blue Quit, and Grass Quits which are finches. **1882–** in OGILVIE and later Dicts. **1894** NEWTON *Dict. Birds* 761.

quit (kwɪt), *sb.*² [f. QUIT *v.*] **1.** A point of departure. *rare.*
1892 H. A. NEWTON in *Astronomy & Astrophysics* Jan. 15 Of the 839 comets..267..will have quits less than 45° from Jupiter's quit, while 38 of them will have quits less than 45° from Jupiter's goal.

2. a. *U.S.* The act or an instance of quitting; one who quits.
1923 J. D. HACKETT *Labor Terms* in *Managem. Engineering* May, *Quit*, a voluntary separation from work by an individual worker, usually without notice of intention. **1976** *Billings* (Montana) *Gaz.* 6 July 8-A/4 The scope of the 'voluntary quits', persons who leave their jobs for any reason is not precisely tabulated. *Ibid.* 8-A/5 Barrett was reluctant to estimate the impact of voluntary quits on the state.

b. *attrib.* and *Comb.*, as ***quit-form***, ***notice***; **quit rate**, the proportion of people in a section of society who voluntarily leave their jobs.
1966 'A. HALL' *9th Directive* xxii. 209 The hospital superintendent..didn't want to release me..but I forced a personal responsibility quit-form out of him and signed it and left. **1976** K. THACKERAY *Crownbird* vi. 111 If..he got a quit notice from the Kenyans, he'd wind up being stateless. **1970** *Women Speaking* Apr. 10/2 For both men and women workers, the lowest quit rates occur among skilled workers and professional and managerial workers. **1973** *N.Y. Law Jrnl.* 26 July 5/3, 41 per cent of married mothers do work; women's 'quit-rate' is lower than men's, making them most dependable workers. **1975** *Sci. Amer.* Jan. 21/1 Let us consider the indicator called the quit rate, which measures the number of people in manufacturing industries (per 100 employed) who voluntarily leave their jobs.

quit (kwɪt), † **quite**, *a.* Forms: α. 3 cwite, 3–6 quyt, (4 qw-), 4–6 quyte, (4–5 qw-), 6 quight, 3–7 quite. β. 4 kuytte, 5 quytt(e, qwytt, qw(h)itte, 6 quitt, 6–7 quitte, 3– quit. [(1) In the α-forms (ME. types *quīte*, *quīt*), a. OF. *quite* = Pr. *quiti*, Sp. *quito*, med.L. *quitus*, unmolested, free, clear, etc., ad. L. *quiētus* QUIET. Hence also OFris. *quyt*, *qwyt* (mod. *quijt*), MDu. *quite*, *quijt* (Du. *kwijt*), MLG. and MHG. *quît* (obs. G. *queit*). (2) In the β-forms (ME. types *quĭtte*, *quĭt*), orig. a. OF. *quitte*, later form of *quite*: cf. med.L. *quittus*, MHG. *quit* (G. *quitt*), ON. *kvittr* (Sw. *qvitt*, Da. *kvit*). The pa. pple. of QUITE *v.* may also have contributed to the use of *quĭt*.

Although there appears to be sufficient evidence for the existence in ME. of forms with a short vowel, clear instances are somewhat rare, as the spelling is often ambiguous or misleading, and the rimes usually show *quīte*, *quīt*. The exact range of *quĭt* is therefore uncertain until the 16th c., when its gradual supersession of *quite* is prob. connected with the similar change in the verb.]

I. In predicative use.

1. Free, clear. (†Occas. ***quite and clear***, ***quite and free***.) ***to be quit for***, to get off with, suffer nothing more than.
a **1225** *Ancr. R.* 6 Sum..mei ful wel beo cwite & paie god mid lesse. *c* **1275** *Pass. Lord* 310 in *O.E. Misc.* 46 Ye nelleþ ..lete me gon quite. *Ibid.* 370 Hit is eur kustume to habbe quyt enne. *c* **1290** *Beket* 812 in *S. Eng. Leg.* I. 129 Þo was þis guode Man quit I-nov. *c* **1330** R. BRUNNE *Chron. Wace* (Rolls) 1224 Þys were our most profit, Wiþ loue & leue he queþe vs quyt. *c* **1400** *Ywaine & Gaw.* 685 Bot so he wend have passed quite. **1470–85** MALORY *Arthur* XIV. vi, Yf thow be ouercome thou shalt not be quyte for losyng of ony of thy membrys. **1509** BARCLAY *Shyp of Folys* (1570) 72 The great fishe are taken..Where as the small escape quite and free. **1577** NORTHBROOKE *Dicing* (1843) 77 What faultes great men alwayes committe Are pardoned still, and goeth quitte. **1609** SKENE *Reg. Maj.* 22 Gif the persewer compeirs nocht ..the defender sall passe quite. **1671** MILTON *P.R.* I. 476, I ..must submiss endure Check or reproof, and glad to scape so quit. **1768** GRAY in *Corr. w. Nicholls* (1843) 72 We..are quit for the fright except the damage above-mentioned. **1817** W. SELWYN *Law Nisi Prius* (ed. 4) II. 761 The judgment shall be against him only..and the other shall go quit. **1852** THACKERAY *Esmond* I. xiii, Harry Esmond was quit for a fall on the grass. **1866** ROGERS *Agric. & Prices* I. v. 124 When the book was restored the borrower [was] declared quit.

b. Free, clear, rid *of* (a thing or person). †Also with omission of prep. (quot. 1630).
a **1225** *Ancr. R.* 90 Ase quite ase ȝe beoð of swuch. *a* **1300** *Cursor M.* 6287 Godd..had mad þam quite Of al þair soru and al þair site. **1340** *Ayenb.* 41 Of these zennes ne byeþ [they] naȝt kuytte. *c* **1375** *Sc. Leg. Saints* xxxiv. (*Pelagia*) 136 Haffand rycht gret delyte Of þare synnis to be quyte. *c* **1450** *Mirour Saluacioun* 1511 Who is qwitte of one temptacionne happily. **1470–85** MALORY *Arthur* X. xxiv, Now my moder is quyte of the. **1596** DALRYMPLE tr. *Leslie's Hist. Scot.* II. 141 Throuch desyre..to be quyte of the glore of a king. *c* **1630** MILTON *On Time* 20 Then all this Earthy grosnes quit,..we shall for ever sit [etc.]. **1741** CHESTERF. *Lett.* (1792) I. 208 Aukwardnesses, which many people contract..and cannot get quit of them. **1840** MISS MITFORD in L'Estrange *Life* (1870) III. vii. 108 To me..it would be a great release to be quit of the trouble and expense. **1875** CROLL *Climate & T.* v. 91 In order that the sea may get quit of its heat.

c. Const. *from*. Now *rare.*
1471 RIPLEY *Comp. Alch.* iii. in Ashm. (1652) 140 Fro feculent feces when hyt ys quytt. *c* **1586** C'TESS PEMBROKE *Ps.* CXIX. i, Quitt and cleere from doing wrong. **1591** SPENSER *Ruins of Rome* viii, Nought from the Romane Empire might be quight. **1660** H. MORE *Myst. Godl.* v. xvii. 209 Nor shall we ever be quit from the crime of slaying the Witnesses. **1845** *Economy* 154 It is the doctor's duty to see you quit from all this.

† **d.** ***to make quit*** (***of***), to do away with, dispose of; to make a clearance. *Sc. Obs. rare.*
c **1470** HENRY *Wallace* VII. 504 The formast sone hym selff sesyt in hand, Maid quyt off hym. **15..** *Droichis Part of Play* 108 in *Dunbar's Poems* (1893) 318 Thair is nocht thair bot tak and slae, Cut throppillis and mak quyte.

† **2.** Destitute, deprived *of* (*from*). *Obs.*
c **1290** *S. Eng. Leg.* I. 399/242 Of ore leoue sones quite we beoth, alas! *c* **1330** R. BRUNNE *Chron.* (1810) 319 Me and many mo, fro our wages ȝede quite. *a* **1352** MINOT *Poems* vii. 124 Now haue þai made þi biging bare, Of all þi catell ertou quite. *c* **1430** *Hymns Virg.* (1867) 35 Of þi blis y were ful qwytt If y hadde aftir þat y haue do. **1573** *Satir. Poems Reform.* xlii. 911 It wald mak vs quyte Of Christis Euangell, our delyte. **1596** DALRYMPLE tr. *Leslie's Hist. Scot.* IV. 232 Ethelfred is maid quyt of ane eye.

† **3.** = QUITS 2. ***double or quit***: see DOUBLE *adv.* 4. *Obs.*
c **1489** CAXTON *Sonnes of Aymon* x. 268, I have yelde you agen that ye had gyven me; we be now quyte. **1596** SHAKS. *Tam. Shr.* III. i. 92 If once I finde thee ranging, Hortensio will be quit with thee by changing. **1607** —— *Cor.* IV. v. 89 To be full quit of those my Banishers Stand I before thee heere. **1687** PRIOR *Epigr.*, '*To John I ow'd*', Sure John and I are more than quit. **1757** MRS. GRIFFITH *Lett. Henry & Frances* (1767) I. 21 But we are now quit; and your generosity is equal to mine.

† **b.** ***to cry quit*** (***with*** one), ***cry one quit*** (cf. QUITTANCE 4). *Obs.*
1626–7 in *Crt. & Times Chas. I*, I. 205 If it would please God..to prosper what we undertake, we might, ere long, cry them quit. **1641** SMECTYMNUUS *Vind. Answ.* I. 5 If we would cry quit with the *Remonstrant*..wee could tell him a Tale.

II. Attributive.

† **4.** Clean, complete. *Obs. rare.*

1583 BABINGTON *Commandm.* viii. (1637) 73 To..the quite marring of all her musicke. **1604** RUDD in *Consid. Peace & Goodw. Prot.* 7 If..there cannot be obtained a quite removall of the Premises. **1607** TOPSELL *Four-f. Beasts* (1673) 487 [This will] make a quit riddance of all their hurts.

quit (kwɪt), † **quite**, *v.* Forms: α. *Infin.* 3–5 quiten, quyten, (5 -yn), 4 quyty, 4–7 quyte, quite, 5 qwite, qwyt(e, qw-, queyt, 5–6 quyt; 5 qu-, qwyght, 6 quight; also *north.* 5 whyte, 6 -tte, 5, 7–9 white, 9 wheyte. *Pa. t.* 4–5 quitte, quyt, 4–6 quit(t, quytte, 5 qwit, 5–6 quyte; 5–6 quyted, 6 quited, quighted. *Pa. pple.* 4–5 iquytt, i-, yquyt(te, yquit; 4 quite, 4–5 quitte, 4–6 quit, quyt, 5 qwit(t(e, *Sc.* quet, 5–6 quyte, qwytt, 6 quitt, *Sc.* quyite; 4 i-quited, 5–7 quited, 6 quyted. β. 4, 7 quitte, 5 quytte, 6 quitt, 4– quit. γ. See QUAT *v.*² [(1) In α-forms (ME. type *quiten*), a. OF. *quiter* = Sp., Pg. *quitar*, It. *quitare*, med.L. *quitare*, ad. med.L. *quiētāre* to make quiet, put in quiet, set free, absolve, etc., f. *quiētus* QUIET (cf. QUIT *a.*). (2) In β-forms (ME. type *quitten*), a. later OF. *quitter* (cf. ON. *kvitta*, Sw. *qvitta*, Da. *kvitte*). The origin of this F. form is obscure; it apparently became common in the 14th c., but med.L. *quittare* is found in documents of the 13th (Du Cange).

The exact range of ME. *quitte(n* is difficult to determine (cf. QUIT *a.*); the usual form was undoubtedly *quite(n*. The pa. t. and pa. pple. of this were usually *quitte, quit* (less commonly *quited*), and this fact may have assisted in the general substitution of *quit* for *quite* which began in the latter part of the 16th c., and was practically complete by 1650. During the first half of the 17th c. the pa. t. and pple. vary between *quit* and *quitted*, the former being freq. employed even by writers who use *quit* in the inf. and pres.; in later use *quitted* is the standard form, *quit* being now chiefly dial. and U.S. colloquial.]

I. † **1. a.** *trans.* To set free, release, deliver, redeem (usually a person; also *absol.*). Const. *from*, *out of*, and occas. with *out* adv. *Obs.*

a **1300** *Cursor M.* 6680 Dei þai sal wit-vten lite, Wit-vten raunscun for to quitte. **1303** R. BRUNNE *Handl. Synne* 9582 Quyte þe weyl oute of borghegang. *c* **1374** CHAUCER *Troylus* IV. 177 (205) Allas! they quitte him out to rathe. *c* **1450** *Mirour Saluacioun* 1352 Crist borne to qwite man out of infernale disese. **1483** CAXTON *Gold. Leg.* 143 b/2 But for al that was not he quyte fro the pryson of helle. *a* **1569** KINGESMYLL *Man's Est.* xi. (1580) 74 They counselled the people to quite Barabbas. **1579** SPENSER *Sheph. Cal.* Feb. 213 For nought mought they quitten him from decay. **1616** R. C. *Times Whistle* vi. 2537 A litle mony from the law will quite thee. **1642** ROGERS *Naaman* 557 Arise therefore, quite thy cause, deliver thy people. **1652** GATAKER *Antinom.* 4 My intent..was..to qit one passage of Scripture from their abuse thereof.

† **b.** To free, clear, rid *of*. *Obs.*

1387 TREVISA *Higden* (Rolls) VI. 317 He delyvered and quitte alle þe cherches..of alle manere kynges tribute. **1530** PALSGR. 677/1, I wyll quyte hym for a grote of all the dettes he oweth. **1593** SHAKS. *2 Hen. VI*, III. ii. 218, I should rob the Deaths-man of his Fee, Quitting thee thereby of ten thousand shames. **1606** G. W[OODCOCKE] *Lives Emperors* in *Hist. Ivstine* I i 5 He quited Ancona and Dalmatia of the Saracens. **1668** PEPYS *Diary* 5 Mar., She..made me resolve to quit my hands of this office. **1715** ROWE *Lady Jane Gray* IV. i, That Mercy, Which quits me of the vast unequal Task. **1798** *Geraldina* II. 201 Two thousand guineas will not quit Revel of the expence.

c. *refl.* To rid (oneself) *of*.

c **1340** *Cursor M.* 11198 (Fairf.) He did alle mennys namys wryte That of this yeld shuld none hem quyte. **1606** G. W[OODCOCKE] *Lives Emperors* in *Hist. Ivstine* I i 5 He quitted himselfe of further trouble. *c* **1665** MRS. HUTCHINSON *Mem. Col. Hutchinson* 10 He quitted himself of his employment abroad. *a* **1703** BURKITT *On N.T., Luke* iv. 30 It was an easy thing for him..to quit himself of any mortal enemies. **1857** RUSKIN *Pol. Econ. Art* 4 It requires some boldness to quit ourselves of these feelings.

† **2. a.** To clear (a suspected or accused person) *from* a charge; to prove (one) innocent *of*. Chiefly *refl.* *Obs.*

a **1300** *Cursor M.* 14857 If it war sli maner wite þat he þar-of ne moght him quite. *c* **1320** *Seuyn Sag.* (W.) 2898 If he haue this day respite, Tomorn he sal himseluen quite. **1533** J. HEYWOOD *Merry Play* (1830) 18, I thought..That he had lovyd my wyfe, for to deseyve me, And now he quytyth hymself. **1590** SPENSER *F.Q.* II. i. 20 He..shall againe be tryde, And fairely quit him of th' imputed blame. **1683** *Apol. Prot. France* iii. 11 Do not conclude before you have quitted the Subjects from that suspicion. **1715** BENTLEY *Serm.* x. 350 Their known Poverty and perpetual Austerities wholly quit them of that suspicion.

† **b.** To absolve, acquit (*of*, *from*). *Obs.*

1303 R. BRUNNE *Handl. Synne* 1337 Þys fals men, þat beyn sysours, þat..wyl..a þefe for syluer quyte. **1451** *Paston Lett.* I. 208 We undirstand he shall not be quyte but before the Justice. **1509** BARCLAY *Shyp of Folys* (1570) 4 There shall be no delayes vntill another Sise, But either quit, or to infernall Gayle. **1584** PEELE *Arraignm. Paris* IV. iv, The man must quited be by heav'ns laws. **1609** BIBLE (Douay) *2 Macc.* iv. 47 Menelaus certes being guiltie of al the evil was quitted of the crimes. **1677** W. HUBBARD *Narrative* (1865) I. 96 Upon Tryal the said Prisoners were all of them quitted from the Fact. **1755** *Monitor* No. 11. I. 84 It will be difficult to quit the advisers of such a misapplication, from a crime.

absol. **1549** COVERDALE, etc. *Erasm. Par. 1 Cor.* 4 Menne maye peraduenture vnrighteously condemne or quyte. **1560** ROLLAND *Crt. Venus* I. 927, I creat ȝow to condampne or to quite, My Iuge deput.

3. *refl.* **a.** To do one's part, behave, bear oneself, (usually in a specified way). Now *arch.*

c **1386** CHAUCER *Frankl. T.* Prol. 1 In feith, Squier, thow hast thee wel yquit. **1455** *Paston Lett.* I. 329 To quyte us lyke men in this querell. **1480** CAXTON *Chron. Eng.* ccxliii. (1482) 291 Manly and knyghtly he quytte hym in al maner poyntes. **1589** *Marprel. Epit.* D ij b, Iohn of London.. could haue quited himselfe no better then this. **1611** BIBLE *1 Sam.* iv. 9 Quit your selues like men, and fight. **1642** ROGERS *Naaman* 188 Labour to quite our selves well in our sufferings. *a* **1716** SOUTH *Serm.* (1744) X. 302–3 This is the fourth means to enable us to quit ourselves in the great duty of peaceableness. **1868** BROWNING *Ring & Bk.* v. 278, I rode, danced and gamed, Quitted me like a courtier.

† **b.** To acquit oneself (well, etc.) *of* a task or duty. *Obs.*

1413 *Pilgr. Sowle* (Caxton 1483) v. xi. 103 Of these.. seuen [signes] ye haue quyte yow well. *c* **1450** *Robin Hood & Monk* lxxvii. in Child *Ballads* III. 100/2, I haue done þe a gode turne for an euyll, Quyte þe whan þou may. **1600** HAKLUYT *Voy.* (1810) III. 383 One which knewe so well to quite himselfe of his charge, that all rancour..ceased.

† **c.** To use (the hands); to play (one's part).

1596 HARINGTON *Metam. Ajax* (1814) 35 That I were as likely to quit my hands in the fray as well as any man. **1603** SHAKS. *Meas. for M.* II. iv. 28 The generall subiect to a wel-wisht King Quit their owne part.

† **4.** To remit (a debt, etc.). *Obs. rare.*

c **1400** *Rom. Rose* 6032 They shall quyte your oth al free. **1523** LD. BERNERS *Froiss.* I. xviii. 22 The lordes dyd quyt me my ransom and prison. **1596** SHAKS. *Merch. V.* IV. i. 381 To quit the fine for one halfe of his goods, I am content. **1671** MILTON *Samson* 509 Perhaps God will relent, and quit thee all his debt. **1693** *Dryden's Juvenal* vii. (1697) 178 For that Revenge I'll quit the whole Arrear.

5. a. To give up, let go, renounce, etc.; to cease to have, use, enjoy, be engaged in or occupied with. (Freq. with implication of sense 7.)

c **1440** *Generydes* 3608 As for the land of Perce..My lord and fader quyte it in his dayes. **1560** ROLLAND *Crt. Venus* I. 900 The copie clene I quite it is sa skant. **1612** SELDEN *To Rdr.* in Drayton's *Poly-olb.*, The Capricious faction will.. neuer quit their Beliefe of wrong. *a* **1661** FULLER *Worthies* (1840) II. 434 It seems that the Christian Britons at the font quitted their native names as barbarous. **1671** *True Nonconformist* 2 That Nonconformists think they may quite the communion of the church, if [etc.]. **1729** BUTLER *Serm. Resentm.* Wks. 1874 II. 100 Resentment has taken possession of the temper,..and will not quit its hold. **1788** FRANKLIN *Autobiog.* Wks. 1840 I. 156 Choosing rather to quit their power than their principle. **1828** D'ISRAELI *Chas. I*, II. ii. 47 Richelieu, once resolved, never quitted his object, till it became his own. **1851** HELPS *Comp. Solit.* xiii. (1874) 236 There are very few men who know how to quit any great office.

b. To give up, yield, hand over *to* another. Now *rare* or *Obs.*

a **1450** *Knt. de la Tour* (1868) 101, I have leuer to quytte yow and gyue yow my parte. **1559** KENNEDY *Lett. to Willock* in *Wodrow Misc.* (1844) 273, I quyte ȝou the haill cause without farther disputatioun. **1627** HAKEWILL *Apol.* (1630) 106 As God had quitted unto them, all dominion over his creatures. **1647** CLARENDON *Hist. Reb.* III. §138 He might wisely quit his Mastership of the Wards to the Lord Say. **1769** ROBERTSON *Chas. V*, XII. Wks. 1826 III. 371 Every argument which..could induce him to quit the Imperial throne to Philip. **1824** J. JOHNSON *Typogr.* I. 551 His father seems to have quitted the trade to him in 1576.

c. To let go (something held or grasped).

1633 G. HERBERT *Temple 122 Love unknown* 11 The servant instantly Quitting the fruit, seiz'd on my heart alone. **1711** ADDISON *Spect.* No. 102 ⁋7 This teaches a Lady to quit her Fan gracefully when she throws it aside. **1808** J. BARLOW *Columb.* VIII. 82 The weak moment when she quits her shield. **1841** ELPHINSTONE *Hist. Ind.* II. 145 A horseman.. sprung from his horse, and, without quitting the bridle, rushed into the tent.

6. a. To cease, stop, discontinue (doing something). Now chiefly *U.S.*

1754 in Picton *L'pool Munic. Rec.* (1886) II. 166 Persons who rent seats..after they quitt sitting in them [etc.]. **1837** W. IRVING *Capt. Bonneville* II. 165 They followed on his trail, nor quit hovering about him..until [etc.]. **1882** A. E. SWEET *Sk. Texas Siftings* 62 The dog-catchers have quit going their rounds. **1892** A. C. GUNTER *Miss Dividends* II. xiv. 208 Quit calling him bishop. He has repented and become a Christian like us! **1917** R. L. ALSAKER *Eating for Health* III. xvii. 237 Quit lunching. Quit taking eggs and milk and olive oil between meals. **1931** T. H. RYNNING *Gun Notches* xviii. 130 So the Judge opened court with the usual formalities, throwing out a couple of drunks who wouldn't quit snoring during the proceedings. **1948** M. LASKI *Tory Heaven* xii. 162 For God's sake, quit arguing politics. **1958** 'A. BRIDGE' *Portuguese Escape* xv. 256 In her anger the Countess's voice took on the rasping accents of the Middle West, and she reverted to her native idiom. 'Quit stalling, Monsignor, and tell me where my daughter *is*?' **1967** *N.Y. Times* (Internat. Ed.) 11 Feb. 4/8 Dr. Higginson quit smoking cigarettes some time ago for, he says, 'the obvious reasons'.

b. *absol.* esp., to give up, renounce, or cease to be engaged in one's employment, or other specified activity. Also *U.S.* with *off*. Now chiefly *N. Amer.*

a **1641** SUCKLING *Why so pale and wan* 11 Quit! quit for shame! this will not move. **1752** H. WALPOLE *Lett.* (1833) III. 25 It is I, that will not act with such fellows..if they are kept, I will quit; and if the Bishop is dismissed, I will quit too. **1773** P. V. FITHIAN *Jrnl.* 27 Nov. (1900) I. 54, I was introduced to one Mr Walker..lately a School-master but has quit. **1807** *Deb. Congress U.S.* (1852) 10th Congress 1 Sess., App. 478 [Robert A. New] inquired of them whether they would stand by Colonel Burr and go on, or quit. **1843, 1889** [see DAY *sb.* 20 b]. **1868** *Morning Star* 10 Mar., The good old maxim for speech-makers, 'Quit when you've done'. **1894** *Chicago Advance* 1 Mar., I don't see how you ever made up your mind to quit off [from study]. **1932** *Atlantic Monthly* Mar. 316/2 The..farmer..let the place run down to almost a raw land value before he quit. **1961** *New Yorker* 12 Aug. 34/3, I came over to tell you I was quitting, Mr Sherman. **1968** *Globe & Mail* (Toronto) 3 Feb. B4/1 It's fine by me; I quit a couple of years ago. **1976** H. NIELSEN *Brink of Murder* xii. 105 Reardon dug out a package of cigarettes..and offered them to Simon. 'I'm quitting,' Simon said... 'I've quit seventeen times this year. .. Right now I need a smoke.' **1977** *News of the World* 17 Apr. 2/3 He has already quit as chairman of the firm.

7. a. To leave, go away or depart from (a place or person); to part or separate from (a thing).

1603 FLORIO *Montaigne* II. ii. (1897) III. 29 Our minde cannot out of her place attaine so high. She must quit it and raise her selfe aloft. **1623** MASSINGER *Dk. Milan* IV. ii, We know our duty, And quit the room. **1653** H. COGAN tr. *Pinto's Trav.* vii. 19 Having quit the river he marched somewhat faster than ordinary. **1732** POPE *Ess. Man* II. 274 Hope travels thro', nor quits us when we die. **1787** WINTER *Syst. Husb.* 306 When the earth is sufficiently dry, so as to quit the hoe. **1805** SCOTT *Last Minstr.* I. iv, They quitted not their harness bright, Neither by day, nor yet by night. **1833** HT. MARTINEAU *Briery Creek* v. 100 It is a serious matter to quit country and family and friends. **1874** GREEN *Short Hist.* v. 242 The labourer was forbidden to quit the parish where he lived.

b. *absol.* To leave the premises which one occupies as a tenant.

1768 [see QUITTING *vbl. sb.*]. **1818** CRUISE *Digest* (ed. 2) IV. 74 A lease..determinable..on giving reasonable notice to quit. **1831** LAMB *Elia* Ser. II. *To the Shade of Elliston*, Thou ..had notice to quit, I fear, before thou wert quite ready to abandon this fleshly tenement.

c. *absol.* To go away. *dial.* and *U.S.*

1839 MARRYAT *Diary Amer.* Ser. I. II. 231 Clear out, quit, and put—all mean 'be off'. **1850** LYELL *2nd Visit U.S.* II. 99 No sooner was I engaged..than all the other workmen quitted. **1883** STEVENSON *Silverado Sq.* 146 He rose at once, and said..he reckoned he would quit. **1977** I. SHAW *Beggarman, Thief* I. v. 59 'Has it ever occurred to you to just pull out?' 'What do you mean?' 'I mean quit... Just pick up and leave.'

8. *intr.* *to quit with*, to part with or from. *rare.*

1635 SHIRLEY *Traitor* I. i, If You can find dispensation to quit with Amidea,..be confident Oriana may be won. **1816** SCOTT *Old Mort.* viii, Ye hae preached twenty punds out o' the Laird's pocket that he likes as ill to quit wi'.

9. *trans.* To remove; to put, take, or send away (also with dat. of person); to dismiss. Now *rare.*

1575 TURBERV. *Faulconrie* 364 This medicine..cureth and quitteth the mangie. **1598** BARRET *Theor. Warres* 116 Having quited and depriued them the preheminence to elect Captaines. **1625** MASSINGER *New Way* II. iii, I'll quit you From my employments. **1649** EVELYN *Mem.* (1857) III. 45 The small intelligence come to us..would have quitted you this trouble. **1755** J. SHEBBEARE *Lydia* (1769) I. 361 Miss Arabella..took it out again, without quitting her hand from it. **1847** *Infantry Man.* (1854) 38 Quit the left hand smartly to the left side.

II. 10. To repay, reward, requite (a person *with* some return *for* something done). *Obs.* exc. *north. dial.* (in phr. *God* etc. *quite*, *white*, *twite*).

13.. *E.E. Allit. P.* A. 595 Þou quytez vchon as hys desserte. *c* **1384** CHAUCER *H. Fame* III. 524 We han well deserued hyt, Therfore is ryght that we ben quyt. *c* **1440** *Generydes* 6975 Thus quyte he them that were to hym so kynd. *c* **1530** LD. BERNERS *Arth. Lyt. Bryt.* (1814) 178 Syth he had done me one displeasure, I shall quite him agayne with two. **1576** WOOLTON *Chr. Manual* C i, Let vs not with like thanks quite almightye God for his greate benefyts bestowed vppon vs. **1599** MASSINGER, etc. *Old Law* II. ii, When I visit, I come comfortably, And look to be so quited. **1664** BUTLER *Hud.* II. i. 448, I understand..how to quit you your own way. **1691** RAY *N.C. Words, White*, to requite; as, 'God white you'. **1790** MRS. WHEELER *Westmld. Dial.* (1839) 16 Odd white..Iustice an king teea, for meakin sic laas.

† **11. a.** To make a return to (a person) for (something done, a benefit or injury received, etc.). *Obs.*

a **1300** *Cursor M.* 4422 Ill es þe quit þi god seruis! *c* **1320** *Sir Tristr.* 2258 Ȝe quite him iuel his swink. *c* **1386** CHAUCER *Manciple's T.* 189 O false theef!..I wol thee quite anon thy false tale! *c* **1440** *Partonope* 1554 His kyndenes so he wole hym quyte. **1509** BARCLAY *Shyp of Folys* (1570) 171 God shall thee heare, and quite thee thy trauayle. **1548** W. PATTEN *Exped. Scot.* Pref. a ij, Since we soo quyt theym their kyndnes, and departed so litle in their det.

b. With omission of personal object: To repay, make a return for (something done to or for one).

c **1350** *Will. Palerne* 325 Alle þi frendes fordedes faire schalstow quite. *c* **1420** *Chron. Vilod.* 1187 His trauelle shalle be ryȝt welle y-quytte. *c* **1470** *Gol. & Gaw.* 1101 As I am cristynit perfite, I sall thi kyndnes quyte. *a* **1533** LD. BERNERS *Huon* liv. 183, I shall quyte your mockes. *c* **1586** C'TESS PEMBROKE *Ps.* CXXXVII. iv, Thou, O Lord, will not forgett To quit the paines of Edoms race. **1607** TOURNEUR *Rev. Trag.* v. iii, The rape of your good Lady has been quited. *a* **1632** T. TAYLOR *God's Judgem.* I. I. ix. (1642) 199 On this manner was the Duke of Orleance death quitted. **1850** BLACKIE *Æschylus* I. 137 Like quit with like, and harm with harm repay. **1879** SIR E. ARNOLD *Lt. Asia* v. xxvii, If I attain I will return and quit thy love.

† **c.** To be a return or equivalent for, to balance; esp. in phr. *to quit* (*the*) *cost*. *Obs.*

c **1420** *Pallad. on Husb.* I. 185 A litel tiled wel wul quyte expence. *c* **1440** *Generydes* 5700 On good turne another quytith. **1523** FITZHERB. *Husb.* §14 The roughe otes be the worste, and it quiteth not the coste to sowe them. **1608–11** BP. HALL *Epist.* I. viii. Wks. (1627) 288 Nothing can quite the cose and labour of trauell but the gaine of wisdome. **1646** J. GREGORY *Notes & Obs.* (1650) 63 The strangeness hath been quitted by an Experience of later daies. **1659** BROME *Eng. Moor* I. i. Wks. 1873 II. 4 It is not grief can quit a father's blood. **1787** JEFFERSON *Writ.* (1859) II. 106 Nor would that country quit the cost of being retained against the will of the inhabitants.

III. 12. a. To pay, pay up, clear off (a debt, etc.).

a **1300** *Cursor M.* 28428, I wit-halden ha my tende, and has it quitte til oþer men. **1340** HAMPOLE *Pr. Consc.* 3920 He may þan In purgatory qwyte alle þe dett. *c* **1386** CHAUCER *Wife of Bath's T.* 152 Koude ye me wisse, I wolde wel quite youre hire. *a* **1450** MYRC 1978 ȝef hys godes to luyte be For to quyte þat oweth he. **1590** SHAKS. *Com. Err.* I. i. 23 A thousand markes..To quit the penalty, and to ransome him. **1649** G. DANIEL *Trinarch., Rich. II*, clvii, Hee meant To quit all scores, after the Parliament. **1677** YARRANTON *Eng. Impr.* 110 I'le pay the reckoning, and quit this honest Countrey-mans Charge. *a* **1800** COWPER *Ep. to R. Lloyd* 22 That I may fairly quit The debt which justly became due. **1854** in Whately *Cautions for Times* 131 The souls in Purgatory..only quit the score of punishment which they have not yet paid in this life.

absol. **1393** LANGL. *P. Pl.* C. XVII. 32 *Operis satisfactio* that ..for alle synnes soueraynliche quiteth.

†**b.** With dat. of person, *esp.* in phr. ***to quite one his meed, hire***, etc. *Obs.*

13.. *Coer de L.* 1420, I schal quyten hym hys mede. *a* **1352** MINOT *Poems* vii. 66 Inglis men..quit þam þaire hire. *c* **1400** *Gamelyn* 512 Ther was non of hem alle..That he ne..quitte him his dette. **1550** CROWLEY *Last Trumpet* 446 Let me take vengeance, saith the Lord, And I wyll quyte them all theyr hyre. **1567** *Satir. Poems Reform.* xiv. 99 All Faithfull hartis quyte thair meid.

†**13. a.** To pay, or give, back; to give in return.

a **1300** *Cursor M.* 27867 (Fairf.) He gas to paine, til wrange tane þing be quite againe. *c* **1380** WYCLIF *Wks.* (1880) 173 þes worldly prestis..quiten not aȝen but stynkynge preiere bifore god. *Ibid.* 215 For o schrewed word a man mot quyte anoþer or moo. **14..** *Good Counsel* in *King's Quair* (S.T.S.) 51 For ilk ynch he wyll the quyte a spane.

†**b.** *absol.* To make return or repayment. *Obs.*

a **1340** HAMPOLE *Psalter* xxxvi. 22 þe synful sall borow and he sall noght quyte. *c* **1460** *Towneley Myst.* xiii. 294 Eft whyte when I may Bot this will I borow.

†**14.** To pay for (a thing). *Obs. rare.*

c **1250** *Soth Sermun* 77 in *O.E. Misc.* 190 Robin wule Gilot leden to þen ale..He mai quiten hire ale. *a* **1300** *Cursor M.* 6685 þe smiter sal quite his lechyng. *c* **1330** R. BRUNNE *Chron. Wace* (Rolls) 11852 Alle oure scaþes schul þey quyte.

quit, variant of COOT *sb.*[2]; obs. form of WHITE.

quital: see QUITTAL.

‖**qui tam** (kwaɪ tæm). *Law.* [L., the first words of the clause *qui tam pro domino rege quam pro se ipso sequitur* 'who as well for the lord the king as for himself sues'.] An action brought on a penal statute by an informer, who sues for the penalty both on his own behalf and on that of the crown. **b.** *transf.* An informer.

1755 CHESTERF. in *World* No. 105 An action popular, or of qui tam, would certainly lie. **1783** *Chron.* in *Ann. Reg.* 213/2 An action was tried brought by qui tam on the statute of usury. **1816** 'QUIZ' *Grand Master* III. 63 While the qui tams abuse each other, From hangman Murtagh to ——.

attrib. **1803** *Med. Jrnl.* X. 170 Whatever certainty is required in an indictment, the same is necessary in a qui tam information. **1812** *Sporting Mag.* XXXIX. 23 Amongst.. these are some qui tam gentry. **1853** T. I. WHARTON *Pennsylv. Digest* (ed. 6) II. 17 Qui tam informations are in the nature of civil suits.

quitance: see QUITTANCE.

quitasol(e: see KITTISOL.

quitch (kwɪtʃ), *sb.*[1] Forms: 1 quice, cwice, etc., 6 quyche, 7–8 quich, 7 cuich, quoich, 6– quitch. See also QUICK *sb.*[2], COUCH *sb.*[2], and TWITCH. [OE. *cwice* = MLG. *kweke* (hence G. *quecke*), Du. *kweek*; usually supposed to be related to *cwic*, QUICK *a.*, in reference to its vitality.]

1. A species of grass. = COUCH *sb.*[2]

a **700** *Epinal Gloss.* 464 *Gramen*, quiquae [*Erfurt* quicae, *Corpus* quice]. *c* **1000** *Sax. Leechd.* I. 182 ȝenym þysse wyrte leaf þe man gramen & oðrum naman cwice nemneð. **1523** FITZHERB. *Husb.* §14 All these maner of otes weare the ground very sore, and maketh it to beare quyche. **1658** SIR T. BROWNE *Hydriot.* 22 Some long roots of Quich, or Dogs-grass wreathed about the bones. **1727** BRADLEY *Fam. Dict.* s.v. *Corn land*, A good fallowing..will kill the Quitch Sorrel, moss and other trumpery. **1816** F. VANDERSTRAETEN *Improved Agric.* p. xv, Destroying weeds, and particularly quitch or dog-grass. **1884** BRITTEN & HOLLAND *Plant-n.* 394.

fig. **1859** TENNYSON *Enid* 1751 The vicious quitch Of blood and custom.

b. Also **quitch-grass** in same sense.

1587 MASCALL *Govt. Cattle, Oxen* (1627) 73 [It] groweth in some Gardens like to a quitch grasse. **1601** HOLLAND *Pliny* II. 206 The Quich-grasse..or Dogs-grasse, is the commonest herbe that groweth. **1712** J. JAMES tr. *Le Blond's Gardening* 66 You avoid Quich-grass, and other Weeds. **1840** BROWNING *Sordello* IV. 23 The thoroughfares were overrun with weed—Docks, quitchgrass.

†**2.** ***quitch-hay*** (see quot.). *Obs. rare*[−1].

1523 FITZHERB. *Husb.* §25 Quyche hey commeth of a grasse called crofote,..and it is the beste hey for horses and beastes, and the sweteste.

†**quitch**, *sb.*[2], obs. variant of TWITCH *sb.*

1600 SURFLET *Countrie Farme* I. xxii. 271 Two straight rules of wood as it were..quitches or pincers.

†**quitch**, *sb.*[3], obs. variant of COACH.

a **1693** AUBREY *Lives, W. Aubrey* (1898) I. 60 He kept his coach, which was rare in those dayes. The Judge told me they then (vulgarly) called it a Quitch.

quitch, variant of QUETCH *v.*

†**quitchineel**, obs. form of COCHINEAL.

1622 FLETCHER *Beggars Bush* I. iii, Indico, Quitchineel choise Chyna stuffs.

quitclaim (ˈkwɪtkleɪm), *sb.* Also 5 -clayme, 7 -claime. [a. AF. *quiteclame* (Godef.), sb. f. *quiteclamer*: see next.] †**a.** A formal discharge or release. *Obs.* **b.** A formal renunciation or giving up of a claim.

1450 *Rolls Parlt.* V. 199/1 Letters Patentes of relesse, quit-clayme and discharge. **1473** *Ibid.* VI. 95/2 Any.. Relesse, Discharge or Quyte clayme. **1611** SPEED *Hist. Gt. Brit.* IX. vii. §19. 517 [He] gaue vnto him for the quit-claime of his sisters Ioyncture, twenty thousand ounces of gold. **1658** PHILLIPS, *Quite claim*, in Common Law, is an acquitting of a man for any action that he hath against him. **1865** NICHOLS *Britton* II. 151 The person to whom the quitclaim was made was not..in seisin of the tenement. **1891** B. HARTE *First Fam. Tasajara* i, There's the papers —the quit-claim—all drawn up and Signed.

attrib. **1893** GUNTER *Miss Dividends* 182 A quit-claim deed..of the Mineral Hill locations.

quitclaim (ˈkwɪtkleɪm), *v.* Forms: see QUIT *a.* and CLAIM *v.* Also 5 quik-, quicke-. [a. AF. and OF. *quiteclamer*, *-claimer*, f. *quite* QUIT, clear, free, etc. + *clamer* to proclaim, declare (see CLAIM *v.* 6). In later use associated with QUIT *v.* and CLAIM *sb.* (see 2 b).]

†**1.** To declare (a person) free; to release, acquit, discharge, etc. *Obs.*

c **1314** *Guy Warw.* (A.) 6654 þai ben out of prisoun y-gon Oþer quite-cleymed ichon. *c* **1450** *Merlin* 19 Quod Merlyn, 'Thow haste quyte claymed [*printed* clayned] my moder...' Quod the Iuge, 'It is soth'. **1456** SIR G. HAYE *Law Arms* (S.T.S.) 167 He suld be content thai quite clamand him in tyme tocum. **1596** SPENSER *F.Q.* VI. ii. 14 Neither will I Him charge with guilt, but rather doe quite clame. **1609** SKENE *Reg. Maj.* 23 b, Everie frie man, haueand natiue bond-men, may quiteclame and make them frie.

2. To renounce, resign, give up (a possession, claim, right, pursuit, etc.).

13.. *Gaw. & Gr. Knt.* 293, I quit clayme hit for euer, kepe hit as his auen. *c* **1400** *Sege Jerus.* (E.E.T.S.) 28/504 þat querel y quik cleyme. **1480** *Bury Wills* (Camden) 66 To reles and quyteclayme all their right, title, and interest in the seid maner. **1508** DUNBAR *Flyting* 62 Quytclame clergie, and cleik to the ane club. **1560** ROLLAND *Crt. Venus* II. 741 For ay mirth clenlie I quitclame. **1639** DRUMM. OF HAWTH. *Mem. State* Wks. (1711) 130 Whether a subject may..give over and quit-claim all right and title [etc.]. **1760** T. HUTCHINSON *Hist. Mass.* (1765) I. 89 Having sold or quit-claimed..a tract for a plantation. **1809** BAWDWEN *Domesday Bk.* 2 The land..which Hugo the Sheriff quitclaimed to Walcherus. **1885** W. ROSS *Aberdour & Inchcolme* ii. 39 He quitclaims the land of Leyis to the Monastery.

b. With *quit* taken as verb. Const. *to.*

a **1706** HOWE in Spurgeon *Treas. Dav.* Ps. xii. 4 We must quit claim to ourselves and look on God as our owner. **1809** R. LANGFORD *Introd. Trade* 108, I, A.B...having remissed, released, and for ever quit claim to C.D...of all..debts. **1886** FOX BOURNE *Eng. Merchants* I. 66 Having..remitted and quitted claim to the king for all..debts.

Hence ˈ**quitclaiming** *vbl. sb.*

1472–3 *Rolls Parlt.* VI. 45/1 For that knowelache, remisyng, quiteclaymyng..the seid William..graunted.. the seid maners.

†**quitclaimance.** *Obs. rare*[−1]. In 4 quiteclamance. [a. AF. *quiteclamance*, *-aunce* (Britton, etc.).] = QUITCLAIM *sb.*

c **1330** R. BRUNNE *Chron.* (1810) 186 Of þat Philip..Mad R. a quite clamance [*so in Langtoft*] fro him & alle hise.

quite (kwaɪt), *adv.* Forms: 4–6 quit, quyte, 5 *Sc.* quhyt, 5–6 quyt, 6 quyght, 6–7 quight, 4– quite. [f. *quite* QUIT *a.*]

I. Completely, wholly, altogether, entirely; to the fullest extent or degree.

1. With verbs, esp. in the pa. pple., denoting the thorough completion of the action. †Formerly also in phr. ***quite and clean***: see CLEAN *adv.* 6.

c **1330** R. BRUNNE *Chron.* (1810) 45 Lyndessie he destroied quite alle bidene. *c* **1375** *Sc. Leg. Saints* iv. (*James*) 288 In þe entent þat þai suld have bene quyt schent. *a* **1529** SKELTON *Phyllyp Sparowe* 706 Comfort had he none For she was quyte gone. **1560** DAUS tr. *Sleidane's Comm.* 273 b, All that was there begonne, was quite dasshed. **1590** SPENSER *F.Q.* III. v. 41 His foule sore..she reduced, but himselfe destroyed quight. **1603** KNOLLES *Hist. Turks* (1621) 204 For now was the Greeke Emperour..quite driuen out of the lesser Asia. **1630** PRYNNE *Anti-Armin.* 133 That I may quite vnuaile the hidden mysteries of this vniuersal grace. **1700** S. L. tr. *Fryke's Voy. E. Ind.* 57 We found our selves forced to Intrench, lest they should have routed us quite. **1785** REID *Wks.* (1863) I. 67/2 My distemper is almost quite gone. **1859** M. ARNOLD *Southern Night* in *Poems* (1869) I. 218 Thy memory, thy pain, tonight..Possess me quite. **1880** JEFFERIES *Gt. Estate* 59 Haws..which often quite cover the hawthorn bushes.

2. With prepositional or adverbial phrases.

c **1375** *Sc. Leg. Saints* xxxiv. (*Pelagia*) 124 It..flaw vpe quyt in þe ayre. *c* **1440** *Generydes* 3048 It ranne down quyte thorough the harnes. **1470–85** MALORY *Arthur* x. lxxix, He smote hym doune quyte from his hors. **1545** BRINKLOW *Compl.* 28 b, He bracke it quyte in pecys. **1551** ROBINSON tr. *More's Utop.* I. (1895) 112 That is..quyte out of remembraunce. *a* **1600** HOOKER *Serm. Sorrow & Fear* Wks. 1888 III. 649 The sword that pierceth their souls quite through. **1638** R. BAKER tr. *Balzac's Lett.* (vol. II) 43, I have done it against the streame of my resolution quite. *c* **1710** CELIA FIENNES *Diary* (1888) 91 Severall nitches for statues quite round it. **1766** GOLDSM. *Vic. W.* xviii, Dryden's and Rowe's manner..are quite out of fashion. *Ibid.* xxi, I had thrown all their power quite away. **1816** J. WILSON *City of Plague* II. ii. 3 Here have I sat..Quite by myself. **1870** E. PEACOCK *Ralf Skirl.* I. 153 The room was not quite without ornament.

3. a. With adjs., and advbs. or sbs. derived from these, denoting that they are to be understood in their fullest or most absolute sense.

c **1375** *Sc. Leg. Saints* xl. (*Ninian*) 1336 Blynd I ame quhyt & fre. **1597** BP. HALL *Sat.* I. iii. 17 Threats, That his poore hearers hayre quite vpright sets. **1604** BP. ANDREWES *Wks.* II. 142 Able to quicken our consideration, if it be not quite dead. **1671** MILTON *P.R.* IV. 317 One regardless quite Of mortal things. **1751** FRANKLIN *Lett.* Wks. 1840 V. 263 By quite dry air, I mean the dryest we have. **1765** A. DICKSON *Treat. Agric.* (ed. 2) 196 The mold-board in the common ploughs is..almost quite straight. **1838** J. KEMPER in *Wisconsin Mag. Hist.* (1925) VIII. 429 It was quite one when we arrived at Lathrop's tavern at Mineral Point. **1860** TYNDALL *Glac.* I. xxiv. 170, I spent that day quite alone upon the Mer de Glace. **1879** R. K. DOUGLAS *Confucianism* iv. 95 A man should be quite certain what he knows and what he does not know. **1927** M. DE LA ROCHE *Jalna* xix. 223 There were quite eight books in the packet.

b. Preceded by def. or indef. article, chiefly with adjs. expressing difference. †***a quite other*** = quite another; †***the quite contrary*** (freq. in 17th c.) = quite the contrary (see next).

1594 CAREW *Huarte's Exam. Wits* 116 In the Spaniards, we discerne the quite contrarie. **1618** BOLTON *Florus* II. vi. 108 Livius marcht..into the quite opposit quarter. **1661** CRESSY *Refl. Oathes Suprem. & Alleg.* 51–2 It speaks a quite other language. **1665** BOYLE *Occas. Refl.* IV. xiii. (1848) 249 Upon a quite contrary account than they intended. **1712** STEELE *Spect.* No. 493 ¶1 In proportion to his deserving the quite contrary. *a* **1774** GOLDSM. *Hist. Greece* I. 251 Into things of a quite opposite nature. **1875** RUSKIN *Fors Clav.* V. lx. 348 When the luxuries are produced, it becomes a quite separate question who is to have them.

c. Preceding the article, chiefly as in prec., and esp. in phr. ***quite another*** (thing, question, etc.); occas. with intervening prep. (cf. 2).

1626 BACON *Sylva* §125 For the Impression of the Sound, it is quite another Thing. **1657** W. RAND tr. *Gassendi's Life Peiresc* II. 262 Trees, quite of another kind. **1664** PEPYS *Diary* III. 91 The comet..is gone quite to a new place in the heavens. **1679** PENN *Addr. Prot.* II. 146 That's quite another thing than being certain. **1716** DAVIES *Athen. Brit.* II. 401 Which was quite the reverse in those two..Prelates. **1751** R. PALTOCK *P. Wilkins* (1883) II. 194 That I did first was quite of a different colour from the leaf. **1810** BENTHAM *Offic. Apt. Maximized, Def. Econ.* (1830) 52 Any such accidental display is quite another business. **1845** M. PATTISON *Ess.* (1889) I. 16 For quite another reason.

d. *colloq.* Expressing appreciation of or agreement with a statement. Freq. ***quite so.***

1892 A. CONAN DOYLE *Adv. Sherlock Holmes* x. 246 'This maid Alice, as I understand, deposes that she..put on a bonnet, and went out.' 'Quite so. And she was afterwards seen walking into Hyde-park.' **1896** [see *so adv.* 5 b]. **1924** GALSWORTHY *White Monkey* II. ii. 131 'I don't hold with it, myself.' 'No, quite!' **1931** WODEHOUSE *If I were You* xxii. 243 'Our likes and dislikes are not the point,' she said. 'The thing's impossible.' 'Quite,' agreed Sir Herbert. **1953** E. SIMON *Past Masters* I. 26 'I didn't know there was a settlement..only a cemetery.' 'The burial ground: quite so.' **1962** D. LESSING *Golden Notebook* I. 131 'I've been supporting policies that should put an end to the whole bloody business.' 'Quite. And quite right.' **1976** K. BONFIGLIOLI *Something Nasty in Woodshed* x. 123 'No takers,' I said. 'Quite. By the way, I'm sorry to say 'quite' all the time but..my work lies amongst Americans and they *expect* Englishmen to say it.'

II. Actually, really, truly, positively (implying that the case or circumstances are such as fully justify the use of the word or phrase thus qualified).

4. a. With adjs. or pa. pples., and derived advbs.

1742 RICHARDSON *Pamela* (1811) III. 311 They tell me she's..quite smart and handsome. **1749** FIELDING *Tom Jones* XIII. v, The widow, quite charmed with her new lodger, invited him..to breakfast. **1805** EMILY CLARK *Banks of Douro* I. 248 She felt..so perturbed..that she was quite ill and restless. **1834** BECKFORD *Italy* I. 326 The gallery immediately before its entrance appeared quite gay. **1848** HERSCHEL *Ess.* (1857) 342 A ship sailing northwards passes quite suddenly from cold into hot water. **1871** RUSKIN *Fors Clav.* iii. 17 You would observe..the quite Anglican character of Richard.

b. Preceding the indef. article. ***quite a few***: see FEW *a.* 2 d.

1756 TOLDERVY *Hist. 2 Orphans* III. 49 It is quite a pleasing, rural,..plentiful retirement. **1799** SOUTHEY *Lett.* (1856) I. 84 Quite a comfortable dwelling. **1843** MILL *Logic* (1865) I. 403 Up to quite a recent period. **1860** KEBLE *Lett.* (1870) 184 They are quite a large party in Edinburgh. **1884** *Manch. Exam.* 3 May 6/1 At quite an early hour.

c. Coupled with *too.*

1763 C. JOHNSTON *Reverie* I. 137 Your offer is quite too low. **1782** MISS BURNEY *Cecilia* VII. i. (1893) 269 Going to Mr. Harrel's again would have been quite too dismal. **1843** J. MARTINEAU *Chr. Life* (1867) 14 Presenting the Creator to us in a relation quite too mean. **1882** H. C. MERIVALE *Faucit of B.* III. II. xii. 47, I quite too awfully near put my foot in it! **1890** BARRÈRE & LELAND *Dict. Slang* II. 164/2 *Quite too nice* (society), expression much used by the aesthetic female portion of society, meaning much the same as 'awfully jolly'. **1897** A. BEARDSLEY *Let.* 26 Apr. (1970) 308 It is quite too nice to be here... Yesterday we had a charming lunch party at Lapérouse. **1909** J. R. WARE *Passing Eng.* p. v, It may be hoped that there are errors on every page, and also that no entry is 'quite too dull'. **1977** P. SCUPHAM *Hinterland* 15 Paquerelle, we fall back on the language of the Aesthetics: Your composition is quite too utterly too too.

d. With superlatives.

1863 F. LOCKER-LAMPSON *London Lyrics* (1870) 106 And all that sort of thing, of which Dear Hawthorne's 'quite' the best describer. **1883** *Harper's Mag.* Nov. 882/1 The auditorium is quite the largest in the world. **1911** G. B. SHAW *Getting Married* 218 Don't you think her letters are quite the best love-letters I get? **1934** W. B. YEATS *Words upon Window-Pane* 36 Exactly: quite the best kind of mediumship if you want to establish the identity of a spirit. **1981** *Country Life* 12 Feb. 409/1 The high degree of accuracy..quite the highest, surely, that *can* be attained.

5. a. With substantives preceded by *a*, or in *pl.* Also in mod. usage, implying emphatic, and occas. ironic, commendation.

c **1586** C'TESS PEMBROKE *Ps.* LXIX. iv, To my kynn a stranger quite, Quite an alien am I grown. **1737** POPE *Hor. Sat.* II. vi. 146 Something..quite a scandal not to learn. —— *Ep.* I. i. 50 Far from a Lynx, and not a Giant quite. **1762** LLOYD *Poet. Wks.* (1774) I. 183 It's quite a journey to come here. **1806–7** J. BERESFORD *Miseries Hum. Life* I. 291 That must have been quite a scene. **1816** JANE AUSTEN *Emma* III. vi. 86 You are an odd creature!.. You are a humourist... Quite a humourist. **1840** THACKERAY *Catherine* i, There's many a girl in the village that at my age is quite chits. **1859** C. M. TUTTLE *Diary* 30 May in *Wisconsin Mag. Hist.* (1931) XV. 78 Council Bluffs is quite a place containing about 3 thousand inhabitants. **1896** T. F. TOUT *Edw. I*, iv. 79 A daughter..who died when quite a child. **1917** *Dialect Notes* IV. 398 An extension of the adverbial use as in 'He is *quite* a lad'. **1938** E. HEMINGWAY *Fifth Column* I. iii. 28 Comrade's quite a word. I suppose I oughtn't to chuck it around. **1950** 'D. DIVINE' *King of Fassarai* xx. 166 We had us a party last night—quite a party. **1962** 'A. GARVE' *Prisoner's Friend* ii. 97 Sheila was in a much happier frame of mind... As he was beginning to think she was quite a girl. *a* **1974** R. CROSSMAN *Diaries* (1975) I. 219 It had been quite a week and I wanted a day of relaxation.

b. With sbs. preceded by *the* (also with adj.).

1762 GOLDSM. *Cit. W.* lxxvii, It [silk] is at once rich, tasty, and quite the thing. **1799** COLERIDGE *Lett.* (1895) 277 Pipes are quite the rage. **1803** in *Spirit Pub. Jrnls.* VII. 20 Quite the tippy for the boxes. **1865** *Sat. Rev.* July 14 The Chancellor is not quite the right man for his..place. **1888** *Poor Nellie* 114 It was quite the thing to be in love.

c. With sbs. preceded by *some*. Chiefly *U.S.*

1894 *Dialect Notes* I. 333 *Quite*..common in C[entral] J[ersey] in such expressions as 'quite some'. **1896** *Ibid.* I. 422 You'll have *quite some* potatoes on the patch. **1931** *Amer. Speech* Oct. 20 It was quite some excitement we had for a while. **1977** *Lancs. Life* Nov. 58/2 A wooden toy..for £125. It was, as you will have gathered, quite some toy.

d. Phr. ***quite something***, a remarkable thing; a good deal. *colloq.*

1958 'N. BLAKE' *Penknife in Heart* iv. 60 Well now, that's quite something. Thank you. **1968** *Guardian* 10 Oct. 7/2 She found out that I was sleeping with someone else and she had to accept the situation which was quite something because it wasn't even a woman. **1971** 'L. BLACK' *Death has Green Fingers* iii. 25 Your village seems to be quite something with the lid off. **1973** *Where* Jan. 27/2 Ideally, of course, all readers should have been included—but the work involved in analysing such a mass of information would have been quite something. **1977** *Lancs. Life* Nov. 74/3 The Women's Institute itself is quite something.

6. With verbs (= 'to go as far as', 'to do as much as').

1770 ELIZ. CARTER *Lett., to Mrs. Montagu* II. 67, I quite longed for you to share my admiration of it. **1819** *Metropolis* I. 213 Lady Mildew..quite haunts us. *Ibid.* 249 A certain upstart commoner..quite made love to me. **1848** J. H. NEWMAN *Loss & Gain* 192 A great personage..quite scoffed at their persisting to hold it. **1866** G. MACDONALD *Ann. Q. Neighb.* xiii. (1878) 285 You can't quite believe there is a God at all.

7. With prep. phrases or advbs.

1846 LANDOR *Wks.* II. 16 There are minerals and instruments quite at hand.

III. 8. In a weakened sense: rather, to a moderate degree, fairly.

This sense has develped out of sense II, and is often difficult to distinguish from it. As a result, sense I is usually felt to be old-fashioned or stilted, and has become less common, except where *quite* is in collocation with certain types of adjective (and their derived adverbs) such as *different, separate, right, wrong, sure, definite*, etc.

1854 THOREAU *Walden* 226 Perhaps I have owed to this employment and to hunting, when quite young, my closest acquaintance with Nature. **1886** *Science* 30 Apr. 403/1 The lithographer has done his work quite, though hardly very, well. **1889** J. K. JEROME *Three Men in Boat* ix. 144 If so, who was the real one that was dreaming, and who was the one that was only a dream: it got quite interesting. **1919** G. B. SHAW *Heartbreak House* II. 54 Theyve been proud of my poverty. Theyve even joked about it quite often. **1931** E. O'NEILL *Homecoming* I, in *Mourning becomes Electra* (1932) 16 Borne on the light puffs of wind this music is at times quite loud. **1952** A. WILSON *Hemlock & After* iii. 58, I quite like queers if it comes to that, so long as they're not on the make like Evelyn's boys. **1958** 'A. BRIDGE' *Portuguese Escape* xvi. 265 You shall..when you have answered one quite small question: where is now Dr. Antal Horvath? **1970** G. F. NEWMAN *Sir, you Bastard* ii. 43 Sneed quite liked DI Johnny Doleman, and the man treated him like an intelligent equal. **1976** C. SARFAS *Space & Space Travel* 19 But the astronauts were wearing their heavy spacesuits and equipment, so even on the moon it was quite hard to move. **1980** J. MCCLURE *Blood of Englishman* xvi. 144, I only said a 'quite' brilliant idea, sir—not a 'very'.

IV. 9. Quasi-*adj. ellipt.* for 'quite a gentleman (lady, etc.)'; socially acceptable. Usu. in neg. Also ***quite-quite***.

1867 TROLLOPE *Last Chron. Barset* I. xlii. 371 Still he wasn't quite,—not quite, you know—'not quite so much of a gentleman as I am'—Mr Walker would have said, had he spoken out freely that which he insinuated. But he contented himself with the emphasis he put upon the 'not quite', which expressed his meaning fully. **1878** —— *Is he Popenjoy?* I. xiv. 195 'I have always liked the Dean personally,' said Lady Sarah... 'But he isn't—he isn't quite—' 'No; he isn't quite—,' said Lord George, also hesitating to pronounce the word which was understood by both of them. **1907** M. E. BRADDON *Dead Love has Chains* vi. 124 Oh, she is quite quite, don't you know... Her father is Sir Michael Thelliston. **1915** V. WOOLF *Voyage Out* xi. 159 Mr. Perrott..knew he was not 'quite', as Susan stated..not quite a gentleman she meant. **1926** *Whispering Gallery* viii. 114 He's not 'quite quite', you know, but he's so clever. **1930** C. WILLIAMS *Poetry at Present* 165 That awful moment when..one feels that one is 'not quite'. **1945** A. HUXLEY *Time must have Stop* xxi. 200 'You'll find him a bit..well, you know, not quite...' The deprecating gesture sufficiently indicated what he quite wasn't. **1956** J. MASTERS *Bugles & Tiger* xv. 182 This was supposed to be not quite quite, and British officers took no part in it. **1960** M. CECIL *Something in Common* 7 'She's a Lady' (acceptable), or 'He's not Quite' (rejected).

‖**quite** ('kite), *sb. Bullfighting.* [Sp.] The action of distracting the bull from a man or a horse by means of elaborate capework.

1926 E. HEMINGWAY *Sun also Rises* xviii. 225 His first 'quite' was directly below us. The three matadors take the bull in turn. **1932** —— *Death in Afternoon* xvii. 184 The spectator..will be liable to..watch the horse and miss the quite that the matador has made. **1957** A. MACNAB *Bulls of Iberia* v. 52 As the picador falls on the sand, the first matador rushes in with his cape, to distract the bull... This rescue job is called making a *quite*. **1967** MCCORMICK & MASCAREÑAS *Compl. Aficionado* ii. 36 We are told that the glory of the early corrida was the emphasis upon cape work in the *quites* necessitated by the large number of pics to the toro. **1975** *Oxf. Compan. Sports & Games* 140/1 The measures take the form of keeping the bull under control at all times..making certain that the animal is not excessively enfeebled during the *suerte de varas* due to tardy *quites*.

quite, obs. form of QUIT *a.* and *v.*; WHITE.

† '**quitely**, *adv. Obs.* [f. QUIT(E *a.* + -LY².]

1. Freely, at liberty.

c **1330** R. BRUNNE *Chron. Wace* (Rolls) 1200 Wheþer þey redden hym for to slo, Oþer quytly let hym go. *c* **1375** *Sc. Leg. Saints* xxvi. (*Nicholas*) 496 Passis one quytly away, & lovis god. *c* **1386** CHAUCER *Knt.'s T.* 934 Lo heere this Arcite, and this Palamon, That quitly weren out of my prison.

2. Completely, altogether. = QUITE *adv.* I.

a **1300** *Cursor M.* 1582 Þe find wend..þat al man kind quitli war his. *a* **1340** HAMPOLE *Psalter* lxxxvii. 5 It semes as þou had whitely [*v.r.* qwitly] forgetten. *c* **1400** *Rom. Rose* 5843 He hath geten a peny or two, That quytely is his owne in holde.

† '**quitement**, *adv. Obs. rare*⁻¹. [a. OF. *quitement* (12th c.), f. *quite*: see QUIT(E *a.*] = prec. 2.

13.. *Coer de L.* 2002 The scull brake with that dent, The right eye flew out quitement.

quiter, obs. f. QUITTER *sb.*¹

quither, obs. f. WHETHER, WHITHER.

quiting, *vbl. sb.*: see QUITTING.

quitli, var. QUITELY *adv.*

quitoure, obs. f. QUITTER *sb.*¹

quit-rent ('kwɪtrɛnt). Also 5–6 quite-, (quyte-, 5 white-, etc.). [f. *quite* QUIT *a.* + RENT.]

1. A rent, usually of small amount, paid by a freeholder or copyholder in lieu of services which might be required of him.

c **1460** *Pol. Rel. & L. Poems* (1866) 24 Consydere what seruyce longyth ther-to And the quyterent that there-of oute shalle goo. **1463** *Bury Wills* (Camden) 24, xijs. of white rente. **1511** FABYAN *Will* in *Chron.* (1811) Pref. p. xi, All the charges and quyterents..goyng owte of the same. **1532–3** in Swayne *Sarum Church-w. Acc.* (1896) 264 To my lorde of Salisbury for quytrent, vijs. iiijd. *a* **1680** CHARNOCK *Attrib. God* (1834) II. 57–8 He that pays not the quit-rent..disowns the sovereignty of the lord of the Manor. **1706** MRS. RAY in *Lett. Lit. Men* (Camden) 208, £40 a year..out of which taxes, repairs, and quit-rent make a great hole. **1776** ADAM SMITH *W.N.* (1869) I. II. iii. 336 The rent they paid was often nominally little more than a quit-rent. **1848** MILL *Pol. Econ.* II. vii. §1 A tenant at a quit rent is to all intents and purposes a proprietor.

b. *transf.* or *fig.*

1607 TOURNEUR *Rev. Trag.* I. i. Wks. 1878 II. 7 Vengence, thou murder's Quit-rent. **1645** QUARLES *Sol. Recant.* III. 54 Is't not enough that we poor Farmers pay Quit-rent to Nature at the very day? **1737** GREEN *Spleen* 657 Fit dwelling for the feather'd throng, Who pay their quit-rents with a song. **1833** H. COLERIDGE *Poems* I. 12 The rose-lipp'd shells Which Neptune to the earth for quit-rent pays.

attrib. **1782** COWPER *Table Talk* 110 The courtly laureate pays His quitrent ode, his peppercorn of praise.

2. A charge upon an estate for some special purpose. ? *Obs.*

1454 *Rolls Parlt.* V. 258/1 Devysed and by his legate ordeyned, vi mark of annuell quyte rente to the sustenaunce of a Prest perpetuall. *a* **1500** *Colyn Blowbols Test.* 180 in Hazl. *E.P.P.* (1864) I. 101 Sauf only a certeyn quyte-rent, Which that I have gevyn with good entent To pay for me, unto my confessour. **1712** ADDISON *Spect.* No. 517 ¶2 The gifts of charity which..he had left as quit-rents upon the estate.

quits (kwɪts), *a.* and *sb.* [Cf. QUIT *a.*, but the origin of the *-s* is obscure; it may be due to a colloquial use of the med.L. *quit(t)us* in receipts (cf. QUITSEST).] **A.** *adj.*

† **1.** Clear, discharged (*of* a liability). *Obs.*

1478 *Croscombe Church-w. Acc.* (Som. Rec. Soc.) 7 Rest to the Wardenes xviijs. ixd. paid them, so quits herof. **1590** *Acc.-bk. W. Wray* in *Antiquary* XXXII. 374 Su[mma] is iiij *li.* iiij *s.* ij *d.*; payd and quits.

2. a. Even or equal (*with* another) by means of repayment or retaliation.

1663 COWLEY *Cutter Colman St.* v. ii, *Wor.* I had quite forgot you... *Joll.* Faith, we're both quits then;..I ha' forgot you. **1675** R. BURTHOGGE *Causa Dei* 127 Revenge.. expressed in common language by 'I will be quits with him'. **1741** RICHARDSON *Pamela* (1824) I. xxix. 47 Do you think, as I had no wages, I may be supposed to be quits? **1816** W. IRVING in *Life & Lett.* (1864) I. 356, I shall be content to be quits with fortune for a very moderate portion. **1879** DIXON *Windsor* II. xx. 215 When all was paid, the young King and the sorceress queen were quits.

b. ***to cry quits*** (cf. QUITTANCE 4).

1639 FULLER *Holy War* III. xi. (1840) 134 To cry quits with them, our English authors impute it to the envy of the French. **1837** MARRYAT *Percival Keene* xix, I should have fired at you, so we may cry quits on that score. **1884** J. GILMOUR *Mongols* 133 On the young man making an apology, the old man had been content to cry quits.

c. ***double or quits***: see DOUBLE *adv.* 4.

d. ***to call (it) quits*** = *to cry quits*; hence, to give up or call off a venture, occas. with suggestion of cutting one's losses.

1898 J. LONDON *Let.* 30 Nov. (1966) 5 Tomorrow I would cut my throat and call quits with the whole cursed business. **1950** *Manch. Guardian Weekly* 16 Mar. 2/2 The old isolationist want to 'call quits' on the whole business. **1963** J. JOESTEN *They call it Intelligence* II. viii. 75 Vic smelled a rat and decided to call it quits. **1972** *Islander* (Victoria, B.C.) 13 Feb. 2/4 Nearly bitten alive with mosquitoes..I called it quits and joined the gang in the [boat].

3. Quit or rid *of*. *rare*⁻¹.

1885 LADY HERBERT tr. *Lagrange's Life Bp. Dupanloup* I. 277 They only wish to be quits of the whole thing.

B. *sb.* **a.** An equivalent, a recompense. **b.** Reprisal, retaliation. *rare.*

1806 SURR *Winter in Lond.* III. 259 Fifty pounds..which ..was to be quits for sister's virtue. **1865** W. G. PALGRAVE *Arabia* I. 38 Not finding the occasion favourable for taking immediate quits.

† **quitsest.** *Obs. rare*⁻¹. [? Colloquial var. of QUIETUS EST: see QUITS.] Release, discharge.

1587 HOLINSHED *Chron.* III. 1170/1 It pleased God to send England..a quitsest from former broiles of a turbulent estate.

† **quit shilling.** *Obs.* [f. QUIT *v.* 2 b.] (See quot.)

1882 J. ASHTON *Social Life Q. Anne* II. 245 Were any one [of the prisoners in Newgate] lucky enough to be acquitted, he had to spend a Quit Shilling for their delight.

quitt, obs. form of QUIT, QUITE.

† '**quittal**, '**quital**. *Obs.* [f. QUIT *v.* + -AL¹.]

a. Requital. **b.** Acquittal.

c **1530** LD. BERNERS *Arth. Lyt. Bryt.* (1814) 178 It is I.. that bereth the hurte, therfore..let me be at the quital therof. **1592** KYD *Sp. Trag.* III. i. 79 Let him vnbinde thee that is bound to death, To make a quitall for thy discontent. **1593** SHAKS. *Lucr.* 236 As in reuenge or quittall of such strife. *a* **1633** AUSTIN *Medit.* (1635) 124 His Doome [is] thy Quittall.

quittance ('kwɪtəns), *sb.* Forms: 3 cwitaunce, 4 quitance, 5 qvyt-, qwyt-, 5–6 quet-, quyt-, 6– quittance (also 5 -awnce, 5–6 -ans, -aunce, and 7 cuttans). [a. OF. *quitance* (later *quittance*), f. *quiter* to QUIT. Cf. med.L. *quit(t)-, quietantia.*]

1. The act of freeing or clearing; release; †acquittal.

In mod. examples perh. associated with sense 5.

a **1225** *Ancr. R.* 126 Wiðute cwitaunce, up of his prisun nis non inumen. *c* **1375** *Sc. Leg. Saints* xxii. (*Laurence*) 702 For quetance scho suld ga one ane heyt yrne. **1426** *E. E. Wills* 71 Þe costes of his qwytaunce of his enditement. **1523** LD. BERNERS *Froiss.* I. xliii. 58 We woll..demaunde of you quytance of our bondes. **1603** *Court Bk. Earl Orkney* 21 June (Jam. Suppl.), Under quittance of the stowt of his nyhbor's peits. **1858** J. ROBERTSON *Poems* 99 Thy work is done..Bless thy good quittance from superfluous life. **1867** TROLLOPE *Chron. Barset* II. xlix. 49 They [quarrels] come very easily,..but the quittance from them is sometimes terribly difficult.

2. A release or discharge from a debt or obligation; a document certifying such discharge; a receipt.

c **1330** R. BRUNNE *Chron.* (1810) 156 Richard ȝald him his right, his tresore & his toun,..To mak certeyn partie, R. a quitance toke. **1464** *Paston Lett.* II. 162 A quetaunce of suche money as ye have receyved. *c* **1500** *Melusine* 356–7 Ye desyre of me quytaunce therof so wyl I haue quytaunce of hym that receyueth it of you. **1600** HAKLUYT *Voy.* II. 272 Hauing paid the custome, it behoueth to haue a quittance. **1628** WITHER *Brit. Rememb.* v. 784, I have thy Quittance, though I am thy Debtor. **1819** SCOTT *Ivanhoe* x, Gurth.. folded the quittance, and put it under his cap. **1863** J. G. MURPHY *Comm., Gen.* xxiv. 5–8 He..obtains a quittance from his oath. **1882** OUIDA *Maremma* I. 248 We let her take our substance and never asked her a quittance.

fig. **1303** R. BRUNNE *Handl. Synne* 10813 Þe fourþe sacrament ys penaunce, þat ys for synne a quytaunce. **1595** *Locrine* v. iv. 188 Soon shall I..with my sword..Seal thee a quittance for thy bold attempts. **1642** QUARLES *Div. Poems* I. 60 Deare Mercy made a Quittance for her sin.

Prov. **1562** J. HEYWOOD *Prov. & Epigr.* (1867) 161 Suffrans is no quittans. **1600** SHAKS. *A.Y.L.* III. v. 133 That's all one: omittance is no quittance.

3. Recompense or requital; repayment; reprisal.

c **1590** MARLOWE *Faust.* Wks. (Rtldg.) 126/1 On his head, in quittance of my wrongs, I'll nail huge forked horns. **1600** HOLLAND *Livy* VII. xix. 262 This execution made quittance with them, for sacrificing the Romanes. **1637** SHIRLEY *Hyde*

Park I. i. Biij b, In quittance of your loving, honest Councell. **1813** BYRON *Corsair* II. vi, Each..sinks outwearied..His last faint quittance rendering with his breath. **1879** BUTCHER & LANG *Odyssey* 18 In quittance whereof ye now work me harm.

Comb. **1862** RUSKIN *Unto this Last* 138 *note*, Tisiphone, the 'requiter (or quittance-taker) of death'.

†**4.** *to cry quittance*, to declare oneself clear or even *with* another; hence, to make full repayment or retaliation. (Cf. QUITS 2 b.) *Obs.*

1579 LYLY *Euphues* (Arb.) 292 Desirous to crye quittaunce for hir present tongue. **1622** MABBE tr. *Aleman's Guzman d'Alf.* I. 234, I thought I had just cause to crie quittance with him. **1679** DRYDEN *Troilus & C.* I. ii, He was struck down yesterday in the Battle, but..he'll cry Quittance with 'em to-day.

5. The act of quitting or leaving. *rare.*

1892 *Black & White* 22 Oct. 462/2 After his quittance of the jail he resumed the editorship.

†**'quittance**, *v. Obs.* [f. prec. sb. Cf. OF. *quittancer* (Godef.).]

1. *intr.* To give a discharge. *rare*⁻¹.

1502 ARNOLDE *Chron.* (1811) 108, I..graunte to my sayd atturnays..to take playnt and arest..and to relece and quitaunce [etc.].

2. *trans.* To give up, cancel. = QUIT *v.* 5.

1592 GREENE *Conny catching* II. 2 b, Shall I be made a slaue because I am bound to you: no no, I can quittance my indenture when I list.

3. To repay, requite (a person, service, injury, etc.).

1590 GREENE *Orl. Fur.* Wks. (Rtldg.) 95 Hate calls me on to quittance all my ills. **1620** *Swetnam Arraigned* (1880) 35 Ere long, It may be in Our power to quittance him. **1624** HEYWOOD *Gunaik.* I. 54 To quittance this He guerdons Midas with his golden wish.

quittasol, variant of KITTISOL.

quitter, quittor ('kwɪtə(r)), *sb.*[1] Now *rare.* Forms: 3–4 quiture, 4 quyt-, 5 quet-, 5–6 quytt-, (5 -ur), 6–7 quitture, (7 -ur); 4 qwetour, quet-, quitoure, 5 quyteour, whitour, whytoure, 7 quittour; 5 quetor, 7–9 quittor; 4–5 quyter(e, quytter(e, 5 quet-, quiter, 6– quitter, (8 coutre). [Perh. a. OF. *quiture, cuiture* cooking, decoction, etc. (but app. not recorded in the specific sense of the Eng. word).]

1. Pus; suppurating matter; a purulent discharge from a wound or sore. *Obs.* except *Jamaican.*

1297 R. GLOUC. (Rolls) 8596 Heo..wess hor vet & clene þe quiture [*v.rr.* qwetour, quetoure] out soȝte. *c* **1305** *St. Edmund* 159 in *E.E.P.* (1862) 75 Moche del his bodi orn in quitoure & in blode. **1382** WYCLIF *Job* ii. 8 [Job] with a sherd scrapide awei the quyture. *c* **1400** *Lanfranc's Cirurg.* 37 Þilke quyttere & blood schulde lette þe helynge of þe wounde. *c* **1440** *Promp. Parv.* 525/2 Whytowre, of a soore, *sanies.* **1543** TRAHERON *Vigo's Chirurg.* Interpret. Strange Wordes, Colde apostemes utteringe quytture or fylthe. **1601** HOLLAND *Pliny* II. 424 The filthy excrements, attyr, and quitter, that gather in sores and wounds. **1686** PLOT *Staffordsh.* 305 The nourishing juice..emptying it self by those corrupted sores in a quitture or Sanies. **1689** HICKERINGILL *Ceremony Monger* Concl. i. Wks. 1716 II. 454 To let the corrupted Quitter out. **1943, 1952** in Cassidy & Le Page *Dict. Jamaican Eng.* **1961** F. G. CASSIDY *Jamaica Talk* i. 4 The ginger-grower in Christiana who spoke of the *quitter* (pus) in a wound..which the OED traces no later than 1689 in this sense.

fig. *c* **1380** WYCLIF *Sel. Wks.* III. 231 So shulde men.. thriste oute þo quyter of hor olde synnes.

2. *Farriery.* = quitter-bone (see 4).

1703 *Lond. Gaz.* No. 3964/4 A Quitter lately taken out of his further Foot behind. **1794** *Sporting Mag.* III. 34 Sandcracks, quittors, strains in the back-sinews. **1843** YOUATT *Horse* xix. 394 Quittor..has been described as being the result of neglected or bad tread, or over-reach. **1900** *Times* 2 Oct. 13/4 He examined the mare and found it suffering from a bad quitter which was discharging matter. **1917** W. OWEN *Let.* 21 Feb. (1967) 437 Certain cases of Thrush, Quitter, and such suppurations go one worse than the battlefield-exhalations.

†**3.** The dross of tin. *Obs. rare*⁻⁰.

1674 BLOUNT *Glossogr.* (ed. 4). **1736** AINSWORTH *Lat. Dict.* [Hence in JOHNSON and mod. Dicts.]

4. *Comb.* †**quitter-bone**, an ulcer or suppurating sore on the coronet of a horse's hoof. *Obs.* (See also TWITTER-BONE.)

1598 FLORIO, *Seta*,..a disease in a horse called a quitter-bone. **1614** B. JONSON *Barth. Fair* II. v, She has..the quitter bone i' the tother legge. **1639** T. DE GRAY *Expert Ferrier* II. xvii. 298 A Quitter-bone..commeth to a horse by some hurt he hath taken in the foot. **1710** *Lond. Gaz.* No. 4771/4 Lately cured of a Coutre Bone on the off Foot behind. **1755** J. SHEBBEARE *Lydia* (1769) I. 337 A roan horse, with..a small quitter bone on the farther leg before. **1798** LAWRENCE *Treat. Horses* II. 520 A quittor, formerly called by our farriers a quittor bone.

Hence †**'quitterish**, †**'quitterous**, †**'quittery** *adjs.*, containing, or of the nature of, pus. *Obs.*

1398 TREVISA *Barth. De P.R.* VII. lxii. (1495) 278 It bredeth a drye scabbe and not quyttery. **1543** TRAHERON *Vigo's Chirurg.* II. i. iii. 48 Apostemes,..quitterous, ful of water. **1582** BATMAN *On Barthol.* xxix. 97 In whom the spettle is quitterie and venemous. **1668** CULPEPPER & COLE *Barthol. Anat.* II. v. 95 Of a quittorish nature.

quitter ('kwɪtə(r)), *sb.*[2] [f. QUIT *v.* + -ER[1].]

†**1.** One who frees, discharges, etc. *Obs. rare*⁻⁰.

1611 COTGR., *Quiteur*, a quitter, acquiter, freer, discharger. [**1736** in AINSWORTH *Lat. Dict.* Hence in JOHNSON, and later Dicts.]

2. orig. *U.S.* One who, or that which, 'quits', goes away, shirks, etc.

1881 *Standard* 7 Sept. 5/2 They may perhaps have a right to the term 'quitter', to stigmatise an animal that will not make a fight. **1887** *Columbus* (Ohio) *Disp.* 31 May, The mighty pressure gives confidence that the [gas] well will not be a quitter. **1897** *Outing* (U.S.) XXIX. 581/1 Leggins may be fat, but he's no quitter. **1908** 'O. HENRY' in *American Mag.* LXVII. 69/2, I can stand the fabulous monster that.. blows hot birds and cold bottles with the same breath. But I can't stand a quitter. **1923** *Auckland Weekly News* 11 Oct. 16/6 He dropped in on me one evening and started to upbraid me for being a quitter. **1931** *Sun* (Baltimore) 12 Jan. 8/6 George Muehlebach..who..became a quitter in the draft fight via the secret mail-vote route is still filled with fight. **1937** G. FRANKAU *More of Us* viii. 94 Stout lad was Jack, and last to play the quitter From lady's side for any casual stares. **1949** *Sat. Even. Post* 15 Oct. 141/3 It's been worn by great battlers in every sport, but never by a quitter or dirty player. **1976** *Billings* (Montana) *Gaz.* 6 July 8-A/5 Records show about 14 per cent of the benefits paid in 1975 were to voluntary quitters.

†**'quitter**, *v.*[1] *Obs.* Forms: 4 quyter, 5 quittur, whytowryn. [f. QUITTER *sb.*[1]] *intr.* To form pus; to fill with pus. Also *pass.* in same sense. Hence **'quittering** *ppl. a.* (in quot. *fig.*).

1382 WYCLIF *Wisd.* vi. 25 Ne with the quyterende enuye weie I shal han. *c* **1400** *Lanfranc's Cirurg.* 9 If þat tweye woundis ben euene I-quytturid. *Ibid.* 207 Whanne þe enpostym is quitturid & sufficiently rotid. *c* **1440** *Promp. Parv.* 525/2 Whytowryn, as soorys, *idem quod* whelyn.

'quitter, *v.*[2] orig. *Sc. arch. rare.* [Prob. of Scand. origin: cf. MSw. *qvitra*, Sw. *qvittra*, Da. *kvidre* to chirp, twitter.] **a.** To twitter. **b.** To flicker, quiver.

1513 DOUGLAS *Æneis* II. viii. 63 With forkit tong intil hir moutht quitterand. *Ibid.* XII. Prol. 241 The gukgo galis, and so quytteris the quaill. **1872** MRS. STOWE *Oldtown Fireside Stories* 64 There was the old tom-turkey a struttin' and a sidlin' and a quitterin', and a floutin' his tail-feathers in the sun. *Ibid.* 156 An old tom-turkey, that'll strut and gobble and quitter, and drag his wings on the ground. **1935** E. R. EDDISON *Mistress* ix. 171 Shall then these ram-cats of Meszria reap all the honour, whiles we of the Queen's true party sit quittering here? *Ibid.* xix. 394 Then strike. Not to stand quittering like quails when the event walketh on razors' edges.

quitter, obs. f. *whiter*, comp. of WHITE.

'quittered, *a. rare.* [f. QUITTER *sb.*[1]] Affected with quitter-bone.

1778 H. BROOKE *Charitable Assoc.* II. i. Wks. 1778 IV. 234 Put the new set of greys to the coach..Old Robin the quitter'd bay..may limp after.

quitting ('kwɪtɪŋ), *vbl. sb.* [f. QUIT *v.* + -ING[1].] The action of the vb. in various senses.

1340 *Ayenb.* 114 Iesu crist ous tekþ zuo to oxi uoryeuenesse and quittinge. **1387** TREVISA *Higden* (Rolls) II. 125 For quytynge þerof he ȝaf to þe bisshop of Lyncolne a real citee. **1519** HORMAN *Vulg.* 271 He was rewarded..for his manly quytynge. **1581** MARBECK *Bk. of Notes* 1115 That such stones did in olde time witnesse the quitting of a man. **1688** WOOD *Life* 1 July (O.H.S.) III. 272 Thanksgiving.. for the deliverance and quitting of the archbishop. **1768** BLACKSTONE *Comm.* III. 211 In case the notice of quitting proceeds from any tenant.

So **'quitting** *ppl. a.*

1886 *Pall Mall G.* 9 Oct. 11/1 The quitting tenant is forbidden to remove..trees and bushes.

'quitting-time. Chiefly *U.S.* Also *Sc.* quating-time. [f. QUITTING *vbl. sb.* + TIME *sb.*] The time at which work is ended for the day.

1835 D. WEBSTER *Orig. Scot. Rhymes* 165 Should he come when crowdie time, Or quating time draws on, Our bairns maun todlin meet wi' him. **1850** H. C. WATSON *Camp Fires Revol.* 111 Every day, he'd come into the workshop, about quitting time, and follow me up to the house. **1888** J. KIRKLAND *McVeys* 203 Once more Strafford sought Phil at the shop at 'quitting-time', after the latter had got in and cleaned his engine. **1906** *Dialect Notes* III. 122 *Quittin time*, regular expression for the time to cease work. **1958** P. OLIVER in P. Gammond *Decca Bk. of Jazz* i. 21 There were, and still are, hollers that told the time of day, that announced 'quitting-time' or summoned the water-boy. **1977** *Rolling Stone* 19 May 18/2 A sign near the kitchen reads: if you don't believe the dead come back to life, you should be here at quitting time.

quittor, -our, -ure: see QUITTER *sb.*[1] (and *v.*).

quittusol, variant of KITTISOL.

quiver ('kwɪvə(r)), *sb.*[1] Forms: 4 quy-, qwyu-ere, 4–7 quiuer, (6 quy-), 5–6 qwyver, (5 -uer, -were), 5– quiver, (5 quy-); 5 whywer, 5–6 -ver. *β. Sc.* 6 quavyr, quauir, 6–7 quaver. [a. AF. *quiveir*, OF. *quivre, quevre* (cu-), *coivre*, etc., app. a. the Teutonic word represented in Eng. by COCKER *sb.*[1]]

1. A case for holding arrows (sometimes also the bow).

α. *a* **1300** *E.E. Psalter* x. 2 Þair bowe þai bent, þair arwes in a quiuer sente. *a* **1340** HAMPOLE *Psalter* x. 2 Þai redied þaire aruys in qwyuere. *c* **1400** *Destr. Troy* 2375 My bow þat was bigge, & my bright qwyuer. **1483** *Cath. Angl.* 417/1 A Whywer for bowes, *architesis.* **1555** EDEN *Decades* 56 When they had emptied theyr quyuers. **1624** CAPT. SMITH *Virginia* II. 25 His arrowes..he wore in a Woolues skinne at his backe for his Quiver. **1740** SOMERVILLE *Hobbinol* III. 170 Fair Virgin Huntress, for the Chace array'd With painted Quiver, and unerring Bow. **1813** SCOTT *Trierm.* III. xx, A quiver on their shoulders lay. **1854** CDL. WISEMAN *Fabiola* II. xxiv. 284 A gaily-painted quiver, full of arrows.

β. **1513** DOUGLAS *Æneis* VIII. iii. 165 Ane courtly quavyr.. Wyth arrowis mayd in Lycia. *a* **1584** MONTGOMERIE *Cherrie & Slae* 114 His quaver..Hang in ane siluer lace.

b. *transf.* and *fig.*

1382 WYCLIF *Ecclus.* xxvi. 15 Aȝen alle arewe [she] shal opene quyuere. **1535** COVERDALE *Ps.* cxxvi[i]. 5 Happie is the man, yᵗ hath his quyuer full of them. **1641** MILTON *Ch. Govt.* I. vi, When the quiver of your arguments..is quite empty, your course is to betake ye to your other quiver of slander. *a* **1711** KEN *Edmund* Poet. Wks. 1721 II. 289 The taper'd Dart, Design'd to make its Quiver in my Heart. **1839** BAILEY *Festus* ii. (1852) 14 Bow of my life, thou yet art full of spring! My quiver still hath many purposes. **1864** TROLLOPE *Small Ho. at Allington* ix, Boyce being a man who had his quiver full of them [children].

c. The contents of a quiver; a quiverful.

1599 SHAKS. *Much Ado* I. i. 274 Nay, if Cupid haue not spent all his Quiuer in Venice, thou wilt quake for this shortly. **1623** WEBSTER *Duchess Malfi* v. ii, Your bright eyes carry a quiver of darts in them sharper than sunbeams.

2. *attrib.* and *Comb.*, as **quiver-bearing** adj.; †**quiver-case** = sense 1; **quiver-tree**, the South African *Aloe dichotoma* (*Treas. Bot.* 1866).

c **1560** A. SCOTT *Poems* (S.T.S.) iv. 47 Sic treitment is a trane To cleive thair quaver caice. **1798** LANDOR *Gebir* VII. 45 Woody Nebrissa's quiver-bearing crew.

quiver ('kwɪvə(r)), *sb.*[2] [f. QUIVER *v.*[1]] **1.** An act of quivering; a tremble; *ellipt.* a trembling of the voice. †Also = QUAVER *sb.* 1.

1715 PENNECUIK *Poems* 73 Cupid..Tun'd all his Crotchets, Quiuers, Semibrieues. **1786** MAD. D'ARBLAY *Lett.* 16 Oct., I was all in a quiver, but gathered courage [etc.]. **1853** C. BRONTE *Villette* xiv, Heaven was..grand with the quiver of its living fires. **1875** JOWETT *Plato* (ed. 2) III. 204 Thrasymachus, I said, with a quiver, have mercy on us.

2. *Comb.* **quiver-grass**, = QUAKING-GRASS.

1860 C. M. YONGE *Hopes & Fears* II. vi. 105 Blue harebells and pale bents of quiver-grass edged the path. **1869** —— *Let.* 6 Aug. in C. Coleridge *C. M. Yonge* (1903) lx. 242 The Norman name for quiver-grass is *Langue de femme.*

quiver ('kwɪvə(r)), *a. Obs.* exc. *dial.* Forms: 1 cwifer, 3 cwiuer, couer, 5 qwy-, 5–6 quyuer, (6 que-), 5–7 quiuer, 6, 9 quiver. [OE. *cwifer, prob. onomatopœic: cf. QUIVER *v.*[2]] Active, nimble; quick, rapid.

c **960** [implied in QUIVERLY]. *a* **1225** *Ancr. R.* 140 Þet fleshs is her et home..ant for þui hit is cwointe & cwiuer [*v.r.* couer]. **1398** TREVISA *Barth. De P.R.* XVIII. xv. (1495) 774 Some wylde oxen ben..moost qwyuer and swyfte. **1519** HORMAN *Vulg.* 281 He or she is a quyuer gester. **1548** UDALL *Erasm. Par. Luke* ii. 34 Of body feble and impotent, but of soule quiuer and lustie. **1567** TURBERV. *Epit.* etc. 46 b, Thy quick and quiuer wings. **1597** SHAKS. *2 Hen. IV*, III. ii. 301 A little quiuer fellow. **1823** E. MOOR *Suffolk Words* 302 We ..use the word in a sense of briskness, smartness—'He's a quiver little fellow.'

quiver ('kwɪvə(r)), *v.*[1] [f. QUIVER *sb.*[1]] *trans.* To put into or as into a quiver. (Chiefly in pa. pple.; cf. QUIVERED 2.)

a **1643** EARL OF CUMBERLAND *Ps.* in Farr *S.P. Jas. I* (1848) 112 Thy galling shafts lye quiuered in my bones. *a* **1711** KEN *Edmund* Poet. Wks. 1721 II. 310 Use Spears, your Arrows quiver, case your Bows. **1866** J. B. ROSE tr. *Ovid's Met.* 137 His thousand arrows lie Quivered around.

quiver ('kwɪvə(r)), *v.*[2] Forms: 5 quyuer, 6 quyver, 6–7 quiuer, 4– quiver. [Prob. onomatopœic: cf. QUIVER *a.* and the vbs. QUAVE, QUAVER.

The existence of an obs. Du. *kuyveren*, given by Kilian as meaning 'to quiver', is not otherwise authenticated.]

1. *intr.* To shake, tremble, or vibrate, with a slight but rapid agitation. (Said of persons, esp. under the influence of some emotion, of things, light, etc.)

1490 CAXTON *Eneydos* xxvii. 103 Dido quyuered & shoke of grete rage. **1530** PALSGR. 677/2 The poore boye quivereth for colde. **1582** STANYHURST *Æneis* III. (Arb.) 73 Scant had I thus spoken, when seats al quiuered about vs. **1620** MIDDLETON *Chaste Maid* I. i. 118 A brave court-spirit makes our virgins quiver. **1670** EACHARD *Cont. Clergy* 55 Do you not perceive the gold to be in a dismal fear, to curl and quiver at the first reading of these words. **1713** ADDISON *Cato* III. ii, O'er the dying lamp th' unsteady flame Hangs quivering. **1752** JOHNSON *Rambler* No. 205 ¶1 The gales quivered among the branches. **1798** WORDSW. *Peter Bell* II. i, Upon the stream the moonbeams quiver. **1853** MAURICE *Proph. & Kings* xxi. 376 This..made his lips quiver and his hands tremble. **1869** FREEMAN *Norm. Conq.* (1876) III. xii. 243 His hand trembled and his flesh quivered.

fig. **1840** ALISON *Europe* (1849–53) VIII. l. §44. 267 The contest was quivering in the balance. **1861** THACKERAY *Four Georges* II. (1862) 86 Scorn and hate quivering in his smile. **1874** S. COX *Pilgr. Ps.* vii. 133 The darkness..quivers on this night with a nameless horror.

2. *trans.* To cause to vibrate or tremble.

1599 MINSHEU *Span. Dict.*, *Blandéar*, to brandish or quiuer a sword. **1789** J. WHITE *Earl Strongbow* II. 146 He had a way of quivering his head and turning up his nose. **1804** GRAHAME *Sabbath* 288 The lark..quivers the wing With more than wonted joy. **1898** R. KEARTON *Wild Life at Home* 53 He then began to quiver his drooping wings.

b. To produce in or by quivering. *rare*⁻¹.

1848 KINGSLEY *Saint's Trag.* IV. iv. 102 The mad air quivered Unutterable music.

Hence **quive'rante** (after *andante*), **quive'ration** (*nonce-wds*). Also **'quiverer**; **'quiverish** *a.*; **'quivery** *a.*

1581 MULCASTER *Positions* xvii. (1887) 77 Wrastling..is daungerous to be delt with in agues, as to vehement and conspiring with the quiuerer. **1582** STANYHURST *Æneis* III. (Arb.) 71 With a quiuerish horror. **1775** SHERIDAN *Rivals* II. i, Such a mistress of flat and sharp, squallante, rumblante, and quiverante! **1812** J. ADAMS *Wks.* (1856) X. 16 My health is..good, excepting a quiveration of the hands... Excuse the word quiveration, which..I borrowed..from an Irish boy. **1877** *Daily News* 11 June 5/5 Like a dreamland that trembles in the quivery air. **1889** 'MARK TWAIN' *Connecticut Yankee* xxvi. 339 The headlines sent a quivery little cold wave through me. **1925** T. DREISER *Amer. Tragedy* I. I. xv. 116 She..hinted of a mood which made Clyde a little quivery and erratic. **1927** *Chambers's Jrnl.* May 315/1 You and he have made my face quite quivery with excitement. **1975** L. GILLEN *Return to Deepwater* viii. 152 'If you kiss me I'll—I'll scream for help,' she said in a small and strangely quivery voice.

quivered ('kwɪvəd), *a.* and *ppl. a.* Chiefly *poet.* [f. QUIVER *sb.*[1] or *v.*[1] + -ED.]

1. Provided or equipped with a quiver.

1634 MILTON *Comus* 422 Like a quiver'd Nymph with Arrows keen. *a* **1661** HOLYDAY *Juvenal* 22 Quiver'd Semiramis th' Assyrian ne're Did thus. **1717** ADDISON tr. *Ovid's Met.* Wks. 1758 I. 169 Diana, with a sprightly train Of quiver'd virgins. **1813** SCOTT *Rokeby* I. xxi, A giant he, With quivered back. **1874** W. BRUCE *Hebrew Odes* 24 Safe from the shout of the quivered foe.

2. Placed or kept in, or as in, a quiver.

1651 SHERBURNE *Rape Helen*, When his quiver'd Shafts she did not see, She knew he was not Love. **1725** POPE *Odyss.* XXII. 4 Full in their face the lifted bow he bore, And quiver'd deaths. **1846** KEBLE *Lyra Innoc.* (1873) 175 If she once unlock her quivered store.

'quiverful. [f. QUIVER *sb.*[1] + -FUL.] As much as a quiver can hold. Usually *fig.* with ref. to Ps. cxxvii. 5 (see QUIVER *sb.*[1] 1 b, quot. 1535).

1861 BUMSTEAD *Ven. Dis.* (1879) 210 Women..who have 'replenished the earth' with many quiverfuls of offspring. **1885** *Manch. Exam.* 18 Feb. 5/2 A quiverful of satirical invectives. **1890** *Longm. Mag.* July 298 She was surrounded by a quiverful of chubby-cheeked children.

b. Used as *adj.* Having one's quiver full.

1869 *Daily News* 20 Mar., The quiverful and luckless Paterfamilias.

quivering ('kwɪvərɪŋ), *vbl. sb.* [f. QUIVER *v.*[2] + -ING[1].] The action of the vb.

1562 TURNER *Herbal* II. (1568) 23 b, The same..is good..for quiueringe or shakinge. **1597** A. M. tr. *Guillemeau's Fr. Chirurg.* 10/1 The Spasmus possessed the whole bodye with shakinge & quiueringe. **1632** MASSINGER *Maid of Hon.* I. ii, Cast not a sheep's eye Upon the quivering of my calf. **1801** SOUTHEY *Thalaba* IX. xxvi, The silver quivering of the element. **1863** GEO. ELIOT *Romola* I. vi, A momentary quivering of the lip. **1884** tr. *Lotze's Logic* 437 The confused notion that..colours [are] merely quiverings of the ether.

quivering ('kwɪvərɪŋ), *ppl. a.* [+ -ING[2].]

1. That quivers; tremulous.

a **1547** SURREY *Æneid* II. 224 Holding..her targe and quiuering spere. **1632** LITHGOW *Trav.* VI. 273 A soft paued lodging for quiuering Goates. **1700** DRYDEN tr. *Ovid's Metam.* XIII. 124 Let his quiv'ring Heart confess his Fear. **1735** SOMERVILLE *Chase* III. 429 The quiv'ring Bog Soft yielding to the Step. **1820** W. IRVING *Sketch Bk.* I. 124 The sequestered pool, reflecting the quivering trees. **1871–4** J. THOMSON *City Dreadf. Nt.* XVII. ii, The quivering moonbridge on the deep black stream.

2. Of the nature of quivering.

1849 NOAD *Electricity* 42 A wide brush of pale ramifications, having a quivering motion. **1882** A. W. WARD *Dickens* iv. 103 The story of experiences..to which his own mind could not recur without a quivering sensitiveness.

quiveringly ('kwɪvərɪŋlɪ), *adv.* [f. prec. + -LY[2].] In a quivering manner; with a quiver in the voice.

1808 HELEN ST. VICTOR *Ruins of Rigonda* III. 164 He started, then quiveringly exclaimed. **1862** R. H. PATTERSON *Ess. Hist. & Art* 365 Pale tremulous rays..shooting quiveringly along the sky. **1876** GEO. ELIOT *Dan. Der.* v. xxxvii, One of those quiveringly-poised natures that lend themselves to second-sight. **1894** *Temple Bar Mag.* CI. 514, 'I did hope' (quiveringly) 'that you knew me better.'

†**'quiverly,** *adv. Obs.* [f. QUIVER *a.* + -LY[2].] Actively, quickly, smartly.

c **960** *Rule St. Benet* (Schröer) 122 Ðonne he wel ðenaþ & ures drihtnes heorde cwiferlice ȝealȝ að & to rihte manað. **1519** HORMAN *Vulg.* 279 b, Thou playest featly at the tynis and very quyuerly. **1637** GILLESPIE *Eng. Pop. Cerem.* Ep. A iv, Whiles our Opposites so quiverly goe about..is it time for us..to sit still?

So †**'quiverness,** activity, etc. *Obs.*

1538 BALE *Thre Lawes* 1323 And toke from me cleane the quyuernesse of bodye. **1581** J. BELL *Haddon's Answ. Osor.* 142 The Goale is not attained by the quyvernes of the person, nor successe of battell by prowesse.

‖**qui vive** (ki viv). [F., lit. '(long) live who?' a sentinel's challenge, intended to discover to which party the person challenged belongs, and properly requiring an answer of the form (*vive*) *le roi, la France*, etc.] ***on the qui vive***, on the alert or look-out.

1726 SWIFT in *Pope's Wks.* (1871) VII. 82 It is imagined that I must be..alway upon the *qui vive* and the slip-slop. **1752** FIELDING *Amelia* Wks. 1775 X. 223 Though he be a little too much on the *qui-vive*, he is a man of great honour. **1833** MARRYAT *P. Simple* lii, This put us all on the *qui vive*. **1883** E. P. ROE in *Harper's Mag.* Dec. 56/1 'What now?' cried Burtis, all on the *qui vive*.

Quixote ('kwɪksət), *sb.* Also 7 -ot, 8 -iot, 9 -otte. [The name of the hero of Cervantes' romance (see DON *sb.*[1] c), = Sp. *quixote*, now written *quijote* (ki'xote) a cuisse.] An enthusiastic visionary person like Don Quixote, inspired by lofty and chivalrous but false or unrealizable ideals.

1648 *Merc. Prag.* No. 1. A ij, The Romance's and Gazetta's of the famous Victories and Exploits of the godly Quixots. *a* **1658** CLEVELAND *Gen. Poems*, etc. (1677) 112 Thus the Quixots of this Age fight with the Windmils of their own heads. **1786–7** BONNYCASTLE *Astron.* i. 17 There are Quixotes and pedants in every profession. **1811** JEFFERSON *Writ.* (1830) IV. 164 What these Quixottes are clamoring for. **1896** *Spectator* 7 Mar. 337/1 Where the more sober thinker fails, the Quixote is often of service.

Comb. **1800** MRS. HERVEY *Mourtray Fam.* IV. 41 Quixote-like, going to fight when he had no occasion.

b. *attrib.* passing into *adj.* = QUIXOTIC.

1708 OZELL tr. *Boileau's Lutrin* IV. (1730) 209 A weak Defence for Quixiot kings. **1757** LADY M. W. MONTAGU *Let. to C'tess Bute* 7 July, The Quixote reputation of redressing wrongs. **1782** H. WALPOLE *Lett. to M. Cole* 14 Feb. (1846) VI. 160 My diet-drink is not all of so Quixote a disposition. **1810** BENTHAM *Packing* (1821) 198 Our Quixote Sheriff.

Hence **'Quixote** *v. intr.* (also with *it*), to act like a Quixote.

1702 VANBRUGH *False Friend* v. i, When you..are upon your rantipole adventures, you shall Quixot it by your self for Lopez. **1803** JANE PORTER *Thaddeus* (1826) I. vi. 131, I will not be the first to tell him of our quixoting.

quixotic (kwɪk'sɒtɪk), *a.* (*sb.*) [f. QUIXOTE *sb.*]

1. Of persons: Resembling Don Quixote; hence, striving with lofty enthusiasm for visionary ideals.

1815 J. ADAMS *Wks.* (1856) X. 157, I considered Miranda as a vagrant, a vagabond, a Quixotic adventurer. **1857** HUGHES *Tom Brown* I. i, This family training..makes them eminently quixotic. **1896** *Spectator* 7 Mar. 336 Any one can exceed, but few can be really Quixotic.

2. Of actions, undertakings, etc.: Characteristic of, appropriate to, Don Quixote.

1851 GALLENGA *Italy* 131 A daring that would seem almost quixotic. **1874** GREEN *Short Hist.* x. 719 A quixotic mission to the Indians of Georgia. **1876** EMERSON *Ess.* Ser. II. vii. 175 All public ends look vague and quixotic beside private ones.

b. *pl.* as *sb.* Quixotic sentiments.

1896 *Spectator* 7 Mar. 337 If..our Quixotics seem foolish or extravagant.

Hence **qui'xotical** *a.*; **qui'xotically** *adv.*; **qui'xoticism** = QUIXOTISM.

1850 *Fraser's Mag.* XLII. 482 No Quixotical redresser of wrong. **1862** *Sat. Rev.* XIII. 660/2 A mathematician who..Quixotically endeavoured to cure him. **1882** *Athenæum* 23 Sept. 410/1 The symbol of his noble quixoticism.

quixotish (kwɪk'sɒtɪʃ), *a. rare.* [f. QUIXOTE *sb.* + -ISH[1].] = QUIXOTIC *a.* 2 a.

1810 SHELLEY *Let.* 20 May (1964) I. 11, I act unlike every other mortal enough in all conscience, without seeking for more Quixotish adventures.

quixotism ('kwɪksətɪz(ə)m). [f. as QUIXOTIC *a.* + -ISM.] Quixotic principles, character, or practice; an instance of this, a quixotic action or idea.

1688 *Pulpit Popery, True Popery* 36 All the Heroical Fictions of Ecclesiastical Quixotism. **1723** *Briton* No. 20 (1724) 86 His Publick Spirit would appear mere Quixotism to a Protestant People. **1793** *Residence in France* (1797) I. 166 If a momentary smile be excited by these Quixotisms. **1858** LYTTON *What will he do?* VIII. vi, In the Quixotism of atonement for your father's fault. **1898** BODLEY *France* II. IV. ii. 345 The scorn which inopportune quixotism provokes.

So **'quixotize** *v.*, (*a*) *intr.*, to act in a quixotic manner; (*b*) *trans.*, to render quixotic.

1831 *Examiner* 226/1 The folly to think of quixotizing through all Europe. **1894** DU MAURIER *Trilby* 99 A thing to Quixotize a modern French masher!

quixotry ('kwɪksətrɪ). Also 8 -ery. [f. as prec. + -RY.] = QUIXOTISM.

[**1718** MOTTEUX *Quix.* (1733) III. 45 Many..cry out Give us more Quixotery.] **1814** SCOTT *Drama* (1874) 217 An adventurous spirit of profligate Quixotry. **1873** H. ROGERS *Orig. Bible* (1874) 411 We may wait for such an objector before indulging in the equal Quixotry of confuting him.

quiyke, obs. form of QUICK *a.*

quiz (kwɪz), *sb.*[1] Also 8 quis. [Of obscure origin: possibly a fanciful coinage, but it is doubtful whether any reliance can be placed on the anecdote of its invention by Daly, a Dublin theatre-manager. Senses 3 and 4 are app. from QUIZ *v.*[1] 1.

The anecdote is given by Smart in his *Walker Remodelled* 1836, but is omitted in the ed. of 1840. The very circumstantial version in F. T. Porter's *Gleanings & Reminiscences* (1875) 32 gives the date of the alleged invention as 1791; but this is later than the actual appearance of the word and its derivative *quizzity*.]

1. An odd or eccentric person, in character or appearance. Now *rare*.

1782 MAD. D'ARBLAY *Early Diary* 24 June, He's a droll quiz, and I rather like him. **1785** *Span. Rivals* 8 Ay, he's a queer Quis. **1793** in W. Roberts *Looker-on* No. 54 (1794) II. 311 Some college cell, Where muzzing quizzes mutter monkish schemes. **1818** EARL DUDLEY *Lett.* 14 Feb. (1840) 196 Nor are we by any means such quizzes or such bores as the wags pretend. **1852** MRS. SMYTHIES *Bride Elect* xiii, If she really means to marry that quiz for the sake of his thousands. **1857** C. BRONTE *Professor* iii, He was not odd—no quiz.

b. An odd-looking thing. *rare*$^{-1}$.

1798 JANE AUSTEN *Northang. Abb.* (1850) 26 Where did you get that quiz of a hat?

†**2.** = BANDALORE, q.v. *Obs.*

c **1790** in Moore *Mem.* I. 12 The Duke..was, I recollect, playing with one of those toys called quizzes. **1792** *B. Munchausen* (1799) II. xi. 137 She darted and recoiled the quizzes in her right and left hand. *a* **1833** MOORE *Mem.* I. 11 A certain toy very fashionable about the year 1789 or 1790 called in French a 'bandalore' and in English a 'quiz'.

3. One who quizzes.

1797 *The Quiz* No. 13. 85 Now, gentlemen, as you have taken to yourselves the name of Quizzes, I request to know [etc.]. **1836** *Ibid.* No. 1. 4/2 A true Quiz is imperturbable: therefore is Talleyrand the Prince of Quizzers. **1870** *Q. Rev.* July 238 She could write letters to Horace Walpole (perhaps because she knew him to be a quiz) in a vein untinctured by narrowness or pharisaism. **1899** *Eng. Hist. Rev.* April 36 Braving the ridicule with which it pleased the quizzes of the day to asperse the husband chosen for her.

4. A practical joke; a hoax, a piece of humbug, banter or ridicule; a jest or witticism.

1807 *Antid. Miseries Hum. Life* 121, I was engaged a few nights ago..in a good quiz for a watchman. **1810** SCOTT *Fam. Lett.* 14 Apr. (1894) I. vi. 171, I am impatient to know if the whole be not one grand blunder or quiz. **1826** —— *Jrnl.* 11 Feb., I should have thought the thing a quiz, but that the novel was real. **1835** WILLIS *Pencillings* II. lxiv. 189 Whipping in with a quiz or a witticism whenever he could get an opportunity. **1840** HOOD *Up the Rhine* 110 Frank said he was travelling for Rundell and Bridge, but I suspect that was only a quiz. **1850** T. A. TROLLOPE *Impress. Wand.* vi. 77 We have..a quiz on all and each of the newly-arisen tribe of journalists.

b. The act or practice of quizzing.

1819 *Quizzical Gaz.* No. 5/1 The Editor..declares this the only article in the Paper devoid of Quiz. *a* **1845** HOOD *Tale Trumpet* xxx, You may join the genteelest party that is, And enjoy all the scandal, and gossip, and quiz. **1870** GREEN *Lett.* III. (1901) 254 What a taste for a quiz a Professorship seems to develop.

quiz (kwɪz), *sb.*[2] orig. *U.S.* [f. QUIZ *v.*[2]] **1. a.** An act of quizzing or questioning; *spec.* an oral examination of a student or class by a teacher; one in written form upon a specified topic. Also, more generally: a set of questions to be answered as an entertainment, etc.; an informal questionnaire.

1867 W. JAMES *Let.* 26 Dec. in R. B. Perry *Thought & Char. W. James* (1935) I. xiv. 254 Occasional review articles, etc., perhaps giving 'quizzes' in anatomy and physiology..may help along. **1891** in *Cent. Dict.* **1895** J. W. BROWN in *Proc. 14th Convent. Instruct. Deaf* 314 My first lesson should be in the form of a quiz. **1907** *Springfield* (Mass.) *Weekly Republican* 7 Feb. 16 For the food chemists the quiz included a study of both French and German. **1931** H. F. PRINGLE *Theodore Roosevelt* I. xvi. 228 This distinguished jurist agreed to lend books and give him a quiz each Saturday. **1941** L. MACNEICE *Poetry of W. B. Yeats* i. 114 We must..in literary criticism be careful not to write as if we were solving a popular Quiz—as if there were a stock set of answers. **1957** *Economist* 19 Oct. 202 To what kind of searching test should an advertiser subject a prospective agent? A friendly personal quiz? **1973** *Houston Chron. Mag.* 14 Oct. 16/4 The teacher erased the board, wrote up new multiplication problems, distributed paper and drilled for the next day's quiz.

b. A form of competitive entertainment, esp. on radio and television, in which questions are put to individuals or to a team.

1941 *Scribner's Commentator* Feb. 86 (*heading*) Quiz by the Quiz kids. **1951** *Ann. Reg. 1950* 415 The quiz mania showed no signs of abatement during the year. **1956** *B.B.C. Handbk.* 1957 70 Archaeology triumphantly holds its special place with its somewhat unexpected quiz presentation of 'Animal, Vegetable, Mineral?' **1958** *Times* 1 Aug. 11/1 In these days of brains trusts, musical quizzes, and increased attention to musical appreciation as a subject for schools and evening classes. **1976** *Loughborough Monitor* 26 Nov., On November 17, Nanpantan [W.I.] were hostesses to Thorpe Acre and Mountfields in a three-cornered friendly quiz, with Mr. Peter Lewis as question master. **1977** *Evening Post* (Nottingham) 24 Jan. 7/9 Tuxford Young Farmers A team defeated their B team in the third round of the county Inter-Club Quiz to reach the semi-finals.

2. *attrib.* and *Comb.* **a.** Simple *attrib.*, as ***quiz compère, game, -paper, party, programme, show, team, -viewer***; ***quiz-type*** adj.

1959 Quiz compère [see HAND *sb.* 15]. **1945** *East Jefferson Sentinel* (Edgewater, Colorado) 26 July 5/4 Mrs Critchfield, chairman and hostess, then conducted three quiz games. **1959** G. FREEMAN *Jack would be Gentleman* i. 7 It was wonderful what you learned from the tee-vee..quiz games, politicians having arguments. **1967** *Listener* 10 Aug. 170/3 The latter sit in the hotel night after night, sipping German beer and watching the quiz games on Indonesian TV. **1914** D. R. CAMPBELL *Proving Virginia* xiii. 226 The black-robed Seniors assembled..to perform the last holy rites over their antique manuscripts, quiz papers, precious testimonials of mid-night toil. **1936** L. C. DOUGLAS *White Banners* viii. 163 It was not easy to concentrate on classroom lectures, student interviews, quiz-papers, and seminars. **1949** 'J. TEY' *Brat Farrar* vi. 47 He..had always come to an examination paper with the same faint pleasure that an addict brings to a quiz party. **1942** D. POWELL *Time to be Born* (1943) ii. 41 Five hundred rags and that tags that..were nothing more than cues in a quiz program. **1947** AUDEN *Age of Anxiety* (1948) i. 28 And now Captain Kidd in his Quiz Programme How Alert Are

You. **1952** W. R. Burnett *Vanity Row* (1953) xiv. 97 'What time did Ilona Vance call you last night?'..'I don't like the quiz programme type of conversation.' **1960** *Guardian* 18 Oct. 10/4 Big-money winners on American television quiz programmes. **1972** *Language* XLVIII. 341 Elicitory question intonation..presupposes that there is information being withheld, and hence is easily associated with teachers or quiz-program M.C.'s. **1946** F. Wakeman *Hucksters* ii. 17 Vic had heard a story of how he went to a sponsor all primed to sell a quiz show. **1954** G. Marx *Let.* 16 Aug. (1967) 93 The gibbering idiots on panel shows, quiz shows, and other half hours of tripe. **1961** A. Miller *Misfits* ii. 18 Just say it: it doesn't have to be true. It's not a quiz show, it's only a court. **1974** P. De Vries *Glory of Hummingbird* (1975) xi. 149 Like all of us watching quiz shows I would call out answers I knew. **1957** R. Hoggart *Uses of Literacy* vi. 155 The typically outspoken member in a radio quiz-team represents both the old-style 'card' and this modern allegorical figure, the 'idiosyncratic hero'. **1976** *Lancs. Evening Post* 7 Dec. 2/4 Preston's BBC Radio 2 quiz team to meet Blackpool's in a broadcast competition. **1963** *Times* 19 Jan. 4/6 It was Sound, after all, which invented several other quiz, or quiz-type, programmes. **1959** *New Statesman* 24 Jan. 107/2 Its audience was almost certainly enlarged this week by the unconscious sadism, latent in all quiz-viewers, which such entertainments harmlessly release and satisfy.

b. Special Combs.: **quiz kid** orig. *U.S.* [after whizz-kid], a child, usu. one of a team, chosen on account of his or her intelligence to answer extempore questions submitted by the audience of a quiz; also *transf.*, an ostentatiously intelligent person; **quiz-master**, (*a*) (see quot. 1889); (*b*) one who presides over a quiz-game, esp. on radio or television; = *question-master* s.v. question *sb.* 7 d.

1941 Quiz kid [see sense 1 b above]. **1941** F. Brown in *Unknown Worlds* Aug. 120/1 If the episode had become known..Herbie would..get more acclaim even than a quiz kid. **1959** *Encounter* July 38/2 He [*sc.* Northcliffe] was a true child of the age—the first and greatest of all quiz-kids. **1972** *Times* 19 Oct. 10/3 He suppresses his taste for swanky, quiz-kids words (telangiectatic, ichor, fastigiate). **1889** *Cent. Dict.*, *Quiz-master*, the teacher or leader of a quiz-class. **1949** *Radio Times* 15 July 15/1 Round Britain Quiz... Quiz-Master, Gilbert Harding. **1952** *News Chron.* 15 Jan. 1/4 In 'What's My Line' on TV last night..Elizabeth Allan introduced Harding as 'the Ace of Quizz-masters'. **1964** C. Barber *Ling. Change in Present-Day Eng.* ii. 20 B.B.C. announcers may be less influential than comedians, quizmasters, compères, and 'personalities'. **1976** J. van de Wetering *Corpse on Dike* ii. 19 The voices of the comics.. the quiz masters and the newscasters.

quiz (kwɪz), *v.*^{1} [Cf. quiz *sb.*^{1}]

1. *trans.* To make sport or fun of (a person or thing), to turn to ridicule; occasionally, to regard with an air of mockery.

1796 *Campaigns* 1793–4, II. viii. 51 And quiz every blockhead accounted a boar. **1802** Mar. Edgeworth *Moral T.* (1816) I. iv. 19 He spent his time in..ridiculing, or, in his own phrase, *quizzing* every sensible young man. **1825** C. M. Westmacott *English Spy* I. 231 Quizzing the little daughter of Terpsichore through his eye-glass. **1833** Marryat *P. Simple* (1863) 113 Young gentlemen are apt to quiz; and I think that being quizzed hurts my authority with the men. **1874** Green *Short Hist.* v. 214 Chaucer..quizzes in the rime of Sir Thopaz the wearisome idleness of the French romance.

absol. **1815** *Sporting Mag.* XLV. 161 All were sneering at Sam, and they quizz'd and they gaz'd. **1870** Green *Lett.* iii. (1901) 254 What a charming tongue Latin is for quizzing in.

†**2.** *intr.* To play with a quiz (*sb.*^{1} 2). *Obs.*

a **1800** Moore in *Mem.* I. 11 The ladies too, when in the streets,..Went quizzing on, to show their shapes and graceful mien.

quiz (kwɪz), *v.*^{2} orig. *dial.* and *U.S.* Also quizz, *dial.* quies. [Prob. a transferred use of prec., by association with *question* or *inquisitive*.] **1.** *trans.* **a.** To question, interrogate (a person); *U.S.* to examine (a student or class) orally (cf. quiz *sb.*^{2}). Also *absol.* **b.** To find *out* (a thing) by questioning.

1847 Southey *Doctor* VII. 85 She com back an' *quiesed* us. **1886** Elworthy *W. Som. Word-bk.* s.v., Her on't be very long 'vore her'll quiz it all out. **1893** Fergusson *My Village* xi. 99 She would gossip..and quiz her visitors as to what was going on in the village. **1922** *History* Apr. 72 Only 43·4 per cent. of the teachers quiz in class. **1928** J. Sykes *M. A. Disraeli* viii. 79 So far forgot his good manners as to quiz Mrs. Disraeli at the dinner-table. **1958** *Daily Mail* 24 Feb. 12/1 To find him I had to drive to the sleepy Sussex town of Pulborough, quiz the locals, [etc.]. **1978** J. Irving *World according to Garp* xiii. 248 He quizzed him about emergency phone numbers.

2. *trans.* and *intr.* To watch or examine closely, to peer (at).

1906 Hardy *Dynasts* II. ii. vi. 199 Better quiz evils with too strained an eye Than have them leap from disregarded lairs. **1909** —— *Time's Laughingstocks* 77 The stars..Quiz downward curiously. **1911** C. Mackenzie *Passionate Elopement* 26 But somehow it was no longer amusing to quizz the young woman..through his ivory rimmed perspective.

quiz (kwɪz), *v.*^{3} *rare*$^{-1}$. [Echoic.] *intr.* To make a whizzing sound.

1866 *Village on Cliff* xiii. in *Cornhill Mag.* Nov. 526 There was a sound of grasshoppers quizzing at their feet.

'**quizzable**, *a.* [f. quiz *v.*^{1} + -able.] That may be quizzed. Hence **quizza'bility**.

1797 *The Quiz* No. 13. 85 Every body seems to set me down as a butt made on purpose to be ridiculed,..as if I had 'This man is quizable', pasted in large letters on my back. **1849** *Blackw. Mag.* LXVI. 687 It may be something satirical, if they see anything quizzable—something about yourself. **1858** Carlyle *Fredk. Gt.* v. vii. I. 616 Even book-men..are good for something, more especially if rich mines of quizzability turn-out to be workable in them.

So **qui'zzacious** *a.*, given to quizzing. **quizza'torial** *a.*, of a quizzing character. **qui'zzee**^{1}, one who is quizzed.

1810 Bentham *Packing* (1821) 179 Another epigram, still more pointed and quizzatorial than the Italian one. **1825** R. P. Ward *Tremaine* I. xxiv. 184 For quizzing to take effect, there must be two parties,..the quizzer and quizzee. *c* **1830** Bentham *Wks.* (1838–43) X. 285, I made a little quizzacious attack upon the bishop. **1840** *New Monthly Mag.* LVIII. 526 Taking care to make their remarks..loud enough to be heard by the quizzees.

quizzee^{2} (kwɪ'ziː). [f. quiz *v.*^{2} + -ee^{1}.] A panellist on a radio or television quiz programme.

1940 *Words* VI. 107/1 *Quizzee*, one who undergoes questioning. **1947** *N.Y. Times* 7 Dec. X13/1 Asking questions of eager quizzees. **1966** *New Statesman* 23 Dec. 947/3 Sheer ignorance about reality (had Mr Livings..ever actually watched a TV quiz?), and an ideology dependent on sentimentality (children being led past 'surgical booths'.. indicated the quizzee's deficient life).

quizzer ('kwɪzə(r)). [f. quiz *v.*^{1} + -er^{1}.]

1. One who quizzes or is given to quizzing.

1797 *The Quiz* No. 13. 84 At every corner, I am accosted by some of these Quizzers. **1810** Scott *Let. to Ellis* in *Lockhart* xx, This said Kehama affords cruel openings for the quizzers. *a* **1845** Hood *Tale Trumpet* xvii, The mischievous quizzers, Sharp as knives, but double as scissors. *a* **1876** Ht. Martineau *Autobiog.* (1877) II. 306 My lectures were maliciously misrepresented by a quizzer here and there.

2. = quizzing-glass. *rare*$^{-1}$.

1806 Surr *Winter in Lond.* II. 83 'You must have a quizzer.' 'What is that?' said Edward. 'Oh, an eye-glass.'

quizzery ('kwɪzərɪ), *sb.*^{1} [f. quiz *v.*^{1} + -ery.] The practice of quizzing; an instance of this.

1821 *Examiner* 348/1 A law..destructive to mirth and quizzery. **1825** T. H. Lister *Granby* lvi. (1836) 394 He began with a little gentle quizzery of the Ladies Manvers. **1841** Caroline Fox *Old Friends* (1882) 122 Of Mrs. Carlyle's quizzeries, he thinks [etc.].

'**quizzery**, *sb.*^{2} *joc.* [f. quiz *sb.*^{2} + -ery.] A collection of quizzes; quizzes collectively.

1957 *Daily Tel.* 24 Dec. 6/6 (*heading*) Quizzery for all. This starts with the easy ones, and gets more specialised as you go on. **1963** *Ibid.* 9 Feb. 8/7 Their answers would therefore belong to the inferior realm of quizzery, in which knowledge of facts is valued for its own sake and not as a passport to wisdom.

'**quizzible**, *a.* and *sb. rare.* [f. quiz *v.*^{1} + -ible.] **a.** *adj.* = quizzable. **b.** *sb.* Something quizzable.

1816 Moore *Let. to Byron* 29 Feb., There is so much of the quizzible in all he writes. **1822** J. Wilson in *Blackw. Mag.* XI. 479 On the whole the book wants vigour, and it is full of quizzibles.

quizzical ('kwɪzɪkəl), *a.* [f. quiz *sb.*^{1} and *v.*^{1}]

1. Of the nature of a quiz or oddity; causing amusement; comical.

1800 Mrs. Hervey *Mourtray Fam.* II. 47 Nothing but a little joke of mine, at his quizzical figure. **1812** *Sporting Mag.* XL. 263 Whilst they were quizzing others, they.. made themselves quizzical. **1842** Motley *Corr.* (1889) I. iv. 101 One of the most quizzical of old-fashioned towns of quizzical Germany. **1873** Holland *A. Bonnic.* xi. 188 With a quizzical expression of countenance, as if he were puzzled to know exactly what his feelings were.

Comb. **1834** *Tait's Mag.* I. 440/2 Some quizzical-looking fellow-countryman in a seedy coat.

2. Given to quizzing; pertaining to, or characterized by, quizzing.

1801 *Sporting Mag.* XVII. 140 One of our quizzical correspondents remarks, that this is the age for producing fat beasts and lean men. **1844** Alb. Smith *Adv. Mr. Ledbury* viii. (1886) 24 The 'after party', which is always so amusing to discuss with people of slightly quizzical powers.

Hence **quizzi'cality**, '**quizzicalness**.

1821 *New Monthly Mag.* I. 574 The *ne plus ultra* of unbecoming quizzicality. **1825** *Engl. Life* I. 76 Cornelia pouring forth her badinage and her quizzicalness. **1831** *Fraser's Mag.* IV. 85 Somewhat of quizzicality began to be associated with the phrase.

quizzically ('kwɪzɪkəlɪ), *adv.* [f. quizzical + -ly^{2}.] In a quizzical manner.

1849 C. Brontë *Shirley* xvii, Somewhat quizzically scanning Shirley's..countenance. **1867** Carlyle *E. Irving* in *Remin.* (1881) II. 95 A sharp man, with mouth rather quizzically close. **1878** M. C. Jackson *Chaperon's Cares* II. viii. 87 Looking at me quizzically through those eye-glasses of his.

quizzifi'cation. [f. as next: see -fication.] The action of quizzing; a quiz.

1800 Mar. Edgeworth *Belinda* (1832) I. xi. 207 After all, ..the whole may be a quizzification of Sir Philip's. **1856** *Chamb. Jrnl.* VI. 179 It is sure to be made a subject of quizzification.

quizzify ('kwɪzɪfaɪ), *v. rare*$^{-1}$. [f. quiz *sb.*^{1} + -(i)fy.] To make into a quiz.

1834 Southey *Doctor* cxii. (1862) 270 The caxon quizzifies the figure, and thereby mars the effect [etc.].

'**quizziness**. *rare*$^{-1}$. [f. quizzy *a.*^{1} + -ness.] Eccentricity, oddness.

1798 Mad. D'Arblay *Lett.* Mar. VI. 187 His singularities and affectation of affectation..and his spirit of satire are mere quizziness.

quizzing ('kwɪzɪŋ), *vbl. sb.* [f. quiz *v.*^{1} + -ing^{1}.] The action of the vb.

1797 *The Quiz* No. 31. 208 On Quizzing. **1802** G. Rose *Diaries* (1860) I. 508 *note*, He made a most brilliant speech with much quizzing on Mr. A. **1830** D'Israeli *Chas. I*, III. v. 75 A remarkable instance of..persiflage, or what we now call quizzing. **1862** Shirley [J. Skelton] *Nugæ Crit.* ix. 402 That indirect and gentlemanly quizzing,..so much relished by the House of Commons.

Comb. **1805** *Edin. Rev.* VI. 184 He acquits himself of all share in a quizzing scene. **1806–7** J. Beresford *Miseries Hum. Life* (1826) xviii. 213 Thinking his Critic a capital Quizzing-stock.

quizzing ('kwɪzɪŋ), *ppl. a.* [f. as prec. + -ing^{2}.] That quizzes.

1797 *The Quiz* No. 31. 208 The supposed robber, was no other than a quizzing fellow. **1806** Surr *Winter in Lond.* III. 197 A subject of mirthful wonder to several quizzing beaux. **1808** Scott *Let. to Gifford* 25 Oct. in *Lockhart*, A notable subject for a quizzing article. **1866** Felton *Anc. & Mod. Gr.* II. v. 348 Attacked by the older students..with all sorts of quizzing questions.

'**quizzing-glass**. [f. quizzing *vbl. sb.*] A single eye-glass; a monocle. Cf. quizzer 2.

1802 *Europ. Mag.* June 500 The prizes consisted of shawls, parasols, handkerchiefs, quizzing glasses, &c. **1840–1** S. Warren *Ten Thousand a Year* (ed. Warne) 96/2 A quizzing-glass was stuck in his right eye. **1885** J. Payn *Talk of Town* I. 152 He wore round his neck what was then called a quizzing-glass, held by the hand.

'**quizzingly**, *adv.* [f. quizzing *ppl. a.* + -ly^{2}.] In a quizzing manner.

1831 *Fraser's Mag.* IV. 147 A lady who was quizzingly condoling with him. **1865** Carlyle *Fredk. Gt.* xvii. ii. (1872) VII. 23 Friedrich..answers quizzingly: 'Island of Tobago?'

quizzish ('kwɪzɪʃ), *a.* ? *Obs.* [f. quiz *v.*^{1} + -ish.] = quizzical 1. Also *Comb.*

1792 J. Budworth *Fortn. Ramble* i. 2 A very quizzish looking man threw himself into a knowing attitude. **1797** Mrs. A. M. Bennett *Beggar Girl* IV. ii. 51, I cant help laughing to think how quizzish the old Doctor will look when he finds my lord has got the girl.

'**quizzity**. *rare*$^{-1}$. [f. quiz *sb.*^{1}] Oddity.

1788 Anna Seward *Lett.* (1811) II. 91 His height and proportion mighty slender..nor are his sharp features..a whit behind them in quizzity.

quizzy ('kwɪzɪ), *a.*^{1} [f. quiz *sb.*^{1}] = quizzical 1.

1797–1805 S. & Ht. Lee *Canterb. T.* V. 13 She had taken all this trouble for some quizzy old bachelor. **1835** *Blackw. Mag.* XXXVII. 84 A quizzy couple, self-proclaimed as man and wife.

quizzy ('kwɪzɪ), *a.*^{2} [f. quiz *v.*^{2} + -y^{1}.] Inquisitive.

1933 M. Lowry *Ultramarine* iii. 158 'You're either one way or the other!' 'A quizzy little bitch, anyhow!' '—that's unfair.' **1955** D'A. Niland *Shiralee* 86, I don't want to be quizzy, Mac, but, if it's a fair question what's the drum? **1959** I. & P. Opie *Lore & Lang. Schoolch.* x. 183 Quizzy flies never grow wise. **1968** 'J. Le Carré' *Small Town in Germany* vi. 99 Still quizzy:..he had to know exactly what each of us was up to. **1978** O. White *Silent Reach* xii. 127 Don't be so quizzy, David..Mr. Sinclair needs a drink, not a cross-examination.

Qum (kuːm). Also **Quoom**. Name of a city in N.W. Iran, used *attrib.* and *ellipt.* to designate a type of rug produced there.

1953 A. C. Edwards *Persian Carpet* xvi. 340/1 The charm of the Qūm carpet lies primarily in its designs, rather than in its quality or colour. **1962** C. W. Jacobsen *Oriental Rugs* 273 (*heading*) *Qum rugs* (*Also spelled Qom, Gum, Goum, Ghum*). *Ibid.*, Qums are made in the sizeable town of Qum, which is some 90 miles South of Ispahan... When rug weaving began in Qum some 20 years ago, their designers preferred the all over designs. **1973** *Guardian* 1 Mar. 21/1 Afghan Carpet..Silk Quoom..Pakistan Bokhara.. Itamadan Carpet. **1974** *Evening Standard* 12 Feb. 48/5 (Advt.), Superb oriental carpets & rugs. Including:..Silk Quoom rugs exceptionally finely knotted in precious Caspian silk. **1975** 'E. Lathen' *By Hook or by Crook* ix. 87 They joined Barney in genial contempt for a job lot of Hamadans, outdid him in admiring two spectacular Qums.

Qumran (kʊm'rɑːn). The name of a region on the western shore of the Dead Sea, used attrib. to designate (*a*) a collection of ancient Jewish scrolls (the 'Dead Sea Scrolls'), discovered in caves there in 1947, or the contents of these scrolls; and (*b*) a religious community which inhabited a site (Khirbet Qumran) in this region, and to which the scrolls belonged. Hence **Qum'ranite** *sb.*, a member of the religious community of Qumran; also as *adj.*

1954 *Biblical Archaeologist* XVII. 8 Represented..is a fragment of the 'Zadokite work'. This document, long an enigma to scholars, had been recognized as related to the Qumran sectarian works as soon as the finds of 1947 became known. **1955** H. H. Rowley *Dead Sea Scrolls & their Significance* I. 8 The type of Biblical text which was used by the Qumran community. *Ibid.* 11 Palaeographically these appear to be later than the Qumran texts. **1961** T. F. Glasson *Gk. Influence in Jewish Eschatology* viii. 55 Dupont-Sommer thinks that the Essenes (whose identity with the Qumranites he accepts) were originally influenced by Zoroastrianism. *Ibid.* 53 The Qumranite community connected with the Dead Sea Scrolls..is thought to have been either Essene or a very closely related movement. *Ibid.* 55 The Qumranite library evidently welcomed a number of the apocalyptic and other non-biblical writings. **1963** *Times Lit. Suppl.* 22 Feb. 138/3 Influence of the sect on the church is recognized, though without making the church into a daughter of the Qumran sect. **1967** H. Chadwick *Early Church* i. 15 The New Testament writings and the Qumran Scrolls mutually illuminate one another. **1971** R. T. France *Jesus & Old Testament* v. 173 The Qumran sect was not a major influence in first century AD Palestine. *Ibid.* 194 Neither the Pseudepigrapha nor the Qumran literature show any use of this passage. **1976** *Jrnl. Theol. Stud.* Oct. 533 For them [*sc.* the Christian Jews], as for the Qumran community, the communal meal replaced the animal sacrifices of the Temple and was endowed with spiritual meaning.

quo, obs. variant of WHO.

quo', abbrev. of QUOTH.

‖**quoad** ('kwəʊæd). [L., 'so far as', 'as much as', 'as to', f. *quō* where, whither + *ad* to.] To the extent of, as regards, with respect to.

1742 Gilbert *Reports of Cases in Equity* 3 To supply the Defect of the Will *quoad* that Daughter. **1807** Vancouver *Agric. Devon* (1813) 462 It will operate beneficially, *quoad* the quantity applied. **1839** Arnold in *Life* (1844) II. ix. 149 The Order of Deacons, which has been long, *quoad* the reality, dead. **1872** E. Braddon *Life in India* iii. 58 His peculiar position..*quoad* the natives subject..to him.

b. quoad hoc, to this extent, as far as this, with respect to this.

1601 J. Chamber *Agst. Judic. Astrol.* iv. 24 It followeth, that these figure-flingers may sometime hit, and sometime misse *quoad hoc.* **1737** *Common Sense* I. 219 Infinite are the Numbers of minor Coxcombs, who are Coxcombs *quoad hoc.* **1779** Hunter in *Phil. Trans.* LXIX. 281 That which they do have must..render the hermaphrodite imperfect *quoad hoc.* **1884** *Law Times* LXXVIII. 169/2 The Bankruptcy and Insolvent Court Act..which *quoad hoc* is unrepealed.

c. quoad sacra ('seɪkrə), 'as far as concerns sacred matters', used esp. in Scotland with ref. to parishes constituted for purely ecclesiastical purposes (as contrasted with parishes *quoad civilia*); hence *attrib.* with *church*, *minister*, *parish*.

The usual Sc. pron. is ('kwoad) or (kwɔd 'sakrə).

1825 Dunlop *Treat. Law Scot.* §125 When a part of a parish is disjoined, or annexed, *quoad sacra* merely [etc.]. **1845** *New Statist. Acc.* XV. *Caithness* 163 The *quoad sacra* parish of Keise was erected 1833. **1882** J. Cunningham *Ch. Hist.* (ed. 2) xxx. 534 The *quoad sacra* ministers in general lost nothing by the Secession.

quoat, obs. f. QUOTE *v.*

quob, dial. var. QUAB *sb.*[2] and *v.*

quobb(e, var. of QUAB *sb.*[1], burbot.

quobmire, dial. var. QUABMIRE.

quock obs. pa. t. QUAKE *v.*

quock, var. QUAWK *sb.*

quocken, dial. var. QUERKEN.

quocyent, obs. f. QUOTIENT.

quod (kwɒd), *sb.*[1] *slang.* Also quad. [Of uncertain origin; commonly regarded as identical with *quod* QUAD *sb.*[1], but there is no evidence that this is really the case. See quot. *a* 1700.] Prison; *spec.* in phr. *in quod.*

a **1700** B. E. *Dict. Cant. Crew, Quod,* Newgate; also any Prison, tho' for Debt. **1752** Fielding *Amelia* I. xii, There is not such a pickpocket in the whole quad. **1795** in *Spirit Pub. Jrnls.* IV. 226 Coming home, was cast in quod Till subjects paid his ransom. **1848** Thackeray *Van. Fair* liv, She's..grudged me a hundred pound to get me out of quod. **1862** Wraxall tr. *Hugo's 'Misérables'* IV. x. (1877) 7 Do you know I have been in quod for a fortnight? **1872** G. P. Burnham *Mem. U.S. Secret Service* p. vi, *In quod,* in prison; committed, permanently. **1884** [see FIDDLING *vbl. sb.* 3]. **1917** Kipling *Holy War* 2 A tinker out of Bedford, A vagrant oft in quod. **1933** *Sun* (Baltimore) 11 July 1/5 According to the representations of the other four Mr. Fullerton was in no way responsible for the incident which put them in quod. **1968** *Listener* 18 July 72/3 Now, one of this chap's maternal uncles..has got to pay a 50 quid debt or go to quod.

Comb. **1812** J. H. Vaux *Flash Dict., Quod-cove,* the keeper of a gaol.

†**quod**, *sb.*[2], obs. var. COD *sb.*[1] 7, a cocoon.

1615 tr. *De Montfort's Surv. E. Indies* 32 They lay so many [silkworms] on it, leauing them there without any more adoe, except it be to gather the quods, when they are ready to be spunne.

quod (kwɒd), *v.* [f. QUOD *sb.*[1]] *trans.* To put in prison.

1812 J. H. Vaux *Flash Dict.* s.v., To quod a person is to send him to gaol. **1823** in *Spirit Pub. Jrnls.* 282 Since Carlile's been quoded, We wanted some shopman about of your size. **1850** Thackeray *Ballad of Eliza Davis,* The cell where she was quodded, In the Close of Clerkenwell. **1888** J. Runciman *Chequers* 80 A woman answered, 'You've struck me, you swine; and if I've got a black eye I'll quod you, sure as I'm yere. Ain't I lushed you, and fed you, and found your clobber long enough?' **1923** D. L. Sayers *Whose Body?* iii. 60 That's her story. Sugg's delighted,..and quodded Thipps on the strength of it. **1930** R. H. Mottram *Europa's Beast* v. 136 In England the police would have 'quodded' her.

quod, quod-a, obs. varr. QUOTH, QUOTHA.

†,**quoda'mmodo,tative**, *a.* and *sb. Obs.* [f. L. *quōdam modō* in a certain way + -(T)ATIVE.]

a. *adj.* Existing in a certain manner. **b.** *sb.* A thing that exists in a certain way.

1656 Stanley *Hist. Philos.* VIII. I. xiii. (1687) 437/1 Things are subdivided into foure Genus's, Subjects, and Qualitatives and Quodammodotatives in themselves, and Quodammodotatives as to others. *Ibid.* xvii. 438/2 Aristo..defined Quodammodotative-Relatives to be those, whose being is..their Quodammodotative being to one another.

'**quoddity.** *rare.* [f. L. *quod* (that) which, neut. of *quī* who + -ITY.] A quasi-scholastic term formed on the anal. of QUIDDITY, q.v.

1682 H. More *Annot. Glanvill's Lux O.* 191 He is..armed with the affrightful terms of Quoddities and Quiddities. **1902** *Union Mag.* Feb. 66/1 He turned over in his mind his instances, his quiddities and his quoddities.

'**quoddle**, *v.* Now *dial.* (quaddle). [var. of WADDLE: cf. *quag* and *wag.*] To waddle.

1662 Stillingfl. *Orig. Sacr.* III. i. §16 You will presently see..the Duck quoddling into a pool. **1886** Elworthy *W. Som. Word-bk., Quaddle,* to waddle.

quod(d)le, quodgell, obs. forms of CODDLE, CUDGEL.

‖**quodlibet** ('kwɒdlɪbɛt). Also 6 quot-. [a. L. *quodlibet* (f. *quod* what + *libet* it pleases (one)), or ad. med.L. *quodlibetum*: cf. F. *quolibet* (13th c.).]

1. Any question in philosophy or theology proposed as an exercise in argument or disputation; hence, a scholastic debate, thesis, or exercise on a question of this kind (chiefly *pl.* in University use, *esp.* in phr. *to do quodlibets*). Now only *Hist.*

1377 Langl. *P. Pl.* B. xv. 375 Of diuinite maistres, That shulde..answere to argumentz and also to a quodlibet..if suche weren apposed. **1526** *Pilgr. Perf.* (W. de W. 1531) 164 As saynt Thomas wytnesseth in his thyrde quodlibet. **1529** More *Dyaloge* III. Wks. 246/1 Among other such as himselfe to kepe a quotlibet & a pot parlament vpon. **1603** P. Stringer in Plummer *Elizab. Oxford* (O.H.S.) 257 At the same hower also there were, in other Common Schooles, disputations called 'Quodlibets' by Masters of Arts and Bachelors in Art. **1631** Weever *Anc. Fun. Mon.* 806 A man of great repute in the Vniuersitie of Oxford for his Quodlibets, ordinary questions, and his Interpretations of the sacred Scriptures. **1687** Wilding in *Collect.* (O.H.S.) I. 265 For doing Qdlibets..00 07 06. **1717** Prior *Alma* III. 347 All his quodlibets of Art Could not expound its [the heart's] pulse and heat. **1868** Milman *St. Paul's* iii. 70 He was also an author, of theological lectures and quodlibets.

2. *Mus.* A fanciful combination of several airs; a fantasia, medley.

1845 E. Holmes *Mozart* 38 The young musician wrote a symphony and a Quodlibet for the Installation festival of the Prince of Orange.

'**quodlibetal**, *a. rare.* [f. prec. + -AL[1].] = QUODLIBETICAL.

1839 tr. *Hugo's Nôtre Dame* I. i, Down with the cardinal and quodlibetal disputations. **1883** *Manch. Guard.* 26 Dec. 7/2 Who chose to consult him on things spiritual, temporal, and quodlibetal. **1975** Alluntis & Wolter tr. Duns Scotus (*title*) God and creatures: the quodlibetal questions.

quodlibe'tarian. [f. as next + -AN.]

†**a.** = QUODLIBETARY A. b. *Obs.* **b.** One who discusses quodlibets.

1727 Bailey vol. II, *Quodlibetarian,* one who follows the Dictates of his own Fancy. **1791–1823** D'Israeli *Cur. Lit.* (1858) I. 60 The works of the scholastics, with the debates of these Quodlibetarians, at once show the greatness and the littleness of the human intellect. **1943** Beerbohm *Lytton Strachey* 22 That agile and mellifluous quodlibetarian, Dr. Joad. **1966** *Duckett's Reg.* Feb. 14/2 The clever quodlibetarians called it an obvious strategic move.

'**quodlibetary**, *sb.* and *a. rare.* [f. L. *quodlibet* QUODLIBET + -ARY.]

†**A.** *sb.* **a.** ? A quodlibetical argument. **b.** (See quot. 1656.) *Obs.*

a **1631** Donne *Lett.* (1651) 162 So, he having made use of all the quodlibetaries, imputations against the other, cannot be obnoxious himself in that kinde. **1656** Blount *Glossogr., Quodlibitaries,* those that run after their own fancy or imagination, and do what they list.

B. *adj.* Pertaining or relating to quodlibets.

1895 tr. *Hugo's Nôtre Dame* I. i, Down with the disputations, cardinal, and quodlibetary.

quodli'betic, *a. rare.* [f. as prec. + -IC.] = next.

1659 Gauden *Tears Ch.* 681 How partial are the principles..of some Quodlibetick Presbyters! **1831** Sir W. Hamilton *Discuss.* (1852) 406 The halls of the Faculty of Arts, in which..the Quodlibetic Disputations were still annually performed.

quodlibetical (kwɒdlɪ'bɛtɪkəl), *a.* [f. as prec. + -AL.] Of the nature of, connected or concerned with, a quodlibet or quodlibets.

1580 Fulke *Answ. P. Frarine* 1 The president of the Quodlibeticall disputations of Louane. **1600** Watson (*title*) A Decacordon of Ten Quodlibeticall Questions concerning Religion and State. *c* **1665** R. Carpenter *Pragm. Jesuit* 47/2 Quodlibetical Brains have Consciences of all sorts and sizes. **1710** tr. *Dupin's Eccl. Hist. 16th C.* I. III. 401 He publicly read Divinity upon those that they [call] Quodlibetical Questions. **1791–1823** D'Israeli *Cur. Lit.* (1858) I. 62 They at length collected all these quodlibetical questions into enormous volumes.

Hence **quodli'betically** *adv.*

1657 J. Sergeant *Schism Dispach't* 174 His Divisionary art, in which it is his common custome to talke quodlibetically. **1682** Sir T. Browne *Chr. Mor.* ii. (1756) 58 Many positions seem quodlibetically constituted.

†,**quodlibe'tificate**, *v. trans.* To deal quibblingly with. *nonce-wd.* So also †'**quodlibetting** *a.*, dealing in quodlibets. †'**quodlibetist**, one who deals in quodlibets. *Obs.*

1610 Cooke *Pope Joan* in *Harl. Misc.* (Malh.) IV. 96 Watson, the quodlibetting priest. **1626** W. Fenner *Hidden Manna* (1652) 22 These heretical Opinionists, schismatical Quodlibetists. ? **1743** in M. Pennington *Mem. Eliz. Carter* (1816) II. 147 To..quodlibetificate any word into a pun.

quodling, obs. form of CODLING[2], apple, etc.

†**quods**, ? var. Cods. (Cf. *Od's buds*, etc.)

1593 Nashe *4 Lett. Confut.* 84 Quods, quods giue mee my Text pen againe, for I haue a little more Text to launce.

quoff, obs. Sc. variant of COFF, to buy.

quohog, variant of QUAHAUG.

quoice, local var. (also *pl.*) of QUEEST, ring-dove. Hence **quoice-neck** (see quot.).

1883 Gresley *Gloss. Coal-mining, Quoiceneck,*..greyish black clay with shining surfaces, and streaked.

quoich, var. QUAICH.

quoif(e, quoiff, quoiffure, obs. ff. COIF, COIFFURE *sb.*

quoi hai, var. QUI-HY.

quoik, obs. Sc. pa. t. QUAKE *v.*

quoil, obs. f. COIL.

'**quoiler.** *dial.* Also quiler. [Cf. COILER[2].] *pl.* The breech-harness of a cart-horse. Also *attrib.* as *quoiler-harness*, *-horse.*

1697 *Lond. Gaz.* No. 3317/4 A black Horse..the Hair rubbed off behind with the Quilers. **1876** *Surrey Gloss., Quoilers,* the breeching of a cart-harness. Quoiler-harness or thill-harness is the trace-harness. **1901** *Kentish Express* 13 July 12/4 Good Quoiler Horse.

quoin (kɔɪn), *sb.* Forms: 6 quoyne, 6–8 quoyn, 7 quoine, 7– quoin; 7 quain; 7–8 quine. [var. spelling of COIN, formerly used in all senses of that word, but now restricted to the following uses, in which *coin, coign* are also occasionally employed.]

1. *Build.* **a.** An external angle of a wall or building; also, one of the stones or bricks serving to form the angle; a corner-stone. = COIN *sb.* 1.

rustic quoin, one projecting from the general surface of the wall, usually with bevelled edges.

1532 in W. H. Turner *Select. Rec. Oxford* 114 The quoyne of the wall of a tenement. *c* **1640** J. Smyth *Lives Berkeleys* (1883) II. 66 The walls, vautes, quines of doors and windows they razed and tear a down. **1663** Gerbier *Counsel* 71 Flowers for the Cross work in the gallace in these quains. **1670** L. Stucley *Gospel-Glass* xxxiv. 365 So many quoines to lock together all parts of the building into one. **1703** Moxon *Mech. Exerc.* 261 At an upright Quine..lay a three quarter Bat at the Quine in the stretching course. **1725** Bradley *Fam. Dict.* s.v. *Wall,* Certain courses, ledges, or Quoins of more strength than the rest, must be interlaid like bones to strengthen the whole fabrick. **1820** W. Irving *Sketch Bk.* II. 197 It is a large building of brick, with stone quoins. **1862** Ansted *Channel Isl.* I. ii. (ed. 2) 29 The walls are of island Sand-stone, with quoins of Caen stone.

b. An internal angle or corner, as of a room. *hollow quoin,* a recess in the walls at each end of a canal lock, to receive the heel-post of the gate.

1825 J. Nicholson *Operat. Mechanic* 627 If a room consists of more than four quoins, the additional corners must be allowed at per foot run. **1838** Simms *Pub. Wks. Gt. Brit.* ii. 6 The joint between the heel-post and hollow quoin is made watertight by the gate being..worked backwards and forwards.

2. A wedge, or wedge-shaped block, used for various special purposes. **a.** *Printing.* A short wedge used to lock up a form.

1570 Levins *Manip.* 215/17 A Printers quoyn, *cuneus, cuneolus.* **1683** Moxon *Mech. Exerc., Printing* viii, Quoyns are..of different Lengths, and different Breadths. *Ibid.* x. ¶9 The extuberancies of Nail-heads would hinder the free sliding of the Quoins. **1727–41** Chambers *Cycl.* s.v. *Printing,* The compositor..unlocking the form..by knocking out or loosening the quoins. **1824** J. Johnson *Typogr.* II. xv. 534 When the form gets out of register..by the starting of the quoins which secure the chase. **1880** *Printing Times* 15 Feb. 30/1 The form having been properly planed..slightly slacken the quoins.

b. *Gunnery.* (*a*) A wedge-shaped piece of wood, with a handle at the thick end, used to raise or lower a gun. (*b*) = QUOINER. ? *Obs.* (*c*) A small wedge used in fixing the breech of a gun.

1627 Capt. Smith *Seaman's Gram.* xiv. 65 Quoines..are great wedges of wood with a little handle at the end to put them forward or backward for leuelling the Peece. **1707**

Gloss. Angl. Nova, *Quoin*, a wedge fastned on the Deck, close to the Breech of the Carriages of the great Guns, to keep them firm up to the Ship's sides. **1711** *Milit. & Sea Dict.* (ed. 4) s.v., The Quoyns the Gunners use under the Guns, to mount them higher or lower. **1805** in Nicolas *Disp. Nelson* (1845) VII. 171 *note*, Our people took the quoins out, and elevated their guns. **1881** GREENER *Gun* 476 For the larger cannon Sir W. G. Armstrong uses a quoin tightened by a screwed breech-plug.

c. *Naut.* A wedge used to prevent casks from rolling. ***cantic quoin, standing quoin*** (see quot. 1711, and cf. CANTIC *a.*, CANTING *ppl. a.*[1]).

1711 *Milit. & Sea Dict.* (ed. 4) s.v., Cantick Quoyns, being short, with three Edges, to put betwixt the Cask at the Bildge Hoops, to keep the Cask steady from rowling, and labouring one against another... The standing Quoyns,..a fit Length to be driven across betwixt the Buts..to keep the Chine of the But steady from jogging. **1769** FALCONER *Dict. Marine* (1776) Y y iij, Quoins or coins used in the stowage of a ship's hold. **1867** in SMYTH *Sailor's Word-bk.*

d. *Build.* The key-stone, or any one of the wedge-shaped stones (voussoirs) of an arch. *rare.*

1730 A. GORDON *Maffei's Amphith.* 306 In the middle, at the Key-Stone or Quoin. **1873** TRISTRAM *Moab* ii. 20 Over the doorway..was let in an old quoin on which was cut an Arabic inscription.

3. An angle, or angular object. *rare.*

1838 SIMMS *Pub. Wks. Gt. Brit.* 36 The quantity thus cut off from the acute quoin is gradually diminished to the opposite or obtuse quoin. **1868** KINGLAKE *Crimea* (1877) IV. ix. 230 It is only by an isthmus..of high land that the triangular quoin remains joined to the bulk of the Chersonese. **1878** GURNEY *Crystallogr.* 30 Similar quoins or solid angles are such as are contained by the same number of plane angles.

4. *Comb.*, as **quoin-drawer, -post, -stone** (see quots.); **quoin-wedge** = sense 2.

1688 R. HOLME *Armoury* III. 111/2 Quine stones..are Stones laid in a Brick wall at the corners of a House—a yard long and three Brick in thickness. **1875** J. SOUTHWARD *Dict. Typogr.* 117 *Quoin-drawer*, a drawer in the frame of the imposing-stone in which the quoins are kept. **1875** KNIGHT *Dict. Mech.* 1849/2 *Quoin post*, the heel-post of a lock-gate. **1923** D. H. LAWRENCE tr. *Verga's Mastro-don Gesualdo* I. iv. 71 We want more man-power—a crane!—or tie a pulley-wheel up there to the beam of the roof—then a quoin-wedge underneath.

quoin (kɔɪn), *v.* [See prec. and COIN *v.*[2]]

1. *trans.* To secure or raise with a quoin or wedge. Also with *up.*

1683 MOXON *Mech. Exerc., Printing* xxiv. ¶7 He..then Quoins up the two ends of the Chase. **1769** FALCONER *Dict. Marine* (1776), *Caler* also signifies to quoin or wedge up any thing. **1854** JACOB ABBOTT *Wallace* vii. 138 What Mr. Grey meant by quoining up, was filling in the spaces under the large stones..and thus wedging them up to their proper level. **1875** J. SOUTHWARD *Dict. Typogr.* 117 *Quoining a Forme*, the fitting of the quoins in a forme so that when it is locked up they shall..wedge up and secure the types.

2. To provide with quoins or corners.

1834 *Gentl. Mag.* CIV. I. 96 A well, curiously quoined with stone.

quoinage, obs. form of COINAGE.

†**quoine**, obs. variant of COIN *v.*[1]

1786 MRS. A. M. BENNETT *Juvenile Indiscr.* III. 181 He lend you money! he must quoine it I believe if he does.

†**'quoiner.** *Obs. rare.* In 7 quoyn-. [f. QUOIN *v.* + -ER.] A wedge used to secure a gun.

1669 STURMY *Mariner's Mag.* v. 64 In Ships..if the Ropes be suspected not to be good, they nail down Quoyners to the Fore-Trucks of heavy Guns, that he may not have any play; and if Britchings, and Tackles, and Quoyners should give way in foul weather, presently dismount her.

quoining ('kɔɪnɪŋ). Also 6 quenynge. [f. QUOIN *sb.* + -ING[1]. Cf. COINING *vbl. sb.*[2]] The stone or brick-work forming the quoin of a wall, or the manner in which this is placed.

1562–3 in Willis & Clark *Cambridge* (1886) II. 567 Stone ..new wrought..to ashler and quenynge. **1848** RICKMAN *Styles Archit. Eng.* App. p. iv, There is a peculiar sort of quoining,..consisting of a long stone set at the corner and a short one lying on it, and bonding one way or both into the wall. **1876** *Archæol. Cant.* X. lii, The quoining of the nave and chancel.

quoining, obs. form of COINING *vbl. sb.*[1]

quoit (kɔɪt, kwɔɪt), *sb.* Forms: α. 4–7 **coyte**, 5–6 (9) coite, 6 c(h)oytte, 7 coyt, coight, 6– coit. β. 7 quoite, quoyt(e, 6– quoit. γ. 6–7 quaite, 7 quayte, queit, 8 quait. [Of obscure etym.; the variation of form between *coit*, *quoit*, and *quait* prob. indicates a French origin.

Derivation from OF. *coitier*, *quoitier* 'to prick, spur, incite, hasten', has been suggested, but it does not appear that this vb. had also the sense 'to throw, hurl', which would be necessary to make the connexion probable; and the sb. *coite*, *quoite* means only 'prick (of spur), encounter, haste'.]

1. a. In orig. and widest sense (now only with ref. to the Greek and Roman discus), a flat disc of stone or metal, thrown as an exercise of strength or skill; *spec.* in mod. use, a heavy flattish ring of iron, slightly convex on the upper side and concave on the under, so as to give it an edge capable of cutting into the ground when it falls, if skilfully thrown. Also, the ring of rope, rubber, etc. used in *deck-quoits* and similar games (see 2).

α. *c* **1440** *Promp. Parv.* 86/1 Coyter, or caster of a coyte, *petreludus.* Coyte, *petreluda.* *c* **1449** PECOCK *Repr.* I. xx. 120 That men..schulden pleie..bi casting of coitis. **1530** PALSGR. 206/2 Coyte to playe with, *palet.* Coyte of stone, *bricoteav.* **1591** HARINGTON *Orl. Fur.* XIII. xxxiv, This like a coight at them Orlando tost. **1657** R. LIGON *Barbadoes* (1673) 28 There is no part of it so broad, but you may cast a Coyte over it. **1711** ADDISON *Spect.* No. 56 ¶4 Some of them were tossing the Figure of a Coit. **1807** CRABBE *Par. Reg.* II. 393 Tossed the broad coite or took th' inspiring ale.
β. *c* **1611** CHAPMAN *Iliad* XXIII. 388 Nestors sonne..got as farre before, As any youth can cast a quoyte. **1715–20** POPE *Iliad* XXIII. 712 Tho' 'tis not thine to hurl the distant Dart, The Quoit to toss. **1783** CRABBE *Village* I, Who..made the pond'rous quoit obliquely fall. **1843** LYTTON *Last Bar.* I. i, They had learned to wrestle,..to pitch the bar or the quoit. **1870** BRYANT *Iliad* II. XXIII. 360 As far as flies a quoit Thrown from the shoulder of a vigorous youth.
γ. **1560** [see b]. **1658** J. JONES tr. *Ovid's Ibis* 144 If Queit thou cast into the open air, let Queit thee kill like Hyacinth the fair. **1711** J. GREENWOOD *Eng. Gram.* 188 Coit, quait.

†**b.** Phr. ***a quoit's cast, distance***, the distance to which a quoit is commonly thrown. *Obs.*

a **1490** BOTONER *Itin.* (1778) 147 Distans per spacium coytys cast. **1560** WHITEHORNE *Ord. Souldiours* xxiv, It would scant be able to drive their pellettes a quaites caste. *a* **1604** HANMER *Chron. Irel.* (1633) 10 The Welch Prophet could not see a quoits cast from him. **1644** MILTON *Areop.* (Arb.) 57 Every acute reader..will be ready..to ding the book a coits distance from him. **1791** COWPER *Iliad* XXIII. 648 Menelaus..fell A full quoit's cast behind.

c. A curling-stone. *rare.*

1827 HONE *Every-day Bk.* II. 164 The stones used are called *coits*, or *quoits*, or *coiting*, or *quoiting-stones.*

2. *pl.* (rarely *sing.*) The sport of throwing the quoit or of playing with quoits; in one modern form of this the quoit is aimed at a pin stuck in the ground, and is intended to fall with the ring surrounding this, or to cut into the ground as near to it as possible. ***deck-quoits***, an imitation of this game, played on shipboard with rings of rope.

1388 *Act 12 Rich. II*, c. 6 §1 Les jeues appelez coytes dyces [etc.]. **1477** *Rolls Parlt.* VI. 188/1 No persone shuld use any unlawfull Pleys, as Dise, Coyte, Foteball. **1527** *Galway Arch.* in *10th Rep. Hist. MSS. Comm.* App. V. 402 Plainge at choyttes or stonis. **1551** ROBINSON tr. *More's Utop.* I. (1895) 57 Lewde, and vnlawfull games, as..tennyes, bolles, coytes. **1592** LYLY *Galathea* II. iv, I will now..play at quaites abroade. **1621** BURTON *Anat. Mel.* II. ii. IV. 342 Keelpins, tronkes, coits..are the common recreations of countrey folks. **1708** W. KING *Cookery* 117 He..From Nine-pins, Coits, and from Trap-ball abstains. **1841** *Q. Rev.* LXVII. 355 Devoting hours on hours to quoits, cricket, and so forth. **1847** TENNYSON *Princ.* III. 199 Quoit, tennis, ball—no games? **1892** E. REEVES *Homeward Bound* 22 One of the best amusements provided on shipboard is 'Quoits'.

3. *transf.* †**a.** A quoit-shaped stone or piece of metal. *Obs. rare.*

1593 P. NICHOLS *Drake Revived* (1628) 78 Thirteene bars of siluer, and some few quoits of Gold. *Ibid.* 79 Promising to give him a fine quoit of gold. *a* **1635** CORBET *Iter Bor.* 114 No pompous weight Upon him, but a pebble, or a quayte.

b. The flat covering stone of a cromlech or cist; also, by extension, a cromlech or cist as a whole.

1753 BORLASE in *Phil. Trans.* XLVIII. 87 A flat rock ..(which in our country [Cornwall] we call a quoit). *Ibid.*, On the top of this quoit there is a remarkable incision. **1827** G. HIGGINS *Celtic Druids* Pref. 49 Under this Quoit I caused to be sunk a pit. **1867** MAX MÜLLER *Chips* (1870) III. xiii. 291 In Bosprennis Cross there was a very large coit or cromlech. **1887** BARING-GOULD *Red Spider* I. ii. 18 A rude granite slab..[which] had been the 'quoit' of a great prehistoric dolmen or cromlech.

c. The backside, the buttocks. Phr. ***to go for one's quoit***, to hurry. *Austral. slang.*

1941 BAKER *Dict. Austral. Slang* 58 *Quoit*, the buttocks. *Ibid.*, *Go for one's quoits*, to travel quickly, go for one's life. **1951** E. LAMBERT *Twenty Thousand Thieves* x. 165 See those jokers sitting on their quoits over there? **1952** J. CLEARY *Sundowners* i. 42 Going for the lick of his coit up the street. **1954** T. A. G. HUNGERFORD *Sowers of Wind* xiv. 176 Gawd, he blew the tripes outa me for nothing at all, and then he kicks a Nip in the coit. **1972** J. BAILEY *Wire Classroom* x. 82 'I think he needs a good kick up the coit,' says Cromwell.

†**4.** A cast or throw. *Obs. rare*$^{-1}$.

1706 *George a Green* in Thoms *Prose Rom.* (1858) II. 165 With such a tumbling quait, as we call a back somerset.

5. *attrib.* and *Comb.*, as ***quoit-cast, -pitcher, -player, -playing, -thrower***, etc.; ***quoit-like*** adj.

1538 LELAND *Itin.* VI. 56 A Coyte or Stone Cast beneth the Kinges Bridge. **1818** KEATS *Endym.* I. 306 They might watch the quoit-pitchers, intent On either side. **1871** ALABASTER *Wheel of Law* 169 The quoit-like weapon (chakra) the emblem of power of India. **1887** UPCOTT *Introd. Gk. Sculpt.* iv. 57 The most familiar of Myron's works is the Quoit-thrower. *Ibid.*, The quoit-player, who is stooping forward in attitude to throw.

quoit (kɔɪt, kwɔɪt), *v.* Forms: 5 coytyn, 6 coyte, quayt-, 7 coit, quait, 7– quoit. [f. the sb.]

1. *intr.* To play at quoits. *rare.*

c **1440** *Promp. Parv.* 86/1 Coytyn, *petriludo.* **1530** PALSGR. 488/2 Let us leave all boyes games, and go coyte a whyle. **1570** LEVINS *Manip.* 216/18 To coyte, *discum mittere.* **1684** DRYDEN *Ovid's Met.* I. 599 To Quoit, to Run, and Steeds and Chariots drive. **1871** L. W. M. LOCKHART *Fair to See* II. xi. 15 The quoiters quoited.

2. *trans.* To throw like a quoit. Also with advbs. as *away*, *down*, *off*, *out.*

1597 SHAKS. *2 Hen. IV*, II. iv. 206 Quoit him downe..like a shoue-groat shilling. **1630** J. TAYLOR (Water P.) *Brave Sea-fight* Wks. III. 39/2 So neere, as a man might quoit a Bisket Cake into her. **1660** SHIRLEY *Andromana* I. v. 47 Tis more impossible for me to leave thee, Then for this carkase to quait away its grave-stone. **1681** COTTON *Poet. Wks.* (1765) 326 If you coit a Stone. **1791** COWPER *Iliad* XXIII. 1042 Leonteus..quoited it next. **1822** LAMB *Elia* Ser. I. *Praise Chimneysweepers*, One unfortunate wight..was quoited out of the presence with universal indignation. **1870** THORNBURY *Tour Eng.* I. iv. 77 It was just beyond..where Falstaff was quoited into the Thames.

'quoiter. [f. QUOIT *v.* + -ER[1].] **a.** One who plays at quoits; a quoit-thrower.

c **1440** *Promp. Parv.* 86/1 Coyter, or caster of a coyte, *petreludus.* *c* **1515** *Cocke Lorell's B.* 11 Bowlers..and quayters. **1656** W. D. tr. *Comenius' Gate Lat. Unl.* 265 Quoiters throw quoits and other things that are to be flung. **1884** *Sporting Times* 9 June 4/6 The death of William Eagle, ..well known amongst quoiters.

b. A curler.

1833 J. CAIRNIE *Essay on Curling & Artificial Pond Making* 93 He was a grand quoiter, he never missed a shot. **1899** J. KENNEDY *Compl. Sc. & Amer. Poems* (ed. 3) 128 May quoiters' joys be mair an' mair.

'quoiting, *vbl. sb.* Forms: 5–7 coyt-, 6 koyt-, quait-, quayt-, 7 coit, 7– quoit-. [f. as prec. + -ING[1].] **a.** The action or game of playing at quoits. Also, = CURLING *vbl. sb.*[1] 2.

1467 *Nottingham Rec.* II. 264 Luserunt ad quendam ludum illicitum et prohibitum vocatum 'le coytyng'. **1532** MORE *Confut. Tindale* Wks. 574/2 Suche prety playes..as chyldren be woont to playe, as cheristone, mary bone,..or quayting. **1541** *Act 33 Hen. VIII*, c. 9 §11 Any common house, aley or place of boulynge, coytynge [etc.]. **1563** B. GOOGE *Eglogs* vii. (Arb.) 58 Suche thynges, wherin we Shepeheardes haue delyght, As in Quaiting. *a* **1619** FOTHERBY *Atheom.* II. i. §8 (1622) 188 Running, Wrestling, Leaping, Coyting. **1799** E. DU BOIS *Piece Family Biog.* I. 16 Wrestling, running, quoiting,..and every description of rural sport. **1811** J. RAMSAY *Acct. Game Curling* 20 From one end of Scotland to the other, it was always named *kuting*, to curl, meaning nothing more than to slide upon the ice. In some parts of Ayrshire..it is pronounced *coiting*. **1836** LYTTON *Athens* (1837) I. 179 At first only the footrace was exhibited, afterwards were added wrestling, leaping, quoiting. **1884** J. TAYLOR *Curling* 74 He had seen Bryan o' the Sun Inn and the deil *quitin'* (curling) on the Auld Water.
Comb. **1530** PALSGR. 488/2, I Coyte. I play with a coyting stone. **1827** [see QUOIT *sb.* 1 c]. **1853** W. WATSON *Poems* 71 The lee-side was cheer'd by the quoitin'-stane roar. **1897** CROCKETT *Lads' Love* xviii. 189 He..fairly dragged me into the quoiting-ground. *Ibid.* 195 The matter of the quoiting-match. **1969** R. WELSH *Beginner's Guide Curling* ii. 15 Kuting stones, channel stanes or loofies are the oldest curling implements known to us.

†**b.** A method of cheating at dice. *Obs. rare*$^{-1}$.

1545 ASCHAM *Toxoph.* I. (Arb.) 54 If they be true dise, what shyfte wil they make to set ye one of them with slyding, with cogging,..with coytinge as they call it.

quok(e, obs. pa. t. of QUAKE *v.*

quokka ('kwɒkə). [Aboriginal name.] A small short-tailed wallaby, *Setonix brachyurus*, found in restricted coastal areas of south-western Australia.

1863 J. GOULD *Mammals Austral.* II. 38 At Augusta..its [the short-tailed wallaby's] native name, Quăk-a, is the same as at King George's Sound. **1943** C. BARRETT *Austral. Animal Bk.* xi. 96 The quokka or short-tailed pademelon.. inhabits the coastal districts of South-western Australia. **1963** *Spectator* 25 Jan. 102/2 The quokka, indigenous to Western Australia, is a 'species of rat', albeit rather friendly. **1968** *New Scientist* 29 Feb. 455/2 At night the place [*sc.* Rottnest Island] quivers with wallabies about the size of hares. They are what the Aborigines call quokkas. **1976** *Nature* 1 Jan. 42/1 Female quokkas mate soon after giving birth.

quoll (kwɒl). [Aboriginal name.] The 'native cat' (*Dasyurus macrurus*) of Australia.

1770 HAWKESWORTH *Voy.* (1773) III. 626, I can add only one more [animal], resembling a polecat, which the natives call Quoll. **1855** in OGILVIE *Suppl.* **1924** *Truth* (Sydney) 27 Apr. 6 *Quoll*, aboriginal name of native cat. **1970** *Courier-Mail* (Brisbane) 15 June 12/5 In 1955, during intensive searches for taipans in scrubs and huge lantana thickets at Chatsworth near Gympie, I was astonished when I captured a savage little quoll (native cat) almost a thousand miles south of what I thought was its home country. **1978** *Ibid.* 18 Feb. 18/8 And talking of this native cat or Quoll, it is a marsupial and a carnivore and it is a clever and persistent hunter.

quom, obs. form of WHOM.

†**quominus, quo minus.** *Obs. Law.* [L., 'by which the less' (viz. one may exercise a right, or perform a duty).] **a.** A writ to restrain a person from committing waste in a wood after granting 'housebote and haybote' to another. **b.** An Exchequer writ available for a steward or debtor to the King against one indebted to himself.

1595 RASTELL *Termes Lawes* 156. *Ibid.* (1598) 160 b. **1623** in *10th Rep. Hist. MSS. Comm.* App. IV. 433 [Paid] to Mr. Hill for suinge out several Quominuses and for his fee, 34*s.* 8*d.* **1642** *Perkins' Prof. Bk.* i. §5. 3 He shall have a *Quo minus* against the vendre in the Exchequer.

‖**quomodo** ('kwəʊmədəʊ), **quo modo** (kwəʊ 'məʊdəʊ). [L. 'in what way?'] ***the quomodo***, the manner, way, means.

1671 EVELYN *Corr.* (1879) III. 383 The difference between us and the Church of Rome consists chiefly in the definition of the manner of the change; the *quomodo* or *modus.* **1749** FIELDING *Tom Jones* VII. xv, Northerton was desirous of departing and nothing remained for him but to contrive the *quomodo.* **1791** *Burke's Corr.* (1844) III. 318, I cannot persuade myself that the obstacle is not to be removed. The *quomodo* is the thing to be considered. **1828** *Congress Debates* IV. II. 2724 (Stanf.) The *quo modo* of executing it is left to the wisdom of the government.

†,**quomodo'cunquize**, *v. nonce-wd.* [f. L. *quomodocunque* in whatever way (with allusion to Horace *Ep.* I. i. 66) + -IZE.] *intr.* To make money in any possible way.

1652 URQUHART *Jewel* Wks. (1834) 213 Those quomodocunquizing clusterfists and rapacious varlets.

quon, variant of WHONE, few. *Obs.*

quondam ('kwɒndəm), *adv.*, *sb.*, and *a.* Also 6 condam. [L., 'formerly'.]

A. *adv.* At one time, formerly, heretofore, 'whilome'. *rare.*

1537 WRIOTHESLEY *Chron.* (1875) I. 63 An Abbott condam of Fountens, of the order of pyed monkes. **1611** CORYAT *Crudities* 648 That..most faithful attendant *quondam* vppon the right Worshipfull Sir Edward Phillips. **1841** CATLIN *N. Amer. Ind.* (1844) II. liii. 162 Mr. C. Jennings quondam of the city hotel in New York.

B. *sb.* The former holder of some office or position; one who has been deposed or ejected; see also quot. 1962.

1535 *Lett. Suppress. Monast.* (Camden) 93 The kinges fowndation thus to be mangellede by the quondam, I have petie; the prior now is..a goode clerke. **1549** LATIMER *4th Serm. bef. Edw. VI* (Arb.) 107 Make them quondammes, out with them, cast them out of ther office. **1583** STUBBES *Anat. Abus.* (1882) II. 54 Let him be..Jacke out of office, make him a Quondam. **1888** A. BLOMFIELD *Let.* in H. H. Henson *Retrospect* (1942) I. II. 30 My dear Henson (If I may as a quondam thus familiarly address you). **1962** A. SAMPSON *Anatomy of Britain* xiii. 214 The most worldly college has been All Souls... The fellows and ex-fellows (called Quondams) are supposed to be the cream of Oxford intellectuals... Lord Curzon, the Viceroy of India, 'an enthusiastic quondam'.

C. *adj.* That formerly was or existed:

a. of persons (the most frequent use).

1586 WARNER *Alb. Eng.* III. xiv. (1612) 65 In Albanie the quondam King at eldest Daughters Court was setled scarce, when she repynes. **1615** BRATHWAIT *Strappado* (1878) 86, I see thy quondam friend, Hath cause to say his hopes are at an end. **1675** COCKER *Morals* 47 Quarles, quondam Poet, for rare Lines Divine. **1728** MORGAN *Algiers* II. ii. 234 This aspiring quondam Consort of his grew apace. **1825** BENTHAM *Offic. Apt. Maximized* (1830) 13 A quondam country Gentleman with thirty years of..experience. **1874** RUSKIN *Fors Clav.* xxxvii. (1874) IV. 3 The loquacious and speculative disposition..of all my quondam friends.

b. of things, qualities, etc.

1588 SHAKS. *L.L.L.* v. i. 6, I did conuerse this *quondam* day with a companion of the kings. **1600** S. NICHOLSON *Acolastus* (1876) 34 Marke..How euery thing in quondam sort appeares. **1642** VICARS *God in Mount* (1644) 44 The heighth of their quondam pride and cruelty. **1717** BP. NICOLSON in Ellis *Orig. Lett.* Ser. II. IV. 318 His quondam diocese of Derry. **1795-6** WORDSW. *Borderer* I. 79 The tale of this his quondam Barony Is cunningly devised.

Hence '**quondamly** *adv.*, formerly; †'**quondamship**, the state of being out of office. *Obs.*

1549 LATIMER *4th Serm. bef. Edw. VI* (Arb.) 108 As for my quondamshyp I thancke God that he gaue me ye grace to come by it so honest a meanes as I dyd. **1814** *Sporting Mag.* XLIV. 53 Certain gentlemen smiths, who have been quondamly in habits of wearing such articles.

quondary, variant of QUANDARY.

quoner, compar. of WHONE, few. *Obs.*

quonet, variant of QUANNET.

†'**quoniam**. *Obs. rare*⁻¹. [? Some allusive use of L. *quoniam* whereas.] (See quot.)

1609 HEALEY *Disc. New World* 69 The drinke is sure to go, be it out of Can, Quoniam, or Iourdan. [*Note.* A Quoniam is a glasse..well knowne in Drink-allia.]

Quonset, quonset ('kwɒnsɪt). orig. and chiefly *U.S.* Also (erron.) quanset. [f. the name of *Quonset* Point, Rhode Island, where the article was first made.] Used *attrib.* and *ellipt.*, esp. in ***Quonset hut***, of a kind of prefabricated building consisting of a semi-cylindrical corrugated metal roof on a bolted steel foundation.

A proprietary name in the U.S.

1942 *Collier's* 19 Sept. 21/1 The boys practiced erecting on deck their 'Quonsett huts', queer little igloos, the roofs of which are designed to catch rainwater to be saved for a sunny day. **1943** *Pop. Mechanics* Apr. 61/1 'Quonset Huts', those portable barracks, begin replacing the tent city. **1946** *New Yorker* 16 Mar. 22/1 The first American-made Nissens, or Quonsets, were sent to England under lend-lease in June, 1941. **1946** *Official Gaz.* (U.S. Patent Offie) 19 Nov. 287/2 Great Lakes Steel Corporation, Wilmington, Del... Filed Mar. 15, 1946. *Quonset.* For readily erectable buildings, knock-down buildings, portable buildings, and prefabricated buildings. Claims use since September 1941. **1949** 'P. MICHAELS' *This Perverse Generation* viii. 67 From sturdy, roomy architectural loveliness to quonset hut—civilization marches on! **1957** J. KEROUAC *On Road* xiii. 90 A tremendous aluminum Quonset warehouse. **1959** E. TUNIS *Indians* 32/2 There seems to have been a quonset-shaped house, too, in Virginia and North Carolina. **1966** T. PYNCHON *Crying of Lot 49* iv. 82 She parked in an enormous lot next to a quonset building painted pink and about a hundred yards long. **1972** E. STAEBLER *Cape Breton Harbour* ii. 24 A long scalloped row of traps made of raw wood slats, shaped like a quanset hut. **1973** 'B. MATHER' *Snowline* iii. 30 Nissen and Quanset huts hastily erected in World War II. **1974** *Spartanburg* (S. Carolina) *Herald-Jrnl.* 21 Apr. A6/5 The family's quonset hut home on Oahu Island's north shore was washed away by a swollen river. **1977** *Time* 27 June 48/2 The final dozen hippies..last week evacuated their grimy quonset hut on the edge of town.

quonundrum, obs. variant of CONUNDRUM.

quony, variant of COYNYE. (See QUIDRATHE.)

quook(e, obs. north. pa. t. QUAKE *v.*

Quoom, var. QUM.

quop (kwɒp), *v. Obs.* exc. *dial.* [Later form of QUAP *v.*] To beat, throb, palpitate.

a **1658** CLEVELAND *Model New Relig.* 32 How Quops the Spirit? In what Garb or Air? **1679** DRYDEN *Limberham* III. ii, Oh, my Eyes grow dim! my Heart quops, and my back aketh. **1681** *Ballad Dk. Monmouth* in *Shaksp. Cent. Praise* 387 His great Heart quops his Courage fails. **1848** A. B. EVANS *Leicestersh. Words, Quop*, to throb (used also in Gloucestershire) as in the suppuration of boils and abscesses. **1889** GISSING *Both of this Parish* I. v. 103 It makes a body's heart quop to hear tell of such a history.

quor, quore, obs. variants of WHERE, CORE.

quorate ('kwɔːrət), *a.* [f. QUOR(UM + -ATE².] Of a meeting: attended by a quorum (and thereby constitutional). Hence **in'quorate** *a.*, not attended by a quorum.

1969 *PI* (University College London, Students' Union) 20 Oct. 3/2 Even barely quorate General Meetings could be dominated by an organised minority. **1971** J. HENDERSON *Copperhead* xv. 192 This meeting is now closed. We're quorate without you. **1973** *Times Higher Educ. Suppl.* 11 May 14/1 In a tiny department of three, what happens if the head is wed to one of the other two? The department meeting becomes quorate during intercourse. **1974** *Times* 13 May 17/6 The meeting..was an inquorate one and therefore had no validity and was entirely unofficial. **1976** *Cherwell* 30 Jan. 2/3 A barely quorate JCR passed a motion..that freshmen at the college should 'fag' for second and third year men. **1978** *Evening News* 22 Apr. 4/3 The motion was passed but there were several people who were in strong disagreement and walked out making the meeting inquorate.

quorister, obs. form of CHORISTER.

Quorn (kwɔːn). The name of a village in Leicestershire (now Quorndon), used *attrib.* and *ellipt.* to denote a famous hunt centred there.

1867 'OUIDA' *Under Two Flags* I. iv. 74 It lay in the Melton country, and was equally well placed for Pytchley, Quorn, and Belvoir. **1904** A. E. W. MASON *Truants* ii. 16 He hunted with the Quorn that winter. **1933** KIPLING in *Strand* Feb. 126, I..was a Gentleman in Red When all the Quorn wore woad, Sir. **1966** J. BETJEMAN *High & Low* 23 The rumble of the railway drowned The thunder of the Quorn. **1971** *Guardian* 30 Sept. 16/8 Melton was frequented by many of the nobility and gentry who came for the Quorn hunting season. **1972** *Country Life* (Suppl.) 26 Oct. 11/1 *Hotel*..in the heart of the Quorn countryside.

†**quorse**, ? obs. variant of CORSE.

1462 in Ellacombe *Bells of Ch.* ix. (1872) 469 Wan they rynge for any quorse or obiit.

‖**quorum** ('kwɔːrəm). [L., lit. 'of whom', from the wording of commissions in which certain persons were specially designated as members of a body by the words *quorum vos...unum* (*duos*, etc.) *esse volumus* 'of whom we will that you...be one (two, etc.)'.]

1. Orig., certain justices of the peace, usually of eminent learning or ability, whose presence was necessary to constitute a bench; latterly the term was loosely applied to all justices.

1455 *Rolls Parlt.* V. 334/1 The Justicez or Justice of the Pease of the Quorum yn the same Shire. **1495** *Act 11 Hen. VII.* c. 2 §5, ij of the Justices of the peas wherof one shalbe of the Quorum. **1559** *Mirr. Mag., R. Tresilian* vii, At sessions & at syses..In patentes & commissions of Quorum. **1581** LAMBARDE *Eiren.* I. ix. (1602) 46 So that the one of those two [Justices] be of that select number, which is commonly tearmed of the *Quorum*. For these of the *Quorum* were wont..to bee chosen, specially for their knowledge in the Lawes of the lande. **1625** MASSINGER *New Way* I. i, Old Sir John Wellborn, Justice of Peace and Quorum. **1691** WOOD *Ath. Oxon.* II. 274 George Wither..a Justice of Peace in Quorum for Hampshire. **1728** VANBR. & CIB. *Prov. Husb.* II. i. 43 I'm o' th' Quorum—I have been at Sessions. **1855** MACAULAY *Hist. Eng.* xxi. IV. 705 A squire who was one of the quorum.

Comb. **1619** HUTTON *Foll. Anat., Ixions Wheele* E iij b, The Gods..Quorum Iustice warrants sent by poast.

b. *transf.* Applied to similarly distinguished members of other bodies; hence, a select company.

1602 WARNER *Alb. Eng.* IX. xlvi. (1612) 216 The Hellish Potentates..a new Commission framed, Narcissus ghost and Ecchos voice therein of Quorum named. *a* **1661** FULLER *Worthies* (1840) III. 187 He was afterwards of that quorum in the translating of the Bible. **1678** MARVELL *Growth Popery* Wks. 1875 IV. 329 [They are] so small a scantling in number, that men can scarce reckon of them more than a *quorum*. **1747** *Scheme Equip. Men of War* 24 A *Quorum* of Surgeons..should be ordered to..examine them. **1859** GREEN *Oxf. Stud.* ii. §10 (O.H.S.) 128 The deepest sot among the topers of the quorum.

Comb. **1659** A. BROME *Panegyr. Verses* in *R. Brome's Wks.* II, These would-be Quorum-Wits, and by their own Commission, do invade Apollo's throne.

2. A fixed number of members of any body, society, etc., whose presence is necessary for the proper or valid transaction of business.

1616 in Row *Hist. Kirk* (1842) 81 The Assemblie appoynts twenty Commissioners nominat, whereof six a quorum, to attend the King's Majestie's ansuer. **1669** EVELYN *Diary* 19 May, It was order'd that 5 should be a quorum for a Council. **1720** *Wodrow Corr.* (1843) II. 524 The Commission should have met this day; but we have not a quorum in the forenoon. **1800** COLQUHOUN *Comm. Thames* xiii. 369 At the Meetings of the Directors, five Members shall be a quorum, capable of acting. **1873** BURTON *Hist. Scot.* V. lvii. 163 Six were to be a quorum, of whom the chancellor must always be one.

†3. Necessary materials. *Obs. rare.*

1650 FULLER *Pisgah* I. vi. 12 Salt, Bread and Wine..(all of the Quorum to every feast). **1655** —— *Ch. Hist.* III. xiv. §12 Fullers earth..a great Commodity of the Quorum to the making of good Cloath.

quos(e, obs. forms of WHOSE.

quosher, var. COSHERY. (See QUIDRATHE.)

quo-so, obs. form of WHO-SO.

†**quoss**, obs. var. COSS, to barter, exchange.

1515 *Burgh Rec. Prestwick* (1834) 47 þe said George allegit he had gottyn it [a sword] in quossyn fra þe said James.

quosshon, quost, obs. ff. CUSHION, COAST.

quot (kwɒt), *pa. pple. dial.* Also 7 quotted, 8 quott. [f. *quot* QUAT *v.*¹ 1 b.] Sated, cloyed.

1674-91 RAY *S. & E.C. Words, Quotted*, cloyed, glutted. *Suss. c* **1741** ELIZ. CARTER *Let.* in *Mem.* (1808) I. 27, I believe I am grown *quott* of assemblies, &c. **1887** *Kentish Gloss., Quot*, cloyed, glutted.

†**quot**, *sb. Sc.*: see QUOTE *sb.*¹ 2 b.

quot, variant of QUAT *a.*, squat.

quota ('kwəʊtə), *sb.* [med.L. *quota* (sc. *pars* 'how great a part'), fem. of *quotus*, f. *quot* how many.]

1. The part or share which is, or ought to be, paid or contributed by one to a total sum or amount; in early use chiefly with ref. to contributions of men, money, or supplies, from a particular town, district, or country. (Cf. CONTINGENT *sb.* 5.) Also *Eccl.*, the proportion of the funds of a parish that is contributed to the finances of the diocese; in full ***diocesan*** (formerly ***parochial***) ***quota***.

1668 TEMPLE *Lett., Ld. Arlington* Wks. 1731 II. 165 Some certain Quota's upon the several Parts of the Empire. **1691** LUTTRELL *Brief Rel.* (1857) II. 236 If his master doe not speedily remitt the money promised, and quota of officers and engineers. **1712** ADDISON *Spect.* No. 439 ⁋2 Newsgatherers and Intelligencers.. who bring in their respective Quotas. **1756** NUGENT *Gr. Tour, Germany* II. 391 They have often balls and feasts, where every one pays their quota. **1769** ROBERTSON *Chas. V*, XII. III. 378 The Papal troops were far inferior in number to the quota stipulated. **1844** DISRAELI *Coningsby* I. vi, The host..always contributed his quota to the general fund of polished sociability. **1887** JESSOPP *Arcady* i. 13 It is the village huckster who has to pay his heavy quota towards the rate. **1911** *Archbishops' Committee on Church Finance Rep.* IV. 45 We recommend... That a system of parochial assessment.. should be adopted... That the amount of this apportionment or contribution (which may conveniently be called the Parochial Quota) should from time to time be fixed by the Diocesan Board of Finance. **1919** W. B. INCLEDON *Vicar Reconstructs* vi. 27 So the Diocesan Finance Committee has been worrying you about the diocesan quota. My advice is to let them worry until you have your parochial finance scheme in proper working order. **1936** W. K. L. CLARKE *Almsgiving* II. i. 82 The diocesan income in its turn is raised by assessing the parishes, each of which is expected to pay its 'quota'. *Ibid.* vi. 115 In many parishes the diocesan quota is paid reluctantly. **1976** *Church Times* 2 July 12/1 Any extra money raised by a parish for some specific occasion..is engulfed by the diocese by an increase in quota. **1978** *Ibid.* 29 Sept. 12/5 Parishes are already struggling to meet vastly increased quotas.

2. a. The part or share of a total which belongs, is given, or is due, to one.

a **1700** B. E. *Dict. Cant. Crew*, s.v., *Tip me my Quota*, give me my Part of the Winnings, Booty, Plunder, &c. **1726** SHELVOCKE *Voy. round World* 227 Sometimes would not allow me a quota of the fish that was caught. **1753** HANWAY *Trav.* (1762) II. I. xii. 61 They have great magazines of East-India goods, this city having its quota of that trade. **1806-7** J. BERESFORD *Miseries Hum. Life* (1826) I. Introd., If nerves are necessary to a boiling fit of rage, I must have my full quota of them. **1883** SHAW *Local Gov. Illinois* 17 Having collected the total amount, the collector disburses to each proper authority its respective quota.

b. In a system of proportional representation, the minimum number of votes required to elect a candidate.

1857 T. HARE *Machinery of Representation* 17 No person shall be returned as a member to serve in parliament for whom there shall not be recorded the full quota or number of votes specified. **1930** C. F. STRONG *Mod. Polit. Consititutions* viii. 177 Instead of having to gain an absolute majority, the candidate needs only to reach the *quota*, i.e. the number of votes cast divided by the number of seats to be filled. **1943** J. F. S. ROSS *Parliamentary Representation* xxiii. 219 The *quota* has next to be determined: this is done by dividing the grand total of votes by a number which is one more than the number of members to be elected. The quota is the whole number next above the result of this division. **1955** LAKEMAN & LAMBERT *Voting in Democracies* v. 91 If the number of envelopes containing..the Socialist list amounts to one d'Hondt quota, the Socialist candidate whose name appears first on the list is declared elected. **1973** *Irish Times* 2 Mar. 8/1 Carlow-Kilkenny. Seats, 5... Valid vote, 46,717; ..Quota, 7,787. **1975** H. BERRINGTON in S. E. Finer *Adversary Politics & Electoral Reform* 281 Neither Labour nor the Conservatives would have 'wasted' many votes—the Tories would have polled two quotas, with little to spare, and Labour would have accumulated three.

3. The maximum number (of immigrants or imports) allowed to enter a country within a set period; a regulation that imposes such a restriction on entry to a country. Also *transf.*

1921 *Washington Post* 21 May 4/5 North European countries may not furnish the full 20 per cent of their entire quotas each month. **1921** *U.S. Congr. House Report* No. 169. 1 The law provides that not in excess of 20 per cent of the yearly quota allotted to any country may come in one month. **1930** W. K. HANCOCK *Australia* xii. 239 In recent years we have extended its operation by instituting 'quotas', which limit the immigration from Southern Europe. **1931** *Foreign Affairs* Apr. 401 On the score of its domestic economic consequences alone, the wisdom of an embargo or fixed import quota is disputable. **1931** *Contemporary Review* Aug. 221 It has not yet been realised, even by some Free Traders, how insidious and dangerous a form of protection is that latest expedient of the tariff-mongers, known as the 'Quota'. **1932** E. BOWEN *To North* xxi. 224 'I have decided to go to America.'.. 'You couldn't stay more than six months, though, because of the quota.' **1949** [see IMMIGRATION]. **1973** *Nation Rev.* (Melbourne) 31 Aug. 1448/2 The board doesn't call for quotas on imports. **1976** *Survey* Winter 128 Quotas upon Jews in higher education had, to be sure, been a staple of the Soviet scene since the postwar period.

4. *attrib.* and *Comb.*, as *quota act*, *film*, *immigrant*, *immigration*, *law*, *limit*, *period*, *plan*, *restriction*; **quota-bill**, a Parliamentary bill passed in March, 1795, under which each county and (by a supplementary bill passed in April) each port had to supply its quota of men to the navy; so also **quota-bounty**, **-man** (see quots.); **quota method**, the statistical method of using quota samples (usu. for opinion polls); **quota quickie** [QUICKIE 1 a], a cheap cinematographic film, rapidly made outside the United States to offset American films shown in other countries; **quota sample**, a sample that is chosen so that various categories of individual (when classified by age, sex, social class, and the like) are represented in the same proportions as in the general population; **quota sampler**, one who devises or uses quota samples; **quota sampling**, the use of the quota method; **quota system**, a law or custom restricting the number or proportion of persons or goods that may be admitted to a country or an institution; also, one prescribing the minimum number of persons to be admitted.

1938 *Times* 22 Feb. 19/3 British film production has made considerable progress during the past ten years as a result of the first Quota Act. **1867** quota-bill [see *quota-man* below]. **1823** BRENTON *Naval Hist. Gt. Brit.* I. 49 The quota-bounty given in 1795, 1796, and 1797..for manning the fleet. **1939** 'N. BLAKE' *Smiler with Knife* ii. 29 Those extras, dressed up to look like rustic ancients for a British quota film. **1974** R. HARRISON *Rex* ii. 29 The British film industry had only just begun to stir [in 1927], with Gaumont Films, and then with American quota films—'quota quickies' made over here by American companies, on a budget of £1 per foot of film and never mind the quality, so that they could then unload their Hollywood products on England. **1924** *U.S. Laws & Statutes* (1925) XLIII. 155 When used in this Act the term 'quota immigrant' means any immigrant who is not a non-quota immigrant. **1965** *Listener* 2 Sept. 340/2 Some [Australian] commentators advocate quota immigration for Asians. **1922** *Proc. Conf. Social Work* XLIX. 460 Just what effect the quota law has had on immigration..cannot be accurately determined. *Ibid.* 465 Under the quota law..we have exclusion for the first time on the basis of numbers alone. **1975** J. CLEARY *Safe House* 10 Every country..had a quota limit when..asked to extend its sympathy into acceptance of the Jews as immigrants. **1823** BRENTON *Naval Hist. Gt. Brit.* I. 49 There were few, if any, seamen among them; and the term 'quota-man', or 'lord-mayor's man', was supposed to comprise every thing that was base and contemptible among sailors. **1867** SMYTH *Sailor's Word-bk.*, *Quota-Men*, those raised for the navy..by Pitt's quota-bill, in 1795 under bounties of from £20 to £60. **1946** HAUSER & LEONARD *Govt. Statistics for Business Use* xii. 356 A commonly used type of sample design is that usually referred to as the 'quota' or 'in-ratio' method of sampling. **1953** W. G. COCHRAN *Sampling Techniques* v. 105 Sampling theory cannot be applied to quota methods which contain no element of probability sampling. **1971** *Guardian* 9 June 13/4 Teams of interviewers were sent out to a random sample of areas to find certain numbers of consumers determined by sex, age, and social class. This is known as the quota method of sampling. Random sampling—where lists are drawn from an 'unbiased' source such as the electoral register—is more rigorous, but much more expensive and is rarely used for commercial work. **1958** *Economist* 18 Oct. 280/1 For the first two quota periods (6 months) of the current year, the permitted output averaged 118 tons per month. **1977** *Grimsby Even. Tel.* 13 May 1/5 It showed we have no confidence in him and his quota plans. **1936** *Economist* 5 Dec. 456/2 The primary objective of the Board of Trade..was the complete extirpation of the 'quota quickie'. **1948** H. WILSON in *Hansard Commons* 21 Jan. 226 To protect this section of the industry against the so-called 'quota quicky' shorts. **1976** *Oxf. Compan. Film* 574/1 'Quota quickies'—cheap programme-fillers made with local personnel and technical resources but financed from the US—kept standards down while fulfilling legal requirements. **1924** J. S. HUXLEY in *Spectator* 20 Dec. 981/1 The 1924 Immigration Law takes the quota idea as its basis... The quota restrictions do not apply to Canadians. **1938** *Ann. Reg. 1937* 17 In Great Britain there were no exchange controls and no quota restrictions save in the case of iron and steel imports. **1952** *Economist* 20 Sept. 689 (Advt.), Checking the quota sample against a random sample. **1974** *Times* 15 Feb. 5/7 The Gallop Poll..plans to do a mixture of random and quota samples. **1952** *Jrnl. R. Statistical Soc.* A. CXV. 412 Quota samplers invariably attempt, as one of their controls, an economic or social breakdown of the sample. **1958** C. A. MOSER *Survey Methods Social Investigation* vi. 105 Quota samplers generally claim that instructions to, and constraints on, interviewers are sufficient to guard against the main dangers of selection bias. **1944** *Jrnl. Marketing* July 26/2 The current method, perhaps most-widely employed in the selection of respondents in market surveys and in polls of opinion, is that of 'in ratio' or 'quota sampling'... The essentials of this method consist in:..(3) the fixing of quotas for each enumerator in such a way that the respondents..will include the specified proportion of each class of the population agreed upon. **1944** *Ibid.*, 29/1 One of the most important advantages of area sampling over..quota sampling is that which reduces the dependence of the investigator on knowledge of the characteristics of the population. **1950** M. PARTEN *Surveys, Polls, & Samples* i. 31 Up to 1946, the nationwide tabulations were usually based on about 3,000 cases selected according to a stratified quota sampling procedure. **1973** *Guardian* 27 Oct. 13/5 Quota sampling sets the interviewer the..task of finding people who are socially representative... Random means what it says, and should..be based on the picking of names at random from the electoral register. **1924** *N.Y. Times* 8 Dec. 17/1 A bill amending the immigration law and abolishing the quota system is being drafted for presentation to Congress. **1934** A. G. MACDONELL *How like an Angel* II. v. 86 It was the business of the All-British Company to produce seventeen exceptionally bad and cheap films every year in England in order to allow two hundred and forty-six exceptionally bad and expensive films to be imported every year into England from Hollywood. This is called the Quota System. **1936** *Discovery* Dec. 374/1 Under the quota system ..2,894 Japanese were entitled to admission [to Brazil] during 1935. **1966** *Guardian* 25 Apr. 8/5 Under the quota method..people are interviewed in the street... The random sample, which involves contacting named individuals..is much more expensive than the quota system. **1969** *Listener* 14 Aug. 201/1 *The quota system.* Thirty per cent of first features shown in this country have to be made here. **1976** *National Observer* (U.S.) 14 Feb. 11/5 Demanding what amounts to a quota system for college and university faculty hiring.

Hence **'quota** *v. trans.*, to impose in quotas. Also **'quotaing** *vbl. sb.*

1784 E. GERRY in *New Eng. Hist. & Gen. Reg.* (1895) XLIX. 431 Troops to be required and quotied [*sic*] on the several States by Congress. **1786** JEFFERSON *Writ.* (1859) I. 593 A convention..by which the burthen of the war might be quotaed on them, according to their respective wealth. **1798** *Ibid.* (1896) VII. 267 This is to avoid the quotaing. *Ibid.*, Requeries under a quotaing law.

quotable ('kwəʊtəb(ə)l), *a.* [f. QUOTE *v.* + -ABLE.] Capable of being quoted; suitable for quoting.

1821 *Examiner* 27/1 Passages of a still more quotable nature. **1849** THOREAU *Week Concord Riv.* Thurs. 326 The Spectators and Ramblers have not failed to cull some quotable sentences. **1883** *Manch. Exam.* 27 Nov. 4/6 There is no quotable change at any of the spot markets.

Hence **quota'bility**, **'quotableness**. Also **'quotably** *adv.*, in a quotable manner, so as to be quoted.

a **1849** POE *Marginalia* Wks. 1865 III. 500 It is the prosaicism of these two writers to which is owing their especial quotability. **1881** *Daily News* 17 Jan. 3/3 Cotton yarns are not quotably dearer. **1888** *Athenæum* 24 Nov. 693/2 This uncouthness interferes with the quotableness.. of not a few anecdotes amusing enough in themselves.

†**'quotal**, *a. Obs. rare*$^{-1}$. [f. L. *quot-a* (*pars*) + -AL[1]: see QUOTA.] = ALIQUOT.

a **1696** SCARBURGH *Euclid* (1705) 177 A Quotal part measures the whole: which is then called a Multiple of that part.

†**quo'tannal**, *a. Obs. rare*$^{-1}$. [f. L. *quotann-is* every year + -AL[1].] Yearly, annual.

1651 BIGGS *New Disp.* 170 A quotannal recidivation.

So †**quo'tannual** *a.* (after *annual*). *Obs.*

1658 J. ROBINSON *Eudoxa* x. 55 There would be a fear of ..a quotannuall Phaetontick combustion.

quotation (kwəʊ'teɪʃən). Also 6–8 **cotation**. [ad. med.L. *quotātiōn-em*, n. of action f. *quotāre* to QUOTE. Cf. obs. F. *quotation* (Godef.).]

†**1.** A numbering, number. *Obs. rare*$^{-1}$.

1456 SIR G. HAYE *Law Arms* (S.T.S.) 100 Here efter followis the chapitris of the ferde buke efter the quotaciouns of the Rubricis.

†**2. a.** A (marginal) reference to a passage in a book: see QUOTE *v.* 2. *Obs.*

1532 MORE *Confut. Barnes* VIII. Wks. 776/1 His quotacion is in the mergent in this maner. *De pene. dis. ii. Si in glossa.* **1557** *N.T.* (Genev.) To Rdr. **iii. Then is it noted with this starre *, as the cotations are. **1574** WHITGIFT *Def. Aunsw.* 793 Although the wordes in the texte be altered, yet the quotations in the margent remayne still. **1664** H. MORE *Apology* 508 The Quotation of the place from whence this Objection is taken is here omitted, but I question not but that it aimes at that passage, Chap. 4. Sect. 3. Book 6. which runs thus [etc.]. **1683** MOXON *Mech. Exerc., Printing* 388 That the Compositer may..Justifie his Notes or Quotations exactly against the designed Line of the Page.

b. *Typog.* (ellipt. for *quotation-quadrat.*) A large (usually hollow) quadrat used for filling up blanks (orig. the blanks between marginal references).

1683 MOXON *Mech. Exerc., Printing* xxii. 224 He Justifies his Stick-full just to the breadth of the Wooden Letter with Quadrats or Quotations. *Ibid.* 236 He sets..a row of Quotations almost down the length of the Page. **1771** P. LUCKOMBE *Hist. Printing* 287 Justifiers, as well for broad as narrow Quotations, are cast, from Double Pica to all the Regular Bodies. **1808** STOWER *Printers' Gram.* 97 Quotations are cast to two sizes, and are called broad and narrow... Quotations should not be cast so high as they sometimes are. **1888** JACOBI *Printers' Vocab.* 109 *Quotations*, large quadrats, generally of four-line pica.

3. a. The action or practice of quoting.

1646 SIR T. BROWNE *Pseud. Ep.* 279 This Translation..is often followed..by our Saviour himselfe in the quotations of the Old Testament. **1765** *Museum Rust.* IV. lxiii. 286 Nothing can be more unfair than false quotation. **1781** JOHNSON in *Boswell* 8 May, Classical quotation is the *parole* of literary men all over the world. **1875** EMERSON *Lett. & Soc. Aims, Quot. & Orig.*, Quotation confesses inferiority.

b. A passage quoted from a book, speech, etc.

1690 LOCKE *Hum. Und.* IV. xvi. (1695) 383 He..cannot doubt how little Credit the Quotations deserve, where the Originals are wanting. **1711** STEELE *Spect.* No. 11 ¶1 He.. enforced his Arguments by Quotations out of Plays and Songs. **1771** *Junius Lett.* xlvi. 245 After giving a false quotation from the journals..he proceeds. **1828** D'ISRAELI *Chas. I*, I. viii. 249 That prodigal erudition which delights in inexhaustible quotations from writers whom we now deem obscure. **1887** BOWEN *Virgil* Pref. (1889) 7 Hundreds of Virgil's lines are for most of us familiar quotations.

c. A short passage or tune taken from one piece of music to another or quoted elsewhere.

1906 E. NEWMAN *Elgar* v. 147 The clarinet softly gives out a quotation..from Mendelssohn's 'Calm Sea and Prosperous Voyage' overture. **1942** G. ABRAHAM *Beethoven's Second-Period Quartets* 42 A note-for-note quotation of a figure much used in the first movement of Mozart's great Quartet in C major, K.465. **1960** *New Oxf. Hist. Music* III. v. 156 The following quotation will..serve to show the extent to which the late Gothic composers intentionally subordinated the natural verbal rhythm to the rhythmic compulsion of the music. **1972** *Jazz & Blues* Oct. 26/3 Flashes of humour in the form of oblique quotations.

†**4.** A note or observation; a matter noted. *Obs.*

1608 MIDDLETON *Family of Love* v. iii, Your wife can furnish you with notes out of her cotations. *a* **1635** NAUNTON *Fragm. Reg.* (Arb.) 51 It were not amisse to take into observation two notable quotations. The first was, a violent indulgencie of the Queen [etc.].

†**5.** Share, QUOTA. *Obs. rare*$^{-1}$.

1613 J. CHAMBERLAIN *MS. Let. to Sir D. Carleton* (T.), That they should not be able to answer their quotations (as they call them), or payments to the general charge.

6. The amount stated as the price of stocks or any commodity for sale.

1812 *Examiner* 21 Sept. 608/2 Sales..sustain the last quotation. **1861** GOSCHEN *For. Exch.* 56 To give any exact or definite quotation of the price of long-dated paper. **1883** *Pall Mall G.* 7 Apr. 5/2 Manufacturers..are disposed rather to increase than to decrease their quotations.

7. *attrib.* and *Comb.*, as (sense 3 b) *quotation-capping* (see CAP *v.*[1] 5), *-monger*; (sense 2 b) *-justifier*, *-quadrat*; **quotation-marks**, signs used in writing or printing to mark the beginning and end of a quotation; in English, single or double inverted commas (see COMMA 4) and apostrophes are employed.

1683 MOXON *Mech. Exerc., Printing* xxii. 236 Then he sets his Notes..and with Quotation Quadrats of proper Bodies, Justifies them up. **1750** *Student* I. 284 The Author shews his skill and address as a quotation-monger. **1771** P. LUCKOMBE *Hist. Printing* 287 Quotation quadrats require to be dressed and finished as carefully as any other sort. **1885** *Pall Mall G.* 11 Apr. 5/1 Characters who..indulge themselves in a little bout of quotation-capping. **1888** JACOBI *Printers' Vocab.* 109 *Quotation justifiers*, spaces for justifying lines of quotations. **1897** *Century Mag.* 563/1, I must put play in quotation-marks to express the sarcasm of it.

Hence **quo'tational** *a.*, of or pertaining to a quotation or quotations; **quo'tationally** *adv.*, by way of quotation, as a quotation; **quo'tationist**, one who (habitually) makes quotations.

1643 MILTON *Divorce* To Parlt. Eng., Let the Statutes of God be..considered not altogether by the narrow intellectuals of Quotationists. **1829** *Blackw. Mag.* XXVI. 443 The quotationist..never saw even the Parthian back of the lucky fugitive. **1862** *Sat. Rev.* 13 Sept. 308 He then observed quotationally, 'Men cannot determine [etc.]'. **1869** EADIE *Galatians* 239 It is only a quotational illustration of the truth announced in the previous verse. **1878** J. W. EBSWORTH *Introd. Brathwait's Strappado* xv, The phrase.. has the imperfect quotational marks before it.

quotatious (kwəʊ'teɪʃəs), *a.* [f. QUOTATI(ON + -OUS.] Fond of using quotations; inclined to quote.

1903 *Daily Chron.* 10 Apr. 3/2 The myriad quotations of that most 'quotatious' of authors are identified every one —no easy task with such a perverter of phrases as Hazlitt. **1910** *Ibid.* 29 Jan. 6/1 A certain person endeavoured to quench my flaming optimism by a stream of frigid quotation... I sought knowledge from the quotatious person.

quotative ('kwəʊtətɪv), *a.* [See QUOTE *v.* and -ATIVE.] **1.** Relating to quoting; inclined to quote.

1812 *Sporting Mag.* XL. 25 What do you think of my quotative powers. **1891** *Sat. Rev.* 12 Sept. 304/1 Mr. Liddell, though still quotative, is straightforward.

2. Of a construction or expression: indicating that the speaker is quoting a word, phrase, etc., attributed to another person.

1927 L. BLOOMFIELD in *Amer. Speech* II. 438/2 Whatever is hearsay and not the speaker's own experience has the predicate verb or particle in a special *quotative* form. **1957** D. L. BOLINGER in *Publ. Amer. Dial. Soc.* XXVIII. 26 A reflex .. may be re-worded to make it less quotative. **1975** *Language* LI. 804 Normally a sentence containing the quotative clitic translates with 'one says'.

quotative ('kwəʊtətɪv), *sb.* [f. the adj.] A quotative word or expression (see prec.).

1902 *Amer. Anthropol.* IV. 401 The quotative *wAnsū'ga*, 'they say', is used extensively in the Skidegate dialect. **1957** D. L. BOLINGER in *Publ. Amer. Dial. Soc.* XXVIII. 95 With other verbs, notably the outright quotatives that connote the adoption or assertion of a view .. concord gives a different meaning. **1965** *Language* XLI. 68 A few further elements — pseudo-constitutes .., multiple constitutes .., and quotatives. **1975** *Ibid.* LI. 804 The first example is provided by quotatives in Luiseño.

'quotativeness. [f. QUOTATIVE *a.* + -NESS.]

a. Fondness for the use of quotations. **b.** The quality of being quotative (sense 2).

1886 G. B. SHAW in *Pall Mall Gazette* 26 July 5/1 A certain facetiousness and quotativeness. **1957** D. L. BOLINGER in *Publ. Amer. Dial. Soc.* XXVIII. 27 The quotativeness of the echo suggests that it be classed as a frag Q.

† **quote,** *sb.*[1] *Obs. rare.* Also 5 quoote, 6 cote; *Sc.* 6 quoitt, 6–7 quott, 7 coitt, 8 quot. [a. OF. *cote*, *quote* QUOTA.]

1. a. An aliquot part.

1460 CAPGRAVE *Chron.* 3 This noumbir eke of sex is praysed for his particuler noumberes, whech be on, too, thre; and these be cleped cote.

b. A quotient.

1676 COLLINS in Rigaud *Corr. Sci. Men* (1841) II. 9 By the second remainder divide the second divisor, reserve the quotes. **1694** E. HALLEY in *Phil. Trans.* XVIII. 250 Divide the Minutes of the said first Æquation and the Quote shall be the Æquation of Num. II. **1767** MURDOCH *ibid.* LVIII. 26 The terms .. must involve a common factor; by which being divided, the quote may be [etc.].

2. = QUOTA 1.

1451 *Rolls Parlt.* V. 222/1 Any part or parcell of any Dysmes, or other Quoote what so ever it be. **1491** *Act 7 Hen. VII*, c. 5 §1 Quinzimes and dismes and other quotes taxes and tallages. **1619** SIR J. SEMPILL *Sacrilege Handled* 78 Paul .. did not settle the Medium, nor name the Quote.

b. *Sc. Law.* 'The portion of the goods of one deceased appointed by law to be paid for the confirmation of his testament, or for the right of intromitting with his property' (Jamieson).

1526 *Sc. Acts Jas. V* (1814) II. 306 The nerrest of þar kyne .. sall have þar gudis, without preiudice to þe ordinaris anent þe cote of thar testamentis. **1666** *Acts Sederunt* 28 Feb., Twelve pennies of every pound of the dead's part shall be the quote of all testaments .. which shall be confirmed. [**1754** ERSKINE *Princ. Sc. Law* (1809) III. ix. §11.]

attrib. **1564** *Acts Sederunt* 13 Apr., The Queins writting of the 1600 lib. of the quoitt silver.

quote ('kwəʊt), *sb.*[2] [f. QUOTE *v.*]

† **1.** A (marginal) reference; a note. *Obs.*

1600 TOURNEUR *Trans. Metamorph.* Author to Book 2, O were Thy margents cliffes of itching lust, Or quotes to chalke out men the way to sin. **1611** COTGR., *Quote*, a quote, or quoting; a marke, or note vpon an article.

2. a. A quotation. Also ***quote mark*** = b.

1885 *Pall Mall G.* 23 Jan. 6/1 The 'interviewer' (.. has not the time come for leaving out the quote marks?) **1888** *Ibid.* 12 Dec. 11/2 Stodgy 'quotes' from the ancients? **1922** T. S. ELIOT *Let.* ? Jan. in E. Pound *Lett.* (1951) 236 Do you mean not use the Conrad quote or simply not put Conrad's name to it? **1950** G. B. STERN *Ten Days of Christmas* i. 27 The title must be a quote. **1959** *Times Lit. Suppl.* 23 Jan. 45/4 The blurb .. and 'quotes' selected from the American Press inaccurately suggest brashness. **1968** *Listener* 25 July 108/2 Don't ask me questions, since I have no wish to figure as the father of all the quotes in your stories. **1978** *Guardian Weekly* 15 Oct. 7/3 A quote from Dayan is painted on one of the twisted gun doors: 'The Bar-Lev line looks like a piece of cheese with a hole in it.'

b. A quotation mark.

1888 JACOBI *Printers' Vocab.* 109. **1891** *Scot. Leader* 2 Apr. 6 The portion of this quotation which we have put within quotes. **1895** *Nation* (N.Y.) 14 Mar. 191 Lodge's "Americanism" .. will get the "double quotes" every time. **1920** WODEHOUSE *Coming of Bill* I. ii. 24 Below the signature, in what printers call 'quotes', a line .. 'Bear the torch and do not falter.' **1937** *Daily Express* 4 Feb. 6/3 New use for 'quotes' ('inverted commas') came to light at the Scottish Literary luncheon in London yesterday. **1955** T. H. PEAR *Eng. Social Differences* iii. 90 The upper class fashion of speaking in 'quotes'—'I don't mind if I do' (in a pronounced Cockney accent). **1969** 'J. MORRIS' *Fever Grass* ii. 24 He'd have witnesses if I put him in the dock. Witnesses in quotes, I mean. **1976** *New Yorker* 16 Feb. 37/1 Freezes over close quote, paragraph.

3. = QUOTATION 6.

1959 *Daily Mail* 8 June 2/3 'Quotes' for readers. The following list of prices is a selection from readers' requests for quotation of some of their shares which do not fluctuate sufficiently to be quoted daily. **1965** E. GUNDREY *Foot in Door* xii. 91 She was shown a long list of things that needed doing .. and was given a quote for 'about £28'. **1970** *Globe & Mail* (Toronto) 25 Sept. 4/4 The Duke price was consistently lower than other quotes. **1976** J. DRUMMOND *Funeral Urn* iv. 14 Do the work, will I? .. I'll give you a quote before I get stuck in. **1980** *Daily Tel.* 3 Jan. 15/6 Yesterday .. he was appointed chairman of construction company Tebbitt, which has a market value of £1·3 million. 'It is a small start, but I needed a vehicle with a quote and Tebbitt is exactly right.'

quote (kwəʊt), *v.* Also 4–7 cote, 6 cott, quoate, 6–7 coat. [ad. med.L. *quotāre* to mark the number of, distinguish by numbers, f. *quot* how many, or *quota* QUOTA. Cf. F. *coter*, †*cotter* (15th c.), whence prob. the obs. forms *cote*, *cott*.]

I. † **1. a.** *trans.* To mark (a book) with numbers (as of chapters, etc.), or with (marginal) references to other passages or works. *Obs. rare.*

1387 TREVISA *Higden* (Rolls) VIII. 205 Stevene þe archbisshop .. coted [L. *quotavit*] þe Bible at Parys, and marked þe chapitres. **1570** FOXE *A. & M.* 1394/2, I was desirous to see it agayne, .. and beyng sent to me the second tyme, it was thus coted [**1596** quoted] in yᵉ margent as ye see.

† **b.** To mark (*with* lines). *Obs. rare*$^{-1}$.

F. *coter* is similarly used by Amyot, 'cicatrisez et cottez de poinctes et picqueures' (Godef. *Compl.*).

1601 WEEVER *Mirr. Mart.* C ij, Thou faire frame, with azure lines thick quoted, Bright heauen.

† **2. a.** To give the reference to (a passage in a book), by specifying the page, chapter, etc. where it is to be found. *Obs.*

1574 WHITGIFT *Def. Aunsw.* 800 They quote for that purpose in the margent the .10. of Matth. verse . 14 . 15. **1581** J. HAMILTON in *Catholic Tract.* (S.T.S.) 104 Quhy haue ye not cottit the places of your bybill, quhair out thaj ar drauin. **1638** FEATLY *Transubst.* 46 If you have read .. the passages which you cote out of Jewell. **1651** HOBBES *Leviath.* III. xlii. 280 What needed he to quote any places to prove his doctrine?

fig. **1588** SHAKS. *L.L.L.* II. 246 His faces owne margent did coate such Amazes.

† **b.** *absol.* To set down references; to refer *to*.

1580 LYLY *Euphues* (Arb.) 270 He .. desired few parentheses or digressions or gloses, but the text, where he him-self was coting [*later eds.* coating] in the margant. **1657** F. COCKIN *Div. Blossomes* 119 Another Book by the same Authour, to the which this Quotes, and would be of great use to go along with this.

3. † **a.** To cite or refer to (a book, author, etc.) for a particular statement or passage. *Obs.* **b.** To copy out or repeat a passage or passages from. Also, to repeat a statement by (someone); to give (a person's name) as the authority for a statement. Freq. in phr. ***don't quote me.***

1589 *Pasquil's Ret.* c, *Mar.* .. in other places he quoates Scripture. *Pas.* He coateth Scriptures indeed. **1692** WASHINGTON tr. *Milton's Def. Pop.* M.'s Wks. 1738 I. 495 Pope Zachary .. in a Letter of his to the French, which you your self quote. **1710** STEELE *Tatler* No. 197 ¶6 He shall quote and recite one Author against another. **1781** WILKES in Boswell *Johnson* 8 May, Upon the continent they all quote the Vulgate Bible. Shakspeare is chiefly quoted here. **1849** MACAULAY *Hist. Eng.* iii. I. 391 One series .. will be occasionally quoted in the course of this work. **1871** JOWETT *Plato* IV. 61 He still quotes the poets. **1953** A. CHRISTIE *Pocket Full of Rye* ii. 12 Of course, I *may* be wrong—don't quote me, for Heaven's sake. **1965** *Word Study* Apr. 6/2 We might happen to have such a quotation from Public Enemy No. 1, and we wouldn't hesitate to quote him. **1973** *Times* 15 Feb. 18/5 They won't be here at all in three years time. And you can quote me on that too. **1976** 'R. MACDONALD' *Blue Hammer* xviii. 150 'Who had reason to kill him?' 'I don't know. His wife, perhaps... Don't quote me, but I wouldn't put it past her.'

4. a. To copy out or repeat (a passage, statement, etc.) from a book, document, speech, etc., with some indication that one is giving the words of another (unless this would otherwise be known). Also *transf.*, of a composer or musical composition: to reproduce or repeat (a passage or tune that forms part of another piece of music).

a **1680** BUTLER *Upon Plagiaries* 102 'Twas counted learning once .. what men understood by rote, By as implicit sense to quote. **1712** ADDISON *Spect.* No. 333 ¶1, I omitted quoting these passages in my Observations on the former books. **1771** *Junius Lett.* liv. 283 He quotes verses without mercy. **1860** TYNDALL *Glac.* II. xxvii. 378, I quote the following passage from this paper. **1878** R. W. DALE *Lect. Preach.* v. 142 The rest of the sermon it is unnecessary to quote. **1946** E. BLOM *Everyman's Dict. Mus.* 138/1 Dies irae. The 2nd section of the Requiem Mass, orig[inally] assoc[iated] with a distinct plainsong theme which has been frequently used or quoted by var[ious] comp[oser]s. **1954** *Grove's Dict. Mus.* (ed. 5) II. 955/1 Var. XIII [of the 'Enigma Variations'] quotes from Mendelssohn's 'Calm Sea and Prosperous Voyage' Overture. **1975** R. S. GOLD *Jazz Talk* 213 *Quote*, .. of a vocalist or soloing instrumentalist to insert a phrase from another tune into the one being played.

b. *absol.* To make quotations (*from* a book, author, etc.).

1787 BURNS *Extempore in Crt. Session*, He clench'd his pamphlets .. He quoted and he hinted. **1827** LYTTON *Pelham* xiv, [He] had a peculiar art of quoting from each author he reviewed. **1874** GREEN *Short Hist.* iii. §5. 142 He .. quotes largely from state documents, .. and exchequer rolls.

c. ***quote .. unquote***: a formula used in dictation to introduce and terminate a quotation. Freq. *transf.*, in speech or writing, introducing and terminating words quoted (or ironically imagined to be quoted) from the speech or writing of another.

1935 E. E. CUMMINGS *Let.* 3 Oct. (1969) 145 The Isful ubiquitous wasless&-shallbeless quote scrotumtightening unquote omnivorously eternal thalassa pelagas or Ocean. **1950** 'S. RANSOME' *Deadly Miss Ashley* xvii. 198 She says, quote, 'What girl wouldn't?' unquote. **1956** *Times* 5 Dec. 1/5 (Advt.), Today, America, you sure are quote in the Big Time unquote. **1958** B. HAMILTON *Too Much of Water* xi. 245 But he did have, quote, a jolly good reason for bumping off one special person, unquote. **1961** P. USTINOV *Loser* viii. 140 He expressed the personal opinion that the picture was quote great for America unquote. **1973** D. ROBINSON *Rotten with Honour* 8 The British .. see too many people like you in London... East Germans, Bulgarians, and Rumanians, all of them quote diplomats unquote.

II. † **5. a.** To write down; to make a note or record of, set down, mention in writing. *Obs.*

1573 TUSSER *Husb.* (1878) 9 New lessons then I noted, and some of them I coted. **1589** GREENE *Menaphon* (Arb.) 76 Her browes are pretie tables of conceate, Where Love his records of delight doth quoate. **1612** WEBSTER *White Devil* Wks. (Rtldg.) 27/2 It is reported you possess a book Wherein you have quoted by intelligence The names of all offenders. *a* **1635** NAUNTON *Fragm. Reg.* (Arb.) 34 It is already quoted, they were such as awakened her spirits.

fig. **1595** SHAKS. *John* IV. ii. 222 A fellow by the hand of Nature mark'd, Quoted, and sign'd to do a deede of shame. **1599** MIDDLETON *Micro-cynicon* III, Fine madam Tiptoes .. That quotes her paces in characters down.

† **b.** To take mental note of; to notice, observe, mark, scrutinize. *Obs.*

1588 SHAKS. *Tit. A.* IV. i. 50 Note how she quotes the leaues. **1592** —— *Rom. & Jul.* I. iv. 31 What care I What curious eye doth quote deformities. **1607** BEAUMONT *Woman Hater* III. iii, I'll quote him to a tittle, let him speak wisely, and plainly, .. or I shall crush him. **1640** GENT *Knave in Gr.* I. i. B iij, My knowledge coated, and all Italy spoke of a Damosell called Cornelia.

absol. **1573** TUSSER *Husb.* (1878) 137 Who minds to cote, vpon this note, may easily find ynough. **1605** B. JONSON *Volpone* II. i, To obserue, To quote, to learne the language, and so forth.

† **c.** To mention in speaking. *Obs. rare*$^{-1}$.

1612 *Pasquil's Night-Cap* (1877) 23 Here could I cote a rabble of those wiues, That you would wonder but to heare them nam'd.

6. † **a.** To regard, look on, take *as* something; to note, set down (a person or thing) *for* something; to speak of, mention, bring forward *for* having done something. *Obs.*

1588 SHAKS. *L.L.L.* IV. iii. 87 Her Amber haires for foule hath amber coted. *Ibid.* V. ii. 796 Our letters .. shew'd much more then Iest... *Rosa.* We did not coat them so. **1601** —— *All's Well* V. iii. 205 He's quoted for a most perfidious slaue. *a* **1635** NAUNTON *Fragm. Reg.* (Arb.) 42 They quote him for a person that loved to stand too much alone. **1691** T. H[ALE] *Acc. New Invent.* p. xxxiii, Dr. Robert Wood .. hath not been by any Author .. so much as quoted for his illuminating us. **1722** DE FOE *Relig. Courtsh.* I. ii. (1840) 61 We can't quote our fathers for anything that is fit to be named.

b. To bring forward, adduce, allege, cite *as* an instance of or *as* being something.

1806–7 J. BERESFORD *Miseries Hum. Life* (1826) I. Introd., As I will evidence in a few instances already quoted. **1855** BAIN *Senses & Int.* II. i. §6 (1864) 77 No impression from without can be quoted as originating this contraction. **1858** W. PORTER *Knts. Malta* 277 This has, in more than one case, been quoted as an excuse. **1863** COWDEN CLARKE *Shaks. Char.* vii. 173 Few instances of concentrated disdain could be quoted as more pungent.

7. To state the price of (a commodity). Also, to name a racehorse *at* specified odds; *absol.* or with a person as *obj.*, to give (someone) a quotation for goods or services.

1865 *Atlantic Monthly* May 575/1 The artist is like the stock which is to be quoted at the board and thrown upon the market. **1866** ROGERS *Agric. & Prices* I. xx. 493 There are entries of shingle-nails, though no shingles are quoted. **1884** *Law Rep.* 9 *App. Cases* 7 The Leeds securities had been quoted, and to a large amount sold, upon the .. exchanges. **1888** *Economist* (Chicago) 3 Nov. 4/3 The effect of quoting Gas Trust upon the ticker .. has been to stimulate trade in this stock here. **1934** *Collier's* 11 Aug. 48/2 Black Gold was quoted at 200 to 1 for the Coffroth event. **1938** *Times* 29 Sept. 19/1 War Loan .. was being quoted 95 middle in inter-office dealings. **1971** *Timber Trades Jrnl.* 14 Aug. 71 (Advt.), Your machines .. reconditioned, re-installed... Let us quote you.

Hence **'quoted** *ppl. a.* **quo'tee**, one who is quoted. **'quoteless** *a.*, 'that cannot be quoted' (Wright). **'quoteworthy** *a.*, worthy of being quoted. **'quoting** *vbl. sb.* **'quotingly** *adv.*

1608 MIDDLETON *Mad World* I. ii, Let him find Some book lie open .. And *coted scripture. **1858** J. B. NORTON *Topics* 4 The perusal of quoted as well as original matter. **1861** *Sat. Rev.* 14 Dec. 600 The quoted prices merely tell us that buyers or sellers .. are on the increase. **1813** W. S. WALKER *Let. to Sir Walter Scott* in *N. & Q.* (1961) Jan. 19/2 You see I am addicted to comparisons, like your *quotee Fluellen. **1821** *Examiner* 461/1 Quotations of us between inverted commas without naming the quotee. **1926** *Eng. Jrnl.* May 395 The quotee protests. Professor Baker has asked that attention be called to a quotation by Professor Campbell .. which he feels does not present his meaning fairly. **1973** *Publishers' Weekly* 7 May 19/2 Ruland was not a manufactured quotee. **1870** F. JACOX *Rec. Recluse* II. xii. 241 [His] description .. is curious, and (to coin a phrase) *quoteworthy. **1580** LYLY *Euphues* (Arb.) 320, I see thou art come .. from *coting of ye Scriptures to courting with Ladies. **1714** FORTESCUE-ALAND *Pref. Fortescue's Abs. & Lim. Mon.* 56 Like quoting of Dacier, for a Verse in Horace. **1657** J. SERGEANT *Schism Dispatch't* Post-scr., Their old method of talking preachingly, *quotingly and quibblingly.

quote, variant of QUOT *sb.*, WHOOT *v.*

quo'tennial, *a. rare*$^{-1}$. [f. L. *quotannis*, after *biennial*, etc.; cf. QUOTANNAL.] Yearly.

1878 SIMPSON *Sch. Shaks.* I. 60 Hugh Stucley was in this state of quotennial warfare with his cousin.

quoter (ˈkwəʊtə(r)). [f. QUOTE *v.* + -ER[1].] One who quotes.

1589 *Pasquil's Ret.* Biij, They are great quoters of common places. **1674** BOYLE *Excell. Theol.* II. v. 194 Small Tracts,..being preserv'd in such a quoter or abridger. *a* **1732** ATTERBURY (J.), I propose this passage entire, to take off the disguise which its quoter put upon it. **1846** LANDOR *Imag. Conv.* Wks. II. 26 A quoter is either ostentatious of his acquirements or doubtful of his cause. **1875** EMERSON *Lett. & Soc. Aims, Quot. & Orig.*, Next to the originator of a good sentence is the first quoter of it.

quoth (kwəʊθ), *v.* (*pa. t.*) Now *arch.* or *dial.* [Pa. t. of QUETHE *v.* to say.] Said.

1. Used with sbs., or pronouns of the first and third persons, to indicate that the words of a speaker are being repeated.

The vb. is always placed before the subject, and the clause is commonly inserted parenthetically towards the beginning of the words quoted, but may also precede or follow the whole sentence or speech.

α. 3 **cwað**, 3–4 **quað**, **quad**, (3 **quat**, **hwat**), 3–5 **quaþ**; 3 *pl.* **queþen**.

c **1200** *Vices & Virtues* 67 'Hlauerd,' cwað he, 'hwat mai ic don [etc.].' *c* **1250** *Gen. & Exod.* 1313 Quat abraham, 'god sal bi-sen [etc.].' *Ibid.* 3331 Quad moyses, 'loc! her nu bread.' *c* **1290** *S. Eng. Leg.* 432/41 'Leoue Moder,' queþen þe sones. *c* **1305** *Andrew* 33 in *E.E.P.* (1862) 99 Hou miȝte hit beo, quaþ þe Iustise, þat his wille were þerto. **1362** LANGL. *P. Pl.* A. I. 41 'A Madame Merci!' quaþ I 'me likeþ wel þi wordes.'

β. 3 *pl.* **quoðen**; 4 **quoþ**, **coþe**, **coth**, **cuth**, 4– **quoth**, (6 **qwoth**).

c **1250** *Gen. & Ex.* 2993 Quoðen ðo wiches clerkes 'ðis fortoken godes gastes is.' *a* **1300** *Cursor M.* 7575 (Cott.), þou es, coth golias, bot ded. **13..** *Gaw. & Gr. Knt.* 776 'Now bone hostel' coþe þe burne. **1508** DUNBAR *Tua mariit wemen* 161 To speik, quoth scho, I sall nought spar. **1581** NOWELL & DAY in *Confer.* I. (1583) Eiiij b, The fyre (quoth wee) hathe heate and lyght. **1655** FULLER *Ch. Hist.* III. vii. §6 No, Quoth the King, I will not be both party and judg. *c* **1705** POPE *Jan. & May* 222 'I say,' quoth he, 'by heav'n the man's to blame.' **1782** COWPER *John Gilpin* 25 Quoth Mrs. Gilpin, 'That's well said'. **1829** HOOD *Eng. Aram* xiii, 'And well' quoth he, 'I know for truth.' **1838** LYTTON *Alice* 146 'I know no man I respect more than Maltravers,' quoth the admiral. **1884** BROWNING *Ferishtah's Fancies, Mihrab Shah* I Quoth an inquirer, 'Praise the Merciful!'

γ. 4 **quot**, **cod**, 4–7 **quod** (the prevailing form *c* 1350–1550).

13.. *Cursor M.* 5005 (Gött.), 'Say me,' quot iacob, 'hou es þis?' *Ibid.* 19311 (Edinb.) 'Lauerdingis, it es selcuþe,' cod þai. **1362** LANGL. *P. Pl.* A. II. 5 'Loke on þe lufthond,' quod heo 'and seo wher [he] stondeþ.' *c* **1420** *Sir Amadace* (Camd.) xxxviii, Quod the quite knyȝte, 'Quat mon is this?' *c* **1470** HENRY *Wallace* VI. 133 'Quhom scornys thow?' quod Wallace, 'quha lerd the?' **1513** DOUGLAS *Æneis* VIII. Prol. 122 Quod I, Lovne, thou leis. **1549** COVERDALE etc. *Erasm. Par. 1 Tim.* 2, I haue not chosen (quod he) out of an other mannes flocke. *c* **1620** A. HUME *Brit. Tongue* (1865) 18 Be quhat reason? quod the Doctour.

δ. 5 **quo**, 6 **ko**, **ka**, 8 *Sc.* **co'**, 8–9 **quo'**.

c **1450** *Merlin* 33 'In feith,' quo the oon, 'I sholde suffer grete myschef er he had eny harm.' *a* **1553** UDALL *Royster D.* III. iii. (Arb.) 44 Bawawe what ye say (ko I)..Nay I feare him not (ko she) **1756** TOLDERVY *Hist. 2 Orphans* I. 39 Marry (quo' she) I think it is the province of our elder brother. *a* **1774** FERGUSSON *Iron Kirk Bell* Poems (1845) 44 Quo' he..'This bell o'mine's a trick'. **1818** SCOTT *Rob Roy* xxiv, Whae's Mr. Robert Campbell, quo' he? **1893** CROCKETT *Stickit Minister* 127 'Horse or mule,' quo' she [etc.].

†**b.** Used at the end of a piece to introduce the name of the author. *Obs.* (Chiefly *Sc.*)

a **1500** *King's Quair* (S.T.S.) 48 Explicit, &c. Quod Jacobus Primus. **1508** DUNBAR *Lament* *101 Quod Dunbar quhen he was seik. *c* **1550** *Lusty Juventus.* Finis. Quod R. Weuer. **1583** *Satir. Poems Reform.* xlv. *118 Finis. Quod R. S. [**1788** BURNS *Friars Carse* 55 Quod the Beadsman of Nith-side.]

†**2.** Used interrogatively with a pronoun of the second person, with the same force as QUOTHA. *Obs.*

The form *quothee* may be a var. of QUOTHA.

a **1553** UDALL *Royster D.* I. ii. (Arb.) 17 Enamoured, quod you?.. Enamoured ka? *Ibid.* III. iv. 54 Scribler (ko you). **1573** *New Custom* I. ii, Primitiue Constitution (quodes stowe) as much as my sleeve! **1583** STUBBES *Anat. Abus.* II. (1882) 12 Rich, quoth you? They are rich indeede toward the deuill and the world. *a* **1600** *Grim, the Collier of Croydon* II. iv. (1662) 30 As it falls! quoth ye, marry a foul fall is it. **1681** T. FLATMAN *Heraclitus Ridens* No. 5 (1713) I. 28 *Earn* ..And what Trade do they intend to drive? *Jest.* What Trade, quothee?

¶ Hence (erroneously) ˈ**quothing**, saying.

1864 SIR F. PALGRAVE *Norm. & Eng.* III. 402 The owner had the power of transmitting the possession to an heir by bequest, by quothing or speaking forth the name of his intended successor to the lord.

quotha (ˈkwəʊθə), *int.* Now *arch.* Also 6 **catha**, **quod a**, **quodha**. [For *quoth he* (see A *pron.*).] The phrase 'said he?', used with contemptuous or sarcastic force in repeating a word or phrase used by another; hence = indeed! forsooth!

1519 *Interl. Four Elem.* (Percy Soc.) 24 Thre course dysshes, quod a. **1528** *Rede me*, etc. (Arb.) 86 *Wat.* Hath Christ amonge theym no place? *Jef.* Christ catha? *c* **1550** *Lusty Juventus* Cii b, Lawfull, quodha, a, foole, foole. **1600** HEYWOOD *1st Pt. Edw. IV* Wks. 1874 I. 33 Forbid, quotha? I, in good sadness. **1680** DRYDEN *Span. Friar* III. ii, A novice quotha! you would make a novice of me too, if you could. **1773** GOLDSM. *Stoops to Conq.* I. i, Learning, quotha! a mere composition of tricks and mischief. **1835** WILLIS *Pencillings* II. xliii. 38 The 'fickle moon,' quotha! I wish my friends were half as constant. **1884** BROWNING *Ferishtah's Fancies, Mihrab Shah* 99 Attributes, quotha? Here's poor flesh and blood. **1917** W. OWEN *Let.* 4 Feb. (1967) 432 Distaste? Distaste, Quotha? **1958** L. DURRELL *Mountolive* v. 111 A fellow-romantic quotha!

†**quothe, quoath**, obs. varr. COTHE *v.* to faint.

1567 GOLDING *Ovid's Met.* v. (1593) 107 He quothing as he stood Did looke about where Atys lay. *Ibid.* VII. 179 She quoath'd, and with her bloud Her little strength did fade.

quothernicke: see COTHURNIC.

‖**quot homines tot sententiae** (kwɒt ˈhɒmɪneɪz tɒt sɛnˈtɛntɪaɪ). [L.] An observation on the diversity of opinions, deriving from Terence *Phormio* II. iv. 14 *quot homines tot sententiae*: *suus cuique mos* 'there are as many opinions as there are men: to each his own way'.

1539 R. TAVERNER tr. *Erasmus's Proverbes or Adagies* f. xiii, Quot homines, tot sentenciæ. So many heades, so many iudgementes. **1575** G. GASCOIGNE *Certayne Notes of Instruction concerning Making of Verse or Ryme in English*, And therwithall I pray you consider that *Quot homines, tot Sententiæ*, especially in Poetrie. **1602** W. WATSON *Quodlibeticall Questions concerning Relig. & State* 343 They follow each one of them their owne priuate foule spirits of deceit and error, & so *quot homines tot sententiæ*, So many men so many minds. **1869** *Fraser's Mag.* LXXX. 68/1 Here all is to be pleasure. The opinions as to what is pleasure vary as a matter of course. *Quot homines tot sententiæ.* **1969** *Listener* 13 Nov. 680/2 A visitor from another planet might well have marvelled at the fertility of the human race in generating opinion—*quot homines tot sententiae* with a vengeance. **1975** *Times* 13 Nov. 17/6 No one has ever agreed entirely about Kipling; *Quot homines, tot sententiae.*

†**quoˈtidial**, *a. Obs.* In 6 cotidial, -yall, 7 quotidiall. [f. L. *cot-*, *quotīdiē* daily + -AL[1].] Daily.

1502 ARNOLDE *Chron.* (1811) 125 Mekly besecheth..your cotidial oratur. **1540** BOORDE *The boke for to Lerne* Cj b, Many other cotidyall expences. **1609** W. M. *Man in Moone* Dij b, Deuoting your selfe to quotidiall daliance.

†**quoˈtidially**, *adv. Obs.* Also 5–6 cotidi-, 6 cotydy-. [f. as prec. + -LY[2].] Day by day.

c **1430** LYDG. *Min. Poems* (Percy Soc.) 63 The monke.. thought he wolde..Cotidially withe hem only oure lady please. **1542** BOORDE *Dyetary* x. (1870) 226 Cotydyally remembryng your bountyful goodnes. **1547** —— *Brev. Health* cxiv. 43 Then cotidially..use stufes wet and dry. **1623** COCKERAM II, *Continually*, Sempeternally,.. Quotidially.

quotidian (kwəʊˈtɪdɪən), *a.* and *sb.* Forms: 4, 6 **cotidien**, (4 **-ene**); 4–6 **cotidian**, **-ane**, (5 **-yan**, **cotydian**, **-yan**, 6 **-yane**); 4– **quotidian**, (6 **-ane**, **-ene**, **quotydian**). [a. OF. *cotidien*, *-ian* (13th c., mod.F. *quotidien*), or ad. L. *cot-*, *quotīdiān-us*, f. *cot-*, *quotīdiē* every day, daily.]

A. *adj.* **1. a.** Of things, acts, etc.: Of or pertaining to every day; daily.

c **1380** WYCLIF *Wks.* (1880) 62 ȝif þei preien, þat is.. comunly for offrynge & cotidian distribucion. **1406** HOCCLEVE *La Male Regle* 25 My grief and bisy smert cotidian. **1432–50** tr. *Higden* (Rolls) V. 307 He made the preface quotidian. **1483** CAXTON *Gold. Leg.* 274 b/2 [A] cotidyan fornays is oure tonge humayne. **1513** BRADSHAW *St. Werburge* I. xx. 5 The cotydyane labours her body to chastyce. **1550** VERON *Godly Sayings* (ed. Daniel) 55 Though your sinnes be daily and quotidian, let not them be deadly. **1603** HARSNET *Pop. Impost.* xxiii. 158 A Quotidian imaginarie oblation of a Sacrifice. **1635** QUARLES *Embl.* I. xi. (1718) 45 And brazen lungs belch forth quotidian fire. *a* **1711** KEN *Hymns Evang.* Poet. Wks. 1721 I. 29 Thence our Quotidian Raptures were begun. **1849** LONGFELLOW *Kavanagh* xi. 53 Five cats..to receive their quotidian morning's meal. **1861** THACKERAY *Philip* xvi, Every man who wishes to succeed at the bar..must know the quotidian history of his country.

b. *spec.* of an intermittent fever or ague, recurring every day. Cf. B. 1.

In early use placed after the sb.; cf. QUARTAN.

1340 HAMPOLE *Pr. Consc.* 2987 Som for pride..Sal haf.. a fever cotidiene. **1390** GOWER *Conf.* II. 142 A Fievere it is cotidian, Which every day wol come aboute. **1530** PALSGR. 209/1 Cotidien axes, *fievre quotidienne.* **1561** HOLLYBUSH *Hom. Apoth.* 41 b, Of the dayly ague or fever quotidiane. **1656** RIDGLEY *Pract. Physick* 37 In chronical diseases, as Quartane and Quotidian diseases. **1718** POPE *Let. to R. Digby* 31 Mar., That spirit..which I take to be as familiar to you as a quotidian ague. **1876** tr. *Wagner's Gen. Pathol.* (ed. 6) 17 If the attack of fever returns every day we have what is called a Quotidian rhythm or type.

fig. *a* **1548** HALL *Chron., Hen. VI* 177 b, This noble realme ..shall never be unbuckeled from her quotidian fever. **1663** COWLEY *Verses & Ess., Obscurity*, We expose our life to a Quotidian Ague of frigid impertinencies.

transf. **1723** COWPER in Ld. Campbell *Chancellors* (1857) V. cxvii. 343 John's drunkenness seems a tertian..except that on Friday it proved quotidian.

2. Of persons: Performing some act, or sustaining some character, daily. *rare.*

1456 SIR G. HAYE *Law Arms* (S.T.S.) 152 Sa that he be wount..to be cotidiane at Goddis service. **1618** BOLTON *Florus* I. xi. (1636) 31 The Æqui and Volscians were..(as I may call them) quotidian enemies. **1714** J. WALKER *Suffer. Clergy* Pref. 37 The weekly writers (and therefore much more the diurnal or quotidian hirelings).

3. Of an everyday character; ordinary, commonplace, trivial.

1461–83 *Liber Niger* in *Househ. Ord.* (1790) 61 Not [to] trouble the seyde soveraynes..in smalle accustomed and cotidyan thinges and questions. **1534** WHITINTON *Tullyes Offices* I. (1540) 59 Tully treateth of two maner of speches, the one after the rhetoricyen eloquent, the other quotydian and vulgare. **1625** W. B. *True School War* 11 So ordinarie and so quotidian procurements of wantonnesse. **1665** J. SPENCER *Vulg. Proph.* 53 Common and quotidian thoughts are beneath the grace of a Verse. *a* **1763** SHENSTONE *Economy* I. 149 To scorn quotidian scenes, to spurn the bliss Of vulgar minds. **1816** W. TAYLOR in *Monthly Mag.* XLII. 423 This (adds Wieland) is very quotidian scepticism. **1837** CARLYLE *Fr. Rev.* III. II. viii, Pastry-cooks, coffee-sellers, milkmen sing out their trivial quotidian cries. **1978** *Studies in Eng. Lit.: Eng. Number* (Tokyo) 121 Malory..omits many of the 'quotidian' actions of chivalric life.

B. *sb.* **1.** A quotidian fever or ague.

a **1400** *Stockh. Medical MS.* ii. 50 in *Anglia* XVIII. 309 þat coueryth þe cotidyan mythilyke. *c* **1400** *Rom. Rose* 2401 Cotidien, ne quarteyne, It is not so ful of peyne. *c* **1491** *Chast. Goddes Chyld.* 21 The fyrst feuere is callid a cotydian. **1547** BOORDE *Brev. Health* cxxxvii. 50 b, In Englyshe it is named a quotidiane the which doth infest a man every daye. **1663** BOYLE *Usef. Exp. Nat. Philos.* II. v. ix. 211, I myself was strangely cured of a violent quotidian. **1732** ARBUTHNOT *Rules of Diet* 324 Tertians sometimes redouble their Paroxysms so as to appear like Quotidians. **1822–34** *Good's Stud. Med.* (ed. 4) I. 607 The quotidian has a longer interval than the tertian.

fig. **1430–40** LYDG. *Bochas* IX. xxxviii. (1554) 217 Trusting ..your liberal largesse Of thys quotidian shall releuen me. **1600** SHAKS. *A.Y.L.* III. ii. 383 He seemes to haue the Quotidian of Loue vpon him. **1643** MILTON *Divorce* II. xvi. Wks. (1847) 150/1 A quotidian of sorrow and discontent in his house.

2. A daily allowance or portion. *rare.*

1828 CAROLINE FRY *Scripture Reader's Guide* vii. 87 The Psalms are..more mechanically chosen for our quotidian of reading than any other part of Scripture. **1894** C. M. CHURCH *Chapt. Early Hist. Church of Wells*, Bishop Jocelin ..increases the quotidians to all members of the Church of St. Andrew in Wells.

So †**quoˈtidianary** *a.* (*obs. rare*[−1]); **quoˈtidianism**.

1719 *Free-thinker* No. 139 ¶3 Quotidianary Words and Actions..do not rise above the Powers of Mechanism. **1920** A. HUXLEY *Limbo* 261 'It is our cheap press. The ephemeral overwhelms the permanent, the classical.' 'This journalism,' I agreed, 'or call it rather this piddling quotidianism, is the curse of our age.'

quoˈtidianly, *adv. rare.* [+ -LY[2].] Daily.

1447 BOKENHAM *Seyntys* (Roxb.) 180 Ryht cotydyanly Aungelys lyftyn sevene sythys up me. *c* **1470** HARDING *Chron.* LXXIV. vi, Princes..That auentures then sought cotidianly. **1652** KIRKMAN *Clerio & Lozia* 121 Consolate a Lover who dyeth quotidianly. **1840** *Tait's Mag.* VII. 384 Epics..are quotidianly placed before us.

†**quotidiˈarian.** *nonce-wd.* [f. L. *quotīdiē* (see QUOTIDIAN), as rendering of Gr. ἐφημερευτής.] A daily official (among the Essenes).

a **1641** BP. MOUNTAGU *Acts & Mon.* (1642) 434 At warning given by one whom they call *Ephemereutes* or *Quotidiarian* they all meet together.

quotient (ˈkwəʊʃənt). Forms: 5 **quocient**, (**quocyens**), 6– **quotient**. [f. L. *quotiens* how many times, how often (f. *quot* how many), erron. taken as a ppl. stem in *-ent*; cf. F. *quotient* (earlier *quotiens*), It. *quoziente*, Sp. *quociente*.]

1. *Math.* **a.** The result obtained by dividing one arithmetical or algebraic quantity by another; the number of times one number is contained in another as ascertained by division.

14.. *Mann. & Househ. Exp.* (Roxb.) 439 Owt of that nowmber take as many tymes clx. as ye may, beyinge for euery tyme a quocyens. *c* **1430** *Art Nombryng* (E.E.T.S.) 12 The nombre that shewith þe quocient. **1542** RECORDE *Gr. Artes* 129 Then I seke howe often the diuisor maye be founde in the diuident, and that I fynde 3 tymes, then set I 3 in the thyrde lyne for the quotient. **1614** T. BEDWELL *Nat. Geom. Numbers* i. 8 The quotients of 60, by 1, 2, 3,..are 60, 30, 20. **1695** ALINGHAM *Geom. Epit.* 73 If..I divide 54 by 3 the quotient is 18. **1727–41** CHAMBERS *Cycl.* s.v. *Division*, For 3 being only contained twice in 8, the last number in the quotient will be 2. **1840** LARDNER *Geom.* 124 Multiply *b* by *c* and divide the product by *a*, and the quotient will be *d*. **1884** A. PAUL *Hist. Reform* ii. 29 The total was to be divided by 558, and the quotient to be deemed the proportion of voters entitled to elect one member.

b. *attrib.*, as ***quotient figure***, ***line***, ***number***, ***ring***; ***quotient representation*** (see quot. 1884 above); **quotient group** = *factor group* s.v. FACTOR *sb.* 9.

c **1430** *Art Nombryng* (E.E.T.S.) 12 Above þat figure..me most sette a cifre in ordre of the nombre quocient. **1542** RECORDE *Gr. Artes* 48 b, That is called the quotiente numbre. **1557** —— *Whetst.* Kij, The roote .2. I sette behind the quotiente line. **1709** J. WARD *Introd. Math.* I. xi. §7 (1734) 139 You must Increase..the Divisor with Thrice the Quotient Figure. **1889** *Universal Rev.* 7 Jan., Equal electoral districts, quotient representation of the population,..are a deduction from the democratic principle. **1893** *Bull. N.Y. Math. Soc.* III. 74 The quotient-group of any two consecutive groups in the series of composition of any group is a simple group. **1911** W. BURNSIDE *Theory of Groups of Finite Order* (ed. 2) iii. 39 Herr Hölder has introduced the symbol *G*/*H* to represent this group; he calls it the quotient of *G* by *H*, and a factor-group of *G*. **1958** R. V. ANDREE *Mod. Abstract Algebra* iv. 101 The order of the quotient group is the order of *G* divided by the order of *H*, providing *G* is finite. *Ibid.* viii. 188 The term *quotient ring* is also used because of the similarity to the concept of quotient groups. **1965** PATTERSON & RUTHERFORD *Elem. Abstract Algebra* iii. 101 If *S* is an ideal in the ring *R*.. The set of all cosets of *S* in *R* is a ring:..this is called the..quotient ring of *R* by *S*. **1972** F. J. BUDDEN *Fascination of Groups* xxi. 409 A group which resolves into a succession of *cyclic* quotient groups in this way is called a 'soluble' group.

†**2. a.** = QUOTUM. *Obs. rare.*

1621 Bp. Mountagu *Diatribæ* 511 The first of their Apples were offered to other gods: and for the quotient, it was a Tenth. **1641** H. L'Estrange *God's Sabbath* 63 The fourth Commandment..declareth also his will concerning the quotient..so that one [day] in a week he must have.

†**b.** Number, total. *Obs. rare*⁻¹.

1659 T. Pecke *Parnassi Puerp.* 82 God is but One. Hells Quotient, none assign.

'**quotientive**, *a. rare*⁻¹. [f. as prec. + -ive.] Indicating how often.

1871 *Public Sch. Lat. Gram.* 73 Quotientive Adverbs,.. answering the question Quoties, how often?

quotiety (kwəʊ'taɪətɪ). [f. L. *quot* how many, on anal. of words in *-iety*.] Condition in respect of number; relative frequency.

1862 Latham *Compar. Philol.* 731 One, two, three, and the other numerals convey the attribute of Quotiety, or Howmanyness.

quoting, quotingly: see quote *v.*

quotity ('kwɒtɪtɪ). *rare.* [a. F. *quotité* (16th c.) or f. L. *quot* how many, *quot-us* of what number or amount (see quota) + -ity. Cf. *quantity*.]

1. = quotum.

1613 F. Robarts *Revenue Gosp.* 128 What needeth this contending for the quotity or determinate tenth? **1894** *Jrnl. R. Agric. Soc.* June 360 It is not a fixed quantity..but a fixed quotity of produce.

2. A certain number (*of* individuals, etc.).

1837 Carlyle *Fr. Rev.* I. iv. ii, These are the thrice-famed 'Brigands': an actual existing quotity of persons. **1858** —— *Fredk. Gt.* I. v. vi. 600 Assisting Prussia..with a like quotity of thousands.

quott(ed: see quot *pa. pple.*

†**quotto**, obs. form of coaita.

1667 G. Warren *Surinam* 11 The inhabitants of the trees are Baboons, Quottoes, Monkeys [etc.].

‖**quotum** ('kwəʊtəm). [L., neut. sing. of *quotus*: see quota.] A number or quantity considered in its proportional relationship to a larger number or amount of which it forms part; a quota.

a **1660** Hammond *Wks.* (1674) I. 89 The exact proportion or *quotum*, I cannot prescribe you, the Scripture.. intimating that there is no set proportion to be defined. **1696** Bp. Patrick *Comm. Exodus* xiv. (1697) 262 Observing that Seventh Day..not for the quotum of one Day in Seven.. but for the designation of that day. *a* **1716** Blackall *Wks.* (1723) I. 394 Not a greater Sum..than a poorer Man..may spare to give away with as little Inconvenience..as the richer Man can give away his larger quotum. **1859** Max Müller *Sc. Lang.* Ser. i. (1864) 382 The number of names which are really formed by an imitation of sound, dwindle down to a very small quotum if cross-examined by the comparative philologist. **1881** A. Rimmer *Old Country Towns* 172 The quotum [of ships] Hythe had to furnish.

†**quotuple.** *Obs. rare*⁻¹. [f. L. *quot* how many, after *quadruple*, etc.] = 'What multiple'.

a **1696** Scarburgh *Euclid* v. i. (1705) 201, I say, that Quotuple AB is of E, Totuple shall AB, CD together, be of E, F together.

quouk, obs. Sc. pa. t. quake *v.*

†**quow**, obs. Sc. form of cow *sb.*¹

1583 *Satir. Poems Reform.* xlv. 715 He had na mair grace ..Nor it had bene ane hieland quow.

quow, obs. form of how *adv.*

‖**quo warranto** (kwəʊ wɒ'ræntəʊ), *sb.* [Med.L. 'by what warrant'.] A King's Bench writ formerly in use, by which a person or persons were called upon to show by what warrant he or they held, claimed, or exercised an office or franchise.

[**1292** Britton i. xx. §2 Nos brefs..del *Quo warranto.*] **1535** tr. *Littleton's Nat. Brev.* 211 (Stanf.) A wryt de Quo warranto. **1555** in W. H. Turner *Select. Rec. Oxford* 224 To make answere to the Quo Warranto. **1621** Elsing *Debates Ho. Lords* (1870) 5 He conceived noe charge against Yelverton for theis 3201 quo warrantos. **1681** Luttrell *Brief Rel.* (1857) I. 153 A writt of quo warranto is delivered to the sheriffs of London against the charter of the citty. *a* **1734** R. North *Life of Lord Keeper North* (1742) 129 That famous Practice..of *Quo Warranto's* against some Corporations. **1805** Jeffrey in *Edin. Rev.* VI. 19 We would also move for a *Quo Warranto* against the spirits of the river and the mountain.

Hence †**quo wa'rranto** *v.*, in *pass.*, to be served with a writ of *quo warranto*. *Obs.*

1690 J. Palmer in *Andros Tracts* I 60 It can..render them liable to be questioned and *Quo warranto'd* for their Malefesance. **1691** C. Mather *ibid.* II. 331 Nor could you have proceeded again as formerly upon your charter, without being quo-warrantoed.

quowke, obs. Sc. pa. t. quake *v.*

quoy, Sc. variant of quey, heifer.

quoy(e, obs. ff. coy *a.* and *v.*¹

†**quoy-duck**, obs. form of coy-duck.

1602 Boys *Wks.* 389 The best trick yᵉ fouler hath is to bring game to his snare by a stale or quoy duck.

quoyl(e, obs. ff. coil *sb.*², *sb.*³

quoyn(e, obs. ff. coin, coyn, quoin.

quoynt(e, quoyntaunce, obs. ff. quaint *a.*, quaintance.

quoyt(e, obs. ff. quoit.

†**quoz.** *Obs.* [App. a fanciful formation: cf. quiz.] **a.** A queer or absurd person or thing (also as *pl.*). **b.** Used as an ejaculation or retort, to express incredulity, contempt, etc.

1790 *Bystander* 93 Mr. World [the newspaper] might retort that Mr. Herald was a Quoz, and a low print. **1796** Mad. D'Arblay *Camilla* vii. xiii. 200 Upon my honour,.. the quoz of the present season are beyond what a man could have hoped to see! **1802** in *Spirit Pub. Jrnls.* VI. 197 At length it was announced, that *Pic-Nic*, like *Quoz*, which was chalked some years ago on windows and doors, really meant nothing. **1841** C. Mackay *Mem. Pop. Delus.* I. 325 Many years ago the favourite phrase (for, though but a monosyllable, it was a phrase in itself) was Quoz.

Quran, Qur'an, Qur(')anic. A frequent esp. scholarly variant spelling of Koran¹, Koranic *a.* Cf Q.

1876 T. P. Hughes in A. Qâdir *Qurán, Transl. into Urdu Language* p. iii, There is no *authorized* translation of the Qurán in any language. **1885** —— *Dict. Islam* 483/2 *Qur'ān* .., the sacred book of the Muhammadans. **1905** W. St. Clair Tisdall *Orig. Sources of Qur'ân* iii. 63 The *Source* of the rest of the Qur'ânic account of the murder is the legend in the *Pirqêy Rabbî Eli'ezer*. **1919** H. U. W. Stanton *Teaching of Qur'ān* 5 The best studies on quranic theology in English are the pamphlets by Rev. W. R. W. Gardner. **1931** *Times Lit. Suppl.* 11 June 459/2 The tales..vary from Qur'anic legends to popular stories of the most ribald and grotesque description. **1932** *Ibid.* 17 Mar. 185/1 He had forgotten the Quran and could not recite one of the suras. **1939** L. H. Gray *Foundations of Lang.* 363 *Arabic*, famous as the language of the Qur'ān. **1954** *Scott. Jrnl. Theol.* VII. 334 The non-expert will find this an eminently readable and absorbing book, and one that might well stimulate to a lasting interest in the Qur'an and the Islamic world. *Ibid.*, Again, the book is the fruit of a lifetime's devotion to Qur'anic studies. **1971** *Nigerian Jrnl. Islam* II. 45 Thus, the emphasis in the Quranic School is on the moral development of the child. **1972** *Computers & Humanities* VI. 195 Arabic, the native language of 100 million people, is also used by many more millions as the language of the Quran and Islamic Law. **1976** *Daily Tel.* 6 Apr. 11/3 Their loans have been supplemented by Qur'ans from the British Library's own collection. **1980** *Oxf. Diocesan Mag.* Feb. 9/1 The total restriction of women to their homes..has been a matter of social custom, not Quranic law.

qussyon, obs. form of cushion.

†**quu-**, obs. (chiefly early ME.) var. of qu- and wh-, as in *quuad* quoth, *quuam* whom, *quuan* when, *quuat* what, *quue* cue, *quuen* queen, *quuo* who, *quuor* where; also *quuow* how.

quuik, obs. Sc. pa. t. of quake *v.*

quurt, variant of quirt *v.*² *Obs.*

quy, obs. form of quey, why.

†**quy-**, a common ME. variant of qui-. Examples (exclusive of mere doublets of forms already given under qui-) are *quyach* queyock, *quyc(c)he* quetch, *quye* quey, *quylet* quelet, *quyn* whin, *quynce* quinsy, *quyndesyn*, *-dezim* quindecim, *quyner* coiner, *quynkill* quinkle, *quynnancy* quinsy, *quynnyble* quinible, *quynse* quince, *quynsine*, *-syn(n)e* quinzine, *quyntans* quaintance, *quyral* coral, *quyras* cuirass, *quyschile* whistle, *quysht* queest, *quysper* whisper, *quysseux*, *-ewes* cuisses, *quyteour*, *-er(e*, *-ure* quitter.

†**quye**, obs. form of coy *sb.*¹

1688 R. Holme *Armoury* ii. 312/1 A Decoy, vulgarly called a Quye, [is] a place made to take wild Fowl in.

†**quyn(e** obs. forms of queen *sb.*

1505 *Mem. Hen. VII* (Rolls) 248 Hit was saied that bothe the Kynge and the Quyn wold come by the see. *Ibid.* 249 In the liffe of the quyne.

†**quyne**, variant of coyn, quince. *Obs.*

c **1450** *Two Cookery-bks.* 69 Quynes bakyn. *c* **1532** Du Wes *Introd. Fr.* in *Palsgr.* 914 Quyne aple tre. **1575** [see coyn].

qv-, occasional ME. var. of qu- (and wh-), as in *qvan* when, *qvare*, *qvayr* quire, *qvarelle* quarrel. *qveise* quease, *qverel* quarrel, *qvycchyn*, *qvyhchyn* quetch, *qvysperyn* whisper, *qvytaunce* quittance, *qvytchyn* quetch, *qvyrlebone* whirlbone; etc.

So also **qvh-**, var. of quh-, as *qvhischen* = *whishen* cushion, *Qvhissonday* Whitsunday.

†**qw-**, freq. ME. (esp. northern) var. of qu- (and wh-), as *qwa* = *qua* who, *qwal* = *qual* whale, *qwarell* quarrel, etc. (see the forms with qu-). Also *qwaintan* quintain, *qwalester* chorister, *qwarto* whereto, *qwatteer* quarter, *qwaylle* whale, *qwe* whew, *qweasse* quease, *qweel* wheel, *qwelke* whelk, *qwenock* whinnock, *qweschyn*, *qweseyn* cushion, *qwinaci* quinsy, *qwissel* whistle, *qworle* whorl.

So **qwh-**, var. of quh-, as *qwhele* wheel, *qwhen* when, *qwhete* wheat, *qwhite* white, *qwhylum* whilom; etc. Also **qwy-**, var. of *quy-*, qui-, as *qwy(e* quey, *qwyce* quice, *qwych(e* which, *qwynne* whin, *qwynse* quinsy, *qwysschewes* cuisses, *qwyuer* quiver; etc. (See the forms with qui-.)

QWERT, QWERTY, qwerty (kwɜːt, kwɜːtɪ). Part of the series of letters that label the first row of letter keys on typewriters in English-speaking countries; also **qwert yuiop**, the full series in that row. Also (in form *qwerty*) used *attrib.* or as *adj.* to designate a keyboard or machine that incorporates this type of non-alphabetical lay-out.

1929 *Times Lit. Suppl.* 11 July 552/2 The 'qwerty' keyboard appears first on the Yost in 1887. **1961** *Courier-Mail* (Brisbane) 5 June (*heading*) 'QWERTS' girls are in demand. **1962** *Which?* Dec. 356/2 The keyboards of all the machines were laid out in the traditional—and irrational—pattern, sometimes called 'qwert yuiop', which gives the left hand a lot of work to do, and its little finger too big a share of that. **1967** *Crescendo* Dec. 15/1 As soon as I had the virgin sheet of paper threaded into my type-writer I discovered that I was at peace with the world. Not a single hostile thought came to mind. I wrote QWERT a couple of times and gazed at my brain-child. **1975** *Nature* 16 Oct. 556/1 Input is usually by Qwerty keyboard, either direct entry or off-line, using punched tape. **1976** *Times* 9 Nov. 16/7 Mutterings..are to be heard among non-French secretaries employed by the European Commission in Brussels over plans to introduce a standardized typewriter based on the French AZERTY keyboard... The Commission..points out that if English QWERTY machines had been chosen.. this decision would have been just as open to accusations of discrimination. Germans..operate QWERTZ machines, while Italians..prefer QZERTY.

qy., abbrev. of query.

1819 M. Edgeworth *Let.* 17 Apr. (1971) 195 We had been presented to the (Qy.) Duchess of Sussex. **1838** *Civil Eng. & Arch. Jrnl.* I. 390/1 Qy. Is this pitch the Trinidad asphalte?

R

R (ɑː(r)), the eighteenth letter of the modern and seventeenth of the ancient Roman alphabet, is derived through early Greek Ɽ, P from the Phoenician ᑫ, representing the twentieth letter of the early Semitic alphabet. In general the character denotes an open voiced consonant in the formation of which the point of the tongue approaches the palate a little way behind the teeth; in many languages this is accompanied by a vibration of the tongue, in which case the *r* is said to be 'trilled'. This trill is almost or altogether absent in the *r* of modern standard English, which moreover retains its consonantal value only when it precedes a vowel; in other positions it has been vocalized to an (ə-) sound, and even this is entirely lost after certain vowels. The earlier history of these sounds is somewhat obscure, as scholars differ in their views as to the formation of *r* in OE. times. In Scotland *r* is still strongly trilled in all positions, and other varieties of the sound are characteristic of certain districts, as the burred *r* of Northumberland and the reverted *r* of the south-west. By southern speakers *r* is frequently introduced in hiatus, esp. in the phrase *the idea(r) of*; in vulgar speech it is heard even in such forms as *draw(r)ing*.

In all periods of English, *r* has exercised a marked effect upon a preceding vowel. In OE., *e* and *a* before *r* + consonant became *eo*, *ea*, as in *steorfan* starve, *deorc* dark, *heorte* heart, *eorðe* earth; *hearm* harm, *wearp* warp. In late ME. and early mod.E. *er* usually became *ar*, *ear*, as in (*sterve*) starve, (*derk*) dark; (*herte*) heart, (*erthe*) earth, the date and extent of the change varying in different dialects. In a few cases (as *clerk*, *sergeant*, *Derby*) the spelling with *er* has been retained, while *ar* (ɑː) is pronounced. In mod.E. (prob. from about 1650) *e* (or *ea*) and *i* before *r* in close syllables have fallen together in one obscure vowel (ɜː), as in *berth*, *birth* (bɜːþ), *dearth* (dɜːþ), *dirt* (dɜːt), often not distinguished from the sound in *bur* (bɜː(r)), *burn* (bɜːn). The vowel-lengthening exemplified in these words is common to all cases in which *r* is not followed by a vowel, as *far* (fɑː(r)), *farm* (fɑːm), *for* (fɔː(r)), *horse* (hɔːs). The effect of *r* is also seen in the use of open vowels instead of the normal close ones, as in *care* (kɛə(r)), *here* (hɪə(r)), *moor* (mʊə(r)), *floor* (flɔə(r)) (these last two now frequently monophthongized (mɔː(r)), (flɔː(r))). In a few words the vowel may have been affected by a preceding *r*, as in *break* (breɪk), *great* (greɪt), *broad* (brɔːd).

OE. *r* usually represents Germanic *r*, but in some cases takes the place of Germ. *z* (Goth. *z* or *s*), as in *éare* ear (Goth. *ausô*), *mâra* more (Goth. *maiza*), *hord* hoard (Goth. *huzd*); hence the variation in verbal forms, as *léosan*, *loren*; *céosan*, *coren*. It was rarely dropped (as in *specan* to speak, for usual *sprecan*); but metathesis was frequent, and many of the forms resulting from this have been retained in the later language, as *beornan* to burn, *berstan* to burst, *hors* horse, *fryhtu* fright, North. *þirda* third. In some Scottish texts of the 15–16th c. there is a similar tendency to transpose *r* (as *trage* targe, *rehress* rehearse, *scruge* scourge), and it is sometimes neglected in rimes (as *large*: *age*).

Among the native words beginning with *r* in modern Eng. are a certain number which in OE. have initial *hr-*, as *hring* ring, *hræfn* raven, *hréod* reed. This *h* was usually written down to the close of the OE. period, but had probably been dropped in speech at a somewhat earlier date; in the northern Gospels it is often erroneously prefixed, as in *hræst* rest, *hreafere* reaver, *hrioppa* reap. On the other hand, *w* before *r* was retained so late (being still pronounced in some Scottish dialects) that confusion between *wr-* and *r-* is comparatively rare, chiefly occurring with the words *rack*, *wrack*, and *rap*, *wrap*.

I. 1. a. Illustrations of the literary use of the letter or its name.

c **1000** ÆLFRIC *Gram.* iii. (Z) 6 *Semivocales* syndon seofan: ..*r*, *s*, *x*. ? **1460** in *Archæologia* (1842) XXIX. 331 There was an V and thre arres to-gydre. *c* **1460** *Pol. Rel. & L. Poems* 2, iij ares for iij Richardes þat bene of noble fames. **1530** PALSGR. 34, R in the frenche tonge shalbe sounded as he is in latyn without any exception. **1599** H. BUTTES *Dyets drie Dinner* M viij b, Oysters..in those Moneths that have the letter R. in their names. **1636** B. JONSON *Eng. Gram.* (1640) 47, R is the Dogs Letter and hurreth in the sound. **1727–41** CHAMBERS *Cycl.* s.v., The Hebrews allow the *r* the privilege of a guttural; that is, they never double it. *a* **1854** CAROLINE B. SOUTHEY *Poet. Wks.* (1867) 21, R's whose lower limbs Beyond the upper bulged unseemly out. **1888** *Cornh. Mag.* Oct. 365 The letter R is not yet menaced with extinction in Washington.

b. ***the 'r' months***: Those months in the name of which an *r* occurs (September to April), during which oysters are in season (cf. quot. 1599 above). So also ***r-less month***.

1764 CHESTERF. *Lett.* cccxlvi, Here is no domestic news of changes and chances in the political world, which, like oysters, are only in season in the R months, when the Parliament sits. **1856** LOWELL *Lett.* (1894) I. iv. 301, I don't believe even the oysters found out what r-less month it was. **1888** *Pall Mall G.* 21 Sept. 7/2 The 'r' months have, however, opened at Brussels in the usual way; the Zeeland and Ostend oysters..made their welcome appearance.

c. Phonetics. ***r-less*** adj.; ***r-colour***, the modification of a vowel sound caused by a following *r*, as in the U.S. pronunciation of *bird*, etc.; hence ***r-coloured*** adj., ***r-colouring***. Also ***intrusive r*** (see introductory note above); ***linking r***: see LINKING *ppl. a.* d.

1887 *Trans. Philol. Soc. 1885–6* 3 The intrusive *r* has actually produced an additional syllable in modern English. **1902** H. L. WILSON *Spenders* xxiv. 277 Her speech bore just a hint of the soft r-less drawl of the South. **1909** O. JESPERSEN *Mod. Eng. Gram.* I. 372 In literature the intrusive *r* is frequently indicated as a characteristic mark of vulgarity; the oldest example, perhaps, is in Smollett. **1928** I. C. WARD *Phonetics of Eng.* xiii. 130 There is no doubt that the intrusive r is spreading; even in districts where it has not been known, the younger generation is using it. **1935** J. S. KENYON *Amer. Pronunc.* (ed. 6) 158 In Southern American speech, instead of accented ɜ, an 'r-colored' vowel varying to ɝ is often heard. *Ibid.* 191 The retroflexion is slight, or replaced by raising and retraction of the tongue, but..the vowel is still 'r-colored', giving the impression of an *r* sound. *Ibid.* 193 In South England..the 'r color' itself disappeared, leaving the sound ɜ. **1940** *Maître Phonétique* Oct.–Dec. 63 ðə nouteiʃnz..witʃ dinout prisaisli vauəlz wið r-kʌlariŋ. **1941** *Language* XVII. 240 This occurs frequently in the mixed dialect of those who have both 'r-pronouncing' and 'r-less' forms in their speech. **1950** D. JONES *Phoneme* xvi. 82, r-colouring, when vowels are said with simultaneous lowering of the soft palate. *Ibid.*, r-coloured vowels are found with significant function in various types of American and British English. **1965** *Canad. Jrnl. Linguistics* XI. 1. 65 Nine free vowels occur under stress in all dialects..; a tenth occurs only in *r*-less dialects. **1977** P. STREVENS *New Orientations Teaching of English* xii. 151 In American English, in all words spelled with *r* there is an *r* sound which occurs simultaneously with the vowel before it. (..The vowels in such cases are said to be *r*-coloured.)

2. Used to denote serial order, as 'R Battery', 'MS. R', etc., or as a symbol of some thing or person, a point in a diagram, etc.

II. Abbreviations.

1. Of Latin words or phrases. **a.** †**R** (in mediæval notation) = 80. **R.** = *rex* king, *regina* queen. In medical prescriptions: **R**, **℞** = *recipe* take. **b. R.I.P.** = ***requiescat in pace***, 'may he (or she) rest in peace'; or ***requiescant in pace***, 'may they rest in peace'; also (occas.) as *v. intr.*

1816 *Catholicon* II. 264 Obituary... On the 24th inst. Mr. Cornelius Peter Murphy..possessed of a heart glowing with the most generous sentiments, he contracted his illness by the devotedness of his friendship to a deserving youth, from whom, during the course of his long and fatal malady, he could not be separated. R.I.P. **1917** A. G. EMPEY *Over Top* 306 'R.I.P.' In monk's highbrow, 'Requiescat in pace', put on little wooden crosses over soldier's graves... Tommy says like as not it means 'Rest in pieces', especially if the man under the cross has been sent West by a bomb. **1962** *Punch* 5 Sept. 334/1 We had a field mouse RIP-ing under the cupboard. **1976** *Liverpool Echo* 22 Nov. 4/1 Fortified by rites of Holy Church (R.I.P.). Requiem Mass Thursday, November 25.

2. Of English words and phrases: **a. R.** = various proper names, as Richard, Robert, etc.; **R.** = Rabbi; **R.** = radius; **R.** = Railway; **R** = RAND *sb.*[2] 2; **R.** = Reaumur; **R.** = †rest; **R**, restricted (rating) (*U.S.*); **R**, reverse (as on the selector mechanism in a vehicle with automatic transmission); **R.** = River; **R.** = †rogue; **R** (*Bacteriol.*) = ROUGH *a.* 1 e; **R.** = Royal; **R.** (*Naut.*), run (see quots. 1706 and 1867); **R.** = rupee; **℟** = response (to a versicle); **®**, registered (of a trademark: incorporated in *Statutes at Large U.S.A. 1946* (1947) LX. I. 436); **R, r**, right; also *spec.* of a stage; **r** = radius vector; **r** (*Naut.* in log-book) = rain; **R.A.** = Rear Admiral; **R.A.** (*Astron.*), right ascension; **R.A.**, Royal Academy or Academician (hence ***R.A.-ship***); **R.A.**, Royal Artillery; **R.A.A.F.**, Royal Australian Air Force; **R.A.C.**, Royal Armoured Corps; **R.A.C.**, Royal Automobile Club; **R.A.E.**, Royal Aircraft Establishment; **R.A.F.** [G. *Rote Armee Fraktion*], Red Army Faction (in West Germany); **R.A.F.V.R.**, Royal Air Force Volunteer Reserve; **RAM** (*Computers*), random-access memory; **R.A.M.**, Royal Academy of Music; **R.A.M.C.**, Royal Army Medical Corps; **R and B, R & B, R'n B, r'n'b** = ***rhythm and blues***; **R and D, R & D**, research and development (chiefly *U.S.*); **R and R, R & R**, rest and recreation (leave) (orig. *U.S.*); **R. and R., R.'n'R., r'n'r** = ROCK AND ROLL; **R.A.O.C.**, Royal Army Ordnance Corps; **R.A.P.**, Regimental Aid Post; **R.A.S.C.**, Royal Army Service Corps; **R. Aux. A.F.**, Royal Auxiliary Air Force; **R.B.C.**, red blood cell or corpuscle; red blood (cell) count; **R.B.E.**, relative biological effectiveness (of radiation); **R.B.I.** (*Baseball*), run batted in; **R.C., r.c.**, reinforced concrete; **RC** (*Electronics*), resistance/capacitance (or resistor/capacitor); **R.C.**, Roman Catholic; **R.C.A.**, Radio Corporation of America; **R.C.A.F.**, Royal Canadian Air Force; **R.C.M.**, radio (or radar) counter-measures; **R.C.M.P.**, Royal Canadian Mounted Police; **R.D.**, refer (also loosely understood as return) to drawer (of cheque); **R.D.C.**, Rural District Council; **R.D.F.**, radio direction-finding, -finder (in quots., referring to radar); also as *v. trans.*, to employ R.D.F. against; **RDV, rdv** = RENDEZVOUS *sb.* (orig. *U.S.*); **R.E.**, religious education; **R.E.**, Royal Engineers; **r.f., R.F.**, radio-frequency; **R.F.**, representative fraction; usu. *attrib.*; **R.F.A.**, Royal Field Artillery; **R.F.A.**, Royal Fleet Auxiliary; **R.F.C.**, Royal Flying Corps; **R.F.D.**, rural free delivery (of letters) (*U.S.*); **R.G.A.**, Royal Garrison Artillery; **R.G.N.**, Registered General Nurse; **Rh**, rhesus (blood group); usu. *attrib.*; **R.H.** = Royal Highness; **R.H.A.**, Royal Horse Artillery; **R.I.**, religious instruction; **RIAA**, Record (since 1970, Recording) Industry Association of America; **R.I.A.F.**, Royal Indian Air Force; **R.I.B.A.**, Royal Institute of British Architects; **R.I.C.**, Royal Irish Constabulary; **R.I.N.**, Royal Indian Navy; **R.K.**, religious knowledge; **R.M.**, Reichsmark; **R.M.**, Resident Magistrate; **R.M.**, Royal Marines; **R.M.A.**, Royal Marine Artillery; **R.M.C.**, Royal Military College (at Sandhurst); **R.M.L.I.**, Royal Marine Light Infantry; **r.m.s., R.M.S.** (chiefly *Electr.*), root mean square; usu. *attrib.*; **R.M.S.**, Royal Mail Steamer (also Ship); **R.N.**, Registered Nurse; **R.N.**, Royal Navy; **R.N.A.S.**, Royal Naval Air Service; **R.N.D.**, Royal Naval Division; **R.N.L.I.**, Royal National Life-boat Institution; **R.N.R.**, Royal Naval Reserve; **R.N.V.R.**, Royal Naval Volunteer Reserve; **R.N.Z.A.F.**, Royal New Zealand Air Force; **ROA** [Russ. *Rússkaya osvobodítel'naya ármiya*], the Russian Liberation Army; **R.O.C.**, Royal Observer Corps; **R.O.K., Rok** (rɒk), Republic (also Relief) of Korea; also *pl.*, soldiers of the Republic of Korea; **ROM** (*Computers*), read-only memory; **R.O.P., rop**, run of paper (as of advertisements not booked for a specific position in a newspaper); also *fig.*; also in colour printing (see quot. 1967); **ROSLA** (also with pronunc. ('rɒzlə), raising of the school-leaving age; **RoSPA** ('rɒspə), Royal Society for the Prevention of Accidents; **RP, rp** = ***received pronunciation*** s.v. RECEIVED *ppl. a.* 1 b; **R.P.M., r.p.m.**, resale price maintenance; **r.p.m., R.P.M.**, revolution(s) per minute; **RPV**, remotely piloted vehicle (orig. *U.S.*); **R.Q.** (*Med.*), respiratory quotient; **rRNA**, ribosomal RNA; **R.S., rs**, received standard; formerly, received speech; **R.S.** = Royal Society; **R.S.A.**, Royal Society of Arts; also *pl.*, R.S.A. examinations; **R.S.F.S.R.** [Russ. *Rossíĭskaya Sovétskaya Federatívnaya Sotsialistícheskaya Respúblika*], the Russian Soviet Federative Socialist Republic; **RSJ**, rolled steel joist; **RSLA**

= *ROSLA* above; **R.S.M.**, Regimental Sergeant Major; **R.S.P.B.**, Royal Society for the Protection of Birds; **R.S.P.C.A.**, Royal Society for the Prevention of Cruelty to Animals; **R.S.V.**, Revised Standard Version (of the Bible); **RSV** (*Biol.* and *Med.*), Rous sarcoma virus; **R/T, R.T.**, radio-telegraph or -telephone; usu. *attrib.*; **RTE**, Radio Telefis Eireann, the official broadcasting authority of the Republic of Ireland; **R.T.O.**, Railway Transport(ation) Officer, Railroad Transportation Officer; **R.T.U.** (*Mil.*), returned to unit; **R.U.C.**, Royal Ulster Constabulary; **RV**, rateable value; **RV** (earlier **RecV**), recreational vehicle, as a motorized caravan (*U.S.*); hence *RVer*; *RVing* ppl. adj.; **R.V., r.v.** = RENDEZVOUS *sb.* and *v. intr.*; **R.V.** = Revised Version (of the Bible); **R.W.** = Right Worthy or Worshipful. See also R.A.D.A., R.A.F., RDX, REM *sb.*², R.E.M.E., RNA, R.O.T.C. (as main entries).

*c*1330 R. BRUNNE *Chron.* (1810) 156 To mak certeyn partie, *R. a quitance toke. **1662** STILLINGFL. *Orig. Sacr.* II. iv. §3 R. Solomon makes this hill to be Kirjath-jearim. **1819** *Pantologia* X. F j b, Then the radius vector *r* is expressed by either of the following formulæ. **1625** MASSINGER *New Way* IV. ii, My hand hissing..with the letter R printed upon it. **1961** *Times* 27 Jan. 19/4 Offers of 'one-ninetyfour' and 'one-ninetyfive'..were chalked up as 'R1.94' and 'R1.95'. **1961** *Africana Notes & News* Mar. (recto rear cover), Subscription R2 per annum..Holt, B. Place-Names of the Transkeian Territories, 1959, R0-75. **1971** J. MCCLURE *Steam Pig* iv. 40 She kept her money in the post office, just over R200. **1925** *Registration of Trade-Marks* (U.S. Congress Senate, Comm. on Patents) 20–1 Jan. 8 It shall be the duty of the registrant to accompany a registered trade-mark with the words 'Registered in U.S. Patent Office',..or by letter 'R' in a circle, thus ®. **1977** *Gloss. Terms Unfair Competition* (U.S. Trademark Assoc.), ®, one of several notices prescribed by law to indicate that a mark is registered in the U.S. Patent and Trademark Office. **1588** J. MELLIS *Briefe Instr.* Dvj, Set the same down..on this Creditor side..with an R before it, signifying rest. **1965** *Acronyms & Initialisms Dict.* (Gale Research Co.) 589 R.. Restricted (Military document classification). **1972** *Daily Colonist* (Victoria, B.C.) 6 Feb. 2/3 The Strawberry Statement, the MGM version of a campus rebellion..was rated R (no one under 17 admitted without parent or guardian). **1976** *New Yorker* 12 Jan. 70/2 Peckinpah was forced to trim 'The Killer Elite' to change its R rating to a PG. *Ibid.*, Many of these theatres wouldn't have taken it if it had an R and the kids couldn't go by themselves. **1951** R = reverse [see L = low s.v. L 7]. **1846** J. R. PLANCHÉ *Bee & Orange Tree* ii. 7 On (R.) a Cavern. Tempest. A Vessel is seen in distress. When it is out of sight, enter (R.) from Cavern, Princess Amy. **1893** G. B. SHAW *Let.* 27 Apr. (1965) I. 392 The old style—the Princess & the audience grouped R, and Adrienne beginning L in profile. **1976** M. S. HOQUE *Hunger* I. i. 1, Moina and Latif appear—R. They are just visible by the door. **1977** *Rolling Stone* 24 Mar., (*caption*) (Opposite, l to r): John, Mick, Christine McVie, Lindsey Buckingham and Stevie Nicks. **1920** J. A. ARKWRIGHT in *Jrnl. Path. & Bacteriol.* XXIII. 359 The R form grows in colonies which have a more or less jagged outline, are flatter and often have an irregular, rough, or dull surface and are slightly opaque. **1973** KLAINER & GEIS *Agents of Bacterial Dis.* i. 23 Rough (R) colonies have a dry, flat, irregular, wrinkled appearance and are generally formed by cells that lack a capsule. **1706** *Lond. Gaz.* No. 4216/3 All such Seamen.., that are made Run, for not repairing to their Duty, shall have their R's taken off. **1867** SMYTH *Sailor's Word-bk.*, *R.* in the muster-book means run, and is placed against those who have deserted, or missed three musters. **1885** KIPLING *Let.* 30 July in C. Carrington *Rudyard Kipling* (1955) iv. 67 One Proprietor offered My Mother Rs 1,000 for an Anglo-Indian story. **1971** *Shankar's Weekly* (Delhi) 4 Apr. 9/3 'It won't cost much.' 'No, about Rs. 10,000.' **1813** *Examiner* 17 May 316/1 Far above the mediocrity of most of our *R.A.'s. **1829** J. CONSTABLE *Let.* 5 Apr. (1965) III. 21, I beg my best regards to Mrs Leslie—I am always dear Leslie. / your obliged friend / John Constable R.A. **1881** *Athenæum* 5 Nov. 603/2 The year of his R.A.-ship. **1890** LLOYD GEORGE *Let.* 10 June (1973) 28 He had numerous R.A.'s & in fact I should fancy his picture gallery alone must have aggregated £10,000 in value. **1970** *Oxf. Compan. Art* 547/2 He was trained as a chorister in the Chapel Royal, and later received an allowance..to study at the R.A. Schools. **1815** J. KANE *List Officers R. Regiment Artillery* 65 List of Subaltern Officers of the Corps of *R.A. Drivers. **1955** *Times* 16 June 4/3 Both achieved a creditable rate of bangs per minute, the R.E. with various demolitions and a set piece assault by flail tanks, the R.A. with gunfire. **1936** *Age* (Melbourne) 5 May 13 (*caption*) Aircraftsmen making adjustments to fuselage and bomb racks on the *R.A.A.F. Hawker Demon at the Exhibition. **1955** *Times* 21 June 9/5 Melbourne, June 20... Four hundred soldiers, police and bushwalkers, helped by R.A.A.F. Dakota aircraft are searching 5,000ft. Mount Baw Baw for Mihran Haig. **1973** *Parade* (Melbourne) Sept. 22/1 The RAAF Lockheed Hudson, carrying a VIP load, was about to land at Canberra from Melbourne. **1942** PARTRIDGE *Dict. Abbrev.* 81/1 **R.A.C.*, Royal Armoured Corps; armoured fighting vehicles and tanks. **1950** *Jrnl. R. United Service Inst.* XCV. 289 The Royal Armoured Corps, as such, did not come into being until April 1939 (A.O. 58/1939)... In the same Army Order it was also stated that on transfer to the R.A.C. the R.T.C. would be re-designated Royal Tank Regiment. **1908** *Autocar Handbk.* (ed. 2) xxvi. 201 Members of most of the best clubs require only one proposer when joining the *R.A.C. **1934** *Glasgow Herald* 11 Apr. 13/3 The R.A.C. will continue to press for a regulation that all pedal cyclists should be compelled to carry red rear lamps. **1977** J. BINGHAM *Marriage Bureau Murders* v. 61 A large, respectable hotel, mentioned in the A.A. and R.A.C. handbooks. **1926** *Encycl. Brit.* I. 20/2 (*heading*) The *R.A.E. Bubble Sextant. **1977** *R.A.F. News* 11–24 May 11/2 Over at the R.A.E.'s Air Transport Flight. *Ibid.* 11/3 The Experimental Flying Squadron..is widely referred to as the sharp end of RAE flying. **1977** *Time* 19 Sept. 8/3 It was signed 'Kommando Siegfried Hausner, *R.A.F.'—referring to a terrorist who died after a 1975 attack on the West German embassy in Stockholm. **1980** C. MOOREHEAD *Fortune's Hostages* viii. 155 The freeing of six jailed 'RAF' prisoners. **1938** *Times* 2 Feb. 18/6 (*heading*) New branch of *R.A.F.V.R. **1951** *Sunday Pictorial* 21 Jan. 13/6 (Advt.), They must undertake to fly with the R.Aux.A.F. or R.A.F.V.R. during their subsequent reserve service. **1957** R. K. RICHARDS *Digital Computer Components & Circuits* vii. 347 'Random access storage' (or *RAM, for 'random access memory'). **1977** *Design Engin.* July 15/2 The MM5799..contains 1,536 8-bit instructions in its ROM, and its RAM can store 96 BCD digits of 4 bits each. **1891** G. B. SHAW in *World* 23 Dec. 15/2, I am not in the habit of advising novices to lay the foundations of their vocal methods in the *R.A.M. **1954** *Grove's Dict. Mus.* (ed. 5) 271/1 The R.A.M. continues its own separate examination in London..of music teachers and performers. **1900** *Morning Post* 25 July 5/6 Surgeon-Captain Rupert Fawssett, *R.A.M.C. *a*1944 K. DOUGLAS *Alamein to Zem Zem* (1946) 128 Presently an R.A.M.C. warrant officer came. **1971** S. HILL *Strange Meeting* i. 67 Dick's in the R.A.M.C. but he's gone out to Egypt. [**1949** *Billboard* 12 Nov. 110/2 Could score in pop as well as b & r mart.] *Ibid.* 31 Dec. 83, I Ain't Fattening Frogs for Snakes..with its catchy tag, could have a pop as well as *r and b future. **1955** L. FEATHER *Encycl. Jazz* (1956) 70 Today's top R & B artists, contemporary equivalents of the Bessie Smiths and other 'race record' favourites of the 1920s. **1967** L. DEIGHTON *London Dossier* i. 30 Deafening foreground music is provided by a giant jukebox. This is where the working City mod goes for his mid-day transfusion of R'n B. **1973** *Publishers Weekly* 14 May 48/3 Devoted to r'n'b groups, blues and r'n'b vocalists. **1977** *Rolling Stone* 13 Jan. 55/1 'Autobiography'..and 'Shakey Ground' have no doubt been formulated by producer David Rubinson to bring Snow into an R and B-flavored pop mainstream. **1952** POHL & KORNBLUTH in *Galaxy* Aug. 129/1 'How's Research and Development doing on the Venus question?'..'*R. and D. is in there punching.' **1966** *Inland* (Inland Steel Co., Chicago) Autumn 5/1 The American iron and steel industry alone will spend $200 million on R & D this year. **1978** *Nature* 2 Mar. 2/2 A reprocessing plant for throughput of about 1,000 tons per annum will cost in excess of £500 million, including radioactive waste storage, some R & D expenditure (say 5% of the total) and a decade of operating costs (perhaps 25% of the total). **1953** *Britannica Bk. of Year* 639/2 A similar idea is contained in the expression *R. and R., the initials standing for 'Rest and Recreation'. **1966** *New Statesman* 14 Oct. 549/2 R & R = Rest and Recreation. Local leave for American troops, mostly in Hong Kong, Bangkok and Singapore. **1968** *Telegraph* (Brisbane) 3 May 1/7 American troops visiting Australia on R and R leave are to be briefed on the exploits of Diggers in Vietnam. **1977** J. GARDNER *Werewolf Trace* xv. 129 Tonight was for R & R, tomorrow he would have another go at her to get the facts straight. **1955** *Life* 18 Apr. 168 On a list of 10 top juke box best-selling records last week, six were *r'n r. **1958** *Listener* 9 Oct. 572/1 The musical basis of R.'n'R...is the blues. **1973** *Publishers Weekly* 10 Dec. 39/1 This fat collection is devoted solely to writing about music (though not restricted to r'n'r). **1977** *Sounds* 1 Jan. 4/3 From head-bashing r&r, through Sixties pop..to an exquisite kick-in-the-teeth for Definitive Punk Rock. **1918** *Times* 28 Nov. 9/3 (*heading*) R.A.S.C., R.A.V.C., and *R.A.O.C. **1930** *War Office Regulations for Equipment of Army (Provisional)* II. 3 Scabbards, bayonet, No. 1... R.A.O.C. on mobilization *if especially ordered.* **1971** S. MILLIGAN *Adolf Hitler* III. 75 Thirty Signallers drove to the R.A.O.C. Depot at Reigate in a three-ton truck. **1942** E. WAUGH *Put out More Flags* ii. 154 'I don't think you mentioned the *R.A.P., did you, Smallwood?' 'R.A.P. sir. No, sir, I'm afraid I don't know where it is.' **1948** E. H. SMITH *Guns against Tanks* 29 The 26th Battalion's Medical Officer..who earned the admiration of the gunners by bringing his RAP truck to within fifty yards of the forward positions. **1954** J. MASTERS *Bhowani Junction* xix. 174, I came to the R.A.P., swallowed, and went down to report to Captain Chaney. **1918** *R.A.S.C. [see R.A.O.C. above]. **1955** *Times* 12 Aug. 4/7 In the permanent hutment camp by the wartime airfield..the Army Emergency Reserve transport columns of the R.A.S.C. are carrying out in succession their annual 15 days' training. **1976** *Daily Mail* (Hull) 16 Dec., Kenneth William Tully Bodfield, T.D., Major late R.A.S.C. **1948** *R.A.F. Rev.* Jan. 19/1 The short title of the Royal Auxiliary [Air Force] will be *R. Aux. A.F. **1972** L. HUNT *Twenty-One Squadrons* 12 It was on 16th December 1947 that King George VI gave permission for the 'Royal' prefix and from that date until the squadrons disbanded in March 1957 they were R Aux AF units. **1922** *Indian Med. Gaz.* LVII. 126/2 The results of blood examination before treatment of soamin was *R.B.C. 3,000,000, W.B.C. 3,500. **1968** PASSMORE & ROBSON *Compan. Med. Stud.* I. xxvi. 2/2 The red cell count (RBC) ranges from 4·5–6·5 million/mm³ in men and 3·9–5·6 million/mm³ in women. **1978** *Nature* 16 Feb. 674/2 Ageing of circulating RBC. **1954** P. E. SMITH in A. J. Fleming et al. *Mod. Occupational Med.* xiii. 179 When irradiation with two different types of radiation requires different doses to achieve the same biological effect, the radiations are said to have a relative biological effectiveness (*R.B.E.) different from one. The R.B.E. is the inverse of the dosage ratio required for equal effect. **1961** G. R. CHOPPIN *Exper. Nuclear Chem.* ii. 10 The RBE (relative biological effectiveness) is defined as the ratio of the absorbed dose in rads of gamma radiation to the absorbed dose of the given radiation which is required to give the same biological effect. **1975** S. C. BUSHONG *Radiologic Sci. for Technologists* xvi. 286 Diagnostic x-rays have an RBE of approximately 1·0. **1951** *Sun* (Baltimore) 6 Oct. B-1/7 (*heading*) Yankee hurler says own *R.B.I. gave him biggest thrill. **1976** *Billings* (Montana) *Gaz.* 1 July 4-E/1 Rusty Staub..had three RBI's, including a two-run homer on Monday. **1979** *Honolulu Advertiser* 8 Jan. C-2/5 Ahu got his six R.B.I.s on three hits, including two doubles and a grand-slam homer. **1932** C. L. BOLTZ *Everyman's Wireless* x. 190 The stage gain from an *R.C. stage is E/e, where E is the voltage (A.C.) developed across the anode resistance and *e* is the voltage (A.C.) applied between grid and filament. *Ibid.*, A 2-valve circuit incorporating detector and one stage of L.F. amplification with R.C. coupling. **1965** *Wireless World* July 326/1 RC coupling has been employed throughout, in preference to direct coupling, to minimize drift and facilitate the setting up procedure while still preserving the lower audio frequencies. **1932** *Civil Engin.* Sept. 17 Each column is supported by two vibro piles capped with a small *R.C. slab. The whole area between the pile caps is covered with a 4 in. R.C. slab. **1953** *Archit. Rev.* CXIV. 305/1 Floors are of r.c. slab with a lightweight screed containing embedded heating coils. *a*1762 LADY M. W. MONTAGU in *Lett.* (1967) III. 92 If the S[cripture] is true the *R.C. Religion is false because contrary. **1820** J. MILNER *Suppl. Mem. Eng. Catholics* II. 176 If it be true, that the Lords Grenville and Grey had any arrangements..inconsistent with the integrity and safety of the R.C. Religion, we declare, that we consider such arrangements as foreign to the obvious meaning of the Resolution we have signed. **1860** QUEEN VICTORIA *Let.* 7 Jan. in R. Fulford *Dearest Child* (1964) 227 Dear good Leopold Hohenzollern arrived... Oh! if only he were not a R.C.!! **1977** *Belfast Telegraph* 24 Jan. 10/1 (Advt.), R.C. Gent, of good family background, with means, wishes to meet teacher, nurse, or respectable farmer's daughter. **1922** *Radio enters Home* (Radio Corp. of Amer.) 7/1 The distributors of *R.C.A. sets and apparatus have been selected carefully. **1938** *Rev. Sci. Instruments* IX. 219/1 (*caption*) The tube is an RCA 32. **1967** COX & GROSE *Organization & Handling Bibl. Rec. by Computer* II. 48 Both Linotron and RCA Digiset have this facility for checking enlarged characters. **1924** *Pay & Allowance Regulations R. Canad. Air Force* IV. 14 Officers..not carried on the General List, *R.C.A.F., but..attached to the Royal Canadian Air Force for flying duty. **1943** *Times* 13 Dec. 2/2 A Royal Canadian Air Force Sunderland of Coastal Command with a mixed R.C.A.F. and R.A.F. crew. **1958** 'CASTLE' & 'HAILEY' *Flight into Danger* ii. 27 'I know it looks a bit like RCAF,' Dun was saying, fingering his great bush of a moustache. **1945** *Electronic Industries* Sept. 222 **RCM*, radar counter measures. **1947** *Jrnl. R. Aeronaut. Soc.* LI. 432/2 The job of the R.C.M. aircraft of the new Group was to impair these systems... Consequently we developed a jamming screen for the purpose of blinding the enemy's early warning system. **1978** R. V. JONES *Most Secret War* xxxiii. 289, I was amazed to sit through meetings of the Radio Counter Measures Board right up to the end of 1942 discussing whether it was advisable for us to start an 'R.C.M. War'. **1920** *Globe* (Toronto) 9 Feb. 3/4 The great increase in the membership of the force consequent of the extensions of its duties to Eastern Canada and the absorption of the Dominion Police within the organization of the *R.C.M.P. **1967** *Canad. Ann. Rev. 1966* 21 Prime Minister Pearson had asked for any information in the RCMP files which indicated impropriety or wrongdoing. **1977** *Financial Times* 11 Nov. 5/5 Prime Minister Pierre Trudeau ordered a Royal Commission to investigate the RCMP's activities. **1913** W. T. ROGERS *Dict. Abbrev.* 163/2 **R.D.* (bank.), refer to drawer (of cheque). **1938** N. MARSH *Death in White Tie* iii. 41 One of my cheques has been returned R.D. **1974** M. BUTTERWORTH *Man in Sopwith Camel* ii. 24 No..girl was going to rest a wet RD stamp on one of Stryvers' cheques by accident! **1904** *Local Govt. Jrnl.* 2 Jan. 3/1 (*heading*) Contracts open. 3/2 Granite.—The Clerk, *R.D.C., Midhurst. *a*1974 R. CROSSMAN *Diaries* (1975) I. 114 At the time, I wasn't too alarmed when Alderman Reeves, the chairman of the R.D.C., called the decision the worst he had ever seen. **1938** F. A. LINDEMANN 8 Mar. in R. V. Jones *Most Secret War* (1978) iv. 40 Lest too much reliance be placed upon the *R.D.F. methods, it is perhaps worth pointing out that certain difficulties may easily be encountered in actual use. **1942** E. WAUGH *Put out More Flags* i. 28 We've got a most valuable invention called R.D.F. *Ibid.*, The German air-bases are too far away for them to be able to attack us. If they do, we'll R.D.F. them out of the skies. **1963** L. DEIGHTON *Horse under Water* xxiii. 101 Just behind me on the bridge Singleton was admiring the R.F.D. and the electronic depth-gauge. **1975** S. JOHNSON *Urbane Guerilla* III. 147 We didn't RDF him... The trouble is RDF-ing, radar direction finding, requires a cross-bearing. **1976** *Oxf. Compan. Ships & Sea* 685/2 In its earliest days, radar in Britain was known as RDF, the initial letters of radio direction finding, but the name was changed early in the Second World War to avoid confusion with H/F D/F, high frequency direction finding. **1955** R. J. SCHWARTZ *Compl. Dict. Abbrev.* 152/3 **RDV*, rendezvous (US Army). **1973** 'A. HALL' *Tango Briefing* iv. 45 I'm speaking from base. We shall need a little more time to set up the radio, so the next rdv is for 15.00 hours tomorrow. **1963** R. ACLAND *We teach them Wrong* 9, I told the deputy head master that I was a Lay Reader in the Church of England and could perhaps help with *R.E. lessons. **1972** *Guardian* 29 Aug. 13/7 RE has been crippled by dogmatism and an arid biblicism. **1978** *Times* 3 Oct. 15/7 Some LEA's have been bold enough to recast their RE curriculum... The RE Council keeps a monitoring eye on emerging methodologies for RE. **1848** *Brit. Army Despatch* 24 Nov. 307/3 Captain Chapman, *R.E., has returned to Zante from Cephalonia. **1877** *Army Circular* Dec. App. 18 Each Officer of R.E. below the rank of Major..is allowed 2 public horses. **1921** V. E. INGLEFIELD *Hist. 20th (Light) Div.* iii. 37 Rations, R.E. material, etc., had to be brought up a long way from the dumps under very difficult conditions. **1959** I. JEFFERIES *Thirteen Days* xi. 175 If that's all you have to say you can get out. This is the R.E. office. **1918** W. H. ECCLES *Wireless Telegr. & Teleph.* (ed. 2) 471 The *r.f. generator 1 and microphone 2 induce currents in circuit 5. **1930** *Proc. IRE* XVIII. 1339 A relatively simple outfit is used comprising an r-f oscillator of variable frequency. **1931** *Electronics* July 17/1 A new impregnation compound for r.f. transformers affords better protection in humid atmosphere. **1956** *Proc. CERN Symposium* I. 64/2 Synchrotron oscillations (if an rf is present) are damped. **1967** *Electronics* 6 Mar. 2 (Advt.), Sweep Oscillators with RF and marker plug-ins meet virtually all of your swept frequency testing requirements. **1886** H. D. HUTCHINSON *Military Sketching made Easy* i. 12 A French map may show a scale of mètres, but to be generally useful to Englishmen it would be necessary to add to it a scale of yards with the same *R.F. **1969** G. C. DICKINSON *Maps & Air Photographs* vii. 102 In countries using the metric system scales of so many centimetres to a kilometre usually also give R.F.s with convenient round numbers. **1900** W. S. CHURCHILL in *Morning Post* 27 Mar. 7/7, 1 battery Corps artillery (*R.F.A.). **1974** A. PRICE *Other Paths to Glory* vi. 71 See how those casualties in the first two years [of the First World War] came from the..8th Hussars and the RFA—I'll bet they were all regulars. **1911** *Shipping World* 15 Mar. 276/1 (*caption*) The *R.F.A. 'Burma'. **1931** *Jane's Fighting Ships* 84/2 Oilers (R.F.A.). **1913** *Flight* 12 Apr. 404/1 (*heading*) Motto for the *R.F.C. **1933** V.

BRITTAIN *Testament of Youth* II. vii. 293 As we left the harbour a transport of the R.F.C. cheered us. **1977** *R.A.F. News* 27 Apr.–10 May 2/2 The final meeting of the North West Royal Flying Corps Association..was attended by Mr. Walter Sumner, a member who is now the sole RFC veteran to be a pensioner at the Royal Hospital, Chelsea. **1903** (*title*) *R.F.D. news; devoted to the interests of the Rural Free Delivery Carriers of the U.S. **1903** *R.F.D. News* Feb. 21/2 Pa doesn't go to town for mail; we've got the R.F.D. **1974** M. HOYT *Thirty Miles for Ice Cream* xv. 187 Our mail used to be delivered by an R.F.D. mailman riding behind a horse in a sort of outhouse on wheels, painted red, white and blue, and lettered U.S. Mail. **1907** *Field Service Pocket Bk* vi. 120 *R.G.A. **1909** *Army & Navy Gaz.* 6 Feb. 140/1 Sir F. D. Blake, Bt., late Northumberland R.G.A. (Mil.). **1924** *Nursing Mirror Pocket Encycl. & Diary 1924* 85 **R.G.N.*, Registered General Nurse (Scotland). **1975** *Irish Independent* 27 May 16/5 (Advt.), Resident R.G.N., or S.E.N., required for day duty in nursing home in Dublin south east. **1940** LANDSTEINER & WIENER in *Proc. Soc. Exper. Biol. & Med.* XLIII. 223 The capacity possessed by some rabbit immune sera produced with blood of Rhesus monkeys, of reacting with human bloods that contain the agglutinogen M has been reported previously. Subsequently it has been found that another individual property of human blood (which may be designated as *Rh) can be detected by certain of these sera. **1954** A. E. MOURANT *Distribution Human Blood Groups* iii. 12 The *Rh* blood groups depend upon three very closely adjacent loci on each of a pair of chromosomes, which may be called the *C*, *D* and *E* loci. **1958** L. P. STREAN *Birth of Normal Babies* iv. 60 If the fetus is Rh-positive and the mother is Rh-negative, then the mother is actually immunized by the developing child's blood and she develops antibodies against the Rh-positive factor. **1968** PASSMORE & ROBSON *Compan. Med. Stud.* I. xxvi. 19/2 Only the ABO and Rh blood group systems contribute significantly to isoantibody incompatibility in the giving of blood transfusions. **1654** SIR E. NICHOLAS in *N. Papers* (Camden) II. 48 Beseech her *R.H. that nothing that comes from me may in any kinde be taken notice. **1854** *Times* 20 Oct. 7/1 Captain Maude's Battery, *R.H.A., was most useful. **1916** LD. E. HAMILTON *First Seven Divisions* 27 The 119th Battery R.F.A. was at this time just south-west of Eloges, and L Battery R.H.A. just north-east of Andregnies. **1962** M. CARVER *El Alamein* iv. 51 While F Battery R.H.A. put down a 'stonk' the carriers counter-attacked and drove the enemy infantry back. **1961** *Where?* III. 16/2 *Religious instruction* (*RI): The only subject which state schools are obliged to teach by law: in county and voluntary controlled schools. **1976** *Evening Post* (Nottingham) 15 Dec. 13/3 (Advt.), A teacher required in January and April for Independent School..(3) R.I. with an interest in general counselling for girls 11 and over. **1952** *Billboard* 16 Feb. 18/1 Selection of an executive secretary for *RIAA..was put off until early next week. **1971** J. EARL *How to choose & use Pickups & Loudspeakers* iii. 90 It is often necessary to attenuate the signal from a piezo cartridge before applying it to the RIAA amplifier input. **1975** *Gramophone* Jan. 1421/3 Also the RIAA correction curve for discs shows only the slightest deviation from the ideal playback curve. **1946** *Civil & Milit. Gaz.* 2 June 11/3 Disciplinary standards in the R.A.F. and *R.I.A.F. **1971** R. RUSSELL tr. *A. Ahmad's Shore & Wave* xv. 161 On one side stood Hasan, looking very smart in his R.I.A.F. uniform. **1913** W. T. ROGERS *Dict. Abbrev.* 167/1 **R.I.B.A.* (Soc.), Royal Institute of British Architects. **1938** *Times* 7 Feb. 9/2 The article consists of a memorandum by the Public Relations Committee of the R.I.B.A. and correspondence therein between the Minister of Health and the R.I.B.A. Council. *a* **1974** R. CROSSMAN *Diaries* (1975) I. 86, I had a difficult task when I had to go to the R.I.B.A. and give the certificates and prizes for the best-designed houses of the year. **1903** SOMERVILLE & 'ROSS' *All on Irish Shore* 196 Two tall constables of the *R.I.C. stood at the door of the cottage. **1972** A. HEZLET *'B' Specials* i. 4 The I.R.A. issued a proclamation referring to the R.I.C. as spies and traitors. **1978** J. CARROLL *Mortal Friends* I. iv. 47 He saw a private soldier, not an RIC Auxiliary, but an honest to God Tommy. **1946** *Civil & Milit. Gaz.* 2 June 11/3 *R.I.N. ratings. **1959** *R. K. [see *physical torture* s.v. PHYSICAL *a.* 7]. **1968** G. MITCHELL *Three Quick & Five Dead* i. 24 'Edward teaches history and something he calls R.K.' 'Religious Knowledge,' said Laura. 'They used to call it Scripture in my young day.' **1875** *Anglo-Brazilian Times* 23 July 6/1 On Hamburg the rates for Bank paper at 90 days have been 442 Reis per *R.M. **1963** L. DEIGHTON *Horse under Water* 251 Peterson had a *Reisepass*..and 200 RM. **1888** V. MARTIN *Diary* 24 June in M. Collis *Somerville & Ross* (1968) iv. 56 Jostled as to our seat by Brady *R.M. **1899** SOMERVILLE & 'ROSS' (*title*) Some experiences of an Irish R.M. **1947** *Daily Gleaner* (Kingston, Jamaica) 3 Nov. 12/5 Some cases before the R.M. Court... His Hon. Mr. S. T. B Sanguinetti, R.M. observed that he had left over the case from last week. **1827** J. WRIGHT *Let.* 13 Nov. in P. H. Nicolas *Hist. Record of Royal Marine Forces* (1845) II. viii. 313 (*heading*) Deputy Adjutant-general's office, *R.M. **1923** *Admiralty Fleet Order No. 1643* 22 June The R.M. Artillery at Eastney, and the R.M.L.I. at Forton will be combined into the Portsmouth Division, R.M. *Ibid.*, *Shoulder Letters.*— Letters 'R.M.' to be worn by all ranks. **1962** S. BASSETT *Royal Marine* iii. 69 If I got high marks, I'd be appointed Superintendent RM Signals, a Corps appointment. **1883** A. COOPER KEY *Let.* in L. Conway-Gordon *Case of Lt. Lewis Conway-Gordon* (1884) 17, I might be able to give you a final answer to your request as to the removal of the names of the two Officers from..the list of Lieutenants, *R.M.A. **1931** *Times Lit. Suppl.* 26 Mar. 246/3 After 1894 the R.M.A. were no longer sent to sea in small craft, but assigned only to first-class ships and flagships. **1893** W. S. CHURCHILL *Let.* 10 Sept. in R. S. Churchill *W. S. Churchill* (1967) I. Compan. I. vii. 412 Tonight I go back to *RMC. **1956** J. MASTERS *Bugles & Tiger* ii. 36 Bert King..led me up the steps and into the low grey pile before me—the Royal Military College, Sandhurst. From that moment..I was Gentleman Cadet John Masters, of No. 5 Company of the R.M.C., as I soon learned to call it. **1968** A. POWELL *Military Philosophers* i. 55 Chu enjoyed the RMC so much he wants to go to Eton. **1889** W. RICHARDS *Her Majesty's Army* II. 195 Lieutenant H. Earle, *R.M.L.I., was sent as an envoy to the King of Dekra. **1916** 'TAFFRAIL' *Pincher Martin* ix. 166 He..hastily told the marine corporal of the watch to turn out twenty marines..and then to inform Captain Hannibal Chance, R.M.L.I., that a Zeppelin was in sight. **1930** *Times Lit. Suppl.* 3 July 542/3 It is the evacuation of the Y Beach at Gallipoli, in which the 1st Battalion was concerned, with one company of the 2nd South Wales Borderers and the Plymouth Battalion R.M.L.I. (consisting entirely of men specially enlisted for the War). **1980** *Globe & Laurel* July/Aug. 241/1 The original Forton RMLI Cadet Band was disbanded on amalgamation of the RMLI and RMA. **1897** A. HAY *Princ. Alternate-Current Working* vii. 93 When we speak of so many volts of an alternating P.D., or so many amperes of an alternating current, we thereby mean their *R.M.S. values. **1940** *Jrnl. Acoustical Soc. Amer.* XI. 278/1 Peak and r.m.s. pressures in one-eighth-second intervals..from the voices of six men and five women. **1945** *Electronic Engin.* XVII. 737/3 The oscillator output voltage was 20V R.M.S. **1977** S. A. BOOK *Statistics* ii. 40 The standard deviation is the square root of the mean of the squared deviations. (In some applied contexts, it is referred to as the 'root-mean-square deviation' or the 'rms deviation'.) [**1852** *Nautical Mag.* XXI. 91 To the Secretary R.M.S.P. Company.] **1870** *Weekly Standard* (Buenos Aires) 12 Jan. 1/3 The *R.M.S. La Plata arrived in port..with the following passengers. **1936** *Discovery* June 181/2 R.M.S. '*Queen Mary*', the greatest achievement of British shipbuilding. **1976** *Oxf. Compan. Ships & Sea* 684/1 *R.M.S.*, the prefix, short for Royal Mail Ship, placed before the name of a British merchant ship with a licence to carry the Royal Mails. **1938** *Amer. Speech* XIII. 228/2 She is an '*R.N.', which means *registered nurse*—one who has graduated from an accredited school of nursing. **1974** *Publishers Weekly* 11 Feb. 62/2 Irish Katie, R.N. in a nursing home. **1846** H. D. CHADS *Let.* in *Madras Artillery Record* VI. 323 [signed] H. D. Chads, Captain *R.N. **1946** 'TACKLINE' *You met such Nice Girls in Wrens* xiii. 144 It is very strange..why R.N. officers are so much meaner with their clothing-coupons than R.N.V.R. officers. **1975** 'J. BELL' *Victim* iv. 52 Wing-Commander Redfern, Late R.A.F., his wife, Amanda, and Commander Pilcher, R.N., retired. **1918** W. S. CHURCHILL *Let.* 10 Sept. in M. Gilbert *W. S. Churchill* (1975) IV. vii. 144 How much flying, for instance, is done by the *RNAS for the 45,000 first-rate fighting men and skilled men they employ? **1977** *Air Mail* Spring 21/1 So this RAF phrase, like 'port' and 'starboard', came with the RNAS when the flying sailors merged with the RFC in 1918 to become the Royal Air Force. **1914** R. BROOKE *Let.* 24 Sept. (1968) 619 The nucleus of the *R.N.D. is marines, Naval Reserve, etc.—more or less trained men. **1916** W. S. CHURCHILL *Let.* 29 Nov. in M. Gilbert *W. S. Churchill* (1977) IV. Compan. I. 34, I rejoiced to read of the glorious achievements of the RND. **1924** *Life-Boat: Centenary Number* 33 Small wonder that its sister-organization in little Holland has kept its eye upon the largest and oldest organization, the *R.N.L.I. **1948** *Life-Boat* Mar. 157 The R.N.L.I. Roadless Tractor..can take the boat over all types of beach. **1977** *Navy News* June 1/2 The Merchant Navy and fishing fleets will be represented, as well as organizations like the R.N.L.I., Trinity House and H.M. Coastguard. **1868** *Times* 1 July 2/2 (Advt.), John Gray, *R.N.R., Commander. **1902** C. J. C. HYNE *Mr. Horrocks, Purser* 85 What's the use of being R.N.R. if you don't let people know it? **1977** *Stornoway Gaz.* 27 Aug. 3/1 As were many other Lewismen, Alick was a member of the R.N.R. **1905** *Text Book for Royal Naval Volunteer Reserve* 3 The smartness, efficiency, and the credit of the *R.N.V.R. depend upon the following principles. **1934** *Brassey's Naval & Shipping Ann.* 25 New rules were notified in Fleet Orders dated April 6, 1933, respecting the rank of Commodore in the R.N.R. and R.N.V.R. **1977** *Listener* 25 Aug. 241/2 Lambert was given a commission in the RNVR. *c* **1944** *Mod. Jun. Dict.* (Whitcombe & Tombs) 454/1 *R.N.Z.A.F., Royal New Zealand Air Force. **1947** *Air Force News* (Cairo) 14 Jan. 1/2 The first two senior RNZAF officers nominated for participation in the exchange scheme with the RAF. **1959** *Listener* 23 July 146/2 We follow the fortunes of Vlasov's Army of Liberation, the *ROA, during the last months of the war. **1974** T. P. WHITNEY tr. *Solzhenitsyn's Gulag Archipelago* I. I. vi. 253 As for the leaflets reporting the creation of the ROA, the 'Russian Liberation Army', not only were they written in bad Russian, but they were inbued with an alien spirit that was clearly German. **1942** PARTRIDGE *Dict. Abbrev.* 84/2 **R.O.C.*, Royal Observer Corps..A civilian body that scans the skies. Modest and selfless. **1947** *R.A.F. Rev.* Sept. 20/2 We hope to live up to its claim, as did the R.O.C. **1950** *N.Y. Times* 2 July IV. 1/6 The man who took over direction of operation *ROK—Relief of Korea—in these dire circumstances was General MacArthur. **1950** *Life* 11 Sept. 51/2 (*heading*) The Durable Roks. *Ibid.*, But the Rok (for Republic of Korea) army was more durable than anybody thought. **1972** P. M. BARTZ *South Korea* 2/2 South Korea's correct title is the Republic of Korea, usually abbreviated R.O.K. **1966** *IEEE Trans. Electronic Computers* XV. 502/1 Transformer memories are read-only memories (*ROM) which make use of magnetic coupling..between a set of interrogation lines and a set of sense lines. **1975** *Sci. Amer.* May 37/3 ROM's are non-volatile: their contents cannot be altered during the operation of the computer, and the retention of stored data does not depend on a supply of power. **1979** *Personal Computer World* Nov. 82/1 Monitors are held in ROM so that they are available and running as soon as the computer is started. **1947** K. M. WELLS *Owl Pen Reader* (1969) I. 97 Our goats..were neither registered, accredited, pure-bred, or *R.O.P. **1955** R. J. SCHWARTZ *Compl. Dict. Abbrev.* 155/3 *rop*, run of paper (advertising). **1961** *Penrose Ann.* LV. 110 Only in recent years was the reproduction of colour transparencies taken up by means of ROP printing, where the full range of colours is produced by superimposing the three basic colours. **1967** E. CHAMBERS *Photolitho-Offset* 276 *R.O.P.*, an American term (run of paper) applying when colour half-tones are printed at the same time as the type matter. **1972** J. R. BRIDGE in *Mathematics in School* Sept. 8 (*title*) *ROSLA and after. *Ibid.* 9/2, I believe ROSLA will be rewarding for groups 2 and 3. **1977** *Jrnl. R. Soc. Arts* CXXV. 300/1 When the additional ROSLA year operated, the prospect of a further year of standard education seems to have been unpalatable to some of the potential beneficiaries. **1948** *Fire Protection & Accident Prevention Year Book 1948–49* III. 139 The Royal Society for the Prevention of Accidents (*RoSPA)... The aim of the Society is the prevention of accidents of all kinds. **1955** *Proc. National Industrial Safety Conf.* 7 Attract new members to your local groups, encourage them to become members of RoSPA. **1965** *Autocar* 24 Sept. 609/1 The leaflet recently published by RoSPA in conjunction with the Ministry of Transport. **1889** A. J. ELLIS *Early Eng. Pronunc.* v. 6 Other Abbreviations in Frequent Use... *rp., received pronunciation, or that of pronouncing dictionaries and educated people. **1964** R. H. ROBINS *Gen. Linguistics* ii. 57 The pronunciation characteristic of this type of English has been called 'received pronunciation' or 'R.P.'. **1964** *English Studies* XLV. 26 There is no Standard Accent of English, and almost the only people who think there *is* are a small number of RP speakers who feel that their accent is..in some way superior. **1977** P. STREVENS *New Orientations Teaching of English* xi. 138 In Britain, the non-regional accent is RP. **1960** *Times Rev. Industry* Mar. 3/2 In the absence of price competition, distributors may compete by offering extra services. *R.p.m. does not guarantee that they do. **1964** *Financial Times* 31 Jan. 6/4 However, the pending abolition of R.P.M. has confused some M.P.s in deciding their attitudes. **1966** J. F. PICKERING *Resale Price Maintenance* i. 15 In a number of trades r.p.m. was enforced privately through the mechanism of the relevant trade association. **1978** *Bookseller* 17 June 3183/1 In Australia and in Sweden the abolition of r.p.m. has had these very effects. **1906** *Trans. Inst. Engineers & Shipbuilders in Scotland* XLIX. 30 Especially should this be done in cases where.. the weight increases more rapidly in inverse proportion to the *R.P.M. and the diameter than it does with other types. **1931** *Discovery* Nov. 344/2 Running the engine at a higher r.p.m. **1950** *Down Beat* 5 May 16 (*heading*) Here's LP, 45 RPM jazz list. **1966** R. THOMAS *Spy in Vodka* (1967) xix. 218 The engine was responding nicely..and I was estimating the rpm's needed for the next bend. **1970** *Air Force Mag.* Oct. 40/2 This study of the Remotely Piloted Vehicle (*RPV) potential consisted of detailed examinations of presently available technologies. **1972** *Observer* 13 Aug. 1/6 Remotely Piloted Vehicles (RPVs) that promise a bizarre kind of 'bloodless' warfare. **1977** *Time* 23 May 33/3 That will make being a pilot a cushy job: he sits at a TV console 200 miles away and gets the RPV to provide surveillance or relay radio messages or pinpoint targets for precision bombing. **1905** W. H. HOWELL *Textbk. Physiol.* xxxviii. 632 In connection with other data,..the *R.Q. may be used to throw light upon the character of the nutrition. **1968** PASSMORE & ROBSON *Compan. Med. Stud.* I. xlii. 4/2 Ingestion of glucose within minutes restores the blood glucose concentration and the working ability, without changes in the RQ. **1967** *Jrnl. Molecular Biol.* XXIII. 149 Abbreviations used: *rRNA, ribosomal RNA. **1977** *Nature* 8 Dec. 473/3 It is probable that no rRNA gene is integrated into the chromosomal DNA of the macronucleus [of *Tetrahymena*]. **1889** A. J. ELLIS *Early Eng. Pronunc.* v. 3 They all spoke 'received speech' (abbreviated to *rs.) in 'received pronunciation' (abbreviated to rp.). **1934** H. C. WYLD *S.P.E. Tract* XXXIX. 605 With this type [of spoken English]..I contrast what, for want of a better name, I call *Received Standard* (henceforward referred to in this paper by the initials *R.S.). **1964** C. BARBER *Ling. Change Present-Day Eng.* ii. 22, I shall use the expression Received Standard (R.S.) to refer to all aspects of the language. **1676** GLANVILL *Ess. Philos. & Relig.* title-p., Joseph Glanvill..Fellow of the *R.S. **1920** *R. Soc. Arts Syllabus Examinations, 1921* p. xviii (Advt.), A selection from many books suitable for *R.S.A. examinations. **1973** M. AMIS *Rachel Papers* 64 Not that age was a helpful grouping criterion, the elder lot ranging as they did from fifteen (a delinquent ghoul studying for RSAs) to nineteen (myself). **1980** *Jrnl. R. Soc. Arts* Feb. 145/1 Nor is the RSA alone. **1923** *Nation* 31 Jan. 130/1 The Russian Socialist Federated Soviet Republic (*RSFSR).. and the Transcaucasian Socialist Federated Soviet Republic (Georgia, Azerbaijan, and Armenia) are concluding the present treaty on their consolidation into one united state. **1975** *Whitaker's Almanac 1976* 956/1, By the 1947 Peace Treaty with Finland, the district of *Petsamo*..was added to the territory of the R.S.F.S.R. **1940** *Chambers's Techn. Dict.* 733/1 **R.S.J.*, rolled steel joist. **1954** *Archit. Rev.* CXV. 334 The extension has a reinforced concrete frame with the exception of the top floor of the main block, which has a RSJ portal frame and a flat roof of asbestos cement decking. **1978** *Private Eye* 17 Mar. 15 We had..three RSJs put across the ceiling to stop the upstairs coming downstairs. **1971** *Circular* (Dept. Educ. & Sci.) No. 8. 1 The effect of raising the school leaving age (*RSLA) is to substitute 16 for 15 in all the provisions of the Education Acts which deal with the upper limits of compulsory school age. **1979** *Rep. on Educ.* (Dept. Educ. & Sci.) No. 95. 1/1 The raising of the school leaving age to 16 (RSLA)—on 1 September 1972 with effect from 1 September 1973—marked the achievement of a long held objective. **1913** W. T. ROGERS *Dict. Abbrev.* 170 **R.S.M.* (tit.), Regimental Sergeant-Major. **1955** E. WAUGH *Officers & Gentlemen* I. ix. 107 The RSM sent up the rocket which announced the start of the exercise. **1978** R. V. JONES *Most Secret War* x. 90 The Grenadiers had sent an R.S.M. to Dover to pick up any Grenadiers and drill them. **1907** *Bird Notes & News* II. 52/2 In our parish nearly all belong to the *R.S.P.B. **1937** *Discovery* Jan. 21/2 We are not planning to have our own bird sanctuaries with watchers to protect them, as this work is already being carried out with great success by the R.S.P.B. **1979** *Birds* Summer 34/1 The RSPB has seven reserves with major reedbeds. **1870** *Animal World* (Suppl.) 1 July 177/1 (*heading*) Annual report of the *R.S.P.C.A. **1924** FAIRHOLME & PAIN *Century of Work for Animals* iii. 53 At the present time the R.S.P.C.A., working in England and Wales, alone employs two hundred and three full-time inspectors. **1978** *Daily Tel.* 18 July 1/8 The RSPCA is to launch an investigation today after about 2,800 of a cargo of 4,000 mink were found dead at Manchester airport. **1961** F. F. BRUCE *English Bible* xiv. 186 The *R.S.V. dispenses with one of the most distinctive features of what English-speaking people have come to regard as 'Bible language'. **1974** *Oxf. Dict. Chr. Ch.* (ed. 2) 171/2 The RSV is widely used not only in America but also in Britain..and other English-speaking countries. **1956** *Jrnl. Nat. Cancer Inst.* XVI. 365 Lesions of the central nervous system produced by a duck variant of the Rous sarcoma virus (*RSV). **1974** J. D. ACTON et al. *Fund. Med. Virol.* xxiii. 301 Some strains of RSV will induce transformation of mammalian (mouse, rat, hamster, primate, human) fibroblast cells. **1942** *Tee Emm* (Air Ministry) II. 64 If the *R/T transmission is a bit distorted, 'Say again' is a set expression. **1971** 'D. HALLIDAY' *Dolly & Doctor Bird* xiii. 180 The R/T isn't functioning, and neither are the radar or echo sounder. **1975** J. WYLLIE *Butterfly Flood* (1977) xxxii. 156 Keep within R.T. range of us. **1969** W. B. EMERY *Nat. & Internat. Syst. Broadcasting* vi. 117 *RTE now has a repertory company of twenty-eight actors.

1979 J. J. LEE *Ireland 1945–70* 173 Over 50 per cent of RTE television broadcasting featured imported programmes at the end of the 1960s. **1917** *B.E.F. Times* 8 Sept. (1918) 4/2 There is also a rumour that the *R.T.O. of Bath has not got a decoration in the new list. **1919** G. S. GORDON *Let.* 20 June (1943) 95 We then drove over to the Gare de Lyon, where we hung about the R.T.O.'s office till 11, getting tickets made out, and our luggage registered. **1930** *Amer. Speech* V. 385 *R.T.O.*, Railroad transportation officer. **1955** E. WAUGH *Officers & Gentlemen* I. v. 45 Guy sought aid of the RTO and was rebuffed. **1978** LD. LOVAT *March Past* I. viii. 132 His last appointment was that of Railway Transport Officer (RTO) at Euston Station. **1917** KIPLING *Book of Words* (1928) 147 I'm not defending ragging—I've known cases where everyone who took part in it ought to have been *R.T.U. **1976** K. BONFIGLIOLI *Something Nasty in Woodshed* ix. 103 Mortdecai [*sic*] would never wear the coveted red tabs on his khaki. 'RTU' (Returned to Unit) would follow his name for ever. **1922** M. GILBERT *Winston S. Churchill* (1977) IV. Compan. III. 1948 The Secretary of State for the Colonies.. stated that the *RUC were not up to strength. **1941** T. J. CAMPBELL *Fifty Years of Ulster* xxii. 322 The R.U.C. are an armed force, provided with revolvers and rifles. **1977** *Irish Times* 8 June 11/8 Last night the injured RUC man was stated to be seriously ill in hospital. **1975** *Irish Times* 9 May 24/1 (Advt.), Long Lease. G.R. £12·50. *R.V. £25. **1976** *Dumfries & Galloway Standard* 25 Dec. 17/7 (Advt.), Modernised ground floor flat... R.V. to be reassessed. **1967** *Wheels Afield* June 42 (*heading*) Handling your *RV in traffic. **1968** *Trailer Life* June 52/2 For early Rec V construction the terms cracker box or bullets served as type designation. **1978** *Sunday Sun-Times* (Chicago) 1 Jan. 120/2 The RV industry.. has regained its feet. **1973** *Trailer Life* Apr. 134/2, I sure wish there was some way to allow *RVers to utilize those great areas. *Ibid.* 194/2 An *RVing woman's luck in being able to take along a wardrobe for every occasion. **1942** PARTRIDGE *Dict. Abbrev.* 86/1 *r.v.* or *R.V.*, (place of) rendezvous. (Common to all three services.) **1973** C. EGLETON *Seven Days to Killing* xiv. 163 He had no way of knowing whether Tarrant would have set up a fail-safe RV or not. **1975** N. LUARD *Travelling Horseman* vi. 162 We'll r.v... in the boozer, and I'll take him over to the garage. **1896** *Expositor* Aug. 126 Here the *R.V. ..has rightly translated.

b. ***the three R's***: Reading, (W)riting, (A)rithmetic. See also quots. 1879, 1892.

The phrase is said to have originated with Sir W. Curtis (1752–1829) who proposed it as a toast.

1825 *Mirror* V. 75/1 The three R's—Reading, Writing, and Rithmetic. **1828** *New Jersey Eagle* (Newark, N.J.) 23 May 3/3 The three R's—honest 'Rithmetic, Reading & 'Riting I think I can say, I'm no fool in. **1864** *Reader* 30 Jan. 134 Middle-class schools, in which education is pushed beyond the three 'R's'. **1879** *Athenæum* 5 Apr. 431/1 Romanism, Ritualism, and Rationalism, the three 'r's' of theological controversy. **1892** *Academy* 31 Dec. 602/3 Rhetoric, reflexion, and repetition—those three R.s of the inexperienced book-maker. **1976** *Times* 26 Mar. 6/3 In some primary and secondary schools the three Rs have been neglected or devalued. **1979** *Jrnl. R. Soc. Arts* CXXVII. 483/1 Writing is, after all, one of the three R's on which education is based.

3. R.S.V.P., abbrev. of the French phrase *répondez, s'il vous plaît*, 'reply, if you please': commonly placed in one of the corners of invitation-cards. Also *attrib.* or *v. intr.*

a **1845** BARHAM *Ingol. Leg.* III. *House Warming* 289 Quadrilles in the afternoon, R.S.V.P. **1883** ANNIE THOMAS *Mod. Housew.* 92 Attend strictly to the R.S.V.P. corner of your 'at home' cards. **1969** R. V. BESTE *Next Time I'll pay my Own Fare* viii. 111 The Duchess de Santine Miorna requests the pleasure of Detective-Inspector John Gage's company to dinner tonight... R.S.V.P... Gage R.S.V.Ped in Spanish. **1978** *Observer* 19 Feb. 7/1 The printed invitations to 27 journalists were delivered... We all RSVP'd.

4. R or **r** (*Physics*): abbrev. of *roentgen* (*unit*) s.v. ROENTGEN 2. Also ***r-unit***.

1922 *Physics Abstr.* A. XXV. 508 The instrument is calibrated in terms of a unit R (the Röntgen), i.e. the ionisation produced in 1 sec. by 1 gm. of Ra at a distance of 20 mm. after filtration by 0·5 mm. of Pt. **1938** R. W. LAWSON tr. *Hevesy & Paneth's Man. Radioactivity* (ed. 2) iv. 58 The γ-radiation from 1 mg. Ra.. supplies 8·6 *r* per hour at a distance of 1 cm. *Ibid.* xxiv. 260 The maximum permissible daily dosage of neutrons is estimated to be one-tenth that for γ- or X-rays, or 0·01 *r* unit. **1962** *Newnes' Conc. Encycl. Nuclear Energy* 205/1 Thus for X- and γ-radiation of energy between 0·3 and 3 MeV, 1 *r* is nearly equivalent to 1 rad in water or soft tissue. **1973** KAYE & LABY *Tables of Physical & Chem. Constants* (ed. 14) iii. 285 The unit of exposure is the roentgen (R) which is equal to 2·58 × 10^{-4} coulomb per kilogram of air.

III. As a symbol. **1.** *Chem.* [Initial letter of *radical*.] R is used in chemical formulæ to represent an unspecified radical or group of radicals (usu. organic).

1866 WATTS *Dict. Chem.* IV. 219 In these formulæ, R+ represents a positive organic radicle, and R− a negative radicle: no negative organic radicle as such, has yet been introduced into these compounds. *Ibid.* 227 Stannic compounds of the form $Sn^{iv}R^4$+ are colourless mobile liquids. **1872** [see POLYMERIZATION]. **1909** C. A. KEANE *Mod. Org. Chem.* viii. 130 In the formula for ketones, the radicals R and R′ may be either like or unlike. **1932** I. D. GARARD *Introd. Org. Chem.* vi. 74 The aldehydes have one of these valences attached to carbon and one to hydrogen, so that for any hydrocarbon radical, R the aldehyde is R−C=O (with H below C). **1950** N. V. SIDGWICK *Chem. Elements* I. 30 It can be shown that the cyanamides $H_2N{\cdot}CN$ and HRN·CN are highly associated in benzene, while $R_2N{\cdot}CN$ is monomeric. **1966** WILLIAMS & FLEMING *Spectrosc. Methods in Org. Chem.* ii. 38 The absorption maximum of the nitroaniline XXXVI (R = Me) is at 385 mμ.. showing a red shift and marked reduction in intensity from that of the parent compound XXXVI (R = H) at 375 mμ.

2. *Physical Chem.* R is used to denote the *gas constant*, i.e. the constant of proportionality in the equation of state for an ideal gas, $PV = NRT$, where P = pressure, V = volume, n = the number of moles of gas, and T = absolute temperature; now usu. taken to be 8·314 joule $kelvin^{-1}$ $mole^{-1}$. [Arbitrary: first used by J. D. Van der Waals 1873, *Over de Continuitet van den Gas- en Vloiestoestand* (Leiden) 58.]

1880 *Phil. Mag.* IX. 393 In relation to pressure, volume, and temperature, gases follow.. with a certain degree of approximation, the laws of Mariotte and Gay-Lussac, which can in common be expressed by the following equation—pv = RT.. wherein.. R is a constant dependent on the nature of the gas. **1895** C. S. PALMER tr. *W. Nernst's Theoret. Chem.* I. i. 31 The factor R is only conditioned by the unit of measure chosen, but is independent of the chemical composition of the gases in question. **1940** GLASSTONE *Textbk. Physical Chem.* ix. 654 The value of *R* for solutions is thus very close to that of *R* usually accepted for a gas, namely 0·0821 liter-atm.., so that it is possible to write $\Pi V = RT$, where *R* may be taken as the gas constant [and Π = osmotic pressure]. **1978** P. W. ATKINS *Physical Chem.* 13 In this expression *R*, the gas constant, is another fundamental constant with the value 8·3 J K^{-1} mol^{-1}.

3. *Biol.* **a.** *r* is used in formulæ and elsewhere to denote the rate of increase of a population, usually representing the factor by which its size is multiplied in each generation; or the value which this factor would have if resources (food etc.) were unlimited.

1918 *Q. Publ. Amer. Statistical Assoc.* XVI. 123 Where *b* = birth rate per head per annum, *r* = natural rate of increase per head per annum... The formulae thus obtained give the relationship between *b* and *r*. **1954** ANDREWARTHA & BIRCH *Distribution & Abundance of Animals* iii. 33 In nature, one or several components may predominate to determine the *actual* rate of increase, which we shall call *r*. **1967** MACARTHUR & WILSON *Theory of Island Biogeogr.* vii. 150 Clearly.. *r* will be increased by a habitat or food shift which increases the density of available food. **1971** A. S. BOUGHEY *Fundamental Ecology* iii. 97 The biotic potential is usually expressed by a factor representing the intrinsic rate of natural increase *r*. **1977** J. L. HARPER *Population Biol. of Plants* i. 3 There is a growing tendency to talk and write about *r*-phases in the life of a population—phases when it explodes with near-exponential growth after a disaster or after a new colonization into an unexploited environment.

b. ***r selection***, the form of natural selection which acts on populations having ample resources and little or no competition.

1967 MACARTHUR & WILSON *Theory of Island Biogeogr.* vii. 149 In an environment with no crowding (*r* selection), genotypes which harvest the most food (even if wastefully) will rear the largest families and be most fit. **1973** P. A. COLINVAUX *Introd. Ecology* 618/2 *r-Selection*, selection for an opportunist strategy leading to an opportunist species. Traits are preserved which use energy to obtain a high natural rate of increase 'r'. **1976** *Nature* 12 Feb. 478/2 MacArthur & Wilson coined the terms *r* selection and *K* selection to describe two general kinds of selection they believed could be functioning in nature (*K* refers to carrying capacity and *r* to maximal intrinsic rate of natural increase, r_m). **1979** *Sci. Amer.* Jan. 26/3 The poles of evolutionary adaptation, *r* selection increasing the number of offspring (the prodigal mackerel roe with half a million eggs) and *K* selection ensuring survival (the proverbial royal litter, only one cub born at a time, but that one a lion).

4. *Spectroscopy.* *R* is used to denote the *Rydberg constant* s.v. RYDBERG 1.

1920 *Phil. Mag.* XXXIX. 47 If the nucleus be a simple point-charge, the negatived total energy *W* belonging to any one of the stationary orbits is given by $W/ch = \kappa^2 R/n^2$,.. where *n* is an integer, *c* the light velocity in vacuo, *h* Planck's constant, and *R* the Bohr expression of Rydberg's constant. **1926** G. BIRTWISTLE *Quantum Theory of Atom* ii. 21 In 1913, Niels Bohr.. gave a theory of the hydrogen spectrum which ..led.. to an expression for the Rydberg constant *R* in terms of known physical constants. **1965** R. N. DIXON *Spectroscopy & Struct.* ii. 31 Since the lowest energy level has $n = 1$, and the highest $n = \infty$, the Rydberg constant R_H corresponds to the minimum energy required for the removal of the electron. **1978** P. W. WATKINS *Physical Chem.* xiv. 427 Balmer.. pointed out that the wavelength of the light in the visible region.. fitted the expression $1/\lambda = R(\frac{1}{4} - 1/n^2)$, $n = 3, 4$.. where *R* is a constant now called the Rydberg constant, and having the value 109 677 cm^{-1}, or 3·289 8 × 10^{15} Hz.

5. *Psychol.* *R*, or *r*, is used in some methods of factor analysis in which traits or abilities are the variables (see quots.); also *attrib.*, as ***R, r technique***. Cf. Q III. 4.

1925 *Brit. Jrnl. Psychol.* July 75 Where *R* is the matrix of the *r*-correlation coefficients. **1927** C. SPEARMAN *Abilities of Man* vi. 73 The form recently preferred is given below. In it, as usual, the letter *r* stands for any correlation, whilst its two subscripts indicate the two abilities (tests, school marks, etc.) that are correlated. **1936** *Brit. Jrnl. Psychol.* Apr. 345 It is convenient to designate all previous factor analysis as *r* technique, and this new inverted form as *Q* technique. **1950** R. B. CATTELL *Personality* ii. 30 In *R* technique one would point to a particular trait-indicator test and say, 'This is the test measure of the surface trait or factor in question'. **1974** W. B. ARNDT *Theories of Personality* viii. 99 In an actual application of the procedure just described, fifty or more measurements would be made on one hundred or more subjects. This technique, based on normative data, is called the *R-technique*.

6. *Chem.* [Abbrev. of L. *rectus* right.] *R* is used to designate (compounds having) a configuration about an asymmetric carbon atom in which the substituents, placed in order according to certain rules, form a clockwise sequence when viewed from a particular direction. Opp. *S* (see S 13).

1956 R. S. CAHN et al. in *Experientia* XII. 83/2 The suggested indications for asymmetry leading, under the sequence and conversion rules, to a right- and left-handed pattern, are capital italic *R* and *S* respectively, where *R* derives from the Latin *rectus*, meaning 'right', and *S* from *sinister*... For the description of pseudo-asymmetric atoms, it is proposed to employ the corresponding lower-case italic symbols, *r* and *s*. *Ibid.* 85/2 The simplest case may be exemplified by bromochloroacetic acid (XV). Priority of the groups (a, b, c, d) is here determined simply by the atomic numbers as Br, Cl, C (of CO_2H), H. Hence, by the conversion rule.. formula (XV) represents an (*R*)-form. **1966** RAKOFF & ROSE *Org. Chem.* xiv. 477 Going from OH to CHO to CH_2OH traces a clockwise path, so the configuration about the asymmetric center in D-glyceraldehyde is rectus, and the compound would be designated (R)-glyceraldehyde. **1971** *Sci. Amer.* Aug. 46/3 One enantiomeric form of carvone, *R*-carvone, has a strong odor of spearmint; the other form, *S*-carvone (which is geometrically a mirror image..) has the odor of caraway. **1973** *Times* 20 Jan. 16/6 Most of the tests were therefore carried out using the R analogue which seemed to be free from side effects.

7. *Astr.* [Initial letter of *rapid*.] ***r-process***: a process believed to occur in stars in circumstances of high neutron flux (e.g. in supernova explosions), in which heavy atomic nuclei are formed from lighter ones by a combination of rapid neutron captures and slower beta decays.

1956 F. HOYLE et al. in *Science* 5 Oct. 612/2 We have distinguished two conditions under which the Neutron capture can take place, a slow (*s*) process and a rapid (*r*) process. *Ibid.*, The *r*-process we associate with the explosion of supernovae, the time scale being as small as 10 to 100 seconds. **1975** *Nature* 2 Oct. 362/1 The measured charge distribution in the vicinity of the Earth at ~0·5 GeV per nucleon strongly favours synthesis of these cosmic rays by the r-process (rapid neutron capture) within the last 10^7 yr. **1977** J. NARLIKAR *Struct. Universe* ii. 49 Whereas the s-process produces proton-rich nuclei, the r-process produces neutron-rich nuclei.

8. *Microbiology.* [Initial letter of *resistance*.] *R* is used to denote certain plasmids which confer drug-resistance on bacteria and can be transferred to other bacteria by conjugation.

1961 *Gunma Jrnl. Med. Sci.* X. 59 It is strongly suggested that there is a transmissible drug-resistance factor (R) which makes R^- cells drug resistant when infected with R^+ cells following cell-to-cell contact. **1962** *Jrnl. Bacteriol.* LXXXIV. 902/2 *R* or *R factor* is a general term for the infectious drug-resistance factors (Mitsuhashi, 1960; at the Meeting of Microbial Genetics at Mishima, Japan, it was agreed by investigators in this field to use the term 'R' for the multiple drug-resistance factor). **1967** *Jrnl. Gen. Microbiol.* XLIX. 97 Genetic alterations resulting in the loss or acquisition of F or R pili are strictly correlated with loss or gain of ability to transfer the chromosome by conjugation. **1969** A. M. CAMPBELL *Episomes* iii. 41 Cells harboring R can transfer it to other cells. **1975** *Sci. Amer.* July 28/3 Antibiotic-resistant *E*[*scherichia*] *coli* isolated in many parts of the world.. were found to contain plasmids, designated *R* factors.. carrying the genetic information for products that in one way or another could interfere with the action of specific antibiotics.

†**ra**[1]. *Sc. Obs.* Also 6 **rae, raye.** [= ON. *rá* (Da. and Sw. *rå*), Du. *ra* (Kilian *rae, rha, rah*), MLG. *râ*, MHG. *rahe* (G. *rahe, raa*):—Comm. Teut. **rahā* pole, stake. In Sc. prob. adopted from ON., or Du.] A sail-yard.

1494 *Accts. Ld. High Treasurer Scot.* (1877) I. 253 Ane gret mast, ane ra. *Ibid.*, Thir rais and the takling. **1513** DOUGLAS *Æneis* v. xiv. 8 Thai.. Set in a fang, and threw the ra abak. **1566** KNOX *Hist. Ref.* (1846) I. 109 Our Schotish schippis war stayed, the sayles tackin from thare rayes. **1589** *Munim. Irvine* (1890) I. 76 To fens and arreist the same schipis.. and take the saillis fra the rais.

‖**ra**[2] (rɑː). *Physical Geogr.* Pl. **ras,** ‖**raer.** [Norw.] One of the terminal moraines near the coast in southern Norway and Sweden that are in the form of long ridges of gravel and clay with a covering of large stones.

1902 *Geol. Mag.* Decade IV. IX. 319 Outside the terminal ra, that is, between the moraine and the coastline,.. there is a widely spread deposit of clay. **1957** J. K. CHARLESWORTH *Quaternary Era* II. xxx. 627 The radially dispersed erratics and diverging striae transverse to the morainic *Raer*.. finally overcame both prejudice and honest conviction. *Ibid.* xlii. 1172 The *Ras*, traceable as far as Stavanger, have been correlated with the double moraines observed in many fjords and fjord-valleys.

ra, obs. f. RAW; obs. north. f. ROE.

raack, obs. f. RACK *sb.*[7]

‖**raad** (rɑːt), *sb.*[1] *S. Afr.* [Du., = council; freq. as shortening of HEEMRAD, VOLKSRAAD, etc.] A council, an assembly; *spec.* (usu. with capital initial) the legislative assembly of one of the former Boer republics (*Hist.*).

1850 R. GRAY *Jrnl.* 8 May in *Jrnl. Bishop's Visitation Tour in 1850* (1851) 25 These men have formed themselves into a Republic, and have their 'Raad' (Council). **1856** C. J. ANDERSSON *Lake Ngami* v. 57 He laid his complaint before the chief of the tribe; and a 'raad', or counsel, was held. **1873** F. BOYLE *To Cape for Diamonds* xii. 153 The gentlemen.. obtained their grant under solemn seal and bond of the Transvaal Parliament, or *raad*. **1930** *Times Lit. Suppl.* 7 Aug. 635/2 The tribal council has become a 'raad' consisting of the chief, ex-officio, and of members elected at the mass meeting. **1940** F. B. YOUNG *City of Gold* 261 So the Raad sat ..voting Burgers down. **1963** S. CLOETE *Rags of Glory* vi. 53 Field Kornet Adriaan de la Rey, the member of the Raad who had been against the war. **1973** *Hansard S. Afr.* 8 Feb. 297 The Minister of Labour..says that in no circumstances will he sit in the same 'raad' as a non-white.

raad (rəˈɑːd, rɑːd), *sb.*[2] [Arabic.] The electric cat-fish, *Malapterurus electricus*, belonging to the family Malapteruridæ, found in the Nile and other rivers of central and western tropical Africa, and distinguished by electric cells in the fatty tissue just beneath the skin.

In quot. 1878 = TORPEDO *sb.* 1 a.

1869 A. GÜNTHER in J. & B. H. Petherick *Trav. Cent. Afr.* II. 240 (*Raad* or *Raasch.*) The electric Silurus is spread over the whole of tropical Africa. **1878** *Encycl. Brit.* VIII. 8/2 The Arabians had long before given this fish [*sc.* the torpedo] the name of *raad* or lightning. **1931** J. R. NORMAN *Hist. Fishes* viii. 149 This species is used by the Arabs for food, and they refer to it as the Raad or Thunder-fish. **1957** E. LE DANOIS *Fishes of World* iv. 130 The electric cat-fish.., the raad or thunder-fish, lives in African rivers.

raad, var. RAD *a.*[2] *Obs.*

raaf, obs. f. RAFF *sb.*[3]

raak, obs. f. RAKE *sb.*[1]

raas(e, obs. forms of RACE *sb.*[1], RASE *v.*[1]

rab[1] (ræb). [ad. F. *rabot* in same sense; cf. RABBIT *sb.*[3]] A wooden beater, formed like a crutch, used for mixing the ingredients of mortar.

a **1825** FORBY *Voc. E. Anglia.* **1860** WORCESTER cites LEONARD. **1875** KNIGHT *Dict. Mech.* 1850/1.

rab[2]. *dial.* = RAD *sb.*[2] (q.v.).

1830 LOUDON *Cottage Arch.* §840 Cob is used for filling in the framework, which is previously lathed with stout slit oak... This sort of work is called rab and dab.

rab[3]. Chiefly Cornish (orig. *dial.*). [Shortened f. Cornish *rabman*, *-men* in the same sense. Ultimate origin obscure. Also recorded from Wales (quot. 1910).

There is no apparent connection with Scottish and Northumberland dial. *raab*, *rab* (the fall of a cliff, a mass of broken rock, etc.), which is of Scandinavian origin (see e.g. S.N.D.).]

Rough or stony subsoil; rubble, gravel.

[**1769** W. BORLASE *Antiquities Cornwall* 452/1 *Rabman*, rubble; that mixture of clay and stone which has not been moved since the flood, and generally lies over the karn. **1868** *Proc. Soc. Antiquaries London* IV. 164 The floor..is composed of the hard subsoil of the country, called by the Cornish 'rabman'.] **1880** COURTNEY & COUCH *Gloss. Words Cornwall* 46/1 *Rab*, decomposed granite used for mending roads. **1910** W. M. MORRIS *Gloss. Demetian Dial.*, *Rab*, rough, stony soil; sub-soil. **1912** *Antiquity* XXVI. 90 The site of the hut was cleared and levelled by cutting back into the hillside and spreading the excavated rab over the lower part of the floor. **1928** *Jrnl. Brit. Archaeol. Assoc.* XXXIV. 153 The paving stones had been laid on the rab or subsoil. **1961** E. CLARK *Cornish Fogous* ix. 68 A drain passes from the fogou to the outer wall, the floor of which is composed of the natural rab... The floor of the main structure is of stoneless rab. **1962** *Punch* 30 May 836/3 Clutching for dear life at the poor rab (the local name for the pink subsoil) this tree has grown.

rabab, rababa, varr. REBAB.

rababoo, var. RUBBABOO.

†ˈ**raband**. *Sc. Obs.* Also rai-. [f. RA[1] + BAND: cf. Da. and Sw. *råband*, Du. *raband* (Kilian *raeband*), G. *rah-*, *raaband*, and ON. *rábenda* to bend a sail.] A roband or robbin.

1513 DOUGLAS *Æneis* III. iv. 110 Do lows the rabandis, and lat doun the sail. **1549** *Compl. Scot.* vi. 40 Cut the raibandis, and lat the mane sail and top sail fal.

rabanet, variant of RABINET.

rabanna (rəˈbænə). [Malagasy.] A fabric woven from raffia.

1883 *Encycl. Brit.* XV. 172/2 The chief articles of export being..rôfia palm cloths (*rabànnas*) and fibre. **1969** R. T. WILCOX *Dict. Costume* (1970) 281/1 *Rabanna*, a textile imported from Madagascar. Used for hats and bags.

rabap, var. REBAB.

rabarber, obs. form of RHUBARB *sb.*

†**rabat**, *sb.*[1] *Obs. rare*$^{-0}$. Also 5 rabet. [a. F. *rabot* = Pg. *rabôte*.] A carpenter's plane.

c **1440** *Promp. Parv.* 421/2 *Rabet*, yryne tool of carpentrye, *runcina*. **1530** PALSGR. 260/1 Rabat an yrone for a carpentar, *rabot*. **1572** HULOET, *Rabat*, a playne that carpenters vse, *runcina*.

rabat, *sb.*[2] *Obs.* exc. *Hist. rare.* Also 6 rabbat. [a. F. *rabat* a turned-down collar.] **a.** = REBATO.

(Recent Dicts. give *rabat* in senses of the mod.F. word.)

1578 *Inv. R. Wardr.* (1815) 231 Huidis quaiffis collaris rabattis. *Ibid.* 234 Ane rabbat of hollane claith. **1865** F. B. PALLISER *Hist. Lace* viii. 126 Suddenly, at the court of Henry [III of France], the fraise gave way to the rabat, or turn-down collar. **1953** M. POWYS *Lace & Lace-Making* vii. 77 With the coming of the wig or natural long curled hair the ruff was given up and men wore their lace in front falling under the chin in the form first of a cravat or Rabat and later in ruffles.

b. A type of turned-down clerical collar. Also, = STOCK *sb.*[1] 44 b. Also, a similar garment worn by a layman.

1889 in *Cent. Dict.* **1931** D. ATTWATER *Catholic Encycl. Dict.* 441/1 *Rabat*... Part of the dress of the French secular clergy. A white *rabat* is worn by the Brothers of Christian Doctrine, university professors, magistrates, barristers and attorneys. **1936** J. G. COZZENS *Men & Brethren* 122 You can go courting, if you like; but you have to go in a rabat, so to say. **1966** H. KEMELMAN *Saturday the Rabbi went Hungry* (1967) ii. 18 In spite of the clerical collar and black silk rabat, he looked more like a football player than an Anglican minister. **1975** *New Yorker* 3 Feb. 23/1 He is dressed in an ultra-attractive robin's-egg-blue rabat and brown velvet suit.

rabat (rəˈbæt), *v. Geom.* Also rebat(e. [ad. F. *rabattre* to lower, fold back, rabat.] *trans.* To rotate (a plane) about its line of intersection with another plane, *spec.* the horizontal plane, until the two coincide. Hence **raˈbatted** *ppl. a.*, **raˈbatting** *vbl. sb.* Also **raˈbatment**, the process of rabatting.

1885 *Encycl. Brit.* XIX. 801/1 In rabatting the plane π_3 its trace OB with the plane π_2 will come to the position OD. **1908** L. N. G. FILON *Introd. Projective Geom.* i. 7 For practical purposes..it is convenient to rotate one of the two planes about *x* until it coincides with the other plane. A figure in the former plane rotates with it, but is fixed in it. Such a process is termed rabatting. *Ibid.*, If..we rabat the figure 2 upon the plane a_1 we obtain a new figure 3 in the plane a_1. *Ibid.* 10 Locus of vertex of projection during rabatment. **1931** A. H. JAMESON *Contour Geom.* i. 13 A.. way to find the true angle between two lines or the true shape of any figure drawn on a plane, is to 'rebate' the plane in which the two lines or the figure lies, i.e. to rotate the plane into a horizontal position about one of the contour lines as axis. Draw a vertical section across the plane at right angles to the contours and draw circular arcs.., giving the rebated contours. *Ibid.* (*heading*) Rebatement. **1949** N. L. REECE *Newnes Building Geom.* 206 A rebattement is the name given to the construction when a figure lying in an inclined plane is turned or 'rebatted' so as to lie in the horizontal plane. **1950** G. A. HANBY *Geometry* viii. 92 Find the true shape of the surface *abcdef* by rabatment. *Ibid.* 93 The true shape of the section is rabatted to the left to keep it clear of the plan, so with *T* as centre, rabat *b'c'* to B'C'.

rabat, obs. form of RABBET *sb.*

†**rabate**, *sb. Obs. rare.* Also rabbate. [a. OF. *rabat*, *rabbat* sb. to *rabattre*: see next, and cf. REBATE *sb.*] Diminution; lessening, drawing in.

1589 PUTTENHAM *Eng. Poesie* II. xi[i]. (Arb.) 109 In his altitude he wil require diuers rabates to hold so many sizes of meetres. *Ibid.* III. xi. 173 Your figures of rabbate be as many [as the 'figures of addition'.]

†**rabate**, *v. Obs.* Also 6 rabbate. [a. F. *rabattre* to beat down, etc.; the more usual form in Eng. is *rebate*.] = REBATE *v.* in various senses.

1489 *Sc. Acts Jas. IV* (1814) 222 And samekle..to be defalkit and Rabatit in þe price of þe said siluer. **1530** PALSGR. 677/2, I rabate a porcyon out of a great somme. **1585** A. POULET *Letter-bk.* (1874) 69 Rabating so many of my number..cannot be any way chargeable. **1632** GUILLIM *Heraldry* III. xx. (ed. 3) 228 She [a Hawk] is sayd to Rabate, when by the motion of the bearers hand she recouerth the fist.

Hence †**rabated** *ppl. a.*; †**rabating** *vbl. sb.*

1589 PUTTENHAM *Eng. Poesie* III. xi. (Arb.) 173 Sometimes by adding sometimes by rabbating of a sillable or letter. *Ibid.* xxv. 310 The full and emptie euen, extant, rabbated, hollow, or..other figure and passion of quantitie.

rabate, obs. form of RABBET *sb.* and *v.*

rabatine. *rare*$^{-1}$. [app. f. F. *rabat* RABAT *sb.*[2] + -INE.] A low collar.

1821 SCOTT *Kenilw.* xxiii, Reform..that precise ruff of thine for an open rabatine of lace and cut work.

rabato, variant of REBATO *Obs.*

†**rabattued**, *a. Obs. rare*$^{-1}$. [f. F. *rabattu* (pa. pple. of *rabattre* RABATE) + -ED.] Blunted.

1562 J. SHUTE tr. *Cambini's Turk. Wars* 1 b, Scanderbeg.. delighted..with his companiones to use the launce, and the rabattued sworde.

rabbat, rabbate, varr. RABAT *sb.*[2], RABATE. *Obs.*

rabbatte, obs. form of RABBIT *sb.*[1]

rabbenet, obs. form of RABINET.

rabbet (ˈræbɪt), *sb.* Forms: 5 rabit, 5–8 rabet, 6 rabat(e, -att, -ett, rabbott-, 8–9 rabbit, 7– rabbet. See also REBATE. [a. OF. *rabat*, *rabbat* the act of beating down, a check, abatement in price, recess in a wall, etc., sb. from *rabattre* to beat back or down: see REBATE *v.*]

I. 1. a. A channel, groove, or slot (usually of rectangular section) cut along the edge or face of a piece (or surface) of wood, stone, etc., and intended to receive the edge or end of another piece or pieces, or a tongue specially wrought on these to fit the groove. **b.** A rectangular recess made along a projecting angle or arris.

Both forms are extensively used in Carpentry in joining or framing wood, the two pieces being commonly either in the same plane or at right angles to each other. In a *double rabbet* (b) the shoulder on one piece fits into the rabbet of the other. In Masonry, a rabbet (b) is often made to receive the edge of a door, window, etc.; in picture-frames the rabbet receives the edges of the glass.

1404 [see *rabbet-stock* in 3]. *c* **1425** WYNTOUN *Cron.* III. ii. 332 Thare he made than rak & rak Quhyll conyhe and rabet bath he brak. *c* **1440** *Promp. Parv.* 421/2 Rabet, in a werke of carpentrye, *runctura*, *incastratura*. **1538** LELAND *Itin.* I. 55 By pulling one or all wold cum downe, briste high in rabettes, and serve for Deskes. **1593–4** in Swayne *Sarum Church-w. Acc.* (1896) 299 Yotting in of the hookes and hewinge of the Rabbottes. **1663** GERBIER *Counsel* 68 Oaken Windows with a double Rabet. **1711** W. SUTHERLAND *Shipbuild. Assist.* 46 Cut the Rabbit of the Keel, Stem and Stern-post the exact Bigness of your Plank. **1793** SMEATON *Edystone L.* §51 The windows, shutters and doors..falling into a rabbet, when shut, their outside formed a part of the general surface. **1830** HEDDERWICK *Marine Arch.* 257 The rabbet is cut out in form of a V, having its breadth equal to the thickness of the garboard-plank. **1870** H. MEADE *New Zealand* 324 The parts are joined by scarfing with a bevelled rabbet at the juncture.

2. †**a.** A tongue to fit into a groove. *Obs.* **b.** One of the sides of a rabbet made in an arris; a shoulder, a ledge.

1678 MOXON *Mech. Exerc.* I. 103 Upon this Rabbet rides a Block with a Groove in its under side..made fit to receive the Rabbet on the Planck. **1728** DESAGULIERS in *Phil. Trans.* XXXV. 606 A square Hole..to receive a Piece..shutting close with a Rabbet or Shoulder. **1826** KIRBY & SP. *Entomol.* l. IV. 544 So as to form a cavity all round of a proper width to closely receive the rabbet. **1867** J. HOGG *Microsc.* I. iii. 188 The dotted ring shows the rabbet on which the centre-piece rests.

3. *attrib.*, as ***rabbet-iron***, ***-joint***, ***measure***, ***-plane***, ***-saw***, †***-stock***; **rabbet-head** (see quot.).

1830 LOUDON *Cottage Arch.* §282 The *rabbet-head of a window is a Scotch term for what in England is called the reveal of a window. **1552** HULOET s.v. *Rabat. Runcina* is the *rabet iron. **1832** WEBSTER, *Rabbeted*, united by a *rabbet joint. **1838** J. BRITTON *Dict. Archit.* 387 The junction thus effected being called a rabbet-joint. **1886** *Pall Mall G.* 26 July 4/2 A frame whose '*rabbet' measure is 96 by 72 inches. **1678** MOXON *Mech. Exerc.* I. 67 The *Rabbet-plain..is to cut part of the upper edge of a Board..square down into the Board. **1881** YOUNG *Every man his own Mechanic* 92 The rabbet or rebate plane. **1875** KNIGHT *Dict. Mech.* 1850/1 *Rabbet-saw. **1404** *Durham Acc. Rolls* (Surtees) I. 396, j *rabitstoke cum ij scrwes. **1573**, **1688** [see CLAVESTOCK].

II. †**4.** *Fencing.* The act of beating down an opponent's weapon. *Obs. rare*$^{-1}$.

c **1450** *Fencing with two handed Sword* in *Rel. Ant.* I. 309 Thy stoppis, thy foynys..Thy spryngys, thy quarters, thy rabetis also.

5. An elastic beam fixed so as to give a rebound to a large fixed hammer; a spring-pole.

1825 J. NICHOLSON *Operat. Mechanic* 335 The hammer in its ascent strikes against this beam, called the rabbit, which by its elasticity reacts upon the hammer [etc.]. **1831** J. HOLLAND *Manuf. Metal* I. 241 An elastic rabbet or spring pole to give a rebound to the hammer. **1852** MORFIT *Tanning & Currying* (1853) 231 Two vertical pieces, supporting horizontally a rabbit, or wooden spring.

rabbet (ˈræbɪt), *v.* Forms: 4, 8 rabit, 5 rabat, -yt, 5–9 rabet, (7 -ett), 6 rabate, rabbat, -ott, -itt, 8 rabbit, 7– rabbet. [app. f. RABBET *sb.*, but found earlier than this in the vbl. sb. *rabityng* (Wyclif), the second vowel of which makes direct adoption of F. *rabattre* unlikely.]

1. *trans.* To join or fix by means of a rabbet or rabbets. Also with *in*.

1565 COOPER *Thesaurus*, *Trabes compactiles*,..Joygned or rabbated one within the other. **1620** BEST *Farm. Bks.* (Surtees) 153 Hee is..to sawe the rayles and postes, and sett them in a groundsell, and rabbitt them in to the rayle above. **1693** EVELYN *De La Quint. Compl. Gard.* II. *Orange-Trees* ii. 5 A double Cloison made of Boards well Rabetted. **1829** *Nat. Philos.* I. *Heat* x. 60 (U.K.S.) It should have a wooden cover, rabbeted in.

2. To form a rabbet in; to provide with a rabbet; to cut *away* or *down* as in making a rabbet.

1572 HULOET, To rabate or make suche chaumfreyes in any thing. **1667** PRIMATT *City & C. Build.* 63 Suppose that a Window hath four lights, and double rabbetted for Ornament. **1679** MOXON *Mech. Exerc.* I. 148 The Window Frame hath every one of its Lights rabbetted on its outside about half an Inch into the Frame. **1711** W. SUTHERLAND *Shipbuild. Assist.* 25 When that is trim'd, scarf'd, and rabbited, mind to set it very streight. **1794** W. FELTON *Carriages* (1801) I. 12 The middle rails are..rabbetted on the top for the boarding or pannels. **1877** COUES & ALLEN *N. Amer. Rod.* 229 The general face is rabbeted down externally. *Ibid.* 532 The outer portion is rabbeted away.

3. *intr.* To join *on* or lap *over* by means of a rabbet.

c **1850** *Rudim. Navig.* (Weale) 101 The upper piece rabbeting on the lower piece. *Ibid.* 119 It rabbets over the ends of the deals.

rabbet, obs. form of RABBIT *sb.*[1]

rabbeted (ˈræbɪtɪd), *ppl. a.* [f. RABBET *v.*] In which a rabbet is cut.

1797 *Monthly Mag.* III. 145 The door shuts without noise, by means of a spring affixed in the rabitted jamb. *c* **1850** *Rudim. Navig.* (Weale) 101 Built with rabbeted or ciphered plank. **1869** SIR E. REED *Shipbuild.* ii. 19 The.. steam-ship 'Persia'..has also a solid rabbeted keel.

rabbeting (ˈræbɪtɪŋ), *vbl. sb.* [f. RABBET *v.* + -ING[1].] The process of grooving boards, etc. by cutting rabbets, or of fitting rabbeted boards together; also the groove or rabbeted portion of such boards.

1382 WYCLIF *Exod.* xxxvi. 22 Two rabitynges weren bi eche tables, that the tone to that other myȝt be ioyned. *c* **1440** *Promp. Parv.* 421/2 Rabetynge to-gedyr of ij. bordys, *supra in* knyttynge, or ioynynge. **1463** *Mann. & Househ. Exp.* (Roxb.) 193 Settyng in of hedys of pypys and barells, and rabating of xl. ber pypys. **1530** PALSGR. 260/1 Rabettyng of bordes, *rabetture.* **1658** PHILLIPS, *Rabbetings*, a term in Navigation, the letting in of the planks to the keel. **1678** MOXON *Mech. Exerc.* I. 67 When two Boards are thus lapped on the edges over one another, this lapping over is called Rabbetting. **1769** FALCONER *Dict. Marine* (1776), *Assembler*, to unite the several pieces of a ship, as by rabbeting, scarfing, scoring, tenanting, &c. **1869** SIR E. REED *Shipbuild.* iii. 48 The rabbeting has now been almost universally dispensed with.

rabbett(e, obs. forms of RABBET, RABBIT.

rabbi (ˈræbaɪ, ˈræbɪ), *sb.*[1] Forms: 4–5 rabi, 4–6 raby, 5 rabe, 7 rabbie, 8 rabby, 6– rabbi. [a. (orig. through L. *rabbi*, Gr. ῥαββί) Heb. *rabbī* 'my master', f. *rabh* master, with pronominal suffix. Cf. OF. *rabi, rabbi* (mod.F. *rabbin*).]

1. A title of respect (in use since the first century B.C.) given by the Jews to doctors of the law.

a. As a form of address. (In English use only in translations or echoes of N.T. passages.)

c **1000** *Ags. Gosp.* John i. 38 Hi cwædon to him 'rabbi', þæt is ȝecweden & ȝereht lareow, 'hwar eardast þu?' *a* **1300** *Cursor M.* 15766 Iudas..lepe him to, 'Aue rabi', coth he. **1377** LANGL. *P. Pl.* B. XVIII. 50 'Aue, rabby!' quod that ribaude, and threw redes at hym. *c* **1386** CHAUCER *Sompn. T.* 479 God liketh nat that Raby men vs calle. *c* **1450** HOLLAND *Howlat* 94 Befor the Pape..on kneis he fell; said 'Aue Raby'. **1526** TINDALE *Matt.* xxiii. 8 Ye shall not suffre youre selves to be called Rabi. *a* **1550** *Image Hypocr.* I. 172 in *Skelton's Wks.* (1843) II. 416/1 Wher they may haue metinge With lordes and with ladyes, To be called Rabyes. **1611** BIBLE *John* i. 38 They said vnto him, Rabbi, (which is to say being interpreted, Master) where dwellest thou?

b. Prefixed to personal names.

1340 HAMPOLE *Pr. Consc.* 7685 Raby Moryses says alle þis. **1387** TREVISA *Higden* (Rolls) III. 365 Avicenna preyseþ hym wel..and Raby Moyses. **1541** R. COPLAND *Guydon's Quest. Chirurg.* Y iij b, Rabymoyses..approued water dystylled of a leane gotes mylke. **1587** GOLDING *De Mornay* xxix. 470 The same man whom..the Chronicle of the Iewes calleth Rabbi Iohanan. **1677** HALE *Prim. Orig. Mank.* III. vii. 285 The Blew and Red Men of Rabbi Elcha, that came out of the Mountains of Armenia. **1727–41** CHAMBERS *Cycl.* s.v., Rabbi Juda is said to have composed the Mischna..in the IId century. **1838** *Penny Cycl.* XII. 92/2 The Jerusalem Talmud appears to have been compiled..by Rabbi Jochonan.

2. a. A Jewish doctor of the law. In mod. Jewish use properly applied only to one who is authorized by ordination to deal with questions of law and ritual, and to perform certain functions.

When used in pl. as the designation of a class (*the rabbis*), the reference is usually to those Jewish teachers or writers who have more commonly been called *rabbins*.

1484 CAXTON *Fables of Alfonce* i, A Rabe of Lucanye sayd to his sone in this maner. **1599** SANDYS *Europæ Spec.* (1632) 226 Each Synagogue hath has Rabbi, to expound their Law. **1641** MILTON *Animadv.* ii. Wks. (1851) 207 The gowned Rabbies..were of opinion that hee was a friend of Beelzebub. **1688** R. HOLME *Armoury* III. 221/1 The Jews.. are Married in the open Aire, either in the Streets or Gardens, by their Rabbies. **1788** GIBBON *Decl. & F.* l. (ed. Milman) V. 22 The dreams and traditions of the Jewish rabbis. **1838** LYTTON *Leila* IV. v, I have been summoned into the presence of their chief rabbi. **1838** *Penny Cycl.* XII. 92/2 The Rabbis of Tiberias and Babylon wrote numerous commentaries upon it [the Mishna]. **1897** *Allbutt's Syst. Med.* II. 391 The early and almost universal seizures of medical officers, of the clergy and rabbis.

b. *transf.* One whose learning, authority, or office is comparable to that of a Jewish rabbi. (Freq. contemptuous.)

1553 BALE *Gardiner's 'De vera Obed.'* To Rdr. A vij b, Yf these ruffling rabbies in theyr Sermons & aduised Orationes said and wrote the truthe. **1629** L. OWEN *Spec. Jesuit.* 1 These great Rabbies that call themselues Iesuites. **1647** N. BACON *Disc. Govt. Eng.* I. ii. (1739) 3 The deep obligement of the People unto these their Rabbies [the Druids]. **1691** WOOD *Ath. Oxon.* II. 175 This book..pusled the Presbyterian Rabbies for a time. **1855** MACAULAY *Hist. Eng.* III. xi. 98 One of the great Presbyterian Rabbies..might well doubt whether..he should be benefited by a comprehension. *a* **1894** STEVENSON *Weir of Hermiston* (1896) i. 24 'I can't see it,' said the little Rabbi... 'No, I cannae see it.' **1932** *Amer. Speech* VII. 278 [New York Post Office] *Rabbi*, one who aids in the securing of a special privilege or favor. **1969** *New Yorker* 3 May 64/2, I asked him if he had done any thinking lately about..violence... 'Mitch Ginsberg has been my rabbi in that,' the Mayor answered. **1972** B. F. CONNERS *Don't embarrass Bureau* (1973) II. 192 You're damn lucky. You came out of the thing pretty clean. You got a rabbi down at the Bureau?

3. *Comb.*, as ***rabbi-like*** adj.

1611 COTGR., *Rabinique*, Rabbie-like, of the Rabbies.

Hence †**ˈrabbi** *v. trans.*, to call 'Rabbi'. *Obs.*

1583 STUBBES *Anat. Abus.* I. K iv, He who hath moni enough shalbe rabbied and maistered at euery word.

rabbi (ˈræbɪ, ˈræbaɪ), *sb.*[2] [Corruption of RABAT[2].] = STOCK *sb.*[1] 44 b. Cf. RABAT[2] b.

1909 J. A. NAINFA *Costume of Prelates* iii. 50 Our Roman Collar..consists of two parts, a starched circle of white linen —the collar, and a piece of cloth or silk to which the collar itself is fastened by means of buttons, hooks, etc., and has been given the..name of 'rabbi'. **1948** H. J. MCCLOUD *Clerical Dress & Insignia of R.C. Ch.* viii. 74 The rabbi is a loose breast piece of silk or woolen material. **1978** J. CARROLL *Mortal Friends* IV. ii. 386 Father McShane..was carefully decked out, too, but clerically and with such fastidiousness as to seem almost the dandy. He wore his black suit and rabbi, of course, with the spotless high collar which was too tight.

rabbin (ˈræbɪn). Also 6 rabbyn, 6–7 -ine, 7 -yne; 6 rabyne, 6–7 -ine, 7–8 -in. [a. F. *rabbin* or ad. med.L. *rabbinus*: cf. It. *rabbino*, Pg., Sp. *rabino*.

The source of the *n* in these forms is obscure: it may have originated in pl. forms (*rabbins, rabbini*) on the supposition that the pl. of the Heb. word was **rabbin* (cf. *assassin, bedouin*, etc.).]

a. = RABBI 2 a (but mainly used in *pl.* to designate the chief Jewish authorities on matters of law and doctrine, the most important of whom flourished between the second and thirteenth centuries of the Christian era).

1579 E. K. in *Spenser's Sheph. Cal.* Gen. Argt., According to the opinion of the best Rabbins..God made the worlde in that Moneth. **1612** BREREWOOD *Lang. & Relig.* 239 The Talmud and Targum..and the books of the latter rabbines. **1676** GLANVILL *Ess. Philos. & Relig.* v. 22 'Tis said in the Talmud, If two Rabbins differ [etc.]. **1741** WATTS *Improv. Mind* I. iv. §1 For a lawyer to learn Hebrew and read the Rabbins. **1832** W. IRVING *Alhambra* II. 23 Instructed..in the language of birds, by a Jewish Rabbin. **1852** THACKERAY *Esmond* I. xi, All the parsons, cardinals, ministers, muftis, and rabbins in the world.

†**b.** = RABBI 2 b. *Obs.*

1531 ELYOT *Gov.* III. xxv, Some of those Rabines..which in comparison of the sayde noble doctours be..unethe lettered. **1531** TINDALE *Exp. 1 John* 5 We remayne all blynde generally, as well our great Rabynes..as the lay people. **1606** in *Crt. & Times Jas. I* (1848) I. 65 Their masters and rabbins, the Jesuits. **1632** LITHGOW *Trav.* I. 35 She is both the Spouse, and the mother of God, saith a Rabbin of theirs.

c. Used as *pl.* (see etym. note).

1826 SIR W. DRUMMOND *Orig.* iii. 105 Many of the Rabbin have understood by Baal Berith the Lord of the Covenant. **1860** MOTLEY *Netherl.* (1868) I. v. 146 A match for the doctors, bishops or rabbin of Europe.

rabbinate (ˈræbɪnət). [f. prec. + -ATE: cf. F. *rabbinat.*] **a.** The office or dignity of a rabbi. **b.** The period during which some one is a rabbi. **c.** *coll.* Rabbis as a body or class.

1702 C. MATHER *Magn. Chr.* IV. ii. §8. 146 He..seemed inclinable to the Jewish Rule about the Rabbinate. **1881** *Encycl. Brit.* XIII. 681 Gradually the Talmud..was abandoned almost entirely to candidates for the rabbinate. **1890** *Jewish Intelligence* Mar. 35 During the Rabbinate of Dr. Adler. **1892** ZANGWILL *Childr. Ghetto* I. 27 The Rabbinate was invited to address the philanthropists.

rabbindom (ˈræbɪndəm). [f. as prec. + -DOM.] The rule and government of rabbis; the sphere of rabbinical authority.

1889 BRUCE *Kingd. God* xi. 266 The state of matters which prevailed in Rabbindom. **1890** E. JOHNSON *Rise Christendom* 32 The twelfth century is the great age of early Rabbindom.

rabbinet, obs. form of RABINET.

rabbinic (rəˈbɪnɪk), *a.* and *sb.* [f. RABBIN + -IC, prob. after med. or mod.L. *rabbinic-us*. Cf. F. *rabbinique* (1611), It. *rabbinico*, Pg., Sp. *rabinico*.]

A. *adj.* = RABBINICAL.

1612 SELDEN *Illustr. Drayton's Poly-olb.* v. 168 The Rabbinic conceit upon the Creation. **1678** CUDWORTH *Intell. Syst.* I. iv. §30. 469 Those Rabbinick Writers commonly interpret certain places of the Scripture to this sence. *a* **1711** KEN *Hymnarium* Poet. Wks. 1721 II. 146 To extract from Mud rabbinick Gold. **1879** FARRAR *St. Paul* I. 136 Illiterate men, untrained in the schools of..rabbinic wisdom.

B. *sb.* **1.** Rabbinical Hebrew.

1832 in WEBSTER. **1878** *Academy* 606/3 A good means of, and help in, practising Rabbinic.

2. *pl.* The study of the writings or doctrines of the rabbins.

1905 *Jewish Encycl.* XI. 93/2 In 1892 Schechter was elected reader in rabbinics [at Cambridge]. **1973** *Jewish Chron.* 2 Feb. 16/5 Dr Nicholas de Lange, lecturer in rabbinics at Cambridge University. **1976** *N.Y. Times* 30 Dec. 26 A Russian-born professor of rabbinics.

rabbinical (rəˈbɪnɪkəl), *a.* [f. as prec. + -AL[1].]

1. Of things: Pertaining to, or characteristic of, the rabbins, their learning, writings, etc.

1622 BOYS *Wks.* 4 It is a Rabinicall conceit, that the last Psalme hath thirteene Halleluiahs [etc.]. **1713** ADDISON *Guard.* No. 138 ¶7 A Rabbinical story which has in it the oriental way of thinking. **1779–81** JOHNSON *L.P., Cowley* (1790) I. 37 In the following verses we have a Rabbinical opinion concerning Manna. **1856** STANLEY *Sinai & Pal.* I. i. 34 The grotesqueness and absurdity of the Rabbinical interpretations.

b. *spec.* of the later form of the Hebrew language or character used by the rabbins.

1727–41 CHAMBERS *Cycl.* s.v. *Hebrew*, Modern, or Rabbinical Hebrew character, is a good neat character, formed of the square Hebrew by rounding it. *Ibid.*, The rabbinical Hebrew must be allowed a very copious language. **1817** COLERIDGE *Biog. Lit.* 55 Of the Hebrew..the remainder seemed to be in the Rabbinical dialect.

2. Of persons: Belonging to the class of rabbis or rabbins; resembling a rabbi; occupied with or skilled in rabbinical literature.

1642 MILTON *Apol. Smect.* i. Wks. (1851) 282 The Masoreths and Rabbinicall Scholiasts. **1711** ADDISON *Spect.* No. 221 ¶10 We had a Rabbinical Divine in England. **1828** SYDNEY SMITH *Serm. Charity* Wks. 1859 II. 248/1 A very short..apologue, taken from the Rabbinical writers. **1838–9** HALLAM *Hist. Lit.* II. II. viii. §45. 349 Hugh Broughton was a deeply learned and rabbinical scholar.

Hence **raˈbbinically** *adv.*, in a rabbinical manner.

1684 N. S. *Crit. Enq. Edit. Bible* App. 286 Vossius..who so greedily catches at dreams more than Rabbinically. *a* **1751** BOLINGBROKE *Fragm.* lxi. Wks. 1754 V. 456 If he [the apostle] understood it as Locke did, he reasoned very rabinically. **1833** *New Monthly Mag.* XXXVII. 149 Responding most rabbinically to the serjeant on this knotty matter.

†**ˈrabbinish**, *a. Obs. rare*[−1]. = RABBINICAL.

1652 GAULE *Magastrom.* 123 Errors of paganish, rabbinish, and other magicians and astrologers.

rabbinism (ˈræbɪnɪz(ə)m). [f. RABBIN + -ISM: cf. F. *rabbinisme*, Pg., Sp. *rabinismo*.]

1. The teaching or doctrines of the rabbins.

1652 GAULE *Magastrom.* 43 The key of doctorall and magisteriall rabbinismes and cabalismes. **1833** *Blackw. Mag.* XXXIII. 628 Rabbinism has continued full of trivial observances. **1887** *Spectator* 1 Oct. 1307 The history of mediæval rabbinism.

2. A rabbinical expression; a peculiarity of the language of the rabbins.

1832 in WEBSTER.

rabbinist (ˈræbɪnɪst). [f. as prec. + -IST: cf. F. *rabbiniste*, It. *rabbinista*, Pg., Sp. *rabinista*.] An adherent or follower of the rabbins; *esp.* among the Jews, one who accepts the teaching of the Talmud and the rabbins, in contrast to the Karaites, who reject tradition.

1599 *Broughton's Lett.* x. 35 You..shew you are a great Rabbinist. **1609** BP. HALL *Pharis. & Chr.* (1627) 408 At deadly fevd with the other Iewes, which they now call Rabbinists. **1727–41** CHAMBERS *Cycl.* s.v. *Caraite*, If a Caraite would become a rabbinist, he should never be received by the other Jews. **1863** J. G. MURPHY *Comm. Gen.* i. 4 According to the Pharisees and Rabbinists. **1882** FARRAR *Early Chr.* II. 66 *note*, The Rabbinists also felt this.

Hence **rabbiˈnistic, rabbiˈnistical** *adjs.*

1599 *Broughton's Lett.* vii. 24 Glorying of your reading Rabbinisticall. **1676** *Doctrine of Devils* 174 What-ever besotted Rabbins, and Rabbinistical men prate..I care not. **1888** B. PICK in *Librar. Mag.* Mar. 247 The last Doctors of the Law in the chain of Rabbinistic succession.

rabbinite (ˈræbɪnaɪt). [f. as prec. + -ITE[1].] = RABBINIST.

1832 in WEBSTER.

Hence **rabbiˈnitic** *a.*

1884 SCHAFF *Encycl. Relig. Knowl.* III. 2095/2 The Pharisaic-rabbinitic system of tradition.

rabbinize (ˈræbɪnaɪz), *v. rare.* [f. as prec. + -IZE: cf. F. *rabbiniser*.]

1. *intr.* To adopt or conform to rabbinism. ? *Obs.*

a **1641**, **1652** [see *Rabbinizing* ppl. a.].

2. *trans.* To imbue with rabbinism.

1835 J. HARRIS *Gt. Teacher* (1837) 54 The whole of their law had become rabbinized and overlaid with traditions.

Hence **ˈrabbinized, ˈrabbinizing** *ppl. adjs.*

a **1641** BP. MOUNTAGU *Acts & Mon.* (1642) 110 A man thoroughly enspired with a Rabbinising spirit. **1652** GAULE *Magastrom.* 44 The rabbinizing and Christianizing magicians and astrologers. **1894** BRUCE *Paul's Concept. Chr.* xx. 377 The bane to be dreaded is a rabbinised church.

ˈrabbinship. *rare.* [f. as prec. + -SHIP.] Rabbinate; the personality of a rabbi.

1599 *Broughton's Lett.* ix. 29 How knoweth your Rabbinship that he is no Grecian? **1852** [see RABBISHIP].

rabbious, variant of RABIOUS.

†**ˈrabbish**, *a. Obs.* Forms: 4 **rabbisshe**, 5 **rabbishe, -isch, -yshe, rabyssh, -sch.** [? f. OF. *rabi, rabbi* rabid, raging + -ISH, or directly from the OF. fem. *rabice, rabiche*, the ending being associated with *-ish*.] Unruly, turbulent; inconsiderate, rash; rough or precipitate in action.

1387 TREVISA *Higden* (Rolls) VIII. 85 Þan þe rabbisshe peple..up wiþ staves, battes, and stoones. **1398** —— *Barth. De P.R.* II. xix. (1495) 45 By rabbyssh foole hardynesse he takyth moore vpon hym than he maye doo. **1494** FABYAN *Chron.* VII. 357 Many of the rabbishe and wylde commoners, were in full purpose to haue defended the cytie.

Hence †**ˈrabbishly** *adv.*; †**ˈrabbishness**. *Obs.*

1387 TREVISA *Higden* (Rolls) VIII. 147 A manere kyndeliche rabbischness of wit. *c* **1400** *Harl. Contin.* ibid. VII. 523 Me wondreth gretlich that ȝe demeth ȝoure bischop so rabbischlich. *c* **1475** *Partenay* 4690 He..A chambre perceiued, in went rabbishly. **1494** FABYAN *Chron.* V. cxxxvi. 123 The kynge handelyd the body of Seynt Denys so rabbysshely, ȳt he brake one of his armes.

rabbiship (ˈræbaɪ-, ˈræbɪʃɪp). [f. RABBI + -SHIP.] The office of rabbi.

1669 PENN *No Cross* Wks. 1782 II. 81 He came..to overthrow their rabbyship. **1702** C. MATHER *Magn. Chr.* IV. ii. §8. 146 The Jewish Rule, about the Rabbinate, Love the Work, but Hate the Rabbiship [ed. **1852** rabbinship]. **1886** *Daily News* 23 Dec. 5/7 His two sons quarrelled for the Rabbi-ship.

rabbit (ˈræbɪt), *sb.*[1] Forms: 5–6 rab(b)ette, 5–7 rabet, 6–8 rabbet, (6 -atte), 7 rabytt, 8 -it, 8–

rabbit. [app. of Northern French origin: cf. Walloon *robett* (Remacle). The primitive seems to occur in Flem. *robbe* (Kilian, De Bo; the latter also gives *ribbe*, *rubbe*), dim. *robbeke(n*; the ultimate etym. is unknown. If F. *rabouillère* (the burrow made by the female rabbit to kindle in) is connected, the ME. *rabet* may be more primitive in form than the Walloon and Flem. words.]

1. a. A common burrowing rodent of the hare-family (*Leporidæ*), esp. the common European species, *Oryctolagus cuniculus*, which is naturally of a brownish-grey colour, but in domestication also white, black, or pied. †Orig. applied only to the young animal, the full-grown one being called a CONY. Also, one of several North American animals of the same family, esp. the varying hare, *Lepus americanus*.

1398 TREVISA *Barth. De P.R.* XVIII. lxvii. 277 Conynges.. bringeþ forþe many rabettes & multiplieþ ful swiþe. *c* **1440** *Anc. Cookery* in *Househ. Ord.* (1790) 457 Then take conynges parboyled, or elles rabets, for thai are better for a lorde. **1502** *Privy Purse Exp. Eliz. York* (1830) 13 A present of Rabettes and quayles. **1576** TURBERV. *Bk. Venerie* lxiii. 178 The Conie beareth her Rabettes xxx dayes, and then kindeleth. **1607** TOPSELL *Four-f. Beasts* (1658) 89 If two males be put to one female, they fight fiercely; but they will not hurt the rabbets. **1634** W. WOOD *New Englands Prospect* vi. 22 The Rabbets be much like ours in England. **1653** WALTON *Angler* viii. 171 Take the flesh of a Rabet or Cat cut smal. **1743** M. CATESBY *Nat. Hist. Carolina* II. p. xxviii, The Monax. This animal is about the bigness of a wild rabbet. **1768** PENNANT *Brit. Zool.* I. 91 Rabbets will breed seven times a year. **1831** J. J. AUDUBON *Ornithol. Biogr.* I. 268 Small hares, or, as we usually call them, Rabbits, are also frequently caught. **1842** [see ORKNEYMAN]. **1846** J. BAXTER *Libr. Pract. Agric.* (ed. 4) I. 334 The rabbit lives to the age of eight or nine years. **1872** R. L. DASHWOOD *Chiploquorgan* 88 There is a species of hare.. mis-called a rabbit, which is numerous but hardly eatable. **1885** E. CLARK in *Nature* XXXI. 264/1 Large tracts are still honeycombed by the ubiquitous biscacha, a gigantic rabbit. *c* **1897** 'MARK TWAIN' *Autobiogr.* (1924) I. 97 The sumptuous meals—well, it makes me cry to think of them. Fried chicken,.. squirrels, rabbits, pheasants. **1907** *St. Nicholas* July 835/1 Sometimes rabbits and prairie-dogs scampered among the bushes. **1958** J. G. MACGREGOR *North-West of 16* v. 69 Many an Alberta farmer and business man is alive today because of rabbits. **1969** M. M. FIRESTONE in Halpert & Story *Christmas Mumming in Newfoundland* 64 Many 'rabbits' (varying hares) are caught in snares.

b. *to buy the rabbit* (slang), to conclude a transaction unfavourably, to fare badly.

1825 J. NEAL *Bro. Jonathan* II. xviii. 156 If that air invoice aint ready soon, thee'll buy the rabbit, I guess! **1935** A. J. POLLOCK *Underworld Speaks* 52/2 *He bought the rabbit*, a criminal case in court poorly handled by attorney; got the worst of it in a business deal.

c. Used (freq. *fig.* or allusively) with reference to the conjuring trick of producing a rabbit from a hat (cf. HAT *sb.* 5 c).

1877 E. SACHS *Sleight of Hand* xviii. 183 The production of.. rabbits from a hat is always very startling. **1906** KIPLING *Puck of Pook's Hill* 99 I've seen a man take rabbits out of a hat, and he told us we could see how he did it, if we watched hard. **1932** L. GOLDING *Magnolia Street* II. iv. 322 His wife.. gave the impression of having emerged like a rabbit from the Conjurer's top-hat. **1938** M. ALLINGHAM *Fashion in Shrouds* vii. 108 There you are... Once more the veteran conjuror staggers out with the rabbit. **1940** A. CHRISTIE *Sad Cypress* II. ii. 121 You want me.. to be the conjuror. To take out of the empty hat rabbit after rabbit. **1965** 'D. SHANNON' *Death by Inches* (1967) xx. 245 Well, you pulled the rabbit out of the hat. **1967** *Guardian* 21 Sept. 7/1 Will man.. control or stop the ever increasing flow of white rabbits.. out of our technological top hats? **1975** *Times* 20 Sept. 6/5 Almost any of the Poirots of the 1930s.. produce the authentic rabbit-from-the-hat shock that is the whole aim of their sort of book.

d. *pl.* Also ***white rabbits***. Repeated as a good-luck charm, esp. on the first day of a month (see quots.).

1920 'D. YATES' *Courts of Idleness* II. ii. 195 On the first day of the month you have to say 'Rabbits'. If you say it to me first, I have to give you a present, and if I say it to you first, you have to give me a present. **1949** H. NICOLSON *Diary* 31 Dec. (1968) 178, I hear the clock strike midnight and say 'rabbits'... That is the end of 1949. **1959** I. & P. OPIE *Lore & Lang. Schoolch.* xiii. 299 'On the first morning of the month,' notes a typical informant, 'before speaking to anyone else, one must say "White rabbits, white rabbits, white rabbits" for luck.' Subject to minor modifications the utterance of this spell appears to be the accepted routine throughout Britain. Some children feel it is enough just to cry 'Rabbits'. **1972** EVANS & THOMSON *Leaping Hare* xvi. 233 A Claydon (Suffolk) woman told us she used to say *Hares, Hares* before going to bed on the last day of the month, and *Rabbits, Rabbits*, when she got up in the morning. **1977** *Times* 20 Aug. 12/2, I took the opportunity of asking them what was the magic word which they.. should have said, first thing that morning... They replied 'Rabbits' except for a few.. who said 'White Rabbits'.

2. *transf.* **a.** Applied contemptuously to a person. *spec.* (slang) a poor performer at any game; a novice; also *attrib.* **b.** A shadow resembling the form of a rabbit, cast by the hands upon a wall. **c.** (See quot. 1878.) **d.** (See quot. 1882.); also in *gen.* use of a horse. *slang.* See also WELSH RABBIT.

1597 SHAKS. *2 Hen. IV*, II. ii. 91 Away, you horson upright Rabbet, away. **1849** *Plymouth Her.* 21 Apr., Shadows.. strong enough for children to make *rabbits* with their fingers upon a wall. **1878** BESANT & RICE *By Celia's Arbour* xxx, Even if you did happen to have a 'rabbit', that is one of the coats lined with white fur. **1882** *Standard* 4 Sept. 6/2 Though somewhat of a 'rabbit', as a horse that runs 'in and out' is sometimes called. **1900** F. P. DUNNE *Mr. Dooley's Philos.* 170 'Well,' says th' horse rayporther, 'they's a couple iv rabbits goin' to sprint around th' thrack at th' fair groun's,' he says. **1904** *Daily Mail* 29 Jun. 4/6 Terms now used in describing the game of cricket... 'Googlies, rabbits'. **1906** *Westm. Gaz.* 8 May 1/3 Nearly every eleven has a 'rabbit' or two at the end. **1908** A. W. MYERS *Compl. Lawn Tennis Player* 184 There was no draw at all, the manager.. merely selecting the four semi-finalists and filling in the gaps with the other players, most of them 'rabbits'. **1924** *Punch* 4 June 620 (*caption*) *Nervous beginner* (*to caddy*). 'I-er-suppose you get an occasional 'rabbit' here?' **1927** *Observer* 17 Apr. 17/2 Fencing is no more considered to be a feeble pastime for 'Rabbits', for those boys who cannot play the more vigorous games of youth. **1930** A. E. M. FOSTER *Contract Bridge for All* 7 Many people of the 'rabbit' class, and even average Auction players, are deterred from giving it a trial at all. **1932** A. J. WORRALL *Eng. Idioms* 12 That girl is a rabbit. She's afraid to say 'Boo' to a goose. **1932** *Sun* (Baltimore) 24 Sept. 20/2 He found the appearance of the young women improved by abandonment of 'rabbit rules'. .. Freshman girls were required.. to refrain from using cosmetics... But now the 'rabbits' can appear in all their glory of pink lips and powdered noses. **1940** W. FAULKNER *Hamlet* ii. 47 He lifted his own reins. 'Come up, rabbits,' he said. 'Let's hit for town.' **1947** *People* 22 June 7/4 Engines roar and the four 'rabbits' get away as best they can, but definitely not in the style of champions. **1952** E. O'NEILL *Moon for Misbegotten* I. 10 I'll bet you're a mile away by now, you rabbit! **1957** *Sun* (Baltimore) 9 Apr. 20-B/3 'I think we owe it to the sponsors,' Ford explained after his remarkable closing 66... 'They help us when we're rabbits (a term for novices) and we should help them when we become winners.' **1974** J. I. M. STEWART *Gaudy* v. 95, I must have been accustomed to think of wee Dreichie as what we called a rabbit, meaning a timid boy wholly without aptitude either for games or for ragging around. **1976** *0–10 Cricket Scene* (Austral.) 41/2 Dennis Amiss.. will have a special desire to prove to the Australian public that he is no longer Dennis Lillee's 'rabbit'. *a* **1976** A. CHRISTIE *Autobiogr.* (1977) VI. iv. 320 He could get no fun out of playing [golf] with a rabbit like me. **1979** *Daily Tel.* 14 Apr. 13/2 In '*Rabbits Review*' B. P. Floyd aims.. to cater with a light touch for the poorer player.

e. Liquor; a bottle of beer. ***to run the rabbit***: see quots. 1916, 1941. *Austral. slang.*

1895 E. GIBB *Thrilling Incidents Convict System in Australasia* 46 'Ikeing the rabbit for a fake for his Bingy, and making a coil of a conkey myrnionger'... Convict slang.. it may be freely translated as having surreptitiously concealed some liquor under the excuse that one was ill and it was required for medicine, and ('making a coil') complaining loudly of some fancied grievance on the part of a ('conkey myrnionger') contemptible or ignorant newly-arrived convict. **1916** C. J. DENNIS *Songs of Sentimental Bloke* Gloss. 124 *Rabbit, to run the*, to convey liquor from a public-house. **1941** BAKER *Dict. Austral. Slang* 58 *Rabbit*, a bottle of beer. *Ibid.* 62 *Run the rabbit*, to secure liquor, often illegally, e.g. after hours.

f. A smuggled or stolen article (see also quot. 1945). *Naut.* and *Austral. slang.*

1929 F. BOWEN *Sea Slang* 109 *Rabbit*, property stolen from the Royal Dockyards, most frequently used in Devonport. **1945** BAKER *Austral. Lang.* viii. 163 *Rabbit*, an article made by a sailor at sea as a gift to a friend or girl. As verb, to scrounge. **1955** G. FREEMAN *Liberty Man* I. i. 11 All at once he remembered his presents for them. 'Rabbits' they called them in the navy. **1958** *Times* 10 Feb. 11/6 'Making rabbits' is a collective term for seamen's 'hobbies'. **1961** F. H. BURGESS *Dict. Sailing* 167 *Rabbit*, an article unlawfully obtained and smuggled ashore.

g. [Shortening of *rabbit-and-pork*.] A conversation, a talk. Also, a lingo. *slang.*

1941 [see *rabbit-and-pork* below]. **1950** P. TEMPEST *Lag's Lexicon* 173 To have a 'rabbit' = to have a pow-wow. **1958** F. NORMAN *Bang to Rights* III. 155 We still had quite a heated rabbit about it. **1962** R. COOK *Crust on its Uppers* i. 20 Moody rabbits in Spanish bars. **1976** E. WARD *Hanged Man* xxvii. 171 Touchy old place, Glasgow.. you can't understand that Scotch rabbit they talk.

h. = PIG *sb.*[1] 9.

1949 *Amer. Speech* XXIV. 33 The piece of steel or iron dropped or pushed through racked pipe to remove obstructions is known as a rabbit. **1975** G. ANDERSON *Coring* v. 95 The core is not completely out of the barrel until a metal slug, called 'the rabbit', appears.

i. A pneumatically or hydraulically propelled container used to convey material into a nuclear reactor or other place where it is to be irradiated.

1950 S. GLASSTONE *Sourcebk. Atomic Energy* xiii. 356/2 The study of the delayed-neutron emitters of short life is facilitated by the use of a device referred to colloquially as a 'rabbit'; by this means a sample of fissionable material, after exposure to a high density of neutrons,.. is rapidly transferred to a counter where the emission of the delayed neutrons is registered automatically. **1954** R. STEPHENSON *Introd. Nuclear Engin.* x. 367 The rabbit (holder for the material to be irradiated) is rapidly shot into and out of the reactor by about 100 lb pressure of filtered air or carbon dioxide. **1967** J. G. WILLS *Nuclear Power Plant Technol.* 318 'Rabbits' often consist of small cylinders of aluminium or plastic, moved by air pressure through a long pipe.

3. *attrib.* and *Comb.* **a.** Simple attributive, as ***rabbit-blood***, ***-burrow***, ***-cleve***, ***farm***, ***fence***, ***fur***, ***†-hay***, ***-hole***, ***-house***, ***-hutch*** (also *fig.*), ***netting***, ***-paw***, ***-pie***, ***-run***, ***-skin***, ***snare***, ***soup***, ***-stock***, ***trap***, ***-warren*** (also *fig.*), ***wire***.

1923 D. H. LAWRENCE *Birds, Beasts & Flowers* 207 Eagle of the Rockies.. Lifting the *rabbit-blood of the myriads up into something splendid. **1964** M. HYNES *Med. Bacteriol.* (ed. 8) xxviii. 438 Culture is effected on Novy and McNeal's medium or in the water of condensation at the bottom of a rabbit-blood agar slope. **1752** SIR J. HILL *Hist. Anim.* 423 Deserted *rabbet-burrows, or any other hollows of a like kind. **1883** E. PENNELL-ELMHIRST *Cream Leicestersh.* 420 A gallant fox getting to ground in a rabbit-burrow. **1869** BLACKMORE *Lorna D.* xiii, I went all along on the ridge of the *rabbit-cleve. **1900** J. K. JEROME *Three Men on Bummel* v. 106 A man starting a *rabbit farm with twelve selected rabbits.. must, at the end of three years, be in receipt of an income of two thousand a year. **1939–40** *Army & Navy Stores Catal.* 982/1 1½" Mesh for *Rabbit fences, proof against the smallest Rabbits. **1944** F. CLUNE *Red Heart* 53 Colson travelled on to Birdsville, crossing the old rabbit fence (built in 1886) to keep vermin out of Queensland. **1873** *Practical Mag.* I. 282 (*heading*) *Rabbit fur as a substitute for wool and cotton. **1973** 'D. HALLIDAY' *Dolly & Starry Bird* iii. 37 A long coat of gray glacé snake-skin, edged.. with lime green rabbit fur. **1725** BRADLEY *Fam. Dict.* s.v. *Woodcock*, Your Net must be like your *Rabbet-Hays. **1705** BERKELEY *Cave Dunmore* in Fraser *Life* (1871) 507 The earth turned up at the entrance of a *rabbit-hole. **1885** LADY BRASSEY *The Trades* 264 We were assured.. that there were no rabbit-holes in the fields. **1743** W. ELLIS *Mod. Husb.* June xviii. 141 An old *Rabbit hutch, that had several Rooms in it. **1839** W. CHAMBERS *Tour Belgium* 77/1 A little garden.. containing a rabbit hutch. **1859** [see *penny plain* adj. s.v. PENNY 12 c]. **1905** *Pall Mall Mag.* July 28/2 The *concierge* in his 'rabbit hutch' down below smiles and even sometimes whistles in tune. **1965** G. MCINNES *Road to Gundagai* ix. 134 Hurstbridge station was a low gravel platform with a small rabbit hutch of a booking office. **1977** P. G. WINSLOW *Witch Hill Murder* II. 135 The collection of rabbit hutches that was now the Manor. **1907** *Yesterday's Shopping* (1969) 664/2 *Rabbit and Hare Nettings.. 4 ft. wide, for half grown rabbits. **1915** KIPLING *Let.* 22 Aug. in C. Carrington *Rudyard Kipling* (1955) xvii. 436 Don't forget the beauty of rabbit netting overhead against hand-grenades. **1973** *Country Life* 1 Mar. 511/1 The only solution is a deer fence.. using large mesh, light-gauge wire above the ordinary rabbit netting. **1851** in *Life A. Fonblanque* (1874) 499 A principal ingredient in this *rabbit-pie. **1876** T. HARDY *Ethelberta* xxxiii, Every detail of barrow, path, and *rabbit-run. **1829** RICHARDSON *Zool. Brit. Amer.* I. 218 The winter skins of this animal [the American Hare] are imported by the Hudson's Bay Company under the name of *rabbit-skins. **1848** DICKENS *Dombey* vi, He hung the rabbit-skin over his left arm. **1861** R. F. BURTON *City of Saints* 590 They were dressed in the usual rabbit-skin cape. **1907** *Yesterday's Shopping* (1969) 664/3 *Rabbit snares.. A few made up ready for use generally in stock. **1978** P. O'DONNELL *Dragon's Claw* viii. 159 There was a noose of wire round his neck which.. tightened like a rabbit snare. **1845** E. ACTON *Mod. Cookery* i. 37 (*heading*) *Rabbit soup à la reine. *Ibid.* 38 (*heading*) Brown rabbit soup. **1960** *Good Housek. Cookery Bk.* (rev. ed.) 65/2 (*heading*) Rabbit soup. **1805** DICKSON *Pract. Agric.* II. 1204 *Rabbit-stock demands, on the whole, but little regard. **1824** *Cobbett's Weekly Register* 27 Mar. col. 797 It is the invariable practice of the farmers to have a number of *rabbit-traps constantly set on the farms. **1856** C. PATMORE *Angel in Ho.* II. Prol. 3 But she turn'd pale, for now the beast Found stock-still in the rabbit-trap,.. Unglobed himself. **1976** J. B. HILTON *Gamekeeper's Gallows* vii. 61 Brunt.. came upon a rabbit trap. **1766** SMOLLETT *Trav.* I. 32 Open downs, where there is a *rabbit warren. **1775** ASH, *Rabbit-warren*. **1800** MAR. EDGEWORTH *The Will* i, There is that rabbit-warren near Clover Hill. **1821** M. WILMOT *Let.* 10 Apr. (1935) 104 This Rabbit Warren in the air. **1892** E. REEVES *Homeward Bound* 295 It is almost as thickly populated as a rabbit warren. **1905** *Birmingham Institute Mag.* Oct. 187 The Institute has been graphically.. described as a rabbit-warren. **1973** 'S. HARVESTER' *Corner of Playground* III. vii. 219 Their dull dusty sunless offices in the chaotic rabbit-warren of officialdom. **1906** KIPLING *Puck of Pook's Hill* 259 A quick movement of the hand as though he were pegging down a *rabbit-wire. **1945** N. COLLINS *London belongs to Me* III. xxxix. 301 The special visitors' room where they saw their loved ones through a screen of rabbit-wire. **1973** 'M. CAMPBELL' *Halfbreed* iv. 30 We took Daddy's rabbit wire and strung it across two small green trees on either side of the footpath.

b. Objective and obj. genitive, as ***rabbit-breeder***, ***-breeding***, ***-catcher*** (also *transf.*), ***-chase***, ***-chasing*** (sb. and adj.), ***-courser***, ***-coursing***, ***-destroyer***, ***-fancier***, ***farmer***, ***-farming***, ***-hunting***, ***-inspector***, ***-keeper***, ***-management***, ***-rearer***, ***-shooting***, ***-trapper***, ***-trapping***; ***rabbit-hunt*** vb.

1885 *Census Instruct.*, *Rabbit Breeder, Catcher, Destroyer. **1848** MAUNDER *Treas. Nat. Hist.* 560/1 Otherwise.. will *Rabbit-breeding turn out a losing speculation. **1724** SWIFT *Wks.* (1941) X. 146 *Rabbet Catcher. I'll Ferret him. **1885** [see *rabbit breeder* above]. **1955** *Sun* (Baltimore) 23 Feb. 5-B/2 Engineers.. have stretched a nylon tennis net across a miniature landing field and are 'serving' Model F86 Sabre Jets into it. The purpose of the experiment is to test a new device, called a 'rabbit catcher'. **1897** *Outing* (U.S.) XXIX. 456/1 A genuine *rabbit-chase. **1885** *Ibid.*, The season of *rabbit-chasing begins.. in October. **1895** *Ibid.* XXVI. 426/2 The *rabbit-chasing pups. **1875** *Rabbit-courser [see *dog-racer* s.v. DOG *sb.*[1] 19 a]. **1900** J. K. JEROME *Three Men on Bummel* v. 106, I have never met a rabbit farmer myself worth two thousand a year. **1891** *Pall Mall G.* 23 Dec. 6/3 Fond of what they call *rabbit-coursing. **1885** *Rabbit destroyer [see *rabbit breeder* above]. **1848** MAUNDER *Treas. Nat. Hist.* 560/1 The ingenuity of *rabbit-fanciers has been shown in the production of various breeds. **1889** G. F. MORANT (*title*) Hutch *rabbit-farming in the open [in K. W. Knight *The book of the rabbit*]. **1943** J. STUART *Taps for Private Tussie* xvii. 172 Uncle Mott cut wood for the fireplace in the mornins and *rabbit-hunted in the afternoons. **1873** *Trans. Illinois Dept. Agric.* X. 65 They prevailed on him to suspend his *rabbit-hunting, and 'show them 'round'. **1953** N. TINBERGEN *Herring Gull's World* iv. 27 Rabbit-hunting is a regular feature in the Dutch North Sea sand dunes. **1936** F. CLUNE *Roaming round Darling* xiii. 114 They were collected by the *rabbit-inspector a number of years ago. **1848** *Chambers's Inform. People* I. 628/2 Experienced *rabbit-keepers conceive too frequent breeding to be injurious. **1805** DICKSON *Pract. Agric.* II. 1203 The hazard and uncertainty of *rabbit-management. **1848** *Chambers's Inform. People* I. 629/1 The duty of the *rabbit-rearer. **1819** *Pantologia* X. s.v., An occasional reduction.. is found necessary.. in which case *rabbit-shooting is a pleasant diversion. **1978** H. Wouk *War & Remembrance* xxxix. 400 The slaughter that ensued was mere rabbit-shooting by our aircraft and submarines. **1888** G. M. Fenn *Dick o' the Fens* 326 'Ay', said the *rabbit-trapper. **1880** W. Carnegie *Practical Trapping* 20 The same sort of gins, the use of which I advocated for *rabbit-trapping, will do. **1935** *Discovery* June 168/1 Gamekeepers in winter in Rossshire often come across wild-cat tracks in the snow when rabbit-trapping.

c. Similative and parasynthetic, as ***rabbit-mouth***, ***-shoulders***; ***rabbit-backed***, ***-coloured***, ***-eared***, ***-faced***, ***-hearted***, ***-like***, ***-mouthed***, ***-scared***, ***-toothed*** adjs.; ***rabbit-wise*** adv.

1778 Foote *Trip Calais* III. Wks. 1799 II. 370 Red-faced, *rabbet-back'd. **1885** W. J. E. Crane *Bookbinding for Amateurs* 71 The book will be 'rabbit-backed'. **1953** R. Graves *Poems* 18 Such gross-headed, *rabbit-coloured litters As soon they shall be happy to desert. **1835–40** Haliburton *Clockm.* (1862) 185 That little..*rabbit-eared runt of a pig. **1939** *Times Lit. Suppl.* 30 Dec. 756/1 Once there was a hasty glimpse of the rabbit-eared bandicoot. **1977** *Jersey Even. Post* 26 July 4/1 And the rabbit-eared bandicoots, small marsupials, only come out to feed at night. **1905** E. F. Benson *Image in Sand* i. 12 He was a *rabbit-faced little man. **1920** *Chambers's Jrnl.* Dec. 812/1 '*Rabbit-hearted' is an expression commonly used not only by white races, but also by red and brown people. **1836–9** Todd *Cycl. Anat.* II. 52/2 The light *rabbit-like hyrax. **1849** *Sk. Nat. Hist., Mammalia* IV. 6 Body short, thick, and rabbit-like. **1833** Disraeli 29 June in *Corr. w. Sister* (1886) 21 Handsome..but with one great fault, a *rabbit mouth. **1909** *Cent. Dict.* Suppl., *Rabbit-mouthed,..having a rabbit-mouth; harelipped. **1956** H. Gold *Man who was not with It* (1965) xxix. 272 His soft and rabbit-mouthed touchiness. **1936** *Partisan Rev.* III. 21/1 Standing there, his big gun smoking, *Rabbit-scared, alone. **1971** *Maclean's Mag.* Oct. 3/2 We've never seemed so rabbit-scared as a nation as we did in August. **1784** J. Barry in *Lect. Paint.* ii. (1848) 94 The excesses and deficiencies in the human form,..*rabbit shoulders, pot belly. **1800** D. Wordsworth *Jrnl.* 14 May (1941) I. 37 The grassy-leaved *rabbit-toothed white flower. **1963** D. Lessing *Golden Notebk.* II. 246 His mouth is a rabbit-toothed hole, and his eyes are sunk in scar tissue. **1980** 'T. Hinde' *Sir Henry & Sons* iv. 33, I am round-faced and stocky... I became rabbit-toothed. **1846** Mrs. Gore *Eng. Char.* (1852) 139 A starveling cat roasted *rabbit-wise.

d. instrumental, as ***rabbit-browsed***, ***-haunted***, ***-nibbled*** adjs.

1923 Kipling *Land & Sea Tales* 81 A little *rabbit-browsed clearing of turf. **1921** F. B. Young *Black Diamond* iv. 38 Evening visits to *rabbit-haunted banks. **1947** W. de la Mare *Coll. Stories for Children* 30 The rabbit-*nibbled turf.

4. Special combs.: **rabbit-and-pork** *Rhyming slang* = talk *sb.*, *v.* (usu. *ellipt.*: see sense 2 g above and rabbit *v.* 6); **rabbit ball** *U.S.*, a baseball that is springy in construction and lively in action; also *fig.*; **rabbit-bandicoot**, a small Australian marsupial belonging to the genus *Macrotis* of the family Peramelidæ, living in a burrow and having rabbit-like ears; cf. *rabbit-eared* in sense 3 c above; **rabbit-beagle**, a beagle used for the hunting of rabbits; so **rabbit-beagling** *vbl. sb.*; **rabbit berry**, a deciduous North American shrub, *Shepherdia argentea*, of the family Elæagnaceæ, or its red berries; **rabbit brush**, **bush**, a western North American shrub of the genus *Chrysothamnus*, esp. *C. nauseosus*, belonging to the family Compositæ and bearing clusters of yellow flowers; **rabbit drive** *U.S.*, a driving together of jack rabbits for slaughtering; **rabbit fever**, a vernacular name for tularæmia; **rabbit-fish**, the name of several fishes having points of resemblance to a rabbit, as (*a*) the British fishes *Chimæra monstrosa* and the striped rock-gurnard; (*b*) *U.S.*, the smooth puffer, *Lagocephalus lævigatus*, or the spotted balloon fish, *Cyclichthys schoepfi*; (*c*) a small herbivorous fish belonging to the family Siganidæ, found in tropical Indo-Pacific seas and bearing venom glands on the fins; **rabbit flea**, one of several fleas which infest rabbits, esp. the European rabbit flea, *Spilopsyllus cuniculi*, or the North American rabbit flea, *Cediopsylla simplex*; **rabbit food** (also **rabbit's food**), food such as is eaten by rabbits; hence (*slang*), lettuce; green salad; **rabbit-foot**: see rabbit's foot; **rabbit-hawk** *U.S.*, the red-tailed hawk, *Buteo jamaicensis*, or the hen harrier, *Circus cyaneus*; **rabbit-moth**, a N. American bombycid moth, *Lagoa opercularis*; **rabbit-mouth sucker**, a N. American fish (see quot.); **rabbit('s) pea** *U.S.*, a perennial herb, *Tephrosia virginiana*, belonging to the family Leguminosæ and bearing white, pink, or yellow flowers; also called goat's rue and wild sweet pea; **rabbit-proof** *a.*, proof against rabbits; esp. of a fence, that excludes rabbits (in Austral. *spec.* such a fence marking a border between States); *ellipt.*, such a fence; **rabbit-rat**, an Australian rodent belonging to either of the genera *Mesembriomys* and *Conilurus*, distinguished by long ears and a bushy tail, esp. the white-footed tree rat, *C. albipes*, the only one not restricted to northern parts of the country; **rabbit-root**, the wild sarsaparilla, *Aralia nudicaulis*; **rabbit-spout** *dial.*, a rabbit-burrow; **rabbit-squirrel**, a S. American chinchilla, esp. *Lagidium Cuvieri*; †**rabbit-starter**, a young rabbit; **rabbit test**, a pregnancy test in which rabbits are used; **rabbit tobacco** *U.S.*, the sweet everlasting, *Gnaphalium obtusifolium*, belonging to the family Compositæ, and bearing clusters of fragrant white flowers; also, the dried flowers of this plant, used as a substitute for tobacco; **rabbit tooth** *slang* = buck-tooth (usu. *pl.*); **rabbit-weed**, a N. American plant.

1941 G. Kersh *They die with their Boots Clean* i. 27 He uses slang... Talk is Rabbit, or *Rabbit-an'-Pork. **1960** *Spectator* 4 Mar. 326 We only allow ourselves a second to remember that rabbit-and-pork is talk. **1971** *National Times* (Austral.) 13 Dec. 20/1 (*heading*) Cockneys lay claim to their rabbit and pork. **1922** *N.Y. Times* 5 June 10/3 The officials who control the destiny of the big leagues let it be known at the opening of the current season that the '*rabbit' ball had seen its day. **1937** *Sun* (Baltimore) 18 Aug. 8/3 There does not seem to be any question of the changes that have been worked in baseball by the lively rabbit ball. **1973** *Times* 15 Aug. 7/3 The rabbit-ball..jumps like a rabbit. **1977** *Time* 11 Apr. 17/1 Rawlings Co. now makes the official major league baseball.., and the scuttlebutt is that Rawlings is turning out a rabbit ball. **1832** Bischoff *Van Diemen's Land* II. 28 (Morris) There are two kinds, the rat and the *rabbit bandicoot. **1896** Spencer *Thro' Larapurta Land* 34 The white tips of the tails of the rabbit-bandicoot. **1923** F. W. Jones *Mammals S. Austral.* I. 154 The animal..is usually termed the Common Rabbit-Bandicoot, but it would be most misleading to apply the term 'common' to it to-day. **1941** E. Troughton *Furred Animals Austral.* 69 The very descriptive name of rabbit-bandicoot was provided by the early colonists who regarded them with a certain amount of tolerance because of their extremely useful share in the destruction of mice and insects. **1970** W. D. L. Ride *Guide Native Mammals Austral.* vii. 104 There are generally thought to be only two species, the Common Rabbit Bandicoot and the small Central Australian Yallara or Lesser Rabbit Bandicoot. **1824** *Sporting Mag.* XIV. 312/2 There is no prettier sport for youth than rabbit beagling... *Rabbit beagles should never be permitted to run hare. **1888** H. Dalziel *Brit. Dogs* (ed. 2) I. xvi. 226 Beagles may be fairly classed as Hare-Beagles and Rabbit-Beagles, other distinction than size being minor. **1804** J. Whitehouse *Jrnl.* 24 Aug. in *Orig. Jrnls. Lewis & Clark Exped.* (1905) VII. ii. 52 We found some red berreys which they call *Rabbit berrys. **1807** P. Gass *Jrnl.* 30 Small red berries, the Indian name for which in English means rabbit berries. **1891** [see *mountain tea* s.v. mountain 9 d]. **1952** A. G. L. Hellyer *Sanders' Encycl. Gardening* (ed. 22) 454 *S[heperdia] argentea*, 'Rabbit Berry', 'Buffalo Berry',..scarlet fruits. **1914** E. Stewart *Lett. Woman Homesteader* 18 Our horse was midside deep in *rabbit brush, a shrub just covered with flowers that look and smell like goldenrod. **1927** W. Cather *Death comes for Archbishop* 95 The sandy soil of the plain..was splotched with masses of blooming rabbit brush. **1946** D. C. Peattie *Road of Naturalist* i. 17 The burro bush and rabbit brush are the natural sons of the desert. **1955** *Daily Progress* (Charlottesville, Va.) 2 Nov. 11/5 That's rabbit-brush, a hearty range perennial that moves in quickly when other vegetation is killed. **1980** *Blair & Ketchum's Country Jrnl.* Oct. 46/3 The first mule I ever owned was rescued from a prairie dog town in southern Colorado, where she had lived for who knows how long on fresh air and rabbit-brush. **1852** H. Stansbury *Expl. & Survey Valley of Gt. Salt Lake* 235 The only vegetation today has been a little dwarf artemisia, grease-bush, *rabbit-bush. **1861** R. F. Burton *City of Saints* 591 An expanse of white sage and large rabbit-bush. **1972** R. & R. Wright *Cariboo Mileposts* 16 Grass and trees are scarce, with only sage and rabbit bush covering the ground. **1979** *Tucson* (Arizona) *Citizen* 28 Apr. 3A/9 Pollen count (yesterday)..Rabbit bush 4. **1887** *Lisbon* (N. Dakota) *Star* 23 Dec. 7/1 Several hundred people.. assembled to engage in the *rabbit drive. **1963** R. Symons *Many Trails* xii. 119 A hunt in the manner of the California rabbit drives. **1977** *New Yorker* 11 July 43/3 We have rabbit drives there. Drive the rabbits from one end of the island to the other and kill them. **1925** *Jrnl. Amer. Med. Assoc.* 25 Apr. 1244/1 A man..working in the Washington, D.C., market went to his physician..in 1921, for treatment for what he informed the physician was '*rabbit fever', adding that 'rabbit fever' was well known among market men... This was the first case of tularemia to be reported for the eastern United States. **1955** *Sci. News Let.* 16 July 43/1 Some species of ticks are occasional spreaders of Rocky Mountain spotted fever and tularemia (rabbit fever). **1973** *Daily Colonist* (Victoria, B.C.) 29 July 2/2 Then he mentioned that he had been doing some squirrel hunting and the doctor immediately ordered a blood test which showed he had tularemia, or 'rabbit fever'. **1828** J. Fleming *Hist. Brit. Animals* 173 The specimen [of *Chimæra*], from which the preceding description was taken, was sent from Unst, where it is termed the *Rabbit-fish. **1842** J. E. DeKay *Zool. N.Y.* iv. 330 The Lineated Puffer..is called Rabbit-fish, according to Schoepfi, on account of the whiteness of its flesh. **1848** Maunder *Treas. Nat. Hist.* 560/1 *Rabbit-fish*, a local name for the Northern Chimæra, or King of the Herrings. **1880** Day *Fishes Gt. Brit.* I. 57 Streaked gurnard, ..rock gurnard, rabbit fish. **1883** Simmonds *Dict. Usef. Animals*, *Rabbit-fish*, a name for *Tetrodon lævigatus*..an American fish. **1884** *Bull. U.S. Nat. Museum* No. 27. 428 Spiny Box-fish; Rabbit-fish; Swell Toad. East coast of the United States. **1897** *Rep. N.Y. Forest, Fish, & Game Comm.* II. 224 Rabbit-fish; Smooth Puffer.—Occasionally taken in the fall in Gravesend Bay. **1905** D. S. Jordan *Guide to Study of Fishes* II. xxiv. 423 In the [American] rabbit-fishes..the body is box-shaped. **1925** J. T. Jenkins *Fishes Brit. Isles* 349 From its great cutting teeth it [sc. *Chimæra monstrosa*] is known to the Shetlanders as the Rabbit-fish. **1941** R. Faherty *Big Old Sun* xi. 255 'I'm a blow-puffing rabbitfish,' he sputtered. **1953** J. L. B. Smith *Sea Fishes S. Afr.* 328 Rabbitfishes. Compressed ovate body with slippery skin and minute concealed scales... Curious small herbivorous fishes of reefs and weeds of the tropical Indo-Pacific. **1962** K. F. Lagler et al. *Ichthyol.* iv. 32 Non-fatal but nevertheless painful to man..are stings of the venomous sharks,..rabbitfishes, and dragonets. **1973** *Aquaculture* I. 361 Rabbitfish are widely spread throughout the Indian and the western and central Pacific oceans. **1975** *Times* 5 Dec. 12/3 The deep-sea species..can be portrayed as menacing horrors. The specific name for one of them, rabbitfish, is Chimaera Monstrosa. **1904** *Proc. U.S. Nat. Museum* XXVII. 368 In the United States the cat, dog, and *rabbit fleas..will readily attack the human being. **1925** A. D. Imms *Gen. Textbk. Ent.* III. 663 The rabbit flea.. commonly affects the ears of hares and rabbits. **1963** O. Breland *Animal Life & Lore* i. 26 In some regions, it [*sc.* myxomatosis] is transmitted by rabbit fleas. **1967** J. M. Brownjohn tr. *Grzimek's Four-Legged Australians* xii. 250 For some years, European rabbit-fleas refused to propagate themselves in Australian research centres. **1975** *Times* 23 June 4/2 The rabbit flea..spreads myxomatosis. **1907** *Yesterday's Shopping* (1969) 58/1 *Rabbit Food..Pigeon Food..Foal Food. **1936** *Amer. Speech* XI. 44/2 *Rabbit's food*, lettuce. **1941** J. Smiley *Hash House Lingo* 45 *Rabbit food*, lettuce. **1959** I. & P. Opie *Lore & Lang. Schoolch.* ix. 163 Tomatoes are generally 'squashers', and 'rabbit's food' is any green salad. **1972** A. Price *Colonel Butler's Wolf* ix. 98 You can both come back with me and eat pounds of rabbit food. **1851** *De Bow's Rev.* XI. 54 1st, *Rabbit hawk. **1880** G. W. Cable *Grandissimes* vii. 43 A great rabbit-hawk sat alone in the top of a lofty pecan-tree. **1904** 'O. Henry' *Heart of West* 64 The other eye noticed a rabbit-hawk sitting on a dead limb in a water-elm. **1964** *Publ. Amer. Dial. Soc.* XLII. 22 Rabbit-hawk. The marsh hawk (*Circus cyaneus*), so called because of its flying low over the pastures in search of rodents. **1882** Jordan & Gilbert *Syn. Fishes N. America* 144 *Quassilabia lacera*, Hare-lip Sucker..*Rabbit-mouth Sucker. **1938** M. K. Rawlings *Yearling* xvii. 199 A *rabbit-pea vine was in blossom. **1976** *Hortus Third* (L. H. Bailey Hortorium) 1101/1 *Tephrosia..virginiana*..Goat's rue, catgut, rabbit's pea. **1832** *Useful & Ornamental* in *Brit. Husbandry* (1840) III. III. 26 The fence of a forest-tree nursery requires to be *rabbit-proof. **1894** W. Robinson *Wild Garden* (ed. 4) xv. 209 Periwinkle, which is named amongst rabbit-proof plants, is generally eaten to the ground in severe weather. *a* **1902** H. Morant in *Penguin Bk. Austral. Ballads* (1964) 212 But once we're through the rabbit-proof..it's 'West-by-North' again. **1957** R. Stow *Bystander* 29 That's the coldest little bitch this side of the rabbit-proof fence. **1961** *Times* 19 Apr. 14/7 Her rabbit-proof fence is not high enough. **1976** D. Hewett *Bonbons & Roses for Dolly* 28 Best little ticket takers this side of the rabbit-proof. **1837** G. Bennett *Catal. Specimens Nat. Hist. Austral. Mus.* 6 The *Rabbit Rat of the Colonists. Habitat, Interior of Australia. **1863** J. Gould *Mammals Austral.* III. 1 White-footed Hapalotis... The Rabbit Rat of the Colonists. **1879** A. R. Wallace *Australasia* iii. 55 Bandicoots and rabbit-rats, are small animals with sharp nose and long claws, allied to the kangaroos. **1941** E. Troughton *Furred Animals Austral.* 305 The various species..are sometimes called 'rabbit-rats' in reference to the rather large ears. **1970** W. D. L. Ride *Guide Native Mammals Austral.* ix. 142 Little is known of the White-footed Tree-rat of eastern Australia; early settlers called this the Rabbit Rat because of its rounded form and long ears. It has not been seen alive in this century. *a* **1833** Richardson in Hooker *Flor. Bor. Amer.* I. 274 The Crees use the root of this plant..under the name of..(*Rabbit-root). **1886** *Field* 27 Feb. 266/3 Here they..run him into a *rabbit-spout in the gorse. **1651** Weldon *Crt. Jas. I.* 125 Little children did run up and downe the King's Lodgings, like little *Rabbit-starters about their boroughs. **1949** S. T. De Lee *Safeguarding Motherhood* 133 (Index), *Rabbit test. **1958** H. Speert *Obstetr. & Gynecol. Milestones* xxviii. 244 The urine of pregnant women contains a gonadotrophic substance simulating the secretion of the anterior pituitary in its effect on the mouse ovary. Applying this observation to the rabbit, Friedman proceeded to develop the pregnancy test known by his name, popularly as the 'rabbit test'. **1977** E. Leonard *Unknown Man No. 89* i. 7 The guy was a gynecologist. So he went in with Rita for her rabbit test, the concerned hubby. **1880** J. C. Harris *Uncle Remus* xiii. 66 'Den he drawd de rockin'-cheer in front er de fier, he did, en tuck a big chaw terbarker.' 'Tobacco, Uncle Remus?' asked the little boy, incredulously. '*Rabbit terbarker, honey.' **1909** 'O. Henry' *Options* 200, I don't give a pipeful of rabbit tobacco whether Queen Sophia Christina or Charlie Culberson rules these fairy isles. **1936** M. Mitchell *Gone with Wind* xxix. 488 'You all got any chewing tobacco, Scarlett?' 'Nothing but rabbit tobacco. Pa smokes it in a corn cob.' **1937** *Amer. Speech* XII. 235/1 On all the poor land in the middle and far West there is a weed known as.. rabbit tobacco. **1964** *Publ. Amer. Dial. Soc.* XLII. 22 Rabbit tobacco. Life everlasting.., used in many folk remedies for catarrh; also chewed and smoked by boys. **1800** *Rabbit tooth [implied in *rabbit-toothed* above]. **1915** W. Owen *Let.* 4 Apr. (1967) 330 Will he be 13 or 14 next birthday?.. Are his rabbit-teeth humanising? **1980** E. Leather *Duveen Let.* viii. 98 He was tall, thin, with large rabbit teeth. **1750** G. Hughes *Nat. Hist. Barbados* VI. 172 The Thistle, or *Rabbit-weed. **1884** E. Ingersoll in *Harper's Mag.* Sept. 502/2 Sorry bunch-grass and sad rabbit-weed.

†**'rabbit**, *sb.*[2] *Obs.* Also rabit. [Of obscure origin.] A wooden drinking-vessel.

1685 Meriton *Praise Yorksh. Ale* 1 Stronge Beer in Rabits and cheating penny Cans. *a* **1700** B. E. *Dict. Cant. Crew*, *Rabbits*, Wooden Kanns to Drink out of, once used on the Roads, now almost laid by.

'rabbit, *sb.*[3] [a. F. *rabot.*] = rab[1] (q.v.).

1850– in Ogilvie and later Dicts.

rabbit ('ræbɪt), *v.*[1] [f. rabbit *sb.*[1]]

1. *intr.* To hunt for or catch rabbits. Chiefly in *pres. pple.*

1852 *Meanderings of Mem.* I. 20 Beer never bound him rabbiting again. **1861** Hughes *Tom Brown at Oxf.* xxx, She liked..coming to look at them fishing or rabbiting. **1873** G. W. Kitchin *Hist. France* I. III. viii. 341 This man caught three Flemish students rabbiting in his warren.

2. *intr.* To crowd *together* like rabbits.

1892 *Sunday Mag.* Sept. 602 The common people.. rabbit together in miserable warrens.

3. *intr.* To go; to move quickly; to run away. *dial.* and *colloq.*

1887 *Rep. & Trans. Devonshire Assoc.* XIX. 77 Miss —— du rabbut 'bout en awl wethurz. **1937** D. JONES *In Parenthesis* IV. 71 You can't find the lane—the one way—you rabbit to and fro. **1960** WENTWORTH & FLEXNER *Dict. Amer. Slang* 416/1 *Rabbit..v.i.*, to move quickly, to run; specif., to flee, to escape. **1962** J. F. STRAKER *Coil of Rope* iii. 22 Susan ..kept skipping from one side of David to the other... David said irritably, 'For heaven's sake stop rabbiting around!' **1972** J. WAMBAUGH *Blue Knight* (1973) ii. 33, I noticed another junkie watching me. He was trying to decide whether to rabbit or freeze.

4. To copulate. *rare.*

1919 J. MASEFIELD *Reynard the Fox* 16 I'll learn 'ee rabbit in my shed.

5. *trans.* To borrow or steal. *Austral. Naut. slang.* Cf. RABBIT *sb.*^{1} 2 f.

1943 BAKER *Dict. Austral. Slang* (ed. 3) 63 *To rabbit*, to borrow, 'scrounge'. (R.A.N. slang.) **1953** K. TENNANT *Joyful Condemned* xxi. 198 Why were Australian Navy men better at 'rabbiting' little valuable articles than Americans?

6. [See *rabbit-and-pork* s.v. RABBIT *sb.*^{1} 4.] *intr.* To talk, to discourse volubly; to gabble. Freq. const. *on. colloq.*

1950 P. TEMPEST *Lag's Lexicon* 173 One who 'rabbits' all the time is one who never stops talking. **1959** *Encounter* Mar. 63/1 The next thing I knew, I was rabbiting away to a geezer. **1960** *News Chron.* 16 Feb. 6/6 She don't want to stand rabbiting away about colourful denizens. **1963** 'A. GARVE' *Sea Monks* iii. 108 Then stop rabbitin' an' get that wall cleaned. **1967** A. DIMENT *Dolly Dolly Spy* iv. 39, I let him rabbit on about the twilight hours of the Third Reich. **1976** J. BINGHAM *God's Defector* vii. 99 You go into a pub with a short-back-and-sides and people stop rabbiting and stare at you. **1977** *Guardian Weekly* 9 Oct. 20/3 A girl reporter from Rolling Stone rabbits on idiotically about the Maharishi.

rabbit ('ræbɪt), *v.*^{2} *Vulgar.* [Prob. a fanciful alteration of *rat* in *od rat* (OD^1), *drat.*] A meaningless word used as an imprecation = DRAT, etc. Also, ***drabbit, od(d) rabbit*** (see OD^1 1 b).

1742 FIELDING *J. Andrews* III. viii, 'Rabbit the fellow' cries he. **1768** GOLDSM. *Good-n. Man* III, Rabbit me, but little Flanigan will look well in anything. **1787** GROSE *Provinc. Gloss., D'rabbit it*, a vulgar exclamation or abbreviation of God rabbit it, a foolish evasion of an oath. N. **1831** ROBY *Trad. Lancash.* Ser. II. (1879) II. 196 Rabbit thee, Will, but the luggage will break thy back. **1880** MRS. PARR *Adam & Eve* xxix. 397 Drabbit the maid! **1889** DOYLE *Micah Clarke* 302 Rabbit me! but you are to be envied.

rabbit, variant of RABBET *sb.* and *v.*

rabbiter ('ræbɪtə(r)). [f. RABBIT *v.*^{1} + -ER^1.] One who hunts rabbits; a rabbit-catcher. Also of a dog (quot. 1883).

1872 BLACKMORE *Maid of Sk.*, The five young rabbiters. **1883** C. READE in *Harper's Mag.* June 97/1 He's the best rabbiter you ha' got. **1887** *Blackw. Mag.* Dec. 826 These rabbiters insisted on being shifted out to more rabbity country.

rabbiting ('ræbɪtɪŋ), *vbl. sb.* [f. as prec. + -ING^1.] Hunting, shooting, or catching rabbits.

1841 J. T. HEWLETT *Parish Clerk* I. 99 A day's rabbiting or rat-catching. **1875** W. S. HAYWARD *Love agst. World* 27 The day's 'rabbitings' on the heath with Giles' ferrets and Giles' terriers.

b. *Comb.* in sense 'useful for rabbiting'.

1884 *Western Morning News* 5 Sept. 2/5 White Rabbiting Spaniels. **1889** *Dogs* ii. 12 A capital rabbiting dog.

rabbitish ('ræbɪtɪʃ), *a.* [f. RABBIT *sb.*^{1} + -ISH.] Characteristic of a rabbit.

1834 BECKFORD *Italy* II. 14 My nose having lost all relish for rabbitish odours. **1851** in *Life A. Fonblanque* (1874) 498 That is just the most rabbitish thing you could do. **1941** E. R. EDDISON *Fish Dinner* xiii. 225 Young man a bit rabbitish by the look of him: doesn't seem to know quite what to do. **1978** J. SYMONS *Blackheath Poisonings* I. 24 Bertie, who was fair and pale, with pinkish eyes, had a slightly rabbitish appearance.

'rabbit-o. *Austral. slang.* Also Rabbit-O, rabbit-oh. [f. RABBIT *sb.*^{1} + -O^2.] An itinerant seller of rabbits as food. Also *attrib.*

[**1908** T. E. SPENCER *Budgeree Ballads* 84 When I ought to think of bizness, I can only think of you, And instead of 'Rabbit-oh!' I sings out 'Liza!'] **1911** A. WRIGHT *Gambler's Gold* 75 Engaged in the hopeless task of trying to win the Rabbit-O man's money. **1945** K. TENNANT *Time enough Later* x. 150 Mrs. Drew knew all about her neighbours from the butcher and the grocer and the rabbit-o. **1975** *Sydney Morning Herald* 9 Apr. 1 Now 65, he is probably the last rabbit-oh in Sydney.

'rabbit punch. Also rabbit's punch. [f. RABBIT *sb.*^{1} + PUNCH *sb.*^{2}] A sharp, chopping blow to the back of the neck delivered with the side of the hand. Also *fig.*

1915 E. CORRI *30 Years Boxing Referee* 175 The occipital punch is well described by its other name, the 'rabbit-punch', derived from the way in which a gamekeeper puts a rabbit out of pain. **1936** *Daily Tel.* 30 Jan. 20/7 The only incident to which any exception could be taken was Petersen's habit of using the 'rabbit punch'—a cuff downwards on the back of the neck. **1958** *Daily Mail* 7 June 5/7 Simpson admitted to the police that he had killed the dog. He said he..gave it a 'rabbit punch'. **1959** I. & P. OPIE *Lore & Lang. Schoolch.* x. 202 A 'Rabbit's Punch' is delivered by pulling a child's head forward, usually by his hair, and slicing the back of his neck with the side of the hand. **1968** A. DIMENT *Bang Bang Birds* iii. 27 Another gust of warm wind caught me in a rabbit punch. **1973** G. SIMS *Hunters Point* xiii. 123 As he toppled forward Buchanan delivered a murderous rabbit punch.

So **'rabbit-punch** *v. trans.*; **'rabbit-punching** *ppl. a.* and *vbl. sb.*

1936 R. CHANDLER in *Black Mask* Jan. 18/2 Somebody rabbit-punched him from behind. **1940** DYLAN THOMAS *Portrait of Artist as Young Dog* 72 The strange boy rabbit-punched me twice. **1968** T. STOPPARD *Real Inspector Hound* (1970) 11, I dream of champions chopped down by rabbit-punching sparring partners. **1971** *Times* 16 Feb. 8/5 A controversial disqualification for rabbit punching. **1972** T. COE *Don't lie to Me* (1974) xx. 161 He rabbit-punched me in the back of the neck.

rabbitry ('ræbɪtrɪ). [f. RABBIT *sb.*^{1} + -RY.]

1. A place in which rabbits are kept; a collection of rabbits. Also, rabbit-breeding.

1838 LOUDON *Suburban Gardener* 712 The Rabbitry.—.. The warren may either be close to the rabbit-house, or at any covenient distance. **1854** WOOD *Anim. Life* (ed. 2) 299 A curious circumstance occurred in my rabbitry. **1886** *Poultry*, etc. 17 Sept. 463 Rye flour may be used to an advantage in the rabbitry. **1968** *Punch* 12 June 858/3 Anyone with distressful childhood memories of pet does unconcernedly making away with their blind and naked young may like to know that commercial rabbitry has just about eradicated such uneconomic vice.

2. *slang.* In sport, poor performers (*collect.*). Also, poor play or performance in any game. Cf. RABBIT *sb.*^{1} 2 a.

1930 *Observer* 25 May 16 The rabbitry..is faithful to the definition of the game [*sc.* golf] as 'pedestrianism round the margin of the links'. **1932** A. MARSHALL *Mrs. Jim* v. 44 Her two younger girls..were made welcome at these [tennis] parties, so that Mrs. Gurdon's rabbitry should not be put to shame.

rabbit's ear. Also rabbit ear. [f. RABBIT *sb.*^{1} + EAR *sb.*^{1}] **1.** A perennial herb, *Stachys olympica* (formerly *S. lanata*), belonging to the family Labiatæ, distinguished by greyish foliage and dense white tomentum covering the whole plant; usually called lamb's ears.

1928 V. WOOLF *Let.* 15 Oct. (1977) III. 545 Might I beg some Saviour's flannel or rabbit ear? *Ibid.* 22 Oct. 547 A thousand thanks for the rabbits ears. **1949** H. NICOLSON *Let.* 15 June (1968) 171, I think of it [*sc.* a garden] as *cineraria* in masses, Rabbit's Ears in masses,..predominantly grey.

2. An indoor television aerial consisting of a base supporting two stiff wires that form a V. *U.S.*

1967 *Boston Sunday Herald Mag.* 16 Apr. 32/2 (Advt.), Top back lifts for rabbit ears—doors fold flat against sides for televiewing. **1972** T. KENRICK *Tough One to Lose* ii. 30 There wasn't much... A TV set in the corner that needed rabbit's ears. **1978** *Tucson Mag.* Dec. 37/1, I use rabbit ears with my set and get a perfect picture.

'rabbit's foot. [RABBIT *sb.*^{1} 4.] Also **rabbit-foot.**

1. The foot of a rabbit carried to bring luck; also *transf.* Phr. ***to work the rabbit('s)-foot*** (U.S.), to cheat, to trick.

1879 L. HEARN *Amer. Miscell.* (1924) I. 185 After the girl told that [ghost] story, Banjo Jim seldom passed along the row at night without a rabbit's foot in the breast pocket of his woolen shirt. **1902** W. N. HARBEN *Abner Daniel* 309 Pole worked the rabbit-foot on them back there. **1922** *Sunset* Dec. 10/2 Presently the word went round that I was a 'rabbit's foot'—a bringer of good luck—and the gamblers began to give me money to place for them. **1948** *Salt Lake Tribune* 17 Dec. 34/6 A dimestore rabbit's foot paid off with one of 1948's biggest football surprises and landed his team in the Delta bowl. **1972** C. WESTON *Poor, Poor Ophelia* (1973) viii. 45 Don't you know a charm when you see one? This is my rabbit's foot.

2. Special combs.: **rabbit('s) foot (clover)** = HARE'S FOOT 1; **rabbit's foot (fern)** *U.S.*, an epiphytic fern, *Polypodium aureum*, native to tropical America and cultivated elsewhere as a house plant; **rabbit('s) foot grass**, an annual grass, *Polypogon monspeliensis*, distinguished by soft hairs on its flower-head, native to Europe and widely naturalized elsewhere.

1817 A. EATON *Man. Bot.* 84 *Trifolium..arvense* (field clover, or *rabbit-foot) heads cylindric. **1850** S. F. COOPER *Rural Hours* 125 The downy 'rabbit-foot', or 'stone-clover', the common red variety..[is] introduced. **1878** H. M. JACKSON *Bits of Travel at Home* 186 [There grows] Rabbit's foot, May-weed, shepherd's purse. **1884** MILLER *Bot. Dict., Trifolium arvense*, Hare's foot Clover or Trefoil, Rabbit-foot, of N. America. **1889** *Cent. Dict.* s.v. Clover. Other species, mostly weeds of little value, are the yellow or hop clover,..the stone, hare's-foot, or rabbit-foot clover. **1954** *Amer. Speech* XXIX. 15 *Trifolium arvense*, a cosmopolitan woolly-headed clover,..is known in America both as the rabbitfoot (clover) and hare's-foot (clover)... Rabbitfoot clover is the commonest designation in the United States, whereas hare's-foot is the usual British term. **1968** PETERSON & MCKENNY *Field Guide to Wildflowers N. Amer.* 246 Rabbit's-foot Clover... The soft silky foliage and the fuzzy, grayish-pink heads of bloom are unmistakable. **1972** G. BEINE *Land of Coyote* 90 These are rattle boxes, and there, some rabbitsfoot clover. **1951** E. GRAHAM *My Window looks down East* vii. 63 The *rabbit's foot fern and all the other green things looked so radiant and fresh. **1964** F. G. FOSTER *Gardener's Fern Bk.* 182 Golden Polypody... Commonly called 'rabbit's-foot' fern. Actually, the 'rabbit's foot' is a colorful orange-brown or white, scaly rhizome. **1973** J. L. FAUST *N.Y. Times Bk. House Plants* 107 Ferns.. best for indoors are..coarse-leaved polypody..and rabbit's-foot. **1935** A. S. HITCHCOCK *Man. Grasses U.S.* 350 *Polypogon monspeliensis*..*Rabbitfoot Grass. **1954** C. E. HUBBARD *Grasses* 285 Annual Beard-grass. *Polypogon monspeliensis*... Known in N. America as 'Rabbitfoot Grass'. **1968** F. W. GOULD *Grass Systematics* v. 172 Most common and widespread is..rabbitfoot grass, present in moist areas along streams. **1973** *Times* 20 Oct. 16/7 Upright 'rabbits' [*sic*] foot', cock-spur or barnyard grasses have been common.

†rabbit-sucker. *Obs.* [Properly an appositive comb., but in some of the transf. uses *rabbit* may have been taken as objective.]

1. A sucking rabbit, a very young rabbit.

c **1460** J. RUSSELL *Bk. Nurture* 457 Rabettes sowkers, þe furþer parte from þe hyndur, ye devide. *Ibid.* 697 Rabettes sowkere. **1591** LYLY *Endym.* Wks. 1858 II. 70, I preferre an olde cony before a rabbet sucker, and an ancient henne before a young chicken peeper. **1605** *Tryall Chev.* v. ii. in Bullen *Old Pl.* 1884 III. 350 If Dicke Bowyer be not writ a bountifull benefactor in hell..I am a rabbit sucker. **1630** J. TAYLOR (Water P.) *Gt. Eater of Kent* 6 This same noble Nicke..hath made an end of an hogge all at once, as if it had bin a rabbet-sucker.

2. *transf.* (See quots.)

1608 DEKKER *Lanth. & Candlelight* E, The commodities that are taken vp are cald Pursenets.. They that take up are the Rabbet-suckers. **1663** COWLEY *Cutter of Colman St.* IV. vi, I'm..mistaken if thou beest not cheated of it all..by such Rabbet-suckers as these. *a* **1700** B. E. *Dict. Cant. Crew, Rabbet-suckers*, young Unthrifts taking up Goods upon Tick at excessive rates. **1725** *New Cant. Dict., Rabbet-sucker*,.. also a Name given to Pawn-brokers and Tally-men.

rabbity ('ræbɪtɪ), *a.* [f. as prec. + -Y^1.] Abounding in rabbits; somewhat like a rabbit. Also, suggestive or characteristic of a rabbit. Also *Comb.*, as ***rabbity-faced, -looking*** adjs.

1887 [see RABBITER]. **1892** *Field* 10 Dec. 883/2 Any gamey or rabbity district. **1897** W. C. HAZLITT 4 *Generations* II. 207 The legs are the only edible part..and..are of a rabbity flavour. *a* **1930** D. H. LAWRENCE *Last Poems* (1932) 98 There are too many people on earth Insipid, unsalted, rabbity, endlessly hopping. **1931** D. L. SAYERS *Five Red Herrings* xvi. 177 The rabbity-faced fellow in the train. **1937** C. DAY LEWIS *Starting Point* III. iv. 284 Darling, you're not going to turn me into a rabbity little wage-earner, are you? **1963** AUDEN *Dyer's Hand* 120 A leporello who, in real life, is a rabbity-looking..professor. **1965** M. SHADBOLT *Among Cinders* xi. 96 I'd been starving on rabbity salads. **1974** T. P. WHITNEY tr. *Solzhenitsyn's Gulag Archipelago* I. II. ii. 544 But somehow this is hard for our rabbity brains to grasp. **1976** *Gramophone* Nov. 878/3 My own family's verdict on the book [sc. *Watership Down*] was that it was 'extraordinarily rabbitty'. **1978** G. GREENE *Human Factor* III. v. 144 He thought he recognised all the faces except for one woman in a shabby rabbity fur.

rabble ('ræb(ə)l), *sb.*^{1} (and *a.*). Forms: 4 rabel, -ul, 6 rabell, -il(l, -yll, rabbell, 6–7 rable, 6– rabble. [Possibly connected with RABBLE *v.*^{1}, the root-notion being that of hurry and confusion; but the respective dates of sb. and vb. make the relationship somewhat uncertain. In early examples the idea of a string or series seems to be prominent.]

A. *sb.* **†1.** A pack, string, swarm (of animals). *Obs.*

13.. *Gaw. & Gr. Knt.* 1703 [The dogs] runnen forth in a rabel. *Ibid.* 1899 Renaud com..& alle þe rabel..ry3t at his helez. **1513** DOUGLAS *Æneis* XI. ix. 29 The rawk vocit swannis in a rabyll. *a* **1529** SKELTON *P. Sparowe* 1313 He brought out a rable Of coursers and rounses. **1591** SYLVESTER *Du Bartas* I. v. 909 Flies, Butterflies, Gnats, Bees, and all the rabbles Of other Insects.

2. a. A tumultuous crowd or array of people, a disorderly assemblage, a mob.

1513 DOUGLAS *Æneis* XIII. iv. 63 In lang rabill the wemen ..fled. *a* **1529** SKELTON *E. Rummyng* 382 Now in cometh another rabell. Fyrst one with a ladell [etc.]. *a* **1568** ASCHAM *Scholem.* I. (Arb.) 69, I sawe..cum out of London..a great rable of meane and light persons. **1667** PEPYS *Diary* (1879) IV. 349 At last the rabble broke up and so I away. **1713** BERKELEY *Guard.* No. 39 ¶ 5 They seemed rather a confused rabble than a regular army. **1756** C. LUCAS *Ess. Waters* III. 332, I narrowly escaped the insolence..of an inraged rabble. **1840** THIRLWALL *Greece* VII. 249 He was accompanied..by a mixed rabble of strangers and disfranchised citizens. **1858** FROUDE *Hist. Eng.* III. xiv. 194 He went unwillingly, with followers little better than a rabble.

b. Applied contemptuously to a class or body of persons, imagined as collected in a mob.

1529 MORE *Dyaloge* III. Wks. (1557) 228/1 That we should not haue such a rabell [of priests]. **1560** DAUS tr. *Sleidane's Comm.* 249 b, Monkes and Freers and all that relygious rabbell. **1652–62** HEYLIN *Cosmogr.* I. (1682) 285 That rabble of 39 Kings..mentioned by Hector Boetius. **1671** J. WEBSTER *Metallogr.* ii. 29 The numerous, and almost innumerable rabble of the School-men. **1741** WARBURTON *Div. Legat.* II. iv, Jupiter, Mercury, Bacchus, Venus, Mars, and the whole rabble of licentious deities. **1792** BURKE *Pres. St. Aff.* Wks. 1826 VII. 100 To class himself with that rabble of murderers. **1847** TENNYSON *Princ.* VI. 290 To mob me up with all The soft and milky rabble of womankind.

c. ***the rabble***, the common, low, or disorderly part of the populace (†or of a company); the mob.

1553 BALE *Vocacyon* in *Harl. Misc.* (Malh.) I. 357 Than was all the rable of the shippe..called to the reckeninge. **1581** J. BELL *Haddon's Answ. Osor.* 215 b, The meane and inferiour subjectes, even the rascall rable and multitude. **1635** N. R. *Camden's Hist. Eliz.* I. 101 A few of the rabble of the people raising a tumult. **1676** MARVELL *Mr. Smirke* Wks. 1875 IV. 80 None but the noisy rabble love to hear anything scurrilous or railing. **1711** ADDISON *Spect.* No. 18 ¶ 6 It is not the Taste of the Rabble, but of Persons of the greatest Politeness. **1813** SHELLEY *Q. Mab* VII. 166 His name unheard, Save by the rabble of his native town. **1873** SYMONDS *Grk. Poets* Ser. I. iii. 86 Theognis complains that the rabble rule the state with monstrous laws.

transf. **1691** T. H[ALE] *Acc. New Invent.* p. xlvi, As to the Rabble of Readers.. Water would have served their turns as well.

d. Without article: Persons of the lowest class. **1726** De Foe *Hist. Devil* II. v. (1840) 235 The devil makes use of scoundrels and rabble, beggars and vagabonds. **1734** T. Sheridan in *Swift's Lett.* (1768) IV. 67 You live in Dublin among a parcel of rabble. **1856** Mrs. Stowe *Dred* II. xxxii. 321 There is always an abundance of excitable rabble to be got for a drink of whiskey.

3. A disorderly collection, a confused medley (of things). **a.** Of material things. *rare.*

1514 Barclay *Cyt. & Uplondyshm.* (Percy Soc.) p. xxxiii, The boorde or table, With dishes charged twentie in a rable. **1555** R. Smith *Let.* in Foxe *A. & M.* (1583) 1699/2 Builde they neuer so strongly: yet downe shall theyr rabble fall. **1581** J. Bell *Haddon's Answ. Osor.* 40 A wonderfull rabble of wormeeaten pictures. **1803** W. Taylor in *Ann. Rev.* I. 431 A rabble of books of all ages, sizes [etc.].

b. Of immaterial things. (In later use only with direct reference to sense 2.)

1549 Coverdale, etc. *Erasm. Par. Rom.* 14 All oure desyres of transitorye pleasures, whose whole rable maye well be called the body of synne. **1562** Jewel *Apol. Ch. Eng.* v. ix. (Parker Soc.) 89 Pardons, crosses, censings, and an endless rabble of ceremonies. **1633** Hart *Diet of Diseased* Introd. 26 A rabble of remedies, which may so easily be abused. **1768–74** Tucker *Lt. Nat.* (1834) II. 401 Reason.. overpowered by the rabble of appetites, passions, and opinions. **1847** H. Rogers *Ess.* I. v. 259 A seditious rabble of doubts. **1861** Emerson *Soc. & Solit., Old Age* Wks. (Bohn) III. 134 We live in youth amidst the rabble of passions.

†**4. a.** A long string or series *of* words, etc., having little meaning or value. *Obs.*

c **1388** *Wyclif's Sel. Wks.* III. 466 Nouþer God ne alle his seintus willen heren men for no rabul of wordis, ne curiouse florischynge in ryme. **1545** Brinklow *Lament.* (1874) 88 A rable of vncommaunded tradicions. **1589** Puttenham *Eng. Poesie* III. xxiii. (Arb.) 271 Such a rable of scholasticall precepts which be tedious. **1641** Earl Monm. tr. *Biondi's Civil Warres* v. 170 Hee told them a long rabble of reasons, why hee had sate downe in that place. **1656** —— tr. *Boccalini's Advts. fr. Parnass.* I. vi. (1674) 10 So horribly tedious did that rabble of discourse appear.

b. A rigmarole. (Cf. rabble *v.*[1]) Now *dial.*

1592 Chettle *Kind-harts Dr.* (1841) 20 When I had read this rabble, wherein I founde little reason, I laide it by. *c* **1600** Forbes *Defence* 65 (Jam.) Such doting dreames.. fitter to bee an addition to rables..then to be reputed profound pointes of Christian wisedome. **1649** J. H. *Motion to Parl. Adv. Learn.* 28 This would amount to a long rabble, and degenerate into some Satyre or Pasquill. **1876** *Mid-Yorksh. Gloss.* s.v., He made sike a rabble on it, I couldn't understand a word he said.

c. Hurried or confused talk or reading.

1868 Browning *Ring & Bk.* IV. 34 To hear the rabble and brabble, you'd call the case Fused and confused past human finding out.

5. *Comb.*, as ***rabble-driver***; ***rabble-charming***, ***-chosen***, ***-courting*** adjs.

1686 South *Serm.* (1693) 455 With this powerfull, senseless Engine the Rabble-driver shall be able to carry all before him. *a* **1716** *Ibid.* (1727) VI. 56 The Rabble-charming words, which carry so much Wild-fire wrapt up in them. **1839** *Times* 10 Apr., Wounded the pride of this rabble-courting despot. **1853** T. N. Talfourd *Castilian* II. iii, A council rabble-chosen.

B. *attrib.* passing into *adj.*

1. Of persons: Forming a rabble; of or belonging to the rabble.

1549 Latimer *3rd Serm. bef. Edw. VI* (Arb.) 93 You my rable people that are wronged in the world, aske of my father in your distresses. **1656** Earl Monm. tr. *Boccalini's Advts. fr. Parnass.* I. lxxix. (1674) 107 To procure them that number of followers of the rabble sort of people. *a* **1683** Oldham *Wks.* (1685) 9 Let rabble Souls..Stoop their vile Necks. **1778** *Heroic Ep. to Unfort. Monarch* 7 Silent, and watchful of the rabble-band. **1831** *Lincoln Herald* 23 Dec. 4/5 This old war-cry of the Newark blues, or rather the rabble part of them. **1885** Lowe *Bismarck* I. 548 His only resource left was..to concentrate his rabble army around.. Sedan.

2. Of things, actions, etc.: Characteristic of, appropriate to, the rabble.

1603 Florio *Montaigne* II. xii. (1632) 317 In the rabble case-canvasing of our plea-courts. **1692** Dryden *Cleomenes* Pref., To gratifie the barbarous Party of my Audience, I gave them a short Rabble-Scene. *a* **1734** North *Exam.* (1740) 306 How could any one of English Education.. swallow such a low Rabble Suggestion. **1780** Johnson *Let. to Mrs. Thale* 10 June, To burn the jails..was a good rabble trick. **1848** Anna Jameson in Mrs. Macpherson *Mem.* (1878) 248 There are some disturbances here..mere rabble-work.

3. ***rabble-fish***, the worthless or less valuable fish of a catch. (Cornwall.)

1862 Couch *Fishes* I. 85 Other fishes..are collectively known by the name of rabble-fish, as being rejected from the market. **1880–4** Day *Fishes Gt. Brit.* II. 335 Things are altered now, much of this rabble-fish going to Billingsgate and other large inland markets.

rabble ('ræb(ə)l), *sb.*[2] Also 7 rabil, 9 ravel. [a. F. *râble*, earlier *roable*, *rouable*:—med.L. *rotabulum*, L. *rutābulum* fire-shovel, f. *ruĕre* to rake up.]

†**1.** A kind of shovel used by charcoal-burners to remove the covering from the burned pile. *Obs.*

1664 Evelyn *Sylva* xxx. 102 Two or three days it will only require for cooling, which..they assist, by taking now off the outward covering with a Rabil or Rubber.

2. 'A kind of rake' (Halliwell).

3. An iron bar sharply bent at the end, used for stirring and skimming molten metal in puddling; also, a steam-pipe used for the same purpose.

1864 *Q. Jrnl. Sc.* I. 493 A stirring tool called a rabble by which the workman stirs the melted iron. **1868** Joynson *Metals* 67 The steam tube, or 'rabble', being bent on the end, so as to inject the steam on the liquid metal. **1877** Raymond *Statist. Mines & Mining* 385 The slag is now drawn with a rabble into molds prepared for it. **1881** Greener *Gun* 221 The scraps were then cut into pieces of the same size, and placed in a furnace until of a white heat, gathered into a bloom with ravels, and the mass placed under a tilt hammer.

4. *Comb.*, as **rabble-arm** = sense 3.

1905 *Electrochem. & Metall. Industry* May 194/1 The upper four hearths are provided with two rabble-arms each, the sixth and seventh with three rabble-arms, in order to increase the stirring and discharge rather on one side of the furnace.

rabble ('ræb(ə)l), *v.*[1] *Obs.* exc. *dial.* Forms: 5–6 rable, 8 *Sc.* raible, 9 rabble. [= Du. *rabbelen* to speak indistinctly, (L)G. *rabbeln* to talk hurriedly and thoughtlessly; also, to struggle, wriggle, Sw. *rabbla upp* to rattle over.]

1. a. *trans.* To utter (words or speech) in a rapid confused manner. Also with *forth*, *off*, *out*, *over*. **b.** *intr.* To speak or read in this fashion; to gabble. (Cf. rabble *sb.*[1] 4.)

14.. *Prov. Solomon* in *MS. Cantab. Ff.* ii. 38 lf. 24 (Halliw.) Let thy tunge..rable not wordes recheles owt of reson. *c* **1410** Love *Bonavent. Mirr.* xviii. 44 (Sherard MS.) In the seyinge of the pater noster they..rablen it forth with oute deuocioun. **1450–1530** *Myrr. our Ladye* 53 [Do] not rable them out togyther as though ye wolde say them all at ones. **1583** Foxe *A. & M.* 1663/2 Thus father Traues you may see my rashnes to rable out the scriptures without purpose, ryme, or reason. **1627** J. Carter *Plain Expos.* 60 The Lords prayer is rabled ouer without..vnderstanding or reuerence. **1785** Burns *Holy Fair* xvii, Wee Miller.. Orthodoxy raibles. **1869–** In various northern glossaries.

2. *intr.* To work in a hurried slovenly manner. *dial.* **b.** *trans.* To rattle *up*.

1862 Mrs. H. Wood *Channings* i. 5 'It looks as though it had been rabbled up for the purpose', cried Hurst in his schoolboy phraseology. **1869** *Lonsdale Gloss.*, *Rabble*,..in sewing, to take too long stitches, and without due care to finish the work neatly. **1880** *Jamieson's Dict.*, *Rabble*,..to do any kind of work in a careless and hurried manner.

rabble ('ræb(ə)l), *v.*[2] Also 8 rable. [f. rabble *sb.*[1] 2.]

1. *trans.* To attack or assail (a person or his property) as, along with, or by means of, a rabble; to mob. ***to rabble out of***, to drive from (a place) in this way.

The word was especially used to describe the attacks made upon the Episcopalian clergy in Scotland by bands of Presbyterians in the last few days of 1688 and early months of 1689, and is frequently employed by historical writers in reference to this.

1644 Howell *Twelve Treat.* (1661) 132 The same kind of riotous Rascals which rabbled the K. out of Town. **1690** *Acc. Pres. Persec. Ch. Scot.* 26 Some who were then very active in rabbling the Clergy. **1694** Gibson in *Lett. Lit. Men* (Camden) 227 He fail'd not to cast in his mite when the Episcopal Clergie were rabbl'd. *c* **1714** *Culloden Papers* (1815) 336 The magistrates thought fitt to stirre up a mob and rable them. **1818** Scott *Hrt. Midl.* vii, The aughty-nine, when I was rabbled by the collegeaners. **1860** A. L. Windsor *Ethica* iv. 199 He was continually receiving missives threatening to rabble his house.

2. *intr.* To become a rabble. Also, to behave as a rabble; to go *off* as a rabble.

1813 Sir R. Wilson *Priv. Diary* II. 448 We rabbled, while he [the enemy] never loosened his solidity. *a* **1861** T. Winthrop *John Brent* (1883) ix. 76 He dismissed his audience with an..injunction to keep closer to the train.. and not be 'rabbling off to catch grasshoppers'. **1970** O. Chadwick *Victorian Church* II. vi. 355 The agitators began to disturb and rabble at services.

Hence **'rabbled** *ppl. a.*

1855 Macaulay *Hist. Eng.* xviii. IV. 186 William.. thought that the rabbled curates had been hardly treated.

rabble ('ræb(ə)l), *v.*[3] Also ravel. [f. rabble *sb.*[2]] *trans.* To stir, skim, or rake with a rabble.

1860 C. Tomlinson *Useful Arts & Manuf.* 2nd Ser. II. 17 The door of the furnace is removed, and the liquid mass well *rabbled* or stirred. **1877** Raymond *Statist. Mines & Mining* 392 Just before tapping it is rabbled for five minutes. **1894** Bowker in *Harper's Mag.* Jan. 420 The molten metal is thoroughly stirred, or 'rabbled' to make it uniform. **1923** *Discovery* Nov. 291/2 The other furnace..in which the flames actually play over the surface of the mundic which is 'ravelled' from the side by a pole some eight or nine feet long.

rabblement ('ræb(ə)lmənt). Also 6 rabel-, 6–7 rablement. [f. rabble *sb.*[1] + -ment.]

1. = rabble 2. Now *dial.*

1548 Udall, etc. *Erasm. Par. Mark* i. 10 Thither flocked a great rablement of souldiers. **1586** J. Hooker *Girald. Hist. Irel.* in *Holinshed* II. 96/1 Two or three field peeces.. scattered Thomas and his rablement. **1665** J. Webb *Stone-Heng* (1725) 127 We are not then to wonder, that..such a promiscuous Rabblement were in great Confusion. **1833** Lamb *Elia* II. *Productions Mod. Art*, A rabblement at the heels of Rosinante. **1837** *New Monthly Mag.* LI. 118 A rude and noisy rabblement whom he could not command. **1877–** In various dial. glossaries (Northumb., Lanc., Som.).

†**b.** = rabble 2 b. *Obs.*

1549 Chaloner *Erasm. on Folly* M iii, Dunsmen, and.. Albertistes, together with the whole rablement of Sophistrers. **1605** Camden *Rem.* (1637) 199 Church-robbers, Traitours, and other of the same rabblement. **1674** Bp. Brownrig *Serm.* I. xxi. 284 Usurers, Brokers, and the like rabblement of City-thieves.

transf. **1599** Nashe *Lenten Stuffe* 25 All the foure footed rablement of herbagers and grasse champers.

c. = rabble 2 c. Now *rare.*

1601 Shaks. *Jul. C.* I. ii. 245 As hee refus'd it, the rabblement howted. **1612** *Trav. Four Englishm.* 95 Messengers..sent to raise vp all the whole rabblement thereabout vpon us. **1748** Thomson *Cast. Indol.* II. xlv, The hubbub of the rabblement. **1813** Ld. Thurloe *Poems* 23 The rudest rabblement With their ill darts upon her bosom glanc'd. **1841** H. Smith *Moneyed Man* I. i. 12 Some of the passing rabblement ordered him to desist.

d. Confusion, disturbance, or tumult like that of a rabble; riotous conduct. *rare.*

1590 Spenser *F.Q.* I. xii. 9 The raskall many..Heaped together in rude rablement. **1731** *Gentl. Mag.* I. 125 Rabblement, Brabblement, or Squabblement. **1888** Stevenson *Black Arrow* 177 This impulse of rabblement was not restrained without a certain clamour of voices.

†**2.** = rabble 3 b. *Obs.*

c **1550** *Will of Deuyle* (Collier) 8 The rablement of..feined and domme ceremonies. **1607** *Scholast. Disc. agst. Antichr.* I. ii. 66 The rabblement of Roman rites which Augustine.. brought in. **1652** G. Collier *Vindic. Sabbath* (1656) 44 The rabblement of Romish holi-daies.

†**3.** = rabble 4. *Obs.*

1545 Joye *Exp. Dan.* ix, An hole rabblement of significations and signes of an abominable desolation. **1581** Marbeck *Bk. of Notes* 845 Prayer consisteth not in a rabblement of words. **1612** tr. *Benvenuto's Passenger* I. i. §19. 73 An whole rablement of flim flam tales. **1714** Gay *Sheph. Week* Proem, A rout and rabblement of critical gallimawfry.

b. = rabble 4 b. Now only *dial.*

1547 Recorde *Judic. Ur.* 1, I wyll..overpasse the greate rablement, only taking one generall sentence. **1654** Gataker *Disc. Apol.* 85 In both his Rabblements fraught with Ribaldrie. **1665** J. Webb *Stone-Heng* (1725) 54 To reckon up the rest of the Rabblement is needless. **1855** Robinson *Whitby Gloss.*, *Rabblement*, a long random discourse.

rabbler[1] ('ræblə(r)). *rare.* [f. rabble *v.*[2] + -er[1].] One who rabbles; one of a rabble.

1634 J. Canne *Necess. Separ.* (1849) 150 The scourges of all God's people, ravening rabblers. **1692–1712** Fountainhall in W. P. Brown *Decis. Suppl.* (1826) IV. 356–7 (Jam.) He had there publicly called him a rabler and a robber. **1693** *Apol. Clergy Scot.* 5 Such of the Presbyterians as..directed the Methods that the Rabblers were to take.

'rabbler[2]. [f. rabble *v.*[3]] **a.** One who uses a rabble. **b.** An instrument for rabbling.

1877 Raymond *Statist. Mines & Mining* 398 The upper hearths are not very accessible to the rabblers. **1883** Nasmyth *Autobiog.* xx. 368 My patent hollow steam Rabbler is at work, producing iron of superior quality.

rabble-rouser ('ræb(ə)lraʊzə(r)). [f. rabble *sb.*[1] + rouser.] **a.** One who practises rabble-rousing; a demagogue.

1843 'R. Carlton' *New Purchase* I. xxii. 211 Nothing surpasses the munificent promises..of a genuine rabble rouser, just before an election. **1926** *Even. Standard* 12 July 3/2 You need not be a Tammany politician to know the meaning of boodle, gerrymander, carpet-bagger, wirepuller, rabble-rouser. **1959** 'M. M. Kaye' *House of Shade* xiv. 190 The murder of a rabble-rouser would probably be considered as of little account. **1972** *Listener* 28 Dec. 899/1 Thomas Paine..was never a rabble-rouser. **1978** J. A. Michener *Chesapeake* 543 Paul..astounded the more conservative Steeds by prevailing upon an itinerant Methodist rabble-rouser to spend five days at Devon.

b. Something, esp. music, that excites an audience.

1958 *New Statesman* 1 Feb. 133/3 The symphony ends with a noisy finale which seemed no more than an unusually prolonged rabble-rouser. **1965** G. Melly *Owning Up* iv. 38 They chose their fastest, loudest numbers, 'rabble rousers' was the trade name, in the hope of making some impact on the audience.

rabble-rousing ('ræb(ə)lraʊzɪŋ), *a.* and *sb.* [f. rabble *sb.*[1] + rousing *ppl. a.* and *vbl. sb.*[1]]

A. *adj.* Tending to arouse the emotions of a rabble or disorderly crowd, esp. for political ends; demagogic, inflammatory, excitatory.

1802 Syd. Smith *Wks.* (1859) I. 10/2 Vulgar violence and the eternal repetition of rabble-rousing words. **1933** *Sun* (Baltimore) 8 Aug. 8/2 They are as old as rabble-rousing nationalism itself. **1951** T. Sterling *House without Door* xi. 126 Mouthing the rabble-rousing opinions of Communist filth. **1969** *N.Y. Rev. Bks.* 30 Jan. 12/4 Convinced that this was a rabble-rousing exaggeration, Booth set out to compile his own statistics. **1976** *Eastern Even. News* (Norwich) 9 Dec. 2/1 Mussolini made a rabble-rousing appearance in Milan after the Allies had landed in the south.

B. *sb.* The act or process of arousing the emotions of a crowd; demagoguery, trouble-stirring.

1933 *Sun* (Baltimore) 18 Sept. 8/2 It is not necessary to pay a great deal of attention to this form of economic rabble rousing. **1962** D. H. Laurence in G. B. Shaw *Platform & Pulpit* p. xii, He was not concerned with rabble-rousing or spell-binding. **1974** A. Ross *Bradford Business* 9 Heated rabble-rousing in our seats of learning.

Hence (as a back-formation) **'rabble-rouse** *v. intr.*, to arouse the emotions of a crowd by a demagogical harangue.

1959 *Time* 15 June 36/3 He rabble-rouses more fluently in English than in Chinese. **1971** *Guardian* 1 July 11/6 Did he [*sc.* Oswald Mosley] make speeches in such a way as to rabble-rouse?

rabble rout (ˈræb(ə)lraʊt). [f. RABBLE *sb.*[1] + ROUT.] = RABBLE 2, 2b.

1599 MIDDLETON *Micro-Cynicon* Wks. (Bullen) VIII. 129 A crew of fiddling knaves abject, The very refuse of that rabble rout. **1639** FULLER *Holy War* I. xii. (1840) 20 Besides these well-meaning people, there went also a rabble-rout. **1768** WESLEY *Jrnl.* 3 June (1827) III. 327 A more rude rabble-rout I never saw. **1822** W. IRVING *Braceb. Hall* xvi. 134 There was a rabble rout on foot. **1881** BESANT & RICE *Chapl. of Fleet* I. 158 The president of the rabble rout was no other than the doctor himself.

b. = RABBLE 2c. Now *rare* or *Obs.*

1654 EARL MONM. tr. *Bentivoglio's Warrs Flanders* 38 The rabble rout now will, and anon will not. *c* **1680** in Somers *Tracts* (1748) I. 213 Those Republicans who..lead the Rabble-rout by the plausible Cry of Religion. **1748** THOMSON *Cast. Indol.* II. xli, With feigned respect he bade give back The rabble rout.

rabbling (ˈræblɪŋ), *vbl. sb.*[1] [f. RABBLE *v.*[2] + -ING[1].] The action of the verb. Also, a particular instance of this.

1690 *Acc. Pres. Persec. Ch. Scot.* 26 Rabbling has been all along in fashion, and continues to this moment. **1692** *Sc. Presbyt. Eloq.* (1738) 89 All the Evidences of their Moderation, are rabbling, robbing, beating. **1693** *Apol. Clergy Scot.* 2 To ward off the blame of the barbarous Rabblings of the Clergy. **1874** GREEN *Short Hist.* viii. 527 The rabbling of the bishops proved that there was 'no free Parliament'.

rabbling (ˈræblɪŋ), *vbl. sb.*[2] [f. RABBLE *v.*[3] + -ING[1].] The action of the verb. Also *attrib.*, as ***rabbling-door***, ***-machine***.

1864 *Q. Jrnl. Sc.* I. 493 After 'rabbling' the puddled ball is ready for shingling. **1877** RAYMOND *Statist. Mines & Mining* 397 The long reverbatory with rabbling-doors on the side. **1882** *Engineer* 24 Feb. 133/2 The puddling furnaces..on the top of each is fitted a rabbling machine.

ˈrabbling, *a. Obs.* exc. *dial.* [f. RABBLE *sb.*[1]] Disorderly, rowdy.

1575 R. B. *Appius & Virg.* in Hazl. *Dodsley* IV. 143 O false Judge Appius, rabbling wretch. **1576** NEWTON *Lemnie's Complex.* (1633) 162 A rabbling rout of idle Louts. **1652** WADSWORTH tr. *Sandoval's Civ. Wars Spain* 301 The report..made a number of rabbling people join. **1887** *S. Chesh. Gloss.*, *Rabblin'*, rowdy, noisy.

rabbonet, rabbott, rabbyn(e, obs. ff. RABINET, RABBET, RABBIN.

rabdo-, see RHABDO-.

rabe, rabel, obs. ff. RABBI, RABBLE.

†**Rabelaic**, *a. Obs. rare.* = next.

a **1768** STERNE *Fragment* i, Longinus Rabelaicus (who is certainly..as Rabelaic a fellow as ever existed).

Rabelaisian (ræbəˈleɪzɪən), *a.* (and *sb.*). Also -æsian. [f. the name of the French author François *Rabelais* (*c* 1490–1553) + -IAN.]

A. *adj.* Pertaining to, characteristic of, or resembling Rabelais or his writings, which are distinguished by exuberance of imagination and language, combined with extravagance and coarseness of humour and satire.

1817 LADY MORGAN *France* II. viii. 167 He talked of recovery,..and still emitted some of those sparks of Rabelaisian humour, attributed to him by contemporary wits. **1857** *Sat. Rev.* 2 May 404/2 The publications of the two Brunets on Rabelæsian bibliography. **1864** —— 5 Mar. 300 Persons of a Rabelaisian turn of mind, who relish La Fontaine and Boccaccio. **1876** LOWELL *Among my Bks.* Ser. II. 132 [Skelton] was truly Rabelaisian before Rabelais. **1876** F. HARRISON *Choice Bks.* (1886) 177 The Rabelaisian redundancy of his humour.

B. *sb.* A student or admirer of Rabelais.

1882 HARDY *Let.* 17 May (1978) I. 106 We Rabelaisians have not as yet reached the state of enlightenment which distinguishes you Noviomagians, & do not include ladies in our company. **1893** *Athenæum* 10 June 729/3 Modern Rabelaisians, anxious concerning the mission of the master.

Hence **Rabeˈlaisianism**, the characteristic style or attitude of Rabelais; a Rabelaisian feature or characteristic. So also **Rabeˈlaism**.

1865 WRIGHT *Hist. Caricat.* xix. (1875) 342 Rabelaism, did not, during the sixteenth century, make much progress beyond the limits of France. **1886** *Athenæum* 23 Jan. 131/3 Rabelaisianism..and Voltairean mockery. **1908** A. BENNETT *Old Wives' Tale* II. ii. 166 The robust Rabelaisianism of his more private conversation. **1922** *Times Lit. Suppl.* 5 Jan. 9/1 His [*sc.* Balzac's] mere Rabelaisianisms sometimes bring a later accent into what should be a very simple atmosphere.

rabell, obs. form of RABBLE *sb.*[1]

rabet, variant of RABAT plane.

rabet(t, obs. form of RABBET; var. RABITE.

‖**Rabfak** (ˈræbfæk). Also rabfac. [a. Russ. *rabfák*, f. *rab(óchiĭ) fak(ul'tét)* workers' school.] A workers' school, established after the Russian Revolution, to prepare workers and peasants for higher education. Also *attrib.*

1928 *Observer* 19 Feb. 12 Among the candidates for admission to the local 'rabfac', or workers' high school, appeared a young woman..who announced herself as 'Sheem Sheem', daughter of Sun-Yat-sen. **1943** E. M. ALMEDINGEN *Frossia* ix. 316 'Rabfaks?' she asked. 'Oh yes, I have heard of them. Workers' Faculties, are they not?' *Ibid.* 337 A few [teachers] deplored the Rabfak system—always in cautious undertones. **1960** *Twentieth Cent.* June 573 In 1922 he [*sc.* Kruschschev] was sent by the Party for a three-year adult education course at a 'Rabfak' school.

‖**rabi** (ˈræbiː). See also RUBBEE. [Urdū *rabī* (ad. Arab. *rabīˁ* Spring.] The most important of the three grain crops of Hindustan, sown in September and reaped in the Spring. Also *attrib.* as ***rabi-crop***, ***-harvest***.

1882 HUNTER *Ind. Empire* 385 According to the system of classification in Upper India, wheat ranks as a *rabí* or spring crop, being reaped at the close of the cold weather in April and May. **1886** A. H. CHURCH *Food Grains Ind.* 99 Where indigo is grown in the kharif, barley is its usual accompaniment in the rabi. **1898** *Agric. Ledger* V. No. 12. 16 Before the rabi-harvest.

rabi, obs. form of RABBI.

†**ˈrabiate**, *a. Obs. rare*[−1]. [a. med.L. *rabiāt-us*, pa. pple. of *rabiāre* to be mad: see RABIES.] Rabid.

c **1470** *Lament. Mary Magd.* xxxiv, Ah ye Jewes, worse than dogges rabiate.

ˈrabiator. *Sc. rare.* [Perh. a later form of RUBIATOR, by assoc. with *rabid.*] 'A violent, noisy, greedy person' (Jam.).

a **1814** *Watch-house* II. i in *New Brit. Theatre* I. 60 They a' barkit at me, like sae many rabiators. **1830** GALT *Lawrie T.* I. vii. (1849) 22 One morning that rabiator, Mr. Lapstone, came into the shop.

rabic (ˈræbɪk), *a.* [f. L. *rab-iēs* + -IC. Cf. F. *rabique.*]

1. Pertaining to, or caused by, rabies.

1885 LADY HAMILTON *Life Pasteur* 295 The saliva loses its rabic virulence in twenty-four hours. **1897** *Allbutt's Syst. Med.* II. 699 Rabic symptoms..induced by the inoculation of milk from affected animals.

2. Affected with rabies.

1887 DOLAN *Hydrophobia* 33 Out of the 38 Russians bitten by wolves, 3 died rabic.

†**ˈrabical**, *a. Obs. rare*[−1]. [f. *rabi* RABBI + -ICAL.] Pertaining to a rabbi (in quot. *transf.*).

1716 M. DAVIES *Athen. Brit.* II. 395 He is willing also to be contented with some bare Rabical Preferment amongst the Elementary Baptists.

rabid (ˈræbɪd), *a.* [ad. L. *rabid-us*, f. *rabĕre* to rave, rage, be mad.]

1. Furious, raging; madly violent in nature or behaviour. Also *transf.* of things or parts of the body.

c **1611** CHAPMAN *Iliad* XXI. 129 As my brows were fork'd with rabid horns. **1615** —— *Odyss.* XII. 428 All the rabide flight Of winds that ruine ships are bred in night. **1695** BLACKMORE *Pr. Arth.* IV. 501 He licks his rabid Jaws. **1722** WOLLASTON *Relig. Nat.* vii. 146 Some men are naturally.. thievish, pugnacious, rabid. **1818** SHELLEY *Rev. Islam* V. vii, Like rabid snakes, that sting some gentle child Who brings them food. **1848** DICKENS *Dombey* x, He was made so rabid by the gout.

b. Of feelings, passions, disease, etc.

1647 CRASHAW *Ps.* xxiii. Poems 34 He..Strokes and tames my rabid grief. **1700** DRYDEN *Ovid's Met.* XV. 512 With rabid Hunger feed upon your kind. **1858** GLADSTONE *Homer* I. 141 She has not the rabid virulence against Troy which distinguishes Juno. **1878** H. M. STANLEY *Dark Cont.* II. xii. 361 The itch disease was rabid..about a dozen of the men were fearful objects of its virulence.

c. Of persons: Having some quality, feeling, view, etc., in a violent degree.

1820 LAMB *Elia* I. *Christ's Hosp. 35 Yrs. ago*, B. was a rabid pedant. **1841–4** EMERSON *Ess., Nom. & Real.* Wks. (Bohn) I. 256 The rabid democrat, as soon as he is senator and rich man [etc.]. **1884** EDNA LYALL *We Two* xiii, He is very rabid on the subject.

2. *spec.* Of beasts (rarely of human beings): Affected with rabies; mad.

1804 *Med. Jrnl.* XII. 388 Persons who have had reason to believe, that they were bitten by a rabid animal. **1822** *Good's Stud. Med.* III. 347 A rabid young man. **1833** FORBES, etc. *Cycl. Pract. Med.* II. 489/1 The disease named hydrophobia usually arises from the bite of a rabid dog. **1880** *Med. Temp. Jrnl.* July 147 Bites of rabid animals.

b. Pertaining to, of the nature of, rabies.

1806 *Med. Jrnl.* XV. 412 Nothing characteristic of rabid hydrophobia. **1822** *Good's Stud. Med.* III. 375 Their plan of abstracting rabid blood from the system. **1887** DOLAN *Hydrophobia* 8 An accompaniment of the rabid virus.

Hence **raˈbidity**; **ˈrabidly** *adv.*; **ˈrabidness**.

1649 JER. TAYLOR *Gt. Exemp.* xv. §27 The furies and rabidness of their passion. **1831** DISRAELI *Young Duke* V. vi. 174 At any rate he must get rid of his rabidity. **1860** PUSEY *Min. Proph.* 409 Wolves..going forth to prey when urged to rabidness by hunger. **1864** CARLYLE *Fredk. Gt.* IV. 505 Brühl's rabidities of appetite. **1877** KINGLAKE *Crimea* VI. vi. §xiv. (1894) 272 Men shouting and rabidly yelling.

rabies (ˈreɪbiːiːz, now usu. ˈreɪbiːz, -ɪz). [a. L. *rabiēs*, f. *rabĕre* to rage, rave. Cf. RAGE.] Canine madness; hydrophobia: a contagious virus disease of dogs and other warm-blooded animals, which produces paralysis or a vicious excitability and in man causes a fatal encephalitis with throat spasm upon swallowing and convulsions. Also *fig.*

1598 J. FLORIO *Worlde of Wordes* 307/2 Rabbino, Rabi, Rabis, the Rabbies. **1661** LOVELL *Hist. Anim. & Min.* 333 The rabies, which is a madnesse, caused by some peculiar poyson. **1753** CHAMBERS *Cycl. Supp.* s.v. *Madness*, Dr. James relates the cure be made of dogs that were mad, and how he preserved others from the rabies. **1828** LYTTON *Pelham* I. xx. 152 Finding Lord Vincent so disposed to the biting mood, I immediately directed his *rabies* towards Mr. Aberton. **1846** J. BAXTER *Libr. Pract. Agric.* (ed. 4) II. 284 Whenever rabies appears it is inevitably fatal. **1884** *Graphic* 22 Nov. 531/2 The alleged epidemic of rabies in South London. **1967** SWAIN & DODDS *Clinical Virol.* xiii. 184 Eradication of rabies can be achieved only when the total elimination of the reservoir of animal infection is possible. It has been achieved in Great Britain by rigid quarantine laws which govern the importation of all livestock. **1977** D. A. WARRELL in C. Kaplan *Rabies: the Facts* iii. 32 In man the disease called rabies is a severe inflammation of the brain and spinal cord..associated with invasion of these tissues by rabies virus. **1980** *Sci. Amer.* Jan. 109/1 Fox rabies is particularly serious in Europe, where the disease has spread steadily at the rate of about 30 kilometers per year from east to west since World War II.

attrib. **1886** *Pall Mall G.* 17 Nov. 5/1 The mad dog with his rabies virus. **1887** *British Med. Jrnl.* 8 Jan. 82/2 A discussion on Pasteur's rabies-inoculations. **1976** *Daily Tel.* 20 July 3/3 A 32-year-old teacher, fined £300 at Uxbridge for contravening the rabies regulations had the penalty reduced on appeal to £100 yesterday. **1976** T. HEALD *Let Sleeping Dogs Die* ii. 30 'But surely he got an injection?' 'Not even anti-tetanus. Let alone a rabies jab. It was only a little bite.'

Hence **rabiˈetic** *a.*, affected with rabies, rabid; **raˈbific** *a.*, causing rabies.

1879 DOLAN *Rabies or Hydrophobia* (ed. 2) 213 The total extinction of the rabific contagion. **1886** *Encycl. Brit.* XX. 202 Rabific virus..obtained from a rabbit.

rabil(l, obs. forms of RABBLE *sb.*

rabin(e, obs. forms of RABBIN.

ˈrabinet. *Obs.* exc. *Hist.* Forms: 6 rabbinet, 7 -enet, rabanet, -init, 9 -onet, 6- rabinet. [App. later form of ROBINET (q.v.).] A small variety of cannon (see quot. 1644).

Smith *Seaman's Gram.* (1627) gives the diameter of bore as 1 inch, and the charge as half-a-pound.

1587 [see ROBINET]. **1596** HARINGTON *Apol. Ajax* A 4 They made a sore batterie, with Rabbinets, minions, Sakers, and Demicannons. **1598** BARRET *Theor. Warres* V. i. 124 Peeces that shoot bullet of waight from seuenteene pound downeward..euen to the Rabinet. **1627** CAPT. SMITH *Seaman's Gram.* ii. 11 Rabinits to cleare the Decks fore and aft. **1644** NYE *Gunnery* I. (1647) 98 The Rabanet hath in diameter at the bore one inch and an halfe, the weight of the shot 8 ounces of Iron, and of Lead 12, the weight of the peece 300, the length 5 foot and an halfe, the charge in powder three quarters. **1727–41** CHAMBERS *Cycl.*, *Rabinet*, a small piece of ordnance, between a falconet and a base. [**1802** JAMES *Milit. Dict.* s.v. *Cannon*, Rabinet, which carried a ball of 16 ounces. **1894** C. N. ROBINSON *Brit. Fleet* 220 Falconets, and rabonets.]

rabiˈosity. *rare*[−1]. [f. as next + -ITY.] Rabies.

1824 H. C. KNIGHT *Letters from South & West* 70 Near Loretto, they have a reputed remedy against canine rabiosity.

†**ˈrabious**, *a. Obs.* Also rabb-. [ad. L. *rabiōs-us*, f. *rabiēs* RABIES. Cf. obs. F. *rabieux*, *-euse* (Godef.).] Rabid.

1613–18 DANIEL *Coll. Hist. Eng.* (1626) 15 Edmond.. surnamed Ironside..was imployed against this rabious inuader. **1646** BUCK *Rich. III*, II. 61 Their cruell Swords, so rabious in their execution. **1689** HARVEY *Curing Dis. by Expect.* xi. 76 Ignorant Arabian (or rather mad rabious) Impostors.

rabit, obs. form of RABBET, RABBIT.

†**rabite.** *Obs.* Forms: 4 rabit, -yt, 4–5 -yte, -yght, -et(t. [Aphetic for *Arabite* (in *Gen. & Exod.* 1203), f. ARAB + -ITE[1]. So also med.L. *rabītus* or *rabīta* (Du Cange), MHG. *râvît*, ON. *rábít-r.*] An Arab steed. Also *attrib.*

13.. *Coer de L.* 2323 In the world nas not..Steed rabyte, ne camayl, That ran so swift. *c* **1320** *Sir Beues* (A.) 4475 Sire Gii lep on a rabit [*varr.* rabyt, -yte, -yght], þat was meche & noþing lite. *a* **1400** *Octouian* 1415 Thys ys a stede of Arabye, ..A rabyte..Therto was mare. *a* **1400–50** *Alexander* 1320 Be rawe of þar rabetis he ruschid to þe erthe.

raˈbitic, *a.* [Irreg. f. RABIES: cf. RABIETIC.] Rabid.

1888 WHITMARSH *Pasteur Treatm.* 33 Rabitic dogs generally take three days before they die.

‖**Rabkrin** (ˈræbkrɪn). [a. Russ. *rabkrín* f. *rab(óche)-kr(est'yánskaya) in(spéktsiya)* worker-peasant inspectorate.] An organization established in 1920 by Lenin to examine the conformity of state organizations to official policy.

1928 *Observer* 18 Mar. 19/5 The Rabkrin (the Russian abbreviation for the Commissariat of Workers' and Peasants' Inspection) is a supreme controlling and auditing department, which is supposed to expose deficiencies in the work of State and industrial institutions. **1949** I. DEUTSCHER *Stalin* vii. 230 The Rabkrin, as the Commissariat was called, was set up to control every branch of the administration.

rable, obs. form of RABBLE *sb.*[1] and *v.*

rablin, obs. form of RAVELIN.

†**rabone.** *Obs. rare.* [? ad. Sp. *rábano*, f. *raba* RAPE.] A radish. Also *attrib.*

1597 GERARDE *Herbal* II. v. §4. 184 Radish is called..in English Radish, and Rabone. **1611** COTGR., *Raifort*, the raddish, or the Rabone, root (or hearb).

raboyt, obs. Sc. form of REBUT *v.*

rabscallion, obs. variant of RAPSCALLION.

rabuke, obs. form of REBUKE, ROEBUCK.

rabul, obs. form of RABBLE *sb.*[1]

†**'rabulane.** *Obs. rare*$^{-1}$. [Of obscure formation: cf. RABONE.] ? A radish.

1593 MUNDAY *Def. Contraries* 97 The Rabulanes, Onions and Beanes of these seuerall Soiles.

†**'rabulous,** *a. Obs. rare*$^{-1}$. [f. L. *rabula* a brawling or wrangling advocate.] Scurrilous.

1538 *State Papers* (1834) III. 1 He hath..rayled and raged ayenste me, calling me heritike and begger, with other rabulouse revilinges.

rabut, obs. Sc. var. REBUT *sb.* and *v.*

raby, obs. f. RABBI.

rabyll, obs. f. RABBLE *sb.*[1]

rabyne, obs. f. RABBIN.

rabysch, -yssh, varr. RABBISH *Obs.*

rabyt(e, -yght, varr. RABITE.

rabytt, obs. f. RABBIT.

rac, obs. f. RACK *sb.*[1], *sb.*[2]

Racah ('rækɑː). *Physics* and *Chem.* The name of Giulio *Racah* (1909–65), Italian-born Israeli physicist, used *attrib.* with reference to his work in quantum mechanics, as ***Racah coefficient*** or ***parameter***, either of two coefficients representing electrostatic interactions within a system of equivalent charged particles, esp. electrons within an atom.

1952 *Physical Rev.* LXXXVIII. 581/2 The coefficients of the transformation have been given by Racah..in terms of his *W* function and are called the Racah coefficients. **1959** *Astrophysical Jrnl.* CXXIX. 441 By means of a few simple formulae, all multiplet strengths..can be expressed in terms of only two basic quantities, viz., the Racah coefficients and the coefficients of fractional parentage. **1962** COTTON & WILKINSON *Adv. Inorg. Chem.* xxvi. 595 The Racah parameters are measures of the energy separations of the various Russell-Saunders states of an atom. **1966** PHILLIPS & WILLIAMS *Inorg. Chem.* II. xxiii. 162 The total electron-electron repulsion energy of each *LS* state arising from a d^n configuration can be calculated and expressed in terms of so-called Racah parameters. **1968** A. B. P. LEVER *Inorg. Electronic Spectroscopy* vii. 207 The Racah inter-electronic parameter *B* (and to a lesser extent *C*) is a function of ligand, central ion and stereochemistry. **1975** *Physics Bull.* Apr. 169/3 The classification of particle and nuclear properties uses techniques such as spinors and Racah algebra which are not for the first degree student.

racand, obs. f. RACKAN.

rac-a-pee, var. RACKAPEE.

racare, obs. f. RAKER.

racch(e, varr. RACHE.

racckee, obs. f. RAKI.

‖**ra'ccolta.** *Obs.* Also 7 re-, ro-, 7–8 racolta; 6 *pl.* raccolte. [It., = fem. pa. pple. of *raccogliere* to collect (f. L. *re-* + *ad-* + *collĭgĕre*).] A gathering, collection; harvest; crop.

1591 *Garrard's Art Warre* 65 That at all times he may make Raccolte, and gather his souldiers togither. *a* **1625** JAS. I in Hacket *Abp. Williams* I. (1693) 115 This motion.. carries all my Raccolta's, my Counsels at the present, and my prospects upon the Future, with it. **1748** in Hanway *Trav.* (1762) I. v. lxxv. 345 To invest it in raw silk cannot be done in less than three racoltas.

†**racco'mmode,** *v. Obs.* Also 8 racomm-, raccomode. [ad. F. *raccommoder*, f. *re-* + *accommoder* to ACCOMMODATE.] *trans.* To restore to good relations (*with* a person); to set right.

1673 DRYDEN *Marr. à la Mode* v. i, My dear French sir, stay but a minute, till I raccommode myself with the princess. **1754** H. WALPOLE *Lett.* (1846) III. 60 If you will take this occasion to write him a line of joy, I am persuaded it will raccomode everything. **1756** MRS. F. BROOKE *Old Maid* No. 16 (1764) 130, I..deranged the right wing a little, but Betty has racommoded it passablement bien.

†**raccom(p)t, raccount**, obs. varr. RECOUNT. (Cf. F. *raconter* and RACONTEUR).

1560 DAUS tr. *Sleidane's Comm.* 300 In the beginning is raccomted, how oftentymes the Emperour hath desired a counsell. *Ibid.* 316 Kynge Ferdinando raccompteth, how he ..made truse with the Turke. **1663** *Flagellum or O. Cromwell* (1672) 18, I have seen it r'accounted by a Worthy and Learned hand.

raccoon, variant of RACOON.

ra'ccourcy, *a. Her.* ? *Obs.* 8 -ci. [ad. F. *raccourci*, pa. pple. of *raccourcir*, f. *re-* + *accourcir* to shorten, f. *court* CURT.] = COUPED 2.

1727–41 CHAMBERS *Cycl.*, *Raccourcy*, in heraldry, signifies the same as *coupy*, that is, cut off, or shortened. **1780** EDMONDSON *Compl. Body Heraldry* II. Gloss., *Raccourcy*, or *Recourcie*, is the same as *Coupée*.

race (reɪs), *sb.*[1] Forms: 3–4 ras, 4–5 raas, 4–6 rase, *Sc.* raiss, 5 *north.* rass, 6 *Sc.* raice, rais, rays, 4– race. [a. ON. *rás* (Norw. and Sw. dial. *rås*), running, race, rush (of water), course, channel, row, series = OE. *rǽs* RESE; of obscure etym. Orig. a northern word, coming into general use about the middle of the 16th c.]

I. 1. a. The act of running; a run. Freq. in phr. ***in, on, with a race.*** Now *Sc.*

c **1325** *Metr. Hom.* 141 To the bischope in a ras He ran. **1340** HAMPOLE *Pr. Consc.* 8938 Assahelle..thurgh rase wald turne bath buk and ra. **1375** BARBOUR *Bruce* v. 638 In a raiss to the king he ran. *c* **1460** *Towneley Myst.* xxii. 145 Thyn apostels full radly ar run from the a rase. **1535** STEWART *Cron. Scot.* II. 118 This nobill Dongard..Than with ane raice amang thame entert in. **1557** *Tottell's Misc.* (Arb.) 199, Chast Diane..And all her maides that sue her in the race. *a* **1637** B. JONSON *Discov.* Wks. (Rtldg.) 756/1 In the contention of leaping, they jump farthest, that fetch their race largest. **1687** DRYDEN *Hind. & P.* I. 46 The bristled baptist Boar..mountains levelled in his furious race. **1810** SCOTT *Lady of L.* I. v, The noble stag..Held westward with unwearied race. *Mod. Sc.* If ye're to jump that, ye'll need to tak' a race.

fig. **1553** T. WILSON *Rhet.* 48 Talking of faith, thei have fetcht their ful race from the xii signes in the zodiake. **1579** GOSSON *Sch. Abuse* (Arb.) 20 Blocks of the Diuel that are cast in our wayes, to cut off the rase of toward wittes. **1642** MILTON *Apol. Smect.* Introd., Wks. (1851) 273 This loose rayler,..having once begun his race, regards not how farre he flies out beyond all truth and shame.

†**b.** Phr. ***to rue a*** (or ***one's***) ***race.*** Chiefly *fig.*, to repent of the course one has taken. *Obs.*

c **1440** *York Myst.* xxx. 214 Rugge hym in ropes, his rase till he rewe. *c* **1470** HENRYSON *Mor. Fab.*, *Wolf & Sheep* xiv, Ye sall rew this rais. Quhat was the caus, ye gaif me sic ane catche? **1560** ROLLAND *Seven Sages* (1837) 32 He knew That it wald caus ane greit Offence, Kend weill that race that he wald rew.

c. *fig.* The course of life or some portion of it.

1513 DOUGLAS *Æneis* III. x. 122 The prince Eneas,..The fatis of goddis and rasis mony ane Rehersing schew. **1559** W. CUNNINGHAM *Cosmogr. Glasse* 1 The Race that euery man in this his transitory life haue to runne. **1667** MILTON *P.L.* XII. 505 Thir Ministry perform'd, and race well run,.. They die. **1671** —— *Samson* 597 My race of glory run, and race of shame. **1697** DRYDEN *Virg. Georg.* IV. 301 Thus thro' the Race of Life they [bees] quickly run. **1709** WATTS *Hymn*, '*Awake, our Souls*' i, Awake, and run the heavenly Race. **1784** COWPER *Tiroc.* 315 The well-known place Whence first we started into life's long race. **1850** TENNYSON *In Mem.* ix, My Arthur, whom I shall not see Till all my widow'd race be run.

†**2.** A rush, onset, charge; a raid. *Obs.*

1535 STEWART *Cron. Scot.* I. 498 Fulgentius, with mony Pecht and Scot,..Full mony raice attour the wall hes maid. **1560** ROLLAND *Crt. Venus* IV. 621 The sowr persute, and syne the resistance, The rigorous rais. **1587** FLEMING *Contn. Holinshed* III. 1986/1 Badlie yet could they make their rase, by reason the furrowes laie trauerse to their course.

†**3.** Rapid action, haste, hurry. *Obs.*

a **1300** *Cursor M.* 26732 Ne tell noght [þi dedis] ouer wit renand ras, als dos þis men þat penis tas. *c* **1400** *Sowdone Bab.* 489 'Arise vp', he saide in a ras, 'We bene elles alle I-take'. *a* **1400–50** *Alexander* 1996 And þaim redes on a rase he & rechez to þe sedes. *c* **1440** *Partonope* 846 [She] ryseth vp in a grete raas.

†**4. a.** The act of riding rapidly on horseback; a course in a tournament (cf. 7 b). *Obs.*

a **1400** *Sir Perc.* 1145 In he rydes one a rase Or that he wiste where he was. *c* **1500** *Lancelot* 3088 Thir sevin in a Ras Deliuerly com prekand our the feldis. **1596** SPENSER *F.Q.* IV. vi. 3 Scudamour..issewed, To have rencountred him in equall race. **16..** *Tom Potts* 286 in Child *Ballads* II. 445/2 Then they turned their horsses round about, To run the race more egarlye.

†**b.** A journey or voyage. *Obs.*

c **1400** *Laud Troy Bk.* 4252 Prothesaly the formast was Off alle the schippis In that ras. **1513** DOUGLAS *Æneis* III. vi. 22 To me all devote goddis wychtis Schew we suld haue a prosper rais. *Ibid.* IV. x. 48 Sall I..Bid thaim mak sail anone, and a new rais? **1557** *Tottell's Misc.* (Arb.) 212 A Man may ..Thrise wander out Vlisses race: Yet neuer finde Vlisses wife.

II. 5. a. Onward movement of a thing, as the heavenly bodies, a vehicle, etc.; running or rush of water (cf. 6). ? *Obs.* †Also, a sudden deviation from a line (quot. 1670).

a **1300** *Cursor M.* 23588 Sun and mon, and water and stern, þat rinnes nu wit ras sa yern. **13..** *Childh. Jesus* 845 in *Archiv neu. Spr.* LXXIV. 338 Twa stremys..That neuermare of rase salle blyne. **1480** *Robt. Devyll* 948 He spyed a great race of bloude in Robertes face. **1557** N.T. (Genev.) *2 Tim.* ii. 9 *note*, The worde of God hath it race and increaseth. **1581** MARBECK *Bk. of Notes* 164 The Chariot came nigh unto them with a great race and mightie force. **1586** BRIGHT *Melanch.* xiii. 66 Some wheeles passing swifter than other some, by divers rases. **1633** D. R[OGERS] *Treatise of Sacraments* i. 168 Your streame weake;..and the staves of your wheele which should support the race of it pittifully broken. *a* **1649** WINTHROP *New Eng.* (1853) I. 4 The tide set in with so strong a race. **1670** NARBOROUGH *Jrnl.* in *Acc. Sev. Late Voy.* I. (1711) 76 It points off with a Race from the other Mountains..into the Channel.

b. *esp.* The daily (or annual) course of the sun through the heavens. Similarly of the moon.

Chiefly by conscious metaphor from sense 1, and usually with vb. *to run.*

1590 SPENSER *F.Q.* I. v. 44 The mother of dredd darkness ..took her wonted way To ronne her timely race. *Ibid.* XI. 33 Titan rose to runne his daily race. **1662** TUKE *Adv.* 5 *Hours* II, The sun..ere half his race be run. *c* **1742** GRAY *Ignorance* 11 Thrice hath Hyperion roll'd his annual race. **1784** COWPER *Task* VI. 126 Should God again..interrupt the race Of the undeviating and punctual sun. *a* **1822** SHELLEY *Hom. Sun.* 10 The immortal Sun, Who, borne by heavenly steeds, his race doth run Unconquerably.

c. The course of time. (Chiefly used as in b.)

1595 SHAKS. *John* III. iii. 39 If the mid-night bell Did.. Sound on into the drowzie race of night. ? **1630** MILTON *On Time* 1 Fly envious Time, till thou run out thy race. **1697** DRYDEN *Virg. Past.* IV. 15 Majestick Months set out..to their appointed Race. *a* **1729** CONGREVE *Imit. Horace, Odes* II. xiv. 1 Eternity! that boundless race Which Time himself can never run.

†**d.** The course or progress of events, or of a narrative. *Obs. rare.*

c **1590** BRUCE *XI Serm.* i. (1591) 6 Gif ȝee..consider the race of the historie. *a* **1626** BACON *On War with Spain* 7 The Prosecution and Race of the Warre, carrieth the Defendant, to assaile and inuade, the..Patrimony of the first Aggressour.

†**e.** Impact; a shock, blow. *Obs. rare.*

c **1400** *Sowdone Bab.* 1349 He raught a stroke to Ferumbras..It brast his hawberke at þat ras. **1535** STEWART *Cron. Scot.* I. 124 Sum gat ane rais gart all hir ribbis rak.

6. a. A strong current in the sea or a river.

Perh. partly ad. F. *raz*, *ras* in same sense, commonly regarded as a. Breton *râz*, a strait, narrow channel.

1375 BARBOUR *Bruce* III. 697 By the mole thai passyt ȝar, And entryt sone in-to the rase. *c* **1400** *Sowdone Bab.* 774 Wynde him blewe..over the salte flode And over the profounde rase. **1506** *Kalender of Sheph.* H ij, Amonge the waues perylous on rases holowe. **1597** J. PAYNE *Royal Exch.* 33 In your Sea stormes,..cross tydes, dangerouse races. **1625** N. CARPENTER *Geog. Del.* II. vii. (1635) 130 Hee found a strong race, a Tide running sometimes Eastward, sometimes Westward. **1697** DAMPIER *Voy.* (1729) I. 82 A short cockling Sea, as if it had been a Race, or place where two Tides meet. **1720** DE FOE *Capt. Singleton* xiv. (1840) 238 Among innumerable islands,..without any pilot that understood the channel and races between them. **1828** PLANCHÉ *Desc. Danube* 72 The river narrows, and a slight fall, or what our sailors call a race, ensues. **1884** *19th Cent.* Feb. 245 We were able to head the races that spun out from submerged trees.

transf. **1894** CLARK RUSSELL *Good Ship Mohock* I. 15 The sky was a race of large torn cloud, white as milk.

b. Used in the names of special currents.

1375 BARBOUR *Bruce* III. 687 Quhar als gret stremys ar rynnand,..As is the raiss of Bretangȝe. *c* **1530** *Hickescorner* B iij, I sawe them all drowned in the rase of Irelande. **1596** FITZ-GEFFRAY *Sir. F. Drake* (1881) 80 In that faire palace neere the milken race. **1697** *Lond. Gaz.* No. 3317/4 He saw 5 Sail of Ships standing through the Race of Fountney. **1769** FALCONER *Dict. Marine* (1776) Eee ij b, The race of Portland. **1862** ANSTED *Channel Isl.* I. ii. 18 Through this channel, the sea, at high spring tides, sweeps at the rate of eight miles an hour... This passage is called the Race (or Ras) of Alderney.

III. 7. As a portion of time or space:

†**a.** A space of time; a while. *Obs. rare*$^{-1}$.

13.. *K. Alis.* 7830 They lyved here bote lite ras; And sone echon forgete was!

†**b.** The distance or space between two points. ***knight's race*** (from 4 a): see quot. 1562. *Obs.*

1562 LEIGH *Armorie* 58 b, Alciatus saith that a man shall discerne colour, if he may come within a knights rase of any banner, but I neuer hard of any man, that came within an 100 rases of the Sun. *Le*: What is a knights rase? *Ge*: It is lx. foote of assise in length, of the field, and is of Here-haughts so called. **1600** HOLLAND *Livy* 1348 The plaine and base plot of the cittie..comprehendeth a Diameter or race almost of 8 Stadia.

c. A piece of ground suitable for running or racing (see 10). *rare.*

1612 DRAYTON *Poly-olb.* III. 23 Nor yet the level South can shew a smoother race. *a* **1783** *Fair Annie* 64 in Child *Ballads* II. 75/1, I wish that they were seven hares To run the castle race. **1890** R. BRIDGES *Shorter Poems* II. 7 Perilous in steep places Soft in the level races.

†**8. a.** The course, line, or path taken by a person or a moving body. Also *fig. Obs.*

? *c* **1400** *Ser. J. Mandevelle & Gt. Souden* 17 in Hazl. *E.P.P.* I. 155 Your prestes that suld tech vertus trace, They ryn rakyll out of gud race. **1513** DOUGLAS *Æneis* V. xiv. 84 Prince Enee persauit by his rais, Quhow that the schip did rok and tailȝevey. **1555** EDEN *Decades* 28 He diuerted from his accustomed rase which was by the Ilandes of Canarie. **1570** DEE *Math. Pref.* 3 Of the auncient Mathematiciens, a Line is called the race or course of a Point. *c* **1580** SIDNEY *Ps.* XXVI. i, I have made my race Within the boundes of innocence to bide.

†**b.** A reach (of a river). *Obs. rare*$^{-1}$.

1611 SPEED *Theat. Gt. Brit.* xxxix. (1614) 77/1 A long race of the river Ouse.

c. The channel or bed (of a stream); *esp.* an artificial channel leading water to or from a point where its energy is utilized, as in a mill or a mining claim. See also HEAD-, MILL-, TAIL-RACE.

It is not clear whether there is any connexion between this sense and OF. *rase*, *rasse*, *raze* (15th c. in Godef.), watercourse, trench, ditch, (mill-) race.

1565–73 *Durham Depos.* (Surtees) 212 The [law-] suit.. for the raic[e] of the said water corne myln. **1777** *Wallingfen Inclos. Act* 45 The beck, race, water, or watercourse. **1796** MORSE *Amer. Geog.* I. 536 The race,..a canal 20 to 30 feet wide, and carried..through rocks and hills. **1805** *West's Antiq. Furness* 74 There has been also a subterraneous passage, leading from the race of the rivulet. **1868** *Rep. U.S. Commissioners Agric.* (1869) 334 The bottoms of the races are covered with small stones and a layer of fine gravel. **1890** 'R. BOLDREWOOD' *Col. Reformer* (1891) 293 The water, brought through races by miles of fluming, spouted clear and strong over heaps of auriferous earth. **1901** M. FRANKLIN *My Brilliant Career* xiv. 117 They have cut races between the two creeks. **1912** B. E. BAUGHAN *Brown Bread* 99 Little runnels and 'races' of water led through the plain from the mountain rivers. **1941** I. L. IDRIESS *Great Boomerang* xxxi. 243 We would take the water from a creek on one side of a mountain and by means of a race (channel) take it completely around the mountain. **1976** *Jrnl. Lakeland Dial. Soc.* 35 Ah thowt Ah wud ga up t' race an' then cross t' beck on t' steppin steans.

d. *Weaving.* The path or channel in the lay or batten along which the shuttle moves in crossing the web; the board or other support on which the shuttle slides.

1855 [see *lay-race* s.v. LAY *sb.*[8]]. **1875** KNIGHT *Dict. Mech.* 1263/1 The picker.. which strikes the fly-shuttle and drives it along the race. **1879** BARLOW *Weaving* 87 The warp threads are pressed down upon the race.

e. A circular path for a horse employed in driving machinery.

1833 J. C. LOUDON *Encycl. Archit.* 470 The back wall of the barn is to be sunk sufficiently deep for the wheel of the threshing-mill and the race (horse-course) from it. **1862** [see *gin-race* s.v. GIN *sb.*[1] 12].

f. *Austral.* and *N.Z.* (See quot. 1872.)

1865 M. A. BARKER *Station Life in N.Z.* (1870) v. 34 The newly-shorn [sheep].. have passed thro' a narrow passage, called a 'race'. **1872** *Rtldg.'s Ev. Boy's Ann.* 53/2 Each lamb was driven through the narrow hurdle-passage.. called a race. **1878** E. S. ELWELL *Boy Colonists* 214 They made a 'lead' in the stockyard for branding the cattle. This was something like a 'race' for drafting sheep, with a swing gate. **1934** T. WOOD *Cobbers* iv. 41 'Bullicks come aboard along a *race.* This is a race,' and he pointed to narrow gang-ways, railed in on both sides, which sloped from the main deck down to the cattle deck. **1950** *N.Z. Jrnl. Agric.* Apr. 373/3 The units [of the pig house] are usually placed side by side under one continuous roof, a service race being provided along the front. **1963** A. LUBBOCK *Austral. Roundabout* 180 The cattle were in the yards and the drovers and dogs were putting them through a 'race'—two rows of wooden fencing with a swing gate at the end. **1977** *N.Z. Herald* 8 Jan. 4-7/9 (Advt.), At present dairy and beef. Good race and fencing, tidal boundary, ample hay storage.

g. *Mech.* The space in which a drum or wheel revolves. (Cf. *wheel-race.*)

1825 J. NICHOLSON *Oper. Mech.* 104 The stones of the race are hewn to a mould, and laid in their places with great care. **1883** GRESLEY *Gloss. Coal-mining* 197.

h. Each of the two grooved rings of a ball or roller bearing.

1903 *Sci. Amer. Suppl.* 2, Feb. 22689/1 The rollers are made to fit the inner and outer treads of the roller race. **1907, 1908** [see *ball-race* s.v. BALL *sb.*[1] 22]. **1930** *Engineering* 4 Apr. 462/1 There are two rings of rollers running side by side between hardened and ground inner and outer races. **1960** [see COIN *v.*[1] 3 b]. **1968** *Autocar* 25 Jan. 49/2, I drove the 2-litre car at Monte Carlo and we had transmission trouble there which was bad luck because it was a ball race that broke. **1971** B. SCHARF *Engin. & its Language* xii. 135 Ball bearings.. consist of.. an inner race, which is a grooved ring firmly attached to the shaft, and an outer race in the stationary housing. The balls which are free to rotate between the races are kept apart by means of a cage. **1980** *Dirt Bike* Oct. 33/1 You may even need to replace the balls and races if they're dented or worn.

9. *Mining.* 'A small thread of spar or ore' (Raymond *Gloss. Mining* 1881).

1580 FRAMPTON *Dial. Yron & Steele* 144 If.. of brimstone and quicksilver they were ingendred, there would be some rase of them, in the mynes of golde and silver. **1747** HOOSON *Miner's Dict.* K iv b, This Keckle-Meckle Stuff has the Ore run with it in small Strings and Races.

b. A row or series. *dial.* and *techn.*

1880 *E. Cornwall Gloss.*, *Race*, a string, *e.g.* of onions. **1883** GRESLEY *Gloss. Coal-Mining* 197 *Race.* See *Journey.* [= 'A train or set of trains all coupled together.'] **1894** *Northumbld. Gloss.*, *Race*, a range or series. A race of pits. **1901** *Scotsman* 8 Mar. 5/1 They were run into by a race of runaway hutches.

IV. 10. a. The act of running, riding, sailing, etc. in competition with one or more rivals; a contest of speed; in *pl.* usually denoting a series of horse-races held at a fixed time on a regular course.

1513 DOUGLAS *Æneis* v. vii. 1 Eftir thir raissis done, and giftis gif. **1582** BIBLE (Rheims) *1 Cor.* ix. 24 They that runne in the race, al runne in deede, but one receiueth the price. **1641** BROME *Joviall Crew* II. Wks. 1873 III. 372 In Hide-Park, to see the Races, Horse and Foot. **1667** MILTON *P.L.* IX. 33 To indite Warrs.. or to describe Races and Games. **1715-20** POPE *Iliad* XXIII. 429 Young Nestor leads the race; Eumelus then. **1781** COWPER *Truth* 13 He that would win the race must guide his horse Obedient to the customs of the course. **1840** DICKENS *Old C. Shop* xvii, We're going on to the races. **1860** LONGF. *Wayside Inn, K. Olaf* II. xi, Swimming, skating, snow-shoe races.

transf. and *fig.* *a* **1592** H. SMITH *Serm.* (1637) 518 A race, wherein they run striving who shall come first to the devill. **1751** EARL ORRERY *Remarks Swift* (1752) 61 Every competitor in the race of wit is left behind him. **1821** SHELLEY *Hellas* 856 Ere thou Didst start for this brief race whose crown is death. **1871** FREEMAN *Norm. Conq.* (1876) IV. xvii. 86 The two nations which, if last in the race of political freedom, were foremost in the race of material civilization.

b. *slang.* A bet on a horse-race.

1894 ASTLEY *50 Years Life* II. 196, I had a fair race on Sir Bevys, L. Rothschild's horse, for the Derby.

c. *fig.* An electoral contest for public office. Phr. ***to make the race***, to run for public office (see also quot. 1881). *U.S.*

1855 I. C. PRAY *Mem. J. G. Bennett* 288 He had been the first to start many of them upon the ground for a successful political race. **1881** H. W. PIERSON *In Brush* 132 To 'make the race' was to secure an election. *Ibid.* 133 This pursuit of office was always spoken of as a 'race'. **1903** *N.Y. Even. Post* 17 Sept. 1 Mr. Cutting ran up stairs to tell Dr. Gould.. that Mr. Gront would make the race. **1949** *Dallas Morning News* 1 May 1/7 He might perhaps consider making the Senate race. **1976** *National Observer* (U.S.) 6 Nov. 24/3 New totals for.. U.S. Senate races and gubernatorial races will churn out every five minutes.

d. As the second element in Comb. with a defining sb., as ***armament race***, ***arms race***, ***moon race***, ***space race***, etc.: see under the first word.

e. In colloq. phr. ***to be in the race***, to have a chance. Usu. in neg. contexts. *Austral.*

1945 M. TRIST *Now that we're Laughing* x. 73 With you and Daffy dressed up, none of us others will be in the race. **1953** T. A. G. HUNGERFORD *Riverslake* x. 227 'See that bloke?' He pointed down the road after the vanished car. 'A few years ago he wouldn't have been in the race to own a car like that.' **1956** J. T. LANG *I Remember* vi. 34 The trade unions realised that if the Chinese could get away with long hours and low pay they would not be in the race to get better conditions.

f. *Electronics.* In a switching circuit, a condition in which the time a component secondary circuit or device takes to operate has to be taken into account (as when two are required to operate simultaneously, though in practice one will operate before the other). Freq. *attrib.*

1954 *Jrnl. Franklin Inst.* CCLVII. 170 In a composite transition matrix the presence of two or more of the digits 'I' indicates that at least two of the secondary relays are simultaneously unstable, and that a race condition exists. **1958** S. H. CALDWELL *Switching Circuits* xii. 469 The race condition in this instance can lead to false operation and we designate this as a critical race. **1969** J. J. SPARKES *Transistor Switching* vii. 161 It is customary to arrange the logic so that all races are removed or rendered non-critical. **1975** J. C. BOYCE *Digital Logic* ix. 267 Races are characterized by arrows that skip rows on flowtables, since more than one gate must change at the same time to allow the operating point to follow the arrow.

V. 11. *attrib.* and *Comb.* **a.** General combs. (sense 10), as ***race-boat***, ***-colt***, ***driver***, ***-dust***, ***fund***, ***-ground***, ***list***, ***-manager***, ***mare***, ***-meeting***, ***-nag***, ***night***, ***record***, ***report***, ***-rider***, ***-riding***, ***-runner***, ***-time***, ***-week***, ***-winner***; 'used or worn by one who rides in a horse-race', as ***race-cap***, ***-jacket***, ***-saddle***; 'intended for wearing at races', as ***race-cloak***, ***-coat***, ***-dress***, ***-gown***, ***-hat***; (sense 8 f) ***race gate***, ***shed***. **b.** Special combs., as **race-ball**, a ball held in connexion with a race-meeting; **race-board**, (*a*) a gang-board, (*b*) the board on which a shuttle slides (see 8 d); **race card**, a printed card giving information about races; **racecaster** orig. *U.S.*, a radio or television broadcaster who reports on horse-racing; **race-circle**, the course of a spindle in a braiding machine; **race-cloth**, a cloth used with a racing-saddle, having pockets to hold the weight required by the rules of the course (Knight *Dict. Mech.* 1875); **race-cup**, a cup or other piece of plate given as a prize to the winner of a race; **race game**, a board game simulating a horse-race in which rival counters proceed at the throw of a dice; also *transf.*; **race gang**, a group of petty criminals who frequent race-meetings; **race-glass** (now usu. in *pl.*), a field-glass for use at races; hence ***race-glassed*** adj.; **race-goer**, a frequenter of race-meetings; also **race-going** *a.* and *sb.*; **race-mark**, a mark attached to pigeons before a particular race; hence **race-mark** *v. trans.*, to supply (pigeons) with race-marks; **race-path**, (*a*) a race-track; (*b*) the channel along which water flows to a mill-wheel; **race-plate** = RACER 4 (see also CURB *sb.* 9 c); **race-reader**, (*a*) one who forecasts the performance of horses in a given race; (*b*) (see quot. 1953); also, a race commentator; hence **race-reading**; **race stand**, a stand at a race-course; **race tankard** (cf. *race-cup*); **race-track** orig. *U.S.* = RACE-COURSE 1 a; also *transf.* and *attrib.*; **race train**, a special train which runs to and from a race-meeting; **race-trough**, a plank with raised edges along which goods are passed in loading or unloading ships or wagons; **race walking**, the act or practice of competing in a walking race; hence **race walker**; **race walk** *v. intr.* See also RACE-COURSE, -DAY, -HORSE.

1775 SHERIDAN *Rivals* II. i, At our last *race ball. *c* **1838** W. H. MURRAY in M. R. Booth *Eng. Plays of 19th Cent.* (1973) IV. 162, I saw Charlotte at the race-ball, and fell over head and ears in love with her. **1808** ASHE *Travels* III. 260 Ships have *race boards to the bank, which gives them an access so easy, that they are often visited from the shore. **1879** BARLOW *Weaving* 97 The middle shuttle boxes are.. lowered to the level of the race-board. **1839** *Spirit of Times* 15 June 177/1 It is most probable we would still have continued to get our *race boats from Philadelphia. **1866** 'ARGONAUT' *Rowing & Training* 7 The modern single-straike race-boat is composed.. of two parts. **1972** C. MUDIE *Motor Boats & Boating* 144 The race boat hull form is not of great value for cruising boats. **1851** MAYHEW *Lond. Labour* (1861) I. 265 This trade (with *race-cards) is not carried on in town. **1967** *Listener* 14 Sept. 325/3, I got hold of a race-card and I said to him: 'This one's got a marvellous chance.' **1979** D. FRANCIS *Whip Hand* ii. 23 It took a course in the country to.. run out of racecards. **1938** *Amer. Speech* XIII. 239/2 *Newscaster* and *sportscaster* are now common terms in *Variety*. *Racecaster is also found. **1969** *Australian* 24 May 35/1 The caller will be 3DB's race-caster, Bill Collins. **1875** KNIGHT *Dict. Mech.* 355/2 The *race-circles, in which the spindles are caused to move. **1850** 'M. TENSAS' *Odd Leaves Life Louisiana 'Swamp Doctor'* 47 She couldn't 'tend races, and have a *race-colt of her own to comfort her 'clinin' years. **1777** SHERIDAN *Sch. Scand.* III. iii, All the family *racecups and corporation bowls. **1935** A. G. KENNEDY *Current Eng.* xiv. 613 In a recent issue of a widely read city paper.. the following headings appeared.. '*Race Driver Pinned under Flaming Car.' **1972** *N.Y. Times* 3 Nov. 45/2 Look at that guy jumping lanes... You have race drivers the same way, but they never amount to nothin'. **1850** MRS. BROWNING *Poems* I. 216 Electric Pindar, quick as fear, With *race-dust on his cheeks. **1840** WHYTE *Hist. Turf* I. 200 The shareholders will receive five per cent... the remainder to go to the *race fund. **1895** *Montgomery Ward Catal.* 235/2 The Grand *Race Game, consists of a substantially cloth bound, folding board.. printed in colors to represent a race track... Has six colored cardboard horses and riders.. two wooden dice cups and two dice. **1903** J. M. FALKNER *Nebuly Coat* xiii. 187 A 'race-game' where the little leaden horse is moved steadily forward. **1930** A. P. HERBERT *Water Gipsies* xiv. 196 In that light the hare seemed tinier and the greyhounds toys... The place might have been some monstrous nursery 'race-game'. **1973** *Daily Tel.* (Colour Suppl.) 29 June 40/2 Backgammon is a race game.. and the precursor of every modern board-pieces-and-dice game. **1931** M. ALLINGHAM *Look to Lady* xxiv. 250 Gipsies and *race gangs always hate each other. **1937** E. RICKMAN *On & off Racecourse* xii. 271 The term 'race gang' is still a very favoured one by newspaper sub-editors. **1930** L. G. D. ACLAND *Early Canterbury Runs* 1st Ser. x. 251 He once asked Moore why he didn't put *race gates into his yards. **1865** *Let.* 11 June in Ld. W. Lennox *My Recoll.* (1874) II. 153 General Fleury almost forced a *race-glass into the hands of the Emperor. **1938** F. D. SHARPE *Sharpe of Flying Squad* xix. 204 From the coach descended a number of the boys one of whom was carrying a pair of race-glasses. **1974** D. FRANCIS *Knock Down* (1976) xii. 137 The runners went down the far side and we lifted race-glasses to watch. **1868** *Daily Tel.* 27 May, Some *race-glassed and blue-veiled traveller. **1880** *Baily's Monthly Mag.* Feb. 71 *Race-goers are not, as a rule, early drinkers. **1948** *Sunday Pictorial* 18 July 13/4 It has now been in operation for some time, and many race-goers are fed up with it. **1975** D. FRANCIS *High Stakes* i. 9 Racegoers were hurrying towards the stands to watch the imminent steeplechase. **1848** *Sporting Life* 2 Sept. 324/2 A great favourite with the *race-going public. **1929** S. ERTZ *Galaxy* xv. 332 He had always been so busy with his.. shooting, his race-going, and latterly his horses. **1963** *Times* 23 Jan. 3/5 Waiting for any crumbs that may be going are the racecourses, the owners and the racegoing public. **1977** D. FRANCIS *Risk* ii. 12 Near the course the crawling racegoing jams would mean half an hour for the last mile. **1698** J. COLLIER tr. Tertullian in *Profaneness & Immorality Eng. Stage* vi. 253 We have nothing to do with the Frensies of the *Race-Ground.. or the Barbarities of the Bear-Garden. **1727** in *Maryland Hist. Mag.* (1912) VII. 400 This Vestry Resolve to meet on Thursday.. at the race Ground near Mr Bensons. **1802** S. CHIFNEY *Genius Genuine* 52, I was the next morning on the race ground. **1840** WHYTE *Hist. Turf* I. 260 The principal rooms overlooking the race-ground. **1856** H. H. DIXON *Post & Paddock* xiii. 228 As plentiful now as ..'garters' in later years, among the list of *race-jackets. **1833** *New Sporting Mag.* V. 398 Chancing to have the *race list in my hand. **1812** *Sporting Mag.* XL. 154 *Race-manager, or keeper of the stud-book at Newmarket. **1853** *Southern Lit. Messenger* XIX. 70/1 He brought with him a small *race mare which excited the acquisitiveness of his father. **1976** *Times Lit. Suppl.* 15 Oct. 1296/2 Park Top.. began to emerge as the outstanding race-mare of her decade. **1890** *Homing News* 3 Jan. 14/3 (Advt.), He is not certain about the *race marks. **1928** *Sunday Dispatch* 8 July 22/3 Birds competing in the.. race from Marennes,.. will be *racemarked at No. 5 platform. **1809** *Sporting Mag.* XXXIII. 108 This almost universal success at the *race-meetings. *a* **1634** RANDOLPH *Poems* (1875) II. 539 Keep his *race-nags, and in Hyde Park be seen. *a* **1687** COTTON *Wks.* (1765) 119 The base Hag Can of a Cudgel make a Race-Nag. **1795** T. WILKINSON *Wandering Patentee* I. 241 The assembly-rooms keep the ladies entirely away the three *race nights. **1837** *Knickerbocker* X. 413 The only *race-path known in this new settlement was that on which the husband and wife contended for the prize of domestic comfort. **1853** F. W. THOMAS *J. Randolph* 84 Along the devious narrow race-path to the mill-dam. **1951** E. RICKMAN *Come racing with Me* iii. 23 Some practised *race-readers tend to become ridiculously self-opinionated. **1953** P. G. BERG *Dict. New Words* 133/1 *Race reader*,.. an expert attached to a radio commentator who helps in giving a broadcast of a horse-race. **1955** *Radio Times* 22 Apr. 29/3 Racing at Newmarket. .. Commentary by Raymond Glendenning, assisted by Tom E. Webster as race-reader. **1968** 'J. WELCOME' *Hell is where you find It* ii. 33 'Mountpatrick still well clear,' came the race-reader's voice. 'Then Blue Soldier, Mark Twain, Kitchener.. all in a group together.' **1963** 'J. PRESCOT' *Case for Hearing* iv. 60, I think you can rule out.. the gift of *race-reading in advance by looking into a crystal ball. **1976** *Horse & Hound* 10 Dec. 6/3 Michael O'Hehir, whose Telefis Eireann race-reading they [*sc.* the BBC] have taken in previously. **1893** *Outing* XXII. 101/1 Goldsmith Maid left the turf with a *race record never equalled. **1977** *N.Z. Herald* 5 Jan. 1-11/1 He set a race record for the track when he went 1 m 58·5 s. **1934** T. S. ELIOT *Rock* i. 29 Many read nothing but the *race reports. *a* **1700** B. E. *Dict. Cant. Crew* s.v. *Jockeys*.. *Race Riders. **1827** J. F. COOPER *Prairie* p. xxiii, She is no great race-rider. **1973** *Country Life* 22 Feb. 457/2 Lester Piggott came from a family of race-riders and trainers. **1840** WHYTE *Hist. Turf* II. 580 We will now.. describe the 'science of *race-riding', or jockeyship. **1863** LD. W. P. LENNOX *Biog. Remin.* II. 146, I had an opportunity of carrying on my passion for race-riding. **1647** TRAPP *Comm. Heb.* iv. 1 To come lag and late.. as lazy *Race-runners. **1950** *N.Z. Jrnl. Agric.* Apr. 375/2 The *race shed was.. popular many years ago. **1829** P. EGAN *Boxiana* 2nd Ser. II. 30 The *Race-stand, at ten *bob* per *nob*, was opened for their reception. **1860** H. AINSWORTH *Ovingdean Grange* 174 No modern race-stand towered before the stern soldier of the Commonwealth. **1881** J. GRANT *Cameronians* I. i. 10 Indian jars and old silver *race tankards. **1702** LADY VERNEY *Let.* 25 Aug. in M. M. Verney *Verney Lett.* (1930) I. vii. 113 We shall have Company at Claydon, it being our *Race-time. **1893** W. B. YEATS *Celtic Twilight* The race-time came round. **1862** *N.Y. Tribune* 6 Mar. 6/6 We don't think that Tennessee is likely to be much of a battle-ground hereafter. There's more probability of her being a *race-track. **1927** *New Republic* 21 Sept. 120/2 No American town is more completely absorbed in race-track gambling. **1945** *Transit News* (Capital Transit Co., Washington, D.C.) 15 June, I picked an early straight on the race track.. Translated into plain English, the operator said: 'I signed up for a day's work on 16th street.' **1958** *New Scientist* 30 Jan. 18/3 We..began the construction of an aluminium torus of 12-in. bore diameter,..and in it were two straight sections —making the torus into a race-track. **1963** *Times* 24 May 16/6 The problem is best presented in terms of the dimensions of the race-tracks round which nuclear particles ..are caused to circle repeatedly while gaining energy at each circuit. **1973** D. MacKenzie *Postscript to Dead Letter* 15 A set of Dufy racetrack prints on the walls. **1938** F. D. Sharpe *Sharpe of Flying Squad* xx. 223 The gymer gets out of the *race train and boards the Underground railway. **1977** *Times* 18 June 12/8 The race train from Waterloo to Sandown Park. **1842** Carlyle in *Cornh. Mag.* (1922) Oct. 496 A huge high pier of wood..lowered down upon us a long *race-trough of wood, by the side of which at due distances some four men stationing themselves [etc.]. **1973** F. Wakefield et al. *Track & Field Fundamentals for Girls & Women* (ed. 3) 253 Because some people do not want to *race walk, the field of competition is small. **1962** *Sport of Race Walking* (Race Walking Assoc.) 34 Race-Walking can only be as strong as its Judges... To this end they have striven.. to select men of integrity, mainly former *race-walkers themselves. **1972** Pickering & Harris *Olympics* 74/2 The difference between the fast, fair race walker and the ordinary person at $3\frac{1}{2}$ miles per hour is the straight leg action. **1954** *Times* 20 Sept. 3/3 Delegates [to the annual meeting of the Road Walking Assoc.] decided to change the name to *Race Walking Association following the Amateur Athletic Association's authority to develop track walking. **1976** *Cumberland News* 26 Nov., The Olympic Games authorities seem hell bent on pushing race walking into the distant background. **1716** *Lond. Gaz.* No. 5436/4 To be fought all the *Race-Week. **1814** *Sporting Mag.* XLIV. 181 In the race-week, a long main of cocks was fought. **1894** Astley *50 Years Life* II. 198 We both got back to Newmarket a few days before the race week. **1823** Byron *Juan* xiii. lxxxvii, Sir Henry Silvercup, the great *race-winner.

race (reɪs), *sb.*[2] Also 6–7 rase. [a. F. *race*, earlier also *rasse* (1512), a. It. *razza* = Sp. *raza*, Pg. *raça*, of obscure origin.]

I. A group of persons, animals, or plants, connected by common descent or origin.

In the widest sense the term includes all descendants from the original stock, but may also be limited to a single line of descent or to the group as it exists at a particular period.

1. a. The offspring or posterity *of* a person; a set of children or descendants. Chiefly *poet.*

1570 Foxe *A. & M.* II. 1841/1 Thus was the outward race & stocke of Abraham after flesh refused. **1606** Shaks. *Ant. & Cl.* iii. xiii. 107 Haue I..Forborne the getting of a lawfull Race, And by a Iem of women. **1667** Milton *P.L.* x. 385 High proof ye now have giv'n to be the Race Of Satan. **1712** Pope *Messiah* 65 Their Vines a shadow to their Race shall yield. **1784** Cowper *Task* iv. 384 Her infant race..sit cow'ring o'er the sparks. **1842** Tennyson *Locksley Hall* 168, I will take some savage woman, she shall rear my dusky race.

transf. and *fig.* **1594** Hooker *Eccl. Pol.* iv. v, Such, as either we must acknowledge for our own forefathers or else disdain the race of Christ. **1728** Pope *Dunc.* i. 70 How Tragedy and Comedy embrace, How Farce and Epic get a jumbled race. **1820** Shelley *Orpheus* 110 Blackthorn bushes with their infant race Of blushing rose blooms.

†**b.** Breeding, the production of offspring. *Obs.*

1607 Topsell *Four-f. Beasts* (1658) 234 It behooveth therefore that the mares appointed for race be well compacted, of a decent quality. **1653** Greaves *Seraglio* 141 He hath also stables of stallions for race. **1667** Milton *P.L.* vii. 530 Male he created thee, but thy consort Femal for Race.

†**c.** A generation. *Obs. rare.*

1549–62 Sternhold & H. *Ps.* cii. 12 Thy remembrance euer doth abide from race to race. **1727–41** Chambers *Cycl.* s.v., In several orders of knighthood..the candidates must prove a nobility of four races or descents. [**1790** Burke *Fr. Rev.* 51 If the last generations of your country appeared without much lustre in your eyes, you might have..derived your claims from a more early race of ancestors.]

2. a. A limited group of persons descended from a common ancestor; a house, family, kindred.

a **1600** Wynne *Hist. Gwydir Family* (1878) 33 Some affirme Jevan ap Meredith to be the elder brother, and soe doth all the race that are of him contend. **1653** Holcroft *Procopius* i. 7 No Government to be conferr'd upon strangers in blood; but such onely to have the place, to whose race it did belong. **1734** Mrs. Delany *Autobiog. & Corr.* (1861) I. 431 Lady Weymouth's person bears away the bell, even from the Marlborough race. **1768** Sterne *Sent. Journ.* (1778) I. 4 (*Calais*) The Bourbon is by no means a cruel race. **1833** Tennyson *Sisters* 1 We were two daughters of one race. **1883** Green *Conq. Eng.* 418 [Eadmund Ironside] shared, no doubt, the weak constitution of his race.

b. A tribe, nation, or people, regarded as of common stock.

a **1600** Wynne *Hist. Gwydir Family* (1878) 20 Llewelyn ap Gruffith last Prince of Wales of the Brittish race. **1667** Milton *P.L.* i. 780 That Pigmean Race Beyond the Indian Mount. **1715** Pope *Iliad* iv. 51 Troy's whole race thou wouldst confound. **1726–46** Thomson *Winter* 499 A mighty people come! A race of heroes! **1827** D. Johnson *Ind. Field Sports* 140 The worst race of people inhabiting that part. **1863** Fr. A. Kemble *Resid. in Georgia* 11 The..proscription under which their whole race is placed.

c. A group of several tribes or peoples, regarded as forming a distinct ethnical stock.

1842 Prichard *Nat. Hist. Man* 150 No two races of Men can be more strongly contrasted than were the ancient Egyptian and the Syro-Arabian races. **1868** Kingsley *Heroes* Pref. 10 They were all different tribes and peoples of the one great Hellen race. **1883** Green *Conq. Eng.* 54 Courage..was a heritage of the whole German race.

d. One of the great divisions of mankind, having certain physical peculiarities in common.

The term is often used imprecisely; even among anthropologists there is no generally accepted classification or terminology.

1774 Goldsm. *Nat. Hist., Animals* xxxiii, The second great variety in the human species seems to be that of the Tartar race. **1839** *Penny Cycl.* XIV. 361/2 Considerable differences occur in the general stature of the several races of mankind. **1861** Hulme tr. *Moquin-Tandon* i. v. 27 Blumenbach proposed to establish five races: 1st, the Caucasian; 2nd, the Mongolian; 3rd, the Ethiopian; 4th, the American; 5th, the Malay. **1936** *Nature* 18 Apr. 636/2 The races or types into which the anthropologist groups the varieties of *Homo sapiens* are ideal types. **1959** *New Biol.* XXIX. 69 From the U.N.E.S.C.O. statement we can define 'race' as 'a division of man, the members of which, though individually varying, are characterized as a group by certain inherited physical features as having a common origin'. **1971** R. M. & F. M. Keesing *New Perspectives in Cultural Anthropol.* 51 It is at this point that the term 'race' becomes relevant. Though in popular usage it is emotionally charged and imprecise, it has a straightforward and important meaning in evolutionary biology. A race is a geographically separated, hence genetically somewhat distinctive, population within a species.

3. a. A breed or stock of animals; a particular variety of a species.

1580 Blundevil *Horsemanship* i. iii. Bj, Of all the races in Græce, both the Horses and Mares of Thessalia..are most celebrated. **1641** Hinde *J. Bruen* vii. 26, I have seene a Gentleman..very carefull to have his horse of a generous race. **1745** Pococke *Descr. East* II. i. 196 There is a race of sheep in this country with four horns. **1781** Gibbon *Decl. & F.* II. 57 The plains..bred a generous race of horses. **1839** *Penny Cycl.* XIV. 362/2 In the most highly domesticated races, as the spaniel, the cranium is more fully developed. **1880** Huxley *Crayfish* 292 In this manner, a variety, or race, is generated within the species.

†**b.** A stud or herd (of horses). *Obs.*

1547 *Privy Council Acts* (1890) II. 86 Persons having custodie of a studde or race of mares. **1596** Shaks. *Merch. V.* v. i. 72 Doe but note a wilde and wanton heard Or race of youthful and vnhandled coltes. *a* **1626** Fletcher *Double Marriage* i. i, The rases of our horses he takes from us. **1667** Duchess of Newcastle *Life Duke of N.* (1886) II. 152 All this stock was lost, besides his race of horses.

c. A genus, species, kind of animals.

1605 Shaks. *Macb.* ii. iv. 15 Duncans Horses.. Beauteous, and swift, the Minions of their Race. **1687** Dryden *Hind & P.* i. 160 The wolfish race Appear with belly gaunt and famished face. **1727–46** Thomson *Summer* 388 Slow move the harmless race [sheep]. **1774** Goldsm. *Nat. Hist.* (1776) VII. 190 The generality of mankind regard this formidable race [serpents] with horror. *a* **1822** Shelley *Hom. Merc.* lii, I wish the race of cows were perished.

4. A genus, species, or variety of plants (cf. quot. 1880).

1596 Spenser *F.Q.* v. i. 1 The wicked seede of vice Began to spring..But evermore some of the vertuous race Rose up. **1712** Addison *Spect.* No. 387 ¶7 The Seeds by which the several Races of Plants are propagated and continued. **1804** Knapp *Brit. Grasses* Pl. 119 The whole race of British grasses now before us. **1880** Asa Gray *Struct. Bot.* ix. §1. 320 A race in this technical sense of the term, is a variety which is perpetuated with considerable certainty by sexual propagation.

5. One of the great divisions of living creatures:

a. Mankind. In early use always ***the human race, the race of men*** or ***mankind***, etc.

c **1580** Sidney *Ps.* xxi. x, From among the humane race [thou shalt] Roote out their generation. **1607** Shaks. *Timon* iv. i. 40 His hate may grow To the whole race of Mankinde. **1667** Milton *P.L.* ii. 348 The happy seat Of som new Race call'd Man. **1727–46** Thomson *Summer* 36 The flux of many thousand years, That oft has swept the toiling race of men.. away. **1781** Cowper *Charity* 22 That every tribe..Might feel themselves allied to all the race. **1850** Tennyson *In Mem.* vi, One writes..That 'Loss is common to the race'. **1871** Morley *Voltaire* (1886) 2 It was one of the cardinal liberations of the growing race.

b. A class or kind of beings other than men or animals.

1667 Milton *P.L.* ii. 194 Shall we then live thus vile, the race of Heav'n Thus trampl'd. **1679** Dryden *Ovid Met.* i. 250 There dwells below a Race of Demi-Gods. **1781** Cowper *Anti-Thelyphthora* 199 The Fauns and Satyrs, a lascivious race. **1820** Shelley *Prometh. Unb.* i. 244 The voice With which our pallid race hold ghastly talk In darkness.

c. One of the chief classes of animals (as beasts, birds, fishes, insects, etc.)

1726–46 Thomson *Winter* 137 The plumy race, The tenants of the sky. **1728–46** —— *Spring* 123 Insect armies.. A feeble race. **1819** Shelley *Cyclops* 110 And who possess the land? The race of beasts? *Ibid.* 244 The sacred waves and all the race of fishes.

6. Without article:

a. Denoting the stock, family, class, etc. to which a person, animal, or plant belongs, chiefly in phr. *of* (*noble*, etc.) *race*.

1559 Sackville *Induct. Mirr. Mag.* vi, Som were Dukes, and came of regall race. **1590** Spenser *F.Q.* i. x. 8 Una.. Whom well she knew to spring from hevenly race. *Ibid.* 60 Thou, faire ymp, sprong out from English race. **1611** Shaks. *Wint. T.* iv. iv. 95 [A] bud of Nobler race. **1660** Stanley *Hist. Philos.* ix. (1701) 362/1 Who, in Race, and Honour, and Wealth, excelled all the rest of the Citizens. **1703** Pope *Thebais* i. 685 A fate..unworthy those of race divine! **1754** Gray *Progr. Poesy* 105 Two Coursers of ethereal race. **1873** Dixon *Two Queens* I. i. i. 5 His ablest servants were of Oriental race.

b. The fact or condition of belonging to a particular people or ethnical stock; the qualities, etc. resulting from this.

1849 Macaulay *Hist. Eng.* i. I. 16 In no country has the enmity of race been carried farther than in England. **1856** Emerson *Eng. Traits, Race* Wks. (Bohn) II. 21 Race in the negro is of appalling importance. **1890** *Spectator* 25 Jan., They are separated by language, by degree of civilisation, and by the indefinable aggregate of inherent differences which we call 'race'.

†**7.** Natural or inherited disposition. *Obs. rare.*

1603 Shaks. *Meas. for M.* ii. iv. 160 Now I giue my sensuall race, the reine. **1610** —— *Temp.* i. ii. 358 Thy vild race..had that in't, which good natures Could not abide to be with.

II. A group or class of persons, animals, or things, having some common feature or features.

8. a. A set or class of persons.

1500–20 Dunbar *Poems* xxvi. 50 Bakbyttaris of sindry racis. *a* **1568** Ascham *Scholem* i. (Arb.) 66 His onely example had breed such a rase of worthie learned ientlemen, as this Realme neuer yet did affourde. *c* **1580** Sidney *Ps.* xii. i, Ev'n the race of good men are decai'd. *a* **1611** Beaum. & Fl. *Maid's Trag.* iv. ii, You preserve A race of idle people here about you, Facers and Talkers. **1712** Budgell *Spect.* No. 404 ¶3 To this Affectation the World owes its whole Race of Coxcombs. **1748** Thomson *Cast. Indol.* i. lii, The race of learned men, Still at their books. **1821** Lamb *Elia* Ser. i, *The Two Races of Men*, The men who borrow, and the men who lend. **1875** Jowett *Plato* (ed. 2) V. 56 There arose a new race of poets..who made pleasure the only criterion of excellence.

b. One of the sexes. *poet.*

1590 Spenser *F.Q.* iii. v. 52 In gentle Ladies breste and bounteous race Of woman kind. **1711** Steele *Spect.* No. 113 ¶4 She is beautiful beyond the Race of Women. **1725** Pope *Odyss.* xi. 349 Three gallant sons..but of the softer race, One nymph alone.

†**c.** The line or succession of persons holding an office. *Obs. rare*$^{-1}$.

1570–6 Lambarde *Peramb. Kent* (1826) 306 The whole race of the Bishops succeeding Iustus in this See.

9. a. A set, class, or kind of animals, plants, or things. Chiefly *poet.*

1590 Spenser *F.Q.* ii. xii. 8 Seagulles..And Cormoyraunts, with birds of ravenous race. **1648** Herrick *Hesper., On Spalt* (1869) 226 Of pushes Spalt has such a knottie race. **1715–20** Pope *Iliad* v. 66 Expert..In woods and wilds to wound the savage race. **1783** Johnson *Let. to Mrs. Thrale* 20 Nov., I hope [her disease] is not of the cephalick race. **1823** Scott *Peveril* xxv. (*motto*), Amidst the faded race of fallen leaves.

†**b.** One of the three 'kingdoms' of nature. *Obs. rare.*

1697 Dryden *Virg. Georg.* iv. 224 Of all the Race of Animals, alone The Bees have common Cities of their own. **1707** *Curiosities in Husb. & Gard.* 184 All the Offsprings that are produc'd in the Race of Vegetables and in the Race of Animals. *Ibid.* 227 They can..extract from Water Minerals, Vegetables, and Animals, and give new Creatures to these three Races of Nature.

10. a. A particular class of wine, or the characteristic flavour of this, supposed to be due to the soil. (Cf. raciness a, racy 1.) ? *Obs.*

1520 Whitinton *Vulg.* (1527) 15 This is a cup of good romney, and drynketh well of the rase. **1625** Massinger *New Way* i. iii, A pipe Of rich Canary..Is it of the right race? *c* **1645** Howell *Lett.* (1650) I. 370 One cannot pass a day's journey but he will find a differing race of wine. *a* **1682** Sir T. Browne *Misc. Tracts* (1684) 25 A pure and flosculous race or spirit. **1779–81** Johnson *L.P., Thomson* Wks. 1787 IV. 178 'Race'..applied to wines, in its primitive sense, means the flavour of the soil. **1835** *Tait's Edin. Mag.* II. 350/1 Like certain wines and fruits..in removal, much of the *race*, or peculiar flavour of the soil, is sure to be lost.

b. *fig.* Of speech, writing, etc.: A peculiar and characteristic style or manner, *esp.* liveliness, sprightliness, piquancy. (Cf. raciness b, racy 3.)

1680–90 Temple *Ess., Learning* Wks. 1731 I. 166, I think the Epistles of Phalaris to have more Race, more Spirit, more Force of Wit and Genius, than any others I have ever seen, either ancient or modern. **1711** P. H. *View 2 last Parlts.* 185 Mr. Dolben..pursu'd the Charge with a peculiar Race of Spirit. **1779–81** Johnson *L.P., Thomson* Wks. 1787 IV. 178, I know not whether they [Thomson's Poems] have lost part of what Temple calls their 'race'. **1831** Macaulay *Ess., Boswell* (1860) I. 369 We know no production of the human mind which has so much of what may be called the race, so much of the peculiar flavour of the soil from which it sprang. **1875** McCosh *Scot. Philos.* xxxi. 247 His conversation had a race and flavour peculiarly its own.

11. a. Now found in almost unlimited *attrib.* and *Comb.* uses: caused by, based on, of or pertaining to race, as ***race-aversion, -blood, -brood, -character, -characteristic, -conflict, culture, -difference, discrimination, -distinction, division, equality, -experience, -feeling, -hatred, -heritage, -history, -improvement, -inheritance, instinct, law, line, -maintenance, -mixture, -name, -patriarch, -poem, -portrait, prejudice, pride, problem, quarrel, -question, relationship, -skull, solidarity, superiority, -survival, tension, -type, war***; ***race-begotten, -conscious, -hating, -maintaining, -perpetuating, -proud, -wide***, adjs.

1897 'MARK TWAIN' *Following Equat.* xxi. 207 It must have been *race-aversion that put upon them a good deal of the low-rate intellectual reputation which they bear. **1878** B. TAYLOR *Deukalion* II. ii. 62 The *race-begotten child Is its own father's lord. **1906** W. H. FLEMING *Slavery* 37 The one is based on a supposed duty to God; the other on a supposed duty to one's *race-blood. **1583** STANYHURST *Æneis* III. (Arb.) 93 Agragas..steeds courrageous with *racebrood plentiful offred. **1866** *Pall Mall G.* 3 Jan. 5/2 It was absurd to ignore all distinctions of *race-character in governing them [negroes]. **1875** WHITNEY *Life Lang.* ii. 8 The theory of a language as a *race-characteristic. **1880** A. W. TOURGÉE *Invis. Empire* xii. 513 Any one who asked the support of colored men as against a Democratic nominee was precipitating a *race-conflict. **1949** *Caribbean Q.* I. II. 28 Countless little stories..about..present life, in country and town..in race-conflict, and class-conflict. **1927** *Observer* 5 June 5/3 Frenchmen are not so *race-conscious as either Englishmen or Americans. **1977** P. JOHNSON *Enemies of Society* viii. 106 Nigger..is now frequently employed by the more race-conscious blacks, but only among themselves. **1909** C. W. SALEEBY (*title*) Parenthood and *race culture. An outline of eugenics. **1875** WHITNEY *Life Lang.* i. 4 Far greater *race-differences are met with among the speakers of one language. **1917** *Cases Argued U.S. Supreme Court: Lawyers' Ed.* (1918) 155/2 Plaintiff is not in a position to raise the issue of *race discrimination, not being himself a negro. **1883** GREEN *Conq. Eng.* 117 *Race distinctions perpetuated themselves in the group of little townships. **1906** *Westm. Gaz.* 21 Feb. 2/3 That simple principle [of One Vote One Value]..at once supplies a strong motive for those who once had everything to gain from the *race-division to talk about 'bringing both races together'. **1974** *Race* XV. 462 The present race divisions are projected into the past as though they were always a feature of South African society. **1911** G. SPILLER *Papers on Inter-Racial Problems* I. 31 It becomes a vital matter to grapple with the problem of *race equality. **1890** O. WILDE in *19th Cent.* Sept. 443 The imagination is the result of heredity. It is simply concentrated *race-experience. **1888** KIPLING *City of Dreadful Night* (1891) 18 A casual reference to Hindus and Mahometans... There is *race-feeling, to be explained away. **1944** J. S. HUXLEY *On Living in Revolution* 169 The actual physical kinship, which is frequently claimed as 'race feeling', must be fictitious. **1941** AUDEN *New Year Let.* III. 68 Self-respect drives negroes from The one-crop and *race-hating delta. **1882** *Times* 15 Mar., The furious *race-hatred that has been raging over the South. **1901** *Times* 5 Aug. 7/2 The object of these documents has usually been..to fan the race-hatred of the Dutch in South Africa. **1935** *Economist* 27 July 175/2 The new excesses are confined to the special domains of class hatred, race hatred and hatred of religion. **1976** *Birmingham Post* 16 Dec. 5/2 Intent to stir up race hatred. **1911** W. JAMES *Some Probl. Philos.* i. 4 Philosophy, thus become a *race-heritage, forms in its totality a monstrously unwieldy mass of learning. **1894** *Psychol. Rev.* Nov. 651 The one criticism which I would venture to make upon this paper..is that it neglects the phylogenetic point of view, the considerations from *race-history. **1907** W. JAMES *Pragmatism* v. 169 The most primitive ways of thinking..may remain as indelible tokens of events in our race-history. **1903** *Daily Chron.* 29 July 4/5 We have a great deal yet to learn on matters bearing upon *race-improvement. **1909** W. JAMES *Meaning of Truth* viii. 214 Dr. Schiller has shown that all our truths, even the most elemental, are affected by *race-inheritance with a human co-efficient. **1901** —— *Let.* 3 Mar. (1920) II. 141 Empire anyhow is half crime by necessity of Nature, and to see a country like the United States..perversely rushing to wallow in the mire of it, shows how strong these ancient *race instincts be. **1942** 'G. ORWELL' *War-time Diary* 22 Mar. in *Coll. Ess.* (1968) II. 412 German propaganda is..offering..emancipation to the Kaffirs and stricter *race laws to the Boers. **1960** *Twentieth Century* Nov. 407 Race-laws make camps almost impossible within the Union. **1978** G. GREENE *Human Factor* II. i. 62 'I fell in love.' 'Yes. So I see. With an African girl... You broke their race laws.' **1883** G. W. WILLIAMS *Hist. Negro Race* II. xxviii. 543 *Race lines must be obliterated. **1891** *Congress Rec.* App. 17 Jan. 101/1 At Marion, Ind.,..when the Democrats were attempting to have a rally,..they were attacked by the colored people, the race line being distinctly drawn by that race. **1879** H. SPENCER *Data of Ethics* ii. §5. 15 *Race-maintaining conduct, like self-maintaining conduct, arises gradually out of that which cannot be called conduct. *Ibid.* 16 This conduct which furthers *race-maintenance. **1905** O. JESPERSEN *Growth & Structure Eng. Lang.* iii. 47 There we had a real *race-mixture, where people speaking two different languages were living in actual contact in the same country. **1935** HUXLEY & HADDON *We Europeans* ix. 278 From what has been said, it will be clear that 'race-mixture' has in the past been beneficial. **1924** *Race-name [see ATESTINE *a.* and *sb.*]. **1950** PARTRIDGE *Here, There & Everywhere* 17 The other self-confident Asiatic race-names are fully qualified. **1859** R. B. ANDERSON tr. *Rydberg's Teut. Mythol.* 106 The songs learned by Saxo in regard to the northern *race-patriarch. **1915** R. LANKESTER *Diversions of Naturalist* xxi. 194 Natural automatically-growing mechanisms of life-saving or *race-perpetuating importance. **1888** *Literary World* (Boston) 29 Sept. 314/3 The Kalevala..a *race-poem whose enduring charm is its artlessness and spontaneity. **1875** TYLOR in *Encycl. Brit.* II. 111/1 The coloured *race-portraits of ancient Egypt. **1890** O. WILDE in *19th Cent.* Sept. 457 Criticism will annihilate *race-prejudices, by insisting upon the unity of the human mind in the variety of its forms. **1913** J. LONDON *Let.* 25 Aug. (1966) 395 First of all..by stopping the stupid newspaper from fomenting race prejudice. **1920** H. CRANE *Let.* 6 Mar. (1965) 35, I am as anti-Semitic as they make 'em, but Frank's comments cannot afford to be ignored merely because of race prejudice. **1942** E. PAUL *Narrow St.* xii. 91 Guy delivered a concise impassioned talk against race prejudice. **1956** L. KUPER *Passive Resistance in S. Afr.* 18 Then Dr. Naicker commented on..the United Party's pandering to race-prejudice to catch votes. **1905** W. BAUCKE *Where White Man Treads* 276 On our side race prejudice, *race pride, preaching honesty, yet unblushingly swindling him and each other. **1973** A. DUNDES *Mother Wit* 2/1 The relationship between folklore and race pride..corresponds to the relationship between folklore and nationalism in the nineteenth century. **1890** A. W. TOURGÉE *Pactolus Prime* xi. 141 If every one could do as much, the *race-problem would soon be solved. **1923** O. SCHREINER *Thoughts on S. Afr.* vii. 296 To..attempt to comprehend or deal rationally with race-problems. **1980** *Bananas* Aug. 7/1 Talking about Korea, Chicago, war, the race problem. **1937** E. MUIR *Coll. Poems* (1960) 72 Now I am shackled to a Grecian dolt, Pragmatic, *race-proud as a pampered colt. **1931** F. L. ALLEN *Only Yesterday* iii. 68 If a white man stood up for a Negro in a *race quarrel, he might be kidnapped and beaten up. **1889** *Boston Jrnl.* 26 Dec. 2/4 Time only can solve the *race-question in the South. **1920** L. STODDARD *Rising Tide of Color* xi. 293 She [*sc.* Japan] should not allow her immigration to be treated as a race-question. **1908** R. S. BAKER *Following Colour Line* x. 217, I have found a sharper feeling and a bitterer discussion of *race relationships among the Negroes of the North than among those of the South. **1864** J. HUNT tr. *Vogt's Lect. Man* vii. 194 More of the Simian type than any other known *race-skull. **1942** Z. N. HURSTON in A. Dundes *Mother Wit* (1973) 25/1 '*Race Solidarity' looked like something solid in my childhood, but like all other mirages, it faded as I came close enough to look. As soon as I could think, I saw that there is no such thing as Race Solidarity in America with any group. **1901** E. A. ROSS in *Ann. Amer. Acad. Pol. Sci.* XVIII. 67 (*title*) The causes of *race superiority. **1951** J. MASTERS *Nightrunners of Bengal* v. 58 She was goading herself to wipe out a sense of race superiority she presumed him to have... She wanted..him to acknowledge beauty in an Indian woman. **1933** A. N. WHITEHEAD *Adventures of Ideas* vi. 97 We can observe insects performing elaborate routine actions..which yet are essential either for their own individual survival or for *race-survival. **1954** P. MASON *Ess. Racial Tension* iii. 45 One would expect *race tensions to be most acute..in the country where there is a temperate climate. **1974** *Allendale* (S. Carolina) *County Citizen* 24 Apr. 6/3 We found ourselves discussion-slanted toward race tension and struggles. **1864** W. D. WHITNEY in *Ann. Rep. Board of Regents Smithsonian Inst. 1863* 113 The kind and amount of modification which external circumstances can introduce into a *race-type is as yet undetermined. **1892** KIPLING *Lett. of Travel* (1920) 30 Seven million negroes..their race-type unevolved. **1927** PEAKE & FLEURE *Priests & Kings* 181 'Race-type' in a general sense is a very difficult matter to define. **1897** *Chicago Tribune* 28 July 3/7 This gave the negroes an excellent chance to start a '*race' war. **1977** P. JOHNSON *Enemies of Society* xix. 247 He realized he was taking part in a race-war, as well as a class-war. **1893** J. H. BARROWS *World's Parlt. Relig.* I. 72 An event of *race-wide and perpetual significance.

b. Of, pertaining to, or designating a style of music, originating among Blacks of the Southern U.S. (cf. RACE *sb.*² 6b), freq. in a twelve-bar sequence (see also quot. 1938).

1926 H. NILES in W. C. Handy *Blues* 31 Listen to the 'race records', for this craft is *sui generis*. **1927** *Jrnl. Abnormal & Social Psychol.* Apr.–June 12 'Race blues'..are not always what they seem. **1935** *Vanity Fair* (N.Y.) Nov. 71/3 Negro bands play 'race music' (a curious euphemism spread by phonograph companies). **1938** *Collier's* 30 Apr. 24/4 We were afraid to advertise Negro records. So I listed them in the catalogue as 'race' records and they are still known as that. **1942** PARTRIDGE *Usage & Abusage* 208/2 'Race (phonograph) *recordings*' for recordings made by Negroes. **1946** R. BLESH *Shining Trumpets* (1949) vi. 145 It was considered authentic enough for the uncritical Victor Company to issue in its race catalogue. **1946** MEZZROW & WOLFE *Really Blues* (1957) ix. 161 Preaching blues was strictly race music. **1952** B. ULANOV *Hist. Jazz in Amer.* (1958) iv. 32 Their masterpieces appeared on the so-called 'race' labels of the record companies. **1968** P. OLIVER *Screening Blues* 5 In the ensuing months more stores carried Race records, specially pressed for the Negro market... Race records from jazz to vaudeville to rural blues reached the remotest districts. **1976** A. MURRAY *Stomping Blues* iv. 50 The period of the race catalogs was also the decade of the so-called revolution in race consciousness known as the Harlem Renaissance. **1977** *Times* 17 Aug. 14/4 Negro styles traditionally stigmatized as 'race' music.

c. Special combs., as **race consciousness**, emotionally based awareness of those differences between people or social groups that can be ascribed to racial factors; the supposed intuitive awareness of a common heritage shared by members of a race or culture; **race-gap**, a difference between racial groups; **race man** *U.S. colloq.*, a Black, esp. one who advocates the rights of Blacks; **race memory**, (a) subconscious memory of events in the history of one's race or of the human race which, it is suggested, is transmitted genetically; **race relations**, a term for such social contacts between racial groups living within a particular area as arise from or are affected by differences in cultural origin or skin colour; freq. *attrib.* or as *adj.*; **race riot**, a riot that results from racial hostility; hence **race rioting**; **race suicide**, the self-extinction of a racial group through failure to reproduce itself sufficiently, esp. of one with high cultural standards and a low birth-rate in competition with a racial group having lower standards and a high birth-rate; the self-destruction of a race; also *attrib.*; **race theory**, a hypothetical assertion that some racial groups are endowed with specific 'superior' qualities; hence **race theorist**, an advocate of a race theory; **race-thinking** (see quot. 1937); also **race-thinker**.

1905 *Race consciousness [see AMALGAMATION 2]. **1926** G. CALLAWAY *Native Probl. in S. Afr.* 2 It is conceivable that the Native people of South Africa might have lived alongside of the Europeans without developing a strong race consciousness. **1968** *Internat. Encycl. Social Sci.* XIII. 269 Relationships which are capable of producing race conflict and race consciousness. **1890** W. JAMES *Will to Believe* (1897) 260 We here..catch the only glimpse it is allotted to us to attain of the working units themselves, of whose differentiating action the *race-gaps form but the stagnant sum. **1936** R. L. ABBOT in *Chicago Defender* 13 June 16/5 One *Race man, finding out this outrage, fired on the officers. **1942** Z. N. HURSTON in A. Dundes *Mother Wit* (1973) 25/1 A 'Race Man' was somebody who always kept the glory and honor of his race before him... It was a mark of shame if somebody accused: 'Why, you are not a Race Man (or woman).' People made whole careers of being 'Race' men and women. They were champions of the race. **1969** *Publ. Amer. Dial. Soc.* LI. 29 Names used..by both Negroes and Whites [for Negroes who demand equal status with whites]..civil rights man, mau mau, race man. **1974** YI-FU TUAN *Topophilia* xiii. 209 The upper shadies can identify emotionally with the ghetto poor; they are recognized by the poor as Race Men, that is, supporters of black causes. **1904** *Folk-Lore* XV. 349, I have heard this belief referred to a '*race-memory' of antediluvian reptiles. **1912** A. CONAN DOYLE *Lost World* i. 10 That race-memory which we call instinct. **1934** R. KNOX *Still Dead* xi. 138 A cave has, for all of us, an atmosphere of..terrifying mystery. The anthropologists would tell us..that it is due to race-memory. **1950** [see OLDEST *a.* 3]. **1972** C. FREMLIN *Appointment with Yesterday* xiv. 110 A race-memory of the days when servants weren't quite real, and so it didn't matter what they heard. **1911** *Pol. Sci. Q.* XXVI. 193 (*title*) *Race relations in the Eastern Piedmont region of Georgia. **1925** *Scribner's Mag.* July 12/2 On two occasions great intercollegiate conventions of students have dealt with race-relations,..and war itself. **1934** *Race Relations* I. 32/1 We have to deal in this country not only with relations between English and Dutch but also between Jews and Gentiles, and between Whites and Coloured, Whites and Indians, as well as between Whites and Bantu... Hence, we decided to invite certain men..to give us their views on how race relations problems strike them. **1965** *Act 13 & 14 Eliz. II* c. 73 (*heading*) Race Relations Act 1965... An Act to prohibit discrimination on racial grounds in places of public resort; to prevent the enforcement or imposition on racial grounds of restrictions on the transfer of tenancies; to penalize incitement to racial hatred. *Ibid.* §2 For the purposes of securing compliance with the provisions of..this Act..there shall be constituted a board to be known as the Race Relations Board, consisting of a chairman and two other members appointed by the Secretary of State. **1970** *Oxf. Univ. Gaz.* 30 Apr. Suppl. 14 During the course of the year two visiting Fellows in Race Relations were appointed in collaboration with St. Antony's College. **1977** *Whitaker's Almanack 1978* 348/2 A Lords amendment to the Race Relations Bill..was reversed in the Commons on Oct. 27. **1890** *Our Day* May 406 *Race Riots in the South. **1921** *Palestine Weekly* 2 Dec. 779/2 With regard to the actual question as to which side initiated the race riot, the Commission speaks with definiteness and precision. **1928** F. HURST *President is Born* xxiv. 250 Race-riots out in Chicago. **1958** *Daily Mail* 3 Sept. 6/6 After three nights of race-riots in their streets the people who live in Notting Hill have been asked to put themselves under a voluntary curfew. **1979** *Dædalus* Spring 103 Race riots broke out in Marseilles in 1973 that left six Algerians dead. **1968** *Economist* 20 July 43/1 The second problem is the emergence of *race rioting as a regular, not to say an annual, occurrence. **1901** E. A. ROSS in *Ann. Amer. Acad. Pol. & Social Sci.* July 88 The American farm hand, mechanic and operative might wither away before the heavy influx of a prolific race from the Orient... For a case like this I can find no words so apt as '*race suicide'. **1904** *Daily Chron.* 9 June 3/2 I'm with the President on this race-suicide question. **1936** M. PLOWMAN *Faith called Pacifism* 14 If war has become race suicide by a perfectly natural process of evolution, why should we continue to call it 'war'? **1945** C. F. MCCLEARY (*title*) Race suicide. **1921** *Times Lit. Suppl.* 25 Aug. 543/1 In defiance of the German *race-theorists, and similar superficial or prejudiced observers, Dr. Curtius insists that French culture..cannot be dismissed with the formulae 'esprit' and 'décadence'. **1949** KOESTLER *Promise & Fulfilment* 334 With the exception of the 'race-theorists' nearly all modern authorities hold that Jewish characteristics are a product of sustained environmental pressure. **1895** W. D. BABINGTON (*title*) Fallacies of *race theories. **1945** KOESTLER *Yogi & Commissar* II. ii. 192 Within a century or two..race-theory and Jew-baiting would have shrunk to episodes of the past. **1937** J. BARZUN *Race: Study in Mod. Superstition* x. 263 Then came the 'biological revolution' and *race-thinkers pinned their hopes on anatomy. *Ibid.* i. 17 We must..see what men who have thought and written about race think it is. Their ideas form, not a definition of race, for they all disagree among themselves, but a type of thinking, which I shall call *race-thinking. **1965** *Listener* 11 Nov. 740/2 This kind of thinking involves what are, in fact, vague figures. It has been described as 'race thinking'. People who think this way..are becoming racists.

race (reis), *sb.*³ [var. of RASE *sb.* (q.v.). Cf. RACE *v.*³] A cut, slit, mark, scratch. Now only *techn.* (see quot. 1819).

c **1500** *Robt. Devyll* in Thoms *Prose Rom.* (1858) I. 40 Robert had a race in his face. **1587** MASCALL *Govt. Cattle, Oxen* (1627) 19 Yee must launce his feete gently round on the edge of his hoofes, with small races not deepe. **1601** HOLLAND *Pliny* (1634) II. 572 That sand cutteth smooth and cleane as it goeth, and leaues no race at all in the work. **1683** MOXON *Mech. Exerc., Printing* xiii. ¶4 He, with the Tooth of the Gage makes a Mark or Race on the side of the Face. **1819** REES *Cycl.* XXIX. *Race*, the mark made on timber, &c. by a tool called a racing-knife.

attrib. **1705** *Lond. Gaz.* No. 4145 She hath had a little Race Sore upon one of her hind Gambrels.

race (reis), *sb.*⁴ *Obs.* exc. *dial.* [f. RACE *v.*⁴: cf. PLUCK *sb.*] The heart, liver, and lungs, *esp.* of a calf.

1661 LOVELL *Hist. Anim. & Min.* 25 The destilled water of the race [of a calf]..helpeth cold. *c* **1818** *Yng. Woman's Companion* 1–2 The head and inwards are called the pluck; in some places they are called the calf's race. **1825** BRITTON *Beauties Wiltsh.* III. (E.D.S.). **1879–** In dial. glossaries (Shropsh., Leic., Wilts, etc.).

†**race**, *sb.*[5] *Obs.* Also 6–7 rase, 7 raice. [Of obscure origin; cf. RACHE *sb.*[2]] A (white) mark down the face of a horse (or dog).

1523 FITZHERB. *Husb.* §73 A whyte rase or a ball in the foreheed. **1674** *Lond. Gaz.* No. 841 A young black.. Dog, with..a little rase of white down his Face and Nose. **1679** *Ibid.* No. 1423 A sorrel Stonehorse..with a white Star and raice down his face. **1707** *Ibid.* No. 4304 A Pair of..black Coach-Mares, with Races in their Foreheads.

race (reɪs), *sb.*[6] Also 6 rase, raze. [ad. OF. *rais, raiz* = Sp. *raiz*:—L. *rādīc-em*: see RADISH, RADIX.] A root (of ginger).

1547 BOORDE *Brev. Health* §16. 324. 105 Take and eate a race of grene ginger. **1627** CAPT. SMITH *Seaman's Gram.* xv. 75 A few stewed Prunes, a race of greene Ginger. **1665** *Sir T. Roe's Voy. E. Ind.* in J. Havers *P. della Valle's Trav. E. India* 361 Ginger..the large races whereof, are there very excellently well preserved. **1750** G. HUGHES *Barbadoes* 233 Its roots are those flattish digitated Races called Ginger. *c* **1825** *Houlston Tracts* II. xlvii. 8 A race of ginger you shall surely have. **1879** in *Cassell's Techn. Educ.* II. 91/2 The ginger of commerce is the dry, wrinkled rhizomes of the plant, which are called 'races'.

attrib. **1832** WEBSTER, s.v. Race-ginger.

race (reɪs), *sb.*[7] [Origin unknown.] A calcareous concretion found in nodules in brick-clay.

1728 WOODWARD *Fossils* 16 There's one sort of this found commonly among the clay us'd for making Tyles and Bricks; which the Workmen call Race or Rance. **1798** MIDDLETON *View Agric.* 311 The calcarious matter is chalk..in very small pieces..which the brickmakers about town call *race.* **1824** *Ann. Reg.* 238* By contact with these bones the clay is converted into nodules of a blueish white substance, called by the workmen race. **1885** *Proc. R. Soc.* XXXIX. 213 What were at first supposed to be pebbles..prove on examination to be calcareous concretions ('race' or 'kunkur').

†**race**, *a. Obs. rare.* [a. F. *ras* shaven, bare, etc., ad. L. *rās-us*, pa. pple. of *rādĕre* to scrape, shave; cf. RASE *v.* and RAZEE.]

1. Of ships: Lying low in the water. Hence ***race-building, -built.***

There is app. no authority for Kingsley's explanation.

1622 SIR R. HAWKINS *Voy. S. Sea* (1847) 199 Whether the race or loftie built shippe bee best for the merchant. *Ibid.* 220 This race building, first came in by overmuch homing in of our shippes. [**1855** KINGSLEY *Westw. Ho.* II. xii. 322 The Spanish fashion..was..to build their men-of-war flush-decked, or, as it was called, race.]

2. Of measure: Bare, without addition.

1736 PEGGE *Kenticisms* (E.D.S.), Full measure is 21 to the score, as of corn, coals, &c.; and race measure is but 20... When the bushel is upheap'd 'tis full; when struck with the strickle and even'd, 'tis race measure.

race (reɪs), *v.*[1] [f. RACE *sb.*[1]]

1. a. *intr.* To run a race (*with*), to compete (*with*) in speed.

1680, 1741–3 [see RACING *vbl. sb.*]. **1818** KEATS *Endym.* I. 534, I who..would race With my own steed from Araby. **1830** TENNYSON *Conf. Sensitive Mind* 158 The lamb.. raceth freely with his fere. **1855** BROWNING *Love among the Ruins* iv, A burning ring..the chariots traced As they raced.

b. To practise or engage in horse-racing.

1827 LYTTON *Pelham* lvii, 'And young A——?'.. 'Has an expensive mistress, and races'. **1881** H. SMART *Race for Wife* iii, I've been racing now getting on fifty years.

2. a. *intr.* To run, ride, sail, etc. swiftly. (In some examples perh. with suggestion of sense 1.)

1757 DYER *Fleece* I. (1761) 81 Those snow-white lambs.. Skip on the green, and race in little troops. **1821** CLARE *Vill. Minstr.* I. 133 Scampering beetles rac'd away. **1847** TENNYSON *Princ.* v. 107 Inward raced the scouts With rumour of Prince Arac hard at hand. **1879** BROWNING *Pheidippides* 12 Run, Pheidippides, run and race, reach Sparta for aid! **1887** BOWEN *Virg. Æneid* III. 191 [We] Spread to the gale our canvas, and race on the waves once more.

transf. or *fig.* **1874** BLACKIE *Self-Cult.* 46 There is a class of people who do not walk through life, but race.

b. Of inanimate things.

1808 SCOTT *Marm.* III. Introd., Like streamlet..racing forth. **1845** DE QUINCEY *Afflict. Childhood* Wks. 1897 I. 51 April, that sometimes cares little for racing across both frontiers of May. **1883** OUIDA *Wanda* I. 31 The north wind is racing in from the Polish steppes.

c. Of a steam engine, screw propeller, wheel, etc.: To run or revolve with uncontrolled speed, when resistance is diminished while the driving power continues the same. Also of an electric motor, car engine, etc.

1862 *Illustr. Catal. Internat. Exhib.* II. XII. 2/1 The 'governor' prevents the engines from racing in heavy weather. **1893** R. KIPLING *Many Invent.* 158 The Rathmines stood poised, her screw racing and drumming. **1893** S. R. BOTTONE *How to manage Dynamo* ii. 29 The dynamo..if shunt-wound..will race and go much faster than usual. **1900** *Daily News* 5 Nov. 7/2 The loss of the propeller caused the engines to 'race' so fiercely that the shaft broke. **1907** C. W. BROWN *Petrol Engine* i. 3 Neglect of this matter will cause the engine to develop a knocking sound, especially..when 'racing' with the governor out of action. **1980** *Sci. Amer.* Jan. 118/3 If the load on the turbine was suddenly removed, then unless the turbine was shut down promptly it would pick up speed and race, conceivably until it flew to pieces.

3. a. *trans.* To race with; to try to beat in running. Also *refl.*

1809 W. IRVING *Knickerb.* iv. (1820) 187 Fought cocks, and raced their neighbours' horses. **1832** R. H. FROUDE in *Rem.* (1838) I. 291 She had two servants a-head, who.. raced him, and..contrived to keep a head. **1847** TENNYSON *Princ.* II. 230, I..Flung ball, flew kite, and raced the purple fly. **1886** C. SCOTT *Sheep-Farming* 203 If he [a dog] lacks speed in racing a sheep [etc.]. **1963** *Daily Tel.* 17 July 1/4 He said he got the impression that America was 'racing herself' in this quest [to the Moon].

b. To hold, 'bring *off*' (a race).

1897 *Westm. Gaz.* 31 Aug. 7/2 A match open to the fourteen feet boats..will be raced off.

4. a. To cause to move swiftly or to make rapid progress; to cause to run a race or races.

c **1860** *Miriam May* xv, Whilst he will race horses, it is as well that he should..separate himself from holy things. **1862** H. KINGSLEY *Ravenshoe* III. ii. 24 That quiet looking commander of hers was going to race her out under steam the whole way. **1896** *Daily News* 9 June 7/4 No attempt would be made by the Government to race the Bill through. **1906** E. DYSON *Fact'ry 'Ands* ii. 17 She raced her work. **1945** *ABC of Cookery* (Ministry of Food) vii. 22 Take care not to race the boiling or the eggs may crack.

b. ***to race away***: to lose by racing.

1856 *Leisure Hour* V. 818/1 He raced all his money away. **1887** RUSKIN in *Pall Mall G.* 8 June 1 It is of infinite importance..that the ancient Lords of England should.. not gamble and race their estates away.

c. To convey swiftly. *rare.*

1896 R. KIPLING *Song of the English* iv, The clippers.. that race the Southern Wool.

d. To cause (an engine) to race; to 'rev'.

1932 *New Yorker* 23 July 14/3 The cop got on his machine, raced his engine,..and throttled down. **1973** W. MCCARTHY *Detail* ii. 117 He started the car and raced the engine noisily.

e. ***to race off***, to seduce (a woman); to hurry (a woman) away in order to seduce her. *Austral. slang.*

1965 W. DICK *Bunch of Ratbags* xii. 185 Three of Knuckles's boys had raced Sharon off to the park to see if they could do any good for themselves. **1967** M. WILDING *Coast to Coast 1965–6* 250 Perhaps Peter thought he would try to race her..off. He relished the phrase, race off. He had not heard it in England. **1969** W. MOXHAM *Apprentice* vii. 87 'That's one bird you won't race off,' Rufe said. 'I know her and the bloke she's with.' **1978** *TV Week* (Austral.) 24 June 46/4 Luckinbill blabs to his wife Cannon that he raced off most of her best friends.

5. To suspend (a wheel, grindstone, etc.) in the proper position for running.

1870 READE *Put yourself in his place* II. 40 The master provides the stone, but the grinder hangs and races it.

†**race**, *v.*[2] *Obs. rare*[−1]. [a. F. *racer*, f. *race* RACE *sb.*[2]] *intr.* Of a parent-bird: To impart its nature to its offspring.

1727–41 CHAMBERS *Cycl.* s.v. *Race sb.*, D'Hervieux observes, that..the male usually races more than the female, i.e. the young ones take more after the male.

race (reɪs), *v.*[3] [var. of RASE (RAZE) *v.*[1], in common use *c* 1400–*c* 1650, now only *techn.* in sense 1.]

1. *trans.* To scratch or tear with something sharp; to cut or slash. Now *techn.*

c **1440** CAPGRAVE *Life St. Kath.* IV. 907 Lete hem take vengeavnce now vp-on me,..lete hem my body race. **1545** ASCHAM *Toxoph.* (Arb.) 108 Buckles and agglettes at vnwares, shall race hys bowe. **1588** PARKE tr. *Mendoza's Hist. China* 327 Al the men and women haue their faces raced, and their legs and armes. **1617** MARKHAM *Caval.* VII. 54 The cure is, with a sharpe knife to race him alongst his gummes. **1703** MOXON *Mech. Exerc.* 24 Drawing, or racing with a Point of hardned Steel, a bright Line by the side of the Ruler. **1794** *Rigging & Seamanship* I. 20 Every butt must be..raced across from side to side. **1819** [see RACER[2]]. **1867** SMYTH *Sailor's Word-bk.* 557 *To Race*, applies to marking timber with the race-tool.

†**b.** *spec.* To cut or slash (shoes or clothes) in an ornamental fashion. *Obs.*

1430–40 LYDG. *Bochas* IX. ix. 24 b, Their shone were raced freshly to the tone. **1583** STUBBES *Anat. Abus.* (1877) 58 [Shoes] raced, carued, cut, and stitched all ouer with silk. **1613** WITHER *Abuses*, *Vanity* 696 Apparel..shall be gathered, stitcht, or lac't, Else plated, printed, iag'd, or cut and rac't. **1653** GREAVES *Seraglio* 128 His shoes..are raced, and painted like childrens shoes.

†**c.** To force (a way) by tearing or cutting.

c **1611** CHAPMAN *Iliad* XI. 287 As when two chaced Bores Turne head gainst kennels of bold hounds, and race way through their gores.

†**2.** *intr.* **a.** To cut a way; to pierce, penetrate.

c **1403** LYDG. *Temple Glas* 756 A world of beaute compassid in hir face, Whose persant loke doþ þuruȝ myn hert[e] race. **1412–20** —— *Chron. Troy* III. xxii, The head of stele..Through plate and mayle mightly gan to glace But to the skinne for nothing might it race. **1447** BOKENHAM *Seyntys* (Roxb.) 31 So depe they dede in race Tyl at the laste a chest they founde.

†**b.** Of boars: ? To slash with the tusks. *Obs.*

1470–85 MALORY *Arthur* VII. xvii, They yede to bataille ageyne tracyng racyng foynyng as two bores.

†**3.** *trans.* To scrape *out*, erase. *Obs.* (Now written RASE or RAZE.)

c **1403** LYDG. *Temple Glas* 1238 Wiþoute merci, shal falle þe vengeaunce Forto be raced clene out of my bokes. **1447** BOKENHAM *Seyntys* (Roxb.) 96 They ordeynyd hys name.. From noumbyr of popys racyd to be. *a* **1541** WYATT in *Tottell's Misc.* (Arb.) 72 The wound alas happe in some other place: From whence no toole away the skar can race. **1596** SPENSER *F.Q.* v. ix. 26 Bon, that once had written bin, Was raced out, and Mal was now put in. **1704** *Providence Records* (1894) V. 220 The three words..Raced out in the thirty fift line.

†**b.** *transf.* and *fig.* (cf. ERASE and RASE). *Obs.*

It is difficult to decide whether some instances of *race out* belong here or to RACE *v.*[4]

1579 TOMSON *Calvin's Serm. Tim.* 215/2 The remembraunce..shoulde bee vtterly raced out of the worlde. **1588** SHAKS. *Tit. A.* I. i. 451 To massacre them all, And race their faction, and their familie. **1630** LORD *Banians & Persees* 89 The Lord utterly raced out all of the Tribe or Cast of the Cutteryes. **1705** STANHOPE *Paraphrase* II. 596 It had made little Impression upon their Minds, or if it had, Grief and Disorder had quite raced them out.

†**4.** To alter (a writing) by erasure. *Obs.*

c **1440** *Promp. Parv.* 421/2 Racyng bokys, or oþer lyke, *rado, abrado.* **1530** PALSGR. 678/1 This indenture is raced, all the worlde may se it. **1577** HARRISON *England* II. viii. (1877) I. 176 The instrument is still wholie or in part raced or reformed. **1614** in *Bury Wills* (1850) 165 The last will and testament of..William Cooke, beinge in noe part therof raced or interlyned.

†**5.** To level with the ground; to RAZE. *Obs.*

c **1565** ABP. PARKER *Psalter* lxxix, Thy holy house they haue defylde, Hierusalem is raced. **1594** PLAT *Jewell-house* I. 16 Hee had sentence giuen him to haue his house raced. **1637** RALEIGH *Mahomet* 50 Such Castles and strengths as hee was jealous of were raced. **1679** G. R. tr. *Boaystuau's Theatre World* 112 Destroyed Cities, raced Fortresses.

†**race**, *v.*[4] *Obs.* See also RASE *v.*[2] [Aphetic form of ARACE: cf. OF. *racher, -ier* for *arrachier* ARRACHE.]

1. *trans.* To tear, snatch, pluck *off, away, from, out, down, up*; to root *out.*

c **1350** *St. Agatha* 148 in Horstm. *Altengl. Leg.* (1881) 47 When hir pappes war raced hir fro. *a* **1400** *Relig. Pieces fr. Thornton MS.* iv. 219 Þay..racede of all þe skyne þat tyde. *c* **1400** tr. *Secreta Secret., Gov. Lordsh.* 91 He þat racys it vp by þe rote, and etys þe flour. *c* **1430** LYDG. *Min. Poems* (Percy Soc.) 162 Lat every man doon his besy cure, To race out pride. *c* **1470** HENRY *Wallace* x. 670 Sone to ground the baner doun he race [*pa. t.*]. **1545** ASCHAM *Toxoph.* I. (Arb.) 89 As wild horses at a brunte doth race and pluck in pieces many a stronge carte. **1596** SPENSER *F.Q.* v. v. 11 Thinking at once both head and helmet to have raced.

2. *intr.* To tear, go in pieces. *rare*[−1].

a **1375** *Lay Folks Mass Bk.* App. iv. 137 So radli he gon hit Rogge þat al þe Rolle gon race.

raceable (ˈreɪsəb(ə)l), *a.* [f. RACE *v.*[1] + -ABLE.]

a. Of a racehorse: capable of being raced.

1965 D. FRANCIS *For Kicks* iii. 40, I might well be given a raceable horse to look after.

b. Of a racecourse: fit for horse-racing.

1976 *Daily Record* (Glasgow) 4 Dec. 27/7 It is raceable at present. **1976** *Horse & Hound* 10 Dec. 6/1 He got to Chepstow [racecourse] only to find..that although the ground there was raceable thick local fog meant that proceedings could never get off the ground.

ˈ**raceabout.** *U.S. Naut.* [f. RACE *v.*[1] + ABOUT *adv.*] A sloop-rigged racing yacht with a smaller keel and larger sailyards than those of a knockabout (see KNOCK-ABOUT, KNOCKABOUT *a.* 3 b). Also *attrib.*

1897 *Forest & Stream* 6 Mar. 194/2 The next size, the 'raceabout', or the *fin de siècle* perversion of the knockabout, promises to be more popular and numerous. **1899** *Ibid.* 25 Feb. 157/1 The yacht will have two rigs, knockabout and raceabout, which can be shifted one for the other in half an hour. **1905** *St. Nicholas* Aug. 865 There were other prizes, of course: the much-coveted silver cup,..pennants for the raceabouts and halfraters, and a first money prize of twenty-five dollars for the fishermen's sloops. **1907** *Forest & Stream* 30 Nov. 863/1 The old jib and mainsail sand-bag rig has been replaced by the modern raceabout. **1927** E. P. MORRIS *Fore & Aft Rig in Amer.* 75 It [*sc.* the knockabout rig] has been somewhat diverted from its original purpose by being used on small racing boats, which are not knockabouts in the strict sense and have been ironically called 'race-abouts'.

race-building, -built: see RACE *a.*

ˈ**race-course.** [f. RACE *sb.*[1] + COURSE.]

1. a. A piece of ground laid out with a track for horse-racing.

1764 in Fletcher *St. Leger* (1902) 32 That the Corporation raise the sum of £50 to be run for upon Doncaster Race Course. **1828** DARVILL *Treat. Race-horse* xi. 253 Race-courses..are sometimes made in the form of the figure 8. **1835** *Encycl. Brit.* (ed. 7) XI. 624/1 The nature and form of race-courses. **1863** *Sat. Rev.* 23 May 656 Those who knew no more than had been seen on race-courses.

attrib. **1896** A. MORRISON *Child of the Jago* 114 A race-course adventure involving bodily risk.

b. The course for a boat-race.

1866 'ARGONAUT' *Rowing & Training* 57 The usual length of racecourses for eights, and all other descriptions of boats, varies from 1½ to 2⅔ miles.

2. *Weaving.* A shuttle-race.

1839 URE *Dict. Arts* 1285 The weaver..sheds the warp.. and opens a pathway or race-course for the shuttle to traverse the middle of the warp.

3. A water-way, mill-race.

1841 BREES *Gloss. Civil Eng.* 192 *Race*, or *Race Course*, the cut or canal along which the water is conveyed to and from a water-wheel.

4. *Building.* ? A string-course.

1883 MARGERISON *Calverley Registers* II. 23 The old race-course,..seen on the tower wall inside the church.

†**raced**, *ppl. a. Obs. rare.* [f. RACE *v.*[3] 1 + -ED[1].] Scratched; cut, slashed.

1576 BAKER *Jewell of Health* 8 b, A wyer wreathed rounde ..caused the Glasse..to cracke at the same raced place. **1600** SURFLET *Countrie Farme* v. xxii. 722 Many raced and checkered draughts, after the manner of small squares. **1602** SHAKS. *Ham.* III. ii. 288 With two Prouinciall Roses on my rac'd Shooes.

ˈrace-day. [f. RACE *sb.*[1]] The day on which a race or set of races is held.

1620 in *Maitland Club Misc.* I. 198 The horse..salbe obleist to be present..befoir the said raice day. **1680** COTTON *Compl. Gamester* xxxv. (ed. 2) 147 Saddle your Horse on the Race-day in the stable. **1838** *Civil Eng. & Arch. Jrnl.* I. 263/2 The numbers of persons conveyed by this railway..during three of the race days. **1866** 'ARGONAUT' *Rowing & Training* 51 He cannot look after his boat too much or too carefully, especially on a race-day.

ˈracehorse. Also race-horse. [f. RACE *sb.*[1] + HORSE.]

1. a. A horse bred or kept for racing.

a **1626** MIDDLETON *Wom. beware Wom.* III. ii, I will allow you..Your race-horses. **1657** R. LIGON *Barbadoes* (1673) 105 Another pleasure, the better sort of the people of England take delight in,..is Race-Horses. **1754** *Ess. Manning Fleet* 42 A Race Horse is..generally computed to stand his Owner in 100l. a Year. **1797** *Encycl. Brit.* (ed. 3) XV. 774/2 Race-horses have been for some time an object of taxation. **1859** DARWIN *Orig. Spec.* i. 26 English racehorses have come to surpass in fleetness and size the parent Arabs. **1878** SMILES *Robt. Dick.* v. 41 With the speed of a race-horse.

attrib. **1839** DICKENS *Let.* 25 Nov. (1965) I. 605 Barnaby moves—not at racehorse speed. **1868** H. WOODRUFF *Trotting Horse* ii. 47, I do not undertake to disparage the method pursued by the race-horse men. **1870** *Regul. Rlwy. Clearing-house* §298 The charges for Race Horses conveyed in Race Horse Vans. **1962** D. FRANCIS *Dead Cert* iii. 27 Pete Gregory, racehorse trainer. **1973** *N.Y. Law Jrnl.* 1 Aug. 11/6 An arrest of other persons..who were involved in 'racehorse policy' gambling activities.

b. *pl.* A gambling game in which small models of horses are used.

1853 LD. MALMESBURY *Mem.* (1884) I. 414 We played at race-horses after dinner.

2. A logger-head or steamer duck.

1773 HAWKESWORTH *Voy.* I. 406 Other Indians..brought with them some of the birds called Race-horses. **1777** G. FORSTER *Voy. round World* II. 520 Five large ducks of the short-winged sort, which our sailors called race-horses. **1845** DARWIN *Voy. Nat.* ix. (1873) 200 These ducks were called, from their extraordinary manner of paddling or splashing upon the water, race-horses.

3. *transf.* and *fig.* Anything racy, sleek, or speedy. Also *attrib.*

1845 W. G. SIMMS *Wigwam & Cabin* 1st Ser. 32 He had the sanguine, the race-horse temperament. **1903** [see *monthly ship* s.v. MONTHLY *a.* 4]. **1953** K. TENNANT *Joyful Condemned* xviii. 164 He sat rolling a very thin cigarette, known as a 'racehorse'. **1974** *State* (Columbia, S. Carolina) 15 Feb. 5-B/2 Freshman flash Adrian Dantley triggered a racehorse offense for Notre Dame with 27 points. **1978** *English Jrnl.* Dec. 72/1 What Charles Cooper refers to as 'race-horse studies'..often compared tactics for forcing students through the hoops handed down from the textbook writers.

4. racehorse lizard, a small Australian lizard, *Amphibolurus caudicinctus*, the ring-tailed dragon.

1937 *Discovery* May 137/1 The Racehorse or Cycling Lizard..runs at an incredible speed. *Ibid.*, Place a Racehorse Lizard on a pink handkerchief and it will quickly assume that colour. **1978** O. WHITE *Silent Reach* iv. 50 The little racehorse lizards skittering away through the spinifex with their tails up.

Hence **ˈrace-horsing** *vbl. sb.* and *ppl. a.*

1745 H. WALPOLE *Lett.* (1846) II. 69 A silly race-horsing boy. **1894** *Westm. Gaz.* 7 June 2/3 Preferring supreme race-horsing to the supreme political office which he holds.

race-knife. [f. RACE *v.*[3]] A cutting tool with a bent lip used for marking on timber, etc.; a race-tool. Also *ellipt.*

1875 in KNIGHT *Dict. Mech.* **1923** G. STURT *Wheelwright's Shop* vi. 30 The various points for cross-cutting the tree were scratched with a 'race'—a sort of knife with point turned back and sharpened at the bend for this especial purpose. **1964** H. HODGES *Artifacts* vii. 109 A row of wedge-pits or triangular slots was cut with an axe-shaped tool (race, gad or jad). **1969** E. H. PINTO *Treen* 401 The saddler's race or race knife,..used for marking leather, is the same tool that is also used by coopers, lumbermen, and carpenters to mark or scribe logs or timber sections, or to register tallies.

racemate (ˈræsɪmət). *Chem.* [f. RACEM-IC + -ATE[4].] **a.** A salt of racemic acid. Hence **ˈracemated** *a.*, containing a proportion of racemic acid.

1835 *Rec. Gen. Sci.* II. 101, 3.20 grs. of neutral racemate of lead. **1838** T. THOMSON *Chem. Org. Bodies* 68 Some of the principal tartrates and racemates. *Ibid.* 74 Racemated suboxide of mercury. **1857** W. A. MILLER *Elem. Chem.* III. 333 The racemate of lime is soluble in hydrochloric acid. **1868** WATTS *Dict. Chem.* V. 37 Alkaline racemates form a green precipitate with cupric salts.

b. A racemic (sense b) form of a compound.

1907 *Jrnl. Chem. Soc.* XCI. I. 906 In the case of substances known only in the liquid state, no general method has as yet been obtained to establish in a sufficiently convincing manner the existence of liquid racemates. **1936** *Discovery* Nov. 341/2 A solution of the racemic form (or racemate as it is sometimes called) is treated with the active form of a Base ..obtained from Nature. **1953** *Jrnl. Amer. Chem. Soc.* LXXV. 4587/2 The possibility of strong *intra*molecular hydrogen bonding in the case of α-phenethyl phthalate would offer an alternative explanation for the similarity in the spectra of the enantiomorphs and racemate. **1973** C. H. SNYDER *Introd. Mod. Org. Chem.* viii. 129 Since attack by bromide ion is equally likely at either carbon, the product is a racemate. **1973** D. WHITTAKER *Stereochem. & Mechanism* i. 8 Racemates..often have different melting points from the optical isomers.

†raceˈmation. *Obs.* [ad. late L. *racēmātiōn-em* (Tertull.), f. *racēmus* RACEME.]

1. The gleaning or gathering of grapes.

1623 in COCKERAM. **1656** in BLOUNT [citing *Hist. K. Chas.* = quot. 1654 in 2 b]. **1685** BURNET *Life Bp. Bedell* 220 Some curious Instruments out of Italy for Racemation, Engrafting, and Inoculating.

2. *concr.* **a.** A small number or quantity still remaining, as grapes to be gleaned; also, what is gleaned, gleanings.

1650 FULLER *Pisgah* I. ix. 31 He suffered a small racemation to remain, still preserving..the solemn Jury of the twelve Tribes. **1655** —— *Hist. Camb.* 5 Yet a racemation at least of Scholars..remained in Cambridge. **1660** GAUDEN *Brownrig* 4 His racemation, or after-gatherings [would be] beyond their proudest Vintages.

b. A collection or cluster (of things or persons).

a **1641** BP. MOUNTAGU *Acts & Mon.* (1642) 389 Meere Racemations, or Collections from the Writings of elder Fathers then himselfe. **1646** SIR T. BROWNE *Pseud. Ep.* III. xxviii. (1686) 147 The whole racemation or cluster of Eggs. **1654** H. L'ESTRANGE *Chas. I* (1655) 115 Such a racemation and cluster of abominations, as were never heard of before.

raceme (rəˈsiːm). *Bot.* [ad. L. *racēm-us* a cluster of grapes: cf. F. *racème.*] A simple inflorescence in which the flowers are arranged on short, nearly equal, lateral pedicels, at equal distances on an elongated axis.

compound raceme, one having the lower pedicels developed into secondary racemes.

1785 MARTYN tr. *Rousseau's Botany* xxiii. (1794) 321 The flowers also grow in a raceme. **1835** KIRBY *Hab. & Inst. Anim.* I. App. 352 Each germ looks like what botanists call a raceme of bell-shaped flowers. **1857** HENFREY *Bot.* §127 The raceme differs only from the spike in having the flowers distinctly stalked. **1880** C. R. MARKHAM *Peruv. Bark* 293 The *Berberis Mahonia*, with its..long slender racemes of yellow flowers.

Hence **raˈcemed** *a.*, disposed in racemes.

1830 LINDLEY *Nat. Syst. Bot.* 292 Flowers..arranged in a spiked, racemed, or panicled manner. **1870** HOOKER *Stud. Flora* 225 Flowers racemed drooping..Hare-bell.

racemic (rəˈsɛmɪk, rəˈsiːmɪk), *a. Chem.* [f. as prec., ad. F. (*acide*) *racémique* (printed *racenique*) (J. L. Gay-Lussac *Cours de Chimie* (1828) XXIV. 23).] **a.** Derived from grapes or grape-juice.

racemic acid, an acid existing in certain tartars, isomeric with tartaric acid, but differing from it in several respects, esp. in its optical properties. (Discovered by Kestner in 1822, and also called *paratartaric acid.*) ***racemic camphor***, a product of the oxidation of borneol. ***racemic ethers***, the acid racemates of ethyl and methyl (Watts 1868).

1835 *Rec. Gen. Sci.* II. 97 The term racemic acid given by the French is preferable. **1838** T. THOMSON *Chem. Org. Bodies* 66 The term *racemic acid*, given it by M. Gay-Lussac in 1828. **1857** W. A. MILLER *Elem. Chem.* III. 333 The ordinary salts of racemic acid occur in symmetrical crystals. **1876** tr. *Schützenberger's Ferment.* 7 It might be thought that ..it resulted, like racemic acid, from the union of two active but opposed molecules. **1894** MORLEY & MUIR *Watts' Dict. Chem.* I. 672/2 The 'racemic' camphor, bromo-camphor, and camphoric acid were also prepared by mixture.

b. Composed of dextro- and lævorotatory isomers of a compound in equal molecular proportions, and therefore optically inactive.

1892 *Jrnl. Chem. Soc.* LXII. II. 822 The fact that the racemic modification of gulolactone cannot be obtained by crystallisation from water is of general interest, but not without analogy. **1894** G. M'GOWAN tr. *Bernthsen's Text-bk. Org. Chem.* (ed. 2) 39 Optically inactive modifications, which result like racemic acid from the conjunction of two active components, are termed 'racemic' modifications. **1926** H. G. RULE tr. *J. Schmidt's Text-bk. Org. Chem.* 37 In a few instances it is possible, by allowing a solution of the racemic mixture to crystallise under certain conditions, to obtain the two enantiomorphs depositing individually. **1947** *Endeavour* VI. 97/2 Pasteur not only showed that the effect on polarized light was due to asymmetry of molecular architecture, but devised methods of resolving racemic mixtures. **1964** N. G. CLARK *Mod. Org. Chem.* iii. 34 The racemic modification of a substance is sometimes said to be 'externally compensated' because its optical inactivity is due to the balancing of two equal and opposite rotations which do not occur within the same molecule. **1971** *Sci. Amer.* May 6/1 L-Leucine has a bitter taste, D-leucine has a sweet taste and the racemic mixture (both) is tasteless.

Hence **†ˈracemism**, the state of existing in a racemic form; **†ˈracemoid** *a.* = RACEMIC *a.* b.

1896 *Proc. Chem. Soc.* 23 Apr. 97 The ethereal salts.. were examined for racemoid compounds, but the quantity found was not sufficient to account for the low activity. **1897** *Jrnl. Chem. Soc.* LXXI. 990 Notwithstanding these marked differences, which may be accepted as conclusive evidence of racemism, this modification of the inactive acid has the same melting point as the active compound. **1902** *Proc. Chem. Soc.* XVIII. 198 Amygdalic acid is racemoid with respect to its asymmetric carbon atom. **1904** *Science* 5 Aug. 178/2 In the cases of some double nuclei (as the camphor group) racemism appears to be impossible, owing to the peculiar molecular structure.

racemiferous (ræsɪˈmɪfərəs), *a. rare.* [f. L. *racēmifer* cluster-bearing (f. *racēm-us* RACEME) + -OUS: see -FEROUS.] Bearing racemes or clusters.

1656 in BLOUNT *Glossogr.* [Hence in Bailey, Johnson, etc.] **1813** J. FORBES *Oriental Mem.* III. 76 A twig of the racemiferous fig tree. **1819** H. BUSK *Banquet* I. 250 The vine its racemiferous branches spread.

raˈcemiform, *a.* [f. L. *racēm-us* + -(I)FORM.] Having the form of a raceme (*Cent. Dict.* 1891).

racemization (ˌræsəmaɪˈzeɪʃən). *Chem.* [f. RACEMIC *a.* + -IZATION.] Conversion of an optically active substance into a racemic form.

1895 A. EILOART in *Sci. Progress* III. 503 If the temperature of racemisation[2] lies below the ordinary temperature, the difficulty of separating the active isomers is accounted for. [*Note*] [2] This term is used to indicate the formation of the inactive aggregate from two isomers of opposite activity. **1927** ARNALL & HODGES *Theoret. Org. Chem.* II. vi. 59 Pinene and limonene undergo racemisation on simple heating. **1950** R. C. FUSON *Adv. Org. Chem.* vi. 111 When L-2 iodoöctane is treated with sodium iodide in acetone solution..racemization occurs. **1966** PHILLIPS & WILLIAMS *Inorg. Chem.* II. xxix. 455 The complexes $[Cr(C_2O_4)_3]^{3-}$ and $[Co(C_2O_4)_3]^{3-}$ will not exchange oxalate with radioactive oxalate in aqueous solution under conditions in which complete racemization takes place. **1975** *Kingston* (Ontario) *Whig-Standard* 5 Sept. 7/5 The ages were obtained by the so-called racemization method. This records the extent to which molecules of aspartic acid in a specimen have altered their configuration from the form that occurs in living bones to its mirror image.

racemize (ˈræsəmaɪz), *v. Chem.* [f. as prec. + -IZE.] **a.** *trans.* To convert (an optically active substance) into a racemic form. **b.** *intr.* To undergo conversion to a racemic form.

1896 [implied in RACEMIZED *ppl. a.* below]. **1902** *Proc. Chem. Soc.* XVIII. 198 The author concludes that in alkaline solution the glucoside is racemized by the catalytic action of the hydroxyl ions. **1913** *Jrnl. Chem. Soc.* CIII. 607 The hydrogen *d.* camphorate..racemises within twenty hours of making up the aqueous solution. **1938** G. H. RICHTER *Textbk. Org. Chem.* xvii. 335 Many natural products which occur only as one optical antipode may be racemized and resolved into both optical antipodes. **1965** G. HALLAS *Org. Stereochem.* ii. 35 Several compounds are known to racemize via non-ionic planar intermediates. **1971** *Nature* 12 Mar. 107/1 In fossil material..the free or bound amino-acids slowly racemize. **1976** LOWRY & RICHARDSON *Mechanism & Theory Org. Chem.* v. 218 The excess of rate of loss of optical activity..over rate of product formation.. means that some process racemizes the substrate more rapidly than the substrate can form products.

Hence **ˈracemized** *ppl. a.*, **ˈracemizing** *vbl. sb.*

1896 *Proc. Chem. Soc.* 23 Apr. 97 Examining..for the presence of racemised salt by converting it into zinc lactate. **1904** *Jrnl. Chem. Soc.* LXXXV. 1253 The racemising effect of the alkali during hydrolysis of the esters. **1940** *Biochem. Jrnl.* XXXIV. 300 Small amounts of partially racemized aspartic acid, as well as of glutamic acid, can be isolated from both normal and malignant tissue protein material. **1951** C. R. NOLLER *Textbk. Org. Chem.* xvii. 273 The racemizing action of halide ion was known to Kekulé in 1864. **1972** S. J. WEININGER *Contemp. Org. Chem.* vii. 158, 2-Octyl bromide in aqueous ethanol forms, among other products, 2-octanol that is partly racemized.

racemo- (rəˈsiːməʊ), used as combining form of L. *racēmus* RACEME in certain chemical terms, with the sense of 'containing a proportion of racemic acid', as ***racemo-carbonate, -methylate, -vinate***; ***racemo-carbonic, -oxalic, -vinic*** adjs.

1838 T. THOMSON *Chem. Org. Bodies* 177 M. Guerin-Varry discovered racemovinic acid. *Ibid.* 178 Racemovinate of potash. *Ibid.* 184 Racemomethylate of potash. **1868** WATTS *Dict. Chem.* V. 40 The ethylic racemo-carbonate may be converted by heating with carbonate of potash. *Ibid.*, Racemocarbonic acid is tribasic.

racemose (ˈræsɪməʊs), *a.* [ad. L. *racēmōs-us* clustering, f. *racēm-us* RACEME: see -OSE.]

1. *Bot.* **a.** Of flowers: Arranged in racemes. **b.** Of an inflorescence or a vegetable growth generally: Having the form of a raceme.

1698 J. PETIVER in *Phil. Trans.* XX. 315 It has a racemose Flower. **1806** GALPINE *Brit. Bot.* 419 Stem cross-branching, ..Fl. racemose. **1860** TYAS *Wild Fl.* 176 A lengthened racemose spike of many closely crowded flowers. **1882** VINES *Sachs' Bot.* 179 A racemose system occurs when the monopodial mother-shoot continues to develope more strongly than all the lateral shoots, and when the lateral shoots of each successive order behave in the same manner in respect to their mother-shoot.

2. *Anat.* Having the form of, arranged as, a cluster (esp. as an epithet of compound glands).

1835-6 TODD *Cycl. Anat.* I. 559/1 The ovisacs are racemose or connected in bunches. **1841-71** T. R. JONES *Anim. Kingd.* (ed. 4) 785 The viscus assumes a distinctly racemose appearance. **1860** SIR H. THOMPSON *Dis. of Prostate* (1868) 34 They are not crowded upon it so as to form a compact mass, as in other racemose glands.

Hence **ˈracemosely** *adv.*, in a racemose manner.

1840 PAXTON *Bot. Dict.*, *Racemosely-corymbose.*

racemous (ˈræsɪməs), *a. Bot. rare.* [f. as prec.: see -OUS.] = prec. 1. Hence **ˈracemously** *adv.*, in the manner of a raceme.

1657 TOMLINSON *Renou's Disp.* 279 Their fruits small, round, and racemously coherent. **1806** J. GALPINE *Brit. Bot.* 181 *Berberis*, Fl. racemous. **1821** W. P. C. BARTON *Flora N. Amer.* I. 79 In this case, the floriferous ramuli must be considered as racemous branches.

racemule (ˈræsɪmjuːl). *Bot.* [ad. L. type **racēmul-us*, dim. of *racēm-us*: see RACEME and -ULE.] A small raceme (Ogilvie 1882).

raˈcemulose, *a. Bot.* [See prec. and -OSE.] Resembling a racemule; somewhat racemose.

1864 WEBSTER cites HENSLOW.

racer[1] (ˈreɪsə(r)). [f. RACE *v.*[1] + -ER[1].]

1. One who races or takes part in a race.

1649 LOVELACE *Poems* 30 Flye on, flye on swift Racer. **1717** BERKELEY *Tour in Italy* 22 Jan. Wks. 1871 IV. 533 Two towers where the racers used to prepare themselves. **1743** BULKELEY & CUMMINS *Voy. S. Seas* 150 They rode backwards and forwards like Racers. **1818** KEATS *Endym.* II. 932 Some breathless racers, whose hopes poise Upon the last few steps. **1879** BROWNING *Pheidippides* 94 Henceforth be allowed thee release From the racer's toil.

fig. **1742** YOUNG *Nt. Th.* IX. 2388 Leave the racers of the world their own, Their feather, and their froth.

2. a. A race-horse.

1670 EVELYN *Diary* 22 July, The jockeys breathing their fine barbs and racers. **1719** D'URFEY *Pills* IV. 13 On Pads, Hawkers, Hunters, on Higlers and Racers. **1768** R. WALL (*title*) A Dissertation on breeding Horses,..an attempt to promote thereby the Breed of Racers and Horses in general. **1833** MARRYAT *P. Simple* (1863) 211 As much difference.. as there is between a racer and a cart-horse. **1887** MISS BRADDON *Like & Unlike* i, He hasn't a racer's head.

b. Any animal having great speed, or fit for racing; *spec.* a North American snake belonging to the genera *Coluber* or *Masticophis*, esp. a variety of *C. constrictor*, and as the name of a sand-crab, and of some varieties of American lake-trout.

1699 DORSET *To Mr. E. Howard* 22 All the swift-finn'd Racers of the Flood. **1711** SHAFTESB. *Charac.* (1737) II. 303 'Tis thus the aerial racers are able to perform so rapid and strong a motion. **1823** E. JAMES *Acct. Exploring Exped. Pittsburgh to Rocky Mts.* I. 267 *Coluber constrictor*—Racer. **1864–5** WOOD *Homes without Hands* 90 Another Land Crab, which..is popularly called the Racer,..is a native of Ceylon. **1866** J. C. GREGG *Life in Army* 18 This species, were called racers on account of their great speed. **1884** GOODE *Nat. Hist. Usef. Aquatic Anim.* 488 Two varieties [of lake-trout] are also recognized, one..known as 'Reef Trout', or when very large are called 'Racers'. **1898** *Westm. Gaz.* 25 Oct. 5/1 The 'carrier' pigeon has become a show bird; so have the 'Antwerp', which succeeded it as a racer, and the 'homer'. **1900** *Ann. Rep. Bd. Regents Smithsonian Inst. 1898* 794 The *Zamenis constrictor* is the 'black snake' of the East and the 'blue' and 'green racer' of the West. **1926** J. K. STRECKER in J. F. Dobie *Rainbow in Morning* 76 W. S. Blatchley..speaker of many 'lies' about the blue racer, or blacksnake. **1946** J. STUART *Tales from Plum Grove Hills* 85 They slid to the foot of the mountain like racer snakes before a new-ground fire. **1954** R. C. STEBBINS *Amphibians & Reptiles Western N. Amer.* 373/2 When foraging, like most racers, the head and neck are held well above the ground. **1969** A. BELLAIRS *Life of Reptiles* I. iii. 103 Even the fastest snakes such as the North American racers and whip-snakes ..cannot exceed more than about four miles an hour.

3. a. Anything used for racing, as a bicycle, yacht, etc.; anything capable of great speed.

1793 COWPER *A Tale* 30 A ship!.. This racer of the sea. **1885** *Cyclist* 19 Aug. 1107/1 Bicycles... Rudge racer, only ridden in ten races. **1895** *Westm. Gaz.* 15 Aug. 3/2 No train ..is timed to do the journey quicker than the above racers. **1903** *Sci. Amer.* 8 Aug. 96/1 Barney Oldfield, on the Ford-Cooper racer..has been steadily lowering track records. **1923** [see CHIRPILY *adv.*]. **1935** A. J. CRONIN *Stars look Down* III. viii. 553 They swooped and soared and dived from giddy heights on the Giant Racer until the whole glittering Fun Fair spun around them in one glorious daze. **1974** D. RAMSAY *No Cause to Kill* II. 158, I wanted a bicycle, and she ran right out and bought me an English racer. **1978** *Dumfries Courier* 20 Oct. 11/1 The newcomers range from fairly basic family saloons to the exotic Mazda RX7 and BMW's M1 sports racer.

b. *Mech.* A part of a machine having an unusually rapid motion.

1875 KNIGHT *Dict. Mech.* 355/2 When the braid is to be laid up flat,..each racer, as the spindle holders are called, makes a single course. **1882** *Standard* 23 Aug. 2/4 The 'racer', which is a half circle, and attached to the machinery, came down with terrific force.

4. *Gunnery.* A rail, forming a horizontal arc, on which the carriage or traversing-platform of a gun is moved.

1861 *Times* 30 May, The carriages work on raised racers —that is, semi-circular lines of metal raised about 1½ inch above the terre-pleine. **1879** *Man. Artill. Exerc.* 255 The racer is secured to the bedding-plate by steel bolts. **1883** NARES *Constr. Ironclad* 9 If a broadside ship, racers and gun ports are fitted.

5. An article of clothing designed in a racing style; *spec.* (*pl.*) a pair of swimming trunks (*Austral.* and *N.Z.*).

1969 *New Yorker* 20 Sept. 149/2 (Advt.), Baby him with our soft, zip-front creepers... Racer in medium blue. **1971** *Telegraph* (Brisbane) 21 Sept. 18/1 (Advt.), Ash boys racers in bright florals..and plain colours. **1977** *N.Z. Herald* 8 Jan. 2–4/8 (Advt.), Speedo togs in quick-drying Bri-nylon. Racers, boys..$4.75.

racer[2] ('reɪsə(r)). *rare.* [f. RACE *v.*[3]]

†**1.** A scalpel, RAZOR *sb. Obs. rare*[−0].

1570 LEVINS *Manip.* 72 A racer, *scalprum.*

2. *Hort.* (See quot.)

1819 REES *Cycl.* XXIX, *Racer*, in Gardening, a name applied to a sort of sward-cutter, or cutting implement, used in racing out or cutting through the surface of grass sward.

race-tool. [f. RACE *v.*[3]] = RACE-KNIFE.

1867 [see RACE *v.*[3] 1.].

raceway ('reɪsweɪ). Chiefly *U.S.* [f. RACE *sb.*[1]]

1. a. A passage or channel for water; the bed of a canal, etc. Cf. RACE *sb.*[1] 8 c.

1828 in S. Jenkins *Story of Bronx* (1912) ix. 199 Fourteen mill sites, each fifty by one hundred feet, were mapped out along the raceways. **1837** *Knickerbocker* IX. 254, I was jerked out with great spite, and, with an imprecation, thrown into the raceway. **1868** *Rep. U.S. Commissioners Agric.* (1869) 335 The sand and gravel which covers the bottom of the raceway. **1877** RAYMOND *Statist. Mines & Mining* 292 From No. 1 the water is carried through a raceway into tank No. 2.

transf. **1873** LOWELL *Poems, Orient Apol.* xvii, A mere Auricular canal or raceway to be fed..From their vast heads of milk-and-water-power.

b. An artificial channel of running water for the rearing of fish.

1897 *Man. Fish Culture* (U.S. Comm. Fish & Fisheries) 74 The object of these boards is to form four avenues leading to the raceway, so that one or two pugnacious fish can not command the approach and keep back spawning fish inclined to enter. **1913** W. E. MEEHAN *Fish Culture* vii. 104 There has been a tendency in recent years for fish-culturists to abandon raceways. **1953** H. S. DAVIS *Culture & Dis. Game Fish* ii. 21 Raceways for holding small fingerlings are usually constructed of concrete. **1972** *Aquaculture* I. 229 Water requirements for 'raceway' production of turbot would be very low compared with the requirements in current trout farming practice. **1976** *San Antonio* (Texas) *Express* 23 Sept. 8-G/1 The facility includes a laboratory, office building, 20 ponds, eight concrete raceways and two wells.

2. A course or passage for a shuttle. Also, a groove in a type-setting machine along which types are moved; also, a groove in which ball-bearings run.

1875 KNIGHT *Dict. Mech.* 1355/2 s.v. *Loom*, A roller imparting a vibratory motion to the lay, in which is a raceway for the shuttle. **1898** *Inland Printer* Nov. 178/1 This machine will select the type, place them in a raceway and move them along until a line is set up. **1946** *Richmond* (Va.) *Times-Dispatch* 8 Dec. IV. 6-D/1 The balls are held in place by two concentric steel rings. They run in grooves or 'raceways' cut in the rings. A retainer or separator is usually inserted to keep them from rubbing against each other.

3. A metal pipe or plastic tube enclosing electrical wires; piping or tubing so used.

1897 F. C. MOORE *How to Build* iv. 58 Conduits or raceways for carrying wires through the house should be of iron or other metal. **1964** R. F. FICCHI *Electrical Interference* ix. 168 Metal boxes, cabinets and fittings, or noncurrent-carrying metal parts of other fixed equipment, if metallically connected to grounded cable armor or metal raceway, are considered grounded by such connections. **1976** LIEBERMAN & RHODES *Compl. CB Handbk.* v. 105 Stick the snake through the 'raceway' (the space in which the tail-light wires run through the trunk).

4. A track or circuit on which harness races, etc., take place; a racecourse. Also *attrib.*

1936 *Sun* (Baltimore) 19 Oct 12/6 Topping..had purchased the Maserati car which Philippe Etancelin, of France, drove in the Roosevelt raceway test. **1942** *Ibid.* 24 Aug. 11/4 Saratoga Raceway's new harness racing venture. **1958** *Washington Post* 30 Aug. A12/5 Raceway officials told the commission the plant would be ready for night racing by next March 1. **1968** *Globe & Mail* (Toronto) 17 Feb. 43 (*heading*) Greenwood Raceway. Saturday, Feb. 17. **1979** *Beautiful Brit. Columbia* Winter 33 The fans..turning to the racing form for the next race in to-night's harness racing card at Cloverdale Raceway.

rachch, obs. f. RATCH *v.*

rache, ratch (rætʃ), *sb.*[1] *Obs.* exc. *arch.* Forms: 3–6 **racch-**, (5 **rachch-**), 4–5 **rach**, 4–7, 9 **rache**; 5–6 **ratch-**, 7–8 **ratch**. [OE. *ræcc*, related to ON. *rakki* dog.] A hunting-dog which pursues its prey by scent.

After *c* 1530 only in Sc. use: cf. quot. 1576.

c **1000** *Ags. Voc.* in Wr.-Wülcker 276/4 *Molosus*, roþhund. *Unfer*, grīȝhund. *Bruccus*, ræcc. *c* **1200** ORMIN 13505 Rihht alls an hunnte takeþþ der Wiþþ hise ȝæpe racchess. *c* **1275** *Serving Christ* 71 in *O.E. Misc.* 92 þe ronke racches þat ruskit þe ron. **1390** GOWER *Conf.* II. 274 Brocours that renne aboute Lich unto racches in a route. **1433** LYDG. *St. Edmund* II. 881 With blast of hornys, with rachchis & with houndys. *c* **1440** *Promp. Parv.* 422/1 Ratche, howynde, *odorinsecus*. **1526** SKELTON *Magnyf.* 592 Here is a leysshe of ratches to renne a hare. *c* **1550** *Satir. Poems Reform.* xviii. 23 Throw out this Realme lyke Ratches se ȝe range. **1576** FLEMING tr. *Caius' Eng. Dogges* (1880) 7 Albeit some of this sort in English be called Brache, in Scottishe Rache, the cause hereof resteth in the shee sex and not in the generall kinde. [**1602** *2nd Pt. Return fr. Parnass.* II. v. 873 Small Ladies puppies, raches, and Bastards.] *a* **1733** RAMSAY *Highland Lassie* iv, With cockit gun and ratches tenty, To drive the deer out of their den. **1829** SCOTT *Demonol.* iv. 131 Three raches, or hounds of scent, followed her closely. **1875** J. VEITCH *Tweed* 56 By her side seven raches running free.

transf. **1597** J. MELVILL *Diary* (1842) 428 Craftie men.. Wha houndit furthe these ratches under night.

Comb. **1732** MACFARLANE *Geneal. Coll.* (1900) 306 Three Wolves Heads erased supported by two Ratch hounds.

Hence †**ratchet** (? after *brachet* from BRACH).

1563 BECON *Acts Christ & Antichr.* Wks. III. 400 Antichrist hunteth the wilde dere..with houndes and ratchettes ronning.

rache, ratch (reɪtʃ, rætʃ), *sb.*[2] *Obs.* exc. *dial.* Forms: 6 **ratche**, 6–8 **rache**, 8 **raich**, 7, 9 **rach**, 9 *dial.* **raitch, ratch.** See also REACH. [Of obscure etym.; cf. RACE *sb.*[5] and RAKE *sb.*[2]] A (white) line or streak down a horse's face.

1523 FITZHERB. *Husb.* (1598) §68 Of markes..a white snyp, or a white rache is good. *Ibid.*, A blacke Horse, so he haue white feet, white ratche, and white feather. **1558** *Wills & Inv. N.C.* (Surtees 1835) 173 My blacke geldinge hauing a white Rache in his forehead. **1610** MARKHAM *Masterp.* I. x. 27 A blacke with white starre, white rache or white foote. **1689** *N. Riding Rec.* VII. 99 One bay guelding with..a white rache down his face. **1725** *Lond. Gaz.* No. 6403/3 A black Filly,..with a Raich down her face. **1811** *Sporting Mag.* XXXVII. 135 He is a good chesnut, no white, except a rach down his face. **1833** *New Sporting Mag.* V. 278/2 A dingy looking bay filly, with a great white ratch down her face. **1855** ROBINSON *Whitby Gloss.*, *Raitch*, a white line down a horse's face.

†**rache**, *v.*[1] *Obs. rare.* [Of obscure origin.] *intr.* and *refl.* ? To hasten, make ready in haste.

a **1400–50** *Alexander* 1239 Meliager with hys men.. rachen with þair route & ryden bott a while. *Ibid.* 2031 Alexander..Rachez hym radly to ride.

†**rache**, *v.*[2] *Obs.*[−1] [a. OF. *racher*, aphetic f. *arracher* ARRACHE.] *trans.* To pull off.

c **1400** *Laud Troy Bk.* 5689 His hed was bare, his helme was rached.

rache, obs. f. REACH *v.*

racheat, obs. f. RECHEAT.

rachel (rə'ʃɛl). Also **Rachel**. [f. *Rachel*, the stage-name of Elisa Félix (1820–58), French actress.] A light, tannish colour (used orig. and chiefly of face-powder). Also *attrib.* or as *adj.*

1887 *Illustr. London News* 6 Aug. 163/1 (Advt.), Toilet powder... In three tints: Blanche, for fair skins; Naturelle, for darker complexions; and Rachel, for use by artificial light. **1907** [see PAPIER]. **1907**, **1927–8** [see NATURELLE *a.*]. **1936** M. KENNEDY *Together & Apart* IV. 320 'If you must use powder at your age, do at least find a more becoming shade.'.. 'It's not dead white,' muttered Elisa furiously. 'It's Rachel.' **1970** 'D. HALLIDAY' *Dolly & Cookie Bird* xii. 195 She has facial plates like a rachel armadillo.

rachen, var. *rechen* RECHE.

rachet, var. RATCHET; obs. f. ROCHET.

rachetic, irreg. var. RACHITIC.

rachi- ('reɪkɪ), **rachio-** ('reɪkɪəʊ), comb. forms of RACHIS, used in some (chiefly recent) terms of *Anat.* and *Path.* relating to the spine or vertebral column. (Also written **rha-**: see below and RACHIS, etc.) **rachi'agra** (see RACHISAGRA). **rachi'algia** [Gr. -αλγία pain], pain in or due to the spine; painter's colic; hence **rachi'algic** *a.* **rachial'gitis** [see -ITIS], inflammation of the spinal chord, myelitis (Dunglison 1893). **rachi'glossate** *a.* [Gr. γλῶσσα tongue], of certain mollusca: having a median row of teeth on the odontophore (*Cent. Dict.* 1891). **'rachiodont** *a.* [Gr. ὀδοντ- tooth], of a genus of serpents (*Rachiodon*): having vertebral processes which penetrate the gullet and serve as teeth (*Cassell's Encycl. Dict.* 1887). **ˌrachi(o)pa'ralysis**, paralysis of the spine (Craig 1848). **'rachiotome** [Gr. -τόμος cutting], a dissecting instrument for cutting open the spinal canal (Knight *Dict. Mech.* 1875). **rachi'otomy** [Gr. -τομία cutting], the operation of cutting into the spinal canal (Dunglison 1893). **ra'chischisis** (-skɪsɪs) [Gr. σχίσις cleavage] = MYELOCELE 1 b. **'rachitome**, (*a*) = *rachiotome* (Ogilvie 1882); (*b*) *Palæont.*, a labyrinthodont belonging to the suborder Rhachitomi; usu. written *rh-*. **ra'chitomous** *a.*, (*a*) of vertebræ: segmented, as in batrachians and other low vertebrate types; (*b*) having segmented vertebræ; usu. written *rh-*.

1811 HOOPER *Med. Dict.*, *Rachialgia. **1822–34** *Good's Stud. Med.* (ed. 4) II. 472 This disease was..a modification of rhachialgia. *Ibid.* I. 172 Without any *rhachialgic pains. **1890** BILLINGS *Med. Dict.* 427/2 *Rachischisis, congenital posterior fissure of spinal column, a form of spina bifida. **1900** *Boston Med. & Surg. Jrnl.* CXLIII. 458/2 (*heading*) A case of rhachischisis. **1901** T. M. ROTCH *Pediatrics* (ed. 3) v. 301 Rhachischisis is one of the principal forms of congenital defects of the spine. It is characterized by a deficiency of the vertebral arches either complete or partial. **1963** K. M. LAURENCE in A. P. Norman *Congenital Abnormalities in Infancy* ii. 26 Myelomeningocoeles, myelocystocoeles, hydromyelocoeles, and syringomyelocoeles, localized rachischisis and myelocoeles are all essentially the same lesion, and best regarded as myelocoeles. **1966** WRIGHT & SYMMERS *Systemic Path.* II. xxxiv. 1234/2 Spina Bifida... The severest and rarest form is rachischisis, in which the spinal canal is open to the exterior, either for a short distance or over its whole length. **1947** *Bull. Museum Compar. Zoöl. Harvard Coll.* XCIX. 103 In the skull roof [of *Edops*], a primitive character is the presence of a distinct intertemporal element, lost in characteristic *rhachitomes. **1964** *Jrnl. Animal Morphol. & Physiol.* XI. 7 The temnospondyls, forming the 'main line' of labyrinthodont evolution, began with Carboniferous types of primitive structure but with rhachitomous vertebrae, evolved in the later Carboniferous and Permian into typical rhachitomes, and eventually gave rise to stereospondylous forms. **1971** E. C. OLSON *Vertebr. Paleozool.* IV. iv. 591 In the Lower Carboniferous limestone of Scotland..is the Gilmerton ironstone from which a number of labyrinthodonts have come:..*Loxomma*, a rhachitome; and..an anthracosaur, *Crassigyrinus*. **1882** E. D. COPE in *Amer. Naturalist* XVI. 334 (*heading*) The *rhachitomous Stegocephali. **1884** —— in *Ibid.* XVIII. 30 Rachitomous vertebræ from the same locality are of larger size and resemble those of Eryops. **1887** E. D. COPE *Orig. Fittest* 317 The reptiles, in their primary representative order,..have been probably derived from the rhachitomous Batrachia. **1947** *Bull. Museum Compar. Zoöl. Harvard Coll.* XCIX. 102 The skull pattern is typically rhachitomous in key features, such as the firm fusion of cheeks and table. **1964** [see *rachitome* above]. **1971** E. C. OLSON *Vertebr. Paleozool.* IV. iv. 591 Although rhachitomous amphibians occur early, in the upper Mississippian, the limbs from this age have not been worked out.

rachial ('reɪkɪəl), *a.* [f. RACHI-S + -AL[1].] Characterized by a rachis.

1848 MACDONALD in *Proc. Zool. Soc.* 140 The Rachidian development..is the longest, and forms the Rachial type.

rachidian (rə'kɪdɪən), *a.* Also **rha-**. [f. *r(h)achid-*, assumed stem of Gr. ῥάχις RACHIS + -IAN. Cf. F. *rachidien.*] Of or pertaining to a rachis, chiefly in sense 2 b. So also **ra'chidial** *a.*

1848 [see RACHIAL]. **1851** WOODWARD *Mollusca* iv. 27 The rachidian teeth sometimes form a single series. **1866** R. TATE *Brit. Mollusks* iii. 51 Each transverse row consists of one median or rachidian tooth. **1880** MACDONALD in *Jrnl. Linn. Soc.* XV. 167 If the rhachidian series is suppressed.

rachiform ('reɪkɪfɔːm), *a. Bot.* [f. RACHI- + FORM.] Having the form of a rachis (1 a).

1866 J. SMITH *Ferns Brit. & For.* (1879) 274 Fertile segments rachiform, compound paniculate.

rachill, var. RATCHEL.

‖**rachilla** (rə'kɪlə). *Bot.* [mod.L. dim. of RACHIS.] (See quot. 1842.)

1842 BRANDE *Dict.*, *Rachilla*, a branch of inflorescence; the zigzag centre upon which the florets are arranged in the spikelets of grasses. **1881** BENTHAM in *Jrnl. Linn. Soc.* XVIII. 367 The rhachilla present, but not exceeding the glume.

‖**rachis** ('reɪkɪs). Also **rha-**. Pl. **rachides** ('reɪkɪdiːz). [mod.L., a. Gr. ῥάχις spine, ridge, rib (of a leaf), etc. The more precise spelling *rhachis* is chiefly confined to sense 2. The pl. *rachides* is erroneous, as the stem of ῥάχις is not ῥαχιδ- but ῥαχι-.]

1. *Bot.* **a.** The axis of an inflorescence in which flower-stalks occur at short intervals from each other, as in grasses.

1785 MARTYN *Rousseau's Bot.* xiii. (1794) 146 The teeth of the rachis or receptacle of the spike bearded. **1830** LINDLEY *Nat. Syst. Bot.* 258 Terminal flowers sessile upon a 2- or 3-branched rachis. **1861** S. THOMSON *Wild Fl.* II. (ed. 4) 132 The grass blossoms are arranged upon a central stem or rachis. **1875** BENNETT & DYER tr. *Sachs' Bot.* 544 The ebracteate flowers stand on the rachis of the inflorescence.

b. The axis of a pinnately compound leaf or frond, corresponding to the midrib of a simple leaf.

1832 LINDLEY *Introd. Bot.* I. ii. 107 The term rachis is applied by Willdenow and others..to the petiole and costa of Ferns. **1861** MISS PRATT *Flower. Pl.* VI. 139 The stalk [of fern] is often called the rachis, but strictly speaking, it is composed of two parts. That part which bears the green leaf is the rachis. **1880** C. & F. DARWIN *Movem. Pl.* 86 The rachis of the bracken fern..rises above ground under the form of an arch.

2. *Anat.* The vertebral column, or the primitive cord from which it develops.

1842 BRANDE *Dict.*, *Rachis*, a term applied by Illiger and other zoologists to the vertebral column of mammals and birds. **1878** BELL *Gegenbaur's Comp. Anat.* 428 The separation of the rachis into skull and vertebral column is not completely effected in Amphioxus.

b. The median part of the odontophore of a mollusc, resembling a series of vertebræ.

1851 WOODWARD *Mollusca* iv. 27 The tongue, or lingual ribbon, usually forms a triple band, of which the central part is called the rachis. **1866** TATE *Brit. Mollusks* iii. 50 The central area is called the rachis, and the teeth form usually a single series.

c. A cord of protoplasmic matter in the ovary of nematoid worms, round which ova are developed.

1877 HUXLEY *Anat. Inv. Anim.* xi. 640 An axile cord of protoplasmic substance—the rhachis—and peripheral masses, each..connected by a stalk with the rhachis.

3. *Ornith.* The stem or shaft of a feather, especially the part bearing the vexillum, as distinguished from the quill.

1874 COUES *Birds N.W.* 607 The central pair..form an angle of 45° with the rachis. *Ibid.* 616 Rhachides of the first two or three primaries pure white. **1893** NEWTON *Dict. Birds* 245 In *Casuarius* each primitive feather consists of a long and slender rhachis bearing two series of rami.

rachi'sagra. *Path.* [Irreg. f. Gr. ῥάχις RACHIS, after χειράγρα, ποδάγρα PODAGRA. Some recent medical dicts. also give *rachidagra* and (correctly) *rachiagra.*] Pain in the spine; spinal gout.

1753 in CHAMBERS *Cycl.* Supp.

rachitic (rə'kɪtɪk), *a.* Also **rh-**, and (irreg.) **-etic**. [f. RACHIT-IS + -IC. Cf. F. *rachitique.*]

a. Affected with rickets, rickety. **b.** Connected with, pertaining to, rickets.

1797 NICHOLSON *Jrnl. Nat. Phil.* I. 175 The nature of rachitic acid. *Ibid.* In general the bile is wanting in rachitic infants. **1822–34** *Good's Stud. Med.* (ed. 4) II. 486 A constitution naturally feeble and rachetic. **1855** *Household Wds.* 25 Aug. 89 Unfortunate little objects..with rachitic limbs. **1876** BRISTOWE *Th. & Pract. Med.* (1878) 919 The shape of the chest in rachitic children becomes remarkably modified.

transf. **1864** R. F. BURTON *Dahome* I. 25 The youngest, and the most rachitic of Great Britain's large..family of colonies.

‖**rachitis** (rə'kaɪtɪs). [mod.L., a. Gr. ῥαχῖτις (f. ῥάχις RACHIS + -ῖτις -ITIS), properly meaning 'inflammation of the spine', but adopted by Gleeson, 1650, in his work *De Rachitide* as a learned form of *rickets.*] **1.** = RICKETS.

1727–41 in CHAMBERS *Cycl.* **1799** UNDERWOOD *Treat. Dis. Childr.* (ed. 4) I. 339 It was named Rachitis, from the Greek, implying that the spina dorsi is particularly affected by it. **1830** R. KNOX *Béclard's Anat.* 241 The vertebral column presents this softening in a very marked degree in cases of rachitis. **1847–9** TODD *Cycl. Anat.* IV. 712/2 In rachitis, the bones may be bent in any direction. **1876** tr. *Wagner's Gen. Pathol.* (ed. 6) 14 Phthisis and rachitis, which usually last for years.

2. *Bot.* 'An abortion of the fruit or seed'.

1864 WEBSTER cites HENSLOW.

rachitogenic (rækɪtəʊ'dʒɛnɪk), *a.* [f. RACHIT(IS + -O + -GENIC.] Tending to cause rickets.

1932 *Biochem. Jrnl.* XXVI. 202 The rachitogenic property of Steenbock's diet is due to its high value for Ca/P together with its lack of vitamin D. **1976** *Lancet* 20 Nov. 1132/2 The rachitogenic activity of oatmeal.

Rachmaninovian (ˌræxmænɪ'nəʊvɪən), *a.* and *sb.* [f. the name of Sergei Vasilyevich *Rachmaninov* (1873–1943), Russian pianist and composer.] **A.** *adj.* Of or resembling the style or the works of Rachmaninov. **B.** *sb.* An admirer of Rachmaninov.

1958 *Times* 3 Nov. 14/4 In their recital..there was only one original composition, a Toccata by Murgatroyd Farrar, which made suitably Rachmaninovian noises. **1962** *Times* 5 July 15/1 A verbose Rachmaninovian Scherzo by John White. **1973** *Times* 27 July 15/4 Mr Previn drew the right pliable phrasing from the LSO without overdoing the succulence (like some older Rachmaninovians one could name). **1976** *Gramophone* May 1816/3 The Rachmaninovian flavour of 'Whitechapel'..making a delightful treasure of sound. **1977** *Ibid.* Nov. 874/1 What Rachmaninovians ought to be shouting for now, however, is a recording of the *Liturgy*, Op. 31.

Rachmanism ('rækmənɪz(ə)m). [f. the name of Peter *Rachman* (1919–62), a London landlord + -ISM.] Exploitation of slum tenants by unscrupulous landlords. Hence '**Rachman**, any such unscrupulous landlord. Also '**Rachmanite** *a.*, of or resembling a Rachman, and other nonce or occasional derivatives.

1963 H. WILSON in *Guardian* 23 July 2/3 The disease of Rachmanism is to buy controlled properties at low prices, and to use every means..to bring about evictions which..have the effect of decontrolling the property. **1963** *Daily Tel.* 23 July 10/2 (*Editorial*) Emotion appeared to get the better of precision in Mr. Harold Wilson's opening contribution to the Rachman debate yesterday... More powers..will not remove the basic conditions in which the Rachmans of this world can thrive. That can only be done by increasing the supply of housing space and bringing down rents. **1963** *Guardian* 7 Aug. 8/3 (*heading*) Rachmanship lives on. *Ibid.* 8/5 The sprawling, sordid acres of what has become known as Rachmanland. **1963** *Daily Tel.* 30 Aug. 19/3 Bringing Rachman-type racketeers to heel. *Ibid.* 22 Nov. 28/4 'Rachman-like' landlords illegally withheld deposits totalling more than £1,400. **1965** *Economist* 6 Mar. 976/2 The poorer tenants who have suffered most from Rachmanite and neo-Rachmanite intimidation. **1968** *Guardian* 13 Sept. 3/3 Rachmanism—harassment of unwanted tenants—has simply grown more subtle since the 1965 Rent Act. **1969** D. WIDGERY in Cockburn & Blackburn *Student Power* 137 The same crisis which forces council rents up and allows the domination of the Rachmans of Islington, Moss Side and Liverpool 9. **1973** C. MULLARD *Black Britain* II. iv. 46 Rachman-type landlords offered as little as they could for as much as they could get. **1973** *Times* 29 Dec. 11/4 Rachmanite landlords..make millions out of office blocks and luxury flats. **1975** *Times* 8 Jan. 15/3 On a fair rents basis..the transaction..would not be attractive to the speculative builder or the Rachman. **1977** *Jrnl. R. Soc. Arts* CXXV. 116/2 Recently, we have added to the problem by extending the area of control to include furnished tenancies. Mr. Tilbe of *Shelter* will no doubt tell you in two weeks time that this was necessary to prevent Rachmanism. **1981** *Times* 9 Feb. 17/5 The long-term tenant's legitimate need for protection against the Rachmanite landlord.

racht, obs. Sc. pa. t. of REACH, RECK.

rachter, obs. Sc. form of RAFTER *sb.*[1]

racial ('reɪʃɪəl, -ʃəl), *a.* [f. RACE *sb.*[2] + -IAL.] Belonging to, or characteristic of, race.

A word of considerable frequency in the 20th century. The examples that follow illustrate some of the more usual collocations.

1862 R. H. PATTERSON *Ess. Hist. & Art* 448 These racial diversities are reflected in the character of the religion. **1883** S. WELLS WILLIAMS *Mid. Kingd.* (ed. 2) I. iv. 199 The racial distinction between the Mongols and Manchus. **1885** CLODD *Myths & Dr.* I. viii. 131 The light which this has thrown upon the racial connection of peoples. **1889** [see NURTURAL *a.*]. **1892** F. W. GAGE *Negro Problem* iii. 56 If it be demonstrated that individual members of the race under favourable circumstances are capable of mature mental development, then the question of racial development is settled. **1899** A. NUTT in *Folk-Lore* June 146 In determining the relative importance of either element for racial discrimination in folklore, I was guided by observation of man in the civilized stage. **1899** C. WALDSTEIN *Expansion of Western Ideals* 141 An historical basis for German unity was not enough; an ethnological, racial unity had to be established. **1914** G. K. CHESTERTON *Wisdom of Father Brown* ix. 266 An attitude we must always remember when we talk of racial prejudices. **1929** H. MILES tr. *P. Morand's Black Magic* I. 63 He supported..racial equality. **1935** HUXLEY & HADDON *We Europeans* ix. 286 Ethnic intercrossing and culture-contacts have proceeded so far that 'racial purity', like complete isolationism or self-sufficiency, is impossible of attainment. **1942** H. A. WALLACE *Century of Common Man* (1944) vi. 32 In June of 1941 he [*sc.* Roosevelt] issued an executive order prohibiting racial discrimination in the employing of workers by national defence industries. **1942** Z. N. HURSTON in A. Dundes *Mother Wit* (1973) 32/2, I did not have to consider any racial group as a whole. **1943** E. H. BROOKS *Bantu in S. Afr. Life* ii. 3 When I say 'a similar point of view', I mean the doctrine of racial domination: there are Africans who still think that the Europeans can be driven into the sea. **1947** 'G. ORWELL' in *Tribune* 7 Feb. 12/2, I should like to think that the position of the racial minorities could be safeguarded. **1954** H. GIBBS *Background to Bitterness* 7 Racial conflict between the groups has not been witnessed on a major scale for many years. **1954** *Harvard Law Rev.* XXIV. 80 Judge Edgerton wrote that as the Supreme Court had..recognized that enforced racial segregation in housing was unconstitutional, it followed that enforced racial segregation in schooling was even more so. **1955** B. SCHWARTZ *Amer. Constitutional Law* ix. 224 There has been a profound change in recent years in the attitude of that tribunal [*sc.* the Supreme Court] toward racial discrimination. **1958** *Spectator* 22 Aug. 239/1 The Little Rock High School must resume racial integration when the new term began. **1960** J. RAE *Custard Boys* II. xix. 210 You think this is a case of racial prejudice and you're probably right. **1960** 'I. Ross' *Murder out of School* i. 7 There's none of what the papers like to call 'racial tension' at Mark Hopkins [School]. **1967** *Boston Sunday Herald* 7 May III. 4/1 'Racial imbalance in Parochial Schools' is the topic for a panel discussion. **1971** R. BENDIX in A. Bullock *Twentieth Cent.* xv. 357/1 Racial minorities..constitute a lower class as women obviously do not. **1971** *Publishers' Weekly* 2 Aug. 46 Mr. Fuller finds that the anthology's one story by a black author—an Eldridge Cleaver story first published in *Playboy*—is racial tokenism. **1976** *CRC Jrnl.* July 3/1 All of the recent immigration debates..have connected the general anxiety about immigration with the current racial tension. **1977** *Whitaker's Almanack 1978* 595 South African Government declared that where feasible there should be an end to racial segregation on buses. **1979** MILES & PHIZACKLEA *Racism* i. 17 A reaction by blacks in Britain to racial discrimination and violence.

racialism ('reɪʃəlɪz(ə)m). [f. RACIAL *a.* + -ISM.] Belief in the superiority of a particular race leading to prejudice and antagonism towards people of other races, esp. those in close proximity who may be felt as a threat to one's cultural and racial integrity or economic well-being.

1907 *Daily Chron.* 2 Jan. 6/5 The two principal planks in the party platform are opposition to all racialism and co-operation with the Government. **1910** *Westm. Gaz.* 11 Apr. 10/3 What appears to me to be the greatest results of the Botha-Smuts Government is the abolition of Racialism and the construction of roads. **1925** E. S. JONES *Christ of Indian Road* ii. 67 Amid the racial clash and bitterness there stands one who is the Son of man. Racialism withers at his touch. **1934** R. MACAULAY *Going Abroad* xv. 127 A Cape Afrikander..had renounced Dutch racialism and the detestation of the English. **1938** *Sun* (Baltimore) 2 Sept. 10/1 The Italian Jews are thus to be added to the victims of Hitler's imbecile 'racialism', now adopted by Mussolini as a sop to superior force. **1940** R. BENEDICT *Race: Science & Politics* vii. 215 Racialism has become involved in scientific absurdities under the Third Reich. **1955** *Times* 20 Aug. 5/5 The Prime Minister spoke on race relations, commenting that in the last session of Parliament there had been less racialism in debate and more moderation. **1960** *Spectator* 6 May 650/1 The two main convictions of racialism are, firstly..'The highest aim of human existence is the conservation of the race..the maintenance of the racial stock unmixed'..and secondly, that once a man's mind is made up about this, he can never think of changing it. **1971** S. ABBOTT *Prevention of Racial Discrimination* i. 16 Britain's long history of colonialism over-seas does not sufficiently explain the present racialism in this country. **1975** *Daily Tel.* 13 Nov. 16/3 Racism, or racialism, or racial discrimination,..covers everything from a vile form of monomania to the innocent preference of human beings for association with their own kind. **1977** P. JOHNSON *Enemies of Soc.* ii. 25 Racialism was linked to wishful-thinking, and almost deliberate self-deception.

racialist ('reɪʃəlɪst), *sb.* and *a.* [f. RACIAL *a.* + -IST.] **A.** *sb.* A partisan of racialism; an advocate of a racial theory.

1917 *Deb. House of Commons Canada* 5870/2 We all become nationalists in the true sense of the word, as distinguished from provincialists and racialists. **1930** *Observer* 22 June 13/4 Some of its characters said things that were calculated to make the blood of headstrong racialists boil. **1937** *Discovery* July 224/2 Curiously enough.., the 'nigger' is much more likely to be treated with contempt by the half-educated in England than among the politically-organised racialists of Germany. **1939** A. TOYNBEE *Study Hist.* IV. 19 We can even drive the racialists out of their one remaining Italian stronghold by finding an alternative explanation for the rise of the Roman Republic. **1940** R. BENEDICT *Race: Science & Politics* i. 6 The racialists have rewritten history to provide the scion of such a race with a long and glamorous group ancestry. **1958** *Times Lit. Suppl.* 28 Mar. 164/3 It is easy today for Britain to see Hertzog as a bitter, anti-British racialist, who deprived the remaining Cape Africans of their vote. **1960** *Spectator* 6 May 650/1 A racialist..lives according to what most people think is a fantasy. **1977** M. WALKER *National Front* iv. 85 He [*sc.* A. K. Chesterton] went on to warn of the perils of racialist extremism, while wholeheartedly agreeing with the racialists' arguments about '..mongrelization'.

B. *adj.* Of, pertaining to, or characterized by racialism.

1946 W. S. KNICKERBOCKER *20th Cent. Eng.* 81 It would be, however, an error to consider this Nazi literary history simply as racialist. **1952** B. DAVIDSON *Rep. S. Afr.* I. vii. 75 Members even of the highly racialist Electors' Union of Kenya..have expessed to me their horror at the explosive possibilities induced by white policy in South Africa. **1960** [see *Africanistic* s.v. AFRICANIST *sb.* (and *a.*)]. **1971** E. POWELL *Let.* in *Observer* 14 Mar. 8/6 The adjective 'racialist' has gained a strange sort of currency in recent years and seems to wear all sorts of meanings. I have even once or twice heard it applied to myself.

Hence **racia'listic** *a.*

1960 *Guardian* 14 Dec. 16/2 The extreme racialistic African leaders. **1969** *Daily Tel.* 18 Jan. 18/4 Coomaraswamy was more than a little influenced by the sort of racialistic sentiment applied to art that has become one of the curses of the 20th century. **1977** P. Johnson *Enemies of Society* xix. 248 The statement is purely racialistic.

racialization (ˌreɪʃəlaɪˈzeɪʃən). [f. racial *a.* + -ization.] The process of making or becoming racialist in outlook or sympathies. Hence **'racialize** *v. trans.*

1918 *Encycl. Relig. & Ethics* X. 557/2 Why should the most progressive Muslim populations be affected most powerfully by 'racialization', which is clearly a retrogressive tendency? **1930** *Month* Dec. 485 A Catholic, following St. Paul, will repudiate this attempt to racialize the universal genius of Christianity. **1977** M. Banton *Idea of Race* 18 There was a social process, which can be called racialization, whereby a mode of categorization was developed.

racially ('reɪʃəlɪ), *adv.* [f. racial *a.* + -ly^{2}.] In respect of race. Freq. linked with a ppl. adj. to form adjs., as ***racially-blended, -integrated, -selected.***

1885 Clodd *Myths & Dr.* i. viii. 133 [They] were.. probably racially connected with the complex group of peoples embracing the Tatar-Mongolians. **1914** 'Saki' *When William Came* x. 170 The record of your racially-blended supper-party. **1921** J. Bryce *Mod. Democracies* I. xiv. 163 Where a racially distinct body of unwilling subjects is included within a State.. are they to be reckoned as part of the people? **1962** Racially-integrated [see colour-blindness b]. **1976** *Drum* (E. Afr. ed.) Sept. 13/2 The team pulled out of the Olympics.. in protest against New Zealand sending a rugby team to play in South Africa against racially-selected sides. **1976** E. K. Francis *Interethnic Relations* xxii. 280 Particular populations that are racially distinct from their social environment occasionally show typical mental and cultural differences.

raciation (reɪsɪˈeɪʃən). [f. race *sb.*^{2} + -ation; cf. speciation.] The evolutionary development of distinct biological races.

1952 *Sat. Rev.* (U.S.) 5 July 16/3 The methods he [*sc.* Edgar Anderson] describes are very like those used by the anthropologist interested in tracing the wanderings of peoples, their mixture, and 'raciation'. **1971** *Nature* 28 May 250/1 This approach to microsystematics has been of particular value in the study of raciation.. in commercially important marine fishes.

racily ('reɪsɪlɪ), *adv.* [f. racy *a.* + -ly^{2}.] In a racy manner or style.

1843 J. T. Coleridge in Stanley *Arnold* I. i. 17 His language was quaintly and racily pointed with phrases from [Aristotle]. **1899** *Westm. Gaz.* 15 Apr. 3/1 We have.. quoted largely from Major Y.'s racily-written pages.

† **ra'cine.** *Obs. rare*$^{-1}$. [a. F. *racine*:—pop.L. *rādicīna dim. of *radix*: see radix.] A root.

c **1400** *Rom. Rose* 4881 Of ech synne it is the rote Unlefulle lust.. And of alle yvelle the racyne.

raciness ('reɪsɪnɪs). [f. racy *a.* + -ness.] The fact or condition of being racy:

a. Of wine, fruit, etc.

1682 *Art & Myst. Vintners* (1703) 51 Nutmegs and Cloves.. give a kind of Raciness. **1823** Lamb *Lett., to B. Barton* xiii. 122 My jargonels.. were of exquisite raciness. **1829** De Quincey in 'H. A. Page' *Life* (1877) I. xii. 265 New potatoes of celestial earthiness and raciness.

b. Of speech, writing, manner, etc.

1778 Johnson *L.P., Milton* I. 247 His images and descriptions.. do not seem.. to have the freshness, raciness, and energy of immediate observation. **1798** W. Taylor in *Monthly Rev.* XXVI. 545-6 That raciness, that taste of the soil, which can alone endear any laws to a free people. **1834** De Quincey in *Tait's Mag.* I. 200/2 An apparent strength of character.. and a raciness of manner. **1884** W. J. Courthope *Addison* ix. 188 Using the language with a raciness and rhythm probably unequalled in our literature.

racing ('reɪsɪŋ), *vbl. sb.*^{1} [f. race *sb.*^{1} or *v.*^{1} + -ing^{1}.]

1. The action of race *vb.*^{1} in its various senses.

1680 Cotton *Compl. Gamester* (ed. 2) xxxv. Of Racing. **1753** Chambers *Cycl.* Supp., *Racing*, the riding heats for a plate or other premium. **1808** Scott *Marm.* v. xii, There was racing and chasing on Cannobie Lee. **1832** Lieder *Encycl. Amer.* X. 474/1 Subsequent sovereigns have also encouraged racing. **1856** Emerson *Eng. Traits, Aristocracy* Wks. (Bohn) II. 86 Yet gaming, racing, drinking,.. bring them down. **1901** *Chambers's Jrnl.* Apr. 221/2 The *Turbinia* has been run.. in almost all states of the sea, and on no occasion has the slightest symptom of racing occurred. **1912** G. Greenhill *Dynamics of Mech. Flight* v. 106 Racing of the screw is due chiefly to variation of axial flow. **1980** G. M. Fraser *Mr American* xviii. 336 Pip's method of travel was.. constant racing of the engine.

2. *attrib.* and *Comb.*, (some functionally indistinguishable from *racing* used as ppl. adj.) as ***racing bicycle, -boat, canoe, car, change*** (change *sb.* 1 g), ***club, colt, correspondent, cycle, cyclist, driver, eight, establishment, -gig, -glass, guide, jacket, man, motor-car, motorist, outrigger, pace, page, -path, place, result, rig, saddle, season, stable, stud, -track, -whip, world, yacht; racing-like, -tyred*** adjs.; † **racing-bell**, a small spherical bell formerly given as a prize in a horse-race (see bell *sb.*^{1} 7); **Racing Calendar**, a yearly publication giving particulars of horse-races run or to be run; **racing colours**, the colours (colour, color *sb.* 6a) by which an owner's racehorses are identified; **racing demon** (see demon 2f); **racing dope** *U.S.*, information about races contained in a *dope-sheet* (see dope *sb.* 5); **racing flag** *Naut.* (see quot. 1961); **racing game** = *race-game* s.v. race *sb.*^{1} 11b; † **racing-loser**, one who loses in or by horse-racing; **racing pigeon**, a homing pigeon taking part in competitions to complete a specific journey as quickly as possible; **racing-plate** (see quot.); **racing-tail**, the tail of natural length worn by race-horses; hence ***racing-tailed*** a.

1910 *Encycl. Brit.* III. 915/1 Wood rims are used on *racing bicycles. **1959** I. & P. Opie *Lore & Lang. of Schoolchildren* x. 191 Who's teacher's pet boy and was given a racing bicycle? **1850** Kingsley *Alton Locke* xii, I stood.. gazing across the river, heedless of the *racing-boats. **1861** Hughes *Tom Brown at Oxf.* I. 68 The flooring, lines, and keel of a racing boat. **1709-** (*title*) The *Racing Calendar. **1838** De Quincey *Wks.* 1863 XV. 114 He would suppose himself reading the 'Racing Calendar'. **1876** *Racing-canoe [see *long-spooned* s.v. long *a.*^{1} 16]. **1932** *Man* May 106 The coffin is placed in a large racing canoe. **1909** *Racing car [see *power producer* s.v. power *sb.*^{1} 18]. **1977** M. Kenyon *Rapist* iv. 44 He said he.. had been an important racing car driver. **1959** I. Fleming *Goldfinger* vii. 86 James Bond flung the DB III through the last mile of straight and did a *racing change down into third. **1840** Whyte *Hist. Turf* I. 191 Members of a *racing or fox-hunting club. **1907** *Yesterday's Shopping* (1969) 302/2 About seven days required to execute orders for *Racing Colours. **1955** W. Gaddis *Recognitions* i. v. 196 She handed a folded twenty-dollar bill to a boy wearing her racing colors. **1961** A. Clarke *Later Poems* 87 At Maynooth, instead of skulls, His racing colours were displayed. **1828** Darvill *Treat. Race horse* 454 On breaking *racing colts. **1961** E. Waugh *Unconditional Surrender* iii. ii. 240 His brief experience as a *racing correspondent seemed irrelevant to the zeitgeist. **1976** 'J. Welcome' *Grand National* i. 11 That is Andrew Mostyn, our chief racing correspondent. **1976** *Eastern Even. News* (Norwich) 22 Dec. 11/3 (Advt.), *Racing cycles at discount prices. **1974** *Times* 29 Oct. 17/4 Scores of club *racing cyclists. **1945** N. Mitford *Pursuit of Love* ix. 74 The Kroesigs obviously longed for bridge, and did not seem to care so much for *racing demon when it was offered as a substitute. **1977** *Times* 24 Dec. 10/2 Try racing demon for the party card game if you have a large table and fast-playing, shouting screaming players. **1931** F. L. Allen *Only Yesterday* iv. 81 Workmen forgot to be class-conscious as they.. studied the *racing dope about Morvich. **1961** *Daily Tel.* 21 May 10, I used to be a *racing driver. **1977** 'D. Cory' *Bennett* iii. 88 Shop girls identify themselves with film stars, bank clerks with racing drivers. **1866** 'Argonaut' *Rowing & Training* 12 Length of boat (*Racing eight) 56 feet. **1811** J. Steele *Let.* 29 Jan. in *Papers* (1924) II. 649 There is nothing.. which wd. afford me greater pleasure than to see a respectable *racing establishment at this place. **1828** Darvill *Treat. Race horse* 6 The home stables of a large public racing establishment. **1860** 'Vanderdecken' *Yarns* 135 Cut the *racing flag clear, and send a hand aloft to lash it to the stump as a signal that you'll fight to the last. **1961** F. H. Burgess *Dict. Sailing* 167 *Racing flag*, a private flag hoisted when racing, instead of the burgee; it is hauled down only on retiring, or when a race is completed. **1860** C. M. Yonge *Hopes & Fears* I. i. v. 123 She beheld his sister.. at the *racing game... Honor waited, however, till the little white horseman had reached the goal. **1890** —— *More Bywords* 154 The 'racing game',.. which was now spread on the dining-table, with all the young people playing in high glee. **1884** *Harper's Mag.* Feb. 344/1 A long *racing-gig swept by us. **1882** *Graphic* 25 Oct. 437/3 Putting off the shibboleth of the turf with his *racing-glasses. **1909** A. L. Bruce *Bridge-Fiend* 12 A peppery, red-faced old gentleman, who was reading a *racing-guide.. was then appealed to. **1833** *New Sporting Mag.* V. 398 The *racing jacket, with fancy buttons and velvet collar. *Ibid.* 132 The *racing-like style in which he did his work. **1852** R. S. Surtees *Sponge's Sp. Tour* (1893) 290 Sound, springy, racing-like turf. **1680** Cotton *Compleat Gamester* (ed. 2) xxxv. 148 The woful experience of too many *Racing-losers. **1828** Darvill *Treat. Race horse* 218 *Racing men endeavour.. to keep the secrets of their stables. **1909** *Westm. Gaz.* 21 Oct. 5/1 Fewer accidents have happened to aviators in proportion to their numbers than to *racing-motor-car drivers in the same period. **1906** *Chambers's Jrnl.* Apr. 347/1 The trophy which is the prize for which *racing-motorists compete. **1866** 'Argonaut' *Rowing & Training* 56 A regular *racing outrigger may be substituted for the tub. **1828** Darvill *Treat. Race horse* 172 To come a long length at a *racing pace. **1948** 'J. Tey' *Franchise Affair* xiv. 156, I went to rest every afternoon with.. the *racing page of the daily paper. **1978** *Islands* (N.Z.) Aug. 78, I got the paper of course. For the racing page really. **1884** *Longm. Mag.* Mar. 484 The feats accomplished.. on the *racing-path. **1910** A. H. Osman *Pigeon Bk.* xiii. 148 It is impossible to say what breeds have and have not been used to 'make' the *racing pigeon. **1933** *Discovery* Nov. 344/1 Racing and homing pigeons are often captured. **1960** *Farmer & Stockbreeder* 26 Jan. 4/2 Demand is expected to broaden as the racing-pigeon season approaches. **1977** *Wandsworth Borough News* 16 Sept. 15/5 Literally rescued from the teeth of a predatory cat, a blue racing pigeon now awaits a claimant at the home of Mr. I. A. McWilliam. **1741-3** Pococke *Descr. East* I. 10 The *racing place, call'd the Hippodromus. **1958** J. Hislop *From Start to Finish* 174 **Racing-plate*, a light shoe (usually made of some form of aluminium) with which horses are shod when they race. **1926** *Racing result [see *bedtime story* s.v. bedtime]. **1976** 'J. Welcome' *Grand National* ii. 27 He turned on the radio to get the racing results. **1906** Conrad *Mirror of Sea* viii. 39 Of those three varieties of fore-and-aft rig, the cutter—the *racing rig *par excellence*—is of an appearance the most imposing. **1828** Darvill *Treat. Race horse* 22 Racks and pegs for the *racing saddles. **1840** Whyte *Hist. Turf* II. 600 The conclusion of the *racing season. **1828** Darvill *Treat. Race horse* p. v, Any one who has not been brought up in *racing stables. **1981** E. Ward *Baltic Emerald* xxiv. 189 A racing stable with high pasturelands for gallops. **1828** T. Creevey *Let.* in *Creevey Papers* (1963) xii. 241 We started about 3 for Petworth.. Sefton's object being to see Lord Egremont's *Racing Stud before dinner. **1840** Whyte *Hist. Turf* I. 36 Oliver Cromwell.. kept a racing stud. **1863** Ouida *Held in Bondage* (1870) 51 She will cost.. more than a racing stud. **1843** Thackeray *Jérôme Paturot* 361 A great floundering *racing-tailed horse. **1913** *O.E.D.* s.v. *Track* sb. 6b, *Racing-track. **1917** [see morning *sb.* 7¶]. **1929** W. E. Collinson *Spoken Eng.* 72 They've built a greyhound racing-track just near the house. **1891** *Pall Mall G.* 29 Oct. 1/3 A Clincher *racing-tyred Humber safety. **1864** *Reader* No. 97. 568/2 A *racing-whip he had brought. **1841** 'Wildrake' *Cracks of the Day* 212 The grand emporium of the year [1838] in the *racing world, was the Epsom Races. **1885** *Royal River* xii. 338 The *racing yachts are clearing for action.

† **'racing,** *vbl. sb.*^{2} *Obs.* [f. race *v.*^{3}] The action of scratching, cutting, or scraping out.

1576 Baker *Gesner's Jewell of Health* 8 b, A waxed threede was fastened about that place.. for the strayghter and evener racing of the Glasse. **1592** West *1st Pt. Symbolæogr.* §56 C ij b, Ingrossed in paper or parchment, without blotting, racing, interlyning. **1633** Hart *Diet of Diseased* iii. ix. 264 By meanes of scarification or racing of the skinne.

attrib. **1794** *Rigging & Seamanship* I. 8 *Racing-knife*, a small tool to race with. **1819** [see race *sb.*^{3}].

racing ('reɪsɪŋ), *ppl. a.* [f. race *v.*^{1} + -ing^{2}.] That races, in various senses of the vb.

1720 Pope *Iliad* xxiii. 342 The Prizes.. decreed To the brave Rulers of the racing Steed. **1811** W. R. Spencer *Poems* 23 How swift from left and right, The racing fields and hills recede. **1876** G. Meredith *Beauch. Career* xxxii, Levelling his telescope to sight the racing cutters.

Racinian (rəˈsiːnɪən), *a.* and *sb.* Also **Racinean**. [f. the name of Jean *Racine* (1639-99), French dramatic poet.] **A.** *adj.* Of, pertaining to, characteristic of, or resembling Racine or his writings. **B.** *sb.* An admirer or imitator of Racine.

1927 *Sunday Times* 13 Mar. 8/3 He [*sc.* Otway] still remains the most Racinian of all our poets. **1931** *Times Lit. Suppl.* 1 Jan. 1/3 Shakespearian, Racinian or Sheridanesque convention. **1946** *Month* May-June 229 His brilliant and enthusiastic appreciation of the great cycle of tragedies, above all *Athalie*, will please the most ardent Racinian. **1950** M. McCarthy in *Reporter* 18 July 37/2 This Racinean world, where stepmother Phèdre and grandmother Athalie queened it. **1948** L. Spitzer *Linguistics & Lit. Hist.* 178 The Racinian, the Vergilian power of poetic alchemy whereby brute reality is transmuted. **1962** *Listener* 30 Aug. 315/2 This Racinian reading of modern life which is dramatized in terms of passion versus reason, will versus duty. **1974** *Ibid.* 8 Aug. 185/2 *A Month in the Country*.. harks back to Racine. There is the Racinian web of emotional incompatibilities.

raciology (reɪsɪˈɒlədʒɪ). [f. race *sb.*^{2} + -ology; cf. F. *raciologie*.] The study of the races of man. Hence **racio'logical** *a.*; **raci'ologist**, a student of raciology.

1924 *Glasgow Herald* 7 Feb 6/5 Societies were formed for the study of their language and raciology, just when the authentic gipsies themselves had begun to disappear. **1926** *Ibid.* 27 Jan. 10/4 A new and searching process of selection.. will result in a revisal of our preconceived notions of African raciology. **1939** C. S. Coon *Races of Europe* viii. 286 Von Eickstedt, the most articulate of the modern German raciologists. **1950** E. W. Count *This is Race* 703 For a commentary on Buffon's raciology, see Scheidt. *Ibid.* 734 The Russian raciologists were very actively engaged.. in combating.. 'bourgeois' racism in general. *Ibid.* 735 Some other works of Fleure have a raciological bearing.

racism ('reɪsɪz(ə)m). [f. race *sb.*^{2} + -ism; cf. F. *racisme* (Robert 1935).] **a.** The theory that distinctive human characteristics and abilities are determined by race. **b.** = racialism.

1936 L. Dennis *Coming Amer. Fascism* 109 If.. it be assumed that one of our values should be a type of racism which excludes certain races from citizenship, then the plan of execution should provide for the annihilation, deportation, or sterilization of the excluded races. **1938** E. & C. Paul tr. *Hirschfeld's Racism* xx. 260 The apostles and energumens of racism can in all good faith give free rein to impulses of which they would be ashamed did they realise their true nature. **1940** R. Benedict *Race: Science & Politics* i. 7 Racism is an *ism* to which everyone in the world today is exposed. **1952** M. Berger *Equality by Statute* 236 Racism, tension in industrial, urban areas. **1952** *Theology* LV. 283 The idolatry of our time—its setting up of nationalism, racism, vulgar materialism. **1960** *New Left Rev.* Jan./Feb. 21/2 George Rogers saw fit to kow-tow to the incipient racism of his electorate by including a line about getting rid of 'undesirable elements'. **1964** Gould & Kolb *Dict. Social Sci.* 571/2 *Racism* is a newer term for the word *racialism*... There is virtual agreement that it refers to a doctrine of racial supremacy. **1971** *Ceylon Daily News* (Colombo) 18 Sept. 8/5 Mr. Seneviratne is welcome to his ideal of inter-racial marriages as panacea for Racism. **1972** J. L. Dillard *Black English* iii. 90 In the British sailors' reactions to the slaves.., the very early existence of racism is as well documented as the difference in language. **1974** M. Fido *R. Kipling* 50/2 In *The Story of Muhammad Din* he wrote one of the most economical and bitter attacks on British racism ever penned. **1976** *Plain Dealer* (Cleveland, Ohio) 4 Mar. A2/4 The Vatican radio said,.. 'Racism might have different faces but it will always be reprehensible.' **1977** M. Walker *National Front* vi. 155 A strike of the Asian workers against racism in the factory.

racist ('reɪsɪst), *sb.* and *a.* [f. race *sb.*^{2} + -ist.] **A.** *sb.* = racialist *sb.*

1932 M. Eastman tr. *Trotsky's Hist. Russ. Revol.* i. 27 This brief comment completely finishes off not only the old philosophy of the Slavophiles, but also the latest revelations of the 'Racists'. **1934** H. G. Wells *Exper. Autobiogr.* I. iii. 107 So much for the Hitlerite stage of my development, when I was a sentimentalist, a moralist, a patriot, a racist. **1940** R. Benedict *Race: Science & Politics* vii. 214 Classic German racists..ascribed all achievements beyond the Alps to infiltrations of northern blood. **1959** *New Statesman* 30 May. 754/2 They see nothing to be gained..if they are dismissed and replaced by fanatical racists. **1965** *San Francisco Examiner* 15 Apr. 34/5, I recently heard a man denounced as a racist for having observed that the rate of illegitimacy in New York is 14 times as high among the Negro population as among the white. **1973** A. Dundes *Mother Wit* p. xii, Folklore has been used as the tool of racists.

B. *adj.* = racialist *a.*

1938 E. & C. Paul tr. *Hirschfeld's Racism* xv. 201 Elective affinity laughs at the maxims and prohibitions of racist wiseacres. **1938** *Mag. Digest* Aug. 22 The racist revue, *Archiv für Biologie und Rassengesellschaft*, one of the organs of the National Socialist Party, published an article..on 'The utility of aerial bombardments from the point of view of racial selection and social hygiene'. **1938** *Sun* (Baltimore) 14 Nov. 6/2 On Thursday..Rome approved new decrees increasing the severity of Italian Fascism's new 'racist' principles. **1940** R. Benedict *Race: Science & Politics* vii. 188 The racist traditions..of the fair, blue-eyed narrow-heads. **1957** P. Worsley *Trumpet shall Sound* App. 268 Racist doctrines and rule by force 'worked' to a degree in the short run of Nazidom, they failed in the (not very) long run. **1960** *Guardian* 23 Mar. 8/2 The President is trying to knock out the racist props from under the present immigration law. **1970** E. Bullins *Theme is Blackness* (1973) 167 I'm too mature and sophisticated to get sucked in by racist arguments. **1979** *Globe & Mail* (Toronto) 28 Nov. 8/4 [Mr. Levesque] can't bear any suggestion that he or his party could be racist, could treat non-francophones as second-class citizens.

Hence **ra'cistic** *a.* (*rare*).

1950 E. W. Count *This is Race* 734 Combating racistic theories. **1963** *Observer* 7 Apr. 22/2 This society is dedicated to pleasure and not over-concerned with the big racistic abstractions.

rack (ræk), *sb.*[1] Forms: 4 rac, 4–5 rakke, 4–6 rak, (5 rake), 6–7 racke, 5– rack. [Chiefly a northern word, and perh. of Scandinavian origin; cf. Norw. and Sw. dial. *rak* (Sw. *vrak*, Da. *vrag*) wreck, wreckage, refuse, rubbish, etc., f. *reka* to drive, reke.

The only form recorded in ON. is *rek* wreckage, but the forms cited above seem to indicate an ON. **rak*, parallel to OE. *wræc* from *wrecan* wreak. The history of the word is not quite clear, however, and some of the senses may have a different origin.]

†**1.** A rush, shock, collision, ? hard blow or push. Also, a noise as of a shock; a crash. *Obs.*

a **1300** *Body & Soul* in *Map's Poems* (Camden) 335 Thouȝ me lete have rap and rac. *c* **1330** *Arth. & Merl.* 3476 (Kölbing) Vlfines launce tobrac. Þe þre come þo gret rac. *c* **1400** *Melayne* 1249 Thay ruysschede Samen with swilke a rake That many a Saraȝene laye on his bake. *c* **1470** *Gol. & Gaw.* 918 The bernys bowit abak, Sa woundir rude wes the rak. **1508** Dunbar *Gold. Targe* 240 Thay fyrit gunnis..The rochis all resownyt wyth the rak. **1513** Douglas *Æneis* xi. xii. 41 Thai meyt in melle with a felloun rak.

†**2.** A rush of wind; a gale, storm. *Obs. rare.*

c **1400** *Destr. Troy* 1984 There a tempest hom toke..A rak and a royde wynde rose in hor saile. **1513** Douglas *Æneis* x. v. 127 Thai fle the weddris blast and rak of wynd.

3. a. Clouds, or a mass of cloud, driven before the wind in the upper air. (The main use.)

13.. *E.E. Allit. P.* C. 176 What my gome trawe, Bot he þat rules þe rak may rwe on þose oþer? *c* **1440** *York Myst.* xvi. 7 The rakke of þe rede skye fulle rappely I ridde. *c* **1450** Lonelich *Grail* xxxv. 386 The Schipe wente..Swiftere than þe Rakke In þe Eyr. **1590** Greene *Never too late* (1600) 34 The welkin had no racke that seemed to glide. **1626** Bacon *Sylva* §115 The Windes in the Vpper Region (which moue the Clouds aboue which we call the Racke). **1697** Dryden *Virg. Georg.* I. 435 With such a force the flying rack is driv'n. **1789** E. Darwin *Bot. Gard.* II. (1791) 53 Now a speck is seen! And now the fleeting rack obtrudes between! **1808** Scott *Marm.* iv. Introd., Along the sky, Mix'd with the rack, the snow mists fly. **1840** Thackeray *G. Cruikshank* (1869) 317 A great heavy rack of clouds goes sweeping over the bridge. **1886** Hall Caine *Son of Hagar* I. viii. 150 The stars struggled one by one through a rack of flying cloud.

fig. **1641** *Curates' Confer.* in *Harl. Misc.* I. 499, I am almost at the same ebb: but let us hope better: things will not always ride in this rack.

Comb. **1618** S. Ward *Jethro's Justice* (1627) 57 It is the ground wind, not the rack-winde, that driues mils and ships. **1620** T. Scott *God & King* (1633) 16 It is for me to observe the ground-winde, not the rack-winde.

†**b.** Driving mist or fog. *Obs.*

13.. *Gaw. & Gr. Knt.* 1695 In rede rudede vpon rak rises þe sunne. **1418–20** *Siege Rouen* 993 in *Archæologia* XXII. 373 The clothis..Kepte hem there from rayne and rack. **1513** Douglas *Æneis* vii. Prol. 131 Wyth cloudy gum and rak ourquhelmyt the air. **1606** Shaks. *Ant. & Cl.* iv. xiv. 10 That which is now a Horse, euen with a thoght the Racke dislimes, and makes it indistinct.

fig. **1610** Shaks. *Temp.* iv. i. 156 The great Globe it selfe ..shall dissolue, And..Leaue not a racke behinde. [**1874** Pusey *Lenten Serm.* 100 The most plausible will not leave a rack behind.]

4. a. A (narrow) path or track. (Cf. rake *sb.*[3])

The identity of the south-western word (cf. also b) with the northern is somewhat doubtful. With some of the senses cf. also Du. *rak* a stretch (of road, river, etc.).

a **1400–50** *Alexander* 3383 Oute of þe rakke [*v.r.* rake] of rightwyssnes rynne shuld he neuer. **1825–46** Brockett *N.C. Gloss* (ed. 3) II. 86 *Rack*, a narrow path, a track, a trace. **1879–** In dial. glossaries (Shropsh., Glouc., Wilts, etc). **1899** H. T. Timmins *Nooks & Corners of Shropshire* 65 We go down a rough footpath, or 'rack', as they call it here-abouts. **1904** G. A. B. Dewar *Glamour of Earth* v. 81, I came down the rack—the narrow path which is cut through ripe underwood fifteen years old, and marks the end of one lot and the beginning of another. **1919** T. Wright *Romance of Lace Pillow* xii. 110 What a relief..to be absolutely free for a few hours; to be able to..roam the ridings, racks, and glades of Yardley Chase. **1957** *Brit. Commonw. Forest Terminol.* II. 149 *Rack*, (*a*) A narrow woodland track maintained for inspection and communication and for extraction of poles, etc. by hand or animal haulage.

b. The track made by an animal; *esp.* that of a deer, as marked by gaps in hedges, etc.

1611 Cotgr., *Les passées d'un Cerf*, His racke, or passages; the places which he has gone through, or by. **1817** J. Mayer *Sportsm. Direct.* 23 Rabbits are taken in various ways... If they lie in hedge-rows..plant one or two guns at the end where the racks meet. **1862** C. P. Collyns *Notes Chase Wild Red Deer* 79 Can he find the 'rack' or place where the deer broke the fence into the wood?

c. *Sc.* A ford in a river. **d.** *Sc.* The course in curling (Jam.). **e.** *north.* A reach of a river.

c. ? **16..** *Kinmont Willie* iv. in Child *Ballads* III. 472/1 They led him thro the Liddel-rack, And also thro the Carlisle sands.

e. 1832 J. F. Watson *Historic Tales of Olden Time N.-Y. City.* 27 The 'Racks' so called, along the [Hudson] river, were Dutch names for Reaches. **1838** T. Wilson *Keelman's Tribute* (Northumbld. Gloss.), The keelman's dues tiv iv'ry rack..knew Faddy. **1930** *Amer. Speech.* V. 164 The Dutch navigators divided the Hudson into *racks* or *reaches*. The former word remains in Claverack.

f. *rack of (the) eye*: (see quots.). *dial.*

a **1796** Pegge *Derbicisms* (E.D.S.) 117 To judge of the value of a thing by 'the rack o' th' eye', by view or sight, without weighing or measuring. **1869** *Lonsdale Gloss.*, *Rack of eye*, to work by. To be guided by the eye in the execution of work done. **1886–7** in Cheshire glossaries.

rack (ræk), *sb.*[2] Forms: 4–5 rekke, rakk(e, 5 rak, 5–7 racke, 6– rack; also 5–6 rake. [App. a. MDu. *rec*, *reck-* (Du. *rek*, *rekke*) or MLG. *rek*, *rekke*, *rik* (LG. and G. *reck*, *recke*; hence Da. *række*, Sw. *räck*, *räcke*), applied to various contrivances (as a horizontal bar or pole, a framework, shelf, etc.) on which things are hung or placed, a henroost, rail, etc., prob. f. *recken* to reach, stretch; see rack *v.*[3] The usual vowel of the Eng. word appears also in Du. *rak*, (L)G. *rack*, variants of *rek*, *reck*, but may have been developed independently.]

†**1.** ? An iron bar or framework to which prisoners were secured. *Obs.*

The exact sense in the first quot. is doubtful.

c **1305** *St. Cristopher* 192 in *E.E.P.* (1862) 64 O womman he let honge, Heuye rekkes bynde to hire fet. **1502** Arnolde *Chron.* (1811) 92 Ye warde must haue a racke wt ij. longe cheynes of yrne. **1572** *Nottingham Rec.* IV. 145, viij. lb. of eyron to the town's rackes and mendyng. **1590** Spenser *F.Q.* ii. iv. 14 Both his hands fast bound behind his backe, And both his feet in fetters to an yron racke.

2. A bar (usu. in *pl.*) or set of bars of iron or wood (see quot. 1617) used to support a spit or other cooking utensil. *Obs.* exc. *dial.*

1390 *Earl Derby's Exped.* (Camden) 18 Pro ij paribus rakkes pro caudrons pendendis. **1424** *E.E. Wills* (1882) 56 Too spytes, and a peyre rakkes of yryne, and to branderes. *Ibid.* 102 Also a rake of yren forto rost on his eyren. **1467** *Mann. & Househ. Exp.* (Roxb.) 399 In makenge of rakkes of tre to roste one, xij d. **1564** *Wills & Inv. N.C.* (Surtees 1835) 223 Toynges, gibcrokes, rakincroke, and rackes. **1617** Minsheu, a *Racke* or Cobborne to lay the broch in at the fire. .. A racke is properly that which is of yron which hath a long ranke of barres in it, and a Cobborne or Coleburne are the little ones of wood. *a* **1643** Cartwright *Lady Errant*, v. i, Spits, Andirons, Racks and such like Utensils. **1706** Phillips, *Rack*, a Wooden Frame..to lay Spits on in a Kitchin. **1888** *Sheffield Gloss.*, *Rack*, a piece of iron to hang a spit on.

3. a. A frame made with upright bars of wood or metal to hold fodder for horses and cattle, either fixed in a stable, or movable so as to be placed where desired in a field or farmyard; a heck.

14.. in *Tundale's Vis.* (1843) 124 To se that lord in a racke lye That hathe hevon under hys poste. **1443** *Pol. Poems* (Rolls) II. 212 In a streiht rakke lay ther the kyng of pees. **1494** Fabyan *Chron.* v. lxxxiii. 61 The Calfe..forthwith ete haye with the dame at the Racke. **1540–54** Croke *xiii. Ps.* (Percy Soc.) 9 Bynde fast theire iawes vp to the racke. **1607** Markham *Caval.* iii. (1617) 21 You shall put into his racke a..bottle of hay. **1697** Dryden *Virg. Georg.* iii. 606 Salt Herbage for the fodd'ring Rack provide. **1781** Cowper *Charity* 173 He breaks the cord that held him at the rack. **1859** Dickens *T. Two Cities* ii. ix, The horses in the stables rattled at their racks. **1886** C. Scott *Sheep-Farming* 65 A rack nine feet long will accommodate twenty sheep... Whenever the racks are taken out to the fields [etc.].

b. Coupled with *manger*.

1391 *Earl Derby's Exped.* (Camden) 205 Pro factura de rakks et mangers in diuersis stabulis. *c* **1450** *Bk. Curtasye* 610 in *Babees Bk.*, Euery horse schalle so muche haue, At racke and manger. *c* **1475** *Partenay* 913 Both rekke and manger at their ease gan make. **1573** Tusser *Husb.* (1878) 35 A racke and a manger, good litter and haie. **1707** Ld. Raby in Hearne *Collect.* 14 Sept. (O.H.S.) II. 42 His Horses stand ..wthout either Racks or Mangers. **1868** *Regul. & Ord. Army* §570 To prevent infection from glanders..the rack and manger are to be scoured.

fig. **1577** Harrison *England* ii. ii. (1877) i. 44 Canturburie was said to be the higher racke, but Winchester..to be the better mangier.

c. Phr. ***at rack and manger***: in the midst of abundance or plenty, wanting for nothing. †Also rarely without prep. (Cf. heck *sb.*[1] 3.)

c **1380** Wyclif *Wks.* (1880) 435 It is yuel to kepe a wast hors in a stable..but it is worse to have a womman wiþ-ynne or wiþ-oute at racke & at manger. **1592** Warner *Alb. Eng.* viii. xli. (1612) 200 A Queane coriuall with a Queene? Nay kept at Racke and Manger? **1593** *Bacchus Bountie* in *Harl. Misc.* (1809) II. 275 Plaine rack and manger, where euery one dranke himself out of danger. **1679** Mrs. Behn *Feign'd Curtizan* iii. i, Danger,..once o'recome, I lie at rack and manger. **1843** Carlyle *Past & Pr.* ii. i, John Lackland.. tearing out the bowels of St. Edmundsbury Convent..by living at rack and manger there.

d. Hence ***rack and manger***, want of proper economy or management, waste and destruction. (? Associated with *rack and ruin*.) Now *dial.*

1687 Miege *Gt. Fr. Dict.* ii. s.v., To leave all at Rack and Manger, *laisser tout à l'abandon.* **1731** Fielding *Grub St. Op.* iii. ii, The moment my back is turned, everything goes to rack and manger. **1785** Grose *Class. Dict. Vulgar Tongue* s.v. *Rackrent*, To lye at rack and manger, to be in great disorder. **1883** in *Hampsh. Gloss.*

e. ***to stand*** (or ***come***) ***up to the rack***: to face or bear the consequences of what one has undertaken; to take one's share of hard work or responsibility. *U.S.*

1834 D. Crockett *Narrative of Life* iv. 61, I was determined to stand up to my rack, fodder or no fodder. **1835** —— *Col. Crockett's Tour* 69 It was a hard row to hoe; but I stood up to the rack. **1837** R. M. Bird *Nick of Woods* II. xiv. 183 But, you see, captain, there's a bargain first to be struck between us, afore I comes up to the rack. **1848** J. F. Cooper *Oak Open.* II. iii. 43 The English used to boast that the Americans wouldn't 'stand up to the rack', if the baggonet was set to work. **1890** *Stock Grower & Farmer* 12 July 4/2 For several years cattlemen have been severe losers but most of them have stood pluckily to the rack.

4. a. A framework (varying greatly in form as used for various purposes) in or on which articles are placed or suspended.

Freq. with defining word prefixed as ***bacon-***, ***bottle-***, ***case-***, ***cheese-***, ***galley-***, ***hat-***, ***plate-rack*** (see the first element).

1537 *Bury Wills* (Camden) 130 The tramely yn the chemney, and the rackes on the soler. *c* **1590** Greene *Fr. Bacon* iii, When we haue..set our cheese safely vpon the rackes. **1683** Moxon *Mech. Exerc.*, *Printing* xix. ¶7 Every Stick-full [of letters] is set up upon the Racks, ready for the Dresser to Dress. **1694** Motteux *Rabelais* v. xxvii. (1737) 120 Having laid their Boots and Spurs on a Rack. **1842** Dickens *Amer. Notes* (1850) 2/1 A rack fixed to the low roof, and stuck full of drinking glasses and cruet stands. **1869** E. A. Parkes *Pract. Hygiene* (ed. 3) 323 A wooden rack round the centre pillar receives the rifles. **1871** C. Gibbon *Lack of Gold* xviii, The dishes on the rack above.

b. *spec.* One on which items of clothing are transported and displayed for sale. Phr. ***off the*** (or ***a***) ***rack*** = *off the peg* adv. phr. s.v. peg *sb.*[1] 1 e.

1948 H. McClennan *Precipice* (1949) ii. 189 Shipping clerks pushing racks of women's dresses. **1962** W. Schirra in *Into Orbit* 47, I acted as a kind of consultant tailor on the pressure suit. It is not possible just to walk in and buy one off the rack. **1976** 'R. Boyle' *Cry Rape* xx. 91, I chose a simple navy shirtmaker dress from the $20-and-under rack. **1976** *Times* 2 Nov. 12/2 In the women's outfitting department, there was..a scramble around the racks of camel coats. **1978** R. Ludlum *Holcroft Covenant* xxxiii. 385 His suit was off a rack.

5. In various special or technical uses.

a. An openwork side for a cart or wagon. ? *Obs.* **b.** A framework set in a river to obstruct the passage of fish. **c.** *Naut.* (see quots.); also = halyard-rack (halyard 2) and = fiddle 3 a. **d.** An inclined frame or table on which tin-ore is washed (cf. wreck). **e.** In organ-building = pipe-rack. †**f.** Part of a moulding-machine (see quot.). *Obs.*

a. 1593 Hollyband *Dict. Fr. & Eng.*, *Bers de chariot*, the sides or racks of a wagon. **1687** Miege *Gt. Fr. Dict.* ii. s.v., The Racks of the Cart are broken.

b. 1735 *Col. Rec. Pennsylv.* IV. 24 That Racks are a much greater Obstruction to Navigation than Wears.

c. 1769 Falconer *Dict. Marine* (1776), *Rack*,..a frame of timber, containing several sheaves, and usually fixed on the opposite sides of a ship's bowsprit. **1794** *Rigging & Seamanship* I. 171 *Rack*, a short thin plank, with holes made through it, containing a number of belaying-pins. *Ibid.* 172 *Rack*, a long shell, containing a number of sheaves, formerly fixed over the bowsprit to lead in the running rigging. **1841** Dana *Seaman's Man.* 119 *Rack*,..a *fair-leader* for running rigging.

d. 1839 Ure *Dict. Arts* 1244 The rough [tin ore] is washed in buddles;..the slimes..upon a kind of twin tables, called racks. **1893** *Longm. Mag.* Feb. 375 *note*, A mine-girl that works at a 'rack', and who separates the particles of tin from the finely crushed ore.

f. 1678 Moxon *Mech. Exerc.* I. 104 To this Engine belongs a thin flat peece of Hard wood, about an Inch and a quarter broad..called the Rack. It hath its under flat cut into those fashioned waves..your work shall have.

g. A large, vertical, metal framework, usu. of standardized dimensions, for supporting items of telephonic or electronic equipment and allowing ready access to them.

1893 Preece & Stubbs *Man. Telephony* xix. 311 An even more effective contrivance for cable racks..is shown in fig. 240. **1906** J. Poole *Pract. Telephone Handbk.* (ed. 3) xxi. 299 Condenser Rack.—This frame is for the accommodation of the 2½-microfarad condensers used in connection with the incoming junction lines... The frame is 7 feet 3½ inches wide and 7 feet 10 inches high. **1930** *Proc. IRE* XVIII. 1320 The amplifiers are mounted on relay racks and connected by twin lead wire pulled in rigid conduit. **1951** *Short Wave Mag.* May 179/1 The left-hand rack, No. 1, starting at the bottom, contains the filament supplies for all transmitters; the 1000 v. HT supply for the 430 and 144 mc exciters; [etc.]. **1977** *Gramophone* June 118/2 In the professional world it is common practice for tuners, preamplifiers, power amplifiers, equalizers, etc. to be mounted on slotted panels, which are mounted vertically into racks. Now several domestic manufacturers are also mounting their units in neat vertical racks, but usually they are less than the professional 48cm (19-inch) width.

h. *U.S.* (See quots.)

1903 *Nation* (N.Y.) 6 Aug. 115/2 Another Americanism we miss under Racks, the technical name for the side plankings or buffers of our ferry slips. **1905** *N.Y. Even. Post* 20 Dec. 1 Three of the Lackawanna 'racks', as the arrangement of piles to fit the ferryboats are called, were left intact.

i. *N. Amer.* A set of antlers. Also *attrib.*

1945 *Richmond* (Va.) *Times-Dispatch* 27 July 14/1 There is no real means of comparing a rack of antlers killed in Bath County and one in New Kent, unless they are placed side by side. **1958** *Outdoor Life* Sept. 34/1 I'd shot moose in British Columbia but never a really big one. This trip I was determined to get a trophy rack. **1971** D. C. BROWN *Yukon Trophy Trails* i. 22 'Wow, he's sure got a big rack,' someone else yelled. **1976** *Listener* 15 Apr. 466/2 The moose..had a rack of five points, which meant that it was five years old and almost fully grown. **1978** L. L. RUE *Deer N. Amer.* iv. 66 A deer with more than four points is called a rack buck... Some racks are large but have few points, some are small but have more points.

j. *U.S. Naut. slang.* (See quot. 1962.)

1955 C. KENTFIELD *Alchemist's Voyage* I. iii. 68 'Where's D'Alessio?' 'In his rack.' **1962** *Amer. Speech* XXXVII. 288 A Marine's bed is not a *sack*, but a *rack*. He *hits the rack* or *puts in rack time*. **1963** *Ibid.* XXXVIII. 78 The term *rack* was borrowed by the Marines from the Navy, and it began to supersede *sack* as the popular term in Marine speech during the early 1950s.

6. *Mech.* A bar, straight or slightly curved, having teeth or indentations on the side or edge, which gear into those of a wheel, pinion, or worm (for the conversion of circular into rectilinear motion or vice versa), or serve to hold something in a desired (and easily alterable) position.

1797 *Encycl. Brit.* (ed. 3) IX. 19 The teeth of these four wheels take alternately into the teeth of four racks. **1805** R. W. DICKSON *Pract. Agric.* I. 39 The friction-bar..being connected..to the front [of the cart] by a closely notched or toothed rack. **1830** LOUDON *Cottage Arch.* §630 The writing-board, or flap, might be made to rise with a rack and horse. **1881** YOUNG *Every man his own Mechanic* 238 The inner jaw is immovable and to the bottom of it a steel rack is fastened.

b. Coupled with *pinion*.

1814 BUCHANAN *Millwork* (1823) 85 The rack and pinion should be made upon the principles of spur geers. **1858** LARDNER *Hand-bk. Nat. Phil.* 32 Sliding shutters, which are raised and lowered by racks and pinions. **1965** G. MCINNES *Road to Gundagai* ix. 134 Up again, straining on the rack-and-pinion of the Rigi.

c. Hence *rack-and-pinion* used attrib., with *adjustment*, *movement*, etc.

1837 GORING & PRITCHARD *Microgr.* 217 Various ingenious contrivances..retaining the rack-and-pinion movement. **1892** *Photogr. Ann.* II. 283 Rack and pinion focussing. *Ibid.* 285 Rack and pinion adjustment. **1903** *Baedeker's Northern Italy* 13 From Capolago to the Monte Generoso, rack-and-pinion railway in 56 minutes. **1958** R. LIDDELL *Morea* II. ii. 55, I took the rack and pinion railway up to Calávryta. **1969** *Observer* (Colour Suppl.) 23 Mar. 29 Rack-and-pinion steering 'can be twirled from lock to lock with the flat palm of one hand'. **1972** *Modern Railways* Sept. 334 This was overcome on the BOB [*sc.* Berner Oberland Bahn] by the use of rack-and-pinion operation with gradients as steep as 1 in 8. **1973** *Country Life* 18 Oct. 1172/1 The Haflinger, a forward-control platform truck..seems to wind on inexorably, rather like a rack and pinion train climbing a mountain. **1978** *Daily Tel.* 16 Aug. 10/6 The ride is on the firm side with the handling being safe and predictable from the rack and pinion steering.

7. In lace-making: (see quots.). Also *attrib.*

1831 MORLEY in Ure *Cotton Manuf.* (1861) II. 356 A rack is a certain length of work counted perpendicularly, and contains 240 meshes or holes. **1832** BABBAGE *Econ. Manuf.* xxx. (ed. 3) 296 The introduction of the 'rack', which counts the number of holes in the length of the piece. **1839** URE *Dict. Arts* 733 A 24 rack piece..is now sold for 7*s*.

8. a. Abbrev. of RACK-DEAL.

1835 WHITE in *Parl. Rep. Timber Duties* 206 The merchants would not sell a cargo without taking some rack and some seconds..and generally the timber merchants had a great many of what were called second rack.

b. = *rack-rail* in sense 9.

1909 *Westm. Gaz.* 7 Aug. 7/2 The greater part of the line would traverse exceedingly difficult country, necessitating ..possibly a few short lengths of rack.

9. *attrib.* and *Comb.*, as **rack-block** *Naut.* (see quot. and cf. sense 5 c); **rack-board**, one of the boards forming the pipe-rack of an organ (also *attrib.*); **rack-calipers**, calipers fitted with a rack and pinion (Knight *Dict. Mech.* 1875); **rack car**, (*a*) a railway-car having open-work sides (cf. sense 3); (*b*) *U.S. Logging*: see quot. 1958; **rack chain**, a chain by which a horse is fastened to the rack in a stall; **rack chase** *Printing*, a chase having racked sides into which fit two adjustable bars; **rack-compass**, a pair of compasses fitted with a rack (sense 6), so also **rack-easel**; **rack-hook**, a hooked lever which catches into the rack in the striking mechanism of a clock; **rack-hurdle, -hurry** (see quots.); †**rack lever**, a lever terminating in a rack formerly employed in the escapement of a clock; **rack-meat**, fodder placed in racks for horses; **rack mounting** *vbl. sb.*, the use of the standardized racks for supporting telephonic or electronic equipment; so **rack mount** *sb.* and *v. trans.*; **rack-pillar**, one of the small upright pieces of wood supporting the rack-boards in an organ; **rack pole**, one of the bars or staves forming a rack (sense 3); **rack-rail**, a cogged rail, into which a cogged wheel on a locomotive works; **rack railway**, a railway having a rack-rail laid between or beside the bearing-rails; **rack-rod** = RACK-BAR; **rack saw**, (*a*) a saw with wide-set teeth (Simmonds *Dict. Trade* 1858); (*b*) see quot. 1971; **rack-side**, one of the horizontal bars of a rack (sense 3); **rack-spring**, the spring attached to the rack in a clock; **rack-stave**, one of the upright staves of a rack (sense 3); **rack-table** = sense 5 d; **rack-tail**, an appendage to the rack in a clock; **rack-tube**, a tube (in a microscope) worked by a rack (sense 6); **rack-way**, (*a*) = *rack-rail*; (*b*) a path through a wood, *esp.* one used for timber extraction; **rack-wheel**, a cog-wheel; **rack-work**, mechanism of the nature of, or containing, a rack (sense 6); **rack-yard**, a stock-yard provided with racks (sense 3).

1794 *Rigging & Seamanship* I. 156 **Rack-blocks* are a range of small single blocks, made from one solid. **1867** SMYTH *Sailor's Word-bk.* 557. **1855** E. J. HOPKINS *Organ* 39 Some thin planks of wood, called *rack-boards..laid parallel with, but four or five inches above, the upper boards. *Ibid.*, Through these rack-board-holes the lower and narrrow ends of the pipe-feet pass. **1881** C. A. EDWARDS *Organs* 57 The Rack-boards..are frames by which the pipes are supported in a perpendicular position over the upper boards. **1875** KNIGHT *Dict. Mech.* 1863/1 [Railway-cars] had four wheels, no springs, and no roof; similar cars, termed '*rack-cars', are still in use. **1958** W. F. MCCULLOCH *Woods Words* 145 *Rack car*, a railroad car specially equipped with stakes or racks to handle pulpwood. **1828** DARVILL *Treat. Race horse* 55 A *rack-chain may be fixed in the centre of the stall. **1958** J. HISLOP *From Start to Finish* iv. 20 Do not leave your horse tied up by the rack-chain, in your hurry to get away. **1963** E. H. EDWARDS *Saddlery* xxii. 167 Usually a rope..to the rear of a head collar is best for tying up unless one has rack chains. **1882** J. SOUTHWARD *Practical Printing* vi. 72 *Rack chases for fixing small formes on presses are made the size of a press table, and obviate the use of furniture. **1898** —— *Mod. Printing* I. ix. 66 Rack chases.. are made to fit the carriage of a press and the bed of a machine. **1859** GULLICK & TIMBS *Paint.* 199 The square '*rack' easel which allows the painter greater facility in raising or lowering his picture. **1875** KNIGHT *Dict. Mech.* 1852/1 **Rack-hook*. **1884** F. J. BRITTEN *Watch & Clockm.* 251 The rack hook is lifted free of the first tooth only at the half-hour. **1770–4** A. YOUNG in A. Hunter *Georg. Ess.* (1803) III. 145 *Rack-hurdles, which are made..[by] leaving the middle rail out and nailing spars across. **1888** *Berksh. Gloss.*, *Rack-hurdles*, hurdles of substantial lathing or split wood. **1788** J. RITSON *Borrowd. Letter* (Cumb. dial.), They feed em [Sea-Nags = ships] wie beck-sand,..but nut out o' *rack-hurries. **1899** *Cumbld. Gloss.*, *Rack-hurry*,..a rack formed of iron bars fixed in the shoot or hurry, which allowed the small coal..to drop through. **1884** F. J. BRITTEN *Watch & Clockm.* 219 The *rack lever is said to have been invented by the Abbé Hautefeuille. **1743** W. ELLIS *Mod. Husbandman* Dec. vii. 46 To..further their Fattening, by enough of dry, hearty Trough and *Rack-meat in Time. **1849** G. A. DEAN *Essays on Construction of Farm Buildings & Labourers' Cottages* 23 Many persons consider that the racks are best placed by the sides of the mangers..others, that horses who work hard should have no rack-meat given to them, considering that they satisfy their hunger much quicker..from the manger. **1965** *Wireless World* July 2 (Advt.), Series 'Y' instruments are housed in strong metal cases and, in some instances, can be *rack-mounted. **1976** *Physics Bull.* Jan. 9 Available in either a rack-mount or a cabinet configuration, it is designed to be used by persons with little or no previous experience with signal averagers. **1978** *Chicago* June 106/1 Rack mounts, for instance, are 'in'. .. These racks will hold pre-amps, amps, equalizers, tuners and tape decks. Some can even accommodate a turntable. **1940** *Chambers's Techn. Dict.* 697/1 **Rack mounting*, the use of standard racks..for mounting panels carrying apparatus ..with a uniform scheme of wiring. **1977** *Gramophone* June 118/1 A Sony rack mounting amplifier using pulse width modulation. **1979** *Sci. Amer.* June 8/2 (Advt.), The 5315B is essentially the same instrument housed in a metal case for rack mounting or stacking. **1881** C. A. EDWARDS *Organs* 57 Rack-boards..are supported by *rack-pillars. **1662** GERBIER *Principles* 32 The *Rack Poles three Inches asunder and upright. **1838** WOOD *Pract. Treat. Rail-roads* (ed. 3) 281 The toothed or *rack rail, was only laid on one side of the road. **1918** *Chambers's Jrnl.* Jan. 13/1 See hazardous bridges being built, and the rack-rail employed to surmount steep gradients. **1931** *Times Educ. Suppl.* 21 Feb. p. iii, An engraving showing a Blenkinsop rack-rail engine and train. **1884** KNIGHT *Dict. Mech.* Suppl. 734/1 **Rack Railway*. **1895** *Daily News* 1 Mar. 5/3 Tourists..who 'do' the Alps in rack railways. **1913** *Chambers's Jrnl.* Jan. 128/2 This railway introduces a cheaper means of ascending rugged mountains than the rack-railway laid upon the ground. **1931** *Times Educ. Suppl.* 21 Feb. p. iii, John Blenkinsop, the inventor of the rack railway, died 100 years ago. **1973** C. BONINGTON *Next Horizon* xii. 183, I..plunged through the deep powder snow..down to the rack-railway track that led up to Kleine Scheidegg. **1839** URE *Dict. Arts* 360 A pushing rod..that passes behind the *rack rod. **1898** *Daily News* 8 Feb. 3/5 The *rack saw, with its 50-feet running platform. **1971** F. C. FORD-ROBERTSON *Terminol. Forest Science* 209/2 *Rack saw*, a head saw (circular or band) with a travelling table operated by rack-and-pinion. **1830** LOUDON *Cottage Arch.* §1103 The *rack sides (top and bottom rails) to be 4 inches by 2 inches and a quarter, and to be fitted in with turned rack-staves. **1892** F. J. BRITTEN *Watch & Clockm.* (ed. 8) 87 If the spring is weak, and the *rack spring strong, it sometimes gives a little. **1587** MASCALL *Govt. Cattle, Sheep* (1627) 202 Their racks to be made..with *rack-staues set nigh together of a good length. *a* **1639** W. WHATELEY *Prototypes* I. xvi. (1640) 166 Them that tie their horses to the rack-staves. **1830** [see *rack-side*]. **1839** URE *Dict. Arts* 1245 The slope of the *rack-table for washing the roasted tin ore is 7¾ inches in the 9 feet. **1875** KNIGHT *Dict. Mech.* 1852/1 **Rack-tail*. **1892** F. J. BRITTEN *Watch & Clockm.* (ed. 8) 87 Rack Tail—A frequent source of trouble in some old clocks is the spring tail to the rack. **1867** J. HOGG *Microsc.* I. ii. 61 So adjusted that its reservoir may be close against the end of the *rack-tube. **1727** D. EATON *Let.* 16 May (1971) 120 The *rack ways in Priors Haw are all brush'd up regularly... I was yesterday in Priors Haw whilst Mr. Goods servant was tything the brush-wood that was cut out of the rack ways. **1825** J. NICHOLSON *Operat. Mechanic* 439 The teeth of the rack-way are of the same pitch as the teeth of a wheel whose axle is in the machine. **1969** *Gloss. for Landscape Work* (*B.S.I.*) v. 40 *Rackway*, a narrow unpaved pathway left or cut through a tree crop to give access and to facilitate the extraction of timber to a wider ride or road. *a* **1824** A. SCOTT in *Trans. High. Soc.* (1824) VI. 33 On the same axis..are fixed the two *rack-wheels, whose teeth will act on the teeth of the racks. **1842** BISCHOFF *Wool. Manuf.* II. 498 This cloth-beam..is furnished with a rack-wheel for the purpose of letting in or winding on the cloth. **1769** *Phil. Trans.* LIX. 189 My telescope..was..governed by *rack-work. **1861** *All Year Round* 13 July 369 There was an unusual quantity of rackwork and windlass tackle about. **1772** *Ann. Reg.* 120/2, 20 horses and 7 cows; the latter in a house or *rack yard. **1877** *N.W. Linc. Gloss.*, *Rack-yard*, a fold-yard.

rack (ræk), *sb.*^{3} Forms: 5–7 racke, 6 rakke, (*Sc.* rak, ract), 6– rack; 6–8 **wrack**. Also 5–7 **rake**. [Related to RACK *v.*^{3}, and perh. formed from it in Eng., but cf. also G. *recke*, more commonly *recke-*, *reck-*, or *rackbank*, a rack for drawing wire, stretching leather, inflicting torture, etc.

An obs. Du. *racke* 'tormentum, fidiculæ, equuleus' is alleged by Kilian, but its genuineness is doubtful, esp. as Kilian also cites the Eng. word.]

1. An instrument of torture formerly in use, consisting (usually) of a frame having a roller at each end; the victim was fastened to these by the wrists and ankles, and had the joints of his limbs stretched by their rotation. (See also quot. 1632.)

c **1460** *Towneley Myst.* xxiii. 88 He wold haue turnyd an othere croke Myght he haue had the rake. **1481** CAXTON *Reynard* (Arb.) 24 Your hows shal be byseged al aboute and ther shal be made to fore it galowes and racke. **1560** DAUS tr. *Sleidane's Comm.* 312 Streight waies was he put upon the Racke, and examined by torture. **1581** CAMPION in *Confer.* I. (1584) Cib, He..had bene twise on the Racke, and.. racking was more grieuous then hanging. **1632** LITHGOW *Trav.* x. 463 A Pottaro or Racke is..made of three plankes of Timber, the vpmost end whereof is larger then a ful stride; the lower end being narrow. *a* **1711** KEN *Blandina* Poet. Wks. 1721 IV. 520 Then on the Rack the Saint they stretch, Her Limbs with Screws and Pulleys retch. **1827** HALLAM *Const. Hist.* (1876) I. iii. 148 The rack seldom stood idle in the Tower for all the latter part of Elizabeth's reign. **1875** STUBBS *Const. Hist.* III. xviii. 281 The rack which bore the name of the duke of Exeter's daughter.

Phr. **1587** HOLINSHED *Chron.* III. 1326/2 The chiefe matter..is as yet vnreuealed, and come racke, come rope, neuer shall that be discouered.

b. *transf.* and *fig.* That which (*rarely* one who) causes acute suffering, physical or mental; also, the result produced by this; intense pain or suffering.

1591 GREENE *Maidens Dr.* xxxvi, Her outward woes betrayed her inward rack. **1607** DEKKER *Knt.'s Conjur.* (1842) p. vi, They that haue once or twice lyen vpon the rack of publicke censure. *a* **1641** SUCKLING *Goblins* v. (1646) 55 What a racke have I within me to see you suffer. **1718** PRIOR *Power* 142 The gout's fierce rack, the burning fever's rage. **1792** S. ROGERS *Pleas. Mem.* II. 49 The racks of thought, and freezings of despair. **1826** DISRAELI *Viv. Grey* IV. iv, There is yet an intellectual rack of which few dream. **1848** THACKERAY *Van. Fair* vi, What is the rack in the punch, at night, to the rack in the head of a morning.

c. Phr. *on the rack*: In a state of acute physical or mental suffering; in keen anxiety or suspense.

1596 SHAKS. *Merch. V.* III. ii. 25 Let me choose, For as I am, I liue vpon the racke. **1668** TEMPLE *Lett.*, *Marq. de Castel Rodrigo* Wks. 1731 II. 116 To see him keep us three or four Days on the Rack till the Affair was just breaking. **1711** ADDISON *Spect.* No. 170 ¶5 A cool Behaviour sets him on the Rack. **1737** *Common Sense* I. 178 He was upon the Rack to be satisfied. **1863** KINGLAKE *Crimea* (1876) I. vii. 104 When for some time men's minds had been kept on the rack, it became known [etc.].

d. *to put* or *set* (faculties, †words, etc.) *on the rack*, to strain to the utmost. So *to be on the rack*, to be at full stretch or strain.

1606 HIERON *Wks.* I. 65 My text very naturally, without setting it vpon the racke, occasioneth the vrging of that duty. *a* **1680** BUTLER *Rem.* (1759) I. 86 Sometimes I set my Wits upon the Rack. **1693** R. FLEMING *Disc. Earthquakes* 23 Men are so much on the Rack how to solve all by natural Demonstration. **1778** MAD. D'ARBLAY *Diary* Aug., They have both worn themselves out by being eternally on the rack to give entertainment to others. **1818** BYRON *Juan* I. clxix, Antonia's skill was put upon the rack. **1856** HUGHES *Tom Brown* II. iii, Martin's ingenuity was therefore for ever on the rack to supply himself with a light.

2. A frame on which cloth is stretched. *Obs.* exc. *dial.*

1519 in Money *Hist. Newbury* (1887) 458 All the Rakkys and teynters as thei now stonde. **1533–4** *Act 25 Hen. VIII*, c. 18 §5 Euerie suche clothe [shall]..be meated both length and brede..before they be set vpon the racke and dried. *a* **1633** AUSTIN *Medit.* (1635) 281 A Web [is]..sometimes upon the Tenters sideswayes, and sometimes on the Racke endwayes. **1678** *Lond. Gaz.* 1281/4 Lost..off from the Racks, 24 yards of Cloth. **1886** ELWORTHY *W. Som. Word-bk.*, *Rack*, a long upright frame on which woollen cloths are stretched while drying.

†**3.** A windlass or winch for bending a crossbow. *Obs.*

1512 *Test. Ebor.* (Surtees) V. 36 My bigge crosbowe w^t the rakke of it. **1578** *Lanc. Wills* (1857) II. 60 One crosse bowe wth the racke to the same. **1630** [see GAFFLE 1]. **1648** WILKINS

Math. Magick I. xiii. 91 The force of racks, which serve for bending of the strongest bows. **1672** [see GAFFLE 1]. **1687** MIEGE *Gt. Fr. Dict.* II. s.v., To set up a Cross-bow with a Rack.

fig. *a* **1628** LD. BROOKE *Alaham* IV. Chorus iv, Your safest racke to winde us up is Loue.

4. = RACK-RENT (see also quot. 1688). Now *rare* or *Obs.*

1605 SANDYS *St. Relig.* O ij b, The parish Priestes in Italie, who have not the Tenthes, which..considering the great rents and rackes would be vnsupportable. **1688** R. HOLME *Armoury* III. 70/1 Such as hold Lands and Livings..upon the Rack, or half-Rack, that is upon the Yearly value, or half value..avoiding at the Landlords pleasure. **1720** *Lond. Gaz.* No. 5895/3 Of the Value of 1500*l.* per Annum on the Rack. **1818** JAS. MILL *Brit. India* II. v. iii. 387 When the revenues were farmed to the Zemindars, these contractors were induced to turn upon the ryots..the same rack which was applied to themselves.

5. That which racks or strains; stress of weather; a storm.

1806 H. SIDDONS *Maid, Wife & Widow* I. 40 These she had preserved amid the frowns of adversity and the rack of wealth. *c* **1865** W. WHITMAN *Leaves of Grass* (1884) 262 O Captain! my Captain!.. The ship has weather'd every rack. **1891** *Daily News* 17 June 5/1 A strong voice, unworn by age and the rack of various seas.

6. *attrib.* and *Comb.*, as ***rack-bent, -proof*** adjs.; **rack-master**, an officer having charge of the rack.

1694 MOTTEUX *Rabelais* IV. xxxi. (1737) 127 A..*rack-bent Cross-Bow. **1582** in J. H. Pollen *Acts Eng. Mart.* (1891) 223 The old *rackmaster, Mr. Topcliffe. **1602** T. FITZHERBERT *Apol.* 4 The crvelty of the Rackmaisters in England. **1886** J. GILLOW *Lit. & Biog. Hist. Eng. Cath.* II. 397 The rack-master of the Tower, a most cruel torturer of priests. **1654** SIR E. NICHOLAS in *N. Papers* (Camden) II. 125 It was to deepe a policy..unless he had bin *rack proofe.

rack (ræk), *sb.*[4] Now *rare.* [Of obscure origin: cf. RACKBONE.

Sometimes referred to *hreacca, hrecca* used to render L. *occiput* in the earliest OE. glosses, but this is prob. an error for *hnecca* neck.]

1. a. A neck, or fore-part of the spine, *esp.* of mutton or pork.

1570 FOXE *A. & M.* 1191/1 A brothe made with the fore-part of a racke of Mutton. **1585** *Good Huswife's Jewell* II. 1 You may boyle Chynes and racks of Veale in all points as this is. **1630** B. JONSON *New Inn* I. i, A poor quotidian rack of mutton. *a* **1648** DIGBY *Closet Open.* (1677) 163 Cut a rack of mutton into tender steaks. **1665** MAY *Accompl. Cook* 167 To carbonado a Rack of Pork. *a* **1796** in PEGGE *Derbicisms* (E.D.S.). **1880-** In various dial. glossaries. **1964** J. MASTERS *Trial at Monomoy* iii. 101 Mary Tolley began to serve the main course, a rack of lamb. **1972** *New York* 12 June 63 Purée of cold carrot soup, rack of lamb, cauliflower provençale. **1974** *Observer* (Colour Suppl.) 22 Sept. 60/3 (Advt.), Fresh river trout followed by rack of highland lamb. **1977** *Time* 21 Nov. 44/3 Recently he ordered a hotel restaurant billboard repainted after noticing that the rack-of-lamb dinner on it 'looked raw'.

b. At Winchester School: A rib of mutton.

1870 MANSFIELD *Sch.-Life Winchester Coll.* 84 All these 'Dispars' had different names;..the ribs 'Racks'. **1893** W. TUCKWELL *Anc. Ways Winchester* 35 The saddles, legs, shoulders, supplied the higher tables; the juniors had the 'racks'.

†**2.** A segment of the backbone or *os sacrum. Obs.*

1615 CROOKE *Body of Man* 899 The marrow concluded within the rackes of the Holy-bone. *c* **1720** W. GIBSON *Farrier's Guide* I. v. (1722) 65 Their Use is to bend the Racks of their Loins.

3. a. The bones of a dead horse. **b.** A horse consisting of 'skin and bone'.

1851 H. MAYHEW *Lond. Labour* I. 181 The bones (called 'racks' by the knackers) are chopped up and boiled. **1878** *Daily News* 16 Sept. 3/1 Among the horses are some fine specimens of racks, that is fleshless horses.

c. *U.S. colloq.* **rack of bones**, a skeleton; an emaciated person or animal. Also ***rackabone, rackerbone, rack-o'-bones***.

1804 J. ORDWAY in Lewis & Ordway *Jrnls. Western Explor.* (1916) 128 We saw the rack of Bones of a verry large fish. **1854** M. J. HOLMES *Tempest & Sunshine* iv. 58 Turn that old rackerbone of yourn straight round, and turn down that ar street. **1856** G. D. BREWERTON *War in Kansas* xxxi. 314 Indeed she was to all appearances but a mere rack of bones, over whose unpicturesque outline nature had condescended to draw an angular wrinkling of skin. **1877** J. HABBERTON *Jericho Road* xvi. 146 Ain't it bad enough to be a good-for-nothin' rack of bones that's no comfort to myself? **1900** *Congress. Rec.* XXXIII. App. 6 Mar. 117/2 A Western farmer had a college-bred son who went off preaching... He came back with an old rackabone. **1911** J. C. LINCOLN *Cap'n Warren's Wards* ix. 140 If she fell on that poor rack-o'-bones,..'twould be a final smash. **1949** *Sat. Even. Post* 2 Apr. 97/2 Mount that rack o' bones you call a horse and ride in front o' me.

rack (ræk), *sb.*[5] [Variant of WRACK, WRECK in various senses.]

1. a. Destruction; chiefly in phr. *to go* (etc.) *to rack* (***and ruin***).

1599 in Fowler *Hist. C.C.C.* (O.H.S.) 349 In the mean season the College shall goe to rack and ruin. *a* **1609** BP. ANDREWES *Serm.* (1841) II. 249 Between Jehu and Jeroboam Solomon's seed went to rack. **1667** MILTON *P.L.* XI. 821 A World devote to universal rack. **1782** ELIZ. BLOWER *Geo. Bateman* II. 126 Everything would soon go to sixes and sevens, and rack and ruin. **1859** G. MEREDITH *R. Feverel* xxxix, If the world's not coming to rack. **1874** BURNAND *My Time* xxxiii. 346 His academicals..run to..utter rack and ruin.

†**b.** A crash as of something breaking. *Obs.*

1671 MILTON *P.R.* IV. 452, I heard the rack as Earth and Skie would mingle.

2. †**a.** A wrecked ship. *Obs. rare*$^{-1}$.

a **1658** CLEVELAND *Wks.* (1687) 365 Ten thousand Racks, Cast on the Shore of the Red Sea.

b. What is cast up by the sea; wrack.

1882 OUIDA *Maremma* I. 102 Well, go, rake some seaweed together or any other rack of your precious sea that one can burn.

c. *U.S.* **rack-heap**, (*a*) a heap of wreckage; (*b*) (see quot. 1958).

1883 'MARK TWAIN' *Life on Miss.* xxiii. 258 There was only one boat advertised..a Grand Tower packet... She was a venerable rack-heap, and a fraud to boot. **1889** P. BUTLER *Personal Recollections* vii. 72 There were in the river heaps of drift-wood, called 'rack-heaps', dangerous places into which the water rushed with great violence. **1892** 'MARK TWAIN' in *Sun* (N.Y.) 13 Mar. 18/2 Fridolin entered ..with a tall skeleton stalking in his rear... The testimony of this wandering rackheap of unidentified bones. **1909** —— *Is Shakes. Dead?* i. 18 When the *Pennsylvania* blew up and became a drifting rack-heap freighted with wounded and dying. **1958** W. F. MCCULLOCH *Woods Words* 145 *Rackheap. a.* A piled-up drift or heap of logs and trees in a river. *b.* Sometimes applied to a heap of logs piled up ready to be splashed down a river.

rack (ræk), *sb.*[6] Also 9 **wrack**. [Related to RACK *v.*[4], and perh. formed from it.] A horse's gait in which the two feet on each side are lifted almost simultaneously, and the body is left entirely without support between the lifting of one pair and the landing of the other. Now only *U.S.*

1580 BLUNDEVIL *Horsemanship* I. iii. Bj b, Their [Turky horses'] trauelling pace is neither amble, racke, nor trot; but a certaine kinde of easie traine. **1607** MARKHAM *Caval.* II. (1617) 135 Exercise him..first vpon an ordinarie rack or foot-pace, then vpon a slow trott. *Ibid.* IV. 5. **1683** *Lond. Gaz.* No. 1846/4 A full trust Nag, a good Trot, short Rack. **1832** FR. A. KEMBLE *Girlhood* III. 257 The Americans..like a horse to have a shambling sort of half-trot, half-canter, which they judiciously call a rack. **1893** E. MUYBRIDGE *Descr. Zoopraxogr.* 35 The rack is an ungraceful gait of the horse, and disagreeable to those who seek comfort in riding.

fig. **1641** HINDE *J. Bruen* lix. 198 All the ease of such a rack will be no other, but..to gallop to the divel.

rack (ræk), *sb.*[7] Also 7 **racke, raack.** [Aphetic form of ARRACK: so also G. *rack.*] = ARRACK. *fool rack*, see FOOL *sb.*[1] Also *attrib. as* ***rack-house***, RACK-PUNCH.

1602 SIR J. LANCASTER in Purchas *Pilgrims* III. (1625) 154 The King..dranke oft to the Generall in their Wine, which they call Racke. **1602-5** E. SCOT *Ibid.* 184 We..draue them into a Racke-house [*Margin.* Racke house where hot drinks are sold]. **1663** BOYLE *Usef. Exp. Nat. Philos.* II. ii. 105 This rack..is often drunk in hot weather. **1719** DE FOE *Crusoe* I. iv, Five or six gallons of rack. **1795** SIR J. DALRYMPLE *Let. to Admiralty* 11 Their common beverage, water, and rack bad and new. **1821** BYRON *Juan* IV. liii, I would take refuge in weak punch, but rack..Wakes me next morning with its synonym. **1848** [see RACK *sb.*[3] 1 b]. **1871** M. COLLINS *Mrq. & Merch.* I. ix. 291 Rooker took..a glass of 'rack'.

b. (See quot.)

1773 *Encycl. Brit.* III. 525/1 *Rack*, a spirituous liquor made by the Tartars of Tongusia. This kind of rack is made of mare's milk, which is left to be sour [etc.].

†**rack**, *sb.*[8] *Obs. rare*$^{-1}$. [? Related to RAKE *v.*[1] Cf. Icel. and Sw. dial. *rak* rakings.] A rick.

A doubtful form: ed. 1566 has *reake.*

1574 WITHALS *Dict.* 21/1 A ricke or racke of hay, *strues. Extruo*, to make up in rokes [*sic*] or rackes.

rack (ræk), *sb.*[9] [Of obscure origin.] The skin of a young rabbit (see quots.).

1805 R. W. DICKSON *Pract. Agric.* II. 1204 There is annually a great loss in what are termed half skins, quarter skins, and racks, sixteen of which are only allowed for as one whole skin. **1878** *Ure's Dict. Arts* IV. Suppl. 380 The rabbit skins are..sorted into four kinds,..racks, or young rabbits about two months old, which have not lost their first coat.

rack (ræk), *v.*[1] [f. RACK *sb.*[1] 3.]

1. *intr.* Of clouds: To drive before the wind. *to rack up*, to clear up, said of the sky (Jam.).

1590 [see RACKING *ppl. a.*[1]]. ? *a* **1611** BEAUM. & FL. *Four Plays in One, Tri. Honour* iv, Stay, clouds, ye rack too fast. **1631** *Celestina* XIX. 187 Looke on the cloudes and see how speedily they racke away. **1678** BUNYAN *Pilgr.* I. 32, I..saw the Clouds rack at an unusual rate. **1812** SCOTT *Rokeby* I. i, Racking o'er her [the Moon's] face, the cloud Varies the tincture of her shroud. **1833** M. SCOTT *Tom Cringle* ii. (1858) 63 A thin fleecy shred of cloud racking across the moon's disk.

fig. **1626** T. H[AWKINS] *Caussin's Holy Crt.* 289 A fayth floating, and racking vp, and downe, like clouds.

†**2.** *trans.* Of the wind: To drive (clouds). *Obs.*

1596 *Edw. III*, II. i, Inconstant clouds, That, rack'd upon the carriage of the winds, Increase or die.

rack (ræk), *v.*[2] [f. RACK *sb.*[2]]

1. *trans.* To fit up (a stable), with racks. *rare*$^{-1}$.

1583 in W. H. Turner *Select. Rec. Oxford* 432 The same stable to be planked and racked at the charges of this Cytie.

†**2.** *transf.* ? To feed as at a rack. *Obs. rare*$^{-1}$.

1659 *Burton's Diary* (1828) IV. 268 They look upon them [negroes] as their goods, horses, &c., and rack them only to make their time out of them, and cherish them to perform their work.

3. *to rack up.* **a.** *intr.* To fill a stable-rack with hay or straw before leaving the horse or horses for the night.

1778 [W. MARSHALL] *Minutes Agric.* 22 Nov. 1775 The hay is meant merely to rack-up with. *Ibid.* 5 Feb. 1776 On the hills of Surry, the Farmers rack up with straw. **1888** in *Berksh. Gloss.*

b. *trans.* To fill the rack for (a horse).

1743 W. ELLIS *Mod. Husbandman* Dec. iv. 29 When the Landlord came to rack up the Horse for all Night. **1798** MIDDLETON *View Agric.* 361 They must be taken into the stable, and..be racked up with tare hay at night. **1834** *Brit. Husb.* I. 232 Pea-haulm is..employed in cart-stables for racking up the horses. **1893** *Times* 20 May 11/5 The younger generation find it intolerably irksome to return after supper to the stables to 'rack up' the horses. **1960** G. E. EVANS *Horse in Furrow* ii. 43 The baiters' mates..were expected..to *rack the horses up* for the night—that is, to fill their racks with fodder.

fig. **1844** J. T. HEWLETT *Parsons & W.* xix, You might have racked yourself up more comfortably.

c. To fasten (a horse) to the rack.

1856 'STONEHENGE' *Brit. Rural Sports* 330/2 The lad first racks up his horse, so that he cannot lie down, but can reach his manger. **1886** ELWORTHY *W. Som. Word-bk.*, *Rack up*, to fasten up a horse with a short chain so that he cannot lie down. **1886** *Sat. Rev.* 6 Mar. 327/2 It is stupid of a groom to rack a horse short up while he is feeding.

d. *fig.* To chalk up, to notch up; to achieve, to score. *N. Amer.*

1961 in WEBSTER. **1970** *Globe & Mail* (Toronto) 28 Sept. 18/3 The winners won the statistical battle by a wide margin, racking up 22 first downs to 16 for the losers. **1974** E. MCGIRR *Murderous Journey* 82 I've got some leave of absence piled up... I would have racked up close on a month. **1976** *Billings* (Montana) *Gaz.* 16 June 3-c/1 Billings began racking up runs in the fourth and fifth innings, while Missoula managed only one more run. **1977** *Time* 14 Nov. 25/1 Over the short run the U.N. vote may even have played into the hands of South African Prime Minister John Vorster, who is anxious to rack up a big majority in the country's Nov. 30 elections. **1978** G. VIDAL *Kalki* vi. 139 CBS had racked up a Nielsen rating of 36.3, the highest ever in that particular time slot. **1979** *Sci. Amer.* Dec. 30/3 She professionally ferries light aircraft (very often Beeches), the number of engines your choice, out of the U.S. to anywhere at all, having racked up almost 350 ocean crossings in 17 years of action.

4. a. To place (a thing) in or on a rack. *spec.* in the *Oil Industry*, to place (lengths of drill pipe) in a pipe rack or derrick.

1855 E. J. HOPKINS *Organ* 39 Most of the metal flue pipes ..are racked in this manner. **1897** *Daily News* 8 Nov. 3/1 The Manhattan Beach Cycle Track have racked 1,000 Cycles. **1949** *Our Industry* (Anglo-Iranian Oil Co. Ltd.) (ed. 2) ii. 39 When the drill pipe is being withdrawn, it is uncoupled in 'stands' of three 30-ft. lengths, these 90-ft. 'stands' being racked upright in the derrick. **1970** W. A. SMITH *Gold Mine* xxix. 81 Big King..wiped down his glossy shoes and racked them. **1971** C. BONINGTON *Annapurna South Face* xiii. 163 Mick got ready for the next pitch,.. racking his pitons on karabiners slung to one side so that he could free them easily. **1973** J. W. JENNER in Hobson & Pohl *Mod. Petroleum Technol.* (ed. 4) iv. 120 The floormen.. swing the bottom end of the stand away from the table and it is lowered on to the rig floor, at which time the derrickman ..pulls the top of the stand over and racks it against the side of the derrick. **1974** *BP Shield Internat.* Oct. 18/2 The second noise was..the drilling pipe being racked in the derrick.

b. *Mining.* To wash on the rack (sense 5 f).

1891 in *Cent. Dict.*

5. a. To move, extend, etc. by means of a rack and pinion. **b.** *intr.* To be moved in this way.

1867 J. HOGG *Microsc.* I. ii. 62 By racking up the condenser for the best light. **1890** *Anthony's Photogr. Bull.* III. 94 A Double Extension Camera..where the front racks out. *Ibid.* 295 The camera is racked to a certain distance. **1906** *Westm. Gaz.* 18 Aug. 14/2 If the image is too big, rack out the camera a little and bring the board nearer. If too small, rack in and push the board away.

6. To give (a thing) the form of a rack; to make as a rack.

1891 in *Cent. Dict.*

rack (ræk), *v.*[3] Also 5 **rakke**, 6 *Sc.* **rak**, 6-7 **racke**, 7 **wrack**, *pa. pple.* **ract.** [Prob. a. MDu. *recken* (Du. *rekken*) or MLG. *recken*, OHG. *recchan* (LG. and G. *recken*) to stretch, draw out, = OE. *reccan*: see RECCHE.

A MLG. *racken* is also recorded, and Kilian has *racken* 'torquere, tendere, tormentis exprimere'. Cf. also G. *racken* to vex, torture (Grimm).]

1. *trans.* To stretch the joints of (a person) by tugging or pulling, esp. with intention to cause severe pain, and *spec.* by means of a special apparatus (see RACK *sb.*[3]).

1433 LYDG. *St. Edmund* II. 277 Worthi to been enhangid bi the hals Or to be rakkid with a broke chyne. **1526** *Pilgr. Perf.* (W. de W. 1531) 135 Some drowned,..some racked, some hanged on a gybet. **1582** STANYHURST *Æneis* III. (Arb.) 71 You rack no forrener owtcast, You rent a Troian. **1632** LITHGOW *Trav.* x. 467 This they did..to make me beleeue I was going to be rackt againe. **1675** BROOKS *Gold. Key* Wks. 1867 V. 89 His legs and hands were violently racked and pulled out to the places fitted for his fastenings. **1712** E. COOKE *Voy. S. Sea* 437 The Pirates exercis'd the most barbarous Cruelty, racking them inhumanly. **1829** SCOTT *Demonol.* viii. 275 Their mouths were stopped, their throats choked, their limbs racked. **1876** GREEN *Stray Stud.* 146 A drummer who had joined in the attack was racked mercilessly.

transf. **1835** LYTTON *Rienzi* I. ix, The winds and storms torture and rack the sea. **1875** MAINE *Hist. Inst.* vi. 183 Their country was racked with perpetual disturbance.

b. To affect with pain similar to that caused by use of the rack. (Said esp. of diseases.)

1588 FRAUNCE *Lawiers Log.* Ded. q ij b, Which..did yet so racke my raunging heade, and bring low my crased body. **1610** SHAKS. *Temp.* I. ii. 369 Ile racke thee with old Crampes, Fill all thy bones with Aches. **1674** ABP. LEIGHTON in

Lauderdale Papers. (Camden) III. xlvi. 76, I keep not bedd much, nor am..rack't with sharp and tormenting diseases. **1742** GRAY *Eton* 85 This racks the joints, this fires the veins. *a* **1859** MACAULAY *Biog.* (1867) 138 A cruel malady racked his joints.

c. To inflict mental pain or torture on (a person); to torture, distract, lacerate (the mind, soul, etc.).

1601 SHAKS. *Twel. N.* v. i. 226 How haue the houres rack'd, and tortur'd me, Since I haue lost thee? **1602** *2nd Pt. Return fr. Parnass.* IV. ii. 1747 Till with my verses I haue rackt his soule. **1647** COWLEY *Mistr.*, *Dialogue* vii, The Sin Will rack and torture us within. **1709** STEELE *Tatler* No. 98 ¶3 How must she be racked with Jealousy. **1771** FLETCHER *Checks* Wks. 1795 II. 243 O how does..guilty horror rack their breasts! **1838** LYTTON *Alice* 380, I regret no more the falsehood that so racked me for the time. **1865** DICKENS *Mut. Fr.* III. xiii, Mr. Fledgeby meant him to be racked.

†**d.** *transf.* To examine searchingly, as by the application of torture. *Obs. rare*[−1].

1581 J. BELL *Haddon's Answ. Osor.* 126 There is nothing so holy in workes, but..must needes be unsavorie in the sight of God, if without Christ it bee racked with exact scrutyne of Gods severe Judgement.

†**2.** To stretch, pull out, increase the length of (a thing, period of time, etc.). *Obs.*

1463–4 [see RACKING *vbl. sb.*[3]]. **1558** *Act 1 Eliz.* c. 12 *Preamble*, Certayne..persons..cast the peeces of cloth ouer a beame..and..racke, stretche and drawe the same. **1565** JEWEL *Def. Apol.* (1611) 302 Heere perhaps yee will set Faith vpon the Last, and racke her to a larger sise. **1613** PURCHAS *Pilgrimage* I. x. 48 The Chaldæan Kalendar, which yet they racke higher to fowre hundred three score and tenne thousand yeres. **1642** FULLER *Holy & Prof. St.* II. xiv. 102 He gives them their true dimensions, not racking them for one, and shrinking them for another.

b. To pull or tear apart, to separate by force, to break up. *Obs.* exc. *dial.*

1549 COVERDALE, etc. *Erasm. Par. Eph.* 7 No more than we see the membres of the body not agre or to be racked one from an other because thei be not indifferently apte al to one vse. **1560** BECON *New Catech.* III. Wks. 1564 II. 327 b, They ..racke that one tente commaundement into two for to supply the nomber. **1608** TOPSELL *Serpents* (1658) 595 Some thinke the putride backe-bone in the grave rack'd.. the shape of snakes to take. **1848** A. B. EVANS *Leicestersh. Words*, *Rack* and *Rack up*, to break up. 'Why didn't ye get at it, and rack it up'.

c. To shake (a thing) violently; to strain; to injure by shaking or straining. Also *absol.*

1840 R. H. DANA *Bef. Mast* xxviii. 93 A dreadful cough, which seemed to rack his whole shattered system. **1865** A. L. HOLLEY *Ordnance & Armor* 134 To waste no power in racking the whole side of the ship. **1867** *Pall Mall G.* 27 July 10 We assumed that the American guns specially constructed to 'rack' would 'rack' as intended. **1873** SYMONDS *Gk. Poets* Ser. I. vii. 194 The Erinnyes leap upon the palace of Atreus, and rack it like a tempest.

d. *intr.* To undergo stretching, strain, or dislocation. Chiefly *Sc.*

1508 DUNBAR *Tua mariit wemen* 350, I gert the renȝeis rak, et rif into sondir. **1535** STEWART *Cron. Scot.* I. 124 Sum gat ane rais gart all hir ribbis rak. **1695** BLACKMORE *Pr. Arth.* III. 47 The Earth's grip'd Bowels with Convulsions rack. **1721** PERRY *Daggenh. Breach* 12 The weight of Earth..usually subjects them [Sluices] to rack and settle down at the Foundation. **1825** JAMIESON s.v., He has a conscience that will rack like raw plaiding. **1890** SERVICE *Notandums* 125 Lang or they win this length..their chafts are like to rack wi' the gantin'.

†**3.** To strain the meaning of (words, etc.); to give a forced interpretation to. *Obs.*

In quot. 1711 with allusion to sense 1.

1549 LATIMER *Serm. Ploughers* (Arb.) 17 This is one of the places yat hath ben racked, as I tolde you of rackynge scriptures. **1599** THYNNE *Animadv.* (1875) 42 How yo[u] may seme to force and racke the worde to Chaucers meaninge, I knowe not. **1645** FULLER *Good Th. in Bad T.* (1841) 21 Grant that I may never rack a scripture simile beyond the true intent thereof. **1692** BENTLEY *Boyle Lect.* ix. 328 The native and naked Letter, which is not to be racked and wrested from its obvious meaning. **1711** 'J. DISTAFF' *Char. Don Sacheverellio* 4 He racks a Text to make it confess a Meaning it never dream'd of.

†**b.** To strain or wrest (law or justice). *Obs.*

1580 LYLY *Euphues* (Arb.) 452 Not racking the lawes to extremitie, but mittigating the rigour with mercy. **1607** J. DAVIES *Summa Totalis* I. 4* So, God doth iudge, and neuer Iustice Rack.

c. To strain, task severely, put pressure upon (the mind, brain, etc.).

1583 W. BYRD in Farr *S.P. Eliz.* (1845) I. 224 Racke not thy wit to winne by wicked waies. *c* **1680** BEVERIDGE *Serm.* (1729) I. 193 They rack their brains..they hazard their lives for it. **1713** STEELE *Guard.* No. 47 ¶7 She racked her invention to no purpose. **1768** MAD. D'ARBLAY *Early Diary* 20 May, I have rack'd my brains half-an-hour—in vain. **1831** *Society* I. 216 Fanny was racking her brains for something to say. **1880** L. STEPHEN *Pope* iv. 82 Racking his wits to contrive exquisite compliments.

†**d.** To force, constrain *to* an action or feeling.

1602 MARSTON *Antonio's Rev.* v. iii, The court is rackt to pleasure; each man straines To faine a jocund eye.

†**e.** To stretch or raise beyond the normal extent, amount or degree (cf. 4). *Obs.*

1596 SHAKS. *Merch. V.* I. i. 181 My credit..shall be rackt euen to the vttermost. **1603** FLORIO *Montaigne* III. xii. 598 Striving about my ransome, which they racked so high [etc.]. **1618** CHAPMAN *Hesiod* II. 22 Hasten thy labours, that thy crowned fields, May load themselues to thee, and rack their yeelds.

4. To raise (rent) above a fair or normal amount. Cf. RACK-RENT.

1553 *Primer Edw. VI*, P v b, [That they] may not racke and stretche oute the rentes of their houses and landes. **1598** BP. HALL *Sat.* IV. ii. 20 They racke their rents vnto a treble rate. **1657** TRAPP *Comm. Job* xxxi. 39 If I have caused..the poor Rent-holders (by racking their rents) to misse of a subsistence. **1778** *Phil. Surv. S. Irel.* 311 Racked the rents to a pitch above the reach of the old tenant. **1826** *Q. Rev.* XXXIV. 214 He racked no rents to maintain the expenses of his establishment.

b. To charge an excessive rent for (land). ? *Obs.*

1581 RICH *Farew.* (1846) 11 Landes be so racked at such a rate. **1628** WITHER *Brit. Rememb.* VII. 751 Yet stand their Farmes already rackt so high, That they have begger'd halfe their Tenantry. **1641** BROME *Joviall Crew* Wks. 1873 III. 356 What Acre of your thousands have you rack'd? **1766** *Museum Rusticum* VI. 145 Open fields may be as high racked as inclosures.

c. To oppress (a person) by extortions or exactions, *esp.* of excessive rent; to bear hard upon (one's purse, etc.).

1584 T. LUPTON *Dreame Devil & Dives*, Wo woorth the time that ever we rackt our tenants. **1594** *1st Part Contention* (1843) 34 Because I would not racke the needie Commons. **1600** HEYWOOD *1st Pt. Edw. IV*, Wks. 1874 I. 69 Oh, good Sir Humfrey, do not rack my purse. **1624** CAPT. SMITH *Virginia* VI. 210 Here are no hard Landlords to racke vs with high rents. *a* **1674** CLARENDON *Hist. Reb.* x. §122 The declared Delinquents [were] racked to as high compositions. **1791** NEWTE *Tour Eng. & Scot.* 124 The same increase of luxury which would induce the landlord to rack his tenant [etc.]. **1862** J. A. ST. JOHN *Four Conq. Eng.* II. 303 Racking the people with impost, and collecting treasure from all parts. **1883** S. C. HALL *Retrospect* II. 315 Implying that tenants were to be racked to the utmost.

absol. **1774** CUMBERLAND in *Westm. Mag.* II. 600 In vain the steward racks, the tenants rave. **1823** BYRON *Juan* IX. xv, Let *this* one toil for bread—*that* rack for rent.

†**d.** To extort (money, etc.). *Obs.*

1591 SPENSER *M. Hubberd* 1306 Each place..fild with treasure rackt with robberies. **1622** FLETCHER *Sea-Voy.* I. i, Here lies all..The money I ha' rack'd by usury. *a* **1680** BUTLER *Rem.* (1759) I. 310 When there is no more to be racked out of the People upon any other Pretence.

absol. **1603** H. CROSSE *Vertues Commw.* (1878) 58 It is neither right, nor honest, to racke, extort, and purloyne from other.

e. To exhaust (tenants, land, etc.) by exactions or excessive use. Also with *out.*

1778 *Family In-compact* 6 Her Lands and Tenants almost rack'd. **1850** *Jrnl. R. Agric. Soc.* XI. II. 717 Soon after it was enclosed it was racked out by over-cropping. **1856** FROUDE *Hist. Eng.* (1858) II. x. 410 It was thought, too, that they had racked their estates. *Ibid.* III. xv. 283 Using..their last opportunity of racking out their properties.

†**5.** *to rack a horse's wind*: to open his lungs. *Obs. rare.*

1607 MARKHAM *Caval.* III. (1617) 45 The first chase will (as the Northerne man saies) racke your Horses winde, and so prepare him to his labor. **1614** —— *Cheap Husb.* I. i. 8 Trauaile moderately in the morning, till his winde be rack'd, and his limbes warmed.

rack (ræk), *v.*[4] [Of obscure origin: cf. RACK *sb.*[6] The F. *racquassure*, by which Palsgr. renders 'racking', appears to be otherwise unknown.]

a. *intr.* Of animals, *esp.* horses: To move with the gait called a rack. Also *trans.* with a distance as object.

1530 [see RACKING *vbl. sb.*[4]]. **1589** PEELE *Eclogue to Earl Essex* xii, His rain-deer racking with proud and stately pace. *c* **1626** *Dick of Devon* I. iii. in Bullen *Old Pl.* (1883) II. 23 Ile ..trott up hill with you and racke downewards. **1671** *Lond. Gaz.* No. 627/4 Bay Gelding..trots and racks. **1829** *Sporting Mag.* XXIII. 266 There can be little doubt of his having racked a mile in even less than I stated. **1843** MARRYAT *M. Violet* xx. 157 No one ever saw him trotting or galloping; he only racks. **1887** E. CUSTER *Tenting on Plains* vi. 187 He [*sc.* a horse] is very affectionate, and he racks a mile inside of three minutes. **1935** H. DAVIS *Honey in Horn* xi. 175 He saddled and bridled the mare..and racked out on the road. *Ibid.* xv. 254 When the wagon went out of sight.. he spurred up and racked after it.

fig. *a* **1661** FULLER *Worthies, Northampton.* (1662) 292 He was thorough-paced in all Spiritual Popery..but in secular Popery..he did not so much as rack.

b. Used *transf.* of vehicles or of persons. *to rack off* (Austral.), to go missing, 'get lost'.

1935 Z. N. HURSTON *Mules & Men* I. iv. 95 Pretty soon the log-train came racking along. **1975** *Sun-Herald* (Sydney) 29 June, [*title of record*] Rak Off Normie. **1980** *Courier-Mail* (Brisbane) 10 Apr. 36 (*caption*) 'Gimme ya money mate or I'll shoot ya!' 'No... Now rack off!'

rack (ræk), *v.*[5] [ad. Prov. (Gascon) *arracar* in same sense, f. *raca* the stems and husks of grapes, thick dregs: cf. obs. F. *vin raqué* 'small or course wine, squeezed from the *marc* or dregs of the grapes' (Cotgr.).]

1. *trans.* To draw off (wine, cider, etc.) from the lees. Also with *off.*

c **1460** J. RUSSELL *Bk. Nurture* 115 The reboyle to Rakke to þe lies of þe rose, þat shalle be his amendynge. **1519** [see RACKED *ppl. a.*[4]]. **1633** *Naworth Househ. Bks.* (Surtees) 330 To the cooper for rackinge 2 hogsheads of sack. **1694** FALLE *Jersey* ii. 71 [To] ferment, rack and bottle our Cidar. **1741** *Compl. Fam.-Piece* I. v. 275 Rack off your Wine into another Vessel. **1846** J. BAXTER *Libr. Pract. Agric.* (ed. 4) II. 416 Whenever the wine becomes dry, rack off the clear into a clean and sulphured cask. **1880** *Act 43 & 44 Vict.* c. 24 §64 The proprietor of spirits..may..vat, blend, or rack them in the warehouse.

absol. **1830** M. DONOVAN *Dom. Econ.* I. 303 It will be necessary to rack off from one cask to another.

transf. **1683** A. SNAPE *Anat. Horse* I. xxviii. (1686) 64 Serving as a Pipe to rack the Urine as it were out of the Bladder of the Young.

b. *fig.* in various senses.

1653 GAUDEN *Hierasp.* 74 Rack him off further, and refine him from the lees of sensual and inordinate lusts. **1696** BROOKHOUSE *Temple Open.* 17 Christ Racks off his Truth from Vessel to Vessel. **1809** MALKIN *Gil Blas* v. i. ¶73 Every morning I wrote down in my pocket-book such anecdotes as I meant to rack off in the course of the day. **1861** SALA in *Temple Bar Mag.* II. 302 His speech was of the finest jackeen just racked through a cask of Cork whisky.

†**2.** To empty (a cask) by racking. *Obs. rare.*

1626 BACON *Sylva* §306 Rack the one Vessell from the Lees. **1703** *Art & Myst. Vintners* 65 Rack your Cask very clean, and let it remain full of water all night.

rack (ræk), *v.*[6] *Naut.* [Of obscure origin: perh. a use of *v.*[2] or *v.*[3]] (See quots.)

1769 FALCONER *Dict. Marine* (1776), *Racking*, the fastening two opposite parts of a tackle together, so as that any weighty body suspended thereby shall not fall down, although the rope..should be loosened by accident. **1841** DANA *Seaman's Man.* 119 *Rack*, to seize two ropes together, with cross-turns. **1882** NARES *Seamanship* (ed. 6) 131.

rack (ræk), *v.*[7] *Building.* [var. RAKE *v.*[3]] *trans.* To build (a brick wall) by stopping each course a little short of the one below, so that the end slopes (usu. temporarily until the work is completed). Usu. with *back.* Cf. RAKING *vbl. sb.*[3]

1873 F. ROBERTSON *Engin. Notes* ii. 35 In repairing masonry where there is a crack or junction, or where new work is to be connected with old, the adjoining ends should be racked back from each other, as it were in ascending steps, and the resulting wedge-shaped void subsequently built in. **1904** C. F. & G. A. MITCHELL *Brickwork & Masonry* ii. 77 (*caption*) Angles of walls racked preparatory to building. *Ibid.* 78 The base of the corner is extended along the wall, and is racked back as the work is carried up. **1945** E. L. BRALEY *Brickwork* iii. 58 Usually five or seven courses are built at each corner, the work being racked back, e.g. first of all three stretchers, then four headers and one closer, then two stretchers, two headers and a closer, one stretcher, and finally the heading face of the top brick. **1972** S. SMITH *Brickwork* iv. 17 When building a wall, it is usual to raise the 'quoins' (corners) first, 'racking back' the work as necessary.

rack, obs. var. RAKE *sb.*[4], *v.*[1] and *v.*[3]; obs. north. and Sc. f. RECK; pa. t. of REKE *v.* *Obs.*

†**racka**, obs. form of ARECA.

1625 PURCHAS *Pilgrims* III. 304 Their lading..was principally dryed Coco Nuts..and Racka Nuts.

rackan ('ræk(ə)n), **reckon** ('rɛk(ə)n). *Obs.* exc. *north. dial.* Forms: 1 **racente, racete,** 4 **rakente,** 5 **rakende, racand,** 6 **raken, racon,** 9 **rackan;** 4 **recawnt,** 5–6 **rekand,** 5 **rekande, rekanth, -enth,** 6 **reckand, -en, recon,** 7 **reckan,** 9 **reckon.** [OE. *racente* wk. f. = ON. *rekendi* (usually in pl. *rekendr* as if from sing. **rekandi*), OHG. *rahchinza* (Graff): cf. RAKENTEIE. In ME. and later use only north. dial., and chiefly in forms *rek-*, *reckan(d*, which app. represent the Scand. rather than the OE. word (but forms with *rak-*, *rack-*, prevail in the comb. *rackan-crook*).]

†**1.** A chain, fetter. *Obs.*

c **888** K. ÆLFRED *Boeth.* xvi. §2 þæt he wearð ȝebunden mid hira racentum. **971** *Blickl. Hom.* 43 Hie hine hæfdon ȝeþreatodne mid fyrenum racentum. *a* **1050** *Liber Scintill.* (1889) 59 ȝebeorscipas swylce racetan..forfleo lusta. **13..** *E.E. Allit. P.* C. 188 Þer ragnel in his rakentes hym rere of his dremes. *a* **1400–50** *Alexander* 5128, I send ȝow..twa hundred & ten..of rekanthes of rede gold. **14..** *Sir Beues* (MS. N.) 1636 Þe jailers liggen bothe dede & Beues liþ bounde in rakende.

2. A chain or other apparatus by which cooking vessels are suspended over a fire; now usually a vertical bar pierced with holes, into one of which the pot-hook is inserted.

1400 *Test. Ebor.* (Surtees) I. 268 Unum recawnt de catenis ferreis. **1445** *Ibid.* II. 194, j. rekand de ferro. **1485** *Ibid.* III. 300, j pare of coberdis, ij potte-hyngyls, j racand. **1534** in Peacock *Eng. Ch. Furniture* (1866) 186 Thre racons wt a peire of galows of yron. **1566** *Richmond. Wills & Inv.* (Surtees) 184, j paire of tongs, j iron scummer and one recken. **1582** BEST *Farm. Bks.* (Surtees) 172 One recon,.. one fier shole, one pare of tanges. **1674–91** RAY *N.C. Words* 58 *Reckans*, Hooks to hang Pots or Kettles on over the Fire. **1876** *Mid-Yorksh. Gloss.* s.v., A pot-hook..sliding through a hole in the bottom piece of the reckon.

rackan-crook. *north. dial.* Forms: 5–6 **raken-,** 6 **rakon-, racon-, rackyn-, rayckin-, rakin(ge)-,** 6, 9 **rackin-,** 7–9 **racken-,** 9 **rackan-, rack-an'-;** 7 **rekin-,** 7–9 **reckin-,** 9 **reckon-.** [f. prec. + CROOK. *Rackan-hook* is used in the same sense in mod. dial.] A rackan serving as a pot-hook, or a pot-hook used with a rackan.

1469–70 *Durham Acc. Rolls* (Surtees) 280 In repar..unius rakencroke, iiijd. **1564** *Wills & Inv. N.C.* (Surtees 1835) 223 Gibcrokes, rakincroke, and racks,..two Rayckincrokes and iiij spetes. **1648** *Lancash. Tracts Civil War* (Chetham Soc.) 254 The very racken crocks and pot hooks. **1684** MERITON *Yorksh. Dialogue* 39 Hing the Pan ore'th fire ith Rekin-Creauk. **1781** J. H. *Gloss. N.E. Words* (E.D.S.), *Rannle-balk*, a piece of wood in a chimney, from which is hung the pot-crook, or racken-crook. **1869-** In dialect glossaries (Lonsdale, Rochdale, Sheff., Northumb.).

rackan hook. Also reckon hook (the usual form). [f. RACKAN + HOOK *sb.*] = RACKAN-CROOK.

1645 *Essex County* (Mass.) *Probate Rec.* (1916) I. 50 Estate of William Goog of Lynn... One gridiron & recke hookes [etc.]. **1647** *Ibid.* 99 Estate of John Jarrat of Rowley.. Reckon hooks & some small things, 4s. **1867** B. BRIERLEY *Marlocks of Meriton* 41 His eyes still intent upon the 'rackan'-hook' hanging in the kitchen. **1961** M. W. BARLEY *Eng. Farmhouse & Cottage* III. v. 175 In such houses as these, cooking was usually done in the house body. There, along with the iron range and the reckon hook, were the bakestone and the wooden boards..with which oatcakes were made.

rackarock ('rækərɒk). [f. RACK *v.*^{3} + A *a.*^{2} + ROCK *sb.*] An explosive consisting of potassium chlorate and nitrobenzol. Also *attrib.*

1885 *Daily News* 12 Oct., A six-pound cartridge of rackarock. **1891** *Times* 8 Oct. 5/4, 200 lb. of rackarock powder..were set off. **1891** THORPE *Dict. Appl. Chem.* I. 84/2 The rackarock cartridges were not fired electrically.

rackat, obs. form of RACKET.

'rack-bar.

1. *Mech.* [f. RACK *sb.*^{2} 6.] A bar fitted with a rack or racks.

a **1824** A. SCOTT in *Trans. Highl. Soc.* (1824) VI. 31 The teeth of these two spur-wheels are to work..into the teeth of the rack-bars. **1879** *Cassell's Techn. Educ.* IV. 395/1 A strong semicircle of cast iron, with which the telescope is connected by a rack-bar.

2. *Naut.* [f. RACK *v.*^{3}] (See quot.)

1867 SMYTH *Sailor's Word-bk.*, *Rack-bar*, a billet of wood used for twisting the bight of a swifter round, in order to bind a raft firmly together.

rack-bolt, variant of RAG-BOLT.

1793 SMEATON *Edystone L.* §58 Of trenails, screws, and rack-bolts 2500 each.

† **'rack-bone.** *Obs.* [RACK *sb.*^{4}] A vertebra.

1615 CROOKE *Body of Man* 775 The transuerse processes of the racke-bones of the necke. *Ibid.* 800 The last spondels or rackbones of the chest. **1656** W. D. tr. *Comenius' Gate Lat. Unl.* (1659) 259 The chine or back bone..is made up of four and thirty rack-bones. *c* **1720** W. GIBSON *Farrier's Guide* I. v. (1738) 67 The Rack-bones that are between the sixth Vertebrae of the Chest, and the middle of the Os sacrum. **1831** W. YOUATT *Horse* ix. 153 The other neck, or *rack*-bones, as they are denominated by the farrier,..are of a strangely irregular shape.

rackcoone, obs. form of RACOON.

'rack-deal. [f. RACK *sb.*^{2}] Deal set up in a rack or framework and dried by exposure to the air.

1807 C. VANCOUVER *Agric. Devon* (1813) 96 The floor above is made of rack deal, or any soft wood plank. **1835** WHITE in *Parl. Rep. Timber Duties* 206 By being cut out with the sap running to them, they would be both sappy and slabby; those are what we call rack deals. **1887** *Dict. Archit.* s.v. *Rack*, The name of the framework in which deals or boards are placed on end for air-drying... Hence the term 'rack deals'.

racked (rækt), *ppl. a.*^{1} [f. RACK *v.*^{1} + -ED^{1}.] Driven along, as clouds by the wind.

1858 KINGSLEY *Poems* 150 Winds, upon whose racked eddies, far aloft, My thoughts in exultation held their way.

racked (rækt), *ppl. a.*^{2} [f. RACK *sb.*^{2} or *v.*^{2} + -ED.] Fitted with a rack or racks.

1890 *Anthony's Photogr. Bull.* III. 128 A metal racked frame to fit inside a plain wooden box.

racked (rækt), *ppl. a.*^{3} [f. RACK *v.*^{3} + -ED^{1}.]

1. That is racked, in various senses of the vb.; stretched, strained, tortured by stretching, etc.

1571 GOLDING *Calvin on Ps.* iv. 1 Wheras some translate thys woord (for ever)..I do reject as a racked translation. **1583** STUBBES *Anat. Abus.* II. i. (1882) 24 They will be sure to make price of their racked cloth, double and triple more than it cost them. **1611** CHAPMAN *Widowes T.* Wks. 1873 III. 59 Much more worth than the rackt value. **1632** LITHGOW *Trav.* x. 484 The maintayning of my Lame and Racked body. **1867** TROLLOPE *Chron. Barset* I. i. 11 He endeavoured to tell the truth, as far as his poor racked imperfect memory would allow him. **1894** HALL CAINE *Manxman* v. xix. 341 The torn heart and racked brain could bear no more.

2. Of rent: Raised to excess. Cf. RACK-RENT.

1583 STUBBES *Anat. Abus.* II. i. (1882) 29 He might haue it freely for this racked rent. **1668** R. L'ESTRANGE *Vis. Quev.* (1708) 164 Impositions, hard Services, and Rackt Rents. **1725** RAMSAY *Gentle Sheph.* II. i, Never did he stent Us in our thriving with a racket rent. **1799** J. ROBERTSON *Agric. Perth* 404 Racked rents..disable the tenant to improve.

b. Of men, their living, etc.: Oppressed by or subjected to extortion or excessive rent.

1628 WITHER *Brit. Rememb.* II. 1713 That Crew of Spend-thrifts..Were now, among their racked Tenants faine To seeke for shelter. **1643** PRYNNE *Sov. Power Parl.* II. 30 Weekely or monethly assessements and contributions.. exceeding many mens racked incomes. **1781** COWPER *Expost.* 304 Thy racked inhabitants repine, complain.

3. racked-out, (*a*) completely exhausted; (*b*) passed through with suffering.

1870 SIR S. NORTHCOTE in *Life* (1890) II. xii. 30 The old racked-out tobacco and corn lands. **1900** W. A. ELLIS *Life Wagner* 332 The harvest of the last outlived, or rather racked-out Summer.

racked (rækt), *ppl. a.*^{4} [f. RACK *v.*^{5} + -ED^{1}.] Drawn off or emptied by racking.

1519 HORMAN *Vulg.* 294 b, Whither so euer I go: I haue with me racked wyne. **1563** T. GALE *Antidot.* II. 83 In the latter drinke we haue vsed to put in rackte Renishe Wyne. **1626** BACON *Sylva* §306 Powre the Lees of the Racked Vessell into the vnracked Vessell. **1764** *Mass. Gazette* No. 3149/4 Good rack'd and refin'd Cyder.

rackee, obs. f. RAKI.

racken, north. and Sc. var. RECKON.

racken-, var. RACKAN-CROOK.

rackensak ('rækənsæk). [Prob. altered form of *Arkansan.*] *U.S. colloq.* A native of Arkansas. ? *Obs.*

1845 [see CORN-CRACKER 1]. **1854** *Putnam's Mag.* III. 665/2 Artillerists and dragoons, suckers and rackensacks, were all mixed up in confusion.

racker^{1} ('rækə(r)). [f. RACK *v.*^{3} + -ER^{1}.]

1. One who racks, in senses of the vb.

1565 COOPER *Thesaurus*, *Contortor legum*, a racker of lawes. **1607** DEKKER *Knt.'s Conjur.* (1842) 72 Landlords dare not quarter themselves here, because they are rackers of rents. *a* **1656** HALES *Gold. Rem.* (1688) 15 These Rackers of Scripture are by St. Peter stiled Unstable. **1725** RAMSAY *Gentle Sheph.* II. i, Rackers aft tine their rent. **1820** SOUTHEY in *Q. Rev.* XXIII. 568 The constant employment of rackers and executioners.

† **2.** (See quot.) *Obs. rare*$^{-1}$.

1688 R. HOLME *Armoury* III. 70/1 The Farmer, or Racker, or Dairy-Man..hold Lands..from the Lords thereof upon Rack or half-Rack, that is upon the yearly value or half value, having no certain term of holding [etc.].

racker^{2} ('rækə(r)). [f. RACK *v.*^{4} + -ER^{1}.] A racking horse.

1829 *Sporting Mag.* XXIII. 266 The racker comes to us from our North Western territory. **1856** THOREAU *Lett.* (1865) 146 The swiftest equine trotter or racker. **1891** *Harper's Mag.* Aug. 366/1, I have seen more than one racker of true Norman blood. **1903** A. D. MCFAUL *Ike Glidden* xiv. 108 Lickety got ter puffin' up his ole hoss, soze you'd a thought it was the Millbridge Racker.

racker^{3} ('rækə(r)). [f. RACK *v.*^{5} + -ER^{1}.]

1. One who racks wine or other liquor.

1611 COTGR., *Frelateur*, a racker of wine. **1865** *Pall Mall G.* 1 Apr. 8 Harris was what is called a racker.

2. An apparatus for racking.

1846 TIZARD *Brewing* (ed. 2) xx. 551 The Floating Racker. [Description follows.]

† **'racket**, *sb.*^{1} *Obs. rare.* Also 4–5 **raket**. [Etym. obscure.] Some game played with dice.

c **1374** CHAUCER *Troylus* IV. 432 (460) Canstow pleyen raket, to and fro, Netle in, dokke out, now this, now that, Pandare? **1387-8** T. USK *Test. Love* I. ii. (Skeat) 166, I haue not plaid raket, Nettle in, Docke out. **1430-40** LYDG. *Bochas* V. xxix. (1554) 140 Kyng Phrahartes, in token he was unstable, Sent him three dees, forged square of golde, To play racket as a chylde chaungeable.

racket ('rækɪt), *sb.*^{2} Forms: 6 **rackat, -it**, *Sc.* **rakkett, rakcat**, 6–7 **rackette**, 8 **-ett**, 5– **racket**; 6–9 **raquet**, 7 **-ett**, 9 **racquet**. See also RAQUETTE. [a. F. *raquette* (16th c.) = Sp., Pg. *raqueta*, It. *racchetta*, *lacchetta*, of uncertain origin (see Littré and Devic): hence also Du. *raket* (in Kilian *racket*), G. *rakete*, *-ette*.]

1. a. A bat used in the games of rackets, tennis, etc., consisting of a network of cord or catgut stretched across a somewhat elliptical frame formed of a bent strip of wood, metal, etc. to the base of which a handle is attached.

1500-20 DUNBAR *Poems* xiv. 66 Sa mony rakkettis, sa mony ketche-pillaris. **1540** [see b]. **1574** NEWTON *Health Mag.* 6 Striking and receaving the balle with a raquet. **1624** CAPT. SMITH *Virginia* II. 27 The Beaver..His taile somewhat like the forme of a Racket. **1690** LOCKE *Hum. Und.* xxi. §9 A Tennis-Ball, whether in motion by the stroke of a Racket, or lying still at rest. **1763** C. JOHNSTON *Reverie* II. 206 He was seated at table with a parcel of shuttle-cocks before him, and mending a racket. **1805** SCOTT *Last Minstr.* II. xxxi, Like tennis-ball by raquet tossed. **1808** PIKE *Sources Mississ.* (1810) 100 [In Lacrosse] one catches the ball in his racket, and..endeavors to carry it to the goal. **1828** D'ISRAELI *Chas. I*, I. ii. 22 In the tennis-court he toiled with the racquet. **1890** C. G. HEATHCOTE *Lawn Tennis* 208 The main object of modern lawn tennis is to meet the ball with a full racket.

fig. **1589** GREENE *Menaphon* (Arb.) 51 Finding opportunitie to giue her both bal and racket. **1610** HEALEY *St. Aug. Citie of God* (1620) 616 Friuolous pamphlets, the very rackets wherewith Greece bandieth ignorant heads about. **1705** HICKERINGILL *Priest-cr.* II. iii. 38 Antichrist is the common Tennis-Ball that every malicious Racket bandies and tosses against each other. **1809** MALKIN *Gil Blas* VIII. ix. ¶9 You have a racket for every ball; nothing comes amiss to you.

b. A game of ball played by two persons, who strike the ball alternately with their rackets and endeavour to keep it rebounding from a wall. Now always *pl.* Also *fig.*

1529 LYNDESAY *Compl.* 175 Sum gart him raiffell at the rakcat: Sum harld hym to the hurly hakcat. **1540** HEYWOOD *Four P.P.* 882 All the soules were playnge at racket. None other rackettes they hadde in honde [etc.]. **1610** GUILLIM *Heraldry* IV. xii. 221 Such [games] are.. Racket, Balloone. **1748** RICHARDSON *Clarissa* (1811) III. xxxii. 191 All his address and conversation is one continual game at racquet. **1822** HAZLITT *Table-t.* II. vii. 161 Rackets..is, like any other athletic game, very much a thing of skill and practice. **1890** E. O. P. BOUVERIE *Rackets* 359 The game of rackets is now exclusively played in a court enclosed in four walls.

† **2.** A military engine (see quot.). *Obs. rare*$^{-1}$.

1535 COVERDALE *1 Macc.* vi. 51 He made all maner ordinaunce: handbowes, fyrie dartes, rackettes to cast stones.

3. a. A snow-shoe made after the fashion of a racket (sense 1), as used in Northern America.

1613 PURCHAS *Pilgrimage* VIII. iv. 753 Their Dogges.. haue rackets tied vnder their feet, the better to runne on the snow. **1677** W. HUBBARD *Narrative* II. 130 Unless they carried Rackets under their Feet, wherewith to walk upon the Top of the Snow. **1758** *Michmakis & Maricheets* 55 Much more capable with their legs only, than we with our rackets. **1790** BEWICK *Hist. Quadrup.* (1792) 111 The sportsman pursues in his broad rackets or snow-shoes. **1875** TEMPLE & SHELDON *Hist. Northfield, Mass.* 84 Travel was next to impossible, except upon rackets.

b. A broad wooden shoe for man or horse to enable them to walk over marshy ground.

1846 P. J. DE SMET *Oregon Missions* (1847) XIV. 193 The savages travel over these marshy places in *Rackets*. **1864** in WEBSTER.

4. *Ornith.* A bird's tail-feather shaped like a racket, a spatule. (*Cassell's Encycl. Dict.* 1887.)

5. *attrib.* and *Comb.*, as (sense 1) ***racket-frame***, ***-maker***, ***-seller***; ***racket-like*** adj.; (sense 1 b) ***racket-ball***, ***-bat***, ***-court***, ***-ground***, ***-match***, ***-player***; (sense 3) ***racket-string***; **racket-press** (see quot.).

1651 OGILBY *Æsop* (1665) 164 Like *Racket-Bals with Argos's I sport And the whole Ocean is my Tennis-Court. **1837** THACKERAY *Ravenswing* vi, Who hit [him] across the shoulders with a *racket-bat. **1604** MIDDLETON *Father Hubbard's T.* Wks. (Bullen) VIII. 103, I am no day from the line of the *racket-court. **1860** *All Year Round* No. 66. 366 It is thoroughly inconvenient and defective as a racket-court. **1837** DICKENS *Pickw.* xli, This area..was the *racket-ground. **1893** NEWTON *Dict. Birds* 168 The outermost pair [of feathers] are enlarged at the end in a *racquet-like form. **1611** COTGR., *Raquetier*, a *Racket-maker. **1838** JAS. GRANT *Sk. Lond.* 57 Employed to supply the *racket-players with balls. **1890** C. G. HEATHCOTE *Lawn Tennis* 204 Among those [implements] which..are useful, may be mentioned the *racket press to keep the racket from warping. **1808** PIKE *Sources Mississ.* (1810) 75 The pressure of my *racket strings brought the blood through my socks and mockinsons.

racket ('rækɪt), *sb.*^{3} Also 8–9 **racquet**. [Prob. onomatopœic. Gael. *racaid*, sometimes cited as the source, is no doubt from Eng.]

1. a. Disturbance, loud noise, uproar, din; usually such as is produced by noisy or disorderly conduct on the part of one or more persons.

In quot. 1597 with pun on RACKET *sb.*^{2}

1565 ABP. PARKER *Corr.* (Parker Soc.) 234, I send you a letter sent to me of the racket stirred up by Withers. **1597** SHAKS. *2 Hen. IV*, II. ii. 23 But that the Tennis-Court-keeper knowes better then I, for it is a low ebbe of Linnen with thee, when thou kept'st not Racket there. *a* **1641** BP. MOUNTAGU *Acts & Mon.* (1642) 323 Antonius..hearing what racket the Parthians kept in Syria. **1712** STEELE *Spect.* No. 336 ¶3 After all this Racket and Clutter [etc.]. **1792** *Elvina* II. 98 We wanted quiet, not racket. **1877** BLACK *Green Past.* xlii. (1878) 336 A quiet country life—no racket except the roosters in the morning.

b. With *a* and *pl.* An instance of this.

1622 MABBE tr. *Aleman's Guzman d'Alf.* II. 261 Then will shee keepe a racket, and cry out. **1683** *Pol. Ballads* (1860) I. 243 And made such a riot..That never before such a racket was known. **1741** RICHARDSON *Pamela* (1824) I. 53 Your daughter has made a strange racket in my family. **1777** MAD. D'ARBLAY *Early Diary* 7 Apr., The drums and trumpets again made a racket. **1824** SCOTT *St. Ronan's* i, Such dashers occasioned many a racket in Meg's house.

fig. **1855** J. H. NEWMAN *Callista* (1890) 87 There is such a racket and whirl of religions on all sides of me.

c. A noisy expression of opinion or feeling; clamour, outcry; excitement or fuss (*about* something, or *with* a person).

1652 CULPEPPER *Eng. Physic.* 182 What a noise Authours have made of Roses, what a 'Racket' they have kept up. **1755** J. SHEBBEARE *Lydia* (1769) II. 270 She was astonished..at the racket which was made about a son of such a creature. **1789** CHARLOTTE SMITH *Ethelinde* (1814) I. 11 Though her father has always made such a racket with her.

2. a. The noise and whirl of society; excessive social excitement or dissipation.

1784 R. BAGE *Barham Downs* I. 118 Charm'd with dress and trumpery, with racket and dissipation. **1822** SCOTT 4 Sept. in *Fam. Lett.* (1894) II. xviii. 149, I did not wish for you in the midst of all this racquet of mirth and war. **1850** THACKERAY *Lett., to Mrs. Brookfield*, With all this racket and gaiety, do you understand that a gentleman feels very lonely? **1886** *Spectator* 6 Feb. 175/1 Dr. Johnson..did not live in the racket of Society.

b. A large or noisy social gathering.

1745 ELIZA HEYWOOD *Female Spect.* No. 12 (1748) II. 269 She told me, that when the number of company for play exceeded ten tables, it was called a racquet. **1750** JOHNSON *Rambler* No. 97 ¶4 To idle amusements, and to negligence of domestic business, to wicked rackets. **1876** T. HARDY *Ethelberta* (1890) 402 She'll have her routs and her rackets as well as the high-born ones.

c. A dance: see quots.

1882 L. O. CARPENTER *J. W. Pepper's Universal Dancing Master* 33 *Racquette*..Make three galop steps or slides to the left, throwing the foot out in second position... Slide to right [etc.]. **1882** P. V. CARTIER *Practical Illustrated Waltz Instructor* 45 *The Racquet*..Take two long galop slides with left foot on accent, and as right foot is brought up to left foot for second time, rest, and hold left foot in air. Repeat by sliding with right foot, etc. **1885** A. DODWORTH *Dancing* vii. 51 Racket Waltz (One-Slide Racket in Waltz Time). *Ibid.* 52 Changes are made..by alternating the one-slide racket with the three-slide. **1935** D. N. CROPPER *Dance Dict.* 54 *Racket*, popular 6/8 number of the 'nineties'. Basic step: a waltz form with leap (1) slide (&) change-cut (2).

3. *slang.* **a.** A trick, dodge, scheme, game, line of business or action. Now usually, any scheme or procedure which aims at obtaining money or effecting other objects by unusual, illegal, and

often violent means; a distinctive form of organized crime.
1812 J. H. VAUX *Flash Dict.*, *Racket*, some particular kinds of fraud and robbery are so termed. **1851** MAYHEW *Lond. Labour* I. 224/1, I did wear a shovel hat when the Bishop of London was our racket. **1884** *Bread-winners* 183 That's just our racket. **1928** *Daily Express* 14 Sept. 1/1 The 'racket' has for years been distinctively a Chicago institution; and it has been found to be such a profitable form of crime there that it is spreading to the other large cities of the Middle West. **1931** *Sun* (Baltimore) 4 Apr. 1/4 One racket in New York State alone—that of fake securities— is known to total approximately $100,000,000 a year. **1940** E. GILL *Autobiogr.* vii. 259 It [*sc.* politics] is all a confused business of ramps and rackets—pretended quarrels and dishonest commercial schemings, having no relation to the real interests of peoples, neither to their spirtual nor their material welfare. **1944** M. LASKI *Love on Supertax* xii. 117 You organised all this Black Market racket, didn't you? **1950** G. BRENAN *Face of Spain* ii. 54 Of all the rackets recorded in history, the Spanish Inquisition, during the first hundred years of its career, was perhaps the most mean and repulsive. **1956** 'C. BLACKSTOCK' *Dewey Death* iv. 83 Mr. Wilson is now telling everybody that I.L.D.A. is the secret headquarters of the drug racket. **1974** J. GARDNER *Return of Moriarty* 31 All our family is affected if we start to lose in any racket, any lay. **1977** *Times* 29 Nov. 14/2 Ulster by the middle of 1974 was suffering from rackets and violent crime on a scale equal to some of Europe's most notorious cities.
b. In more weakened senses: an activity, a way of life; a line of business.
1891 KIPLING & BALESTIER *Naulahka* vi, What's your lay? What's your racket? **1907** R. DUNN *Shameless Diary of Explorer* xviii. 251 The Professor is working his faith-in-God-and-self, and line-of-least resistance racket, a mite too strong. **1916** J. BUCHAN *Greenmantle* i. 4, I thrive on the racket and eat and sleep like a schoolboy. **1927** *Vanity Fair* (N.Y.) XXIX. 132/3 'What's your racket?' meaning 'What do you do for a living?' **1930** *Sun* (Baltimore) 12 Feb. 10/7 My satisfaction would be complete if there were a 100 per cent rush for the doors that would entirely eliminate the encore racket. **1931** F. L. ALLEN *Only Yesterday* vii. 172 At the beginning of the decade advertising had been considered a business..by the end of the decade many of its practitioners..were beginning to refer to it—among themselves—as a racket. **1936** *Amer. Speech* XI. 274/2 Nowadays a *racket* may be a legitimate business... A man may say..'I rather like the racket I'm in', referring to his business. **1938** *Downside Review* LVI. 100 It is true that the phrase 'muscling in on the culture racket' reflects a development of English word-usage from which the present reviewer had perhaps been preserved by monastic seclusion. **1942** *R.A.F. Jrnl.* 3 Oct. 11, I sold insurance, and..that's the racket to develop your wits. **1944** J. S. HUXLEY *On living in Revol.* 23 What with football, racing, the cinema, the theatre, popular literature, and holiday resorts, recreation is today one of the most profitable commercial rackets. **1978** J. UPDIKE *Coup* (1979) vi. 239, I am in the insurance racket. I am a claims adjuster.
4. An exciting or trying situation or experience; an ordeal. ***to stand the racket***, (*a*) to hold out against strain or wear and tear; (*b*) to face the consequences of an action; (*c*) to pay.
1823 'J. BEE' *Dict. Turf*, '*Racket*—to stand the', when one of a set stands forward to bear all the blame. **1827** T. WILSON *Pitman's Pay* II. 63 Sic tussels nobbit pluck could settle, For nowse less could the racket stand. **1837** WHITTOCK *Bk. Trades* (1842) 404 (*Shoemaker*) Upon this.. preparation depends his work standing the racket of adverse seasons. **1846** *Swell's Night Guide* 132/2 *Stand the racket*, treat, pay for all. **1878** BESANT & RICE *Celia's Arb.* xxxii. (1887) 237, I escaped and came out of the whole racket unwounded. **1904** G. K. CHESTERTON *Napoleon of N.H.* III. iii. 168 'Can we do fifteen hundred pounds?' 'I'll stand the racket.' **1905** *Pall Mall Mag.* Dec. 678/2 If there is trouble, it will be for Great Britain to stand the racket. **1930** *Punch* 19 Feb. 204/3 If her..friend had been a sportsman he'd have stood the racket himself.
5. *Sc.* A hard blow; a severe slap.
1710 RUDDIMAN *Douglas Æneis, Gloss.* s.v. *Rak*, More frequently..we use Racket, as he gave him a racket on the lug, i.e. a box on the ear. **1810** *Cock's Simple Strains* 135 (Jam.) The wabster lad bang'd to his feet, An' gae 'im a waefu racket.
6. *attrib.* and *Comb.*, as ***racket-buster***, ***-busting*** (sb. and adj.), ***-ridden*** (adj.), ***ring***.
1940 *Sun* (Baltimore) 21 Nov. 1/2 Sol Gelb..had been assigned by the New York 'racket-buster' to watch the hearing. **1959** *Times Lit. Suppl.* 30 Jan. 55/4 Mr Danforth was senior investigator..from 1935–1951, when former Governor Thomas E. Dewey was the courageous D.A... and his famous racket-busting took place. **1972** 'H. HOWARD' *Nice Day for Funeral* iv. 58 Until the motive is established beyond doubt this case remains part of the DA's racket-busting programme. **1978** *Time* 3 July 55/2 Died. Luther W. Youngdahl, 82, unflappable federal judge who.. was appointed to the bench in 1951 after five years as a racket-busting Republican Governor of Minnesota. **1931** F. D. PASLEY *Muscling In* v. 138 New York stood revealed as the most racket-ridden city in the country. **1973** *Black Panther* 5 May 2/2 It is widely known that Inman is himself a king pin in the city's organized crime and racket rings.

† ˈ**racket**, *v.*[1] *Obs.* Also 7 rackat. [f. RACKET *sb.*[2]]
1. *trans.* To strike with, or as with, a racket; to toss or bandy about. Chiefly *fig.*
1603 FLORIO *Montaigne* III. ix. (1613) 540 The Gods perdie doe reckon and racket us men as their tennis balles. **1609** B. JONSON *Case is Altered* IV. iv, Then think, then speak,..And racket round about this body's court These two sweet words, 'tis safe. **1631** R. H. *Arraignm. Whole Creature* xiv. §2. 244 They are moveable as Shittlecockes, or Tennis Balls, now rackated here, now there. **1705** G. SCROPE *Epit. on himself* (St. Michael's, Coventry), Here lyes an Old Toss'd Tennis ball Was Racketted from Spring to Fall.
b. ***to racket away***: To lose (money) in playing with a racket. Also *transf.*
1612 WEBSTER *White Devil* II. i, I shall not shortly Racket away five hundred crowns at tennis But it shall rest upon record! **1861** F. W. ROBINSON *No Church* I. iv. 95 An improvident young man, who..would racket away all the money he might be able to leave her.
2. ***to racket it***: To carry a racket. *rare*$^{-1}$.
1605 CHAPMAN, etc. *Eastw. Hoe* I. i, There's thy fellowe Prentise, as good a Gentleman borne as thou art.. But does he pumpe it or Racket it?

racket (ˈrækɪt), *v.*[2] [f. RACKET *sb.*[3]]
1. *intr.* To live a gay life, to take part in social excitement. Also with *about*.
1760 GRAY *Lett., to Dr. Clarke*, Poems (1775) 282 Company and cards at home, parties by land and water abroad, and..racketing about from morning to night. **1792** *Elvina* II. 132 Sir Edward will not allow Elvina to racket any more for some time. **1833** MACAULAY in *Life & Lett.* (1880) I. 346, I have been racketing lately, having dined twice with Rogers and once with Grant.
2. *intr.* To make a noise or racket; to move about in a noisy way. Also const. *about*, *along*, *around*.
1827 CAPT. HARDMAN *Waterloo* 16 A ball from their infantry went through my jacket, Took the skin off my side, and made me racket. **1851** S. JUDD *Margaret* xvii. 151 The wind blazed and racketed through the narrow space between the house and the hill. **1885** B. POTTER *Jrnl.* 6 May (1966) 141 How is it these high-heeled ladies who dine out..can racket about all day long, while I..am so tired toward the end of the afternoon that I can scarcely keep my feet? **1897** R. KIPLING *Captains Courageous* iv. 86 The pots and pans.. jarred and racketed to each plunge. **1914** W. OWEN *Let.* 21 Dec. (1967) 309, I racketed about all Saturday making luggage out of lumber. **1916** 'BOYD CABLE' *Action Front* 197 A dozen paces away two of the battalion machine-guns were clattering and racketing in rapid gusts of fire. **1929** M. DE LA ROCHE *Whiteoaks* xiv. 188 Aha..that's what I like to hear! Young lads racketing about! **1936** A. RANSOME *Pigeon Post* vi. 69 But do you think we'll hear it?' said Mrs. Blackett, 'when we're racketing about and busy with other things.' **1967** J. C. HOLMES *Nothing More to Declare* i. 20 We read it in an empty subway car racketing along under the deserted streets. **1970** G. GREER *Female Eunuch* 331 The first significant discovery we shall make as we racket along our female road to freedom is that men are not free. **1977** 'L. EGAN' *Blind Search* i. 12 That girl racketing around heaven knows where or with what sort of characters. **1977** W. M. SPACKMAN *Armful of Warm Girl* 34 Guests..racketing up into the bedroom.
b. To get *up* with noise and confusion.
1847 ALB. SMITH *Chr. Tadpole* lii. (1879) 445 They're.. obliged to racket up too early in the morning to catch the train, to take anything.
3. *trans.* To keep lively, to disturb, destroy (also with *away*), etc. by racketing. *rare.*
1753 RICHARDSON *Grandison* (1781) VI. xxvii. 166 Dearly do we love racketing; and, another whisper, some of us to be racketed. **1777** LADY S. LENNOX in *Life & Lett.* (1901) I. 261 The racketting their health so entirely away. **1827** HONE *Every-day Bk.* II. 820 A racketty life had racketted his frame. **1886** H. WARD BEECHER in *Hom. Rev.* May 421 We hear the whole land racketed with the disturbance produced by labor and capital.

racket, var. RACKETT.

racketeer (rækɪˈtɪə(r)), *sb.* orig. *U.S.* [f. RACKET *sb.*[3] + -EER.] A member of a gang or association of criminals practising extortion, intimidation, violence, and other illegal acts on a large scale; any person making easy money by such means. Also *transf.*, one who achieves an easy result by illegitimate means.
1928 *Time* 9 July 14 In the old days it was a mark of distinction to be seen at gangster funerals, but during the Loesch prosecutions, probably not even U.S. Senator Deneen of Illinois would care to be seen near the bier of a 'racketeer'. **1928** *Daily Express* 14 Sept. 1/4 'Racketeers'.. now control 150 lines of business in Chicago, and collect an enormous tribute for immunity from their violence. **1929** *Sun* (Baltimore) 15 Nov. 1/6 'Spike' along with six police captains and a dozen politicians and racketeers, is accused of participation in the profits of gambling machines placed in speak-easies. **1931** *Times* 24 Sept. 11/2 The campaign against gangsters and 'racketeers' in New York City has resulted today in the arrest of..one of the most powerful 'labour racketeers' in the city. **1935** J. T. FARRELL *Judgment Day* iv. 76 We got to get a strong man in the White House ..to kick out the bankers and grafting politicians and racketeers. **1939** *Scrutiny* VII. 439 The older generation of middlebrow propagandists, whom *Scrutiny* used to refer to as literary racketeers. **1948** *Sunday Pictorial* 18 July 7/1 The public are completely at the mercy of these racketeers. **1956** 'C. BLACKSTOCK' *Dewey Death* iii. 52 You romantic writers are as much a menace to the community as drug racketeers. **1967** *Wall Street Jrnl.* 24 Apr. 32/2 Rosenberg, according to Illinois authorities, was secretly associated with..an important Chicago racketeer. **1978** *Cornish Guardian* 27 Apr. 3/1 Metrication will be an open invitation for every spiv and racketeer to cheat the British public.

racketeer (rækɪˈtɪə(r)), *v.* *U.S.* [f. the sb.]
a. *trans.* To subject to racketeering. **b.** *intr.* To engage in fraudulent business.
1928 *Time* 30 Jan. 11/2 In 36 years in Chicago I have never been held up, robbed, or racketeered. **1933** G. B. SHAW *Polit. Madhouse in Amer.* 56 What is the use of paying you money to racketeer with? **1934** *Words* Nov. 5/2 *To press-agent,..to service,..to gesture, to racketeer*..are new, and most of them are obviously American.

rackeˈteering, *vbl. sb.* *U.S.* [f. RACKETEER *sb.* + -ING[1].] The business of racketeers; a system of organized crime directed chiefly to extorting money from business firms by intimidation, violence, or other illegal methods. Also *attrib.*
1928 *N.Y. Times* 18 Aug. 15 Two gang murders within the last week prompted Judge Edwin O. Lewis..to order the August Grand Jury to delve to the bottom of 'racketeering' in Philadelphia. **1928** *Daily Express* 14 Sept. 1/4 'Racketeering' is the new word that has been coined in America to describe the big business of organised crime. **1929** *Sun* (Baltimore) 10 Jan. 1/6 The defendants are charged with compelling..manufacturers to pay tribute to them by threatening to call strikes. The indictment was one of the first to be returned here in connection with a Federal investigation of racketeering. **1930** *Observer* 19 Oct. 17 He had hoped..perhaps to introduce and organise 'racketeering' processes. *Ibid.*, The only new detail is the paid protection of blackmail which now exists in many cities, described by the term 'racketeering'. **1931** *Sun* (Baltimore) 29 Jan. 1/6 Another effort is to be made to prohibit congressional nepotism now commonly recognized as 'pay-roll racketeering' on the part of members of both the House and Senate. **1941** L. B. NAMIER *Conflicts* (1942) 163 Look at this Jew! What did he do in the war? Some racketeering? **1959** *Ann. Reg. 1958* 187 Only on three major Bills was the President defeated..the attempt to regulate the affairs of trade unions to cut out racketeering [etc.]. **1978** S. BRILL *Teamsters* ii. 41 It was at the time when he was being charged with racketeering that Bufalino joined Hoffa's legal team.

rackeˈteering, *ppl. a.* [f. RACKETEER *v.* + -ING[2].] Characterized by or engaging in rackets.
1931 *Times* 30 July 11/3 Sometimes employers trying to operate an 'open shop' hire strike breakers... In other cases 'racketeering' gangs take the initiative in intimidating employers with 'open shops'. **1967** *Sunday Times* 8 Oct. 24/8 Kim, at this period, 'gave the impression of being a complaisant passenger in a racketeering upper-class world'.

racketer[1] (ˈrækɪtə(r)). *rare.* Also 6 **rakketter.** [f. RACKET *sb.*[2] + -ER[1].]
1. One who plays with a racket.
1581 MULCASTER *Positions* xxvii. (1887) 105 The rakketters in tennyse play..must shew them selues nymble. **1860** *All Year Round* No. 66. 366 These listless racketers rarely, if ever, hit the ball twice before it dropped.
2. One who wears, or walks on, rackets or snow-shoes (*Funk's Stand. Dict.* 1893).

ˈ**racketer**[2]. *rare.* [f. RACKET *sb.*[3] or *v.*[2] + -ER[1].] A gay or noisy person.
1661 *Sir A. Haslerig's Last Will* 3 The discontented Party ..may find our impregnant City a ready Foster-Mother to nurse these distempers in her ranting Racketers. **1754** RICHARDSON *Grandison* (1781) I. xvi. 109 At a private concert last night..and again to be at a play this night: I shall be a racketer, I doubt.

racketiness (ˈrækɪtɪnɪs). [f. RACKETY + -NESS.] The quality of being rackety; fondness for noise, excitement, etc.
1939 C. DAY LEWIS *Child of Misfortune* III. ii. 270 No doubt racketiness was just part of the fashionable sexual lure then. **1979** *Listener* 1 Nov. 508/2 Her racketiness and smart friends arouse less appreciation.

racketing (ˈrækɪtɪŋ), *vbl. sb.* [f. RACKET *v.*[2] + -ING[1].] The action of the vb., esp. in sense 1; an instance of this.
1753 [see RACKET *v.*[2] 3]. **1795** SCOTT 23 Aug. in *Lockhart*, I wish they may come down soon, as we shall have fine racketting. **1822** —— 25 June in *Fam. Lett.* (1894) II. xviii. 139 Late hours and raqueting. **1843** MIALL in *Nonconf.* III. 745 No racketing of engines to turn his domain into a modern Babel. **1886** BARING-GOULD *Mehalah* 183 There'll be junketings and racketings.

racketing (ˈrækɪtɪŋ), *ppl. a.* [f. as prec. + -ING[2].] That rackets, in senses of the vb.; characterized by racket or racketing.
1763 ELIZ. CARTER in *Mem.* (1808) I. 362 We live a very racketting life at the Hague. **1821** JEFFREY in Cockburn *Life* II. lxxxvi, We have had a racketing feverish life since we came here. **1847** W. IRVING in *Life & Lett.* (1864) IV. 25 One of the most racketing cities in the world. **1895** BESANT *Westminster* iii. 88 A place filled with noisy, racketing, even uproarious life.

racketry (ˈrækɪtrɪ). [f. RACKET *sb.*[3] + -RY.] Systematic or continuous noise or disturbance.
1884 in Bryce *Amer. Commw.* II. 639 The non-voters.. constitute the muscle and sinew of the campaign racketry —a word made indispensable by political conventions. *Ibid.* 640 All this racketry has been going on..for seven months.

rackett (ˈrækɪt). Also racket, ranket(t. [a. G. *rackett*, *rankett.*] **1.** A Renaissance musical instrument of the oboe family, consisting of a squat cylinder containing nine parallel channels joined alternately at top and bottom to form a continuous tube nine times the length of the cylinder.
1876 STAINER & BARRETT *Dict. Mus. Terms* 374/1 *Rackett*, *Rankett*, (1) an obsolete wind-instrument of the double bassoon kind. **1891** C. R. DAY *Catal. Mus. Instr. R. Milit. Exhib. 1890* 100 Racket. This beautiful instrument is constructed in the form of an ivory cylinder, and it is played by means of a rather large double reed. **1910** F. W. GALPIN *Old English Instr. of Music* ix. 167 A yet shorter instrument of bass pitch with a cylindrical-shaped tube..was called the Racket. **1939** A. CARSE *Muscial Wind Instr.* xiv. 206 In the racket or sausage-bassoon the air-passage is doubled and redoubled to such an extent that the sounding-length of the tube is quite nine times as long as the body of the instrument. **1961** A. BAINES *Mus. Instr. through Ages* ix. 232 The deep soft buzz of one racket among recorders, cornetts, etc., made a better effect than a whole consort of them [*sc.*

mixed instruments]. **1966** —— *Europ. & Amer. Mus. Instr.* 98 The *racket* contains a number of short parallel bores connected in series to make up a total windway of a metre or more. **1968** *Radio Times* 26 Sept. 48 A unique collection of medieval instruments—including rackett, rebec, crumhorn. **1970** *Daily Colonist* (Victoria, B.C.) 26 Feb. 28/1 They have chosen to play medieval music on a number of rare and little-used instruments, including the krummhorn, rauschfeiffer, ranket, and baroque oboes. **1976** D. Munrow *Instr. Middle Ages & Renaissance* 46/1 The rackett's narrow cylindrical bore consists of no less than nine parallel channels drilled in a wooden or ivory cylinder and connected alternately top and bottom.

†**2.** An organ stop. *Obs.* exc. *Hist.*

1876 Stainer & Barrett *Dict. Mus. Terms* 374/1 *Rackett, Rankett*..(2) An organ stop of 16 ft. or 8 ft. pitch now obsolete. **1897** H. Riemann *Dict. Mus.* 629/1 *Rackett* (Ranket),..in the organ an obsolete reed-stop almost entirely covered, of quiet tone (16 and 8 feet). **1962** S. Irwin *Dict. Pipe Organ Stops* 160 *Rankett*, a very old form of short-resonatored Reed stop, at 16′ or 8′ on both manual and pedals.

ˈracket-tail. [f. racket *sb.*[2]] A (bird's) tail shaped like a tennis-racket; hence used as a name for various species of humming-birds and motmots having tails of this form.

1851 Jardine *Contrib. Ornith.* 111 The beautiful species *S[pathura] Underwoodii*, with its white boots and racket tail. **1861** Gould *Humming Birds* III. Pl. 162 *Spathura Underwoodi*, white-booted Racket-tail. *Ibid.* 164 *S. Peruana*, Peruvian Racket-tail. **1893** Newton *Dict. Birds* 446 The lateral feathers may..suddenly enlarge into a terminal spatulation as in the forms known as 'Racquet-tails'.

So **ˈracket-tailed** *a.*, having a racket-tail.

1812 Shaw *Gen. Zool.* VIII. i. 317 The Racket-tailed Humming Bird is a rare species, and is a native of South America. **1833** Jardine *Humming-Birds* II. 110 Rough-legged Racket-tailed Humming-Bird. **1894** *Naturalist on Prowl* 178 The ever-changing..notes of the Racket-tailed Drongo.

rackette, obs. form of racket *sb.*[2]

racket-wheel, variant of ratchet-wheel.

1794 W. Felton *Carriages* (1801) I. 78 The brace is fixed to a spindle..and is there confined by a small racket-wheel and ketch. **1837** *Penny Cycl.* IX. 150/1 There is also a racket-wheel to prevent its unwinding.

rackety (ˈrækɪtɪ), *a.* Also -tty. [f. racket *sb.*[3] + -y.]

1. Addicted to making a racket; noisy, gay, fond of excitement.

This and sense 2 are tending to merge.

1773 Berridge *Chr. World Unmasked* (1812) 27 Some players are rude and racketty. **1857** Kingsley *Two Years Ago* I. vii. 192 This strange metamorphosis in the rackety little Irishman. **1885** *Manch. Exam.* 9 Apr. 5/3 The rackety winds of March and April. **1975** I. Murdoch *Word Child* 257 It was raining, and a rackety wind was sweeping the rain in little wild gusts across the windows. **1976** A. Powell *Infants of Spring* v. 80 In the middle age-group of most houses there inclined to occur a cluster of fairly rackety boys, from whom the house-tutor might expect trouble. **1977** *Daily Tel.* 20 Jan. 12/1 Crosby did not much like Harvard, but he seems to have been a fairly conventional undergraduate there, even if wilful and rackety.

2. Characterized by noise, excitement, dissipation, or disturbance.

1827 [see racket *v.*[2] 3]. **1840** Hood *Up the Rhine* 61 Foreign travelling is very racketty work. **1865** Carlyle *Fredk. Gt.* x. ii. (1872) III. 221 He..studies and learns amazingly in such a rackety existence. **1927** C. Connolly *Let.* 11 Feb. in *Romantic Friendship* (1975) 250 One misses the thrilling rackety journey to the wagon restaurant. **1961** A. Ritner *Seize Nettle* 158 The big basket of clothes to be coaxed through the rackety old washer. **1974** C. Milne *Enchanted Places* xix. 129 A room designed—as a nursery should be—for doing things in, messy things, racketty things, rough-and-tumble things. **1975** J. Symons *Three Pipe Problem* xviii. 201 He unlocked the door, switched on the engine, and listened to its rackety coughing.

¶**3.** = rickety.

1824 W. Irving *T. Trav.* I. 55 An old rackety inn, that looked ready to fall to pieces.

ˈrackful. [f. rack *sb.*[2]] The fill of a rack.

1898 C. G. Robertson *Voces Academ.* 190 A rackful of sticks and pipes.

Rackhamesque (rækəˈmɛsk), *a.* [See -esque.] Characteristic of or resembling the drawings of Arthur Rackham (1867–1939), book illustrator.

1935 *Forestry* IX. 15 There was also strong feeling about the way in which Rackhamesque trees of the forest were rapidly being replaced by pines. **1936** 'G. Orwell' *Keep Aspidistra Flying* iv. 88 The trees..twisted themselves into whimsy Rackhamesque attitudes. **1961** S. Gilruth *Drown her Remembrance* iii. 30 A few isolated olive trees, gnarled and twisted into weird Rackhamesque shapes.

rackin-crook, variant of rackan-crook.

ˈracking, *vbl. sb.*[1] [f. rack *v.*[1] + -ing[1].] The action of driving before the wind. *rare*[−1].

1631 *Celestina* Prol. A vj b, Those rackings to and fro of the clouds.

ˈracking, *vbl. sb.*[2] [f. rack *v.*[2]] **1. a.** Fitting with, placing in, etc., a rack or racks. **b.** The washing of ore on a rack (Knight 1875).

1888 *Daily News* 18 July 2/6 Restitution of 'pennies' if the girls do their own racking.

2. Shelving designed to be functional and inexpensive rather than decorative.

1937 G. Frankau *More of Us* viii. 91 While Art Department hummed like dynamo As frenzied hands tore pictures from their racking. **1976** *Gloss. Documentation Terms (B.S.I.)* 52 *Racking*, shelving, usually of a cheaper quality, used for storage purposes in non-public stacks and areas of a library.

racking (ˈrækɪŋ), *vbl. sb.*[3] [f. rack *v.*[3]]

1. a. The action of stretching, extending, straining, etc.; pulling tight or making fast by rack-lashings. Also with *down*.

1463–4 *Rolls Parlt.* V. 501/1 Brode Cloth..after almanere rakkyng, streynyng or teyntyng therof. **1565** Jewel *Repl. Harding* (1611) 364 It cannot be drawen, nor by racking can be stretched to any other sense. **1577** Holinshed *Chron.* II. 1751/2 Thys grieuous racking and extending of this worde Procurement. **1764** Churchill *Gotham* 12 The daily, nightly racking of the brains, To range the thoughts. **1853** Sir H. Douglas *Milit. Bridges* 170 The oars and poles were used as ribands for racking. **1876** Voyle & Stevenson *Milit. Dict.*, *Racking-down*, an operation performed with the aid of rack-lashing in laying a gun or mortar platform.

b. Torturing by means of the rack.

1494 Fabyan *Chron.* vii. 490 Dyuerse tourmentes, as rakkynge, heddynge, and hangynge. **1560** Daus tr. *Sleidane's Comm.* 284 All racking and torture, that exceadeth a meane, is uncerten and perillous. *a* **1653** Gouge *Comm. Hebr.* xi. 36 If racking, if scourging..be reall persecutions, then were theirs reall. **1732** Neal *Hist. Purit.* I. 429 He had condemned racking for grievous offenders, as contrary to Law. **1868** Browning *Ring & Bk.* v. 13 Noblemen were exempt, the vulgar thought, From racking.

c. Raising (of rents) to an excess. Also with *up*.

1581 W. Stafford *Exam. Compl.* iii. (1876) 82 This rackynge and hoyssing vp of Rentes. **1627** Hakewill *Apol.* (1630) 522 By unconscionable racking of rents and wresting from them excessiue fines. **1690** Child *Disc. Trade* (1694) 50 The racking up of rents in the years 1651 and 1652.

2. The undergoing or causing of strain, distortion, or dislocation. *spec.* Distortion of a structure under shear.

1739 Labelye *Short Acc. Piers Westm. Bridge* 18 The Frames could move..without any Danger of racking or straining. **1793** Smeaton *Edystone L.* §306 Nothing to oppose the racking of the frame. **1868** *Rep. Munitions War* 267 The 'Bellerophon' could pass the forts at New York within 200 yards without suffering except by racking. **1869** Sir E. Reed *Shipbuilding* ii. 23 This plan..has the important advantage of opposing the racking of the floor plates longitudinally. **1957** *Brit. Commonw. Forest Terminol.* II. 149 *Racking*, in timber testing, the application of loads to an assembly, tending to deform it in shear. **1976** W. J. Patton *Construction Materials* 386 *Racking*, tendency of a rectangular frame to distort from its rectangular shape due to lack of stiffness against shear forces. **1977** *Engin. Materials & Design* Aug. 17/1 A batch of fifty radiators made in this way have been subjected to tests against thermal shock cycling, pulsating pressure, vibration and racking.

attrib. **1865** A. L. Holley *Ordnance & Armor* 212 The 'racking' system, by means of heavy projectiles at low velocities.

3. Intense pain.

1896 *Allbutt's Syst. of Med.* I. 680 Violent aching of the head..with racking in the bones.

ˈracking, *vbl. sb.*[4] [f. rack *v.*[4]] Of a horse: The action or fact of moving with a rack. Also *attrib.*, as ***racking event, horse***.

1530 Palsgr. 260/2 Rackyng of a horse in his pace, *racquassure*. **1607** Markham *Caval.* iv. 5 Taking his time-keeping from trotting, and his motion of legges from ambling, and so compound this which is called a Traine, or Racking. **1725** Bradley *Fam. Dict.* s.v. *Rules for buying Horses*, Racking..'tis the same Motion as Ambling, only it is a sweeter Time. **1818** J. Palmer *Jrnl. Travels* 51 Racking is a favourite ambling pace. **1974** *Marlboro Herald-Advocate* (Bennettsville, S. Carolina) 18 Apr. 10/3 In ladies racking, Sherry Jean Nolan..rode King to a first-place win. *Ibid.*, Larry Griggs rode King to a first place victory in the junior racking event. **1974** *Greenville* (S. Carolina) *News* 23 Apr. 11/2 Friday performances, beginning at 1 p.m. and 7 p.m., have the pleasure horse classes,..along with three racking horse classes.

racking (ˈrækɪŋ), *vbl. sb.*[5] [f. rack *v.*[5]] Drawing off wine, etc. from the lees.

c **1475** *Liber Niger* in *Househ. Ord.* (1790) 74 The rackinge, coynynge, rebatinge, and other salvations of wynes. **1626** Bacon *Sylva* §305 It is in common Practise, to draw Wine, or Beere, from the Lees, (which we call Racking). **1703** *Art & Myst. Vintners* 23 The usual times for Racking, are Mid-summer and Alhallontide. **1783** B. J. Bromwich *Exper. Bee-keeper* 59 If it does not become fine after the first racking, the operation should be repeated. **1846** J. Baxter *Libr. Pract. Agric.* (ed. 4) I. 169 The manufacture of cider may be divided into twelve heads:..8. The racking.

b. *attrib.*, as ***racking-back, -can, -cellar, -cock, -engine, -faucet, -hose, -pump, -shed, -tap, -vessel***.

1846 Tizard *Brewing* (ed. 2) xx. 547 A more perfect racking-engine than such as are in ordinary use. *Ibid.*, The racking tap. **1890** *Pall Mall G.* 4 Aug. 3/1 The cask..is further cleaned with steam..before being allowed to roll off into the 'racking shed', where it is filled with porter. **1892** H. E. Wright *Handy Bk. Brewers* 37 'Settling backs' or 'racking backs'. *Ibid.* 42 The fermenting or racking vessels. *Ibid.* 503 Racking hose..and racking cocks.

ˈracking, *vbl. sb.*[6] [f. rack *v.*[6]] A piece of spun yarn or other material used for racking ropes.

1711 W. Sutherland *Shipbuild. Assist.* 143 Racking and Seizing for the Parrel. *c* **1860** H. Stuart *Seaman's Catech.* 34 It will greatly assist the spunyarn racking. **1882** Nares *Seamanship* (ed. 6) 116 Cast off the racking.

†**ˈracking,** *vbl. sb.*[7] [f. *rack* wrack *v.* Cf. rack *sb.*[5]] Wrecking, destruction.

1689 *Pol. Ballads* (1860) II. 8 The Queen and Prince banisht for what none dares own, Unless for the racking and ruin o' the state.

ˈracking, *ppl. a.*[1] [f. rack *v.*[1] + -ing[2].]

1. Of clouds: Driving before the wind.

1590 Marlowe *2nd Pt. Tamburl.* iv. iv, Draw my chariot swifter than the racking clouds. **1697** Dryden *Æneid* iv. 361 Drives the racking clouds along the liquid Space. **1808** Scott *Marm.* iii. xxii, Of middle air the demons proud, Who ride upon the racking cloud.

2. Of winds: Driving, carrying along.

1667 Milton *P.L.* ii. 182 The sport and prey Of racking whirlwinds. **1840** Carlyle *Heroes* iii. (1858) 255 The racking winds..whirl them away again.

racking (ˈrækɪŋ), *ppl. a.*[2] [f. rack *v.*[3]]

1. Extortionate; exacting.

1580 Sidney *Arcadia* i. (1598) 2 The court of affection, held by that racking steward, Remembrance. **1636** Featly *Clavis Myst.* vii. 90 Hee layeth the blame on..racking Landlords. **1649** Bp. Hall *Cases Consc.* (1650) 12 Let those ..learn to make no lesse conscience of a racking bargain. **1817** Scott *Search after Happiness* xvi, Cursed war and racking tax Have left us scarcely raiment to our backs.

†**b.** Let at rack-rents. *Obs. rare*[−1].

a **1619** Beaum. & Fl. *Wit without M.* i. i, Your racking Pastures, that have eaten up as many singing Shepherds, and their issues, as Andeluzia breeds.

2. Torturing; causing intense pain, physical or mental.

1667 Milton *P.L.* xi. 481 Maladies Of gastly Spasm, or racking torture. **1693** Congreve in *Dryden's Juvenal* xi. (1697) 296 The most racking Thought, which can intrude. **1752** Hume *Ess. & Treat.* (1777) II. 106 A man lying under the racking pains of the Gout. **1806–7** J. Beresford *Miseries Hum. Life* (1826) vi. xxii, Getting up for a journey with a racking headache. **1873** G. C. Davies *Mount. & Mere* viii. 57, I had been kept awake by a most racking tooth-ache.

3. Straining, dislocating; breaking under strain.

1868 *Rep. Munitions War* 262 To neutralize the vibration, when struck a racking blow on one side. **1874** Thearle *Naval Archit.* 118 Great racking strains are set up, tending to alter the relative positions of the beams to each other and to the ship's side. **1895** R. Kipling in *Pall Mall G.* 25 Oct. 3/2 Spirits, goblins, and witch-people were moving about on the racking ice.

Hence **ˈrackingly** *adv.*, in a racking or exhausting manner.

1857 *Chamb. Jrnl.* VIII. 33 They will certainly become.. monotonous by virtue of being so rackingly relevant.

ˈracking, *ppl. a.*[3] [f. rack *v.*[4]]

1. Of a horse: Moving with a rack.

1562 *Richmond. Wills* (Surtees) 166 One old rackynge nagg. **1585** *Wills & Inv. N.C.* (Surtees 1860) 108 My rackinge blacke nagge. **1817** Paulding *Letters fr. South* (1835) I. 86, I bought a new horse,—one of your capital racking ponies, as they are yclept.

fig. *a* **1661** Fuller *Worthies, Staffordsh.* (1662) 41 He himself became a racking but no thorough-paced Protestant.

2. ***racking pace*** = rack *sb.*[6]

1611 Cotgr., *Amble*,..an ambling, or racking pace. **1676** *Lond. Gaz.* 1138/4 Two Cart-Geldings,..a little racking-pace. **1721** Dudley in *Phil. Trans.* XXXI. 167 A Moose.. shoves along side-ways, throwing out the Feet, much like a Horse in a racking pace. **1819** Rees *Cycl.* XXIX. s.v. *Rack*, The racking pace is much the same as the amble.

ˈracking, *ppl. a.*[4] *Naut.* [f. rack *v.*[6]] That fastens ropes together.

1867 Smyth *Sailor's Word-bk.* s.v. *Nippering*, Fastening nippers by taking turns crosswise between the parts... These are called racking turns. **1882** Nares *Seamanship* (ed. 6) 34 It is..secured with a racking seizing. **1886** J. M. Caulfeild *Seamanship Notes* 3 Secure..reef-pendant to boom with a racking or rolling hitch.

racking, var. raking *vbl. sb.*[3]

†**rack jack.** *Obs. rare*[−1]. A racket.

1582 Stanyhurst *Æneis* i. (Arb.) 22 Dare ye..Too raise such raks iaks on seas, and danger vnorderd?

ˈrack-jobbing, *vbl. sb.* [f. rack *sb.*[2] + jobbing *vbl. sb.*[2] 2.] The supplying of goods to a retailer for display on racks on condition that the supplier undertakes to accept unsold stock after an agreed period. Hence (as a back-formation) **ˈrack-job** *v. intr.* and *sb.* (used *attrib.*). Also **ˈrack-jobber.**

1959 *Economist* 12 Dec. 1090/1 A complete 'rack jobbing' service. Here the supplier takes responsibility for the stock and display from week to week; the retailer simply provides the space, and accepts a lower margin on the goods that are sold. **1964** *Credit Trends* Sept. 5 Some supermarket operators are new to these lines, and the profession of rack-jobbing has grown up. The retailer leases out shelf space to these specialist concessionaires in return for an agreed profit margin related to normal earning for the space used. **1967** *Economist* 15 July 238/3 Smith and other wholesalers can help by teaching them [*sc.* newsagents] and stocking for them—as some paperback publishers already rack-job for the small newsagent or supermarkets. **1968** *Times* 29 Nov. p. iv/5 E.M.I., Decca and Pye have recently set up a joint company called Record Merchandisers to exploit what is referred to in the trade as rack jobbing. This is a system where the servicing company supplies the records for display on racks in non-conventional outlets (such as stationers and supermarkets) taking full responsibility for what is put on display and taking back unsold stock. **1969** *JEMF Quarterly* V. iii. 101 In recent years, the introduction of rack-job merchandising of LPs in supermarket and other retail outlets has obviated the need for printed graphics to complement record distributions. **1977** *Rolling Stone* 19 May 14/4 It further states that Klein instructed 'another person' to sell the records at a profit to wholesalers, rack jobbers and distributors.

'rack-ˌlashing. *Mil.* [f. RACK *v.*[3]] A lashing consisting of a piece of stout rope fastened to a short tapering stick, by means of which it may be twisted tight.

1834–47 J. S. MACAULAY *Field Fortif.* (1851) 74 A piece of smaller scantling is laid on the top of the plank.. to which it is secured with rack-lashings. **1859** F. A. GRIFFITHS *Artil. Man.* (1862) 257.

rackle ('ræk(ə)l), *a.* *Obs.* exc. *Sc.* and *north. dial.* Forms: 4–5 rakel, -il, 4–6 -yl, (5 -yll), racle, 6 ra(c)kle, *Sc.* rakill, 7 rackel, 8 raucle, 9 rackle, rau(c)kle. [Of obscure origin.] Hasty, rash, impetuous, headstrong; rough or coarse in action; also *Sc.* possessed of rude strength, vigorous at an advanced age. **a.** of persons:

a **1300** in Horstm. *Altengl. Leg.* (1875) 37 To rakele þo þei were, ȝware fore þo huy fullen þere. **13..** *E.E. Allit. P.* C. 526 He þat is to rakel to renden his cloþez, Mot efte sitte with more vnsounde to sewe hem togeder. *c* **1430** LYDG. *Min. Poems* (Percy Soc.) 30 To wyving be thou nat racle. **1433** —— *St. Edmund* II. 512 The kyng, nat rakel, but of hih prudence. **1570** LEVINS *Manip.* 129/8 Rakyl, *insolens*. *c* **1670** *Poor Man's Cup* in G. Hickes *Spirit of Popery* (1680) 10 Samson was a Rackel and Rough-handed Saint, ready to Pelt the Philistines on all occasions. **1785** BURNS *Jolly Beggars* 4th Recit., Then niest outspak a raucle carlin. **1826** T. WILSON *Pitman's Pay* I. lxvi, Te guide a rackle ram-stam wife. **1876** WAUGH *Hermit Cobbler* (Lancash. dial.) 29 Is there ony news o' that rackle (reckless) brother o' thine?

b. of things, actions, feelings, etc.

c **1374** CHAUCER *Troylus* III. 380 (429) Eche rakil dede, and eche unbridelid chere. *c* **1386** —— *Manciple's T.* 185 A thousand folk hath rakel Ire Fully fordoon. *Ibid.* 235 Wostow wherof a rakel tonge serueth. **1406** HOCCLEVE *La Male Regle* 83 His rakil wit only to him souffysith. *c* **1550** R. BIESTON *Bayte Fortune* A ij, Thy tounge is racle, thy wit is rechles. **1786** BURNS *Earnest Cry & Prayer* xxii, Auld Scotland has a raucle tongue.

Comb. **1715** *Wodrow Corr.* (1843) II. 39, I suspect this will be a very rackle-handed committee.

? Hence †**rackle** *v. intr.*, to act rashly or roughly. *Obs. rare*[−1].

c **1374** CHAUCER *Troylus* III. 1593 (1642), I nil not rakle as for to greven here.

rackleness ('ræk(ə)lnɪs). *Obs.* exc. *dial.* [f. RACKLE *a.* + -NESS.] †**a.** Rashness, hastiness. *Obs.* **b.** *Sc.* (See quot. 1825).

c **1386** CHAUCER *Manciple's T.* 179 O euery man be war of rakelnesse Ne trowe no thyng withouten strong witnesse. **1549** COVERDALE, etc. *Erasm. Par. James* 29 True godlynes can in no wise agree with racklenes of tongue. **1825** JAMIESON Suppl., (*Rackleness*), *Raucleness*, vigour and freshness in an advanced period of life.

'rackless, *a.* *rare*[−1]. [f. RACK *sb.*[3] + -LESS.] Produced without a rack.

1867 G. GILFILLAN *Night* ix. 310 Rackless torture.

rackless, obs. (north and Sc.) f. RECKLESS.

†**'rackly,** *adv.* *Sc.* *Obs.* *rare*[−1]. In 6 raklie. [? f. RACKLE *a.* + -LY[2].] Rapidly, impetuously.

c **1470** HENRYSON *Mor. Fab.* XI. (*Wolf & Sheep*) xix, Went never hound mair haistelie fra the hand, Quhen he wes rynnand maist raklie at the ra.

'rackman. *U.S.* [f. RACK *sb.*[2] + MAN *sb.*[1]] A man who distributes newspapers from the publishing office to local newspaper racks.

1943 *Sun* (Baltimore) 17 Sept. 20/2 The.. Court of Appeals upheld today a lower court decision that rackmen distributing papers.. for the publishing company of the Baltimore Sun were not engaging in interstate commerce within the meaning of the Fair Labor Standards Act. **1944** *Ibid.* 18 Jan. 17/7 (*heading*) Rackmen decision refused review.

rackoon(e, obs. forms of RACOON.

rack-out, *a.* [f. RACK *v.*[2] 5.] Designed to rack out.

1893 *Photogr. Ann.* 333 This camera is well known. It has double extension leather bellows... The extension is rack-out, but by an ingenious arrangement instantly extended as required.

'rack-pin.

1. [f. RACK *v.*[3]] = RACK-STICK.

1832 *Blackw. Magazine* XXXII. 471 Friend, if thou be'st not nautical, thou knowest what a *rack-pin*, something of the stoutest, is. **1859** J. BROWN *Rab & F.* (1862) 33, I had to brain him wi' a rack-pin.

2. [f. RACK *sb.*[2]] One of the pins supporting the rack-boards in an organ.

1881 W. E. DICKSON *Pract. Organ-building* 91 The rack-board.. may be placed on its rack-pins, and the feet dropped into their places.

rack-punch. [f. RACK *sb.*[7] + PUNCH.] Punch made with arrack.

1713 STEELE *Guard.* No. 143 ¶3 Rack-punch, quickned with brandy and gun-powder. **1752** FIELDING *Amelia* Wks. 1775 X. 155 The governor.. trumpeted forth the praises of his rack-punch. **1848** THACKERAY *Van. Fair* vi, He insisted upon having a bowl of rack punch; everybody had rack punch at Vauxhall.

'rack-rent, *sb.* [f. RACK *v.*[3] 4 + RENT. *Rack-rented* is found in 1591.] A very high, excessive, or extortionate rent; a rent equal (or nearly equal) to the full value of the land.

1607 J. NORDEN *Surv. Dial.* v. 80 An obseruing and painefull husband.. thriueth as well upon his farme of rack rent, as many.. Freeholders. **1715** *Act Reg. Papists* in *Lond. Gaz.* (1716) No. 5455/3 Any Farmer or Tenant at Rack-Rent. **1745** *Season. Adv. Protest.* 18 They steal from their Neighbours, to enable them to pay the Land-Jobber his Rack-Rent. **1818** JAS. MILL *Brit. India* I. II. v. 184 *note*, One third to the cultivator, and two thirds to the proprietor, would be accounted a rackrent in England. **1879** H. GEORGE *Progr. & Pov.* II. ii. (1881) 111 They lived on the potato, because rack-rents stripped every thing else from them.

attrib. **1778** [W. MARSHALL] *Minutes Agric.* 4 Dec. 1775 *Obs.*, The rack-rent Gentlemen of landed property. **1834** *Tait's Mag.* I. 17/1 Every year growing worse than the last in this rack-rent country.

transf. and *fig.* **1608** MIDDLETON *Fam. Love* I. ii, *Nil muliere levius.* Tut, man, every one knows their worth When they are at a rack rent. **1768** *Woman of Honor* II. 178 Subjecting to the rack-rent of avarice and insolence that country of theirs.

'rack-rent, *v.* [f. prec.]

1. *trans.* To subject (a person) to the payment of rack-rent.

1748 RICHARDSON *Clarissa* (1811) I. xiii. 83 It was a maxim with his family.. never to rack-rent old tenants or their descendants. **1879** H. GEORGE *Progr. & Pov.* 105 Who rack-rent the cultivators most mercilessly.

absol. **1856** LEVER *Martins of Cro'M.* 138 He hunted, and drank, and feasted and rack-rented.

2. To let (a farm, etc.) at a rack-rent.

1882 in OGILVIE.

Hence **rack'rentable** *a.*, capable of being rack-rented; **'rack-ˌrented** *ppl. a.* (in quot. 1591 app. f. the sb.); **'rack-ˌrenting** *vbl. sb.* and *ppl. a.*

1591 SYLVESTER *Du Bartas* I. iii. 1154 The needy, hard-rack-rented Hinde. **1663** E. BUTTERFIELD *Let.* 1 Feb. in M. M. Verney *Memoirs of Verney Family* (1899) IV. ii. 43, I hate this rack-renting 'tis worse than usury. **1840** J. S. MILL in *Edin. Rev.* LXXII. 46 Much alteration may be requisite in the system of rack-renting and tenancy at will. **1856** LEVER *Martins of Cro'M.* 398 Is it rack-renting.. would make them popular? **1875** MAINE *Hist. Inst.* vi. 175 They were the first 'tenants at will'.. and.. were always theoretically rackrentable. **1893** PEEL *Spen Valley* 120 The appeal of the poor rack-rented tenantry. **1897** *Westm. Gaz.* 9 Sept. 7/1 Even the most rack-renting of landlords will find .. the impossibility of extortion. **1963** *Economist* 3 Aug. 421/1 The rack-renting of London's tenantry. **1969** *Listener* 12 June 815/3 Communism appeals to hundreds of thousands of peasants who hate corruption, rack-renting and foreign intervention.

'rack-ˌrental. *rare*[−1]. The value (of land) at rack-rent.

1812 SOUTHEY in *Q. Rev.* VIII. 328 The rack-rental of England in that year [1803] was about forty millions.

'rack-ˌrenter.

1. One who pays rack-rent.

1680 *Spirit of Popery* 45 If they were Rack-renters. **1733** TULL *Horse-hoeing Husb.* Pref. 6 'Tis a publick Calamity, that the Lands of a Country must be all or mostly in the Hands of Rack-Renters, whose Interest it is.. that they never may be improv'd. **1807** VANCOUVER *Agric. Devon* (1813) 224 These meadows the rack renters are bound to dress after every third crop of hay. **1826** COBBETT *Rur. Rides* (1885) II. 236 The farmers were real yeomen, and not miserable rack-renters.

2. One who exacts rack-rent.

1880 *Times* 23 Oct. 6/5 Not.. one [landlord] in 500 [will] be found to merit the name of 'rack-renter'.

racks (ræks). *Television slang.* (See quots.)

1960 O. SKILBECK *ABC of Film & TV* 104 *Racks*, colloquial term for the vision control department (T.V.) between cameras and vision mixer. **1974** *Some Technical Terms & Slang* (Granada Televison), *Racks*, the television control area between studio camera and control box.

†**rack-sauch.** *Sc.* *Obs.* *rare*[−1]. [f. RACK *v.*[3] + SAUCH, sallow, willow.] A gallows-bird.

1508 DUNBAR *Flyting* 245 Filling of tauch, rak sauch, cry crauch, thow art our sett.

'rack-staff. ? *Obs.* (See quots.)

1611 COTGR., *Frayoire*, the racke-staffe, or nog of a mill; the little peece of wood which rubbing against the hopper makes the corne fall from it. **1688** R. HOLME *Armoury* III. 340/2 The parts of a Wind-Mill.. The Rack-staff, that shakes the Shough. **1847–78** HALLIWELL, *Rack-staff*, a kind of pole or staff used for adjusting the mill-stones.

'rack-stick. [f. RACK *v.*[3]] A stick used for tightening a rope placed round anything.

1859 F. A. GRIFFITHS *Artil. Man.* (1862) 258 Rack-sticks, and lashings. *Ibid.* 259 The.. officer carries the rack sticks.

rackt, obs. form of *raked*, RAKE *v.*[1]

†**rack vintage.** *Obs.* (See quot. 1617.)

1540 *Act 32 Hen. VIII*, c. 14 For the freight of euery tun wyne at the racke vintage, xvi.*s.* **1617** MINSHEU *Ductor*, *Racke vintage*, An. 32. H. 8. cap. 14, is a second vintage or voyage for wines by our Merchants into Fraunce, &c. [Hence in Blount and later Dicts.]

rack-wind: see RACK *sb.*[1] 3.

rackyn-croke, obs. form of RACKAN-CROOK.

racle, obs. f. RACKLE *a.*

‖**raclette** (raklɛt). [Fr., = scraper.]

1. *Archæol.* [A. Cheynier 1930, in *Bull. Soc. Préhist. Française* XXVII. 488] An end-, or side-scraper, of a type discovered in the valley of the Vézère, dating from the Early Magdalenian age. Also *attrib.*

1931 *Proc. Prehist. Soc. E. Anglia* VI. 322 Dr. André Cheynier,.. working at Badegoule, has obtained from a special layer several hundreds of.. tools, to which he has given the name of Raclettes. **1936** *Nature* 11 July 79/2 (*heading*) An Early Magdalenian 'raclette' industry in the Lower Thames valley.

2. A fondue-like dish consisting of cheese melted before an open fire, scraped on to the plate, and served with potatoes. Also *attrib.*

1949 A. L. SIMON *Dict. Gastron.* 200/2 *Raclette*, the name given in the Valais Canton of Switzerland to the local *Fondue*. **1958** *Times* 15 Nov. 11/6 There is dried meat of the Valais.. and there are *raclettes* and *fondues*. **1961** *Times* 23 Mar. 16/7 The Seiler family arranged an enormous *raclette* party on the slopes of the Riffelalp. **1971** *Vogue* 15 Sept. 118/1 *Raclette*.. is.. a speciality of the Valais... A whole side of cheese is grilled in front of a brazier.. the sizzling bits scraped on to your plate.. served with potatoes boiled in their skins and gherkins. **1974** *Times* 4 Feb. 17/5 Six helpings of raclette cheese with potatoes.

racloir ('ræklwɑː(r)). Chiefly *Archæol.* [Fr., = scraper.] A scraper, esp. of a type discovered amongst the remains of the Mousterian period of the Middle Palæolithic period.

1892 P. L. SIMMONDS *Commercial Dict. Trade Products* 311/2 *Racloir*, a scraper; a grater; an instrument to strike off the heaped corn in a measure. **1923** *Nature* CXII. 118/2 The latest group which is found upon the Stoke Newington 'floor' is a clearly-defined Mousterian industry, with fine examples of both racloirs and of the equally characteristic trimmed-flake points. **1935** *Antiquity* IX. 118 [Flint] blades of Upper Palaeolithic facies, racloirs, tranchets, and carinated fragments. **1956** A. L. ARMSTRONG in D. L. Linton *Sheffield* vi. 94 Zones II and III yielded quartzite hand-axes, racloirs, and scrapers displaying great skill and a refined technique.

racoille, var. RECUEIL *v.*

racolta, var. RACCOLTA.

racommode, var. RACCOMMODE.

racon ('reɪkɒn). orig. *U.S.* [f. RA(DAR + BEA)CON *sb.*] = *radar beacon* s.v. RADAR[2].

1945 *Army & Navy Jrnl.* 18 Aug. 1534/4 *Racon*, radar beacons. Stations which serve as the radar equivalents of lighthouses. **1947** L. A. TURNER in L. N. Ridenour *Radar System Engin.* viii. 246 Beacons of the synchronous sort just described have been variously called 'radar beacons', 'responder beacons', 'racons', and 'transponders'. **1958** *Proc. Inst. Electr. Engineers* CV. B. Suppl. No. 8. 351/1 A racon has recently been developed at the Admiralty Signals and Radar Establishment for use on lightvessels, the intention.. being that a number of such racons shall be fitted around the shores of Great Britain on both lightvessels and lighthouses. **1967** B. KNOX *Blacklight* vii. 142 'The screen was registerin' one o' those blacklight beacons.'.. 'The deep-water racon,' nodded Carrick. **1977** *Globe & Mail* (Toronto) 24 Feb. B16 Lakes shipping.. can also obtain guidance from racons (shore-based radar reflectors).

racon, obs. f. RACKAN.

‖**raconteur** (rakɔ̃tœr). [F., f. *raconter* to relate: see RECOUNT *v.*[1]] One skilled in relating anecdotes or stories.

1828 J. C. YOUNG *Jrnl.* 3 July in *Memoir Charles Mayne Young* (1871) I. v. 169 Sir Charles is a handsome, thoroughbred gentleman, and a capital *raconteur*. **1829** DISRAELI *Yng. Duke* I. xii. (1831) 97 Stamped the illustrious narrator as the most consummate *raconteur*. **1855–6** THACKERAY *Four Georges* (1861) 183 Scott.. the very best *raconteur* of his time. **1885** *Manch. Exam.* 13 Apr. 5/7 He was a good *raconteur*. No one knew more good stories or could tell them so well. **1922** JOYCE *Ulysses* 604 A gifted man, Mr Bloom said of Mr Dedalus senior, in more respects than one and a born *raconteur* if ever there was one. **1937** *Discovery* Oct. 326/1 Mrs. Johnson says little about herself, indulges in no purple passages, and without the conscious effort of the *raconteur* she manages to introduce many good stories and telling anecdotes. **1958** L. DURRELL *Mountolive* xv. 296 The inevitable anecdote of a famous *raconteur* to round off the letter. **1972** J. MOSEDALE *Football* iii. 35 (*caption*) Jimmy Conzelman functioned as quarterback, coach, raconteur, songwriter.. and promoter.

So **raconteuse** (-tøz), a female raconteur.

1863 OUIDA *Held in Bondage* (1870) 46 'There's not one of you men now-a-days like Selwyn', began the old *raconteuse* again. **1892** *Daily News* 2 Aug. 5/1 Let us admit that she is a good *raconteuse*, for the sake of grammar.

racoon, raccoon (rə'kuːn, ræ'kuːn), *sb.* Forms: 7 (see etym. note; also) racoone, -oune, -owne, 7–8 rackoon, (7 rack-, rockoone), 7– raccoon, 8– racoon. See also COON *sb.* and RATTOON. [Powhatan (Virginia) dialect of Algonquian. The following quots. show more precise reproductions of the native word:

1608 CAPT. SMITH *True Relat.* Wks. (Arb.) 19 Couered with a great Couering of Rahaugcums. *Ibid.* 23 Presents of Deare, bread, Raugroughcums. *c* **1610** W. STRACHEY *Virginia* (1849) I. x. 122 There is a beast they call arocoune, much like a badger. *Ibid.* 183 *Dict. Ind. Lang.*, *Arathkone*, a beast like a fox. **1624** CAPT. SMITH *Virginia* II. 27 There is a beast they call Aroughcun, much like a badger. *Ibid.* III. ii. 48 A great robe, made of Rarowcun skinnes.]

a. An American nocturnal carnivore of the genus *Procyon*. The common N. American species is *P. lotor*, a grayish-brown furry animal with bushy tail and sharp snout.

1619 MIDDLETON *Love & Antiq.* 19 Minck, Stote, Miniuer, Racoone, Moashye, Wolverine. **1632** T. MORTON *New Eng. Canaan* v. (1838) 54 The Racowne is a beast as bigg..as a Foxe, with a Bushtayle. **1672** JOSSELYN *New Eng. Rarities* 17 The Raccoon liveth in hollow trees. **1712** E. COOKE *Voy. S. Sea* 326 Of wild Creatures, there are Raccoons, Hares, Rabbits, &c. **1774** GOLDSM. *Nat. Hist.* (1776) IV. 333 The racoon, which some authors have called the Jamaica rat, is about the size of a small badger. **1809** W. IRVING *Knickerb.* (1861) 204 They were gallant bush-whackers and hunters of racoons by moonlight. **1856** BRYANT *Winter Piece* 52 The lighter track Of fox, and the racoon's broad path, were there. **1895** *Outing* (U.S.) XXVI. 434/2 The American raccoon..is practically a bear.

b. The skin or fur of the racoon.

1815 C. WILT *Let.* in J. C. Luttig *Jrnl. Expedition Upper Missouri* (1920) 130 Raccoon from your country will not bring 62½c in Kentucky. **1901–2** *T. Eaton & Co. Catal.* Fall & Winter 42/1 Alaska Sable... Black Persian Lamb... Raccoon. **1976** 'D. HALLIDAY' *Dolly & Nanny Bird* ii. 28 Hefty young men clad in Timberwolf, Raccoon, Scimmia, Tibetan Yak and Natural Unplucked Nutria.

c. *attrib.* and *Comb.*, as ***racoon-hunt, -hunting, -skin***; **racoon-berry** *U.S.*, the May-apple or mandrake (Miller, 1884); **racoon-bridge** (see quot. 1791); **racoon-cap** *U.S.*, a cap made from the dressed skin of the racoon; **racoon dog**, a mammal about the size of a fox, *Nyctereutes procyonoides*, belonging to the family Canidæ, native to eastern Asia, and distinguished by thick greyish-brown fur and black, racoon-like markings on its head; so **racoon-like dog** (in same sense); **racoon oyster** *U.S.*, a small, brown-shelled oyster, *Ostrea frons*, found in clusters off the shores of south-eastern North America.

1791 W. BARTRAM *Carolina* 445 No other bridge than a sapling felled across it, which is called a *raccoon bridge. **1840** *Knickerbocker* XVI. 163 He then made me a rakish *raccoon-cap, with a flaunting tail to it. **1848** in H. Howe *Hist. Coll. Ohio* 151 For..several years after the war, raccoon-caps, with fur outside..were almost universally worn. [**1833** J. E. GRAY *Illustr. Indian Zool.* II. plate 1 (*caption*) Racoon-faced Dog.] **1868** *Proc. Zool. Soc.* 522 *Raccoon Dog. Tail short, bushy. **1876** A. R. WALLACE *Geogr. Distrib. Anim.* I. x. 226 The quadruped figured is the curious racoon dog. **1959** *Times* 23 Feb. 10/5 Two of the strangest members of the dog family arrived recently at the Regent's Park Zoo. They are the maned wolf..and the raccoon-dog from Siberia. **1974** L. E. BUELER *Wild Dogs of World* 217 In Japan..the raccoon dog was once common to all the principal islands. **1864** C. GEIKIE *Life in Woods* xix. (1874) 317, I remember one *racoon hunt. **1809** A. HENRY *Trav.* 131 *Racoon-hunting was my..daily employ. **1890** ST. G. MIVART *Dogs, Jackals, Wolves, & Foxes: Monogr. Canidæ* 135 The *Raccoon-like Dog is an inhabitant of Japan, the valley of the Amoor, and China. **1931** *Proc. Zool. Soc.* 174 A female Raccoon-like Dog..lived..5 years. **1964** L. S. CRANDALL *Managem. Wild Mammals in Captivity* 280 The raccoon-like dog..is a small grayish animal,..with a black facial mask which is the basis for its name. **1834** J. J. AUDUBON *Ornith. Biogr.* II. 504 Shrimps..have been detained at low water on the banks of *racoon oysters, a kind of shell-fish so named under the idea that they are eaten by that quadruped. **1854** W. G. SIMMS *Southward Ho!* iii. 28 They procure the ordinary 'racoon oyster'—the meanest of the tribe. **1883** SIMMONDS *Useful Animals, Raccoon Oysters*, a variety of American oysters from Appalichicola Bay, Florida. **1884** GOODE *Nat. Hist. Usef. Aquatic Anim.* 752 From..overcrowding the shells of the individual Oysters become very narrow and greatly elongated; the peculiar forms which result are known to oystermen as 'Raccoon Oysters' or 'Cats-tongues'. **1885** *Harper's Mag.* Jan. 219/1 When the mangrove grows on the outer edge of the water-line, and drops its aerial roots,..the spat of the raccoon oyster finds a lodgement. **1624** *Racoon skin [see etym. note]. **1670** D. DENTON *Descr. New York* (1845) 2 Bevers, Otter, Raccoon skins, with other Furrs.

Hence **ra'coon** *v. intr.*, to walk about at night, like a racoon. *nonce-wd.*

1855 MRS. GASKELL *North & S.* xiii, She heard him pacing about (racooning, as she and Edith used to call it).. long after she began to listen as she lay in bed.

racord, obs. Sc. form of RECORD.

Racovian (rəˈkəʊvɪən), *a.* and *sb.* [f. *Rakow*, a town in Poland + -IAN.] **a.** *adj.* Of or pertaining to Rakow, or to the Unitarians (Socinians) who made it their chief centre in the 17th century. **b.** *sb.* An adherent of the doctrines taught at Rakow.

1652 (*title*) The Racovian Catechisme. **1768–74** TUCKER *Lt. Nat.* (1834) II. 474 Should another Edwards do me the honour to make another Mr. Locke of me by calling out, Racovian! **1837** HALLAM *Hist. Lit.* III. ii. §39 The Racovian institution was broken up and dispersed in 1638. *a* **1861** CUNNINGHAM *Hist. Theol.* (1864) II. *xxiii. 177 The Racovian Catechism fills very nearly two hundred pages.

racquet, -ette, varr. RACKET *sb.*, RAQUETTE.

racquetball (ˈrækɪtbɔːl). orig. *U.S.* Also **racquet ball**. [f. RACQUET + BALL *sb.*[1]] A game resembling paddle ball played with a light ball and a racket in a four-walled handball court. Also *attrib.* Hence **'racquet,baller**, one who plays racquetball.

1972 WICKSTROM & LARSON (*title*) Racquetball-paddleball fundamentals. **1974** *Wall Street Jrnl.* 12 June 1 Mr. Kendler split with the International Racquetball Association last year to form a rival organization, the National Racquetball Club, which sponsors a professional tour for 16 top-ranked racquetballers. **1976** *Milton Keynes Express* 23 July 17/4 Over the five week period they will include trampoline, squash, volley-ball, racquet ball, gymnastics, football, table tennis, five a side football,.. chess and draughts. **1978** *Monitor* (McAllen, Texas) 29 May 3B/7 The newest indoor sports craze for physical fitness nuts is racquetball. The game is a cross between tennis and handball. **1979** *Tucson Mag.* Apr. 55/1 Racquetball courts and numerous other recreation centers are spotted throughout the city.

ract, obs. Sc. form of RACK *sb.*[1]

racunnis, etc., obs. Sc. forms of RECOGNIZE.

racy (ˈreɪsɪ), *a.* Also 7 racie, razy, 8 razie. [f. RACE *sb.*[2] 10 + -Y[1].]

1. a. Of wine or other liquors, vegetable juices, fruits, etc.: Having a characteristically excellent taste, flavour, or quality. So of taste, flavour, etc.

1654 GAYTON *Pleas. Notes* III. vi. 102 The generous oyle of Sack, nitty, roapy, and razy. **1676** WORLIDGE *Cyder* (1691) 210 If ground early then is the cider more racy. **1756–7** tr. *Keysler's Trav.* (1760) IV. 244 The racy flavour and strong body of this wine. *a* **1774** GOLDSM. *Surv. Exp. Philos.* (1776) II. 243 The juices which are nourished in the vegetable world by the solar heat, are light, pungent, and racy. **1800** MOORE *Anacreon* i. 12 His lip exhaled..The fragrance of the racy tide. **1849** SIR J. STEPHEN *Eccl. Biog.* II. 228 The grapes they yield are ponderous and racy, like the clusters of Eshcoll.

fig. *c* **1650** DENHAM *Progr. Learn.* 68 Might make old Homer's skull the Muses' hive; And from his brain that Helicon distil Whose racy liquor did his offspring fill. **1832** DE QUINCEY *Rhetoric* Wks. 1862 X. 50 English divinity ceased to be the racy vineyard that it had been in ages of ferment and struggle.

†**b.** Of plants: Full of sap, succulent. *Obs.*

1675 EVELYN *Terra* (1729) 25 Some Plants, the most racy, and charg'd with Juice..thrive well amongst Rocks.

2. a. Of persons: Having a distinctive quality or vigour of character or intellect; lively, spirited, full of 'go'. So of actions, qualities, etc.

1668 DRYDEN *Even. Love* II. i, A colony of Spaniards, or spiritual Italians, planted among us, would make us much more racy. **1849** C. BRONTE *Shirley* ix, Yorkshire has such families here and there..peculiar, racy, vigorous; of good blood and strong brain. **1852** MISS MITFORD *Recoll.* II. 147 My friend the rector, raciest of men, is an Oxford divine of the old school. **1864** BLACKMORE *Clara Vaughan* lxi, That genial racy smile, which very few could resist.

b. Of animals or their parts: Showing high breeding or good blood.

1841 'WILDRAKE' *Cracks of the Day* 190 The *racy* Mango won him the St. Leger. **1885** *Century Mag.* XXXI. 118 The Gordon setter..should have..a narrow deep chest with racy front. **1889** *Pall Mall G.* 21 Aug. 2/1 His [a horse's] head having a racy, determined look.

†**c.** Of a sense: Noble, superior. *Obs. rare*$^{-1}$.

1675 R. BURTHOGGE *Causa Dei* 400 There are things Good, and things Evil to this High and Racy Sense, as well as to Inferiour Ones.

3. Of speech, writing, etc.: Having a characteristic sprightliness, liveliness, or piquancy.

a **1667** COWLEY *Answ. Verses fr. Jersey*, Brisk racy Verses, in which we The Soil from whence they came, tast, smell, and see. *c* **1817** GIFFORD *Let.* in Smiles *Mem. J. Murray* (1891) II. xxi. 47 His style is racy and vivid. **1841** D'ISRAELI *Amen. Lit.* (1867) 291 The conversations of Sir Thomas More were racy. **1895** J. HOLLINGSHEAD *My Lifetime* I. xxiv. 232 A rich imagination, and the power of racy narrative. **1901** 'P. BEE' *Vagaries of Men* 107 Women who tell racy stories..can rouse a great deal of enthusiasm in a room full of men. **1955** *Times* 19 Aug. 8/2 Lieutenant-Colonel R. J. T. Hills..contributes to the summer number of the *Household Brigade Magazine* some racy memories of Combermere, the Household Cavalry barracks at Windsor. **1971** D. POTTER *Brit. Eliz. Stamps* xv. 179 Every new Great Britain stamp appears on the front cover in full colour, and there is hardly a week without a racy, but informative piece, on some aspect of Great Britain collecting. **1973** *Nature* 27 July 241/2 The introductory passages are autobiographical in content and colourful, frank and uninhibited in style—racy is the only word.

4. Of pleasure, enjoyment, etc.: Peculiarly agreeable or rich.

1690 SHADWELL *Am. Bigot* 11, 'Tis difficulty makes the pleasure high and racy. **1847** LYTTON *Lucretia* (1853) 166 There was a racy, wholesome gusto in his enjoyment of novelty. **1862** BURTON *Bk. Hunter* (1863) 163 The active racy enjoyments of life—those enjoyments in which there is also exertion and achievement.

5. Of the air: Pure, exhilarating.

1838 LYTTON *Alice* VIII. vii, Theresa's merry laugh sounded clear and musical in the racy air.

6. Phr. ***racy of the soil***, characteristic of a certain country or people (chiefly used with ref. to Ireland).

1870 *Daily News* 16 Feb., It is racy of the soil; and would not admit of transplantation to England or Scotland. **1889** *Spectator* 26 Oct., This popular [Irish] superstition..is so racy of the soil, that it is really deserving of a much wider publicity.

racyn, obs. form of RAISIN.

racyonal, obs. form of RATIONAL.

rad (ræd), *sb.*[1] Also **Rad.** Abbrev. of RADICAL *sb.* 5.

1820 LADY J. CAMPBELL *Let.* 18 Nov. in Duke of Argyll *Intimate Society Lett.* (1910) II. 654 We shut all our shutters for fear our lights shd seem *Rads* too. **1831** *Lincoln Herald* 7 Jan., The tricolor rads of this Borough. **1852** COL. HAWKER *Diary* (1893) II. 344 Hooted at by the scum and rads at this dirty end of the town. **1882** BESANT *All Sorts* (1884) 139 He is the reddest of red-hot Rads and the most advanced of Republicans. **1898** H. N. PAGE *Red Rock* xxxiv. 411 He..was abusing Leech and Still and pretty much all the Rads. **1912** J. GALSWORTHY *Eldest Son* I. ii. 27 Plenty of time to work up the constituency before we kick out these infernal Rads. **1973** R. HAYES *Hungarian Game* viii. 61 A clumsy bribe and a gambit about student rads.

rad, *sb.*[2] [Abbrev. of RADDLE *sb.*[1]] In phr. ***rad and dab***: see RADDLE *sb.*[1] 2.

1887 in *Dict. Archit.* VII.

rad (ræd), *sb.*[3] Abbrev. of RADIAN.

1913 GODFREY & SIDDONS *Four-Figure Tables* 38 Radians and degrees... Rad. **1960** C. L. MCCLURE *Theory of Inertial Guidance* i. 11 The total inertial angular velocity of the terrestrial geoid: $\omega_{EI} = 7{\cdot}2921 \,.\, 10^{-5}$ rad/sec...measured in radians per mean solar second. **1973** *Nature* 6 Apr. 372/3 The Mars 2 and 3 experiments were intended to give a continuous scan of the planet's surface using a field of vision of 0·01 rad (15 km from a distance of 1,500 km).

†**rad** (ræd), *sb.*[4] *Obs.* [f. RAD(IATION.] A unit of X-ray dose (see quots.).

1918 S. RUSS in *Arch. Radiol. & Electrotherapy* XXIII. 226 [I venture to put forward a suggestion for a new unit, by which the dose of X rays administered to a patient may be measured; the new unit is primarily intended for use in what is known as 'deep therapy'.] *Ibid.* 231 The radium capsule, when applied to malignant cells, causes complete inhibition of their proliferation after an exposure thereto for one hour; this latter quantity is the suggested unit, viz., the Rad. **1922** S. RUSS et al. in *Lancet* 4 Feb. 213/1 As yet there is no international unit by which X rays are measured, and during the course of this work we have employed the 'rad' as our working unit—i.e., the minimum dose of X rays which..is needed to prevent the growth of Jensen's rat sarcoma when inoculated into normal rats.

rad (ræd), *sb.*[5] Abbrev. of RADIATOR. Also *attrib.*

1935 F. BRETT YOUNG *White Ladies* v. vi. 558 The rads are stone-cold. **1967** L. DEIGHTON *Expensive Place* xxvii. 169 He..opened up the rad cap. **1975** J. SYMONS *Three Pipe Problem* iii. 28 It was an air bubble, we've bled the rads. **1977** *Hot Car* Oct. 19/2 The fan should be left off and an electric one fitted in front of the rad.

rad (ræd), *sb.*[6] Pl. **rad, rads.** [f. initial letters of *radiation absorbed dose*.] A unit of absorbed dose of ionizing radiation, corresponding to the absorption of 100 ergs of energy per gramme of absorbing material (0·01 joule per kilogramme).

In the International System of Units replaced by the gray, equal to 100 rads.

1954 *Brit. Jrnl. Radiol.* XXVII. 243/1 The rad is the unit of absorbed dose and is 100 ergs per gramme. **1957** *Financial Times Ann. Rev. Brit. Industry* 87/2 For example, a 1,000 curie cobalt source has a total power output of 15 watts and gives a radiation intensity of the order of 100 rads per second of high penetration at a convenient operating distance. **1968** *Times* 16 Dec. 7/4 During the flight the three astronauts are expected to receive radiation doses of less than one rad a man, less than from chest X-ray series. **1971** J. Z. YOUNG *Introd. Study Man* xxviii. 393 The minimum dose of radiation that will produce a doubling of the spontaneous mutation rate is likely to be in the region of 10 rad per 30 years. **1972** 'J. LANGE' *Binary* 64 Two rad cartridges... Bars of plutonium-238 oxide. That's a radioactive isotope. **1976** *Lancet* 6 Nov. 993/1 The intended tumour dose was 4000 rads in four weeks. **1976** *Path. Ann.* XI. 368 (*caption*) Follicular thyroid carcinoma excised 26 years after approximately 700 rad were applied for enlarged tonsils and adenoids.

rad (ræd), *a.*[1] and *adv.* *Obs.* exc. *dial.* Forms: 1 **hrad, hræd**, 1–3 **ræd**, 3–6 **rade**, 3–6 (9 *dial.*) **rad.** [OE. *hrad, hræd* = OHG. *hrad, hrat*, ON. *hrað-r* (MSw. *radh*).]

A. *adj.* Quick, hasty, speedy; active, prompt, ready; eager, elated.

a **700** *Epinal Gloss.* 742 *Percitus*, hraed [*Erfurt* hrad]. *c* **888** K. ÆLFRED *Boeth.* iv, þu þe on hrædum færelde þone heofon ymbhweorfest. *c* **897** —— *Gregory's Past.* xxxviii. 280 Sie æghwelc mon swiðe hræd & swiðe ȝeornfull to ȝehieranne. *c* **1000** *Ags. Gosp.* Matt. xxvi. 41 Se gast is hræd [*Hatton MS.* ræd], þæt flæsc ys untrum. *c* **1205** LAY. 12318 þer fore wes þe king glad & þiderward wes swiðe ræd. *c* **1250** *Gen. & Ex.* 2730 Ðu art of dede and o word to rad. *a* **1310** in Wright *Lyric P.* 45 Wymmen..beoth to rad upon huere red, To love [etc.]. *c* **1400** *Destr. Troy* 917 The freike..raght to his Ryng in a rad haste. *c* **1425** *Seven Sag.* (P.) 1290 The tormentours wer ful rade To do tha[t] the Emperour bade. *c* **1470** HENRY *Wallace* VII. 526 Cast we doun all, we mycht be demyt our rad. **1570** LEVINS *Manip.* 7/41 Radde, *agilis, promptus.* **1876** *Whitby Gloss.* s.v., 'Either too rad or too sad', as a variable person, over-elated or, otherwise, depressed. **1887** *S. Chesh. Gloss., Rad*, quick, ready.

†**B.** *adv.* Quickly, readily, soon. *Obs.*

c **1250** *Gen. & Ex.* 998 Al ðat euere ðe louerd bad dede abraham redi and rad. **13..** *Gaw. & Gr. Knt.* 862 Ryche robes ful rad renkkez hem broȝten. *c* **1400** *Destr. Troy* 9233 He made hym redy full rad, ron to the toun. **1486** *Bk. St. Albans* F j b, Then ar thay glad In hope thay shall hym haue & renne so rad. *c* **1525** *Priests of Peblis* 1190 Thow thocht I was not wort ane prene, And that I am, ful rade on the will be sene.

rad (ræd), *a.*[2] *Obs.* exc. *Sc.* Also 3 **raad**, 3–5, 20 **radd**, 3–5 **rade**, 4–6 **radde**, 6 **raed**; 4, 8 **rede**; 4–8 **red**, 5 **redd**, 6 **redde.** [a. ON. *hrædd-r* (Sw. *rädd*,

Da. *ræd*) frightened, afraid, pa. pple. of *hrǽða* to frighten.] Frightened, afraid, alarmed. Const. *of*, *for*, and infin.

c **1200** ORMIN 2170 Ȝho drefedd wass & radd off Godess enngell. **13..** *Cursor M.* 5097 Bes noght rad bot mas godd chere. *Ibid.* 23024 Þai for him sal be sa redd. *a* **1340** HAMPOLE *Psalter* lxv. 8 All erthly lufers was rad for pyne. **1375** BARBOUR *Bruce* XII. 431 Thai war rad till byd fichting. *a* **1400–50** *Alexander* 2510 Þan am I redd all oure rewme be reft vs for euire. c **1450** *St. Cuthbert* (Surtees) 4627 For few perills were þai radd. **1513** DOUGLAS *Æneis* II. ii. 18 Semyng ful red, Behalding Troiane rowtis on athir hand. c **1600** MONTGOMERIE *Cherrie & Slae* 1392, I am red His hastyness bred us mishap. *a* **1708** *Outlaw Murray* xxvi. in Child *Ballads* V. 192/1, I am right rad of treasonrie. **1791** LEARMONT *Poems* 284, I'm rede I tine the way. **1861** R. QUINN *Heather Lintie* 56 We'd na be rad o' scath frae wather, Though snow was wreathin'. *a* **1870** H. S. RIDDELL *Poet Wks.* (1871) II. 250 That ye might saints and angels meet And no be rad. **1930** in *Sc. Nat. Dict.* (1968) VII. 319/3 I'm radd ye ken mair aboot youres and sick like than yer buiks.

rad, obs. f. RAID *sb.*, obs. pa. t. READ, REDE, RIDE.

R.A.D.A., **RADA**[1] ('rɑːdə). Also **Rada**. [Acronym f. the initials of *R*oyal *A*cademy of *D*ramatic *A*rt, founded in 1904 and granted a royal charter in 1920.] One of the leading acting schools in Britain, at present situated in Gower Street, London. Also *attrib.*

1921 *Times* 19 July 8 (*heading*) R.A.D.A. Ex-Students First Production... The author of the play was Mr. Kenneth Barnes, Director of R.A.D.A., and his maiden effort was a worthy one. **1937** W. S. MAUGHAM *Theatre* xx. 191, I always say you're the greatest actress on the stage. I've learnt more from you than I did all the years I was at the R.A.D.A. **1949** *Listener* 21 Apr. 676/1 They were, in fact, R.A.D.A. students at play. **1962** J. BRAINE *Life at Top* iv. 68 A different voice, the voice of the red-haired girl from RADA whom now I dimly remember talking to earlier. **1965** *Observer* 19 Sept. 1/5 The new man for Rada? **1968** *Listener* 26 Dec. 873/3 The melodies are dim, the lyrics wanly snobbish, the costumes are rainwear ads and the Cockney accents (except Breeze's) RADA-provincial. **1977** L. MEYNELL *Hooky gets Wooden Spoon* xiv. 179 Sergeant Fitt could certainly have won a medal at RADA for.. complete impassiveness.

Rada[2] ('rɑːdə). [App. ad. *Allada*, the name of a former principality of Dahomey (now Benin).] The name of a group of deities of West African derivation venerated in Haiti; the worship of these deities. Also *attrib.*

1929 W. B. SEABROOK *Magic Island* I. i. 11, I knelt at last before the great *Rada* drums. *Ibid.* iii. 43 Some..danced, not the mad *Rada* of the night, but boisterous, gay Congo dances. **1937** M. J. HERSKOVITS *Life in Haitian Valley* viii. 149 When *vodun* deities are discussed in Mirebalais, most often two 'companies' of them are mentioned, the Rada and the Pétro 'squads'. **1941** J. G. LEYBURN *Haitian People* vii. 145 To the spirits..not drawn from Christianity the name 'loa' is applied. There seem in general to be two classes of these: those who have an African origin, and those with a Haitian background only. The former group is called 'Rada', the latter 'Petro'. **1957** *Amer. Anthropologist* LIX. 821 Members of two African-derived religions, Yoruba 'Shango'..and Dahomean 'Rada'..consider themselves also to be Roman Catholics.

radappertization (ræˌdæpətaɪ'zeɪʃən). [f. L. *rad-iāre* to furnish with rays, shine + F. *appertization* kind of heat treatment of food (f. the name of Nicolas-François *Appert* (d. 1841), French inventor: see -IZATION).] The treatment of food with ionizing radiation so as to reduce the number of micro-organisms sufficiently to prevent future spoilage in the absence of recontamination (see quot. 1964). Cf. RADICIDATION, RADURIZATION.

1964 H. E. GORESLINE et al. in *Nature* 17 Oct. 237/2 Type I is the application to food of doses of ionizing radiation sufficient to reduce the number and/or activity of viable organisms to such an extent that very few, if any, are detectable in the treated food by any recognized method (viruses being excepted) while no spoilage or toxicity of microbial origin is detectable no matter how long or under what conditions the food is stored in the absence of recontamination... The following are names we suggest... Type I, radappertization. **1966** *Proc. Internat. Symp. Food Irradiation* 352 Salmonellae could be said to be moderately radiation-sensitive when bacteria are generally considered ..and therefore the dose requirement for their inactivation in food will be very much lower than that needed for radappertization (4·5–5·0 Mrad). **1975** *Appl. Microbiol.* XXX. 811 (*heading*) Low-temperature irradiation of beef and methods for evaluation of a radappertization process.

Hence **ra'dappertize** *v. trans.*, **ra'dappertized** *ppl. a.*

1974 *Jrnl. Food Sci.* XXXIX. 806 The accepted procedure for estimating the 12D dose of radappertized food has shortcomings that ought not to be ignored. **1975** *Appl. Microbiol.* XXX. 811/1 The wholesomeness of beef radappertized..with ^{60}Co gamma rays and with 10 MV electrons. **1977** *Jrnl. Food Sci.* XLII. 338 (*heading*) Variables affecting the acceptability of radappertized ground beef products.

radar ('reɪdɑː(r)). orig. *U.S.* [f. *ra*dio *d*etection *a*nd *r*anging.] **1. a.** A system for detecting the presence of objects at a distance, or ascertaining their position or motion, by transmitting short radio waves and detecting or measuring their return after being reflected; also (*secondary radar*), a similar system in which the return signal consists of radio waves that a suitably equipped target automatically transmits when it receives the outgoing waves. Cf. RADIOLOCATION.

1941 *N.Y. Times* 18 Nov. 8/4 The Navy undertook a special enlistment campaign today to recruit men for training in maintenance of the radio device known as 'Radar', which is used to locate ships and aircraft that are hidden by fog or darkness. **1943** *News Chron.* 9 Feb. 4/6 He described Radar as 'probably the most dramatic new weapon to come out of this war'. **1943** *Times* 24 June 4/6 It is expected also to improve 'radar', the device for detecting enemy aircraft and ships. **1946** *Electronics* Apr. 130/3 Frequency-modulation radar determines the distance to a reflecting surface..by measuring the frequency shift between transmitted and reflected waves. **1957** *Economist* 7 Sept. 831 (Advt.), The performance of modern aircraft must be matched by the radio, radar and Doppler navigational aids necessary for their safe and efficient operation. **1959** K. HENNEY *Radio Engin. Handbk.* (ed. 5) xxv. 34 Secondary radar, or the ATC radar-beacon system, solves the problem of identification of the individual aircraft in air-traffic control. **1960** J. D. HAIGH *Radiolocation Techniques* xiv. 213 Another advantage of secondary radar is that if the 'responding' transmitter is made to radiate on a frequency different from that of the 'interrogating' transmitter, the received picture will be completely free from all permanent echoes and no targets other than those with responding transmitters will be seen. **1962** R. M. PAGE *Origin of Radar* i. 15 The name 'radar' was coined from the words *Ra*dio *D*etection *A*nd *R*anging by two U.S. Naval officers, F. R. Furth and S. M. Tucker. **1971** D. W. SCIAMA *Mod. Cosmol.* i. 2 The distance of the Sun is determined most accurately by radar. **1977** C. MCCULLOUGH *Thorn Birds* xvii. 451 The field which had fascinated him since he first got acquainted with radar: electronics.

b. (An) apparatus or an installation used for this system.

1945 *Electronics* Apr. 92/1 The free-space radar equation relates the power radiated from the radar..to the power delivered to the terminals of the receiver. **1945** *Proc. IRE* XXXIII. 740/2 An army radar, the SCR-270, gave warning of the impending attack on Pearl Harbor. **1959** K. HENNEY *Radio Engin. Handbk.* (ed. 5) xxv. 34 Present-day precision approach radars look only 20 deg in azimuth and 6 deg in elevation. **1967** *Listener* 9 Feb. 185/3 A 'thin area defence' for the whole United States, consisting of a dozen Spartan batteries and the relevant radars, would cost about $4,000 million. **1971** *Sci. Amer.* Oct. 73 (Advt.), APQ-140 is a digitally controlled phased array radar system that does the job formerly requiring several radars. **1977** *Navy News* Aug. 34 (Advt.), We're working on a wide variety of radars for applications throughout the world.

c. *fig.* An intuitive perception or sense of awareness attributed to or regarded as a characteristic of a person.

1950 'D. DIVINE' *King of Fassarai* xxix. 262 Thirty-kid power radar. Nothing ever gets by 'em. **1959** *Listener* 1 Jan. 31/3 With that political radar with which all good Levantine rulers are endowed, he succeeded for years. **1975** D. M. DAVIN *Closing Times* vi. 142 With that radar sense of quality that governed his taste in poetry and other people's clothes, he chose her own favourite scarf. **1976** P. ALEXANDER *Death of Thin-Skinned Animal* xviii. 183 That's what Joan thinks ..intuition, female radar, or maybe she read it in the tea-leaves.

d. *transf.*

1963 [see LIDAR]. **1974** *Physics Bull.* Jan. 11/2 Like ordinary radar, laser radar is based on the detection of a signal scattered from some object. If a laser beam is emitted into the atmosphere, some of the radiation will be absorbed by atmospheric molecules, some will be scattered by them.. and some will be scattered by aerosols. **1974** *Sci. Amer.* Mar. 83/2 One of the more promising instruments is an acoustic-radar detector, in which a noise signal is transmitted from the ground and is deflected by interaction with the vortex.

2. *attrib.* and *Comb.* ***radar altimeter***, ***astronomy***, ***beam***, ***dish*** [DISH *sb.* 4b], ***echo***, ***equation***, ***equipment***, ***eye***, ***operator***, ***reconnaissance***, ***set***, ***signal***, ***station***, ***system***; ***radar-controlled***, ***-directed*** ppl. adjs.; ***radar-ranging*** vbl. sb.; **Radar Alley** (see quot. 1971); **radar beacon**, a radio transmitter that automatically transmits a return signal when it receives a signal from a radar transmitter; *esp.* one that transmits a coded signal enabling it to be identified; **radar fence**, a line of radar stations for giving warning of intrusions into the air space behind it; **radar man, radarman**, a man trained to operate radar equipment; **radar map**, a map compiled from radar observations; hence **radar-map** *v. trans.*, **-mapping** *vbl. sb.*; **radar net**, a network of radar stations, esp. a radar fence; **radar picket**, a picket-ship specially equipped with radar; **radar plotter**, one who plots the direction and course of objects from radar observations; **radar scanner**, a rotatable aerial for transmitting and receiving radar signals; **radar screen**, the screen of a radarscope; also *fig.*; **radar-sonde**, a sonde which can be tracked by radar so that information on the wind may be obtained as well as the usual meteorological information; **radar speed detector, trap**, etc. = *radar trap*; **radar-track** *v. trans.*, to track by radar; also *fig.*; **radar trap**, a speed trap in which speed is measured using radar and the Doppler effect.

1971 M. TAK *Truck Talk* 127 *Radar Alley*, Interstate 90, between Cleveland and the New York line; so named because of the numerous radar traps set on the road. **1976** PERKOWSKI & STRAL *Joy of CB* 174 The name of Radar Alley ..aptly applies to the Ohio Turnpike..that is heavily patrolled by bears. **1946** *Electronics* Apr. 130/2 A detailed description of an f-m radar altimeter may now be given, following the declassification of the model AN/APN-1 altimeter. **1951** *Jrnl. Brit. Interplanetary Soc.* X. 101 This means a vertical descent using reverse rocket braking in conjunction with a radar-altimeter and landing legs. **1978** *Nature* 10 Aug. 540/1 Balloon-borne radar altimeters have also been used to map surface topography in Antarctica. **1959** DAVIES & PALMER *Radio Studies of Universe* i. 3 This discovery laid the foundation for the second branch of the science of radio astronomy, that of radar astronomy which probes the nearest inhabitants in space—the meteors, moon and planets—using the radio-echo technique. **1969** *Sci. News Yearbk.* 83 Radar astronomy had done particularly well with its studies of nearer planets, especially Venus. **1945** *Electronic Engin.* XVII. 685/2 By this means our airborne forces were enabled to direct themselves to any given point in hostile country where an advance party had already installed a 'Radar beacon'. **1958** *Listener* 13 Nov. 779/1 Navigational aids, such as radio stations and radar beacons, are few. **1959** [see sense 1 a above]. **1965** D. K. BARTON in R. S. Berkowitz *Mod. Radar* ii. 12 A modern radar beacon weighing a few pounds can receive signals 100 db below 1 watt and retransmit them as 100-watt pulses, providing tremendous range extension. **1958** *Times* 9 Oct. 10/2 When the rockets burn out,..the missile coasts to the target, riding along the centre of a radar beam which is directed by the pilot of the launching aircraft. **1959** N. MAILER *Advts. for Myself* (1961) 183 The other-directed man is flexible... His movement is 'radar-controlled',..his 'taste' rather than his work the primary concern... He obeys 'the process of paying close attention to the signals from others'. **1978** R. V. JONES *Most Secret War* xxxi. 265 He also concluded that some of the lights were radar-controlled. **1947** CROWTHER & WHIDDINGTON *Science at War* 75 H.M.S. *Warspite* fired her first radar-directed broadside. **1952** *Electronic Engin.* XXIV. 126/1 A 3 centimetre radar installation with a V.H.F., D.F. receiver, the radar dish being mounted on a common rotatable shaft with the D.F. aerial. **1969** *New Yorker* 11 Oct. 51/1 In the gaunt shade of oil rigs and radar dishes. **1946** *Electronic Engin.* XVIII. 149/2 The technique of setting the calibration pip against the radar echo is one which gives surprisingly accurate results. **1962** F. I. ORDWAY et al. *Basic Astronautics* iii. 65 The first radar echoes were returned from the Moon in 1946. **1945** D. G. FINK in *Electronics* Apr. 92/1 The basic factors concerned are the formation and propagation of radio beams, and the reflection of radio waves when they encounter a sudden change in the electrical properties of the transmission medium... The equation which links these factors may be termed appropriately the radar equation. **1966** *McGraw-Hill Encycl. Sci. & Technol.* XI. 200/2 The strength of echo signals is related to the parameters of the radar system by the radar equation. **1944** *Jrnl. R. Aeronaut. Soc.* XLVIII. 103 Tests of various wireless and Radar equipment. **1976** *Daily Mirror* 16 July 2/2 The cases are believed to contain aircraft parts and radar equipment. **1957** R. WATSON-WATT *Three Steps to Victory* xliii. 249 British fighters could entrust themselves to the..far-seeing radar-eye. **1977** *R.A.F. News* 5–18 Jan. 9/1 The Shackleton airborne early warning aircraft of Lossiemouth's 8 Squadron..act as airborne radar eyes searching for low-flying aircraft. **1948** *Sat. Even. Post* 21 Aug. 27/1 There are wide gaps in the Soviet radar fence. Russia is too huge to be rimmed completely with twirling antennas. **1957** R. WATSON-WATT *Three Steps to Victory* (*caption to plate facing p.* 320) The 350 ft. steel lattice masts on 'T' site. Combined with ultra-short-wave-radiation these ensured that the outer edge of the radar fence could be set far enough from the British coasts. **1942** *Radio-Craft* Jan.–Feb. 332/1 'Radar' men will operate the newly perfected radio device which locates planes in flight. **1946** P. CARTER in Aldiss & Harrison *Decade 1940's* (1975) 109 He was at once geologist, radarman, vibration expert and navigator. **1966** M. WOODHOUSE *Tree Frog* x. 75 Pzenica, the radar man from Poland, was standing over me. **1977** *R.A.F. News* 5–18 Jan. 8/2 The Buchan radarmen help to look after the safety of these fliers. **1960** *Sci. Amer.* Aug. 59/1 The radar mapping experiment marks the first trial of this technique. *Ibid.* 59/2 (*caption*) Radar map of the moon. **1962** F. I. ORDWAY et al. *Basic Astronautics* iii. 65 In January, 1960, a preliminary radar map of the Moon was made from 440 mc observations performed with the 84-ft antenna at Millstone Hill, in Massachusetts. **1970** *New Scientist* 19 Feb. 361/1 Each Victor can radar-map the entire Mediterranean in one seven-hour sortie. **1948** *Sun* (Baltimore) 3 June 2/3 Representative Vinson (D., Ga.) introduced a bill to authorize construction of a radar net along the coasts of the United States and Alaska. **1964** G. LYALL *Most Dangerous Game* vi. 48 The border could be flown all right... The Finns didn't have a complete radar net along it, and most pilots knew just where the Finnish radar stations were. **1945** *Yank* 5 Oct. 16/3 Radar operators and observers were known as 'radio operators'. **1967** L. B. ARCHER in Wills & Yearsley *Handbk. Management Technol.* vii. 129 Some of the early experiments [in ergonomics] were to determine the best spacing of markings on instrument dials so that the pilot or gunner or radar operator could read them rapidly and accurately. **1952** *Jane's Fighting Ships 1952–53* p. vii, Among the recent U.S. photographs added to this issue are those of the..radar picket *William T. Powell*. **1966** *McGraw-Hill Encycl. Sci. & Technol.* XII. 264/2 Some U.S. Navy destroyers are specially fitted as radar pickets, and some British ones as aircraft fighter directors. **1957** *Technology* Dec. 358/3 This new principle of design may be contrasted with the old by considering the radar plotter tracking targets on his radar tube. **1978** R. V. JONES *Most Secret War* xxiii. 196 She..had been taken on with two other girls at Bawdsey by Watson-Watt to see whether girls would make good radar-plotters. **1976** *Sci. Amer.* Feb. 51/1 The second astronomical experiment consists of precise radar-ranging measurements of the distance between the earth and the inner planets Mercury and Venus. **1959** *Daily Tel.* 7 Mar. 7/3 An area equal to the whole of the Mediterranean could be covered in a single radar reconnaissance by one aircraft. **1946** *Electronics* Oct. 35 (Advt.), Aircraft radar scanner. **1947** *Daily Progress* (Charlottesville, Va.) 15 Dec. 2/3 New radar scanner to watch the skies for airplanes approaching New York airport is now in experimental operation. **1976** 'A. YORK' *Dark Passage* xiii. 164 Her radio aerial and the radar scanner on her wheelhouse roof remained visible. **1945** *Instruments* XVIII. 745/1 Its beam-splitter..allows operator to view radar reflection in normal manner while image on radar screen is reflected up into camera. **1958** *New Statesman* 18 Jan. 64/1 What is needed is 'patience': the West is to sit behind the radar screens and rocket bases waiting for a change of heart, and perhaps a change of regime, in Russia. **1977** J. BINGHAM *Marriage Bureau Murders* v. 58 He was reluctant to switch from thinking about her... He kept her within the radar screen of his mind. **1946** *Electronic Engin.* XVIII. 2 The operation of a Radar set as a position finder. **1947** *Daily Mail* 22 May 3/6 Radar sets which will 'see' through fog are to be fitted in long-distance passenger trains as soon as materials are available. **1969** *Times* 25 Mar. 12/6 By bouncing radar signals off Venus, scientists from the United States have counted the numbers of electrons in the space between the planets. **1949** *Jrnl. R. Aeronaut. Soc.* LIII. 441/1 At T.R.E. the wind-finding responder is being adapted for use as a 'radarsonde', meteorological instruments to measure pressure, temperature and humidity being mounted towards the top of the responder. **1956** *Nature* 17 Mar. 520/1 Progress was made in the measurement of solar radiation and in the development of the new radar-sonde. **1957** *Times* 4 Oct. 6/4 A London electronics engineer described to Leyland magistrates today the effects of laboratory and outside tests he had carried out on a radar speed detector to assess the effects of extraneous sources on the accuracy of the instrument. **1962** *Daily Tel.* 22 May 24/6 [He] complained through his solicitor that police radar speed traps were 'un-British' when he was fined £10..for speeding... Police said Cadbury went through a radar speed check at 58 mph. **1971** *Observer* 26 Sept. 9/5 Radar speed traps are being planned for a 60-mile stretch of the River Nene..to stop boats from exceeding the seven m.p.h. limit. **1945** *Times* 15 Aug. 5/6 By December 1935, the experimental work was sufficiently advanced for the Air Ministry to decide on establishing a chain of five radar stations on the east coast of England... This was the first operational radar system installed anywhere in the world. **1958** *New Statesman* 22 Feb. 223/2 Radar stations at sea picked up 'blips' suggesting that an air armada was flying at 2,000 mph towards the interior of the United States. **1978** R. V. JONES *Most Secret War* xxiii. 196 It happened that this sortie was also plotted by a German radar station north-west of Brest. **1945** Radar system [see *radar station* above]. **1956** *Tuscaloosa* (Alabama) *News* 31 July 11/6 The Italian Line said the Doria radar-tracked the oncoming Stockholm before the fatal crash. **1973** M. AMIS *Rachel Papers* 24, I felt a hand traverse the lower areas of my back. In seconds—radar-tracked by my whisker-sensitive pubic hairs—it was treading air above my groin. **1962** *Punch* 18 July 74/3 A motorist has been acquitted of a speeding charge because the radar trap that provided the evidence against him could not be put on oath. **1975** *Globe & Mail* (Toronto) 4 June 1/6 A check with the radar trap involved showed the limousine was doing a mere 71 miles an hour in a 70-mile-an-hour zone.

radarscope ('reɪdɑːskəʊp). Also **radar scope**. [f. RADAR + -SCOPE.] A cathode-ray oscilloscope on the screen of which radar echoes are represented for observation; also, the screen itself.

1948 *Nat. Geographic Mag.* Feb. 255/1 Then an operator 'talks them down', watching each plane on the radarscope. **1958** *Observer* 22 June 12/6 The future of mankind might lie at the mercy of an officer reading a radarscope in the Canadian Arctic, who might conceivably mistake an electronic storm..for the trajectory of a Soviet I.C.B.M. **1959** K. HENNEY *Radio Engin. Handbk.* (ed. 5) xxv. 34 Precision Approach Radar... Distance, bearing, and elevation above ground are presented continuously on the face of the radar scope. **1966** M. WOODHOUSE *Tree Frog* xxi. 154, I can never stand by a radarscope..without recalling the Rubaiyat; the moving Finger writes. **1972** *Sci. Amer.* Jan. 52/3 The image..is a direct representation of the scene ahead of the driver rather than the usual maplike plan view of the radarscope.

Radcliffian (ræd'klɪfɪən), *a.* Also **Radcliffean**. [f. the name of (Mrs.) Ann *Radcliffe* (1764–1823), English 'Gothic' novelist.] Of or characteristic of Mrs. Radcliffe or her works.

1801 M. EDGEWORTH *Belinda* II. xx. 265 Here is a Radcliffian tour along the picturesque coasts of Dorset and Devonshire. **1884** *Spectator* 19 Jan. 91/1 There is, too, a Radcliffian eeriness about his castle, with its mysterious noises, secret passages, and buried rooms. **1931** *Times Lit. Suppl.* 26 Feb. 151/3 The 'Radcliffian' novel, or *roman noir*, as the French call it. **1966** *English Studies* XLVII. 287 But symbol, action, and the perceiving sensibility..add to the Radcliffean question, 'what is the mystery of the veil?'

†**radcolle.** *Obs.*$^{-0}$ A radish. (Cf. REDCOLL.)
1483 *Cath. Angl.* 298/1 Radcolle, *raphanus*.

radd(e, variants of RAD *a.*^{1} and *a.*^{2}

radde, obs. f. RAID; obs. pa. t. READ, REDE.

raddish, obs. form of RADISH.

raddle ('ræd(ə)l), *sb.*^{1} *Obs.* exc. *dial.* Also 6 radel(l, -yll, 8 roddle, 8–9 ruddle. [a. AF. *reidele* (Wright *Vocab.* 168), OF. *reddalle*, *ridelle*, *rudelle* (14th c. in Du Cange) a stout stick or pole, the rail of a cart (so mod.F. *ridelle*), of obscure origin.]

1. †**a.** The rail of a cart. *Obs. rare*$^{-0}$.
1530 PALSGR. 260/2 Radyll of a carte, *costee*.

b. *north. dial.* and *U.S.* A wooden bar with upright pegs, used to keep the threads of the warp in place while it is being wound upon the beam.
1848 in WORCESTER. **1883** *Almondbury Gloss.*

2. A slender rod, wattle, or lath, fastened to or twisted between upright stakes or posts to form a fence, partition, or wall (in the latter case usually plastered over with clay, whence the phr. ***raddle and daub*** or ***dab***, applied to walls or houses made in this way).

1577 HARRISON *England* II. x[ii.] in *Holinshed* 84b, The houses of the Brytons were slitely set vppe with a few postes and many radles, the like whereof almost is to be seene in the fenny countries vnto this day. **1686** PLOT *Staffordsh.* 233 Small stakes driven into the ground..and interwoven with broom and other raddles. **1736** PEGGE *Kenticisms* (E.D.S.), *Raddis-chimney*, a chimney made of studs, lathes, or raddles, and covered with lome or lime. **1868** *Sussex Gloss.* in Hurst *Horsham* (1889), *Ruddles*, long supple sticks of greenwood interwoven between upright sticks to make a hedge. **1869–** In dial. glossaries (Lanc., Chesh., Som.).

attrib. **1736** PEGGE *Kenticisms* (E.D.S.), *Raddle-hedge*. **1736** LEWIS *Hist. Thanet* Gloss., *Ruddle-wattle*, a hurl made of small hazle-rods, interwoven. **1778** [W. MARSHALL] *Minutes Agric.*, *Observ.* 167 A live roddle Hedge..is, perhaps, the Ultimate of Farm hedge-making. **1785** HUTTON *Bran New Wark* (E.D.S.) 372 The girl unsneck'd the raddle heck. **1786–1805** H. TOOKE *Purley* (1829) II. 258 A raddle hedge, is a hedge of pleached or plashed or twisted or wreathed twigs or boughs.

3. A piece of wattled work; a hurdle, door, hedge, etc. made with intertwined raddles.

1886 *Cheshire Gloss.* s.v., Long sticks were wound together between the timber, forming a sort of basket-work or raddle. **1892** J. LUCAS tr. *Kalm's England* 398 In only a few places were there any 'Raddles', or wooden hurdles.

raddle ('ræd(ə)l), *sb.*^{2} Also 6 radel, raddell, 7–8 radle. [var. RUDDLE, q.v.: cf. also REDDLE.]

1. Red ochre, RUDDLE.

1523 [see *raddle-mark* below]. **1577** B. GOOGE *Heresbach's Husb.* (1586) 16b, Stone, marble, sande, gravell, raddell, chalke, &c. **1631** J. BURGES *Answ. Rejoined, Lawfuln. Kneeling* 21 The raddle doth signifie more then the brand alone. **1699** T. BROWN in R. L'Estrange *Colloq. Erasm.* (1711) 402 To revive the decay'd Red and White in their cheeks with raddle and chalk. **1757** DYER *Fleece* I. 321 See that thy scrip have store of..marking pitch and raddle. **1805** DICKSON *Pract. Agric.* (1807) I. 360 *note*, Raddle..has lately been used with advantage on some lands. **1853** LANDOR *Last Fruits, Let. Wiseman* vi. 194 He would whistle the sheep into the ancient fold, marking them with his raddle.

transf. **1603** OWEN *Pembrokeshire* (1891) 83 'Nod glas' which in Englishe is blewe radle or blewe markinge stone.

b. A coarse red layer. *nonce-use.*

1860 THACKERAY *Round. Papers* xxxii, To hide..a yellow cheek behind a raddle of rouge.

2. *attrib.* and *Comb.*, as ***raddle-ground***, ***-mark***; ***raddle-red*** adj.

1523 FITZHERB. *Husb.* §52 Se that thy [the sheep] be well marked, both eare-marke, pitche-marke, and radel-marke. **1577** B. GOOGE *Heresbach's Husb.* (1586) 18 A raddell and a stonie grounde is discerned by the eye. **1897** *Contemp. Rev.* June 765 The then new and raddle-red penny postage stamps.

'raddle, *sb.*^{3}, variant of RABBLE *sb.*^{2}
1875 in KNIGHT *Dict. Mech.*

raddle ('ræd(ə)l), *v.*^{1} Also 6 rathel. [f. RADDLE *sb.*^{1}] *trans.* To weave or twist together (like raddles), to intertwine, interlace.

1671 *St. Foine Improved* 18 To wrap or wreath or raddle the spikes or teeth of the Harrow. **1719** DE FOE *Crusoe* II. v, They came at last to build up their Huts..very handsomely; raddling or working it up like Basket-work all the way round. **1747** HOOSON *Miner's Dict.* I j b, They are made of Boards or of Sticks radled together. **1824** in *Craven Dialect.* **1867** SMYTH *Sailor's Word-bk.*, *To raddle*, to interlace; as in making boat's gripes and flat gaskets. **1869–** In dial. glossaries (Yks., Lanc., Som.).

Hence **'raddled** *ppl. a.*^{1}

1562 WITHALS *Dict.* 41 b/1 A hartheled wall, or ratheled ..*paries craticius*. **1876** *Whitby Gloss.*, *Raddled*, wrought or painted in a zigzag pattern.

raddle ('ræd(ə)l), *v.*^{2} [f. RADDLE *sb.*^{2}] *trans.* To paint or mark with raddle; to colour coarsely with red or rouge.

1631 J. BURGES *Answ. Rejoined, Lawfuln. Kneeling* 21 Hee that beside a pitch-brande, doth raddle the heads of his fat sheepe, doth more then marke them. **1848** THACKERAY *Lett.* 1 Nov., A chief raddled over with war-paint. **1879** SALA *Paris herself again* (1880) I. viii. 120 They do not even go so far as to raddle themselves. Rouge is apparently too dear. **1966** J. F. H. THOMAS *Sheep Farming Today* v. 57 Recently there has been introduced a breast harness device which holds a colour marking crayon on rams in lieu of raddling their breast wool with colour.

Hence **'raddled** *ppl. a.*^{2} (also *fig.*, worn, worn out).

1681 CHETHAM *Angler's Vade-m.* iv. §7 (1700) 35 Perhaps within an Hour again the bright ones will be taken, and the radled Worms refused. **1854** THACKERAY *Newcomes* xx, Those whitened and raddled old women. **1901** W. BARRY *Wizard's Knot* vii. 74 Raddled like scabby sheep with red paint. **1922** GALSWORTHY *In Chancery* II. vii. 621 An 'old Johnny' in a gown and long wig, looking awfully like a funny raddled woman, came through a door. **1922** JOYCE *Ulysses* 96 Outside them and through them ran raddled sheep bleating their fear. **1969** *Listener* 30 Jan. 156/2 Ruth Gordon's Minnie might be a typical New York eccentric, a raddled Carmen Miranda. **1975** *Nature* 28 Aug. 738/2 They were all kept in identical conditions of housing and management, and oestrus was detected by raddled vasectomised rams at 0900 daily. **1978** *Time* 3 July 10/3 By day she rests, and her face, without makeup, softens but still retains the raddled quality of hard living.

raddle ('ræd(ə)l), *v.*^{3} *north. dial.* [Perh. f. RADDLE *sb.*^{1} (as if = to beat with a raddle).] *trans.* To beat, thrash.

1688 SHADWELL *Sqr. Alsatia* II. i, I'st raddle the bones o' thee. **1818** SCOTT *Rob Roy* vii, I'se raddle Dick the miller's bones for him. **1855** *Bon Gaultier Ballads* 171 Raddle him well, till he roar again.

†**'raddled**, *a.* *Obs. rare*$^{-1}$. [Of obscure origin.] Fuddled.

1694 MOTTEUX *Rabelais* v. xxxix, A..sottish Fellow, continually raddled, and as drunk as a Wheelbarrow.

'raddleman. [f. RADDLE *sb.*^{2}] A digger of, or dealer in, raddle. †Applied allusively to Rutlandshire, and to a disease in wheat. *Obs.*

1622 DRAYTON *Poly-olb.* xxiii. 268 Little Rutlandshire is tearmed Raddleman. *a* **1661** FULLER *Worthies, Rutland* (1662) 347 Rutland *Raddleman*... *Rad* here is the same with *red* (onely more broadly pronounced)..*Raddleman* then is a *Reddleman*. **1798** *Ann. Agric.* XXVI. 177 *Raddleman*, earcockle, the disease in wheat due to *Vibrio tritici*. *Sal.* **1881** in *Leicestersh. Gloss.*

'raddling, *sb.* *dial.* Also 7, 9 radling. [f. RADDLE *sb.*^{1} + -ING^1.]

1. A raddle, rod, twig, etc.

1616 *Salford Portmote Rec.* (1902) 121 Any sprinkelings radlings or any other woode. **1626** *Manchester Court Leet Rec.* (1886) III. 114 John Wright..got Radlings in the grounds of Elizabeth Mosley. **1736** PEGGE *Kenticisms* (E.D.S.), *Raddles*...in some countries called *raddlings*. *a* **1796** —— *Derbicisms*, *Radlings*, long slender poles for binding hedges. **1841** S. BAMFORD *Life of Radical* I. xxi. 137 A timber frame, filled with raddlings and daub (wicker work, plastered with clay).

2. (See quots.)

1674 RAY *N.C. Words* 38 *Radlings*; Windings of the wall. **1736** NEVE *Builders' Dict.* (ed. 3), *Raddlings*, in Architecture, the Bowings-in, or copeings of Walls. **1824** *Craven Dialect*, *Raddling*, *Rabbling*, the winding or crookedness of a wall.

raddling ('rædlɪŋ), *vbl. sb.* [f. RADDLE *v.*^{2} + -ING^1.] The action of marking sheep with raddle, or some other red substance.

c **1873** J. ALBERY *Fortune* III, in *Dramatic Wks.* (1939) I. 574 Mark 'em [*sc.* sheep] all with two red letters, Johnny; they always do that;—raddling they call it, I think.

raddock, obs. or dial. form of RUDDOCK.

†**raddour**^{1}. *Sc. Obs.* Forms: 5 redur(e, reddure, redoure, 5–6 rad(d)our(e. [f. *red* RAD *a.*^{2} + -OUR, -URE. The formation is unusual (cf. DREADOUR).] Fear, terror.

c **1375** *Sc. Leg. Saints* xviii. (*Egipciane*) 701 Sic redure & sic dowl me tuk, þat to-gyddir I swet & quok. *Ibid.* xix. (*Cristofore*) 391 He fel fore redoure doune. **1456** SIR G. HAYE *Law Arms* (S.T.S.) 118 In raddour thare cummys fayntnes, and failling of hert. **1513** DOUGLAS *Æneis* IX. xii. 67 Of dreidfull raddour trymlyng for affray, The Troianys fled rycht fast.

†**raddour**^{2}. *north.* and *Sc. Obs.* Also 5 -owre, radure. [var. of REDDOUR (q.v.).] Severity, harshness, harsh treatment.

a **1400–50** *Alexander* 2329 (Dubl. MS.) Who þat rekenly vs resaued no raddour tholett. *c* **1425** WYNTOUN *Cron.* VIII. xliv. 6941 Radure in prynce is a gud thyng For but radure all governyng Sall al tyme bot dispysyd be.

raddyk, obs. variant of RADISH.

†**rade**, *sb. Obs. rare.* [ad. L. *radius* RADIUS *sb.*: see also RAY.] One of the arms of a star-fish.

1661 LOVELL *Hist. Anim. & Min.* 283 Those of foure, six, and twelve rades are edible.

rade, var. RAD *a.*; obs. f. RAID; var. RATHE; obs. f. or var. of RED(D, REDE; obs. pa. t. RIDE.

‖**radeau** (rado). [F., a. Prov. *radel*:—L. **ratellus*, dim. of *ratis* raft. Cf. med.L. *radellus* (15th c.).] A raft; *spec.* a floating battery.

1759 *Hist. Eur.* in *Ann. Reg.* 44/1 A great radeau 84 feet in length and 20 in breadth which carried six twenty-four pounders. **1801** SIR H. PARKER 6 Apr. in Nicolas *Disp. Nelson* (1845) IV. 319, I reconnoitred the formidable line of ships, Radeaus, Pontoons [etc.].

†**radegound.** *Obs. rare*$^{-1}$. [App. f. GOUND, with obscure first element.] ? A running sore.

1377 LANGL. *P. Pl.* B. xx. 82 Rewmes, and radegoundes and roynouse scalles.

radel(l, obs. ff. RADDLE *sb.*

radeliche, -ly, varr. RADLY *adv.*

radem(e, obs. Sc. ff. REDEEM.

†**radeur, radour.** *Obs. rare.* [a. OF. *radeur*, *radour*, f. *rade*:—L. *rapid-us* RAPID.] Rapidity, impetus, force.

c **1477** CAXTON *Jason* 30 He smote the king..by such radeur that he lefte him oute of his arsons. *Ibid.* 113 The ship..that saylled by a grete radour and a full sail. *c* **1500** *Melusine* 329 Thenne cam geffray toward the doore, rennyng with a grete radeur.

†**radevore.** *Obs. rare.* Also radi-, rady-, raduore. [? a. OF. **ras de Vor* rash of Vaur (in Languedoc): see Skeat *Notes Eng. Etym.* (1901) 239.] A kind of cloth.

c **1385** CHAUCER *L.G.W.* 2352 *Philomela*, She werken and embrowden kouthe, And weven in the stole the radevore. *c* **1400** '*As ofte as syghes*, etc.' (Tanner MS. 346 lf. 73), As ofte tymes as Penelapye Renewed her werk in the raduore.

radeym, obs. Sc. form of REDEEM *v.*

radfulle, variant of REDEFUL *a.*

†**radge.** *Obs. rare*⁻¹. A species of duck; perh. the gadwall. (Cf. RODGE.)

1620 VENNER *Via Recta* iii. 65 The Radge is next vnto Teale in goodnes: But yet there is great difference in the nourishment which they make... Neither is the Radge so pleasant to the taste..as the Teale.

radgee, obs. form of RAJA(H.

'radiad, *adv. Anat.* [f. RADI-AL + *-ad*; see DEXTRAD.] 'Towards the radial aspect'.

1803 BARCLAY *New Anat. Nomencl.* 165-6. **1808** —— *Muscular Motions* 409 The motions of the metacarp by its own muscles, are Radiad, Thenad.

radiæsthesia, etc., varr. RADIESTHESIA, etc.

radial ('reɪdɪəl), *a.* and *sb.* [a. late L. *radiāl-is* (see Quicherat), F. *radial* (1611 in sense 5), or directly f. RADI-US + -AL¹.] **A.** *adj.*

1. Of light, beams, etc.: Proceeding or issuing as rays from a common centre; also, of or pertaining to light in the form of rays. Now *rare*.

1570 DEE *Math. Pref.* 19 The certaine and determined actiue Radiall emanations. **1637** R. ASHLEY tr. *Malvezzi's David Persecuted* 83 A violent starre, whose radiall beames may be good. **1713** C'TESS WINCHELSEA *Misc. Poems* 69 Enliv'ning Beams might from them fly, To re-inkindle.. The radial sparks. *a* **1774** GOLDSM. *Surv. Exp. Philos.* (1776) II. 353 Place an object that is blue under a yellow ray, the object immediately assumes the radial colour.
transf. **1650** CHARLETON *Van Helmont's Tern. Paradoxes* Proleg. D 1 b, The omnipotent Odor, or radial activity whereof. *Ibid.* D 2, An Influential or Radial activity (so have I taken the liberty to Christen it).

2. a. Arranged like rays or the radii of a circle; having the position or direction of a radius.

1750 FRANKLIN *Lett.* etc. Wks. 1840 VI. 103 Eight concentric circles, and eight radial rows. **1756** BURKE *Subl. & B.* IV. xvi, The contraction of the radial fibres of the iris. **1837** BREWSTER *Magnet.* 115 When the eight open radial spaces were filled up with tin. **1860** TYNDALL *Glac.* I. xv. 100 The glacier of the Rhone..its system of radial crevasses. **1884** BOWER & SCOTT *De Bary's Phaner.* 338 The radial walls of the layer of cells bordering these canals.

b. *radial axle*, an axle (of a railway carriage, tramway car, etc.) which on a curve of the track assumes the position of a radius to that curve; so *radial axle box*.

1883 *Daily News* 6 July 3/7 A system of cars by which.. a truly radial axle is obtained. **1889** G. FINDLAY *Eng. Railway* 104 The compound engines are fitted with 'Webb's radial axle-box.'

c. Pertaining to the radius of a circle.

1869 RANKINE *Machinery & Millwork* 111 The radial pitch [is to be found] by dividing the radius by the same number.

d. *Bot.* and *Timber.* Applied to a longitudinal section or cut along a radius or diameter, and to the surface so exposed. Also as *adv.*, as *radial-sawn* adj.

1881 J. S. GAMBLE *Man. Indian Timbers* 175 Medullary rays fine, equidistant, prominent on a radial section. **1924** HOLMAN & ROBBINS *Textbk. Gen. Bot.* iv. 104 The annual rings appear in radial section as more or less parallel bands which impart to the wood its characteristic grain. **1938** H. E. DESCH *Timber* ii. 19 The rays are usually just visible to the naked eye on radial surfaces, where they appear as narrow, horizontal ribbons. **1958** *N.Z. Timber Jrnl.* Apr. 61/2 Radial sawn. **1969** H. L. EDLIN *What Wood is That?* i. 20 (*caption*) The radial cut through a birch-log, which splits it into two, becomes convex after seasoning. **1972** H. J. DITTMER *Mod. Plant Biol.* viii. 151 Radial or quarter-sawed wood is taken through the radius of the log.

e. Of a road, route, etc.: running directly from the centre of a town or city to an outlying district (usu. as part of a system of such roads). Hence also used of transport services using such routes.

[**1909** H. I. TRIGGS *Town Planning* ii. 88 In cities laid out upon the radial system, the radiating streets form as it were the skeleton of the system.] **1937** [see *parkway* s.v. PARK *sb.* 7]. **1942** *Policy on Rotary Intersections* (Amer. Assoc. State Highway Officials) 1 Each road approaching a rotary hereafter is called 'radial road'. **1948** T. SHARP *Oxford Replanned* 7 Radials. Oxford has a highly developed pattern of radial roads which all centre on Carfax. **1957** *Encycl. Brit.* XXII. 335 Wren suggested the use of radial streets integrated with the rectangular plotting of intervening areas, broad streets and location of industry outside the city limits. **1976** P. R. WHITE *Planning for Public Transport* v. 93 The major growth during the twentieth century was in improvement of principal radial roads beyond the limit of the then built-up areas, and construction of bypasses or ring roads. *Ibid.* 106 Even on the radial Green Line Services, the heaviest loads are often between inner and outer suburban centres.

3. a. Having spokes, bars, lines, etc., extending from a centre; *spec.* applied to certain apparatus or machines having a part or parts thus arranged, as *radial drill*, *drilling-machine*, *plane*, etc.

1762 FALCONER *Shipwr.* I. 174 In his radial wheel the circling Sun Thro bright Astræa and the Scales had run. **1869** SIR E. REED *Shipbuild.* xv. 278 Common radial paddle wheels usually have two shaft bearings. **1875** *Practical Mag.* V. 276/1 Bouhey's radial machine. *Ibid.*, It will be seen that it is a radial drill. **1898** *Cycling* 46 The tangent wheel, as it is called, is immensely stronger than the old-fashioned radial or 'direct' wheel.

b. *radial point* = radiant point (sense a).

1867 J. HOGG *Microsc.* I. ii. 40 The pencil *d n*..having a radial point at *p q*.

c. *radial engine*, a type of internal-combustion engine (used chiefly in aircraft) having its cylinders fixed radially around a rotating crankshaft. Hence *radial-engined* adj.

1909 R. KENNEDY *Flying Machines* vii. 115 Miesse aero-motor: 8-cylinder radial engine, having the cylinders arranged in pairs and in an horizontal position. **1934** *Discovery* Dec. 353/1 The tendency in Great Britain is to develop both types, the large in-line engine being composed of four banks of cylinders forming an H, and the corresponding radial engines with two circles of cylinders one immediately behind the other. **1942** *R.A.F. Jrnl.* 16 May 14/1 Single-seat, low-wing, radial-engined monoplane fighters..are standardised by the Army. **1963** BIRD & HUTTON-STOTT *Veteran Motor Car* 21 The interesting radial-engined Enfield-Allday. **1971** L. J. K. SETRIGHT *Power to Fly* vi. 162 Each of the 9 cylinder banks had its own overhead camshaft, a most uncommon luxury in radial engines.

d. Also *radial-ply*. Denoting a tyre in which the layers of fabric are laid with the cords running at right angles to the circumference of the tyre, and the tread is strengthened by further layers of fabric running round the circumference. Also *ellipt.* as *sb.*

1964 *Economist* 26 Sept. 1191/2 British manufacturers have shied away..from buying components at more than minimal cost. They are changing their attitudes..with the advent of the radial-ply tyre, whose greater expense is.. compensated for by better wear. *Ibid.* 1254/1 Firestone has been experimenting with fibreglass cords for radials. **1966** *Ibid.* 22 Oct. 388/2 Michelin, pioneers of radial-plies, have yet another new tyre. **1967** *Autocar* 5 Oct. 19/2 Radial tyres ..add appreciably to the car's safety margin, especially in the wet. **1971** *Guardian* 23 Mar. 18/4 Patents for radial-ply tyre design were first registered in about 1912. It was not until 36 years later that Michelin..introduced the first radial for commercial sale. **1972** *Practical Motorist* Oct. 82/1 Since July 1 it has been illegal to fit a cross-ply tyre and a radial on the same axle. **1972** C. WESTON *Poor, Poor Ophelia* (1973) viii. 42 His car whirled up, radial tires singing on the glossy pavement. **1976** *Field* 18 Nov. 1021 (Advt.), The.. radial ply tyres produce a very peaceful ride.

4. a. Of immaterial things: Involving or characterized by the divergence of lines or parts from a centre; taking the direction of, acting or moving along, such lines.

1833 HERSCHEL *Astron.* xi. 353 The radial part of the disturbing force. **1862** H. SPENCER *First Princ.* II. xix. §155 (1875) 426 When the blow is violent enough to fracture the mass, we see, in the radial dispersion of its fragments [etc.]. **1872** MIVART *Elem. Anat.* 10 Another form of symmetry which is entirely absent in Man is radial symmetry. **1875** BENNETT & DYER tr. *Sachs' Bot.* 692 The root takes an outward radial direction..the stem an inward radial direction.

†**b.** *radial curve* (see quot.). *Obs. rare*⁻⁰.

1710 J. HARRIS *Lex. Techn.* II. s.v., Radial-Curves are Curves of the Spiral-kind, whose Ordinates, if they may be so called, do all terminate in the Centre of the including Circle, and appear like so many *Radii* or Semi-diameters of that including Circle. [Hence in Bailey, Chambers, Crabb, Worcester, and recent Dicts.]

c. *radial-flow* adj.: being or employing a turbine, pump, or the like in which fluid is forced to move at right angles to an axis of rotation.

1881 *Encycl. Brit.* XII. 527/1 For radial flow turbines the wheel may have the form A or B, fig. 191, A being most usual with inward, and B with outward flow turbines. **1914** W. M. WALLACE *Hydraulics* vii. 101 It is usual to designate turbines as radial flow or parallel flow according as the water flows in a radial or axial direction through the wheel. **1958** *Technology* Mar. 29/3 The basic principles of the Derwent, radial-flow, jet engine are described. **1972** J. M. K. DAKE *Essentials of Engin. Hydraulics* vi. 160 The centrifugal pump and the Francis turbine are examples of radial flow reaction machines.

d. *Astr. radial velocity*, the velocity of a star or other body along the line of sight of an observer.

1895 *Nature* 13 June 155/2 (*heading*) Measurement of radial velocities. **1930** R. H. BAKER *Astron.* viii. 315 Radial velocities of the stars up to 30 km./sec...are usual. **1966** J. D. KRAUS *Radio Astron.* viii. 353 The wisps of nebulosity show a large radial velocity of over 5,000 km sec⁻¹, indicating a rapid expansion. **1977** F. N. BASH *Astron.* iii. 67 The Doppler effect..gives astronomers a way of measuring radial velocity.

e. *Physical Geogr.* Of (a pattern of) drainage: being or involving a pattern of streams flowing outwards from a central dome or other elevated region.

[**1910** LAKE & RASTALL *Text-bk. Geol.* iv. 86 The arrangement of the principal valleys, in most of which are considerable lakes, is distinctly radial.] **1932** W. H. EMMONS et al. *Geol.* vi. 106 (*caption*) A radial stream pattern developed on the surface of the dome-like uplift of the Black Hills in South Dakota. **1939** A. K. LOBECK *Geomorphol.* xv. 513 A radial drainage pattern is characteristic of very young and undissected domes. **1954** W. D. THORNBURY *Princ. Geomorphol.* v. 126 In radial patterns,..the individual stream patterns may well be dendritic or pinnate, and radial designates more their arrangement with respect to each other than it does the stream pattern. **1969** *Geography* LIV. 199 The almost perfect radial drainage developed on the andesite volcano of Mount Egmont.

5. *Anat.* Pertaining to the radius or chief bone of the forearm, esp. in *radial artery*, *nerve*, *vein*.

1741 A. MONRO *Anat. Nerves* (ed. 3) 64 The posterior Branches of the *ulnar* and *radial* Nerve. **1786** J. PEARSON in *Med. Commun.* II. 98 The radial artery. **1830** R. KNOX *Cloquet's Anat.* 352 The section of the radial nerve at the lower part of the arm. **1840** G. V. ELLIS *Anat.* 392 The radial vein commences on the outer side of the back of the hand. **1851** H. MAYO *Pop. Superst.* (ed. 2) 195 The radial (or thumb) edge of the wrist. **1870** ROLLESTON *Anim. Life* 14 The long radial extensor of the metacarpus.

6. *radial energy*: in the writings of Teilhard de Chardin, a form of energy postulated to be independent of the conventional laws of thermodynamics and to tend to produce increasing organization and complexity in both the physical and spiritual worlds; it was held to be manifest, for example, in the evolution of living organisms and in the development of ideas. Cf. *tangential energy*. [Introduced in Fr. *c* 1938 in *Le Phénomène Humain* (1956) 62.]

1959 B. WALL et al. tr. *Teilhard de Chardin's Phenomenon of Man* I. ii. 65 In each particular element this fundamental energy is divided into two distinct components: a tangential energy which links the element with all others of the same order (that is to say, of the same complexity and the same centricity) as itself in the universe; and a radial energy which draws it towards ever greater complexity and centricity—in other words forwards. *Ibid.* iii. 72 Spiritual energy, by its very nature, increases in 'radial' value, positively, absolutely, and without determinable limits, in step with the increasing chemical complexity of the elements of which it represents the inner lining. **1965** *Listener* 15 Apr. 558/2 We really need different kinds of language to deal with the concepts proper to biology and those proper to thermodynamics. One thinks at once of Teilhard's brilliant pioneering neologisms, such as 'radial' and 'tangential' energy, phrases devised precisely to meet some at least of the difficulties. **1969** A. RICHARDSON *Dict. Christian Theol.* 333/1 It is through increase in radial energy that decisive 'critical points' are reached, whether, for example, at the molecular level or at the leap from instinct to thought.

B. *sb.* **1.** *Anat.* A radiating segment of a crinoid, between the stem and the brachials.

1872 NICHOLSON *Palaeont.* 125 A series of two or three rows of plates, which are directly superimposed upon one another, and which form the foundations of the arms... These are termed the 'radials'. **1877** HUXLEY *Anat. Inv. Anim.* ix. 583 The first radial corresponds in direction with the origin of one of the arms, and is followed by a second and third radial.

2. *Anat.* Cuvier's name for the scapula or hypercoracoid bone of a fish.

In recent Dicts.

3. *Anat.* A radial nerve or artery.

1871 TURNER in *Encycl. Brit.* I. 868/2 The radial passes through the forearm to the hand. **1899** *Allbutt's Syst. Med.* VI. 368 Extending the inquiry from the radials of both sides to the brachial and axillary arteries.

4. *Aeronaut.* A radial engine.

1920 G. C. BAILEY *Complete Airman* xii. 93 The rotary is very similar in appearance to the radial. **1944** P. H. WILKINSON *Aircraft Engines of World* 44 The M-11 engine is a 100 h.p. 5-cylinder air-cooled radial which is used in secondary training planes. **1960** C. H. GIBBS-SMITH *Aeroplane* xiv. 110 The 247..was powered by two 550-h.p. Pratt and Whitney *Wasp* radials.

5. a. A radial road or route. **b.** *Canad.* A train or tram running on a radial route.

1948 [see sense A. 2e above]. **1966** *Globe & Mail* (Toronto) 12 Sept. 16 (*caption*) The radials: commuter dream of the auto killed. **1972** J. MOSHER *Adultery* III. xiv. 134 Father had already gone off on the half-past six radial.

6. (See quot. 1956.)

1956 W. A. HEFLIN *U.S.A.F. Dict.* 417/2 *Radial*, any one of a number of lines of position radiating from an azimuthal radio-navigation facility,..identified in terms of the bearing of all points along that line from the facility. **1971** *Flying* Apr. 42/2 Then via the Coyle 270 radial until intersecting the 113 radial of Modena. **1972** R. L. TAYLOR *Instrument Flying* viii. 114 The number that now appears under the OBS index is your course to the station (inbound it will always be the reciprocal of the radial you are on).

7. A radial-ply tyre (see sense A. 3d above).

‖**radiale** (reɪdɪ'eɪliː). Pl. **radialia**. [L., neut. sing. of *radiālis*: see prec.]

1. = RADIAL *sb.* 1.

1877 HUXLEY *Anat. Inv. Anim.* ix. 583 Upon this follow five pieces (first *radialia*) closely united together. *Ibid.* 584 At the third radiale, the series bifurcates into two series of brachialia.

2. The carpal bone or element which lies on the radial side of the carpus.

1888 PARKER in *Proc. Royal Soc.* XLIII. 486 Two well-marked carpals have appeared, one of which—the radiale—lies pre-axiad and slightly proximad of the other.

radialization (ˌreɪdɪəlaɪ'zeɪʃən). [f. as next + -ATION.] The state of being arranged in radiating lines, or the process of producing this.

1889 *Q. Jrnl. Geol. Soc.* XLV. 267 Thus the rocks exhibit much evidence of a silicification (and often of a radialization possibly connected with it).

radialized ('reɪdɪəlaɪzd), *ppl. a.* [f. *radialize vb., f. RADIAL + -IZE.] Arranged in a radial manner.

1889 *Q. Jrnl. Geol. Soc.* XLV. 249 One fragment [of felsite] exhibits part of a large radialized structure. *Ibid.* 260 The radialized crust..follows the stellar points of the interior.

radially ('reɪdɪəlɪ), *adv.* [f. RADIAL *a.* + -LY².] In a radial manner; in the form of radii or rays.

1662 J. CHANDLER tr. *Van Helmont's Oriat.* 274 Its whole did shine only radially on the ignoble parts. **1794** G. ADAMS *Nat. & Exp. Philos.* IV. xlix. 348 The sun..is also continually agitating this fluid either radially or obliquely. *c* **1860** FARADAY *Forces Nat., Electric Light* 189 A number of magnets placed radially upon a wheel. **1878** A. H. GREEN, etc. *Coal* iii. 77 The primary medullary rays extend.. radially from pith to bark. **1884** BOWER & SCOTT *De Bary's Phaner.* 13 The radially arranged apical prolongation of the periblem.

radian (ˈreɪdɪən). *Trig.* [f. RADI-US + -AN.] (See quot. 1879.)

1879 THOMSON & TAIT *Nat. Phil.* I. I. §41 The usual unit angle is..that which subtends at the centre of a circle an arc whose length is equal to the radius;..for brevity we shall call this angle a radian. **1881** HALSTED *Mensuration* 24 The number which expresses any angle in radians also expresses its intercepted arc in terms of the radius.

radiance (ˈreɪdɪəns). Also 7 **radience**. [ad. late or med.L. *radiantia* brightness: see RADIATE *v.* and -ANCE.]

1. a. Light shining with diverging rays; hence, brilliant light, vivid brightness, splendour.

1601 SHAKS. *All's Well* I. i. 99 In his bright radience and colaterall light, must I be comforted. **1605** —— *Lear* I. i. 111 By the sacred radience of the Sunne. **1667** MILTON *P.L.* VII. 194 The Son..with radiance crown'd Of majesty divine. **1728–30** THOMSON *Spring* 191 The rapid Radiance instantaneous strikes Th' illumin'd Mountain. **1795** SOUTHEY *Joan of Arc* VI, Innocuous lightnings round the hallowed banner Wreath'd their red radiance. **1812** J. WILSON *Isle of Palms* I. 214 Well may the moon delight to shed Her softest radiance round that head. **1874** H. R. REYNOLDS *John Bapt.* i. 11 When the sun arose the morning star was lost in his radiance.

fig. **1761** WARTON *Poems* (1777) 10 The radiance of the regal name. **1822** B. CORNWALL *Misc. Poems*, The soul's radiance in a wintry hour Flings a sweet summer halo round us. **1896** MRS. CAFFYN *Quaker Grandmother* 13 It was a soft, luminous radiance of sincerity and sympathy.

b. Brightness of the eye or look.

1748 THOMSON *Cast. Indol.* II. lxxii, Sweet love their looks a gentle radiance lends. **1769** SIR W. JONES *Palace of Fortune* in *Poems* (1777) 8 The mild radiance of her sparkling eye. **1863** GEO. ELIOT *Romola* II. iv, There was a radiance of satisfaction about him not quite usual.

2. = RADIATION.

1800 HERSCHEL in *Phil. Trans.* XC. 294 The..agency of heat in other circumstances than in its state of radiance, or heat-making rays. **1885** CLERK MAXWELL in *Encycl. Brit.* XIX. 2 Thus we have..(3) Theory of radiance. (*a*) Geometrical optics [etc.].

3. The radiant flux emitted by unit area of a source into unit solid angle.

1917 H. E. IVES in *Astrophysical Jrnl.* XLV. 43 If now we divide this radiant intensity in any direction by the projected area of the opening in that direction.., we obtain the specific radiant intensity or radiance in that direction. *Ibid.* 48 'Radiance', as a time-saving word for 'specific radiant intensity', is frankly taken from the dictionary, as the appropriate synonym for 'brightness'. **1944** *Jrnl. Optical Soc. Amer.* XXXIV. 253/2 The luminance of any surface is the product of the radiance of that surface by the absolute luminosity *K* of the energy radiated by the surface. **1951** [see *luminosity curve*]. **1972** *Science* 22 Sept. 1100/1 Radiance gradients determined from data gathered by the infra-red spectrometers aboard the Nimbus III and Nimbus IV satellites.

radiancy (ˈreɪdɪənsɪ). Also 7 **-encie, -ency**. [f. as prec.: see -ANCY.] The quality of being radiant; radiance.

1646 SIR T. BROWNE *Pseud. Ep.* II. (1672) 98 Too high an apprehension [of the Carbuncle] and above its natural radiancy. **1693** J. EDWARDS *Author. O.N. Test.* 243 The radiency, the splendour of Moses's face. **1702** ECHARD *Eccl. Hist.* (1710) 72 The skies were divided with great radiancy. **1813** SHELLEY *Q. Mab* II. 10 The billowy clouds Edged with intolerable radiancy. **1873** SYMONDS *Gk. Poets* vii. 230 Euripides incontestably displays the quality of radiancy.

radiant (ˈreɪdɪənt), *a.* and *sb.* Also 5–6 **radyant**, 6 **-aunt(e, -iaunt**; 6 **radyent**, 7–9 **-ient**. [ad. L. *radiānt-em*, pres. pple. of *radiāre* to emit rays: see RADIUS *sb.* Cf. mod.F. *radiant.*]

A. *adj.* **1. a.** Sending out rays of light; shining brightly.

c **1450** *Cov. Myst.* xli. (Shaks. Soc.) 387 Heyl! radyant sterre, the sunne is not so bryth. *c* **1510** *Gesta Rom.* Add. Stories ii. 433 [Christ's] body yͭ was..more radyent than ony syluer. **1590** SHAKS. *Mids. N.* III. i. 95 Most radiant Piramus, most Lilly white of hue. **1604** DRAYTON *Owl* (R.) The great eagle..Which from the mountain (with a radiant eye) Brav'd the bright cressit of the glorious sky. **1667** MILTON *P.L.* III. 63 On his right The radiant image of his Glory sat, His onely Son. **1742** YOUNG *Nt. Th.* IV. 373 This gloom of night,..with all her radiant worlds. **1812** J. WILSON *Isle of Palms* II. 493 Her little sail beneath the sun Gleams radiant as the snow. **1872** BLACKIE *Lays Highl.* 75 The height which bears The sailor's radiant mark.

fig. **1838** EMERSON *Literary Ethics* Wks. (Bohn) II. 208 The humblest.. in view of these radiant facts, may now theorize and hope. **1874** H. R. REYNOLDS *John Bapt.* iv. §6. 262 The author..treats the Old Testament as radiant with the features and fragrant with the Spirit of the Christ.

b. Represented as sending out rays of light, or having radial projections resembling this. In *Her.* = RAYONNÉ.

1614 SELDEN *Titles Hon.* 138 Which the learned Paschalius interprets for a Crown radiant. **1661** MORGAN *Sph. Gentry* IV. vi. 83 A kind of radiant or pointed Coronet. **1780** EDMONDSON *Compl. Body Heraldry* II. Gloss., *Radiant, Rayonned*..terms used to express any ordinary edged with glittering rays, or shining beams. **1799** G. SMITH *Laboratory* II. 16 The radiant crown, on ancient coin, signifies that the prince was..Deified.

c. Of the eyes or looks: Bright, expressive of lively joy, hope, or the like; beaming.

1794 BURNS *Charming Month of May* 5 The glorious sun ..Out-rival'd by the radiant eyes Of..charming Chloe. **1859** HAWTHORNE *Fr. & It. Jrnls.* II. 287 The most radiant eye that the dull earth ever opened to see heaven withal. **1878** BROWNING *Poets Croisic* clix, Let, through the tumult, break the poet's face Radiant.

d. Designed to send out radiant heat.

1936 FABER & KELLS *Heating & Air-Conditioning* iv. 81 The warming effect of convectors is slower than with the radiant type of heater. **1936** *Economist* 28 Mar. 738/1 Our High Beam fires have proved to be the most efficient radiant gas fires in the world. **1951** *Good Housek. Home Encycl.* 35/2 More recently the use of 'radiant radiators'..has become more common. **1957** *Heating, Ventilating, Air Conditioning Guide* XXXV. 399 Radiant heaters..have a refractory directly above the burners which is heated to incandescence. **1962** *Listener* 13 Sept. 411/3 It [*sc.* an electric cooker] has two radiant plates. **1964** J. J. BARTON *Heating & Ventilating* xii. 318 The principal heat requirements are provided by convection, with a small radiant unit providing sufficient beamed heat for topping-up. **1977** *Direct Electric Heating* (Electricity Council) v. 21/1 Direct electric heating appliances and equipment... They may be divided into four basic groups, namely—(i) Low intensity radiant systems incorporated in the building fabric. (ii) Individual radiant-convector units. (iii) Forced warm air systems. (iv) Hot water radiator systems.

2. a. Issuing or appearing in the form of rays (of light); hence, bright, shining, splendid. Also *transf.* of qualities, as beauty.

1509 HAWES *Past. Pleas.* iii. (Percy Soc.) 15 The radiant bryghtnes of golden Phebus. *Ibid.* xxxv. 112 The mone..is fayre replendysshaunte In the longe nyght with rayes radyaunte. **1548** UDALL *Erasm. Par. N.T.* Pref. C ij b, The clere radiaunt sunnebeames of his holy woorde. **1601** SHAKS. *Twel. N.* I. v. 181 Most radiant, exquisite, and vnmatchable beautie. **1646** SIR T. BROWNE *Pseud. Ep.* v. ix. (1686) 202 With scintillations, or radiant Halo's about their heads. *c* **1750** SHENSTONE *Elegy* ix. 28 All that bears the radiant stamp of Kings. **1781** COWPER *Truth* 61 Meridian sunbeams tempt him to unfold His radiant glories. **1810** CRABBE *Borough* i, Velvet leaf with radiant beauty drest. **1878** M. A. BROWN *Nadeschda* 66 A radiant glow o'erspread Her rigid face.

†**b.** Of heat: Strong, fierce. *Obs. rare*$^{-1}$.

1508 FISHER 7 *Penit. Ps.* cxxx. Wks. (1876) 231 Ionas.. made hym a shadowynge place for his defence agaynst the radyaunt heet of the sonne.

3. a. Moving or operating in a radial manner; esp. ***radiant heat***: see HEAT *sb.* 2 b. Also ***radiant heating***; ***radiant-heated*** adj.

1800 HENRY *Epit. Chem.* (1808) 29 Radiant Caloric exhibits several interesting properties. **1835** KIRBY *Hab. & Inst. Anim.* I. Introd. 40 Both in the vegetable and animal it [Life] is a radiant principle. **1887** CROOKES in *Proc. Royal Soc.* XLII. 111 (*title*) On Radiant Matter Spectroscopy. **1912** *Cassier's Mag.* XLI. 569/1 (*heading*) Radiant heating. *Ibid.* 570/1 The demonstrations were continued..at the experimental works of the Radiant Heating Syndicate. **1962** *Punch* 24 Jan. 178/2 The 'tropical radiant-heated indoor pool'. **1966** *McGraw-Hill Encycl. Sci. & Technol.* XI. 213/1 Any radiant-heating system using a fluid heat conveyor may be employed as a cooling system by substituting cold water or other cold fluid.

b. ***radiant efficiency***, the ratio of the radiant flux emitted to the power consumed; ***radiant energy***, energy in the form of (usu. electromagnetic) radiation; ***radiant flux***, the rate of flow of radiant energy; ***radiant power*** = *radiant flux* above.

1914 *Rep. Brit. Assoc. Adv. Sci. 1913* 435 The true remedy must be sought for in increasing the 'radiant efficiency' of the [gas] fire. *Ibid.* 436 Part of the radiant energy is directly determined..by using a radiation calorimeter. **1917** *Astrophysical Jrnl.* XLV. 44 Through this space radiant energy is passing at a certain rate. This rate constitutes the radiant flux through the space. **1923** *Sci. Papers U.S. Bureau of Standards* No. 475. 132 The ratio of luminosity to radiant power—the luminous efficiency. **1932** HARDY & PERRIN *Princ. Optics* i. 19 If the human eye were uniformly sensitive to radiation of all wave lengths, the radiant power expressed in watts would provide an adequate method of evaluating the flux. **1936** FABER & KELL *Heating & Air-Conditioning of Buildings* iv. 74 Their [*sc.* gas fires'] radiant efficiency is about 50 per cent. (with an additional 10 per cent. convection). **1944** *Jrnl. Optical Soc. Amer.* XXXIV. 252/2 When radiant flux is evaluated with respect to its capacity to evoke the brightness attribute of visual sensation it is called luminous flux. **1970** M. V. KLEIN *Optics* iv. 121 The radiant energy density..is the radiant energy contained in a unit volume of space. Radiant power or radiant flux..is the time rate of change, or rate of transfer, of radiant energy.

4. (Chiefly *Bot.*) Extending in a radial manner; having parts so extending.

1830 LINDLEY *Nat. Syst. Bot.* 153 The radiant stigma of Papaver. **1845** —— *Sch. Bot.* vi. (1858) 84 Flowers either flosculous or radiant. **1847** W. E. STEELE *Field Bot.* 34 Pet[als] obcordate, the outer ones radiant and deeply bifid.

5. Characterized by radiation.

1825 J. NICHOLSON *Operat. Mechanic* 406 Cut into grooves,..in a radiant direction from the centre. **1851** RUSKIN *Stones Ven.* (1874) I. xx. 223 The scallop also is a pretty radiant form. **1881** *Nature* XXIII. 462 A means..for carrying energy in a 'radiant' manner.

6. ***radiant point***: **a.** Any point forming a centre from which rays or radii proceed.

1726 E. STONE *New Math. Dict.* **1727–41** CHAMBERS *Cycl.* s.v., Every radiant point diffuses innumerable rays all round. **1831** BREWSTER *Optics* i. 10 The point of divergence ..or the *radiant point*, as it is called. **1833** N. ARNOTT *Physics* (ed. 5) II. 209 If the distance of the radiant point be very great, they [the rays] really are..nearly parallel.

b. *Astron.* The apparent focal point of a meteoric shower. So ***radiant region***.

1864 A. S. HERSCHEL in *Monthly Notices R. Astron. Soc.* (1865) 33 Two radiant-points of shooting stars..presented themselves in Auriga and in Cetus. **1864** *Brit. Assoc. Rep. Meteors* (1865) 101 Allowing a *radiant-region* of 10° to 15° in diameter for each. **1867–77** G. F. CHAMBERS *Astron.* IX. iii. 799 Herrick regarded the position of the radiant-point as being near the cluster..in the sword-hand of Perseus.

B. *sb.* **1. a.** *Physics.* A point or object from which light or heat radiates.

1727–41 CHAMBERS *Cycl.* s.v., All the rays proceeding from the same radiant continually diverge..Every ray is supposed to carry with it the species, or image, of the radiant. **1800** HERSCHEL in *Phil. Trans.* XC. 295 Our next division comprehends the heat of coloured radiants. **1869** TYNDALL *Notes Lect. Light* §291 All bodies, whether luminous or non-luminous, are radiants; if they do not radiate light they radiate heat. **1880** LE CONTE *Sight* 29 The central rays from all radiants cross each other in the lens.

b. Each of the units in a radiant fire that are designed to radiate heat.

1914 *Rep. Brit. Assoc. Adv. Sci. 1913* 436 A little later a more marked step in the evolution of the new radiating fire consisted in joining the two or three fireclay pieces into one, and thus making the firefront consist of a series of hollow fireclay columns (now known as radiants). **1936** *Economist* 28 Mar. 738/1 Our 'Thermo-XX Beam' radiant..was the first radiant designed to emit an increased proportion of short infra-red rays, and its introduction marked a new stage in the development of the gas fire. **1953** 'N. SHUTE' *In Wet* 173 They sat down in arm chairs before the radiants of the electric fire. **1958** *Woman's Journal* Mar. 20/2, I..sat down by my hissing gas fire. One of the radiants was missing.

2. *Geom.* 'A straight line proceeding from a given point or fixed pole about which it is conceived to revolve' (Brande *Dict. Sci.* 1842).

1842 BRANDE *Dict. Sci.*, etc. 1012 The theory of the description of lines of the second order by the intersection of radiants is given by Newton in the *Principia*. **1846** CLERK MAXWELL in Campbell *Life* (1882) 77, *r* and *r'* being the radients to any point of the curve from the two foci.

3. *Astron.* A radiant point (see 6 b above).

1864 *British Assoc. Rep. Meteors* (1865) 101 Professor Heis..has..divided his meteor-showers and radiants into bi-monthly divisions. **1884** *Athenæum* 20 Dec. 809/3 The meteors from some radiants leave a streak; those from others are swift.

radiantly (ˈreɪdɪəntlɪ), *adv.* [f. prec. + -LY².]

1. In a radiant manner; brightly, splendidly.

1557 PAYNELL *Barclay's Jugurth* 89 The lyght and glorie of the progenitours shineth more radiauntly by virtue of their progeny. **1570** FOXE *A. & M.* 197/1 A certayne vessell ..made of the pretious stone Onichinus, so radiantly wrought, that in it appeared yͤ lyuely corne growing, and mens images walkyng [etc.]. **1819** SHELLEY *Let. to Peacock* 26 Jan., They are of marble, radiantly white. **1877** *Honourable Miss Ferrard* III. i. 28 Helena was looking radiantly lovely. **1880** MRS. FORRESTER *Roy & V.* I. 61 She smiles radiantly at him.

2. = RADIALLY. *rare*$^{-1}$.

1811 PINKERTON *Petral.* II. 409 A porous lava,..mingled with laminæ of mica, radiantly disposed.

3. By means of radiant energy.

1948 R. W. SHOEMAKER *Radiant Heating* i. 11 A radiantly heated room.

radiary (ˈreɪdɪərɪ). *Zool.* [ad. F. *radiaire* or mod.L. *Radiaria* (pl.), f. *radius* ray.] An animal of the class *Radiaria* (comprising certain Invertebrates) in the systems of Lamarck and Owen.

1835 KIRBY *Hab. & Inst. Anim.* I. vi. 199 We may say that in some sense the whales were created for the gelatinous radiaries..and that these gelatinous radiaries were created for the whales. **1846** PATTERSON *Zool.* 43 The anatomist is baffled by the seeming simplicity and uniformity of texture in the gelatinous Radiaries.

‖**radiata** (reɪdɪˈeɪtə). **1.** *sb. pl. Zool.* (Usu. with capital initial.) [neut. pl. of L. *radiātus*, pa. pple. of *radiāre* to furnish with rays: cf. next.] One of the great divisions of the animal kingdom according to the system of Cuvier (afterwards modified and now discarded), consisting of animals with radial structure, as sea urchins, sea anemones and polyps.

1828 STARK *Elem. Nat. Hist.* II. 393 Division IV.— Radiata. **1842** H. MILLER *O.R. Sandst.* xiv. (ed. 2) 295 The radiata cover the bank by thousands. **1855** H. SPENCER *Princ. Psychol.* I. IV. i. (1872) 396 In such so-called Radiata as the Star-fish. **1874** WOOD *Nat. Hist.* 767 A vast..division of living beings, which have no joints whatever, and are called Radiata.

2. *Bot.* [a. the specific epithet of *Pinus radiata* (D. Don 1837, in *Trans. Linn. Soc.* XVII. 442).] In full, ***radiata pine***: = INSIGNIS, *Monterey pine* s.v. MONTEREY.

1953 *N.Z. Jrnl. Forestry* V. 374 The development of major industries, dependent wholly or substantially on radiata pine as a basic raw material, is well advanced. **1959** A. MCLINTOCK *Descr. Atlas N.Z.* p. xiii, Plantation and shelter belts of introduced (exotic) trees, mainly radiata pine and macrocarpa, break up the farmlands. **1963** *Times* 11 Feb. 9/1 At Kaingaroa..273,000 acres of radiata pines were planted during the depression. **1972** *Daily Colonist* (Victoria, B.C.) 24 May 5/4 It was found, however, that the radiata pine (Monterey pine) would flourish in this otherwise 'dead' [volcanic] soil. **1973** T. E. SIMPSON *Kauri to Radiata* vii. 310 By 1959 radiata would have achieved prominence in sawn output over that of our indigenous timbers.

radiate (ˈreɪdɪət), *a.* and *sb.* [ad. L. *radiātus*: cf. next.]

A. *adj.* **1.** Having rays proceeding from a centre, or having parts arranged in this manner. ***radiate animal***, one of the Radiata. ***radiate***

crown: see RADIATED 1. *radiate flower*, a composite flower-head having radial (usually ligulate) florets.

1668 WILKINS *Real Char.* II. iv. 84 Divided leaves; having a Radiate flower. **1751** HURD *Marks of Imitation* Wks. 1811 II. *253 Anciently the Sun was commonly emblematized by a starry or radiate figure. **1769** *De Foe's Tour Gt. Brit.* III. 139 Those Pieces that have radiate Crowns on the Heads of the Effigies, they call Saracens Heads. **1785** MARTYN *Rousseau's Bot.* vi. (1794) 65 In the radiate flowers the disk is often of one colour. **1846** PATTERSON *Zool.* 57 The naturalist who has been an observer of the radiate animals. **1877** HUXLEY *Anat. Inv. Anim.* 591 The apparently radiate *Echinus* or Star-fish.

2. Arranged like rays, diverging from a centre.

1822–34 *Good's Study Med.* (ed. 4) I. 271 A terminal mouth surrounded by two rows of radiate hooks or holders. **1877** BURNETT *Ear* 65 The radiate fibres are strongly developed in comparison with the circular fibres. **1882** VINES tr. *Sachs' Bot.* 131 The thickening tissue placed horizontally..and radially, out of which the radiate tissue is composed.

3. = RADIAL *a.* 4.

1859 J. TOMES *Dental Surg.* 394 The radiate direction followed by the enamel fibres must be borne in mind.

B. *sb.* **1.** A radiate animal; one of the Radiata.

1854 EMERSON *Lett. & Soc. Aims, Poet. & Imag.* Wks. (Bohn) III. 141 From radiate, mollusk,..up to man. **1863** DANA *Man. Geol.* 158 The sub-kingdom of Radiates contains three classes.

2. A ray-like projection, a ray.

c **1885** in *Cent. Dict.*

3. A classical coin with rays issuing from the device.

1939 *Oxoniensia* IV. 61 The coins discovered during the exploration of the Cemetery are listed below... 1 Radiate *Antoninianus*. **1974** *Sci. Amer.* Dec. 122/3 The radiate was by then [*sc.* A.D. 301] reckoned to be equal to two of the seldom-seen *denarii*.

radiate ('reɪdɪeɪt), *v.* [f. L. *radiāt-* ppl. stem of *radiāre* to furnish with rays, to emit rays, f. *radius* a ray, RADIUS *sb.*]

1. a. *intr.* To emit rays of light; to shine brightly. Also *fig.*

1649 HOWELL *Verses pref. Ld. Herbert's Hen. VIII*, Vertues shine more clear In Them, and radiat like the Sun at Noon. **1678** CUDWORTH *Intellectual Syst.* I. iv. §27.454 The Fixed stars..strongly radiate with their light upon our eyes. **1766–74** TUCKER *Lt. Nat.* (1834) I. 475 Everything set forth in our theory radiates, as the saying is, with its own lustre. **1852** D. G. MITCHELL *Dream Life* 17 It radiates like a star, God-ward and earthward. **1865** CARLYLE *Fredk. Gt.* XX. viii. (1872) IX. 158 The..brow of Maria Theresa..did not radiate in response; but gloomed indignantly.

b. Orig., to emit rays of heat. Now more widely, to emit energy of any kind in the form of rays or waves.

1833 N. ARNOTT *Physics* (ed. 5) II. 41 Metal with a scratched or roughened surface radiates or receives much more rapidly than polished metal. **1878** E. CLARK *Visit S. America* 111 Long grass radiates very freely. **1927** I. B. CRANDALL *Theory of Vibrating Systems & Sound* ii. 55 Dissipation due to radiation is usually of much greater importance than dissipation due to friction in the neck of the resonator, provided the resonator is so situated that it can radiate. **1960** *Practical Wireless* XXXVI. 414/2 The VHF transmitter also radiates during daylight but continues throughout the hours of darkness. **1962** A. NISBETT *Technique Sound Studio* iii. 64 Remembering that it is the soundboard that is radiating, an alternative is to move the piano well away from the wall and stand the microphone on a chair at the back. **1978** *Nature* 2 Mar. 37/1 The ability of degenerate dwarfs..to radiate at X-ray wavelengths has created much theoretical interest.

2. *intr.* Of light or heat: To issue in rays.

a **1704** LOCKE *Elem. Nat. Phil.* xi. (1754) 41 Light..as it radiates from luminous bodies directly to our eyes. **1746–7** HERVEY *Medit.* (1818) 263 A richer lustre than that which radiates from thy resplendent orb. **1841** *Penny Cycl.* XIX. 233/2 Heat..which radiates from the glass after having been for a time absorbed in it. **1854** BREWSTER *More Worlds* ix. 158 Those eastern lands,..from which the beams of knowledge first radiated on mankind.

3. a. *intr.* To spread or move in all directions from a centre; to diverge from a central point.

1830 N. S. WHEATON *Jrnl.* 387 The centre whence diligences radiate to every part of this great empire. **1841** T. R. JONES *Anim. Kingd.* 314 One great central brain, from whence nerves radiate to all parts of the body. **1856** STANLEY *Sinai & Pal.* iv. 200 The three valleys that radiate from the uplands of Michmash.

b. Of immaterial things:

In quot. *a* 1619 perh. *fig.* from sense 1.

a **1619** FOTHERBY *Atheom.* II. ii. §8 (1622) 209 The Holy and vndiuided Trinitie..is easily able to fill it, and to radiate into euery corner of it. **1807** J. BARLOW *To Freedom* in *Columb.*, Soul-searching Freedom! here assume thy stand, And radiate hence to every distant land. **1871** SMILES *Charac.* ii. (1876) 41 Philanthropy radiates from the home as from a centre.

c. To converge to or towards a centre. *rare.*

1835 WILLIS *Pencillings* I. iii. 27 Repelling the beggars who radiated to us from every corner. **1866** ROGERS *Agric. & Prices* I. xxi. 543 A circumference of timber firmly mortised together, with spokes radiating to an axle.

d. *Biol.* Of an animal or plant group, to spread from its area of greatest concentration into new habitats.

1923 F. W. JONES *Mammals S. Austral.* I. 24 A stock will become progressively altered by adaptation to its environment as it radiates from its centre of domicile. **1949** W. C. ALLEE et al. *Princ. Animal Ecol.* xxxiv. 661/1 The Australian marsupials..radiated into a great variety of habitats. **1957** P. J. DARLINGTON *Zoogeogr.* ii. 58 Over a longer period of time, the whole of the Ostariophysi may have radiated from the Old World tropics. **1978** *Sci. Amer.* Sept. 111/1 Many of the early amphibian lineages developed rather large body sizes and radiated into the available habitats, becoming herbivores and predators on many food items in aquatic, semiaquatic and terrestrial settings.

4. a. *trans.* To emit (light or heat) in rays. More widely, to emit (energy of any kind) in the form of rays or waves. Also with *away*.

1794 J. HUTTON *Philos. Light*, etc. 226 Whether..the body is thereby made to radiate or emit light. **1860** TYNDALL *Glac.* II. iii. 242 If..we stand before a wall of ice, the wall radiates heat to us, as we also radiate heat to it. **1868** LOCKYER *Elem. Astron.* ii. (1879) 51 The Sun sends out, or radiates, its light and heat in all directions. **1937** *Discovery* Nov. 331/1 It is possible that the Baird video transmitter..will be removed to Birmingham, since only small alterations would be required to make it radiate the signals generated by Marconi-E.M.I. cameras. **1971** *Nature* 29 Jan. 304/1 The compactness of the hot plasma cloud suggests that it is probably gravitationally confined and, as the thermal energy is radiated away in a fraction of a second, continuously replenished in some way. **1978** *Ibid.* 27 Apr. 784/2 Stars radiate their heat away, and must burn nuclear fuel to keep going.

b. To spread or disseminate as from a centre.

1821 SHELLEY *Epipsych.* 325 From her presence life was radiated Through the grey earth. **1872** W. R. GREG *Enigmas of Life* (1873) 271 Those whom he softens and purifies that they may radiate love and serenity around them.

c. To transmit (radio waves); to broadcast.

1923 *Radio Times* 28 Sept. 12/3 A ninety-minute excerpt ..will be simultaneously radiated from all other stations. **1951** *Times* 4 Jan. 7/6 Items, mainly music, are selected from one of the three home services. They are radiated simultaneously by a 25-kw. frequency modulated (f.m.) transmitter..and a standard amplitude modulated transmitter. **1956** *B.B.C. Handbk. 1957* 59 Thirty-nine high-power, short-wave transmitters..radiate the BBC's External Services programmes. **1967** *Listener* 30 Mar. 423/3 All three programmes in the United Kingdom will eventually be radiated in colour on 625 lines. **1972** *Radio Times* 28 Sept. 42/1 World News is also radiated on medium waves.

5. To irradiate, illuminate. *rare.*

1658 *Hewyt's Nine Serm.* To Rdr., That glorious light, which continually..did radiate the souls of his faithful Auditory. **1831** *Fraser's Mag.* III. 482 The..pleasurable feelings which..radiate the broad disk of our..face.

radiated ('reɪdɪeɪtɪd), *ppl. a.* [f. prec.]

1. Furnished with rays; made or depicted with rays issuing from it, esp. *radiated crown.*

1658 SIR T. BROWNE *Hydriot.* (1736) 60 By the Radiated-Crown, this Piece should be coined after his Death and Consecration. *a* **1661** FULLER *Worthies, Suffolk* III. (1662) 57 A Radiated Circle as particular to Canonized Saints. **1702** ADDISON *Dial. Medals* Wks. 1721 I. 466 The radiated head of the Phœnix. **1864** BOUTELL *Her. Hist. & Pop.* xxi. (ed. 3) 368 Az., three clouds, radiated. **1876** HUMPHREYS *Coin-coll. Man.* x. 117 The radiated crown is found on the coins of this prince.

2. Having or consisting of parts arranged like rays or radii. Cf. RADIATE *a.* 1.

1775 J. JENKINSON *Brit. Plants* Gloss., Radiated-flowers, are such as have several semifloscules set round a disk in form of a radiant star. **1796** KIRWAN *Elem. Min.* (ed. 2) II. 292 A radiated ore so light as to float in water. **1807** T. THOMSON *Chem.* (ed. 3) II. 269 It hardens, and a radiated crust forms on its surface. **1845** WHEWELL *Indic. Creator* 68 The symmetry of the radiated zoophytes. **1876** tr. *Haeckel's Hist. Creat.* I. iii. 53 The same holds good..in Molluscous and Radiated animals.

b. *spec.* in *Ornith.* of birds having plumage or markings thus arranged. Also *radiated mole* (see quot. 1781).

1781 PENNANT *Quadrupeds* 488 Radiated Mole. [*Ibid.* 486 Nose long; the edges beset with radiated tendrils.] **1815** *Shaw's Gen. Zool.* IX. I. 281 Radiated Grosbeak (*Loxia lineata*). **1821** LATHAM *Gen. Hist. Birds* I. 222 Radiated Falcon. **1822** *Ibid.* IV. 256 Radiated Creeper. **1848** GOULD *Birds Australia* I. Pl. 16 *Astur Radiatus*, Radiated Goshawk.

3. Arranged like rays. = RADIATE *a.* 2.

1748 HARTLEY *Observ. Man* I. i. §3. 100 The radiated Fibres of the Uvea. **1845** DARWIN *Voy. Nat.* i. (1873) 6 Groups of beautifully radiated fibres resembling arragonite. *Comb.* **1870** BENTLEY *Man. Bot.* (ed. 2) 147 The veins..diverge from each other..as in the radiated-veined variety of reticulated leaves.

4. Characterized by radiation. = RADIAL *a.* 4.

1798 W. BLAIR *Soldier's Friend* 54 Bell tents, in which the men lie in a radiated manner. **1830** LYELL *Princ. Geol.* I. 205 The same combination of concentric and radiated structure. **1848** CARPENTER *Anim. Phys.* 64 Arranged in a circular manner around a common centre, so as to present a radiated or rayed aspect.

radiately ('reɪdɪətlɪ), *adv.* [f. RADIATE *a.* + -LY[2].] In a radiate manner; in the manner of radii or rays.

1846 DANA *Zooph.* (1848) 301 Corallum..below radiately echinulate. **1851–6** WOODWARD *Mollusca* 292 The sides are concentrically furrowed, the posterior slope radiately striated. **1887** SOLLAS in *Encycl. Brit.* XXII. 413/2 From the walls..cæcal processes grow out radiately.

So **'radiateness**, radiality (*Cent. Dict.* 1891).

radi'atiform, *a. Bot.* [f. RADIATE *a.* + -(I)FORM.] (See quot.).

1880 A. GRAY *Struct. Bot.* Gloss. 429 *Radiatiform*, said of a capitulum of flowers which is radiate by enlargement of some of the outer flowers, which however are not truly ligulate, as in species of Centaurea.

radiating ('reɪdɪeɪtɪŋ), *vbl. sb.* [f. RADIATE *v.* + -ING[1].] The action of the vb. Also *attrib.*

1833 N. ARNOTT *Physics* (ed. 5) II. 40 The comparative absorbing powers of the substances and colours were very nearly proportioned to their radiating powers. **1844** W. UPTON *Physioglyphics* ii. 61 It will imply the radiating of right lines over the one barrier or object.

radiating ('reɪdɪeɪtɪŋ), *ppl. a.* [f. as prec. + -ING[2].] That radiates, in senses of the verb.

1. That sends out rays (of light or heat).

1721 BAILEY, *Radiating point*..is that Point from whence the Rays of Light issue. **1841** *Penny Cycl.* XIX. 233/1 The velocity of radiation depends more on the surface than on the nature of the radiating body. **1892** J. TAIT *Mind in Matter* 201 Radiating-points of light to the world at large.

b. Moving in a radial direction.

1841 *Penny Cycl.* XIX. 232/2 The radiating particles falling upon the surfaces of any bodies..are..absorbed in them.

2. Extending in the manner of rays.

1849 MURCHISON *Siluria* x. 232 Furnished with radiating ribs. **1870** HOOKER *Stud. Flora* 15 Stigma discoid or pyramidal with radiating lobes. **1884** BOWER & SCOTT *De Bary's Phaner.* 97 They form a radiating ring round the margin of the flat surface.

3. Characterized by radiation.

1831 R. KNOX *Cloquet's Anat.* 680 They..send twigs in a radiating manner into the pectoralis major. **1869** PHILLIPS *Vesuv.* iii. 67 The mountain became fissured in a radiating direction. **1874** WOOD *Nat. Hist.* 555 Each plate being marked with slight grooves in a radiating fashion.

radiation (reɪdɪ'eɪʃən). [ad. L. *radiātiōn-em* n. of action from *radiāre*: see RADIATE *v.* and cf. F. *radiation* (1469).]

1. a. The action or condition of sending out rays of light. Now *rare* (see note to 2).

1626 BACON *Sylva* §125 So it [sound] paralleleth in so many other things with the Sight, and Radiation of Things visible. **1646** SIR T. BROWNE *Pseud. Ep.* 260 As for Sciotericall Dialls, whether of the Sunne or Moon, they are only of use in the actuall radiation of those Luminaries. **1740** CHEYNE *Regimen* 123 The glorious Appearance and Radiation of our Saviour's Body on the Mount. **1773** *Encycl. Brit.* III. 525/2 *Radiation*, the act of a body emitting or diffusing rays of light all round, as from a centre.

b. A ray or quantity of light emitted by a radiant body (usu. in *pl.*) In mod. use (usu. in *sing.*), energy transmitted in the form or rays, waves, or sub-atomic particles; in non-*techn.* use *spec.* ionizing radiation.

1570 DEE *Math. Pref.* b j, Perspective..demonstrateth the maner and properties, of all Radiations Direct, Broken, and Reflected. **1626** BACON *New Atl.* 39 Wee haue also Perspectiue-Houses, wher wee make Demonstrations of all Lights and Radiations. **1792** DALTON *Meteorol. Obs.* (1834) 64 The beams lost their lateral motion, and were converted ..into the flashing radiations. **1837** BREWSTER *Magnet.* 225 The part of the heavens where all these beams or radiations unite. **1871** TYNDALL *Fragm. Sci.* (1879) II. xvi. 450 Dissolved in a proper vehicle, iodine cuts the visible radiation sharply off. **1896** *Strand Mag.* July 108/1 If a solid object is placed in the path of this [negative] stream..it may become the seat of the production of that..which is variously known as Röntgen radiation or X-radiation. At the solid object the new radiation springs into being, and then travels away from it in all directions, in very much the same way that ordinary light would do. **1899** *Phil. Mag.* XLVII. 109 The remarkable radiation emitted by uranium and its compounds has been studied by its discoverer, Becquerel. **1934** H. M. VERNON *Princ. Heating & Ventilation* iii. 50 The intensity of the radiation from a coal fire varies enormously. **1958** *New Statesman* 25 Oct. 545/3 This week's inquest on the second serviceman to die after the Christmas Island tests reveals once more the astonishing medical and scientific ignorance of the effects of radiation. **1962** A. NISBETT *Technique Sound Studio* iii. 52 With stringed instruments, very little of the sound we hear is directly from the strings; what we are actually listening to is the radiation from a sounding board to which the strings are coupled. **1966** *McGraw-Hill Encycl. Sci. & Technol.* XIV. 265/2 The trapped radiation consists of protons and electrons constrained to bound orbits by the geomagnetic field. **1972** *Daily Tel.* (Colour Suppl.) 3 Mar. 17 Our planet is constantly being bombarded by all kinds of radiation—from natural radio waves to infra-red, visible light, ultraviolet, X-rays and gamma radiation. **1978** *Sci. Amer.* July 82/1 Although bees are most sensitive to ultraviolet radiation, it is not the color that they learn best. To the bee ultraviolet radiation is sky radiation, and it seems not to be expected as a pure color at food sources.

fig. **1652** JER. COLLIER *Eccho* in Benlowes *Theoph.*, The Radiations of the Soul All splendors of the flesh controul. **1750** JOHNSON *Rambler* No. 29 ¶4 As the errors and follies of a great genius are seldom without some radiations of understanding, by which meaner minds may be enlightened. **1871** FARRAR *Witn. Hist.* ii. 83 This life is not a type of any one excellence, but a radiation of them all.

†**c.** *Astrol.* = ASPECT *sb.* 4. *Obs. rare.*

1555 DIGGES *Prognos.* B iv, The Sextile aspecte or radiation..is with in 60 degrees thone from the other. **1688** R. HOLME *Armoury* II. i. 27 Names or Terms used by Astronomers... Aspect or Radiation.

2. Orig., the emission and diffusion of heat-rays. Now, the emission of energy of any kind in the form of rays or waves, esp. electromagnetic waves.

In its widest sense, radiation denotes the manner in which the energy of a vibrating body is transmitted in all directions by a surrounding medium. When this energy is imparted to the ether, it produces waves which, according to their frequency, affect the senses either as light or heat.

1812–16 PLAYFAIR *Nat. Phil.* (1819) I. 229 Heat escapes from bodies..by radiation, or by passing in straight lines through the air with great rapidity. **1845** DARWIN *Voy. Nat.* xi. (1879) 249 The winter is rendered excessively cold by the radiation from a large area of land into a clear sky. **1880** HAUGHTON *Phys. Geog.* ii. 50 This process..goes on in every planet, as long as it is losing heat by radiation. **1908** C. C. F. MONCKTON *Radio-Telegr.* iv. 69 There will be a certain amount of radiation possibly from the tree back towards the radiator, and a consequent distortion of the field. **1934** *Discovery* Dec. 347/2 The noise in aeroplanes can be reduced..; little can be done for reducing the external radiation of noise. **1956** *B.B.C. Handbk.* 1957 9 The radiation of signals from the transmitting aerial.

fig. **1827** HARE *Guesses* Ser. I. (1873) 44 Under the impulses of a mighty passion, he..fuses every object by its intense radiation.

3. a. Divergence from a central point; radial arrangement or structure.

1658 SIR T. BROWNE *Gard. Cyrus* iii. 59 The motion of vegetation upward, and of radiation into all quarters. **1856** RUSKIN *Mod. Paint.* IV. v. xv. §8 The beauty of a crest or bird's wing consists..in the radiation of the plumes. **1868** STANLEY *Westm. Abb.* iii. 129 The radiation of the polygonal chapels round the Choir.

b. One of a set of radiating things or parts.

1843 YOUATT *Horse* vi. (1847) 110 Rays or radiations of bone extend thence in every direction. **1899** *Allbutt's Syst. Med.* VI. 756 Division of the optic radiations was attended by a descending degeneration.

c. *Biol.* The spread of an animal or plant group from an area in which its greatest concentration is or was found. Cf. *adaptive radiation* s.v. ADAPTIVE *a.*

1949 W. C. ALLEE et al. *Princ. Animal Ecol.* xxxiv. 662/2 The early radiation of the orders of insects is even more remarkable than that of the orders of mammals. **1957** P. J. DARLINGTON *Zoogeography* vii. 414 The most profound patterns of geographical radiation, reflecting spread of great, dominant groups from definite centers, are found among the animals which disperse most slowly over land. **1977** *Sci. Amer.* May 28/3 In the course of their wide and long-lasting radiation these apes seem to have encountered increasingly cooler environments. **1978** *Nature* 17 Aug. 662/1 The *Dicroidium* complex, a diverse group of seed ferns characteristic of the Triassic, became nearly entirely extinct and was replaced by a Jurassic radiation of conifers.

4. In mod. use freq. *attrib.* with the sense 'ionizing radiation', as ***radiation dosage, dose, dosimetry, level, meter, monitor; radiation, induced, -proof*** adjs.; in the names of bodily disorders caused by ionizing radiation, as ***radiation cachexia, carcinogenesis, dermatitis, osteitis, ulcer.*** *Comb.* as **radiation accident**, an accident involving potentially hazardous exposure to ionizing radiation; **radiation badge**, a badge that changes its appearance when a prescribed dose of ionizing radiation has been received; cf. *film badge* s.v. FILM *sb.* 7b; **radiation belt** *Astr.*, a region surrounding a planet where charged particles accumulate under the influence of the planet's magnetic field; **radiation burn**, a burn caused by over-exposure to ionizing radiation; **radiation chemistry**, the study of chemical changes arising from the impact of ionizing radiation; (cf. RADIOCHEMISTRY); hence ***radiation-chemical*** adj.; ***radiation chemist***; **radiation counter** = COUNTER *sb.*[2] 3b; **radiation damage**, damage caused by ionizing radiation; **radiation efficiency** *Telecommunications* (see quot. 1977); **radiation field**, an extent of space in which there is radiation; *spec.* the space around an aerial in which there is a continuous outward flow of energy, separated from the aerial by the induction field; **radiation fog**, fog formed when the ground loses heat by radiation and cools overlying moist air; **radiation frost**, frost which occurs when the ground loses heat by radiation; **radiation genetics**, the branch of biology concerned with the genetic effects of ionizing radiation; **radiation hazard**, a risk to health owing to the presence of ionizing radiation; **radiation injury**, an injury caused by over-exposure to ionizing radiation; **radiation pattern**, the way in which the intensity of the radiation from an aerial or other source varies in different directions from it; **radiation pressure**, mechanical pressure exerted by electromagnetic radiation or by sound waves; **radiation pyrometer**, a pyrometer which functions by measuring radiant energy; hence ***radiation pyrometry***; **radiation resistance**, the part of the electrical resistance of an aerial that is due to its radiating properties, being the ratio of the radiated power to the mean square current in the aerial; an analogous property of a sound radiator; **radiation sickness**, disease caused by exposure of the body to ionizing radiation; **radiation therapy, treatment**, medical treatment by means of radiation, such as X-rays or ultraviolet light; **radiation-thermometer**, a thermometer specially adapted for measuring the effects of radiation.

1954 A. HOLLAENDER *Radiation Biology* I. 1255/2 (Index), *Radiation accidents. **1970** PASSMORE & ROBSON *Compan. Med. Stud.* II. xxxiii. 1/1 Further knowledge of the acute effects of high doses of radiation in man has been provided by the outcome of radiation accidents. **1964** C. HODDER-WILLIAMS *Main Experiment* I. i. 18 Some of you are not wearing *radiation badges. **1959** *Times* 14 Feb. 8/4 By a '*radiation belt' is meant a region in which incoming charged particles are trapped and held captive by the magnetic field of the earth. **1959** *Sci. Amer.* Mar. 47/2 The radiation belts obviously present an obstacle to space flight. **1962** *Daily Tel.* 2 May 1/8 American scientists have said it may take 10 or even 100 years before the radiation belts return to their present conditions [after the explosion of a hydrogen bomb]. **1977** F. N. BASH *Astron.* xiii. 398 Jupiter's radiation belts are not only more intense, but also much larger than the similar Van Allen belts that girdle the earth. **1949** *Surg., Gynecol., & Obstetr.* LXXXVIII. 609 (*heading*) Surgical treatment of *radiation burns. **1960** *Gloss. Atomic Terms* (Atomic Energy Authority) 42 Patients subject to intense irradiation, e.g. in cancer therapy by X or gamma rays sometimes get surface or skin radiation burns. **1961** R. D. BAKER *Essent. Path.* vii. 127 Heavy dosages of x-ray, especially to the upper abdomen, may lead to radiation sickness, nausea and vomiting shortly after the radiation; *radiation cachexia, weakness, anemia, and leukopenia several weeks after exposures. **1947** *Radiology* XLIX. 359/2 The question of *radiation carcinogenesis in the lungs cannot be fully dismissed. **1951** *Jrnl. Chem. Educ.* XXVIII. 419/2 From the more theoretical point of view *radiation chemical reactions should be studied to determine how internal conversion and energy transfer affect yields. *Ibid.* 407/2 Not all instruments shown in Table 1 are equally useful for the *radiation chemist. **1940** *Chem. Abstr.* XXXVI. 229 (*heading*) The significance of *radiation chemistry and its procedures for the science and technology of glass. **1951** *Jrnl. Chem. Educ.* XXVIII. 416/2 We may note finally in the radiation chemistry of water the anisotropic distribution of H_3O^+ and OH^- ions, particularly in cases of heavy particle bombardment. **1961** G. R. CHOPPIN *Exper. Nuclear Chem.* xii. 192 Most of the early research in radiation chemistry used natural nuclear emissions. **1974** J. E. WILSON *Radiation Chem. of Monomers, Polymers, & Plastics* iv. 185 A study of the radiation chemistry of small molecules is helpful in understanding the radiation chemistry of polymers. **1979** *Nature* 15 Feb. 583/3 Work was soon under way in the β and γ-ray spectrometry of (mainly) naturally radio-active species, and in radiation chemistry. **1947** *Nucleonics* Sept. 23/1 (*heading*) Crystal and Cerenkov *radiation counters. **1941** *Jrnl. Appl. Physics* XII. 293/1 Cases of severe *radiation damage to the hands of radiologists and technicians. **1957** BENEDICT & PIGFORD *Nuclear Chem. Engin.* iii. 66 The extent to which fuel elements of a power reactor can be irradiated may be limited ..by physical changes in the fuel caused by radiation damage. **1970** PASSMORE & ROBSON *Compan. Med. Stud.* II. xxxiii. 7/2 That harmful mutations may result from radiation seems almost certain... The demonstration of microscopic radiation damage to human chromosomes makes the occurrence of finer damage almost beyond question. **1961** R. D. BAKER *Essent. Path.* xx. 542 *Radiation dermatitis, usually from overexposure to X-rays and less commonly to radium, results in similar atrophic changes in the skin..which, after a number of years, become squamous cell carcinoma. **1934** *Radiology* XXIII. 738 (*heading*) Some mathematical aspects of *radiation dosage. **1922** tr. Friedrich & Glasser in Kroenig & Friedrich *Princ. Physics & Biol. of Radiation Therapy* 241 (*heading*) The distribution of the *radiation dose in intracorporeal radium and mesothorium therapy. **1970** PASSMORE & ROBSON *Compan. Med. Stud.* II. xxxiii. 1/2 Other important aspects of radiation dose are the rate of delivery, whether it is fractionated in time and the duration of the radiation-free periods between doses. **1937** *Brit. Jrnl. Radiol.* X. 600 (*heading*) *Radiation dosimetry. **1968** *Courier-Mail* (Brisbane) 16 Nov. 15 (Advt.), The Australian Atomic Energy Commission is in the process of establishing a programme of research and development in the field of radiation dosimetry and radiation standards. **1913** J. ERSKINE-MURRAY *Handbk. Wireless Telegr.* (ed. 4) xix. 367 (*heading*) A direct experimental method for the determination of the *radiation efficiency, earth resistance and other constants of a transmitter. **1977** S. W. AMOS *Radio, TV & Audio Technical Ref. Bk.* xxi. 5 Antenna radiation efficiency = power radiated by antenna/input power to antenna. **1924** *Physical Rev.* XXIV. 339 The energy which is removed from a *radiation field..by the positive absorption of quanta by *N* oscillators all in $(n - 1)$ quantum states. **1928** STERLING & KRUSE *Radio Man.* 663/1 (Index), Radiation field of antenna. **1948** A. L. ALBERT *Radio Fund.* xiii. 494 At a distance greater than, say, a few wavelengths from the antenna, the induction field approaches zero, and the radiation field exists... The energy in the radiation field does not return to the antenna when the antenna voltage and current die out. **1971** *Nature* 20 Aug. 572/1 The ultra-sonic field was monitored by a small, sensitized, thermistor probe which could be positioned at any point in the radiation field by means of a micromanipulator attached to the irradiation chamber. **1857** HERSCHEL *Meteorol.* (1861) 93 A *radiation-fog once formed tends to its own increase, by radiating off heat from its own particles. **1883** R. H. SCOTT *Elem. Meteor.* 121 A class of fogs, termed by Herschel 'radiation fogs'. **1937** G. T. TREWARTHA *Introd. Weather & Climate* iii. 109 Radiation fog is at its worst in the vicinity of large cities where the air is rich in hygroscopic smoke particles. **1971** W. HILLEN *Blackwater River* xiii. 121 Morning radiation fog shrouded the lake..and filled the lower valley. **1889** *Q. Jrnl. R. Meteorol. Soc.* XV. 23 It was not an ordinary *radiation frost, but one in which the entire valley was filled with an almost uniformly cold atmosphere. **1906** *Daily Chron.* 8 Mar. 7/4 It will surprise many people..to know that a slight radiation frost actually occurred on the grass early yesterday morning. **1945** R. BUSH *Frost & Fruitgrower* iii. 13 Cloud coming up when a radiation frost is beginning sends the temperature up surprisingly quickly. **1959** *Chambers's Encycl.* VI. 93/2 The occurrence of radiation frost at night is associated with the growth of an inversion in the surface layers of air. **1934** *Lancet* 28 July 214/1 A new subject to many members is '*radiation genetics'. **1956** C. AUERBACH *Genetics in Atomic Age* viii. 69 In the twenty-eight years since its beginning, radiation genetics has developed into a large and flourishing branch of research. **1945** H. D. SMYTH *Gen. Acct. Devel. Atomic Energy Mil. Purposes* vii. 73 Two types of *radiation hazard were anticipated—neutrons generated by the pile, and alpha-particles, beta-particles, and gamma rays emitted by products of the pile. **1964** C. HODDER-WILLIAMS *Main Experiment* I. iii. 34 She's batty on the subject of radiation hazards. She used to flirt with the CND. **1946** U.S. Atomic Energy Comm. Rep. MDDC-700 (*title*) *Radiation-induced changes in ultraviolet absorption spectra of urine. **1962** *Times* 12 July 3/1 The effects of radiation-induced mutations on mouse populations. **1971** *Brit. Med. Bull.* XXVII. 66/1 The Survey is occasionally referred to as a source of information about mongols and leukaemia, but never in connexion with radiation-induced cancers. **1942** *Radiology* XXXIX. 663 (*heading*) Influence of the medium on *radiation injury of sperm. **1970** PASSMORE & ROBSON *Compan. Med. Stud.* II. xxxiii. 7/2 In other respects the histological appearance of the tissue are those of a nonspecific inflammatory response although some features suggest a radiation injury. **1955** *Radiation level [see RADIOBIOLOGY]. **1947** *Nucleonics* Sept. 61/1 (*heading*) Beta and gamma *radiation meter. **1961** *Economist* 23 Dec. 1220/2 'Survival biscuits'.., water, first-aid kits and radiation meters. **1951** GRAY & MARTENS *Radiation Monitoring in Atomic Defense* xii. 91 Emergency workers, particularly *radiation monitors, should be equipped with dose meters for their own protection. **1955** [see *film badge* s.v. FILM *sb.* 7b]. **1964** C. HODDER-WILLIAMS *Main Experiment* I. iii. 29 Recessed radiation monitors placed at fifty-foot intervals. **1926** *Acta Radiol.* VI. 399 (*heading*) *Radiation osteitis. **1948** A. L. ALBERT *Radio Fund.* xiii. 496 (*caption*) The *radiation patterns of a half-wave antenna. **1978** *Nature* 5 Jan. 48/2 The radiation pattern of the antenna is similar to that of a half-wave dipole. **1978** *Sci. Amer.* Aug. 120 (*caption*) Flask arrangement for measuring the radiation pattern from a conventional grate. **1901** *Physical Rev.* XIII. 308 *Radiation pressure, from its nature, must reach its maximum value instantly. **1905** [see RADIOMETER 2]. **1926** H. C. MACPHERSON *Mod. Astron.* vi. 96 It is now generally admitted that the chief factor in producing comets' tails is the radiation pressure. **1966** *McGraw-Hill Encycl. Sci. & Technol.* XI. 317/1 Since the radiation pressure is $p = 2E$, where E is the energy of the acoustic wave per unit area, a direct measurement of this pressure will determine the energy of a plane wave. **1976** *Nature* 2 Sept. 15/2 Theoreticians..remained frustrated in their attempts to explain motions in the great straight tails [of comets] by means of solar radiation pressure alone. **1952** B. WOLFE *Limbo '90* (1953) IV. xiv. 220 Heat-proof and *radiation-proof name plates. **1904** *Physical Rev.* XIX. 422 The best types of *radiation pyrometers that are at present available to the experimentalist. **1959** *Techn. Survey Dorman Long (Steel) Ltd.* (Iron & Coal Trades Rev.) 59/2 Each furnace also has two radiation pyrometers focussed on the crown of the roof ten feet on either side of the tap-hole. **1972** G. F. WARNKE in H. H. Plumb *Temperature* IV. I. ii. 503/2 The instrument engineer seeking to employ infrared radiation pyrometers for process temperature measurement and control. **1904** *Physical Rev.* XIX. 422 Under the term *radiation pyrometry may be grouped all those methods in which the temperature of bodies is estimated from the radiant energy emitted, either in the form of visible light radiation or of the longer infra red waves. **1922** GLAZEBROOK *Dict. Appl. Physics* I. 643/1 In radiation pyrometry generally the term 'full radiator' or 'black body' denotes one that will absorb all the radiation it receives. **1913** J. ERSKINE-MURRAY *Handbk. Wireless Telegr.* (ed. 4) xiv. 223 The fourth numeric of the antenna, namely *r*, the radiation coefficient or '*radiation resistance', is that on which transmission actually depends. **1938** F. E. TERMAN *Fund. of Radio* xiv. 389 The magnitude of the radiation resistance depends..upon the point in the antenna system at which the resistance is considered as being inserted. *Ibid.* xvii. 435 The presence of the air in contact with the vibrating diaphragm produces a mechanical radiation resistance.. which varies with frequency. **1975** D. G. FINK *Electronics Engineers' Handbk.* XIX. 55 A loudspeaker designed to resonate at a low frequency combines decreasing velocity with increasing radiation resistance to yield a uniform response within the frequency range where the assumptions hold. **1924** *Lancet* 23 Aug. 365/1 Dodds and Webster have recently summarised the literature of *radiation sickness in *The Lancet*. **1948** *Sci. News* VII. 8 Radiation sickness, its prevention, its treatment, is..a problem for the medical services. **1961** R. D. BAKER *Essent. Path.* vii. 127 Heavy dosages of x-ray, especially to the upper abdomen, may lead to radiation sickness, nausea and vomiting shortly after the radiation. **1978** *Sci. Amer.* May 49/3, 10 percent of the people exposed to 150 rads will die from radiation sickness. **1922** tr. Krönig & Friedrich (*title*) The principles of physics and biology of *radiation therapy. **1961** R. D. BAKER *Essent. Path.* vii. 127 Radiation therapy of the cervix under abnormal circumstances may result in damage to the mucosa of the rectum or of the urinary bladder. **1980** *Daily Tel.* 4 Dec. 6/8 It can implant radioactive seeds by needle when..patients can no longer sustain external radiation therapy. **1868** *Symons's Meteorol. Mag.* III. 7 The sensitiveness of a terrestrial *radiation thermometer. **1924** *Lancet* 4 Oct. 725/1 (*heading*) Chloride metabolism in *radiation treatment. **1968** *Brit. Med. Bull.* XXIV. 190/1 Someone without training using the computer procedure can produce a competent radiation-treatment plan. **1970** PASSMORE & ROBSON *Compan. Med. Stud.* II. xxxiii. 7/2 A *radiation ulcer of the skin often fails to heal.

radiational (reɪdɪˈeɪʃənəl), *a.* [f. prec. + -AL[1].] Of, pertaining to, or involving radiation.

1902 *Encycl. Brit.* XXXIII. 213/1 This wider theory [of the electric telegraph] is founded upon Maxwell's theory of electromagnetic radiation, and may be accordingly termed the radiational theory. **1949** KOESTLER *Insight & Outlook* xi. 156 The 'particles' in the atom..are capable of persisting as functional wholes in the teeth of mechanical, thermal and radiational disturbances. **1964** M. MCLUHAN *Understanding Media* (1967) xix. 198 The wheel and the road expressed and advanced this explosion by a radiational or center-margin pattern. **1969** *Sci. Jrnl.* Jan. 64/2 Analysis of the tides at other localities suggests that the ratio of radiational: gravitational tide of O-2 is fairly typical.

Hence **radiˈationally** *adv.*

1969 R. BUCKMINSTER FULLER *Operating Man. Spaceship Earth* vi. 76, I would like to inventory rapidly the system variables which I find to be by far the most powerful in consideration of our present life-regenerating evolution aboard our spaceship as it is continually refueled radiationally by the Sun and other cosmic radiation.

radiationless (reɪdɪˈeɪʃənlɪs), *a. Physics* and *Chem.* [f. RADIATION + -LESS.] Not involving the emission of electromagnetic radiation.

1919 *Proc. Nat. Acad. Sci.* V. 590 For any real motion, where the velocity is less than that of light,.. radiationless orbits, other than straight lines uniformly described, are impossible. **1931** *Proc. R. Soc.* A. CXXXII. 668 It is uncertain whether these γ-rays are actually emitted or whether the β-ray lines from which their existence is inferred are due to a radiationless transition. **1939** *Trans. Faraday Soc.* XXXV. 142 The radiationless transfer of energy from A to A' is caused by the close electrical coupling (resonance) between the electrons in atoms close together as in crystals. **1974** *Nature* 15 Mar. 196/1 The excited molecule loses its energy, first, by radiationless conversion to the lower excited singlet state and finally by fluorescence from this state at 28,600 cm^{-1}.

Hence **radiˈationlessly** *adv.*

1974 GILL & WILLIS *Pericyclic Reactions* v. 137 However, the BO 'hole' provides a mechanism for the system to relax radiationlessly into the ground state.

radiative (ˈreɪdɪətɪv), *a.* [f. as RADIATE *v.* + -IVE.] **a.** Pertaining to, connected with, radiation; having the quality of radiating. Also, occurring by means of radiation; involving or accompanied by the emission of radiation.

1837 WHEWELL *Hist. Induct. Sc.* (1857) II. 383 In this manner the radiative effect of a body could be more precisely traced. **1870** TYNDALL *Heat* xi. §453. 343 Showing the superior radiative power of this gas over air. **1889** *Nature* 28 Nov. 81 Our own sun falls nearly as far short of the radiative strength of Arcturus. **1894** *Mem. R. Astron. Soc.* LI. 145 There are two causes affecting the distribution of density, which respectively cease at different known points, namely, convection at a uniform distribution, and unequal radiative cooling at the distribution given on p. 144. **1930** *Proc. R. Soc.* A. CXXIX. 2 Radiative transitions in the nucleus resulting in the emission of a γ-ray. **1934** *Nature* 10 Feb. 211/1 The energy of these rays corresponds roughly to that which would be emitted in the radiative combination of a neutron and a proton. **1958** *New Scientist* 16 Jan. 14/1 A radiative heat loss due to this process (technically known as *bremsstrahlung* radiation) is thus an unavoidable feature of a thermonuclear reactor. **1973** W. K. ROSE *Astrophysics* ii. 63 The transport of energy in the interior of a star can be caused by radiative transport, convection, or electron conduction. **1977** J. NARLIKAR *Struct. Universe* ii. 29 The star therefore is no longer completely convective, and it develops a 'radiative core'. That is, the energy transport in the core takes place by radiation rather than convection.

b. ***radiative capture***, capture of a particle by an atomic nucleus with accompanying emission of one or more gamma rays; ***radiative equilibrium***, a state of equilibrium in which the total energy flux emitted is equal to that absorbed; a state of equilibrium in which radiation is the predominant energy transport mechanism.

1926 A. S. EDDINGTON *Internal Constitution of Stars* v. 99 Radiative equilibrium has a natural precedence over convective equilibrium, since in radiative equilibrium convection ceases, whereas in convective equilibrium radiation remains and tends to destroy it. **1934** D. BRUNT *Physical & Dynamical Meteorol.* vii. 138 It is impossible for the upper region of the atmosphere to be kept in an isothermal condition by radiative equilibrium when it is only irradiated from below by long-wave radiation. **1935** *Physical Rev.* XLVII. 508/1 (*heading*) Radiative capture of protons by carbon. **1953** B. STRÖMGREN in G. P. Kuiper *Sun* ii. 40 In regions in radiative equilibrium, i.e., where the transport of energy.. is entirely by radiation, the transport by convection and conduction being negligible by comparison, the temperature gradient is given by equation (4*a*). **1962** *Newnes Conc. Encycl. Nuclear Energy* 287/1 In radiative capture the compound nucleus de-excites through intermediate states to the ground state, each step yielding a γ-ray.

Hence **ˈradiatively** *adv.*, by means of (esp. electromagnetic) radiation; with emission of radiation.

1957 F. HOYLE *Black Cloud* ix. 177 The volume of information that can be transmitted radiatively is enormously greater than the amount that we can communicate by ordinary sound. **1969** *Nature* 16 Aug. 727/1 The permitted lines are probably radiatively excited from the lowest levels. **1973** *Physics Bull.* Apr. 243/1 The introduction of thallium into the crystal allows the exciton to decay radiatively by luminescence.

radiato- (reɪdɪˈeɪtəʊ), used as a comb. form of RADIATE *a.* to modify an adj., with the meaning 'in a radial direction, in the manner of rays', as ***radiato-patent***, ***-porose***, ***-striate***, ***-sulcate***, ***-undulate***.

1819 *Pantologia* X, *Radiato-patent*, in botany. Radiate-expanding: or, spreading out like rays. Applied to the stigma. **1850** DANA *Geol.* App. i. 702 The surface of the cast towards the beak is smooth, and not finely radiato-striate. *Ibid.* 713 Upper and under-surfaces correspondingly radiato-undulate. **1868** tr. *Figuier's Ocean World* v. 119 *Cœloptychium*,.. radiato-porose above, flat and radiato-sulcate below.

radiator (ˈreɪdɪeɪtə(r)). [agent-n. in L. form from RADIATE *v.*] **1. a.** One who or that which radiates; *esp.* anything which radiates light, heat or sound waves.

1836 BRANDE *Chem.* (ed. 4) 516 The polished metals are very imperfect radiators and receivers of heat. **1858** LARDNER *Hand-bk. Nat. Phil., Hydrost.*, etc. 373 The power of thermal rays.. is augmented by raising the temperature of the radiator. **1879** PROCTOR *Pleas. Ways Sc.* xvi. 364 Glass .. is a good radiator, so that dew is freely deposited on glass objects. **1927** *Physics Abstr.* A. XXX. 415 (*heading*) Performance and design of sound radiator consisting of an acoustic transformer and horn. **1936** P. M. MORSE *Vibration & Sound* vii. 240 Few radiators of sound are so much longer than they are wide that they behave like long cylinders, but many radiators behave like spherical sources. **1962** A. NISBETT *Technique Sound Studio* iii. 60 'Cellos and basses differ from violins and violas in that they are much more efficient as radiators in the lower register. **1977** G. PORGES *Appl. Acoustics* xii. 140 A dipole is a less efficient radiator of sound than a monopole, and a quadrupole is even less efficient.

b. A small chamber or compartment heated by means of steam or hot air, and radiating warmth into a room or other place. Now usu. a tank or compact array of pipes, having a large surface area, which is heated usu. by circulating hot water and gives off warmth also by convection. Also applied to various kinds of electric space heater.

1851 C. CIST *Cincinnati* 213 The introduction of evaporatory radiators and registers. **1875** KNIGHT *Dict. Mech.* 1853/1. **1891** W. P. BUCHAN *Ventilation* xv. 166 The so-called steam or hot-water 'radiators' heat principally by conduction, as may be easily proved by suspending one thermometer, say, a foot high right above the 'radiator' and another right in front of it and six inches from it. **1899** *Daily News* 3 June 8/7 In cold weather some form of 'radiator' should always be used by those who can afford it. *a* **1910** 'MARK TWAIN' *Europe & Elsewhere* (1923) 178 The German stove.. is lovely,.. compared with any 'radiator' that has yet been intruded upon the world. **1959** N. MAILER *Advts. for Myself* (1961) 153 She has shut the window and neglected to turn off the radiator. The room is stifling. **1966** N. CHAPMAN *Heating* 37 A storage radiator.. provides the most comfortable conditions in a room early in the morning because the air is warmer from the heat given off during the charging period. **1975** R. H. WARING *All about Home Heating* ii. 14 Modern radiators are usually either of panel type or radiant panel, of relatively slim construction and with inlet and outlet connection at the bottom on each end. Panel radiators have a ribbed surface. Radiant panel radiators consist of a radiator tube attached to the back of a metal sheet.. or sandwiched between two metal sheets for complete enclosure.

c. Part of the cooling system of a liquid-cooled internal-combustion engine, consisting of a large bank of thin tubes in which the circulating fluid (freq. water) is cooled by the surrounding air after passing round the engine.

1900 *Sci. Amer. Suppl.* 25 Aug. 20617/3 The present water circulating plan.. has.. the defect of complicating the mechanism by the addition of tanks, radiators and pumps, causing multiplied trouble. **1905** *Daily Chron.* 6 July 5/2 Lancia had negotiated half of the round when his radiator suddenly burst, and left him stranded. **1932** KIPLING *Limits & Renewals* 80 Private Gillock.. was stage-whispering me for leave to 'put a shot into his radiator'. **1935** C. G. BURGE *Compl. Bk. Aviation* 271/2 In a single-engined aircraft the radiator may be mounted below the fuselage. **1970** K. BALL *Fiat 600, 600D Autobook* iv. 40/2 Maintenance of the cooling system is confined to periodical flushing of the radiator, refilling with antifreeze solutions for cold weather or clean water for warm, [etc.].

d. An aerial for transmitting (and often also receiving) radio waves.

1903 *Sci. Amer. Suppl.* 4 July 23000/3 The 'aerial', or radiator; that was, the tall wire which.. sent electric waves off into the ether. **1947** D. G. FINK *Radar Engin.* v. 303 The radiator forms the radiated beam and presents the absorption area for reception of the echoes. **1952** E. A. LAPORT *Radio Antenna Engin.* ii. 94 The type of radiator that is generally used for medium-frequency broadcasting is the straight uniform vertical with its lower end near ground. **1973** W. E. KOCK *Radar, Sonar, & Holography* ii. 42 In radars and sonars, this ability to steer the beam electrically, that is, without moving the radiator, permits much larger arrays to be used.

2. *attrib.* and *Comb.*, (chiefly sense 1 c), as ***radiator cap***, ***fluid***, ***grill(e***.

1913 *Collier's* 11 Jan. II. 9/1 If it has a new radiator cap or a new form of rear spring suspension.. it is immediately surrounded by a crowd of motor sharps. **1948** M. LASKI *Tory Heaven* ix. 130 James managed to undo the radiator cap and poured the water in. **1979** *Arizona Daily Star* 5 Aug. C 5/3 (Advt.), Includes pressure-checks of radiator cap, hoses and fittings for leaks. **1972** D. E. WESTLAKE *Bank Shot* ii. 16 Glass was broken, chrome was bent, and.. radiator fluid was making a green puddle on the blacktop. **1938** *Decorative Art* 53/2 The floral designs over the book-cases and the radiator grille are hand-painted on wood. **1959** *Motor* 4 Mar. 168/1 Wider than hitherto, the radiator grille is flanked by combined sidelamps and turn-signal flashers. **1973** D. MILLER *Chinese Jade Affair* xxi. 212 Potter was still in the Mini... I kicked the radiator grill in passing.

radiatory (ˈreɪdɪətərɪ), *a.* [f. as RADIATE *v.* + -ORY.] Radiating, radiative.

1865 ALLMAN in *Intellect. Observer* (No. 38) 85 A series of tubular cells.. extending in a radiatory direction from the disc outwards.

radiature (ˈreɪdɪətjə(r)). [f. as prec. + -URE.] Radiation; an act of radiation.

1704 NORRIS *Ideal World* II. iii. 190 The proper business of opticks, to consider the radiature of light. **1883** *Nature* 8 Feb. 351 In these radiatures motion is conveyed through space by transfer of vibratory motions.

radical (ˈrædɪkəl), *a.* and *sb.* Also 5–6 radycall, 5–7 -icall. [ad. late L. *rādīcāl-is* (Augustine), f. *rādīc-* RADIX. F. *radical* (15–16th c. as adj.) is the direct source of sense 4 of the sb.]

A. *adj.* Of or pertaining to a root or to roots.

1. a. ***radical humidity***, ***humour***, ***moisture***, ***sap***: In mediæval philosophy, the humour or moisture naturally inherent in all plants and animals, its presence being a necessary condition of their vitality. So ***radical heat***.

1398 TREVISA *Barth. De P.R.* XVII. xlii. (Bodl. MS.) Radical humouris isente into þe herbe. ? *a* **1412** LYDG. *Two Merchants* 313 Thilke humydite i-called radical. **1471** RIPLEY *Comp. Alch.* VI. xx. in Ashm. (1652) 166 Moysture radycall, whych theyr begynnyng was. **1530** RASTELL *Bk. Purgat.* III. vii. 2 The radycall naturall humour of that appell wyll increase whyle it is growynge. **1601** HOLLAND *Pliny* I. 531 The better will she imploy her radicall sap and moisture to fructifie and yeeld good store of grapes. **1643** SIR T. BROWNE *Relig. Med.* I. §43 Though the radicall humor containe in it sufficient oyle for seventy, yet I perceive in some it gives no light past thirty. **1772** FLETCHER *Appeal* Wks. 1795 I. 46 His intense application hath.. almost dried up his radical moisture. **1818** LADY MORGAN *Autobiog.* (1859) 235 Our wood fire scarcely suffices to keep up the radical heat. **1863** KINGSLEY *Water Bab.* 330 Being a water-baby, his radical humours were of a moist and cold nature. *fig.* **1626** BP. ANDREWES *Serm.* (1856) I. 445 These affections be the radical humour or sap. **1635** QUARLES *Embl.* IV. xii. 230 Whilst thus my sorrow-wasting soule was feeding Upon the rad'cal Humour of her thought. **1655** FULLER *Ch. Hist.* IV. ix. §15 Edward.. took order, that these Aliens should no longer prey on the Radical moisture of this Land.

b. Of qualities: Inherent in the nature or essence of a thing or person; fundamental.

1562 BULLEYN *Def. agst. Sickness, Bk. Sicke men* 69 b, It doeth.. consume, and waste the beste humour, or one of the radical vertues. **1611** TOURNEUR *Ath. Trag.* v. i. Wks. 1878 I. 137 These bodies are depriu'd of all The radicall abilitie of nature. **1663** J. HEATH *Flagellum or O. Cromwell* (ed. 2) 4 [Cromwell's] main policy was a radical and original Hypocrisie. **1775** JOHNSON *Tax. no Tyr.* 23 The radical vigour of the Mother-country. **1806** *Med. Jrnl.* XV. 220 The radical diversity of these rival maladies. **1828** J. M. SPEARMAN *Brit. Gunner* (ed. 2) p. xiv, I have pointed out.. a radical error in the graduation of these scales. **1871** R. H. HUTTON *Ess.* (1877) I. Pref. 12 A sneer at the radical rottenness of human nature.

c. *Philos.* ***radical empiricism***: a name given by W. James (1842–1910) to a philosophical position according to which even underlying postulates are regarded as hypotheses to be verified (see quot. 1897); more generally, a rigorous or sceptical empiricism; hence ***radical empiricist***, one who adopts this position. Similarly ***radical pluralism***, ***pluralist***.

1897 W. JAMES *Will to Believe* p. vii, Were I obliged to give a short name to the attitude in question, I should call it that of *radical empiricism*... I say 'empiricism', because it is contented to regard its most assured conclusions concerning matters of fact as hypotheses liable to modification in the course of future experience; and I say 'radical', because it treats the doctrine of monism itself as an hypothesis. *Ibid.* p. ix, This is pluralism, somewhat rhapsodically expressed. He who takes for his hypothesis the notion that it is the permanent form of the world is what I call a radical empiricist. **1904** —— *Ess. Radical Empiricism* (1912) ii. 90 These are the main features of a philosophy of pure experience... In my own mind such a philosophy harmonizes best with a radical pluralism. **1911** —— *Some Prob. Philos.* x. 164 He concluded that such realities as present beings, past events and causes, steps of change and parts of matter, must needs exist in limited amount. This made of him a radical pluralist. **1949** *Mind* LVIII. 369, I remember well the dismay in an undergraduate philosophical society when one of the members.. announced that he had adopted the 'radical pluralism' of this author [*sc.* Russell]. **1965** P. A. BERTOCCI in B. B. Wolman *Scientific Psychol.* xvi. 295 Radical empiricism, synoptic examination as well as analysis—this is the methodology that alone can provide hypotheses which.. will not lose their anchorage in what is phenomenally given. **1973** K. B. MADSEN in D. Berlyne *Pleasure, Reward, Preference* xi. 286 We expect a radical empiricist to be a materialist rather than a dualist.

2. a. Forming the root, basis, or foundation; original, primary.

1560 ROLLAND *Crt. Venus* Prol. 235 Idilnes is Mother Radycall, Of all vicis, and font originall. **1597** HOOKER *Eccl. Pol.* v. lv. §4 They intimate the radicall cause out of which it groweth. *a* **1639** W. WHATELEY *Prototypes* I. xi. (1640) 94 This grace of faith is the radicall grace, that upon which all other graces grow as on their roote. *a* **1677** HALE *Prim. Orig. Man.* IV. ii. 305 Not.. all those kinds which we now see,.. but only those primitive and radical Species. **1755** JOHNSON *Dict.* Pref. ¶50 When the radical idea branches out into parallel ramifications. **1811** PINKERTON *Petral.* Introd. 30 The position that granite is the universally radical rock. **1871** MORLEY *Crit. Misc.* Ser. I. *Vauvenargues* (1878) 4 A syllabus of the radical articles of the French creed of the eighteenth century.

b. *Anat.* = RADICULAR 2 b.

18.. DUNGLISON (cited by Worcester 1860).

3. a. Going to the root or origin; touching or acting upon what is essential and fundamental; thorough; esp. ***radical change***, ***cure***.

1651 BAXTER *Inf. Bapt.* 294 Out of which Radical Regeneration.. the exercised act of Faith and Graces is wont to be educed. **1735** BOLINGBROKE *On Parties* xviii. 220 Such a Remedy might have wrought a radical Cure of the Evil, that threatens our Constitution. **1751** JOHNSON *Rambler* No. 171 ¶3 Desirous to fit men to his purpose by complete and radical corruption. **1802** *Med. Jrnl.* VIII. 353 A radical and systematic change of that mode of living. **1865** SEELEY *Ecce Homo* iv. (ed. 8) 34 Christ undertook a work more radical than that of Moses. **1874** GREEN *Short Hist.* iv. §2. 171 The financial difficulties of the Crown led to a far more radical revolution in the admission into the Great Council.

b. ***radical reform***, a thorough reform; *esp.* as a phrase of English politics in the end of the 18th and early part of the 19th century.

a **1786** J. JEBB in Disney *Life* Wks. 1787 I. 194 The necessity of a substantial and radical reform in the representation. **1798** *Acme & Septimius* in *Anti-Jacobin* 5 Feb., May success..lead..To one grand Radical Reform. **1815** *Paris Chit-Chat* (1816) I. 54 Every body seems sensible of the necessity of radical reform both in politics and in manners. **1830** Gen. P. Thompson *Exerc.* (1842) I. 227 The actual agent..will be a radical reform in what is called the commons house of parliament.

c. Hence ***radical reformer*** = radical *sb.* 5. Also ***radical reformation.***

1781 C. Wyvill *Polit. Papers* (1794) I. vi. viii. 341 While independent men, supported by large bodies of their fellow citizens, have the virtue thus to resist corruption..the hope of a radical reformation cannot be ill-founded. **1809** *Morning Post* 17 June, Reformer radical! I love thy song. **1819** Scott *Let. to T. Scott* 16 Oct. in *Lockhart*, You will learn enough of the doings of the Radical Reformers from the papers.

d. *Politics.* Advocating 'radical reform' (see sense 3 b above) or any thorough political and social change; representing or supporting the extreme section of a political party; hence, in more recent use (orig. *U.S.*) left-wing, revolutionary. Also in *Comb.* with sense 'radical and ——'.

In Britain in the 19th c., the extreme section of the Liberal party was so designated; on the continent of Europe in the 20th c., parties bearing the title of 'Radical' have in fact freq. tended towards the centre or even a conservative standpoint.

1820 Shelley *Œdipus* i. 12 Kings and laurelled Emperors, Radical butchers. **1832** J. S. Mill *Let.* 17 Sept. in *Wks.* (1963) XII. 117 Several friends of mine, radical-utilitarians of a better than the ordinary sort. **1835** *Knickerbocker* VI. 92 The tendency of Americans, instead of being aristocratic, is decidedly radical. **1837** Disraeli in *Corr. w. Sister* 21 Nov. (1886) 75 Wakley made a most Radical speech and amendment. **1839** *Gentl. Mag.* Nov. 519/1 These Essays are intended to advocate the popular or radical cause. **1840** Carlyle *Chartism* 5 Radical members, above all, friends of the people. **1841** S. Bamford *Life of Radical* I. 58 The presumptuous appearance of a radical hat. **1844** C. M. Yonge *Abbeychurch* xiv. 303 The window..was adorned with all the worst caricatures which had found their way to Abbeychurch, the portraits of sundry radical leaders. **1846** J. W. Croker in *C. Papers* (1884) III. xxiv. 90 If Radical measures were to be carried..they should be carried by Radical men. **1847** *Semi-Weekly News* (Fredericksburgh, Va.) 21 Oct. 2/2 The Barnburners with their 'Radical democracy' can never long govern this great State. **1856** Emerson *Eng. Traits, Truth* Wks. (Bohn) II. 55 The radical mob at Oxford. **1865** *Atlanta Daily Intelligencer* 1 Oct. 3/1 The radical Republicans are now proposing a compromise on the negro-suffrage question. **1884** E. W. Hamilton *Diary* 6 Oct. (1972) II. 699 He is sure the Opposition will insist on our strengthening our Navy and he believes that even the 'Radical Economists' will advocate this. **1890** W. James *Princ. Psychol.* I. 24 The more radical-minded reader can always read 'ideational process' for 'idea'. **1905** *Daily Chron.* 30 June 6/2 It is reported that..a Radical-Protectionist Government will take office. **1908** *Ibid.* 6 Apr. 7/4 Under Mr. Asquith, the balance of power in the Government shifts from the Radical-Socialist to the more moderate Radical side. **1912** W. E. Walling *Socialism as it Is* iii. 166 While one element is growing more radical another is growing more conservative and the breach between the Independents and the other Labourites is widening. **1927** W. Irwin *How Red is America?* ii. 47 The half-century when the radical parties were getting their foothold in Europe and America. **1940** B. Miall tr. *Salvatorelli's Conc. Hist. Italy* xx. 616 Since there was an anti-ministerial movement even in the Radical party, Giolitti resigned. **1950** Theimer & Campbell *Encycl. World Politics* 171/2 The radicals..are associated with..the *Union démocratique socialiste et radicale*, in the *Rassemblement des Gauches*..; they still use the old name of radical-socialists, but are not socialist. **1953** *Manch. Guardian Weekly* 1 Jan. 2 He deplored the 'pinks', 'radical cliques' and other victims of the 'Communist line'. **1965** E. Nolte in Rogger & Weber *European Right* 297 The antigovernmental Right..often attacked Hitler for being a Catholic or insufficiently radical. **1968** *Ann. Reg. 1967* 5 Mr Thorpe represented the radical wing [of the Liberal Party], while Mr Lubbock epitomized the suburban vote. **1969** *Ann. Reg. 1968* 491 British students (with the exception of a radical handful at the London School of Economics in 1967) had been quiet and conservative. **1969** [see Marxist *a.*[1]]. **1969** G. S. Jones in Cockburn & Blackburn *Student Power* 38 A country [*sc.* the U.S.] where the hysteria of the Cold War had previously smothered all radical politics. **1974** A. J. Gregor *Fascist Persuasion in Radical Politics* 16 The Fascist emphasis..on the 'primacy of politics', on a 'collectivistic' rather than a 'liberal' social order..are all emphases that have become more and more characteristic of *all* radical political ideologies.

e. Characterized by independence of, or departure from, what is usual or traditional; progressive, unorthodox, or revolutionary (in outlook, conception, design, etc.).

1921 *Daily Colonist* (Victoria) 20 Mar. 24/1 In appearance the Coats car is attractive, but not at all radical in design. **1928** E. O'Neill *Strange Interlude* i. 15 A natural tendency toward a prim provincialism where practical present-day considerations are concerned (though he is most liberal—even radical—in his tolerant understanding of the manners and morals of Greece and Imperial Rome!). **1938** H. A. Murray *Explor. in Personality* iii. 148 Radical sentiments: the origination, promulgation or defence of sentiments, theories or ideologies that are novel, questionable or opposed to tradition. **1958** *Listener* 23 Oct. 648/1, I would describe as radical paintings that make a difference to our ideas about art. The American contribution to radical art in this sense is particularly to be seen in the big picture. **1962** *New Statesman* 25 May 768/2 A true modernist, a radical functionist, would have rejected this basic proposition. **1971** C. Hampden-Turner *Radical Man* i. 17 While Conservative Man is caused to behave, Radical Man imagines and reasons autonomously. **1977** *Western Mail* (Cardiff) 5 Mar. (Rugby Suppl.) 2/7 The 'radical rugby thinker' Jika Travers from Australia and Oxford University, capped as a war veteran at 27.

f. Special collocations in senses 3 d and e, as ***radical chic***, the fasionable affectation of radical left-wing views or of dress, style of life, etc., associated with such views; also *transf.*, those who embody such an affectation; ***radical feminism***, advocacy of radical left-wing views designed to counter the traditional dominance of men over women; hence ***radical feminist*** adj. and sb.; ***radical left*** = New Left; ***radical right***, extremist conservative or fascist views favouring group action to protect or re-instate certain social traditions.

1970 T. Wolfe in *New York* 8 June 40/2 Radical Chic invariably favors radicals who seem primitive, exotic, and romantic, such as the grape workers..the Panthers..and the Red Indians. *Ibid.* 56/1 Radical Chic..is only radical in style; in its heart it is part of Society and its traditions. Politics, like Rock, Pop, and Camp, has its uses; but [etc.]. **1973** *Guardian* 5 Mar. 20/4 (*heading*) For a taste of radical chic—try a plum jam buttie. **1977** *Rolling Stone* 24 Mar., Right now bisexuality is the big radical chic on campuses. **1977** *Daily Tel.* 16 July 12 The environmental lobby, a cause largely invented by the Manhattan radical chic. **1980** *Church Observer* Apr. 18/2 By translating the actions of ancient Judea into modern radical chic, the whole story [*sc.* *Monty Python's Life of Brian*] comes dangerously close to life today and threatens to upset the safe, neat and tidy arrangement we favour in Sunday morning religion. **1923** A. R. Wadia *Ethics of Feminism* i. 19 These would also have to be studied so as to enable us to judge how far they afford a stable basis for the advocates of radical feminism. **1971** S. Firestone *Dialectic of Sex* ii. 16 In the radical feminist view, the new feminism is not just the revival of a serious political movement for social equality. **1976** *Papers on Patriarchy Conference London 76* 3 Radical feminists/separatists place importance on the subjective, personal perceptions of oppression to provide the guidelines for 'political' action. **1977** *Rolling Stone* 24 Mar., I've read some radical feminist reviews of your book which gripe about your excessive closeness to men. **1969** *N.Y. Times Mag.* 9 Feb. 34/1 They are members of a newly assertive radical left group called Women's Liberation. **1970** *New Yorker* 26 Sept. 136 The Wallace voters and the radical right—often ideologically distinct, though not always—and the radical left. **1977** *Times* 21 Sept. 1/6 Although the 'radical left' are still only a minority in the institutes of higher education, they deserved serious..rebuttal. **1954** T. Taylor *Grand Inquest* (1955) p. xvi, The Communist *Weltanschauung* and conception of the individual's relation to the State have much more in common with the nationalism of the radical right than with the liberal internationalism of the left. **1965** E. Weber in Rogger & Weber *European Right* 20 The violence and brutality of the radical Right became acceptable to conservatives who viewed them as defenders against the threat of a radical Left. **1970** C. Hampden-Turner *Radical Man* (1971) ix. 267 This explains the relative efficiency and speed of organized groups on the Radical Right and the Communist Left. **1977** M. Walker *National Front* v. 117 The [Monday] Club accepts..the name 'Radical Right'.

4. *Math.* **a.** Pertaining to or forming the root of a number or quantity; esp. ***radical sign***, the sign $\surd$ used to indicate that a root of the number to which it is prefixed is to be extracted; † ***radical number*** (see quot. 1557).

Used by itself, the sign $\surd$ indicates that the square root is to be taken; for the cube, biquadratic, etc., appropriate numbers are added, $^{3}\surd$, $^{4}\surd$, etc.

1557 Recorde *Whetst.* Sj, Nombers radicalle, whiche commonly bee called nombers irrationalle... Other men call them more aptly Surde numbers. **1570** Dee *Math. Pref.* 5, I..do giue to this Practise, the name of the Arithmetike of Radicall numbers. **1668** T. Brancker tr. *Rhonii Algebra* 43 In the quotient subjoyn the surd part with its first radical Sign. *a* **1746** MacLaurin *Algebra* (1748) i. viii. 44 Placing above the radical Sign the Number that denominates what kind of Root is required. **1897** H. F. Baker *Abelian Functions* 377 The most important of the radical functions are those which are square roots of rational functions.

b. *Geom.* Used in several terms relating to the intersection of circles and planes, esp. ***radical axis, centre, circle, plane*** (cf. quots.).

1848–55 Salmon *Conic Sect.* (ed. 3) ix. §111 The line *S*–*S′*..has been called [*Note.* By M. Gaulier, of Tours..1813] the radical axis of the two circles. *Ibid.* §113 Given any three circles, if we take the radical axis of each pair of circles, these three lines will meet in a point, and this point is called the radical centre of the three circles. **1889** J. Casey *Spher. Trig.* 101 The circle of the system *S*, whose plane passes through the centre of the sphere, is called the radical circle of the system.

5. *Philol.* **a.** Of or belonging to the roots of words; connected with, based on, roots. ***radical word***, a simple uncompounded word having the form of, or directly based on, a root.

1577 Dee *Relat. Spir.* i. (1659) 75 No word in his radical form is extended. **1605** Bacon *Adv. Learn.* ii. f. 59v, They [*sc.* the Chinese] haue a vast multitude of Characters, as many (I suppose), as Radicall words. **1641** Milton *Animadv.* i. Wks. (1851) 189 They thought it best not to screw the English mouth to a harsh forreigne termination, so they kept the radicall word. **1777** J. Richardson *Dissert. East. Nations* 2 Radical words in any tongue are expressive of certain customs, objects and modes of thinking. **1824** L. Murray *Eng. Gram.* (ed. 5) I. 347 Three great principles of accentuation..the radical, the terminational, and the distinctive. **1838–9** Hallam *Hist. Lit.* II. ii. i. 15 The arrangement of the lexicon is not according to an alphabetical but a radical order. **1861** Max Müller *Sc. Lang.* 275 As long as every word..is felt to express its own radical meaning, a language belongs to the first or radical stage. **1921** E. Sapir *Language* ii. 29 Radical-words may and do occur in languages of all varieties.

b. ***radical letter***, (*a*) an original unchanged letter (so also ***radical sound***); (*b*) a letter belonging to the root of a word.

In sense (*a*) chiefly used of Welsh initial consonants, which are liable to be altered by a preceding word; in (*b*) chiefly of the consonants (commonly three in number) of Hebrew roots, and *spec.* of those which appear in roots only.

(*a*) *c* **1645** Howell *Lett.* (1650) I. 457 Wallia, which the Romans called Gallia, turning *W* into *G*,..yet the Walloon keeps his radical letter to this day. **1724** W. Gambold *Welsh Gram.* (1727) 114 Table of Words and Particles:..shewing what effect They haue on the radical initial Letters of Subsequent Words. **1833** *Ibid.* (ed. 3) 13 After the prefix *gor*, the initials *b, d, g, m, r*, assume their Light sound; but after *tra* the retain their Radical sound; as *gorfod*,..*trablin*.

(*b*) *a* **1653** Gouge *Comm. Hebr.* xi. 11 Sarah hath all the radical letters in it. **1658** Sir T. Browne *Gard. Cyrus* v. 71 Why the radicall Letters in the Pentateuch should equall the number of the Souldiery of the Tribes. **1762** Parkhurst *Heb. Gram.* (1778) 3 Although the radical Letters..are never Servile, yet the servile letters are very often radical. **1831** Lee *Hebr. Gram.* (1832) 222 One of the two last radical letters of any word, when both are the same, may..be rejected.

†**c.** Exhibiting the roots or radical letters. *Obs.*

1623 Lisle *Ælfric on O. & N. Test.* Pref. 7 Huterus..in his Catalogue..before his radicall Hebrew Bible.

†**6.** *Astrol.* Belonging to the radix of an astrological calculation. ***radical question*** (see quot. 1647). *Obs.*

1621 Burton *Anat. Mel.* i. ii. i. iv, Any of those radicall promissors in the geniture. **1647** Lilly *Chr. Astrol.* 121 The Question then shall be taken for radicall, or fit to be judged, when as the Lord of the hour at the time of proposing the Question..and the Lord of the Ascendant or first House, are of one Triplicity, or be one. **1654** Culpepper *Opus Astrol., Aphorisms* §69 A Radical Figure resembles either the nativity or the revolution of the nativity of the Querent. **1679** Moxon *Math. Dict.* 38 The moons coming to the.. Radical place, where she was at the beginning of the sickness.

7. *Mus.* Belonging to the root of a chord, esp. ***radical bass, cadence, number*** (cf. quots.).

1753 Chambers *Cycl. Supp.* s.v., Radical numbers..in the Italian music, are, 2, 3, 4, 5, 6, 7, 8, 9, and sometimes 10, which are often met with in musical compositions, to denote the accords of the thorough basses. **1867** Macfarren *Harmony* iii. 97 According to the radical progression of ascending 4ths. **1873** H. C. Banister *Music* 69 By the root of a chord, or its Radical Bass, is meant its Bass-note in its original, uninverted form.

8. *Bot.* Of or belonging to the root of a plant; *esp.* of leaves or stalks: Springing directly from the root-stock or the stem close to the root.

1753 Chambers *Cycl. Suppl.* s.v. *Leaf*, Radical Leaf, that which grows immediately from the root of a plant, not from the stalk. **1766** *Museum Rust.* VI. 47 From the top of this turnep rise a number of leaves,..which answer to the radical leaves in other plants. **1851** Richardson *Geol.* vii. 203 Leaves..proceeding from the crown or radical plate. **1861** Bentley *Man. Bot.* (1870) 57 On young roots we find cells ..which are of the nature of hairs, and have therefore been termed radical hairs.

†**9.** *Chem.* ***radical vinegar***, an old name for acetic acid. *Obs.*

1797 *Encycl. Brit.* (ed. 3) IV. 592/1 Experience has shown that radical vinegar differs considerably in its properties from the common acid. **1819** *Pantologia* X. s.v., The acid thus obtained..was formerly distinguished by the names of radical vinegar, and vinegar of Venus.

B. *sb.* (elliptical or absolute uses of the adj.)

1. *Philol.* **a.** A root; a word or part of a word which cannot be analysed into simpler elements.

1641 Wilkins *Mercury* xiii. (1707) 57 The Hebrew.. Language consists of fewest Radicals. **1677** Plot *Oxfordsh.* 284 He [Dalgarno] published a Specimen..containing but 500 Radicals, all the Particles being brought from the Radicals by which they are resolved. **1797** *Encycl. Brit.* (ed. 3) V. 463 The Welsh, the Cornish and the Armoric dialects, whose radicals are so much alike [etc.]. **1822** *Good's Study Med.* IV. 592 It has been shown, that the real radical is the Hebrew term..(tsora). **1874** Sayce *Compar. Philol.* i. 54 Words derived from the same radical will often assume different forms in different languages.

b. A radical letter (see 5 b above).

1652–62 Heylin *Cosmogr.* Introd. (1674) 8/2 Divers Cities in that tract, which still preserve the Radicals of Hull or Chull. **1724** W. Gambold *Welsh Gram.* (1727) 2 Ch.. being a radical, is ever attended with *w.* **1784** Henley *Note* in *Beckford's Vathek* (1786) 263 On his forehead the radicals of cafer [or infidel] are said to be impressed. **1870** Helfenstein *Compar. Gram. Teut. Lang.* 410 The radical is either *a* or *ê*... The radical of the perfect is of course modified by the reduplication.

c. One of the set of basic Chinese characters (usu. reckoned to number 214) which, occas. in modified form, constitute elements, freq. with semantic significance, in the composition of other characters and are a means by which characters can be classified and arranged in dictionaries. Cf. phonetic *sb.*

[**1736** R. Brookes tr. *Du Halde's Hist. China* II. 393 As in Hebrew there are radical letters..so likewise the Chinese have their radical characters; for instance the characters of mountains, of trees,..under which must be sought all that belongs to mountains, trees.] **1824** J. Johnson *Typographia* xii. 368 (*heading*) Table of the Chinese Radicals. *Ibid.* 369 Each Radical is placed at the head of a new family of characters. **1834** *Chinese Repository* May 31 The most conspicuous portions of characters were adopted as 'heads of tribes', which in Europe have been called keys and radicals... The radicals..rarely have any relation to the sounds of the characters of which they form component parts. **1874** [see phonetic *sb.*]. **1907** W. Hillier *Chinese Lang.* i. 4 We..divide Chinese characters into two parts—one, the *sound* indicator, to which the name 'phonetic' is generally given; the other, the *idea* indicator, which is commonly called the 'radical'... The radicals are limited in number, there being only 214 of them altogether. **1921** *New*

China Review III. 390 The sign..does not figure..as a phonetic but rather as the genuine hieroglyph, to which a classifying radical has been added. **1948** R. A. D. FORREST *Chinese Lang.* ii. 38 After we have deducted the 'sheep' device from each of the three examples, the part remaining in each case is known as the 'radical', or better, as the 'signific'. **1973** *Sci. Amer.* Feb. 54/1 A dictionary published in 1971..has merged some radicals, reducing the number to 189. **1978** *Nagel's Encycl.-Guide: China* 88 Character 14 was described as consisting of a phonetic and a radical; the phonetic showed the reader that the word was pronounced in much the same way as 'door', and the radical showed that the meaning was linked with 'ear'.

2. a. A basis, a fundamental thing or principle.

1657 VINES *Lord's Supp.* (1677) 357 Covenant-benefits, convenant graces, the radicals, the vitals. **1808** *Med. Jrnl.* XIX. 41 Water doubtless concurs..to produce this effect, by supplying two radicals, which become assimilated to the other nutritive principles. **1833** HOLLAND *Manuf. in Metal* II. 304 With reference to a similar radical, that is to say, the English penny.

b. A root or radicle.

1850 M^cCOSH *Div. Govt.* III. i. (1874) 292 They are roots or radicals supporting all visible truth, but themselves unseen. **1897** *Allbutt's Syst. Med.* III. 380 The..radicals of the portal vein.

3. *Math.* **a.** A quantity forming or expressed as a root of another quantity.

1738 DE MOIVRE in *Phil. Trans. Abridg.* VIII. 271 (title) Of the Reduction of Radicals to more Simple Terms. *a* **1746** MACLAURIN *Algebra* (1748) VI. 117 Multiply any two Radicals as 2 *xy* by 2 *xz*. **1798** HUTTON *Course Math.* II. 298 Expand the radical or fraction..into an infinite series of simple terms. **1868** CAYLEY *Math Papers* (1874) VII. 14 The expression cannot contain any radical such as [etc.].

b. The radical sign.

1780 HUTTON in *Phil. Trans.* LXX. 401 Where the two denominators under the radicals differ by 4. **1882** C. SMITH *Conic Sect.* (1885) 33 It is necessary and sufficient that the quantity under the radical should be a perfect square.

4. *Chem.* An element or atom (*simple radical*), or a group of these (*compound radical*), forming the base of a compound and remaining unaltered during the ordinary chemical reactions to which this is liable. (See also RADICLE.)

Introduced (in French) by G. de Morveau, 1787. When used without adj., 'radical' usually denotes a compound radical, and is thus contrasted with 'element' or 'atom'.

1816 J. SMITH *Panorama Sc. & Art* II. 343 Oxygen is called the radical or base of the gas. **1845** J. E. DAY tr. *Simon's Anim. Chem.* I. 141 If we knew more of the composition of the extractive matters, we should doubtless find a radical common to all of them. **1881** *Nature* No. 618. 415 Compounds of hydrogen with elements or radicals like chlorine.

5. *Politics.* An advocate of 'radical reform' (see A. 3 b); one who holds the most advanced views of political reform on democratic lines. In the 19th c., the name was applied to the extreme section of the Liberal party; now *gen.*, an advocate of any thorough political or social change; one who belongs to the extreme section of a political party; a member or supporter of a radical movement (cf. sense A. 3 d), a left-winger or revolutionary. Also *transf.*

1802 in *Spirit Pub. Jrnls.* VI. 4 The sagacious only could have forseen that he should have become a r—c—l. **1819** SCOTT *Let. to T. Scott* 16 Oct. in *Lockhart*, Radical is a word in very bad odour here, being used to denote a set of blackguards [etc.]. **1822** J. Q. ADAMS *Diary* 16 June in *Memoirs J. Q. Adams* (1875) VI. iii. 22 General Scott..said Archer was a Radical and inclined to be Jacobinical. **1829** *Western Monthly Rev.* II. 593 The schism in the Methodist Church..exists between the sticklers for the ancient structure of episcopalianism..and the *radicals*, who seem to be contending for a more democratic form of church government. **1830** GEN. P. THOMPSON *Exerc.* (1842) I. 269 The term Radical once employed as a name of low reproach, has found its way into high places, and is gone forth as the title of a class, who glory in their designation. **1847** *Semi-Weekly News* (Fredericksburgh, Va.) 21 Oct. 2/2 The Barnburners are the progressives, the radicals. **1862** O. W. NORTON *Army Lett.* (1903) 129, I suppose the radicals have got enough of Burnside now. **1873** H. SPENCER *Stud. Sociol.* xi. 290 It is manifest to the Tory that the Radical does not see the benefit there is in that which he wishes to destroy. **1876** *San Francisco Daily Examiner* 10 Oct. 2/1 The real issue with the Radicals is to divert public attention from the unexemplified corruption of the Radical party during the past eight years. **1888** W. H. DAWSON *German Socialism* i. 22 The association was joined by South German Radicals, North German students... All that came of it was an outbreak..at Frankfort on April 3rd, 1833. **1912** W. E. WALLING *Socialism as it Is* iii. 35 Whether the radical of to-day, the 'State Socialist' favors political democracy or not, depends on whether these 'passive beneficiaries' of the new 'altruistic' system are in a majority. **1921** *N. Amer. Rev.* Aug. 316 Liberals are merely terror-stricken Radicals. **1938** N. M. BUTLER *Family of Nations* vi. 86 There are very few radicals who are liberals; radicals are almost without exception advocates of compulsion in some one of its forms. **1942** E. PAUL *Narrow St.* iv. 35 Some radical that year [*sc.* 1923] (they called them anarchists, not communists, then) had taken a pot shot at Léon Daudet. **1946** E. O'NEILL *Iceman Cometh* (1947) I. 10 There is a foreign atmosphere about him, the stamp of an alien radical, a strong resemblance to the type Anarchist as portrayed, bomb in hand, in newspaper cartoons. **1950** [see sense A. 3 d above]. **1962** S. E. FINER *Man on Horseback* iv. 59 The Egyptian army officers were..right-wing radicals..with motivations much more akin to the Nazi storm-troopers. **1976** *Guardian* 8 Nov. 2/6 Hundreds of police sealed off the red brick social club where the Right-wing radicals gathered. **1977** *New Yorker* 1 Aug. 49/1 A radical—someone who continued to defend the Soviet revolution after other Socialists had turned against it.

fig. **1822** COBBETT *Weekly Reg.* 30 Mar. 779 Love is a great leveller; a perfect Radical. **1831** TRELAWNEY *Adv. Younger Son* xcvii, Gout, apoplexy, dropsy..are in their nature, radicals.

b. *ellipt.* A white hat, formerly affected by Radicals (in consequence of one having been worn by Henry Hunt at various political meetings in 1820).

1828 *Lights & Shades* I. 294 A whity-brown radical on his head, the edges of which are worn down to the brown-paper foundation. (Cf. *radical hat* in c.)

Hence **'radical** *v. intr.*, to act like a radical.

1867 CARLYLE *Remin.* (1881) II. 219 The notions they seemed 'reforming' (and radicalling, and quarrelling with their superiors) upon!

'radicale. *Bot. rare.* [In form = L. *rādīcāle* neut. sing. of *rādīcālis* RADICAL, but perh. intended for *radicle* or *radicule*.] = RADICLE.

1763 GOLDSM. *Misc. Wks.* (1837) II. 544 The radicale or incipient root,..when shot into the ground, imbibes nourishment from thence. **1847** W. E. STEELE *Field Bot.* 158 A large, many-leaved plumule, and an inferior radicale.

'radicalish, *a.* [f. RADICAL *a.* and *sb.* + -ISH[1].] Characterized by, or suggestive of, political radicalism.

1837 R. H. BARHAM *Let.* 29 Apr. (1870) II. 24 There is a sort of Radicalish tone about *Oliver Twist* which I don't altogether like.

radicalism ('rædɪkəlɪz(ə)m). [f. RADICAL *a.* or *sb.* + -ISM.]

1. a. The political views or principles characteristic of radicals.

1820 *Chron.* in *Ann. Reg.* I. 418 You are cherishing in the mind of the multitude the spirit of 'radicalism'. **1852** SMEDLEY *L. Arundel* xxiv. 179 In all cases of incipient radicalism, chartist tendencies, or socialist symptoms, his Grace was an infallible specific. **1870** DICKENS *Lett.* (1880) II. 436, I was determined that my Radicalism should not be called in question.

b. *transf.* Thoroughness of method.

1830 GEN. P. THOMPSON *Exerc.* (1842) I. 306 This is an attempt to carry radicalism into Geometry; always meaning by radicalism, the application of sound reason to tracing consequences to their roots. **1885** MAX MÜLLER in *19th Cent.* XVIII. 921 There is a true radicalism in scholarship, which despises all measures which do not go to the roots of things.

c. Views or principles favouring radical social or political change and reform (see RADICAL *a.* 3 d).

1899 C. B. R. KENT *Eng. Radicals* i. 4 When contentment reigns, and there is satisfaction with the present, then radicalism languishes. **1925** tr. *Trotsky's Lenin* 45 What a contrast Vera Ivanovna, with her indefinite radicalism, her subjectivity, and her confusion presented to Vladimir Ilyich. *Ibid.* 85 The shell of intellectual radicalism. **1938** H. A. MURRAY *Explor. in Personality* iii. 226 The S [*sc.* subject] favours modern art, the rejection of sex taboos, socialism,..progressive schools, the humane treatment of criminals, etc. Radicalism is usually opposed to authority, to any force that restrains liberty. **1960** A. B. ULAM *Unfinished Revol.* iii. 78 The element of ethnic hostility..may become subdued..if that radicalism is assimilated into socialism. Or it may become expanded if the radicalism is absorbed into a revolutionary movement with nationalistic or fascist characteristics. **1968** *Internat. Encycl. Social Sci.* XIII. 299/1 Radicalism is a part of the general theme of the growth of rationalistic ethics. **1974** J. WHITE tr. *Poulantzas's Fascism & Dictatorship* VI. ii. 282 Like the urban petty bourgeoisie, the small-holders are at once drawn towards 'democratic' radicalism, *and*..especially likely..to give massive support to Bonapartist forms of State.

d. *Psychol.* ***radicalism-conservatism***: an axis of attitude measurement sometimes used for personality testing.

[**1930** T. F. LENTZ in *Jrnl. Social Psychol.* I. 537 Since the original purpose was to measure radicalism and conservatism, statements were chosen which would involve this characteristic. The statements used are drawn from various fields of interest: ethics, education, feminism,..sex and marriage, politics, race relations.] **1944** G. MYRDAL *Amer. Dilemma* II. App. II. 1038 The place of the individual scientist in the scale of radicalism-conservatism has always had strong influences upon both the selection of research problems and the conclusions drawn from research. In a sense it is the master scale of biases in the social sciences. **1953** H. J. EYSENCK *Structure of Human Personality* vii. 224 His [*sc.* Carlson's] second factor, radicalism-conservatism, opposed belief in God to an attitude favourable to pacifism and communism. **1965** R. BROWN *Social Psychol.* x. 535 Our problem..is that communism and fascism are opposite extremes on a left to right or radicalism-conservatism dimension.

2. The subject of (Hebrew) roots.

1849 S. R. MAITLAND *Illustr. Mesmerism* I. 61 No point in Hebrew radicalism would have been considered more clear and indisputable.

radicality (rædɪ'kælɪtɪ). [f. as prec. + -ITY.]

1. Radical state or condition; the fact of being radical.

1646 SIR T. BROWNE *Pseud. Ep.* 147 Equivocall seeds and Hermaphroditicall principles, which contain the radicality and power of different formes. **1685** WALLIS *Alg.* xxv. 107, I..prefix the Root of such Power to the note of Radicality. **1727–41** CHAMBERS *Cycl.* s.v. *Radical*, $\surd$ is the character of radicality, and expresses the square root. **1819** JAS. WILSON *Compl. Dict. Astrol.* 269 Numerous and strong testimonies like these prove the radicality of the question. **1979** *Dædalus* Winter 30 The radicality of these changes..had lent credence to the set of beliefs described above.

2. a. = RADICALISM. **b.** The Radicals, or Radical party.

1820 *Blackw. Mag.* VII. 318 The demons of whiggery and radicality. **1832** J. WILSON *ibid.* XXXII. 722 We shall play one section of you against the other this day, and both sections against the radicality the next. **1841** *Ibid.* XLIX. 549 John remained a year or so opposed to Radicality.

radicalize ('rædɪkəlaɪz), *v.* [f. RADICAL *a.* + -IZE.]

1. *trans.* To make radical in politics; to imbue with radical principles.

1830 LD. ELLENBOROUGH *Diary* 31 July (1881) II. 329 He said Yorkshire was quite radicalised by having four members. **1835** GREVILLE *Mem.* 9 Sept. (1875) III. xxix. 313 That the new councils will be Radical, and that their influence will radicalise the boroughs. **1966** *New Statesman* 11 Feb. 185/2 Volunteers returning from two years living with poor people..find that their notions about the world have been radicalised. **1969** *N.Y. Rev. Books* 30 Jan. 17/2 The strongest force for 'radicalizing the campus' may not, after all, be the Cossacks' whips, as many radical tacticians —including those at Columbia—have thought. **1972** *Maclean's Mag.* Sept. 6/2 Being in prison for eight days.. helped to radicalize me, as it did so many others. **1976** *National Observer* (U.S.) 24 Apr. 17/1 After all, isn't economic freedom one very important kind of human freedom? Obviously it is, and yet many college students, most particularly the radicalized students of the late 1960s, have been unable to make the connection. **1979** *Dædalus* Summer 19 It disrupts the delicate balance of pluralistic societies and radicalizes everyone.

2. *intr.* To become Radical in politics; to uphold Radical principles.

1823 *Blackw. Mag.* XIV. 295 Many an honest squire.. rapidly radicalizing against Mr. Canning. **1839** LADY LYTTON *Cheveley* (ed. 2) I. viii. 184 When it [the Reform Bill] and the Catholic question were both carried..Herbert Grimstone radicalized.

Hence **'radicalized** *ppl. a.*; **'radicalizing** *vbl. sb.* and *ppl. a.*; **radicali'zation.**

1885 G. MEREDITH *Diana* III. v. 92 Such is the condition of a rapidly Radicalizing country! **1889** *Pall Mall G.* 27 July 2 A remarkable instance, this, of the Radicalising of the Liberal party. **1891** *Ibid.* 28 Feb. 7 The rapid Radicalization ..of the Tory party. **1905** *Daily Chron.* 1 May 4/5 The united French Socialist party from now henceforward..will draw to itself..all the radicalising elements in the country. **1935** *Communist* XIV. 884 (*heading*) The radicalization of the masses. *Ibid.* 885 The bourgeoisie..are alarmed at the rapid radicalization of the workers. **1953** R. BENDIX in Bendix & Lipsett *Class, Status & Power* 605 The radicalization of people who had not participated actively in party politics..gave a major impetus to the rise of fascism. **1960** *New Left Rev.* Nov.–Dec. 7/2 This is a question of the radicalisation of Labour politics. **1969** G. S. JONES in Cockburn & Blackburn *Student Power* 53 British students.. are for the first time showing a certain radicalization. **1971** *Nature* 19 Feb. 513/1 What might have been a valuable public discussion on the ethical problems of modern biology ..seems to have tailed off into discussion of the process of radicalization of science and even some of the familiar problems of Vietnam. **1973** *Bulletin* (Sydney) 25 Aug. 26/2 It was an amazing revelation and a radicalising one. **1977** *Time* 27 June 21/1 As in so many other places, the suppression of legitimate, moderate opposition leads to radicalization. **1978** *New York* 3 Apr. 34/3 Those themes also spoke to a significant section of the radicalizing, college-educated young, the members of Students for a Democratic Society.

radically ('rædɪkəlɪ), *adv.* [f. RADICAL *a.* + -LY[2].]

1. With reference to root or origin; primitively, originally, naturally.

1624 DONNE *Serm.* ii. 12 Mercy as it is Radically in God and an essentiall attribute of his. **1671** J. WEBSTER *Metallogr.* xii. 175 Gold may be radically separated into Salt, Sulphur, and Mercury. **1796** MORSE *Amer. Geog.* II. 209 The language, which is called the Manks, is radically Erse, or Irish. **1822** *Good's Study Med.* IV. 592 Psora is allowed to import derivatively, what, upon this explanation, it opposes radically. **1884** tr. *Lotze's Logic* 100 That the different subjects..are all radically one common essence.

2. To or from the root or central part; fundamentally; completely, thoroughly.

1609 [BP. W. BARLOW] *Answ. Nameless Cath.* 152 Naturally inclined (at least radically instructed) to disobedience. **1674** R. GODFREY *Inj. & Ab. Physic* Pref., How to cure a cut Finger radically. **1696** TRYON *Misc.* ii. 53 What is more profitable for all Lovers of Health and Wisdom, than Food that is Radically Clean? **1770** BURKE *Pres. Discont.* Wks. 1808 II. 223 If these be radically and essentially vicious..those men are very unhappy. **1783** —— *Rep. Aff. India* Wks. 1842 II. 12 That India should not be radically and irretrievably ruined. **1822** *Good's Study Med.* I. 136 They..have some tendency to correct the disorder radically. **1871** TYNDALL *Fragm. Sc.* (1879) I. xi. 333 Two radically distinct modes of viewing the subject.

3. *Comb.* ***radically-minded*** adj.

1978 J. ANDERSON *Angel of Death* x. 112 He's..radically-minded, and doesn't go much for that old-fashioned religion.

'radicalness. [f. as prec. + -NESS.] The condition of being radical.

1654 CULPEPPER *Opus Astrol., Aphorisms* §70 This is the most absolute way to judge of the radicalness of a Figure. **1727** BAILEY, *Radicalness*, the Quality of being radical, of having Roots, or of being well-founded. **1843** POE *Purloined Letter* Wks. 1864 I. 278 The radicalness of these differences, which was excessive.

radicant ('rædɪkənt), *a.* *Bot. rare.* [a. L. *rādīcant-*, ppl. stem of *rādīcāre* RADICATE. Cf. F.

radicant.] Producing roots; usually said of parts of a plant which produce adventitious roots.

1753 CHAMBERS *Cycl. Supp.* s.v. *Leaf*, *Radicant Leaf*, one which pushes out roots from its summit, as some of the ferns do. **1866** *Treas. Bot.* 954/2.

radicarian (rædɪˈkɛərɪən), *a. rare.* [f. L. *rādīc-* stem of RADIX + *-arian*.] Of or pertaining to roots (of words).

1880 WHITNEY in *Amer. Jrnl. Philol.* I. 338 The strength of the radicarian theory is that it accords with all that we have learned as to the nature of language.

radicate (ˈrædɪkət), *a.* [ad. L. *rādīcāt-us*, pa. pple. of *rādīcāre*: see next and -ATE².]

†**1.** Rooted, deep-seated, firmly established. *Obs.*

1656 H. MORE *Enthus. Tri.* (1712) 27 Their settled and radicate ignorance. **1720** WELTON *Suffer. Son of God* II. xxiv. 643 The Cleansing of their Radicate Sores. **1768** WHITAKER *Two Serm.* ii. (1770) 39 We..have found it..innate, and radicate in the heart.

†**2.** ***radicate vinegar***: (see RADICAL *a.* 9). *Obs.*

1694 SALMON *Bate's Dispens.* (1713) 571/1 Spirit of Vinegar may also be made radicate, and more strong if it be distilled anew upon Sal-armoniack. *Ibid.*, The Uses of the terebinthinated or radicate Vinegar.

3. *Bot.* Having a root (*Treas. Bot.* 1866).

radicate (ˈrædɪkeɪt), *v.* Now *rare.* Also 6 **radycate**, *pa. pple.* 5–6 **radicate**, 6 *Sc.* **-cait**. [ad. L. *rādīcāt-*, ppl. stem of *rādīcāre* or *rādīcārī* to take root, f. *rādīc-* RADIX.]

1. *trans.* To cause to take root; to plant or establish firmly. Usually *fig.* with reference to qualities. Const. *in*.

a. passively, in pa. pple. (orig. in form *radicate*).

c **1470** HENRYSON *Mor. Fab.* Prol. viii, Lust and appetyte ..in thair myndis sa fast is radicate. **1531** ELYOT *Gov.* II. v, He beinge radicate in pride..continued his way to the Senate. **1560** ROLLAND *Crt. Venus* I. 151 Venus Quene, quhair his hart Radicait Was on all time. **1600** W. WATSON *Decacordon* (1602) 264 No doubt the originall cause of religious change, came..to be radicated in the mournefull effects we now behold. **1676** COLE in *Phil. Trans.* XI. 609, I should think the upper of them to be radicated..at the pylorus. **1775** JOHNSON *Let. to Boswell* 14 Sept., My regard for you is so radicated and fixed, that it is become part of my mind. **1873** H. ROGERS *Orig. Bible* ii. (1874) 93 These [actions] will want that quality which can alone crown them, if not radicated in religious principle.

b. actively (less freq. than prec.).

1531 ELYOT *Gov.* I. iv, Often remembrance..of their estate may happen to radycate in theyr hartes intollerable pride. **1627** W. SCLATER *Exp. 2 Thess.* (1629) 6 By radicating or making more firme Graces receiued. **1720** WELTON *Suffer. Son of God* I. xi. 285 Radicate thy Love within me, O my God, Let it be Rooted Deep. **1788** BURKE *Sp. Warren Hastings* Wks. 1822 XIII. 65 That gulf, which manners, opinions and laws have radicated in the very nature of the people. **1873** H. ROGERS *Orig. Bible* i. (1874) 23 Philosophers who did not care to radicate it [morality] in religion.

†**2.** *intr.* To take root, become established. *Obs.*

1656 in BLOUNT *Glossogr.* **1681** RYCAUT tr. *Gracian's Critick* 134 Trees began there to radicate where but lately a shrub wanted moisture.

radicated (ˈrædɪkeɪtɪd), *ppl. a.* [f. prec.]

1. Rooted, established, etc.

a. of qualities, etc. (freq. in 17th c.).

1633 HART *Diet of Diseased* Introd. 10 As for true radicated Consumptions..she was farre from curing any such. **1679** J. GOODMAN *Penitent Pardoned* II. i. (1713) 150 The breaking off old and radicated customs. **1703** KELSEY *Serm.* 235 The radicated Corruption of all Mankind. **1722** DE FOE *Serious Refl.* v. 215 A Mind of radicated Infidelity.

b. of a person. *rare*⁻¹.

a **1661** FULLER *Worthies, Warwickshire* III. (1662) 123 Had he any assurance, that he had been a radicated Romanist.

†**2.** ***radicated vinegar*** (see RADICAL *a.* 9). *Obs.*

1660 tr. *Paracelsus' Archidoxis* I. IV. 52 Pour thereto the Acetum of the Roote, or Radicated Vinegar.

†**3.** *Bot.* Having roots. *Obs.*

1753 CHAMBERS *Cycl. Supp.* s.v. *Leaf.*

radication (rædɪˈkeɪʃən). [n. of action from *rādīcāre*: see RADICATE *v.* and -ATION. Cf. F. *radication.*] The process of radicating or taking root; the fact of being rooted, firmly established, etc.; also, the manner in which a plant, etc., is rooted; an arrangement or system of roots.

†**a.** of veins or arteries. *Obs.*

1615 CROOKE *Body of Man* 856 As the Liuer is the beginning of Radication and Dispensation to the Veines, so is the Heart to the Arteries. **1638** A. READ *Chirurg.* ii. 14 If the vessell be cut..asunder..that part of it which is next the radication of it, shrinketh up.

b. of plants. *rare.*

1658 SIR T. BROWNE *Gard. Cyrus* iv. 59 Whereby they maintained some proportion to their height, in Trees of large radication. **1727–41** CHAMBERS *Cycl.* s.v., A great number of curious observations on the germination and radication of plants. **1775** ELLIS in *Phil. Trans.* LXVI. 5 To shew in what it differs from what is called radication in plants. **1866** in *Treas. Bot.* 954/2.

c. *fig.* of qualities, states, etc. ? *Obs.* (freq. in the 17th c.).

1615 JACKSON *Creed* IV. ii. §1 Faith..different in want of radication and durability. *a* **1658** C. CARTWRIGHT *Except. agst. Baxter* (1675) 21 The confirmation, radication, and further degree of grace. **1707** NORRIS *Treat. Humility* iii. 97 This shews such a deep and settled radication of vice in us.

†**ˈradicative**, *a. Obs. rare*⁻¹. [f. ppl. stem of L. *rādīcāre* RADICATE + -IVE.] = RADICAL *a.* 3.

1727 DOUGLAS in *Phil. Trans.* XXXV. 318 A Palliative Cure..where a radicative Cure could not be expected.

radice, obs. form of RADISH.

radicel (ˈrædɪsɛl). *Bot.* [ad. mod.L. *radicella*, dim. of RADIX. Cf. F. *radicelle.*] A rootlet.

18.. GRAY *Struct. Bot.* (cited by Worcester 1860). **1819** J. LINDLEY tr. *Richard's Observ. Fruits & Seeds* 68 A slight rim round the base of the radicel. **1944** S. PUTNAM tr. *da Cunha's Rebellion in Backlands* i. 31 Their principal roots are atrophied..and in their place is a wide expanse of secondary radicels, clustered in sap-swollen tubercles.

So **radiˈcellar** *a.*, of the nature of rootlets. **radiˈcellate** *a.*, belonging to the *Radicellata*, a class of polyzoans. **ˈradiceˌllose** *a.*, having rootlets.

1831 MACGILLIVRAY tr. *Richard's Elem. Bot.* 295 Through which one or more radicellar tubercles are to issue. **1881** G. BUSK in *Jrnl. Microsc. Sc.* Jan. 12 *Kinetoskias* and many other radicellate forms. **1881** SPRUCE in *Jrnl. Bot.* X. 12 Stems an inch high,..very sparingly radicellose.

radiche, obs. form of RADISH.

radici-, comb. form of L. *rādix, rādīc-em* RADIX, used in a few terms of *Bot.* and *Zool.*, as **radiˈcicolous** *a.*, living on the roots of a plant. **raˌdiciˈflorous** *a.*, flowering from the root. **raˈdiciform** *a.*, having the form of a root. **radiˈcivorous** *a.*, eating roots.

Cf. F. *radiciflore, -forme, -vore* (Littré).

1843 HUMPHREYS *Brit. Moths* II. 85 They are never.. radicivorous in their habits. **1848** LINDLEY *Introd. Bot.* (ed. 4) II. 104 Two or three radiciform prolongations. **1862** MAYNE *Med. Voc.* (ed. 2), Radiciflorous.

radicidation (ˌrædɪsaɪˈdeɪʃən). [f. L. *radi-āre* to furnish with rays, shine + *oc-cid-ere* to strike down, kill + -ATION.] The treatment of food with ionizing radiation so as to reduce the number of micro-organisms in it to an undetectable level (see quot. 1964). Cf. RADAPPERTIZATION, RADURIZATION.

1964 H. E. GORESLINE et al. in *Nature* 17 Oct. 237/2 Type II is the application to foods of doses of ionizing radiation sufficient to reduce the number of viable specific non-spore-forming pathogenic micro-organisms (other than viruses) so that none is detectable in the treated food by any standard method... The following are the names we suggest for these types of treatment:.. Type II, radicidation. **1972** *Poultry Sci.* LI. 277 (*heading*) Poultry feed radicidation. **1973** N. F. LEWIS et al. in *Radiation Preservation of Food* (Internat. Atomic Energy Agency, Vienna) 203 'Radicidation' is synonymous with a 'bactericidal' effect of radiation where a specific pathogenic species is eliminated. Thus, when the process is used solely for destroying enteropathogenic and enterotoxinogenic organisms belonging to the genus *Salmonella*, it is referred to as '*Salmonella* radicidation'.

†**raˈdicity.** *Obs. rare*⁻¹. [f. L. *rādīc-*, stem of RADIX + -ITY.] = RADICALITY.

1651 BIGGS *New Disp.* ¶305 Diseases have not in themselves an essentiall radicity.

radicle (ˈrædɪk(ə)l). [ad. L. *rādīcula* RADICULE; cf. *follicle, ventricle*, etc.]

1. *Bot.* **a.** That part of the embryo of a plant which develops into the primary root.

1671 *Phil. Trans.* VI. 3037 The one is called by him [Grew] the Radicle, being that, which, upon the vegetation of the Seed, becomes the Root [= **1672** GREW *Anat. Veget.* 7]. **1707** *Curiosities in Husb. & Gard.* 31 The..lowermost part is called Radicle; because 'tis the Origin of the Root... The Radicle is likewise called the seminal Root. **1727–41** CHAMBERS *Cycl.* s.v., When in sowing, the radicle happens to light lowest, it is no wonder the root should spread itself under ground. **1796** C. MARSHALL *Garden.* ii. (1813) 15 The substance of seeds appears to be spent first in feeding the radicle. **1880** C. & F. DARWIN *Movem. Pl.* 5 The radicle can be distinguished from the hypocotyl only by the presence of root-hairs and the nature of its covering.

b. A rootlet.

1829 J. L. KNAPP *Jrnl. Naturalist* 122 The radicles penetrate like the finest hairs into the substance. **1856** KANE *Arct. Expl.* II. i. 10 Using the long radicles of a spongy moss for wick.

2. *Anat.* One of the branching subdivisions of veins, nerves, etc. resembling a part of a root.

1830 R. KNOX *Béclard's Anat.* 182 A doubling of a minute artery which becomes a venous radicle. **1880** BASTIAN *Brain* 44 The radicles of a much branched nerve process.

3. *Chem.* = RADICAL *sb.* 4.

Radicle has been preferred to *radical* by some authorities, and was the form formerly employed in the Journal of the Chemical Society, but its introduction appears to have been due to a misunderstanding (see quot. 1862).

1862 W. MILLER *Elem. Chem.* III. 36 Liebig..defined organic chemistry to be the chemistry of compound radicles. [*Ibid.* note, The German term *radikal* is commonly, but inaccurately translated *radical*, which is properly an adjective, the word *radicle* being the appropriate rendering.] **1880** FRISWELL in *Soc. of Arts* 444 The iodides of the alcoholic radicles, methyl and ethyl.

4. *Philol.* (See quot.)

1870 F. A. MARCH *Anglo-Saxon Gram.* 33 Radicles are elementary relational parts of words. They are generally single sounds—oftenest a consonant sound.

ˈ**radicose**, *a. Bot. rare*⁻⁰. [ad. L. *rādīcōs-us*: see RADIX and -OSE.] Having a large root (*Treas. Bot.* 1866).

†**ˈradicous**, *a. Obs. rare.* [cf. prec. and -OUS.] Root-like; pertaining, or appropriate, to a root.

1767 BUSH *Hibernia Cur.* (1769) 78 A..kind of heath, which..vegetates at the bottom into a close and extremely radicous texture. *Ibid.* 84 Of..radicous or lignous composition.

radicular (rəˈdɪkjʊlə(r)), *a.* [f. L. *rādīcula* RADICULE + -AR.]

1. *Bot.* Belonging to the radicle.

1830 LINDLEY *Nat. Syst. Bot.* 72 Radicular end next the hilum. **1831** MACGILLIVRAY tr. *Richard's Elem. Bot.* 288 The radicular body or radicle constitutes one of the extremities of the embryo. **1875** BENNETT & DYER tr. *Sachs' Bot.* 462 The embryo is thick at the radicular end.

2. a. *Path.* Affecting or attacking the roots (of a tooth, nerve, etc.).

1878 T. BRYANT *Pract. Surg.* I. 561 Radicular Odontome has attained the size of a chestnut. **1899** *Allbutt's Syst. Med.* VI. 652 To this form the name of radicular brachial neuritis is given.

b. *Anat.* Belonging to, forming part of, the root of an artery, nerve, etc.

1897 *Syd. Soc. Lex.*, *Radicular arteries, fibres.* **1899** *Allbutt's Syst. Med.* VII. 390 The radicular branches [of arteries] to the bulbar nerves arise from the vertebral.

radicule (ˈrædɪkjuːl). *Bot.* [ad. L. *rādīcula*, dim. of RADIX. Cf. F. *radicule.*] = RADICLE.

1836 LOUDON *Encycl. Plants* Gloss. **1883** *Knowledge* 20 July 43/2 In five or six days the radicules will appear.

Hence †**raˈdiculode** *Bot.* (see quot.). *Obs.* **raˈdiculose** *a.*, having radicles.

1831 MACGILLIVRAY tr. *Richard's Elem. Bot.* 295 The inferior extremity of the blastus..bears the name of radiculode. **1880** GRAY *Struct. Bot.* Gloss. (ed. 6) 430 *Radiculose*, bearing rootlets.

radiculitis (rædɪkjʊˈlaɪtɪs). *Path.* [ad. F. *radiculite*, f. *radicule* radicle (f. L. *rādīcula*, dim. of *rādix* root): see -ITIS.] Inflammation of the root of a spinal nerve.

1907 *Jrnl. Amer. Med. Assoc.* 5 Oct. 1227/2 (*heading*) Radiculitis. **1940** S. A. K. WILSON *Neurol.* xiii. 260 For self-evident anatomical reasons, radiculitis can scarcely occur by itself. *Ibid.* 261 Radiculitis and 'spinal neuritis' will not here be distinguished. **1973** *N.Y. Law Jrnl.* 19 July 12/2 Her physicians testified that she had suffered from severe cervical sprain and cervical radiculitis since the accident.

radie, obs. Sc. form of READY.

radience, -ent, varr. of RADIANCE, RADIANT.

radiescent (reɪdɪˈɛsənt), *a.* [Irreg. f. RADIATE *v.* + -ESCENT.] = RADIANT.

1863 *Reader* 26 Sept. 348/3 The radiescent state of substances is known to originate in three different modes.

radiesthesia (ˌreɪdɪɪsˈθiːzɪə). Also **radiæsthesia**. [ad. F. *radiesthésie*: see RADIO- and ÆSTHESIA.] The detection of radiation by, or by means of, the body: a process believed by some to be responsible for the operation of dowsing rods, pendulums, and the like as means of locating buried substances, diagnosing illness, etc.

1935 *Jrnl. Brit. Soc. Dowsers* II. 337 The field of radiesthesia is beset with many pitfalls for the unwary. **1950** V. D. WETHERED *Radiesthetic Approach to Health & Homeopathy* iv. 30 The term radiesthesia has been given to the detection by human reactions of ultra-fine radiations or influences such as are given off by the body. **1958** B. NICHOLS *Sweet & Twenties* xi. 146 A few doctors who are making the first, hesitant steps into the uncharted science of radiaesthesia. **1960** *Times* 19 July 18/4 Radiaesthesia and radionics were studied and believed in by many persons. **1960** *Spectator* 28 Oct. 653/2 Radiesthesia may be described as the utilising of psychic powers for the diagnosis of disease, with the help of some mechanical apparatus. **1962** M. ASH *Health, Radiation & Healing* iv. 81 The practice of radiesthesia is based on two fundamental facts: first the muscular response of human beings to fields of radiating energy, and secondly the radiating energy emitted by the human body itself. **1975** *Homes & Gardens* Nov. 63/1 More than 20 doctors in this country practise radiesthesia and some belong to the Medical Society for the Study of Radiesthesia.

So **radiesˈthesic** *a.*, radiesthetic; **radiˈesthesist**, a radiesthetist; **radiesˈthetic** *a.*, of or pertaining to radiesthesia; **radiesˈthetically** *adv.*; **radiˈesthetist**, one skilled in the techniques of radiesthesia.

1934 *Jrnl. Brit. Soc. Dowsers* I. 142 *Study of radiesthetic fields*, by Maurice Alby, describes in rather complicated detail the nature and position of fields surrounding underground water. **1936** *Discovery* Dec. 395/2 Radiesthesists have not hesitated to borrow, often irrationally and incautiously, from the terminology of physics. **1939** MABY & FRANKLIN *Physics of Divining Rod* 436 Many investigators have thought that dowsers work radiesthetically. **1950** F. A. ARCHDALE *Elem. Radiesthesia & Use of Pendulum* i. 9 Radiesthesists have different methods, although they achieve the same results or at least hope to, that is to develop and intercept the reflexes resulting from their sensitiveness to radiations emanating from other bodies, either animal, vegetable or mineral. **1957** V. D. WETHERED *Introd. Med. Radiesthesia & Radionics* xiii. 130 A foreign radiesthetist travelling in a train on the Continent was able to diagnose accurately what a fellow traveller was suffering from. **1959** B. COPEN *What Radiesthesia is & What* *it can Do* 15 All Radiesthesic research, diagnosis or therapy does not involve vivisection or cruelty to animals in any way. **1959** M. CLEMENT tr. *A. Mermet's Princ. & Pract. Radiesthesia* iii. 36 No insulating substance is known which can affect radiesthetic radiations. *Ibid.* 37 Some reveal themselves to be radiesthetists at the first attempt, sometimes while undertaking an experiment for fun. **1962** M. ASH *Health, Radiation & Healing* iv. 88 He showed me how he took a radiesthetic reading by allowing a pendulum held in his hand to swing radially away from a patient's body and moving the pendulum gradually outwards until it began to swing in a different direction. **1977** D. V. TANSLEY *Dimensions of Radionics* p. xvii, Out of the investigation we made, there developed in due course his remarkable discovery that it was possible, radiesthetically, to find the archetypal pattern of any substance. **1978** COPEN & KOWA *Pendulum* 7 There are radiesthesists in every country of the world, many who use it [*sc.* radiesthesia] as a hobby, others as a full-time profession.

† **radiferous** (rə'dɪfərəs), *a. Obs.* [f. RADI(UM + -FEROUS.] Containing or yielding radium.

1903 W. J. HAMMER *Radium* 18 They used two small bulbs.., one containing one gramme of radiferous barium chloride. **1913** J. COX *Beyond Atom* vi. 89 Several investigators made a thorough search of all the known radiferous minerals.

radiism ('reɪdɪɪzm). [f. RADI-US + -ISM.] Radiate arrangement; radiation.

1841 E. FORBES *Brit. Starfishes* 243 In the animals of which we have now to treat, Radiism sets and Annulism appears.

radik, radilie, obs. ff. RADISH, READILY.

radio ('reɪdɪəʊ), *sb.* orig. *U.S.* [Independent use of the initial element of RADIO-TELEGRAM, RADIO-TELEGRAPHY, etc.] † **I. 1.** A message sent by wireless telegraphy or telephony; a radio-telegram. *Obs.*

[**1906** *Internat. Radiotelegraphic Convention*: *Regulations* (Internat. Radiotelegr. Conf., Berlin) 34 Radiotelegrams bear the service instruction 'Radio' in the preamble.] **1915** R. H. DAVIS *With Allies* 2 For any exhibition they gave of excitement or concern, the news the radio brought them might have been the result of a by-election. **1920** *Glasgow Herald* 10 Aug. 7 In reply the Polish Government sent the following radio. **1923** R. D. PAINE *Comrades of Rolling Ocean* xiv. 245, I shall have to get a radio off to my wife to come on from Ohio and meet me. **1924** R. KEABLE *Recompence* (1926) i. 18 There's a radio in. The *Balmoral* sailed a fortnight after we did.

II. 2. a. The transmission and reception of radio-frequency electromagnetic waves, esp. as a means of communication that does not need a connecting wire; wireless telephony or telegraphy.

Orig. in *attrib.* use only. *radio-receiver* in quot. 1903 is prob. f. RADIO- 4 and not necessarily to be taken as evidence of a word *radio*.

1903 Radio-receiver [see sense 5 a]. **1907** L. DE FOREST in *Electr. World* 22 June 1270/1 This factor, damping, is of far more vital import than any regulation of wave-lengths... Radio chaos will certainly be the result until..regulation is enforced. **1911** Radio-communication [see sense 5 a]. **1912** Radio station [see sense 7]. **1913** Radio operator [see sense 5 a]. **1914** Radio transmitter [see sense 5 a]. **1917** *Electr. Experimenter* Jan. 650 (*heading*) Election returns flashed by radio to 7,000 amateurs. **1919** *Pop. Sci. Monthly* Mar. 116/3 Instead of taking bearings by known landmarks, the bearings are determined from known wireless stations by means of radio. **1921** *Sci. Amer.* 2 July 5/1 Armstrong became interested in radio and erected a radio station at his home. **1922** C. W. TAUSSIG (*title*) The book of radio: a complete, simple explanation of radio reception and transmission. **1924** *Glasgow Herald* 26 Jan. 11/5 At the time when radio is in its infancy, experimentalists midway in the United States summoned their friends to hear the Atlantic waves and Pacific surf simultaneously. **1948** A. L. ALBERT *Radio Fund.* x. 380 In radio, the feed-back coil of an oscillator is sometimes called a tickler. **1960** C. H. GIBBS-SMITH *Aeroplane* xi. 76 In August [1910], radio was used for the first time between the ground and an aeroplane in flight. **1964** R. H. BAKER *Astron.* (ed. 8) xvii. 505 (*heading*) Tracing of spiral arms by radio. **1975** FINK & MCKENZIE *Electronics Engineers' Handbk.* XVIII. 62 In radio, polarization usually refers to the electric vector. **1976** PERKOWSKI & STRAL *Joy of CB* i. 6 It's the initial onslaught that is difficult to take, and that is somewhat the condition that we find ourselves in today with CB radio.

b. Organized wireless broadcasting in sound; the sound broadcasting network or service as a whole; sound broadcasting considered as a medium of communication or as an art form.

1922 *Sci. Amer.* June 376/2 Radio today is a continuous performance. You purchase your ticket in the form of a receiving set..and then listen in..to the music of today..the news of the minute, stock quotations, and so on. **1944** W. C. GREET *World Words* p.v, For effective radio.. pronunciation is not an opportunity to be elegant but an everyday problem of what to do with..words. **1946** *B.B.C. Year Bk.* 29 Plays were a popular form of radio before the beginning of the war. **1951** *Ann. Reg. 1950* 415 Not only did these forums..make good radio, but they were also excellent publicity for the B.B.C. **1958** *Listener* 25 Sept. 482/1 It [*sc.* a play] was also made into some very good radio by the adaptation of the prologue spoken by Luxury and her daughter Poverty. **1960** *B.B.C. Handbk.* 33 In addition to the series of Party Political Broadcasts, the Budget broadcasts, and the Ministerial broadcasts (on sound radio and television), there were reports on Parliamentary topics ..in the Home Service. **1966** *Listener* 2 June 816/3 Going back over reviews of the past three months I cannot find a dozen productions which were unequivocally radio and nothing else. **1967** *Ibid.* 18 May 653/1 In the evening they will have radio to listen to, television to watch, and darts and billiards as well in a light and attractive recreation room. **1972** G. GREEN *Great Moments in Sport*: *Soccer* xxii. 186 They invited me..to examine the organisational set-up they were planning—for spectators, press, radio, television and the rest. **1977** *Daily Tel.* 9 Feb. 11/2 The programme itself was not an outstanding piece of radio. **1978** *Times* 12 June 3/2 Mainly because of economies, radio had become very run down... Some equipment had not been replaced, studios were becoming less suitable. *Ibid.* 3/3 He welcomed the competition of commercial radio.

c. (Preceded by a proper name, esp. of a place.) A particular radio station or network.

1943 C. J. ROLO *Radio goes to War* xxii. 207 The Berlin radio continued to rely most heavily on divisive propaganda. **1958** *Whitaker's Almanack 1959* 582/1 Moscow radio announced that Russia had launched an earth satellite. **1967** *Listener* 12 Jan. 58/1, I do recall that Cairo radio—as well as many Western sources—had interpreted the Soviet warning to Britain and France requiring them to cease operations as implying a threat to bomb London and Paris by missiles. **1968** *Ibid.* 27 June 824/1 Ask Goose Bay Radio if they have any other traffic in this area. **1975** *Whitaker's Almanack* 593/1 The Ethiopian army took control of the national radio station in Addis Ababa and of the independent Voice of the Gospel Radio owned by the World Lutheran Federation. **1978** *Oxford Mail* 20 Feb. 1, Twelve Egyptian soldiers died and 19 were injured in the commando raid at Larnaca airport, Cyprus radio said today.

d. (With capital initial.) Forming the first part of the proper names of particular radio stations or services (the second part freq. being a place-name); ***Radio 1, 2, 3, 4,*** (also ***Radio One***, etc.), the four national radio networks of the BBC (inaugurated on 30 Sept. 1967 in place of the programme services that had existed previously).

1920 *Wireless World* Jan. 587/2 A new Dutch wireless company, called the Nederlandsche Telegraaf Maatchappij 'Radio-Holland' has been formed... 'Radio-Holland' acquires the rights of wireless installations on Dutch mercantile vessels..and the contracts relating thereto. **1926** *Encycl. Brit.* I. 455/1 In 1924–25 the Cie. Française de Radiophonie set up 'Radio Paris'..and provincial stations at Toulouse and Lyons. **1938** *Ann. Reg. 1937* 161 On New Year's Eve, a message from General Smuts, one of the founders of the League, was transmitted from 'Radio-Nations', the League wireless station at Geneva. **1958** *Economist* 25 Oct. 331/1 Radio Free Europe..concentrates on Poland, Czechoslovakia, Hungary, Rumania and Bulgaria, while Radio Liberation broadcasts to the Soviet Union, in no less than seventeen languages. **1964** *Daily Tel.* 13 May 1/8 Radio Atlanta, Britain's second floating commercial 'pirate' radio station, went on the air with programmes for the first time yesterday. **1967** *Listener* 17 Aug. 194/1 The new 247 metres network will be known as Radio 1. The 1500 metres and VHF network will be Radio 2, and..the present Third Network will become Radio 3 and the Home-Service network Radio 4. **1968** *B.B.C. Handbk.* 29 Our first local station, Radio Leicester, began broadcasting on 8 November 1967, followed shortly afterwards by Radio Sheffield and Radio Merseyside. **1973** P. DICKINSON *Gift* ix. 139 Penny was listening to Radio One. **1976** *Daily Tel.* 30 June 1/4 Radio Uganda, monitored in Nairobi, gave no immediate indication of the 'penalties' involved. **1976** *Times* 29 Sept. 16/6 That all this may be entering the field of immodesty is redeemed by a quick smile and the admission that perhaps Radio 3 takes itself too seriously. **1978** *Bookseller* 1 July 54/1 Mike Stevenson, author of Ward Lock's biography of cricketer *Ray Illingworth*..has been interviewed on Radios Leicester, Leeds, Cleveland, Pennine, Piccadilly, Hallam and City.

3. Radio equipment; *spec.* a receiving set.

[**1913**: cf. *radio operator* in sense 5 a.] **1917** *Electr. Experimenter* May 3/1 When the German spies..found that it was not very healthy to operate their outfits in attics or in house chimneys..they simply put their radios in touring cars, cleverly concealing the aerial wires inside of the car bodies. **1925** H. L. FOSTER *Trop. Tramp with Tourists* 97 It fairly shrieked with the blare of jazz—of jazz from radios, jazz from mechanical pianos. **1936** KING EDWARD VIII in *Manch. Guardian Weekly* 6 Mar. 185/1 Science has made it possible for me..to speak to you all over the radio. **1941** AUDEN *New Year Let.* II. 36 He moves on tiptoe round the room, Turns on the radio to mark Isolde's Sehnsucht for the dark. **1968** *New Society* 22 Aug. 265/2 Non-U *radio*/U *wireless* is no longer true; the U call it a radio too. **1973** J. PATTINSON *Search Warrant* ii. 28 There was a load of noise.. It sounded like a radio going full belt on a pop-music channel.

4. = *radio spectrum* in sense 7 below; radio wavelengths.

1968 *Physical Rev. Lett.* XXI. 1540/1 NGC1275 and 3C120..are a hundred times more luminous in the radio than most of the Seyferts. **1975** *Nature* 3 Jan. 7/1 It [*sc.* the Crab nebula] is unique in that it has been detected over the entire electromagnetic spectrum from radio through infra-red and the visual to X rays and γ rays.

5. *attrib.* **a.** In general uses, as ***radio aerial, antenna, apparatus, beacon*** (= BEACON *sb.* 6 d), ***beam, bearing, black-out, cabinet, communication, countermeasure, detector, fade-out, fix, intercept, link*** (= LINK *sb.*² 3 f), ***marker, mast, message, operator, receiver*** (= in quot. 1903 prob. f. RADIO- 4), ***relay, room, set, shop, traffic, transmission, transmitter, valve.***

1949 E. B. MOULLIN (*title*) Radio aerials. **1968** *Times* 16 Oct. 8/8 It also seems to have a large radio aerial more suitable for a trip to the planets. **1927** B. F. DASHIELL *Popular Guide to Radio* v. 71 (*heading*) The use of radio antennas and grounds. **1972** K. BONFIGLIOLI *Don't point that Thing at Me* xi. 89 It was the same car..but overnight it had..acquired a suit of whitewall tyres and another radio antenna. **1912** *Statutes U.S.A.* XXXVII. I. 303 The President..may cause the closing of any station for radio communication and the removal therefrom of all radio apparatus. **1916** *Lit. Digest* (N.Y.) 1 Jan 13/1 It is conceivable that this small body of men might have neither sending or receiving radio-apparatus. **1919**, etc. Radio beacon [see BEACON *sb.* 6 d]. **1966** D. FRANCIS *Flying Finish* ii. 27, I flew contentedly along..checking my direction by the radio beacons over which I passed. **1923** E. W. MARCHANT *Radio Telegr.* i. 12 A ship coming into harbour will pick up the radio beam at the instant at which its direction is towards the ship. **1966** *McGraw-Hill Encycl. Sci. & Technol.* IX. 20/1 Radio beams that are transmitted from moving aircraft to the ground will have an apparent change of frequency. **1977** Radio beam [see *radio detector* below]. **1978** R. V. JONES *Most Secret War* xvii. 139 Milch, the Head of the Luftwaffe, was advising Goering that the current policy of night attacks was useless without special radio-beam devices, like the new X-Gerät. **1935** Radio bearing [see FIX *sb.* 3]. **1957** *Encycl. Brit.* XVI. 174/1 The accuracy of radio bearings.. [is] dependent upon properly functioning equipment and skilful operation. **1958** *New Scientist* 6 Mar. 8/3 The storm and its associated radio blackout. **1925** *Scribner's Mag.* Sept. 19/1 Have you seen a radio cabinet which..actually does not look like one? **1911** *Statutes U.S.A.* XXXVI. I. 629 (*heading*) An act to require apparatus and operators for radio-communication on certain ocean steamers. **1912** *Ibid.* XXXVII. I. 308 The expression 'radio communication' as used in this Act means any system of electrical communication by telegraphy or telephony without the aid of any wire connecting the points from and at which the radiograms, signals, or other communications are sent or received. **1942** *Electronic Engin.* XV. 116/1 Planck's constant *h*, is a universal one which is applicable to all radiations, including..the wavelengths used in radio-communication. **1947** *Jrnl. R. Aeronaut. Soc.* LI. 425/2 The use of radio counter-measures, introduced for the first time with such telling effect in the last war, will be a prominent feature in all future large-scale conflicts. **1978** R. V. JONES *Most Secret War* xxii. 180 With our nightfighters and guns powerless, radio countermeasures were our only means of defence. **1936** *Discovery* Mar. 70/1 Each of these observatories is equipped..with..a radio detector, which enables the specialist to learn at once which station is transmitting. **1977** C. FORBES *Avalanche Express* x. 106 It takes two radio-detector vans..five minutes to take a fix on a secret transmitter—to plot from two locations the cross-point of the radio beams indicating where the transmission is coming from. **1937** Radio fade-out [see FADE-OUT 3]. **1942** Radio fix [see FIX *sb.* 3]. **1977** C. FORBES *Avalanche Express* xxi. 218 The operator in the radio-detector van..reached for the radio-telephone... 'We have a radio fix, sir... Positive.' **1974** G. MARKSTEIN *Cooler* liv. 192 It was a radio intercept by security monitoring. The message, decoded, read: 'Stand by 24-hourly.' **1928**, etc. Radio link [see LINK *sb.*² 3 f]. **1971** A. DIMENT *Think Inc.* xii. 208 'I love you,' I said and cut the radio link. **1978** *Dumfries Courier* 20 Oct. 10/2 A special Police control room on site at the NEC will have radio links with Police helicopter, car, motor cycle and foot patrols. **1933** *Nat. Geogr. Mag.* May 618/2 Radio-range and radio-marker beacons. **1942** B. A. SHIELDS *Air Pilot Training* xxx. 515 Low-powered radio stations, called radio markers,..are placed along the airways to serve as radio fixes. **1950** 'D. DIVINE' *King of Fassarai* v. 38 The metereological station was completed... The radio masts were put up. **1976** *Cumberland & Westmorland Herald* 27 Nov., The committee approved the Corporation's application to build a radio mast almost 50 ft. high and a modular equipment building. **1916** *Lit. Digest* (N.Y.) 1 Jan 13/2 The radio-message containing this intelligence is flashed over the hills. **1974** M. HASTINGS *Dragon Island* xiii. 112, I have to..send a radio message to Djakarta. **1913** *Year-bk. Wireless Telegr.* 96 The radio operator..must furnish to the inspector evidence that he is 'skilled in the use of the apparatus'. **1925** *Scribner's Mag.* July 44/2 Hank Quiller was rated as chief radio operator on board the S.S. *Omega*. **1974** G. MARKSTEIN *Cooler* lxii. 218 If we find your killer we find your mysterious radio operator. **1903** C. H. SEWALL *Wireless Telegr.* IV. 154 The first radio-receiver in which cause and effect were observed and recognized was devised by Hertz in 1886. **1929** J. H. MORECROFT *Elem. Radio Communication* vii. 220 With coils having a power factor of about 1 per cent, as is the case with the average radio receiver, one tuned circuit will not give sufficient selectivity to eliminate interference. **1976** B. JACKSON *Flameout* (1977) I. 22 They all wore Bellboy radio receivers in their shirt pockets, in case they could not be reached by telephone. **1926** *Wireless World* 1 Sept. 307/1 The wireless signals received in this Radio Relay Office are relayed to the Central Radio Office in the same building. **1927** B. F. DASHIELL *Popular Guide to Radio* xi. 195 The radio relay scheme, whereby a program from a central station is broadcast, received and rebroadcast by other stations, has been successfully tried out. **1966** *McGraw-Hill Encycl. Sci. & Technol.* V. 520/2 Radio relays are used for simultaneous transmission of up to hundreds of telephone conversations over a trunk route. **1921** R. D. PAINE *Comrades of Rolling Ocean* xiv. 244 A message from the radio-room, sir. **1976** 'J. FRASER' *Who steals my Name?* ii. 15 Later..the radio room springs into life, dispatching police cars..over the face of the city. **1913** *Proc. IRE* I. 43 The purpose of this paper is to describe some recent radio sets designed for the Marconi Wireless Telegraph Company of America to meet the new specifications of the United States Navy. **1926** S. LEWIS *Mantrap* ii. 22 How necessary for hardy camp-life are the portable radio set, the pneumatic cushion. **1971** *Daily Tel.* 13 Sept. 1/8 The radio ham..heard two men planning the raid over short-wave radio sets. **1974** E. JONES *Barlow comes to Judgement* 127 He works in a radio shop in Bayswater. **1927** *Jrnl. Franklin Inst.* CCIV. 240 Beam stations are carrying regular radio traffic between England and Canada. **1973** D. KYLE *Raft of Swords* (1974) I. ix. 88 There had been remarkably little radio traffic. So he would sit in the radio room. **1935** C. G. BURGE *Compl. Bk. Aviation* 506/1 The number of channels available for radio transmission is limited. **1974** G. MARKSTEIN *Cooler* li. 181 The interception stations..noted every illicit radio transmission. **1914** R. STANLEY *Text Bk. Wireless Telegr.* xix. 300 The range of a given size of radio transmitter has been greatly increased since the time when coherer detectors were used in conjunction with a Morse tape machine or siphon recorder. **1970** V. CANNING *Great Affair* x. 167 He probably had a secret radio transmitter and receiver somewhere. **1929** *Radio Times* 8 Nov. 434/2 (Advt.), The Radio Valves—with the only filament that has stood the test of time. **1970** P. DICKINSON *Seals* ix. 178 It provided a short-cut in the mass-production of radio valves.

b. Connected with, participating in, or transmitted as part of organized sound broadcasting, as ***radio acting, actor, actress, adaptation, announcer, audience, ballad, broadcast, broadcasting, bulletin, celebrity, comedian, commentator, commercial, company, critic, criticism, drama, dramatist, interview, journalism, journalist, listener, news, organization, personality, play, producer, production, programme, reporter, revue, script, serial, series, spot, star, talk, writer.***

1940 *Radio Times* 23 Aug. 6/4 Frederick Allen.. had also done a considerable amount of radio acting and singing before becoming a BBC announcer. **1968** *Daily Tel.* (Colour Suppl.) 15 Nov. 32/3 He returned to a contract with Mr. Beaumont, radio-acting, poetry recitals, bit parts in films. **1938** *Encycl. Brit. Bk. of Year* 123/1 The widespread unionization of radio actors. **1975** *Times* 20 Sept. 8/4 That uncommon breed, the exceptional radio actor. **1972** P. BLACK *Biggest Aspidistra in World* I. iv. 39 Jenny was played by Lilian Harrison, the leading radio actress of her day. **1931** T. H. PEAR *Voice & Personality* viii. 94 Holt Marvell's radio-adaptation of.. *Carnival*. **1927** *Scribner's Mag.* Apr. 437/2 We must listen to radio announcers who insist that the instant programme is most colorful. **1970** 'T. COE' *Wax Apple* (1973) iv. 29 His voice was deep and resonant, like that of a radio announcer. **1932** *Radio Times* 29 July 251/3 Christopher Stone keeps the radio audience amused with a selection from the new discs. **1972** P. BLACK *Biggest Aspidistra in World* I. vii. 56 Mabel Constanduros, who in 1925 introduced the Buggins family.. aiming.. at the entire radio audience listening in its own family groups. **1960** *Times* 16 Aug. 5/2 Singing the Fishing; radio ballad by Ewan MacColl and Charles Parker. **1956** H. KURNITZ *Invasion of Privacy* xviii. 117 The late radio broadcasts.. had given the Morley case a big spread. *a* **1974** R. CROSSMAN *Diaries* (1976) II. 549 A B.B.C. experiment for live radio broadcasts of extracts from the House of Commons debate. **1922** Radio broadcasting [see RADIOGRAPHY 2]. **1975** *Listener* 25 Dec. 853/3 The poem, with its five voices, is suited to radio broadcasting. **1965** *B.B.C. Handbk.* 65 During the day well over twenty million people listen to at least one radio bulletin. **1948** E. E. CUMMINGS *Let.* 20 Aug. (1969) 184 A charming & handsome & tall & sweet youth named Billy; think he later became a radio-celebrity. **1930** H. NICOLSON *Diary* 18 Oct. (1966) 57, I have become 'famous' as a radio comedian, and shall never be able to live down the impression thus acquired. **1980** S. BRETT *Dead Side of Mike* vi. 60 The programme was merely a showcase for the talents of a once-loved radio comedian. **1938** Radio commentator [see COMMENTATOR 2 c]. **1953** *Manch. Guardian* 21 May 1/4 Raymond Gram Swing was the most powerful and admired radio commentator working between the two major allies during the war. **1978** *Listener* 27 July 111/3 The skilled radio commentator.. was there to tell you what is happening. **1951** M. MCLUHAN *Mech. Bride* (1967) 117/2 The big hefty heartiness of this is very familiar in the radio commercials. **1980** *Broadcast* 7 July 17/2 (Advt.), Production of radio commercials, voice-overs, stereo programmes. **1920** *Sci. Amer.* 24 July 79/1 A leading radio company is about to begin construction of a super-powered radio station. **1938** JOYCE *Let.* 6 June (1966) III. 424 His (my son's) experience of broadcasting in the U.S.A... is that these Radio Companies are all in watertight compartments and that the director who has charge of the singing almost resents even a friendly introduction from the director, say, who controls the sports programme. **1974** *IBA Evidence to Annan Comm.* 46 The local radio companies should retain their creative initiative. **1929** *Vox* 9 Nov. 3/1 Heaven forbid that I should try to emulate the new Radio critics of the *Daily Express* who have apparently been told.. to sit down immediately after tea and listen right through the evening, after which they are expected to discuss their indigestion attractively next morning. **1966** *B.B.C. Handbk.* 14 Every critic (and who is not his own television and radio critic?) would do well to temper his occasional rage with the thought that there is much to admire about the BBC. **1976** *Listener* 15 Jan. 42/1, I stopped being radio critic of the *Guardian*. **1940** R. S. LAMBERT *Ariel & all his Quality* vii. 173 It seemed desirable for the BBC to try and build up a.. solid school of radio criticism. **1978** *Listener* 27 July 111/2, I was writing radio criticisms for *The Listener*. **1925** *Glasgow Herald* 1 Sept. 8 One of the many limitations of radio-drama will be the impossibility of introducing any but audible actions of a simple kind. **1951** M. MCLUHAN *Mech. Bride* (1967) 157/2 Soap operas are written and acted quite as well as the ordinary evening radio drama. **1929** *Radio Times* 8 Nov. 388/2 Conrad has, curiously, attracted the radio-dramatist. **1944** Radio dramatist [see ACTUALITY 4 b]. **1926** G. FRANKAU *My Unsentimental Journey* ii. 37 A new form of torment, the 'radio interview'. **1974** *Guardian* 21 Mar. 1/3 Mr Edward Short, Leader of the House, said in a radio interview. **1968** *Listener* 21 Mar. 380/2 When the war was over Ed Murrow went back home, the 'first authentic original' of radio journalism. **1977** *Times* 14 May 10/5 Mary Goldring is a radio journalist... She has now concluded three reports on contemporary India. **1926** *Public Opinion* 2 July 17/2, 27,000,000 persons are now radio listeners in the United States. **1974** *Listener* 24 Jan. 123/3 Faithful radio listeners were entitled to their regular programmes. **1940** J. FLANNER in *New Yorker* 7 Dec. 60/2 To Parisians, the most trusted radio news is what they get from the American short-wave broadcasts. **1973** A. PRICE *October Men* iii. 46 Not a word in the morning paper.. or on the radio news. **1962** A. NISBETT *Technique Sound Studio* x. 168 At a radio organization such as the BBC it is easy to feel spoilt for choice. **1941** J. W. WELCH in *Listener* (1978) 18 May 626/1 The BBC is now building up Joad as a radio personality. **1972** P. BLACK *Biggest Aspidistra in World* I. vii. 56 Tommy Handley.. in 1929.. was already a radio personality. **1924** *Variety* 24 Dec. 35/4 Gene Rouse, announcer for WOAW, has written a 'radio play'. **1973** M. AMIS *Rachel Papers* 75, I slammed the door, so that the sounds of the radio-play on the kitchen wireless were reduced to an underground rumble. **1955** T. H. PEAR *Eng. Social Differences* ix. 195 'Living by the clock' is a virtue in a radio-producer. **1974** *Listener* 14 Feb. 219/2 The radio producer hears the play over and over again. The lives and all the action become crystal-clear to him. **1959** D. COOKE *Lang. Mus.* iv. 200 A private tape-recording of a radio-production of *King Lear*. **1978** *Listener* 2 Feb. 152/1 *The Beggar's Opera*.. is a splendid new radio production. **1922** *Variety* 10 Mar. 7/2 Among the theatres which will provide acts exclusively for the 'Star's' radio programs are the Shubert, Orpheum,.. Royal and 12th streets. **1925** A. H. MORSE *Radio* v. 78 There need be no limitation of the public enjoyment of the radio programme. **1972** *Sat. Rev.* (U.S.) 27 May 18/2 In Israel I was invited to go on a radio program to discuss the problem. **1926** *Wireless World* 18 Aug. 231/1 The radio reporters are kept busy all the summer, carrying their microphones to the important sporting events, [etc.]. **1975** *Times* 6 Jan. 12/8 Why did Sir Keith tell a radio reporter.. that it [*sc.* a speech] was meant to be 'light-hearted'? **1929** *Radio Times* 8 Nov. 395/3 The brilliant little skit.. which enlivened a recent radio revue. **1941** B. SCHULBERG *What makes Sammy Run?* ii. 30 He had written a radio script. **1962** A. NISBETT *Technique Sound Studio* ix. 156 Such a 'radio script' will probably have to be reinterpreted. **1958** M. KENNEDY *Outlaws on Parnassus* ii. 28 A Dickens novel had to end sometime, whereas a radio serial can go on for ever. **1977** S. BRETT *Star Trap* iv. 40, I can't do Friday... Doing a pilot of a radio series. **1973** *Black Panther* 28 Apr. 11/2 Bobby has layed out his program.. in countless radio spots, interviews and discussions. **1932** *Radio Times* 29 July 279/3 (Advt.), A permanent.. record of your favourite radio stars. **1980** P. ABLEMAN *Shoestring's Finest Hour* i. 11 Lonely women who ring up famous radio stars.. in the hope of getting to sleep with them. **1940** R. S. LAMBERT *Ariel & all his Quality* vii. 173 Experts are able.. to express themselves freely.. about current radio drama, music, talks, and television programmes. **1943** D. POWELL *Time to be Born* i. 8 My days are filled with my war committees and my refugee children and my radio talks. **1977** *Listener* 16 June 800/3 BBC Television now appears to be giving radio talks. **1944** L. MACNEICE *Christopher Columbus* 8 The radio writer has to think of words in the mouths of actors.

c. Designating devices controlled or operated by radio, as ***radio bomb***; vehicles equipped with radio for receiving information, directions, etc., as ***radio cab, car, taxi, van.***

1974 D. SEAMAN *Bomb that could Lip-Read* xxiv. 243 Once they discover it was a radio bomb, they will take this hamlet apart. **1977** *Times* 18 July 1/4 (*heading*) Provisional IRA widen use of radio bombs. **1955** J. B. PRIESTLEY in Priestley & Hawkes *Journey down Rainbow* xii. 173 Most of the taxis down here are like our radio cabs in London, but the voice of the distant operator, calling cabs and giving addresses, is always left turned on. **1977** F. WELDON in *Winter's Tales 23* 190 Maureen's on the phone, calling radio cabs. **1925** *Sci. Amer.* Nov. 308/1 The Yard has seven radio-equipped motor cars attached to the Criminal Investigation flying squad... These radio cars not only aid in detecting crime but also perform a helpful service in regulating heavy traffic along the highways. **1967** *Listener* 19 Jan. 95/2 WINS reporters were there with their radio cars and tape recorders inching the story along every few minutes or so with eye-witness reports, [etc.]. **1973** 'E. MCBAIN' *Hail to Chief* i. 3 Two radio-car cops, on routine patrol. **1962** *Spectator* 13 Apr. 486 Lots of tourist information, though we do have radio-taxis here too. **1977** E. AMBLER *Send no more Roses* x. 215, I had used the time.. to check out the local radio-taxi services. **1950** J. FLANNER in *New Yorker* 8 Apr. 79/1 On the street, crowds had collected and a radio van had arrived. **1974** N. FREELING *Dressing of Diamond* 10 They [*sc.* the police] say they've two radio vans.

d. Chiefly *Astr.* Connected with the natural emission of radio waves (freq. denoting objects or entities which emit radio waves in unusually large quantities or are being considered as sources of radio waves), as ***radio brightness, emission, emitter, flux, galaxy, noise, observatory, sky, source, sun, universe.***

1960 RODMAN & VARSAVSKY tr. *I. S. Shklovsky's Cosmic Radio Waves* iii. 174 The radio brightness of the hypothetical objects, averaged over time, would thus exceed that of the sun by some ten orders of magnitude. **1974** *Sci. Amer.* Aug. 26/3 In the direction of this cloud of ionized gas, designated 30 Doradus, there is a decrease in the radio brightness of the sky. **1949** *Nature* 12 Nov. 816/1 Only a proportion of the flares have associated radio bursts, the bigger flares being the more likely to produce strong radio emissions. **1958** *Listener* 27 Nov. 870/1 One of the earliest of the post-war surprises was the discovery by Appleton and Hey that the sun spots and flares which occasionally appear on the solar surface are associated with large and irregular increases in the solar radio emissions. **1978** *Nature* 14 Sept. 111/1 One of the most important features of the jovian decametric radioemission comes from the geometry of the observed radiation. **1954** *Ann. Reg.* 1953 373 Future accurate measurements of the positions of cosmic radio emitters. **1951** *Monthly Notices R. Astron. Soc.* CXI. 366 The intensity of the radio flux from M31 observed on the Earth at a wavelength of 1·89 metres is 10^{-24} watts/square metre/c.p.s. **1960** RODMAN & VARSAVSKY tr. *I. S. Shklovsky's Cosmic Radio Waves* vi. 356 The relative radio emitting power of radio galaxies is 10^3 and even 10^5 times as great as for normal galaxies. **1973** *Sci. Amer.* Sept. 72/3 Many 'classic' radio galaxies consist of an optically bright galaxy situated halfway between two radio-emitting regions. **1979** *Jrnl. R. Soc. Arts* CXXVII. 582/1 The so-called 'radio galaxies', whose power output in radio waves exceeds the total galactic luminosity of all the stars. **1933** *Gen. Electr. Rev.* XXXVI. 201/1 The radio-noise meter.. detects radio noise, measures its intensity, and locates its source. **1946** *Nature* 17 Aug. 234/1 The solar radio noise from sunspots is also characterized by strong fluctuations. **1977** *New Yorker* 19 Sept. 137/1 In 1964, two radio astronomers.. made the unexpected discovery that there was cosmic radio noise entering their system which they could do nothing to get rid of. **1958** *Ann. Reg.* 1957 472 The principal radio-observatories developed during the previous few years. **1969** *Times* 18 Apr. 12/6 The Parkes radio observatory in New South Wales. **1959** DAVIES & PALMER *Radio Studies of Universe* iv. 46 The early maps of the radio sky were made with small aerials which could not readily distinguish radio sources from the background of radio emission. **1950** *Monthly Notices R. Astron. Soc.* CX. 519 The five major extra-galactic nebulae in the selected area are listed.. together with the radio sources which appear to be associated with them. **1961** *New Scientist* 5 Jan. 50/1 About 30 per cent of the accurately measured and suitably placed radio sources can be identified with visible galaxies. **1971** *Sci. Amer.* May 56/3 Before 1960 radio astronomers had identified and catalogued hundreds of radio sources. **1961** WEBSTER, Radio sun. **1965** M. R. KUNDU *Solar Radio Astron.* i. 1 Decimeter-wave observations of the radio sun during a solar eclipse. **1974** G. L. VERSCHUUR *Invisible Universe* iii. 32 (*heading*) The radio sun and planets. **1960** RODMAN & VARSAVSKY tr. *I. S. Shklovsky's Cosmic Radio Waves* vi. 355 Further investigations of the variations in the cosmic radio-wave background at high galactic latitudes will undoubtedly reveal new peculiarities of the 'radio universe'.

6. *Comb.* (cf. RADIO- 4): ***radio-controlled*** (so ***radio-control*** vb. trans.), ***-emitting, -equipped, -linked, -minded, -receiving, -steered, -transmitting*** adjs.

1959 K. VONNEGUT *Sirens of Titan* vii. 121 Without Boaz, their real commander, to radio-control them, they fought bitterly. **1979** *Amat. Photographer* 30 May 162/3 The Post Office refusing him a license to radio-control a camera. **1936** *Punch* 4 Mar. 273/1 Then possibly another sequel in which the generations are estranged over the question of small rubber electric radio-controlled fish. **1958** I. ASIMOV *Naked Sun* i. 9 The radio-controlled flight would be smooth; there would scarcely be any sensation of motion once the plane was airborne. **1976** L. ST. CLAIR *Fortune in Death* xi. 109 The gates swung wide—radio-controlled. **1960** Radio-emitting [see *radio galaxy* in sense 5 d above]. **1971** *Sci. Amer.* May 56/3 Object 3C 48 was thought to be a unique kind of radio-emitting star in our own galaxy until 1963. **1935** C. G. BURGE *Compl. Bk. Aviation* 499/1 By means of radio and land-line the pilot of a radio-equipped 'plane is to-day in closer touch with the ground than the driver of a normal road vehicle. **1963** A. LUBBOCK *Austral. Roundabout* 36, I wouldn't like to say what my radio-equipped bikes and plane save me in time and labour. **1974** H. R. F. KEATING *Bats fly up for Inspector Ghote* iii. 33 Ghote, in yet a third radio-linked car, would be a useful addition to the team. **1930** *Wireless World* 10 Dec. 655/3 To the housewife anxious to please her radio-minded family I would say fill the Christmas pudding this year with a fair sprinkling of miniature fuse lamps instead of with sixpences. **1922** *Glasgow Herald* 21 Apr. 10 Already the number of radio receiving outfits installed in private houses runs into seven figures. **1936** *Discovery* Mar. 69/2 Some 70 radio-receiving observatories all round the earth. **1917** *Nature* 2 Aug. 442/2 Attempts to develop a radio-steered torpedo. **1935** C. G. BURGE *Compl. Bk. Aviation* 511/1 The purpose of the radio compass is to determine whether or not one is flying directly towards a radio-transmitting station. **1959** *Observer* 3 May 17/5 The Authority has now developed radiotransmitting tide gauges which will continuously relay to Gravesend the height of the water at all points of navigational importance. **1978** R. V. JONES *Most Secret War* xliv. 422 We had not known beforehand of these radio-transmitting samples.

7. Special Combs. (cf. RADIO- 4): **radio altimeter**, an altimeter which functions by emitting a radio signal and measuring the time it takes to be reflected back from the ground; **radio amateur**, one who makes a hobby of picking up, and often also transmitting, radio messages; **radio compass**, a radio direction-finder used for the purpose of navigation; **radio contact**, the state or an instance of being in communication by radio; **radio dial** = DIAL *sb.*[1] 6 e; **radio direction-finder** = *direction-finder*; so **radio direction-finding**; **radio dish** = DISH *sb.* 4 b; **radio echo** = ECHO *sb.* 1 d; **radio energy**, energy transmitted in the form of radio waves; **radio engineering**, the branch of engineering concerned with the design, construction, and operation of radio equipment; so **radio engineer**; **radio ham** *colloq.* [HAM *sb.*[1] 6], = *radio amateur* above; **radio industry**, the radio engineering or sound broadcasting industries; **radio licence**, a licence certificate that owners of radios are required to have; (such licences for radio only were abolished in the U.K. in 1971); **radio-loud** *a. Astr.*, emitting significant quantities of radio waves; **radio man**, (*a*) a man who operates, repairs, or otherwise deals with radios; (*b*) a man employed in sound broadcasting; **radio map** *Astr.*, a diagram showing the strength of the radio emission from different parts of the sky; **radio microphone** (see quot. 1962); also (*colloq.*) **radio mike**; **radio navigation**, navigation by means of radio signals; so **,radio-navi'gational** *a.*; **radio net**, a system of intercommunicating radio sets, operated esp. by a police force or similar body; **radio network**, a system of radio stations for navigation, communication, or broadcasting; a sound broadcasting organization or channel; **radio pager** = PAGER *sb.*[3]; so **radio paging** *vbl. sb.*; **radio-'phonograph** *U.S.* = RADIO-GRAMOPHONE; **radio pill** *colloq.* = *endo-radiosonde* s.v. ENDO-; **radio pirate** = PIRATE *sb.* 4 b; **radio-'quiet** *a.*, emitting a negligible amount of radio waves; hence **radio-'quietness**; **radio-radar**, used *attrib.* of devices, systems, etc., combining radio and radar; **radio range**, (*a*) = *radio spectrum* below; (*b*) a radio beacon transmitting directional radio signals which can be used by aircraft possessing appropriate receiving apparatus to determine the bearing of the transmitter; **radio shack**, a small building housing radio equipment; (esp. *Naut.*) a radio room; **radio show**, (*a*) an exhibition of radio equipment, etc.; (*b*) a radio programme, usu. featuring light entertainment; **radio signal**, a radio message; a group of radio waves transmitted or emitted by any source; **radio silence**, deliberate abstention from radio transmission; failure to communicate by radio; **radio-silent** *a.*, (*a*) maintaining radio silence; (*b*) = *radio-quiet* adj. above; **radio sounding**, the use of radiosondes or radar techniques for investigating the atmosphere, sea bed, or the like; so **radio sounder**; **radio spectrum**, the radio-frequency part of the spectrum of electromagnetic radiation; also, the spectrum of any particular source at these frequencies; **radio star**, any discrete source of radio waves outside the solar system (rarely a star in the usual sense); **radio station**, a radio-transmitting installation or establishment; a sound broadcasting establishment or organization; **radio telescope** *Astr.*, an apparatus or installation for detecting and recording radio waves from the sky with great sensitivity and a high degree of resolution, consisting essentially of a large sensitive directional aerial together with a receiver and recording equipment; (in quot. 1929, a fictitious apparatus in which a 'radio contrivance' is attached to an optical telescope); **radio wave**, an electromagnetic wave having a frequency within the range used for telecommunication; (cf. RADIO-FREQUENCY); usu. *pl.*; so **radio wave-length**.

1940 *Chambers's Techn. Dict.* 698/2 Radio altimeter. **1953** R. CHISHOLM *Cover of Darkness* I. xii. 123 My Mosquito had a radio altimeter, a device which gave absolute readings of height. **1968** *Times* 15 Nov. 8/6 The radio-altimeter, which made only one measurement of the probe's altitude, must have been wrong. **1916** *Lit. Digest* (N.Y.) 1 Jan. 13/1 But there will be a lone radio amateur on the alert who has seen the approaching fleet. **1977** *N.Z. Herald* 5 Jan. I. 1/8 Mr Kilpatrick said radio amateurs—there are almost 4000 in New Zealand—were anxious to have aerial installation defined because of the growing public interest in town planning and the environment. **1918** *Flying* 14 Aug. 150/3 The radio-compass and wireless log signals will doubtless be pressed into service in the age of commercial aviation. **1946** *Happy Landings* July 9/1 A severe thunderstorm can be detected by intelligent use of the Radio Compass. **1966** *McGraw-Hill Encycl. Sci. & Technol.* III. 332/2 The modern radio compass uses a nondirectional antenna in combination with a bidirectional loop antenna to provide a unidirectional bearing indication. **1958** *Times* 18 Jan. 8/7 It will enable the masters or pilots of vessels coming in and out of Southampton to coordinate their movements with other shipping by direct radio contact with the radio information centre. **1962** V. GRISSOM in *Into Orbit* 130, I was in radio contact with..the helicopters which were on their way to pick me up. **1975** T. ALLBEURY *Special Collection* v. 34 He had a long radio contact with London and..gave full details. **1976** H. MACINNES *Agent in Place* xvii. 185 'Emil is sleeping on board.' 'You've radio contact with him?' 'Of course.' **1934** WEBSTER, Radio dial. **1974** *Listener* 7 Nov. 593/3 Twiddling his radio dial to hear what is top of the pops. **1922** *Sci. & Invention* May 10/1 (*caption*) The radio direction finder aboard this vessel can locate the transmitting station within one half a degree accuracy. **1966** *McGraw-Hill Encycl. Sci. & Technol.* IV. 232/2 This ground-based radio direction finder, operating at frequencies of 2 to 20 megacycles, is used mainly for navigational assistance in the long-distance en-route zone. **1920** *Radio Rev.* Oct. 644 Radio direction finding..has become a practical possibility owing to the use of powerful amplifiers. **1974** *Encycl. Brit. Macropædia* XII. 903/2 Radio direction finding..developed in two ways. First, radio transmitters, or 'beacons', were sited..to enable ships or aircraft to fix their positions. Second, ground DF stations that could pick up radio signals sent out by a ship or an aircraft were built. **1960** *Aeroplane* XCVIII. 366/2 The largest steerable radio 'dish' in the World, at Jodrell Bank in England. **1977** *Nature* 9 June 478/1 Australia leapt into the big league of astronomical nations with the building of the giant 64-metre radio dish at Parkes, New South Wales. **1928** Radio echo [see ECHO *sb.* 1 d]. **1947** *Sci. News* V. 36 Radio echoes do not come from the meteors themselves but from the lengthy filament of highly conducting gas which forms their trail or streak. **1975** *Nature* 30 Oct. 780/2 A radio-echo technique gave the surface velocity relative to a layer that reflected electromagnetic waves—evidently from a level close to the base of the ice. **1946** *Proc. IRE* XXXIV. 558/2 Presumably, radio energy could..be focused by means of lenses made of a material such as plastic or glass which is transparent at the transmitter frequency. **1955** *Sci. Amer.* Mar. 36/1 The radio energy given forth by..Cygnus A, startles even astronomers. **1974** F. W. COLE *Fund. Astron. Solar Syst. & Beyond* xiv. 379/1 Certain peculiar galaxies emit thousands of times more radio energy than does an average galaxy. **1912** *Electrician & Mechanic* Aug. 140/1 The Institute of Radio-Engineers comprises the bodies formerly known as the Society of Wireless Telegraph Engineers and the Institute of Wireless Engineers. **1937** *Discovery* Apr. 111/1 Radio engineers have recorded an increasing number of sudden and complete fadings affecting reception on short-wave wireless transmission. **1974** *Encycl. Brit. Macropædia* XV. 429/2 Marconi's faith in the successful commercial operation of the system was more than justified, and radio engineers elsewhere were quick to change from skepticism to enthusiasm. **1917** *Wireless World* Apr. 10 The name 'wireless system' in radio engineering seems now to have no scientific meaning. **1942** P. C. SANDRETTO *Princ. Aeronaut. Radio Engin.* p.v, It is necessary to explain how I determined the point where ordinary radio engineering ends and aeronautical radio engineering begins. **1975** D. G. FINK *Electronics Engineers' Handbk.* p. xiii, This new Handbook is the first to be devoted to the field of electronics engineering at large. Earlier important handbooks..treated the field primarily from the point of view of the first important application in the field—radio engineering. **1928** Radio ham [see HAM *sb.*[1] 6]. **1951** H. M. WATSON et al. *Understanding Radio* (ed. 2) xxvi. 642 The exploits of the radio hams in times of disaster..are well known. **1971** *Daily Tel.* 13 Sept. 1/8 The radio ham..heard two men planning the raid over short-wave radio sets. **1926** *Wireless World* 18 Aug. 229/1 American business men engaged in the radio industry. **1933** *Radio Times* 14 Apr. 94 (Advt.), Mullard valves have always taken the radio industry ahead. **1951** M. MCLUHAN *Mech. Bride* (1967) 22/2 This is not a situation peculiar, for example, to the radio, movie or book industries. **1928–9** *T. Eaton & Co. Catal.* Fall & Winter 245/3 Radio License... The law requires that every radio set be licensed. **1969** *Morning Star* 9 Aug. 5 Heavier fines for TV and radio licence dodgers have been called for by the Postmaster General. **1975** *Times* 26 Sept. 15/4 His father was one of the original radio licence holders. **1978** *Nature* 14 Sept. 91/3 Less than 10% of these [QSOs] are turning out to be 'radio-loud'. **1921** R. D. PAINE *Comrades of Rolling Ocean* iv. 73 The radio man reports storm signals hoisted all the way from Key West to Norfolk. **1928–9** *T. Eaton & Co. Catal.* Fall & Winter 245/3 Our radio goods..are purchased and inspected by qualified radio men. **1945** M. LOWRY *Let.* 6 June (1967) 46 A great friend of mine who was at college with me—a well-known radioman in Canada. **1977** *Time* 3 Jan. 35/2 He lied about his age to get into the Navy and served as a radioman in the Pacific during World War II. **1977** *New Statesman* 2 Sept. 298/1 This is not because Bush has a particularly high quota of veteran radio men. **1978** PASACHOFF & KUTNER *University Astron.* viii. 221 (*caption*) A radio map of the sun made at a wave-length of 2·8 cm with the 100-meter dish of the Max Planck Institute for Radio Astronomy. **1962** A. NISBETT *Technique Sound Studio* 267 *Radio microphone*, microphone and small transmitter sending a signal which can be picked up at a distance of up to perhaps several hundred yards. **1978** *Broadcast* 6 Feb. 12/3 Licences which authorize..mobile radiotelephone, radiomicrophones, radiopaging devices. **1980** J. BALL *Then came Violence* (1981) xvi. 144 He picked up the radio microphone. **1974** *Listener* 14 Mar. 330/3 Rix..had me fitted with a radio mike, which is..a small and highly sensitive transmitter, enabling me to record impressions unobtrusively. **1931** B. JONES *Avigation* xv. 274 (*heading*) Radio navigation. **1951** *Sci. News* XXII. 110 Positions were fixed by radio navigation. **1974** *Encycl. Brit. Macropædia* XII. 908/2 Loran..is a radio-navigation system that permits a ship to locate its position accurately by timing the arrival of pulses from synchronized shore transmitters. **1921** *Brit. Pat.* 161,448 (*title*) Improvements in or relating to radio-navigational systems. **1958** *Times* 18 Aug. 8/3 The Nantucket field had no instrument landing system, no high intensity approach lights, and only a minimum of radio navigational aids. **1978** R. V. JONES *Most Secret War* xxiv. 210 The drive at last started for us to emulate the Germans in their radio navigational techniques. **1941** *Sun* (Baltimore) 15 Oct. 5/5 The Twenty-ninth Division has its full complement of radio nets, and is maintaining its communications of this nature with considerable success. **1976** C. EGLETON *State Visit* ix. 84 A re-broadcast system had been installed which allowed them to monitor the police radio net. **1935** C. G. BURGE *Compl. Bk. Aviation* 503/1 Air transport is essentially international in character, and the organization and control of the radio networks, if they are to benefit air transport, must also be applied on an international basis. **1966** N. WYMER *From Marconi to Telstar* viii. 85 Since the war all the great nations have steadily expanded their overseas services until today the radio network covers the entire world. **1972** J. MOSEDALE *Football* iv. 52 New York..is the communications capital of the world—home to national magazines and the television and radio networks. **1968** Radio pager [see PAGER *sb.*[3]]. **1960** Radio paging [see PAGE *v.*[1] c]. **1978** *Times* 3 Nov. 27/4 The Post Office itself has listed the main telecommunications services..envisaged for the years 1985 and 2000... By 1985 there will be..radiopaging, confravision (conference television), viewphone. **1925** *Scribner's Mag.* Sept. 80 (Advt.), Model 50 Radio-Phonograph Combination. Price $325. **1952** AUDEN *Nones* 18 According to the gospel Of the radio-phonograph. **1979** T. GIFFORD *Hollywood Gothic* (1980) xxi. 216 An ancient Philco radio-phonograph. **1957** *Nature* 4 May 898/1 This 'radio pill', as it is termed, was designed by Dr. V. K. Zworykin and developed by engineers of the Radio Corporation of America at Camden, New Jersey. **1962** *New Scientist* 10 May 288/3 A radio pill contains an electronic circuit that generates a radio frequency signal. **1970** *Sci. Jrnl.* June 84/1 Pressure changes within the vagina and uterus have also been measured, by using a tiny device known as the radio-pill. **1933** Radio pirate [see PIRATE *sb.* 4b]. **1964** *Daily Tel.* 11 May 20 (*heading*) Radio 'pirates' problem for Cabinet. **1965** *Astrophysical Jrnl.* CXLI 1560 Members of the class called here quasi-stellar galaxies..resemble the quasi-stellar radio sources..in many optical properties, but they are radio-quiet. **1977** *Sci. Amer.* Aug. 38/3 Many quasars have no detectable radio emissions. In fact, the great majority of quasars may be radio quiet. **1971** D. W. SCIAMA *Mod. Cosmol.* v. 73 It must be emphasised that the radio-quietness of these new objects is only relative. **1949** *Sun* (Baltimore) 26 July 18/3 The wing tip 'radomes', as the compact radio-radar installation is called, were developed for the Air Force. **1966** M. WOODHOUSE *Tree Frog* viii. 62 A radio-radar control system with a range of seven hundred miles. **1976** G. H. MORRISON in L.-H. Lee *Characterization of Metal & Polymer Surfaces* I. 362 Our laboratory has been involved in an examination of steel strands in the cables suspending a 525-ton feed platform in the world's largest radio-radar telescope at Arecibo, Puerto Rico. **1926** *Physical Rev.* XXVII. 202 The ionic term will be negligibly small compared to the electronic term, except for very long waves outside of the usual radio range. **1929** *Proc. IRE* XVII. 2147 The so-called 'aural' type of directive radiobeacon, or 'radio range' as it is now called, was finally considered to be most applicable to the Airways Service. **1942** P. C. SANDRETTO *Princ. Aeronaut. Radio Engin.* i. 7 By the late fall of 1929, there was installed in the United States a line of radio ranges extending from New Jersey to Iowa. **1949** *Nature* 12 Nov. 816/2 The radio range from about 1 cm. to 20 m. **1951** *Oxf. Jun. Encycl.* IV. 291/1 The Radio Range, a long-range navigational aid..transmits the letters A..and N..in Morse code simultaneously in different directions. If the pilot is flying directly on his proper course, he will be midway between the paths of the two signals. **1960** RODMAN & VARSAVSKY tr. *I. S. Shklovsky's Cosmic Radio Waves* ii. 84 Thus if the sun appears to be the dominating source of radiation at optical frequencies, in the radio range it plays a much more modest role. **1966** *McGraw-Hill Encycl. Sci. & Technol.* XI. 255/2 *Consol*... This radio range navigation aid provides a number of characteristic signal zones that rotate in a time sequence. **1946** R. E. HIGGINBOTHAM *Wine for my Brothers* v. 97 He paused a moment before the door of the radio shack. **1973** D. KYLE *Raft of Swords* (1974) xiv. 152 Bill Harrison was sitting in his radio shack at Bella Bella. **1976** 'M. NELSON' *Crusoe Test* iii. 42 He had veered off into the captain's room..taken the radio shack key... He had only needed seconds in the radio room. **1922** *Moving Picture Stories* 4 Aug. 22/2 When the Women's Radio League of America some months ago asked me to join them and appear at their exhibition at a radio show, I thought it a unique invitation. **1932** *Radio Times* 29 July 239/2 Peter Creswell will produce *Ball and Dance*, a German radio show built up from scenes at famous balls of history. **1940** G. MARX *Let.* 10 Oct. (1967) 26 I'm..discussing a radio show that I might do... A kind of human interest story with a slightly wacky father, who, of course, would be me. **1971** D. NATHAN *Laughtermakers* ii. 50 When the series was over Milligan went to Australia, where he did thirteen radio shows similar to the Goons. **1976** B. TOOK *Laughter in Air* i. 11 Theatre magnates still held the whip hand, making offers they couldn't refuse to Arthur Askey and Jack Warner for stage versions of their hit radio shows. **1923** E. W. MARCHANT *Radio Telegr.* ix. 100 The problem of finding the direction from which a radio signal is coming has been referred to already, and its practical importance..is obvious. **1937** *Discovery* Jan. 3/2 Radio signals can travel round the world and not be lost in space as would be the case if the ionosphere did not exist. **1962** F. I. ORDWAY et al. *Basic Astronautics* iii. 46 The planet [*sc.* Mercury] emits natural radio signals. **1969** *Times* 16 Jan. 4/7 Measurements of the radio signals from sulphur hydride may be a valuable check of estimates of the amount of sulphur in interstellar space. **1974** L. DEIGHTON *Spy Story* xix. 208 That radio signal obliges us to continue with the pick-up. **1946** Radio silence [see RADIOLOCATOR]. **1959** R. COLLIER *City that wouldn't Die* vii. 106 [He] exultantly broke radio-silence: 'I've got two dirty great Huns in my sights!' **1970** A. DEKKER *Divers Diamonds* ii. 15 *Toledo* [*sc.* a submarine] has subsequently maintained total radio silence and has gone without trace. **1977** *Observer* 3 Apr. 1/6 The control tower said sharply, 'Radio silence please, I will continue to call up KLM.' **1978** *Peace News* 25 Aug. 8/2 This 'strike' lasted some three days, and rumour had it that GCHQ feared that the Russians were maintaining 'radio silence', the traditional prelude to offensive action! **1976** B. LECOMBER *Dead Weight* xiii. 154 Filing incomplete flight plans and going radio-silent for long periods is bloody silly. **1977** *Sci. Amer.* Aug. 38/3 Only later, when the sky was searched at optical wavelengths for bright blue and ultraviolet objects, were the radio-silent quasars discovered. **1931** *Flight* XXIII. 278/1 The trials proceeding in America with a radio-sounder have been successful and appear to promise good results. **1969** *Times* 20 Jan. 8/1 Alouette 1, the first of a series of satellites built in Canada.. is equipped with a radio sounder which probes the atmosphere beneath the satellite. **1929** *Bull. Amer. Meteorol. Soc.* X. 220 The radio sounding balloons to be released from the *Graf Zeppelin* will employ a radio sending device developed under the direction of P. A. Moltchanoff. **1936** *Meteorol. Mag.* LXXI. 5 (*heading*) Radio-sounding of the atmosphere. **1958** MILLER & PARRY *Everyday Meteorol.* i. 29 The radio-sounding balloon..has the advantage that it need not be visible. **1963** *Times* 31 May 16/2 A form of radio sounding, similar to radar, may provide a new means of charting the depth of rock surfaces covered by snow and ice, as in Greenland and Antarctica. **1929** *Bell System Techn. Jrnl.* VIII. 313 Fortunately this frequency was so located in the radio spectrum that a band of the desired width..could be obtained. **1932** *Proc. IRE* XX. 96 Ultra-short waves in point-to-point propagation resemble light waves rather than the longer and more conventional waves of the radio spectrum. **1964** R. H. BAKER *Astron.* (ed. 8) iv. 116 The only known emission line in the radio spectrum was first observed..in 1951. **1978** *Nature* 8 June 431/2 Samples of QSOs with flat radio spectra were chosen. **1949** *Sci. Amer.* Sept. 38/1 The small spots are tiny enough to be considered 'radio stars'. **1957** *New Scientist* 27 June 32/1 Ryle concludes that his weak radio stars are evidence of more crowded days when the universe was young. **1963** *Times* 20 Apr. 8/4 The first true radio stars—stars (in the ordinary sense) that emit radio waves at sufficient intensity to be detected and identified by radio telescopes—have been discovered by Sir Bernard Lovell. **1969** *Times* 18 Apr. 12/5 Pulsars, the radio stars whose clock-like regularity has so far eluded explanation. **1912** *Statutes U.S.A.* XXXVII. I. 303 Every Government station on land or sea shall have special call letters designated and published in the list of radio stations of the United States. **1934** JOYCE *Let.* 20 Nov. (1966) III. 328 You don't say what those radio stations pay. **1968** A. DIMENT *Bang Bang Birds* iii. 41 One of the local radio stations gave me the news. **1977** C. MCCULLOUGH *Thorn Birds* xv. 340 Progress had finally come to Gillanbone in the shape of an Australian Broadcasting Commission radio station. **1929** *Amazing Stories* June 202/1 Well, what do you think of it?.. How do you like my radio-telescope? **1948** *Newsweek* 18 Nov. 98/2 The newer radio telescope..is designed to gather radio static in the microwave region. **1953** *N.Y. Times* 19 Apr. E9/5 The foundations of Britain's million-dollar radio telescope..are now being built at Jodrell Bank, Cheshire. **1969** *Times* 25 Mar. 12/6 The experiment was carried out with the giant radio telescope carved out of a natural bowl in the hills of Puerto Rico. **1976** L. DEIGHTON *Twinkle, twinkle, Little Spy* xxiii. 229 Two huge radio telescopes, the dishes about sixty feet across. **1916** *Electr. Experimenter* IV. 486/3 If the radio waves were powerful enough to travel from Mars to the moon, they.. could travel from the moon to Mars. **1946** *Nature* 3 Aug. 150/1 As radio-waves are reflected by obstacles of any kind, they can be used in darkness as well as daylight, in thick fog or other obscuring atmospheric conditions, as light to show whether the way is open or not. **1969** G. LYALL *Venus with*

Pistol xxxiii. 212 The dark air between us slowly started to hum like radio waves. **1977** *Times* 20 June 5/2 Through vibrations, the radio wave can transmit conversation and noise back from the room it is aimed at. **1937** *Proc. Nat. Acad. Sci.* XXIII. 178 The low opacity in the radio wave-lengths, arising from the small relative size of the particles, will selectively permit the escape of these longer wave-lengths. **1972** *Sci. Amer.* Aug. 51/3 Neutral atomic hydrogen emits and absorbs radiation at the radio wavelength of 21 centimeters and can be readily observed by radio telescopes.

radio ('reɪdɪəʊ), *v.* [f. the sb.] **a.** *trans.* To transmit or send (a message or information) by radio. **b.** *intr.* To send a message, etc., by radio; to give information or make a request by radio (with dependent clause). (In both senses freq. with advbs.)

1919 *Pop. Sci. Monthly* Sept. 116/2 He radios the information to the ship. **1926** H. T. Wilkins *Marvels Mod. Mech.* 213 As soon as the observer spots a shoal of fish, he marks a square on the chart,.. and at once radios to the port. **1926** *Glasgow Herald* 20 Dec. 9 The British ship Defender has radioed that it has saved two members of the crew of the schooner Lincoln. **1937** G. Frankau *More of Us* xiii. 136 Let Pink flay Anti-Pink, or vice versa, 'Delicious weather', radio'd still our purser. **1958** *Industr. & Engin. Chem.* Mar. 22A/2 Explorer has radioed back information that the temperature inside is between 20° and 50°C., tolerable enough for a human passenger. **1958** 'Castle' & 'Hailey' *Flight into Danger* ii. 29 Let me know if she gets any worse and I'll radio ahead. **1969** *New Yorker* 12 Apr. 68/2 A satellite..radioed information about the fields of low-energy particles far above the earth. **1970** *Daily Tel.* 14 Oct. 1/3 The lifeboat later radioed back that the dead man and the others were being taken by the trawler to Boulogne. **1972** *Oxford Times* 25 Feb. 1/8 Our beat policemen radio through if congestion is building up anywhere. **1973** J. Rossiter *Manipulators* xxvi. 244 He had to get away before Jackson found Bradley's body and radio'd back. **1977** *Daily Tel.* 18 Mar. 1/7 The police radioed for assistance and a detachment of Irish troops arrived. **1978** J. Irving *World according to Garp* xv. 313 Go radio our position.

Hence **'radioed** *ppl. a.*, transmitted or reported by radio.

1943 J. Flanner in *New Yorker* 29 May 42/3 A radioed appeal from General de Gaulle in London. **1953** A. Huxley *Let.* 9 Aug. (1969) 682 Robots responsive to the radioed will of their masters. **1973** 'A. Hall' *Tango Briefing* xii. 149 London wanted photographs and a full radioed report of the freighter's cargo. **1977** 'W. Wingate' *Fireplay* i. 12 Doneska could have foundered anywhere from her last radioed position off Los Angeles to close by Valparaiso.

radio- ('reɪdɪəʊ).

1. Comb. form of radius *sb. Anat.* Belonging to the radius in conjunction with some other part, as **,radio-'carpal, -'digital, -'humeral, -'muscular, -'palmar, -'ulnar** *adjs.*

1831 R. Knox *Cloquet's Anat.* 133 The external lateral ligament of the radio-carpal articulation. **1845** Todd & Bowman *Phys. Anat.* I. 137 Another example is the superior radio-ulnar articulation. **1858** Holden *Hum. Osteol.* (1878) 160 The lower end of the bones of the fore-arm forms the radio-carpal joint.

2. Comb. form of radiate *v.* or radiation. *Physics.* Connected with rays or radiation, esp. connected with ionizing radiation, as **radio'density**, the degree to which a material will absorb ionizing radiation; radio-opacity; **,radioderma'titis**, dermatitis caused by X-rays or other ionizing radiation; **,radiodiag'nosis**, the diagnosis of disease by means of X-rays or other ionizing radiation; hence **,radiodiag'nostic** *a.*; **radio-e'cology**, the study of the ecological effects of radioactive materials and ionizing radiation; hence **,radio-eco'logical** *a.*; **radio-e'cologist**; **radioge'netics**, the study of the genetic effects of ionizing radiation; hence **radioge'netic, -ical** *adjs.*; **,radiolumi'nescence**, luminescence caused by ionizing radiation; hence **,radiolumi'nescent** *a.*; **,radio-mi'crometer**, an instrument for measuring minute degrees of infra-red or microwave radiation; **radiomi'metic** *a.*, of (the action or properties of) a substance: producing effects upon living cells resembling those produced by ionizing radiation; **,radione'crosis** *Med.*, necrosis caused by excessive exposure to ionizing radiation; **,radio-pasteuri'zation**, pasteurization of food by exposure to ionizing radiation; so **radio-'pasteurized** *a.*; **,radiopharma'ceutical** *a.* and *sb.*, (being or pertaining to) any radioactive compound or preparation which is administered to a patient for the purpose of radiotherapy or diagnosis; **,radiopharma'cology**, the use of drugs in radiology; also, the study of physiology and the metabolism of drugs by means of radiopharmaceuticals; so **,radiopharmaco'logical** *a.*, **-pharma'cologist**; **radio'pharmacy**, the preparation and use of radiopharmaceuticals; a laboratory for this work; so **radio'pharmacist**; **,radio-pro'tection**, the prevention or countering by chemical means of the harmful effects produced in living tissues by ionizing radiation; so **,radio-pro'tective** *a.*, being or possessing this property; **,radio-pro'tector**, a substance possessing this property; **radio-re'sistant** *a.*, resistant to the action of ionizing radiation; so **radio-re'sistance**; **radio'sensitive** *a.*, sensitive to the action of ionizing radiation; so **†radio'sensitiveness, radiosensi'tivity**; **radio'sensitize** *v. trans.*, to make (more) radiosensitive; so **radio'sensitizing** *vbl. sb.*; also **,radiosensiti'zation**; **radio'sensitizer**, a substance which is used to increase the sensitivity of particular organisms or tissues to ionizing radiation; **,radiosterili'zation**, (*a*) the process of rendering sterile by means of ionizing radiation; (*b*) the process of rendering free from micro-organisms by means of ionizing radiation; also (in either sense) **radio'sterilized** *a.*; **radio'surgery**, the use of beams of ionizing radiation in surgery; so **radio'surgical** *a.*; **,radiotrans'lucent** *a.* = radiolucent *a.*; hence **,radiotrans'lucency**.

1936 B. J. M. Harrison *Textbk. Roentgenol.* iii. 62 Of the media of greater radiodensity than the tissues the most commonly used is sulphate of barium. **1977** *Proc. R. Soc. Med.* LXX. 518/2 If the stone is still *in situ* then the chemical composition may be assessed by the radiodensity. **1903** *Progressive Med.* III. 161 Heidingsfeld's case was a bullous radiodermatitis. **1930** *Times Educ. Suppl.* 2 Aug. p. iv/3 The Cross of the Legion of Honour has been conferred on Dr. Jean Chabry, whose experimental work in radiology has resulted in an attack of radiodermatitis, necessitating amputation of his right arm. **1968** A. Rook et al. *Textbk. Dermatol.* xv. 359/2 Chronic radiodermatitis is not an inflammatory process and should strictly be termed roentgen atrophy or perhaps roentgen poikiloderma. **1904** F. P. Foster *Appleton's Med. Dict.* 1676/2 *Radiodiagnosis*, diagnosis by means of Röntgen ray examination. **1910** A. Abrams *Diagnostic Therapeutics* iv. 627 Radio-diagnosis is more accurate than percussion in defining the dimensions of the organ. **1978** *Lancet* 25 Feb. 434/1 The current practice of treating radiodiagnosis as cost-free, risk-free, and done in a flash has seriously affected medical standards over the past three decades. **1907** *Jrnl. Amer. Med. Assoc.* 17 Nov. 1392/2 (*heading*) The correlation of clinical and radio-diagnostic findings. **1961** *Lancet* 29 July 257/1 Dr. C. Pickard..was..critical of past and future planning for radiodiagnostic departments. **1956** E. P. Odum in *Conf. Radioactive Isotopes in Agric.* (U.S. Atomic Energy Comm.) 102/2 Radio-ecological research at AEC installations..has been handicapped by (1) lack of prior knowledge of the environment, and (2) uncontrolled experimental conditions. **1975** *Nature* 3 Jan. p. xiii (Advt.), The successful candidate should have knowledge and some experience in marine radioecological research and related techniques. **1959** E. P. & H. T. Odum *Fund. Ecol.* (ed. 2) xiv. 477 This rather surprising finding, repeatedly documented by radioecologists working at the Nevada Test Site.., is apparently to be explained by the fact that the smaller particles which fall at a distance stick to the leaves of plants and dissolve more readily. **1956** E. P. Odum in *Conf. Radioactive Isotopes in Agric.* (U.S. Atomic Energy Comm.) 100/1 Only now that we have some familiarity with the functional aspects of our ecosystem are we ready to begin controlled experiments in radio-ecology. **1964** *Oceanogr. & Marine Biol.* II. 256 Radioecology or radiation ecology is the branch of ecology which concerns itself with the dispersion and interaction of radionuclides in and with the physical, chemical, and biological environment. **1974** *Nature* 13 Dec. 618/2 The two fundamental problems in radioecology are to determine how radionuclides migrate within biogeological systems and how ionising radiations affect microorganisms, plants and animals. **1971** *Radiation Bot.* XI. 119 (*heading*) Radiogenetic effects of gamma- and fast neutron irradiation on different ontogenetic stages of the tomato. *Ibid.*, Pollen, which has advantages for radiogenetical studies, seems to hold little promise for mutation breeding purposes. **1950** *Genetics* XXXV. 56 (*heading*) On the interpretation of the dose-frequency in radiogenetics. **1955** [see radiobiology]. **1963** *Biol. Abstr.* XLI. 642/2 Valuable data have been obtained in the field of radiogenetics. **1911** *Chem. Abstr.* V. 3059 The intensity of the radioluminescence is proportional to the distance in mm. **1946** *Thorpe's Dict. Appl. Chem.* (ed. 4) VII. 405/2 Radioluminescence of solids induced by X-rays finds considerable technical application in industrial and medical fields. **1966** G. F. J. Garlick in P. Goldberg *Luminescence of Inorg. Solids* xii. 689 It was the existence of the particle-excited radioluminescence of uranyl salts that led Becquerel to the discovery of radioactivity in 1896. **1919** *Chem. Abstr.* XIII. 2806 A long discourse on the underlying principles and the preparation of radioluminescent paints. **1887** C. V. Boys in *Proc. Royal Soc.* XLII. 189 (*title*) Preliminary Note on the 'Radio-Micrometer'. **1888** *Times* 10 May 5/5 Mr. C. V. Boys's Radiomicrometer..consists of a circuit made of antimony, bismuth, and copper. **1908** *Rep. Brit. Assoc. Adv. Sci. 1907* 621 The first thing is to tune up the receiver accurately. This can be done by a Duddell radio-micrometer, which measures the received [radio] energy satisfactorily although it is very small. **1966** *McGraw-Hill Encycl. Sci. & Technol.* XI. 319/1 The radiomicrometer was invented by C. V. Boys in 1887 to avoid the limitations of a separate thermocouple and galvanometer. However, because it is delicate and inconvenient, it has virtually gone out of use. **1947** P. Dustin in *Nature* 14 June 796/2 These effects are remarkably similar to those of ionizing radiations: the mitotic poisons of the trypaflavine type are radio-mimetic. **1965** *New Scientist* 25 Nov. 586/2 The still unidentified agent causing the haemorrhage is a radiomimetic compound—that is, it poisons the bone-marrow very much as radiation does. **1974** R. M. Kirk et al. *Surgery* ii. 9/2 Irradiation and radiomimetic drugs..administered in the treatment of neoplasms, cause delay in wound healing by their damaging effects on dividing cells. **1933** Ward & Smith *Rec. Adv. Radium* viii. 85 In this way radio-necrosis may result in the more radio-resistant tumours without destruction of the tumour. **1963** *New Scientist* 9 May 334/3 Early treatment of certain irradiation accident cases with 'vasodilators' may prevent radionecrosis altogether. **1977** *Lancet* 27 Aug. 460/1 Radionecrosis of the brain may follow therapeutic irradiation of the pituitary. **1959** *Internat. Jrnl. Appl. Radiation & Isotopes* VI. 128/1 Extensive investigations..will be necessary before radio-pasteurization without refrigeration can be recommended for meats. **1968** *Biol. Abstr.* XLIX. 2446/2 Freshly killed pre-rigor fish respond better toward the radio-pasteurization process than do post-rigor fish. **1966** E. R. Killam et al. in *Proc. Internat. Symposium Food Irradiation* 839 A petition was submitted to the FDA on April 29, 1966 for the approval of radio-pasteurized strawberries for public consumption. **1971** *Jrnl. Food Technol.* VI. 82 Blackening in radio-pasteurized shrimps can be effectively controlled by pre-blanching treatment. **1960** *Jrnl. Amer. Med. Assoc.* 10 Sept. 162/1 The production of radiopharmaceutical compounds that concentrate in organs, such as colloidal gold in the liver and chlormerodrin..in the kidneys. **1963** P. F. Belcastro in H. M. Burlage et al. *Physical & Technical Pharmacy* xvii. 701 Radiopharmaceuticals can be used as therapeutic agents for treating specific diseases more efficiently than by traditional methods. **1966** G. V. LeRoy in G. A. Andrews et al. *Radioactive Pharmaceuticals* xxxvii. 669 There is a continuing disagreement about the appropriate dose of almost all the radiopharmaceutical agents currently in use. **1977** *Lancet* 23 Apr. 907/2 Adverse reactions to radio-pharmaceuticals are rare, and are generally due to the carrier portion rather than to the isotope itself. **1973** Radiopharmacist [see radiochemist]. **1963** *Biol. Abstr.* XLIV. 479/2 (*heading*) Radio-pharmacological investigations of the mechanism of action of sympathetic alpha and beta receptors in the region of the cardia of the rabbit. **1960** *Jrnl. Amer. Med. Assoc.* 10 Sept. 165/2 The clinician, biochemist, physiologist, or radiopharmacologist will eventually discover substances that will concentrate in the pancreas and adrenal and parathyroid glands. **1968** *Australasian Radiol.* XII. 239/1 Pancoast, in 1914, appears to have initiated radiopharmacology when he used morphine to stimulate gastric peristalsis. **1976** M. Tubis in Tubis & Wolf *Radiopharmacy* xv. 406 Radiopharmacology ..is concerned with the use of labeled compounds, the 'radiophores' carriers of radioactivity, to demonstrate the distribution, deposition, kinetics of metabolism, turnover, and the excretion. *Ibid.*, Radiopharmacy..is the science and art of preparing and dispensing the labeled compounds of pharmaceutical quality that are used in nuclear medicine for diagnosis and therapy. **1977** K. Kristensen et al. *Quality Control in Nuclear Med.* xxxiii. 271/1 The radiopharmacy should be designed so that dispensing and radioactive waste handling do not interfere with or contaminate each other. **1957** *Brit. Jrnl. Radiol.* XXX. 97/1 This..underlines the importance of the liver in radio-protection. **1975** *Internat. Jrnl. Radiation Biol.* XXVIII. 41 It appears that cystamine may be limiting the availability of reducing equivalents and thus providing radioprotection to lipogenesis. **1956** *Brit. Jrnl. Radiol.* XXIX. 623/1 Scientists..have studied the radio-protective activity of cysteamine and cystamine. **1958** *Ibid.* XXXI. 339/2 All the radio-protective substances effective in mice have the common action of lowering body temperature. **1975** *Biochem. & Biophys. Res. Communications* LXVII. 1170 The increase..in the amount of exogenous superoxide dismutase associated with the eluted bone marrow stem cells was also accompanied by an enhancement in the radioprotective effect of the enzyme on the proliferative capacity of the cells. **1960** *Internat. Jrnl. Radiation Biol.* II. 231 (*heading*) Sub[s]trates as radioprotectors of hexokinase. **1977** *Nature* 3 Nov. 15/3 A significant contribution to radiobiology was the demonstration that SOD is an effective radioprotector exerting a protective role even when administered after radiation doses have been delivered. **1927** *Cancer Rev.* II. 397 The degree of radio-resistance seems to be more marked in proportion as the treatment has been unwisely prolonged. **1957** *Brit. Jrnl. Radiol.* XXX. 97/1 A higher concentration of cysteamine in the liver increases radio-resistance. **1929** *Radiology* XIII. 316/2 Squamous carcinoma, malignancy of varying grades, radioresistant. **1959** *Internat. Jrnl. Appl. Radiation & Isotopes* VI. 157/1 The alkaline phosphatase of milk is extremely radio-resistant. **1977** *Lancet* 27 Aug. 460/1 The endocrine-active adenomas are characteristically more radio-resistant than the endocrine-inactive variety. **1920** *Amer. Jrnl. Roentgenol.* VII. 53/1 Remarkable examples of radio-sensitive tumors are ectodermal and basal-celled epithelioma derived from the basal-celled layers of the epidermis. **1956** C. Auerbach *Genetics in Atomic Age* viii. 80 Tissues in which division is going on are so much more radiosensitive than tissues in which cell division has ceased. **1976** *Nature* 17 June 588/1 If these cells are less radiosensitive, ionising radiation could favour their overgrowth. **1921** *Arch. Radiol. & Electrotherapy* XXV. 348 A further factor in tissues is the blood or lymph content; the more this is, the more is the radio-sensitiveness. **1924** *Brit. Jrnl. Radiol.* XXIX. 270 The radio-sensitivity was found to vary greatly according to the stage of cellular division. **1971** G. G. Luce *Body Time* v. 167 Perhaps the rhythm of radiosensitivity may be traced to cycles of activity in the bone marrow and spleen where blood is formed. **1951** *Jrnl. Chem. Educ.* XXVIII. 414/2 Radiosensitization may be significant in radiation chemistry. **1976** *Radiology* CXIX. 221 This..would ostensibly lead to some degree of tumor reoxygenation ('radiosensitization') as well as direct chemotherapeutic effects. *Ibid.* 725/1 Cetylpyridinium chloride did not radiosensitize bacteria suspended in nutrient broth. **1953** *Brit. Jrnl. Cancer* VII. 316 This compound (Synkavit) has a small but useful effect as a clinical radiosensitiser. **1972** *Lancet* 22 Sept. 638/2 A true radiosensitiser is a chemical which increases the cell-killing effect of a given dose of radiation. **1936** *Biol. Abstr.* X. 1905/1 His researches concern the radio-sensitizing effect of metabolic exchanges and the degree to which substances modifying the metabolism also modify the radiosensitivity. **1953** *Brit. Jrnl. Cancer* VII. 314 A radiosensitising chemical agent..in combination with radiotherapy should produce a mean survival time after treatment double that after radiotherapy only. **1978** *Jrnl. R. Soc. Med.* LXXI. 672 The radiosensitizing properties of the group of nitroimidazoles. **1964** *Jrnl. Econ. Entomol.* LVII. 756/1 For mosquito sterilization..the desired goal of highly competitive, yet permanently sterile, males is more readily attainable with chemosterilization than radiosterilization. **1966** E. R. Killam et al. in *Proc. Internat. Symposium Food Irradiation* viii. 842 The radiosterilization of certain cuts of beef may require irradiation at this temperature [*sc.* −80°C]. *Ibid.*, Future developments in cryogenics should lower the..cost of radiosterilized meat products. **1967** *Jrnl. Econ. Entomol.* LX. 696 (*heading*) Mating competitiveness in radiosterilized males. **1975** *Ibid.* LXVIII. 595/2, 300 radiosterilized ♀ and 4200 radiosterilized ♂ were released each evening. **1933** *O.E.D.* Suppl. s.v. *Radio-* 2, Radio-surgery. **1963** *New England Jrnl. Med.* 19 Sept. 597/2 In 1954 we set out upon a study in clinical medicine in which these high-energy protons and alpha particles have been used in various forms of so-called 'bloodless' surgery, or radiosurgery. **1973** *Internat. Jrnl. Radiation Biol.* XXIV. 229 (*heading*) Split-brain cats prepared for radiosurgery. **1929** *Daily Express* 16 Jan. 9/6 Even if the growth should have extended to the glands, radio-surgical methods would offer a good prospect of eradication. **1959** *Probl. Oncol.* V. 98 (*heading*) Radio-surgical treatment of skin cancer involving a free skin graft. **1973** *Internat. Jrnl. Radiation Biol.* XXIV. 239 A 3 mm beam of protons is too wide for safe radiosurgical use in the rat brain. **1974** A. Henry in R. M. Kirk et al. *Surgery* xv. 295/2 X-rays show an area of radiotranslucency in the metaphysis, which may cross the growth plate to involve the epiphysis. **1959** *New Biol.* XXX. 25 If the process is observed radiologically, the solid lungs become radio-translucent rapidly, as if a light has been turned on. **1964** L. Martin *Clin. Endocrinol.* (ed. 4) iv. 149 Destructive bone lesions..cause sharply demarcated radiotranslucent areas in affected bones.

3. a. Connected with radioactivity, as **ˌradioallergoˈsorbent** *a.* [ALLERG(Y + -O + SORBENT *sb.* (*a.*)], in ***radioallergosorbent test***, a form of radioimmunoassay for measuring antibodies to an allergen (see quot. 1967); **radioˈassay** *sb.*, an assay performed by measuring radioactivity from a radioisotope; also as *v. trans.*; **ˈradio-atom**, an atom of a radioactive substance; **radioˈautograph** = AUTORADIOGRAPH; also **ˌradioautoˈgraphic** *a.*; **radioauˈtography**; **ˌradiochroˈmatogram**, a chromatogram of a radioactively labelled preparation which is recorded or measured by means of a radiological technique; **radioˈcolloid**, a radioactive substance in colloidal form; hence **radiocoˈlloidal** *a.*; **radio-ˈdating** *vbl. sb.*, isotopic dating; **ˈradio-element**, a radioactive element; **radioˈhalo** = *pleochroic halo*; **radio-ˈiodinate** *v. trans.*, to label (a substance) with radio-iodine; so **radio-ˈiodinated** *ppl. a.*; **ˌradio-iodiˈnation**; **ˈradioligand**, a radio-labelled compound that has a strong chemical affinity for a particular receptor; **radio-ˈnuclide**, a radioactive nuclide; **radioˈpurity** = *radio-chemical purity*; **ˈradioscan**, a determination of the distribution of radioactive material (esp. a tracer) in a sample, an organ, etc.; **ˌradioˌstereoˈassay**, any biological assay technique in which the test substance is determined by allowing it to bind to a suitable protein or antibody in competition with a known quantity of radioactively labelled material, the extent of reaction being measured radiologically; (usu. applied to non-immunological methods: cf. *radioimmunoassay* s.v. RADIOIMMUNO-); **radiotoˈxicity**, the property of a radioactive substance of being injurious to a living organism when present in its tissue; hence **radioˈtoxic** *a.*; **radioˈtracer**, a radioactive tracer.

1967 L. Wide et al. in *Lancet* 25 Nov. 1105/2 An in-vitro method, called the radioallergosorbent test, has been developed for the detection of allergen-specific antibodies of a new immunoglobulin class, provisionally called IgND. *Ibid.* 1106/1 The principle of the method, the radioallergosorbent test (R.A.S.T.) is as follows: an allergen coupled to an insoluble polymer is added to the serum to be investigated, if antibodies to the allergen are present they should react with the conjugate; after the removal of all unbound serum components ^{125}I-labelled anti-IgND antibodies are then added, they will bind to the antibodies of the IgND class which have reacted with the polymer-coupled allergen; the uptake of labelled antibodies, measured in terms of radioactivity, on the particles is essentially proportional to the IgND allergen antibodies. **1971** *Internat. Arch. Allergy & Appl. Immunol.* XLI. 443 The radioallergosorbent test (RAST) was applied for quantitative estimation of IgE antibodies to various common allergens. **1977** *Lancet* 22 Oct. 847/2 Radioallergosorbent tests..for specific IgE antibody were also positive. **1951** *Nucleonics* Nov. 60 (*heading*) A simple inexpensive sample changer for the radioassay of..simple samples. **1963** *Analytical Biochem.* V. 89 The radioassay of cholesterol-C^{14} digitonide by gas flow technique..using methanol as the solvent for solution and plating. **1970** *Steroids* XV. 470 The method..requires only a simple extraction and an alumina thin layer chromatographic separation prior to radioassay. **1972** *Nature* 22 Dec. 463/2 Out of a series of a hundred [silver] bars, we have radio-assayed seven bars picked at random. **1905** *Phil. Trans. R. Soc.* A. CCIV. 209 It may..be supposed that occasionally one of the outlying revolving electrons, comprising the radio-atom, lapses into a position which results in a slow loss of energy from the atom in the form of radiation. **1947** *Instruments* XX. 712/1 The qualities which make radio-atoms ('hot' atoms) useful to science and industry make them hazardous to handle. **1941** *Jrnl. Appl. Physics* XII. 328 Slides of radio-autographs showing the distribution of phosphorus in various plant tissues will be shown. **1956** *Sci. Amer.* Nov. 144/2 (*caption*) Radioautographs indicate how Isoniazid is concentrated in brain tissue. **1974** K. N. Prasad *Human Radiation Biol.* xxi. 426 For the radioautographs of soluble materials, the tissue sections must be cut in a frozen state and then dried in a vacuum. **1947** *Radiology* XLIX. 327/2 Extensive radioautographic studies were made of these organs in which a high degree of selective localization took place. **1967** F. O. Schmitt in G. C. Quarton et al. *Neuro-sciences* 211/2 The radioautographic method using tritiated precursors lends itself well to the determination of the fate of axoplasm moving cellulofugally, both down the axon and possibly out along the dendrites. **1978** *Bull. Amer. Acad. Arts & Sci.* Feb. 17 These radioautographic experiments have revealed that in normal female somatic cells, one member of each pair of X chromosomes always replicates much later than all the other chromosomes including the second X chromosome. **1941** *Jrnl. Appl. Physics* XII. 446/1 Stout and his co-workers have followed the metabolism of inorganic phosphate in the leaves and fruit of the tomato plant by..the technique of radio-autography. **1973** *Nature* 20 Apr. 523/2 Whole-body radioautography is a useful method for studying the distribution of radio-labelled compounds among all the organs and tissues of an experimental animal. **1952** F. P. W. Winteringham et al. in *Nucleonics* Mar. 56/1 When the radiochromatogram is plotted as net rate of count against distance along the strip, *w* [*sc.* the total weight of labelled component] is proportional to the area enclosed by the relevant part of the curve. **1972** *Physics Bull.* May 298/1 At the 1971 Physics Exhibition Panax showed a unique rapid imaging system which promised to shorten the time to locate the radioactive regions on thin layer radiochromatograms. **1930** *Chem. Abstr.* XXIV. 1279 Recent expts. on solns. of the 'radiocolloid' Th C (Bi). **1956** *Nature* 28 Jan. 184/1 It is more likely..that the high concentration of chromate ions in the resin promotes the formation of a radio-colloid, which is then adsorbed on the resin. **1977** *Proc. R. Soc. Med.* LXX. 522/2 In the normal subject the radio-colloid is taken up avidly by the mono-nuclear phagocytes of the liver and only a small amount is taken up by other organs. **1936** O. Hahn *Appl. Radiochem.* 275/1 (Index), Radiocolloidal particles, size of... Radiocolloidal thorium X. **1950** *Thorpe's Dict. Appl. Chem.* (ed. 4) X. 433/1 Some portion..of the radiocolloidal phenomena is due to adsorption of the radioactive ions on particles of dust and solid impurities fortuitously present in the solutions. **1969** *New Scientist* 25 Sept. 632/1 Radiodating has revealed..that the lunar samples are at least 3100 million years old. **1975** K. H. Goulding in Williams & Wilson *Biologist's Guide to Princ. & Techniques Pract. Biochem.* vi. 196 The assumptions made in radiodating are sweeping and hence palaeontologists and anthropologists who use this technique can only give very approximate dates to their samples. **1903** *Contemp. Rev.* May 709 In the Periodic table of elements arranged in the ascending order of their atomic weights the three radio-elements are therefore at the extreme end. **1937** *Discovery* Mar. 65/2 A search for new radio elements of very short life whose existence is suspected. **1967** *New Scientist* 15 June 675/1 The main problem here is to ensure that dangerous long-lived radio-elements are not inadvertently produced. **1971** *Science* 20 Aug. 728/1 A new type of composite radiohalo has been found with rings attributable both to the ^{218}Po decay sequence and to ^{212}Po and possibly ^{212}Bi. **1974** *Nature* 13 Dec. 564/1 Polonium radiohaloes occur widely and not infrequently (total about 10^{15}–10^{20}) in Precambrian rocks. **1971** *Ibid.* 4 June 322/1 This protein was radio-iodinated to a specific activity of 0·6 μCi/μg with ^{125}I-iodide. **1955** *Ibid.* 26 Mar. 536/1 (*heading*) Radioiodinated human serum albumin. **1970** *Ibid.* 3 Oct. 58/1 Radioiodinated polypeptide hormones are widely used as tracers for both radioimmunoassay and *in vivo* metabolic studies. **1977** *Lancet* 13 Aug. 355/1 Dr Chait and his colleagues have studied the metabolism of very-low-density lipoprotein (V.L.D.L.) in a patient with type III hyperlipoproteinæmia..by injection of radioiodinated V.L.D.L. from a donor with endogenous hypertriglyceridæmia (type IV). **1957** *Jrnl. Laboratory & Clin. Med.* XLIX. 128 (*heading*) A method for radioiodination of antibody protein. **1974** *Nature* 25 Jan. 175/2 Several groups of investigators have subjected lymphocytes to enzymatic radioiodination of their cell surface proteins. **1972** *Jrnl. Clin. Endocrinol. & Metabolism* XXXIV. 130/1 Radioligand assays enable the biological activity of hormones at the target cell to be evaluated without the additional and variable effect of metabolism *in vivo*. **1978** *Nature* 8 June 472/1 This radio-ligand, which has been used in identifying and quantifying β-adrenoreceptors in a variety of intact and disrupted cell preparations, has enabled us to study cellular cyclic AMP accumulation and binding to β-adrenoreceptors in similar experimental conditions. **1947** T. P. Kohman in *Amer. Jrnl. Physics* XV. 356/2 *Radionuclide* should replace *radioelement* and *radioisotope* in most applications. **1963** *Engineering* 20 Sept. 378/3 The use of short-lived radio-nuclides makes it imperative to transfer the sample from the irradiation area to the activity-measuring location as speedily as possible. **1976** J. Follett *Doomsday Ultimatum* 73 What is the exact nature of the radionuclides stored..and what will happen if they are released? **1977** I. M. Campbell *Energy & Atmosphere* vii. 187 The radionuclide ^{14}C is produced naturally in the atmosphere by cosmic radiation but the level was almost doubled by the atmospheric nuclear-weapon testing of the 1960's. **1956** *Internat. Jrnl. Appl. Radiation & Isotopes* I. 227/2 The only disadvantage of the method of measurement is its extreme sensitivity to gamma-emitting impurities, although this can be turned into an asset in the determination of radio-purity. **1973** *Weed Res.* XIII. 340 The radiopurity of the isolated metabolites was checked by thin-layer chromatography..and autoradiography. **1965** *Amer. Rev. Respiratory Dis.* XCII. 959/2 (*caption*) The per cent of total pulmonary blood flow calculated from the radioscan for the diseased lung. **1966** *Amer. Jrnl. Cardiol.* XVIII. 819/2 The radioscan accurately reflected the pattern of arteriolar-capillary blood flow. **1974** *Nature* 1 Nov. 68/1 The radio-purity of these compounds was determined by radioscan of thin layer chromatograms. **1967** B. E. P. Murphy in *Jrnl. Clin. Endocrinol.* XXVII. 973/2 Such methods have been termed by the author 'competitive protein binding (CPB) analysis' and by R. P. Ekins 'saturation analysis', but because of their basic similarity to radioimmunoassays..the name 'radiostereoassay' has also been suggested [by the writer] as an analogous term which could be applied to both types of assay. **1974** *Nature* 22 Feb. 563/2 Before it can act, vitamin D must first be converted to its 25-hydroxy derivative..in the liver, and this chief circulating metabolite can be measured by radio-stereo-assay, thus providing a precise index of vitamin D nutritional status. **1950** *Nuclear Sci. Abstr.* IV. 398/1 Rat erythrocytes were irradiated with 6,030r and then injected subcutaneously..in order to determine the severity and nature of radiotoxic effects. **1975** *Nature* 27 Mar. 278/3 The dose limit for bone is based on uniformly deposited ^{226}Ra: but Pu, collecting at the bone surface, is considered ~5 times as radiotoxic. **1946** D. Antony et al. *Radiotoxicity of Injected Sr^{89} for Rats, Mice & Rabbits* (U.S. Atomic Energy Comm. Rep. MDDC 1540) 6 Radium, hitherto the only substance of which the radio-toxicity had been extensively studied. **1961** G. R. Choppin *Exper. Nuclear Chem.* ii. 12 Some of the commonly used nuclides are listed..according to their relative radio-toxicities. **1977** S. L. Barker in B. A. Rhodes *Quality Control in Nuclear Med.* xxviii. 243/1 Prepared formulations of long-lived nuclides present no special problems with the exception of possible radiotoxicity. **1950** *Mining Engin.* Mar. 364/2 Radiotracers were demonstrated to be of considerable value in the study of a typical mineral-collector system, dithiophosphate-galena. **1977** *Lancet* 19 Nov. 1072/2 No abnormal localisation of the radiotracer was observed in muscles of any of the controls.

b. Prefixed to the names of chemical elements and compounds: (i) Designating a radioactive isotope (usu. one prepared artificially) of the named element (†occas. of an element other than that named), as ***radio-caesium***, ***-chlorine***, ***-cobalt***, ***-gold***, ***-iron***, ***-potassium***, ***-silver***, ***-sodium***, etc.; †**radio-acˈtinium**, a thorium isotope (mass number 227) which is produced by beta decay of actinium and is an alpha emitter of half-life 18·2 days; **radio-ˈiodine**, esp. iodine 131, an artificial isotope with a half-life for beta decay of about 8 days, which is widely used as a tracer (esp. in investigating thyroid function), and for radiotherapy of the thyroid gland; **radio-ˈlead**, a mixture of isotopes of lead, together with some bismuth and polonium, which constitutes the longer-lived product of the decay of radon; sometimes *spec.* lead 210, the major radioactive component of this mixture, which has a half-life for beta decay of 21 years; **radio-ˈphosphorus**, *spec.* phosphorus 32, an artificial isotope which is widely used as a tracer and decays by beta emission with a half-life of 14·3 days; **radio-ˈstrontium**, *spec.* strontium 90, a beta emitter with a half-life of roughly 28 years which occurs among uranium fission products; (in quot. 1941 referring to strontium 85); †**radio-teˈllurium**, a former name for a polonium isotope of mass number 210 (originally thought to be tellurium), which occurs in the radium decay series and decays by alpha emission with a half-life of 138 days; †**radio-ˈthorium**, thorium 228, an alpha emitter of half-life 1·91 years which occurs in small amounts in natural thorium and is formed by the beta decay of mesothorium II; (see also quot. 1950). Also RADIO-CARBON.

1906 O. Hahn in *Nature* 12 Apr. 560/1, I have found that a new product is present in actinium which is intermediate between actinium and actinium X, and..will be called..'radio-actinium'. **1926** R. W. Lawson tr. *Hevesy & Paneth's Man. Radioactivity* xxiii. 164 The β-radiation of actinium, the existence of which it is necessary to assume in order to explain its transformation into radioactinium, is too weak to be detected. **1955** *Bull. Atomic Scientists* Oct. 287/3 The long-lived useful products radiocaesium and radiostrontium will be separated from the rest of the fission products and concentrated into radioactive sources. **1935** *Physical Rev.* XLVIII. 571/1 During a study of the beta-radiation from a sample of silver radiochloride..it was found possible to follow the decay of the radiochlorine. **1949** *Atomics* Oct. 75/2 Radio-cobalt and radio-strontium have been used to dissipate charge from textile machinery. **1959** *Listener* 22 Oct. 675/2 The new knowledge does not only apply to atomic bombs and radio-cobalt but to the mechanisms of biology as well. **1955** *Sci. News Let.* 19 Mar. 184/3 A gram of radiogold, costing about $25, can irradiate tissues with the power that would be obtained from a $20,000 chunk of radium. **1938** R. W. Lawson tr. *Hevesy & Paneth's Man. Radioactivity* (ed. 2) 303/1 (Index), Radio-iodine. **1940** *Amer. Jrnl. Physiol.* CXXXI. 135 The radio-iodine was prepared by the Berkeley cyclotron and converted to sodium iodide. **1961** *Lancet* 2 Sept. 551/1, 8 mC of radioiodine was administered..to achieve a permanent remission of the hyper-thyroidism. **1970** Passmore & Robson *Compan. Med. Stud.* II. vi. 8/2 The rapidity of uptake and the speed with which the plasma is cleared of radioiodine provide measures of the activity of the thyroid gland. **1960** *Proc. Soc. Exper. Biol. & Med.* CIV. 442/2 This calculation is based on the assumption that loss of radioiron from liver between 0–3 hrs is negligible. **1903** *Phil. Mag.* V. 585 Thus the radio-lead described by Hoffmann and Strauss and by Giesel cannot be regarded as a new element until it is shown that it has permanent activity of a distinctive character. **1910** *Nature* 24 Feb. 492/1 The most natural source of polonium is radium D (radio-lead), which grows polonium and has a period of half-transformation of about twenty years. **1910** A. T. Cameron *Radiochem.* v. 52 The lead obtained from pitchblende was strongly and permanently radioactive—hence the name radio-lead. **1926** R. W. Lawson tr. *Hevesy & Paneth's Man. Radioactivity* xiv. 118 Polonium..can be prepared..from solutions of the salts of radio-lead, which..contains an isotope of bismuth (RaE) and three isotopes of lead (RaD, RaG, Pb). **1941** *Jrnl. Appl. Physics* XII. 440/2 The detection of radio-lead by its radioactivity is more than a million times more sensitive than the ordinary chemical and physical methods. **1938** R. W. Lawson tr. *Hevesy & Paneth's Man. Radioactivity* (ed. 2) x. 122 For every 10^7 α-particles of high energy value..only 6 are effective in the activation of aluminium, i.e. in the production of radio-phosphorus. **1951** *New Biol.* X. 36 Mosquito larvae grown in water containing phosphorus-32 (radiophosphorus) produce radioactive adults whose presence in a swarm can be picked out immediately. **1963** BALL & HOOPER in Schultz & Klement *Radioecology* 227/1 The movement of radiophosphorus through the ecosystem of a cold water stream was studied by adding spikes of approximately 23 millicuries of phosphorus-32 to the water during the summers of 1958, 1959, and 1960. **1973** P. A. COLINVAUX *Introd. Ecol.* xiv. 207 Radiophosphorus has a half-life of 14 days. **1948** *Sci. News* VII. 38 The release of heat from radio-potassium must have been 200 times greater than from uranium and thorium combined. **1938** R. W. LAWSON tr. *Hevesy & Paneth's Man. Radioactivity* (ed. 2) v. 118 A 40-fold yield in the preparation of radio-silver. **1971** *Nature* 10 Dec. 347/1 The reaction $^{109}Ag\ (n, 2n)^{108m}Ag$ does seem to be important in thermonuclear bomb production of radiosilver. **1935** *Physical Rev.* XLVII. 17 Doubtless radio-sodium will find many uses in the physical and biological sciences. **1951** *New Biol.* X. 39 In animals, it has also been shown that radiosodium is actively transferred inwards across a frogskin membrane into a solution of higher sodium concentration than that of the external medium. **1941** *Jrnl. Appl. Physics* XII. 456/2 Radio-strontium has a half-life of 55 days, can be readily prepared in relatively large amounts, and emits very energetic beta-particles. **1946** *Chemistry* Jan. 20/1 The use of radio-strontium in the treatment of metastatic carcinoma in bone and for other diseases can now be tried in a much larger field than was ever possible before. **1957** *New Scientist* 9 May 30/1 He..argues that..the level of radio-strontium in human bones will eventually rise to between 5 and 20 'sunshine units' if test firings of bombs continue indefinitely at their present rate. **1958** *Times* 12 Nov. 4/2 A further report will be published shortly by the Atomic Energy Research Establishment, Harwell, giving the 1957 figures for radiostrontium in soil, herbage, animal bone, and milk samples from the United Kingdom. **1972** GOLDMAN & BUSTAD (*title*) Biomedical implications of radiostrontium exposure. **1904** *Technics* II. 173/1 There is at present a good deal of evidence that the radio-active substance, separated from pitchblende by Marckwald, and called by him radio-tellurium, is in reality the fifth product of the disintegration of the radium atom. **1906** *Phil. Mag.* XII. 361 A bismuth rod coated with radiotellurium was used as a source of α rays. **1962** O. HAHN in *Coll. Papers Ld. Rutherford* I. 168 Eventually it turned out that polonium and radiotellurium were identical, and the latter name had to be dropped, although polonium is in fact a higher homologue of tellurium. **1905** *Jrnl. Chem. Soc.* LXXXVIII. II. 789 The author [*sc.* Ramsay] hence considers it very probable that the radioactive power of thorium is to be attributed to small quantities of this element, radiothorium. **1921** *Phil. Mag.* XLI. 572 A much weaker source of α rays was obtained by dipping a nickel plate for a few seconds in a more dilute solution of radio-thorium. **1950** *Thorpe's Dict. Appl. Chem.* (ed. 4) X. 435/1 The term radiothorium is loosely applied to the mixture of isotopes that can be separated from natural thorium and which contain the bulk of its activity. Such radiothorium consists of a mixture of meso-Th I, meso-Th II, radium, and actinium isotopes, respectively, Th-*X*, a radium isotope, and their decay products, including true radiothorium or ^{228}Th.

(ii) Designating a compound containing a radioactive label.

1935 Radiochloride [see *radiochlorine* in (i) above]. **1951** *New Biol.* X. 40 A sample of blood is withdrawn and mixed with radiophosphate, in the form of sodium or chromium phosphate. **1952** *Ibid.* XIII. 64 The addition of anti-thyroid substances to the incubating fluid resulting in a diminished formation of radiothyroxine and radiodiiodotyrosine. **1963** *Amer. Jrnl. Obstetr. & Gynecol.* LXXXVII. 208/1 One hundred microcuries of sodium radiochromate is added and the mixture allowed to incubate at room temperature for 25 minutes. **1977** *Lancet* 5 Feb. 303/2 We infer that the clots were formed after radio-fibrinogen had been administered.

4. Connected with radio (cf. RADIO *sb.* 6, 7), as †**,radio-con'ductor**, a former term for a coherer; **radio'heliograph** *Astr.*, an interferometric radio telescope system designed to record instantaneous high-resolution pictures of the sun as observed at radio wavelengths; **radio'meteorograph** [METEOROGRAPH] = RADIOSONDE; so **,radiometeo'rography**; **radio-'physics**, the branch of physics concerned with the properties and applications of radio waves; hence **radio'physical** *a.*; **radio-'physicist**; **,radio-tele'metering** *vbl. sb.*, **,radio-te'lemetry**, telemetry by means of radio; hence **,radio-tele'metric** *a.*; **radio-'teletype**, a teletype which transmits and receives information by radio.

1898 *Tit-Bits* 28 May 175/3 M. Branly, whose 'radioconductor' or 'coherer' is used by Marconi in his wireless telegraph. **1906** S. R. BOTTONE tr. *Mazzotto's Wireless Telegr. & Telephony* vii. 166 Branly gave the name of 'radio-conductors' to the tubes with filings, a name which some prefer, as it only points to the fact, leaving the true nature of the phenomenon unexplained. **1962** *Nature* 18 Aug. 649/1 The Ford Foundation has announced the grant of 550,000 dollars to the Radio-physics Division of the Australian Commonwealth Scientific and Industrial Research Organization for the construction of a radioheliograph for photographing the sun in its natural radio emission. **1966** *New Scientist* 7 Apr. 27/1 The main circle of the radioheliograph will observe events in the Sun's atmosphere with all the detail and definition to be expected from a dish aerial of the same diameter. **1973** *Sci. Amer.* Oct. 72/3 Spatial structure in the corona is studied on a second-by-second basis by a radioheliograph composed of 96 linked antennas each 45 feet in diameter at Culgoora in Australia. **1932** *Nature* 31 Dec. 1006/1 What is believed to be the first kind of such radio-meteorograph was devised a few years ago by Prof. Moltchanoff, of Leningrad, records of temperature and pressure being obtained in several test ascents in January, 1930. **1944** C. P. LENT *Rocket Res.* 74/2 Improved balloons and radiometeorographs..are now being developed by meteorologists. **1934** *Monthly Weather Rev.* LXII. 221 (*heading*) Radiometeorography as applied to unmanned balloons. **1974** R. RODMAN tr. *Al'pert's Radio Wave Propagation & Ionosphere* (ed. 2) II. p. ix, Various radiophysical and radio-engineering problems. **1961** *Flight* LXXX. 531/1 From the point of view of Soviet radiophysicists and astronomers the West Ford project, if carried out, may have consequences dangerous to artificial satellites, and especially to those with a man on board. **1929** *Compt. Rend. des Séances des Commissions* (Union Radio Scientifique Internationale) II. 29/2 The Commission of Radiophysics held in Brussels in 1928. **1947** *Nature* 18 Jan. 103/1 The Division of Radiophysics [of the Australian Council for Scientific and Industrial Research] was formed early in the War. **1960** RODMAN & VARSAVSKY tr. *I. S. Shklovsky's Cosmic Radio Waves* i. 11 It is shown in radiophysics that if a receiving antenna is used as a transmitting antenna the power radiated by it in each direction will have the same angular dependence $A(\theta,\phi)$. **1976** *Nature* 24 June 663/1 *The Australian Journal of Physics* has had a reputation..for specialising in radiophysics and high energy physics. **1946** *Trans. Amer. Inst. Electr. Engineers* LXV. 865/1 The accuracy and stability of the airborne radio telemetering equipment depend upon a high degree of stability of the plate supply. **1949** *Electronic Engin.* XXI. 209/1 The data..is transmitted to the ground by radio telemetering methods. **1974** *Physics Bull.* Oct. 443/2 Launch and subsequent collection of data by radiotelemetric methods demand access to major ground facilities. **1976** L. BROWN *Birds of Prey* 60 Advanced radiotelemetric techniques may be the only method of learning much detail about many forest raptors. **1951** *Rev. Sci. Instruments* XXII. 2/1 Almost every application of radio telemetry involves some form of multiplexing—i.e., the transmission of several channels of information by the same radio carrier. **1967** E. L. GRUENBERG *Handbk. Telemetry & Remote Control* iv. 2 The development of radio telemetry has been principally centered around the drone and missile programs of the armed forces. **1974** *Country Life* 13 June 1572/2 Roding behaviour and its purpose are still not fully understood, and until radiotelemetry or a similar technique is used to discover what different individuals are doing, we have to watch and guess. **1939** H. K. MORGAN *Aircraft Radio & Electr. Equipment* xii. 325 It may be that by 1945 it will be considered profitable to equip transports with a tape or page radio teletype. **1949** KOESTLER *Promise & Fulfilment* II. iii. 236 Communications..are rather precarious, depending as they do on the vagaries of the American consul's radio teletype. **1976** *S9* (N.Y.) May/June 137 (*caption*) Bart also monitors RTTY (radioteletype) and amateur radio SST (slow-scan television) signals.

radio-actinium: see RADIO- 3 b (i).

radio'activate, *v.* Also with hyphen. [f. as next + -ATE³.] *trans.* To make radioactive. Also *fig.* So **radio'activated** *ppl. a.*; **radio'activating** *vbl. sb.*

1903 *Electr. World & Engin.* 28 Mar. 529/2 An account of the investigation of the radio-activating process at the foot of waterfalls. **1949** M. MUGGERIDGE *Affairs of Heart* iii. 47 Even the atomic bomb..may prove a great deception, only serving to radio-activate yet another attempt to re-define human rights. **1971** P. KRUGER *Princ. Activation Analysis* vi. 223 The energies of most gamma-ray transitions from radioactivated nuclides are less than 2 MeV. **1978** *N.Y. Times* 30 Mar. c 19/2 Both Russia and America are looking for an excuse to try out on each other a new variation of the neutron bomb that will radioactivate the earth for 1,000 years.

,radioacti'vation. *Chem.* [f. next + -ATION.] The process of making radioactive; freq. *attrib.*; **radioactivation analysis**, chemical analysis in which a sample is made radioactive by exposure to radiation and its components are then identified, and their concentrations measured, by radiochemical methods; also called *activation analysis*.

1938 *Brit. Chem. Abstr.* A. I. 112/2 (*heading*) Artificial disintegration and radioactivation. *a* **1947** CLARK & OVERMAN in *Determination Trace Elem. by Radioactivation Anal.* (U.S. Atomic Energy Comm. Rep. MDDC-1329) (1947) 1 The potential uses of radioactivation analysis for the determination of trace amounts of substances have been recognized for some time. **1950** *Ann. Rep. Progr. Chem.* XLVI. 285 Although radioactivation analysis was first used in 1936, it is still in the early stages of development. **1960** *Times* 19 July (Royal Society Suppl.) p. xv/1 The geochemist is particularly trying..new techniques of analysis such as the isotope dilution and radioactivation methods. **1971** P. KRUGER *Princ. Activation Analysis* iii. 62 The most copious and controllable sources of neutrons for radioactivation are found in nuclear reactors. **1971** *Nature* 15 Oct. 506/2 Radioactivation analysis..is now well established in its own right as an important tool in science and technology.

radioactive (reɪdɪəʊ'æktɪv), *a.* Also with hyphen. [f. RADIO- 2 + ACTIVE *a.*] **1.** Of an atomic nucleus, a substance, etc.: (capable of) undergoing spontaneous nuclear decay involving emission of ionizing radiation in the form of particles or gamma rays; *spec.* of an element: consisting of a radioactive isotope.

1898 *Nature* 28 July 312/1 On a new radio-active substance contained in pitchblende. **1900** PRINCE KROPOTKIN in *19th Cent.* Dec. 932 Material particles projected from the radio-active bodies. **1904** E. RUTHERFORD *Radio-Activity* v. 161 This increase of activity is due to the continuous production by the radium of the radio-active emanation or gas, which is occluded in the radium compound. **1913** *Q. Rev.* July 117 The disintegration of atom after atom of the radio-active element. **1926** R. W. LAWSON tr. *Hevesy & Paneth's Man. Radioactivity* i. 4 We now define a substance as being radioactive when the atoms of which it is composed disintegrate spontaneously, and regardless of whether or not the emission of rays can readily be detected in the process. **1935** *Nature* 9 Nov. 754/1 The radio-active phosphorus in the urine..was then investigated. **1952** *New Biol.* XIII. 63 The introduction of radio-active iodine (I^{131}) has provided a tool..of the greatest value..to the comparative physiologist. **1955** *Times* 18 Aug. 8/6 Radioactive caesium recovered from waste fission products has been made available to the Royal Marsden Hospital..for treatment of deep-seated cancer. **1957** *Times Lit. Suppl.* 15 Nov. p. iv/3 Death waits for us on the zebra crossing; and tomorrow morning's milk may be radio-active. **1959** *Daily Tel.* 10 Mar. 16/3 He also asked the secretary..to advise us of the possibility of any appreciable rise in radioactive content in the river which may result. *Ibid.* 23 Mar. 18/3 The rate of descent from the stratosphere of radio-active debris, including strontium 90, from nuclear explosions. **1961** G. R. CHOPPIN *Exper. Nuclear Chem.* vi. 77 The average time of existence τ of a radioactive atom before decay is the reciprocal of the decay constant. **1966** C. R. TOTTLE *Sci. Engin. Materials* i. 23 Almost all elements of atomic number greater than $Z = 83$ (bismuth) are naturally radioactive. **1969** N. W. PIRIE *Food Resources* v. 127 Marine organisms concentrate several of the radioactive isotopes enormously. **1977** *Nature* 14 Apr. 585/1 Any radio-active chemical which enters one organism may be transported a considerable distance as it travels through the food chain.

2. Of a process, phenomenon, etc.: of, pertaining to, involving, or produced by radioactivity.

1903 *Phil. Mag.* V. 580 These rays have not yet been sufficiently examined to make any discussion possible of the part they play in radioactive processes. **1906** *Nature* 25 Oct. 634/1 The escape of the emanation causes a radio-active contamination of the laboratory which renders delicate experiments on radio-activity or ionisation very difficult. **1919** *Phil. Mag.* XXXVII. 537 Results showed..that..the H atoms from a glass α-ray tube were a product of radio-active disintegration. **1926** R. W. LAWSON tr. *Hevesy & Paneth's Man. Radioactivity* vii. 78 Ions are produced along the tracks of the radioactive rays. **1938** *Ibid.* (ed. 2) iv. 55 (*heading*) Absorption measurements with γ-rays as applied to radioactive analysis. **1956** A. H. COMPTON *Atomic Quest* v. 303 At the instant of the flash there is a burst of radio-active rays of enormous magnitude. **1961** G. R. CHOPPIN *Exper. Nuclear Chem.* i. 3 The formation of a more stable nucleus as a result of radioactive decay is accompanied by a release of energy. **1969** BENNISON & WRIGHT *Geol. Hist. Brit. Isles* i. 6 Only the limitations of radioactive dating..are here dealt with. **1971** *Nature* 6 Aug. 367/2 The dating of the earlier part of the Pleistocene period still presents considerable problems, but further exploitation of the various 'radioactive clocks' should eventually overcome these difficulties. **1977** *Ibid.* 10 Mar. 106/1 Even the most resolute proclaimers of radioactive doom seem to have convinced themselves that fusion power will be gentle and on a homely scale, and that radioactive pollution will be a thing of the past when dirty fission gives way to clean fusion.

3. *fig.* (Possibly also influenced by RADIO- 4.)

1905 S. MACNAUGHTAN *Lame Dog's Diary* x. 128 Eliza has found that London is radio-active, hence enjoyable. And Eliza had only been once to the Royal Institution when she said it! **1909** A. BENNETT *Glimpse* x. 71 She did not begin to live, socially, till her body was at rest... Then her individuality would be radioactive whereas the individuality of Inez spent itself mildly without ceasing in a persuasive appeal to the sight. **1919** D. H. LAWRENCE in *Eng. Rev.* June 477 Our plasmic psyche is radio-active, connecting with all things, and having first-knowledge of all things. **1923** L. P. SMITH *S.P.E. Tract* XII. 57 This radio-active quality of popular idiom, this power to give out life and never lose it. **1934** *Punch* 5 Sept. 280/2 The invalid son, who ultimately comes out at least all even in the contest with the radio-active Audrey. **1955** KOESTLER *Trail of Dinosaur* 12 The logic of expediency leads to the atomic disintegration of morality, a kind of radioactive decay of all values. **1974** *Times* 27 May 6/1 His [*sc.* Byron's] was a radio-active personality that had shattering effects on all who came in contact with him.

4. Special collocations: **radioactive constant**, the average proportion of nuclei of a given radioactive nuclide which will decay in a given time; now usu. called *decay constant*; = *disintegration constant*; **radioactive equilibrium**, a condition in which the quantities of radioactive daughter nuclides in a material remain constant because each is decaying at the same rate as that at which it is being formed; **radioactive indicator** = INDICATOR 2 b (ii); **radioactive series**, a series of radioactive nuclides each member of which decays into the next, together with a non-radioactive end-product; the series of transformations relating such a set of nuclides; (four such series exist among the nuclides heavier than lead: see quot. 1974); **radioactive tracer** (see TRACER¹); **radioactive waste**, waste material that is radioactive, esp. spent nuclear fuel.

1903 RUTHERFORD & SODDY in *Phil. Mag.* V. 581 The law of radioactive change may therefore be expressed in the one statement—the proportional amount of radioactive matter that changes in unit time is a constant... λ may therefore be suitably called the 'radioactive constant'. **1923** GLAZEBROOK *Dict. Appl. Physics* IV. 574/2 λ, the radioactive constant, represents the average fraction of the number of atoms which break up per unit time. **1942** J. D. STRANATHAN *'Particles' of Mod. Physics* viii. 325 (*heading*) Relationships among the several radioactive constants. **1904** E. RUTHERFORD *Radio-Activity* vii. 189 In uranium and thorium compounds there is a continuous production of active matter which keeps the compound in radio-active equilibrium. **1923** GLAZEBROOK *Dict. Appl. Physics* IV. 576/1 If a radioactive mineral is sealed up so that the products of transformation are allowed to accumulate, a stage is ultimately reached in which the amount of each product formed is equal to the amount transformed per unit time throughout the series... Material which has reached this state is said to be in radioactive equilibrium. **1946** *Physical Rev.* LXIX. 672/2 Since the age of the earth is much greater than the life of C^{14} a radioactive equilibrium must exist in which the rate of disintegration of C^{14} is equal to the rate of production. **1968** MUSSET & LLORET *Conc. Encycl. Atom* 95/2 Radioactive equilibrium is also referred to when a radioactive body is produced by nuclear reaction, such as bombarding a target with a beam of particles having a constant intensity. After a certain time, the body formed in the nuclear reaction also acquires a constant radioactivity through the balance of its rates of formation and decay. **1923** *Biochem. Jrnl.* XVII. 439 (*heading*) A contribution to the application of the method of radioactive indicators in the investigation of the change of substance in plants. **1943** Radioactive indicator [see INDICATOR 2 b (ii)]. **1923** *Phil. Mag.* XLVI. 647 There are only four complete radio-active series of the type that is known. **1926** R. W. LAWSON tr. *Hevesy & Paneth's Man. Radioactivity* xxiv. 184 The element thorium is the parent element of a radioactive series. **1956** I. ASIMOV *Inside Atom* v. 85 The entire set of changes is an example of a radioactive series. This particular one we have been talking about is the uranium-238 series. **1974** *Encycl. Brit. Micropædia* VIII. 378/2 *Radioactive series*, any of four independent sets of unstable atomic nuclei that decay through a sequence of nuclear transformations until a stable nucleus is achieved... Three of the sets, the thorium series, uranium series, and actinium series..are headed by naturally occurring species of unstable nuclei whose half-lives are comparable to the age of the Earth... The fourth set, neptunium series.., came to light after the discovery of induced radioactivity (1934). **1947** C. D. CORYELL in C. Goodman *Sci. & Engin. of Nucl. Power* I. vii. 249 In general, radioactive wastes from separation processes must be stored indefinitely in systems free from leaks. **1958** *Engineering* 21 Feb. 236/2 The problem of radioactive waste disposal is finally solved only by the complete natural decay of the constituent fission product activity—a process which may take hundreds of years. **1969** N. W. PIRIE *Food Resources* v. 127 Nuclear power stations discharge slightly radioactive waste into the sea near the shore. **1977** *Nature* 10 Mar. 109/2 One of the major obstacles to have arisen to the expanded use of nuclear power has focused on the reprocessing and storage of radioactive waste.

Hence **radio'actively** *adv.*, by radioactive decay; with radioactive material; by means of a technique dependent upon radioactivity.

1925 J. JOLY *Surface-Hist. of Earth* ix. 147 This method would not be reliable..if the lead was in either case unstable —i.e. ultimately changed radioactively into something else. **1936** O. HAHN *Appl. Radiochem.* vi. 171 In the Kjeldahl determination of nitrogen, the ammonia formed is led into a solution of lead nitrate that has been radio-actively activated. **1948** *Physical Rev.* LXXIV. 279/1 Individual atoms of this isotope transform radioactively. **1959** *Oxf. Univ. Gaz.* 16 Mar. 795/2 In the event of nuclear warfare, farm products, particularly milk, obtained from a radio-actively contaminated soil might be positively harmful. **1968** R. A. LYTTLETON *Mysteries Solar Syst.* ii. 65 The release of radioactively produced energy means that the internal temperatures of the planets will have risen from their initial values. **1976** *Nuclear Sci. Internat.* Nov. 36/2 Direct measurements of bronchial clearance rates (by inhalation of radioactively labelled dust followed by measurements of radiation from the chest) show little difference between smokers and non-smokers.

ˌradioac'tivity. Also with hyphen. [f. RADIO- 2 + ACTIVITY.] **1. a.** The property or condition of being radioactive; (the field of study concerned with) the phenomena displayed by radioactive materials. Hence, the radiation emitted by a radioactive material, or such material itself in a dispersed form.

1899 *Nature* Nov. 71/1 On the radio-activity induced by the Becquerel rays. **1900** PRINCE KROPOTKIN in *19th Cent.* Dec. 932 They communicate radio-activity..to the surface of the bodies. **1902** *Harper's Mag.* Aug. 364/1 For days Professor Curie was unable to approach his electrometers.. owing to his acquired radio-activity. **1920** *Discovery* Apr. 122/1 This was the first discovery in the science which later became known as radio-activity. **1947** *Sci. News* V. 55 Between them, these three series of radioactive elements include the whole of the known natural sources of radioactivity. **1955** *Sci. Amer.* Aug. 35/1 Radioactivity is measured in curies: one curie is equal to the radioactivity from one gram of radium (37 billion atoms disintegrating per second). **1955** *Bull. Atomic Scientists* Sept. 253/1 Radioactivity can travel in the air over large distances, and its very nature and action are unknown and unfamiliar to most people. **1962** S. G. WALEY in A. Pirie *Lens Metabolism Rel. Cataract* 359 When the enzyme is treated with isotopically labelled iodoacetate..and the enzyme is boiled, no radio-activity is released. **1969** *Daily Tel.* 23 Jan. 1/4 A small Swiss nuclear research and training reactor at Lucens was closed yesterday after developing a leak of radio-activity. **1978** L. DEIGHTON *SS-GB* xvi. 135 Do you know what radio-activity is?.. It's the emission of radiation from unstable atomic nuclei—alpha particles, nucleons, gamma rays, electrons and so on.

b. *fig.*

1922 C. E. MONTAGUE *Disenchantment* (1924) xv. 210 In men and women of high mental vitality, in places where any of the radio-activity of gifted teaching breaks out for a while ..the mind is easily delighted. **1928** *Manch. Guardian Weekly* 27 July 74/1 That radio-activity and that consummate technique shine out from poem after poem.

2. The property of emitting radio waves.

1959 *Sci. Amer.* Feb. 66/1 (Advt.), This is Messier 87— one of many galaxies and nebulae radiating radio energy throughout time and space. What primeval force motivates this celestial radioactivity? **1972** *Nature* 20 Oct. 440/2 It seems unlikely that Cygnus X-3 is unique with respect to its radioactivity and it may therefore represent only one member of a large number of objects that exhibit highly variable radio emission, and which may have been overlooked in classical radio surveys. **1978** *Ibid.* 11 May 131/1 We show here that these non-Io-related..decametric radio activities are affected by solar wind conditions around Jupiter.

radioallergosorbent, -assay: see RADIO- 3 a.

radio astronomy. Also with hyphen and as **radioastronomy.** [f. RADIO *sb.* + ASTRONOMY.] The branch of astronomy concerned with the study and interpretation of radio waves reaching the earth from space, and with the astronomical use of radio-echo techniques.

1948 *Sci. News Let.* 1 May 279/1 Radioastronomy is a new branch of astronomy only recently announced, Dr. Shapley stated. By use of high-frequency radio waves meteors are tracked in their flight. **1951** *Sci. News* XXI. 40 There are two basic methods of observing in radio astronomy. In the first, we use the familiar processes of radar to explore space around us... The second method is the one in general use. Radiation of radio wavelengths, emitted.. by extra-terrestrial bodies, is collected. **1951** *Nature* 7 July 17/1 Dr. Alfred Charles Bernard Lovell has been appointed to a newly created chair of radio-astronomy in the University of Manchester. **1958** *Listener* 27 Nov. 869/2 Out of the cataclysm of a world war have emerged two technical developments which are creating a revolution in astronomical observations—radio astronomy and the earth satellite. **1966** *McGraw-Hill Encycl. Sci. & Technol.* XI. 247/1 Large radio antennas designed for radio astronomy are now used for radar, radio communications, and satellite telemetering. **1973** 'D. HALLIDAY' *Dolly & Starry Bird* xiii. 188 Innes is a Steady-State man, having done a sabbatical on radio astronomy at Cambridge. **1977** J. NARLIKAR *Struct. Universe* iii. 66 Radio-astronomy has played an important part in galactic explorations. For example, 21-cm radio wave-length observations are useful for detecting neutral hydrogen. **1978** R. V. JONES *Most Secret War* xlix. 486 We supplied German radar components..to both Bernard Lovell and Martin Ryle, to help them in their start on radio-astronomy.

Hence **radio astronomer**, a person engaged in radio astronomy; **ˌradio-astro'nomical** *a.*, of or pertaining to radio astronomy; obtained by means of radio telescopes.

1949 *Nature* 12 Nov. 815/2 Three British research organizations which have played a major part in radio-astronomical research. **1952** *Ibid.* 1 Mar. 350/1 It appears likely that..experimental radio astronomers will concentrate their attention on devices for achieving increased angular accuracy. **1959** *Listener* 31 Dec. 1152/2 Interest in peculiar galaxies has been stimulated recently by radio-astronomical observations. **1962** *New Scientist* 5 Apr. 827/3 The primary gamma-ray picture of the Universe might resemble the radioastronomical one. **1968** *Times* 26 Oct. 4/4 A new pulsar has been discovered by radio astronomers at Jodrell Bank. **1973** C. SAGAN *Cosmic Connection* vi. 47 We see..in radio-astronomical studies of the interstellar medium, a profusion of simple and complex organic molecules. **1976** *Time* 27 Dec. 37/2 Radioastronomers..have beamed coded signals toward the stars to let any other civilization know that intelligent life exists on earth.

radio-atom, -autograph (etc.): see RADIO- 3 a.

† **radiobe** ('reɪdɪəʊb). *Obs.* [f. RADI(O- 3 + *-obe*, after MICROBE.] A cell-like body observed to form in large numbers in gelatin solutions in the presence of radium salts, which was formerly claimed to be a living organism owing its existence to radioactivity.

1905 J. B. BURKE in *Nature* 25 May 79/2 As these bodies cannot be identified with microbes, on the one hand, nor with crystals on the other, I have ventured..to give them a new name, *Radiobes*, which might..be more appropriate as indicating their resemblance to microbes, as well as their distinct nature and origin. **1905** *Daily Chron.* 20 June 4/4 Tubes of bouillon containing radium and tubes without radium were stopped up with cotton-wool, subjected to a temperature far above the boiling point of water, under pressure, for half an hour. The control tubes which contained no radium were then watched, and 'nothing happened'... But the surface of the beef-gelatine in the other tubes began to show a peculiar 'growth'. This 'growth'..was examined by a very high power of a microscope and found to consist of minute rounded objects which looked like bacteria... Like living cells they contain nuclei and these have been photographed through the microscope... They exhibited a property possessed by no crystals; a property possessed by living things alone... When they reach the maximum size already named, they subdivide... Mr. Burke calls them radiobes. **1908** *Encycl. Relig. & Ethics* I. 26/1 Mr. Butler Burke inclines to the conclusion that they are organisms on the border lines between microbes and crystals, and, provisionally, he names them 'radiobes'. **1920** *Punch* 7 Jan. 7/2 Let scientists on various fronts Indulge in their atomic stunts, Or harness to our prams and punts The puissant radiobe.

radiobi'ology. Also with hyphen. [f. RADIO- 2, 3 + BIOLOGY.] The branch of biology concerned with the effects on living organisms of radiation and radioactivity, and with the application in biology of radiological techniques.

1919 *Med. Sci. Abstr. & Rev.* I. 358 In radio-biology, when we wish to show the selective action of X-rays we usually choose, as an example, one of the glands of external secretion. **1935** *Discovery* Aug. 225/1 A Congress of Radiobiology was held..last year in Venice. **1955** *Times* 18 Aug. 6/1 The organization that he thought necessary would consist of experts in radiophysics and radiobiology, including radio-genetics, and would be empowered to promote essential research in its field and to organize continuous general supervision of the radiation level of the world. **1962** *Lancet* 26 May 1106/2 The subjects cover almost every aspect of radiobiology, from radiation chemistry to straightforward radiotherapy. **1972** *Physics Bull.* Mar. 147/1 Typical of the radiobiology experiments is one carried out by a team at the Ames Laboratory of NASA in which some 56 pocket mice..were irradiated by the 250 MeV/nucleon nitrogen ion beam.

Hence **ˌradiobio'logic** (chiefly *U.S.*), **-'logical** *adjs.*, of or pertaining to radiobiology; **ˌradiobio'logically** *adv.*; **radiobi'ologist.**

1929 *Radiology* XII. 454/2 (*heading*) Radio-biologic investigations on eggs of Ascaris. **1931** *Gen. Electr. Rev.* XXXIV. 98 (*heading*) Instruments for radiometric and radio-biological investigations at the Desert Sanatorium and Institute of Research, Tucson, Arizona. **1945** C. W. WILSON *Radium Therapy* iii. 81 Innumerable radio-biological experiments and clinical studies have shown that ..a number of purely physical factors influence the biological effects produced by high-voltage radiation. **1946** *Nature* 2 Nov. 601/2 Radiobiologists should be grateful for accurate data such as these. **1955** *Times* 18 Aug. 6/1 The problem of extending the present international standards of radiobiological protection from the occupational workers.. was discussed. **1956** *Proc. Internat. Conf. Peaceful Uses Atomic Energy* XI. 3/1 It is our belief that, if we take sufficient care radiobiologically to look after mankind..the rest of nature will take care of itself. **1961** *Ann. N.Y. Acad. Sci.* XCV. 828 (*heading*) Radio-biologic observations on human hemic cells *in vivo* and *in vitro*. **1971** *New Scientist* 8 Apr. 108/2 Even if radiobiologists could quantify the deaths and deformations caused by radiation, planners and government consultants feel that these numbers then need to be translated into economic terms. **1976** *Nature* 22 Jan. 209/1 Among the many important radiobiological findings recently summarised are the following: the mutation rate depends on sex, on the type of germ cell irradiated, on radiation quality (X rays, neutrons), [etc.]. **1977** *Lancet* 20 Aug. 411/1 Complete recovery of thyroid function after prolonged ^{125}I-induced hypothyroidism can be explained radiobiologically.

radio-cæsium: see RADIO- 3 b (i).

radio-'carbon. Also radiocarbon. [f. RADIO- 3 b + CARBON.] **1.** A radioactive isotope of carbon; *spec.* = *carbon 14*, which is formed in trace amounts by the effect of cosmic rays on atmospheric nitrogen. Also *ellipt.* for *radio-carbon dating*.

1940 *Physical Rev.* LVII. 549/2 Large quantities of nitrogenous material have been exposed to neutrons for several months and will be shortly worked up for radio-carbon. **1946** *Ibid.* LXIX. 672/1 The purpose of this letter is to..suggest that radiocarbon might be found in living matter especially in connection with the concentration of C^{13} for tracer uses. **1956** W. F. ALBRIGHT *Archaeol. of Palestine* (rev. ed.) i. 22 Radiocarbon has a 'half life' of some 5,600 years, and the count loses any significance beyond 25,000–30,000 years ago. **1957** *Times* 11 Sept. 6/2 Recent studies using radiocarbon indicated that the yield of photosynthesis by the plankton of the oceans was at least equal to that of the land flora, and might be several times greater. **1963** G. M. B. DOBSON *Exploring Atmosphere* i. 12 The radio-carbon formed in the upper atmosphere becomes radio-carbon dioxide and is gradually mixed throughout the whole atmosphere. **1970** *Nature* 4 Apr. 45/1 The chronology of several glacial stages has been recognized in the microfossils and dated by radiocarbon. **1976** P. L. BROWN *Planet Earth* iii. 77 Radiocarbon then combines with oxygen to form $C^{14}O_2$ which is diffused through the atmosphere and then is absorbed by plants via photosynthesis and ultimately by all living things.

2. *attrib.* and *Comb.* (usu. with reference to radio-carbon dating), as ***radio-carbon age***, ***content***, ***method***, ***year***, etc.; **radio-carbon dating**, a method of isotopic dating which is applicable to dead organic matter and in which the proportion of carbon 14 (which has decreased at a known rate since the death of the sample material), is measured and compared with the known natural abundance of the isotope; hence ***radio-carbon date***; ***radio-carbon-dated*** ppl. adj.

1949 *Antiquity* XXIII. 113 A method of dating dead pieces of formerly living substances (such as wood and bone) by means of their radiocarbon content. **1949** *Science* 23 Dec. 679/2 These results indicate that the two basic assumptions of the radiocarbon age determination method —namely, the constancy of the cosmic radiation intensity and the possibility of obtaining unaltered samples—are probably justified for wood up to 4600 years. **1950** ARNOLD & LIBBY (*title*) Radiocarbon dates. **1951** *Amer. Jrnl. Sci.* CCXLIX. 257 (*heading*) Radiocarbon dating of Late-Pleistocene events. *Ibid.*, All of the dates are of the right order of magnitude, with a few exceptions where it seems likely that the stratigraphic position of the sample, and not the radio-carbon age, has been incorrectly given. *Ibid.* 268 The radio-carbon date, 12,148 ± 700 years. **1956** M. WHEELER in A. Pryce-Jones *New Outl. Mod. Knowl.* 399 A radio-carbon dating gives 7538 B.C. (with a possible error ± of 350 years) for the settlement. **1957** G. E. HUTCHINSON *Treat. Limnol.* I. i. 8 The dating of the events, based primarily on the varve chronology, is in fair accord with the radio-carbon chronology. **1963** D. W. & E. E. HUMPHRIES tr. *Termier's Erosion & Sedimentation* iii. 55 (*caption*) Old peat deposits (radio-carbon-dated to the Early Holocene) dot the area 'drowned' by the Flandrian transgression. **1966** *Radiocarbon* VIII. 534 The result of a radiocarbon determination is commonly expressed as an age given in radiocarbon years. *Ibid.*, The conversion of a radiocarbon age..to a true calendar year makes necessary certain assumptions with respect to: (1) the half-life of C^{14}, (2) the production rate of C^{14} by cosmic rays, (3) the size of reservoirs into which C^{14} is distributed and the exchange rate of this distribution. **1973** *Nature* 1 June 266/1 Three radiocarbon laboratories, at La Jolla, Philadelphia and Tucson, have obtained radiocarbon dates over the past decade for specimens of bristlecone pine already dated dendrochronologically, thereby allowing the 'correction' of the radiocarbon scale. **1973** *Nation Rev.* (Melbourne) 31 Aug. (Suppl.) 2/3 Until 1972 only two radio-carbon-dated remains of Chinese origin were known. **1978** *New Scientist*

2 Mar. 599/2 The dating of carbon in glacier varves would extend the calibration of the radiocarbon dating curve.

radiocast ('reɪdɪəʊkɑːst, -æ-), *sb.* and *v.* *U.S.* [f. RADIO *sb.* + *-cast*, after BROADCAST.] **A.** *sb.* A radio broadcast.

1931 *Daily Progress* (Charlottesville, Va.) 10 Feb. 5/3 J. B. Priestley.. is going to Tahiti, via New York, to write his next novel. He said in a radiocast he'd need a small island to recover from the fright he expects to receive on the gigantic island of Manhattan.

B. *v.* To broadcast by radio; so **'radiocasting** *vbl. sb.*

1931 *Amer. Speech* VI. 253 Where the writer wishes to leave no doubt that he means *to radio-broadcast*, he is taking now to *to radiocast*. **1940** *Christian Sci. Monitor* 16 Mar. (Mag. section) 3/3 (*caption*) From this radiocasting structure, 400 feet high, music without static is being sent to listeners. **1947** PARTRIDGE *Usage & Abusage* 260/1 Both 'to radio' and 'to *broadcast*' are infinitely preferable to either *radiocast* or *radio-broadcast*.

radio'chemical, *a.* (*sb.*) Also with hyphen. [f. RADIO- 3 + CHEMICAL *a.*] **1.** Of, pertaining to, or considered in terms of radiochemistry; ***radiochemical purity***, the state of being free from radioactive impurities. Also as *sb.*, a radioactive chemical.

1915 F. SODDY *Chem. Radio-Elements* (ed. 2) I. 46 In a condition of complete radio-chemical purity. **1946** *Chem. & Engin. News* 10 Dec. 3168/1 Laboratory facilities for radiochemical research are classified according to the level of radioactivity involved in the operations. **1961** G. R. CHOPPIN *Exper. Nucl. Chem.* ix. 129 Radiochemical purity is frequently of greater importance than chemical purity; it may be better to have a milligram of inert impurity in the final sample than 10^{-9} gm of radioactive contaminant. **1971** *New Scientist* 1 Apr. 26/2 The US market is estimated to be worth over $80 million a year with some $25 million spent on radiochemicals, $40 on radiopharmaceuticals, and about $20 million on basic radioisotopes and sealed sources. **1973** D. L. HORROCKS in Moghissi & Carter *Tritium* i. 34 The total fissions are determined by radiochemical assay of a fission product (i.e., ^{140}Ba) of known yield. **1978** *Nature* 11 May p. xii/1 (Advt.), Our supply of radiochemicals of the highest quality and technical specifications.

2. (With hyphen.) Of or pertaining to chemical changes caused by radiant energy. *rare.*

1921 D. H. LAWRENCE *Let.* 2 Mar. (1962) II. 512 The sun is dangerous these months—it has a radio-chemical action on the blood which simply does for me. **1935** *Mind* XLIV. 545 In general, chemical reactions are coming to be conceived in the light of the 'radio-chemical' hypothesis, *viz.* that no structural modification can take place except as the result of quantities of radiant energy imparted in rhythmic pulses.

Hence (sense 1) **radio'chemically** *adv.*, by a radiochemical method or process; in terms of radiochemistry.

1915 F. SODDY *Chem. Radio-Elements* (ed. 2) I. 44 Another and very important sense [of the term 'pure'], which may conveniently be termed 'radio-chemically' pure. **1923** GLAZEBROOK *Dict. Appl. Physics* IV. 590/1 A product may be prepared 'radio-chemically' pure, in which the radio-element may be mixed with a certain amount of inactive matter, but is free from substances chemically analogous to itself. **1957** *Jrnl. Biol. Chem.* CCXXIX. 443 A substance subsequently shown to be radiochemically pure was treated in a similar manner. **1975** *Nature* 1 May 77/1 The plutonium in each right testis was measured radiochemically.

radio'chemistry. Also with hyphen. [f. RADIO- 3 + CHEMISTRY.] The chemistry of radioactive substances; sometimes held to include also *radiation chemistry* s.v. RADIATION 4. Hence **radio'chemist.**

In quot. 1904 perh. = *radiation chemistry*.

1904 *Jrnl. Physical Chem.* VIII. 506 Under chemical energetics we find the mass law relations for equilibrium and reaction velocity,.. electrochemistry, photochemistry and radiochemistry. **1910** A. T. CAMERON (*title*) Radiochemistry. **1911** F. SODDY *Chem. Radio-Elements* 11 A special branch of chemistry, which may be appropriately termed 'Radio-Chemistry' has come into existence. **1938** R. W. LAWSON tr. *Hevesy & Paneth's Man. Radioactivity* (ed. 2) xxiv. 247 The study of the chemical effects of the rays from radium is sometimes called 'radio-chemistry' in the narrower sense... However, we shall confine the use of the term 'radio-chemistry' to the chemistry of the radio-elements, or the study of their chemical properties and reactions. **1952** F. E. ZEUNER *Dating Past* (ed. 3) IV. x. 346 One can confidently expect the radio-chemist to be aware of the difficulties. **1953** E. SIMON *Past Masters* III. 141 A radio-chemist [should] be called in to carry out tests on the stone fabric of this and the other huts in order to determine age. **1971** I. G. GASS et al. *Understanding Earth* ii. 42/1 Direct measurements of long half-lives.. have been carried out in many physics and radiochemistry laboratories. **1973** *Nature* 3 Aug. p. xiii. (Advt.), South African Atomic Energy Board. Radiochemist or Radiopharmacist. Applications are invited.

radio-chlorine to **-element**: see RADIO- 2, 3, 4.

'radio-frequency. Also radio frequency, radiofrequency. [f. RADIO *sb.* + FREQUENCY.] **1.** A frequency in the range used for telecommunication; greater than that of the highest audio-frequency and less than that of the shortest infra-red waves (i.e. between about 10^4 and 10^{11} or 10^{12} Hz).

1915 *Electrician* 2 July 463/1 Mercury arc rectifiers can be operated at a good efficiency even at radio frequencies. **1937** *Discovery* Mar. p. xxiii/1 Loud Speaker output at radio frequencies. **1976** A. WHITE *Long Silence* xi. 95 You can often get close enough.. without them being aware of it, especially if they're listening to a radio frequency.

2. *attrib.* Pertaining to (electromagnetic radiation having) such a frequency; operating at or having such a frequency; employing alternating current having such a frequency.

1915 *Engin. Mag.* XLIX. 253/2 The usual radio frequency transformers. **1919** *Wireless World* May 75/1 The arc transforms.. the 1,500-volt direct current power into radio frequency energy. **1922** *Nature* 20 May 650/2 A six-tube amplifier having three stages of radio-frequency amplification. **1943** *Electronic Engin.* XV. 344/2 When the bridge goes off balance a radio-frequency current flows through the meter. **1946** *Nature* 10 Aug. 194/1 Radio-frequency heating is not an economic proposition for heating stable liquids, but may prevent serious losses of activity in heat-sensitive ones. **1955** J. G. DAVIS *Dict. Dairying* (ed. 2) 828 The use of radio-frequency heating for the pasteurization of milk. **1957** *Endeavour* XVI. 187/1 Electronic equipment to generate the radio-frequency radiation and to measure its absorption by the sample. **1965** *B.B.C. Handbk.* 116 For best results on short waves, a receiver should incorporate a tuned radio-frequency amplifier preceding the frequency-changer stage. **1967** M. CHANDLER *Ceramics in Mod. World* ii. 76. Other methods of drying, of more limited and special application, include infrared and radio-frequency drying. **1970** G. K. WOODGATE *Elem. Atomic Struct.* viii. 148 Many precise measurements of g_J.. have now been made by the methods of radio-frequency spectroscopy.

radiogenetic(al, -ics: see RADIO- 2.

radiogenic (reɪdɪəʊ'dʒɛnɪk), *a.* [f. RADIO- 3, 4 + -GENIC (in sense 1 after *photogenic*).] **1.** Well suited for broadcasting by radio; providing an attractive subject for a radio broadcast.

1928 *Radio Times* 24 Aug. 342/2 Their object is to discover.. a form (or forms) of drama which shall be truly 'radiogenic'. **1931** T. H. PEAR *Voice & Personality* xii. 149 England has greater artistic variety of 'radiogenic' material. **1943** S. LEWIS *Gideon Planish* xxxii. 418 The.. Great Leaders: Governor Blizzard and.. the dazzle-sounding, radiogenic Winifred Marduc Homeward. **1946** *Electronic Engin.* XVIII. 207/3 Transatlantic Quiz, even if radiogenic, is not pictorial and there seems no good reason for transplanting it into television. **1959** *Listener* 27 Aug. 332/2 Radiogenic in the extreme, Miss Jacob led her interlocutors more of a dance than anyone else in this series since Thurber. **1975** *Encounter* Sept. 43 This short play.. has appeared in book form; but so totally radiogenic is its very nature that the printed page cannot represent it.

2. Produced by or resulting from radioactive decay or ionizing radiation.

1935 *Jrnl. Amer. Chem. Soc.* LVII. 470/2 There seems to be no definite trend in the relation of the atomic weight of uranium lead to the period during which the radiogenic lead has been forming. **1947** *Endeavour* VI. 104/1 The present rates of production of radiogenic lead are known with a remarkable degree of accuracy. **1960** *New Scientist* 5 May 1114/3 No evidence of radiogenic mutations has been discovered so far. **1970** *Nature* 5 Dec. 906/1 It could be.. that the Moon is expanding slowly as a result of radiogenic heating. **1971** *Brit. Med. Bull.* XXVII. 68/1 There were about 15 times as many spontaneous cases as radiogenic cases.

Hence **radio'genically** *adv.*, by means of radioactive decay.

1956 *Sci. News* XXXIX. 14 Any helium nuclei produced radiogenically would all be of mass 4. **1970** *Nature* 23 May 692/1 These dykes have been radiogenically aged at 2,420 million years.

radio-gold: see RADIO- 3 b (i).

ˌradiogoni'ometer. Also with hyphen. [f. RADIO- 4 + GONIOMETER.] = GONIOMETER 2. Hence **ˌradiogonio'metric, -'metrical** *adjs.*, of, pertaining to, or by means of a radiogoniometer; **ˌradiogoni'ometry**, direction-finding by means of a radiogoniometer.

1908 L. H. WALTER tr. Bellini & Tosi in *Electr. Engin.* 5 Mar. 348/1 In the present article it is proposed to treat in a more detailed manner the theory and construction of the instruments above referred to, and to which the name of radio-goniometers has been given by the authors. **1913** *Year-bk. Wireless Telegr.* 310 The radiogoniometer.. consists of two coils wound over and at right angles to each other, each coil being connected to one of the directive aerials. **1921** *Nature* 23 June 542/2 Radiogoniometry and atmospheric influences. **1927** *Daily Express* 13 Oct. 11/5 A radiogoniometric aerial, an ingenious piece of wireless apparatus which enables the exact position of an air liner in flight to be located. **1932** *Times Lit. Suppl.* 9 June 429/4 He had several narrow escapes.. before a cleverly-hidden radiogoniometer ran the Whisperer to earth. **1935** C. G. BURGE *Compl. Bk. Aviation* 480/1 Visual radio-goniometry, or the actual wireless compass, will no doubt come into being when a solution is found to a number of the present wireless problems. **1936** *Discovery* Apr. 125/2 Radiogoniometrical control of such a projectile.. is quite beyond accomplishment at present. **1961** *Engineering* 16 June 825/1 A new radiotelephone transmitter-receiver.. may be used with a radiogoniometer unit. **1971** WATSON & WRIGHT *Radio Direction Finding* iv. 46 The radiogoniometer is designed to give maximum accuracy and sensitivity.. to the direction finding equipment. **1978** D. BLOODWORTH *Crosstalk* xvi. 136 Interception and radiogoniometrical checks show irregular traffic on one high-frequency waveband.

radiogram^1 ('reɪdɪəʊgræm). [f. RADIO- + -GRAM.] **1.** = RADIOGRAPH *sb.* 2.

1896 *Photogram* Apr. 105 Another title,.. suggested by Dr. Hill-Norris, appears to us.. much superior.. and we propose to call prints made by radiography 'radiograms'. **1898** ISENTHAL & WARD *Pract. Radiogr.* 101 For developing radiograms, almost any of the usual developers may be employed. **1921** A. V. KNOX in A. V. & R. Knox *Gen. Pract. & X-Rays* I. i. 21 A radiogram may be defined as a shadow-picture of structures lying in different planes reproduced on a flat surface. **1962** G. CREMER-BARTELS in A. Pirie *Lens Metabolism Rel. Cataract* 444 (*caption*) Radiogram after digestion with phosphatase. **1975** B. WOOD *Killing Gift* (1976) I. 13 She could be crippled if that hip is broken and I don't set it. And if I have to set it without a radiogram, I can't be sure of doing it properly.

2. = RADIO-TELEGRAM.

1904 *Prelim. Conf. Wireless Telegr. Berlin 1903* 10 It seems to us inadvisable.. to insist on the interchange of radiograms between ships on the high sea. **1925** H. L. FOSTER *Trop. Tramp Tourists* 172 Radiogram just came in. The railway can only furnish us with six cars. **1929** *Star* 21 Aug. 12/4 The wireless message was in reply to the following radiogram. **1938** E. WAUGH *Scoop* I. v. 90 William hastened to consult him about a radiogram which had arrived that morning. **1949** *Radio Times* 15 July 6/1 I'm from the radio room. Here's a radiogram for you. **1966** *McGraw-Hill Encycl. Sci. & Technol.* XIII. 423/2 In overseas communication, telegraph messages usually are referred to as cablegrams or radiograms, depending on the overseas transmission medium. **1980** L. ST. CLAIR *Obsessions* ii. 58 Helen had replied with her own radiogram: 'What's wrong? No shipboard romance?'

radiogram^2 ('reɪdɪəʊgræm). Abbrev. of next.

1932 G. WILSON *Gramophones* viii. 43 If you have no electricity in your house you should avoid the radio-gram. **1933** *Sunday Referee* 2 July 16/2 In the living-room.. is a ply-wood built-in book-case, at one end of which is.. a built-in electric radiogram and loud-speaker. **1935** M. EGAN *Dominant Sex* III i. 86 She switches on the radiogram and dances gaily for her own amusement. **1938** AUDEN & ISHERWOOD *On Frontier* II. ii. 77 Valerian and Stahl.. are listening to the Leader's speech on the radiogram. **1945** J. BETJEMAN *New Bats in Old Belfries* 31 Softly croons the radiogram, loudly hoot the owls. **1970** J. EARL *Tuners & Amplifiers* i. 21 The old-style radiogram with inbuilt speakers.. rarely yields good stereo reproduction. **1977** *Gramophone* Jan. 1217/1 The widespread development of the music centre as successor to the radiogram.

radio-'gramophone. [RADIO *sb.* + GRAMOPHONE.] A radio and gramophone combined in a single cabinet (with a speaker).

1927 *Wireless World* 19 Oct. 539/1 (*heading*) A combined radio-gramophone installation. **1930** *Times Educ. Suppl.* 15 Feb. p. iv/4 We may reasonably expect a radio-gramophone to work without an outside aerial. **1935** *Economist* 23 Nov. 1042/1 Radio receiving sets and radio-gramophones had formed the largest part of the sales in the home markets. **1976** *Broadcast* 29 Nov. 19/1 Granny and her pre-war radiogramophone.

radiograph ('reɪdɪəʊgrɑːf, -æ-), *sb.* [f. as RADIOGRAM^1 + -GRAPH.]

1. An instrument by which the duration and intensity of sunshine is measured and recorded.

1880 D. WINSTANLEY in *Chem. News* 30 Apr. 205/1, I will now ask your attention to the description of another and much more perfect apparatus, one which continuously records the intensity of thermal radiation in which it is exposed. This instrument I have called the 'Radiograph'. **1881** *Jrnl. Science* XVIII. 221 This instrument, which Mr. Winstanley names the 'Radiograph', is shown.

2. An impression or image of an object produced on a sensitive plate by means of the Röntgen rays. Now also made using other forms of ionizing radiation.

1896 *Westm. Gaz.* 21 Feb. 7/2 A 'radiograph', or shadow picture, of the hand of Mr. Alfred Lyttelton. **1896** *Daily Tel.* 16 Mar. 7/2 A radiograph of the front portion of the foot gave no trace of the needle. **1923** GLAZEBROOK *Dict. Appl. Physics* IV. 618/1 Tool-marks and fine mould-marks often show up in a radiograph. **1948** *Sci. News* VII. 104 A new type X-ray tube permits radiographs to be made with exposures of 1/500,000th second. **1966** *McGraw-Hill Encycl. Sci. & Technol.* XI. 304a/1 Radiographs made with γ-rays have high resolving power because of the absence of scattering. **1971** *Sci. Amer.* Oct. 16/3 Radiographs of the chest in persons on a starvation diet have indicated that the heart shrinks in size. **1972** *Nature* 15 Sept. 157/2 It has been the practice among nuclear physicists to take 'radiographs' with beams of accelerated light nuclei to determine the location of detector targets.. relative to the position of the beam.

†**3.** = RADIO-TELEGRAPH. *Obs.*

1904 *Prelim. Conf. Wireless Telegr. Berlin 1903* 5 It is to him [*sc.* Popoff] that we owe the first radiograph apparatus.

radiograph ('reɪdɪəʊgrɑːf, -æ-), *v.* [f. the sb.] *trans.* To make a radiograph of; to study by radiography. Also *fig.* Hence **'radiographing** *vbl. sb.*

1896 *Daily News* 29 Feb. 5/4 Mr. Stanley Kent photographed, shadowgraphed, electrographed, or radiographed—for the proper verb is still undetermined—a fractured finger bone at St. Thomas's Hospital. **1896** *Photogram* Apr. 108 Our illustration.. is the first complete human skeleton ever radiographed. **1897** *Treatment* I. 43/2 It is almost routine practice.. to radiograph fractures. **1908** *Sci. Abstr.* A. XI. 105, 1M of No. 5 rays will suffice for the radiographing of a hand. **1924** *Observer* 6 Apr. 12/3 He [*sc.* Byron] has been radiographed to the bone. **1940** J. A. ROSS *Handbk. Radiography* xii. 112 Various methods of examination have been devised in an attempt to radiograph movement. **1951** L. P. DUDLEY *Stereoptics* vi. 106 The tube-film distance adopted in radiographing the subject must be the same as that adopted in radiographing the wire model. **1977** *Lancet* 19 Nov. 1059/2 Each section was photographed in colour, radiographed, drawn in black-and-white and compared with the scanner image at the corresponding level.

radiographer (reɪdɪˈɒgrəfə(r)). [f. prec. + -ER¹.] One who practises radiography; a person qualified to operate radiographic equipment.

1896 *Photogram* Apr. 105 The high price of Crookes' tubes is a matter of wonder to many radiographers. **1907** *Oxf. Univ. Gaz.* 19 Feb. 395/2 The Committee for appointment of Honorary Medical Officers will shortly proceed to the Election of a Radiographer. **1917** *Med. Jrnl. Australia* 5 May 386/1 The radiographer, who had made a screen examination, reported the presence of a large aneurysm of the aortic arch. **1958** *Times* 4 Aug. 9/3 Recent figures have revealed a serious shortage of more than 500 radiographers in the National Health Service. **1971** [see RADIOLOGIST]. **1975** E. LAWSON *Seeing through You* i. 16 The radiographer was turned towards her patient, one hand outstretched to guide him safely against the cassette containing the X-ray film.

radiographic (reɪdɪəʊˈgræfɪk), *a.* [f. as prec. + -IC.] **1.** Of, pertaining to, or carried out by means of radiography.

1896 *Q. Rev.* Apr. 501 The internal organs will be brought, it is hoped, within the range of radiographic inspection. **1921** *Lancet* 22 Jan. 175/2 (*heading*) Radiographic appearances of pyorrhœa. **1933** *Jrnl. Franklin Inst.* CCXXVI. 183 The radiographic method is useless.. in detecting cracks in which the two conjugate surfaces are pressed closely together, leaving no open space. **1976** *Offshore Platforms & Pipelining* 167/1 The most effective way to determine weld quality is by radiographic inspection.

†**2.** = RADIO-TELEGRAPHIC *a.* *Obs.*

1904 *Prelim. Conf. Wireless Telegr. Berlin 1903* 5 It was Hughes.. who laid, in 1877, the first stone of radiographic practice by his detailed experiments. **1907** *Liverpool Post* 10 Sept. 7 On Wednesday night.. the Lusitania will.. get into radiographic touch with the American coast.

Also **radioˈgraphical** *a.* (*rare*) = sense 1; also *fig.*; **radioˈgraphically** *adv.*, by means of radiography; as regards radiography.

1898 ISENTHAL & WARD *Pract. Radiogr.* 135 The radiographical study of Obstetrics. *Ibid.* 134 Coins,.. buttons, and so on, have been radiographically traced. **1925** *Jrnl. Anat.* LIX. 149 Dubreuil employed lead pellets, periodically measuring the intervals between the pellets, radiographically. **1931** S. BECKETT *Proust* 63 He describes the radiographical quality of his observation. The copiable he does not see. **1977** *Lancet* 14 May 1053/1 Although similar clinically and radiographically, the two syndromes show marked differences when pulmonary surfactant is examined.

radiography (reɪdɪˈɒgrəfɪ). [f. RADIO- 2 + -GRAPHY.] **1.** The science or process of making radiographs.

1896 *Brit. Med. Jrnl.* 14 Mar. 678 'Radiography' and its more thoroughbred equivalent 'actinography'.. are a trifle vague. **1898** *Ibid.* 7 May 1196 Since the introduction of radiography into surgery, many advances have been made in its application. **1922** G. W. C. KAYE *Pract. Application of X-Rays* vi. 85 When the art of radiography had sufficiently advanced in medicine, it extended its scope to industry. **1948** *Sci. News* VII. 104 Radiography of rapidly-moving enclosed machine parts, such as pistons or the impeller blades of turbines, has become practical. **1948**, etc. [see *neutron radiography* s.v. NEUTRON 2]. **1966** C. R. TOTTLE *Sci. Engin. Materials* vi. 147 With γ-rays, down to 10^{-2}Å, the penetration through metals is even greater; hence the use of X- and γ-rays for radiography. **1971** *World Archaeol.* III. 240 My colleague, Miss Theya Molleson, assisted in the radiography of the skeleton.

†**2.** = RADIO-TELEGRAPHY. *Obs.*

1904 *Prelim. Conf. Wireless Telegr. Berlin 1903* 5 It is due to radiography that communication has been created between parts of the globe which had previously been deprived of it. **1922** *Hotel World* 15 Apr. 6/2 Mr. Eastman, in charge of the radio broad-casting station in Chicago,.. said: 'When I took charge of this work I knew very little about radiography.'

radiohalo, -heliograph: see RADIO- 3 a, 4.

radioimmuno- (ˌreɪdɪəʊˌɪmjuːnəʊ, -ɪˌmjuːnəʊ). [f. RADIO- 2 + IMMUNO-.] Formative element in terms pertaining to analytical techniques combining immunological and radioisotopic methods. (In the following words secondary stresses vary as indicated above, and are not in general marked in each word.)

radioimmunoˈassay, an immunological assay in which the test sample is determined by allowing it to react with a prepared antiserum in competition with a known quantity of radioisotopically labelled antigen, the extent of reaction being measured from the amount of radiation emitted (see quot. 1974); hence **radioimmunoˈassayable** *a.*, capable of determination by radioimmunoassay; **radioimmunoˈchemical** *a.*, deriving both from immunology and from radiochemistry; employing radioisotopically labelled antigens and antibodies as reagents for chemical analysis; hence **radioimmunoˈchemically** *adv.*; **radioimmunoeˌlectrophoˈresis**, immuno-electrophoresis carried out using radioisotopically labelled samples, usu. as a means of studying the formation or binding of proteins; so **radioimmunoeˌlectrophoˈretic** *a.*; **radioimmunoprecipiˈtation**, the use of radioisotopically labelled antigen or antibody in a precipitin test, the radioactivity in any precipitated complex being measured.

1961 *Jrnl. Clin. Investigation* XL. 1086/1 A specific radioimmunoassay of human growth hormone.. has been devised. **1966** *Lancet* 24 Dec. 1389/2 Glucose was measured by the potassium-ferricyanide method.. and insulin by radio-immunoassay. **1974** R. M. KIRK et al. *Surgery* ii. 36 To carry out radioimmunoassay, an antiserum is first raised by injecting the substance repeatedly into laboratory animals, and later withdrawing serum containing antibody. A known concentration of antigen, labelled with a radioactive marker, is placed in competition with the test serum for combination with the antibody. **1977** *Time* 24 Oct. 52/1 Yalow and her late collaborator, Dr Solomon Berson, devised a sensitive new biological analytic technique called the radioimmunoassay (RIA). **1973** *Nature* 27 July 230/1 The serum level of radioimmunoassayable (RIA) growth hormone. **1978** *Ibid.* 12 Jan. 178/2 The radioimmunoassayable enkephalin content of the basal ganglia does not change after cortical ablation. **1968** *Gastroenterology* LV. 317/2 The supernatant solutions were analyzed in triplicate for gastrin by a radioimmunochemical technique *Ibid.* 326/2 The gastrin contents.. were measured radioimmunochemically. **1977** *Lancet* 26 Mar. 666/2 Blood obtained by antecubital-vein puncture was assayed radioimmunochemically for insulin, glucagon, gastrin, and pancreatic polypeptide. **1962** MORSE & HEREMANS in *Jrnl. Laboratory & Clin. Med.* LIX. 893 This method of immunoelectrophoresis, followed by autography, will be referred to as radioimmunoelectrophoresis. **1970** *Nature* 12 Dec. 1086/2 Radioimmunoelectrophoresis was also performed on dialysed supernatant from cell cultures incubated with either amino-acids labelled with ^{14}C or with reconstituted protein hydrolysate similarly labelled. **1975** *Ibid.* 11 Dec. 547/2 Radioimmunoelectrophoresis of serum from snakes injected with HEA revealed that the gamma precipitin line specifically bound HEA^{131}I. **1962** *Jrnl. Immunol.* LXXXIX. 744/2 Similar radio immunoelectrophoretic technique was applied in insulinbinding antibodies from human patients. **1962** *Jrnl. Clin. Investigation* XLI. 260/1 Our observations with radioimmunoprecipitation confirm the information obtained with more orthodox immunologic procedures. **1971** *Jrnl. Immunol.* CVI. 1167/1 The radioimmunoprecipitation test (RIP) was performed by the microtiter method as modified by Sever.. using V-bottom thin plastic plates. **1974** *Nature* 25 Jan. 176/3 In addition the antigen was detected by radioimmunoprecipitation in the supernatant fluid of a few cultures which had been serially passaged.

radioimmunology (ˌreɪdɪəʊɪmjuːˈnɒlədʒɪ). [f. RADIO- 2 + IMMUNOLOGY.] The application of radiological techniques in immunology.

1971 *Biol. Abstr.* LI. Ann. Cum. Index 4200/1 (*heading*) Radio immunology. **1976** *Scand. Jrnl. Immunol.* V. 609 (*heading*) Unified mass-action theory for virus neutralization and radioimmunology.

So **ˌradioimmunoˈlogic** (chiefly *U.S.*), **-ˈlogical** *adjs.*, combining radiological and immunological methods; of or pertaining to radioimmunology; **ˌradioimmunoˈlogically** *adv.*

1965 *Jrnl. Clin. Endocrinol.* XXV. 1043 (*heading*) A radioimmunological assay method for insulin using insulin-^{125}I and gel filtration. *Ibid.* 1457 (*heading*) Radioimmunologic measurement of human placental lactogen in plasma by a double antibody method. **1970** *Ibid.* XXXI. 679/2 HGH antibodies were determined radioimmunologically. **1976** *Science* 24 Dec. 1428/3 Radioimmunologic techniques have markedly increased the sensitivity with which viruses can be detected. **1977** *Lancet* 7 May 1006/2, 194 rural men, aged 55–74 and leading the same agricultural life, were screened for milk antibodies by a radioimmunological method.

radio-iodinate(d, -iodination: see RADIO- 3 a.

radio-iodine, -iron: RADIO- 3 b (i).

radioisotope (reɪdɪəʊˈaɪsətəʊp). Also with hyphen. [f. RADIO- 3 + ISOTOPE.] A radioactive isotope.

1946 *Chem. & Engin. News* 10 Dec. 3168/1 The availability of radioisotopes of nearly all elements in quantities hitherto unachievable. **1950** *Times* 8 May 4/4 Also being shown are the machines and methods used for the extraction and synthesis of C-14, a radio-isotope of carbon, which has many uses in industrial, medical, and biological research work. **1958** *Economist* 8 Feb. 496/2 Radio-isotope departments are being set up in the Royal Hospital in Baghdad and the University of Shiraz for the diagnosis and treatment of disease. **1976** *Daily Colonist* (Victoria, B.C.) 15 Apr. 5/5 A freshly fallen meteorite.. contains radioisotopes which decay in a matter of days or weeks. **1980** *Brit. Med. Jrnl.* 29 Mar. 931/1 The clinical use of radioisotopes has developed over the last 30 years from a technical science into a recognisable clinical specialty.

Hence **ˌradioisoˈtopic** *a.*, **-isoˈtopically** *adv.*

1956 *Nature* 7 Apr. 639/1 The kinetics of biological systems as studied by radioisotopic methods. **1970** *Ibid.* 13 June 1025/1 Detection of regulatory proteins present in such small amounts would probably require radioisotopically labelled proteins of very high specific activity. *Ibid.* 24 Oct. 383/1 Radioisotopic tracer experiments have established that carbonate from seawater is incorporated into the skeleton by many corals. **1978** *Ibid.* 19 Oct. 667/2 We used a radioisotopically labelled complementary DNA probe.. generated from an *in vitro* reverse transcriptase reaction.

radioize (ˈreɪdɪəʊaɪz), *v.* *U.S.* [f. RADIO *sb.* + -IZE.] *trans.* To equip with radio.

1922 *Sci. & Invention* May (Advt., rear cover), Radioize your phonograph with a guaranteed adapter. **1950** *Sun* (Baltimore) 19 July 13/1 Russia is in the middle of an all-out campaign to 'radioize' the entire population of its sprawling Soviet Socialist Republics.

ˈradio-label, *v.* and *sb.* *Biol.* and *Chem.* Also **radiolabel**. [f. RADIO- 3 + LABEL *v.*] **A.** *v.* *trans.* To label with a radioactive isotope (see LABEL *v.* 2). So **ˈradio-labelled** *ppl. a.*, **radio-ˈlabelling** *vbl. sb.*

1953 *Adv. Biol. & Med. Physics* III. 149 It may be possible to demonstrate the existence of such autoantibodies by the use of radio-labeled sera. **1962** *Jrnl. Immunol.* LXXXIX. 559/1 In the present study with poliovirus, this hindrance was overcome by radiolabeling the virus. **1970** *Nature* 16 May 649/1 In radiolabelling experiments, synchronized cultures were incubated with radioactive aminoacids for the required time and radiolabelled γG_{2a} was assayed. **1972** *Science* 16 June 1226/3 The tube is then washed, radiolabeled HBAb is added, and the new mix incubated. **1976** *Chem. in Brit.* XII. 375 (*heading*) Radiolabelling water's courses. *Ibid.* 379/1 Radiolabelling has become the preferred method for studying the metabolic fate of foreign compounds in biological systems.

B. *sb.* A radioactive label (LABEL *sb.*¹ 7 d).

1972 *Science* 16 June 1226/3 The use of a radiolabel makes the technique expensive. **1978** *Nature* 12 Jan. 111/3 That these phenomena are not due to breakdown and reincorporation of the radiolabel is shown by the negligible label in juice if the radiolabelled protein presented is albumin.

‖**Radiolaria** (ˌreɪdɪəˈlɛərɪə), *sb. pl.* *Zool.* [mod.L. f. *radiol-us*, dim. of RADIUS *sb.*] A class of rhizopods (see quot. 1872).

1872 NICHOLSON *Palæont.* 66 The order Radiolaria is defined as comprising those members of the Rhizopoda which possess a siliceous test or siliceous spicules. **1879** tr. *Semper's Anim. Life* 74 Most of the Radiolaria.. bear in their body certain.. particles known as the yellow cells.

radiolarian (ˌreɪdɪəˈlɛərɪən), *a.* and *sb.* [f. prec. + -AN.]

A. *adj.* **a.** *Zool.* Of or pertaining to the Radiolaria. **b.** *Geol.* ***radiolarian chert***, a cryptocrystalline type of radiolarite; *loosely* = RADIOLARITE; ***radiolarian earth***, unconsolidated siliceous rock formed from the remains of radiolaria; ***radiolarian ooze***, a siliceous marine sediment rich in the remains of the tests of radiolarians.

1876 [see OOZE *sb.*² 2 b]. **1877** THOMSON *Voy. Challenger* I. 231 It was found to contain so large a proportion of the tests of radiolarians, that Mr. Murray proposed for it the name 'radiolarian-ooze'. **1889** J. W. GREGORY in *Q. Jrnl. Geol. Soc.* Nov. 646 The Radiolarian deposits include a somewhat variable series of marls. **1890** *Geol. Mag.* VII. 144 (*heading*) Radiolarian chert in the Ballantrae series. **1911** [see OPHIOLITIC *a.*]. **1913** HATCH & RASTALL *Petrology of Sedimentary Rocks* I. iv. 143 One of the most notable instances of the abundant presence of this division of the Protozoa is afforded by the so-called Radiolarian earths of Barbados. *Ibid.* II. iii. 233 An interesting example of the metamorphism of a nearly pure siliceous rock is found in the Galloway district, where certain radiolarian cherts of Arenig age are altered by the Loch Doon granite. **1926** W. H. TWENHOFEL *Treat. Sedimentation* v. 377 Radiolarian ooze is confined to the Pacific and Indian oceans. **1944** A. HOLMES *Princ. Physical Geol.* xv. 317 The siliceous remains persist to greater depths, some of them down to 5,000 fathoms, the average for radiolarian ooze being about 3,000. **1953** *Caribbean Q.* III. III. 179 Barbados.. has a foundation of rocks... On top of this is a layer of deep sea deposit (radiolarian earth) and on top of this a slab of white limestone. **1971** B. W. SPARKS *Rocks & Relief* ix. 306 Certain beds of radiolarian chert.. are sufficiently resistant to form series of hog-back ridges across both outcrops. **1971** [see OOZE *sb.*² 2 b]. **1975** FOX & HEEZEN in Nairn & Stehli *Ocean Basins & Margins* III. x. 430 Piston cores obtained from the base of one escarpment recovered Early Eocene radiolarian ooze.

B. *sb.* One of the Radiolaria.

1877 THOMSON *Voy. Challenger* I. iii. 186 They brought back.. many large radiolarians. **1879** tr. *Semper's Anim. Life* 74 These yellow or sometimes green cells occur in many fresh-water Radiolarians.

radiolarite (reɪdɪəʊˈlɛəraɪt). *Geol.* [a. F. *radiolarite* (F. Jaccard 1904, in *Bull. des Laboratoires de Géol.*, etc. (Univ. of Lausanne) II. viii. 79): see RADIOLARIA *sb. pl.* and -ITE¹.] A type of homogeneous fine-grained siliceous sedimentary rock formed mainly from skeletal remains of radiolarians; also applied loosely to other sedimentary rocks similarly formed.

1910 *Proc. Sect. Sci. K. Akad. Wetensch. te Amsterdam* XII. 141 In the year 1894 I [*sc.* G. A. F. Molengraaff] discovered in the basin of the Upper Kapoewas in Western Borneo cherts and hornstones, consisting almost entirely of tests of Radiolaria, which I described as deep-sea deposits. Such rocks are also known as Radiolarite. **1924** J. G. A. SKERL tr. *Wegener's Orig. Continents & Oceans* ii. 20 The practically non-calcareous 'radiolarites' of the Alps. **1938** HATCH & RASTALL *Petrol. of Sedimentary Rocks* (ed. 3) x. 203 In Great Britain, two principal types of radiolarite may be distinguished, one represented by the jaspers and jasper-like cherts, and the other by the culm type of chert. **1945** M. F. GLAESSNER *Princ. Micropalaeont.* ii. 11 Radiolarite- and serpentine-zones in close association form important structural elements in many folded zones of different age. **1972** *Gloss. Geol.* (Amer. Geol. Inst.) 587/1 *Radiolarite*,.. (a) the comparatively hard, very fine-grained, chert-like, homogeneous, consolidated equivalent of radiolarian earth. (b) Indurated radiolarian ooze. (c) A term that is often applied as a syn. of radiolarian earth. **1977** A. HALLAM *Planet Earth* 254/1 Ancient radiolarian-rich sediments are known as radiolarites, and many of these are believed to be deep-water deposits.

radiole (ˈreɪdɪəʊl). *Zool.* [f. L. *radiolus*, dim. of *radius* RADIUS.] One of the spines or prickles of a sea-urchin. Also ***radiole spine***.

1929 *Encycl. Brit.* VII. 900/2 Primarily radioles serve for protection, but the larger radioles may be used like stilts for locomotion or for digging. **1979** *Nature* 8 Nov. 135/3 Differing feeding processes in echinoids were correlated with differing fine structure of their radiole spines.

radio-lead: see RADIO- 3 b (i).

radioless (ˈreɪdɪəʊlɪs), *a.* [f. RADIO *sb.* + -LESS.] Without radio broadcasting or radio equipment.

1937 *Daily Express* 3 Mar. 8/3 'Wilky' was an R.A.F. war pilot, and after the armistice was one of the heroes to work the radioless, single-engined air-mail service for the Rhineland Army. **1938** *Times Lit. Suppl.* 29 Jan. 69/1 Sir John [Reith] would have liked to impose a radioless Sabbath on the listening public. **1973** H. GRUPPE *Truxton Cipher* xviii. 189 Cutter had been radioless, his ship last reported as destroyed.

radioligand: see RADIO- 3 a.

radiolite (ˈreɪdɪəʊlaɪt). [f. RADIO- + -LITE.]

1. *Conch.* (See quot.)

1839 SOWERBY *Conch. Man.* 91 Radiolites. A family belonging to the order Cephalopoda.. containing the genera Rotalina, Lenticulina, Placentula.

2. *Palæont.* A cretaceous fossil bivalve of the family *Rudista*.

1842 in BRANDE *Dict. Sci.* **1851** WOODWARD *Mollusca* 280 The outer layer of shell in the Hippurite and Radiolite consists of prismatic cellular structure.

3. *Min.* A variety of natrolite with radiated structure.

1855 in ORR *Geol.* etc. 517. **1866** WATTS *Dict. Chem.* IV. 29 Radiolite, from Brevig [in Norway].

ˌradioloˈcation. Also with hyphen. [f. RADIO- 4 + LOCATION.] The term orig. used in Britain for RADAR; the determination of the position and course of ships, aircraft, etc., by means of radar.

1941 *Flight* 26 June 430/1 In the Battle of Britain the advantages of radiolocation were even more apparent. **1941** *Hutchinson's Pict. Hist. War* 14 May–8 July 180 Radiolocation has been described by Air Chief Marshall Sir Philip Joubert as Britain's secret weapon against the German bomber. Rays are sent out and any aircraft or ship in their path immediately reflects a signal. **1942** *R.A.F. Jrnl.* 30 May 30 By what, then, is the R.A.F. kept in the air?.. Its radio-location girls,.. its operations staff? **1947** J. HAYWARD *Prose Literature since 1939* vi. 43 The public should be disabused of the notion that science.. is merely another word for technology; and that its purpose is.. to develop and supply 'modern conveniences'.. in the form of.. radio-location for the General Staff. **1976** M. GILBERT *Winston S. Churchill* V. xxxiii. 659 The existence of 'radar' was not publicly acknowledged until 1941, when it was referred to as 'Radiolocation'.

Hence **ˌradioloˈcate** *v. trans.*, to locate (an aircraft, etc.) by means of radar; **ˌradioloˈcated** *ppl. a.*; **ˌradioloˈcator**, an apparatus for radiolocation.

1941 *Flight* 26 June 430/1 They could rely on the vast radiolocator system to tell them in plenty of time when the enemy were coming and from what direction. **1942** *Times* 20 Jan. 2/2 Members of the A.T.S. have taken over the working of the radiolocators, predictors, and height-finders. **1943** *Times* 25 Oct. 3/4 Many experts are convinced that the attack was.. ordered from a German patrol boat that had radio-located the aircraft. **1945** *Electronic Engin.* XVII. 679/3 It is no exaggeration.. to say that the first object to be radiolocated was the Heaviside layer. **1945** *Jrnl. Inst. Electr. Engineers* XCII. I. 342/1 In this method of determining the distance of a radiolocated object, short radio-frequency pulses are sent out at regular intervals. **1946** P. CARTER in Aldiss & Harrison *Decade the 1940s* (1975) 108 He passed by the radio locator and the radioman. Their jobs would come later, meantime radio silence was enforced. **1947** CROWTHER & WHIDDINGTON *Science at War* 18 The radiolocator requires as strong an echo as possible.

radiologic (reɪdɪəʊˈlɒdʒɪk), *a.* Chiefly *U.S.* [f. as next + -IC.] = next.

1909 in *Cent. Dict.* Suppl. **1914** *Jrnl. Amer. Med. Assoc.* 28 Mar. 980/2 Increased gastric peristalsis has been commonly listed among the radiologic signs of duodenal ulcer. **1945** *Radiology* XLIV. 82/2 His interest in radiology has made him an energetic participant in local and national radiologic organizations. **1975** S. C. BUSHONG (*title*) Radiologic science for technologists. **1978** *Detroit Free Press* 5 Mar. 9/1 Career training offered at Madonna for deaf students includes.. radiologic technology, business administration, [etc.].

radiological (reɪdɪəʊˈlɒdʒɪkəl), *a.* [f. next + -ICAL.] **a.** Of, pertaining to, or concerned with radiology.

1909 *Proc. R. Soc. Med.* II. I. (Electro-Therapeutical Section) 5 Two most interesting papers were those by Béclère, of Paris, and Alban Köhler, of Wiesbaden, on the 'Radiological Exploration of the Liver'. **1923** *Daily Mail* 7 Aug. 5/6 In the radiological department of the hospital there he was shown his hand with the X rays. **1947** *Radiology* XLIX. 345/2 One of the old ideas running through the entire radiological literature is that small doses of X-rays exert a stimulating effect. **1955** *Bull. Atomic Scientists* May 171/1 The composition and possible radiological effects of the super-bomb tested in the Pacific last spring. **1969** P. JACOBS in D. Sutton *Textbk. Radiol.* I. ii. 31/2 Since the surgeon is likely to explore the lesion as soon as it is suspected clinically, one will seldom nowadays observe the radiological phases corresponding to the pathological changes mentioned above. **1976** *Globe Democrat* (St. Louis, Missouri) 18 Sept. 8F/3 Six sections of radiological shield manufactured here.. are being shipped by rail to.. a nuclear power plant.

b. Of warfare, weapons, etc.: involving the deliberate release of ionizing radiation or radioactive material in harmful quantities.

1951 *Britannica Bk. of Year* 686/2 *Radiological warfare*, warfare with radioactive material. **1952** B. WOLFE *Limbo '90* (1953) vii. 79 H-bombs.. supplemented with radiological-warfare dust. **1958** *Ann. Reg. 1957* 478 Radiological warfare was now a distinct possibility through the use of low altitude explosions of high fission energy yield which could contaminate large areas beyond the range of physical damage. **1963** *New Scientist* 28 Mar. 679 (*heading*) A radiological arms race in the Middle East? *Ibid.* 679/3 The radiological bomb would, presumably, come into the same military category as a persistent gas.

Hence **radioˈlogically** *adv.*

1924 *Brit. Jrnl. Dermatol.* XXXVI. 516 When studying radiologically the osseous lesions.. I had been struck by the clear delimitation of the pathological loci. **1955** *Sci. News* XXXV. 87 It was shown radiologically that the sphincter is capable of shutting off the venous return. **1979** *Guardian* 1 May 3/3 The Windscale site is known to be radiologically 'dirty'.

radiology (reɪdɪˈɒlədʒɪ). [f. RADIO- 2 + -LOGY.] **a.** The medical use of X-rays, esp. in diagnosis; also extended to include the diagnostic use of other forms of radiation. †**b.** (See quot. 1905.) Cf. *roentgenology* s.v. ROENTGEN-, ROENTGENO-.

1900 *Pop. Sci. Monthly* May 110/1 An International Congress of Medical Electrology and Radiology has been connected with the International Congress system of the Paris Exposition, 1900. **1905** A. M. CLERKE *Syst. Stars* (ed. 2) vi. 80 The many suggestions of 'radiology' (as the new science of radioactivity might be designated) cannot be inconsiderately set aside. **1928** *Daily Express* 6 Dec. 7/4 A specialist in radiology and electrical treatment. **1938** S. C. SHANKS et al. *Text-bk. X-Ray Diagnosis* I. p. vii, Diagnostic radiology is becoming an increasingly complex specialty, and it is difficult for one person to be equally expert in all its branches. **1959** W. T. MOSS *Therapeutic Radiol.* i. 23 The selective destruction of tissues forms the basis of therapeutic radiology. **1979** BARTRUM & CROW *Case Stud. in Ultrasound* p.v, Even more than in conventional radiology, the satisfactory application of ultrasound requires that the practitioner know the clinical history. **1980** D. SUTTON *Textbk. Radiol. & Imaging* p. vii/1 When the last edition of this book was published in 1975 Radio-isotope Scanning was well established and Ultrasound had already made a major impact on radiology... Nuclear Medicine has also steadily progressed. Imaging, as these new disciplines are usually called, is now a major force which has profoundly influenced the practice of radiology.

Hence **radiˈologist**, a person employing ionizing radiation or radioactive material in any field, esp. a medically qualified practitioner of the diagnostic use of X-rays.

1906 *Arch. Roentgen Ray* XI. 20/1 Hitherto the majority of radiologists have been accustomed to work without any measurement of the Roentgen light. **1926** *Encycl. Brit.* XXXII. 284 This region of the intestinal tract is becoming an open book to the radiologist. **1955** *Sci. News Let.* 11 June 372/2 Because the field of radiation itself is so well-defined, City of Hope radiologists and physicists found it possible to dispense with the customary heavy, lead-lined door. **1958** *Times Lit. Suppl.* 2 May 233/3 The radiologists in their helmets of lead, the scientists tracking down the atom, cast their strange shadows on the Pyramids. **1971** *Lancet* 29 May 1124/1 A radiologist to the N.H.S. is medical and a radiographer non-medical.

radiolucent (reɪdɪəʊˈl(j)uːsənt), *a.* [f. RADIO- 2 + TRANS)LUCENT *a.*] Transparent to X-rays. So **radioˈlucency**, the state or property of being radiolucent.

1917 K. THOMA *Oral Roentgenol.* IV. iv. 197 The Roentgen evidence of alveoloclasia is due to the dissolution of bone and replacement by radiolucent pathological tissue. **1936** B. J. M. HARRISON *Textbk. Roentgenol.* iii. 62 Of the relatively radiolucent substances those used are air, carbon dioxide, and oxygen. **1940** *Bull. Johns Hopkins Hosp.* LXVI. 91 The cutaneous region of the foetus is usually represented by a dark line, due to radiolucency. **1961** *Dental Progr.* I. 177/2 Most of the difficulty in diagnosis was caused by general graininess of the film combined with poor contrast between areas of varying radiolucency. **1973** *Daily Tel.* 22 Oct. 13/6 The plastics used in the modern motor car.. are radiolucent and do not reveal themselves on an X-ray film.

radioluminescence, -ent: see RADIO- 2.

radiolysis (reɪdɪˈɒlɪsɪs). *Chem.* [f. RADIO- 2 + -LYSIS.] Decomposition of a compound by the action of ionizing radiation. Hence **radioˈlytic** *a.*, of, pertaining to, or formed as a result of, radiolysis.

1948 *Jrnl. Physical & Colloid Chem.* LII. 516 The kinetics of the radiolysis of pure water and of indirect action on solutes are discussed. **1950** *Ann. Rev. Physical Chem.* I. 120 Negative ions make important contributions to the general radiolytic process only in special cases. **1951** *Jrnl. Amer. Chem. Soc.* LXXIII. 532/2 H_2O_2 produced in the radiolysis may affect the pH. **1963** DAWSON & SOWDEN *Chem. Aspects of Nuclear Reactors* II. iii. 96 The discovery.. that cupric ion would act as an effective homogeneous catalyst to promote the recombination of radiolytic gas within the reactor core.. was of the highest importance to homogeneous aqueous reactor technology. **1977** J. WEISMAN *Elem. Nuclear Reactor Design* ii. 35 Ions which participate in electron-transfer reactions can combine with H or OH ions thus preventing recombination and leading to an increased radiolysis.

ˈRadiometal. Also radiometal. An alloy consisting largely of nickel and iron in approximately equal proportions and having a high magnetic permeability.

1940 *Chambers's Techn. Dict.* 699/1 *Radiometal*, an alloy of permalloy type. Contains iron 50%, nickel 45%, and copper 5%. **1941** *Jrnl. Brit. Inst. Radio Engineers* II. 101 A group of metallurgists and electrical technicians concentrated on the problem of high permeability materials and carried out intensive research on alloys with 80%, 50% and about 36% nickel content. The outcome of the work was the commercial introduction of the well known alloys Mumetal (78% Ni), Radiometal (48% Ni) and Rhometal (36% Ni). **1946** *Nature* 13 July 54/2 The stator core consists of radiometal laminations 0·010 in. thick. **1951** *Electronic Engin.* XXIII. 330/1 The smoothing choke is wound on a radiometal core. **1957** W. J. JOHN *Mod. Electr. Engin.* I. iv. 116/2 Radiometal, or Permalloy B, has a saturation of 16,000 gauss and a maximum permeability of 10,000 to 30,000 at *H* = 0·3 to 0·4 oersted... Composition: nickel 50 per cent, iron 50 per cent.

radiometeorograph(y: see RADIO- 4.

radiometer (reɪdɪˈɒmɪtə(r)). [f. RADIO- + METER.]

†**1.** An instrument formerly used for measuring angles; a cross-staff, forestaff. *Obs.*

1727–41 in CHAMBERS *Cycl.* **1802** in JAMES *Milit. Dict.*

2. An instrument invented by Sir W. Crookes, with the design of illustrating the transformation of radiant energy into mechanical force. Also, more generally, any device used to detect, or measure the intensity of, electromagnetic radiation (freq. *spec.* infrared). Also extended to instruments (in the first cases adapted from Crookes's device) used to measure the intensity of sound by means of its radiation pressure.

1875 CROOKES in *Proc. R. Soc.* XXIII. 377 The luminous rays.. repel the black surface more energetically than they do the white surface. Taking advantage of this fact, the author has constructed an instrument which he calls a radiometer. **1893** SIR R. BALL *Story of Sun* 256 Highly rarefied gas like that contained in one of Mr. Crookes's radiometers. **1905** R. W. WOOD in *Physical Rev.* XX. 113 It occurred to me that a mill-wheel or radiometer driven by these [sound] waves would be useful for purposes of demonstration in treating of radiation pressure. **1920** *Q. Jrnl. R. Meteorol. Soc.* XLVI. 399 (*heading*) The ether differential radiometer. **1927** I. B. CRANDALL *Theory Vibrating Syst. & Sound* iv. 180 The radiometer is a simple torsion balance; a thin hollow metal box filled with air, on being submerged serves as a very good totally reflecting vane. **1930** R. H. BAKER *Astron.* x. 396 Abbot,.. working with the 100-inch reflector, made use of delicate radiometers, having vanes of blackened bits of fly-wings, to measure the energy in different parts of the spectrum. **1963** G. L. PICKARD *Descriptive Physical Oceanogr.* vi. 92 The downward directed component of the long-wave radiation term.. is determined by means of a radiometer. **1966** *McGraw-Hill Encycl. Sci. & Technol.* XI. 317/1 Other radiometers use the pressure of sound waves to deflect a spherical body. *Ibid.* 317/2 The Crookes radiometer survives in jewelers' windows as a 'perpetual motion' device. **1969** *Times* 19 Feb. 13/6 An infra-red radiometer will map the temperature across the surface of Mars. **1973** *Nature* 20 Apr. 506/2 The radiometer was a load-switched superheterodyne microwave receiver. **1977** *R.A.F. News* 11–24 May 11/1 Radiometers to measure infra-red and solar radiation.

attrib. **1876** *Nature* XIV. 288/2 The friction of the radiometer vanes with the rarefied air of the globe. *Ibid.* 508/1 The radiometer experiments were successful.

3. An instrument for determining the amount of X-radiation administered to a patient.

[**1904** *Sci. Abstr.* A. VII. 362 A 'chromo-radiometer' has been invented by Holzknecht, which consists of two parts —a measurer and a comparative scale.] **1912** *Med. Ann.* 73 The.. method of using Holzknecht's new radiometer for the more exact measurement of the *x*-ray dose. **1918** R. KNOX *Radiogr.* (ed. 2) II. 437 The radiometer is so sensitive that it is possible to measure with accuracy the pastille tint when it has not become nearly such a dark colour as in the case of the Sabouraud method. **1934** H. DAVIES *Pract. X-Ray Therapy* iii. 31 (*caption*) Holzknecht radiometer, showing both halves of the pastille in position.

radiometric (reɪdɪəʊˈmɛtrɪk), *a.* [f. RADIO- 2 + -METRIC.] **1.** Of or pertaining to the radiometer (sense 2) or its use.

1877 *Chem. News* 12 Jan. 21/2 (*heading*) New radiometric experiments. **1883** *Athenæum* 10 Feb. 189/2 The effects of all the different parts of the radiometric apparatus in influencing radiometer motion. **1904** *Electrician* 28 Oct. 58/2 Prof. Nichols also suggests a new radiometric receiver, whose action is based on the electrostatic and electrodynamic action between equal resonators. **1927** H. N. RUSSELL et al. *Astron.* II. xxi. 735 With a suitable thermoelectric device the heat radiation of the stars may now easily be measured and the results expressed as 'radiometric magnitudes'. **1964** *Yearbk. Astron. 1965* 111 For Mars, information about ground temperatures may be obtained from radiometric observations, and the amount of insolation is easily calculable. **1977** A. HALLAM *Planet Earth* 111 Magnetic, electromagnetic and radiometric techniques are commonly adapted to airborne surveys.

2. Of, pertaining to, or involving the measurement of radioactivity or ionizing radiation; ***radiometric dating***, isotopic dating.

1906 *Sci. Abstr.* A. IX. 50 Sabouraud and Noiré.. point out that their radiometric value is not in any way diminished. **1938** R. W. LAWSON tr. *Hevesy & Paneth's Man. Radioactivity* (ed. 2) xviii. 169 This method of 'Radiometric Microanalysis' has rendered it possible.. to carry out a determination of the nitrogen content of organic substances to the order of magnitude of some ten-thousandths of a milligram. **1951** *Engineering* 2 Feb. 148/1

Radiometric methods are frequently used in the investigation of uranium-bearing minerals. **1962** F. I. ORDWAY et al. *Basic Astronautics* v. 191 Gamma ray scintillation spectrometers make radiometric assays. **1968** *Sci. Jrnl.* Oct. 122/3 *Geologic Time* is concerned with how the present knowledge of the Earth's history has been built up;..palaeomagnetism and continental drift; biostratigraphy and radiometric dating. **1969** *Beaver* Summer 34/2 The coal deposits there are overlaid by volcanic ash determined as 72–73 million years old by radiometric dating processes. **1972** *Science* 2 June 977/1 Radiometric ages obtained for the Apollo 14 examples.. cluster around a value of 3·9 × 10^9 years.

Hence (in either sense) **radio'metrically** *adv.*, by a radiometric method.

1920 *Jrnl. Franklin Inst.* CLXXXIX. 27 The energy was determined in the spectrophotometric laboratory, visually on a König-Martens Spectrophotometer, by a substitution method of comparison with a radiometrically calibrated Mazda lamp. **1962** F. P. W. WINTERINGHAM in *Radioisotopes & Radiation in Entomol.* (Internat. Atomic Energy Agency) 117 P^{32} and S^{35} are readily differentiated radiometrically. **1968** *Palaeogeogr., Palaeoclimatol., Palaeoecol.* V. 69 The paleobotanical event has been radiometrically dated at about 12,000,000 years B.P. **1972** *Science* 2 June 978/1 The times of formation of lunar craters have been determined radiometrically. **1973** *Physics Bull.* Apr. 239/3 The centre is equipped with radiometrically and photometrically calibrated sources and a range of calibrated detectors for continuous wave and pulsed radiation.

radiometry (reɪdɪ'ɒmɪtrɪ). [f. RADIO- 2 + -METRY.] The use of a radiometer; *spec.* the detection and measurement of infra-red radiation.

c **1890** A. R. BENNETT (*title*) On some experiments in Radiometry. **1906** *Sci. Abstr.* A. IX. 50 They have used this method of radiometry in 5,000 cases of tinea tonsurous without accident. **1923** GLAZEBROOK *Dict. Appl. Physics* III. 718/2 The second method of attack is by means of thermal radiometry with non-selective receivers. **1934** *Discovery* Oct. 282/2 The combination of visual observation at the telescope with the employment at some of the great observatories of the resources of photography, spectroscopy, radiometry, and polarimetry. **1977** I. M. CAMPBELL *Energy & Atmosphere* iii. 44 One of the methods which has been used to measure the temperature profile of the atmosphere as a function of altitude, namely infrared radiometry from satellites.

radio-micrometer, -mimetic, -necrosis: see RADIO- 2.

radionic (reɪdɪ'ɒnɪk), *sb.* and *a.* [f. RADI(O- 2 + -*onic*, after ELECTRONIC *a.*] **A.** *sb. pl.* (const. as *sing.*) † **1.** *U.S.* Electronics, esp. those aspects of electronics connected with radio. *Obs.*

1943 *Radio News* May 4/2 In its simplest form, radionics would be understood by we Americans as being an all-inclusive term of any equipment or science where the use of vacuum tubes is employed [*sic*]. **1943** *Proc. IRE* XXXI. 192 He [*sc.* Hitler] was stopped because the RAF had gone him one better on the new weapon which had paced his early victories, the only new weapon this war has produced: Radionics.

2. The study and interpretation of radiation believed by some to be emitted by and to characterize living and other substances, and to be detectable by skilled use of various complicated electrical instruments.

1954 *Brit. Jrnl. Radiesthesia* I. III. 18 Radiesthesia.. applied to the use of the pendulum, Radionics..applied to instrumental detection and use, and Dowsing, the use of the Divining Rod. **1960** *Times* 21 June 5/4 The plaintiff alleged that the defendant is an exponent of and practitioner in the pseudo-science of radionics, and that..he fraudulently represented that there were associated with substances distinctive waves, vibrations or radiations capable of affecting a device..called a Delawarr Diagnostic Instrument. **1960** *Spectator* 28 Oct. 653 The founder of what today is known as radionics was Dr. Albert Abrams (1863–1924), a..physician who came to believe that the basis of disease was atomic or electronic..and that disease could therefore be treated by giving healthy radiations to neutralise the unhealthy ones. **1969** B. COPEN *Radionic Computer Handbk.* 8 Radionics is the science of radiation detection which uses the extra sensory perception of the operator..and automatic instruments, of which this computer is but one. Modern Radionics is a combination of the older Radiesthesia (detection with pendulum) and the more modern semi-automatic instruments (Radionics). **1976** T. GRAVES *Dowsing* xii. 124 *Radionics*, the specific form of medical dowsing which uses as its instrument a 'box' containing a number of dials in a particular sequence or pattern, seems to be a compound-word formed from 'radiesthetic electronics'—so the word is another product of the tangle over the assumed physical basis of dowsing.

B. *adj.* **1.** Of or pertaining to radionics (sense 1); electronic. orig. *U.S.*

Quot. 1963 represents an independent use not connected with the orig. use of radionics (sense A. 1 above).

1943 *Radio News* May 75/1 Radio News will use 'radionic' in preference to 'electronic' wherever it is more descriptive. **1943** *Proc. IRE* XXXI. 193 This one [*sc.* war], at the front, is run by radio and radionic devices. **1963** *Spectator* 15 Nov. 616/3 Even in this radionic age, a Prime Minister cannot hope to make his way in the country without establishing his mastery over the House of Commons.

2. Of, pertaining to, or practising radionics (sense 2).

1947 *Radiesthesia* III. 58 The development of a new technique in Radionic Diagnosis. **1969** B. COPEN *Radionic Computer Handbk.* 54 Any potency of the lower order may be chemically analysed, but the higher potencies are non-analytic in nature, by the orthodox system, but are by the Radionic system. **1972** D. V. TANSLEY *Radionics & Subtle Anat. of Man* 7 Today, most if not all radionic practitioners would agree that it is their belief that man does have what is referred to as an etheric body. **1975** *Homes & Gardens* Nov. 63/2 Sometimes a diagnostic box helps to make the diagnoses and may also broadcast the treatment. The instrument is not electrically powered but gains its energy from the patient's witness which is put into the box... The radiesthetist determines the diagnosis and then uses the radionic box to broadcast the selected rate of the remedy.

radionuclide: see RADIO- 3 a.

,radio-o'paque, *a.* Also **radiopaque.** [f. RADIO- 2 + OPAQUE *a.*] Impervious to X-rays. So **,radio-o'pacity, radio'pacity,** the state or property of being radio-opaque.

1917 K. THOMA *Oral Roentgenol.* IV. iv. 197 Unsanitary concretions, such as salivary..calculi, can be seen on account of their radiopacity. **1926** *Jrnl. Amer. Med. Assoc.* 19 June 1883/1 In the stenotic larynx, the extent of the destruction may be visualized by the introduction of radiopaque substances. **1940** *Brit. Jrnl. Radiol.* XIII. 261/2 To determine the depth of the foreign body, the observer places a radio-opaque guide-mark on the skin..; then he moves the X-ray tube horizontally. **1961** *Dental Progr.* I. 178/2 Radio-opacity of the palatal vault blotted out the apices of the maxillary teeth. **1970** H. MCLEAVE *Question of Negligence* xxvii. 228 They had trundled in a portable X-ray machine..injected a radio-opaque substance into a neck artery. They ran off six plates. **1971** G. H. BOURNE *Ape People* vii. 186 A series of cinemagraphs were taken with radiopaque material being injected into different chambers of the heart. **1971** *Brit. Dental Jrnl.* CXXX. 430/1 The localised radiopacity caused by the superimposition of shadows can be very misleading, therefore patients should be instructed to remove their ear-rings before the picture is taken.

radio-pasteurization, -ized: see RADIO- 2.

radiophare ('reɪdɪəʊfɛə(r)). [f. RADIO- 4 + PHARE.] A navigational radio beacon.

1915 W. H. ECCLES *Wireless Telegr. & Telephony* 362 The French Government is installing wireless lighthouses or radiophares round the French coast. **1922** *Nature* 20 May 650/1 Until two or three years ago the radiophares—or radio-beacons as they are called in America—were purely stations for giving ships their positions. **1966** *McGraw-Hill Encycl. Sci. & Technol.* IV. 231/2 Radio stations erected specifically for use with the ADF are known as NDB (non-directional beacons or radiophares).

radiopharmaceutical, -pharmacist, -pharmacology (etc.), **-pharmacy:** see RADIO- 2.

radiophone ('reɪdɪəʊfəʊn). [f. RADIO- + -PHONE.] **1.** An instrument for the production of sound by intermittent radiant energy, such as light or heat; the photophone and thermophone are special forms.

1881 BELL *Sound by Radiant Energy* 32 We have decided to adopt the term 'radiophone', proposed by M. Mercadier, as a general term signifying an apparatus for the production of sound by any form of radiant energy.

2. Also **radio-phone, radio phone.** = RADIO-TELEPHONE.

1919 *Wireless World* May 105/2 (*heading*) Radiophones over London. **1922** *Sci. Amer.* Sept. 160/1 The receiver can be worked on very short waves, well below 200 meters, thus opening up a new field of wave lengths for radio-phone broadcasting. **1926** *Popular Radio* IX. 91 (*caption*) The first radiophone booth on an ocean liner. **1940** N. MONKS *Squadrons Up!* ii. 39 The boys [*sc.* pilots] wisecracked to each other into their radio-'phones. **1971** J. BRUNNER *Honky in Woodpile* xii. 90 A luxuriously-equipped Mercedes convertible—it even boasted a radiophone. **1978** R. LUDLUM *Holcroft Covenant* xxviii. 322 We use a radiophone off Cap Camarat.

radiophonic (,reɪdɪəʊ'fɒnɪk), *a.* [Cf. prec. and -PHONIC.] **1.** Belonging to radiophony.

1881 *Sci. Amer.* 5 Feb., Radiophonic notes, such is the new term, have been obtained by M. Mercadier from ordinary gas lamps. **1881** *Nature* XXIII. 367 The radiophonic sounds result from a direct action of radiations upon the receiving substances.

2. Pertaining to or designating synthetic sound produced by electronic means and the use of tape recorders, usually for use in broadcasting in conjunction with conventional material.

1958 *Times* 24 May 10/2 B.B.C.'s Radiophonic Workshop. A 'workshop' for producing synthetic sounds, partly by electronic oscillators and partly by trickery with conventional sounds recorded on tape has been set up by the B.B.C. at their Maida Vale studios. **1958** *Observer* 22 June 14/3 He [*sc.* Patrick Magee] must be the only actor who can sound as if he's talking through a radiophonic filter. *Ibid.* 6 July 14/2 Those radiophonic plays where an old woman's memories or a young man's nightmares are made the slender excuse for the latest in ghost-train noises. **1960** *BBC Handbk.* 67 Special effects..created..for the occasion by 'radiophonic' devices. **1961** *Listener* 16 Nov. 834/1 Michael Bakewell employed radiophonic effects to communicate the variant senses of time experienced by the normal and the mentally ill characters in this double bill. **1972** *Ibid.* 21 Dec. 872/3 Not a *Goon Show* script, but..one of Michael Mason's radiophonic workshop larks.

Hence **radio'phonicist,** an exponent of radiophonic sound; **radio'phonics** *sb. pl.*, the production and use of radiophonic sound; the sounds themselves; **radi'ophonist** = *radiophonicist* above.

1958 *Listener* 28 Aug. 319/3 Our local radiophonicists and 'concrete' music men have too often seized upon noise in the higher octaves to drive home dramatic nails that would have seemed excruciating even to Jael. **1962** A. NISBETT *Technique Sound Studio* xii. 203 Radiophonics does not in general attempt to assert itself as an art form in its own right; it is always an element in a larger picture. **1963** F. C. BROOKER (*title*) Radiophonics in the B.B.C. **1976** *Listener* 21 Oct. 511/3 The tinkling celeste tune—now, alas, abandoned in favour of radiophonics—that used to introduce *Listen with Mother.* **1977** *Listener* 18 Aug. 217/2 What was crushing to the fond memory was the way the poverty had affected the radiophonics, too. **1977** *Times* 3 Sept. 10/3 Isaac Asimov's *Foundation Trilogy*..on Radio 4 certainly provided a field day for the radiophonists.

radiophony (reɪdɪ'ɒfənɪ). [Cf. prec. and -PHONY.] The theory or method of producing sound by radiant light or heat.

1880 *Athenæum* 25 Dec. 870/3 M. Mercadier brought before the Academy of Sciences a paper on 'Radiophony', as he names the phenomenon of using a ray of light for the conveyance of sound. **1884** *New Eng. Jrnl. Educ.* XIX. 374 Tyndall's experiments in radiophony.

radio-phosphorus: see RADIO- 3 b (i).

radiophoto ('reɪdɪəʊfəʊtəʊ). [f. RADIO- 4 + PHOTO.] A photograph transmitted by means of radio.

1942 *Wireless World* Sept 217/2 The first..radiophoto service between America and Egypt was recently opened. **1961** *New Scientist* 13 July 91/2 If the radiophotos show recognizable evidence of hurricane breeding in the clouds, hurricane-hunting planes will be sent out. **1971** *Encycl. Americana* XXIII. 121n/1 The channel capacity of an HF system is limited to four voice or radiophoto channels.

radiopho'tography. Also with hyphen. [f. RADIO- 2 + PHOTOGRAPHY.] **1.** = RADIOGRAPHY 1 (see also quot. 1939).

1897 *Chem. News* 26 Feb. 102/2 (*heading*) Radiophotography of the soft parts of man and the lower animals. **1934** *Jrnl. R. Anthrop. Inst.* LXIV. 70 It may be demonstrated by radiophotography that bronze, on exposure to the atmosphere, immediately begins to oxidize. **1939** *Jrnl. Amer. Med. Assoc.* 6 May 1844/1 Radiophotography, or indirect radiography, consists in simultaneously photographing the thoracopulmonary images as they are observed at radioscopic examination.

2. The transmission of photographs by means of radio.

1915 *Wireless World* Apr. 60/1 The number of interruptions per second required is very high, as in radio-photography. *Ibid.* 60/2 A system of radio-photography.. would be of great military use.

Hence **radio'photograph** = RADIOGRAPH *sb.* 2; (in either sense) **,radiophoto'graphic** *a.*

1897 *Chem. News* 26 Feb. 102/2 We have been able to place the muscles, the ligaments, and the tendons in such a state that they have yielded radio-photographic images. **1915** *Wireless World* Apr. 60/2 Even were they possessed of radio-photographic apparatus, the received message would be unintelligible unless they knew the exact speed. **1924** *Times* 13 Sept. 12/5 In this section are some radio-photographs showing considerable advance on any hitherto.

radiophysics (etc.): see RADIO- 4.

radio-potassium: see RADIO- 3 b (i).

radio-protection, -protective, -protector: see RADIO- 2.

radio-purity: see RADIO- 3 a.

'radioreceptor. *Physiol.* [f. RADIO- 2 + RECEPTOR.] † **1.** Written **radio-receptor.** A sensory receptor which responds to electromagnetic radiation of any kind. *Obs.*

1927 [see MECHANORECEPTOR]. **1935** *Brit. Jrnl. Psychol.* XXV. 266 As Parsons describes, the receptors differentiated along three main lines, chemo-, radio-, and mechano-receptors.

2. ***radioreceptor assay***, a radiological assay for hormones in which the test sample, together with a known quantity of radioactively labelled hormone, is allowed to bind to a standard preparation containing receptor sites.

1973 *Science* 1 June 968 A radioreceptor assay with a sensitivity of 5 nanograms per milliliter has been developed for mammalian and avian pituitary prolactin, placental lactogenic hormones, and human growth hormones, using a membrane receptor preparation isolated from rabbit mammary glands. **1974** *Nature* 29 Mar. 436/2 At this time the PL concentrations measured by radioreceptor assay were almost entirely due to the cross reaction of pituitary prolactin in the receptor assay. **1978** *Ibid.* 20 Apr. 730/2 The fact that affinity to rat opiate receptors was demonstrated in the plasma using a radioreceptor assay..indicates that a loss of the postulated biological activity by metabolic or other processes can be excluded.

radio-resistance, -ant: see RADIO- 2.

radioscan: see RADIO- 3 a.

radioscopy (reɪdɪ'ɒskəpɪ). [f. RADIO- + -SCOPY.] The examination of objects by means of the roentgen rays. *spec.* = FLUOROSCOPY. So **radio'scopic** *a.*; also † **'radioscope** = FLUOROSCOPE.

1897 [see RADIOTHERAPEUTIC *sb. pl.* and *a.*]. **1897** *Treatment* I. 43/2 It makes his own heart beat faster as the observer sees for the first time thrown upon the radioscopic screen a living heart in action. **1898** ISENTHAL & WARD *Pract. Radiogr.* 114 The latter method..enables us..to practise radioscopy in broad daylight. *Ibid.* 121 The radioscopic or radiographic image. **1898** *Amer. Jrnl. Med. Sci.* CXV. 464 The capsules are readily seen (in thin persons) with the radioscope. **1908** *Chem. Abstr.* II. 229 (*heading*) The radioscope and the radiograph applied to the inspection of tubercular meats. **1915** R. KNOX *Radiogr.* 188 Radioscopy, or the examination of a patient with the fluorescent screen, is a method of great value, as a diagnosis can often be made from it alone, to be subsequently confirmed by radiographic exposures. **1928** B. J. LEGGETT *Theory & Pract. Radiol.* III. x. 459 (*heading*) Radiographic and radioscopic rooms. **1937** M. CAMPBELL in *Brit. Encycl. Med. Pract.* VI. 352 Radioscopy is of great help; the presence of a large left ventricle or of a dilated left auricle in mitral stenosis,..may clinch a doubtful diagnosis. **1946** *Surg. Clinics N. Amer.* Oct. 1286 Such long radioscopic exposures are only possible without danger of dermatitis when a very small radioscopic field is used. **1979** *SLR Camera* Sept. 5/1 Now the holiday season is on us perhaps a word, or two, about the precautions needed to safeguard films from damage by radioscopic screening is pertinent.

radiosensitive(ness, etc.: see RADIO- 2.

radio-silver, -sodium: see RADIO- 3 b (i).

radiosonde ('reɪdɪəʊsɒnd). *Meteorol.* Also **radio-sonde, radio sonde.** [a. G. *radiosonde* (P. Moltchanoff 1931, in *Beiträge z. Geophysik* XXXIV. 36), f. *radio-* RADIO- + *sonde* probe, sounding-line.] A small package of meteorological instruments which is carried through the atmosphere by balloon or other means and automatically transmits measurements of conditions at various heights by radio. Freq. *attrib.* So **radiosondage** (-'sɒndɪdʒ), sounding of the atmosphere by radiosonde.

1937 *Geogr. Jrnl.* XC. 381 The use of the radio-sonde, from which automatically transmitted W/T signals can be transformed into data of temperature and pressure. **1939** *Meteorol. Gloss.* (Meteorol. Office) (ed. 3) 153 Radio-sondages (Radio-soundings). **1940** *Manch. Guardian* 30 Jan. 6/6 The staff of our Meteorological Office..receives great help from an instrument called the radio sonde, which is sent up attached to a small balloon and automatically reports by wireless the air conditions up to a great height. **1946** *Electronics* May 123/3 Several methods of radiosonde tracking have been used in order to determine the speed and direction of the wind at various altitudes. **1948** *Times* 23 Feb. 6/7 The radio-sonde equipment..was insufficiently sensitive to detect the rapid temperature changes within the first few hundred feet of the sea surface. **1951** T. F. MALONE *Compendium Meteorol.* 1215/2 The parachute radiosonde was designed to be launched from a weather-reconnaissance plane. **1955** W. GIRVAN *Flying Saucers & Common Sense* ix. 110 The weather-balloon..crossed the coast near Eastbourne and then burst, the radio-sonde falling into the Channel at approximately 3.30 p.m. after descending slowly by parachute. **1959** H. R. BYERS *Gen. Meteorol.* (ed. 3) vi. 101 Several types of rawinsonde systems, combining radiosondage with tracking of the radiosonde to get wind drift of the balloon, have been developed. **1960** *Times* 19 July (Royal Society suppl.) p. x. 6 Preparations are being made to launch a hydrogen-filled balloon carrying a radiosonde transmitter. **1976** B. JACKSON *Flameout* (1977) xii. 205 The radiosonde balloons from the unnamed Air Force base in Nevada.

radiostereoassay: see RADIO- 3 a.

radiosterilization, -ized: see RADIO- 2.

Radiostol ('reɪdɪəʊstɒl). Also **radiostol.** [f. RADIO- 2 + *-stol.* (f. ERGOSTEROL from which calciferol can be prepared by irradiation with light).] A proprietary name for a preparation of calciferol (vitamin D_2).

1927 *Trade Marks Jrnl.* 27 Apr. 737/1 *Radiostol*... Chemical substances prepared for use in medicine and pharmacy. The British Drug Houses, Limited. **1928** *Daily Express* 27 Jan. 3/3 It is possible to give margarine the rich food value of the best butter by treating it with radiostol. **1934** *Nature* 2 June 821/2 Modifications [in the diet]..were additions of oatmeal, olive oil, cod liver oil or radiostol (irradiated ergosterol), and milk, [etc.]. **1967** *Martindale's Extra Pharmacopoeia* (ed. 25) 258/2 Radiostol (*British Drug Houses*). Calciferol, available as Capsules..; as a Solution [etc.].

radio-strontium: see RADIO- 3 b (i).

radio-surgery, -surgical: see RADIO- 2.

radio-'telegram. [f. RADIO- 4 + TELEGRAM.] A telegraphic message sent by radio.

1902 *Sci. Amer. Suppl.* 15 Nov. 22474/1 The radio-telegrams arrived from Poldhu constantly and surely at the receiver on board the 'Carlo Alberto'. **1904** *Prelim. Conf. Wireless Telegr. Berlin 1903* 16 We desire to grant to existing systems a fair share of the charge to be collected for radio-telegrams. **1913** *Wireless World* Aug. p. xxx (Advt.), Hand your message in at any Telegraph Office, where full particulars concerning radio-telegrams can be obtained. **1920** *Glasgow Herald* 2 Apr. 5/7 The charge for such radio-telegrams is 10½d. per word.

radio-'telegraph. Also **radiotelegraph.** [f. RADIO- 4 + TELEGRAPH *sb.*] A means of sending telegraphic messages by radio rather than along a wire. Usu. *attrib.* So **,radio-tele'graphic** *a.*, **-tele'graphically** *adv.*, **-te'legraphist** (all *rare*); **radio-te'legraphy**, wireless telegraphy.

1898 J. MUNRO in *Electrician* 21 Jan. 428/2 'Wireless telegraphy' is not a bad technical term; but if a more scientific name be desirable would not Radiotelegraphy or Ray Telegraphy be preferable to 'Space Telegraphy'? which Dr. Lodge employs. **1902** *Nature* 25 Sept. 538/2 The creation of a radio-telegraphic station communicating with the stations established..by the Marconi companies in London and in America. **1903** *Ibid.* 23 Apr. 590/1 The establishment on the coast and on the islands off the Italian coast of a system of twelve Marconi radio-telegraph stations of an average range of 300 kilometres. **1906** *Westm. Gaz.* 19 Dec. 2/2 Wireless telegraphy, or 'radio-telegraphy', as it is more technically called. **1907** *Athenæum* 14 Sept. 308/1 The Report and Evidence of the Radiotelegraphic Convention Committee. **1907** *Daily Chron.* 11 Nov. 6/6 The Amalgamated Radio-Telegraph Company, Limited. **1908** J. A. FLEMING *Radiotelegr. & Radiotelephony* p. vi, Expositions of electrical phenomena which are.. unnecessary to the practical radiotelegraphist. **1918** *Wireless World* June 192 (*heading*) Senatore Marconi radiotelegraphically expresses the national sentiment of Italy. **1921** *Jrnl. R. Soc. Arts* 9 Dec. 68/2 Marconi..was able to dispatch wireless messages across the Atlantic which made long-distance radio-telegraphy a demonstrated achievement. **1945** *Sun* (Baltimore) 23 Oct. 1/3 (*heading*) Radio telegraph plan announced. **1955** *Times* 12 Aug. 5/3 A feature of the year has been the development in leased channel operations, that is, in the provision of direct customer-to-customer private radio-telegraph circuits. **1966** *McGraw-Hill Encycl. Sci. & Technol.* I. 364/2 Much of the radiotelegraph traffic of the world uses AM telegraphy, although there had been extensive conversion to frequency-shift (frequency-modulation) telegraphy since 1944. *Ibid.*, Most aviation and marine radiotelegraphy uses AM manual methods.

radio-telemetering, -telemetric, -y: see RADIO- 4.

radio-'telephone. Also **radiotelephone, radio telephone.** [f. RADIO- 4 + TELEPHONE *sb.*] A transmitting and receiving set for radio-telephony.

1909 *Daily Chron.* 15 Feb. 1/2 Mr. Lee De Forest,.. whose radio-telephone system has been adopted by the American navy. **1922** *Encycl. Brit.* XXXII. 1027/2 Compact light-weight sets of radio-telephone transmitters and receivers. **1935** H. G. WELLS *Shape of Things to Come* 15 There will be a radio telephone arrangement on his chest no more obtrusive than a modern breast pocket. **1957** *Practical Wireless* XXXIII. 517/1 Cable and Wireless Ltd. announce that a radiotelephone service has been opened between Saudi Arabia and Bahrein. **1966** P. O'DONNELL *Sabre-Tooth* xiv. 187, I will arrange for you to speak to her briefly over the radio-telephone. **1973** *Sat. Rev. Society* (U.S.) Mar. 52/2 An immaculately uncluttered teakwood desk, flanked by..two telephones, a radio-telephone and an intercom.

So **,radio-tele'phonic** *a.*; **,radio-tele'phonic-ally** *adv.* (*rare*); **radio-te'lephony**, telephony in which the signal is transmitted by radio over part of the route; wireless telephony.

1908 J. A. FLEMING (*title*) Radiotelegraphy and radio-telephony. *Ibid.* 325 We have..in the combined radio-telephonic transmitter and receiver, a wonderful transformation of energy. *Ibid.* 329 Transmitting speech radio-telephonically from Paris..to Dieppe. **1923** *Radio Times* 28 Sept. 12/1 We are most enthusiastic admirers of this remarkable radio-telephonic invention. **1930** *Daily Express* 8 Sept. 3/7 The principal means of communication; both in the brigade and battalions, will be radio-telephony. **1935** *Times* 12 Nov. 20/5 It is a strange thing that in radio-telephony across the Atlantic..some wave-length, which has been behaving admirably, will rather swiftly fade and fail. **1966** *McGraw-Hill Encycl. Sci. & Technol.* I. 364/1 Since radio is the only way to communicate with ships and aircraft, hf AM radiotelephony has remained essential to these operations. **1974** *Guardian* 22 Mar. 13/7 Will you see to it that the cars used by public figures are fitted with.. radio-telephonic methods of communication?

radio-teletype, -tellurium: see RADIO- 4, 3 b (i).

,radiothera'peutic, *sb. pl.* and *a.* Also with hyphen. [f. RADIO- 2 + THERAPEUTIC *a.*] **A.** *sb. pl.* = RADIOTHERAPY. **B.** *adj.* Of, pertaining to, or employing radiotherapy. Hence **,radio-thera'peutically** *adv.*; †**,radiothera'peutist** = RADIOTHERAPIST.

1897 *Treatment* I. 43/1 (*heading*) Radiography, radioscopy, and radiotherapeutics. **1904** *Bristol Medico-Chirurg. Jrnl.* XXII. 43 What this variation is is a question for the radio-therapeutists to solve. **1906** *Arch. Roentgen Ray* XI. 20/1 It is to be hoped that in radiotherapeutic practice the use of the dosimeter may become universal. *Ibid.* 20/2 Radio-therapeutists are divided into..those who believe in the large (so-called) measured dose, and those who administer small unmeasured doses at intervals. **1932** *Discovery* Aug. 255/2 The report urges the establishment of radio-therapeutic centres associated with large general hospitals. **1937** *Amer. Jrnl. Obstetr. & Gynecol.* XXXIV. 50 In the surgically or radiotherapeutically induced menopause, much can be done by prophylactic psychotherapy. **1975** *Nature* 13 Mar. 97/1 The Medical Research Council is to set up a new unit for research in clinical oncology and radio-therapeutics at Cambridge. **1977** *Proc. R. Soc. Med.* LXX. 591/2 This is a very comprehensive review of the present state of knowledge of the investigation and treatment, medical, surgical and radiotherapeutic, of these lesions.

radio'therapy. [f. RADIO- 2 + THERAPY.] The treatment of disease by means of X-rays or other forms of ionizing radiation.

1903 *Boston Med. & Surg. Jrnl.* CXLIX. 325/1 He had been interested in comparing the effects of phototherapy and radiotherapy. **1904** *Westm. Gaz.* 29 Dec. 2/1 A working knowledge of the technique of radio-therapy. **1955** *Bull. Atomic Sci.* Oct. 287/3 These will become available in source strength varying from kilocurie sources of radiocaesium for use in radiotherapy to megacurie sources for industrial applications. **1970** *Sci. Jrnl.* Mar. 62/3 Where a cancer has become disseminated to other areas, treatment with drugs or radiotherapy is used. **1974** 'H. CARMICHAEL' *Motive* iv. 47 Dr. Egan will see you. He's in the Radio-Therapy department.

Hence **radio'therapist**, one who practises radiotherapy.

1918 R. KNOX *Radiogr.* (ed. 2) II. 388 It is easy..to understand the complexity of the problem which confronts the radiotherapist in dealing with morbid growths. **1934** *Lancet* 29 Sept. 697/1 The patient should..be examined in consultation with an expert radiotherapist before any operation on the primary tumour or glands. **1976** *Ibid.* 6 Nov. 992/1 The introduction of improved techniques has enabled radiotherapists to treat relatively large volumes of the body with comparative safety.

radiothon ('reɪdɪəʊθɒn). *U.S.* [f. RADIO *sb.* + -A)THON.] A prolonged radio broadcast by a person or group, usu. as a fund-raising event.

1964 *Richmond* (Va.) *Times-Dispatch* 26 Jan. 6B/1 With only an hour to run, the radiothon had netted the March of Dimes here more than $1,200. **1974** *State* (Columbia, S. Carolina) 15 Feb. 20-A/3 A 15-day try for a world record radiothon is being made by WCOS-AM disc jockeys to benefit the Heart Fund. **1976** *Long Island Traveler-Watchman* 8 July 1/3 (*caption*), The radiothon, to raise funds for Kiwanis youth programs, will be broadcast WRIV.

radiothorium: see RADIO- 3 b (i).

radiotoxic(ity, -tracer: see RADIO- 3 a.

radiotranslucency, -ent: see RADIO- 2.

†**'radious**, *a. Obs.* Forms: 6 **radius, radyuss, -ous,** 6–8 **radious.** [ad. F. *radieux* (15–16th c.), or L. *radiōsus* (Plautus), f. *radius* ray.]

1. Radiant, bright.

1500–20 DUNBAR *Poems* xlviii. 132 A radius croun of rubeis scho him gaif. **1552** LYNDESAY *Monarche* 5350 Thare Radious beymes ar turnit in reik. **1592** R. D. *Hypnerotomachia* 79 Two pleasant radious and glistering eyes. **1610** G. FLETCHER *Christ's Tri.* I. xxxv, His radious head with shamefull thorns they teare. **1678** CUDWORTH *Intell. Syst.* I. iv. §36. 582 That radious effulgency which, immediately encompassing them, is beheld together with them. **1692** O. WALKER *Grk. & Rom. Hist. Illustr.* 334 The Sun (as Constantine) radious.

b. Forming rays of light. *rare.*

1709 BERKELEY *Th. Vision* §90 The Intersection made by the Radious Pencils. **1733** —— *Th. Vision Vind.* §50 The Pictures, so called, being formed by the radious Pencils.. are not so truly Pictures as Images.

2. Belonging to the radius of a circle or sphere; radial. *rare*$^{-1}$.

1678 CUDWORTH *Intell. Syst.* I. iv. §36. 598 The Centre, Radious Distance, and Movable Circumference, may be all said to be Co-Essential to a Sphere.

'radiovision. Also with hyphen. [f. RADIO- 4 + VISION *sb.*] **1.** The combination of a radio programme with a specially prepared film strip or series of slides, esp. as an educational aid. Freq. *attrib.*

1964 *Guardian* 14 Feb. 7/2 The technique..is to issue film strips to accompany selected broadcasts; it is becoming known as 'radiovision'. **1965** *B.B.C. Handbk.* 70 The use of radio-vision in the teaching of languages was the subject of an experiment in fifty schools in the autumn of 1963. **1966** *Listener* 24 Sept. 786/2 In a radiovision talk of great virtuosity..Mr Morris explained the nature of an atmospheric depression. **1971** *Daily Tel.* 4 May 2/2 The radio-vision programmes were more easily taped and film-strips could be stored for parent evenings.

2. Radio broadcasting accompanied by the simultaneous showing of the broadcasters on television.

1980 *Daily Tel.* 6 Nov. 19/4 Miss Monica Sims, controller of Radio 4 and a former head of children's television, has been asked to chair an immediate feasibility study on the possibilities of 'radiovision' and report by next spring to Sir Ian Trethowan, B B C director-general.

radir, obs. form of RATHER.

radish ('rædɪʃ). Forms: α. 1 **redic, rædic,** 3 **redich,** 4 **radiche,** 5 **radik, raddyk.** β. 5 **radissh,** 5–6 **radys(s)he,** 6– **-ishe, -ice, redish,** 6–7 **raddish,** 7 **reddish,** (7–8 *erron.* **rhadish**), 5– **radish.** [In the α-forms ad. L. *rādīc-em*, with subsequent palatalization in southern Eng.; in the 15th c. readopted from F. *radis*, a. Pr. *raditz*, or It. *radice*:—L. *rādīc-em*: see RADIX and RACE *sb.*[6]]

1. a. The fleshy, slightly pungent, root of a widely cultivated cruciferous plant (*Raphanus sativus*), commonly eaten raw as a relish or in salads. **b.** The plant of which this is the root.

wild radish, a field-weed (*R. Raphanistrum*), also called *jointed* or *joint-podded charlock*.

α. *c* **1000** *Sax. Leechd.* II. 64 Wiþ sidan sare..redic, & hwite clæfran wyrc to clame. *c* **1000** ÆLFRIC *Gloss.* in Wr.-Wülcker 135/23 *Raphanum, uel radix*, rædic. *c* **1265** *Voc. Plants* ibid. 556/20 *Raffarium*,..redich. *a* **1387** *Sinon. Barthol.* (Anecd. Oxon.) 36 *Raphanum*, radiche. *c* **1425** *Voc.* in Wr.-Wülcker 645/20 *Raparium*, raddyk.

β. *c* **1420** *Pallad. on Husb.* IX. 30 Now rape and neep in places drie is sowe..and radish last. *Ibid.* 44 Radish female hath litel bitternesse. **1548** TURNER *Names Herbes* (1881) 66 There are two kindes of radice, the one is the commune radice wyth the longe roote..The other kynde hath a rounde roote. **1598** B. JONSON *Ev. Man. in Hum.* I. v, We will have a bunch of redish, and salt, to tast our wine. **1620** VENNER *Via Recta* vi. 99 Some Physitians commend the eating of Radishes before meate. **1649** BLITHE *Eng. Improv. Impr.* (1652) 248 You may Plant your garden with Onions,

Reddishes or any sallet herb. **1718** QUINCY *Compl. Disp.* 158 Radish..is much in Diet amongst our Spring-Sallets, but little used as Medicine. **1784** COWPER *Task* IV. 173 Enjoyed, spare feast! a radish and an egg. **1853** LYTTON *My Novel* IV. viii, It was with some such tract that Lenny was seasoning his crusts and his radishes.

2. *attrib.* and *Comb.*, as ***radish-bed***, ***-oil***, ***-pod***, ***-root***, ***-seed***; ***radish-leaved***, ***-like*** adjs.; **radish communist**, one who professes communism but is not sincerely devoted to it; also *ellipt.*; **radish-fly** (*U.S.*), a small dipterous insect, *Anthomyia raphani*, whose larvæ burrow in radishes (*Cent. Dict.* 1891); **radish tree** = HORSE-RADISH TREE (*b*).

1855 E. S. DELAMER *Kitch. Garden* (1861) 115 The traveller who has no *radish-bed to go to. **1920** *Times* 31 Oct. 11/1 A '*radish' is a man who fervently professes devotion to the Communist cause while harbouring a secret longing for its overthrow. Red outside, but white..inside. The epithet was invented by Trotsky. **1966** *Listener* 29 Sept. 445/1 Stalin would speak disparagingly of Mao's men as being 'not real communists', mere 'margarine communists', 'radish communists'—red on the outside and white on the inside. **1753** CHAMBERS *Cycl. Supp.* s.v. *Sisymbrium*, The short-podded *radish-leaved water-*sisymbrium*. **1711** J. PETIVER in *Phil. Trans.* XXVII. 385 Auriculated, or rather small wing'd *Radish-like Leaves. **1728** E. SMITH *Compl. Housew.* Index, *Radish Pods pickled. **1855** DELAMER *Kitch. Garden* (1861) 134 Radish-pods..make an excellent pickle. **1533** ELYOT *Cast. Helthe* (1539) 25 *Radyshe rootes, haue the vertu to extenuate, or make thyn. **1626** BACON *Sylva* §408 A Beet-Root, a Borrage-Root, and a Raddish-Root. **1868** WATTS *Dict. Chem.* V. 76 Radish-roots contain ..water 959.74 [parts in 1000]. **1538** ELYOT *Dict.*, *Cortinon*, *radyshe seede. **1599** HAKLUYT *Voy.* II. 163 Some others.. that practised to worke that effect by Radish seed. **1626** BACON *Sylva* §401 There were sown in a Bed, Turnip-seed, Radish-seed [etc.]. **1898** MORRIS *Austral Eng.* 378/1 *Radish-Tree, an Australian timber-tree, *Codonocarpus cotinifolius*, called also Poplar in Central Australia.

radishy ('rædɪʃɪ), *a.* [f. RADISH + -Y^1.] Resembling or suggestive of a radish.

1861 H. MAYHEW *London Labour* III. 64/2 The matches were tied..to his [*sc.* the guy's] radishy and gouty fingers.

radium ('reɪdɪəm). [f. L. *radius* ray, RADIUS: see -IUM.] **1.** *Chem.* **a.** [a. F. *radium* (P. Curie et al. 1898, in *Compt. Rend.* CXXVII. 1217).] A radioactive element, chemically a member of the alkaline earth metals, which occurs in small amounts in uranium ores, notably pitchblende; atomic number 88, symbol Ra.

1899 *Chem. News* 6 Jan. 1/2 These different reasons lead us to believe that the new radio-active substance contains a new element, to which we propose to give the name of radium. **1903** *Daily Mail* 11 Sept. 3/1 All the speakers recognised that the discovery of radium, with its apparent power of emitting heat for ever without diminution, has opened the door to something like a new world of science. **1904** *Daily Chron.* 7 Jan. 5/1 It is quite as good as any other assertion to say that an ounce of radium is worth the British Empire; no more having yet been obtained than about the weight of a lump of sugar. **1909** 'O. HENRY' *Roads of Destiny* xxi. 358 'Change the treatment,' says I... 'Call a consultation or use radium or smuggle me in some saws or something.' **1933** BOWING & FRICKE in O. Glasser *Sci. of Radiol.* xv. 281 The paramount advantage of the use of radium in medicine..consists in the proved fact that the rays of radium have a selective action on cancer cells. **1950** *Thorpe's Dict. Appl. Chem.* (ed. 4) X. 446/1 The history of radium refining during the 50 years, 1898–1948,..covers the rise of radium from a scientific curiosity to a commodity of almost fabulous value and wide importance, and its subsequent relegation to a minor role following the development of the atomic pile. **1958** *Daily Express* 11 Mar. 7/1 An escape of radium at a hospital led to the dumping of tons of material down a disused pit shaft. **1974** *Encycl. Brit. Micropædia* VIII. 382/1 Metallic radium has high chemical reactivity. It dissolves in water with vigorous evolution of hydrogen.

b. (Followed by capital letter.) Designating substances (mostly radioactive) subsequently identified as isotopes of other elements, which are formed successively in the radioactive series of radium: ***radium A***, polonium 218; ***radium B***, lead 214; ***radium C***, bismuth 214 together with some polonium 214 (***radium*** C_1 **or** *C′*) and thallium 210 (***radium*** C_2 **or** *C″*); ***radium D***, lead 210; ***radium E***, bismuth 210; ***radium F***, polonium 210; ***radium G***, lead 206, the non-radioactive end-product of the series.

The substances now designated *radium E* and *F* were in the first instances named *radium* D_1 and *E* respectively.

1904 E. RUTHERFORD in *Phil. Mag.* VIII. 636 For convenience, the products in the active deposit will be termed Radium A, Radium B and Radium C, respectively. *Ibid.* 641 Following the nomenclature suggested, radium C gives rise to the β ray product, which will be called Radium D, while radium D changes into the α ray product, which will be called Radium E. **1905** —— in *Nature* 9 Feb. 342 In order to avoid confusion, I have called the new radium product 'radium D_1'. If no further intermediate products of radium are brought to light, it would be simpler to call it radium E and to call the α ray product (polonium) radium F. **1905** —— in *Phil. Mag.* X. 293 This rayless product will be called radium D. The β ray product which arises from it will be called radium E. The α ray product (previously termed radium E) will be called Radium F. **1910** *Westm. Gaz.* 16 Feb. 4/1 Sir William Ramsay's description..of 'Radium D', one of the mysterious products of radium, as 'rather dull-looking, like lead'. **1911** *Phil. Mag.* XXII. 628 Fajans has suggested that the name radium C_2 should be given to the new product of period 1·4 minutes. **1913** *Nature* 28 Aug. 659/2 That radium-G and lead are identical is supported by much indirect evidence, though no direct proof has been advanced. **1933** FAILLA & QUIMBY in O. Glasser *Sci. of Radiol.* xiii. 249 In about a month the equilibrium amounts of radon and radium A, B, and C will have accumulated, and the preparation has a maximum beta and gamma ray activity. **1936** *Discovery* July 218/2 The radium E was produced..through the bombardment of bismuth, with deuterons at an energy of 5,500,000 electron volts. **1966** R. OLIVER *Radiation Physics in Radiol.* vi. 71 Radium then disintegrates to form radon which is a gas at normal temperature and pressure. There follows a long series of disintegrations through nuclides referred to as radium A (RaA), B, C, C′, C″, D, E, F and G. The last nuclide (radium G) is a stable isotope of lead. **1974** *Encycl. Brit. Micropædia* VIII. 382/1 A sample of radium, sealed to prevent the escape of gaseous radon, reaches radioactive equilibrium in about a month and becomes a powerful source of gamma radiation, due especially to radium C (bismuth-214).

2. A smooth, plain fabric with the sheen of silk (see quots.).

1904 *Daily Chron.* 12 Mar. 8/5 The newest ribbon is radium, and what a future lies before it! **1930** *Daily Express* 6 Oct. 5/2 (Advt.), Radium velvet. Rich quality panne velvet giving a fashionable brilliance for afternoon and evening wear. **1957** M. B. PICKEN *Fashion Dict.* 269/1 *Radium*, smooth, pliable lingerie fabric of synthetic yarn in plain weave, with dull finish and natural sheen of silk. **1970** R. T. WILCOX *Dict. Costume* 281/2 *Radium*, a lustrous, plain, smooth silk or rayon, which has crispness, yet supple, draping quality.

3. *attrib.* and *Comb.*, as (sense 1) ***radium atom***, ***bromide***, ***chloride***, ***salt***, ***sulphate***, ***treatment***; (sense 2) ***radium poplin***, ***silk***, ***velvet***; ***radium-bearing***, ***-coloured*** adjs.

1903 *Daily Mail* 11 Sept. 3/1 Illustrating the amazing properties of a radium atom. **1926** R. W. LAWSON tr. *Hevesy & Paneth's Man. Radioactivity* xxiii. 161 St. Joachimstal in the Erzgebirge is the most important source of radium-bearing ores in Europe. **1904** *Chem. News* 24 June 301/1 As radium bromide yields electrolytic gas, containing an excess of hydrogen, the pressure gradually rose. **1913** *Med. Ann.* 647 Each capsule contains ·0002 mgram radium bromide. **1966** P. ASTBURY tr. *G. Amaldi's Nature of Matter* iv. 125 Pierre and Marie Curie..had to examine about seven tons of pitch-blende..in order to prepare a single gram of radium bromide. **1902** *Harper's Mag.* Aug. 360/2 M. Curie possesses about two to three hundredths of a gram of chemically pure radium chloride. **1904** *Daily Chron.* 2 Sept. 8/3 A magnificent mantle fully trained and made of radium-coloured taffetas mousseline, the blue, pink, and moonlight shades of which mingle with one another. **1952** C. W. CUNNINGTON *Eng. Women's Clothing* 296 *Radium poplin*, a silk and wool textile looking like a silk poplin. **1905** KIPLING *Actions & Reactions* (1909) 121 An expense of one hundred and seventy-odd pounds..for radium salts and such trifles. **1956** J. K. ROBERTSON *Radiology Physics* xii. 228 When radium needles are used, the dose delivered to the region treated depends on..the amount of absorption by the materials enclosing the radium salt. **1972** BARNES & REES *Conc. Textbk. Radiotherapy* viii. 178 Radium is prepared as the salt, radium sulphate, and mixed with a suitable filler, it is sealed into thin-walled metal capsules. **1936** *Discovery* Nov. 351/2 Apparatus for radium treatment recently installed at the Hampstead annexe of Westminster Hospital. **1930** Radium velvet [see sense 2 above].

b. Special Combs.: **radium beam**, a beam of gamma radiation from a radium source, used in radiotherapy; **radium bomb**, a container holding a large quantity of radium and used in radiotherapy as a source of a gamma ray beam; **radium burn**, a burn caused by over-exposure to radiation from radium; **radium clock**, a device utilizing the β-rays of radium to charge two electroscopic leaves, which discharge at regular intervals when they diverge sufficiently to touch two earthed metal plates; **radium emanation**, the radon isotope of atomic weight 222, which is the first product of the radioactive decay of radium; cf. EMANATION 2c; **radium needle**, a needle containing radium which can be inserted into tissue for radiotherapy; **radium plaque** = PLAQUE 3; **radium therapy**, radiotherapy using radiation from radium.

1933 *Jrnl. Amer. Med. Assoc.* 12 Aug. 533/2 The work before the radium beam therapy research will be to.. discover how far the present limited field of operation for a mass radium unit..may be extended. **1940** *Ibid.* 16 Mar. 999/1 Treatment of carcinoma of the mouth and throat by the radium beam is at least as satisfactory as by surgery or interstitial radium. **1956** J. K. ROBERTSON *Radiology Physics* xii. 227 In radium beam therapy, the source contains several grams of this radioactive element. **1930** *Brit. Med. Jrnl.* 19 July 98/1 An attempt to measure accurately the gamma radiation field, in air, of the radium 'bomb' in use at Westminster Hospital annexe. **1952** W. M. LEVITT *Handbk. Radiotherapy* iii. 42 It is probable that the radium bomb can do nothing that super-voltage x-ray therapy cannot do at least as well and little that deep x-ray therapy cannot do. **1908** *Jrnl. Amer. Med. Assoc.* 30 May 1871/1 (*heading*) Radium burns of the skin. **1926** R. W. LAWSON tr. *Hevesy & Paneth's Man. Radioactivity* xxv. 211 Radium burns are especially troublesome, because..even if they mend there remains a supersensitiveness of the skin. **1940** S. CADE *Malignant Dis. & Treatm. by Radium* 246 Radium burns of the skin or mucous membrane may take 8 to 10 months to heal. **1905** W. HAMPSON *Radium Explained* 69 We are now able to understand the action of the radium clock. **1905** E. RUTHERFORD *Radio-Activity* (ed. 2) iv. 123 This 'radium clock' should work at a sensibly uniform rate for many years, but..the number of β particles emitted would decrease exponentially with the time, falling to half value in about 1200 years. **1926** R. W. LAWSON tr. *Hevesy & Paneth's Man. Radioactivity* xxv. 211 The so-called 'radium clock'.. illustrates how the rays from radium may be utilized indirectly to give rise to motion. **1901** *Nature* 13 June 157/2 The radium emanation..preserved its radiating power for several weeks. **1910** *Daily Chron.* 17 Feb. 3/3 Take the next product, the gas which it is continually giving off, and which is called radium emanation. That can be worked with because it is only half gone in four days. **1946** F. E. ZEUNER *Dating Past* x. 318. As radium decays, a gas called radium-emanation is formed which, in turn, emits another atom of helium and thereupon changes into a solid substance, called radium A. **1921** *Pennsylvania Med. Jrnl.* XXIV. 218/1 Radium needles should be inserted directly into the glands. **1959** C. L. & J. A. MARTIN *Low Intensity Radium Therapy* iii. 33 Low intensity radium needles still seem to provide the best available medium for interstitial therapy. **1960** A. HUXLEY *Let.* 20 May (1969) 890 For cases like mine, radium needles are now standard procedure at the University of California. **1919** *Amer. Jrnl. Roentgenology* VI. 134/1 It is.. a very simple matter to treat a small lesion with a radium plaque. **1962** J. THEWLIS *Encycl. Dict. Physics* VI. 171/1 Formerly, radium plaques were used as β-emitters, but these have now been almost completely replaced by applicators containing strontium-90. **1904** *Med. Electrol. & Radiol.* V. 336 (*heading*) Radiumtherapy. **1905** *N. Amer. Jrnl. Homœopathy* LIII. 720 It would seem wise to postpone judgment as to the worth of radium therapy in dermatology. **1931** G. B. SHAW *Doctors' Delusions* 28 Nobody would dream of excluding radium therapy from the medical curriculum merely because more nonsense has been written about radium than about the philosopher's yarn to shine. **1964** L. DEIGHTON *Funeral in Berlin* xxix. 152 Began work as a representative [for] radium therapy machinery 1948. Assigned to Northern Spain as radium therapy equipment salesman 1949.

radiumize ('reɪdɪəmaɪz), *v.* [f. RADIUM + -IZE.] *trans.* To subject to the action of radium. Hence **'radiumized** *ppl. a.*

1906 *Jrnl. Amer. Med. Assoc.* 21 July 184/2 Two fine examples of spindle-celled sarcoma..have been thoroughly radiumized. **1914** *Chambers's Jrnl.* Oct. 688/2 The process of radiumising the soil. **1920** *Amer. Jrnl. Roentgenology* VII. 54/1 Such radiumized tissue will not grow when inoculated in mice. **1928** *Daily Tel.* 10 July 9/5 Work..is being pursued upon the immunity conferred upon rats and mice by X-rayed or radiumised tumour tissues. **1939** *Jrnl. Amer. Med. Assoc.* 1 Apr. 1280/1 (*heading*) Radiumized health pad.

radius ('reɪdɪəs), *sb.* Also 7 -ous. Pl. **radii** ('reɪdɪaɪ); also 7–8 **radius's**, 8 **-uses**. [a. L. *radius* a staff or stake, measuring-rod, spoke, ray, etc. (cf. senses below).]

1. A staff, rod, bar, or other straight object.

†**a.** The staff of a cross; hence *Astron.* a CROSS-STAFF. *Obs.*

1597 MORLEY *Introd. Mus.* 174 The Radius or staffe of the crosse containeth like wise two partes in one. [**1727–41** CHAMBERS *Cycl.* s.v., *Radius astronomicus*, an instrument usually called Jacob's staff, or the cross-staff.] **1742** YOUNG *Nt. Th.* IX. 646 With my Radius (the rich Gift Of Thought nocturnal!) I'll point out to thee Its various Lessons.

†**b.** The bony spine or sting near the base of the tail of a sting-ray. *Obs. rare*$^{-1}$.

1661 LOVELL *Hist. Anim. & Min.* 201 Fork-fish... Their Radius only is poysonsome, which being cut off, the rosted may be eaten.

c. *Anat.* The thicker and shorter of the two bones of the forearm in man, extending from the humerus to the thumb side of the wrist; also the corresponding bone of the foreleg in quadrupeds, and of the wing in birds.

The name has also been given to a bone of the pectoral arch in fishes, held to be homologous with the radius of higher vertebrates.

1615 CROOKE *Body of Man* (1618) 782 The whole hand being sustained almost alone by the Radius, hath one and the same motion. **1719** QUINCY *Phys. Dict.* (1722) s.v., Altho the *Ulna* and *Radius* accompany one another, they touch but at their Extremities. **1758** J. S. *Le Dran's Observ. Surg.* (1771) 12 The Radius of the left Arm was..broke. **1827** ABERNETHY *Surg. Wks.* II. 72 The carpal bones were.. driven upwards, some before, and others behind the ends of the radius and ulna. **1841** R. E. GRANT *Comp. Anat.* 65 In the perch..the two succeeding bones [are regarded] as the ulna and the radius. **1881** MIVART *Cat* 94 At its lower end the radius becomes much broadened out. **1896** NEWTON *Dict. Birds* 859 In Birds..there are..only two free carpals —one, generally termed the 'radial',..articulating with the distal end of both radius and ulna.

†**d.** (In full ***radius articulatus***.) The alveolus of the belemnite. *Obs. rare*$^{-1}$.

1753 CHAMBERS *Cycl. Supp.* s.v., Many of these *radii* are found remarkably compressed, bent, or distorted, which is an accident accounted peculiar to the fossils formed in animal moulds.

e. A dorsal fin. *rare*$^{-1}$.

1822 G. A. MANTELL *Geol. Sussex* 229 Dorsal fin, or radius, of a fish allied to the Balistes... It consists of thirteen narrow parallel rays.

2. a. A rod, bar, etc., forming one of a set extending in several directions from one point; a wheel-spoke; a radiating part or filament, etc.

1726 BAILEY, *Radius* (in mechan.), a spoke, or felloe of a wheel, because they issue like rays from the centre of it. **1800** HURDIS *Fav. Village* 169 His fine-spun radii flings from side to side. **1805** SOUTHEY *Madoc* II. x, Equal in number,..The spreading radii of the mystic wheel, Revolve. **1876** *Nature* XIV. 465/1 A horizontal wheel of iron..having six radii. **1878** BELL *Gegenbaur's Comp. Anat.* 41 In the animals built on a radiate plan the number of the ganglia is increased in correspondence with the radii.

†**b.** In fishes: (*a*) *pl.* The branchial lamellæ. (*b*) A fin-ray. *Obs.*

1691 RAY *Creation* I. (1692) 66 These papillæ do well resemble the Aristæ or radii of a Fishes Gills. **1753** CHAMBERS *Cycl. Supp.* s.v. *Radii*, In the mackrel, the radii of the first fin of the back..are absolutely simple.

c. *Bot.* (*a*) The ray or outer whorl of ligulate florets surrounding the disk in a composite flower-head; the border of enlarged petals on a partial umbel; (*b*) a peduncle supporting a partial umbel; (*c*) a medullary ray.

1775 J. Jenkinson tr. *Linnæus Brit. Pl.* Gloss., *Radius*, is the semifloscules that surround the disk. **1796** *Encycl. Brit.* (ed. 3) III. 448/1 *Radius*, the rim or outward part, consisting of irregular florets. **1835** Lindley *Introd. Bot.* (1839) 156 The peduncles which support the partial umbels are named *radii*. [**1866** *Treas. Bot.* 955/1 *Radii Medullares*, the medullary rays.] **1880** Gray *Struct. Bot.* (ed. 6) 430/1 *Ray* (*Radius*), one of the radiating branches of an umbel.

d. *Ent.* One of the radiating subdivisions of a digitate wing.

1826 Kirby & Sp. *Entomol.* IV. 338. **1848** Maunder *Treas. Nat. Hist.*, Gloss.

e. One of the five arched rod-like pieces set radially in the mouth of a sea-urchin.

1877 Huxley *Anat. Inv. Anim.* 576 The Latern consists of twenty principal pieces—five teeth, five alveoli, five rotulæ, and five radii.

f. *Ornith.* One of the processes on the barb of a feather, a barbule.

1893 Newton *Dict. Birds* 240 The radii or barbules are attached in two opposite rows to the thick upper rim of the rami.. Each radius is a thin lamella, about 1 mm. in length.

3. *Math.* a. A straight line drawn to the circumference of a circle or the surface of a sphere from the centre, all lines so drawn being equal in length.

1656 Hobbes *Six Lessons* Wks. 1845 VII. 256 Is the radius that describes the inner circles equal to the radius that describes the exterior? **1672** Boyle *Virtues of Gems* 67 These rows of Planes reaching euery way, almost like so many radious's of a Sphere from the Centre. **1705** Berkeley *Commonpl. Bk.* Wks. 1871 IV. 428 Circles on several radius's are not similar figures. *a* **1721** Keill *Maupertuis' Diss.* (1734) 47 Our first Method of finding the Curves, by Radii and Angles. **1831** Brewster *Optics* iii. 23 Let a small tube.. be so made that it may be attached to the board along any radius. **1853** Herschel *Pop. Lect. Sc.* i. §53 (1873) 41 In a circle 22 miles in radius.. every town and village was destroyed. **1879** Calderwood *Mind & Br.* iii. 70 A series of fibres, some of which are arranged as radii, others in a circular manner.

transf. and *fig.* **1649** G. Daniel *Trinarch., Hen. IV*, xlv, Thus when All Causes are mett, their Radij must Spread. **1710** T. Fuller *Pharm. Extemp.* 201 It [the Glyster].. driveth the Radii of the Miasmi outward. **1856** Dove *Logic Chr. Faith* vi. §5. 369 Phenomena are the radii of Knowledge. **1860** Farrar *Orig. Lang.* (1865) 15 The radii of inference from many other sources all converge to the common centre of a similar hypothesis.

b. A radial line of a curve, drawn from a certain point such as the focus to any point on the curve.

1836 Lardner in *Civil Eng. & Arch. Jrnl.* I. 40/2 This.. is altogether independent of the radius of the curve. *Ibid.*, A curve of large radius. **1849** Salmon *Conic Sect.* (1855) 162 In the hyperbola, the difference of the focal radii is constant. **1875** B. Williamson *Integr. Calc.* 261 The area between two focal radii of a parabola and the curve.

c. Any line in an arrangement of straight lines diverging from a point, and resembling the radii of a circle.

1774 Pennant *Tour Scotl. in 1772*, 358 On a live rock is cut the radii of a dial. **1802** James *Milit. Dict.* s.v., In fortification, the radius is distinguished into exterior, interior, oblique, and right radius... The latter is a perpendicular line drawn from the center of a polygon to the exterior side.

d. In various phrases, as ***radius of concavity***, ***of curvature***, ***of dissipation***, ***of an eccentric***, ***of the evolute***, ***of evolution***, ***of explosion***, ***of gyration***, ***of inversion***, ***of rupture***, ***of torsion*** (cf. quots. and see the second element). ***radius of action***: in *Aeronautics*, the distance that an aircraft can cover so as to leave sufficient fuel for its return to base.

1753 Chambers *Cycl. Supp.* App., *Radius of Concavity*, in Geometry, is sometimes used for the Radius or ray of curvature. *Ibid.*, s.v. *Curvature*, This circle is called the circle of curvature.. and its semidiameter, the ray or radius of curvature. **1758** J. Landen *Resid. Anal.* vii. 75 The right line *CP* is called the radius of evolution corresponding to the point *P*. **1834–47** J. S. Macaulay *Field Fortif.* (1851) 201 In common mines the horizontal radius of rupture is equal to 1⅜ times the line of least resistance... In a vertical direction, this radius is of the same length as the radius of explosion. **1879** Thomson & Tait *Nat. Phil.* I. i. §281 The radius of gyration about any axis is therefore the distance from that axis at which, if the whole mass were placed, it would have the same moment of inertia as before. **1881** Casey *Sequel to Euclid* iii. xx. 41 The point *C* is called the inverse of the point *P*,.. and the constant *R* the radius of inversion. **1887** D. A. Low *Machine Draw.* (1892) 47 The distance from the centre of the sheave to the centre of the shaft is called the radius or eccentricity of the eccentric. **1908** *Aeronaut. Jrnl.* Apr. 44/2 In a 10 hours' run a distance of 300 kilm. (186 miles) might be traversed, the radius [of] action being 150 kilm. **1918** *Flying* 20 Mar. 188/3 The problem of any extension of the radius of action is almost entirely one of increased efficiency.. of modern aircraft.

e. ***radius vector***, a variable line drawn to a curve from a fixed point as origin; in astronomy the origin is usually at the sun or a planet round which a satellite revolves. Also *pl.*

1753 in Chambers *Cycl. Supp.* App. **1816** Playfair *Nat. Phil.* II. 103 The line drawn from the moveable to the immoveable body, (the radius vector), describes areas round the latter proportional to the times. **1841** C. Graves tr. *Chasles' Properties of Cones* 60 The sum or the difference of the two radii vectores. **1872** Proctor *Ess. Astron.* xxx. 373 These cones will have a common axis—namely, the Earth's radius vector.

4. a. A circular area of which the extent is measured by the length of the radius of the circle which bounds it. Also *pl.*

1853 Stocqueler *Mil. Encycl.* s.v. *Grenade*, It bursts into many pieces, scattering death and wounds among all who are within its radii. **1862** Miss Braddon *Lady Audley* xiii. 82, I shall first go to Audley Court, and look for George Talboys in a narrow radius. **1866** Crump *Banking* ix. 180 Restricting its operations to a radius of sixty-five miles from London.

b. *spec.* in London, a circle of four miles in all directions from Charing Cross, outside of which cab-fares are higher.

1889 Baedeker *London* (ed. 7) 28 Beyond the 4-mile radius from Charing Cross the fare is 1*s.* for every mile. **1899** W. Pett Ridge (*title*) Outside the Radius. Stories of a London Suburb.

5. *Comb.*, as ***radius-bearing*** adj.; **radius-bar**, a bar pivoted at one end so that it can move in a circle or arc of a circle, used esp. in the parallel motion of a steam engine; **radius-finder**, an instrument for finding two radii (and thereby the centre) of a circle; **radius rod** = *radius-bar*; **radius-saw**, a circular saw in which the plate is journaled to the end of a radius-bar (Knight *Dict. Mech.* Suppl. 1884).

1839 R. S. Robinson *Naut. Steam Eng.* 75 To these levers are also secured the radius bars, which are rods of wrought-iron, proceeding from the side rods. **1853** Glynn *Treat. Power Water* 140 The radius bar carries a pen, the nib of which is in the line of the radius. **1858** Murray *Marine Engines* (ed. 3) Gloss., *Radius rods* or *bars*,.. are the guiding rods in a parallel motion. **1886** Lockwood *Dict. Terms* s.v., *Radius finder*, a centre square. **1893** Newton *Dict. Birds* 245 In Gallinæ there are from 10 to 12 somewhat stiff radius-bearing rami. **1907** [see *chain case* s.v. CHAIN *sb.* 19]. **1946** *Happy Landings* July 2/1 The inner radius rod of the starboard undercarriage was pulled away from the undercarriage. **1970** K. Ball *Fiat 600, 600D Autobk.* 165/1 *Radius rod*, pivoted arm confining movement of a part to an arc of fixed radius.

radius (ˈreɪdɪəs), *v.* [f. the sb.] *trans.* To round off, make (a corner or end) curved.

1938 J. Healey *Metal Aircraft* ii. 14 Tubular rivets are a reamer fit, so having reamered the hole to size, radius the edge of the metal slightly. **1954** *Electronic Engin.* XXVI. 538/1 All corners and bends should be 'radiused', i.e. finished with as large a radius as possible. **1962** *Engineering* 6 July 10/1 The effect of radiusing the corners is also discussed. **1972** Greer & Howell *Mech. Engin. Craft Stud.* II. iii. 157 (*table*) Millsaw. For sharpening circular saws, radiusing slots etc.

Hence ˈ**radiused** *ppl. a.*

1954 *Archit. Rev.* CXV. 144/1 Radiused blocks are made for use at corners. **1959** *New Scientist* 31 Dec. 1339/2 Sharply radiused members are more expensive than straight members. **1975** *Mariner's Mirror* LXI. 406 A slightly more radiused stem rabbet where it meets the keel.

radix (ˈreɪdɪks, ˈrædɪks). Pl. 7– **radices** (ˈreɪdɪsiːz), 7– **radixes**. [a. L. *rādīx* (stem *rādīc-*) a root.] = ROOT, in various senses.

1. *Math.* †a. A root of a number. *Obs.*

1571 Digges *Pantom.* ii. ii. Mj, The Radix Quadrate of the Product, is the Hypothenusa. **1579** —— *Stratiot.* 13 To find the square Radix, or Roote of any number. **1719** Quincy *Phys. Dict.* (1722) s.v., A Number, which multiplied into it self makes a Square, is called the Root, or Radix.

b. A number or symbol which is made the basis of a scale of numeration.

'The term "radix" is due to Robert Flower (1771)'. A. J. Ellis in *Nature* (1881) XXIII. 379/2.

1798 Hutton *Course Math.* I. 148 When the radix *r* is = 10, then the index *n* becomes the common or Briggs's log. of the number N. **1841** *Penny Cycl.* XIX. 234/2 Ten is the radix of the decimal system of numeration, and the radix of the common system of logarithms. **1888** C. Smith *Algebra* xviii. (1893) 271 To express a number, *N*, in the scale whose radix is *r*.

attrib. **1888** C. Smith *Algebra* xviii. (1893) 273 Radix fractions in any scale correspond to decimal fractions in the ordinary scale. **1950** W. W. Stifler *High-Speed Computing Devices* vi. 80 For any radix arithmetic the basic tables corresponding to the addition and the multiplication tables of decimal arithmetic can be written. *Ibid.* 87 Corresponding representations of the same numbers for radices 2, 3, 4, 5, 8, and 10 are tabulated. **1960** N. R. Scott *Analog & Digital Computer Technol.* vii. 224 To represent the *r* digits in a radix *r* system by *r* binary digits is highly inefficient, and this figure of merit unduly penalizes radices not close to *ε*. *Ibid.* 227 If numbers can have *n* digits to the left of the radix point, the radix complement of a negative number is formed by adding the radix raised to the *n*th power to the negative number. **1969** P. B. Jourdain *Condensed Computer Encycl.* 412 If a number is added to its radix complement, the result is a 1 followed by a 0 for every position in the original number. Radix complement is used in some computers.. and desk calculators for representing negative numbers. **1970** O. Dopping *Computers & Data Processing* xvii. 280 In radix sort, the records usually pass through the sorting device—a computer or a card sorter, as many times as there are digits in the sorting key.

†2. *Astrol.* and *Astron.* A basis of calculation, as a nativity, a certain point in time, position of a planet, etc. *Obs.*

1603 Heydon *Jud. Astrol.* 363 These.. haue euer a principall aime, vnto the position of heauen, at the natiuite, as the Radix, or roote of their operations. **1615** Bedwell *Arab. Trudg.* Tarich., The Astronomers.. do call it *Radix*, whereby they vnderstand some set.. time beginning at some memorable action. **1674** Flamsteed in Rigaud *Corr. Sci. Men* (1841) II. 143, I have pasted new radixes to the meridian of Derby, that so they may comply the better with my solar numbers. **1726** tr. *Gregory's Astron.* I. 469 Every Planet's Radixes are to be settled, not of Longitude thereof,.. but of the Mean Anomaly of the Planet. **1774** J. Kennedy *Expl. &c. Astron. Chron.*, Title, The truth and reality of the orginal Luni-Solar Radix.

3. The source or origin; that in which anything originates.

1607 Heywood *Fair Maid Exchange* Wks. 1874 II. 54 Her wit is all spirit, that spirit fire,.. able to burne the radix of the best invention. **1654** H. L'Estrange *Chas. I* (1655) 111 The radix and ground of this contest was this. *a* **1716** South *Serm.* (1744) XI. i. 5 Concupiscence, I shew, was the radix of all sin. **1822–34** *Good's Study Med.* (ed. 4) III. 26 Hence a separate and specific power has.. been ascribed to the nervous fibres themselves, while the brain has been contemplated as their radix. **1840** De Quincey *Essenes* Wks. 1862 IX. 297 Judaism is the radix of Christianity.

†4. *Philol.* An original word or form from which other words are derived. *Obs.*

1641 E. Legh (*title*) Critica Sacra. Observations on all the Radices, or Primitive Hebrew words of the Old Testament. **1668** Wilkins *Real Char.* iv. vi. 453 Of all other Languages, the Greek is looked upon to be one of the most copious; the Radixes of which are esteemed to be about 3244. **1761** Sterne *Tr. Shandy* IV. xxix, Inasmuch as the radix of each word is hereby torn up. **1771** W. Jones *Zool. Eth.* 102 A quadriliteral word.. compounded of a double radix.

†5. Ancestral root or stock. *Obs. rare.*

1651 C. Cartwright *Cert. Relig.* i. 106, I shall run your pedigree to the radix. **1652** H. C. *Looking Glasse for Ladies* A ij, The two Twins of Grace and Vertue descended from the Radix of your Nobility.

†6. *Mus.* The root of a chord. *Obs. rare*$^{-1}$.

1672 *Phil. Trans.* VII. 5154 Musical Sounds are originally in the Radix or Unison.

7. *Bot.* The root of a plant.

1727–41 in Chambers *Cycl.* **1866** *Treas. Bot.* 955/1.

radja, obs. form of RAJA(H.

radknight (ˈrædnaɪt). *Eng. Hist.* Forms: 1 **rádcniht**, 7– **radknight**, (9 **-cnecht**, **radechnight**). See also RODKNIGHT. [OE. *rádcniht*, f. *rád* riding (see RAID and ROAD) + *cniht* KNIGHT, partially modernized by historical writers. In Domesday Book the word appears as *radchenistre*.] In Old English times, a tenant holding land on condition of performing service on horseback.

c **1025** *Instituta Cnuti* ii. c. 59 in Liebermann *Gesetze der Angels.* I. 73 In domo hominis quem Angli nominant radcniht, alii uero sexhendeman. **1614** Selden *Titles Hon.* 334 Rodknights.. were such as held their lands by the seruice to Ride vp and down with their Lords... They were called also Radknights. **1647** N. Bacon *Disc. Govt. Eng.* xxxi. 76 Others served on horseback, and were called Rad-knights, or Knights riders, as Bracton noteth. **1778** Pennant *Tour Wales* (1883) I. 56 The.. Rad-knights, who by the tenure of their lands, were bound to ride with or for the lord, as often as his affairs required. **1818** Hallam *Mid. Ages* (1872) II. 361 Radechnights, and lesser thanes, seem to be included in this rank. **1861** Pearson *Early & Mid. Ages Eng.* 201 Radknights, or freemen owing commutable service. **1872** [see RADMAN].

radle, radling, obs. forms of RADDLE, -LING.

†ˈ**radly**, *adv.* *Obs.* Forms: 1 **hræd-**, **rædlice**, 2 **radlice**, 4 **radli**, 4–5 **radeliche**, 5 **radely**, 4–6 **radly**, 6–7 **radlie**, **-lye**. [f. RAD *a.*^{1} + -LY^2.] Quickly, promptly, without delay, soon.

Beowulf 356 (Z.) [He] hwearf þa hrædlice þær Hroðgar sæt. *c* **888** K. Ælfred *Boeth.* x, Mine sælða.. nane sælða ne sint, forðam hi swa rædlice ȝewitaþ. *Ibid.* xli. §5 þæt ðu mæȝe hrædlicost cumon.. to þinre aȝenre cyððe. *c* **1131** *O.E. Chron.* (Laud MS.) an. 1127 Swa radlice swa he þær com [etc.]. *c* **1205** Lay. 25603 þes drake and beore.. radliche sone to-gadere heo come. **13..** *E.E. Allit. P.* B. 797 He ros yp ful radly & ran hem to mete. *c* **1400** *Destr. Troy* 6904 Radli on þe right syde Rakit he furth. *c* **1420** *Chron. Vilod.* 126 (Halliw.) That blessud virgyn.. badde hym arys radeliche and blyve. *c* **1477** Caxton *Jason* 104 Therwith was the boote seen approchyng moche radely the Ryuage. **1515** *Scot. Field* 417 in *Chetham Misc.* (1856) II, Every ryncke to his reste full radlie him dressed. *a* **1600** *Floddan F.* vii. (1664) 60 Who radly by the ranks did ride.

radman (ˈrædmən). *Eng. Hist.* [OE. **rádmann*, f. *rád* (ROAD) + MAN.] = RADKNIGHT.

1086 *Domesday Book* (1783) I. 174b/2 Ipsi radmans secabant una die in anno. *Ibid.* 270/1 Sunt in dominio.. vi burgenses et iij radmans. **1628** Coke *On Litt.* i. 5b, Coleberti often also named in Domesday, signifieth Tenants in free socage by free rent, and so it is expounded of.. Radmans.. there also often named. **1778** Pennant *Tour Wales* (1883) I. 56 (Coleshill) had at the Conquest four villeyns, two boors, and a Radman. **1872** E. W. Robertson *Hist. Ess.* 139 A similar character seems traceable in the Radman or Radcnecht of Southumbrian England.

†ˈ**radness**. *Sc.* and *north.* *Obs.* Also 5 *Sc.* **rednase**, **-nes**. [f. RAD *a.*^{2} + -NESS.] Fear, fright.

a **1300** *E.E. Psalter* liv. 4 Radnes of dede felle ouer me. *c* **1375** *Sc. Leg. Saints* iii. (*Andrew*) 1099 þe portare.. come.. but delay, haffand wondir with rednes. ?*a* **1400** *Mort. Arth.* 120 The Romaynes for radnesse ruschte to the erthe. *c* **1425** Wyntoun *Cron.* v. i. 172 Thare Mary wes And Joseph bathe in gret radness.

radome (ˈreɪdəʊm). [Blend of RADAR and DOME *sb.*] A dome or other structure, transparent to radio waves, protecting a radar aerial.

1945 in *Amer. Speech* XX. 310/2 *Radome*, housing enclosing a radar scanner. **1949** *Sun* (Baltimore) 29 Dec. 5/1 Supported by air pressure.., the balloon-like buildings, called radomes, are ideal for the housing of large radar antennae. **1951** *Electronics* Aug. 89/2 The radar antenna is enclosed in a streamlined radome aft of the big bomb bay. **1962** *Guardian* 3 Oct. 3/7 The Air Ministry should.. mitigate the 'nuisance' of a station in the National Park by keeping buildings..away from the main road..and by making the radomes a pale blue to tone with the sky. **1968** *New Scientist* 21 Mar. 631/2 The *Vladimir Komarov* is distinguished by two massive radomes of some 50ft diameter and a smaller radome amidships. **1973** C. MASON *Hostage* x. 136 Radar picket aircraft..with grotesque radomes projecting above and below the fuselages. **1977** *Time* 4 Apr. 13/1 A mushroom-shaped 'radome' 30 ft. in diameter and 6 ft. thick sprouts from the rear of the grey fuselage on two large struts.

radon ('reɪdɒn). *Chem.* [a. G. *radon* (C. Schmidt 1918, in *Zeitschr. f. Anorg. Chem.* CIII. 114): see RAD(IUM and -ON².] **1.** A short-lived radioactive element which belongs to the group of noble gases and occurs naturally in trace amounts as a result of the decay of radium and other radioactive elements; orig. *spec.* the longest-lived isotope, radon 222, having a half-life of 3·82 days. Atomic number 86, symbol Rn (orig. Ro). Cf. *radium emanation* s.v. RADIUM 3 b.

1918 *Jrnl. Chem. Soc.* CXIV. II. 306 Radium emanation is given the name Radon, Ro, which at once indicates its origin and its relationship to the argon group. **1927** *Observer* 3 Apr. 20/2 The Radium Institute sends radium, or rather radon, its active principle, to hospitals all over the country. **1938** R. W. LAWSON tr. *Hevesy & Paneth's Man. Radioactivity* (ed. 2) xxiii. 227 The first five disintegration products of the gas radon are isotopes of the metals polonium, lead, bismuth, or thallium. **1942** S. TOLANSKY *Introd. Atomic Physics* xiii. 218 A body exposed for a short time to radon coats with an active deposit which emits α-, β-, and γ- radiation and exhibits a regular decay. **1974** *Environmental Conservation* I. 24/1 Uranium miners are known to suffer from an increased risk of lung cancer from inhaled radon. **1977** *Time* 22 Aug. 8/2 The radon in these waters is supposed to be good for everything from paralysis to curvature of the spine.

2. Special comb.: **radon seed**, a short tube containing radon that is used in radiotherapy as a source of alpha radiation.

1925 A. E. H. PINCH *Clin. Index Radium Therapy* 61 Treatment by the burying..of numerous unscreened radon 'seeds'..will often prove effective. **1930** *Sunday Times* 12 Oct. 24/2 Medical evidence showed that the child was placed under an anæsthetic and radon seeds..were placed in the growths. **1966** HENSCHKE & HILARIS in G. H. Fletcher *Textbk. Radiotherapy* i. 43/1 Ninety radon seeds each 0·75 cm. were permanently implanted through 17 needles and the uterus was sutured over the implant.

† **ra'dote**, *v. Sc. Obs. rare*⁻¹. [ad. F. *radoter*: see DOTE *v.*] *intr.* To mutter disconnectedly.

1595–6 BUREL *Pilgr.* in Watson *Coll. Sc. Poems* (1709) II. 34 Than softlie did I suoufe and sleep..Radoting, starnoting, As wearie men will do.

radoun, obs. Sc. f. REDOUND.

radour, var. RADEUR.

radres, obs. Sc. f. REDRESS.

‖ **radula** ('rædjʊlə). [L. *rādula* scraper, scraping-iron, f. *rād-ere* to scrape: see RASE *v.*] †**1.** *Surg.* (See quot.) *Obs.*

1753 CHAMBERS *Cycl. Supp.*, *Radula*, the raspatory, a chirurgical instrument used to cleanse foul bones.

2. *Zool.* The odontophore or lingual ribbon of certain molluscs.

1877 HUXLEY *Anat. Inv. Anim.* viii. 488 The radula is a cuticular chitinous product of the epithelium of the sub-radular membrane. **1878** BELL *Gegenbaur's Comp. Anat.* 341 They form the supporting apparatus of the radula and the parts connected with it. **1901** E. STEP *Shell Life* iii. 42 The number of these teeth to one tongue or radula varies to a remarkable extent. **1928** RUSSELL & YONGE *Seas* ix. 202 In common with many other members of the snail family they [*sc.* limpets] possess a very characteristic feeding apparatus consisting of a long horny ribbon, made up of many rows of fine teeth, and known as the 'radula'. **1959** A. C. HARDY *Open Sea* II. vi. 128 A radula is a remarkable structure found in the mouths of all typical gastropods; it is a long ribbon, bearing a vast number of transverse rows of sharp horny teeth. **1975** *Sci. Amer.* Feb. 106/3 The snail combines the functions of teeth and tongue in a single organ: the radula, a toothed, filelike muscle inside the mouth.

Hence **'radular** *a.*, pertaining to the radula; **'radulate, radu'liferous** *adjs.*, provided with, bearing a radula; **'raduliform** *a.*, rasp-like.

1849–52 TODD *Cycl. Anat.* IV. 874/1 The teeth of the sheat-fish present all the gradations between the villiform and raduliform types. **1885** PENNELL *Hist. Brit. F.W. Fish* 34 Teeth..when much shorter than the latter [card-like]..become raduliform, or rasp-like.

radure, var. RADDOUR².

radurization (rædjʊəraɪ'zeɪʃən). [f. L. *radiāre* to furnish with rays, shine + *dur-āre* to make hard, preserve + -IZATION.] The treatment of food with ionizing radiation so as to enhance its keeping qualities by killing many of the micro-organisms in it (see quot. 1964). Cf. RADAPPERTIZATION, RADICIDATION.

1964 H. E. GORESLINE in *Nature* 17 Oct. 237/2 Type III is the application to foods of doses of ionizing radiation sufficient to enhance keeping quality by causing substantial reduction in the numbers of viable specific spoilage micro-organisms... The following are the names we suggest for these types of treatment... Type III, radurization. **1973** N. F. LEWIS et al. *Radiation Preservation of Food* (Internat. Atomic Energy Agency) 201 'Radurization' is essentially a pasteurization treatment that results in prolonging shelf-life of foods by a selective control of spoilage microflora. **1977** *Biol. Abstr.* LXIII. 5003/1 Irradiation preservation of Korean fish: I. Radurization of croaker, yellow corvenia and roundnose flounder.

radwaste ('rædweɪst). orig. *U.S.* Also **rad-waste**. [Short for *rad*ioactive *waste*.] = *radioactive waste* s.v. RADIOACTIVE *a.* 4.

1973 *Trans. Amer. Nucl. Soc.* XVI. 176/1 (*heading*) A cyrogenic approach to fuel reprocessing gaseous radwaste treatment. **1975** *Proc. Symp. on Reliability of Nuclear Power Plants* (Internat. Atomic Energy Agency) 373 A computerized reliability-risk model has been developed to simulate the rad-waste system. **1978** *Times* 28 July 1 Principal components of typical radwaste calcin[ation]. **1979** *Nature* 15 Mar. 219/1 The most popular procedure advocated by the nuclear power establishment during the past 25 yr has been to incorporate the radwaste into a borosilicate glass.

radyll, -y(s)she, obs. ff. RADDLE *sb.*², RADISH.

rae, var. RA¹, ROE.

ræ(c)che: see REACH, RECCHE, RECK.

ræd(e: see RAD *a.*², RED *a.* and *sb.*¹, REDE.

rædi(ȝ, obs. ff. READY.

rædlice, var. RADLY.

ræf, var. REAF, obs. f. REIF.

ræfde, raeff, obs. pa. t. REAVE, RIVE.

ræȝe: see REH *a.*

ræȝ(e)l, obs. f. RAIL *sb.*¹

ræh(ȝe, ræi(h)e: see REH *a.*

ræiȝe: see REH *a.*

ræil, ræin, obs. ff. RAIL *sb.*¹, RAIN.

ræm, var. REAM *sb.*¹

ræmen, var. REME *v.*

ræm(i)en, var. REAM *v.*

raen, var. RANE *v.*, obs. f. REIGN *sb.*

raep, obs. *Sc.* f. RAPE, ROPE.

† **raer**, obs. var. RATHE, RAVE, cart-rail.

1688 R. HOLME *Armoury* III. 339/2 The two Cart Raers, the Railes on the Cart top. The Cart Staves are those that hold the Cart and the Raers together, which maketh the Cart Body.

rætful, var. REDEFUL *a.*

raeth, var. RATHE *sb.*

Rætian, Rætic: see RHÆTIAN, RHÆTIC.

ræue: see REAF.

ræuthe, ræw, obs. ff. RUTH, RUE.

R.A.F. Also (*colloq.*) **raf, raff** (ræf). [f. initial letters of *R*oyal *A*ir *F*orce, founded in 1918 on the amalgamation of the Royal Flying Corps with the Royal Naval Air Service.] The British Air Force or (*collect.*) members of this organization.

1920 M. BARING *R.F.C., H.Q.* xxi. 276 On the 20th of May we started on a long expedition to the R.A.F. Headquarters. **1924** G. BELL *Let.* 2 July (1927) II. xxiv. 701 The most interesting thing which happened during this week was a performance by the R.A.F., a bombing demonstration. **1941** W. S. CHURCHILL *Into Battle* 310 Operating from new Greek bases, the R.A.F. attack Bari and Brindisi, and bomb military objectives in Naples. **1946** 'TACKLINE' *You met such Nice Girls* vii. 73 And it is a peculiar thing, but the Raff and the Wavy Navy do not mix at parties, and in fact the only place the Wavy Navy like the Raff to be is in the air. **1950** C. MACINNES *To Victors the Spoils* ii. 227 They're Raf bods, escaped prisoners. **1954** 'E. C. R. LORAC' *Shroud of Darkness* xvi. 173 I'd fly the plane for you if the Raf'd let me. **1957** M. SWAN *Brit. Guiana* iv. 76 He was a big man, in his late twenties, with an R.A.F. moustache, wearing a bush-hat and a bush-shirt whose breast pockets bulged with papers. **1965** J. PORTER *Dover Two* v. 60 'A decent lad like our Rex..in the Raf.' 'R.A.F., Dad... I've told you before not to call it Raf!' **1974** S. MILLIGAN *Rommel* 186, I never dreamed, one day he, I, and a lone RAF erk called Sellers..would make a sort of comic history. **1980** J. DITTON *Copley's Hunch* I. i. 11 For a Raff bloke, that's good going. You're not trained to make full use of ground cover, are you?

Hence as *v. trans.* (see quot. 1940) and *intr.* (*rare*).

1930 T. E. LAWRENCE *Let.* 8 Jan. (1938) v. 675, I spend innocent days R.A.F.ing. **1940** *Daily Mail* 28 Aug. 3/1 Yesterday I heard: 'He'll get R.A.F.'d if he doesn't mind.' There's surely a rousing neologism in this—to 'raff' the Nazis instead of the old 'strafing Fritz'. Why not say 'Berlin has been raffed to blazes?'

raf, obs. f. RAFF; obs. pa. t. RIVE.

‖ **rafale** (rafal). [Fr., lit. a gust of wind.] A series of bursts of gun-fire; a roll of drums. Also *fig.*

1903 P. DE B. RADCLIFFE tr. *G. Rouquerol's Tactical Employment Quick-Firing Field Artillery* II. i. 33 To obtain the instantaneous effect, to produce that which he [*sc.* Gen. Langlois] vividly termed the *rafale*, or shell-storm, he conceived a special device which he called '*échelon* fire'. **1914** *Sphere* 3 Oct. 8/1 The second diagram shows a 'rafale', or 'shell-storm'. This is the method practised by batteries of French artillery to prevent the advance of infantry. **1916** *Chambers's Jrnl.* Sept. 604/2 The ·75, by rafale and curtain tactics, is able to isolate an attacking force by keeping the supports at bay. **1922** *Public Opinion* 28 July 85/1 If I had a few private batteries I should fire a private rafale in honour of the best book of the year. **1928** *Blackw. Mag.* Jan. 69/1 This was delivered with a slobbering roll of 'r's' like a rafale of water-logged kettle-drums. **1931** E. LINKLATER *Juan in Amer.* II. xii. 137 Now the staccato ear-splitting *rafale* of cheering rowels them afresh.

rafar, obs. f. RAVER.

rafe, obs. f. RAFF, RAVE; obs. pa. t. RIVE.

raff (ræf), *sb.*¹ Also 4–5 (9) raf, 6–7 raffe. [app. the second member in the phrase *riff and raff* one and all, every one, everything: see RIFF and RIFF-RAFF. But senses 3–6 may be (at least in part) of different origin: cf. RAFF *v.* and Sw. *rafs* rubbish, rag-tag.]

1. *north.* and *Sc.* Abundance, plenty. ? *Obs.*

c **1320** *Sir Tristr.* 328 He ȝaf has he gan winne In raf [*rime* ȝaf]. **1768** ROSS *Helenore* II. 90, I thought ay ye wad brak naething aff, I mind ye liked ay to see a raff. **1806** JAMIESON *Dey's Sang* in *Popular Ball.* II. 363 He'll bless your bouk whan far awa,..And scaff and raff ye ay sall ha'.

b. A large number or collection. = RAFT *sb.*²

a **1677** BARROW *Unity of Church* Serm. (1687) 321 The Synod of Trent [was called] to settle a raff of Errours and Superstitions. **1825** BROCKETT, *Raff*,..a great quantity, a great number. 'A raff of fellows', a great many men.

†**2.** A class of persons. *Obs. rare*⁻¹.

c **1330** R. BRUNNE *Chron.* (1810) 136 Fiue þousand marke he gaf, Tille heremites & tille seke men, & oþer of suilk raf.

3. a. Worthless material, trash, rubbish, refuse. Now only *dial.*

c **1420** *Pallad. on Husb.* I. 827 Take chaf & raf [L. *purgamenta*] And ley hit on thy lond..And when thou sist the myst, let brenne vp chaf And raf. **1645** WARD *Serm. bef. Ho. Comm.* 31 Whatever seed is cast in, it returns nothing but Carlock and such like raffe. **1811** WILLAN *Archæologia* (E.D.S.), *Raff*, scum, refuse. **1869–** In dial. glossaries (Lonsd., E. Angl., Cornw.).

b. *spec.* Ore which requires re-crushing; ***raff-wheel***, a wheel for lifting such ore.

1867 *Ure's Dict. Arts* (ed. 6) II. 72 The hopper is continuously charged, and that portion which is not reduced sufficiently fine is returned by the raff wheel to be recrushed. **1902** *Trans. Inst. Mining & Metall.* X. 459 The stuff rejected by..[a cylindrical trommel] is brought back by means of a Raff wheel and re-crushed.

4. *collect.* **a.** The common run (of people); the ruck or rag-tag; the lowest class of the populace.

1673 MARVELL *Corr.* Wks. 1872–5 II. 413 Among the raffe of the meaner and most unexperienced mariners. **1823** C. WESTMACOTT *Points of Misery* 34 The impertinent curiosity of the town raff. **1838** DICKENS *O. Twist* l, Ragged children, and the very raff and refuse of the river. **1876** GEO. ELIOT *Dan. Der.* VI. xlii, The raff and scum go there to be maintained like able-bodied paupers.

b. Without article: Persons of the lowest class.

1811 WOLCOTT (P. Pindar) *Carlton House Fête* Wks. 1812 V. 413 Raff that we Britons with our freedom trust. **1824** *Hist. Gaming* 27 He took to drinking and frequented low houses of Irish raff. **1848** DICKENS *Dombey* ix, Mrs. McStinger immediately demanded whether..she was to be broke in upon by 'raff'.

5. A low worthless fellow.

1785 GROSE *Dict. Vulgar T.*, *Raffs*, an appellation given by the gownsmen of the university of Oxford to the inhabitants of that place. **1800** *Sporting Mag.* XV. 86 Went down into St. Thomas's, and fought a raff. **1827** SCOTT *Two Drovers* ii, You..have behaved to our friend..here like a raff and a blackguard. **1856** F. E. PAGET *Owlet of Owlst.* 184 That raff of a fellow that had 'Swindler' stamped on every feature of his dirty face.

6. *attrib.* or as *adj.* = RAFFISH.

1823 in *Spirit Pub. Jrnls.* 485 My Lady has no disposition To have her name seen..with the raff Opposition. **1848** THACKERAY *Bk. of Snobs* xxx, There is the English raff snob that frequents Estaminets.

† **raff**, *sb.*² *Obs.* [Onomatopœic.] A word used by itself or in combination with similar forms, to denote verse (alliterative or riming) of a rude kind, or in which sound is more prominent than sense.

a **1300** *Body & Soul* 57 in *Map's Poems* 340 For to bere thi word so wyde And maken of the rym and raf. *c* **1386** CHAUCER *Pars. Prol.* 43 (Harl. MS.), I can not geste rum raf ruf by letter. **1418–20** J. PAGE *Siege Rouen* in *Hist. Coll. Citizen Lond.* (Camden) 46 Thys procesce made John Page, Alle in raffe and not in ryme. **1575** GASCOIGNE *Weedes, Gr. Knt.'s Farew. Fansie*, A fansie fedde me ones, to wryte in verse and rime,..To rumble rime in raffe and ruffe. **1600** NASHE *Summer's Last Will* D 3 To hold him halfe the night with riffe, raffe, of the rumming of Elanor.

raff (ræf), *sb.*³ Also 5 raaf, raf, 7 raffe, 9 raft. [? a. G. *raf*, *raff(e*, obs. or dial. ff. *rafe* rafter, beam.] Foreign timber, usually in the form of deals.

c **1440** [see *raff-man*, *-ware* in b]. **1667** *Lond. Gaz.* No. 124/1 The Three Kings, belonging to Stockholm,..laden with Raffe,..about 7000 Deals. **1774** *Hull Dock Act 6* Hemp, iron, flax, yarn, timber, raff. **1794** R. Lowe *View Agric. Notts.* 51 By the Trent are carried..Upwards Raff or Norway timber, hemp, flax, iron. **1894** *Northumbld. Gloss.*, *Raff*, timber, especially in boards and kinds ready for use.

b. *attrib.* and *Comb.*, as ***raff man, -merchant, -ware, -yard*** (also *attrib.*).

c **1440** *Promp. Parv.* 421/2 *Raaf man. [*No Latin.*] **1459** in Kirkpatrick *Relig. Ord. Norwich* (1845) 168 William Norwyche, senior, citizen of Norwich, rafman. **1533** in Blomefield *Topogr. Hist. Norfolk* (1745) II. 148 This year was setled the Order of the Procession of the..Crafts or Companies... 18. The Grocers and Raffmen. **1641** Best *Farm. Bks.* (Surtees) 125 The *raffe-merchant may lawfully stile them good deales. **1885** *Census Instruct.* 20 Raff Merchant. *c* **1440** *Promp. Parv.* 421/2 *Raaf ware. [*No Latin.*] **1606** *Charter* in Brand *Newcastle* (1789) II. 700 Hemp, pitch, tarr, or any other goodes or raffe wares. **1840** *Evid. Hull Docks Comm.* 51 There should be room for *raft-yards and timber-yards. **1886** Linskill *Haven Hill* I. i. 12 Tall, white hanging cranes were gleaming in the raff yards. **1885** *Census Instruct.* 20 Raff yard Labourer.

† **raff**, *sb.*[4] *Obs. rare*[−1]. A grain-measure (see quot. and curnock).

1727 Bradley *Fam. Dict.* s.v. *Dry Measure*, Two curnocks make a quarter seam or Raff.

raff (ræf), *v. Obs.* exc. *dial.* Also 7 **raffe**. [Of obscure origin: cf. obs. F. *rafer* 'to catch, or snatch, also to scrape' (Cotgr.); Sw. *rafsa* 'to sweep together, huddle up'.] *trans.* To sweep together.

1602 Carew *Cornwall* 69b, That Church-ales ought to bee sorted in the better ranke of these twaine, may be gathered from their causes and effects, which I thus raffe up together. **1876** *Mid. Yorksh. Gloss.*, *Raff*,..to brush or rake together promiscuously.

raff, obs. form of raft *sb.*[1]

Raffaelesque, variant of Raphaelesque.

raffan, variant of raffing. *Sc.*

raffe, obs. f. raft *sb.*[1], rave; obs. pa. t. rive.

raffee (ræˈfiː). Also **raffeé**. [Of obscure origin.] (See quots. 1880 and 1891.) Also *attrib.*

1880 D. Kemp *Man. Yacht & Boat Sailing* (ed. 2) 547 *Raffee*, the square topsail set flying on the foretopmast of schooners, and formerly often set on cutters and ketches above the squaresail. Sometimes this topsail is triangular in shape, like a scraper. **1891** H. Patterson *Illustr. Naut. Dict.* 144 *Raffeé Rail*, a sail in the shape of an equilateral triangle ..which is sometimes set over the highest yard... This sail is common to English schooner yachts rigged to carry a squaresail, as the *raffeé* is set over the yard. **1922** *Field* 8 July 59/1 A square sail and a raffee, or the topsail set over it, are such old-fashioned sails that many modern yachtsmen have never seen them. **1942** C. Crockett *House in Rain Forest* i. 18 The southeast trades filling our square-sail and raffee. **1976** *Oxf. Compan. Ships & Sea* 687/1 *Raffee*, another name for the sail in a square-rigged ship known as a moonraker, set only in light weather.

† **ˈraffell, raphell**, ? Sc. ff. *roe-fell* roe-skin.

1474 *Recs. Burgh Edinb.* (1869) 29 Quha that..sellis the samin poyntis for raphell. **15..** *Christ's Kirk* 11 in *Bann. MS.* 282 Thair gluvis wes of the raffell rycht, Thair schone wes of the straitis.

Rafferty (ˈræfətɪ). *Austral.* and *N.Z. slang.* [Eng. dial. corruption of *refractory* (Eng. Dial. Dict.).] Used *attrib.* or in the possessive, as ***Rafferty('s) rules***, no rules at all, esp. in boxing.

The customary initial capital suggests that the word is felt by many to be the Irish surname *Rafferty*.

1928 *Bulletin* (Sydney) 5 Jan. 37/4 M.Q. (and Rafferty) Rules. **1935** *Sydney Morning Herald* 28 Dec. 11 Rafferty rules may suit Mr Keenan and the Communist party, but they are repugnant to the trade union movement. **1941** Baker *Dict. Austral. Slang* 58 *Rafferty rules*, no rules at all, applied to any system, organisation or contest run in slipshod fashion. **1958** A. Wall *Queen's English* xxxii. 112, I do not know that the Queensberry Rules ever acquired any figurative usage; but the 'Rafferty Rules' certainly did. This term means no rules at all; in Australian, and hence New Zealand slang, it means any free and easy way of running things; 'Rafferty' here is thought to be an English dialect corruption of 'refractory'. **1964** H. P. Tritton *Time means Tucker* (ed. 2) 34 The Show adjourned at noon for the races. They seemed to be run on the 'Rafferty Rules' principle, but I heard no complaints. **1974** *Bulletin* (Sydney) 18 May 63 Rafferty's rules predominate. **1977** *Financial Times* 17 May 37/8 Because of the nature of the town and its 'Rafferty's rules' violence is a way of life and it is a well known haunt for criminals and tribal outcasts.

ˈraffery. *rare*[−1]. [f. raff *sb.*[1] + -ery.] Raffish conduct.

1819 Southey in *Life & Corr.* (1850) IV. 343 The college ..is no longer the seat of drunkenness, raffery and indiscipline.

raffia (ˈræfɪə). Also **rafia**. [var. raphia, q.v.]

1. A palm of the genus *Raphia*. In quots. *attrib.*

1897 Mary Kingsley *Trav. W. Africa* 600 A slip of rafia palm drawn..across a notch in another piece of rafia wood. **1906** *Westm. Gaz.* 26 Sept. 8/1 Mr. William H. Hunt.. announced the discovery, in the leaves of the rafia palm, of a product which..may be classed between wax and gum. **1958** C. Achebe *Things fall Apart* I. viii. 57 Obierika was sitting outside under the shade of an orange tree making thatches from leaves of the raffia-palm.

2. The soft fibre from the leaves of *Raphia Ruffia* and *Raphia tædigera*, largely employed by gardeners for tying up plants, cut flowers, etc. Also, extensively employed in the making of baskets, lamp-shades, mats, and similar articles.

1882 J. Smith *Dict. Econ. Plants* 231 The cuticle of the leaves of this palm has of late years been imported into this country in considerable quantities for tying plants,..under the name of Raffia or Ruffia. **1897** *Jrnl. R. Agric. Soc.* Dec. 615 Raffia..is now largely imported for tying purposes. **1901** M. White *How to make Baskets* ii. 11 It is a rare thing to find a material at once so soft and so strong as raffia. **1912** *Educ. Handwork* Nov. 201/1 The materials most suitable for weaving are, wool, bast or raffia, and cane. **1937** A. H. Crampton *Raffia Work & Basketry* 7 Raffia work although allied to the ancient craft of Basket Making, may be termed a modern craft. **1951** 'R. Brinley' *Raffia Work* i. 11 One of the chief advantages of working with raffia is the very low cost of the material. **1978** P. Van Greenaway *Man called Scavener* vi. 84 He noticed a confusion of raffia, macramé and pieces of knitting.

3. *attrib.* and *Comb.*, as (sense 2) ***raffia bag, basket, cloth, fibre, grass, lace, mat, needle, tape, work, workbag***; ***raffia-embroidered*** adj.

1932 S. Gibbons *Cold Comfort Farm* viii. 121 Raffia bags and linen bags embroidered with hollyhocks. **1960** G. Durrell *Zoo in my Luggage* iii. 77, I bent down, picked up a raffia bag and held it aloft. **1914** S. G. Fitzgerald *Priscilla Juniors' Basketry Bk.* 19 (*heading*) Handle for raffia basket. **1977** G. Scott *Hot Pursuit* iii. 25 Dried fish, piled in raffia baskets, on the pavement. **1932** D. C. Minter *Mod. Needlecraft* 59/1 Raffia work is really another form of embroidery... The materials for working on are..hessian, raffia cloth, and woven straw. **1967** E. Short *Embroidery & Fabric Collage* iii. 84 Fabrics with unusual textures, raffia cloth, for instance, can be decorated with simple embroidery such as bands of drawn threads. **1904** *Daily Chron.* 3 May 8/3 A pretty and attractive novelty..is the raffia embroidered cushion. **1906** *Westm. Gaz.* 26 Sept. 8/1 The natives gather the rafia fibre. **1910** M. T. Priestman *Handicrafts in Home* 207 Delicate strands of raffia fibre should be secured for this purpose. **1904** *Daily Chron.* 3 May 8/3 The embroidery is worked with raffia grass dyed in various colours. **1906** *Queen* 5 May 757/1 Raffia lace hats are the choicest things in headgear that ingenuity has ever devised out of vegetable fibre. **1914** S. G. Fitzgerald *Priscilla Juniors' Basketry Bk.* 6 (*heading*) Woven raffia mat. **1953** E. Simon *Past Masters* iv. 263 Raffia mats, cutlery and glasses defined the full number of places. **1976** *Daily Times* (Lagos) 22 Sept. 16/4 To build a crib to store maize harvested from a one-hectare plot requires only six 12-ft (360-cm)-long bamboo poles; another six of such poles of 180 cm length each; 45 raffia mats; [etc.]. **1914** H. C. Walker *Rafia Work* 7 The reasons for urging the claims of rafia work are many... It requires no tools beyond rafia needles, wool needles..and knitting needles. **1932** D. C. Minter *Mod. Needlecraft* 226/2 Use a small packing needle, or a raffia needle, and a backing of Helvellyn canvas with Persian, or Straight, or Shetland rug wool. **1979** *Dryad Catal.* 89/3 Raffia needles..For coiled raffia basketry. **1907** *Daily Chron.* 5 Jan. 9/1 Sometimes the flowers require staking, and this should be done..with stiff, straight wires or sticks, to which the stems should be fastened with West's Raffia Tape. **1939–40** *Army & Navy Stores Catal.* 956/1 Raffia Tape..balls in coloured string nets. **1908** M. E. Morgan *How to dress Doll* vii. 65 Little girls who know how to do raffia work can easily make such a hat. **1974** C. Fremlin *By Horror Haunted* 88 He attended his own classes in Braille and raffia-work. **1928** *Chambers's Jrnl.* 24 Mar. 261/1 From a corner of one of the baskets she unpacked her raffia workbag.

raffinate (ˈræfɪneɪt). [ad. G. or F. *raffinat*, f. G. *raffinieren* (F. *raffiner*) to refine + *-at* -ate[1] (as in *distillate*, *filtrate*, etc.).] The refined fraction which results after removal of impurities by solvent extraction, *spec.* in oil refining. Also *attrib.*

The term was first used in oil refining, in connection with the solvent extraction process invented by the Romanian chemical engineer L. Edeleanu and introduced on a commercial scale at Rouen *c* 1911.

1928 L. Edeleanu *U.S. Pat. 1,661,565* 2/1 The finished hot raffinate is taken from the last evaporator 21 by the pump 23 and passed..to the storage tank. **1932** *Jrnl. Inst. Petroleum Technologists* XVIII. 919 Dr. Edeleanu could lay claim to a further distinction, in having added two words to the English language—the words 'edeleanize' and 'raffinate'—words which, if not already in the dictionary, soon would be. **1941** W. L. Nelson *Petroleum Refinery Engin.* (ed. 2) xxvii. 617 Elaborate equipment is required to distill the solvent (or oil) from the extract and raffinate solutions. **1950** *Jrnl. Amer. Chem. Soc.* LXXII. 12/2 Now the flask in the 'R' position contained penicillin which was emptied into a larger container as raffinate pool. **1958** *Engineering* 14 Feb. 205/2 The presence of this dissolved salt in the fission-product raffinate stream limits the degree of concentration which may be achieved by evaporation while still keeping all the material in solution. **1970** W. G. Roberts *Quest for Oil* ix. 95 The raffinate is given a final sweetening and is ready for use as premium kerosene.

‖ **raffiné** (rafine), *a.* (*sb.*) [Fr.] Of manners or judgement: refined. Also as *sb.*, a person distinguished by the possession of refinement in manners, action, or feeling.

1876 [see méfiance]. **1883** *Atlantic Monthly* Aug. 179/1 The ingenious Catherine—she was a *raffinée*. **1920** D. H. Lawrence *Lost Girl* i. 10 No French marquis..could have been more elegant and *raffiné*. **1943** *Scrutiny* XI. 317 He is an older and wiser Tonio Kröger who has broken away from the precious and the *raffiné*. **1966** *Punch* 2 Feb. 173/1 The waiter, the actor, the communist, the painter all have their says [in a play] but it is through the analyst and the raffiné aristocrat..that we learn of hate-objects. **1970** *New Yorker* 23 May 126/3 He has a tendency..to favor his vigorous vulgarians at the expense of his effete *raffinés*.

ˈraffing, *a. Sc. rare.* Also 8 **raffan**. [Of obscure formation.] Merry, hearty; noisy.

1719 Ramsay *3rd Answ. Hamilton* xiii, Thy raffan rural rhyme sae rare. **1824** Mactaggart *Gallovid. Encycl.* 403 Raffing Fallows—Ranting, roaring, drinking fellows.

raffinose (ˈræfɪnəʊz, -s). *Chem.* [a. F. *raffinose* (D. Loiseau 1876, in *Compt. Rend.* LXXXII. 1058), f. *raffiner* to refine: see -ose[2].] A non-reducing trisaccharide sugar found in sugar-beet, cotton seed, and many cereals.

1876 *Jrnl. Chem. Soc.* XXX. 398 At 20° water dissolves one-seventh of its weight of raffinose. **1881** Watts *Dict. Chem.* 3rd Suppl. 1743 Raffinose..is crystalline, colourless, easily soluble in water, sparingly in alcohol. **1894** Morley & Muir *Watts' Dict. Chem.* IV. 394 In a mixture of cane-sugar and raffinose, the amount of raffinose may be determined by observing the change of rotatory power after hydrolysis. **1934** *Industr. & Engin. Chem.* Apr. 462/1 The cottonseed meal has been the raw material from which most of the small supply of pure raffinose has been obtained. **1950** *Thorpe's Dict. Appl. Chem.* (ed. 4) X. 468/1 The arrangement of the hexoses in raffinose is galactose-glucose-fructose. **1970** A. L. Lehninger *Biochem.* xi. 227 Raffinose (fructose, glucose, galactose) is found in abundance in sugar beets and many other higher plants.

raffish (ˈræfɪʃ), *a.* [f. raff *sb.*[1] + -ish.] Disreputable, vulgar, low.

1801 Jane Austen *Lett.* (1884) I. 295 He is as raffish in his appearance as I would wish every disciple of Godwin to be. **1818** *Blackw. Mag.* III. 527 A raffish sort of a fellow calling himself Menippus. **1879** Miss Braddon *Clov. Foot* xv. 130 An older man, of somewhat raffish aspect.

Comb. **1842** T. Martin *My Namesake* in *Fraser's Mag.* Dec., A raffish-looking youngster.

Hence **ˈraffishly** *adv.*, **ˈraffishness.**

1850 L. Hunt *Autobiog.* xx. (1860) 320 A fine head, but still a beggar. Some were of portentous raffishness. **1887** *Spectator* 5 Nov. 1513 There was nothing of the character of raffishness or Bohemianism in David Kennedy. **1897** Crockett *Lads' Love* xi. 116 Her water-can, raffishly a-dangle at her side.

raffle (ˈræf(ə)l), *sb.*[1] Forms: 4 **rafle**, 5 **rafell**, **raphill**, 7– **raffle**. [a. F. *rafle*, †*raffle* (1399 in Du Cange; also med.L. *raffla* 1362), and *raffe*, *raphe* (Godef. *Compl.*), of uncertain origin.

In later F., *rafle* has also the sense of 'clean sweep', and Diez supposes the related vb. *rafler*, 'to carry off completely, make a clearance of', to be derived from the synonymous MHG. *raffen*; but the existing evidence is against his view that these senses are the original ones.]

† **1.** A game of chance played with three dice, in which the winner was the person who threw the three all alike, or, if none did so, the one who threw the highest pair; also, the throwing of a doublet or triplet in this game. *Obs.* exc. *dial.*

c **1386** Chaucer *Pars. T.* ¶719 Hasardrie with hise apurtenances as tables and Rafles. **1468** in *Records Peebles* (1872) 159 Quhat nychtbur that rasettis playaris at the dyss, other hasart or rafell, in hys hows [etc.]. **1479** in *Eng. Gilds* (1870) 422 The towne clerke to fynde theym Dyce, and to have 1d. of every Raphill. **1656** Blount *Glossogr.*, *Raffle*, a game with three Dice, wherein he that throws the greatest Pair-Royal, wins. **1668** Dryden *Even. Love* iii. i, Most commonly they use Raffle. That is, to throw with three Dice, till Duplets, and a Chance be thrown; and the highest Duplet wins, except you throw In and In, which is call'd Raffle; and that wins all. **1727–41** Chambers *Cycl.* s.v., The raffle is properly the doublet or triplet: a raffle of aces, or duces, carries it against mere points. **1869** *Lonsdale Gloss.*, *Raffles*, plays with dice.

2. A form of lottery, in which an article is assigned by drawing or casting of lots (properly by casting of dice as in sense 1) to one person among a number who have each paid a certain part of its real or assumed value.

1766 [Anstey] *Bath Guide* xv. 24 Balls, Raffles, Subscriptions, and Chairs. **1782** Miss Burney *Cecilia* v. xii, Has there been anything of the nature of a lottery, or a raffle, in the garden? **1855** Macaulay *Hist. Eng.* xx. IV. 489 He.. had made such sums by raffles that he was able to engage in very costly speculations. **1871** C. Gibbon *Lack of Gold* xxx, There was to be a raffle for a silver watch.

transf. **1776** Adam Smith *W.N.* (1869) II. iv. vii. 205 The little prizes which are to be found in what may be called the paltry raffle of colony faction. **1840** Hood *Kilmansegg*, *Courtship* viii, She had won the 'Man of her choice' In a matrimonial raffle!

3. *attrib.*, as ***raffle prize, ticket.***

1976 *Milton Keynes Express* 16 July 9 The raffle prize of a 10 foot canoe went to Mr Sheldrick of Tandra, Bean Hill. **1976** *Jrnl.* (Newcastle) 26 Nov., Mr. Large produced a bundle of official raffle tickets offering Michael's models, which include a gypsy caravan, as prizes.

raffle (ˈræf(ə)l), *sb.*[2] Forms: 5 **rafull**, 7 *Sc.* **raphall**, 7– **raffle**. [? a. OF. *rafle*, *raffle* in phr. *rifle ou rafle* anything whatsoever, *ne rifle ne rafle* nothing at all; cf. raff *sb.*[1]]

1. Of persons. **a.** A rabble. **b.** Raff, riff-raff.

1486 *Bk. St. Albans* F vj b, A Rafull of knauys. **1670** G. H. *Hist. Cardinals* i. i. 12 The Priests, and the Friers, and such other raffle. **1921** G. C. Shedd *Lady of Mystery House* xix. 171 Probably the drunken raffle were seeking far and near to take me.

2. a. Of things: Rubbish, refuse.

1848 A. B. Evans *Leicestersh. Words*, s.v., I have cut the hedge; what shall I do with the raffle? **1899** Kipling *Stalky* 73 Plaster, odd shavings, and all the raffle that builders leave in the waste-room of a house. **1906** *Macmillan's Mag.* Aug.

755 A heavy cattle-boat limping past us..with its raffle of pens and its sour sweet reek. **1977** A. Hunter *Gently Instrumental* iv. 50 It was a pleasant-enough spot up there, in spite of the raffle of the yard below.

transf. **1891** Kipling *City Dreadf. Nt.* 87 The raffle of conversation that a man picks up as he passes. **1895** —— *Day's Work* (1898) 343 He..was pushed and prodded through the slack back-waters of the Lower Fourth, where the raffle of a school generally accumulates.

b. *Naut.* Lumber, débris, a confused tangle of ropes, canvas, broken spars, etc.

1881 Clark Russell *Ocean Free Lance* I. vi. 278 Others were making some half-hearted efforts to clear away the raffle. **1892** Stevenson & L. Osbourne *Wrecker* 208 The loose topsail had played some havoc with the rigging, and there hung..a raffle of intorted cordage.

transf. **1887** Stevenson *Merry Men*, etc. (ed. 2) 285 Huddled from the wind in a raffle of flying drapery.

raffle (ˈræf(ə)l), *sb.*³ *rare.* [a. F. *rafle*, of uncertain origin.] A kind of net used in fowling and fishing. Also ***raffle-net***.

1725 Bradley *Fam. Dict.* II. 5 U iij/1 There is a triple or counter-mesh net, called by some a Raffle, wherewith they likewise catch Birds. **1823** Crabb, *Raffle-net*, a sort of fishing net.

raffle (ˈræf(ə)l), *v.*¹ [a. F. *rafler* in same sense, or directly f. raffle *sb.*¹ An earlier synonym was rifle *v.*²]

1. a. *intr.* To cast dice, draw lots, etc., *for* something; to take part in a raffle.

a **1680** Butler *Rem.* (1759) I. 84 Those Jew troopers, that threw out, When they were raffling for his Coat. **1689** Shadwell *Bury F.* ii, Will you please to raffle for a tea pot. **1711** Swift *Jrnl. to Stella* 10 Apr., I was drawn in..to raffle for a fan,..it was four guineas, and we put in seven shillings a piece. **1811** W. Taylor in Robberds *Mem.* II. 365 It is as rational to raffle for a residence as to choose one. **1849** Lytton *Caxtons* 21 That work-box which you enticed Mrs. Caxton into raffling for, last winter.

b. Hence in pass., of a thing. Const. *for*.

1710 *Lond. Gaz.* No. 4687/3 The winning Horse to be sold or raffled for at the value of 40*l*. **1884** *Graphic* 21 June 595/3 A quilt..to be raffled for at a charitable bazaar.

2. *trans.* To dispose of by means of a raffle. Also const. *off*.

1851 Mayhew *Lond. Labour* I. 372/1, I can't recollect how many ornaments I raffled. **1872** Black *Adv. Phaeton* xxii. 309 Drowned the precentor, and raffled the church bell. **1877** —— *Green Past.* xxix. (1878) 236 We raffled a rug. **1889** 'Mark Twain' *Connecticut Yankee* xv. 175, I shan't know what to do with them: unless I raffle them off. **1976** *Washington Post* 7 Nov. k2/3 We'll raffle off a 'possum and award a prize to the wearer of the biggest beehive hairdo.

ˈraffle, *v.*² *rare.* Also 8 rafle. [? var. ruffle *v.* Cf. Sw. *raffla* to scrape, fret, grate; F. *érafler* to graze.] *trans.* **a.** To indent, serrate (a leaf). **b.** To crumple. **c.** *dial.* To ruffle. Hence **ˈraffled** *ppl. a.*¹, **ˈraffling** *vbl. sb.*²

a. **1712** J. James tr. *Le Blond's Gardening* 134 You must then..part and raffle the Leaves. **1817** Rickman *Goth. Archit.* 26 The best examples have all some trifling difference, principally in the raffling of the leaves. *Ibid.* 32 The first has..water leaves instead of raffled leaves under the volutes. **1895** Burns *Gloss. Archit., Raffling*, the notched edge of foliage in carving.

b. *c* **1728** Earl of Ailesbury *Mem.* (1890) I. 211 He despatched Mr. Carleton..with a bit of paper rafled up.

c. **1868** Atkinson *Cleveland Gloss., Raffle*, to raise the skin slightly by abrasion.

ˈraffle, *v.*³ *north. dial.* [var. ravel *v.*] *trans.* To ravel, entangle. Hence **ˈraffled** *ppl. a.*²

1800 I. Milner in *Life* xii. (1842) 216 A sad raffled letter. *a* **1843** Southey *Doctor* (1847) VII. Interch. xxiv. 80 T' Maister wad wind 3 or 4 clues togedder, for 3 or 4 Bairns to knitt off—that 'at knit slawest raffled tudder's yarn. **1863** in Robson *Bards of Tyne* 86 Pee Dee ran to clear the anchor, 'It's raffled'! right loudly he roar'd. **1876-** In dial. glossaries (Yks., Rochdale, Sheff., Linc., etc.).

†**ˈraffle**, *v.*⁴ *Obs. rare.* [? var. ruffle *v.*] *intr.* To quarrel, wrangle.

c **1750** [implied in raffler²]. *a* **1796** Pegge *Derbicisms*.

raffle ant, variant of rifle ant.

ˈraffle leaf. *Arch.* A raffled leaf (see raffle *v.*² a).

1887 in *Dict. Arch.*

raffler¹ (ˈræflə(r)). [f. raffle *v.*¹ + -er¹.] One who raffles. Also *spec.* (see quot. 1851).

1798 *Poetry* in *Ann. Reg.* 450, I see the rafflers press, by thousands, round; I hear the die's still profitable sound. **1851** Mayhew *Lond. Labour* I. 371 The trade in China ornaments..is carried on both in the regular way and by means of raffles. At some public-houses, indeed, the China ornament dealers are called 'rafflers'.

†**ˈraffler**². *Obs. rare*⁻¹. [f. raffle *v.*⁴ + -er¹.] A quarrelsome person.

c **1750** *Long Meg of Westminster* 24 If any rafler [*var.* raffler] come in, and make a quarel..thrust him out of doors.

Raffles (ˈræf(ə)lz). The name of A. J. *Raffles*, hero of *The Amateur Cracksman* (1899) and other books by E. W. Hornung (1866-1921), used allusively of a gentleman who engages in crime, esp. burglary. Also *attrib.*

1908 'O. Henry' *Gentle Grafter* 142 It's part of my business..to play up to the ruffles when I want to make a riffle as Raffles. **1930** G. Smithson *Raffles in Real Life* i. 16 What an ignominious ending to the ambitious ideas that had filled my mind when I set out on the perilous career of a modern Raffles! *Ibid.* 18 By steady, if somewhat painful, steps, I had graduated from a middle-class cracksman to a Raffles of the gentleman type. **1953** J. Trench *Docken Dead* viii. 113 It [is] a good thing to look to one's way of retreat. Have you thought of that, my good Raffles? **1960** *John o' London's* 31 Mar. 384/3 An educated renegade..in the classic *Raffles* tradition. **1974** *Listener* 21 Feb. 242/3 Damiaen van Doorninck, a Dutch Naval officer, made a reputation..as a cracksman—'the Raffles of Colditz'.

‖**rafflesia** (rəˈfliːʒɪə, -ˈiːzɪə). *Bot.* [mod.L., named after Sir T. Stamford Raffles (1781-1826), British governor in Sumatra, who discovered the plant.] A stemless, leafless, parasitic plant of the genus so called, of the family Rafflesiaceæ, native to Java and Sumatra, and remarkable for the size of its flowers.

[**1818** Raffles *Letter* in *Memoir* (1830) 316 The Sumatran name of this extraordinary production is Petimum Sikinlili or Devil's-Siri (betle) box.] **1821** R. Brown in *Trans. Linn. Soc.* XIII (1822) 206 It is proposed, in honour of Sir Stamford Raffles, to call this genus Rafflesia. **1830** Lindley *Nat. Syst. Bot.* 74 Rafflesia is used in Java as a powerful astringent. **1883** *Good Words* Dec. 788/2 Rafflesia..bears the largest flower of which we have any knowledge. **1933** L. Ainsworth *Confessions Planter in Malaya* 111 This plant..is known as the 'Rafflesia', and is one of the largest parasites in the world. **1954** R. E. Holttum *Plant Life in Malaya* xiv. 192 Rafflesia plants are only found in deeply shaded forest.

raffling (ˈræflɪŋ), *vbl. sb.*¹ [f. raffle *v.*¹ + -ing¹.] The action of the verb.

1684 *Lond. Gaz.* No. 1950/4 To keep Rafflings, Ordinaries, and other publick Games. **1693** Southerne *Maid's last Prayer* ii. i, You have so many rafflings, and whoever throws most you win the prize. **1716** Addison *Freeholder* No. 11 ¶4 Never was a Subscription for a Raffling or an Opera more crowded. **1851** Mayhew *Lond. Labour* I. 371/2 The most lucrative part of the trade is in the raffling.

b. *attrib.*, esp. in †***raffling-shop***.

1682 *Lond. Gaz.* No. 1773/4 A newly invented Lottery, under the name of the Riffling or Raffling Lottery. **1706** Baker *Hampstead Heath* ii. 16 To have Presents made one at the Raffling-Shops. *a* **1732** Gay *Poems* (1745) II. 82 'Twas there the raffling dice false Damar threw; The raffling dice to him decide the prize. **1756** Nugent *Gr. Tour, Netherlands* I. 273 About the pumps..there are raffling shops, coffee-houses, and all other diversions. **1870** in *N. & Q.* 4th Ser. V. 225/2 The last day in January..observed in Newark as a raffling day for oranges.

ˈraffling, *vbl. sb.*²: see raffle *v.*²

rafft, obs. form of raft *sb.*¹

rafftе, obs. pa. t. reave.

ˈraffy, *a.* [? f. raff *sb.*¹ 3.] Of loose texture.

1867 F. Francis *Angling* i. 12 Bad gut is flat, greasy, dull, raffy, or rough and frayed.

rafia, variant of raffia.

‖**rafik** (raˈfik). Also raffik, rafiq. [ad. Arab. *rafīq*.] In Arabia: a companion or escort (see quot. 1920).

1856 R. F. Burton *Pers. Narr. Pilgrimage to El-Medinah* III. 84 The payment of a small sum secures..a 'Rafik', and this 'friend', after once engaging in the task, will be faithful. **1888** C. M. Doughty *Trav. Arabia Deserta* I. viii. 235 The Arabian rafik, often an enemy, is a paid brother-of-the-road, that for a modest fee takes upon him to quit the convoy from all hostile question and encounter of his own tribesmen. **1911** T. E. Lawrence *Let.* 18 June (1954) 170 'Am I not your friend, your raffik?' said the zaptieh. **1913** G. Bell *Let.* 20 Dec. (1927) I. xiii. 314 We have a Rafiq, a comrade of the Ghiyatah with us—we fetched him from Dumeir to stand surety for us if we met his tribe. **1920** *Handbk. of Arabia* (Admiralty) I. 21 The one thing needful is a *rafiq*, i.e. a companion derived from the tribe through whose range one must pass, or from some tribe allied with it or authorized to share its range.

†**rafiol.** *Obs. rare*⁻¹. In 5 *pl.* raffyolys. [a. It. *rafioli* (Florio), var. *ravioli*: see raviol.] A kind of meat-ball in mediæval cookery; a rissole.

c **1440** in *Househ. Ord.* (1790) 442 Raffyolys. Take swynes lire, and sethe hit, and hewe hit smalle, and do therto ȝolkes of egges,..a lytel larde mynced, and grated chese, and pouder of ginger, and of canelle; then take and make balles therof as gret as an appull [etc.].

raflak, variant of reflac. *Obs.*

rafle(r, obs. ff. of raffle *sb.*, raffler².

raft (rɑːft, -æ-), *sb.*¹ Forms: α. 5 rafft, 5-6 rafte, 6- raft. β. 5-7 raff, 6-7 raffe. [a. ON. *rapt-r* (Sw. *raft*, Da. *rafte*) rafter. The form *raff* may be partly due to assoc. with raff *sb.*³]

1. A beam, spar, rafter. Now only *arch.*

c **1420** *Avow. Arth.* xxv, Aythir gripus a schafte Was als rude as a rafte, So runnun thay togedur. **1426** Lydg. *De Guil. Pilgr.* 20396 Maystres off dyvers crafftys Hang out, on polys and on rafftys, Dyuers sygnys. **1650** W. D. tr. *Comenius' Gate Lat. Unl.* §446 Especially if it [a barrel] bee laid upon stalls (Rafts, tressels) somwhat high. **1745** Blomefield *Topogr. Hist. Norfolk* II. 148 Raftermen, those that deal in Rafts or Timber Pieces. **1820** *Blackw. Mag.* VIII. 147 The roof wags its remotest raft. **1854** S. Dobell *Balder* xxviii. 198 Like a Temple, wherein cost Is absolute, dark beam and hidden raft Shittim.

2. A collection of logs, planks, casks, etc., fastened together in the water, so as to be transported from one place to another by floating.

1497 *Naval Acc. Hen. VII* (1896) 249 Cariage of certeyn mastes to the Watyrsyde and ther to be made in a Raff & so to be conveyed to Portesmouth. **1614** Raleigh *Hist. World* ii. (1634) 424 Hiram caused his Servants to bring downe the Cedars and Firres from Libanon to the Sea, and thence sent them in raffes to Joppe. **1685** *New Eng. Hist. & Gen. Register* (1882) XXXVI. 396 By one Raft of boards qt 12500 ft. **1774** Goldsm. *Nat. Hist.* (1776) VII. 119 [Crocodiles] lying as close to each other, as a raft of timber upon one of our streams. **1806** *Gazetteer Scotl.* (ed. 2) 124 At proper seasons, large rafts of trees are constructed, and floated to the sea. **1863** *Life in Normandy* II. 80 [They] work the rafts of timber and floats of tar barrels down the great rivers to the Gulf of Bothnia.

3. a. A flat structure of logs, inflated skins, or other materials, for the conveyance or support of persons or things on water.

α. **1590** Shaks. *Com. Err.* v. i. 348 Where is that sonne That floated with thee on the fatall rafte. **1653** H. Cogan tr. *Pinto's Trav.* lxvi. 267 Before it was day they had made a raft of such planks and beams as came to their hands. **1677** W. Hubbard *Narrative* (1865) I. 88 They..either waded over ..or else wafted themselves over upon small Rafts of Timber. **1719** De Foe *Crusoe* i. iv, This Raft was so unweildy, and so overloaden, that..it overset. **1790** Beatson *Nav. & Mil. Mem.* II. 354 The building of a large raft, or radeau, to carry some heavy artillery. **1855** Macaulay *Hist. Eng.* xx. IV. 509 Eight large rafts, each carrying many mortars, were moored in the harbour.

transf. *a* **1822** Shelley *Hom. Merc.* xiii, For each foot he wrought a kind of raft Of tamarisk. **1853** Kane *Grinnell Exp.* xxxviii. (1856) 353 Using the frozen water as a raft to traverse the open sea. **1890** 'R. Boldrewood' *Col. Reformer* (1891) 375 Such a raft of a place as Rainbar.

β. **1599** Hakluyt *Voy.* II. i. 214 Certaine Zattares or Raffes made of blowen hides or skinnes... These Raffes are bound fast together. **1603** Knolles *Hist. Turks* (1638) 185 Making a little boat, or rather as some suppose a raffe.

b. *Mil.* A floating bridge.

1802 in James *Milit. Dict.* **1876** Voyle & Stevenson *Milit. Dict.* 322/1 Good rafts can be made of casks or barrels, and form a better bridge than baulks of timber.

4. (Chiefly *U.S.*) A large floating mass or accumulation of some material, or collection of materials, as fallen trees, logs, vegetation, ice, etc. Also, a dense flock of swimming birds, *esp.* ducks; similarly, a group of other aquatic animals.

1718 [see *raft-fowl* in 6]. **1802** A. Ellicott *Jrnl.* (1803) 189 The upper raft is of considerable magnitude, and covered with grass and other herbage, with some bushes. **1812** Brackenridge *Views Louisiana* (1814) 48 There is at that point a curious raft, formed of logs and earth, which entirely covers its channel. **1848** W. E. Burton *Waggeries & Vagaries* 70 We've shoals of shad, hull rafts of canvass-back ducks, and no eeend of terrapins. **1852** Mrs. Stowe *Uncle Tom's C.* vii. 43 The descending ice..lodged, and formed a great undulating raft, filling up the river. **1872** *Fur, Fin & Feather* 26 The great collections [of ducks] are termed rafts. **1876** R. F. Burton *Gorilla L.* II. 158 The nymphæa, lotus or water-lily, forms rafts of verdure. **1949** Sprunt & Chamberlain *S. Carolina Bird Life* 135 The Greater Scaup..congregates there in large flocks or 'rafts', as they are called. **1952** *Chambers's Jrnl.* Jan. 19/2 That black mass far away to starboard, what is it—brent geese? And the bigger one over there? It looks like a good raft of wigeon. **1959** E. Collier *Three against Wilderness* xxi. 210 A raft of newly hatched geese had been perched on the beaver house. **1961** *Guardian* 4 Mar. 4/1 Rafts of widgeon cry *wee-too* from the steamer lines. **1972** S. Burnford *One Woman's Arctic* ii. 48 There were long rafts of murres out in the middle. **1975** *Country Life* 16 Jan. 132/3 A tiny band of sea otters..had grown to a raft of 130. **1975** P. A. Johnsgard *Waterfowl N. Amer.* II. 347 Scaup in such rafts do not all forage at the same time.

5. *Building.* A layer of reinforced concrete forming the foundation of a building.

1903 *Engineering* 17 Apr. 517/1 Finally, the Co-operative Wholesale Society resolved to adopt their architect's recommendation to have recourse to a raft of Hennebique ferro-concrete over the whole area of the ground. **1936** *Concrete & Constructional Engin.* XXXI. 423 There are a great many districts where rafts are the best and often the only solution to foundation problems. **1970** R. Jeffries *Dead Man's Bluff* iii. 21 A concrete raft on which was a feeding trough and about fifty Kow Kennels. **1978** *Daily Tel.* 12 May 19/3 All the floors in the houses are dropping out because they were built on a concrete raft. The raft is now sinking into the peat below.

6. *attrib.* and *Comb.*, as ***raft-chain***, ***log***, ***-man***, ***-master***, ***tug***, ***-voyage***, ***-wood***, ***-work***; ***raftlike*** adj.; ***raftwise*** adv.; **raft-breasted** *a.*, of birds: having a keelless sternum (*Cent. Dict.* 1891); **raft-bridge**, a bridge made of a raft, or supported by rafts; **raft-deck**, an under-water protecting deck formerly used to cover the unarmoured parts of some warships; **raft-dog**, an iron bar, having its ends pointed and bent at right-angles, used to secure logs in a raft; **raft-duck**, the scaup or blackhead duck (*Athya marila*), so called from its flocking closely on the water (see also quot. 1824); **raft foundation** = sense 5 above; **raft-fowl** (see quot. 1709); **raft-port** (see quot. 1769); **raft spider**, a spider which makes a floating nest.

1834-47 J. S. Macaulay *Field Fortif.* (1851) 130 When plenty of heavy timber can be procured, a *raft-bridge may be made. **1846** A. Young *Naut. Dict.* 244 An eye..through which the *raft-chains are rove. **1867** Smyth *Sailor's Word-bk.* 559 There are also dog-hooks..by which the raft-chains are secured. **1886** *Encycl. Brit.* XXI. 822/2 But the sailors of 1854-1860 did not take the view that buoyancy and stability ..were the vital parts, needing defence by armour or by a *raft-deck. **1846** A. Young *Naut. Dict.* 244 Secured by means of *raft-dogs, with chains wove through them. **1867** Smyth *Sailor's Word-bk.* 558 A sort of float..fastened together with swifters and raft-dogs. **1824** Latham *Gen. Hist. Birds* X. 302 Scaup Duck..is known in Georgia, and called by some the *Raft Duck. [*Note.* But the Raft Duck, truly so called, is another species.] *Ibid.* 352 Raft Duck (*Anas fuligula*). **1872** E. Coues *Key to N. Amer. Birds* 289 Greater Scaup Duck... Raft Duck. Flocking Fowl. **1975** P. A. Johnsgard *Waterfowl N. Amer.* II. 347 The 'rafting' behaviour of migrant and wintering scaup is well known and indicated by their vernacular names—'raft duck', 'flock duck', and 'troop duck'. **1904** C. F. Marsh *Reinforced Concrete* 541/1 (Index), *Raft foundations. **1910** F. Rings *Reinforced Concrete* iv. 61 For ordinary level or raft foundations wire meshing or expanded metal are extremely useful. **1974** *Encycl. Brit. Macropædia* III. 458/1 Of mat, or raft, foundation, there are two types—the beam-and-slab type and the flat-slab type. **1709** Lawson *Carolina* 150 *Raft-Fowl includes all the sorts of small Ducks and Teal, that go in Rafts along the Shoar. **1865** Tenney *Hist. Rebellion U.S.* 224/2 One of the 11-inch Dahlgrens from the ..tower upon the *raft-like structure. **1753** Washington *Jrnl.* Writ. 1889 I. 38, I fortunately saved myself by catching hold of one of the *Raft Logs. **1776** C. Carroll *Jrnl. Miss. Canada* in B. Mayer *Mem.* (1845) 47 Each one is marked, so that the *raft-men..may easily know their own rafts. **1828** A. Sherburne *Mem.* vi. 234 The raft men had the privilenge [*sic*] of cooking, and sleeping under cover, in the boat. **1847** C. Lanman *Summer in Wilderness* xviii. 111 The principal anglers for this fish are steamboat hands and raftmen. **1903** *Blackw. Mag.* Feb. 228/1 The figures of the raftmen seem to walk magically on the water. **1963** A. Smith *Throw out Two Hands* xv. 153 We wished..to be a raft in the air, and to pay as little attention to our conveyance as raft-men do. **1828** Planché *Desc. Danube* 56 The *Raft-masters of Munich. **1769** Falconer *Dict. Marine* (1776), *Raft-port, a square hole, cut through the buttocks of some ships, immediately under the counter, to receive the planks or pieces of timber ..brought to lade her. **1830** Hedderwick *Marine Arch.* 258 A raft-port in the upper part of the bends and black strakes. **1864–5** Wood *Homes without H.* xxxi. (1868) 597 There is another spider which frequents water, but which only makes a temporary and moveable residence. This is the *Raft Spider (*Dolomedes fimbriatus*). **1879** *Lumberman's Gaz.* 5 Nov., *Raft tugs are in demand to bring more logs down. **1891** 'Mark Twain' *Let.* 1 Oct. (1917) II. 558 A pedestrian tour in Europe doesn't begin with a *raft-voyage for hilarity and mild adventure. **1905** 'Q' *Shining Ferry* I. vi. 61 A hatch opened in her bows, through which the long balks of timber were thrust..to be laid *raftwise and lashed together with chains. **1880** C. R. Markham *Peruv. Bark* 225 One of the rafts..was composed of twelve trunks of *raft-wood. **1892** B. Hinton *Lord's Return* 200 Liking best the *raft-work on the Hudson.

raft (rɑːft, -æ-), *sb.*² orig. *dial.* and *U.S.* [var. RAFF *sb.*¹, perh. by assoc. with prec.] A large collection; a crowd; a lot. Freq. in phr. ***a whole raft of*** (persons or things).

1830 W. A. Ferris *Life in Rocky Mts.* (1940) vi. 29 We.. would have fought a whole raft of them. **1833** 'Maj. Downing' *Lett.* xiv. (1835) 88 Binny, and Everett, and Gallatin, and a raft more of such kinder fellows. **1876** 'Mark Twain' *Tom Sawyer* 235 If you was to go to Europe you'd see a raft of 'em hopping around. **1887–** In dial. glossaries (Kent, Cumb.). **1922** S. Lewis *Babbitt* viii. 116 They say there's a whole raft of stuff being smuggled across at Detroit. **1936** P. Bottome *Level Crossing* xxiv. 298 You've got to stand on what results there are, and not take on a whole raft of things that have nothing to do with it. **1947** 'N. Shute' *Chequer Board* x. 298 There's a whole raft o' things here that I never seen before. **1959** *Sunday Times* 7 June 21/5 Only very rich companies with a raft of employees build them. **1972** *Guardian* 19 Oct. 14/4 A year or two of keeping house, loving and looking after a raft of kids. **1977** *Time* 3 Jan. 36/1 There were a whole raft of programs in the '60s followed by eight years when there was no attempt to work with any degree of compassion. **1977** *Guardian Weekly* 16 Oct. 20/2 It has a raft of actors with the energy and skill to bring humour, depth and resonance to even the smallest parts. **1978** P. Theroux *Picture Palace* ix. 71 There was a whole raft of photographers in New York at the time. **1979** *Amer. Speech* LIV. 44 He reserved what he called 'a great raft' of *Beowulf* materials for a more leisurely time.

raft, *sb.*³, var. RAFF *sb.*³ (q.v.).

raft (rɑːft, -æ-), *v.*¹ [f. RAFT *sb.*¹]

1. *trans.* To transport by water: **a.** in the form of a raft (also *transf.*)

1706 *Wooden World Dissected* (1708) 3 Charon..rafting the poor Souls astern, like Water-cask. **1768** in F. Chase *Hist. Dartmouth Coll.* (1891) I. 104 The stream..(a branch of Merrimack, by which logs are rafted to the sea). **1792** Belknap *Hist. New Hampsh.* III. 207 The lumber..is rafted down that river. **1840** *Evid. Hull Docks Comm.* 84 The ships have to discharge it [timber] in the old dock, and it is rafted round into the harbour. **1881** *Nature* XXIII. 340 All the slabs have been rafted out to sea by the high tide. **1896** Kipling *Seven Seas* 26 With cedars out of Lebanon Which Hiram rafted down. **1921** *Discovery* Feb. 48/1 The water hyacinth..causes an annual loss of one-fourth of the value of the logs rafted down the river. **1961** *Nature* 3 June 856/2 Sial blocks..being rafted to down-welling sites. **1972** *Sci. Amer.* May 62 (*caption*) In this schematic view the lithosphere is thicker under the continent it is rafting toward a subduction zone.

b. on, or by means of, a raft.

1689 H. Kelsey *Jrnl.* 22 July in *Kelsey Papers* (1929) 30 This morning tryed to gett over yᵉ mouth of it but could not so..went up yᵉ river to Raft our selves over. **1766** in W. Smith *Bouquet's Exped.* (1868) 126 The carts, provisions and baggage, may be rafted over, or a bridge built. **1827** J. F. Cooper *Prairie* I. ii. 33 We rafted ourselves across. **1845** Hood *Mermaid of Margate* xxv, There was not a box or a beam afloat To raft him from that sad place. **1847** *Knickerbocker* XXIX. 314 We crossed it on the following day, rafting over our horses and equipage with much difficulty. **1972** *Nat. Geographic* Oct. 469/2 Wielding huge sweeps, Peruvians raft bananas down the Ucayali River.

c. ***to raft off***: To float off (water-casks, or the water in them) from the shore to a ship.

1745 P. Thomas *Jrnl. Anson's Voy.* 174 We now continued to raft off Water. **1748** *Anson's Voy.* III. v. 334 We were obliged to raft off all our cask, and the tide ran so strong, that..we more than once lost the whole raft. **1882** Nares *Seamanship* (ed. 6) 146 The casks must be rafted off to the ship.

2. To form into a raft or rafts. Also with *up*, and in sense 4 of RAFT *sb.*¹

1745 P. Thomas *Jrnl. Anson's Voy.* 120 A couple of Canoes, which we brought..on purpose to raft and carry up Barreecas. **1800** Colquhoun *Comm. Thames* i. 27 These Logs are rafted in the River. **1833** Marryat *P. Simple* (1863) 221 Our first business was to water the ship by rafting and towing off the casks. **1883** J. Fraser *Shanty, Forest & River Life* xxix. 340 The timber is floated in single pieces down all the numerous tributaries of the Ottawa, and then 'rafted-up' at 'the mouth' of each. **1891** C. Roberts *Adrift Amer.* 203 A place..where the logs that came down the Chippewa River were rafted. **1924** R. Campbell *Flaming Terrapin* ii. 38 Stacked with flaming spears Old Ocean shone, as swaying through the Night He rafted up his monstrous chandeliers. **1950** E. Hemingway *Across River* xli. 242 They [*sc.* ducks] must really be rafted up out there, the Colonel thought. **1976** *Yachts & Yachting* 20 Aug. 353/1 In St. Peter Port I have seen yachts rafted-up almost wall-to-wall on the buoys, like the trots used to be at Cowes. **1978** J. A. Michener *Chesapeake* 665 There must have been three thousand ducks rafted there beneath a frozen late-rising moon.

3. To go upon or cross (a river) by means of a raft.

1765 R. Rogers *Jrnls.* (1883) 162 The river St. Francis.. is very still water, and may be easily rafted where you cross it. **1808** Pike *Sources Mississ.* II. (1810) 119 We concluded to raft the river, which we effected with difficulty. **1844** J. C. Frémont *Rep. Exploring Expedition* (1845) 251 We had expected to raft the river. **1955** E. Pound *Classic Anthol.* I. 17 Ready to raft the deep, Wade shallow or dive for gain. **1974** *Marlboro Herald-Advocate* (Bennettsville, S. Carolina) 22 Apr. 6/2 During the four day exercise, members of the 541st engineer company rafted the Rhine river and secured tactical positions.

4. *intr.* To use a raft for some purpose; to work on or direct a raft.

1741 *New Eng. Hist. & Gen. Register* (1879) XXXIII. 330 We met with great difficulty in passing that River, first attempting to wade,..then tried to Raft. **1808** Pike *Sources Mississ.* (1810) 88 We could not cross the river, unless we rafted. **1840** *Evid. Hull Docks Comm.* 122 They cannot raft out of the old dock. **1888** *Academy* XXXIV. 301/2 They canoed, and rafted, and steam-boated.

5. *intr.* Of an ice floe: to be driven on top of or underneath another floe. Also *trans.*, to drive (ice) in this way.

1883 Hatton & Harvey *Newfoundland* III. iii. 301 Or, under pressure of the storm, it frequently happens that the ice is 'rafted', as the sealers call it; that is, the fragments are piled in layers one over the other to the height of thirty or forty feet, being lifted by the swell and hurled forward as if from huge catapults. **1919** E. Shackleton *South* I. 11 In obedience to renewed pressure this young ice 'rafts', so forming double thicknesses of a toffee-like consistency. **1939** *Beaver* Mar. 13/2 On the sea and large lakes ice seldom forms smoothly. Early storms break it and pack it in confusion, and pressure causes it to 'raft'.

raft, *v.*² *rare*⁻¹. [f. RAFT *sb.*¹ 1.] = RAFTER *v.*

1804 *Trans. Soc. Arts* XXII. 70 The roof rafted and thatched by myself.

raft (ræft), *v.*³ *Southern dial.* [Origin unknown.] *trans.* To rouse; to disturb, disquiet, or unsettle. Hence '**rafted** *ppl. a.*², '**rafting** *ppl. a.*²

1851 *Gloss. Provincial Words Dorset* 6 Raft, to irritate. **1895** Hardy *Jude* IV. iv. 290 'I think you are rafted, and not yourself,' he continued. 'Do go back and make up your mind to put up with a few whims.' **1896** —— *Under Greenwood Tree* (rev. ed.) I. iv. 32 They should ha' stuck to strings. Your brass-man is a rafting dog—well and good; your reed-man is a dab at stirring ye—well and good; your drum-man is a rare bowel-shaker—good again. **1904** in *Eng. Dial. Dict.* V. 11/1 When a sick person is at the point of death, old nurses think it wrong to disturb the spirit of the dying by speaking to him, lest by doing so his spirit may be 'rafted', i.e. disturbed by earthly thoughts, and so bereft of the consolation of religion [Hants.]. **1920** Hardy *Coll. Poems* 377 My rafted spirit would not rest.

raft, *ppl. a. rare*⁻¹. [Arch. for REFT.] Torn off.

1818 Keats *Endym.* I. 334 The raft Branch down sweeping from a tall ash top.

raft(e, obs. or arch. pa. t. and pa. pple. REAVE.

rafted (ˈrɑːftɛd, -æ-), *ppl. a.*¹ [f. RAFT *v.*¹ + -ED¹.]

1. Of floating ice: piled up as a result of one floe having been driven on top of another.

1897 J. W. Tyrrell *Across Sub-Arctics of Canada* vii. 92 Toward the north end of the lake we passed great piles of rafted ice on the shore. **1924** R. J. Flaherty *My Eskimo Friends* III. ii. 93 On the tenth of April we came face to face with a gigantic pile of rafted ice. **1960** G. Blanchet *Search in North* viii. 109 Sunlight created strange effects from rafted ice. **1974** L. Deighton *Spy Story* xix. 203 We'll go south until we find the end of the rafted ice.

2. Of swimming birds: gathered into a dense flock.

1962 R. Haig-Brown *Whale People* x. 89 They covered the canoe with brush and allowed it to drift in on the rafted ducks. **1978** J. A. Michener *Chesapeake* 844 With a gentle ..push he launched the skiff toward the rafted geese.

rafted, *ppl. a.*²: see RAFT *v.*³

rafter (ˈrɑːftə(r), -æ-), *sb.*¹ Forms: *α.* 1 ræfter, reafter, 1–3 ræftr-, 1–4 reftr-, 2–4 raftr-, 3–7 refter, 4 raftere, (rafterer), raftyr, 4 (5 *Sc.*) raftre, (7 rafture), 4– rafter. *β.* 6 raughter, *Sc.* rach-, rauch-, rawch-, raychter. [O.E. *ræfter* = MLG. *rafter, rachter*, related to ON. *rapt-r* RAFT *sb.*¹ The Sc. forms with *ch* are prob. from LG.]

1. One of the beams which give slope and form to a roof, and bear, directly or indirectly, the outer covering of slates, tiles, thatch, etc.

angle-, binding-, cushion-, hip-, jack-rafter: see under the first element. ***principal rafter***, a strong beam in a truss, lying under the ***common*** or ***ordinary rafters***.

α. *a* **700** *Epinal Gloss.* 11 *Amites*, reftras. *c* **900** tr. *Bæda's Hist.* III. xiv. [xvi.] (1890) 202 Micelne ád gesomnade on beamum & on ræftrum. *c* **1050** *Byrhtferth's Handboc* in *Anglia* VIII. 324 Þa syllan man fæȝere ȝeleȝð, and þa beamas ȝeleȝþ, and þa ræftras to þære fyrste ȝefæstnað. *c* **1275** Lay. 7839 Þeos reftres stode, hi-hud in þan flode. **1340** *Ayenb.* 175 Þe ypocrites..ysyeþ bet mot ine þe oþres eȝe and ne ysyeþ naȝt þane refter ine hire oȝene eȝe. *c* **1386** Chaucer *Knt.'s T.* 132 He..rente adoun bothe wall, and sparre, and rafter. *c* **1470** Henry *Wallace* VII. 449 Brundis fell off raftreis thaim amang. **1555** Eden *Decades* 159 To lade his neighbours waules with rafters or beames. **1594** Plat *Jewell-ho.* I. 10 The principall postes, the Rafters, and the beames of any house. **1667** Primatt *City & C. Build.* 86 Single Rafter being four foot long, and four and three and a half in thickness. **1726** Pope *Odyss.* XXII. 262 Perch'd like a swallow on a rafter's height. **1823** P. Nicholson *Pract. Build.* 128 Common rafters are inclined pieces of timber, parallel to the principal rafters. **1865** G. Macdonald *A. Forbes* 21 Her eyes rested on nothing but bare rafters and boards.

transf. and *fig.* *c* **1200** *Vices & Virtues* 95 Caritèð..arist up anon to ðe roue, forðan to hire bieð ifastned alle ðe raftres of ðe hali mihtes. *c* **1590** Greene *Fr. Bacon* xi. 13 The rafters of the earth rent from the poles..When Bacon read upon his magic book. **1635** Swan *Spec. M.* iv. §2 (1643) 58 The heaven it self, whose beams or rafters are laid in the waters. **1844** Willis *Lady Jane* II. 150 'Fame's proud temple', build it ne'er so proud, Finds notoriety a useful rafter. **1891** C. E. Norton *Dante's Purgat.* XXX. 193 Even as the snow, among the living rafters upon the back of Italy, is congealed.

β. **1500–20** Dunbar *Poems* xxxiii. 37 His yrnis was rude as ony rawchtir. **1551** *Aberdeen Reg.* V. 21 (Jam.) Ane schip laidnit with rachteris and dalis. **1592** Lyly *Gallathea* I. iii, I will..hang myselfe on a raughter in the house.

†**b.** A large beam such as is used for a rafter.

1553 Brende *Q. Curtius* G j, To the deisturbaunce of the shippes that approched the walles, they devised longe rafters. **1579–80** North *Plutarch* (1676) 584 They left their Rafters or great pieces of timber pinned together, whereupon they had passed over the stream. **1652** Earl Monm. tr. *Bentivoglio's Hist. Relat.* 2 Rampires of Earth, built up with great Stones, Raftures of Wood [etc.]. **1697** Potter *Antiq. Greece* III. xv. (1715) 127 [The Sides of the Ship] were compos'd of large Rafters extended from Prow to Stern.

c. *U.S.* A transverse bar (of wood or iron) in the roof of a railway-car.

1891 in *Cent. Dict.*

2. = *rafter-bird* (see 3).

1802 G. Montagu *Ornithol. Dict.* (1833) 398.

3. *attrib.* and *Comb.*, as ***rafter-end, foot, -frame, -nail, -tree***; ***rafter-wise*** adv.; **rafter-bird**, the beam-bird, spotted flycatcher (cf. sense 2); **rafter-level** (*U.S.*), a kind of level made of long spars of wood; **rafter-ridging** = RAFTERING 2; **rafter-roof**, a roof constructed with rafters; **rafter-timbering** *Mining* (see quot.).

1817 T. Forster *Nat. Hist. Swallowtribe* (ed. 6) 75 *Muscicapa grisola*,..*Rafterbird. **1885** Swainson *Names Birds* 48 From the site of its nest, which is generally placed ..on a beam or rafter of an out-building, this bird is called ..Rafter or Rafter-bird. **1895** *Educat. Rev.* Sept. 118 Rough walls and protruding *rafter-ends. **1825** J. Nicholson *Operat. Mechanic* 567 Framing the *rafter foot into the girder. **1871** B. Taylor *Faust* (1875) II. III. 181 The lofty beam, upholding *rafter-frame and roof. **1834** *Brit. Husb.* I. 534 In America, where it is much used for ascertaining the declination of land, it is called a *rafter-level. **1730** Savery in *Phil. Trans.* XXXVI. 296 The largest Sort of *Rafter-Nails. **1838** Holloway *Prov. Dict.*, *Rafter Ridging, a mode of ploughing land, which is performed as follows [etc.]. *Hants.* **1847** R. & J. A. Brandon *Anal. Goth. Archit.* (1860) I. 92 Sometimes a trussed *rafter-roof spans both the nave and the aisles. **1887** *Dict. Arch.*, s.v. **1881** Raymond *Mining Gloss.*, *Rafter-timbering, timbering in which the pieces are arranged like the rafters of a house. **1819** W. Tennant *Papistry Storm'd* (1827) 210 Ceiling dark and *rafter-treen. **1676** Plot *Oxfordsh.* 251 Wheat..they shock it *rafter-wise, ten sheaves in a shock.

rafter (ˈrɑːftə(r), -æ-), *sb.*² [f. RAFT *sb.*¹ or *v.*¹ + -ER¹.] **1.** One who is employed in rafting timber.

1809 Kendall *Travels* III. 305 That the rafters should relinquish..the earnings of their immediate hands. **1851–61** Mayhew *Lond. Labour* III. 295 The labourers connected with this portion of the trade are rafters or raftsmen. **1891** C. Roberts *Adrift in Amer.* 206 The rafters were engaged in making the rafts up. **1905** 'Q' *Shining Ferry* vi. 70 In fifty strokes he brought her alongside the barque where the rafters—twenty-five or thirty—were at work. **1936** [see CROSS-CUTTER]. **1954** A. M. Bezanson *Sodbusters invade Peace* xxii. 160 Rafters kept coming quite a while. They all finally got tired waiting for God to freeze the rivers again, and came down on rafts.

2. One who travels on a raft.

1978 *TV Bk.* (Detroit Free Press) 16–22 Apr. 21/2 Adventures of a group of white water rafters on the Chatooga River in South Carolina. **1979** *Sunset* Apr. 38 (*caption*) Jagged, glacier-dotted Mount Moran hobnobs with the clouds as rafters laze along Jackson Lake towards shore for Teton camping.

rafter ('rɑːftə(r), -æ-), *v.* Also 6 **raufter.** [f. RAFTER *sb.*[1]]

1. *trans.* To build or furnish with rafters. Also *fig.*

1538 ELYOT *Dict., Contigno,..* to raufter a house. **1611** BIBLE *2 Chron.* xxxiv. 11 Timber for couplings and to floore [*marg.* rafter] the houses. **1853** KANE *Grinnell Exp.* v. (1856) 39 A square inclosure of stone or turf is raftered over with drift-wood or whalebones. **1869** DORA GREENWELL *Carmina Crucis* 36 Ivory palaces raftered with..cedar. **1935** C. DAY LEWIS *Time to Dance* 64 A hungry soul Urged them to try new air-routes, and their skill Raftered the sky with steel.

2. *Agric.* To plough (land) in a certain way (see quot. 1846, and cf. RAFTERING *vbl. sb.* 2).

a **1733** [see RAFTERING *vbl. sb.* 2]. **1794** YOUNG in Driver *Gen. View Agric. Hants* 68 Raftering the land, which is a sort of rest baulk ploughing. **1844** *Jrnl. R. Agric. Soc.* V. I. 173 The land is raftered, and pared with the breast-plough; or raftered again in a cross-direction. **1846** CLARKE in *Jrnl. R. Agric. Soc.* VII. II. 511 To rafter or plough-rafter the land ..is to plough only one-half of the land, turning the furrow ploughed upon the same breadth of land remaining unploughed throughout the field.

3. To form into rafters (Worcester, 1846).

4. *intr.* Of ice: = RAFT *v.*[1] 5. *N. Amer.*

1792 G. CARTWRIGHT *Jrnl.* II. p. vii, Raftering of ice. Ice is said to rafter, when, by being stopped in its passage, one piece is forced under another, until the uppermost ones rise to a great height. **1861** L. DE BOILIEU *Recoll. Labrador Life* viii. 100 It is a sad sight to see a ship on the weather edge of ice not enabled to work off; for when the ice begins to rafter she is thrown up, falls over, and becomes like corn between two millstones, and is literally ground up. **1908** N. DUNCAN *Every Man for Himself* ii. 60 The ice begun t' drive an' grind an' rafter. **1924** R. J. FLAHERTY *My Eskimo Friends* III. iii. 99 Miles and miles of ice, raftering and rearing and overriding us it fought its way to the sea. **1964** *Newfoundland Q.* Spring 16/3 Evidently, just like frozen masses of ice raftered, one layer rising above the other by pressure, the crust of the earth broke and travelled southward.

raftered ('rɑːftəd, -æ-), *ppl. a.* [f. RAFTER *sb.*[1] or *v.* + -ED.] Roofed with or composed of rafters; *esp.* indicating that the rafters are visible as part of the ceiling. Also *transf.*, and in sense 4 of RAFTER *v.*

1732 POPE *Ep. Bathurst* 189 No rafter'd roofs with dance and tabor sound. **1751** T. WARTON *Poet. Wks.* (1802) II. 168 Whose rafter'd hall the crowding tenants fed. **1871** M. COLLINS *Mrq. & Merch.* I. ii. 91 Quaint casements and raftered rooms. **1893** MRS. C. PRAED *Outlaw & Lawmaker* I. 238 Its beamed and raftered ceiling. **1916** N. DUNCAN *Billy Topsail, M.D.* xvii. 130 It was six miles from the edge of the raftered ice to the first island. **1924** R. CAMPBELL *Flaming Terrapin* ii. 32 She skimmed along—Till, raftered by the forest,.. She saw the monsters that the jungle breeds.

raftering ('rɑːftərɪŋ, -æ-), *vbl. sb.* Also 6 **raftre-, raufteryng(e, raftring.** [f. RAFTER *v.* + -ING[1].]

1. Roofing with, or forming of, rafters; the arrangement of rafters; wood for rafters.

1538 ELYOT *Dict., Contignatio,..* the raufterynge. **1542** UDALL *Erasm. Apoph.* 232 Buyldyng an hous euen from the foundacion vnto the vttermost raftreyng and reiryng of the roofe. **1667** PRIMATT *City & C. Build.* 65 How many square of Raftering there will be in a Roof. **1857** tr. *Pliny* (Bohn) VI. 345 The raftering being so contrived as to admit of the beams being removed. **1880** C. R. MARKHAM *Peruv. Bark* 357 The ben-teak yields timber used for raftering and flooring.

transf. *c* **1586** C'TESS PEMBROKE *Ps.* CXXXIX, viii, Thou, how my back was beam-wise laid, And raftring of my ribbs dost know.

2. *Agric.* A certain method of ploughing (see quot. 1851, and cf. RAFTER *v.* 2).

a **1733** In Tull's *Horse-Hoeing Husb.* (1733) ix. 94 By the Paring and Burning the Surface; by Raftering, or Cross Plowing. *Ibid.* (1762) 297, I have seen Land plowed in this manner, where not half of it has been moved, nor better tilled than by Raftering. **1778** [W. MARSHALL] *Minutes Agric.* 7 Dec. 1775 The Plowman..told me, that it is his country-method of plowing, and calls it raftering. **1851** H. STEPHENS *Bk. of Farm* (ed. 2) I. 183/1 There is a kind of ploughing..which bears the name of ribbing in Scotland and of raftering in England... It consists in turning the furrow-slices on their backs upon as much of the firm soil as they will cover.

rafterless ('rɑːftəlɪs, -æ-), *a.* [f. RAFTER *sb.*[1] + -LESS.] Having no rafters.

1854 'G. GREENWOOD' *Haps & Mishaps* vii. 128 This is a picturesque, roofless, rafterless edifice, in a good state of preservation. **1943** L. B. LYON *Evening in Stepney* 20 Who tremble, yet dare not call On the crushed bones to bear witness And rafterless heaven to fall.

'raftery, *a.* [f. RAFTER *sb.*[1] + -Y[1].] Full of rafters.

1872 HOWELLS *Wedd. Journ.* (1892) 50 The roof seemed.. in its coal-smoked, raftery hollow to generate a heat deadlier than that poured upon it from the skies.

rafting ('rɑːftɪŋ, -æ-), *vbl. sb.* [f. RAFT *v.*[1] + -ING[1].] **a.** The action of the vb., in various senses.

1697 H. KELSEY *Jrnl.* 16 Aug. in *Kelsey Papers* (1929) 95 Our 3 boats went to ten shilling creek to rafting. **1753** WASHINGTON *Jrnl.* Writ. 1889 I. 29 Crossing the Creek.. was impossible, either by fording or rafting. *a* **1817** T. DWIGHT *Trav. New Eng.* (1821) II. 167 Their first experiments at rafting..were so often unsuccessful. **1840** *Evid. Hull Docks Comm.* 122 Is not rafting the cheapest mode? **1891** MISS DOWIE *Girl in Karp.* 256 This rafting had a fascination for me. **1905** 'Q' *Shining Ferry* I. vi. 69 'Have they begun the rafting?' 'Bless your life, they've been working all night. There's one raft finished.' **1920** W. T. GRENFELL *Labrador Doctor* ix. 180 On then swept the floe, crashed into the fixed ice, shattered its edge, rose up out of water over it, which is called 'rafting', forced itself on the unfortunate ship. **1967** *Vogue* Jan. 76/1 Jamaica has..skin-diving, rafting, cheap rum. **1975** B. L. FAIRBANK *Cruising Guide to Lake Ontario* 19 Rafting alongside is accepted practice on crowded weekends, although it is good manners to ask permission of the boat you are coming alongside.

b. *Comb.* **rafting chain,** a chain used to bind logs together into a raft; **rafting distance,** the distance that can be traversed in a raft; **rafting-dog,** a raft-dog (RAFT *sb.*[1] 6); **rafting works** (see quot. 1969).

1842 A. LANGTON *Jrnl.* 4 Nov. in *Langton Records* (1904) 319 His errand..was to get a rafting chain. **1846** A. YOUNG *Naut. Dict.* 244. **1904** *Daily Chron.* 29 Jan. 3/3 Unlike Crusoe he has no ship within rafting distance filled with everything he might want. **1931** *Sun* (Baltimore) 20 Mar. 10/6 The Mississippi Logging Company..maintained a boarding house..on the way to the rafting works at West Newton. **1969** L. G. SORDEN *Lumberjack Lingo* 94 *Rafting works*, booming grounds. A place where logs are held.

rafting ('rɑːftɪŋ, -æ-), *ppl. a.*[2] [f. RAFT *v.*[1] + -ING[2].] Of ice: that rafts (see RAFT *v.*[1] 5).

1883 HATTON & HARVEY *Newfoundland* III. iv. 311 When they are in danger from 'rafting' ice, or fragments of floes.. the self-sacrificing affection of the mothers leads them to brave all dangers. **1935** *Discovery* Mar. 77/1 A suitable block-and-tackle is essential in order that the boat may be hauled far enough up the shore to be safe from 'rafting' ice. **1966** *Weekend Mag.* (Montreal) 19 Mar. 34/1 Each year.. seals congregate on the rafting ice pressing in around the shores of Canada's Magdalen Islands.

rafting, *ppl. a.*[2]: see RAFT *v.*[3]

raftre, obs. f. RAFTER *sb.*[1]

raftsman ('rɑːftsmən, -æ-). [f. RAFT *sb.*[1] + -S- + MAN.] One who works on a raft.

1776 C. CARROLL *Jrnl. Miss. Canada* in B. Mayer *Mem.* (1845) 67 A small current begins here, and the raftsmen are not obliged to row. **1846** WHITTIER *Ship-builders* iii, For us the raftsmen down the stream Their island barges steer. **1883** OUIDA *Wanda* I. 13 She wished..he should grow up a raftsman, or a fisherman.

rafture, obs. form of RAFTER *sb.*[1]

rafty ('rɑːftɪ, -æ-), *a.* *Obs.* exc. *dial.*

1. Damp, musty, muggy, raw.

1655 GURNALL *Chr. in Arm.* I. 280 Things kept in a rafty muggish Room, subject them to mould. **1658** J. ROBINSON *Endoxa* 146 The Occidental mansions are, by their moisture, rafty. **1787** MARSHALL *E. Norfolk* (1795) II. Gloss., *Rafty*, damp and musty; as corn or hay in a wet season. **1893** *Essex Rev.* II. 126 A rafty morning is still well understood in North Essex as meaning a raw morning.

2. Stale, rancid (usually said of bacon).

a **1722** LISLE *Husb.* (1752) 347 Shred rafty bacon into it [milk]. **1874** JEFFERIES *Labourer's Daily Life* in *Toilers of Field* (1893) 95 The small bit of fat and rafty bacon.

raftyr, rafull, obs. ff. RAFTER *sb.*[1], RAFFLE.

rafwire ('ræfwaɪə(r)). *Aeronaut.* Also **Rafwire, RAFwire, raf-wire.** [f. the initial letters of the *R*oyal *A*ircraft *F*actory + WIRE *sb.*] A kind of wire having a flattened, semi-streamlined cross-section formerly used as bracing wire on aircraft.

1918 W. E. DOMMETT *Dict. Aircraft* 38 *Rafwire*, wires of flattened section, approaching to streamline shape, designed originally at R.A.F. **1920** *Techn. Rep. Advisory Comm. Aeronaut. 1915–16* 15 Recent Laboratory tests have shown that raf-wires of the type developed at the Factory show little or no aerodynamic disadvantage as compared with wires of stream-line section. **1922** *Encycl. Brit.* XXX. 34/2 The elliptical-section wires were called 'Rafwires', to distinguish them when they were standardized. **1933** *Flight* 4 May 412/2 External bracing is by RAFwire. **1933** *Jrnl. R. Aeronaut. Soc.* XXXVII. 788 The 'singing' of a rafwire when yawed in the wind at an angle greater than the stalling angle is an example of this type of oscillation.

rag (ræg), *sb.*[1] Also 4–7 **ragg(e.** [ME. *ragge*, possibly repr. an OE. **ragg* (cf. *raggiȝ* RAGGY *a.*[1]), ad. ON. *rǫgg* tuft or strip of fur (Norw. and Sw. *ragg* rough hair); the difference in sense between the ME. and ON. sbs. may have been developed through the adjs. *ragged* and *raggy*.]

I. 1. a. A small worthless fragment or shred of some woven material; *esp.* one of the irregular scraps into which a piece of such material is reduced by wear and tear.

c **1310** [see b]. *c* **1375** *Sc. Leg. Saints* xxiv. (*Alexis*) 411 His clathis in ragis he rafe. **1388** WYCLIF *Jer.* xxxviii. 11 Elde clothis, and elde ragges, that weren rotun. **1538** BALE *Thre Lawes* 677 Ragges, rotten bones and styckes. **1609** HOLLAND *Amm. Marcell.* 400 [A coat] over-rotten and run to ragges and tatters. **1667** MILTON *P.L.* III. 491 Cowles, Hoods and Habits..tost And flutterd into Raggs. **1735** B. MARTIN *Philos. Gram.* 151 Dogs, Cats, Rats, Mice &c...expire in half a Minute, and look as thin as a Rag. **1820** SHELLEY *Vis. Sea* 1 The rags of the sail Are flickering. **1848** DICKENS *Dombey* vi, There was a great heap of rags..lying on the floor. **1887** *Brit. Med. Jrnl.* I. 28/1 We believe that rags are frequently disinfected by the owners of paper mills.

b. Used in *pl.* to denote a ragged or tattered garment or clothes; freq. in phr. ***in rags.***

c **1310** *Pol. Songs* (Camden) 150 That er werede robes, nou wereth ragges. **1390** GOWER *Conf.* I. 100 In ragges, as sche was totore, He set hire on his hors tofore. **1500–20** DUNBAR *Poems* xxxix. 27 Honest ȝemen..Ar now arrayit in raggis. **1588** SHAKS. *L.L.L.* IV. i. 84 What, shalt thou exchange for ragges, roabes? **1671** MILTON *Samson* 415 The base degree to which I now am fall'n, These rags, this grinding. **1784** COWPER *Task* I. 568 The sportive wind blows wide Their fluttering rags, and shows a tawny skin. **1851** D. JERROLD *St. Giles* xiv. 137 Such mercy went far to encourage rags and tatters. **1874** RUSKIN *Fors Clav.* xliv. 171 Going in rags through the winter.

fig. *c* **1380** WYCLIF *Serm.* Sel. Wks. II. 226 Cristene men shulden þenke shame to cloþe hem above wiþ raggis, and foule þe worþi suyt of Crist. **1659** PEARSON *Creed* (1839) 262 To put on the rags of our infirmity before the robe of majesty and immortality. **1700** DRYDEN *Wife of Bath's T.* 457, I begin, In virtue cloathed, to cast the rags of sin. **1807** CRABBE *Par. Reg.* III. 936 My moral rags defile me every one. **1843** CARLYLE *Past & Pr.* II. xvii, The superannuated rags and unsound callosities of Formulas.

c. Used (esp. in negative phrases) to suggest the smallest scrap of cloth or clothing.

1590 SPENSER *F.Q.* II. x. 58 Without or robe or rag to hide his shame. *a* **1625** FLETCHER *Faithful Friends* IV. iv, I prize poor virtue with a rag Better than vice with both the Indies. **1782** MISS BURNEY *Cecilia* v. i, Won't leave him a rag to his back nor a penny in his pocket. *a* **1786** N. GREENE in Bancroft *Hist. U.S.* (1876) VI. lvii. 462 Not a rag of clothing has arrived to us this winter. **1873** *Routledge's Young Gentlm. Mag.* May 366/1 The 'week's wash' had disappeared. Every rag of it.

fig. **1663** BUTLER *Hud.* I. i. 562 He had First Matter seen undrest..Before one rag of form was on.

d. Similarly, the smallest scrap *of* sail.

1653 H. COGAN tr. *Pinto's Trav.* xiii. 40 We passed that night..without bearing so much as a rag of sail. **1804** *Naval Chron.* XI. 258 Steering after them with every rag of sail set. **1823** BYRON *Island* II. xxi, I've seen no rag of canvass on the sea.

e. In *sing.* without article, as a material.

1808 *Med. Jrnl.* XIX. 99 Some simple ointment spread on rag. **1825** J. NICHOLSON *Operat. Mechanic* 375 Compressing the fibres of rag together, for the purpose of making them cohere, and thereby giving tenacity to the paper.

f. *pl.* Personal clothing or garments of any kind. Also in *sing.*, a garment, esp. a dress or coat. Cf. *glad rags* s.v. GLAD *a.* 4 f. *colloq.* (orig. *U.S.*).

1855 *Knickerbocker* XLV. 502 Oh! the robe was of *moire antique*, (a very expensive 'rag'). **1883** 'MARK TWAIN' *Life on Mississippi* iii. 43, I stood up and shook my rags off and jumped into the river. **1903** *N. & Q.* Dec. 513/1 'Raggie' is of course diminutive or fond for 'rag', *i.e.* coat, tunic. I remember my uncle, writing to congratulate me on passing into the R.M. Academy, Woolwich, many years ago, asking me if I was 'going to sport the blue rag or the red one'—R.A. or R.E. **1906** E. DYSON *Fact'ry 'Ands* x. 126 In their secon' best baggin', they're sort iv subdood... Look at ther difference when they get inter ther rags. **1966** 'L. LANE' *ABZ of Scouse* II. 88 *Rags*, any form of clothing. **1974** H. L. FOSTER *Ribbin'* iv. 171 *Rags*, clothing.

g. ***(from) rags to riches***: used variously to describe a 'fairy-tale' rise from poverty to wealth; esp. as *attrib. phr.*

1947 R. DE TOLEDANO *Frontiers of Jazz* 148 Goodman was the first real rags-to-riches success in the swing-jazz field. **1953** *Gramophone* Dec. 256/2 The Irish flavour is readily apparent in *Begorrah* as sung by Ray Burns... This is great fun, and infinitely preferable to the more common-place *Rags to Riches* verso. **1954** M. EWER *Heart Untouched* ix. 156 Isn't this a Cinderella story—a rags to riches? **1959** *Times Lit. Suppl.* 13 Nov. 658/2 The story he has to tell is..a classic American rags-to-riches story with nothing lacking. **1965** 'H. CARMICHAEL' *Post Mortem* x. 120 One of those spectacular companies that came up from nowhere. You've heard of them—from rags to riches in five years. **1972** D. LEES *Zodiac* 34 It stands up as a rags to riches yarn. **1977** *Cornish Times* 19 Aug. 9/2 Last week's *Cornish Times* spelt out a success story with the rare theme of rags to riches by sheer hard labour.

2. *transf.* and *fig.* **a.** A fragment, scrap, bit, remnant; a torn or irregularly shaped piece.

c **1440** *York Myst.* xxx. 36 All to ragges schall ye rente hym and ryue hym. **1555** W. WATREMAN *Fardle of Facions* II. ix. 207 Then take thei the dead mannes heade, and pike the braine oute cleane, with all other moistures and ragges. **1611** COTGR., *Chaplis,..* the small peeces that flye from stones in the hewing; we call them rags. **1650** FULLER *Pisgah* I. ii. 6 Some proud Geographer will scarce stoop to take up so small a Ragge of land into his consideration. **1761** *Ann. Reg.* II. 7 Where meat is plentiful they boil the offal to rags. **1820** SHELLEY *Sensit. Pl.* III. 68 A murderer's stake, Where rags of loose flesh yet tremble on high. **1873** BLACK *Pr. Thule* i. 1 Volumes and flying rags of cloud.

b. of immaterial things.

a **1529** SKELTON *Replyc.* 1 A lytell ragge of rethorike, A lesse lumpe of logyke. **1579** E. K. *Ded. Spenser's Sheph. Cal.*, They patched vp the holes with peces and rags of other languages. **1624** DONNE *80 Serm.* ii. 12 First and last are but ragges of time. **1707** *Curiosities in Husb. & Gard.* 29 The Belief..is a Rag of the Peripatetick Philosophy. **1807–8** W. IRVING *Salmag.* (1827) 170 A fierce fellow..tearing the music to rags. **1893** *Times* 22 Apr., They have no rag of evidence to uphold them. **1922** E. SITWELL *Façade* 14 Limp in bright crackling rags of laughter. **1924** R. CAMPBELL *Flaming Terrapin* iii. 45 Their spirits shed their gross Rags of despair. **1963** S. CLOETE (*title*) Rags of glory.

c. of money. ? Hence in *obs. Cant*, a farthing.

1590 SHAKS. *Com. Err.* IV. iv. 89 Monie by me? Heart and good will you might [send], But..not a ragge of Monie. **1613** BEAUM. & FL. *Captain* IV. ii, *Jac.* 'Twere good she had a little foolish mony... *Host.* Not a rag, Not a Deniere. *a* **1700** B. E. *Dict. Cant. Crew, Rag*, a Farthing. **1811** *Lexicon Balatronicum*, s.v. *Rag*,.. Money in general. The cove has no rag; the fellow has no money. **1846** *Swell's Night Guide* 14 The pleasure-seeker may gain admission, if his appearance proclaim that he is in possession of the *rag*—the *tin* to defray the unavoidable demands upon his purse.

d. A familiar name applied to the Army and Navy Club in London. In full ***the Rag and Famish*** (see quot. 1908[1]). *slang.*

1858 TROLLOPE *Three Clerks* II. i. 5 He delighted in the Rag and Famish, and there spent the most of his time. **1908** NEVILL & JERNINGHAM *Piccadilly to Pall Mall* vi. 235 The familiar name of the 'Rag', by which it is generally known, was invented by Captain William Duff, of the 23rd Fusiliers... Coming in to supper late one night, the refreshment obtainable appeared so meagre that he nicknamed the club the 'Rag and Famish'. **1908** 'ONE OF OLD BRIGADE' *London in Sixties* xvii. 224 These touts and store-keepers and bonnet-shop keepers will make the Rag a den of thieves, by Gad. **1941** E. NASH *I liked Life I Lived* iv. 33 Cairnes, who was a most hospitable man, invited me to dine with him once a week at the Rag, while the sales of the book were in full swing... No member of the Army and Navy Club was aware that Cairnes had written the book. **1974** R. McDOUALL *Clubland Cooking* 12 Unlike the clubs on the south side of Pall Mall.. the Junior Carlton and the Rag owned their freeholds.

e. Phr. *to knock all to rags*: to knock senseless. *U.S.*

1889 'MARK TWAIN' *Connecticut Yankee* xxxiii. 432 The blow came crashing down and knocked him all to rags.

3. a. Applied contemptuously to things, e.g. a torn or scanty garment, a flag, handkerchief, theatre-curtain, newspaper, paper-money, etc.; also, a napkin worn during menstruation, a sanitary towel; esp. in phr. *to have the rag(s) on.*

1549 LATIMER *5th Serm. bef. Edw. VI* (Arb.) 154 Another poore womanne was hanged for stealynge a fewe ragges of a hedg. *a* **1734** NORTH *Exam.* II. v. §14 (1740) 323 Would any one expect in Print, upon tolerable Paper, and a clear Character, such Malice and Knavery as lies here, scarce fit for Midnight Grubstreet Rags. **1752** FIELDING *Amelia* II. iv, Young gentlemen of the order of the rag. **1782** J. TRUMBULL *M'Fingal* IV. 97 O'er heaps of rags, he waves his wand, All turn to gold at his command. **1811** *Lexicon Balatronicum*, s.v. *Rag*, bank notes. **1816** *Deb. Congress U.S.* 29 Jan. (1854) 775, I say cash, sir, for we, there, have nothing of that circulating medium which the gentleman from Virginia.. denominates rags. **1817** PAULDING *Letters from South* II. 158 What would be an independence, were it not for the rags in circulation. **1832** *Blackw. Mag.* Jan. 117/1 Under their tri-color—the rascally rag. **1846** *Swell's Night Guide* 129/1, *Rag*, money—I've no rag; meaning, I've no notes. **1859** J. W. COLE *Life & Times C. Kean* I. i. 8 Our old friends of the Dublin gallery, who, in days of yore, never failed to cry, 'Up with the rag!' even before the act-drop, so classically designated, had time to reach the ground. **1885** J. K. JEROME *On the Stage* 76 The 'rag' went up unexpectedly, and discovered the following scene. **1889** *Spectator* 23 Nov. 712/1 Every rubbishy rag now contains the 'news'. **1906** E. DYSON *Fact'ry 'Ands* xvii. 233 Ther revolvin' arm [of a machine] was bent out, 'n' it got home a left lead 'n' er right cross, 'n' ther rag went in from ther Pelican's corner. **1920** J. FERGUSON *Northern Numbers* 101 The lights are lowered and the 'rag' divides. **1929** A. CONAN DOYLE *Maracot Deep* 200 Has your rag commissioned you to obtain an interview? **1948** *Amer. Speech* XXIII. 249/2 *Riding the rag*, menstruating. **1955** D. W. MAURER in *Publ. Amer. Dial. Soc.* xxiv. 115 That working stiff had over two C's in rag on him. **1961** PARTRIDGE *Dict. Slang* Suppl. 1242/2 *Rags (on), have the*, to be having one's period. **1970** G. GREER *Female Eunuch* 51 Male disgust [for menstruation] expressed in terms like *having the rags on.* **1974** *National Skat & Sheepshead Q.* Mar./Apr. 7 The bills [*sc.* paper money] wear out down here very fast due to the humidity. They all become 'rags' in a short period. **1977** J. I. M. STEWART *Madonna of Astrolabe* i. 27 A fugitive rag put out by one of our junior members. **1978** *Maledicta* II. 50 There were several references to menstruous conditions or activities, found equally commonly in both male and female rest rooms ('Sue Ellen's on the rag' [etc.]).

b. Similarly applied to persons.

1566 DRANT *Horace, Sat.* ii. 8 The..rabblement Of ragges and raskalls all Be pensive. **1598** SHAKS. *Merry W.* IV. ii. 194 You Witch, you Ragge, you Baggage. **1649** G. DANIEL *Trinarch., Rich. II*, lxxvii, For not the lowest Ragge of Human race, But in a change will seeke to mend his place. **1875** RUSKIN *Fors Clav.* lv, That rubbishy rag of a girl. **1882** STEVENSON *New Arab. Nts.* (1884) 247 The poet was a rag of a man.

c. Colloq. phrases. (*a*) Miscellaneous, as *to drop the rag* (U.S.): to give the signal, to give notice; *to take the rag off* (*the bush* or *hedge*) (chiefly U.S.): to excel, to surpass everything or everyone; to take the palm. Also *to chew the rag*: see CHEW *v.* 3 g. (*b*) Expressing anger, as *to get one's rag out* and varr.: to become or make angry; *to lose one's rag*: to lose one's temper; *on the rag* (U.S.): angry, irritable.

1810 *Norfolk* (Va.) *Gaz.* 19 Sept. 2/3 This 'takes the rag off the bush' so completely, that we suppose we shall hear no more..about the Chesapeake business. **1837** *Davy Crockett's Almanack Wild Sports of West* I. iii. 40, I can take the rag off—frighten the old folks—astonish the natives—and beat the Dutch all to smash. **1868** *Accrington Times* 16 May 5/3 These three elegant flags ull teck th' rag off th' edge, un ull be mich admir'd bi all them ut's i' th' love o' fine arts. **1880** 'MARK TWAIN' *Tramp Abroad* xx. 194 I've got to stay here, till the old man drops the rag and gives the word,——yes, *sir*, right here in this——country I've got to linger till the old man says *Come!* **1897** *Halifax Courier* 12 June, He's getten his rag drawn. **1901** W. N. HARBEN *Westerfelt* 3 That gal certainly takes the rag off'n the bush. **1902** —— *Abner Daniel* 264 You are a jim-dandy, young man... That's all there is about it. You take the rag off the bush. **1914** D. H. LAWRENCE *Prussian Officer* 185 An' that got your rag out, did it? **1927** W. E. COLLINSON *Contemp. Eng.* 116 Anger is expressed by such phrases as..he got shirty or hairy, he got his rag out, [etc.]. **1938** G. GREENE *Brighton Rock* VII. vii. 329 'I've told you before how I won't stand...' 'You needn't get your rag out,' the Boy said. **1959** I. & P. OPIE *Lore & Lang. Schoolch.* x. 178 They taunt the person [who is easily provoked]:..'Don't lose your bait' ('rag', 'rise', 'wool'). **1960** L. COOPER *Accomplices* I. vi. 60 Roger was definitely shirty about that... He really got his rag out. **1969** *Current Slang* (Univ. S. Dakota) I-II. 65 *On the rag*, in a bad mood.—College males, Arizona. **1975** HILL & THOMAS *Give Little Whistle* x. 95 Allison lost his rag with me over two goals by Leicester's Mike Stringfellow, both of which he considered were offside. **1977** *Rolling Stone* 16 June 31/1 *Time* has Joan Baez on the rag.

†**4.** An alleged name for a 'company' of colts. (From RAGGED *a.* 1.) *Obs. rare.*

c **1470** *Hors, Shepe & G.*, etc. (Caxton 1479, Roxb. repr.) 31 A Stode of mares, a Ragg of coltes. **1486** *Bk. St. Albans* F vj, A Ragg of coltis or a Rake.

5. A sharp or jagged projection. *rare.*

1664 EVELYN *Kal. Hort.* (1720) 190 Cut off slanting above the Bud, with a very sharp knife, leaving no Rags. **1683** MOXON *Mech. Exerc., Printing* xvii. ¶2 He Rubs every side of them on the Stone..to take off the small Rags that may happen on the Shanck of the Letter. *Ibid.* 388 When Letter Cast has a Bur on any of its edges, that Bur is called a Rag. **1872** *Routledge's Ev. Boy's Ann.* 536/1 File off the rags left by the saw.

6. a. *pl.* A kind of moss (*muscus pulmonarius*).

1758 *Phil. Trans.* L. 683 The people in Herefordshire, where this moss is called rags, dye their stockings of a brown colour with it.

b. The fibrous pithy part of an orange, lemon, or other citrus fruit.

1895 *U.S. Dept. Agric. Yearbk. 1894* 196 The fruit resulting is usually of poor quality, inclined to be large and rough, with a thick rind and abundant rag.

7. Short for RAGWORM.

1881 *St. James's Budget* Aug. 12/1 Lastly, there are the two species of mud-worms, the 'lug' and the 'rag', equally nasty to look at.

II. *attrib.* and *Comb.*

8. General combs. **a.** attributive, 'pertaining to, containing, dealing in or with, rags', as *rag-basket, machinery, market, tank*; 'consisting, or made, of rags', as *rag-baby, -ball, -carpet, -carpeting, doll, -mop, -paper, -puppet, -rug, -torch, -wick.* Also *rag-carpeted, -made* adjs.

1809 *Deb. Congress U.S.* 20 Jan. (1853) 1165 If they insist upon dressing up, in their own ways, their *rag-babies,..it is not for me to interfere. **1900** J. DE F. SHELTON *Salt-Box House* xvii. 143 Dolls were almost as mythical as fairies, but a 'rag-baby' was loved. **1837** *Southern Lit. Messenger* III. 333 There was a snug little bed room..and a comfortable good-sized one for Charlotte, with a neat *rag carpet on it. **1904** M. E. WALLER *Wood-Carver of 'Lympus* 72, I have begged Aunt Lize to take up the rag-carpet. **1845** C. M. KIRKLAND *Western Clearings* 185, I led the young gentleman through the shop into the *rag-carpeted sitting-room. **1813** *Niles' Weekly Reg.* III. 329/1, 24 yards *rag carpeting. **1853** J. RUSKIN *Let.* 17 Nov. in *Wks.* (1904) XII. p. xxxiv, She thought me so wise that anybody might make an idol of me ..but when she got to talk to me, I turned out only a **rag doll* after all. **1883** 'ANNIE THOMAS' *Mod. Housewife* 116, I couldn't play with my rag doll here. **1972** M. WOODHOUSE *Mama Doll* xiii. 194 She slumped like a rag doll. **1853** URE *Dict. Arts* (ed. 4) II. 345 Improved *rag machinery. **1885** *Pall Mall G.* 15 May 2/1 The finest *rag-made paper. *c* **1645** HOWELL *Lett.* (1655) I. I. vii. 11 The Dog and *Rag Market is hard by. **1831** *For. Q. Rev.* VIII. 380 *Rag-paper..was also invented in Germany some hundred and fifty years before. **1840** CARLYLE *Heroes* (1858) 308 Those poor bits of rag-paper with black ink on them;—from the Daily Newspaper to the sacred Hebrew Book. **1884** G. MEREDITH *Diana* xxii, How long do you keep me in this *rag-puppet's state of suspension? **1923** E. SITWELL *Bucolic Comedies* 42 The witch's *rag-rug takes its flight. **1937** [see KEWPIE]. **1969** M. HARRIS *Kind of Magic* 30 By the fire stretched a lovely rag rug. **1973** J. THOMSON *Death Cap* xiii. 177 Finch was reminded of his grandmother's bedroom... There had been the same kind of rag rug on the floor; the same marble-topped wash-hand stand. **1894** KIPLING in *To-day* 6 Jan. 5/1 And the doolie-bearers lit the noisome, dripping *rag-torches. *a* **1918** G. STUART *40 Yrs. on Frontier* (1925) I. 31 A tin lamp holding about a quart of lard with a *rag wick in its spout which, when lighted, would cast a strong light for several yards.

b. Objective or objective genitive, as *rag-boiler, -collector, -cutter, -dealer, -gatherer, -grinder, -picker, -raker, -seller, -sifter, -sorter, -stitcher, -washer*; *rag-cleansing, cutting, -grinding, -picking, -sorting, weaving.*

Many of the combs. with agent-nouns (*rag-boiler*, etc.) are applied to mechanical contrivances.

1884 KNIGHT *Dict. Mech.* Suppl. 735/2 The *rag-boiler.. is generally rotative, which gives a continual agitation to the contents. **1873** *Pract. Mag.* I. 147 Sanitary arrangement adopted in *rag cleansing. **1860** *Chambers' Jrnl.* 55/1 The 800 *rag-collecters who come under the notice of the police. **1865** *Sat. Rev.* 21 Jan. 74/2 His fame would have been by this time food for the rag-collectors. **1860** TOMLINSON *Usef. Arts* Ser. I, Paper ii, Another set of women, and sometimes children, called *rag-cutters. **1851** MAYHEW *Lond. Lab.* II. 106/1 My informant, the *rag dealer. **1884** *Cassell's Fam. Mag.* Feb. 156/2 In New York..there are more than 800 rag-dealers. **1704** *Visits from Shades* III. 21 *Rag-gatherers, Cynderwomen, and Oyster Wenches wou'd disclaim her Acquaintance. **1851** MAYHEW *Lond. Labour* II. 139/1 The bone-pickers and rag-gatherers are all early risers. **1831** CARLYLE *Sart. Res.* I. viii. 55, I, the dust-making, patent *Rag-grinder, get new material to grind down. **1860** *Chambers' Jrnl.* XIV. 53/1 Rags and *Ragpickers in France. **1884** *Harper's Mag.* Mar. 648/2, 30,000 rag pickers in Paris thrown out of employment. **1931** 'D. STIFF' *Milk & Honey Route* ix. 101 It is not surprising to find the moper turning to *rag-picking if the notion comes to him to earn a living. **1966** *National Observer* (U.S.) 5 Dec. 15/3 There are ways to hold rag-picking down. One can, for example, specialize in $1 bills. **1614** B. JONSON *Barth. Fair* I. i, None but..one of these *rag-rakers in dunghills..would have been up when thou wert gone abroad. **1700** T. BROWN *Amusem. Ser. Com.* 37, I..was mortally frighted..by the Impudent *Ragsellers. **1887** *British Med. Jrnl.* 12 Feb. 343/1 *Rag-sorters' Disease. **1853** HICKIE tr. *Aristoph.* (1872) II. 574 You gossip-gleaner, and drawer of beggarly characters, and *rag-stitcher.

c. Attrib. phrases, as *rag-and-bone gatherer, -man, merchant, -picker*; *shop, warehouse*; *rag-and-bottle man, merchant, -shop, warehouse*; *rag-and-tatter kind.*

1901 B. S. ROWNTREE *Poverty* iii. 35 *Rag and bone gatherer. Married. One room. One child. **1904** E. NESBIT *Phoenix & Carpet* xii. 236 An insane millionaire who amused himself by playing at being a *rag-and-bone man. **1960** 'H. CARMICHAEL' *Seeds of Hate* xix. 157 Someone had sold them to a rag-and-bone man. **1963** *Times* 6 Mar. 9/3 Four Soviet *rag and bone merchants have been sentenced to death in Azerbaijan for heading a gang which robbed the state of hundreds of thousands of roubles. **1851** MAYHEW *Lond. Labour* II. 139 The state of the shoes of the *rag and bone picker is a very important matter to him. **1870** LOWELL *Study Wind.* 99 The somewhat greasy heap of the literary rag-and-bone-picker is turned to gold by time. **1895** C. M. YONGE *Long Vacation* xix. 188 Transforming the draperies from the aspect of a *rag-and-bone shop to a wonderful quaint and pretty fairy bower. **1939** W. B. YEATS *Last Poems* 31 In the foul rag and bone shop of the heart. **1848** MRS. GASKELL *Mary Barton* I. v. 74 Public-houses, pawn-brokers' shops, *rag and bone warehouses, and dirty provision shops. **1904** E. NESBIT *Phœnix & Carpet* xii. 229 It's the *rag-and-bottle man's day to-morrow... He will take it away. *a* **1902** S. BUTLER *Way of All Flesh* (1903) lv. 254 A *rag and bottle merchant in..the last stage of dropsy. **1851** MAYHEW *Lond. Labour* II. 139 Anything that is saleable at the *rag-and-bottle or marine store shop. **1852** DICKENS *Bleak Ho.* (1853) v. 35 A shop, over which was written, *Krook, *Rag and Bottle Warehouse.* **1886** STEVENSON *Kidnapped* 267 A fine, hang-dog, *rag-and-tatter..kind of a look.

9. Special combs.: **rag-book**, a book for children of which the pages are made of untearable cloth; **rag-box**, (*a*) a box in which rags are contained; (*b*) *slang*, the mouth; **rag-bush**, a bush on which rags are fixed as a superstitious observance; **rag-carrier** (*nonce-wd.*), a contemptuous term for a valet or an ensign; **rag-castle** (*nonce-wd.*), a haunt of beggars; **rag-chawing, -chewing** *vbl. sbs.*, protracted discussion or argument (cf. *to chew the rag* s.v. CHEW *v.* 3 g); also *attrib.*; **rag content**, the proportion of rag in paper; freq. *attrib.*; **rag-dust** (see quot.); **rag end**, the extreme and untidy end of something; cf. FAG-END 2; **rag engine**, a machine for reducing rags to pulp in paper-making (hence *rag engineer*); †**rag-footed** *a.*, ? badly shod (in quot. *fig.*); **rag frame** *Mining* (see quot. 1964); **rag-front**, in a carnival or circus: a façade or banner made of painted canvas; **rag-head** *N. Amer. slang*, one who wears a turban or cloth about the hair; **rag-house**, a building in which rags are stored or prepared for paper-making; **rag-knife**, one of the knives in a rag-engine; **rag-lamp** *U.S.*, a lamp in which a rag serves as a wick; †**rag-manners**, low, ill-bred behaviour (hence *rag-mannered*); **rag-merchant**, a dealer in rags; also (in contempt) a banker or draper; **rag-money** (contemptuously), paper-money; **rag-offering**, a rag or rags suspended or fixed at some spot (esp. a well or standing stone) as an offering for the cure of disease, etc.; **rag running**, whippet-racing; **ragsackman** *nonce-wd.*, a ragman bearing a sack; **rag-shop**, a shop for rags and old clothes; also *fig.*; **rag-store** *U.S.* = *rag-shop*; **ragtop** *U.S. slang*, a convertible car with a soft hood (see also quot. 1971); also *attrib.*; **rag trade**, trade in rags; also *slang* (see quots.); now usu. applied to the manufacture and sale of women's garments; freq. in humorous or ironical use; and *attrib.*; **rag-tree** (cf. *rag-bush* above); **rag turnsole**, turnsole dye which is kept in linen rags impregnated with it; **rag-well** (see quots., and cf. *rag-bush, -tree*); **rag-woman**, a woman who gathers or deals in rags (cf. RAG-MAN); **rag-wool**, wool obtained by tearing rags to pieces. Also RAG-BAG, -BOLT, -FAIR, -MAN[1].

1905 *Athenæum* 16 Dec. 833/1 The improvements recently made in the productions called *rag-books are strikingly exemplified in *Dog Toby*. **1974** P. DICKINSON *Poison Oracle* iv. 111 He had packed..rag books, fruit, favourite toys. **1801** D. WORDSWORTH *Jrnl.* 12 Nov. (1941) I. 79, I put the *rag-boxes into order. **1890** KIPLING in *Scots Observer* 28 June 149/1 Now all you recruities what's drafted to-day, You shut up your rag-box an' 'ark to my lay. **1882** C. ELTON *Orig. Eng. Hist.* 285 There is usually a '*rag-bush' by the well on which bits of linen or worsted are tied as a gift to the spirit of the waters. **1893** E. S. HARTLAND in *Folk-Lore* IV. 453 Pin-wells and Rag-bushes are found all over the British Isles. *a* **1754** FIELDING *New way to keep a Wife at Home* I. iii, I must tug along the empty portmanteau of this shabby, no-pay ensign..What can a man expect who is but the *rag-carrier of a rag-carrier? **1828** CARLYLE *Misc.* (1857) I. 215 A dream, and the very *Ragcastle of 'Poosie-Nansie'. **1885** *Santa Fé Weekly New Mexican* 1 Oct. 1/3 After a few minutes *rag-chawing a verdict of 'came to his death from unknown causes', is promptly rendered. **1904** 'H. McHUGH' *I'm from Missouri* v. 66 The news of the proposed joint debate spread like wildfire, and it soon became patent that whoever won the rag-chewing contest would also win the election. **1937** G. FRANKAU *More of Us* xii. 130 Great work Lord Bubbles put in presently Over their teas and pastries and rag-chewing. **1976** PERKOWSKI & STRAL *Joy of CB* viii.

86 In the evening you can set up your rig at home for extended rag-chewing sessions. **1930** *Official Gaz.* (U.S. Patent Office) 7 Oct. 25/1 *Rag Content Paper Manufacturers. **1957** J. B. CALKIN *Witham's Mod. Pulp & Paper Making* (ed. 3) ii. 20 Rag papers cover a considerable spread of products from 100 per cent rag to the so-called 'rag content' papers which are made from various percentages of wood and rag fibers. **1967** KARCH & BUBER *Offset Processes* xi. 479 The finer, longer-lasting paper, made from cotton and cloth clippings, is called 'rag content', or lately, 'cotton content' paper... Rag content is usually 25 percent, 50 percent, 75 percent, or 100 percent. **1976** *Cincinnati Enquirer* 16 Sept. A-19/3 The documents and letters are as legible as the handwriting of their authors. The high rag content of the paper has preserved them. **1864** WEBSTER, **Rag-dust*, fine particles of rags when torn thoroughly to pieces, used in making *papier-maché*. **1917** E. POUND *Lustra* 192 And the booths Were scattered align, the *rag ends of the fair. **1853** URE *Dict. Arts* (ed. 4) II. 346 The improvement in paper making, for which T.W.W... obtained a patent in 1842, relate [*sic*] to the *rag engine. **1885** *Census Instruct.*, *Rag engineer. **1606** BIRNIE *Kirk-Buriall* (1833) 33 Some *rag-footed resons that we must refute. **1904** *Eng. Dial. Dict.*, *Rag frame. **1920** *Conquest* Nov. 17/1 The stream is dammed and the sludge or slime settles, and is allowed to flow through launders which feed automatically-tilting tables of the most ingenious structure. .. These tables are called rag frames. **1964** A. NELSON *Dict. Mining* 358 *Rag frame*, a broad, slightly inclined wooden frame for the rough concentration of slimes. **1926** *Variety* 29 Dec. 7/4 The outdoor show game with its '*rag front', 'silver men', [etc.]. **1927** K. NICHOLSON *Barker* 150 *Rag front*, painted canvas banners. **1921** *Dialect Notes* V. 111 **Raghead*, a Hindu; any Asiatic. From the turbanned Asiatics who are common on the campus [of the University of California]. **1970** C. MAJOR *Dict. Afro-Amer. Slang* 96 *Raghead*, black male who wears a scarf tied around his head to protect an expensive hairdo. **1975** *Canadian Mag.* 8 Mar. 6/1 East Indians are called 'rag-heads' if they continue to wear the traditional turban of the Sikh religion. **1860** TOMLINSON *Useful Arts* Ser. I. Paper ii, The rags..are conveyed in baskets to the *rag-house. **1889** 'MARK TWAIN' *Connecticut Yankee* xlii. 531 He had re-instituted the ancient *rag-lamp. **1893** —— in *Cosmopolitan* Nov. 59/2 The house was shut up tight and the rag lamps lighted. **1731** *Gentl. Mag.* I. 350 Why charge ye *Rag-manners thus upon the clergy? **1698** COLLIER *Immor. Stage* v. §3. 220 This Young Lady swears, talks smut, and is..just as *rag-manner'd as Mary the Buxsome. **1690** *Lond. Gaz.* No. 2597/4 At the same Prices they have hitherto Paid the *Rag-Merchants. **1821** COBBETT *Rur. Rides* (1885) 17 The country rag-merchants have now very little to do. They have no discounts. What they have out, they owe; it is so much debt. **1838** DICKENS *O. Twist* xxvi, The shoe-vamper and the rag-merchant display their goods. **1862** F. G. TRAFFORD (Mrs. J. Riddell) *Too Much Alone* 124 (Hoppe) Rag-merchant,..the above expression does not refer to a marine-store dealer, but simply to a dealer in Manchester goods, who is frequently thus designated in the City. **1878** *N. Amer. Rev.* CXXVI. 166 The complete disuse and actual repulsion of silver by *rag-money. **1893** *Archæol. Æliana* XVI. 463 Squibs and skits regarding rag-money were issued. **1777** BRAND *Pop. Antiq.* 85 These *Rag-offerings are the Reliques of the then prevailing popular Superstition. **1892** *Folk-Lore* III. 89 The geographical distribution of rag-offerings coincides with the existence of monoliths and dolmens. **1927** *Daily Express* 25 May 12 A little more foresight and push..might have made '*rag running' a very popular entertainment. **1922** JOYCE *Ulysses* 429 A sackshouldered ragman bars his path. He steps left, *rag-sackman left. **1829** P. EGAN *Boxiana* 2nd Ser. II. 643 'It's the Bank of Ireland,' said an Irish swell, 'to a *rag shop.' **1851–61** MAYHEW *Lond. Labour* III. 207 (Hoppe) Writing a squib for a ragshop. **1865** E. C. CLAYTON *Cruel Fortune* I. 143 A ragshop..occupied the basement story. **1894** G. B. SHAW *Let.* 23 Apr. (1965) I. 427 You have a perfect rag shop of old ideas in your head. **1903** —— *Man & Superman* p. xiii, His profligacy and his dare-devil airs have gone the way of his sword and mandoline into the rag shop of anachronisms and superstitions. **1869** 'MARK TWAIN' *Innoc. Abroad* xvi. 157 Filthy dens on first floors, with *rag stores in them (the heaviest business in the Faubourg is the chiffonier's). **1882** Rag store [see *junk store* s.v. JUNK *sb.*[2] 5]. **1955** *Sun* (Baltimore) 27 Aug. B11/1 Every American manufacturer with a '*ragtop' in his line will be represented. **1971** M. TAK *Truck Talk* 127 *Rag top*, 1. a low-sided trailer with metal bows over the top to support a tarpaulin... 2. an open top van with a tarpaulin covering over the top. **1974** D. WESTHEIMER *Olmec Head* xvii. 235 Get a ragtop trailer. That's one with a fabric cover instead of a solid top. **1976** *Springfield* (Mass.) *Daily News* 22 Apr. 4/3 (*caption*) The last U.S. built convertible, a Cadillac Eldorado, rolls along the assembly at the General Motors' plant in Detroit Wednesday. It ended an era for ragtops that began 74 years ago. **1979** T. GIFFORD *Hollywood Gothic* (1980) ix. 100 Eddie's ragtop had a small tear that let the rain draw a bead on the back of the seat. **1843** MARRYAT *M. Violet* xxvii, There is in Galveston a new invented trade, called 'the *rag-trade'..I refer to the purchasing of false bank-notes, which are..palmed upon any stranger suspected of having money. **1875** *Pract. Mag.* V. 221 Parliamentary Reports on the Rag Trade of Foreign Countries. **1890** BARRÈRE & LELAND *Dict. Slang* (1897), *Rag trade*,..the tailoring business. Also the mantle-making trade. **1907** *Daily Chron.* 31 Dec. 8/4 They do an enormous business with the 'rag trade'—that is to say, the wholesale drapers, silk mercers, hosiers, and so on. **1938** *Times Lit. Suppl.* 11 June 405/2 The few years which she spent as fashion-goods buyer in what is known to its members as 'the rag trade'. **1957** J. COATES *Ship of Glass* 241, I know that line. It's going to be fashionable... Forgive the digression but I'm in the rag trade. **1967** *Listener* 2 Feb. 168/3 These delicate and puzzling effects..were seized upon with glee by rag-trade designers and window dressers. **1975** R. BUTLER *Where All Girls are Sweeter* i. 2 I'd sold her to a man in the rag-trade. **1880** M. J. WALHOUSE in *Jrnl. Anthrop. Inst.* IX. 106 The Christmas Trees..are but changed survivals of the Pagan *rag-trees. **1777** BRAND *Pop. Antiq.* 85 A Well in the road to Benton..called The *Rag Well. **1855** ROBINSON *Whitby Gloss.*, *Ragwells*, certain springs in the neighbourhood, held sacred in former days for curing diseases... Rags from the garments of those who recovered, were torn off and hung up as offerings to the patron saint of the well. **1672** WYCHERLEY *Love in a Wood* v. ii, The *rag-women, and cinder-women, have better luck than I. **1723** *Lond. Gaz.* No. 6175/5 Ellen Weeb,..Rag-Woman.

rag (ræg), *sb.*[2] Also 3 **ragghe**, 5–8 **ragge**, 9 **ragg.** [Of obscure etym.; original connexion with prec. seems unlikely, but the idea of 'ragged' stone would naturally suggest itself in later use.]

1. A piece (mass or bed) of hard, coarse or rough stone (cf. 2). *Obs.* exc. *dial.* (see quot. 1877).

1278 *Bursar's Acc. Merton Coll.* (Parker *Dict. Archit.*), Pro ij magnis lapidibus qui vocantur ragghes. **1375–6** *Abingdon Abb. Acc.* (1892) 29 Pro scapulacione xxxij pedes de ragis ij.*s.* viij.*d.* **1601** HOLLAND *Pliny* II. 467 Otherwhiles they meet with rocks of flint and rags, as wel in vndermining forward, as in sinking pits downeright. **1609** —— *Amm. Marcell.* XXXI. x. 417 Taking up their standing upon the craggie rockes and ragges round about. **1769** *De Foe's Tour Gt. Brit.* I. 158 A Kind of Paving Stone, called Kentish-rags. **1778** *Eng. Gazetteer* (ed. 2) s.v. *Nutfield*, A metalline kind of substance (that looks like cast-iron, and is called ragges) much esteemed hereabouts for paving. **1877** *N.W. Linc. Gloss.*, *Rag*, a whetstone.

b. A large coarse roofing-slate.

1825 J. NICHOLSON *Operat. Mechanic* 622 Patent slate.. was originally made from Welsh rags. **1842** GWILT *Archit.* 501 Welsh rags are next in goodness [to Westmorland slates]. **1865** J. T. F. TURNER *Slate Quarries* 15 A large, rough kind, of varying dimensions, having one side uncut. These are termed 'rags', from their ragged appearance.

2. The name given in various parts of England to certain kinds of stone, differing greatly in structure, but chiefly of a hard coarse texture, and breaking up in flat pieces several inches thick.

The best-known varieties are CORAL-RAG, *Kentish rag* (see KENTISH), and *Rowley rag*, a basaltic rock from the Rowley Hills in Staffordshire. With quot. 1751 cf. quot. 1877 in 1, and quot. 1812 under RAGSTONE 1.

c **1420** *Pallad. on Husb.* I. 318 First thy grount assay. If hit be ragge or roche, on hit thow foote In depth a foote or too. **1606** HOLLAND *Sueton.* 230 He laid foundations of piles.. and hewed rocks of most hard flint and rag. **1647** SANDERSON *Serm.* (1681) II. xv. 218 A little Diamond may be more worth than a whole Quarry of Ragge. **1681** *Phil. Collect.* XII. 90 Made of one of the most common sort of Stone, *viz.* of a course Rag, or Milstone-grit. **1751** J. BARTRAM *Observ. Trav. Pennsylv.* etc. 30 A steep hill side, full of excellent flat whet-stones of all sizes... I brought one home..it is as fine as the English rag, but of a blackish colour. **1837** *Civil Eng. & Arch. Jrnl.* I. 72/1 At a depth varying from 5 to 7 feet from the surface, is the first bed of stone called rag; this is a coarse tough stone, rising in large layers from 6 to 9 inches thick. **1847** TENNYSON *Princ.* III. 344 Hornblende, rag and trap and tuff.

rag (ræg), *sb.*[3] *University slang.* [f. RAG *v.*[2]] An act of ragging; *esp.* an extensive display of noisy disorderly conduct, carried on in defiance of authority or discipline. Now usu. a programme of satirical revues, frivolous stunts, etc., organized by students to raise money for charities. Also *attrib.*

Known in Oxford for some years before date of first quot.

1864 H. SIDGWICK in A. & E. M. Sidgwick *Henry Sidgwick* (1906) ii. 111 They enjoy beer, tobacco and students' 'rags'. **1885** *Punch* 5 Dec. 273/1 We had a good rag when he was away. **1892** *Isis* No. 13. 88/2 The College is preparing for a good old rag to-night. **1894** WILKINS & VIVIAN *Green bay-tree* I. 275 It was the usual senseless 'rag' in which Pimlico and his friends were wont to indulge at their convivial gatherings. **1905** *Westm. Gaz.* 25 Apr. 3/3 It [*sc.* Sheridan's 'Critic'] has been left alone of late except for an occasional 'rag' performance at a charity matinée. **1924** *Glasgow Herald* 26 Feb. 9/7 Liberals played up skilfully in their interrogative zest, and the P.M.G...found the 'rag' more embarrassing than any miners' indiscipline. **1930** J. BUCHAN *Castle Gay* iv. 60, I do not wish to have my name associated with an undergraduate—'rag', I think is the word. **1946** L. P. HARTLEY *Sixth Heaven* iii. 76 He organised one or two rags..of the more painful kind. **1958** *Oxford Mail* 15 Feb. 1/1 A 1902 James and Browne vintage car removed from the Imperial College, South Kensington, London, by students of Southampton University for their 'rag' day. **1974** *Times* 4 Nov. 14/6 The university's Rag Week..[with] the 24-hour piano-playing marathon..and the joke kidnapping of the president of the athletic union.

†**rag**, *sb.*[4] *Obs. rare.* In 8 **ragg.** (See quot.)

Perh. a chain-pump, worked by a *rag-wheel*, sometimes called a 'rag-and-chain pump'.

1747 HOOSON *Miner's Dict.* Q ij, Those common Pumps used in the Mines, such as Raggs, Churns, Sweaps, Forces, for drawing of Water, these are so well known to every one that it is..needless to describe them.

rag (ræg), *sb.*[5] orig. *U.S.* [Of obscure origin: perh. f. RAGGED *a.*[1] 3; see RAGTIME.] **1.** A dance or ball; esp. a variety of dance performed to ragtime music. ? *Obs.*

1896 *Dialect Notes* I. 423 *Rag*, dance, ball. 'We can go to *rags*.' **1899** *Musical Rec.* (Boston) 1 Apr. 158/1 The negroes call their clog-dancing, 'ragging', and the dance, a 'rag'. **1914** 'HIGH JINKS, JR.' *Choice Slang* 17 *Rag*, one of the newer gyrations now included under the category of dancing. **1923** *Dialect Notes* V. 218 *Rag*,..dance.

2. A musical composition written in ragtime, a ragtime tune.

1897 W. H. KRELL (*song-title*) The Mississippi rag two-step: the first rag-time two-step ever written. **1897** T. TURPIN (*song-title*) Harlem rag: two step. **1916** *Variety* 25 Aug. 8 Ash..is seen daily on the streets playing rag dance numbers. **1922** T. S. ELIOT *Waste Land* ii. 21 But O O O O that Shakespeherian Rag—It's so elegant So intelligent. **1947** G. SKLAR *Two Worlds J. Truro* iii. 24 They listened to rags and stomps, to fox trots and marches. **1957** G. LASCELLES in S. Traill *Concerning Jazz* 77 Few of the original rags were written, and those which were, had often no bass part added beyond the conventional harmonies. **1977** *New Yorker* 19 Sept. 96/2 She would play some Menotti, Barber, and Gershwin, a piece by Paul Tufts, a Seattle composer, and some Scott Joplin rags.

3. *attrib.* and *Comb.* in sense 'ragtime', as ***rag music, musician, rhythm; rag-flavoured*** adj.

1959 'F. NEWTON' *Jazz Scene* vi. 103 Rag-flavoured numbers also became part of the staple repertoire of New Orleans jazz. **1934** C. LAMBERT *Music Ho!* II. 95 The *Rag-time*, like the piano *Rag Music*, is an abstract pattern created out of the raw material of certain syncopated devices. **1955** R. DAVIES in J. McCarthy *Jazzbk. 1955* 37 They left the Crescent City..intending to disseminate through the dance halls of Chicago the rag music they had created. **1976** R. SANDERS in D. Villiers *Next Year in Jerusalem* 198 One of the great Negro rag musicians, Ben Horney, a composer and singer. **1923** R. H. MYERS *Mod. Music* 65 Darius Milhaud has sought, by the use of rag-rhythms, to evoke the exotic yet intensely human atmosphere of the Bar and its inhabitants.

rag (ræg), *v.*[1] Also 7 **ragge.** [f. RAG *sb.*[1]]

1. *trans.* †**a.** To tear in pieces. *Obs.* **b.** To make ragged; to tear in a ragged manner.

c **1440** *York Myst.* xxxvi. 120 On roode am I ragged and rente, þou synfull sawle, for thy sake. **1521** FISHER *Serm. agst. Luther* Wks. (1876) 322 Martyn luther..so malycyously contemneth and setteth at nought and all to raggeth the heed of chrystes chyrche. *a* **1603** CARTWRIGHT *Confut. Rhem. N.T.* (1645) 331 The other testimony of Augustine, wherewith they have garded or rather ragged their margent. **1879** *Cassell's Techn. Educ.* IV. 117/2 There was a burr left at the hinder end of the thread which 'ragged' the wood. **1894** HALL CAINE *Manxman* 246 The steel of the drum ragging me sideways.

2. *intr.* †**a.** To become ragged. *Obs. rare.*

1641 BEST *Farm. Bks.* (Surtees) 13 The woll of such sheepe will immediately beginne to rise, ragge, and fall of. *a* **1661** FULLER *Worthies* (1840) II. 312 Leather, thus.. tanned,..will prove serviceable which otherwise will quickly fleet and rag out. **1683** MOXON *Mech. Exerc.*, *Printing* xvi, If they do not [fit exactly], the Mold will be sure to Rag.

b. To sort needles by means of a rag.

1861 WYNTER *Soc. Bees* 189 Little children 'rag' with inconceivable rapidity.

c. *U.S. slang. to rag out*, to dress well.

1865 'ARTEMUS WARD' *Trav.* xi. 92 We air goin' right straight through in these here clothes,..We ain't goin' to rag out till we get to Nevady.

rag (ræg), *v.*[2] *dial.* and *slang.* [Of obscure origin: cf. *bally-*, BULLYRAG.]

1. *trans.* **a.** To scold, rate, talk severely to. Also, to examine or question.

1739 *Proc. Sessions of Peace* June 107/2 On Monday Night Bird and Clark came to their House to ragg (scold) her Grandfather for what he had talk'd of, concerning them. *a* **1796** PEGGE *Derbicisms* Ser. II, 'To rag a person', to scold and abuse him. **1808** in JAMIESON. **1878–** In dial. glossaries (Cumb., Hants., Som., etc.). **1895** F. ANSTEY *Lyre & Lancet* vii. 70 You..used to rag me for not readin' enough. **1899** T. M. ELLIS *Three Cat's-eye Rings* 116 She'll keep her head, and I hope rag 'em well. **1908** A. S. M. HUTCHINSON *Once aboard Lugger* I. iv. 47 Not one had ever worked. Each had been 'ragged' on a subject of which he knew absolutely nothing.

b. To annoy, tease, torment; *spec.* in *University slang*, to annoy or assail in a rough or noisy fashion; to create wild disorder in (a room). Cf. RAG *sb.*[3]

1808 JAMIESON, *To rag*, to rally. **1877–** In dial. glossaries (Yks., Linc., etc.). **1894** HALL CAINE *Manxman* v. iv. 293 Nothing much—nothing to rag you at all. **1891** *Spectator* 3 Jan. 3/2 The revellers went round and 'ragged' several men in their rooms. **1897** J. WELLS *Oxford* 111 A..man..was so trying that, according to Oxford custom, the future Archbishop proceeded to 'rag' him. **1956** 'C. BLACKSTOCK' *Dewey Death* vii. 156 You're always ragging me, and I know you think I'm an ass. **1975** *Times* 30 Dec. 4/2 The President is now ragged mercilessly on national television, by talk show hosts, by comics, and in cartoons.

absol. **1896** *Isis* No. 112. 100/2 The difficulty of 'ragging' with impunity has long been felt.

2. *intr.* To wrangle *over* a subject.

1889 'J. S. WINTER' *Mrs. Bob* (1891) 275 If it is constantly discussed and ragged over between us, we shall have only a miserable life.

rag (ræg), *v.*[3] [Of obscure origin: cf. RACK *v.*[3]] *trans.* To break up (ore) with a hammer, preparatory to sorting.

1875 *Ure's Dict. Arts* II. 76 In spalling such portions as have been ragged, an additional quantity of refuse should be excluded. *Ibid.* 78 After these stones are washed they are ragged.

†**rag**, *v.*[4] *Sc. Obs. rare*[−1]. (Meaning obscure.)

a **1585** POLWART *Flyting w. Montgomerie* 790 Buttrie bag, fill knag! thou will rag with thy fellows.

rag (ræg), *v.*[5] orig. *U.S.* [f. RAG *sb.*[5]] **1.** *intr.* To play, sing, or dance in ragtime. Also const. *it.*

1905 *Dialect Notes* III. 152 *Rag*,..to dance. 'Everybody *rag* as pooty (puti) as you can.' **1923** R. D. PAINE *Comrades of Rolling Ocean* viii. 137 They were dancing on the pavement of the public market or ragging it on the smooth white streets. **1928** F. SCOTT FITZGERALD in *Sat. Even. Post* 29 Sept. 118/3 Oh, listen!.. Do you know how to rag? **1946** B. TREADWELL *Big Bk. Swing* 125/1 *Rag*, to play the blues and jazz. **1971** C. C. ADAMS *Boontling* 237 *Rag*, to dance in 'ragtime' form, considered indecent in valley dance halls in the Boontling era.

2. *trans.* To convert (a melody, etc.) into ragtime; to play ragtime music on (an instrument).

1917 *Lit. Digest* 25 Aug. 28/2 The jazz bands take popular tunes and rag them to death to make jazz. **1922** H. L. Foster *Adventures Trop. Tramp* v. 47 The camp victrola was broken and..I was the only man in camp that could rag the piano. **1949** R. Blesh *Shining Trumpets* viii. 181 The violin played the melody straight while Bolden ragged it. **1956** G. P. Kurath in A. Dundes *Mother Wit* (1973) 108/1 The slaves ragged and syncopated their clog dances. **1960** [see anti-[1] 2 c].

rag, var. raga.

raga (ˈrɑːgə). Also **raag, rag** (rɑːg). [a. Skr. *rāga*, colour, passion, melody; Hindi *rāg*, a mode in music, music.] **1.** In Indian music, a melodic type which provides a framework for improvised melodies; such an improvised melody. Also *fig.*

1788 W. Jones in *Asiatick Researches* I. 264 The beautiful allegories of the Hindus in their system of musical modes, which they call Rágás, or Passions, and suppose to be Genii or Demigods. **1807** *Asiatick Researches* IX. 447 The Indian Rágas and Ráginis are fixed respectively to particular seasons of the year and times of the night or day. **1891** C. R. Day *Music & Mus. Instr. S. India & Deccan* ii. 23 Mode and râga are..perfectly distinct from each other. *Ibid.* 24 In almost all these works a somewhat similar classification of the râgs and râginis has been adopted. **1924** E. M. Forster *Passage to India* vii. 80 The song is composed in a raga appropriate to the present hour, which is the evening. **1934** C. Lambert *Music Ho!* v. 289 Although the scales of folk music may vary from the simple pentatonic scales of the Hebridean to the complicated ragas of the Hindu, the same outlook on tonality is implied. **1944** W. Apel *Harvard Dict. Mus.* 332/2 The ragas fall under the classification of melody-types... A raga is a much more specialized tonal frame than a mode; it prescribes..not only a scale and a center-tone (*amsa*), but also the avoidance of certain tones. **1958** *Times* 30 May 16/5 The Indian *raga* provides the structure for an improvisatory kind of music which..approaches the articulation of speech. **1962** I. Holst *Tune* iv. 53 It is impossible to memorize fragments of a raga during a performance. **1967** 'La Meri' *Spanish Dancing* (ed. 2) v. 67 The *Rag* (roughly, melody) has a definite mood throughout. **1969** *Sunday Standard* (Bombay) 3 Aug. (Magazine Section) p. iv/6 Instead of outlining the form of his 'raag' in sinuous, unbroken contours he seems to have preferred segment sketching. **1970** W. Burroughs *Speed* vii. 151 On stage, a couple of young guys played a mediocre raga. **1971** J. Mandelkau *Buttons* vii. 81 'The Truth is the Only Law!' It's sewn on the inside shoulder of William's jacket and has become my daily prayer. My holy raga. **1972** P. Holroyde *Indian Music* 277 *Ragas* developed as an arrangement of intervals so that seven notes are in a certain relationship with each other and thus define a melody. **1975** *Guardian Weekly* 25 Jan. 21/3 The score by Alan Lloyd can best be described as Schubertian raga, a non-stop prelude (vamp till ready) to the verbal fugues on the stage. **1977** Y. Menuhin *Unfinished Journey* xii. 258 A *raga* is a scale-cum-melody, a given sequence of notes whose interrelationships are already determined.

2. *attrib.* and *Comb.*, as ***raga form, quality, system***; **raga rock**, rock music characterized by improvisation, etc., in the style of a raga.

1968 *Jrnl. Mus. Acad. Madras* XXXIX. 7 The classical music of India has thus for its aim the delineation of the Raga-forms. **1972** *Last Whole Earth Catalog* (Portola Inst.) 3/1 Fuller's lectures have a raga quality of rich nonlinear endless improvisation full of convergent surprises. **1966** *Melody Maker* 30 Apr. 12/1 America's..Byrds come up with a new formula! Raga-rock, based on Eastern musical forms. **1967** P. Welles *Babyhip* (1968) xv. 108 'Leave me alone,' she said, 'you're some kind of sex fiend. And anyway, I'm looking for raga rock.' She turned the station to another. **1957** A. Bake in *New Oxf. Hist. Mus.* I. iv. 213 In the classical *râga* system such a new creation usually bears the name of its parents, as, for instance, *Megh-Malhâr*.

raga, obs. form of raja(h.

ragabash (ˈrægəbæʃ), *sb.* and *a. Sc.* and *north. dial.* Forms: 7–9 **raggabash**, 8–9 **rag(g)abrash**, 9 **ragabash**, (**ragabosh**, *Sc.* **rag-a-buss**). [App. f. rag *sb.*[1], with fanciful ending.]

1. An idle worthless fellow; a ragamuffin.

1609 Healey *Discov. New World* i. v. 81 They are the veriest Lack-latines, and the most Vn-alphabeticall raggabashes that euer bred lowse. **1781** J. Hutton *Tour to Caves* (ed. 2) Gloss., *Raggabrash*, an idle ragged person. **1825** in Jamieson Suppl. **1855-** In various northern glossaries.

2. *collect.* Rabble, riff-raff.

1824 Mactaggart *Gallovid. Encycl.* 267 The ragabash were ordered back. **1859** Sala *Tw. round Clock* (1861) 361 This scum of frantic knavery and ragabosh. **1891** Hall Caine *Scapegoat* xxv, The raggabash of the Sultan's following had slunk away ashamed.

3. *attrib.* or as *adj.* Beggarly.

1818 Hogg *Brownie of Bodsbeck*, etc. II. 47 He thought proper to ascribe it a' to his ragabash prayer. **1829** J. Wilson in *Blackw. Mag.* XXV. 802 The ragabash rascals, who sham being ministers.

ragacyoun, obs. form of rogation.

ˈragalet. *rare.* [Obscurely related to raggle *sb.*[1]; cf. raglet.] = raggle *sb.*[1]

1833 Loudon *Encycl. Archit.* §940 Ragalets (grooves), 2 inches deep into the walls, are to be made under these stones, to receive the ends of the slates. **1887** *Dict. Archit.*, *Ragalet*, the Scotch term for a groove.

†**ˈragamuff.** *Obs. rare.* = next.

1591 Horsey *Trav.* (Hakluyt Soc.) 190, I was..taken by raggamouff souldiers, whoe used me verie ruffly. [**1863** Sala *Capt. Dangerous* I. vii. 217 Even thou art a Gentleman, little Ragamuff.]

ragamuffin (ˈrægəmʌfɪn), *sb.* and *a.* Forms: α. 4 **ragamoffyn, -muffyn, -mofin**, 5 **ragomofin**, 6 **rag of muffin**, 6–9 **ragga-**, 7 **ragge-**, 7–8 **rag-a-**, 9 *Sc.* **rag-o-**, 7– **ragamuffin**; 7–9 **ragamuffian**, (8 **ragga-**). β. 7 **raggede-**, 9 *dial.* **ragg'dmuffin**. [Prob. from rag *sb.*[1] (cf. ragged 1 c), with fanciful ending.]

†**1.** The name of a demon. *Obs. rare*[−1].

1393 Langl. *P. Pl.* C. xxi. 283 Ac rys vp ragamoffyn and reche me alle þe barres, That belial þy bel-syre beot with þy damme.

2. A ragged, dirty, disreputable man or boy.

1581 G. Pettie tr. *Guazzo's Civ. Conv.* (1586) iv. 187 b, Others there are..who care not how like slouens and raggamuffins they goe. **1607** Dekker & Webster *Westw. Hoe* D.'s Wks. 1873 II. 350 What set of Villaines are you, you perpetuall Ragamuffins? **1622** T. Scott *Newes fr. Pernassus* 48 It is no marvaile if I be spoyled to clothe so many Raggedemuffins. **1704** Swift *Batt. Bks.* Misc. (1711) 243 Rogues and Ragamuffins, that follow the Camp for nothing but the Plunder. **1764** *Mem. G. Psalmanazar* 152, I soon persuaded half a dozen of my fellow ragamuffians to follow me. *c* **1817** Hogg *Tales & Sk.* V. 178 Come out, ye vile rag-o-muffin. **1840** Dickens *Barn. Rudge* xxxv, A set of ragamuffins comes a-shouting after us, 'Gordon for ever!' **1894** Jessopp *Rand. Roam.* ii. 32 A caretaker..to warn off ragamuffins.

b. *attrib.* or as *adj.* Rough, beggarly, good-for-nothing, disorderly.

1602 Rowlands *Greenes Ghost* 37 There are a certaine band of Raggamuffin Prentises about the towne, that will abuse anie vpon the smallest occasion that is. **1668** Evelyn tr. *Freart's Idea Perfect. Paint.* 105 He rather chose to resemble a ragamuffin Vagabond than a Philosopher. **1772** Graves *Spir. Quix.* viii. xxiii. (1783) II. 262 Mr. Aldworth ..turned over the rest of this ragamuffin assembly to the care of his Butler. **1812** H. & J. Smith *Rej. Addr.*, *T. Drury Lane* (Revival), Many a raggamuffin clan With trowel and with hod. **1858** R. S. Surtees *Ask Mamma* xxiv. 92 Look at a shooter, — what a ragamuffin dress his is.

3. *dial.* The long-tailed titmouse.

1885 Swainson *Names Birds* 31.

Hence **ragamuffinery** = *ragamuffinry*. **ragamuffiness**, a female ragamuffin. **ragamuffinism**, the world of ragamuffins. **ragamuffinize** *v. trans.*, to render disreputable. **ragamuffinly** *a.*, beggarly. **ragamuffinry**, (*a*) the disreputable classes of society; (*b*) depraved actions or conduct.

1831 *Fraser's Mag.* IV. 5 A fair specimen of the manner in which the *ragamuffinery will manage their members. **1868** Helps *Realmah* xvii, Six or eight *ragamuffinesses..began to dance. **1859** Masson *Brit. Novelists* ii. 95 He..knew the very face of the mob and *ragamuffinism in its haunts. **1832** *Blackw. Mag.* XXXI. 668 You will not object..to *ragamuffinize that House a little. **1890** Jessie Fothergill *March in Ranks* I. x. 154 His attire was..shabby, not to say *ragamuffinly in the extreme. **1831** *Fraser's Mag.* III. 745 Hunt..is jostled by every-day compeers in *ragamuffinry. *Ibid.* IV. 131 The whole..of the ragamuffinry of the town proceed to the fight. **1851** *Life Bunyan* in *Scott's Pilgr. Progr.* 6 He never committed theft or ragamuffinry of any kind.

‖**ragazzo** (raˈgattso). Pl. **ragazzi**; fem. **ragazza**. [a. It. *ragazzo* boy, *ragazza* girl.] In Italy: a youngster; a lad or a young girl.

1862 Borrow *Wild Wales* I. xxiv. 283 When I was a ragazzo I knew many from the Lake of Como, who dressed much like yourself. **1897** A. T. Ritchie *Let.* Mar. (1924) xi. 239 Two nice little ragazzi showed us the way. **1906** W. De Morgan *Joseph Vance* xliv. 404 In a day or two Beppino was bored, and..I noticed that he was keeping at a respectful distance from every ragazza. **1957** 'N. Culotta' *They're Weird Mob* (1958) ii. 24 'What please is a sheila?' 'A sheila? A bint. A ragazza.' **1975** *Publishers Weekly* 27 Jan. 230/1 A novel concerning a *ragazza* of the streets grown to movie star.

ˈrag-bag, *sb.* **1. a.** A bag in which rags or scraps of cloth are collected or stored.

1820 M. Wilmot *Let.* 7 Aug. (1935) 76 Well, and well and well, what have I got to say in my *ragbag* of a brain? I have a hundred odds and ends. **1850** Dickens *Dav. Copp.* xlviii. 490 Sheets in the rag-bag. **1853** C. Brontë *Villette* I. ix. 174 Your mind..seems..chaotic as a rag-bag. **1861** Dickens *Gt. Expect.* xl, An animated rag-bag whom she called her niece. **1873** Miss Braddon *Str. & Pilgr.* iii. xii. 360 Her brain was..a chaos of many-coloured scraps and shreds, like a good house-keeper's rag-bag. **1884** *Cassell's Fam. Mag.* Feb. 155/1 Many people..would..be surprised if they could see the contents of a rag-bag. **1917** E. Pound *Lustra* 181 And that the 'modern world' Needs such a rag-bag to stuff all its thought in. **1964** A. Sexton *Sel. Poems* 57, I hid in the kitchen under the ragbag.

b. *transf.* and *fig.* A motley collection. Also *spec.* a sloppily-dressed woman, a slattern. *slang.*

1864 Lowell *Wks.* (1890) V. 156 The Convention was a rag-bag of dissent. **1885** A. Dale *Jonathan's Home* 108 That indescribable medley of houses, a ragbag of dwellings. **1888** Kipling *Under Deodars* 70 If I were a man I would perish sooner than be seen with that rag-bag. **1937** Partridge *Dict. Slang* 683/2 *Rag-bag*,..a slattern. **1973** 'W. Haggard' *Old Masters* vi. 75 Lord Tokenhouse was no sort of economist, indeed he despised the whole ragbag whole-heartedly. **1976** P. Cave *High Flying Birds* iii. 31 She was neither attractive nor plain; not a raver or a ragbag. **1980** *Jrnl. R. Soc. Arts* Feb. 149/2 The design courses are in danger by their very existence of joining Art, Music and Technical Drawing in the ragbag of the system.

2. *attrib.*

1907 *Daily Chron.* 13 Mar. 8/4 The association of wealth and rag-bag poverty in London is one of her most remarkable features. **1948** *Life* 13 Sept. 152/2 In the old days..some of them little 'rag-bag' shows used to carry a lot of grift. **1953** S. Kauffmann *Philanderer* vi. 104 The living-room, with its rag-bag summer cottage furnishings. **1968** *Listener* 31 Oct. 583/2 There is certain to be some inherent weakness in the direction of generalisation and 'rag-bag' proliferation of studies that I deplore. **1980** *Jrnl. R. Soc. Arts* Feb. 154/1 That is what I call the ragbag attitude.

ˈrag-bolt. [? f. rag *sb.*[1] 6.] A bolt having barbs directed towards the head, so that it cannot be easily withdrawn after it is driven in; a jag-bolt or barb-bolt.

1627 Capt. Smith *Seaman's Gram.* ii. 5 Rag bolts are so iaggered that they cannot be drawne out. **1691** T. H[ale] *Acc. New Invent.* 47 The Ragg-bolts eaten away to nothing. **1769** Falconer *Dict. Marine* (1776) Y 2, A rag-bolt is retained in it's situation by..barbs. **1836** in *Civil Eng. & Arch. Jrnl.* (1838) I. 150/2 Additional ties were..put in at every other oak pile, and..secured down by rag-bolts.

Hence **ˈrag-bolt** *v. trans.*, to fasten *down* by rag-bolts.

1836 in *Civil Eng. & Arch. Jrnl.* (1838) I. 150/2 It even became necessary..to place stringers outside of the sheet piles..and to rag bolt them down.

rag-burned. A term applied to tin-witts which have undergone the first roasting. So **rag-burning.**

1875 *Ure's Dict. Arts* III. 1003 Instead of being at once completely roasted, the 'whits' from the stamps are sometimes first 'rag' (or partially) burnt, for about six or eight hours. **1881** Raymond *Mining Gloss.*, Rag-burning.

rage (reɪdʒ), *sb.* Also 5 **rag**, 6 **raige, rayge**, *Sc.* **raig, rege.** [a. F. *raige, rage* (11th c.) = Prov. *ratje*:—**rabje*:—*rabia* late L. form (cf. Sp., Pg. *rabia*, It. *rabbia*) of *rabies* rabies.]

1. a. Madness; insanity; a fit or access of mania. *Obs.* exc. *poet.*

c **1325** *Metr. Hom.* 141 Snakes and nederes..lep upward til his visage, And gert him almast fal in rage. **1390** Gower *Conf.* I. 40 Wher that wisdom waxeth wod, And reson torneth into rage. *c* **1400** Maundev. viii. (1839) 89 He felle in a rage, and oute of his Wytt. **1552** Lyndesay *Monarche* 5137 Thocht sum de Naturally, throuch aige, Fer mo deis raiffand in one raige. **1590** Shaks. *Com. Err.* iv. iii. 88 The reason that I gather he is mad, Besides the present instance of his rage [etc.]. **1605** —— *Lear* iv. vii. 78 Be comforted good Madam, the great rage You see is kill'd in him. **1700** Dryden *Pal. & Arc.* i. 542 Museful mopings, which presage The loss of reason and conclude in rage. **1819** Shelley *Peter Bell 3rd* vii. xv, To wakeful frenzy's vigil rages, As opiates, were the same applied.

†**b.** Madness, folly, rashness; an instance of this, a foolish act. *Obs.*

13.. *K. Alis.* 4336 Alisaundre..bad non have the rage Theo water to passe of Estrage. *c* **1320** *Cast. Love* 197 Thus is Adam, thorwh rufull rage I-cast out of his eritage. *a* **1400** *R. Brunne's Chron. Wace* (Rolls) 11598 Ffor loue men doþ gret outrage [*Petyt MS.* many rage]. **1412–20** Lydg. *Chron. Troy* i. vi, It were a rage a man from him to chase Wilfull fortune whan she is beninge.

†**c.** Rabies. *Obs.*

1558 Warde tr. *Alexis' Secr.* (1568) 28 Agaynst the bytyng of a madde dogge, and the rage or madnesse that followeth the man after he is bitten. **1595** Duncan *Appendix Etymol.*, *Rabies*, rage of a dogge.

2. Violent anger, furious passion, usually as manifested in looks, words or action; a fit or access of such anger; †angry disposition.

a. of persons:

1297 R. Glouc. (Rolls) 4415 In is wod rage he wende Vor to awreke is vncle deþ. *c* **1330** *Arth. & Merl.* 2422 (Kölbing) þe king com wiþ his barnage & tounes brent in gret rage. ? *a* **1366** Chaucer *Rom. Rose* 156 A-midde saugh I Hate stonde..grinning for dispitious rage. *a* **1548** Hall *Chron.*, *Hen. VI* 163 b, He could not appeace the furious rage of the common people. **1607** Shaks. *Cor.* v. iii. 85 Desire not t'allay My Rages and Reuenges, with your colder reasons. **1697** Dryden *Virg. Georg.* iv. 652 The Seer, who could not yet his Wrath asswage, Rowl'd his green Eyes, that sparkled with his Rage. **1773** Mrs. Chapone *Improv. Mind* (1774) II. 19 The sharpest accusation excites pity or contempt, rather than rage. **1810** Scott *Lady of L.* v. xv, The foe..Foil'd his wild rage with steady skill. **1862** Carlyle *Fredk. Gt.* x. i. (1872) III. 208 Liable to rages, to utterances of a coarse nature.

b. of animals:

13.. *K. Alis.* 555 Theo lady gede to theo drake, He lette his rage for hire sake. **1390** Gower *Conf.* III. 267 Riht as Leon in his rage, Which of no drede set acompte. *c* **1500** *Lancelot* 3173 In his ferss curag Of armys, as o lyoune in his rag. **1611** Bible *Job* xxxix. 24 [The horse] swalloweth the ground with fiercenesse and rage. **1687** Dryden *Hind & P.* i. 305 The Wolf, the Bear, the Boar..Their rage repressed, ..stand aloof, and tremble. **1720** Pope *Iliad* xvii. 609 So looks the Lion o'er a mangled Boar, All grim with Rage. **1810** Scott *Lady of L.* vi. xxii, The prison'd eagle dies for rage.

†**3. a.** Vehement, violent or impetuous action (of persons); vigour, rapidity, haste. *Obs.*

13.. *K. Alis.* 980 That othres flowen with gret rage. **13..** *Seuyn Sag.* (W.) 480 Sche to-cragged hire visage, And gradde, 'Harow!' with gret rage. **1390** Gower *Conf.* III. 219 Til that thei sihe time, and knewe, That thei be fled upon the rage. *c* **1485** *Digby Myst.* (1882) iii. 1331 Masengyr, owt of þis town with a rage!

†**b.** An act of violence; a fight. *Obs. rare.*

c **1330** R. Brunne *Chron. Wace* (Rolls) 16173 þys byword was longe y-told, þys þey seide at ilka rage. —— *Chron.* (1810) 114 Whan Rauf herd him so seie, he dight him to þat rage.

4. *transf.* **a.** Violence, violent operation or action, 'fury' (of things, e.g. wind, the sea, fire, etc.).

c **1320** *Sir Beues* (MS. A.) 4580 þe wind blew hardde wiþ gret rage. **1340** *Ayenb.* 142 Uor þe rage and uor þe tempeste of euele tongen. c **1400** *Rom. Rose* 1916 The arwis were so fulle of rage. **1513** Douglas *Æneis* x. xii. 19 The fors..of the hevynnis and byr of seis rage. **1562** Pilkington *Expos. Abdyas* Pref. 8 The rage of fyre is swaged with water. **1634** Sir T. Herbert *Trav.* 39 Bodies..exposed to the Sunnes fiery rage. **1770** Armstrong *Imitations* 85 Every petty brook ..mocks the river's rage. **1822** Shelley *Calderon* ii. 64 In contempt of the elemental rage A man comes forth in safety.

b. A flood, high tide, sudden rising of the sea.

1390 Gower *Conf.* III. 103 Thilke almyhty hond Withdrouh the water fro the lond, And al the rage was aweie. **1538** Leland *Itin.* IV. 23 At Ragis of Spring Tydes. **1577** B. Googe *Heresb. Husb.* (1586) 173 The old Water lying vnder the leuell of the Sea, will not out againe, except a greater rage come in. **1885** Lady Brassey *The Trades* 361 These apparently unaccountable risings of the waves are called by the natives [of the Bahamas] 'rages'.

†**c.** A fierce blast of wind. *Obs. rare*$^{-1}$.

c **1386** Chaucer *Knt.'s T.* 1127 And ther out came a rage and suche a veze That it made al the gate for to rese.

†**5.** Extravagant, riotous, or wanton behaviour; sport, game; jest, jesting talk. *Obs.*

c **1320** *Sir Beues* (MS. A) 2967 An erneste & a rage [He] euer spekeþ frensche laungage. c **1330** *Arth. & Merl.* 4618 (Kölbing) þou schust leten þi folye, þi rage & þi ribaudye. a **1400** *Roberd of Cisyle* (Vernon MS.) 190 þer nas in court grom ne page þat of þe kyng ne made rage. c **1425** *Seven Sag.* (P.) 2177 The knave..bygan onnoon hys rage, And cast watyr oppon the kage.

6. a. A violent feeling, passion, or appetite. Also, violence, severity, height (*of* a feeling, etc.).

1390 Gower *Conf.* III. 237 Sardanapallus..Was..Falle into thilke fyri rage Of love. **14..** in *Tundale's Vis.* 96 Whom a sarpent falsly dyd exyle Of fals malice in a soden rage. **1513** Douglas *Æneis* iv. ii. 33 Quhat helpis to vesy templis in luiffis raige? *Ibid.* viii. iv. 1 Eftir that stanchit was the hungris rage. **1570** Foxe *A. & M.* 1767/1 If the rage of the payne were tolerable..he should lift vp his handes. **1593** Shaks. *Lucr.* 424 His rage of lust by gazing qualified. **1691** Lady R. Russell *Lett.* II. 95 The present rage of your sorrow. **1709** Steele *Tatler* No. 34 ¶2 It is in vain to give it when the Patient is in the Rage of the Distemper. **1784** Burns *Man was made to Mourn* ii, Does thirst of wealth thy step constrain Or youthful pleasure's rage. **1833** Tennyson *Miller's Dau.* 192 You must blame Love. His early rage Had force to make me rhyme in youth.

b. Violent desire; sexual passion; heat.

? a **1366** Chaucer *Rom. Rose* 1657 Whan I was with this rage hent That caught hath many a man and shent. **1390** Gower *Conf.* III. 271 That ilke fyri rage In which that thei the lawe [of Mariage] excede. **1500–20** Dunbar *Poems* lxxxiv. 8 Quhone the biche is jolie and on rage. **1552** Lyndesay *Monarche* iii. 4706 [Personis] lyke Rammis in to thair rage. **1602** Shaks. *Ham.* iii. iii. 89 When he is drunke asleepe: or in his Rage. **1697** Dryden *Virg. Georg.* iii. 381 'Tis with this Rage, the Mother Lion stung, Scours o'er the Plain..Demanding Rites of Love.

†**c.** Violent sorrow; a fit of this. *Obs. rare.*

c **1386** Chaucer *Frankl. T.* 108 Hir grete sorwe gan aswage; She may nat alwey duren in swich rage. c **1530** Ld. Berners *Arth. Lyt. Bryt.* (1814) 51 Than Florence stepped forth all in a rage, and piteously cried and sayd. c **1586** *Epit. Sidney* in *Spenser's Wks.* (Globe) 571/2 Silence augmenteth grief, writing encreaseth rage.

†**d.** Violent pain. Hence humorously suggested as a name for a set of teeth. *Obs. rare.*

1486 *Bk. St. Albans* F vij, A Rage [= set] of the teethe. **1520** *Calisto & Melibæa* C i, *Mel.* I ask the how long in this paynfull rage He hath leyn. *Cel.* He hath be in this agony this .viii. days. **1561** Hollybush *Hom. Apoth.* 17 b, As sone as he had taken it, furthwyth had he suche a rage and grepyng wythin hym.

†**e.** Extreme hunger. *Obs. rare*$^{-1}$.

a **1533** Ld. Berners *Huon* cix. 375 We haue no thynge to ete nor drynke, wherfore we shal dye for famyne and rage.

7. a. A vehement passion *for*, desire *of*, a thing. Also const. *after*, *infin.*, or *absol.*

1593 Shaks. *Lucr.* 468 This moves in him more rage..To make the breach. **1671** Milton *Samson* 836 Call it furious rage To satisfie thy lust. **1697** Dryden *Virg. Georg.* iv. 299 Such Rage of Honey in their Bosom beats. **1750** H. Walpole *Lett.* (1846) II. 359 You can't conceive the ridiculous rage there is of going to Newgate. **1758** Johnson in Boswell xii, Warburton..has a rage for saying something, when there's nothing to be said. **1790** *Loiterer* 2 Jan. 4 This prevailing rage after knowledge. **1820** Shelley *Witch Atl.* xviii, The earth-consuming rage Of gold and blood. **1882** A. W. Ward *Dickens* iii. 65 The rage which possesses authors to read their writings aloud.

b. (*all*) *the rage*: said of the object of a widespread and usually temporary enthusiasm.

1785 *Europ. Mag.* VIII. 473 The favourite phrases..The Rage, the Thing, the Twaddle, and the Bore. **1802** *Monthly Mag.* 1 Oct. 253/1 The *rage* for the dotting style of engraving ..is on the decline. **1811** Byron *Let.* 15 Dec. (1973) II. 149 Tomorrow, I dine with Rogers & am to hear Colridge, who is a kind of rage at present. **1834** Lytton *Last Days of Pompeii* I. i. 173 Sylla is said to have transported to Italy the worship of the Egyptian Isis. It soon became 'the rage'—and was peculiarly in vogue with the Roman ladies. **1836** T. Hook *G. Gurney* I. 52 At that period it was the rage to parodize tragedies. **1837** Marryat *Perc. Keene* ii, In a short time my mother became quite the rage. **1861** K. Stone *Jrnl.* 28 Aug. in *Brokenburn* (1955) 48 Plaiting palmetto for baskets has been the rage for several days. **1870** Ld. Malmesbury in *Athenæum* 4 June 734 In 1776, the game of 'Commerce'..was 'all the rage'. **1881** [see colloquialism 2]. **1940** Graves & Hodge *Long Week-End* iii. 38 After the war the new fantastic development of Jazz music and the steps that went with it, became, in the comtemporary phrase, 'all the rage'. **1951** [see dead *a.* 30].

8. Poetic or prophetic enthusiasm or inspiration; musical excitement.

c **1600** Shaks. *Sonn.* xvii, So should..your true rights be term'd a poet's rage. c **1611** Chapman *Iliad* i. 66 His prophetic rage Given by Apollo. **1713** Pope *Prol. Addison's Cato* 44 Assert the stage, Be justly warm'd with your own native rage. **1795** Wolcott (P. Pindar) *Lousiad* 11, The ragged Warblers pour their tuneful rage. **1811** Scott *Don Roderick* i. iii, For Homer's rage A theme. **1857–69** Heavysege *Saul* (1869) 173 Beat out harsh rhythms with augmenting rage.

9. Martial or high spirit, ardour, fervour, manly enthusiasm or indignation.

1591 Shaks. *1 Hen. VI*, iv. vi. 13 Leaden Age, Quicken'd with Youthfull Spleene, and Warlike Rage. **1700** Dryden *Pal. & Arc.* i. 117 The soldiers shout around with generous rage. **1720** Pope *Iliad* xvii. 305 Merion burning with a Hero's Rage. **1850** Tennyson *In Mem.* xxvii, I envy not in any moods The captive void of noble rage.

10. Excitement or violence *of* an action, operation, etc.; also, the acutest point or heat of this.

1593 Shaks. *Lucr.* 145 All for one we gage; As life for honour in fell battle's rage. **1725** N. Robinson *Th. Physick* 124 This Fever..assaults with all the Rage and Fury of Burning. **1756** Burke *Vind. Nat. Soc.* Wks. 1842 I. 7 Great carnage did in those times and countries ever attend the first rage of conquest. **1784** Cowper *Task* iii. 519 As time subdues The rage of fermentation. **1831** Macaulay *Let. to Sister* in Trevelyan *Life* (1876) I. iv. 233 The rage of faction at the present moment exceeds any thing that has been known in our day.

†**11.** An alleged name for a company of maidens.

1486 *Bk. St. Albans* F vj b, A Rage of Maydenys; a Rafull of Knauys.

12. *attrib.* and *Comb.*, as ***rage-infuriate***, ***-swelling*** adjs.; †***rage-apples*** (see raging *ppl. a.* b).

1578 Lyte *Dodoens* iii. lxxxv. 438 Of Madde Apples, or Rage Apples. **1632** Lithgow *Trav.* i. 14 The violent force of his rage swelling courtesie. **1806** J. N. White *Poems* 54 A rage-infuriate train.

†**rage**, *a. Obs.* [f. rage *sb.* or *v.*; cf. outrage *a.*] Mad, raging; wanton.

13.. *Coer de L.* 828 Sche gahchyd herself in the vysage, As a wymman that wolde be rage. c **1330** *Amis & Amil.* 1945 The gode man wende he hadde ben rage. **1426** Lydg. *De Guil. Pilgr.* 16367 The Rage Floode off worldly Tribulacion kometh. c **1430** —— *Reas. & Sens.* 6988 Swifter also of passage, More than any Tigre rage. **1573** Tusser *Husb.* (1878) 214 Cocking Dads make sawsie lads In youth so rage, to beg in age.

rage (reɪdʒ), *v.* Also 6 *Sc.* **raige, rege.** [ad. F. *rager* (13th c.), f. *rage* rage *sb.*]

†**1.** *intr.* To go mad; to be mad; to act madly or foolishly. *Obs.*

a **1300** *Cursor M.* 6986 þai..lefte þe lagh of hei drihtin.. Qua herd euer men sua rage! a **1533** Ld. Berners *Huon* cxvii. 423 Shortely delyuer vs, for we rage for famyne. **1567** *Gude & Godlie B.* (S.T.S.) 203 Thay ar with dolour pynde, And lyke to raige out of thair mynde.

2. To show signs of madness or frenzy; to rave in madness or fury; to act or speak wildly or furiously; to storm; *Sc.* to scold. Also, to have frenzied or angry feelings, to be full of anger.

a **1300** *Cursor M.* 7621 Saul..Als he was won bi-gan to rage. **13..** *Coer de L.* 2106 The emperour began to rage; He grunte his teeth and fast blewe. **1528** Tindale *Obed. Chr. Man* Wks. (1573) 120 Then fume we and rage and set vp the bristels and bend owrselues to take vengeaunce. **1631** Gouge *God's Arrows* i. §71. 119 Some..that are affected therewith, rage and rave. **1667** Milton *P.L.* xi. 444 Whereat hee inlie rag'd, and as they talk'd, Smote him. **1710** Steele *Tatler* No. 217 ¶11 If..the Beauteous could but rage a little before a Glass, and see their pretty Countenances grow wild. **1815** Shelley *Demon of World* 282 They did rage horribly, Breathing..fierce blasphemies. **1868** Tennyson *Lucretius* 272 She heard him raging, heard him fall.

b. Const. *against*, *at*, *upon*, †*with*.

1519 Horman *Vulg.* 61 He suffereth men all to rayle and rage vpon hym. **1535** Coverdale *2 Kings* xix. 27, I know.. that thou ragest agaynst me. **1591** Spenser *M. Hubberd* 1088 The Tygre, and the Bore,..with the simple Camell raged sore In bitter words. **1596** —— *State Irel.* Wks. (Globe) 614/1 The lawes themselves they doe specially rage upon. **1642** Rogers *Naaman* 8 A patient raging at his Physitian. **1855** Tennyson *The Letters* 26, I raged against the public liar. **1866** Mrs. Carlyle *Lett.* III. 325 Hayward was raging against the Jamaica business.

†**c.** Of poets: To be under inspiration. *rare*$^{-1}$.

1611 Beaum. & Fl. *Maid's Trag.* i. ii, Poets, when they rage, Turn gods to men, and make an hour an age.

†**3.** To behave wantonly or riotously; to take one's pleasure; to play. Const. *with* (a person).

a **1300** *Body & Soul* in *Map's Poems* 347 Body, miht thou nouht lepen to pleyen ant rage. **1303** R. Brunne *Handl. Synne* 7896 To pley wyþ wommen and to rage. **1390** Gower *Conf.* I. 101 Sche began to pleie & rage. c **1430** *Syr Gener.* (Roxb.) 7107 Ye shul haue youre will Of my maden, al youre fill; And rage with hir ye shal. **1508** Dunbar *Tua Mariit Wemen* 386 Quhen he ane hail ȝear was hanyt, and him behuffit rage. **1597** Shaks. *Lover's Compl.* 160 When we rage, advice is often seen By blunting us to make our wits more keen.

b. Const. *in* (an action, practice, etc.).

a **1300** *Cursor M.* 48 A saumpul her be þaem I say þat rages in þare riot ay. **1567** *Gude & Godlie B.* (S.T.S.) 151 Man was sa wylde and nyce, And rageing in all vyce. **1599** Shaks. *Much Ado* iv. i. 62 Those pampred animalls, That rage in sauage sensualitie. **1645** Quarles *Sol. Recant.* iii. 28 One while we plunge in teares; and by and by, We rage in laughter.

4. *transf.* of things (e.g. wind, the sea, etc.): To be violent and boisterous; to move or rush furiously.

1535 Coverdale *Ps.* xlvi. 3 The waters of the see raged. **1590** Shaks. *Two Gent.* ii. vii. 26 The Current that with gentle murmur glides..being stop'd, impatiently doth rage. **1611** Bible *Jer.* xlvi. 9 Come vp ye horses, and rage yee charets. **1667** Milton *P.L.* vi. 211 The madding Wheeles of brazen Chariots rag'd. **1795–1814** Wordsw. *Excurs.* iv. 536 Rage on, ye elements! let moon and stars Their aspects lend. **1819** Shelley *Cenci* iv. i. 114, I see a torrent of his own blood raging between us. **1832** Tennyson *Sisters* 21 The wind is raging in turret and tree.

b. Of passions, feelings, etc.: To have or reach a high degree of intensity.

1583 Stubbes *Anat. Abus.* i. E iij b, Els it [pride] could neuer so rage as it dooth. **1605** Shaks. *Lear* i. ii. 178 His displeasure, which at this instant so rageth in him, that..it would scarcely alay. **1671** Milton *Samson* 963 Thy anger, unappeasable, still rages. **1810** Scott *Lady of L.* i. xxxv, Wild were the heart whose passion's sway Could rage beneath the sober ray! **1818** Shelley *Rev. Islam* iii. xxi, Thirst raged within me. **1849** Macaulay *Hist. Eng.* vi. II. 64 The passion for play raged in him without measure.

c. Of a disturbed state of things (as a storm, battle, etc.): To have course, to continue or prevail, without check or with fatal effect; to be at the height. ***to rage out***, to break out violently.

1667 Milton *P.L.* i. 277 On the perilous edge Of battel when it rag'd. **1705** Addison *Italy* 7 Sudden Tempests rage within the Port. **1720** Ozell *Vertot's Rom. Rep.* I. iii. 159 Discord raged out again with more Fury than ever. **1784** Cowper *Task* iv. 309 The frost, Raging abroad, and the rough wind. **1871** L. Stephen *Playgr. Eur.* iv. (1894) 98 The gale..evidently raged above our heads.

d. Of a disease or pain: To be violent. Also *transf.*

1602 Shaks. *Ham.* iv. iii. 68 Like the Hecticke in my blood he rages. **1611** Beaum. & Fl. *Maid's Trag.* ii. i, Some fever rages in thy blood. **1671** Milton *Samson* 619 My griefs not only pain me As a lingring disease, But..ferment and rage. **1756** C. Lucas *Ess. Waters* I. 217 All his former complaints rage with more than double fury. **1800**, **1840** [see raging *ppl. a.* 1 b].

e. Of a tooth †or sore: To ache violently.

1567 Turberv. *Epit.* etc. 616 That..doth cause my ranckling sore to rage. **1604** [see raging *ppl. a.* 1 c]. **1710** Swift *Tatler* No. 238 ¶3 Old Aches throb, your hollow Tooth will rage. **1806** [see raging *ppl. a.* 1 c].

5. To be widely prevalent, or to spread widely, in a violent or virulent form.

1563 Winȝet *Four Scoir Thre Quest.* Wks. 1888 I. 57 Manifest rebellioun raigeing at this præsent aganis Godis plane word. **1737** Pope *Hor. Ep.* ii. i. 254 Triumphant Malice rag'd thro' private life. **1774** Goldsm. *Nat. Hist.* (1776) VII. 160 These dangers..in other parts of the world ..still rage with all their ancient malignity. **1784** Cowper *Task* iii. 682 Vicious custom, raging uncontrolled Abroad, and desolating public life.

b. *esp.* of epidemical diseases.

1584 Cogan *Haven Health* ccxliii. (1636) 320 The same kinde of agew raged in a manner over all England. **1667** Wood *Life* (O.H.S.) II. 124 The small pox rageth much about the kingdom. **1732** Berkeley *Alciphr.* iii. §16 Where an epidemical distemper rages. **1816** J. Wilson *City of Plague* iii. i. 168 The Plague That rages round us. **1893** Tout *Edw. I*, iii. 49 Sickness..raged throughout the camp.

6. To act with fury, ardour, or vehemence; to move furiously *over* (a place) or *about*.

1593 Shaks. *3 Hen. VI*, ii. iii. 26 Why stand we..heere, Wayling our losses, while the Foe doth Rage. **1665** Manley *Grotius' Low C. Warres* 68 Those Northern Nations raged over all these parts of the World. **1884** Symonds *Shaks. Predec.* iii. 110 The Devil leapt from the cart to rage about among the people.

†**b.** To exercise one's rage *on*, *upon*. *Obs.*

c **1540** tr. *Pol. Verg. Eng. Hist.* (Camden No. 36) 143 Yet these rude raskalls..raged on the dead carkas. **1603** Knolles *Hist. Turks* (1621) 867 With the same [cruelty] he also raged upon the meaner sort of the citizens.

†**7.** With various constructions: To be violently bent *upon*, to be furiously eager *to* (with inf.), to be impatient *for*. *Obs. rare.*

1509 Hawes *Past. Pleas.* xlii. (Percy Soc.) 206 Insaciately upon covetyse to rage. **1611** Beaum. & Fl. *Maid's Trag.* i. i, My Lord, the Maskers rage for you. **1671** Milton *Samson* 1275 Violent men..raging to pursue The righteous.

†**8.** *trans.* (in *pa. pple.*) To enrage. *Obs. rare.*

1593 Shaks. *Rich. II*, ii. i. 70 Young hot Colts, being rag'd do rage the more.

9. *refl.* To bring into a certain state by raging.

1831 Carlyle *Sart. Res.* ii. ix, The hot Harmattan wind had raged itself out. **1839** Bailey *Festus* xvi. (1852) 199 The strong passions..Soon rage themselves to rest.

rage, obs. f. rag *sb.*¹

ragea, obs. f. raja(h.

ragee, variant of ragi.

rageful (ˈreɪdʒfʊl), *a.* [f. rage *sb.* + -ful.]

†**1.** Mad, frantic, frenzied. *Obs. rare.*

1580 Sidney *Arcadia* iii. (1598) 280 Then Sorrow lost the witte of utterance, and grew ragefull, and madde. **1635** A. Stafford *Fem. Glory* (1869) 143 Any other desperate signe of ragefull sorrow.

2. Full of rage or furious anger.

1580 Sidney *Arcadia* (1622) 142 With ragefull eyes shee bad him defend himselfe. **1599** Sandys *Europæ Spec.* (1632) 184 The right Zelez,..are as malicious and ragefull against the Protestants as ever. a **1639** W. Whateley *Prototypes* ii. xxix. (1640) 144 That bloudy and ragefull murder. **1741**

RICHARDSON *Pamela* II. 245 Her fiery Eyes, and rageful Countenance, made me lose all my Courage. **1855** SINGLETON *Virgil* II. 187 Allecto doffs grim face and rageful limbs. **1885** TENNYSON *Anc. Sage* 269 Nor be thou rageful, like the handled bee.

3. *transf.* of things: Full of furious activity.

1597 BEARD *Theatre God's Judgem.* (1612) 68 The furie of that ragefull storme. *a* **1619** FOTHERBY *Atheom.* I. xii. §4 (1622) 129 As if ragefull windes should bring this ratling sound. **1668** H. MORE *Div. Dial.* III. i. (1713) 182 Some Chymical Liquors..mingled together will be in such a rageful Fermentation, that the Glass will grow hot. **1855** SINGLETON *Virgil* II. 523 A rageful show'r hath washed it down.

Hence **'ragefully** *adv.*

a **1615** DONNE *Ess.* (1651) 123 Ragefully tempested with storms of persecution. **1865** *Day of Rest* Oct. 585 The Israelite was ragefully indignant. **1874** LISLE CARR *Jud. Gwynne* I. vii. 204 Again he stared ragefully and viciously.

'rageless, *a. rare.* [f. RAGE *sb.* + -LESS.] Devoid of rage.

1578 T. PROCTOR *Gorg. Gallery* in *Heliconia* (1815) I. 112 With Rageles moodes they suffer wronge. **1948** R. GRAVES *Coll. Poems* 218 My self reversed, my rage-less part, a slimy yellowish cone.

Hence **'ragelessness,** absence of rage or rages.

1904 E. F. BENSON *Challoners* v. 101 London, tired with its spinster ragelessness, rose at them as trout rise in the days of May fly.

rageman, -ment, -mon, var. RAGMAN.

rageous ('reɪdʒəs), *a. Obs.* exc. *dial.* Also 5 rageouse, 5–6 ragyous, 5–8 ragious, 6 ragius. [a. OF. *rageux, -euse* (Godef.), f. *rage* RAGE *sb.*: see -OUS.] Furious, mad, full of passion: **a.** of persons, their attributes, actions, utterances, etc.

1440 in *Wars Eng. in France* (1864) II. 453 The grete trouble..begonne..by the rageous demenyng of thayme of Basyle. **1490** CAXTON *Eneydos* xxii. 81 Tourned from herself for grete sorowe in to a rageouse franesye. **1536** *Rem. Sedition* 1 Suche ragious outcries of souldiours, noyse and brayeng of horses. **1579** J. JONES *Preserv. Bodie & Soule* I. vii. 12 Pithagoras..quenched..the lusting minde of a ragious yong man. **1686** G. STUART *Joco-Ser. Disc.* II. 30 The Rageous Pangs that I ha' tane Wou'd e'en have burst'n a Heart o' Stane. *a* **1796** PEGGE *Derbicisms* Ser. II, *Ragious*, full of rage or anger, very angry. **1869–** In northern glossaries (Lonsd., Whitby, Linc., etc.). **1891** ATKINSON *Last of Giant-Killers* 57 There was a shrill peal of laughter such as to make Mr. Wolfwald shivery as well as rageous.

†**b.** *transf.* of things (sea, fire, etc.). *Obs.*

1430–40 LYDG. *Bochas* I. ii. (1544) 5 The boystruous wyndes and the ragious skie. **1532** MORE *Confut. Tindale* Wks. 520/1 Fierce & ragyous fire, whyche shall consume the aduersaryes. *c* **1555** HARPSFIELD *Divorce Hen. VIII* (1878) 177 The rageous insurges of the wind and water.

Hence †**'rageously** *adv.*; †**'rageousness.** *Obs.*

1509 FISHER *Serm. 10 May* Wks. (1876) 278 They ragyously and furyously gape. **1540** HYRDE tr. *Vives' Instr. Chr. Wom.* (1592) D d vj, What a ragiousnes is it, to set thy chastity common like an harlot, that thou maiest gather riches? **1600** SURFLET *Countrie Farme* VI. xvi. 758 If there bee any water it..will boile ragiouslie.

rager ('reɪdʒə(r)). Also 5 raiare. [f. RAGE *v.* + -ER[1].] **a.** One who, or that which, rages.

c **1440** *Promp. Parv.* 422/1 Raiare (*K.* ragere), *rabiator, rabulus.* **1622** S. WARD *Woe to Drunkards* (1627) 6 Wine is a rager and tumultuous make-bate. **1925** G. MURRAY tr. *Aeschylus' Eumenides* 4 The ragers sleep: the Virgins without love.

b. *spec. Austral.* 'An old and fierce bullock or cow that always begins to rage in the stock-yard' (Morris *Austral Eng.* 1898).

1884 'R. BOLDREWOOD' *Melb. Mem.* xiv. 105 Amongst them was a large proportion of bullocks, which declined with fiendish obstinacy to fatten. They were what are known by the stock-riders as 'ragers' or 'pig-meaters'. **1890** —— *Col. Reformer* (1891) 223 The 'rager' cuts through the opposing ranks like a dragoon through Chinese infantry.

†**'ragery.** *Obs.* In 4–5 ragerie, -ye. [a. OF. *ragerie* (Godef.): see RAGE *sb.* and -ERY.] Raging; wantonness, etc.; a frolic.

c **1386** CHAUCER *Wife's Prol.* 455, I was yong and ful of ragerye. **1390** GOWER *Conf.* II. 337 Diane..Was come, and in a ragerie Sche seide that sche bathe wolde. **1422** HOCCLEVE *Jonathas* 221 Fro your fyngir mighte it fall, Or plukkid of been in a ragerie.

ragesome ('reɪdʒsəm), *a. U.S. rare.* [f. RAGE *sb.* + -SOME.] Rageful, angry.

1913 G. STRATTON-PORTER *Laddie* xvii. 580 He can be awful ragesome when he's excited.

Rag-fair. [f. RAG *sb.*[1] + FAIR *sb.*[1]] A market for the sale of old clothes, held at Houndsditch in London.

1722 DE FOE *Col. Jack* (1840) 14 I'll go into Rag fair, and buy me a pair of shoes. **1805** TURNBULL in *Naval Chron.* XIV. 193 The cellars of Rag-fair. **1855** DICKENS *Dorrit* ix, Such threadbare coats and trousers..never were seen in Rag Fair. **1894–5** *Dickens' Dict. Lond.* 135 s.v. *Jews*, Rag Fair,..the greatest old clothes market of the metropolis, is held in a open space close to Houndsditch. Sunday morning is its busiest time.

attrib. **1722** DE FOE *Col. Jack* (1840) 14 We bought..a pair of Rag fair stockings. **1788** WOLCOTT (P. Pindar) *B. Peter to B. Tom* Wks. 1812 I. 535 Bartering like Rag-fair Jews. **1840** LOUISA S. COSTELLO *Summer amongst Bocages* II. 246 Quantities of ready-made clothes..all of coarse materials..giving a Rag-fair effect, anything but pleasing. *fig.* **1831** CARLYLE *Sart. Res.* III. iii, The tatters and rags of ..worn-out Symbols (in this Ragfair of a World).

b. *slang.* (See quots.)

1785 GROSE *Dict. Vulg. Tongue, Rag Fair*, an inspection of the linen and necessaries of a company of soldiers, commonly made by their officers on Mondays, or Saturdays. **1890** BARRÈRE & LELAND *Slang Dict.* (1897), *Rag-fair*.., kit inspection.

rag-fallow, -faugh. *Sc.* [The sense of *rag* is not clear.] (See quots.) So **rag-fallowing.**

1793–5 G. ROBERTSON *Agric. Surv. Mid. Lothian* 3 (Jam.) Rag-fauch is ground ploughed up, and prepared for wheat, that has been two years in grass, and generally gets three furrows. **1805** R. SOMERVILLE *Agric. Surv. E. Lothian* 110 Rag-fallow..consists in ploughing the clover down immediately after the first cutting. **1855** STEPHENS *Bk. Farm* (ed. 2) II. 266/1 A kind of fallowing, technically named rag-fallowing,..consists in pulverising lea ground in summer as a preparation for wheat in autumn.

ragg: see RAG *sb.*[2]

raggabash, -brash, variants of RAGABASH.

raggamouff, obs. variant of RAGAMUFF.

raggamuffian, -muffin, obs. ff. RAGAMUFFIN.

‖**raggare** ('ragarə). Pl. -(s). [Sw., f. *ragga* to pick up (girls).] In Sweden: a member of a gang of youths who cruise about in cars; a street-tough, a teddy-boy.

1964 *Pix* 25 Jan. 45/3 By midnight even most of the 'raggare'—Sweden's beatniks—have disappeared from the streets. **1971** *Daily Tel.* 2 Aug. 4/8 About 300 'raggares'—Sweden's motorised teddy boys—clashed with 90 police in ..Stockholm yesterday. **1977** *Time* 25 July 10/1 To their bitterest enemies, a group of restless young toughs known as the Raggare, the Assyrians are despised 'black-skulls', to be attacked with chains and clubs.

ragged ('rægɪd), *a.*[1] Forms: α. 3–5 ragget, 5 -eth, 4–9 *Sc.* -it, 6 -at; 4 raggede, (-ud, 4–5 -id, 5–6 -yd, 6 -ued), 6 wragged, 3– ragged. β. 5 ragyt, 5–6 -it; 4–6 raged, (5 -ud, 5–6 -yd). γ. 6 ragd(e, 6–7 rag'd, 8–9 *north. dial.* ragg'd, raggt. [f. RAG *sb.*[1] + -ED; but the early uses (senses 1 and 2) are not directly based on the prominent sense of the sb., and may have retained an older and more general meaning of the word (cf. RAGGY, and Norw. *ragget* shaggy).]

I. 1. a. Of animals, their fur, etc.: Rough, shaggy, hanging in tufts.

13.. *K. Alis.* 684 His men him brought..A grisly best, a ragged colt. *Ibid.* 4471 A raggid wolf. *a* **1400** *Octouian* 839 That fole, Raggeth, and hegh, and long of swere. *c* **1450** *Arth. & Merl.* L 1585 (Kölbing) His tayle was ragged [*v.r.* raggud] as a feond. **1579** SPENSER *Sheph. Cal.* Feb. 5 My ragged rontes all shiver and shake. **1697** DRYDEN *Virg. Past.* III. 1 What Shepherd owns those ragged Sheep? **1786** BURNS *Dream* xi, Aft a ragged cowte's been known To mak a noble aiver. **1791** 'G. GAMBADO' *Ann. Horsem.* (1809) Pref. 55 To preserve a ragged flock of sheep from the rot. **1859** KINGSLEY *Misc.* (1860) II. 237 A pair of ragged ponies.

†**b.** Of the Devil or devils, imagined as shaggy like beasts. *Obs.* (Cf. RAGAMUFFIN, RAGMAN[1].)

a **1300** in *Map's Poems* (Camden) 338 A thousend develene..thei weren ragged, roue, and tayled. *c* **1320** LANGTOFT *Chron.* (Rolls) II. 248 The devel I them bikenne That ragged sit in helle. *c* **1460** *Towneley Myst.* viii. 414 Help! the raggyd dwyll, we drowne!

c. Of birds: Having the feathers broken, or irregularly disposed. *rare.*

1508 DUNBAR *Flyting* 57 Revin, raggit ruke, and full of rebaldrie. **1611** COTGR., *Faulcon halbrené*, a Faulcon thats ragged, or broken-feathered.

2. Of a rough, irregular, or straggling form; having a broken jagged outline or surface; full of rough or sharp projections.

a. of roots, branches, plants, trees, etc.

13.. *Gaw. & Gr. Knt.* 745 With roȝe raged mosse. **1362** LANGL. *P. Pl.* A. x. 120 Out of a ragged roote and of rouwe breres. **1390** GOWER *Conf.* II. 177 That was to day a ragged tre, To morwe..Stant in the temple wel besein. *c* **1470** *Gol. & Gaw.* 854 As roise ragit on rise. **1598** SYLVESTER *Du Bartas* II. I. IV. 104 The ragged Bramble With thousand scratches doth their Skin bescramble. **1664** EVELYN *Kal. Hort.* (1729) 195 Rosemary thrives better by cutting off the Sprigs, than by ragged slips. **1794** COWPER *Needless Alarm* 14 Wide yawns a gulf beside a ragged thorn. **1860** RUSKIN *Mod. Paint.* V. VI. x. §12. 97 Leaves rent into alternate gaps ..give the expression to foreground vegetation which we feel and call 'ragged'.

b. of stones, rocks, cliffs, buildings, etc.

c **1400** *Destr. Troy* 12559 Roches full rogh, ragget with stones. *c* **1435** *Torr. Portugal* 194 Ther lay a gret Ragyd ston. **1579** LYLY *Euphues* (Arb.) 120 One may..weare the precious Diamonde though he dispise the ragged bricke. **1595** SPENSER *Col. Clout* 114 That auncient Cittie..Whose ragged ruines breed great ruth. **1632** LITHGOW *Trav.* x. 447 [Toledo] is situate on a ragged Rocke. **1695** J. EDWARDS *Perfect. Script.* 285 This ragged pile was of much antienter date. **1742** COLLINS *Ecl.* iv. 19 Yon ragged cliff, whose dang'rous path we tried. **1860** TYNDALL *Glac.* I. xviii. 128 I descended..through a second ragged fissure.

c. of a stretch of ground or country.

1555 EDEN *Decades* 350 The toppe of the mountayne sheweth very ragged. **1607** J. NORDEN *Surv. Dial.* v. 203 Euen the best meddowes will become ragged and full of unprofitable weeds, if it bee not cut and eaten. **1697** DAMPIER *Voy.* (1729) I. 256 To the West of this ragged Land is a Chain of Mountains. **1796** MRS. E. PARSONS *Myst. Warning* III. 188 A ragged and unfrequented part of the hill. **1867** TROLLOPE *Chron. Barset* II. l. 65 A path led through a ragged garden.

d. of other things.

a **1400–50** *Alexander* 5133 Rynoseros, a roghe best with raggid tyndis. **1598** SHAKS. *Merry W.* IV. iv. 31 Herne the Hunter..with great rag'd-hornes. **1664** POWER *Exp. Philos.* I. 53 A right line either printed or drawn never so neatly upon paper appears all ragged, indented, and discontinued. **1821** SHELLEY *Prometh. Unb.* III. ii, Through the thick ragged skirts Of the victorious darkness. **1873** BLACK *Pr. Thule* vii. 112 The wind sent ragged bits of yellow cloud across the shining blue.

†**e.** *absol.* as *sb.* The rough part, roughness.

a **1300** *Ancr. R.* 284 *note* (MS. C.), þe file fret of þe irn þe rust & tet ragget, & makeð hit hwit & smeðe.

3. *transf.* of immaterial things (in some cases perh. directly associated with sense 5):

a. Faulty, imperfect, irregular.

c **1500** *Priests of Peblis* 1044, I am red that my count be ovir raggit. **1579** E. K. *Ded. Spenser's Sheph. Cal.* ¶ij, Theyr rough sounde would make his rymes more ragged and rustical. **1621** QUARLES *Argalus & P.* (1678) 110 Aid me and inspire My ragged rhimes, with thy diviner fire. *a* **1864** HAWTHORNE *Eng. Note-bks.* (1879) I. 133 Uttering one rough, ragged, and shapeless sentence after another. **1888** MRS. H. WARD *R. Elsmere* IV. xxx, His work..He saw it all as the merest nothing, a ragged beginning. **1894** *Times* 6 Mar. 7/2 Began to row at 33 strokes a minute. The work was done in ragged fashion.

b. Of sounds: Harsh, discordant, rough.

1600 SHAKS. *A.Y.L.* II. v. 15 My voice is ragged; I know I cannot please you. **1633** G. HERBERT *Temple, Redemption*, I heard a ragged noise and mirth Of Theeves and Murderers. **1840** DICKENS *Barn. Rudge* viii, A voice as ragged as the head.

4. *Her.* = RAGULY.

1562 LEIGH *Armorie* (1597) 31 b, He beareth Geules, a long crosse ragged and trunked Argent. **1727–41** CHAMBERS *Cycl.* s.v. *Raguled, Ragged* differs from indented, in that the latter is regular, and the former not.

II. 5. a. Of cloth, garments, etc.: Rent, torn, frayed, in rags.

c **1325** *Alexis* 155 in Horstm. *Altengl. Leg.* (1881) 177 Full raggid and riuen wase his clathis. **1377** LANGL. *P. Pl.* B. XI. 33 Recchelesnes stode forth in ragged clothes. *c* **1400** *Destr. Troy* 13525 A Roket full rent, and Ragget aboue. **1567** *Add. MS.* 6167, lf. 203 b, in Gross *Gild Merch.* II. 92 Which booke is so ragged, torne, and rent one peece from another. **1599** SHAKS. *Hen. V*, IV. ii. 41 Their ragged Curtaines poorely are let loose. **1709** STEELE *Tatler* No. 37 ¶3 Are your Petticoats ragged? **1745** POCOCKE *Descr. East* II. I. 166 Their sheik..came out to us in a ragged habit of green silk, lined with fur. **1870** DICKENS *E. Drood* i, He draws back the ragged curtain.

b. Of places: Dilapidated, broken-down. *rare.*

1805 WORDSW. *Prelude* III. 465 Ragged villages and crazy huts. **1851** S. JUDD *Margaret* xv. 124 A small, low, ragged room.

6. Of persons: Wearing ragged clothes; dressed in rags. Hence of appearance, etc. Also of mood or condition: tired, run-down. Colloq. phr. ***to run*** (one) ***ragged*** (orig. *U.S.*): to exhaust or debilitate (a person).

c **1375** *Sc. Leg. Saints* xlvi. (*Anastas*) 186 Fra þat place þan vald he ga, raggit & rent & blak alswa. *c* **1530** *Court of Love* 478 To wander lich a dulled ass, Ragged and torne, disgysed in array. **1570** GOLDING *Justin* XXVIII. 127 No better but a sort of ragged Shepeheardes. **1642** VICARS *God in Mount* (1644) 78 A ragged regiment of malignant and ill-affected persons. **1781** GIBBON *Decl. & F.* xxxi. III. 215 A swarm of dirty and ragged plebeians. **1850** L. HUNT *Autobiog.* xx. 319 These coadjutors were..the raggedest fellows in Genoa. **1876** BESANT & RICE *Gold. Butterfly* Prol. ii, He was in no way discomfited by any sense of false shame as to his ragged appearance. **1925** *New Yorker* 5 Sept. 10/3 This eighteen-year-old youngster ran Bill Johnston, the Californian, ragged. **1951** W. STEVENS *Let.* 26 Mar. (1967) 712 This is simply typical of the sort of thing that runs one ragged. **1969** M. PUGH *Last Place Left* xxix. 213 Sorry, sir, I'm pretty ragged. Is Miss Drummond okay? **1970** A. DRAPER *Swansong for Rare Bird* v. 35 We really ran the teachers ragged. **1977** P. HILL *Liars* (1978) iii. 36 All four of them were now feeling mentally ragged.

7. *Combs.* and *phrases*, as ***ragged-edged, -looking*** adjs.; †**ragged-apples** (see quot.); **ragged edge** *U.S. slang*: in phr. ***on*** (also ***in***) ***the ragged edge***, on the extreme edge or verge; also *transf.*, in a state of distress or resourcelessness; **ragged hip,** in a horse: a hip standing away from the backbone (hence ***ragged-hipped*** adj.); **ragged-jacket,** †**regiment** (see quots.); **ragged r** (see quots.); **Ragged Robert** (see quot.); **ragged school,** a free school for children of the poorest class. See also RAGGED ROBIN, RAGGED STAFF.

1601 HOLLAND *Pliny* XV. xiv. 438 The *ragged-apples *Pannucea* take this name, for that of all others they soonest be riveld. **1885** *N.Y. Mercury* 10 Jan. 4/7 It seems fair to assume that father, daughter and her child sailed yesterday for Paris, leaving poor Tom on the *ragged edge. **1889** 'MARK TWAIN' *Connecticut Yankee* xvi. 196 He was always on the ragged edge of apprehension. **1892** —— *Amer. Claimant* ii. 28 It was away out in the ragged edge of Washington and had once been somebody's country place. **1935** A. J. POLLOCK *Underworld Speaks* 84/1 *On the ragged edge*, slight chance to make good; down and out. **1916** 'BOYD CABLE' *Action Front* 164 The face of one house was marked by a huge splash, with solid centre and a *ragged-edged outline of radiating jerky rays. **1799** *Sporting Mag.* XIV. 185 The goose-rump as well as the *ragged hip [is] another angular infringement of Hogarth's curve of beauty. **1843** YOUATT *Horse* xvii. 353 Many a *ragged-hipped horse has possessed both fleetness and strength. **1898** J. A. GIBBS *Cotswold Village* 345 Well ribbed up, he is at the same time rather 'ragged-hipped'. **1884** GOODE *Usef. Aquatic Anim.* 62 The young [of the Harp Seal] when first born, are called by the Newfoundland sealers 'White-coats'; later, during the first molt, '*Ragged-jackets'. **1833** F. WITTS *Diary* 8 Apr.

(1978) 91 One tract of common over which we passed is called Coalpit-heath, a *ragged-looking spot. **1884** 'H. Collingwood' (W. J. C. Lancaster) *Under Meteor Flag* 3 Dull, dirty, ragged-looking clouds. **1755** J. Smith *Printer's Gram.* iv. 117 Black letter..has two different r's, one of which is called the *ragged r [ꝛ], and is particularly used after letters that round off behind. **1969** H. Carter *View of Early Typogr.* iii. 62 The ragged r—the r that followed letters that had once been round. **1770** in *Archæologia* I. 37 *note* This table of pictures is fixed over the press [in Westminster Abbey] wherein the effigies of the kings vulgarly called, The *ragged regiment, are placed. **1765** Layard in *Phil. Trans.* LVI. 18 The herb *Geranium Robertianum*, commonly called *Ragged Robert. **1843** *Times* 18 Feb. 1/3 Advt. [headed] '*Ragged Schools'. **1847** Cockburn *Jrnl.* II. 172 There was a public meeting here on the 9th instant [April] in favour of what are now called 'ragged schools'.

Hence '**raggedish** *a.*, somewhat ragged.

1837 *New Monthly Mag.* XLIX. 235 A large, rather raggedish, arm-chair.

ragged (rægd), *a.*² (or *pple.*) *dial.* [Of obscure origin; connexion with prec. is not clear.] Covered with fruit; thickly laden.

1661 Hickeringill *Jamaica* 16 A sort of Cabbage trees, rag'd with berries. *a* **1796** Pegge *Derbicisms* Ser. I. **1877-** In dial. glossaries (Yks., Linc.).

ragged (rægd), *ppl. a.*¹ [f. rag *v.*³] Subjected to the process of ragging (*vbl. sb.*³).

1875 *Ure's Dict. Arts* II. 76 In the process of cobbing, either ragged or spalled work.

ragged (rægd), *ppl. a.*² [f. rag *v.*²] That has suffered ragging, teasing, or annoyance.

1903 *Westm. Gaz.* 11 May 6/2 The 'ragged' officer was allowed leave of absence and has not yet returned to duty.

ragged (rægd), *ppl. a.*³ [f. rag *v.*⁵] Of music: that has been converted to ragtime.

1956 G. P. Kurath in A. F. C. Wallace *Men & Cultures* (1960) 155 They represent the following steps:..Two-step (ragged). **1958** C. Wilford in P. Gammond *Decca Bk. Jazz* ii. 40 Ragtime lives on in jazz, for all jazz is based on ragtime, though it is true some parts are more ragged than others.

raggedemuffin, obs. form of ragamuffin.

raggedly ('rægɪdlɪ), *adv.* [f. ragged *a.*¹ + -ly².] In a ragged manner.

1552 Huloet, Raggedly arayed, *pannose.* **1586** J. Melvill *Let.* in *Wodrow Misc.* (1844) 438 He spake raggatly the rough truth. **1592** Ld. Vaux in Ellis *Orig. Lett.* Ser. iv. IV. 109, I am come upp raggedlie suted and clothed. **1691** *Meeting at Hague* in *Coll. Poems* 37 All raggedly torn, this Mobb of Commanders. **1854** Thoreau *Walden* (1884) 293, I heard the foxes..barking raggedly and demoniacally like forest dogs. **1881** J. Hawthorne *Fortune's Fool* i. v, The grass grew tall and raggedly in the shaded corners.

raggedness ('rægɪdnɪs). [f. ragged *a.*¹ + -ness.] The fact or condition of being ragged.

1. Roughness; irregularity of form, surface, etc.

1538 Elyot *Dict.*, *Lamæ*, the raggydnesse of rockes. **1601** Holland *Pliny* xxxii. x. 448 The grosse pickle sauce called Alex..cureth the raggednesse of nails. **1610** Donne *Lett.* (1651) 224 You have been so long used to my hand that I stand not to excuse the hasty raggednesse of this letter. **1658** Evelyn *French Gardiner* (1675) 71 Pared away the raggednesse which the saw hath left. **1725** Bradley *Fam. Dict.* s.v. *Shoeing of Horses*, The raggedness also on the outside of the coffin should be fil'd away.

2. Ragged state of clothing or persons.

1580 Sidney *Arcadia* iii. (1598) 297 His decking..being cut out into the fashion of very rags: yet all so daintily ioyned together with precious stones, as it was a braue raggednesse. **1605** Shaks. *Lear* iii. iv. 31 Your lop'd, and window'd raggednesse. **1728-9** Swift *Lett.*, to *Worrall* 13 Jan. (1766) II. 89 My raggedness will soon force me away. **1816** W. Taylor in *Monthly Rev.* LXXXI. 121 That ignoble raggedness with which Aristophanes reproaches this tragedian. **1859** Sala *Tw. round Clock* (1861) 96 His silk gown is shabby, almost to raggedness.

3. *fig.* Want of coherence, connexion, etc. *rare.*

1590 C. S. *Right Relig.* 32 These painted clothes bewray the raggednesse of their religion. **1616** Hieron *Wks.* I. 586 The more aduised, holding it vp (as it were) against the light, see the rawnesse and raggednesse and independance of that which is deliuered.

4. Irregularity, lack of uniformity.

1885 *Manch. Guard.* 28 Mar. 6/6 The most noticeable faults of the Cantabs are bad time and raggedness of feather. **1894** *Times* 4 June 11/5 The most remarkable feature of the shooting was the raggedness of the volleys.

ragged robin. [See robin.] One of the popular names of a well-known English flower, *Lychnis Floscuculi.* Also *attrib.*

1741 *Compl. Fam.-Piece* ii. iii. 401 *Lychnis Coronaria*, Spiderwort, ragged Robbin. **1777** [see cuckoo-flower]. **1821** Clare *Vill. Minstr.* II. 133 The ragged-robins by the spinney lake. **1872** Black *Adv. Phaeton* II. xx. 92 The viscid petals of the Ragged Robin glimmered a bright crimson. **1875** Ruskin *Fors Clav.* V. 279, I have been quietly drawing ragged-robin leaves.

b. *transf.* A ragged person.

1826 Scott *Woodst.* ii, I took thee up when thou wert but a ragged Robin, made a keeper of thee and so forth. **1859** Tennyson *Geraint* 724 The Prince Hath pick'd a ragged-robin from the hedge, And..brought her to the court.

ragged staff. [ragged *a.*¹ 2.]

1. A staff with projecting stumps or knobs; chiefly in reference to the badge or crest of the Earls of Warwick.

1449 *Pol. Poems* (Rolls) II. 222 The Bere..hath lost his ragged staffe. **1556** *Chron. Gr. Friars* (Camden) 73 The pepulle sayd dyvers that ther was the ragyd staffe. **1593** Shaks. *2 Hen. VI*, v. i. 203 Old Neuils Crest, The rampant Beare chain'd to the ragged staffe. **1685** Temple *Ess., Gardens* Wks. 1731 I. 185 [Vines] should be left but like a Ragged Staff, not above two or three Eyes at most upon the Bearing Branches. **1778** *Eng. Gazetteer* (ed. 2) s.v. *Penrith*, A town-house..beautified with bears climbing up a ragged staff. **1856** Emerson *Eng. Traits, Aristocracy* Wks. (Bohn) II. 78 The black ragged staff, his badge.

2. *Naut.* (See quot.)

1805 W. Hunter in *Naval Chron.* XIII. 13, I was one day watering at the ragged Staff. [*Note.* So called from the Stump Mast..fitted into the Launch, when sent to get water, in order to hoist the Casks in and out.]

raggedy ('rægɪdɪ), *a.* Chiefly *U.S.* and *dial.* Also 9- **raggety**; **raggity.** [f. ragged *a.*¹ + -y¹.]

1. Of a ragged form or appearance.

a. Of persons. Cf. ragged *a.*¹ 6.

1890 J. W. Riley in *Century Mag.* Dec. 318/2 Oh, the Raggedy Man! He works fer Pa; An' he's the goodest man ever you saw! **1894** Crockett *Raiders* 211 Fore and aft of the herd there were raggety boys holding the beasts in check. **1939** J. Steinbeck *Grapes of Wrath* xxiv. 462 A raggedy kid with no shoes. **1959** *Encounter* Dec. 17/2 The covey of raggety small boys. **1960** C. Day Lewis *Buried Day* iii. 38 The bridge..was lined..with raggedy men. **1975** *New Yorker* 1 Dec. 48/2 A lady's..raggedy kids lined up by the track where they'd put pennies.

b. Of clothing. Cf. ragged *a.*¹ 5 a.

1893 *Trans. Devonshire Assoc. Adv. Sci., Lit., & Art* XXV. 201 My smock's a-got cruel raggety, I sim. **1929** D. Runyon in *Hearst's Internat.* Oct. 62/2 Mostly she is wearing raggedy clothes and busted shoes. **1967** H. Porter in *Coast to Coast 1965-6* 171 Underwear got more raggedy. **1978** J. Carroll *Mortal Friends* iii. v. 322 It serves me right for asking what raggedy clothing you'd flung off.

2. Of a rough, irregular, or straggling form. Cf. ragged *a.*¹ 2. **a.** *gen.*

1896 'Mark Twain' in *Harper's Mag.* Aug. 358/1 Raggedy white patch between the shoulders..looked like some-body had hit him with a snow-ball. **1899** *Pall Mall G.* 26 Dec. 2/1 A man with..unpleasant-looking, raggedy teeth. **1938** L. Mumford *Whither Honolulu?* v. 16 Cities throughout America have been..over-extending themselves in raggedy fragments. **1955** J. Masters *Coromandel!* i. 23 Voy sucked his raggedy moustache.

b. Of branches, plants, etc.

1912 J. Stephens *Crock of Gold* v. 40 There was a raggedy blackberry hedge all round the field. **1927** D. H. Lawrence *Mornings in Mexico* 12 Like rather raggedy green buds climbing to the sun.

3. Of music or rhythm: irregular, uneven, broken. Cf. ragged *a.*¹ 3 b.

1949 R. Blesh *Shining Trumpets* viii. 186 The tempo is buoyant, the beat is alive, and the rhythm is very *raggedy.* **1975** *New Yorker* 19 May 113/2 A casual encounter between a boy and a girl who compete to the piled-up, off-center rhythms of many raggedy dances.

4. *Comb.*, as **Raggedy Andy** *U.S.*, a rag-doll, the male counterpart of Raggedy Ann (see next); **Raggedy Ann** orig. *U.S.*, a rag-doll with short, mop-like, red hair; also *attrib.*; **raggedy-ass(ed)** *a. U.S. slang* (orig. *Mil.*) [cf. ass *sb.*²], of persons: inexperienced, raw; also *transf.*

1920 J. Gruelle *Raggedy Andy Stories* 2 Gran'ma had told Daddy..that at the time Raggedy Ann was made, a neighbor lady had made a boy doll, *Raggedy Andy. **1974** *News & Reporter* (Chester, S. Carolina) 22 Apr. 5-A/1 He was honored with a family party at his home with guests enjoying Raggedy Andy Cake. **1918** J. Gruelle *Raggedy Ann Stories* Pref., To the millions of children and grown-ups who have loved a Rag Doll, I dedicate these stories of *Raggedy Ann. **1957** M. B. Picken *Fashion Dict.* 124/2 *Raggedy Ann costume*, costume taken from child's story book about a stuffed doll. Consists of bright colored patched skirt, patched apron, simple white blouse, white socks and black shoes. Usually worn with ragged woolen wig. **1966** J. S. Cox *Illustr. Dict. Hairdressing* 124/2 *Raggedy Ann Bob*, a short hair style for women similar to the wind-blown bob. **1967** *Southerly* XXVII. 209 Katrina..brushed the short, raggedy-ann hair until it shone. **1970** *New Yorker* 14 Nov. 50/3 She removed the clothes from a Raggedy Ann doll and stuck a pin..into the center. **1976** *Times* 8 July 12/1 (*caption*) Raggity Ann patched up trousers. **1977** *Redbook* Mar. 81/2 Kim wanted a Raggedy Ann cake. **1930** T. Fredenburgh *Soldiers March* vii. 50 The *Raggedy Ass Cadets are out today. **1956** B. Holiday *Lady sings Blues* (1973) vi. 57 I'd have to travel five hundred to six hundred miles on a hot or cold raggedy-ass Blue Goose bus. **1967** E. Liebow in T. Kochman *Rappin' & Stylin' Out* (1972) 406 A nice woman does not dress in 'raggedy-ass clothes'. **1969** J. A. McPherson *Hue & Cry* 58 Who taught you the moves when you were just a raggedy-ass waiter? **1929** in J. J. Niles et al. *Songs My Mother never taught Me* 182 The *raggedy assed cadets are on parade. **1971** R. Flanagan *Maggot* 252 Respect what man, you raggedy-assed little fuck?

raggee, var. ragi.

raggeman, -muffin, obs. ff. ragman, ragamuffin.

'**ragger**¹. [f. rag *v.*¹ 2 b.] One who sorts needles by means of a rag.

1861 Wynter *Soc. Bees* 189 Heads and points still lie together, and in order to put them all in the same direction, the 'ragger' is employed.

ragger². [f. rag *v.*² + -er¹.] One who rags or teases; *spec.* a participant in a student rag.

1903 *Speaker* 7 Feb. 451/1 There is much to be said in favour of the 'raggers'. Mere 'ragging' as distinguished from ..persistent and brutal bullying..never yet did a youngster any harm. **1905** *Westm. Gaz.* 15 May 7/3 One of the raggers received a bullet in the mouth, and is seriously injured. **1909** H. G. Wells *Ann Veronica* xi. 220 Ann Veronica decided that 'hoydenish ragger' was the only phrase to express her. She was always breaking rules. **1930** *Daily Express* 6 Nov. 1/2 Guys were then thrown on the blazing piles amid the wild shrieks of the 'raggers'.

raggery ('rægərɪ). *rare.* [f. rag *sb.*¹ + -ery.] **a.** Ragged people. **b.** Rags, collectively.

1843 Thackeray *Irish Sk.-bk.* viii, Round the coach came crowds of raggery, and blackguards fawning for money. **1854** —— *Newcomes* xxxv, Grim portentous old hags.. draped in majestic raggery.

ragghe, obs. f. rag *sb.*²

raggi, var. ragi.

raggie ('rægɪ). *Mil.* Also **raggy.** [f. rag *sb.*¹ + -ie.] †**1.** A mess jacket. *Obs.*

1843 F. J. Bellew *Mem. Griffin* I. ix. 126 As for myself, in my scarlet raggie, brimstone facings,..and regulation sword, in my own opinion, I looked quite the god of war. **1903** *N. & Q.* 26 Dec. 512/2 In India, in the early part of last century,..the scarlet 'shell' jacket, or mess jacket—almost the only uniform then worn in that country—was invariably called a 'raggie', and this not jocularly or as slang, but seriously and as a matter of course.

2. *Naval slang.* (See quot. 1912.)

1912 'Aurora' *Jock Scott* xiv. 170 A 'raggy' is a friend whom you know so intimately that you feel you could with confidence keep your brass-rags in the same bag as his. **1914** 'Bartimeus' *Naval Occasions* xiv. 111 'If I don't get no letter this mail—so 'elp me I stops me 'arf pay,' he confided grimly to a 'Raggie'. **1916** 'Taffrail' *Carry On!* 27 Men who are friendly with each other are 'raggies', because they have the free run of each others' polishing paste and rags; but if their friendship terminates they are said to have 'parted brass-rags'. **1946** J. Irving *Royal Navalese* 143 *Raggie*, a very close friend.

'**ragging**, *vbl. sb.*¹ *rare*⁻¹. [f. rag *v.*¹] *concr.* Ragged edges or projections.

1683 Moxon *Mech. Exerc., Printing* xvi, To Justifie the Mold, and clear it from Ragging.

'**ragging**, *vbl. sb.*² [f. rag *v.*²] The action of scolding, annoying, etc.; an instance of this. Also *attrib.*

1796 Grose *Dict. Vulg. Tongue* (ed. 3) s.v. *Rag*, She gave him a good ragging. **1888** E. Dowson *Let.* Nov. (1967) 19 After a good deal of ragging with Chitty J. two days ago, the affair was settled. **1893** *Daily News* 25 Sept. 5/3 Commemoration Week exercises at Oxford furnished..the most audacious examples of 'ragging'. **1899** T. M. Ellis *Three Cat's-eye Rings* 114 What a ragging we should get! **1920** *Chambers's Jrnl.* 1 May 337/1 An ugly ragging mood was astir. **1932** *Daily Tel.* 8 Oct. 12/4 Ragging in the army, such as we have at home (this was said just after one of the so-called 'ragging scandals' in the Guards) would be impossible here. **1942** *R.A.F. Jrnl.* 2 May 31, I miss the comradeship, the ragging, the talks in Mess.

ragging, *vbl. sb.*³ [f. rag *v.*³]

1. (See quot. and cf. rag *v.*³)

1875 *Ure's Dict. Arts* II. 78 *Ragging*..consists simply in reducing the stones to a smaller size, and rejecting as many of the sterile stones as can be readily picked out.

attrib. **1875** *Ure's Dict. Arts* II. 76 The ragging hammer should..be brought into free requisition. **1878** *Ibid.* IV. (Suppl.) 618 Steel ragging sledge, 7lb. weight.

2. Ore of a certain class (see quots.). Also *pl.*

1860 C. Tomlinson *Useful Arts & Manuf.* 2nd Ser. *Dressing ores* 10 That portion [of a dredging] occupying the bottom of the sieve, called ragging, which is also in a marketable state. **1878** *Ure's Dict. Arts* IV. (Suppl.) 618 The ores are divided into four classes: (1) Cobbed ore; (2) Sieve raggings; (3) Fine Raggings; (4) Slimes. **1890** Lock *Mining & Ore-dressing Mach.* 395 The mixed product of the jiggers..called chatts or ragging, must be separately treated.

3. = straggling *vbl. sb.*²

1850 [see straggling *vbl. sb.*²].

'**ragging**, *vbl. sb.*⁴ orig. *U.S.* [f. rag *v.*⁵] The act or practice of playing, singing, or dancing in ragtime.

1899 [see rag *sb.*⁵ 1]. **1913** *Collier's Mag.* 15 Feb. 6/2 The worst of these dance halls..are habitually frequented by people of the fashionable and so-called decent class, who go ..for the purpose of joining in the 'ragging'. **1914** 'High Jinks Jr.' *Choice Slang* 17 *Ragging*, the act of doing the 'Rag'. **1936** *Harper's Mag.* 3 Apr. 570/2 'Jamming', 'cat-time', 'swing', 'riffing', 'getting off', 'going to town', 'ragging', 'gut-bucketing',..are names for the *hot* performance, which is the heart and soul of jazz. **1958** *Life* (Internat. ed.) 13 Oct. 96/2 The rhythm was called ragtime (after a Negro clog dance sometimes called 'ragging').

raggle ('ræg(ə)l), *sb.*¹ *Sc.* [Of obscure origin and history: cf. the vb.] A groove cut in stone, esp. on a wall to receive the end or edge of a roof.

1835 in *Sc. Nat. Dict.* (1968) s.v. *Raggle* v.¹, n.¹ **1881** D. H. Fleming *Guide St. Andrews* 55 The raggle of the roof and the ragged marks of the wall are still seen on the west front of the tower. **1895** E. M. Chalmers *St. Ninian's Candida Casa* 9 The raggle cut in the stone for the roof. **1956** *Scotsman* 22 Sept. 9/1, I am..taken aback by the nonchalance with which these..men stroll about among the chimney pots..uttering deep thoughts about raggles and sarking, flashing and skews and Raffit verges.

† **'raggle**, *sb.*[2] *Sc. Obs.*$^{-1}$ Straggling order.
1594 in Tytler *Hist. Scot.* (1864) IV. 222 [Marching, as described by an eye-witness] at raggle and in plumps without order.

'raggle, *sb.*[3] *U.S.* [f. RAG *sb.*[1] + -LE.] A rag, a strip (of fur, etc.).
1888 *Cosmopolitan* (quoted in *Cent. Dict.*).

raggle ('ræg(ə)l), *v.* [? f. RAGGLE *sb.*[1]; but the vbl. sb. is found much earlier than this.] **a.** *trans.* To cut a raggle in (stone). **b.** = HOUSE *v.* 4 d.
1808 JAMIESON, *To raggle*..in architecture, to jagg, to make a groove in one stone for receiving another. **1833** LOUDON *Encycl. Arch.* §1066 All the treads and risers to be raggled (housed) into strings.

raggle-taggle ('ræg(ə)l,tæg(ə)l), *a.* and *sb.* Also **wraggle-taggle.** [App. fanciful var. RAG-TAG.]
A. *adj.* Of a group of persons: ragged, rambling, straggling; disreputable, unorganized (freq. used in allusion to the song referred to in quot. 1904). Hence of a person and in extended use of appearance, etc.
1904 in Sharp & Marson *Folk Songs from Somerset* 1st Ser. 19 What care I for my house and my land? What care I for my money, O? What care I for my new wedded lord? I'm off with the wraggle taggle gipsies, O! **1913** C. MACKENZIE *Sinister St.* I. I. ii. 29 He made up his mind..that it was better to be a raggle-taggle wanderer than anything else. **1923** J. BUCHAN *Midwinter* i. 34 My companions are the moor-men and..the raggle-taggle gypsies. **1933** W. STARKIE *Raggle-Taggle* ii. 7 It was no easy task to convince my family of my sanity in wishing to follow the raggle-taggle Gypsies. **1936** C. DAY LEWIS *Friendly Tree* 132 Like the lady who ran away with the wraggle-taggle gipsies. **1942** C. BARRETT *On Wallaby* vi. 122 It was a Paddy's market day and a raggle-taggle crowd had gathered to bargain shrewdly and noisily. **1970** N. BAWDEN *Birds on Trees* v. 83 It's not easy for someone of my generation to accept this raggle-taggle look, we had a bit more self-respect. **1977** O. JACKS *Autumn Heroes* viii. 118 How would you rate your raggle-taggle band of poorly armed warriors?
B. *sb.* **a.** A wanderer, a rover. **b.** A straggling, unorganized, or disreputable collection of persons.
1933 W. STARKIE (*title*) Raggle-taggle. **1958** *Times* 19 Mar. 7/4 President Nasser's permanent Afro-Asian guests—that Cairo raggle-taggle ranging from the permanent representatives of the Algerian National Liberation Front on the one hand to the office of the Deputy Imam of Oman on the other. **1972** 'H. CALVIN' *Take Two Popes* ii. 18 The Curia..considered *all* non-Italians as an unfortunate raggle-taggle.

'raggling. Also 5 raggalyne, 7- raglin(e, ragling.
a. *Build.* = RAGGLE *sb.*[1]
1500 in *Sc. Nat. Dict.* (1968) s.v. *Raggle* v.[1], n.[1] **1683** MARTINE *Reliq. Divi Andreæ* (1797) 183 The chaple hath had at several times three roofes, as appears by the raggling in the body of the chaple eastward. **1704–1898** in *Sc. Nat. Dict.* (1968) s.v. *Raggle* v.[1], n.[1] **1833** LOUDON *Encycl. Arch.* §983 Common rafters 3 inches by 2 inches and a half; rafflings, 3 inches and a half by 2 inches. **1929** H. MARWICK *Orkney Norn* 137/1 *Raglins*, the top of the side walls of a house, the space between top of wall and the slates. **1964** J. S. SCOTT *Dict. Building* 255 *Raglet* or *raggle* or *raglin*, a thin groove, in stone often dovetailed, cut in stone or in a mortar joint of brickwork to receive the end of a lead flashing, which is fixed by burning in or wedging.
b. *Mining.* (See quot. 1886.)
1839 URE *Dict. Arts* 985 There is a simple mode of conducting air from the pit bottom to the forehead of the mine, by cutting a ragglin, or trumpeting, as it is termed, in the side of the gallery. **1886** J. BARROWMAN *Gloss. Scotch Mining Terms* 53 *Raggling*, a channel cut in the side of a mine and covered with boarding to serve as an airway.

† **raggmall.** *Obs. rare*$^{-1}$. ? = RAGAMUFFIN.
1581 J. BELL *Haddon's Answ. Osor.* 276 New straunge stragglers, bussardly blynde and unknowne Raggmalles.

raggy ('rægɪ), *a.*[1] Also 4 raggi, 6–7 raggie. [OE. *raggiʒ*, app. f. **ragg* RAG *sb.*[1] (q.v.). Cf. Sw. *raggig* shaggy, rough.] = RAGGED *a.*
a **1100** in Napier *O.E. Glosses* 131/5191 *Setosa*,..raggie, loc[code]. (Cf. *ibid.* 155/30 *Setosa*, racgige.) *c* **1320** LANGTOFT *Chron.* (Rolls) II. 248 The roghe raggi sculke Rug ham in helle! **1483** *Cath. Angl.* 299/1 Raggy, *fractillosus.* **1567** DRANT *Horace, Ep.* II. i. G viij, Raggie rugged rymes. **1601** HOLLAND *Pliny* XIV. vi, Upon a stony and raggie hill. **1750** RUTTY in *Phil. Trans.* LI. 472 A sediment..partly white and raggy. **1822** *Blackw. Mag.* XII. 785 [It] sent up only weeded, raggy, and mixed crops. **1876** SMILES *Sc. Natur.* ii. (ed. 4) 38 His clothes were thin and raggy.
Comb. **1600** E. BLOUNT *Hosp. Incur. Fooles* 8 His traine of three or fower raggie heeld followers.

raggy ('rægɪ), *a.*[2] *slang.* [f. RAG *v.*[2] + -Y[1].] Annoyed; irritated.
1900 G. SWIFT *Somerley* 21 He was jolly raggy about us taking his old gee.

raggy ('rægɪ), *a.*[3] orig. *U.S.* [f. RAG *sb.*[5] + -Y[1].] Of music: pertaining to or resembling ragtime; characterized by ragtime.
1933 *Fortune* Aug. 92/1 At sixteen he began to play raggy music for Washington society with Louis Thomas' orchestra. **1944** W. RUSSELL in M. T. Williams *Art of Jazz* (1960) iv. 36 His feeling for a joyful, raggy, and stompy rhythm. **1952** B. ULANOV *Hist. Jazz in Amer.* (1958) xv. 181 Duke wove tricky, raggy, endlessly inventive variations around the Miley theme. **1958** in P. Gammond *Decca Bk. Jazz* xv. 185 Arthur Schutt, whose raggy piano sounded on many a Mole or Nichols session. **1972** *Jazz & Blues* Dec. 30/2 Billie's very raggy piano.

raggy, var. RAGGIE.

raght(e, raȝt(e, obs. ff. pa. t. REACH.

ragi ('rɑːgiː), **raggy** ('rægɪ). Also **rag(g)ee, raggi.** [Hindī (Skr.) *rāgī.*] One of the food-grains of India (*Eleusine coracana*).
1792 in G. R. Gleig *Life Sir T. Munro* (1830) III. 92 (Y.) The season for sowing raggy, rice, and bajera. **1800** *Asiat. Ann. Reg., Misc. Tr.* 178/2 A small quantity of dry grain, such as raggy and Indian corn. **1869** E. A. PARKES *Pract. Hygiene* (ed. 3) 228 Raggy or Ragee..is largely used in Southern India. **1889** *Daily News* 3 July 4/8 The prices of rice and ragi are still rising.

ragia, obs. form of RAJA(H.

raging ('reɪdʒɪŋ), *vbl. sb.* [f. RAGE *v.* + -ING[1].] The action of the vb. in various senses.
c **1320** *Sir Beues* (MS. A) 1673 Ase þai sete in here raging, In at þe dore Beues gan spring. *c* **1430** *Freemasonry* 768 Lawȝe thou not..Ny make no ragynge with ey-body. **1561** HOLLYBUSH *Hom. Apoth.* 21 Thys alayeth the heate and ragynge of the heade. **1604** E. G[RIMSTONE] *D'Acosta's Hist. Indies* III. xiii. 161 The tempests and raging of the sea. **1631** GOUGE *God's Arrows* I. §66. 110 Let not..the present raging of this plague too much daunt us. **1711** *Fingall MSS.* in *10th Rep. Hist. MSS. Comm.* App. V. 193 He fell into a fitt of rageing a little before he dyed. **1810** SOUTHEY *Kehama* XX. vi, The travellers hear The raging of the flood. **1892** ZANGWILL *Bow Mystery* 137 His most ungentlemanly raging and raving.

raging ('reɪdʒɪŋ), *ppl. a.* [f. as prec. + -ING[2].]
1. a. That rages, in various senses of the vb.
1483 *Cath. Angl.* 298/2 Ragynge, *rabians, rabidus.* **15..** *Jerusalem, reioss* in *Dunbar's Poems* (1893) 322 The regeand tirrant that in the rang, Herod, is exilit. **1535** COVERDALE *Wisd.* xiv. 1 Beginnynge to take his iourney thorow yᵉ raginge see. **1591** SPENSER *Tears of Muses* 374 Those bitter stounds Of raging love. *a* **1680** BUTLER *Rem.* (1759) I. 116 Man, with raging Drink inflam'd, Is far more savage and untam'd. **1697** VANBRUGH *Relapse* v. ii, Behold this raging lion at your feet. **1727–46** THOMSON *Summer* 432 'Tis raging noon; and vertical, the sun Darts..his forceful rays. **1866** G. MACDONALD *Ann. Q. Neighb.* xxx. (1878) 523 Beyond the reach of all the raging storms.
Comb. **1562** PILKINGTON *Expos. Abdyas* Pref. 8 Summer is raging hoate. **1592** SHAKS. *Ven. & Ad.* 1151 Loue..shall be raging mad, and sillie milde.
b. Of a disease or pain: Violent.
1695 *New Light Chirurg. put out* 58 Brought the Gentleman into a raging Fever. **1800** MRS. HERVEY *Mourtray Fam.* III. 234, I have such a raging head-ache. **1840** DICKENS *Old C. Shop* lxiii, Mr. Richard..was stricken with a raging fever.
c. Of a tooth: Aching furiously.
1604 SHAKS. *Oth.* III. iii. 414 Being troubled with a raging tooth, I could not sleepe. **1806** H. SIDDONS *Maid, Wife, & Widow* III. 246 Some opium I had concealed for a raging tooth.
d. Highly successful, tremendous; also as a mere intensifier. ***raging favourite***, 'hot' favourite. *colloq.*
1886 H. BAUMANN *Londinismen* 151/2 A raging favourite. **1889** 'MARK TWAIN' *Connecticut Yankee* xxxi. 398 He..was doing a raging business. **1894** —— in *St. Nicholas* Mar. 400/2 A raging lot of sand. **1977** *Hongkong Standard* 12 Apr. 12/2 Raging favourite Orange Peel was pushed to the limit by Glynn Parry.
†**2. raging (love) apples**, = 'mad apples' (q.v.). **raging nightshade** (see quot.). *Obs.*
1578 LYTE *Dodoens* III. lxxxv. 438 There be two kindes of Amorus or Raging loue apples. *Ibid.* 439 They be called.. Raging or mad Apples. *Ibid.* xcii. 447 The other [kind] is called *Solanum Manicum*, that is to say, Mad, or Raging Nightshade.

ragingly ('reɪdʒɪŋlɪ), *adv.* [f. prec. + -LY[2].] In a raging manner, vehemently, furiously.
1549 COVERDALE, etc. *Erasm. Par. Eph.* vi. (1551) 14 The enemyes and foes of Christe, whose champions and instrumentes those are, that ragingly assault vs. **1600** SURFLET *Countrie Farme* I. viii. 35 If the winde called Typhon..doe blow ragingly. *a* **1677** MANTON *Serm. Ps.* cxix, lxxxvi. Wks. 1872 VII. 232 Pestilence doth not ragingly spread. **1840** GALT *Demon of Destiny* VIII. 57 Satan glared ragingly. **1879** G. MEREDITH *Egoist* I. v. 77 He had wooed her rageingly; he courted her becomingly.
So †**'ragingness**, fury. *Obs. rare*$^{-1}$.
1621 MOLLE *Camerar. Liv. Libr.* II. xviii. 132 The ragingnesse of the dogs upon the poore and naked.

‖**ragini** ('rɑːgiːniː). [a. Skr. *rāgiṇī*, lit. coloured, impassioned.] In Indian music, a modification of a raga.
1788 W. JONES in *Asiatick Res.* I. 264 The Nymphs of Musick are the thirty Râginis or Female Passions. **1807**, **1891** [see RAGA]. **1944** W. APEL *Harvard Dict. Mus.* 333/1 The theoretical system..knows 6 (main) ragas and 30 *raginis*, each of which are duplicated according to the sa-grama or the ma-grama scheme (perfect or augmented fourths). **1948** B. BOSE *Acre of Green Grass* 41 In classical Indian music..words are no more than pleasing containers of the *ragini*, or the melodic pattern. **1954** *Grove's Dict. Mus.* (ed. 5) IV. 457/1 Seven were chosen in the end..to serve as basic modes or pure *jâtis*. From these seven *jâtis* the whole elaborate structure of *râgas* and *râginis* was eventually developed. **1968** *Indian Mus. Jrnl.* V. 33 He minutely studied the nature of various *rāga-s* and *rāginī-s*, to find out their suitability for expressing different emotions.

ragipou, ragius, obs. ff. RAJPUT, RAGEOUS.

raglan ('ræglən). Also with capital initial. [f. the name of Lord Raglan, the British commander in the Crimean war.] **a.** An overcoat without shoulder seams, the sleeve going right up to the neck. (See also quot. 1881.) Also *attrib.*
1863 'G. HAMILTON' *Gala-Days* 27 A thousand considerations, in the shape of raglans..induce you to modify your view. **1864** in WEBSTER. **1867** F. H. LUDLOW *Little Brother* 44 Distant visions of black whiskers and big Raglans. **1881** JEFFERSON DAVIS *Rise & Fall Confed. Govt.* II. 701, I picked up what was supposed to be my 'raglan', a waterproof, light overcoat, without sleeves. **1898** *Tailor & Cutter* Dec. 162/1 (*heading*) The Raglan Overcoat. **1926** *Daily Colonist* (Victoria, B.C.) 5 Jan. 2/6 (Advt.), Overcoats. .. Some with half belts, full belters and raglan-back styles. **1948** M. LASKI *Tory Heaven* xii. 166 A thick raglan overcoat over his dinner jacket. **1976** 'J. Ross' *I know what it's like to Die* ii. 11 His thick raglan overcoat.
b. *attrib.* Applied to the shoulder or sleeve of any (esp. knitted) garment designed after the style of a raglan. Also *absol.*, a garment with such sleeves.
1906 *Daily Chron.* 4 Oct. 3/4 As for the Raglan shoulders they are only to be worn with sporting clothes. **1930** M. STORY *Individuality & Clothes* II. ii. 204 Raglan and kimono sleeves tend to increase the breadth of the figure. **1957** M. B. PICKEN *Fashion Dict.* 269/2 *Raglan sleeve*, sleeve with long armhole line extending to neckline. **1966** *Illustr. London News* 26 Feb. 5 (Advt.), The knitwear is made of Shetland wool and is fully fashioned with raglan sleeves. **1969** *Sears Catal.* Spring/Summer 26 *Cardigan sweater* interlock knit of Orlon acrylic... Rib knit cuffs on the long sleeves, raglan shoulders. **1978** *Detroit Free Press* 2 Apr. 5D/1 One reason for the great popularity of 'knit-from-the-neck-down' raglans is the fact that there are no sleeves to set in. **1980** *Times* 11 Nov. 10/5, I liked..the reversible coats with raglan shoulders.
c. *Comb.*, as ***raglan-coated, -sleeved*** adjs.
1975 J. SYMONS *Three Pipe Problem* xviii. 207 Twenty yards ahead..stalked the raglan-coated figure of Sheridan Haynes. **1974** S. MARCUS *Minding Store* (1975) iv. 81 The first raglan-sleeved fur coat.

† **'ragler.** *Obs.* Also -lar, -lor. [ad. W. *rhaglaw* deputy, f. *rhag* before + *law* hand. In L. documents of the 14–15th c. the form *rag(e)lotus* is used; also *rag(e)lotia, ragloria* raglership.] The chief officer in a Welsh commot; a sheriff or constable. Hence †**'raglership.** *Obs.*
1408 in Rymer *Fœdera* (ed. 2) VIII. 547 L'office de Raglore de les Commotes de Generglyn & Hannynyok. **1485** *Rolls of Parlt.* VI. 353/2 The Raglorships of the Advowres of the same Counties. **1577** in *Archæologia* (1829) XXII. 330 An Abstract of the Office of Raglershipp. **1579** *Ibid.* 334 The..profytt of the Office of Ragler.

'raglet. *rare*$^{-1}$. [f. RAG *sb.*[1] + -LET.] A small rag or scrap.
1836–48 B. D. WALSH *Aristoph., Acharnians* II. iv. 45 Give me a raglet out of your old play.

ragly, obs. form of RALLY *v.*[1]

ragman[1] ('rægmən). Also (sense 1) 4 **raggeman, rageman, -mon,** 6 *Sc.* **ragmen.** [f. RAG *sb.*[1] + MAN.]
†**1.** A name given to the Devil, or one of the devils. (Cf. RAGAMUFFIN 1, RAGGED *a.*[1] 1 b, and Sw. *Ragg-en*). *Obs. rare.*
1377 LANGL. *P. Pl.* B. XVI. 89 Go robbe that raggeman and reue the fruit fro hym. **1393** *Ibid.* C. XIX. 122 To ransake that rageman and reue hym hus apples. **15..** in *Bannatyne MS.* 76 [Christ] that ransonit ws vpoun the rude Fra ruffy ragmen and his route. *Ibid.* 302 Ruffy Ragmen with his taggis Sall ryfe thair sinfull saule in raggis.
†**2.** A ragged person. *Obs. rare*$^{-0}$.
c **1440** *Promp. Parv.* 421/2 Ragmann, or he that goythe wythe iaggyd [*v.r.* raggyd] clothys, *pannicius.*
3. a. A rag-gatherer, rag-dealer.
1586 DAY *Eng. Secretary* (1625) 110 He is become a sworne brother of the rag-mans number. **1660** BURNEY *Κέρδ. Δῶρον* (1661) 99 They were too base to make Gunpowder on, and below the Market of a Ragman. **1732** BERKELEY *Alciphr.* ii. §2 He sets the Paper-mills at work, by which the poor Rag-man is supported. **1763** T. PRICE *Life B. M. Carew* 217 Happening to meet with a brother ragman..they joined company. **1833** *Boston Herald* 19 Mar. 4/4 The ragman came up, and began to call me about the cards. **1966** F. SHAW et al. *Lern Yerself Scouse* 24 *De ragman*, the old-clothes man. **1976** *New Yorker* 23 Feb. 39/2 The street down which will sometimes come, on his rattling wagon, a ragman.
b. Contemptuously, a banker. (Cf. RAG *sb.*[1] 3.)
1821 COBBETT *Rur. Rides* (1885) I. 18 [Tax collectors] will receive the country rags, if the rag-man can find, and will give security for the due payment of his rags.
4. [See RAG *sb.*[5]] A musician who plays ragtime music.
1938 J. R. MORTON in *Downbeat* Sept. 4/1 Blues players who could play nothing else... What we call 'ragmen' in New Orleans. **1950** BLESH & JANIS *They all played Ragtime* (1958) vi. 108 Following 1907–8 there comes a second generation of ragmen. **1970** C. MAJOR *Dict. Afro-Amer. Slang* 96 Ragmen, jazzmen who play that type of music.

† **'Ragman**[2]. *Obs.* Forms: 3–5 **rageman,** 4 **-mon, -ment;** 4, 6 **raggeman;** 4–7 **ragman,** 5 **-man(n)e;** 5–7 *Sc.* **ragment,** (6 **-men).** [Of obscure origin and history. In the absence of any plausible etym. the development of senses can only be conjectural, and is perh. not properly illustrated by the existing material.
In early examples the invariable spelling is *rageman*, app. implying three syllables; but the form *ragman* is clearly proved for the 15th c. by the rimes in the *Towneley Myst.*]

1. The name given to a statute of 4 Edw. I (appointing justices to hear and determine complaints of injuries done within 25 years previous), and to certain articles of inquisition associated with proceedings of *Quo Warranto* under this statute.

See *Placita de Quo Warranto* (1818) pp. xvi–xvii.

1276 in *Statutes Realm* I. 44 Statutum de justic'. assign'.; quod vocatur Rageman. **1280** *Assize Roll* (P.R.O.) No. 670 Placita de Ragemannis et de Quo Warranto coram J. de Vallibus et sociis suis, justitiariis itinerantibus in comitatu Notinghamiae. **1292** in *Placita de Quo Warranto* (1818) 378 Juratores de Ragemann' præsentaverunt quod [etc.]. *Ibid.* 382 b, De hiis quae praesentata sunt in le Rageman.

2. A roll, list, catalogue. Also *Roll of Ragman* = RAGMAN ROLL.

c **1394** *P. Pl. Crede* 180 þer is none heraud þat haþ half swich a rolle, Riȝt as a rageman haþ rekned hem newe. *c* **1450** *Pol. Poems* (Rolls) II. 228 Pite for to here the people.. riken up the ragmanne of the hole rowte, That servyth silvyre and levyth the law oute. *c* **1460** *Towneley Myst.* xxx. 224 Here a rolle of ragman of the rownde tabille, Of breffes in my bag, man, of synnes dampnabille.

b. *Sc.* A long discourse, rhapsody, rigmarole.

1506 DUNBAR *Tua Mariit Wemen* 162, I sall a ragment reveil fra [the] rute of my hert. **1513** DOUGLAS *Æneis* VIII. Prol. 147 He raucht me a roll: to reyd I begane The riotest ane ragment wyth mony rat rane. **1536** LYNDESAY *Answ. King's Flyting* 1 Redoutit Roy, ȝour ragment I haue red. *a* **1585** POLWART *Flyting w. Montgomerie* 142, I laugh to see the bluiter Glor in thy ragments, rash to raill.

3. A game of chance, app. played with a written roll having strings attached to the various items contained in it, one of which the player selected or 'drew' at random.

In one form the game was a mere amusement, the items in the roll being verses descriptive of personal character: see Wright *Anecd. Lit.* (1844) 76–82 and Hazlitt *E. Pop. Poetry* (1864) I. 68. But that of quot. 1377 was probably a method of gambling, forbidden under penalty of a fine. In the other quots. the word may be a proper name, as in b.

c **1290** *MS. Digby* 86, lf. 162 [Heading of a set of French verses.] Ragemon le bon. **1377** *Durham Halmote Rolls* (Surtees) 140 De Thoma Breuster et Ricardo de Holm quia ludaverunt ad ragement contra pœnam in diversis Halmotis positam 20s. condonatur usque 2s. **1390** GOWER *Conf.* III. 355 Venus, which stant.. In noncertein, but as men drawe Of Rageman upon the chance.

b. ***King Ragman***, feigned to be the author of the roll used in playing the game.

c **1400** *MS. Fairfax* 16 in Hazl. *E.P.P.* I. 69 This rolle which.. Kynge Ragman bad me sowe in brede... Drawith a strynge [etc.]. *c* **1500** *Lenvoy of Prynter* in Dodsley *O. Pl.* (1827) XII. 308 Go lytyl rolle.. Excuse thy prynter.. Layenge the faute on kynge Ragman holly, Whiche dyde the make many yeres ago.

4. A document (contract, agreement, indenture, etc.) with seals attached.

App. by transference from sense 3, the pendent seals being compared to the strings, etc. attached to the roll used in the game: cf. quot. *a* 1350 in b.

1362 LANGL. *P. Pl.* A. Prol. 72 [The pardoner] rauhte with his ragemon ringes and broches. **1376** *Rolls Parlt.* II. 324/2 Une lettre.. sealees des sealx des plusours Seignurs de Bretaigne, appellee Ragman. *Ibid.*, Le dit Rageman. **1399** in Rymer *Fœdera* (ed. 2) VIII. 109 De Raggemannis Comburendis. *Ibid.*, Per diversa Scripta, Cartas sive Literas Patentes, vocata Raggemans sive Blank Chartres, Sigillis eorumdem Subditorum separatim consignata. *c* **1425** WYNTOUN *Cron.* VI. xvii. 1722 Thai consentyd than And mad apon this a ragman Wyth mony sellys off lordys. *c* **1470** HENRY *Wallace* x. 1149 The Bruce and he completyt furth thar bandis; Syn that samyn nycht thai sellyt with thar handis. This ragment left the Bruce with Cumyn thar.

b. *spec.* The document by which the Scottish nobles in 1291 acknowledged Edward I as their overlord (given up by Edward III in 1328).

a **1350** *Chron. Lanercost* 261 (an. 1327) A Scottis, propter multa sigilla dependentia, Ragman vocabatur. *c* **1420** *Chron. Thomas Otterbourne* (1732) I. 114 (an. 1328) Redditis regi & regno Scotiæ juribus.. et litera quæ vocatur Ragman, cum sigillo de homagio facto nobili regi Edwardo I°. **1480** CAXTON *Chron. Eng.* 216 An endenture was made of the scottes vnto kyng Edward.. whiche endenture they called it rageman. **1559** *Mirr. Mag.*, *Two Rogers* vi, Causde the kyng to yelde the Skot,.. the charter called Ragman.

Ragman('s) roll. *Obs.* exc. *Hist.* [f. prec. + ROLL.]

†**1.** The roll used in the game of Ragman. *Obs.*

c **1400** *MS. Fairfax* 16 in Hazl. *E.P.P.* I. 68 Here begynnyth Ragmane roelle. *c* **1500** in Dodsley *O. Pl.* (1827) XII. 308 Explicit Ragmannes Rolle.

†**2.** A list, catalogue, etc. = RAGMAN[2] 2. *Obs.*

α. **1523** SKELTON *Garl. Laurel* 1490, I did what I cowde.. Apollo to rase out of her ragman rollis. **1556** OLDE *Antichrist* 87 b, The noble ragge man rolle of those most holy fathers. **1599** NASHE *Lenten Stuffe* (1871) 48 The whole ragman roll of fasting days. *a* **1603** T. CARTWRIGHT *Confut. Rhem. N.T.* (1618) 286 A ragman roule, of numbers of rogues.

β. **1532** MORE *Confut. Tindale* Wks. 653/2 All the heresies that they haue in all theyr whole raggemans rolle. **1553** BECON *Reliques of Rome* (1563) 195 Many other raggemans roules could I here haue placed. *a* **1610** HEALEY *Disc. New World* 175 The ragman's rolles of porters and panierists.

3. †**a.** = RAGMAN[2] 4 b. *Obs.*

1570 FOXE *A. & M.* 470/1 Their indenture which was called the Ragman role. **1611** SPEED *Hist. Gt. Brit.* IX. xii. §13. 671 There was also deliuered to them that famous Euidence called the Ragman-Roll. **1641** BAKER *Chron.* (1660) 227 The King.. restores.. the famous Evidence called Ragmans Roll.

b. A set of rolls (formerly preserved in the Tower of London, now in the Public Record Office), in which are recorded the instruments of homage made to Edward I by the Scottish King (Balliol), nobles, etc., in 1296.

This application of the term seems to be comparatively modern: older writers apply it only to the original document given back to the Scots by Edward III (see above).

1710 RUDDIMAN *Gloss. Douglas' Æneis* s.v. *Ragmen*, Hence the famous Ragman's row or roll, i.e. a collection of those deeds.. recorded in four large rolls of parchment [etc.]. **1834** *Instrumenta Publica*, etc. (Bann. Club) p. xv, They are the same instruments that have been usually known under the uncouth appellation of the Ragman Rolls.

So †**Ragman('s) rew** (see quots.). *Obs.*

1542 UDALL *Erasm. Apoph.* 244 b, Augustus had written a greate ragmans rewe, or bille to bee soung on Pollio in derision and skorne of hym. *Ibid.* 245 A ragmans rewe, or, a bible... So dooe we call a longe ieste that railleth on any persone by name, or toucheth a bodyes honestee somewhat nere. **1570** LEVINS *Manip.* 95/2 Ragmanrew, *series*.

†**ragmas, -mersshe.** *Obs. rare.* Some kind of cloth. Also *attrib.*

Perh. the same word as OF. *racamaz* in a document of 1350 quoted by Du Cange.

1403 in Rymer *Fœdera* (ed. 2) VIII. 296 Un entire Vestiment.. de Drap d'Or ragmas rouge & bloy. **1488** in *Jrnl. Archæol. Assoc.* XXXIII. 317 A pelow couered with ragmersshe sylke.

†**rag'matical,** *a. Obs. rare.* [? f. RAG *sb.*[1], after PRAGMATICAL.] ? Wild, ill-behaved, riotous.

1742 FIELDING *J. Andrews* I. vii, I think him the ragmaticallest fellow in the family. **1771** SMOLLETT *Humph. Cl.* 19 May ii, I won't be Rogered.. by any ragmatical fellow.

ragmen(t, obs. Sc. forms of RAGMAN[2].

Ragnarök ('ragnarœk). Also 8 **Ragnarockur; Ragnarok, Ragnarökr.** [ON. *ragna rök*, f. *ragna* gen. of *regin* the gods + *rök* destined end (a conventional usage in this phrase of *rök* the course of events from origin to end, their causes and consequences); properly as above, but the form *Ragna rökr* (*rökr* twilight, a more readily comprehensible substitute for the archaic *rök*) occurs in the prose Edda, and the mod. sense is freq. founded upon this (see Cleasby-Vigfusson ed. 2).] In Scandinavian mythology, the destruction of the gods or the twilight of the gods; *spec.* the last battle of this world, in which gods and men will be defeated by monsters and the sun will grow dark. Also *fig.*

1770 T. PERCY tr. *Mallet's Northern Antiquities* I. vi. 119 The end of the world, that is,.. the time of that universal desolation of nature which was to be followed by a new creation, and what they called *Ragnarockur*, or the Twilight of the Gods. **1866** *Chambers's Encycl.* 525/2 This terrible age of destruction, the Ragnarök, or twilight of the gods, will be marked by a three years' winter of hard frost. **1887** A. LANG in *Contemp. Rev.* Nov. 693 If the battle between the crocodile of Realism and the catawampus of Romance is to be fought out to the bitter end—why, in that Ragnarök, I am on the side of the catawampus. **1899** A. H. YAPP *Cuckoo* III. 178 The ragnarok of the cuckoos—the last band of the migrating males. **1933** A. THIRKELL *High Rising* xi. 199 Zeus dethrones Chronos.. Ragnarok swallows up the Gods. **1953** G. TURVILLE-PETRE *Origins Icelandic Lit.* i. 15 The giant.. predicts the *Ragnarǫk* (Fall of the Gods) and the manner of Oðinn's death. *Ibid.* ii. 57 The treacherous Loki was bound in chains, but he will break them when the gods' Doomsday (*Ragnarǫk*) draws near. **1965** H. M. SMYSER in Bessinger & Creed *Medieval & Linguistic Stud.* 110 It is not the place where Odin's *einherjar* fight daily as they await Ragnarøkr. **1978** *Islands* (N.Z.) Aug. 86 Ragnarök and Loki's frames Lie curing in the dust.

rag(o)muffin, etc. obs. ff. RAGAMUFFIN.

ragoo, -ou(e, obs. forms of RAGOUT *sb.* and *v.*

ragosie: see ARGOSY.

ragout (rə'guː), *sb.* Forms: α. 7 **ragust,** 7–8 **ragoust.** β. 7– **ragout,** 8–9 **ragoût.** γ. 7 **ragoue, ragow,** 7–8 **ragou,** 7–8 (9) **ragoo.** [F. *ragoût*, †*ragoust* (1642 in Hatz.-Darm.), f. *ragoûter* to revive the taste of, f. *re* back + *à* to + GOÛT.]

1. A dish usually consisting of meat cut in small pieces, stewed with vegetables and highly seasoned.

α. **1664** BUTLER *Hud.* II. i. 598 Season her, as French Cooks use Their Haut-gusts, Buollies, or Ragusts. **1673** S. C. *Art of Complaisance* 59 Producing.. the same effect which salt does in a ragoust. **1727** SWIFT *Modest Proposal* Wks. 1755 II. II. 61 It will equally serve in a *fricassé*, or a *ragoust*.

β. **1656–7** DAVENANT *Rutland Ho.* Wks. (1673) 357 Your Pottages, Carbonnades, Grillades, Ragouts,.. and Entremets. **1698** J. CRULL *Muscovy* 34 That Ragout which the Italians call Cavayar. *a* **1764** R. LLOYD *Cobler of Cripplegate's Lett.* Wks. 1774 II. 102 Borrows fine shapes, and titles new, Of fricasee and rich ragoût. **1842** BARHAM *Ingol. Leg.* Ser. II. *Nell Cook*, For soups and stews and choice *ragoûts* Nell Cook was famous still. **1859** WRAXALL tr. *R. Houdin* xxi. 310 A rich soup, roast fowls, various ragoûts which I cannot describe.

γ. *a* **1687** VILLIERS (Dk. Buckhm.) *Timon* Wks. (1752) 116 As for French kickshaus, cellery, and champain, Ragous and fricasses, in troth we 'ave none. **1692** LOCKE *Educ.* §37 Sauces and Ragoos, and Food disguis'd by all the Arts of Cookery. **1730** SWIFT *Panegyr. on Dean*, She sent her priest in wooden shoes From haughty Gaul to make ragoos. **1747–96** MRS. GLASSE *Cookery* v. 38 Put the collops into the ragoo. [**1885** A. DOBSON *At the Sign of Lyre* 123 He classed your Kickshaws and *Ragoos* With Popery and Wooden Shoes.]

b. *transf.* or *fig.*

1672 MARVELL *Reh. Transp.* I. 83 These being Conceits too trivial, though a Ragoust fit enough for Mr. Bayes his palate. **1717** MRS. CENTLIVRE *Bold Stroke for Wife* II. 21 She has an odd Ragoût of Guardians, as you will find when you hear the Characters. **1739** CIBBER *Apol.* (1756) I. 34 A mere ragoust, toss'd up from the offals of other authors.

†**2.** A sauce or relish. *Obs.*

1741 *Compl. Fam.-Piece* I. ii. 148 Pour on it a Ragoo, and Garnish with Orange and Lemon. **1750** E. SMITH *Compl. Housew.* 29 A ragoo for made dishes.

fig. **1673** [R. LEIGH] *Transp. Reh.* 28 A Couplet in a Song gives a better Ragoust to a Controversial Discourse. **1698** L. MILBOURNE *Notes Dryden's Virgil* 67 The Translator puts in a little Burlesque now and then, for a Ragout for his cheated Subscribers. **1734** tr. *Rollin's Rom. Hist.* (1827) IV. IV. 240 Hunger was their only ragout.

ragout (rə'guː), *v.* Forms: 7 **ragoust;** 8– **ragout;** 8 **ragoo,** 8–9 **ragou.** [f. prec. or ad. F. *ragoûter*.]

1. *trans.* To make a ragout of, to stew with highly flavoured seasoning.

1748 MRS. HARRISON *House-Keeper's Pocket-bk.* ii. (ed. 4) 5 Breast of Veal ragou'd, with Mushrooms. *a* **1756** MRS. HEYWOOD *New Present* (1771) 163 To ragout a Leg of Mutton. **1833** *Westm. Rev.* Jan. 33 To allow beef to be ragouted in small kitchens.

†**2.** *transf.* To give piquancy or variety to; to enrich or improve. *Obs.*

1749 FIELDING *Tom Jones* I. i, We shall.. hereafter hash and ragoo it, with all the high French and Italian seasoning of affectation and vice. **1753** *Scots Mag.* Sept. 458/2 Pin a stomacher bib on, Ragout it with cutlets of silver and ribbon.

†**3.** ? To have a relish of, to understand. *Obs.*

1673 HICKERINGILL *Gregory Father Greybeard* 142 If there be, Within you so much Repartee, As to ragoust now what I mean.

Hence **ra'goued, ra'goo'd** *ppl. a.*

1755 SMOLLETT *Quix.* (1863) IV. 71, I would not have you touch these ragoo'd rabbits. **1810** *Splendid Follies* I. 73 He handed his plate to the butler for some ragoued pigeon.

'ragstone. [f. RAG *sb.*[2]]

1. = RAG *sb.*[2] 2.

1350 in Riley *Lond. Mem.* (1868) 262, [2 boatloads of] ragston. *c* **1420** *Pallad. on Husb.* II. 139 Ragstoon & thinges hard.. bereth vyneyerdes grete. [**1573** in Willis & Clark *Cambridge* (1886) I. 174 Item for Ramsey stone free and ragge.] **1695** WOODWARD *Nat. Hist. Earth* (1723) 10 Free-stone, Ragg-stone, Lime-stone. **1759** B. STILLINGFLEET tr. *Biberg's Econ. Nat.* in *Misc. Tracts* (1762) 42 The upper parts consist of rag-stone, the next of slate, the third of marble. **1812** J. SMYTH *Pract. of Customs* (1821) 242 Rag stone.. is used by artificers, for the purpose of giving a fine edge to knives, chissels, and other tools, which have previously been sharpened upon stones of a coarse texture. **1881** YOUNG *Every man his own Mechanic* §1309. 602 The famous Kentish ragstone so much used in bold rubble work for churches, houses, walls.

attrib. **1846** MCCULLOCH *Acc. Brit. Empire* (1854) I. 197 The soil of the lower, or ragstone ridge, varies much.

2. = RAG *sb.*[2] 1.

1565 COOPER *Thesaurus*, *Cæmentitius*, Made of rubbell or ragge stones. **1565** JEWEL *Def. Apol.* (1611) 352 The great ragge stones at Stonage, or Long Compton. **1698** W. KING tr. *Sorbière's Journ. Lond.* 11 All the Streets are Paved with Pebbles, and Flints and Rag Stones. **1766** ENTICK *London* IV. 265 A handsome walk paved with rag stones. **1840** J. DEVLIN *Shoemaker* I. 113 Rag stones for pointing awls. **1872** *Archæol. Cantiana* VIII. 11 Some large squared ragstones, and beneath them some human bones.

rag-tag ('rægtæg), *sb.*(*a.*) [f. RAG *sb.*[1] + TAG. The older expression was *tag and rag* (very common in 16–17th c.).]

A. *sb.* **1. a.** *coll.* The ragged disreputable portion of the community; the raff or rabble. **b.** One of the individuals forming this class.

1879 MARG. LONSDALE *Sister Dora* viii. (1880) 199 She visited all classes—from the respectable, down to what she called the 'ragtags' of the town.

2. ***rag-tag*** (or ***rag, tag***) ***and bob-tail*** = 1 a. Also *transf.*; sometimes = 'the whole lot'.

1820 *Blackw. Mag.* VII. 318 This Journal cuts up the rag-tag and bobtail of the faction. **1882** H. SEEBOHM *Siberia in Asia* 100 Ragtag-and-bobtail of the great Arctic army. **1887** T. A. TROLLOPE *What I remember* II. vi. 95 He shall have them all, rag, tag, and bobtail.

attrib. **1882** F. M. CRAWFORD *Mr. Isaacs* 3 Regular rag-tag-and-bobtail cut-throat moss-troopers.

B. Passing into *adj.* Of form or appearance: ragged, raggle-taggle; disreputable; disorderly, unorganized, straggling.

a. Of persons, etc.

1883 *Glasgow Weekly Herald* 23 Apr. 8/4 These are the shapes sold by certain rag-tag drapers at 3*d*. **1884** *American* VIII. 46 We are hemmed in by.. rag-tag Arabs. **1969** *Telegraph* (Brisbane) 19 Aug. 19/4 In unison a ragtag band of motorcyclists drank a toast. **1978** S. BRILL *Teamsters* ix. 322 These were by and large a ragtag group of overaged ne'er-do-wells.

b. Of things.

1922 BLUNDEN *Shepherd* (ed. 2) 30 When on the green the rag-tag game had stopd. **1969** *Jrnl. Amer. Chem. Soc.* XCI. facing p. 4946 (Advt.), Such rag-tag, sometimes illegible copies probably stay in your files.. permanently. **1977** *Rolling Stone* 5 May 11/1 The audience was evenly divided between under-18s in ragtag street wear and those first-generation rock fans now moving into Sisley jeans affluence.

ragtime ('rægtaim). orig. *U.S.* Also **rag-time.** [Prob. f. RAG *sb.*[5] + TIME *sb.*] **1. a.** A musical rhythm characterized by a syncopated melodic line and regularly-accented accompaniment, evolved among American Negro musicians in the 1890s; hence, music (esp. for the banjo and piano) of this character, the immediate precursor of jazz.

1897 W. H. Krell *Mississippi Rag* (title-page of sheet-music), The first rag-time two-step ever written. **1898** *Étude* Oct. 285/3 'Rag time' is a term applied to the peculiar, broken, rhythmic features of the popular 'coon song'... Unfortunately, the words to which it is allied are usually decidedly vulgar, so that its present great favor is somewhat to be deplored. **1899** *Musical Rec.* (Boston) 158/1, I feel safe in predicting that rag-time has come to stay. **1900** *Musical Courier* 23 May 20/2 'Rag-time' is a rhythm which is the most characteristic feature of what may be called American negro music. **1906** 'O. Henry' *Four Million* 238 They sing 'Home Sweet Home' in rag-time. **1916** A. Huxley *Let.* 7 Aug. (1969) 109, I have been sleeping out on the roof.. spending most of the night in conversation or in singing folk-songs and rag-time to the stars. **1934** C. Lambert *Music Ho!* III. 206 Jazz, or to be pedantically accurate, 'ragtime',..has suddenly achieved the status of a 'school'. **1938** *Sun* (Baltimore) 6 Sept. 8/7 Under their ministrations, the simplest ragtime becomes jazz. **1956** B. Edwards in S. Traill *Play that Music* 59 Rag-time, to give it its contemporary title [in 1920], was absolute anathema to both my parents. **1957** G. Lascelles in S. Traill *Concerning Jazz* 76 In the late nineteenth century there started a music which was a rather modern development of the old dance rhythms such as the schottische and polka... This development was later to be known as 'rag-time', and was essentially piano music. **1968** *Blues Unlimited* Nov. 23 Ragtime one probably loves or loathes. **1976** *New Yorker* 8 Mar. 32/3 He started to play, and before long he was lost in some wildly effervescent ragtime.

†**b.** A piece of music in rag-time; = rag *sb.*[5] 2. *Obs.*

1914 G. B. Shaw *Misalliance* p. cviii, If they [*sc.* our young people] had learnt what can be done with syncopation from Beethoven's third Leonora overture, they would enjoy the ragtimes all the more. **1916** *Oxford Song Bk.* p. iii, An authority has just informed me that 'rag-times are "back numbers" now'.

2. a. *attrib.* and *Comb.*, as ***ragtime accompaniment, band, melody, music, party, rage, record, saloon, singer, song, sound, tune, wedding***.

1901 *Sage Leaf* Apr. 6 The coon song, with its rag-time accompaniment. **1911** I. Berlin (*song-title*) Alexander's Ragtime Band. **1949** R. Blesh *Shining Trumpets* vii. 156 Buddy Bolden's Ragtime Band of 1893, generally considered the first jazz band. **1906** *Westm. Gaz.* 23 Apr. 7/2 He is amusing the crowd with rag-time melodies. **1921** R. D. Paine *Comrades of Rolling Ocean* v. 75 Through an open hatch rose the rag-time melodies of a piano. **1897** Ade *Pink Marsh* 159 He told of his belief that the angels in heaven played 'rag-time' music. **1977** *Monitor* (McAllen, Texas) 9 Jan. 5c/3 Tichenor..says *ragtime music* peaked in the 1920s and died in the Depression. **1960** *Times* 29 Sept. 16/6 She pushes him downstairs during a ragtime-party. **1900** *Musical Courier* 23 May 20/1 (*heading*) The rag-time rage. **1906** Taylor & Gibson *Extra Dry* 71 Putting a ragtime record in the graphophone he pulls the throttle wide open. **1903** *Outing* Aug. 552/1 He has as many eyes for the ragtime saloon. **1917** E. Wallace *Kate plus Ten* (1930) v. 74 A peer of the realm and a ragtime singer. **1914** Ragtime song [see *high kick* s.v. high *a.* 21]. **1927** *Jrnl. Abnormal & Social Psychol.* XXII. 19 The earliest ragtime songs, like Topsy, 'jes' grew'. **1974** *Times* 27 Apr. 9/8 We've ended up with a ragtime sound you might even have heard from the piano accompanying the silent movies. **1913** Kipling *Diversity of Creatures* (1917) 282 The boys and girls at the piano played the rag-time tunes of their own land. **1922** F. Scott Fitzgerald *Beautiful & Damned* II. i. 131 Kept telling me she wished this was a ragtime wedding.

b. *attrib.*, passing into *adj.* Ragged; irregular, inferior, disorderly; disreputable, mean. *slang.*

1919 H. Crane *Let.* 17 June (1965) 20 Your remarks 'about the ladies' really hurt me with a kind of ragtime vulgarity. **1926** F. M. Ford *Man could stand Up* ii. 119 A Hun up against a Tommie looked like a Holbein *lansknecht* fighting a music-hall turn. It made you feel that you were indeed a rag-time army. *c* **1926** 'Mixer' *Transport Workers' Song Bk.* 47 Note the constant drop in wages.. Endorsed by every rag-time press That the master-class command. **1929** *Papers Mich. Acad. Sci., Arts & Lett.* X. 317/2 *Ragtime Army*, the Australasian forces. **1940** Graves & Hodge *Long Week-End* ii. 26 The topic of 'this rag-time f——g peace' succeeded that of 'this bloody f——g war'. *Ibid.* iii. 38 The more extravagant 'rag-time' dances had not been socially approved. 'Rag-time' was an adjective of reproach; a rag-time regiment was a disorderly and untrustworthy one. **1948** V. Palmer *Golconda* ii. 14 But what if some really big concern swallowed up the three ragtime companies and planned to open up the whole mountain? **1974** P. Wright *Lang. Brit. Industry* xiv. 142 Hated shifts in that [electrical engineering] industry are the *rag-time* or *spare-shift*, one necessary to make up the required number of hours for the week.

Hence **'ragtimer**, one who plays ragtime; **'ragtim(e)y** *a.*, suggestive of ragtime; **'ragtiming** *a.*

1912 G. Frankau *One of Us* x. 92 Where the Rat Mort's rag-timing Ethiope Dins in one's ears. **1915** D. O. Barnett *Let.* 7 Jan. 37 Been making out forms of times. Feel rather ragtimy. **1927** *Daily Tel.* 1 Nov. 9/3 Most nimble of rag-timers at the piano. **1950** Blesh & Janis *They all played Ragtime* (1958) i. 26 Under Joplin he quickly became an adept ragtimer and was soon playing at dances in and around Sedalia. **1952** B. Ulanov *Hist. Jazz in Amer.* (1958) xxii. 306 They played their ragtimey work..with a finish and polish. **1974** *Country Life* 7 Nov. 1360/1 The ragtime music chosen..was the least..heard of Scott Joplin, supplemented by less well-known ragtimers such as.. Joseph Lamb.

ragulé, variant of raguly.

†**raguled**, *a. Her. Obs.* Also 6 **ragueled**. [f. as next, with native termination.]

1. = raguly.

1572 Bossewell *Armorie* II. 24b, This noble Baron beareth Argent, a Crosse ragueled Sable. **1610** Guillim *Heraldry* III. iv. 95 He beareth Argent, two Billets Raguled and Truncked. **1661** Morgan *Sph. Gentry* II. i. 10 The field is pearl, a cross Raguled and trunked Diamond. **1727–41** Chambers *Cycl.*, *Raguled*, or *Ragged*, in heraldry, is applied to an ordinary, *e.g.* a cross, whose out-lines are jagged or knotted.

2. = couped, coupé. *rare*$^{-0}$.

1727–41 Chambers *Cycl.* s.v., *Raguled* is sometimes also used in the sense of truncated or couped, and applied to a branch that is sawed from the tree, or a stock sawed from its root.

raguly ('rægjʊlɪ), *a. Her.* Also 9 **ragulé(e**. [Of obscure formation: perh. based on *rag*, *ragged*, or *raggy*.] Of a cross or other bearing: Having short oblique projections resembling the stumps of branches cut off close to the stem. Hence of a division between parts of the field: Having alternate projections and depressions like a battlement, but set obliquely.

1658 Guillim *Heraldry* II. vii. 83 He beareth Ermine, a Cross, Raguly, Gules. **1780** *Encycl. Brit.* (ed. 2) V. 3585/1 Lines may be either straight or crooked... There are 14 distinct kinds... 6. The raguly. **1864** Boutell *Her. Hist. & Pop.* xvii. (ed. 3) 262 Staff ragulée sable. **1872** Ellacombe *Bells of Ch.* vii. 366 A crucifix attached to a cross raguly.

Ragusan (rə'gu:zən), *sb.* and *a.* Also †**Ragusian**.

A. *sb.* **a.** An inhabitant of Ragusa, now Dubrovnik, on the Adriatic coast of Yugoslavia. **b.** An extinct dialect of Dalmatian, spoken formerly by inhabitants of Ragusa.

1652 Heylin *Cosmogr.* II. 197 Languste, environed about with very high Mountains, in which are the Ragusians Farms. **1905** *Westm. Gaz.* 29 Apr. 4/1 The advent of Napoleon I. early in the nineteenth century deprived Ragusans for ever of their freedom. **1933** [see Dalmatian *sb.* and *a.* 2]. **1967** D. S. Parlett *Short Dict. Lang.* 38 Ragusan extinct since beginning C17.

B. *adj.* Of or pertaining to Ragusa.

1788 Gibbon *Decl. & F.* V. vi. 613 The Apulian and Ragusian vessels fled to the shore. **1799** R. Smelt *Let.* 6 Dec. in B. Ward *Dawn Catholic Revival* (1909) II. xxxi. 220 We sailed from Palermo on Saturday night, November ye 2nd: altogether seventeen sail, Imperial, Sicilian, Ragusian and American. **1932** *Times Lit. Suppl.* 14 Jan. 27/1 If all the Ragusan men knew Italian, most of the ladies to whom their love poems were dedicated spoke only Slovinski. **1971** *Textile Hist.* II. 10 In 1420 the Ragusan government arranged for a colony of traders from the Italian textile town of Prato to live in Ragusa.

ragust, obs. form of ragout *sb.*

ragusye, obs. form of argosy.

†**rag-water.** *Obs. Cant.* (See quot.)

a **1700** B. E. *Dict. Cant. Crew*, *Rag-water*, a common sort of Strong-waters.

'ragweed. [Cf. ragwort.]

1. = ragwort[1] 1.

1658 Sir T. Browne *Gard. Cyrus* iii. 48 Accounting upward is often observable in furre, pillitorry, Ragweed, [etc.]. **1682** Wheler *Journ. Greece* III. 222 The Leaves are.. something like ragweed. **1765** A. Dickson *Treat. Agric.* xiii. (ed. 2) 113 The yellow rag-weed, by which light land, when laid out in grass, is very much infested. **1846** J. Baxter *Libr. Pract. Agric.* (ed. 4) II. 387 Clearing his land of charlock, rag-weed,..&c. **1881** Blackie *Lay Serm.* v. 162 A grand growth of rushes, dock, and rag-weed.

attrib. **1785** Burns *Addr. to Deil* ix, Wither'd hags,..on ragweed nags, They skim the muirs.

2. *U.S.* A plant belonging to the genus *Ambrosia*, esp. *A. trifida* and *A. artemisiæfolia*.

1866 *Treas. Bot.* 956/2 Ragweed, *Ambrosia trifida*. **1883** *Century Mag.* Aug. 487/2 Buck-wheat, the seeds of grasses, and the rag-weed.

attrib. **1894** *Outing* (U.S.) XXIII. 397/1 All around this rag-weed patch their innumerable little footprints run.

'rag-wheel. [f. rag *sb.*[1]]

1. A wheel having projections which catch into the links of a chain passing over it, as in a chain-pump; a sprocket-wheel.

1812 *Niles' Reg.* II. 393/2 A rag wheel [of a mill machine] of three feet diameter is kept in complete motion. **1829** *Nat. Philos.* I. *Mechanics* v. 21 (U.K.S.) An endless chain..is made to revolve on two wheels..called rag-wheels. **1830** Kater & Lardner *Mech.* xviii. 249 In some cases the teeth of the wheel work in the links of a chain. The wheel is then called a rag-wheel. **1848** *Rep. Comm. Patents 1847* (U.S.) 79 The feeding is usually effected by a band taking into a ratchet, or rag wheel. **1873** J. M. Bailey *Life in Danbury* 9 He employed a carpenter from a place twenty miles distant to make a new rag-wheel.

2. A polishing wheel composed of rags.

1884 Knight *Dict. Mech.* Suppl. 736/1.

'ragwork[1]. [f. rag *sb.*[1]] The process of making a fabric out of rags by weaving, sewing, or other means; the fabric thus made.

1891 in *Cent. Dict.*

'ragwork[2]. [f. rag *sb.*[2]] Masonry composed of flattish pieces of ragstone, having an undressed surface.

1840 Parker *Gloss. Arch.* (ed. 3) I. 173.

'ragworm. [f. rag *sb.*[1]] A polychæte worm belonging to the family Nereidæ, esp. *Nereis diversicolor*, found in sand or under stones and often used as bait for fish.

1865 J. C. Wilcocks *Sea-Fisherman* 99 The larger Rag Worms, are found by digging in stoney ground. **1884** *St. James's Gaz.* 18 Jan. 6/2 The bait used is that damp kind of centipede called a ragworm. **1894** *Blackw. Mag.* Sept. 426/2 One of the best known baits is a live rag-worm. **1906** *Daily Chron.* 6 Jan. 8/6 An enormous specimen of the king ragworm has been found by a bait-digger at Southend-on-Sea. **1928** Russell & Yonge *Seas* 34 It [sc. *Nereis diversicolor*] is frequently used as a bait, being known as 'rag-worm' in many parts. **1967** *Daily Tel.* 21 Oct. 14/6 There were other ways of catching bass than with ragworm or sandeels. **1978** B. Gledhill *Cod Fishing* ii. 58 The ragworm likes hard ground usually.

'ragwort[1]. [Prob. f. rag *sb.*[1], in reference to the ragged form of the leaves.]

1. The popular name of several species of the genus *Senecio*, esp. the common ragwort, *Senecio Jacobæa*. (See also ragweed.)

The first quot. may belong to sense 2.

c **1450** *M.E. Med. Bk.* (Heinrich) 205 Tak lytwort.. plantayne, Ragwort [etc.]. **1597** Gerarde *Herbal* II. xxvi. 218, S. Iames his woort: the countrey people do call it..also Ragwoorte. *Ibid.* 219 Lande Ragwoort groweth euerywhere in vntilled pastures and fieldes. **1678** Phillips *Ragwort* (Jacobæa), an Herb of Mars of a bitter, discussing and cleansing quality. **1753** Chambers *Cycl.* Supp. s.v. *Jacobæa*, The species of Ragwort enumerated by Mr. Tournefort are these [etc.]. **1792** Burns *Let. to Grose* Prose Wks. (1869) 210 A crew of men and women, who were busy pulling stems of the plant Ragwort. **1862** Ansted *Channel Isl.* II. viii. (ed. 2) 176 In drier places, the handsome foxglove is beautifully contrasted with the golden yellow of the ragwort. **1885** Runciman *Skippers & Sh.* 104 When the yellow moths began to twirl round the ragworts.

b. ***African ragwort*** = othonne. *rare*$^{-0}$.

1760 J. Lee *Introd. Bot.* App. 324. **1866** *Treas. Bot.* 956/2.

†**2.** The wild parsnip. *Obs. rare*$^{-0}$.

1570 Levins *Manip.* 173/29 Ragworte, *elephabascum*. [For *elaphoboscon* (Pliny) = Gr. ἐλαφοβόσκον.]

†**ragwort**[2]. *Obs.* [ad. G. *ragwurz*, f. *rag* stiff: see Grimm s.v.] = gandergoose (*Orchis mascula*).

1552 Elyot, *Orchis*,..some call it in English gandergoose some raggewoorte. **1578** Lyte *Dodoens* II. lvi. 222 In English some cal it also Orchis,..Ragworte, Priest pintell. **1601** Holland *Pliny* II. 265 As for Ragworts [*margin*, Orchis] they cure morimals also, either drie or greene.

ragyous, obs. form of rageous.

rah (rɑ:), *int.* and *sb. U.S.* Also **ra**. Aphetic for hurrah.

1870 D. J. Kirwan *Palace & Hovel* xxiv. 372 The 'Rah, 'Rah, 'Rah, of Harvard pierces the air... Oxford has just got into her careless, easy swing. **1887** *Harper's Mag.* Feb. 395/1 The junior class filed into the green enclosure amidst the 'rahs of their friends. **1889** 'Mark Twain' *Connecticut Yankee* xxxiii. 421 'Rah for protection—to Sheol with free-trade! **1894** R. H. Davis *Eng. Cousins* 120 An American misses the rah-rahs and the skyrocket cries. **1905** *N.Y. Even. Post* 29 June, Harvard almost immediately increased her stroke, and the way their cut-water slid along called forth the nine long 'rahs again and again. **1917** R. Frost *Let.* 3 Dec. (1972) 20 Rah rah rah for some other college than Wellesley. **1924** H. T. Lowe-Porter tr. *Mann's Buddenbrooks* II. vii. iv. 24 A voice..shouts suddenly: 'Heine Seehas is 'lected—'rah for Heine Seehas!' **1942** Ade *Let.* 1 Feb. (1973) 227 We didnt play basket-ball or foot ball [at school in the 'seventies and eighties'] and we never learned to stand up on our hind legs and let out a rah-rah. **1972** 'E. Lathen' *Murder without Icing* (1973) iv. 41 'Way to go, Billy!' 'Rah! Rah! Billy Siragusa!' **1977** *Lancashire Life* Mar. 56/1 Ra-ra-ra! Give a cheer from the sidelines for Accrington, the town that is instilling new life into American baseball.

†**rahate**, obs. variant of rate *v.*, to scold.

1542 Udall *Erasm. Apoph.* 77b, He neuer lynned rahatyng of those persones [etc.]. *Ibid.* 84b, To bee chidden and rahated of all the worlde.

‖**rahat lokum** ('rɑ:hæt lɒ'kʊm). Also **rahat lakoum, lahkoum, lakuhm**, etc. [a. Turk. *rahat lokum*, ad. Arab. *rāḥat al-ḥulqūm* throat's ease.] Turkish delight. Also (occas.) *ellipt.* as *rahat*. Cf. locoum.

1856 R. F. Burton *Personal Narr. Pilgrimage to El-Medinah* III. 362 Squares of Rahah, a comfiture highly prized in these regions, because it comes from Constantinople. **1861** *Punch* 12 Jan. 12/1 Rahat lahkoum, or lumps of delight! **1894** [see delight *sb.* 4]. **1900** *Confectioners' Union Handbk.* 167 Butter-Scotch, nougat, rahat lakuhm. *Ibid.* 169 Hawes, J., & Son... Rahat Lakoum and water mould fancies. **1907** *Yesterdays' Shopping* (1969) 32/1 Rahat La Koum or Turkish Delight. **1931** A. J. Cronin *Hatter's Castle* I. vii. 126 They come off to the ship in boats at Port Said and sell very good rahat-lakoum which is an excellent sweet. **1931** *Discovery* Nov. 359/2 Today the Turks here [on the island of Ada Kaleh] live by some gardening and fruit cultivation, a little cigar manufacture, the preparation of rahat ('Turkish Delight') and mild catering for the few individuals who visit the island. **1935** M. Morphy *Recipes of All Nations* 767 The Turks are extremely fond of sweetmeats..and among the most popular is *rahat el halkum*. Make a thick syrup..adding.. lemon juice..starch..almonds, pistachio nuts..hazel nuts ..cut into squares. **1945** C. S. Forester *Commodore* xviii. 198 He had eaten Westphalian ham and Italian beccaficoes and Turkish rahat lakoum. **1960** *Times* 24 Oct. (Financial Rev.) p. xiv/6 The sweetmeat was called Rahatlokum, but today it is better known as Turkish delight. **1963** *Punch* 20 Nov. 748/2, I..went for coffee and rahat lakoum. **1968** C.

RODEN *Bk. Middle Eastern Food* xv. 295 *Rahat Lokum*, Turkish Delight. This little sweet epitomizes luxury, pleasure and leisure. **1970** [see LOCOUM].

rahatour, variant of REHATOR. *Obs. Sc.*

‖**'rahdar.** *Anglo-Ind.* [Urdū (Pers.) *rāhdār*, f. *rāh* road.] **a.** a road-keeper, toll-gatherer. †**b.** *erron.* = RAHDAREE a. *Obs.*

1623 *St. Papers, Colon.* 1622–4, 178 The rahdars or duties at Daita, &c., shall be remitted. **1753** HANWAY *Trav.* (1762) II. xv. ii. 412 The rahdars were ordered to examine passports. **1764** *Ann. Reg.* 188 To all governors, officers, .. rahdars .. in the provinces of Bengal.

Hence †**'rahdarage** (in 7 rhadorage) = RAHDAREE a. *Obs.*

1698 FRYER *Acc. E. India & P.* 222 Safe Travelling .. for which Rhadorage, or high Imposts, are allowed by the Merchants.

‖**'rahdaree.** In 7 rattar(r)ee, 9 rahdarry. [Urdū (Pers.), f. RAHDAR.]

a. A transit-duty, toll; a tax paid to secure safety in travelling. Also *attrib.* **b.** = RAHDAR a.

1685 HEDGES *Diary* 15 Dec. I. 213 Here we were forced to compound with the Rattaree-men, for the Dutys on our goods. **1686** *Ibid.* 13 Feb. I. 218 Here we paid Rattarree. **1804** WELLINGTON in Gurw. *Disp.* (1844) II. 1182 A rahdarry will go to you this day for the convoy.

'rahing, *vbl. sb.* = HURRAHING *vbl. sb.*

1904 *Daily Chron.* 25 July 7/7 There was not nearly so much 'rahing' and flag-waving as in 1899.

rah rah (rɑː rɑː), *sb.* and *a. slang* (orig. *U.S.*). Also **rah rah rah, ra ra.** [Reduplication of RAH *int.*] **A.** *sb.* A shout of support or encouragement, as for a college team: see RAH *int.* and *sb.* **B.** *adj.* with hyphen. Of or pertaining to college, collegiate; (of behaviour, etc.) characteristic of college students; marked by the generation of enthusiasm or excitement, as in cheer-leading, etc. *U.S.*

1911 [see CUT-UP *sb.* 1 b]. **1914** S. LEWIS *Our Mr. Wrenn* iii. 41 Bunches of rah-rah boys wanting to cross .. to England. **1924** *Public Opinion* 15 Feb. 152/1 When father was a rah-rah boy and wore those comedy clothes. **1945** L. SHELLY *Jive Talk Dict.* 31/2 *Rah rah drapes*, collegiate clothing. **1948** *Landfall* II. 312 Of course, it was all eyewash —rah-rah publicity if you like. **1959** *Economist* 27 June 1151/1 If there is an October election there will be time only for a two-day ra-ra conference before going into battle. **1960** I. CROSS *Backward Sex* iii. 72 The team and three bus-loads of their ra-ra supporters arrived about midday. **1970** *People* (Austral.) 25 Mar. 24/3 The possible solution to the growing world-wide problem of football game disorder comes clad in a delightfully brief skirt and twirls a baton. In America she is known as a 'Rah-Rah girl', in Australia as a Drum Majorette. **1972** *Sat. Rev.* (U.S.) 24 June 18/2 People .. are real rah-rah, knocking on doors and asking you to come to parties. **1974** *Sunday Sun* (Brisbane) 18 Aug. 5/4 The rah-rah teams, Brothers, University and GPS have won 28 of the past 30 grand finals. **1976** *National Observer* (U.S.) 3 July 8/2 'In spite of all the rah-rah rhetoric about recycling's merits, a large market share eludes recycling,' says M. J. Mighdoll, executive vice president.

Hence **rah-'rahing** *ppl. a.*, **rah-'rahism.**

1892 *Outing* Oct. 37/1 He no longer felt stage-fright surrounded by the 'rah-'rahing mob'. **1930** *Chicago Daily Maroon* 9 Dec. 4/1 Students engage in rah-rahism because it gives them a certain simple amount of enjoyment.

raht(e, obs. forms of pa. t. REACH.

Rai (raɪ), *sb.* and *a.* [Native name.] **A.** *sb.* **a.** A member of a tribe of eastern Nepal; this people collectively. **b.** The language of the Rai people. **B.** *adj.* Of or pertaining to the people or their language.

1906 E. VANSITTART *Gurkhās* xi. 128 In the history of Nēpāl it is stated that the Rāis conquered the Nēpāl Valley. *Ibid.* 129 It would be merely a repetition .. to enter into details regarding Rāi customs. **1928** NORTHEY & MORRIS *Gurkhas* xv. 216 Khambus and Yakhas .. are now both regarded as Rais. They both speak the Rai language. **1957** F. TUKER *Gorkha* v. 37 For every Rai a different language, the Gurkhas say. **1962** D. FORBES *Heart of Nepal* xi. 119 Beyond .. lies the territory of the tribes .. the Magars and Gurungs to the west, Rais and Limbus to the east. **1970** L. CAPLAN *Land & Social Change in E. Nepal* v. 96 The land was repossessed .. and re-pledged to a Rai landholder. **1974** *Encycl. Brit. Macropædia* XII. 954/1 The languages of the north and east belong predominantly to the Tibeto-Burman family. These include Magar, Gurung, Rai, [etc.]. **1975** C. VON FÜRER-HAIMENDORF *Himalayan Traders* iii. 63 Grain which the Sherpas brought from the Rai country.

rai, variant of RAY *sb. Obs.*

‖**raia** ('reɪə). *Zool.* Also **raja.** [L. *raia* (pl. *raiæ*).] = RAY (the fish).

1633 P. FLETCHER *Purple Isl.* IV. xii, His fashion like the fish a Raia nam'd. **1646** SIR T. BROWNE *Pseud. Ep.* 169 The severall sorts of Raia's, Torpedo's, Oysters. **1752** HILL *Hist. Anim.* 304 The apertures of the gills in the Raia are five on each side. **1804** *Med. Jrnl.* XII. 550 The rajæ .. are provided with glandulous grains. **1878** BELL *Gegenbaur's Comp. Anat.* 500 There is a pseudo-electric apparatus in Raja.

raia(h, -aw, obs. ff. RAJA(H.

raiah, obs. f. RAYAH.

raiat, var. RAYAT.

raiband, var. RABAND.

raible, var. RABBLE *v.*[1]

raice, obs. f. RACE *sb.*[1]

raich, obs. f. RACHE *sb.*[2], RASH *sb.*

raicke, obs. f. RAIK *v.*

raid (reɪd), *sb.* Forms: 5–6 **rade,** 7 **radde,** 5 **raide,** 5–6, 9 **raid.** [Sc. form of OE. *rád* ROAD, revived by Scott and subsequently adopted in general use, with extension of meaning. In sense 4 perh. partly a. F. *rade*, †*radde*: see also REID.]

I. 1. a. A military expedition on horseback; a hostile and predatory incursion, properly of mounted men; a foray, INROAD.

c **1425** WYNTOUN *Cron.* VIII. xxxiv. 5034 Schyr Andrew syne wyth stalwart hand Made syndry radis in Ingland. **1528** in Tytler *Hist. Scot.* (1864) II. 348 *note*, The said Erle .. procurit divers radis to be maid upon the brokin men of our realme. *a* **1578** LINDESAY (Pitscottie) *Chron. Scot.* (S.T.S.) I. 61 The Scottis maid dywerse incurtiouns and raidis in Ingland. **1805** SCOTT *Last Minstr.* v. xxviii, In raids he spilt but seldom blood. **1818** —— *Rob Roy* Introd., A war which opened the low country to the raids of the clan Gregor. *a* **1839** PRAED *Poems* (1864) II. 14 His Highland plaid, Long borne in foray and in raid. **1868** G. DUFF *Pol. Surv.* 215 The people of Uruguay accuse the Rio Grandians of making raids into their territory.

attrib. **1806** JAMIESON *Pop. Ball. & Songs* I. Pref. 7 A parcel of raid ballads of the Border.

b. A 'lifting' *of* cattle by means of a raid. *rare.*

1867 LADY HERBERT *Cradle L.* v. 153 A 'raid' of cattle .. by the tribe of whom their escort was composed.

c. = AIR-RAID. Also *attrib.* and *Comb.*

1908 H. G. WELLS *War in Air* xi. 354 The Asiatics endeavoured to establish .. fortified centres from which flying-machine raids could be made. **1916** MRS. BELLOC LOWNDES *Let.* 2 Nov. (1971) 77 The Raid night was *horrid*. .. Every moment we expected to hear the bombs drop close by or *on* us, for the machines sounded overhead. **1917** R. FRY *Let.* 6 Oct. (1972) II. 417 There was a scare of a raid on Monday while I was hanging at Heal's. We were all shepherded down into the basement. **1939** H. NICOLSON *Diary* 3 Sept. (1966) 422 We learn afterwards that the whole raid-warning was a mistake. **1940** [see AUXILIARY *a.* 1 b]. **1942** 'N. SHUTE' *Pied Piper* i. 9, I thought of ringing her up, but it's not a very good thing to clutter up the lines during a raid. **1953** C. DAY LEWIS *Italian Visit* ii. 31 Recall how flyers from a raid returning, Lightened of one death, were elected for another. **1974** *Listener* 7 Feb. 176/3 My father .. had the idea that we were being shelled from the river—no one thought anything about a raid from above. *Ibid.* 177/1 By the autumn of 1915, there had been 19 zeppelin raids... They were raids intended to bring Britain to her knees.

2. *transf.* and *fig.* **a.** An invading troop or company, as of raiders.

1826 SCOTT *Jrnl.* 8 Apr., We expect a raid of folks to visit us this morning.

b. A rush, charge, hurried movement.

1861 N. A. WOODS *Tour Pr. Wales Canada* 50 In the reckless indiscriminate raid made to all parts of the States, emigrants often commit the most ruinous mistakes. **1877** A. B. EDWARDS *Up Nile* iii. 51 A rapid raid into some of the nearest shops, for things remembered at the last moment.

c. A sudden or vigorous descent, onset, or attack *upon* something which it is intended to seize, suppress, or destroy. Also, = *police raid* s.v. POLICE *sb.* 6.

1873 SMILES *Huguenots Fr.* I. ii. (1881) 14 There was .. a general raid upon Protestant literature all over France. **1878** MORLEY *Diderot* I. 106 A stern raid was made upon all the scribblers in Paris. **1892** A. W. PINERO *Magistrate* III. 109 *Lugg*. .. (*Reading*) 'Raid on a West End Hotel. At an early hour this morning——' *Wormington*. Yes .. a case of assault upon the police. *a* **1922** T. S. ELIOT *Waste Land Drafts* (1971) 5 We've only had a raid last week, I've been warned twice. **1924** J. BUCHAN *Three Hostages* xv. 215 It would never do for him to be caught in a raid on a dance-club. **1973** W. MCCARTHY *Detail* iii. 264 We're making a raid and will need your help. Can you have your cars and sheriffs' cars block all the roads from Palm Springs?

d. A forceful or insistent attempt at making a person or group provide something. Const. *on*, *upon*.

1931 *Economist* 10 Jan. 58/1 Although he is willing to ask for a further $100,000,000 to $150,000,000 for constructional and other public works, he is averse to spectacular raids on the Treasury for relief purposes. **1940** T. S. ELIOT *East Coker* v. 14 Each venture Is a new beginning, a raid on the inarticulate With shabby equipment always deteriorating In the general mess of imprecision of feeling. **1967** *Listener* 23 Mar. 404/2 Here .. we have .. one who has .. devoted long years .. to a series of attempts, raids upon the articulate, at making available to the English tradition this least accessible of German poets.

e. ***dawn raid*** (Stock Exchange slang), a swift operation effected early in trading whereby a stockbroker obtains for his client a markedly increased shareholding in a company (freq. preparatory to a take-over) by clandestine buying from other substantial shareholders.

1980 *Times* 28 May 17/6 'Dawn raids', in which a stock-market raider suddenly buys a substantial stake in a company and possibly denies non-professional shareholders the opportunity to sell at a price above that in the market, were causing a 'great deal of anxiety'. *Ibid.* 22 July 17 De Beers went into the market on the morning of February 12 and bought another 11·6 per cent in a 'dawn raid'. **1981** *Bookseller* 21 Feb. 568/3 Following his 'dawn raid' last July, which gained him 29·4 per cent of BPC, Robert Maxwell .. clearly plans to secure and consolidate his control of the group.

II. †**3.** A roadstead for ships. *Obs.* Cf. ROAD.

1445 *Recs. Burgh Edinb.* (1869) 8 Shipps that commys in the havin or in the raide. *c* **1470** HENRY *Wallace* IX. 264 Be this the schippis was in the Rochell raid. **1535** STEWART *Cron. Scot.* I. 10 Sone tha let saill and straik into the raid, And ankeris cast. **1609** SKENE tr. *Reg. Maj.* 122 (*Burrow Lawes* c. 27) His shippe is in the radde. **1636** *Charter* in Maitland *Hist. Edin.* (1753) III. 264 The aforesaid Port, .. Harbour, Soil, and Raid of Leith.

raid (reɪd), *v.* Also 8 **rhaad.** [f. prec. sb.]

1. a. *intr.* To go upon, or take part in a raid.

1865 *Intell. Observ.* No. 38. 104 To raid in the surrounding country. **1879** *Academy* 11 Oct. 261/2 English sportsmen who raid with rifle and hound among the Rocky Mountain game. **1885** *Manch. Exam.* 28 May 4/6 He hides in the mountain fastnesses .. whence he raids into the settlements.

b. Of speculators in a market or stock-exchange: To act so as to depress prices or create uncertainty as to values.

1889 *Times* 9 Mar., A further decline .. due to a 'bear' clique raiding.

2. *trans.* To make a raid on (a place, person, cattle, etc.). ***to raid the market*** (see 1 b).

1880 *New Virgin.* II. 208 Their apple and peach orchard had been 'raided'. **1887** J. HATTON *Old Ho. at Sandwich* I. III. vii. 200 The police had raided the house almost simultaneously with my entrance. **1894** [see RAIDER a]. **1902** R. MACHRAY *Night Side of London* xi. 173 Such dens have been raided by the police out of existence. **1908** H. G. WELLS *War in Air* xi. 351 The Germans were .. already raiding London and Paris when the advance fleets from the Asiatic air-parks .. were reported. **1930** L. G. D. ACLAND *Early Canterbury Runs* 1st Ser. vi. 138 A cowboy of his brought a disastrous career to an end by raiding the pantry. **1940** C. MILBURN *Diary* 1 July (1979) 49 It is a few days since the Channel Islands were raided. **1953** K. TENNANT *Joyful Condemned* ii. 12 This place .. is .. never raided... The Vice Squad are always in and out of the place two doors down—but us—we never seem to have them. **1970** *Daily Tel.* 2 June 1/7 The Israeli Air Force yesterday raided Egyptian military positions near Port Said, killing five soldiers and wounding eight.

Hence **'raided** *ppl. a.*; **'raiding** *vbl. sb.*

1785 W. HUTTON *Bran New Wark* 40 What debateable wark, what rhaading, and watching, and warding .. alang the Border Service. **1824** J. HODGSON in Raine *Mem.* (1858) II. 29 Such a race as figured in it during the border raiding. **1891** *Daily News* 16 May 6/1 To arrest .. every person .. who might be found on the raided premises.

raid, obs. variant of RED(D, spawn. *Sc.*

raid, obs. Sc. pa. t. RIDE, RAY.

raider ('reɪdə(r)). [f. RAID *v.* + -ER[1].] **a.** One who raids; a plundering invader, a marauder. Also *transf.*

1863 *Boston Commonwealth* (U.S.) 30 Oct., Governor Bramlette of Kentucky .. telegraphs that the rebel raiders are within forty miles of his capital. **1870** MORRIS *Earthly Par.* II. III. 481 Hearkening the raiders call The cattle o'er the meads. **1878** JEFFERIES *Gamekeeper at H.* 142 There are three kinds of poachers, the local men, the raiders coming in gangs from a distance—and the mouchers. **1894** 'MARK TWAIN' in *Century Mag.* XLVII. 776/2 It's perfectly plain that the thief took advantage of the reception .. to raid the vacant houses... It's the same old raider. **1976** *Daily Record* (Glasgow) 4 Dec. 26/1 Seldom do we find Irish raiders at the Market Rasen track, but trainer Moore has sent two over in a bid for a winning double. **1979** *Austral. Financial Rev.* 7 Aug. 1/1 (*caption*) Raider [*sc.* a stock-exchange speculator] hits Ansett.

b. An aircraft on a bombing operation. Hence phr. ***raiders passed*** (or ***past***), the 'all clear' signal given by sirens, etc., after an air-raid.

1908 H. G. WELLS *War in Air* viii. 248 He is now in the act of bombarding the chief manufacturing city .. by means of three raider airships. **1917** 'CONTACT' *Airman's Outings* II. iii. 258 Certainly they do not include speculation about the men who man the raiders. **1940** *New Statesman* 19 Oct. 372/1 The 'Raiders Passed' went and the tens of thousands of East Londoners poured out of the shelters. **1941** *Ann. Reg. 1940* 69 The damage inflicted by the raiders was little less serious. **1942** *R.A.F. Jrnl.* 13 June 27 When the 'raiders past' had sounded .. we emerged, coughing, from our subterranean dens. **1943** G. GREENE *Ministry of Fear* I. i. 22 Three flares came sailing .. down... Yet another raider came up from the south-east. **1966** A. POWELL *Soldier's Art* ii. 158 'That one didn't take long.' .. 'Another tip-and-run raider,' said Pilgrim.

raider, dial. var. RATHER.

'raiding, *ppl. a.* [f. RAID *v.* + -ING[2].] **a.** In senses of the verb. **b.** ***raiding party***, a small military group taking part in an organized foray into enemy territory, esp. in order to seize prisoners or supplies.

1865 R. H. KELLOGG *Life & Death in Rebel Prisons* iii. 97 All communications were interrupted by our '*raiding parties*'. **1866** J. B. ROSE tr. *Ovid's Met.* 45 Jove now circuits heaven and taketh note Of raiding flames. **1885** *Harper's Mag.* Mar. 611/1 Washington detailed soldiers to guard them from British raiding parties. **1892** M. A. JACKSON *Life & Lett. Gen. Jackson* xxiii. 462 The raiding-parties of the enemy were operating all through the intervening country. **1914** G. BELL *Let.* 21 Jan. (1927) I. xiii. 327 They had spied us as we passed under the Thlaithuwât and, taking us for a raiding party, had followed us to see where we were going. **1918** E. A. MACKINTOSH *War* iv. 126 The raiding party dispersed each to a dug-out to feed at other people's expense. **1923** KIPLING *Irish Guards in Gt. War* I. 220 Raiding-parties dove in and out of the front lines. **1931** *Times Lit. Suppl.* 16 Apr. 300/2 When he saw a German raiding-party approaching he forgot in his excitement to take off his safety-catch. **1977** B. LUCAS tr. *C. De Foucauld's*

Lett. from Desert vii. 140 He was killed on 13 December.. by a raiding party of thirty horsemen who then disappeared.

raie, obs. f. RAY.

‖**raie ultime** (rɛ yltim). *Spectroscopy.* [Fr. (A. de Gramont 1907, in *Compt. Rend.* CXLIV. 1101), f. *raie* line + *ultime* ultimate, last.] An emission line in the spectrum of an element which is the last (or one of the last) to remain detectable as the concentration of that element is decreased.

1922 W. F. MEGGERS et al. in *Sci. Papers U.S. Bureau of Standards* XVIII. 239 The raies ultimes are the most sensitive spectral lines of an element. **1923** F. TWYMAN *Wavelength Tables for Spectrum Anal.* 79 It is in the ultra-violet that the 'Raies Ultimes' almost always lie. **1937** C. CANDLER *Atomic Spectra* II. xvii. 120 As the proportion of calcium in the powder is diminished step by step, the weaker lines successively disappear until finally only one is left; this is known as the *raie ultime*. **1948** G. R. HARRISON et al. *Pract. Spectroscopy* xv. 429 The *raie ultime* is the last line of an element to disappear as the quantity of the element burned in a sample is decreased to the vanishing point. **1962** WALKER & STRAW *Spectroscopy* I. i. 94 The identification of the persistent (the *raies ultimes*) lines proves without doubt the presence of the corresponding element.

raif(f, obs. Sc. f. RAVE, REEVE, REIF, REIVE; obs. pa. t. RIVE.

†**raiffell**, *v. Sc. Obs. rare.* (Meaning not clear.)
? Cf. north. dial. *raffle* to lounge about, dissipate.
1529 LYNDESAY *Compl.* 175 Sum gart hym raiffell at the rakcat.

†**raifort.** *Obs.* Also 6 rayf(f)ort, -ert; *Sc.* raphorte, 7–8 ri-, ryfart, 9 reefort. [a. F. *raifort*, †*reff-*, *riffort* (16th c. Littré and Godef.), f. *raiz* root, RACE *sb.*⁶ + *fort* strong.] Horse-radish.

1541 R. COPLAND *Galyen's Terap.* D iv, He.. fyrste of all vsed his salue of mustarde,.. & than his vomyte of rayffort. **1578** LYTE *Dodoens* v. xxxvii. 599 Mountayne Radish or Rayfort hath great brode leaues, in fashion lyke to the great Docke. *a* **1700** in *Sempill's Poems* (1849) 69 With sybows and rifarts and carlings. **1808** JAMIESON, *Reefort.*

raig(e, obs. forms of RAGE *sb.* and *v.*

†**raign**, *v. Obs.* Forms: 5–6 **rayn-**, **reyn-**, 5 **raygn-**, 5–6 **reygne**, 6 **reign**, **rain**. [Aphetic form of ARRAIGN *v.*¹] *trans.* To arraign.

1444 *Rolls of Parlt.* V. 116/2 He shall.. be punysshed be prisounement, and rayned at the Kynges will. **1480** CAXTON *Chron. Eng.* cclii. (1482) 323 Iohan hume [etc.].. byfore the mayer the lordes and chyef Iustyce of Englond were rayned and dampned. **1526** *Pilgr. Perf.* (W. de W. 1531) 97 b, Reigned before Pylate & iudged. **1581** MARBECK *Bk. of Notes* 374 Yᵗ same false faith in their owne works, raineth yᵉ mercy promised to the merits of their own works.

So †'**raignment**, arraignment. *Obs. rare*⁻¹.
1570 FOXE *A. & M.* 1637/1 Hauyng somewhat.. to declare touching the raynment and death of the Duke of Suffolke.

raign(e, obs. forms of REIGN *sb.* and *v.*

'**raiiform**, *a. rare*⁻¹. [f. RAI-A + -(I)FORM.] Having the form of a ray (the fish).
1884 F. DAY *Fishes Gt. Brit. & Irel.* II. 331 These fishes .. possess a squaliform stage, a raiiform stage, and a torpediform stage.

raijpout, obs. form of RAJPUT.

raik, *sb.* Now *rare* or *Obs.* Forms: 5 **rayk**, **reyke**, 5–6 **rayke**, 5–7 (9) **raike**, 6 (9) **raik**. [a. ON. *reik* (Norw. dial. *reik*), walking, strolling, etc., related to *reika* RAIK *v.* In ME. distinct from RAKE *sb.*³; at a later period the two coalesced, and the spelling *raik* became unusual.]

1. The act of going, walking about, etc.; course, way; journey.

? *a* **1400** *Morte Arth.* 2985 Sir Gawaynne.. Rydes one a rawndoune, and his rayke holdes. *c* **1425** WYNTOUN *Cron.* III. i. 98 To the dure.. Scho tuk hyr rayk rycht hastyly. *c* **1440** *Promp. Parv.* 427/2 Reyke, or royt, ydylle walky[n]ge abowt (*S.* reyke or royke), *discursus, vagacio.* **1535** STEWART *Cron. Scot.* I. 284 Cesus Nausica.. with his raikis all that land ouir raid. **1570** LEVINS *Manip.* 198/17 Rayke, *ambulacrum.* **1808** JAMIESON s.v., It is said of a horse, that takes a long step, or moves actively, that he has a great raik of the road. **1813** HOGG *Queen's Wake, Kilmeny* xxiv, The wolf and the kid their raike began.
fig. **1401** *Pol. Poems* (Rolls) II. 73 That ȝe myȝten have ȝour reyke and prechen what ȝou list.

†**2.** The space of ground over which animals, esp. cattle, usually move or pasture; a piece of pasture-land, etc. *Obs.* Cf. RAKE *sb.*³

c **1425** WYNTOUN *Cron.* VII. vi. 104 That land, thai oysyd all The Barys rayk all tyme to call. **1591** *Manor Records* in *N.W. Linc. Gloss.* (1877) s.v., There was a place in the Manor of Scotter called Long Rayke. **1641** *N. Riding Rec.* IV. 212 A place called le Cow Raikes.

3. = RAKE *sb.*³ 4. *rare.*
1623 in *Records Peebles* (1872) 412 To bring vp the vther tua trieis with his hors and his oxine, pryce ewerie raike thretie tua *s.* **1808** JAMIESON s.v., He brings twa, thrie, &c. raik a day; applied to dung, coals, &c... as equivalent to draught.

†**raik**, *v. Obs.* Forms: 3–5 (9) **raike**, 4–6 **rayk(e**, 5 **raicke**, 5–6 **reyke**, 3–6 **raik**. [a. ON. *reika* (Norw. dial. *reika*, MSw. *reka*) to walk about, stroll, wander. In ME. distinct from RAKE *v.*², in which it was subsequently absorbed.]

1. *intr.* To go, proceed, make one's way; to walk, stroll, wander, etc.

a. of persons. = RAKE *v.*² 1 a.
c **1340** *Hampole's Wks.* (1895) I. 140 þas þat eauer raikis aboute to fede þaire wittis with vanitees and lustis. **13..** *E.E. Allit. P.* C. 89 þenne he ryses radly, & raykes bylyue Ionas toward port Iaph. *a* **1400–50** *Alexander* 5555 þan raikis he by þe reede see & rides ay þe sannd. **1535** STEWART *Cron. Scot.* III. 40 The men of weir.. In gude array come raikand fra the schoir. **1596** DALRYMPLE tr. *Leslie's Hist. Scot.* VI. 349 He raikis throuch the hail realme.
fig. *a* **1300** *Cursor M.* 20798 It es better to be stell, þan raik on reson þat es will. **1340–70** *Alex. & Dind.* 467 We raiken to oure romauncus & reden þe storrius.

b. of things. = RAKE *v.*² 1 b.
13.. *E.E. Allit. P.* A. 112 þe water con swepe Wyth a rownande rourde raykande aryȝt. **1375** BARBOUR *Bruce* III. 627 Thar schip.. Raykit slidand throw the se. *c* **1475** *Rauf Coilȝear* 212 Lat the cop raik for my bennysoun.
fig. *a* **1340** HAMPOLE *Psalter* lxxxv. 5 þai suffire þaire hert to rayke in ydel thoghtis. *c* **1400** *Destr. Troy* 3048 Hir chekes .. as the chalke white, As the rose, was the rud þat raiked hom in.

c. of cattle, deer, etc. = RAKE *v.*² 1 c.
a **1225** [see RAIKING *ppl. a.*]. *c* **1470** HENRYSON *Robene & Makyne* 12, I.. keipis my scheip undir yone wude, Lo! quhair thay raik on raw. **1530** LYNDESAY *Test. Papyngo* 643 The fallow deir, to see thame raik on rawe.

2. *refl.* To betake oneself. *rare.*
13.. *E.E. Allit. P.* B. 465 þe rauen raykez him forth. **13..** *Gaw. & Gr. Knt.* 1735 þe lady.. ros hir vp radly, rayked hir þeder.

3. *trans.* **a.** To make, pursue, (one's way). *rare.*
c **1425** WYNTOUN *Cron.* V. x. 3477 The dede body ras.. And raykyt off the kyrk hys way.

b. To wander through or over (a place).
1813 HOGG *Queen's Wake, Kilmeny* vii, Lang haif I raikit the world wide. *Ibid.* xxiv, To raike the lanely glen.

Hence †'**raiker**, a stroller, vagabond; †'**raiking** *vbl. sb.* and *ppl. a. Obs.*
a **1225** *Ancr. R.* 140 *note* (Titus MS.), As mon dos þe custel to the ku, oðer to þe beast, þat is to raikinde. **13..** *E.E. Allit. P.* B. 382 Neuer cowþe stynt.. þe raykande wawez. *c* **1340** *Hampole's Wks.* (1895) I. 140 Thre maners of occupacions are, as.. Raykyng aboute. **1596** DALRYMPLE tr. *Leslie's Hist. Scot.* I. 121 Reiuers, Raikers, Herrieris of the ground.

raik(e, obs. Sc. ff. RAKE, RECK.

raikn-, obs. Sc. f. RECKON.

†**rail**, *sb.*¹ *Obs.* Forms: 1 **hræȝ(e)l**, **hreȝl**, etc., 2 **ræȝ(e)l**, **reil**, 3 **reȝel**, 5 **reile**, 6 **raill**, **rayll**, **rale**, 6–7 **raile**, **rayl(e**, 7–8 (9 *Sc.*) **rail**. [OE. *hrægl*, *hrægel* = OFris. *(h)reil*, OHG. *(h)regil*, *hrecil*, of obscure etym.]

1. A garment, dress, mantle, cloak.
a **700** *Epinal Gloss.* 84 *Amiculo*, hraecli [*Erf.* hræȝl, *Corpus* hreȝli]. *c* **897** K. ÆLFRED *Gregory's Past.* xiv. 82 Ðæt hræȝl .. sceolde bion ȝeworht of purpuran. *c* **1000** *Ags. Gosp.* John xiii. 4 He.. lede his reaf & nam linen hræȝel [*Hatton MS.* rail]. *c* **1175** *Lamb. Hom.* 5 þa oðre men þe reil nefden. *a* **1250** *Owl & Night.* 562 þu art lutel and unstrong And nis þi reȝel nowiht long.

b. A woman's gown (? misuse of sense 2).
c **1817** HOGG *Tales & Sk.* (1837) II. 15 She was dressed in a plain white rail.

2. A piece of linen or other cloth formerly worn about the neck by women; a neckerchief. See also NIGHT-RAIL.
1482 *Act 22 Edw. IV*, c. 1 They shall not suffer their wives to weare any reile called a kercheffe, whose price exceedeth twentie pence. **1530** PALSGR. 260/2 Rayle for a woman's neck, *crevechief en quattre doubles.* **1592** NASHE *P. Penilesse* (ed. 2) 8 A course hempen raile about her shoulders. *a* **1635** CORBET *Poems* (1807) 232 Ladyes, that weare black cipress-vailes Turn'd lately to white linnen-rayles. **1678** PHILLIPS (ed. 4) s.v., The.. gathered piece of Cloth which Women throw about their necks, when they dress them.. is also called a Rail. **1710** RUDDIMAN *Gloss. Douglas' Æneis* s.v. *Ralis*, A womans rail or collar-body, as Scot. Bor. call it.
Comb. **1558** *Richmond Wills* (Surtees) 126 Fower crepings .. iiij railbandes.

rail (reɪl), *sb.*² Forms: 4–6 **raylle**, 4–7 **raile**, 5 **reyle**, 5–7 **rayl(e**, 6–7 **rale**, 4, 7– **rail**. [a. OF. *reille* (1334):—pop. L. **regla*, L. *rēgula* straight stick, bar, rod, etc. (see RULE): the mod. Norm. form is *raîle* (Moisy). (M)Du., (M)LG., and Sw. *regel*, OHG. *rigil* (G. *riegel*) bar, bolt, etc., are prob. also of Latin origin.]

1. a. A bar of wood, fixed in a horizontal position for hanging things on, or for other purposes. Now chiefly in combs., as ***copping-***, ***hat-***, ***towel-rail.***
c **1320** [see *rail-tree* in 6 a]. **1390** GOWER *Conf.* III. 75 Into an Egle he gan transforme, And flyh and sette him on a raile. **1497** *Naval Acc. Hen. VII* (1896) 313 Cloffeborde & Raylles for the seyd ship. **1609** HOLLAND *Amm. Marcell.* 222 The master of the Engine.. setteth open the rayles that contain the binding of the whole worke. **1683** MOXON *Mech. Exerc., Printing* xi. ¶22 These Racks.. are hung a-thwart two Rails an Inch thick.. which Rails are fastned.. by Stiles perpendicular to the Ceiling. **1710** STEELE *Tatler* No. 174 ¶3 All the Volumes.. shall be from Time to Time placed in proper Order upon the Rails of the unhoused Booksellers. **1793** [see COPPING-RAIL]. **1883** [see *hat-rail*, s.v. HAT *sb.* 8].

b. Used to support vines or other plants.
1389 *Helmingham MS.* 21, lf. 17 b, Forkis & railis to bere up þe vyne. *c* **1420** *Pallad. on Husb.* IV. 287 Helpe hem [gourds] vp with rayles, as they growe. **1548** ELYOT *Dict.*, *Cantherius*, the raile of a vine borne vp with forkes & postes. **1600** SURFLET *Countrie Farme* I. ii. 2 A frame of railes in forme of an Arbor for vines to runne vpon. **1777** MASON *Eng. Garden* II. 290 To defend Their infant shoots, beneath, on oaken stakes, Extend a rail of elm.

c. Forming part of the sides of a cart.
1530 PALSGR. 260/2 Rayle for a carte, *coste.* **1611** COTGR., *Ridelle*, the rayle of a Cart or waine; and more particularly, the vppermost of the three. **1797** *Encycl. Brit.* (ed. 3) XVIII. 697/2 The chest or body of the waggon, having the staves or rails fixed thereon. **1851** STEPHENS *Bk. Farm.* (ed. 2) II. 357/1 The outer rails support the sheaves of corn over the wheels.

d. *Naut.* ***rails of the head***: (see quot. 1769).
1769 FALCONER *Dict. Marine* (1776), *Rails of the head*, certain curved pieces of timber extending from the bows on each side to the continuation of the ship's stem. **1867** SMYTH *Sailor's Word-bk.* 375 The short rails of the head, extending from the back of the figure to the cat-head.

e. In various (mainly *U.S.*) phrases: ***to split a rail***, to split timber for rails; ***to ride a rail*** (see quot. 1836); ***to ride*** (someone) ***on a rail***, to punish someone by carrying him about astride a rail to be mocked; ***as thin*** (or ***lean***) ***as a rail***.
1714 J. HEMPSTEAD *Diary* in *Coll. New London Hist. Soc.* (1901) I. 38, I was at home al day spliting Railes & holing Posts. **1820** *Niles' Reg.* XVIII. 256/1 At 97 he went into the woods and split 100 chesnut rails in less than a day. **1907** *St. Nicholas* Oct. 1078/1 You never split a rail in your life.
1834 *New England Mag.* VII. 455 The mill-men resolved to bestow public honors on Dominicus Pike, only hesitating whether to tar and feather him, ride him on a rail, or refresh him with an ablution at the town-pump. **1836** T. POWER *Impressions of Amer.* I. 180 Here I enjoyed my first lesson in .. riding a rail;.. The term is derived from a fence-rail being occasionally used to supply the place of a broken thoroughbrace, by which all these stages are hung. **1853** 'MARK TWAIN' in *Hannibal* (Missouri) *Jrnl.* 23 May 3/1 The gentleman ought to be ducked, ridden on a rail, tarred and feathered. **1900** *Congress. Rec.* 5 Feb. 1521/2 Up in Maine .. they mobbed two preachers, tarred and feathered them, and rode them on a rail because they preached the doctrine of Jesus Christ.
1872 'MARK TWAIN' *Roughing It* xv. 125 You'll marry a combination of calico and consumption that's as thin as a rail. **1927** W. E. COLLINSON *Contemp. Eng.* 117 Here I will insert a few current comparisons which are in frequent colloquial use:.. as thin as a lath or rake or rail. **1934** 'J. S. STRANGE' *For Hangman* xvi. 183 He was a bright looking boy of about sixteen.. and thin as a rail. **1939** *Amer. Speech* XIV. 261 A skinny person [in Indiana] is 'thin as a rail'. **1946** W. S. MAUGHAM *Then & Now* viii. 39 Machiavelli, himself as lean as a rail, did not like fat men. **1967** G. JACKSON *Let.* 30 Sept. in *Soledad Brother* (1971) 131, I am getting thin as a rail, feel all right, however.

2. a. A horizontal bar of wood or metal, fixed upon upright supports (posts) as part of a fence. (In *pl.* freq. = b.)
1494 *Nottingham Rec.* III. 272 For sawyng reyleyes [*sic*] to the pale. *a* **1548** HALL *Chron., Hen. VIII* (1550) 59 This Gardeyn was towred at euery corner and railed with railes gilt. **1616** SIR R. BOYLE in *Lismore Papers* (1886) I. 115, I agreed with my carpenter to mak my postes and Rayles of my Park. **1732** LEDIARD *Sethos* II. VII. 91 The rails which inclos'd the sanctuary. **1792** BELKNAP *Hist. New Hampsh.* III. 117 The wood.. makes durable rails for fences. **1861** N. A. WOODS *Pr. Wales Canada* 315 Mr. Lincoln.. began his career in life as a splitter of rails. **1891** *Law Times* XC. 395/1 Placing wooden rails on the side next the glebe land.
fig. **1614** DAY *Dyall* ix. (1613) 246 The law hath made rayles and barres about thee.

b. A continuous series of bars forming the horizontal part of a fence; also, by extension, a fence or railing, whether constructed of posts and rails, or of some other form.
1541 *Act 33 Hen. VIII*, c. 38 Reparacions nedefull to be done in and vpon any pale, rayle and lodge, within any of the saide parkes. **1600** SURFLET *Countrie Farme* VII. xix. 833 These seuerall grounds.. must be separated one from the other by a strong rale, through which deere or sheepe (but no greater cattell) may passe. **1650** T. B[AYLEY] *Worcester's Apoph.* 31 As we were going along by the Churchyard Rayle. **1726** LEONI *Alberti's Archit.* II. 62/2 The rail or side-wall of the Bridge. **1871** L. STEPHEN *Playgr. Eur.* iii. (1894) 88 The dangerous place is guarded by a wooden rail.

c. The HAND-RAIL of a stair.
1453 *Mem. Ripon* (Surtees) III. 160 Pro emendacione de le grece et le reyle infra aulam. **1663** GERBIER *Counsel* 15 Carpenters do frame their Railes to Ballesters to meet on the Pedestals. **1778** *Encycl. Brit.* (ed. 2) I. 618/2 The three dotted lines drawn from the rail to the pitch board represent the width of the rail. **1825** J. NICHOLSON *Operat. Mechanic* 600 Every level straight line, directed to the axis of the well-hole, from every point of the side of the rail. **1842** GWILT *Encycl. Arch.* §2182 In the upper ramp.. produce the top of the rail.. to P.

d. An altar-rail (see ALTAR *sb.* II).
1641 MILTON *Prel. Episc.* 10 Unlesse a man be within the rayls, or enclosure of the Altar. **1711** HEARNE *Collect.* (O.H.S.) III. 231 In the Chancell just on this side the Rayle. **1874** MICKLETHWAITE *Mod. Par. Churches* 90 The rail was introduced in the seventeenth century as a fence to the altar.

e. *Naut.* (See quot. 1804.)
1804 A. DUNCAN *Mariner's Chron.* Pref. 19 Rails are narrow planks nailed for ornament on several parts of a ship's upper works, as drift-rails, fife-rails, sheer-rails. **1840** R. H. DANA *Bef. Mast* xxxi. 112 Our ship had.. high bulwarks and rail. **1867** SMYTH *Sailor's Word-bk.* 264 Those parts where the sheer is raised, and the rails are cut off.

f. The fence or railings forming the boundary of a racecourse. Hence phr. ***on the rails***, beside the rails, on the track nearest the rails. Also *fig.*
1928 GALSWORTHY *Swan Song* II. iii. 122 On the rails they were almost opposite the winning post. **1930** *Times* 24 Mar. 4/2 Rubicon II and War Mist were running side by side with Porthaon, the last-named being on the rails. **1931** *Daily*

Express 21 Sept. 15/4 Smirke followed the Wootton tradition and secured the rails. **1931** T. H. Dey *Leaves from Bookmaker's Bk.* ii. 34 He achieved a great success amongst the 'swells', who formed the bulk of his clientèle 'on the rails' at the principal race meetings. **1951** 'J. Tey' *Daughter of Time* vii. 89 It's as reliable as a bookie's tips would be. He's on the wrong side of the rails. **1962** D. Francis *Dead Cert* xiii. 144 The bookmakers on the rails—those..who stand along the railing between Tattersall's and the Club enclosures,..send out weekly accounts. **1975** H. Carvic *Odds on Miss Seeton* (1976) vii. 87 Stay here till the jockeys are up, then..get close up to the rails so you can see properly. **1977** *Irish Press* 29 Sept. 13/4 She is drawn on the rails, and on her immediate right is Sprightly Peg.

g. *Surfing.* (See quot. 1962.) Also **rail turn** (see quot. 1969).

1962 T. Masters *Surfing made Easy* 65 *Rails*, the edge of the surfboard. **1965** *N.Z. Listener* 17 Dec. 5/2 You crouch down, grab a rail (side of board) and get shot like a catapult. **1968** W. Warwick *Surfriding in N.Z.* 3/2 He also screwed beading around the outside rail to prevent him sliding off the board. **1969** *Observer* 3 Aug. 35/1 He may execute the spectacular 'rail turn', during which the whole of one edge or rail is buried in the face of the wave.

3. *Carpentry.* **a.** One of the horizontal pieces in a door or other framework.

1678 Moxon *Mech. Exerc.* I. 106 In Wainscoting of Rooms..the Upper and Lower Rails have also the same breadth with the Margent of the Stile. **1823** P. Nicholson *Pract. Build.* 160 All the cross pieces (of a frame) are denominated rails. **1834–47** J. S. Macaulay *Field Fortif.* (1851) 81 This gate..is usually composed of two upright stiles, and two horizontal rails, framed together.

†**b.** A string of a stair. *Obs.*

1679 Moxon *Mech. Exerc.* I. 154 The Rail these Steps are built upon..must..be framed into the next Post.

†**c.** (See quot.) *Obs. rare*$^{-0}$.

1688 R. Holme *Armoury* III. 100/1 Raile is a piece of Timber 6..foot or more long, and carrieth four inches broad, and an inch or more thick. A Raile is an half Spare.

4. a. A bar or continuous line of bars (now usu. of iron or steel) laid on or near the ground (commonly in pairs) to bear and guide the wheels of a vehicle, and enable them to run more easily. Usu. *pl.*

a **1734** North *Life Lord Keeper North* (1742) 136 Laying Rails of Timber, from the Colliery, down to the River, exactly streight and parallel; and bulky Carts are made with four Rowlets fitting these Rails. **1789** Brand *Newcastle* I. 687 *note*, Upon these sleepers, other pieces of timber called rails, of 4 or 5 in. square are laid. **1834** N. W. Cundy *Inland Transit* 34 These iron bars, which are called rails, are firmly connected end to end. **1866** *Engineering* I. 255/2 Steel rails have so much more stiffness in a vertical direction than iron. **1932** G. Greene *Stamboul Train* I. i. 3 A wilderness of rails and points. **1954** J. Masters *Bhowani Junction* I. i. 17 The coal train..ran off the rails. **1976** *Illustr. London News* Nov. 53/4 One gets a much greater thrill from speeding on rails at 300 kmh than from flying in Concorde.

b. Phr. ***off the rails*** (freq. *fig.* = out of the proper or normal condition). Also opp., ***on the rails***.

1848 G. E. Jewsbury *Let.* Mar. (1892) 242, I was very worried, and I felt as if the least thing would throw me off the rails. **1859** Gen. P. Thompson *Audi Alt.* II. xcv. 80 At the arrival of a general election England therefore may be considered as 'off the rails'. **1883** E. W. Hamilton *Diary* 1 Aug. (1972) II. 467 'To be on the rails', as Mr. G. said this morning, 'and to be off the rails are two different things'. **1886** Gurney, etc. *Phantasms of Living* I. 499 A sane, healthy, waking mind can really get momentarily off the rails. **1916** J. Buchan *Greenmantle* i. 5 He told me just how and why and when Turkey had left the rails. **1935** B. Malinowski *Coral Gardens* II. vi. v. 235 Where Durkheim 'goes off the rails', so to speak, is in reducing his sound conception to a very narrow formula of the direct emotional experience of the crowd and of the influences of crowd phenomena on the individual. **1938** E. M. Forster in *Nation* 16 July 68/1 They [*sc.* citizens] are obliged to be born separately and to die separately and, owing to these unavoidable termini, will always be running off the totalitarian rails. **1953** K. Amis *Lucky Jim* xxii. 228 He resolved not to run off the rails again. He cleared his throat, found his place, and went on in a clipped tone. **1954** T. S. Eliot *Confidential Clerk* II. 63, I make decisions on the spur of the moment, But you'd never take a leap in the dark; You'd keep me on the rails. **1955** G. Greene *Quiet American* II. ii. 132 All my conversations with Pyle seemed to take grotesque directions. Was it because of his sincerity that they so ran off the customary rails? **1971** *Daily Tel.* 20 Oct. 12/7 They are proud, stubborn and steady—even if dad appears to have gone off the rails. **1975** M. Babson *There must be Some Mistake* xvi. 128 Would John have gone off the rails like this if she had been paying enough attention?

c. *N. Amer.* A railwayman.

1938 L. M. Beebe *High Iron* 223/2 *Rail*, railroad man. **1960** [see *biscuit-toss* s.v. biscuit 3 b]. **1974** *Maclean's Mag.* Jan. 16/2 She spent too much time..listening to a bunch of young 'rails' repeat lies handed down over the years.

d. *Electronics.* A conductor which is maintained at a fixed potential and to which other parts of a circuit are connected.

1960 in H. Carter *Dict. Electronics* 255. **1965** *Wireless World* Aug. 399 The common rail for input signals is the positive line, while the common connection to the thyristor is the negative line. **1977** *Gramophone* Feb. 1344/1 Gramophone inputs are to feedback pairs on a 25-volt rail giving a reasonable overload margin. **1979** *Personal Computer World* Nov. 3 (Advt.), 30 Amp, 8v power supply, 5 Amps on ± 16v rails (all rails are separately fused).

5. a. = railway, now chiefly in phr. *by rail*, and on the Stock Exchange in *pl.* = railway shares. *spec.* **British Rail**, the name of the national railway of Britain.

1843 Syd. Smith in Lady Holland *Mem.* (1855) II. 495 The rail..has brought us within fifty miles of London. **1843** *Ainsworth's Mag.* III. 361 My lord and lady start, per rail, To London for the Season. **1848** J. J. Ruskin *Let.* 17 Mar. in M. Lutyens *Ruskins & Grays* (1972) xi. 98 For God-sake be done with Rails and Shares—or you will not have a Business, for who will confide in Railway people I am not clear. **1858** Queen Victoria *Let.* 8 May in R. Fulford *Dearest Child* (1964) 103 We went by rail, nice, quick! **1867** in 'Mark Twain' *Innoc. Abr.* (1869) i. 21 They can by rail go on to Florence. **1872** Black *Adv. Phaeton* xi. 149 He had come on by rail to pay us a visit. **1884** E. W. Hamilton *Diary* 5 Aug. (1972) II. 666 His solution of the financial difficulty is that we should guarantee 'the Rails', the slang phrase for the Preference Debt to which the Railroads are assigned. **1892** B. Potter *Jrnl.* 30 July (1966) 243 The Volunteers broke up and several companies went off by rail. **1893** *Westm. Gaz.* 25 Feb. 8/1 The public have lost nearly all confidence in American rails. **1926** *Daily Colonist* (Victoria, B.C.) 15 July 17/1 The advance in rails has slowed up temporarily, although a strong investment demand is reported for several of the high grade issues. **1935** *Economist* 27 July 191/1 Rails and utilities..have hardly participated at all in this week's upward movement. **1965** *Evening Standard* 4 Jan. 9/3 (*heading*) Now it's British Rail—Beeching's last new look for trains, stations, men. *Ibid.*, A new image for British Railways—'British Rail'—is being launched tonight when Dr. Beeching opens an exhibition showing the new symbols, train liveries and uniforms at the Design Centre in the Haymarket. 'There's been a lot of criticism about the new name,..' Mr. George Williams, the railways Director of Industrial Design, said at a preview of the exhibition today. 'Personally I think that passengers..will soon find themselves saying British Rail.' **1965** *Observer* 31 Jan. 12/8 British Rail officials admit there appears to be an injustice. **1976** *Illustr. London News* Nov. 52/4 Fruit and vegetables now tend to go increasingly by road..where a few years ago they travelled by rail. *Ibid.* 53/3 The productivity a head has more than quadrupled since 1945, whereas..for British Rail [it has] only doubled. **1981** *Daily Tel.* 3 Mar. 18/2 Lucky evening travellers tonight..will each be presented with a miniature of British Rail sherry.

b. Railway journey.

1857 E. FitzGerald *Lett.* (1889) I. 242 So as the Atlantic should have been no greater Bar between us than the two hours rail to Oxford.

c. Usu. *pl.* A railway station.

1854 *Poultry Chron.* I. 117/2 The middle and humble classes..are oft times virtually prohibited from attending if bad weather sets in; more especially if out of the way of rails. **1939** H. Hodge *Cab, Sir?* xv. 222 The 'Rails' are railway stations, as distinct from the Underground.

6. *attrib.* and *Comb.* **a.** In senses 1 and 2, as ***rail-mould, -piece, -post, -splitter*** (U.S.), ***-splitting*** (U.S.), ***-work***; ***rail-under*** (poet. adv.); **rail-bird** *U.S.*, (*a*) the American spotted cuckoo; (*b*) one who watches from the rails or sidelines (*lit.* and *fig.*); †**rail-cloth**, ? a cloth for the altar-rail; **rail-cut**, a length of timber cut off for a rail; **rail-ridden**, compelled to 'ride' on a rail, as a punishment; †**rail-stair**, a stair with a railing; †**rail-tree**, a rail. Also rail-fence.

1797 *Encycl. Brit.* (ed. 3) V. 596/2 The nævius, spotted cuckow, or *rail-bird, is about the size of a field-fare... It inhabits Cayenne... This..is seen often perched upon gates and rails, whence its name. **1931** *Daily Progress* (Charlottesville, Va.) 26 Mar. 13/7 Louisville's railbirds are ..watching and clocking the workouts of Derby eligibles. **1947** *Sun* (Baltimore) 4 Nov. 16/1 With the grandstand crowded when regular railbirds pushed their way into the shelters, betting dropped away. **1957** [see cookie 4]. **1959** *Washington Post* 8 Oct. A21 Political rail-birds out here suspect that Brown is beginning to think of himself as something more than a favorite son. **1971** *Daily Colonist* (Victoria, B.C.) 27 May 54/3 He gave them a three-week course of instruction in lacrosse fundamentals, banned railbirds who might make the boys feel self-conscious then turned them loose in lacrosse games. **1531** *MS. Acc. St. John's Hosp., Canterb.*, Paid for a lyne to the *rale cloth. **1836** D. B. Edward *Hist. Texas* IV. 69 The farmers often get it measuring two *rail cuts in length. **1881** *Scribner's Monthly* Feb. 503/2 The pole fence was laid after the same fashion of a rail fence only the poles were longer than rail-cuts. **1778** *Encycl. Brit.* (ed. 2) I. 618/2 If the sides of the twisted part of the rail be shaped by the *rail-mould. **1816** *Mechanic* I. 487 The under edge of the blade may coincide with the top or winding surface of the *rail-piece. **1825** J. Nicholson *Operat. Mechanic* 600 A parallel piece of thin wood..bent to the side of the rail-piece. **1875** Knight *Dict. Mech.* 1860/1 **Rail-post*, a newel post for a staircase or balustrade. **1865** *Morn. Star* 19 July, A Woman Tarred and *Rail-ridden. **1865** *Macm. Mag.* Nov. 7 Earned his life as *rail-splitter, deck-hand, farm-labourer, clerk. **1863** Dicey *Federal St.* I. 164, I am not practically acquainted with *rail-splitting. **1589** in *Recs. Burgh Glasgow* (1876) I. 148 With ane *raill galrie stair and ane turlies upoun the northmest windo therof. *c* **1320** *Sir Beues* (MS. A.) 3217 Þanne was before his bed itiȝt..A couertine on *raile tre, For noman scholde on bed ise. **1825** Jamieson Suppl., *Rail-tree*, a large beam, in a cow-house, fixed about two feet above the heads of the cows, into which the upper ends of the stakes are fixed. Teviotdale. **1930** J. Masefield *Wanderer of Liverpool* 23 The ship..Beaten *rail-under by tempest and deluged by billows. **1828** *Lights & Shades* I. 287 A little green cross-barred *railwork for mignonette.

b. In sense 4, in a large number of compounds, mostly of recent origin, as ***rail-bed, -bender, -borer, -chair, -clamp, -joint, -layer, -laying, -maker, -making, -mill, -parallel, -trade***, etc.; **rail bond**, an electrical connection between consecutive lengths of rail in a railway or tramway.

1880 'Mark Twain' *Tramp Abroad* xxix. 306 There was no level ground at the Kaltbad station; the *railbed was as steep as a roof. **1969** E. W. Morse *Fur Trade Canoe Routes* II. vi. 78 The portage is rough, and at its western end leads into an abandoned rail-bed once used for logging. **1875** Knight *Dict. Mech.* 1859–60 **Rail-bender*, etc. **1893** in K. Hedges *Amer. Electr. Street Railways* (1894) iii. 22 Each joint of the rails is supplied with two *rail bonds of No. 0000 copper wire, each only 12 inches long. **1907** Wilson & Lydall *Electr. Traction* I. vi. 107 The 'Protected' rail bond is made by fusing terminals of solid copper upon a loop of flattened copper wire. **1884** Knight *Dict. Mech.* Suppl. 737 **Rail-borer*, etc. **1864** Webster, **Rail-joint*. **1835** Barlow *2nd Rep. Direct. Lond. & B'ham Railw.* 49 Both sides being alike, the *rail-layers may select the side that fits best. **1838** *Civil Eng. & Arch. Jrnl.* I. 166/1 In all present systems of *rail-laying the supports..simply rest upon the ground. **1835** Barlow *2nd Rep. Direct. Lond. & B'ham Railw.* 22 The *rail parallel weighing 42 lbs. per yard.

c. In sense 5, as ***rail-bank, -bridge, -car, -carriage, charges, distance, -end, -fare, -head, operations, -service, -side, tanker, -track, -waggon***; ***rail-borne, -minded, -mounted*** adjs.; **rail-bus**, (*a*) a vehicle resembling a bus but running on a railway track; (*b*) in Denmark, etc.: a tramcar running on tram-lines set in the road; **rail-car**, (*a*) = car *sb.* 2; (*b*) (see quot. 1949); **railcard**, a pass entitling the holder to reduced fares on the railway; **rail-cutting**, the destruction of railway communications; **rail-head**, (*a*) the furthest point reached by a railway; (*b*) the point on a railway from which branch-line or road transport of supplies begins; hence ***railhead facilities***; also *fig.*; **rail-line**, a railway line; **rail link**, a railway service joining two established transport systems; **rail-motor**, a passenger train which consists of a single coach attached to a small locomotive or having its own engine; a rail-car; also *attrib.*; **railplane** (see quots.); **railsickness**, sickness caused in a passenger by the motion of a train.

1852 Wiggins *Embanking* 67 Shaping the material for the *rail-bank. **1928** *Britain's Industr. Future* (Liberal Industr. Inquiry) IV. xxiii. 313 In Germany the tonnage of canal and river traffic is equivalent to one-fifth or one-sixth of *rail-borne traffic. **1976** *Illustr. London News* Nov. 52/4 The trend has been for rail-borne freight to lose ground to passenger traffic and to road transport. **1963** *Times* 8 June 14/3 Two-day talks between English and French Government officials on whether there should be a Channel *rail bridge or road and rail tunnel ended in London yesterday. **1978** H. R. F. Keating *Long Walk to Wimbledon* IV. 59 The massive yellow-brick rail-bridge. **1933** *Morning Post* 30 Aug. 10/4 The London and North-Eastern Railway Company will put the new..stream-lined Diesel-electric '*railbus' into regular service on the suburban and outlying railway systems round Newcastle, within the next two weeks. **1956** *Railway Mag.* Mar. 195/1 The 'railbus' advocated for branch-line use by a correspondent in your January issue may have disadvantages. **1968** *Drive* Spring 37/2 British Rail could save many of their rural routes by introducing rail buses—a sort of single-decker diesel tramcar, operated by a driver-conductor not as a train but as if the vehicle were on the open road. **1976** J. Tate tr. *Bodelsen's Operation Cobra* viii. 42 The access road..is to be blocked..where the rail-bus cuts across it. *Ibid.* x. 54 The empty road along which the rail-bus ran. *Ibid.* xi. 56 Frederik cycled across the rail-bus tracks. **1977** *Modern Railways* Dec. 485/3 An early example was the German MAN railbus built in 1932, which remained in service for 30 years. **1834** *Knickerbocker* III. 112 After two hours past in this fair presence on *rail-cars, I returned with my head running most uncomfortably upon this new acquaintance. **1843** Whittier *Pr. Wks.* (1889) I. 352 Steam-boats and rail-cars. **1860** J. S. C. Abbott *South & North* ix. 206 Thence, in rail-cars..through the heart of Alabama. **1934** *Discovery* Nov. 314/1 The term railcar is a convenient one to apply to the fast self-contained passenger units now running on many of the world's railways. **1949** *Richmond* (Virginia) *Times-Dispatch* 27 Oct. 4/2 This new-fangled transport is called a 'rail-car'.., principally for the reason that it is built compactly into a single unit... It operates much on the same principle as a streetcar, with controls at each end so that it can travel in either direction. The car, with a seating capacity of 90 persons, is especially designed for local passenger traffic. **1959** A. McLintock *Descr. Atlas N.Z.* 63 New Zealand Railways: Some Facts..Wagons 18,650.. Railcars 23. **1963** *Times* 27 Feb. 5/1 Fiat was the first to start mass production of railcars. Its products are used by the railways not only of Italy but of a number of other countries. Fiat railcars are in service in Spain, Portugal, Egypt, Greece, Yugoslavia, Argentina, Brazil, Mexico, Venezuela, India and elsewhere. **1971** *Railway World* Mar. 116 There are also several diesel locomotives and a couple of railcars. **1976** *Sci. Amer.* Jan. 27/2 After the cooling period the fuel will in the future be shipped in specially protected trucks or railcars to a chemical-reprocessing plant. **1977** *Times* 16 Mar. 6/4 The senior citizens' *Railcards will become available from April 1 for a full year regardless of the date of purchase. **1978** *Oxford Consumer* Mar. 18/1 Railcards for the 14–17 yr olds will be able to be purchased at most local stations from the above mentioned date. **1867** G. Musgrave *Nooks Old France* II. 204 A hybrid combination of *rail-carriage, omnibus and diligence. **1880** *Q. Rev.* CXLV. 319 On the question of *rail charges a good deal might be written. **1899** *Westm. Gaz.* 9 Dec. 5/3 We shall hear a good deal more of *rail-cutting operations on the part of the enemy. **1944** Rail-cutting [see interdiction 4]. **1882** E. FitzGerald *Lett.* (1889) I. 489 An hour's *Rail distance from here. **1869** W. Barnes *Early England* 106 When the railway was taken into the hands of more learned men, we had..the *terminus* instead of the *rail-end. **1955** R. W. & M. L. Settle *Saddles & Spurs* xii. 205 The first rail was laid in Sacramento October 26, 1863. Two years later rail-end had reached Colfax, fifty-five miles away. **1976** S. Hynes *Auden Generation* vii. 229 Details of landscape—the mountains, the pass, the rail-end—take on symbolic meanings. **1974** *Times* 22 Oct. 14/4 I'll pay *rail fares, of course. Second class. **1976** B. Williams *Making of Manchester Jewry* vi. 157 If the synagogue was prepared to pay the rail fare of a Jewish pauper as far as Hull, the society undertook to see him across the North Sea. **1896** *Daily News* 13 May 9/3 The advanced base camp has been transferred to the vicinity of the *rail head. **1905** *Daily Chron.* 14 June 4/2 The political rail-head ..has not got beyond Balfour Junction, and there are no definite lines of policy laid down beyond that point. **1905** *Athenæum* 24 June 781/2 When Lord Kitchener, during the operations of the Soudanese war, sternly relegated the war correspondents to the railhead, he earned the hostility of those who regard the distribution of news as of more importance. **1915** A. D. GILLESPIE *Lett. from Flanders* (1916) 243 There are some hills not far away, beyond the rail-head from which I marched in February. **1941** I. L. IDRIESS *Great Boomerang* xvii. 119 Now mineral wealth comes in—copper at the Duchess, with a railhead at Dajarra. **1955** *Times* 22 July 9/7 The Indian Government pays for the long, expensive haul from Pathankot, the rail-head on the plains. **1961** *Times* 30 June 9/4 Railwaymen have come to talk of such goods stations as 'railheads'. **1972** *Oxford Times* 5 May 4/1 Culham, Clifton Hampden, Stadhampton and Little Milton are all on the route from the Didcot railhead —and lorries are due to start rolling in three weeks' time... No-one..expected Didcot to be the railhead for the materials. **1973** *Times* 29 Nov. 16/7 Every factory and warehouse and all the rest—is provided with railhead facilities. **1974** *Times* 8 Jan. 2/5 We have said we would go ahead provided all those who wanted a railhead were prepared to make good the financial shortfall. **1979** *Jrnl. R. Soc. Arts* CXXVII. 412/2 This was in general only temporary until the pipeline, gathering stations and railhead installations..had all been fully run in. **1961** E. F. MCKINNEY *Educ. in Violence* 365 Garrard's Covington raid and Rousseau's Opelika raid cut two-thirds of the *rail lines he had to break. **1976** *Jrnl.* (Newcastle) 26 Nov., Holly Avenue, a quiet street sandwiched endways between Osborne Road and the rail-line. **1978** *Amer. Poetry Rev.* Nov./Dec. 6/3 The linear travel of the rail-line has become three-dimensional. **1975** *Guardian* 21 Jan. 12/1 The *rail link from Folkestone to London. **1976** *Illustr. London News* Nov. 52/1 The first rail link with Britain by train and boat had been opened with the Calais Docks station in 1849. **1963** *Times* 23 May 13/7 Switzerland is the most *rail-minded country in the world. **1906** *Westm. Gaz.* 5 June 5/3 An excursion train on the Great Western line colliding..with an empty *rail-motor coach. **1927** *Observer* 13 Nov. 13/3 'Rail motors' or 'motor trains', may either take the form of self-contained vehicles having a steam or petrol engine built into the coach, or of trains hauled by very small engines and arranged to be driven from either end. **1962** *Coast to Coast 1961–62* 202 Rattling along on a rail-motor somewhere south-west of Bundaberg, recollection nagged busily and painfully. **1967** G. F. FIENNES *I tried to run a Railway* iii. 24 They allocated a *railmounted gun..to Norfolk. **1969** *Jane's Freight Containers 1968–69* 241/3 All these cranes are rail-mounted, pneumatic tyred cranes will not be used. **1855** CARLYLE in *E. FitzGerald's Lett.* (1889) I. 235 The end of my shrieking, mad, (and to me quite horrible) *rail operations. **1933** *Sun* (Baltimore) 25 Sept. 6/8 A *railplane car, built along the lines of airplane architecture and designed to carry passengers over railroad tracks at ninety miles an hour, was announced today by the Pullman Car and Manufacturing Corporation. **1968** S. E. ELLACOTT *Everyday Things in Eng. 1914–68* xii. 185 A gallant pioneer effort..to revolutionize rail travel by suspending a carriage on an overhead rail..was the invention of a Scot, George Bennie, who built his first railplane in 1929... Ironically, a monorail service was running with apparent success in Tokyo in 1957. **1976** *Illustr. London News* Nov. 29/2 The most effective way of providing a 'rapid transit' is to improve the *rail service. **1892** SWINBURNE *Lett.* (1962) VI. 30, I have got over the unnerving effects of *railsickness. **1928** *Daily Tel.* 17 July 4/5 Freehold *railside factory. **1959** *Listener* 8 Jan. 50/1 Iron ore is brought down to rail-side by country carts from the nearby mountains. **1958** *Times Rev. Industry* Feb. 74/1 *Railtankers standing in readiness then loaded up and took the crude oil the remaining 250 miles to the sea at Philippeville for storage. **1979** *Jrnl. R. Soc. Arts* CXXVII. 406/1 The oil would be transmitted by pipeline to a rail terminal for transmission by rail tanker. *a* **1824** ROBERTSON in *Trans. Highland Soc.* VI. 68 The *rail-track was now made of cast-iron and concave. **1858** HAWTHORNE *Fr. Note-bks.* (1883) 42 On our left, the rail-track kept close to the hills. *a* **1824** A. SCOTT in *Trans. Highland Soc.* VI. 30 Simple as the common *rail-waggon convoy may appear [etc.].

Hence **'railage**, conveyance by rail, or the charges for this; also *attrib.*; **'railery** *nonce-wd.*, travelling by rail; **'raily** *a. nonce-wd.*, railway-like.

1852 LD. COCKBURN *Circuit Journ.* (1883) 373 Too much railery is an unbecoming thing for an aged judge. **1859** SALA *Tw. round Clock* (1861) 42 These vegetable Titans are of the rail, and raily. **1891** *Auckland* (N.Z.) *Star* 1 Oct. 4/2 Labour, cartage, and railage. **1903** *Daily Chron.* 19 June 5/2 Food and forage..are continually coming forward from the coast at high cost for railage. **1907** *Westm. Gaz.* 19 Jan. 7/1 Welsh smokeless coal is now 19s. per ton at the pit's mouth, and to that has to be added 8s. 4d. per ton for railage to London. **1955** *Times* 3 June 10/6 Further increases in the cost of commodities and stores, the latter resulting largely from the higher railage rates introduced in recent years. **1972** P. NEWTON *Sheep Thief* i. 14, I would require two horses..and I would like to take my own. This would involve the cost of railage.

rail (reɪl), *sb.*^{3} Forms: 5–7 **rayle**, 5, 8 **rale**, 6–7 **raile**, 7– **rail**. [a. F. *râle* (Picard *reille*), OF. *raale* (13–14th c.), of uncertain origin. Hence also G. *ralle*, med.L. *rallus*.] A bird of the family *Rallidæ* and especially of the genus *Rallus*: see LANDRAIL, WATER-RAIL.

c **1450** *Two Cookery-bks.* 69 Votrellez, Rales, Quayles. **1483** *Cath. Angl.* 299/1 A Rayle, *glebarius*. *a* **1529** SKELTON *Col. Cloute* 870 Some..by the barres of her tayle Wyll knowe a raven from a rayle. **1615** MARKHAM *Eng. Housew.* (1660) 76 Sauce for a Quail, Raile, or any fat big bird. **1755** *Mem. Capt. P. Drake* II. xviii. 273 We diverted ourselves in the Meadows, where my Lord shot some Rales. **1843** LEVER *J. Hinton* xxxv, All was hushed and still, save the deep note of the rail. **1885** G. S. FORBES *Wild Life in Canara* 207 The rails tried all they knew to stop the cobra.

attrib. **1573** BARET *Alvearie*, A Raile bird, *rusticula*. **1808** T. ASHE *Trav.* II. 67 Rail-bird, *Rallus Virginianus*.

rail (reɪl), *sb.*^{4} *rare*. Also 6 **rayle**. [f. RAIL *v.*^{4}] An act of railing or reviling.

a **1529** SKELTON *Caudatos Anglos* 30 With thy versyfyeing rayles How they haue tayles. **1596** SPENSER *F.Q.* IV. i. 43 All carelesse of his taunt and bitter rayle. **1869** MANNING *Petri Privileg.* (1871) II. 9 Some half-educated minds..who keep up the old rail against the Catholic religion.

rail (reɪl), *sb.*^{5} *Sc. rare*$^{-1}$. [f. RAIL *v.*^{1}: cf. quot. 1887 in sense 2.] A row (of nails).

1776 C. KEITH *Farmer's Ha'* v, They..set about their heels wi' rails O' clinkin tackets.

rail (reɪl), *sb.*^{6} [Origin uncertain: cf. RAIL *sb.*^{2}] A hot-rod or dragster.

1962 *Punch* 17 Oct. 560/2 A dragster, or rail, is the most skeletal vehicle of all. **1965** *Daily Mail* 2 Oct. 5/5 There is no lonelier place on earth than the cockpit of a rail... A rail? That is race-jargon for a dragster. **1977** *Hot Car* Oct. 42/2 A reasonable crowd showed to watch rails, gassers, comp altered, and street saloons race together.

rail (reɪl), *v.*^{1} *Obs.* exc. *Sc.* Also 4 **raill-**, 4–6 **rayl(e**, 5 **rayll(e**, 6 *Sc.* **ralye**. [a. OF. *reiller*:—pop. L. **reglare*, L. *rēgulāre*, f. *rēgula*: see RAIL *sb.*^{2}]

†**1.** *trans.* To set in order or array; to arrange; to regulate. *Obs.*

a **1310** in Wright *Lyric P.* xiii. 43 The rose rayleth hire rode. *a* **1352** MINOT *Poems* iv. 83 Both alblast and many a bow Was redy railed opon a row. *c* **1440** CAPGRAVE *Life St. Kath.* IV. 1020 Soo weel can oure mayden hir proporsyons rayll. *Ibid.* v. 1168 Whan that no counseill may yow reden ne rayle. *c* **1530** LD. BERNERS *Arth. Lyt. Bryt.* (1814) 181 Than his people rayled theym togyther.

†**b.** To tie or fasten in a string or row. *Obs. rare.*

1622 BACON *Hen. VII* 141 [The rebels] were brought to London, all rayl'd in Ropes, like a Teame of Horses in a Cart. **1634** FORD *Perk. Warb.* III. i, The ringleaders of this commotion, Railed in ropes, fit ornaments for traitors Wait your determinations.

2. To array, adorn, set (*with* something).

c **1350** *Will. Palerne* 1618 Eche a strete was..realy railled wiþ wel riche cloþes. ? *a* **1400** *Morte Arth.* 3264 The rowelle whas rede golde..Raylide with reched and rubyes inewe. *c* **1430** LYDG. *Reas. & Sens.* 2561 To conserve hyt, and to Raylle With fresh and lusty apparaylle. **1542** *Inv. R. Wardr.* (1815) 85 Ane cott of blak sating ralyeit with gold and silver. **1887** *Jamieson's Scot. Dict.* Suppl. 317 *To rail shoon*, to fill the soles with rows of iron nails.

fig. *c* **1440** CAPGRAVE *Life St. Kath.* III. 1230 Wyth many ioyes I wyl ȝow newly rayle.

rail (reɪl), *v.*^{2} Also 4–7 **rayle**, **raile**, 7 *Sc.* **raill**. [f. RAIL *sb.*^{2}]

†**1.** *trans.* To provide (vines, etc.) with rails; to train on rails. *Obs.*

1389 *Helmingham MS.* 21, lf. 17 b, þe vyne..schal wax wilde but if she be railid. *c* **1420** *Pallad. on Husb.* I. 805 Now rayle hem, and of closure is no doute. **1495** *Trevisa's Barth. De P.R.* XVII. clxxvii. 717 Vynes ben perched and rayled and bounde to trees that ben nye to them.

2. a. To furnish or enclose (a place) with rails.

c **1374** CHAUCER *Troylus* II. 820 (771) This yerd was large, and rayled alle the aleyes. *c* **1400** *Beryn* 291 Al the Aleyis feir ..I-raylid. **1587** *Nottingham Rec.* IV. 215 Chayney Pooll the syde towardes Est Crofte to be rayled. **1641** W. MOUNTAGU in *Buccleuch MSS.* (Hist. MSS. Comm.) I. 286 All the streets are railed for the advantage of the show. **1679–88** *Secr. Serv. Money Chas. & Jas.* (Camden) 125 In rayling the walke called Swinley Rayles, in the forest of Windsor. **1726** AYLIFFE *Parergon* 173 The Church-yard.. ought to be fenced in and railed. *a* **1817** T. DWIGHT *Trav. New Eng.*, etc. (1823) I. 456 The sides of the causeys are stoned, capstained, and railed.

b. With adverbs, esp. ***to rail in***, to enclose (a space or thing) with rails; ***to rail off***, to separate by a railing.

1423 JAS. I *Kingis Q.* xxxi, Ane herbere grene, with wandis long and small Railit about. **1576** GASCOIGNE *Kenelworth* A iij, A bridge, the which was rayled in on both sides. **1604** *Manchester Court Leet Rec.* (1885) II. 205 Raphe Hulme hath Rayled in a parcell of land. **1711** ADDISON *Spect.* No. 112 ¶2 Sir Roger has..railed in the Communion-Table. **1802** MAR. EDGEWORTH *Moral T.* (1816) I. 221 A space was railed in for the reception of the..jurors. **1856** FROUDE *Hist. Eng.* (1858) I. v. 451 The footpaths were railed off along the whole distance.

†**c.** To confine (sheep) by rails. *Obs. rare*$^{-1}$.

1641 BEST *Farm. Bks.* (Surtees) 84 Yett some will perswade to rayle them a little before they goe to field.

3. To provide (a hedge, bench, etc.) with a rail or rails. Also with *about*, *in* (cf. 2 b). *rare.*

1577 B. GOOGE *Heresb. Husb.* (1586) 50 The common hedge made of dead wood, well staked and thicke plashed or railde. **1683** MOXON *Mech. Exerc.*, *Printing* xi. ¶11 The Inck-Block..is Railed in on its farther and hinder-sides.. with Wainscot Board. *Ibid.* xx. ¶3 The Bench hath its farther Side, and both ends, railed about with slit Deal about two Inches high.

4. To lay with rails (in sense 4 of the sb.).

1888 *Harper's Mag.* LXXVII. 125 One hundred and fifty miles of new road graded last year, which was to receive its rails this spring, will not be railed.

5. To convey by rail.

1865 *Pall Mall G.* 4 Sept. 10/1 Fat cattle and fat sheep.. to be railed to market. **1916** E. W. HAMILTON *First Seven Divisions* 142 Four Army Corps were railed up from the eastern frontier. **1936** R. C. K. ENSOR *England, 1870–1914* ix. 299 It cost as much at that time to rail coal from the Rhondda to North Dorset as to ship it 3,000 miles to Alexandria. **1973** *Sunday Times* 7 Oct. 46 Forty-four-thousand gallons of sterile milk are daily railed from Anand to Bombay. **1975** *Times* 27 Dec. 9/7 Next year's Motorail brochure has just come... For many years I railed my car to Scotland. Not again, at £100 a time.

6. *intr.* To travel by rail. Also with *it*.

1842 LADY GRANVILLE *Lett.* (1894) II. 337 We rail to Munich to-morrow. **1853** VISC. STRATFORD DE REDCLIFFE in Lane-Poole *Life* II. 243 Next day we railed it away through Gratz and Laibach.

7. To fish with a hand-line over a boat's rail.

1889 *Nature* XLI. 180 In England, the summer fishing for mackerel is carried on by means of hand lines, and small boats may be seen 'railing' or 'whiffing' amongst the schools of mackerel.

†**rail**, *v.*^{3} *Obs.* Forms: 5 **raylle**, **rayl**, **reyle**, 5–6 **rail(e**, **rayle**, 6 *Sc.* **rale**. [Of obscure origin.] *intr.* To flow, gush (*down*). Usu. said of blood.

c **1400** *Laud Troy-bk.* 6842 Thei mette so well..That the blod fro hem rayled. *c* **1440** CAPGRAVE *Life St. Kath.* V. 1720 Ffro thi eynez lete the water now be thi cheekis reyle. **1513** DOUGLAS *Æneis* XI. xiii. 172 The blude haboundantly furth ralis. **1591** SPENSER *Vis. Bellay* 155, I saw a spring out of a rocke forth rayle. **1600** FAIRFAX *Tasso* IV. lxxiv, A tempest railed downe her cheekes amaine.

rail (reɪl), *v.*^{4} Forms: α. 5–7 **rayl**, 6 *Sc.* **ral-**, **raill**, 6–7 **rayle**, **rayll**, 6– **rail**; β. 6 *Sc.* **ralȝe**, **railȝe**, **relȝie**. [a. F. *railler* (15th c.), of uncertain origin. Cf. RAILLY, RALLY.]

1. a. *intr.* To utter abusive language.

1460–70 GREGORY *Chron.* (Camden) 229 He raylyd soore and grevysly to fortefy hys bretherynys sayyngys. *a* **1529** SKELTON *Caudatos Anglos* 63 Walke, Scot, Walke, sot, Rayle not to far. *c* **1560** A. SCOTT *Poems* (S.T.S.) iii. 44 Be ȝe rank quhen thay begin to relȝie. **1624** CAPT. SMITH *Virginia* III. xi. 86 To force you from your Idlenesse, and punish you if you rayle. **1735** BERKELEY *Def. Free-think. Mathemat.* §8 To see you rail and rage at the rate you do. **1781** COWPER *Charity* 500 Satire..Too often rails to gratify his spleen. **1871** B. TAYLOR *Faust* (1875) I. xiv. 152 You rail, and it is fun to me.

b. constr. *against*, *at*, †*of*, *on*, *upon*, †*with*.

1470–85 MALORY *Arthur* x. lxxi, Sire Dynadan rayled with sir Tristram. **1519** HORMAN *Vulg.* 61 He is so pacient, that he suffereth men all to rayle and rage vpon him. **1560** DAUS tr. *Sleidane's Comm.* 23 [He] raileth against all the discipline of the church. *Ibid.* 47 The Masse is railed on. **1588** BABINGTON *Prof. Exp. Lord's Pr.* (1596) 267 They rayle of al compulsion to the contrarie. **1602** MARSTON *Ant. & Mel.* v. Wks. 1856 I. 60 Hee railes at mee beyond reason. **1611** BIBLE *Mark* xv. 29 And they that passed by, railed on him. *Ibid. Luke* xxiii. 39 And one of the malefactors..railed on him, saying, If thou be Christ, save thy selfe and us. **1660** WOOD *Life* Dec. (O.H.S.) I. 369 Who rayl'd more..than he, against both Presbyterians and Independents? **1771** *Junius Lett.* lv. 291 Enemies..rail at him for crimes he is not guilty of. **1819** SHELLEY *Cyclops* 98, I am the same, but do not rail upon me. **1855** MACAULAY *Hist. Eng.* III. xii. 213 His very soldiers railed on him in the streets of Dublin. **1866** MISS BRADDON *Lady's Mile* i. 6 Don't rail against the women. **1872** BAGEHOT *Physics & Pol.* (1876) 195 We are beginning to see this, and we are railed at for so beginning.

†**2. a.** To jest, to rally. Also const. *with*. *Obs.*

1508 DUNBAR *Tua Mariit Wemen* 480 Sum rownis; and sum ralȝeis, and sum redis ballatis. **1530** PALSGR. 678/1, I rayle, I jeste meryly, *je me gaudis*. **1590** BUREL in Watson *Coll. Poems* (1709) II. 12 Let no man me esteme to raill, Nor think that raschelie I report. **1685** EVELYN *Mrs. Godolphin* (1888) 98 Severall Ladyes..were railing with the Gallants trifleingly enough.

†**b.** To brag or boast. *Obs. rare*$^{-0}$.

1530 PALSGR. 678/1, I rayle in bostyng, *je me raille*. He doth naught els but rayle at the ale house all daye.

3. a. *trans.* To bring (a person) *into* a certain condition by railing. Also rarely with a thing as obj. in other constructions.

1596 SHAKS. *Merch. V.* IV. i. 139 Till thou canst raile the seale from off my bond Thou but offend'st thy Lungs to speake so loud. **1606** —— *Tr. & Cr.* II. i. 17, I shal sooner rayle thee into wit and holinesse. **1642** SIR T. BROWNE *Relig. Med.* II. §4 Noble natures..are not railed into vice. **1823** LOCKHART *Reg. Dalton* I. xiii. (1842) 88 Trying..to rail his old English heart out of his bosom?

b. With adj. expressing the result. *rare*$^{-1}$.

1676 OTWAY *Don Carlos* v. i, You spightfully are come to rail me dead.

†**rail**, *v.*^{5} *Obs. rare.* [Of obscure etym.] *intr.* To go about, wander, roam.

c **1400** *Laud Troy Bk.* 6845 Aboute Ector euere thei rayled. *Ibid.* 7432 Ther come two kynges In that batayle, That saw Ector aboute rayle, As faucoun flees afftir drake. **1530** PALSGR. 678/1, I rayle, I straye abrode, *je trace, je tracasse*. He doth naught els but rayle here and there.

rail (reɪl), *v.*^{6} [Prob. echoic.] *trans.* and *intr.* To rattle.

1770 ARMSTRONG *Imitations* 85 Every petty brook that crawled..Railing its pebbles. **1844** [see RAILING *ppl. a.*^{3}].

railed (reɪld), *ppl. a.* [f. RAIL *sb.*^{2} and *v.*^{2}]

1. Enclosed with a rail or rails (sense 2). Also with advb., as ***railed-in***, ***-off***.

1639 *Rec. Dedham, Mass.* (1892) III. 58 One litle parcell of meadow..within a Rayled neck of Land. **1832** G. DOWNES *Lett. Cont. Countries* I. 205 The railed inclosure of the altar. **1868** E. YATES *Rock Ahead* II. iii, The crowds kept pouring in to the railed-off space. **1892** ZANGWILL *Bow Myst.* 97 A woman..standing before a railed-in grave. **1930** *Times Educ. Suppl.* 23 Aug. 364/4 A railed-off enclosure. **1973** 'D. HALLIDAY' *Dolly & Starry Bird* ix. 119 The man we were following..gazed..at the railed-off pieces of terrazzo on the pavement.

2. Laid with rails (sense 4).

1769 *De Foe's Tour Gt. Brit.* III. 276 The..Waggons.. are easily pushed by a Man, on a railed Way, to a Stage over the Canal. **1800** in Picton *L'pool Munic. Rec.* (1886) II. 235

A waggon way or Railed Road for conveying stone from the quarry.

railer^{1} ('reɪlə(r)). [f. RAIL *v.*^{4} + -ER^{1}.] One who rails; a reviler.

1513 DOUGLAS *Æneis* VIII. Prol. 66 The railȝear raknis na wordis, but ratlis furth ranis. **1575–85** ABP. SANDYS *Serm.* xiv. 242 He is a railer, he doteth, he wanteth discretion. **1642** MILTON *Apol. Smect.* Introd., I go on to shew you the unbridl'd impudence of this loose rayler. **1726** POPE *Odyss.* xx. 328 Dread not the railer's laugh, nor ruffian's rage. **1810** CRABBE *Borough* xiii, Thou writ'st of living men, And art a railer and detractor then. **1859** SMILES *Self-Help* (1860) 216 The grumblers and the railers against fortune.

railer^{2} ('reɪlə(r)). [f. RAIL *v.*^{2} + -ER^{1}.] **1.** A rail-maker; one who fits or furnishes with rails.

1882 in OGILVIE. (Cf. *stair-railer*.)

2. One who travels by rail.

1874 J. ALBERY *Two Roses* I. 12 Wherever you go there's Stone before you... Stone's a railer. **1889** F. E. GRETTON *Memory's Harkback* 103 Your constant 'railers' are blindly ignorant of the localities they scud over.

3. *Racing.* A runner that stays close to the rail.

1958 *Times* 29 Nov. 7/7 A 'railer' will always stick to the rails and a slow starter will always be such.

† **'railer**^{3}. *Obs. rare*$^{-1}$. = RAIL *sb.*^{2} 1.

14.. *Sir Beues* (MS. M.) 149/3217 Iosyan made On her gurdill a knott rennand..ouer a rayler sche it drew.

railery, obs. form of RAILLERY.

rail-fence. orig. *U.S.* [f. RAIL *sb.*^{2} + FENCE *sb.*] **1.** A fence made of wooden posts and rails. Hence ***rail fencing***.

1649 *Charlestown* (Mass.) *Land Rec.* (1878) 110, I doe sell ..five Akers of planting Land,..Bounded on the..North by the ould raile fence. **1725** *Manchester* (Mass.) *Town Rec.* (1889) 166 For making a rail fence from yᵉ s[ai]d pound. **1807** *Salmagundi* 15 Oct. 331 Some..enjoy the varied and romantick scenery of..rail fences..potatoe patches, and log huts. **1848** WEBSTER, *Rail-fence*. *a* **1864** HAWTHORNE *Grimshawe* xii. (1891) 142 Simple and rustic as the gap in a rail fence. **1870** LOWELL *Study Wind.* 18 One of the male birds accompanies me, flitting from post to post of the rail-fence. **1902** S. E. WHITE *Blazed Trail* xxxix. 355 It was near the 'pole-trail', which was less like a trail than a rail-fence. **1924** LAWRENCE & SKINNER *Boy in Bush* i. 7 Her easy indifference to English rail-fences. **1945** J. HORN in B. A. Botkin *Lay my Burden Down* 181 He was so fat he couldn't git through the fence. You know what sort of fence, a rail fence it was. **1968** J. ARNOLD *Shell Bk. Country Crafts* v. 101 Rail fencing usually consists of cleft or sawn oak posts set at 9 ft intervals, each mortised to take three rows of rails. **1973** L. RUSSELL *Everyday Life Colonial Canada* ii. 32 Easiest to construct was the rail fence... Rails were about six inches in thickness and something like 12 feet long. **1979** *Yale Alumni Mag.* Apr. 24/3 The rail fence, the center of campus life for many years, was originally erected in the 1830s.

2. *Cryptology.* A cipher or code obtained by splitting the plaintext between two or more lines in a zig-zag pattern (see quot. 1963). Also ***rail-fence cipher***.

1939 H. F. GAINES *Elementary Cryptanalysis* iii. 12 Passing on to irregular types [of cryptogram], we find these in all degrees of difficulty, from the very simple 'rail fence' to the formidable 'U.S. Army' double transposition. **1943** J. M. WOLFE *First Course in Cryptanalysis* (rev. ed.) II. x. 1 During the Civil War the *rail fence* transposition was one of the cryptographic systems used as a field cypher. **1963** D. KAHN *Plaintext* 16 *The rail-fence cipher* can extend the number of lines in which the plaintext is distributed beyond two... If the key is 3, the cipher is still a rail-fence.

railȝe, -ȝear, obs. Sc. ff. RAIL *v.*^{4}, RAILER^{1}.

railing ('reɪlɪŋ), *vbl. sb.*^{1} [f. RAIL *v.*^{2}]

†**1.** The training of vines upon rails. **b.** A shoot of a vine so trained; also *attrib.* *Obs.*

1382 WYCLIF *Ps.* lxxix. 12 [lxxx. 11] He straȝte out his braunchis vnto the se; and vnto the flod his railingus [L. *propagines*]. —— *Isa.* xvi. 8 His railing braunches [L. *propagines*] ben forsaken, thei passeden the se. **1495** *Trevisa's Barth. De P.R.* XVII. xviii. 614 Balsamum.. spredyth as a vyne wythout raylyng and vndersettinge.

2. The action of making fences, or enclosing ground with rails. Also *railing-in*.

1543 *Act 35 Hen. VIII*, c. 17 § 6 To..take any of the same [coppies woodes] for palyng raylyng or enclosing of parkes. **1641** MILTON *Ch. Govt.* II. iii, The railing in of a repugnant and contradictive mount Sinai in the gospel. **1679–88** *Secr. Serv. Money Chas. & Jas.* (Camden) 139 Expended in.. rayling and paleing in Bushy Parke.

b. *concr.* (also in *pl.*) A fence or barrier made of rails, or in some other fashion.

1471–2 *Durham Acc. Rolls* (Surtees) 94 Pro factura lxiiij rod' del Ralyng. **1826** SCOTT *Woodst.* i, The gilded railing, which was once around it, was broken down. **1852** MRS. STOWE *Uncle Tom's C.* xii. 105 Tom..stood listlessly gazing over the railings.

transf. **1860** TYNDALL *Glac.* I. xviii. 125 From roof to ledge stretched a railing of cylindrical icicles.

c. Material for railings.

1812 SIR J. SINCLAIR *Syst. Husb. Scot.* 336 Railing must be nailed across the boss..but when railing is not at hand, a strong straw rope is commonly used in its stead. **1847** SMEATON *Builder's Man.* 147 Bars of fancy railing, and balusters of stairs consist of cast iron.

3. The laying of rails; a set or line of rails.

1825 J. NICHOLSON *Operat. Mechanic* 655 The railing must..be set out in levels, or in lines nearly level.

4. *Comb.* **railing-line**, a hand-line used over the rail of a boat.

1626 CAPT. SMITH *Accid. Yng. Seamen* 5 Rayling lines for Mackerell. **1883** *Fisheries Exhib. Catal.* 12 Handlines and Long Lines..railing Lines for Mackerel.

Hence **'railinged** *a.*, enclosed by a railing; also ***railinged off***.

1862 *Temple Bar Mag.* V. 181 A turfed and railinged square. **1938** *Archit. Rev.* LXXXIV. 104 The plain railinged balcony outside the first floor windows was replaced, for obvious aesthetic as well as structural reasons, by balconettes related in style to many which adorn the Adelphi. **1974** K. ROYCE *Trap Spider* ii. 37 The houses were railinged off, with sub-basements. *Ibid.* vii. 120 The squares were big..with a railinged green in their middle.

railing ('reɪlɪŋ), *vbl. sb.*^{2} [f. RAIL *v.*^{4} + -ING^{1}.] The action of the vb.; abusing, abuse.

1470–85 MALORY *Arthur* x. lxxii, For this entente syr Dynadan said alle this raylynge and langage ageynst sir Tristram. **1533** FRITH *Another Bk. agst. Rastell* ii. (1572) 66/2 He recounteth it to be rayling, gesting, and scolding. *c* **1580** SIDNEY *Ps.* XXXI. vii, I understand what railing greate men spredd. **1681** DRYDEN *Abs. & Achit.* 555 Railing and praising were his usual Themes. **1769** *Junius Lett.* xviii. 77 Railing is usually a relief to the mind. **1873** DIXON *Two Queens* II. XI. vi. 255 He was proof against the railing of a mob.

pl. **1526** TINDALE *1 Tim.* vi. 4 Stryfe, realinges [**1534** raylinges], evyll surmysinges. **1612** T. TAYLOR *Comm. Titus* ii. 8 Hee heard raylings and reproaches of many. *a* **1704** T. BROWN *Satire Antients* Wks. 1730 I. 17 The gall, the railings ...which made these satires take with so much applause. **1854** MACAULAY *Biog.* (1867) 30 It does not appear..from the railings of his enemies, that he ever was drunk in his life.

railing ('reɪlɪŋ), *ppl. a.*^{1} [f. as prec. + -ING^{2}.] That rails; characterized by railing.

1526 TINDALE *Jude* 9 Michael..durst nott geve raylynge sentence. *c* **1586** C'TESS PEMBROKE *Ps.* LXXIV. ix, The wrong Of thy reviling railing foe. **1697** DRYDEN *Virgil* Life (1721) I. 53 The railing Eloquence of Cicero in his Philipics. **1724** POPE *Lett.* 10 Sept., The railing Papers about the Odyssey. **1821** BYRON *Sardanap.* I. ii, The railing drunkards! why, what would they have?

† **'railing**, *ppl. a.*^{2} [f. RAIL *v.*^{3}] Flowing.

1590 SPENSER *F.Q.* III. iv. 57 Instead of rest thou lendest rayling teares.

'railing, *ppl. a.*^{3} [f. RAIL *v.*^{6}] Rattling.

1844 LEVER *T. Burke* II. 163 The railing crash of falling branches, and the deep baying of the storm.

railingly ('reɪlɪŋlɪ), *adv.* [f. RAILING *ppl. a.*^{1} + -LY^{2}.] In a railing manner.

1547–64 BAULDWIN *Mor. Philos.* (Palfr.) 132 When wee do railingly burst out against any man into slanderous and contentious words. **1684** BUNYAN *Pilgr.* II. 65 They will railingly return them answer.

rai'lipotent, *a.* *nonce-wd.* [f. RAIL *v.*^{4}, after *omnipotent*.] Powerful in railing.

1593 G. HARVEY *Pierce's Super.* Prol. **4 b, Spare me, o super-dominering Elfe, And most Railipotent for euer raine.

raillery ('reɪlərɪ). Also 7 **railery**. [a. F. *raillerie*, f. *railler* to rally: cf. RALLERY, a form which represents the older pron. ('rælərɪ), given by Sheridan, Walker, Smart, etc., and still used by some (esp. *U.S.*) speakers.]

1. Good-humoured ridicule, banter.

1653 R. LOVEDAY *Lett.* (1663) 245 The word Raillery you return'd me for interpretation..is now grown here so common with the better sort, as there are few of the meaner that are not able to construe it. **1656** COWLEY *Misc.* Pref., I am not ignorant, that by saying this of others, I expose my self to some Raillery. **1756–82** J. WARTON *Ess. Pope* II. xi. 257 The raillery is carried to the very verge of railing, some will say ribaldry. **1806–7** J. BERESFORD *Miseries Hum. Life* (1826) VII. x, A company in which you have been galled by the raillery of some wag by profession. **1871** R. ELLIS *Catullus* lxi. 127 The countryman's Ribald raillery.

b. With *a* and *pl.*: An instance of this.

1654 SIR E. NICHOLAS in *N. Papers* (Camden) II. 100 He sayes Sir E. H. found fault with the meat and such like railleries. **1683** D. A. *Art Converse* 100 An Innocent Raillery is their greatest delight. **1710** ADDISON *Whig-Exam.* No. 1 ¶ 1 There is a shocking familiarity both in his railleries and civilities. **1829** LYTTON *Devereux* I. ii, All his purposed railleries deserted him.

†**2.** Railing, reviling. *Obs. rare.*

1709 HEARNE *Collect.* (O.H.S.) II. 180 He fell into a great Passion, and began to call Names..He continu'd his Raillery. *Ibid.* 193 The very stile, wᶜʰ is nothing but Raillery and Billingsgate.

railless ('reɪllɪs), *a.* [f. RAIL *sb.*^{2} + -LESS.] Devoid of rails; having no railway.

1887 HISSEY *Holiday on Road* vii. 123 The railless, almost roadless downs. **1897** *Daily News* 25 Jan. 3/1 The slippery and railless gangway. **1905** *Westm. Gaz.* 11 Mar. 7/2 Considerable amusement was created among the crowded audience by the pictures of bygone 'railless engines'. **1981** *Daily Tel.* 6 June 11/3 It will be sad..to see the rail-less cutting and the crumbling station.

‖ **railleur.** *Obs.* Also 7–8 **raillieur**. [Fr., f. *railler* to rally.] One who practises raillery.

1667 SPRAT *Hist. R. Soc.* 417 The Family of the Railleurs is deriv'd from the same Original with the Philosophers. **1675** WYCHERLEY *Country Wife* II. Wks. (Rtldg.) 75/2 His acquaintance were all wits and raillieurs. **1751** J. BROWN *Shaftesb. Charac.* 62 *note*, Setting aside all raillery, advising the railleurs to be serious.

† **'raillier.** *Obs.* Also 8 **-yer**. [f. RAILLY *v.* + -ER^{1}.] = RALLIER^{2}.

1711 SHAFTESB. *Charac.* (1737) III. 288 An airy Gentleman of the World, and a thorow Raillyer. **1754** RICHARDSON *Grandison* IV. vi. 50 The free, gay, Raillier..of all our Sex's Foibles.

'railly, *sb.* *Sc.* *rare*$^{-1}$. [f. RAIL *sb.*^{1} + -Y.] A woman's jacket.

1818 SCOTT *Br. Lamm.* xii, What's the colour o' her hair? —and does she wear a habit or a railly?

† **'railly**, *v.* *Obs.* Also 7 **rayly**, **raillie**. [ad. F. *railler* to RALLY *v.*^{2}]

1. a. *intr.* To rally, to jest.

1635–56 COWLEY *Davideis* I. Note 18 He would not railly with the God from whom he hoped for Relief. **1673** O. WALKER *Educ.* v. 45 If they railly, droll, and speak evil of others. *a* **1760** I. H. BROWNE *Poems* (1768) 111 Train'd up to laugh,..And railly with the prettiest air.

b. *trans.* To rally, ridicule, tease (a person).

1673 *Lady's Call.* I. v. §26 The jollier [sort] that would railly them out of their faith. **1740** CIBBER *Apol.* (1756) I. 269 He began to railly himself with..much wit and humour.

2. *intr.* To mock, scoff, or jeer *at*.

1678 WOOD *Life* 11 Dec. (O.H.S.) II. 426 Barnesley a Jesuit..came then through Oxford..attended by a guard and a tipstaff; raylied at by the boyes.

Hence **'raillying** *vbl. sb.* *rare*$^{-1}$.

1760 STERNE *Tr. Shandy* III. Auth. Pref., There would be ..scoffing and flouting, with raillying and reparteeing.

raillyer, obs. form of RAILLIER.

railman ('reɪlmən). [f. RAIL *sb.*^{2} 6 c.] A person employed on a railway; a railwayman.

1923 *Weekly Dispatch* 11 Feb. 3 (*heading*) Lord Lascelles and the Railmen. *Ibid.* 25 Mar. 1 (*heading*) Railmen forbidden to obey the French. **1927** *Sunday Times* 6 Mar. 15/6 (*heading*) Duke and the railmen. **1967** *Guardian* 11 Dec. 1/1 Management proposes to replace the many dozens of [railway] job classifications..by four broad and flexible grades. They would be called Railmen..Leading Railmen ..Senior Railmen..and Chargemen. **1976** *Milton Keynes Express* 11 June 5/4 Wolverton Works this week scotched rumours that psychological tactics were being used in an attempt to squeeze out any of the local railmen involved in the closed shop row. **1977** *Listener* 2 June 703/1 Our industry is always associated with rattling a begging bowl. Some railmen are even embarrassed about going into the pub.

† **railodok** ('reɪlədɒk). *Obs.* Also **-doc**, **-dock**, **R-**. The name given to an observation car, running on rails and conveying visitors round the British Empire Exhibition at Wembley in 1924. Also *attrib.*

1924 *Glasgow Herald* 31 May 8 (*heading*) Railodok Tour of the Exhibition. *Ibid.*, Her Majesty..toured the Exhibition in a railodok car. **1924** *Times* 29 July (Brit. Empire Suppl.) p. xxi/6 The Railodok cars..travel from point to point and make circular tours. *Ibid.*, It is possible for goods to be taken right up to the stalls..inside the bigger halls by Railodok trolley. **1924** *British Weekly* 21 Aug. 446/3, I made the complete tour in the railodoc. **1925** *Ibid.* 9 July 331/3 Boats on the lake were well patronised, and the railodok cars were partly full. **1927** W. E. COLLINSON *Contemp. Eng.* 16 The terms for the various vehicles to take visitors round like the railodocks are probably doomed to extinction.

† **railophone** ('reɪləfəʊn). *Obs.* Also with capital initial. [f. RAIL *sb.*^{2} + -O + PHONE *sb.*^{2}] A telephone in a train. Also *attrib.* Hence as *v. trans.*, to telephone by means of such a phone.

1911 *Times* 8 Feb. 25/2 Any train fitted with the Railophone can be instantly spoken to. **1911** *Chambers's Jrnl.* Apr. 268/1 (*heading*) The Railophone system of wireless telephony on trains. **1912** *Morning Post* 29 June 10/7 Last year the first public installation of the railophone ..was made on the Stratford-on-Avon and Midland Junction Railway, and the process of telephoning to and from moving trains and the sending of messages from stations to trains and *vice versa* was then clearly demonstrated. *Ibid.*, These instruments are electrically connected with two large insulated copper coils mounted in a wooden casing called the railophone frames. *Ibid.*, Messages to and from passengers can be railophoned with ease.

railroad ('reɪlrəʊd), *sb.* Also 8–9 **rail road**, **rail-road**. [f. RAIL *sb.*^{2} 4. Now chiefly *U.S.*, the usual term in Great Britain being RAILWAY.]

1. a. = RAILWAY 1.

1757 in *Trans. Hon. Soc. Cymmrodorion 1897–98* (1899) Laying rails or making a railroad to the pits from the main or great road. **1771** T. PENNANT *Tour in Scotl. 1769* 29 The collieries lie at different distances..and the coal is brought down in waggons along rail roads. **1775** SMEATON *Rep.* (1837) II. 411 It seems perfectly practicable to carry the coals upon a rail-road. **1793** —— *Edystone L.* §167 *note*, The timber road, commonly called at the Collieries, where they are used, a Rail Road. **1805** *Trans. Soc. Arts* XXIII. 318 A horse employed on a rail-road. **1832** *Act 2 & 3 Will. IV*, c. 64 Sched. O. 40 Along Smithsons railroad to the point at which the same meets the Dewsbury road. **1855** 'Q. K. P. DOESTICKS' *Doesticks what he Says* xvi. 138 Every stitch was as long as a railroad. **1873** 'MARK TWAIN' *Gilded Age* xvii. 163 Yes, this is the railroad, all but the rails and the iron-horse. **1888** RUSKIN *Praeterita* III. iv. 174 You enterprised a railroad..you blasted its rocks away... And now, every fool in Buxton can be at Bakewell in half-an-hour, and every fool in Bakewell at Buxton. **1949** *Sun* (Baltimore) 28 Sept. 14/5, I came along the old railroad to town this morning.

b. = RAILWAY 1 b.

1852 CAROLINE FOX *Old Friends* (1882) 276 The speculum [of Lord Rosse's telescope]..has its own little railroad, over which it runs into the cannon's mouth.

2. a. = RAILWAY 2.

1825 T. TREDGOLD *Rail-Roads & Carriages* i. 15 The Surrey rail-road commences on the south bank of the Thames, near Wandsworth..and proceeds..to Croydon, and from thence..to Merstham, making a total distance of about 18 miles. **1830** M. EDGEWORTH *Let.* 18 Oct. (1971) 419 A regular communication goes on now by trains of cars on this railroad backwards and forwards to Liverpool and Manchester. 1831 SCOTT *Ct. Robert* Introd., The giddiness attendant on a journey on this Manchester railroad. 1835 MOORE *Mem.* (1856) VII. 95 To Liverpool by the railroad; a grand mode of travelling. 1856 RUSKIN *Mod. Paint.* III. IV. xvii. §35 Your railroad..is only a device for making the world smaller. 1969 *New Statesman* 4 July 23/3 I'd also like to know whether the late Peter Arno coined, or merely repeated, three of his cartoon captions..'What a way to run a railroad'. 1976 *New Yorker* 16 Feb. 75/1 Here, at last, is an explanation of why the railroads in the United States have been decaying.

fig. 1847 HAMILTON *Let. to De Morgan* 5 Mathematicians ..leaving the level railroad of their own [science].

b. *pl.* Railway shares.

1848 J. J. RUSKIN *Let.* 17 Mar. in M. Lutyens *Ruskins & Grays* (1972) xi. 98 If you do not..deceive yourself or are led to plunge farther into Railroads—your situation is much better than I expected. 1916 C. SANDBURG *Chicago* in *Poetry* Mar. 191 Hog Butcher for the World, Tool Maker, Stacker of Wheat, Player with Railroads and the Nation's Freight Handler. 1957 [see DOW-JONES]. 1964 *Financial Times* 12 Mar. 3/1 All the Dow Jones Indices made headway, with new all-time closing peaks again recorded by Industrials and Railroads.

3. *attrib.* and *Comb.* (cf. RAILWAY 3).

a. attrib., as ***railroad agent, bill, bookstand, box-car, brakeman, camp, car, carriage, charge, coach, companion, company, conductor, conveyance, crew, cut, depot, detective, engineer, equipment, fare, hat, hotel, land, line, man, map, omnibus, pace, pass, police, president, security, shares, speed, spur, station, town, track*** (also as *v. trans.*), ***train, travelling, tunnel, whistle.***

1859 REDPATH & HINTON *Handbk. Kansas Territory* ii. 24 Select your route before buying your ticket, without consulting any *railroad agent. 1838 *Civil Eng. & Arch. Jrnl.* I. 296/1 The Aylesbury and Thame *Railroad Bill. 1847 F. A. KEMBLE *Rec. Later Life* (1882) III. 289 One of those pale green volumes headed, 'Reading for Travellers', to be found on all the *railroad bookstands. 1976 *Billings* (Montana) *Gaz.* 4 July 1-c/3 'Beet shacks' vary in luxury. But few are as primitive as the old *railroad boxcars that once housed migrants and still dot the area. 1898 *Kansas City Star* 18 Dec. 2/3 Grant Meade became a *railroad brakeman. 1976 *Washington Post* 19 Apr. C1/2 When Mack was born in 1902 in Greeley, Colo., his father, a railroad brakeman, named him William Edward Maguiness. *a* 1927 F. M. CANTON *Frontier Trails* (1930) ii. 33 Stolen cattle were driven into *railroad camps and sold to contractors at half their value. 1977 H. FAST *Immigrants* 11 He was nursed in railroad camps while his father drove spikes and handled steel rails. 1830 *Mechanics' Press* (Utica, N.Y.) 17 Apr. 183/3 Prizes..are offered on the following subjects: Iron castings,..Steam Carriages, *Rail Road Car, [etc.]. 1863 B. TAYLOR *H. Thurston* v. 71 We ask that his boasted chivalry be put into practice, not merely in..giving us his seat in a railroad-car. 1923 C. R. COOPER *Under Big Top* i. 4 A circus ..has its own railroad cars. 1967 *N.Y. Times* (Internat. Ed.) 11–12 Feb. 4/6 The snow, loaded in 14 railroad cars, arrived here yesterday as Chicago officials sought to clear out some of the nearly 40 inches that has fallen there since Jan. 26. 1839 PARKIN in Barlow *Railw. Eng. Wheels* (1848) 26 Improvements in *railroad and other carriages. 1865 RUSKIN *Sesame & Lilies* I. 85 Your *one* conception of pleasure is to drive in railroad carriages round their aisles. 1979 A. HOLLAR tr. *W. Schivelbusch's Railway Journey* (1980) vi. 92 The entirely different development of the railroad and the railroad carriage in the United States. 1848 *Amer. Railroad Jrnl.* 29 July 481/1 We wish to call attention to the subject of **railroad charges, for passengers* and *freight*. 1833 *Niles's Reg.* XLIV. 98/2 Comfortable naps may be taken in the *rail-road coaches, if desired. 1839 BOWDLER *Sunday Trains* 15 Proprietors of Railroad coaches. 1848 J. H. NEWMAN *Loss & Gain* 363 The troubled thoughts from which his *railroad companion had extricated him. 1815 *New Jersey Acts* 69 The New-Jersey Rail Road Company. Said president and directors so to be chosen shall be called The New-Jersey *Rail Road Company. 1825 HONE *Every-day Bk.* I. 173 Twenty Rail Road Companies. 1903 E. JOHNSON *Railway Transportation* 73 The railroad company derives its powers from a charter granted to it by the State. 1979 A. HOLLAR tr. *W. Schivelbusch's Railway Journey* (1980) ii. 35 The railroad companies' *monopoly* on transportation. 1842 *Liberator* (Boston) 21 Jan. 10/1 The kingly power of a *rail-road conductor. 1942 E. PAUL *Narrow St.* vii. 61 The time came for Mariette to marry the railroad conductor of her choice. 1967 Railroad conductor [see BRAKESMAN 2]. 1825 WOOD *Pract. Treat. Railroads* Introd. 1 The acknowledged importance of *Railroad conveyance. 1976 *Times* 23 July 11/6 Buffalo Bill..had been ..buffalo hunter for a contractor supplying food to the Kansas Pacific *railroad crews. 1862 *Rebellion Rec.* V. II. 403 On Friday morning we held the ridge, in front of which runs an incomplete *railroad-cut. 1940 *Quiz on Railroads & Railroading* (Assoc. Amer. Railroads) Quest. 13 What is a railroad cut? When the right-of-way of a railroad is cut through a hill, knoll or slope to provide a roadway, the excavation is called a cut. 1836 *Southern Lit. Messenger* II. 735 Away we whirled with great rapidity to the *railroad depot, where the cars were ready to receive us. 1980 L. ST. CLAIR *Obsessions* i. 36 Companies of Red troops..were marching toward the railroad depot. 1903 R. L. MCCARDELL *Conversations Chorus Girl* 78 Aunt Em says the *railroad detectives seen him in a saloon. 1942 Z. N. HURSTON *Dust Tracks on Road* xii. 229 De white man..he was a *railroad engineer. 1976 A. WHITE *Long Silence* vi. 44 The signals office contained the latest *railroad equipment. 1910 *N.Y. Even. Post* 17 Dec. 7 The round-trip *railroad fare will be $6.80. 1957 J. KEROUAC *On Road* I. iii. 15 All the men were..wearing *railroad hats, baseball hats. 1869 *Bradshaw's Railway Manual* XXI. 427 *Expended* ..*Railroad hotel—$6,082. 1872 F. F. VICTOR *All over Oregon & Washington* xvi. 188 The *railroad lands will be mostly taken in the foot-hills. 1872 *Newton Kansan* 17 Oct. 3/3 Mr. Wm. B. Blake..having purchased railroad land east of town, is about building a fine residence thereon. 1908 *Pacific Monthly* Jan. 6/1 The people on the railroad lands began to want deeds. 1841 *Punch* 16 Oct. 165/2 The infernal smashes that have recently taken place on several *railroad lines. 1979 A. HOLLAR tr. *W. Schivelbusch's Railway Journey* (1980) vi. 98 American railroad lines proceed by curves. 1845 THOREAU *Jrnl.* 14 July in *Writings* (1906) VII. 366 *Railroad men who take care of the road. 1980 L. ST. CLAIR *Obsessions* i. 21 The yard superintendent tells us you are a good railroad man. 1976 J. LEE *Ninth Man* 70 He would need *railroad maps and timetables. 1858 C. M. YONGE *Christmas Mummers* i. 9 They had actually hopes of being able to hire the *railroad omnibus. 1838 DICKENS *Let.* 20 May (1965) I. 400, I hope to make a great dash tomorrow, however, to proceed at *railroad pace. 1840 THACKERAY *Catherine* i, Hope, glory,..and such subjects,..whirled through their brains at a rail-road pace. 1895 W. H. CHAMBLISS *Diary* 48, I did not come out on one of those *railroad passes especially designed for the accommodation of senators. 1976 *New Yorker* 15 Nov. 41/3 They also included bookplates, letterheads, railroad passes, commercial paperweights and music sheets. 1913 J. LONDON *Valley of Moon* in *Cosmopolitan* July 241/1 Up Pine Street..was coming a rush of *railroad police..firing as they ran. 1914 *Sat. Even. Post* 4 Apr. 52/3 The train slowed down. The Kid swung off. He feared the railroad police in the terminal yards. 1892 'MARK TWAIN' *Amer. Claimant* xiv. 134 There isn't a lawyer, doctor, editor, author, tinker, loafer, *railroad president, saint..in the United States that wouldn't jump at the chance. 1949 *Chicago Daily News* 9 Aug. 10/5 His chance of becoming an American railroad president is probably about one in ten million. 1912 *Railroad security [see KILLING *vbl. sb.* 2]. *a* 1839 PRAED *Poems* (1864) II. 221, I ask the price of *rail-road shares. 1840 [R. E. HILL] *Pinch of Snuff* 59 Intellect and refinement ..now progress at *rail-road speed. 1859 C. E. DELONG in *Calif. Hist. Soc. Q.* (1931) X. 45 Committee convened.. hurried through at rail road speed. 1976 *National Observer* (U.S.) 12 June 4/2 It includes..construction of a *railroad spur into the plant. 1978 S. SHELDON *Bloodline* xvi. 191 A nest of research buildings, manufacturing plants, experimental laboratories, planning divisions, and railroad spurs. 1837 *Civil Eng. & Arch. Jrnl.* I. 77/2 Entrance to a *Rail-road Station. 1875 RUSKIN *Fors Clav.* lvii. 250 The main railroad station at Birmingham. 1923 R. HERRICK *Homely Lilla* xi. 172 She passed the county building on her way from the railroad station. 1976 *National Observer* (U.S.) 22 May 19/3 Sadly, a beautiful stone railroad station in the hamlet of Slingerlands is gone, replaced by a fire station. 1872 F. F. VICTOR *All over Oregon & Washington* xvi. 188 Some parcels, lying along the lines of the roads, or near *railroad towns, will increase considerably in value during the current year. 1834 *Knickerbocker* V. 53 *Rail-road tracks are projecting in all directions. 1858 O. W. HOLMES *Aut. Breakf. T.* i. (1859) 11 Boys that put coppers on the railroad tracks. 1947 *Southern Folklore Q.* Dec. 265 One of the most vivid of these images is one which describes a person's squirming 'like a country mule hitched beside the railroad track'. 1973 M. R. CROWELL *Greener Pastures* 54 Apple maggots have railroad-tracked the flesh of others [*sc.* apples]. 1836 *Amer. Jrnl. Sci. & Arts* XXX. 382 The vibrating effects of a passing *rail road train. 1922 C. SANDBURG in *Bookman* (U.S.) LV. 151 The little flivs of women, ready to throw themselves in front of *railroad trains for men they love. 1837 HT. MARTINEAU *Soc. Amer.* II. 180 *Railroad travelling in America is very fatiguing and noisy. 1836 *Amer. Jrnl. Sci. & Arts* XXIX. 73 The length of this *Rail Road tunnel is eight hundred and seventy-seven feet. 1854 A. M. MURRAY *Lett. from U.S.* (1856) 149 It does seem an extraordinary recklessness which causes these dreadful occurrences, when *railroad whistles would guard against them.

b. objective and obj. gen., as ***railroad director, manager, proprietor, scalper*** (see quot.), ***-wrecking*** adj.; ***railroad-building*** vbl. sb.

1873 'MARK TWAIN' *Gilded Age* xxiii. 216 Philip devoted himself day and night..to the science of *railroad-building. 1849 J. J. RUSKIN *Let.* 4 June in M. Lutyens *Ruskins & Grays* (1972) xxiii. 211 We have not heard a word from Scotland..of John's Book... If *Railroad Directors ever trouble themselves with such work, I should like to hear their notion of it. 1848 *Amer. Railroad Jrnl.* 29 July 482/3 In a short time, the *railroad managers found that it would be convenient to grant to this company the use of their canal. 1839 BOWDLER *Sunday Trains* 16 The *Railroad proprietors are men of property. 1892 STEVENSON & L. OSBOURNE *Wrecker* 43 He became a *railroad-scalper..its essence appears to be to cheat the railroads out of their due fare. 1898 *Engineering Mag.* XVI. 71 The *railroad-wrecking plant, especially the heavier types of steam derricks, will be found of great value.

c. railroad bull, a policeman or detective on a railroad; **railroad bunk-car**, an old sleeping-car used as quarters for railway workers; **railroad commission**, a committee appointed to guard the public interest in relation to railroads; so **railroad commissioner**; **railroad-creeper** = *railway-creeper*; **railroad euchre**: see EUCHRE *sb.* 1; **railroad fever**, (*a*) enthusiasm for the construction of railroads; (*b*) a passion for riding on trains; **railroad flat** *U.S.*, a flat consisting of a series of long, narrow rooms; **railroad guide**, a railway timetable; **railroad king**, a leading business man in the railroad industry; **railroad service**, in real tennis, an overhead service (see quot. 1961[1]); **railroad tie**, a railway sleeper; **railroad worm**, the larva or the adult female of the South American beetle, *Phrixothrix tiemanni*, of the family Phengodidæ, which bears luminous red and green patches on its body.

1941 S. LONGSTREET *Last Man around World* xxxiii. 357 Hobo and *railroad bull..and people who once shook hands with Warren G. Harding..fill the land. 1945 Railroad bull [see MESQUITE, MESQUIT[2] 1 b]. 1961 H. GARNER *Ten for Wednesday Night* 131 It had probably been some native-born jerk in a *railroad bunk-car or construction boarding-house..who had named him. 1887 *Statutes at Large U.S.A.* XXIV. 384 Investigate any complaint forwarded by the railroad commissioner or *railroad commission of any State or Territory. 1913 R. M. LA FOLLETTE *Autobiogr.* vi. 238 He was now making a dogged fight for a railroad commission to regulate rates. 1914 *Cycl. Amer. Govt.* III. 109/1 At the beginning of the twentieth century, nearly every state in the United States had a railroad commission. 1845 *Massachusetts Acts & Resolves* 582 The Governor..shall appoint..five persons, who shall, together, constitute 'the Board of *Rail-road Commissioners'. 1946 S. H. HOLBROOK *Lost Men of Amer. Hist.* xii. 262 He was made railroad commissioner of Iowa. 1891 KIPLING & BALESTIER *Naulahka* v, The mauve *railroad-creeper on the station. 1852 *Oregon Statesman* 20 Jan. 1/6 The people up country are likewise agitated with the *railroad fever. 1880 *Bradstreet's* 15 Sept. 8/1 A railroad fever is pervading various portions of the state. 1899 'J. FLYNT' *Tramping with Tramps* I. ii. 53 The tramp's theory of them [*sc.* runaway boys], is that they are possessed of the 'railroad fever'. 1956 B. MALAMUD in *New Yorker* 22 Sept. 149/1 A five-room *railroad flat above a butcher store. 1962 S. J. PERELMAN *Rising Gorge* 283 His apartment, a railroad flat... Halfway down its central corridor, Barber flung open a door. 1859 L. D. TIERNEY *Hist. Gold Discoveries on South Platte River* 25 Persons starting from points east of Chicago, by obtaining a *railroad guide, can easily estimate the distance and cost of travel for themselves to that point. 1868 *Commercial & Financial Chron.* VI. 295/1 The *railroad kings..have entered the lists. 1871 MRS. STOWE *My Wife & I* xvi. 176 He is a rail-road king—a prince of stocks—a man going with a forty thousand steam power through New York waters. 1890 W. JAMES *Princ. Psychol.* I. xiv. 579 Such new attributes as make up the notions of a 'railroad king'. 1903 T. M. TARBELL in *McClure's Mag.* Jan. 254/2 The acquiescence of the 'railroad kings'..was followed by an unwilling promise to break the contracts with the company. 1898 KENNEDY & COHEN in W. A. Morgan *'House' on Sport* I. 421 His *railroad service did not have nearly the effect he expected. 1959 *Times* 6 May 4/3 Hampel who set up a promising attack based on a railroad service. 1961 J. S. SALAK *Dict. Amer. Sports* 352 *Railroad service* (court tennis) —an overhead service delivered by the server standing near the wall between the last gallery and the dedans wall. 1961 *Times* 13 Jan. 16/2 Each showed skill in handling the other's rail-road service. 1856 *Railroad tie [see DOUGLAS[1]]. 1877 [see *fencing post*]. 1927 [see BOHUNK]. 1935 Z. N. HURSTON *Mules & Men* I. iv. 86 They were accustomed to strange women dropping into the quarters, but not in shiny gray Chevrolets. They usually came plodding down the big road or counting railroad ties. 1977 R. E. HARRINGTON *Quintain* viii. 78 The railroad-tie steps that led down to the terrace. 1979 *Arizona Daily Star* 5 Aug. (Advt. Section) 9/5 Railroad ties, $9 ea. 1944 E. N. HARVEY in *Jrnl. Cellular & Compar. Physiol.* XXIII. 31 (*heading*) The nature of the red and green luminescence of the South American '*railroad worm'. 1973 C. A. VILLEE et al. *Gen. Zool.* (ed. 4) iv. 79/2 One of the more spectacular luminescent creatures is the 'railroad worm' of Uruguay, the larva of a beetle, which has a row of green lights on each side of its body and a pair of red lights on its head.

Hence **ˌrailroadiˈana**, matters pertaining to railroads; **ˈrailroadish** *a.*, resembling a railroad in speed; **ˈrailroadship**, *nonce-wd.*, connexion by means of railroads.

1838 (*title*) Railroadiana. A New History of England. 1855 SMEDLEY *H. Coverdale* i. 3 A little too railroadish, perhaps, unless a man's in an awful hurry. 1883 *National Baptist* (U.S.) XIX. 700 Connecting the three Americas..in one bond of railroadship.

railroad (ˈreɪlrəʊd), *v.* [f. prec. sb.]

1. *trans.* **a.** To furnish (a country) with railroads. **b.** To engross (the mind) in railroads. **c.** *transf.* To mark with parallel lines.

a 1847 ELIZA COOK *Poems* II. Pref. 5 The public mind seems nearly as much railroaded as the country. 1893 A. ROBERTSON *Fra Paolo Sarpi* 26 The modern practice of 'railroading' Bibles. 1894 *Blackw. Mag.* Dec. 788/2 Nearly every country except China has been railroaded.

2. a. To transport by means of the railroad.

1893 LELAND *Mem.* II. 69 We were marched and railroaded back to Philadelphia.

b. orig. *U.S.* To accomplish (an action) with great speed; to 'rush' (a person or thing) *to* or *into* a place, *through* a process, occas. *from* a position, etc. Also const. without prep., to hustle, to coerce.

1884 *Amer. Law Rev.* in *Law Times* LXXVII. 104/2 The way men are railroaded to the gallows in that country. 1898 *Educat. Rev.* (U.S.) XV. 465 This process of railroading a pupil through school. 1917 E. H. HADLOCK *Journalism & Authorship* 23 'Rail-road' means to rush matter through without the usual precautions against typographical errors. 1924 P. C. MACFARLANE *Tongues of Flame* xxv. 222 They railroaded it [*sc.* the bill] through the senate before I was awake. 1934 J. M. CAIN *Postman always rings Twice* xi. 123 If all cases were railroaded through that quick, it would do more to prevent crime than passing a hundred laws. 1952 *Manch. Guardian Weekly* 12 June 3 The most ruthless block railroads its man into the nomination. 1958 M. DICKENS *Man Overboard* x. 151 How had he let himself be railroaded into this? 1961 A. HUXLEY *Let.* 5 May (1969) 911 I'm very thankful I didn't let myself be railroaded..into having half my tongue and a quarter of my neck cut out. 1963 J. N. HARRIS *Weird World Wes Beattie* vii. 83 Paget..had been primarily responsible for railroading the case through the magistrate's court. 1967 *Boston Sunday Herald* 7 May (Show Guide) 17/2 It is..unbelievable that he would railroad his alcoholic daughter..into a mental hospital. *a* 1974 R. CROSSMAN *Diaries* (1976) II. 223 The timetable was fixed and it was railroaded through the Cabinet. 1974 *News & Courier* (Charleston, S. Carolina) 21 Apr. A-1/1 Nixon's accusers then would be vulnerable to the charge they were trying to railroad him from office. 1975 B. GARFIELD *Death Sentence* xi. 59 Take all the time you want. Nobody wants to railroad him.

c. To send (someone) to a place of punishment with summary speed or by means of false evidence.

1877 *N.Y. Herald* 9 Mar. 8/4 'Railroaded!' Joe Coburn takes the cars for his ten years' home [*i.e.* Sing Sing]. **1900** [see FAIR *sb.*² 1 c]. **1930** *Sat. Even. Post* 26 July 26/2 He broke up the best gang of counterfeiters the country ever saw... He went into the post-office department and rail-roaded six of the smartest mail workers that ever hit a prison. **1935** A. J. POLLOCK *Underworld Speaks* 94/1 *Railroaded*, sentenced to prison when innocent. **1942** E. PAUL *Narrow St.* xv. 108 It was no new thing to the French to have undesirables railroaded and executed on one flimsy pretext or another. **1964** C. CHAPLIN *Autobiogr.* xxvii. 464 In spite of the absurdity of the charges there lurked in the back of my mind the possibility that I might be railroaded. **1974** *Black Panther* 27 Apr. 9/1 Concrete evidence smashed American military intelligence attempts to illegally railroad eleven Black sailors in U.S. military court here.

3. *intr. U.S.* To travel by rail.

1889 *Lit. World* (Boston) 8 June 190/3 Now steaming along the coast, now railroading along the shore.

4. *intr. U.S.* To work on the railroad.

1887 C. B. GEORGE *40 Yrs. on Rail* iv. 69 A couple of fast runs that were made while I was railroading in Vermont. **1893** GUNTER *Miss Dividends* 52, I was born in Chicago,.. and railroaded ever since I was corn high.

Hence **railroaded** *ppl. a.*

a **1847** ELIZA COOK *Rhymes by Roadside* i, Time, with deep railroaded brow, Changes all things but horses now.

railroader ('reɪlrəʊdə(r)). *U.S.* [f. prec. sb. or vb. + -ER.] One who is employed in the management or the working of a railroad.

1856 *Iroquois Republican* (Middleport, Illinois) 8 May 3/2 A scuffle between young Walker, a railroader, and Cochran, a rail ripper. **1881** *Lewisburg Chron.* No. 1938 Experienced railroaders.. soon placed them again upon the rails. **1895** *Outing* (U.S.) XXVI. 369/2 We had a most vigilant brakeman on the train,.. I called the attention of this railroader. **1907** *Daily Chron.* 20 Sept. 3/2 Here are particulars of some of the new novels which Messrs. Cassell will publish in October:-.. 'Caleb Conover, Railroader', by Mr. A. P. Terhune. **1973** *Sunday Bull.* (Philadelphia) 14 Oct. (Parade Suppl.) 20 (Advt.), *The Old West*.. shows you the people who met its most extraordinary challenges, people who became *The Forty-Niners, The Trailblazers, The Railroaders.* **1977** *Modern Railways* Dec. 461/1 On the one hand he rages that the railroad's proposal to pay by the hour instead of by the mile would lower the American railroader to the social and economic level of his Soviet counterpart.

railroading ('reɪlrəʊdɪŋ), *vbl. sb.* Chiefly *U.S.* [f. as prec. + -ING¹.]

1. Travelling by rail. Also *attrib.*

1842 F. A. KEMBLE *Let.* 16 June in *Rec. Later Life* (1882) II. 258 An hour's railroading from London has brought me into a lovely country. **1855** LOWELL *Lett.* I. 251 A quiet Sunday.. after a week's railroading. **1872** MARK TWAIN *Innoc. Abr.* 77 It is hard to make railroading pleasant. *Ibid.* xxvii. 217 These matter-of-fact railroading and telegraphing days. **1905** *Daily Chron.* 9 Feb. 33 Automobilism has been taken too much as a matter of course, though its position is obviously midway between cycling and rail-roading.

2. The business of making or working railroads.

1882 PIDGEON *Engineer's Holiday* I. 228 Mountain railroading is much easier at its highest than at its lower levels. **1887** M. ROBERTS *Western Avernus* 203 Railroading is considered by all who do not follow it as a 'low-down job'. **1907** *Daily Chron.* 20 Feb. 4/7 [Bad management] has brought American railroading into the position of being the most slovenly of all our great business enterprises. **1915** *Lit. Digest* 4 Sept. 458/1 The New Haven was wrecked by excessive capital issues either alien to the business of railroading or for properties and purposes without equivalent value. **1945** H. HUBBARD *Railroad Avenue* ii. 7 The prevalence of Joneses in railroading, as elsewhere, is shown by the fact that in 1944 there were 1,078 Joneses on the Canadian National pay roll. **1977** *Modern Railways* Dec. 460/3 Precious little has been heard of how they order things in the land of—still largely—free enterprise railroading. **1979** *Tucson Mag.* Apr. 47/3 His re-creation of early British railroading will warm the cockles of every train buff's heart.

3. The action of 'rushing' things. In quot. *attrib.*

1884 *American* VIII. 104 A conviction secured in an hour.. the 'railroading' feature.. produces a painful feeling.

4. *Printing.* In proof-correcting, a method of indicating by parallel lines that words are to be transferred to the next line; overrunning.

1882 J. SOUTHWARD *Pract. Printing* 153.

rail-splitter. *U.S.* [f. RAIL *sb.*² + SPLITTER *sb.*²] One who splits wood for rails; used *transf.* of Abraham Lincoln. Hence *fig.*, a Republican. Also *attrib.* in apposition.

1860 *Congress Globe* 36th Congress 1 Sess. App. 462/2 They call him 'Uncle Abe', 'Old Abe', 'Honest old Abe', 'The old rail-splitter', 'The flat-boatman', &c. **1864** A. GUROWSKI *Diary* 17 Sept. (1866) III. 350, I rejoice that Lincoln's mind is not befogged by that limited scholarship; and.. I prefer the railsplitter to any narrow, classical hairsplitter. **1865** *Harper's Mag.* July 227/2 His [*sc.* Lincoln's] national reputation as a rail-splitter. **1885** *Mag. Amer. Hist.* Mar. 298/1 Clubs of 'Rail-Splitters' were formed during the campaign. **1887** J. D. BILLINGS *Hardtack & Coffee* i. 19, I had taken an active part in the torchlight parades of the 'Wide-awakes' and 'Rail-splitters', as the political clubs of the Republicans were called. **1901** W. CHURCHILL *Crisis* I. v. 150 What they seemed proudest of was that he had been a rail-splitter. **1903** J. G. NICOLAY in *Cambr. Mod. Hist.* VII. xvi. 548 Both classes very naturally doubted whether a rail-splitter candidate.. possessed the wisdom and the strength of will to conquer a formidable rebellion. **1925** *Scribner's Mag.* Oct. 361/1 Did Lincoln say that to America? He was only a rail-splitter. He had reason to think that he might not count. **1952** *Manch. Guardian Weekly* 17 July 3 The patron saint of the Republicans is an uncouth rail-splitter. **1960** B. KEATON *My Wonderful World of Slapstick* i. 11 James Agee described my face as ranking 'almost with Lincoln's'. I can't imagine what the great rail splitter's reaction would have been to this.

† **rail timber.** *U.S. Obs.* [f. RAIL *sb.*² + TIMBER *sb.*¹] Timber suitable for making rails.

1662 *Portsmouth* (New Hampsh.) *Rec.* (1901) 396 He is to preserve all the Rayle timber. **1681** *Town Rec. Topsfield, Mass.* (1917) I. 36/2 There shall be noe raile timber feled. **1786** G. WASHINGTON *Diary* 30 Oct. (1925) III. 131 The Wood part, of wch. there is a good deal, is tolerably full of rail timber and wood. **1816** U. BROWN *Jrnl.* in *Maryland Hist. Mag.* (1915) X. 281 A poor stony rocky Country.. with an abundance of good Chestnut rail Timber. **1843** N. BOONE *Jrnl.* 23 July in L. Pelzer *Marches of Dragoons* (1917) 233 There being a great scarcity of water and no building or rail timber. **1860** H. GREELEY *Overland Journey* v. 65 The squatter can give you a hundred good excuses for his miserable condition:.. he has no good rail-timber [etc.].

rail-train. [f. RAIL *sb.*² 4 and 5.] **a.** A railway-train. **b.** (See quot. 1881).

1855 E. FITZGERALD *Lett.* (1889) I. 233 There are Rail-Trains to Ipswich from Shoreditch. **1872** TALMAGE *Sermons* 139 It is a rail-train.. run into by a Bangor express. **1881** RAYMOND *Mining Gloss.*, *Rail-train*, a train of rolls for reducing iron piles or steel ingots or blooms to rails.

railway ('reɪlweɪ), *sb.* Also **rail-way, rail way.** [f. RAIL *sb.*² 4 + WAY. Cf. RAILROAD, at one time equally (or more) common in Great Britain and still usual in America.

1838 *Civil Eng. & Arch. Jrnl.* I. 275/1 *Railway* seems now we think the more usual term.]

1. a. A way or road laid with rails (originally of wood, in later times usually of iron or steel), on which the wheels of wagons containing heavy goods are made to run for ease of transport; also, the way composed of rails thus laid.

Railways (or railroads) of this kind were app. first used at Newcastle in the beginning of the 17th c. Cast-iron rails were introduced about the middle of the 18th c., and wrought-iron ones about 1820. Although this use of the words is not obsolete, it has now a very restricted currency in comparison with sense 2.

1776 *Act 16 Geo. III*, c. 32 To make.. a rail-way from hence to or near Caledon.. and to make other rail-ways. **1798** *Term Rep.* VII. 599 To the sleepers or dormant timbers they affixed railways or waggon ways. **1825** J. NICHOLSON *Operat. Mechanic* 655 Five tons to a horse is the average work on railways, descending at the rate of three miles per hour.

b. Any line or set of rails intended to facilitate the motion of wheels or other apparatus.

1835 URE *Philos. Manuf.* 177 To turn the wheel round at such rates that the spindles will not take up faster than the carriage moves on its rail-way. **1945** G. MILLAR *Maquis* ii. 30 On the side of the aircraft near the hole there were several little metal railways for holding the fixed end of the static lines. **1979** W. GOLDING *Darkness Visible* iii. 39 The place [*sc.* a shop] grew a spider's web of wires along which money trundled in small, wooden jars.. the overhead railway.

2. *spec.* A line or track consisting of iron or steel rails, on which carriages or wagons conveying passengers or goods are moved by a locomotive engine. Hence also, the whole organization necessary for the conveyance of passengers or goods by such a line, and the company of persons owning or managing it. ***British Railways***: formerly, the name of the national railway system of Great Britain. Cf. *British Rail* s.v. RAIL *sb.*² 5 a.

The great extension of railways from their original limited use (see sense 1) began with the opening of the line between Stockton and Darlington in 1825, and that between Liverpool and Manchester in 1830.

1812 (*heading*) Map of the railways in the Newcastle on Tyne Coal Field in 1812 [reproduced in A. Hollar tr. *W. Schivelbusch's Railway Journey* (1980) i. 6]. **1830** M. EDGEWORTH *Let.* 18 Oct. (1971) 418 We were invited.. to go on the Liverpool railway in the very carriage in which the Duke of Wellington went... 4 of these cars similar in size and shape.. were linked together on the rail way. **1832** COBBETT *Rural Rides* 2 Oct., They have begun to make a rail-way from Carlisle to Newcastle. **1842** TENNYSON *Locksley Hall* 166 In the steamship, in the railway, in the thoughts that shake mankind. **1868** G. DUFF *Pol. Surv.* 45 The construction of a railway would encounter no great difficulties. **1889** G. FINDLAY (*title*) The Working of an English Railway. **1892** B. POTTER *Jrnl.* 13 Sept. (1966) 260 To Perth with Papa, the first time I have been on the railway since we have been here. **1955** *Times* 9 May 4/5 The start of a new era for the railways. **1964** *Ann. Reg. 1963* 12 British Railways, a weary and over-extended system, had been slithering ever deeper into deficits since 1953. **1965** *Ann. Reg. 1964* 486 British Railways signed an agreement in January with the Central Electricity Generating Board for the delivery of coal by continuously moving merry-go-round trains to selected power stations. **1976** *Illustr. London News* Nov. 51/3 The first iron railway in France was designed, as in Britain, for the transport of coal from the mines to the water... But it used horse traction as often as steam.

3. *attrib.* and *Comb.*

a. attrib., as ***railway accident, act, age, arch, bank, bill, book, bookstall, bridge, bus, cab, car, carriage, cat, company, contractor, cottage, cutting, director, economics, engine, enthusiast, excursion, fare, garden, horse, interest, journey, junction, labourer, line, man, manual, map, marshalling yard, office, platform, police, policeman, porter, poster, sandwich, servant, share, shareholder, siding, signal, speed, stall, station, stock, switch, system, tea, terminus, ticket, timetable, town, track, train, traveller, travelling, truck, tunnel, viaduct, wagon, worker, works.***

The great development of railways in the 19th c., leading to an extensive use of the word in various connexions, has given rise to many attributive collocations of a more or less permanent character, while the number of those which may be formed at will is infinite. The examples given here have been selected mainly as being instances of some of the more usual combinations.

1837 *Civil Eng. & Arch. Jrnl.* I. 43/1 *Railway accidents, by An Old Engineer. **1850** J. H. NEWMAN *Christ upon Waters* 23 You know what a sensation railway accidents occasion. **1939** T. S. ELIOT *Family Reunion* I. i. 43 We know about the railway accident. **1829** in Wood *Pract. Treat. Railroads* (ed. 3) 305 The provisions of the *railway act, 7 Geo. IV. **1877** E. BLANCHARD in E. Farjeon *Nursery in Nineties* (1935) IV. i. 162 In this *railway Age.. Fresh lines are still appearing. **1976** A. PRICE *War Game* I. v. 99 The railway age was.. part of bygone history. **1892** B. POTTER *Jrnl.* 9 Sept. (1966) 257 A charming game of 'bolting the pony' under the *railway arch. **1976** A. POWELL *Infants of Spring* v. 79 We were making for the open country beyond the railway arches that link Windsor with the main line. **1894** B. POTTER *Jrnl.* 25 Sept. (1966) 346 Our nerves were rather startled by the sight of some cattle up the *railway bank between Sprouston and Kelso. **1819** *Rep. Darlington & Stockton Railw. Petit.* 3 Any Agent for the Darlington *Railway Bill. **1854** C. M. YONGE *Heartsease* I. II. ii. 142 It was a green *railway book. Theodora made me read it. **1893** *Railway bookstall [see BIG *a.* 3 e]. **1974** in A. Briggs *Ess. Hist. of Publishing* 289 The first railway bookstall was opened at Euston by W. H. Smith in 1848. **1837** *Civil Eng. & Arch. Jrnl.* I. 55/2 About 140 men are employed at the fallen *railway bridge. **1892** B. POTTER *Jrnl.* 26 July (1966) 239 He [*sc.* a dog] used to be very much in evidence.. until safely hoisted on to the top of the *railway bus in front of the luggage. **1893** YONGE & COLERIDGE *Strolling Players* xxviii. 254 A *railway cab dashing up to the door. **1828** *Deb. Congress U.S.* 9 Apr. 2249 The *rail way car at Charleston, South Carolina.. weighs upwards of one ton. **1830** M. EDGEWORTH *Let.* 18 Oct. (1971) 418 Francis was prevented from going in the common train of *railway cars* from Liverpool to Manchester. **1894** *Harper's Mag.* July 316/1 Railway cars for transporting the army were appropriated at Omaha. *a* **1824** A. SCOTT in *Trans. Highland Soc.* (1824) VI. 57 If springs.. were fixed to the front of *railway-carriages. **1939** T. S. ELIOT *Old Possum's Bk. Pract. Cats* 40 (*heading*) Skimbleshanks: the *Railway Cat. *Ibid.* 41 You can leave all that to the Railway Cat, The Cat of the Railway Train! **1824** R. STEVENSON in *Trans. Highland Soc.* (1824) VI. The first Public *Railway Company seems to have been instituted at Loughborough, in the year 1789. **1976** A. WHITE *Long Silence* vi. 43 Five shunting engines were.. presented to the railway company. **1846** SHAW *Gauge Question* p. xxviii, Carriers, miners, and *railway contractors. **1962** M. DUFFY *That's how it Was* ii. 22 The warren of *railway cottages run up at the end of the nineteenth century. **1976** *Milton Keynes Express* 23 July 2/6 Time is running out for the Bradwell residents who have petitioned against the preservation of the town's railway cottages. **1842** BRANDE *Dict. Sci.* etc. 1017/2 The strata through which *railway cuttings are made. **1878** *Q. Jrnl. Geol. Soc.* XXXIV. 496 Railway-cuttings and other workings made since the date of the survey have exposed masses of rock not then known to exist. **1976** A. WHITE *Long Silence* xviii. 147 The road that led to the railway cutting. **1837** *Civil Eng. & Arch. Jrnl.* I. 43/1 The discouragement given by *railway directors to railway improvements. **1845** *Punch* VIII. 101 The old maxim that civility costs nothing, seems to be utterly repudiated by Railway Directors. **1976** *Illustr. London News* Nov. 53/3 One aspect of *railway economics in which the SNCF has made remarkable progress in recent years is productivity. **1838** WOOD *Pract. Treat. Railroads* (ed. 3) 726 The Stanhope and Tyne *railway engines. **1950** *Oxf. Jun. Encycl.* IX. 399/2 Ian Allan ..brought into being the first club for young *railway enthusiasts who wished to collect the numbers of locomotives. **1976** *Scotsman* 20 Nov. (Weekend Suppl.) 5/8 Information and photographs are wanted from railway enthusiasts about historic rail buildings, either extant, demolished or adapted. **1853** *Punch* XXIV. 92/2 Railway Maxims,.. After a *Railway excursion, the Doctor. **1885** *List of Subscribers, Classified* (United Telephone Co.) (ed. 6) 181 Railway Excursion Agents.. Cook Thomas & Son. **1891** KIPLING *Life's Handicap* 30 Ye might give me my *railway fare. **1980** A. MORICE *Death in Round* xxi. 169 The idea of thumbing a lift was reasonable... The railway fare is quite steep. **1892** B. POTTER *Jrnl.* 26 July (1966) 239 It [*sc.* a hedgehog] was gobbling up little spring cabbages in a promising little *Railway Garden. **1976** *Field* 18 Nov. 994/1 (*caption*) Nationalization came that year [*sc.* 1947] and this was almost the end of a long *railway-horse tradition. **1869** *Bradshaw's Railway Manual* XXI. p. xi, The *railway interest in parliament, etc. **1864** BURTON *Scot Abr.* I. i. 36 Who prefer economy and a sea-voyage to a *railway journey. **1845** A. H. CLOUGH *Sic itur* in *Poems* (1862) 24 As, at a *railway junction, men Who came together, taking then One the train up, one down, again Meet never! **1977** V. S. PRITCHETT *Gentle Barbarian* iii. 45 When Dickens stayed there with the Viardots he complained that.. the place.. was like a railway junction where people were changing trains. **1845** WORDSWORTH *At Furness Abbey* in *Poetical Wks.* (1954) III. 63 Well have you *Railway Labourers to *this* ground Withdrawn for noontide rest. **1838** *Civil Eng. & Arch. Jrnl.* I. 143/2 The survey of the *Railway line between England and Scotland. **1880** G. MEREDITH *Trag. Com.* (1881) 3 The bare railway line of their story. **1976** *Illustr. London News* Nov. 29/2 London is adequately served with railway lines.. either by London Transport or British Rail. **1845** SIDNEY *Gauge Evidence* (1846) 13 An experienced *railway man. **1906** *Daily Chron.* 30 Apr. 3/1 Near the junction of the northern and western railway lines,.. two stones and a piece of iron had been placed on the rails. They were removed by a railwayman. **1938** F. D. SHARPE *Sharpe of Flying Squad* xxiv. 251, I could see by their 'railwaymen's' trousers that they were country splits. **1976** W. GREATOREX *Crossover* 194 They found a pub.. packed with railway porters and shunters... A couple of railwaymen moved out to make room. **1863** (*title*) Bradshaw's *railway manual. **1845** *Punch* IX. 163 (*heading*) A *railway map of England. **1853** J. E. Millais *Let.* Sept. in M. Lutyens *Millais & Ruskins* (1967) 90 My face..would be lined like a Bradshaw railway map. **1907** *Yesterday's Shopping* (1969) 1106/2 District Railway Map..0/9. **1976** A. White *Long Silence* vii. 53 The *railway marshalling yards we were to disable were crescent-shaped. **1831** W. Dalton *Let.* 16 Oct. in *N. & Q.* (1920) 11 Dec. 461/2 We drove to the *railway office at Warrington. **1976** A. White *Long Silence* vi. 44 She had no other thought than to seek employment in the railway office. **1922** C. Mackenzie *Altar Steps* xix. 218 While Father Rowley was speaking the Bishop of Silchester had been looking like a man on a *railway platform who has been ambushed by a whistling engine. **1846** *Punch* XI. 11/1 The corps of *Railway police was next put through its exercise. **1972** J. Wainwright *Requiem for Loser* viii. 165 The man.. in charge of the goods yard police activity was a uniformed Railway Police inspector. **1838** *Penny Mag.* 31 Aug. 331/2 The *railway policeman, holding up at intervals red or white flags. **1972** M. Gilbert *Body of Girl* i. 9 A very big consignment of used notes..was coming up for pulping... There were two railway policemen to meet it. **1890** P. Geddes in *Scots Mag.* Aug. 192 The student..needs a better greeting than the *railway porter's when he arrives at his destination. **1978** Ld. Drogheda *Double Harness* xiii. 132 His father..obliged him to take a job as a railway porter. **1926** *Scribner's Mag.* Aug. 221/2 Byron was too grandiose to travel well. He founded the *railway-poster style of description. **1931** D. L. Sayers *Five Red Herrings* xiv. 153 A board which displayed time-tables and railway posters. **1948** M. Laski *Tory Heaven* xii. 159 There were some benches round the walls..and a lot of gaudy railway posters. **1847** Dickens *Dombey* (1848) xv. 155 There were railway plans, maps, views, wrappers, bottles, *sandwich-boxes, and time tables. **1868** Trollope *He knew he was Right* (1869) I. xxxvii. 292 The real disgrace of England is the railway sandwich. **1915** J. Buchan *Thirty-Nine Steps* vii. 177, I never ate a meal with greater relish, for I had had nothing all day but railway sandwiches. **1972** Railway sandwich [see *railway tea* below]. **1840** *Act 3 & 4 Vict.* c. 97 §13 *Railway servants guilty of misconduct. **1837** *Civil Eng. & Arch. Jrnl.* I. 27/2 Questions respecting the sale of *railway shares. **1876** 'L. Carroll' *Hunting of Snark* III. 30 You may seek it with thimbles—and seek it with care; You may hunt it with forks and hope; You may threaten its life with a railway-share; You may charm it with smiles and soap. **1837** *Civil Eng. & Arch. Jrnl.* I. 43/2 The anxiety.. for *railway shareholders to commence business. **1942** C. Milburn *Diary* 26 Feb. (1979) 130 The King and Queen slept in *our* *railway siding on Tuesday night. **1976** A. White *Long Silence* vi. 43 The railway sidings became one of the principal marshalling yards. **1838** *Civil Eng. & Arch. Jrnl.* I. 358/1 A *railway signal erected at the Grand Junction station. **1836** T. Barlow (*title*) A Trip to Rome at *Railway Speed. **1866** Geo. Eliot *Let.* 11 Sept. (1956) IV. 309 My 6/- editions are never on the *railway stalls. **1838** *Civil Eng. & Arch. Jrnl.* I. 358/1 Fire at the London and Birmingham *Railway Station. **1849** De Quincey in *Blackw. Mag.* Oct. 492/1 Interesting personal communications,..revelations of impressive faces..could not have offered themselves amongst the hurried and fluctuating groups of a railway station. **1892** B. Potter *Jrnl.* 25 Aug. (1966) 252 A large proportion of the seven thousand spectators poking away through the small Railway Station. **1964** G. L. Cohen *What's Wrong with Hospitals?* vi. 115 Their baronial board-room..dignified by a staircase for consultants only, in Railway Station Gothic. **1852** *Jewish Chron.* 10 Dec. 78/2 The poor..are induced to go..from town to town; each congregation..assisting to pay a portion of the dividends on *railway-stock, under the name of.. charity. **1863** H. Fawcett *Pol. Econ.* III. xv. 504 The possessor of railway stock is part owner of the railway itself. **1838** *Civil Engin. & Archit. Jrnl.* Oct. 358 *Railway Switch Signal. **1824** R. Stevenson in *Trans. Highland Soc.* VI. 3 An offer of a reward for the advancement of the *Railway-system. **1872** Geo. Eliot *Middlem.* III. lvi. 227 The infant struggles of the railway system. **1981** *Times* 10 Feb. 6/6 The railway system and the port of Mombasa have..benefited from the growing volume of tea exports. **1972** 'G. North' *Sgt. Cluff rings True* iv. 31 Travellers..reviving themselves with *railway tea and railway sandwiches. **1845** *Punch* VIII. 101 An applicant for information at a *Railway Terminus. **1942** E. Waugh *Put out More Flags* iii. 228 They reached the classic columns of the railway terminus. **1976** G. Seymour *Glory Boys* iv. 42 The big railway termini of North London. **1839** F. Witts *Diary* 4 May (1978) 158 Meantime the passengers receive a *railway ticket to London which purports to be worth 5s 6d. **1895** E. Lear in *Nonsense Songs & Stories* 87 On his nose there was a Cricket,—In his hat a Railway-Ticket. **1912** W. Owen *Let.* 4 June (1967) 140 Does the Railway Ticket Problem assume a different aspect now? **1977** *Lancashire Life* Dec. 60/2 In those wartime days, holiday-period railway tickets were at a premium. **1847** *Railway timetable [see *railway sandwich* above]. **1932** D. L. Sayers *Have his Carcase* xxvi. 352 Do you happen to have a railway time-table on you? **1980** *Times* 12 Aug. 10/1 He wants the centre of the British railway system moved from London to Birmingham..to rewrite the entire railway timetable around Birmingham. **1881** A. Begg *Gt. Canadian N.W.* 106 The railway is constructed to a point on the eastern side of the river opposite Selkirk, so that there is every chance of its becoming a *railway town. **1888** *Lippincott's Monthly Mag.* XLII. 783 There stood close to the opposite wall a large piano of the class known as the 'grand', rare enough among the railway towns west of the Mississippi States. **1943** *Sun* (Baltimore) 13 Dec. 5/2 The Peiping Hankow railway town of Sinyang. *a* **1824** A. Scott *Ibid.* 43 All public lines of railway will require two distinct sets of *railway-tracks. **1976** A. White *Long Silence* vi. 44 She propelled the creaking vehicle..up and down the railway tracks. **1841** Brees *Gloss. Civil Eng.* 196 The effect of high winds upon a *railway train is very considerable. **1891** *Murray's Handbk. India & Ceylon* p. xv, In Bombay, the Indian *A.B.C. Guide* and the *Indian *Railway Travellers' Guide* ..give..the railway routes for all India. **1980** G. M. Fraser *Mr American* xxvi. 552 The vaguely hostile silence of the British railway traveller. **1842** W. F. Cooke *Telegr. Railw.* 3 The comparatively high-degree of safety now attained in *Railway travelling. **1838** *Civil Engineer* I. 390/1 A new *Railway Truck, the invention of Mr. Robert Grant, of Maine. **1839** F. Witts *Diary* 4 May (1978) 158 There the carriages are placed each on a railway truck. **1841** Dickens *Let.* 13 June (1969) II. 302 One is hoisted bodily, carriage and all, on a Railway Truck. **1836** in *Civil Eng. & Arch. Jrnl.* (1837) I. 27/1 Improvements in the Construction and Arrangement of *Railway Tunnels. **1867** Queen Victoria *Jrnl.* 22 Aug. in D. Duff *Victoria in Highlands* (1968) 223 We went by the side of Eildon Hills, past an immense *railway viaduct. **1976** C. Dexter *Last seen Wearing* xxi. 162 He..slept beneath a railway viaduct. *a* **1824** Robertson in *Trans. Highland Soc.* (1824) VI. 88 A *railway-waggon..has two axles to sustain the burden. **1976** A. White *Long Silence* xiv. 121 They might hide themselves in a railway wagon. **1943** J. Flanner in *New Yorker* 29 May 45/1 The Nazis..had decided to kill the French railroad men's resistance movement..by inviting twelve thousand French *railway workers to go to Germany. **1979** P. Alexander *Show me Hero* xv. 161 Crumbling terraced cottages, once occupied by railway workers. **1869** *Bradshaw's Railway Manual* XXI. 371, 17,500,000 *thalers* were to be applied to *railway works. **1976** *Milton Keynes Express* 16 July 7/7 The part time station at the Wolverton is still dependent on men from the railway works.

b. objective and instrumental, as ***railway-borne*** adj., ***railway-making***.

1843 (*title*) Examples of Railway Making (Weale). **1881** *Daily News* 9 Sept. 2/6 An inland market for..railway-borne fish.

4. Special combs.: **railway beetle** = *railroad worm* s.v. railroad *sb.* 3 c; **railway bull** = *railroad bull* s.v. railroad *sb.* 3 c; **railway-creeper**, a plant conspicuous at railway stations in India; **railway crossing** = *level crossing* s.v. level *a.* 3 b; **railway edition**, a cheap edition of a book suitable for reading on a railway journey; **railway guide**, a train timetable; **railway hotel**, an hotel sited near to a railway station for the convenience of travellers; **Railway Institute**, a (social) club building for railway workers, esp. in India; **railway label**, an address or destination label stuck on a passenger's luggage; **railway letter** (see quot. 1933); **railway novel**, a light novel, suitable for reading on a railway journey; **railway pass**, a ticket authorizing the holder to travel by rail; **railway rug**, a rug used for warmth during railway journeys; **railway sickness** = *railsickness* s.v. rail *sb.*[2] 6 c; **railway spine**, an affection of the spine produced by concussion in a railway accident; **railway time**: see as main entry; **railway volume** = *railway edition*; **railway warrant** = *railway pass*; **railway whistle**, a whistle blown by the guard as a signal to the driver to start the train; **railway wrapper**, a travelling-cloak.

1915 E. R. Lankester *Diversions of Naturalist* 234 A peculiar grub-like female glow-worm, three inches long, is found in South America, which produces a red light at each end of the body and numerous points of green light on each side of it. It is called the '*railway-beetle' in Paraguay. **1973** B. Broadfoot *Ten Lost Years* ii. 17 [To] the town cop or the *railway bull..you automatically became a criminal. **1895** Mrs. Croker *Village Tales* (1896) 47 Verandahs, embowered in pale lilac '*railway' creeper. **1907** *Yesterday's Shopping* (1969) 1040/2 *Railway Crossing, finely japanned, to be opened and shut..8 in. long. **1937** *Discovery* May 144/2 A railway crossing west of Scarborough. **1859** G. H. Lewes in *Blackw. Edin. Mag.* July 101/1 Twice or thrice have the *railway editions been out of print. *c* **1838** W. H. Murray in M. R. Booth *Eng. Plays of 19th Cent.* (1973) IV. 161 That woman..[is] as difficult to understand as an Act of Parliament, or a *Railway Guide, or a Weather Almanack. **1855** Mrs. Gaskell *North & South* II. vii. 87 One of the very common mistakes in the 'Railway Guide' as to the times when trains arrive at the smaller stations. **1932** D. H. Lawrence *Etruscan Places* i. 13 The inestimable big Italian railway-guide says the station is Palo. **1847** F. A. Kemble *Rec. Later Life* (1882) III. 265 To this Hull *Railway Hotel is attached a magnificent Railway Station (or rather *vice versâ*). **1871** Geo. Eliot *Let.* 20 Aug. (1956) V. 179 There is a palatial bedroom here, but if you reject that, there is a Railway Hotel, just opposite the station. **1911** Beerbohm *Zuleika Dobson* ii. 13 She took a night's sanctuary in some railway-hotel. **1972** *Country Life* 5 Oct. 799/1 The Great Northern, designed by Lewis Cubbitt..was far more restrained than any of the railway hotels of the next decade. **1937** K. Blixen *Out of Afr.* iv. 299 The High Court was set in Nakuru, in the *Railway Institute. **1954** J. Masters *Bhowani Junction* I. v. 42 There were two Railway Institutes ..one for Europeans and Anglo-Indians, and one for Indians... Ours was a fine big building with a dance floor and card rooms and a bar. **1979** *Times* 26 Nov. 14/7 Giving song recitals at the Railway Institute at Lahore. **1909** Beerbohm *Yet Again* 125 *Railway-labels are..crudely coloured, crudely printed. **1917** *Science Progr.* XI. 685 The railway labels jealously preserved on travellers' portmanteaux. **1933** *Post Office Guide* Jan. 42 The following Railway Companies..under agreement with the Postmaster-General, accept and convey letters, both on week-days and on Sundays, by the next available train or ship, either to be called for at the Station of address or to be transferred there to the nearest Post Office letter box. Such letters are called *Railway Letters. **1971** D. Potter *Brit. Eliz. Stamps* xii. 132 In 1969 two other railway lines decided to avail themselves of the privilege of accepting and carrying railway letters. **1857** C. M. Yonge *Dynevor Terrace* I. ii. 12 'Reading... See here', as he held up maliciously a *railway novel. **1871** *Routledge's Ev. Boy's Ann.* June Suppl. 3/1 Two or three..Railway novels. **1896** B. Matthews *Bookbindings* IV. i. 239 In England the railway novel is incased in boards sheathed in paper. **1981** V. Powell *Flora Annie Steel* i. 6 The yellow-backed novels..known as 'railway novels' and bought to beguile the long haul from Harrow to the West of Argyll. **1901** Kipling *Kim* vii. 178 Colonel Creighton's *railway pass lay in his hand, and Kim..was still lord of two rupees seven annas. **1915** W. B. Yeats *Reveries* 5 An uncle called me out of bed one night, to ride..to Rosses Point to borrow a railway-pass from a cousin. **1853** *Illustr. London News* 12 Nov. 409/2 Blankets and *railway rugs have formed the chief protection against the low temperature. **1858** Simmonds *Dict. Trade*, *Railway-rug*. **1883** G. H. Boughton in *Harper's Mag.* Apr. 688/1 With a railway rug around one. **1895** Swinburne *Lett.* (1962) VI. 85, I am now sufficiently recovered from *railwaysickness. **1878** tr. *H. von Ziemssen's Cycl. Med.* XIII. 353 *Railway-spine of the English. **1888** *Pall Mall G.* 29 Nov., It is now stated..that the Tzar is suffering from 'railway spine'. **1895** G. B. Shaw in *Liberty* 27 July 6/2 The connection between degeneration and 'railway spine'. **1954** W. Mayer-Gross et al. *Clin. Psychiatry* iv. 135 The days of neurasthenia and railway-spine at the time of Beard. **1869** D. G. Rossetti *Let.* Aug. (1965) II. 710 In the above year [1862] Messrs. Routledge reprinted it as a shilling *railway volume. **1919** J. Buchan *Mr. Standfast* ix. 183, I..emerged in the uniform of a British private... I had a *railway warrant made out in my name for London. **1978** T. Allbeury *Lantern Network* ii. 30 He had been released..with a railway warrant to Southampton. **1854** Dickens *Seven Poor Travellers* in *Househ. Words* VIII. Extra Christmas No. 4/1 A..young man connected with the Fly department, and well accustomed to the sound of a *railway whistle which Ben always carries in his pocket. **1847** *Railway wrapper [see *railway sandwich*, sense 3 a]. **1860** Dickens *Uncomm. Trav.* (1861) i. 1 No hotel-room tapestried with great-coats and railway wrappers is set apart for me. **1866** G. M. Hopkins *Let.* 14 Dec. (1956) 34 Tell Anne to pack my railway-wrapper (which will help to keep the books fr. jolting).

Hence **'railwayize** *v. trans.*, to furnish with a railway; **'railwayless** *a.*, having no railway.

1873 M. Collins *Squire Silchester* III. xii. 118 He is getting up a company to railwayize you quiet folk at Silchester. **1860** *Chamb. Jrnl.* XIV. 338 Many a day's hard galloping in the railwayless East.

railway ('reɪlweɪ), *v.* [f. prec. sb.]

1. *intr.* **a.** To make railways. **b.** To travel by rail.

1839 Carlyle *Chartism* viii. 168 The Saxon kindred burst forth into cotton-spinning,..railwaying. **1855** Sir J. G. Simpson in *Mem.* xi. 359, I was railwaying hither or thither. **1860** Mrs. Carlyle *Lett.* III. 36 Sailing, which he prefers infinitely to railwaying.

2. *trans.* To deprive *of*, by making a railway.

1844 J. T. Hewlett *Parsons & W.* i, A house now, alas! railwayed of its glories.

3. To provide with railways.

1917 H. Macfall *Germany at Bay* xii. 243 When Russia was gunned and munitioned and well railwayed, she was more than a match for the Germans.

railwayana (ˌreɪlweɪ'ɑːnə). [f. railway *sb.* + ana *suffix*.] Material pertaining to railways; railway relics.

1970 *Sunday Mail Mag.* (Brisbane) 7 June 9/3 In the wake of steam's demise, the collection of railway relics has become almost a national obsession. Enthusiasts have invented a new word—Railwayana... On May 21, Sotheby's held its 'first sale of Railwayana'. **1970** *Railway Mag.* Oct. 541/2, I discovered, in one of the many stalls selling 'railwayana', a line-drawing of Highland Railway No. 103. **1972** *Times* 30 Dec. 14/1 When it proved possible to buy a section, preservationists realized there was more to 'railwayana' than static museums. **1975** *Times* 15 Jan. 15/5 British Rail might do better to invest their pension funds in their own surplus railwayana. Steam locomotive nameplates..now change hands at £200–300 each.

railwaydom ('reɪlweɪdəm). [f. railway *sb.* + -dom.] Railways considered collectively; the railway world.

1881 *Punch* 17 Sept. 132/1 The public ought to devise some means of putting the screw on railwaydom. **1885** *Ibid.* 10 Oct. 170/2 For one of the ways By which Railwaydom pays Is to keep us at work day & night, my dear!

railway time. [railway *sb.*] A standard time adopted throughout a railway system to supersede local time for railway operations (in Great Britain, London time before the adoption of Greenwich Mean Time).

1847 Dickens *Dombey* (1848) xv. 155 There was even railway time observed in clocks, as if the sun itself had given in. **1851** *London at Table* i. 19 A private note,..has been sent out, naming eight, railway time, and at that hour to a minute the guests are seated. **1898** *Murray's Handbk. India* (ed. 3) p. xvi, Railway time throughout India is Madras time... Karachi time is 52 min. behind railway time... Allahabad [time is] 7 min. before railway time. **1959** *Chambers's Encycl.* XIII. 641/1 Till the end of the first half of the 19th century local time was largely used in Great Britain, but the development of railways caused a need for a common system of time-keeping throughout Great Britain, thus the use of 'railway' i.e. Greenwich time became fairly general. **1968** *Guardian* 17 Feb. 8/4 A 24-hour electric clock was built into a wall at Greenwich, and this master clock controlled, by 'galvanism', another clock at London Bridge station, and all the other stations followed London Bridge. Greenwich Mean Time, or Railway Time, as it was called, prevailed. **1975** *Times* 21 June 12/2 From 1840 Greenwich or 'London' time began to be used as 'railway time' throughout Great Britain.

†**railwifery.** *Obs. nonce-wd.* [f. *rail(ing) wife* + -ery.] Abusive scolding.

1695 J. Sage *Article* Wks. 1844 I. 319 He was infinitely far from Gilbert Rules railwifery.

†**railya.** *Sc. Obs. rare*$^{-1}$. ? Striped, rayed.

1542 *Inv. R. Wardr.* (1815) 78 Ane nycht gown of blak sating railya lynit with mertrikis.

†**railyet.** _Sc. Obs. rare_$^{-1}$. [Of obscure etym.] 'Prob., bands, ribbons, ties' (Jam.).

1561 _Inv. R. Wardr._ (1815) 148 Item, sevin quaiffis of claith of silvir cordonit with blak silk, and the railyettis of the same.

†**raim,** _v. Obs._ Forms: 4 **raim(e, reyme,** 4–5 **rame, rayme,** (4 **-mi**), 5 **raym.** [a. OF. _raim-, reim-_ (_raem-, reaim-_, etc.), stem of _raimbre, reimbre_, etc. (see _raembre_ in Godef.):—L. _redimere_ to REDEEM. (Cf. Skeat _Notes Engl. Etym._ 241.)

An app. instance of _raim_ (_rayme_) sb. in _Alexander_ 4563 is perh. a scribal error for _rauine_, RAVIN(E.]

1. _trans._ To ransom, redeem, deliver (a person); to recover (a heritage). _rare._

_a_ **1300** _Cursor M._ 23156 Þai sal be dempt al wit þe wick ..þat al þis werld þaim mai not raim. _c_ **1330** R. BRUNNE _Chron._ (1810) 185 We clayme þis our heritage..& þorgh hard woundes of þam salle reyme it eft.

2. To put to ransom, exact ransom from; hence, to spoil, plunder, deprive (_of_).

_c_ **1330** R. BRUNNE _Chron._ (1810) 43 Eilred has no þing. Eilred is so reymed [F. _raynt_] of his tresorie. **1340** _Ayenb._ 44 Sergons þet accuseþ..þet poure uolc and ham doþ raymi [F. _raembre_] and kueadliche lede. _a_ **1400–50** _Alexander_ 2488 Þis souerayn..þoȝt to ride & to rayme þe regions of barbres. _c_ **1460** _Towneley Myst._ xiii. 16 We ar so hamyd, Fortaxed, and ramyd.

b. To take away from a person. _rare._

_a_ **1400–50** _Alexander_ 2510 Þen am I raddest all our realme be raymed vs first.

c. ? To treat with violence, to torment. _rare_$^{-1}$.

_c_ **1380** WYCLIF _Wks._ (1880) 185 False marchauntis.. preisen hym most þat foulest rayme þ alle þe membris of crist falsly.

3. a. _absol._ To take at will. **b.** _trans._ To get possession of; to have control of; to rule over.

_c_ **1325** _Pol. Songs_ (Camden Soc.) 150 Thus me pileth the pore and pyketh ful clene, The ryche raymeth withouten eny ryht. _c_ **1330** R. BRUNNE _Chron._ (1810) 263 If he had.. gyuen þam..þer wynnyng ilk a dele, þat þei mot reyme & gyue. **1362** LANGL. _P. Pl._ A. I. 93 Kynges and knihtes scholde..rihtfuliche raymen the realmes a-bouten. **1393** _Ibid._ C. XIV. 96 Al that the ryche may reyme and ryghtfulliche dele.

raim, variant of RAME _v._, to cry.

raiment ('reɪmənt), _sb._ Forms: 5–7 **rayment,** (5–6 **-e**), 6 **rement,** 6– **raiment.** [Aphetic form of ARRAYMENT: cf. RAY _v._] Clothing, clothes, dress, apparel. Now _rhet._

_c_ **1440** _Promp. Parv._ 422/1 Rayment, or arayment.., _ornatus._ **1470–85** MALORY _Arthur_ VIII. xxviii, They brouȝt hym thyder in a fysshers rayment. **1523** FITZHERB. _Husb._ §151 An other symple man..seynge him to weare suche rayment, thynketh..that he maye were as good. _a_ **1625** FLETCHER _Women Pleased_ I. ii, Do you think to..keep me like an alms-woman in such rayment, Such poor unhandsome weeds? **1695** WOODWARD _Nat. Hist. Earth_ I. (1723) 72 Provision for Food, Rayment, and the like. **1781** COWPER _Truth_ 235 You..cast his filthy raiment at them all. **1814** CARY _Dante, Par._ XXV. 96 The white raiment destined to the saints. **1868** MISS BRADDON _Dead Sea Fr._ I. i. 3 Bright with the holiday raiment of busy multitudes.

fig. **1581** SIDNEY _Apol. Poetrie_ (Arb.) 41 The masking rayment of Poesie. _c_ **1600** SHAKS. _Sonn._ xxii, All that beauty that doth cover thee Is but the seemly raiment of my heart. **1819** SHELLEY _P. Bell 3rd_ Prol. 5 Wrapped in weeds of the same metre, The so long predestined raiment [etc.].

†**b.** With _a_ and _pl._: An article of clothing, a garment, a dress. _Obs._

1483 CAXTON _Cato_ F ij, Thou oughtest not to haue..ouer precyous Jewellys ne raymentes. **1527** _Lanc. Wills_ (1857) I. 6 The residue of my raymentes not beqwhethed. **1590** SPENSER _F.Q._ I. vi. 9 With ruffled rayments, and fayre blubbred face. **1655** STANLEY _Hist. Philos._ III. (1701) 122/1 A new Rayment for your use this Winter.

fig. **1662** STILLINGFL. _Orig. Sacr._ I. i. §7 Error seldom walks abroad the world in her own raiments.

Hence †**'raiment** _v. trans._, to clothe; **'raimented** _ppl. a._, clothed (_lit._ and _fig._); **'raimentless** _a._, destitute of raiment.

1656 S. H. _Gold. Law_ 57 He robes, raiments, and ornaments him from head to foot. **1833** TENNYSON _Poems_ 16 All raimented in snowy white. **1861** BP. G. SMITH _Ten Weeks Japan_ xix. 272 Raimentless, naked, tattooed bodies. **1887** D. C. MURRAY & HERMAN _Traveller Returns_ ix. 132 No woman of Coerlea had ever before her been so gorgeously raimented.

raimondite ('reɪməndaɪt). _Min._ [Named in 1866 after A. _Raimondi_, an Italian scientist: see -ITE.] A hydrous sulphate of iron, occurring in hexagonal yellow crystals.

1872 WATTS _Dict. Chem._ 1st Suppl.

rain (reɪn), _sb._[1] Forms: 1 **reȝn, ræȝn,** 1–2 **rén,** 2 **rien,** 2–4 **rein,** (3 **-e**), 3 **reȝȝn,** 3–5, **rayn,** (4–6 **-e**), 3–6 **reyn,** (4–6 **-e,** ? 5 **reynne**), 4 **rene,** 4–5, 6 _Sc._ **rane,** 4–7 **raine,** 3– **rain.** [Comm. Teut.: OE. _reȝn, rén_ = OFris. _rein_ (mod. _reijn_), OS. _regan, -in_ (Du. _regen_), OHG. _regan_ (MHG., G. _regen_), ON. (Sw., Da.) _regn_, Goth. _rign._ There are no certain cognates outside of Teut.]

1. a. The condensed vapour of the atmosphere, falling in drops large enough to attain a sensible velocity; the fall of such drops.

_c_ **825** _Vesp. Psalter_ cxlvi. 8 Se oferwirð heofen mid wolcnum & ȝearwað eorðan reȝn. _a_ **1000** ÆLFRIC _Gen._ vii. 4 Ic..sende ren nu..ofer eorðan. **1154** _O.E. Chron._ (Laud MS.) an. 1117 Mid þunre & lihtinge & reine & haȝole. _a_ **1200** ORMIN 8622 Wel hallf feorþe ȝer..comm na reȝȝn onn eorþe. _c_ **1250** _Gen. & Ex._ 3265 Ðhunder, and leuene, and rein ðor-mong God sent. _c_ **1330** R. BRUNNE _Chron. Wace_ (Rolls) 6827 Þe arewes come so þykke so reyn. _c_ **1386** CHAUCER _Monk's T._ 183 In reyn with wilde beestes walked hee. —— _Prioress' T._ 222 Hise salte teeris trikled doun as reyn. _c_ **1449** PECOCK _Repr._ II. ii. 146 To couere him fro reyne and fro othir sturne wedris. **1535** STEWART _Cron. Scot._ III. 257 Fers as ane eill war new tane in the rane. **1635** SWAN _Spec. M._ iv. §2 (1643) 58 The rain, proceeding from those vapours which we call the clouds. **1710** ADDISON _Tatler_ No. 218 ¶2 A black Cloud falling to the Earth in long Trails of Rain. **1752** HUME _Ess. & Treat._ (1777) II. 90 There is a certain uniformity in the operation of the sun, rain, and earth. **1810** SCOTT _Lady of L._ V. xv, Fierce Roderick.. shower'd his blows like wintry rain. **1878** HUXLEY _Physiogr._ 41 We may fairly expect the formation of rain to be preceded by that of cloud.

b. In proverbial and allusive expressions. Also in fig. phr. _**to know enough to come in out of the rain**_, and varr., to be sensible enough to act prudently in a given situation (cf. RAIN _v._ 1).

_c_ **1250** _Long Life_ 3 in _O.E. Misc._ 156 Fair weder turneð ofte into reine. _c_ **1386** CHAUCER _Wife's Prol._ 732 Er þat thonder stynte, comth a reyn. **14..** in _Rel. Antiq._ I. 323 After droght commyth rayne. **1484** CAXTON _Fables of Æsop_ II. viii, After the rayne cometh the fair weder. **1599** H. BUTTES _Dyets drie Dinner_ B iv, Fooles..have the wit to keep themselves out of the raine. **1670** RAY _Eng. Prov._ 135 Small rain lays great dust. **1777** [see RAIN _v._ 3]. **1848** F. A. DURIVAGE _Stray Subjects_ 95 _Ham_ was one of 'em—_he_ was! He 'knew sufficient to get out of the rain'. **1884** 'MARK TWAIN' _Huck. Finn_ xiv. 122 De man dat think he kin settle a 'spute 'bout a whole chile wid a half a chile doan' know enough to come in out'n de rain. **1894** STEVENSON & OSBOURNE _Ebb-Tide_ I. vi. 102 You seem to think underwriters haven't got enough sense to come in out of the rain. **1920** 'SAPPER' _Bull-Dog Drummond_ ii. 47 Either, James, I am a congenital idiot, and don't know enough to come in out of the rain; or we've hit the goods. **1932** 'A. GILBERT' _Body on Beam_ i. 23 A girl who's lived..in Menzies Street knows when to come in out of the rain. **1941** B. SCHULBERG _What makes Sammy Run?_ i. 9 He didn't know enough to come in out of the rain and he died of..dumbness. **1973** J. WAINWRIGHT _Devil you Don't_ 47 Come on in, out of the rain, Sugden—your brain is growing moss.

c. _**rain or shine**_: see SHINE _sb._[1] 3 b.

2. _pl._ **a.** Showers of rain; rainfalls.

_a_ **900** _O.E. Martyrol._ 20 Mar. 40 Þære lyfte ȝecynd is þæt heo tehð to þa renas of þæm sealtan sæ. **971** _Blickl. Hom._ 51 Þas windas & þas reȝnas syndon ealle his. **1154** _O.E. Chron._ (Laud MS.) an. 1098 Þurh mycele renas þe ealles ȝeares ne ablunnon. _c_ **1200** _Vices & Virtues_ 143 Godd..wiðheld alle reines þrie hier & six moneþes. _a_ **1340** HAMPOLE _Psalter_ civ. 30 He set þaire raynys haghil. _c_ **1400** MAUNDEV. (Roxb.) vii. 23 Þare es na trubling of þe aer thurgh raynes. **1556** _Chron. Gr. Friars_ (Camden) 2 Thys yere felle gret raynes. **1625** N. CARPENTER _Geog. Del._ II. i. (1635) 5 The extraordinary Raines and showers which those places suffer. **1738** GRAY _Tasso_ 10 Swoll'n with new force and late descending rains. **1878** HUXLEY _Physiogr._ 48 The heavy tropical rains are usually confined to definite periods.

Prov. **1846** DENHAM _Prov._ (Percy Soc.) 54 Many rains, many rowans.

b. In India, the rainy season.

1616 SIR T. ROE _Jrnl._ (Hakluyt Soc.) I. 247 A storme of rayne called the Oliphant, vsuall at goeing out of the raynes. **1707** _Let._ in Orme _Hist. Fragments_ (1805) p. vi, We are heartily sorry that the rains have been so very unhealthy with you. **1776** _Trial of Nundocomar_ 65/2 Was it..before the rains that the army came there? **1879** SIR E. ARNOLD _Lt. Asia_ VIII. (1881) 236 Forty-five rains thereafter showed he those..and gave Our Asia light. **1895** MRS. CROKER _Village Tales_ (1896) 125 One rains he died.

c. _Naut._ A part of the Atlantic Ocean (see quots.), in which rain is frequent.

1727–41 CHAMBERS _Cycl._, _Rains_, in the sea-language, denote all that tract of sea to the northward of the equator, between 4 and 10 degrees of latitude; and lying between the meridian of Cape Verde, and that of the easternmost islands of the same name. **1803** VINCE in _Naval Chron._ X. 145 There are..constant calms in that part of the ocean called the _Rains._ **1867** SMYTH _Sailor's Word-bk._, _Rains_..exist between the north-east and south-east trade-winds, changing their latitude several degrees.

3. With indef. article: †**a.** A shower of rain. _Obs._

_a_ **1225** _Ancr. R._ 246 A muchel wind aliþ mid a lutel rein. _c_ **1250** _Gen. & Ex._ 3326 First he wenden it [manna] were a rein. _c_ **1385** CHAUCER _L.G.W._ 2411 _Phyllis_, Behynde him come a wynde and eke a rayne. _c_ **1420** _Pallad. on Husb._ III. 442 At euery rayn Do delue vp smal the mold. _a_ **1533** LD. BERNERS _Huon_ xiv. 39 A small rayne abatyth a grete wynd. **1597** MORLEY _Introd. Mus._ 69 It is no maruayle to see a Snayle after a Rayne to creep out of his shell.

b. A (specified) kind of rain (or shower).

1699 _Phil. Trans._ Abridg. (1731) III. 495 A small drizling Rain..increased to a very plentiful shower. **1711** SWIFT _Jrnl. to Stella_ 1 Aug., The queen and I..were both hindered by a sudden rain. **1782** _Encycl. Brit._ (1797) XV. 779/1 If the vapours..rise a little higher, we have a mist or fog. A little higher still, and they produce a small rain. **1853** G. J. CAYLEY _Las Alforjas_ II. 51 Set off in a mizzling rain. **1963** C. D. SIMAK _They walked like Men_ xxiv. 142 It was raining. Not much of a rain, just the beginning of a rain, cold and miserable.

4. a. _transf._ The descent of liquid or solid particles or bodies falling in the manner of rain; the collective particles or bodies thus falling. Also _fig._

1388 WYCLIF _Ecclus._ xliii. 20 An herte dredith on the reyn therof [snow]. _a_ **1541** WYATT in _Tottell's Misc._ (Arb.) 39 A rayne of teares, a clowde of darke disdayne. **1648** J. BEAUMONT _Psyche_ I. xxxviii, Wealth it self doth roll In to her bosom in a golden Rain. **1753** CHAMBERS _Cycl. Supp._ s.v., These rains of frogs always happen after very dry seasons. **1821** SHELLEY _Hellas_ 381 The batteries blazed, Kneading them down with fire and iron rain. **1847** TENNYSON _Princ._ Prol. 62 The fountain..playing, now A twisted snake, and now a rain of pearls. **1935** T. S. ELIOT _Murder in Cathedral_ ii. 75 A rain of blood has blinded my eyes. **1942** _R.A.F. Jrnl._ 2 May 4 The continuous rain of pamphlets in all languages told of the enemy's defeats. **1975** J. G. EVANS _Environment Early Man Brit. Isles_ iv. 81 It is difficult to work out vegetational structure from the pollen record due to the wide area from which the pollen 'rain' derives.

b. _fig._ of immaterial things.

1821 SHELLEY _Prometh. Unb._ III. iii. 119 The dew-mingled rain Of the calm moonbeams. **1820** —— _Skylark_ 35 From thy presence showers a rain of melody. **1893** MRS. C. PRAED _Outlaw & Lawmaker_ II. 229 To shield herself from the rain of kisses.

c. _spec._ A composition used in rockets, producing a shower of bright-coloured sparks.

1749 _Descr. Machine for Fireworks_ 12 Explosions of Serpents, Rains, and Stars. **1853** MORTIMER _Pyrotechny_ (ed. 2) 94 Golden Rain..Silver Rain.

5. _attrib._ and _Comb._ **a.** attributive or appositive, as _**rain-bag, -blast, -blur, -cloud, -course, -cult, -curtain, -dew, -ditch, -drift, -dust,**_ †_**-frost, -gem, -land, -light, -mist, -pearl, -pipe,**_ †_**-rift, -shine, -song, -spout, -squall, -stain, -storm, -tear,**_ †_**-time, -vapour, -washing,**_ †_**-weather, -world.**_

1634–5 BRERETON _Trav._ (Chetham Soc.) 66 Rain-water preserved in *rain-bags. **1863** G. M. HOPKINS _Poems_ (1967) 12 But if the *rain-blasts be unbound And from dank feathers wring the drops. **1930** E. POUND _XXX Cantos_ vii. 27 Passion to breed a form in shimmer of *rain-blur. **1839** _Trans. Meteorological Soc._ I. 40 _Nimbus_, or *_Rain Cloud_, is accumulated layers of the stratus, which dissolving falls as rain. **1846** RUSKIN _Mod. Paint._ I. II. III. iv. §2 The nearness of the rain-cloud..makes its hue of grey monotonous. **1812** SCOTT _Rokeby_ II. xiv, Hid in the shrubby *rain-course now. **1923** L. SPENCE _Gods of Mexico_ i. 11 We shall..attempt to descry..an incipient *rain-cult. **1926** M. LEINSTER _Dew on Leaf_ II. iii. 159 The *rain-curtain that swayed like a grey chiffon veil before Rhona's window. **1954** J. R. R. TOLKIEN _Fellowship of Ring_ I. viii. 146 Frodo heard a sweet singing running in his mind: a song that seemed to come like a pale light behind a grey rain-curtain. **1922** JOYCE _Ulysses_ 416 The air is impregnated with *raindew moisture. **1949** E. POUND _Pisan Cantos_ lxxiv. 12 Tovarish blessed without aim wept in the *rainditch at evening. **1910** W. DE MORGAN _Affair of Dishonour_ xiii. 207 The *rain-drift..strengthened ever from the seaward. **1912** GALSWORTHY _Inn of Tranquility_ 48 The mist had thickened to a white, infinitesimal *rain-dust. _a_ **1300** _Fragm. Pop. Sc._ (Wright) 232 Of hawel, of deu, of *reyn-forst, and hor-forst. **1931** BLUNDEN _To Themis_ 27 The impulses of April, the *rain-gems, the rose-cloud. **1930** T. S. ELIOT _Ash-Wednesday_ 18 Not On the mainland, in the desert or the *rain land. **1957** LD. HAILEY _Afr. Survey_ xiv. 1011 Subject to a fixed annual payment to the former 'rainland landholders'. **1904** W. H. HUDSON _Green Mansions_ x. 143 This subdued *rain-light did not last long. **1893** KIPLING _Seven Seas_ (1896) 76 Then softly as a *rain-mist on the sward, Came to the Rose the Answer of the Lord. **1936** _Discovery_ Aug. 242/2 A leaf which is slightly damp with dew or rain-mist. **1968** 'HAN SUYIN' _Birdless Summer_ vi. 136 The peaks were shrouded in rain-mist. **1879** O. WILDE in _Time_ Apr. 30 Brush the *rain-pearls from the eucharis. **1926** M. LEINSTER _Dew on Leaf_ II. iv. 191 Eastern music..was to him..as soft as whispered words of love, delicate as tumbling rain-pearls. **1889** F. A. KNIGHT _By Leafy Ways_ 12 It rouses the ire of the householder by stopping up the *rain-pipe. **1913** J. MASEFIELD _Daffodil Fields_ 92 The water..gurgled through the rain-pipe to the butt. **1969** _Sears, Roebuck & Co. Catal._ Spring/Summer 924/2 All guttering and rainpipes have double-locked seams and rolled edges for added strength. **13..** _E.E. Allit. P._ B. 368 Mony clustered clowde clef alle in clowteȝ, To-rent vch a *rayn-ryfte & rusched to þe vrþe. **1960** C. DAY LEWIS _Buried Day_ i. 15, I am still haunted by the *rainshine of orchards in the vale of Evesham. **1907** N. CURTIS _Indians' Bk._ 365 The Rain-Youth made the *rain-songs and gave them to the Navajos. **1954** J. R. R. TOLKIEN _Fellowship of Ring_ I. vii. 140 It seemed plain to them that the song was a rain-song, as sweet as showers on dry hills, that told the tale of a river from the spring in the highlands to the Sea far below. **1922** JOYCE _Ulysses_ 470 Boys from high school are perched on the..*rainspouts, whistling and cheering. **1962** _Publ. Amer. Dial. Soc._ XXXVIII. 38 _Rain spouts_ and _water spouting_ predominate in Midland territory. **1978** J. A. MICHENER _Chesapeake_ 488 The two Steeds, tumbling from their widow's walk, had caught momentarily on rainspouts edging the roof, and then fallen heavily into flowerbeds. **1849** N. KINGSLEY _Diary_ (1914) 80 A few *rain squalls headed off this forenoon to the NE. **1902** CONRAD _Youth_ 40 Before sunset a thick rain-squall passed over the two boats ..and that was the last I saw of them for a time. **1930** _Times Educ. Suppl._ 24 May 4/2 Dense rain-squalls forced her to deviate from her course. **1923** W. DE LA MARE _Riddle_ 183 The mosses and *rain-stains and frost-flowerings of centuries of autumns and winters. **1952** DYLAN THOMAS _Let._ 6 Nov. (1966) 381 This tumbling house whose every rain-stain..I know in my sleep. **1816** COLERIDGE _Lay Serm._ 348 The rainbow on a fast-sailing *rain-storm. **1905** _Macmillan's Mag._ Nov. 42 Everything European was washed off, as is paint off a woman's face in a rain-storm. **1979** 'A. BLAISDELL' _No Villain need Be_ ix. 147 Sunday morning broke bright and clear..which was normal for Southern California after a rainstorm. **1909** E. POUND _Personae_ 13 Cloud and *rain-tears pass they fleet! _c_ **1425** _St. Mary of Oignies_ I. ix. in _Anglia_ VIII. 142/33 She..in þe *rayne-tyme come home ageyne vntouched. **1922** JOYCE _Ulysses_ 416 Those burgeoning stars overhead, rutilant in thin *rainvapour. **1886** HARDY _Mayor Casterbr._ II. xxii. 306 The walls..had been worn by years of *rain-washings to a lumpy crumbling surface. _c_ **1520** L. ANDREWE _Noble Lyfe_ in _Babees Bk._ 219 In fayre weder he reioyseth sore, but whan it is *rayne weder, than it singeth selden. **1970** T. HUGHES _Crow_ 43, I am the uncrowned Of the *rainworld.

b. Instrumental, chiefly with pa. pples., as _**rain-affected, -awakened, -beat, -beaten, -bedraggled,**_ †_**-berun, -bleared, -blown,**_

-blurred, -born, -bound, -bright, -bruised, -burdened, -cold, -darkened, -dishevelled, -drenched, -fed, -filled, -flawed, -fragrant, -gorged, -heavy, -laden, -laid, -logged, -loud, -molested, -murmured, -pitted, -pocked, -rusted, -scented, -shimmery, -sleeked, -slicked, -soaked, -sodden, -stained, -starred, -streaked, -sunken, -sweet, -swept, -varnished, -washed, -weathered, -wet, -worn adjs.

1905 *Daily Chron.* 26 July 1/7 A brilliant innings by Darling was the redeeming feature of Australia's batting on a *rain-affected wicket at Manchester. **1962** *Times* 30 Aug. 3/3 Essex won the toss, decided to bat on a rain-affected wicket. **1976** J. SNOW *Cricket Rebel* 26 The rain affected wicket was a little suspect all through. **1820** SHELLEY *Skylark* 58 *Rain-awakened flowers. **1598** BP. HALL *Sat.* IV. iii. 22 Figures halfe Obliterate In *rain-beat Marble. *a* **1450** *Fysshynge w. Angle* (1883) 2 *Reyn beton..and hys clothes torne. *a* **1529** SKELTON *Col. Cloute* 55 Though my ryme be ragged,..Rudely rayne beaten. **1606** J. REYNOLDS *Dolarnys Primerose* D iv b, T'haue deckt, and trim'd, this now rainbeaten face. **1914** W. B. YEATS in *Poetry* (Chicago) May 60 The pale unsatisfied ones Appear and disappear..With all their ancient faces like rain-beaten stones. **1932** D. GASCOYNE *Roman Balcony* 7 From the rain-beaten roses under the balcony. **1909** *Daily Chron.* 21 Aug. 1/2 (*heading*) *Rain-bedraggled Suffragettes removed by Police. **1922** JOYCE *Ulysses* 434 Her dark den furtive, rainbedraggled. *c* **1420** *Pallad. on Husb.* VII. 73 In londis wete, or ellis *rayn bironne. **1849** M. ARNOLD *Strayed Reveller*, Grey, *rain-blear'd statues. **1917** R. GRAVES *Fairies & Fusiliers* 24 I'm away to the *rain-blown hill. **1901** 'L. MALET' *Hist. Sir R. Calmady* V. i. 384 Actuality of *rain-blurred, wind-scourged town without, and anger-begetting memories of Brockhurst within. **1965** M. MORRIS in *Overland* XXXI. iii. 11 A gateway that still bore, rain-blurred and tattered, the printed notices. **1862** G. M. HOPKINS *Poems* (1967) 114 Then while the *rain-born arc glows higher Westward on his sinking sire. **1864** D. G. MITCHELL *Sev. Stor.* 45 A stranger who is *rain-bound in the opposite inn. **1818** MILMAN *Samor* 344 Freshens the circuit of the *rain-bright grove. **1916** D. H. LAWRENCE *Amores* 130 The *rain-bruised leaves are suddenly shaken. **1932** D. GASCOYNE *Roman Balcony* 15 Clouds rear, Dark and ominous, *rain-burdened. **1916** E. POUND *Lustra* 22 Grey olive leaves beneath a *rain-cold sky. **1928** V. WOOLF *Orlando* v. 224 Her eyes slowly lowered themselves down and down till they came to the *rain-darkened earth. **1962** I. MURDOCH *Unofficial Rose* i. 13 Her bright hair..hidden now except where a few rain-darkened ends clung to her neck. **1917** D. H. LAWRENCE *Look! We have come Through!* 56, I listen For the sluicing of their *rain-dishevelled petals. **1853** TALFOURD *Castilian* V. iv, Not a scent Of *rain-drench'd flower. **1901** *Contemp. Rev.* Mar. 437 This process of disafforesting is ruinous in a rain-drenched country. **1932** D. GASCOYNE *Roman Balcony* 75 To wait in the weary, rain-drenched queues. **1979** *Arizona Daily Star* 5 Aug. C1/4 The drive found the rain-drenched fairway. **1892** KIPLING *Barrack-Room Ballads* 192 Till he heard as the roar of a *rain-fed ford the roar of the Milky Way. **1979** *Nature* 27 Sept. 251/3 Some good progress has certainly been made in research on dry-land farming, largely aimed at reducing risks in cultivation in rainfed areas. **1942** W. FAULKNER *Go down, Moses* 356 The tent-flap falling on the same out-waft of faint and *rain-filled light. **1963** A. LUBBOCK *Austral. Roundabout* 4 Across the paddock the sheen of water glittered from the rain-filled dams. *a* **1918** W. OWEN *Poems* (1963) 95 Or be you in the gutter where you stand, Pale *rain-flawed phantom of the place. **1916** JOYCE *Portrait of Artist* (1969) 228 The brother's face was bent upon her fair *rainfragrant hair. **1917** KIPLING *Diversity of Creatures* 404 Rain on *rain-gorged channels raised the water-levels round them. **1943** D. GASCOYNE *Poems 1937–1942* 59 Beside the stolid opaque flow Of rain-gorged Thames. **1942** W. FAULKNER *Go down, Moses* 240 Now the woods ahead of them and the *rain-heavy air were one uproar. **1916** JOYCE *Portrait of Artist* (1969) v. 176 The *rainladen trees of the avenue evoked in him, as always, memories of the girls and women in the plays of Gerhart Hauptmann. **1921** W. DE LA MARE *Mem. Midget* viii. 47 We..mounted into a four-wheeled cab, and once more were in motion in the *rain-laid dust. **1970** G. E. EVANS *Where Beards wag All* viii. 90 On some Suffolk farms it was used in the 'fifties, though admittedly for special jobs like..the saving of wind- or rain-laid crops. **1960** T. HUGHES *Lupercal* 27 *Rain-logged, wind-unroofed, The manor farm hulked its last use As landmark. **1926** A. HUXLEY *Two or Three Graces* 173 Peddley broke the *rain-loud silence. **1845** LONGFELLOW *To Old Danish Songbook* in *Poems* (1846) 377 Yellow are thy time-worn pages, As the russet, *rain-molested Leaves of autumn. **1942** W. FAULKNER in *Story Mag.* May–June 51/2 The tent, the *rain-murmured canvas globe, was filled with it once more. **1916** H. G. WELLS *Mr. Britling* II. iii. 285 Men shouted and women sobbed and cowered, and flares played upon the *rain-pitted black waves. **1931** V. WOOLF *Waves* 227 One bone lay *rain-pocked and sun-bleached. **1947** AUDEN *Age of Anxiety* (1948) ii. 49 O the drains are clogged, *Rain-rusted, the roofs of the privies Have fallen in. **1818** KEATS *Endym.* I. 100 *Rain-scented eglantine. **1905** *Academy* 21 Oct. 1103/1 The rabbit that scuttled before us, the league-footing hare That shot from her form with tawny and *rain-sleeked coat. **1964** *Listener* 9 Jan. 67/1 In darkness outside Foxes and rain-sleeked stones and the dead. **1970** *Globe & Mail* (Toronto) 28 Sept. 12/4 She braked and skidded on *rain-slicked pavement but had no real chance to stop. **1789** WOLCOTT (P. Pindar) *Subj. for Painters* Wks. 1812 II. 135 Drooping *rain-soak'd fowls. **1890** KIPLING *Departmental Ditties* (ed. 4) 94 The rotten, rain-soaked *khud.* **1975** N. LUARD *Robespierre Serial* iii. 11 They'd gathered in his suite at the Vendôme as soon as they got back from the Loti, without even pausing to change their rain-soaked clothes. **1904** *Westm. Gaz.* 10 May 2/1 The Cossacks were drawn up on a large, *rain-sodden, muddy field. **1978** *Cornish Guardian* 27 Apr. 4/8 In the second half it was the clay club who played the game to suit the rain-sodden conditions. **1895** M. PEMBERTON *Impregnable City* II. xiii. 270, I..watched for a while the sleeping island through the *rain-stained glass. **1958** L. DURRELL *Balthazar* iii. 62 The gonfalons bellied like sails in the *rain-starred afternoon. **1956** H. GOLD *Man who was not with It* (1965) xii. 100 The carnival smelled the same, and The *rain-streaked sign swung there. **1980** *Jrnl. R. Soc. Arts* July 530/1 She made an artificial stone, but this was nothing like the dismal, rain-streaked concrete of today. **1916** BLUNDEN *Harbingers* 20 *Rainsunken roof, grown green and thin For sparrows' nests and starlings' nests. **1913** W. DE LA MARE *Peacock Pie* 127 Feathered birds in the *rain-sweet sky. **1932** BLUNDEN *Face of England* 177 Those blackening *rain-swept fields. **1978** R. LUDLUM *Holcroft Covenant* xxxi. 366 His last assignment had been at Kennedy Airport during a rainswept night when a cordon of police surrounded the glistening fuselage of a British Airways 747. **1867** J. R. LOWELL in *Atlantic Monthly* July 99 The candle she held in the door, From *rain-varnished tree-trunk Flashed fainter. **1870** MORRIS *Earthly Par.* III. iv. 231 The *rain-washed fields from hedge to hedge are bare. **1965** *New Statesman* 19 Nov. 803/1 We shared a rainwashed picnic with some shy, boyish chaps. **1940** J. BETJEMAN *Old Lights for New Chancels* 39 The *rain-weathered streets of adjacent Rumsaa. **1916** D. H. LAWRENCE *Amores* 49 All round the yard it is cluck, my brown hen, Cluck, and the *rain-wet wings. **1928** E. SITWELL *Five Poems* 16 The airs like rain-wet shrinking petals curl. **1904** W. DE LA MARE *Henry Brocken* vi. 51 She trod with cautious foot and peering eye the green, *rainworn paths. **1968** T. KINSELLA *Nightwalker* 11 A rain-worn, delicate Stone shape.

c. Objective, etc., as ***rain-bearer, -giver; rain-aboding, -bearing, -bringing, -dropping, -repellant, -repelling, -resistant, -resisting*** adjs.; also ***rain-tight.***

1640 G. ABBOTT *Job Paraphr.* 229 A *rain-aboding wind gives fore-knowledge of it. **1878** HUXLEY *Physiogr.* 42 South-west winds act as the chief *rain-bearers to our islands. **1922** W. G. KENDREW *Climates of Continents* v. 25 But in the south, south-west winds begin to make their appearance and the southern limit of the [Sahara] desert is found about 18° N. lat. where these *rain-bringing winds become predominant in summer. **1946** F. E. ZEUNER *Dating Past* vii. 203 The secondary effects of the glaciation.. affected the Mediterranean, through the deviation of many rain-bringing depressions. **1632** LITHGOW *Trav.* x. 429 There Fabrickes are..of smoake-torne straw..and *Raine-dropping watles. **1922** W. G. KENDREW *Climates of Continents* xx. 110 The south-west monsoon is essentially the *rain-giver of India. **1927** P. M. LARKENS in *Sudan Notes & Rec.* IX. 46 But in spite of this it is Liwa's spirit, and not *Mbali*, that is supposed to be the rain-giver here. **1968** *Daily Tel.* 4 Nov. 11/5 Best outfits..included a gleaming parchment kid coat, *rain-repellant. **1892** C. M. YONGE *Old Woman's Outlook* 178 Sheaves..built up in the *rain-repelling arrangements. **1958** *Times* 6 Oct. 13/1 And all the tweeds are mothproofed as well as *rain-resistant. **1963** *Economist* 20 July 256/2 Novelties (such as 'rain-resistant' petunias..from Japan). **1952** R. LEIGHTON *Compl. Bk. Dog* (rev. ed.) viii. 126 The outer-coat [of the Alsatian] is also close,..so that it is *rain-resisting.

6. Special Combs.: **rain-ball** *dial.* (see quot.); **rain-band**, a dark band in the solar spectrum, caused by the presence of water-vapour in the atmosphere; **rain-bath**, a shower- or spray-bath; **rain-belt**, a stretch of land much subject to rain; also *fig.*; **rain bonnet** chiefly *U.S.*, a plastic fold-up bonnet worn as a protection against the rain; **rain boot** *U.S.* (see quot. 1975); **rain-box**, a contrivance used in a theatre for imitating the sound of rain; **rain-cap**, a cap worn as a protection against rain (so ***rain-cloak, -clothes***, etc.); **rain-cape**, a waterproof cape (CAPE *sb.*[2] 3) furnishing protection from rain; hence **'raincaped** *a.*, wearing a rain-cape; **rain-chamber**, in metal-working, a compartment in which noxious fumes are condensed by the action of spray (Knight *Dict. Mech.* 1875); **rain-charm**, an object, action, or incantation used by a rainmaker to summon rain; **rain-chart** = *rain-map*; **rain check, cheque** chiefly *U.S.*, (*a*) a ticket given to a spectator at an outdoor event providing for a refund of his entrance money or admission at a later date, should the event be interrupted by rain; *transf.*, a ticket allowing one to order an article before it is available, and to collect it when it becomes so; (*b*) *fig.* (see quot. 1930); also, esp. in phr. *to take a rain check on*, to reserve the right not to take up a specified offer until such time as it should prove convenient; **raincoat**, a coat worn as a protection against rain; used *attrib.* of someone or something thought to be lewd or unseemly, esp. in phr. ***raincoat brigade***, disreputable, raincoat-clad, frequenters of cinemas that show pornographic films (also in extended use); hence **'raincoated** *a.*, wearing a raincoat; **rain crow** *U.S.*, the yellow-billed or black-billed cuckoo, *Coccyzus americanus* or *C. erythrophthalmus*; cf. RAINBIRD 2; **rain-cuckoo** = RAIN-BIRD 2; **rain dance**, a dance performed by a tribal group in the hope of summoning rain; **rain date** *U.S.*, an alternative date upon which an outdoor activity can be held if rain should cause the intended date to be unsuitable; **rain-day** *Meteorol.*, a day, commencing for statistical purposes at 9 a.m. G.M.T., on which the recorded rainfall is not less than 0·01 inch or 0·2 mm.; **rain-doctor**, one who professes to bring rain by incantations; **rain dog** (see DOG *sb.*[1] 10 a and quot.); **rain-door**, an outside door in Japanese houses; **rain-fly**, a blood-sucking, greyish fly, *Hæmatopota pluvialis*, of the family Tabanidæ; **rain frog**, a name used in North and Central America for a small tree frog or spring peeper belonging to the genus *Hyla*; **rain-gauge**, an instrument measuring the amount of the rain-fall; **rain-glass**, a barometer; **rain-god**, the god who has control of the rain; also **rain-goddess**; **rain-goose** (also *rein goose*), the red-throated diver (*Colymbus septentrionalis*); **rain-hat, hood**, a head-covering designed spec. to afford protection against the rain; **rain jacket**, a short raincoat designed in the shape of a jacket; also, a small protective covering worn by a dog; **rain-jungle** = RAIN FOREST; **rain-king**, rain personified as a king; **rain load**, the weight of rain on an airship; †**rain-machine** = *rain-gauge*; **rain-map**, a map showing the distribution of the rainfall over a certain area; **rain-mark, -pit**, an indentation made in the ground by a rain-drop (so ***rain-pitting, -print, -spot***); **rain-plover** (see quot.); **rain-procession**, a ceremonial procession made in the hope of obtaining rain; **rain-quail**, the Indian and African quail (*Coturnix coromandelicus*), abundant in some parts of India during the rainy season; **rain-shadow**, an area of small annual rainfall, brought about because it is sheltered from prevailing rain-bearing winds by a range of hills (see also quot. 1955); hence **rain-shadowing**, the action of producing a rain-shadow; **rain-stone**, a stone believed to possess certain qualities and used in primitive rain-making rituals; **rainsuit**, a jacket and leggings designed to protect one against the rain; **rain-temple**, a temple in which supposedly rain-provoking rituals are enacted; **rain-tree**, (*a*) an evergreen shrub, *Brunfelsia undulata*, of the family Solanaceæ, native to Jamaica and bearing white, bell-shaped flowers; (*b*) = GUANGO, SAMAN[2]; †**rain-vault**, a compluvium; **rain-wash**, the effect of rain in washing away earth, etc.; also, the matter thus washed away; **rainwear** (see quot. 1953). See also RAIN-BIRD, -BOW, -DROP, -FALL, FOREST, -FOWL, -SHOWER, -WATER.

1888 R. ABERCROMBY *Weather* iii. 78 In Lancashire, the festoons [of cloud] are called '*rainballs', and are only considered a sign of rain. **1882** PIAZZI SMYTH in *Knowledge* II. 294 That water-vapour band..has, therefore, been called, the '*rain-band'. *Ibid.* 'Rain-band spectroscopes' have been specially constructed by..opticians. **1887** *Nature* XXXV. 588/2 The intensity of the rainband is observed and recorded. **1896** *Allbutt's Syst. Med.* I. 340 Hip-baths, shower or *rain-baths. **1878** R. J. HINTON *Handbk. Arizona* vii. 201 The Santa Cruz [Valley], up to Tubac, marks the western limit of a notable *rain-belt. **1948** E. WAUGH *Loved One* 69 Water played everywhere from a buried network of pipes, making a glittering rain-belt waist-high. **1968** *Punch* 19 June 892/3 Weinsoff can have his name on his key tag.. hatband and sponge (and Mrs. Weinsoff on her pot holder, thimble and *rain bonnet). **1975** S. LAUDER *Killing Time on Corvo* vi. 53 She grinned chummily, tucking strands beneath the rain bonnet. **1951** *Sun* (Baltimore) (B ed.) 23 May 7/6 (Advt.), The only *rainboot made of Norlon, the wonder plastic!.. Folds neatly and compactly in a fit-in-your-purse plastic pouch. **1975** *Listener* 25 Dec. 845/1 American rain boots..are a kind of mid-calf galoshes which pull over your shoes. **1881** *Era Almanack* 38, I had pulled the rope connected with the '*rain-box'. **1827** CARLYLE *Germ. Rom.* I. 25 She drew a *rain-cap over her face. **1921** *Daily Colonist* (Victoria, B.C.) 1 Oct. 3/5 (Advt.), Children's good quality tan colored *raincapes to fit girls 4 to 12 years; made with lined hood. **1922** D. H. LAWRENCE in *Dial* Jan. 54 Fat cab-men, whose rubber rain-capes flapped like wings in the wind. **1976** *Southern Even. Echo* (Southampton) 1 Nov. (Advt. section) 8/6 Cindico Pushchair Raincape, royal blue, new, unwanted gift. **1977** *Observer* (Colour Suppl.) 7 Aug. 41/2 Dress properly for riding a bike... Avoid rain capes that flap about the wheels. **1922** JOYCE *Ulysses* 406 They hear the heavy tread of the watch as two *raincaped shadows pass the new royal university. **1973** A. PRICE *October Men* iii. 41 The rain-caped policeman materialised out of a gap in the hedge to stop the car. **1890** J. G. FRAZER *Golden Bough* I. iii. 403 The story that the body of Osiris enclosed in a coffer was thrown by Typhon into the Nile perhaps points to a custom of throwing the body of the victim, or at least a portion of it, into the Nile as a *rain-charm. **1936** E. E. EVANS-PRITCHARD in *Essays Soc. Anthrop.* (1962) viii. 188 On one occasion, at Tambura, a rainmaker buried his rain charm with the body of his son, in revenge for the latter's death, which he suspected to have been caused by magic. **1884** *St. Louis* (Missouri) *Post-Dispatch* 26 May 8/2 The heavy rain yesterday threw a damper over local operations. At each of the parks the audience had to be content with three innings and *rain checks. **1919** *Nat. Geogr. Mag.* Aug. 103 Even the sport-loving Britons are said to have admired and wondered at the American dough-boy..issuing occasional rain-checks in mid-inning when the downpour of bursting shells became too distracting. **1930** J. LAIT *Big House* 6 A parole is a 'rain check'. **1939** R. CHANDLER *Big Sleep* xi. 83 The Sternwoods have money. All it has bought them is a rain cheque. **1959** P. H. JOHNSON *Humbler Creation* xviii. 120 Westlake said, 'I'll take a rain-check. Be back.' Maurice, not certain of this idiom which he vaguely knew to be American, watched him go. 'Has he had enough?' he asked Kate... 'I should make a guess that he has to have a drink.' **1970** *Washington Post* 30 Sept. D3/5 (Advt.), If our stores cannot perform this work within the time indicated we will give you a raincheck enabling you to have work done within 30 days at the advertised price. **1976** L. DEIGHTON *Twinkle, Twinkle Little Spy* xiv. 141 'Let me take a rain-check.' 'On a love affair?' I said. **1976** *New Yorker* 26 Apr. 31/1 Levin's project is to array miniature open-air versions of a hundred New York restaurants side by side along the Central Park Mall on Saturday, May 22nd (rain check for Sunday). **1977** *Time* 14 Nov. 41/3 Unless he can cash his rain check by early 1978, the President will run smack into France's March elections. **1830** J. F. WATSON *Ann. Philadelphia* App. 52 As a defence from rain, the men wore '*rain coats', and the women 'camblets'. **1871** A. B. MITFORD *Tales Old Japan* II. 3 The farmers, dressed in their grass rain-coats. **1897** *Sears, Roebuck Catal.* 187/1 Men's Double Texture Mackintosh Rain Coats.. Made from good quality diagonal cloth.. suitable to wear in place of an overcoat. **1925** *Scribner's Mag.* Sept. 238/2 His raincoat was split up the back, under his belt. **1976** *Vogue* Jan. 22/4 Raincoats in rust, khaki and navy blue.. £74. **1976** *Times Lit. Suppl.* 9 July 842/2 The serious press in England is still being penalized for having so long tolerated less high-minded efforts at disclosure by the raincoat press. **1976** *Observer* 12 Dec. 24/4 Mindful of its duty to the raincoat brigade, however, the film abandons investigation at regular intervals to provide the expected, and inordinately protracted, bouts of titillation. **1977** *New Yorker* 23 May 33/2 O.K. for the raincoat brigade, but rather bland for the longhairs. **1930** W. FAULKNER *As I lay Dying* 74 Slowly he strokes his hands on his *raincoated thighs. **1974** D. FRANCIS *Knock Down* i. 10 The rain-coated assembly looked.. miserable. **1806** M. LEWIS *Jrnl.* 16 July in *Orig. Jrnls. Lewis & Clark Exped.* (1905) V. 205, I saw both yesterday and today the Cookkoo or as it is sometimes called the **rain craw*. **1831** J. J. AUDUBON *Ornith. Biogr.* I. 19 The Dutch farmers of Pennsylvania know it [*sc.* the yellow-billed cuckoo] better by the name of Rain Crow. **1872** E. COUES *Key to N. Amer. Birds* 190 American cuckoos ..are..noted for their loud jerky cries, which they are supposed to utter most frequently in falling weather, whence their popular name, 'rain crow'. **1880** G. W. CABLE *Grandissimes* xxviii. 237 The dismal ventriloquous note of the rain-crow. **1899** B. TARKINGTON *Gentleman from Indiana* viii. 118 The rain-crow that sat on the fence. **1917** T. G. PEARSON *Birds Amer.* II. 130/1 Both species are known as the 'Rain Crow' because of the belief—especially among farmers—that their guttural cry predicts rain. **1935** H. DAVIS *Honey in Horn* xv. 237 A rain-crow..sang like clanking a little copper bell. **1946** G. STIMPSON *Bk. about Thousand Things* 55 The American cuckoo is known to country people as the rain or storm crow because its plaintive note..is regarded as a sign of rain or storm. **1782** LATHAM *Gen. Syn. Birds* I. II. 535 Long-billed *Rain Cuckow. **1930** J. M. BUTTREE *Rhythm of Redman* 89 It is the privilege of all to improvise the new song for each *rain dance. **1968** E. MCCOURT *Saskatchewan* 6 Old Chief Sheepskin, nominally a Christian, summoned his braves to perform a rain dance. **1977** *Time* 18 Apr. 25/1 When the wet season in Northern California turned up bone dry, about 2,000 San Franciscans staged a modern rain dance in the Hyatt Regency Hotel. **1972** *Village Voice* (N.Y.) 1 June 34/5 The Blue Mountain Paper Parade will present choreographer Barbara Roan's latest work, 'Waystation/Truckers Only,' on Saturday, June 3, at 3 p.m. on the Brooklyn Heights Promenade... The *rain date is June 4. **1975** *New Yorker* 7 July 11/3 Wednesday, July 2, at 8:30 (rain date, July 3), 'La Traviata'. **1978** *Chicago* June 201/2 It's open house at the Durant's on June third.. Stop in between ten a.m. and five p.m. $1.50 admission. Rain date is June fourth. **1906** *Brit. Rainfall 1905* 123 This improvement may be traced by the steady increase in the number of *rain days reported. **1928** *Nature* 14 Apr. 591/2 The variations of the number of rain-days over the British Isles are much less than the corresponding variations of rainfall. **1976** *Southern Even. Echo* (Southampton) 2 Nov. 13/6 According to meteorological office statistics, rainfall in the city was more than double the average and the number of 'rain-days' ranked as the highest in 50 years. **1843** *The Rain Cloud* 213 Should rain happen to fall, the credit is given to the *rain-doctor. **1857** LIVINGSTONE *Trav.* (1861) 17 The chief Sechele was himself a noted rain-doctor. **1866** 'MARK TWAIN' in *Sacramento Union* 24 Aug. 3/2 What the sailors call '*rain dogs'—little patches of rainbow—are often seen drifting about the heavens in these latitudes. **1888** *Pall Mall G.* 12 Sept. 2/1 The *amado*, or outside *rain-doors, were slid in front of all the houses. **1921** E. STEP *Brit. Insect Life* 231 This is the Clegg or *Rain-fly.., the grey, dusty-looking Fly that you have no suspicion is sitting on your hand or neck until its sharp lancet is thrust into your flesh. **1952** E. F. DAGLISH *Name this Insect* 277 Rain-fly or Clegg... Common in fields, meadows, woods, and about hedgerows. **1958** J. CAREW *Black Midas* v. 79 A money-spider was struggling with a rain fly. **1971** *Country Life* 21 Oct. 1035/1, I am not partial to the bite of the rainfly. **1827** T. L. MCKENNEY *Sk. Tour to Lakes* 158 We found the few people who live near its mouth..[with] *rain frogs on the logs of their huts to sing them to repose. **1938** M. K. RAWLINGS *Yearling* i. 6 A rain frog sang a moment and then was still. **1958** J. CAREW *Wild Coast* iv. 59 Outside, rain frogs were complaining to the stars. **1962** S. WYNTER *Hills of Hebron* v. 70 From the dark hollows rain-frogs cracked sharp sad notes. **1769** HEBERDEN in *Phil. Trans.* LIX. 359 The *rain-gage..was fixed so high, as to rise above all the neighbouring chimnies. **1860** MAURY *Phys. Geog.* (Low) v. 105 Rivers are the rain-gauges of nature. **1862** *Athenæum* 26 July 121 The following may be depended upon as a *rain-glass. **1864** *Rain-god [see MGANGA]. **1884** A. J. EVANS in *Archæologia* XLIX. 108 The hill which is supposed to be the Rain-God himself. **1968** *New Larousse Encycl. Mythol.* 438 (*caption*) Tlaloc, the Aztec rain god enjoyed a similar popularity and was also one of the chief gods of the pantheon. **1904** *Rain-goddess [see *Earth-Mother* s.v. EARTH *sb.*[1] II.]. **1967** J. R. CRAWFORD *Witchcraft & Sorcery in Rhodesia* xii. 188 We go to *Hosana*, that is the rain goddess, and appeal to *Hosana* for rain. **1793** *Statist. Acc. Scot.* VII. 573 The birds are, eagles, marrots or auks, kingfishers, *rain geese, muir fowls. **1882** *Standard* 22 Aug. 2/5 Rein geese and brent geese were seen. **1921** *Daily Colonist* (Victoria, B.C.) 28 Oct. 7/1 (Advt.), Women's and children's *rain hats at $1.50 each. **1955** E. POUND *Classic Anthol.* IV. 208 With a crowd of rain-hats And clicking hoes Out goes the weed To mulch and rot. **1967** *Punch* 21 June 907/1 Prizes for the best set of answers include restrung celebrity-used rackets, foldaway rain hats and transistor radios for getting the cricket commentaries. **1977** *Chicago Tribune* 2 Oct. XIII. 4/1 Besides, you have only a mile and a half to go, and you have boots, raincoat, and rain hat. **1964** 'E. PETERS' *Flight of Witch* ii. 34 Did she go off wearing her *rain-hood, and her heavy shoes, a night like this? **1977** P. KEMP in P. Collenette *Winter's Tales 23* 49 She was busy.. untying a transparent plastic rain-hood that she was wearing over a rayon head-square. **1975** *Country Life* 29 May 1424/2 The newest thing in rainwear is the suit... Next to the suit, the *rain jacket is very much around. **1976** *Evening Times* (Glasgow) 1 Dec. 26/6 Rain jackets, royal, sky, red and yellow, all sizes from £8·99. **1960** *Spectator* 30 Sept. 493/2 The Brookes..stayed a hundred years as landgraves of an impoverished swatch of *rain-jungle. **1964** R. PERRY *World of Tiger* i. 3 There are..less than four thousand scattered over India,..from Goa to the rain-jungles of Assam. **1880** BLACK *White Wings* xx, There is a deeper gloom overhead; the *rain-king is upon us. **1928** C. F. S. GAMBLE *Story N. Sea Air Station* xv. 249 *Rain load also had to be reckoned with, which may go as far as 3,000 kg. **1767** HUXHAM in *Phil. Trans.* LVII. 446 One of the Thermometers is kept.. without Doors in the *Rain Machine. **1878** HUXLEY *Physiogr.* 46 A general view of the rainfall..is presented by the accompanying *rain-map. **1867** LYELL *Princ. Geol.* II. xv. I. 335 Tracks of worms..occasionally pass under the middle of a *rain-mark. **1841** *Penny Cycl.* XIX. 270/2 Foot-prints, *rain-pits, and hollows of every kind. **1871** A. C. RAMSAY in *Q. Jrnl. Geol. Soc.* XXVII. 250 The presence of sun-cracks and *rain-pittings in the Longmynd beds. **1879** *Encycl. Brit.* X. 294/1 *Sun-cracks, Rain-pittings*, &c. —Proofs may not infrequently be found that during deposition aqueous strata have been laid bare to air and sun. **1817** T. FORSTER *Nat. Hist. Swallowtribe* (ed. 6) 86 *Charadrius pluvialis*. Golden plover..*Rainplover. **1859** PAGE *Geol. Terms* *Rain-Prints. **1882** GEIKIE *Text-bk. Geol.* IV. i. 486 Ripple-marks, rain-prints, or sun-cracks. **1884** A. J. EVANS in *Archæologia* XLIX. 106 The Roman *rain-procession,..described by Petronius. **1902** H. J. MACKINDER *Britain & Brit. Seas* 165 This dryness to leeward of the heights has been termed their *rain-shadow. **1955** *Sci. News Let.* 2 Apr. 212/1 Prevailing winds..smack against the mountains, and are then forced down the eastern slopes. These winds are so strong they keep warm, moist air from the Gulf of Mexico from penetrating deep inland. The air is sinking rather than rising. Result: no moisture falls. Weathermen call this effect the rain shadow. **1974** M. PEISSEL *Great Himalayan Passage* vi. 112 This entire area is within what is known as the 'rain-shadow' of the Himalayas, a sheltered spot where clouds never break. **1936** *Geogr. Jrnl.* LXXXVII. 11 Valley routes have certain advantages as well as disadvantages for air travel. Among their advantages I would put..the finer weather, owing to local *rain-shadowing. **1897** *Allbutt's Syst. Med.* IV. 530 Round depressions resembling the impress of *rain-spots on soft sand. **1897** W. E. ROTH *Ethnol. Stud. N.-W.-Central Queensland Aborigines* xii. 167 The rain-stick, *koo-roo-mun-do*, is formed of a thin piece of a species of 'white' wood, about 20 inches long, on to the top of which is fixed a mass of the ordinary cementing-substance: into this the three '*rain-stones', pieces of white quartz-crystal, are stuck. **1932** *Times Lit. Suppl.* 1 Dec. 915/2 Such rain-stones may be of quartz, of which the transparency is suggestive of water. **1975** *Islander* (Victoria, B.C.) 2 Feb. 3/1 When the medicine man..wishes to produce rain he plunges his rain-stone in water, takes a split-top peeled cane in hand and beckons with it to the clouds. **1965** *Harper's Bazaar* Feb. 39 *News now, the *rainsuit*, newer still if it's trousers. **1966** *Daily Tel.* 14 Nov. 10/7 Not certain of the weather? Then for town or country a rainsuit could be the answer. **1974** M. HOYT *30 Miles for Ice Cream* x. 114 So I, for one, wear the rubber pants of a rain suit when I'm shanty-fishing. **1977** *New Yorker* 27 June 74/2 Six miles downstream, I had added..a rain suit, hood to heel. **1907** R. S. RATTRAY *Some Folklore Stories & Songs in Chinyanja* II. ix. 118 Next morning at dawn everyone comes together and they go to the *rain temple. **1911** J. G. FRAZER *Golden Bough: Magic Art* (ed. 3) I. v. 250 When the rains do not come..the people of Central Angoniland repair to what is called the rain-temple. **1878** *Nature* XVII. 349/1 The Tamia-caspia, or *rain tree of the Eastern Peruvian Andes. **1879** *Bull. U.S. Nat. Mus.* No. 13. 75 *Brunefelsia pubescens* Rain-tree... Flowers odorous before rain. **1911** *Chambers's Jrnl.* Feb. 206/1 The rain-tree ..can withstand extreme climatic fluctuations, needs but little care in its cultivation, and grows rapidly. **1924** RECORD & MELL *Timbers Trop. Amer.* 204 The 'samán' or rain tree ..belongs to this genus. **1939** R. C. MARSHALL *Silviculture Trinidad & Tobago* 119 Rain Tree..is a short-boled tree with an enormous wide spreading crown. **1961** *20th Cent.* Jan. 64 Rain-trees, whose leaves close up at night, enfolding moisture which in the morning the unfurling foliage discharges. **1963** [see GUANGO]. **1969** [see *monkey-pod (tree)* s.v. MONKEY *sb.* 18 b]. **1975** *Bangladesh Observer* 25 July 5/6 Rain-tree..is found in abundance all over Bangladesh. **1976** *Hortus Third* (L. H. Bailey Hortorium) 185/2 *Brunfelsia.. undulata*..Rain tree. Slender, evergreen shrub. **1552** HULOET, *Rayne volte, *Compluuius lacus*. **1876** A. H. GREEN *Phys. Geol.* iii. §2. 112 These accumulations of rain-borne decomposed rock go by the general term of '*Rain-wash'. **1896** *Geol. Mag.* Oct. 466 The rain and rain-wash loosen the light soil below and about the roots. **1942** Rain-wash [see BAD LANDS]. **1965** G. J. WILLIAMS *Econ. Geol. N.Z.* vii. 80/1 In his view all the components of the schist except the quartz and gold and such resistant heavy minerals as zircon were reduced to clay and generally removed by rain-wash. **1977** A. HALLAM *Planet Earth* 81/1 Because of the dominance of rainwash over other erosional forces, these features are most common in warmer climates. **1953** P. C. BERG *Dict. New Words* 134/1 **Rainwear*, garments suited for wearing in rain; e.g. 'Britain's Best Rainwear'. **1958** *People* 4 May 15/7 (Advt.), Have your suit for £1 down and add whatever else you need—rainwear, shoes, shirts, sportswear, etc. to your account. **1975** *Country Life* 6 Feb. 347/3 Ismat also sell..T-shirts and rainwear. **1977** J. AIKEN *Last Movement* i. 33 It was still pouring, so..Gina..put herself back into her red plastic rainwear.

rain (reɪn), *sb.*[2] *Obs.* exc. *dial.* Forms: 5–7 reyne, 6 raine, rayn(e, 9 *dial.* rein, rain. See also REAN. [a. ON. *rein* (Norw. *rein*, Sw. and Da. *ren*) = MLG. *rein*, OHG. *rain*, *rein* (G. *rain*), strip of land, esp. one left unploughed between fields or ridges, a balk, etc. Da. *ren* has also the sense of 'furrow' which is prominent in Eng.]

1. A strip of land, a ridge; a division between lands or fields.

1481 in *Ripon Ch. Acts* (Surtees) 346 Layland Raynes—Lidale Rayne—Turff-car Rayne—&c. **1541** *Mem. Ripon* (Surtees) III. 194 Et in decasu firmæ unius Rane voc. Sayntwilfryd Rane ad 10s. per annum 10s. 4d. **1608** in Peel *Spen Valley* (1893) 125 Followinge a certaine rayne or hedge devydinge Gomersall and Liversedge. **1819** in *Sheffield Gloss.* s.v., A line across meadows where has formerly been a hedge or a road is called the *rain*.

2. A furrow between the ridges or lands in a field.

1523 FITZHERB. *Husb.* §7 He seeth not, whether the plough go in rydge or rayne. *a* **1600** WYNNE *Hist. Gwedir Fam.* (1878) 54 They reaped the corne that grew in the raine ..as the corne in the ridge was not readie. **1611** COTGR., *Seillon*,..the narrow trench, reyne, or furrow, left betwene butt and butt for the drayning thereof. **1844** PALIN in *Jrnl. R. Agric. Soc.* V. I. 59 Commencing in the rein of the former butts and making the former ridges into reins.

†**b.** A small stream or ditch. *Obs. rare*−0.

1611 COTGR., *Ardoüe*, a little brooke, or reyne, that gently runnes along a field.

rain (reɪn), *v.* Forms: 1 (h)reᵹnian, 2–3 rein-, 3 reȝȝn-, 4 regne, reigne, reine, 4–5 reyne, 4–6 rayne, 4–7 *Sc.* rane, 4–7 raine, 5 reyn, reygne, (6 raigne, 7 reign), 3– rain. [OE. *reᵹnian* (rare) = MDu. *reghenen* (Du. *regenen*), OHG. *reganôn* (MHG. *regenen*, *regnen*, G. *regnen*), ON. *regna* (Sw. *regna*, Da. *regne*), f. *reᵹn* RAIN *sb.*[1] The usual form in OE. was the causative *riᵹnan*, *rínan* RINE *v.*]

I. Intransitive senses.

1. a. Impersonally. *it rains*: rain falls. Also in proverbial phr. ***it never rains but it pours***. ***to go*** (or ***come***) ***in when it rains*** (*U.S.*): to take measures for one's own safety; to exercise ordinary prudence; to shift for oneself (cf. RAIN *sb.*[1] 1 b).

c **1200** ORMIN 8694 He badd o Drihhtin Godd þat itt ta shollde reȝȝnen. **13..** *K. Alis.* 6450 Whan hit snywith, other rayneth. *c* **1380** WYCLIF *Sel. Wks.* III. 380 þof hit rayne on þo auter of þo parische chirche. **1430–40** LYDG. *Bochas* III. xxiv. 95 It may nother blowe thereon, nor reyn. **1523** LD. BERNERS *Froiss.* I. ccvii. 244 For moost part day and night it reyned without cease. **1697** DAMPIER *Voy.* I. 13 It rained very hard. **1711** SWIFT *Lett.* (1767) III. 151 It rained so this evening again, that I thought I should hardly be able to get a dry hour to walk home in. **1854** EARL CARLISLE *Diary* 115 It has really taken to rain rather frequently. **1882** OUIDA *Maremma* I. 197 If it would only have rained, how welcome it would have been.

Phr. **1726** ARBUTHNOT (*title*) It cannot rain but it pours; or London strow'd with rarities. *a* **1852** F. M. WHITCHER *Widow Bedott Papers* (1856) iii. 36 He was a *saftly* feller—dident scarcely know enough to go in when it rained. **1866** 'MARK TWAIN' *Lett. from Sandwich Islands* (1937) 84 A.. majority..that knew just about enough to come in when it rained. **1873** —— *Choice Humorous Wks.* III. 524, I perceive that thou art none of them that know not to come in when it doth rain. **1893** EARL DUNMORE *Pamirs* I. 292 As it never rains but it pours, news of another disaster was rife in the city in the evening. **1906** *Springfield* (Mass.) *Weekly Republ.* 12 July 2 Every citizen of Vermont who is capable of going in when it rains ought to understand [etc.]. **1923** E. F. WYATT *Invis. Gods* I. ii. 19 Hetherington Marshfield, who doesn't know enough to go in when it rains!

b. In indirect passive. Const. *on*, *upon*.

1382 WYCLIF *Ezek.* xxii. 24 Thou art the vnclene loond, not reynyd togidir [COVERDALE, etc. rayned vpon] in the dai of woodnes. **1561** WINȜET *Cert. Tractates* Wks. 1888 I. 14 Ane vnclene land, quhilk is not raynit vpon. **1840** [R. E. HILL] *Pinch of Snuff* 129 Carrying a duck in a rained-upon sedan chair. **1925** R. TORRENCE *Hesperides* 60, I was weak as a rained-on bee. **1937** *Burlington Mag.* June 262/1 Rained-on, as it were, by Nature. **1972** J. GORES *Dead Skip* xvi. 113 Two big recently rained-on cardboard boxes of trash.

2. Of the Deity, the sky, clouds, etc.: To send or pour down rain.

c **950** *Lindisf. Gosp.* Matt. v. 45 He..hreᵹnað [*Rushw.* reᵹneð] ofer soðfæsta & unsoðfæste. *c* **1290** *S. Eng. Leg.* 284/235 þat weder bi-gan to reinie faste. *c* **1374** CHAUCER *Troylus* III. 502 þe walken shop hym for to reyne. **1382** WYCLIF *Gen.* ii. 5 The Lord God forsothe had not reyned vpon the erthe. *a* **1550** *Droichis Part of Play* 35 in *Dunbar's Poems* (1893) 315 The skyis raind quhen he wald [scowle]. **1605** SHAKS. *Lear* III. vii. 62 Poore old heart, he holpe the Heauens to raine. **1697** DRYDEN *Æneid* Ded. b 4, They make Æneas..a kind of a St. Swithen Heroe, always raining. **1833** TENNYSON *Lady of Shalott* IV. i, Heavily the low sky raining Over tower'd Camelot.

fig. **1597** SHAKS. *2 Hen. IV*, II. iii. 59 To raine vpon Remembrance with mine Eyes, That it may grow, and sprowt. **1642** FULLER *Holy & Prof. St.* II. xv. 107 Good reason therefore Northern Scholars should be most watered there, where Northern Benefactours rained most.

transf. **1883** GRESLEY *Gloss. Coal-mining* 198 An underground place is said to rain when water drops freely from the roof.

3. Of rain: To fall.

a **1300–1400** *Cursor M.* 1835 (Gött.) þis rain rained euer onane. **1377** LANGL. *P. Pl.* B. XVII. 333 The reyne þat reyneth þere we reste sholde. *c* **1440** *Gesta Rom.* lvi. 239 (Harl. MS.) Yf..þe Reyne Rayne vppon boþe myn yen [etc.]. **1523** [see GOSLING 1. *Prov.*]. **1601** SHAKS. *Twel. N.* V. i. 401 The raine it raineth every day. **1777** BRAND *Pop. Antiq.* 53 Happy (says the Proverb) is..the Corpse the Rain rains on.

4. *transf.* **a.** Of substances other than water: To fall from the sky or through the air in the manner of rain, esp. in small particles.

c **1200** *Trin. Coll. Hom.* 99 God let hem reine manne. *c* **1330** R. BRUNNE *Chron. Wace* (Rolls) 2623 þre dayes in his tyme reyned blod. *c* **1450** *Mirour Saluacioun* 1477 Manna also yt in desert reynyde. **1655** FULLER *Ch. Hist.* II. iii. §33 Bloud reigned in some parts of the Land. **1820** SHELLEY *Vis. Sea* 29 The intense thunder-balls which are raining from heaven. **1842** TENNYSON *Sir Galahad* 12 Perfume and flowers fall in showers, That lightly rain from ladies' hands.

b. Of tears: To fall like rain.

c **1374** CHAUCER *Troylus* V. 1336 The terys which þat fro myn eyen reyne. **1602** SHAKS. *Ham.* IV. v. 166 On his graue raines many a teare. **1667** MILTON *P.L.* IX. 1122 They sate them down to weep, nor onely Teares Rained at thir Eyes. **1860** THACKERAY *Lovel* vi, Genuine tears rained down her yellow cheeks.

c. Of immaterial things: To descend, fall, come, etc., in a manner comparable to the fall of rain.

1393 LANGL. *P. Pl.* C. xv. 24 Grace groweth nat til goode wil gynne reyne. **1412–20** LYDG. *Chron. Troy* I. v, The foyson & plente Of kyngly fredom.. So fulsomely gan there to reygne and snowe. **1535** COVERDALE *Job* xx. 23 God shal ..cause his battayll to rayne ouer him. **1602** MARSTON *Antonio's Rev.* III. ii, The curse of Heaven raines In plagues unlimited through all his daies. **1801** J. ADAMS *Wks.* (1854) IX. 585 Ennui, when it rains on a man in large drops, is worse than one of our north-east storms. **1847** TENNYSON *Princ.* v. 490 As from a giant's flail, The large blows rain'd.

5. *it rains in*: rain enters or penetrates. Also *transf.* with other subjects (cf. 4).

1596 *Vestry Bks.* (Surtees) 270 Mendinge the church porch and over hed above where it did rayne in. **1664** J. WEBB *Stone-Heng* (1725) 95 The Impluvium or open Part where it rained in. **1771** FOOTE *Maid of B.* II. Wks. 1799 II. 222 The house..is a little out of repair; not that it rains in.. at above five or six places. **1865** W. G. PALGRAVE *Arabia* I. 72 Invitations rained in on all sides.

II. Transitive senses.

6. a. Impersonally. *it rains*: There is a shower of (something falling from above or through the air).

a **1225** *Ancr. R.* 98 (MS. C) þach hit reine arewen, ich habe a nede erende. *c* **1275** LAY. 3895 þreo daiȝes hit reinede blod. *a* **1400–50** *Alexander* 566 þen rekils it vnruydly & raynes doune stanys. **1535** COVERDALE *Luke* xvii. 29 It rayned fyre and brymstone from heauen. **1596** BARLOW *Three Serm.* iii. 141 In Bauaria it rained corne, of which much bread was baked. **1653** WALTON *Angler* vii. 152 It should rain none but water Frogs. **1738–** [see CAT AND DOG 2]. **1753** CHAMBERS *Cycl. Supp.* s.v. *Rain*, [They] acounted it a miracle that it rained earth and sulphur upon them. **1821** SHELLEY *Hellas* 604 It has rained blood. **1871** W. D. HOWELLS in *Atlantic Monthly* Dec. 722/2 It was raining one of those cold rains.

fig. **1596** SHAKS. *1 Hen. IV*, v. i. 47 It rain'd downe Fortune showring on your head. **1606** —— *Ant. & Cl.* III. xiii. 85 Bestow'd his lips on that vnworthy place, As it rain'd kisses. **1746** H. WALPOLE *Lett.* (1857) II. 24 Why, it rains princes. **1876** C. M. DAVIES *Unorth. Lond.* (ed. 2) 110 It has positively rained tracts.

b. Phr. ***if it should rain porridge, he would want his dish*** and varr., denoting a person's recurrent bad luck or management.

1670 J. RAY *Coll. Eng. Proverbs* 191 If it should *rain* pottage, he would want his dish. **1732** T. FULLER *Gnomologia* 112 If it should rain Porridge, he'd want a Dish. **1889** C. H. SPURGEON *Salt-Cellars* 257 If it rained porridge, the lazy man would have no basin. **1950** K. S. PRICHARD *Winged Seeds* ii. 29 Unluckiest man ever I knew. If it was raining pea soup, he'd only have a fork. **1970** R. BEILBY *No Medals for Aphrodite* (1971) v. 169 Gawd, we're an unlucky battalion, we are. If it was rainin' virgins we'd be washed away with a poofta, dinkum!

7. a. Of personal or other agents: To pour or shower down (something falling through the air like rain).

a **1300** *Cursor M.* 2841 Ouer lauerd raind o þam.. Dun o lift, fire and brinstan. **1390** GOWER *Conf.* II. 183 The myhti god began to reyne Manna fro heuene doun to grounde. **1542** UDALL *Erasm. Apoph.* 166b, Iupiter in fourme of a shoure raynyng droppes of golde. **1598** SHAKS. *Merry W.* v. v. 21 Let the skie raine Potatoes. **1697** DRYDEN *Virg. Georg.* IV. 119 Nor shaken Oaks such Show'rs of Acorns rain. **1768–74** TUCKER *Lt. Nat.* (1834) II. 312 He could have rained us food from heaven. **1818** KEATS *Endym.* II. 427 Another [Cupid]..Rain'd violets upon his sleeping eyes. **1855** MACAULAY *Hist. Eng.* xxi. IV. 591 He rained shells and redhot bullets on the city. **1939** *Ann. Reg. 1938* 260 Air-raids rained bombs on Barcelona, Tarragona, and a number of peaceful seaside towns where there was no trace of any military objective. **1977** *Time* 14 Mar. 53/1 Fans rained bottles and cans on to the ground.

fig. **1882** BLUNT *Ref. Ch. Eng.* II. 9 Raining coronets upon their heads and wealth into their coffers.

b. To shed (tears) copiously.

1588 SHAKS. *L.L.L.* v. ii. 819 Raining the teares of lamentation. **1820** SHELLEY *Ode to Liberty* viii, What if the tears rained through thy shattered locks Were quickly dried? **1875** JOWETT *Plato* (ed. 2) I. 240 His eyes rain tears.

c. With immaterial object.

a **1340** HAMPOLE *Psalter* xvii. 13 Prechours, þe whilk.. raynes down godis word till oþer. **1382** WYCLIF *Job* xx. 23 That he..reyne vp on hym his bataile. *c* **1586** C'TESS PEMBROKE *Ps.* LXIX. x, Downe upon them fury raine. **1632** MILTON *L'Allegro* 122 Ladies, whose bright eies Rain influence. **1726** POPE *Odyss.* XVII. 49 Rains kisses on his neck, his face, his eyes. **1820** SHELLEY *Skylark* 30 The moon rains out her beams, and heaven is over-flowed. **1878** BOSW. SMITH *Carthage* 152 The blows rained by practised pugilists on one another.

8. a. In *passive*: To be showered down. *rare.*

1647 HAMMOND *Power of Keys* vii. 140 Manna ceased to be rain'd from heaven. **1756** C. LUCAS *Ess. Waters* II. 28 Sometimes salt instead of fresh water has been rained in different places.

b. *pass.* and *intr.* Of particulate matter: to be removed from the atmosphere as a result of being incorporated into raindrops as they form. Cf. RAIN-OUT.

1975 *Nature* 13 Nov. 134/2 The importance of this observation is that it makes nonsense of the assumption.. that practically everything that can..be rained out as air ascends into the stratosphere, actually is rained out and thus removed. **1979** *McGraw-Hill Yearbk. Sci. & Technol.* 153/1 The ^{3}H generated was largely injected into the upper atmosphere, from which it 'rained out' into the oceanic-hydrologic system.

9. a. With complement: To bring into a specified condition by raining.

a **1340** HAMPOLE *Psalter* cxlii. 6 My saule..draghis til þe noght til þe warld, þat may noght wete it, forþi þou rayne it ful of grace. *c* **1440** *Gesta Rom.* lvi. 239 (Harl. MS.) Yf..þe Reyne Rayne vppon boþe myn yen, yee, me hadde leuer let hit Reyne hem oute of the hede, than I turnid me. *a* **1903** *Mod.* It will probably rain itself out before morning. **1924** C. MACKENZIE *Old Men of Sea* ii. 17 The sky had rained itself out. **1944** T. D. CLARK *Pills, Petticoats & Plows* 88 Behind him at home was a cotton crop which had been rained out. **1976** G. MOFFAT *Short Time to Live* ix. 85 She was a walker rained off the hill.

b. ***to be rained out*** (U.S.) or ***off***, of an outdoor event (esp. a match), an airline flight, etc.: to be terminated or cancelled because of rain. So **rained-off** *a.*

1928 *Chicago Tribune* 18 June 27/7 (*heading*) Sox, Boston series final is rained out. **1937** *Sun* (Baltimore) 18 May 17/8 Today's [baseball] game was rained out. **1955** *Times* 24 May 10/2 An open-air meeting was rained off, but pickets patrolled the dock entrances carrying sandwich boards. **1960** C. DAY LEWIS *Buried Day* i. 20 Their tiny tragedies —a rained-off picnic, a broken toy. **1964** *Observer* 12 Jan. 32/1 Rain check..is the receipt or counterfoil of a ticket taken for a baseball game which entitles you to see another match if the one you wanted to see is 'rained off'. **1969** 'E. LATHEN' *When in Greece* ix. 98 Unfortunately the planes are rained out, but the train should get her here before midnight. **1974** *Union* (S. Carolina) *Daily Times* 19 Apr. 6/1 In the American League..Minnesota clipped California 3–2 and Baltimore's game at Detroit was rained out. **1977** 'J. LE CARRÉ' *Hon. Schoolboy* xvi. 399 Watching a rained-off cricket match where the contestants wanted only to go back to the pavilion. *Ibid.* xxii. 525 The match was rained off... Another date would be fixed. Stand by, they said.

†10. To wet with rain. *Obs. rare*$^{-1}$.

c **1440** *York Myst.* xiv. 18 þe walles are doune on ilke a side, þe ruffe is rayned aboven oure hede.

rain, var. RAIGN *v. Obs.*; obs. f. RANE *sb.*, REIGN, REIN *sb.* and *v.*

'rain-bird. [f. RAIN *sb.*[1] + BIRD *sb.*]

1. The green woodpecker, *Picus viridis.*

1555 GESNER *Hist. Anim.* III. 675 *Picus*, Anglis a specht, *uel* a Vuodpecker, *uel* raynbyrde. **1601** HOLLAND *Pliny* II. 214 The Rainbird, Woodpeck or Hickway, called Picus Martius. **1843** YARRELL *Brit. Birds* II. 136 The Green Woodpecker..[is] said to be vociferous when rain is impending, hence their name of Rain-bird. **1913** H. K. SWANN *Dict. Eng. & Folk-Names Brit. Birds* 187 Rain-bird, Rain-fowl, or Rain-pye: The Green Woodpecker... It is still a country belief that when the cry of this bird is much heard rain will follow. **1979** *Country Life* 20 Sept. 829/3 Now I hardly ever hear the rainbird, as the green woodpecker is called.

2. A Jamaican cuckoo (cf. quots. 1852 and 1894).

1725 SLOANE *Jamaica* II. 312 It makes a noise generally before rain, whence it had its name of Rain Bird. **1756** P. BROWNE *Jamaica* 467 The Rain-Bird..is seldom seen, but when it flies it takes a thousand turns in its flight. **1852** SCHLATER in Jardine *Contrib. Ornith.* 83 Rain-Birds (a modification of *Saurotheræ*, Motmots..). **1894** NEWTON *Dict. Birds* 654 *Old Man*, the name in Jamaica for *Hyetornis pluvialis*, one of the Cuckows which is also called Rain-bird, as are others of the family.

3. In Australia: (see quots.).

1860 G. BENNETT *Gather. of Naturalist* 283 The Australian Shrike or Butcher-bird, also called Rain-bird by the colonists (*Vanga destructor*). **1898** MORRIS *Austral Eng.* s.v., The rain-bird of Queensland and the interior is the great Cuckoo or Channel-bill.

rainbow ('reɪnbəʊ), *sb.* Forms: see RAIN *sb.*[1] and BOW *sb.*[1] (also 5 -*bawe*, 6 -*boll*, -*boaw*). [OE. (*reȝn-*), *rénboȝa* = OHG. *reginbogo* (MHG. *regenboge*, G. -*bogen*; Du. -*boog*), ON. *regnbogi* (Sw. -*båge*, Da. -*bue*).]

1. a. A bow or arch exhibiting the prismatic colours in their order, formed in the sky opposite to the sun by the reflection, double refraction, and dispersion of the sun's rays in falling drops of rain. Also, a similar arch formed in the spray of cataracts, etc. Hence in phr. ***all the colours of the rainbow***. Also ***the end of the rainbow, the rainbow's end***: with allusion to the proverbial belief in the existence of a crock of gold (or something else of great value) at the end of a rainbow (cf. *rainbow-chase* at sense 5d below).

lunar rainbow, one formed by the moon's rays, rarely seen. *marine* or *sea rainbow*, one formed on sea-spray. *secondary* or *supernumerary rainbow*, a fainter one formed inside or outside the primary by double reflection and double refraction, and exhibiting the spectrum colours in the opposite order to that of the primary.

c **1000** ÆLFRIC *Gen.* ix. 13 Ic sette minne renboȝan on wolcnum. *a* **1175** *Cott. Hom.* 225 þanne bið atáwed min rén bóge. *c* **1250** *Gen. & Ex.* 637 God..taunede him in ðe walkene a-buuen Rein-bowe, men cleped reed and blo. *a* **1300** *Cursor M.* 1976 þou sal fra now mi rainbow see. **1387** TREVISA *Higden* (Rolls) I. 337 A ston..callede Iris, whiche putte to the sonne causethe a reynebawe to appere in the aier. **1471** RIPLEY *Comp. Alch.* Ep. in Ashm. (1652) 188 Pekoks fethers in Color gay, the Raynbow whych shall overgoe. **1526** TINDALE *Rev.* iv. 3 There was a rayne boll aboute the seate. **1555** EDEN *Decades* 246, I sawe a whyte raynebowe abowt mydnyght. **1698** FROGER *Voy.* 169 This same night, we beheld a Rain-bow cross the heavens, which ..had a very lively red colour. **1753** HOGARTH *Anal. Beauty* xi. 84 Any two opposite colours in the rainbow, form a third between them. **1813** SCOTT *Trierm.* II. iii, As wilder'd children leave their home, After the rainbow's arch to roam. **1860** TYNDALL *Glac.* I. ii. 12 In front of us a magnificent rainbow, fixing one of its arms in the valley.

Phr. **1598** SHAKS. *Merry W.* IV. v. 119, I was beaten myselfe into all the colours of the Rainebow. **1834** J. W. CROKER in *C. Papers* 10 June (1884), The women dressed in all the colours of the rainbow. **1836** W. D. COOPER *Gloss. Provincialisms Sussex* 16 Go to the end of the rainbow, and you'll find a crock of money. **1916** R. E. BEACH (*title*) Rainbow's end. **1971** A. DIMENT *Think Inc.* ii. 21 Every wornout hack of an agent retires there... It's the end of the rainbow for every British spy. **1973** R. LEWIS *Blood Money* i. 12 He'd found the jackpot again, the end of the rainbow. **1976** *Times* 9 Aug. 10/5 Until recently West Germany has [been]..relegating reunification to the dream world at the rainbow's end. **1977** *Times* 27 Apr. 11/1 Holyhead could do with some oil at the end of the rainbow... It has seen a substantial decline in trade.

b. *fig.* (occas. with allusion to Gen. ix. 13–16).

1742 YOUNG *Nt. Th.* II. 234 Has Death his fopperies? Then well may Life Put on her plume, and in her rainbow shine. **1813** BYRON *Br. Abydos* II. xx, Be thou the rainbow to the storms of life! **1876** SAUNDERS *Lion in Path* iii, He has seen in the tears of the nation a new rainbow of hope.

c. *Her.* A representation of a rainbow.

1780 EDMONDSON *Compl. Body Her.* II. Gloss., *Rainbow* is represented in armory as a semi-circle of various colours, arising from clouds. **1780** *Encycl. Brit.* (ed. 2) V. 3599/2 'Argent, a Rainbow with a Cloud at each end'... This is part of the crest to the earl of Hopeton's coat-of-arms.

2. *transf.* a. A brightly coloured arch, ring, etc., resembling a rainbow.

1715 tr. *Pancirollus' Rerum Mem.* I. II. xvii. 113 [A vessel made of Electrum] discovers Poison, by a Rain-bow in the Cup. **1788** COWPER *Mrs. Montagu* 4 The peacock sends his heavenly dyes, His rainbows and his starry eyes. **1842** TENNYSON *Vision of Sin* 32 Purple gauzes, golden hazes, liquid mazes, Flung the torrent rainbow round.

†b. *spec.* The iris of the eye. *Obs. rare.*

1615 CROOKE *Body of Man* 748 The horny tunicle neere vnder the Rain-bow in the great Circle. **1634** T. JOHNSON *Parey's Chirurg.* XIII. xiii. (1678) 315 [An Ulcer] about the circle of the Iris or Rain-bow.

c. *Boxing slang.* A discoloured bruise.

1811 *Sporting Mag.* XXXVII. 100 A violent blow on the forehead, by which he picked up a handsome rainbow.

3. a. A South American humming-bird of the genus *Diphlogena* (esp. *D. Iris*).

1861 GOULD *Monogr. Trochilidæ* IV. pl. 247.

b. Short for *rainbow-trout.*

1779 P. FRENEAU in *U.S. Mag.* Feb. 85 The rainbow cuts the deep of varied green. **1897** *Daily News* 30 Aug. 2/4 The fish included a number of Rainbows, a species of trout not hitherto introduced to the river..Thames. **1909** *Westm. Gaz.* 13 Feb. 16/2 If there is a river in which rainbows should grow large and wax fat it is the Thames. **1940** R. PERTWEE *Master of None* v. 27, I caught a sizeable rainbow with it [*sc.* a rod] last season. **1963** *Times* 8 June 13/2 The rainbow is a fish of American origin. **1977** F. PARRISH *Fire in Barley* iii. 33 The Mullett family had eaten a good many of his fat rainbows. **1979** *Fisherman's Weekly* 21 June 5/4 Top fish was a rainbow of 7lb. 7oz. taken by Eddy Ouslie of Exeter.

4. A capsule containing the barbiturates Amytal and Seconal, one end of which is red and the other blue. *slang* (orig. *U.S.*).

1968–70 *Current Slang* (Univ. S. Dakota) III–IV, 100 *Rainbows*, n. A type of barbiturate in red and blue capsules. (Drug users' jargon.) **1972** *Sunday Sun* (Brisbane) 2 July 14/3 The barbiturate addict takes red devils..rainbows..all 1972 junkie names for various drugs. **1972** J. WAMBAUGH *Blue Knight* (1973) xvi. 303 One lousy time I dropped a red devil and a rainbow with some guys at school, and that's all the dope I ever took. **1976** M. MILLAR *Ask for me Tomorrow* xiv. 115 Getting their kicks by mixing drinks and drugs, like ..the high school kid carrying a flask of vodka to wash down the rainbows.

5. *attrib.* and *Comb.* a. attributive, in senses 'of or belonging to a rainbow', 'having the shape or colours of a rainbow', as ***rainbow colours, crown, curve, dyes, flower, hue, light, path, -pinions, -shower, sister, -space, tint, -vapour.***

1753 CHAMBERS *Cycl. Supp.* s.v. *Iris*, A peculiar species of spring crystal, remarkable for its giving the *rainbow colours in reflection. **1810** SOUTHEY *Kehama* XI. ix, A cataract..Hung with many a *rainbow crown. **1795–1814** WORDSW. *Excurs.* VII. 743 The inglorious football..shaped a *rainbow curve. **1860** C. LANGSTER *Hesperus* 53 Queenly beauty diademed with *rainbow dyes. **1816** SHELLEY *Alastor* 599 Nurses of *rainbow flowers and branching moss. **1928** BLUNDEN *Retreat* 67 What angel dropped her rainbow-flowers In that horizon blue of ours? **1816** SHELLEY *Alastor* 334 The beams of sunset hung their *rainbow hues [etc.]. **1813** —— *Q. Mab* I. 54 Those lines of *rainbow light. **1854** THOREAU *Walden* 218 It was a lake of rainbow light, in which, for a short while, I lived like a dolphin. **1924** R. GRAVES *Mock Beggar Hall* 78 Then since laws move in rainbow-light Let faith be therefore strong. **1812** HEBER tr. *Pindar* ii. 127 To walk the *rainbow paths of heaven. **1839** BAILEY *Festus* xix. (1852) 303 *Rainbow-pinions coloured like yon cloud. **1804** *Edin. Rev.* V. 103 The globules in a *rainbow-shower being all nearly of the same dimensions. **1818** BYRON *Ch. Har.* IV. lxi, Where Sculpture with her *rainbow sister vies. **1918** E. SITWELL *Clowns' Houses* 14 A glassy ball that clowns have hurled Through the *rainbow-space of laughter. **1812** BYRON *Ch. Har.* II. xlviii, Where'er we gaze.. What *rainbow tints, what magic charms are found! **1840** BROWNING *Sordello* II. Wks. 1896 I. 128/2 Whose shape divine, Quivered i'the farthest *rainbow-vapour.

b. attributive, in various *fig.* senses, as ***rainbow-hint, -presence, promise, -welcome.***

a **1806** K. WHITE *Time* 121 There's not a wind that blows but bears with it Some rainbow promise. *a* **1835** MRS. HEMANS *Poems, To the New-Born*, A rainbow-welcome thine has been, of mingled smiles and tears. —— *Genius Singing of Love*, The light thy rainbow-presence throws Over the poet's dream. **1861** DICKENS *Lett.* 17 Nov. (1880) II. 158 Precious to me as a rainbow-hint of your friendship.

c. instrumental, parasynthetic, and similative, as ***rainbow-coloured, -edged, -gay, -girded, -happy, -large, -like, -painted, -sided, -skirted, -sweet, -tailed, -tinted, -winged*** adjs.

a **1711** KEN *Hymnotheo* Poet. Wks. 1721 III. 191 A loose ..*Rainbow-colour'd Vest. **1860** G. A. SPOTTISWOODE in *Vac. Tour* 82 Clouds of rainbow-coloured spray. **1840** BROWNING *Sordello* I. Wks. 1896 I. 124/1 Lucid dew-drops *rainbow-edged. **1893** KIPLING *Seven Seas* (1896) 69 O *rainbow-gay the red pools lay that swilled and spilled and spread. *c* **1611** CHAPMAN *Iliad* II. 699 To Troy the *rainbow-girded Dame right heavy news relates. **1940** BLUNDEN *Poems 1930–1940* 190 How comes the *rainbow-happy shower! **1818** KEATS *Endym.* I. 755 My higher hope Is of too wide, too *rainbow-large a scope. **1847** LD. LINDSAY *Chr. Art* I. 119 Five concentric *rainbow-like semicircles. **1750** WARTON *Ode* vii. Poet. Wks. 1802 I. 159 Through the sunshine and the shower, Descry the *rainbow-painted tower. **1818** KEATS *Endym.* II. 110 Fish, Golden, or *rainbow-sided. **1821** SHELLEY *Prometh. Unb.* III. iii. 116 With *rainbow-skirted showers, and odorous winds. **1942** L. HUGHES *Shakespeare in Harlem* 20 So if you want to know beauty's *Rainbow-sweet thrill, Stroll down luscious, Delicious, *fine* Sugar Hill. **1929** *Oxf. Poetry* 32 Conjure..rich waterlilies lightly to be embraced by *rainbowtailed delirious dragonflies. **1827** DISRAELI *Viv. Grey* IV. VI. vi. 196 The sun..lent additional brilliancy to the *rainbow-tinted birds of paradise. *a* **1835** MRS. HEMANS *Poems, Tale of Fourteenth Cent.*, Fancy's rainbow-tinted dreams. **1897** E. L. VOYNICH *Gadfly* viii. 352 The surplices of the choristers gleamed, rainbow-tinted, beneath the coloured windows. **1819** SHELLEY *Prometh. Unb.* II. iv. 130, I see cars drawn by *rainbow-wingèd steeds.

d. Special combs., as **rainbow agate, chalcedony**, iridescent varieties of these stones; **rainbow-bird** *Austral.*, the bee-eater, *Merops ornatus*, a small, brightly coloured bird belonging to the family Meropidæ and native to northern Australia; **rainbow boa**, a large iridescent snake, *Epicrates cenchris*, of the family Boidæ, found in forest areas of northern South America; **rainbow cactus**, a small, cylindrical cactus, *Echinocereus pectinatus*, native to southwestern North America and bearing red flowers and spines in bands of various colours; **rainbow-chase** *fig.*, a quest which is rendered pointless by the illusory nature of its object; hence **rainbow-chaser, -chasing; rainbow coalition** orig. *U.S.*, a political grouping of minority peoples and other disadvantaged elements, esp. for the purpose of electing a candidate; also in extended use; **rainbow crystal** = IRIS 3 b; **rainbow darter**, an American fish of the genus *Pœcilichthys*, esp. *P. cœruleus*; **rainbow-fish**, a name given to several brightly-coloured fishes of America and Australia; also, a brightly coloured wrasse belonging to the family Labridæ; **rainbow-flower**, the Iris; **rainbow pitta**, the *Pitta Iris* of Australia; **rainbow rash** = *rainbow-worm*; **rainbow-serpent**, in Australian aboriginal mythology, a large snake associated with water; **rainbow-stone** = IRIS 3 b; **rainbow trout**, a Californian species of trout, *Salmo irideus*, recently introduced into British rivers; **rainbow tub**, a tub used in calico-printing to produce rainbow-colours; **rainbow-worm**, a species of tetter; **rainbow wrasse**, a brilliantly-coloured labroid fish (*Julis vulgaris* or *Coris Julis*).

1911 J. A. LEACH *Austral. Bird Bk.* 107 *Rainbow-bird, Aust. Bee-eater,.. Spinetail, Pintail, *Merops ornatus*. **1933** *Bulletin* (Sydney) 11 Oct. 21/3 One of the loveliest birds of N. Australia..is the rainbow-bird, which, with its green coat, black tail, and bright orange throat, well deserves its name. **1944** A. RUSSELL *Bush Ways* v. 28 The mutton-birds make underground nesting burrows, and so, too, do the rainbow-bird..and the white-backed swallow. **1963** A. LUBBOCK *Austral. Roundabout* 167 A rainbow-bird darted across the road, a brilliant flash of emerald, blue and orange. **1975** I. ROWLEY *Bird Life* 253 Hole-nesting birds such as pardalotes, kingfishers, rainbow-birds, parrots, mutton-birds and penguins can all be captured while they are visiting the nest. **1910** R. L. DITMARS *Reptiles of World* IV. 231 The *Rainbow Boa..derives its name from a gorgeous iridescence playing over the scales of a healthy example. **1937** A. H. VERRILL *Strange Reptiles* ix. 120 We found two of the lovely iridescent rainbow boas, one barely five feet in length, the other a trifle over six feet. **1958** J. CAREW *Black Midas* vi. 119 On our way back I saw a rainbow boa coiled around a branch. **1965** R. & D. MORRIS *Men & Snakes* viii. 198 But what *is* the true life span of a snake?.. An anaconda managed 28 years, a rainbow boa 27. **1972** M. RICHARDSON *Fascination of Reptiles* vii. 79 A relation [of the Cuban boa] is the rainbow boa..found between the south of Mexico and northern Argentina. **1892** J. G. LEMMON in G. W. James *In & Around Grand Canyon* (1900) xxxi. 325 *Rainbow cactus, with bright-coloured zones. **1930** J. M. BREAZEALE *Color Schemes of Cacti* 14 (*caption*) A flower of the rainbow cactus ..about three-fourths natural size. **1976** *Express-News* (San Antonio, Texas) 27 Nov. 10-C/1 We..saw a spiny little cactus growing upright out of the ground like a fat ear of corn. Its bands of colors were the colors of the rainbow—and that's its name—the rainbow cactus. **1865** PAGE *Geol. Terms* (ed. 2) 382 *Rainbow Chalcedony. **1886** *St. James's Gaz.* 2 June 10 A fact which had led Mr. Rylands off a *rainbow-chase after a visionary Chancellorship. **1892** *Courier-Jrnl.* (Louisville, Kentucky) 1 Oct. 1/8 The *rainbow chasers of the Administration are not idle these days. **1925** D. SENIOR *Rainbow Chasers* iii. 33 'We are all Rainbow-Chasers in youth,' I retorted. 'And even in old age the hope of finding the Crock of Gold is hard to kill.' **1904** *N.Y. Even. Post* 1 Sept. 7 Early in the campaign he had told his associates that it was of no use to go *rainbow chasing after Massachusetts, Wisconsin, or Illinois. **1908** *Hampton's Broadway Mag.* Nov. 599/1 We had no business whatever to go rainbow chasing. **1982** *Austin* (Texas) *Amer. Statesman* 15 Apr. 88/1 Hightower boasts he will beat the incumbent with the help of 'The *Rainbow Coalition: the blacks, the browns, the white liberals and the Yellow Dog Democrats'. **1983** *N.Y. Times* 14 Nov. 18/5 Unity among the white poor, minorities and women will create a 'Rainbow Coalition' that can have a significant impact on our process of government. **1985** *Times* 26 Mar. 5/7 The careers of all the important black politicians are directly linked to the Democratic Party. Mr Jackson's idea of drawing other minority groups into a 'rainbow coalition' has failed. **1986** *Today* 6 May 16/7 The Alliance's best chance of something spectacular is in Liverpool where they hope to gain minority control by forming a 'rainbow' coalition with Labour opponents of council deputy leader Derek Hatton. **1748** SIR J. HILL *Hist. Fossils* 179 The Iris, or *Rain-bow Crystal of authors. **1882** JORDAN & GILBERT *Syn. Fishes N. America* 514 *Pœcilichthys Agassiz*, *Rainbow Darters. **1888** G. B. GOODE *Amer. Fishes* 205 In this limpid pool were many gorgeously-colored species, the angel-fish, the parrot-fish, the *rainbow-fish. **1908** E. J. BANFIELD *Confessions of Beachcomber* I. iv. 156 In the rainbow and parrot fishes they [*sc.* pharyngeal teeth] are highly specialised. **1927** [see GUPPY[1]]. **1955** I. S. R. MUNRO *Marine & Fresh Water Fishes Ceylon* 183 Rainbow Fish, Wrasses... Mostly brilliant coloured species. **1962** D. W. TUCKER tr. *Sterba's Freshwater Fishes of World* 807 Dwarf Rainbowfish, Blacklined Rainbowfish. Northern Australia. **1973** *Stand. Encycl. S. Afr.* IX. 237/2 Rainbow-fishes... Tropical fishes, known also as wrasses, mostly living about coral reefs in warm seas. **1977** J. M. THOMSON *Field Guide Sea & Estuary Fishes Austral.* 92 The female Rainbow Fish is less colourful than her mate. **1848** GOULD *Birds of Australia* IV. pl. 3 The *Rainbow Pitta differs..from all other known species of this lovely tribe of birds. **1926** A. R. RADCLIFFE-BROWN in *Jrnl. R. Anthrop. Inst.* XXIX. 19 There is found in widely separated parts of Australia a belief in a huge serpent which lives in certain pools or water-holes. This serpent is associated, and sometimes identified, with the rainbow... Hence the *rainbow-serpent may come to occupy an important place in the beliefs and customs relating to medicine-men and the practice of magic. **1930** *Oceania* I. 270 It [*sc.* the snake represented] is both the rainbow-serpent who brings spirit babies into water-holes, and also a 'quiet' python which is eaten. **1950** ELKIN & BERNDT *Art in Arnhem Land* i. 17 A diffusion from the south of Rainbow Serpent mythology. **1965** R. & D. MORRIS *Men & Snakes* i. 19 By far the most spectacular snakes in Australian aboriginal art are the mythical rainbow serpents. These usually live deep in waterholes during the dry season, but take to the thunder clouds when the rains come, sometimes appearing in the sky as rainbows. **1977** *Bulletin* (Sydney) 22 Jan. 65/1 At the foot of the monolith is an extensive Aboriginal art gallery including an ochre rock painting of the sacred rainbow serpent. **1797** *Encycl. Brit.* (ed. 3) XII. 270/1 The iris, or *rainbow-stone, seems to be no other than a moon-stone. **1882** JORDAN & GILBERT *Syn. Fishes N. America* 312 S[*almo*] *irideus*—California Brook Trout, *Rainbow Trout. **1885** *Census Instruct.*, *Rainbow Tub Maker. **1822–34** *Good's Study Med.* (ed. 4) IV. 475 The *Rainbow-Worm, or tetter, is of a rare occurrence... [Willan] called it a rainbow rash. **1836** W. YARRELL *Hist. Brit. Fishes* I. 291 (*heading*) The *Rainbow Wrasse. **1854** BADHAM *Halieut.* 86 The..rainbow wrasse in his gay harlequin dress of green and blue. **1864** COUCH *Fishes* III. 51 The usual size of the Rainbow Wrass is in length from four to six or seven inches. **1972** *Oxf. Bk. Vertebrates* 62/1 *Coris julis* (Rainbow Wrasse), common in the Mediterranean and adjacent Atlantic, appears only rarely in British waters.

rainbow (ˈreɪnbəʊ), *v.* [f. prec.] *trans.* To brighten or span with, or as with, a rainbow; to produce like a rainbow.

1807 J. BARLOW *Columb.* IV. 264 His sword, high waving, ..rainbow'd far the spray. **1860** *Athenæum* 26 May 719 A life whose hopes and fears are rainbow'd out from tears! **1892** *Times* 15 Apr. 3/3 The sails..rainbowed with small signalling flags.

Hence **ˈrainbowed** *ppl. a.*

1846 KINGSLEY *Saint's Trag.* I. iii, See him stand Before the altar, like a rainbowed saint. **1865** E. BURRITT *Walk to Land's End* 420 The rainbowed mist of poetic fiction.

ˈrainbowy, *a.* [f. RAINBOW *sb.* + -Y.] Of the nature of a rainbow.

1830 W. TAYLOR *Hist. Surv. Germ. Poetry* I. 292 A misty glory, an intangible rainbowy lustre. **1852** H. R. REYNOLDS in *Life* (1898) II. 69 It..tosses itself in..rainbowy spray.

† **rainbreed,** *a. nonce-wd.* Producing rain.

1582 STANYHURST *Æneis* I. (Arb.) 42 Thee rainebreede seunstars, with both the Trionical orders.

raindeer, obs. form of REINDEER.

ˈraindrop, rain-drop. [OE. *regndropa* = OHG. *regentropho* (G. *-tropfen*), MSw. *rägndropi* (Sw. *regndroppe*): see RAIN *sb.*[1] and DROP *sb.*]

1. A single drop of rain.

c **1000** *Sax. Leechd.* III. 278 Hagol cymð of ðam rendropum þonne hi beoð gefrorene up on ðære lyfte. [*c* **1290** *S. Eng. Leg.* 442/380 þare þis holie man stod Ne fel neuere a reynes drope.] *c* **1400** *Solomon's Bk. Wisdom* 11 Who schulde þe rein-dropes telle. **1560** PILKINGTON *Expos. Aggeus* 180 The teares like rayn droppes come tricklinge doune his cheekes. **1698** KEILL *Exam. Th. Earth* (1734) 163 We must not imagine, that rain drops have the same form and density in the Clouds with which they arrive at the ground. **1805** WORDSW. *Waggoner* I. 156 Large rain-drops on his head Fell. **1860** TYNDALL *Glac.* I. x. 65 The rounded rain-drops had solidified during their descent.

attrib. **1860** G. H. K. in *Vac. Tour* 117 Sprinkling sweet odours and sparkling raindrop gems. **1879** DANA *Geol.* (ed. 3) 84 Rill-marks, mud-cracks, and rain-drop impressions.

2. The dropping of rain or rain-water. *rare.*

a **1400** *Minor Poems fr. Vernon MS.* xxiv. 108 Of reste he is vr tabernacle To schilde vs from reyn-drope. **1880** MUIRHEAD *Gaius* II. § 14 *a*, Urban servitudes are..the rights of roof-gutter and rain-drop.

raine, obs. form of RAIN, REIGN, REIN.

ˈrainer. [f. RAIN *v.* + -ER[1].] One who rains.

a **1845** HOOD *To St. Swithin* v, Mother of all the Family of Rainers! Saint of the Soakers! **1889** MAX MÜLLER *Nat. Relig.* xv. 484 The human mind must think a rainer behind the rain.

† **Raines.** *Obs.* Forms: *α.* 4–6 **reynes,** 5 **raynez, -ys, raygnes,** 5–6 **raynes,** 6 **rein(e)s,** *Sc.* **rence,** 6–7 **rains,** 6–8 **raines.** *β.* 5 **rayne.** [f. *Raynes*, obs. f. *Rennes*: see def.

The place-name occurs in the form *Raynes c* 1460 in the *Play Sacram.* 107: also 1489 in *Paston Lett.* (1897) III. 358.]

1. *cloth of Raine(s)*, a kind of fine linen or lawn made at Rennes in Brittany. Also with *a* or *one*: a piece of this.

c **1369** CHAUCER *Dethe Blaunche* 255 Many a pelowe, and euery bere Of clothe of reynes. **14..** *Sqr. lowe Degre* 842 Your shetes shall be of clothe of rayne. **1485** in J. M. Cowper *Churchw. Acc. St. Dunstan's, Canterbury* p. xi, j cloth of raynez for the lectron. **1526** *Pilgr. Perf.* (W. de W. 1531) 281 b, Clothed in purpull & cloth of reynes. **1558** MORWYNG *Ben Gorion* (1567) 61 Upon the beere was also a cloth of raynes.

b. Similarly with names of garments or other articles made of this cloth.

1395 *E.E. Wills* (1882) 4 A peyre schetes of Reynes. *a* **1400–50** *Alexander* 1550 All samen of a soyte in surples of raynes. *c* **1460** J. RUSSELL *Bk. Nurture* in *Babees Bk.* (1868) 130 þan take a towaile of Raynes. **1560** ROLLAND *Crt. Venus* I. 127 [A] noble seme was on his sark of Rence.

2. *absol.* = Cloth of Raines.

1526 TINDALE *Luke* xvi. 19 Clothed in purple, and fyne raynes. *a* **1571** JEWEL *On 2 Thess.* (1611) 141 That great City that was clothed in reines, and scarlet, and purple. **1607** J. CARPENTER *Plaine Mans Plough* 26 The which in the Apocalips are called the pure raines of the Bride. **1721** C. KING *Brit. Merch.* I. 283 Boulteel Raines, 368 Pieces.

raine-sacking, obs. f. RANSACKING *ppl. a.*

ˈrainfall. [f. RAIN *sb.*[1] + FALL *sb.*]

1. A fall or shower of rain.

1848–58 KINGSLEY *Poems* 15 Pawing the spray..till a fiery rainfall..Sparkled and gleamed. **1884** *Manch. Exam.* 6 June 4/6 Early in the game there was a smart rainfall.

2. The quantity of rain falling in a certain time within a given area, usually estimated by inches (in depth) per annum.

1854 H. MILLER *Sch. & Schm.* iii. (1860) 139 The Rainfall of this year..must have stood..above even this average. **1880** C. R. MARKHAM *Peruv. Bark* 282 There is one arid region, with a normal rainfall of less than fifteen inches.

attrib. **1868** *Symons's Meteorol. Mag.* III. 204 Rainfall Registration. **1869** *Ibid.* IV. 133 Report of the Rainfall Committee. **1872** MELDRUM in *Q. Jrnl. Meteorol. Soc.* (1873) I. 131 The rainfall tables of land-stations.

rainforce, ? obs. Sc. form of REINFORCE.

rain forest. Also with hyphen. [tr. G. *regenwald* (A. F. W. Schimper *Pflanzengeographie* (1898) III. iii. 281): see RAIN *sb.*[1] and FOREST *sb.*] A dense forest in an area of high rainfall with little seasonal variation, esp. a tropical forest characterized by a rich variety of plant species. Also *attrib.*

1903 W. R. FISHER tr. *Schimper's Plant-Geogr.* I. iii. 260 The Rain-forest is evergreen, hygrophilous in character, at least thirty meters high, but usually much taller, rich in thick-stemmed lianes, and in woody as well as herbaceous epiphytes. **1922** W. G. KENDREW *Climates of Continents* 327 The air is always moist, and the forests are very luxuriant. Dense rain-forest, with rubber, vanilla, and cacao, flourishes up to about 4,000 feet. **1926** T. F. CHIPP in Tansley & Chipp *Aims & Methods in Study of Vegetation* x. 207 The tropical rain forest is a type developed under abundant water supply, with high temperature of little variation, and but a short, if any, dry season. **1937** ALLEE & SCHMIDT *Hesse's Ecol. Animal Geogr.* xxi. 428 This rain-forest reaches its largest continuous extent in South America. **1952** P. W. RICHARDS *Tropical Rain Forest* i. 1 The name 'Rain forest' is commonly given, not only to the evergreen forest of moist tropical lowlands..but also to the somewhat less luxuriant evergreen forest found at low and moderate altitudes on tropical mountains, and to the evergreen forests of oceanic subtropical climates. **1956** *Nature* 25 Feb. 367/2 A detailed entomological survey..has been commenced in and around Ilobi, a typical rain-forest belt village fifty miles from Lagos. **1960** N. POLUNIN *Introd. Plant Geogr.* xiv. 430 In lowland rain forest any luxuriant herbaceous ground-vegetation is found chiefly in clearings ..where illumination is above the average. **1973** *Sci. Amer.* Dec. 59/1 Sizable areas of rain forest still stand in Amazonia, Africa, Borneo and New Guinea, but..the rain forest is retreating. **1974** *Country Life* 9 Oct. 894/3 Apes, monkeys, rhinoceroses, okapis, bongoes, tapirs and antelopes are just some of the other rain forest animals dependent on this habitat for their survival. **1978** *Vole* Dec. 25/1 Tropical rain forests are one of the world's main remaining wild places.

'rain-fowl. ? *Obs.* **1. a.** = RAINBIRD I.

c **1440** *Promp. Parv.* 428/1 Reyn' fowle, bryd (or Wodewale, or Wodehake), *gaulus.* **1678** RAY *Willughby's Ornith.* 135 The green Woodpecker..called also the Rain-fowl. **1769** J. WALLIS *Northumberland* I. 321 The lesser spotted Woodpecker..Our common people call them Pick-a-trees, also Rain-fowl, from their being more loud and noisy before rain.

b. The Mistletoe Thrush.

1817 T. FORSTER *Nat. Hist. Swallowtribe* (ed. 6) 70 *Turdus viscivorus*..Stormcock, Stormbird,..Rainfowl.

2. = RAINBIRD 2.

1694 RAY in *Lett. Lit. Men* (Camden) 200 The referring of the Old-men, or Rain-fowls, to the Cuckow.

3. = RAINBIRD 3.

1849 tr. *Cuvier's Animal Kingdom* 215 The Australian Rain-fowl (*Scr. australasia*), a grey bird of the size of a crow.

'rainful, *a.* [f. RAIN *sb.*[1] + -FUL.] Rainy.

1484 CAXTON *Fables of Æsop* v. viii, This yere shalle be raynfull and grete habondaunce of waters shalle falle. **1877** BLACKIE *Wise Men* 126 Dionysus, born Of rainful Jove.

rainge(r, obs. forms of RANGE(R.

'rainily, *adv.* [f. RAINY *a.* + -LY[2].] In a rainy manner; with rain falling.

1835 *New Monthly Mag.* XLIII. 495 The day now went very rainily and pleasantly on. **1887** BOWEN *Virg. Æneid* III. 516 Palinurus..observes..the Hyads rainily bright.

raininess ('reɪnɪnɪs). [f. RAINY *a.* + -NESS.] The fact or condition of being rainy.

1727 in BAILEY, vol. II. **1849** KINGSLEY *Misc. N. Devon* II. 298 The very raininess of the climate..leaves the clear air..all the more pure.

raining ('reɪnɪŋ), *vbl. sb.* [f. RAIN *v.* + -ING[1].] The action of the vb.

1557 *Tottell's Misc.* (Arb.) 190 As shinyng sunne refreshe the frutes When rainyng gins to cease. **1611** BIBLE *Ecclus.* xliii. 18 The heart is astonished at the raining of it [snow]. **1633** P. FLETCHER *Elisa* I. xlix, So high her eye-banks swell'd with endlesse raining. **1753** CHAMBERS *Cycl. Supp.* s.v. *Rain*, Preternatural rains, such as the raining of stones, of dust, of blood..and the like.

'raining, *ppl. a. rare.* That rains, rainy.

1523 LD. BERNERS *Froiss.* I. ccvii. 244 The season was sore reyning and weyt. **1647** FULLER *Good Thoughts in Worse T.* 17 A husbandman at plow in a very raining day. **1829** *Amer. Jrnl. Science & Arts* XV. 170 Raining Trees... There has been found in Brazil a tree the young branches of which drop water.

†'rainish, *a. Obs. rare* $^{-0}$. [f. RAIN *sb.*[1] + -ISH.] Somewhat rainy.

1530 PALSGR. 322/1 Raynisshe, belongyng to rayne, *pluuial.* **1598** FLORIO, *Piouaiuolo*, rainish, waterish, shourish.

raink, obs. Sc. form of RANK.

rainless ('reɪnlɪs), *a.* [f. RAIN *sb.*[1] + -LESS. Cf. G. *regenlos*, Sw. *regnlös.*] Destitute of rain.

1557 *Tottell's Misc.* (Arb.) 177 Gaping ground that raineles can not close. **1596** J. NORDEN *Progr. Pietie* (1847) 104 No shaft, no shot, no rainless cloud, Can daunt his spouse with woe. **1605** SYLVESTER *Du Bartas* II. iii. III. *The Law* 528 Rainlesse their soyl is wet. **1842** J. WILSON *Chr. North* (1857) I. 242 An hour of rainless sunshine. **1854** H. MILLER *Sch. & Schm.* (1858) 457 The sandy deserts of the rainless districts of Chili.

Hence **'rainlessness.**

1879 MISS BIRD *Rocky Mntns.* 2 The look of long rainlessness, which one may not call drought.

'rainmaker, rain-maker. [f. RAIN *sb.*[1] + MAKER.] **a.** A member of a tribal community believed or claiming to be able to procure rain by the use of magic. **b.** One who attempts to cause rainfall by a technique such as seeding. Hence **'rain-making** *sb.* and *a.*

1775 ADAIR *Amer. Ind.* 89 The old women were less honest in paying their rain-makers. **1775** J. ADAIR *Hist. Amer. Indians* 87 Rain-making, in the Cheerake mountains, is not so dangerous an office, as in the rich level lands of the Chikkasah country, near the Mississippi. **1856** SIR B. BRODIE *Psychol. Inq.* I. i. 25 The poor African, who..seeks the conjurations of the rainmaker. **1889** RIDER HAGGARD *Allan's Wife* 158 This old rain-making savage. **1890** J. FRAZER *Golden Bough* I. i. 13 The third, who was called 'the rain-maker', had a bunch of twigs with which he sprinkled water from a vessel. **1903** *Folk-lore* Sept. 252 The sorcerers ..are capable of rain-making, sun-making, and wind-making. **1930** E. R. B. GRIBBLE *40 Yrs. with Aborigines* ix. 87 One old fellow was a noted rain-maker. **1934** V. G. CHILDE *New Light Most Anc. East* i. 10 These are ruled by rain-maker magicians or by divine kings who were until recently ritually slain. **1960** *Times* 22 Apr. 9/2 The rainmaker must try to induce artificially the formation of ice crystals. **1971** *Islander* (Victoria, B.C.) 18 July 12/3 Here in Canada, where lawmakers are now eyeing rainmakers suspiciously, I might not have been able to try at all. **1976** G. A. BROWNE *Slide* (1977) 14 The Air Force had been conducting rain-making manoeuvres above the Mojave and Death Valley. **1978** D. BATES in C. Allen *Tales from Dark Continent* vi. 88 They took chickens or pots of beer to a rain-maker in order to pray for rain.

rainment, rains: see RAIGNMENT, RAINES.

'rain-out. Also rainout. [f. RAIN *v.* + OUT *adv.*]

1. *U.S.* The termination or cancellation of an outdoor event because of rain. Cf. RAIN *v.* 9 b.

1947 *Richmond* (Va.) *Times-Dispatch* 1 June 12-c/3 Barring professional uncertainties such as rainouts, wrecks, engine trouble, etc., a racer has a chance for good money. **1967** *Boston Sunday Herald* 14 May II. 3/5 National League figures show the senior circuit was hit hardest with 20 rainouts compared with 11 for the same period last year. **1977** *New Yorker* 15 Aug. 24/3 The day after the rainout, the sun emerged, and that evening Jimmy Buffett and his band, the Coral Reefers, finally made it to Wollman Memorial Rink, in Central Park.

2. [After FALL-OUT.] Incorporation into raindrops of radioactive debris from a nuclear explosion and its localized deposition on the Earth's surface (see quot. 1974).

1954 *Science* 7 May 619/1 The extent of the rainout was much greater than that detected in the area from any previous nuclear detonation. *Ibid.* 620/1 Although there were several days of rain immediately after the rainout, the activity was firmly adsorbed on the pavement and disappeared at a rate about equal to that for decay alone. **1955** *Sci. News Let.* 25 June 406/3 'Rain-out' might take place instead of fallout, Dr. Lapp suggested, thus producing localized areas of contamination 'hotter' than the surrounding region by a factor of ten or more. **1974** *Population Dose Evaluation* 492 Several mechanisms have been conceived for deposition from the atmosphere to the earth's surface. In addition to dry deposition, there is washout by rain falling through a cloud of activity in the atmosphere, or rainout in which the activity is incorporated into rain drops at the time of their formation.

'rainproof, rain-proof, *a.* (and *sb.*). [f. RAIN *sb.*[1] + PROOF *sb.*] Impervious to rain. Hence as *sb.*, a rainproof garment, esp. a raincoat. Also **'rain-proofed,** (*a*) rendered impervious to rain; (*b*) wearing a rainproof; **'rainproofer,** a manufacturer of rain-proof fabrics.

1831 CARLYLE *Sart. Res.* II. vii, Their old Temples..for long have not been rainproof. **1870** EMERSON *Soc. & Solit.* vii. 131 Rain-proof coats for all climates. **1902** *Daily Chron.* 7 Jan. 6/3 The greatcoat is to be made of rain-proofed drab-mixture cloth. **1908** *Ladies' Field* 25 July p. iii/3 (Advt.), J. W. Elvery & Co., waterproofers and rain-proofers,.. London, W. **1923** W. DEEPING *Secret Sanct.* xiii. 136, I was a wiser virgin than you. I did take a rainproof with me. **1960** *News Chron.* 6 May 8/4 His identically rainproofed escorts prepare to shoot him. **1965** D. FRANCIS *For Kicks* ii. 29 Everything from under-clothes to washing things, jodhpur boots to rainproof, jeans to pyjamas. **1967** N. FREELING *Strike Out* 34 The figure wears a black track-suit now gone greenish, with khaki rainproof trousers and an English suède windcheater. **1977** M. KENYON *Rapist* xii. 165 George in rainproof hat.

'rain-shower. [OE. *rénscúr* = ON. (Sw., Da.) *regnskúr*, G. *regenschauer*: see RAIN *sb.*[1] and SHOWER.] A shower of rain.

c **1000** ÆLFRIC *Hom.* II. 16 Se ðe..sylð renscuras ðam rihtwisum & ðam unrihtwisum. **1340** HAMPOLE *Pr. Consc.* 4317 Fra heven he sal do falle rayne-shours. **1513** DOUGLAS *Æneis* v. viii. 76 Als fast as rayne schour rappis on the thak. **1868** LOSSING *Hudson* 40 Towards morning there was a rain-shower. **1910** W. OWEN *Let.* 29 Dec. (1967) 66 We have been prevented from going this morning by the first rain-shower of the week. **1981** L. DEIGHTON *XPD* xxvi. 214 London..The chilly climate with frequent rain showers.

'rain-water. [OE. (*reȝn-*), *rénwæter* = Du. *regenwater*, MHG. *regenwazzer* (G. *-wasser*), ON. *regnvatn* (Sw. *-vatten*, Da. *-vand*): see RAIN and WATER.] **a.** Water that falls from the clouds as rain.

c **1000** *Sax. Leechd.* II. 26 ðefylle þonne mid ren wætere. *c* **1200** *Trin. Coll. Hom.* 151 þe teares þe man wepeð for longenge to heuene ben cleped rein water, oðer deu water. *c* **1420** *Pallad. on Husb.* I. 770 Let make a stewe With rayn watir, thyn herbis to renewe. **1481** CAXTON *Godfrey* clxxiv. 257 The Cysternes where as was rayn water. **1563** W. FULKE *Meteors* (1640) 49 The raine water doubtlesse doth more encrease and cherish things growing on the earth, than any other water. **1600** SURFLET *Countrie Farme* I. iv. 12 The best and most wholesome water..is raine water falling in sommer. **1748** *Anson's Voy.* II. vii. 214 To caulk the decks.. of the Centurion, to prevent the rain-water from running into her. **1827** FARADAY *Chem. Manip.* iii. 50 As pure or purer than rain-water. **1869** E. A. PARKES *Pract. Hygiene* (ed. 3) 6 Rain-water is collected from roofs.

pl. **1692** RAY *Dissol. World* v. (1693) 299 We daily see, that the Rain-waters wash away the Superficies of the Mountains.

b. *attrib.* and *Comb.*, as ***rain-water butt, cistern, pipe, spout, tank***; **rain-water goods,** exterior pipework, guttering, etc., designed to conduct rain-water from a building; **rain-water head,** a collecting piece, freq. ornamental in design, at the top of a drainpipe.

1836-9 DICKENS *Sk. Boz* v. (1850) 18/1 An open rain-water butt on one side. **1842** GWILT *Archit.* 1023 *Rain-water pipe*, one usually placed against the exterior of a house to carry off the rain-water from the roof. **1851** STEPHENS *Bk. Farm* (ed. 2) II. 540/2 The form of a rain-water cistern. *Ibid.* 533/1 Rain-water spouts, or rones as they are commonly termed. **1876** W. P. BUCHAN *Plumbing* xiii. 86 Fig. 149 shows conductor with rain-water head, carrying off water from gutter. **1884** *Meteorology in rel. to Health* 30 With regard to this rain-water tank. **1936** P. E. THOMAS *Mod. Building Pract.* IV. 225 The lower end of a gutter..can be formed so as to discharge direct into a rain-water head. **1949** J. F. L. D'ESTÉ in A. C. Martin *Mod. Pract. Plumber* (ed. 3) III. xiv. 321 (*caption*) Surveyor's dimensions for quantities of rainwater goods. **1955** *Times* 8 July 3/3 The Government would have to look at the restrictive practices and rings in the building industry, particularly in the rain-water goods section. **1963** *Times* 8 May 6/2 Mr. Lipton (Brixton, Lab.) asked if the Minister would give a list of the persons whose initials were inscribed on the rainwater heads in the new buildings in Downing Street. **1981** *London (North) Telephone Directory: Yellow Pages* Jan. 401/1 Bond & White Ltd. Suppliers—sanitary ware—plumbing—rainwater goods.

'rainworm. [OE. (*reȝn-*), *rénwyrm* = Du. *regenworm*, MHG. *reginwrm* (G. *regenwurm*): see RAIN *sb.*[1] and WORM.] The common earth-worm.

c **1000** ÆLFRIC *Gloss.* in Wr.-Wülcker 122/22 *Lumbricus*, renwyrm, *uel* angeltwicce. **1731** MEDLEY *Kolben's Cape G. Hope* II. 184 In the Cape countries there is a sort of Rain-worms that are altogether like the Rain-worms of Germany. **1902** *Westm. Gaz.* 23 May 10/2 Putting a live rain worm between the halves of a stoned black plum.

rainy ('reɪnɪ), *a.* Forms: 1 **réniȝ**, 4-5 **reyny**, (4 -i, -ie), 5-6 **rayny**, (5 -eny, 6 **raynye**, **-ney**, *Sc.* **rany(e)**, 6-7 **rayn-**, **rainie**, 6- **rainy**. [f. RAIN *sb.*[1] + -Y[1]. Cf. Sw. *regnig.*]

1. Of weather or climate: Characterized by rain.

a **1000** *Riddles* i. 10 (Gr.) þonne hit wæs reniȝ weder. *c* **1380** WYCLIF *Serm.* lxxiii. Sel. Wks. I. 235 Ofte tyme, in reyny wedir, chirchis don good on halidai. *c* **1449** PECOCK *Repr.* II. viii. 183 In reyny and wyndy wedris. **1535** COVERDALE *Ezra* x. 13 It is a raynye wether, & they cannot stonde here without. **1604** ROWLANDS *Looke to it* 26 An Almanacke..To search and finde the rainy weather out. **1748** *Anson's Voy.* II. vii. 214 A rainy climate. **1828** J. H. MOORE *Pract. Navig.* (ed. 20) 128 When the wind was easterly, the weather was gloomy, dark, and rainy.

2. a. Of periods of time: During or within which rain is falling, or usually falls.

In Meteorology, a ***rainy day*** is one having at least one millimetre (formerly one hundredth of an inch) of rain.

c **1000** *Sax. Leechd.* III. 162 þonne bið..windiȝ lengten & reniȝ sumer. *c* **1460** *Launfal* 169 Upon a rayny day hyt befel, An huntynge wente syr Launfel. **1481** CAXTON *Godfrey* cciv. 299 The moneth of Iuyll, whiche is moche rayny customably in that countrey. **1555** EDEN *Decades* 28 The fyrst day was fayre: but all the other, clowdy & rayny. **1660** T. BLOUNT *Boscobel* 40 The night was very dark and rainy. **1719** DE FOE *Crusoe* II. iv, The rainy season came on. **1816** J. SMITH *Panorama Sc. & Art* II. 60 An unproductive year mostly succeeds a rainy winter. **1865** TROLLOPE *Belton Est.* xviii. 207 Monday and Tuesday were rainy days.

b. *fig.* ***a rainy day***: a time of need.

c **1580** J. JEFFERIE *Bugbears* III. ii. in *Archiv Stud. neu. Spr.* (1897) 23 Wold he haue me kepe nothyng agaynst a raynye day? **1677** YARRANTON *Eng. Impr.* 115 In the Time of Plenty, they lay up for a Rainy-day. **1768-74** TUCKER *Lt. Nat.* (1834) II. 300 It behoves us to provide against a rainy day while the sun shines. **1865** CARLYLE *Fredk. Gt.* III. VIII. vi. 53 The massive silver did prove a hoard available, in after times, against a rainy day.

c. ***rainy season***: in certain, esp. tropical, regions, an annually recurring season of heavy rain (in *Meteorol.*, of at least one month's duration).

1720 DEFOE *Capt. Singleton* 135 We could not expect to reach it till an other rainy Season would be upon us. **1817** S. R. BROWN *Western Gazetteer* 13 The rainy season.. commences after midsummer. **1872** R. G. MCCLELLAN *Golden State* xxii. 294 December..and the succeeding months until May are termed winter, or the 'rainy season', in California. **1910**, **1922** [see BAI-U]. **1977** 'J. LE CARRÉ' *Hon. Schoolboy* xvii. 410 'This [tarmac road is] where he lands?' 'Only in the rainy season.'

3. a. Of places: In which it rains or is raining; where rain is frequent; subject to rain.

1432-50 tr. *Higden* (Rolls) I. 333 þe lond is nesche, reyny, and wyndy. **1697** DRYDEN *Virg. Georg.* III. 437 Southward to the Rainy Regions. **1845** FORD *Handbk. Spain* I. 1 The north western provinces are more rainy than Devonshire. **1885** R. L. & F. STEVENSON *Dynamiter* vi. 91, I wandered bedless in the rainy streets.

b. Of an action: Done in the rain. *rare*$^{-1}$.

1599 SHAKS. *Hen. V*, IV. iii. 111 Besmyrcht With raynie Marching in the painefull field.

4. a. Of clouds, mist, etc.: Bringing rain; laden with rain; of the nature of rain; connected with rain. **†*rainy bow***, the rainbow.

1390 GOWER *Conf.* I. 65 The colour of the reyni Mone With medicine upon his face He set. *Ibid.* 312 The reyni Storm fell doun algates. **1513** DOUGLAS *Æneis* VII. Prol. 27 Rany Orioune wyth his stormy face. **1563** *Mirr. Mag.*, *Lord Hastings* II. 108 As beastes forshew the drought or rayny dropps. **1604** JAS. I *Counterbl.* (Arb.) 104 The raynie clouds are often transformed and euaporated in blustering winds. *a* **1649** DRUMM. OF HAWTH. *Poems* Wks. (1711) 56/2 The seas we may not plow, Ropes make of the rainy bow. **1818** SHELLEY *Prometh. Unb.* I. 217 As rainy wind [sweeps] through the abandoned gate. **1876** GIBBON *Robin Gray* iv, A white rainy mist lowered upon the water.

b. *fig.* of the eyes: Shedding tears; tearful.

1563 *Mirr. Mag.*, *Compl. Dk. Buck.* xcvii, With rainy eine and sighes cannot be told. **1633** P. FLETCHER *Pisc. Ecl.* iv. 1 Why drop thy rainie eyes? **1774** J. ADAMS *Diary* 5 Mar. Wks. 1850 II. 332 A pathetic..performance. A vast crowd, rainy eyes, &c. **1871** R. ELLIS *Catullus* lxiii. 48 O'er the waste of ocean with a rainy eye he gazed.

5. ***rainy-shimmery, -sounding, -wet*** adjs.

1930 J. DOS PASSOS *42nd Parallel* 27 Through the rail of the bridge we can look way down into the cold rainy shimmery water. **1896** A. E. HOUSMAN *Shropshire Lad* xxvi. 37 Overhead the aspen heaves Its rainy-sounding silver leaves. **1952** R. CAMPBELL tr. *Baudelaire's Poems* 70 There the suns, rainy-wet, Through clouds rise and set.

raioid ('reɪɔɪd), *a.* and *sb.* [f. RAI-A + -OID.] **a.** *adj.* Resembling, or related to, the *Raiæ* or rays. **b.** *sb.* A fish of this type. (In recent Dicts.)

raion, var. RAYON[2].

raip, north. and Sc. var. ROPE.

raipe, obs. Sc. var. REAP.

rair, obs. Sc. f. RARE, ROAR.

raird, var. REIRD.

rais, obs. Sc. f. RACE *sb.*[1], RASE *v.*[1]; var. REIS; obs. pa. t. RISE.

raisable ('reɪzəb(ə)l), *a.* Also 9 **raiseable.** [f. RAISE *v.*[1] + -ABLE.] Capable of being raised.

1644 *New Eng. Hist. & Gen. Reg.* (1850) IV. 51 A third of the clear profitts raised or raisable of all my other lands. **1739** LORD HARDWICKE in Atkyns *Rep. Cases* (1781) I. 512 The infant, dying..makes this legacy not raisable. **1855** M. H. BLOXAM *Fragm. Sepulch.* iv. 83 An interior lid..raisable by means of two iron rings. **1858** R. S. SURTEES *Ask Mamma* xliii. 188 The time soon arrived when the rent was not raiseable.

raise (reɪz), *sb.*[1] Also 5 reise, 6 rayse. [f. RAISE *v.*[1]]

†**1.** A levy. *Obs. rare*[−1].

c **1500** *Three Kings' Sons* 91 Than may ye make a newe reise, bothe of people & tresour.

†**2.** The act of raising; uplifting, elevation. *Obs.*

1538 BALE *God's Promises* III. in Hazl. *Dodsley* I. 301 The sure health and raise of all mankind. *c* **1560** ABP. PARKER *Ps.* cxli. 405 My rayse of handes: as sacrifice,..let it bee. **1626** BACON *Sylva* §699 In Leaping with Weights..the Hands goe backward before they take their Raise.

3. A rising passage or road. *spec.* in *Mining*, a sloping shaft excavated from the lower end. Cf. RISE *sb.* 10 b.

1877 RAYMOND *Statist. Mines & Mining* 197 We are.. engaged in running a raise up from west drift on eighth level. **1887** HALL CAINE *Deemster* xxxiii. 222 Sometimes at the top of a long raise they stopped to breathe the horse. **1898** S. J. TRUSCOTT *Witwatersrand Goldfields* xiii. 293 It being usual in that mine for the man who is driving the levels with machines to come back and put up the raises. **1930** *Economist* 26 Apr. 951/2 The work done by means of drives, winzes, raises and incline shafts to open up new ground. **1973** L. J. THOMAS *Introd. Mining* vi. 167 Most raises are in the orebody and follow the footwall in grade in narrower stopes.

4. *to make a raise* = RAISE *v.*[1] 27. *U.S.*

1837 NEAL *Charcoal Sketches* (Bartlett), I made a raise of a horse and saw, after being a wood-piler's apprentice for a while. **1845** J. J. HOOPER *Some Adventures Simon Suggs* iv. 48 The chances were altogether favourable for making a 'raise'. **1878** J. H. BEADLE *Western Wilds* II. 41 At last I made a little raise..and concluded to come home. **1900** S. HANDSAKER *Pioneer Life* (1908) 35 The two brothers 'made quite a raise' in the California mines soon after their discovery. **1914** 'HIGH JINKS, JR.' *Choice Slang* 15 Make a raise, to secure a loan.

5. a. An increase in amount. Also, an increase in the price, rate, or value of a thing. Cf. RISE *sb.* 16 a.

1728 *Maryland Hist. Mag.* (1923) XVIII. 335 You wil certainly find Crops short this year..which I hope may contribute to the Raise of that on hand. **1883** 'MARK TWAIN' *Life on Mississippi* xxxix. 366 France and Italy..cracked on such a rattling impost that cotton-seed olive-oil couldn't stand the raise. **1891** A. WELCKER *Wild West* 21 By continued raises, Potlatch had everything which he possessed..at stake. **1894** WILKINS & VIVIAN *Green bay tree* I. 108 Pimlico had obtained a raise of the limit to £20. **1904** [see JACK *v.*[1] 1 b]. **1931** W. G. MCADOO *Crowded Yrs.* xxx. 469 A gigantic raise in [freight] rates would have added materially to the inflation.

b. An increase of a stake or bet at poker; in Bridge, a higher bid in the same denomination as a previous bid by one's partner.

1821 *Hoyle's Games Improved* 164 The player who last goes the double, raise, or brag, has the right, in his turn, of increasing either. **1887** 'S. CUMBERLAND' *Queen's Highway* vi. 277 You feel certain that every 'raise' he makes will be his last. **1887** J. W. KELLER *Draw Poker* 11 Limit, a condition made at the beginning of the game limiting the amount of any single bet or raise. **1921** C. E. MULFORD *Bar-20 Three* vii. 86 He had a reputation to maintain, and he saw the raise and returned it. **1923** [see PRE-EMPTIVE *a.* 2]. **1929** [see GOOD *a.* 22 j]. **1959** [see LIMIT *sb.* 2 g (*b*)]. **1964** *Official Encycl. Bridge* 192/2 A raise to two spades would be appropriate when one spade has been overcalled by two hearts. **1976** SCOTT & KOSKI *Walk-In* (1977) xxxii. 236 They were making another raise in that poker game, they were threatening to break off diplomatic relations.

c. An increase in wages or salary. Cf. RISE *sb.* 15 b. Chiefly *U.S.*

1898 *Scribner's Mag.* Oct. 489/1 A. J. Packer..had begun to ponder doubts of his wisdom in agreeing to the second 'raise'. **1902** G. H. LORIMER *Lett. Merchant* xiii. 187, I earmarked Charlie for a raise and a better job right there. **1921** H. L. MENCKEN *Amer. Lang.* (1922) iv. 131 When her wages are increased she does not get a *raise*, but a *rise*. **1934** T. WILDER *Heaven's my Destination* 28, I keep getting raises all the time. **1956** S. ERTZ *Charmed Circle* xiii. 217 She could go on working. She had lately had a raise. **1968** *Globe & Mail* (Toronto) 3 Feb. 37/1 'Stay in shape and I'll give you a raise next season,' advised coach George Imlach. **1971** C. FICK *Danziger Transcript* (1973) 25 My bureau..were delighted that I got to Cambodia... I got a raise..when I went back to Cuba. **1977** *Time* 10 Jan. 46/2 Workers strike like clockwork to protest high prices, and nearly always win raises from management.

raise (reɪz), *sb.*[2] *north. dial.* [a. ON. *hreysi* (Norw. *röys, rös*, Sw. *röse*), cairn.] A pile of stones, a cairn. (Freq. in place-names in Cumbria.)

1695 KENNETT *Par. Antiq.* (1818) I. 50 Such risings as are caused by the burial of the dead; which in the northern parts are called raises. **1794–8** HUTCHINSON *Hist. Cumbld.* (Halliwell), There are yet some considerable remains of stones which still go by the name of raises. **1869** A. C. GIBSON *Folk Sp. Cumbld.* 7 Dunmail Raise is t' biggest cairn i' t' country.

†**raise**, *sb.*[3] *Obs.* (See REISE.)

raise (reɪz), *v.*[1] Forms: α. 3 reisen, reȝȝsenn, 4 reys(en, 5 -yn, 4–6 reise, reyse, 5 rese, reze, 6 reyze, rease; β. 4 raisin, 4–8 rayse, 4–7 rais, 8 raize, 4– raise; γ. 4 rase(n, 4–6 ras, 8 raze. [a. ON. *reisa* (used in most of the main senses of the Eng. word; Sw. *resa*, Da. *rejse*) = Goth. (*ur*)*raisjan*, OE. *rǽran* (:—**raizjan*), causative f. *rais-* ablaut-variant of **rīs-* to RISE.

First prominent in the *Ormulum*, in which it occurs freely in various senses. In the Wyclif Bible, up to the end of Jeremiah, the earlier version regularly has *rear*, while the later has *raise*; but from Ezekiel onwards *raise* appears in both versions. From an early period the word has been extensively used in a great variety of senses, the exact development of which is not always perfectly clear. The main senses (here distinguished by Roman numerals) are distinct enough in themselves, but tend to pass into each other in transferred uses, while with certain objects more than one idea may be present. The addition of *up* to strengthen the verb is less common now than formerly.]

I. To set upright; to make to stand up.

1. a. *trans.* To set (a thing) on end; to lift up one end or side of (a post, stone, etc.) so as to bring into or towards a vertical position; to restore (a fallen thing) to its usual position.

Occasionally with suggestion of sense 8 or 17.

a **1240** *Wohunge* in *Cott. Hom.* 283 A, nu raise þai up þe rode. *a* **1350** in Horstm. *Altengl. Leg.* (1881) 170/527 þe Emperoure..Gert þir wheles be smertly graid & on þe thrid day þam rayse. **1388** WYCLIF *Jer.* li. 12 Reise ȝe a signe on the wallis of Babiloyne. **1500–20** DUNBAR *Poems* xxxviii. 4 The signe trivmphall rasit is of the croce. **1530** PALSGR. 684/1 Reyse this speare and set it agaynst the wall. **1592** SHAKS. *Rom. & Jul.* v. iii. 299, I will raise her Statue in pure Gold. **1791** MRS. RADCLIFFE *Rom. Forest* ii, La Motte and Peter endeavoured to raise the carriage. **1813** SCOTT *Trierm.* I. vii, Stones of power By Druids raised in magic hour. **1847** R. & J. A. BRANDON *Anal. Gothic Archit.* (1860) 99 It [a door] consists of battens slightly raised towards the centre.

b. *fig.* To set up, establish, restore, etc.

c **1200** ORMIN 5327 To swelltenn bliþeliȝ Forr Crisstenndom to reȝȝsenn. *Ibid.* 5685 To reȝȝsenn rihhtwisnesse. **1388** WYCLIF *Ruth* iv. 5 Thou owist to take ..the wijf of the deed man, that thou reise the name of thi kynesman in his eritage. **1535** COVERDALE *Ecclus.* xxxvi. 15 Geue wytnes vnto thy creature..and rayse vp the prophecies that haue bene shewed in thy name. **1559** ABP. HETHE *Sp.* in Strype *Ann. Ref.* (1824) I. II. App. vi. 400 We ..are muche..inclined to rayse uppe the errors and sects of ancyent and condemned heretickes. **1654** GAYTON *Pleas. Notes* IV. xx. 268 He undertook to raise up the almost-perished name of Chivalry.

c. *spec.* To set up (paste, crust) without the support of a dish.

1594 *Good Huswifes Handmaide* 17 To make Paste and to raise Coffins. **1681** W. MOUNTAGU in *Buccleuch MSS.* (Hist. MSS. Comm.) I. 335 Tom Cooke can neither tie brawn nor raise past[e]. **1712** STEELE *Spect.* No. 306 ¶8 Miss Liddy can dance a Jig, raise Paste. *a* **1756** MRS. HEYWOOD *New Present* (1771) 187 Make the flour and butter into a pretty stiff paste ..then raise it for the pastry. **1845** MISS ACTON *Mod. Cookery* xvi, 346 The paste must be sufficiently stiff to retain its form perfectly after it is raised.

2. a. To lift (a person or animal) and place in a standing posture; to assist (one) to rise from the ground, etc. (Freq. in *fig.* context.)

c **1220** *Bestiary* 671 Mitte helpe of hem alle ðis elp he reisen on stalle. *Ibid.* 676 Ðus fel Adam..Moyses wulde him reisen. *a* **1300** *Cursor M.* 19792 (Edin.) To saint petir sco raȝt hir hande, ande he hir raisid for to stande. **1382** WYCLIF *Amos* v. 2 She is cast doun in to hir erthe, ther is not that shal reyse hir. **1413** *Pilgr. Sowle* (Caxton 1483) III. vi. 54, I felle to the ground, but full soone myn Aungell reysed me and sette me on my fete. **1530** PALSGR. 683/2 If you fall you shall nat be reysed for me. **1611** BIBLE *2 Sam.* xii. 17 The Elders of his house..went to him, to raise him vp from the earth. **1667** MILTON *P.L.* VIII. 258 Rais'd By quick instinctive motion up I sprung..and upright Stood on my feet. **1749** FIELDING *Tom Jones* VII. xii, [They] had raised up the body of Jones, but..again let him fall. **1841** LANE *Arab. Nts.* I. 113 Therefore, liberate them, and come, and take my hand, and raise me.

b. *refl.* = To rise, get up.

c **1200** ORMIN 504 Whillc tott himm shollde reȝȝsenn To cumenn inntill Ȝerrsalæm. **1603** SHAKS. *Meas. for M.* v. i. 231 Let me in safety raise me from my knees. **1630** PRYNNE *Anti-Armin.* 119 We..haue all a vniuersal strength..to raise our selues being fallen. [**1715** POPE *Iliad* II. 127 The king of kings his awful figure raised.] **18..** HOGG *Field of Waterloo* Poet. Wks. 1838–40 II. 161 Our soldier raised him from the sod, And..leaned upon his bloody wrist.

3. a. To restore (a dead person or animal) to life.

Orig. implying the lifting up of the dead, or enabling them to rise to their feet, but freq. also including the idea of bringing up out of the grave, and thus associated with sense 17. Also with *again* = resurrect.

a **1300** *Cursor M.* 9156 Helias..was þe first,..þat ded man raisd in form dais. *a* **1350** in Horstm. *Altengl. Leg.* (1881) 38/343 þe moder him prayd to rays hir sun. *c* **1420** *Prymer* 69 Lord, þat reisidist stynkynge lazer fro his graue. **1566–7** L. WAGER *Marie Magd.* (1902), At Naim a dead chylde agayne he did rayse. **1667** MILTON *P.L.* III. 296 So Man.. Shall..dying rise, and rising with him raise His Brethren. *a* **1770** JORTIN *Serm.* (1771) I. ii. 27 God was able to raise him from the dead. **1850** TENNYSON *In Mem.* xxxi, Behold a man raised up by Christ!

b. So with body, bones, etc. as obj.

a **1300** *Cursor M.* 194 O lazar ded..Iesus raised his licam. **1610** BEAUM. & FL. *Maid's Trag.* IV. i, They must restore him flesh again, and life, And raise his dry bones to revenge this scandal.

c. Hence, *to raise from death, to life.* Cf. 19.

a **1300** *Cursor M.* 22374 Quen þai ha lien tua dais, Til liif vr lauerd sal þam rais. *a* **1340** HAMPOLE *Psalter* xvi. 14 Take out my saule fra þe wicked deuel, raisand me fra ded. *c* **1375** *Sc. Leg. Saints* viii. (*Philip*) 52 Fra ded to lyfe..he raysit þame. **1530** PALSGR. 683/2 Christ dyd rayse Lazar from deth to lyfe. **1885** *Catholic Dict.* (ed. 3) 584/1 If he had raised their dead bodies to life.

4. To cause (a person or animal) to rise or stand up:

a. To rouse from sleep; to make (one) waken up or get out of bed. ? *Obs.*

c **1200** ORMIN 5843 O þe þridde daȝȝ itt iss Waccnedd off slæp & reȝȝsedd. **1382** WYCLIF *John* xi. 11 Lazarus..slepith, but I go for to reyse him fro slepe. *a* **1400–50** *Alexander* 5174 þe duke..Fand him slowmand on slepe & sleely him rayses. **1530** PALSGR. 683/2, I reyse one out of his bedde. *Je le fays leuer.* By my fayth, if you wyll nat ryse I wyl rayse you. **1573** TUSSER *Husb.* (1878) 17 To raise [*v.r.* rise] betimes the lubberlie..Hob and Margerie. **1653** H. MORE *Antid. Ath.* III. ix. §2 *Schol.*, Then he would raise his Amanuensis to write down his dictates. **1731** DERBY in *Phil. Trans.* XLI. 229 The Houses of all the Town were so shock'd, as to raise the Inhabitants. **1781** J. MOORE *View Soc. It.* (1790) I. i. 16 Raising the people at midnight.

b. To rouse (a beast or bird) from a lair, retreat, or covert.

14.. *Kyng & Hermyt* 216 in Hazl. *E.P.P.* I. 21 A dere we reysed in that stonds, and gave chase. **1484** CAXTON *Fables of Poge* iv, They be dogges whiche are good for to serche and fynde partryches & quaylles. And whan they haue reysed them, my sperehawke taketh them. **15..** *Tayis Bank* (Bann. MS.) 25 Raising the birdis fra thair rest. **1607** TOPSELL *Four-f. Beasts* (1658) 31 This being effected, they raise the Bear. *Ibid.* 122 These are taught by falconers to retrive and raise partridges. **1721** BAILEY, To *spring* (in Fowling), to raise a Partridge or Pheasant. **1874** J. W. LONG *Amer. Wild-Fowl Shooting* ix. 157 Watch this old fool of a duck coming, and see me 'raise her'. **1976** *Globe & Mail* (Toronto) 21 Jan. 36/1 A jack rabbit was loping his way. It was only 250 yards from where he first raised it.

c. To cause or compel (a person) to rise from a seat. (Cf. 31.)

c **1460** *Towneley Myst.* xiii. 302 So farys A huswyff..To be rasyd thus betwene. **1542** UDALL *Erasm. Apoph.* 111 He ..that reaseth one sittyng on his taill, to arise out of his place. **1590** SHAKS. *Com. Err.* IV. iv. 36, I am wak'd with it when I sleepe, rais'd with it when I sit. **1785** BURNS *Death & Dr. Hornbook* xxxi, The auld kirk-hammer strak the bell ..Which rais'd us baith. **1824** SCOTT *St. Ronan's* vii, When he wan to the lee-side of a bowl of punch there was nae raising him.

5. a. To rouse or stir up (a number of persons, a district, etc.) for the purpose of common action, esp. for attack or defence.

c **1374** CHAUCER *Troylus* v. 1471 To sle þis bor was al þe contree reysed. ? *c* **1480** *Three 15th Cent. Chron.* (Camden) 76 The quene reysed all the northe and all oþer pepull by the wey. **1510** *Virgilius* in Thoms *Prose Rom.* (1858) II. 23 And forthewith he caused his kynsfolke to reyse theyr people. **1674** COTTON tr. *Montluc's Comm.* 363, I then dispatcht away Captain M..giving him order..to raise all the people of the Valleys and Villages. **1725** DE FOE *Voy. round World* (1840) 157 The mother crying and raising her neighbours. **1849** MACAULAY *Hist. Eng.* v. I. 544 Danvers undertook to raise the City.

b. Const. *against, upon.*

1382 WYCLIF *Amos* vi. 2 Loo! Y shal reyse a folc vpon ȝou ..and it shal to gydre breke ȝou. —— *Ezek.* xxiii. 22, Y schal reyse alle thi loueris aȝens thee. **1608** *Yorksh. Trag.* I. vii, It shall be my charge To raise the town upon him. **1854** TENNYSON *Geraint* 457 He..Raised my own town against me in the night. **1882** FLOYER *Unexpl. Baluchistan* 190 The whole country was raised upon him.

c. To stir up, incite, instigate (one or more persons) *to* do something or *to* some feeling.

1581 J. BELL *Haddon's Answ. Osor.* 106 b, To rayse up all men in every place, to the dewe feare of Gods law. **1667** MILTON *P.L.* I. 99 That fixt mind And high disdain..That with the mightiest rais'd me to contend. **1711** *Fingall MSS.* in *10th Rep. Hist. MSS. Comm.* App. V. 127 This suggestion raysed the Prince on a resolution to undertake the Irish expedition. **1814** BYRON *Lara* II. viii, A word's enough to raise mankind to kill.

d. To excite, agitate, provoke, rouse to excitement or anger. Chiefly *Sc.* Also *raised-like.*

1768 ROSS *Helenore* 17 Up there came twa shepherds.. Rais'd like. *Ibid.* 39 She ran aff as rais'd as onie deer. **1786** BURNS *To Auld Mare* ii, He should been tight that daur't to raize thee, Ance in a day. **1828** SCOTT *F.M. Perth* xxxvi, His countenance was wild, haggard, and highly excited, or, as the Scottish phrase expresses it, much *raised*. **1889** 'R. BOLDREWOOD' *Robbery under Arms* vii, When she was a little raised-like you'd see a pink flush come on her cheeks.

6. a. To rouse up, to give or add vigour to (the mind, spirit, etc.); to animate, stimulate.

In later use associated with the ideas of elevating (the heart, spirit, etc.) and increasing (courage, etc.).

1388 WYCLIF *Ezra* i. 5 Ech man whos spirit God reiside [L. *suscitavit*] for to stie to bilde temple of the Lord. **1470–85** MALORY *Arthur* II. ii, Balen..sawe this adventure werof hit reysed his herte. **1508** FISHER *7 Penit. Ps.* Wks. (1876) 39

The prophete..wyllynge to excyte and reyse vp the myndes of synners. **1567** *Gude & Godlie B.* (S.T.S.) 231, I will speik planelie, to rais ȝour hartis quiklie. **1641** Hinde *J. Bruen* xlvi. 146 Much after this manner did this faithful Servant of Christ raise up his thoughts and quicken his soule. **1719** De Foe *Crusoe* I. xvi, His spirits being a little raised with the dram I had given him, he was very cheerful. **1728** Pope *Dunc.* II. 223 To move, to raise, to ravish ev'ry heart, With Shakespear's nature or with Jonson's art. **1839** Thirlwall *Greece* xxii. III. 251 The immediate effect was to raise the spirit of the Athenians.

†**b.** To encourage, inspire (a person) *with* courage, confidence, hope, etc. *Obs.*

1533 Bellenden *Livy* III. xxi, The horsmen..rasit þare futemen with new curage. **1652** Needham tr. *Selden's Mare Cl.* Ep. Ded. 12, I am raised with more than ordinary confidence, that the same Spirit of Justice will carrie you on. **1697** Dryden *Virg. Georg.* IV. 555 Rais'd with so blest an Omen, she begun, With Words like these, to chear her drooping Son.

7. ***to raise the wind***: to cause the wind to blow; hence *fig.* (with ref. to wind as a motive power), to procure money or necessary means.

a **1350** in Horstm. *Altengl. Leg.* (1881) 33/421 þan deuils ..raysed þe wynd with weders wik. *a* **1515** *Droichis Part of Play* in *Dunbar's Poems* (1893) 316 At Norway coist scho raisit the wynd. **1880** T. A. Spalding *Eliz. Demonol.* 113 Charged..with having raised the wind.

fig. **1789** *Loiterer* No. 42. 10 He..never offered to pay earnest. I suppose, poor fellow, he could not raise the Wind. **1857** Trollope *Three Clerks* xxxiv, He came to me this morning to raise the wind. **1885** *Manch. Even. News* 23 June 2/2 A large number of people still rush to such methods of raising the wind.

II. To build up, construct, create, produce, etc.

8. a. To lift up and put in position the parts of (a structure); to construct by piling up, building, or fitting together; *spec.* in *U.S.* to set up the wooden framework of (a house or other building).

c **1200** Ormin 15591 Unnbindeþþ all þiss temmple, & icc Itt i þre daȝhess reȝȝse. *c* **1330** R. Brunne *Chron. Wace* (Rolls) 6059 Engyns dide þe Bretons reyse, & mangenels. *c* **1386** Chaucer *Sompn. T.* 394 Many a Muscle and many an oystre..Hath been oure foode, our cloystre for to reyse. **1458** *MS. Christ's Hosp., Abingdon* in Turner *Dom. Archit.* III. 42 They reysid up the archeys be gemeotre in rysyng. **1579** Gosson *Sch. Abuse* (Arb.) 37 The Carpenter rayseth not his frame without tooles. *c* **1615** Sir W. Mure *Misc. Poems* ix. 9 So shall my Muse rich trophes rayse. **1657** in *Essex Inst. Hist. Coll.* (1865) VII. 40/1 The said John norman is..to be paid in corne & cattell the one halfe att or before the house be raised. **1697** Dryden *Virg. Georg.* III. 19 Of Parian Stone a Temple will I raise. **1712** S. Sewall *Diary* 15 July (1879) II. 355, I, and Mr. Gerrish went to Hog-Island and saw the Barn Rais'd. **1735** B. Lynde *Diary* (1880) 144 Mr. Fisk's people..raised a new meeting house. **1779** J. Moore *View Soc. Fr.* (1789) I. xl. 342 Encouraging them to raise magnificent churches. **1846** *Knickerbocker* XXVIII. 338 After the usual amount of eating, drinking, swearing, and joking, the house..was raised and covered in. **1874** Green *Short Hist.* iii. §4. 129 In the fields to the north the last of the Norman Kings raised his palace. **1879** *Harper's Mag.* June 142/1 If a man raised a house or barn, the rum flowed freely. **1943** W. Faulkner in *Sat. Even. Post* 13 Feb. 70/3, I told you we would meet here tomorrow to roof a church... We'll meet here in the morning to raise one.

†**b.** *Math.* To construct or draw (a figure or line) *upon* a certain base. *Obs.*

1660 Barrow *Euclid* I. ii, Join *AC*; upon which raise the equilateral triangle *ADC*. **1706** J. Ward *Introd. Math.* III. (1734) 294 To Erect or Raise a Perpendicular upon the End of any given Right-line. **1712** J. James tr. *Le Blond's Gardening* 85 Raising a Square..is, when, upon a strait Line ..you cause another Line to fall..perpendicular.

c. To found, build up, make or construct (a scheme, plan, description, etc.) ? *Obs.*

1652 J. French *Yorksh. Spaw* ii. 14 Neither is it rais'd upon that account of condensation, & rarefaction [etc.]. **1706** J. Ward *Introd. Math.* v. (1734) 431 From hence we may also raise a Theorem for finding the Frustum..of the last Figure. **1712** Addison *Spect.* No. 339 ¶6 What a beautiful Description has our Author raised upon that Hint in one of the Prophets. **1802** James *Milit. Dict.*, To Raise a plan of a fortress.

d. To form (a small projection or elevation), to cause (a blister, etc.) to rise or form.

1551 Turner *Herbal* (1568) *iij, Medicines that are hote in the fourth degre, rayse vp bladders. **1688** Holme *Armoury* III. 14/1 Shavings of Leather..of wich a Heel is raised. **1712–14** Pope *Rape Lock* IV. 68 Spoil a grace, Or raise a pimple on a beauteous face. **1810** Henry *Elem. Chem.* II. 371 Acetic acid, thus prepared..raises a blister when applied to the skin. **1867** Smyth *Sailor's Word-bk.*, *Raising a Mouse*, the process of making a lump on a stay.

e. *U.S.* To form, appoint (a committee). (Perh. orig. in sense 28).

1816 Pickering *Vocab. Amer.* 160 A member moves that a committee should be raised..and a committee is accordingly raised.

9. a. To bring into existence, to produce, beget (offspring). Now *rare*.

c **1200** Ormin 9852 Drihhtin haffde mahht inoh To reȝȝsenn off þa staness Rihht aþell streon till Habraham. *a* **1300** *Cursor M.* 1199 Ur lord had aghteld yete A child to rais of his oxspring. **1388** Wyclif *Gen.* xxxviii. 8 Entre thou to the wijf of thi brothir..that thou reise seed to thi brothir. **1599** Shaks. *Hen. V*, v. ii. 476 Take her, faire Sonne, and from her blood rayse vp Issue to me. **1667** Milton *P.L.* XII. 123 God..from him will raise A mightie Nation. **1711** H. Martyn *Spect.* No. 180 ¶11 Will any man think of raising children without any assurance of clothing for their backs? **1869** Freeman *Norm. Conq.* (1876) III. xii. 79 It was before all things needful that William should raise up sons of his own.

b. To produce a supply of (persons of a certain class); to breed (animals).

1601 R. Johnson *Kingd. & Commw.* (1603) 89 France wanteth shipping..can raise no good Sailers. **1632** Massinger *City Madam* II. ii, Some innocent country-girl ..That could give directions..when to raise up goslings. **1798** Wordsw. *Last of Flock* iv, From this one, this single ewe, Full fifty comely sheep I raised. **1891** E. Kinglake *Australian at Home* 154 We 'raise' our own ministers and judges.

10. a. To foster, rear, bring up (a person). Now chiefly *U.S.*, and commonly in pass. with specification of place.

1744 M. Bishop *Life & Adv.* 268 The Child..she..says ..is the Picture of his Father, and that she would endeavour to raise it for his Sake. **1795** *Fate of Sedley* II. ix. 104 My dissolution will be made more sweet by dying in the arms of one whom I raised. **1817** Paulding *Lett. fr. South* (1835) I. 85 You know I was raised, as they say in Virginia, among the mountains of the north. **1824** A. Hodgson *Lett. from N. Amer.* II. 208 One of my young Canadian female companions..was *raised*, as they say here, in Portsmouth. **1837** Haliburton *Clockm.* (1862) Pref. 6, I don't know as ever I felt so ugly afore since I was raised. **1846** J. Hall *Wilderness & War Path* 160 'I can't back out,' said he, 'I never was raised to it, no how.' **1870** Marcy *Border Rem.* (1872) 117 A second lieutenant..was born and 'raised' in the wilds of Indiana. **1882** G. C. Eggleston *Wreck of Red Bird* 3 Maum Sally was born and 'raised', as she would have said, in 'Ole Firginny'. **1929** D. Runyon in *Hearst's International* Oct. 63/1 She slips this baby off to her sister in a little town in Spain to raise up. **1953** *Manch. Guardian Weekly* 15 Jan. 13/3 It [*sc.* Wenatchee, Wash.] is a pleasant town of sixteen thousand home-loving people, mostly engaged in raising nice children and very good eating apples. **1977** 'J. Le Carré' *Hon. Schoolboy* xv. 354 The American wife asked Jerry where he was *raised* and..where his *home* was.

b. To rear or bring up (animals).

1767 G. White *Selborne* 9 Sept., The young of the barn-owl are not easily raised. **1859** Marcy *Prairie Traveler* iv. 111 Horses which have been raised exclusively upon grass.

c. To cause or promote the growth of (plants), to grow (fruit, vegetables, flowers, etc.).

1669 Worlidge *Syst. Agric.* (1681) 99 The Alaternus..is raised from Seeds. **1719** De Foe *Crusoe* II. v, I..got into the method of planting and raising my corn. **1780** Coxe *Russ. Disc.* 7 Greens and other vegetables are raised with great facility. **1802** Mar. Edgeworth *Moral T.* (1816) I. viii. 59 A rose..raised in a conservatory. **1875** *Encycl. Brit.* I. 301/1 No notice is taken of either clover or turnips as crops to be raised.

d. Said of the soil producing the plants.

1720 Swift *Modern Education*, The dung-hill having raised a huge mushroom of short duration, is now spread to enrich other men's lands. **1797** J. A. Graham *Pres. St. Vermont* 31 The soil is excellent, and raises vast supplies of wheat, Indian corn.

e. *transf.* To produce (manure). *rare*$^{-1}$.

1792 *Trans. Soc. Arts* (ed. 2) III. 58 They [Hogs] would certainly, in a yard properly littered, raise dung enough to manure one acre very amply.

11. To cause (a person of specified character) to come into existence or appear: **a.** of God.

1382 Wyclif *Zech.* xi. 16 Y shal reyse a sheperd in erthe. **1388** —— *Deut.* xviii. 15 Thi Lord God schal reise a prophete of thi folk. **1568** H. Charteris *Pref. Lyndesay's Wks.* (E.E.T.S.) 6* God raisit vp in Ingland, Iohne Uicleif. **1611** Bible Pref. ¶11 We acknowledge them to haue been raised vp of God, for the building and furnishing of his Church. **1667** Milton *P.L.* XII. 318 Provoking God to raise them enemies. **1785** Burns *Cotter's Sat. Nt.* xxi, [Do Thou] still the patriot, and the patriot-bard, In bright succession raise. **1883–97** *Catholic Dict.* (ed. 5) 632/1 Great saints are raised up in different ages to renew the fervour of Christians.

b. of persons or impersonal agencies.

c **1717** Pope *Ep. Craggs* 11 Nor [do thou] wish to lose a Foe these Virtues raise. **1765** H. Walpole *Otranto* i, Her gentleness had never raised her an enemy. **1821** Shelley *Hellas* 597 The sins of Islam Must raise up a destroyer even now. **1881** Stubbs *Early Plantag.* ii. (ed. 3) 19 In trying to make himself friends he raised up persistent enemies.

c. To establish contact with (a person, etc.) by radio or telephone.

1929 *Amer. Speech* V. 49 *Raise*, to secure [radio] communication with. **1969** 'J. Morris' *Fever Grass* xxii. 208 Raise McKay on that [radio] set of yours. **1974** 'M. Hebden' *Pride of Dolphins* III. i. 210 She's gone off the air... We can't raise her. **1976** G. Seymour *Glory Boys* vii. 87 She raised Jimmy, still waiting beside the receiver. **1979** *Daily Tel.* 3 Jan. 1/1 A British Airways plane which tried to get into Teheran had to turn back to Kuwait when it could not raise air traffic control.

12. To produce, bring into existence or action (various natural phenomena or forces; also *fig.*).

c **1375** *Sc. Leg. Saints* xxvi. (*Nycholas*) 303 It a fyre mad alsone þat broynt þe watir, & lo rasyt. **1401** *Pol. Poems* (Rolls) II. 109 The sterne stormes that reufulli ȝe reisin. **1513** Douglas *Æneis* v. xiii. 58 Sa maisterfull storme amyd the Libyan see Scho raisit sone. **1560** Daus tr. *Sleidane's Comm.* 469 These sedicious persones, which as certen bellouse seke to reyse up flame. **1654** Gayton *Pleas. Notes* IV. xx. 269 The joyfull departure of their suspected guest, rais'd this merry showre in their eyes. **1741–2** Gray *Agrip.* 91 One..may still With equal power resume that gift, and raise A tempest. **1820** Scott *Monast.* i. *motto*, I will as soon believe..That old Moll White..raised the last night's thunder. **1884** W. E. Norris *Thirlby Hall* v, All she can do is to raise a storm in a tea-cup.

13. a. To utter (a cry, etc.) with loud voice; to produce (a loud noise) by shouting or otherwise.

a **1350** in Horstm. *Altengl. Leg.* (1881) 100/261 A hidose cry þan raysed þai. *c* **1470** Henry *Wallace* v. 40 Gret noyis & dyne was rayssit thaim amang. **1582** Stanyhurst *Æneis* II. (Arb.) 68, I stoutly emboldned with night shade raysed an howting. **1611** Bible *Job* iii. 8 Let them curse it..who are ready to raise vp their mourning. **1671** Milton *Samson* 1124, I only with an Oak'n staff will meet thee, And raise such out-cries on thy clatter'd Iron. **1748** Thomson *Cast. Indol.* II. xliv, Th' inferior demons of the place Rais'd rueful shrieks and hideous yells. **1808** Scott *Marm.* VI. xxxiv, To tell red Flodden's dismal tale, And raise the universal wail. **1845** M. Pattison *Ess.* (1889) I. 18 The Frank warriors.. raised a fierce shout of indignation.

b. Hence simply, to utter or produce (a sound).

1590 Spenser *F.Q.* I. xi. 7 Fayre Goddesse,..to my tunes thy second tenor rayse. **1602** Shaks. *Ham.* II. i. 94 He rais'd a sigh, so pittious and profound. **1743** Garrick *Lethe* I. Wks. 1798 I. 5 I'll raise music shall dispel their fears.

c. To sing; also, to begin to sing, to strike up.

1653 Milton *Psalm* vii. 62 Then will I Jehovah's praise According to his justice raise. **1727–8** Pope *Mem. of P.P.* in *Swift's Wks.* (1751) IV. 230 When I raised the psalm, how did my voice quaver for fear! **1808** Scott *Marm.* III. Introd., I love the license..In sounds now lowly, and now strong, To raise the desultory song. **1856** Olmsted *Slave States* 25 An old negro,..who raised a hymn, which soon became a confused chant.

14. To cause, originate, give rise to, bring about, set going. Used with a variety of objects, as:

a. strife, dissension, or other disturbance (*among* or *between* persons, *in* a place, etc.). Cf. 16 a.

c **1380** Wyclif *Wks.* (1880) 185 þei..reisen debatis & enemytes bitwene weddid men & here wiwes. *c* **1400** *Cursor M.* 27728 (Cott. Galba) Wreth es raysand..missaw, flit, and malisoune. **1533** Gau *Richt Vay* 17 Thayme quhilk rasis discord amangis nichtburs. **1560** Daus tr. *Sleidane's Comm.* 4 So muche contention is reysed in these oure daies about matters of learnyng. *Ibid.* 13 But in case we preferre Charles ..what tumultes shall we raise up in Italy. **1667** Milton *P.L.* v. 226 Thou hear'st what stir on Earth Satan..Hath raisd in Paradise. **1719** Ramsay *Richy & Sandy* 58 How the ill sp'rit did the first mischief raise. **1781** Cowper *Table Talk* 317 Liberty..Shall raise no feuds for armies to suppress. **1843** Mill *Logic* I. iii. §7 There are metaphysicians who have raised a controversy on the point. **1875** Jowett *Plato* (ed. 2) III. 384 Do not raise a quarrel.. between Thrasymachus and me.

b. a report or rumour, slander, etc.

a **1350** in Horstm. *Altengl. Leg.* (1881) 29/91 þai said he suld a sklaunder rays Of God. **1576** [see 16 b]. **1611** Bible *Exod.* xxiii. 1 Thou shalt not raise a false report. **1678, 1685** [see 16 b]. **1711** Addison *Spect.* No. 13 ¶5 A groundless Report that has been raised, to a Gentleman's Disadvantage.

c. a feeling, idea, etc.

c **1380** Wyclif *Wks.* (1880) 40 þat noon euyl suspecion may be reysed of hem. **1513** Douglas *Æneis* x. xiii. 2 Thus awfull Mars..The sorow rasit apon athyr hand. **1596** Dalrymple tr. *Leslie's Hist. Scot.* x. 385 Quhilk rumour in Scotland rayset not lytle invie in ffrance. **1600** Shaks. *A.Y.L.* IV. iii. 51 If the scorne of your bright eine Haue power to raise such loue in mine. **1667** Milton *P.L.* IV. 806 Thence raise..discontented thoughts, Vain hopes, vain aimes, inordinate desires. **1729** Butler *Serm. Resentm.* Wks. 1874 II. 94 Momentary anger is frequently raised.. without any apparent reason. **1855** Pusey *Doctr. Real Pres.* Note A. 2 Opponents have succeeded in raising an almost insurmountable prejudice.

d. the expression of some feeling.

1654 Gayton *Pleas. Notes* IV. vi[i]. 207 The publique worship..rais'd a condemning, but selfe-absolving blush into her cheeks. **1726–46** Thomson *Winter* 652 The comic muse..raises sly the fair impartial laugh. **1781** Cowper *Table Talk* 658 They raised a smile At folly's cost. **1892** G. S. Layard *C. Keene* viii. 176 He never fell into the habit of raising a laugh at the expense of individuals.

e. an action, process, condition, etc.

c **1425** Wyntoun *Cron.* VIII. xl. 3 The Kyng off Frawns set hym to ras And set a sege befor Calays. **1560** Daus tr. *Sleidane's Comm.* 28 b, Suche as eyther Reyse up new customes, or extorte that is forboden. **1611** Bible Pref. ¶2 They raise vp a tragedie, and wish..the Temple had neuer bene built. **1671** Milton *Samson* 625 Thoughts my Tormenters..raise Dire inflammation. **1706** E. Ward *Wooden World Diss.* (1708) 86 The Rogue..has rais'd such a Funk in the Forecastle. **1765** A. Dickson *Treat. Agric.* (ed. 2) 145 The application of such manures as raise a fermentation. **1831–3** E. Burton *Eccl. Hist.* iii. (1845) 54 The watchword..was sufficient to raise a ferment from one end of Jerusalem to the other. **1876** Paton in *Encycl. Brit.* IV. 688/1 The requisite heat for the dyeing operation is raised and maintained. **1890** Kipling *Barrack-Room Ballads* (1892) 53 Ship me somewheres east of Suez, where the best is like the worst, Where there aren't no Ten Commandments an' a man can raise a thirst. **1892** *Speaker* 3 Sept. 278/2 The outbreak has raised a demand for restriction [etc.]. **1930** 'Sapper' *Finger of Fate* 79 He grinned and said, 'We're not all savages, Mrs. Dankerton. Even though there aren't no Ten Commandments, and a man can raise a thirst.'

15. a. *Law.* To draw up, frame (a summons, letter, etc.), institute (an action or suit), establish (a use).

1546 *Reg. Privy Council Scot.* I. 45 Raising of new letteres for halding of siclik courtis justiciare. **1609** Skene *Reg. Maj.* 109 b, The name of the Judge, at quhais command the summons is raised, and directed. **1632** in *Star Chamber Cases* (Camden) 126 He..out of one cause ill begunne, raysed 20 severall actions. **1752** J. Louthian *Form of Process* (ed. 2) 85 Criminal Letters, raised at the Instance of D.F. his Majesty's Advocate. **1766** Blackstone *Comm.* II. xx. 330 A use could not be raised without a sufficient consideration. **1877** *Act 40 & 41 Vict.* c. 50 §8 Actions relating to questions of heritable right..raised in a Sheriff Court.

b. To bring up (a question, point, etc.); to bring or put forward (a difficulty, objection, etc.); to put forward, advance (a claim).

1647 Gentilis tr. *Malvezzi's Chiefe Events* 159 In raising difficulties hee makes them easie. **1722** Steele *Conscious Lovers* II. i. (1723) 26 This will certainly give me occasion to raise Difficulties. **1855** Macaulay *Hist. Eng.* xiii. III. 285 The question of the union therefore was not raised. *Ibid.* xv.

602 A day was appointed for considering the point raised by Crone. **1881** STUBBS *Early Plantag.* iv. (ed. 3) 70 John the Marshal..raised a claim touching one of the archiepiscopal manors.

16. With various constructions:

a. To begin, make, institute, direct, etc. *against* a person or thing.

a **1300** *Cursor M.* 1071 Allas!..A-gain abel he raysed strijf. **1513** DOUGLAS *Æneis* VIII. x. 98 Thar most thou behald The weris rasit aganis Romanis bald. **1546** *Reg. Privy Council Scot.* I. 29 The summondis raisit be the said Lord aganis the said James. **1560** DAUS tr. *Sleidane's Comm.* 262 He..raysed warre against us, and was taken therin. **1611** BIBLE *Acts* xiii. 50 The Iewes..raised persecution against Paul and Barnabas. **1822** SCOTT *Pirate* Advt. 6 A variety of sham suits, raised against him by Newgate solicitors. **1873** MAX MÜLLER *Sc. Rel.* 356 The objections which have been raised against this view.

b. To bring, send, or direct *on* or *upon* one.

a **1300** *Cursor M.* 7949 Iuel he sal apon þe rais. **1375** BARBOUR *Bruce* VI. 276 Fra thai had rasit on him the cry. **1388** WYCLIF *Jer.* li. 1 Y schal reise on Babiloyne..as a wynd of pestilence. **1535** COVERDALE *Amos* v. 9 He rayseth destruccion vpon the mightie people. **1576** *Oppress. Orkney & Shetland* (1859) 49 Gif ane brute be rasit upon thame. **1678** CUDWORTH *Intell. Syst.* I. v. 846 This was..a meer Slander raised upon Atheists. **1685** *Acct. Execution Dk. Monmouth* 2, I have had a Scandal raised upon me.

c. To draw, obtain, derive (one thing) *out of* or *from* another. *rare.*

1627 DONNE *Serm.* v. (1640) 48 Moses third excuse, raised out of a naturall defect. **1732** POPE *Ess. Man.* II. 245 Heav'n's great view..Virtue's ends from Vanity can raise. **1772** PRIESTLEY *Inst. Relig.* (1782) I. Pref. 12 Abstruse speculations..have been raised from every branch of my speculations.

III. To remove to a higher position.

* *To lift up by direct effort.*

17. a. To lift as a whole, to put or take higher, to elevate. Also, to pull up, hoist (sail, etc.).

a **1300** *Cursor M.* 22109 þof þou þe rais up intil heven, To hell depe sal þou be driuen. *a* **1350** in Horstm. *Altengl. Leg.* (1881) 88/685 Angels..rayses hir vp into þe ayre. **1375** BARBOUR *Bruce* XVI. 692 Thai rasit salys but abaid. **1500–20** DUNBAR *Poems* lxxii. 71 Him all nakit on the tre Thai raisit on loft. **1590** SPENSER *F.Q.* I. i. 18 She..all attonce her beastly body raizd. **1593** SHAKS. *2 Hen. VI*, I. i. 254 Then will I raise aloft the Milke-white-Rose. **1728** POPE *Dunc.* II. 39 Such a bulk as no twelve bards could raise. *a* **1771** GRAY *Dante* 1 The griesly Felon raised His Gore-dyed Lips. **1805** SCOTT *Last Minstr.* II. Concl., He raised the silver cup on high. **1814** —— *Ld. of Isles* II. xxxii, The train..Embark'd, raised sail, and bore away. **1867** TROLLOPE *Chron. Barset* II. liii. 100 Should he try to catch her eye, and then raise his hat? **1886** FROUDE *Oceana* 296 She could have struck him, and had her arm raised to do it.

b. *spec.* To draw or bring up (water, minerals, etc.) to the surface of the ground.

1745 POCOCKE *Descr. East* II. I. xvi. 61 The oxen raise the water by a bucket and rope. **1759** B. MARTIN *Nat. Hist. Eng.* I. 65 Much Ore has been formerly raised on this Hill. **1851** *Blackw. Mag.* Dec. 639 The coal raised in 1829 was 37,000 tons. **1872** R. B. SMYTH *Mining Statist.* 44, 12,656 tons of quartz..raised from depths between 240 and 690 feet.

c. In various special uses: (see quots.).

1753 CHAMBERS *Cycl. Supp.*, *Raise* is likewise used for placing a horse's head right, and making him carry well, and hindring him to carry low, or to arm himself. **1775** A. BURNABY *Trav.* 87 When the trees are fallen, they..drag them along the snow. It is exceedingly difficult to put them first in motion, which they call raising them. **1867** SMYTH *Sailor's Word-bk.*, *To raise the metal*, to elevate the breech, and depress thereby the muzzle of a gun. *To raise tacks and sheets*, the Lifting the clues of the courses, previously to bracing round the yards in tacking or wearing.

d. To turn (the eyes or look) upwards.

1388 WYCLIF *Ps.* cxx. 1, I reiside myn iȝen to the hillis. **1599** JONSON *Ev. Man out of Hum.* II. iii, Gentle friend be merry, raise your lookes out of your bosome. **1703** ROWE *Fair Penit.* I. i, Wherefore are your Eyes Severely rais'd to Heav'n? **1818** SHELLEY *Rev. Islam* v. xxii, Nor spoke..nor raised his looks to meet The gaze of strangers. **1859** TENNYSON *Vivien* 787 He raised his eyes and saw The tree.

e. Fig. phr., *to raise its (ugly) head*, to make an (unwelcome) appearance; to present itself as a (troublesome) subject for attention. Cf. REAR *v.*[1] 10 b.

1822 SCOTT *Peveril* II. i. 27 The ancient superstition..is raising its head. **1930** WODEHOUSE *Very Good, Jeeves!* ix. 230, I am starving on my feet. Well, when I tell you that it's weeks since a beefsteak pudding raised its head in the house, you'll understand what I mean. **1966** *Listener* 28 July 141/3 The subject of money for the arts raised its head again when *New Release*..investigated the facts behind the Authors' Society recent publication about the stipends of professional writers. **1971** WODEHOUSE *Much Obliged, Jeeves* xiii. 133 The snag which had raised its ugly head was one of formidable—you might say king-size—dimensions.

f. Other phrases. *to raise one's eyebrow(s)*: see EYEBROW 1 c; *to raise the roof*: see ROOF *sb.* 1 e (*a*).

18. *fig.* **a.** To promote or advance (a person, people, etc.) to a higher rank, office or position; to exalt in dignity or power.

c **1200** ORMIN 9611 Forr to reȝȝsenn alle þa þatt follȝhenn soþ meocnesse. *a* **1300** *Cursor M.* 22281 He sal him rais sua hei on hight, þat men sal wen þat he es dright. *a* **1350** in Horstm. *Altengl. Leg.* (1881) 42/13 In þe kinges hows sethin was he To ofice and to reuerence raysed. *c* **1440** *Gesta Rom.* lxv. 291 (Harl. MS.) He resede þe poore man fro filthede..to sette him among princis. **1559** *Mirr. Mag.*, *Dk. Suffolk* xvii, How high, how soone, she did me raise. **1667** MILTON *P.L.* XII. 162 A Son whose worthy deeds Raise him to be the second in that Realme of Pharao. **1752** YOUNG *Brothers* IV. i, They'll say the subtile statesman plann'd this marriage To raise his blood into his master's throne. **1810** CRABBE *Borough* iii, Theirs is a gracious bounty, form'd to raise Him whom it aids. **1874** GREEN *Short Hist.* ii. §6. 90 Charter after charter..raised the townsmen of boroughs from mere traders..into customary tenants.

†**b.** To promote *to* some privilege. *rare*$^{-1}$.

c **1400** *Apol. Loll.* 11 As sone as mony is ȝeuen þei reysen þe synnars to þe takyng of þe sacraments.

c. To exalt (one's name, state, etc.) *rare.*

a **1425** *Cursor M.* 2373 (Trin.) þere shal þi name reised be And alle þo heires þat comen of þe. **1593** SHAKS. *3 Hen. VI*, IV. i. 68 It pleas'd his Maiestie To rayse my State to Title of a Queene. **1732** POPE *Ep. Bathurst* 202 Of qualities deserving praise, More go to ruin fortunes than to raise. **1820** SCOTT *Monast.* xix. *motto*, Farewell each hope of..raising thy low rank.

d. To extol, laud. *rare.*

c **1631** MILTON *Arcades* 8 Fame that her high worth to raise Seem'd erst so lavish. **1735** POPE *Prol. Sat.* 211 While Wits and Templars ev'ry sentence raise, And wonder with a foolish face of praise.

19. *fig.* **a.** To elevate (persons) to a higher moral or mental condition. (In early use perh. from 2.)

c **1200** ORMIN 4373 He ras o þehhtennde daȝȝ To reȝȝsenn uss off sinne. *a* **1300** *Cursor M.* 18674 Iesus him kidd til þaim..vtte o wan-hope for to rais [*Trin. MS.* hem to reise]. *a* **1340** HAMPOLE *Psalter* Prol., þai rays þaim in til contemplatyf lyf. *c* **1560** A. SCOTT *Poems* (S.T.S.) xxxiv. 149 Thir ressonis ar to raiss ȝow Fra crymes vndir coite. **1605** BACON *Adv. Learning* II. xxiv, I cannot but be raised to this persuasion, that [etc.]. **1758** S. HAYWARD *Serm.* xvii. 530 Oh stupid creatures that are not raised with the description of..his infinite excellencies! **1848** R. S. WILBERFORCE *Doctr. Incarnation* v. 95 The Incarnation of Christ our Lord has raised us..above the carnal anthropology of the Greeks. **1863** FR. A. KEMBLE *Resid. in Georgia* 14 They are doing their best to raise and improve the degraded race.

b. To elevate (the thoughts, mind, etc.), to make higher or nobler.

c **1340** *Hampole's Wks.* (1895) I. 69 He..rayses þar thoght abouen all erthly thyng. **1590** SPENSER *F.Q.* I. Introd. iv, Raise my thoughtes, too humble and too vile. **1667** MILTON *P.L.* I. 23 What in me is dark Illumine, what is low raise and support. **1786** BURNS *Despondency* iii, While praising, and raising His thoughts to Heav'n on high. **1871** MORLEY *Voltaire* (1886) 2 Its great glory was to have raised the moral dignity and self-respect of the many to a level which had hitherto been reached only by a few.

c. To elevate (a subject, style, diction).

1668 DRYDEN *Def. Ess. Poesy* Essays 1900 I. 114 He does so raise his matter in that prose, as to render it delightful. **1712** ADDISON *Spect.* No. 289 ¶ 11 Milton has put in practice this method of raising his language. **1737** LD. HERVEY *Memoirs* (1848) II. 361 His words are well chosen, his diction extremely raised.

d. *spec.* in relation to consciousness: to heighten (sensitivity or awareness).

1970 K. MILLETT *Sexual Politics* (1971) I. ii. 38 The hope of seeking liberating radical solutions of their own seems too remote for the majority to dare contemplate and remains so until consciousness on the subject is raised. **1976** *Spare Rib* Dec. 22/2 We're raising consciousness, affecting some concrete issues like age discrimination, putting lousy pay on the agenda too. **1977** *Rolling Stone* 7 Apr. 53/3 My efforts to raise the consciousness of whites who are so against Indians in the States were bound to be stopped by the FBI sooner or later.

20. *Phonetics.* To articulate (a vowel) with the tongue closer to the roof of the mouth. Cf. RAISING *vbl. sb.* 1 d.

1874 H. SWEET *Hist. Eng. Sounds* in *Trans. Philol. Soc.* *1874* 506 To assume that the low-narrow [ẹ̀] was first widened, and then raised to the mid position, would be to ignore the fundamental laws of short vowel change. **1914** H. C. WYLD *Short Hist. Eng.* vii. 136 Old tense *ē* was raised to [ī] at least by the end of the first third of the sixteenth century. **1934** C. DAVIES *Eng. Pronunc.* 5 ME *ă*. Was early fronted and raised to [ĕ]. **1957** E. J. DOBSON *Eng. Pronunc. 1500–1700* II. 612 The view that ME *ę̄* tended to be raised to ME *ę̄* is strongly supported by the parallel case of ME *ǭ*, which is shown by seventeenth-century evidence and by that of the modern dialects to have been raised to ME *ǭ*, ModE [u:]. **1959** A. CAMPBELL *Old Eng. Gram.* 122 By the tenth century *æ* of whatever origin had been raised to *ē* in Kt. [*sc.* Kentish]. **1968** CHOMSKY & HALLE *Sound Pattern Eng.* III. 255 The environments where /ī/ and /ū/ are lowered to [ē] and [ō] are distinct from those where /ē/ and /ō/ are raised to [ī] and [ū].

** *To cause to rise or mount up.*

21. a. To cause (a spirit) to appear, esp. by means of incantations.

a **1350** in Horstm. *Altengl. Leg.* (1881) 98/152 Experimentes þan ordand he; And raised deuils grete plente. **1375** BARBOUR *Bruce* IV. 243 The erll Ferrandis moder was Ane nygramansour, & Sathanas Scho rasit. **1513** DOUGLAS *Æneis* I. Prol. 212 Like as the spreit of Samuell..Rasit to Kinge Saul was by the Phitones. **1583** *Leg. Bp. St. Androis* 296 in *Satir. Poems Reform.* 362 Reasing the devill with invocationes. **1671** MILTON *P.R.* IV. 430 Grisly Spectres, which the Fiend had rais'd. *c* **1725** RAMSAY *To Malloch* viii, He that could in tender strains Raise Margaret's plaining shade. **1785** BURNS *Addr. to Deil* xiv, Masons' mystic word an' grip, In storms an' tempests raise you up. **1826** DISRAELI *Viv. Grey* III. ii, Then the magician..raised the once-laid ghost of Cleveland's ambition.

b. *to raise the Devil, the mischief*: to make a disagreeable disturbance; to create trouble, uproar, or confusion. Also, *to raise Cain* [CAIN[2] 1 b]; *to raise Ned* (U.S. slang); *to raise hell*: see HELL *sb.* 10 n, q; *to raise hob*: see HOB *sb.*[1] 2 b.

[**1705** VANBRUGH *Confed.* v. ii, Sir, give me an Account of my Necklace, or I'll make such a Noise in your House I'll raise the Devil in't.] **1840**, etc. to raise Cain [see CAIN[2] 1 b]. **1841** LEVER *C. O'Malley* lxiii, He was going to raise the devil. **1848** J. R. LOWELL *Biglow Papers* 1st Ser. 69 Your fact'ry gals..'ll go to work raisin' promiscoous Ned. **1852** MRS. STOWE *Uncle Tom's C.* xx. 212 Topsy would hold a perfect carnival of confusion..in short, as Miss Ophelia phrased it, 'raising Cain' generally. *c* **1865** 'MARK TWAIN' *Sketches* i. *Mr. Bloke's Item* (1900) 217 The head-editor has been in here raising the mischief and tearing his hair. **1904** J. C. LINCOLN *Cap'n Eri* ii. 28 The boy sort of run loose, as yer might say. Went to school when he had to, and raised Ned when he didn't, near's I can find out.

22. To make (the voice) heard. Also *fig.*

1388 WYCLIF *Ps.* xcii. 3 The flodis han reisid [L. *elevaverunt*] her vois. **1581** SIDNEY *Apol. Poetrie* (Arb.) 46 Who sometimes rayseth vp his voice to the height of the heauens. **1697** DRYDEN *Virg. Past.* VI. 42 He rais'd his Voice, and soon a num'rous throng Of tripping Satyrs crowded to the Song. **1738** GRAY *Propertius* iii. 31 The Tyrant Love permit me raise My feeble voice. **1849** MACAULAY *Hist. Eng.* vi. II. 31 Many voices were boldly raised in menace and accusation. **1868** FREEMAN *Norm. Conq.* (1876) II. x. 472 Not a voice was raised in opposition. **1921** H. CRANE *Let.* 1 Oct. (1965) 65 It will be time for me to raise my voice in praise of Anderson soon, as his new book ..is on the market.

23. a. To cause (dust, vapour, smoke, water, etc.) to ascend or rise; to send or force up, to stir up. See also DUST *sb.*[1] 5, SAND *sb.*[2] 7 c.

1422 HOCCLEVE *Jonathas* 57 Sholde y a neewe smoke now vp reyse. **1581** G. PETTIE tr. *Guazzo's Civ. Conv.* I. (1586) 27 b, They doe nothing else but raise a dust. **1646** SIR T. BROWNE *Pseud. Ep.* III. xxii. (1686) 130 Camels to make the water sapid do raise the mud with their feet. **1686** W. HARRIS tr. *Lemery's Course Chym.* (ed. 2) 43 Sublime is to raise by Fire any Volatile matter to the top of the Cucurbit or into its Head. **1719** DE FOE *Crusoe* II. viii, The wine..raise[d] disagreeable fumes from the stomach into the head. **1732** BERKELEY *Alciphr.* VII. §3 We may perhaps raise a dust and dispute about tenets purely verbal. **1807** J. BARLOW *Columb.* I. 34 The drizzly fogs from dull Pisuerga raised. **1891** T. HARDY *Tess* i, And where do we raise our smoke... I mean, where do we D'Urbervilles live?

†**b.** To render (tin) volatile. *Obs. rare*$^{-1}$.

1686 W. HARRIS tr. *Lemery's Course Chym.* (ed. 2) 96 To Sublime Tinn is to raise and Volatilize it by means of a Volatile Salt.

24. *Naut.* **a.** To come in sight of (another ship, land, a whale, etc.).

1556 W. TOWRSON in Hakluyt *Voy.* (1589) 98 At 11. of the clocke wee raysed the Isle of Madera. **1633** T. JAMES *Voy.* 28 We hull'd off, North North-east, but still raised land. **1634** SIR T. HERBERT *Trav.* 12 The last of June we raised the Antarticke Pole. **1775** ROMANS *Hist. Florida* App. 61, I would not come nearer than just to raise the land. **1851** H. MELVILLE *Moby Dick* I. xxxv. 259 Whosoever of ye raises me a white-headed whale..he shall have this gold ounce. **1890** *Century Mag.* May 516 In October 1832, the ship Hector of New Bedford raised a whale and lowered for it. **1928** BELLOC *Chanty of Nona* 1 Before it was morning he raised Lundy Light.

b. To give a higher appearance to (a ship, etc.) by coming nearer.

1574 BOURNE *Regiment for Sea* xiii. (1577) 39 In going to the North, you doe rayse the Pole, and lay the Equinoctiall. **1700** MOXON *Math. Dict.* 46 So many Degrees you approach towards it, so much you are said to Raise the Pole. **1769** FALCONER *Dict. Marine* (1776), *Hausser un vaisseau*, to raise a distant ship by approaching her gradually in chace. **1796** NELSON 21 Sept. in Nicolas *Disp.* (1845) II. 279, I saw a Spanish Frigate coming..who, when she raised our hull hauled her wind to the eastward.

25. To make (a horse) rise in leaping or rearing. ? *Obs.*

1753 CHAMBERS *Cycl. Supp.*, *Raise*, in the manege, is used for working; thus to raise a horse upon corvets, caprioles, and pesades, is to make him work at corvets, caprioles, &c.

26. To reach the crest or summit of (a hill, ridge, etc.). *U.S.*

1804 J. ORDWAY in Lewis & Ordway *Jrnls. Western Explor.* (1916) 168 We raised a Steep bank back of this bottom. **1866** 'MARK TWAIN' *Lett. from Hawaii* (1967) 291 We 'raised' the summit of the mountain and began to canter along the edge of the crater. **1872** —— *Roughing It* xli. 287, I 'raised the hill' overlooking the town. **1934** J. R. BARROWS *Ubet* 280 Every time I would raise a ridge, I expected to see him; for the signs were fresh.

*** *To collect by lifting; to levy.*

27. a. To levy (a tax, etc.); to collect (rents or other charges); hence, to bring together, obtain, procure by means of collecting or in any other way. †Const. *on* (a person).

c **1330** R. BRUNNE *Chron.* (1810) 55 þorgh alle his lond þe Kyng his sonde sent, Forto raise þe treuage, þat on þe lond was sette. **1389** in *Eng. Gilds* (1870) 30 It schal ben reysed and gadered be ye alderman and his felas. **1463** *Bury Wills* (Camden) 43, I wil the mony y[t] is reysid and reseyvyd be delyueryd. **1511** *Waterf. Arch.* in *10th Rep. Hist. MSS. Comm.* App. V. 325 Noo man..shall reise keiage of noo kaye ..except it be buylded as a keay. **1546** *Suppl. of Commons* 16 What yearelye rentes may be clearlye reased therof. **1651** HOBBES *Leviath.* II. xxix. 173 The difficulty of raising Mony, for the necessary uses of the Common-wealth. **1689** J. MATHER in *Andros Tracts* II. 5 Impowered to make Laws and raise money on the Kings Subjects. **1708** J. C. *Compleat Collier* (1845) 19 If no Profit can be raised, I see no reason why any Man should Adventure his Money. **1760** C. JOHNSTON *Chrysal* (1822) I. 30, I immediately raised all the money I possibly could. **1821** BYRON *Juan* III. xiv, Let not his mode of raising cash seem strange. **1838** J. W. CARLYLE *Let.* 28 Nov. (1903) I. 71 We have..*raised* (as dear Mary used to say) a capital easy chair. **1852** THACKERAY *Esmond* I. xiv, The correspondence..related to a new loan my lord was raising. **1875** W. S. GILBERT *Tom Cobb* 1, Me so pinched for money till I can hardly raise an egg for breakfast. **1948** 'N. SHUTE' *No Highway* vi. 171, I..told Miss Learoyd to see if she could raise two cups of tea. **1973** M. WOODHOUSE *Blue Bone* xv. 162 Would you please see if you can raise us all a drink? **1976** *Daily Mirror* 16 July 3/4 He..was living on what his wife Susan could raise by selling her furniture and jewellery.

b. *transf.* To obtain, procure (advantage, pleasure, praise, etc.).

1633 Bp. Hall *Hard Texts, N.T.* 89 We cannot hope to raise any advantage to ourselves by our utmost endeavours. **1645** Quarles *Sol. Recant.* xii. 79 What pleasure shall thy great Creator raise From thy breath-tainted, and unsav'ry praise? **1781** Cowper *Retirement* 805 Content if..I may raise A monitor's, though not a poet's praise.

c. Of articles sold: To bring, fetch (a certain price). *rare*$^{-1}$.

1791 Newte *Tour Eng. & Scot.* 241 The few firs..cut for deals raise from eight pence to twelve pence per foot.

d. To succeed in procuring.

1841 'Wildrake' *Cracks of Day* 184 Mango could scarcely raise a gallop.

28. To levy, collect, gather, bring together (an army, troops, etc.).

In early use perh. to be taken in sense 5.

1388 Wyclif *Jer.* l. 9 Y schal reise, and brynge in to Babiloyne the gaderyng togidere of grete folkis. *a* **1400–50** *Alexander* 829 Nicholas..Had rasyd vp a rode hoste. **1473** Warkw. *Chron.* (Camden) 7 Alle his peple he reysyd were fledde fro hym. **1567** *Satir. Poems Reform.* iii. 90 Our Quene ..Into this Realme did rais ane ryall rout. **1596** Dalrymple tr. *Leslie's Hist. Scot.* x. 282 Raseng an airme thame cruellie he persewis. **1643** *Decl. Commons* (Reb. Ireland) 63 Lord Barnewall..hath a Commission for a Troupe of horse, and is now gone into Wales to raise them. **1759** H. Walpole *Corr.* (ed. 3) III. cccxliv. 324 We continue to militate and to raise light troops. **1839** Marryat *M. Violet* xxxix, A mob was raised in 1833, and expelled the whole Mormon body. **1863** H. Cox *Instit.* iii. ii. 594 The Sovereign has the sole power of raising..fleets and armies.

******** *To remove by, or as by, lifting up.*

29. a. To put an end to (a siege or blockade) by withdrawing the investing forces.

1375 Barbour *Bruce* xx. 64 Thus maid wes pes..And syne the assegis rasit wair. *c* **1477** Caxton *Jason* 27 b, He hadde not entencion for to disloge him ne to reyse his siege. **1560** Daus tr. *Sleidane's Comm.* 83 He raised his siege and departed without his purpose. *a* **1671** Ld. Fairfax *Mem.* (1699) 62 Our men..put the enemy to a total rout, upon which he raised the siege. **1769** Robertson *Chas. V*, xi. Wks. 1813 III. 274 He gave orders immediately to raise the siege. **1835** *Penny Cycl.* IV. 531 If the blockade shall be found to be raised.

b. To remove, rescind (a prohibition, etc.).

1887 *Mind* XII. 257 The Sorbonne raised the prohibition it had so long laid upon the works of the Grecian philosopher. **1893** Gunter *Miss Dividends* 141 He will be.. happy..to raise the injunction, which..has crippled you.

30. a. To end (a siege, etc.) by compelling the investing forces to desist or remove.

c **1489** Caxton *Sonnes of Aymon* vii. 163 Gyve me some parte of your men, And I shall goo reyse the siege of Cologne. **1523** Ld. Berners *Froiss.* I. cccxxiii. 503 They were all determyned to go and reyse vp the siege, and to refresshe and vitayle the castell. **1603** Drayton *Heroic. Ep.* vii. 155 He is besieg'd, the Siege that came to raise. **1800** Wellington in Gurw. *Desp.* I. 181, I..have taken from him one place of consequence, and I have raised the siege of another. **1811** *Ibid.* VII. 518 The enemy are still close to us, but they have made no progress in raising the blockade. **1855** Macaulay *Hist. Eng.* xvii. IV. 14 William had still some faint hope that it might be possible to raise the siege.

†**b.** To cause (the besieger) to abandon a siege.

1592 Wyrley *Armorie* 39 The King of England..Hearing declar'd his friends besieged so..hasts himselfe to go To rease the Duke. **1611** Cotgr. s.v. *Lever, Il leur fit lever le cul à*, he raised them, or their siege, from.

31. To set in motion (an army or camp).

Perh. originally related to 4 c.

c **1470** Henry *Wallace* i. 79 His ost he rasd, and come to Werk on Twede. **1569** Stocker tr. *Diod. Sic.* iii. xviii. 135 Lysimachus..in a foule and raynie night raysed hys Campe. **1640** Yorke *Union Hon.* Battles 41 Edward loth to loose time about one Cities Siege, raiseth his Army and departeth. **1684** J. Peter *Siege Vienna* 7 The Grand Visier raising His Camp, followed the Christians. **1824** P. Ogden *Jrnl.* 20 Dec. in *Publ. Hudson's Bay Rec. Soc.* (1950) XIII. 5 The Kootonnies & Flat Heads are likewise here waiting our arrival intending to raise Camp together. **1837** W. Irving *Rocky Mts.* I. vi. 78 On the following morning, just as they were raising their camp, they observed a long line of people pouring down a defile of the mountains. **1855** A. Ross *Fur Hunters of Far West* II. xi. 61 The next morning on raising camp, I ordered Martin's horses to be loaded and we set off.

IV. To make higher or greater.

32. a. To increase in height or bulk; to cause to rise up or swell; to give a higher level to.

c **1450** Lydg. & Burgh *Secrees* 2670 Shuldrys sharpe I mene not reysed with slevys. **1485** Caxton *Chas. Gt.* 26 He had hys nose reysed vpon a roundnes. **1513** Douglas *Æneis* i. ii. 30 The fadir..gaif the power..To meis the flude, or rais with stormes hie. **1596** Raleigh *Discov. Gviana* 51 All the..riuers which fell into Orenoque were raised with such speed [etc.]. **1611** Tourneur *Ath. Trag.* iv. iii, Why could not he ha' suffer'd me to raise The mountaines o' my sin with one as damnable As all the rest? **1692** Ray *Dissol. World* v. (1693) 295 That the Mountains do daily diminish..that the Valleys are raised..no man can deny. **1720** Pope *Iliad* xxiii. 640 The Corselet..Whose glitt'ring Margins rais'd with Silver shine. **1836** Macgillivray tr. *Humboldt's Trav.* xx. 290 Raising the flesh in alternate bands from the ankle to the top of the thigh.

†**b.** *to raise in flesh*: to make plump. *Obs.*

1608 Topsell *Serpents* (1658) 797 These Tortoises..are given to Horses, for by them they are raised in flesh, and made much fatter. **1615** Latham *Falconry, Words of Art expl.* (1633), Raised in flesh, is when a Hawke grows fat, or prospereth in flesh.

†**c.** To make up the height of. *Obs. rare.*

1662 Gerbier *Princ.* 24 Four of them (together with the Morter thereunto belonging) may raise a Foot. **1663** —— *Counsel* 56 The fittest bigness of a good brick; is..two Inches, a quarter and a half thick, which will raise a foot in the Morter with four bricks.

33. In various technical uses:

a. To bring up (the nap of cloth) by carding with teazles, etc.; to make a nap on (cloth).

1481–90 *Howard Househ. Bks.* (Roxb.) 320 [The] fuller.. shall dresse..vij. brode clothes; that is to say reyse, skore them, barbe them. **1494** *Act 11 Hen. VII*, c. 27 They raise up the Cotton of such Fustians. **1633** J. Anchoran tr. *Comenius' Gate Latin Unl.* §503 *marg.*, The shear-man.. raiseth the nap. **1727–41** Chambers *Cycl.* s.v. *Cloth*, The cloth..is..given, all wet, to the carders, to raise the hair, or knap, on the right side, with the thistle, or weed. **1797** *Encycl. Brit.* (ed. 3) VI. 45/1 Teazel..is of singular use in raising the knap upon woollen cloth. **1835** Ure *Philos. Manuf.* 195 The pile is also said to be more perfectly raised. **1879** *Cassell's Techn. Educ.* IV. 343/1 Cloth is usually 'raised' twice and 'cropped' several times.

b. To cause (dough, bread) to expand and become light, as by the use of yeast. Also *absol.*

1611 Bible *Hos.* vii. 4 The baker: who ceaseth from raising after he hath kneaded the dough, vntill it be leauened. **1789** *Trans. Soc. Arts* I. 178 For fermenting liquors, and raising bread. **1845** E. Acton *Mod. Cookery* xxiii. 509 All light cakes require a rather brisk oven to raise and set them.

c. To cause (hides) to increase in thickness.

1581 Lambarde *Eiren.* iv. 164 If any tanner have raised with any mixture any hide to bee converted to backes, bend-leather [etc.]. **1777** Macbride in *Phil. Trans.* LXVIII. 127 When you find your hides sufficiently raised, put them directly into the ooze. **1852** Morfit *Tanning & Currying* (1853) 196 The skins..have not yet been raised sufficiently to prepare them for tanning.

d. To give (metal) a rounded form.

1846 Holtzapffel *Turning* I. 398 In raising the metals by the hammer [etc.]. *Ibid.* 410 Thimbles, which are slightly conical are raised at five or six blows. **1879** *Cassell's Techn. Educ.* IV. 299/1 Brings down upon them a..globular punch, which domes them up—in technical parlance, 'raises' them.

34. a. To increase the amount of, to heighten (rent, taxes, prices, etc.). Also *Cards* (orig. *U.S.*), to lay a higher stake than (one's opponent); to increase (a stake or bid); freq. *absol.* and with partner as obj. Hence *to raise out*, to cause (a player) to withdraw from a game by making the stake too high for him. Also *fig.* Cf. raise *sb.*[1] 5 b.

1500–20 Dunbar *Poems* xvii. 13 Mailis and gersomes raisit ouir hie. **1548** Forrest *Pleas. Poesye* 358 Too reyse his Rent alas it neadethe not. **1596** Shaks. *Merch. V.* iii. v. 26 This making of Christians will raise the price of Hogs. **1607** Heywood *Fayre Mayde Exch.* Wks. 1874 II. 28 Once already have you prisoned me, To my great charge..And somewhat raisde the debt by that advantage. **1700** T. Brown tr. *Du Fresny's Amusem. Ser. & Com.* 78 One side endeavours to raise, and the other to beat down the Market Price. **1820** J. Gifford *Compl. Eng. Lawyer* ii. viii. (ed. 5) 167 Journeymen who refuse to work, in consequence of a combination to raise their wages. **1821** *Hoyle's Games Improved* 163 After the first three cards are dealt, but before taking in, the eldest hand after seeing his cards, may raise the ante. **1864** W. B. Dick *Amer. Hoyle* 165 When *any* player makes a bet, it is the privilege of the *next player to the left* to *raise him*, or..to deposit in the pool the amount already bet by his adversary, and make a still higher bet. **1872** 'Mark Twain' *Roughing It* 332 'I have to pass, I judge.' 'How?' 'You've raised me out, pard.' **1885** *Manch. Exam.* 16 May 5/1 It is proposed to raise the duty on rye. **1890** Champlin & Bostwick *Young Folks' Cycl. Games & Sports* 269/1 The third player may stay out, see, or raise the second player. **1894** Maskelyne *Sharps & Flats* 57 You can bet against that particular player, continually raising the stakes, until all the other players are 'raised out'. **1901** R. F. Foster *Poker* 40 Twice the amount of the blind is the amount of the ante, unless some player has raised it. **1951** E. Culbertson *Bidding & Play in Duplicate Contract Bridge* v. 55 In rubber bridge he might take a chance and raise partner to three of the minor suit. **1959** T. Reese *Bridge Player's Dict.* 142 North opens one spade and South..raises to two spades. **1965** *Listener* 4 Nov. 735/2 The only course open to him therefore is to raise to Four Clubs. **1981** P. Van Greenaway *'Cassandra' Bell* xv. 183 I'll raise you. Any odds you care to name I walk out of here a free man.

b. To increase, add to (one's reputation, interest, credit, etc.).

1654 Gayton *Pleas. Notes* iv. viii. 219 The circumforaneous Emperick rais'd his Fame. *a* **1715** Burnet *Own Time* (1724) I. 474 His being thus divested of his Commissions..would raise his interest in the Nation. **1849** Macaulay *Hist. Eng.* ix. II. 446 Promises and services which, if discovered, would not have raised his credit at Whitehall. **1871** Morley *Voltaire* (1886) 3 Each did much to raise the measure of worth.

c. *Math.* To increase (a number or quantity) by multiplication into itself.

1706 J. Ward *Introd. Math.* ii. ii. §5 (1734) 157 To Raise the Binomial Root $a + b$ to the Seventh Power. **1798** Hutton *Course Math.* I. 201 To involve or raise Surd Quantities to any Power. **1893** S. L. Loney *Anal. Trig.* 22 Raise each of these quantities to the pth power.

35. To increase the value, price, or rate of. *to raise the market*: to charge a higher price. Also *absol.*

1535 Lyndesay *Satyre* 3186 The markit raisit bene sa hie. **1596** Bacon *Maxims & Uses Com. Law* viii. 33 If..the King ..doth raise monies, that the weight of silver in the piece now of sixpence should goe for twelve pence. **1662** Petty *Taxes* p. xix, The effects of the various species of coins,..as also of raising or embasing them. **1751** R. Paltock *P. Wilkins* (1884) II. 279 'Tis all one to her..so she can raise but the market by a change. **1763** Foote *Mayor of G.* ii. Wks. 1799 I. 181 How comes it about that you have rais'd it a penny a quart? **1822** Scott *Pirate* ii, Sweyn Erickson had gone too far in raising the market upon Mr. Mertoun (.. charging the rock codfish at a penny instead of a halfpenny a-piece). **1869** 'Mark Twain' *Lett. to Publishers* (1967) 25, I had a bargain about concluded for the purchase of an interest in a daily paper and when everything seemed to be going smoothly, the owner raised on me.

36. To increase the degree, intensity, or force of.

a. To make (the voice or its sound) louder; to give a higher pitch to.

1638 R. Baker tr. *Balzac's Lett.* (vol. II.) 145 An honest man never raiseth the sound of his Voyce, to get advantage of them that speake not so loud. **1654** Gayton *Pleas. Notes* iv. xvi. 254 Raise thy clear notes so high, That labouring birds may die. *c* **1783** Cowper *Mutual Forb.* 16 'You are so deaf', the lady cried (And raised her voice..). **1886** Froude *Oceana* 84 They do not raise the voice at the end of a sentence, as the Americans do.

b. To make keener, to intensify (sensations).

1697 Dryden *Virg. Georg.* iii. 608 These raise their Thirst. **1699** Dampier *Voy.* II. i. 93, I think my appetite was raised by seeing so much food. *a* **1704** T. Brown *Sat. agst. Woman* Wks. 1730 I. 55 To raise thy pain, be Strephon ne'er forgot. **1813** Shelley *Q. Mab* viii. 139 Lending their power to pleasure and to pain, Yet raising, sharpening, and refining each.

c. To brighten (colours), *esp.* in dyeing.

1814 Jane Austen *Lady Susan* xxiii. (1879) 253 His complexion was raised and he spoke with great emotion. **1874** Crookes *Dyeing & Calico-printing* 607 Steam-greens after printing are frequently brightened, or 'raised' as it is technically called. **1884** *Girl's Own Paper* 8 Mar. 353 The first pigment..when mingled with any other colour raises its tone—that is to say, lightens it.

d. To cause (the pulse) to beat faster; to make (a fire) burn up better; to make hotter; etc.

1707 Floyer *Physic. Pulse-Watch* 222 Burning heats a part, and raises the Pulse. **1715–20** Pope *Iliad* ix. 277 Meanwhile Patroclus sweats the fire to raise. **1758** Reid tr. *Macquer's Chym.* I. 381 After you raise the fire in order to melt the mixture. **1863** Tyndall *Heat* i. 10 Raised to incandescence by friction against our atmosphere.

V. 37. *intr.* To rise, in various senses. *Obs.* exc. *U.S.*

1470–85 Malory *Arthur* xx. xxii, Syr Gauwayns hors fete reysed and so the hors and he fyl to the erthe. **1490** Caxton *Eneydos* vii. 32 The delectable name of hir cyte grewe & reysed in praysing. **1654** Gayton *Pleas. Notes* iv. xxii. 273 Iust as imprison'd windes, when once broke forth, One against the other raiseth. **1666** *Ormonde MSS.* in *10th Rep. Hist. MSS. Comm.* App. v. 12 They never raised in rebellion against his Majestie. **1702** *Eng. Theophrast.* 240 His reputation abroad will raise or sink as his affairs go well or ill at home. **1727** *Philip Quarll* (1816) 57 The fowl..launched itself into the pond, but raised more easily, which gave him time to take his aim. **1761** Hume *Hist. Eng.* II. xxix. 145 The artisans, finding their profits to raise by the favour of their Customers, increase..their skill. **1770** C. Carroll *Let.* 5 Sept. in *Maryland Hist. Mag.* (1918) XIII. 61, I am quite indifferent whether Stephenson takes or Refuses the tob[acc]o, as I think the Price will raise again. **1785** G. Washington *Diary* 22 Sept. (1925) II. 415 The Water having raised,..I could form no accurate judgment of the progress. **1808** in J. H. Beadle *Undevel. West* (1873) xxi. 410 Should the accused person or persons raise up with arms in his or their hands. **1819** T. Forsyth in *Minnesota Hist. Coll.* (1880) III. 143 As the Mississippi was raising, the current was very strong. **1861** *Trans. Illinois Agric. Soc.* IV. 102 The milk sours before the cream all raises. **1911** H. P. Fairchild *Greek Immigration to U.S.* 70 About 1,000 houses are vacant in Athens, and yet the prices of rent have raised 15 to 20 per cent.

38. *raising* = being raised.

1642 *Royal Commission* in *Buccleuch MSS.* (Hist. MSS. Comm.) I. 527 There are now..moneys raising by way of contribution and otherwise. **1743** T. Jones *ibid.* 405 'Tis said magazines are raising for us at Coblentz. **1758** Goldsm. *Mem. Protestant* (1895) I. 225 There was raising a new Regiment in his Province. **1802** H. Martin *Helen of Glenross* II. 180, I see money is raising in all possible ways —by all possible means. **1864** Tennyson *Enoch Arden* 175 Annie seemed to hear Her own death-scaffold raising.

39. *intr. Mining.* To drive a raise (raise *sb.*[1] 3).

1898 S. J. Truscott *Witwatersrand Goldfields* xiii. 294 With machine drills it costs slightly more to sink a winze than to raise. **1973** L. J. Thomas *Introd. Mining* i. 9 The connections may be made by driving upwards, known as rising or raising, or working downwards, known as winzing.

†**raise**, *v.*[2] *Obs.* Also 5 *Sc.* rais, 6 rayse. [var. of raise *v.*[1]; the spelling may be partly due to association with prec.; cf. raised *ppl. a.*[2]]

1. *trans.* To tear; to scratch, to cut.

In some cases perh. with idea of 'raising' or lifting a portion of the surface.

c **1475** *Rauf Coilȝear* 550, I sall rais thy Ryall array. **1590** R. Harvey *Pl. Perc.* 6 If you strike his face, you can raise no skin, for his forhead is brasse. **1601** Hakluyt tr. *Galvano's Discov.* 23 They tilled and raised the ground with oxe hornes. **1641** Best *Farm Bks.* (Surtees) 48 That hee lay strawe in the barne floore..to prevent the wheeles from breakinge and raysinge the floore. **1677** *Lond. Gaz.* No. 1223/3 [Having] his Skin only raised.

2. To erase or raze.

1530–1 *Act 22 Hen VIII*, c. 15 Excepted always..all raysynge of recordes. **1588** A. King in *Cath. Tract.* (S.T.S.) 216/16 To raise the diett of ane instrument. **1601** R. Johnson *Kingd. & Commw.* (1603) 165 In the year 1241 they raised [1630 razed] Kiouia the chiefe city of the Rutheni. **1645** *Answ. to Pref.* 130 If there had been any such church robberie of raising the recordes.

3. To graze, touch.

1591 Spenser *Vision Bellay* xiv, It seem'd her top the firmament did rayse.

raise, obs. pa. t. rise *v.*

raised (reizd), *ppl. a.*[1] [f. raise *v.*[1] + -ed[1].]

1. a. Set erect; restored to life; roused up.

1604 Shaks. *Oth.* i. ii. 29 Those are the raised Father, and his Friends. **1697** G. Keith *2nd Narr. Proc. Turner's Hall*

32 The Raised Saints shall neither need Candle, nor Light of the Sun.

b. ***raised pie***: a pie having a 'raised' crust (see RAISE *v.*[1] 1 c).

1747–96 MRS. GLASSE *Cookery* xiii. 191 Raised pies should have a quick oven, and well closed up. **1844** ALB. SMITH *Adv. Mr. Ledbury* iii. (1886) 11 [He] entered a neighbouring shop, where he purchased a raised pie. **1865** BEETON *Dict. Cookery* 282/1 Raised Pie of Veal and Ham... Plenty of practice [should be] given to the making of raised pies.

2. Set on foot, instituted. *rare.*

1604 SHAKS. *Oth.* I. i. 159 Lead to the Sagitary the raised Search.

3. a. Lifted up, elevated, exalted, high. *lit.* and *fig.* Also ***raised eyebrows***, eyebrows raised in censure or query (see EYEBROW 1 c).

1627 FELTHAM *Resolves* I. xli. (1709) 101 From the Pismire .. to the Monarch on the raised Throne. **1662** STILLINGFL. *Orig. Sacr.* II. iii. §2 Such as are of more raised and inquisitive minds. *a* **1708** BEVERIDGE *Thes. Theol.* (1711) III. 11 High and raised apprehensions of God's goodness. **1818** SHELLEY *Rev. Islam* III. xi, A stroke on my raised arm and naked head. **1875** JOWETT *Plato* (ed. 2) III. 400 Between the fire and the prisoners there is a raised way. **1968** P. DURST *Badge of Infamy* v. 39 'I'll bet that causes some raised eyebrows,' Gina said. **1974** E. AMBLER *Dr. Frigo* II. 82, I expected another violent reaction. None came. He merely glanced with raised eyebrows at Delvert, who nodded.

Comb. **1662** STILLINGFL. *Orig. Sacr.* III. iii. §2 The more raised-spirited Moralists.

b. ***raised beach***, a former beach, now situated above sea-level; ***raised bed***, a flower-bed, at a higher level than the adjacent garden; ***raised bog***, an area of acid, peaty soil, esp. that developed from moss, in which growth is most rapid at the centre, giving rise to a domed shape.

1834 *Proc. Geol. Soc.* II. 102 These are the only instances which the author could discover of a raised beach on this part of the coast. **1842** H. MILLER *O. R. Sandst.* i. (ed. 2) 37 A raised beach of the Moray Frith. **1863** A. C. RAMSAY *Phys. Geog.* i. (1878) 11 On all continents and on many large islands raised beaches occur. **1910** L. B. MEREDITH *Rock Gardens* ii. 25 The best and most usual form [of small rock garden] is a raised bed. **1938** *New Phytol.* XXXVII. 425 Since the primary lakes are frequently of glacial origin, raised bogs have generally proved to be extremely satisfactory sources of long continuous profiles illustrative of post-glacial forest and climatic history. **1946** *Proc. Prehist. Soc.* XII. 4 Raised-bogs very commonly occur in peri-glacial regions, often upon the sites of lakes created by the laying down of terminal moraines across glaciated valleys. **1959** J. D. CLARK *Prehist. S. Afr.* vi. 164 The earliest Middle Stone Age is probably that associated with the 20-foot raised beach at Blind River, East London. **1959** C. SPRY *Favourite Flowers* xxiii. 166, I wanted a raised bed of well-drained agreeable soil. **1966** F. H. BRIGHTMAN *Oxf. Bk. Flowerless Plants* 88 Sometimes fen becomes choked with vegetation, and acid conditions develop at the top, so that species of Sphagnum can grow on the surface, forming 'raised bog'. **1969** BENNISON & WRIGHT *Geol. Hist. Brit. Isles* xvi. 366 The evidence of uplift is found in the form of marine-cut erosion platforms, or raised beaches where these erosion surfaces have a cover of beach material. **1974** *Country Life* 21 Mar. 650/1 Raised beds housing all manner of plants became characteristic features. **1976** *Nature* 23 Sept. 281/1 Raised bogs represent a special type of peat bog... They.. have their own water regime, with all of the moisture supplied from the atmosphere.

4. a. Increased in height or size; made larger, thicker, or more prominent; standing out; etc.

1582 STANYHURST *Æneis* I. (Arb.) 21 Soom wights vp-floating on raisd sea wyth armor apeered. **1599** MINSHEU *Span. Gram.* 77 Imbrodered with imbost or raisd golde and pearle. **1676** WISEMAN *Chirurg. Treat.* v. ix. 380 The raised-up Lip might be troublesome to the Chirurgeon in his work. **1772** T. NUGENT tr. *Hist. Friar Gerund* II. 339 Two scapularies ornamented with tinsel raised-work. **1777** MACBRIDE in *Phil. Trans.* LXVIII. 127 The lime-water ooze penetrates raised leather. **1836** *Penny Cycl.* V. 240 The type required for printing in raised characters. **1873** *Young Englishwoman* Aug. 406/2 The medallions are worked on brown American cloth.. in raised embroidery. **1882** CAULFEILD & SAWARD *Dict. Needlework* 416 Raised Embroidery.. consisting of working raised flowers upon a flat foundation. **1900** E. JACKSON *Hist. Hand-made Lace* 216 *Raised work*, in bobbin lace this term denotes the raised edge worked down one side of leaves and flowers. Honiton and Duchess each have occasionally raised work, which heightens the effect of the lace considerably. **1960** B. SNOOK *Eng. Hist. Embroidery* 86 Stump work originally was known as 'raised work', its present name probably not being used before 1894.

Comb. **1632** HAYWARD tr. *Biondi's Eromena* 55 They laid downe the Beere upon a rais'd-worke mourning Coverlet. **1879** SIR G. SCOTT *Lect. Archit.* II. 177 Square and oblong spaces were vaulted.. on the raised-ridge principle.

b. Increased in amount or degree.

1706 J. WARD *Introd. Math.* II. ii. §5 (1734) 157 The intermediate Terms in the new Raised Power. **1809** PINKNEY *Trav. France* 58 His wife came in, hearing my raised voice. **1826** MISS MITFORD *Village* Ser. II. 122 To speak of him as dead, seemed to her raised feelings, like murder. **1846** *P. Parley's Ann.* VII. 232 With smiling face, indeed, but with a raised complexion.

c. ***raised bands*** (see quots.).

1835 J. ARNETT *Bibliopegia* I. 23 The old mode of sewing on raised bands combined many advantages. **1846** G. DODD *Brit. Manuf.* 6th Ser. iv. 96 'Raised bands'.. are sometimes used for ornament in the better kinds of books; they consist of little strips of leather or cord pasted across the back of the book before it is covered. **1875** [see PANEL *sb.*[1] 8 c]. **1901** D. COCKERELL *Bookbinding* i. 26 The public having become accustomed to raised bands on the backs of books, and the real bands being sunk in the back, the binders put false ones over the 'hollow'. **1952** J. CARTER *ABC for Bk.-Collectors* 147 When a book is bound.. the gathered sections are sewn on to horizontal cords or bands... When the boards are covered, these cords (unless sunk in grooves to make a flat spine) will stand out in the form of ridges. These are known as raised bands. **1972** P. GASKELL *New Introd. Bibliogr.* 148 The cords themselves could be placed either outside the backs of the folded sheets, where they would show as raised bands across the spine of the book, or in slots sawn into the folds.

d. Of a cake, biscuit (see U.S. sense s.v. BISCUIT 1), etc.: made with baking-powder or other raising agent. *U.S.*

1889 R. T. COOKE *Steadfast* xvii. 189 Then it [*sc.* the election cake] wore only the style of 'raised cake'. **1890** *Harper's Mag.* Oct. 707/1 I've got raised biscuit for supper. **1907** *N.Y. Even. Post* (semi-weekly ed.) 18 July 5 The ever-lasting repetition of salt meats, potatoes, and raised biscuit in their bill of fare. **1914** G. ATHERTON *Perch of Devil* i. 28 I've got fried chicken.. and raised biscuit. **1937** E. K. HAINES *Cook Bk.* xii. 360 *Raised muffins*.. A good old-fashioned change from the modern quick muffin.

5. *Naut.* ***raised upon***: having a framework added to increase the height of the sides.

1799 NELSON in Nicolas *Disp.* (1845) I. 3, I exerted myself to have the command of a four-oared cutter raised upon. **1867** SMYTH *Sailor's Word-bk.* 559.

6. *Phonetics.* Articulated with the tongue in a higher position.

[**1888** H. SWEET *Hist. Eng. Sounds* 2 Intermediate positions are: *retracted*.. and *advanced*, *raised*.. and *lowered*.] **1942** J. S. HALL *Phonetics Gt. Smoky Mountain Speech* (Amer. Speech Repr. & Monogr. No. 4) 15 There is a tendency in some speakers to use a tense, slightly raised [ɪ˔]. **1957** E. J. DOBSON *Eng. Pronunc., 1500–1700* II. 614 The struggle of the raised ME ẹ̄ to replace the normal ME ę̄ was in StE [*sc.* Standard English] a long-drawn-out process. *Ibid.* 642 The raised pronunciation was not accepted in any but careless speech in the seventeenth century. **1972** M. L. SAMUELS *Linguistic Evol.* iii. 44 There is often a process of systemic regulation.. by the selection of raised variants.

raised, *ppl. a.*[2] (and *pa. pple.*). [f. RAISE *v.*[2]; now associated with prec. Cf. RASED *ppl. a.*]

1. Of cloth: †**a.** Having the pile cut close. (Cf. *velours ras, drap d'or ras* in Cotgrave.) *Obs.* **b.** Having the pile (apparently) cut away in such a manner as to leave a raised pattern.

c **1550** *Fabric Rolls York Minster* (Surtees) 311 A greene cushion of raised velvet. **1578** *Inv. R. Wardr.* (1815) 222 Ane uther [gowne] of raisit claith of silver. **1870** ROCK *Textile Fabrics* Introd. lxxiii, Some [art-velvets] are raised or cut, the design being done in a pile standing well up by itself from out of a flat ground of silk. *Ibid.* 200 The fabric .. now known as cut or raised velvet.

†**2.** Of shoes: Having designs cut in the leather.

1688 R. HOLME *Armoury* III. 14/2 Pinked or raised shooes, have the over leathers grain part cut into Roses, or other devices.

†**raise-devil**, *a.* *nonce-wd.* [f. RAISE *v.*[1] 21.] Devil-raising.

c **1661** *Mrq. Argyle's Last Will* in *Harl. Misc.* (1746) VIII. 27/1 That.. it may by the same raise-Devil Directory be conjured up again.

'raisedly, *adv.* *Obs.* exc. *dial.* [f. RAISED *ppl. a.*[1] + -LY[2].] In an elevated or excited manner.

1611 FLORIO, *Rileuatamente*, raisedly. **1651** H. MORE *Enthus. Tri.* (1712) 39 Enthusiasts.. have spoken very raisedly and divinely. **1887** JAMIESON Suppl., *Raisitly*, excitedly.

'raisedness. ? *Obs.* [f. as prec. + -NESS.] The state of being raised, elevated, or exalted.

1645 W. JENKYN *Stil-Destroyer* 32 Others neglect the Sacrament.. in comming with little raisednesse of soule, dead affections. **1646** H. LAWRENCE *Comm. Angells* 33 Thirdly, you shall know what they know, and as they know it; whence you see what raisednes of your conditions will bee. **1693** R. FLEMING *Disc. Earthquakes* 57 Such a Raisedness and Security of a Christians Soul in an extraordinary Hour of Tryal.

raiser ('reɪzə(r)). [f. RAISE *v.*[1] + -ER[1].]

1. a. One who raises, in various senses of the vb. Also, a nurseryman who breeds or cultivates new varieties of plants.

13.. *Evang. Nicod.* 1162 in Herrig *Archiv* LIII. 413 To þe, Ihesu, we pray, Rayser tyll lyfe fro ded. **1388** WYCLIF *Judith* xiv. 9 That Holofernes schulde awake not of the reiseris. *c* **1460** *Towneley Myst.* xxii. 37 Rasars of slanderyngys. **1570** BUCHANAN *Admonitioun* Wks. (1892) 24 Rasaris of rebellioun. **1577** B. GOOGE *Heresbach's Husb.* (1586) 47 b, In no wyse to be a rayser or enhaunser of rentes. **1607–12** BACON *Ess., Parents & Childr.* (Arb.) 272 They that are the raysers of their houses are most indulgent towardes theire Children. **1611** BIBLE *Dan.* xi. 20 Then shall stand vp in his estate a raiser of taxes. **1665** MANLEY *Grotius' Low C. Warres* 624 The raysers of the War were scattered here and there. **1704** NORRIS *Ideal World* II. vii. 367 The great raiser and improver of the optical science. **1707** J. MORTIMER *Whole Art of Husbandry* xvi. 315 A planter or raiser of trees ought to consider the under soil, as well as the superficies of the earth. **1741** MIDDLETON *Cicero* I. vi. 459 Cæsar was the author and raiser of all that storm. **1845** *Florist's Jrnl.* VI. 198 For the beginner, whose chance of competing with the more established raiser is so remote, this suggestion holds forth the most flattering hopes. **1847** TENNYSON *Princ.* Concl. 87 A raiser of huge melons and of pine. **1874** *Act 37 & 38 Vict.* c. 94 §42 The raisers of such inhibitions.. may again record the same. **1884** *Harper's Mag.* June 53/2 A disappointed raiser of church debts. **1921** *Sat. Westm. Gaz.* 10 Sept. 16/2 We owe this new race [of freesias] largely to Continental raisers. **1970** *Daily Tel.* 17 Oct. 9/1 New roses from the same raiser.. are Golden Times and Rosy Mantle.

b. So ***raiser-up***.

a **1425** *Cursor M.* 16705 (Trin.) Heil þou temple caster doun:.. And reiser vp. **1580** HOLLYBAND *Treas. Fr. Tong*, *Resusciteur de proces vuidez*, a raiser vp of matters alredy decided and iudged. **1879** MISS BRADDON *Vixen* III. 89 She had been.. the raiser-up of many a sickly child.

2. That which raises; *spec.* an elevator muscle; also, leaven or yeast.

1758 J. S. *Le Dran's Observ. Surg.* (1771) Expl. Fig. v, The Raiser of the *Scapula.* **1838** LYTTON *Alice* x. ii. 357 His excited fancy was the sole and real raiser of the spectre. **1908** *Animal Managem.* 121 The utility of boiled foods in the service is limited to their occasional use as condition raisers for horses which require fattening.

3. *Carpentry.* **a.** A riser (of a stair). **b.** A start or shoulder of a water-wheel bucket.

1679 MOXON *Mech. Exerc.* I. 152 You would by supporting each Step with a Raiser have the model of a true pair of Winding Stairs. **1825** J. NICHOLSON *Operat. Mechanic* 85 All the grooves for starts or raisers, and buckets, were cut out before it was removed. **1875** KNIGHT *Dict. Mech.* 1874/1 *Raiser*, the front of a step.

4. *Bridge.* **a.** A player who increases his partner's bid. **b.** A card or combination of cards which justifies the increase by a player of his partner's bid. Cf. RAISE *v.*[1] 34 a.

1912 F. IRWIN *Fine Pts. Auction Bridge* 89 No guarded queens nor guarded jacks in side-suits, may be counted as raisers. **1929** M. C. WORK *Compl. Contract Bridge* iv. 34 In the latter case the raiser must have Hearts stopped at least once. *Ibid.* v. 100 It is impossible to translate each individual element directly into raisers. **1964** *Official Encycl. Bridge* 447/1 *Raiser*, the player who bids for a greater number of tricks in a suit first bid by his partner.

†**raise-velvet**, *a.* *Obs.* *rare*$^{-1}$. Superfine.

Cf. *raised velvet* s.v. RAISED *ppl. a.*[2]

1603 *Patient Grissil* (Shaks. Soc.) 19 'The sintheresis of the soul', and such like raise-velvet terms.

†**raish.** *Obs.* *rare*$^{-1}$. [Echoic.] A harsh swish.

1710 *Last Distemper Tom Whigg* II. 38 A Couple of undone Ravens, cutting the Air at every Stroke of their rank Wing with a Raish [etc.].

raisin ('reɪz(ə)n). Forms: α. 3 raycin, 4–5 -syn, 4, 6–7 -son, 4, 7 -sin, (5 -sing), 6 -sen; 4, 6– raisin, 6–8 -son. β. 4 racyn, 4–6 rasyn(g, 5 rason, razin, 5–6 rasin, 6 -en. γ. 4–5 reysyn(g, (5 reyssyng), 4–6 reysin, (5 -ing), 4–7 -on, (5 -one, -oun); 4–5 reisyn, 6 -on, 6–7 reisin, 7 -en. δ. 4 resyn(g, 5–7 -on, (6 -onn); 5 reasyng, 6 -en, 7 -in, 6 reazin, 6–7 (9) reason. ε. 5 royson. [a. OF. *raiz-*, *razin*, *reis-*, *resin*, *roisin*, etc. (F. *raisin*) = Prov. *razin*, *razim*, Sp. *racimo*:—pop. L. **racīm-um*, L. *racēm-um* RACEME.

The five main forms of the word are all of Fr. origin; that with *oi* is rare in Engl., but is the base of G. *rosine*, Du. *rozijn*, Da. *rosin*, Sw. *russin*. The pron. ('riːz(ə)n) remained current after the spelling *reason* had been dropped, and is still defended by Webster in 1828 (cf. quot. 1807 in 2 δ); Sheridan, however, gives ('reɪz(ə)n) in 1789.]

†**1. a.** A cluster of grapes; a grape. *Obs.*

1382 WYCLIF *Lev.* xix. 10 Ne in thi vyne ȝeerd the reysonus and cornes fallynge down thow shalt not gedere. *c* **1400** MAUNDEV. (1839) xv. 168 The peper growethe, in maner, as dothe a wylde Vyne... and the Fruyt thereof hangethe in manere as Reysynges. **1484** CAXTON *Fables of Æsop* IV. i, A foxe.. beheld the raysyns that grew vpon a hyghe vyne. **1614** RALEIGH *Hist. World* I. (1634) 103 The fruit of the Vine or Raysin, did not grow naturally in that part of Armenia.

†**b.** = *raisin-grape* (see 3). *Obs.* *rare*$^{-1}$.

1573 TUSSER *Husb.* (1878) 76 Of trees or fruites to be set or remooued.. 20 Respis. 21 Reisons.

2. a. A grape partially dried, either in the sun or by artificial means. (Chiefly *pl.*)

α. [**1278** *Durh. Acc. Rolls* (Surtees) 486 In.. ficubus, Raycinys, et novem lagenis vini.] **13..** *Coer de L.* 1549 Off froyt here is gret plenté! Fyggys, raysyns, in frayel. *c* **1400** tr. *Secreta Secret., Gov. Lordsh.* 74 Old wyn and swete raysyns. **1533** ELYOT *Cast. Helthe* (1539) 20, Raysons do make the stomake firme and strong. **1616** B. JONSON *Devil an Ass* II. i, Is not that strange, S[r], to make wine of raisins? **1651** JER. TAYLOR *Serm. for Year* I. vii. 81 A man is.. so exposed to calamity, that a raisin is able to kill him. **1703** *Lond. Gaz.* No. 3971/4 Their Cargoes, consisting of.. Brandys, Prunes, Raisons. **1841** LANE *Arab. Nts.* I. 123 A sweet drink composed of water with raisins.

β. *c* **1400** tr. *Secreta Secret., Gov. Lordship* 77 Seuyn dragmes of pressyd rasynges. *c* **1450** *Mirour Saluacioun* 1771 Figes, Razines and Nuttes and apples. **1536** *MS. Acc. St. John's Hosp., Canterb.*, Payd for a pound of Rasens iijd. **1551** TURNER *Herbal* (1568) II. 144 The frayles.. that figges and rasines are carried better in.

γ. **13..** *K. Alis.* 5193 It wil al fruyt ete, Applen, noten, reisyns, and whete. **1422** tr. *Secreta Secret., Priv. Priv.* 245 Vse in this tymes.. fygis, datis, and reysyns. **1596** J. SMYTHE in *Lett. Lit. Men* (Camden) 90 To suppe.. with bread and reysins.

δ. [**1348–9** *Durh. Acc. Rolls* (Surtees) 549 In duabus libr. de Resyns sanz pepyn.] **14..** *Voc.* in Wr.-Wülcker 621/8 *Vua passa*, resonn. **1544** in R. G. Marsden *Sel. Pl. Crt. Adm.* (1894) I. 127 Venturyn.. ladyth ij butts saying therein to be reasens of Damask. **1645** HOWELL *Lett.* lix. (1650) 241 With Figs and Reasons allur'd litill Children. [**1807** H. J. PYE *Comm. Commentators Shaks.* 225 Reason and raisin.. are pronounced alike in the age of George the Third, by every person who speaks without affectation.]

†**b.** ***great raisins***, the dried fruit of the common vine, as distinguished from ***small raisins*** = *raisins of Corinth* (see CURRANT 1 a). *Obs.*

c **1420** *Liber Cocorum* 16 Sethe þenne oþer raysyns grete In rede wyne. *c* **1430** *Two Cookery-bks.* 33 Þen caste þer-to Roysonys of Coraunce, Dates y-talid, grete Roysonys. **1485**

Inv. in *Ripon Ch. Acts* (Surtees) 366 In small reasynges, 1½*d.* **1584** COGAN *Haven of Health* cvii. (1612) 95 Great Raysons, and small Raysons, otherwise called Corans. **1598** *Epulario* B iij b, Take a few small Reasons and an Onion.

c. ***raisins of the sun***, sun-dried grapes.

1544 PHAER *Regim. Lyfe* (1553) I vj b, A litle quantitie of raisins of the sunne. **1612** WOODALL *Surg. Mate* Wks. (1653) 166 Currants and Reysons of the Sun are likewise very good [in Scurvy]. **1780** J. T. DILLON *Trav. Spain* 376 The raisins of the sun..are still more delicate. **1841** *Penny Cycl.* XIX. 274/1 Muscatels, blooms,..raisins of the sun.

d. The dark purplish-brown colour of raisins.

1909 *Westm. Gaz.* 4 Sept. 3/2 The long-suffering mole is to find serious rivals in coal-dust grey, elephant's breath, and a purplish black called raisin. **1927** *Daily Express* 7 Mar. 6 (Advt.), Light mulberry, new blue, raisin, rosewood. **1971** *Guardian* 7 Sept. 9/1 A choice of colours: greengage,..fig, raisin, grape, black.

3. *attrib.* and *Comb.*, as ***raisin-brandy, bread, brew, cake,*** **†*-frail, -grape, pudding, -vine, -wine; raisin-coloured*** adj.; **raisin-tree** (see quots.).

1753 CHAMBERS *Cycl. Supp.*, *Raisin brandy,..a very clean and pure spirit, obtained from raisins. **1902** A. BENNETT *Anna of Five Towns* xii. 316 The delicacies which differentiate high tea from tea..hot toast, sardines with tomatoes, *raisin-bread, currant bread [etc.]. **1965** W. R. HARDING *Days of Henry Thoreau* x. 183 Thoreau experimented frequently with his bread making and soon learned that an unleavened variety was the simplest. When he added raisins to the dough, it was said that he became the inventor of raisin bread. **1980** A. AUSWAKS *Trick of Diamonds* iii. 80 Toasted raisin bread and butter. **1919** H. CRANE *Let.* 27 Dec. (1965) 28, I got dreadfully drunk on dreadful *raisin brew. *Ibid.* 29 This fellow of the raisin brew is another poor soul like myself, in Akron exile from N.Y. **1907** *Yesterday's Shopping* (1969) p. lii/1 *Raisin cakes. **1973** M. AMIS *Rachel Papers* 83 Two kinds of sandwiches, raisin cake, sliced ham, unlimited tea. **1939** SPENDER & GILI tr. *Lorca's Poems* 47 *Raisin-coloured shoes. **1669** EVELYN *Vintage* (1675) 48 Putting the cluster into a *raisin-frail or bag of hair-cloth. **1676** WORLIDGE *Cyder* (1691) 225 The *Raisin-grape is a large and long grape. **1767** J. ABERCROMBIE *Ev. Man his own Gard.* (1803) 674/2 Tokay, red, white, Alexandrian, Raisin [Grapes]. **1883** *Cheltenham Examiner* Suppl. 19 Sept. 1/3 Berries and apricots often yield still more profit to the acre than raisin grapes. **1767** J. WOODFORDE *Diary* 24 July (1924) I. 64, I gave them a fine ham..and a good rich *raisin pudding. **1861** MRS. BEETON *Bk. Househ. Managem.* 671 (*heading*) Baked raisin pudding (plain and economical). **1548** TURNER *Names Herbes* (E.D.S.) 86 Rhibes..is called in some places of Englande a *Rasin tree. **1887** NICHOLSON *Dict. Gardening, Raisin-tree, Japanese*, a common name for *Hovenia dulcis*. **1597** GERARDE *Herbal* II. cccxxiii. (1633) 875 We may call it in English *Raisin Vine. **1664** EVELYN *Kal. Hort.* (1729) 234 Cluster Grape, Parsley, Raisin [Vines]. **1723** J. NOTT *Cook's & Confectioner's Dict.* sig. Ff1v (*heading*) To make *raisin wine. **1769** MRS. RAFFALD *Eng. Housekpr.* (1778) 319 To make Smyrna Raisin Wine. **1845** E. ACTON *Mod. Cookery* xxvi. 541 Raisin Wine. **1976** 'TREVANIAN' *Main* (1977) viii. 165 The proprietor of the Greek restaurant..keeps refilling her glass with raisin wine.

raisin, variant of RASEN, wall-plate.

raising (ˈreɪzɪŋ), *vbl. sb.* [f. RAISE *v.*[1] + -ING[1].]

1. a. The action of the vb., in various senses; *spec.* in *Curling*, driving a partner's stone into one of the circles round the tee.

a **1350** in Horstm. *Altengl. Leg.* (1881) 134/216 It was bigun..Thurg raising of þe kinges sun. **1388** WYCLIF *Judith* xiv. 9 Thei..ymagyneden by craft vnrestfulnesse for cause of reisyng. **1455** *Charter* in *Liber Eccl. de Scon* (Bann. Cl.) 185 In the lifting and raising of the saidez fourti schillingis ȝerly. **1511** GUYLFORDE *Pylgr.* (1851) 25 The very hooly crosse was prouyd by reysinge of a deed woman. **1591** PERCIVALL *Sp. Dict.*, *Descerco*, the raising of a siege. **1622** MISSELDEN *Free Trade* 106 The dearenesse of things, which the Raising of Money bringeth with it. **1706** J. WARD *Introd. Math.* II. ii. §5 (1734) 154 Involution is the Raising or Producing of Powers from any proposed Root. **1781** COWPER *Lett.* 8 Apr., I send you a cucumber, not of my own raising. **1828** SCOTT *F.M. Perth* ii, A sign from Catharine, if that slight raising of her little finger was indeed a sign. **1842** DICKENS *Amer. Notes* II. ii. 58 Down Easters, and men of Boston raising. **1892** J. KERR in *Skating, Curling*, etc. 350 Every competitor shall play four shots at..raising, and chipping the winner. **1929** M. C. WORK *Compl. Contract Bridge* p. xv, Any advice given for bidding, raising, etc., applies when the score is 'love-all'. **1967** *Gloss. Mining Terms (B.S.I.)* IX. 11 *Raising*, the process of excavating a shaft from the bottom upwards. **1978** *Sci. Amer.* July 112/3 Raising (making a new bet by putting more money into the pot than is required for calling).

b. So ***raising up***.

c **1440** *Promp. Parv.* 428/1 Reysynge vp, *elevacio.* **1530** PALSGR. 260/2 Raysing up of a thyng, *leuee.* **1597** GERARDE *Herbal* III. lxxxviii. 1256 Almonds..serue for the raising vp of flegme and rotten matter. **1684** BUNYAN *Pilgr.* II. 69 The reason of raising up of that Stage. **1929** D. RUNYON in *Hearst's International* Oct. 63/1 Madame La Gimp figures a baby is not apt to get much raising-up off of her as long as she is on Broadway. **1972** J. S. HALL *Sayings from Old Smoky* 113 In my raisin' up two or three besides your own would set up with sick people.

c. With *a* and *pl.* An instance of this; *spec.* in *U.S.* a house-raising (see RAISE *v.* 8).

c **1380** WYCLIF *Sel. Wks.* III. 361 Suspendingis, enterditingis, cursingis, and reisingis of croiserie. **1388** —— *Ps.* xcii. 4 The reisyngis of the see ben wondurful. **1609** HOLLAND *Amm. Marcell.* XXVII. xii. 324 Sapor,..by way of open reises and raisings of booties wasted all Armenia. **1651** *Rec. Waterhouse, Mass.* (1894) I. I. 29 [For] raising of the howse. **1711** J. GREEN *Jrnl.* 6 June in *Essex Inst. Hist. Coll.* (1869) X. I. 91, I went to ye raising ye New Meeting House at Col. Gardner's. **1772** M. CUTLER in *Life, Jrnls. & Corr.* (1888) I. 38 At Robert Dodge's, at a raising. **1856** G. DAVIS *Hist. Sketch Stockbridge & Southbridge, Mass.* 174 Raisings were also considered as an affair of similar interest, followed by an entertainment of good things. **1861** TRENCH *Comm. Ep. 7 Churches* 11 Such raisings from the dead as that of the widow's son.

d. *Phonetics.* Articulation (of a vowel) with the tongue closer to the roof of the mouth; an instance of this. Cf. RAISE *v.*[1] 20.

1874 H. SWEET *Hist. Eng. Sounds* in *Trans. Philol. Soc. 1874* 533 The short vowels do not seem to have changed much in the last few generations. The most noticeable fact is the loss of *æ* among the vulgar. It is modified by raising the tongue into the mid-front-wide, resulting in the familiar *ceb* for *cæb*. This anomalous raising of a short vowel is gradually spreading among the upper classes. **1909** O. JESPERSEN *Mod. Eng. Gram.* I. viii. 231 The great vowel-shift consists in a general raising of all long vowels with the exception of the two high vowels. **1934** C. DAVIES *Eng. Pronunc.* 7 From the fourteenth century on this vowel [*sc.* ME. ǭ] underwent a gradual raising and rounding. **1957** E. J. DOBSON *Eng. Pronunc. 1500–1700* II. 635 There are parallels enough for isolative raisings occurring in spite of, but hardly any for a combinative raising because of, a following *r*. **1959** A. CAMPBELL *Old Eng. Gram.* 71 Just as all back vowels are subject to fronting by *i*-umlaut, so certain front vowels are subject to raising. **1972** M. L. SAMUELS *Linguistic Evol.* iii. 44 In ME..we find widespread new raisings to /ɪ/. **1975** *Language* LI. 307 The asymmetry between front and back vowels is due to the raising of /æ̅/.

2. Anything that is raised; a raised place.

1572 HULOET, Raysing, or going vp of a hyll, *accliuitas.* **1611** COTGR., *Condol*, a ridge or raising of earth. **1658** A. FOX *Wurtz' Surg.* II. xxviii. 196 The place..is hard and red, and a raising is there. **1742** LEONI *Palladio's Archit.* I. 64 The floor of the Chambers is raised thirteen foot from..the ground..; and below under the raising of the thirteen foot, are the Cellars. **1858** *Skyring's Builder's Prices* (ed. 48) 46 If raised panels, add from whence the article arises. If moulded raisings, add [etc.].

3. a. A crop raised. **b.** *Mining* = GET *sb.*[1] 1 b.

1857 *Hunt's Merchants' Mag.* XXXVI. 755 Mr. Pease claimed it [*sc.* the tobacco] as his own raising and pointed to his mark to corroborate his statement. **1869** *Daily News* 8 Dec., Its most important 'raisings' are in wheat, oats, maize, tobacco, grapes, &c. **1883** GRESLEY *Gloss. Coal-mining* 198.

4. *attrib.* and *Comb.*, as ***raising-cord, -gin, -machine, -motion, -tool, -vat, -wheel***; **raising-bee** (*U.S.*), a gathering of neighbours to give assistance in raising the framework of a house or other building; **raising-board**, a corrugated board used in raising the grain of leather (Knight *Dict. Mech.* 1875); **raising-dinner** (*U.S.*), a dinner given at a 'raising'; **raising-gig** = GIG-MILL (Knight *Dict. Mech.*); **raising-hammer**, a hammer used in giving metal a rounded form (see RAISE *v.* 33 d); **raising-knife** (see quots.); **†raising-pair**, a framework used in mining (see quot.); **raising-room**, a room where cloth is raised.

1836 *Backwoods of Canada* 121 Neighbours who assemble at your summons to raise the walls of your house..: this is termed a '*raising bee'. *a* **1859** W. IRVING *Knickerb.* VII. ii. (1900) 254 'Raising bees' also were frequent. **1839** URE *Dict. Arts* 1230 The dots, spots, or ciphers which denote the *raising cords. **1702** *New Eng. Hist. & Gen. Reg.* (1879) XXXIII. 176 *note*, Provide a *Raysing Dinner for the Raysing the Schoolmasters House. **1952** *Chambers's Jrnl.* Aug. 455/2 For really fine-quality face cloths..nothing has yet been found to equal the slower and less rigorous action of the traditional west of England teazle *raising-gig. **1497** *Naval Acc. Hen. VII* (1896) 104 Shipping crane with a *Reysing gynne. **1846** HOLTZAPFFEL *Turning* I. 404 Figure 277 shows the narrow edge of the *raising-hammer, in the act of descending. **1725** BRADLEY *Fam. Dict.* s.v. *Green plot*, They put the *Raising Knife under the Turf and raise it up. **1875** KNIGHT *Dict. Mech.* 1874/1 *Raising-knife*, a knife employed by coopers in setting up the staves in form for a cask. **1885** *Census Instruct.*, *Raising Machine Minder. **1839** URE *Dict. Arts* 1230 The *raising motion is effected by coupling the leaf to one end of its correspondent top lever. **1747** HOOSON *Miner's Dict.* Q iij, *Raising-Pair... The use for these is, when we begin at the Bottom of any wide Pit at the Day to Sink, we rise with these Pair upwards. **1835** URE *Philos. Manuf.* 203 The cloth passes several times to and from the *raising and cutting-rooms. **1884** *B'ham Daily Post* 23 Feb. 3/5 Steel-pen Trade.—Wanted, a *Raising-Tool Maker. **1852** MORFIT *Tanning & Currying* (1853) 197 The last *raising-vat, which contains the strongest tan-liquor. *a* **1824** DOUGLAS in *Trans. Highland Soc.* VI. 105 The crank must revolve nearly 13 times to give the *raising-wheel one revolution.

ˈraising, *ppl. a.* [-ING[2].] That raises.

1609 W. M. *Man in Moone* (1849) 20 Their followers; who, by the raising hand of their lord's assistance, have ascended many high and loftie steppes of dignity.

ˈraising-piece. [f. RASEN *sb.* (q.v.), associated with RAISING *vbl. sb.*] A wall-plate.

a **1548** HALL *Chron.* XII, *Hen. VIII* 605 From the firste water table to the raysyng or resun pieces. **1663** GERBIER *Counsel* 66 Oake Roofing raysing pieces. **1679** MOXON *Mech. Exerc.* I. 143 Wall plates, or Raising Pieces and Beams. **1736** NEVE *City & C. Purchaser* s.v. **1842** GWILT *Archit.* §1023 *Raising Piece*, one which lies under a beam or beams and over the posts or punchions.

So **ˈraising-plate.**

1679 MOXON *Mech. Exerc.* I. 137 They frame the Raising-plates just as the Ground-plates are framed; and then frame the Roof into the Raising-plates. **1825** J. NICHOLSON *Operat. Mechanic* 571 Wall-plates are sometimes called raising plates.

raisiny (ˈreɪzɪnɪ), *a.* [f. RAISIN + -Y[1].] Like or suggestive of (the taste of) raisins. Also *Comb.*

1864 J. A. GRANT *Walk across Afr.* 157 Plantain-wine..is a sweet raisiny-tasting wine; if aerated, nearly equal to sparkling hock in richness of flavour. **1975** *Times* 5 Apr. 11/5 Fortified dessert wines—rather more raisiny than port.

raison, obs. form of RAISIN, variant of RASEN.

raison, -able, obs. ff. REASON, REASONABLE.

‖**raison d'état** (rɛzɔ̃ deta). [Fr.] = *reason of state* s.v. REASON *sb.*[1] 5 b.

1869 MILL *Subj. Women* iii. 92 The *raison d'état*, meaning the convenience of the government,..was deemed a sufficient explanation and excuse for the most flagitious crimes. **1939** A. TOYNBEE *Study of Hist.* VI. 38 The god who was worshipped by the Imperial Dynasty was not..a product of *raison d'état.* **1958** E. H. CARR *Socialism in One Country* I. i. 6 *Raison d'état* is tough enough to emerge unscathed from the revolutionary turmoil. **1965** *New Statesman* 23 Apr. 648/2 The Third Reich, whose ideologists preferred the declamatory pathos of Fichte to Hegel's dispassionate concern with *raison d'état.* **1976** *Times Lit. Suppl.* 26 Nov. 1483/2 Hanged, on very dubious law, for raisons d'état by a post-war Labour Lord Chancellor. **1977** *Times* 14 Jan. 17/4 The Elysée's short-sighted conception of *raison d'état.*

‖**raison d'être** (rɛzɔ̃ dɛtr). [Fr.] 'Reason of being'; rational ground for existence.

1864 J. S. MILL *Let.* 18 Mar. (1910) II. 3 Modes of speech which have a real *raison d'être.* **1867** MORLEY *Burke* 208 Plunder in three forms..was the very *raison d'être* of the power of the [East India] Company. **1880** *Standard* 29 Nov., The Royal Society has almost ceased to have a *raison d'être.* **1889** A. JAMES *Diary* 14 Dec. (1964) 67 The French ladies of the 18th century..whose whole *raison d'être* was the graceful, and the light. **1927** C. CONNOLLY *Let.* 5 May in *Romantic Friendship* (1975) 301 With Desmond gone I have no *raison d'être.* **1959** J. BRAINE *Vodi* vii. 102 There were a few trees and fields, and even a small colony of expensive privately-built houses, which was rare for a place for which the raison d'être now was Rimelby Main [colliery]. **1975** J. G. EVANS *Environment Early Man Brit. Isles* v. 104 A possible *raison d'être* for these sites was the chert, a desirable raw material.

‖**raisonné** (rɛzɔne), *a.* [Fr., pa. pple. of *raisonner* to reason, etc., f. *raison* REASON.] Reasoned out, logical or systematical. Cf. CATALOGUE RAISONNÉ.

1777 H. WALPOLE *Lett.* (1857) VI. 492 This is my creed.. I think it is *raisonné.* **1845** THACKERAY *Misc. Ess.* (1885) 102 French Cookery is not..*approfondi* or elaborately described, but nobly *raisonné.*

‖**raisonneur** (rɛzɔnœr). [Fr., lit. 'one who reasons or argues'.] A character in a play, etc., who gives expression to the author's message, standpoint, or philosophy. Also *transf.* and (*nonce-wd.*) as *v. intr.*

1903 M. BEERBOHM in *Sat. Rev.* 5 Dec. 700/2 There is an old man [in Gorki's *Lower Depths*]..in whom we dimly descry a 'raisonneur'. **1913** G. B. SHAW *Quintessence of Ibsenism* 177 Poins, who was originally meant to be the *raisonneur* of the piece, and the chief figure among the prince's dissolute associates. **1950** E. H. CARR *Bolshevik Revol.* I. ii. 38 The Mensheviks..were primarily men of theory; in Bolshevik terminology they were *raisonneurs*, 'dry-as-dust archivists', the 'party intelligentsia'. **1955** *Times* 24 May 3/3 The *raisonneur*, for example, the family friend who announces the thesis of the play, draws the moral, and preaches his little sermons to the parties concerned, is bound to strike us as something of a nuisance. **1959** *Listener* 29 Oct. 749/1 He is clearly introduced as the play's *raisonneur*, the doughty exponent of a radical viewpoint. **1963** WODEHOUSE *Stiff Upper Lip, Jeeves* xii. 97, I saw that the time had come to be a *raisonneur*... 'Are you sure,' I said, raisonneuring like nobody's business, 'that you were altogether wise in confining him to spinach and what not?' **1969** M. R. BOOTH *Eng. Plays of 19th Cent.* II. 345 It seems rather unfair that..the worldly *raisonneurs*..are responsible for breaking up love affairs between young people and..forcing unhappy wives to stay with unpleasant and incompatible husbands, yet are themselves blessed with the hands in marriage of comely widows of means. **1980** *Times Lit. Suppl.* 23 May 581/1 Dottie..is a scatterbrained raisonneur, on stage throughout, directing her two lovers.. to their respective concealment in kitchen or spare bedroom.

raiss, obs. Sc. f. RACE *sb.*[1]

raistit, obs. var. REISTIT *Sc.*

raisty, var. REASTY, RESTY *Obs.*

†**ˈraisure.** *Obs. rare.* [f. RAISE *v.*[1] + -URE.] Elevation.

1613 MARKHAM *Eng. Husbandman* I. II. xvi. (1635) 203 Where by meanes of such raisure, you shall want mould.. you shall supply that lacke. **1677** GALE *Crt. Gentiles* III. 2 The highest raisures of natural or moral endowments.

rait, obs. f. RATE; Sc. pa. pple. RAY *Obs.*; var. RET *v.*

raitch, dial. var. RACHE *sb.*[1]

raiter, obs. var. REITER *sb.*[1]

raith (reːθ). *Sc.* (†and *north.*) Also 4 **rath(t, raþe,** 4, 8 **rathe,** 8 **reath.** [a. OIr. *ráthe, ráithe*, or Gael. *ràith* in same sense (cf. QUIDRATHE). The appearance of the word in the *Cursor M.* is remarkable.] A quarter of a year; three months.

a **1300** *Cursor M.* 16166 (Gött.) Herodes had grenid him to se, þar forwid mani ratht. *Ibid.* 23833 Said it es gane mani rath [etc.]. *c* **1375** *Sc. Leg. Saints* xl. (*Ninian*) 772 Men fastis it..thryse ilke rath of þe ȝere. **1768** ROSS *Helenore* I. 6 Howsoon as the jimp three raiths was gane. *a* **1774** FERGUSSON *Rising of Session* Poems (1807) 277 Little mair than half a reath. **1871** W. ALEXANDER *Johnny Gibb* (1873) 57, I wuntit him to gie Sawney a raith at lan' mizzourin'.

raith, obs. Sc. f. RATHE *a.* and *adv.*

raithe, dial. var. RATHE *sb.*

raither, dial. var. RATHER.

raive, Sc. pa. t. RIVE *v.*

raivel, Sc. var. RAVEL *sb.* and *v.*

raiyat, var. RAYAT.

raize, Sc. var. RAISE *v.*[1] (5 d).

‖**raj** (rɑːdʒ). Also 8 raje. [Hindī *rāj*: cf. RAJA(H.] **a.** Sovereignty, rule; kingdom.

1800 *Asiatic Ann. Reg., Misc. Tr.* 261/2 An account of the revenues of this raje, and a chart of the country. **1858** J. B. NORTON *Topics* 58 A very faint sample of what must have universally happened had any new 'Raj' been established.

b. *spec.* the British dominion or rule in the Indian sub-continent (before 1947). In full, *British raj*. Also *transf.*

1859 M. THOMSON *Story of Cawnpore* xvi. 229 But Delhi had fallen when these gentlemen threw their strength into the tide of revolt, and they were too late for a decisive superiority over the British *râj*. **1876** *Hansard Commons* 16 Mar. 141 Without upsetting the British Raj. **1890** *Athenæum* 13 Sept. 348/1 That standing miracle, the maintenance of the British *raj* [in India]. **1908** *Daily Chron.* 21 June 4/4 The Indian agitators who represent the British raj as the author of the plague. **1955** *Times* 25 Aug. 9/7 It was effective against the British raj in India, and the conclusion drawn here is that the British knew that they were wrong. **1969** R. MILLAR *Kut* xv. 288 Sir Stanley Maude had taken command in Mesopotamia, displacing the raj of antique Indian Army commanders. **1971** *Illustr. Weekly India* 18 Apr. 4/2 Though it appears paradoxical, in the last days of the Raj, the British were the only people who wished to keep India united. **1975** H. R. ISAACS in H. M. Patel et al. *Say not the Struggle Nought Availeth* 251 The post-independence régime in all its incarnations since the passing of the British Raj.

‖**raja, rajah** (ˈrɑːdʒə). Forms: 6–7 (8) raia, 7 raiah, raiaw, raya; 7 raga, ragea, 8 ragia; 7 radgee, 8 radja; 7– raja, 7– rajah. [Hindī *rājā*, Skr. *rājan* king, etc., f. *rāj* to reign, rule; cognate with L. *rēx, rēg-is*, OIr. *rī, rīg* king (see RICH).]

Originally the title given in India to a king or prince; in later times extended to petty chiefs or dignitaries (as Zemindars) or conferred as a title of nobility on Hindus, and adopted as the usual designation of Malay and Javanese rulers or chiefs (cf. quot. 1777).

1555 EDEN *Decades* 224 The Kyngs name was Raia Colambu and the Prince was cauled Raia Siagu. **1608** W. HAWKINS in Purchas *Pilgrims* (1625) III. vii. §2. 209 A Raga, who was absolute Lord of a Prouince. **1608** FINCH *Ibid.* IV. §4. 424 A small King or Raiaw, a Gentile. **1630** LORD *Banians & Persees* 68 The Raiahs..did procure the Bramanes to make it an act of Religion [etc.]. **1665** SIR T. HERBERT *Trav.* (1677) 65 This Castle [Rota] for many Ages acknowledged the Radgee her Governour. **1735** SOMERVILLE *Chase* II. 331 Potent Rajahs who themselves preside O'er Realms of wide Extent. **1777** MILLER in *Phil. Trans.* LXVIII. 167 Their Radjas (by which name they call every freeman that has property, of which there are sometimes one, sometimes more, in one Compong, and the rest are vassals). **1810** SOUTHEY *Kehama* VII. xi, The power Of the dread Rajah, terrible alike To men and Gods. **1844** H. H. WILSON *Brit. India* I. i. 99 The Raja of Bhurtpore had become..an ally of the British Government. **1878** C. STANFORD *Symb. Christ* i. 13 A chieftain so different from the fiery rajahs around.

attrib. *a* **1843** in Southey *Comm.-pl. Bk.* Ser. II. (1849) 486 The whole race of Kettris, the Rajah-tribe of India.

b. *attrib.* in bird-names, as ***raja(h) lory, shrike***.

1812 G. SHAW *Gen. Zool.* VIII. 537 Raja Lory. Psittacus Raja..Scarlet Lory, with gold-yellow wings. **1822** LATHAM *Gen. Hist. Birds* II. 63 Rajah shrike. *Ibid.* 226 Rajah Lory. Size of the Purple-capped Lory..Inhabits the Moluccas, and there called Rhadia, and is a rare species.

raja, variant of RAIA.

rajah-poot, obs. form of RAJPUT.

‖**rajahship** (ˈrɑːdʒəʃɪp). [f. RAJAH + -SHIP.]

1. The territory of a rajah.

1698 J. FRYER *Acc. E. India & Persia* 166 They are only said to be a petty Rajaship in the Plain. **1763** SCRAFTON *Indostan* (1770) 14 There are a number of Rajahships interspersed throughout India, which..have..never been subdued. **1862** BEVERIDGE *Hist. India* I. III. iv. 430 The two rajahships or Hindoo states of Trichinopoly and Tanjore.

2. The rank or power of a rajah. Also as a title.

1825 *Blackw. Mag.* XVII. 706 The gentle Hindoo cared not how the Rajahship was disposed of. **1859** LANG *Wand. India* 86 It was the acceptance of the 'Rajahship' which led to the confiscation of his estates. **1867** *Gd. Words* 336/1 His Rajahship rose.

Rajasthani (rɑːdʒəˈstɑːnɪ), *sb.* and *a.* [f. the name *Rajasthan* (see below) + -I.] **A.** *sb.* A collective term for the dialects spoken in Rajasthan, a state in north-west India; also, a member of the people of Rajasthan. **B.** *adj.* Of or pertaining to this language or people; *spec.* used of a style of dancing.

1901 [see JAIPUR]. **1933** L. BLOOMFIELD *Lang.* iv. 63 A number of dialect areas..cover the larger part of India and include such great languages as..Panjabi (16 millions), Rajasthani (13 millions),..Bihari (36 millions). **1957** [see JAIPUR]. **1958** [see MEWATI *sb.* and *a.*]. **1967** D. C. COOKE *C/o Amer. Embassy* (1968) v. 40 The Rajasthani women labourers. **1969** [see KATHAK]. **1972** W. B. LOCKWOOD *Panorama Indo-Europ. Lang.* xii. 198 The language Rajasthani..is essentially a linguist's term to denote a theoretical concept. *Ibid.* 203 Rajasthanis normally practice literacy through Hindi/Urdu. **1975** A. B. SHAH in H. M. Patel et al. *Say not the Struggle Nought Availeth* 105 Rajasthanis have settled down in all parts of the country without coming into conflict with the local people. **1976** H. R. F. KEATING *Filmi, Filmi, Inspector Ghote* vi. 50 Some simple Rajasthani peasant girl in *ghagra* and *choli*. *Ibid.* vii. 64 Tiny mosaic fragments of purple and gold Rajasthani enamel work.

raja yoga (ˈrɑːdʒə ˈjəʊgə). Also with capital initials. [Skr., f. *rājan* king + *yoga* YOGA.] A form of Yoga by which the practitioner attains control over his mind and emotions. Also *attrib.* Hence ‖**raja-yogin**, one who practises raja yoga.

1885 M. N. DVIVEDI *Râja Yoga* I. 44 The Vedântic process..of attaining to this state of Brahma generally described as *Râjayoga* is purely mental, and deals entirely with rules for restraining the mind. **1911** [see HATHA-YOGA]. **1913** E. F. BENSON *Thorley Weir* v. 167 For those three years he..lived a life of meditation that would have done credit to a student of Râja Yoga attaining Samâdhi. **1956** E. WOOD *Yoga Dict.* 127/2 *Rāja-yoga*, the system of yoga in which the man within asserts himself as the king (*rāja*) of all his mental and bodily possessions and powers. **1960** J. HEWITT *Yoga* 14 Others of the Raja Yoga school consider only a little Hatha necessary. *Ibid.* 15 Raja Yoga is designed to..put our mental house in order and concentrate our scattered energies. **1960** R. ROLLAND in *Ibid.* 95 It [is] astonishing that Western reason has taken so little into account the experimental research of Indian Raja-yogins. **1962** [see KARMA-YOGA]. **1977** C. MACFADDEN *Serial* (1978) xviii. 42/1 She had like *mutated* over the years through..hatha and raja yoga.

raje, obs. form of RAJ.

Rajmahali (ˈrɑːdʒməhɑːlɪ), *sb.* and *a.* Also Rajmahal. [f. the name of the *Rajmahal* hills of northern India + -I.] = MALER *sb.* and *a.*

1848 *Jrnl. Asiatic Soc. Bengal* XVII. II. 553 Comparative Vocabulary of the Aboriginal languages of Central India... 5. Múndala. 6. Rájmahali. 7. Góndi. **1853** J. R. LOGAN in *Jrnl. Indian Archipelago* VII. 49, I now proceed to the south Gangetic or Vindyan tribes, the Male or Rajmahali, the Kol, the Khond and the Gond. **1856** R. CALDWELL *Compar. Gram. Dravidian Lang.* 21 There are two uncultivated idioms of Central India, the Ûrâon and the Râjmahal, which contain..many Drâvidian roots of primary importance. **1872** E. T. DALTON *Descr. Ethnol. Bengal* VIII. ii. 272 The Rájmaháli version of the Oráon ceremony called the 'rog-pelowa', expulsion of an evil spirit. **1873, 1885** [see MALER *sb.* and *a.*]. **1906** G. A. GRIERSON *Linguistic Survey of India* IV. 446 The Maler also call themselves Sauriā, and their language is also known under the name of Rājmahālī, *i.e.*, the language of the Rajmahal Hills.

‖**rajpramukh** (ˈrɑːdʒprəmʊk). [Hindi, f. *rājya* state + *pramukh* chief.] In the Republic of India between 1948 and 1956, a governor of a state which was formerly a princely state or which resulted from the unification of several princely states.

1949 *Britannica Bk. of Year* 339/1 The remainder [of the Indian states] were grouped under the aegis of a *Rajpramukh* or presiding prince into 30 homogeneous groups, the rulers retaining their titles, dignities, and personal estates [in 1948]. **1950** G. N. JOSHI *Constitution of India* VII. 232 The head of a Part B State is called the Rajpramukh. *Ibid.* XIX. 342 As the executive heads of the Union and the State, the President and the Governor or Rajpramukh are given immunity from proceedings in court. **1957** *Listener* 5 Dec. 925/1 The Ruler..has since become..Rajpramukh of Rajasthan. **1958** G. MIKES *East is East* 171 He [*sc.* the Nizam of Hyderabad] became *rajpramukh*—appointed democratic governor—of his own state and all has gone well ever since. **1962** *Times* 26 Jan. (India Suppl.) p. xx/4 The office of *Rajpramukh* was abolished.

‖**Rajput** (ˈrɑːdʒpuːt). Forms: α. 6 reysbuto, 7 resbuti (*pl.*), rashboot(e, -bout, -poot, rasboute, reshpout, 8 rasspout. β. 7 ratspuche, razbooche. γ. 7 ragipou, 8 raijpout, rajah-, rajepoot, 9 rajapoote, -put, raujepoot, rajpoot, rajput. [Hindī *rājpūt*, f. Skr. *rāja* king + *putra* son. The form *rashbūt* is found in an Oriental writer of the 16th c. (Yule); *reysbuto* came through Pg., and *ragipou* through Fr.] A member of a Hindu caste, claiming descent from the original Kshatriyas, and distinguished by its military spirit.

α. **1598** tr. *Linschoten's Voy.* xxvii. 48 Reysbutos of Cambaia doe yet liue by robbing and stealing, and those of Cambaia pay tribute to the saide Reysbutos. **1615** E. TERRY in Purchas *Pilgrims* (1625) IX. vi. §4. 1479 The Rashbootes eate Swines-flesh most hatefull to the Mahometans. **1689** DAMPIER *Voy.* (1697) I. 507 Our Seamen..calling the Idolaters, Gentous, or Rashbouts. **1727** A. HAMILTON *New Acc. E. Ind.* I. xii. 134 Those Rasspouts..are all Gentlemen of the Sword,..well trained in the Art of killing.

attrib. **1616** SIR T. ROE *Jrnl.* 9 Oct. (Hakluyt Soc.) II. 282 In the handes of a Rashboote Gentile.

β. **1612** COPLAND in Purchas *Pilgrims* (1625) IV. viii. §1. 467 A Castle kept by the Ratspuches. **1612** WHITHINGTON *Ibid.* §3. 482 A Castle of the Razbooches (which were before the Mogolls Conquest, the Nobles of that countrey now liuing by robbery).

γ. **1678** J. PHILLIPS tr. *Tavernier's Trav.* II. I. iv. 34 The Ragipou's, who are the best Souldiers among the Indians. **1763** SCRAFTON *Indostan* (1770) 7 The Soldiers are commonly called Rajah-poots. **1800** *Asiatic Ann. Reg., Chron.* 47/2 A remarkable strong Rajepoot, selected for the purpose. **1829** J. TOD *Rajast'han* I. 137 The poorest Rajpoot of this day retains all the pride of ancestry, often his sole inheritance. **1836** N. WISEMAN *Lect. Doctr. Cath. Ch.* I. vi. 174, I consider the soul of the meanest and poorest in the lowest caste, equal, in the estimation of God, to that of the Rajpoot. **1841** ELPHINSTONE *Hist. Ind.* I. i. 103 The Rájpúts still loudly assert the purity of their descent from the Cshetriyas. **1864** TREVELYAN *Compet. Wallah* (1866) 67 Coer Sing, who was recognised as chieftain by the Rajpoots, or soldier caste, of that region. **1971** *Illustr. Weekly India* 4 Apr. 8/3 The non-Vedic and non-Aryan Kshatriyas..had been admitted to the military class by Shankaracharya. These (along with certain other families who claimed descent from Raja Ram Chandra) became the masters of Rajputana. Their royal families acquired the title of Rajputra or *Rajanya*, which ultimately became 'Rajput'.

attrib. **1878** A. C. LYALL in *Fortn. Rev.* XXX. 543 (*heading*) A Rajput Chief of the old School. **1931** *Times Lit. Suppl.* 18 June 482/3 They [*sc.* hill paintings] differ not only from the metropolitan art of the Mughal Court, but from the Rajput paintings of other parts of India. **1937** [see *candy pink*]. **1974** *Encycl. Brit. Micropædia* VIII. 396/3 *Rajput painting*, the art of the independent Hindu feudal states in India, as distinguished from the court art of the Mughal emperors.

‖**Rajya Sabha** (ˈrɑːdʒjə ˈsɑːbə). Also Raj Sabha. [Hindi, f. *rājya* state + *sabhā* assembly, council.] The upper house of the central Indian parliament.

1948 *Whitaker's Almanack* 772/1 The Union Constitution Committee of the Constituent Assembly recommended the bicameral union of the legislature on the British model with two Houses to be called 'Lok Sabha'..and 'Raj Sabha' or the House of States. **1954** BINANI & RAMA RAO *India at Glance* (rev. ed.), (Index), Rajya Sabha (Council of States). **1955** M. P. SHARMA *Govt. Indian Republic* (ed. 2) vii. 144 The Parliament..consists of the President and the two Houses—the Council of States and the House of the People now formally styled as Rajya Sabha and Lok Sabha respectively. **1969** *National Herald* (New Delhi) 29 July 4/3 The two Rajya Sabha seats from UP for which by-elections are due on August 13. **1972** *Times of India* 28 Nov. 8/2 (*heading*) Rajya Sabha to debate world situation. **1979** *Ibid.* 17 Aug. 1/5 Those in the alignment were willing to accommodate Mr. Mahadev Prasad Varma of the Charan Singh faction as deputy leader of the party in the Rajya Sabha, but not Mr. Amin.

rak, obs. f. RACK, RAKE *sb.*[1]; obs. Sc. f. RECK.

Rakah (ˈrɑːkə, ‖ˈrakax). [mod. Heb., acronym f. *Reshimah Komunistit Ḥadashah*, New Communist List (of candidates).] One of the two communist parties in Israel, formed in 1965.

1969 W. LAQUEUR *Struggle for Middle East* ix. 166 From July 1967 RAKAH was recognized as the official Israeli Communist party by the Soviet bloc. *Ibid.* 167 RAKAH demanded the unconditional surrender of all the Israeli-occupied territories. **1970** A. DERSHOWITZ in *Commentary* Dec. 76/2 They [*sc.* some Israeli Arab citizens] may..belong to the Maoist-oriented Rakah party which has eight members in the Knesset. *Ibid.* Sharing office space with an older Arab lawyer active in Rakah. **1974** N. CHOMSKY *Peace in Middle East?* v. 176 One of the communist parties (Rakah) is 'pro-Arab', a testimonial to Israeli democracy. *Ibid.*, Sabri Jiryis..describes Rakah as 'the Communist sector of the Israeli establishment'. **1977** *Hongkong Standard* 14 Apr. 9/4 Until now, discontent has been expressed through voting for Rakah, the pro-Moscow Israeli Communist Party whose membership is overwhelmingly Arab.

rakcat, obs. form of RACKET *sb.*[1]

rake (reɪk), *sb.*[1] Forms: 1 raca, racu, 4 raak, 5 rak, 5–6 *Sc.* raike, 4– rake. [OE. *raca* m., *racu* f. = MLG., MDu. *rāke* (Du. *raak*), (M)Sw. *-raka*, Da. *-rage*, related by ablaut to MLG. *rēke*, OHG. *rehho*, *recho* (MHG. *reche*, G. *rechen*) rake, ON. *reka* spade, shovel, f. root **rek-* (Goth. *rikan*, OHG. *rehhan*) to gather, heap up.]

1. a. An implement, consisting of a bar fixed across the end of a long handle and fitted with teeth which point downwards, used in field-work for drawing together hay, grass, or the like, and in gardening for similar purposes or for breaking up, levelling, and smoothing the surface of the ground (a *hand-rake*). Also, a larger agricultural implement of the same character, mounted on wheels and drawn by a horse (a *horse-rake*), or one of the bars with teeth in a tedding-machine.

a **725** *Corpus Gloss.* 25 Rastrum, ræce. *c* **1000** ÆLFRIC *Gloss.* in Wr.-Wülcker 105/1 *Rastrum, uel rastellum*, raca. *a* **1100** *Gerefa* in *Anglia* IX. 263 He sceal habban..bytel, race, ȝeafle, hlædre [etc.]. **1387** TREVISA *Higden* (Rolls) III. 55 Fabius slowȝ Remus..wiþ an herdes rake [*v.r.* raak]. *c* **1420** *Pallad. on Husb.* I. 837 Take thy spadis, rakis, knyf, and shoule. **1523** FITZHERB. *Husb.* §24 A good husbande hath his forkes and rakes made redye in the wynter before. **1603** KNOLLES *Hist. Turks* (1638) 105 All his mattockes, forkes, rakes, syths [etc.]. **1697** DRYDEN *Virg. Georg.* I. 233 The land with daily Care Is exercis'd, and with an Iron War Of Rakes and Harrows. **1727–46** THOMSON *Summer* 359 Infant hands Trail the long rake..Wide flies the tedded grain. **1841–4** EMERSON *Ess., Prudence* Wks. (Bohn) I. 98 Keep the rake, says the hay-maker, as nigh the scythe as you can, and the cart as nigh the rake. **1844** STEPHENS *Bk. Farm* (1855) II. 228/2 A skeleton carriage, having a series of revolving rakes, occupying the place of the body.

b. Phr. *as lean* (also *thin*, †*rank*) *as a rake*.
c **1386** CHAUCER *Prol.* 287 And leene was his hors as is a rake. *c* **1450** HOLLAND *Howlat* 216 The Ravyne..Was dene rurale to reid, rank as a raike. *a* **1529** SKELTON *P. Sparowe* 913 Odyous Enui..His bones crake, Leane as a rake. **1694** MOTTEUX *Rabelais* v. iv, All these sorts of Birds..grow in an instant as fat as Hogs, tho' they came as lean as Rakes. **1823** E. MOOR *Suffolk Wds.* s.v., 'Thin as a rake' is not an infrequent comparison with us.

c. *transf.* A very lean person.
1582 STANYHURST *Æneis* III. (Arb.) 89 A meigre leane rake with a long berd goatlyke. **1607** SHAKS. *Cor.* I. i. 24 Let vs reuenge this with our Pikes, ere we become Rakes.

2. a. An implement, similar to the above, used for various purposes, sometimes having a flat blade in place of the bar with teeth. *spec.* (*a*) an implement with a blade instead of teeth for gathering money or chips staked in a game of chance; (*b*) (see quot. 1966).
1530 PALSGR. 260/2 Rake for the Kenell, *rasteau*. **1574** SCOT *Hop. Gard.* (1578) 51 A Rake fashioned like a Coale rake, hauing in stede of teeth a boorde. **1671** [see *rake-man* in 5]. **1825** J. NICHOLSON *Operat. Mechanic* 606 The tools of the plasterer consist of..a rake, with two or three prongs, bent downwards..for mixing the hair and mortar together. **1851** GREENWELL *Coal-Trade Terms Northumb. & Durh.* 41 A rake, with about 8 teeth..is used by the hewer in working coal by separation. **1865** TROLLOPE *Can you forgive Her?* II. xxv. 280 The money..was all drawn back by the croupier's unimpassioned rake. **1868** *Rep. U.S. Commissioner Agric.* (1869) 342 The tongs [in oyster fishing] are composed of two iron rakes attached to..poles. **1884** [see CROUPIER 2]. **1907** *Yesterday's Shopping* (1969) 109/3 Aluminium Combs—Dressing or Rakes..each 1/6... Rakes, Vulcanite..1/3. **1937** [see PASSE *sb.*[2]]. **1966** J. S. COX *Illustr. Dict. Hairdressing & Wigmaking* 125/1 *Rake*, a strong comb with large even-sized teeth. Used for removing tangles in long hair. **1972** D. LEES *Zodiac* 47 If you don't want Françoise to blue in all her winnings..you'd better get her away from the table. The way she's going the croupier's going to have to send out for a bigger rake. **1973** 'R. MACLEOD' *Burial in Portugal* vi. 117 A blonde..was the only player to avoid the croupier's rake on the first couple of spins of the wheel.

b. A kind of rasp or scraper. (? For RAPE *sb.*[5])
1727 BRADLEY *Fam. Dict.* s.v. *Hoof bound*, With a Rake or Drawing-Iron, file or draw away the old Hoof somewhere near. **1845** *Penny Cycl.* Supp. I. 624/2 In the preparation of hares' fur for the hatter, the skin..is rubbed with a kind of saw called a rake. **1878** *Ure's Dict. Arts* IV. 380 The skin is first carded with a rake, which is the blade of an old shear or piece of a scythe, with large teeth notched into its edge.

3. = *rake-hook* (see 5).
1797 JOHNSTON *Beckmann's Invent.* III. 152 The same craft in avoiding rakes and nets is ascribed to that fish.

4. An act of raking.
1869 'MARK TWAIN' *Innoc. Abr.* xii. 114 The first rake of his razor loosened the very hide from my face. **1961** Y. OLSSON *Syntax Eng. Verb* vii. 207 (From garden talk:) Let me have a rake!

5. *attrib.* and *Comb.*, as **rake-backed** adj., **rake-handle, -head,** †**-man, -shaft, -shank, -stem, -teeth, -tine, -wheel; rake-comb** = RAKE *sb.*[1] 2 a (*b*); **rake-dredge**, a dredge fitted with a rake, used for collecting natural history specimens; †**rake-fetter**, ? a maker or mender of rakes; **rake-hook**, a set of hooks fixed on a bar which is dragged along the bottom of a river or lake so as to catch fish by the body; †**rake-lean** *a.*, lean as a rake; **rake-steel**, a rake-handle (now *dial.*); **rake-up**, something concocted; a fabrication.
1629 GAULE *Holy Madn.* 324 Gaunt-belly'd, *Rake-backt. **1790** *Rake-comb [see *dressing-comb* s.v. DRESSING *vbl. sb.* 5 a]. **1969** E. H. PINTO *Treen* 364 The boxwood H comb is an 18th-century type barber's comb, used on wigs after the coarse or 'rake' comb. *c* **1500** *Cocke Lorell's B.* 11 Schouyll chepers, gardeners, and *rake fetters. **1644** *Essex County, Mass. Probate Rec.* (1916) I. 39 Rakes and *rake hedds, 7s. 8d. **1780** EDMONDSON *Body Heraldry* II. Gloss., Rake-head, as borne in armory. **1844** STEPHENS *Bk. Farm* (1855) II. 229/2 As there are 8 rake-heads, there will be..36 contacts with the substance..to be lifted. **1884** T. SPEEDY *Sport* viii. 120 The fines imposed for illegal fishing, or for having leisters, *rake-hooks, or nets. **1891** *Daily News* 28 May 4/8 They kill fish by 'sniggling', or rake hooks, by the gaff or cleek. **1593** NASHE *Christ's T.* 32 b, Through theyr garments theyr *rake-leane rybbes appeared. **1618** BRATHWAITE *Descr. Death* in Farr *S.P. Jas. I* (1848) 270 His rake-leane body shrinking underneath. **1671** *Phil. Trans.* VI. 2112 The *Rake-man..constantly moves the Tin with his Rake. **1641** BEST *Farm. Bks.* (Surtees) 33 With her *rakeshafte to throw up the sweath. **1892** H. E. WRIGHT *Handy Bk. Brewers* 484 The horizontal rake-shaft has a number..of wrought iron rakes bolted on. **1878** *Cumbld. Gloss.*, *Rake-steel*, **Rake-shank*, the handle of a rake. *c* **1386** CHAUCER *Wife's T.* 93 That tale is nat worth a *rake stele. *c* **1440** CAPGRAVE *Life St. Kath.* IV. 2009 Youre resons, lady, avayle not a rake-stele. **1880** HARDY *Trumpet-Major* II. xxiii. 160 For use at home as *rake-stems, benefit-club staves, and pick-handles. **1844** STEPHENS *Bk. Farm* (1855) II. 229/1 Bringing the *rake-teeth nearer to, or farther from the ground. *Ibid.* 230/1 All the *rake-tines are lifted from the ground by one operation. **1957** M. SPARK *Comforters* v. 95 On the front of the [cigarette] case was a tiny raised crest... 'It's the Hogarth crest. Only a Victorian *rake-up, I imagine.' **1844** STEPHENS *Bk. Farm* (1855) II. 229/1 The two *rake-wheels..are of very light construction.

†**rake**, *sb.*[2] *Obs.* Forms: 1 hræce, 3 rake. [OE. *hræce, hrace, -u*, f. *hraca* m. = OHG. *rahho* (MHG. *rache*, G. *rachen*), MLG. *rāke*, Du. *raak* throat.] The throat, jaws.
c **825** *Vesp. Psalter* v. 11 Byrȝen open is hræce heara. *c* **1000** *Sax. Leechd.* II. 62 Stinge him ȝelome on þa hracan þæt he maȝe spiwan. *a* **1225** *St. Marher.* 11 The rode the arredde me so redlich of his reowliche rake. *c* **1250** *Death* 214 in *O.E. Misc.* 180 þer is sathanas..redi wið his rake.

rake (reɪk), *sb.*[3] *Sc.* and *north. dial.* (exc. in sense 8). [a. ON. *rák* stripe, streak (Norw. dial. *raak* footpath, stripe or streak, channel, string of cattle, etc.), f. **rák-* ablaut var. of *rek-* to drive: see RACK *sb.*[1] In later use also in part repr. ME. *rayk*, RAIK *sb.*]

1. A way, path; *esp.* a rough path over a hill, a narrow path up a cleft or ravine.
13.. *Gaw. & Gr. Knt.* 2144 Ryde me doun þis ilk rake, bi ȝon rokke syde. *a* **1400-50** *Alexander* 5070 Lene to þe left hand, For þe rake on þe riȝt hand þat may na man passe. ? *c* **1600** *Hodgson MS.* in *Northumbld. Gloss.* s.v., Two brode waies or rakes commonly used occupied and worne with cattal brought out of Scotland. **1869** *Lonsdale Gloss.*, *Rake*, ..A strip of ground..lying in the side of a hill, and sunk below the level of the neighbouring parts. **1872** JENKINSON *Guide Eng. Lakes* 303 A method of ascent..is by the 'Lord's Rake', a narrow cleft a short distance from the ridge.
fig. *a* **1400-50** *Alexander* 3383 Out of þe rake..of riȝtwysnes ren suld he neuire.

2. a. A run, rush; speed. *rare.*
c **1460** *Towneley Myst.* xvi. 65 Fast afore wyll I hy radly on a rake. **1768** ROSS *Helenore* II. 91 Their milk white lads..At a gueed rake were running on before.

†**b.** A pass in fencing. *Obs. rare.*
c **1450** *Fencing w. two handed Sword* in *Rel. Ant.* I. 309 Thy rakys, thy rowndis, thy quarters abowte, Thy stoppis, thy foynys, lete hem fast rowte.

3. Course or path, *esp.* of cattle in pasturing; hence, pasture-ground, right of pasture.
a **1640** JACKSON *Creed* XI. xii. § 8 In that region wherein the clouds have their rake. **1688** MIEGE *Grt. Fr. Dict.*, *Sillage*,..Course, the Rake or Run of a Ship, her Way forward on. **1724** *MS. Survey, Lower Brunton* in *Northumb. Gloss.*, It pays 13*s.* 4*d.*..yearly for what is call'd a Rake for their cattle in Tuggle Moore. **1728** in Best *Farm. Bks.* (Surtees) 174 *note*, This walk or rake for my tenants' sheep upon Cottom Pry or Monk Lees. **1863** MRS. TOOGOOD *Yorksh. Dial.*, The cattle had a good rake ower yon common.
attrib. **1744** *N. Riding Rec.* VIII. 111 A rake-rent of 10s. for leave to graze their cattle upon Raskelf Moor.

4. A single journey in conveying anything from one place to another; hence, the amount so carried by a person, horse, cart, or railway train; a 'gang'.
a **1779** D. GRAHAM *Writings* (1883) II. 59 I'll gar haf-a-crown and haf-a-mutchkin or a rake o' coals do it a'. **1792** A. WILSON in *Poems*, etc. (1876) II. 25 He kend..How mony rake wad lave the ocean toom. **1862** D. WINGATE in *Blackw. Mag.* Mar. 377 The ponies had their rakes brought in, And been stabled one by one. **1894** CROCKETT *Raiders* 192 To fetch a rake of water from the well. **1930** *Times Educ. Suppl.* 20 Sept. 397/3 When the boys of the Clachan had finished dinner, their customary task was to fetch the day's 'rake' of water to their homes. **1934** T. WOOD *Cobbers* v. 69 Before we could board, however, they said we must see the Rake for the Day go by: all the trees we had seen felled. **1976** *Indian Express* 23 Jan. 5/4 The first rake of 1000 tonnes for Iran was despatched from the Bhilai Steel Plant yesterday. **1979** *Times of India* 17 Aug. 10/2 Actual daily arrivals, according to food department sources, has recently been two rakes or one and half rakes less than what it should be.

5. a. A leading vein of ore, having a more or less perpendicular lie; a rake-vein.
Hooson *Miner's Dict.* (1747) limits the term to a vein which is in process of being worked.
1634 in Pennant *Tour in Wales* (1778) I. 74 A grant, made ..by Charles I. of all the mines of lead, or rakes of lead, within the hundreds of Coleshill and Rudland. **1653** MANLOVE *Rhymed Chron.* 2 If any..find a Rake, Or sign, or leading to the same. *Ibid.* 260 Main Rakes, Cross Rakes,.. Randum of the Rake. **1759** MARTIN *Nat. Hist.* I. 66 It runs along after the Rakes, and not crossing them as the leading Vaults do. **1884** J. A. PHILLIPS *Ore Deposits* 1. 64 It is now well known that the true fissure veins, or rakes, pass through these igneous rocks.

b. *rake-soil*, the deads or rubbish of a vein. ? *Obs.*
1653 MANLOVE *Rhymed Chron.* 271.

†**6.** = RACE *sb.*[5], RACHE *sb.*[2] *Obs. rare*$^{-1}$.
1685 *Lond. Gaz.* 2023/4 A little Spaniel Bitch brown and white spotted..and a white Rake on the Forehead.

7. A rut, groove.
1781 J. HUTTON *Tour to Caves* (ed. 2) Gloss., *Rake*, rut, crack, or crevice. **1789** *Trans. Soc. Arts* VII. 199 Heavy loads..made almost as deep a rut, or rake, as ever. **1812-16** J. SMITH *Panorama Sc. & Art* I. 110 The blade..is covered with rakes or small grooves close to each other.

8. A row, series. = RACE *sb.*[1] 9 b. *spec.* a series of wagons or carriages on a railway or of wagons or trucks in a mine or a factory (in this sense, no longer restricted to *Sc.* and *north. dial.*).
1901 *Daily Record* (Glasgow) 28 Nov. 3/2 A number of lads were riding on a rake of hutches. **1909** *Daily Chron.* 11 Dec. 4/5 In reaching the shaft some of the men got on to the top of a loaded rake of hutches. **1921** H. FOSTON *At Front* viii. 60 The ballast engine, with her 'rake' of empty trucks. **1940** L. A. G. STRONG *Sun on Water* 224 The train I join is made up locally. The rake of carriages does be waiting at the station, and a tank engine comes in. **1949** D. M. DAVIN *Roads from Home* II. vii. 175 Geordie Smith on his shunter had just given a rake of meat waggons a bit of a nudge. **1961** *Trains Illustrated* Dec. 762/2 A special seven-car rake of B.R. standard stock provided the final services, hauled alternatively by Class E1 4-4-0 No. 31739 and Class Q1 0-6-0 No. 33029. **1962** *Times* 26 Oct. (Spencer Steelworks Suppl.) p. xviii/3 The operator uses a Beetle to bring forward the first rake of 15 wagons. **1969** *Sunday Standard* (Bombay) 6 July 1/7 Only 27 rakes were available out of the normal complement of 31 rakes for running the scheduled number of trains. **1973** C. D. GARRATT *Masterpieces in Steam* 108 The engine was bringing its last rake of wagons through the colliery yard. **1977** *Modern Railways* Dec. 492/1 Positioning two cars at one end of the train would lead to excessive buckling forces when propelling, hence the central position which was also claimed to provide two relatively-short virtually-identical rakes of trailer cars for operational flexibility.

rake (reɪk), *sb.*[4] Also 7 rack(e. [? f. RAKE *v.*[3]]

1. *Naut.* **a.** The projection of the upper part of a ship's hull at stem and stern beyond the corresponding extremities of the keel (distinguished as *forerake* and *sternrake*). Hence, the slope of the stern or stern-post, or of the rudder.
1626 CAPT. SMITH *Accid. Yng. Seamen* 9 The lengths, breadthes, depthes, rakes, and burdens. **1664** E. BUSHNELL *Compl. Shipwright* 7 Had we given 5 foot more Racke. **1690** LEYBOURN *Curs. Math.* 83, 55 Foot..for the length by the Keel,..16 Foot..for the Rack forward. **1706** PHILLIPS (ed. Kersey), s.v. The Rake of the Rudder. **1711** W. SUTHERLAND *Shipbuild. Assist.* 60 Looking on the Rake of the Stern of any Ship. **1815** BURNEY *Falconer's Mar. Dict.* s.v. *Rudder*, Rake of the Rudder, a term used to signify the fore part of the rudder, which depends entirely upon the rake of the stern-post. **1833** RICHARDSON *Merc. Mar. Arch.* 9 It also shows the round aft of the stern on the rake. **1867** SMYTH *Sailor's Word-bk.* 559.

b. The deviation (usually towards the stern) of a ship's masts from a perpendicular to the keel.
1815 BURNEY *Falconer's Mar. Dict.* s.v. **1842** LEVER *J. Hinton* xxxvi, The rake of her low masts, and the long boom. **1882** W. H. WHITE *Naval Archit.* (ed. 2) 506 It is customary to have the greatest rake in the aftermost mast.

2. *transf.* **a.** The inclination of any object from the perpendicular or to the horizontal; slope.
1802 *Trans. Soc. Arts* XX. 287 The stems are segments of a circle, with considerable rakes. **1825** J. NICHOLSON *Operat. Mechanic* 602 To find the face-mould of a staircase, so that when set to its proper rake it will be perpendicular to the plan. **1881** *Gard. Chron.* XVI. 657 The arrangement of the plants follows the rake of the roof. **1893** *Building News* 10 Feb. 189 The stage floor..rises from the foot-lights..at a rake of half an inch to the foot. **1932** *Pictorial Weekly* 19 Mar. 223/2 Most stages have to rise in floor level towards the back in order to make the action visible to the audience... This is known as the 'rake'. **1939** JOYCE *Finnegans Wake* (1964) 560 Spotlight working wall cloths. Spill playing rake and bridges. **1951** [see COSSACK 2 e]. **1955** *Times* 10 May 7/7 The front seat is immediately adjustable over a range of 5 in., and further adjustments for rake and height are provided. **1967** *Oxf. Compan. Theatre* (ed. 3) 40/2 The Chicago Opera House..was a tamed Bayreuth, with a flattened rake and a wedge auditorium. **1973** *Country Life* 22 Feb. 468/3 Front seats have ample adjustment for reach and rake. **1974** B. FORBES *Notes for Life* xii. 92 The rake on the stage of the Theatre Royal, Brighton, is a violent one.

b. The inclination of an edge or face of a cutting tool (or other tool) with respect to some line or plane (freq. to a line perpendicular to the surface of the work). Also ***angle of rake, rake angle.***
1888 *Lockwood's Dict. Terms Mech. Engin.* 276 *Rake.* (1) A term usually applied to signify the angles of metal turning tools, as side rake, front rake, &c. (2) The amount of forward angle, or pitch of saw teeth. **1901** *Shop & Foundry Practice* (Colliery Engineer Co., Scranton, Pa.) I. v. 8 This tendency to spring is greatly increased when the tool has insufficient side rake or clearance. **1903** W. H. VAN DERVOORT *Mod. Machine Shop Tools* xv. 198 The cutting edge of the lathe tool..has what we term an angle of clearance A and an angle of rake B. *Ibid.*, A tool may have front rake..or side rake... A tool without rake requires greater force to drive it through the cut as it tears rather than cuts the metal. *Ibid.* 550/1 (Index), Rake angles. **1923** T. R. SHAW *Mechanisms of Machine Tools* i. 71/1 With a flat top face either so much metal has to be removed that the tool is weakened or the rake angle must be so slight that there would be no proper cutting action. **1938** R. T. KENT *Kent's Mech. Engineers' Handbk.* (ed. 11) III. xxi. 41 Rake angle of a milling cutter..is defined as the angle by which the face of the tooth is displaced back of the radial line drawn from the center of rotation to the cutting edge. **1964** S. CRAWFORD *Basic Engin. Processes* v. 119 Rake angles influence chip formation, tool wear, cutting force, surface finish, and permissible cutting speed. **1975** *Drilling Technol. & Collet Chuck* (Bristol Erickson Ltd.) 3 Figures 1 & 2 illustrate the variation in normal rake angle across the cutting edge of a standard ½" diameter drill. *Ibid.* 11 Helic angle is the angle between the outer edge of the drill land and the drill axis, and is equivalent to the top rake of a flat cutting tool.

rake (reɪk), *sb.*[5] [abbrev. of RAKEHELL.]
a. A man of loose habits and immoral character; an idle dissipated man of fashion.
1653 H. MORE *Antid. Ath.* III. vii. §13 *Schol.*, These dissolute Rakes endeavour to extinguish the memory of the narrations. **1710** LADY M. W. MONTAGU *Let. to Bp. Burnet* 20 July, There are more atheists among the fine ladies than the loosest sort of rakes. **1775** SHERIDAN *Duenna* II. iii, Is he not a gay dissipated rake who has squandered his patrimony? **1836** HOR. SMITH *Tin Trump.* (1876) 89 An old rake who has survived himself is the most pitiable object in creation. **1880** L. STEPHEN *Pope* iv. 83 Pope..had tried to assume the airs of a rake.
Comb. **1892** TENNYSON *Dawn* iii, Rake-ruin'd bodies and souls go down in a common wreck.

b. A woman of similar character.
1712 STEELE *Spect.* No. 336 ¶3 These Rakes are your idle Ladies of Fashion. *a* **1777** GOLDSM. *Gift* 1 Cruel Iris, pretty rake, Dear mercenary beauty. **1832** L. HUNT *Sir R. Esher* (1850) 367 How superior did she seem to all the fair rakes of the Court. [**1886** BYNNER *A. Surriage* xxxi. 373 A plentiful sprinkling of rakes of both sexes.]

c. Phr. ***rake's progress*** [the title of a series of engravings (1735) by William Hogarth: see

HOGARTHIAN *a.*]: a course of dissipation; a progressive degeneration or decline.
1849 THACKERAY *Pendennis* I. xx. 183 (*heading*) Rake's progress. **1925** T. E. LAWRENCE *Let.* 13 June (1938) 476 If you want to trouble yourself still with the rake's progress of this deplorable work. **1937** H. G. WELLS *Brynhild* x. 202 I'd have been ashamed not to have been her lover. Another score in the rake's progress. **1950** A. HUXLEY *Themes & Variations* 250 If the Western Powers had a positive instead of a mainly negative international policy, they would come forward with a plan to check this rake's progress towards human and planetary bankruptcy. **1959** *Listener* 17 Sept. 451/3 The later rake's progress toward corruption, aggression, humiliating subjection to Hitler, pathological megalomania and final catastrophe. **1961** *Times* 9 Feb. 15/2 A literary rake's progress from false materialist to fake romantic. **1976** *Times* 20 Feb. 19/4 Mr Healey has described the course of Britain's recent financial history as a 'rake's progress'.

rake (reɪk), *sb.*[6] *rare*⁻¹. [f. RAKE *v.*[1] 9.] The act of raking with shot.
1810 *Naval Chron.* XXIII. 97 The frigate..gave her the rake astern.

†**rake**, *sb.*[7] *Obs. rare*⁻¹. A herd (of colts).
1486 *Bk. St. Albans* F vj, A Ragg of coltis or a Rake.

rake, obs. form of RACK *sb.*[1], *sb.*[2], *sb.*[3]

rake (reɪk), *v.*[1] Also 7 rack; *pa. pple.* 4 **rake**, 6 *Sc.* **raik**, 4, 8 **raken**. [a. ON. *raka* (Sw. *raka*, Da. *rage*) to scrape, shave, rake, etc. = (M)LG., (M)Du. *raken*, f. the root **rak-*: see RAKE *sb.*[1], on which later uses may to a large extent be directly based.]

I. † **1.** *trans.* To scrape away. *Obs. rare*⁻¹.
c **1250** *Gen. & Ex.* 2132 Al ðat ðise first .vii. [years] maken, Sulen ðis oðere vii. rospen & raken.

2. a. To draw together, collect, gather (scattered objects) with, or as with, a rake.
c **1250** *Gen. & Ex.* 3324 Ðor migte euerilc man fugeles taken, So fele so he wulden raken. **1456** in Gross *Gild Merch.* (1890) II. 345 No man..Rake yn ony mannes lond ane Corne yn harvestyme. **1530** PALSGR. 678/2 Rake this corne. **1598** GRENEWEY *Tacitus, Ann.* XII. ii. (1622) 157 Her exceeding greedines in raking mony. **1627** MAY *Lucan* VII. 846 There gold rak'd in Spaine, There th' Easterne Nations treasuryes remaine. **1796** MORSE *Amer. Geog.* I. 772, 3 or 400 go annually to Turk's Island, to rake salt.
absol. **1642** ROGERS *Naaman* 173 A spirit of the world, lusting to rake and scrape.

b. So with *together.* (Commoner than prec.)
1550 [see RAKING *vbl. sb.*[1] 1]. **1570–6** LAMBARDE *Peramb. Kent* (1826) 137 Odo raked together great masses of silver and gold. **1663** BUTLER *Hud.* I. i. 676 But now a Sport more formidable Had rak'd together Village Rabble. **1840** DICKENS *Barn. Rudge* x, Leaving the window now and then to rake the crackling logs together. **1874** GREEN *Short Hist.* ix. §4. 629 Raking together every fault in the Chancellor.

3. To draw or drag in a specified direction with, or as with, a rake (freq. with implication of sense 2). Const. with various preps. and advbs., as:

a. with *out, out of.* ***to rake out a fire***: to clear the embers out of the grate.
1412–20 LYDG. *Chron. Troy* I. ii, His hyd iniquitee He out gan rake that hath he hyd so long. **1602** MARSTON *Antonio's Rev.* II. i, A slave rak't out of common mud. **1691** WOOD *Ath. Oxon.* II. 318 All the bad things..which Prynne could pick and rake out of Histories. **1838** PRESCOTT *Ferd. & Is.* (1846) III. xxiii. 341 Endeavouring to rake a good claim for Castile out of its ancient union with Navarre. **1853** 'C. BEDE' *Verdant Green* iv. (ed. 4) 33 To see that your fire was safely raked out at night.

b. with *up.* Used esp. of searching for and bringing forward all that can be said or charged against a person.
1581 J. BELL *Haddon's Answ. Osor.* 398 The Pope..raketh uppe unto him..that which was geven to the whole Church. **1680** ALLEN *Peace & Unity* 27 By raking up, and then scattering abroad all the evil they can. **1729** in Keble *Life Bp. Wilson* xx. (1863) 698 Raking up and ransacking.. several articles of illegal and arbitrary practices. **1813** *Gen. Hist.* in *Ann. Reg.* 20 This evidence is to be raked up in order to condemn. **1831** *Note Bk. Oxonian* 215 Should the black win, the bankers..rake up the money from off the red. **1865** TROLLOPE *Can you forgive Her?* II. xxviii. 224 The croupier raked it [*sc.* money] all up, and carried it all away. **1868** FREEMAN *Norm. Conq.* (1876) II. vii. 144 The old charges.. were again raked up against him. **1913** W. OWEN *Let.* 9 Apr. (1967) 182 Unless I raked up matter from the past,..I have had nothing to deliver myself of. **1939** 'N. BLAKE' *Smiler with Knife* ii. 33 Had tea? No? Good, I'll see what Mrs. Raikes can rake up.

c. with *into,* (†*un*)*to, over* preps., *in* adv. ***to rake in the shekels***: see SHEKEL 2.
1581 J. BELL *Haddon's Answ. Osor.* 298 [They] did rake unto themselves a certeyne Heavenly power out of the very Heavens. **1583** STUBBES *Anat. Abus.* II. (1882) 54 By which kind of theft,..they rake in great somes of mony. **1637** R. HUMPHREY tr. *St. Ambrose* I. 6 Bind up thy speech..lest by much talke it rake into thy bosome many sinnes. **1684** BUNYAN *Pilgr.* II. (1900) 184 The man..raked to himself the Straws. **1851** *Oquawka* (Illinois) *Spectator* 22 Oct. 1/4 Then, of course, they 'dropped the gate' upon them and 'raked in the pile'. **1888** WHITTIER *Maud Muller* Pref., She strove to hide her bare feet by raking hay over them. **1893** 'MARK TWAIN' *Lett. to Publishers* (1967) 343 We are at a heavy expense, now, in breaking up housekeeping and raking-in old bills. **1926** *Punch* 22 Dec. 682/2 His having been raked in to complete the officers' team at the last minute in place of an absentee. **1959** *Economist* 11 Apr. 153/2 The Bank of France has 'raked in' part of the working balances of foreign currency held by the French commercial banks. **1969** *Observer* 21 Dec. 28/3 He's raking it in already. Writes 'think pieces' for *Honey* magazine.

d. with *away, down, off* advbs. ***to rake down***: (esp.) to win (money) at cards, etc. (*U.S. slang*).
1623 GOUGE *Serm. Extent God's Provid.* §13 Yet were those ashes raked away. **1839** *Spirit of Times* 13 July 223/3 If he has anything like as good a horse as the balance, he is certain to *rake down the corn.* **1843** *Ibid.* 18 Nov. 431 She [*sc.* a horse] is a perfect wax figure and all believed that she would rake down the socks. **1846** S. F. SMITH *Theatr. Apprenticeship* 151 With one hand he gracefully turned over *four Kings* and a Jack, and with the other tremblingly 'raked down' the pile of bank notes, gold and silver. **1853** J. G. BALDWIN *Flush Times Alabama* 8 What lots of 'Ethiopian captives' and other plunder he *raked down* vexed Arithmetic to count. **1854** RONALDS & RICHARDSON *Chem. Technol.* (ed. 2) I. 312 The charge..is..raked down on to the lower level. **1859** R. THOMPSON *Gard. Assist.* 123 Wooden rakes..are required for raking off grass and leaves. **1882** B. HARTE *Flip & Found at Blazing Star* 164 You kin rake down the pile now.

II. †**4. a.** To cover with, or bury under, something brought together with, or as with, a rake. *Obs.*
c **1386** CHAUCER *Monk's T.* 143 (*Hercules*) In hoote coles he hath hym seluen raked. *c* **1430** *Hymns Virg.* 89/23 Whanne þi soule is went out, & þi bodi in erþe rakid. **1483** CAXTON *Gold. Leg.* 374/1 He toke the yarne..and rakyd it in the fyre. *c* **1580** SIDNEY *Ps.* VII. v, Then in the dust lett hym my honor rake. *a* **1644** QUARLES in Farr *S. P. Jas. I* (1848) 136 If hidden wages..doe lie Rak't in her furrowes. **1786** BURNS *Toothache* 21 Worthy friends rak'd i' the mools, Sad sight to see!

†**b.** So with *up. Obs.*
1576 FLEMING *Panoplie Ep.* 277 The deade bodie of her childe..put into the sepulchre, and raked vp in clods of earth. **1605** JONSON *Volpone* Ded., By faults which charity hath raked up, or common honesty concealed. **1622** J. REYNOLDS *God's Revenge* III. Hist. xv, Their remembrance of him was wholy raked up, and buried in the dust of his grave.

5. *spec.* **a.** To cover (a fire) with ashes or small coal in order to keep it in without active burning. Now *dial.* Also in *fig.* context.
1412–20 LYDG. *Chron. Troy* I. vi, Many man..Can..rake falsly the wycked couert fire. **1513** DOUGLAS *Æneis* VIII. vii. 90 The puir wyf quhilk at evin had raik Hyr ingill, risis for to beit hyr fyr. **1697** DRYDEN *Virg. Georg.* I. 390 To work by Night, and rake the Winter Fire. *a* **1796** PEGGE *Derbicisms.* **1829–** in many dial. glossaries.
fig. **1601** MUNDAY in Hazl. *Dodsley* VIII. 185 The abbot's malice, rak'd in cinders long Breaks out at last. **1615** BRATHWAIT *Strappado* (1878) 71 Yet shall not..those accomplisht parts..Lie rak't in Ashes.

b. So with *up.*
1530 PALSGR. 678/2 Rake up the fyre and come to bedde. **1629** *Bk. Meery Riddles* A iij, The fire that burneth brigh[t] all the day, and at night is raked vp in his ashes. **1742** YOUNG *Nt. Th.* I. 109 Slumbers, rak'd up in dust, ethereal fire. **1866** LOWELL *Biglow P.* Introd., Such a one..called hell 'the place where they did n't rake up their fire nights'.
fig. **1650** R. STAPYLTON *Strada's Low C. Warres* VII. 81 His Indignation, then raked up in Embers, would in time breake out.

III. 6. a. To go over with a rake, so as to make clean, smooth, etc., or to find something. Also with *up, over.*
1523 FITZHERB. *Husb.* §28 Whan the barley is ledde away, the landes muste be raked, or els there wyll be moche corne loste. **1583** BABINGTON *Commandm.* iv. (1637) 38 O filthy savour that ariseth out of this lothsome channell, thus raked up into the nostrils of the Lord! **1693** EVELYN *De la Quint. Compl. Gard.* II. 199 We rake it over five or six times with an Iron Rake, to make the Seed enter into the Ground. **1727–46** THOMSON *Summer* 365 They rake the green-appearing ground. **1854** WHITTIER *Maud Muller* 2 Maud Muller..Raked the meadow, sweet with hay.
fig. **1676** MARVELL *Mr. Smirke* 18 To be raked and harrowed thorow with so rusty a saw! **1810** CRABBE *Borough* i, The billows..take their grating course, Raking the rounded flints. **1835** WORDSW. *Death of Hogg* 21 Clouds that rake the mountain-summits.

b. *transf.* To search, etc., as with a rake.
1618 L. PARSONS in *Lismore Papers* Ser. II. (1887) II. 154 For feare he rake me for more mony. **1670** EACHARD *Cont. Clergy* 35 They rake Lilly's Grammar; and if they can but find two or three letters of any name [etc.]. **1727** SWIFT *On Dreams*, The statesman rakes the town to find a plot. **1884** *Manch. Exam.* 19 June 5/3 To rake history ancient and modern for proofs of the wickedness of Dissenters.
absol. **1735** in *Swift's Lett.* (1766) II. 219 Mr. Curll will rake to the dunghill for your correspondence.

†**c.** In phr. ***to rake hell.*** *Obs.* Cf. RAKEHELL.
1542 UDALL *Apophth. Erasm.* 116b, Suche a feloe as a manne should rake helle for. **1677** W. HUGHES *Man of Sin* II. xii. 215 Should you rake Hell and Scum the Devil (as our Country speakes) they will hardly be outmatch'd. **1880** TENNYSON *Village Wife* xii, Ya wouldn't find Charlie's likes ..Not thaw ya went fur to raäke out Hell wi' a small-tooth coämb.

d. With complement: To make *clean, clear, level,* etc. by, or as by, raking.
1399 *Pol. Poems* (Rolls) I. 363 The long gras that is so grene, Hit most be mowe, and raked clene. **1573** TUSSER *Husb.* (1878) 121 See feeld ye rake cleene. **1641** [see RAKER[1] 1]. **1816** SCOTT *Old Mort.* ix, Raking this country clear o' whigs and roundheads. **1851** STEPHENS *Bk. Farm* (ed. 2) II. 235/2 The second field-worker..rakes clean the half ridge he has cleared. **1856** DELAMER *Fl. Gard.* (1861) 53 Rake the surface perfectly level.

7. a. To scratch or scrape.
1609 BP. HALL *Serm.* v. 31 That Head..is all raked and harrowed with thorns. **1662** *Act 13 & 14 Chas. II*, vii. §7 Divers Tanners do shave cut and rake..the Necks of their Backs, and Butts, to the great impairing thereof. **1754** RICHARDSON *Grandison* (1781) I. xxvii. 195 His sword a little raked my shoulder. **1821** CRAIG *Lect. Drawing* vii. 380 The plate..is first raked, notched, or punched all over. **1866** M. ARNOLD *St. Brandan*, Sand raked his sores from heel to pate.

b. *intr.* or *absol.*
1621 BURTON *Anat. Mel.* To Rdr. 41 Thou..stingest like a Scorpion, rakest like a Wolfe. **1740** R. BROOKES *Art of Angling* I. iv. 22 As you will be oblig'd to play the Fish for some time, the Line must rake against his Teeth.

8. a. *Farriery.* To clean (a costive horse or its fundament) from ordure by scraping with the hand.
1575 *Gamm. Gurton* III. iv. 18 Chil see what deuil is in her guts, chil take the paines to rake her! *Ibid.* 20 Did not Tom Tankard rake his curtal toure day. **1607** TOPSELL *Four-f. Beasts* (1658) 270 If he be costive, let his fundament be raked, or else give him a glyster. *c* **1720** W. GIBSON *Farmer's Dispens.* x. (1721) 234/2 If the Horse be first raked very well, which is..necessary.., that room may be made for the Clyster. **1805, 1842** [see RAKING *vbl. sb.*[1] 2].

b. *Sc.* To rub the rheum from (the eyes). *rare.*
1708 M. BRUCE *Lect.* etc. 26 Love..will put you in pursuit after Christ, or ever other Folk rake their Eyes.

9. a. *Mil.* and *Naut.* To sweep or traverse with shot; to enfilade; *spec.* to send shot along (a ship) from stem to stern (in full ***to rake fore and aft***).
1630 J. TAYLOR (Water P.) *Braue Sea Fight* Wks. III. 39/1 Wee gaue him a whole broad side, euery shot raking him fore and after. *c* **1642** in *Glover's Hist. Derby* (1829) I. App. 71 When there was no other expectation but of rakeing the towne, instead of being seconded, we were called off. **1734** tr. *Rollin's Anc. Hist.* (1827) VI. xv. vi. 82 Coming forward in boats and raking the dike on each side. **1800** NELSON 18 Feb. in Nicolas *Disp.* (1845) IV. 189 Captain Peard..lay across his hawse, and raked him with several broadsides. **1874** GREEN *Short Hist.* iv. §6. 207 The English archers were thrown forward to rake the Scottish squares. **1939** JOYCE *Finnegans Wake* (1964) 349 Spraygun rakes and splits them from a double focus: grenadite, damnymite, alextronite, nichilite. **1959** 'B. MATHER' *Achilles Affair* I. ii. 22 The Nazi patrol..could have raked us with their Schmeissers. **1967** *Boston Sunday Globe* 23 Apr. 17/2 Artillery and air strikes raked the Communist positions in the battle. **1973** *Times* 13 Feb. 7/1 Mr Rashad al-Shawa, the former mayor of Gaza town, narrowly escaped today when his car was raked by automatic weapon fire.
transf. **1636** G. SANDYS *Paraphr. Ps.* lxxviii. (1648) 130 Thy thunders..rake the Skies. **1785** BURNS *Jolly Beggars* 7th Recit., The fiddler rak'd her, fore and aft, Behint the chicken cavie. **1858** RUSKIN *Arrows of Chace* (1880) I. 131 [Pictures hung] with their sides to the light, so that it 'rakes' them. **1884** *Christ. Treasury* Feb. 69/1 Every wandering wind..seemed to take peculiar pleasure in raking it.

b. To command, dominate, overlook.
1842 MRS. F. TROLLOPE *Vis. to Italy* I. i. 11 [An] edifice ..so placed as easily to rake the road in all directions. **1895** *Jrnl. R. Inst. Brit. Architects* 14 Mar. 350 Care should be taken that the front door be not too much raked by the principal windows.

c. To sweep with the eyes; to look all over.
1848 THACKERAY *Van. Fair* lxvii, George took the glass again and raked the vessel. **1894** A. ROBERTSON *Nuggets*, etc. 164, I raked him across the bows with my two black eyeballs.

d. *Hawking.* Of a hawk: To strike (the game) in the air. Also ***to rake off.***
1763 J. BELL *Travels from St. Petersburg* II. 78 The hawks generally raked in the pheasants while flying. **1773** J. CAMPBELL *Mod. Faulconry* 211 When she sees the fowl fluttering, she is apt to come down rapidly, in order to rake it off. *Ibid.* 232 When the hawk is well acquainted with the sport, she will be..ready to rake the fowl as it rises. **1896** A. AUSTIN *England's Darling* II. iii. 42 Until the unseamed falcon learned to wing its way..And, binding, rake its quarry to the ground.

10. *Dyeing.* To stir or mix (liquor) with a rake.
1816 J. SMITH *Panorama Sc. & Art* II. 534 The weld..is to be stirred with a rake. The vat..is raked again for half an hour. **1837** WHITTOCK *Bk. Trades* (1842) 192 (*Dyer*) The liquor..is said to be raked, because it is mixed with a 'rake'.

†**IV. 11.** To draw along like a rake. *Obs. rare.*
1581 J. BELL *Haddon's Answ. Osor.* 156b, They..are alwayes rakyng their nayles upon that scabbe (as the Proverbe sayth). **1646** FULLER *Wounded Consc.* (1841) 282 Satan rakes his claws in the blood of a wounded conscience.

V. *intr.* or *absol.* **12. a.** To use a rake; to scrape with the fingers or similar means; to make search with, or as with, a rake. Const. *in, among* (that which is scraped or searched).
1575 *Gamm. Gurton* I. iv. 11 As thou sawest me raking in the asshes. *a* **1633** AUSTIN *Medit.* (1635) 176 It is not for every bodies fingers to be raking in Christs Side. *a* **1708** BEVERIDGE *Priv. Th.* I. (1730) 122 If I must needs be raking in other Mens Sores, it must not be behind their Backs, but before their Faces. **1842** TENNYSON *Will. Waterpr.* xvi, The Cock..raked in golden barley. **1856** FROUDE *Hist. Eng.* (1858) II. xi. 505 It has been no pleasure to me to rake among the evil memories of the past.

b. Const. *after, for* (the object of search).
1581 J. BELL *Haddon's Answ. Osor.* 259b, You busye yourselfe about a straunge matter as though you were raking after the Moone. **1599** SHAKS. *Hen. V*, II. iv. 98 If you hide the Crowne Even in your hearts, there will he rake for it. **1670** COTTON *Espernon* II. v. 236 The people..never fail, after a storm to rake all along the Shoar for this Commodity.

c. *fig.* To make search or investigation, to poke, *into.* Also with *for* as in b.
1637 R. HUMPHREY tr. *St. Ambrose* Pref., I will rake no deeper into this kennell. **1658–9** in *Burton's Diary* (1828) III. 569 It is not prudence for us to rake into the proceedings of the former Parliaments. **1790** BURKE *Fr. Rev.* 206 To rake into the histories of former ages..for every instance of oppression and persecution. **1877** MRS. OLIPHANT *Makers Flor.* i. 2 Students rake into the dust of old histories for further particulars of those street riots.

13. To move *on* or *over* like, or with the effect of, a rake; to scrape *against.*
1598 SYLVESTER *Du Bartas* I. iii. 21 Whose pow'rful breath..constrains..Seas' salt billows 'gainst Heav'n's

vaults to rake. **1628** Digby *Voy. Medit.* (1868) 91 A mighty growne sea that continually raked ouer our shippe. **1814** Southey *Warning Voice* ii. ii, Like the sound of the sea Where it rakes on a stony shore.

14. To come *up* when raked. *rare.*

1778 [W. Marshall] *Minutes Agric.* 24 Jan. 1775 What rakes up is chiefly fern.

†**15.** (See quots.) [Perh. a different word.]

a. **1753** Chambers *Cycl. Supp.* s.v., A horse rakes, when being shoulder-splait, or having strained his fore-quarter, he goes so lame, that he drags one of his fore-legs in a semi-circle.

b. **1819** Rees *Cycl.* s.v. *Racing*, If it be perceived that their [horses] wind begins to rake hot, and they want a sob, the business is to keep them up to that speed.

c. **1725** *New Cant. Dict.*, *To Rake*, signifies also to stick, as, *To rake in the Throttle*; To stick in the Throat.

rake (reɪk), *v.*[2] [OE. *racian*, perh. = Sw. *raka* to run, rush, slip, etc. In later use also in part repr. ME. *rayk*, *raik* RAIK *v.*]

1. *intr.* To go, proceed, move forward, esp. with speed. Also (esp. in later use), to go or wander *about*, to roam, stray. Now only *dial.*

a. of persons. = RAIK *v.* 1 a.

a **1023** Wulfstan *Hom.* xxxii. (1883) 155 Ne biþ na ȝeborhlic..þæt he to hrædlice into godes huse æfter þam racige. *c* **1205** Lay. 18058 Vtheres cnihtes..mid sweorden heom to rakeden. *c* **1330** *Arth. & Merl.* 8038 (Kölbing) As þai þus togider spake, Fresche paiens on hem com rake. *c* **1470** Henry *Wallace* vi. 429 Furth fra his men than Wallace rakit rycht. **1579–80** North *Plutarch* (1676) 357 As they..came raking by the Romans camp. *c* **1645** T. Tully *Siege Carlisle* (1840) 21 From thence they raked towards Botcherby, along ye Riverside. **1714** Mandeville *Fab. Bees* (1723) I. 305 Keep their Children in awe, and never suffer them to rake about the Streets, and lie out a-nights. **1869** Gibson *Folk-Speech Cumbld.* Gloss. 219 They ga rakin aboot widoot ayder eerand or aim.

†**b.** of things. *Obs.* = RAIK *v.* 1 b.

c **897** K. Ælfred *Gregory's Past.* xxxviii. 274 He his tungan ȝehealde ðæt heo ne raciȝe on unnytte spræce. *c* **1400** M. Kildare in *Rel. Ant.* II. 193 So wo and wrake sal fram the rake. **1511** Guylforde *Pilgr.* (Camden) 75 The same sayde galye..fell in rakynge, and so draggyd and droffe by force and vyolence of the sayde tempest. **1572** *Schole-ho. Wom.* 395 in Hazl. *E.P.P.* IV. 120 The wife would have a tail Come raking after.

c. of animals. = RAIK *v.* 1 c. In later use, of horses and dogs: To go at a rapid pace.

c **1400** *Beryn* 2743 If that thy blowing of þat othir [leopard]..be spyed, Anoon he rakith on the. **1513** Douglas *Æneis* xii. Prol. 177 The bustuus bukkis rakis furth on raw. **1717** *N. Riding Rec.* VIII. 100 For permitting John Thompson's sheep to rake upon the forest. **1862** Whyte-Melville *Inside the Bar* xi, I followed.., Tipple Cider raking and snatching at his bridle in disagreeable exuberance of spirits. **1883** E. Pennell-Elmhirst *Cream Leicestersh.* 357 The pack are raking onwards, and momentarily there is more danger of losing them.

2. *spec.* **a.** Of hawks: To fly along after the game; also = *to rake out* (*off*, *away*), to fly wide of (or away from) the game; sometimes said of the game itself.

1575 Turberv. *Faulconrie* 121 She will the lesse delyght to rake out after a checke. *Ibid.* 151 Your hawke will learne to giue ouer a fowle that rakes out. **1677** N. Cox *Gentl. Recreat.* ii. 191 Whistle her off your Fist, standing still to see.. whether she will rake out or not. **1797** *Encycl. Brit.* (ed. 3) VIII. 344/2 It frequently happens, that they escape from the hawk, and she, not recovering them, rakes after them. **1852** R. F. Burton *Falconry in Valley of Indus* iii. 28 When the bird mounts, the hawk rakes along after it. *Ibid.* 31 She 'checked' first at one bird, then at the other,..and lastly,.. she 'raked off'. **1855** Salvin & Brodrick *Falconry* 46 A Hawk is particularly liable to 'rake away', and amuse itself with an occasional stoop at any bird that may pass. **1859** Tennyson *Merlin & V.* 125 She is too noble..to check at pies, Nor will she rake.

b. Of hunting dogs (see quots.).

1819 J. B. Johnson *Shooter's Companion* 84 A dog that rakes (that is, runs with his nose close to the ground). **1877** C. Hallock *Sportsman's Gaz.* 466 All young dogs are apt to rake; that is, to hunt with their noses close to the ground, following their birds by the track rather than by the wind.

rake (reɪk), *v.*[3] Also 7 **rack.** [Of obscure origin: Sw. *raka*, to project, has been suggested, but this (like Da. *rage*) is prob. ad. G. *ragen*. Cf. RAKE *sb.*[4]]

1. *intr.* **a.** Of a ship, its hull, timbers, etc.: To have a rake at stem or stern.

1627 Capt. Smith *Seaman's Gram.* ii. 4 She rakes so much forward. **1692** *Ibid.* ii. xv. 122 Suppose a Ship..did Rack it with the Stem forwards 13 foot. **1711** W. Sutherland *Shipbuild. Assist.* 35 Let your long Timbers..rake forward one after another. **1833** Richardson *Merc. Mar. Arch.* 6 To rake aft two inches to every foot length of the sternpost. *transf.* **1865** Swinburne *Poems & Ballads*, *Time of Order* 12 The wind holds stiff And the gunwale dips and rakes.

b. Of masts or funnels: To incline from the perpendicular.

1691 T. H[ale] *Acc. New Invent.* 126 The dimensions of the Masts..and..the reasons of their raking aft. **1769** Falconer *Dict. Marine* (1776) s.v. *Tomber, le mât tombe en arrière*, the mast hangs, or rakes aft. **1882** P. Fitzgerald *Recreat. Lit. Man* (1883) 192 Their..ghastly white chimneys..raking back. **1883** R. Jefferies in *Pall Mall G.* 5 Nov. 2/1 Two lines of masts, one raking one way, the other the other.

2. *trans.* To cause to incline. In *pa. pple.*

1842 J. Gwilt *Encycl. Archit.* ii. iii. 635 If dwarf wainscoting be framed with two panels in height, add ·016 to the rate... When raked to stairs, ·023 extra. **1860** Dickens *Uncomm. Trav.* iv, With every face in it commanding the stage, and the whole..admirably raked and turned to that centre. **1898** *Cycling* 60 The 'Rational Ordinary' [bicycle] has the front forks 'raked'. **1930** W. Faulkner *As I lay Dying* 100 The broken hat raked at a swaggering angle. **1964** *Listener* 23 Apr. 664/2 Two of the best modern theatres, merely for the fact that the auditorium is steeply raked. **1977** *Transatlantic Rev.* lx. 83 He spoke with the microphone.. his TWA captain's hat raked across one eyebrow.

rake (reɪk), *v.*[4] [f. RAKE *sb.*[5]] *intr.* To be a rake; to live a dissolute or dissipated life.

1700 Farquhar *Constant Couple* iv. i, I'll..Swear and Rant, and Rake..with the best of them. **1714** Rowe *Jane Shore* Epil., To see your Spouses Drinking, Gaming, Raking. **1824** *Examiner* 456/2 The battered youth..rakes, games, makes love. **1846** Geo. Eliot in Cross *Life* I. 147 We have been to town but once, and are saving all our strength to 'rake' with you.

rakeage (ˈreɪkɪdʒ). *rare.* [f. RAKE *v.*[1] + -AGE.] That which is raked together.

1851 Mayhew *Lond. Labour* II. 205 Engaged in removing the Scrapeage or Rakeage..from the surface of the streets.

raked (reɪkt), *ppl. a.*[1] [f. RAKE *v.*[1] + -ED[1].] Drawn together, covered up, etc.

1513 Douglas *Æneis* viii. ix. 3 The sloknyt fyris hes he gart, The rakyt harthis and ingill ȝistir nycht,..bet and kyndill brycht. *c* **1586** C'tess Pembroke *Ps.* lxxviii. ix, The raked sparkes in flame began t'appeare. **1851** Stephens *Bk. Farm* (ed. 2) II. 230/2 The latter may make as many ricks along one ridge as the raked grass will admit.

raked (reɪkt), *ppl. a.*[2] [f. RAKE *v.*[3] + -ED[1].] Inclined from the perpendicular or from the horizontal; also, swept-*back*.

1948 H. Innes *Blue Ice* iv. 96 A single raked-back funnel. **1955** *Times* 5 July 5/6 The well-raked steering wheel gives a sense of precise control at speed without being heavy in manoeuvring. **1972** *Soviet Weekly* 22 Apr. 13 Lecturers use portable TV cameras, and students have screens over their heavily raked desks. **1976** B. Jackson *Flameout* xi. 185 The clean aerodynamic form of the airliner:..the raked-back wings..supporting streamlined engine pods. **1977** *Time* 21 Feb. 41/2 The action is carried out on a raked stage.

†**raked table.** *Obs.*[−0] [Of obscure origin.] (See quot. and cf. RAKING-TABLE.)

1704 Harris *Lex. Techn.* s.v. *Table*, Raked Table, is that which is hollow'd in the Square of a Pedestal, or elsewhere.

rakee, variant of RAKE.

rake-hell (ˈreɪkhɛl), *sb.* Now *arch.* Also 6 **rack-**. See also RAKEL. [See RAKE *v.*[1] 6 c.]

1. A thorough scoundrel or rascal; an utterly immoral or dissolute person; a vile debauchee or rake. (In common use *c* 1550–1725.)

1554 Bale *Declaration* (1561) Pref. Aj b, After the mischeuous example of Cain, and the other rake hels. **1581** J. Bell *Haddon's Answ. Osor.* 315 Momish Monckes, flatteryng Fryers, and others such lyke Religious Rackhells. **1603** H. Crosse *Vertues Commw.* (1878) 87 Al the rake-hels and loose vagabonds in a countrey. **1690** J. Mackenzie *Siege London-Derry* 2/1 These Rake-hells (who were the very scum of the Countrey). **1766** Anstey *New Bath Guide* (1776) 131 Brother Simkin's grown a rakehell, Cards and dances ev'ry day. **1870** Thornbury *Tour Eng.* I. ii. 43 The wild son of a baronet, a rake-hell who had been brought up at Eton.

†**b.** Applied to a place. *Obs. rare*[−1].

1560 Daus tr. *Sleidane's Comm.* 17 b, Rome..is the most filthy sinke of al the places in the Uniuersall worlde, and a rakehell heaped of all mischief [L. *inexhausta colluvies*].

2. *attrib.* or as *adj.* = RAKEHELLY 1.

1556 Olde *Antichrist* 186 Most filthie rakehell masse priestes. **1596** Spenser *F.Q.* v. xi. 44 Amid their rakehell bands, They spide a Lady. **1682** *Sec. Plea Nonconf.* 28 A reviling sort of Rake-hell Scriblers. **1782** Cowper *Progr. Err.* 314 Some lewd earl, or rakehell baronet.

transf. **1895** Crockett *Cleg Kelly* xvi, [A] rake-hell cat skirmishing across from area-railing to area-railing.

†**b.** of things. = RAKEHELLY 2. *Obs. rare.*

a **1547** Surrey in *Tottell's Misc.* (Arb.) 11 The rakehell lyfe that longes to loues disporte. **1589** *Pappe w. Hatchet* B ij, If Martin haue not barrelde vp all rakehell words.

Hence **ˈrakeˌhellish** *a.* = RAKEHELLY; †**rakeheˈllonian**, one of the 'sect' of rakehells.

a **1704** T. Brown *Wks.* (1730) II. 313, I have been.. admitted into the family of the rakehellonians. **1824** *New Monthly Mag.* XI. 240 Not to be in bed before midnight was ..esteemed a rakehellish practice.

rakehelly (ˈreɪkˌhɛlɪ), *a.* and *sb.* [f. prec. + -Y[1].] See also RAKELY.

A. *adj.* **1.** Of persons: Of the nature of, or resembling, a rakehell, or rakehells.

1579 E. K. *Ded. Spenser's Sheph. Cal.*, The rakehellye route of our ragged rymers. **1698** Farquhar *Love & Bottle* ii. i, I am a Rakehelly Rascal not worth a Groat. *a* **1766** Mrs. F. Sheridan *Sidney Bidulph* IV. 103 Her ladyship has the misfortune of having a rakehelly young fellow to her son. **1841** *Blackw. Mag.* Apr. 439 They were..repulsive in appearance—rakehelly, slovenly in dress.

2. Appropriate to, characteristic of, rakehells.

1594 O. B. *Quest. Profit. Concern.* 13 Reuiling..his mother and me with such rakehelly words & hellish oathes. *c* **1700** tr. *B. Jonson's Leges Convivales* x, Breaking of windows,..And spoiling the goods for a rakehelly prank. **1825** J. F. Cooper *Lionel Lincoln* II. iv. 89 They needn't think to frighten the people with their rake-helly noises. **1888** J. Payn *Myst. Mirbridge* vii, Those dissipated, not to say rakehelly countenances.

B. *sb.* = RAKE-HELL 1.

a **1762** Lady M. W. Montagu *The Lover* iii, No pedant, yet learned; no rake-helly gay. **1825** J. F. Cooper *Lionel Lincoln* II. iv. 95 Let the rake-hellies go up to Breeds; the people will teach them the law!

rakeism. *rare*[−1]. [f. RAKE *sb.*[5]] = RAKERY.

1775 S. J. Pratt *Liberal Opin.* cxvii. (1783) IV. 94 One of the greatest raptures of rakeism.

†**ˈrake-ˌkennel.** *Obs. rare*[−1]. A scavenger.

1716 [W. Darrell] *Gentleman Instr.* (ed. 2) 445 A Committee of Gold-finders, or a Club of rake-kennels.

ˈrakel. *Obs.* exc. *dial.* Abbrev. of RAKE-HELL.

1622 Boys *Wks.* 413 This rakel-like behauiour is not in imperfect words only, but in scornful gestures of contempt. *a* **1661** Fuller *Worthies* (1840) III. 207 In Cambridge, where (when a youth) he was a Rakel in grain. **1670** Cotton *Espernon* iii. xi. 545 A Cooper that had put himself in the head of a crew of Rakels of his own profession. **1886** *Cheshire Gloss.*, *Rakell*, a thoroughly bad man.

rakel, obs. form of RACKLE *a.*

rakeles, obs. north. and Sc. form of RECKLESS.

rakeless (ˈreɪklɪs), *a.* [f. RAKE *sb.*[4] + -LESS.] Having no rake; having perpendicular forks.

1886 *Wheeling* 2 June 172/2 Very few would care to ride a rakeless machine constantly.

†**ˈrakely**, *a.* *Obs. rare.* [f. RAKEL + -Y[1].] = RAKEHELLY 1.

1694 Southerne *Fatal Marriage* i. i, I saw just now a glimpse of my rakely son. **1713** Shadwell *Hum. Army* i. (1713) 4 Our rakely young Fellows, live as much by their Wits as ever.

†**ˈrake-mould.** *Obs. rare*[−1]. [f. RAKE *v.*[1]] *attrib.* Mould-collecting.

1676 J. Beaumont in *Phil. Trans.* XI. 732 In the Courses, ..betwixt the clifts I find of these Plants growing up in the gristy clay,..being rooted on the rake-mold stones.

raken, obs. f. RECKON, REKEN.

raken(te, obs. f. RACKAN.

†**rakenteie.** *Obs.* Forms: α. 1 racentéah (-téaȝ-), (h)rac(c)en-, racon-, 2 rachenteȝe, 4 rakenteie. β. 1 racetéaȝ-, 2–3 raketeie, -tehe, 3 -teȝe, 3–4 -teye, 4 -tiȝe, 5 rakketye. γ. 4 raketyne, 6 rakentyn. [OE. *racentéah*, f. *racente* chain, RACKAN + *téah*, *téaȝ-* TIE *sb.*] A chain.

c **950** *Lindisf. Gosp.* Mark v. 3 Ne hraccenteȝum [*Rushw.* racent-, racont-]..æniȝ monn hine mæhte ȝebinda. **971** *Blickl. Hom.* 209 Glæsen fæt on seolfrenre racenteaȝe ahangen. *c* **1000** *Ags. Gosp.* Mark v. 4 He..to slat þa raceteaȝa [*Hatton MS.* raketeȝen]. *c* **1154** *O.E. Chron.* an. 1137 In mani of þe castles wæron lof & grin, ðæt wæron rachenteȝes [etc.]. *a* **1225** *Juliana* 46 A great raketehe þat heo wes mide ibunden. **1297** R. Glouc. (Rolls) 3001 An raketeie [*v.rr.* raketyne, raketiȝe] of hire in is hond he nom. *c* **1320** *Sir Beues* (A.) 1636 Now er þai ded, þe geilers tweie, & Beues liþ to þe rakenteie [*MS. E.* raketeye]. **1517** *Nottingham Rec.* III. 138 Unum par galefurcarum de ferro cum les rakentyns eisdem.

ˈrake-off. *slang* (orig. *U.S.*). Also **rakeoff**, **rake off.** [Cf. RAKE *sb.*[1] 2 a (*a*).] A share (of the winnings in gambling, of profits, etc.), a 'cut'; commission. (Freq. with derogatory overtones.)

1888 *Texas Siftings* 28 Jan. 16/1 We always give him a rake-off, so he makes a good enough thing of it. **1890** J. P. Quinn *Fools of Fortune* 188 This percentage is technically known as the 'rake-off', and insures the proprietors of the establishment a handsome royalty on all winnings. **1899** B. Tarkington *Gentleman from Indiana* vii. 95 In oil it's the farmer that gets the rake-off. **1903** *Sun* (N.Y.) 2 Nov. 3 This is a day of rake-offs. The boss..gets his rake-off from every service he renders to his party. The laborer gets his rake-off for selling his vote. **1905** D. G. Phillips *Plum Tree* 61 It means a big rake-off for Dunkirk. Politics is on a money basis nowadays. **1914** 'J. H. Keate' *Destruction of Mephisto's Greatest Web* ii. 60 The slot that receives the 'rake off', or percentage. *Ibid.* iii. 91, I would do my best to prepare him a meal. This I was willing to do, as my 'rake off' for the night had only been ten cents. **1926** E. Wallace *Yellow Snake* xxvii. 224 This was something more profitable than the smuggling of cocaine,..a quicker way to fortune than the rake-off of coppers from a forbidden game of fantan. **1929** M. A. Gill *Underworld Slang* 10/1 *Rake-off man*, nickel taker at dice game. **1934** J. T. Farrell *Young Manhood* viii. 121 'Hey, Hugo, what undertaker's giving you a rakeoff?' interrupted Arnold Sheehan. **1934** *Punch* 26 Dec. 722/2 Why don't you make the cost of The Club Dinner inclusive of wines and spirits? I suppose it is because the hotel where you are having the meal won't give you a rake-off on all liquor served? **1936** [see *football pool*]. **1951** *Proc. Prehistoric Soc.* XVII. 174 The Burmese ones are reputed better, and always fetch a higher price—in fact they must do so or they would never reach the western villages, as the rake-off from passing them on would be inadequate. **1959** J. Cary *Captive & Free* lxix. 315, I didn't say fifty to you. Sorry. But the agency would give me a rake off on reprints. **1968** *Globe & Mail* (Toronto) 3 Feb. 11/1 Police and politicians in Vancouver may be getting a rake-off from the ring. **1973** 'D. Rutherford' *Kick Start* viii. 174 The vendors were waiting... Obviously the courier would receive a handsome rake-off. **1977** *Time* 31 Oct. 23/3 The President again assailed the big oil companies, charging that deregulation of natural gas prices would produce 'big profit rake-offs and huge cost increases to the American consumers'.

raker[1] (ˈreɪkə(r)). Also 4 **rakyer.** [f. RAKE *v.*[1]]

1. One who rakes. Also with *after*, *up*.

1563 Foxe *A. & M.* 37/1 Not repairers of peace, but rakers for money. **1619** Hieron *Minoritie of Saints* Wks. 1632 II. 35 This cryeth shame vpon the rakers and scrapers of this world. **1641** Best *Farm. Bks.* (Surtees) 36 Rakers-after should have charge given that they rake cleane. **1823** J. Wilson *Trials Marg. Lyndsay* xxix. 76/1 She used, half in work, half in pastime, to join the merry band of rakers. **1854**

MILMAN *Lat. Chr.* VIII. vii. 422 Greedy rakers up of gold. **1865** E. EDWARDS *Libraries* 425 To rake from a dead man's private diaries and memoranda passages which it is hoped by the raker will cause pain.

2. *spec.* A scavenger, street-cleaner. Now *arch.*

1362 LANGL. *P. Pl.* A. v. 165 A ribibor, a ratoner, a rakere [*v.r.* rakyer] of Chepe. **1469** *Churchw. Acc. St. Mich. Cornhill*, Paid to the raker for caryng awey of the chirche dust. **1535** in *Vicary's Anat.* (1888) App. iii. 170 The Raker .. shall have a horne, & blowe at euery mannes doore .. to lay owt theyre offal. **1665** *Orders of Ld. Mayor Lond.* in De Foe *Plague* (Rtldg.) 63 That the Sweeping .. of Houses be .. carry'd away by the Rakers. **1766** ENTICK *London* IV. 17 A wharf used for a laystall, to which the rakers carry street-soil. **1817** *Act 57 Geo. III*, c. 29 §59 The scavengers, rakers, or cleansers of the streets and public places. **1851** in Mayhew *Lond. Labour* II. 210 Sewers' Office, Guildhall, London, Rakers' Duties, Midsummer, 1851, to Midsummer, 1852.

3. †**a.** A gun so placed as to rake an enemy's vessel. *Obs. rare*[−1].

a **1625** FLETCHER *Double Marr.* II. i, Every man to his charge, man her .. wel, And place your rakers right.

b. *Mining.* (See quot.)

1883 GRESLEY *Gloss. Coal-mining, Rakers*, shots placed round sumpers.

4. An implement for raking: *spec.* **a.** A tool used by charcoal-burners. ? *Obs.* **b.** An iron tool having pointed steel ends bent at a right angle in opposite directions, used in removing old mortar from the joints of walls. **c.** A salt-rake. **d.** (See quot. 1887.) **e.** A gill-raker (see GILL *sb.*[1] 5).

1727 BRADLEY *Fam. Dict.* s.v. *Charcoal*, Lastly, they do with the Handles of their Rakers, &c. make Vent-holes thro' the Stuff that covers the Heap. **1812–16** J. SMITH *Panorama Sc. & Art* I. 194 The raker .. is employed to rake or scrape loose and decayed mortar out of the joints of walls. **1842** GWILT *Archit.* §1890 The tools used by the bricklayer .. are .. 10. The raker. **1886** *Cheshire Gloss., Raker*, .. a piece of flat iron at the end of a long handle, used for raking the salt off the fires and to the sides of the pan. **1887** *Dict. Archit., Raker*, an implement used in mixing lime and hair for plaster, or in making parget.

5. = *raking-coal* s.v. RAKING *vbl. sb.*[1] 3. *dial.* Cf. RAKE *v.*[1] 5.

1858 GEO. ELIOT *Scenes Clerical Life* II. 250 The kitchen fire .. was kept in under a huge 'raker'—a possibility by which the coal of the midland counties atones for all its slowness and white ashes. *c* **1909** D. H. LAWRENCE *Collier's Friday Night* (1934) iii. 87 Ernest has come from the cellar with a large lump of coal, which he pushes down in the fireplace so that it shall not lodge and go out... He puts the candle on the table, and puts some coal on the fire, round the 'raker'.

6. An inclined beam or strut.

1882 C. H. STOCK *Treat. Shoring & Underpinning* ii. 5 The outer shore is called the top raker, the middle shore the middle raker, and the lowest is called the bottom shore. **1887** G. H. BLAGROVE *Shoring* ii. 32 The foot of the middle raker thrusts against a cleat bolted to the foot of the bottom shore. **1956** *Archit. Rev.* CXX. 327/2 The existing balcony rakers, the main roof and the back stage parts were retained, but the stalls floor .. was rebuilt. **1963** M. J. TOMLINSON *Foundation Design & Construction* vii. 404 A large pile cap is provided to counteract the uplift on the backward raker.

raker[2] ('reɪkə(r)). *colloq.* [f. RAKE *v.*[2] (cf. RAKING *ppl. a.*[2]), but prob. vaguely associated with prec.]

1. a. An extremely fast pace.

1876 *Coursing Calendar* 38 Poacher, going a raker from Cannobie lea, never let the latter next the hare in a well-run course of good length. **1895** *Daily News* 8 July 8/6 The pace home was a raker, the three boats throwing up great sheets of white water.

b. A good stroke at golf.

1899 *Golf Illustr.* 15 Sept. 393/2 Vardon drove a 'raker' from the first tee, nearly hole high.

2. *Sporting slang.* A heavy bet, a 'plunge'.

1869 BRADWOOD *The O.V.H.* (1870) 339 His Lordship has gone a 'raker' for Lord of the Valley.

rakery ('reɪkərɪ). Now *rare.* [f. RAKE *sb.*[4] + -ERY.] Rakish conduct; debauchery, dissoluteness; social excitement.

1728 FIELDING *Love in Sev. Masques* I. v, O if that be the malady, I would prescribe to the gentleman a course of rakery. *a* **1734** NORTH *Lives* (1826) II. 233 He .. instructed his Lordship in all the rakery and intrigues of the lewd town. **1850** L. HUNT *Autobiog.* I. vi. 241 He looked .. like the man who could bear rakery and debauch.

†**rakes.** *Obs. rare*[−1]. A term of abuse.

1575 *Gamm. Gurton* III. iii. 25 Thou slut, thou kut, thou rakes, thou iakes! will not shame make the bide?

rakeshame ('reɪkʃeɪm). Now *rare* (? *U.S.*). [f. RAKE *v.*[1] + SHAME *sb.*; perh. suggested by RAKEHELL.] One who covers himself with shame; an ill-behaved, disorderly, or dissolute fellow. (Common in 17th c.)

1599 *Broughton's Lett.* v. 15 It is an easie matter for euery rakeshame to reuile an innocent. **1621** BP. MOUNTAGU *Diatribæ* 446 Such roysters and rake-shames as Mars is manned with. **1682** MRS. BEHN *City Heiress* 39 Marry you! a Rakeshame .. without Money or Credit. **1718** OZELL tr. *Tournefort's Voy.* I. 353 The Caimacan .. gave strangers a permission to defend themselves against these disorderly Rake-shames. *c* **1840** WHITTIER *Tales & Sk., Dr. Singletary* vi, There's not a more drunken, swearing rakeshame in town than Tom Osborne.

Hence †**'rake-shamed** *a.*, disreputable, disgraceful. *Obs.*

1635 *Long Meg of Westminster* (1816) 6 Away, you foule rake-sham'd whore, quoth he. **1662–3** PEPYS *Diary* 21 Feb., These fellows, which are called the commissioners, but are the most rake-shamed rogues that ever I saw in my life.

rake-soil: see RAKE *sb.*[3] 5 b.

raket, obs. form of RACKET *sb.*[1]

raketehe, -teie, etc., varr. RAKENTEIE. *Obs.*

'rake-vein. [f. RAKE *sb.*[3] 5.] A leading vein of ore (cf. quots. and RAKE).

1813 BAKEWELL *Introd. Geol.* (1815) 274 Rake veins or perpendicular veins resemble mineral dykes in position, but not in their contents. **1874** J. H. COLLINS *Metal Mining* 24 Rake-veins or Lodes appear to occupy fissures in the earth, sometimes parallel to, sometimes cutting across, the general bedding, and even the cleavage of the rocks.

raki (rə'kiː, 'rækiː). Forms: 7 racckee, 8 rakia, 8–9 rakie, 9 rackee, ra(k)kee, 7– raki. [a. Turkish *rāqī* (whence also mod. Gr. ρακή, ρακί) brandy, spirits.] *Orig.*, an aromatic liquor made from grain-spirit, or from grape-juice, used in Greece and the Levant. Now also used of a liquor made from other ingredients (see quot. 1959) in various countries of eastern Europe and the Middle East; a drink of glass of this.

1675 TEONGE *Diary* (1825) 96 [We] drinke to our friends in England in racckee at night. **1775** R. CHANDLER *Trav. Asia Minor* lxxv. 255 Not far from us were booths of the Turcomans... Some of them joined us, and one or two wanted rakí or brandy. **1777** *Ann. Reg.* II. 47 They distil from the fruits of trees .. a sort of brandy, called rakie. **1835** MARRYAT *Pacha* i, Sherbet I cannot drink, rakee I must not. **1845** E. WARBURTON *Crescent & Cross* I. xxvi. 295 Their dram is distilled from rice, and called *Raki.* **1873** TRISTRAM *Moab* x. 192 The only levy on our stores had been four bottles of raki. **1919** E. H. JONES *Road to En-Dor* iii. 34, I .. poured myself out a tot of Raki from Alec's bottle. **1933** 'G. ORWELL' *Down & out in London & Paris* xvi. 122 Raki, the Arab drink, was very cheap. **1941** 'R. WEST' *Black Lamb* (1942) I. 410 Raki, the colourless brandy loved by Slavs. **1956** R. MACAULAY *Towers of Trebizond* xii. 125 We had supper at the khan, and sat on there smoking and sipping raki .. while Turks played tric-trac at little tables beneath the trees. **1959** W. JAMES *Word-bk. Wine* 154 *Raki*, a fairly general name for spirits in Balkan countries; it may be made from wine, grain, molasses, potatoes, plums, and so on; in Turkey it is a spirit resembling Pernod, which goes milky when diluted. **1969** J. MAVOR *Voyage to Atlantis* ix. 206 The old woman with two eye-teeth brought us raki or tsipuro, a 40-proof sort of grappa. **1980** M. BAR-ZOHAR *Deadly Document* ix. 158 He sat down and ordered a *raki.*

‖**rakia** (ra'kija, 'rakia). Also **rakija.** [a. Bulg. *rakíya*, Serbo-Croat *ràkija*: cf. RAKI.] In the Balkan countries: brandy, liquor; = prec.

1845 *Encycl. Metrop.* XXV. 1290/2 *Rakia* is a Dalmatian spirit, drawn from the murk of the wine-press, mingled with aromatics. **1926** *Blackw. Mag.* Apr. 526/1 It was a large scent-bottle filled with *rakija.* **1932** G. GREENE *Stamboul Train* IV. i. 179 Ninitch sipped his glass of *rakia*; the heavy plum wine brought tears to his eyes. **1950** V. CANNING *Forest of Eyes* iii. 62 He took the *rakia* bottle from his desk drawer and set two glasses. **1959** F. MACLEAN *Back to Bokhara* ii. 103 Rakia, the plum brandy of Bosnia. **1966** *New Statesman* 11 Nov. 705/2 A Montenegrin town, in 1943, is garrisoned by a tattered Venetian legion... The garrison stifles in rock heat, bloats on rakija. **1980** J. HONE *Flowers of Forest* I. 21 Playing chess over a bottle of rakia somewhere in Yugoslavia.

rakil(l, obs. ff. RACKLE *a.*

rakily ('reɪkɪlɪ), *adv. rare.* [f. (*rakey f.) RAKE *sb.*[5] + -LY[2].] In a rakish manner; rakishly.

1904 C. HAMILTON *Passing of Arthur* xx. 167 His newly-ironed tall hat was rakily cut, and he wore an immaculate light grey frock coat and waistcoat.

rakin, obs. f. RACKAN.

rakin(e, obs. ff. RECKON *v.*

raking ('reɪkɪŋ), *vbl. sb.*[1] [f. RAKE *v.*[1] + -ING[1].]

1. a. The action of the vb., in various senses.

c **1440** *Promp. Parv.* 422/2 Rakynge, *rastratura.* **1474–5** *Durham Acc. Rolls* (Surtees) 95 Pro .. le rakyng circa muros coquinæ. **1550** CROWLEY *Waie to Wealth* 528 Howe you have obeyed the lawe in rakeinge together of fermes. **1654** GAYTON *Pleas. Notes* III. xi. 150 There would be foul raking in the dust. **1702** *Eng. Theophrast.* 377 That which some call good-husbandry, industry, and providence, others call raking, avarice, and oppression. **1769** FALCONER *Dict. Marine* (1776) s.v., This is frequently called raking fore and aft. **1851** MRS. BROWNING *Casa Guidi Wind.* 111 The raking of the guns across The world. **1942** *R.A.F. Jrnl.* 18 Apr. 8 There should be full scale raking down of land and sowing.

b. With *a*: An instance of this.

c **1700** *Battle of Pentland Hills* in Child *Ballads* VII. 242 Such a raking was never seen As the raking o' the Rullien Green. **1883** *Jrnl. Educ.* (U.S.) XVIII. 136 The average common-school received a raking.

c. *concr.* (in *pl.*). That which is collected with a rake. Also *fig.*

1641 BEST *Farm. Bks.* (Surtees) 46 A fewe of those rakins will serve to blacken and spoyle a greate deale of better corne. **1698** SIR J. HOLT in *12 Mod. Rep.* Case 399. 235 One may libel in the spiritual courts for tithe of rakings of corn. **1851** STEPHENS *Bk. Farm* (ed. 2) II. 341/2 The rakings should not exceed from four to five per cent of the crop. **1868** in *Trans. Illinois State Agric. Soc.* (1870) VII. 434 The supply of hogs .. appeared to be made up of the rakings and sweepings of the country. **1977** *Times* 24 Dec. 14/5 A series of ovens had been cut into the back of the rampart, their rakings being deposited in the abandoned ditch of the superseded marching camp.

d. A rebuke or scolding. Also with *down*, = a 'dressing down'. Chiefly *U.S.*

1854 *La Crosse* (Wisconsin) *Democrat* 17 Jan. 2/4 Mr. Wright .. gave Smith a small raking down. **1883** J. D. SHIELDS *Life & Times S. S. Prentiss* 125 He cheerfully paid it, vowing that the 'raking down' which Prentiss had given his prosecutor was worth that. **1897** G. BARTRAM *People of Clopton* iii. 80 He got such a terrific raking-down from Aunt that his long black shadow never darkened our doors again. **1907** *Black Cat* Jan. 7 I'll bet somebody has got a raking for losing it.

2. *spec.* **a.** *Farriery.* (See RAKE *v.*[1] 8.)

1805 *Trans. Soc. Arts* XXIII. 108 Clysters and raking afford much relief. **1842** SPOONER *White's Vet. Art* 527 In some cases .. the straight gut is so loaded with hard dung that raking is a necessary operation.

b. *Billiards.* (See quot. 1788.)

1670 COTTON *Gamester* (1680) 22 Have a care of raking, for .. it is a fault, hardly excusable. **1788** in BENNETT & 'CAVENDISH' *Billiards* (1873) 7 Trailing [or raking], that is, following the ball with the mace to such a convenient distance from the other ball as to make it an easy hazard.

3. *attrib.*, as ***raking machinery, operation***; **raking-coal** (see quot. 1883).

1866 *Engineering* I. 340 Raking Machinery for the River Hooghly. *Ibid.*, A steamer to be used in the raking operations. **1883** GRESLEY *Gloss. Coal-mining, Raking-coal*, a large lump of hard coal placed upon a fire .. for the purpose of just keeping it burning, or rather smouldering.

raking ('reɪkɪŋ), *vbl. sb.*[2] [f. RAKE *v.*[2] + -ING[1].] The action of the vb. (in sense 2).

1828 SIR J. S. SEBRIGHT *Hawking* 47 Buzzards, Sparrow-hawks .. fly near the ground, and take their prey by what is called raking.

raking ('reɪkɪŋ), *vbl. sb.*[3] [f. RAKE *v.*[3] + -ING[1].] The fact of sloping or causing to slope. *spec.* in *Building* (usu. written **racking**), the action of RACK *v.*[7]; also, the resulting arrangement of bricks or stones, and in phr. ***racking back.***

1873 A. M. LANG *J. G. Medley's Roorkee Treat. Civil Engin. in India* (ed. 3) I. xvii. 345 (*heading*) Racking back. *c* **1880** *Dict. Archit.* s.v. *Jump*, Instead of making abrupt jumps, it is better to let the brickwork rise gradually in step courses. This operation is called 'raking back'. **1894** C. F. MITCHELL *Building Construction* iii. 132 Racking is the term applied to the method of arranging the edge of a brick wall, part of which is unavoidably delayed while the remainder is carried up. **1902** *Encycl. Brit.* XXVI. 437/1 The foundations must be spread below the column bases... This is accomplished by rackings of stone or brickwork. **1945** E. L. BRALEY *Brickwork* iii. 60 Racking back is the best method of executing this particular job, as by this means the bonding bricks can be perfectly bedded. **1946** HOLGATE & MCDOUGALL *Bricklaying* vi. 88 Corbling and raking are also largely used in the building of chimney flues. Since a chimney flue always runs upwards at an angle, raking is necessary on one side and corbling on the other. **1964** J. S. SCOTT *Dict. Building* 254 The normal way of building a *brick* wall consists of first building the corners or ends .. in steps rising one course at a time from the middle part of the wall. The gradual increases of height to the corner are called racking back.

raking ('reɪkɪŋ), *vbl. sb.*[4] [f. RAKE *v.*[4] + -ING[1].] Playing the rake; dissolute living.

1700 FARQUHAR *Constant Couple* I. i, [He] usurps Gentility, where he may die by Raking. **1722** DE FOE *Col. Jack* (1840) 63 Something .. kept me from the other degrees of raking and vice. **1828** *Lights & Shades* I. 124, I didn't waste my health and my money in drinking and raking. **1874** GREEN *Short Hist.* ix. §1. 589 Duelling and raking became the marks of a fine gentleman.

raking ('reɪkɪŋ), *ppl. a.*[1] [f. RAKE *v.*[1] + -ING[2].] That rakes, in senses (esp. 2 and 9) of the vb.

1500–20 DUNBAR *Poems* lix. 2 A refyng sone of rakyng Muris. **1611** SPEED *Hist. Gt. Brit.* IX. ix. (1632) 624 Daily did he send his raking Clerkes .. to delude the King and purloine his Subiects. **1666** DRYDEN *Ann. Mirab.* lxxxii, Raking chase-guns through our sterns they send. **1797** SIR J. JERVIS in Nicolas *Disp. Nelson* (1845) II. 404 *note*, The Launch .. was sunk by a raking shot from the Enemy's gun boats. **1840** DICKENS *Barn. Rudge* i, Being exposed to this raking fire of eyes.

raking ('reɪkɪŋ), *ppl. a.*[2] [f. RAKE *v.*[2] + -ING[2].] Fast-going. Also *Comb.*

1862 WHYTE-MELVILLE *Inside the Bar* ii, A well-bred, raking-looking sort of mare. **1883** C. J. WILLS *Land Lion & Sun* 61 A big, coarse, raking chestnut, that took all the boy who rode him could do to hold him.

raking ('reɪkɪŋ), *ppl. a.*[3] [f. RAKE *v.*[3] + -ING[2].]

a. Slanting, sloping.

1711 [see b]. **1778** *Encycl. Brit.* (ed. 2) I. 618/2 The square of the rail, with the raking line of the pitch-board drawn through the middle. **1801** *Sketch Paris* I. vi. 36 A pediment, whose raking columns are composed of two stones only. **1840** R. H. DANA *Bef. Mast* ix. 20 A long, sharp brig, .. with raking masts. **1872** C. KING *Mountain. Sierra Nev.* x. 208 Short boots, with high, raking heels.

b. In special phrases:

raking arch, a rampant arch. ***raking bond*** (see quot. 1876); also, ***raking stretcher bond. raking-mould***, in hand-railing = face-mould. ***raking-piece***, (*a*) part of the supports of a bridge-centering; (*b*) a low sloping piece of stage-scenery. ***raking plate, prop, work*** (see quots.).

1711 W. SUTHERLAND *Shipbuild. Assist.* 61 A *Raking Arch. **1842** GWILT *Encycl. Arch.* §1413 The model of a raking arch. **1876** P. G. L. SMITH *Notes Building Construction* II. xiii. 221 *Raking Bond is of two kinds, *Diagonal* and *Herringbone.* In both the bricks in the interior of the wall are placed in directions oblique to the face. A course or two of raking bond is sometimes introduced at intervals in thick walls built in English bond. The proportion of stretchers in a brick wall diminishes according to its thickness... The raking courses are therefore useful in giving longitudinal strength to thick walls which are deficient in stretchers. In both kinds of raking bond alternate courses rake in opposite directions. **1937** P. E. THOMAS *Mod. Building Pract.* III. 294 The direction of the diagonal or raking bond is changed in each course to further strengthen the bond of the wall. **1974** *Bricks: Their Prop. & Use* (Brick Devel. Assoc.) I. 29 *(caption) Raking Stretcher bond.* Economical and more interesting than normal Stretcher Bond. Joints tend to become very prominent unless mortar colour is chosen with care. **1825** J. NICHOLSON *Operat. Mechanic* 600 The face-mould.. is also called the *raking-mould. **1875** KNIGHT *Dict. Mech.* 1877/2 **Raking-pieces*, pieces laid upon sills supported by the footings or impost of a pier. Above them are the striking-plates. **1884** Raking-piece [see *cut cloth* s.v. CUT *ppl. a.* 12]. **1898** 'P. McGINNIS' *Bohem. Girl* 124 The theatre was like a barn, and we had to get to our dressing-room up a raking-piece with ribs nailed across it. **1887** *Dict. Archit.*, **Raking plate*, for housing a step in a partition. **1883** GRESLEY *Gloss. Coal-mining*, **Raking Props*, short wooden props used in sinking for supporting the curbs during the excavation of the sides of the shaft. **1736** NEVE *City & C. Purchaser*, **Raking-Work*, that which (..in Mouldings, etc.) is to be join'd by Mitering exactly.

raking ('reɪkɪŋ), *ppl. a.*⁴ [f. RAKE *v.*⁴ + -ING².] Dissolute, dissipated.
a **1704** T. BROWN *Praise Poverty* Wks. 1730 I. 98 A thoughtless, raking, roaring, drinking scoundrel. **1760** C. JOHNSTON *Chrysal* (1822) III. 116 Procuring the living for one of his raking companions. **1803** MAR. EDGEWORTH *Manufacturer* ii, Mrs. Germaine, thanks to the raking hours she keeps,.. looks ten years older than she is.

rakinge-crok, obs. variant of RACKAN-CROOK.

† **raking-table** *Obs.*⁻⁰ = RAKED TABLE.
1736 NEVE *City & C. Purchaser* s.v., Raking-table, among Architects, a Member hollow'd in the Square of a Pedestal, or elsewhere.

rakish ('reɪkɪʃ), *a.*¹ [f. RAKE *sb.*⁵ + -ISH.]
1. Of persons: Having the character, appearance, or manners, of a rake.
1706 MRS. CENTLIVRE *Love at a Venture* IV, The grave, serious, formal lover, or the gay rakish soldier. **1758** JOHNSON *Idler* No. 33 ¶25 Some rakish fellow-commoner in the next room. **1811** BYRON *Hints from Hor.* 165 A..rakish youngster wild from school. **1840** THACKERAY *Paris Sk.-bk.* (1872) 226 The knavish valets, rakish heroes.
2. Of things: Characteristic of, appropriate to, a rake. **a.** of talk, manners, mode of life, etc.
1722 WOLLASTON *Relig. Nat.* vi. 142 Impertinent simile's and rakish talk. **1784** BURNS *Song, O leave novels*, That feeling heart but acts a part, 'Tis rakish art in Rob Mossgiel. **1876** *World* No. 116. 6 The rakish ways of the medical student of Albert Smith.
b. of appearance, carriage, etc.
1706 FARQUHAR *Recruiting Officer* IV. i, I take a bold Step, a rakish Toss, a smart Cock and an impudent Air. **1816** J. SCOTT *Vis. Paris* (ed. 5) 93 With keen proud looks,.. and a rakish dissolute carriage. **1859** KINGSLEY *Misc.* (1860) II. 123 The rakish swagger.. of the coxcombs.
transf. **1860** TYNDALL *Glac.* I. xxv. 186 The wild and rakish appearance of the sky.
c. of material things: Having a rakish look.
1847 L. HUNT *Men, Women & B.* II. xi. 275 He does not wear so rakish a wig. **1876** HOLLAND *Sev. Oaks* ii. 25 With a basket.. in the back of the rakish little wagon.
3. *Comb.*, as ***rakish-looking***.
1861 HUGHES *Tom Brown at Oxf.* II. 322 In a few minutes a rakish-looking stable-boy came round for his horse. **1897** *Daily News* 26 May 9 Four or five stalwart young fellows in rakish-looking broad brimmed hats.

rakish ('reɪkɪʃ), *a.*² [See notes below.]
1. *Naut.* Of a ship: Having an appearance indicative of smartness and fast sailing, freq. with suggestion of suspicious or piratical character.
The precise origin is not clear: it may orig. be a transferred use of *a.*¹ (cf. sense 2 c there), but recent dicts. associate it with the raking masts of pirate-vessels.
1824 W. IRVING *T. Trav.* II. 242 A little rakish, musquito-built vessell, that could run into all kinds of waters. **1835** MARRYAT *Jac. Faithf.* xxxix, A low schooner, sir, very rakish indeed, black sides. **1884** *Pall Mall G.* 22 Aug. 3/1 A yacht of grand proportions and rakish beauty.
Comb. **1838** POE *Narr. A. G. Pym of Nantucket* in *Wks.* (1902) III. 146 She was a long, low, and rakish-looking schooner. **1868** WHYTE-MELVILLE *White Rose* II. xi. 138 They found.. that the beautiful, rakish-looking schooner was averse to piracy.
2. Of a hawk's wings: Smart-looking.
Perh. suggested by RAKE *v.*² 2 a.
1855 SALVIN & BRODRICK *Falconry* 62 This Tiercel.. has a short strong body, with remarkably rakish wings, which accounts for its great speed.

rakishly ('reɪkɪʃlɪ), *adv.* [f. RAKISH *a.*¹ + -LY².] In a rakish manner, jauntily.
1838 DICKENS *O. Twist* xxxvii, Mr. Bumble took his hat.. putting it on, rather rakishly, on one side. **1884** E. P. ROE *Nat. Ser. Story* iv, A.. little atom of a bird, with his tail pointing rakishly toward his head.
So **'rakishness**, the quality of being rakish.
1832 in WEBSTER. **1866** GEO. ELIOT *F. Holt* (1868) 31 On the stupid rakishness of the original heir.. he had calculated rashly. **1878** H. IRVING *Stage* 25 These pieces.. inoculate the feminine mind with rakishness.

rakk(e, obs. ff. RACK, RECK.

rakkee, obs. f. RAKI.

rakkett, rakkin, obs. Sc. ff. RACKET *sb.*¹, RECKON.

rakle, obs. f. RACKLE *a.*

rakles, obs. Sc. and north. f. RECKLESS.

raklie: see RACKLY.

raknit, obs. Sc. pa. t. RECKON.

rakon-cruke, obs. f. RACKAN-CROOK.

‖**rakshasa** ('rɑːkʃasa). Also **raksasa, rakshas**; fem. **rakshasi**. [a. Skr. *rākshasa* demon, f. *rakshas* something to be guarded against or warded off.] In Hindu mythology, a malignant demon, esp. one of a band at war with Rama and Hanuman. Also, an artistic representation of such a demon.
1866 *Chambers's Encycl.* VIII. 101/1 *Rakshas*, or *râkshasa*, is, in Hindu Mythology, the name of a class of evil spirits or demons,.. imagined.. more frequently as mischievous, cruel, and hideous monsters, haunting cemeteries, [etc.]. **1899** F. H. GROOME *Gypsy Folk-Tales* p. lxxiv, In the folk-tales of India.. a *rakshasi* makes nothing of polishing off the entire population of a city. **1917**, etc. [see PISHACHI]. **1937** M. COVARRUBIAS *Island of Bali* vii. 178 The most complete statue is that of a wild *raksasa* crowned with skulls. *Ibid.* viii. 239 The giant Rawana, the *raksasa* king, a monster of wickedness and lechery. **1967** SINGHA & MASSEY *Indian Dances* x. 106 A pair of enormous discs are often held by an unseen helper on either side of the face of a rakshasa or demonic character [in Kathakali dancing]. **1972** *Daily Tel.* (Colour Suppl.) 12 May 58/3 The most feared Indian vampire, the Rakshasa, was all powerful; it animated dead bodies, snatched babies,.. could change into any form and lengthen its arms to 80 miles.

‖**rakshi** ('rɑːkʃiː). Also **raksi**. [a. Nepali *raksi*; cf. Tibetan *rag-śi*.] In Nepal and Tibet, a liquor distilled from rice or grain.
1877 D. WRIGHT *Hist. Nepal* ii. 30 The Newârs, and most of the lower castes consume a considerable quantity of a coarse spirit called Rakshī, which is distilled from rice and wheat. **1954** W. NOYCE *South Col.* v. 72 Hospitably entertained with tea.. and a not very good *rakshi* or rice spirit. **1959** *Times* 23 May 7/7 We spent half a day at the famous monastery of Thyangboche, where we were entertained to dinner by the head lama and sampled his excellent *rakshi*, the local distillation. **1966** C. BONINGTON *I chose to Climb* x. 124 The Sherpas had settled down to a celebratory binge, consuming huge quantities of rakshi, a potent spirit distilled from barley or rice. **1971** —— *Annapurna South Face* iv. 50 And then supper—chicken and rice washed down by *raksi*, the local spirit made from distilled millet. *Ibid.* vii. 81 Meanwhile, Pasang had taken the unwise step of making a *raksi* issue to some of them.

‖**raku** ('raku). Also **Raku**. [Jap., lit. ease, relaxed state, enjoyment: see quot. 1882.] A kind of lead-glazed Japanese pottery, often used as tea-bowls and similar utensils. Also *attrib.*
1875 AUDSLEY & BOWES *Keramic Art Japan* I. 52 Raku is occasionally covered with lacquer, and it is made in other places than in Kioto. **1882** C. DRESSER *Japan* II. iv. 371 Shôgun Taikosama.. honoured this particular manufacture with a golden seal, on which the character 'raku' (meaning enjoyment) was engraved... The competition for objects specially valued (as some of these black raku cups) was such that wars were often waged between Daimios with the sole view of possessing certain coveted goods. **1890** B. H. CHAMBERLAIN *Things Japanese* 278 The *Raku-yaki* of Kyōto is the parent of all the rest... The *Raku* faience owed much of its popularity to the patronage of the 'tea clubs'. **1960** B. LEACH *Potter in Japan* ii. 51 One bowl was old Corean and the other, used alternately, was a 'Doniu' black raku. **1970** *Oxf. Compan. Art* 610 The famous *Raku* is a very soft glazed ware widely used for deliberately misshapen vessels. **1979** C. McCARRY *Better Angels* II. i. 105 The elegant old man pouring tea into Raku bowls.

rakyer, obs. f. RAKER¹.

† **'rakyl**. *Obs. rare*⁻¹. ? var. of *rakent* RACKAN. (Jamieson (1808) has '*Rackle*, a chain'.)
c **1430** LYDG. *Min. Poems* (Percy Soc.) 113 He dyght hym in a dyvelles garment,.. He cam in at the chyrch dore.. Rynnyng, roryng, wythe hys rakyls, as devilles semyd to doo.

rakyl(l, obs. forms of RACKLE *a.*

rakyn, obs. Sc. form of RECKON *v.*

‖**râle** (rɑl). *Path.* Also **rale**. [F. *râle*, †*rasle* (Cotgr. 1611), vbl. sb. from *râler*, †*raller* (16th c.), of uncertain etym.; connexion with LG. and Du. *ratelen*, Eng. *rattle* is doubtful.] An abnormal sound additional to that of respiration, heard on auscultation of the lungs when these are not in a perfectly healthy condition.
1828 *Glasgow Med. Jrnl.* I. 72 The respiratory murmur is often rendered fainter, and it is accompanied and obscured by certain *râles*, or unnatural sounds. **1829** *Good's Study Med.* (ed. 3) I. 537 'For want' says he [Laennec] 'of a better or more generic term, I use the word râle, rattle, or rhoncus, to express all the sounds, besides those of health, which the act of respiration occasions'. **1853** MARKHAM tr. *Skoda's Auscult.* 130 The moist and dry cavernous râles, as well as the blowing râle of the bronchial tubes. **1894** DOYLE *Round Red Lamp* 7 The difference between a mitral murmur and a bronchitic rale. **1963** *Lancet* 12 Jan. 76/1 There were a few dry rales at the right lung base. **1977** *Ibid.* 17 Dec. 1265/2 At this stage there are usually rales in the chest but no definite signs of lung consolidation.

rale (reɪl), *a. U.S.* and *dial.* var. of REAL *a.*²
1835 D. CROCKETT *Acct. Col. Crockett's Tour* 60 Folks need not go out of Boston to find rale hospitality. **1873** C. M. YONGE *Pillars of House* II. xvi. 108 A fellow that.. makes verses—rale, superior, iligant articles. **1901** M. FRANKLIN *My Brilliant Career* xxviii. 237 'Wot's she like?' 'Oh, a rale little bit of a thing.' **1922** E. O'NEILL in *Hearst's Internat.* Mar. 47/1 It was.. aisy for a rale man with guts to him, the like of me. **1940** *Amer. Speech* XV. 46 Characteristic of those encountered in the Cumberlands and Ozarks are.. *rale*, real.

rale, obs. f. RAIL.

raleiff, ralȝe, obs. Sc. ff. RELIEVE, RAIL *v.*⁴

† **'raling**, *vbl. sb. Obs. rare.* [? f. RAIL *v.*⁵] Flying away, straying.
1618 LATHAM *2nd Bk. Falconry* (1633) 21 Although they fall to raling or soaring quite away from them. *Ibid.* 41 Shee will not stay, but forthwith will fall to raling; neuer once looking backe to her Keeper.

rall (ræl). *Mus.* Abbrev. of RALLENTANDO.
1876 STAINER & BARRETT *Dict. Mus. Terms* 374/1 *Rall.*, abb. for rallentando. **1886** [see A TEMPO]. **1959** *Collins Music Encycl.* 530/1 *Rallentando*,.. often abbreviated *rall.*

‖**rallen'tando** (rallen'tando). *Music.* [It., pres. pple. of *rallentare*: see RELENT.] A musical direction indicating that the time is gradually to be made slower. Also *transf.*
1811 in BUSBY *Dict. Mus.* (ed. 3). **1861** GEO. ELIOT *Let.* 6 Oct. (1954) III. 456 Our violoncello.. is.. a man who is all assent and perpetual rallentando. **1926** *Brit. Weekly* 27 May 161/2 The beauty of the theme was heightened by a perfect rallentando. **1946** A. CHRISTIE *Come, tell me how you Live* i. 24 Its [*sc.* the Orient Express's] tempo.. gradually slows down in a *rallantando* [*sic*] as it proceeds eastwards. **1965** A. T. HATTO *Nibelungenlied* 349 The strophe of the *Nibelungenlied* is normally a balanced and self-contained unit with a marked *rallentando* in the last half-line owing to its extra filled bar. **1978** R. DONINGTON in J. M. Thomson *Future of Early Music in Britain* 13 What sort of rallentandos and how many of them.

† **'rallery**. *Obs.* Also 7 **ralliary, -ie.** [var. RAILLERY; for the spelling cf. RALLY *v.*²]
1. Banter, etc. = RAILLERY 1.
1651 EVELYN *Char. England* (1659) 53 That innocent, yet salt and pleasant diversion, which in France we call Ralliary. **1693** DENNIS *Imp. Crit.* iii. 28 Curse of this unseasonable Rallery: Can anything be more insipid than an untimely Jest? *a* **1754** FIELDING *Fathers* I. i, I admit rallery.
b. With *a* and *pl.* = RAILLERY 1 b.
1654 tr. *Scudery's Curia Pol.* 164 Prince Bajazet, was sometimes called the Shepherd, by a tart Ralliarie. **1707** *Curios. in Husb. & Gard.* 169 Ready and pleasant Ralleries are the Delights of the Mind in.. Conversations.
2. A jesting or playful action. *rare.*
1653 LD. VAUX tr. *Godeau's St. Paul* 49 All these were ralleries rather of a Monster then a Man. **1654** *Nicholas Papers* (Camden) II. 57 He thought she tooke them up in rallery and that, if he gave her good words, he might have them againe.

'ralliance. [f. RALLY *v.*¹; cf. *dalliance.*] The act of rallying.
1826 T. JEFFERSON *Writings* (1854) IX. xlviii. 510 The good Old Dominion.. will then.. become a centre of ralliance to the States whose youth she has instructed. **1848** in WEBSTER.

ralliarie, -ry, variants of RALLERY.

Ralli-car, -cart. [See def.] A form of light two-wheeled driving-trap for four persons, introduced by C. S. Windover & Co. in 1885 and named after the first purchaser.
1890 *Coach Builders' Jrnl.* XI. 181 The remaining exhibit.. by this firm was a specimen of their famous Ralli Car with basket body. **1890** *Cornhill Mag.* Oct. 417 Little ladies and gentlemen who are driven in in the morning for instruction, in governess and ralli carts.

rallied ('rælɪd), *ppl. a.*¹ [f. RALLY *v.*¹ + -ED¹.] Reassembled in order to make a stand.
1663 J. SPENCER *Prodigies* (1665) 359 Brennus.. was by some rallyed forces of his defeated enemy, quite vanquished. **1704** OLDMIXON *Blenheim* xxii, His great Brother.. At Bleinheim holds a rally'd Rout at Bay. **1818** SHELLEY *Rev. Islam* VI. v, Soon came pouring there New multitudes, and did those rallied bands o'erbear.

'rallied, *ppl. a.*² *rare.* [f. RALLY *v.*² + -ED¹.] Subjected to raillery or banter.
a **1704** LOCKE *Educ.* (1705) 255 The rallied Person also finds his account, and takes part in the diversion.

'rallier, *sb.*¹ [f. RALLY *v.*¹ + -ER¹.] One who reassembles, etc.
1887 in *Cassell's Encycl. Dict.* **1904** F. LYNDE *Grafters* i. 11 They.. presently found themselves in the thick of the crowd of debarking ralliers.

rallier ('rælɪə(r)), *sb.*² Now *rare.* [f. RALLY *v.*² + -ER¹.] One who banters.
1678 BUTLER *Hud.* III. i. 759 Ralliers in their Wit or Drink. **1719** *Freethinker* No. 131 ¶4 A noted Rallier generally delights in galling the inoffensive. **1732** SWIFT *Beasts Conf.* Pref., The Wits, the ralliers, the smart fellows.

†**'rallier**, *v. Obs. rare*[−1]. [a. F. *rallier*: cf. RALLY *v.*[1]] *trans.* To rally.
1619 T. MILLES tr. *Mexia's Treas. Anc. & Mod. T.* II. 564/1 Lysias ralliered together his scattered troopes.

†**'ralliment.** *Obs. rare.* Also rally-. [ad. F. *ralliement*: see RALLY *v.*[1] and -MENT.] Rallying.
1655 EARL ORRERY *Parthen.* (1676) 532 He made it the place of Ralliment. **1677** —— *Treat. Art War* 183 When you come to Rally, you make your Rallyment of those onely who are of your own Troops.

ralline ('rælaɪn), *a. Ornith.* [f. mod.L. *rall-us* RAIL *sb.*[3] + -INE[1].] Pertaining to, related to, or resembling the rail, or the family *Rallidæ*.
1885 C. F. HOLDER *Marvels Anim. Life* 159 A long-billed, flightless ralline bird. **1892** W. H. HUDSON *Nat. La Plata* 19 Of rails, or ralline birds, there are ten or twelve.

rally ('rælɪ), *sb.*[1] [f. RALLY *v.*[1]]
1. a. A rapid reunion for concentrated effort, *esp.* of an army after repulse or disorganization.
1651 DAVENANT *Gondibert* I. v. 27 Yet soon with Rallys he reviv'd the warre. **1695** KENNETT *Par. Antiq.* iii. 7 After this defeat, and a second unsuccessful rally, they still retir'd. **1751** JOHNSON *Rambler* No. 96 ¶15 They yielded at last.. with frequent rallies, and sullen submission. **1808** SCOTT *Marm.* VI. xxv, Recoil and rally, charge and rout. **1865** KINGSLEY *Herew.* xvii, She told him.. of the last rally of the men. **1928** *Observer* 19 Feb. 27/1 In a belated rally Ivor Jones scored and converted his own try for Llanelly.
fig. **1674** N. FAIRFAX *Bulk & Selv.* 120 This darting force or rally of stirring springs, is shotten or propagated also.
b. *Mil.* The signal for rallying.
1897 SIR E. WOOD *Achievem. Cavalry* i. 14 A relieving force coming out, the 'Rally' was sounded.
2. a. A quick recovery from a state of exhaustion, a renewal of energy, *esp.* a (temporary) recovery of strength during illness.
1826 SCOTT *Jrnl.* 24 Sept., I made a rally to-day and wrote four pages. **1855** KANE *Arct. Expl.* (1856) II. v. 63 The constant rally of its energies to meet the calls of the hour. **1896** *Allbutt's Syst. Med.* I. 302 The improvement was but temporary, though the rally might be repeated more than once before death.
b. *spec.* a rapid rise in share prices after a fall.
1930 *Economist* 22 Nov. 965/1 Despite all the bad news, a rally in prices made some headway after the liquidation of Monday. **1979** *Daily Tel.* 6 Oct. 23/1 The Index fell.. to be 478.8 (down 2.6 at 1 p.m.), but some new account demand after the official close of the market brought an encouraging rally to 480.4.
3. a. *Theat.* A general mêlée, scramble, or chase, of the characters in a pantomime.
1870 J. H. FRISWELL *Mod. Men of Lett.* i. 8 Character degenerates to caricature, and fun to pantomimic romp and 'rally'. **1882** SERJT. BALLANTINE *Exper.* xxiii. 230 A storm of carrots.. and turnips.. terminated the act, technically termed, I believe, a 'general rally'.
b. orig. *U.S.* A political mass-meeting. Also, a mass-meeting of the supporters of any specified cause.
1840 *Niles' Reg.* 12 Sept. 20/3 Rally of the democracy of Niagara. **1878** E. EGGLESTON *Roxy* I. v. 58 The grand rally of each party had been held in the village of Luzerne. **1886** MRS. H. BURNETT *Lit. Ld. Fauntleroy* v, He described the Republican Rally in all the glory of its banners. **1921** *Proc. 3rd Nat. Country Life Conf.* 48 Funds for the school are obtained through rallies held in the churches on the fifth Sunday. **1930** A. P. HERBERT *Water Gipsies* iii. 27 At an annual rally of the Boy Scouts.. the band was playing the National Anthem. **1960** M. LAURENCE in *Tamarack Rev.* Autumn 8 'Hey, you Sabina!' Mammi Ama shouted. 'Were you at the rally?' **1973** D. AARONS *Unwritten War* III. viii. 129 His passions were literary, not political. He disliked speeches, rallies, meetings.
c. *dial.* A crowd of persons, a large group.
1837 M. PALMER *Dialogue in Devonshire Dialect* II. 16 There was a whole rally of us at the Pigeons. **1892** S. HEWETT *Peasant Speech Devon* 116 There's a turrabul rally aw'm down there. **1908** *Daily Chron.* 16 Jan. 8/5 There's a whole rally of us driving over in Peter's wagonette.
d. Also **rallye** [Fr.]. A competitive event for motor vehicles, usu. over a long distance on public roads.
1932 *Radio Times* 29 July 267/1 Some of the big motoring events of the year—the Ulster Motor Rally, [etc.]. **1949** C. A. N. MAY *'Wheelspin' Abroad* v. 79 There can be no guarantee of a 1949 Rallye actually taking place. **1963** P. DRACKETT *Motor Rallying* i. 9 The true progenitor of the rally was the reliability trial. **1973** E. LEMARCHAND *Let or Hindrance* viii. 90 He seemed more interested in cars than in girls. Went to rallies, and so on.
4. a. *Boxing.* A separate bout. Also, a sustained flurry of blows in a boxing match.
1825 *Sporting Mag.* XVI. 332 The workmen, whose 'Gee-up', it seems, was a signal for a 'rally'. **1829** P. EGAN *Boxiana* 2nd Ser. II. 20 A terrible rally was the finishing stroke of the round. **1857** HUGHES *Tom Brown* II. v, The two stand to one another like men; rally follows rally. **1885** G. B. SHAW in *Mag. of Music* Nov. 178/3 Exciting pantomime music to what is called by stage managers and prize-fighters a rally.
b. *Lawn Tennis.* The series of strokes made by both players between the service and failure to return the ball. Also used in similar games.
1887 J. HAMILTON *A Splendid Rally* xiii. 83 Just then the players were in the heat of an exciting 'rally'. **1899** MILES *Lessons in Lawn Tennis* 82 Something which shall (*a*) produce a level game.. (*b*) produce good rallies. **1955** *Times* 9 May 15/3 Kershaw was now increasing his own pace of stroke which led to many long rallies [Real Tennis]. **1977** 'S. WOODS' *Law's Delay* III. 125 [The bell] chimes in the hall... We might not have heard it if we were in the middle of a rally [Table Tennis].
5. *attrib.* and *Comb.*, as (sense 3 b) ***rally-goer***; (sense 3 d) ***rally atmosphere, car, coat, driver, -driving, motorist, plate, seat, wheel, winner***; ***rally-bred, -prepared, -proved, -sickened, -toughened*** adjs.
1952 W. LEONARD *Rallies & Races* i. 19 We touched the real Rally atmosphere. **1977** *Belfast Telegraph* 17 Jan. 10 (Advt.), Safe rally-bred handling, failsafe disc braking all round, safety cage construction. **1976** *Morecambe Guardian* 7 Dec. 18/7 A young Morecambe man had been drinking and was well over the limit for driving when his high-powered rally car smashed into a tree, an inquest at Preston was told on Tuesday. **1973** *Perthshire Advertiser* 17 Feb. 10/1 (Advt.), Gent's rally coats. Concealed hood. 2 inside pockets. **1952** W. LEONARD *Rallies & Races* 14 They are rather nice chaps, these Rally-drivers. **1976** *Cumberland News* 3 Dec. 21/3 Even the hardened rally drivers.. said it was the worst spectator behaviour they had ever seen. **1954** C. MEISL tr. *J. A. Grégoire's Best Wheel Forward* 121 The future racing driver passes through three well-defined phases: rally driving, hill climbs and endurance tests. **1973** *Guardian* 26 Jan. 13/1 Monte Carlo Rally drivers.. should have been able to check in.. on time without having to resort to full-blooded rally driving techniques. **1960** *Ibid.* 11 July 6/7 There were few of the familiar, regular rally-goers. **1955** *Times* 9 Aug. 7/7 In making their cars comfortable living places for several days on end, rally motorists have 'invented' several ideas which could add to the comfort and convenience of the ordinary motorist. **1949** C. A. N. MAY *'Wheelspin' Abroad* iii. 40 One car.. carrying the official Rallye plates. **1968** *Autocar* 25 Jan. 30/1 Like all the rally-prepared cars we have tried, the Triumph handled beautifully. **1961** *Times* 5 Oct. 11/6 You get the rally-proved, highly-praised Anglia engine. **1976** *Liverpool Echo* 22 Nov. 15/4 (Advt.), Mini 1000, blue, Rostyle wheels, rally seats etc. **1961** *Times* 4 Aug. 11/6 To visit any of Britain's several hundred rally-sickened villages during the sport's 'close' season is an edification that regular rally teams should not miss. **1963** P. DRACKETT *Motor Rallying* iv. 52 From a rag-bag of memories one recalls the blush brought to the rally-toughened countenance of Gregor Grant. **1966** *Motor Trends* Dec. 52/1 (*caption*) Our great Rally II wheels... Wider white-walls are available. **1951** S. C. H. DAVIS *Rallies & Trials* viii. 108 The Rally winner is rarely decided by the acceleration and brake test.

rally ('rælɪ), *sb.*[2] *rare.* [f. RALLY *v.*[2]] A piece of rallying or banter.
1832 in WEBSTER. **1863** COWDEN CLARKE *Shaks. Char.* xvi. 404 It is after this friendly rally that the grave Merchant.. turns to Bassanio.

rally ('rælɪ), *v.*[1] Also 6–7 **rallie**, 7 **r'ally, ralley,** (**ragly**). [ad. F. *rallier*, f. *re-* + *allier* to ALLY. The form *r'ally* (as if for RE-ALLY) prob. implies the same stressing as Milton's *ra'llied*. See also RELY, used earlier in the same sense.
The precise sense is not clear in the earliest example, viz. **1591** PERCIVALL *Sp. Dict.*, *Rehazer*, to renewe, to rallie.]
I. *trans.* **1.** To reassemble, bring together again (an army or company which has been, or is, scattered). Also with *up, back*.
1604 R. CAWDREY *Table Alph.*, *Rallie*, gather together men dispersed, and out of order. **1632** MASSINGER *Maid of Hon.* I. i, The great Gonzaga,.. rallying up Her scattered troops. **1723** DE FOE *Col. Jack* (1840) 238 Their troops, being rallied by the dexterity of their generals, came on again to the charge. **1824** CAMPBELL *Theodric* 348 Oh! were he there.. to rally back One broken band. **1868** E. EDWARDS *Ralegh* I. xxv. 622 Young Ralegh was the first to rally his men under the unexpected charge.
2. a. To collect, bring together (persons) to one's assistance or for concentrated action.
1603 FLORIO *Montaigne* I. Ded., Yet did your honoured name r'ally to my succour the forces of two deare friends. **1678** EARL OF LINDSEY in *12th Rep. Hist. MSS. Comm.* App. v. 50, I make no question butt your Lordship too will rally your friends. **1874** GREEN *Short Hist.* vii. §2. 361 Even this blow failed to rally the Country round the Queen. **1883** *Manch. Exam.* 1 Dec. 5/2 He does not believe that the Mahdi will rally to his banners the pure Arab tribes.
†**b.** To collect (things). *Obs.*
1643 CARYL *Sacr. Covt.* 7 The Lord doth r'ally all the promises of mercy made to us, which lie scattered. **1674** N. FAIRFAX *Bulk & Selv.* 131 To rally together all those sparks of life, that lay asunder in a clammy dew.
c. To drive (cattle) in a close herd. *rare*[−1].
1889 'R. BOLDREWOOD' *Robbery under Arms* (1890) 31 Now you rally the cattle well after me.
3. To drive (a vehicle) in a motor rally. *colloq.*
1969 *Guardian* 18 Aug. 10/2 He drove it around, occasionally attending vintage meetings, but never rallying the car. **1976** L. DEIGHTON *Twinkle, Twinkle Little Spy* xxii. 220 You want to buy a car?.. One owner. Never raced or rallied. **1977** *Drive* Sept.–Oct. 113/1 The punter-hunter fills his advert with euphemisms. Such as: *1974 model* made in 1973;.. *never raced nor rallied.*
4. a. To concentrate or revive (a faculty, etc.) by a strong effort of the will. Also with *up*.
1667 MILTON *P.L.* VI. 786 His hapless Foes.. to rebellious fight rallied thir Powers. **1702** J. LOGAN in *Pa. Hist. Soc. Mem.* IX. 157, I can say no more,.. having rallied my memory for that to the utmost. *a* **1716** SOUTH *Serm.* (1823) IV. 371 Let a man rally up his best attention, his severest and exactest thoughts. **1791** MRS. RADCLIFFE *Rom. Forest* ii, She rallied her drooping spirits. **1837** PRESCOTT *Ferd. & Is.* II. vii. 542 He rallied his strength for a final blow. *a* **1859** MACAULAY *Hist. Eng.* xxv. V. 288 He rallied the last energies of his failing body and mind.
b. To pull together, revive, rouse, stimulate (a person or animal).
1790 BURNS *Tam o' Shanter* 191 Scarcely had he Maggie rallied, When out the hellish legion sallied. **1832** R. & J. LANDER *Exped. Niger* I. vii. 261, I endeavoured.. to rally him, but he was scarcely able to stand. **1856** KANE *Arct. Expl.* I. xvi. 188 They were sinking with fatigue and hunger, and could hardly be rallied enough to tell us the direction.
refl. **1818** SCOTT *Br. Lamm.* xxii, The Lord Keeper with difficulty rallied himself so far as to explain. **1863** MRS. GASKELL *Sylvia's L.* xxxiv. III. 85 Philip rallied himself, and tried to speak up to the old standard of respectability.
c. *Boxing.* To attack vigorously.
1812 *Sporting Mag.* XXXIX. 139 Molineux rallied him with quickness.
d. *Sporting.* To harry.
1808 COL. HAWKER *Diary* (1893) I. 12 While the others rallied his covers.
II. *intr.* **5. a.** To come together again, to reassemble, *esp.* in order to renew the conflict; to return in a body to the fray or contest.
1655 FULLER *Ch. Hist.* I. v. §12 This Conquerour.. now routed the Remnant, which began to ralley and make head again. *a* **1680** BUTLER *Eleph. in Moon* 83 The Battle's desperately fought: The gallant Subvolvani rally. **1723** DE FOE *Col. Jack* (1840) 237 The battalions rallied and came boldly on to charge a second time. **1774** GOLDSM. *Nat. Hist.* (1776) III. 384 The dogs.. instantly turn tail,.. and no exhortations can ever bring them to rally. **1849** MACAULAY *Hist. Eng.* v. I. 583 The Whigs, few and weak as they were, attempted to rally. **1887** BOWEN *Virg. Æneid* II. 716 Severed asunder at starting, we there shall rally at last.
b. Of a single person: To return and renew the attack; *spec.* in *Boxing*. (Cf. RALLY *sb.*[1] 4 a.)
1813 H. & J. SMITH *Horace in Lond.* 21 Long may'st thou rally, hit, and stop.
†**6.** Of things: To come *together*, to collect.
a **1694** TILLOTSON *Serm.* (1728) I. 17 Innumerable parts of matter chanc'd just then to rally together, and to form themselves into this new world.
7. a. Of persons: To come together in a body; to unite for a common purpose, *esp.* to assist or support some one. Usu. const. *round*.
1818 COBBETT *Pol. Reg.* XXXIII. 106 The people would have rallied round the Bill. **1849** MACAULAY *Hist. Eng.* ii. I. 263 The majority of the upper and middle classes hastened to rally round the throne. **1853** J. H. NEWMAN *Hist. Sk.* (1873) II. I. iv. 174 The veterans of Sylla.. refused to rally round Pompey in his war with Cæsar. **1866** GEO. ELIOT *Felix Holt* I. iii. 87 People were told they must 'rally' at the coming election. **1905** R. FRY *Let.* 21 Jan. (1972) I. 233, I find that these people will rally and do all they can. **1915** J. WEBSTER *Dear Enemy* 201 His friends rallied about the babies, sold.. the studio fittings.. paid off the debts. **1940** 'N. BLAKE' *Malice in Wonderland* II. ix. 123 Those who were loudest.. are now.. the first to rally round. **1963** P. WILLMOTT *Evolution of Community* vii. 75 When one of the neighbour's children married a little while ago we all rallied round. **1978** J. BARNETT *Head of Force* iii. 19 The demonstrators marched.. to Trafalgar Square where they planned to rally, sing the National Anthem and dismiss.
b. Const. *to*. (Also said of a single person.)
1879 G. BARNETT SMITH *Life Gladstone* I. iv. 85 Mr. Gladstone, amongst others, rallied to the support of the Government. **1888** BRYCE *Amer. Commw.* I. xi. 142 Some of these senators.. rally to the cry.
c. ***to rally round the flag***: of a group, to demonstrate loyalty to a cause, as at a moment of impending danger. Also as *attrib. phr. U.S.* (orig. in Civil War use).
1862 G. F. ROOT *Battle Cry of Freedom* (song) 3 Yes we'll rally round the flag, boys, we'll rally once again, Shouting the battle-cry of Freedom. **1957** M. SHULMAN (*title*) Rally round the flag, boys! **1964** *New Yorker* 4 Jan. 77 Much of the book is written in a tough, choppy, emotional style, but this approach disguises a spurious rally-round-the-flag vision. **1968** *Listener* 8 Feb. 164/2 The immediate reaction of the American people is to rally round the flag and demand that its honour be upheld.
8. a. To revive, recover, acquire or assume fresh vigour or energy.
1744 ELLIS *Mod. Husbandman* Jan. vi. 60 After the first Mowing.. they do not *rally*, as we call it, *i.e.* they do not grow again to much Profit. **1792** H. NEWDIGATE *Let.* Feb. in A. E. Newdigate-Newdegate *Cheverels* (1898) viii. 111 Sally Rally'd last night and sang Charmingly. **1840** MACAULAY *Ess., Ranke's Hist.* (1851) II. 144 Catholicism had rallied, and had driven back Protestantism even to the German Ocean. **1871** FREEMAN *Norm. Conq.* (1876) III. xi. 9 At last his flagging powers rallied. **1878** BROWNING *Poets Croisic* xlix, The red fire.. winks, Rallies, relapses, dwindles.
b. To recover in part from an illness.
1853 MRS. CARLYLE *Lett.* (1883) II. 220 Dr. Carlyle thinks it probable enough she may not rally again. **1855** THACKERAY *Newcomes* II. 160 She never rallied, or, we believe, spoke, after the first fatal seizure. **1880** MCCARTHY *Own Time* IV. lvi. 209 He rallied indeed and grew much better.
c. To recover *from* some misfortune.
1863 *Sat. Rev.* 8 Aug. 173/1 It is possible that the Confederates may rally from their heavy disasters.

rally ('rælɪ), *v.*[2] [ad. F. *railler*, of uncertain origin: cf. RAIL *v.*[4] and RAILLY *v.*]
1. *trans.* To treat or assail with banter, pleasantry, or good-humoured ridicule; to make fun or game of.
a. a thing. ? *Obs.*
1679 OLDHAM *Adv. Satyr on Jesuits* Wks. (1686) 1 The gravest Fathers have rallied the fopperies and superstitions of the Heathen. **1713** SWIFT *Cadenus & Vanessa*, They rally'd next Vanessa's dress. **1716** *Town Talk* 6 Jan. (1790) 40 The sanguine temper which precipitates people into excesses.. was most admirably rallied in an Epilogue.
b. a person.
1691 BENTLEY *Phal.* xi. (1699) 298 Euripides.. is pleasantly burlesqu'd and rally'd on this very account. **1770** LANGHORNE *Plutarch* (1879) I. 132/2 He rallied Simonides for his absurdity. **1806–7** J. BERESFORD *Miseries Hum. Life* (1826) XI. Sigh 3, Being rallied by a facetious gentleman.

1878 G. MACDONALD *Phantastes* II. xiii. 4 Rallied by his fellow-students On his wretched looks.

c. With complement.

1668 SEDLEY *Mulb. Gard.* v. Wks. 1722 II. 71 'Twas only a Trick he put upon us, and let's rally it off. **1782** MISS BURNEY *Cecilia* IX. xi, I will not..be rallied from my purpose. **1788** WESLEY *Wks.* (1872) VII. 22 These..reason, and rally, and laugh you out of it.

2. *absol.* or *intr.* To employ banter or pleasantry against one. Also constr. *at*, *with* (a person), *upon* (a thing). ? *Obs.*

1668 SHADWELL *Sullen Lovers* I. i, Sure you rally with me all this while. **1676** D'URFEY *Mad. Fickle* II. i, I see Madam you are disposed to rally. **1758** MRS. LENNOX *Henrietta* II. v. (1761) I. 130, I could not help humorously rallying upon some of her notions. **1792** *Elvina* II. 185 She would have rallied, but he stopped her short.

'rally, *v.*[3] *dial.* Also 8 ralley. [? Echoic.] *intr.* To make a loud or sharp noise.

1728 *Calendar Virginia State Papers* (1875) I. 215 We were like a sow that had lost her pigs, would ralley for a little time and then have done. **1821** CLARE *Vill. Minstr.* I. 29 All in chorus rallied out amain. **1894** *S.-E. Worcestersh. Gloss.*, *Rally*, to crack or 'smack' a whip.

rallycross ('rælıkrɒs). [f. RALLY *sb.*[1] 3 d + AUTO)CROSS.] A form of motor racing combining elements of rallying and autocross. Also *attrib.*

1967 *Daily Mirror* 26 Aug. 9/5 What is the sport that scales down motor rallying to a seven-minutes sensation?.. Rallycross, which combines the thrills of autocross where old 'bangers' tackle mud-covered hills—with the ordeals of the Monte Carlo rally. **1968** *Observer* 21 Apr. 7/4 (Advt.), 'It's got these ingredients that cut the corrosion cars suffer from when they're left hanging about.' Roger Clark, leading Ford rally driver and rallycross man. **1978** *Morecambe Guardian* 14 Mar. 11/1 Motor sport is having trouble finding suitable space for short track speedway racing and rallycross.

rallying ('rælıŋ), *vbl. sb.*[1] [-ING[1].] **a.** The action of RALLY *v.*[1] Also, the action or practice of participating in a rally (in senses of RALLY *sb.*[1]).

1845 LD. CAMPBELL *Chancellors* (1857) III. li. 3 Noble rallyings from his disgrace. **1850** LYNCH *Theo. Trinal* ii. 22 The rallying of the world's love and hope. **1864** DICKENS *Let.* 25 Oct. (1880) II. 222 Occasional [family] rallyings coming off here. **1960** S. TURNER *Rallying* i. 12 There are four levels of rallying: Closed, Restricted, National and International. **1971** 'D. RUTHERFORD' *Clear Fast Lane* 39 The usual changes needed before a production car is ready for rallying. **1978** *Times* 4 July 19/2 He [*sc.* Nastase] mixed the pace and pattern of his rallying with..nonchalant grace.

b. *attrib.*, as ***rallying cry, place, point, round, shout, sign, square, word.***

In some of these the word may be regarded also as ppl. adj., in transitive sense.

1818 SHELLEY *Rev. Islam* VI. iii, *Rallying cries of treason and of danger. **1879** M. ARNOLD *Mixed Ess., George Sand* 338 France which has made equality its rallying cry. **1820** W. IRVING *Sketch Bk.* (1859) 135 The paternal hearth [is] the *rallying-place of the affections. **1799** WASHINGTON *Lett.* Writ. 1893 XIV. 140 It would be a *rallying-point for the timid. **1855** MACAULAY *Hist. Eng.* xx. IV. 408 He thought his star a good rallying point for his own troops. **1814** *Sporting Mag.* XLIV. 167 A most determined *rallying round, commenced by Burn. **1930** WODEHOUSE *Very Good, Jeeves!* iii. 69 Cold and haughty. No symp. None of the rallying-round spirit which one likes to see. **1810** SCOTT *Lady of L.* II. xvii, The rapid charge, the *rallying shout. **1840** CARLYLE *Heroes* (1858) 270 Shakspeare,..the noblest, gentlest, yet strongest of *rallying-signs. **1847** *Infantry Man.* (1854) 63 Form the *rallying square. **1818** HALLAM *Mid. Ages* (1872) I. 383 The *rallying word of faction. **1845** JAMES *Arrah Neil* ii, It's my battle-cry, my rallying word.

rallying ('rælıŋ), *vbl. sb.*[2] [-ING[1].] The action of RALLY *v.*[2]

1673 DRYDEN *Assignation* III. i, There was one thing amiss in it, that was your rallying of Religion. **1698** JER. COLLIER *Short View Eng. Stage* 160 Rallying, no less than Railing, ought to be under the Discipline of Law. **1834** HT. MARTINEAU *The Farrers* ii. 28 Bore rallying on preferring.. negus and sweet cake. **1884** E. P. ROE *Nat. Ser. Story* viii, He replied to her..rallyings.

attrib. **1710** SHAFTESB. *Charac.* (1737) I. 62 Whither this rallying Humour will at length carry us. **1741** MIDDLETON *Cicero* I. vi. 485 Cicero being in a rallying humor, made the petition..ridiculous.

rallying ('rælıŋ), *ppl. a.*[1] [f. RALLY *v.*[1] + -ING[2].] That rallies (reassembles, revives, etc.).

1896 *Daily News* 11 June 2/4 Sir Wilfrid saw signs of encouragement in the rallying spirit of the Liberal party.

rallying ('rælıŋ), *ppl. a.*[2] [f. RALLY *v.*[2] + -ING[2].] That rallies, banters, etc.

1678 BUTLER *Hud.* III. I. 1398 These Rallying Devils do no hurt. **1868** HOLME LEE *B. Godfrey* lxii. 361 'You took my strawberries so prettily', said Basil with rallying fondness.

Hence **'rallyingly** *adv.*

1669 R. MONTAGU in *Buccleuch MSS.* (Hist. MSS. Comm.) I. 424 He..rallyingly thanked me for the good news I told him. **1838** MOORE *Mem.* (1856) VII. 220 The 'Evêque de Lombaz' wrote to Petrarch rallyingly, that all his love for Laura was a mere fiction.

rallyist ('rælııst). [f. RALLY *sb.*[1] + -IST.] One who competes in a motor rally or rallies.

1961 *Times* 4 Aug. 11/7 With some common sense.. rallyists could avoid strangling their own lusty child. **1963** P. DRACKETT *Motor Rallying* ii. 28 Another outstanding rallyist, John Sprinzel, writes a regular column for the monthly *Motor Racing*. **1972** *Sci. Amer.* Jan. 11/1 Since becoming involved in this task I've met a fascinating variety of nonacademic types—automobile wreckers, automobile racers, rallyists, manufacturers of technical equipment.

rallyment: see RALLIMENT.

ralstonite ('rɔːlstənaıt). *Min.* [Named (1871) after J. G. *Ralston* its discoverer: see -ITE.] (See quot. 1875.)

1875 WATTS *Dict. Chem.* 2nd Suppl. 1038 *Ralstonite*, a hydrated aluminium fluoride containing traces of sodium and calcium from the cryolite formation of Arksut Fjord in Greenland. **1882** *Jrnl. Amer. Sci.* CXXXII. 380 (*title*) The Chemical Compositon of Ralstonite.

ram (ræm), *sb.*[1] Forms: 1 rom(m, 1-2 ramm, 4-7 ramme, 5-6 rame, rambe, 1- ram. [OE. *ram(m, rǫm(m* = (M)Du., (M)LG., OHG. and MHG. *ram (ramm-)*: cf. G. *ramme* rammer, naval ram. Perh. related to ON. *ramm-r* strong.]

1. a. A male sheep; in domestication, one kept for breeding purposes, a tup.

c **825** *Vesp. Ps.* lxiv. 14 Ȝeȝerede sind rommas scepa. *c* **1000** ÆLFRIC *Gen.* xxii. 13 Abraham..ȝeseah þær anne ramm..be þæm hornum ȝehæft. *c* **1200** ORMIN 1136 Þe ramm wass offredd forr þe preost. **13..** *K. Alisaunder* 388 His heved, and his scholdron fram, He dyghte in forme of a ram. *c* **1400** tr. *Secreta Secret., Gov. Lordsh.* 104 Ffor man ys hardy as a lyon..rebell as a rambe. **1470-85** MALORY *Arthur* I. xxiii, They wente to the batayl ageyne and so hurtled to gyders lyke two rammes. **1523** FITZHERB. *Husb.* §39 The better shall the ewe take the ramme agayne. **1575** TURBERV. *Venerie* 30 You must couple him with a ramme or a stoute Sheepe. **1697** DRYDEN *Virg. Georg.* III. 594 Ev'n though a snowy Ram thou shalt behold, Prefer him not in haste, for Husband to thy Fold. **1727-46** THOMSON *Summer* 411 The sturdy boy Holds by the twisted horns, the indignant Ram. **1790** BEWICK *Hist. Quadrup.* (1792) 49 The Ram lives to the age of about fifteen years, and begins to procreate at one. **1842** BISCHOFF *Woollen Manuf.* II. 328 We would recommend the introduction of..English rams amongst the Indian ewe flocks.

fig. *a* **1529** SKELTON *Col. Cloute* 157 To kepe..theyr spiritual lammes Sequestred from rammes. **1840** BARHAM *Ingol. Leg., St. Nicholas* xi, Holy Church denieth all search 'Midst her sanctified ewes and her saintly rams.

†**b.** As the reward given to the victor in a wrestling match. *Obs.*

c **1386** CHAUCER *Prol.* 548 The Millere was a stout carl.., At wrastlynge he wolde haue alwey the Ram. *c* **1400** *Gamelyn* 184 Her be side, brother is cried a wrastlynge, And þer fore shal be sette a ram and a rynge.

c. *transf.* A sexually aggressive man; a lecher. *colloq.*

1935 *N. & Q.* 23 Nov. 366/2 *Ram*, a male, sexual enthusiast. **1946** *Penguin New Writing* XXVIII. 185 'Yes, it's the Chalk all right,' Willie said. 'The old ram!' he added, happily. **1977** J. WAINWRIGHT *Do Nothin' till You hear from Me* viii. 128 One day, May will rise up on the ram she has for a husband and pan him in the chops.

2. *Astron.* (with cap.). The zodiacal sign ARIES.

c **1050** *Byrhtferth's Handboc* in *Anglia* VIII. 307 Þe ys aries, þæt ys ram genemned. *c* **1386** CHAUCER *Prol.* 8 Whan ..the yonge sonne Hath in the Ram his halfe[e] cours yronne. *c* **1470** HENRY *Wallace* IX. 18 Quhen conryet [*read* aryet] the hot syng coloryk, In to the Ram quhilk had his rowmys ryk. **1563** B. GOOGE *Eglogs.* i. (Arb.) 31 The Ram doth cause to spring, eche herbe and floure. **1669** STURMY *Mariner's Mag.* VI. 95 Here in the Zodiack begins The Ram, the Bull, the loving Twins. **1697** DRYDEN *Virg. Georg.* III. 476 Till the new Ram receives th' exalted Sun. **1868** LOCKYER *Guillemin's Heavens* (ed. 3) 330 Between the square of Pegasus and the Bull we meet with two constellations, the Fishes and the Ram.

3. a. = BATTERING-RAM.

c **897** K. ÆLFRED *Gregory's Past.* xxi. 160 Besittað hie utan ..& ðerscað ðone weall mid rammum. *c* **1000** ÆLFRIC *Gram.* vi. (Z.) 12 Aries byð..ram to wealȝeworce. **1513** DOUGLAS *Æneis* XII. xii. 27 The barmkin law smait with the rammis fast. **1569** STOCKER *Diod. Sic.* III. viii. 113/2 He had also many other engines called Rammes very large and great to batter any wall. **1593** DONNE *Sat.* ii. 19 Rammes, and slings now are silly battery. **1727-41** CHAMBERS *Cycl.* s.v. *Aries*, Pliny assures us, the ram was invented at the siege of Troy. **1858** GREENER *Gunnery* 5 A 68 lb. shot has all the force that could be given even to that famous ram of Vespasian. **1884** *Manch. Exam.* 14 Oct. 5/7 They brought planks, and by using them as rams, broke open one of the reserved doors.

fig. **1606** SHAKS. *Ant. & Cl.* III. ii. 30 Let not the peece of Vertue which is set Betwixt vs,..be the Ramme to batter The Fortresse of it. **1648** HERRICK *Hesper., Panegyr. Sir L. Pemberton*, The iron and rock, Which tryes, and counter-stands the shock, And ramme of time. **1829** CARLYLE *Misc.* (1857) II. 47 Concede him this, and his ram swings freely to and fro through Space.

b. *Naut.* A solid point or beak projecting from the bows of a war-vessel, and enabling it to ram and batter in the side of an opponent.

1865 TENNEY *Hist. Rebellion U.S.* 223/2 The Merrimac soon crushed her iron horn or ram into the frigate.. knocking a hole in the side near the water-line. *c* **1869** LD. C. E. PAGET *Autobiog.* (1896) 335 There was but little damage done to them by shot or shell. The ram was the deadly weapon.

c. *Naut.* A battleship fitted with a ram.

1862 ELLET in Tenney *Hist. Rebellion U.S.* 169/1 After.. the gunboats and one of my rams had passed below. **1869** SIR E. REED *Our Iron-Clad Ships* Introd. 23 The chapters on the cost of our iron-clad fleet, and upon the deeply important question of 'Rams'. **1898** C. A. DANA *Recoll. Civil War* iii. 37 First came seven ironclad turtles and one heavy armed ram.

d. *Shipbuilding.* (See quot.)

1867 SMYTH *Sailor's Word-bk.*, *Ram*, a long spar, iron-hooped at the ends, used for driving out blocks from beneath a vessel's keel, and for driving planks an end while only wedged to the ship's side.

e. *U.S. Naut.* (See quot. 1961.)

1909 *Sun* (Baltimore) 1 Aug. 14/2 Capt Andrew Hubbard, who later, with all hands, was lost at sea, saw the queer craft coming down stream. He shouted at Captain Insley 'That's certainly a Nanticoke ram.' **1953** *Sun Mag.* (Baltimore) 25 Oct. 30/5 Rams which once hauled lumber are now summer cruise ships. **1961** J. E. MARVIL *Sailing Rams* 9 *Ram*, 3 masted bald headed schooner, flat bottom, straight sides without jib boom built and sailed mainly on Chesapeake Bay.

f. *Eton slang.* (See quot. 1977.)

1922 S. LESLIE *Oppidan* xvii. 200 A strange procession... There was no variation in the *ram*, as it was called by a football metaphor. **1930** *Daily Tel.* 1 Dec. 21/2 On the last occasion Lori-Phillip touched a rouge, but the ram failed. **1942** J. LEES-MILNE *Ancestral Voices* (1975) 30 Then to evensong in [Eton] College Chapel where the traditional ceremonial is invariable. The 'ram' marches in the same deliberate, self-conscious manner. **1977** A. J. AYER *Part of My Life* ii. 44 After scoring a rouge the attackers could gain an extra point by charging in column and bundling their opponents and the ball into the goal. The column was known as a ram, which was also the name given to the twin columns of Colleger and Oppidan sixth-formers, as they processed into Chapel.

g. An underwater projection from an iceberg or other body of ice.

1952 *Functional Gloss. Ice Terminol.* (U.S. Navy Hydrogr. Office) 22 More rapid melting at the water line than above and below causes a notch to be formed at the water line below which is the ram. **1974** *Encycl. Brit. Macropædia* IX. 160/2 In the Labrador current, sailing at one or two knots toward the North Atlantic shipping routes, this iceberg had a ram (underwater projection), as most icebergs do by the time they enter the warmer waters near the Gulf Stream. **1976** *Jrnl. R. Soc. Arts* CXXIV. 644/1 Ice headlands are elevated because the underwater 'ram' at the seaward side gives more buoyancy.

4. a. The weight of a pile-driving machine, which is raised to a height by pulleys, and being released is so guided as to fall on the head of the pile which is being driven; a monkey.

1440 in C. Welch *Tower Bridge* (1894) 55 The 'great Gebet-ram', the 'Lesser Rennyng ram'. **1462** *Ibid.*, Drawing the Gebet-ram in pylyng by stadelles next the bridge. **1587** FLEMING *Contn. Holinshed* III. 536/2 Some of those piles were..driven into the maine rocke of chalke, with a great engine called a ram. **1739** C. LABELYE *Short Acc. Piers Westm. Bridge* 21 Supposing the Ram or Weight to be 1700 lb. **1776** G. SEMPLE *Building in Water* 36 The Ram and Follower resting on the Head of the Pile. **1853** SIR H. DOUGLAS *Milit. Bridges* (ed. 3) 306 If..the piles are.. driven by heavy rams till they will sink no further.

b. A steam-hammer used in setting-up a bloom of metal.

1875 KNIGHT *Dict. Mech.*

c. A paviour's RAMMER.

1885 *Antiquary* Oct. 146/1 Each man..threw down the ram with a thud.

5. a. An automatic water-raising machine, in which the raising power is supplied by the concussion of a descending body of water in a pipe.

1808 YOUNG in *Phil. Trans.* XCIX. 22 Almost in the same manner as a stream of water strikes on the valve of the hydraulic ram. **1851** STEPHENS *Bk. Farm* (ed. 2) I. 27/1 The ram may be described as a sloping pipe in which the stream runs [etc.].

b. The piston of the large cylinder of a hydrostatic press.

1816 J. SMITH *Mechanic* II. 396 It is desirable..to make use of the larger pump rod to raise the ram as expeditiously as possible. **1839** URE *Dict. Arts* s.v. *Press*, The hollow cylinder of the press, which, as well as the ram, is made of cast iron. **1858** LARDNER *Hand-bk. Nat. Phil., Hydrost.*, etc. 10 The ram, the immediate object that receives and transmits the pressure.

c. A hydraulic lifting-machine.

1861 *Times* 7 Oct., There were several men engaged in pumping water into the ram. I observed..that they were lifting the girder with one ram. **1862** *Catal. Intern. Exhib.* II. x. 9/2 The hydraulic rams will safely lift a dead weight of 6000 tons.

d. The plunger of a force-pump.

1883 GRESLEY *Gloss. Coal-mining*, *Forcer*, a pump by which the water is raised with a ram or plunger.

e. The reciprocating arm on which the tool is mounted in a shaping or slotting machine.

1864 D. K. CLARK *Exhibited Machinery of 1862* III. §1. ii. 133 Machines..for shaping levers, cranks, connecting rods. .. The ram is moved by means of a peculiar crank-motion, with a quick return. **1935** *Buck & Hickman Ltd. Gen. Catal. Tools & Supplies* 126 Hand shaping machine... There are nine different working positions of handle, the ram having three holes and the handle three holes. **1964** S. CRAWFORD *Basic Engin. Processes* viii. 216 Most shaping machines are of the crank type... The ram is located in the top slideway of the body and is reciprocated by the crank mechanism. **1977** *Buck & Hickman Catal. 1977-1979* High speed shaping machine... The ram, carriage and table are all mounted in dovetail guides.

6. *attrib.* and *Comb.* **a.** (sense 1) ***ram-breeding, -faced*** adj., ***-horn*** (also *attrib.*), ***-lamb, -like*** adj., ***-mutton, -supporters, -tender, trade.***

1875 *Encycl. Brit.* I. 393/2 Pure Leicesters..are now confined to a few *ram-breeding flocks. **1921** R. GRAVES *Pier-Glass* 49 *Ram-faced lecher, the blood on his own beast head! **15..** *Wooing of Jok & Jynny* 65 (Bann. MS.) Ane trene truncheour, ane *ramehorne spone. **1725** RAMSAY *Gentle Sheph.* v. ii, His ram-horn spoons and kitted whey. **1824** MACTAGGART *Gallovid. Encycl.* Introd. 5 Ill-tongued tinklers, with..their hampers, and their ram-horns. **1573** TUSSER *Husb.* (1878) 81 Geld bulcalfe and *ramlamb, as soone as they fall. **1601** HOLLAND *Pliny* I. 227 If his right cullion or stone be tied vp, hee getteth ewe lambes; but if the left be taken vp, hee getteth ramme lambes. **1886** C. SCOTT

Sheep-Farming 63 The ram-lambs..are slightly heavier than the ewe lambs. **1851** C. L. SMITH tr. *Tasso* XI. xxxvii, The ram..Whose *ram-like head is armed with iron plates. **1632** MASSINGER *Maid of Hon.* III. i, A huge shoulder Of glorious fat *ram-mutton. **1837** HALIBURTON *Clockm.* 168 A few half-starved pigs,..some ram mutton. **1864** BOUTELL *Her. Hist. & Pop.* xxx. (ed. 3) 451 In addition to the *ram-supporters, rams' heads are several times sculptured. **1611** SHAKS. *Wint. T.* IV. iv. 805 An old Sheepe-whistling Rogue, a *Ram-tender. **1886** C. SCOTT *Sheep-Farming* 154 The history of the *ram trade.

b. *Naut.* (sense 3 b), as ***ram-bow, cruiser, fleet, -steamer, -stem, -vessel***; (sense 3 e) ***ram schooner***; ***ram type*** adj.

1869 SIR E. REED *Shipbuild.* xv. 292 Ships with *ram-bows in which the distance from the catheads to the hawseholes is considerable. **1895** *Chambers' Encycl.* VII. 417/1 *La Gloire*..was built with a ram-bow. **1892** *Daily News* 16 Dec. 5/6 The *ram cruiser Empress Elisabeth. **1865** TENNEY *Hist. Rebellion U.S.* 169/1 Col. Ellet commanding the *ram fleet. **1904** *Naut. Gaz.* 14 Apr. 211/1 Geo. K. Phillips & Co., Bethel, Del., have on the stocks a three-masted *ram schooner 140 ft. long. **1897** R. KIPLING *Captains Courageous* 128 The *ram-steamer *Arctic* that breaks the ice. **1869** SIR E. REED *Our Iron-Clad Ships* i. 19 The 'Warrior' is much more than an ordinary ship..having a massive solid forged *ram-stem. **1956** *Sun* (Baltimore) 19 Apr. 38/8 Mr. Katz said he would prove the captain of the ill-fated '*ram type' schooner ran for shelter when hurricane winds were predicted. **1878** *N. Amer. Rev.* CXXVII. 381 All fleets should be attended upon by *ram-vessels.

7. Special combs.: **ram-block** *Naut.*, a dead-eye (†also *ram's block*); †**ram('s)-ciche**, the common chick-pea (*Cicer arietinum*); **ram-coupler**, a form of coupler used between closely-set organ manuals; †**ram-engine**, a battering-ram; †**ram-fish**, some kind of sea-monster (L. *aries*, Pliny); **ram-getter**, a ram kept for breeding rams; **ram-goat**, †a he-goat; also, a low-growing shrub (*Fagara microphylla*) of the W. Indies and S. America; **ram-house**, a shed for protection in working a battering-ram; **ram-letting**, the letting-out of rams for breeding purposes; **ram-reel**, a dance of men only, a bull-dance; **ram-riding**, a form of popular punishment; †**ram-sheep**, the common sheep.

1611 COTGR., *Cap de mouton*, (in a ship is) a certaine flat peece of wood bored full of holes..; we call it, the *Rammes-blocke. **1601** HOLLAND *Pliny* II. 143 The blacke ciches..called *Ram-ciches. **1611** COTGR. s.v. *Belier*, *Chiches de belier*, Rammes Citches, blacke Citches. **1881** W. E. DICKSON *Pract. Organ-Building* xii. 156 The *ram-coupler can be used between manuals arranged too closely to admit of tumblers. **1632** HAYWARD tr. *Biondi's Eromena* 150 Don Peplasos..caused a *Ram-engine to be landed, which, together with its testude, they setled on its wheels. **1601** HOLLAND *Pliny* I. 262 Of the *Ram-fish. This fish is a very strong theef at sea, and makes foule work where he comes. **1790** MARSHALL *Rural Econ. Midl. C.* I. 429 Getting Rams, to be let out again to inferior tupmen, as *ram-getters. **1837** YOUATT *Sheep* 317 Strength of frame..was the distinction between the 'ram-getter' and the 'wedder-getter'. **1575** TURBERV. *Faulconrie* 136 The flesh of a *Ram goat. **1634** SIR T. HERBERT *Trav.* 8 In Angola..some adore the Deuill in forme of a bloudie Dragon, others a Ram-goat. **1864** GRISEBACH *Flora Brit. W. Indian Isl.* Index, Ram-goat. **1882** in *Smithsonian Misc. Collect.* XXIII. No. 13. 38 Ramgoat-bush... The whole plant has a strong smell. **1878** GOSSE *Rivers of Bible* 152 The *ram-house, and part of the tower, are covered with hurdles or hides. **1861** *Times* 17 Sept., The *ram lettings in progress..show..a great development of enterprise on the part of sheep breeders. **1813** D. ANDERSON *Poems* 122 (Jam.) The chairs they coup, they hurl an' loup, A *ram-reel now they're wantin. **1891** Q. [COUCH] *Noughts & Crosses* 100 They had seized the woman ..and were hauling her along in a *Ram Riding..the men..had to drag her, her feet trailing, and the horns and kettles dinning in her wake. **1797** *Encycl. Brit.* (ed. 3) XIII. 562/1 Linnæus enumerates three species..1. The *ovis aries*, or *ram-sheep.

ram, *sb.*[2] *rare.* Ore. ***black ram***, bog-iron.

1683 PETTUS *Fleta Min.* II. iii. 114 The rich Gold Ram or Slick (out of which Gold is quickened). **1807** VANCOUVER *Agric. Devon* (1813) 76 Large quantities of black ram (i.e. bog iron) are found dispersed through all the moors and low-grounds.

ram, *sb.*[3] *Naut.* Length 'over all' of a boat. Also, the centre plank of a coble.

1723 *Lond. Gaz.* No. 6224/5 A Vessel 27 Foot and half upon the Keel, 33 Foot Ram. **1889** *Whitby Gaz.* 2 Aug. 4/6 The charge for any boat exceeding 17 feet in the ram, that is to say anything after the style of a coble. **1933** *Yachting Monthly* LVI. 108/1 The centre plank [of a coble] is called the 'ram'. **1970** E. J. MARCH *Inshore Craft Gt. Brit.* I. iv. 137 The true coble is built up on a 'ram plank' not a keel. **1973** W. ELMER *Terminol. Fishing* iv. 113 The *ram* denotes the broad central bottom plank in the cobles, which have no keel.

ram (ræm), *sb.*[4] [f. RAM *v.*[1]] **1. a.** The act or process of ramming.

1897 *Westm. Gaz.* 7 May 2/1 The prescribed course of alternate cram and ram proved entirely successful.

b. ***ram and dam(n)***, jocularly applied (*attrib.* or *absol.*) to a muzzle-loading gun.

1866 *Cornhill Mag.* Sept. 342 Old sportsmen..who still use and prefer the old 'ram and d—n' which they wielded so effectively in their youth. **1899** *Pall Mall Mag.* Jan. 116 A pot-hunter..considering the condition of his ancient ram-and-dam gun.

2. a. The compressive effect experienced by air which is constrained to enter a moving aperture or restricted space (*spec.* the intake of a jet engine); (cf. RAMJET). orig. and freq. *attrib.*, as ***ram compression, effect, pressure***.

1944 *Jrnl. R. Aeronaut. Soc.* XLVIII. 445 Air is led from the intake A, under full ram due to the forward speed of the aircraft, to the compressor B. **1945** P. H. WILKINSON *Aircraft Engines of World* 343 Ram effect in flight compresses air to more than atmospheric pressure. **1948** C. E. CHAPEL *Aircraft Power Plants* iii. 30/2 Ram pressure is that developed in the carburetor air scoop by the forward speed of the airplane. **1953** J. LISTON *Power Plants for Aircraft* ii. 65 Compression is obtained by utilizing the forward motion of the aircraft to produce a dynamic pressure or 'ram' in the diverging inlet section of the engine. **1960** D. G. SHEPHERD *Introd. Gas Turbine* (ed. 2) iii. 84 This increase of temperature and pressure due to aircraft speed is called the ram effect, or simply ram. **1969** W. THOMSON *Thrust for Flight* 43 At the high forward speeds made possible by jet propulsion the pressure in the turbine compressor intake can be raised by ram effects to such an extent that the turbines of fast aircraft become very efficient. *Ibid.* 53 Increase of pressure by ram is not a free gift. **1971** P. J. MCMAHON *Aircraft Propulsion* iii. 111 All the compression needed for it [*sc.* the ramjet] to operate as a heat engine comes from ram compression in the intake due to forward motion.

b. Special Combs.: **ram air**, air which is constrained to enter a moving aperture; freq. *attrib.*; **ram-wing**, a wing-like structure on an air-cushion vehicle which generates lift by means of a ram effect, compressing air between itself and the ground or water surface as it moves.

1953 JENNINGS & ROGERS *Gas Turbine Analysis & Practice* i. 9 Ram air slightly compressed by the forward progress of the airplane enters the impeller, where the pressure of this air is increased by some 10 to 20 in. Hg. **1962** *Engineering* 31 Aug. 258/2 If..all the engines were out, two ram-air turbines provide electric and hydraulic power for essential flying control and aircraft services. **1978** A. WELCH *Bk. of Airsports* vi. 92/2 The Para-Foil, or ram-air 'chute, was developed in the late 1960s by Domina Jalbert. **1962** *Air-Cushion Vehicles* Oct. 70/2 Of particular interest..is a Kawasaki ram-wing craft now being built. **1968** ELSLEY & DEVEREUX *Hovercraft Design & Construction* i. 13 The ram wing is another type of aerodynamic craft... This is essentially a low-aspect-ratio wing with its trailing edge virtually touching the surface and with endplates sealing the tips to the surface. Suction pressures are developed on the upper surface together with ram or dynamic pressure underneath.

ram (ræm), *v.*[1] Also 4–7 **ramme**, 7 **ramb**, 8 **ramm.** [ME. *rammen* = MHG. *rammen* to batter, drive in, etc. Perh. f. RAM *sb.*[1] (as if, to butt or strike like a ram), but the earliest uses in Eng. do not clearly show this.]

1. a. *absol.* To beat down earth with a heavy implement, so as to make it hard and firm.

*c***1330** *Arth. & Merl.* 533 (Kölbing) Sum rammed & doluen snel & gun þat castel fair & wel. *c***1440** *Promp. Parv.* 422/2 Rammyn' wythe an instrument, *trudo, tero, pilo.* **1651** W. BACON *Disc. Govt. Eng.* II. xvii. (1739) 94 An instrument ..that in laying a sure Foundation, doth as well ram down as raise up. **1796** C. MARSHALL *Gardening* iii. (1813) 35 It is best to lay a few yards of gravel only at a time before ramming or treading. **1846** J. BAXTER *Libr. Pract. Agric.* (ed. 4) I. 239 Throw in six more inches of clay, and ram well over.

b. *trans.* with *ground*, etc. as object.

1596–7 S. FINCHE in Ducarel *Acct. Croydon* App. (1783) 153 Small stone, and brickbats..rammed stronglye, course upon course. **1664** GERBIER *Counsel* 26 The Brick-layers to lay no Foundation except the ground be first Ram'd. **1703** MOXON *Mech. Exerc.* 128 If the Ground be hollow or weaker in any place, he strengthens it, sometimes by well ramming it down. **1757** MILLES in *Phil. Trans.* L. 26 They are obliged to pave and ramm the bed of the river. **1823** P. NICHOLSON *Pract. Build.* 338 The space between being filled with clay or chalk closely rammed.

transf. **1873** HOLLAND *A. Bonnic.* xiii. 214 Mr. Mullins..rammed down his shirt bosom again.

c. To fix or make (a thing) firm by ramming the surrounding soil.

1565 GOLDING *Cæsar* 190b, Greate postes of streight timber..are let into the grounde..and rammed surely with a great deale of earth. **1882** *Garden* 11 Mar. 169/2 The plants may be well rammed and top-dressed with stiff loam.

2. a. To force or drive *down* or *in* by heavy blows; to drive (piles, etc.) *into* the soil in this way.

1519 HORMAN *Vulg.* 240 A quauery..foundacion, must be holpe with great pylys of alder rammed downe. **1530** PALSGR. 678/2, I ramme, as workmen ramme in pyles... They have rammed syxe pyles this mornynge. **1621** T. WILLIAMSON tr. *Goulart's Wise Vieillard* 85 Euen, as it were, pyles of wood rammed into the earth. **1708** J. C. *Compl. Collier* (1848) 22 Stiff Clay..is forc'd and ram'd in next the Sand. **1840** *Evid. Hull Docks Com.* 37 We ram some concrete between the piles. **1881** WHITEHEAD *Hops* 36 Men pitch holes..and ram the poles down into them.

b. To force (a charge) into a fire-arm by means of a ram-rod. ***to ram home***: see HOME *adv.* 4.

1598 BARRET *Theor. Warres* III. i. 34 To ramme the same [bullet] with paper, tow or such like. **1627** CAPT. SMITH *Seaman's Gram.* xiv. 66 A Rammer is a bob of wood..to ramme home the Powder. **1700** S. L. tr. *Fryke's Voy. E. Ind.* 72, I..loaded again with a double Charge.., which I took care to ram down as hard as ever I was able. **1781** THOMPSON in *Phil. Trans.* LXXI. 269 The recoil of a musket is greater when its charge is rammed than when it is not. **1878** BESANT & RICE *Celia's Arb.* xxii, You had better ram in your charge.

absol. **1859** F. A. GRIFFITHS *Artil. Man.* (1862) 112, No. 2 searches, sponges, rams home.

c. To cram, stuff, thrust (a person or thing) *into* something (*lit.* and *fig.*).

1582 STANYHURST *Æneis* II. (Arb.) 44 In this od hudge ambry they ramd a number of hardye Tough knights. **1640** SIR E. DERING *Sp. on Relig.* 14 Dec. 13 They have rammed a prodigious ungodly oath into them. **1682** DRYDEN & LEE *Duke of Guise* v. i, By Heaven I'le ramm thee in some knotted Oak. **1840** LADY C. BURY *Hist. of Flirt* xxvi, I always ram my clothes into a box. **1869** C. GIBBON *Robin Gray* xxxvi, In a hurry to ram his head into the noose.

d. To push firmly *down*; to pen *up* closely.

1602 MARSTON *Antonio's Rev.* I. iv, Ramm't quicklie downe, that it may not rise up. **1768** FOOTE *Devil* I. iii, Consider, ramm'd up in this narrow compass [a bottle], I can't be much at my ease. **1887** SIR R. H. ROBERTS *In the Shires* ii. 25 He rams his old hat down on his head.

3. a. To force in or compress the charge or contents of (a gun, etc.) by ramming.

1581 STYWARD *Mart. Discipl.* I. 13 Euerie peece to haue his gonner,..to wade, ram,..and coole the peeces. **1796** PEGGE *Anonym.* (1809) 280 It made a flash and a sharp crack, like that of a gun high charged and hard rammed. **1799** G. SMITH *Laboratory* I. 9 Having rammed a rocket. **1894** HALL CAINE *Manxman* IV. xvii. 265 He took out his pipe, and rammed it with his forefinger.

b. To cram or stuff hard *with* something.

1590 SPENSER *F. Q.* I. vii. 13 That divelish yron Engin,..With windy Nitre and quick Sulphur fraught, And ramd with bollet rownd. **1601** B. JONSON *Poetaster* v. i, His poesie, tis so ramm'd with life. **1721** RAMSAY *To R. H. B.* iii, If ram'd wi' red, they rant and rair, Like mirthfu' men. **1838** *Civil Eng. & Arch. Jrnl.* I. 237/1 The intervening space being well rammed with saw-dust.

4. To stop, stuff, or block *up*. Also const. *with*.

*a***1548** PATTEN *Exped. Scotl.* B vij b, These kepers had rammed vp their outer dores. **1620** QUARLES *Feast for Wormes* (1638) 3 Ramme up thine eares,..Be deafe to them. **1691** WOOD *Ath. Oxon.* II. 518 A back stair..ramb'd up with earth to prevent any passage. **1843** CARLYLE *Past & Pr.* IV. iii, Ædiles; who would..have rigorously seen rammed up into total abolition many a foul cellar.

5. †**a.** *intr.* To batter *at* with a ram. *Obs. rare.*

1599 HAKLUYT *Voy.* II. 134 So was it impossible that the wals of Iericho should fall doune, being neither vndermined, nor yet rammed at with engines.

b. *trans.* To dash violently against, to strike with great force; esp. *Naut.* to strike (a ship) with the ram.

1864 *New York Picayune* in *Daily Tel.* 30 Aug., The Tennessee was rammed by the Hartford. **1893** *Times* 24 June 7/5 The Victoria had been rammed six miles off Tripoli. **1897** *Allbutt's Syst. Med.* II. 1071 In blood so treated it is easy to observe the filariæ ramming the sheath and hitting their way out.

absol. *c***1869** LD. C. E. PAGET *Autobiog.* x. (1896) 334 The Kaiser..rammed four successive times. **1898** *Tit-Bits* 26 Mar. 492/2 When the order to ram is given, everybody throws himself flat on the deck.

6. a. To dash, force or drive (one thing *on*, *at*, or *into* another); *Sc.* to punish (a person) by dashing against a wall (quot. 1854).

1715 RAMSAY *Christ's Kirk Gr.* III. xxiii, Some ramm'd their noddles wi' a clank..On posts that day. **1854** H. MILLER *Sch. & Schm.* (1858) 228 The disputants..were prepared to assist in ramming each the other; and so rammed they both were. **1858** R. S. SURTEES *Ask Mamma* xxiii, Ramming his horse well at it, he gets through. *c***1869** LD. C. E. PAGET *Autobiog.* x. (1896) 334 The gallant Petz, who rammed the old two-decker..into an Italian ironclad.

b. Of a ship: to force *a way* by ramming.

1914 *Times* (Weekly ed.) 10 Apr. 293/1 The Bellaventure was nine hours yesterday in ramming her way through four miles of ice.

†**7.** ***to ram oneself***: to say 'rammee' (q.v.). *Obs.*

1667 WATERHOUSE *Fire Lond.* 126 His Proclamations and Manifests against Prophaneness..disobeyed by..those who will Ram and Damn themselves to be his best friends.

†**ram**, *v.*[2] *Obs. rare.* [f. RAM *sb.*[1] 1.] *trans.* To leap (the ewe).

1688 R. HOLME *Armoury* II. vii. 134/1 A Ram, Rutteth or Rammeth the Ewe. **1694** MOTTEUX *Rabelais* v. (1737) 222 They will not be ridden, tupp'd, and ramm'd.

-rama: see -ORAMA.

ramada (rə'mɑːdə). *U.S.* [Sp.] In the Western U.S.: an (orig. temporary) arbor or similar structure; a porch.

1869 B. I. HAYES *Pioneer Notes from Diaries* (1929) viii. 289, I paid them a dollar for my bath, at the rustic bathing establishment they have constructed, consisting of two goods' boxes sunk in the ground, sheltered by a *ramada*. **1911** H. B. WRIGHT *Winning of Barbara Worth* 201 Every evening under the ramada Barbara sat with her father, often alone. **1949** *Desert Mag.* Apr. 24/1 In a brush ramada the Navajo women weave their blankets while the older children tend the sheep. **1957** G. SHIRREFFS *Rio Bravo* (1972) i. 8 Someone walked across the boardwalk beneath the *ramada* in front of the building. **1976** *Arizona Republic* (Phoenix, Arizona) 27 May B-15/3 Desert Foothills Scenic Drive..a 17-mile desert drive with ramadas and rest rooms. **1979** *Arizona Daily Star* 5 Aug. (Advt. Section) 17/1 Common areas with playgrounds and ramada.

‖**Ramadan** (ræmə'dɑːn). Forms: α. 7 **ramm-, rom-, rummadan, ramdam,** 7–9 **ramadhan,** 8 **-dam, ramandan,** 8–9 **rham-,** 7– **ramadan.** β. 7 **ram-jan, ramizam,** 7–8 **ramezan,** 8 **-esan,** 9 **r(h)amazan(i, ramadzan, ramzaun,** 6– **ramazan.** [a. Arab. *ramaḍān* (hence Turk. and Pers. *ramazān*), f. *ramaḍa* to be heated or hot (see note to def.).] The ninth month of the Muslim year, rigidly observed as a thirty days' fast, during the hours of daylight, by all Muslims.

The lunar reckoning of the Muslim calendar brings the fast eleven days earlier each year, so that in a cycle of about thirty-three years it passes through all the seasons successively; but it is supposed originally to have been one of the hot months.

α. **1601** W. BIDDULPH in T. Lavender *Trav. Four Englishmen* (1612) 95 The Turkes Romadan, which is their Lent, being ended. **1695** MOTTEUX *St. Olon's Morocco* 43 On the Eve of that Ramadan, they prepare themselves for its observation by public Rejoycings. **1757** HUME *Ess. & Treat., Nat. Hist. Relig.* (1777) II. 463 The Rhamadan of the Turks.. must be more severe than the practice of any moral duty. **1865** WHITTIER *David Watson* Pr. Wks. 1889 I. 316 At the season called Ramadan, he was left at leisure for a whole week. **1927** C. CONNOLLY *Let.* Mar. in *Romantic Friendship* (1975) 279 It is Ramadan at present and nobody eats till the evening. **1976** *Hanna* (Alberta) *Herald* 16 June 10/5 During one month each year the Muslims observe Ramadan.

transf. **1822** DE QUINCEY *Confess.* II. 126 A Lent or Ramadan of abstinence from opium.

β. **1599** HAKLUYT *Voy.* II. 203 The Mahumetans observe a kinde of lent continuing one whole moone.. called in their tongue Ramazan. **1698** J. FRYER *Acc. E. India & P.* 379 In their Ramzan, or on a Journey, they often expire for want of it [opium]. **1706** *Lond. Gaz.* No. 4205/1 This being the Moon of Ramezan, during which it is the Custom of the Turks to fast by Day and feast by Night. **1812** BYRON *Ch. Har.* II. lx, Ramazani's fast Through the long day its penance did maintain. **1815** ELPHINSTONE *Acc. Caubul* (1842) I. 279 The fast of the Ramzaun is.. strictly observed; and.. is felt as a real hardship. **1935** H. EDIB *Clown & his Daughter* xli. 67 He has been back for some time, and is getting ready to open his shop for Ramazan.

attrib. **1653** GREAVES *Seraglio* 112 The Ramazan time, which is their lent, and lasteth a whole moon. **1884** J. PAYNE *Tales fr. Arabic* I. 49 *note*, The orthodox Muslim, whose only meals in Ramazan-time are made between sun-set and dawn-peep. **1971** *Sun* (Colombo) 17 Sept. 3 November 8... Ramazan Festival Day.

† **ramage**, *sb.*¹ *Obs. rare.* [f. RAMAGE *a.*; the OF. sb. is not recorded in the same senses.]

1. Wildness, high spirit, courage.

In first quot. perh. an adj. (qualifying *woodnes*).

1456 SIR G. HAYE *Law Arms* (S.T.S.) 285 Malice or hete, woodnes, ramage, or pride orguillous. *a* **1500** *Promp. Parv.* 422/2 (MS. H.) Ramage, or corage, *coragium.* **1618** LATHAM *2nd Bk. Falconry* (1633) 107 The Lanner.. is nothing inferiour to the other in ramage and wildenesse.

2. A ramage hawk. *rare*$^{-1}$.

1612 SELDEN *Illustr. Drayton's Poly-olb.* v. 304 The Goshawk taken at the source by the Falcon soone fell down at the King's foot, which performance in this ramage made him yearly afterward send hither for eyesses.

ramage (ˈræmɪdʒ), *sb.*² Also 7 ramm-. [a. F. *ramage* = Prov. *ramatge*:—late L. **rāmāticum*, f. *rāmus* branch: see RAMUS and -AGE.]

1. a. The collective branches of a tree or trees. *arch.*

1656 BLOUNT *Glossogr.*, *Ramage*, Boughes, Branches, or any thing that belongs thereto. **1855** BAILEY *Mystic*, etc. 85 That beneficent stem.. From leaf and ramage sheddeth cool bright showers.

b. *Anthrop.* A corporate descent group which includes members of both maternal and paternal lineages.

1936 R. FIRTH *We, the Tikopia* x. 371 One term that might be employed to characterize such kinship groups is 'ramage', for which there is literary authority, though it has fallen out of use. *Ibid.* xvi. 586 The patrilineal principle of descent in the ramage ('joint family' is the translation given of the native term *hoa*) is modified. **1957** —— in *Man* LVII. 6/1 In former publications I have used *ramage* to include the Tikopia unilineal descent group. This, I think, is better described functionally as a lineage. *Ibid.* 6/2 Ramage would then be defined as a corporate descent group of a non-unilinear (ambilineal) character, membership being obtained ambilaterally.. according to circumstances. **1963** *Brit. Jrnl. Sociol.* XIV. 24 The word *ramage* has been used to mean a corporate group in which membership may be acquired through either parent. **1976** HUNTER & WHITTEN *Encycl. Anthropol.* 330/1 *Ramage*, nonunilineal descent group composed of individuals who are descended from one ancestor through any combination of male and female links.

† **2.** The song or cry of birds. *Obs. arch.*

1616 DRUMM. OF HAWTH. *Poems* II. x, My Lute bee as thou wast when thou didst grow.. in some shadie Groue,.. And Birds on thee their Ramage did bestow. *a* **1693** URQUHART *Rabelais* III. xiii, The barking of currs, bawling of mastiffs,.. rammage of Hawks.

Ramage (ˈræmɪdʒ), *sb.*³ The name of Adam *Ramage* (1770–1850), a printer of Philadelphia, used *attrib.* to denote a (usu. wooden) printing-press, or part of one, designed by him.

1827 *Hallowell* (Maine) *Gaz.* 20 June 4/3 For Sale, a small font of Brevier, nearly new; also a Printing Press with a new Ramage Screw. **1874** B. F. TAYLOR *World on Wheels* I. iii. 24 The cargoes of those boats.. was something wonderful,.. plows, axes and Bibles, teachers, preachers and Ramage presses. **1923** L. E. YOUNG *Founding of Utah* xxxiii. 349 The old Ramage press had a lever which the printer pulled in the printing of each page. **1949** *Mississippi Valley Hist. Rev.* Mar. 634 It was.. printed on a small wrought-iron Ramage press.

† **ˈramage**, *a.* *Obs.* Also 6–7 (9) **rammage**, 7 **ramadge**; 6–7 **ramege**, 7 **rammege**. [a. OF. *ramage*:—late L. **rāmāticus*: see prec. and cf. RAMMISH *a.*², RAMMIST *a.*]

1. Of hawks: Having left the nest, and begun to fly from branch to branch (cf. BRANCHER²); hence, wild, untamed, shy.

1390 GOWER *Conf.* I. 361 The faucon which that fleth ramage And soeffreth nothing in the weie, Wherof that he mai take his preie. **1483** CAXTON *G. de la Tour* A viij, Take a sperhauke ramage and calle hym curtoysly and ye shall make hym come frely to yow. **1575** TURBERV. *Faulconrie* 31 The seconde name is a ramage falcon, and so she is called when she hath departed and left the eyrie. **1616** SURFL. & MARKH. *Country Farme* 708 Iias-hawkes are nothing so valiant as those which are taken long time after, and are called ramadge hawkes. *a* **1682** SIR T. BROWNE *Tracts* (1683) 118 Nor must you expect from high Antiquity the distinctions of Eyess and Ramage Hawks. **1773** J. CAMPBELL *Mod. Faulconry* 201 It is best to give them [stones] at night to haggards and ramage-hawks.

b. *transf.* of persons.

1567 TURBERV. *Epit.* etc. 15 b, You are become so wylde and rammage.. As though you were a haggard Hawke. **1589** GREENE *Menaphon* (Arb.) 42 She left from being so rammage, and.. came to the fist, and granted me those favours she might affoord. **1652** MAINE *Epig. from Donne* vi. 89 Though ramage grown, Th' art still for carting fit.

2. Of animals: Wild, untamed, unruly, violent.

c **1290** *MS. Laud* 108 fol. 11 þe wolfues þat weren ramage. **1387–8** T. USK *Test. Love* I. iii. (Skeat) l. 49 Nothyng is werse then the beastes, that shoulden been tame, if thei catche her wildenesse, and ginne again waxe ramage. *c* **1430** LYDG. *Reas. & Sens.* 2858 At wylde bestis for to shete,.. Whan she seeth hem to savage, Hygh of gres, or to Ramage. **1580** BLUNDEVIL *Art of Riding* D i b, A horse that is.. of nature ramege or restiffe. **1639** T. DE GREY *Compl. Horsem.* 12 Horses.. becomming wild, rammage and unruly.

b. Of persons: Furious, frenzied.

c **1470** HARDING *Chron.* XCVII. vi, Some woode, some ramage went. [**1824** MACTAGGART *Gallovid. Encycl.* 406 When a man is rammaged, that is.. craz'd.. with drink.]

3. Of places: Full of thickets, rough.

c **1475** *Partenay* 527 Cerching, enquering in wodes ramage. **1809** *Christmas Ba'ing* in Skinner *Misc. Poet.* 127 He rumbl'd down a rammage glyde.

4. Of velvet: (see quot. and cf. BRANCHED 2 b).

1727–41 CHAMBERS *Cycl.* s.v. *Velvet*, Ramage or branched velvet, representing long stalks, branches, &c. on a sattin ground.

† **ˈramageness.** *Obs.* [f. RAMAGE *a.* + -NESS.] Wildness, wantonness; high spirit.

c **1440** *Promp. Parv.* 422/2 Ramagenesse, or coragyowsnesse, *luita.* **1575** TURBERV. *Faulconrie* 147 When your Falcon will come a far off vnto the lewre.. wᵗout any coynesse or ramagenesse. **1607** MARKHAM *Caval.* III. i. 5 This.. takes from him [the horse] two vices, barbarous ramegnesse and fantasticke restifnesse. **1686** R. BROME *Gentl. Recreat.* II. x. 33 In her making, a little rest will cause her [the hawk] to return to her first ramageness.

† **ˈrameageous**, *a.* *Obs.* Also 5 -geouse, -gyous, -gous, -geus, 6 -gious. [a. OF. *rameageous* (Godef.), f. *ramage* RAMAGE *sb.*] = RAMAGE *a.*

1398 TREVISA *Barth. De P.R.* XII. iii. (Bodl. MS.) 115 b, The goshauke.. bi moche mete.. waxiþ ramageouse oþer slowȝ. **1412–20** LYDG. *Chron. Troy* I. ii. 162 Bullis full vnmilde With brasen fete ramageous and wilde. *a* **1450** *Knt. de la Tour* (1868) 14 A sparhauke, be he never so ramageus. ? *c* **1530** *Remedy of Love* xlvii, Now is he tame that was so ramagious.

† **ˈramager.** *Obs. rare*$^{-1}$. [f. RAMAGE *a.*, perh. after BRANCHER.] A ramage hawk.

1686 R. BROME *Gentl. Recreat.* II. 46/2 There is more danger in heating a Hawk taken out of the Mew, than one newly taken being a Ramager.

ramail(e, obs. forms of RAMMEL *sb.*¹

ramakin, variant of RAMEKIN.

ramal (ˈreɪməl), *a.* [f. L. *rām-us* branch.]

1. *Bot.* Of or belonging to a branch; growing on or out of a branch.

1856 HENSLOW *Bot. Terms.* **1861** BENTLEY *Man. Bot.* 135 The leaves which arise from the main stem are called cauline; those from the branches ramal.

2. *Anat.* and *Zool.* Pertaining to a ramus; of the character of a ramus.

1891 in *Cent. Dict.*

ramal, obs. f. RAMMEL *sb.*¹

ramallie, obs. f. RAMILLIE.

† **ramalling.** *Obs. rare*$^{-0}$. [ad. F. *ramaillage*, f. *ramailler* (see def.).] The process of scraping the hair from the skins in the manufacture of chamois leather.

1727–41 CHAMBERS *Cycl.* s.v. *Shammy.* Kid and goats-skins.. when brought from the mill.. undergo a particular preparation, called ramalling; the most delicate and difficult of all the others. [Description follows.]

Raman (ˈrɑːmən). *Chem.* and *Physics.* Also (*rare*) **raman**. The name of Sir Chandrasekhara Venkata *Raman* (1888–1970), Indian physicist, used *attrib.* and in *Comb.* with reference to the Raman effect he discovered, as ***Raman band, line, shift*** (so ***Raman-shifted*** adj.), ***spectrometer, spectroscopy***, etc.; **Raman-active** *a.*, capable of giving rise to Raman scattering; **Raman effect, scattering**, the scattering of light by a substance with a change in the frequency of the light by an amount which is characteristic of the scattering substance and represents a change in the vibrational, rotational, or electronic energy of the substance; occas. with ellipsis of *effect*; **Raman spectrum**, a spectrum of scattered light showing additional bands produced by the Raman effect.

1928 *Nature* 29 Sept. 477/2 (*heading*) The Raman effect in crystals. **1929** *Ibid.* 24 Aug. 301/1 The Raman spectra for various liquids. **1937** *Jrnl. Amer. Chem. Soc.* LIX. 1139/1 It is generally admitted that the 3654 cm^{-1} Raman band of water vapor corresponds to the symmetric.. vibration. **1945** G. HERZBERG *Infrared & Raman Spectra of Polyatomic Molecules* iii. 243 All three vibrations of non-linear symmetric.. XY_2 are Raman active as well as infrared active. **1947** *Nature* 11 Jan. 60/2 The principal feature noticeable in the spectra is the appearance of a whole series of sharply defined Raman lines. **1947** *Thorpe's Dict. Appl. Chem.* (ed. 4) VIII. 190/1 Fundamental frequencies will be active in Raman scattering only when the mode of vibration of the molecule associated with that fundamental frequency causes an equiperiodic variation in the polarisibility of the molecule. **1950** W. J. MOORE *Physical Chem.* xi. 332 Since the Raman spectra are studied with light sources in the visible or ultra-violet, they provide a convenient means of obtaining the same sort of information about molecular structure as is given by the infrared spectra. In many cases, the two methods supplement each other, since vibrations and rotations that are not observable in the infrared.. may be active in the Raman. **1958** *Oxf. Univ. Gaz.* 23 Apr. 881 Application of raman spectra to chemical problems. **1962** *Times* 9 Mar. 2/6 (Advt.), The successful applicant will work in one of the following fields:.. ultra-violet, infra-red and Raman spectroscopy of aromatic, *N*-heterocyclic and tautomerizable substances. **1966** D. H. WHIFFEN *Spectroscopy* ix. 110 The Raman lines are always extremely weak with respect to the incident light intensity. **1967** L. A. WOODWARD in H. A. Szymanski *Raman Spectroscopy* I. i. 16 In practice, the pure rotational Raman shifts are small.. and it is necessary to use a spectrograph of high dispersion and resolving power. **1970** GILSON & HENDRA *Laser Raman Spectroscopy* ii. 21 In the basic Raman spectrometer, the sample under examination is subjected to irradiation from a suitable monochromatic source, and the Raman spectrum is observed by use of a system comprising a monochromator, detector, and recorder. **1974** *Nature* 8 Mar. 124/1 Raman-shifted backscatter of laser radar radiation from atmospheric constituents in the troposphere has been reported. **1976** *Jrnl. Chem. Soc. Dalton Trans.* 1148/2 Five of the six Raman-active vibrations of the two octahedral anions.. were clearly observed. **1978** P. W. ATKINS *Physical Chem.* xvii. 563 The molecule is active in the Raman because the end-over-end rotation modulates its polarizability as viewed by a stationary observer.

ramanand, obs. Sc. var. REMANENT.

ramanas (ˈræmənəs). [perh. f. Jap. *ranman* full bloom.] ***ramanas rose*** = RUGOSA.

1876 *Garden* 3 May 452/2 (*heading*) The Ramanas Rose of Japan. **1955** N. D. G. JAMES *Forester's Compan.* xxii. 246 Shrubs of value for food and cover.. Ramanas rose (*Rosa rugosa*). **1956** [see *Japanese rose* s.v. JAPANESE *a.* b].

ramandan, obs. f. RAMADAN.

Ramapithecus (ˌrɑːməˈpɪθiːkəs). [mod.L. (G. E. Lewis 1934, in *Amer. Jrnl. Sci.* CCXXVII. 162), f. *Rāma*, the name of an Indian prince of Ayodhyā + Gr. πίθηκος ape.] A fossil anthropoid ape, sometimes considered a hominid, belonging to the genus so called and known from remains found in northern India and East Africa. So **ramaˈpithecine** *sb.* and *a.*, a fossil anthropoid closely related to *Ramapithecus*; pertaining to or resembling an anthropoid ape of this kind.

1934 *Discovery* July 197/2 The other [ape], *Ramapithecus*, is represented by an upper jaw in which the teeth are set in a rounded V, approaching the human form, instead of the U-shape characteristic of the anthropoids. **1965** *Folia Primatologica* III. 90 No finds of *Ramapithecus* or any other dryopithecine or hominid have ever been made in the Tatrot or Pinjor zones. **1968** D. PILBEAM in *Nature* 28 Sept. 1337/1, I would argue.. that *Ramapithecus* is probably a hominid,.. even if fossil evidence were produced which showed that it was not yet a habitual biped. **1969** J. E. PFEIFFER *Emergence of Man* ii. 47 Imagine an adventurous hominid or prehominid, a primitive *Ramapithecus* perhaps, looking for food in the savanna. **1971** [see KENYAPITHECUS]. **1973** *Listener* 10 May 604/3 Some anthropologists would boldly put *Ramapithecus* among the hominids. **1976** R. ARDREY *Hunting Hypothesis* 35 Were the ramapithecines close to the common ancestor of chimp and man? **1977** *Sci. Amer.* May 31/1 Kretzoi now recognizes his fossils as being 'ramapithecine' even if they are not generically *Ramapithecus.* **1978** *Nature* 5 Jan. 12/1 It is of interest and of uncertain significance that not all ramapithecines have been found in woodland deposits.

ramaquin, var. RAMEKIN.

ramarama (ˈrɑːməˌrɑːmə). Also **ramiram**, **rummyrum**. [Maori.] An evergreen New Zealand shrub or small tree, *Myrtus* (or *Lophomyrtus*) *bullata*, belonging to the family Myrtaceæ and bearing small white flowers followed by dark red berries.

1843 E. DIEFFENBACH *Travels in N.Z.* II. III. 382 Rama rama—name of a tree (*Myrtus bullata*). **1851** H. W. RICHMOND *Let.* 15 June in *Richmond-Atkinson Papers* (1960) I. ii. 97 A letter might be written about the tapitap so useful for hammer handles.. and the ramiram for ramming in the posts in fencing. **1882** W. D. HAY *Brighter Britain!* II. vi. 196 The Rama-rama.. has a good hard wood. **1889** T. KIRK *Forest Flora N.Z.* 273 The ramarama is the largest and most attractive of the New Zealand myrtles. *Ibid.*, The wood of the ramarama is red, straight, and compact. **1928** H. H. ALLAN *N.Z. Trees & Shrubs* 131 Ramarama.. Bushy shrub up to 15 ft; branchlets tomentose. **1946** *Jrnl. Polynesian Soc.* LV. 157 Ramarama, a tree.., often corrupted to rummyrum. **1970** M. E. FISHER et al. *Gardening with N.Z. Plants* I. 75 The ramarama is easily distinguished from all other native plants by its reddish-brown leaves, the spaces between the veins of which are inflated.

†**ramass**, *sb. Sc. Obs. rare*⁻¹. [a. F. *ramas* (1549) heap, collection, etc., f. *ramasser*: see next.] A summary, résumé.

1606 BIRNIE *Kirk-Buriall* (1833) 32 This ramasse of these reasons in the bygone discourse being thus made.

†**ramass**, *v.*¹ *Obs.* Also 7 remass, ramash, rammass. [ad. F. *ramasser* (1539), f. *re-* RE- + *amasser* AMASS.] *trans.* To gather together.

1589 HAKLUYT *Voy.* To Rdr. *3 b, Those wearie volumes ..most vntruly and vnprofitablie ramassed and hurled together. **1613-18** DANIEL *Coll. Hist. Eng.* 199 Phillip..had ramassed one of the fayrest Armies..that ever was seene in France. **1650** T. VAUGHAN *Anthroposophia* 54 If I will but ramash all that be. **1659** *World in Moon* (Halliwell, s.v.), When they have ramast many of several kindes and tastes.. they open one vessel, and then another.

ramass, *v.*² *rare.* Forms: 6 ramassh, 8 rammass. [ad. F. *ramasser* (1606), f. *ramasse* sledge of branches, ad. It. *ramazza*, f. *ramo*, L. *rāmus* branch.] *trans.* To convey on a sledge of branches such as is used in certain parts of the Alps for descending snow slopes.

1511 GUYLFORDE *Pilgr.* (Camden) 80 From the hyght of the mounte downe to Lyuyngborugh I was ramasshed, whiche is a right straunge thynge. **1792** A. YOUNG *Trav. France* 257 When arrived at the precipice..the mule is dismissed, and the rammassing begins.

Ramayana ('rɑːmɑːjænə). Also †Ramayuna, -unu. [a. Skr. *Rāmāyaṇa*, f. *Rāmā* Rama, the seventh incarnation of Vishnu + *ayana* a going.] An ancient Hindu epic, ascribed to the poet Valmiki. Also *attrib.*

1788 *Asiatick Researches* I. 351 The first Indian Poet was Válmíci, author of the Rámáyana, a complete Epick Poem on one continued, interesting, and heroick, action. **1806** CAREY & MARSHMAN tr. *Ramayuna* I. p. ii, The Committee ..have made choice of the Ramayuna of Valmeeki to be the first in the series of translations from the Sungskrit. **1811** W. WARD *Acct. Hindoos* I. p. viii, Next follow Translations of the Contents of the Mŭhabharŭtŭ, the Ramayŭnŭ, and the Shrēē-Bhagŭvŭtŭ. **1841** *Penny Cycl.* XX. 401/1 There are three pieces of his, one in which a domestic subject is treated ..and two others taken from the cycle of traditions of the Râmâyana. **1870** F. RICHARDSON *Iliad of East* p. vii, The Râmâyana comprises in all some twenty-four thousand verses, or *slokas.* **1937** M. COVARRUBIAS *Island of Bali* viii. 235 The great epics of the Hindus, the famous *Ramayana* and *Mahabharata*..came by way of Java as propaganda for the ancient Hindus and as part of their religious teachings. **1974** *Times* 5 Nov. 11/4 The play is a stirring episode from the Hindu *Ramayana* epic: Rama's courtship of the lustrous Siti Dewi.

ramayle, obs. f. RAMELL *sb.*²

ramayn, -and, obs. Sc. ff. REMAIN, REMANENT.

ramazan, var. RAMADAN.

ramb, obs. f. RAM *v.*¹

rambai ('rambaɪ). Also †rambé, rambeh. [Malay.] An evergreen tree, *Baccaurea motleyana*, or a closely related species, belonging to the family Euphorbiaceæ, native to Malaysia, and bearing large dark green leaves and racemes of tiny yellowish-green flowers; also, the fruit of this tree, which is an oval about two inches long with white flesh and pale brown seeds in a smooth brownish-yellow skin. Also *attrib.*

1811 W. MARSDEN *Hist. Sumatra* (ed. 3) 101 The *chupak, ayer-ayer*, and *rambé* are species or varieties of the same fruit [*sc.* lanseh]. **1820** J. CRAWFURD *Hist. Indian Archipelago* I. IV. 432 The *Langseh, Rambeh*, and *Dukuh* are indigenous fruits. **1839** T. J. NEWBOLD *Straits of Malacca* I. ii. 53 In the valley grow various fruit-trees, such as..the rambai. **1911** [see LANGSAT]. **1924** H. N. RIDLEY *Flora of Malay Peninsula* III. 250 *B[accaurea] Motleyana*... The Rambeh, cultivated all over the peninsula. **1940** E. J. H. CORNER *Wayside Trees of Malaya* I. 241 In habit, trunk, bark and strings of buff-coloured fruits with green seeds and white pulp, the *Rambai* and *Langsat*..are very much alike. **1975** B. M. ALLEN *Common Malaysian Fruits* 11 Rambai is native to Malaysia and is commonly cultivated in the lowlands. *Ibid.*, Rambai fruits are easily confused with Duku and Langsat.

†**ramband.** ? error for *rampand* f. RAMP *v.*

a **1300** *Cursor M.* 24447 (Cott.) Apon mi tas oft-sith i stod, Roles ramband [*Gött.* raxland] to þe rode.

†**rambarre**, *v. Sc. Obs. rare.* [a. F. *rembarrer*, f. *re-* RE- + *embarrer* EMBAR.] *trans.* To beat or force back.

1644 HUME *Hist. Doug.* 290 They were quickly rambarred, and beaten back by those that had been left of purpose in the Court. **1819** W. TENNANT *Papistry Storm'd* (1827) 165 To rambarre The shock o' that near-comin' war.

rambe, obs. form of RAM.

‖**ramberge.** *Obs. rare.* Also 7 -barge. [obs. F. *ram-, rem-, rauberge* (Godef.), ad. Eng. ROW-BARGE.] A long, narrow, swift war-vessel formerly used by the English.

Described by Du Bellay (*Memoires* x., an. 1545).

[**1656** in BLOUNT *Glossogr.*, copying Cotgr.] *a* **1693** *Urquhart's Rabelais* III. li. 416 The huge Rambarges, mighty Gallioons, the large Floyts [etc.].

‖**rambla** ('ræmbla). [Sp., ad. Arab. *ramla*, lit. 'sandy ground'.] **1.** A Spanish ravine, usu. waterless; the dry bed of an ephemeral stream.

1829 W. IRVING *Conq. Granada* I. xii. 97 Sometimes their road was a mere rambla, or dry bed of a torrent. **1845** R. FORD *Hand-bk. Spain* I. 398/2 Three long L[eagues], by a *rambla* of red rocks, lead to Berja. **1923** *Blackw. Mag.* Oct. 509/2 Before we reached this *rambla*, coming around a series of sharp bends down a hillside to a lower level, we were tempted by a combination of sun, dust, and the fortuitous appearance of a wayside venta to halt the Colonel. **1960** *Geogr. Rev.* L. 60 Long stretches of drainage channels have been filled up..with erosion debris of rock fragments, gravel, and sand. Such debris-choked channels are called *ramblas.* **1977** *New Yorker* 16 May 34/3 On the perimeter of the terrace were a four-foot-high chain-link fence, then a narrow *rambla*, and then another..fence.

2. A broad street in a city of eastern Spain, built on a shallow watercourse; *spec.* (now usu. in *pl.*) a broad avenue in Barcelona.

1829 A. S. MACKENZIE *Year in Spain* i. 37 Our fonda was situated..upon the Rambla, an immense highway through the city, the chief thoroughfare and promenade of Barcelona. **1873** *Amer. Cycl.* II. 304/1 Foremost among its numerous promenades is the Rambla (so called from the Arabic *raml*, sand, applied to a dry river bed, used as a road). **1893** *Johnson's Universal Cycl.* I. 497/1 The city is divided into the old and the new town by a beautiful promenade called La Rambla. **1923** *Blackw. Mag.* Aug. 197/1 The rambla turned into a narrow valley. **1968** *Encycl. Brit.* III. 154/2 Cutting through the old city to the west is the street called the Ramblas leading from the Puerta de la Paz to the Plaza de Cataluña, the centre of the modern Barcelona where are numerous banking houses. **1975** D. BEATY *Electric Train* 34 She had seen the boys and girls promenading up and down in the evening on the *ramblas.*

ramblage ('ræmblɪdʒ). *Manx law.* [f. RAMBLE *v.* + -AGE.] Chiefly in phr. ***right of ramblage***, the right to ramble over land in addition to passing across it.

1887 *Peel City Guardian* 17 Sept. 5/2 The public will not only be able to claim right of way but also right of ramblage over the whole of the headlands down to the shores. **1898** *Ibid.* 19 Feb. 3/5 The defendant claimed right of ramblage for the people of Rushen. *Ibid.* 3/6 His Honour said that was ramblage. **1930** *Times* 11 Nov. 10/5 Surely the word 'ramblage' is as worthy of preservation as 'the right of ramblage' itself.—The Rev. T. G. Phillips, Wesley Manse, Peel, Isle of Man.

ramble ('ræmb(ə)l), *sb.*¹ [f. the vb.]

1. An act of rambling; a walk (†formerly any excursion or journey) without definite route or other aim than recreation or pleasure.

1654 GAYTON *Pleas. Notes* IV. xx. 268 Witches are confin'd in their night rambles, to egge shels. **1662** PEPYS *Diary* 30 June, So through bridge to Blackfryers, and home; she being much pleased with the ramble in every particular of it. **1725** BERKELEY *Let. to Prior* 15 Oct. Wks. 1871 IV. 115, I have been these five weeks in a ramble though England. **1791** BOSWELL *Johnson* an. 1776, 21 Mar., Next morning..we set out in a post-chaise to pursue our ramble. **1810** CRABBE *Borough* xxiv, Then walks were made, Not a sweet ramble, but a slow parade. **1854** B'NESS BUNSEN in Hare *Life* (1879) II. iv. 173 A most delightful ramble up a dell.

transf. and *fig.* **1659** H. MORE *Immort. Soul* III. xiv. §10. 479 This wild and audacious ramble from a more secure state. *a* **1700** in Somers *Tracts* (1748) I. 269 This Ramble of Imagination is not altogether a Dream. **1818** KEATS *Endym.* I. 932 A brook—Whose silver ramble..Tracing along,—it brought me to a cave.

b. Phr. ***on*** or ***upon the ramble*** = rambling.

1700 T. BROWN *Amusem. Ser. Com.* 19, I will set both his and my Imagination on the Ramble. **1733** SWIFT *Corr.* (1841) II. 714 Since I left that place..I have been still upon the ramble. **1792** CHARLOTTE SMITH *Desmond* III. 167, I.. shall be upon the ramble for some time.

2. Rambling, incoherence. *rare.*

a **1716** SOUTH *Sermons* (1737) II. 107 Put off with ramble and confused talk, babble, and tautology. *Ibid.* 159 Their prayers; so full of ramble and inconsequence.

'**ramble**, *sb.*² *Coal-mining.* Also ram(m)ell. [? var. of RAMMEL *sb.*²; but cf. Sw. *ramla* to fall down.] A thin bed of shale lying above a coal-seam, which falls down as the coal is taken out, and requires to be separated from it. Also *Comb.*

1851 GREENWELL *Coal-Trade Terms* 41 At some collieries, an extra allowance..is made for hewing with ramble. **1893-4** *Labour Commission, Gloss.* 66 An extra allowance.. called 'ramble-money'.

ramble ('ræmb(ə)l), *v.* Also 7 ramel. [Of obscure formation: cf. *cramble, scramble.* An earlier form appears to have been *romble* RUMBLE.]

1. a. *intr.* Of persons: To wander, travel, make one's way about (now usually to walk) in a free unrestrained manner and without definite aim or direction. †Formerly sometimes conj. with *be.*

1620 T. PEYTON *Paradise* in Farr *S. P. Jas. I* (1848) 178 Hauing rambled in the sacred keele About the world. **1672** R. MONTAGU in *Buccleuch MSS.* (Hist. MSS. Comm.) I. 521, I go tomorrow towards Italy, where I will ramble for two or three months. **1711** STEELE *Spect.* No. 96 ¶2, I.. went out of the House to ramble wherever my Feet would carry me. **1754** WARBURTON in W. & Hurd *Lett.* (1809) 165 He is rambled into Staffordshire. **1807-8** W. IRVING *Salmag.* (1824) 260 A delightful piece of wood and water, where he might ramble on a summer's noon. **1880** L. STEPHEN *Pope* iv. 89 He was often rambling about on horseback.

b. *fig.* with ref. to mental pursuits or studies.

1650 T. VAUGHAN *Anthroposophia* 2, I studied several Arts, and ramel'd over all those Inventions which the folly of man call'd Sciences. **1669** STURMY *Mariner's Mag.* Ep. Ded., Then I rambled over all these Mathematical Inventions. **1726** BOLINGBROKE *Lett. Stud. Hist.* v. (1752) 140 We must not ramble in this field without discernment or choice, nor even with these must we ramble too long.

c. *transf.* of things (material and immaterial).

1665 BOYLE *Occas. Refl.* IV. i. (1848) 167 My roving Thoughts were in various Dreams, rambling to distant places. **1800** WORDSW. *Seven Sisters* vi, The stream..As through the glen it rambles, Repeats a moan. **1858** GLENNY *Gard. Every-day Bk.* 37/1 If they [plants] be neglected until they have rambled about.

2. *intr.* To wander in discourse (spoken or written); to write or talk incoherently or without natural sequence of ideas.

1640 [see RAMBLING *vbl. sb.*]. **1692** DRYDEN *St. Euremont's Ess.* 27, I should then ramble from the Subject I have proposed to my self. **1710** SWIFT *Jrnl. to Stella* 19 Oct., My pen is apt to ramble when I think who I am writing to. **1825** COBBETT *Rur. Rides* 282 He rambled on in a childish sort of way. **1850** KINGSLEY *Alt. Locke* xi, He rambled off into a long jumble of medical-officers.

3. *trans.* To wander over. *rare.*

1810 E. WEETON *Let.* 4 June (1969) I. 265 If my time were my own, [I] would ramble the country over. **1825** in Hone *Every-day Bk.* I. 291, I ramble the rough highland hills. **1930** V. WOOLF in *Death of Moth* (1942) 19 The greatest pleasure of town life in winter—rambling the streets of London.

ramble, variant of RAMMEL *sb.*²

†**ramble-berry.** *Obs. rare*⁻¹.

App. a prepared dish; cf. *ale-, bread-berry.*

1658 *Phillida flouts me* in *Wit restored* 166 Curds and Cream,..Wigge and whay..And ramble-berry.

†'**ramble-,headed**, *a. Obs. rare*⁻¹. [f. RAMBLE *sb.* or *v.*] Of a wandering, giddy disposition.

a **1761** RICHARDSON *Grandison* (1902) VI. i. 2 Lord, how we ramble-headed [1754 rambling-headed] creatures break in upon ourselves.

rambler ('ræmblə(r)). [f. RAMBLE *v.* + -ER¹.]

a. One who rambles. In later use, one who walks through the countryside on a specified route, freq. in company with others.

1624 MASSINGER *Parl. Love* IV. iii, My young rambler, That thought to cheat me..I have in the toil already. **1750** LADY M. W. MONTAGU *Let. to C'tess Bute* 17 Oct., You will think me a great rambler, being at present far distant from the date of my last letter. **1808** SCOTT *Marm.* I. xxv, I love such holy ramblers. **1846** LANDOR *Imag. Conv.* Wks. II. 207 It collects all ramblers and gamblers. **1888** C. F. WARDLEY (*title*) The rambler's guide to Buxton and neighbourhood, specially compiled for pedestrians. **1932** *Ramblers' Federation Handbk.* III. 15 Many ramblers have made acquaintance with the Batham Gate on visits to the Peak Forest district. **1955** *Times* 11 July 7/1 Such acts of vandalism, said an official of the Peak Park Board, turned the farmers and villagers against genuine ramblers. **1977** *Times* 5 Oct. 14/5 The animal is..in a very unsuitable field and frightening the wits out of innocent ramblers.

b. A rose which straggles or climbs freely, esp. the ***crimson rambler.*** Also *attrib.*

1837 T. RIVERS *Rose Amateur's Guide* 43 Dundee Rambler is..one of the best. *Ibid.*, Lovely Rambler, or the Crimson Ayrshire, is..semi-double. **1895** *Westm. Gaz.* 16 July 4/3 The Queen..inspected the new crimson rambler rose.

c. A type of house, usu. a single-storey suburban building; a ranch house. *U.S.*

1958 *Washington Post* 16 Aug. B1/4 These 3-bedroom, full-basement ramblers and split-foyer ramblers will be sold on terms of no money down to qualifying G.I. buyers. **1967** T. BAIRD *Finding Out* x. 88 The houses in lots..Cape Cod cottages, ramblers, colonial split-levels, random provincials. **1975** P. MOYES *Black Widower* ii. 20 She would not have traded their tiny frame house..for a modern split-level rambler in any smart suburban development. **1976** *Washington Post* 19 Apr. C17/2 (Advt.), Forestville—Rambler, 3-br. $325.

'**ramble-'scramble**, *a.* [f. RAMBLE *v.* + SCRAMBLE *v.*] Wanting in system; confused.

1833 ARNOLD in Stanley *Life* (1844) I. vii. 306 The Penny and Saturday Magazines are all ramble-scramble. **1864** KNIGHT *Passages Work. Life* II. xv. 322 The engravings were superior; the writing was less ramble-scramble.

rambling ('ræmblɪŋ), *vbl. sb.* [f. RAMBLE *v.* + -ING¹.] The action of the vb., in its various senses. Also in *pl.*

1624 MASSINGER *Parl. Love* v. i, For this gallant, sir, I do confess I cooled him—spoiled his rambling. **1640** W. S[TYLE] tr. *De Antisco Span. Gallant* 126 Hee..ought to provide, that hee doe not often repeate the same words, ..(which is that which is called rambling). *a* **1704** T. BROWN *Imit. 1st Sat. Persius* Wks. 1730 I. 54 When such wild ramblings got him some poor fame. **1745** POCOCKE *Descr. East* II. II. iii. 277 Rambling makes little alteration in the mind, unless proper care be taken to improve it. **1833** TENNYSON *Miller's Dau.* 105 Oft in ramblings on the wold, ..I saw the village lights below. **1897** *Allbutt's Syst. Med.* II. 543 Rambling of the mind and delirium.

b. *attrib.* and *Comb.*, as ***rambling age, club***, etc.

1673 WYCHERLEY *Gent. Dancing-Master* I. i, To confine a woman just in her rambling age! **1902** *Encycl. Brit.* XXXII. 682/2 Sketching clubs and rambling clubs are formed among young people. **1974** *Country Life* 7 Mar. 471/3 Many rambling clubs..[are] printing on their club programmes that dogs must be kept on a lead on farm land.

rambling ('ræmblɪŋ), *ppl. a.* [f. as prec. + -ING².] That rambles, in various senses of the vb.

1. a. Of persons or things: Wandering, moving about, straying from one place to another.

1623 MASSINGER *Bondman* II. i, Your rambling hunt-smock feels strange alteration. *a* **1652** J. SMITH *Sel. Disc.* iii. 53 How these moveable and rambling atoms come to place themselves so orderly in the universe. **1711** ADDISON *Spect.* No. 129 ¶1 Hunting about the whole Town after a rambling Fellow. **1741** RICHARDSON *Pamela* I. xvi. (1824) 257 A kind of rambling rheumatism. **1819** SHELLEY *Cyclops* 58 Get along, you horned thing, Wild, seditious, rambling.

b. Of life, etc.: Characterized by wandering.

1699 DAMPIER *Voy.* II. Pref., My first Entrance upon this Rambling kind of Life. **1718** LADY M. W. MONTAGU *Let. to Abbé Conti* 19 May, I am on the point of removing. Such is my rambling destiny. **1787** COWPER *On Bill Mortality* i, All these, life's rambling journey done, Have found their home, the grave.

2. a. Of the thoughts, mind, etc.: Straying from one subject to another; unsettled.

1635 QUARLES *Embl.* IV. xii, What unwonted way Has 'scap'd the ransack of my rambling thought. **1700** ASTRY tr. *Saavedra-Faxardo* II. 194 Those Means which their rambling and unquiet Minds prompt 'em to. **1719** DE FOE *Crusoe* I. i, My Head began to be fill'd very early with rambling Thoughts. *a* **1839** PRAED *Poems* (1864) II. 14 An opiate for a rambling head.

b. Similarly of speech, discourse, writings, etc.

c **1645** HOWELL *Lett.* (1650) I. 345 It may seem a rambling wild speech at first view. **1691** BENTLEY *Phal.* Introd. (1699) 17 A Man of much rambling Learning. **1713** STEELE *Guard.* No. 34 ¶1 The conversation..was so very rambling that it is hard to say what was talked of. **1837** DISRAELI *Venetia* I. x, A long rambling ghost story. **1872** BLACK *Adv. Phaeton* viii. 120 Rambling reminiscences of theatres.

c. Of persons: Given to wandering in thought or discourse.

1693 J. EDWARDS *Author. O. & N. Test.* 124 The usual mistake of the rambling poets. **1774** J. BRYANT *Mythol.* II. 365 Nonnus is a rambling writer and unacquainted with method. **1899** *Allbutt's Syst. Med.* VII. 681 The patient became mildly demented, rambling in speech, and defective in memory.

3. Of plants: Straggling, spreading or climbing freely and irregularly.

1728–46 THOMSON *Spring* 795 O'er his ample sides the rambling sprays Luxuriant shoot. **1807** CRABBE *Sir Eustace Grey*, I've hung upon the ridgy steep Of cliffs and held the rambling briar. **1882** *Garden* 11 Feb. 93/1 One of the creeping or rambling species.

4. Having an irregular straggling form or plan.

c **1702** C. FIENNES *Journeys* (1947) 152 There are no good houses but what are old rambling ones [in Bury St. Edmunds]. **1790** *Loiterer* 2 Jan. 10 C—— Castle is a wretched, irregular, heavy, and rambling pile of building. **1816** JANE AUSTEN *Emma* III. vi. 93 The house was.. rambling and irregular. **1836** F. WITTS *Diary* 12 July (1978) 115 A large rambling mansion first built in the close of the 17th century. **1849** C. BRONTE *Shirley* I. x. 288[The house] was antique, rambling, and incommodious. **1858** HAWTHORNE *Fr. & It. Note-bks.* (1872) I. 16 This narrow, crowded, and rambling street.

ramblingly ('ræmblɪŋlɪ), *adv.* [f. prec. -LY².] In a rambling manner.

a **1641** BP. MOUNTAGU *Acts & Mon.* (1642) 232 Our Lords kinsmen, of whom Africanus, Epiphanius, and the Jesuit talk so ramblingly. **1686** GOAD *Celest. Bodies* III. ii. 422 All that I shall ramblingly note here. **1855** DORAN *Hanover Queens* II. xi. 207 He..ran his fingers ramblingly over his harpsichord.

So **'ramblingness**.

1835 JAMES *Gipsy* I. vi. 163 Mrs. Falkland's house had a certain ramblingness of construction. **1890** *Sat. Rev.* 7 June 690/1 A general ramblingness, so to speak, which used to be characteristic of the female intellect.

rambo¹ ('ræmbəʊ). *U.S.* [See RAMBURE.] A variety of eating or cooking apple which ripens late in autumn and has yellowish, red-streaked skin. Also *attrib.*

1804 J. MEASE in A. F. M. Willich *Domestic Encycl.* (Amer. ed.) III. 113/1 Rambo. From Delaware; a fine fall apple. **1817** W. COXE *View of Cultivation of Fruit Trees* 116 Rambo, or Romanite. This apple is much cultivated in Delaware, Pennsylvania, and New Jersey. **1867** *Hours at Home* V. 318/1 There, too, was the 'rambo-row'—alas! how it is thinned out. **1880** *Harper's Mag.* Aug. 355/1 Outside there were great orchards..with old fashioned Baldwins and Rambos. **1898** M. DELAND *Old Chester Tales* 178 Its apples..were poor enough—hard, gnarly russets, or small, bitter rambos. **1906** *N.Y. Even. Post* (Saturday Suppl.) 5 May 3/2 There were still the meetings of an evening.. beneath the rambo apple tree. **1913** G. STRATTON-PORTER *Laddie* xi. 329 There was a teasing fragrance in the spiced vinegar for pickles, a reminder of winesap and rambo in the boiling cider. **1942** C. WEYGANDT *Plenty of Pennsylvania* 64 The Rambo apple is not generally raised nowadays.

Rambo² ('ræmbəʊ). The name of the hero of David Morrell's novel *First Blood* (1972), popularized in the films *First Blood* (1982) and *Rambo: First Blood Part II* (1985), a Vietnam war veteran represented as macho, self-sufficient, and bent on violent retribution: used allusively. Hence **Rambo'esque** *a.*, resembling Rambo, his attitude, or behaviour; **'Ramboism**, conduct or attitudes resembling those of Rambo; **Rambo-like** *a.*

[**1982** *N.Y. Times* 22 Oct. c6/5 Mr. Stallone's Rambo isn't a cold-blooded killer. He's almost a Boy Scout.] **1985** *Washington Post* 6 July A19 Given the bomb-'em-kill-'em suggestions pulsing from the typewriters of 100 literate Rambos, a boycott of the airport was the most reasonable act suggested. *Ibid.* 9 July A2/5 To lawyers, as to other Americans, Ronald Reagan apparently has become the stars and stripes for ever. By his own oft-stated, Rambo-like standards, the hostage crisis was a downer. There was none of the threatened 'swift and effective retribution'. **1986** *Christian Science Monitor* 6 Jan. 18/3 Ramboism is becoming pervasive enough. **1986** *Washington Post* 12 Jan. D5/4 [Metzenbaum] was a critic of the 'rogue elephant' that the CIA became during the years of targeting a Lumumba or a Castro for 'elimination with extreme prejudice'... Metzenbaum repeated his Ramboesque bombshell in an interview with the Cleveland Plain Dealer. **1986** *N.Y. Times* 21 Apr. D12/4 Clercq..described American trade policy as 'Rambo-like diplomacy'. **1986** *Punch* 11 June 18 Malcolm 'Rambo' Rifkind—as the lean and very hungry-looking Scottish secretary has come to be called.

rambootan, variant of RAMBUTAN.

†**rambooz(e, -buze.** *Obs.* (See quot. 1656.)

There is no evidehce of connexion with RUMBOOZE.

1656 BLOUNT *Glossogr.*, *Rambooz*, a compound drink, at Cambridge, and is commonly made of Eggs, Ale, Wine and Sugar; but in Summer, of Milk, Wine, Sugar, and Rose water. **1668** WILKINS *Real Char.* II. xii. §4. 296 Other made Drink, as..Rambooz, Syllabub, etc. **1815** *Hist. John Decastro* I. 226 Giving directions for a hot pot of rambooze.

rambostan, -boteen varr. RAMBUTAN.

rambunctious (ræm'bʌŋkʃəs, 'ræm,bʌŋkʃəs), *a. colloq.* (orig. and chiefly *U.S.*). Also **rambunkshus, rumbunctious,** etc. [Origin unknown: cf. RUMBUSTIOUS *a.*] Of a person: rumbustious, exuberant; boisterous, unruly; flamboyant; of an animal: wild, high-spirited. Also *transf.* Hence **ram'bunctiously** *adv.*, **ram'bunctiousness.**

1830 *Boston Transcript* 1 Sept. 3/1 If they are 'rumbunctious' at the prospect, they will be 'riprorious' when they get a taste, for a 'copious acquaintance' with Vinegar. **1859** 'Dow, Jr.' *New Patent Sermons* 120 Some [men] are mild and peaceable as lambs, while others are as uproarious and rambunctious as tigers. **1866** C. H. SMITH *Bill Arp* 54 A plan was set on foot to procure a fierce and rambunkshus animal from the mountains of Hepsidam. **1886** *Galaxy* 1 Oct. 275 'Rampunctious' is belligerent. **1899** *Century Mag.* Aug. 623/1 Och, Misther McGeever, now.. I niver heerd no man accuse you of bein' anyway rambunkshus about yer nabor's house. **1902** KIPLING *Traffics & Discoveries* (1904) 181 'The petrol will light up and the boiler may blow up.' 'How rambunkshus!' **1904** E. ROBINS *Magnetic North* I. 123 And it hasn't thought of sleetin'..or anything else rambunksious. **1914** *Blackw. Mag.* July 123/1 Our western bronco retains much of his primitive rambunctiousness. **1922** JOYCE *Ulysses* 146 Those slightly rambunctious females. **1926** 'J. J. CONNINGTON' *Death at Swaythling Court* xvi. 284, I was a bit worried and not feeling particularly rambunctious. **1928** W. A. WHITE *Masks in Pageant* 442 Outside of Vermont, in these expansive, more rambunctious United States, economy is a low virtue ordinarily. **1962** J. E. HARTSHORN *Politics & World Oil Econ.* xiii. 193 In the United States these companies, and a host of smaller, even more rambunctiously 'free enterprisers' in the domestic oil business there, get on very comfortably thank you with state agencies. **1962** *Guardian* 4 May 16/5 It then seemed that Mr Fulbright's opponent would be..Dale Alford, a weak but rambunctious man who had promising connections with the Walkerites, the Indignationists, the Birchites. **1971** G. H. BOURNE *Ape People* xi. 247 This animal was a rough, tough, rambunctious creature. **1976** *Time* 27 Dec. 13/2 Brezhnev inherited many problems from his rambunctious, buccaneering predecessor, Nikita Khrushchev. **1977** *New Yorker* 8 Aug. 47/3 The club that initiated the championship was Prestwick, which occupies a rambunctious stretch of duneland on the east shore of the Firth of Clyde. **1980** *Daily Tel.* 19 Feb. 17/4 J. Edgar Hoover, the then-director of the FBI and the man in charge of all counter-intelligence operations in the United States, personally ordered the probe into Flynn's off-screen activities after the rambunctious star was accused in California of sexually assaulting two under-age girls.

‖**rambur(e.** *Obs.* Also 8 -bourg. [F. *rambour* (Cotgr. *rambure*), f. *Rambures* near Amiens.] A large kind of cooking apple.

1600 SURFLET *Countrie Farme* III. xlix. 535 Sharpe sowre apples..as ramburs. **1657** TOMLINSON *Renou's Disp.* 370 All curtipendulous apples, rambures and the like. **1706** LONDON & WISE *Retir'd Gard.* x. 43 The Frank Rambourg is a large Apple of a broad Figure, having a Coat streaked with Red.

†**ramburse,** *v. Sc. Obs. rare*⁻⁰. [ad. F. *rembourser*, f. *re-* + *embourser* IMBURSE.] *trans.* To reimburse. Hence **rambursing** *vbl. sb.*

1582 *Burgh Rec. Edinb.* (1882) 229 The obligatioun..for rambursing to the guid towne of the xᵐ merkis lent to the Kingis Grace.

rambustious, variant of RUMBUSTIOUS *a.*

rambutan, -bootan (ræm'bu:tən). Also 8 **rum-, rambostan, rambustine,** 9 **rambotan, ramboutan, ramboteen.** [a. Malay *rambūtan*, f. *rambut* hair, in allusion to its villose covering.] The fruit of *Nephelium lappaceum*, a tree of the Malay archipelago, having a reddish coat, covered with soft spines or hairs, and pulp of a subacid flavour. Also, the tree bearing this fruit, which belongs to the family Sapindaceæ.

The forms with *s* are prob. due to association with MANGOSTEEN, which also exhibits the substitution of *-ine*, *-een* for *-an* in the last syllable, as in *rambustine, -boteen.*

1707 FUNNELL *Voy.* x. 286 The Rumbostan is about the bigness of a Walnut. **1779** T. FORREST *Voy. N. Guinea* 323 They have also..Mangoes, Mangustines, Rambustines. **1772–84** COOK *Voy.* (1790) I. 281 The rambutan contains a fruit within which is a stone, that is perhaps the finest acid in the world. **1795** tr. *C. P. Thunberg's Travels* (ed. 2) II. 277 The Rambutan (*Nephelium lappaceum*) grows in large clusters and is very generally eaten. **1815** W. THORN *Conq. Java* 212 The Ramboutan is..of a very pleasant taste. **1839** T. J. NEWBOLD *Straits of Malacca* I. ii. 53 In the valley grow various fruit-trees, such as the mangostin,..the rambotan, etc. **1852** F. A. NEALE *Resid. Siam* xii. 194 The bilimby, the ramboteen and the sour-sop. **1880** *Nature* XXIII. 143/2 The mango, pine-apple, durian, rambutan. **1895** *Natural Sci.* VI. 25 He came upon a brisk fight between a large number of Kras and about half a dozen Lotongs (*Semnopithecus*) for the possession of a Rambutan tree..in fruit. **1920** W. POPENOE *Man. Tropical Fruits* x. 328 The rambutan is eaten fresh. **1940** E. J. H. CORNER *Wayside Trees of Malaya* I. 592 Mangosteen, Durian and Rambutan generally flower together. **1962** B. HARRISSON *Orang-Utan* iii. 106 The only alternatives were some rambutan trees in the back of the garden... We were little surprised that the new trees, though they had only a small supply of ripe rambutan, stimulated a bout of nest-building. **1966** [see JACK *sb.*⁴ b]. **1969** *Oxf. Bk. Food Plants* 100/2 The rambutan is limited to tropical lowlands and requires a high rainfall. **1976** 'G. BLACK' *Moon for Killers* ix. 125, I had two helpings and followed them with a couple of rambutans. **1977** *Borneo Bull.* 7 May 2/2 The corn potential is shown in the centre's annual report for 1976, which also underlines pepper and rambutans as two other valuable income-earning crops.

rambuze, variant of RAMBOOZ(E *Obs.*

'ram-cat. Now only *dial.* [f. RAM *sb.*¹: see CAT *sb.*¹ 1 b.] A male cat.

1672 JOSSELYN *New Eng. Rarities* 16 The Ounce or Wild Cat, is about the bigness of two lusty Ram Cats. **1751** SMOLLETT *Per. Pic.* (1779) II. xlviii. 103 The skin and feet of a special ram-cat, newly flayed. **1802** WOLCOTT (P. Pindar) *Gt. Cry & Lit. Wool* Wks. 1816 IV. 264 He.. already has kill'd one Ram Cat. **1809** W. IRVING *Knickerb.* vii. (1820) 414 Like two furious ram cats on the very point of a clapper-clawing. **1880-** in dial. glossaries (Som., Devon, Cornwall).

ramdam, obs. form of RAMADAN.

ramdohrite ('ræmdɔəraɪt). *Min.* [ad. G. *ramdohrit* (F. Ahlfeld 1930, in *Centralbl. f. Min.*, etc. A. 367), f. the name of Paul *Ramdohr* (b. 1890), Ger. mineralogist: see -ITE¹.] A sulphide of lead, silver, and antimony found as long, grey-black prisms.

1931 *Chem. Abstr.* XXV. 2940 Ramdohrite is found as bluish, grey-black prisms in quartz with accompanying pyrite, stannite, sphalerite, jamesonite and pyrargyrite at the Chocaya la Vieja mine, Potosi [Bolivia]. **1954** *Amer. Mineralogist* XXXIX. 161 Most specimens of andorite are syntaxic intergrowths of two distinct species, which have also been observed separately... We propose to call them andorite IV and andorite VI... Ramdohrite = andorite VI. **1972** *Mineral. Abstr.* XXIII. 128/2 The dark phase is thus andorite whereas the light-coloured phase gives a new formula; the formula previously assumed for ramdohrite ($Ag_2Pb_3Sb_6S_{13}$) occupies an exactly intermediate position. .. The name 'ramdohrite' must be transferred to the Pb-rich phase with formula $AgPb_2SbS_7$. **1975** *Amer. Mineralogist* LX. 621 Another solid solution includes the compositions of andorite ($PbAgSb_3S_6$), ramdohrite ($Pb_3Ag_2Sb_6S_{13}$), and fizelyite ($Pb_5Ag_2Sb_8S_{18}$).

rame (reɪm), *sb.*¹ Now only *dial.* [Perh. = MDu. *rame* (Du. *raam*), OHG. *rama* (MHG. *ram, rame*, G. *rahm, rahmen*) frame, framework.] **a.** (Chiefly *pl.*) The bones or skeleton (of a human being or animal). **b.** *dial.* The mere skeleton or framework (of a thing); also, dried stalks.

1497 *Will of Otteley* (Somerset Ho.), Where my wif lieth buried so that the bones of her be not digged up but to ly upon the Rame of the same bones. **1581** J. BELL *Haddon's Answ. Osor.* 40 b, Naturall fooles do detest the stincking Rames..of that Rebellious traytour. *Ibid.* 460 b, Would any man dought but that her Rames [L. *ossa*] would have bene bragged upon. **1847** in HALLIWELL. **1880-** in south-western glossaries (Glouc., Som., Devon, Cornwall).

rame (reɪm), *sb.*² *rare.* [a. F. *rame*:—L. *rāmus* branch, RAMUS.] A branch of a tree or shrub; also *transf.* of a nerve, etc.

1578 BANISTER *Hist. Man* VIII. 109 [This] braunch [of nerve]..is reflected aboue the wrest, there into three proper rames specially deuided. [**1858** O. W. HOLMES *Aestivation* i. in *Aut. Breakf.-t.* 255 The foles, languescent, pend from arid rames.] *a* **1893** T. HENEY *Wood Notes* xi. (Funk), The Wattles crown With golden down Their sombre rames.

rame (re:m), *sb.*³ *Sc.* Also **rhame.** [f. RAME *v.*¹] A cry; a continuous repetition of the same words or sound. (Cf. RANE *sb.*)

1808 JAMIESON s.v., It is said of one, *He has ay ae rame*, when he continues to cry for the same thing or to repeat the same sound. **1822** HOGG *Perils of Man* I. 244 The poet can bring out naething but rhames o'..nonsense.

rame (reːm), *v.*[1] *Sc.* and *north. dial.* Also 6 raym, 9 rhame, raim, ream. [Prob. f. ON. *hreim-r* a scream, cry.]

1. *intr.* To shout, cry aloud, scream; *dial.* to keep up the same cry, to continue repeating the same thing. (Cf. RANE *v.*)

c **1470** *Gol. & Gaw.* 693 The roy ramyt for reuth. **1513** DOUGLAS *Æneis* VII. x. 76 Thay rame and cry fast on the King Latyne. *c* **1560** A. SCOTT *Poems* (S.T.S.) xxxiv. 51 Ȝe rame as ȝe wer rent. **1808** in JAMIESON. **1829** in BROCKETT. **1876-** in northern glossaries (Yks., Northumb.).

2. *trans.* †**a.** To obtain by persistent asking. *Obs.*

1500-20 DUNBAR *Poems* lx. 33 Sum ramyis ane rokkat fra the roy.

b. To repeat, run *over*.

1818 HOGG *Brownie of Bodsbeck* II. 76 She'll rhame o'er bladds o' scripture to them. **1822** —— *Perils of Man* II. 262, I heard Will.. rhaming o'er the names o' a' the saints he had ever heard of.

Hence †**'raming** *vbl. sb. Obs.*

1513 DOUGLAS *Æneis* v. vi. 94 With loude ramyngis and with mony a schout. **1551** *Sc. Acts Mary* (1814) 487 Nane of thame may pas throw the streittis for raming and crying vpone thame.

†**rame,** *v.*[2] *Obs. rare*[−1]. (Sense not clear.)

c **1205** LAY. 7854 Þa Rom-leoden rameden ȝeond uþen.

rame, obs. form of RAM.

‖**ramé** ('ræmeɪ), *a. Her.* [F., f. *rame* branch.] = ATTIRED *ppl. a.* 4.

1878 in BURKE *General Armory* p. xliv.

rameal ('reɪmiːəl), *a. Bot.* [a. F. *raméal*, f. *rame* branch.] = RAMAL.

1852 GRAY in *Smithsonian Contrib. Knowledge* V. VI. 77 Leaves 12 to 18 lines long.. the smaller rameal ones sometimes contracted at the base.

rameal, -mel, app. erron. ff. CARAMEL.

1584 *Bk. of Rates*, Ramels the c[wt.].. x *li.* **1660** *Ibid.*, Melasses or Rameales the hundred weight.. 01 *l.*

Ramean ('reɪmiːən), *a.* and *sb.* [f. *Ramus* (see RAMIST) + -(E)AN.] **a.** *adj.* Belonging to, connected with, Ramus. **b.** *sb.* A Ramist.

1710 tr. *Bayle's Dict.* (1735) IV. 842/1 A dissertation for the Ramean Philosophy. **1838-9** HALLAM *Hist. Lit.* I. vii. §13 *note*, The sixth stage of Aristotle's fortune Launoy reckons to be the Ramean controversy. *a* **1880** J. MCCLINTOCK & J. STRONG *Cycl. Bib. Lit.* VIII. 900 The faults of the Ramean system of dialectics have long been acknowledged.

ramed, *a. Naut.* [? f. RAME *sb.*[1]] (See quot.)

1867 SMYTH *Sailor's Word-bk.* 559 *Ramed*, the state of a ship on the stocks, when all the frames are set upon the keel, the stem and stern-post put up, and the whole adjusted by the ram-line.

ramed(e, obs. Sc. ff. REMEDE.

ramee, var. of RAMIE.

ramefy, obs. f. RAMIFY.

ramege, var. RAMAGE *a.*

rameid, obs. Sc. f. REMEDE.

ramekin ('ræməkɪn). Forms: 8 ramme(l)kin, 8- ramequin, 9 ramakin, -aquin; 9- ramekin. [ad. F. *ramequin* (1690) of dub. etym. Cf. obs. Flem. *rammeken* toasted bread (Kilian).] **a.** A small quantity of cheese, with bread-crumbs, eggs, etc., usually baked and served in a special mould. Chiefly *pl.*

1706 PHILLIPS, *Ramequin* (Fr. in Cookery), toasted Cheese and Bread, a Toast and Cheese. Ramequins are also small slices of Bread-crum cover'd with a Farce made of pounded Cheese, Eggs and other Ingredients bak'd in a Pie-pan. **1754** *Connoisseur* No. 19 Toasted cheese is already buried in rammelkins. **1819** H. BUSK *Banquet* II. 647 Your ramekins too rich.. Your fricassee too fat. **1864** A. B. KIRWAN *Host & Guest* 198 At large dinners in London, cheese is oftenest eaten in the form of ramequins, or grated Parmesan, and other preparations. **1879** *B'ham Weekly Post* 8 Feb. 1/4 We had hot cheese, like ramakins.

attrib. **1894** *Westm. Gaz.* 2 June 8/2 Butter some small ramekin moulds. **1894** C. H. SENN *Pract. Gastron.* 551 Fill the mixture in little French china ramaquin cases.

b. A dish in which ramekins or other portions of food are baked and served.

1895 in *Funk's Stand. Dict.* **1946** *Farmhouse Fare* 19 Flake fish... Mix well and pile into buttered ramekins. **1957** *Housewife* Sept. 89/2 Scandinavian saucepan in oven-proof pottery. There is a ramekin.. in the same design. **1974** M. BABSON *Stalking Lamb* xviii. 129 Sybilla was standing beside the oven, having just transferred the ramekins into it. **1976** *Field* 18 Nov. 1028 (Advt.), These superb oven proof ramekins each depict a different game bird of Great Britain.

ramel, obs. form or var. of RAMBLE *sb.*[2] and *v.*, RAMEAL, and RAMMEL *sb.*[1]

†**'ramelande.** (Of obscure form and meaning.)

Perh. written for *ramel* (= rammel, rubbish) *ande*.

a **1320-30** *E.E. Allit. P.* C. 279 Nowhere he fyndez No rest ne recouerer, bot ramelande myre.

†**'ramelet.** *Obs. rare*[−1]. [f. F. *rame* branch + -LET.] A small branch, twig. In quot. *fig.*

1652 URQUHART *Jewel* Wks. (1834) 200 For better understanding whereof, with all its dependant boughs, sprigs, and ramelets, I have set down [etc.].

ramell, obs. form of RAMMEL *sb.*[1]

ramellie(s, obs. variant of RAMILLIE.

ramellose ('ræmələʊs), *a.* [f. mod.L. *rāmell-us*, dim. of *rāmus* (cf. RAMULUS) + -OSE.] Bearing, or having the form of, small ramuli.

1852 *Smithsonian Contrib. Knowl.* V. v. 205 Branches excessively divided, ramellose. **1872** H. C. WOOD *Fresh-Water Algæ* 207 Fasciculi of extreme branches densely ramellose.

ramembrance, obs. Sc. f. REMEMBRANCE.

ramenas ('ramə,nas). *S. Afr.* Also ramnas. [Afrikaans, f. Du. *ram(m)enas* black radish.] The wild radish, *Raphanus raphanistrum*, belonging to the family Cruciferæ; also, formerly, the wild mustard, *Sinapis arvensis*, a similar plant also belonging to the family Cruciferæ.

[**1896** R. WALLACE *Farming Industries of Cape Colony* vi. 117 Charlock, wild mustard, or 'rominas', *Sinapis arvensis*, L., is a widely prevalent weed of the corn-fields of Cape Colony.] **1913** C. PETTMAN *Africanderisms* 391 Ramenas .. *Raphanus raphanistrum*—Wild mustard is known by this name in the Western Province. **1932** WATT & BREYER-BRANDWIJK *Medicinal & Poisonous Plants S. Afr.* 56 *Raphanus raphanistrum* L., an introduced species known as Charlock (jointed), Ramenas, Ramnas, and Knopherik, is used by Europeans in the treatment for gravel. **1950** *Cape Times* 8 Aug. 9/6 Weeds such as 'wilde ertjies', ramenas and sorrel,.. are regarded by farmers as their biggest enemies. **1953** *Ibid.* 20 May 8 The ramnas, the wild radish of the Cape .. is a weed of cultivation also introduced from Europe.

rament ('reɪmənt). [ad. L. RAMENTUM.]

†**1.** *pl.* Scrapings. *Obs. rare.*

1670 W. SIMPSON *Hydrol. Ess.* 143 A saxum nitrosum, or raments of stone. **1675** E. W[ILSON] *Spadacr. Dunelm.* 38 This Liquor thus replenish'd.. with the raments of Iron.

2. *Bot.* = RAMENTUM 2.

1819 in *Pantologia* X.

ramentaceous (ræmən'teɪʃəs), *a. Bot.* [f. RAMENT-UM + -ACEOUS.]

1. Covered with ramenta or scales.

1816 KEITH *Phys. Bot.* I. 75 A branch or stem that is covered with thin and dry scales or flaps is said to be ramentaceous. **1845** LINDLEY *Sch. Bot.* ix. (1858) 154 Leaves simple,.. with a ramentaceous stalk. **1866** *Treas. Bot.* 957/1.

2. Resembling ramenta.

1861 BENTLEY *Man. Bot.* 48 Other modifications.. are the ramenta or ramentaceous hairs so abundant upon Ferns.

ramen'tiferous, *a. Bot.* [f. as prec. + -(I)FEROUS.] Bearing ramenta.

1886 *Athenæum* 27 Nov. 711/2 The ramentiferous surfaces not extending to the apex.

‖**ramentum** (rə'mɛntəm). Chiefly in pl. ramenta. [L., f. *rādere*: see RASE *v.*[1]]

1. A fragment scraped off; †an atom, mote.

1662 RAY *Three Itin.* (1846) 124 Common, or rain, water falling upon a stone, doth continually carry away some insensible ramenta, or atoms, of it. **1678** CUDWORTH *Intell. Syst.* I. iii. §14. 115 Those Ramenta that appear in the air when the sun-beams are transmitted through cranies. **1822-34** *Good's Study Med.* (ed. 4) I. 73 Sir Gilbert Blane.. considers the salivary glands as one of the outlets for the ramenta of the bones.

2. *Bot.* A thin membraneous scale formed on the surface of leaves and stalks.

1819 in *Pantologia* X. **1832** LINDLEY *Introd. Bot.* 41 Ramenta.. are particularly numerous.. upon the petioles and the backs of the leaves of Ferns. **1872** NICHOLSON *Palæont.* 480 Rhizomata.. covered with hairs or ramenta.

rameous ('reɪmiːəs), *a. Bot.* [f. L. *rāmus* branch + -EOUS.] Of or belonging to branches.

1760 LEE *Introd. Bot.* III. iv. (1765) 172 *Rameous*, belonging to the Branches. **1832** LINDLEY *Introd. Bot.* 416. **1866** *Treas. Bot.* 957/1.

ramequin, variant of RAMEKIN.

ramera, rames, obs. ff. REMORA, RAMS.

ramesan, obs. form of *ramazan*, RAMADAN.

Ramessid ('ræməsɪd), **-ide** (-aɪd), *sb.* and *a.* Also Rameside. [ad. Gr. type *Ῥαμεσσίδης, f. Ῥαμέσσης Rameses + -ίδης, patronymic suffix.] A member of the Egyptian royal family during the 19th and 20th dynasties.

1854 C. H. COTTRELL tr. *Bunsen's Egypt's place in Univ. Hist.* II. 571 The Ramessides of this [20th] Dynasty have generally been made use of for completing the 19th. **1875** S. BIRCH *Egypt fr. Earliest Times* iv. 154 The Theban line of the Ramessids appears to have been broken up [etc.].

b. *attrib.* or as *adj.*

1859 C. H. COTTRELL tr. *Bunsen's Egypt's place in Univ. Hist.* III. 160 The confusion of the Sesostride and Rameside legends. **1864** *Athenæum* No. 1937. 786/1 The great Pharaohs of the Ramesside dynasty. **1875** S. BIRCH *Egypt fr. Earliest Times* iv. 154 A princess.. of the Ramessid line.

ramet ('reɪmət). [f. L. *rāmus* branch + -ET.] An individual plant belonging to a clone.

1929 A. B. STOUT in *Jrnl. N.Y. Bot. Garden* XXX. 33 It is here suggested that the word 'ramet'.. be used for a member of the clon. **1938** *Jrnl. Ecology* XXVI. 379 *Silene maritima* was remarkable for the quick completion of first flowering by all ramets on sand and chalky clay as contrasted with the slow completion by ramets on calcareous sand and Potterne soil. **1963** DAVIS & HEYWOOD *Princ. Angiosperm Taxonomy* x. 345 Cloning has obvious advantages in that the vegetative divisions or ramets are genetically identical. **1977** J. L. HARPER *Population Biol. Plants* i. 24 The 'ramet' is the unit of clonal growth.

‖**'ramex.** *Med. Obs.* [L.] A rupture, hernia.

1608-9 MIDDLETON *Widow* IV. ii, I thought 't had been some gangrene, fistula, Canker, or ramex. **1753** CHAMBERS *Cycl.* Supp., *Ramex*, a word used by some as a name for hernia or rupture.

ramezan, obs. form of *ramazan*, RAMADAN.

ram'feezled, *a. Sc.* Worn out, exhausted.

1785 BURNS *2nd Ep. J. Lapraik* 13 The tapetless ramfeezl'd hizzie. **1890** SERVICE *Notandums* ix. 63 He wrocht awa till he was ramfeezled.

†**ramforce,** *v.*[1] *Obs.* Chiefly *Sc.* Also 6 -forse. [var. RANFORCE, q.v.] *trans.* To fortify, strengthen (a wall, rampart, etc.); to block up, barricade (a gate or door).

1570 *Burgh Rec. Edinb.* (1875) 269 The counsall ordanis the baillies.. to caus ramforce the Walter Yait. **1583** STOCKER *Civ. Warres Lowe C.* IV. 56 Thei beganne to.. ramforce the Rampares, and Vauntmures. **1644** *Privy Council Decreta* 2 Oct. 331 She.. caused ramforce the doores of the kirk with clog stones and otheris the like materiallis ..[and] debarred the people from accesse.

fig. **1581** *Satir. Poems Reform.* xliv. 141 His boss bellie, ramforsit with creisch and lie, Will serue to be a gabion.

b. ? To stop or jam up (cannon).

1632 LITHGOW *Trav.* III. 104 They scaled the walles, slue the watches, and vnhappily ramforced all the Canon.

Hence †**ramforced** *ppl. a. Obs.*

1589 A. HUME *Hymns* vii. 76 Wks. (S.T.S.) 54 Of mightie walls and ramforst towers so hie.

ramforce ring, var. RANFORCE RING.

1669 STURMY *Mariner's Mag.* v. 48 (*plate*).

ram'gunshoch, *a. Sc.* Harsh, ill-tempered.

1721 KELLY *Sc. Prov.* 348 What makes you so Ramgunshoch to me? **1795** BURNS *Had I the wyte* ii, Our ramgunshoch glum gudeman Is out.

†**'ram-head.** *Obs.* [f. RAM *sb.*[1]]

1. One who has a head like a ram; a dull, thick-witted, or obstinate person; also, a cuckold.

1605 *Play Stucley* in Simpson *Sch. Shaks.* (1878) I. 196 Drum,.. make the ram-heads hear that are within. **1630** J. TAYLOR (Water P.) *Taylor's Pastorall* 54 To be cald Ramhead is a title of honour. **1632** MASSINGER & FIELD *Fatal Dowry* II. i, Were it my father's trunk, The tyrannous ram-heads with their horns should gore it.

2. *Naut.* A halyard block: see RAM'S HEAD 2.

1514 in Oppenheim *Adm. Royal Navy* (1896) I. App. A. Ramehedes with ij shevers of Brasse. **1626** CAPT. SMITH *Accid. Yng. Seamen* 11 The ram heads, the Knights. **1704** in HARRIS *Lex. Techn.*

3. Part of the arm of a crane.

1611 COTGR., *Mollette*,.. the ram-head of a fearne, or windlesse. **1686** *Lond. Gaz.* No. 2183/4 Stolen,.. a Crane Rope cut, and the Ram-head of Iron. **1729** DESAGULIERS in *Phil. Trans.* XXXVI. 200 The End of the Gibbet *g* with the Ram-head *r*, and the Weight hanging at it.

Hence †**'ram-head** *v. trans.*, to give horns to, to make a cuckold of. *Obs.*

1713 *Poor Robin* (N.), For fear you should be this day wedded, And on the next day be ram-headed.

'ram-,headed, *a.* Having the head of a ram; *fig.* thick-headed.

1813 SCOTT *Let. to Morritt* 12 Jan. in *Lockhart*, To enlighten the understanding of an old ram-headed sheriff who was usually named Leather-head. **1865** J. H. INGRAHAM *Pillar of Fire* (1872) 213 The worship of.. the sacred ox at On, and of the ram-headed Ammon at Thebes.

rami, pl. of RAMUS.

†**'Ramic,** *a. Obs. rare*[−1]. [f. *Ram-us* (see RAMIST) + -IC.] = RAMEAN.

1653 R. SANDERS *Physiogn.* 165 The Aristotelick and Ramick Philosophy.

ramicle ('ræmɪk(ə)l). *Zool.* [ad. L. type **rāmiculus*, dim. of *rāmus* branch.] A small branch (of a zoophyte).

1846 DANA *Zooph.* (1848) 463 Ramicles much crowded.

ramicorn ('ræmɪkɔːn), *sb.* and *a.* [ad. L. type **rāmicornis*, f. *rāmus* branch + *cornu* horn.]

A. *sb. Ornith.* The horny sheath of the rami of the lower mandible.

1866 COUES in *Proc. Acad. Nat. Sc. Philadelphia* 176 The ramicorn which covers the sides of the rami of the lower mandible is chiefly noticeable for the peculiar outline of its base.

B. *adj. Ent.* Having ramified antennæ. (In recent Dicts.)

ramiculose (rə'mɪkjʊləʊs), *a. Zool.* [ad. L. type **rāmiculōsus*, f. **rāmiculus*: see RAMICLE and -OSE.] Characterized by ramicles.

1846 DANA *Zooph.* (1848) 465 Erect arborescent, stem.. laterally ramiculose.

ramie (ˈræmiː). Also ramee, rami (rami). [Malay *rāmī*.] **a.** A Chinese and East Indian plant of the nettle family, *Bœhmeria nivea*, called also *rhea* and *grass-cloth plant*. **b.** The fine fibre of this plant, extensively employed in weaving.

[**1817** RAFFLES *Java* I. 7 Among plants, the *widúri* and *râmi*, the fibres of the latter afford very strong and durable cords.] **1832** W. ROXBURGH et al. *Flora Indica* III. 590 Rami, the Malay name in the Island of Pulo Pinang. A native of the Island of Sumatra, where it is cultivated for its bark, which abounds in fibres of very great strength and fineness. **1839** T. J. NEWBOLD *Straits of Malacca* I. vii. 444 The Rámi Rámi.., the fibres of which the Malays twist into fishing lines, cordage, etc., flourishes on the peninsula. **1868** A. GRAY *Field, Forest & Garden Bot.* 299 Ramie, or the Grass-Cloth Plant of China,..is recently planted S.W. for its very valuable textile fibres. **1888** *Times* 22 Sept. 6/6 The best machine for extracting the fibre of ramie in a green state. **1895** [see FILASSE]. **1897** *Westm. Gaz.* 3 July 6/2 The canvas is made of Indian ramee. **1909** *Chambers's Jrnl.* Nov. 699/2 The future of the mantle lies in the discovery of some material which can take the place of cotton or ramie. **1955** *Sci. News Let.* 2 Apr. 213/2 Ramie..produces a strong silky fiber used to make upholstery material. **1963** R. R. A. HIGHAM *Handbk. Papermaking* xiii. 264 Ramie..and hemp ..were used prior to the third century AD. **1976** *Times* 29 Apr. 8/8 A wall hanging made in..herdwick, swaledale, Welsh kemp, raw and treated ramie, flax, alpaca, mohair. **1978** *Nagel's Encycl.-Guide: China* 277 China produces tobacco (400,000 tons in 1956) and fibre-bearing plants—jute, ramie, hemp.

attrib. and *Comb.* **1874** *Rep. Comm. Agric. 1873* (U.S. Dept. Agric.) 262 A treatise has been prepared by Émile Lefranc, of the 'Southern Ramie-Planting Association'. **1884** KNIGHT *Dict. Mech. Suppl.* 742/1 Ramie Machinery. **1890** HOSIE *West China* 73 The cloth is manufactured from Ramie-fibre. **1906** *Westm. Gaz.* 21 July 5/3 The ramie plant—a tall, bushy member of the nettle family. *Ibid.*, The ramie undergarments are so light and..occupy so little space that they make one covetous on a hot July day. **1909** *Public Ledger* (Philadelphia) 24 June 5/6 (Advt.), Ramie-cloth and natural linen. **1949** *Sun* (Baltimore) 11 Mar. 7/2 The pioneer ramie producers and manufacturers. **1965** 'HAN SUYIN' *Crippled Tree* ii. 22 The weavers of ramie cloth along the water courses are Hakkas ('guest people').

c. A garment woven of ramie fibre.

1922 *Chambers's Jrnl.* Mar. 145/1 Mrs. Godfrey, insufficiently but comfortably clothed in a *rami*, sat under the shade of her veranda. **1928** *Funk's Stand. Dict.*, *Ramie*, ..3. (Papua.) A skirt, waist-cloth, or kilt of ramie.

ramiˈfactive, *a.* [f. L. *rāmus* branch + FACTIVE.] Forming, or developing into, a branch.

1766 *Museum Rust.* VI. 210 We are ignorant what, in the natural..state of a tree, determines a bud to form a ramifactive, instead of a fructiferous shoot.

ramiferous (rəˈmɪfərəs), *a. rare.* [f. L. *rām-us* branch + -(I)FEROUS.] Bearing branches.

1819 H. BUSK *Banquet* I. 249 The broad elm, ramiferous o'er head. **1856** W. CLARK *Van der Hoeven's Zool.* I. 83 Shaft knotty, genicula tumid, ramiferous.

ˈramificate, *v. rare*$^{-1}$. [Latinized form of RAMIFY, after next.] *intr.* To branch out.

1844 *Fraser's Mag.* XXX. 518/1 It is surprising how the family tree ramificates and widens.

ramification (ˌræmɪfɪˈkeɪʃən). [n. of action f. med.L. *rāmificāre* RAMIFY, perh. after F. *ramification* (16th c.).]

1. The action or process of ramifying.

1760 J. LEE *Introd. Bot.* III. xiii. (1765) 200 Ramification is the Manner in which a Tree produces its Branches. **1785** MARTYN *Rousseau's Bot.* xxxi. (1794) 485 The mode and degree of ramification in leaves and branches. **1865** MOZLEY *Mirac.* i. 207 The ramifications and migrations of the human race. **1881** WESTCOTT & HORT *Grk. N.T.* Introd. §12 Transmission ceases..to retain exclusively the form of diverging ramification.

b. The branches of a tree collectively.

1821 CRAIG *Lect. Drawing* v. 283 This character.. pervades..trunk, ramification, bark, and foliage.

2. A subdivision or single part of a complex structure analogous to the branches of a tree, *esp.* of veins, arteries, and other parts in animals and plants, and of rivers. Cf. BRANCH *sb.* 2.

1677 HALE *Prim. Orig. Man.* I. ii. 65 A ramification of the *nervus intercostalis* is also inserted into the Muscle of the Heart. **1677** PLOT *Oxfordsh.* 122 In congelations..we frequently find curious ramifications, as on Glass-windows in winter. **1775** ADAIR *Amer. Ind.* 284 From the small rivers ..the far-extending ramifications are innumerable. **1813** SIR H. DAVY *Agric. Chem.* iii. (1814) 56 The root.. terminating in minute ramifications and filaments. **1834** R. MUDIE *Brit. Birds* (1841) I. 14 All feathers are subdivided till the ultimate ramifications are exceedingly minute. **1879** A. R. WALLACE *Australasia* ii. 23 Like the Amazon, it sends out forks and ramifications.

b. *transf.* Of immaterial things.

1755 JOHNSON *Dict.* Pref., When the radical idea branches out into parallel ramifications. **1800** COLQUHOUN *Comm. Thames* Pref., The numerous ramifications of a Commercial intercourse of unexampled extent. **1849** MACAULAY *Hist. Eng.* v. I. 596 One of the ramifications of the Whig plot had extended thither. **1866** DK. ARGYLL *Reign Law* i. (ed. 4) 27 Like all central truths, its ramifications are infinite.

ramified (ˈræmɪfaɪd), *ppl. a.* [f. RAMIFY *v.* + -ED^1.] Branched, characterized by ramification.

1672 GREW *Idea Philos. Hist. Pl.* §6 As of Roots, in being Thick or Slender,..Stringed or Ramified. **1799** J. ROBERTSON *Agric. Perth* 329 Their horns..are solid, cylindrical and ramified. **1863** H. SPENCER *Ess.* II. 205 The ramified consequences that laws have produced.

ramiˈflorous, *a. Bot.* [f. L. *rāmus* branch + *flōr-*, *flōs* flower + -OUS. Cf. F. *ramiflore*.] Flowering on the branches.

1880 A. GRAY *Struct. Bot.* Gloss.

ramiform (ˈræmɪfɔːm), *a.* [f. as prec. + -FORM: cf. F. *ramiforme*.] Branch-like; ramified.

1822–34 *Good's Study Med.* (ed. 4) II. 556 The ramiform expansion of a minute vein. **1853** KANE *Grinnell Exp.* xlviii. (1856) 449 The water gorges were more ramiform.

ramify (ˈræmɪfaɪ), *v.* Also 6 **ramefy, -ifye, -yfye,** 6–7 **ramifie.** [ad. F. *ramifier* (1314), ad. med.L. *rāmificāre*, f. *rāmus* branch: see -FY.]

1. *intr.* Of trees and plants or their parts: To form branches, to branch out, extend in the form of branches.

1576 NEWTON *Lemnie's Complex.* (1633) 212 Those Trees and Sprayes that doe not burgen and ramifie. *a* **1735** ARBUTHNOT *Aliments* iii. 64 When they [asparagus plants] are older, and begin to ramify, they lose this Quality. **1842** LANCE *Cottage Farmer* 18 The roots are allowed to ramify and collect additional nourishment.

2. *intr.* To extend or spread in a number of subdivisions or offshoots analogous to branches; esp. *Anat.* of veins, nerves, etc.

1578 BANISTER *Hist. Man* VIII. 109 That [nerve] which runneth inward..ramifieng to that first Muscle. **1646** SIR T. BROWNE *Pseud. Ep.* II. v. (1672) 97 Whether..some [Corals]..were able even in their stony natures to ramifie and send forth branches. **1787** HUNTER in *Phil. Trans.* LXXVII. 419 The branches of the bronchiæ which ramify into the lungs. **1822–34** *Good's Study Med.* (ed. 4) I. 223 [Cholera] spread..to Panwell, where it ramified north and south. **1861** MAY *Const. Hist.* (1863) II. xiv. 428 Dissent had grown and spread and ramified throughout the land. **1888** BRYCE *Amer. Commw.* I. xxviii. 443 The machinery of the National government ramifies over the whole Union.

3. *intr.* To break up, divide, into branches or analogous parts.

1541 R. COPLAND *Guydon's Quest. Chirurg.* Gj b, Yet agaynwarde they ramyfye in to two partyes. **1805** W. SAUNDERS *Min. Waters* 12 A system of cylindrical vessels generally ramifying into minute branches. **1822–34** *Good's Study Med.* (ed. 4) I. 177 Esculent colic may be justly contemplated as ramifying into the three following varieties. **1856** OLMSTED *Slave States* 93 The road, which for a short distance further was plain enough, soon began to ramify.

4. *trans.* To cause to shoot out, spread, or extend after the manner of branches. (Somewhat rare in active voice; the passive is freq. in 19th c.)

1565 J. HALL *Crt. Vertue* 31 b, But we O Lorde, that be alyue, Thy prayse wyll spreade and ramifye. **1578** BANISTER *Hist. Man* v. 78 The braunches..are ramified abroad through the thinne Membran. **1620** T. GRANGER *Divine Logike* 296 The seede, or roote out of which all the specials following..are as it were procreated, and ramified. **1767** GOOCH *Wounds* I. 273 The vessels, which are ramefied in, and upon the plicatures of the *pia Mater*. **1825** MACLAREN *Railways* 27 Railways..may be ramified over a whole country. **1860** TYNDALL *Glac.* II. xxiv. 357, I have seen the internal liquefaction ramify itself like sprigs of myrtle.

5. To separate into branches or analogous divisions. Also *absol.*

1800 JEFFERSON *Writ.* (1859) IV. 313 Some of these articles are too much for one professor and must therefore be ramified. **1822–34** *Good's Study Med.* (ed. 4) I. 543 The variations of the pulse [have] been ramified into so many divisions and sub-divisions. *Ibid.* II. 105 In dividing them into two distinct sub-species,..he ramifies very unnecessarily.

Hence **ˈramifying** *vbl. sb.* and *ppl. a.*

1682 GREW *Anat. Leaves* iv. §17 The Distribution of the Threds which the Vessels compose, is not the Ramifying of Greater Pipes into Less. **1822–34** *Good's Study Med.* (ed. 4) III. 108 Fanaticism..may..rage with all the ramifying power of an epidemic. **1884** BOWER & SCOTT *De Bary's Phaner.* 62 Branch-endings of ramifying conical hairs.

ramigerous (rəˈmɪdʒərəs), *a. Bot.* [f. L. *rām-us* + -(I)GEROUS.] = RAMIFEROUS.

In recent Dicts.

†**ˈramillet.** *Obs. rare*$^{-1}$. [ad. Sp. *ramillete*.] A bouquet or nosegay of flowers.

c **1620** T. ROBINSON *Mary Magd.* 364 Faire ramillets and posies hee preepares.

ramillie (ˈræmɪlɪ). *Obs.* exc. *Hist.* Also 8 **ramallie, -ellie(s,** 8–9 **ramilie,** 9 **ramil(l)ies.** [From *Ramillies* in Belgium, the scene of Marlborough's victory in 1706.]

1. *attrib.* Applied **a.** to a wig having a long plait behind tied with a bow at top and bottom (so also with *tail*); **b.** to a method of cocking the hat.

c **1740** A. ALLEN *MS. Dict.*, Ramellies-Cock... So a Ramilie wig i. the twisted Tail Wig. **1767** STERNE *Tr. Shandy* IX. ii, Putting my uncle Toby's great ramallie wig into pipes. **1858** CARLYLE *Fredk. Gt.* v. iii. (1872) II. 83 Drinking champagne in ramilies wigs.

2. *absol.* A ramillie wig or tail.

1752 *Monthly Rev.* Feb. 121 A head of fine flaxen hair.. braided into a ramillie. **1816** SCOTT *Antiq.* xvii, Sir Arthur's ramilies being the positive, his own bob-wig the comparative. **1885** A. DOBSON *At Sign of Lyre* 118 Giving his Ramillie a whisk.

Hence **ˈramillied** *a.* = RAMILLIE 1 a.

1792 BUDWORTH *Fortn. Ramble* ii. 10 Decorated with a ramillied peruke.

ramin (ræˈmiːn). [Malay.] A tree of the genus *Gonystylus*, esp. *G. bancanus*, belonging to the family Thymelæaceæ and native to fresh-water swamps of Malaysia, Sarawak, and the Philippines; also, the light-coloured hardwood obtained from this tree.

1955 *World Timbers* (Timber Development Assoc.) III. 94 There are very large stands of ramin in Sarawak. The timber is comparatively new to the European market, the first shipment being in 1949. **1955** F. G. BROWNE *Forest Trees of Sarawak & Brunei* II. 340 *Ramin* can be sawn without difficulty. **1959** *Archit. Rev.* CXXVI. 13 The wall is pale yellow ramin, the floor maple. **1970** *Timber Trades Jrnl.* 21 Mar. 54/1 Ramin, too, is becoming more expensive and shipments increasingly extended. **1977** *Ibid.* 17 Dec. 30/1 The slight improvement in demand has helped prices in the Far East. Ramin remains rather weak, but kerning has started to firm up.

ramiparous (rəˈmɪpərəs), *a. Bot.* [f. L. *rām-us* + -(I)PAROUS.] That produces branches.

1866 *Treas. Bot.* 957/1.

ramiram, erron. form of *ramizam*, RAMADAN.

ramisection (ræmɪˈsɛkʃən). *Surg.* [f. L. *rami-*, comb. form of *rāmus* (see RAMUS) + *sectio*, *section-* cutting.] Section of some of the *rami communicantes* so as to prevent sympathetic nervous impulses from reaching some region of the body.

1924 *Med. Jrnl. Australia* 14 June 589/1 After ramisection of the second, third and fourth ganglia has been effected, the cord is divided below the fourth ganglion and the operation completed. **1930** *Lancet* 19 July 127/2 The operation of ramisection, or division of the sympathetic rami to the limbs, was devised by J. I. Hunter and N. D. Royle in the course of some experimental observations upon muscle tone in animals. **1954** E. L. FARQUHARSON *Textbk. Operative Surgery* iv. 104 The operation of pre-ganglionic rami-section came to be recommended in place of ganglionectomy for denervation of the upper limb.

ramisectomy (ræmɪˈsɛktəmɪ). *Surg.* [f. as prec., blended with -ECTOMY.] = prec.

1924 N. D. ROYLE in *Med. Jrnl. Australia* 26 Jan. 85/2 Sympathetic ramisectomy is a procedure which deals with efferent nerve fibres and prevents discharge from the central nervous system into the affected muscles. **1935** H. P. JENKINS *Terminol. of Operations* vi. 35 Section of nerve roots includes..Ramisectomy.

ramish, obs. form of RAMMISH *a.*

Ramism (ˈreɪmɪz(ə)m). [f. *Ramus* (see next) + -ISM.] The logical system of Ramus.

1710 tr. *Bayle's Dict.* (1735) IV. 842/2 Ramism had been introduced into the universities of Holland, if Scaliger and some others had not prevented it. **1882** R. ADAMSON in *Encycl. Brit.* XIV. 803 Cambridge alone..was a stronghold of Ramism.

Ramist (ˈreɪmɪst), *sb.* (and *a.*). [f. the name of *Ramus* (Pierre de la Ramée, 1515–1572) + -IST.]

A. *sb.* A follower of Ramus, as the author of a system of logic opposed in various respects to the Aristotelian.

1605 CAMDEN *Mem.* (1636) 112 To reduce surnames to a methode is matter for a Ramist. **1702** C. MATHER *Magn. Chr.* III. iii. (1852) 539 He was an acute Ramist, but yet he professed himself a lover of a Trichotomy. **1837** K. H. DIGBY *Mores Catholici* VIII. vi. 194 Petrus Ramus, to whom adhered Francis Fabricius, the poet Milton, and others, who obtained the title of Ramists, applied himself [etc.]. **1876** BOURNE *Locke* I. i. 45 At Oxford, in Locke's day, the Ramists and anti-Ramists fought out their interminable battle. **1976** *Times Lit. Suppl.* 2 July 812/4 The same idea had already been popularized on the Continent long before Bacon wrote. As McRae has pointed out, for example, the Ramists had already stressed that knowledge ought to be 'for use'.

B. *attrib.* or as *adj.* Of, pertaining to, characteristic of, Ramists or Ramism.

1852 H. L. MANSEL *Artis Logicæ Rudimenta* (ed. 2) p. xl, The mixed school represented by Keckermann, Aristotelian in matter, Ramist in method. **1863** W. C. DOWDING *Life Calixtus* vi. 40 It is the Ramist party that the allusion points to. **1882** R. ADAMSON in *Encycl. Brit.* XIV. 803 Bacon with well-grounded objection to much of the Ramist method, expounds the system of logic with unmistakable reference to the Ramist principles. **1955** D. DAVIE *Brides of Reason* 38 But Wesley's sermons could be methodized According to a Ramist paradigm.

Hence **Raˈmistic** *a.*, pertaining to Ramus or his system; also †**Raˈmistical** *a.* †**ˈRamistry**, Ramism.

1594 HOOKER *Eccl. Pol.* I. vi. §4 *margin*, Ramystry. **1627** HAKEWILL *Apol.* (1630) 261 Even Hooker himselfe (though otherwise no friend to Ramystry) acknowledgeth that it is of marveilous quicke dispatch. **1636** FEATLY *Clavis Myst.* xxi. 277 Whose day after a ramisticall dichotomy being divided into forenoone and afternoone. **1962** *Listener* 5 July 19/1 Behind Bacon stands not only the Ramistic Cambridge of his youth, but also the body of London craftsmen and scientists. **1965** K. CHARLTON *Educ. in Renaissance Eng.* v. 153 Ramistic texts..poured from the presses.

ˈram-ˈjam, *adv. dial.* and *slang.* [f. RAM *v.* + JAM *v.*] ***ram-jam full***, crammed full.

1879 WAUGH *Chimney Corner* 46 If I wur ram-jam full o' sixpences, I shouldn't feel comfortable. **1897** *Outing* (U.S.) XXX. 487/2 It's truly a royal game, ram-jam full of pluck.

ramjet (ˈræmdʒɛt). Also **ram-jet, ram jet.** [f. RAM *v.*^{1} + JET *sb.*^{3}; see also RAM *sb.*^{4} 2.] A simple

form of jet engine in which the air used for combustion is compressed solely by the forward motion of the engine. Also *attrib.* and *Comb.*
1942 in *29th Ann. Rep. U.S. Nat. Advisory Comm. Aeronaut. 1943* (1948) 407/2 An experimental investigation of an idealized ram-jet propulsion system was conducted in the..wind tunnel at the Langley Memorial Aeronautical Laboratory in March 1941. **1945** *Sci. News Let.* 17 Nov. 317/3 A ramjet motor of new and unusual design. **1947** *Sun* (Baltimore) 3 Sept. 20/7 He had been working on the development of the supersonic ram jet engine. **1948** *Times* 2 Feb. 3/2 An aerial missile driven by a 'ram-jet' engine is reported, on its first flight over the desert at Inyokern, California, to have 'far exceeded' the speed of sound. **1955** *Sci. Amer.* Jan. 38/2 Probably the simplest helicopter built so far is the Hiller Hornet. It is powered by ramjets, mounted in the tips of the rotor blades. **1957** *Jane's Fighting Ships 1957–58* 439/3 The ramjet-propelled 'Talos' is capable of engaging both supersonic and subsonic targets. **1967** M. CHANDLER *Ceramics in Mod. World* vi. 177 The ramjet engine..is little more than a plain tube with a very high-temperature fire inside it. **1974** *Encycl. Brit. Micropædia* VIII. 407/2 Ramjets work best at speeds of Mach 2..and higher. **1977** *Times* 5 Nov. 4/5 (*caption*) Five turbojet engines would power it from take-off until it reached 600 mph when five ramjet engines using liquid hydrogen fuel would take over.

‖**ramkie** ('ramki). *S. Afr.* Also **raamakie, ramkee,** etc. [Afrikaans, ad. Nama *ramgi-b*, prob. ad. Pg. *rabequinha* dim. of *rabeca* fiddle.] A stringed instrument, roughly resembling a guitar, played by the Hottentots and Bushmen of Southern Africa.
[**1790** E. HELME tr. *Le Vaillant's Trav. Afr.* II. vii. 128 The *rabouquin*..is, indeed, a kind of guittar [*sic*].] **1805** *Gleanings in Afr.* xxvii. 232 Others were busily employed in dancing to the music of the ramky, (as they call it,) and seemed highly delighted with their exertions. **1827** G. THOMPSON *Trav. & Adv. Southern Afr.* I. 391 In the evening we were entertained by a Bushwoman..playing on the *Raamakie*—an instrument about forty inches long by five broad, and having the half of a calabash affixed to one end, with strings somewhat resembling those of a violin. **1835** J. W. D. MOODIE *Ten Yrs. S. Afr.* I. 224, I have often listened with great pleasure to the wild and melancholy notes of the 'gorah' and 'ramkee'. *Ibid.* 226 The 'ramkee' is constructed on the same principle as a guitar, by stretching six strings along a flat piece of thin board, with the half of a gourd or 'calabash' at one end, over which a piece of dried skin is strained, on which the bridge is placed. It is played after the manner of a guitar; and in the hands of a skilful performer, makes no contemptible music. **1934** P. R. KIRBY *Mus. Instr. of Native Races of S. Afr.* x. 249 Another stringed instrument, the name of which is familiar to most South Africans, is the *ramkie*. **1969** J. M. WHITE *Land God made in Anger* 41 There is everything here..from the two-note whining of the Bushman *ramkie* to Schönberg. **1970** P. OLIVER *Savannah Syncopators* 109 *Ramkie, remkie*, three- or four-stringed guitar related to the Portuguese *rabequinha* brought from Malabar to South Africa and developed by the Cape Hottentots. Also *rabekin, ramakienjo, raamakie, ramki*. **1972** *Stand. Encycl. S. Afr.* V. 609/1 Besides stringed instruments, such as the *!goura* (gorah), the *!guba* and the *ramgyb* (ramkie), they [*sc.* the Hottentots] used a set of reed-pipes.

†'**ramkin.** *Obs. rare*⁻¹. A young ram.
1638 FORD *Fancies* IV. i, This ramkin hath tupp'd my old rotten carrion mutton.

Ramlila, Ram Lila ('rɑːm,liːlə). *India.* [Hindi, f. *Rām* the god Rama (cf. RAMAYANA) + *līlā* sport, deeds.] A drama, representing episodes from the *Ramayana* and commemorating the victory of Rama over Ravana, performed during the festival of Dusserah. Also *attrib.*
1880 *Encycl. Brit.* XI. 474/2 The principal religious fairs are the following:—At Bilgrám, in September, on the occasion of the *Rám Lila* festival, lasting ten days and attended by about 40,000 persons. **1894** J. C. OMAN *Great Indian Epics* I. iii. 71 A large space for the performance of the Ram Lila was kept clear by sepoys. **1935** L. S. S. O'MALLEY *Popular Hinduism* ii. 59 In North India the *Ramlila* thrills multitudes of villagers every year with the moving story of Rama and Sita. **1953** L. IREMONGER in *Caribbean Anthol. Short Stories* 20 There was a *Ram Lila*, and they went. They did not often leave their fields. But one must go to a *Ram Lila*. Dharam and Dharup dressed up..in European shirts and Indian *dhotis*. **1968** *Indian Mus. Jrnl.* V. 32 Omkar..also performed as an actor..in a Rāmlīla party. **1969** *Cultural News from India* Nov. 28 Both shows were largely attended and are now as much a part of the Delhi scene as the yearly 'Ramlila'.

ram-line. [? f. RAM *sb.*³] (See quots.)
1664 E. BUSHNELL *Shipwright* 14 A line stretched from the middle of the Sterne-Post to the middle of the Stem, called by Ship-wrightes, a Ram-line. **1711** W. SUTHERLAND *Shipbuild. Assist.* 27 A Ram-line made fast on the Stem and Stern-post, and weighed by some Device or other to steddy it. **1794** *Rigging & Seamanship* I. 8 *Ram-line*, a long line (thicker than common) used to gain a straight middle-line upon a tree or mast. **1815** BURNEY *Falconer's Mar. Dict.*, *Ram-line*, a small rope, or line, sometimes used to form the sheer of a ship, and to set the beams of the deck fair.

ramm, obs. form of RAM *sb.* and *v.*

rammadan, obs. form of RAMADAN.

rammage, -al(e: see RAMAGE, RAMMEL *sb.*¹

†**rammasche,** ? var. RAMAGE *a. Obs. rare*⁻¹.
Explained by Leyden (1801) as F. *ramassé*, collected.
1549 *Compl. Scot.* vi. 38, I herd the rumour of rammasche foulis ande of beystis that maid grite beir.

rammass, variant of RAMASS *v. Obs.*

ramme, obs. form of RAM *sb.* and *v.*

rammed (ræmd), *ppl. a.* [f. RAM *v.*¹ + -ED¹.] Forced in, beaten hard, etc.
1582 STANYHURST *Æneis* III. (Arb.) 77 With ramd cramd garbadge, theire gorges draftye be gulled. **1656** EARL MONM. tr. *Boccalini's Advts. fr. Parnass.* I. xc. (1674) 123 A Musket loaded with ram'd bullets. **1833** LOUDON *Encycl. Arch.* §753 Partitions..of rammed earth or of cob. **1859** R. THOMPSON *Gardener's Assist.* 677 The roots do not penetrate through the rammed chalk.

†'**rammee.** *Obs. rare.* Euphemism for DAMME.
1652 *Total Rout* in *Commw. Ball.* (Percy Soc.) 133 With dammees and rammees you addle his brains.

rammege, variant of RAMAGE *a. Obs.*

rammekin, obs. form of RAMEKIN.

rammel ('ræm(ə)l), *sb.*¹ Now only *dial.* Forms: 5 **ramail, -ayle, -al,** 5–6 **ramel(le,** 4–6, 9 **ramell;** 6 **rammal(e, -ald,** 6–7 **rammell,** 6–9 **rammel, -il.** [In senses 1 and 2 app. a. OF. *ramaille* branches (Godef.), f. *rame* branch. But the remaining senses are not clearly developed from these, and may really represent a different word.]
†**1.** *north.* and *Sc.* Brushwood, underwood, small trees or bushes. *Obs.*
1373 *Durh. Halm. Rolls* (Surtees) 121 Pro transgressione facta in Elden, viz. succidend' ramell'. **1513** DOUGLAS *Æneis* X. vii. 112 The hyrd..Amang the scroggy rammell settis the fyre. **1590** BUREL *Descr. Queen's Entry* in Watson *Coll. Sc. Poems* (1709) II. 1 In Tapestries ye micht persaue, Young Ramel, wrocht like lawrell treis.
attrib. **1542** *Surv. Cheviot* in *MS. Cott. Calig.* B 8, fol. 73 b, By the ryuers these growyth many allers and other rammell wood. **1549** *Compl. Scot.* vi. 37 There vas ane grene banc ful of rammel grene treis.
2. Small, crooked, or rubbishy branches, *esp.* from trees which have been felled and trimmed.
c**1420** *Pallad. on Husb.* III. 292 The ramail from the fressher bough to leson Is good. **1611** *Inv.* in *Chesh. Gloss.* (1880) s.v., It. ffyve wayne loads of Coles, some Ramell, Kids, pooles, & a stone trough. a**1796** PEGGE *Derbicisms*, *Rammel*, small spray-wood left after the cordwood, stakes, and all the larger stuff is taken out. **1886–** in dial. glossaries (W. Som., Chesh., Northumb.).
3. Rubbish of any kind.
1370–71 *Acc. Rolls Durham* (Surtees) 209 De ramell petrarum rem. de ecclesia del Magdeleynes. **1475** *Waterf. Arch.* in *10th Rep. Hist. MSS. Comm.* App. V. 312 That no..man..putte no manere dunge, ramell or fylth into the ryvere. **1569** *Chron. St. Martin's Leicester* (1866) 172 For Caryinge yᵉ stones & Rammell away where yᵉ Crosse stoode. **1616** *Nottingham Rec.* (1889) IV. 348 For..clensinge the streetes, and caryinge away the rammell..xlvijs. **1766** *Ch. Acc.* in *Rutland Gloss.* s.v., For Raming Rammil out of the church porch 6*d.* **1832** *Boston Herald* 6 Mar. 4 Some rammel which had been most improperly placed in Broad-street. **1870** E. PEACOCK *Ralf Skirl.* I. 194 Tak' that rammil [= money] back; I don't want none on it. **1877–** in dial. glossaries (Linc., Rutl., Warw., etc.).
attrib. **1433** *Fabric Rolls York Minster* (Surtees) 51 De 4*d.* de magistro Ricardo Morton pro ramelstone sibi vendito.
4. *W. Midland dial.* A hard infertile earth.
1834 *Brit. Husb.* I. 405 A grey sand, mixed with coarse clay—which the farmers call rammel. **1844** *Jrnl. R. Agric. Soc.* V. I. 80 A few inches of an unwholesome rammel, under which is a stiff marl subsoil. **1894** BARING-GOULD *Queen of Love* III. 37 The fold was apparently of 'rammel'..and grew nothing but a little stunted broom.

'**rammel,** *sb.*² *Sc.* Also **ramble.** [Of obscure origin: prob. not identical with prec.] A mixture of barley and common bear formerly sown in Fife.
1793 *Statist. Acc. Scotl.* IX. 441 (Crail). **1794** *Ibid.* XII. 531 (Markinch).

†'**rammel,** *v. rare*⁻⁰. [app. f. RAMMEL *sb.*¹ 3; but cf. Sw. *ramla* in same sense.] (See quot.)
1611 FLORIO, *Franáre*, to breake in sunder, to rammell or moulder in pieces as sometimes mud walles or great masses of stones will doe of themselues.

rammelkin, obs. form of RAMEKIN.

'**rammelly,** *a. dial.* [f. RAMMEL *sb.*¹ 4 + -Y.] Of the nature of rammell.
1879 MISS JACKSON *Shropsh. Word-bk.* **1883** GRESLEY *Gloss. Coal-mining* 199 *Rammelly*, mixed argillaceous and sandy rocks.

rammelsbergite ('ræməlzbɜːgaɪt). *Min.* [ad. G. *rammelsbergit* (W. Haidinger *Handb. der bestimmenden Mineral.* (1845) 560), f. the name of K. F. *Rammelsberg* (1813–99), German mineralogist: see -ITE¹.] An arsenide of nickel, $NiAs_2$, that occurs as white granular or fibrous masses.
1854 J. D. DANA *Syst. Min.* (ed. 4) II. 61 Rammelsbergite. .. Trimetric... Slightly ductile. **1913** [see MAUCHERITE]. **1939** [see *pararammelsbergite* s.v. PARA-¹ 2c]. **1963** [see MAUCHERITE]. **1973** SORREL & SANDSTROM *Rocks & Minerals of World* 106 Rammelsbergite..is found with loellingite, skutterudite minerals, sulfides, and other arsenides in medium-temperature veins.

rammer ('ræmə(r)). Also 6 **-ar, -or.** [f. RAM *v.*¹]
1. An instrument for ramming or beating down earth, or forcing stones into the ground, consisting of a heavy piece of wood held upright, the blow being given with the lower end.
1497 *Naval Acc. Hen. VII* (1896) 89 Paving rammers of tymbre. **1530** PALSGR. 260/2 Rammer for husbandrie. **1600** SURFLET *Countrie Farme* II. liv. 372 You may beate it [the earth] downe with a rammer of wood. **1641** BEST *Farm. Bks.* (Surtees) 107 The rest have rammers for ramminge and beatinge of the earth downe into the hole. **1766** *Museum Rust.* VI. 318 One person may be employed with a rammer, to follow five or six mowers. **1876** VOYLE & STEVENSON *Milit. Dict.* 325/2 Compressing, by means of rammers, the loose earth used in building parapets.
b. A similar implement used for other purposes; a pestle or stamp.
1643 HORN & ROB. *Gate Lang. Unl.* xxxiii. §402 They stamped it [barley] with a rough rammer in a bake house. **1755** *Gentl. Mag.* XXV. 361 Ramming them [ashes]..with a small light rammer, as tight as you can, without bursting the vatt. **1837** WHITTOCK *Bk. Trades* (1842) 254 (*Fuller*) Very heavy pointed 'rammers' fall upon the cloth. **1852** MORFIT *Tanning & Currying* (1853) 499 The skins..are beaten out with the mace, or rammer. **1879** *Cassell's Techn. Educ.* IV. 338/1 When full to the brim the salt is worked about with a short thick stick, the 'rammer'.
c. Applied in contempt to a heavy, clumsy shoe.
1810 *Splendid Follies* I. 127 If you had but a pair of pink slippers on instead of those confounded rammers.
2. A cylindrical block of wood fixed at the end of a staff, used to drive home the charge of a cannon; †the ramrod of a fire-arm.
1497 *Naval Acc. Hen. VII* (1896) 125 Rammers for gonnes. **1581** STYWARD *Mart. Discipl.* I. 44 A good and sufficient peece, flaske,..mould, rammor. **1627** CAPT. SMITH *Seaman's Gram.* xiv. 66 A Rammer is a bob of wood at the other end [of the sponge] to ramme home the Powder and the Waddings. **1669** STURMY *Mariner's Mag.* v. 68 Then with the Rammer put the Powder home gently. **1778** HUTTON in *Phil. Trans.* LXVIII. 68 The powder was forced up with only one stroke of the rammer. **1833** MARRYAT *P. Simple* (1863) 247 As the men withdrew the rammer, a shot from the enemy entered the muzzle. **1879** *Man. Artillery Exerc.* 8 Overbank carriages, jointed rammers, &c., for our siege guns.
b. A ramming instrument used in chemical experiments, or in blasting operatons.
1660 BOYLE *New Exp. Phys. Mech.* xxiii. 185 The lower end of the Glass rammer (if we may so call it). **1709** *Phil. Trans.* XXVI. 262, I ramm'd them strongly down with a Rammer, whose Basis was very little less than the Bore of the Tube. **1799** G. SMITH *Laboratory* I. 6 The rammer one diameter shorter than the mould. **1868** FAIRLEY *Gloss. Terms Coal-Mining* II, *Rammer*, an iron instrument used in filling a hole..previous to firing the powder.
†**3.** A battering-ram. *Obs. rare.*
1546 LANGLEY *Pol. Virg. De Invent.* II. vii. 47 b, The rammer called in Latin Aries wherwith walles be ouerthrowen was made by Epeus at Troye.
4. A pile-driver, or similar device.
1688 R. HOLME *Armoury* III. 480/2 A Rammer, or an Instrument to Drive Piles into the Ground. **1775** FALCK *Day's Diving Vess.* 27 The next implement was a rammer, with which the blocks were to be driven into the object. [Description follows.] **1853** J. NICHOLSON *Operat. Mechanic* (ed. 4) 313 The rammer made use of to drive piles.
5. One engaged in ramming earth.
1876 VOYLE & STEVENSON *Milit. Dict.* 326/1.
6. *attrib.* and *Comb.*, as (sense 1) ***rammer-beaten*** adj., (sense 2) ***rammer-head, rod.***
1549 *Privy Council Acts* II. 349/1 Rammers and ramer-hedes, xvj dousen. **1692** *Capt. Smith's Seaman's Gram.* II. xi. 106 Make a mark upon the Rammer-head. **1774** COOK in *Phil. Trans.* LXIV. 411 The shock forced the musket out of his hand, and broke the rammer rod. **1834** LANDOR *Exam. Shaks.* Wks. 1846 II. 276 The groundwork and religious duty not being well rammer-beaten and flinted. **1876** VOYLE & STEVENSON *Milit. Dict.* 325/2 Rammer-heads for..siege guns are not attached to the sponge staves.

rammes, rammil, obs. ff. RAMS, RAMMEL *sb.*¹

rammies ('ræmiːz), *sb. pl. Austral.* and *S. Afr. slang.* [Origin unknown: cf. RAMIE c.] Trousers.
1919 W. H. DOWNING *Digger Dial.* 41 *Rammies*, breeches. **1933** *Bulletin* (Sydney) 26 Apr. 20/1 Old Bill watched the youngest jackeroo disrobing... 'If I was you, young feller,' he said, 'I'd leave them rammies on.' **1953** T. A. G. HUNGERFORD *Riverslake* ii. 42 Elastic for the old girl's rammies. **1961** *Personality* 16 May 27 Narrow trousers have ceased to be 'drain-pipes' and are now identified..as 'rammies'.

ramming ('ræmɪŋ), *vbl. sb.*¹ [f. RAM *v.*¹ + -ING¹.] The action of the vb. in its various senses. Also with *adv.*
c**1440** *Promp. Parv.* 422/2 Rammynge, of a grownde. **1464** *Nottingham Rec.* (1883) II. 371 For makyng of holes and rammyng..iiijd. **1591** PERCIVALL *Sp. Dict.*, *Maçoneria*, ..ramming in. **1854** H. MILLER *Sch. & Schm.* ix. 177 The cry arose..'A ramming! a ramming!'.. He was poised like an ancient battering-ram, and driven headlong against the wall of the kiln. **1876** VOYLE & STEVENSON *Milit. Dict.* 325/2 Ramming is essential for the stability of the ramparts.
attrib. **1775** FALCK *Day's Driving Vess.* 27 At the top [of a rammer] was a ring to hold the ramming rope.

†**ramming,** *vbl. sb.*² ? *Obs.* [f. RAM *sb.*¹ + -ING¹.] The copulation of sheep. Only *attrib.* in ***ramming-time.***
1590 SWINBURNE *Treat. Testaments* 163 The spotted stickes being laide before Labans sheepe at the ramming time. **1607** TOPSELL *Four-f. Beasts* (1658) 487 By the behaviour of Sheep at their Rutting or Ramming time the Shepherds observe tempests.

ramming ('ræmɪŋ), *ppl. a.* [f. RAM *v.*¹]
1. *slang.* Forcible, 'go-ahead'.
1825 *Sporting Mag.* XVII. 38 The most ramming, cramming, jamming cove you ever saw perform.

2. *dial.* Very big, huge.
1864 J. C. ATKINSON *Stanton Grange* 226 He worried a great, ramming rat. **1877-** in northern glossaries.

† **'rammis,** *a. Sc. Obs.* = RAMMIST *a.*
c **1450** *Craft of Deyng* 113 in *Ratis Raving* 4 Sa mony of thir men gangis rammys.

† **'rammis,** *v. Sc.* Now *rare* or *Obs.* Also 6 -ise, -eis, 7 -ish. [prob. a back-formation from RAMMIST *a.*] *intr.* To behave frantically, to rush wildly about.
a **1585** MONTGOMERIE *Flyting w. Polwart* 511 [They] rammeist redwood, and raveld in their reeles. **1596** DALRYMPLE tr. *Leslie's Hist. Scot.* VII. 1 He began..to rammise and rin wylde. **1607** in C. K. Sharpe *Pref. Law's Mem.* (1818) 55 She maid their two Kye run mad and rammish to deid. **1808** JAMIESON, *Rammis*, to go about in a state approaching to frenzy.

rammish ('ræmɪʃ), *a.*[1] Now *dial.* Also 4-6 -issh, -yssch, etc., 6-8 **ramish**. [app. f. RAM *sb.*[1]]
1. a. Of smell, taste, etc.: Rank, strong, highly disagreeable.
c **1386** CHAUCER *Can. Yeom. Prol. & T.* 334 They stynken as a goot Hir sauour is so rammyssh and so hoot. **1562** TURNER *Herbal* II. 62 b, Sampharitik..hath a rammishe or buckishe styngkyng smell. **1657** W. COLES *Adam in Eden* cclxvii, Purging away thereby the ranke and rammish savour. **1719** D'URFEY *Pills* V. 269 Butchers..sell a lump of Ramish scent; For Weather Mutton.
b. Having a rank smell or taste.
c **1430** LYDG. *Reas. & Sens.* 3378 Whan she is hoot, Rammysh taraged as a goot. **1530** PALSGR. 322/1 Rammysshe, yll savoured as a man or beest that is to rancke. **1600** SURFLET *Countrie Farme* VII. xxii. 838 Blacke dogs.. delight most in coursing the rammish and strong sented beastes, as wilde bores, foxes [etc.]. **1677** PLOT *Oxfordsh.* 94 Cats, or such like ramish creatures. **1863** MRS. TOOGOOD *Spec. Yorksh. Dial.*, This cheese..is rather rammish. **1894** CLARK RUSSELL *Good Ship Mohock* I. 140 Open that sky-light..Its growing durned rammish down here.
c. *fig.* of persons, things, qualities, etc.
1610 *Histrio-m.* III. 310 Fat Ignorance, and rammish Barbarisme. *c* **1611** CHAPMAN *Iliad* III. Comm. (1857) 79 In this poesy, redundant I affirm him, and rammish. **1656** EARL MONM. tr. *Boccalini's Advts. fr. Parnass.* I. xxiii. (1674) 25 Those preambles, which smelt so rammish.
†**2.** ? Lascivious, lustful. *Obs.*
Perh. belongs to RAMMISH *a.*[2] (cf. sense 2 there).
1577 STANYHURST *Descr. Irel.* in *Holinshed* (1809) VI. 32 Rutting wives make often rammish husbands, as our proverb dooth inferre. **1635** QUARLES *Embl.* II. i. 29 Goe, Cupids rammish Pandar, goe.
Hence **'rammishly** *adv.*
1567 J. MAPLET *Nat. Hist.* 63 At haruest time his leaues smel rammishly, in maner like the Goate. **1623** COCKERAM I, *Hircosically*, smelling rammishly. *a* **1693** *Urquhart's Rabelais* III. xii. 95 More rammishly lascivious than a Buck.

rammish ('ræmɪʃ), *a.*[2] Now only *dial.* Also 6 -ysshe, 7-9 **ramish**. [Alteration of RAMAGE *a.*, perh. after prec., but cf. RAMMIST.]
†**1.** = RAMAGE *a.* 1. *Obs.*
1526 SKELTON *Magnyf.* 1831 My hawke is rammysshe. **1593** *Tell-Troth's N. Y. Gift* 88 The rammish hauke is tamd by carefull heed. **1653** WALTON *Angler* i. 12 The Ramish Hawk, the Haggard, and the two sorts of Lentners.
2. Wild, violent. Now only *dial.*
Perh. to some extent associated with RAM *sb.*[1]
1607 MARKHAM *Caval.* I. 67 Stond horses naturally..are exceeding rammish, & vnruely. **1807** J. STAGG *Poems* 134 What avail'd their ramish routs, Wi' Sampson leyke exertions. **1869** in *Lonsdale Gloss.*

rammish, variant of RAMMIS *v. Sc.*

rammishness ('ræmɪʃnɪs). [f. RAMMISH *a.*[1] + -NESS.] The fact or condition of being rammish.
1552 HULOET, Rammishness, *hircus.* **1591** PERCIVALL *Sp. Dict.*, *Rancioso*, rustie, ful of rammishnes. **1617** R. FENTON *Serm.* in *Treat. Ch. Rome* 107 The killing of the rammishnesse of our affections. **1660** HEXHAM, *Guelscheydt*, an unpleasant Tast,..or Smell, or Rammishnesse.

'rammist, *a. Sc.* Now *rare.* Also 5 -ysd. [? Alteration of RAMAGE *a.* Cf. also RAMMIS *a.* and *vb.*] Mad, crazy, frantic.
1456 SIR G. HAYE *Law Arms* (S.T.S.) 245 A woodman, a ramysde fule that for lytill gude wuld sett his lyf in perile. **1536** BELLENDEN *Cron. Scot.* (1821) I. 186 The residew.. come..as rammist and wod creaturis, to have revengit the slauchter of their freindis. [Still used in Orkney and Shetland dial.]
Hence †**'rammistness**, madness, frenzy. *Obs.*
1456 SIR G. HAYE *Law Arms* (S.T.S) 227 The quhilk duk ..takis a woodnes and a ramysdness in his hede.

rammy ('ræmɪ), *a.* Now chiefly *north. dial.* [f. RAM *sb.*[1] + -Y.] Characteristic of, resembling (that of) a ram; *esp.* = RAMMISH *a.*[1] 1.
1607 TOPSELL *Four-f. Beasts* (1658) 482 That Rammy humour and rank moistness which is found in the Male-sheep. **1621** BURTON *Anat. Mel.* II. ii. I. i, That rammy mutton, which is in Turkey and Asia Minor. **1652** BROME *City Wit* IV. ii, Thou rammy nastinesse. **1882-** in dial. glossaries (Yks., Lanc., Chesh.). **1884** BOURKE *Snake Dance Moquis* xxvii. 295 Herds of goats skipped nervously past us, the leader giving his rammy bleat of warning.

rammy ('ræmɪ), *sb. Sc. slang.* [? f. Sc. *rammle* row, uproar, var. RAMBLE *sb.*[1]: see *S.N.D.* s.v. *rammle.*] A brawl, a fight (esp. between gangs); a quarrel.
1935 MCARTHUR & LONG *No Mean City* iv. 45 Evidence about a 'rammy' is always conflicting, never reliable and frequently perjured. **1938** *Evening Standard* (Glasgow) 1 Apr. 17 Gallaher had the body, he was Irish, he laid out two slops in the last rammy. **1944** *Scots Mag.* Oct. 46 Not so long ago, in a dance hall rammy, a fella had laid hands on Hardy. **1967** 'H. CALVIN' *DNA Business* iv. 49, I enjoy a good rammy... I think I must have an adrenalin hunger. **1973** J. WOOD *North Beat* vi. 82 He'd had a rammy with his missus. **1977** *Time Out* 28 Jan.-3 Feb. 10/3 Still, the Villiers at Charing Cross plans a rammy where the only authentic ingredients missing will be the blood and hair on the walls.

rammyn, ramne, ramnus: see RHAMN, RHAMNUS.

rammys, obs. f. RAMS.

ramnas, var. RAMENAS.

‖**ramolade.** *Obs.* A kind of sauce for fish, made of parsley, 'chibols', anchovies, and capers, with other seasoning.
1706 in PHILLIPS. **1736** BAILEY *Househ. Dict.*, Having dress'd the fillets in a proper dish, they are to be sprinkled with this ramolade.

‖**ramollissement** (ramɔlismɑ̃). *Path.* [F., f. *ramollir* to soften: see MOLLIFY.] A morbid softening of some part of the body.
1822-34 *Good's Study Med.* (ed. 4) I. 357 *note*, The black ramollissement or disease, in which the liver is reduced to a dark-coloured mass, of very little consistence. **1880** AITKEN *Pract. Med.* (ed. 7) II. 474 In thirteen cases of ramollissement of the cerebellum..motion was greatly affected.

ramon: see RAMOON.

‖**Ramon Allones** (ra'mon a'ʎones). The proprietary name of a brand of cigar. Also *attrib.*
1907 *Yesterday's Shopping* (1969) 65/2 *Havana cigars* ..'Ramon Allones.' ('Flor fina.') **1913** *Trade Marks Jrnl.* 22 Jan. 122 Ramon Allones... Havana cigars and Havana cigarettes. Allones, Limited,..London,..cigar manufacturers. **1965** V. CANNING *Whip Hand* xv. 173 He pulled out a cigar... It was certainly Havana, and probably Ramon Allones. **1973** 'M. INNES' *Appleby's Answer* i. 11 His droopy moustache held the particular tinge of brown.. known to proceed only from the smoking of *Ramon Allones* (or would it be *Romeo y Julieta*?) cigars.

ramonda (rə'mɒndə). Also **ra(y)mondia**. [mod.L. (A. Richard in C. H. Persoon *Synopsis Plantarum* (1805) I. 216), f. the name of L. F. *Ramond* (d. 1827), French botanist and traveller + -A or -IA[1].] A small perennial herb of the genus so called, belonging to the family Gesneriaceæ, native to mountainous regions of Europe, and having hairy leaves in a basal rosette and single stems of white, pink, or violet flowers.
c **1828** B. MAUND *Bot. Garden* I. 83 (*heading*) Borage-leaved Ramonda. **1865** M. EYRE *Lady's Walks in South of France* xxiv. 267 Mrs. Nash took a small *terrine* with a *Raymondia* in it with her to Switzerland. **1907** R. FARRER *My Rock-Garden* xv. 243 Much more beautiful..to my mind, is the Queen of all Ramondias, Queen Natalie's Ramondia. **1931** *Discovery* Nov. 354/1 We stopped..at the gorge of the Treska river to collect ramondia. **1942** T. G. MANSFIELD *Alpines* i. 80 Ramonda... The name is frequently mis-spelt Ramondia. **1955** L. D. HILLS *Alpine Gardening* vii. 248 All the Ramondas like a soil that is both leafy and limy. **1971** D. BARTRUM *Rock Gardens* iii. 113 Grow Ramondas in low crevices of a rock wall.

‖**ramoneur** (ramɔnœr). [F., f. *ramoner* to sweep, f. *ramon* broom, ultimately from L. *rāmus* RAMUS.] **a.** A chimney-sweep. **b.** A machine for sweeping chimneys. Also *attrib.* **c.** A colour resembling that of soot.
1835 *Court Mag.* V. p. ii/1 Velvet and satin hats of a new colour called ramoneur (it is a dingy shade of brown, approaching nearly to black). **1859** SALA *Tw. round Clock* (1861) 39 Smoke has been merciful to Covent Garden Market, and its cornucopia is not as dingy as a ramoneur's sack. **1861** MAYHEW *Lond. Labour* II. 373 Cleansing Chimneys with the Patent Ramoneur Machine.

ramoon (rə'mu:n). Also **ramon**. [Sp. *ramon*, f. *ramo* branch; cf. prec.] The tops and leaves of a West Indian and Central American tree (*Trophis Americana*), used as fodder for cattle. Chiefly in comb. ***ramoon-tree***.
1756 P. BROWNE *Jamaica* 357 The Ramoon tree. The leaves and tops of this tree make an agreeable wholesome fodder for all sorts of cattle. **1843** *Penny Cycl.* XXV. 302/2 *T. americana*, the Ramoon-tree, is twenty feet high... The drupes are about the size of grapes, and have a pleasant flavour. **1885** *Harper's Mag.* Feb. 374/2 They go half buried under a load of ramon. (The ramon-tree serves as fodder for horses.)

ramord, variant of REMORD *v. Obs.*

ramose (rə'məʊs), *a.* [ad. L. *rāmōsus*: see RAMUS and -OSE.] = RAMOUS 1.
1689 H. MORE *Answ. Psychop.* 139 They are long, smooth, flexible Parts whereas those of Oil are more ramose. **1707** SLOANE *Jamaica* I. 66 This Fungus..begins very narrow, growing in breadth to its end, where it is flat, ramose, or deeply cut. **1804** *Phil. Trans.* XCIV. 43 Either in the form of layers, or of mamillae, or in the ramose form of stalactites. **1870** STONE *Invit. Heeded* 184 Churches..springing into vigorous ramose existence.
Hence **ra'mosely** *adv.*; † **ra'mosity** *Obs.*$^{-0}$
1656 BLOUNT *Glossogr.*, *Ramosity*, fulness of Boughes, boughiness. **1872** H. C. WOOD *Fresh-Water Algæ* 21 A gelatinous stratum..here and there ramosely divaricate.

ramoso- (rə'məʊsəʊ), combining form of prec., as in ***ramoso-palmate, -subdivided, -subpinnate.***
1846 DANA *Zooph.* (1848) 615 Erect,..irregularly ramoso-palmate. *Ibid.* 662 The viminalis..is described as ramoso-subpinnate. *Ibid.* 707 Minutely ramoso-subdivided.

ramous ('reɪməs), *a.* Now *rare.* [ad. L. *rāmōsus*: see RAMOSE and cf. F. *rameux* (16th c.).]
1. Branching, ramose: **a.** of plants, or plant-like forms. Also *fig.* of a pedigree.
1562 LEIGH *Armorie* (1597) 120 b, Genealogies discending, and Ramous. **1668** WILKINS *Real Char.* II. iv. 84 Marigold..having a ramous leavy stalk. **1676** J. BEAUMONT in *Phil. Trans.* XI. 732 A Mine, where well near all the *Entrochi*..grew tapering and ramous. **1793** SIR J. E. SMITH in *Mem.* (1832) I. 409 A very beautiful, large, ramous shrub.
b. Applied (after ancient physics) to the particles of viscous or rigid bodies.
1674 *Phil. Trans.* IX. 105 The Rigidity of the Ramous parts of the Air proceeds from the Nitro-aerial corpuscles therein infixed. **1742** *London & Country Brewer* I. (ed. 4) 38 Hops..whose Particles are active and rigid, by which the viscid ramous Parts of the Malt are much divided. **1813** T. BUSBY *Lucretius* I. II. *Comm.* p. xx, The ramous and incurvated seeds..must inlock each other universally.
2. Belonging to, characteristic of, branches.
1813 T. BUSBY *Lucretius* II. v. *Comm.* p. xxxii, They arose from the ramous friction of groves and woods. *a* **1845** HOOD *Elm Tree* II. xiv, In ramous wrestlings interlaced—A Forest Läocoon.

ramowd: see *raw-mouthed* s.v. RAW *a.*

† **ramp,** *sb.*[1] *Obs.* Also 5-6 **rampe**. [? f. RAMP *v.*[1] 4.] A bold, vulgar, ill-behaved woman or girl.
a **1450** *Knt. de la Tour* (1868) 25 A woman that dede ansuere her husbonde afore straungeres like a rampe, with gret uelonis wordes. *a* **1548** HALL *Chron.* (1809) 148 [She] was a rampe of suche boldenesse, that she would course horsses and ride theim to water. **1573** G. HARVEY *Letter-bk.* (1884) 113 An insatiable rampe, Of Messalines stampe. **1611** MIDDLETON & DEKKER *Roaring Girl* III. iii, The bouncing ramp, that roaring girl my mistress. **1728** DENNIS *Pope's Rape Lock* 16 The Author..represents her likewise a fine, modest, well-bred Lady:..And yet in the very next Canto she appears an arrant Ramp and a Tomrigg. [**1896** A. LANG *Monk Fife* 62 All men..mocked the Pucelle for a bold ramp, with a bee in her bonnet.]

ramp (ræmp), *sb.*[2] [Of obscure origin in sense 1; in sense 2 abbrev. of RAMPION; in sense 3 a back-formation from RAMPS.]
†**1.** The plant Wake Robin (*Arum maculatum*).
1548 TURNER *Names Herbes* 16 Arum is called..in english Cuckopintell, Wake Robin, or Rampe. **1578** LYTE *Dodoens* III. vii. 323. **1611** COTGR., *Iarrus*, Wake-robin,..Rampe.
2. The garden rampion. Also *attrib.*
1598 FLORIO, *Ramponzoli*, a kind of roote vsed in sallads called rampes [**1611** Rampe-rootes vsed much in salades]. **1846** MCCULLOCH *Acc. Brit. Empire* (1854) I. 105 The ramps of the garden are the roots of Campanula rapunculus. **1854** S. THOMSON *Wild Fl.* III. 305 The root of the *Campanula rapunculoides* was formerly cultivated under the name of ramps.
3. a. The wild garlic, ramsons. (See RAMPS.)
1826 SOUTHEY *Vind. Eccl. Angl.* 18 The ramp and the stinkard will continue to be as offensive and as rank, although we should dignify them by their Linnaean appellations. **1869** in *Lonsdale Gloss.*
b. *U.S.* A small, wild onion, *Allium tricoccum.* Cf. RAMPS 2.
1923 A. PRICE *Dreams* 102 A gorge of trout and hot corn pone, Mountain dew that would float a stone, All topped off by a mess of ramps. **1939** *Sun* (Baltimore) 11 Feb. 5/6 Ramps are tiny, green, onion-like bulbs that dot West Virginia's slopes each spring, taste like the food of the gods and smell..a dozen times worse than limburger cheese and burning rubber. **1952** R. BISSELL *Monongahela* iii. 40 We boys would go out on what we called the Hogback near the fort to hunt ramps. **1967** *National Observer* (U.S.) 10 Apr. 6/3 Back in the hills of West Virginia it's ramp season again. **1976** *Daily Colonist* (Victoria, B.C.) 9 Mar. 3/7 The ramps are sprouting and requests are coming in from ramp lovers in many states.

ramp (ræmp), *sb.*[3] [f. RAMP *v.*[1]] The act of ramping, in senses of the vb.
1671 MILTON *Samson* 139 The bold Ascalonite Fled from his Lion ramp. **1798** COLERIDGE *France* iii, Her arm made mockery of the warrior's ramp. **1872** BROWNING *Fifine* lxxvii, No pompous stag..with toss of horn, and brag Of bray, and ramp of hoof.
†**b.** *pl.* Romps. *Obs. rare*$^{-1}$.
1747 CARTE *Hist. Eng.* I. 325 Dunstan..breaking abruptly into the room, found him playing at ramps with his wife and her mother.

ramp (ræmp), *sb.*[4] [a. F. *rampe*, f. *ramper* RAMP *v.*[1]]
I. 1. a. A slope; an inclined plane connecting two different levels, *esp.* in fortifications. Also, *spec.* a movable slope or passageway which may be positioned to admit access to another level, as on to a boat or aeroplane.
1779 FORREST *Voy. N. Guinea* 233 A ramp of masonry was the ascent, but only to one door of this vast apartment. **1832** SOUTHEY *Hist. Penins. War* III. 419 They were employed in

..destroying the ramps of the covered way. **1881** PALGRAVE *Visions Eng.* 238 Like hornets they swarm up the ramp, Lancing a breach through the long palisade. **1893** KIPLING *Day's Work* (1898) 2 At either end rose towers of red brick, loopholed for musketry and pierced for big guns, and the ramp of the road was being pushed forward to their haunches. **1901** 'LINESMAN' *Words by Eyewitness* xii. 230 They [*sc.* animals] are then led out..down the slippery ramp, stepping gingerly, much afraid of man's extraordinary devices. **1908** *Animal Managem.* 267 The only difficulty which occurs is from the nervousness of some horses to step across or up the ramp. **1909** *Cent. Dict.* Suppl., *Ramp*, an inclined traveling platform or carrier for transferring freight from a boat to a dock or warehouse. **1938** *New Yorker* 24 Sept. 29/2 Meek-eyed parents hasten down the ramps To greet their offspring, terrible from camps. **1961** WEBSTER, *Ramp*,..the stairway by which passengers enter the main door of an airplane. **1976** *Lancs. Evening Post* 7 Dec. 1/7 They..were driving off the ramp of the landing craft type vessel when the accident happened.

b. *Railways.* (*a*) The tapering end of a conductor rail, provided to guide the collector shoe on to or off the rail. (*b*) An apparatus used to replace derailed rolling stock on the track.

1922 F. W. CARTER *Railway Electr. Traction* v. 218 Ramps are provided at the ends of each length of conductor rail, in order that the shoes may be brought to the contact surface without shock. **1926** *Chambers's Jrnl.* Aug. 539/1 The turned up edge of the ramp guides the wheels of the vehicle back to the rail... Four ramps are used, one for each wheel. **1927** R. E. DICKINSON *Electr. Trains* vii. 161 Sudden re-application of motor current occurring at ramps caused pressure surges. **1956** R. A. HAMNETT *Brit. Rail Track* iv. 191 At the ends of sections of conductor rail, ramps are provided to pick up the shoe. **1960** *Chemins de Fer* (Bureau Internat. de Documentation des Chemins de Fer) 212/3 Rerailing ramp.

c. An inclined slip road leading on to or off a main highway. Cf. OFF-RAMP. *N. Amer.*

1952 [see EXPRESSWAY]. **1965** *Tamarack Rev.* Winter 10 The town must be five or six miles off the highway and one of the county roads connects. One of these days I'll take the ramp, turn off north. **1979** *Upper Valley Progress* (Mission, Texas) 9 Aug. 1/4 Frontage road traffic shall yield the right of way to traffic..leaving an off-ramp on controlled access highways.

d. (See quots.)

1940 *Highway Engin. Terms* (*B.S.I.*) 12 *Ramp*, a short slope formed to overcome differences in level or for some other special purpose. **1961** WEBSTER, *Ramp*,..a contrivance (as of blocks or wedges of wood) laid parallel in a roadway for passing traffic over lines of hose.

e. A low platform from which competitors leave successively at timed intervals at the start of a motor rally.

1963 P. DRACKETT *Motor Rallying* iv. 57 The start was in Blackpool, from a Mille Miglia type ramp. **1971** *E. Afr. Standard* (Nairobi) 13 Apr. 1/3 There were 107 starters from the ramp outside City Hall, Nairobi, on Thursday.

2. The difference in level between the abutments of a rampant arch.

1725 W. HALFPENNY *Sound Building* 4 Raise a Perpendicular..equal to the Ramp of the Arch. **1842** GWILT *Archit.* §1943 To describe a rampant pointed arch, whose span..and the height of the ramp are given.

3. a. Part of the handrail of a stair, having a concave or upward bend (freq. continued in a knee or convex bend), as at a landing.

1778 *Encycl. Brit.* (ed. 2) I. 618/1 The manner of drawing the *ramp*, which is to rise equal to the height of the first step of the next flight. **1842** GWILT *Archit.* §2182 In the upper ramp..produce the top of the rail..to P. **1862** *Catal. Internat. Exhib.* II. XXXI. 24 Model of Stable Fittings..showing the..division railing and ramps.

Comb. **1859** *Carriage Builders' Jrnl.* I. 184/2 The iron ramp-rail,..with the stable-stall-post,..is a most neat and desirable division.

b. A slanting (straight or curved) shoulder connecting two levels of the coping of a wall. Also, the sloping part of a stair parapet.

1842 GWILT *Archit.* 1023. **1882** *Standard* 15 Apr. 2/6 Falling over the coping or ramp of the steps.

4. orig. *U.S.* The point or area at an airport where unloading and loading of aircraft takes place; the 'apron'. Freq. *attrib.*

1947 M. B. BAKER *Airline Traffic & Operations* viii. 205 We're not too bothered with other aircraft parked on the ramp. **1961** *New Scientist* 13 Apr. 15/2 On stages up to 1,000 miles in length the turboprop is equal to the jet in ramp to ramp speeds. **1971** *Daily Colonist* (Victoria, B.C.) 24 Aug. 7/1 We are flying at 33,000 feet, the outside temperature is 24 degrees and our expected ramp time in Los Angeles is..oh..about 3.30. **1974** P. S. SMITH *Air Freight* x. 399 Ramp handling is the operation of loading and unloading freight on and off an aircraft and moving it across the apron.

II. 5. *Electronics.* An electrical waveform in which the voltage increases linearly with time. Freq. *attrib.*, as **ramp function**, a mathematical expression of the shape of a ramp.

1957 J. D. RYDER *Engin. Electronics* xviii. 618 The response of the first-order system to a so-called ramp input θ_i..is also of interest. **1959** J. MARKUS *Handbk. Electronic Control Circuits* 281/1 An output pulse begins when the ramp voltage starts increasing and terminates when the ramp and signal voltages are equal. *Ibid.* 281/2 The flip-flop opens a transistor switch, allowing the ramp generator to begin generating a linearly rising voltage. **1962** HUSKEY & KORN *Computer Handbk.* xviii. 31 The stability is a function of..the stability of the ramp function itself. **1965** *Wireless World* Aug. 399 By the introduction of an integral of the ramp voltage as a feedback term it should be possible to generate an ultra-linear ramp. **1976** *Austral. Jrnl. Physics* XXIX. 187 A second phase-sensitive detector yielding a ramp-function output is used to indicate, by the positive or negative gradient of the ramp, the sense of the Doppler frequency shift, i.e. decreasing or increasing. **1980** *Sci. Amer.* Mar. 73/1 To compensate for echo decay over longer distances, receiver sensitivity is enhanced by ramp gain and a Q filter.

III. 6. *Comb.*, as **rampway** *N. Amer.*, a sloping passageway formed by a ramp between different levels.

1970 I. PETITE *Meander to Alaska* II. xi. 105 Then we walked up the long, cleated rampway to the sidewalk above. **1976** B. BOVA *Multiple Man* (1977) vi. 68 We stepped through one of these rampways into a different building.

ramp, *sb.*[5] *slang.* [f. RAMP *v.*[2] 2.] **a.** A swindle †(see also quot. 1812); *spec.* the act or practice of obtaining profit or benefit fraudulently, as by the unwarranted increase of the price of a commodity.

1812 J. H. VAUX *Vocab. Flash Lang.* in *Mem.* (1964) 261 *Ramp*, to rob any person or place by open violence or suddenly snatching at something and running off with it... A man convicted of this offence, is said to have been done for a *ramp*. This audacious *game*, is called by *prigs*, *the ramp*. **1888** *Standard* 27 June 6/1 How often do we hear people say that such-and-such a race was a fearful ramp. **1895** J. CAMINADA *Twenty-Five Years of Detective Life* 161 Watching them perform the 'ramp'—a sudden rush and bustle in which robberies are committed. **1902** *Standard* 29 Apr. 4/5 Being president of a swindle—'a ramp' they called it. **1915** *Truth* 2 June 890/2 The ramp in connection with the shares of the East Rand Amalgamated Gold Estates. **1922** *Daily Mail* 20 Nov. 8 (Advt.), Is there a coal 'ramp'? Miners, middlemen and merchants in the coal trade all blame one another for the high price of coal. **1934** R. MACAULAY *Going Abroad* xxiii. 195 If I had my way, you would sign a paper..confessing that your whole business is a ramp and a fraud. **1956** *People* 13 May 8/3 From Manchester, Glasgow and Bristol, examples of this growing ramp have reached 'The People'. *a* **1966** 'M. NA GOPALEEN' *Best of Myles* (1968) 228 You know the limited edition ramp. **1976** W. G. KERR *Scottish Capital on Amer. Credit Frontier* iii. 77 On their arrival in Dallas, Wellesley and Renshaw discovered that some serious 'ramps', or swindles, had been going on there.

b. bankers' ramp (see quot. 1932). Also *transf.*

1931 J. R. MACDONALD in *Times* 26 Aug. 12/3 We are told that this is a bankers' 'ramp', or a conspiracy, or something of the kind, against a Labour Government. **1932** *Ann. Reg. 1931* 68 Mr. Hayday..elaborated the theory of what was known in Labour circles as 'the bankers' ramp'—a financial crisis deliberately engineered for the purpose of forcing Britain to curtail its expenditure on social services, and so remove one of the chief barriers to a reduction of the wage level. **1958** *Times* 10 July 13/2 The orthodox Labour version is that the second Labour Government was broken by a 'bankers' ramp'. **1976** LD. ROBBINS *Against Inflation* (1979) xx. 98 What I hope your Lordships will agree is a pure fallacy; namely, the suggestion that what has happened recently is all a pure conspiracy, a banker's ramp and so on.

ramp (ræmp), *a. Sc.* [Of obscure origin; perh. a corrupt form of RANK *a.*, after RAMP *v.*]

1. Wanton, riotous. ***ramp rider*** = rank rider.

1715 PENNECUICK *Tweeddale* 27 When frank Miss John came first into the camp With his fierce flaming sword, none was so ramp. **1759** FOUNTAINHALL *Decis.* I. 2 (Jam.) The other a gentleman, and young, and known to be ramp. *a* **1800** in Child *Ballads* IV. 198/2 Ride out, ride out, ye ramp rider! **1819** W. TENNANT *Papistry Storm'd* (1827) 62 The mob were ramp already.

2. Strong, rank.

1824 MACTAGGART *Gallovid. Encycl.* s.v., A ramp smell, a strong smell, the smell of a he-goat. **1887** *Suppl. Jamieson's Dict.* s.v. *Let*, A barbarous, cruel method of reducing the ramp flavour of the flesh of animals.

ramp (ræmp), *v.*[1] Forms: 4–5 **raunp-**, 4–6 **raump-**, (9 *dial.* **rawmp**), 6–7 **rampe**, 4– **ramp**. [a. OF. *ramper* (12th c.) to creep, crawl, climb, of uncertain origin: cf. It. *rampare*.]

I. † 1. *intr.* To creep or crawl on the ground. *rare.*

1390 GOWER *Conf.* III. 76 A litel Serpent on the ground, Which rampeth al aboute round. *c* **1430** *Pilgr. Lyf Manhode* I. xli. (1869) 25, I make briddes flee, bestes go, fisshes swymme, dragowns raunpen. **1594** T. B. *La Primaud. Fr. Acad.* II. 409 Beastes ramping on the earth, or marching vpon all foure.

2. a. To climb, scramble. Now only *dial.*

1523 LD. BERNERS *Froiss.* I. cxci. 227 First there entred, raumpynge vppe lyke a catte, Bernard de la Salle. **1601** HOLLAND *Pliny* x. xviii, These birds will rampe up with their bellies to the tree, bending backward. **1653** URQUHART *Rabelais* I. xxiii. 106 He would..ramp and grapple after this fashion up against a window of the full height of a lance. **1886** H. CUNLIFFE *Rochdale Gloss.*, *Rawmp*, to climb or reach over things in a careless manner.

transf. and *fig.* **1578** T. PROCTER *Gorg. Gallery* P iii, One ryme too low, another rampes too hye. **1641** MILTON *Animadv.* v. Wks. (1851) 224 Surely the Prelates would have Saint Pauls words rampe one over another, as they use to clime into their Livings and Bishopricks.

b. Of plants: To climb (*up*, or *upon* some support). Now chiefly *dial.*

1597 GERARDE *Herbal* II. l. §2. 266 It rampeth vpon whatsoeuer is neere vnto it. *Ibid.* lvii. §1. 277 The great With-winde that rampeth in hedges. **1657** W. COLES *Adam in Eden* clxiv, The Vine, ramping and taking hold of any thing it meeteth with. **1691** RAY *Wisd. God* I. (1692) 102 Ramping upon Trees, Shrubs, Hedges or Poles, they [plants] mount up to a great height. **1766** *Museum Rust.* VI. 198 Black Bindweed..frequently ramps up in hedges. *Ibid.* 443 The great Bindweed which ramps in the hedges. **1877** *N.W. Lincs. Gloss.*, *Ramp up*, to climb as a plant.

c. Of non-climbing plants: To grow rankly or luxuriantly, to shoot up rapidly.

1607 [see RAMPING *ppl. a.* 4 b]. **1610** W. FOLKINGHAM *Art of Survey* I. xi. 38 Jesamines rampe vp in a rotten earth. **1733-** [see RAMPING *ppl. a.* 4 b]. **1820** CLARE *Rural Life* (ed. 3) 70 The cow-boy seeks the sedge, Ramping in the woodland hedge. **1895** *E. Anglian Gloss.*, *Ramp*,..to grow rapidly and luxuriantly. It is applied to the rank growth of plants supporting themselves. **1921** [see FLETCHERIAN *a.*]. **1959** *Listener* 29 Oct. 754/3 The schizanthus..is ramping away and will need potting.

3. a. Of beasts (real or depicted, as in *Her.*): To rear or stand on the hind legs, as if in the act of climbing; to raise the fore-paws in the air; hence, to assume, or be in, a threatening posture. (Chiefly said of lions.) Also of persons: To raise, or gesticulate with, the arms; †to clutch wildly *at*.

a **1300** *Cursor M.* 7104 A lion quilpe..Rampand to sampson he stert. *c* **1330** R. BRUNNE *Chron.* (1810) 305 þei sauh kynge's banere, raumpand þre lebardes. **14..** *Tundale's Vis.* 134 Fowle fendys ay grennyng And as wyld wolfis thei cam rampyng. *c* **1450** HOLLAND *Howlat* 416 A lyoun crovnit with gold, Of siluir ȝe se shold To ramp in array. **1549-62** STERNHOLD & H. *Ps.* xxii. 13 Like a Lyon roaring out, and ramping for his pray. **1590** SPENSER *F.Q.* I. v. 28 Their bridles they would champ, And trampling the fine element would fiercely ramp. **1641** HINDE *J. Bruen* xlvii. 151 The Bish. was glad to lay hold on the boy, ramping at the windows to have gotten out that way. **1774** J. BRYANT *Mythol.* II. 363 The lion ramped: the pard sported. **1822** W. IRVING *Braceb. Hall* xxvii. 245 My Lady Lillycraft's little dogs ramped and barked. **1883** LD. R. GOWER *Reminisc.* I. iv. 48 Above the fireplace ramps the Royal Lion of Scotland. **1922** E. R. EDDISON *Worm* xiv. 203 It stamped with its silver hoofs, flapping its wings, ramping like a lioness. **1924** R. CAMPBELL *Flaming Terrapin* v. 79 Panthers..And tigers..And lions..They ramped in the morning light. **1974** R. ADAMS *Shardik* xv. 100 Kelderek..remained constantly near the bear, observing all that it did, attentive to its moods and ways—its frightening habit of ramping from side to side in excitement or anger; [etc.].

† b. To trample in triumph. *Obs. rare*[−1].

1579-80 NORTH *Plutarch* (1595) 906 To exceede the bonds of modestie so farre, as to rampe in manner with both their feete vpon the dead, and to sing songs of victorie.

4. a. Of persons: To storm or rage with violent gestures; to act in a furious or threatening manner.

c **1386** CHAUCER *Monk's Prol.* 16 Whan she comth home she rampeth in my face, And crieth false coward, wrek thy wyf. *c* **1470** HENRY *Wallace* VII. 458 The peple beryt lyk wyld bestis..Within the wallis, rampand on athir sid. *a* **1605** MONTGOMERIE *Devot. Poems* ii. 1 Quhy doth the Heathin rage and rampe? **1642** FULLER *Holy & Prof. St.* v. xiv. 414 By this time the long dormant Usurer ramps for the payment of his money. **1648** *Regall Apol.* 39 He saw the House of Commons begin to ramp upon him. **1809** W. IRVING *Knickerb.* (1861) 168 The lion-hearted Peter roared and ramped. **1860** GEN. P. THOMPSON *Audi Alt.* III. cxli. 120 They had ramped and sworn that drawing by the tail was an 'institution'.

b. *transf.* of things. Also with *it*.

a **1605** MONTGOMERIE *Misc. Poems* xxviii. 41 Watring wauis and huge, Quhilk ramping ouer his rigging ryds. *a* **1734** NORTH *Exam.* (1740) II. Pref. 1 'Impartial' ramps it on the Title Page. **1864** H. C. COOTE *Neglected Fact Eng. Hist.* 108 Though Christianity flourished..heathenism ramped by its side. **1874** HOLLAND *Mistr. Manse* xiv. 197 Ramping from his hiding place Roared the wild Thunder.

5. † a. To go about in a loose, immodest way. *Obs.*

1530 PALSGR. 678/2, I rampe, I playe the callet. *Je ramponne. a* **1553** UDALL *Royster D.* II. iv. (Arb.) 37 Is all your..ioy In whiskyng and ramping abroade like a Tom boy. **1611** COTGR., *Gadriller*, (a wench) to raump, or play the rig.

b. = ROMP *v.* Now *dial.*

1657 [see RAMPING *vbl. sb.*[1]]. *a* **1700** B. E. *Dict. Cant. Crew*, *To Ramp*, to Play rude Horse-Play. **1720** SWIFT *Irish Feast*, They dance in a round, Cutting capers and ramping. **1741** [see RAMPING *vbl. sb.*[1]]. *a* **1825** in FORBY. **1951** DYLAN THOMAS *Poems* (1971) 206 Wherever I ramped in the clover quilts.

6. a. To bound, rush, or range about in a wild or excited manner.

1627 FELTHAM *Resolves* II. lxxxii. (1677) 333 Such wild Cattel as ramp up and down on the earth. *a* **1800** *Kempy Kay* vii. in Child *Ballads* I. 302/2 She rampit out, and she rampit in, She rampit but and ben. **1853** HAWTHORNE *Tanglewood T.*, *Minotaur* 18 The great sow had been an awful beast while ramping about the woods and fields. **1890** D'OYLE *Notches* 88 The bronchos, by 'ramping' across the storm, had found good shelter for themselves.

refl. a **1857** *Jovial Hunter Bromsgrove* in Child *Ballads* I. 212/2 The wild boar..Thrashed down the trees as he ramped him along.

b. To sail swiftly, to scud. Also with *along* and *transf.*

1872 BLACKIE *Lays Highl.* 61 The rocks..Saw thy daring Norsemen, Haco, Ramping o'er the Scottish tide! **1889** *Blackw. Mag.* CXLVI. 187/2 We were ramping along under a brilliant sun. **1933** P. A. EADDY *Hull Down* 283 *Ramp along*, sailing with all sails drawing to the wind. **1941** J. CARY *House of Children* xxxv. 153 It won't waste your time because you'll learn more too—it's a place for teaching stupid young men how to pass into the army, so you'll simply ramp along.

II. 7. *Arch.* Of a wall: To ascend or descend from one level to another. (Cf. RAMP *sb.*[4] 3 b.)

1855 *Ecclesiologist* XVI. 342 Sections of wall 'ramping' from its cornice line to the north and south extremities of the half screen. **1858** SPURDEN *Suppl. Forby* 40 A wall so formed is said to ramp. **1876** in *Surrey Gloss.*

8. a. *trans. Mil.* and *Arch.* To furnish with a ramp, to build with ramps.

1848 A. B. EVANS *Leicestersh. Words* s.v., On slopes the wall is generally so 'ramped' or 'ramped off' at intervals.

1897 LD. ROBERTS *41 Yrs. India* xlvi. (1898) 354 The banks of the numerous nullas..had to be ramped before the guns and baggage could pass over them.

b. (See quot.)

1847 HALLIWELL, *Ramp*,..(5) Bending a piece of iron upwards to adapt it to wood-work, of a gate, &c. is called ramping it.

ramp (ræmp), *v.*² [Of obscure origin.

In sense 1 perh. a misuse of prec., as Wyclif and Trevisa render L. *rapiens* and *rapax* by 'rampant'. Sense 2 may be a different word.]

†**1.** *trans.* To snatch, tear, pluck. *Obs.*

1567 GOLDING *Ovid's Met.* VIII. (1593) 206 She the gag-toothd elfe did spie,..ramping up the grasse With uglie nailes and chanking it. **1570** LEVINS *Manip.* 18/39 To rampe, *rapere.* **1626** SANDYS *Ovid's Met.* XII. 243 Amycus..down ramps A brazen cresset. **1633** J. DONE *Hist. Septuagint* 99 It is not lawfull to vexe and trouble any person ..nor rampe away his Goods by force.

2. *slang.* **a.** To rob or swindle; *spec.* to force (one) to pay a pretended bet. (Cf. RAMPER².)

1812 J. H. VAUX *Flash Dict.*, *Ramp*, to rob any person or place by open violence or suddenly snatching at something and running off with it. **1887** *Daily News* 12 Oct. 7/1 If you have seen me ticket-snatching and 'ramping' why did you not take me in charge? **1892** *Chamb. Jrnl.* 13 Aug. 517/2 The neighbour who's ramped the man that trusted him. **1897** *Daily News* 3 Sept. 3/5 Charge of 'ramping' a book-maker.

b. To search (a prisoner) in jail. Also of a prison cell. *Austral.*

1950 *Austral. Police Jrnl.* Apr. 117 *Ramp*, search a prisoner in gaol, as distinct from a search anywhere else. **1979** *Courier-Mail* (Brisbane) 2 Aug. 9/3 He heard noises from Gage's cell, but presumed the cell was being 'ramped' (searched).

ramp, *v.*³ *Obs.* exc. *dial.* Also 6 **raumpe**. [Imitative.] *trans.* To eat greedily or noisily.

1542 UDALL *Erasm. Apoph.* 73 Ye maye take some parte, with me, were my woordes, and not to raumpe them vp on that facion. **1894** *Northumbld. Gloss.*, *Ramp*, to eat with a gnashing sound.

ram'pacious, *a. rare.* [var. *rampageous*, as if f. RAMP *v.*¹ + -ACIOUS.] = RAMPAGEOUS.

1837 DICKENS *Pickw.* xxii, A stone statue of some rampacious animal with flowing mane and tail, distantly resembling an insane cart-horse. **1894** *Daily News* 20 Apr. 5/4 A dog and a cat and three rampacious children.

ram'paciously, *adv. rare.* [f. RAMPACIOUS *a.* + -LY².] In a rampacious or unruly manner.

1915 V. O'CONNOR *Mary's Meadow Papers* x. 127 During such a wet summer the grass had grown rampaciously.

rampage (ræm'peɪdʒ, 'ræm-), *sb.* [f. the vb.] A state of excitement or violent passion; the act of behaving or rushing about in a reckless or riotous fashion; esp. in phr. ***on the rampage*** and in U.S. colloq. phr. ***to ride (a) rampage***. Also *fig.*

1861 DICKENS *Gt. Expect.* ii, She's been on the Ram-page this last spell, about five minutes. **1872** BLACK *Adv. Phaeton* xi. 147 She leaves his charming society to go off on a wild rampage through the country. **1891** *Spectator* 10 Oct. 487 The Irish Members..think a rampage will guarantee their seats. **1906** 'MARK TWAIN' in *Harper's Mag.* Aug. 335 The raven..sets on her shoulder often when she rides her breakneck rampages. **1927** H. CRANE *Let.* 19 Dec. (1965) 313 Her drunken and exclamatory rampage through *Edificios Blancos* [*sc.* H. Crane's *White Buildings*]. **1955** *Times* 29 Aug. 10/5 Mr. Jack Warner, representing Scotland Yard, is indeed a comfort to have at hand when Things are on the rampage. **1967** *Boston Sunday Herald* 2 Apr. (T.V. Mag.) 57/1 A gang on a rampage through Matt Dillon's territory.

rampage (ræm'peɪdʒ), *v.* Also 9 *Sc.* **-auge**. [Orig. *Sc.*, of obscure formation, but perh. based on RAMP *v.*¹ The stressing '*rampage* also occurs.]

1. *intr.* To behave violently or furiously; to storm, rage wildly.

1715 RAMSAY *Christ's Kirk Gr.* II. xvii, His wife did reel, And rampage in her choler. *c* **1720** —— *Marriage of Earl Wemyss* xii, Were Jove rampaging in the air. *a* **1784** Ross *Helenore* (1789) 64 He rampaged red wood, And lap and danc'd, and was in unco mood. **1824** SCOTT *Redgauntlet* let. xi, He came down here, rampauging like a lion. **1898** J. ARCH *Story of Life* ix. 232 He rampaged like a lunatic, and fairly lost his head.

2. To go about in an excited, furious, or violent manner; to rush wildly hither and thither.

1808 J. MAYNE *Siller Gun* IV. 137 Friends feghting friends, rampaged about. **1831** GEN. P. THOMPSON *Exerc.* (1842) I. 360 Our sailors would have been 'rampaging' over the world. **1861** DICKENS *Gt. Expect.* ii, She made a grab at Tickler, and she Ram-paged out.

transf. **1892** HUXLEY in *Life* (1900) II. xx. 331, I hear you have influenza rampaging about the Camp.

3. *trans.* To rampage about or over (a place).

1905 E. M. ALBANESI *Brown Eyes of Mary* i. 7 Where is the beast now? Is she rampaging the premises?

Hence **ram'paging** *vbl. sb.* and *ppl. a.*

1824 SCOTT *Redgauntlet* ch. xi, There was a set of rampauging chields in the country then that they called rebels. **1876** F. E. TROLLOPE *Charming Fellow* II. iv. 63 Religion is one thing and rampaging is another.

rampageous (ræm'peɪdʒəs), *a.* Also **-ious**. [f. RAMPAGE *sb.* + -OUS.]

1. Violent; unruly; boisterous.

1822 GALT *Provost* xv. 115 The primitive ages of a rampageous antiquity. **1840** MRS. F. TROLLOPE *Widow Married* xxiii, She must be careful not to be too frolicsome and rampageous. **1888** MRS. H. WARD *R. Elsmere* I. v, A rampagious class of hundreds of Scotch lads.

2. *transf.* Glaring, outrageous.

1889 *Harper's Mag.* LXXIX. 200 The ornamentation is for the most part rampageous rocaille style.

Hence **ram'pageously** *adv.*; **ram'pageousness**.

1840 LADY C. BURY *Hist. of Flirt* xxiii, He swears so rampageously, it upsets me. **1883** *St. James's Gaz.* 19 May 5 They..have good cause for rampageousness.

rampair(e, obs. variants of RAMPIRE.

†**ram'pallion.** *Obs.* Also 6-7 **-alion**, 7 (9) **-allian**. [Perh. based on RAMP *v.*¹ Cf. *rapscallion, tatterdemallion.*] A ruffian, villain, scoundrel.

1593 NASH *4 Lett. confut. Strange Newes* I, Pocket not up this abuse at a rakehell rampalions hands. **1613** BEAUM. & FL. *Honest Man's Fortune* II. i[i], Out upon them rampallions. I'll keep my self safe enough out of their fingers. **1639** R. DAVENPORT *New Trick to Cheat Devil* I. ii, And bold Rampallion like, swear and drinke drunke. **1822** SCOTT *Nigel* xxvi, I was almost strangled with my own band by twa rampallians.

b. Applied to a woman. *rare*⁻¹.

1602 S. ROWLANDS *Greene's Ghost* D 3 Here was..an aged Rampalion put besides her schoole-tricke.

rampancy ('ræmpənsɪ). [f. next: see -ANCY.] The fact or condition of being rampant.

1664 H. MORE *Exp. 7 Epist.* Pref. b iv b, The Temporal Power being quite in a manner evacuated by the Rampancy of the Spiritual. **1699** COLLIER *2nd Def. Short View* (1730) 373 Is Rampancy and Lewdness the Character of Breeding? **1844** DICKENS *Mart. Chuz.* viii, He may be said to have exhibited, at the moment, a sort of moral rampancy himself. **1892** H. R. REYNOLDS in *Life* (1828) xix. 468, I am considerably moved by the rampancy of much of this Old Testament criticism.

rampant ('ræmpənt), *a.* (*sb.*) Also 5 **raump-**; 4-6 **-aunt**, (5 **-awnt**), 5-6 **-and**. [a. F. *rampant*, pres. pple. of *ramper* RAMP *v.*¹

By Wyclif and Trevisa inaccurately employed to render L. *rapiens* and *rapax*. In northern Eng. and Sc. prior to 1600 *rampand* is properly the pres. pple. of RAMP.

In early use freq. placed after the sb., as in French; now only in *Her.*, or with suggestion of this.]

A. *adj.* **1.** Of beasts, esp. lions: Rearing or standing with the fore-paws in the air.

1382 WYCLIF *Ps.* xxi. 14 Thei openeden vp on me ther mouth; as a leoun rampaunt [L. *rapiens*] and rorende. ? **14..** *Leg. Rood* 145 þe deuel stod lyk A lyon raumpaunt. **1509** HAWES *Past. Pleas.* XVIII. (Percy Soc.) 79 Rampande lyons stode up wondersly. **1601** HOLLAND *Pliny* VIII. xvi, When he chaseth and followeth after other beasts, hee goeth alwaies saltant or rampant. **1667** MILTON *P. L.* VII. 466 The Tawnie Lion..Rampant shakes his Brinded main. **1735** SOMERVILLE *Chase* I. 196 Then on their Haunches rear'd, rampant they seize Each other's Throats. **1876** GEO. ELIOT *Dan. Der.* I. vi, Careful how he moved his lion paws lest he should crush a rampant..mouse.

transf. **1698** FRYER *Acc. E. India & P.* 52 The one part of them wearing naked Swords rampant in one Hand.

Comb. **1852** MUNDY *Antipodes* (1857) 185 The rampant-looking rocks of the 'Cavallos'.

b. *spec.* in *Her.* 'Standing on the Sinister hind-leg, with both forelegs elevated, the Dexter above the Sinister, and the head in profile' (Cussans).

14.. *Sir Beues* 177/3480 (M.) Syr Beuys bare of colour poymant A rede lyon of golde rampant. **1562** LEIGH *Armorie* (1597) 45 You must note heere the difference [of] the Lyon rampande, and this Lyon [saliant]. **1593** SHAKS. *2 Hen. VI*, v. i. 203 Old Neuils Crest, The rampant Beare chain'd to the ragged staffe. *a* **1667** COWLEY *Ess., Agric.* Wks. 1710 II. 709 Lillies, and Lions Rampant, and Spread Eagles in Fields d'Or. **1724** RAMSAY *On Royal Comp. Archers* 21 Well pleas'd the rampant Lyon smooths his mane. **1814** SCOTT *Wav.* xi, The chosen crest of our family, a bear, as ye observe, and rampant.

transf. **1633** T. ADAMS *Exp. 2 Peter* iii. 12. 1346 God is no Iudge Dormant, nor Demurant, nor Rampant. **1641** BROME *Joviall Crew* II. Wks. 1873 III. 376 Couchant and Passant, Guardant, Rampant Beggars.

c. Given to ramping; of a fierce disposition.

1387 TREVISA *Higden* (Rolls) IV. 447 Bestes rampaunt [L. *rapaces*] spare her owne kynde. **1579** SPENSER *Sheph. Cal.* July 21 The rampant Lyon hunts he fast, With dogges of noysome breath. **1641** J. JACKSON *True Evang. T.* I. 66 To make the condemnation of these ravenous Wolves, and Lion rampants, more just.

d. Exhibiting fierceness or high spirits by ramping or similar movements. Also const. *with.*

a **1529** SKELTON *Agst. Scottes* 135 The Whyte Lyon, there rampaunt of moode, He ragyd and rent out your hart bloode. **1684** BUNYAN *Pilgr.* II. 155 The Monster at first was very Rampant and looked upon these Enemies with great Disdain. **1748** THOMSON *Cast. Indol.* II. lviii, The younglings frisk along the meads..Rampant with life. **1843** *P. Parley's Ann.* IV. 235 A wild boar, rampant from a forest.

2. *transf.* **a.** Of persons: Violent and extravagant in action, opinion, etc. (esp. in the manner implied by the sb.).

1628 EARLE *Microcosm., Player* (Arb.) 42 He is tragicall on the Stage, but rampant in the Tyring-house, and sweares oathes there which he neuer con'd. **1709** in Hearne *Collect.* (O.H.S.) II. 324 *note*, The Whiggs are rampant, and thinke to carry all before them. **1848** THACKERAY *Bk. Snobs* xvii, The English Snob rampant always does this to the present day. **1858** HAWTHORNE *Fr. & It. Note-bks.* II. 137 The crowd has not spirit and self-consciousness enough to be rampant. **1877** DAWSON *Orig. of World* xiii. 264 Some very rampant theorists of some ethnological schools.

b. Of things: Unchecked, unrestrained, aggressive, etc.; *esp.* of a quality, belief, state of things, etc.: Having full sway or unchecked course in the individual or (more commonly) in general society.

1619 SIR R. NAUNTON in *Fortescue Pap.* (Camden) 95 In whom theyr hope is now growen rampant. **1642** FULLER *Holy & Prof. St.* v. xviii. §4 It grieved him to see ignorance and impiety so rampant. **1673** GREW *Acc. Veget. Roots* §66 The Sulphureous or Oyly Parts, which were before concentred, are now more or less rampant. **1718** *Wodrow Corr.* (1843) II. 392 The great thing I fear..is, that Arianism turn rampant. **1795-7** SOUTHEY *Juvenile & Minor Poems* Wks. 1838 II. 227 Iniquity abounds, and rampant Vice..taints The herd of humankind. **1856** KANE *Arct. Expl.* I. xvi. 186 The tide was low, the ice rampant. **1877** MRS. OLIPHANT *Makers Flor.* ii. 31 This curious outbreak of rampant democracy.

†**3.** Lustful; vicious. *Obs.*

c **1680** BEVERIDGE *Serm.* (1729) I. 36 Lest his body should grow rampant..the church orders him to fast. **1732** FIELDING *Miser* IV. xiv, The young fellows of this age are so rampant, that even degrees of kindred can't restrain them. **1812** H. & J. SMITH *Rej. Addr., Archit. Atoms*, The rampant lessons of the stews.

4. Of plants or their growth: Rank, luxurious.

1764 *Museum Rust.* II. 298 Where a fine sheep-walk is wanted, the sweeter and less-rampant grasses will, of course, be chosen. **1796** C. MARSHALL *Garden.* xvi. (1813) 271 A rich [soil]..makes them [nasturtiums] too rampant and less fruitful. **1867** D. G. MITCHELL *Rural Stud.* 34 Its rampant growth will cover your trellised porch in a pair of seasons.

5. *Arch.* Of an arch or vault: Having the abutments or springing lines on different levels.

1725 W. HALFPENNY *Sound Building* 5 To draw a Rampant Semicircular Arch. **1842** GWILT *Archit.* §1943 To draw a rampant pointed arch, whose span,..and the height of the ramp are given.

†**B.** *sb.* = RAMP *sb.*¹ *Obs. rare*⁻¹.

1671 *Prol. to Shadwell's Humorists*, These Rampants have a hungry Worm indeed.

rampantly ('ræmpəntlɪ), *adv.* [f. prec. + -LY².] In a rampant manner.

1426 LYDG. *De Guil. Pilgr.* 12760 Rampawntly she gan to go Vn-to me-ward, off cruelte. **1697** COLLIER *Immor. Stage* vi. (1730) 183 Their Songs are often rampantly lewd. **1897** *Atlantic Monthly* Oct. 546 A town so rampantly democratic.

rampar, var. RAMPER¹, obs. var. RAMPIRE.

rampart ('ræmpɑːt), *sb.* Also 6 **-arte**, **-arde**, **-erd**, 6-7 **-ard**, 7 **-ert**. See also RAMPIRE *sb.* [ad. F. *rempart*, †*rempard*, *rampart*, etc. (16th c.), f. *remparer* RAMPIRE *v.*]

1. *Fortif.* A mound of earth raised for the defence of a place, capable of resisting cannon-shot, wide enough on the top for the passage of troops, guns, etc., and usually surmounted by a stone parapet.

1583 STOCKER *Civ. Warres Lowe C.* IV. 64 b, This daie was begunne a Rampart, at Northe newe Gate. **1585** T. WASHINGTON tr. *Nicholay's Voy.* I. viij. 7 b, Strong walles, ramperdes, ditches. **1641** EARL MONM. tr. *Biondi's Civil Warres* v. 134 The Rampard betweene the two townes was covered with blood. **1667** MILTON *P. L.* I. 678 To trench a Field, Or cast a Rampart. **1774** PENNANT *Tour Scotl. in 1772*, 91 The camps united to each other by a rampart. **1777** WATSON *Philip II* (1839) 233 The fort of Sparendam, the rampart of which stood on the dyke along which the troops must pass. **1810** [see 3]. **1880** OUIDA *Moths* II. xvii. 235 It was rather a rampart than a terrace, and the waves beat and fretted the wall below.

transf. and *fig.* **1611** BIBLE *Nahum* iii. 8 That had the waters round about it, whose rampart was the sea. **1675** TRAHERNE *Chr. Ethics* 185 As the laws are the rampart of mens estates, justice is the rampart of the law. **1748** GRAY *Alliance* 96 The rocky ramparts round they see. **1818** SHELLEY *Rev. Islam* VI. xi, Flesh and bone Soon made our ghastly ramparts. **1867** SMILES *Huguenots Eng.* x. (1880) 159 Louis XIV..could not prevail against the impenetrable rampart of conscience.

2. *Canad.* A steep bank of a river or gorge. Usu. *pl.*

a **1853** R. CAMPBELL *Two Journals* (retyped from MS, Vancouver Publ. Libr.) 112 Yesterday and today we have been passing through what they call the ramparts—rocks and steep banks along the river. **1921** W. A. FRASER *Red Meekins* I. iii. 32 Cast high on a rampart by a thrust of the waters lay the stern half of their canoe. **1940** *Beaver* June 29/1 After forty miles more came to the ramparts, a large canyon or gorge where for seven miles the river flows between perpendicular cliffs of limestone from one hundred to two hundred feet high. The channel is very deep here —three hundred feet in places. **1973** D. ANDERSEN *Ways Harsh & Wild* i. 48 Here in the upper ramparts there were steep cliffs and mountains rising on each side of the river.

3. *attrib.* and *Comb.*, as ***rampart-base***, ***communication***, ***-height***, ***-line***, ***-walk***.

1799 CAMPBELL *Pleas. Hope* Wks. (1837) 13 On the rampart-heights array'd His trusty warriors. **1810** WELLINGTON in Gurw. *Desp.* VI. 11 To fill up the rampart in the bastions, and to make a good rampart communication from both. **1852** TENNYSON *Ode Wellington* 105 The vast designs Of his labour'd rampart-lines. **1915** G. FRANKAU *Tid'apa* v. 25 Green-dark to the rampart-bases, save where, like a wild beast's eye One red light glowered and glimmered in the shadow-tracery, stretched jungle. **1923** R. G. COLLINGWOOD *Roman Britain* ii. 30 Along the top [of Hadrian's wall] was a rampart-walk, patrolled by the sentries, and reached by stairs either at a fort, a milecastle, or a turret.

rampart ('ræmpɑːt), *v.* [f. prec.] *trans.* To fortify or surround with, or as with, a rampart.

Orig. only in ppl. form, perh. directly from the sb.

1585 T. WASHINGTON tr. *Nicholay's Voy.* II. x. 44 The castle..ramparded & ditched. **1611** SPEED *Hist. Gt. Brit.* IX. xv. §57. 792 A Field well trenched, and ramparted with strong Gates. **1796** COLERIDGE *Ode Departing Year*, Those glittering dells Proudly ramparted with rocks. **1822** LAMB *Elia* Ser. I. *Distant Corr.*, I stood ramparted about with so many healthy friends. **1882** G. MACDONALD *Castle Warlock* I. i. 9 The hills that ramparted the horizon.

Hence **'ramparted, 'ramparting** *ppl. adjs.*

1837 CAMPBELL *On the Camp Hill* in *Poems* 297 The ramparted ground With a vision my fancy inspires. **1850** BROWNING *Christmas Eve* iv, The ramparted cloud-prison, ..built up in the West. **1881** F. T. PALGRAVE *Vis. England* 250 The ramparting rocks their darkness uprear.

rampauge, Sc. variant of RAMPAGE.

rampeare, obs. variant of RAMPIRE.

ramped (ræmpt), *ppl. a.* [f. RAMP *v.*[1] 8.] Made with a ramp or rise.

1825 J. NICHOLSON *Operat. Mechanic* 604 Hand-railing.. whether ramped, swan-necked,..or wreathed. **1833** LOUDON *Encycl. Archit.* §752 A cast-iron ramped cap..to the partition between the stalls. *Ibid.*, The ramped iron copings.

†**'rampen**, *v. Obs. rare.* [? cf. G. *rampeln*, *rempeln* to push, shove.] *trans.* To force, ram.

13.. *Propr. Sanct.* (Vernon MS.) in *Archiv neu. Spr.* LXXXI. 84/109 Þe Rode-tres þei liften vp anon, Rampned hit harde in a ston. *Ibid.* 84/117 Vre Cake on Crois þei knede Rampned hit harde aȝeyn þe Roode.

ramper[1] ('ræmpə(r)). *dial.* Also 8 rampar. [Prob. a corruption of LAMPREY.] **a.** The lamprey. Usu. *ramper-eel.* **b.** (see quot. 1865.)

1792 *Statist. Acc. Scotl.* IV. 217 *note*, These spotted eels are called Rampar Eels. **1818** R. JAMIESON *Notes Burt's Lett.* I. 122 The ramper-eel, lamprey, or nine eyes, is held in abhorrence. **1865** J. COUCH *Brit. Fishes* IV. 408 *Myxine*. Hagfish. Ramper eel. Poison Ramper. **1894** *Northumbld. Gloss., Ramper* [N.], the lamprey.

ramper[2] ('ræmpə(r)). [f. RAMP *v.*[2] + -ER[1].] One who ramps; *spec.* (see quot. 1887.)

1819 *Sporting Mag.* V. 123 The cup-and-ball Macers, the Nob-Pitchers, and the Rampers. **1886** *Gd. Words* 247 A 'ramper'..is engaged with other roughs to get up the disturbances, under which 'welshers' seek to..secure their retreat. **1887** *Daily News* 12 Oct. 7/1 He knew the prisoners as 'rampers', i.e. men who claimed to have made bets to bookmakers, and hustled and surrounded them if they refused to pay.

ramper, obs. or dial. var. RAMPIRE.

ramperd, -ert, obs. ff. RAMPART.

ramphoid, var. RHAMPHOID.

rampiar, obs. f. RAMPIRE.

rampick ('ræmpɪk), *a. Obs.* exc. *dial.* Also 6–7 ran-, 9 *dial.* raun-; 6 ranpike. [Of obscure origin: cf. RAMPIKE.] Of a tree or bough: Partially decayed or dead; bare of leaves or twigs.

1593 DRAYTON *Ecl.* i. 23 Rowland, leaning on a Ranpike Tree. [*Margin.* A tree with age beginning to decay at the top.] **1594** BARNFIELD *Affect. Sheph.* xxvii, When their fleeces gin to waxen rough, He combs and trims them with a rampicke bough. **1627** DRAYTON *Agincourt*, etc. 181 The night-Crow sometimes, you might see, Croking to sit vpon some Ranpick-tree. **1881** *Leicestersh. Gloss., Raunpick*, bare of bark or flesh, looking as if pecked by ravens.

So **'rampicked** *a.* = RAMPIKED.

1836 WILBRAHAM *Chesh. Gloss.*, A Rampicked tree is a stag-headed tree.

rampier, variant of RAMPIRE.

rampike ('ræmpaɪk). *dial.* and *N. Amer.* Also 9 ran-, raun-. [Of obscure formation: the second element may be PIKE. Cf. RAMPICK.] A decaying or dead tree; a spiky stump or stem of a tree. Also *attrib.*

1853 S. STRICKLAND *Twenty-Seven Years in Canada West* II. 198 The recently burnt fallow, with its blackened stumps and rampikes did not contribute much to improve the landscape. **1865** in *Warwicksh. Gloss.* (1896) *Ranpike* or *Raunpike*, a tree beginning to decay at the top from age, and having bare dead branches in consequence. **1881** W. F. RAE *Newfoundl. to Manitoba* iii. 93 The sight of these bare and lifeless poles is a common one here; the poles are termed 'rampikes'. **1894** PHILLIPPS-WOLLEY *Gold, Gold in Cariboo* 90 Cruel fire-hardened rampikes, which tore the skin to rags. **1908** C. MAIR *Through Mackenzie Basin* 146 The 'rampike' country would be..converted from a burnt-wood region to a bare one. **1936** J. MASEFIELD *Letter from Pontus* 19 With blackened rampikes from old forest fires. **1955** *Jrnl. Canad. Ling. Assoc.* Oct. 6 Apparent survivals from various Scottish and English dialects, such as *bultow*, *drake*, *glitter*, *knap*, *rampike*. **1961** R. M. PATTERSON *Buffalo Head* vi. 220 There they stood—three gaunt, upstanding rampikes of charcoal with the humus burnt away from their roots.

Hence **'rampiked** (8 ran-, 9 rawn-) *a.*, of the nature of a rampike.

1775 T. CAMPBELL *Diary* in Napier *Johnsoniana* (1884) 246 The trees were stunted and ranpiked, as they call it in Ireland. **1875** T. E. PAGET *Student Penitent* vii, One of the old oaks in his park—erect and majestic even in decay, though scathed and rawnpiked and leafless.

†**rampin.** *Obs. rare.* In 5 -yn. [obs. F. (in Godef. from *Melusine* only).] A kind of ship.

c **1500** *Melusine* 117 The Rampyn then, or Caruell, saylled thither. *Ibid.* 168 He made a rampyn or smal galeye.

ramping ('ræmpɪŋ), *vbl. sb.*[1] [-ING[1].] The action of RAMP *v.*[1] in its various senses.

1580 HOLLYBAND *Treas. Fr. Tong, Grimpure*, a ramping or grasping. **1656** JEANES *Mixt. Schol. Div.* 20 His very ramping and roaring might terrify him, that is farre enough out of his reach. **1657** G. THORNLEY *Daphnis & Chloe* 53 That wanton, untoward, malepert ramping and hoytie-toitie which he kept in the grove. **1741** RICHARDSON *Pamela* (1824) I. cii. 490 An over-free, and even indecent degree of ramping, as it is called. **1870** DICKENS *E. Drood* vi, Swaggering fighting men had had their centuries of ramping and raving about Minor Canon Corner.

'ramping, *vbl. sb.*[2] (See quot. and RAMP *v.*[2])

1830 LYTTON *Paul Clifford* I. viii. 150 Before this initiatory process, technically termed 'ramping'..had reduced the bones of Paul..to the state of magnesia, [etc.]. **1891** *Times* 16 Oct. 8/4 The trick..was technically known in sporting circles as 'ramping', which had been extensively practised during the past season on bookmakers.

ramping ('ræmpɪŋ), *ppl. a.* (and *adv.*) [-ING[2].] That ramps, in senses of RAMP *v.*[1]

The obs. northern and Sc. form *rampand* may also be taken as a variant of RAMPANT.

†**1.** Creeping, crawling. *Obs. rare*[−1].

c **1440** *Bone Flor.* 845 Syr Garcy went crowlande for fayne, As rampande eyen [?] do in the rayne.

2. Of beasts: Standing erect, rearing, showing fierceness.

1382 WYCLIF *Gen.* xlix. 27 Beniamyn, a wulf raumpynge. **1509** HAWES *Past. Pleas.* XXXIII. (Percy Soc.) 162 A rampynge lyon of fyne golde so pure. **1596** SHAKS. *1 Hen. IV*, III. i. 153 A couching Lyon, and a ramping Cat. **1743** WESLEY *Wks.* (1872) XIII. 191 The mob..were as so many ramping and roaring lions. **1862** G. MEREDITH *Mod. Love* I, Thundering like ramping hosts of warrior horse.

fig. **1850** BLACKIE *Æschylus* II. 238 Lest our pride of ramping riches kick our sober weal in the dust.

3. Of persons, their actions, etc.: Violent, extravagant, unrestrained; †romping.

1483 CAXTON *G. de la Tour* B vj, Wymmen that ben chydars and rampynge. **1582** STANYHURST *Æneis* III. (Arb.) 88 With ramping bounce clapping..Fierce the waters ruffle. **1595** SHAKS. *John* III. i. 122 What a foole art thou, A ramping foole, to brag, and stamp, and sweare, Vpon my partie! **1675** E. PHILLIPS *Theat. Poet.* Pref. ** 8 A style not ramping, but passionately sedate and moving. **1697** VANBRUGH *2nd Pt. Æsop* ii. 237 I've a great ramping daughter, that stares like a heifer. **1745** J. MASON *Self-Knowl.* I. xiv. (1853) 106 The maddest Sallies and the most ramping Reveries of the Fancy. **1876** BLACKIE *Songs Religion & Life* 241 Race not with a ramping might. **1891** HANNAH LYNCH *G. Meredith* 86 The wild ramping life of the colonies.

4. † **a.** Climbing, clasping. *Obs. rare*[−1].

1578 LYTE *Dodoens* IV. xx. 475 Foure or fiue griping or ramping claspers, whereby the Pease doth take holde.

b. Growing luxuriantly. Now *dial.*

1607 *Barley-Breake* (1877) 28 A Pipe made of a ramping Oate. **1733–4** MRS. DELANY *Lett., to Mrs. A. Granville* 428 White ground with great ramping flowers in shades of purples, reds, and greens. **1821** CLARE *Vill. Minstr.* I. 203 Picking from the ramping grass Nameless blossoms as I pass. **1829** —— *Ode to Autumn*, With ramping sallows lined, and crowding sedge.

5. As *adv.* Exuberantly. *rare*[−1].

1886 J. M. CAULFEILD *Seamanship Notes* 2 These sails are to be ramping full.

rampion[1] ('ræmpɪən). [Prob. ad. some form of the Romance name, which appears as F. *raiponce* (†*reponce*, etc.), Sp. *reponche*, *ruiponce*, Pg. *ruiponto*, etc., It. *rap-*, *ramponzolo*; cf. G. *rapunzel*. The etym. of these forms is obscure: connexion with L. *rāpum* RAPE *sb.*[5] is doubtful.]

1. A species of bellflower, *Campanula Rapunculus*, of which the white tuberous roots are sometimes used as a salad.

1573 TUSSER *Husb.* (1878) 94 Herbes and rootes for sallets and sauce..Radish..Rampions. Rokat. **1578** LYTE *Dodoens* V. xxxv. 597 The litle Rampion flowreth in June and July. **1622** DRAYTON *Poly-olb.* xx. 60 The Rampion rare..the hardly gotten Gourd. **1725** BRADLEY *Fam. Dict.* s.v. *Saller*, Others mingle Endives, Succory and Rampions without Distinction. **1785** MARTYN *Rousseau's Bot.* xvi. (1794) 187 Rampion, which was formerly cultivated for its roots to eat in sallads. **1820** L. HUNT *Indicator* No. 28 (1822) I. 224 The rampions grew so thickly. **1883** *St. James's Gaz.* 20 Dec. 2/2 The rampion..with its roots shining as ivory and its flavour recalling the filbert.

2. A plant of the genus *Phyteuma.*

1760 J. LEE *Introd. Bot.* App. 324 Rampions, Horned, *Phyteuma*. **1790–1820** SOWERBY *Eng. Bot.* VI. 6 Spiked Rampion, *Phyteuma spicatum*. *Ibid.*, Round-headed Rampion, *Phyteuma orbiculare*. **1882** G. ALLEN *Colour of Flowers* iv. 73 The rampions (*Phyteuma*) vary from blue to white; so do many of the campanulas.

†**3.** The Lobelia. *Obs.*

1733 MILLER *Gard. Dict.* s.v. *Rapuntium*, Greater Rampions with a Crimson-spiked Flower, commonly call'd the Scarlet Cardinal's Flower. **1760** J. LEE *Introd. Bot.* App. 324 Rampions, Crested, *Lobelia*.

†**rampion**[2]. *Obs. rare*[−1]. [Of obscure origin.] A certain kind or colour of wine.

1519 *Interl. Four Elem.* (Percy Soc.) 22 Ye shall have spayneshe wyne and Gascoyn, Rose coloure, whyt, claret, rampyon.

rampire, -pier ('ræmpaɪə(r)), *sb.* Now *arch.* Forms: α. 6 rampair(e, -are, -eare, 6–7 rampar, rampere, 6–7 (9 *dial.*) ramper. β. 6 rampyre, 6– rampire, rampier, (7 -iar, -yer). [a. obs. F. *rampar* (Godef. *Compl.*), var. *rempar*, *rempart* RAMPART. The origin of the β-forms is not clear; cf. *hampire*, *-ier* obs. forms of HAMPER *sb.*[1] and *camphire* CAMPHOR *sb.* Sheridan (1789) gives *rampyr*, and marks the final syllable as short.]

1. = RAMPART.

α. *a* **1548** PATTEN *Exped. Scotl.* A vj, My lordes grace, walking vpon the Rampere of the tounewalles [etc.]. **1557** N. T. (Genev.) *Luke* xix. 43 Thy enemies shalt cast rampars about thee. **1560** DAUS tr. *Sleidane's Comm.* 396 A certain piece of the wall and Rampeare was falled downe. **1599** HAKLUYT *Voy.* II. I. 125 The battered earth, which fell in the ditches from the rampaire. **1604** E. GRIMSTONE *Hist. Siege Ostend* 133 The dike,..Rampars and defences. **1689** *Def. Liberty agst. Tyrants* 56 Fortifying..by Ravelins, Ditches, and Rampers, the Temple of God.

β. *a* **1557** VAUX in *Tottell's Misc.* (Arb.) 172 Good will the master of the shot, Stode in the rampyre braue and proud. **1579** DIGGES *Stratiot.* 93 He ought to have knowledge in Fortification, especially in the manner of making Trenches and Rampiers. **1603** KNOLLES *Hist. Turks* (1638) 82 The Venetians..built a strong tower of wood, higher than the wals and rampiars of the towne. **1665** MANLEY *Grotius' Low-C. Warres* 97 They begin to fortifie their City with strong Bulwarks and Rampires. **1747** CARTE *Hist. Eng.* I. 110 It is fenced with an high treble rampire. **1813** SCOTT *Trierm.* I. xiii, Buttress, and rampire's circling bound. **1870** F. R. WILSON *Ch. Lindisf.* 71 On its wide summit there is a strong rampier built of stone.

†**b.** A dam, barrier. *Obs.*

1586 T. B. *La Primaud. Fr. Acad.* 604 To strengthen with rampires the banks of rivers. **1611** CORYAT *Crudities* 257 The great long banke..which is interjected as a strong Rampier betwixt the Adriatique sea and the citie. **1764** GOLDSM. *Trav.* 286 Sedulous to stop the coming tide, Lift the tall rampire's artificial pride.

c. *dial.* A raised road or way; the highway.

1848 in EVANS *Leic. Gloss.* **1864** in *Mem. Tennyson* (1897) II. i. 9 When I canters my 'erse along the ramper I 'ears proputty, proputty, proputty. **1881** *Gd. Words* Nov. 752 Along the rutted ramper Thory wheels His barrow.

2. *transf.* and *fig.* A thing or person resembling or comparable to a rampart.

1567 TURBERV. *Epit.* etc. 37 A Patrone to the poore, a Rampire to the rest. *a* **1586** SIDNEY *Arcadia* v. (1598) 443 Fortifying courage with the true Rampier of patience. **1592** KYD *Sp. Trag.* I. ii. 50 With a swelling tide, It beats upon the rampiers of huge rocks. **1611** SIR W. MURE *Misc. Poems* i. 16 To siege, and sack the Rampier of my ressoune. **1627** E. F. *Hist. Edw. II* (1680) 58 Makes himself a Rampire of all his Servants, Friends and Kindred. **1700** DRYDEN *Iliad* I. 401 The son of Thetis, rampire of our hosts. **1880** SWINBURNE *Stud. Song* 116 The rampire of water in front is erect. **1881** —— *Mary Stuart* IV. i, Of those claims..have you made The stoutest rampire of your rule.

3. *attrib.* and *Comb.*, as ***rampire bank, bar, -like*** adj., ***-mound, wall.***

1555 PHAER *Æneid* II. 39 The fomy flood whose *rampier banks are torne. **1776** MICKLE tr. *Camoens' Lusiad* 112 Dash'd the fierce monarch on a *rampire bar. **1635** J. HAYWARD tr. *Biondi's Banish'd Virg.* 179 That sinuous Region..is ever..calme; thanks to the *rampire-like sheltring rocks and cragges. **1866** CONINGTON *Æneid* 6 Banks them round With sand as with a *rampire-mound. **1688** R. HOLME *Armoury* III. 457/1 A *Rampiar Wall..or Coffer worke.

rampire, -pier ('ræmpaɪər), *v.* Now *arch.* Forms: α. 6–7 rampar(e, -air, -er. β. 6 rampyer, -iere, 6–7 rampier, 6–7 (9) rampire. [a. F. (†*ramparer*), *remparer* (15th c.) to fortify, etc., f. *re-* RE- + *emparer* to take possession of, ad. Prov. *amparar*, f. L. *ante-* + *parāre* (cf. *prepare*).]

†**1.** *trans.* To strengthen, increase the strength of (a bulwark, gate, etc.) against attack; to block *up* (a gate) for this purpose, *esp.* by piling earth behind it; to close *up* (an opening). *Obs.*

1552 EDW. VI. *Lett.* (Roxb.) 81 We find the bulwarkes chargeable, massie, wel rampared. **1557** in Strype *Eccl. Mem.* (1721) III. II. App. lxxix. 275 The Englishmen within, looking for the siege, had rampered up the gates. **1596** R. H. tr. *Lavaterus' Ghostes* 83 A brasen gate being fast rampired with barres. **1622** J. REYNOLDS *God's Revenge* II. 81 He sees..the draw-bridges and approches drawn up, and rampired up with Barricadoes. **1632** LITHGOW *Trav.* II. 48 The walls [of the city] are strongly rampired with earth.

2. To fortify, strengthen, or protect (a place), *esp.* by a rampart. Now only *arch.*

1550 in Hodgson's *Hist. Northumb.* III. II. 200 That side to be massively rampiered with earth. **1553** BRENDE *Q. Curtius* F viij, Havinge rampared the prores for defence of the souldiers that were behinde. **1614** RALEIGH *Hist. World* V. i. §10 (1634) 574 The fort of Elsenour; which at that time was not so well rampard, as now perhaps it is. *a* **1656** USSHER *Ann.* (1658) 221 His Camp was no better rampiered than it should be. **1855** SINGLETON *Virgil* I. 238 Rampire with abundant power Long Alba.

transf. and *fig.* **1614** RALEIGH *Hist. World* II. (1634) 254 Knowing the strength of his owne Countrey,..rampir'd with high and sharpe Mountains. **1631** MASSINGER *Believe as you List* III. iii, There is no touch of moral honesty Though rampired in your soul, but will fly from you.

b. To shut *up* or *out* as with a rampart. *rare.*

1566 SIR H. SIDNEY in *Four C. Eng. Lett.* 24 Nature hath rampired up (as it were) the tongue with teeth, lips, yea and hair without the lips. **1606** N. BAXTER *Sir P. Sidney's Ourania* M i, Within a branchie filme there lyeth the braine, Close rampir'd vp with Barracados twaine. **1873** LYTTON *Kenelm. Chil.* V. iv. (1878) 312 Trees..which rampired out all horizon beyond.

†**3.** To fix or establish firmly. *Obs. rare.*

1555 EDEN *Decades* 5 Hyghe trees, sette close together and fast rampaired in the grounde. *a* **1670** HACKET *Cent. Serm.* (1675) 396 When men have ramparcd witty shifts against truth, it is in vain to tell them [etc.].

Hence **'rampired** *ppl. a.*, **'rampiring** *vbl. sb.*

1582 STANYHURST *Æneis* I. (Arb.) 26 With thick bulwarck shal he fence thee rampired Alba. **1657** REEVE *God's Plea*

168 Where there is unity there needeth no barricadoing nor rampering. **1776** MICKLE tr. *Camoens' Lusiad* VII. 311 Rampired walls lie smoaking on the ground. **1873** BROWNING *Red Cott. Nt.-Cap* 1381 Grass..contemptible Compared with solid rock, the rampired ridge.

†**'rampish**, *a. Obs. rare.* [f. RAMP *v.*[1] + -ISH.] Given to ramping or romping.

1530 PALSGR. 322/1 Rampysshe as beest is or a yonge wenche, *ramponneux.* **1573** TUSSER *Husb.* (1878) 214 Not rampish toie, of girle and boie,..good end doth frame. **1661** W. K. *Conf. Charact.* To Rdr. (1860) p. xii, Rampish lust and damnable pride.

†**'rampling**, ? alteration of RAMPING *vbl. sb.*[1]

c **1580** JEFFERIE *Bugbears* v. ix. in *Archiv Stud. neu. Spr.* (1897), With ramplynges, with tramplynges [etc.].

†**'ramplish**, *v. Obs. rare*[−1]. [ad. F. *rempliss-*, *remplir* to fill, etc.] *trans.* To cover.

1494 in *Lett. Rich. III & Hen. VII* (Rolls) I. 396 A lion of gold,..sett in maner of a curnalles with plumesses whit and grene, and ramplyshed with spangils.

'ramplor. *Sc.* [? f. RAMP *v.*[1]] **a.** *sb.* A rover, a restless person. **b.** *adj.* Roving, restless.

1821 GALT *Ann. Parish* 162 He was a ramplor, roving sort of a creature. **1822** —— *Sir A. Wylie* I. xxv. 226 A mischievous clever ramplor.

†**rampone.** *Obs. rare*[−1]. = LAMPAS *sb.*[1]

1580 HOLLYBAND *Treas. Fr. Tong, Lampas,* or *lampast*, a disease and swelling rising in the mouth of horses, being holpen by letting the bloud, and pricking the same with an horne, the rampone.

ramps (ræmps). [Var. of RAMS; cf. G. *rampe(n* in same sense.]

1. *north. dial.* and *Sc.* Ramsons.

1538 TURNER *Libellus*, Arisaron..puto hodie a nostris dici rammes aut rampes. **1663** BLAIR *Autobiog.* iii. (1848) 53 All things smelling of a root called ramps. **1824** MACTAGGART *Gallovid. Encycl., Ramps*, wild leeks, common on shores. **1869–** in northern dial. glossaries (Cumb., Lanc., Northumb.).

2. *U.S.* = RAMP *sb.*[2] 3 b.

1939 *Jrnl. Tennessee Acad. Sci.* XIV. 280 One kind [of wild onion] is much sought after by mountain folk, who call it 'ramps', and gather and eat its bulb with great relish. **1960** *Washington Post* 29 Apr. 12/1 It [*sc.* a smell] will emanate from the cooking of ramps—a wild plant somewhat like an onion. **1976** *Amer. Speech 1974* XLIX. 21 'There's a wild onion, smells like ramps, you know.'

rampsman ('ræmpsmən). *slang.* [f. RAMP *sb.*[5] + MAN *sb.*[1]: cf. *cracksman*, etc.] One who commits robbery with violence.

1859 HOTTEN *Dict. Slang* 80 *Rampsman*, a highway robber who uses violence when necessary. **1862** H. MAYHEW *Lond. Lab.* Extra vol. 31/2 The '*Rampsman*' or '*Cracksman*' plunders by force; as the burglar, footpad, etc. **1882** *Sydney Slang Dict.* 7/2 *Rampsmen*, burglars, highway robbers. **1932** H. WALPOLE *Fortress* III. iv. 467 The perils of London—the cracksmen, the rampsmen, the snorrers and thimble-screwers. **1975** M. CRICHTON *Great Train Robbery* xiii. 72 Barlow was a reformed buzzer turned rampsman—a pickpocket who had degenerated to plain mugging.

rampsoun, obs. form of RANSOM *v.*

rampyer, -pyre, obs. forms of RAMPIRE.

'ram-race. *Sc.* and *north. dial.* Also 6 **-rays**, 7 (9) **-raise.** [f. RAM *sb.*[1] + RACE *sb.*[1]]

1. A headlong rush, like that of a ram. Also *fig.*

1513 DOUGLAS *Æneis* XI. xvii. 49 Sum..Can with a ram rays to the portis dusche. **1821** *Blackw. Mag.* IX. 163 Poor man! he ran at last a ram-race, and was taken before the session.

2. A short run preparatory to a jump.

1695 KENNETT *Par. Antiq.* II. Gloss., *Ram-raise.* *c* **1815** HOGG *Connel of Dee* xxviii, With ram-race he cleared at a bensil the wall. *c* **1817** —— *Tales & Sk.* II. 158 They took a short race of about twelve or fourteen paces, which they denominated the ramrace.

ram-riding: see RAM *sb.*[1] 7.

ramrod ('ræmrɒd). [f. RAM *v.*[1] + ROD.]

1. A rod used for ramming down the charge of a muzzle-loading fire-arm. (The earlier word was RAMMER.)

1797 *Encycl. Brit.* (ed. 3) VIII. 246/1 If the ball has been forcibly driven down with an iron ramrod..the piece will almost certainly burst. **1859** *All Y. Round* No. 4. 87 The invention of the iron ramrod by the Prince of Dessau,.. doubled the value of the fire of infantry.

2. *transf.* †**a.** *Cricket.* (See quots.) *Obs.*

1870 R. B. MANSFIELD *School-Life at Winchester College* 228 *Ramrod, Raymonder*, names given to a ball bowled all along the ground. **1880** *Baily's Monthly Mag.* Feb. 93 It [*sc.* a quick underhand ball] must be very straight so as to ensure a L.B.W., and provided it pitches half-way—for 'ramrods' are *not* cricket proper—the more irregular the pitch the better.

b. A foreman or manager. *N. Amer.*

1881 E. W. NYE *Bill Nye & Boomerang* 60 John Humpfner, the ram-rod of the New York House, feared that the explosion might break the large French plate glass windows of his palatial hotel. **1905** *Dialect Notes* III. 92 *Ramrod*, main-stay, manager, superintendent. **1942** *Amer. Speech* XVII. 75/1 The man in charge of a herd on the trail [in Nebraska] is the *trailboss* or *ramrod.* **1973** R. SYMONS *Where Wagon Led* I. i. 10 Jake..acted in between times as a sort of foreman, or in western parlance, 'ramrod' of the outfit.

c. With sexual connotations.

1951 DYLAN THOMAS *Poems* (1971) 206 Sighed the old ram rod, dying of women. **1974** H. S. KAPLAN *New Sex Therapy* i. 17 The glans also becomes enlarged. It does not become hard, however, thus guarding against the possibility that the female will be hurt by the ramrod of the phallus.

3. a. *attrib.* and *Comb.*, as ***ramrod-maker***, ***spring***; ***ramrod-backed***, ***-like***, ***-rigid***, ***-stiff***, ***-straight*** adjs.; **ramrod roll** *U.S.* (see quot.).

1939 'N. BLAKE' *Smiler with Knife* ii. 33 The major or his ramrod-backed housekeeper. **1861** MUSGRAVE *By-roads* 264 A ramrod-like descent of pelting rain. **1860** TOMLINSON *Arts & Manuf.* II. *Gun-Barrels*, The bayonet and ramrod maker. **1961** *Countryman* LVIII. 515 We lay ramrod rigid. **1936** M. MITCHELL *Gone with Wind* xxviii. 477 The men added as dessert some 'ramrod rolls'..and this was the first time Scarlett had ever seen this Confederate article of diet. .. The soldiers mixed their ration of corn meal with water, and salt too when they could get it, wrapped the thick paste about their ramrods and roasted the mess over camp fires. **1841** *Ordnance Man. for Use of Officers of U.S. Army* (U.S. Ordnance Dept.) 120 In the musket of the model of 1840, the trigger screw and trigger are taken off after the guard, then the pin for the ramrod spring and the ramrod spring. **1961** *Times* 6 Dec. 17/3 A ramrod-stiff naval officer. **1979** G. HAMMOND *Dead Game* xii. 150 A slim man, ramrod-straight.

b. *attrib.*, passing into adj. Rigid, inflexible; solemn, formal.

1905 *Pall Mall Gaz.* 18 Dec. 2 Under the pretence that, apart from such ramrod rule, the nation would tumble to pieces. **1920** D. H. LAWRENCE *Lost Girl* vii. 137 He was a tall Swiss with..a flattish face and a rather stiff, ramrod figure. **1932** *Times Lit. Suppl.* 19 May 366/3 Mrs. Stainlit, an elderly lady of the ramrod breed. **1978** J. A. MICHENER *Chesapeake* 74 He saw him as..a man of petty foibles and ramrod rectitude.

Hence **'ramrod** *v. trans.*, to force or drive (something), as with a ramrod; *spec.* (*U.S.*), to manage, direct (a ranch, event, etc.); also, to beat or thrust in the form of a ramrod; (*nonce-wds.*) **'ramroddy** *a.*, stiff, unbending; **'ramrodism**, military stiffness.

1880 SIR W. BUTLER *Far Out* 12 The Mosaic ramrodism of the German Emperor's face and figure. **1886** *Harper's Mag.* May 888 Ramroddy and uncompromising. **1948** *Popular Western* June 15/2 This is Tex Grant, the star-toter who ramrods this burg. **1955** R. HOBSON *Nothing too Good* vi. 50 You're Rich Hobson, ramrodding the Batnuni end of Frontier Company. **1966** S. HEANEY *Death of Naturalist* 39 A volley of cold blood ramrodding the current. **1973** R. SYMONS *Where Wagon Led* I. vii. 118, I ramrodded the Circle Diamond for quite a few years after that. **1976** *Publishers Weekly* 1 Mar. 84/1 The skittish livestock Kingman must ramrod to a distant army post. *Ibid.* 8 Mar. 57/1 Railroad builders par excellence who ramrod tracks across the virgin countryside. **1979** *Tucson* (Arizona) *Citizen* 20 Sept. 11A/3 Scores of volunteers rallied around this charitable event which was ramrodded by the city of Tucson.

rams (ræmz). Now only *dial.* Forms: 1 **hramsa, -se, (hromsa, ramese)**, 5 **rammys,** *pl.* **ramsis, -zys,** 6 **ram(m)es,** 8–9 **rams,** 9 *Sc.* **ramsh.** [OE. *hramsa, -se* = MLG. *ramese*, G. *rams* (with many dial. variants: see Grimm), Da., Sw., and Norw. dial. *rams* (Sw. *rams-lök*), cognate with OIr. *crem* (Ir. and Gael. *creamh*, W. *craf*), Lith. *kermùszė*, Russ. *cheremsha* wild garlic, Gr. *κρόμυον* onion.] Wild garlic, ramsons.

Some mod. dialects treat *rams* as a pl. form, with sing. *ram* or *rame*. See also RAMPS, RAMSEY, RAMSON.

a **700** *Epinal Gloss.* 59 *Actula (accitula)*, hramsa [*Corpus* hromsa]. **10..** *Ags. Voc.* in Wr.-Wülcker 296/3 *Acetula*, ramese. *c* **1440** *Promp. Parv.* 422/2 Ramzys, herbe (*H.* ramsis, *K., S.* rammys), affodyllus. **1548** TURNER *Names Herbes* (E.D.S.) 10 The third kinde [of garlick] is called in latin *Allium vrsinum*, and in english Ramsey, or bucrames or rames. **1551** —— *Herbal* I. (1568) B v, The third kynd is called in Englysh rammes. *a* **1796** PEGGE *Derbicisms* Ser. II. *Rams*, rampions [? ramsons]. **1818** *Trans. Antiq. Soc. Scotl.* II. 70 On these hills [P. of Monivaird] is found a mountain leek, or ramsh, as it is here named. **1876** *Whitby Gloss.*, *Rams*, wild garlic, flavouring the cow's milk that eats it.

ram-sammy (ˌræm'sæmɪ). *slang* (orig. *dial.*). [Origin unknown.] **a.** A family quarrel; a noisy gathering. **b.** A fight; a scrap.

1891 *N. & Q.* 12 Sept. 206/1 'A ram sammy' = [in the W. country] a family quarrel or, in variation, a noisy gathering. **1902** *Western Morning News* 22 Apr. 5/5 A 'ram sammy' was a family quarrel. **1967** H. W. SUTHERLAND *Magnie* v. 70 She'd sent for Big Hughie in case there was a ram sammy. Magnie was no match for Big Hughie. **1976** J. WAINWRIGHT *Walther P. 38* 98, I was there, at this jazz club..in a cramped basement... Some people might have called it a 'jam session'. Some people might have called it a 'ram-sammy'.

Ramsauer ('ræmzaʊə(r)). *Physics.* The name of Carl Wilhelm *Ramsauer* (1879–1955), Ger. physicist, used *attrib.* with reference to the Ramsauer effect, as ***Ramsauer cross-section***, ***free path***; **Ramsauer effect**, the sharp decrease, almost to zero, of the scattering cross-section of atoms of inert gases for electrons with energies below a critical value (first described by Ramsauer in 1921 and independently by Townsend in 1922; now usu. called the Ramsauer–Townsend effect: see next); **Ramsauer minimum**, the minimum in the scattering cross-section for electrons exhibiting the Ramsauer effect.

1930 *Chem. Abstr.* XXIV. 5218 An historical and critical review of the Ramsauer effect. **1938** L. B. LOEB *Atomic Structure* xix. 338 The Ramsauer cross sections..vary in some cases over wide ranges with electron energy. *Ibid.*, Ramsauer's pioneer measurements and the later ones of Ramsauer and Kollath have been carried to such perfection that we today speak of the electron free paths as Ramsauer free paths. **1960** *Physical Rev.* CXVII. 1416/2 For argon, krypton, and xenon $\sigma_t(\epsilon)$ is approximately proportional to ϵ except below the Ramsauer minimum. **1963** *Ibid.* CXXX. 1021/1 This method of analysis might be characterized as a short circuiting of the procedure used by Holtzmark in his remarkable analysis of the Ramsauer cross sections for argon and krypton. **1972** A. GILARDINI *Low Energy Electron Collisions in Gases* iv. 338 Argon has a large Ramsauer minimum at $\sim$0·3 eV, so that electrons experience far fewer collisions with molecules at these energies than at lower and higher energies. **1974** G. REECE tr. *Hund's Hist. Quantum Theory* xi. 146 It was possible to explain the Ramsauer effect qualitatively in terms of the diffraction of long waves by small spheres.

Ramsauer–Townsend ('ræmzaʊə 'taʊnzɛnd). *Physics.* The names of C. W. *Ramsauer* (see prec.) and John Sealy Edward *Townsend* (1868–1957), Irish physicist, used *attrib.* with reference to the Ramsauer effect (see prec.).

1952 MASSEY & BURHOP *Electronic & Ionic Impact Phenomena* i. 9 The remarkable transparency of the heavier rare gases atoms towards electrons of energy 1 eV or so..will be referred to as the Ramsauer–Townsend effect. *Ibid.* iii. 115 It is now of interest to consider the contribution from higher-order cross-sections. These are very small at the Ramsauer–Townsend minimum. **1963** *Physical Rev.* CXXX. 1022/2 It might be guessed that the Ramsauer–Townsend minimum should occur at approximately the same place in both scattering and momentum transfer cross sections. **1977** P. G. BURKE *Potential Scattering in Atomic Physics* vii. 73 The balance of this repulsion with the long range r^{-4} attraction caused by the polarization of the atom in the field of the incident electron is the cause of the Ramsauer–Townsend effect.

ramsayite ('ræmzeɪaɪt). *Min.* [ad. Russ. *ramzait* (E. E. Kostyleva 1923, in *Compt. Rend. de l' Acad. des Sci. de Russie* A. 55), f. the name of Wilhelm *Ramsay* (1865–1928), Finnish geologist: see -ITE[1].] A silicate of sodium and titanium, $Na_2Ti_2Si_2O_9$, occurring as orthorhombic crystals.

1924 *Mineral. Abstr.* II. 250 (*heading*) On a new mineral—ramsayite from the Khibinsky and Lovozersky tundras. **1967** *Norsk Geol. Tidsskr.* XLVII. 249 Ramsayite is an important constituent of the mosandrite pseudomorphs... The crystals range in length from about 0·1 mm to 1·5 mm. They are colourless to greyish.

ram'scallion. Chiefly *north. dial.* [Of obscure formation: cf. *rapscallion*, *rampallion.*] A mean wretched fellow.

1733 FIELDING *Don Quixote in Eng.* I. i, The Don is just such another lean ramscallion as..his Rozinante. **1855–6** in northern glossaries (Yks., Lonsd.).

ramsdellite ('ræmzdəlaɪt). *Min.* [f. the name of Lewis S. *Ramsdell* (1895–1975), U.S. mineralogist + -ITE[1].] An oxide of manganese, MnO_2, similar to pyrolusite, occurring as orthorhombic crystals and platy masses of a grey to black colour.

1943 FLEISCHER & RICHMOND in *Econ. Geol.* XXXVIII. 278 Ramsdellite. [*Note*] This is the first use of this name in print. The mineral was described in 1932 by Ramsdell..as a possible dimorph of pyrolusite. **1965** G. J. WILLIAMS *Econ. Geol. N.Z.* xiii. 190/2 Coombs (in Reed, 1959) mentioned the existence of ramsdellite (a polymorph of pyrolusite) at Taieri Mouth in ore which consists of pyrolusite with minor manganite. **1969** *Econ. Geol.* LXIV. 221/2 Ramsdellite can very easily be mistaken for pyrolusite. **1972** *Mineral. Rec.* III. 210 Ramsdellite, a relatively common mineral in the Chihuahua geodes, is found as fibrous dendritic masses on quartz but is more commonly found growing as well developed crystals on goethite blades in two different habits.

Ramsden ('ræmzdən). The name of Jesse *Ramsden* (1735–1800), English instrument-maker, used *attrib.* and in the possessive to designate an eyepiece commonly used in astronomical telescopes (see quot. 1847) which he described in 1783 (*Phil. Trans. R. Soc.* LXXIII. 94).

1787 *Phil. Trans. R. Soc.* LXXVII. 55 The telescope.. was an achromatic object-glass of Dollond, of 16 inches focal length, and 2 inches aperture; with a Ramsden's eye-glass, magnifying about 25 times. **1847** R. POTTER *Elem. Treat. Optics* I. vii. 117 Ramsden's eyepiece is formed of a plano-convex and a convexo-plane lens of equal focal lengths, set at a distance of about two-thirds of the focal length of either. **1900** R. A. HERMAN *Treat Geom. Optics* vi. 137 Both Huyghens' and Ramsden's eye-pieces have convergent powers, and the image appears inverted. **1923** GLAZEBROOK *Dict. Appl. Physics* IV. 77/1 When a Ramsden eyepiece is employed even pronounced apparent distortion is of no importance for exact measurements. **1971** SMITH & THOMSON *Optics* viii. 133 The focal plane of eyepieces of the Ramsden type is close to the first lens.

rams(d)en, dial. variants of RAMSON.

ramsey ('ræmzɪ). Now *dial.* Forms: *pl.* 5, 7 **ramseys**, (6 **-eyes**), 6–7, 9 **ramsies**; *sing.* 6, 9 **ramsey**, 9 **ramsy.** [f. RAMS, prob. by a wrong analysis of the pl. *ramsis*, *ramses.*] = RAMSON.

1499 *Promp. Parv.* 422/2 (Pynson) *Ramseys*, affodyllus. **1548** [see RAMS]. **1655** MOUFET & BENNET *Health's Impr.*

(1746) 325 Ramseys are of the like Power with Garlic. **1882** *Devon Plant Names, Ramsey, Ramsies,* or *Ramson.*

ramshack (ˈræmʃæk), U.S. Black English var. RANSACK *v.*

1901 W. CHURCHILL *Crisis* III. vi. 413 Supper, Miss Jinny. Lawsy, if I ain't ramshacked de premises fo' you bof. **1935** in Z. N. Hurston *Mules & Men* (1970) 323 Me and my buddy and two three more, Going to ramshack Georgy everywhere we go. **1962** W. FAULKNER *Reivers* i. 13 Now you got to ramshack the country to locate another back window you can crawl in.

ramshackle (ˈræmʃæk(ə)l), *a.* and *sb.* Also -shacle. [Later var. of RAMSHACKLED.]

A. *adj.* **1.** Loose and shaky, as if ready to fall to pieces; rickety, crazy, tumble-down. (Said chiefly of carriages and houses.)

1830 MISS MITFORD *Village* Ser. IV. (1863) 215, I could shake the old chaise to pieces with one jerk, it's so ramshackle. **1847** THACKERAY *Cane-bottom'd Chair,* The rickety, ramshackle, wheezy spinet. **1865** *Athenæum* No. 1978. 400/3 A huddle of ramshackle lath-and-plaster houses. **1889** D. C. MURRAY *Danger. Catspaw* 78 There was J. P.'s ramshackle figure on the pathway.

2. Of persons, actions, etc.: Unsteady, irregular, disorderly, rude. (Chiefly *dial.*)

1855 ROBINSON *Whitby Gloss.* **1870** E. PEACOCK *Ralf Skirl.* II. 121 What ramshackle wark ha' ye been after? **1880** 'VERNON LEE' *Italy* II. ii. 26 Fine talent..ruined..by a disorderly character, a ramshackle career.

B. *sb.* **1.** *dial.* A thoughtless or reckless fellow.

1824 LOCKHART *Reg. Dalton* I. 199 This will learn ye, again, ye young ramshackle. *Ibid.* III. 267 An ignorant ramshackle, no question. **1877** in *N.W. Linc. Gloss.*

2. *nonce-use.* A ramshackle object.

1865 *Even. Standard* 28 Mar., Our own..purchased hulks and general congregation of naval ramshackles.

Hence **ˈramshackle** *v. trans.*, to 'rattle up'.

1865 *Daily Tel.* 27 Oct. 5/6 If their dwellings were not 'ramshackled' or 'run up' by some..speculative builder.

ramshackled (ˈræmʃæk(ə)ld), *ppl. a.* Also 7 ranshacled, 8 -shackled, 9 *Sc.* -shachled. [Perh. f. *ram-, ranshackle* RANSACKLE *v.*, as if = 'wrecked or destroyed by plundering'; but cf. Sc. CAMSHACHLE, to distort.] = RAMSHACKLE *a.* 1.

1675 S. SEWALL *Diary* 31 July, A window which was all ranshacled. **1703** —— *Let.* 5 Jan., Barn and outhousing ranshackld. **1789** *Loiterer* No. 39. 12 The house itself was ..such a ranshackeld old place that it must be pulled down. **1883** *Amer. Missionary* Dec. 367 [The Chinese Wall] a barbaric, ramshackled old thing of a great many centuries.

So **ˈramshackling** *a.*

1868 LD. HOUGHTON *Let.* in *Life* (1890) II. 196 The house is a ramshackling old place, without a fine room in it. **1951** DYLAN THOMAS *Poems* (1971) 211 And the tusked, ramshackling sea exults.

ramshackledom (ˈræmʃæk(ə)ldəm). [f. RAMSHACKLE *a.* + -DOM.] = next.

1962 L. G. PINE (*title*) Ramshackledom: a critical appraisement of the Establishment. **1962** *Listener* 15 Nov. 835/2 Originality he [*sc.* Berlioz] possessed..but it does not consist in hopeful random ramshackledom (almost a principle of composition nowadays). **1963** *Guardian* 1 Feb. 9/1 The condition of British ramshackledom exceeds anything hitherto known.

ramshackleness (ˈræmʃæk(ə)lnɪs). [f. RAMSHACKLE *a.* + -NESS.] Ramshackle character or state.

1922 'R. WEST' in *Public Opinion* 17 Nov. 486/2 These Houses of Parliament are the symbol of a real miracle, a real mixture of ramshackleness and nobility.

ˈramshackly, *a.* [f. RAMSHACKLE + -Y, after *rickety, shaky,* etc.] **1.** = RAMSHACKLE *a.* 1.

1857 READE *Course True Love, Clouds & Sunshine* ix. 266 Immeasurably fond of the old ramshackly house. **1892** J. PAYN *Mod. Whittington* I. 166 Lawrence was ashamed of.. the ramshackly dwelling. **1897** E. A. BARTLETT *Battlefields of Thessaly* xii. 262 There was also the araba with our baggage, a very ramshackly weather-beaten old carriage. **1924** E. M. FORSTER *Passage to India* xxiv. 217 The chuprassies..filed into the ramshackly room with a condescending air, as if it was a booth at a fair. **1939** in B. A. Botkin *Treas. S. Folklore* (1949) I. iii. 59 The cabin was ramshackly.

2. = RAMSHACKLE *a.* 2.

1910 E. M. FORSTER *Howards End* v. 38 Helen, you must not be so ramshackly. You took this gentleman's umbrella away from Queen's Hall, and he has had the trouble of coming round for it. **1927** —— *Aspects of Novel* i. 28 In the rather ramshackly course that lies ahead of us, we cannot consider fiction by periods. **1976** *Daily Tel.* 8 July 16 The accelerating shift to the Left which has rendered that great ramshackly confederation [*sc.* the Labour party] increasingly vulnerable to the subversive activities of Marxists.

ramshandry (ræmˈʃændrɪ), *a.* *nonce-wd.* [Fanciful combination of RAM-STAM *a.* and SHANDY *a.*] Thoughtless; light-headed; precipitate.

1907 W. DE MORGAN *Alice-for-Short* xxviii. 280 Don't you go making a runaway match with a ramshandry sort o' half-French girl.

ram's head. Also ram's-head. [f. RAM *sb.*[1]; cf. RAM-HEAD.]

1. a. Used *attrib.* to designate the ordinary chick-pea, *Cicer arietinum.* ? *Obs.*

1601 HOLLAND *Pliny* I. 570 There is a second kind named Columbinum... These are white, round, light, lesse than the former Rams-head ciches. **1866** *Treas. Bot.* 957/2.

b. The American plant *Cypripedium arietinum,* a species of Lady's Slipper. (*Treas. Bot.* 1866.)

2. †**a.** *Naut.* (See quot.) *Obs.* Cf. RAM-HEAD 2.

1627 CAPT. SMITH *Seaman's Gram.* ii. 7 The Ramshead is a great blocke wherein is three shiuers into which are passed the halyards, and at the end of it in a hole is reued the ties, and this is onely belonging to the fore and maine halyards.

b. (See quots.)

1944 L. T. C. ROLT *Narrow Boat* 206 *Ram's head,* the boatman's name for the wooden rudder post of a narrow boat; usually it is bound with pipe-clayed Turk's-head knots, and occasionally decorated with a horse's tail. **1947** S. WOOLFITT *Idle Women* ii. 26 The tiller is called the 'ram's head' and is curved like a swan's neck towards the steerer. It is metal, on the motor, and is painted in sections with..red, white and blue. *Ibid.* Gloss. 222 *Ram's Head,* in the butty, the post at the top of the rudder, usually highly decorated with Turk's heads and/or horse-hair; in the motor, the steering column. **1976** A. HILL *Summer's End* i. 12 The ram's head was part of the tiller, and by putting our hands to it we got the 'feel' of boat-steering.

†**3.** (See quots.) *Obs.* Cf. RAM-HEAD 3.

1611 COTGR., *Louve de fer,* a Rammes head; or, the (pinser-like) hook of a Crane, &c. **1727** BOYER *Dict. Royal* II. s.v. *Ram,* Ram's Head, (an Iron Pincher to heave up great Stones with).

ram's horn. Also ram's-horn. [f. RAM *sb.*[1]]

1. The horn of a ram; the material of this. Also *transf.* and *fig.*, and in proverbial phr. ***as †right (straight, crooked,*** etc.) ***as a ram's horn.***

c **1320** in Wright & Halliwell *Reliquæ Antiquæ* (1843) II. 19 As ryt as ramis orn. **1522** SKELTON *Why not to Court* 87 As ryght as a rammes horn. **1611** BIBLE *Josh.* vi. 6 Let seuen Priests beare seuen trumpets of rammes-hornes. **1658** MENNIS & SMITH *Wit Restor'd* 102 Straight as a rams horne is thy nose. **1751** R. PALTOCK *P. Wilkins* (1884) I. 178 The thing I made..was composed of old hat, pieces of rams-horn [etc.]. **1816** SCOTT *Antiq.* xxii, Sir Arthur drew from his pocket a large ram's-horn, with a copper cover. **1834** C. A. DAVIS *Lett. J. Downing* XXXVI. 324 As crooked as a ram's horn. **1842** [see SHEEP'S EYE(s 2]. **1878** HARDY *Return of Native* II. III. iii. 107 I'm as stiff as a ram's horn, stooping so long. **1914** C. MACKENZIE *Sinister Street* II. III. v. 588 A ramshorn of snuff and glasses of mead waiting for casual callers. **1947** *S. Folklore Q.* Dec. 263 More conventionally.. a seasoned reprobate is characterized as 'old as the hills and crooked as a ram's horn'.

attrib. and *Comb.* **1589** T. NASHE *Anat. Absurd.* Wks. (Grosart) I. 71, I know the learned wil laugh me to scorne, for setting down such Rams horne rules of direction. **1820** LAMB *Elia, Christ's Hospit. 35 Yrs. ago,* A young ass..blew such a ram's horn blast, as..set concealment any longer at defiance. **1840** MRS. F. TROLLOPE *Widow Married* xxiii, My old ramshorn aunt Betsy. **1897** *Allbutt's Syst. Med.* II. 1081 They form a long ram's-horn-like projection. **1897** *Sears, Roebuck Catal.* 612/2 *Handle bars,*..up or down or ram's horn as desired. Our ram's horn bar is the neatest and most comfortable made. **1909** *Daily Chron.* 17 Aug. 7/4 A great silver-mounted ram's-horn snuffbox. **1934** *Archit. Rev.* LXXVI. 64/3 Material [*sc.* timber] possessing 'ram's horn' figure, is also met with, and 'stripe' or 'ribbon-grain' is relatively common. **1964** J. S. SCOTT *Dict. Building* 256 *Ram's horn figure*.., a ripple like *fiddleback.*

b. A form of scroll ornament.

1842 FRANCIS *Dict. Arts, Ram's Horn,* a particular kind of scroll ornament, the origin of which is from the skull and horns of the ram.

†**2.** An ammonite or nautilus (*Nautilus spirula*). Also *ramshorn sailor. Obs.*

1798 NEMNICH *Polyg. Lex.* V. II. 865.

3. *Mil.* (See quot.)

1802 JAMES *Milit. Dict., Rams-horns,*..are a kind of low works made in the ditch, of a circular arc; they were invented by M. Belidor, and serve instead of tenailles.

4. A vessel in which fish are washed.

1809 *Naval Chron.* XXI. 21 The fish [cod] are thrown into what is called a ram's-horn (a square wooden thing, perforated with holes, to admit the water to pass), when the fish are tumbled about and well washed. **1883** *Fisheries Exhib. Catal.* (ed. 4) 175 Washing Fish in a Ram's-Horn.

b. *dial.* 'A winding-net supported by stakes, to inclose fish that come in with the tide. *Somerset.*' (Halliwell.)

5. *dial.* The plant *Orchis Morio.* Also *attrib.*

1884 in BRITTEN & HOLLAND *Plant-Names.* **1889** JEFFERIES *Field & Hedgerow* 115 Soon after the May garlands the meadow orchis comes up,..and after that the 'ram's-horn' orchis, which has a twisted petal.

6. In full, ***ram's-horn (pond) snail.*** A herbivorous aquatic snail belonging to the family Planorbidæ, esp. *Planorbis planorbis* or *P. corneus.*

1901, 1926 [see *flat-coil* s.v. FLAT *adj.* 15]. **1950** *Sci. News* XV. 101 These absorption bands have not got precisely the same wave-lengths in the blood of man and in that of the ramshorn pond snail. **1952** J. CLEGG *Freshwater Life Brit. Isles* xvi. 254 The larger species of Ram's Horn Snails..live at least two or three years. **1960** *Times* 4 Aug. 1/3 (Advt.), Pond Naturalist would gratefully acknowledge information where to collect Ramshorn Snails. **1971** *Oxf. Bk. Invertebrates* 68 The ramshorns can possibly live in more stagnant conditions than other water-snails.

ramsin, -sioun, obs. ff. RAMSON, RANSOM.

†**ram-skyt.** *Obs. rare*[−1]. A term of abuse.

c **1460** *Towneley Myst.* iii. 217 We! hold thi tong, ram-skyt or I shall the still.

ramson (ˈræmsən). Forms: 1 ramesan, hrameson, 5 ramsyn, 6 -sin, 6–7, 9 -som, 6, 9 *dial.* -sen, 9 ransom, (9 *dial.* ramsden), 6– ramson. [OE., pl. of *hramsa, -se* RAMS (the *-n* being retained as in *oxen, hosen,* etc.), but in later use taken as a sing., with pl. *ramsons.*] The broad-leaved garlic, *Allium ursinum*; the bulbous root of this plant, used as a relish. Chiefly in *pl.*

c **1000** ÆLFRIC *Gloss.* in Wr.-Wülcker 134/7 *Ramusium,* ramesan. *c* **1000** *Durham Gloss.* in *Sax. Leechd.* III. 304/2 *Ramuscium,* Hrameson. **14..** *Voc.* in Wr.-Wülcker 561/13 *Acticola,* ramsyn. **1547** BOORDE *Brev. Health* xv. 12 b, They muste eat no salades, garlyke, ramsons, onyons, chybolles, or scalyons. **1657** TOMLINSON *Renou's Disp.* 29 That poysonous medicament..such as be Ramsons, Savine, Leeks, &c. **1733** MILLER *Gard. Dict.* (ed. 2), *Allium, sylvestre latifolium,* Ramson's. **1805** *Medical Jrnl.* XIV. 65 Ramsons. Ramson garlic. **1879–** in south-western dial. glossaries.

ramson, obs. form of RANSOM.

ram-stam (ˈræmˈstæm), *a., sb.,* and *adv. Sc.* and *north. dial.* [A riming comb., perh. based on RAM *sb.*[1] and dial. *stam* to stamp.]

A. *adj.* Precipitate, headstrong.

1786 BURNS *To Jas. Smith* xxviii, The hairum-scairum, ram-stam boys, The rattlin squad. **1824** MACTAGGART *Gallovid. Encycl.* Introd. 8, I scamper along rather in the 'ram stam' manner. **1893** CROCKETT *Stickit Minister* 81 He's young an' terrible ram-stam. **1934** M. WATT *Visitors at Birkenbrae* 12 John's that ram-stam..he wad be sure tae come oot wi' something. **1976** *Scottish Rev.* Spring 19 In 'The Steeple Bar, Perth'..his [*sc.* Sydney Goodsir Smith's] ram-stam bacchanalian voice is heard, as naturally as if he had been attuned to spoken Scots from childhood. **1976** *Ibid.* Summer 32 This is a rather ramstam, happy-go-lucky, whimsical procedure.

B. *sb.* A thoughtless person. *rare.*

1823 GALT *Entail* III. 70 Walky, who is a lad of a methodical nature, and no a hurly-burly ramstam.

C. *adv.* Precipitately, headlong.

1818 SCOTT *Rob Roy* xxviii, The least we'll get, if we gang ramstam in on them, will be a broken head. **1895** CROCKETT *Men of Moss-Hags* xxiv. 178 Was there ever a Gordon that would not go ram-stam at the boar. **1910** *Blackw. Mag.* Jan. 31/1 He proposed, ramstam, by telegraph; was accepted, and the lady came home..that he might marry her. **1922** T. S. CAIRNCROSS *Scot at Hame* 54, I left my gless a meenit, ran ram-stam. **1967** 'H. CALVIN' *Nice Friendly Town* ix. 136 The way young folk nowadays go ram-stam at things without a by-your-leave.

ramsyn, obs. form of RAMSON.

ramtil (ˈræmtɪl). [Bengālī *rāmtil,* f. *rām* pleasing, beautiful, excellent (freq. prefixed to names of plants, etc. to denote special kinds or varieties) + *til* TIL.] A plant (*Guizotia Abyssinica* or *oleifera*) largely cultivated in various parts of India for the oil which is expressed from the seeds (*niger* or *ramtil seeds*). Sometimes called *black til.*

1858 in SIMMONDS *Dict. Trade.* **1873** DRURY *Usef. Plants India* (ed. 2) 238 The Ramtil oil is sweet-tasted, and is used for the same purposes as the gingely oil.

ramuff, obs. Sc. form of REMOVE *v.*

ramulet (ˈræmjʊlɪt). *rare.* [f. RAMUL-US + -ET[1].] = RAMULUS.

1671 GREW in *Phil. Trans.* VI. 3042 The purest sap, imbosom'd in the ramulets of the Seed branch. **1829** *Westm. Rev.* July 111 The branches and ramulets of the trunk.

ramuli, pl. of RAMULUS.

ramuˈliferous, *a.* [See next and -(I)FEROUS.] Bearing ramuli. (In recent Dicts.)

ramulose (ˈræmjʊləʊs), *a. Bot.* and *Zool.* [ad. L. *rāmulōsus* (applied by Pliny to veined leaves); see RAMULUS and -OSE.] Characterized by ramuli.

1753 CHAMBERS *Cycl. Supp.* s.v. *Leaf, Ramulose Leaf,* a kind of compound leaf, in which there are several foliola sustained on a branched petiole. **1872** H. C. WOOD *Fresh Water Algæ* 207 Fascia..densely clothed with penicillately ramulose fasciculi.

Hence ***ramuloso-pinnate, -verrucose*** adjs.

1846 DANA *Zooph.* (1848) 650 Flabellate and ramuloso-pinnate. *Ibid.* 520 Corallum with the branchlets subulate, ramulose-verrucose above.

So **ˈramulous** *a.* [see -OUS.]

1664 POWER *Exp. Philos.* I. 29 About the joynts and ramulous divisions. **1846** DANA *Zooph.* (1848) 607 Carnose Alcyonidæ, ramulous or fruticulose.

‖**ramulus** (ˈræmjʊləs). *Bot.* and *Anat.* Pl. ramuli (-laɪ). [L., dim. of RAMUS.] A small branch or ramus.

c **1783** W. STARK in *Med. Commun.* I. 367 Those [vessels] may be traced..to the smaller ramuli. **1872** H. C. WOOD *Fresh Water Algæ* 207 Primary branches..densely ramellose with the ramuli lanceolate.

‖**ramus** (ˈreɪməs). Pl. rami (ˈreɪmaɪ). [L. *rāmus* branch, etc.]

1. *Anat.* **a.** A process of a bone, *esp.* of the ischium and pubes, and of the jaw-bone.

1803 *Med. Jrnl.* IX. 394 The transverse space existing between the rami of the ischium. **1843** J. G. WILKINSON *Swedenborg's Anim. Kingd.* I. i. 22 Between the rami of the lower jaw, and the base of the tongue. **1855** RAMSBOTHAM *Obstetr. Med.* 5 The ischium is connected..with the pubis at the junction of the rami.

b. A major branch of a nerve; ***ramus communicans*** (pl. *rami communicantes*), a branch of one nerve that joins another; *esp.* one of those joining a sympathetic ganglion with a spinal nerve.

1811 J. BELL *Anat. Human Body* (ed. 3) II. 515 Whilst it [*sc.* the tibial nerve] is yet in the hollow behind the joint formed by the hamstring tendons, it gives off a nerve which comes out from the ham, and descends superficially on the back of the leg. This has been called ramus communicans tibialis. *Ibid.* 517 When it [*sc.* the fibular nerve] arrives at the anular ligament, it is much diminished. Here it divides into the ramus dorsalis pedis profundus, and superficialis. **1893** H. ST. J. BROOKS in H. Morris *Treat. Human Anat.* v. 864 Each of the thoracic ganglia is connected to the corresponding spinal nerve by two rami communicantes, a white and a grey. The white ramus communicans consists of medullated fibres... The grey ramus communicans or revehent nerve is formed of non-medullated fibres. *Ibid.* 865 Occasionally the number of rami is increased to five or six. **1927** W. KEILLER *Nerve Tracts* I. 147 The spinal nerves distal to the root ganglia divide almost immediately into anterior and posterior rami. **1946** *Gray's Anat.* (ed. 29) 1078 The sensory root [of the ciliary ganglion] is formed by a ramus communicans from the nasociliary nerve. **1964** A. J. BERGER *Elem. Human Anat.* v. 84 The definitive spinal nerve is very short because it splits into two main branches (or rami) almost as soon as it is formed. The smaller dorsal primary ramus innervates the deep back muscles. **1967** G. M. WYBURN et al. *Conc. Anat.* iii. 93/1 Incise one or two intercostal spaces to expose the intercostal nerves and find their slender connections with the sympathetic trunk, i.e. the grey and white rami communicantes. **1972** C. R. & T. S. LEESON *Human Structure* iii. 11/1 Immediately after emerging from an intervertebral foramen, the spinal nerve divides into a posterior primary ramus and an anterior primary ramus.

2. *Ornith.* = BARB *sb.* 6.

1882 H. GADOW in *Proc. Zool. Soc.* 411 The series of radii or barbules on either side of the rami or barbs.

3. *Zool.* In the mastax of rotifers, each of the two articulated parts of the incus that are attached to the fulcrum.

1856 *Phil. Trans. R. Soc.* CXLVI. 426 The incus.. consists of distinct articulated portions. The principal are two stout rami..resting on what appears to be a slender pedicel (fulcrum, *h*). **1886**, etc. [see FULCRUM 2 c]. **1972** M. S. GARDINER *Biol. Invertebrates* vii. 236/2 The wall [of the mastax]..is extended into seven firm, sclerotized pieces, the trophi, moved by small individual muscles. These pieces are a single median fulcrum and three pairs of lateral ones, two rami, two unci, and two manubria.

†**ramuscle.** *Obs.* = next.

1677 in *Phil. Trans.* XII. 902, I could see those manifold little vessels with their ramuscles, which were all very feeble, and by the least touch broke asunder.

ramuscule (rəˈmʌskjuːl). *Biol.* [ad. late L. *rāmusculus*, dim. of *rāmus* RAMUS: see -CULE. Cf. F. *ramuscule.*] A small branch.

1831 R. KNOX *Cloquet's Anat.* 644 From the aorta..arise secondary trunks, branches, twigs and ramuscules in great number. **1881** P. M. DUNCAN in *Jrnl. Linn. Soc.* XV. 323 These branch.., and terminate in minute ramuscules.

So ‖**raˈmusculus** (pl. -culi).

1842 E. WILSON *Anat. Vade M.* (ed. 2) 263 They inosculate..with the terminal ramusculi of the arteries. **1866** *Treas. Bot.* 957/2 *Ramusculi*, the mycelium of certain fungals.

†**ramverse**, *v. Obs.* [ad. F. *renverser*, f. *re-* + *envers* INVERSE.]

1. *trans.* To overturn, overthrow. Also *fig.*

1412–20 LYDG. *Chron. Troy* II. xiii, He hath aye ioye theyr honour to ramuerse. **1593** NASHE *Christ's T.* (1613) 28 They seeke to drowne and ramuerse euery ship.

2. To reverse, withdraw.

1632 LITHGOW *Trav.* x. 461 He could not Ram-verse the Wedges. **1662** PETRIE *Ch. Hist.* xiii. I. 391 Thus he did ramverse the priviledge granted by Pope Honorius the III.

Hence †**ramvert** *v.* (after *convert, invert*, etc.).

1632 LITHGOW *Trav.* v. 189 A guilty conscience.. ramverts most of them, either ouer in a torment of melancholy, otherwise in the extasie of madnesse.

ramyfye, obs. f. RAMIFY.

ramysde, var. RAMMIST *a.*

ramzaun, var. *ramazan* RAMADAN.

ramzys, obs. pl. RAMS.

ran (ræn). [Of unknown origin.]

1. A certain length of twine (see quots.).

1794 *Rigging & Seamanship* 56 *Ran*, twenty cords of twine, wound on a reel, and every cord so parted by a knot as to be easily separated. **1880** *Plain Hints Needlework* 104 For netting, the ordinary common twine runs three-quarters of a pound to a 'ran'.

2. *dial.* A certain width of a net (see quot.).

1887 *Kent. Gloss.*, *Ran*, a Folkestone herring net, which is about thirty yards long, is made four rans deep; and there are sixty meshes to a ran.

ran, pa. t. and obs. pa. pple. of RUN *v.*

ran, Sc. variant of RAWN, roe.

Rana (ˈrɑːnə). [Nepali and Hindi *rānā* prince, f. Skr. *rājana* royal: cf. RAJA, RAJAH.] The title used by members of the family which virtually ruled Nepal from 1846 to 1951. Also *attrib.*

1951 *Britannica Bk. of Year* 462/2 Although the relations between the exiled members of the ruling Rana family with the hereditary prime minister..had been unfriendly [etc.]. **1959** *Manch. Guardian* 18 Aug. 5/1 The Ranas married their daughters to Rajput princes. **1971** C. BONINGTON *Annapurna South Face* iii. 32, I could pick out Rana palaces with spacious courtyards and rusty, corrugated-iron roofs. *Ibid.* 37 The Ranas have lost their power but many of them still hold high office, particularly in the armed forces. However, most of the old Rana palaces..have now been turned into offices or hotels. **1971** K. KENT in *Ibid.* 311 In early 1951 a democratic form of government [in Nepal] was established by proclamation. It kept the existing Rana, Sir Mohan Chamsher, as Prime Minister, but in November 1951 a revision replaced this last Prime Minister with Mr M. P. Koirala of the Congress Party. **1977** *Times* 15 Nov. 15/1 The overthrow of the Rana regime in 1951.

ranai, var. LANAI.

Ranal (ˈreɪnəl), *a.* and *sb. Bot.* [f. mod.L. name of order *Ranales* (J. Lindley *Nixus Plantarum* (1833) 9), f. RAN(UNCULUS + L. *-āles*, pl. of *-ālis* -AL.] **A.** *adj.* = RANALIAN *a.* **B.** *sb.* A ranalian plant.

1839 T. BASKERVILLE *Affinities of Plants* 73 We shall find there a collection of orders constituting the Ranal and Anonal alliances. **1846** J. LINDLEY *Veget. Kingdom* 416 In appearance Ranals are singularly different in the same Order.

ranalian (rəˈneɪlɪən), *a. Bot.* Also **Ran-**, **-ean.** [f. as prec. + -IAN.] Of or pertaining to a plant of the order Ranales or the group as a whole.

1915 C. E. BESSEY in *Ann. Missouri Bot. Garden* II. 116 The opposite-leaved class..is the first to emerge from the cycadean phylum, appearing as the ranalean complex. *Ibid.* 127 Ranalean evolution has..been one of more and more simplification of flower structure. **1926** *Jrnl. Bot.* LXIV. 83 In following the lead of those who assume a common Ranalian origin for Angiosperms, Mr. Hutchinson has burnt his boats. **1931** A. M. JOHNSON *Taxonomy of Flowering Plants* i. 11 We have thus a phylogenetic tree of three main branches radiating from the polycarpellate, apocarpous, hypogynous, Ranalian base. **1959** FOSTER & GIFFORD *Compar. Morphol. Vascular Plants* xviii. 458 It is clear that these ranalian plants are primitively vesselless. *Ibid.* 480 It is only by such laborious procedures that we shall be able to test the importance of recent investigations on ranalean families. **1972** *Nature* 14 Apr. 353/2 The Magnoliidae association corresponds with the 'Ranalian' and the Hamamelidae-Dilleniidae associations with the 'Rosalian' cluster as conceived above.

raˈnarian, *a. nonce-wd.* [f. as next.] 'Froggy'.

1814 T. L. PEACOCK *Sir Proteus* i. *note*, Ranarian minstrels of all ages and nations have entertained a high opinion of their own melody.

ranarium (rəˈnɛərɪəm). [Mod.L., f. *rāna* frog: see -ARIUM.] A place in which frogs are kept.

1889 *Lancet* 27 Apr. 862 The [Berlin] institute..possesses a ranarium, in which are 700 frogs.

ranc, obs. form of RANK *a.*

rance (rɑːns, -æ-), *sb.*[1] Also 7 **rauns, raunce, ranse.** [Prob. of F. origin, but not recognized in the leading F. dicts.] A kind of variegated marble (see quot. 1887). Also *attrib.*

Described by Larousse (*Dict. Univ. XIX Siècle*, s.v.) as 'un marbre blanc et rouge brun, veiné de blanc cendre et de bleu'.

1598 SYLVESTER *Du Bartas, Triumph of Faith* (title-p.), A Tomb..With Ivorie Pillars mixt with Jet and Rance. **1632** QUARLES *Div. Fancies* IV. liii, No Launce can pierce it, it is grown More heard than Raunce, or th' Adamantine stone. **1686** PLOT *Staffordsh.* 107 Yielding Coal, Lead, Copper, Rance Marble, and Mill-stones. **1703** T. N. *City & C. Purchaser* 107 Chimney-pieces..of Rance, or Liver-colour'd-marble. **1723** J. SMITH *Art Paint. Oyl* (ed. 5) 1 The Stone must be a hard Rance, Marble, or some other of a close grain. **1887** *Archit. Publ. Soc. Dict.*, *Rance*, a marble obtained from Hainault in Belgium, of a dingy red colour varied with veins and spots of blue and white.

fig. **1598** SYLVESTER *Du Bartas* II. iv. I. *Tropheis* 1110 What living Rance, what rapting Ivorie Swims in these streams?

rance, ranse (ræns), *sb.*[2] Chiefly *Sc.* [Perh. a. F. *ranche* pole, bar, rung (see Hatz.-Darm., and Du Cange s.v. *ranchonum*).] A bar or baton; a prop or support.

1808 JAMIESON, *Rance*, 1. a prop, a wooden stake employed for the purpose of supporting a building. 2. The cross-bar which joins the lower part of the frame of a chair together. 3. The fore-part of the roof of a bed, or the cornice of a wooden bed. **1855** AINSLIE *Land Burns* (1892) 243 Our Cadger..shot the muckle door slot, Made a ranse o' a big racking pin. **1867** SMYTH *Sailor's Word-bk.*, *Rance*, the strut or support of a Congreve rocket. **1883** GRESLEY *Gloss. Coal-mining* 199 *Rance*, a pillar of coal—a large stoop.

Hence **rance** *v. trans.*, to bar, prop, etc.

1808 JAMIESON, *To rance*, to prop with stakes. **1887** MᶜNEILL *Blawearie* 54 Did ye sit..wi' a foot ranst against the wa' face. *Ibid.* 119 We have 'ransed' the cage with crossbars.

†**rance**, *sb.*[3] *Obs.* Nasalized form of RACE *sb.*[6]

1570 LEVINS *Manip.* 21/8 A rance of ginger, *zinziber.*

†**rance**, *sb.*[4] *Obs.* Nasalized form of RACE *sb.*[7]

1728 [see RACE *sb.*[7]].

rance, obs. Sc. form of RHENISH.

rancel, ransel (ˈræns(ə)l), *v. Orkn. & Shetl.* Also 8 rancell, 8–9 -cil. [App. a back-formation from RANCELMAN.] *intr.* 'To search throughout a parish for stolen or for insufficient goods; also, to inquire into every kind of misdemeanour' (Jamieson). Hence **ˈrancelling** *vbl. sb.*

The main sense is that of ON. *rannsaka* RANSACK *v.*, but the form can scarcely be derived from this.

1615 *Act 10* in Barry *Orkney* App. (1805) 460 Anent Rancelling of Theft. **1725** *Act 26* in Gifford *Hist. Descr. Zetland* App. (1876) 91 Upon any suspicion of theft, two or three Rancelmen may..go to the neighbour parish and rancell. **1733** GIFFORD *Hist. Descr. Zetland* (1876) 41 To enter any house within the parish at all hours of the day or night, and search the house for stolen goods, which they call ranciling.

ˈrancellor. [f. as prec. + -OR.] = next.

The form *rauzellaar* (for *ran-*) used by Scott app. implies an idea that the word was of Dutch origin.

1644 *Act 46* in Barry *Orkney* App. (1805) 477 That the seaverall rancellors in every paroch [be] solemnly sworn upon their great oath. **1822** SCOTT *Pirate* ii. 26 The old Rauzellaar of the village, who had the voice most potential in the deliberations of the township.

ˈrancelman, ˈranselman. Also 8 -cell-, 9 -cil-, -zel-. [? a. ON. **reynslu-maðr* (acc. *-mann*), f. *reynsla* trying, searching, f. *reyna* to try, examine, search into + *maðr* MAN.] A local officer formerly appointed in Orkney and Shetland to inquire into thefts and petty offences, and otherwise preserve good order in his district.

1752 *Act 26* in Gifford *Hist. Descr. Zetland* App. (1876) 89 A list of such honest men in the parish as are fit to be rancelmen. **1822** SCOTT *Pirate* v. **1892** G. GOUDIE in *Proc. Soc. Ant. Scot.* XXVI. 189 *heading*, The Founds, Lawrightmen, and Ranselmen of Shetland Parishes.

ranˈcescent, *a. rare*$^{-0}$. [ad. L. pres. pple. of *rancēscĕre.*] Becoming rancid. (Webster, 1832.)

ranch, *sb.*[1] *rare.* [Nasalized var. RACE *sb.*[3]; cf. RANCH *v.*[2]] A scratch.

1611 COTGR., *Griffade*, a clawing; a scratch or gripe with the clawes; a ranche, or clinch with a beasts paw. *a* **1825** FORBY *Voc. E. Anglia*, *Ranch*, a deep and severe scratch, a flesh wound.

ranch (rɑːn(t)ʃ, rænʃ), *sb.*[2] orig. *U.S.* Also **ranche.** [Anglicized form of RANCHO.]

1. a. A hut or house in the country.

1808 PIKE *Sources Mississ.* III. (1810) 254 When we arrived at the Ranche, we soon had out a number of boys, who brought in the horse. **1867** DIXON *New Amer.* iv. (ed. 6) 42 A white frame house—on this side of the river called a ranch —peeps out..from beneath the foliage.

b. A single-storey or split-level house.

1960 'E. MCBAIN' *Killer's Payoff* xi. 111 Some real estate agent had decided to give the title 'ranch' to any house that had all of its living space on one floor. **1965** H. HOOD in *Tamarack Review* Winter 12 Our house was the first California-redwood ranch in the town of Mount Royal. **1965** 'L. EGAN' *Detective's Due* (1966) 10 Big newish expensive homes. The one they wanted turned out to be a split-level ranch with a lot of synthetic stone on its front. **1974** R. B. PARKER *God save Child* (1975) x. 73 A one-story house..a low ranch built on a slab.

2. a. A cattle-breeding establishment, farm, or estate. Also, the persons employed or living on this, and *transf.* Phr. ***meanwhile, back at the ranch***: orig. used in Western cowboy stories and films, introducing a subsidiary plot.

Quot. 1831 may belong to sense 1.

1831 J. O. PATTIE *Personal Narr.* 221 [At] a ranch..I procured a horse for three dollars. **1847** B. LUNDY *Life* x. 58 We set off at day-break, and went twenty-one miles to a *ranche.* **1870** J. C. DUVAL *Adventures Big-Foot Wallace* xl. 247 When I have got through with..my 'inheritance', I shall come back to my ranch here, put on my old buckskins, and run after stock and fight Indians for a livelihood the balance of my life. **1872** RAYMOND *Statist. Mines & Mining* 278 Large ranches for beef-cattle and horses. **1881** *Chicago Times* 4 June, There are already three thousand cows in this ranch. **1887** *Scribner's Mag.* II. 509/2 The American herder speaks of his companions collectively as the 'ranch' or the 'outfit'. **1888** R. W. BUCHANAN *Heir of Linne* II. xx. 121 I've got a cattle ranche in the wild west. **1933** J. D. HIGINBOTHAM *When West was Young* 201 A ranch frequently takes the name of the horse or cattle brand of its owner... Other ranches took the name of a locality. **1950** *Sun* (Baltimore) 2 Mar. 8/5 A New Zealander has swopped his cow pastures for a 'whale ranch'... The 'ranch' has been set up in a bay of Arapawa Island off Wellington by Gill Perano, who carries out his 'round-ups' by motor boat. **1958** L. VAN DER POST *Lost World of Kalahari* iv. 72 He went out to East Africa to one of its remote frontier areas and started a ranch of his own. **1963** J. CRIST in *N.Y. Herald Trib. Sunday Mag.* 24 Nov. 40/2 Kramer keeps any number of old 'meanwhile, back at the ranch' side adventures going. **1972** *Buenos Aires Herald* 2 Feb. 7/6 He..seduced several women after promising he would marry them later in Venezuela where he said he owned several ranches. **1978** *Observer* (Colour Suppl.) 29 Jan. front cover (*caption*) Meanwhile, back at the ranch...

b. A farm (arable, fruit-growing, etc.); *spec.*, one on which foxes or mink are bred and raised for their fur.

1865 'MARK TWAIN' in *Californian* 28 Oct. 5/3, I have a ranch of quite unknown extent, Its turnips great, its oats without compare. **1890** *Stock Grower & Farmer* 12 July 5/1 They are pasturing on the Alfalfa ranches. **1900** *Sci. Amer.* 21 Apr. 242/3 There are..no less than thirty-five [Alaskan] islands occupied by proprietors of fox ranches. **1948** [see *mink ranch* s.v. MINK 4]. **1953** A. R. M. LOWER *Unconventional Voy.* 146 The Okanagan with its pleasant little towns and its fruit ranches—everything is a ranch in B[ritish] C[olumbia]. **1958** H. B. ALLEN in *Publ. Amer. Dialect Soc.* xxx. 6 *Ranch*, denoting an establishment for cattle-raising..although the somewhat prestigious nature of the word has spread it eastward through its adoption by farmers who have large wheat-farms. **1976** *Billings* (Montana) *Gaz.* 4 July 8-D/2 (Advt.), Experienced worker ..for dryland grain & livestock ranch South of Billings.

3. a. *attrib.* and *Comb.*, as ***ranch-boarding, -building, company, country, dog, experience, girl, guitar, hand, hide, -house, -hut, job, -land, -life, -mark, -overseer, -owner, -woman; ranch-owning*** adj.; **ranch egg**, a fresh egg; **ranch mink**, mink bred on a ranch, or its fur; also *ellipt.*, a coat made of ranch mink fur; **ranch wagon**, (*a*) a horse-drawn wagon used on a ranch; (*b*) = *estate car* s.v. ESTATE *sb.* 14.

1976 *Rhyl Jrnl. & Advertiser* 9 Dec. 22/3 (Advt.), Reclaimed and new timber for sale..Perspex corrugated sheets, Target board, plywoods, ranch boarding, chipboard, melamine etc. **1926** D. H. LAWRENCE *Plumed Serpent* vi. 109 The telephone was in the old ranch-building. **1884** *Daily News* 19 Dec. 3/1 Ranche companies are quite modern institutions. **1885** *Weekly New Mexican Rev.* 22 Jan. 2/5 Texas..is still as good, if not a better ranch country, than New Mexico. **1895** *Rev. of Rev.* Aug. 167 The ranch country where his herds graze. **1897** E. HOUGH *Story of Cowboy* 227 In the Indian Nations the writer has been out with a pack of greyhounds, which included a good pack of ranch dogs. **1923** D. H. LAWRENCE *Birds, Beasts & Flowers* 156 Now you've come sex-alive, and the great ranch dogs are all after you. **1908** *Sunset* Dec. 792/2 If you were working with ranch eggs, store eggs or yard eggs, it might be different. **1966** 'L. HOLTON' *Out of Depths* xv. 149 Two ranch eggs with ham. **1976** *Billings* (Montana) *Gaz.* 4 July 8-D/2 (Advt.), Must have Animal Science or Animal Husbandry degree. Previous sales, ranch or feed lot experience preferred. *c* **1894** C. HOYT *Texas Steer* I, in M. J. Moses *Representative Amer. Dramas* (1925) 17 Oh, I do so want to be something besides a Texas ranch girl. **1951** M. MCLUHAN *Mech. Bride* (1967) 148/1 There is a story about a little ranch girl. **1947** R. TAYLOR *Bar Nothing Ranch* xvi. 190 She'd cuddle the ranch guitar and croon heartbreakingly. **1951** GILLIS & MYLES *North Pole Boarding House* 6 A minister to the spiritual needs of the husky ranch-hands in Alberta's godless foothills. **1977** *Herald* (Melbourne) 17 Jan. 18/7 (Advt.), Sheepskin car seat covers and rugs, ranch hides, kangaroo and calf skin. **1978** *Lancashire Life* Mar. 70 (Advt.), The seating area is in hard wearing ranch hide. **1862** *Harper's Mag.* June 14/1 Having awakened my mule I rode on about five miles further, where I reached a small ranch-house. **1872** C. KING *Mountain. Sierra Nev.* ii. 28 The roads..are flanked by small ranch-houses. **1933** J. STEINBECK in *North Amer. Rev.* Nov. 423/2 At the ranch house, he found his mother sitting on the porch. **1930** R. MACAULAY *Staying with Relations* xix. 273 At El Refugio,..there's a tiny ranch-hut where I tried for a drink of Mexicali. **1976** *Billings* (Montana) *Gaz.* 4 July 7-D/7 (Advt.), Competent college girl for summer ranch job. **1933** *Times Lit. Suppl.* 9 Feb. 94/2 The arrival of a stranger on the ranchlands of Clinton Prescott coincided with a fierce snowstorm. **1979** *Time* 8 Jan. 40/2 In Texas, Prince Franz Joseph..bought 16,000 acres of ranch land. **1899** 'MARK TWAIN' in *Harper's Monthly Mag.* (1914) Dec. 4/2 It told me where to begin to talk ranch-life in Carson Valley. **1903** A. M. BINSTEAD *Pitcher in Paradise* iv. 110 Sleep, someone, whose name and ranchmarks I have forgotten, once observed, is much overrated. **1952** S. ELLIN *Key to Nicholas Street* I. i. 10 A ranch mink that is worth laying your life down for. **1960** *Bull. Retail Trading-Standards Assoc.* Nov. 2 Ranch Mink should..be so described unless it is a mutation mink. **1964** *Harper's Bazaar* Nov. 83 Ranch mink hat. **1976** *Daily Record* (Glasgow) 23 Nov. 18/2 Ranch mink brushes expensive mohair and the whole atmosphere is narcotic and totally unreal. **1926** D. H. LAWRENCE *Plumed Serpent* vi. 112 He was not really an hotel manager, but a ranch-overseer. **1888** *Cent. Mag.* Feb. 500 The ranch-owners differ more from each other than do the cowboys. **1977** *New Yorker* 29 Aug. 46/3 Harlow comes from a ranch-owning family whose roots were established in northern California over several generations. **1886** T. ROOSEVELT in *Outing* July 387, I took along the ranch wagon, drawn by four shaggy horses. **1970** *Globe & Mail* (Toronto) 26 Sept. 48/1 (Advt.), 69 Ford 6-passenger ranch wagon, finished in a rich dark blue. **1975** *Country Life* 2 Jan. 32/1 One feature of these New World ranch wagons..is the tailgate. **1877** BLACK *Green Past.* xxxii. (1878) 255 In the company of a ranchwoman, a farmeress.

b. Of a modern building: built in the style associated with a ranch; single-storey; as ***ranch bungalow, dormitory, home, house***; also ***ranch-style, -type*** adjs.

1966 *Globe & Mail* (Toronto) 30 June 30/5 (Advt.), Rustic 7 room ranch bungalow on ½ acre lot, trees galore! **1973** *Irish Times* 2 Mar. 22/6 (Advt.), Delightful American ranch bungalow..in exceptional position and close to all amenities. **1974** *Country Life* 21 Feb. Suppl. 36/1 American Ranch Bungalow in Surrey..£60,000. **1976** *Columbus* (Montana) *News* (Joliet Suppl.) 27 May 2/3 Housing [malefactors] in ranch and dairy dormitories. **1973** *N.Y. Law Jrnl.* 26 July 16/8 (Advt.), Mini-farm, 19 acres, neat 5 room ranch home, almost borders Summit Lake. **1978** *Detroit Free Press* 16 Apr. F9/1 (Advt.), Bar with 2 bdrm ranch home & soft ice cream business. **1952** H. INNES *Campbell's Kingdom* I. ii. 33 The Fergus home was a low, sprawling ranch-house building. **1959** N. MAILER *Advts. for Myself* (1961) 378 Eitel's rented ranch-house in the desert. **1975** *Woman's Jrnl.* Sept. 62/1 Today..she lives in style in a palatial ranch-house in Beverly Hills. **1961** J. MITFORD in *Life* 4 Aug. 8/2 Motels..may be Tudor, Queen Anne, Colonial, Knotty Pine, Ranch Style, or Futuristic in décor. **1962** E. SNOW *Other Side of River: Red China Today* lx. 461 To people who live in American ranch-style bungalows, all the new multiple dwellings in China would seem primitive. **1970** *Cape Times* 28 Oct. 19/9 (Advt.), Outstanding architect designed, owner built ranch style house on high foundation. **1978** *Detroit Free Press* 16 Apr. (Parade) 20/2 Just before Christmas, Dan Scarborough, the senior state senator from northeast Florida, was entertaining some friends in his family's sprawling ranch-style home. **1956** W. H. WHYTE *Organization Man* 11 It is difficult to see the three-button suit as more of a strait-jacket than overalls, or the ranch-type house than old law tenements. **1976** J. PHILIPS *Backlash* (1977) III. 118 [She] lived in a modern ranch-type house about a mile out of town.

Hence **'ranchless** *a.*, devoid of ranches.

1888 *Home Missionary* (N.Y.) May 15 We were away out on even the ranchless plains.

ranch, *v.*[1] [f. RANCH *sb.*[2]] **1. a.** *intr.* Also with *it.* To conduct a ranch.

1866 B. HARTE in *Californian* 26 May 1/1 Ranchin' out this way? **1872** 'MARK TWAIN' *Roughing It* xxxiv. 242 He had been farming (or ranching as the more customary term is) in the Washoe District. **1890** *Anthony's Photogr. Bull.* III. 32 The jolly fellows who ranch it in the West. **1976** *Billings* (Montana) *Gaz.* 28 June 5-A/2 The bridegroom graduated..with a degree in agriculture. The newlyweds will ranch near Boyes. **1976** *Laurel* (Montana) *Outlook* 30 June 14/1 He farmed and ranched at Acton until 1974.

b. To let land for grazing.

1910 *Blackw. Mag.* July 126/2 He is 'ranching', that is, letting grazing on the eleven months' system.

2. *trans.* **a.** To put (an animal) on a ranch.

1873 J. H. BEADLE *Undevel. West* xxx. 663 Six hundred miles..had worn out my horse, and on the 16th instant I 'ranched him' twenty miles south of Beaver. **1916** *Yukon Territory* (Canada Dept. Interior) x. 177 Foxes should be ranched in woodland areas. **1935** *Discovery* Feb. 50/2 Animals so purchased will be ranched and tended by the vendor. **1980** *Times* 18 Mar. 14/8 Mink being ranched, humanely killed and kept in a life of luxury.

b. To use (land) as a ranch.

1901 B. HARTE *Under Redwoods* 74 It caused her to remove to Santa Ana, where her old father had feebly ranched a 'quarter section' in the valley. **1927** *Daily Tel.* 23 Aug. 11/6 The large arable farms..must..be grassed down, and ranched at a nominal rent. **1965** F. SYMINGTON *Tuktu* 13 If the central Arctic were being systematically 'ranched' with caribou herds.

Hence **ranched** *ppl. a.*, of an animal: confined to or bred on a ranch; also *transf.*, of the fur of a ranched animal.

1954 *Economist* 20 Feb. 567/1 Ranched Russian mink. *Ibid.*, Wild furs and ranched furs. **1970** *Daily Tel.* 10 Oct. 14 Tourists who visit emergent countries do so to see the animals in their natural environment—not confined and 'ranched'. **1977** *Harpers & Queen* Sept. 65 Very dark natural ranched mink coats from £2,750.

ranch (rɑːnʃ, -æ-), *v.*[2] *Obs.* exc. *dial.* Also 5 **ransch**, 7 **raunch**. [Nasalized form of RACE *v.*[3]; compare GLACE *v.* with *glanch* GLANCE *v.*] *trans.* To tear, cut, scratch, etc.

c **1430** *Two Cookery-bks.* 39 Þan take a longe Pecher, al a-bowte ouer alle þat it be ransched. *c* **1460** *Play Sacram.* 813 How thys paynfulle passyon rancheth myn hart. *c* **1611** CHAPMAN *Iliad* v. 856 A javelin..his belly graz'd upon.. and ranch'd the flesh. **1700** DRYDEN *Fables, Meleager & Atalanta* 140 [The boar] ranch'd his hips with one continu'd wound. *a* **1825** FORBY *Voc. E. Anglia*, *Ranch*, to scratch deeply and severely, as with a nail.

absol. **1699** GARTH *Dispens.* v. (1706) 89 Emetics ranch, and keen Catharticks scour.

Hence **'ranching** *ppl. a.*

1620 SHELTON *Quix.* II. IV. xix. 233 Fierce Whelps, which shall imitate the ranching paws of their valorous Father.

†**ranch**, *v.*[3] *Obs. rare.* In 6 raunch. [Var. RACE *v.*[4]; cf. prec.] *trans.* To pull, pluck.

1579 SPENSER *Sheph. Cal.* Aug. 99 Hasting to raunch the arrow out. **1593** NASHE *Christ's T.* (1613) 65 Not a weede sprung vp, but..was weeded and rauenously rauncht vp.

'rancher. orig. and chiefly *U.S.* [f. RANCH *sb.*[2] + -ER[1].]

1. A ranchman.

1836 *Papers of M. Buonaparte Lamar* (1921) I. 337 Capt King went..to Lopes..for the purpose of chastising some ranchers. **1866** *Rep. Indian Affairs* (U.S.) 189 Teamsters, packers, herders, ranchers and miners all over the country have become exasperated. **1885** *Manch. Exam.* 13 Aug. 4/7 This..prevents ranging by other ranchers. **1953** *Manch. Guardian Weekly* 18 June 3 The surviving farmers and ranchers have bought up the land from the men who went away. **1958** *Publ. Amer. Dialect Soc.* xxx. 6 A man with such a dual [*sc.* wheat and cattle] establishment in central Nebraska..is more likely to identify himself as a rancher rather than as a farmer. **1961** L. VAN DER POST *Heart of Hunter* I. vii. 112 One of the foremost ranchers near Gemsbok Pan was in the Union and coming back by truck across the desert. **1973** *Sunday Advocate-News* (Barbados) 21 Jan. 14/1 There are a few ranchers.. on the Brazilian border, a few miners, a few lumberjacks. **1976** *Billings* (Montana) *Gaz.* 4 July 1-A/5 Z—— C—— was born into a family of ranchers who had come to Montana from Canada a few years before the first Yegen arrived.

2. A modern single-storey house.

1965 *Sun* (Vancouver) 8 Aug. 47/7 (Advt.), Rancher.. close to Burnaby Park and swimming pool. **1968** H. WAUGH *Con Game* ii. 23 The Demarest home was a rancher in the $25,000 class. **1970** *Globe & Mail* (Toronto) 28 Sept. 24/3 (Advt.), Lovely buff brick rancher on wide 80 ft. lot. **1978** *N.Y. Times* 29 Mar. B8/6 (Advt.), Beautiful rambling Rancher. 2 yrs old, 7 spac rms, [etc.].

rancheral (rɑːn'ʃɛərəl, -æ-), *a. rare.* [f. RANCHERO + -AL.] Of or pertaining to rancheros.

1847 G. F. A. RUXTON *Adventures in Mexico* xiii. 94 Of these eight mozos, he who bore away the palm of rancheral superiority..was the third son.

‖**rancheria** (rantʃe'ria). Also **rancheree**, **rancherie** ('rɑːnʃəriː, ræn-). [Sp., f. *rancho* RANCHO.] In Spanish America and Western U.S., a collection of Indian huts; a place or house where a number of rancheros live.

1600 HAKLUYT *Voy.* III. 678 Here the Spaniardes haue seated their Rancheria of some twentie or thirtie houses. **1760–72** *Juan & Ulloa's Voy.* (ed. 3) I. 134 Several Rancherias, or assemblages of Indian huts, are under the jurisdiction of a village. **1851** MAYNE REID *Scalp Hunt.* ix. 70 Indians crowd in from the neighbouring rancherias. **1854** C. E. DE LONG in *Calif. Hist. Soc. Q.* (1929) VIII. 200 Anderson & I fell in with an Indian Rancheria. **1872** C. KING *Mountain. Sierra Nev.* ii. 37 The rancheria was astir when we arrived. **1872** R. B. JOHNSON *Very Far West Indeed* 197 I'd take a dozen Injuns straight out of the rancherie, an' make a better government out of 'em than they've got up thar. **1901** *Canad. Mag.* XVIII. 179/1 Jim is the policeman at the Indian rancheree. **1901** *Daily Colonist* (Victoria, B.C.) 15 Oct. 3/2 A heavy cargo, including everything from shipments of lumber for Bella Coola and Kitimaat, to new gravestones for various Indians at Northern rancheries. **1914** A. H. FITCH *Junipero Serra* iii. 222 There were many rancherias on the banks of the Colorado. **1955** *Sci. News Let.* 16 Apr. 245/3 These [South American] Indians..live in very small communities called 'rancherias', consisting of from two to 15 individuals. **1963** R. SYMONS *Many Trails* vii. 71 Although they own small reserves—which they call rancheries—most of them prefer a nomadic life. **1976** *Islander* (Victoria, B.C.) 27 June 2/3 Sent their logs downstream to a booming ground near the Indian rancherie.

‖**ranchero** (ran'tʃero). [Sp., f. as prec.] One employed on a ranch as herdsman or overseer; the owner of a ranch; a ranchman. Also *attrib.*

1826 J. E. B. AUSTIN *Let.* 31 Oct. in C. Barker *Austin Papers* (1924) I. II. 1482 The old Ranchero was much surprised, but overjoyed to see me. **1836** C. J. LATROBE *Rambler in Mexico* ii. 27 You have here..every degree from the substantial *Ranchero*, or proprietor, bespurred,.. embroidered vest, and gaudy *serape*,..or the trusty *arriero*, with his long string of mules. **1840** R. H. DANA *Bef. Mast* (1854) 118 A law was passed..declaring all the Indians free and independent Rancheros. **1846** *Times* 16 June 8/2 The Rancheros, part of the material of the Mexican army, are half Indian and half Spanish in their extraction. **1883** STEVENSON *Silverado Sq.* 25, I think we passed but one ranchero's house in the whole distance. **1927** W. CATHER *Death comes for Archbishop* III. 78 He and the *rancheros* had run their church to suit themselves, making a very gay affair of it. **1947** M. LOWRY *Under Volcano* iii. 90 The orange juice and ranchero eggs. **1963** *Punch* 20 Feb. 285/2 Women have gone overboard for their ranchero hats. **1968** *Esquire* July 99/3 John Weitz..designed this yellow-and-black-striped blazer suit. With it, Ranchero tie over a neckband shirt. **1973** *Country Life* 6 Dec. 1970/1 The Mexican heavy knit woollen jacket..worn by *rancheros*... The coat looks good on either sex. **1977** *Times Lit. Suppl.* 21 Jan. 88/5 In the ranks of the Cristeros [in Mexico 1926–29] there figure small landowners, rancheros, Indians.

ranchette (rɑːn'ʃɛt, -æ-). *U.S.* [See -ETTE.] A small, modern, single-storey or split-level house.

1956 R. A. HEINLEIN in *Mag. of Fantasy & Sci. Fict.* Oct. 23/2, I wanted a ranchette near the plant; she favored a flat in Town. **1966** *Punch* 9 Nov. 692/2 Their split-level Graeco-Moorish ranchette, set on teetering stilts above the green Los Angeles smog. **1979** *Tucson* (Arizona) *Citizen* 3 Oct. 18C/3 (Advt.), 1½ to 2 commercial acre Ranchettes overlooking the city.

'ranching, *vbl. sb.* orig. and chiefly *U.S.* [f. RANCH *sb.*[2] + -ING[1].] Stock-raising or cattle-breeding on a ranch. Also, the raising of game and other animals.

1863 E. R. MEREDITH *Let.* May in *Frontier & Midland* (1937) XVII. 288/1 A ranch is properly a grazing farm and the term 'ranching' sometimes means farming but is generally applied in this country [*sc.* Idaho] to taking care of stock. **1870** J. C. DUVAL *Adventures Big-Foot Wallace* xlvi. 302 We would try our hands at 'ranching'. **1873** J. H. BEADLE *Undevel. West* xv. 267 'Ranching' came next, and all this industry is not lost. **1882** *Contemp. Rev.* Aug. 232 Ranching or stock-raising on a colossal scale has already begun. **1916** [see *mink ranching* s.v. MINK 4]. **1950** *Manch. Guardian Weekly* 5 Jan. 10 Teamsters carried it through the ranching country. **1971** *Inside Kenya Today* Mar. 52/2 Arrangements have also been finalized for the establishment of a ranching scheme at Jaldesa. **1974** *Listener* 2 May 572/3 [The land] is all earmarked for ranching development. **1975** *Nature* 5 June 449/2 Interest in game ranching of natural animal populations as a food source goes back a long way. **1980** *Daily Tel.* 30 Dec. 7/2 Salmon ranching, inshore fishing and tourism are the immediate projects for economic development.

ranchito (ran'tʃito). Also **ranchita**. [Sp., dim. of RANCHO.] In the Western U.S., a small ranch or farm.

1850 L. H. GARRARD *Wah-to-Yah* xvii. 231 To the Ranchita is something less than a mile. **1906** A. ADAMS *Cattle Brands* 92 He had sent to a nearby ranchito for a man who had at least the reputation of being quite a hunter. **1976** *New Yorker* 26 Apr. 122/2 Many descendants of the *pobladores* still live in villages that seem dominated by cracked adobe or on tiny *ranchitos* with a garden patch and a few head of cattle.

'ranchman. [f. RANCH *sb.*[2] + MAN *sb.*[1]] The owner of a ranch; a man employed on a ranch.

1856 *Spirit of Times* 4 Oct. 75/1 The dusty, rusty, rough-clad, huge-pawed creatures, known as ranch-men. **1872** RAYMOND *Statist. Mines & Mining* 287 The ranchmen of Colorado. **1879** MISS BIRD *Rocky Mount.* 84 The ranchman, who is half hunter half stockman. **1926** J. F. DOBIE *Rainbow in Morning* (1965) 97 A barbecue required the coöperation of the substantial citizens of the country, for they furnished the beef to barbecue. A ranchman might contribute a calf, a yearling, or steer; or he might contribute money. **1949** *Daily Ardmoreite* (Ardmore, Oklahoma) 4 Dec. 10/1 The ranchmen are piling up hay in strategic places to feed stock if the severe cold comes again. **1959** T. D. CLARK *Frontier America* xxvii. 640 A ranchman could homestead 160 acres in his own name... A ranchman could purchase public lands outright.

‖**rancho** ('rantʃo). [Sp. *rancho* a mess, a company of persons who eat together; in Sp. America applied to the huts occupied by herdsmen or labourers. Cf. Skeat *Notes Engl. Etym.* 241.]

1. a. In Spanish parts of America: A rudely-built house, a hut or hovel; also, a collection of huts, a hamlet or village.

1845 DARWIN *Voy. Nat.* iv. (1873) 71 We took up our residence in the rancho, or hovel, of an old Spaniard. **1860** *Merc. Marine Mag.* VII. 37 To the westward..there is a rancho of 8 or 9 huts. **1887** E. F. KNIGHT *Cruise Falcon* (ed. 4) 107 Every native likes if possible to have a little wooden saint of his own in his rancho. **1931** *Times Lit. Suppl.* 19 Mar. 214/2 To live in a mud 'rancho', eat frugally..was no hardship for this class of immigrant.

b. *spec.* A hut or shed, or a collection of these, put up for the accommodation of travellers. Hence, in extended use, a roadhouse or inn.

1808 PIKE *Sources Mississ.* III. (1810) 260 Marched early and at nine o'clock arrived at a Rancho. **1846** G. GARDNER *Brazil* 455 Ranchos are large sheds generally open at the sides..for the accommodation of travellers. **1849** J. T. BROOKS *Four Months Among Gold-Finders in Alta California* ii. 8 Bradley urged us to proceed a few miles farther, where we could take up our quarters at a rancho belonging to a friend of his. **1854** C. E. DE LONG in *Calif. Hist. Soc. Q.* (1929) VIII. 199 Took Dinner at the Empire Rancho. **1869** R. F. BURTON *Highl. Brazil* I. 102 The Rancho represents the 'Traveller's Bungalow' lacking, however, cot, chair, and table.

c. (See quots.)

1957 P. KEMP *Mine were of Trouble* iii. 45 *Rancho*, usually some form of stew, was at half past twelve... And, at six-thirty, the evening *rancho*. **1976** *National Observer* (U.S.) 17 July 10/1 A 23-inch TV is in the dining room, and most of the population are able to eat the *rancho*—the Mexican native meals—because it is very good.

2. In the Western U.S., a cattle-farm, a ranch.

1840 R. H. DANA *Bef. Mast* xiv. 35 The nearest house, they told us, was a rancho, or cattle-farm, about three miles off. **1872** C. KING *Mountain. Sierra Nev.* v. 105 There they had taken up a rancho, a quarter-section of public domain.

†**ranch-sieve.** *Obs. rare*[−1]. = RANGE *sb.*[2]

1669 DIGBY *Closet Opened* (1677) 40 Lade out the water (letting it run through a Ranch-Sieve).

ranchy ('rɑːnʃɪ, -æ-), *a. U.S. slang.* [Perh. var. RAUNCHY *a.*] Dirty, disgusting, indecent.

1903 A. M. BINSTEAD *Pitcher in Paradise* xii. 283 Then they brought the monkey in—the sad-faced, bare-based, flea-ranchy old monk. **1959** LD. KINROSS *Innocents at Home* xxii. 196 The bridegroom, an Englishman, declared his intention of having the English as opposed to the American marriage service. This included..the worshipping of her with his body. There was an embarrassed pause at this; and then one of the bridesmaids remarked, 'A bit ranchy, that.'

rancid ('rænsɪd), *a.* Also 7 **rancide**. [ad. L. *rancid-us* stinking, rank, whence also obs. F. *rancide* (mod.F. *rance*). Cf. RANCOUR.]

1. Having the rank unpleasant taste or smell characteristic of oils and fats when no longer fresh. Hence of tastes or smells.

1646 SIR T. BROWNE *Pseud. Ep.* 114 A garous excretion or a rancide and olidous separation. **1731** ARBUTHNOT *Aliments* iv, The Oils, with which Fishes abound often turn rancid.. and affect the very Sweat with a rancid Smell. **1766** SMOLLETT *Trav.* 200 The oil thus procured is apt to grow rancid. *a* **1813** A. WILSON *Foresters* Poet. Wks. (1846) 215 The black wet bread, with rancid butter spread. **1889** JESSOPP *Coming of Friars* ii. 90 It must have been only too common to find the bacon more than rancid.

2. *fig.* Nasty disagreeable, odious. Also as *sb.*

1833 J. CONSTABLE *Let.* 3 Apr. (1965) III. 98 He is too fond, of *rancid old art*. **1883** *Gd. Words* 109 Their unctuous, rancid words about their Christian affection. **1884** STEVENSON *New Arab. Nts.* 219 He's a rancid fellow. **1892** 'MARK TWAIN' *Amer. Claimant* xv. 156 He couldn't get his breath at first. When he did get it, it came rancid with sarcasm. **1912** B. PAIN *Locris of Tower* in *Stories in Grey* 195 Black kid gloves, the most rancid form of gloves. **1924** E. F. BENSON *David of King's* v. 79 'When Milton talked of a pansy, he called it "freaked with jet".' 'O Lord, did he really?' said David. 'How frightfully rancid!' *a* **1930** D. H. LAWRENCE *Old Men* in *Last Poems* 251 The rancid old men that don't die because the gods don't want them..Old people fixed in a rancid resistance to life, fixed to the letter of the law. **1941** E. P. O'DONNELL *Great Big Doorstep* ix. 125 If she ain't a rancid! She's sweet as sugar to Evvie jiss to get Evvie in a good humor, then she turn around and talk sarcastic. **1973** *Times Lit. Suppl.* 16 Mar. 304/3 The movement was sufficiently vague for any rancid provincial mediocrity to come to believe that he was himself at the centre.

Hence '**rancidly** *adv.*; '**rancidness**. Also †**ran'ciduous** *a.*, rancid.

1664 H. MORE *Myst. Iniq.* I. xxii. 86 These false Apostles having abused the belief..so grossely and rancidly. **1688** R. HOLME *Armoury* II. 388/1 The Ranciduous, or Mouldy Scent is..from things corrupted. **1755** JOHNSON, *Rancidness*. **1789** G. WHITE *Selborne* xliv, From this food their flesh has contracted a rancidness which occasions them to be rejected by nicer judges of eating.

rancidity (ræn'sɪdɪtɪ). [f. prec. + -ITY. Cf. F. *rancidité*.] The quality or state of being rancid.

1654 H. L'ESTRANGE *Chas. I* (1655) 195 To smell out the rancidity, the ill savour of their intentions. **1774** GOLDSM. *Nat. Hist.* (1776) VI. 43 Neither boiling nor bleaching can divest them of their oily rancidity. **1869** E. A. PARKES *Pract. Hygiene* (ed. 3) 240 The rancidity of butter is chiefly owing to changes in the fat.

rancîéite (rænsiː'eɪaɪt). *Min.* Also **rancieite**, †**rancierite**. [ad. F. *rancierite* (A. Leymerie *Cours de la Minéralogie* (1857) II. 329), f. Rancié (formerly also Rancier), name of the mountain near Vicdessos, Ariège, France, where it was first found: see -ITE[1].] A hydrated oxide of calcium and manganese, $(Ca,Mn^{II})Mn^{IV}{}_4O_9 \cdot 3H_2O$, occurring as soft flakes and as compact or friable masses.

1861 H. W. BRISTOW *Gloss. Mineral.* 313/1 *Rancierite*... Occurs in earthy masses of a deep brown colour. Soils the fingers. **1907** *Mineral. Mag.* XIV. 408 *Rancieite*. (Collection de Minéralogie du Muséum d'Histoire Naturelle, Paris, Guide du Visiteur, 2nd edit., 1900, p. 29 (Rancîéite).) The correct spelling of rancierite (A. Leymerie), a variety of wad. **1923** *Mineral. Abstr.* II. 144 A mineral found by G. Friedel in the haematite of Villerouge, Aude, was identified as rancieite of Lacroix. **1943** *Econ. Geol.* XXXVIII. 594 The manganese is in the form of rancîéite, a finely flaky, soft, brownish-black, hydrous calcium-manganese oxide, mixed with calcium carbonate in the form of calcareous tuffs. **1969** *Mineral. Abstr.* XX. 225/2 Rancîéite, from old workings at Rancié, forms soft brown scales with metallic lustre;.. pleochroic yellow to deep brown. **1979** *Nature* 12 July 137/1 That rancieite belongs to the birnessite group (family) has been established by Bardossy and Brindley.

ranck(e, obs. f. RANK.

rancken, var. RANKEN *v.*

ranckle, rancle(n, obs. ff. RANKLE.

ranckor, obs. form of RANCOUR.

†**rancon.** *Obs. rare*[−1]. [a. obs. F. *rancon, ramcon* (Godef.).] A kind of pike or bill.

1547 in Merrick *Anc. Armour* (1824) III. 14 Rancons with staves garnyshed with velvett and fringed..56.

ranconter, obs. form of RENCONTRE.

rancorous ('ræŋkərəs), *a.* Also 6–7 **ranckor-**, 7 **ranker-**. [f. RANCOUR *sb.* + -OUS. Cf. OF. *rancorus, rancurus* (Godef.).]

1. Of feelings: Having, or partaking of, the nature of rancour.

1590 SPENSER *F.Q.* I. xi. 14 So flam'd his eyne with rage and rancorous yre. **1627** P. FLETCHER *Locusts* II. xiii, Her gracious love weighs downe our ranck'rous spight. **1771** *Junius Lett.* I. 261 Malice..feasting with a rancorous rapture upon..distress. **1867** FREEMAN *Norm. Conq.* (1876) I. App. 665 This excited rancorous envy in the breast of his uncle.

transf. **1800** WEEMS *Washington* (1877) 71 A wound of such rancorous malignity.

2. Of actions, etc.: Proceeding from, or characterized by, rancour.

1590 SHAKS. *Com. Err.* I. i. 6 The enmity and discord which of late Sprung from the rancorous outrage of your Duke. **1667** H. MORE *Div. Dial.* IV. xxxvii. II. 206 The rancorous attempts of the Romish adherents. **1784** *De Lolme's Eng. Constit.* Advt. p. xx, Those lasting and rancorous divisions. **1849** W. IRVING *Mahomed* vii. (1853) 36 Mahomet was keenly sensible of the rancorous opposition of this uncle.

3. Of persons (the mind, heart, etc.): Feeling or displaying rancour.

1592 MARLOWE *Edw. II*, II. ii, Can you..display such rancorous minds? **1597** SHAKS. *Rich. III*, I. iii. 50 Because I cannot flatter..I must be held a rancorous Enemy. *a* **1656** BP. HALL *Rem. Wks.* (1660) 108 Even hatred itself, to a rancorous stomack, hath a kinde of wicked pleasure in it. **1797** BURKE *Regic. Peace* iii. Wks. 1826 VIII. 324 Throwing themselves and their sovereign at the feet of a wicked and rancorous foe. **1879** M. ARNOLD *Mixed Ess., Falkland* 235 In that age of harsh and rancorous tempers.

†**4.** Of a wound or sore: Festering, inflamed, full of corruption. *Obs.*

1660 GAUDEN *Brownrig* 243 Our wounds are so deep, so rankerous, and incurable. **1667** H. MORE *Div. Dial.* IV. xxxvii. (1713) 393 This rancorous sore sticks more especially ..on those marked Vassals of the Beast.

Hence '**rancorously** *adv.*, '**rancorousness**.

1727 BAILEY, Vol. II, *Rancorousness*. **1767** *Junius Lett.* xxiii. (1804) I. 155 He would not at one moment rancorously persecute, at another basely cringe, to the favourite of his Sovereign. **1845** DARWIN *Voy. Nat.* xix. (1879) 443 The whole community is rancorously divided into parties.

rancoun, obs. variant of RANSOM.

rancounter, -re, obs. ff. RENCOUNTER *sb.* and *v.*

rancour ('ræŋkə(r)), *sb.* Forms: 4–6 **rankor, -our**, (5 **-oure, -owre, -ure**), 6 **ranckor**, 6–7 **ranker**; 4 **rauncour**, 5–6 **rancoure**, 3– **rancor**, 4– **rancour**. [a. OF. *rancor, -cour, -cuer, raunkour*, etc.:—L. *rancōr-em* rancidity, rankness, hence (in the Vulgate) bitter grudge.]

1. Inveterate and bitter ill-feeling, grudge, or animosity; malignant hatred or spitefulness.

[*a* **1225** *Ancr. R.* 200 Þe oðer kundel is Rancor siue odium: þet is, hatunge oðer great heorte.] **13..** *E.E. Allit. P.* B. 756, I schal..my rankor refrayne for þy reken wordez. *c* **1380** *Sir Ferumb.* 5759 Fyrumbras..prayede him cesse of his rauncour. **1413** *Pilgr. Sowle* II. xlv. (1859) 51 Wretched folke and irous, ful of venym, of rancour, and of hate. *c* **1440** *Jacob's Well* 249 Whanne þou mercyfully forȝeuyst þi wrongys, wyth-oute wreche & rankure in herte, þat is mercy. *a* **1533** LD. BERNERS *Huon* lxxxiv. 266, I..pardon you of all myn yll wyll, and put al rancoure fro me. **1547** J. HARRISON *Exhort. Scottes* A iv b, Peace in their mouthes, and all rancor and vengeaunce in their hartes. **1605** WILLET *Hexapla Gen.* 234 Yet doe retaine ranker and seedes of malice in their heart. **1667** MILTON *P.L.* x. 1044 Rancor and pride, impatience and despite. **1725** POPE *Odyss.* III. 182 Each burns with rancour to the adverse side. **1828** D'ISRAELI *Chas. I*, II. vii. 174 To envy..Charles traced their personal rancour to the friend of his heart. **1865** MAFFEI *Brig. Life* II. 37 The gratification of private rancour, and personal revenge.

b. *transf.* and *fig.* of things.

1582 STANYHURST *Æneis* I. (Arb.) 22 Billows theire swelling ranckor abated. **1605** CAMDEN *Rem.* 207 Through the rancor of the poyson, the wound was iudged incurable. **1663** BUTLER *Hud.* I. i. 364 The peaceful Scabbard..The Rancor of its edge had felt. **1719** D'URFEY *Pills* (1872) I. 48 Let the frozen North its rancour show. **1860** EMERSON *Cond. Life, Power* Wks. (Bohn) II. 333 The rancour of the disease attests the strength of the constitution.

†**2.** Rancid smell; rancidity; rankness. *Obs. rare.*

c **1400** *Laud Troy Bk.* 6028 Ther come of hem a foul savour And smot to hem a gret rancour. *c* **1420** *Pallad. on Husb.* XI. 111 Lest rancour oil enfecte, do fier away. **1567** J. MAPLET *Naturall Hist.* 33 b, It is also said somtime through the rancor of grounds to come vp vnsowne.

Hence '**rancourless** *a.*, free from rancour.

1886 H. JAMES *Bostonians* II. II. xx. 26 She was too rancourless,..too free from private self-reference.

'**rancour**, *v.* Now *rare* or *Obs.* [f. prec.]

1. *intr.* To have rancorous feelings; to rankle.

1530 PALSGR. 679/1, I ranker by wrathe or anger, *je rancune*. **1640** HABINGTON *Edw. IV* 130 Unlesse some malice rancord in the genius of our Nation against the French.

2. *trans.* To infect with rancour; to make rancorous.

1654 R. BOREMAN *Triumph of Faith* Ep. Ded., Men (not rancord with envy) usually love in others what they see in themselves. *a* **1711** KEN *Edmund* Poet. Wks. 1721 II. 313 Despite and Fury ranker'd Hanguar's Breast.

Hence '**rancoured** *ppl. a.*; '**rancouring** *vbl. sb.* and *ppl. a.*

1567 J. MAPLET *Naturall Hist.* 10 b, It kepeth the place of vstion, free and cleare from yll smelling and rancoring. **1600** W. WATSON *Decacordon* (1602) 129 Thou kept the venime in thy rankred hart. **1611** SPEED *Hist. Gt. Brit.* IX. viii. §36. 553 The King..esteemed the Popes..loue as most rancored hatred. **1728** MORGAN *Algiers* II. i. 217 The vanquished Moors swarmed over into Africa, bearing rancoured Hearts against the successful Spaniards. *a* **1814** *Forgery* II. iii. in *New Brit. Theatre* I. 452 Her detested vile inconstancy Which with a rancoring silence I must bear.

rancune, obs. variant of RANSOM.

rand (rænd), *sb.*[1] Also 7 (in sense 3 a) **rann**. [OE. *rand, rǫnd* brink or bank, shield-boss, shield = ON. *rönd* shield-rim, shield, stripe (Sw. and Da. *rand* rim, border, etc.), OHG. *rant* shield-boss (G. and Du. *rand* bank, beach, brink, field-border, rim, margin, etc.).

The orig. sense of the word is app. 'border, margin, rim', although there is very little evidence for this in the older literatures, in which the word is almost entirely poetic and restricted to the shield.]

1. A border, margin, or brink (of land). *Obs.* exc. *dial.* and *regional* in specific senses (see latest quots.).

The E. Anglian word is usually ROND q.v.

Beowulf 2538 Aras ða bi ronde rof oretta. [**903** in Kemble *Cod. Dipl.* II. 259/8 Of ðam fulan broce wið westan randes æsc.] **13..** *E.E. Allit. P.* A. 105 Þe playn, þe plonttez, þe spyse, þe perez, & rawez & randez & rych reuerez. **13..** *Gaw. & Gr. Knt.* 1710 At þe last bi a littel dich he lepez ouer a spenné, Stelez out ful stilly by a strothe rande. **1840** SPURDENS *Suppl. Forby, Rand*. A reed-rand, on our rivers and broads is a margin overgrown with reeds. **1868** ATKINSON *Cleveland Gloss., Rands*,..the borders round fields left unploughed and producing rough grass: applied loosely to the grass in question. **1895** *Daily News* 22 Apr. 7/4 The rands, skirts, and walls thereof, and fens and reed grounds appertaining thereto. **1958** *New Biol.* XXVI. 92 The underlying fen peat acts as a reservoir of wetness while the margins of the peat-filled basin insulate the raised centre from the soil water which is draining into the basin... Such a bog is called a raised bog, the sloping slides being called the rand, and the insulating zone round the edge the lagg.

2. A strip or long slice: **a.** of meat (see quots. 1611 and 1895). Now only *dial.*

c **1394** *P. Pl. Crede* 763 Wiþ þe randes of bakun his baly for to fillen. **1530** PALSGR. 260/2 Rande of befe, *giste de beuf*. **1611** COTGR., *Giste de bœuf*, a rand of beefe; a long, and fleshie peece, cut out from betweene the flanke and buttocke. **1669** DIGBY *Closet Opened* (1677) 124, I like to add to this a rand of tender briskit Beef. **1838** in HOLLOWAY *Prov. Dict.* **1895** *East Anglian Gloss.*, Rand..[seems] to signify any fleshy piece from the edges of the larger divisions of the hind quarter, the rump, loin, or leg.

b. of fish (esp. sturgeon). Now *rare*.

1572 in Turner *Select Rec. Oxford* (1880) 345 Item, thre rands of sturgion..xij[s]. **1622** *Jrnl. Eng. Plant.* in Arber *Story Pilgrim Fathers* (1897) 429 We saw it was a grampus which they were cutting up. They cut it into long rands or pieces, about an ell long and two hands full broad. **1655** MOUFET & BENNET *Health's Impr.* (1746) 264 Being cold, they [sturgeon] are divided into Jouls and Rands. **1820** T. MITCHELL *Aristoph.* I. 83 A rand Of tunny fish.

3. a. A strip of leather placed under the quarters of a boot or shoe, to make this level before the lifts of the heel are attached. (Cf. G. *rand* welt.)

1598 FLORIO, *Tornara*,..the rande of a shooe. **1647** *New Haven Col. Rec.* (1857) I. 347 The deffendant was faine to take those rands to make welts for the plaine shooes. **1688** R.

HOLME *Armoury* III. 14/1 Parts of a Shooe.. The Rann [is] the Leather as holds the Heel quarters and Vamp to the Soles. **1823** E. MOOR *Suffolk Words* s.v., The rand and welt being stitched to the superior and inferior portions, strengthen the work. **1862** *Catal. Internat. Exhib.* II. xxvii. 56 Box cork boot, without rand or stitch in sole.

attrib. and *Comb.* **1840** J. DEVLIN *Shoemaker* 91 The single rand-pricker then in use (the forerunner of our present rand-wheel). *Ibid.* 113 One rand iron, a tool for setting up the rand before stitching. **1875** KNIGHT *Dict. Mech.* 1879/2 A rand-guide, by which the rand-coil or ribbon is directed. **1882** *Worc. Exhib. Catal.* III. 31 Rand turning machine.. delivers the rands.. in a horse shoe form ready for use.

b. A strip of iron.

1831 J. HOLLAND *Manuf. Metal* I. 212 The sheet iron.. is cut into strips or rands.

c. *Basketry.* (See quots. 1910 and 1912.)

1903 R. M. JACOT *Useful Cane Work* I. p. ix/2 *Trade or workshop terms*,.. randing, or a 'rand'. **1910** *Encycl. Brit.* III. 482/2 The chief strokes used in constructing an ordinary basket are:—the 'slew'—two or more rods woven together; the 'rand', rods woven in singly. **1912** T. OKEY *Introd. Art of Basket-Making* v. 20 The next section is formed by a *Rand*—one single rod worked alternately in front of and behind each Stake. **1959** D. WRIGHT *Baskets & Basketry* vi. 136 *Rand*: a single rod worked in front of one stake and behind the next.

†**4.** A piece or mass of ice. *Obs. rare.*

1633 T. JAMES *Voy.* 18 As thick rands of Ice, as any we had yet seene. *Ibid.* 104 The Ice lyes.. in rands and ranges. **1702** C. MATHER *Magn. Chr.* (1852) II. App. 195 They kept labouring.. among enormous rands of ice.

5. [a. G. and Da. *rand.*] A rim, margin. *rare.*

1830 W. TAYLOR *Hist. Surv. Germ. Poetry* II. 356 A rusty, brazen, oval vase... 'Should there be nought within the rand', Thinks he, 'I'll take it to the brazier'. **1868** STEPHENS *Runic Mon.* I. 182 The raised rands and upstanding carved ridges have been left in their original.. glitter.

rand (rænd, ‖rɑːnt), *sb.*[2] *S. Afr.* Also **randt**, **rant.** Pl. **rands**, ‖**rande.** [Afrikaans, a. Du. *rand(t)* edge, margin: rel. to RAND *sb.*[1]] **1. a.** In South Africa: a rocky ridge or area of high sloping ground, esp. overlooking a river-valley. **b.** *spec.* ***the Rand***, the Witwatersrand, a notable gold-mining area of the Transvaal.

1839 J. COLLETT *Diary* 27 May in *Voorloper* (1976) 663 Finished making New Kralls to day on Willow fountain rant. **1856** F. FLEMING *Southern Africa* v. 109 The country, lying between the Rand and the Fish River, is thickly populated with Fingoes. **1890** *Digger's Doggerel* 28 The best Crushing Spec.. on the Rand. **1891** B. MITFORD *Romance of Cape Frontier* iv. 23 He stood on the top of the *randt* for a brief blow after his exertions. **1899** G. B. SHAW *Let.* c 26–30 Dec. (1972) II. 124 The conflict that was inevitable from the moment that gold was discovered in the Rand.. had to come. **1900** A. H. KEANE *Boer States* iii. 22 We can here speak of 'rands', that is, ridges of moderate elevation, which, however, are sometimes high enough to form water-partings. **1928** E. WALKER *Hist. S. Afr.* xii. 413 Mining areas were proclaimed on the Rand. **1947** H. C. BOSMAN *Mafeking Road* 3 'I don't think they [*sc.* the stars] would be good for growing mealies on, though,' I answered, 'they look too high up, like the rante of the Sneeuberge, in the Cape.' **1953** D. LESSING *Five* iii. 129 He thought of the old prospectors.. panning gold.., washing the grit for those tiny grains that might proclaim a new Rand. **1972** D. FRANCIS *Smokescreen* ix. 123 Most of Johannesburg sank about three feet.. after all the reef was out... The Rand gold fields are shallower.

2. (freq. with capital initial.) Pl. *rand* or *rands.* [f. with ref. to sense 1 b.] A unit of decimal currency, orig. equivalent to ten shillings sterling, and containing 100 cents, adopted by the Republic of South Africa in 1961, and subsequently by certain other southern African countries. Also *attrib.*

1961 *Times* 27 Jan. 19/4 There was a boom on the Johannesburg Stock Exchange last night... The occasion was the second dress rehearsal for trading in rand and cents when decimalization overtakes South Africa on the second Tuesday of next month. **1961** *Guardian* 26 May 3/3 A two-rand (formerly one pound) postal order bought in a Capetown post office. **1970** *Daily Nation* (Nairobi) 16 Jan. 14/5 Lesotho's currency is the South African Rand. **1972** P. DRISCOLL *Wilby Conspiracy* ii. 37 You want wine? It'll cost you two rands a bottle. **1978** J. PAXTON *Dict. European Econ. Community* (rev. ed.) 21 In March 1976 the E.E.C. agreed to provide Botswana with about 90m. Rand in aid over four years.

rand (rænd), *v.*[1] [f. RAND *sb.*[1]]

†**1.** *trans.* To cut into rands (sense 2 b). *Obs.*

1630 J. TAYLOR (Water P.) *Jack-a-Lent* Wks. I. 117/1 The Sturgeon is keg'd, randed, and iold about the eares.

2. a. *intr.* To cut rands (sense 3). **b.** *trans.* To fit with rands. **c.** *trans.* and *intr.* To weave by randing (sense 1 b). Hence **'randing** *vbl. sb.*[1] (used *attrib.* in ***randing-machine, -tool***).

1875 KNIGHT *Dict. Mech.* 1879. **1959** D. WRIGHT *Baskets & Basketry* ii. 45 After the initial pairing the base may be randed. **1962** *Punch* 1 Aug. 170/3 The basket workers.. still keep their rhymed boast: I can rand At your command.. Wale all right And keep my stakes in order.

†**rand,** *v.*[2] *Obs. rare.* [a. obs. Flem. *randen*, var. *ranten* to RANT.]

1. *intr.* To rave, to rant.

1601 B. JONSON *Poetaster* III. iv, He will teach thee to tear and rand. **1607** DEKKER & WEBSTER *Northw. Hoe* IV. D.'s Wks. 1873 III. 54, I..rau'd and randed, and raild.

2. *trans.* (with *out.*) To utter in a furious manner.

1609 ROWLEY *Search for Money* (Percy Soc.) 21 After Coller had procured a foaming vent, he randed out these sentences—Money? vengeance and hell so soone as money!

Hence **'randing** *vbl. sb.*[2] and *ppl. a.*

1609 ROWLEY *Search for Money* (Percy Soc.) 31 An audatious mouthing-randing-impudent.. rascal. **1633** T. ADAMS *Exp. 2 Peter* iii. 3 For a hypocrite to decline open randing.. and revels, it is no wonder. **1714** C. JOHNSON *The Country Lasses* v. ii, Here will be brave randing, i' faith: all the steeples in the County are to rock.

rand (rænd), *v.*[3] *dial.* [Of obscure origin: cf. RANDY *v.*[1]] *trans.* and *intr.* To canvass. Hence **'randing** *vbl. sb.*[3]

1740 SIR C. H. WILLIAMS *Wks.* (1822) I. 69, I in plain English will the country rand, And shake each good freeholder by the hand. *Ibid.* 70 Freeholders with such language well dispense,.. Therefore, be wise, go home, and rand no more. **1842** in *Glouc. Gloss.* (1890), *Randing.*

†**rand,** *v.*[4] *Sc. Obs. rare*$^{-0}$. [ad. F. *rend-*, stem of *rendre* RENDER; cf. *rand* 'a melting' (of tallow) in *Suppl. Jamieson's Dict.* (1887).] *trans.* To melt (tallow). Hence **'randing** *vbl. sb.*[4]

1583 *Burgh Rec. Edinb.* (1882) 313 Ane suspect pair for randing of talloun and sending the sam away furth of the realm.

†**randall,** obs. var. *randon* RANDOM.

1599 PORTER *Angry Wom. Abingdon* (Percy Soc.) 108 Least striking vp and downe at randall the roge might hurt me.

randall-, variant of *randle-* RANNEL-.

randan (ræn'dæn), *sb.*[1] [? var. of *randon* RANDOM, with assimilation of the vowels.]

1. Riotous or disorderly behaviour; a spree.

c **1710** CELIA FIENNES *Diary* (1888) 180, I had the trouble of.. ye Randan they made in the publick houses. **1826–7** HONE *Every-day Bk.* II. 820 He had seen a deal of 'ran-dan', and a racketty life had racketted his frame. **1893** STEVENSON *Catriona* 164 He was fond of a lass and fond of a glass, and fond of a ran-dan.

b. In phr. ***on the randan***, 'on the spree'.

1764 *Low Life* 16 Young Fellows, who have been out all Night on the Ran-Dan, stealing Staves and Lanthorns. **1894** STEVENSON *St. Ives* xxvii. (1898) 203 They were a' on the ran-dan last nicht!

2. A riotous person. *rare.*

a **1809** MRS. COWLEY *Who's the Dupe* I. ii, The most extraordinary youth... None of your randans, up all night —not drinking..—No.. poring, and reading.

randan (ræn'dæn), *adv.*, *sb.*[2] (and *a.*). [Of obscure origin: connexion with prec. is not apparent.] **a.** *adv.* Applied to a style of rowing in which the middle one of three rowers pulls a pair of sculls, stroke and bow an oar each. **b.** *sb.* A boat for rowing in this fashion. **c.** *attrib.* or *adj.*

1828 *Sporting Mag.* XXII. 251 Pulling what is termed 'Ran-Dan', that is, a pair of sculls and a pair of oars. **1857** P. COLQUHOUN *Compan. Oarsman's Guide* 20 Four is the best number, and randan the best style, for an up-country trip. **1884** YATES *Recoll.* iv, Had a randan gig built for us. **1885** *Act 48 & 49 Vict.* c. 76 §29 The term 'vessel' shall include any.. house-boat, boat, randan, wherry [etc.].

randan, *sb.*[3] *dial.* or *techn.* (See quots.)

1750 ELLIS *Mod. Husb.* VI. ii. 65 (E.D.S.) *Ran-dan*, the coarsest wheat flour that is made. *a* **1825** FORBY *Voc. E. Anglia*, *Randan*, the produce of a second sifting of meal. **1858** SIMMONDS *Dict. Trade*, *Randan*, a miller's name for the finest parts of the bran or outside skin of the wheat. **1886** *Cheshire Gloss.* 281 *Randan*, the very coarsest flour, or rather the very finest bran, ground almost as fine as flour.

†**ran'dan,** *v. Obs. rare*$^{-1}$. [? f. RANDAN *sb.*[1]] *trans.* To abuse, vituperate.

1764 T. BRYDGES *Homer Travest.* (1797) I. 30 Atrides he did so randan, He call'd him all but gentleman.

randan, obs. form of RANDOM.

ran-dan, var. RAN-TAN *v.*

randanite ('rændənaɪt). *Min.* Also **-dann-.** [f. *Randanne*, Puy de Dôme, France, its locality + -ITE.] (See quots.)

1862 DANA *Elem. Geol.* 67 Randanite, a kind of opal made of infusorial remains. **1868** WATTS *Dict. Chem.*, *Randanite*, an earthy hydrate of silica, occurring near Pont Gibaud.

randa-uou, obs. form of RENDEZVOUS.

randed, *a. Basketry.* [f. RAND *sb.*] Woven by randing (sense 1 b).

1907 *Yesterday's Shopping* (1969) 153/1 Basket, fine randed buff wicker. **1912** T. OKEY *Introd. Art of Basket-Making* ix. 91 The chief difference to be noted in the methods of Randed work are: that fine White or Buff is normally used. **1959** D. WRIGHT *Baskets & Basketry* ii. 42 For a Randed base.. an extra short stick will be needed to make an odd number.

randem ('rændəm), *adv.*, *sb.* (and *a.*). Also **randem-tandem, random.** [Prob. based on RANDOM, on the analogy of TANDEM.] **a.** *adv.* Applied to a style of driving in which three horses are harnessed tandem. **b.** *sb.* A carriage or team driven in this fashion. **c.** *attrib.* or as *adj.*

c **1805** MAR. EDGEWORTH *Wks.* (Rtldg.) I. 185 To.. go down.. to Marryborough, in his dog-cart, randem-tandem. **1818** T. L. PEACOCK *Nightmare Abbey* i, His fellow-students.. who drove tandem and random in great perfection. **1870** J. PAYN *Like Father, like Son* iv, The Squire's jovial friends used, for the most part, strange conveyances, such as tandems and randems. **1883** *Illustr. Sport. & Dram. News* 10 Feb. 542/2 'A randem team'. That randems should be uncommon is natural enough.

'rander. *rare*$^{-1}$. [f. RAND *v.*[1] + -ER[1].] One who cuts into rands.

1757 W. THOMPSON *R.N. Advoc.* 42 Under the Randers and Messers Coarses in cutting up, I have.. seen the stinking oily Substance of the Flesh, fly up to the Beams of the Cutting House.

rander, obs. f. RENDER *v.*

randeuou(ce, -devoo, -vous, etc., obs. ff. RENDEZVOUS.

randge, obs. f. RANGE *v.*

randie, var. RANDY.

randing ('rændɪŋ), *sb.* [? f. RAND *sb.*[1]]

1. a. *Mil.* A kind of basket-work used in fortification in making gabions.

1834–47 J. S. MACAULAY *Field Fortif.* (1851) 66 The randing or basket-work is continued to near the top of the pickets. **1876** in VOYLE & STEVENSON *Milit. Dict.* 326/1.

b. *Basketry.* The action or process of weaving rands (sense 3 c); randed work.

1903 R. M. JACOT *Useful Cane Work* I. p. x/2 The basket maker.. would speak of driving down the stakes.. into the 'randing' or 'pairing' of a bottom. **1912** T. OKEY *Introd. Art of Basket-Making* ix. 91 Randing is sub-divided into Coarse, Slight, Light, Fine and Close. **1946** N. WYMER *Eng. Country Crafts* vii. 73 He now fills in the sides by weaving single willows.. a stage known as 'randing'. **1964** H. HODGES *Artifacts* x. 146 The simplest weave, *randing*, was done with a single rod passed behind one stake and in front of the next.

2. 'A narrow frieze running along the edge of a knife handle' (*Sheffield Gloss.* 1888).

randing, *vbl. sbs.*: see RAND *v.*[1]–*v.*[4]

‖**randjie** ('rɑːntji). *S. Afr.* Also **randje, rantjie.** [Afrikaans, ad. Du. *rand(t)je*, *rantje*, dim. of *rand(t)* RAND *sb.*[2]] A narrow ridge of rocky ground, not as high as a kopje.

1889 *'Argus' Ann. & S. Afr. Directory* 849/1 Stony hills and knolls—known locally as *randjes* and *spitskops.* **1914** L. H. BRINKMAN *Breath of Karroo* i. 17 Here and there a few kopjes relieved the monotony of the view, and every few miles, randjes, or low stony hills, stretched across the plains. **1939** S. CLOETE *Watch for Dawn* 31 The small path that runs along the randjie. **1944** V. POHL *Adventures Boer Family* i. 11 There were roebuck in the *rantjies.* **1949** M. LEIGH *Cross of Fire* v. 99 The track climbed the randjie on which we stood and petered down again into the darkness and the gloom towards Matzana's kraal.

‖**randkluft** ('rantklʊft). [Ger., lit. 'edge crevice'.] A crevasse between the head of a glacier and a surrounding rock wall.

1934 C. F. MEADE in S. Spencer *Mountaineering* vi. 122 Another sort of chasm closely related to the bergschrund is the *randkluft*. This is the name given to the gap between the glacier and the bare rock-wall of a peak. **1958** *Polar Record* IX. 91 *Bergschrund*, the crevasse which occurs at the head of a cirque or valley glacier and which separates the moving glacier ice from the rock wall and the ice apron attached to it. When the ice apron is absent the gap is known as a Randkluft. **1970** R. J. SMALL *Study of Landforms* xi. 380 Temperature changes such as these seem insufficient to cause powerful shattering of the rock, and in any case they are presumably still less pronounced in the crack ('randkluft') between the névé and the headwall.

randle-balk, -tree: see RANNEL-.

Randlord ('rændlɔːd). *slang.* Also with small initial. [f. RAND *sb.*[2] + LORD *sb.*, after LANDLORD *sb.*] The owner or manager of a gold-field on the Rand in South Africa.

1904 *Daily Chron.* 21 Mar. 5/5 The Randlords' proposal really drives the British workman out of the Transvaal. *Ibid.* 14 May 4/7 Recent newspaper writers, in coining the word Randlords—have they not all done what they could to popularise a wrong pronunciation of Rand? **1936** R. J. M. GOOLD-ADAMS *S. Afr. To-day & To-morrow* ii. 54 The black man may.. die a premature death, but that—so the Rand-lords say—is not the fault of the mines in which he worked. **1938** J. CARY *Castle Corner* v. 255 There's no religion any more—no honesty either—it's all money—these randlords, as they call 'em. **1955** L. HOTZ in Saron & Hotz *Jews in S. Afr.* xix. 357 Among the leading figures from Kimberley who quickly assumed a commanding position on the gold-fields, the so-called Randlords, were Barnato, the Joels, Alfred Beit, Albu, and Lionel Phillips.

random ('rændəm), *sb.*, *a.*, and *adv.* Forms: *α.* 4 randun, 4–6 -doun (also 4 ren-, 6 *Sc.* rayn-), 5 -down, 5–6 -downe, -doune; 4–6 -done, 4–7 -don, (7 -dan.). *β.* 4–5 raundoun, 5 -done, 5–6 -don; 5 rawndoune, *Sc.* -down. *γ.* 6 raundom, 6–8 randome, -dum, 5– random. [a. OF. *randon* (*rendon*, etc.), f. *randir* to run fast, gallop. The change of final *-n* to *-m* is independent of the very rare OF. form *random*: cf. RANSOM.] **A.** *sb.*

I. †**1. a.** Impetuosity, great speed, force, or violence (in riding, running, striking, etc.); chiefly in phr. ***with*** (or ***in***) ***great randon*** (= OF. *de* or *a grant randon*). Also, with *a*, an impetuous rush, a rapid headlong course; chiefly in phr. ***in*** (***on***, or ***with***) ***a randon*** (= OF. *en un randon*); hence *Sc.* a straight course, direct line. *Obs.*

In common use from *c* 1300 to the early part of the 16th c.

c **1305** *Land Cokayne* 132 in *E.E.P.* (1862) 159 Þe monkes liȝtiþ noȝt adun. Ac furre fleeþ in o randun. **1375** BARBOUR *Bruce* v. 632 He..Raucht him sic rout in randoun richt. *c* **1450** *Merlin* vii. 118 Than thei..ronnen a-gein hym with as grete raundon as their horse myght hem bere. *c* **1477** CAXTON *Jason* 57 The ship..hurtlyd againe the ground in suche a random and force that hit was all to broken. **1513** DOUGLAS *Æneis* I. vi. 149 Behald tuelf swannis in randoun glaid and fair [L. *ordine longo*]. **1523** LD. BERNERS *Froiss.* I. clvii. 191 The frenchmen..came on them with great randon, their speares in their restes. **1594** *2nd Rep. Dr. Faustus* in Thoms *Prose Rom.* (1858) III. 396 Two great waves..meeting together by long randome. **1600** HOLLAND *Livy* VII. xxiv. 265 The barbarous people..fled in this randon beyond their tents. **1611** SPEED *Hist. Gt. Brit.* IX. xx. (1632) 964 The Kings vantgard..giuing in among them with full randon, slew first such Captaines as resisted. **1889** 'MARK TWAIN' *Conn. Yankee* xv. 180 Two knights came together with great random.

†**b.** A rush or stream (*of* words, fire). *Obs.*

c **1440** *Promp. Parv.* 423/1 Randone, or longe renge of wurdys, or other thyngys,..*haringga*. *c* **1450** *Merlin* 219 The dragon..caste oute of his throte so grete raundon of fiere in-to the aire..that it semed all reade.

2. Phr. ***at*** (***the***) ***randon*** or ***random***.

†**a.** *Hawking.* (See quot. 1486). *Obs.*

1486 *Bk. St. Albans* D j b, If the fowle spryng not bot flee a long after the Reuer and the hawke nym it then ye shall say she slew it at the Raundon. **1600** W. WATSON *Decacordon* (1602) 145 They [Jesuits] haue, like great fawcons or hawkes of the Tower, firmely seazed vpon the pray, kild, at randon, wing, or souce.

†**b.** *Mil.* Applied to some method of encounter in a tournament (contrasted with *at the tilt*). *Obs.*

1538 ELYOT, *Decursio*, Iustes, as at the tylte or randon. **1587** HOLINSHED *Chron.* III. 833/2 At the randon and turneie the duke of Suffolke hurt a gentleman. *a* **1648** LD. HERBERT *Hen. VIII* (1683) 52 The Laws on Horse-back were, that with Sharp Spears they should run fiue Courses at Tilt, and fiue more at Randon.

†**c.** ? At full speed. *Obs. rare*⁻¹.

1632 LITHGOW *Trav.* VI. 264 Wee found twelve..Turkes, ready to receiue vs,..who foorthwith opened at randon the two great Brazen halfes of the Doore.

3. Phr. ***at random***, orig. at great speed, without consideration, care, or control; hence, **a.** with vbs. of action or occurrence: At haphazard, without aim, purpose, or fixed principle; heedlessly, carelessly, etc. (Cf. also sense B. 1 b.)

Chiefly used with verbs of moving, striking, throwing, speaking, thinking, or taking; in early use esp. in the phr. *to run at random* (very common down to *c* 1650).

1565 JEWEL *Replie Harding* viii. §16 Leaste he happen..to renne at randon. **1591** SHAKS. *1 Hen. VI*, v. iii. 84 He talkes at randon: sure the man is mad. **1592** —— *Ven. & Ad.* 940 Hatefully at randon doest thou hit. **1616** DRUMM. OF HAWTH. *Poems* I. C j b, Psyche's louer hurles his Darts at randon. **1662** GERBIER *Principles* 16 Not to Build at Randome, as the Custome of too many ill Builders is. **1729** BUTLER *Serm. Hum. Nat.* ii. Wks. 1874 II. 32 Man cannot be considered as a creature left by his Maker to act at random. **1796** H. HUNTER tr. *St. Pierre's Stud. Nat.* (1799) I. Pref. 9 A few passages, not selected, but picked up at random. **1833** J. HOLLAND *Manuf. Metal* II. 33 This composition is then dropped upon the surface..at random, leaving the effect to chance. **1862** SIR B. BRODIE *Psychol. Inq.* II. vi. 193 Eclipses..formerly were supposed to occur at random. **1898** W. A. WHITWORTH *Expectation of Parts* 7 If a magnitude *s* be divided at random into *n* parts, the expectation of each part is *s*/*n*. **1921** *Biometrika* XIII. 309 An event happens at random once in a period *m*, therefore its chance of occurring in an interval of time or space δt is $\delta t/m$. **1931** H. JEFFREYS *Scientific Inference* iii. 24 We select at random *m* of the objects... We need a definition of what we mean by *at random*. We mean that every possible selection of *m* objects from the original *n* is equally probable. **1951** *Jrnl. Ecol.* XXXIX. 172 The principle of contagion..is that the groups are distributed at random and that the number of individuals in each group is also random.

b. Similarly with sbs. Somewhat *rare*.

a **1653** GOUGE *Comm. Hebr.* xiii. 20 To shew that Christ is a Shepherd not at random for any sheep, but that he hath a peculiar flock belonging unto him. **1667** MILTON *P.L.* IV. 930 Thy words at random, as before, Argue thy inexperience. **1784** COWPER *Task* II. 522 Their answers, vague And all at random, fabulous and dark.

c. (*to leave*) in a neglected or untended condition. Now *rare*.

1582 N. LICHEFIELD tr. *Castanheda's Conq. E. Ind.* 162 b, The Caruell,..being thus left at randon,..fell vpon certaine Rockes. **1642** ROGERS *Naaman* 537 Leaving thy flock and charge at random. **1848** KEBLE *Serm.* Pref. 12 How can there be any comparison of safe or unsafe, if all be left at random?

†**d.** (*to leave* or *live*) at liberty, free from restraint or control. *Obs.*

1569 in Bolton *Stat. Irel.* (1621) 313 Libertie to..liue at randan. **1590** SPENSER *F.Q.* III. x. 36 The gentle Lady, loose at randon lefte, The greene-wood long did walke. **1632** LITHGOW *Trav.* IX. 388 There was not a Bandit left at randon in all Sicilia. **1694** R. L'ESTRANGE *Fables* (J.), In the days of old the birds lived at random in a lawless state of anarchy.

4. A random course (now *rare*). Also, that which is random; random state, randomness.

In early use perh. directly from sense 1, but latterly influenced by the phr. *at random*.

1561 SACKVILLE & NORTON *Gorboduc* I. ii. 127 When such beginning of such liberties..Shall leaue them free to randon of their will. *c* **1624** LUSHINGTON *Serm. Resurr.* in *Phenix* (1708) II. 480 We follow not the random of their roving, but take the sum of their saying. **1670** COTTON *Espernon* I. II. 58 Making stories, as it is his custom at the random of his own passion, and fancy. **1813** G. EDWARDS *Meas. True Pol.* 86 As if the ant and bee..had..proceeded in chaotic randoms upon points actually unascertained in nature. **1929** R. BRIDGES *Testament of Beauty* II. 44 As when a high moon thru' the rifted wrack gleameth upon the random of the windswept night. **1969** *Listener* 13 Nov. 678/3 'There's a lot of random in our songs,' says Paul [McCartney].

II. *techn.* †**5.** *Gunnery.* The range of a piece of ordnance; properly, long or full range obtained by elevating the muzzle of the piece; hence, the degree of elevation given to a gun, and *spec.* that which gives the utmost range (45°). *Obs.*

1571 DIGGES *Pantom.* Pref. A iij b, Science in great Ordinance especially to shoote exactly at Randons. **1588** LUCAR tr. *Tartaglia's Colloq. Shooting* 4 How a Table of Randons may be made for any peece of ordinance. **1661** S. PARTRIDGE *Double Scale Proport.* 85 How far will a Cannon carry her Bullet at her best Random, that carrieth it at point-blank 360 paces. **1669** STURMY *Mariner's Mag.* v. 71 The next Shot was at five degrees Random, and at that mounture the shot was conveyed 416 Paces. **1731** J. GRAY *Gunnery* 81 The random and direction of a piece on the plane of the horizon being given..find it's random on an inclined plane.

fig. **1667** DENHAM *Direct. Painter* I. 26 The Duke himself..was not out of dangers random set. **1697** J. SERGEANT *Solid Philos.* A iv, Fancy let loose to fly at its full Random, and driven forward with a quick Wit.

†**b.** Phr. ***at random***, at any range other than point-blank. *Obs.*

1588 LUCAR tr. *Tartaglia's Colloq. Shooting* App. 62 To know how he shoote in the said peece at randon. **1612** CAPT. SMITH *Map Virginia* 24 Forty yards will they shoot level or very neare the mark, and 120 is their best at Random. **1669** STURMY *Mariner's Mag.* v. 67 How to make a good Shot either of Point-blank, or at Random. **1698** FRYER *Acc. E. India & P.* 137 Two unshapen Sakers..one of which at random killed a Rajah some four months ago.

6. *Mining.* The direction (*of* a rake vein, etc.).

1653 MANLOVE *Lead Mines* 261 Break-offs, and Buckers, Randum of the Rake. **1747** HOOSON *Miner's Dict.* D ij b, Observe whether such leading keep its course according to the Randome of the Vein already cut. **1866** *Durham Mining Lang.*, We must lower the sump from yon level down to the random of Wiregill lower-level.

7. (From B. 3.) **a.** *Building.* Stone of irregular sizes, or a piece of this.

1886 in *Rochdale Gloss.*

b. *Dyeing.* Clouded yarn.

1874 W. CROOKES *Dyeing & Calico-Print.* xii. 102 Scarlet Random [etc.].

8. *Printing.* (See quots.)

1888 C. T. JACOBI *Printers' Vocab.* 110 Random, a special frame used by compositors in making-up. **1898** J. SOUTHWARD *Mod. Printing* I. iv. 29 Making-up Frames..consist of an ordinary whole frame, fitted with a 'random'—that is, a sloping board, corresponding to a case, with ledges running along it transversely. **1910** A. BENNETT *Clayhanger* I. xii. 101 Under the furniture rack was the 'random', full of galleys. **1922** W. H. SCLATER *What Compositor should Know* I. 82 Randoms, on which new composition is placed for the purpose of being 'made up' into column form or page form. **1960** G. A. GLAISTER *Gloss. Bk.* 341/2 *Random*, the sloping work-top of a composing frame.

B. *adj.* (from phr. *at random*: see A. 3).

1. a. Not sent or guided in a special direction; having no definite aim or purpose; made, done, occurring, etc., at haphazard.

1655 FULLER *Ch. Hist.* IX. vii. §29 In vain do staid heads make serious comments on light mens random-expressions. **1697** DRYDEN *Æneid* IV. 95 The watchful Shepherd..Wounds with a random Shaft the careless Hind. **1728** POPE *Dunc.* I. 275 She shews..How random thoughts now meaning chance to find. **1764** BURN *Poor Laws* 190 Leaving the poor to be supported by random charity. **1827** ROBERTS *Voy. Centr. Amer.* 172 The random and ill-directed fire of the Spaniards. *a* **1845** HOOD *Song, 'O Lady, leave thy silken thread'* i, Stoop where thou wilt, thy careless hand Some random bud will meet. **1877** E. R. CONDER *Bas. Faith* iii. 102 The random working of our..intellect.

b. *Statistics.* Governed by or involving equal chances for each of the actual or hypothetical members of a population; also, produced or obtained by a random process (and therefore completely unpredictable in detail); ***random distribution***, a probability distribution, esp. the Poisson distribution; ***random error***: see ERROR 4 d; ***random noise*** (see quot. 1954); ***random number***, a number selected from a given set of numbers in such a way that all the numbers in the set have the same chance of selection; also, a pseudorandom number; ***random process***, (a process characterized by) a sequence of random variables (see also quot. 1937); ***random sample***, a sample drawn at random from a population, each member of it having an equal or other specified chance of inclusion (sometimes contrasted with *quota sample* s.v. QUOTA *sb.* 4); so ***random sampling***; ***random selection***, a random sample; random sampling; ***random variable***, ***variate***, a variable whose values are distributed in accordance with a probability distribution; ***random walk***, the movement of something in successive steps, the direction, length, or other property of each step being governed by chance independently of preceding steps.

1898 *Phil. Trans. R. Soc.* CXCI. 230 Every artificial or even random selection of a group out of a community changes not only the amount of variation, but the amount of correlation of the organs of its members as compared with those of the primitive group. **1900** *Phil. Mag.* L. 157 (*heading*) On the criterion that a given system of deviations from the probable in the case of a correlated system of variables is such that it can be reasonably supposed to have arisen from random sampling. *Ibid.* 164 The question we wish to determine is whether the sample may be reasonably considered to represent a random system of deviations from the theoretical frequency distribution of the general population. **1905** K. PEARSON in *Nature* 27 July 294/2 (*heading*) The problem of the random walk. **1924** *Bell Syst. Technical Jrnl.* III. 88 (*heading*) Deviation of random samples from average conditions. **1925** F. C. MILLS *Statistical Meth.* xvi. 552 Great care is generally needed in securing a purely random selection. The obvious procedure of picking the most readily available cases would by no means meet the condition of random selection. **1927** *Tracts for Computers* xv. p. iii, In order to form this table of random numbers 40,000 digits were taken at random from census reports and combined by fours to give 10,000 numbers. *Ibid.*, These numbers, if truly random, could be used in a very great variety of ways for artificial sampling. **1933** *Forestry* VII. 149 As far as possible a random arrangement of replicated treatments and controls was adopted. **1936** *Jrnl. Ecol.* XXIV. 232 The simplest assumption, and the one most frequently made, concerning the distribution of the individuals of a plant species, is that it is random, i.e. that the chance that an individual shall occur in a given spot is the same for all spots... The chances that 0, 1, 2, 3,.. individuals shall occur in a sample area large enough to contain very many individuals, are given by the terms of the Poisson series. *Ibid.* 240 Fig. 5 illustrates the divergence from random distribution. **1937** H. CRAMÉR (*title*) Random variables and probability distributions. *Ibid.* viii. 90 The set of variables Z_τ will be said to define a homogeneous random process if, for $\tau_1 \geqq 0$, $\tau_2 > 0$, the difference $U_{\tau_1 \tau_2} = Z_{\tau_1 + \tau_2} - Z_{\tau_1}$ is a random variable which is independent of the variable Z_{τ_1} and has a d[istribution] f[unction] which is independent of τ_1. **1938** *Jrnl. R. Statist. Soc.* CI. 147 In colloquial speech the word 'random' is applied to any method of choice which lacks aim or purpose; and this usage is also found in certain sciences. In statistics, however, the word has a somewhat different and more definite significance, closely related to probability. **1939** *Jrnl. Franklin Inst.* CCVII. 747 Corresponding to the constrictions in the vocal passages from which are made the unvoiced sounds the Voder contains an electrical 'random noise' source which by itself produces a continuous hissing sound. **1946** C. E. WEATHERBURN *First Course in Math. Statistics* ii. 21 The method thus uses the similarity of the marbles to ensure that the selection is random. **1948** *Tracts for Computers* xxv. (*title*) Random normal deviates. *Ibid.* p. iii, They may be regarded as fair random samples from a normal universe having a zero mean and a unit standard deviation. **1949**, etc. [see PSEUDORANDOM *a.*]. **1951** *Jrnl. Ecol.* XXXIX. 172 In a random distribution the variance is equal to the mean, and the variance divided by the mean..can be used to test departures from a random distribution. **1952**, etc. [see *quota sample*]. **1953** J. B. CARROLL *Study of Language* vii. 204 Communication theory is forced to regard messages as random processes. *Ibid.* 245 We use the term *random process* in the statistical sense: a random process is the sampling at random from a population of *potential* events. **1954** T. W. ANDERSON in P. F. Lazarsfeld *Math. Thinking in Social Sci.* i. 35 Since each individual's sequence of opinions is a random variable (i.e., there is a probability attached to each possible sequence), the total number of individuals holding a given sequence is a random variable. **1954** L. L. BERANEK *Acoustics* xiii. 393 Random noise is an acoustical quantity (*e.g.*, sound pressure) or an electrical quantity (*e.g.*, voltage) whose instantaneous amplitudes occur, as a function of time, according to a normal (Gaussian) distribution curve. A common random noise is that resulting from the random motion of molecules of the air... Random noise need not have a flat (uniform) frequency spectrum. *Ibid.*, White noise need not be random. **1959** *Oxf. Univ. Gaz.* 5 Mar. 678/1 Random variates, probability, and likelihood. **1963** B. FOZARD *Instrumentation & Control of Nuclear Reactors* vii. 71 Radioactive disintegrations are truly random, *i.e.* the probability of a disintegration is independent of the occurrence of other events. **1967** C. BERNERS-LEE in Wills & Yearsley *Handbk. Managem. Technol.* 5 In an agricultural experiment to determine the effect of two different fertilizers, *N* and *P* for instance, the classical approach would be to compare unfertilized plots with suitably chosen random selections of plots fertilized with *N*; also to compare with the unfertilized plots a number of plots fertilized only with *P*. **1967** G. WILLS in *Ibid.* 186 Random samples..ensure that if we are drawing a sample from the 27,000 paint retailers in the United Kingdom each retailer would have an equal chance of being selected. This is *not* what is generally meant in common parlance by 'random', but it is what the statistician means. **1968** P. A. P. MORAN *Introd. Probability Theory* i. 6 A random variable is also sometimes called a 'variate'. *Ibid.* x. 459 The study of random walks is the study of the sums of random variables, these variables varying in complexity from simple independent distributions in one dimension to random variables of a much more complicated character. **1970** W. B. DAVENPORT *Random Processes* ix. 299 Such an infinite family of random variables is commonly called a random sequence or random process (or stochastic sequence or stochastic process). **1971** [see *quota method*]. **1973** LORD & ROBINSON tr. *Kuttruff's Room Acoustics* viii. 211 The room under investigation..is excited by stationary random noise..with a large frequency bandwidth. **1973** F. E. FISCHER *Fund. Statistical Concepts* vii. 139 We can think of most discrete random variables as counts (how many heads, children, spades, or accidents?) and most continuous random variables as measures (how tall, long, heavy, or intelligent?). **1975** R. B. ELLIS *Statistical Inference* ii. 17 What counts is making sure that the sample really is random, that at any time any item in the population has as much chance of being chosen as any other item in the population. **1975** *Sci. Amer.* May 48/3 A series of numbers is random if the smallest algorithm capable of specifying it to a computer has about the same number of bits of information as the series itself. **1977** *Private Eye* 1 Apr. 5/2 The naive random walk theory..rules out the application of any device based upon the movement of past prices in the market. **1978** *Sci. Amer.* Apr. 71/2 One way to test for the role of chance in such a situation is to devise a Monte Carlo computer program, which generates random numbers to determine the distances and angles between consecutive directional changes of simulated tracks.

c. *Psychol.* Of activity, movements, etc.: seeming to be without purpose or direct relationship to a stimulus, sometimes thought of as an organism's initial reaction to unfamiliar stimuli, and giving way to directed action as learning takes place.

1905 *Psychol. Bull.* II. 251 Fuhrmann noted prevalence of predicative association and of the egocentric factors; moreover, especially in the beginning of tests, random association. **1911** E. L. THORNDIKE *Animal Intelligence* vi. 242 If the movements are really random, they occur by virtue of some force that works at random. **1927** J. ADAMS *Errors in School* x. 304 The knowledge the psycho-analyst acquires by random-answering is knowledge-by-the-way so far as the instructor is concerned. **1927** M. K. THOMSON *Springs of Human Action* v. 74 *Undifferentiated activity* (random movement), among the native tendencies none is more primitive and fundamental than activity. **1934** CROZIER & HOAGLAND in C. Murchison *Handbk. Gen. Exper. Psychol.* 20 It is to be noted that there is obtainable in this way a *measure* of 'random' movements and a key to their interpretation. **1935** K. KOFFKA *Princ. Gestalt Psychol.* xiii. 629 Trial and error may then mean that he gets a 'hunch' from the data... This would no longer be random activity, but activity determined by the nature of the task. **1935** E. L. THORNDIKE *Psychol. of Wants, Interests & Attitudes* ii. 13 The fact of multiple response or varied reaction..has led to the error of assuming that man at least had a tendency to make responses that were random. *Ibid.*, There doubtless is a residuum of behavior that may be called random. **1948** E. R. HILGARD *Theories of Learning* v. 116 Although it was often convenient to talk about 'random' or 'spontaneous' responses, it was not doubted that stimuli were present to elicit them.

2. Of persons: Living irregularly. *rare.*

c **1825** *Houlston Tracts* II. No. 60. 6 'In my time, Sir', said he, 'I've been random and free, But I now prefer order and quiet'. **1873** H. SPENCER *Stud. Sociol.* xv. 371 Continually we remark that men who were random grow steady when they have children to provide for.

3. *techn.* **a.** Said of masonry, in which the stones are of irregular sizes and shapes. Cf. C. 2 b.

1823 P. NICHOLSON *Pract. Build.* 339 Random Courses—Unequal courses, without any regard to equi-distant joints. **1886** *Chesh. Gloss.* s.v., A random wall.

b. Of tooling: (see DROVE *v.*[3]).

1842 GWILT *Archit.* §1914 Droving is the same as that called random tooling in England, or boasting in London.

c. Of yarn = CLOUDED 2 a.

1874 W. CROOKES *Dyeing & Calico-Print.* xii. 102 On the large scale the random yarns are coloured in machines.

4. ***random shot***, a shot fired at random (orig. in sense 5 b of the sb., but latterly apprehended as in sense 1 of the adj.).

1693 LUTTRELL *Brief Rel.* (1857) III. 9 One of their random shotts killed lieutenant coll. Jackson. **1708** *Lond. Gaz.* No. 4422/7 The nine Sail stood in fair with us near random Shot. **1788** GIBBON *Decl. & F.* lxviii. (1869) III. 716 The first random shots were productive of more sound than effect. **1806** A. DUNCAN *Nelson* 109 The..ship..had approached within random shot of the Leander. **1849** MACAULAY *Hist. Eng.* ix. II. 457 A random shot or the dagger of an assassin might in a moment leave the expedition without a head.

fig. **1785** BURNS *To J. Smith* vi, The star that rules my luckless lot..Has blest me with a random-shot O' countra wit. **1809** MALKIN *Gil Blas* VII. vi. ¶2 The random shot of ..self-created guides in matters of taste.

5. ***random access*** (Computers): used to designate a memory or file all parts of which are directly accessible, so that it need not be read sequentially; esp. one in which the access time for any item is effectively independent of the location and the access time of the item last accessed.

1953 *Proc. IRE* XLI. 1264/2 The random-access property also makes it easier to operate input, output, and external storage devices out of synchronism with the central computer. **1967** *New Scientist* 5 Oct. 13/1 This type of memory, in which all addresses are directly accessible, is known as random-access, to distinguish it from the slower but cheaper type which is scanned sequentially, used for backing stores. **1969** P. B. JORDAIN *Condensed Computer Encycl.* 414 The true random-access devices are static memories: core, thin film, electrostatic cathode-ray tubes, electronic. Most of the so-called random-access devices—drum, disk, tape loop, magnetic card file..—are really cyclic access devices. **1971** *Publishers' Weekly* 9 Aug. 24/3 The advantage of random access disc storage is that all required files for a specific application will be on-line to the computer when that application is being processed. **1975** T. W. PRATT *Programming Languages* iii. 87 A random access file is organized as a set of unordered records. Access is through an address that indicates the position of the record on the external device.

C. *adv.* †**1.** = At random. *Obs. rare.*

1618 BOLTON *Florus* (1636) 96 The third lightnings of Annibal flew randome at us by Trasimenus lake. *a* **1619** FOTHERBY *Atheom.* II. xi. §2 (1622) 313 Neither doe they runne randon, nor are they rolled, beside their ancient order.

2. *Comb.*, as ***random-blown, -cast, -fashioned, -rubbed*** adjs.; ***random-wise*** adv.

1790 R. MERRY *Laurel Liberty* (ed. 2) 7 Random-cast, beside some stream,..Thou ponder'st. **1839** DARLEY *Introd. Beaum. & Fl.'s Wks.* (1839) I. 26 Most imaginative authors, perhaps, commence random-wise,..and save themselves the trouble of a total invention at first. **1862** *Illustr. Catal. Internat. Exhib., Industr. Dept., Brit. Div.* II. No. 2253 Castellated circular turret, random rubbed; white quartz. **1871** TENNYSON in *Contemp. Rev.* XIX. 12 Tristram ..sank Down on a drift of foliage random-blown. **1906** HARDY *Dynasts* II. v. viii. 287 Ephemeral at the best all honours be,..So random-fashioned, swift, perturbable!

b. ***random-jointed*** (see quot. 1833 and B. 3 a).

1833 LOUDON *Encycl. Archit.* §185 Rubble stone, or random jointed ashlar work (free stone, rough as it comes from the quarry, laid in irregular courses). **1848** [J. C. WHARTON] *Quarrendon Church* 7 The external walls are built with random-jointed squared ashlar.

Hence **'randomish** *a.*, somewhat random; **'randomly** *adv.*; **'randomness**; also **rando'micity** = prec.

1824 in *Spirit Pub. Jrnls.* (1825) 136 My son Jonathan is but a randomish sort of a chap. **1865** *Ch. Times* 2 Sept. 276/3 Each rode his own hobby..so randomly and violently [etc.]. **1866** J. VENN *Logic of Chance* ii. 30 We must also idealize the 'randomness' of the throwing of the penny. **1872** BLACKMORE *Maid of Sker* 166 If any one cares for that sort of thing, who knows mankind's great randomness. **1891** G. MEREDITH *One of our Conq.* I. xii. 228 He talked randomly of money. **1921** J. M. KEYNES *Treat. Probability* xxiv. 281 Many important differences of opinion in the treatment of probability have been due to confusion or vagueness as to what is meant by Randomness. **1936** *Rev. Sci. Instruments* VII. 459/2 Fluctuations to be expected due to the randomicity of the counting. **1938** *Nature* 14 May 881/2 Four tests for randomness..were applied to these numbers, with satisfactory results in each case. **1957** P. GREIG-SMITH *Quantitative Plant Ecol.* iii. 51 Departure from randomness of distribution of a species indicates that one or few factors are determining the performance or survival of the species. **1959** *New Scientist* Dec. 1144/3 An interesting point of this arrangement is that the lengths of the delays can be chosen randomly. **1963** H. M. MORRIS *Twilight of Evolution* ii. 44 The natural tendency of all change is to create a greater degree of disorder and randomness. **1963** T. & P. MORRIS *Pentonville* iv. 75 Half the men in each group were randomly selected on the basis of throwing dice. **1972** *Science* 27 Oct. 392/3 Environmental randomicity of various kinds may have important implications in triggering evolutionary sequences that would be impossible or unlikely in non-stochastic environments. **1980** *Jrnl. R. Soc. Arts* Feb. 138/1 The cosmos will end in heat death with all matter randomly diffused.

random ('rændəm), *v. rare.* [f. the sb.] *intr.* To do something at random, to occur at random.

1889 'MARK TWAIN' *Conn. Yankee* xxvii. 349 A thought came randoming overthwart this majestic dream. **1921** R. FROST *Let.* 15 Apr. (1964) 127 She wasn't experimenting, poor thing. She was randoming, as Alisande hath it.

randomization (ˌrændəmaɪ'zeɪʃən). [f. next + -ATION.] The action, process, or result of randomizing.

1926 *Jrnl. Min. Agric.* XXXIII. 510 A process of randomization by which one is selected at random out of the total number of Latin Squares possible. **1934** *Math. Gaz.* XVIII. 294 The process of randomisation has in recent years come to play such a central part in experimental design that it is of some interest to find that it affords a means of resolving one of the oldest paradoxes which arose in discussions of gaming. **1946** G. W. SNEDECOR *Statistical Methods* (ed. 4) 253 The degree of randomization is no longer evident, but the weekly heights and the block differences are brought into prominence. **1960** *Daily Tel.* 23 Aug. 16/5 Because the experiments were made over five years, using a 'randomisation' method, the Australian results were considered by other experts at the conference to be the first to be absolutely conclusive. 'Randomisation' means that clouds are selected in a completely random manner. **1966** *Lancet* 24 Dec. 1371/2 We tested the randomness of these four groups; except for age-distribution, randomisation was satisfactory. **1980** *Times Lit. Suppl.* 15 Feb. 160 A 'genuinely open society' is, presumably, one in which relative mobility chances have been equalized. But how?.. By the randomization of access to the labour market?

randomize ('rændəmaɪz), *v.* [f. RANDOM *sb.*, *a.*, and *adv.* + -IZE.] *trans.* To render unpredictable, unsystematic, or random in order or arrangement; to employ random selection or sampling in (an experiment or procedure).

1926 *Jrnl. Min. Agric.* XXXIII. 509 The distinction between errors eliminated in the field, and the errors which are to be carefully randomized in order to provide a valid estimate of the errors which cannot be eliminated, may be made most clear by one of the most useful and flexible types of arrangement, namely, the arrangement in 'randomized blocks'. **1939** H. JEFFREYS *Theory of Probability* iv. 192 Most physicists, of course, will envy workers in subjects where uninteresting systematic effects can be randomized. **1958** *New Scientist* 21 Aug. 659/3 Having produced a beam of the required energy, the Oak Ridge group then try to randomise it by firing it into a magnetic bottle produced by two mirror coils. **1959** *Test House Rep.* No. OTL/M1/5/59 (Inspectorate of Fighting Vehicles & Mech. Equipm. Test House. Oil Test Lab.) 4 A programme of two tests on each of the seven oils was arranged and the tests randomised to eliminate bias. **1967** *Listener* 26 Jan. 134/2 A number of years ago Sir Ronald Fisher made a statistical analysis of the problem and came to the unexpected conclusion that the best rule in each case was not to have any fixed rule at all, but to randomize one's actions by an appeal to chance. **1971** *Jrnl. Gen. Psychol.* LXXXV. 172 The order of these pronouns was randomized. **1977** *Sci. Amer.* Sept. 42/2 Assume that the deck of cards is finite, so that an umpire can indeed randomize them.

Hence **'randomized** *ppl. a.*, chosen at random; deliberately made random or unpredictable; **'randomizing** *ppl. a.*, generating random output; **'randomizing** *vbl. sb.*, the act of rendering random.

1926 Randomized [see RANDOMIZE *v.*] **1936** *Nature* 15 Feb. 253/1 It is with applications of the principle of testing null hypotheses by means of randomised and replicated experiments that the first nine chapters of this book deal. **1936** *Jrnl. R. Statist. Soc.* Suppl. No. 3. 118 The tendency of deliberate randomizing is to increase the error. **1938** *Nature* 14 May 881/1 M. G. Kendall and B. B. Smith have designed a randomizing machine. **1955** *Sci. Amer.* Feb. 81/2 The idea is to let chance play a role in the choice of strategy, that is, to use a randomized or 'mixed' strategy. **1962** *Times Lit. Suppl.* 2 Feb. 73/3 To randomized numbers where no fancy boggles The Great Boondogglers go. **1968** P. A. P. MORAN *Introd. Probability Theory* i. 44 Decimal digits which were obtained by a 'randomizing machine'. **1970** *Nature* 12 Dec. 1113/1 Each block of twenty trials contained all possible combinations of test stimuli presented in randomized sequence. **1978** *Lancet* 14 Jan. 72/2 The claim that an upright maternal posture during labour improves the efficiency of the uterus to the benefit of both mother and fetus has been investigated in a randomised prospective study.

randomizer ('rændəmaɪzə(r)). [f. prec. + -ER[1].] A device which generates random output.

1974 *Sci. Amer.* Apr. 112/2 It is very easy to use a penny as a randomizer for deciding between two alternatives with probabilities expressed by rational fractions. **1976** *Times Lit. Suppl.* 13 Feb. 172/4 Chickens..which appear capable of influencing mentally an electronic randomizer controlling the switching mechanism of a lamp.

†**'randon,** *v. Obs. rare.* Also 7 **-ome.** [f. the sb.; in earliest quot. perh. a. OF. *randonner.*]

1. *intr.* ? To flow swiftly. *rare*[−1].

Or perh. *trans.* 'to set in line' referring to the walls.

c **1470** *Gol. & Gaw.* 248 Apone that riche river, randonit full evin, The side-wallis war set, sad to the see.

2. *intr.* To fly at random.

1602 *Narcissus* (1893) 735 Lett not your iudgments randome. **1605** CAMDEN *Rem.* (1637) 204 That it [the bullet of a sling] pierceth helmet and shield, that it reacheth farther, that it randoneth lesse.

randon(e, -doun(e, -down(e, obs. ff. RANDOM.

‖**randori** (ræn'dɔːrɪ). [Jap., lit. 'informal practice'.] A (session of) informal practice in Judo.

1913 E. J. HARRISON *Fighting Spirit of Japan* iv. 65 The non-esoteric branches of *judo* are called *randori*, in which the pupil freely applies his knowledge in open practice..with others. **1932** —— *Art of Ju-Jitsu* iii. 30 It is not absolutely necessary for the pupil to master all these details..before beginning '*randori*' practice. **1954** E. DOMINY *Teach Yourself Judo* vi. 63 In 'randori' which is free practice you never find an opponent who is willing to lie passively on his back. **1972** *Oxf. Mail* 1 Aug. 10/3 This initial practice very soon develops into 'randori', the form of training in which most players spend most of their judo time. This involves moving about with a partner.

randring, obs. Sc. pr. pple. RENDER.

randsom, obs. form of RANSOM.

randum, -dun, obs. forms of RANDOM.

randy ('rændɪ), *a.* and *sb.*[1] orig. *dial.* and *Sc.* Also 7–9 **randie.** [Perh. f. RAND *v.* + -Y: but the original sense of the word is not quite clear.]

A. *adj.* **1.** *Sc.* Having a rude, aggressive manner; loud-tongued and coarse-spoken.

In early use always of beggars, and probably implying vagrant habits as well as rude behaviour. Now applied only to women.

1698 *Culross Kirk Session Minutes* 18 Sept., Seven pounds Scots..distributed to the randie beggars. **1723** MESTON *Poems, Knight* (1767) 6 A rambling, randy errant Knight. **1785** BURNS *Jolly Beggars* 1st Recit., A merry core O' randie, gangrel bodies. **1816** SCOTT *Old Mort.* xxvii, It was him and his randie mother began a' the mischief in this house. **1894** CROCKETT *Raiders* (ed. 3) 42 Hearing what the pair of old randy wives had to say to me.

2. a. *dial.* Boisterous, riotous, disorderly, dissipated; wild, unruly, unmanageable.

1787 in GROSE *Prov. Gloss.* **1874** SIR J. KAY-SHUTTLEWORTH *Ribblesdale* I. 21 Mind you long-horned cattle..they are apt to be randy. **1876-** in dial. glossaries (Yks., Linc., Chesh., Shropsh., etc.). **1884** *Punch* 8 Mar. 118/1 That young bay you'll find a little randy, With rather more of 'devil' than comes handy.

b. Wanton, lustful, lewd. orig. *dial.*

1847 in HALLIWELL. **1881-** in dial. glossaries (Yks., Leic., Warw., etc.). *c* **1888–94** *My Secret Life* III. 280 She'll be randy directly her belly is filled. **1922** [see PUSSY *sb.* 6]. **1939** J. STEINBECK *Grapes of Wrath* vi. 69 Fust time I ever laid with a girl..snortin' like a buck deer, randy as a billygoat. **1957** W. CAMP *Prospects of Love* II. v. 62 Suffers from too much sex, if anything—he's a randy old man. **1965** F. SARGESON *Mem. Peon* iv. 87, I was randy myself at your age. But be careful. These native girls can put you right into hospital if you don't take care. **1978** K. J. DOVER *Greek Homosexuality* ii. 38 The gangs or clubs of randy and combative young men.

3. *Comb.*, as (sense 2 b) ***randy-arsed*** adj.; also with sbs. forming attrib. compounds, as ***randy-dog.***

1968 Randy-arsed [see LENGTH *sb.* 11 c]. **1963** *Times Lit. Suppl.* 18 Jan. 37/4 Harold Barlow is an Amis character.. with that special randy-dog flavour. **1973** M. AMIS *Rachel Papers* 173 Tom, Geoffrey's analogue of my own Sebastian: sixteen, wealthy in pustules, randy-dog smells, sebum-moist hairline, and other adolescentiana.

B. *sb.*[1] *Sc.* and *north. dial.* **a.** A sturdy rude-mannered beggar; a thorough vagrant.

1788 BURNS *Louis, what reck* ii, Reif randies, I disown ye! **1792** *Statist. Acc. Scotl.* II. 515 Many Randies (sturdy vagrants) infest this country. **1811** WILLAN *W. Riding Gloss.* (E.D.S.), *Randies*, itinerant beggars and ballad-singers. **1884** *Gd. Words* 161 She's a regular randy, nigh as bad as a gipsy. She's never in the house.

b. A loud-tongued, coarse-mannered woman; a scold, virago, termagant.

1816 SCOTT *Old Mort.* viii, The daft speeches of an auld jaud..a daft auld whig randy. **1850** CARLYLE *Let. to Wife* 19 Aug. in Froude *Life in London* (1884) II. xviii. 52 Do not let that scandalous randy of a girl disturb you. **1878-** in dial. glossaries (Cumbld., Northumb., Antrim).

Comb. **1822** GALT *Steam-boat* ix. 179 A randy-like woman.

Hence **randy** *v.*[3] *trans.*, to render (a person) lascivious (*nonce-use*); **'randiness**, the quality or condition of being randy (sense 2 b); lustfulness.

1911 *Conc. Oxf. Dict.*, Randiness. **1953** W. COOPER *Ever-Interesting Topic* 145 Attending Dr Foy's series of lectures on sex was inducing in the boys a distinctly higher-than-usual state of—there is no other word for it—randiness. **1967** A. WILSON *No Laughing Matter* III. 305 This bloody randiness always threatened to suck him down into the vast, empty emotional gulf of Ted's shapeless life. **1976** W. GREATOREX *Crossover* 103 He didn't like randy old sods. He thought randiness should be forbidden after the age of, say, forty. **1961** A. WILSON *Old Men at Zoo* v. 278 You've randied him into the looney bin now..the highest-minded little whore that ever almost gave herself out of charity.

'randy, *sb.*[2] *dial.* [cf. RANDY *v.*[2]] A noisy merry-making or revel. Also ***randy-go*** and ***on the*** (or ***a***) ***randy***, 'on the spree'.

Perh. abbrev. of RENDEZVOUS, used in various dialects (in forms *randivoo*, *-bew*, *-bow*, *-voose*, etc.) in a similar sense. But cf. RANDY *a.* 2.

1825 in JENNINGS *Dial. West Eng.* **1856** THOMPSON *Hist. Boston* Gloss. s.v., 'He was at the randy'. Rendezvous. **1877** E. PEACOCK *Gloss. Words Manley & Corringham, Lincolnshire* 202/1 Bill's on the *randy* to-day. **1881** MISS YONGE *Lads & Lasses Langley* iv. 159 He was trained on by the music, and got into that there randy go up in the park. **1891** T. HARDY *Tess* (1900) 78/2 A rattling good randy wi' fiddles and bass-viols complete. **1934** L. MACNEICE *Poems* (1935) 18 Over the randy of the theatre and cinema I hear songs. **1940** DYLAN THOMAS *Portrait of Artist as Young Dog* 67 'Hush! hush! your mother'll be waiting. You must come home.' 'No she won't. She's gone on a randy with Mr Robert.'

†**'randy,** *v.*[1] *Obs. rare.* [Cf. RAND *v.*[2]] *intr.* To canvass. Hence **'randying** *vbl. sb.*

a **1720** T. GORDON *Cordial Low Spirits* 57 Who advised him, as soon as ever he came to the randying ground, to bray with all his might. **1733** FIELDING *Don Quix. in Eng.* II. iii, He was here..randying for a knight of his acquaintance, with no less than six hundred freeholders at his heels.

'randy, *v.*[2] *dial.* [cf. RANDY *sb.*[2]] *intr.* To be 'on the spree'.

1832 *Boston Herald* 4 Dec. 4/3 A number of labouring bankers were 'randying' at the Woolpack inn. **1870** E. PEACOCK *Ralf Skirl.* III. iv. 62, I fetch him hoome fra' that big hoose yonder, after he's been randyin' ower long.

randy, *v.*[3] see RANDY *a.* and *sb.*[1]

'randy-'dandy. Redupl. form of RANDY *sb.*[2]

1917 J. M. BARRIE *Old Lady shows her Medals* 34, I have a theatre tonight, followed by a randy-dandy.

rane (reːn), *sb. Sc.* Now *rare.* Also 5 **rayne,** 6 **reane,** 8 **rain.** [Of obscure origin. With sense 2 cf. RAME *sb.* and *v.*]

†**1.** ***in a rane***, continuously, without cessation.

c **1375** SC. LEG. SAINTS iii. (*Andreas*) 989 Bot ay þe bischope in a rane beheld hyr bewte, and nocht fane. *Ibid.* xxxix. (*Cosm. & Dam.*) 251 He..cryit ay in til a rane. **1560** ROLLAND *Seven Sages* 250 Thay rattill ay in a rane. *a* **1585** MONTGOMERIE *Flyting w. Polwart* 501 All the ky in the countrey..roaring, they wood ran, and routed in a reane.

2. A prolonged cry or utterance; a long string of words; a rigmarole.

c **1425** WYNTOUN *Cron.* II. ix. 883 Swa suld I dulle hale yhoure delyte, And yhe sulde call it bot a rane. **1513** DOUGLAS *Æneis* VIII. Prol. 66 The railȝear raknis na wordis, but ratlis furth ranis. **1710** RUDDIMAN *Gloss. Douglas' Æneis* s.v., You're like the Gowk,..you have not a rain but one. **1825** in Child *Ballads* II. 82/1 It was, as she described it, a 'lang rane' of her mother's.

Hence **rane** (also 9 **raen**), *v.* †(*a*) *trans.*, to demand with a continuous cry. *Obs.* (*b*) *intr.*, to wail or complain incessantly.

1513 DOUGLAS *Æneis* VII. x. 90 Thar the detestable weris, evyr in ane, Agane the fatis all, thai cry and rane. **1899** J. COLVILLE *Scott. Vernacular* 17 She tholed much from the wheenging raenin' bairn.

rane, obs. Sc. form of RAIN; obs. pa. t. RUN.

ranedeer, obs. form of REINDEER.

‖**ranee** ('rɑːniː). Also 7 **ranna,** 8 **r(h)anny,** 9 **rannee, ráni, (ranie, -y).** [Hindī *rānī* = Skr. *rājnī* fem. of *rāja*(*n* RAJAH.] A Hindu queen.

1698 FRYER *Acc. E. India & P.* IV. iii. 162 The Ranna, the relict of Sham Shanker Naig; who now Rules in her Son's Minority. **1781** POPHAM in Jas. Grant *Hist. India* (1876) I. xlix. 254/1 The Rhanny is allowed to reside in this province. **1818** JAS. MILL *Brit. India* II. v. vii. 614 The Rannee, that is, the widow of the deceased Rajah. **1841** ELPHINSTONE *Hist. India* II. 495 He dispatched the ráni and her infants in disguise. **1858** BEVERIDGE *Hist. India* I. III. iv. 431 He made the ranee prisoner.

ranegate, obs. form of RENEGATE.

ranet, obs. form of *roe-net*: see ROE *sb.*[1]

Raney ('reɪnɪ). *Chem.* The name of Murray *Raney* (1885–1966), U.S. engineer, used *attrib.* in **Raney nickel,** a form of nickel catalyst first prepared by him (see quot. 1932) which has a high surface area and is used in organic hydrogenation reactions.

First described by Raney in U.S. Patent 1,628,190 (1927).

1932 *Jrnl. Amer. Chem. Soc.* LIV. 4116 The Raney catalyst is prepared by alloying equal parts of nickel and aluminum and dissolving out the latter with aqueous sodium hydroxide. **1940** *Ibid.* LXII. 1687/1 The catalytic hydrogenation of azo compounds at normal temperature and pressure over Raney nickel is not only of scientific interest, but also of considerable practical value. **1964** G. H. HAGGIS et al. *Introd. Molecular Biol.* xii. 325 The cysteine was then converted to alanine with the aid of a catalyst called Raney nickel. **1977** L. F. & M. FIESER *Reagents for Org. Synthesis* VI. 54 The corresponding 1,4-diketones can be obtained by hydrolysis catalyzed by mercuric chloride or by treatment with Raney nickel.

†**ranforce,** *v. Obs.* Also 6 **-forse.** [ad. F. *renforcer* RENFORCE; cf. RAMFORCE *v.*]

1. *trans.* To strengthen, fortify. Hence **ranforcing** *vbl. sb.*

1547 *Register Privy Council Scot.* (1877) I. 79 Our auld ynemeis of Ingland..hes ranforsit the samin, and..perseveris in thair bigging and ranforsing of the saidis places. **1590** SIR J. SMYTH *Disc. Weapons* Ded. 5 Newe supplies of men and munitions from time to time to ranforce his Armie or Armies. *Ibid.* 6 Light Harquebuzes well formed of conuenient length, and ranforced.

¶**2.** To force, break open.

1637 MONRO *Exped.* I. 51 With a huge great ladder and the force of men we ran-forced the doore and entred.

Hence †**ranforce-ring.** *Obs.* (See quot. and REINFORCE *sb.*)

1706 PHILLIPS, *Ranforce-Ring of a Gun*, that which is next before the Touch-hole, between it and the Trunnions.

rang. *Sc.* Now *rare* or *Obs.* Also 9 **raing.** [a. F. *rang*: see RANGE *v.*] A range, rank.

In earliest quots. perh. written for *range*.

c **1470** HENRY *Wallace* IV. 681 The rang in haist thai rayit. *Ibid.* IX. 875 In till a rang. **1580** J. HAYE *Demands* in *Cath. Tract.* (S.T.S.) 51 Mony..of your secte, yea ministers of the first rang. *Ibid.* 64 Ministers..nocht in the lawest rang. **1808** JAMIESON, *Rang, raing*, a row, a rank.

rang, obs. f. RANK *a.*; see also RING *v.*[1], *v.*[2]

†**rangale.** *Obs.* Chiefly *Sc.* Forms: 4 **rengaile,** 4–5 **rangale, -all,** 6 **-ald, ringald.** See also RANGAT[2]. [ad. OF. *ringaille* (Wace, etc.).]

1. The ranks or main body of an army. *rare*[−1].

c **1330** R. BRUNNE *Chron.* (1810) 116 He bad, þat non alone breke out of þe rengaile.

2. *Sc.* Rabble, *esp.* of an army; camp-followers.

1375 BARBOUR *Bruce* XI. 111 Men on fut and small rangale, That ȝemyt harnas and vittale. *c* **1425** WYNTOUN *Cron.* VIII. xxxvi. 35 Ane hundreth armyd jolyly Off knychtis and sqwyeris, but rangale. **1513** DOUGLAS *Æneis* VI. xii. 73 Gret rout with rangald, in ledis he.

b. The common herd (of deer).

1513 DOUGLAS *Æneis* I. iv. 57 First the ledaris thre,..Smertlie he slew, syne all the rangald persewis.

'rangant, *a. Her.* [F., for *rangeant*, pr. pple. of *ranger* to RANGE.] = FURIOSANT (q.v.).

†**'rangat**[1]. *Sc. Obs.* [Of obscure origin.] Disorder, disturbance, noise.

1500–20 DUNBAR *Poems* lxvi. 30 Gude rewle is banist our the Bordour, And rangat ringis but ony ordour. **1535** STEWART *Cron. Scot.* III. 294 For feiring of thair fo, Tha tuke the gait without rangat till go.

†**'rangat**[2]. *Sc. Obs.* [var. *rangald* RANGALE, perh. after prec.; but cf. the Sc. pron. of the surname *Donald* as *Donnat.*] Rabble.

1535 [see RINGAT-RANGAT.] **1606** BIRNIE *Kirk-Buriall* (1833) 20 At first they held their Abbay burials royall, yet in the end they were for pryce exposed to the rangat.

‖**rangatira** (ranga'tira). *N.Z.* Also *erron.* **rangitira.** [Maori.] A Maori chief (male or female), a noble.

1820 *Gram. & Vocab. Lang. N.Z.* (Church Missionary Soc.) 200 *Ránga tira*, a gentleman or lady. **1824** H. WILLIAMS *Let.* 27 Jan. in H. Carleton *Life of Henry Williams* (1874) I. 35 We told him that *rangatiras* [gentlemen] do not steal. **1843** E. DIEFFENBACH *Travels in N.Z.* II. I. vii. 112 The principal person in a tribe is the Ariki; but as he is *per se* a Rangatira, he is rarely called by the former name. **1855** V. LUSH *Jrnl.* 23 Sept. (1971) 165 This addition to the Native Ministry is a fine, tall and highly intelligent man, and being by birth a Rangatira (a Chief) he has far, far more influence among his countrymen than Rota has, who formerly was but a slave. **1863** F. E. MANING *Old N.Z.* i. 6 The chief..having made some inquiries..such as, whether I was a *rangatira*. **1882** W. D. HAY *Brighter Britain!* I. 253 The caste styled tana, or chieftains, a degree above that of rangatira, or simple gentlemen-warriors. **1903** *Daily Chron.* 21 Sept. 5/1 This lad, Victor Huia, was born in New Zealand thirteen years ago, and by the Maoris was formally created a native chief, or rangatira, being duly decorated with the sacred feather of the huia. **1936** R. HYDE *Check to your King* 146 Maori *rangatira*..promise that in future jury trial shall be observed. **1937** N. MARSH *Vintage Murder* xxii. 242 My grandfather was a deeply-instructed rangitira. **1943** —— *Colour Scheme* ii. 37, I am a *rangatira*. My father attended an ancient school of learning. He was a *tohunga*. **1962** M. K. JOSEPH *Pound of Saffron* iv. 65 I'd like to see old Blennerhassett in a flax mat—some rangatira he'd make. **1967** A. & D. REID *Paddle Wheels on Wanganui* 69 According to local history a rangatira had in decades past been buried in a certain upriver area. **1978** B. MASON in *Islands* Aug. 18 In the past of our people, he would have been a splendid *rangatira*, a glory to his *taua*.

range (reɪndʒ), *sb.*[1] Forms: 4–7 **raunge,** (5 *Sc.* **rawnge,** 6 **rawng),** 5 **rangh, raynge,** 6–8 **rainge,** 6 **randge,** 4- **range.** [a. OF. *range* row, rank, file (Godef.), sb. f. *ranger* to RANGE *v.* See also RENGE *sb.*]

I. 1. A row, line, file or rank, of persons (†*spec.* of hunters or fighting men) or animals. Now *rare.* † ***on range***, in file.

a **1300** *Cursor M.* 23109 (Cott.) þe first range [*Gött.* rau]..sal be o wreches mistruand. **1375** BARBOUR *Bruce* x. 379 Thai..on range [*E.* rawnge] in ane rod can ga. *c* **1470** HENRY *Wallace* III. 259 Na chyftane was that tyme durst tak on hand, To leide the range on Wallace to assaill. **1513** DOUGLAS *Æneis* I. vi. 153 Behald twelf swannis..Now with lang range to lycht thai bene adrest. *Ibid.* IV. iii. 56 Quhen that the rangis and the faid..Dynnis throw the gravis, sersing the woddis wyde. **1585** T. WASHINGTON tr. *Nicholay's Voy.* I. vi, A little further were in a range the kings slaues. **1640** YORKE *Union Hon.* 45 King Richard..made firm the Range of his owne Battaile. **1677** W. HUBBARD *Narrative* (1865) I. 274 The Indians were laid in one Range by several Fires. **1760–72** H. BROOKE *Fool of Qual.* (1809) III. 134 Two brilliant ranges of foreign and British ladies. **1847** TENNYSON *Princ.* II. 89 There sat along the forms..A patient range of pupils.

2. A row, line, or series of things.

a. of objects in general. (Now usually expressed by *row*; in 17–18th c. freq. used of trees.)

1511 GUYLFORDE *Pilgr.* (Camden) 36 There be .iiij. rowes or ranges of pylers thrughout yᵉ church. **1578** LYTE *Dodoens* IV. viii. 461 The grayne or cornes are placed..in foure ranges or moe lines. **1652** NEEDHAM *Selden's Mare Cl.* 77 A Galley with one range of Oares. **1695** BLACKMORE *Pr. Arth.* III. 539 Trees on their Banks in goodly Ranges grow. **1786** tr. *Beckford's Vathek* (1868) 113 A range of brazen vases surrounded the elevation. **1832** HT. MARTINEAU *Life in Wilds* ix. 123 His present was a range of beehives. **1863** GEO. ELIOT *Romola* I. xii, The walls were..covered with ranges of books in perfect order.

b. of buildings or parts of these. Also, a continuous stretch of building.

1600 in Willis & Clark *Cambridge* (1886) II. 259 In this rawng now erecting..it wilbe well..that the thyrd story may be..higher than it is in the north rawng. **1618** *Ibid.* I. 206 Concerninge a Range of buildinge to be erected. **1705** ADDISON *Italy* 11 The New-Street is a double Range of Palaces from one end to the other. **1771** BENTHAM *Ely Cath.* (1812) 33 Two, and sometimes three ranges of pillars, one over another. **1834** H. MILLER *Scenes & Leg.* xix. (1850) 280 The range had been inhabited..by a crew of fishermen and their families. **1863** P. BARRY *Dockyard Econ.* 227 Turning from these buildings, this further range of brick and mortar is the engine factory and foundries.

c. of large natural objects, *esp.* of mountains.

Hence in *pl.* 'the usual word in Australia for mountains' (Morris *Austral Eng.* 1898), though the sing. form is also used.

1705 ADDISON *Italy* 451 The Town..has its Views bounded on all Sides by several Ranges of Mountains. **1748** ANSON *Voy.* III. v. 344 The Ladrones will be only one small portion of a range of Islands. **1791** W. BARTRAM *Carolina* 197 This range or chain of morasses. **1839** J. MORPHETT in J. Stephens *Land of Promise* ii. 17 We passed the range at the point where the shingle-splitters have their settlement. **1846** F. DUTTON *S. Australia & its Mines* xi. 297 The Ranges, immediately at the back of Adelaide, are at present the principal locality where this ore has been met with in great abundance. **1859** JEPHSON *Brittany* xix. 311 A magnificent range of cliffs. **1864** J. ROGERS *New Rush* 31 How merrily passes the digger's life..To live in the ranges free from strife. **1871** L. STEPHEN *Playgr. Eur.* iv. 228 Those gigantic ranges which surpass even the Alps in magnitude. **1901** M. FRANKLIN *My Brilliant Career* v. 31 The furnace-breath wind which roared among the trees on the low ranges at our back. *Ibid.* viii. 60 Those trees are Five-Bob Downs—see, away over against the range. **1946** K. TENNANT *Lost Haven* (1947) 6 Alec's father..set up a farm for himself far enough off in the ranges to be out of reach of his father's interference. **1966** 'J. HACKSTON' *Father clears Out* 11 There's a big fire burning left of the ranges. *Ibid.*, It's over the range now.

d. *N. Amer.* A series of townships, six miles in width, extending north and south parallel to the principal meridian of a survey.

Ranges were established by the U.S. Congress on 20 May 1785.

1785 *Jrnls. Continental Congress U.S.* (1933) XXVIII. 376 The geographer shall designate the townships..by numbers progressively from south to north; always beginning each range with number one. **1790** *Deb. Congress U.S.* 27 Dec. (1834) 1832 Mr. Clymer wished to know how much land these seven ranges included. **1811** R. SUTCLIFF *Jrnl.* 28 Nov. in *Trav. N. Amer.* (1811) ix. 148 They meted out the tract into divisions and ranges, which are numbered. **1837** J. M. PECK *Gazetteer Illinois* (ed. 2) I. 76 In numbering the townships east or west from a principal meridian they are called ranges, meaning a range of townships. **1843–56** BOUVIER *Law Dict. U.S.* (ed. 6) II. 419 In patents from the United States to individuals they are described as being within a certain range. **1882** *Contemp. Rev.* Aug. 233 These townships are numbered..in Roman numerals, I., II., III., &c., in what are called ranges westward from the principal meridians. **1960** DAVIES & VAUGHAN *Beyond Old Bone Trail* iii. 23 The land had been split up into townships, ranges, sections, and quarter-sections. Townships and ranges were six miles square. **1977** *Chicago Tribune* 2 Oct. II. 14/6

(Advt.), Section 23 in Chapel Hills Garden South of the North West quarter of Section 21, Township 37 North, Range 13, East of the Third Principal Meridian.

e. *Math.* A set of points on a straight line.

1858 Cayley *Wks.* (1889) II. 577 The theories of ranges and pencils..are in fact a single theory. **1872** J. M. Wilson *Solid Geom.* 65 The points *A*, *B* are said to be conjugate to one another in the harmonic range *ACBD*.

3. Rank, class, order. *rare.*

1625 Markham *Bk. Honour* II. v. §1 The Eternall Maiestie, who..hath created and placed in Heauen these seuerall Rankes and Raunges of Honor. **1677** Hale *Prim. Orig. Mankind* IV. iii. 310 The lowest rank or range of Intellectual and Immaterial Beings. **1874** Stubbs *Const. Hist.* I. vii. 211 The cohesion of the nation was greatest in the lowest ranges.

4. a. Line, direction, lie.

Perh. to some extent connected with branch II.

1677 Moxon *Mech. Exerc.* 23 Keep the outside flat of the Bolt on the Range. **1712** J. James tr. *Le Blond's Gardening* 84 Direct all the other Stakes according to the Range of the first. **1788** M. Cutler in *Life, Jrnls. & Corr.* (1888) I. 393 The range of the hills and valleys is nearly from north to south. **1849** Murchison *Siluria* xvii. 416 The low ridges clearly exhibit the strike or range of the strata. **1858** *Merc. Marine Mag.* V. 190 Keeping the two Buoys in range with the Lighthouse.

†**b.** quasi-*adv.* In range or line. *Obs. rare.*

1678 Moxon *Mech. Exerc.* 111 The side of any work that runs straight, without breaking into angles, is said to run Range. **1683** *Ibid., Printing* x. ¶7 The Hind-Posts may stand Range or even with the outer-sides of the Cheeks.

II. 5. a. The act of ranging or moving about. Now *rare* in literal sense. † ***at range***, at random.

1470–85 Malory *Arthur* IV. xviii, Syre Marhaus.. departed fro them to fetche his raunge. **1568** T. Howell *Arb. Amitie* (1879) 22 Thou runst at rainge: and needes restraint. **1598** Manwood *Forest Lawes* xxiv. (1615) 240/1 When the said Regardors haue made their range. **1693** Luttrell *Brief Rel.* (1857) III. 30 The French had made a range into the country of Wirtemburgh. **1720** Gay *The Toilette* 51 I'll dress, and take my wonted range Through evr'y India shop. **1803** *Naval Chron.* IX. 70 The ship taking a sudden range, the cable parted. **1850** Tennyson *In Mem.* xciii, From thy sightless range With gods..Descend. **1856** 'Stonehenge' *Brit. Sports* I. I. iii. §6 Then, not letting him [the dog] dwell any longer, cry 'Hold up' and proceed with the range.

transf. and *fig.* c**1380** Wyclif *Wks.* (1880) 332 Summe prestis seyne simply 'I assoyle þe of þi synnes'..Summe prestis seyne a more raunge. **1540–54** Croke *13 Ps.* (Percy Soc.) 25 Thy range, Thy course, thy yeres, shall knowe none ende. **1784** Cowper *Tiroc.* 174 This blest exchange Of modest truth for wit's eccentric range. **1878** R. W. Dale *Lect. Preach.* ix. 283 Sometimes our hymns should take a wider range.

b. Opportunity or scope for ranging; liberty to range.

1793 *Minstrel* I. 95 A boy drove out a herd of cows, who, pleased with the range, ran kicking and scampering along. **1858** Kingsley *Misc.* (1859) I. 180 The boa, alligator, shark, pike,..will..attain an enormous size, give them but range enough. **1865** *Jrnl. R. Agric. Soc.* Ser. II. I. II. 246 The ewes have range over the stubbles..during the day.

c. The application of the file to each notch in the entire length of a saw-blade.

1846 Holtzapffel *Turning* II. 693 In this first range each notch has only received one stroke of the file; but three or four ranges..are required to bring the teeth up sharp.

6. a. An area, space, or stretch of ground, over which ranging takes place or is possible; *spec.* †the course in a tournament (*obs.*), and orig. *U.S.*, an extensive stretch of grazing or hunting ground.

1470–85 Malory *Arthur* x. xli, Sir Launcelot came in to the raynge [*printed* rayeng]. *Ibid.* xlix, Thenne sire Launcelot made sire Galyhodyn to lede hym thorugh the raunge. **1640** *Essex Inst. Hist. Coll.* (1863) V. 170/1 The range of the cattle at the fforest river head. **1707–8** in *Sheffield Gloss.* Suppl. s.v., One other range or parcell of wood in two cloases called the Parke Bottoms. **1808** Pike *Sources Mississ.* III. App. (1810) 30 At the crossing of this river there is a range for the horses of St. Antonio. **1827** J. F. Cooper *Prairie* I. ii. 30 [I] seldom pass more than a month at a time on the same range. **1851** S. Stephens *Jrnl.* 18 Apr. (typescript) II. 507 There is plenty of grass for [stock] there [*sc.* Wairau, N.Z.] and an extensive range, more suited for growing young stock..than the more limited boundary of the farm. **1856** Froude *Hist. Eng.* (1858) I. i. 27 In most parishes..there were large ranges of common and unenclosed forest land. **1911** *Daily Colonist* (Victoria, B.C.) 6 Apr. 8/3 Here they were able to learn something about a country where the sheep growers are able to raise their herds on expansive ranges. **1946** *Richmond* (Va.) *Times-Dispatch* 24 Nov. II. 1/4 Turkeys in the Valley of Virginia generally are raised 'on the range', which means that after they're nine weeks..old, in the Summer they're put out in fenced fields with a few shelters or roosts and plenty of room to wander about. **1949** J. Nelson *Backwoods Teacher* iii. 29 He..steals hogs off the range for winter meat. **1963** R. Symons *Many Trails* v. 52 When a rancher spoke of his 'range', he meant the natural grazing area around his holdings.

b. orig. *U.S.* Without article: Grazing ground.

1626 in *Virginia Mag. Hist. & Biog.* (1894) II. 52, 300,000 acres of land, which will feed such nombers of people, with plentifull range for Cattle. **1766** J. Bartram *Jrnl.* 12 Feb. in Stork *Acc. E. Florida* 67 There is good pine-woods, and fine range for cattle. **1812** Brackenridge *Views Louisiana* (1814) 117 The want of wild pasturage, or range, as it is called, for their cattle. **1959** *Times* 18 May 10/4 There are plenty of range rearers who annually take their pullets off range into straw yards without trouble. **1961** *Guardian* 17 May 3/5 There was insufficient land in Britain to keep sufficient birds on range. **1977** in *Fremdsprachen* (1979) XXIII. 131/1 After a maximum of two years in lay birds on range continue to lay for a further two or three years.

7. a. *Bot.* and *Zool.* The geographical area over which a certain plant or animal is distributed. Also, the period of time during which it has existed on the earth; the limits of depth between which a marine animal is found.

1856 Kane *Arct. Expl.* I. viii. 80 The reindeer, who is even less Arctic in his range than the musk ox. **1866** A. Murray *Geogr. Distrib. Animals* ii. 19 Even birds are subject to the same law, although it cannot be expected that rivers should often limit their ranges. **1887** *Life Darwin* I. 300 The habits and ranges of the birds which were described by Gould. **1900** B. D. Jackson *Gloss. Bot. Terms* 221/1 *Range*, the region over which a given form grows spontaneously. **1951** *Jrnl. Ecol.* XXXIX. 205 By 'range' is intended the geographical area within which, at a given time, a taxon or a plant community is to be found. **1963** Davis & Heywood *Princ. Angiosperm Taxonomy* xiii. 425 Species tend to occur in more restricted, and often more extreme, habitats at the edge of their range than in the centre of it. **1975** P. A. Johnsgard *Waterfowl N. Amer.* II. 346 No specific information on home ranges of the greater scaup is available. **1980** *Nature* 3 Jan. 15/2 The recurring theme was the problem of identifying the stresses and stratagems of animals exposed in different parts of their range to widely differing environmental conditions.

b. The area or period over or during which the occurrence of something is possible.

1830 Lyell *Princ. Geol.* I. xviii. 325 Not wholly beyond the range of earthquakes in Northern Italy.

8. a. The area or extent covered by, or included in, some thing or concept.

1661 J. Fell *Hammond* 98 The range and compass of his [Hammond's] knowledge fill'd the whole Circle of the Arts. **1732** Pope *Ess. Man* I. 207 Far as Creation's ample range extends, The scale of sensual, mental pow'rs ascends. **1742** Young *Nt. Th.* VII, Thro' nature's ample range, in thought, to strole. **1805** Wordsw. *Prelude* II. 176 Daily the common range of visible things Grew dear to me. **1841** E. Miall in *Nonconf.* I. 1 The whole range of politics, domestic and foreign. **1870** Huxley *Lay Serm.* x. (1874) 217 Through the whole range of geological time. **1942** [see level *sb.* 4 c]. **1966** *Oxf. Univ. Gaz.* 23 Dec. 430/1 Important general questions of constitutional arrangements..down to those individual points with which you are familiar... That is the range we have at present.

b. A series, number, or aggregate.

Perh. to some extent connected with sense 1.

1847 Tennyson *Princ.* III. 161 The day fled on thro' all Its range of duties to the appointed hour. **1856** Emerson *Eng. Traits, Race* Wks. (Bohn) II. 23 The English derive their pedigree from such a range of nationalities.

9. Sphere or scope of operation or action; the extent to which energy may be exerted, a function discharged, etc. **a.** of immaterial things. †*Naut.* = Range of vision.

1666 Bunyan *Grace Abound.* §156 He would not suffer them to fall without the range of Mercy. **1706** *Lond. Gaz.* No. 4215/3 The Marlborough, and the Dover..joined them yesterday in our Range. **1835** I. Taylor *Spir. Despot.* VII. 314 Affirming..the unrestricted range of ecclesiastical jurisdiction. **1867** Freeman *Norm. Conq.* (1876) I. iv. 244 A variety of circumstances brought them within the range of French influences.

b. of instruments; *esp.* of musical instruments (and so of the voice) with reference to variation of pitch in the sounds produced; compass, register.

1825 J. Nicholson *Operat. Mechanic* 43 Both the sensibility and the range of the instrument [the tachometer] may be infinitely increased. **1833** Tennyson *Dream Fair Wom.* xlii, Her..voice, a lyre of widest range. **1872** Huxley *Phys.* vii. 183 The range of any voice depends on the difference of tension which can be given to the vocal chords.

c. of persons, in respect of knowledge, ability, etc.

1847 Emerson *Repr. Men, Shakespeare* Wks. (Bohn) I. 352 Great men are more distinguished by range and extent, than by originality. **1876** Trevelyan *Life Macaulay* I. iv. 188 Macaulay who knew his own range.

10. a. The extent to which variation is possible; the limits between which a thing may vary in amount or degree.

1818 L. Howard *Climate Lond.* II. 48 The average annual range [of the barometer] is very nearly 2 inches. **1875** Bedford *Sailor's Pocket Bk.* v. (ed. 2) 168 The height from low water to high water is called the range of the tide.

b. A series or scale (of sounds, temperatures, prices, etc.) extending between certain limits.

1812 Sir H. Davy *Chem. Philos.* 85 Air at a range of temperature such as we can command below our common temperatures. **1871** B. Stewart *Heat* §25 Between 0° and 100°, and for a range extending not too far beyond. **1892** *Photogr. Ann.* II. 549 Three sets..of apparatus which will prove.. to give a range for demonstrating purposes that will embrace most experiments that are required. **1895** *Chambers' Encycl.* I. 100 Beef and mutton..have at last come down to a much lower range of prices. **1921** *Glasgow Herald* 7 Nov. 11 Manufacturers were called upon to make far too many patterns. In preparing their ranges for the particular season, manufacturers are guided largely by the experience of the seasons which have just gone. **1967** E. Short *Embroidery & Fabric Collage* ii. 45 Today there is a wide range of beads and sequins on the market.

c. *Statistics.* The difference observed in any sample between the largest and the smallest values of a given variate.

1911 G. U. Yule *Introd. Theory Statistics* viii. 133 The simplest possible measure of the dispersion of a series of values of a variable is the actual range, *i.e.* the difference between the greatest and least values observed... The range is..subject to meaningless fluctuations. **1948** G. Herdan *Quality Control* ii. 22 The range is the difference between the greatest and smallest dimensions in one sample of *n* specimens. **1975** A. K. S. Jardine et al. *Statistical Methods for Quality Control* ii. 15, 1. Range = class mark of highest class − class mark of lowest class; *or* 2. Range = upper class limit of highest class − lower class limit of lowest class... It can be seen that range is not uniquely defined in such cases. **1978** *Nature* 3 Aug. 490/2 Seven normal volunteers (four males, three females; mean age 25 yr, range 21–30) were studied.

d. *Math.* The set of values that the dependent variable of a function can take; the set comprising all the second elements of the ordered pairs constituting some given set.

1914 [see domain *sb.* 4 e]. **1959** J. G. Kemeny et al. *Finite Math. Structures* ii. 70 Let $f(x)$ be the age of x, expressed to the nearest year. The range of f consists of a set of whole numbers, starting with 0, presumably including all integers up to 100, and even having a few integers above 100 in the set. **1968** E. T. Copson *Metric Spaces* i. 19 The set of all points..which are images of points of E is called the range of the mapping. **1977** C. B. Allendoerfer et al. *Elem. Functions* iii. 49 The values of the dependent variable constitute a subset of the reals called the range of the function. *Ibid.* 50 It is often difficult to determine the range.

11. a. The distance to which a gun, rifle, etc. is capable of sending a ball or bullet; the space which any projectile or missile can be made to traverse. Also, the distance of the object aimed at. More widely, the distance anything can travel, as (*a*) *Nucl. Physics*, the maximum distance which an ionizing particle of a given energy can travel in a given medium; (*b*) the maximum distance at which a radio transmission may reliably be received; (*c*) the distance which an aircraft can travel without refuelling, normally under stated assumptions regarding factors such as speed, air speed, and altitude; (*d*) the distance on the earth's surface which a rocket or missile can traverse from launch to landing.

Technically defined in *Weaponry* as 'the distance from the muzzle of the piece to the (second) intersection of the trajectory with the line of sight'.

1591 Digges *Pantom.* 163 Any two Peeces of Battery Ordinance..shall euer make their Profundities of pearcing Proportionall to their leuell Randges Horizontall. **1692** *Capt. Smith's Seaman's Gram.* II. xxvi. 138 The Horizontal Rainge of that Peece will be found to be 374 Paces. *Ibid.* xxx. 142 The drying of the Powder..doth help..the Rainge of the Shot. **1769** in Falconer *Dict. Marine* (1776). **1838** Thirlwall *Greece* xxxvii. V. 20 He..approached so near the walls, as to be within the range of the..missiles from the battlements. **1860** W. H. Russell *Diary in India* I. 268 The enemy have got the range of our camp. **1884** *Times* (weekly ed.) 8 Feb. 1/4 The rebels were visible; but they were altogether out of range. **1904** *Phil. Mag.* VIII. 725 The first breakdown of the radium atom is responsible for the α particle of..the least range. **1906** G. Eichhorn *Wireless Telegr.* vi. 37 Bearing in mind..the enfeebling influence of obstructions and the curvature of the earth, the range of normal installations is reduced to about 300 miles. **1924** *Harmsworth's Wireless Encycl.* 1635/2 It is a common experience for ship sets of only one and a half kilowatts to transmit over a range of 1,000 miles. **1926** R. W. Lawson tr. *Hevesy's Man. Radioactivity* vii. 78 Fig. 25..shows the tracks of individual α-particles. Almost without exception they are rectilinear, and the ionization produced by the rays ceases quite suddenly, which indicates that they have a definite range. **1928** V. W. Pagé *Mod. Aircraft* xix. 818 *Range at economic speed*, the maximum distance a given aircraft can cover while cruising at the most economical speed and altitude at all stages of the flight. *Range at full speed*, the maximum distance a given aircraft can cover at full speed at sea level. **1947** C. F. Toms *Introd. Aeronautics* iii. 141 The range..depends on the air-speed, on the initial all-up weight.., and.. on the bomb-load. **1947** *Jrnl. Inst. Electr. Engineers* XCIV. I. 176/1 On the Plan Position Indicator these objects will appear in their correct relative position provided we correct for the fact that radar measures slant range and not plan range. **1949** G. P. Sutton *Rocket Propulsion Elements* viii. 246 Altitudes above 250 miles and ranges over 300 miles can generally be attained only with single-step missiles having small payloads or multiple-step missiles. **1965** [see sense 11 c below]. **1965** Stuhlinger & Mesmer *Space Sci. & Engin.* xvi. 191 The range of a particle can be obtained directly by integrating the reciprocal of the stopping power over the appropriate energy range. **1967** Ketcham & Martin *Propulsion* ix. 197 It is possible to make an approximation for the maximum range of a ballistic missile from the geometry of the elliptical flight path and the intersections with the spherical earth surface. **1968** Sands & Tellet *VHF-FM Marine Radio* i. 21 The range of VHF transmissions is limited to a little more than line-of-sight distance. **1970** M. Smith *Aviation Fuels* xxxvii. 256 When boiling occurs, the loss of fuel can be serious both from the viewpoint of lost range and from danger to the aircraft structure from excessive tank pressures.

transf. **1687** *Refl. Hind & Panther* 21 That's a Flight of Fancy at its full Range.

b. The position of a gun in firing (see quot. 1704). †Also, the direction of a shot. *Obs.*

1669 Sturmy *Mariner's Mag.* v. 69 For Shooting in a Right-line called the Right Range of a Bullet. **1692** *Capt. Smith's Seaman's Gram.* II. xxix. 140 The Gun being..upon a Level Rainge. **1704** Harris *Lex. Techn.* s.v., If the Bullet go in a Line parallel to the Horizon, it is called the Right or Level-Range; if the Gun be mounted to 45 Degr., then will the Ball have the highest or utmost Range,..all others between 45 Degr. and 00 are called the Intermediate Ranges. **1867** Smyth *Sailor's Word-bk.*

c. A place or piece of ground having a target and other fittings, used for practice in shooting. Also, a strip of land or sea used for testing rockets or missiles in flight between their launch and return to earth.

1862 *St. Andrews Gaz.* 3 Oct. 3/4 At the rifle range, the corps was divided into two squads, the one party firing against the other. **1873** *Queen's Regul. & Orders, Army* VIII. §64 Fences for cavalry, and ranges, butts, &c. for rifle-practice. **1900** KIPLING *Let.* 24 July in C. Carrington *R. Kipling* (1955) xiii. 315 We've started a rifle-club in the village... We've got a 1,000 yards range among the downs. **1947** *Jrnl. Brit. Interplanetary Soc.* VI. 191 Some details have appeared of an American rocket-testing range comparable to the projected Anglo-Australian one. **1955** *Times* 19 Aug. 4/6 The crofters last night unanimously agreed to a six-point resolution protesting that the range, which is expected to absorb crofting land in Benbecula and North and South Uist, represented a threat to the Hebridean way of life. **1965** L. E. FOSTER *Telemetry Systems* vii. 283 The range of these vehicles requires an accurate real-time 'picture' of the vehicle position to assure that it does not go beyond the safety corridor of the range and impact on some populated territory. **1971** GREEN & LOMASK *Vanguard* viii. 133 In the fall of 1955 the 15,000-acre missile firing range on the snake-infested and palmetto-covered sand dunes of the Florida flatlands was completing its sixth year as the.. Proving Ground for American guided-missile development.

III. 12. a. A form of fire-grate, fire-place, or cooking apparatus. Hence *spec.* a fire-place having one or more ovens at the sides, and closed on the top with iron plates having openings for carrying on several cooking operations at once. Also, a gas or electric cooker, typically with a grill, ring burners or plates, and one or more ovens. Now chiefly *U.S.*

The precise meaning in some of the older instances of the word is not clear. With quot. 1574 cf. *roasting-range*, which is perh. the sense of the earliest quots. In mod. Linc. dial. *range* denotes a high fender or fire-guard.

1446–7 *Durham Acc. Rolls* (Surtees) 84 De 34*s.* 1*d.* rec. de feodo de le rangh et exitibus animalium. **1471–2** *Ibid.* 93 Pro iij kirsettes ferri empt. pro le Raunge. *a* **1548** HALL *Chron.* (1809) 607 Chimnays, Ranges and such instrumentes. **1574** R. SCOT *Hop Gard.* (1578) 36 Then you must lay these Poales vpon a couple of forked stalkes.. as Spittes vpon Raunges. **1611** BIBLE *Lev.* xi. 35 Whether it be ouen, or ranges for pots, they shalbe broken downe. **1660** PEPYS *Diary* 19 July, An iron of our new range which is already broke. **1736** NEVE *Builder's Dict.* (ed. 3) s.v. *Building*, We have occasion for larger Ranges, or Chimneys, and more ample Kitchens. **1862** *Catal. Internat. Exhib.* II. XXXI. 49/1 The whole top of the range is a flat iron platform, which may be covered with vessels for boiling, stewing, etc. **1895** *Montgomery Ward Catal.* Spring & Summer 423/2 Gas range... This range.. has four top burners.. and is fitted with movable ovens. **1908** *Sears, Roebuck Catal.* 529/2 Ranges,.. gas.. oil. **1929** *T. Eaton & Co. Catal.* Spring & Summer 416/2 Acme Electric Range... One of the most efficient cooking devices of its kind. **1935** *Words* Jan. 31/2 (Advt.), Entirely automatic gas ranges.. with.. aluminum cooking burners;.. fuel saving oven; sanitary high burner tray (porcelain); choice of closed or open top cooking surface; Astrogril broiler in rollout drawer. **1959** *Sears, Roebuck Catal.* Spring & Summer 932/2 Our best Kenmore kerosene-burning range. **1970** *Washington Post* 30 Sept. B13/4 (Advt.), We have everything you'll need to transform your kitchen, including the fantastic Modern Maid flameless electric range with all the newest, most wanted features. **1973** *Sunday Express* (Trinidad) (Suppl.) 1 Apr. 2/5 Today's squared off ranges are designed for a close fit. **1977** *Sci. Amer.* Dec. 51/2 Between them, in ascending order, are a washing machine, a dishwasher, a color television set, a free-standing electric range, a gas clothes dryer, a freestanding gas range, an electric clothes dryer and a refrigerator.

†**b.** Dripping, 'kitchen-fee'. *Obs. rare*$^{-1}$.

Ellipt. for *range-fee* (cf. quot. 1446–7 above).

1469 in *Househ. Ord.* (1790) 95 As for the raunge that comyth of rosted meate, to be feable.

13. The name of various articles (see quots.).

a. **1563–4** in Willis & Clark *Cambridge* (1886) II. 571 For xij Arms and lxxij greate paynted quarrells and xij Ranges.

b. **1688** R. HOLME *Armoury* III. 243/2 In the Cow-House.. a Range either for Oxe or Cow to which they are tyed. [Cf. **1886** *Cheshire Gloss.*, *Range Stake*, the wooden stake to which cows are tied in the shippon.]

c. **1726** BAILEY, *Range*,.. a Beam which is betwixt two Horses in a Coach. **1847** HALLIWELL, *Range*,.. (3) the shaft of a coach. *Devon.*

d. *Naut.* **1644** MANWAYRING *Sea-man's Dict.*, *Ranges*, there are two, one aloft upon the fore-castle.. the other in the beak-head. **1704** HARRIS *Lex. Techn.*, *Ranges*, in a Ship, are two pieces of Timber going a-cross from Side to Side. **1711** W. SUTHERLAND *Shipbuild. Assist.* 163 *Ranges*, pieces fitted to the Ship to belay or fasten the Main and Fore Sheets. **1769** FALCONER *Dict. Marine* (1776) Hiij, The cleats, kevels, and ranges, by which the ropes are fastened. *c* **1850** *Rudim. Navig.* (Weale) 140 *Ranges*, horned pieces of oak, like belaying cleats, but much larger... Also those pieces of oak plank fixed between the ports, with semicircular holes in them, for keeping shot in.

14. A length or stretch of something.

†**a.** *pl.* A fence, enclosure. *Obs.* **b.** (see quot.) **c.** An unbroken stretch of railing, balustrade, etc. ? *Obs.* **d.** *Naut.* (see quot.) ? *Obs.* **e.** A strip of glass. **f.** A strip of leather. **g.** *Coal-mining* (see quot.). **h.** (See quot.)

a. **1537** BIBLE (Matthew) *2 Kings* xi. 8 Whosoeuer cometh wyth in the ranges shale dye for it. **1611** BIBLE *2 Chron.* xxiii. 14 Haue her foorth of the ranges.

b. **1703** T. N. *City & C. Purchaser* 158 There are several Appellations given to the various Dimensions, &c. of Quarries, viz. 1. The Range, which is a Perpendicular let fall from one of the Obtuse Angles to the opposite side.

c. **1723–4** CHAMBERS tr. *Le Clerc's Treat. Archit.* I. 114 The Ranges.. ought to terminate in half Balusters joyn'd to the Pedestals. **1770** *Ann. Reg.* 171 A whole range of the east battlement of Westminster-hall gave way.

d. **1769** FALCONER *Dict. Marine* (1776), *Range*, a sufficient length of the cable, drawn up on deck, before the anchor is cast loose from the bow, to let it sink to the bottom, without being interrupted.

e. **1726** *Maryland Hist. Mag.* (1923) XVIII. 216, 20 tables Crown glass cutt into Ranges 7 inches high. **1825** J. NICHOLSON *Operat. Mechanic* 636 The square is used in cutting the squares from the range, that they may with greater certainty be cut at right angles.

f. **1878** *Ure's Dict. Arts* IV. 110 The 'butt' is first cut into long strips known as 'ranges'.

g. **1892** *Daily News* 29 Aug. 5/4 There are two main roads.. from which there branch off.. what are known as 'ranges', in which the coal winning principally goes on.

h. **1923** *Daily Mail* 28 Apr. 8 Eighty ranges, the young wood of ten acres—a range consists of all but the grown timber of twenty rods—had passed under the hammer.

15. *Shoemaking.* The lie or line of the upper edge of the counter in a top-boot, corresponding to (and continued in) that of the vamp.

1840 J. DEVLIN *Shoemaker* 63 Remedying every fault that may be in the cutting, the range, the position, the back catch of the counter. *Ibid.* 65 A further closing may then follow, beginning at the turn of the.. counter, and going right round, along the range, and up the tongue.

IV. 16. *attrib.* and *Comb.*

a. in senses 6 and 7, as ***range base, boss, cow, district, end, horse*** (see quot.), ***-land, -man, management, mark, rider, tree.*** **range egg**, an egg laid by a hen which has ranged outdoors for its food; **range war** *U.S.*, a struggle for the control and use of a cattle or sheep range.

1895 C. DIXON *Migrat. Brit. Birds* ii. 27 Three fairly well defined *range bases or refuge areas. **1893** W. L. CHITTENDEN *Ranch Verses* 94 The *range boss's outfit rides in through the herd. **1922** *Short Stories* Feb. (early issue) 70/2 He dominates everybody but Ben Whitman and.. dad's range-boss. **1894** *Outing* (U.S.) XXIV. 336/2 Their '*range' cows and razor-backed hogs climb the steep hills like goats. **1887** *Q. Rev.* July 49 In the *range districts the proportion of loss has been much higher. **1963** *Punch* 19 June 891/1 We.. keep hens and if they pack up buy '*range' eggs. **1470–85** MALORY *Arthur* x. xlii, As sire Palomydes came in to the felde syr Galahalt.. was at the *raunge ende. **1859** MARCY *Prairie Trav.* iv. 111 Horses which have been raised exclusively upon grass.. or '*range horses', as they are called in the West. **1931** *Sun* (Baltimore) 23 Dec. 15/1 Ranchers in the district are unable to care for them [*sc.* starving horses] and the *rangeland is covered with snow. **1949** *Daily Progress* (Charlottesville, Va.) 26 Jan. 1/3 The winter snows have.. laid the foundation for a good growth of rangeland grasses next summer. **1958** *Yearbk. Agric. 1957* (U.S. Dept. Agric.) 765/2 *Range* (or *rangeland*), land that produces primarily native forage plants suitable for grazing by livestock, including land that has some forest trees. **1961** *Times* 7 Feb. 3/1, 40 million acres of rangeland north of Brisbane. **1969** *Science & Technology* Jan. 49/2 Rangelands is an American term now used throughout the world to describe areas where rainfall is too low or too unreliable for crops or sown pastures. **1976** *Billings* (Montana) *Gaz.* 11 July 1-D/5 The fires apparently were started by lightning and began on the rangeland two miles south of Interstate 90 on the Big Horn-Yellowstone County line. **1979** *Arizona Daily Star* 5 Aug. A4/4 Four fires.. destroyed more than 3,100 acres of timber and range land in western and central Oregon. **1887** *Q. Rev.* July 49 The high-handed conduct of the *range-men. **1972** *Agric. Handbk.* (U.S. Dept. Agric.) No. 435. 1/1 Values for each of the *range management practices were determined from published sources and from experience of USDA Forest Service experts in this field. **1979** *Arizona Daily Star* 1 Apr. (Advt. Section) 3/9 Natural resource manager.. 2 years experience, preferably in range management. **1700** *Providence* (R.I.) *Rec.* (1893) IV. 139 From it to turne and Range East and be southward to a heape of stones laid for a *Range marke. **1890** *Stock Grower & Farmer* 28 June 3/4 A few years more will see all the last of the *range rider. **1909** 'O. HENRY' *Roads of Destiny* xxii. 368, I slapped that old captive range-rider half across his little garden. **1955** *Radio Times* 22 Apr. 44/2 A programme of films... 'The Range Rider' with Jack Mahoney and Dick West. **1703** *Ibid.* (1894) V. 95 A blacke Oake tree marked for a *Range tree. **1908** MURRAY & MILLER *Round-Up* xiv. 288 We don't want no range-war. **1939** C. W. TOWNE *Her Majesty Montana* 89 In the days of the big ranges there never was any trouble between the cattlemen and the sheepmen, and there never was a '*range war' between them in Montana. Many of the cattlemen also had bands of sheep. **1976** A. PRICE *War Game* i. 67 It was a typical feud situation—like a range war in the Wild West.

b. in sense 11, as ***range-board, -holding*** adj., ***-indicator, -officer, -plate, -tables***; *spec.* in radar, as ***range(-amplitude) display, gate, mark, -marker, measurement, resolution, ring, step.***

1946 *Jrnl. Inst. Electr. Engin.* XCIII. IIIA. 1559/1 The *Range or Type A display is one of the basic forms of presentation of radar information. **1948** K. ULLYETT *How Radar Works* vii. 101 Range-amplitude, or type A, display on the CRT of a radar receiver would be of very little use with many modern systems, as the information it gives is not sufficiently accurate, nor can it be deciphered sufficiently speedily. **1876** VOYLE & STEVENSON *Milit. Dict.* 326/2 **Range Board*, this nature of board.. has the distances painted on it of prominent objects within the range of the guns mounted on the works. **1967** G. J. WHEELER *Radar Fund.* v. 55 A *range gate.. is a switch which opens at a time coinciding with a prescribed range and closes at a set time later. **1973** MEYER & MAYER *Radar Target Detection* ii. 29/2 The majority of operational radar detection devices have some collapsing loss. The loss can be caused by.. improper range gate width. **1977** *Electronics Lett.* XIII. 416/1 The range gate first resets the tunnel diode D, and any subsequent transition of D which is within the range gate produces a 1 output at the AND gate. **1865** *Sat. Rev.* 21 Jan. 72/1 The rights enjoyed by the *range-holding Corps. **1916** 'BOYD CABLE' *Action Front* 131 When the *range-indicator told that it was within reach of their shells the first gun opened with a trial beltful. **1948** J. L. HORNUNG *Radar Primer* iii. 69 A simple kind of range-indicator consists of a cathode-ray tube with a time-base voltage applied to the left and right deflection plates and echo-pulse voltages connected to the top and bottom plates. **1945** *Electronic Industries* Sept. 222/3 **Range mark*, a mark on the CRT screen which indicates distances from the radar set of the various echoes appearing on the screen of the CRT. **1949** H. E. PENROSE *Princ. & Pract. Radar* xv. 281 In the simplest calibrating system a generator (range mark generator).. produces at equal intervals of time, short sharp signals or pips.., and these are imposed upon the trace just as though they were incoming signals. **1944** *Princ. Radar* (Mass. Inst. Technol. Radar School) ii. 3 A very common method [of range determination] for search-type sets is the use of *range markers generated in the timer. **1977** J. FRENCH *Small Craft Radar* ii. 69 Two types of range markers are in common use, the variable range marker giving only one ring which can be set by the operator, and fixed rings which appear at fixed distances usually preset by the Range switch. **1949** H. E. PENROSE *Princ. & Pract. Radar* i. 1 When velocity is a known constant and time can be measured, distance can be calculated = velocity × time. This is the basis of *range measurement. **1978** R. V. JONES *Most Secret War* xxi. 177 Only later did I find that there was no foundation to our original reasoning that the Y system would involve a beam and a range measurement. **1891** *Daily News* 27 July 3/4 Permitted by their *range officer.. to violate the regulations. **1876** VOYLE & STEVENSON *Milit. Dict.* 326/2 **Range Plates*, plates of brass attached to the brackets of.. field carriages. They are marked with three columns of figures, showing the range in yards.. with the corresponding elevations. **1959** R. L. SHRADER *Electronic Communication* xxix. 833 *Range resolution is the ability to distinguish two or more targets in the same direction but at different distances. **1970** G. KENNEDY *Electronic Communication Systems* xv. 625 Another argument in favor of short pulses is that they improve the range resolution, which is the ability to separate targets whose distance from the transmitter differs only slightly. **1956** D. G. LANG *Marine Radar* vii. 80 Range pulses are applied to the P.P.I. [*sc.* plan position indicator], but as the P.P.I. is intensity modulated and the trace rotates around the screen's centre, the pulses appear as rings encircling the centre of the screen... Fixed rings are known as calibration or *range rings, and a variable ring is known as a variable-range marker. **1977** J. FRENCH *Small Craft Radar* ii. 71 The output from this circuit is added to the video amplifier, often via a Brightness control or on/off switch so that the operator can check for the possible presence of echoes under the range rings. **1946** *Princ. Radar* (Mass. Inst. Technol. Radar School) (ed. 2) i. 23 Higher precision with a Type A indicator may be attained by the addition of a *range step. The horizontal sweep is displaced vertically, producing the effect of a step in the sweep. **1873** *Queen's Regul. & Orders, Army* VIII. §40 Proper *range-tables for each battery must be prepared.

c. in sense 12, as ***range-cock, -stove*** (Knight 1875); ***range-fitter.***

1884 *B'ham Daily Post* 24 Jan. 3/4 Range fitter, Wanted, used to Patterns.

d. Special Comb. **range beacon** = *radio range* (*b*) s.v. RADIO *sb.* 7; **range-finder**, a device used for the estimation of the distance separating the observer from an object; *spec.* (*a*) *Mil.*, usu. attached to a weapon, to estimate the range of a target; (*b*) *Photogr.*, as an aid to focusing a camera, freq. coupled to the lens (see quot. 1958); so **range-finding** *vbl. sb.* (also *transf.*); **range-heads** *Naut.*, the windlass bitts (Smyth 1867); **range-plate**, a ring-burner inset on the surface of a gas or electric range; **range-proof** *a.* (*U.S.*), unbreakable by heat from a ring burner on a gas or electric range; **range safety crew**, a team of persons responsible for ensuring the safety of people and structures should a rocket deviate from its intended path after launching by destroying it in flight if necessary; **range safety officer**, the principal member of a range safety crew; **range work**, (*a*) work having a straight face; (*b*) masonry laid in level courses; (*c*) practice in shooting at a range; **range-zone** *Palæont.* (see quots.).

1931 P. V. H. WEEMS *Air Navigation* xiv. 271 Range beacons may be of the aural type, which operate an ordinary aural receiving set with head phones, or of the visual type which operate vibrating reeds in a special visual indicator. **1935** C. G. BURGE *Compl. Bk. Aviation* 503/1 The system.. employs a number of beacons whereby the pilot approaching the aerodrome along the route marked by range beacons is advised of the locality of the 'drome by first an approach marker beacon and secondly by a boundary marker beacon. **1940** A. BLACK *Story of Flying* xvii. 183 Each range-beacon signal is interrupted every 30 seconds by an identification characteristic. **1872** *Daily News* 16 July, A very simple and useful instrument.. called a range-finder. **1876** VOYLE & STEVENSON *Milit. Dict.* 326/2 *Range-finder*, an instrument for ascertaining the range of a piece of ordnance or small-arm. **1916** 'BOYD CABLE' *Action Front* 38 He.. was.. followed by his trumpeter and a man with the six-foot tube of a range-finder strapped to the saddle. **1930** *Pop. Sci. Monthly* Dec. 33/3 A new 'gravity range finder' that clips to the camera bed eliminates guesswork in judging the distance. **1934**, **1935** [see COUPLE *v.* 2 e]. **1958** *Oxf. Mail* 19 May 7/2 *Coupled rangefinder.* This means a rangefinder which you work usually by making two images coincide. It is coupled to the lens, so that when you have focussed the image on the rangefinder the lens is automatically focussed. **1973** *Times* 1 Oct. 16/5 Exactly what the cost of the new tank will be is anyone's guess. One estimate is that it might cost as much as £200,000 by the time one has installed the £50,000 fire control system with its laser range-finder and computer. **1977** J. HEDGECOE *Photographer's Handbk.* 13/1 The range-finder focusing system uses two windows,.. one the actual viewfinder and another placed further along the camera body. *Ibid.* 13/2 The Leica CL.. is a sophisticated direct vision 35 mm camera with coupled rangefinder. **1890** SIR F. ABEL *Addr. Brit. Assoc.* 11 The applications of electricity in connection with range-finding. **1946** *Jrnl. Inst. Electr. Engineers* XCIII. I. 378/2 A corresponding advance in precision of range-finding was achieved by Pollard in work.. on the radiolocation equipment for the laying of heavy anti-aircraft artillery. **1971** *Nature* 16 Apr. 460/2

Range-finding experiments have shown that the maximal tolerated doses of propylene imine and propane sultone, in distilled water, .. were 20 mg/kg and 56 mg/kg, respectively. **1954** *Archit. Rev.* CXVI. 270 72B 'Main' gas rangeplate in cast iron and pressed steel, finished in cream vitreous enamel. **1969** *New Yorker* 29 Nov. 109/1 The ware is ovenproof but not rangeproof. **1966** *Electronics* 17 Oct. 37/1 Range safety crews must monitor the handling and launch of a rocket on the ground, and then watch such flight parameters as critical velocity, position and impact prediction for signs of danger. **1965** L. E. FOSTER *Telemetry Systems* vii. 284 During the transition from aerodynamic to ballistic missiles, the range safety officer found he had need of an impact predictor. **1971** GREEN & LOMASK *Vanguard* ix. 162 The displays in the Central Control room gave the range safety officer a second-by-second picture of the path the vehicle was following. **1678** MOXON *Mech. Exerc.* I. 112 The side that falls away from the Foreside of any Straight or Range-work is called the Return. **1884** KNIGHT *Dict. Mech.* Suppl. 742/1 Range work .. is usually backed up with rubble masonry. **1908** *Daily Chron.* 16 Apr. 4/6 Some 200 of the London Scottish will be quartered at Aldershot for range work and field exercises, their sergeants sharing the mess of the Gordon Highlanders. **1957** E. D. MCKEE et al. in *Bull. Amer. Assoc. Petroleum Geologists* XLI. 1880 Vertical and horizontal limitations in the absolute three dimensional distribution of individual taxonomic entities in the rocks of the earth's crust provide the basis for biostratigraphic subdivision of strata into range-zones or zones comprising the total body of strata through which specimens of a particular taxonomic entity .. range or occur. **1976** H. D. HEDBERG *Internat. Stratigr. Guide* vi. 53 A biostratigraphic range-zone may represent the stratigraphic range of some one taxonomic unit .., or of a grouping of taxons, or of a lineage or segment of a lineage, or of any particular paleontological feature whatsoever.

range (reɪndʒ), *sb.*[2] *Obs.* exc. *dial.* [Goes with RANGE *v.*[2], and may be identical with prec., but the history is not clear. Cf. RANCH-SIEVE and RENGE *sb.*[2] (the earlier form).]

A kind of sieve or strainer. †Also ***range-sieve***.

1545 ELYOT, *Sisacthea*, a rayeng [*sic*] sieue. **1615** MARKHAM *Eng. Housew.* (1660) 187 You shall have Boulters, Searses, Ranges, and Meal-sives of all sorts, both fine and coorse. **1616** SURFL. & MARKH. *Country Farme* v. xvii. 549 If it be sifted and cleansed through a fine raunge, searce, or boulter. **1886** ELWORTHY *W. Som. Word-bk.*, *Range*, a sieve used for straining liquids and not for sifting dry matter. In cider making, the juice is strained through a range; so in cheese making.

†**range**, *sb.*[3] *Obs. rare.* Also 8 **rainge**. [? Nasalized var. of RACHE *sb.*[2]] = RACE *sb.*[5]

1685 *Lond. Gaz.* No. 2079/4 A large well quartered Chesnut Coloured Mare, with .. a range down her face. **1723** *Ibid.* No. 6197/3 A brown Bay Mare .. having a Star and Range in her Forehead.

range (reɪndʒ), *v.*[1] Forms: 4-5 *Sc.* **raung**, (9 *dial.*) **rawnge**, 5-7 **raunge**; 4-7 **raynge**, 7 **rainge**; 6 **randge**, 4- **range**. [a. F. *ranger* (12th c.), f. *rang* var. *ranc* RANK *sb.* See also RENGE *v.*]

I. *trans.* **1. a.** To place, set, or station (persons, rarely animals) in a row, line, or rank; to draw up, arrange (an army, etc.) in ranks. Chiefly *pass.* and *refl.*

1375 BARBOUR *Bruce* XI. 431 Thai stude than rangit all on raw. *Ibid.* XVII. 348 Quhen thai saw [That] menȝe raynge thame swa on raw. *c* **1400** *Destr. Troy* 5678 The Troiens .. Bowet euyn to þe banke .. Out of rule or aray raungit on lenght. *c* **1450** HOLLAND *Howlat* 244 Quhen thai [birds] war rangit on rawis. **1523** LD. BERNERS *Froiss.* I. xviii. 24 The Englishe oste dislodged, .. and raynged theyr battelles. **1598** FLORIO Ep. Ded. 5 An armie ranged in files is fitter for muster then in a ring. **1671** tr. *Frejus' Voy. Mauritania* 57 Yet .. would they not be perswaded to range themselves and make us way. **1717** LADY M. W. MONTAGU *Let. to C'tess Mar* 18 Apr., Her she-slaves, finely dressed, were ranged on each side. **1842** MACAULAY *Horatius* xii, All the Etruscan armies Were ranged beneath his eye. **1877** A. B. EDWARDS *Up Nile* xi. 292 A double file of men .. ranged themselves along the ropes.

b. To place (a person or persons) in a specified position, situation, or company. Const. with preps. and prep. phrases, as *against*, *among*, *around*, *on the side of*, *under*, *with*. Chiefly in *pass.* and *refl.*, and commonly *fig.*

1598 B. JONSON *Ev. Man in Hum.* III. i, The most fatal and dangerous exploit that euer I was rang'd in, since I first bore Arms. **1711** ADDISON *Spect.* No. 55 ⁋4 The Father of a Family would often range himself under the Banners of Avarice, and the Son under those of Luxury. **1796** BURKE *Let. Noble Lord* Wks. 1826 VIII. 8 To range myself on the side of the Duke of Bedford. **1818** JAS. MILL *Brit. India* II. v. ii. 358 A similar contention .. ranged one of the rivals on the side of Ragoba. **1874** STUBBS *Const. Hist.* (1897) I. x. 318 The Norman baronage .. ranging themselves with the king or against him.

†**c.** To reduce or bring *under* obedience, or *to* something. *Obs.*

Renderings of F. *ranger sous* (*l'obéissance*), and *ranger à* (*la raison*, etc.).

1601 HOLLAND *Pliny* I. 169 Hauing .. subdued Africke, and raunged it vnder the obedience of Rome. **1608** D. T. *Ess. Pol. & Mor.* 75 He .. tells Fortune shee did well to range him to the gowne, and to the studie of Philosophie. **1622** BACON *Hen. VII* 55 If it be no more but to range his subjects to reason. **1659** B. HARRIS *Parival's Iron Age* 9 Duke Charles .. ranged the Finlanders .. under obedience to himself.

2. a. To set or dispose (things) in a line or lines; hence, to arrange, put in order. Also as in 1 b.

a **1400** *Pistill of Susan* 112 The rewe, þe rubarbe, rawnged fulle ryghte In rees. **1594** PLAT *Jewell-ho.* I. 19 Those they couch and range in the earth. **1628** HOBBES *Thucyd.* (1822) 106 The quiet life can never be preserved if it be not ranged with the active life. **1658** EVELYN *Fr. Gard.* (1675) 163 You may range the first at the very edg of the trench. **1711** ADDISON *Spect.* No. 37 ⁋1 Her Books .. were ranged together in a very beautiful Order. **1816** BENTHAM *Chrestom.* 25 The component particles of water .. have to range themselves in such a manner as to form a surface. **1860** TYNDALL *Glac.* I. ii. 16 All the images will be ranged upon the circumference.

b. To set or lay out (a line or curve).

1712 J. JAMES tr. *Le Blond's Gardening* 100 Fix a line upon the Stake F, and .. range it by the Stakes F and D. **1847** BRODIE (*title*) Rules for ranging railway curves with the theodolite.

c. To make straight, even, or level.

1846 HOLTZAPFFEL *Turning* II. 690 The little facet thus exposed by the process of topping or ranging the teeth. **1888** JACOBI *Printers' Vocab.*, *Range matter*, to make lines in composing range equally at either or both ends of the stick.

d. *Naut.* To lay out (a cable) so that the anchor may descend without check.

1833 MARRYAT *P. Simple* xv. (1873) 103 Which cable was ranged last night. **1882** NARES *Seamanship* (ed. 6) 157 Too much chain should not be ranged. **1886** J. M. CAULFEILD *Seamanship Notes* 4 If chain lockers are forward, do not range cables.

e. To provide with a row or rows of something.

1858 HAWTHORNE *Fr. & It. Note-bks.* II. 259 The upper one of these floors .. is ranged round with the beds.

3. To place (persons or things) *in* a certain class or category; to divide *into* classes; to classify, arrange, etc.

1601 HOLLAND *Pliny* VII. xlv. 179 The late Emperour Augustus, whome all the world raungeth in this ranke of men fortunate. **1662** GERBIER *Principles* 4 Those who have Marshald the Orders of Colombs .. have Ranged the Toscan to be the Supporter of a Building. **1688** R. HOLME *Armoury* II. 131/2 All four-footed Creatures are Ranged into two sorts. **1730** A. GORDON *Maffei's Amphith.* 240 Divinities to be ranged in the same Rank. **1762** MILLS *Pract. Husb.* I. 16 The subdivisions of different soils .. may .. be ranged under two general heads. **1805** WORDSW. *Prelude* II. 223 To range the faculties In scale and order.

4. *refl.* (ad. F. *se ranger*.) To adopt a more regular mode of life.

1855 THACKERAY *Newcomes* xxviii, You tell me to marry and range myself. **1880** MRS. LYNN LINTON *Rebel of Family* III. vii. 144 He had no intention of marrying and ranging himself just yet. **1903** M. BEERBOHM in *Sat. Rev.* 16 May 615/2 Suppose that, when he disembarked at S. Helena, Napoleon so 'ranged himself' as to become a gentle, agreeable, .. old gentleman.

II. *intr.* **5. a.** Of things, *esp.* buildings or their parts, or large natural objects: To stretch out or run in a line, to extend.

1607 SHAKS. *Cor.* III. i. 206. **1613-39** I. JONES in Leoni *Palladio's Archit.* (1742) II. 43 A Wall ranges along the Cell to bear up the Roof. *Ibid.*, This Cornice only ranges along the Cell. **1703** *Providence Rec.* (1894) V. 95 From the said black oake tree to Range away northeastward to a stake. **1770** *Easington Incl. Act* 7 Such parcel of land adjoining to the sea and ranging along the same. **1862** ANSTED *Channel Isl.* I. iv. (ed. 2) 61 A formidable group of rocks and islands, ranging north-east and south-west.

b. To extend or lie in the same line or plane (*with*); esp. in *Printing*, of type, lines, or pages.

1599 SHAKS. *Much Ado* II. ii. 7 Whatsoeuer comes athwart his affection, ranges euenly with mine. **1664** E. BUSHNELL *Compl. Shipwright* 20 That the backside of the upper end may randge faire. **1712** J. JAMES tr. *Le Blond's Gardening* 84 If one Stick stand half a Foot higher than another .. it matters not, so they range directly. **1771** LUCKOMBE *Hist. Printing* 391 So that they may not range against each other. **1816** SCOTT *Antiq.* vi, I have a copy at home that stands next my twelvemo copy of the Scots Acts, and ranges on the shelf with them very well. **1883** *Academy* 20 Jan. 40/3 Many of the sonnets on opposite pages have not been made to 'range'.

6. a. To take up or occupy a place or position. Const. as in 1 b. Also, of a number of persons: To draw up in rank or order. (*rare.*)

1596 SHAKS. *1 Hen. IV*, I. iii. 169 The Predicament Wherein you range vnder this subtill King. **1613** —— *Hen. VIII*, II. iii. 20 Tis better to be lowly borne, And range with humble liuers in Content. **1697** DRYDEN *Virg. Georg.* I. 687 The neighb'ring Cities range on sev'ral sides. **1774** REYNOLDS *Disc.* vi. (1876) 401 He would .. have ranged with the great pillars and supporters of our Art. **1832** TENNYSON *Œnone* 79 When all the full-faced presence of the Gods Ranged in the halls of Peleus. **1841** R. OASTLER *Fleet Papers* I. iv. 29 That would range under the head of 'news'. **1852** THACKERAY *Esmond* I. xii, In the unhappy matrimonial differences .. Mistress Beatrix ranged with her father. **1877** G. H. LEWES *Let.* 27 Feb. in *Geo. Eliot Lett.* (1956) VI. 345 When do you think we ought to issue the 7/6 edition? It would of course be made to range with the edition I speak of.

b. *Naut.* of ships. Also *trans.*

1709 *Lond. Gaz.* No. 4521/2 The Comodore .. came ranging along our Larboard-side. **1797** NELSON in A. Duncan *Life* (1806) 41 The Excellent ranged up within two feet of the San Nicholas. **1841** R. H. DANA *Seaman's Man.* 79 She [*sc.* a ship] may be ranged a little ahead, or deadened, by filling or backing the cross-jack yards. **1855** MOTLEY *Dutch Rep.* I. ii. (1866) 102 Ten English vessels .. ranging up .. as close to the shore as was possible, opened their fire.

III. *intr.* **7.** To move hither and thither over a comparatively large area; to rove, roam, wander, stray. Const. with various advbs. and preps. (see quots.), and sometimes including the idea of searching (*for* something).

a. of persons (also *Naut.* = to cruise, sail about), animals (*esp.* of hunting dogs searching for game), and material objects.

1547 BOORDE *Introd. Knowl.* 170 Out of my countre I do syldome randge. **1591** SPENSER *M. Hubberd* 630 Brave beasts .. In the wilde forrest raunging fresh and free. **1618** LATHAM *2nd Bk. Falconry* 142 She .. attends the Falconer and his Spaniels as they range. **1628** DIGBY *Voy. Medit.* (1868) 85 The Dunkerkers ranged much and in great fleetes about our channell. **1666** BAXTER *Call to Unconverted* 213 Its easie to catch such greedy fish that are ranging for a bait. **1727** DE FOE *Hist. Appar.* iv. (1840) 29 That all the planets should seem to be made for nothing but to range about the waste. **1772-84** COOK *Voy.* (1790) V. 1699 We bore away to leeward, and ranged along the S.E. side of the coast. **1838** THIRLWALL *Greece* xlii. V. 219 It was his habit in summer to range over the Thracian woodlands. **1866** ROGERS *Agric. & Prices* I. xxi. 525 The custom of allowing sheep to range prevailed. **1875** 'PATHFINDER' *Breaking & Training Dogs* 118 The dog should range no nearer than five .. yards from the gun.

fig. **1561** NORTON *Calvin's Inst.* III. 246 Hipocrites .. that wildly range with licentiousnesse of sinnyng. **1581** J. BELL *Haddon's Answ. Osor.* 67 b, To raunge in the bookes of Philosophie. **1751** JOHNSON *Rambler* No. 153 ⁋10 By ranging through all the diversities of life. **1885** TENNYSON *Locksley Hall 60 Yrs. After* 217 While we range with Science, glorying in the time.

b. of immaterial things.

1574 tr. *Marlorat's Apocalips* 50 Whose heresie began .. to raunge through the Churches of Asia. **1581** J. BELL *Haddon's Answ. Osor.* 28 There raunged at that tyme a certeine outragious burnyng feaver. **1667** MILTON *P.L.* IX. 134 That destruction wide may range. **1781** COWPER *Conv.* 438 The Mind .. Should range where Providence has blessed the soil. **1814** SCOTT *Ld. of Isles* IV. xxviii, How would his busy satire range. **1880** GOLDWIN SMITH in *Atlant. Monthly* No. 268. 208 You will hardly restrain our thoughts from ranging beyond an earthly abode.

c. of the eye: To 'move' from one object of sight to another; to reach in this way.

1622 J. REYNOLDS *God's Revenge* I. 8 Shee .. checks her eyes from ranging beyond the lists of modestie and discretion. **1721** RAMSAY *Morning Interview* 93 Her unfix'd eyes with various turnings range. **1857** LIVINGSTONE *Trav.* xxvii. 548 Landscapes which permit the eye to range over twenty or thirty miles. **1872** JENKINSON *Guide Eng. Lakes* (1879) 351 As far as the eye can range.

d. *Gunnery.* Of projectiles: To traverse, go (a specified distance).

1644 NYE *Gunnery* (1670) 34 By noting how many paces a shot rangeth. **1798** HUTTON *Course Math.* (1828) II. 208 Some of those which in the air range only between 2 and 3 miles. **1846** GREENER *Sc. Gunnery* 324 Projectiles are made heavy under the impression they will range further.

e. To make search. Now *Sc.*

1551 T. WILSON *Logike* (1580) 60* Whensoeuer he shall seeke out the truthe of any cause, by diligent searche, and raungyng in these corners. **17..** RAMSAY *Twa Cut-Purses* 24 The ferly quickly chang'd, When throw their empty fobs they rang'd.

8. To change from one attachment to another; to be inconstant.

1596 SHAKS. *Tam. Shr.* III. i. 91 If once I finde thee ranging, Hortensio will be quit with thee by changing. **1706** *Lond. Gaz.* No. 4190/4 My Mind is fixt, I will not range, I like my Choice too well to change. **1807** BYRON *To Sighing Strephon* v, 'Tis, true, I am given to range; If I rightly remember, I've loved a great number.

9. *Bot.* and *Zool.* Of plants and animals: To extend (i.e. to occur, be found) over a certain area or throughout a certain period of time.

1859 DARWIN *Orig. Spec.* xiii. (1873) 359 The lower any group of organisms stands, the more widely it ranges. **1886** PRESTWICK *Geol.* I. 67 The Entomostraca range from the Lower Cambrian up to the present day. **1895** C. DIXON *Migrat. Brit. Birds* ii. 31 We find .. Ethiopian types ranging right up the Nile valley to the shores of the Mediterranean.

10. To vary within certain limits; to form a varying set or series.

1835 SIR J. ROSS *Narr. 2nd Voy.* v. 71 Ranging between two and twelve. **1857** LIVINGSTONE *Trav.* xxiv. 484 The thermometer early in the mornings ranged from 42° to 52°. **1876** *Nature* XIV. 22/2 Of Prime Movers alone there are 66 groups, ranging through many forms from a collection of the Original Models of Steam Engines .., downwards.

IV. *trans.* **11. a.** To traverse, to go over or through (a place or area) in all directions. (Sometimes including the idea of searching or examining.)

1533 FRITH *Another Bk. agst. Rastell* B iij, In the seconde chaptre, he rangethe the felde, and sercheth out .. what worde I haue spoken. **1601** R. JOHNSON *Kingd. & Commw.* (1603) 3 The French did raunge Italy at their pleasure under Charles the eight. **1715** POPE *Iliad* II. 62 The king despatch'd his heralds with commands To range the camp. **1781** COWPER *Charity* 301 To traverse seas, range kingdoms. **1850** TENNYSON *In Mem.* Concl. 96 Out we pass To range the woods, to roam the park.

transf. *c* **1572** GASCOIGNE *Fruites Warre* Poems (1831) 211 Warre seemes sweete to such as raunge it not.

b. *Naut.* To sail along or about (a country, the coast, etc.).

1603 R. SALTERNE in *Capt. Smith's Wks.* (1819) I. 108 As they ranged the coast .. they were kindly vsed by the Natiues. **1624** CAPT. SMITH *Virginia* I. 1 John and Sebastian [Cabot] .. ranged a great part of this vnknowne world. **1748** *Anson's Voy.* III. v. 342 These vessels .. are fitted for ranging this collection of Islands called the Ladrones. **1834** BANCROFT *Hist. U.S.* I. i. 10 Gaspar Costereal ranged the coast for .. six or seven hundred miles.

c. To cast (one's eyes) over a series of objects.

1862 MRS. H. WOOD *Channings* I. i. 11 The master ranged his eyes round the circle.

12. a. To pasture (cattle) on a range.

1857 OLMSTED *Journ. Texas* 184 They ranged their cattle over as much of the adjoining prairie as they chose.

b. To place (a telescope) in position.

1860 TYNDALL *Glac.* I. xxvii. 213 Ranging the telescope along the line of pickets, I saw them all standing.

c. To throw (a projectile) a specified distance.

1858 GREENER *Gunnery* 53 They say it ranges the projectile double the distance.

d. *absol.* To give a gun a certain range.

1892 *Black & White* 12 Mar. 342/1 The guns were all laid for the leading line, there was no question of ranging at all.

†**13.** Of a cannon: To throw (a bullet of a specified weight). *Obs.*$^{-1}$

1643 in Jos. Lister's *Autob.* (1842) 68 Their ordnance.. played upon us, one of them ranged an 8 pound bullet.

14. To cut (glass) into strips.

1825 J. NICHOLSON *Operat. Mechanic* 636 Ranging of glass is the cutting it in breadths as the work may require, and is best done by one uninterrupted cut from one end to the other.

range, *v.*² *Obs.* exc. *dial.* [Of doubtful origin; cf. RANGE *sb.*²] *trans.* To sift (meal).

1538 ELYOT, *Acerosus panis*, browne bredde not ranged. *Ibid.*, *Cernere*, to syfte or range floure of corne. **1623** COCKERAM, *Succernate*, To bolt or range meale. **1891-2** in *Eng. Dial. Dict.* (Devonshire).

fig. **1694** MOTTEUX *Rabelais* v. xxi. 94 She used to sift, searse, boult, range, and pass away time with a.. Sieve.

‖**rangé**, *a. Her.* [F., pa. pple. of *ranger* RANGE *v.*¹] **1.** (See quots.)

1780 EDMONDSON *Compl. Body Her.* II. Gloss., *Range* [sic] is a French term signifying many mullets, or other charges, placed in bend, saltire, fesse, cross etc. **1894** GOUGH & PARKER *Gloss. Heraldry* 489 *Rangé*, (fr.): arranged in a line.

2. Domesticated, orderly, regular, settled. Also in fem. form **rangée**.

1893 A. ATKINSON *Let.* 6 Feb. in F. Stark *Traveller's Prelude* (1950) ii. 29 He is stolider than ever and getting fat—looked terribly rangé and bourgeois. **1906** W. DE MORGAN *Joseph Vance* xviii. 149 It [*sc.* a public house] is still the George the Fourth, but the gas-jets no longer sow wild oats of lamp-black—they are *rangés*. **1927** *Observer* 17 July 14/3 Beckmesser (Bruce Anderson) displayed a fine voice, .. and was amazingly quick on his legs for a tolerably *rangé* mastersinger. **1931** *Times Lit. Suppl.* 29 Oct. 838/2 Experiences that left her mature, to enter, possibly, on the next stage of her life definitely *rangée*. **1934** 'A. BRIDGE' *Ginger Griffin* iv. 46 It's possible for girls to be too *rangées*. **1935** *Essays & Studies* XX. 117 The best printers, whose spelling was far more *rangé* than that of even the most scholarly and learned writers. **1941** 'R. WEST' *Black Lamb & Grey Falcon* (1942) I. 195 That bias would make it very difficult for Slavs ever to settle down under a government, and lead a *rangé* political life. **1951** R. F. HARROD *Life of J. M. Keynes* iii. 131 By comparison with Strachey he was *rangé*. **1952** 'J. TEY' *Singing Sands* v. 78 He listened.. to the talk of the two fellow sheep-farmers... Nothing hounded these large *rangé* creatures. **1977** A. WILSON *Strange Ride* vii. 334 Kipling was a.. respected writer in France, particularly in *rangé* circles.

range, dial. var. RINSE *v.*, obs. pa. t. RING.

ranged (reɪndʒd), *ppl. a.*¹ [f. RANGE *v.*¹ + -ED¹.] **1.** Set in line, ranked. †*a* **ranged battle**: a pitched battle.

1530 PALSGR. 678/2 It is a goodly thyng to se a ranged bataylе. **1609** DANIEL *Civ. Wars* VIII. xvi, The ranged horse breake out. **1680** G. HICKES *Spirit of Popery* 11 That Army of Saints, which fought the Kings Forces on Pentland-hills in a ranged Battel 1666.

2. *transf.* Systematically arranged; ordered.

1869 TENNYSON *Pelleas & Ettarre* 152 in *Idylls of King* 313 Whose lightest whisper moved him more Than all the ranged reasons of the world.

3. = RANGÉ *a.* 2.

1899 G. KEGAN PAUL *Memories* v. 142, I have loved less many more ranged and orderly men.

†**ranged**, *ppl. a.*² *Obs.* [f. RANGE *v.*²] Sifted; made of sifted flour.

1538 ELYOT, *Panis secundarius*, raunged bread, or chete breadde, or crybell breade. **1559** *Will of P. Kedwellye* (Somerset Ho.), To be made in penye Ranged bread. **1598** FLORIO, *Pane di ceruita*,.. choise bread, ranged bread.

'**rangeful.** [f. RANGE *sb.*¹] The fill of a range.

1616 *Trav. Eng. Pilg.* in *Harl. Misc.* (Malh.) III. 324 Some two hundred persons are owners of one rangeful [of eggs placed in furnaces for hatching].

'**rangeless**, *a. rare.* [f. RANGE *sb.*¹ + -LESS.] That has no range or limit.

1838 S. BELLAMY *Betrayal* 166 A fornix vast, that rangeless from the eye Ran wildering.

†'**rangement.** *Obs. rare.* [= F. *rangement* (1630): see RANGE *v.*¹ and -MENT.] Arrangement.

1674 N. FAIRFAX *Bulk & Selv.* 55 Without aiming at any better rangement for them. *a* **1740** WATERLAND *Wks.* (1823) IV. 468 General abstract ideas.. formed by the mind for the better.. rangement, and adjustment of our other ideas.

†'**rangen.** *Obs. rare*$^{-0}$. (See quot.)

1688 R. HOLME *Armoury* II. 182/1 The Kernells.. are little bunches rising in the throat, and unto this Disease belongs another called the Rangen.. it is a swelling in the lower part of the chap of the swins mouth.

ranger ('reɪndʒə(r)), *sb.*¹ Also 5-7 **raunger**, (5 -ier), 7 **randg-**, **rainger**. [f. RANGE *v.*¹ + -ER¹.] One who or that which ranges, in senses of the vb.

1. a. A rover, wanderer; †a rake. Also *spec.* = BUSH-RANGER.

1593 BRETON in *Phœnix Nest* (Grosart) I. 6/1 The Rookes, no raungers out of raie The Pawnes, the pages [etc.]. **1599** *Broughton's Let.* v. 17 Accusing his father.. for an whoremaster and.. a raunger. **1636** HEYWOOD *Love's Mistr.* Epil. Wks. 1874 V. 88 Mercury shall flie.. Upon your errands, prove your happy ranger. *a* **1711** KEN *Hymnarium* Poet. Wks. 1721 II. 119 The Rangers in the wild just God design'd [etc.]. **1818** KEATS *Endym.* IV. 274 I've been a ranger In search of pleasure throughout every clime. **1840** *Sydney Herald* 9 Sept. 2/3 It seems as though the constabulary there, are either too weak-handed or hearted!—for the rangers are still there, and at large. **1862** *Mudgee* (N.S.W.) *Liberal* 28 Nov. 2/6 Down on his knees pops our repentant ranger, and earnestly pleads for mercy for the sake of his wife and babes. **1865** NEALE *Hymns Parad.* 28 On this sea my bark, poor ranger, Is from pirates sore in danger. **1918** C. FEATHERSTONHAUGH *After Many Days* 364 The rangers then went on to the store... 'We have come to bail you up, young man.'

b. Applied *spec.* to certain animals (see quots.).

1686 R. BROME *Gentl. Recreation* II. 33/1 Four or five Couple of Spaniels that are good Rangers. **1832** WEBSTER, *Ranger*, a dog that beats the ground. **1855** F. MARRYAT *Mountains & Molehills* xi, I had two horses; one was an old grey 'Texian Ranger'. **1867** F. FRANCIS *Angling* x. (1880) 343 Following up the military lead, we come to the Rangers [a kind of salmon-flies]. **1884** GOODE *Nat. Hist. Aquatic Anim.* 58 The Harbor Seal. *Phoca vitulina*. The young are there [Newfoundland] also called 'Rangers'. **1887** *N. & Q.* 7th Ser. IV. 278 The Sp. *besugo*, a kind of sea-bream, is called in English ranger. **1890** H. H. *Dogs for Gun* III. iii. 103, I took him [a pointer] out with five high rangers in a 200 acre field.

attrib. **1895** *Outing* (U.S.) XXVII. 214/2 We.. secured a fine young ranger seal.

c. A wave of unusual height and force.

1891 *Pall Mall G.* 31 Aug. 4/3 The character of the great wave is a mystery... The sailors declared that it was a not unfamiliar phenomenon, and called it 'a ranger'.

2. a. A forest officer, a gamekeeper. Subsequently, the official title of the keepers of the royal parks. Now esp., a warden of a park or resort.

1455 *Rolls of Parlt.* V. 318/1 Almaner and singuler Offices of Foresters and Raungers of oure said Forestes. **1579** SPENSER *Sheph. Cal.* Sept. 159 [Wolves] walk not widely, as they were woont, For fear of raungers, and the great hoont. **1632** *High Commission Cases* (Camden) 288 The lopps and topps were all worth but 46ˢ, and he agreed with the Ranger of the Forrest for them. **1697** DRYDEN *Æneid* VII. 486 Tyrrheus chief ranger to the Latian King. **1788** H. WALPOLE *Reminisc.* 131 We afterwards recollected that lord Bute was ranger of the park. **1813** SCOTT *Rokeby* III. iv, He heard the rangers' loud halloo, Beating each cover.. As if to start the sylvan game. **1895** *Whitaker's Almanack* 169/2 St. James's, Green, and Hyde Parks—Ranger, H.R.H. the Duke of Cambridge. **1938** R. D. FINLAYSON *Brown Man's Burden* 40 The rangers had spotted them spearing the trout. **1943** *Amer. Speech* XVIII. 242 As the years went on, the rangers and other forest officers began to help with the good work [of map revision]... One name.. was 'Pomas Creek', submitted by Ranger Jim McKenzie. **1966** *Weekly News* (N.Z.) 3 Aug. 7/4 Fiordland's chief ranger.. emphasises that the authority's huts are 'spartan'. **1970** *Cape Times* 28 Oct. 3/2 (*heading*) Rangers wanted. *Ibid.*, the Simonstown Town Council is inviting applications from people to act as beach rangers during the summer season at R20 a week. **1973** *Sun-Herald* (Sydney) 26 Aug. 85/3 It is no easy job being a national park ranger. **1976** J. VAN DE WETERING *Tumbleweed* xiii. 132 He became a ranger on a nature reserve. **1978** *Nature* 26 Jan. 343/1 According to accounts of the rangers at Volcan Poas National Park, bushes at the high plateau level, 300-500 m. above the lake, were set on fire.

b. orig. *U.S.* An officer who rounds up straying domestic animals or livestock.

1744 *Pennsylvania Gaz.* 15 Nov. 3/3 Any Person or Persons, who have lost one or more of the following Strays, by applying to William Hartley, of Charles Town, Chief-Ranger for Chester County,.. may be informed where to find them. **1796** in G. Imlay *Topogr. Descr. W. Territory N. Amer.* (1797) 535 [The county court] shall also have power to appoint one register and ranger for the county, who shall hold their offices during good behaviour. **1828** *Cherokee Phoenix* (New Echota, Georgia) 27 Mar. 1/2 The ranger shall be entitled to one dollar for every horse so posted. **1886** *Buck's Handbk. Med. Sci.* II. 304/1 In Mississippi the coroner is also the county ranger, and performs the duties of that office. **1886** [see POUND-KEEPER]. **1926** A. WEBB *Miss Peters' Special* 50 The ranger's got the cow.

3. a. *pl.* A body of mounted troops, or other armed men, employed in ranging over a tract of country. Also in *sing.*

Chiefly *U.S.*; in the British Army the title is given to one regular regiment, the Connaught Rangers.

1670 *Massachusetts Hist. Soc. Coll.* (1800) VI. 211, [I] saw one of captain Willet's rangers coming on post on horseback. **1692** *Calendar Virginia State Papers* (1875) I. 38 [Petition of Lefᵗ David Straughan and] 'eight Rangers' [for pay for services]. **1713** *Colonial Rec. Carolina* (1886) II. 32, I have ordered all our Rangers.. to march that way. **1733** *Colonial Rec. Georgia* (1905) III. 90 Captain Macpherson with fifteen of the Rangers.. cover'd and protected the new Settlers. **1742** *State Prov. Georgia* (1897) 15 For the defense of the colony now, it is necessary to have.. rangers who can ride the woods. **1789** in O. Browning *Despatches from Paris* (1910) II. 169 The strongest proof is given of His disinterestedness by His proposing to resign the Office of Ranger (Capitainerie) of different Districts. **1796** STEDMAN *Surinam* I. iv. 81 The rangers in Virginia, who were sent out against the Cherokee Indians. **1835** W. IRVING *Tour on Prairies* ii. in *Crayon Misc.* (1863) 22 We learnt that a company of mounted rangers, or rifle-men, had departed but three days previous. **1882** DE WINDT *Equator* 34 The 'Sarawak Rangers'.. are recruited from Malays and Dyaks. **1906** *Westm. Gaz.* 2 June 8/3 Governor Ysabel, of the Mexican province of Senora [*sic*],.. will be met there by a force of American rangers from Bisbee... It is thought that the arrival of the Rangers from Bisbee will restore order. **1909** 'O. HENRY' *Roads of Destiny* xvi. 257 Standifer himself had served the commonwealth as Indian fighter, soldier, ranger, and legislator.

b. Chiefly *U.S.* A member of an élite American military unit established in 1941 for close combat and raiding; = COMMANDO 3 a. Also *attrib.*

1942 *N.Y. Times* 20 Aug. 1/5 The first American troops to receive a baptism of fire in Europe in this war were the men of the United States Ranger Battalion who fought in the Dieppe raid today. It was the first time the name Rangers had appeared in a war communiqué anywhere. **1942** *Newsweek* 31 Aug. 21/3 Mention in last week's communiqués of a detachment of a 'United States Ranger battalion' that had taken part in the Dieppe raid was the first disclosure of the existence of these Commando-type American troops... All Rangers are volunteers, they reported. *Ibid.* 22/1 The Rangers were named after Rogers's Rangers, the rough and crafty Indian fighters of colonial days who battled near the Canadian border. **1961** B. FERGUSSON *Watery Maze* vii. 180 The Commandos had a number of Rangers, their American counterparts, attached to them for experience. **1976** R. MOORE *Dubai* ii. 22 A newly organized unit.., the U.S. Army Special Forces.. made up of soldiers who were paratroopers, rangers, and combat men from World War II.

4. One who sets in order. *rare*$^{-1}$.

1611 BIBLE *1 Chron.* xii. 33 *marg.*, Rangers of battell.

5. In full now ***Ranger Guide***. A member of the Girl Guides Association who is in the section for older girls, aged between 14 and (usually) 18. ***Ranger Guider***, a leader of a unit of Ranger Guides. Cf. GUIDE *sb.* 2 d.

1921 G. I. J. POTTS *Girl Guide Badges* 2 The Service Star for Guiders and Rangers is worn on a red cloth ground. **1929** *Second Bk. of Ranger Games* 72 This is a favourite game with Rangers. **1944**, **1969** [see *Guider* s.v. GUIDE *sb.* 2 d]. **1969** [see GUIDE *sb.* 2 d]. **1976** *Ulverston* (Cumbria) *News* 3 Dec. 1/4 She has kept up her membership of the Ranger Guides and still finds time for some needlework. **1977** *National Trust* Spring 21/3 The Ranger Guides of S.E. England were invited to steward, usher and sell programmes. *Ibid.* 21/4 The smartness, efficiency and good humour of the Rangers .. evoked most favourable comment. **1977** *Daily Tel.* 2 June 18 Early photographs showing the Queen, Princess Margaret and other members of the Royal family as Brownies, Guides or Rangers will be among the exhibits. *Ibid.*, The exhibition.. also marks the diamond jubilee of the Ranger Guide section. **1977** *Guider* July 319/2 An enthusiastic Ranger Guider will invite older Guides to some of the interesting Ranger activities as 'tasters'.

†'**ranger**, *sb.*² *Obs.* [f. RANGE *v.*²] A sieve.

1485 in Kitchin *Rolls St. Swithin's* 383, j Ranger. **1498** *Ibid.* 387 In j Fyne Ranger empto, x d. In iiij Cours Rangers emptis, xviij d. **1601** HOLLAND *Pliny* II. 100 Rushes so big, that they will serue to make sieues, rangers, and vans.

‖**ranger** (rɑ̃ʒe), *v.*¹ [a. F. *se ranger* (also used) to settle down.] *refl.* To settle down. Cf. RANGÉ *a.* 2.

Used only in the infinitive form.

1854 THACKERAY *Newcomes* I. xxxii. 320 It is high time that Kew should *ranger* himself... I am sure he will make the best husband.. in England. **1883** W. JAMES *Let.* 2 May in R. B. Perry *Tht. & Char. W. James* (1935) I. 753 The time had come that I should *ranger* myself. **1924** J. BUCHAN *Three Hostages* xiii. 182, I heard somewhere you were goin' to be married... What do you call it—*ranger* yourself? **1979** A. BUCHAN *Scrap Screen* iii. 40 He desired to *se ranger* himself, having sown his wild oats.

ranger ('reɪndʒə(r)), *v.*² [f. RANGER *sb.*¹] *intr.* To be a ranger.

1909 'O. HENRY' *Roads of Destiny* xvi. 263 We fought Kiowas, drove cattle, and rangered side by side nearly all over Texas. **1979** P. L. SANDBERG *Stubb's Run* ii. 9 He had rangered in the Sawcut for seventeen years.

rangerine ('rændʒəraɪn), *a. Zool.* [f. F. *ranger* (*-gier*) reindeer + -INE.] Resembling the reindeer.

1852 J. E. GRAY *Catal. Mamm. Brit. Mus.* III. 185 The Rangerine Deer have a large, basal anterior snag to the horns, close to the crown or bur, and no muffle.

rangership ('reɪndʒəʃɪp). [f. RANGER *sb.*¹ + -SHIP.] The office of ranger of a forest or park.

1464 *Rolls of Parlt.* V. 533/2 The Office of the Raungership of the Chace of our said Castell. **1697** LUTTRELL *Brief Rel.* (1857) IV. 216 Lord Dursley.. quitted the same for a rangership of a forest which the duke of Beauford had. **1788** H. WALPOLE *Reminisc.* i. 12 Queen Anne had bestowed the rangership of Richmond New Park on her relations the Hydes. *a* **1859** MACAULAY *Hist. Eng.* xxv. V. 274 Garters, gold keys, white staves, rangerships,.. were now intercepted by aliens.

rangette (reɪn'dʒɛt). *N. Amer.* and *N.Z.* [f. RANGE *sb.*¹ 12 a + -ETTE.] A small gas or electric cooker.

1959 *Sears, Roebuck Catal.* Spring & Summer 934/1 Kenmore 20-inch Gas Rangettes. **1968** *Globe & Mail* (Toronto) 5 Feb. 25/9 (Advt.), Wanted to buy. Household furniture, fridge, stove, washer, rangette, urgent. **1977** *N.Z. Herald* 5 Jan. 1-20/4 She cooks on an electric rangette.

rangey, **rangily**: see RANGY *a.*

rangh, obs. form of RANGE *sb.*¹

ran'giferine, *a. Zool.* [f. med.L. *rangifer* (F. *rangifère*) reindeer + -INE.] Rangerine; belonging to the genus *Rangifer*, which includes the reindeer. (In recent dicts.)

ranginess ('reɪndʒɪnɪs). [f. RANGY *a.* + -NESS.] **1.** Capacity for ranging.

1872 *Rep. Vermont Board Agric.* I. 213 A 1100 or 1200 lb horse, with bone, ranginess and endurance.

2. The state of being tall and slender.

1965 G. McInnes *Road to Gundagai* xiv. 257 He was..of a Gary Cooper ranginess.

ranging (ˈreɪndʒɪŋ), *vbl. sb.* [f. Range *v.*[1]]

1. The action of the vb. **a.** in transitive senses; *spec.* the action of measuring the distance to an object by radar or other means.

1622 Markham *Decades War* iv. ix. 155 These Corporals haue the raunging of Battels. **1710** Addison *Whig Exam.* No. 4 When an author..imposes upon us by the sound and ranging of his words. **1846** Trench *Mirac.* xviii. (1862) 313 A ranging of men in their true ranks. **1919** *Sci. Amer.* 17 May 511/3 Sound-ranging is a vast improvement [for]..locating hostile points of fire. **1946** *Jrnl. Inst. Electr. Engineers* XCIII. i. 378/2 The foundation for precision radar ranging in fire control was firmly laid in 1938. **1965** Filipowsky & Muehldorf *Space Communications Techniques* ii. 136 The reference frequency of 29⅝ or 32 Mc is transmitted..over the microwave link to the receiver where the ranging equipment is situated. **1970** *Nature* 12 Dec. 1024/2 The Smithsonian Astrophysical Observatory has..smaller instruments for satellite ranging.

b. in intransitive senses.

c **1610** *Women Saints* 38 After many perills and long ranging..they arriued at Colen. **1651** Hobbes *Leviath.* i. iii. 9 This wild ranging of the mind. **1719** D'Urfey *Pills* (1872) VI. 44 Cupid it is my Name, I live by ranging. **1862** *Catal. Internat. Exhib.* II. xxviii. 123 Their inequality of size and consequent irregularity of ranging. **1890** H. H. *Dogs for Gun* iii. i. 80, I have seen four months' old pups go in for ranging.

2. *attrib.* and *Comb.*, as ***ranging company***, †***wise***; **ranging-lath**, a lath employed to guide the tool in cutting glass; **ranging-line, -pole, -rod, -stick**, a line, pole, etc. used in surveying or measuring, for setting out straight lines; **ranging-timber** (?).

1779 L. McIntosh in Sparks *Corr. Amer. Rev.* (1853) II. 285, I..authorized the Lieutenants to raise a *ranging company. **1825** J. Nicholson *Operat. Mechanic* 636 The *ranging lath must be long enough to extend rather beyond the boundary of the table of glass. **1712** J. James tr. *Le Blond's Gardening* 82 The Legs and *Ranging-sticks are tied up together in a Bundle. **1796** Morse *Amer. Geog.* I. 394 Ship timber, *ranging timber, plank, deals. **1563–87** Foxe *A. & M.* (1596) 92/2 Neither yet in *ranging wise wander the starres to what place of the world they list.

ranging (ˈreɪndʒɪŋ), *ppl. a.* [f. as prec. + -ing[2].] That ranges, in senses of the vb.

1559 *Mirr. Mag., Dk. Clarence* xxix, A raynles ranging horse. **1560** A. L. tr. *Calvin's Foure Serm. Songe Ezech.* iv. 62 Though we haue many ranging woordes in our prayer. **1655** Sir E. Nicholas in *N. Papers* (Camden) II. 337 Only fit for one of..his ranging spaniells to finde where the game lyes. **1700** Prior *Carm. Sec.* xvii, She thro' the ranging Ocean now Views him advancing his auspicious Prow. **1887** Bowen *Virg. Æneid* vi. 161 Many the troubled thoughts that in ranging talk they pursue.

†**ˈranging sieve.** *Obs. rare.* = Range *sb.*[2]

1548 Elyot, *Sisacthea*, a rangeyng sieue. **1601** Holland *Pliny* viii. xliv. 224 That no corne-maisters..should beat this Mule away from their raunging sives.

rangiora (raŋiˈɔra). [Maori.] An evergreen New Zealand shrub or small tree, *Brachyglottis repanda*, belonging to the family Compositæ, and bearing large ovate leaves with white tomentum on the under side and terminal panicles of small greenish-white flowers. Also *attrib.*

1868 W. Colenso in *Trans. N.Z. Inst.* I. iii. 38 For wounds..they used the large leaves of the Pukapuka, or Rangiora. **1882** *Trans. N.Z. Inst.* XIV. 357 The Maoris also distinguish the two plants by different names, the present plant being known as Rangiora. **1921** H. Guthrie-Smith *Tutira* vii. 51 Later, appeared slender matapo [*sic*]..and rangiora. **1933** *Bulletin* (Sydney) 9 Aug. 21/2 The large leaves of the rangiora bushes growing near tracks. **1966** *Encycl. N.Z.* II. 785/2 Gums and resins..were obtained from kauri,..rangiora..and wharangi.

ˈrangle, *sb. rare.* [Of obscure origin.] Small stones or gravel given to hawks, usually to improve their digestion.

1678 in Phillips (ed. 4). **1852** R. F. Burton *Falconry Valley Indus* vii. 75 The Bazdar gives his falcons bits of rangle the size of a pea in order to prevent their laying eggs.

†**ˈrangle**, *v. Obs.* [Of obscure origin; cf. ramble. Mod. S.W. dial. has *rangle* to twine, of climbing plants.] *intr.* To rove, wander, stray.

1567 Turberv. *Epit.* etc. 15 Such as..neuer rangle farre abroade against the keepers will. **1575** —— *Faulconrie* 23 These Eagles..doe roue and rangle abroade. **1591** Harrington *Ariosto* xix. lvi, They scaped best that here and thither rangled.

Hence †**ˈrangler**, a rover; †**ˈrangling** *vbl. sb.*

1575 Turberv. *Faulconrie* 9 No inwarde Eagle but a fugitive and a rangler. **1594** Willobie *Avisa* (1880) 138 The rangling rage that held from home Vlisses all too long.

rangle, obs. form of wrangle.

ˈrangled, *ppl. a.* Also (? *Obs.*) **wrangled**. [Cf. rangle *v.*] Wreathed; twisted; injured by twisting.

a **1560** Phaer *Æneid* viii. (1562) B b iij, Both noise and feare thei mingled through their work, and wrangled wrathes of following flame. **1807** in *Spirit Pub. Jrnls.* XI. 17 The stump..was harder than his head; and his arm was a little wrangled, as we may say, by pitching on it. **1924** A. J. Small *Frozen Gold* x. 220 The trail led through four miles of rugged, rangled bushland to the Yukon water edge. **1929** R. Bridges *Testament of Beauty* iii. 84 Nor the rangled shroud that she wove for his sire.

Rangoon (ræŋˈguːn). The name of the capital of Burma, used *attrib.* in **Rangoon bean**, the Lima bean, *Phaseolus lunatus* var. *limensis* (see Lima); **Rangoon creeper**, a tropical climbing shrub, *Quisqualis indica*, belonging to the family Combretaceæ, native to south-east Asia, and bearing spikes of white, pink, or red flowers having an elongated calyx tube.

1877 G. M. Woodrow *Hints on Gardening in India* (ed. 2) 110 *Quisqualis Indica* (Rangoon Creeper). A straggling shrub, which may be trained to cover a wall..; flowers vary in colour, from white to rose. **1901** L. H. Bailey *Cycl. Amer. Horticulture* III. 1486/2 This [genus] includes the Rangoon Creeper, a tender woody plant with 5-petaled red flowers. **1922** Joyce *Ulysses* 289 The extremely large wains bring foison of the fields, flaskets of cauliflowers, floats of spinach, pineapple chunks, Rangoon beans, strikes of tomatoes. **1928** K. Gough *Garden Bk. for Malaya* viii. 111 Kopsia and Rangoon creeper are respectively a shrub and a creeper with flowers that shade from pale-pink to deep red-pink. **1971** C. Flieger in E. L. Wardman *Bermuda Jubilee Garden* viii. 163/2 Rangoon creeper. A deciduous clambering shrub with very attractive drooping spikes of elongated pink and red flowers, and a perfume that suggests a mixture of ripe fruits. **1972** Y. Lovelock *Veg. Bk.* i. 55 A variety known as Lima bean.., also Tonga, Burma, Rangoon, Java and Madagascar bean, bears large white seeds which are dried, canned and marketed under the names wax or butter beans.

Rangri (ˈrɑːŋgriː). Also **Rangree**. A form of the Malvi dialect of Rajasthani.

1823 J. Malcolm *Mem. Central India* II. xiv. 166 In Central India they learn the Rangree or Hindui dialect, in which business is commonly transacted. **1878** R. N. Cust *Mod. Languages of E. Indies* ii. 49 Sir J. Malcolm..alludes to Rangri as the Dialect of Hindi taught in the schools of Central India... By Rangri he meant at that time Dialects of Hindi, spoken all over Central India, and now resolved into separate Tribal and Political subdivisions. **1908** G. A. Grierson *Ling. Survey of India* IX. ii. 52 The form of Mālvī spoken by Rajputs of Malwa proper is called Rāṅgṛī. It is distinguished by its preference for Mārwāṛī forms. *Ibid.* 53 As stated above, Mālvī, in the Malwa country, has two forms, *viz.*:—Rāṅgṛī..or Rāj-wāṛī, spoken by Rajputs, and Mālvī.., spoken by the rest of the population. **1920** —— *Index of Language-Names* 172 Rāngṛī... A form of the Mālvī Dialect.

†**ˈrangy**, *sb. Obs. rare*[−1]. = range *sb.*[1] 13 c.

1657 C. Beck *Univ. Charac.* K iij, A rangy or beam between horses in a Coach.

rangy (ˈreɪndʒɪ), *a.* Formerly chiefly *U.S.* Also **rangey**. [f. range *sb.* or *v.* + -y.]

1. Of animals: **a.** Adapted for or capable of ranging; having a shape indicative of this.

1868 H. Woodruff *Trotting Horse* xlvii. 381 The latter was a fine, rangy gelding. **1885** T. Roosevelt *Hunting Trips of Ranchman* 21 The ponies..used for the circle riding in the morning have need rather to be strong and rangey. **1891** *Harper's Mag.* Aug. 365/2 The former trots by on his rangy thoroughbred. **1895** *Century Mag.* Aug. 627/2 How the dogs, like the race-horse, have grown lighter, more rangy in form, smaller, solider in bone. **1936** F. Clune *Roaming round Darling* xxiv. 252, I counted over four score of rangy mangy looking racehounds all capable of running a kangaroo to earth. **1955** *Times* 20 May 10/5 Some bulls—black and white beasts of the Holmogorky breed, somewhat like British Friesians, but rather bigger and rangier. **1977** J. Bingham *Marriage Bureau Murders* iii. 30 She had been out cubbing one autumn on a great rangy beast. **1977** *Time* 19 Sept. 61/1 The royal government provided no housing materials and no food beyond a few rangy cattle.

b. Of a long, slender form. Also of persons.

1876 *Rep. Vermont Board Agric.* III. 215 They were..light colored, rather rangy sheep. **1886** C. Scott *Sheep-Farming* 22 The short close-made ewe is not..as prolific a breeder, as those more rangy and of greater length. **1899** G. Ade *Doc' Horne* 42 He was considerably over six feet tall, raw boned and rangy. **1910** *Daily Chron.* 18 Apr. 8/3 Truxton King is a tall, raw-boned, 'rangy' American—notice particularly the 'rangy', as it seems to be his chief characteristic—though we don't quite know what it means. **1932** L. C. Douglas *Forgive us our Trespasses* (1937) x. 197 You're rangy enough. Tall as Craig, himself. **1956** C. Willock *Death at Flight* iv. 51 The Americans..would describe such a man as 'rangy'. **1968** J. Lock *Lady Policeman* viii. 76 He's tall, rangy, with skin-tight pants, long dark hair and plum-coloured lipstick. **1971** *Guardian* 28 Aug. 9/1 A rangy 26-year old Australian who walks and talks with equal stamina. **1977** *Time* 3 Jan. 36/3 A freewheeling, gregarious politician, the rangy (6ft. 2in.) Bergland is married to a farmer's daughter and is the father of six children. **1977** J. F. Fixx *Compl. Bk. Running* i. 4 Carver is tall, rangy and sturdily built, but at thirty-three he was out of shape.

2. Of places: Giving scope for ranging; spacious.

1880 Lanier *Sunrise* 79 in *Poems* (1892), Breathe it free, By rangy marsh, in lone sea-liberty.

3. *Austral.* Mountainous.

1880 Sutherland *Tales of Goldfields* 89 The most rangy and inaccessible regions of the Colonies. **1890** 'R. Boldrewood' *Robbery under Arms* 144 The hills on the south were wild and rangy enough.

Hence **ˈrangily** *adv.*, in a rangy fashion.

1976 'S. Woods' *My Life is Done* 62 He was..very tall..and rangily built.

rani, var. ranee.

ranid (ˈreɪnɪd), *sb.* and *a.* [ad. mod.L. family name *Ranidæ*, f. L. *rāna* frog + -id[3].] **A.** *sb.* A frog of the family Ranidæ, which includes typical amphibious frogs. **B.** *adj.* Of, pertaining to, or designating a frog of this family.

1888 *Proc. Zool. Soc.* 509 Our attention was early arrested by the general similarity between the proximal syndesmoses in the Hylids and Ranids and the knee-joint in the higher Vertebrata. **1901** *Ibid.* I. 58 (*heading*) On abnormal ranid larvae from North-Eastern India. **1946** *Nature* 23 Nov. 749/2 In *L[eptodactylus] pentadactylus*..both the uteri and the Wolffian ducts run separately throughout their course as in ranid frogs. **1957** P. J. Darlington *Zoogeogr.* iii. 170 Ranids have evolved in the main part of the Old World tropics. **1974** H. R. Heusser in B. Grzimek *Animal Life Encycl.* V. vi. 397 In true frogs or ranids..the presacral vertebrae are typically amphicoelous.

raniform (ˈreɪnɪfɔːm), *a.* [f. *rāni-* comb. form of L. *rāna* frog + -form.] Frog-shaped.

1852 Wyman in *Smithsonian Contrib. Knowl.* V. iv. 46 Dissections of other than Raniform Batrachians. **1875** Huxley in *Encycl. Brit.* I. 751/2 No raniform Labyrinthodonts have yet been discovered.

ranikaboo: see rannygazoo.

raninal, *a. rare*[−1]. = ranine 1.

1822–34 *Good's Study Med.* (ed. 4) I. 93 The necessity for deep incisions has been superseded by bleeding from the raninal veins.

ranine (ˈreɪnaɪn), *a.* [ad. mod.L. *rānīnus*, f. *rāna* frog: see -ine.]

1. *Anat.* Belonging to the under side of the tip of the tongue (the part liable to be affected by ranula); in ***ranine artery*** (the terminal branch of the lingual artery), ***ranine vein***.

Cf. F. *veine ranine* (Cotgr.), *artère ranine* (Littré).

1819 *Pantologia* X, *Ranine artery*,.. the second branch of the external carotid. **1831** R. Knox *Cloquet's Anat.* 740 It anastomoses with the ranine vein. **1840** G. V. Ellis *Anat.* 198 The continuation of the gustatory nerve to the tip of the tongue, together with the ranine artery.

2. Pertaining to a frog; frog-like. *rare.*

1840 in Smart.

raninian (rəˈnɪnɪən), *a.* and *sb.* [f. as prec. + -ian.] **a.** *adj.* Pertaining to the *Raninidæ*, an order of frog-crabs. **b.** *sb.* One of the *Raninidæ*.

1841 *Penny Cycl.* XIX. 298/1 *Raninians*, the name by which M. Milne Edwards designates the fourth tribe of the family *Apterura*.

ranite, the correct form of rauite.

raˈnivorous, *a.* [f. *rani-* (see *raniform*) + -vorous.] Frog-eating.

1821 Latham *Gen. Hist. Birds* I. 181 Ranivorous Falcon. **1878** *Fraser's Mag.* XVIII. 504 Frenchmen..were not the ranivorous and capering creatures they supposed.

‖**ranjau** (ˈrændʒaʊ). Also 8–9 **ranjow**. [Malay.] A stake or caltrop of bamboo or iron placed in the ground to pierce the feet or body of an enemy.

1783 W. Marsden *Hist. Sumatra* 278 *Ranjows* are sharp pointed stakes of *bamboo*, of different lengths, stuck into the ground, in order to penetrate the naked feet, or body, of an enemy. **1839** T. J. Newbold *Straits of Malacca* II. xii. 210 A Malay considers himself completely armed with..the tombak (spear), and a quiver of ranjows, or caltrops, at his back. **1936** G. B. Gardner *Keris* x. 118 While the chiefs might have used horses for purposes of display, on account of the *ranjau* or pointed stakes planted in the passes they could not have been employed effectively.

rank (ræŋk), *sb.*[1] Also 6 *Sc.* **raink**, 6–7 **ranke**, 6–8 **ranck**, (6–7 -e), 7 **ranque**. [a. obs. F. *ranc* (mod. *rang*), var. *renc*, usually supposed to be a. OHG. *hrinc*, *hring* ring.]

1. a. A row, line, or series of things.

In common use *c* 1580–1610, esp. with ref. to teeth and trees; now rare in general sense, but used *spec.* of cabs or carriages (sense 1 c), and *techn.* of organ-pipes and in *Teleph.*

1570 Levins *Manip.* 24/21 A rank of things, *turba, caterua*. **1576** Fleming *Panopl. Epist.* 249 Such a rancke and rowe of litigious causes..hange one vppon another, as linckes in a long chaine. **1590** Spenser *F.Q.* i. xi. 13 In either jaw Three ranckes of yron teeth enraunged were. **1600** Shaks. *A.Y.L.* iv. iii. 80 The ranke of Oziers by the murmuring streame. **1693** Evelyn *De la Quint. Compl. Gard.* II. 149 A Rank of Baskets..one at the tail of the other, beginning the Rank or Row where the Bed is to end. **1811** Busby *Dict. Mus.* s.v. *Stop*, Furniture Stop..comprising two or more ranks of pipes. **1881** Edwards *Organs* xxi. 153 The most useful mixture for a small organ is one of three ranks. **1888** Jacobi *Printers' Vocab.* s.v., Composing frames are generally arranged in rows or ranks. **1924** *Brit. Stand. List Terms Telegraphs & Telephones* 13 *Rank of switches*,..the switches which provide for any one stage of call selection. **1929** *P.O. Engin. Dept. Techn. Instr.* XXV. ii. 6 The number of ranks of selectors is one less than the required number of digits to call a number on the exchange. **1969** S. F. Smith *Telephony & Telegraphy A* v. 119 If more than 1000 numbers are required, another rank of group selectors can be used.

†**b.** ***on a rank***: On end, continuously. *Obs.*

1574 Hellowes *Gueuara's Fam. Ep.* (1577) 360 Hee went to fast..xl. dayes and xl. nights on a rancke.

c. A row of public vehicles waiting to be hired, or the place where these stand; a taxi-rank.

c **1843** J. R. Planché *Extravaganzas* (1879) II. 240 My Minstrel Boy for a cab is gone, In the ranks no doubt he'll find one. **1851** Mayhew *Lond. Lab.* III. 353 [The] small masters..are amongst the most respectable men of the ranks. **1903** *Daily Chron.* 29 Sept. 3/1 These proposals include the use of such large ranks as that in Berkeley-square as feeders for smaller ones in the vicinity. **1922** *Daily Mail*

Year Bk. 1923 74/2 One London firm having an air-garage with machines waiting for hire always on its 'rank'. **1930** D. L. SAYERS *Strong Poison* i. 21 The taxi-driver Burke, who was standing on the rank in Guilford Street, was approached by Philip Boyes. **1962** S. BECKETT in *Evergreen Rev.* Jan.-Feb. 16, I learnt there were still some cabmen who spent their day snug and warm inside their cabs on the rank. **1974** 'J. ROSS' *Burning of Billy Toober* ix. 88 She returned.. by taxi... The driver..picked her up at the rank in the town square. **1978** *Taxi* 16 Feb. 2/2 On Alf's return to the forecourt the dozen cabmen who had gathered decided that a protest boycott was necessary and they began picketing the rank.

2. a. A row or line of persons. Now *rare* (cf. 3).

1571 GOLDING *Calvin on Ps.* xlii. 5 David ment ranks: bycause they went..in orderly rowes when they came to the Tabernacle. **1597** HOOKER *Eccl. Pol.* V. lxxix. §14 A miserable ranke of poore, lame and impotent persons. **1697** DRYDEN *Æneid* II. 1044 A ranck of wretched youths, with pinion'd Hands. **1728** POPE *Dunciad* IV. 107 Courtiers and Patriots in two ranks divide, Thro' both he pass'd, and bow'd from side to side. **1870** B. TAYLOR *2nd Pt. Faust* III. 440 Chorus..dancing nimbly..in interlinking ranks.

†**b.** Phr. ***in*** or ***of a rank***, in a line or file. ***on a rank***, abreast. *Obs.*

1570 *Satir. Poems Reform.* xxii. 6 A gyde to blind men in a rank. **1581** PETTIE *Guazzo's Civ. Conv.* III. (1586) 157b, All the women in the towne runne thether of a ranke, as it wer in procession. **1588** PARKE tr. *Mendoza's Hist. China* 182 The hie wayes are verie brode, that twentie men may ride together on a ranke and one not hinder an other.

†**c.** Movement in line or file. *Obs. rare.*

1600 SHAKS. *A.Y.L.* III. ii. 103 It is the right Butter-womens ranke to Market.

3. *Mil.* A number of soldiers drawn up in line abreast. Hence in *pl.* freq. = forces, battalion, army (also in phrases as ***ranks of death, of war***). ***to close ranks***: see CLOSE *v.* 10 b. Also *fig.*

1574 H. G. tr. *Cataneo's Briefe Tables* F iij, Let 44 ranckes of unarmed Pikes..be bestowed behind these armed ranckes. **1595** SHAKS. *John* IV. ii. 244 My State is braued,.. with rankes of forraigne powres. **1668** CULPEPPER & COLE *Barthol. Anat.* IV. xx. 356 They resemble a rank of Souldiers in battle array. **1732** LEDIARD *Sethos* II. IX. 320 The march was to be by ten in a rank. **1738** GRAY *Propertius* iii. 33 To paint the Hero's Toil, the Ranks of War. **1781** COWPER *Table T.* 768 'Twould thin the ranks of the poetic tribe. **1813** SCOTT *Rokeby* I. xii, On Marston heath Met, front to front, the ranks of death. **1796–7, 1873** [see CLOSE *v.* 10 b]. **1855** PRESCOTT *Philip II*, II. (1857) 274 He at once enrolled himself in the ranks of the opposition. **1874** GREEN *Short Hist.* vii. §6. 399 Scholars like Hooker, gentlemen like George Herbert, could now be found in the ranks of the priesthood. **1875** JOWETT *Plato* (ed. 2) I. 82 When the ranks are broken and you have to fight singly. **1941** 'G. ORWELL' *Lion & Unicorn* I. iii. 35 England..is a family... It has its private language and its common memories, and at the approach of an enemy it closes its ranks. **1948** W. CHURCHILL *Gathering Storm* I. xxi. 382 The tide of events brought with it a closing of the ranks between England and France, and also at home. **1974** G. HUBBARD *Quaker by Convincement* II. i. 68 Some Friends occasionally suggest that a creed might help to clarify our thoughts... At this suggestion the majority close their ranks, and hold firm to their beliefs, which are not to be contained in the strait-jacket of a creed. **1977** *Oxford Mission Quarterly Paper* Jan.-Mar. 16 When surrounded by astronomical numbers of non-Christians, Christians tend to show their solidarity by closing their ranks.

transf. **1577** BRETON *Flourish upon Fancie* II. (Grosart) I. 10/1 A Garde of Geese and Ganders, in one rancke. **1625** J. GLANVILLE *Voy. to Cadiz* (Camden) 15 To enjoyne our ffleete to advance & fight att Sea, much after the maner of an Armie at land, assigneing every shipp to a perticular division, ranke, file, and station.

b. *pl.* The body of private soldiers; the rank and file (see 5 b). Also *transf.* ***to rise from the ranks***, of a private or non-commissioned officer: to receive a commission, to become a commissioned officer; freq. *transf.*, to rise from a lowly social, etc., position. Cf. OTHER *a.* 5 f.

1809 WELLINGTON *Let. to Beresford* 25 June in Gurw. *Desp.* (1837) IV. 464 The irregularity of Colonel Blunt having three servants from the ranks. **1845** *Punch* VIII. 127 I've flattered Peel; he smiles back thanks... But still he keeps me in 'the ranks'. **1853** RUSKIN *Let.* 6 Nov. in M. Lutyens *Millais & Ruskins* (1967) 106 Mr. Beveridge [has] ..been effecting singular cures..and rose from the ranks — as Jephson did. **1858** TROLLOPE *Dr. Thorne* I. iii. 67 A native of Barchester, having risen from the world's ranks. **1897** *Daily News* 16 June 7/7 Native ranks, except three, doing well. **1936** B. KELLERMANN *Tunnel* II. iii. 84 There was no doubt about the fact that Woolf had risen from the ranks. **1958** J. WAIN *Contenders* ii. 27 Baxter, a harmless bore of about thirty-five, had risen from the ranks, so to speak. **1977** *Times* 2 June 15/7 St. George..is acclaimed as a soldier who rose from the ranks to become a tribune.

c. *Chess.* One of the lines of squares stretching across the board from side to side. Also ***in rank***, on one of these lines (cf. 4).

1597 G. B. *Ludus Scacchiæ* D iij b, Mouoing a Pawne from left hand side, which on the fourth ranke stood. **1672** BARBIER *Saul's Chesse play* ix, [The King's move is] to the next House or place, in File or rancke, of any side. **1894** J. MASON *Princ. Chess* 4 The rank upon which the player's Pieces are ranged is his first rank.

d. *fig.* of things.

1593 SHAKS. *Lucr.* 1439 Simois..Whose waves to imitate the battle sought..and their ranks began To break upon the galled shore. **1697** DRYDEN *Virg. Georg.* IV. 514 At once the Ranks of swelling Streams divide. **1842** TENNYSON *Amphion* 33 The linden broke her ranks and rent The woodbine wreaths that bind her.

4. Without article: Line, order, array. In phr. as ***in*** (***into***) or ***out of rank***, ***to keep*** or ***break rank***.

1572 HULOET s.v., Goe in rancke, or raye, *incede ordine.* To come into rancke, or raye, *incurrere in ordinem.* **1598** BARRET *Theor. Warres* II. i. 25 He must be carefull that his souldiers breake not out of ranke. **1607** TOPSELL *Four-f. Beasts* (1658) 249 The Horse-men had broken rank and were asunder. **1611** BIBLE *1 Chron.* xii. 33 Fifty thousand, which could keep rank. **1647** N. BACON *Disc. Govt. Eng.* I. xv. (1739) 29 The Legate..soon reduced him into rank. **1711** *Fingall MSS.* in *10th Rep. Hist. MSS. Comm.* App. V. 167 The entrance is too narrow, as not capable of above four men in ranck. **1850** TENNYSON *In Mem.* xiv, [To] see thy passengers in rank Come stepping lightly down the plank. **1880** BROWNING *Echetlos* ii, No man but..kept rank and fought away In his tribe and file.

transf. **1623** MASSINGER *Bondman* IV. iv, A part of your honour's ruff stands out of rank.

5. ***rank and file***: **a.** (see quot. 1802 and FILE *sb.*[2] 7). Chiefly *pl.* or without article in phr. ***in rank and file*** (cf. 4). Also *transf.*

1598 BARRET *Theor. Warres* III. i. 34 To learne to keepe his ranke and file orderly. **1600** HOLLAND *Livy* XXXV. v. 891 This tempest and storme of Cavallerie..brake their rankes and files cleane. **1632** MASSINGER *Maid of Hon.* IV. i, See the soldiers set In rank and file. **1697** DRYDEN *Virg. Georg.* II. 375 Extend thy loose Battalions..Opening thy Ranks and Files on either Side. **1781** COWPER *Truth* 422 His books well trimmed..Like regimental coxcombs rank and file. **1802** JAMES *Milit. Dict.*, *Ranks and files*, are the horizontal and vertical lines of soldiers when drawn up for service. *a* **1822** A. BOSWELL *Skeldon Haughs*, The Crawfords march'd in rank and file.

transf. **1784** BURNS *1st Ep. to Davie* xi, The words come skelpan, rank and file.

b. *collect.* (The) common soldiers; (the) privates and corporals. Now freq. hyphened. Cf. RANK-AND-FILE *a.*

1796 *Campaigns* 1793–4 I. I. vi. 51 It may not be amiss.. to state..that rank and file means, in Gazette returns, the corporals and private soldiers. **1814** WELLINGTON 15 May in Gurw. *Disp.* XII. 13 A corps consisting of about 12,000 rank and file of British infantry. **1894** WOLSELEY *Life Marlborough* II. lii. 84 Unless the Rank and File are interested in their work, there will be no enthusiasm.

transf. **1860** MILL *Repr. Govt.* (1865) 64/2 One of the mere rank and file of a party. **1888** BRYCE *Amer. Commw.* I. xv. 212 For other committees there remains only the rank and file of the House. **1927** *New Republic* 12 Oct. 205/2 The rank and file have grown tired of the persistent effort of the Communists to subvert trade-union discipline. **1939** H. NICOLSON *Diary* 14 Mar. (1966) 392 The ignorance of the Tory rank-and-file in regard to foreign policy is as terrifying as the prospect of a gardener suddenly driving a Rolls Royce. **1972** *History Workshop Pamphlet No. 6* 37 In the depression of the later 1870s the demand from the rank-and-file for a policy of restriction became very strong. **1976** E. MACLAREN *Nature of Belief* ix. 91 Professional theologians might refine beyond recognition the bald credal outlines demanded of the rank-and-file. **1976** tr. Wang Chin-fu et al. in *Yenan Seeds & other Stories* 113 You'd better go to the rank-and-file to find out what they think.

†**6.** A class, set, kind (of persons or things). *Obs.*

1585 T. WASHINGTON tr. *Nicholay's Voy.* I. xxi, The most part of them were put to the ranke of criminels forsworn. **1610** WILLET *Hexapla, Daniel* 294 The diuers opinions.. may be sorted into three ranks. **1660** STANLEY *Hist. Philos.* IX. III. 47 A Pythagorean of the Acousmatick ranck. **1725** WATTS *Logic* II. iii. (1736) 221 The Authority of Men is the Spring of another Rank of Prejudices.

7. One of several rows or lines of things placed at different levels. ? *Obs.*

1577 B. GOOGE *Heresbach's Husb.* (1586) 179b, It is enough to haue three rankes of them, one aboue the other. **1667** MILTON *P.L.* IV. 140 As the ranks ascend Shade above shade, a woodie Theatre. **1693** EVELYN *De la Quint. Compl. Gard.* I. 178 One single rank or story of roots is enough. **1734** tr. *Rollin's Anc. Hist.* V. 13 Ranks of oars in the modern galleys.

8. a. A number of persons forming a distinct class in the social scale, or in any organized body; a grade of station or dignity, an order; hence, (one's) social position or standing. Also in phrases ***of high*** (etc.) ***rank***.

1596 DALRYMPLE tr. *Leslie's Hist. Scot.* VI. 347 He was bot of the mid ranck of nobles. **1611** TOURNEUR *Ath. Trag.* I. i, To put me in the habite of my ranque. **1651** HOBBES *Leviath.* II. xxx. 180 The aydes they give to men of inferiour rank. **1732** BERKELEY *Alciphr.* III. §17 Reasonable and well-educated men of all ranks. **1781** GIBBON *Decl. & F.* xxxv. (1869) II. 306 The boldest chieftains aspired to the rank of kings. **1791** MRS. RADCLIFFE *Rom. Forest* vi, An air of dignity which declared him to be of superior rank. **1853** LYTTON *My Novel* II. v, His descendants..took rank among the first commoners in England. **1873** MAX MÜLLER *Sc. Relig.* 347 Few men commanded greater respect in all ranks of Greek society.

b. High station in society, etc.; social distinction. Also in professional, military, and other walks of life. *concr.* persons of high position. Phr. ***to pull rank***: see PULL *v.* 20 g.

1742 SHENSTONE *Schoolmistress* 140 Some with rank she grac'd (The source of children's and of courtier's pride). **1776** *Trial of Nundocomar* 91/1, I heard..several persons of rank had been to pay salams. **1830** D'ISRAELI *Chas. I*, III. v. 75 The pride of rank was attended by one of its peculiar infirmities. **1883** FREEMAN *Impress. U.S.* 172 The rank and fashion of the older country does not shut itself up in a town. **1964** M. BANTON *Policeman in Community* iv. 116 One Carolina City officer had served in a United States army unit which was stationed alongside the Black Watch..and he commented: 'Why, a man with one stripe in that outfit had more rank than a master-sergeant in ours.' **1968** J. LOCK *Lady Policeman* xv. 129 Most days we wouldn't see any rank. **1972** J. R. T. POLLARD in G. W. Knight *Jackson Knight* 10 One who stood above rank,..and took just as much interest in the problems and activities of the..College domestic staff as he did in those of the students and his fellow academics. **1977** *Transatlantic Rev.* LX. 21 Why doesn't he wear his rank on his coat, he had once asked his mother.

9. a. A class (of persons, animals, or things) in a scale of comparison; hence, relative position or status, place. *spec.* in *Statistics*, position in a numerically ordered series; the number specifying the position. Cf. RANK *v.*[1] 3 b.

1605 SHAKS. *Macb.* III. i. 103 If you haue a station in the file, Not i' th' worst ranke of Manhood, say't. **1639** T. BRUGIS tr. *Camus' Mor. Relat.* 144 A Castle bearing such ranke as few are before it, but divers behind it in magnificence. *a* **1674** CLARENDON *Hist. Reb.* XI. §151 The Convertine, a Ship of the second Rank, that carried seventy Guns. **1774** GOLDSM. *Nat. Hist.* (1776) IV. 64 If we look through the different ranks of animals, from the largest to the smallest. *Ibid.* V. 107 The first rank in the description of birds, has been given to the eagle. **1851** RUSKIN *Stones Ven.* I. Pref. (1874) 8 To place in its true rank the general Gothic of the 13th century, in Italy. **1874** GREEN *Short Hist.* iii. §4. 128 Oxford stood in the first rank among English towns. **1883** F. GALTON *Inquiries into Human Faculty* 53 We are often called upon to define the position of an individual in his own series... In reckoning this, a confusion ought to be avoided between 'graduation' and 'rank', though it leads to no sensible error in practice. *Ibid.* 54 All..ranks stand half a degree short of the graduation bearing the same number. *Ibid.*, His rank of No. 5 will correspond to the graduation 4°.5. **1904** *Amer. Jrnl. Psychol.* XV. 81 Rank has..the useful property of allowing any two series to be easily and fairly combined into a third composite one. **1907** *Drapers' Company Res. Mem.* (Biometric Ser.) IV. 10, I term rank the actual position in order of an individual with regard to any variate in a given series obtained by measurement or observation. If v_1 be the 'rank' of an individual for a given character this signifies that in the observed population there are $v_1 - \frac{1}{2}$ individuals with character greater than x. **1936** *Ann. Math. Statistics* VII. 32 Continuous variates expressing these qualities are likely not to be normally distributed... We may therefore resort to the ranks, ignoring any exact values that have been assigned. **1943** M. G. KENDALL *Adv. Theory Statistics* xvi. 390 The ranks are ordinal numbers and cannot without justification be operated on by the laws of cardinal arithmetic. **1976** T. D. V. SWINSCOW *Statistics at Square One* x. 60 The ranks for the two samples are..added separately and the smaller total is used. *Ibid.* xii. 74 Boys K, L, and M are tied at rank 12.

b. *Linguistics.* The position of a unit in a grammatical or phonological hierarchy.

1961 *Word* XVII. 251 The units of grammar form a hierarchy... The relation among the units, then, is that.. each 'consists of' one, or of more than one, of the unit next below... The scale on which the units are in fact ranged.. may be called 'rank'. **1964** M. A. K. HALLIDAY et al. *Linguistic Sci.* 27 The term used to name the hierarchical relation among the units is *rank*; they can be arranged on a scale, and this is known as the 'rank scale'. **1965** J. C. CATFORD *Linguistic Theory of Translation* i. 6 The units of grammar or of phonology operate in hierarchies—'larger' or more inclusive units being made up of 'smaller' or less inclusive units. They form a scale of units at different ranks. .. The sentence is a unit of higher rank than the clause. *Ibid.* 9 The concept of rank..is an important one both in theoretical linguistics and..translation-theory. **1971** R. A. HUDSON *Eng. Complex Sentences* ii. 70 What a grammar will contain..is not a number of different system-networks, each for a different 'rank' (clause, phrase, etc.) or a different environment (subject, main verb, etc.), but a single network which includes all the grammatical systems needed for the language. **1977** *Language* LIII. 192 Although admitting that a sentence could be regarded as a special type of clause, she in fact treats them as distinct ranks.

10. *Math.* Used variously, at the discretion of the author, to denote some integer that characterizes the entity being discussed.

1835 *Rep. Brit. Assoc. Adv. Sci. 1834* 528 *i* in the denominator..names, according to the author's nomenclature, the 'order' of the logarithm, and *i*, in the numerator, its 'rank' in that order. **1913** C. E. CULLIS *Matrices & Determinoids* ix. 265 The rank of the matrix *A* is the greatest order which a non-vanishing derived determinant can have. **1914** H. HILTON *Homogeneous Linear Substitutions* ii. 50 Suppose that..the determinant itself and all the 1st, 2nd,.., $(m - r - 1)$-th minors vanish, but that not all the $(m - r)$-th minors vanish. Then the determinant is said to be of rank *r*. If the determinant does not vanish, it is of rank *m*; if the determinant vanishes but not every first minor vanishes, the determinant is of rank $m - 1$', and so on. **1941** [see NULLITY 6]. **1953** N. JACOBSON *Lect. Abstr. Algebra* II. i. 22 Any two maximal linearly independent subsets of a set *S* have the same cardinal number. We call this number the rank of the set *S*. **1965** J. J. ROTMAN *Theory of Groups* xi. 241 If *F* is a free group, the rank of *F*, $r(F)$, is the number of elements in a free set of generators. **1972** R. J. WILSON *Introd. Graph Theory* viii. 121 The rank $\rho(A)$ of a subset *A* of *E* is defined as the number of elements in the largest partial transversal of $\mathscr{S}$ contained in *A*. **1979** *Proc. London Math. Soc.* XXXVIII. 532 Let *G* be a reduced torsion-free abelian group of finite rank.

11. *Petrol.* The degree of metamorphic maturity or hardness, esp. of coal.

1914 *Bull. U.S. Bureau of Mines* No. 38. 4 The higher rank ('grade') of coal differs from the respective lower rank of the same genetic type by the effects of the greater metamorphism and devolatilization to which the higher rank of coal has been subjected. **1928** *Jrnl. Chem. Soc.* 2971 What we have termed the 'degree of coalification' of a coal is sometimes..termed its 'rank', a coal of lowest rank being one in which the processes of coalification..have had least result. **1948** *Mem. Geol. Soc. Amer.* No. 30. 55 Metamorphic rank and grade are synonymous terms denoting the stage of metamorphism reached. **1964** A. NELSON *Dict. Mining* 360 Lignite is a low-rank coal whilst anthracite is a high-rank coal. *Ibid.* 89 Coal rank indicates the stage of coalification which any particular coal deposit has reached between peat at one end of the scale and anthracite at the other. *Ibid.* 218 Hitt..came to the conclusion that in a vertical succession at any point in the coalfield the rank of the coals increased with the depth. **1976** *Nature* 1 July 48/1 Coals of various ranks have been treated in electrical arcs. **1979** *Sci. Amer.* Jan. 29/3 When adjustments are made for the inferior heating value of the lower ranks, the recoverable tonnage comes to about 600 billion tons of hard-coal equivalent, enough for more than 200 years' consumption at current rates.

12. *attrib.* and *Comb.*, as (sense 1) *-wise* adv.; (sense 3) ***rank-closing***, ***-fellow***; ***rank-breaking***, ***-worshipping*** adjs.; (sense 8) ***rank badge***, ***-class***, ***-distinction***, ***-holder***, ***-mark***, ***tab***; (sense 9 b) ***rank-scale***, ***-unit***; ***rank-based***, ***-bound*** adjs.; **rank correlation** *Statistics*, the correlation between two ways of assigning ranks to the members of a set; **rank difference** *Statistics*, the difference between two ranks assigned to the same thing; freq. *attrib.*; †**rank-toothed** *a.*, having a row of teeth; †**rank-work**, work set in straight lines. Also RANK ORDER.

1961 *Men Only* June 37/2 His eyes flicked contemptuously to the *rank badges on his right sleeve. **1975** T. ALLBEURY *Special Collection* v. 32 Wehrmacht men ..with their insignia and rank badges torn off. **1966** G. N. LEECH *Eng. in Advertising* ii. 11 A *rank-based description avoids these confusions, because of the insistence that each sentence should be fully described at all ranks. **1965** J. C. CATFORD *Linguistic Theory of Translation* ii. 25 The cruder attempts at Machine Translation are *rank-bound in this sense..; that is, they set up word-to-word or morpheme-to-morpheme equivalences, but not equivalences between high-rank units such as the group, clause or sentence. **1968** *Meta* XIII. 7 *Replacement* ..may be *rank-bound* (as when only word-to-word equivalences are sought) or unbounded (as when equivalences occur between higher rank units such as sentences). **1887** R. BROWN *Trilog. Life to Come* 76 *Rank-breaking Achilles. **1930** C. G. SELIGMAN *Races of Africa* ix. 221 The Akamba have age-grades, and within them *rank-classes. **1966** *New Society* 12 May 5/3 *Rank-closing had generally made the seamen as solid as a filled-in ditch... But there was more to the solidarity than just the rank-closing. **1907** *Drapers' Company Res. Mem.* (Biometric Ser.) IV. 25 No two *rank correlations are in the least reliable or comparable unless we assume that the frequency distributions are of the same general character..provided by the hypothesis of normal distribution. *Ibid.* 3 Dr. Spearman has suggested that rank in a series should be the character correlated, but he has not taken this rank correlation as merely the stepping stone..to reach the true correlation. **1943** M. G. KENDALL *Adv. Theory of Statistics* xvi. 391 A second coefficient of rank correlation which has certain advantages may be obtained as follows. *Ibid.* 408 Up to this point we have considered the problem of rank correlation without reference to any variate system which might underlie the rankings. **1977** S. A. BOOK *Statistics* xi. 427 The technique, called the Spearman test of 'rank correlation', requires us to rank each set of data and then compute the correlation coefficient of the ranks. **1904** *Amer. Jrnl. Psychol.* XV. 86 (*heading*) Method of *rank differences. **1907** *Drapers' Company Res. Mem.* (Biometric Ser.) IV. 39 Mean square of rank differences will be more accurate than mean positive rank difference. **1972** KAGAN & HAVEMANN *Psychol.* xiii. 485 In some cases it is convenient to use the rank-difference method, which produces a different coefficient of correlation called ρ. **1895** tr. *Ratzel's Hist. Mankind* I. 54 When the two halves of the race..show no recognition of *rank-distinctions. **1591** *Garrard's Art Warre* 84 Keeping his *ranck-fellowes justlie on both sides. **1951** S. F. NADEL *Found. Social Anthropol.* i. 18 As a *rank-holder.. features of social life on lower levels may be closed to you. **1928** C. F. S. GAMBLE *Story N. Sea Air Station* iv. 76 They were entitled to wear the 'curl' on their gold lace *rank-marks. **1964** *Rank scale [see sense 9 b above]. **1970** G. C. LEPSCHY *Survey of Structural Linguistics* vii. 124 Along the rank scale five grammatical units (sentence, clause, phrase, word, morpheme) and four phonological units (tone group, foot, syllable, phoneme) are used in English. **1974** 'G. BLACK' *Golden Cockatrice* xii. 212 Janey, in her neat uniform without *rank tabs. **1578** LYTE *Dodoens* III. xlvi. 381 Each leafe is *ranke toothed or snipt round about. **1968** *Rank unit [see *rank-bound* above]. **1677** CARY *Chronology* II. I. xx. 154 Several were in posture of time standing abreast, or *rank-wise. **1703** MOXON *Mech. Exerc.* 114 Any Straight or *Rank-work [*ed.* 1678 Range-work]. **1869** *Sat. Rev.* 25 Sept. 421/2 The *rank-worshipping mammas of the period.

†**rank**, *sb.*[2] *Obs. rare*$^{-1}$. [? cf. G. *rank* quinsy, garget.] A disease of birds.

1708 *Brit. Apollo* No. 97. 2/1 Many [birds] dye of the *Pip*, the *Rank*, &c.

rank (ræŋk), *a.*, (*sb.*[3],) and *adv.* Forms: 1–3 ranc, (3 rannc, rang), 3–5 ronke, 4–6 ronk, (5 rong), 4–7 ranke, (4 raunke, 7 rawnke), 6–7 rancke, (7 wrancke), 6–8 ranck, 4– rank. [OE. *ranc*, = (M)LG. *rank* long and thin, tall and slender (hence prob. Da. *rank* erect, upright, Sw. *rank* slender), ON. *rakkr* slender, bold.

The ultimate etym. is uncertain, but the stem may be an ablaut-var. of OS. *rink*, OE. *rinc* man (? full-grown man), warrior. The root-idea appears to be that of growing or shooting up, taken in its fullest sense in Eng., but in LG. (and ON.) restricted to height or length without corresponding breadth. The development of the word in Eng. is, however, far from clear, as the OE. uses are not quite the primitive ones. In ME. also it chiefly occurs in alliterative verse, app. more for convenience than to express definite meanings. In the later language the chief difficulty is to decide which of the more original senses are represented in the transferred uses.]

A. *adj.* **I.** †**1.** Proud, high-minded, haughty; froward, rebellious. *Obs.*

In OE. also proud or showy in dress: see Bosw.-Toller.

c **1000** ÆLFRIC *Deut.* xxi. 18 ȝif ænig man hæbbe modiȝne sunu and rancne [L. *protervum*]. *c* **1200** ORMIN 9622 Heh follc & rannc onn eorþe. *c* **1300** *Havelok* 2561 Yif þat ani were so rang [*rime* þank] That he þanne ne come anon..he sholde maken him þral. **13..** *E.E. Allit. P.* B. 455 þat was þe rauen so ronk þat rebel was euer. *c* **1440** *York Myst.* xxvi. 33 Þer is a ranke swayne Whos rule is noȝt right. *c* **1560** A. SCOTT *Poems* (S.T.S.) i. 188 This ȝeir..sall aryse Rowtis of þe rankest þat in Europ ringis.

2. a. Stout and strong. *Obs.* exc. *dial.* (in later use chiefly in ***rank wing***; cf. 3).

c **1122** *O.E. Chron.* (Laud MS.) an. 1006 þær mihton [hi] ȝeseon..rancne here & unearhne. *c* **1330** R. BRUNNE *Chron. Wace* (Rolls) 13,805 Was þer non helm wiþ stel so rank þat his swerd þorow-out ne sank. *c* **1400** *Destr. Troy* 4701 þere arof all the rowte with þere Ranke shippes. *Ibid.* 4709 A tried castell..[with] Ranke men with in. *c* **1470** *Gol. & Gaw.* 691 Ryngis of rank steill rattillit and rent. **1536** BELLENDEN *Cron. Scot.* v. vi. (1821) I. 177 Certane wycht and rank men tuke him be the middil. **1656** EARL MONM. tr. *Boccalini's Advts. fr. Parnass.* II. lxxvi. (1674) 228 That Pidgeon, which ..hath the rankest wing. **1710** *Last Distemper of Tom Whigg* II. 38 Ravens, cutting the Air at every Stroke of their rank Wing. **1824** R. GILCHRIST *Local Songs* (ed. 2) 5 Archy lang was hale an' rank, the King o' laddies braw.

b. Firm, strong. *rare*$^{-0}$.

1848 WEBSTER, *Rank*, strong, clinching. Take rank hold.

3. a. Having great speed or force; swift; impetuous; violent. Also const. *of*.

a **1225** *Ancr. R.* 268 His strencðes & his stronge [*T.* ronke] turnes. *c* **1275** *Serving Christ* 71 in *O.E. Misc.* 92 þe ronke racches þat ruskit þe ron. *a* **1300** *E.E. Psalter* lxxvii. 44 [He] turned in blode þar stremes ranke. **13..** *E.E. Allit. P.* A. 1166 Of raas þaȝ I were rasch & ronk, ȝet rapely þerinne I was restayed. **1560** ROLLAND *Crt. Venus* IV. 700 The rank riding, and the greit turnament. **1565** JEWEL *Repl. Harding* (1611) 340 M. Harding findeth him so farre, and so ranke of his side, that he is faine to checke him of too much riot, and to call him back. **1635** QUARLES *Embl.* v. ix. 278 The Hawlk ..makes a rank Bate from her forsaken Block. **1769** R. CUMBERLAND *Brothers* I. i, It blows a rank storm. *a* **1803** *May Collin* iv. in Child *Ballads* IV. 442/1 They came to a rank river, Was raging like the sea.

†**b.** ***rank rider***, a rapid, headlong, or reckless rider; a moss-trooper, highwayman. (Freq. in 17th c.) So ***rank-runner***. *Obs.*

1590 R. HARVEY *Pl. Perc.* (1860) 11 When a Rancke rider hath put his horse to a hedge and lay in the ditch for his labor. **1603** FLORIO *Montaigne* II. xxii. (1632) 382 Sure he was a rancke-runner: for where any river hindred his way, he swam it over. **1641** HINDE *J. Bruen* xi. 38 A good rule for our horse-racers, rank riders, and hot-spurre hunters..to measure their actions by. *a* **1700** B. E. *Dict. Cant. Crew*, *Rank-rider*, a High-way-man, also a Jockey.

fig. **1603** DEKKER *Wonderf. Yeare* A iv, Those ranck-riders of Art that haue spur-gald your lustie wingd Pegasus.

II. Full, large or gross in size, quantity, etc.

†**4.** Full-grown: mature. *Obs. rare.*

c **1000** ÆLFRIC *Saints' Lives* xxxv. 52 He funde..fif mædena..wlitiȝe and rance. **13..** *E.E. Allit. P.* B. 869 In Sodamas..non semloker burdes, Hit arn ronk, hit arn rype & redy to manne. **1536** BELLENDEN *Cron. Scot.* (1821) I. lvii, Al rank madinnis and wiffis, gif thay war nocht with child, yeid als weill to battall as the men.

5. Vigorous or luxuriant in growth. In later use: Growing too luxuriantly; large and coarse. Hence of growth, etc., and freq. as complement with *grow* or similar verbs.

In ***rank weed*** also with implication of sense 15.

c **1250** *Gen. & Ex.* 2105, .vii. eares wexen fette of coren, On an busk ranc and wel tidi. **13..** *Gaw. & Gr. Knt.* 513 Blossumez bolne to blowe, Bi rawez rych & ronk. **1398** TREVISA *Barth. De P.R.* XIV. iii. (1495) 470 Grasse and herbes that growe in valeyes..ben generall more ranke and fatte. **1526** *Pilgr. Perf.* (W. de W. 1531) 54 b, Our vyne waxeth ranke & must nedes be cutte. **1544** PHAER *Bk. Childr.* (1553) T iij, Take a good handful of ranke & lusty rew. **1605** SHAKS. *Lear* IV. iv. 3 Crown'd with ranke Fenitar, and furrow weeds. **1697** DRYDEN *Virg. Georg.* II. 340 Moist Earth produces Corn and Grass, but both Too rank and too luxuriant in their Growth. **1777** ROBERTSON *Hist. Amer.* IV. Wks. 1813 I. 257 The woods are choked with its rank luxuriance. **1832** R. & J. LANDER *Exped. Niger* II. xi. 148 We found the road to be overgrown with rank grass and luxuriant vegetation. **1850** R. G. CUMMING *Hunter's Life S. Afr.* (ed. 2) I. 195 The male lion is adorned with a long, rank, shaggy mane. **1892** *Speaker* 3 Sept. 290/1 This year the roses grew a little rank, and with an over-abundance of leaves.

fig. **1606** SHAKS. *Tr. & Cr.* I. iii. 318 The seeded Pride That hath to this maturity blowne vp In ranke Achilles.

†**6. a.** Excessively great or large; *esp.* swollen, puffed up, grossly fat, too highly fed. *Obs.*

c **1330** R. BRUNNE *Chron. Wace* (Rolls) 9720 He wax al blak, & bolned rank, & deyde. *c* **1400** *Destr. Troy* 1991 The flode..Rose vpon rockes as any ranke hylles. **1530** PALSGR. 322/1 Rammysshe, yll savoured as a man or beest that is to rancke. **1568** *Jacob & Esau* II. iv, Is that meate for you? nay, it would make you to ranke. Nay, soft brother mine, I must kepe you more lanke. **1612** DRAYTON *Poly-olb.* vii. 238 Teame lastly thither com'n with water is so ranke.

transf. **1597** SHAKS. *2 Hen. IV*, IV. i. 64 To dyet ranke Mindes, sicke of happinesse. *c* **1600** —— *Sonn.* cxviii, A healthful state Which, rank of goodness, would by ill be cured. **1631** T. POWELL *Tom All Trades* 167 For an over-flowing, and Ranker disposition.

†**b.** of immaterial things. *Obs.*

13.. *E.E. Allit. P.* C. 490 Is þis ryȝt-wys, þou renk, alle þy ronk noyse. *a* **1400** *Isumbras* 200 Nowther of tham myghte other stille, Thaire sorowe it was fulle ranke. *c* **1400** *Destr. Troy* 13902 þan the ruerde wax ranke of þat rught fare. **1633** HEYWOOD *Eng. Trav.* III. Wks. 1874 IV. 44 To stop this clamor ere it grow too wrancke.

c. High or excessive in amount. *Obs.* exc. *Law.*

1602 SHAKS. *Ham.* IV. iv. 22 Nor will it yield..A ranker rate, should it be sold in fee. **1765** BLACKSTONE *Comm.* II. iii. §3. 30 The *modus* must not be too large, which in law is called a *rank modus*. **1885** *Law Times Rep.* LII. 536/2 The modus..was rank, that is to say, that is was a pecuniary payment greater than the value of the tithes.

†**7. a.** Abundant, copious. *Obs.*

1303 R. BRUNNE *Handl. Synne* 5095 In sum man vnkynde-hede ys so rank þat he ne may cunne no man þank For no gode dede. **13..** *E.E. Allit. P.* A. 843 Wolle quyte so ronk & ryf. *c* **1400** *Destr. Troy* 8511 He hade no ruthe of hor remyng, ne þe rank teris. *a* **1568** ASCHAM *Scholem.* II. (Arb.) 112 Soch a rancke and full writer must use, if he will do wiselie, the exercise of a verie good kinde of epitome. **1579** SPENSER *Sheph. Cal.* July 211 When folke bene fat, and riches rancke, It is a signe of helth. **1632** LITHGOW *Trav.* VII. 301 The rank serene or dew of the night..refresheth all kindes of growing things.

†**b.** Abounding in, full *of*. *Obs.*

a **1300** *Cursor M.* 21024 O reson was nan sa ranc. *c* **1400** *Destr. Troy* 9204 Of Rent, & of Riches, rankir þan I. **1575** R. B. *Appius & Virg.* B ij, I neuer heard one so rancke of rudeness. **1652** C. B. STAPYLTON *Herodian* IV. 29 Rank of successe he was so puft with pride.

8. a. In close array, crowded together; thick, dense. *Obs.* exc. *north. dial.*

a **1400–50** *Alexander* 1319 Alexander..Ridis euen þurȝe þe route þar rankest þai were. **1513** DOUGLAS *Æneis* III. ix. 4 Than suddanlie, furth of the woddis ronk, We se a strange man. **1579** SPENSER *Sheph. Cal.* July 4 A goteheard..Whose straying heard them selfe doth shrowde Emong the bushes rancke. **1788** MARSHALL *Yorksh.* Gloss. (E.D.S.), *Rank*, standing in close order; thick upon the ground, as corn in the field, or trees in a wood. **1823** SCORESBY *Acc. Whale Fish.* 240 Endangered, while among rank ice, by a gale of wind. **1864** MRS. LYNN LINTON *Lake Country* 200 Where the sheep are 'rank' on the fell sides.

b. Numerous, frequent. *Obs.* exc. *north. dial.*

1545 ASCHAM *Toxoph.* I. (Arb.) 93 The Archers of England should not be only a great deale ranker, and mo then they be; but also a good deale bygger and stronger. **1551** ROBINSON tr. *More's Utop.* I. (1895) 43 Theues..were in euery place so ryffe and ranke. **1642** ROGERS *Naaman* To Rdr. b 3 b, Eighteene of this rable, all rife and ranke among us. **1868** ATKINSON *Cleveland Gloss.*, *Rank*, numerous, abundant, of frequent occurrence.

9. *techn.* Projecting, standing out.

1678 MOXON *Mech. Exerc.* 111 The Iron of a Plain is said to be set Ranck, when its edge stands so flat below the Sole of the Plain, that in working it will take off a thick shaving. **1727–41** CHAMBERS *Cycl.* s.v. *Keel*, When a ship has a deep keel, she is said to have a rank keel. **1867** F. FRANCIS *Angling* i. (1880) 19 The barb is so rank..that it often takes some time to unhook the fish. **1884** *Sci. Amer.* 17 July 32 Whether the tool used was a roughing tool with rank feed or a finish tool with fine feed.

III. Of a luxuriant, gross or coarse quality.

10. Covered or filled with a luxuriant (and coarse) growth of grass or plants.

rank pasture may also be taken in sense 5.

a **1400–50** *Alexander* 3060 As fele..As risonis in a ranke fild quen riders it spillen. **1538** STARKEY *England* I. iii. 98 When they [sheep] are closyd in ranke pasturys. **1612** DRAYTON *Poly-olb.* xiii. 398 Meadowes hugely ranke. **1735** SOMERVILLE *Chase* II. 29 In hopes Of plenteous Forage, near the ranker Mead. **1821** GALT *Sir A. Wylie* I. 44 A small garden rank with aplerings and other fragrant herbs. **1890** G. A. HENTY *Lee in Virginia* 209 The patch..though now rank with weeds, had evidently been carefully cultivated.

11. Grossly rich, heavy, or fertile; liable to produce rank vegetation.

c **1420** *Pallad. on Husb.* I. 104 Take the fatte and moyst is myn auise; Aftir hit the thikke and ronke is best. **1523** FITZHERB. *Husb.* §17 The moystnes of the dounge shall cause the grounde to be ranke ynoughe. **1615** G. SANDYS *Trav.* 151 Full of flowrie hils ascending leisurely, and not much surmounting their rancker vallies. **1760** BROWN *Compl. Farmer* II. 22 Where land is rank, it is not good to sow wheat after a fallow. **1789** G. WHITE *Selborne* i. (1853) 12 A rank clay that requires the labour of years to make it mellow. **1895** *Tablet* 9 Nov., The land is at first too 'rank' to grow corn or even root crops.

12. a. Having an offensively strong smell; rancid. †Also, smelling strongly *of*.

a **1529** SKELTON *E. Rummyng* 540 She brought a bore pygge; The fleshe therof was ranke. **1615** G. SANDYS *Trav.* 148 They are generally fat, and ranke of the sauors which attend vpon sluttish corpulency. **1656** RIDGLEY *Pract. Physick* 346 After that, add Discussives, as rank nuts. **1725** DE FOE *Voy. round World* (1840) 84 Our men made some butter..but it grew rank and oily. **1800** COLERIDGE *Piccolom.* I. iv, Pirates,..crowded in the rank and narrow ship. **1878** B. TAYLOR *Deukalion* I. ii. 24 The incense rank in censers burned, which seem to mask some odour of decay.

fig. **1602** SHAKS. *Ham.* III. iii. 36 Oh my offence is ranke, it smels to heauen. **1664** H. MORE *Myst. Iniq.* Apol. 545 To smell too rank of down-right Atheism.

b. Of smell: Offensively strong.

1570 LEVINS *Manip.* 24/28 Ranke smell, *magnus odor, olidus*. **1576** FLEMING *Panopl. Epist.* 274 Some ranke stinking sauour. **1697** DRYDEN *Virg. Georg.* III. 628 With that rank Odour from thy Dwelling-place To drive the Viper's Brood. **1735** POPE *Hor. Sat.* II. ii. 28 A stench.. Rank as the ripeness of a rabit's tail. **1834** PRINGLE *Afr. Sk.* viii. 268 The smell of the hyæna crocuta is so rank and offensive that scarcely any animal will come near the carcase.

†**13.** Lustful, licentious; in heat. *Obs.*

c **1520** *Mayd Emlyn* 289 in Hazlitt *E.P.P.* IV. 92 She was full ranke..In Venus toyes Was all her joyes. **1596** SHAKS. *Merch. V.* I. iii. 81 The Ewes being rancke,..turned to the Rammes. **1611** —— *Cymb.* II. v. 24 Lust, and ranke thoughts [are] hers. **1701** DE FOE *Trueborn Eng.* I. 289 Their Rank Daughters.. Receiv'd all Nations with Promiscuous Lust. **1765** *Treat. Dom. Pigeons* 25 A merry rank hen will sometimes shew and play almost like a cock.

14. a. Gross, highly offensive or loathsome; in later use *esp.* grossly coarse or indecent.

13.. *E.E. Allit. P.* B. 760, I tene hem no more, But relece alle þat regioun of her ronk werkkez. *c* **1400** *Destr. Troy* 11775 Couetous..That rote is & rankist of all the rif syns. *a* **1529** SKELTON *Agst. Scottes* 172 The rude ranke Scottes, lyke dronken dranes. **1611** SHAKS. *Wint. T.* I. ii. 277 My Wife..deserues a Name As ranke as any Flax-Wench, that puts to Before her troth-plight. **1742** YOUNG *Nt. Th.* v. 41 Hand in hand lead on the rank debauch. **1871** MORLEY *Voltaire* (1886) 5 The rank vocabulary of malice and hate.

b. Corrupt, foul; festering.

1579 Gosson *Sch. Abuse* (Arb.) 17 Yeelding the ranke fleshe to the Chirurgions knife. **1597** Shaks. *2 Hen. IV*, iii. i. 39 Then you perceiue..what ranke Diseases grow. **1634** Milton *Comus* 17 The rank vapours of this Sin-worn mould. **1727–46** Thomson *Summer* 1016 The scent Of steaming crowds, of rank disease, and death. **1862** Stanley *Jewish Ch.* (1877) I. ii. 26 Corrupt civilisation had growen up in the rank climate of that deep descent.

15. a. Of a strongly marked, violent, or virulent type; absolute, downright, gross. (Used to add force to terms implying the existence of bad qualities in a person or thing.)

1513 Douglas *Æneis* ii. iv. 37 Full of vennome and rank poyson. **1528** Roy *Rede me*, etc. (Arb.) 41 This is rancke heresy. **1550** Bale (*title*) The Apology of Johan Bale agaynste a ranke Papyst. *c* **1613** Middleton *No Wit like a Woman's* i. iii, 'Tis a most rank untruth. **1676** Marvell *Mr. Smirke* 12 The meanest Varlet, the dullest School-boy, the rankest Idiot. **1711** Addison *Spect.* No. 105 ¶5 What are these but rank Pedants? **1766** Fordyce *Serm. Yng. Wom.* (1767) I. iv. 148 Rank treason against the royalty of Virtue. **1809** Wellington in Gurw. *Desp.* (1837) V. 150 General Eguia's plan is rank nonsense. **1822–34** *Good's Study Med.* (ed. 4) II. 610 Those who are actually labouring under the disease, and in its rankest form. **1880** W. Day *Racehorse in Training* v. 40 A horse..which turned a rank roarer.

b. Grossly apparent. *rare.*

1624 Massinger *Parlt. Love* iv. i, 'Tis rank! The sight of my wife hath forced him to forget To counterfeit! **1784** Cowper *Tiroc.* 564 His pride resents the charge, although the proof Rise in his forehead, and seem rank enough.

†**B.** *sb.*[3] Rankness, strength. *Obs. rare*$^{-1}$.

13.. *E.E. Allit. P.* C. 298 Þurȝ mony a regioun ful roȝe, Þurȝ ronk of his wylle.

C. *adv.* †**1.** = rankly. *Obs.*

1590 Spenser *F.Q.* ii. iii. 6 The seely man, seeing him ryde so ranck..fell flatt to ground for feare. **1596** *Ibid.* iv. v. 33 The sound Of many yron hammers beating ranke.

2. With adjs.: Completely, extremely.

1607 Marston *What you Will* i. i, He's irrecoverable; mad, ranke madde. **1888** in *Sheffield Gloss.*

D. *Comb.* **a.** Parasynthetic adjs., as ***rank-brained, -leed, -minded, -scented, -winged.***

1614 Chapman *Masque Mid. Temple* Pref. A iij b, Insania, is that which euery *Ranck-brainde writer; and iudge of Poeticall writing, is rapt withal. **1703** *Art & Myst. Vintners* 18 The ill savour of *Rank-lee'd French wine. **1593** Harvey *Pierce's Super.* 147 Sweet Gossip,..the dunghill is your freehold:..I know none so *rank-minded. **1567** Golding *Ovid's Met.* x. (1593) 257 *Rankesented mints to make Of womens limmes. **1638** Junius *Paint. Ancients* 154 Some such like faces were painted neere the rank-sented mangers. **1637** T. Morton *New Eng. Canaan* (1883) 196 These [Lannarets] are most excellent Mettell, *rank winged, well conditioned. *a* **1700** B. E. *Dict. Cant. Crew, Rank-wing'd* Hawk, that is a slow Fligher.

b. With pa. pples., as ***rank-grown***, †***-rode, -set***, †***-smelt.***

1642 Vicars *God in Mount* (1644) 6 This evill weed so *rank-grown in the garden of the Kingdom. *c* **1611** Chapman *Iliad* iv. 414 The *rank-rode Cadmeans.. Lodg'd ambuscadoes for their foe. **1615** Brathwait *Strappado* (1878) 87 Flora..them did put In her embrodred skirts which were *rancke set, With Prime-rose, Cow-slip, and the violet. **1823** P. Nicholson *Pract. Builder* 229 The edge of the iron of a plane is said to be rank-set when it projects considerably below the sole. **1595** Barnfield *Pecuniæ* xxxi, Thy chafing hath begot A *ranke-smelt sauour.

c. With pres. pples., as ***rank-feeding, -riding, -scenting, -smelling, -springing, -swelling, -tasting.***

c **1820** *Philos. Recreat.* 20 The skins of large, or *rank-feeding birds. **1612** Drayton *Poly-olb.* iii. 40 The *rank-riding Scots upon their Galloways. **1735** Somerville *Chase* iv. 171 O'er Plains with Flocks distain'd *Rank-scenting. **1904** W. de la Mare *Henry Brocken* vii. 71 Near by me grew some *rank-smelling waterside plant. **1919** 'K. Mansfield' *Let.* 21 Nov. in *Lett. to J. M. Murry* (1951) 401, I remember standing in a rank-smelling field. **1816** Scott *Old Mort.* i, *Rank-springing grass. *a* **1649** Drumm. of Hawth. *Poems* Wks. (1711) 36 Loud-bellowing Clyde ..*Rank-swelling Annan. **1921** D. H. Lawrence *Sea & Sardinia* ii. 63 A massive yellow omelette..cooked in the usual *rank-tasting olive oil.

d. ***rank-old*** adj.; †**rank-goat** *Obs. rare*$^{-0}$ (see quot.).

1611 Cotgr., *Blanche-putain*, the hearbe *Ranke-goat, or stinking Motherwort. *a* **1889** G. M. Hopkins *Poems* (1967) 179 What being in *rank-old nature should earlier have that breath been.

rank (ræŋk), *v.*[1] Also 6–7 ranke, ranck, (7 rancke). [f. rank *sb.*[1]]

1. a. *trans.* To arrange or draw up (persons, *esp.* soldiers) in a rank or in ranks.

1573 *Satir. Poems Reform.* xxxix. 2 To ring ȝour drummis and rank ȝour men of weir. **1632** Lithgow *Trav.* v. 206, I haue seene hundreds of them after this manner, lie ranked like durty swine. **1667** Milton *P.L.* vi. 604 In view Stood rankt of Seraphim another row. **1726** Swift *Gulliver* iii. vii, We passed..between servants of the same sort, ranked on each side as before. **1814** Scott *Ld. of Isles* v. xiv, Upon the sand Let every leader rank his band. **1884** *Harper's Mag.* Nov. 884/2 The prisoners were then drawn up.., ranked six deep.

refl. **1612** Capt. Smith *Wks.* (Arb.) I. 72 These..ranked themselves 15 a breast, and each ranke from another 4 or 5 yards. **1686** tr. *Chardin's Trav. Persia* 88 They rank themselves, either in a circle, or side by side. **1726** Cavallier *Mem.* i. 99 My Men stood to their Arms, and ranked themselves in a fit Posture to receive them. **1865** Carlyle *Fredk. Gt.* vii. vii. (1872) II. 329 They all ranked themselves round me.

†**b.** = dress *v.* 4 a. *Obs. rare*$^{-1}$.

1604 Edmonds *Observ. Cæsar's Comm.* 131 The leader of the left hand file..with the leader of the right hand file do alwaies in their marching and imbattelling rectifie or rancke the whole front of the battallion.

2. a. To arrange (things) in a row or rows; to set in line; to put in order.

1590 Spenser *F.Q.* iii. vi. 35 And every sort is in a sondry bed Sett by it selfe, and ranckt in comely rew. **1650** Earl Monm. tr. *Senault's Man bec. Guilty* 304 He sought for stone..he ranked them with Symmetry. **1697** Dryden *Virg. Georg.* iv. 213 He knew to rank his Elms in even Rows. **1778** Reynolds *Disc.* viii. (1876) 453 A plain space in the middle, and the groups of figures ranked round this vacuity. **1833** *Fraser's Mag.* VIII. 62 Exerting all his mind in ranking up flower-pots. **1871** W. Alexander *Johnny Gibb* v. 45 The fishers gettin'..the nets rankit oot.

refl. **1707** *Curiosities in Husb. & Gard.* 331 Little Plants.. rank'd themselves in order around the sides of the Vial.

†**b.** To divide or form *into* ranks or classes. *Obs.*

1630 Prynne *Anti-Armin.* 123 An equipage..which all Diuines haue rancked into different orders. **1690** Locke *Hum. Und.* iii. iii. §19 Those Things we are acquainted with, and have ranked into Bands, under distinct Names.

†**c.** In *pa. pple.*, of a place: Surrounded or bounded with rows or ranks. *Obs.*

1607 Shaks. *Timon* i. i. 65 The Base o' th' Mount Is rank'd with all deserts, all kinde of Natures. **1623** J. Reynolds *God's Revenge* iii. xii. 79 A curious walk, ranked about with many rowes of Sycamore trees. **1698** Fryer *Acc. E. India & P.* 38 The Streets are sweet and clean, ranked with fine Mansions.

3. a. To place, locate; to give a certain position or station to; to class or classify. With various constructions. Also *refl.*

1592 Shaks. *Rom. & Jul.* iii. ii. 117 If sower woe..needly will be rankt with other griefes. **1612** Brinsley *Lud. Lit.* 7 To ranke euery head in the right order and proper place. **1666** Dryden *Ann. Mirab.* Pref., Wks. (Globe) 38 Those who rank Lucan rather among historians in verse than epic poets. **1713** Berkeley in *Guardian* No. 49 ¶6 A stranger would be apt to rank me with the other domestics. **1777** Miss Burney *Evelina* xxviii, Arguments, which..will rather rank me as an hermit. **1847** Tennyson *Princ.* ii. 32 Aftertime..Will rank you nobly, mingled up with me. **1875** Jowett *Plato* (ed. 2) III. 525 In ranking theories of physics first in the order of knowledge.

b. *Statistics.* To assign a rank to (rank *sb.*[1] 9 a).

1907 *Drapers' Company Res. Mem.* (Biometric Ser.) IV. 25 It is easier to rank individuals than to measure their attributes accurately. **1944** *Jrnl. Anat.* LXXVIII. 185/1 The severity of the inflammation can easily be ranked, i.e. given an ordinal number. **1951** Brookes & Dick *Introd. Statistical Meth.* ix. 221 It is possible to rank depths of colour without requiring some form of graduated scale, and to rank dimensions of objects..by comparing one with another and arranging them in sequence. **1977** [see *rank correlation* s.v. rank *sb.*[1] 12].

4. *Sc. Law.* To place (orig. in order of precedence) on the list of claims, or of those having claims, on a bankrupt estate.

1695 [see ranking *vbl. sb.*[1] b]. **1711** *Acts Sederunt* 23 Nov. (1790) 251 The creditors shall..name the Lord..before whom their severall rights and interests are to be ranked. **1735** *Ibid.* 29 July (1790) 306 All creditors..shall come in, and be ranked *pari passu* upon the moveable estate. **1859** J. Lorimer *Handbk. Law Scot.* (1862) 307 All arrestments and poindings..shall be ranked *pari passu.*

5. a. orig. and chiefly *U.S.* To take precedence of.

1841 *Southern Lit. Messenger* VII. 766/1, I have Mr. Sanford under my command—I *rank* him,..and then I have charge of the *whole* ship. **1860** *Congress. Globe* 10 Dec. 27/3, I shall..submit a few reasons for this opinion..but not until other Senators are heard who rank me in age, experience, and wisdom. **1865** *N.Y. Herald* in *Morning Star* 27 May, 'That's right', politely observed Grant, 'the President ranks us both'. **1893** J. Strong *New Era* 153 A growing class of idle rich,..who..rank Solomon himself in luxury. **1904** *Delineator* Dec. 933 The Secretary of State ranks all the other members of the Cabinet. **1907** [see importance 2 b]. **1976** J. Wainwright *Who goes Next?* 177 Bear..ranked Sullivan, neck-and-neck—they were both deputy chief constables.

b. *U.S. Mil.* To deprive or turn (someone) *out* of quarters, etc., by virtue of superior rank.

1872 F. M. A. Roe *Army Lett.* (1909) 66 Faye has been turned out of quarters—'ranked out', as it is spoken of in the Army. **1891** C. King *Trials of Staff Officer* 184 We were 'ranked' out of those quarters presently. **1932** L. H. Nason *Among Trumpets* 13 What's the good of havin' three stripes if you can't rank somebody out of a bunk or horse or something?

c. *U.S. Blacks.* (See quots.) Cf. ranking *vbl. sb.*[1] c.

1971 C. Mitchell-Kernan in A. Dundes *Mother Wit* (1973) 316/2 'Barbara was trying to *rank* Mary', to put her down by typing her. **1974** H. L. Foster *Ribbin', Jivin', & Playin' Dozens* iv. 171 *Rank*, to insult someone. **1978** *English Jrnl.* Dec. 56/1 'We're ranking people out'..'What does that mean?' I asked...'We're saying things about other people to put them down,' answered one helpful student.

6. a. *intr.* To form a rank or ranks; to stand in rank; to take up a position in a rank.

1582 Stanyhurst *Æneis* ii. (Arb.) 58 Soom bands of Troians..Ranck close too geather, thee Greeks most manlye repealing. **1605** Marston *Dutch Courtezan* iv. i, Harke they are at hande, ranke handsomly. **1796** Southey *Hymn to Penates* 11 In your holy train Jove proudly ranks. **1865** S. Ferguson *Forging of Anchor* i, Fitfully you still may see the grim smiths ranking round.

b. To take or have a place in a certain rank or class; to have rank or place. Const. as in 3. Also in phr. ***to rank high.***

1599 Shaks. *Hen. V*, v. ii. 474, I pray you..Let that one Article ranke with the rest. **1745** *Observ. conc. Navy* 45 Colonels dispute the Right of Captains of Men of War ranking with them. **1784** Cowper *Tiroc.* 465 A principle.. That..Ranks as a virtue, and is yet a vice. **1805** Mrq. Wellesley in Owen *Desp.* (1877) 499 Holkar never had ranked among the states of India. **1824** Macaulay in *Knight's Q. Mag.* II. 357 Ovid, Catullus, Tibullus, Horace, and Propertius, in spite of all their faults must be allowed to rank high in this department of the art. **1828** Carlyle *Crit. & Misc. Ess.* (1840) I. 157 This play should rank high among that class of works. **1850** Merivale *Rom. Emp.* (1865) II. xi. 17 Surenas ranked next to the king in birth, wealth and distinction. **1885** *Nature* 8 Jan. 223/2 The man who ranks 5th from the bottom of a class of 100 males would rank 10th from the top in a class of 100 females. **1932** *N.Y. Times Book Rev.* 3 Jan. 9/5 Nevertheless, as an imaginative humorist he ranks very high, and his omnibus can be warmly recommended to those who have hitherto been unfamiliar with his work. **1973** *Daily Tel.* (Colour Suppl.) 13 July 9/1 Diplomats caught have ranked up to ambassador.

c. *Law.* Of creditors or claims (see 4). Also, to qualify *for.*

1883 *Law Times Rep.* XLIX. 75/2 It was contended..that they were..creditors entitled to rank next after the outside creditors (if any), or even with them. **1891** *Law Times* XCII. 106/2 Burdens arising after the first registration of the land rank in the order of their registration. **1899** I. Pitman *Commercial Corresp.* xix. 197 Statement of Affairs: Cross Liabilities; Liabilities as Estimated by Debtor; Expected to Rank; [etc.]. **1928** *Daily Mail* 3 Aug. 18/2 The new shares did not rank for the interim dividend. **1930** *Daily Express* 22 May 7/4 Mr. Bottomley's amended statement of affairs showed gross liabilities £116,769, ranking at £115,899. **1976** *Milton Keynes Express* 11 June 13/1 There may well be very considerable sums to be spent on essential repairs which will not rank for subsidy aid.

7. *intr.* To move or march in rank; chiefly *Mil.* in ***to rank past, off.***

1832 *Prop. Reg. Instr. Cavalry* iii. 59 In ranking past by Threes there is to be a horse's length from croup to head. **1833** *Regul. Instr. Cavalry* i. 64 They rank off alternately. **1840** Carlyle *Heroes* ii. (1858) 236 Your cattle..come ranking home at evening-time.

8. *trans. U.S. slang.* **a.** To betray (a person), to give away (in quot. *refl.*). Also, to apprehend in the act of committing a crime.

1929 [see fuzz *sb.*[3]]. **1955** D. W. Maurer in *Publ. Amer. Dial. Soc.* xxiv. 175 *Whiz dicks* are on the lookout..to *rank* a pickpocket.

b. To spoil or thwart (an action), esp. in phr. ***to rank the play.***

1937 C. Himes *Nigger* in *Black on Black* (1973) 125 The landlady..had sent Mr. Shelton on up to catch him there in the hopes of ranking Fay's play. **1968–70** *Current Slang* (Univ. S. Dakota) III–IV. 101 *Rank*, to spoil.

Hence **ˈranking** *ppl. a.* (freq. in sense 5 of the vb.).

1863 *Yale Lit. Mag.* XXIX. 80 His two ranking officers both gone. **1865** *Bill of Confed. States Amer.* in *Morning Star* 2 Feb., An officer..designated as General-in-Chief, who shall be the ranking officer of the army..of the Confederate States. **1885** E. Custer *Boots & Saddles* xiii. 137 The ranking lady had a sabre which her chief had received as a present, and this she waved over the others in command. **1895** *Daily News* 27 Aug. 2/7 The total ranking liabilities may amount to between 15,000*l.* and 20,000*l.* **1906** *Westm. Gaz.* 4 Apr. 7/2 It was estimated that his [*sc.* the bankrupt's] ranking indebtedness would be about £2,280. **1925** T. Dreiser *Amer. Tragedy* (1926) II. ii. xlvii. 73 These tall, close, ranking pines. **1931** *Publishers' Weekly* 20 June 2849/1 The publishing industry of this country.. now takes a ranking place in the economic structure. **1962** Plano & Greenberg *Amer. Polit. Dict.* vii. 141 *Ranking member*, that member of the majority party on a legislative committee who ranks first after the chairman in number of years of continuous service (seniority) on the committee. **1970** E. R. Johnson *God Keepers* xii. 132 There was a lot of merit in having the ranking man right where the heat was going to be. **1974** P. Gore-Booth *With Great Truth & Respect* 315, I learned it on the afternoon of a Sunday on which we had arranged for a dinner in honour of Sir James Cassels, the new British Chief of the General Staff. The ranking guest was to be General Muchu Chaudhuri, the Indian Commander-in-Chief. **1976** *Washington Post* 19 Apr. B6/5 Six ranking generals carried the coffin to the simple military grave. **1976** H. Wilson *Governance of Britain* vii. 150, I approached Sir John Arbuthnot, then, as the Americans would have put it, 'ranking' Conservative Member on the Committee. **1978** R. Ludlum *Holcroft Covenant* xv. 175 The offspring of a ranking member of the Third Reich's High Command.

rank, *v.*[2] *rare.* Also 3 ronke. [f. rank *a.*]

†**1.** *intr.* To grow rank; to rankle. *Obs. rare.*

a **1325** *Prov. Hending* xi. in *Anglia* IV. 193 Wel is him þat sunne hateþ, And þat hit leteþ and forsakeþ, Er hit ronke in rote. **1330** R. Brunne *Chron.* (1810) 205 An alblastere.. smote him in þe schank..It began to rank, þe querelle Envenomed was. **1606** J. Davies *Sel. 2nd Husband* (Grosart) 9 T'will swell vnseene, Which ranking inward, outward shews thy teene.

2. *trans.* To cause to project. (Cf. rank *a.* 9.)

1867 F. Francis *Angling* xiv. 410 The point of the hook being ranked outwards slightly.

†**rank,** *v.*[3] intr. *Obs. rare.* (Origin and precise sense not clear.)

a **1529** Skelton *Caudatos Anglos* 56 That dronke asse, That ratis and rankis..On Huntley bankes. *a* **1783** *Gil Brendon* lxi. in Child *Ballads* I. 69/2 An ay she ranked, an ay she flang, Till a' the tokens came till her han.

†**rank**, *v.*[4] *Obs. rare.* [ad. late L. *rancāre* (al. *raucāre*, *raccāre*).] *intr.* Of a tiger: To roar. Hence †'**ranking** *vbl. sb.* and *ppl. a.*

1607 TOPSELL *Four-f. Beasts* 708 The voice of this beast is cald Ranking, according to this verse: *Tigrides indomitæ rancant. Ibid.*, A tame Tiger.. by her ranking and crying voice.. made signes to her keeper for other meate. *Ibid.* 709 She maketh.. great lamentation upon the Sea shoare howling, braying and rancking.

'**rank-and-file**, *a.* [f. *rank and file*: RANK *sb.*[1] 5 b.] **a.** *Mil.* Of or belonging to the rank and file; private; ordinary.

1885 [see CHEW *v.* 3 g]. **1904** *Westm. Gaz.* 27 Feb. 2/3 Those who know the rank-and-file men of the Russian army will agree. **1907** *Daily Chron.* 19 Dec. 3/3 The memoirs of a rank-and-file man like this are very touching and painful reading. **1966** *Times* 9 July 9/7 Command Orders say.. Rank and File Mess is altered to 'soldiers' mess'.

b. *transf.* Of, pertaining to, or designating an ordinary member of a group (as a political party, union, etc.) as opp. to a leader or principal.

1887 *Century Mag.* Nov. 42/1 Some rank-and-file chairs besides. **1931** *Times Lit. Suppl.* 4 June 437/2 He always assumed that the rank-and-file politician was actuated by his own high motives. **1945** KOESTLER *Yogi & Commissar* III. i. 131 The absence of any rank-and-file influence on the party-line. **1955** *Times* 2 May 17/4 He came in for much criticism for not being in touch with the rank-and-file members of his union. **1974** *Times* 19 Sept. 1/1 No party leader or rank-and-file MP can exclude.. the possibility.. that.. the electorate may once again create a parliamentary deadlock. **1976** *Church Times* 15 Oct. 13/1 More than twenty years ago a refreshing, highly competent and, for rank-and-file Christians in the parishes, most stimulating and encouraging publishing event took place. **1977** *Times* 7 Sept. 4/3 That might be because many rank-and-file union members are unenthusiastic about the so-called war on Grunwick.

,**rank-and-'filer.** orig. *U.S.* [f. as prec. + -ER[1].] A member of the rank and file; an ordinary member (of a group, society, etc.).

1940 *Sat. Even. Post* 27 Jan. 82/1 Others assert he never in his life toiled as an active rank-and-filer. **1943** *Sun* (Baltimore) 1 June 10/2 Many of the AFL transit rank and filers—perhaps even many of their union leaders—agree at heart with Messrs. Green and Katz. **1950** E. H. CARR *Bolshevik Rev.* I. ii. 33 Lenin's followers were rank-and-filers with scarcely a known name among them. **1959** *Encounter* Aug. 74/2 No 'ordinary people', no John Doe, Tommy Atkins, rank-and-filer, man-in-the-street. **1966** *New Statesman* 13 May 680/1 Some 30 members of the union's executive are sea-going ex-rank-and-filers. *a* **1974** R. CROSSMAN *Diaries* (1976) II. 63 Three of the rank-and-filers were ultra-left-wingers and my part of the programme developed into a futile shouting match. **1978** S. BRILL *Teamsters* i. 25 Barkett was more involved in the union than most rank-and-filers.

ranked (ræŋkt), *ppl. a.*[1] [f. RANK *v.*[1] + -ED.]

1. Drawn up in ranks.

1786 BURNS *Toothache* v, And ranked plagues their numbers tell In dreadfu' raw. **1837** CARLYLE *Fr. Rev.* II. II. vi, The ranked Regiments hear it in their meadow. **1897** H. N. HOWARD *Footsteps Proserpine* 106 A woman.. Braves the ranked cohorts.

2. *Statistics.* Assigned a position in a series.

1907 *Drapers' Company Res. Mem.* (Biometric Ser.) IV. 36 The actual size of organ corresponding to a bracket rank may differ widely from the size really belonging to the ranked organ. **1931** *Biometrika* XXIII. 396 The mean interval between any two individuals in a ranked series. **1937** YULE & KENDALL *Introd. Theory Statistics* (ed. 11) xiii. 247 We arrange the students *in order* of their ability... We then allot to each student a number which indicates his position... The students are then said to be *ranked*, and the number of a particular individual is his rank.

†'**ranked**, *ppl. a.*[2] *Obs.* [f. RANK *a.*] Rancid.

1660 HEXHAM, *Vergarst*, Ranked, or Growne mustie.

rankel(l, obs. forms of RANKLE *sb.* and *v.*

†'**ranken**, *v. Obs. rare.* Also 7 **ranckn-**. [f. RANK *a.* + -EN.] *trans.* To make rank.

1614 C. BROOKE *Ghost Rich. III, Tragedie* xxix, My barren heart.. ranckned with sinn's ayre.. brought thornes of sharp despaire. **1651** BAXTER *Inf. Bapt.* 135 To dispatch men out of the world.. and to ranken Church-Yards.

ranker ('ræŋkə(r)). [f. RANK *sb.*[1] and *v.*[1] + -ER.]

1. One who arranges in ranks (Webster 1832).

2. One (esp. a soldier) in the ranks.

1890 [see GENTLEMAN 7]. **1891** *Daily News* 13 Mar. 3/5 Rankers in the Navy have thus had an object lesson presented to the world in their interests. **1898** *Echo* 5 Jan. 1/7 In the list of officers who have been 'rankers'.

3. An officer who has risen from the ranks.

1878 BESANT & RICE *Celia's Arb.* II. xiii. 112 Every regiment has its 'rankers'; every ranker has his story. **1881** *Echo* 21 Mar. 1/5 This most deserving class of officers are 'rankers' to a man. **1905** *Daily Chron.* 11 May 4/7 The 'ranker' officer.. has been explaining how his bankruptcy was due to expenses connected with his promotion. **1926** A. BENNETT *Lord Raingo* I. xxxi. 143 He regretted his humorous remarks to her about the war.. for they took no account of the daily torture of millions of young men, including Delphine's own promoted ranker. **1943** J. W. DAY *Farming Adventure* (1949) xviii. 210 The village and the Army discussed ranker-officers with great candour. There had been two of them at the Hall with a previous unit —an ex-farmer and an ex-sergeant-major.

rankest ('ræŋkɪst), *a. colloq.* (chiefly *U.S.*). Now *rare.* [Irreg. f. RANK *sb.*[1] + -EST, as adj. of superlative degree; cf. RANK *v.*[1] 5 and RANKING *ppl. a.*] Of the highest rank; most senior, 'rankingest'.

1907 B. M. CROKER *Company's Servant* xxiv. 257 All the 'Rankest' or senior ladies, had received their due meed of attention. **1926** *Sat. Even. Post* 6 Mar. 154 As he's the rankest man he'll have to take charge while I'm gone. **1930** T. FREDENBURGH *Soldiers March!* 86 It's very hard on a self-respecting Corporal to be seen publicly with the rankest soldier in the outfit.

ranket(t, var. RACKETT.

†'**rankfully**, *adv. Obs. rare*⁻¹. Rankly.

1607 TOPSELL *Four-f. Beasts* 755 The Sabel.. at that time stincketh very rankefully.

rankil(l, obs. forms of RANKLE *v.*

Rankine ('ræŋkɪn). [The name of William John Macquorn *Rankine* (1820–72), Scottish physicist and engineer.] **1.** Used *attrib.* or in the possessive to designate concepts propounded by Rankine or arising out of his work, as **Rankine cycle**, a thermodynamic cycle which describes the operation of an ideal composite engine worked by steam or another condensable vapour, and is used as a standard of efficiency; **Rankine efficiency**, the efficiency of an engine relative to that of an ideal engine following the Rankine cycle; **Rankine's** (occas. **Rankine**) **formula**, any of a number of formulæ derived by Rankine in his work in various fields; *spec.* (see quot. 1940).

1868 J. BOURNE *Treat. Steam-Engine* (ed. 8) i. 86/1 (*heading*) Rankine's formula. **1891** S. ANGLIN *Design of Structures* xi. 209 Apply Rankine's formula to determine the breaking weight of a wrought-iron hollow cylindrical column, its length being 10 feet, [etc.]. **1896** R. H. THURSTON in *Jrnl. Franklin Inst.* CXLII. 444 Comparing the efficiency of the best modern steam-engine employing saturated steam, about 0·20, with the Rankine cycle, which is that ideal cycle which constitutes the closest approximation to its method of steam distribution, the ideal case giving an absolute efficiency, 0·25, it is found to have, measured by this latter standard, a relative efficiency of 80 per cent. **1897** J. A. EWING *Steam-Engine* (ed. 2) iv. 120 Rankine's formula ought to be applicable when the amount of superheating is very great. **1907** W. H. P. CREIGHTON *Steam Engine* viii. 196 This engine is one which follows the Rankine cycle, where steam at a constant pressure is admitted into the cylinder with no clearance, and after the point of cut-off is expanded adiabatically to the back pressure. **1913** J. DUNCAN *Appl. Mech. for Engineers* x. 237 At present, most designers rely on the Rankine formula coupled with a liberal factor of safety. **1930** *Engineering* 6 June 739/3 The new Barton turbine is $8\frac{1}{2}$ per cent. more efficient relative to the Rankine cycle than the older units. **1933** T. H. TAFT *Elem. Engin. Thermodynamics* ix. 130 (*heading*) Effect on the Rankine efficiency of changing conditions. **1940** *Chambers's Techn. Dict.* 702/2 *Rankine's formula*, an empirical formula giving the collapsing load for a given column. **1954** L. PILBOROUGH *Appl. Heat & Heat Engines* xviii. 313 The Rankine efficiency may be used when determining the efficiency ratio of a steam plant. **1967** *Trans. Inst. Engineers & Shipbuilders in Scotland* CX. 21 As turbine efficiency increases with superheat and decreases with pressure the Rankine efficiency gains are modified accordingly. **1976** T. J. REYNOLDS et al. *Struct. Steelwork* (ed. 14) xi. 237 Using Rankine's formula, find the safe axial load for a 308 × 305 × 97 kg universal column 3·3 m high —to be regarded as having ends fixed—using the usual constraints for mild steel and adopting a factor of safety of 4. **1978** *Jrnl. R. Soc. Arts* CXXVI. 608/2 We have not, however, been complacent about more advanced thermodynamic cycles. We have studied a number of possibilities of achieving higher thermal efficiency than the Rankine cycle used in most of our existing plant.

2. Used *attrib.* to designate a temperature scale in which the zero is identified with absolute zero and the degrees are equal in size to those on the Fahrenheit scale. Also ***degree Rankine*** (or ***Rankine degree***), a degree of this scale; ***Rankine temperature***, a temperature expressed in terms of this scale.

1941 H. T. WENSEL in *Temperature* (Amer. Inst. Physics) i. 10 The Rankine Scale is essentially the same scale [as the Kelvin]. Temperatures on the Rankine Scale are simply 9/5 of temperatures on the Kelvin Scale. **1941** L. S. MARKS *Mech. Engineers' Handbk.* (ed. 4) 295 Degrees Rankine (R) = degrees Fahrenheit + 459·69. **1962** J. THEWLIS *Encycl. Dict. Physics* VII. 207/1 On the Rankine scale, absolute zero is zero degree Rankine, the freezing point of water is 491·7° and the boiling point of water 671·7°. **1963** EASTOP & MCCONKEY *Appl. Thermodynamics* i. 8 Note that 1 Kelvin degree is equivalent to 1·8 Rankine degree. **1974** P. L. MOORE et al. *Drilling Practices Manual* v. 131 T_s = Temperature at surface, degrees Rankine.

ranking ('ræŋkɪŋ), *vbl. sb.*[1] [f. RANK *v.*[1]] **a.** The action of placing in rank, arranging, etc. Also, the outcome of such action; ordering, classification. Also *attrib.*

1625 J. GLANVILL *Voy. to Cadiz* (Camden) 16 The nameing and rankeing of the shipps. **1693** EVELYN *De la Quint. Compl. Gard.* Pref., They are ill contrived in the Disposition and Ranking of the things contained in them. **1903** *Daily Chron.* 29 Sept. 3/1 The provision of additional ranking accommodation [for cabs] in suitable places. **1909** *N.Y. Even. Post* 31 Dec. 4/5 William A. Larned.. and Hackett and Alexander.. lead the tennis players, according to the official ranking. **1926** W. S. BRUCE *Salt & Sense* viii. 64 The men of money are supposed to be above the men of mind. That ranking is entirely wrong. **1939** A. E. TRELOAR *Elem. Statistical Reasoning* iii. 38 Arrangement of a series of values in order of magnitude is known as ranking. **1948** *Sporting Mirror* 21 May 14/1 According to American world ranking he places one higher than our own Alan Paterson. **1962** C. L. BARBER in F. Behre *Contrib. Eng. Syntax* 28 The complete ranking-order of the ten tenses in my material is as follows: 1. Present Simple Active (64%). 2. Present Simple Passive (25%) [etc.]. **1969** C. DAVIDSON in Cockburn & Blackburn *Student Power* 345 The question of ranking and university complicity with the Selective Service System needs to be tied to a general anti-draft and 'No Draft for Vietnam' movement. **1978** *Taxi* 16 Feb. 17/2 All the Airport hotels refused.. to allow ranking facilities on their premises.

b. *Sc. Law*, with ref. to creditors or claims on an estate (see RANK *v.*[1] 4 and 6 c); also in phr. ***ranking and sale*** (cf. quot. 1711).

1695 *Acts Sederunt* 2 Nov. (1790) 215 The ranking of the creditors.. shall proceed. **1711** *Ibid.* 23 Nov. (1790) 249 Act anent Bankrupts, the Ranking of their Creditors, and Sale of their Estates. *Ibid.*, The raiser of a process of sale and ranking. **1773** ERSKINE *Inst. Law Scot.* I. II. xii. 409 An action of ranking and sale, which is calculated for the common interest of all the creditors. **1882** WATSON *Bell's Dict. Law Scot.* 800 Ranking and sale.. is now practically superseded by the simpler procedure provided by the Bankruptcy Act.

c. *U.S. Blacks.* (See quot. 1958.) Cf. RANK *v.* 5 c.

1958 W. B. MILLER in *Jrnl. Social Issues* XIV. III. 16 The term 'ranking', used to refer to the pattern of intra-group repartee, indicates awareness of the fact that this is one device for establishing the intra-group hierarchy. **1974** H. L. FOSTER *Ribbin', Jivin', & Playin' Dozens* v. 183 In a Brooklyn, New York, secondary school the terms ranking and sounding are still used.

ranking, *vbl. sb.*[2]: see RANK *v.*[4]

rankinite ('ræŋkɪnaɪt). *Min.* [f. the name of G. A. *Rankin* (1884–1963), U.S. physical chemist + -ITE[1].] A white, monoclinic polymorph of a calcium silicate, $Ca_3Si_2O_7$, of which kilchoanite is another polymorph.

1942 C. E. TILLEY in *Mineral. Mag.* XXVI. 194 For the new mineral the name rankinite is now proposed in honour of Mr. G. A. Rankin, who has contributed so much to our knowledge of the binary and ternary systems in which it was first discovered as a constituent phase. **1961** [see KILCHOANITE]. **1966** W. A. DEER et al. *Introd. Rock-forming Minerals* I. 77 Rankinite occurs at contacts between limestone and basic igneous rocks, as at Scawt Hill, Northern Ireland, and Ardnamurchan. **1974** *Mineral. Abstr.* XXV. 322/1 Rankinite occurs in the metasomatic formations of the Anakitsk trap massif, in the Lower Tunguska area [of the U.S.S.R.], where it is associated with other high-temperature phases.

†'**rankish**, *a. Obs. rare.* [f. RANK *a.* + -ISH.] Somewhat rank.

1398 TREVISA *Barth. De P.R.* XVII. clxviii. (1495) 711 Fatte and rankysshe whete and heuy of weyghte. **1589** FLEMING *Virg. Georg.* II. 31 These able are for rankish soile. **1661** LOVELL *Hist. Anim. & Min.* 225 They have an unpleasant smell and taste, or rankish.

†'**rankle**, *sb.*[1] *Obs. rare.* In 4 rancle, 6 *Sc.* rankel. [a. OF. *rancle* (*raancle*, *raoncle*) a fester, ulcer, var. *drancle*, *draoncle* (see Godef.) = med.L. *dranculus* and *dracunculus*, which in form is a dim. of *draco* dragon: see Skeat *Notes Eng. Etym.* (1901) s.v.] A festering sore.

c **1380** in *Rel. Ant.* I. 52 The rancle sal abate.. the sare sal slake. **14..** *Stockh. Medical MS.* i. 160 in *Anglia* XVIII. 298 þanne wyl þis playster al rancles slon. *a* **1585** POLWART *Flyting w. Montgomerie* 556 With scartes and scores athort his frozen front, In rankels run.

'**rankle**, *sb.*[2] [f. RANKLE *v.*] A rankling thought or feeling. Also without article, rankling, bitterness.

1795 EARL MALMESBURY *Diaries & Corr.* III. 220, I could see it did not please, and left a rankle in his mind. **1913** H. SUTCLIFFE *Open Road* xviii. 275 She won't get the rankle out of her mind. **1922** *Blackw. Mag.* June 710/2, I had come prepared to find they loved us as much as we loved the Germans—or perhaps the rankle might be unkinder, for we did not lose the war. **1941** B. WEBB *Why does God permit Evil?* 117 Suffering ill borne causes rankle in the soul.

rankle ('ræŋk(ə)l), *v.* Forms: 4–5, 7, (9) **rancle**, 6 **rankel(l**, **-kil(l**, **-kyll**, 6–7 **ranckle**, 7– **-el**, 6– **rankle**; *erron.* 7 **wranckle**, 8–9 **wrankle**. [a. OF. *rancler*, *raoncler*, var. *draoncler* (Godef.): see RANKLE *sb.*[1]]

I. *intr.* **1.** To fester, esp. to a degree that causes pain. †**a.** of a wounded or diseased part of the body; also *rarely* of a person. *Obs.*

c **1320** *Sir Beues* 2832 (MS. A.) Þar þe venim on him felle, His flesch gan ranclen. *c* **1425** *Orolog. Sapient.* v. in *Anglia* X. 363/5 Þe handes vnweldy bigynnen to rancle. **1486** *Bk. St. Albans* A iij b, It will.. maake the legges to rancle. *c* **1592** MARLOWE *Jew of Malta* II. ii, Therewithal their knees would rankle. **1616** T. ADAMS *Taming of Tongue* Wks. (1629) 153 A Leaper shut vp in a Pesthouse, ranckleth to himselfe, infects not others. **1646** SIR J. TEMPLE *Irish Rebell.* (1746) 206 Her hand grew black and blew, [and] rankled.

b. of a wound, sore, disease, etc. In later use chiefly *fig.*

1523 LD. BERNERS *Froiss.* I. xciii. 115 His soores rankeled and.. within a shorte space after he dyed. **1553** BRENDE *Q. Curtius* G vij, The wound.. beganne to swele and rancle as the bloud waxed colde. **1642** ROGERS *Naaman* 336 Which makes their disease to ranckle in them. **1741** RICHARDSON *Pamela* (1824) I. 204 The wound.. is but skinned over, and rankles still at the bottom. *a* **1828** H. NEELE *Lit. Rem.* (1829) 331 When the heart's wounds Rankle the sorest. **1875**

STUBBS *Const. Hist.* III. xviii. 49 The king forgave Mowbray ..but the sore rankled still.

c. of things.

1746, 1768 [see RANKLING *ppl. a.* a]. **1855** BROWNING *Childe Roland* xxvi, Now blotches rankling, coloured gray and grim. **1860** E. P. HOOD in Spurgeon *Treas. Dav. Ps.* lxxiv. 16 Forms that rankle..contract around themselves loathsomeness and disgust.

†**2.** To inflict a festering wound; to cause a painful festering. *Obs.*

1575 TURBERV. *Venerie* 207 Their biting is venemous and rancleth sore. **1580** LYLY *Euphues* (Arb.) 266 This vile Dog Loue will so ranckle where he biteth. **1644** BULWER *Chirol.* 181 Two venemous weapons, and apt to wranckle where they fasten. **1698** DRYDEN *Æneid* IV. 100 Still the fatal Dart Sticks in her side; and rankles in her Heart.

transf. **1584** LYLY *Sapho* II. iv. 84 Honney ranckleth, when it is eaten for pleasure.

3. a. Of persons: To have a painful feeling; to fret or chafe angrily. *rare.*

1582 STANYHURST *Æneis* II. (Arb.) 46 With choloricque fretting I dumpt, and ranckled in anguish. **1894** GLADSTONE *Odes of Horace* IV. iv. 63 Alcides, rankling to be foiled, Saw the lopped limbs grow quick again.

b. Of a bitter or malignant feeling: To have course, or continue in operation, with an effect like that of a festering sore.

1508 [see RANKLED *ppl. a.*]. **1590** [see RANKLING *ppl. a.*]. **1789** JEFFERSON *Writ.* (1859) II. 583 The ill humor on account of the Dutch revolution continues to rankle here. **1838** THIRLWALL *Greece* V. 263 Animosity had long been rankling between Thebes and Phocis. **1874** DIXON *Two Queens* III. XVII. iii. 265 A bitter feeling rankled in his heart.

c. Of experiences, events, etc.: To continue to cause painful, bitter, or venomous feelings.

1735 BOLINGBROKE *Lett. Stud. Hist.* ii. (1752) 36 The passages of King Charles the Second's reign might rankle still at the hearts of some men. **1792** *Anecd. Pitt* III. xliv. 195 Such a mode of warfare would rankle in the heart of America. **1855** MACAULAY *Hist. Eng.* xxi. IV. 584 The mock embassy..was doubtless still rankling in his mind. **1868** FREEMAN *Norm. Conq.* (1876) II. x. 486 The sight of the palace of the English King..rankled in his soul.

4. To change *to*, pass *into*, by, or as by, festering.

1741–2 GRAY *Agrip.* 74 Sweets of kindness lavishly indulg'd Rankle to gall. **1831** MACKINTOSH *Sp. Ho. Comm.* Wks. 1846 III. 562 Discontent will rankle into disaffection.

II. *trans.* **5. a.** To cause (flesh, wounds, etc.) to fester; to make painful. Also with *up*.

1530–77 H. RHODES *Bk. Nurture* 32 in *Babees Bk.* (1868) 83 Vyce..dulleth wits, ranckleth flesh. **1609** BP. W. BARLOW *Answ. Nameless Cath.* 96 Hee would needes rankle vp againe so old sores. **1640** QUARLES *Enchirid.* III. xxxiv, Hasty words ranckle the wound. **1761** HUME *Hist. Eng.* I. x. 218 He..rankled Richard's shoulder by pulling out the arrow. **1865** SIR J. K. JAMES *Tasso* x. xiv, His wounds were chilled By the night breeze, which rankled them still more.

b. To embitter, envenom (feelings); to cause painful irritation in (a person). Also const. *into* (quot. 1796). In recent use, chiefly *N. Amer.*

1606 *True & Perfect Relat.* X x iv, A Prince..more willing to solicite union, then to ranckle hate. **1629** MAXWELL tr. *Herodian* (1635) 365 Which horrid facts did infinitely rankle and fester the affections of all Estates. **1659** MILTON *Hirelings* 57 A fierce reformer once, now ranckl'd with a contrary heat. **1711** *C.M. Lett. to Curat.* 79 That not so much as the Difference of a Ceremony from the English might rankle them. **1796** *Hist. Ned Evans* II. 21 Envy..has ..rankled his base soul into hatred against you. **1850** MCCOSH *Div. Govt.* III. ii. (1874) 396 Whatever rankles the mind—and nothing so much rankles it as an unappeased conscience. **1962** E. LUCIA *Klondike Kate* vii. 142 It probably rankled a great many of them just to patronize his theatres. **1971** *Daily Colonist* (Victoria, B.C.) 31 Oct. 4/1 The demonstrations of glee..which understandably rankled President Nixon. **1976** *National Observer* (U.S.) 19 June 7/2 Rome's unbending attitude towards mixed marriages of Roman Catholics and non-Catholics rankled Anglicans. **1978** *National Geographic* Nov. 627/1 The low sum [of money] rankles many Yakimas, who complain of poor management.

†**c.** To poison, destroy (one's credit). *Obs.*

1615 T. ADAMS *White Devill* 7 His teeth rankle the womans credit. **1633** —— *Exp. 2 Peter* ii. 3 Do they never.. rankle another's credit with malicious report.

6. To conceive or nourish (a bitter feeling).

1819 *Metropolis* III. 16 His heart rancled hatred in the extreme for the cruel act.

Hence **'rankled** *ppl. a.*

1508 DUNBAR *Tua Mariit Wemen* 163 A roust that is sa rankild quhill risis my stomok. **1590** SPENSER *F.Q.* III. iii. 36 Then shall the Britons..avenge their ranckled ire. **1631** WEEVER *Anc. Funeral Mon.* 464 The rankled wound..was iudged incurable. **1756** HOME *Douglas* II. 28 I've known a follower's rankled bosom breed Venom most fatal.

'rankless, *a. rare.* [f. RANK *sb.* + -LESS.] Not drawn up in ranks.

1843 *Tait's Mag.* X. 566 Like a flood He..swept the rankless tens away.

rankling ('ræŋklɪŋ), *vbl. sb.* [-ING¹.] The action of the vb. RANKLE.

14.. *Stockh. Medical MS.* i. 310 in *Anglia* XVIII. 303 Al þe rancelynge schall owyr gon. *Ibid.* 316 þe rank[l]ynge schal swage away. *c* **1450** *M.E. Med. Bk.* (Heinrich) 224 Hyt wolle aswage ranclyng of woundes. **1578** LYTE *Dodoens* I. xlix. 71 Corruption, festering or inward ranckling. **1614** MARKHAM *Cheap Husb.* (1623) 127 To preuent the ranckling and impostumation of the soare. **1719** DE FOE *Crusoe* I. xx, His limbs..swelled with the rankling of his..wounds. **1795–1814** WORDSW. *Excurs.* IV. 212 Ill-governed passions, ranklings of despite. **1832** MACAULAY *Ess., Hampden*, A rankling which may last for many years.

rankling ('ræŋklɪŋ), *ppl. a.* [f. as prec. + -ING².] That rankles: **a.** In intransitive senses.

1528 ROY *Rede me*, etc. (Arb.) 25 One rancklynge member [putrifieth] the whole boddy. **1590** SPENSER *F.Q.* I. vi. 44 Two Bores, with rancling malice mett. **1631** GOUGE *God's Arrows* III. §95. 363 The daily licking of his ranckling wounds. **1746** SMOLLETT *Reproof* 98 Thy rankling pen produces nought but gall. **1768** BEATTIE *Minstrel* I. xli, Dark error's den, whose rankling slime First gave you form. **1868** FARRAR *Silence & Voices* ix. (1875) 152 It was not the rankling wound of an enemy.

b. In transitive senses.

1635 QUARLES *Embl.* II. xi, Whose ranckling pricks are sharp, and fell. **1742** GRAY *Ode Eton Coll.* 66 Jealousy with rankling tooth, That inly gnaws the secret heart. **1821** JOANNA BAILLIE *Met. Leg., Colum.* xlii, His rankling chain. **1846** O. W. HOLMES *Rhymed Lesson* (1883) 72 Shall I wound with satire's rankling spear?

Hence **'ranklingly** *adv.*

1860 SIR B. BURKE *Viciss. Fam.* Ser. II. 128 The high-hearted boy..ranklingly nurtured that mixture of fiercely vengeful and patriotic spirit.

rankly ('ræŋklɪ), *adv.* [f. RANK *a.* + -LY².] In a rank manner, in various senses of the adj.

c **1000** *Canons of Ælfric* §35 in Thorpe *Laws* II. 358/6 Ne eower reaf ne beo to ranclice ʒemacod. *c* **1050** *Byrhtferth's Handboc* in *Anglia* VIII. 312/18þæt hiʒ maʒon þe ranclicor þas þing heora clericum ʒeswutelian. **13..** *E.E. Allit. P.* C. 431 Herk renk! is this ryʒt so ronkly to wrath. **1549** COVERDALE, etc. *Erasm. Par. Titus* 28 Slowe belyes whiche ..lyue in ydlenes and rankly. **1590** R. HARVEY *Pl. Perc.* 10 Prid and venime, if they had so ranckly possessed his hart [etc.]. **1661** LOVELL *Hist. Anim. & Min.* 157 It's best when young, it smelling rankely when old. **1743** *Lond. & Country Brewer* II. (ed. 2) 109 Because their Back, Tuns, or Tubs are not rankly damaged. **1824** *Hist. Gaming Houses* 57 If his Lordship found that he had been cheated rankly, he soon retaliated in kind. **1846** HOLTZAPFFEL *Turning* III. 1146 Tools for brass and gun-metal, when left from the grindstone, cut too rankly. **1871** R. ELLIS tr. *Catullus* lxiv. 42 Steals a deforming rust on ploughs left rankly to moulder.

rankness ('ræŋknɪs). [f. RANK *a.* + -NESS.] The quality of being rank, in senses of the adj.

a **1400–50** *Alexander* 3350 Ronkenes of wynes. *a* **1485** *Promp. Parv.* 423/1 (MS. S.) Rankenesse, *crassitudo.* **1523** FITZHERB. *Husb.* §58 Murren..commeth of a ranknes of bloudde. **1555** EDEN *Decades* 122 The rankenesse and frutefulnesse of the grounde. **1640** FULLER *Joseph's Coat* i. (1867) 110 Experience had..corrected the rankness of his spirit. **1692** R. L'ESTRANGE *Fables* ccxxxiv. (1708) 252 The Crane's Pride is in the Rankness of her Wing. **1751** SMOLLETT *Per. Pic.* (1779) II. xlviii. 103 The dish had a particular rankness of taste. **1850** R. G. CUMMING *Hunter's Life S. Afr.* (ed. 2) I. 265 The rankness of his flowing mane. **1873** SYMONDS *Gk. Poets* i. 36 Weeds lovely in their rankness.

rank order, *sb. Statistics.* Also **rank-order.** [f. RANK *sb.*¹ + ORDER *sb.*] An arrangement of the members of a set in order, with consecutive integers assigned to them. Also *attrib.*

1920 *Amer. Jrnl. Psychol.* XXXI. 32 We are left..with the rank-orders of our psychological quantities, given by reference to a fixed but arbitrary extra-psychological scale. **1959** SCHUELL & JENKINS in Saporta & Bastian *Psycholinguistics* (1961) 441/1 Table 3 presents the rank-order correlation coefficients between the order of difficulty of the tests for the entire group, and for each of the subgroups. *Ibid.*, Table 4 presents the tests on which rank-orders of the three subgroups differed by three or more ranks. **1973** *Jrnl. Genetic Psychol.* CXXIII. 79 Rank-order correlations were obtained by correlating the rank of each student on the original test with his rank on the retest. **1975** Z. GOVINDARAJULU *Sequential Statistical Procedures* iii. 259 One can derive an explicit expression for the probability of a rank order.

Hence **rank-order** *v. trans.*, to arrange in such a way.

1972 *Jrnl. Social Psychol.* LXXXVIII. 169 The concepts are rank-ordered in terms of the pre-GSRI attitude change correlations.

'rankshift, *sb. Linguistics.* [f. RANK *sb.*¹ + SHIFT *sb.*] A downward shift in the rank of a grammatical unit (see quot. 1966).

1961 M. A. K. HALLIDAY in *Word* XVII. 251 The theory allows for downward 'rank shift': the transfer of a (formal realization of a) given unit to a lower rank... It does not allow for upward rank shift. **1966** G. N. LEECH *Eng. in Advertising* ii. 20 *Embedding* is a shift in rank, whereby a group acts as a word, or a word acts as a morpheme, etc... The nominal genitive is another case of double rank shift: (((Mary)'s aged grandmother)'s faithful servant). The nominal groups 'Mary' and 'Mary's aged grandmother' act as morphemes. **1969** —— *Towards Semantic Descr. Eng.* iii. 52 Rank-shift or downgrading, as forms of subordination, introduce an extra factor of order into semantic structure, so that by reversing the relation of dependence between two predications, one may account for a difference of meaning. **1972** M. L. SAMUELS *Linguistic Evolution* iv. 59 Many later additions to the inventory of English prepositions resulted from a similar process of historical rankshift, e.g. *concerning, regarding, according to, owing to,* and (more recently) *due to.* **1977** *Language* LIII. 192 Although *the men's halls and the women's halls* is a group consisting of two smaller groups, B does not regard this as an instance of 'rankshift': this is restricted to cases where an element of a multivariate structure is filled by an expression of higher or equal rank.

Hence as *v. trans.*, to assign an inferior rank or function to a unit in a grammatical structure. Also **'rankshifted** *ppl. a.*; **'rankshifting** *vbl. sb.*

1964 M. A. K. HALLIDAY et al. *Linguistic Sci.* 27 In English some clauses are rankshifted and work inside the pattern of a group. If I say 'where I live it always rains', this sentence consists of two clauses, which together make up the structure of the sentence. But if I say 'the house where I live is very damp', the sentence consists, *in its structure,* of only one clause; the clause 'where I live' is rankshifted and operates in the structure of the *group* 'the house where I live'. **1969** *Eng. Studies* L. 36 We shall not go into the question of whether examples here quoted under the heading of headlines with FB structure do not really belong in the section rankshifted clauses. **1969** G. N. LEECH *Towards Semantic Descr. Eng.* ii. 26 There is no defined limit of tolerance to the depth of constituent structure produced by rank-shifting one predication inside another. **1972** *Language* XLVIII. 451 Limitations of space permit both L [*sc.* G. N. Leech] and myself only to raise, but not to answer, the question whether one can express within the notation of logic the operations of rank-shifting and down-grading. **1973** G. W. TURNER *Stylistics* iii. 82 'If you expect to get something good, for nothing, you are likely to get something good for nothing'..in the second clause 'good for nothing' is rank-shifted to behave as one word and become a single qualifier. **1977** *Language* LIII. 192 It follows that *from Glasgow* is rankshifted in *the man from Glasgow,* where it functions as qualifier in a multivariate nominal group.

'ranksman. *rare.* [f. RANK *sb.*¹] **a.** (See quot. 1880.) **b.** One drawn up with others in a rank.

1880 JAMIESON, *Ranksmen,* a name given to two or more boats' crews fishing together and dividing the catch equally. Shetl. **1898** T. HARDY *Wessex Poems* 89 Hosts of ranksmen round.

†**'rankum.** *Obs. rare*⁻¹. ? A noisy chorus.

1693 SOUTHERNE *Maid's Last Prayer* IV. iii, Pox a' this scraping and tooting; shall we eclipse, Tom, and make it a Rankum.

rankyll, obs. form of RANKLE *v.*

‖**rann** (ræn). [Ir.] A verse, a strain.

1843 CARLETON *Traits Irish Peas.* I. 338 The ranns, an' prayers, an' holy charms. *a* **1849** J. C. MANGAN *Poems* (1859) 388 [To] chant aloud the exulting rann of jubilee. **1895** W. B. YEATS *Poems, To Ireland* 234 Who sang to sweeten Ireland's wrong, Ballad and story, rann and song.

rannc, ranndon, rannee, rannegald, obs. ff. RANK *a.*, RANDOM, RANEE, RANNIGAL.

'rannel-balk. *north. dial.* = RANNEL-TREE.

1790 GROSE *Provincial Gloss.* (ed. 2) sig. K4, *Rannel-tree,* cross-beam in a chimney, on which the crook hangs; sometimes called *Rannebauk*; North. **1817** *Edin. Monthly Mag.* June 241 The rusticity of their benisons amused me. —One wished them, 'thumpin luck and fat weans'; another, 'a bien rannle-bauks, and tight thack and rape o'er their heads'. **1859** A. WHITEHEAD *Legends of Westmorland* (1896) 11 Fair shack'd the rannel bawk et swang The keayle pot ower the grate. **1906** H. D. RAWNSLEY *Months at Lakes* 236 A great cauldron of spiced ale..hung on the 'rannel bowk', and was ladled out from time to time into basins and presented to the guests. **1910** W. G. COLLINGWOOD *Dutch Agnes* 47 In the chimney at this time of the year mutton-hams hanging from the rannelbalk. **1931** H. S. WALPOLE *Judith Paris* II. i. 218 He was aware of..sides of bacon hanging, the oak settle screened by the 'heck', the 'rannel-balk' or great wooden beam across the chimney.

†**'rannell**, *sb. Obs.* A hussy, jade.

1573 G. HARVEY *Letter-bk.* (Camden) 113 A beastely rannell, A filthy cannell. **1592** —— *Pierce's Super.* 146 Though she were a lustie bounding rampe..yet was she not such a roinish rannell..as this wainscot-faced Tomboy.

'rannel-tree. *Sc.* and *north. dial.* Also 9 **rannell-, randle-, rangel-,** 8–9 *Sc.* **rantle-tree.** [App. of Scand. origin; cf. the synonymous Norw. dial. *randa-tre* and *rand-aas,* f. *rand* the space above the fire-place. But the appearance of *l* in all the English forms is difficult to account for.] A horizontal bar of wood or iron fixed across a chimney, on which the pot-hooks or rackans are hung.

Rannel-perch is also common in north. dial.; see also RANNEL-BALK.

1755 R. FORBES *Jrnl. fr. Lond.* 4 The lum o' a house that wanted baith crook an' rantle-tree. **1785** HUTTON *Bran New Wark* (E.D.S.) 380 A seaty rattencreak hang dangling fra a black randle tree. **1790** GROSE *Prov. Gloss., Rannel-tree.* **1818** SCOTT *Hrt. Midl.* xviii, An unguent to clear our auld rannell-trees. **1829–** in northern glossaries. **1887** HALL CAINE *Deemster* xix. 113 Over the rannel-tree shelf a huge watch was ticking.

transf. **1815** SCOTT *Guy M.* xxvi, If ever I see that auld randle-tree of a wife again.

'rannigal. *Sc.* and *north. dial.* Also *Sc.* 6 **rannegald,** 9 **rannygill.** [? Alteration of *renegade.*] (See quots.)

15.. KENNEDY *Flyting w. Dunbar* 401 (Bann. MS.) Rawmowd rebald, rannegald [*ed.* 1508 renegate] rehatour. **1825** JAMIESON *Suppl., Rannygill,* a bold, impudent, unruly person... Roxb. **1847–78** HALLIWELL, *Rannack,* a worthless fellow. *Rannigal* is also used. **1878** *Cumbld. Gloss., Rannigal,* a masterful child or animal.

ranny ('rænɪ). *Obs.* exc. *dial.* Also 9 **-ey.** [App. ad. L. *araneus mūs* (Colum. and Pliny) 'a kind of small mouse, acc. to some the shrew mouse'.] The shrew mouse, or field mouse.

1559 W. CUNNINGHAM *Cosmogr. Glasse* 173 Venomous beastes, and Wormes, as Ranny, Tode, Edder. **1646** SIR T. BROWNE *Pseud. Ep.* 153 Sammonicus and Nicander do call the Mus-Araneus, the shrew or Ranny, blinde. **1787** in MARSHALL *Norfolk* (1795) II. Gloss. **1823** MOOR *Suffolk Words, Ranny,* the long-nosed, small-eyed, fetid shrew or field mouse... Hence anything long nosed is called ranny-nosed.

ranny, Sc. var. RANDY *a.*, obs. f. RANEE.

rannygazoo (ˌrænɪgəˈzuː). Chiefly *U.S. dial.* or *slang.* Also **ranikaboo, reinikaboo, renicky-boo.** [Origin unknown.] A prank, trick; horseplay, 'nonsense'. (See also quots. 1901, 1940.)

1901 *Dial. Notes* II. 146 *Reinikaboo*.., a newspaper story which is midway between a fake and a statement of fact; a statement of news out of all proportion and almost out of relation to the facts, yet having a certain origin and shadowy foundation. **1907** S. E. WHITE *Arizona Nights* iii. 255 'You—bluffer!' shouted a voice, 'don't you think you can run any such ranikaboo here!' **1917** *Dial. Notes* IV. 328 *Renicky*..or *renicky-boo.* 'He wants to run some sort of bluff or *renicky* on us.' **1924** WODEHOUSE *Bill the Conqueror* xi. 204 I'll hang around for a while just in case friend Pilbeam starts any rannygazoo. **1940** *Time* 14 Oct. 28 Wilkie went to N.Y.C. to tour Democratic Brooklyn... Still he refused to make a.. speech, stil turned down..pleas..to let loose with a ring-tailed, rabble-rousing rannygazoo. **1947** *Sun* (Baltimore) 20 Jan. 1/2 A ranikaboo in Arizona would be known as a prank in other states. **1974** WODEHOUSE *Aunts aren't Gentlemen* vii. 59 Her lips were tightly glued together, her chin protruding, her whole lay-out that of a girl who intended to stand no rannygazoo.

ran-pick, -pike(d: see RAMPICK, -PIKE(D.

ranque, obs. form of RANK *sb.*

ransack (ˈrænsæk), *sb.* [f. the vb. Cf. ON. *rannsak.*] The act of ransacking.

1589 PUTTENHAM *Eng. Poesie* II. xi[i]. (Arb.) 118 In the ransacke of the Cities of Cartagena and S. Dominico. **1635** QUARLES *Embl.* IV. xii. (1818) 241 What unwonted way Has 'scap'd the ransack of my rambling thought? **1649** EARL MONM. tr. *Senault's Use Passions* (1671) 137 His Choler committed no less ransack. **1887** BLACKMORE *Springhaven* (ed. 4) III. xv. 208 'There are no official papers here', he said, after another short ransack.

ransack (ˈrænsæk), *v.* Forms: 3–7 **ransake**, (3 **-en**, 5 **-yn**; 4 **ron-**, 5 ? **raun-**; also 5 **ransek**, ? **runsik**, 6 **ransik, -sike**), 5–7 **ransacke**, (8 **-sac**), 6– **ransack.** [a. ON. *rannsaka* (Sw. *ransaka*, Da. *ransage*), f. *rann* house (= Goth. *razn*, OE. *ærn*) + *-saka*, ablaut-var. of *sœkja* to seek; cf. *saka* to blame, accuse, harm. Guernsey dial. *ransaquer*, Gael. *rannsaich* are from Eng. or ON.

ON. *rannsaka* is esp. used in the legal sense of searching a house for stolen goods: cf. senses 1 and 2 below.]

†**1.** *trans.* To search (a person) for something stolen or missing. *Obs.*

c **1250** *Gen. & Ex.* 1773 Ðu me ransakes als an ðef. *Ibid.* 2323 He gan hem ransaken on and on, And fond it ðor sone a-non. **1393** LANGL. *P. Pl.* C. XIX. 122 Filius..flegh..To ransake that rageman and reue hym hus apples. **1493** *Festivall* (W. de W. 1515) 22 They..sayd it was not so, and he [Joseph] ransaked them by and by.

2. To make thorough search in or throughout (a place, receptacle, collection of things, etc.) *for* something (in early use, something stolen: cf. 1). Also (rarely) with *up.*

a **1300** *Cursor M.* 4893 (Gött.) ȝon er theues..Foluis þaim and ransakis [*Cott.* ripe] þair ware. **1530** PALSGR. 679/1 He hath ransaked all the chystes I have for his beades. **1532** MORE *Confut. Tindale* Wks. 595/2 He sayth..that the woman had lost her money, though by ransaking vp her howse and seking she founde it at last agayne. **1592** GREENE *Art Conny catch.* 30 The Knight sat downe with him and fell a ransacking his budget. **1644** H. PARKER *Jus Populi* 42 We have ransacked the bosome of Nature for all species of Power. **1739** CIBBER *Apol.* (1756) II. 80, I am ransacking my memory for..scraps of theatrical history. **1805** WORDSW. *Prelude* v. 255 She scratches, ransacks up the earth for food. **1867** FREEMAN *Norm. Conq.* (1876) I. iii. 135 The Latin language is ransacked for strange and out-of-the-way terms.

b. *absol.* To make thorough search. Now *rare.*

c **1386** CHAUCER *Knt.'s T.* 147 To ransake in the tas of bodyes dede..The pilours diden bisinesse and cure. *c* **1440** *York Myst.* xlvi. 215, I shall renne and reste not to ransake full right. **1598** SYLVESTER *Du Bartas* I. v. 749 We..ransack deeply in her bosom tender. **1732** NEAL *Hist. Purit.* I. 253 This raised a clamour as if the Queen intended to ransack into mens consciences.

3. To examine thoroughly, to subject to close scrutiny; to overhaul and investigate in detail.

a **1300** *E.E. Psalter* lxiii. 6 þai ransaked wicnesse, and iuel thinge. *a* **1400** *Minor Poems fr. Vernon MS.* 684/40 Hou schulde a leche this mon releeve But ȝif he miȝte ronsake the wounde. *c* **1440** *Jacob's Well* 109 þere is no man, & he raunsake his conscyens, but he schal fynde..manye [sins], to schryuen him of. **1470–85** MALORY *Arthur* XIII. xiii, Anone he ransakyd hym & thenne he saide vnto syr galahad I shal hele hym of this wounde. **1533** MORE *Apol.* xlii. Wks. 912, I purpose not to ransake and rebuke either the tone lawe or the tother. **1612** T. TAYLOR *Comm. Titus* i. 9 Reade then this booke..and thou shalt ransacke the affections, yea and consciences of the hearers. **1684** J. GOODMAN *Old Relig.* (1848) 160 Ransacking a man's own heart in secret. **1850** HAWTHORNE *Scarlet L.* xx. (1852) 207 She ransacked her conscience..and took herself to task..for a thousand imaginary faults. **1872** RUSKIN *Eagle's N.* §66 In astronomy, the fields of the sky have not yet, indeed, been ransacked by the most costly instruments.

†**b.** *fig.* of things: To search, explore, penetrate. Also *intr. Obs.*

1562 PHAER *Æneid* IX. Bb iij b, The sword..Had ransakt through his ribs. **1579** GOSSON *Sch. Abuse* (Arb.) 38 One dramme of Eeleborus ransackes euery vaine. **1590** SPENSER *F.Q.* III. v. 48 The mightie ill, which, as a victour proud, gan ransack fast His inward partes.

4. To search (a place, person, etc.) with intent to rob; hence, to rob, plunder, pillage (*of*).

1390 GOWER *Conf.* II. 331 He can the packes wel ransake, ..Thus Robberie goth to seke. **1465** MARG. PASTON in *P. Lett.* II. 251 They stode uppon the hey awter, and ransackyd the images and toke a way such as thay myght fynd. **1522** MORE *De quat. Noviss.* Wks. 94 In what painefull plight they shall lye a dying, while theyr executours afore their face ransake vp theyr sackes. **1638** R. BAKER tr. *Balzac's Lett.* (vol. II) 110 Hee hath beene robbed and ransacked in France. **1686** tr. *Chardin's Trav. Persia* 145 That poor country had been pillag'd, plunder'd and ransack'd by the Persians. **1755** J. SHEBBEARE *Lydia* (1769) II. 413 Those whose houses are ransacked by invading enemies. **1809** MALKIN *Gil Blas* VII. xv. ¶4 They rob, ransack, and devour me. **1878** BOSW. SMITH *Carthage* 109 The palaces were ransacked of their valuables and then ruthlessly set on fire.

absol. **1598** BARRET *Theor. Warres* V. iii. 179 To robbe.. and ransack, whereby to sustaine themselues. **1642** *Lancash. Tracts Civil War* (Chetham Soc.) 46 The Souldier hath ransakt and pillag'd..in the country thereabouts. **1726** LEONI tr. *Alberti's Archit.* II. 53 A furious and insolent enemy ransacking among the Sepulchres of their Ancestors.

b. To search for and take (*away*) or carry off as plunder. Also with *up.* Now *rare.*

c **1400** *Beryn* 3652 Hanybald shall..delyvir the good ageyn, þat from ȝewe was ransakid. **1523** [COVERDALE] *Old God & New* (1534) F ij b, The nations dyd ransake away whatsoeuer thinges they myght. **1621** BP. MOUNTAGU *Diatribæ* 463 To spoyle the whole Countrey: and rake and ransake vp all things that are for mans vse. **1634** SIR T. HERBERT *Trav.* 57 Refined gold, which greedy Antiochus thought to haue ransackt. **1867** LADY HERBERT *Cradle L.* viii. 218 Even scented soap and toilette-vinegar..were ransacked from his stores.

†**5.** To visit with harshness or violence; to assail, drag, shake, etc. roughly. *Obs.*

c **1375** *Cursor M.* 15825 (Fairf.) Forþ his maister þai drogh & ronsaked him vnrekenli baþ ouer hil & seogh. *c* **1400** *Laud Troy Bk.* 7967 Many a knyȝt fel to the grounde. Ful sorily he hem ransaked. *c* **1422** HOCCLEVE *Learn to Die* 92 A yong man..Whom deeth so ny ransakid had, & soght.

ransacked (ˈrænsækt), *ppl. a.* [f. prec. + -ED¹.] Searched into, explored, plundered, etc.

c **1440** *Promp. Parv.* 423/1 Ransakyd, *investigatus, perscrutatus.* **1581** MULCASTER *Positions* xxxix. (1887) 194 The spoile of the ransaked pouertie. **1659** SPRAT *Plague of Athens* (1790) 249 The ransack'd memory Languish'd in naked poverty. **1697** DRYDEN *Æneid* II. 1040 The Spoils which they from ransack'd Houses brought. **1862** LYTTON *Str. Story* II. 175 A Flora and a Fauna which have no similitudes in the ransacked quarters of the Old World.

ransacker (ˈrænsækə(r)). Also 4 **raunsaker.** [f. as prec. + -ER.] One who ransacks; a pillager.

c **1340** HAMPOLE *Prose Tr.* 42 Raunsaker of þe myghte of Godd. **1609** BIBLE (Douay) *Judg.* ii. 14 Our Lord.. delivered them into the handes of ransackers. **1862** GLADSTONE in *Times* 8 Apr. 9/1 He is a ransacker of Hansard.

ransacking (ˈrænsækɪŋ), *vbl. sb.* [f. as prec. + -ING¹.] The action of the verb RANSACK.

a **1300** *E.E. Psalter* lxiii. 6 þai waned..of ransakinge. **1435** MISYN *Fire of Love* 60 Be ransakynge of rightwys mens lyfis fro all pryde þi self refreyn. **1579** E. K. *Gloss.* in *Spenser's Sheph. Cal.* Oct. 65 He came to ransacking of king Darius coffers. **1656** EARL MONM. tr. *Boccalini's Pol. Touchstone* (1674) 262 Naples..is now brought to utter desolation..by the general ransacking of the Vice Roys. **1691** T. H[ALE] *Acc. New Invent.* 28 Their Ransackings, Groundings, Dockings, and Repairings. **1708** J. CHAMBERLAYNE *St. Gt. Brit.* II. I. ii. (1710) 349 (*Orkneys*) They..make search for the Theft, which is called Ransaking. **1955** H. ROTH *Sleeper* i. 10 What..happened before the ransacking?

ransackle, *v. Obs.* exc. *north. dial.* Forms: 7 ransacle, 8 -shakle, 9 -s(h)ackle (also ram-). [f. RANSACK *v.* + -LE.] *trans.* To ransack.

1621 B. JONSON *Gipsies Metam.* II. vi, They ha'.. ransacled me of every penny. *a* **1802** *Jamie Telfer* iv. in Child *Ballads* IV. 6/1 They..ranshakled the house right weel. **1825** in BROCKETT *N.C. Gloss.* **1877** in *Holderness Gloss.*

ranse, variant of RANCE *sb.*² and *v.*

ransel, ranselman: see RANCEL, -MAN.

ransom (ˈrænsəm), *sb.* Forms: α. 3–4 **ransun**, (4 **-coun, -cun-e, -scun, -scon**), 4–6 **ransoun**, 4–7 **ranson**, (5, 7 **-sone**); 4 **raunsun**, (**-scun, -ceoun, -zoun**, etc.), 4–5 **raunson, -soun** (also 4 **ron-**, 5 **rawn-, rawun-**, etc.). β. 4 **rans(o)um, -scum, -scome**, 6–7 **ransome**, (7 **randsom**), 4– **ransom**, (4 **rauns(o)um**, 4–6 **rawnsom-e**, 4–6 **raunsom**, 6 **-some, raundsom, -sum**). γ. 4 **raymson**, 4–5 **raumso(u)n**, 4–6 **ramson.** δ. 5 **raen-, reanson, reaunceoune.** [a. OF. *rançon, ran-, raunson, raençon, -son, ra(a)nceun, rampçon*, etc. (see Godef.):—**re(d)empçon*:—L. *redemptiōn-em*: see REDEMPTION. For the change of *-on* to *-om*, which appears quite early, cf. *randon*, RANDOM.]

1. The action of procuring the release of a prisoner or captive by paying a certain sum, or of obtaining one's own freedom in this way; the fact or possibility of being set free on this condition; the paying of money to this end.

In older use freq. in phrases †*to make ransom*, †*to let* or *take to ransom.* In the 19th c. the sense appears to have been revived by Scott, and now occurs chiefly in the phr. *to hold to ransom.*

a **1300** *Cursor M.* 9772 (Cott.) Angel ne might wit na resun Mak for adam his ranscun [*Gött.* raunsum]. **1340** HAMPOLE *Pr. Consc.* 2834 'In helle', he says, 'es na raunceon'. For na helpe may be in þat dungeon. **1375** BARBOUR *Bruce* XIII. 72 Slayand thame without ransoune. *c* **1430** LYDG. *Min. Poems* (Percy Soc.) 102 Whan he for man the raunsom on hym tooke. **1456** SIR G. HAYE *Law Arms* (S.T.S.) 60 Four consules, the quhilkis the inymyes wald nocht lat to ransoun. *c* **1489** CAXTON *Blanchardyn* 89 He wolde take to raenson þe knyght that was a straunger. **1568** GRAFTON *Chron.* II. 295 They slue many a man that could not come to raunsome. **1819** SCOTT *Ivanhoe* xxvii, An honourable imprisonment..as is due to one who is in treaty for ransom. *Ibid.* xxxii, Let us put the Jew to ransom. **1859** JEPHSON *Brittany* xvi. 261 Gwesklen, taken prisoner by Chandos, was held by him to ransom.

2. a. The sum or price paid or demanded for the release of a prisoner or the restoration of captured property. ***a king's ransom***, a large sum. †***man of ransom***, one able to pay ransom, or for whom ransom will be paid.

a **1225** *Ancr. R.* 124 A mon þet leie ine prisune, & ouhte muche raunsun. **1297** R. GLOUC. (Rolls) 6046 þis folc bisette kaunterbury..& gret raunson of hom wiþinne esste. *c* **1350** *Will. Palerne* 1251 Y am prest as þi prisoun to paye þe my ransum. **1390** GOWER *Conf.* III. 220 A gaz made gret beheste Of rancoun which he wolde yive. *c* **1470** HENRY *Wallace* II. 150 His kyn mycht nocht him get..Mycht thai hawe payit the ransoune of a King. **1542** UDALL *Erasm. Apoph.* 163 b, Thei had been leat..without any peny of raunsome paiyng to escape. *c* **1590** MARLOWE *Faust.* vi, I'll not speak another word for a King's ransom. **1636** MASSINGER *Bashf. Lover* II. vii, I know him: he's a man of ransom. **1697** DAMPIER *Voy.* (1729) I. 145 Here we staid till the sixth day, in hopes to get a Ransom for the Town. **1718** LADY M. W. MONTAGU *Lett.* (1887) I. 239 Her brother.. sent the sum of four thousand pounds sterling as a ransom for his sister. **1802** MAR. EDGEWORTH *Moral T.* (1816) I. 208 Like all..prisoners of war, she must..pay her ransom in gold. **1829** MRS. HALL *Sketches Irish Char.* I. 75, I couldn't look upon the babby's face for a king's ransom. **1882** OUIDA *Maremma* I. 11 The stranger had been waiting for a ransom to be sent.

b. *fig.*, in religious use, of Christ or His blood.

a **1300** *Cursor M.* 21731 On cros godd boght ur saul liues þar-on he gaf him-seluen ranscun. **1483** CAXTON *Gold. Leg.* 290 b/2, O crosse..which only were worthy to bere the raunson of the world. *a* **1569** KINGESMYLL *Confl. Satan* (1578) 37 Looke, Christe is called a ransome, that is, a price of redemption. **1667** MILTON *P.L.* x. 61 Sending thee..his Mediator..Both Ransom and Redeemer voluntarie. *a* **1711** KEN *Christophil* Poet. Wks. 1721 I. 511 A Price inestimable paid, The Blood of God our Ransom made. *a* **1854** H. REED *Lect. Eng. Lit.* vii. (1878) 236 A soul..not unworthy the awful ransom of the Redeemer's blood.

†**c.** A large sum. *Obs. rare*⁻¹.

a **1400–50** *Alexander* 1665 Besands to þe bischop he bed out of nounbre, Reches him of rede gold ransons many.

d. *Sc.* An exorbitant price, rent, etc.

1816 SCOTT *Antiquary* I. iii. 59 Could a copy [of Caxton's 'Game of Chess'] now occur..Lord only knows what would be its ransom. **1824–7** MOIR *Mansie Wauch* i, Grannie.. sold the milk..at the ransom of a ha'penny the mutchkin. **1875** W. ALEXANDER *Sk. Life among my Ain Folk* viii. 133 Some said Sandy Mutch had taken the farm 'at a ransom'. **1932** A. J. CRONIN *Three Loves* II. xviii. 352 But the price of things... It's shameful. Everything a ransom now.

†**e.** The thing ransomed. *Obs. rare*⁻¹.

a **1300** *Cursor M.* 28023 Fra godd his ful dere ranscon yee stele, þat es þat ilk saul þat he Cost wit his ded.

†**3. a.** The action or means of freeing oneself from a penalty; a sum of money paid to obtain pardon for an offence; a fine, mulct. *Obs.*

a **1300** *Cursor M.* 1970 Qua þat slas or man or wijf þar gas na ransun bot liue for lijf. *c* **1330** R. BRUNNE *Chron.* (1810) 329 Som gaf raunson after þer trespas. *c* **1386** CHAUCER *Wife's Prol.* 411, I wolde no lenger in the bed abyde... Til he had maad his raunson vn to me. **1491** *Act 7 Hen. VII*, c. 22 §1 To abyde in prisone therfor unto the tyme he have made fyne and raunsom for the same. **1526** *Pilgr. Perf.* (W. de W. 1531) 42 Pardons payeth most properly the raunsom of payne due in purgatory. *c* **1585** *Faire Em* III. 768 Thy death should pay the ransom of thy fault. **1647** N. BACON *Disc. Govt.* I. xxxix. (1739) 59 Then might that Penance be reduced to a Ransom (according to the grain of the offence). **1769** BLACKSTONE *Comm.* IV. 373 This is the reason why fines in the king's court are frequently denominated ransoms.

†**b.** A sum paid as a tax or tribute. *Obs.*

c **1320** *Sir Tristr.* 935 Mani man wepen sare For ransoum to yrland. Marke schuld ȝeld..þre hundred pounde of gold. *a* **1327** *Poem Time Edw. II* 302 in *Pol. Songs* (Camden) 337 If the King in his lond maketh a taxacioun, And everi man is i-set to a certein raunzoun.

4. A ransom bill or bond (see 5 b).

1747 *Col. Rec. Pennsylv.* V. 75 The St. Christopher arrived, whose Crew..had taken and dismissed on a Ransome for Four thousand Dollars an English Frigate.

5. *attrib.* and *Comb.*, as ***ransom-free*** adj.; ***ransom demand, -gift, -gold, -money, package, -payer, -price, purchase.***

1976 R. L. BOYER *Giant Rat of Sumatra* (1977) x. 150 None of the staff..were aware of the *ransom demand. *c* **1560** A. SCOTT *Poems* (S.T.S.) xxxvi. 76 Thy haly grave, Quhilk makis ws *ransome fre. **1715** TICKELL *Homer* 8 Till Ransom-free the Damsel is bestow'd. **1848** BUCKLEY *Iliad* 107 My sire will bestow on thee countless *ransom-gifts. **1815** SCOTT *Ld. of Isles* v. xxiv, He proffer'd *ransom-gold to pay. **1722** DE FOE *Col. Jack* (1840) 198 We bilked the captain of his *ransom money. **1848** BUCKLEY *Iliad* 351 Two men contended for the ransom-money of a slain man. **1969** B. MALAMUD *Pictures of Fidelman* iii. 69 The insurance company..would at once kick in with the ransom money. **1976** T. HEALD *Let Sleeping Dogs Die* vii. 130 These particular villains were interested in ransom money, not selling. **1974** *Aiken* (S. Carolina) *Standard* 24 Apr. 5-A/3 Police said a dummy *ransom package with a note asking the alleged abductors for more time was delivered according to the instructions Dantzler said his kidnapers had given him. **1645** RUTHERFORD *Tryal & Tri. Faith* (1845) 186 You shame the glory of the *ransom-payer. **1872** J. H. INGRAHAM *Pillar of Fire* 329 The King may be redeemed..with a vast *ransom-price. **1865** BUSHNELL *Vicar. Sacr.* v. (1868) 113 To be the *ransom purchase of others.

b. ransom-bill, -bond, an engagement to redeem or pay ransom, in later use esp. for a vessel captured by the enemy; **ransom note**, a letter sent by a kidnapper or kidnappers to interested parties demanding ransom money or other satisfaction, and specifying the consequences should this not be forthcoming.

1575 CHURCHYARD *Chippes* (1817) 7 Releasing many of his fellow-captives, on his own ransom-bond. **1764** *Ann. Reg.* 138 The ransom bills for preserving Manilla from pillage. **1767** BLACKSTONE *Comm.* III. 436 The privileges of embassadors, hostages, or ransom-bills. **1896** *Daily News* 29 Feb. 6/2 The Alabama burned fifty-seven ships besides releasing on ransom-bond a great many with neutral cargo on board. **1935** M. M. ATWATER *Murder in Midsummer* xiv. 135 Maybe it's a kidnapping, but there's no ransom notes. **1975** D. PITTS *This City is Ours* viii. 28 That ship might explode if it's tampered with. That's what the ransom note says, and I believe it.

ransom ('rænsəm), *v.* Forms: see the sb. (also 4 **raunsene**, 5 **rampsoum**, 6 **ramsion**, *Sc.* **ransson**; *pa. t.* 4 **raunsede**). [a. OF. *ransonner*, *-çonner*, etc. f. *ranson*: see prec.]

1. *trans.* To redeem (from captivity or punishment); to procure the release of (a person) or restoration of (a thing) by payment of the sum or price demanded. Also *fig.*

1377 LANGL. *P. Pl.* B. x. 420 A robbere was yraunceouned, rather than thei alle. **1387** TREVISA *Higden* (Rolls) VI. 211 Withbrandes kyng of Longobardes.. raunsoned [*v.r.* raunsede] þe relikes of seint Austyn. *c* **1470** HENRY *Wallace* VIII. 452 Quha ȝeildis him, sall neuir ransownd be. **1513** *Galway Arch.* in *10th Rep. Hist. MSS. Comm.* App. V. 395 That no dweller of this towne become suertie for no gent of the countrey, ne ramson none of them. **1624** CAPT. SMITH *Virginia* VI. 215 Their Canowes.. they ransomed for Beuer skinnes. **1667** SPRAT *Hist. R. Soc.* 434 To randsome the minds of all mankind from Slavery. **1839** THIRLWALL *Greece* VI. 73 They were obliged to ransom not only their prisoners but their dead. **1868** FREEMAN *Norm. Conq.* (1876) II. viii. 280 His wife ransomed him at a heavy price.

b. To redeem, deliver, in religious sense.

a **1300** *Cursor M.* 9784 If godd had wroght anoþer man For to ransun wit adam. **1414** BRAMPTON *Penit. Ps.* (Percy Soc.) 28 Cryist, that deyid up on the rood, To raunsoun synfull creature. **1557** N. T. (Genev.) Epistle **j, He was solde to ransom vs. **1667** MILTON *P.L.* III. 297 His Brethren, ransomd with his own dear life. **1784** COWPER *Tiroc.* 128 We.. learn with wonder how this world began, Who made, who marr'd, and who has ransom'd man. **1859** TENNYSON *Guinevere* 677 Poor sick people, richer in His eyes Who ransom'd us.. than I.

c. To purchase (life or liberty) by a ransom.

1630 DEKKER *2nd Pt. Honest Wh.* Wks. 1873 II. 170 If my life May ransome thine, I yeeld it to the Law. **1697** DAMPIER *Voy.* (1729) I. 75 The Men.. made them send ashoar for Cattle to ransom their Liberties. **1801** *Lusignan* III. 82 The design she had long meditated.. of endeavouring to ransom his liberty.

d. To atone or pay for, to expiate; †to procure respite of (time); to bring *into* by ransoming.

a **1300** *Cursor M.* 14427 þat he suld flexs take.. For to ranscun wit adam sin. *c* **1375** *Sc. Leg. Saints* xxxiii. (*George*) 77 To ransone þe tyme & to sauf þame fra his venyme. *c* **1600** SHAKS. *Sonnets* xxxiv, Those tears.. are rich and ransom all ill deeds. **1604** —— *Oth.* III. iv. 118 Nor my Seruice past, nor present Sorrowes,.. Can ransome me into his loue againe. **1796** JEFFERSON *Writ.* (1859) IV. 152 Its moments of extasy would be ransomed by years of torment and hatred.

2. a. To permit to be ransomed; to admit to ransom; to set free on payment of a sum of money; †to fix one's ransom *at* a certain sum.

1375 BARBOUR *Bruce* II. 466 Off othir, that war takyn than, Sum thai ransownyt, sum thai slew. **1442** in *Proc. King's Council Irel.* (Rolls) 274 He.. put him in greet duresse of prisoun, and rampsoumed him at c. marcs. **1494** FABYAN *Chron.* VII. 348 That he were streyght put in pryson, and not to be raunsomyd nor delyuered tyll the Kyngys pleasure were forther knowen. *a* **1578** LINDESAY (Pitscottie) *Chron. Scot.* (S.T.S.) I. 228 Stewin Bull ranssonat the skiparis, and held money of the marienaris presonaris. **1599** BRETON *Will of Wit* III. i. Wks. (Grosart) 37/2 The souldiours entred, slewe a number, some they raunsommed. **1819** SCOTT *Ivanhoe* x. Leaving it with your nobleness to retain or to ransom the same, according to your pleasure.

b. To demand ransom from or for; to exact payment from; †hence, to oppress with exactions. Also *absol.*

c **1380** WYCLIF *Wks.* (1880) 66 Many.. ben dede bi þe weie, what wiþ traueile & cold.. & enemyes & ofte raunsonyd. ? *a* **1400** *Morte Arth.* 100 Why thow has redyne and raymede, and raunsound þe pople. **1495** *Act 11 Hen. VII*, c. 9 *Preamble*, People.. be.. caried into Scotland and their raunsomed to ther.. utter empoverysshing for ever. **1525** LD. BERNERS *Froiss.* II. 3 All suche landes as he had rule of, he raunsomed them.. greuously, and wolde taxe the men two or three tymes in a yere. **1590** SIR J. SMYTH *Disc. Weapons* 7 b, By fleecing and ransoming of their soldiers being men of wealth. **1819** SCOTT *Ivanhoe* xix, Who is it that rifle, and ransom, and make prisoners in these parts. **1888** in *Times* 17 Aug. 7/6 These gentlemen contend that unfortified towns will never be bombarded or ransomed.

3. To pay ransom to (a person). Also *absol.*, to pay ransom for oneself. *rare*$^{-1}$.

1722 CAPT. OGLE in *Lond. Gaz.* No. 6091/2 They had all ransomed at the Rate of eight Pounds Weight of Gold each; an English Ship, for refusing to ransom the Pyrates had been burnt.

ransomable ('rænsəməb(ə)l), *a.* [f. prec. + -ABLE.] Capable of being ransomed.

c **1611** CHAPMAN *Iliad* I. 22 To dissolve the ransomable chain Of my lov'd daughter's servitude. **1641** EARL MONM. tr. *Biondi's Civil Warres* IV. 79 He made a scrutiny of the prisoners, he detained such as were ransomable. **1718** MOTTEUX *Quix.* (1733) II. 164 The King's Slaves, which are ransomable, are not obliged to go out to Works.

ransomed ('rænsəmd), *ppl. a.* [f. as prec. + -ED[1].] Freed by means of a ransom, delivered, redeemed. Also *absol.*

c **1400** *Prymer* 12 Folkis raunsoned, reioice ȝe. *c* **1440** *Promp. Parv.* 424/2 Rawnsomyd, *redemptus.* **1533** BELLENDEN *Livy* V. xxiii, þe goddis.. wald nocht suffir þat romanis suld leif as redemit or ransound pepil. **1611** BIBLE *Isa.* xxxv. 10 The ransomed of the Lord shall returne. **1760–72** H. BROOKE *Foole of Qual.* (1809) III. 107 A man then demanded.. if I was one of the ransomed? **1846** TRENCH *Mirac.* xxviii. (1862) 387 Here is.. a ransomed and a Ransomer. **1850** TENNYSON *In Mem.* lxi, If.. Thy ransom'd reason change replies With all the circle of the wise.

ransomer ('rænsəmə(r)). [f. as prec. + -ER[1].]

1. One who ransoms; a redeemer.

a **1300** *Cursor M.* 15043 Crist and king and ransconer [*Gött.* ransuner] O folk o godds lai. *c* **1375** *Sc. Leg. Saints* iii. (*Andrew*) 682 Thru þe wes myn ransoner. **1500–20** DUNBAR *Poems* xi. 45 Thy Ransonner, with woundis fyve. **1571** GOLDING *Calvin on Ps.* xxxiv. 23 Ere God can appeere to bee their raunsomer. **1678** J. BROWN *Life of Faith* (1824) I. vii. 129 A Ransomer.. will be most tender of them. **1802** J. JAMIESON *Use Sacr. Hist.* I. I. 86 Elihu speaks of the Messiah as a Ransomer. **1870** R. C. JEBB *Sophocles' Electra* (ed. 2) 9/1 A ransomed prisoner-of-war and his ransomer.

2. *spec.* **a.** One of the representatives of the Order of our Lady for the redemption of captives, founded by St. Peter Nolasco in 1223 (see quot.).

1745 A. BUTLER *Lives of Saints* (1821) I. 462 Two members of the Order should be sent together among the infidels to treat about the ransom of christian slaves, and they are hence called Ransomers.

b. A member of a Roman Catholic guild which aims at the conversion of England to the Roman Catholic faith.

1890 *Pall Mall G.* 1 Apr. 6/2 The Guild was inaugurated about two years ago.. and already numbers 12,000 members, called 'Ransomers'. **1896** *Westm. Gaz.* 1 June 9/2 An enormous gathering of ordinary lay Catholics, including 'Ransomers', whose special mission is to pray for the conversion of England.

3. A person held as security for the payment of ransom for a ship. ? *Obs.*

1707 *Lond. Gaz* No. 4326/3 This Privateer had on Board eight Ransomers for Vessels taken in this Chanel. **1761** *Ann. Reg.* 157 The Courageux.. had ransomers on board for five prizes, amounting to 8200*l.* **1782** *Chron.* in *Ann. Reg.* 199/1 A flag of truce arrived here last week with some ransomers.

ransoming ('rænsəmɪŋ), *vbl. sb.* [f. as prec. + -ING[1].] The action of the vb. RANSOM.

a **1300** *Cursor M.* 4420 In kinges prisun for to lij, Wit na raunsuming to bij. *c* **1375** *Sc. Leg. Saints* ix. (*Barthol.*) 128 þe manere of oure ransonynge. **1442** in *Proc. King's Counc. Irel.* (Rolls) 287 þe taking, imprisonyng and rampsonyng of the Priouer of Conale. **1525** LD. BERNERS *Froiss.* II. 52 He.. dyde great domage to the countre.. by raunsomynge of the townes. **1575** *Galway Arch.* in *10th Rep. Hist. MSS. Comm.* App. V. 425 For redeming and ramsoning of the Illes of Aren. **1790** BEATSON *Nav. & Mil. Mem.* I. 295 All the articles relative to the ransoming of the town. **1899** STALKER *Christol. Jesus* v. 180 Such cases show clearly what ransoming was.

ransomite ('rænsəmaɪt). *Min.* [f. the name of F. L. *Ransome* (1868–1935), U.S. mining geologist + -ITE[1].] A hydrated sulphate of copper, ferric iron, and aluminium, $Cu(Fe,Al)_2(SO_4)_4{\cdot}7H_2O$, formed as blue monoclinic crystals in a mine fire.

1928 C. LAUSEN in *Amer. Mineralogist* XIII. 221 Ransomite occurs as crusts lining cavities in the crushed rocks and also as small tufts of radiating crystals. **1970** *Ibid.* LV. 729 Ransomite.. occurs only in the United Verde mine at Jerome, Arizona where it formed as the result of a mine fire.

ransomless ('rænsəmlɪs), *a.* [f. RANSOM *sb.* + -LESS.] Without ransom.

1588 SHAKS. *Tit. A.* I. i. 274 Ransomlesse heere we set our Prisoners free. **1645** MILTON *Tetrach.* (1851) 160 (Gen. ii. 18) A ransomles captivity. **1676** HOBBES *Iliad* I. 98 Till she be to her Father sent.. ransomless. **1796** ANNA SEWARD *Lett.* (1811) IV. 265 Fingal.. releases him ransomless. **1846** H. W. TORRENS *Rem. Milit. Hist.* 145 As ransomless prisoners after a battle. **1873** SYMONDS *Grk. Poets* viii. 244 The Athenians released Dorieus ransomless and scatheless.

rant (rænt), *sb.* [f. the vb.]

1. A high-flown, extravagant, or bombastic speech or utterance; a piece of turgid declamation; a tirade.

1649 G. DANIEL *Trinarch., Hen. IV*, cxl, 'Tis a brave Costly Rant th' Hesperian King vtters with many Titles. **1668** DRYDEN *Maiden Queen* Epil., I left my Client yonder in a Rant Against the Envious, and the Ignorant. **1717** ATTERBURY *Let. to Pope* 8 Nov., What I look'd upon as a Rant of Barrow's, I now begin to think a serious Truth. **1787** MAD. D'ARBLAY *Diary* 6 Mar., Then broke forth one of his most flighty rants of compliments. **1849** MACAULAY *Hist. Eng.* vi. II. 139 He sometimes,.. in his rants, talked with Norman haughtiness of the Celtic barbarians.

†**b.** A violent scolding. *Obs. rare.*

1663 PEPYS *Diary* 14 Mar., A great rant I did give to Mr. Davis.. and others about their usage of Michell. **1725** RAMSAY *Gentle Sheph.* I. ii, If canker'd Madge, our aunt, Come up the burn, she'll gie's a wicked rant.

c. A ranting state or condition.

1722 DE FOE *Col. Jack* (1840) 207 Her former behaviour was a kind of rant, or fit. **1801** C. GADSDEN in *J. Adams's Wks.* 1854 IX. 579 The uncommonly extravagant ravings of our own times.. still in the highest rant. **1876** C. M. DAVIES *Unorth. London* (ed. 2) 42, I set out one May evening to see the Tabernacle 'on the rant'.

2. Extravagant or bombastic language or sentiments; magniloquent and empty declamation.

1708 J. PHILIPS *Cyder* (1807) 99 Nought is heard But din, and various clamor, and mad rant. **1762** KAMES *Elem. Crit.* xvii. (1833) 234 The following passages are pure rant. **1820** SCOTT *Abbot* xxxi, He.. need not plead his cause with the commonplace rant of romantic passion. **1861** J. G. HOLLAND *Lessons in Life* viii. 119 They strain their brains.. and wear themselves out repeating the rant of their sect and the cant of their schools.

b. A declamatory way of speaking. *rare*$^{-1}$.

c **1742** JOHNSON in *Boswell* an. 1744, The players, Sir, have got a kind of rant, with which they run on, without any regard either to accent or emphasis.

3. *north. dial.* and *Sc.* A boisterous, riotous frolic or merry-making; a spree. Also *transf.*

1675 in THORESBY *Ducatus Leodensis* (1715) App. 617 In December the same Year was an Epidemick Distemper profanely called the Jolly Rant; it was a severe Cold, and violent Cough. **1703** *Lond. Gaz.* No. 3944/4 The Yearly Fox and Hare Hunting, famous by the Name of Dalton Rant. **1786** BURNS *Scotch Drink* viii, Thou art the life o' public haunts; But thee, what were our fairs and rants? **1816** SCOTT *Bl. Dwarf* ii, A rant amang the lasses, or a splore at a fair. **1876** *Mid-Yorks. Gloss.* s.v., The feast-days of Nidderdale localities are called *rants*.

4. (Chiefly *Sc.*) A lively, noisy, or irregular tune or song.

1725 RAMSAY *Gentle Sheph.* I. i, How heartsome is't.. To hear the birds chirm o'er their pleasing rants! **1830** SIR J. BARRINGTON *Pers. Sk. Own Times* (ed. 2) II. 166, I think our rants and planxties would have answered just as well without either symphonies or chromatics. **1898** MUNRO *John Splendid* xi. 112 A tune they call 'The Galley of the Waves,' a Stewart rant.

rant (rænt), *v.* [a. obs. Du. *randten*, *ranten* (also *randen*: see RAND *v.*) to talk foolishly, to rave; cf. G. *ranzen* to frolic, spring about, etc.]

1. *intr.* (†or with *it*). To talk or declaim in an extravagant high-flown manner; to use bombastic language.

1602 SHAKS. *Ham.* v. i. 307 Nay, and thou'lt mouth, Ile rant as well as thou. **1664** H. MORE *Myst. Iniq.* xii. 40 Those that talk at this rate rant it, and speak unintelligible riddles. **1747** in Doran *Mann & Manners* (1876) I. xi. 250 As an Actress.. she does extremely well.. She rants a little too much whilst she is in woman's cloaths. **1781** COWPER *Table-t.* 299 In such a cause I grant An English poet's privilege to rant. **1864** KNIGHT *Passages Work. Life* II. viii. 169 Pretended teachers of political economy.. were ranting in popular assemblies.

†**b.** To storm or scold violently. Const. *at*, *against*. *Obs.*

1647 COWLEY *Mistr., Rich Rival* i, They say you're angry, and rant mightily. **1664** PEPYS *Diary* 5 Feb., Which I ranted at him for when he came in. **1667** POOLE *Dial. betw. Protest. & Papist* (1735) 63, I have heard some of your Priests ranting highly against our Translation. **1710** PALMER *Proverbs* 206 Children and servants must never be suffer'd to.. insult and rant at one another.

2. *intr.* (†or with *it*). To be jovial, boisterous, uproariously gay or merry; to lead a gay or dissolute life; also, to sing loudly.

1598 [see RANTING *ppl. a.*]. **1641** BROME *Joviall Crew* (1651) 15 The more the merrier, I am resolv'd to Rant it to the last. **1657** THORNLEY tr. *Longus' Daphnis & Chloe* 84 He permitted them securely to rant and be joviall as in peace. **1700** FARQUHAR *Constant Couple* IV. i, I'll Court, and Swear and Rant, and Rake. **1785** BURNS *Jolly Beggars*, 1st Recit., Wi' quaffing and laughing, They ranted and they sang. **1821** CLARE *Vill. Minstr.* II. 95 The birds that ranted in the hedge-row boughs. **1824** SCOTT *Redgauntlet* let. x, If ye expect to be ranting among the queans o' lasses.., Ye will come by the waur.

3. *trans.* To utter in a declamatory and bombastic manner; to mouth. Also with *out*.

1650 W. SAUNDERSON *Aul. Coquin.* 97 He hath ranted his Stories of Mansell.. and of the peace. **1788** MAD. D'ARBLAY *Diary* 13 Feb., To hear a man rant such stuff. **1805** T. HARRAL *Scenes of Life* III. 34 Ranting out some speeches of Hamlet. **1865** MORLEY *Mod. Characteristics* 150 Ranting Carlyle and Emerson by the volume.

rant, obs. form of *rent*, pa. pple. REND *v.*

rant, var. RAND *sb.*[2]

ran-tan ('ræntæn), *sb. slang* or *dial.* [Echoic: in sense 2 perh. for RANDAN.]

1. A word expressive of a loud banging noise; hence *sb.* as a name for this, and †*attrib.* = noisy.

1630 J. TAYLOR (Water P.) *Wks.* I. 110 There is ran tan Tom Tinker and his Tib. *c* **1640** SHIRLEY *Capt. Underwit* III. iii. in Bullen *O. Pl.* (1883) II. 366 Ran tan: enough,—you must not waste your lunges Too much at once. **1837** CARLYLE *Fr. Rev.* III. VII. v. Beating sharp ran-tan, To arms, To arms! **1869** *Lonsdale Gloss.*, *Rantan*, a loud and long knocking at a door.

2. A riot, drinking bout. ***on the ran-tan***, on the spree, on the 'randan'.

1853 DICKENS in *Househ. Words* 24 Sept. 75 For the one word drunk,.. I find.. beery, winey, slewed, on the ran-tan. **1886** *Rochdale Gloss.*, *Ran-tan*, riot, involving the idea of breaking furniture, when the actor is drunken. **1936** I. L.

IDRIESS *Cattle King* v. 43 When sober, he worked miracles with his limited materials. When 'on the ran-tan', which was every three months, Charlie did the cooking. **1959** G. SLATTER *Gun in my Hand* iv. 42, I remember you on that trip to Nelson for the footie. You really got on the rantan. I bet you never been back to that pub! **1963** A. PRIOR *Z Cars Again* (1964) ii. 22 Wilson had been out on the ran-tan, came home late.

ran-tan ('ræntæn), *v. north. dial.* Now *rare.* Also **ran-dan.** [f. the sb.] *intr.* To make a noise with unruly singing, and the beating of pots and kettles, at the house of a man who has beaten his wife. Also *trans.*, with husband as obj. Hence ˌ**ran'tanning** *vbl. sb.*

1866 J. E. BROGDEN *Provincial Words & Expressions Lincs.* 163 *Ran-dan*, to ride the stang (or pole) connected with agricultural lynch-law, usually applied to husbands who have beaten their wives. **1886** *Folk-Lore Jrnl.* IV. 262 He'd ought to be *ran-dan'd* out o' the town. **1891** *Lincolnshire N. & Q.* II. vi. 186 As the news spreads, 'So-and-so threshed his wife yisterday mornin',' it is accompanied by the comment, 'We must 'ran-tan' him to-night.' **1928** *Observer* 26 Feb. 17/2 Seventeen villagers of Lincolnshire have been fined for 'rantanning'... Rantanning is the 'rough music' of kettle and pan, in which the rustic moralist conveys his sense of outraged propriety.

†**rantantingly** *adv.* App., extravagantly.

Perh. a misprint for *rantingly*, but cf. RAN-TAN *sb.*

1599 NASHE *Lenten Stuffe* 15, I would not..haue it cast in my dishe that therefore I prayse Yarmouth so rantantingly, because I never elsewhere bayted my horse.

rantepole, obs. form of RANTIPOLE.

ranter ('ræntə(r)), *sb.* [f. RANT *v.* + -ER[1].]

1. One who rants, declaims noisily or bombastically, esp. in preaching (cf. 2).

1649 CROMWELL *Let.* 14 Nov. (Carlyle), There went also, with this party, Sir Thomas Armstrong, Colonel Trevor, and most of their great ranters. **1675** TRAHERNE *Chr. Ethics* 339 How empty these self, but shallow-conceited ranters are,..they place all gallantry and worth in valour. **1786** *Gentl. Mag.* LVI. i. 305 Some other ranters and rhapsodists. **1826** SCOTT *Woodst.* xxii, A wild ranter in religious opinions. **1889** JESSOPP *Coming of Friars* i. 48 Rome has found a place for the dreamiest mystic or the noisiest ranter.

†**2.** A noisy, riotous, dissipated fellow; a rake.

1654 SIR E. NICHOLAS in *N. Papers* (Camden) II. 81 A very sober and honnest understanding man, noe drinker nor ranter. **1681** T. JORDAN *London's Joy* in Heath *Grocers' Comp.* (1869) 548 We sing, dance, and trip it, as frolick as Ranters. **1712** ADDISON *Spect.* No. 486 ¶1 The Hazards of a Town full of Ranters and Debauchees. **1828** SCOTT *F.M. Perth* xii, It was never your mother's custom, and it shall never be mine, to take up with ranters.

b. *Sc.* A lively singer or player.

17.. *Maggie Lauder* (Sc. Song) 10 I'm a piper to my trade, My name is Rob the Ranter. **1812** W. TENNANT *Anster F* I. 10, I see the Ranter with bagpipe on back.

3. *spec.* (With capital initial; chiefly *pl.*). **a.** Applied to the members of a sect of Antinomians which arose *c* 1645. Now only *Hist.*

1651 BROME (*title*), The Joviall Crew, or the Devill turn'd Ranter: a Comedie, containing a true Discovery..of a Sect (lately sprung up amongst us) called Ranters. **1667** L. STUCLEY *Gospel-Glass* xxxii. (1670) 319 Seekers, Ranters, and Quakers, have took occasion to cry down the Office of the Ministry. **1722** B. STAR tr. *Mlle. de St. Phale* vii. 192 Had they been born Ranters, or Papists, or Jews, they would not have changed their Religion. **1856** R. A. VAUGHAN *Mystics* (1860) II. 217 The priests and magistrates were not more violent against him [G. Fox] than the Ranters.

b. Applied to members of the Primitive Methodist body, which originated in 1807–10.

The statement in quot. 1823 connects this use of the term with sense 2 of the vb. (cf. 2 b above).

1823 H. BOURNE *Hist. Primitive Methodists* 49 When these ..meetings were closed, the praying people, in returning home, were accustomed to sing through the streets at Belper. This circumstance procured them the name of Ranters; and the name of Ranter, which first arose on this occasion [in 1814], afterwards spread very extensively. **1827** SYD. SMITH *Wks.* (1867) II. 129 The Ranters do not cost us a farthing, because they are not disqualified by ranting. **1839** *Penny Cycl.* XV. 143/1 The Primitive Methodists, who are sometimes known as Ranters, originated in Staffordshire. **1862** SIR B. BRODIE *Psychol. Inq.* II. v. 174 Those having a too lively imagination..become Mormonites and Ranters.

ranter ('ræntə(r)), *v. dial.* and *techn.* [ad. F. *rentrer*, *rentraire* in same sense: see RENTER *v.*]

1. *trans.* To darn, mend. Also *transf.*

1673–88 LD. FOUNTAINHALL in M. P. Brown *Decis. Suppl.* (1826) III. 86 (Jam.) He bade the defender ranter the two ends of an inconsistency he was urging together. **1808** in JAMIESON. *a* **1825** in FORBY. **1848** in EVANS *Leicest. Gloss.*

2. To join (two edges of cloth) with fine stitching (see also quot. 1902).

1902 M. PRINCE BROWNE *Pract. Work of Dressmaking & Tailoring* II. iii. 87 *Rantering.*—This is a stitch used for joining cloth, and the two edges to be joined are put together—level..with the right side of each piece facing; they must then be neatly 'back-stitched' together by hand, as *near* to the edge of the cloth as possible... A cloth which is too thin to join by 'fine drawing', can be 'rantered' together. **1933** J. E. LIBERTY *Pract. Tailoring* iii. 24 (*caption*) Seaming and rantering. An alternative to stoting for use on loose materials (tweeds, etc.).

Hence †**ranter-drawed** *a.*, darned. *Obs.*

1655 J. BARNES *Gerania* (1675) 69 His very cloaths were so neatly ranter-draw'd, that no man living cou'd ever discern they had been torn.

Ranterism ('ræntərɪz(ə)m). [f. RANTER *sb.* + -ISM.] The practices or doctrines of Ranters.

1673 PENN *Spir. Alexander the Coppersmith Rebuked* 9 It is an absolute Inlet to Ranterism. **1697** G. KEITH *Sec. Narr. Proc. Turn.-Hall* 26 The bottom of it is Ranterisme, and wild Notion and Fancy. **1841** *Englishman's Mag.* 1 Mar. 32 Methodism and Ranterism.

ranterpike ('ræntəpaɪk). Now *Hist.* Also **rantipike.** [Origin unknown.] (See quot. 1948.) Also *attrib.*

1892 L. ANDERSON *Among Typhoons & Pirate Craft* 38 Like the *Ranterpikes*, that used to ply between Liverpool and Glasgow, before the day of steamers, there was no taking in sail here as long as she would stand up to it. **1929** *Mariner's Mirror* XV. 316/1 They were two of the famous Ranterpikes employed carrying pig-iron and heavy castings to Liverpool. *Ibid.*, The correct name is Ranterpike, not Rantipike. **1948** R. DE KERCHOVE *Internat. Maritime Dict.* 579/2 *Ranterpike*, three-masted topsail schooner or brigantine of the River Clyde of about 250 tons... These vessels were generally engaged in the transportation of pig iron from Glasgow to Liverpool. The type is now extinct. Also called *rantipike.* **1973** D. R. MACGREGOR *Fast Sailing Ships* iii. 91/3 The ranterpike rig is rarely referred to but apparently necessitated that one of the upper masts on the fore mast was stepped abaft the other.

ranting ('ræntɪŋ), *vbl. sb.* [-ING[1].] **1.** The action of the vb. RANT in various senses.

1653 *Nissena* 40 [He] was the scandal of all Nicocia, though his ranting..made him [etc.]. **1672** GREGORY in Rigaud *Corr. Sci. Men* (1841) II. 231, I am afraid ye will find these Cogitationes..to be but ranting. **1768–74** TUCKER *Lt. Nat.* (1834) II. 116 The bigot has been..terrified by the rantings of some gifted preacher. **1785** BURNS *Addr. to Deil* xx, A certain Bardie's rantin, drinkin..will send him..To your black pit. **1843** LEFEVRE *Life Trav. Phys.* III. III. viii. 187 The scene..was nobly acted, without ranting.

2. *attrib.*, as *ranting ground.*

1814 JANE AUSTEN *Mansfield Park* I. xiv. 276 There was some very good ranting ground in [the part of] Frederick.

ranting ('ræntɪŋ), *ppl. a.* [-ING[2].]

1. That rants, in senses of the verb.

1598 SHAKS. *Merry W.* II. i. 196 Looke where my ranting Host of the Garter comes..hee lookes so merrily. **1706** FARQUHAR *Recruiting Officer* IV. i, I fancy my Breeches wou'd become me as well as any ranting Fellow of 'em all. **1771** WESLEY *Wks.* (1872) V. 149 Some of the wild, ranting Antinomians. **1838–9** HALLAM *Hist. Lit.* III. III. vi. §103. 347 Marston is a tumid and ranting tragedian.

2. Characterized by, of the nature of, ranting.

a **1656** USSHER *Ann.* VI. (1658) 470 [He] sent to Jonathan ..a ranting challenge to meet him if he dared. **1665** BUNYAN *Holy Citie* (1669) 199 It looks too like Ranting Opinions, and contradiction to Scripture, for me to believe. **1681–6** T. SCOTT *Chr. Life* (1747) III. 599 Flat Impertinence or ranting Enthusiasm. **1814** SCOTT *Wav.* xxx, Is this a day, to be singing your rantin fule sangs in? **1824** —— *Redgauntlet* let. xi, The ranting suppers in Redgauntlet Castle. **1894** 'MARK TWAIN' *Pudd'nhead Wilson* 333 'Bob Riley' is a common rackety slam-bang secular song, one of the rippingest and rantingest and noisiest there is. **1929** *Oxford Poetry* 40 The ranting numbers do not pierce your ear.

3. †**a.** Unruly, restive. †**b.** Flaunting. *Obs.* **c.** *Sc.* Blazing, roaring.

1658 OSBORN *Jas. I* (1673) 478 Horses, that are far less ranting, and easier brought to an even temper. *c* **1685** *Bagford Ball.* App., Her Kitchin-stuff she often will sell, to purchase that Ranting Attire. **1725** RAMSAY *Gentle Sheph.* IV. i, I'll mak a rantin' fire, and merry sall we be. **1880** WATT *Sketches* 75 (E.D.D.) A red rantin' fire.

Hence '**rantingly** *adv. Sc.*

1733 RAMSAY *South Sea Sang* i, [We] rantin'ly ran up and down, In rising stocks to buy a skair. **1794** BURNS *Mc Pherson's Farewell*, Sae rantingly, sae wantonly, Sae dauntingly gaed he.

rantipike, var. RANTERPIKE.

rantipole ('ræntɪpəʊl), *sb.* (and *a.*) Also 8 **rante-, -pol**; *dial.* 9 **ranty-, -pow(l.** [? A fanciful formation on RANT *v.*: cf. FRAMPOLD.]

1. A romp; a wild, ill-behaved or reckless person; a scold, termagant. Now *rare.*

In southern dial. also applied to the wild-carrot, and in the north to the game of see-saw.

a **1700** B. E. *Dict. Cant. Crew*, *Rantipole*, a rude wild Boy or Girl. **1719** D'URFEY *Pills* (1872) I. 6 Good buye to the Change Where Rantepoles range. **1790** R. TYLER *Contrast* III. i. (1887) 55 There was a poor, good-natured, curse of a husband, and a sad rantipole of a wife. **1829** MARRYAT *F. Mildmay* xv, I was always considered as a rantipole.

2. *attrib.* or as *adj.* Wild, disorderly, rakish.

1700 CONGREVE *Way of World* IV. x, [To] comport your self at this Rantipole rate. **1728** VANBR. & CIB. *Prov. Husb.* V. i. 93 Another rantipol Dame of Quality. **1842** S. LOVER *Handy Andy* xxiv. 212 My house is respectable..none o' your rantipole places, Sir. **1863** SALA in *Temple Bar* Dec. 9, I never knew such a set of rantipole maniacs. **1866** *Hansard Commons* 27 Apr. 91 But, notwithstanding all the statements that are made—notwithstanding this rantipole rhetoric—it is not true that the North of England is superior in population or property to the South. **1970** *Times* 7 Jan. 9/7 Four rantipole businessmen lament the problems faced by the wolfish married man. **1976** *Times Lit. Suppl.* 12 Mar. 297/4 [Marlborough's] letters to the duchess are intact and ample but allowances have to be made for anyone writing to that rantipole lady.

rantipole ('ræntɪpəʊl), *v.* [f. prec. *sb.*] *intr.* To go *about*, or behave, in a romping, rude or noisy fashion. †Also with *it.*

1712 ARBUTHNOT *John Bull* II. iv, She used to Rantipole about the House, pinch the Children, kick the Servants. **1760** MURPHY *Way to Keep Him* I. ii, Lord bless you, ma'am, they rantipole it about this town. **1841** *Blackw. Mag.* XLIX. 494 When they have once run rantipoling over the country after bullocks.

Hence '**rantipoling** *vbl. sb.* and *ppl. a.*

1754 RICHARDSON *Grandison* VII. xliii, They go on without rantipoling, in the ordinary course of reasonable creatures. **1850** E. WARBURTON *R. Hastings* I. 6 Fitter for honest men than for the like of us rantipoling cavaliers.

†'**rantism**[1]. *Obs. rare.* [ad. Gr. ῥαντισμ-ός, n. of action f. ῥαντίζ-ειν RANTIZE.] A sprinkling.

a **1626** BP. ANDREWES 96 *Serm.* xix. (1661) 394 But an handful to their heap; but a rantisme to their baptisme. **1701** WHITEHEAD *Truth Prevalent* 116 For Sprinkling is Rantism, and not Baptism... I would not have these Men offended at the word Rantism, it being as much English as the word Baptism.

†'**Rantism**[2]. *Obs. rare.* [f. RANT *v.* + -ISM.] The practice of ranting, *spec.* after the manner of those called Ranters; Ranterism.

1665 *Truth Vindicated* 13 John had not then..gotten into a perfect state of Rantisme. *a* **1670** BP. RUST *Disc. of Truth* xi. (1682) 181 The Foundations of Rantism, Debauchery, and all Dissoluteness of Life. **1691** WOOD *Ath. Oxon.* II. 362 This person [F. Cheynell] who had ran through most, if not all, religions, even to rantism.

†**rantize**, *v. Obs. rare.* [ad. Gr. ῥαντίζ-ειν to sprinkle.] *trans.* To sprinkle. (Used with reference to baptism by sprinkling instead of immersion: cf. RANTISM[1].)

1644 *Mock. Majesty* in *Harl. Misc.* (Malh.) V. 455 To the intelligent reader, baptised or rantised. Thou must excuse me for this pretty new stamped word... It is not a week since I first met with it. **1653** S. FISHER *Baby Baptism* 5 It is..no true visible Church of God because it Rantizes Infants. **1701** WHITEHEAD *Truth Prevalent* 118 In Rantizing, or sprinkling and crossing Childrens Faces.

rantle, dial. var. ROWAN-TREE.

rantle-tree, Sc. var. RANNEL-TREE.

†'**rantling**, *vbl. sb. Obs. rare*[−1]. Squeaking.

a **1693** *Urquhart's Rabelais* III. xiii. 107 The barking of Currs, bawling of Mastiffs,..rantling of Rats.

†**rantoon(e.** *Obs.* A form of tricycle formerly in use (see quot. 1869).

1869 R. CRAWLEY *Manly Games for Boys* 439 The Rantoone has a small wheel in front, and two larger wheels behind. It is guided by means of the front wheel. **1870** H. KINGSLEY *Boy in Grey* 1 A Noah's Ark, in which the elephant..would serve for a rantoone.

rantree, -try, dial. variants of ROWAN-TREE.

†**rantum-scantum**, *int.*, *sb.*, and *a. Obs.* Also 8 **-skantum.** [A riming comb., perh. suggested by RANT *v.*]

A. *int.* and *sb.* (Precise sense not clear; cf. quots.)

1600 HEYWOOD *1st Pt. Edw. IV*, I. iv. Wks. 1874 I. 19 Rantum, scantum, rogues, follow your leader! **1667** DAVENANT & DRYDEN *Tempest* IV. iii, I found her..singing Tory Rory, and Rantum Scantum, with her own natural brother. **1760** *Did you ever see such Damned Stuff?* Title-p., Rantum-skantum is the Word, and Nonsense shall ensue. **1772** BRYDGES *Homer Trav.* (1797) I. 78 Jove and his queen have had their quantum Of jaw, and such-like rantum-scantum.

B. *adj.* Harum-scarum, disorderly.

1727–8 MRS. DELANY *Lett., to Mrs. A. Granville* 164 Don't think me the maddest thing in the world for writing such a rantum scantum letter. *c* **1780** M. MONSEY *Let. to Mrs. Montague* in *Bk. about Drs.* (1860) II. iv. 83, I shall find rantum scantum work at Cyprus, Paphos, and Cythera.

So **rantum-scootum** *a.* (U.S.)

1885 *Harper's Mag.* Mar. 614/1 He's a deal sight more serious-minded than most of the rantum-scootum boys.

ranty ('ræntɪ), *a. Sc.* and *north. dial.* [f. RANT *sb.* or *v.* + -Y[1].] Wildly excited; riotous, boisterous, lively; inclined to rant.

1783 in *Eng. Dial. Dict.* **1790** J. FISHER *Poems on Various Subjects* 115, I us'd to be right ranty, An' mak the youngsters spring like bucks. **1867** 'H. LEE' *Mr. Wynyard's Ward* I. I. iii. 94 Master'll be ranty again. We once afore got as much gowld as was worth a pound or two, and you'd have thought we'd found a Californy to hear him talk. **1913** D. H. LAWRENCE *Let.* 10 Feb. in F. Lawrence *Not I but the Wind* (1934) 81 Well, do write about what you think—say Dehmel is ranty and tawdry.

rantypole, variant of RANTIPOLE.

ranty-tanty. *north. dial.* and *Sc.* 'A weed which grows among corn, with a reddish leaf' (Jam.); also, 'broad-leaved sorrel' (ibid.).

1725 RAMSAY *Scornfu' Nansy* ii, With crowdymowdy they fed me, Langkail and ranty-tanty. **1829** BROCKETT *N.C. Wds.* (ed. 2), *Ranty-tanty*.. There is a troublesome weed in corn fields of this name. **1893** T. F. HENDERSON *Old World Scotland* 51 Ranty-tanty, carrots and turnips.

‖**ranula** ('rænjʊlə). *Path.* [L. *rānula* a little frog, a little swelling on the tongue of cattle (Vegetius), dim. of *rāna* frog. Cf. F. *ranule.*] A cystic tumour under the tongue, caused by the obstruction of the salivary ducts or glands.

'The term is derived either from an imaginary resemblance of the swelling to a frog, or from the peculiar croaking noise which the patient makes when affected by it' (Craig).

[*c* 1400 *Lanfranc's Cirurg.* 262.] **1657** in *Physical Dict.* **1661** LOVELL *Hist. Anim. & Min.* 348 The ranula under the tongue, which is a tumour in forme like a frog. **1727–41** in CHAMBERS *Cycl.* **1834** *Good's Study Med.* (ed. 4) I. 94 When a ranula has been opened, the surgeon should always examine with a probe [etc.]. **1879** *St. George's Hosp. Rep.* IX. 266 The only case of ranula was treated by snipping out a fair-sized piece of cyst-wall.

Hence '**ranular** *a.* **a.** = RANINE 1. (So F. *ranulaire.*) ? *Obs.* **b.** Of or pertaining to ranula.

1656 in BLOUNT *Glossogr.* s.v. *Vein.* **1784** W. CULLEN *First Lines Pract. Phys.* cccv. Wks. 1827 II. 35 The opening of the ranular veins seems to be an insignificant remedy.

ranunculaceous (rəˌnʌŋkjʊˈleɪʃəs), *a. Bot.* [f. RANUNCUL-US + -ACEOUS.] Belonging to the Natural Order *Ranunculaceæ*, of which Ranunculus is the typical genus.

1833 *Penny Cycl.* I. 88/1 From all other ranunculaceous plants, Aconitum is at once known [etc.]. **1882** G. ALLEN *Colours of Flowers* ii. 35 Among the higher ranunculaceous plants.. we get the fullest and richest colouration.

‖**ranunculus** (rəˈnʌŋkjʊləs). *Bot.* Pl. **-culuses**, (7–8 **-us's**, 8 **-usses**) and **-culi**. [L., a little frog, tadpole; also a medicinal plant, perh. crowfoot (Pliny); dim. of *rāna* frog.] **a.** (With capital initial.) A genus of plants (also called CROWFOOT) widely diffused in temperate regions; the common species with yellow flowers are popularly known by the name of BUTTERCUPS; the usual cultivated species is *R. asiaticus*. **b.** A plant belonging to this genus.

[**1562** TURNER *Herbal* II. 114 Ranunculus is called.. in Englishe Crowfoot or kingcup.] **1578** LYTE *Dodoens* III. lxxii. 415 There be foure kindes of Ranunculus, or Crowfoote. **1663** BOYLE *Usef. Exp. Nat. Philos.* II. ii. 42, I have made.. even a ranunculus itselfe, to grow.. with water. **1712** tr. *Pomet's Hist. Drugs* I. 39 A Root divided by Lumps or Clods, like the Ranunculus. **1767** J. ABERCROMBIE *Ev. Man his own Gardener* (1803) 45 Plant ranunculuses and anemonies in mild, dry, open weather. **1855** E. S. DELAMER *Flower Garden* (1861) 68 The florists' Ranunculus is the *R. Asiaticus*; but the genus is large, and several of the species, in their double varieties, are cultivated as border flowers.

attrib. **1702** *Lond. Gaz.* No. 3786/4 Divers kinds of double Ranunculos [*sic*] Roots. **1845** *Florist's Jrnl.* 5 Although worms are always troublesome.. in a garden, there is no bed .. they are likely to deface more than the ranunculus bed.

ranungard, obs. Sc. f. RENEGADE.

ranverse, var. RENVERSE *v.*

Ranvier (rɑ̃vje). *Anat.* [The name of Louis Antoine *Ranvier* (1835–1922), French histologist.] ***node of Ranvier*** (also ***Ranvier('s) node***): each of the interruptions of the myelin which occur regularly along the sheaths of myelinated nerves; (described by Ranvier in *Leçons sur l'Histologie du Système Nerveux* (1878) vii. 110–12).

1881 T. E. SATTERTHWAITE *Man. Histol.* ix. 110 Each fibre has a double contour and is divided at tolerably regular intervals by transverse divisions, which are now known as Ranvier's nodes. **1885** [see NODE 3 c]. **1912** J. D. LICKLEY *Nervous Syst.* ii. 11 On the outside of the medullary sheath ..is a thin structureless membrane known as the neurilemma... It is a continuous sheath and is not interrupted at the nodes of Ranvier. **1966** *McGraw-Hill Encycl. Sci. & Technol.* VIII. 198/2 The all-or-nothing nerve impulse.. was shown to arise at the first Ranvier node adjacent to the ending. **1968** PASSMORE & ROBSON *Compan. Med. Stud.* I. xiv. 4/1 Generally, the greater the diameter of the fibre the less frequent are the nodes of Ranvier, so that the internodal length of a nerve fibre 5 μm in diameter is about 0·5 mm while that of a 10 μm fibre is about 2 mm.

rany, obs. f. RANEE.

ranye, obs. Sc. f. RAINY *a.*

‖**ranz-des-vaches** (rɑ̃(s) de vaʃ). Also †**rens de vache**, *erron.* **-vach**. [Swiss dial. of Fribourg, f. *ranz*, of doubtful origin and meaning + 'of the cows'.] One of the melodies peculiar to Swiss herdsmen, usually played on an Alpine horn, and consisting of irregular phrases made up of the harmonic notes of the horn. Also *transf.*

1773 C. BURNEY *Present State of Music in Germany* II. 125 His lordship next confirmed to me, the account of the *Maladie du Païs* or home-sickness, being brought on by the tune called the *Rens de Vache*, if heard by any of the Swiss troops in foreign service. **1801** *Encycl. Brit.* Suppl. II. 492/1 Every Senn has an harmonious set of at least two or three bells, chiming in with the famous *ranz des vaches*. **1841** *Penny Cycl.* XIX. 299/1 The bands of the Swiss regiments in foreign service were forbidden to play the Ranz des Vaches. **1841** C. LEVER *Charles O'Malley* I. xxxvi. 201 Your wild countrymen [*sc.* Irish troops] have heard their *Ranz des vaches*, it seems. **1857** LONGF. in *Life* (1891) II. 557 The sound of his voice was like a *Ranz des Vaches* to her ears.

Rao (raʊ). Also **Raw, Row.** [Hindi *rāo* chief, prince, f. Skr. *rājan* king: see RAJA, RAJAH.] In W. and N.W. India: a title given to a chief or prince, and affixed to the names of other distinguished persons.

1799 *Asiatick Researches* VI. 67 The Raw or Rajah is of the tribe Nirooka, and a feudatory of the Rajah of Jynagur. **1801** *Ibid.* VII. 129 The districts adjoining to the eastern parts of the Mahratta territory, were at this term under Inkut Row, a Goand chief. **1845** *Encycl. Metrop.* XIII. 468/2 Mohammed Ali had also allured into his service the famous Morari Rao, chief of the Mahrattas. **1887** QUEEN VICTORIA *Let.* 27 Aug. in D. Duff *Victoria in Highlands* (1968) 362 Fritz.. kindly helped me in receiving the Rao of Kutch... The Rao is most amiable, gentle, and unaffected. **1927** *Blackw. Mag.* Sept. 395/1 At the head of each valley squats the domed and generally crumbling fortress of the local 'Rao'. **1978** 'M. M. KAYE' *Far Pavilions* xiv. 224 The Rao Sahib, a brother of the late Maharajah.

Raoult (raul(t)). *Physical Chem.* [The name of François-Marie *Raoult* (1830–1901), French physical chemist.] ***Raoult's law***: (*a*) the freezing point and boiling point of an ideal solution are respectively depressed and elevated relative to that of the pure solvent by an amount proportional to the mole fraction of solute; (*b*) the vapour pressure of an ideal solution is proportional to the mole fraction of solvent.

The two statements are closely related. In recent use *Raoult's law* usu. refers to (*b*).

1892 BEDSON & WILLIAMS tr. *L. Meyer's Outl. Theoret. Chem.* 137 The molecular weights of other bodies.. can be determined by aid of Raoult's Law in the following manner. **1899** R. A. LEHFELDT *Text-bk. Physical Chem.* vi. 269 This result is included in Raoult's law of the lowering of vapour pressure. **1950** W. J. MOORE *Physical Chem.* vi. 133 An example exhibiting a positive deviation from Raoult's Law is the system carbon bisulphide-methylal, whose vapor-pressure-composition diagram is shown. **1966** GUCKER & SEIFERT *Physical Chem.* xvii. 465 In the last two diagrams dotted lines represent partial pressures calculated from Raoult's law. **1977** MONCRIEFF & JONES *Elem. Physical Chem.* xvii. 379 An ideal binary solution is defined as one in which both components obey Raoult's law over the entire concentration range.

rap (ræp), *sb.*[1] Forms: 4–6 **rappe**, (8 **wrap**), 6– **rap**. [Prob. of echoic origin (cf. *clap, flap, slap, wap*), appearing in the 14th c. together with the related verb (RAP *v.*[1]). Da. *rap*, Sw. *rapp* agree in meaning, but there is no evidence of primitive Scand. origin.]

I. 1. a. A blow or stroke, esp. one inflicted on a person. Orig. applied to severe blows with weapons, etc., now restricted to a sharp or smart stroke with a stick or the like, not causing serious hurt.

1340–70 *Alisaunder* 348 To riden into the route rappes to deale. *a* **1400** *Octouian* 334 To the ape anoon he gert Wel many rappys. *c* **1460** *Emare* 660 The wawes.. On the bote faste they thronge, With mony unsemely rappes. *a* **1548** HALL *Chron., Edw. V* 14 b, He clapped hys fyste on the borde a great rappe. **1549–62** STERNHOLD & H. *Ps.* lxxiv. 11 Lord.. be not slacke, to geue thy foes a rap. **1601** HOLLAND *Pliny* II. 571 Paris caught a rap vpon the mouth with a marble stone. **1711** STEELE *Spect.* No. 260 ¶5 She pulled off her Shoe, and hit me with the Heel such a Rap. **1875** JOWETT *Plato* (ed. 2) V. 56 The boys, and the audience in general, were kept in order by raps of a stick.

b. A sharp and pretty loud knock, such as is produced by striking on a wooden surface with something hard; *esp.* a knock at a door, or (in recent use) one supposed to be made by a spirit.

1637 RUTHERFORD *Lett.* lxxxviii. (1862) I. 227 His first knock or rap at the door. **1727** SWIFT *Further Acc. E. Curll* Wks. 1755 III. I. 156, I hear the rap of Mr. Curll's ivory-headed cane upon the counter. **1785** SARAH FIELDING *Ophelia* I. xvii, The peculiarity of a footman's rap startled me. **1853** *Spirit Rappings* 4 'Hush!' she exclaims, 'I think I hear a rap.' The spirit-seeker stretches his neck and intently listens, and a sound like the dripping of water is distinctly heard. **1870** EMERSON *Soc. & Solit., Success* Wks. (Bohn) III. 119, I hate this shallow Americanism which hopes to get .. knowledge by raps on midnight tables.

†**2.** = CRACK *sb.*[3] *Obs.*

c **1500** *Mery geste Frere & Boye* 119 in Hazl. *E.P.P.* III. 66, I wolde she sholde let a rappe go, That myght rynge ouer all the place. **1589** PUTTENHAM *Eng. Poesie* III. xxiii. (Arb.) 274 Flamock hauing his belly full.. gaue out a rappe nothing faintly.

3. *Sc.* A moment. Cf. CLAP *sb.*[1] 7.

1768 ROSS *Helenore* III. 112 Honest Jean brang forward in a rap Green horn cutties. **1813–** in *Eng. Dial. Dict.*

II. *transf.* **4. a.** A rebuke; an adverse criticism.

1777 in *Amer. Pioneer* (Cincinnati) (1843) Jan. 17 The post master general.. has lately had a rap, which I hope will have a good effect. **1803** P. CANVAS (*title*) A rap for the P.R.A., or three words to Mr. West on his late attempt to pass off an old lady of 76 for a beauty of eighteen hundred and three. **1932** 'A. ROLLS' *Lobelia Grove* x. 227 It's up to us to keep a damn sharp look-out, my boy... We've had a bit of a rap over it, between you and me. **1976** *Cumberland News* 3 Dec. 16/9 A top Carlisle haulage firm got a council room rap yesterday for jumping the gun over planning. **1977** *National Observer* (U.S.) 22 Jan. 16/7 'Mr Fixit' is coming to town, and that is no rap on Jimmy Carter. More than anything else, the American people want government to work.

b. A criminal accusation, charge. Freq. in phr. ***bum rap***, a false charge, an undeserved punishment (cf. BUM *a.*); also *fig. slang* (chiefly *U.S.*).

1903 H. HAPGOOD *Autobiogr. of Thief* (1904) xii. 265 'What makes you look so glum?'.. 'Turned out of police court this morning.' 'What was the rap, Mike?' 'I'm looking too respectable. They asked me where I got the clothes.' **1910** *New England Mag.* July 587 A complaint or charge of crime is a 'rap' and the complainant is the 'rapper'. **1926** J. BLACK *You can't Win* (1927) xii. 165 We've got two tough raps... In the first place a hypo ain't supposed to be found within a block of police headquarters... In the second place, a hypo ain't allowed to leave Chinatown. **1927** CLARK & EUBANK *Lockstep & Corridor* vii. 45 Edgar is now.. in prison for what I honestly believe is a bum rap. **1930** *Sat. Even. Post* 26 July 145/1 We ran into a funny rap out there, kid. On some fool income-tax trick, they locked up seven of my best men. **1936** J. CURTIS *Gilt Kid* 229 There was no burglary rap because the offices had not been inhabited. **1946** 'P. QUENTIN' *Puzzle for Fiends* xxv. 239, I couldn't.. leave them to face the rap for three murders they hadn't committed. **1970** R. D. ABRAHAMS *Positively Black* iii. 79, I was standing on the corner, wasn't even shooting crap, When a policeman came by, picked me up on a lame rap. **1978** S. BRILL *Teamsters* i. 21 The 1961 kidnap-murder rap would move toward trial. **1980** *Outdoor Life* (U.S.) (Northeast ed.) Oct. 138/1 Two years ago a local chapter of the National Rifle Association hung a bum rap on Udall as 'likely to vote for gun registration'.

c. An identification (see quot. 1926). *Criminals' slang.*

1914 JACKSON & HELLYER *Vocab. Criminal Slang* 68 *Rap*, .. an identification; a charge of guilt. **1926** *N.Y. Times* 30 May 2/3 In order to understand the news of the day the innocent must.. familiarize themselves with new words from the bright lexicon of crime. The newest is 'rap', meaning identification. When one is singled out from a line of suspects as the dip who slid the ticktick, one is the victim of a 'rap'.

d. A prison sentence. *slang* (chiefly *U.S.*).

1927 *Amer. Speech* II. 281/1 *Rap*, sentence imposed by law. **1935** 'E. QUEEN' *Spanish Cape Mystery* xiv. 300 You're in a tough spot. Do you know what the rap for blackmail is in this State? **1956** B. HOLIDAY *Lady sings Blues* (1973) xii. 108, I might explain the first rap was a freak accident. But the second was tougher.

e. Phrases: ***to beat the rap*** (chiefly *U.S.*), to escape punishment, esp. a prison sentence; ***to get the rap***, to suffer a rebuke or scolding; to receive the blame; ***to hang*** (***pin, tie***) ***the rap on***, to charge (a suspect), showing (occas. dishonestly) that circumstantial evidence is incontrovertible; ***to take the rap***, to accept responsibility and the consequent punishment (orig. for a crime).

1865 *Atlantic Monthly* Mar. 297/2 He who has the bad taste to meddle with the caprices of believers.. gets the rap and the orders of dismissal. **1927** CLARK & EUBANK *Lockstep & Corridor* vii. 42, I told him that the only way for his brother to beat the 'rap' was to.. furnish bond and beat it. **1930** E. H. LARINE *Third Degree* ii. 17 Good, honest cops will often take a 'rap' or complaint,.. rather than.. testify against a fellow cop. **1932** 'SPINDRIFT' *Yankee Slang* 58 Pin the rap on him and make it 'stick'. **1936** J. CURTIS *Gilt Kid* xxvi. 265 You're not going to hang a bum rap on me. **1943** P. CHEYNEY *You can always Duck* iv. 75 You can't hang any murder rap on me. **1952** *Chambers's Jrnl.* May 309/1 Groteman was quite calm. 'Arresting me? Nonsense! In any case, what about you? Do you think I would leave you here to take the rap? I wouldn't do that, Rudolf.' **1953** W. BURROUGHS *Junkie* viii. 78 At the time, he was out on bail, but expected to beat the rap on the grounds of illegal seizure. **1962** WODEHOUSE *Service with Smile* vi. 88 Keep saying 'Is zat so?'.. confident that she can never pin the rap on you. **1965** H. GOLD *Man who was not with It* xxvi. 245 How do I know the fuzz aren't waiting back here to tie on a rap for Aiding and Abetting? **1969** J. MCPHERSON *Hue & Cry* 56 Damn if I'm takin' the rap for you niggers. **1970** N. FLEMING *Czech Point* ii. 39 He could have pinned that rap on the Australian girl in the PVC outfit any day he cared. **1972** 'H. HOWARD' *Nice Day for Funeral* iii. 51 Suppose somebody gets the rap for killing Frankie? What good will that do her? **1978** S. BRILL *Teamsters* iv. 143 He thought Sammy Provenzano had made a deal with Briguglio to get him to take the rap. **1978** M. PUZO *Fools Die* xx. 226, I even felt that Frank might beat the rap.

5. a. Conversation, talk, chat. *dial.*

1898 R. BLAKEBOROUGH *Wit N. Riding Yorks.* 433 Lets 'ev a pipe an' a bit o' rap.

b. Among American Blacks, a special style of verbal display, repartee, etc. (see quot. 1967). More generally, impromptu dialogue, talk, or discussion. *colloq.* Cf. RAP *v.*[1] 3 d.

1967 J. HORTON in *Trans-Action* Apr. 6/1 Sometimes used synonymously with street conversation, 'rap' is really a special way of talking—repartee... For example, one needs to throw a lively rap when he is 'putting the make on a broad'. **1970** D. LEE *We walk Way of New World* 52 The national rap deliberately continues, 'wipe them niggers out'. **1970** *New Yorker* 8 Aug. 36/1 Around Jane Fonda you may call it a rap, but here it's still called a powwow. **1971** *Black Scholar* Jan. 17/2 The indigenous, enduring black folk rap, then, is populated with witches, tyrants, befrienders of young children, the strong, the stoic, the quick-witted. **1972** *Last Whole Earth Catalog* (Portola Inst.) 183/3 Ordinarily the talk about their Uncle Emmit would have led D.R. and Marcella on into a general rap about other relatives. **1973** S. HENDERSON *Understanding New Black Poetry* p. xi, An extension of this is the emergence over the past few years of the 'rap' as an authentic Black literary form. **1974** *Black World* Sept. 55/2 The percussion group introduces Roach's rap, whose text is ministerial on 'the power of love'. **1974** H. L. FOSTER *Ribbin'* ii. 51 George is sitting on the steps in the school running a strong rap with a number of girls. **1975** *Time Out* 7 Feb 43/2 Although their rap between songs seems more suited to a family variety show it can at least be excused as 'professionalism'. **1976** *New Musical Express* 31 July 6/4 Five minutes into the rap and the singer who replaced Ian Gillan three years ago seems prepared to reveal a damn sight more than one of the original members. **1977** *Zigzag* Apr. 46/1 'Dum Dum Boys' opens with a 'whatever happened to me mates' rap. **1978** *Amer. Poetry Rev.* July/Aug. 44/3 Each section of the book.. is an interlude, a rap, a seeming improvisation on some aspect of the blues. **1978** *Verbatim* Feb. 10/1 Each sees Black English as richly metaphoric and imagistic, its speakers adept at creative compounds and the double entendre, frequently extraordinarily skilled in traditional verbal battles and games which are integral to their world, a world in which the baddest dude is often the one with the best rap. (A word.. whose meaning in Black English differs from the meaning it took on when assimilated into White English.)

6. A commendation, 'boost'. *Austral. colloq.*
1939 K. Tennant *Foveaux* II. iv. 176 Everyone wants to be seen with a high-up feller. When I pass the time of day to a cove he feels that's a rap for him, see? **1973** K. Dunstan *Sports* 229 And if someone does something good, takes a good mark, give him a rap. Tell him.

7. *attrib.* and *Comb.* (chiefly *U.S. colloq.*), as (sense 4 d) ***rap partner***; **rap centre**, the meeting-place of a rap group; **rap club**, a club that ostensibly provides companionship and conversation but is really a brothel; **rap group**, a group that meets to discuss problems; **rap parlour** = *rap club*; **rap session**, a group discussion; **rap sheet**, a police record.
1973 *Tucson* (Arizona) *Daily Citizen* 22 Aug. 28/1 Those turned off by rap centers, afraid of encounter groups and frightened to death by pillows-on-the-floor revelations may be seeking someone to listen to them. **1976** *National Observer* (U.S.) 16 Oct., The committee decided we needed a sort of rap center for teenagers with the exhibit, and we wanted to do something that would be appealing to them. **1973** *N.Y. Post* 22 June 7 In the face of a crackdown on street prostitution many of the girls..are taking shelter in 'rap clubs'—which have replaced massage parlors in the sex-for-sale world. **1970** *Time* 30 Aug. 18 The heart of the [women's liberation] movement is made up of hundreds of 'rap groups', usually formed on an *ad hoc* basis. **1971** *N.Y. Times* 12 June 28 The New York chapter of the Vietnam Veterans Against the War instituted weekly 'rap groups' where men meet and talk about their experiences and feelings. **1972** *Listener* 31 Aug. 270/1 We created..a kind of anti-war community consisting of veterans and professionals. To avoid clinical terminology, we called the programme we established 'rap groups' rather than 'therapy groups'. **1978** *Chicago* June 82/3 Women's center—for lesbians and other women... Rap-group organizing, info on pregnancy testing, birth control etc. **1975** *N.Y. Times* 4 Oct. 1/8 'Rap' parlors, 'sensitivity training' centers and other establishments that use imaginative covers for illicit sex other than the pretense of being a massage parlor would not be affected by the measure. **1971** *Black Scholar* Sept. 37/1 He thought about..the four rap partners he had on his last beef. **1970** *Time* 24 Aug. 12 In every major city, women, most of them young, gather for 'consciousness-raising' rap sessions, the awareness rituals of The Sisterhood. **1973** *Publishers Weekly* 18 June 9 (Advt.), Secret tapings of rap sessions where seven suburban wives tell with startling candor of their search for personal identity. **1974** *Greenville* (S. Carolina) *News* 23 Apr. 16/1 Special-interest rap sessions will be conducted by Campus Scouts from Furman University. **1976** *Sunday Times* (Lagos) 3 Oct. 13/2, I drive straight to the NBC studios for a recording of my rap session on the weekly programme for youths. **1977** *Times Lit. Suppl.* 18 Feb. 179/2 For years Americans have been participating in rap sessions and consciousness-raising groups. **1980** *Underground Grammarian* Mar., The ensuing rap session will be quite long enough to provide yet another day's respite from the tedious and dehumanizing study of language and thought. **1960** *Washington Post* 3 Dec. A3 You will not find violence on his rap sheet. **1976** G. V. Higgins *Judgement D. Hunter* xvi. 179 He was convicted... Two charges..were dismissed, but remained on his rap sheet as having been brought.

rap (ræp), *sb.*[2] [Of obscure origin; there is no evidence of connexion with G. *rappe*, the name of a small coin.]

1. a. A counterfeit coin, worth about half a farthing, which passed current for a halfpenny in Ireland in the 18th c., owing to the scarcity of genuine money. Now only *Hist.*
1724 Swift *Drapier's Lett.* Wks. 1755 V. II. 14 Copper halfpence or farthings..have been for some time very scarce, and many counterfeits passed about under the name of raps. **1776** R. Twiss *Tour Irel.* 73 The beggars..offering a bad halfpenny, which they call a rap. **1827** J. Wilson *Noct. Ambr.* Wks. 1855 I. 182 Ane o' the bawbees o' an obsolete sort..what they ca' an Eerish rap.

b. Taken as a type of the smallest coin; chiefly in negative phrases, esp. ***without*** or ***not a rap***.
1823 Byron *Juan* XI. lxxxiv, I have seen the Landholders without a rap. **1830** Marryat *King's Own* xxxv, 'You must fork out'. 'Not a rap'. **1881** Miss Braddon *Asphodel* xiv. 158 A man who dies and leaves not a rap behind him.

c. *fig.* An atom, the least bit. Chiefly as prec., and esp. ***not to care a rap***.
1834 Ainsworth *Rookwood* III. v, For the mare-with-three-legs [the gallows], boys, I care not a rap. **1875** *Punch* 18 Sept. 113/2 It don't matter a rap whether it's rough or fine. **1882** Miss Braddon *Mt. Royal* III. iv. 79 If I thought you cared a rap for me, I should stay.

2. ***rap halfpenny***: A bad halfpenny.
1864 *Blackw. Mag.* Oct. 392 It is not of very great moment to me that I am now and then imposed on by a 'rap halfpenny'. **1878** in *Cumbld. Gloss.*

3. *transf.* A worthless person, rascal, good-for-nothing.
1771 R. Cumberland *Let.* 4 July in D. Garrick *Private Corr.* (1831) I. 426 Assisted by a jury of printers, compilers, devils, hawkers, and raps of all sorts. **1842** S. Lover *Handy Andy* xix. 168 What do you mean, you rap?—do you intend to say I'm drunk? **1949** M. Molloy *King & Friday's Men* in *Plays of Year 1949* (1950) 400 (Murty drags her violently across the room and flings her on to the sofa.) *Murty* (savage and scared): Biddy, watch over this rap.

rap (ræp), *sb.*[3] Now *dial.* [f. rap *v.*[4]] An exchange (esp. of horses).
1755 T. H. Croker *Ariosto* xxx. v, I, for your nag, incline To make a rap of this same mare of mine. **1886** in dial. glossaries (Linc., Som.).

rap (ræp), *sb.*[4] [Of obscure origin.] A skein containing 120 yards of yarn.
1776-7 *Act 17 Geo. III*, c. 11 §11 Every..hank of..yarn shall..contain seven raps or leas, and..every such rap or lea shall..contain eighty threads. **1875** Knight *Dict. Mech.*

rap (ræp), *sb.*[5] Now *dial.* [Of obscure origin.] A strip, *esp.* of land.
1710 *Lond. Gaz.* No. 4714/4 A Rapp of Ground ranging along from the Mills. **1886-93** in south-western dial. glossaries (Som., Wilts).

rap (ræp), *v.*[1] Also 4-6 **rappe**, (7 **wrap**). [Related to rap *sb.*[1]; cf. also *frap* vb. and G. *rappeln* to rattle. Sw. *rappa* to beat, drub, is of obscure history.]

1. a. *trans.* To strike, smite (*esp.* a person); now, to strike smartly without causing serious hurt (cf. rap *sb.*[1] 1). Also *absol.*
1377 Langland *P. Pl.* B. I. 95 Kynges & kniȝtes shulde.. Riden and rappe down in reumes aboute. *c* **1400** *Destr. Troy* 13007 All the Rebellis full rad [he] rappit to dethe. *c* **1490** *Promp. Parv.* 423/2 (MS. H) Rappyn, or smytyn, *percucio*. **1530** Palsgr. 679/1, I shall rappe you on the costarde if you playe the knave. **1577-87** Holinshed *Chron.* I. 13/2 It [a toad] suddenlie reculed backe, as though it had beene rapt in the head. **1600** Holland *Livy* xxxiv. xv. 863 If he espied any one to step out of his rank, he would..rap him with his light javelin. **1676** Hobbes *Iliad* 175 So thick they did the Trojan armours rap. **1873** Ouida *Pascarel* I. iii. 34 Fortunato could rap both feet and hands sharply enough with his bow.

b. Phr. ***to rap (one's) fingers*** or ***knuckles***, to check or punish smartly.
a **1677** Barrow *Serm.* Wks. 1716 I. 219 He that will have a scickle in another's corn,..no wonder if his fingers be rapped. **1681** J. Flavel *Right. Man's Refuge* 257 Every objection with which he will rap thy fingers. **1759** [see knuckle *sb.* 2 b]. **1824** De Quincey *Falsif. Eng. Hist.* Wks. 1859 XII. 327 If that bishop were not dead, I would here take the liberty of rapping his knuckles.

c. To charge, prosecute; to apprehend with a view to prosecution. *slang.*
1904 'No. 1500' *Life in Sing Sing* 252/1 *Rap*,..to prosecute. **1960** 'M. Cronin' *Begin with Gun* viii. 93 If I [*sc.* a policeman] hear that Kehely has been getting in our way ..I'll have to rap him.

d. To criticize adversely; to rebuke; to mention unfavourably. orig. *U.S.*
1906 *N.Y. Even. Post* 23 Nov. 5 Football was sharply rapped and rowing was highly praised by President Eliot in his address. **1926** J. Kerney *Political Educ. Woodrow Wilson* 105 In screamer headlines the conference was rapped as a secret and reprehensible thing. **1967** *Boston Globe* 20 May 2/2 (*heading*) Teachers rapped for failure to understand their pupils. **1973** *Trinidad & Tobago Overseas Express* 28 May 21/3 (*heading*) Bar body raps Sir Hugh for attack. **1976** *Abingdon Herald* 9 Dec. 5/2 (*heading*) Parties united to rap county.

2. To drive, dash, knock, etc. with a rap. Const. *against*, *in*, *on*, †*to*. orig. chiefly *Sc.*
a **1400** *Octouian* 1439 In the stedes mouth he rapte An huge brydel. *c* **1440** *Promp. Parv.* 423/2 Rappyn', or smytyn' a thynge a-ȝen' a-noper, *collido*, *allido*. **1539** *Extracts Aberd. Reg.* (1844) I. 161 Thai..tuk him be the hair and rappit his heid to the wall. **1596** Dalrymple tr. *Leslie's Hist. Scot.* x. 367 A great ship..quhilk albeit rapit on a craig chaipet safe. **1838** Rodger *Poems* 46 Ilk thing against whilk my head I might rap. **1861** Geo. Eliot *Silas M.* I. iv. 69 Dunstan, as he went along..was always rapping his whip somewhere. **1968** *Globe & Mail* (Toronto) 15 Jan. 19/6 Keon rapped in Mahovlich's rebound to make it 5-0 and Oliver tipped in Hillman's slap shot during a power play to complete the scoring.

3. †a. *Sc.* To send *forth* with a clap. *rare*$^{-1}$.
1513 Douglas *Æneis* III. iii. 96 The brokin skyis rappis furth thunderis levin.

b. Usually with *out*: to utter, 'let off' (*esp.* an oath) sharply, vigorously, or suddenly. Also in weakened sense: to say, talk.
1541 Wyatt *Defence* 267, I am wont sometime to rap out an oath in an earnest talk. **1609** Holland *Amm. Marcell.* xxvii. ii. 305 In bragging wise rapping out nothing but vaine sounds and noyses of threats. **1635** Quarles *Embl.* I. x. 41 One raps an oath; another deales a curse. **1742** Fielding *J. Andrews* III. ii, Adams then rapped out a hundred Greek verses. **1815** W. H. Ireland *Scribbleomania* 208 *note*, My orator raps out a pun. **1879** *Macm. Mag.* Oct. 501 A reeler came up to me and rapped (said), 'Now—you had better guy,..or else I shall give you a drag (three months in prison).' **1880** Browning *Clive* 203 Out he rapped Such a round of oaths. **1887** J. W. Horsley *Jottings from Jail* 1. 7 So I said, 'All right,' but he rapped, 'It is not all right.' **1929** *Sat. Even. Post* 12 Jan. 72/3 'Remember now, don't rap anything to Swinnerton.'..'I'm not goin' to talk,' Barr answered. **1951** M. McLuhan *Mech. Bride* (1967) 60/2 An indignant girl who raps out, 'You've *had* it!' **1975** *High Times* Dec. 22/3 All those veteran comedians..used to rap about the drunk. **1976** K. Royce *Bustillo* xv. 215 'Bustillo still has to get out,' rapped Susumu mildly. **1977** C. McCullough *Thorn Birds* ii. 31 That dry old voice rapped a curt question at her.

†c. *slang.* To swear (a thing) *against* a person. Also *intr.* To swear; to perjure oneself. *Obs.*
1733 Budgell *Bee* I. 207 He ask'd me what they had to rap against me, I told him only a Tankard. *Ibid.* 213 We will get them that will rap the Tankard was your grandmother's. **1752** Fielding *Amelia* II. x, I scorn to rap against a lady. **1818** Scott *Hrt. Midl.* xx, It's..hard, when three words of your mouth would give the girl the chance.., that you make sure scrupling about rapping to them.

d. *intr.* In more informal contexts than sense 3 b: to talk or chat in an easy or discursive manner. Freq. const. *with*. *colloq.* (chiefly *U.S.*). Cf. rap *sb.*[1] 5 b.
1929 D. Runyon in *Hearst's Internat.* Oct. 65/2, I wish Moosh a hello, and he never raps to me but only bows, and takes my hat. **1965** E. Cleaver *Let.* 19 Sept. in *Soul on Ice* (1968) I. 46 In point of fact he is funny and very glib, and I dig rapping (talking) with him. **1967** *Time* 7 July 17/1 Hirsute, shoeless hippies huddled in doorways, smoking pot, 'rapping' (achieving rapport with random talk), or banging beer cans. **1968** *Negro Digest* Jan. 4/2 Karenga is a spokesman..with the power to rap in a manner thoroughly black. **1971** P. Kavanagh *Triumph of Evil* iv. 35 It really helped me to talk to you, Miles. You're the only older person I know that I can rap with. **1973** S. Henderson *Understanding New Black Poetry* 26 The younger poet will usually rap or declaim or sing, but if he wants to create a Black character..he usually turns to drama or the short story. **1975** *Times Lit. Suppl.* 13 June 675/2 Eavesdropping on..Ishmael Reed when he raps along quite disingenuously about a press dominated by white reviewers. **1978** *Detroit Free Press* 16 Apr. F6/4 Can you rap with students? **1979** *Tucson* (Arizona) *Citizen* 20 Sept. 7A/1 Obviously relishing the opportunity to rap with what Jordan called the 'press biggies from out of town'. **1979** *Quarto* Oct. 3/3 Like a good investigative journalist, Wolfe has raided official sources and rapped with those in the know. **1980** *Oxford Times* 4 Jan. 15/2 She 'raps' (i.e. talks) in the intimate style of Millie Jackson.

4. a. *intr.* To knock sharply (*esp.* at a door).
c **1440** Capgrave *Life St. Kath.* III. 312 þer nedyth þe noght neyther ryng ne rap, The gate shal open lightly. **1470** Harding *Chron.* III. lxxvi, Doores and wyndowes al clapped ..Opened and sparred al by theim selfs fast rapped. *a* **1510** Douglas *K. Hart* II. 13 He rappit at the ȝet, but courtaslie. **1613** Hayward *Norm. Kings* 15 Here he continued rapping at the gate..vntill it was opened. **1750** Gray *Long Story* 55 The heroines..Rap'd at the door nor stay'd to ask [etc.]. **1860** *All Year Round* No. 66. 372 The spirits only rapped when the younger medium was present. **1867** Trollope *Chron. Barset* II. xlv. 6 One morning..the squire rapped at the window of the drawing-room. **1950** [see *crystal-gaze* vb. s.v. crystal *sb.* and *a.* B. 2 c]. **1972** S. Chance *Septimus & Minster Ghost* (1974) vii. 72 He went into a trance and rapped away like mad.

b. *trans.* To strike with a rap; to rap at or on.
1712-14 Pope *Rape Lock* IV. 130 He spoke, and rapp'd his box. **1718** Prior *Dove* 33 With one great peal they rap the door, Like footmen on a visiting day. **1784** Cowper *Task* VI. 292 He notes it in his book, then raps his box. **1865** Dickens *Mut. Fr.* III. v, Sharply rapping the table.

c. *trans.* ***to rap out***, to knock out; also (*esp.* of spirits), to declare by means of raps.
1841 J. T. Hewlett *Parish Clerk* II. 192 All three rapped the unconsumed tobacco out of their pipes. **1860** *All Year Round* No. 66. 373 The spirits rapped out their dismissal, and the séance was at an end.

5. *intr. Sc.* a. To fall sharply or smartly; to fall in pattering drops.
1508 Dunbar *Gold. Targe* 195 The schour of arowis rappit on as rayn. **1535** Stewart *Cron. Scot.* I. 69 The dartis ..rappit on sa rudlie with greit reird. **1768** Ross *Helenore* I. 64 By this time the tears came rapping down. **1819** W. Tennant *Papistry Storm'd* (1827) 34 Tears rappit down the dreamer's cheeks.

b. To go *off* with a sharp sound.
1818 Scott *Rob Roy* xxxvi, The pistols and the carabines of the troopers..rappit aff the tane after the tother.

Hence **rapped** (ræpt), *ppl. a.*; also ***rapped-out***.
1899 A. Hope *King's Mirror* xxviii. 308 The little girl's bare, red, rapped knuckles. **1906** *Daily Chron.* 7 June 6/1 There was certainly nothing theatrical about the sound, stately, straight-backed, rapped-out rowing of those Eton eights.

†**rap**, *v.*[2] *Obs.* In 5 **rappe**. [App. related to G. dial. *rappen* (Da. *rappe*, Sw. *rappa*), used reflexively in the sense 'to make haste, hurry'; cf. (M)LG., Du., Sw. *rap*, *rapp* quick.]

1. *intr.* To move with speed; to hasten, rush.
13.. *Coer de L.* 2206 All that he hit he all to-frapped; The Griffons away fast rapped. *c* **1320** *Sir Beues* (MS. A) 1900 Beues is swerd anon vp swapte, He and þe geaunt togedre rapte. **1362** Langl. *P. Pl.* A. IV. 23 Resun with him rideþ rappynge swiþe. *c* **1420** *Filius Regis Mortuus est* 45 in *Pol. Rel. & L. Poems* 206 þe clawdes gan clappe, The elements gonne to rusche & rappe.

2. *trans.* To hurry or huddle *up*. *rare*$^{-1}$.
1450-1530 *Myrroure our Ladye* 55 They rappe vp theyr seruyce as faste as they can, for haste to be at their worke.

rap (ræp), *v.*[3] Now *rare*. Also 6-7 **rappe**, 7 **rapp**. [In sense 1 perh. related to MLG. (and G.) *rappen* (Sw. *rappa*) to seize, snatch; but in 2 app. a back-formation from rapt *pa. pple.*]

†1. *trans.* To seize or snatch for oneself; to take or get by snatching or stealing. *Obs.*
1564 Grindal *Funeral Serm.* Bj, I knew a Priest, who had rapped together foure, or fiue benefices. **1581** Marbeck *Bk. of Notes* 402 Thinges which are founde must be restored. Which thing if thou doe not, thou hast rapt them. **1689** T. R. *View Govt. Europe* 2 Their work was by hook and crook, to rap and bring all under the Emperours power. *a* **1754** Fielding *Voy. Lisbon* Wks. 1784 X. 246 Every man spunges and raps whatever he can get.

b. In alliterative phrases, esp. ***rap and rend*** (common in 16-17th c.). Now *arch.* or *dial.* Cf. rape *v.*[2] 1 b.
1528 Roy *Rede me*, etc. (Arb.) 74 Acustumed to rappe and rende All that commeth in their fingrynge. **1570** Foxe *A. & M.* 983 Thinke you..they will not plucke from you what soeuer They can rappe or reue? **1678** Marvell *Growth Popery* 23 Contributing all that we could rap and rend of Men, or Amunition. **1712** Arbuthnot *John Bull* IV. ii, An Eating-house, where the whole Tribe of them spend all they can rap or run. **1842** Barham *Ingol. Leg.*, *St. Aloys*, From foe and from friend He'd 'rap and he'd rend'. **1872** Browning *Fifine* Epil. iv, Let them.. Make and mend, or rap and rend, for me! **1877** Leigh *Cheshire Gloss.*, *Rap and*

ring, scrape together. **1877** *N.W. Linc. Gloss.*, Rap and rear, to gather together by any means.

†**c.** *intr.* To snatch *at. Obs. rare*⁻¹.

1669 W. SIMPSON *Hydrol. Chym.* 209 Through a confident ignorance, he rapps at the prediction, and at a venture.

2. a. To take up and carry off, to transport, remove. Now *rare.*

1599 *Warn. Faire Wom.* I. 41 To rack a thought,.. Until I rap the senses from their course. **1613** HEYWOOD *Silver Age* II. i. Wks. 1874 III. 110 With my sudden greeting, Il'e rap her soule to heauen. **1654** H. L'ESTRANGE *Chas. I* (1655) 90 He was rapp'd and hurried into another world by an abrupt and untimely death. **1771** WESLEY *Wks.* (1872) V. 351 God is pleased..sometimes to rap them up, as it were, into the third heavens. **1872** S. MORTON in *Mem. Tennyson* (1897) II. 119 The burning impressions..which rap the poet into the lyrical heaven.

b. To affect with rapture; to transport, ravish (with joy, etc.).

1599 B. JONSON *Ev. Man out of Hum.* I. i, Is't a prognostication raps him so? **1685** R. BAXTER *Paraphr. N.T.*, *Matt.* xvii. 4 A glympse of glory is enough to rap a Soul into extasie. **1726** POPE *Odyss.* XIX. 43 The Prince.. rap'd with ecstacy the Sire address'd. **1751** YOUNG *Nt. Th.* IX. 774 God..seizes man; Seizes, and elevates, and raps.

rap (ræp), *v.*⁴ *dial.* and *slang.* [Of obscure origin; cf. RAP *sb.*³] To exchange, barter.

a **1700** B. E. *Dict. Cant. Crew*, *Rap*, to Swop or Exchange a Horse or Goods. *a* **1796** PEGGE *Derbicisms* Ser. II, *Rap*, to swap, with which it is often joined; to exchange. **1879-** in dial. glossaries (Shropsh., Chesh., Glouc., W. Som., Dorset, Warwicksh., E. Angl.).

rap, obs. pa. t. REAP *v.*, obs. f. ROPE *sb.*, WRAP *sb.* and *v.*

rap, used imitatively: see RAP *sb.*¹ and *v.*¹

1760 GOLDSM. *Cit. W.* xxxix, Rap, went the footman at the door, bounce went my heart. **1833-74** [see RAP-TAP]. **1889** MCNEILL *Blawearie* 165 Eighteen hutches of coal were winded rap dash to the pithead.

rapable ('reɪpəb(ə)l), *a.* Also **rape-able.** [f. RAPE *v.*² + -ABLE.] Of a person: regarded as a suitable object for sexual pursuit or assault.

1972 J. ROSSITER *Rope for General Dietz* xiii. 183 He looked so eminently rape-able with his spaniel's brown eyes. **1976** K. BONFIGLIOLI *Something Nasty in Woodshed* vii. 75 I've no intention of distributing cantrips and costly crucifixes to every rapable woman in the Parish. **1977** J. I. M. STEWART *Madonna of Astrolabe* xi. 155 The virgin bloom remained, Duncan. You were very rapable still.

rapacious (rə'peɪʃəs), *a.* [f. L. *rapāci-*, *rapax* grasping (f. *rapĕre*: see RAPE *v.*²) + -OUS.]

1. Giving to grasping or taking for oneself; inordinately greedy. Also const. *of*, and *inf.*

1651 JER. TAYLOR *Serm.* xxii. (1653) 287 We may be diligent in the conduct of souls though we be not rapacious of estates. **1663** COWLEY *Ess.*, *Liberty* (1684) 80 Who more rapacious in robbing, who more profuse in giving? **1752** YOUNG *Brothers* IV. i, To keep rapacious Rome, from seizing Thrace. **1848** LYTTON *Harold* v. i, By the side of Harold stands Tostig, rapacious to grasp. **1871** FREEMAN *Norm. Conq.* (1876) IV. xvii. 37 Even this small fragment of former wealth came into the hands of the rapacious stranger.

b. *transf.* of things.

1706 E. WARD *Wooden World Diss.* (1708) 13 But sometimes he meets with a gruff Subaltern, that snarls at his rapacious Stomach. **1776** SEIFERTH tr. *Gellert's Metall. Chym.* 36 A rapacious-ore..in the fire destroys more or less of the metalline particles. **1818** KEATS *Endym.* II. 332 Deliver me from this rapacious deep.

c. of qualities, modes of action, etc.

1663 COWLEY *Ess.*, *Avarice* (1669) 127 The rapacious Appetite of Gain. **1727** S. SWITZER *Pract. Gardiner* I. v. 47 Vegetables of a more rapacious nature. **1769** ROBERTSON *Chas. V*, VIII. Wks. 1813 III. 109 Heavy fines..which he levied with most rapacious exactness. **1847** MRS. A. KERR *Hist. Servia* 201 Falling under the rapacious domination of the Fanariotes.

2. Of animals: Subsisting by the capture of living prey; raptorial.

1661 LOVELL *Hist. Anim. & Min.* Introd., The nailes..of the rapacious [quadrupeds are] aduncate. **1726** GAY *Fables* I. Introd. 12 Rapacious animals we hate: Kites, hawks, and wolves, deserve their fate. **1774** GOLDSM. *Nat. Hist.* (1776) V. 79 Of Rapacious Birds in General. **1874** COUES *Birds N.W.* 330 Marsh Hawks..were the most abundant..of all the rapacious birds.

rapaciously (rə'peɪʃəslɪ), *adv.* [f. prec. + -LY².] In a rapacious manner; greedily.

1730-6 in BAILEY (fol.). **1742** *Lond. & Country Brew.* II. (ed. 4) 112 Rapaciously impregnating the Salt and Sulphur ..with the Liquor. **1772** FOOTE *Nabob* III. Wks. 1799 II. 322 What has been treacherously and rapaciously gained. **1894** *Chicago Advance* 1 Mar., Mohammedanism..rules so ignorantly and rapaciously.

ra'paciousness. [f. as prec. + -NESS.] The quality of being rapacious; rapacity. Now *rare* (freq. in 18th c.).

1659 *Gentl. Calling* iv. §27 He that hath the rapaciousness of a wolf. **1711** ADDISON *Spect.* No. 55 ¶2 Raising fresh Supplies of Money, by all the Methods of Rapaciousness and Corruption. **1781** GIBBON *Decl. & F.* xviii. II. 77 The opposite yet reconcileable vices of rapaciousness and prodigality. **1829** SOUTHEY *Sir T. More* (1831) II. 34 Its wealth exposes it to envy and rapaciousness.

rapacity (rə'pæsɪtɪ). [ad. L. *rapācitāt-em*, f. *rapax* RAPACIOUS. Cf. F. *rapacité* (16th c. Littré).] The quality or fact of being rapacious; the exercise of rapacious tendencies.

1543 BECON *Policy of War* Wks. 1564 I. 136 The rapacite of wolues, the violence of Lyons. **1641** J. JACKSON *True Evang. T.* I. 73 Our rapacity,..our snatching, and catching, at far more then is our own. **1790** BURKE *Fr. Rev.* 75 The great masses..which excite envy, and tempt rapacity. **1868** FREEMAN *Norm. Conq.* II. viii. 187 An act of wanton rapacity was presently punished.

‖**rapa'dura.** [Pg., lit. 'scraping', f. *rapar* to scrape.] A coarse sugar, in cakes or lumps, made in Mexico and S. America.

1846 G. GARDNER *Brazil* 188, I had often an opportunity of seeing the manner in which Rapadura is made. **1933** P. FLEMING *Brazilian Adventure* I. xvii. 146 *Rapadura*..is a product of sugar-cane, and is manufactured in rectangular blocks six inches long. It looks exactly like a huge slab of home-made toffee.

rapakivi (ræpə'kiːviː, 'ræpəkiːviː). *Petrol.* Also †**Rapa-, -kiwi.** [a. Finn. *rapakivi* crumbly stone, f. *rapa* mud + *kivi* stone.] A form of granite characterized by plagioclase mantles surrounding large crystals of potash feldspar; orig. *spec.* that occurring in southern Finland. Usu. *attrib.*

[**1784** R. KIRWAN *Elem. Mineral* I. viii. 149 A stone of this sort which moulders by exposures to the air, is found in Finland, and is said to contain sometimes saltpetre, and sometimes common salt, it is there called Rapakivi.] **1795** *Ibid.* (ed. 2) I. 345 The aggregate of felspar and mica is called Rapakivi. **1906** J. P. IDDINGS *Rock Minerals* II. 487 Quartz ..may often be the darkest mineral visible megascopically, as in some varieties of rapakiwi from Finland. **1933** R. A. DALY *Igneous Rocks* viii. 141 Sederholm concluded that the Rapakivi granite in southern Finland is a thick flow, poured out on the surface of a fault trough or graben, the liquid rising along one or more of the faults concerned. **1944** *Proc. Geologists' Assoc.* LV. 74 The typical rock, the rapakivi granite proper, is characterised by abundant large ovoids.. of potash-felspar which lie in a matrix of quartz, potash-felspar, plagioclase and dark mica, and, sometimes, hornblende; often the potash-felspar ovoids are mantled by a ring made up of small oligoclases, and it is this striking phenomenon which is usually in mind when the rapakivi granites are considered. **1976** *Nature* 10 June 482/2 The granites locally display the well developed rapakivi texture characteristic of anorogenic granites throughout the world.

†**rap and run,** *adv. Obs. rare*⁻⁰. (See quot.)

1598 FLORIO, *Allarappa*,..shiftingly, rap and run.

raparal, Sc. var. REPAREL *Obs.*

rapare, obs. Sc. f. REPAIR *v.*

raparee, var. RAPPAREE.

†**rape,** *sb.*¹ *Obs.* Also 3 rap. [Related to RAPE *v.*¹] Haste, speed, hurry; chiefly in phrases *to have rape* and *in rape.*

a **1300** *K. Horn* 1532 Horn him wok of slape, So a man þat hadde rape. *c* **1330** *Arth. & Merl.* 2368 (Kölbing), He stirt vp al in rape. *Ibid.* 4850 Fleand oway with gret rape. *c* **1374** CHAUCER *To Scriv.* 7 Al is thorugh thy neclygence and rape. *c* **1400** *Laud Troy Bk.* 1644 Thei saw come many a lord,.. With mychel spede and mychel rape. *c* **1400** *Promp. Parv.* 423/2 Rape, or hast, *festinacio.*

Prov. c **1300** *Prov. Hending* xxxi. in *Salomon & Sat.* (1848) 278 Ofte rap reweþ, quoþ Hendyng. **1473** MARG. PASTON in *P. Lett.* III. 78 Bydde hym that he be not to hasty of takyng of orderes..for oftyn rape rewith.

b. With *a*, in phr. *in a rape*, in a hurry.

c **1320** *Sir Beues* (MS. A.) 642 Beues slouȝ hem in a rape. *c* **1400** *Destr. Troy* 5633 Row forthe in a rape right to the banke, Tit vnto Troy, tary no lengur.

rape (reɪp), *sb.*² [a. AF. *rap*, *raap*, *rape* (Britton, etc. in sense 3), prob. a back-formation from L. *rapĕre*: see RAPE *v.*²]

†**1.** The act of taking anything by force; violent seizure (of goods), robbery. Also with *a*: A case or instance of this. *Obs.*

In later use perh. *transf.* from 2 or 3.

c **1400** *Destr. Troy* 4926 Right, þat vs riches for rape of our godes. **1526** *Pilgr. Perf.* (W. de W. 1531) 238 All vnlawfull vsurpyng..of the temporall goodes of ony persone, by rape, pykyng..or ony other maner of stelyng. **1596** SPENSER *F.Q.* IV. vii. 5 He liu'd all on rauin and on rape Of men and beasts. **1646-8** G. DANIEL *Poems* Wks. 1878 I. 204 Soe farre Humanitie enforces..In the Sterne Rape of Power. **1706** DE FOE *Jure Divino* XI. 246 When Kings their Crowns without Consent obtain, 'Tis all a mighty Rape, and not a Reign. **1712** POPE (*title*) The Rape of the Lock.

2. The act of carrying away a person, *esp.* a woman, by force.

Sometimes (as in quot. 1436) involving also sense 3.

c **1400** *Destr. Troy* 3539 Menelay..was told Of the rape vnrightwis of his Riche qwene. **1436** *Rolls of Parlt.* I. 497 There the seid Besecher [he] felonousely and moste horribely ravysshed, and her..ledde with him into the wylde and desolate places of Wales; of the which rape, he.. is endited. **1588** SHAKS. *Tit. A.* I. i. 405 Rape call you it.. to cease [seize] my owne, My true betrothed Loue. **1616** R. C. *Times' Whistle* Cert. Poems (1871) 128 So death is cruell,.. of all he makes his rape. **1697** DRYDEN *Virg. Georg.* IV. 490 All the Rapes of Gods, and ev'ry Love. **1763** J. BROWN *Poetry & Mus.* v. 77 He..sung the Rape of Proserpine by Pluto. **1829** SCOTT *Rob Roy* Introd. 31 We need not refer to the rape of the Sabines.

3. a. Violation or ravishing of a woman. Also, in mod. usage, sexual assault upon a man.

1481 CAXTON *Reynard* (Arb.) 95 There rauysschyd he and forcyd my wyf..See my lorde thys fowle mater, this is murdre rape and Treson. **1588** SHAKS. *Tit. A.* IV. i. 48 This ..treates of Tereus treason and his rape, And rape I feare was roote of thine annoy. **1667** MILTON *P.L.* XI. 717 Marrying or prostituting, as befell, Rape or Adulterie. **1768** BLACKSTONE *Comm.* IV. 15 An attempt to rob, to ravish, or to kill, is far less penal than the actual robbery, rape, or murder. **1869** LECKY *Europ. Mor.* II. i. 69 The rape of a slave woman was also in this reign punished like that of a free woman, by death. **1976** *Listener* 27 May 683/1 The brutal assault with flagellation and homosexual rape. **1981** *Times* 9 Mar. 4/8 The president of the National Viewers' and Listeners' Association..is bringing a summons against the director of the play..over the scene of homosexual rape.

b. With *a* and *pl.* An instance of this.

1577 tr. *Bullinger's Decades* (1592) 190 Let adulteries,.. rapes, and incestes bee put to exile. **1616** R. C. *Times' Whistle* VI. 2460 The daunger of the lawe, which for a rape Awardeth death. **1709** STEELE *Tatler* No. 84 ¶1 At the Old-Bailey when a Rape is to be try'd. **1757** BURKE *Abridgm. Eng. Hist.* II. iii. Wks. (1812) 283 Rapes, and vows of perpetual chastity, succeeded each other in the same persons. **1834** *Cycl. Pract. Medicine* III. 583/1 An assault, with intent to commit a rape. **1977** *New Yorker* 24 Oct. 64/3 Hardly a year goes by without a gang rape at Green Haven. On New Year's Eve, 1976,..a..man was forcibly assaulted and sodomized.

c. *transf.* and *fig.* (Freq. in 17th c.)

1595 SHAKS. *John* II. i. 97 Thou hast..done a rape Vpon the maiden vertue of the Crowne. **1642** FULLER *Holy & Prof. St.* I. v. 13 When they set Abel to till the ground, and send Cain to keep sheep..they commit a rape on nature. **1677** GILPIN *Demonol.* (1867) 76 If thou yield, will not God account it a rape upon thine integrity? *a* **1704** T. BROWN *Sat. French King* Wks. 1730 I. 60 Old Jerom's volumes next I made a rape on. **1975** *Times Lit. Suppl.* 10 Oct. 1217/5 It is his job to save Juli from the hangman and, in the final court scene, he does it by the public rape of the boy's secret personality and the destruction of his genius.

4. *concr.* One (*esp.* a woman) who is raped. ? *Obs.*

1586 WARNER *Alb. Eng.* I. II. viii. (1589) 29 And hauing brought his trembling Rape into a vallie, said: Se Deianira how thy Loue an end of me hath made. **1621** G. SANDYS *Ovid's Met.* III. (1626) 45 The God, arriuing with his Rape At sacred Creet, resumes his heauenly shape. *a* **1683** OLDHAM *Wks.* (1686) 20 Ravish at th' Altar,..Make them your Rapes, and Victims too in one.

5. *attrib.* and *Comb.*, as ***rape fiend, hound, -novel, -scene; rape-happy*** adj.; **rape artist,** one who successfully plans and executes a rape or rapes.

1974 *News & Courier* (Charleston, S. Carolina) 28 Apr. E-2/1 The majority result from spur-of-the-moment urges, although 'rape artists' who plan their assaults ahead of time and attack on a regular basis, do exist. **1935** N. ERSINE *Underworld & Prison Slang* 61 *Rape fiend, rape hound*, a person serving time on a rape *rap*. He is held in contempt by all *cons* on other charges. **1973** C. HIMES *Black on Black* 40 You dirty, lying rape fiend, I hope they beat you up. **1953** 'M. SPILLANE' *Kiss Me, Deadly* i. 7 Damn rape-happy dame. You think all guys are the same? **1961** R. WILLIAMS *Long Revolution* 336 The horror-film, the rape-novel. **1961** *John o' London's* 3 Aug. 163/2 A truly Moravian rape-scene in a ruined church. **1981** *Times* 11 Mar. 14/8 The rape scene is handled with a casual certainty that robs it of all offence.

rape (reɪp), *sb.*³ *Obs.* exc. *dial.* [a. F. *râpe* †*raspe* RASP *sb.*¹] A rasp, rough file.

1502 ARNOLDE *Chron* (1811) 245 The toel yᵗ belongeth to my crafte, as saues,..hameres, rapis, filis. **1546** LANGLEY *Pol. Verg. de Invent.* II. xii. 56 b, Ciniras also deuised the tonges, fyle or rape, leuer and stithe. **1639** T. DE GREY *Compl. Horsem.* 101 Take a rape, or a drawing-iron, and with eyther of these make the coffin of the hoofe fine and thin. **1725** BRADLEY *Fam. Dict.* s.v. *Shoeing of horses*, The Raggedness also on the out side of the Coffin, should be filed away with a Rape. **1888** in *Sheffield Gloss.*

attrib. **1610** MARKHAM *Masterp.* II. cii. 385 The best cure is with a fine rape-file to smooth the wrinckles away.

rape (reɪp), *sb.*⁴ Also 1 rap, 4 rope. [Of unknown etym.; first found in Domesday Book, but possibly of OE. origin.

The form of the word is decisive against any connexion with Icel. *hreppr* poor-law district, parish, which is freq. given as the source. Advocates of this etym. have further attempted to explain the term as meaning land measured by the 'rope' (OE. *rāp*, ON. *reip*); but the one suggestion necessarily excludes the other. The latter is phonetically possible, but there is no positive evidence for it.]

One of the six administrative districts into which Sussex was divided, each comprising several hundreds.

c **1086** *Domesday Bk.* II. 17 b, De his hiðis jacent .III. hiðæ ..in Rap de Hastinges. **1376** *Rolls of Parlt.* II. 348/1 En les Rapes de Cicestre & Arundell. **1380** *Ibid.* III. 95/2 Le Rope d'Arundell', en quele Rope sont contenuz pluseurs Hundredes. **1495** *Ibid.* VI. 500/1 The Ferme and Issues of the Rape of Chichestre. **1588** FRAUNCE *Lawiers Log.* I. xii. 52 b, Lathes, Rapes, and Wapentakes, be so called of the divisions of partes of shires. **1611** SPEED *Theat. Gt. Brit.* v. (1614) 9/2 This country is principally divided into six Rapes, containing a river, a castle, and forrest in themselves. **1717** GAY *To William Lowndes Esq.* 12 Great Lownds his praise should swell the trump of fame, And rapes and wapentakes resound his name. **1832** *Act 2 & 3 Will. IV*, c. 64 §22 Such Eastern Division shall include..the several rapes of Lewes, Hastings, and Pevensey. **1888** *Archæol. Rev.* Mar. 59 In West Sussex the rape also survives for the important purpose of liability to the repair of bridges.

b. *Comb.*: †**rape reeve,** the official charged with the administration of a rape. *Obs.*

1765 BLACKSTONE *Comm.* I. 116 These had formerly their lathe-reeves and rape-reeves acting in subordination to the Shire-reeve.

rape (reɪp), *sb.*⁵ [ad. L. *rāpum* neut., *rāpa* fem., a turnip. In sense 2 perh. partly from Du. *raap* turnip, rape; cf. G. (now obs. or dial.) *rape, rabe(n, räbe(n* turnip.]

† **1.** (With *a* or in *pl.*) **a.** A turnip (? or radish). **b.** A plant of rape (2 b). *Obs.*

In 15th c. glossaries *rape* is used to render both *rāpa* and *raphanus*. In *K. Alis.* (Weber) 4983 *rabben* is not a form of *rape*, but an error for *crabben* of the MS.

? *c* **1390** *Form of Cury* in Warner *Antiq. Culin.* (1791) 4 Take rapus, and make hem clene..parboile hem [etc.]. *c* **1440** *Anc. Cookery* in *Househ. Ord.* (1790) 426 Take rapes and scrape hom wel..and then cut hom on peces. **1551** TURNER *Herbal* II. 112 Rapum..is called in English of them of the South countre, turnepe, of other countre men a rape. **1577** B. GOOGE *Heresbach's Husb.* (1586) 25 Plinie would not haue Rapes sowen, but in very well dunged ground. **1597** GERARDE *Herbal* II. ii. 179 Wild Turneps or Rapes haue long, broad, and rough leaues like those of Turneps. **1634** W. WOOD *New Eng. Prosp.* (1865) 15 This land likewise affoards Hempe and Flax..with Rapes if they bee well managed. **1667** 'EPHELIA' *Females Poems* 46 Filberts, or Strawberries, or the Roots of Rapes. **1714** AINSWORTH *Lat. Dict.* 11, *Nāpus*,..Turnep, or naphew, naphew gentle, or long rapes.

2. As a plant-name. † **a.** The common turnip. *Obs.* **b.** An annual or biennial yellow-flowered herb, a variety of *Brassica napus* or a closely related species, belonging to the family Cruciferæ, widely cultivated in Europe, North America, and Japan and used as cattle fodder or the source of a seed yielding an edible oil; also known as cole or coleseed.

There has been much confusion between *rape* and *coleseed*, either plant being known under both names; the former is sometimes called *winter rape* and the latter *summer rape*. The older writers usually distinguish the turnip and rape by the adjectives *round* and *long(-rooted)* respectively.

1398 TREVISA *Barth De P.R.* XVII. cxxxviii. (Bodl. MS.), Of sede of þe Rape and also of þe Raphane is oile made. **1548** TURNER *Names Herbes* (E.D.S.) 55, I haue hearde sume cal it [*napus*] in englishe a turnepe, and other some a naued or nauet, it maye be called also longe Rape or nauet gentle. **1551** —— *Herbal* II. 113 The great round rape called commonly a turnepe groweth..more about London than in other place of England that I knowe of. *Ibid.*, The long rooted rape groweth very plenteously a litle from Linne where as much oyle is made of the sede of it. **1597** [see RAPE-OIL]. **1651** R. CHILD in *Hartlib's Legacy* (1655) 9 To sow Turneps, Carrets,..Pease, Rape. **1760** STERNE *Tr. Shandy* IV. xxxi, It was plain he should reap a hundred lasts of rape ..the very first year. **1796** C. MARSHALL *Garden.* xvi. (1813) 272 Rape or coleseed is sown for a sallad herb to be eat in the seed leaf. **1842** BISCHOFF *Woollen Manuf.* II. 91 The nominal duty on the cake made from rape was reduced. **1889** G. S. BOULGER *Uses of Plants* III. 133 Rape..yields from its seeds an oil still largely used for lamps and lubricating. **1937** A. F. HILL *Econ. Bot.* ix. 218 The rape..is extensively cultivated in Europe. **1958** GILL & VEAR *Agric. Bot.* ix. 119 Rapes are forms with..rather small leaves. **1970** J. G. VAUGHAN *Structure & Utilization of Oil Seeds* 49 The rapes and mustards are crops adapted to temperate regions and also to certain subtropical areas. **1976** *Western Producer* (Saskatoon) 24 June C7/2 On the other hand a field of rape shining glowing and bright—as yellow as any field of mustard.

† **c.** Ellipt. for RAPE-OIL. *Obs. rare*$^{-1}$.

1641 HEYWOOD *Reader. Here you'l plainly see* 6 When our sope of sweetest oyle was made..These by an ingrost Patent coveting gaine Compos'd it all of stinking rape and traine.

3. *wild rape*, Charlock or Field-Mustard.

1551 TURNER *Herbal* II. 112 The thyrde [kind] whiche is called the wilde rape..rinneth furth a long. **1597** GERARDE *Herbal* II. ii. 179 Charlocke or the wild Rape, hath leaues like vnto the former [the wild Turnip] but lesser, and not so rough. **1766** *Museum Rust.* VI. 272 *note*, The wild rape or charlock, and wild navew, or bunias, which have both been used in making oil; and are frequently confounded under the name of rape-seed. **1805** DICKSON *Pract. Agric.* I. 563 The rough-leaved charlock, or wild mustard; the smooth-leaved, or wild rape.

4. *attrib.* and *Comb.*, as ***rape crop, culture, field, -leaf, -leaved*** adj., ***-mill, plant, root, -shearing, -thresher, -threshing***; **rape-cloth**, a cloth on which rape is threshed; † **rape-cole**, the turnip-cabbage, KOHLRABI; † **rape crowfoot**, *Ranunculus bulbosus*; **rape-dust**, rapeseed ground to powder and used as manure; † **rape radish**, the round radish; † **rape violet**, *Cyclamen europæum*. Also RAPE-CAKE, -OIL, -SEED.

1765 *Museum Rust.* IV. 212 The size of our *rape-cloths is so great, that [etc.]. **1597** GERARDE *Herbal* xxxvii. 251 The first kinde of *Rape Cole hath one single long roote [etc.]. **1610** W. FOLKINGHAM *Art of Survey* I. xi. 37 The Coley-florey, Rape-cole, Muske-melon, Cucumber. **1788** W. MARSHALL *Yorksh.* II. 49 There have been instances..in which the produce of the *rape crop has been equal to the purchase-value of the land. **1578** LYTE *Dodoens* III. lxxiii. 421 We may call it *Rape Crowfoote. **1597** GERARDE *Herbal* II. ccclxviii. (1633) 957 St. Anthonies Rape may be called in English Rape Crowfoot. **1856** EMERSON *Eng. Traits* v. 99 The fens of Lincolnshire..have been drained, and put on equality with the best for *rape-culture and grass. **1807** *Beverley & Kexby Road Act* 6 Mould, dung, *rape-dust, soot, compost or manure. **1580** HOLLYBAND *Treas. Fr. Tong*, *Vne Navitiere*, a *Rape field. **1765** *Museum Rust.* IV. 212 People who have rape-fields bespeak them [rape-cloths] long before. **1538** ELYOT, *Rapacia*, *rape leaues. **1816–20** GREEN *Herbal* II. 521/2 *Salvia Napifolia*, *Rape-leaved sage. **1634–5** BRERETON *Trav.* (Chetham Soc.) 43 Hence we went to see a *rape-mill turned by an horse at Swammerdam. **1766** *Museum Rust.* VI. 271 The *rape plant ..is a species of wild turnep. **1842** LANCE *Cottage Farmer* 15 The Rape Plant is of the cabbage kind, and is good feed for sheep. **1548** TURNER *Names Herbes* (E.D.S.) 67 This maye be called in englishe, an Alman radice, or *rape radice. **1533** ELYOT *Cast. Helthe* (1539) 24 b, *Rape rotes and Nauews. The iuyce made by them, is very grosse. **1606** HOLLAND *Suetonius* 241 In a seditious commotion: there were Rape-rootes [*marg.* Or Turneps] flung at his head. **1765** *Museum Rust.* IV. 206 A great *rape-shearing in our constablery. *Ibid.* 212 The disconcerting of the whole series of *rape-threshers. *Ibid.* 206 Description of a *rape-threshing..in the North-Riding of Yorkshire. **1548** TURNER *Names Herbes* (E.D.S.) 33 It might well be called in englishe *Rape Violet because it hath a roote lyke a Rape & floores lyke a Violet. **1552** ELYOT, *Cyclaminus*..is named in english rape violet.

rape (reɪp), *sb.*[6] Also 7 **rappe**. [In branch I a. F. *râpe* = Prov. and Sp. *raspa*, It. *raspo*, med.L. *raspa* (1202 in Du Cange). In II properly *rapé*, a. F. *râpé* (:—OF. *raspeit*, 12–13th c.) f. *râpe*.]

I. 1. The stalks of grape-clusters, or refuse of grapes from which wine has been expressed, used in making vinegar. Also *pl.* in same sense.

1657 *Bk. of Values*, Rape of grape, the tun..*l.* 06. **1682** *Art & Myst. Vintners* (1703) 64 Then wash your Rapes clear out, and put it in the Hogshead. **1725** BRADLEY *Fam. Dict.* s.v. *Vinegar*, Put in some Rape, or Husks of Grapes,..then letting the Rape settle, draw off the liquid Part. **1830** M. DONOVAN *Dom. Econ.* I. 321 The rape used in this process is kept for a succession of other processes. **1875** KNIGHT *Dict. Mech.* 1880/2 It derives its name from being charged with rapes.

2. A vessel used in the manufacture of vinegar.

1805 SHANNON *Brewing* III. 64 Small rapes..that do not but hold but from 1500 to 3000 gallons, whereas the rapes in general hold 20,000 gallons. **1885** GARDNER *Acetic Acid* 68 This operation [of filtering vinegar] is performed in large casks with false bottoms called 'rapes'.

3. *attrib.*, as ***rape-shed, tun, -vinegar***.

1747–96 MRS. GLASSE *Cookery* xix. 299 If you can get rape-vinegar, use that instead of salt and water. **1811** A. T. THOMSON *Lond. Disp.* (1818) 7 These rape tuns are worked by pairs. **1845** G. DODD *Brit. Manuf.* 5th Ser. iv. 76 In a building called the 'rape-shed' are some enormous wooden vessels called 'rapes'.

II. † **4.** (More fully ***rape wine***, = F. *vin râpé*.) Wine made either from the rape (sense 1 above) by addition of water, or from fresh grapes and light wine placed together in a cask. *Obs.*

1600 SURFLET *Countrie Farme* VI. xvi. 756 He shall make it in this sort after the manner of a rappe vine. **1656** BLOUNT *Glossogr.*, *Rape wine* [copying Cotgr. s.v. *râpé*]. **1726** in BAILEY. **1733** MILLER *Gard. Dict.* (ed. 2) s.v. *Vitis*, Concerning Rapes, or New Wines. They make a Rape of Cuttings only, without any mixture of Grapes.

† **5.** The grapes used in making *vin râpé* (see 4).

1704 RAY *Creation* (ed. 4) 31 The Juice of Grapes is drawn as well from the Rape, where they remain whole, as from a Vat, where they are bruis'd.

† **rape**, *a.* and *adv. Obs. rare.* [? Back-formation from RAPELY *adv.*] **a.** *adj.* Quick, hasty. **b.** *adv.* Hastily.

c **1400** *Gamelyn* 101 Than bispak his brother, that rape was of rees, 'Stond stille, gadelyng'. *c* **1400** *Rom. Rose* 6516, I sey, and swere him ful rape, That riche men [etc.]. *a* **1585** MONTGOMERIE *Cherrie & Slae* 884 Then Will, as angrie as an ape, Ran ramping, sweiring, rude and rape.

† **rape**, *v.*[1] *Obs.* Also *inf.* 3–4 **rapen**, 5 **rapyn**. [a. ON. *hrapa* (MSw. *rapa*) to hasten.]

1. *refl.* To betake (oneself) in haste or with speed.

c **1250** *Gen. & Ex.* 2376 He..bad hem rapen hem homward swiðe. *c* **1330** R. BRUNNE *Chron. Wace* (Rolls) 7748 A-wey þey scaped, Ouer se til oþer land þeym raped. **1377** LANGL. *P. Pl.* B. v. 399 'What! awake, renke!' quod repentance, and rape þe to shrifte'. *a* **1450** *Le Morte Arth.* 2665 He wolle rape hym on A Resse..to the holy londe.

b. Const. with *infin.*

c **1250** *Gen. & Ex.* 1221 Abraham rapede him sone in sped for to fulfillen godes reed. **1362** LANGL. *P. Pl.* A. IV. 7, I comaunde þe..þat þou Rape þe to ride. *a* **1460** *Play Sacram.* 659, I shalle rape me redely anon To plucke owt the naylys.

c. *trans.* To cause to hasten, to hurry on.

c **1330** R. BRUNNE *Chron.* (1810) 284 ȝour clerke ȝe þider rape with our messengere. *Ibid.* 309 þe tyme he will not rape, no set a certeyn day.

2. *intr.* To hasten, hurry, make haste.

c **1330** *Arth. & Merl.* 7474 (Kölbing) Of hem fiue þousand, þat wald scape Toward king Oriens gan rape. *c* **1400** *Destr. Troy* 1897 Pas fro my presens..And rape of my rewme in a rad haste. *c* **1430** *Syr Gener.* 122 To his felows he gan to rape.

rape (reɪp), *v.*[2] [Prob. ad. L. *rapĕre* to seize, take by force: cf. AF. *raper* (1400 in Godef.), obs. and dial. F. *raper* (ibid.). The relationship of (M)LG. and (M)Du. *rāpen* in the same sense is not clear (cf. RAP *v.*[3]).]

1. a. *trans.* To take (a thing) by force. Also *absol.*, *transf.* and *fig.* (in some examples, also influenced by sense 3).

1388 WIMBLETON *Serm.* in *MS. Hatton* 57 fol. 16 Rauenous fisches han sum mesure; whanne þei hungren thei rapyn; whanne þei ben ful þey sparyn. **1526** *Pilgr. Perf.* (W. de W. 1531) 140 To rape & deuour the..sustenaunce of the poore seruauntes of god. **1596** DRAYTON *Legends* iv. 749 What their Fathers gave her..The Sonnes rap'd from her with a violent Hand. **1635** HEYWOOD *Hierarch.* 349 As before, They rape, extort, forsweare,..Oppresse. **1807** J. BARLOW *Columb.* v. 693 So Leda's Twins from Colchis raped the Fleece. **1863** COWDEN CLARKE *Shaks. Char.* xvii. 421 Steadily clutching all that he had raped. **1927** *Blackw. Mag.* Apr. 494/2 The stone walls on either side pressed close, threatening to rape from us our faithful caravan. **1949** WYNDHAM LEWIS *Let.* 6 Aug. (1963) 502 Their women *rape* 'culture' (clubs, 'circles' for weekly absorption of potted literature etc). **1950** D. GASCOYNE *Vagrant* 27 Rockets released tonight rush up to rape the grapebloom sky. **1976** *Bookseller* 14 Feb. 811 (Advt.), Browning, whose life he saved in 1944, is now his rival, raping the Great Land with oil-wells and pipelines. **1977** *Undercurrents* June–July 41/2 We are not going to 'subsistence production' because the capitalists have raped our land and resources. **1978** G. VIDAL *Kalki* ii. 30 Dr Ashok's eyes had a tendency to pop whenever he wanted to rape your attention.

b. In alliterative and riming phrases, as † ***rape and renne, rend, wring*** (obs.); ***rape and scrape*** dial. (Cf. RAP *v.*[3] 1 b.)

c **1386** CHAUCER *Can. Yeom. Prol. & T.* 869 Al that ye may rape and renne. **1555** W. WATREMAN *Fardle Facions* II. x. 217 Thei euer couete, and..rape and rende from other. **1610** HOLLAND tr. *Camden's Brit.* I. 259 To scrape and rape money to himselfe. **1622** MABBE tr. *Aleman's Guzman d'Alf.* I. 230 Whatsoever I could rape or wring from them. **1655** FULLER *Ch. Hist.* IV. i. §12 She..snatched all she could rape and rend, unto herself. **1887** *S. Cheshire Gloss.*, *Rape an' scrape*, to rake and scrape together.

† **c.** To pull *down*. *Obs. rare*$^{-1}$.

1597 J. KING *On Jonas* (1618) 78 They..rend and rape downe tackles, sailes, all implements.

d. To rob, strip, plunder (a place). Also used with a group of people as object.

a **1721** D'URFEY *Ariadne* I. ii, I can..Rape the tow'ring Eagle's Nest. **1892** R. KIPLING *Barrack-r. Ballads* 177, I raped your richest roadstead, I plundered Singapore. **1972** *Business Week* 18 Mar. 70/1 'Our underwriter raped us,' reports the president of a small New York company that sold $250,000 in stock in 1968. **1973** *Black Panther* 21 July p. B, The Reading administration will continue to rape the poor.

2. To carry off (a person, *esp.* a woman) by force. ? *Obs.*

1590 SPENSER *F.Q.* III. x. *heading*, Paridell rapeth Hellenore; Malbecco her poursewes. **1598** B. JONSON *Ev. Man in Hum.* II. v, These houshold precedents; which are strong And swift to rape youth, to their precipice. *a* **1649** DRUMM. OF HAWTH. *Poems* Wks. (1711) 46/2 The flower of virgins..By ruthless destiny is ta'ne away, And rap'd from earth. **1715–20** POPE *Iliad* XIII. 782 A princess raped transcends a navy storm'd.

3. To ravish, commit rape on (a woman). Also, with a man as the sexual object and a man or woman as the subject.

1577 *Test. 12 Patriarchs* (1604) 45 *marg.*, The Sichemites raped Dina; persecuted strangers; ravished their wives. *a* **1641** BP. MOUNTAGU *Acts & Mon.* (1642) 343 To..torment their bodies, rape their wives and daughters. **1861** *Times* 18 July, She charged that..he had violently assaulted and raped her. **1885** *Law Times* LXXVIII. 240/2 Females who have been raped or indecently assaulted. **1928** D. H. LAWRENCE *Let.* ? 28 Oct. (1962) II. 1096 Why do men only thrill to a woman who'll rape them? **1971** *Southerly* XXXI. 6 The first of the series of sexually voracious women who seek virtually to rape him. **1972** *Times* 31 Oct. 2/4 The girls had taken their clothes off and intended to rape him. **1977** *New Society* 1 Sept. 449/2 These women have been confined for a variety of offences, chief among which are soliciting and manslaughter. When a man finds his way into their midst, he is promptly raped. **1977** *New Yorker* 24 Oct. 64/3 A man..claimed he had been assaulted and raped by four other prisoners.

4. To transport, ravish, delight. Now *rare*.

1613 DRAYTON *Ecl.* v. 60 To rape the fields with touches of her string. **1675** BAXTER *Cath. Theol.* I. III. 91 This grace ..rapeth the will so that it is scarce perceived to act. **1852** *Meanderings of Mem.* I. 87 With art's refinement he would ..rape the soul.

Hence **raped** *ppl. a.*[1]

1675 PENN *Eng. Pres. Interest* 41 There is no such Excitement to Revenge, as a rap'd Conscience. **1960** O. MANNING *Great Fortune* xiv. 180 The raped boys who, once corrupted, sold themselves for a few *lei*. **1977** *Sunday Times* 30 Jan. 38/1 Squads of sexologists, whole studios full of raped girls, etc., etc.

rape, *v.*[3] *Obs.* exc. *dial.* [a. F. *râper*, f. *râpe* RAPE *sb.*[3]] *trans.* To rasp. (In mod. south-western dial., to scratch.)

1596 BARROUGH *Meth. Physick* (ed. 3) 369 Take and rape it [wood]. *Ibid.*, After you have raped it. **1633** [J. PARTRIDGE] *Treas. Hid. Secrets* cxvii, Put into the pot one pound and halfe of your Wood small raped.

Hence **raped** *ppl. a.*[2], **raping** *vbl. sb.*

1596 BARROUGH *Meth. Physick* (ed. 3) 369 Take one pound of the raped wood. *Ibid.*, The last proofe of this wood is, to boile the rapings thereof.

† **rapé.** *Obs.* Also 4 **rapee, rapy**, 5 **rapey(e**. [a. F. *râpé*, pa. pple. of *râper* to scrape, grate: cf. RAPPEE[1].] A dish in mediæval cookery, composed of many ingredients grated, stamped, or pounded, and highly seasoned.

1381 *Anc. Cookery* in Warner *Antiq. Culin.* (1791) 49 For to make rapee. Tak the crustys of wyt bred, and reysons, and bray hem wel in a morter. *c* **1430** *Two Cookery-bks.* 25 Rapeye of Fleysshe. Take lene Porke y-sode & y-grounde smalle. *c* **1467** *Noble Bk. Cookry* (1882) 118 To mak rape of fisshe tak luces and tenches or other fisshe and fry them in oile [etc.].

rape, obs. form of REAP *sb.* (sheaf).

rape, Sc. and north. f. ROPE.

'rape-cake. [f. RAPE *sb.*[5]] **a.** A flat cake made of rapeseed pressed into this form after the oil has been extracted from it. **b.** The substance of which these cakes are composed.

1660 *Bk. of Rates*, Rape cake the thousand, xs. **1732** W. ELLIS *Pract. Farmer* II. 51 Several make use of Rape-cakes, Ground..into Powder. **1766** *Museum Rust.* VI. 269 Cattle are not fed with rape cakes, because they refuse to eat them: and those cakes are therefore sold for manuring the ground.

1869 E. A. PARKES *Pract. Hygiene* (ed. 3) 283 Pepper is adulterated with linseed..rape cake, and ground rice.

rapee, variant of RAPÉ, RAPPEE^1.

†**'rapeful**, *a. Obs.* [f. RAPE *sb.*^{2} + -FUL.] Given to, or characterized by, rape or violence.
1605 CHAPMAN *Byron's Trag.* IV. i, To teach the rapefull Hyrcans mariage. **1633** *Costlie Whore* I. i. in Bullen *O. Pl.* IV, His suite, Which he in rapefull manner oft hath sought.

†**'rapely**, *adv. Obs.* Also 3 -like, 4 -liche. [a. ON. *hrapaliga* hurriedly, f. *hrapa* RAPE *v.*^{1}] Hastily, in haste, quickly. (Cf. RAPLY *adv.*)
c **1220** *Bestiary* 240 Ðe mire..renneð rapelike. *a* **1352** MINOT *Poems* vi. 67 Gold..made him rapely ride. **1377** LANGL. *P. Pl.* B. XVI. 273 With that sawe I an other Rapeliche renne forth. *c* **1400** *Gamelyn* 420 Adam took Gamelyn, And ladde him into spence rapely and anon.

rapent, obs. Sc. form of REPENT *v.*

'rape-oil. [f. RAPE *sb.*^{5} Cf. Du. *raapolie.*] A thick brownish-yellow oil expressed from rapeseed, used chiefly for lubricating and in the manufacture of soap and india-rubber.
1545 *Bk. of Values*, Rape oyle the last, viiil. **1597** GERARDE *Herbal* II. ii. 179 There be three sorts of wilde Turneps; one our common Rape which beareth the seed whereof is made rape-oil. **1640** PARKINSON *Herbal* 861 Rape oyle that is used in Lampes and therefore called Lampe Oyle. **1712** tr. *Pomet's Hist. Drugs* I. 10 Rape-Oil is sweet, and on the contrary the Linseed bitter. **1723** J. NOTT *Cook's & Confectioner's Dict.* sig. Kk3^v Fry it [*sc.* a sturgeon] in four Gallons of Rape-oil clarified. **1839** H. T. DE LA BECHE *Rep. Geol. Cornwall* xv. 601 The undermentioned articles are included under the head of Materials and Water-cost.. Coals..Rape-oil..Books and Stationery. **1866** *Public Ledger* 10 Jan. 3/2 Rape-oil is only in limited request. **1913** V. B. LEWES *Oil Fuel* vi. 177 The number of seconds taken by the oil to flow up to the 50 c.c. mark on the flask is noted, and the results brought into comparison with the viscosity of rape oil, that being the oil with which the apparatus is standardised. **1926** [see HYDROXAMIC *a.*]. **1937** A. F. HILL *Econ. Bot.* ix. 218 Cold-pressed rape oil is also edible.
attrib. and *Comb.* **1766** *Museum Rust.* VI. 272 The uses, to which the rape-oil cakes are applied for the feeding of cattle. **1885** *Census Instruct.*, Rape Oil Refiner, Maker.

raper ('reɪpə(r)). [f. RAPE *v.*^{2} + -ER^1.] One who rapes. Also *fig.*
1927 *Contemp. Rev.* July 85 In woman's eyes this magic creature was phallic man, 'old Adam', the raper, who started life. **1930** L. W. MEYNELL *Camouflage* vii. 102 Notorious in the countryside as the attempted raper of women. **1951** M. MCLUHAN *Mech. Bride* (1967) 129/2 It is the savage dream of Mistah Kurtz..the raper and rifler of nations and continents. **1959** M. BRADBURY *Eating People is Wrong* iv. 114 He's sexually unpleasant, Stuart. I call him The Solitary Raper. He's like a walking phallic symbol. **1971** L. P. HARTLEY *Mrs Carteret Receives* 178 Some women locked theirs [*sc.* bedroom doors] even when there was no threat of a nightly visitant, burglar, marauder, raper, or such-like.

raper, obs. form of RAPIER, ROPER.

raperee, obs. form of RAPPAREE.

'rapeseed. [f. RAPE *sb.*^{5} Cf. Du. *raapzaad.*] The seed of the RAPE (esp. *Brassica campestris oleifera*), used chiefly for the production of oil.
1577 B. GOOGE *Heresbach's Husb.* (1586) 29 b, Amongest the Winter seedes, Rape seed dooth chalenge his place, whiche I take to be the seede of the Rape which Plinie maketh for his third kinde. **1634–5** BRERETON *Trav.* (Chetham Soc.) 44 A..mill-stone, upon which the rape-seed being thrown was ground. **1712** tr. *Pomet's Hist. Drugs* I. 10 The seed of a Kind of wild Colly-flower, which they call..Rape-seed. **1812** SIR J. SINCLAIR *Syst. Husb. Scot.* I. Add. 4 As rape-seed is so much larger than turnip-seed, the drill should be wider. **1842** BISCHOFF *Woollen Manuf.* II. 90 There is another oil made from rapeseed, also used in the coarse woollen manufacture.
b. Used as a name for the plant itself (cf. COLESEED). Now *rare.*
c **1532** DU WES *Introd. Fr.* in Palsgr. 915 Rape side, *nauette.* **1597** GERARDE *Herbal* II. ii. 180 Wilde Turnep is called in Latine *Rapistrum*..in English Rape, and Rape seed. **1666** in F. L. Hawks *Hist. N. Carolina* (1858) II. 39 The meadows are very proper for rice, rape-seed, linseed, &c. **1766** *Museum Rust.* VI. 272 *note*, The common rape-seed is a wild species..called in authors *Bunias* and *Napus sylvestris.* **1865** tr. *Erckman-Chatrian's Waterloo* 141 And these rape seed,..this colza,..how they all are at work, living and growing.
c. *attrib.*, as ***rapeseed-cake, -oil, stubble.***
1634–5 BRERETON *Trav.* (Chetham Soc.) 177 The rape-seed cakes I observed laid up. **1816** J. SMITH *Panorama Sc. & Art* II. 638 Its seed..by expression yields an oil called rapeseed-oil. **1840** J. BUEL *Farmer's Companion* 118 To sow a green crop..in the rape-seed stubble. **1854** SIMMONDS *Comm. Products Veg. Kingd.* v. 564 The export of linseed and rapeseed cakes from Stettin.

rapey(e, variant of RAPÉ *Obs.*

rap full, *a. Naut.* (See quot.)
1867 SMYTH *Sailor's Word-bk.* s.v., 'Keep her rap full!' means, do not come too close to the wind, or lift a wrinkle of the sail.

†**'rapfully**, *adv. Obs. rare*$^{-1}$. [f. RAP *sb.*^{1} + -FUL + -LY^2.] With resounding blows; violently.
1582 STANYHURST *Æneis* III. (Arb.) 88 A seabelch grounting on rough rocks rapfulye frapping.

rapha, obs. form of RAPHE^2.

Raphaelesque (ˌræfeɪə'lɛsk), *a.* Also raffaell-. [f. the name of *Raphael* (It. *Raffaello*), one of the great artists (1483–1520) of the Italian Renascence, + -ESQUE.] After the style of Raphael.
1832 *Edin. Rev.* XXXVIII. 455 He may be competent to expatiate upon..Raphaelesque expression. **1841** W. SPALDING *Italy & It. Isl.* II. 406 An almost Raffaellesque purity of outline. **1887** LAYARD *Kugler's Italian Schools* II. 469 Timoteo's manner might be called 'Raphaelesque' were he not the teacher and Raphael the pupil.
So **'Raphaelhood** *nonce-wd.*, the artistic nature of Raphael's work; **Rapha'elic** *a.*, *nonce-wd.*, concerned with Raphael; **'Raphaelism**, the principles of art introduced by Raphael; his style or method.
1851 MRS. BROWNING *Casa Guidi Wind.* 25 If any should ..Gaze scorn down from the heights of Raffaelhood, On Cimabue's picture. **1859** HAWTHORNE *Marb. Faun* vi. (1883) 77 Thus they convert themselves into..Raphaelic machines. **1877** SYMONDS *Renaiss. It., Fine Arts* III. x. (1882) 490 In a style of over-blown but gorgeous Raphaelism.

'Raphaelite. Also Raf-. [f. *Raphael* (see RAPHAELESQUE *a.*) + -ITE, in some cases in contrast to PRE-RAPHAELITE *sb.* and *a.*] One who adopts the principles or follows the style of Raphael. So **'Raphaelitism** = RAPHAELISM.
1851 RUSKIN *Pre-Raphaelitism* 59 And thus Pre-Raphaelitism and Raphaelitism, and Turnerism, are all one and the same, so far as education can influence them. **1905** W. HOLMAN HUNT *Pre-Raphaelitism* I. 137 The artists who thus servilely travestied this prince of painters at his prime were Raphaelites. **1928** GALSWORTHY *Swan Song* I. xii. 89 Harold is the only Rafaelite... He'll be the last, too.

†**'raphane.** *Obs. rare.* [ad. L. *raphanus* radish.] The radish.
1398 TREVISA *Barth. De P.R.* XVII. cxxxviii. (1495) 694 Of the sede of the rape and also of sede of Raphane is oyle made that is nedefull in many vses.

‖**raphania** (rə'feɪnɪə). *Path.* [mod.L., f. *raphanus* radish + -IA^1.] A name given by Linnæus to a form of ERGOTISM, on the supposition that it was due to the use of grain containing seeds of species of Raphanus.
1799 *Med. Jrnl.* I. 63 Palsy of the tongue, raphania,..the hooping cough [etc.]. **1847** tr. *Feuchtersleben's Med. Psychol.* 51 At the beginning of the eighth decennium, raphania.. became particularly prevalent.

‖**raphanus** ('ræfənʌs). *Bot.* [L., a. Gr. ῥάφανος = ῥαφανίς radish.] A genus of cruciferous plants, of which the common radish (*R. sativus*) is the most important species.
1730–6 in BAILEY (fol.). **1778** *Encycl. Brit.* (ed. 2) III. 1795/1 Charlock, the English name of the Raphanus,..is a very troublesome weed among corn. **1897** *Allbutt's Syst. Med.* II. 796 It has since been shewn that the raphanus is never poisonous.

†**raphe**^{1}. *Obs. rare.* [ad. L. *raphanus*: see prec. Cf. obs. F. *raphe* (Cotgr.).] The radish.
c **1420** *Pallad. on Husb.* II. 204 The raphe is roote, al other in letuce Vpgooth. *Ibid.* 212 The raphe outake, and lappe hit faire in donge.

‖**raphe**^{2} ('reɪfiː). Also 8 **rapha**, 8–9 **rhaphe**, 20 **raphé**. Pl. **raphæ**. [mod.L., a. Gr. ῥαφή seam, suture (of the skull, a wound, etc.).]
1. *Anat.* A line of union between the two halves of an organ or part of the body, having the appearance of a seam. Also, a median plane between two halves of a part of the brain, esp. that of the medulla oblongata and that of the tegmentum of the mid-brain.
1753 CHAMBERS *Cycl. Supp.*, *Rapha*, in anatomy, the ridge or line which..divides the scrotum and perinæum in two. **1758** J. S. *Le Dran's Observ. Surg.* (1771) 257 An Abscess was formed in the *Scrotum*, on the right Side near the *Rhaphe.* **1811** J. BELL *Anat. Human Body* (ed. 3) II. 410 Betwixt these salient lines there is..a kind of rut, called sometimes the rapha, or suture,..which..forms the accurate division of the two sides of the whole brain. **1830** R. KNOX *Béclard's Anat.* 43 This line even appears defined in some places, where it forms what are called raphæ or seams. **1858** GRAY *Anat.* 462 Along the middle line [of the corpus callosum] is a linear depression, the raphe. **1882** *Quain's Elements Anat.* (ed. 9) II. 297 Traced backwards into the raphe, the deep arcuate fibres appear to cross obliquely to the other side of the medulla. **1884** MACKENZIE *Dis. Throat & Nose* II. 476 Along the middle line of the nose there was a raphe projecting to the extent of about one millimetre. **1890** A. HILL tr. *Obersteiner's Anat. Central Nervous Organs* 215 All the way up to the third ventricle the median plane of the brain-stem is occupied by fibres which cross one another at an acute angle, but the area in which this decussation occurs is reduced to a vertical plate, termed the raphe. **1939** O. LARSELL *Textbk. Neuro-Anat.* xvi. 191 Some of these masses of cells in the tegmentum are sufficiently distinct to have individual names, but little is known of their individual functions. The most important are the..tegmental nuclei, the reticulotegmental nucleus, the superior central nucleus, and the dorsal nucleus of the raphé. **1971** *Nature* 23 Apr. 532/2 Adult rats of both sexes..were anaesthetized..and a bipolar steel stimulating electrode was placed stereotaxically in the caudal mid-brain raphé. **1976** SMYTHIES & CORBETT *Psychiatry* xiv. 266 Lesions of the raphe nuclei of the lower brain stem cause a profound disturbance of sleep.

2. *Bot.* **a.** In certain ovules, a cord connecting the hilum with the chalaza, and usually appearing as a ridge. **b.** In the Umbelliferæ, the line of junction or suture between the carpels. **c.** A median line or rib on the valves of diatoms.
1830 LINDLEY *Nat. Syst. Bot.* 123 Raphe and chalaza usually very distinctly marked. **1870** HOOKER *Stud. Flora* 105 Ovules..pendulous with a ventral raphe, or ascending with a dorsal one.
3. *Ornith.* The groove along the under-side of the rachis of a feather.
1859 TODD *Cycl. Anat.* V. 480/1.

raphell: see RAFFELL.

raphia ('reɪfɪə). *Bot.* [Malagasy: see ROFIA.] A genus of palms, containing three main species, with short stems and long pinnate leaves. Also *attrib.* as ***raphia grass*** = RAFFIA.
1866 *Treas. Bot.* 959/2. **1885** J. RICHARDSON *Malagasy-Eng. Dict.* s.v. *Rofia*, The fibre from the young leaves is used as string, for which purpose it is exported under the name of Raphia grass.

raphide ('reɪfaɪd). *Bot.* [a. F. *raphide*, f. stem of Gr. ῥαφίς.] = RAPHIS.
1884 BOWER & SCOTT *De Bary's Phaner.* 139 The elongated or spindle-shaped raphide-bearing sacs, which are common, e.g. in the Aroideæ. *Ibid.* Hanstein's raphide-containing sac-vessels.

raphi'diferous, *a. Bot.* [f. *raphid-* RAPHIS + -(I)FEROUS.] Bearing raphides.
1870 [see RAPHIS. *Comb.*].

raphilite ('ræfɪlaɪt). *Min.* [f. Gr. ῥαφίς needle + -LITE.] = TREMOLITE.
Given as *raphylite* in 1835 by C. N. Shepard (*Minerals* II. 329 App.), prob. through communication with Thomson.
1836 T. THOMSON *Outlines Min.* I. 153 *Raphilite.* I have given this name to a mineral from the township of Perth, Upper Canada. **1868** WATTS *Dict. Chem.*, *Raphilite*, asbestiform tremolite from Lanark, in Canada.

raphill, obs. form of RAFFLE *sb.*^{1}

‖**raphis** ('reɪfɪs). *Bot.* Also rha-. Pl. **raphides** ('ræfɪdiːz). [Gr. ῥαφίς, ῥαφιδ- needle.] One of the minute crystals, usually of acicular form, found in the cells of many plants.
The name was suggested by De Candolle (1826). The sing. is rarely used, and *raphides* may sometimes be intended as pl. of RAPHIDE.
1842 BRANDE *Dict. Sci.*, *Raphides.* **1854** J. HOGG *Microsc.* II. i. (1861) 233 Among the cell-contents of some plants are beautiful crystals called Raphides. **1876** HARLEY *Mat. Med.* (ed. 6) 393 Many spiral vessels may be detected in these scales by the microscope, as well as numerous acicular raphides.
Comb. **1870** BENTLEY *Man. Bot.* (ed. 2) 33 The orders to which it applies should be named raphis-bearing or raphidiferous.

raphorte, variant of RAIFORT *Obs.*

rapic ('reɪpɪk), *a. Chem.* [f. RAPE *sb.*^{5} + -IC.] Belonging to the rape. In ***rapic acid*** (see quot.).
1894 MORLEY & MUIR *Watts' Dict. Chem.* IV. 394 Rapic Acid..occurs as glyceride..in rape-seed oil.

rapid ('ræpɪd), *a.*, (*adv.*), and *sb.* [ad. L. *rapidus*, f. *rapĕre* to seize, carry off, etc.: see -ID^1. Cf. F. *rapide* (1611 in Cotgr.).]
A. *adj.* **1.** Moving, or capable of moving, with great speed; swift, very quick.
1634 T. CAREW *Cœlum Brit.* iv. 29 Be fix'd you rapid Orbes, that beare The changing seasons of the yeare On your swift wings. **1667** MILTON *P.L.* II. 532 Part..shun the Goal With rapid wheels. *c* **1742** GRAY *Ignorance* 34 Her rapid wings the transient scene pursue. **1791** COWPER *Iliad* XVII. 847 On rapid feet Sped to Achilles. **1832** DE LA BECHE *Geol. Man.* (ed. 2) 213 This river was at first by no means rapid, and afterwards acquired considerable velocity. **1866** G. MACDONALD *Ann. Q. Neighb.* xxvii. (1878) 466 A space.. sufficient to show the persons even of rapid riders.
2. Characterized by speed: **a.** of motion.
1697 DRYDEN *Virg. Georg.* IV. 533 With rapid Course [Po] seeks the sacred Main. **1730–46** THOMSON *Autumn* 683 Turn we a moment Fancy's rapid flight To vigorous soils. **1815** SHELLEY *Alastor* 522 With rapid steps he went Beneath the shade of trees. **1860** TYNDALL *Glac.* I. xxvii. 212, I observed a rapid movement on the part of the remaining three men.
b. ***rapid eye movement***, a type of jerky, binocular movement of the eyes of a sleeping person that is associated with a distinctive kind of sleep (REM sleep: see REM *sb.*^{2}).
1916 [see SACCADIC *a.* 1]. **1953** ASERINSKY & KLEITMAN in *Federation Proc.* XII. 6/2 Rapid eye movements..were observed to appear from 2 to 5 hr...after the onset of sleep in 10 subjects. **1955** —— in *Jrnl. Appl. Physiol.* VIII. 3/1 As a nomenclature..is lacking, the first type of movement will be referred to as slow eye movement and the second type as rapid eye movement. **1968** *Brit. Med. Bull.* XXIV. 257/1 There is a reduction in the amplitude of the evoked response during rapid eye-movement sleep as compared with slow wave sleep. **1971** J. Z. YOUNG *Introd. Study Man* x. 134 In man phases of sleep somewhat similar to the paradoxical ones of the cat are accompanied by rapid eye movements. **1977** *Listener* 16 June 787/2 What he calls 'active sleep' (which used to be called 'rapid eye movement' sleep). **1980** *Brit. Med. Jrnl.* 29 Mar. 896/1 Only one of the..patients had an episode of sleep apnoea during stage II sleep as opposed to rapid eye movement sleep.
c. of speech: Extremely quick.

1761 STERNE *Tr. Shandy* V. iii, My father's eloquence was too rapid to stay for any man. **1835** BROWNING *Paracelsus* v, I heard my name among those rapid words.

3. a. Quick in action, discourse, etc.

1791 COWPER *Iliad* II. 136 On that he leaned, and, rapid, thus began. **1818** SHELLEY *Rev. Islam* III. vii, Ere with rapid lips and gathered brow I could demand the cause. **1826** DISRAELI *Viv. Grey* v. iv. 180 He saw the student was a rapid drinker. **1861** M. ARNOLD *Translating Homer* i. 11 Homer is eminently rapid.

b. *techn.* Said of photographic lenses, plates, or subjects, requiring only a short exposure.

1878 ABNEY *Photogr.* (1881) 292 A magnifying lens, which takes the form known as 'the rapid rectilinear'. **1890** *Anthony's Photogr. Bull.* III. 28 When I speak of subjects impossible to the draughtsman, I do not mean merely very rapid subjects. **1892** *Photogr. Ann.* II. 38 Your long exposure was not on the most rapid plate you had with you.

4. a. Taking place with speed; accomplished, attained, etc., within a short time; coming quickly into existence or to completion.

1780 HARRIS *Philol. Enq.* Wks. (1841) 479 The rapid victories of these Eastern conquerors soon carried their empire from Asia even into the remote regions of Spain. **1796** H. HUNTER tr. *St.-Pierre's Stud. Nat.* (1799) III. 166 As it's growth is very rapid, it attained three years after to the height of twenty feet. **1809–10** COLERIDGE *Friend* I. vii, Bristol has, doubtless, been injured by the rapid prosperity of Liverpool. **1874** GREEN *Short Hist.* viii. §5. 504 Charles had good ground for this rapid confidence in his new minister.

b. Of a slope: Descending quickly.

1890 *Gd. Words* 133/2 The slope [is] so rapid that you can scarcely find footing when once off the beaten road.

5. quasi-*adv.* Rapidly, with rapidity.

1791 COWPER *Iliad* VIII. 381 Ajax,.. advancing rapid, stalk'd Around him. **1810** *Splendid Follies* II. 59 The hours winged away uncommonly rapid with Freelove.

6. *Comb.*, as ***rapid-footed, -mannered; rapid-breeding, -closing, -firing, -flowing, -growing, -hardening, -running, -selling, -travelling*** adjs.; ***rapid-fire*** (used *attrib.*); **rapid-transit** (usu. *attrib.*) orig. *U.S.*, (a system of) carriage of persons by fast public transport, esp. within a heavily built-up area.

1922 T. S. ELIOT in *Dial* (Chicago) Dec. 662 The encouragement of the cheap and rapid-breeding cinema. **1969** *Jane's Freight Containers 1968–69* 238/3 An interior rapid-closing floor valve NW 32. **1890** NOBLE in *Rep. Brit. Assoc.* 944 The increased importance of rapid-fire guns. **1900** F. P. DUNNE *Mr. Dooley's Philos.* 61 Th' paapers says th' rapid fire gun'll make war in th' future impossible. *Ibid.* 185 In him th' counthry loses a valu'ble an' acc'rate citizen, th' state a lile an' rapid firin' son. **1925** C. CONNOLLY *Let.* 27 June in *Romantic Friendship* (1975) 94 Will you start a rapid fire of postcards etc. if I do, just for a bit? **1969** *Times* 25 Mar. 9/1 The new play relies for its theatrical effect on rapid-fire repartee. **1976** *All about Games* (Com. Org. des Jeux Olympiques) 76 The competition now includes.. small-bore rifle shooting, rapid-fire pistol shooting. **1976** *New Yorker* 15 Nov. 120/2 The classic symptoms of stuttering.. include rapid-fire repetitions of consonant or vowel sounds. **1896** *Daily News* 28 Apr. 3/2 Loaded with rapid-firing and machine guns. **1848** BUCKLEY *Iliad* 265 The rapid-flowing current of eddying Xanthus. **1749** G. WEST tr. *Pindar* (1753) I. 6 If.. the rapid-footed Steed Could with joy thy Bosom move. **1907** *Westm. Gaz.* 22 Mar. 2/3 These creatures.. are chickens fed so generously that they are marketable.. three weeks before the most rapid-growing Aylesbury duckling is saleable. **1964** A. BATTERSBY *Network Analysis* v. 58 For example, even if expensive rapid-hardening cement is used for laying foundations, they must have at least a day to harden. **1967** *Gloss. Highway Engin. Terms (B.S.I.)*, *Rapid-hardening Portland cement*, a Portland cement which has the property of attaining a high early strength. **1820** G. HAKE *Mem. 80 Yrs.* lxiii. 262 A young Bavarian officer of the rapid-mannered kind. **1797** BEWICK *Birds* I. Pref. 6 Its business being.. among rapid-running streams. **1962** E. GODFREY *Retail Selling & Organization* ii. 20 Generally speaking, rapid-selling stock is placed on open fixtures. **1873** *Daily Graphic* (N.Y.) 26 Mar. 3/3 In addition to the accommodations which are afforded the citizen of New York in the way of rapid transit.. our elevated road will be the great 'accommodator'. **1904** *N.Y. World Mag.* 21 Aug. 5/1 But the cars buzz on, heedless, as they do at the beck of a private citizen, and the great General must feel, unless his nerves are iron, that rapid transit gloria mundi. **1961** L. MUMFORD *City in Hist.* xiv. 425 Señor Soria y Mata .. boldly proposed to make the new city a function of a spinal rapid-transit system. **1968** *Economist* 2 Nov. 50/3 There will also be 75 per cent grants available for big new passenger projects (e.g. new rapid transit system, such as the one investigated at Manchester). **1976** *Illustr. London News* Nov. 29/2 A rapid transit system is essentially one with an exclusive right of way. **1977** *Chicago Tribune* 2 Oct. II. 30/1 Closed by the strike were two Pullman-Standard plants in Hammond, which manufacture railroad freight and passenger cars, and the plant at 720 E. 111th St., which manufactures rapid-transit cars. **1932** *World Today* Feb. 213/2 By ten o'clock the narrow strip of timber some three miles long and an eighth of a mile wide was well aflame and had arrived at the rapid-travelling stage.

B. *sb.* **1.** A part of a river where the bed forms a steep descent, causing a swift current. (Originally *U.S.* and usually in *pl.*; cf. F. *rapides.*) Also *fig.*

1765 G. CROGHAN *Jrnl.* 2 June in R. G. Thwaites *Early Western Trav.* (1904) I. 136 What is called the Fall here, is no more than rapids. **1776** C. CARROLL *Jrnl.* (1845) 84 Took boat and went down Hudson's river, through all the rapids, to Albany. **1803** GOUV. MORRIS in Sparks *Life & Writ.* (1832) I. 483 In this condition we descend the rapid. **1820** SHELLEY *Witch* xli, Mortal boat In such a shallow rapid could not float. **1856** STANLEY *Sinai & Pal.* vii. (1858) 282 It plunges through twenty-seven rapids, through a fall of a thousand feet. **1900** G. B. SHAW *Let.* 11 Apr. (1972) II. 157 We steered the Society safely through a rapid in which it might have been wrecked. **1911** CHESTERTON *Innocence of Father Brown* x. 265 She was already in the rapids of an ethical tirade about the 'sickly medical notions'. **1979** P. L. SANDBERG *Stubb's Run* xxvii. 174 They were in the middle of the rapid, picking up speed.

2. Usu. *pl.* Rapid-fire shooting.

1913 A. G. FULTON *Notes on Rifle Shooting* 20 A man who is a good deliberate shot can, with very little practice, become good at 'rapids'. **1923** KIPLING *Irish Guards in Gt. War* II. 142 They indulged the enemy.. with five minutes' 'rapid' of Lewis-guns or rifles. **1932** J. A. BARLOW *Elements of Rifle Shooting* v. 62 It is this conflict between the desire to have the aim correct before firing, and the desire to let the round off before too much time is wasted, which is the most usual cause of bad rapids.

‖**rapide** (rapid). [Fr.] A French express train.

1904 A. E. W. MASON *Truants* i. 14 No 'Rapide' passed from France on its way to Italy during his leisure hours. **1923** W. J. LOCKE *Moordius & Co.* xxi. 288 She had lost the *rapide* from Cannes, the only train she knew of. **1946** G. MILLAR *Horned Pigeon* xix. 306 They only appeared to be stopping passengers who were catching the *rapide* for Marseilles. **1979** *Business Traveller* Mar.–Apr. 60/1 The landing.. took us within 50 yards of the connecting 'rapide'.

rapidity (rəˈpɪdɪtɪ). [ad. L. *rapiditāt-em*, f. *rapidus*: see RAPID and -ITY. Cf. F. *rapidité* (1611 in Cotgr.).] The quality of being rapid; celerity; velocity; swiftness of motion or action.

[**1616** BULLOKAR *Eng. Exp.*, *Rapiditie*, a snatching, a catching.] **1654** BUTLER *Elephant in Moon* 301 The rapidity Of both their motions cannot be But so prodigiously fast [etc.]. **1701** BRAND *Descr. Orkney* (1883) 73 The quickness and rapidity of the Tide. **1783** WATSON *Philip III*, II. (1839) 123 He advanced towards them with the utmost rapidity. **1871** TYNDALL *Fragm. Sci.* (1879) I. xxi. 492 There are other actions which far transcend in rapidity that of the rifle-bullet.

pl. *a* **1774** GOLDSM. *Surv. Exp. Philos.* (1776) I. 337 The water at the surface of a river, and that at its bottom, are often found to have very different rapidities. **1867** TYNDALL *Sound* i. (1871) 4 It is conveyed with different rapidities in three different directions.

rapidly (ˈræpɪdlɪ), *adv.* [f. RAPID + -LY².] In a rapid manner, with rapidity; swiftly, quickly. (Sometimes hyphened to ppl. adjs.)

1727 in BAILEY. *a* **1751** BOLINGBROKE *Ess. Hum. Reas.* ii. §7 Thales is said to have held, that mind.. was the swiftest of things, and pervaded rapidly the universe. **1784** COWPER *Task* I. 130 Our years, As life declines, speed rapidly away. **1838** T. THOMSON *Chem. Org. Bodies* 272 The crystals are deposited rapidly. **1847** LEWES *Hist. Philos.* (1867) II. 118 Carried along by the rapidly-swelling current of their age. **1887** BOWEN *Virg. Æneid* I. 90 Lightnings rapidly flash.

ˈrapidness. Now *rare.* [-NESS.] = RAPIDITY.

a **1656** USSHER *Ann.* (1658) 733 The passage seemed very difficult, by reason of the.. rapidnesse of the river. **1719** DE FOE *Crusoe* I. xiii. (1858) 199 With the same rapidness of the currents. **1782** PAINE *Let. Abbé Raynel* (1791) Introd. 6 Rapidness of thinking, and quickness of sensation. **1863** EDITH J. MAY *Stronges of Netherstronge* 239 This man's folly .. will lose all that rapidness might have won.

‖**rapido** (ˈrapido), *adv.*, (*a.*), and *sb.* [It.]

A. *adv. Mus.* With rapidity. Also quasi-*adj.*

1876 STAINER & BARRETT *Dict. Mus. Terms* 374/2 *Rapido (It.)*, with rapidity. **1955** *Times* 6 June 9/2 The veiled purity of his pianissimo singing touch, and the jewelled evenness of his *rapido* flourishes in Chopin.

B. *sb.* An Italian express train.

1957 *Punch* 7 Aug. 163/1 In the restaurant car of the *Rapido* from Rome to Florence next day there was one of his private clients. **1964** P. JONES *Month of Pearl* vii. 65 An early evening train, a Rapido scheduled to stop only at Latina on its way to Rome. **1980** *Cook's Internat. Timetable* Nov. 209 Excess fare is charged for Rapido trains.

rapier (ˈreɪpɪə(r)). Also 6 raper(e, -yer, -yre; *Sc.* and *north dial.* 6–, 20 **rapper**; 8 -ier. [a. F. *rapière* (1474 in Du Cange) of unknown origin.]

a. Originally, a long, pointed, two-edged sword adapted either for cutting or thrusting, but chiefly used for the latter. In later use, a light, sharp-pointed sword designed only for thrusting; a small sword.

1553 EDEN *Treat. Newe Ind.* (Arb.) 20 A rede is to them in the stede of sworde, rapyre & iauelyne. **1590** SIR J. SMYTH *Disc. Weapons* 3 b, Rather.. Rapiers of a yard and a quarter long the blades, or more, than strong short arming Swords. **1622** MABBE tr. *Aleman's Guzman d'Alf.* II. 227 They would ..pricke me in the body with their Rapiers points. **1709** STEELE *Tatler* No. 88 ¶12, I went up Stairs with my Hand upon the Hilt of my Rapier. **1727–41** CHAMBERS *Cycl.*, *Rapier*.. In a modern sense among us, usually denotes a small sword, as contradistinguished from a back-sword, or cutting sword. **1818** SCOTT *Rob Roy* xxviii, Aware of the superiority of my weapon, a rapier or small-sword, [I] was little afraid of the issue of the contest. **1889** GROVE *Fencing* etc. (Badminton) Introd. 5 When there is a public exhibition of fencing, an assault with rapiers is very frequently announced.

1911 C. J. SHARP *Sword Dances Northern Eng.* 9 The long-sword Yorkshire dances differ very considerably from those gathered in the more northern counties, where the short-sword or 'rapper' is used. **1933** E. K. CHAMBERS *Eng. Folk-Play* 126 A long sword, found in Yorkshire, and a short sword or 'rapper', found in Durham. **1956** N. MARSH *Off with his Head* (1957) iii. 62 Hand over thik rapper.. Us'll take the edge off of it.

fig. **1890** 'R. BOLDREWOOD' *Col. Reformer* (1891) 304 This smiling satirist with his society talk and ready rapier of repartee.

†**b.** Coupled with *dagger*; also *fig.* and *Comb.*

1591 HARINGTON *Orl. Fur.* Pref. i, Hercules.. fought with a club, and not at the rapyer and dagger. **1597** *1st Pt. Return fr. Parnass.* IV. i. 1236 This bracchidochio,.. this meere rapier and dagger. **1603** SHAKS. *Meas. for M.* IV. iii. 15 Mr Starue-Lackey the Rapier and dagger man.

c. *attrib.* and *Comb.*, as ***rapier blade, hilt, point; rapier-girdled, -like, -pointed, -snouted, -thin*** adjs.; **rapier dance**, a sword-dance; also **rapier-sword dance**; hence **rapier-sword dancer**; †**rapier-fish** *Obs.*, the sword-fish.

1590 SIR J. SMYTH *Disc. Weapons* 4 *Rapier blades being so narrow.. do presently breake. **1811** WILLAN in *Archæologia* (1814) XVII. 154 *Rapier Dance. **1960** *Times* 16 Jan. 12/5 A Tyneside rapper dance. **1681** GREW *Musæum* I. v. i. 86 The head of the *rapier-fish; called Xiphias.. Grows sometimes to the length of five yards. **1908** C. W. WALLACE *Children of Chapel* xiv. 177 The local and personal drives have caused my *rapier-girdled courtier and fine gentleman to avoid the public theatres. **1599** B. JONSON *Ev. Man out of Hum.* v. iv, I will make thy blood flow on my *rapier hilts. **1975** R. BARCLAY *Ernest Bevin & Foreign Office* ii. 42 Quite untrue, of course, and not exactly *rapier-like diplomacy, but it effectively crushed the Ambassador. **1884** L. GRIFFIN in *Fortn. Rev.* Mar. 387 The conclusions.. pierce the soul.. with so true and acute a *rapier-point. **1816** KEATS *To Ch. C. Clarke* 65 The sharp, the *rapier-pointed epigram. **1906** *Daily Chron.* 11 Oct. 3/6 This *rapier-snouted fish [sc. *Belone vulgaris*] consorts with the mackerel. **1937** *Times Lit. Suppl.* 20 Feb. 155/3 Long-sword dances, *Rapper-sword dances. **1977** *Sunday Mail* (Brisbane) 6 Feb. 10/4 An ancient English dance came to Brisbane yesterday as Moreton Bay rapper sword dancers rehearsed for the Folk Music Festival. **1961** *Times* 7 Apr. 18/3 The acting, though it may broaden some of the *rapier-thin parts, is as good as can be demanded.

Hence **ˈrapiered** *a.*, wearing or furnished with a rapier; sharp-pointed; **ˈrapier** *v. trans.*, with direct speech: to comment or query pointedly (*nonce-use*).

1683 *Roxb. Ball.* (1885) V. 454 A nimble thrust of Rapier'd Wit. **1854** LOWELL *Cambridge 30 Yrs. Ago* Pr. Wks. 1890 I. 94 The scarlet-coated, rapiered figures. **1957** O. NASH *You can't get there from Here* 151 Has the moment come, rapiered Mr. Webster, to abjectly surrender to journalese?

‖**raˈpilli.** [It., pl. of *rapillo.*] Small fragments of pumice-stone. Cf. LAPILLI.

1809 WILSON *Hist. Mountains* II. 620 The first ejections ..were simply ashes, pieces of pumice stone and rapilli. **1871** C. KINGSLEY *At Last* I. ii. 46 Soils of still unexhausted fertility, save when—as must needs be in a volcanic region —patches of mere rapilli and scoriæ occur. **1882** A. GEIKIE *Text-bk. Geol.* 162 Lapilli (rapilli).—Ejected fragments of lava.

‖**rapin** (rapɛ̃). [Fr.] In France: an apprentice in an artist's studio; an (unruly) art student.

1891 M. S. VAN DE VELDE tr. *H. Lavedan's Mamzelle Vertu* in *French Fiction of To-day* I. iv. 88 Nothing disturbed her, neither the stifled laughter of a group of *rapins* in front of a Hercules, or the 'shocking' bleated by a herd of female English visitors. **1894** G. DU MAURIER *Trilby* I. II. 94 From the kind of laughter with which the points were received by the 'rapins' in Carrel's studio he guessed these little songs were vile.

rapine (ˈræpɪn, ˈræpaɪn), *sb.* Forms: 5–6 **rapyne**, 6– **rapine**, (7 **-in**). [a. F. *rapine* (12th c.) or ad. L. *rapina*, f. *rapĕre* to seize: see RAPE *v.*² and -INE⁴. The popular form in OF. was *ravine* RAVIN(E.] **a.** The act or practice of seizing and taking away by force the property of others; plunder, pillage, robbery.

a **1420** HOCCLEVE *De Reg. Princ.* 4834 Is it Knyghtly to live on rapyne? nay. **1509** HAWES *Past. Pleas.* XI. (Percy Soc.) 41 For these thre vyces abhominable.. For his pryde, avaryce, and also rapyne. **1586** A. DAY *Eng. Secretary* (1625) 44 What rapine, what theft,.. was in him throughly planted? **1637** R. HUMPHREY tr. *St. Ambrose* Pref., Countries layed open to their furious rapin. **1699** BURNETT *39 Art.* xxxvii. (1700) 390 All the Rapine and Bloodshed that is occasioned by their Pride and Injustice. **1769** ROBERTSON *Chas. V*, I. Wks. 1813 V. 66 The lawless rapine of banditti.. rendered a journey of any length a perilous enterprise. **1879** H. PHILLIPS *Notes Coins* 9 The robber city, founded by outlaws and living by rapine.

fig. **1879** GEO. ELIOT *Theo. Such* xi. 202 Angry at his conversational rapine.

b. *pl.* Acts of violent robbery or pillage. (Freq. in 17th c., now *rare.*)

1494 FABYAN *Chron.* (1516) II. 45 b/2 The good Cristen people, whiche they had harmed by meanes of their Rapynes & extorcions. **1514** BARCLAY *Cyt. & Uplondyshm.* (Percy Soc.) 56 Nought is in warfar save.. murder and mischiefe, rapines and cowardise. **1631** WEEVER *Anc. Fun. Mon.* 363 Such were the Popes rapines and enormous proceedings in those dayes. *a* **1711** KEN *Hymnotheo* Poet. Wks. 1721 III. 31 A lawless Band, Infesting with their Rapines all the Land. **1826** SOUTHEY *Vind. Eccl. Angl.* 348 The Judges complained to the king of the frequent thefts, rapines, and homicides.

c. ***beast*** (etc.) ***of rapine***: beast of prey.

1612 SELDEN *Illustr. Drayton's Poly-olb.* iv. 252 To haue terrible crests or ingraven beasts of Rapine.. hath been from inmost antiquity continued. **1648** GAGE *West Ind.* xii. (1655) 44 For hawking fowles, and fowles of rapine. **1859** TENNYSON *Merlin & V.* 578 That foul bird of rapine whose whole prey Is man's good name.

†**ˈrapine,** *v. Obs. rare.* [f. prec. or a. F. *rapiner* (1507).] **a.** *intr.* To commit rapine. **b.** *trans.* To plunder, or carry away, by rapine.

1580 HOLLYBAND *Treas. Fr. Tong*, *Rapiner*, to rapine, to robbe, and spoile. **1646** BUCK *Rich. III*, v. 134 A Tyrant doth not onely rapine his Subjects, but Spoils and robs Churches and Church-men. **1660** F. BROOKE tr. *Le Blanc's*

Trav. 323 In their dealings these people are lawlesse, trading in slaves..which they rapine from all parts.

So **'rapiner**, one who commits rapine. *rare*⁻¹.

1843 LYTTON *Last Bar.* IV. v, Are not the king's officers and purveyors licensed spoilers and rapiners?

†**'raping**, *ppl. a. Obs. rare.* [f. RAPE *v.*²]

1. *Her.* Of animals: Devouring or tearing prey.

1660 GUILLIM *Heraldry* III. xv. 179 Lyons Bears, Wolves and other Beasts of ravening kind, when they are borne in Armes feeding, you must term them in Blazon, Raping, and tell whereon.

2. Transporting, ravishing.

1613–6 W. BROWNE *Brit. Past.* I. iv. 69 O, had I Virgil's verse or Tullie's tongue, Or raping numbers like the Thracian's Song! *Ibid.* v. 94 Raping notes.

'raping, *vbl. sb.* [f. RAPE *v.*²] The action of the vb.; rape, ravishment.

1961 *Life* 15 Dec. 33 Presently the well-armed members of the *Force Publique*..erupted in mutiny, rioting, raping and looting. **1972** *Daily Tel.* 3 Nov. 19/8 The raping of a 14-year-old Girl Guide at Totton, Hants, last May..led to jail sentences being imposed on three Hells Angels.

†**'rapinous**, *a. Obs.* [f. RAPINE *sb.* + -OUS, or ad. OF. *rapineus, -eux* (14th c. in Godef.).] Given to rapine; rapacious.

1483 CAXTON *G. de la Tour* F viij, He maketh the noble men to be rapynous & tyraunts. **1627** W. SCLATER *Exp. 2 Thess.* (1629) 277 What is that liuing other than vnjust, rapinous, and..iniurious? **1682** *Lond. Gaz.* No. 1735/3 The Rapinous hands and power of wicked..Men.

b. *transf.* Carrying or sweeping away.

1632 LITHGOW *Trav.* x. 505 One of these tides..will carry any Vessel backward,..the length of its rapinous current.

rapist ('reɪpɪst). orig. *U.S.* [f. RAPE *sb.*² + -IST.] One guilty of rape. Also *fig.*

1883 *National Police Gaz.* (U.S.) 5 May 6/4 (*heading*) The stalwart resistance a married woman offered a would-be 'nigger' rapist. **1889** *Columbus* (Ohio) *Dispatch* 13 June, Two horse thieves and a rapist were sentenced..this morning. **1901** *Nation* (N.Y.) 18 Apr. 313/1 A bill having been passed by the State legislators, March 20, 1901 'providing for the public execution of convicted rapists'. **1937** *Sun* (Baltimore) 16 July 1/4 The State demanded the chair for Norris as 'a warning to other rapists and a protection for the womanhood of the State'. **1938** I. KUHN *Assigned to Adventure* vi. 54 Men had lived with death so long that they seized upon life with a rapist's lust. **1949** *Time* 19 Dec. 23/3 We follow a system which amounts to rape of the land. We are no careful husbandmen—not husbands but rapists. **1953** R. CHANDLER *Long Good-Bye* xxiv. 153 Take your hands off me, you goddamned rapist. **1959** *Guardian* 20 Oct. 9/1 A convicted kidnapper and rapist. **1975** *Daily Mirror* 14 Apr. 5/2 Hooded rapist claims victim no 6... The rapist who is terrorising a city's bed-sitter girls struck again yesterday.

'rap-jacket. *Southern U.S.* [f. RAP *v.*¹] (See quot. 1893.) Also *transf.* Now *rare* or *Obs.*

1893 H. A. SHANDS *Some Peculiarities of Speech in Mississippi* 52 *Rap-jacket*,..a term used by all classes to mean a game of whipping, in which two boys are given switches, and whip each other with all of their might until one says 'enough'. They both thus have their jackets thoroughly rapped, if they happen to have on those garments. Two boys who have been fighting at school are very frequently punished by the teacher's making them play *rap-jacket* until he tells them to stop. **1904** *Westm. Gaz.* 12 Feb. 2/1 He up en say dat he be dad blame ef he ain't gwineter play at rap-jacket wid de whole-hoggers ef he kotch um.

†**'rapless**, *a.* [f. RAP *sb.*¹] Free from blows.

a **1400** *Minor Poems fr. Vernon MS.* 477/14 We ne mowe raples þorw þo þre To Bere þe croune to-fore þe kyng.

raploch ('ræplɔx), *sb.* and *a. Sc.* Also 6 rep-, roploch, rapploch, -lack, raplach, -lock. [Of obscure origin.]

A. *sb.* Coarse, homespun, undyed woollen cloth.

1530 LYNDESAY *Test. Papyngo* 1045 Thay haue renuncit russat and roploch quhyte. **1535** —— *Satyre* 1995 Thair vmest clayis, that was of rapploch gray. **1831** SCOTT *Cast. Dang.* ix, I will owe you a kirtle of the best raploch grey. **1832** VEDDER *Native Parish* i. in *Poems*, etc. (1878) 348 Ophelias in woollen raplochs, and Desdemonas in linsey woolsey frocks.

B. *adj.* Coarse, rough, homely.

1724 RAMSAY *Tea-t. Misc.* (1733) II. 183 The rost was teugh as raploch hodin. **1785** BURNS *Ep. Davie* vii, The Muse, poor hizzie! Tho' rough an' raploch be her measure, She's seldom lazy. **1894** R. REID *Poems, Songs & Sonnets* 134 Rough and raploch mountain cheer. **1927** *Scots Observer* 21 May 16/1 Thistle and lily are alike admirable though one be raploch and the other circumspect.

†**'raply**, *a. rare.* [Cf. next.] Hasty, hurried.

a **1400** *Body & Soul* (Vernon MS.) 149 To harme was thi raple res. *c* **1400** *St. Alexius* (Cotton MS.) 353 She com Forthe with A raply rese.

†**'raply**, *adv. Obs.* Also 4 -li, -liche, -lych. [= MSw. *raplika* in the same sense, perh. related to RAP *v.*², but cf. RAPELY.] Hastily, hurriedly.

c **1325** *Metr. Hom.* 32 This reul thai gert me rapli rede. **1362** LANGL. *P. Pl.* A. v. 176 Thei rise vp raply [*v.r.* rapliche]. *c* **1440** *York Myst.* xvi. 7 The rakke of þe rede skye full rappely I ridde.

rapok, obs. form of RAPPOCK *dial.*

rapontik: see RHAPONTIC.

raporie, obs. form of RAPPAREE.

raport, obs. form of RAPPORT, REPORT.

rapparee (ræpə'riː). Forms: α. 7 rappery, *pl.* -ies, rap(p)ories. β. 7–8 raparee, 8 rapperee, 7– rapparee. [a. Ir. *rapaire* 'a short pike, a raparee' (O'Reilly; cf. *ropaire* 'a rapier, a treacherous violent person', ibid.); the β-forms app. originated in the pl., after the southern Irish pl. *rapairídhe* (-ijə).]

†**1.** A half-pike. *Obs. rare*⁻¹.

1690 *Lond. Gaz.* No. 2529/3 Both Horse and Foot are very ill Armed, the latter having for the most part only Scythes, or Half Pikes called *Rapories*.

2. *Hist.* An Irish pikeman or irregular soldier, of the kind prominent during the war of 1688–92; hence, an Irish bandit, robber, or freebooter.

α. **1690** T. HARRISON in Ellis *Orig. Lett* Ser. II. IV. 212 The fugitive Irish, or Rapperies, who steal in the night. *a* **1700** B. E. *Dict. Cant. Crew, Rapparies*, Wild Irish Robbers, and Out-laws.

attrib. **1690** *Lond. Gaz.* No. 2596/3 Another of our Parties have cut off a Rappery Colonel, with 50 of his Men.

β. **1690** MACKENZIE *Siege London-Derry* 2/2 These were afterwards called Rapparee's, a sort of Irish Vultures that follow their Armies to pray on the spoil. **1692** *Siege Lymerick* 3 This day several notorious Rapparees were brought Prisoners into our Camp. **1707** *Act 6 Anne* 11 An Act for the more effectual suppression of..robbers and rapparees. **1745** BERKELEY *Let. to Gervais* 24 Nov. in Fraser *Life* viii. 304 We have been alarmed with a report that a great body of rapparees is up in the county of Kilkenny. **1855** MACAULAY *Hist. Eng.* xvii. IV. 73 The English complained that it was no easy matter to catch a Rapparee.

attrib. **1834** AINSWORTH *Rookwood* IV. vi, O'Hanlon.. That o'er the broad province of Ulster, the Raparee banner unfurled. **1888** H. D. TRAILL *William III* 87 The rapparee Irish levies who formed the bulk of James's force.

b. *fig.*, or extended to persons of similar character in other countries.

1693 J. EDWARDS *Author. O. & N. Test.* 397 These zealots, these Jewish rapparees and assassins. **1720** J. JOHNSON *Canons Eng. Ch.* I. Eej b, Let..Rapperees and Freebooters, incur the severest Wrath of God. **1816** SCOTT *Antiq.* xiii, This rapparee promised him mountains of wealth. **1833** MARRYAT *P. Simple* xiii, By that time we had arrived at the door..I paid the rapparee, and in I popped.

rappee¹ (ræ'piː). Also 9 rapee. [ad. F. (*tabac*) *râpé*, pa. pple. of *râper* to RASP (see def.).] A coarse kind of snuff made from the darker and ranker tobacco leaves, and originally obtained by rasping a piece of tobacco. Also †*rappee-snuff*.

c **1740** *Wimble's Snuffs* in F. W. Fairholt *Tobacco* (1876) 268 English Rappee, Scented Rappee [etc.]. **1758** JOHNSON *Idler* No. 34 ⁋24 Made some rappee-snuff. **1785** CRABBE *Newspaper* Wks. 1834 II. 128 He May tell their honours that he sells rappee. **1859** THACKERAY *Virgin.* lx, He started back, and must have upset some of his rappee, for Macbeth sneezed thrice.

ra'ppee². *nonce-wd.* [f. RAP *v.*¹ + -EE¹.] One who raps or knocks; a rapper. (In quot., with punning allusion to RAPPEE.)

1819 KEATS *Let.* 27 Sept. (1958) II. 216, I heard a rap at the door... There came a louder rap... A little girl in the house was the Rappee—I assure you she had nearly made me sneeze.

rappel, *sb.* [F., f. *rappeler* to recall, REPEAL.]

‖**1.** (rapɛl). The roll or beat of a drum to summon soldiers to arms.

1848 W. H. KELLY tr. *L. Blanc's Hist. Ten Y.* I. 125 Then came drums of the national guard beating the *rappel* and the *générale*. **1861** W. H. RUSSELL in *Times* 29 July, A strong body of drummers on the French model beat some noisy rappel.

transf. **1866** MISS THACKERAY *Village on Cliff* xiv, He.. beat the *rappel* with his spoon upon the tablecloth.

2. (ræ'pɛl). *Mountaineering.* (The technique of) descending a steep face by means of a doubled rope fixed above the climber; = ABSEIL. Also *attrib.*

1931 *Times Lit. Suppl.* 19 Feb. 129/3 On it [*sc.* Mont Blanc], climbing guideless, they practise every modern refinement, the use of crampons, scarpetti and the rappel. **1943** E. SHIPTON *Upon that Mountain* iv. 84 We could only proceed by a series of *rappels*. This is a method of 'roping down'. **1950** Rappel sling [see LINE *sb.*² 1]. **1952** MORIN & SMITH tr. *Herzog's Annapurna* viii. 119 We..fixed our spare rope for a rappel... Terray went down first on the doubled rope. **1959** S. CLARK *Puma's Claw* xii. 143 In 1956 the two of us had used the technique of 'abseil' or 'rappel' for seven hours continuously on a descent in the Alps. **1965** A. BLACKSHAW *Mountaineering* viii. 240 Roping down... This involves:..pulling the rope round the anchor and down (the '*rappel*' from which the manœuvre takes its name). **1971** D. HASTON in C. Bonington *Annapurna South Face* xvii. 209 The descent took only twenty minutes as I was so enraged with myself. I caught Nick up on the last rappel. *Ibid.* 218 Don was already fixing a rappel peg.

rappel (ræ'pɛl), *v.* [ad. F. *rappeler*: see REPEAL *v.*]

†**1.** *trans.* To recall (a hawk). *Obs. rare.*

1575 TURBERV. *Faulconrie* 62 A fearfull goshawke..[will] not willingly repayre to any devise wherwith she is called and rappelde after hyr flight.

2. *intr. Mountaineering.* To make a steep descent on a doubled rope; to rope down. Hence **ra'ppelling** *vbl. sb.*

1957 P. MANSFIELD *Final Exposure* xvi. 239 He *rappelled* downwards, with the feel of good rock beneath his feet and the bite of the rope at his back. **1969** *Time* 22 Aug. 8/2 It is a stirring demonstration ranging from scuba diving.. to archery and rappelling (descending a cliff on a double rope). **1974** *Telegraph* (Brisbane) 7 Aug. 23/3 There goes Harry Garner Haskell Jr. rappelling down the side of Abercrombie and Fitch.

rappely, variant of RAPLY *adv. Obs.*

‖**rappen** ('rapən). Also (anglicized) rap(p). [Ger., pl. as sing. f. *rappe* raven.] In the German-speaking cantons of Switzerland: the Swiss centime.

1838 *Murray's Hand-bk. Travellers Switzerland* p. viii, 1 batz contains 10 rappen, and = 1½*d.* (nearly) English. The Swiss coins most frequently met with are pieces of 5 batzen, or ½ a Swiss franc; 1 batz, ½ batz, and rappen. *Ibid.* p. ix, 1 French franc = (commonly) 7 batzen or exactly 6 batzen 8 rapps. **1864** *Baedeker's Switzerland* ii. p. xix, The Swiss monetary system has since 1854 been assimilated to that of France. Coins of 5, 2, 1 and ½ fr. in silver; 20, 10 and 5 Rappen (centimes) in plated copper; 2 and 1 Rappen in copper. 1 fr. = 100 Rappen = ..9⅗d. **1911** *Encycl. Brit.* XIX. 907/2 Like Belgium, Switzerland had before her adhesion to the Latin Monetary Union adopted the French system, with the franc of 100 centimes or rappen as the unit of value. **1938** *Baedeker's Switzerland* iii. p. xvii, The monetary unit is the *Swiss franc* (fr.) of 100 *Centimes* (c.) or *Rappen* (in the German-speaking cantons). **1960** H. HAYWARD *Antique Coll.* 233/2 *Rappen*, small Swiss copper coin of late 18th and early 19th cent. with types of shield in wreath and value and date. **1962** R. A. G. CARSON *Coins* 326 In 1798 Switzerland was invaded by the revolutionary armies of France and a Helvetic republic was established and a new unified and decimal coinage was instituted with the franc as the unit, divided into 10 batzen, the batz divided in turn into 10 rappen. The system included pieces of 32 and 16 francs in gold; 40, 20, 10 and 5 batzen in silver and in billon the batz, its half and the rap. **1973** *Daily Tel.* 4 Aug. 15/2 In Zurich..the dollar lost 1 rappen to 2·84½.

rapper ('ræpə(r)). [f. RAP *v.*¹ + -ER¹.]

1. a. One who raps or knocks; a spirit-rapper.

1755 in JOHNSON. **1857** P. CARTWRIGHT *Autobiogr.* xix. 276 There is a dark, motley crowd of..spiritual rappers, so called.

†**b.** *slang.* One who tells a downright lie; a professional perjurer. Cf. sense 3 a and RAPPING *vbl. sb.*¹ 2 b. *Obs.*

1840 in Fielding *Jonathan Wild* (new ed.) p. lxii, The rapper, I think (as the cant phrase has it), is the most necessary man for your purpose.

c. *U.S. slang.* A complainant, plaintiff; a prosecutor. Cf. RAP *v.*¹ 1 c.

1904 'No. 1500' *Life in Sing Sing* 252/1 *Rapper*, prosecutor; complainant. **1910** *New England Mag.* July 587 A complaint or charge of crime is a 'rap' and the complainant is the 'rapper'. **1926** *Clues* Nov. 158/2 *Lam* up to the *pagey* and see the *rapper*. **1935** *Jrnl. Abnormal Psychol.* XXX. 364 *Rapper*, the complainant in the case. **1955** D. W. MAURER in *Publ. Amer. Dial. Soc.* XXIV. 108 A *rapper* is a mark who prefers charges against a pickpocket; sometimes he can be bought off with a return of his money. 'If the law won't take, the next thing is to try the rapper.'

d. An itinerant purchaser of antiques; esp. one who buys valuable objects cheaply from credulous householders. Cf. KNOCKER 2 e.

1914 H. A. VACHELL *Quinneys'* x. 146 Gossip had it that he had begun life as a 'rapper'. **1928** *Daily Express* 29 Feb. 14 The rapper frequently adopts the Aladdin method of offering new lamps for old, undertaking, for example, to give the innocent owner of a little old Queen Anne bureau a brand-new chest of drawers and a cash sum in exchange.

e. *U.S. slang.* A talker; a chatterer. Cf. RAP *v.*¹ 3 d.

1971 *Time* 22 Feb. 38 Boulez clearly hopes there will be as many rappers as listeners. **1972** C. WESTON *Poor, Poor Ophelia* iii. 18 Let's you and me talk like crazy. You look like a rapper, and I feel like rapping. **1973** C. MILNER *Black Players* i. 8 He is recognized as among the best talkers or 'rappers' in the hustling world.

2. Anything used for rapping; *spec.* †**a.** A door-knocker. *Obs.* **b.** A rattle or clapper. *rare.* **c.** *Coal-mining* (see quot. 1851).

1640 *Outlandish Proverbs* §916 An old mans staffe is the rapper of deaths doore. **1767** STERNE *Tr. Shandy* IX. xvi, He stood with the rapper of the door suspended for a full minute in his hand. **1810** *Splendid Follies* I. 16 Cavendish Square, where the rapper first roused her from the deepest.. ruminations. **1834** SOUTHEY *Doctor* I. (1862) 116 He was not disturbed..by the watchmen's rappers, or clap-sticks. **1851** GREENWELL *Coal-trade Terms, Northumb. & Durh.* 41 *Rapper*.—A lever, placed at the top of a shaft or inclined plane,..to give signals, when every thing is ready at the bottom for drawing away. **1869** *Pall Mall G.* 8 Oct. 8 The connection to each rapper and battery was to be made by means of a small button.

3. a. An arrant lie; a downright falsehood. Now only *dial.*

1611 COTGR., *Bourdes*, fibs, rappers, lyes. **1681** T. FLATMAN *Heraclitus Ridens* No. 38 (1713) I. 252 Care has told as many Rappers for the Dissenters as he thinks good. *a* **1734** NORTH *Exam.* II. v. §139 (1740) 402 What a Rapper is it then to say further [etc.]. **1890** in *Gloucestersh. Gloss.*

b. A great oath. Now only *dial.*

1678 DRYDEN *Limberham* IV. i, If you can swear such Rappers too, there's hope of you. *a* **1734** NORTH *Lives* (1826)

III. 225 When he was very angry..he was apt to let go a rapper or two. **1890** in *Gloucestersh. Gloss.*

†**4.** Something remarkably good or large. *Obs.* (Cf. RAPPING *ppl. a.* 2.)

1653 SIR E. NICHOLAS in *N. Papers* (Camden) II. 34 Tell my deerest Lord Norwich he shall have a rapper [of a letter] next week. **1672** MARVELL *Reh. Transp.* I. 203 There remains but one Flower more that I have a mind to; but that indeed is a Rapper. 'Tis a Flower of the Sun.

rapper, -ier, dial. forms of RAPIER.

rapperee, -y, obs. forms of RAPPAREE.

rapping ('ræpɪŋ), *vbl. sb.*[1] [f. RAP *v.*[1]]

1. The action of striking or knocking sharply; = SPIRIT-RAPPING. Also *transf.*

c **1400** tr. *Secreta Secret., Gov. Lordsh.* 97 A rappyngge togedre of stones. *a* **1548** HALL *Chron., Edw. V* 4 b, When he was with hasty rappyng quickely let in. *c* **1611** CHAPMAN *Iliad* XII. 162 Stones..on the helms..Kept such a rapping, it amaz'd great Asius. **1710** *Tatler* No. 160 ¶1, I heard a great Rapping at my Door. **1848** M. Fox in A. Conan Doyle *Hist. Spiritualism* (1926) I. iv. 62 The children, who slept in the other bed in the room, heard the rapping, and tried to make similar sounds by snapping their fingers. **1860** EMERSON *Cond. Life, Worship* Wks. (Bohn) II. 397 In creeds never was such levity; witness the..deliration of rappings. **1894** A. LANG *Cock Lane* 29 The facts of rappings, ghosts, clairvoyance..are very doubtful facts after all. **1923** *Times Lit. Suppl.* 6 Dec. 853/3 He writes in short snappy sentences, the persistent rapping of which makes it very difficult for the reader to keep up his attention for long. **1954** J. F. RINN *Searchlight on Psychical Res.* vi. 56 'What are the points of your coming exposé?' asked Creelman. 'First the rappings,' Mrs. Kane smiled. **1974** *Encycl. Brit. Macropædia* XVII. 513/1 The spirits,..it is alleged, use different methods [of communication].., such as rappings, table tippings, [etc.].

2. a. Utterance (of an oath). †**b.** Perjury. *Obs.*

1611 COTGR., *Iurement*,..a rapping out of an oath. **1754** FIELDING *Jonathan Wild* I. xiii. (1840) 551 He was a pitiful fellow who would stick at a little rapping for his friend.

c. *colloq.* (orig. *U.S.*). The action or practice of talking or chatting; conversation, gossip. spec. *U.S. Blacks*, repartee, banter. Cf. RAP *v.*[1] 3 d.

1969 *Observer* 16 Feb. 40/6 Pendennis boogaloos, falls by cats into numbers, and lays down heavy outasight rapping. Translation: Pendennis arranges events, calls on people in the money, and produces a lot of fantastic gossip. **1969** T. KOCHMAN in *Trans-Action* Feb. 27/1 While often used to mean ordinary conversation, rapping is distinctively a fluent and lively way of talking, always characterized by a high degree of personal style. *Ibid.* 27/2 Rapping between men and women often is competitive and leads to a lively repartee. **1972** M. J. BOSSE *Incident at Naha* i. 60 After this failure of communication, our rapping dragged on like that of two old ladies. **1973** *Black World* Mar. 85 Jiving, bopping, rapping, signifying, sounding—all modes of Afro-American expression—seek to affirm the vitality of the Black American experience. **1977** *Rolling Stone* 13 Jan. 60/2 (Advt.), Multi-racial magazine features workable self-help articles, rapping, fiction.

3. *attrib.*, as **rapping bar**, a pointed iron bar used in founding for loosening patterns from moulds; **rapping iron**, an implement used in basketry to tap the rows of weaving into the desired position; **rapping plate** *Founding*, a metal plate attached to a pattern in order to prevent damage to the pattern when it is loosened from the mould.

1888 *Lockwood's Dict. Mech. Engin.* 277 Rapping bar. **1948** H. W. BAKER *Mod. Workshop Technol.* I. iii. 60 For a wood pattern the rapping bar may be pointed and driven into the wood itself; or special rapping plates with suitable holes may be fixed to it. **1960** R. LISTER *Decorative Cast Ironwork in Gt. Brit.* ii. 31 The rapping bar is tapped with a mallet to loosen the pattern. **1924** C. CRAMPTON *Cane Work* 12 Rapping iron to tap the rows of weaving to make the work quite level. **1979** *Dryad Catal.* 87/1 Canework tools..Rapping iron for levelling (or regulating) cane weaving. **1885** *Pattern Making* xxii. 158 (*heading*) Rapping plates. **1894** W. J. LINEHAM *Textbk. Mech. Engin.* ii. 67 Rapping plates have become necessary in order to prevent injury to the pattern by the moulder. **1948** Rapping plate [see *rapping bar* above]. **1960** R. LISTER *Decorative Cast Ironwork in Gt. Brit.* ii. 25 To further facilitate the withdrawal, metal rapping and lifting plates are available.., ready drilled and countersunk for screwing to the pattern, and tapped to receive the lifting screw.

†**'rapping,** *vbl. sb.*[2] *Obs.*$^{-1}$ [f. RAP *v.*[2]] The practice of seizing or taking.

1541 PAYNELL *Catiline* i. 1 In rappynge and catchynge he was auaritious.

rapping ('ræpɪŋ), *ppl. a.* [f. RAP *v.*[1]]

1. That raps or knocks.

1855 SMEDLEY *Occult Sciences* 191 After all that has been written on the subject of the rapping spirits. **1933** N. FODOR *Encycl. Psychic Sci.* 321/2 *Rudolf of Fulda*, a chronicle dating from 858 A.D. speaks of communications with a rapping intelligence.

2. Uncommonly big or striking. Now *dial.*

1658 BRAMHALL *Consecr. Bps.* vi. 146 Some others who fathered this rapping lie upon him. **1720** STRYPE *Stow's Surv.* (1754) I. I. xvii. 100/1 He maketh a voluntary confession of three other rapping crimes. **1728** W. SMITH *Univ. Coll.* 181 Next comes a rapping Lye. **1847-78** HALLIWELL, *Rapping*, large. *Var. dial.*

Rappist[1] ('ræpɪst). *U.S.* [See def.] A member of an American religious sect named from its leader, George Rapp.

1845 G. STRUTHERS in *Ess. Chr. Union* xii. 372 The Rappists, Shakers, Mormons..and other small sects. **1882-3** SCHAFF *Encycl. Relig. Knowl.* III. 1994 The Rappists emigrated to Economy, 17 m. northwest of Pittsburg.

So **'Rappite.**

1832 S. A. FERRALE *Ramble through U.S.A.* 92 The Rappites had been in possession of the place for six years. **1864** T. L. NICHOLS *40 Yrs. Amer. Life* II. 20 The Rappites ..were the followers of a religious zealot, who yielded implicit obedience to his commands.

rappist[2] ('ræpɪst). [f. RAP *sb.*[1] or *v.*[1] + -IST.]

a. One who believes in spirit-rapping. **b.** A supposed spirit that 'raps'.

1853 *Tait's Mag.* XX. 417 Clairvoyants, rappists, connoisseurs in ghostology, and such-like mystery-mongers. **1888** *Pall Mall G.* 10 Sept. 2/2 The 'rappists', whoever they might be, apparently followed with close attention the conversation that went on in the room.

rapplack, -loch, obs. forms of RAPLOCH.

rapply, variant of RAPLY *adv. Obs.*

'rappock. *north dial.* In 4 **rapok,** 9 **rappak, -uck.** An ill-behaved person.

c **1350** *Ipomadon* 7006 By none suche rapokys will I sitt. **1878** *Cumbld. Gloss.*, *Rappak*, a pet name for an unruly child. **1881** J. SARGISSON *Joe Scoap* 144 (Cumbld. Gloss.) Them rappucks at cuh creepan aboot t' back dooar.

rapporie, obs. form of RAPPAREE.

rapport (ræ'pɔə(r), ‖rapɔr; formerly rə'pɔət), *sb.* Also 7 **raport.** [F., f. *rapporter*: see RE- and APPORT *v.*]

†**1.** Report, talk. *Obs. rare*$^{-1}$.

1539 CROMWELL in Merriman *Life & Lett.* (1902) II. 194, I perceyve by his rapport that your grace shewed unto hym that the yong duck of Cleves was decessed.

2. a. Reference, relationship; connexion, correspondence, conformity. Also, harmonious accord, co-ordination. Now freq. used of relations between persons. ***in rapport***: (see 3.)

The quots. show that Johnson was mistaken in supposing that Temple was the introducer and sole user of the word.

1661 in BLOUNT *Glossogr.* **1662** J. DAVIES tr. *Mandelslo's Trav.* 226 Between whose Languages there is no more rapport, then the English hath to the Greek and Arabian. **1680-90** TEMPLE *Ess., Learning* Wks. 1731 I. 167 'Tis obvious enough, what rapport there is..between the Thoughts and Words. **1697** J. SERGEANT *Solid Philos.* 26 It has no Rapport at all to the Line of Knowledge. [**1755** JOHNSON, *Rapport*..A word introduced by the innovator, Temple, but not copied by others.] **1821** *Sporting Mag.* IX. 3 The rapports of conformity which naturally exist between the male and the female. **1894** DOYLE *S. Holmes* 169 As a proof that I had been in rapport with you. **1915** 'W. N. P. BARBELLION' *Jrnl.* Apr. in *Enjoying Life* (1919) 67 It wounds my self-esteem not to be..in direct telepathic rapport with the universe and its beauty. **1919** *Lancet* 8 Feb. 206/2 A lack of complete *rapport* between the muscles and the brain nerve centres. **1934** C. LAMBERT *Music Ho!* III. 175 This lack of rapport between the tune and harmony is particularly noticeable in some of the later works of Bartók. **1941** A. WHITE *Let.* 7 Feb. in *Hound & Falcon* (1969) 114 It was one of our good 'rapports' that I should have hit on Huvelin's admirable sayings just as you had written to me quoting some of them. **1957** J. KEROUAC *On Road* (1958) III. xi. 247 Dean's second baby, the result of a few nights' rapport. **1969** *Morning Star* 18 Nov. 2 The animal kingdom is in rapport with its environment, but man is not, unless he makes it so by taming his planet and remaking it to suit his needs. **1976** J. I. M. STEWART *Memorial Service* vii. 104 Jiffy temperately signalled the gratification proper to be felt on establishing this sort of *rapport* with a stranger.

b. *spec.* A state in which mesmeric action can be exercised by one person on another. Hence, a feeling of sympathy and co-operation between therapist and patient or tester and subject that is considered necessary for successful therapy or psychological testing. Also *attrib.* and *Comb.*

1845 POE in *Amer. Rev.* Dec. 564/2, I endeavored to place each member of the company in mesmeric *rapport* with him. **1848** CROWE *Night Side of Nature* I. 345 The somnambule reads the thoughts not only of his magnetiser, but of others, with whom he is placed in rapport. **1849** H. ROGERS *Ess.* (1874) II. vi. 293 Every work of genius, by coming, as it were, into mesmeric rapport with the affinities of kindred genius,..is itself the parent of many others. **1894** CREIGHTON & TITCHENER tr. *Wundt's Lect. Human & Animal Psychol.* xxii. 331 There then arises what the animal-magnetism school term the *rapport* of the medium with the magnetiser. **1923** J. T. MACCURDY *Probl. Dynamic Psychol.* xi. 121 Manipulation of *rapport* is thus made the core of psychoanalytic treatment. **1924** J. RIVIERE tr. *Freud's Coll. Papers* I. 293 In his treatment of her case Breuer could make use of a very intense suggestible rapport on the part of the patient. **1954** A. ANASTASI *Psychol. Testing* iii. 50 It is apparent that the establishment of rapport, prior to the administration of the test, is generally an important part of the testing procedure. **1965** F. M. LOPEZ *Personnel Interviewing* i. 12 Then there are the *rapport* behaviors that help the interviewer to establish a bond of communication with the interviewer. **1970** A. MAGONET *Psychotherapy by Hypnosis* i. 3 Mesmer discovered that it was important that there should exist between physician and patient a close interest in and sympathy for each other. He described this as rapport. **1971** D. B. PESKIN *Human Behavior & Employment Interviewing* vii. 170 If the response seems neutral, the interviewer applies more of the same rapport-producing small talk and humor. **1976** A. ANASTASI *Psychol. Testing* (ed. 4) ii. 34 The training of examiners covers techniques for the establishment of rapport.

3. In Fr. phr. ***en rapport***, in a state of rapport or close and harmonious relation; in sympathy, in harmony. Usu. of persons.

1818 LADY MORGAN *Autobiog.* (1859) 98 During his government as First Consul, I was frequently *en rapport* with him. **1846** GEO. ELIOT *Let.* Apr. in J. W. Cross *George Eliot's Life* (1885) I. ii. 116 See what it is to have a person *en rapport* with you, that knows all your thoughts. **1851** MAYNE REID *Rifle Rangers* xxviii, Sympathetic natures, who only needed to be placed *en rapport* to 'like each other mightily'. **1884** *Proc. Soc. Psychical Res.* II. 127 A mesmerised 'subject' who is sufficiently *en rapport* with his mesmeriser. **1933** WODEHOUSE *Mulliner Nights* v. 151 'I fear we were not exactly *en rapport*,' sighed Sacheverell.

†**4.** *Comb.* **rapport-work** (tr. F. *ouvrage de rapport*), inlaid or mosaic work. *Obs.*

1686 tr. *Chardin's Trav. Persia* 407 The Workmanship is of several pieces of rapport-work after the Mosaic manner.

†**ra'pport,** *v. Obs. rare*$^{-1}$. [See prec.] *intr.* To relate *to.*

1649 JER. TAYLOR *Gt. Exemp.* II. §10 Which duty.. r'apports to God and touches not the Man.

‖**rapportage** (ræpɔː'tɑʒ, ‖rapɔrtaʒ). [Fr., 'tale-telling': Eng. usage is influenced by REPORTAGE.] The reporting or describing of events in writing; mere description, uncreative accounting. Also *transf.*

1903 *Independent* 22 Jan. 210/2 It has nearly disabled prose fiction..by making of it a trade or handicraft, an affair of *rapportage*. **1935** S. SPENDER *Destructive Element* i. 26 James's earlier books are much fuller of descriptive writing and *rapportage* than the later books. **1957** *Times Lit. Suppl.* 8 Nov. 667/2 In describing his visits to the three North African territories in 1956 he has produced the modern counterpart to those brilliant pieces of pre-war *rapportage*. **1960** K. CLARK *Looking at Pictures* 145 The *Snowstorm* is very far from rapportage. It is the essence of all that Turner had discovered about himself and his art during forty years of practice. **1966** C. MACKENZIE *My Life & Times* V. 141, I decided it was too soon to write a novel about the war. Experience which had not been 'cooled a long age' might produce *rapportage* instead of genuine creative work.

rappor'teur. [a. F. *rapporteur*, f. *rapporter*: see RAPPORT *sb.*] †**1.** A reporter. *Obs. rare*$^{-1}$.

c **1500** *Melusine* 190 With drawe not rapporteurs of wordes toward you.

‖**2.** A person who prepares an account of the proceedings of a committee, etc., for a higher body. Cf. REPORTER 1 c.

1791 LD. PALMERSTON *Diary* 13 July in O. Browning *Despatches Earl Gower* (1885) 290 The Rapporteur said that the Committees did not consider the king's flight as a constitutional crime in him. **1927** *Daily Tel.* 8 Mar. 11/5 The representative of Holland, as the rapporteur, submitted a report of the Permanent Mandates Commission which was adopted by the Council. **1937** *Nature* 17 Apr. 683/1 Two *rapporteurs* were appointed to summarize the papers. **1949** I. DEUTSCHER *Stalin* v. 143 At the conference he was the *rapporteur* on the problem of nationalities. **1955** *Times* 1 July 8/5 The congress..has appointed five *rapporteurs* on economic and financial policy, agriculture, foreign affairs, and the French oversea territories. **1964** *Ann. Reg. 1963* 175 The recommendation submitted by the Defence Committee's rapporteur..urged full nuclear co-operation between Britain and France. **1977** *Daily Tel.* 24 May 16 Normanton is to be the rapporteur of a study into the industrial and economic aspects of buying arms through a Common Market agency.

‖**rapprochement** (raprɔʃmɑ̃). [F., f. *rapprocher* (f. *re-* + *approcher* APPROACH) + -MENT.] A coming or bringing together, an establishment of harmonious relations.

1809 *Edin. Rev.* XIV. 228 One of the opinions..deserves to be mentioned, as exhibiting a curious *rapprochement*. **1888** *Times* (weekly ed.) 6 July 8/3 A rapprochement between the Russian and Austrian governments. **1905** *Daily Chron.* 19 Jan. 4/3 The retiring Premier is fully justified in claiming as a distinctive mark of his Government that it aimed at a 'rapprochement between peoples'. **1934** C. LAMBERT *Music Ho!* III. 207 The same rapprochement between highbrow and lowbrow..can be seen in literature. **1940** [see ARTIFY *v.*]. **1955** *Times* 17 May 9/5 They should not assume that a Soviet-Yugoslav *rapprochement* was outside the framework of current conciliatory developments. **1958** L. DURRELL *Mountolive* xii. 228 With some half-formulated idea of offering the silent figure another chance to open up a discussion with him or seek a *rapprochement*, he rode his horse into the courtyard. **1974** J. WHITE tr. *Poulantzas's Fascism & Dictatorship* IV. iii. 211 It was only with the split in the Socialist Party, in October 1922, that rapprochement with the Maximalists was attempted. **1979** *Dædalus* Winter 78 The Community's structures were designed..to accommodate the Franco-German rapprochement.

rapreiff, obs. Sc. form of REPROVE.

rapscallion (ræp'skæliən). Also 8 **rabs-.** [Later form of RASCALLION.] A rascal, rogue, vagabond, scamp.

1699 E. WARD *London Spy* No. 5. 10 A parcel of Poor ragged Rapscallions, mounted upon Scrubbed Tits. **1748** SMOLLETT *Rod. Rand.* xxv, Go your ways, you rapscallion. **1837** HOWITT *Rur. Life* IV. ii. (1862) 335 Those ragged rapscallions that abound in the streets of towns,.. uncultivated, neglected. **1885** RUNCIMAN *Skippers & Sh.* 214 A set of ferocious-looking rapscallions had boarded the steamer.

b. *attrib.* or as *adj.*

1711 E. WARD *Quix.* I. 380 Such a strange Rapscallion fellow. **1777** in F. Moore *Songs & Ball. Amer. Rev.* (1856) 172 From him who..calls all Congresses Rabscallion. **1869** TROLLOPE *He knew*, etc. xii. (1878) 66 He is dressed in such a rapscallion manner.

Hence **rap'scallionly** *a.*, rascally; **rap'scallionry**, rascals collectively.

1832 *Blackw. Mag.* XXXII. 245 A 'rapscallionly part' there is in every community. **1858** *Times* 30 Nov., I suppose this rapscallionry will 'quit' soon. **1899** G. B. SHAW *Let.* 29 Sept (1972) II. 106. There being between Maggie [*sc.* Margaret Hobhouse] & myself a sort of rapscallionly freemasonry.

rap'scallionism. *rare.* [f. RAPSCALLION + -ISM.] Rapscallions collectively; the conduct or condition of rapscallions.

1920 GALSWORTHY *In Chancery* III. ix. 288 Soho seemed more than ever the disenchanted home of rapscallionism.

†'rapshin. *Obs. rare.* [f. RAP *v.*^{1} + SHIN.] A kind of fetter contrived to strike against a horse's leg, and so prevent it from running away.

1677 *Dulwich College MSS.* Ser. II. 30 (28 July), 4 pins for the horses rapshins. **1683** KENNET tr. *Erasm. on Folly* 54 The Penalty of his Jaws being curbed, his Tail dock'd, his Rapshin and Fetters when he runs a-Grass.

rapsodie, -ist, -y, obs. ff. RHAPSODIST, -Y.

†'rapster. *nonce-wd.* [f. RAP *v.*^{1} + -STER.] One who raps.

1772 T. BRYDGES *Homer* (1797) I. 309 Then at another stroke this rapster Settled Calisius, his tapster.

rapt (ræpt), *sb.* Now *rare.* [ad. L. *raptus*, n. of action f. *rapĕre* to seize. Cf. F. *rapt.*]

1. A trance, ecstasy, rapture.

1526 *Pilgr. Perf.* (W. de W. 1531) 272 A rapt, or a rauysshynge of the soule. **1555** EDEN *Decades* 182 He seemeth to lye as thoughe he were in great payne or in a rapte. **1669** WOODHEAD *St. Teresa* I. xxiv. 165 There came a Rapt upon me, so sudden, that it took me, as it were, out of myself. **1751** LAVINGTON *Enthus. Meth. & Papists* III. (1754) 72 Being much indisposed, I took up my Rosary, and insensibly fell into a Rapt. **1826** SOUTHEY *Vind. Eccl. Angl.* 138 In one of his rapts the Angels, who conducted his spirit ..bade him look down upon the earth.

†2. *Sc.* = RAPE (abduction or ravishing). *Obs.*

1535 STEWART *Cron. Scot.* II. 121 Adulterie and fornicatioun, Rapt and incest. *c* **1614** SIR W. MURE *Dido & Æneas* I. 48 Fair Helen's rapt, and Paris' prowd offence. *a* **1693** *Urquhart's Rabelais* III. xlviii. 387 A Vagabond Stranger..by an open Rapt snatcht away before their own eyes their..Daughters.

†b. An abducted woman. *Obs. rare*$^{-1}$.

1632 LITHGOW *Trav.* II. 70 [Helen is] the inordinate patterne of all willing and licentious rapts.

†3. The act or power of carrying forcibly away; sweep; force, current. *Obs.*

1632 LITHGOW *Trav.* VIII. 341 Neither may reason find place in the violent rapt of such passions. **1645** RUTHERFORD *Tryal & Tri. Faith* iv. (1845) 149 Nor are we to think that God doth all with an immediate rapt. **1682** SIR T. BROWNE *Chr. Mor.* I. §24 Move by the Intelligences of the superiour Faculties, not by the Rapt of Passion.

†4. Violent robbery, rapine. *Obs. rare*$^{-1}$.

1641 *Sc. Acts Chas. I* (1814) V. 425 [He] brought away from thame ane kow whairof he never made restitutione as yet, quhilk is manifest rapt and oppressioune.

rapt (ræpt), *pa. pple.* (and *pa. t.*). Also 5–6 rapte, 7 rap't. [ad. L. *rapt-us*, pa. pple. of *rapĕre* to seize, RAPE *v.*^{2}

Chiefly employed as a pa. pple. passive (rarely active), but also occas. in poetry (from *c* 1600) as a pa. tense. The use of RAP *v.*^{3} to supply an inf. and pres. was formerly common (cf. also RAPT *v.*), but is now extremely rare.]

I. As *pa. pple.* passive. (The ordinary use.)

1. (Also with *up.*) Taken and carried up *to* or *into* heaven (either in literal or mystical sense).

a **1400** *Vernon MS.* in *O.E. Misc.* 223 Þe visions of seynt poul wan he was rapt into paradys. **1412–20** LYDG. *Chron. Troy* II. xiv, In this wyse were the bretheren twayne To heauen rapt, as thes poetes fayne. **1432–50** tr. *Higden* (Rolls) III. 25 Helyas was rapte in this tyme. **1526** *Pilgr. Perf.* (W. de W. 1531) 25 Whan he was rapt & taken vp in to the thyrde heuen. **1610** GUILLIM *Heraldry* III. ii. (1660) 99 To this place..were Enoch, Elias and Paul rapt up before their deaths. **1667** MILTON *P.L.* III. 522 Rapt in a Chariot drawn by fiery Steeds. **1760–72** H. BROOKE *Fool of Qual.* (1809) IV. 71 They are..rapt, perhaps, like Elijah, alive into Heaven. **1866** KINGSLEY *Herew.* I. Prel. 12 He was rapt up on high and saw S. Peter.

2. a. Carried away *in spirit*, without bodily removal.

c **1470** *Monk of Evesham* (Arb.) 15 How a certeyn deuowt person..was rapte in spirite by the wille of god. **1550** BALE *Image Both Ch.* I. C iij, I..was in the spirite rapte, and clerely taken vp from all wordlye affectes. **1669** WOODHEAD *St. Teresa* I. xxxvi. (1671) 272 Being in Prayer.., and rapt in Spirit. **1712** POPE *Messiah* 7 Rapt into future times, the Bard begun. **1878** S. COX *Salv. Mundi* ix. (ed. 3) 198 St. Paul when he was rapt in the spirit into Paradise.

b. With various const., as *beside*, *beyond*, *out of* (oneself), *into* (a certain state).

1549 CHALONER *Erasm. on Folly* T. iij, They are wholy distraught and rapte out of theimselves. **1576** FLEMING *Panopl. Epist.* 289 Doe I seeme..to be frentique, and rapt beside my selfe. **1621** BURTON *Anat. Mel.* III. ii. III. iii. (1651) 476 Anthony was amazed and rapt beyond himself. **1691** RAY *Creation* I. (1692) 160 How would he have been rapt into an Extasie of Astonishment. **1795–1814** WORDSW. *Excurs.* I. 215 Rapt into still communion. **1879** HESBA STRETTON *Through a Needle's Eye* I. 182 He had been rapt away into a trance of spiritual ecstasy.

3. Transported with some emotion, ravished, enraptured. Also const. *with*, *by*, or *away.*

1539 TAVERNER *Gard. Wysed.* II. 3 With this noble corage, with this ardent zele..he is thus rapte. **1596** SPENSER *F.Q.* IV. ix. 6 With the sweetnesse of her rare delight The prince halfe rapt began on her to dote. **1680** CROWNE *Misery Civ. War* IV. 50, I am so rapt I mind not what she says. **1713** ADDISON *Cato* IV. iii, I..Am rapt with joy to see my Marcia's tears. **1795–1814** WORDSW. *Excurs.* IV. 187 From such disorder free, Nor rapt, nor craving, but in settled peace. **1814** SCOTT *Wav.* xxvi, I am not, like him, rapt by the bustle of military preparation. **1860** MAURY *Phys. Geog. Sea* vi. §313, I have stood on the deck under those beautiful skies gazing, admiring, rapt. **1924** A. D. SEDGWICK *Little French Girl* II. xii. 194 The heir..stood with his little shoulders screwed up, his elbows in his hands, rapt away from shyness and self-consciousness by his sincere delight.

4. Deeply engaged or buried *in* (a feeling, subject of thought, etc.); intent *upon.*

1509 HAWES *Past. Pleas.* XXIX. (Percy Soc.) 137 For a woman rapt in love so marveylously. **1601** R. JOHNSON *Kingd. & Commw.* (1603) 222 As men rapt in deep contemplation. **1682** H. MORE *Belshazzar* I. 66 Rapt in prophetic vision, I behold Things hid as yet from mortal sight. **1769** GRAY *Installat. Ode* 18 Rapt in celestial transport they. **1846** TENNYSON *Golden Year* 69 As if the seedsman, rapt Upon the coming harvest, should not plunge His hand into the bag. **1847** —— *Princ.* VI. 203 Ida spoke not, rapt upon the child. **1882** FARRAR *Early Chr.* I. 416 Rapt in adoring contemplation.

5. Of a woman: Carried away by force; raped.

1432–50 tr. *Higden* (Rolls) I. 197 Sekenge Europa his sustyr,..whiche was rapte by Iupiter. *c* **1550** *Life Bp. Fisher* in Wks. (E.E.T.S.) II. p. xliv, Provided alwaies that you.. Catherine were not rapt against your will. **1594** DRAYTON *Idea* 497 By Proserpine's sad Teares, When she was rapt to the infernall Bower. *a* **1634** RANDOLPH *Poems* (1638) 11 Euridice..From Orpheus rapt.

6. a. Carried or removed from one place, position, or situation to another. (Chiefly said of persons.) With various const.

1552 LATIMER *Godly Serm.* (1562) 113 b, They..shal be rapte vp into the ayre. **1615** SANDYS *Trav.* 206 The house of the blessed Virgin..was rapt from thence, and set in the woods of Picenum. *a* **1639** WOTTON in *Reliq.* (1651) 506 From Oxford I was Rapt by my Nephew..to Redgrave. **1715–20** POPE *Iliad* V. 113 Rapt through the ranks he thunders o'er the plain. **1820** W. IRVING *Sketch Bk.* I. 212 The aspiring family was rapt out of sight in a whirlwind. **1870** MYERS *Poems* 82 That face,..Lo, while we looked on her, was rapt away.

b. Taken *away* by death.

1820 W. IRVING *Sketch Bk.* (1859) 121 His only daughter had been rapt away to the grave. **1865** CARLYLE *Fredk. Gt.* X. viii. (1872) III. 297 Looking back..upon such a Father now rapt away for ever.

†c. Snapped *up* (by purchasers). *Obs. rare*$^{-1}$.

1567 DRANT *Horace, Epistles* To Rdr. *v, Flim flames and gue gawes..are soner rapte vp thenne..Clarkly makinges.

II. 7. As *pa. pple.* active. *rare.*

1509 HAWES *Past. Pleas.* XVI. (Percy Soc.) 59 The mynde inwarde Venus had rapte and taken fervently. **1605** B. JONSON *Volpone* Ded., This it is, that hath..rap't me to present indignation. **1671** MILTON *P.R.* II. 39 What accident Hath rapt him from us?

III. 8. As *pa. t.* Chiefly poetic, and now *rare.*

1594 *2nd Rep. Faustus* (1828) 76 He..rapt him up by his long hair out of the water unto the land. **1621** H. KING *Serm.* 54 Else some whirle-wind rapt him, and bare him to the house. **1651** R. WARING *Verses prefixed Cartwright's Comedies*, He rapt us, too: 't was Heaven but to heare. **1797** MRS. RADCLIFFE *Italian* xi, A pleasing melancholy, that rapt all her attention. **1821** SHELLEY *Adonais* xxiii, Sorrow and fear So struck, so roused, so rapt Urania. **1876** SWINBURNE *Erechtheus* 617 As the wild God rapt her from earth's breast lifted.

rapt (ræpt), *ppl. a.* [See prec.]

1. Entranced, ravished, enraptured, etc.

1555 EDEN *Decades* 182 The spirite answereth by the mouth of the rapte Piaces. **1632** MILTON *Penseroso* 40 Thy rapt soul sitting in thine eyes. **1732** POPE *Ess. Man* I. 278 The rapt Seraph that adores and burns. **1841** EMERSON *Addr. Meth. Nature* Wks. (Bohn) II. 221 The rapte saint is found the only logician.

2. Indicating, proceeding from, characterized by, a state of rapture. (Freq. in later 19th c. use.)

1797 MRS. RADCLIFFE *Italian* i, He listened..with a rapt attention. **1851** J. P. NICHOL *Archit. Heav.* (ed. 9) 300 The rapt language of the Psalmist. **1874** L. STEPHEN *Hours in Library* (1892) I. iv. 167 It is not the poetry of deep meditation or of rapt enthusiasm.

†3. Due to being carried along. *Obs. rare*$^{-1}$.

1603 SIR C. HEYDON *Jud. Astrol.* xxi. 432 The Moone by her diurne rapt motion from East to West.

†rapt, *v. Obs.* [f. RAPT *pa. pple.*; cf. RAP *v.*^{3}, RAPE *v.*^{2}]

1. *trans.* To carry away by force.

1577 NORTHBROOKE *Dicing* (1843) 86 The women of Saba ..were rapted and rauished by the Romaines. **1601** DANIEL *Civ. Wars* VII. xcvii, The Libyan lion,..Out-rushing from his den, rapts all away. **1619** SIR A. GORGES tr. *Bacon's De Sap. Vet.* 159 This spirit is fained to be rapted by the Earth. *Ibid.*, The ayre is rapted by the water.

2. To transport, enrapture.

1598 SYLVESTER *Du Bartas* II. iv. I. *Trophies* 441 The Prophet rapting his soule's soule a space. *a* **1619** FOTHERBY *Atheom.* II. xii. §2 (1622) 337 It euen rapteth the soule, and abstracteth it from it selfe.

Hence **†'rapted** *ppl. a.*, **†'rapting** *vbl. sb.*

1586 WARNER *Alb. Eng.* I. v. (1589) 16 Hercules..in rescue of the rapted Bride did runne. **1592** tr. *Junius on Rev.* xxi. 9 His rapting up by the Spirit. *a* **1619** FOTHERBY *Atheom.* II. xii. §2 (1622) 337 Tuning rarely right, Vnto the rapting Spirit, the rapted spright.

rap-tap, etc., *int.* An imitation of the sound produced by rapping on a door.

1833 MARRYAT *P. Simple* i, Rap, tap, tap! 'There's your master',..screamed the lady. **1874** A. G. MURDOCH *Sandy M'Tartan* 3 Rap, tap, tirrap, went the Tweezer's knuckles against the pannelling of the door.

'rap-'tap, *v.* [Cf. RAP-TAP *sb.*] *intr.* To make a rapping noise. Hence **'rap-'tapping** *ppl. a.*

1821 CLARE *Vill. Minstr.* I. 36 The tuteling fife, and hoarse rap-tapping drum. **1859** CAPERN *Ball. & Songs* 142 Thrice happy cot, if there the bard should stray By some kind chance, and rap-tap at its door.

rapta'torial, *a.* [f. L. type **raptātōri-us* (f. *raptāre* to seize) + -AL^1.] = RAPTORIAL.

1861 in *Smithsonian Misc. Collect.* IV. I. Gloss. **1880** GÜNTHER *Fishes* 296 A raptatorial fish organised to live at a depth of between 500 and 800 fathoms.

So **'raptatory** *a.* (In recent Dicts.)

†'rapter. *Obs.*$^{-1}$ [f. RAPT *v.*] A ravisher.

1612 DRAYTON *Poly-olb.* x. 149 Chaste Winifrid; who chose..To haue her harmlesse life by the leud Rapter spilt.

†'raptery. *Obs. rare*$^{-1}$. [f. RAPT *pa. pple.* + -ERY.] Rapture.

1640 BP. REYNOLDS *Passions* iv. 18 To quicken and rayse the Minde with a kind of heat and rapterie.

†'rapting, *ppl. a. Obs.* [f. RAPT *v.* + -ING^2.] Transporting, enrapturing, ravishing. (Not uncommon in 17th c.)

1598 SYLVESTER *Du Bartas* I. vi. (1641) 57/2 Come and see Womans rapting features. **1610** *Histrio-m.* i. 35 In flowing straynes, and rapting Symphonie. **1676** D'URFEY *Mad. Fickle* II. ii, He eager of such rapting Bliss, awak'd her with a kiss. **1721** —— *Operas*, etc. Ded., Sing then, Apollo, touch thy rapting Lyre.

†'raption. *Obs. rare*$^{-1}$. [ad. L. *raptiōn-em* (Terence), n. of action f. *rapĕre* RAPE *v.*^{2}] The fact of being snatched up.

1548 UDALL *Erasm. Par.* Pref. A iiij b, Of feigned visions, of lying in traunces, of rapcions, euen unto the third heauen. **1623** in COCKERAM. [**1644** condemned in *Vindex Anglicus* 5–6.]

'raptly, *adv.* [f. RAPT *ppl. a.* + -LY^2.]

†a. Quickly. *Obs.* **b.** Rapturously. *rare.*

1646 J. GREGORY *Notes & Obs.* (1650) 74 That part of the Spheare is most raptly moved, which is most remote from the Poles. **1890** S. J. DUNCAN *Social Departure* 225 Just the thing, she whispered to me raptly.

c. Intently, concentratedly, absorbedly.

1924 E. POWER *Medieval People* ii. 52 The crowd of Venetian prisoners and Genoese gentlemen, raptly drinking in all the wonders of Kublai Khan. **1971** *Daily Tel.* 13 Feb. 7/1 There was a delightful sequence of a 7 year-old girl 'cellist playing raptly and well for her judges.

'raptness. *rare.* [f. as prec. + -NESS.]

†a. Swiftness. *Obs.* **b.** Rapt condition.

1597 A. M. tr. *Guillemeau's Fr. Chirurg.* 52 b/2 With more festination & more raptnes. **1891** *Cornh. Mag.* Feb. 182 That look which such raptness wears.

raptor ('ræptə(r)). [a. L. *raptor*, agent-noun f. *rapĕre* RAPE *v.*^{2}]

1. A ravisher; an abductor. *rare.*

1609 HEYWOOD *Brit. Troy* XIV. xcv, Oh! had the Raptor in his cradle dide, Millions of liues had in his death beene sau'd. **1709** J. JOHNSON *Clergym. Vade M.* II. 30 If the virgin had been engaged to another,..the raptor had been guilty of adultery. **1884** ADDIS & ARNOLD *Cath. Dict.* 436/1 The councils..prohibit subsequent marriage between the raptor and his victim. **1975** *Daily Tel.* 12 Aug. 12 What I had in mind was the ruling that there was no rape provided the raptor believed..that the woman consented.

†2. A plunderer, robber. *Obs.*

1667 WATERHOUSE *Fire Lond.* 32 They that took away goods in a sort wrongfully will prove themselves preservers not raptors. **1720** J. JOHNSON *Canons Ch. Eng.* II. H h j b, Some Raptors rather than Rectors of Churches.

3. *Ornith.* One of the *Raptores* (see 4). Also *attrib.* and *fig.*

1873 W. CORY *Lett. & Jrnls.* (1897) 324 We wake the echoes of the rocks so well stocked with raptors. **1892** W. H. HUDSON *La Plata* 93 Some raptors never attack birds, others only occasionally. **1933** *Condor* XXXV. 19 (*heading*) Food habits of Southern Wisconsin raptors. *Ibid.*, The ex post facto recording of raptor kills encountered in the field should not be regarded as a proper source of quantitative data. **1963** D. P. MANNIX *All Creatures Great & Small* vi. 86 Raptors (birds of prey) do not have the nervous, active minds of the Corvidæ. **1974** *Sci. Amer.* Dec. 156/3 A cruel human raptor..boasted of killing golden eagles with a sawed-off shotgun as he flew beside them. **1976** *Nature* 23 Sept. 321/1 Other relevant predators such as large raptors or felids do not occur on these islands. **1980** *Observer* (Colour Suppl.) 6 Jan. 57/1 Hundreds of thousands of raptors—birds of prey such as stork, buzzard, kite and eagle—commute across this corner of north-western Turkey.

4. In Lat. pl. **Raptores** (ræp'təʊriːz), as the name of an order of birds of prey, including the eagle, hawk, buzzard, owl, etc.

1823 VIGORS in *Trans. Linn. Soc.* XIV. 405 *note*, The term *Raptatores* of that naturalist [Illiger] I have ventured to alter to *Raptores*, which appears to me more classical. The former I believe is not in use. **1854** BADHAM *Halieut.* 157 Representatives of all the raptores, or birds of prey, vultures, falcons, and owls.

raptorial (ræp'təʊrɪəl), *a.* (and *sb.*) [f. L. type **raptōri-us* (cf. prec.) + -AL^1.]

1. a. Given to seizing prey, predatory; esp. ***raptorial bird*** = prec. 4.

1825 VIGORS & HORSFIELD in *Trans. Linn. Soc.* XV. 177 The first order..is the Raptorial Order, or the Birds of Prey. **1854** OWEN *Skel. & Teeth* in Orr *Circ. Sc., Organ. Nat.* I. 226 Raptorial birds take a horizontal position when suspended in the air. **1892** W. H. HUDSON *La Plata* 158 Bringing a raptorial insect and a firefly together. **1919** T. A.

COWARD *Birds Brit. Isles* I. 330 Most raptorial birds are variable in plumage. **1931** —— *Life of Birds* vi. 46 The flesh-eating or raptorial birds kill birds which we call useful as well as those which are troublesome. **1968** *Nature* 14 Dec. 1098/1 Declining populations of raptorial and fish-eating birds. **1976** *Field* 30 Dec. 1281/1 Goats shot this year have helped to nourish a foundation stock of ten white-tailed eagles, brought over from Norway by special arrangement with the government of that country in an attempt to reintroduce a raptorial bird once native to Britain.

b. as *sb.* A bird of prey. (Ogilvie 1882.)

2. Pertaining to, or characteristic of, predatory birds or animals; adapted for seizing prey. Also *fig.*

1839 JARDINE *Brit. Birds* II. 53 With raptorial or predacious manners. **1870** H. A. NICHOLSON *Man. Zool.* I. 219 In others the first pair of legs are greatly developed, and form powerful raptorial organs, as in the *Mantis*. **1916** *Sci. Progress* XI. 245 'Canto di cigno'..—a droll metaphor having regard to Spallanzani's raptorial countenance. **1933** *Condor* XXXV. 19 Erroneous impressions obscure the true proportions of one prey species to another in raptorial diets. **1955** W. GADDIS *Recognitions* II. vii. 620 At that instant the room was pierced by a raptorial cry like that of the bird descending. **1973** *Nature* 20 July 179/2 Planktonic crustacea exhibit selective feeding behaviour ranging from passive size selection in *Daphnia* to raptorial feeding in cyclopoid copepods.

So **rap'torious** *a.*

1819 G. SAMOUELLE *Entomol. Compend.* 300 Anterior legs raptorious. **1835** KIRBY *Hab. & Inst. of Anim.* II. xv. 59 The raptorious fore leg of the Squillæ.

'raptril. ? *pseudo-arch.* App. = RASCAL.

1843 LYTTON *Last Bar.* I. vii, The raptril vulgar..who hiss one day what they applaud the next. *Ibid.* IV. v, Heard you the name the raptrils shouted.

rapture ('ræptjʊə(r)), *sb.* Also 7 wrap-. [f. RAPT *pa. pple.* + -URE. Cf. *capture.*]

†**1.** The act of seizing and carrying off as prey or plunder. *Obs.*

1608 SHAKS. *Per.* II. i. 161 Spite of all the rapture of the sea, This jewel holds his building on my arm. *c* **1611** CHAPMAN *Iliad* XXII. 271 Look how an eagle from her height Stoops to the rapture of a lamb. **1639** G. DANIEL *Ecclus.* xliv. 6 Who did Realmes subdue.. Were wise in Councell, and in Rapture strong.

2. The act of carrying, or fact of being carried, onwards; force of movement. Now *rare.*

1615 CHAPMAN *Odyss.* XIV. 428 Our Ship..'gainst a Rocke, or Flat, her Keele did dash With headlong rapture. **1625** N. CARPENTER *Geog. Del.* II. vi. (1635) 98 A receiued opinion amongst Philosophers..that the sea by the rapture of the heauens should be moued round..in a diurnall course. **1667** MILTON *P.L.* VII. 299 Wave rowling after Wave, where way they found, If steep, with torrent rapture. **1888** LOWELL *Agassiz* VI. i. 21 With the rapture of great winds to blow About earth's shaken coignes.

†**3. a.** The act of carrying off a woman. *Obs.*

1600 DEKKER *Fortunatus* Wks. 1873 I. 151 That feare Which her late violent rapture cast upon her. **1662** J. BARGRAVE *Pope Alex. VII* (1867) 117 A flat piece of brass, with the rapture of Proserpine by a Centaure. **1728** NEWTON *Chronol. Amended* i. 114 Under which of the Kings happened the rapture of Europa.

†**b.** = RAPE *sb.*² 3. *Obs.* Also *fig.*

1615 CHAPMAN *Odyss.* XX. 485 My women servants dragg'd about my house To lust and rapture. **1649** G. DANIEL *Trinarch., Hen. V*, cccxxix, Though the Representative committ Rapture vpon his heart, in well-drawne Smiles.

4. The act of conveying a person from one place to another, *esp.* to heaven; the fact of being so conveyed.

1647 WARD *Simp. Cobler* 19 Horrid raptures downe to the lowest hell. **1693** J. EDWARDS *Author. O. & N. Test.* 193 Elias's rapture to heaven. **1842** MANNING *Serm.* viii. (1848) 139 In the book of the prophet Ezekiel we read of his rapture to Tel-abib. **1895** A. NUTT *Voy. Bran* I. 273 *note*, The rapture of the hero, by the heroine, to the Underworld.

5. a. Transport of mind, mental exaltation or absorption, ecstasy; now *esp.* ecstatic delight or joy.

1629 MILTON *Nativity* 98 Such musick sweet..As all their souls in blissfull rapture took. **1655** STANLEY *Hist. Philos.* III. (1701) 86/1 His Contemplative Rapture at the same time was no less worthy Admiration. **1717** LADY M. W. MONTAGU *Let. to C'tess Mar* 18 Apr., Women always speak in rapture when they speak of beauty. **1818** MRS. SHELLEY *Frankenst.* iii. (1865) 58 The astonishment..soon gave place to delight and rapture. **1863** GEO. ELIOT *Romola* II. xxiv, He felt in that moment the rapture and glory of martyrdom without its agony.

b. With *a* and *pl.* An instance of this. (In mod. use the pl. is freq. in the phr. (*to be*) *in*, or (*to go*) *into raptures.*)

1605 DRAYTON *Bar. Wars* III. lviii, With such brave raptures from her words that rise, She made a breach in his impressive breast. **1642** MILTON *Apol. Smect.* iii. Wks. (1851) 287 This man..sees truth as in a rapture, and cleaves to it. **1738** WESLEY *Hymns*, '*Again the kind revolving Year*' iv, If aught can there enhance their Bliss Or raise their Raptures higher. **1760** GOLDSM. *Cit. W.* xi, He is instantly in raptures at so great an improvement. **1862** MISS BRADDON *Lady Audley* i, A place that strangers fell into raptures with. **1866** GEO. ELIOT *F. Holt* (1868) 19 The mother's early raptures had lasted but a short time.

c. A state of passionate excitement; a paroxysm, fit. *rare* (now *dial.*).

1607 SHAKS. *Cor.* II. i. 223 Your pratling Nurse Into a rapture lets her Baby crie. **1634** SIR T. HERBERT *Trav.* 24 Then in rage and sudden rapture drew out his knife. **1895** W. C. FRASER *Whaups of Durley* xii, The laddies used to pit her into terrible raptures when they misca'ed her.

d. A strong fit or attack *of* (some emotion or mental state).

1795–1814 WORDSW. *Excurs.* VI. 488 A rapture of forgetfulness. **1871** W. ALEXANDER *Johnny Gibb* ii. 19 'Eh, that's the sea!' exclaimed the lassie in a rapture of admiration.

e. *rapture(s) of the deep* or *depths*, nitrogen narcosis.

1953 J. Y. COUSTEAU *Silent World* ii. 14 (*heading*) Rapture of the deep. *Ibid.* 21 We called the seizure *l'ivresse des grandes profondeurs* (rapture, or 'intoxication', of the great depths). **1955** R. & B. CARRIER *Dive* iii. 77 This nitrogen narcosis or 'rapture of the depths'..seems to have varying effects on different types of people. **1955** J. SWEENEY *Skin Diving & Exploring Underwater* vii. 89 It has not been established with absolute certainty how nitrogen causes a narcotic effect ('raptures of the deep') when breathed under high pressure. **1962** [see *nitrogen narcosis*]. **1971** J. F. BERNARD tr. *Cousteau's Life & Death in Coral Sea* 261 The diver's threshold of susceptibility to rapture of the depths can be pushed back..by replacing the nitrogen in one's breathing mixture by a lighter gas, such as helium. **1974** *Petroleum Rev.* XXVIII. 672/1 Nitrogen narcosis, popularly called 'raptures of the deep' but perhaps more accurately described as 'the uglies', is the malady caused by nitrogen under pressure, interfering with the normal function of the nervous system.

6. The expression of ecstatic feeling in words or music; a rhapsody.

1620 MELTON *Astrolog.* 27 The cause of such Musicall and Harmonious Raptures. **1667** MILTON *P.L.* III. 369 With Præamble sweet..they introduce Thir sacred Song, and waken raptures high. **1763** J. BROWN *Poetry & Mus.* vi. 102 When the first Fire of Enthusiasm had vented itself in the Rapture of Hymns and Odes. **1835** LYTTON *Rienzi* IX. iv, The people..shouted raptures as he passed. **1845** BROWNING *Home Th. fr. Abroad* 14 The first fine careless rapture [of the thrush].

7. *Comb.* **a.** Instrumental, as *rapture-bound, -bursting, -lightened, -rising, -smitten, -touched, -trembling* adjs.

1842 FABER *Styrian Lake* 26, I see Mary *rapture-bound, And the lily-flowers around. **1824** T. FENBY *Four Temperam.* IV. xv, Its *rapture-bursting joys. **1799** CAMPBELL *Pleas. Hope* Wks. (1837) 6 Turn..thy *rapture-lighten'd eye To Wisdom's walks. **1842** SIR AUBREY DE VERE *Song of Faith* 219 With *rapture-rising heart, and a thanksgiving tongue. **1799** CAMPBELL *Pleas. Hope* Wks. (1837) 23 Who hath not own'd with *rapture-smitten frame The power of grace. **1820** T. MITCHELL *Aristoph.* I. 209 Your bard shall depart With a *rapture-touch'd heart. **1794** COLERIDGE *Relig. Musings* vi, Cherubs and *rapture-trembling Seraphim.

b. Objective, as *rapture-breathing, -giving, -moving, -speaking* adjs.

1777 POTTER *Æschylus* Suppl. 111 The muses' *rapture-breathing shell. **1787** BURNS *Answ. Verses by Guidwife of Wauchope* iv, The saul o' life, the heav'n below, Is *rapture-giving woman. **1801** ELIZABETH SCOT *Alonzo & Cora* 81 Her *rapture-moving voice. **1799** CAMPBELL *Pleas. Hope* Wks. (1837) 4 The *rapture-speaking tear.

Hence **'raptural** *a.*, **raptu'ration.** *nonce-wds.*

1695 BP. SPRAT *Disc. Clergy* 46 Such raptural (if I may so call it) or Enthusiastical Spirit of Preaching. *a* **1814** *Gonzanga* II. i. in *New Brit. Theatre* III. 110 I'll tell you. Now prepare for rapturation.

rapture ('ræptjʊə(r)), *v.* [f. the sb.] **a.** *trans.* To enrapture. Also const. *with.* (Chiefly in *pass.*, common *c* 1700–50.) Now *rare.*

1637 HEYWOOD *Royal Ship* 27 Shee hath (no doubt) raptured our Undertaker. **1710** STEELE *Tatler* No. 224 ¶7 The highest compounded Spirit of Lavender..which..raptures the Spirits. **1748** RICHARDSON *Clarissa* (1811) V. 308 How will Lord M. be raptured when he sees her. **1818** KEATS *Endym.* II. 947. **1892** INGERSOLL in *Pall Mall G.* 16 Apr. 7/1 While yet in love with life and raptured with the world, he passed to silence.

b. *intr.* To express oneself in raptures; to take rhapsodic delight *in* or display ecstatic excitement *over* something.

1908 A. LIPDEGRAFF in *Smart Set* June 133, I rapture in some lonely night-bird's cries. **1965** E. O'BRIEN *August is Wicked Month* i. 12 She went out and raptured over the tent and said what a genius he was.

raptured ('ræptjʊəd), *ppl. a.* [f. prec. sb. and vb.] Ecstatic, enraptured. (Freq. in 18th c.)

1682 SIR T. BROWNE *Wks.* (1836) I. 343 The meeter of the rapturd pædagogue. **1725** POPE *Odyss.* I. 558 In his raptured soul the vision glows. **1748** THOMSON *Cast. Indol.* II. xlvi, Light o'er the chords his raptur'd hand he flung. **1830** TENNYSON *Ode to Memory* v, Large dowries doth the raptur'd eye To the young spirit present.

'raptureless, *a. rare*⁻¹. Devoid of rapture.

1811 SCOTT *Don Roderick* I. iii, Weak minstrels of a laggard day,..Timid and raptureless.

†**'rapturist.** *Obs. rare.* [f. RAPTURE *sb.* + -IST.] An enthusiast.

1663 SPENCER *Prodigies* (1665) 43 Swarms of prophets and rapturists. **1783** MAD. D'ARBLAY *Diary* 13 Jan., Dr. Warton ..is what Dr. Johnson calls a rapturist.

rapturize ('ræptjʊəraɪz), *v.* [f. RAPTURE *sb.* + -IZE.] *intr.* To fall into ecstasies. Also (*nonce-use*), to say in an ecstatic way.

1822 MRS. E. NATHAN *Langreath* I. 25 'I would not miss this fête for the world!' rapturized the Earl. **1832** DARWIN in *Life* (1887) I. 232, I will not rapturize again, but I give myself great credit in not being crazy out of pure delight.

rapturous ('ræptjʊərəs), *a.* Also 7–8 *poet.* rapt'rous. [f. RAPTURE *sb.* + -OUS.]

1. Characterized by, expressive of or partaking of, rapture.

1678 CUDWORTH *Intell. Syst.* I. iv. §36. 549 A kind of Rapturous and Ecstatick Union with..The One and The Good. **1695** BLACKMORE *Pr. Arth.* I. 441 Here rapt'rous Converse he with Heav'n maintains. **1756** BURKE *Subl. & B.* I. viii, The pleasure..is of a lively character, rapturous and violent. **1802** MAR. EDGEWORTH *Moral T.* (1816) I. xx. 178 The joy of the..master..was rapturous and voluble. **1853** KINGSLEY *Hypatia* xxii. 279 A shout of rapturous applause greeted this announcement.

2. Feeling or exhibiting rapture.

1754 GRAY *Pleasure* 18 Rise the rapturous choir among. **1851** HELPS *Comp. Solit.* iv. (1874) 42 A rapturous imaginative girl. **1871** R. ELLIS tr. *Catullus* xxv. 17 Muse more rapturous, you, than any Sappho. **1885–94** R. BRIDGES *Eros & Psyche* June xxvi, [We] see thee now so glad and rapturous.

rapturously ('ræptjʊərəslɪ), *adv.* [f. prec. + -LY².] In a rapturous manner.

1664 H. MORE *Myst. Iniq.* 293 Mere Prophetick Ellipsis.. spoken rapturously and ecstatically. *a* **1711** KEN *Sion* Poet. Wks. 1721 IV. 375 When Tears..so rapturously glide. **1845** LD. CAMPBELL *Chancellors* (1857) VI. cxxix. 174 The speech ..was rapturously praised as a fine specimen of judicial eloquence. **1873** BURTON *Hist. Scot.* VI. lxxi. 246 They crowded rapturously round the princely boy.

So **'rapturousness.**

1880 G. MEREDITH *Trag. Com.* (1881) 271 All that he has dreamed of rapturousness and blessedness.

‖**raptus** ('ræptəs). [L., vbl. sb. f. *rapĕre* to seize: cf. RAPT, RAPTURE, etc.]

1. *Path.* A seizure. (Craig, 1848.)

Chiefly in L. phrases, as *raptus melancholicus, nervorum.*

2. A state of rapture or excitement. Also, an instance of this.

1844 MARG. FULLER *Wom. 19th C.* (1862) 106 How graceful she is in her tragic raptus the chorus shows. **1888** *Scott. Leader* 17 Nov. 4 Did he not lash up the raptus over the extension of the franchise? **1902** W. JAMES *Var. Relig. Exper.* xvi. 412 In the condition called *raptus* or ravishment by theologians, breathing and circulation are so depressed that it is a question among the doctors whether the soul be or be not temporarily dis-severed from the body. **1964** L. WOOLF *Beginning Again* I. 32 Beethoven, every now and again, used to have what his faithful disciple called 'a raptus', a kind of volcanic creative outburst... The raptus or inspiration is clearly only a rare and wonderful form of a well-known everyday mental process. **1977** A. SHERIDAN tr. *J. Lacan's Écrits* vi. 207 The subject had his first attack of anxious confusion with suicidal raptus.

rapy, var. RAPÉ *Obs.*

rapyer, -yre, obs. ff. RAPIER.

rapyne, obs. f. RAPINE.

raquer, obs. f. REQUIRE.

raquest, obs. Sc. f. REQUEST.

raquet, var. RACKET *sb.*¹

‖**raquette** (ra'kɛt). Also racq-. = RACKET *sb.*² (esp. in sense 3 a).

c **1665** P. E. RADISSON *Voyages* (1885) 66 We found snowes in few places, saving where the trees made a shadow, wᶜʰ hindred the snow to thaw, wᶜʰ made us carry the raquetts. **1760** T. JEFFERYS *Nat. & Civil Hist. French Dominions* I. 57 The texture of the raquette or snow-shoe, consists of straps of leather about two lines in breadth, bordered with some light wood hardened in the fire. **1849** J. E. ALEXANDER *L'Acadie* II. 19 It was ludicrous to witness the mishaps of those who figured on the broad racquettes for the first time. **1861** J. G. SHEPPARD *Fall Rome* xiii. 744 The bishop calls for his raquette, and engages in a game at tennis. **1897** *Outing* (U.S.) XXIX. 362/1 When the racquette is fastened the heel and toe are free. **1965** *Canad. Geogr. Jrnl.* Feb. 62/2 The 'raquettes' of today are strung, usually, with especially prepared cowhide, rather than the original deerhide.

†**raquitable,** *a. Obs. rare*⁻¹. [a. OF. (*rente*) *raquitable* (Godef.): see next.] Redeemable.

1682 WARBURTON *Hist. Guernsey* (1822) 92 If the inheritance shall be sold for rent raquitable, that is to say, rent afterwards to be bought off, or..passed away by deed of gift..or for wares..received.

†**raquite,** *v. Obs. rare*⁻¹. [a. OF. *raquiter* to recover, to pay (Godef.): see RE- and ACQUIT.] *trans.* To redeem.

1454 *Rolls of Parlt.* V. 255/2 To leye in plege all my grete Jowellys, and the most partie of my Plate not yit raquited.

rar, obs. form of ROAR.

ra-ra, var. RAH-RAH *a.*

‖**rara avis** ('rɛərə 'eɪvɪs, 'rɑːrə 'ævɪs). Pl. **rara avises,** ‖**rarae aves.** [L., 'rare bird' (Juvenal *Sat.* vi. 165; cf. also Persius *Sat.* i. 46).] **1.** A person of a type seldom encountered; an exceptional person, a paragon. Occas. without article.

1607 G. WILKINS *Miseries Inforst Mariage* sig. A3ᵛ, And by that, thou hast beene married but three weekes, tho thou shouldst wed a *Cynthia rara avis*, thou wouldest be a man monstrous: A cuckold, a cuckold. [**1654** E. GAYTON *Pleasant Notes Don Quixot* IV. xv. 251 But all to Donna Clara The judges daughter yield, shee's *Avis rara*.] **1748** SMOLLETT *R. Random* II. li. 166 Calling my Lord Strutwell by the appellations of Jewel, Phœnix, *Rara avis*. **1749** FIELDING

Tom Jones III. viii. i. 150 A single instance.. is not sufficient to justify us, while we are writing to thousands who never heard of the person, nor of any thing like him. Such Raræ Aves should be remitted to the epitaph-writer. **1813** Southey *Let.* 30 Nov. (1856) II. 338, I sent them, thinking that a char in London must be like a tortoise-shell Tom cat, a *rara avis.* **1825** Mill in *Jrnl. Adult Educ.* (1929) IV. 54 A good doubter may as yet be truly pronounced to be *rara avis,* etc. **1852** 'G. Greenwood' *Haps & Mishaps* (1854) iv. 91 A pretty Irish peasant girl we found the rarest of *rara avises.* **1892** D. H. Tuke *Dict. Psychol. Med.* 854 A good nurse for neurotic patients is a *rara avis* indeed. **1919** V. Woolf *Night & Day* xii. 154 'But I do read De Quincey.., more than Belloc and Chesterton, anyhow.' 'Indeed!' exclaimed Mrs Cosham... 'You are, then, a *rara avis* in your generation.' **1931** 'G. Trevor' *Murder at School* i. 13 That *rara avis,* the headmaster who was also a man of the world. **1955** *Times* 23 May 3/3 The harpist is a *rara avis* among recitalists. **1975** *Listener* 31 July 140/1 Peter Jay is the *rara avis* of broadcasting. He is the high-flyer who descends from the thunderous crags of the *Times* to perch, with no hint of condescension, on the television aerials of the nation.

2. That which is seldom found; an unusual occurrence, etc.; something very remarkable.

1884 J. J. Hissey *Old-Fashioned Journey* vii. 99 A perfect day with us is somewhat of a *rara avis.* **1906** [see redouble *sb.*^{2}]. **1942** *Burlington Mag.* Feb. 50/2 Truly a *rara avis* among books of memoirs! **1979** *Guardian* 15 Mar. 11/1 It is a moving document, not to say a *rara avis.*

3. *lit.* A rare bird.

1891 H. M. Smith in *Proc. U.S. Nat. Museum* XIII. 171 The Dick Cissel [*sc.* a bird].. is now a veritable *rara avis.*

†**rarachose,** *a. Obs. rare*$^{-1}$. [ad. F. *rare chose* rare thing.] Rare, unusual.

1676 Marvell *Mr. Smirke* 20 He is ravisht in Contemplation how Rarachose it is, to see or hear a material Question in Theology defended in the University Schools.

raræ show, obs. form of raree-show.

rardess, obs. form of reredos.

rare (rɛə(r)), *a.*^{1} (*adv.*^{1} and *sb.*) Also 6-7 *Sc.* rair. [ad. L. *rār-us* or a. F. *rare* (14th c.).]

1. a. Having the constituent particles not closely packed together. (Opposed to *dense.*) In later use chiefly of the air or gases (see sense 5 f).

c **1420** *Pallad. on Husb.* i. 99 The londis fatte, or lene, or thicke, or rare. **1595** Spenser *Sonn.* lv, Not ayre; for she is not so light or rare. **1610** W. Folkingham *Art of Survey* i. viii. 16 Distinguishing betweene open and rare soyles, and such as are condense and close. **1669** Sturmy *Mariner's Mag.* v. 47 All pure and rare bodies ascend, as the Fire more than the Air. **1732** Arbuthnot *Rules of Diet* 275 A denser Fluid is hotter than a rarer. *c* **1790** Imison *Sch. Arts* I. 100 As the air rises above the earth's surface, it grows rarer, and consequently lighter, bulk for bulk. **1862** H. Spencer *First Princ.* ii. v. §55 (1875) 181 A projectile would travel a far greater distance through a rare medium like air, than through a dense medium like water.

fig. **1820** Shelley *Let. to Maria Gisborne* 7 Spinning.. From the fine threads of rare and subtle thought.

†**b.** Of colour: Thin, faint. *Obs. rare*$^{-1}$.

1750 tr. *Leonardus' Mirr. Stones* 111 Those are reckoned the best, whose colour is neither too thick nor too rare.

†**2. a.** Having the component parts widely set; of open construction; in open order. *Obs. rare.*

c **1420** *Pallad. on Husb.* xi. 494 A multitude of reysouns puld they take, And into rushy frayels rare [L. *rariore contextu*] hem gete. **1622** Sir R. Hawkins *Voy. S. Sea* (1847) 197 They being rare shippes, and without any manner of close fights, in bourding with us, their men were all open unto us, and we under covert and shelter. **1647** May *Hist. Parl.* iii. v. 100 One rare and slender ranke were to receive all the storme without seconds.

†**b.** Thinly attended or populated. *Obs. rare.*

1610 J. Forbes *Cert. Rec.* x. (1846) 387 The Assemblie was so rare that they were not exceeding the number of nineteen Commissioners. *c* **1789** Gibbon *Autobiog.* (1854) 61 Our immediate neighbourhood was rare and rustic.

†**3. a.** Placed or stationed at wide intervals; standing or keeping far apart. *Obs.*

c **1420** *Pallad. on Husb.* i. 1033 Bowis ore it trayn So lough and rare, on hem that bees may dwelle. *Ibid.* iv. 183 Cvcumber in this mone is sowen rare. **1667** Milton *P.L.* vii. 461 Among the trees in pairs they rose, they walk'd; Those rare and solitarie, these in flocks.

†**b.** Seldom appearing or seen. *Obs.*

c **1450** tr. *De Imitatione* i. viii. 9 Be rare amonge yonge peple & straunge folkes. **1784** Cowper *Task* ii. 383 Frequent in Park with lady at his side,.. But rare at home.

†**c.** Sparing. Const. *in. Obs. rare*$^{-1}$.

1526 *Pilgr. Perf.* (W. de W. 1531) 56 b, Pacyent in aduersytees, rare & sobre in wordes.

d. Infrequent. *rare.*

1707 Floyer *Physic. Pulse-Watch* 128 The Pulse becomes.. more languid, rare, slow. **1859** Tennyson *Elaine* 164 He.. Chose the green path that show'd the rarer foot.

4. (With pl. sbs.) Few in number, and widely separated from each other (in space or time); forming a small and scattered class.

1555 *Act 2 & 3 Phil. & Mary,* c. 13 The Fertility of the Ground is not apt to bring forth any Corn nor good Grass, but in rare Places. **1654** Bramhall *Just Vindication* iv. (1661) 65 And the Legations from Rome were almost as rare as appeals to Rome,.. untill the Norman conquest. **1698** Fryer *Acc. E. India & P.* 199, I never saw but one Grey-ey'd and therefore I suppose them rare. **1784** Cowper *Tiroc.* 700 Are such men rare? Perhaps they would abound Were occupation easier to be found. **1820** Shelley *Let. to Maria Gisborne* 263 Clouds sail o'er the inverse deep,.. And the rare stars rush through them. **1885** *Manch. Exam.* 15 May 5/6 Brake appliances, to the development of which we mainly owe it that railway accidents are now so rare.

5. a. Of a kind, class, or description, seldom found, met with, or occurring; unusual, uncommon, exceptional.

1542 Udall *Erasm. Apoph.* 171 It is a veraye rare thyng in princes to feele the mocions and pangues of the graces. **1560** Daus tr. *Sleidane's Comm.* 378 An Olyphaunt of Inde,.. a rare spectacle, and a beast not often sene in Germany. **1611** Bible *Pref.* ¶ 15 Many rare names of certaine birds, beastes and precious stones. **1709** Hearne *Collect.* (O.H.S.) II. 269 The Book being very rare in England. **1755** *Man* No. 15. 4 It is comparatively rare for brutes to die of sickness. **1779** Forrest *Voy. N. Guinea* 139 The white bird of Paradise is the most rare... The first sort is very rare. **1812** J. Wilson *Isle of Palms* iv. 399 Gathering rare shells, delighted children stray. **1863** Fr. A. Kemble *Resid. in Georgia* 42 How very rare it is to see a well-formed face. **1870** E. Peacock *Ralf Skirl.* III. 182 It was a rare event for Mrs. Skirlaugh to go from home.

b. *it is rare that...* (Cf. F. *il est rare que...,* and see rarely *adv.* 2 d.)

1788 T. Taylor *Proclus* (1792) I. 34 It is very rare that philology and philosophy are united in the same person. **1855** Prescott *Philip II,* I. ii. ii. 163 It was rare that the tone of remonstrance was heard in the halls of Castilian legislation.

c. ***rare earth*** (Chem.), any naturally occurring oxide of an element of the lanthanide series (usu. including lanthanum and freq. also scandium and yttrium); also (*loosely*), any of these elements themselves; a lanthanide. Hence ***rare-earth element, metal.***

In earliest examples used in a less restricted sense, including oxides of other metals.

1875 *Jrnl. Chem. Soc.* XXVIII. 1001 (*heading*) The quantivalence of the metals of the rarer [*sic*] earths [= tr. G. seltenen Erdmetalle]. **1877** *Ibid.* XXXI. 49 (*heading*) The quantivalence of the rare earth-metals. **1878** *Chem. News* 13 Sept. 136/2, I found nearly one-half of the known elements represented, and separated a group of oxides belonging to the rare earths. **1902** *Encycl. Brit.* XXVI. 710/1 Helium has since been extracted from a variety of minerals consisting of salts of uranium, yttrium, thorium and other rare earths. *Ibid.* 710/2 In the case of the rare-earth metals, the elements from air and the radio-active elements, the discovery of new elements has frequently been consequent on the introduction of novel methods. **1933** *Discovery* Jan. 1/1 Samarium has an atomic number 62 and a mass of about 150. Chemically it is a 'rare earth'. **1937,** etc. [see lanthanide]. **1958** *Optima* Mar. 22b/2 Thorium occurs chiefly in association with the rare-earth elements in monazite ore. **1959** *Nomencl. Inorg. Chem.* (I.U.P.A.C.) 6 The name rare-earth metals may be used for the elements Sc, Y, and La to Lu inclusive. **1965** D. Abbott *Inorg. Chem.* i. 36 The third transition series is interrupted after lanthanum by a set of elements known as the Rare Earths or Lanthanons. **1968** *Times* 18 Oct. 16/8 Gadolinium belongs to the little known family of minerals called the rare earths... The name rare earth is something of a misnomer, since many of the minerals in the family are widely distributed throughout the earth's crust. **1972** *Nature* 31 Mar. 197/1 Also concentrated in this liquid are a group of trace elements, including barium, yttrium, rare earths, zirconium, hafnium, phosphorus and niobium, about which are centred many of the geochemical arguments concerning the differences between terrestrial and lunar rocks.

d. ***rare bird*** = rara avis 1, 2.

1890 G. B. Shaw in *Star* 21 Feb. 2/5 She [*sc.* the perfect dancer] is the rarest of rare birds. **1912** R. Lynd *Rambles in Ireland* i. 45 In Ireland.. one drunk man is as conspicuous as a thousand sober ones... But he is, comparatively speaking, a rare bird and an exception for all the show he makes. **1934** C. Day Lewis *Hope for Poetry* x. 66 The true lyric poet is a very rare bird indeed. **1950** W. Saroyan *Assyrian* 21 The writer who is only a writer is a rare bird these days, most writers having taken posts at universities, [etc.]. **1962** *Which? Car Suppl.* Oct. 141/1 The foreign cars are still somewhat rare birds. **1977** *Times* 20 Oct. 16/3 That rare bird, a historian who was also a history-maker.

e. ***rare book,*** a book which is in demand and made valuable by its actual or prospective rarity. Also *attrib.*

[**1862** J. H. Burton *Book-Hunter* ii. 210 David Clement.. lays it down with authority, that 'a book which is difficult to find in the country where it is sought ought to be called simply rare'.] **1895** W. Roberts *Rare Bks.* 7 This is a very unusual contingency even in the history of rare books. **1910** A. W. Pollard in *Encycl. Brit.* IV. 223/1 The Boccaccio.. went to Earl Spencer (d. 1834) for £750, to pass with the rest of his rare books to Mrs Rylands in 1892. **1930** R. Curie *Collecting Amer. First Editions* vi. 168 (*heading*) Rare books still obtainable. **1941** B. Schulberg *What makes Sammy Run?* v. 97 One of the finest collections of rare books in the country. **1948** J. Carter *Taste & Technique in Book-Collecting* p. ix, I am the first member of the rare book trade to have been appointed Sandars Reader. **1952** —— *ABC for Book-Collectors* 148 The First Folio Shakespeare and the Gutenberg Bible are certainly 'rare books' as the term is generally understood. **1967** E. Grierson *Crime of one's Own* i. 12 The 'rare book' trade, which he was trying to build up. **1976** 'O. Bleeck' *No Questions Asked* ii. 22 The Library of Congress is an interesting place... The reading room of the Rare Book Division turned out to be a peaceful place. **1980** *Times* 29 Jan. 14/6 It was a characteristic out-of-season sale, containing faulty copies of rare books.

f. ***rare gas*** (Chem.) = *inert gas* (*b*) s.v. inert *a.* 1 c. (Cf. sense 1 a.)

1901 M. W. Travers *Exper. Study Gases* xi. 116 Mercury, which somewhat resembles the rare gases with regard to its low boiling-point and monatomic character, would be chemically inactive at 1000° C. **1937** *Discovery* Aug. 227/2 The separation of the 'rare gases' from the atmosphere. **1963** J. H. Pomeroy in H. H. Hyman *Noble-Gas Compounds* iii. 125, I.. suspect that the discovery of the rare-gas compounds has been greeted with particular enthusiasm by the producers of textbooks in chemistry, since it gives them.. a sort of windfall of unplanned obsolescence. **1972** *Nature* 8 Dec. 345/2 Radon (^{222}Rn)—a radioactive rare gas emanating essentially from large continental land areas.

6. a. Unusual in respect of some good quality; of uncommon excellence or merit; remarkably good or fine; †distinguished (quot. 1685).

1483 Caxton *Cato* 2 b, Therin they fonde many noble and rare bookes. **1570** *Satir. Poems Reform.* x. 140 Of quhais rair bewtie scho did sumpart farlie. **1594** Plat *Jewell-ho.* iii. 27 One of the rarest Mathematicians of our age. **1639** Fuller *Holy War* iii. xxv. (1840) 164 A more substantial tower was built, the rarest piece in that kind the world ever saw. **1685** Baxter *Paraphr. N.T.* Matt. x. 42 It is not only Charity to Preachers and rare Persons, but to the least Christians. **1779** Cowper *Yearly Distress* 57 A rarer man than you In pulpit none shall hear. **1818** Shelley *Rev. Islam* i. xxiii, A boat of rare device, which had no sail. **1874** Bancroft *Footpr. Time* i. 67 This rare nation knew how to adapt its governments to its needs.

b. *colloq.* Splendid, excellent, fine.

Distinguished from prec. merely as applied to more trivial objects or employed in less dignified context. Intermediate applications are not uncommon in the 17th c.

1596 Shaks. *Merch. V.* ii. ii. 116 Maister Bassanio, who indeede giues rare new Liuories. **1667** Dryden *Sir Martin Mar-All* v. iii, *Mill.* You and I will disguise too... *Mood.* That will be most rare. **1706** E. Ward *Wooden World Diss.* (1708) 59 He's a rare Fellow for giving a bad Captain a good Word. **1791** 'G. Gambado' *Ann. Horsem.* xviii. (1809) 140 My horse must have had a rare bit of bone in his back. **1812** *Sporting Mag.* XXXIX. 283 The prisoner said it would be a rare thing to get at that mare which was first favourite. **1878** Mrs. H. Wood *Pomeroy Abbey* I. 172 Guy will about die of it I expect. Rare fun if he does.

†**c.** Interjectionally in ***O rare!***

1596 Shaks. *1 Hen. IV,* i. ii. 72 Shall I? O rare! Ile be a braue Iudge. *a* **1688** Villiers *Rehearsal* iv. i, O rare! this is the most natural, refined fancy that ever I heard. **1761** Sterne *Tr. Shandy* VI. xxxvi, "*Evye!*" O rare! 'tis fine reasoning, Sir, indeed! **1786** Burns *Ordination* vii, Oh rare! to see our elbucks wheep.

d. *colloq.* in ironical use.

1600 Rowlands *Let. Humours Blood* i. 48 Vttring rare lyes to be admired at. **1712** Arbuthnot *John Bull* iii. x, Well, John, thou are got into rare company! One has a dumb devil [etc.]. **1789** Gouv. Morris in Sparks *Life & Writ.* (1832) I. 323 This is a rare situation, for which they must thank themselves. **1837** Mrs. Sherwood *Henry Milner* iii. v. 95 And do you mean always to go to bed at nine o'clock?.. If that a'n't rare.

e. *colloq.* as an intensive, with sbs. and adjs. (also ***rare and*** with adjs.).

1833 Ht. Martineau *Loom & Lugger* ii. vi. 121 They put me in a rare passion. **1848** Mrs. Gaskell *Mary Barton* ix. 49 We got a good supper, and grew rare and sleepy. **1877** Mrs. Hungerford *Phyllis* xxvii. (1884) 308 That's a rare good sign. **1879** Stevenson *Trav. Cevennes* 61, I was rare and hungry.

7. *absol.* or as *sb.* †**a.** A rare thing; a rarity. *Obs.*

1566 *Banquett of Dainties* A vj b, Of dainties these let me not fayle, with other rares among. **1611** T. Bastard *Paneg. Verses* in *Coryat's Crudities,* Put downe, put downe, Tom Coryate, Our latest rares.

b. What is rare.

1656 Earl Monm. tr. *Boccalini's Advts. fr. Parnass.* i. v. (1674) 8 Of all other things which the rest had mentioned of rare in the State of Venice, this was to be preferred. **1813** Scott *Trierm.* iii. xxxvii, That bower, the gazer to bewitch, Hath wondrous store of rare and rich.

†**8.** As *adv.* = rarely. *Obs.*$^{-1}$

1721 Ramsay *Content* 213 Rare she appears, unless on some fine day She grace a nuptial.

9. *Comb.,* as ***rare-featured, -painted, -qualitied, -shaped*** adjs.; ***rare-spring*** attrib. Also used advb. (mainly *poet.*) with adjs. or ppl. adjs. ***rare-bred, -coming, -composed, -dear, -feathered, -felt, -grown, -seen, -spoken, -veined.***

1877 *Coursing Calendar Autumn 1876* 327 Westeria.. was put out in a bad trial. She is a rare-bred one, being by Contango out of Joan-of-Arc. **1937** Blunden *Elegy* 90 Where the dogs.. regard The rare-coming stranger in the yard An excitement not to be missed. **1601** Marston *Jack Drums Entertainment* sig. A2^v, If he could.. distill the quintessence of heauen In rare composed Sceanes. **1876** G. M. Hopkins *Wreck of Deutschland* xxxv, in *Poems* (1967) 63 Let him [*sc.* our King].. be a crimson-cresseted east, More brightening her, rare-dear Britain, as his reign rolls. **1904** *Westm. Gaz.* 19 Nov. 9/2 The class for pied, albino, or rare-feathered British birds contains a pure yellow, pink-eyed, yellow-hammer. **1607** Wilkins *Mis. Enforced Marriage* F iv b, They are the moste rare featur'd.. rare qualitied.. gentlewoman. **1785** T. Dwight *Conquest of Canäan* iv. 97 A rare-felt joy inspir'd the friendless band. **1922** Blunden *Shepherd* 85 And rare-grown daisy in the meadow. **1818** Scott *Rob Roy* xi, O rare-painted portrait!.. Vandyke was a dauber to you. **1794** T. Dwight *Greenfield Hill* I. 18 The rare-seen felon startles every mind And fills each mouth with news. **1882** De Windt *Equator* 37 The Deli pony is a rare-shaped little animal.. with immense strength, and very fast. **1915** D. H. Lawrence *Rainbow* i. 8 A rare-spoken, almost surly man. **1641** Howell *Vote* in *Lett.* (1650) II. 142 No Pistolls or som rare-spring Carrabins. **1879** G. M. Hopkins *Duns Scotus's Oxford* in *Poems* (1967) 79 Of realty the rarest-veinèd unraveller.

rare (rɛə(r)), *a.*^{2} [Later form of rear *a.*^{1}] †**a.** Of eggs: Left soft in cooking. *Obs.* **b.** Of meat (now usu. of beef): Underdone. Also *Comb.*

In sense b, formerly often regarded as an Americanism, although it was current in many English dialects (cf. rear), and used by English writers in the first half of the 19th c.

a. 1655 Moufet & Bennet *Health's Improv.* 137 A rare Egg any way drest is lightest of Digestion, a hard Egg is most rebellious. *Ibid.,* Eggs.. being rare-roasted in embers.. make thickest and strongest blood. **1836** *Public Ledger* (Philadelphia) 19 Apr. 1/3 [Certain persons] in calling for boiled eggs, instead of ordering them to be done rare, order them to be '*boiled soft*'. **1856** *Knickerbocker* XLVII. 249 'Do you like your eggs done rare?' asked the good landlady.

b. **1784** in *Life Longfellow* (1891) II. xvii. 414 The lean should be quite rare, not so the fat. **1820** LAMB *Elia* Ser. I. *Christ's Hosp. 35 Yrs. Ago*, The same flesh, rotten-roasted or rare, on the Tuesdays. **1830** M. DONOVAN *Dom. Econ.* II. 289 The meat was in all cases a little rare at its centre. **1861** G. F. BERKELEY *Sportsm. W. Prairies* 26 The wood-cock and snipe..should be underdone or what the Americans call 'rare'. [**1890** LOWELL *Introd. Biglow Papers* Ser. II. in *Poems* II. 181 The earliest form of the word with us was, and the commoner now in the inland parts still is, so far as I can discover, *raredone*.] **1904** *N.Y. Sun* 6 Aug. 5 The waiter took his order for a sirloin rare. **1911** E. FERBER *Dawn O'Hara* ii. 20 I've devoured rare porterhouse and roast beef day after day for weeks. **1940** R. CHANDLER *Farewell, my Lovely* xxv. 186 Would you like your steak rare or medium, sir? **1977** *Times* 24 Aug. 14/8 A reader ordered a steak, rare, at a Yorkshire roadside café.

rare (rɛə(r)), *a.*[3] and *adv.*[2] *Obs.* exc. *dial.* [Var. of RATHE *a.*[1]: cf. RARE-RIPE.] Early.

1574 W. BOURNE *Regiment for Sea* iii. (1577) 12b, Sometime in the yeare you shall see the Moone rarer than at some other time, as this for example, from January to June you shall see the Moone within .24. houres after the chaunge. **1615** CHAPMAN *Odyss.* VI. 422 Rude mechanicals, that rare and late Work in the market-place. **1847** HALLIWELL, *Rare*,..early. *Devon.* **1880** in *W. Cornwall Gloss.*

rare, *v.* orig. *U.S.* and *dial.* [Var. of REAR *v.*[1]]

1. a. *intr.* = REAR *v.*[1] 15.

1833 *Sketches & Eccentricities D. Crockett* vii. 92 He just *rared* up upon his hind legs. **1898** H. S. CANFIELD *Maid of Frontier* 100 Break 'em with a curb an' they have an' fall back on you. **1938** [see JES, JES'].

b. colloq. ***to be raring to*** (*go*, etc.), to be extremely eager or fully ready to (do something). Also *transf.*

1909 E. BANKS *Mystery F. Farrington* iv. 13/2 They make me raring, tearing mad to look at 'em. **1927** F. N. HART *Bellamy Trial* i. 10 Both sides are rarin' to go, and they are not liable to touch their peremptory challenges [of jurymen]. **1935** WODEHOUSE *Luck of Bodkins* xv. 167 Keep it crisp, because I'm raring to go. **1957** A. MACNAB *Bulls of Iberia* viii. 79 The bull was a *toro de bandera*, the bravest of the brave,..and was 'rarin' to fight'. **1971** J. TYNDALL *Death in Lebanon* vii. 114 He's laid it on that the preacher makes some inflammatory remarks..so that the congregation..will be rarin' to go. **1979** *Church Times* 9 Feb. 9/1 We were at the starting-gate and raring to go.

2. *trans.* = REAR *v.*[1] 9.

1901 M. FRANKLIN *My Brilliant Career* v. 24 It was my duty to 'rare the poddies'. **1961** 'F. O'BRIEN' *Hard Life* ix. 67 Well, there's no doubt about it, we rare up strange characters in this country.

rare, obs. form of REAR, ROAR.

rarebit: see WELSH RABBIT.

†**raree-fine**, *a.* *Obs. rare*[−1]. [f. RAREE (see next) + FINE *a.*] ***raree-fine show*** = next.

1736 FIELDING *Pasquin* v. i, All the raree-fine shows exhibited to them in what they call entertainments.

raree-show (ˈrɛəriːʃəʊ). Also 7–8 rary-, 8 raræ-. ['This word is formed in imitation of the foreign way of pronouncing *rare show*' (Johnson).

It has also been suggested that *raree* may represent *rarity* (cf. G. *raritäten-kasten*), but Johnson's statement is prob. correct; the early exhibitors of peep-shows appear to have been usually Savoyards, from whom the form was no doubt adopted.]

1. A show contained or carried about in a box; a peep-show.

[*c* **1681** (*title*) Raree Show, or the true Protestant Procession.] *a* **1704** T. BROWN *Sat. French King* Wks. 1730 I. 61 May Savoy with thee hither pack And carry a raree-show upon his back. **1730** FIELDING *Tom Thumb* III. iv, Why dost thou speak Like men who carry raree-shows about? **1822** SCOTT *Peveril* xli, Fitter..by his size and appearance, for the inside of a raree-show, than the mysteries of a plot. **1849** E. FITZGERALD *Lett.* (1889) I. 198 A showman whom one gives a shilling to once a month to see his raree-show.

2. *transf.* **a.** A show or spectacle of any kind.

1684 *Hist. Acct. Gt. Frost* 22 Thames becomes a kind of raree-show. **1719** RAMSAY *To Arbuckle* 66 [A] poet, or an airy beau, Or ony twa-legg'd rary-show. **1747** CHESTERF. *Lett.* cxxx. (1792) I. 349 Those who only mind the raree-shews of the places which they go through, such as steeples, clocks, town-houses, etc. **1824** J. SYMMONS tr. *Æschylus' Agam.* 75, I long have mark'd Life's raree-show before me in a mirror. **1883** *Chr. World* 22 Nov. 813 He is averse to taking part in such a raree-show upon the Sunday. **1931** BLUNDEN *To Themis* 22 Colours flying, drums drubbing, boys run miles for the raree-show. **1955** W. GADDIS *Recognitions* II. vii. 634 He'll show you... He'll put up a real maudlin raree-show for you. **1971** *Daily Tel.* 8 Nov. 9/1 Religious people today protest against 'Jesus Christ Superstar' as a vulgar raree-show cashing in on an adolescent fad.

b. Spectacular display.

1809 SCOTT 16 July in *Fam. Lett.* (1894) I. v. 137 Those immense London Stages fit only for pantomime and raree-show.

3. *attrib.*, as ***raree-show-box***, ***-man*** (hence ***-manism***), ***-performance***.

1737 *London Mag.* June 324/2, I presume that he [*sc.* Punch] will not be tolerated, either upon the Stage, or even in a *Raree-shew Box. **1765** STERNE *Tr. Shandy* VIII. xxiv, Thou didst look into it with as much innocency of heart, as ever child look'd into a raree-shew-box. **1806–7** J. BERESFORD *Miseries Hum. Life* (1826) xx. ii, Two men at two of the holes of a raree-show-box. *a* **1700** B. E. *Dict. Cant. Crew*, *Raree-show-men. **1756** C. LUCAS *Ess. Waters* III. 329 A rary-shewman..always takes care to tell he had the honor [etc.]. **1864** C. KNIGHT *Passages Work. Life* II. xiii. 269 The raree-showman is no more. **1812** S. JONES *Baker's Biographia Dramatica* (rev. ed.) III. 306 A frivolous *raree-show performance. **1842** MOORE *Mem.* (1856) VII. 311 S——l, too, upon Romanism Will sport his *raree-showmanism.

rarefaction (rɛərɪ-, rærɪˈfækʃən). Also 7–8 rari-. [Noun of action f. L. *rārēfacĕre*: see RAREFY *v.* Cf. F. *raréfaction* (14th c., Oresme).] The action of rarefying, or process of being rarefied; diminution of density. (Now chiefly of the air or gases, or *Path.* of bones.)

1603 HOLLAND *Plutarch's Mor.* 1318 To clense and purifie the aire by this rarefaction and subtilization. **1626** BACON *Sylva* §30 In Gunpowder, the Force of it hath been ascribed to Rarefaction of the Earthy Substance into Flame. **1707** FLOYER *Physic. Pulse-Watch* 69 In those Persons who have the best Tempers, the Blood and Spirits have a moderate Rarifaction. **1869** E. A. PARKES *Pract. Hygiene* (ed. 3) 466 In ascending mountains there is rarefaction, i.e. lessened pressure of air. **1898** *Allbutt's Syst. Med.* V. 605 In others there is..thickening or rarefaction of skull bones.

fig. **1672** MARVELL *Reh. Transp.* (1675) II. 249 Lest they [laws]..lose in strength what they gain by extension and rarefaction. **1873** SYMONDS *Grk. Poets* vi. 171 Arriving at monotheism by a process of rarefaction and purification.

b. With *a* and *pl.* An instance of this.

1834 MRS. SOMERVILLE *Connex. Phys. Sc.* xvi. (1849) 144 A regular series of condensations and rarefactions. **1873** W. LEES *Acoustics* I. i. 10 An undulation or wave..consists of two parts—a condensation and a rarefaction.

rarefactional (rɛərɪˈfækʃənəl), *a.* [f. RAREFACTION + -AL.] Characterized by rarefaction.

1909 in *Cent. Dict.* Suppl. **1971** I. G. GASS et al. *Understanding Earth* xix. 272/1 On either side of the fault, the first waves to leave the source are compressions in the direction of motion and rarefactions away from it. This gives the symmetrical distribution of compressional and rarefactional first motions shown. **1972** *Sci. Amer.* May 58/3 After an earthquake one finds that the seismological stations that have received the first waves can be assigned to one of four geographic quadrants. In two of the quadrants, lying opposite each other, the first waves are compressional; in the other two quadrants the first waves are rarefactional.

rareˈfactive, *a.* and *sb.* [ad. L. type **rārēfactīvus*, f. *rārēfacere* to RAREFY. Cf. F. *raréfactif* (16th c.).]

A. *adj.* Having the quality of rarefying; characterized by rarefaction. (In recent use only *Path.* of diseases of bones.)

1656 [? J. SERGEANT] tr. *T. White's Peripat. Inst.* v. xiv. 313 'Tis plain..that an Intelligence, by that one rarefactive Vertue, can operate whatever is to be done by Bodies. **1664** POWER *Exp. Philos.* II. 114 Hence it appears, that Ayr, besides its gravity, has a nobler rarefactive faculty. **1889** *Lancet* 6 Apr. 684/2 A rarefactive disease of the whole bone. **1899** *Allbutt's Syst. Med.* VI. 551 The microscopic appearances are those of a rarefactive osteitis.

†**B.** *sb.* (See quot.) *Obs. rare*[−0].

1727–41 CHAMBERS *Cycl.*, *Rarefactives*,..in medicine, remedies which open and inlarge the pores of the skin.

†**rarefiable**, *a.* *Obs. rare.* In 7 rarifi-, -fy-. [f. RAREFY *v.* + -ABLE; cf. F. *raréfiable*.] Capable of being rarefied.

1656 [? J. SERGEANT] tr. *T. White's Peripat. Inst.* 57 Any dense body that is rarifiable. **1680** BOYLE *Exper. Chem. Princ.* II. 64 That so inconsiderable a proportion of that liquor, should be rarifiable into so much ardent spirit.

rarefiˈcation. *rare.* Also 7–8 rari-. [Noun of action, after L. types, from RAREFY *v.*] = RAREFACTION.

1616 in BULLOKAR *Eng. Expos.* **1727** BRADLEY *Fam. Dict.* s.v. *Bee hive*, Its Whiteness is increased by this Rarification. **1794** SULLIVAN *View Nat.* I. 209 It carries the point of greater rarefication on the same side of the equator. **1893** SIR J. C. BROWNE in *Times* 3 Oct. 9/5 Rarefication in quality of two orders of impressions.

ˈrarefied, *ppl. a.* [f. RAREFY *v.* + -ED.] That is made less dense. (Chiefly of air). Also *transf.* and *fig.*

1634 PEACHAM *Gentl. Exerc.* III. 140 The higher parts of the ayre, which..are more rarified and pure then the neather. **1665** GLANVILL *Scepsis Sci.* i. 17 That a Bullet should be moved by the rarified fire. **1785** FRANKLIN *Lett.* Wks. 1840 VI. 506, I need not explain to you,..what is meant by rarefied air. **1855** PRESCOTT *Philip II*, II. iv. (1857) 243 The brisk and rarefied atmosphere of Madrid proved favourable to Charles's health. **1899** *Allbutt's Syst. Med.* VIII. 482 Mast-cells closely packed in columns in a rarefied tissue. **1961** *Blackw. Mag.* Oct. 290/1 From the light of common day into the rarified atmosphere of the late eighteenth century. **1977** G. MICHANOWSKY *Once & Future Star* iv. 33 In the rarefied world of cuneiform scholarship, it is known as BM—86378. **1978** N. MOSS *What's the Difference?* (ed. 2) 93 *Professor, n*—a less rarefied post than at a British university, since there are usually several professors to a department.

ˈrarefier. *rare.* [f. RAREFY *v.* + -ER[1].] That which rarefies.

1686 GOAD *Celest. Bodies* I. ii. 6 Such infinite variety of Rarefiers and Condensers. **1798** HUTTON *Course Math.* (1807) II. 240 The air-pump, or rarefier.

rarefy (ˈrɛərɪfaɪ, ˈrærɪfaɪ), *v.* Also 5–6 rere-, 5–9 rari-, 7 reri-. [a. F. *raréfier* (14th c., Oresme), or ad. L. *rārēfacĕre* (Lucretius), f. *rār-us* RARE *a.*[1] + *facĕre* to make; the form (for *rārifacĕre*) is perh. on analogy of *ārefacĕre*).

The pron. now usual in England has the vowel of *rare* adj.; the older usage, with the short vowel, is still favoured in America and Scotland (not *dial.*); cf. RARITY.]

1. *trans.* To make rare or thin, esp. by expansion; to lessen the density or solidity of (a substance, now usually air or, in *Path.*, bone).

1398 TREVISA *Barth. De P.R.* III. xv. (Tollem. MS.), To hot sunne þat rarefieþ [**1535** rerefieth] and openeþ þe pores ouer mesure. **1477** NORTON *Ord. Alch.* v. in Ashm. *Theat. Chem. Brit.* (1652) 77 Water rarified becomes Ayre againe. **1523** SKELTON *Garl. Laurel* 651 The clowdis gan to clere, the myst was rarifiid. **1659** W. CHAMBERLAYN *Pharonnida* III. iv. (1820) 67 Whilst choice music rarifies the air. **1677** W. HARRIS tr. *Lemery's Course Chym.* I. xiv. (1686) 347 A Coral rarefied and opened by the Spirit of Vinegar. **1756** C. LUCAS *Ess. Waters* I. 44 Higher degrees of heat rarefy and expand water. **1871** TYNDALL *Fragm. Sci.* (1879) I. v. 135 The hot wire rarefied the air in contact with it. **1897** *Allbutt's Syst. Med.* III. 149 The osseous structure..is absorbed, rarefied and softened.

absol. **1697** DRYDEN *Virg. Georg.* I. 566 As Rains condense, and Sunshine rarifies.

2. *fig.* **a.** To make less gross or material, to refine, to purify.

1599 B. JONSON *Ev. man out of Hum.* II. iii, You see..how their wits are refinde and rarefi'd! **1626** T. H. *Caussin's Holy Crt.* 24 Raryfying the most grosse thoughts, as the sun-beames doth the vapours of the earth. **1720** WELTON *Suffer. Son of God* I. xi. 282 It is Prayer that..rarifies his Soul into an Essence of Divine Love. **1818** HAZLITT *Char. Shaks.* (1838) 142 Love is a gentle flame that rarefies and expands her whole being.

b. To make (an idea) subtle.

a **1699** STILLINGFL. *Serm.* (R.), Plain truths lose much of their weight when they are rarify'd into subtilities. **1875** JOWETT *Plato* (ed. 2) IV. 149 In some parts of the argument the abstraction is so rarefied as to become..fallacious.

†**c.** To palliate, extenuate (a fault). *Obs.*

1622 H. SYDENHAM *Serm. Sol. Occ.* (1637) 222 There is something in this way, which may rarifie or extenuate an offence, nullify it cannot.

d. *intr.* To discourse exaltedly. *nonce-use.*

1928 BLUNDEN *Undertones of War* iv. 44, I remember how Limbery-Buse and myself chirped and rarefied over some crayfish and a great cake.

†**3.** To reduce the number of (trees); to thin (a wood). *Obs. rare.*

1650 FULLER *Pisgah* 411 Cedars were so rarified in Libanus, that modern travellers saw but four and twenty in their passage over this mountain. *a* **1661** —— *Worthies* (1840) III. 244 There needed no iron mills to rarify the woods of this county.

4. *intr.* To become less dense; to be thinned. *rare.*

a **1658** CLEVELAND *Committee* 34 Bodies at the Resurrection are On Wing, just rarifying into Air. **1750** tr. *Leonardus' Mirr. Stones* 132 When it is kindled by fire, it rarifies, and is violently dilated. **1847** DE QUINCEY *Span. Mil. Nun* Wks. 1862 III. 57 Like the mist sometimes rarefying into sunny gauze.

Hence **ˈrarefying** *vbl. sb.* and *ppl. a.*

1648 HAMMOND *Serm.* iii. Wks. 1683 IV. 487 This rarifying power of flames and judgments. *a* **1660** *Ibid.* xxiv. 641 This rarifying and purifying of the fancy. **1898** *Allbutt's Syst. Med.* V. 9 The common atrophic rarefying emphysema.

rarely (ˈrɛəlɪ), *adv.* [f. RARE *a.*[2] + -LY[2].]

†**1. a.** Thinly, scantily. *Obs. rare.*

1523 CROMWELL *Sp.* in Merriman *Life & Lett.* (1902) I. 40 How should we be Able to possede the large Cuntreye of Fraunce which haue our owne Realme so meruelous rarely storyd of inhabytauntes and hable men.

†**b.** In a wide-set or open manner. *Obs.*

a **1547** SURREY *Æneid* IV. (1557) E i, The hayes so rarely knit [L. *retia rara*]. **1622** SIR R. HAWKINS *Voy. S. Sea* (1847) 196 Shee..being rarely built, and utterly without fights or defences..wee cleered her decks in a moment.

2. Seldom, infrequently, in few instances.

Formerly compared *rarelier*, *rareliest* (quots. 1640, 1656).

1552 HULOET, Rarelye, *raro.* **1570** in LEVINS *Manip.* *a* **1618** RALEIGH *Rem.* (1664) 121 Benefits are sometimes acknowledged, rarely requited. **1640** BOLTON *Comf. Affl. Consc.* (ed. 3) Ep. Ded., They are rarelier, and hardlier wrought upon by the Word. **1656** EARL MONM. tr. *Boccalini's Advts. fr. Parnass.* I. xxxix. (1674) 51 Those precious Stones are most esteemed of, which are rareliest found. **1712** BUDGELL *Spect.* No. 277 ¶6 She was not Talkative, a Quality very rarely to be met with in the rest of her Country-women. **1756** C. LUCAS *Ess. Waters* II. 3 They rarely, if ever..are perfectly frozen. **1861** FLO. NIGHTINGALE *Nursing* 7 The windows are rarely or never opened. **1880** GEIKIE *Phys. Geog.* ii. §11. 85 How rarely does the air seem to be perfectly motionless!

b. With *ever* added.

1694 W. WOTTON *Anc. & Mod. Learn.* (1697) 403 The most verbose Mathematicians have rarely ever said any thing for Saying sake. **1709** MRS. MANLEY *Secret Mem.* II. 167 They..rarely ever examin into the true Motive. **1728** RAMSAY *Health* 355 Who rarely ever cures, but often kills. **1857** [see EVER *adv.* 7c].

c. ***rarely or ever***, by confusion of 'rarely if ever' and 'rarely or never'. Cf. EVER *adv.* 7b.

1768 *Woman of Honor* I. 139 But those schemes..rarely or ever answer the end. **1811** SYD. SMITH *Wks.* (1850) 200/1 The contest would rarely or ever take place, where the friends of the Establishment were not numerous enough.

d. ***it is rarely that*** = It is rare or seldom that. (See RARE *a.* 5b.)

1753 CHAMBERS *Cycl. Supp.* s.v. *Louse*, He observes, that it is rarely that flies are found infested with them. **1825** G. N. COLLINGWOOD in *Parr's Wks.* (1828) I. 505 It was rarely indeed that any such request was denied.

3. Unusually or remarkably well; finely, splendidly, beautifully. (Freq. in 17th c.)

1590 SHAKS. *Mids. N.* I. ii. 31, I could play Ercles rarely. **1602** MARSTON *Antonio's Rev.* v. i, I could belch rarely, for I am all winde. **1667** DRYDEN *Sir Martin Mar-all* v. i, I'll instruct him most rarely, he shall never be found out. **1703** MAUNDRELL *Journ. Jerus.* (1732) 136 A stately Architrave, and Cornish rarely carv'd. **1786** BURNS *Dream* x, Down Pleasure's stream, wi' swelling sails I'm tauld ye're driving rarely. **1860** GEO. ELIOT *Mill on Floss* III. iii, You can write rarely now, after all your schooling, I should think.

4. In an unusual degree; exceptionally.

1606 SHAKS. *Ant. & Cl.* v. ii. 158 Villain, Dog. O rarely base. **1661** BOYLE *Spring of Air* II. v. (1682) 56 It will agree rarely-well with the Hypothesis. **1681** R. KNOX *Hist. Ceylon* 15 It is rarely sweet and pleasing to the pallat. **1853** KANE *Grinnell Exp.* xxii. (1856) 174, I was one of the oarsmen, and sweated rarely. **1882** JESSIE FOTHERGILL *Kith & K.* xxx, I believed him to be rarely good and wise.

b. With (ppl.) adjs. used attributively.

1668 CULPEPPER & COLE *Barthol. Anat.* I. vii. 16 The rarely learned Marcus Aurelius Severinus. **1860** G. H. K. in *Vac. Tour* 117 Bits of rarely-scented shrub here and there. **1866** *Macm. Mag.* Apr. 521 Investigated by.. That rarely-gifted Scholar.

rareness (ˈrɛənɪs). [f. RARE *a.*[1] + -NESS.] The fact or quality of being rare.

†**1.** Thinness; fewness, scantiness. *Obs. rare.*

1588 WHITEHORNE tr. *Machiavel's Arte of Warre* III. 43 The Hastati.. retyred by a litle, and litle, by the rarenes of thorders betweene the Principi. **1610** J. FORBES *Cert. Rec.* x. (1846) 390 The said Assemblie.. having weighed the rareness of their own number [etc.].

2. = RARITY 2.

1614 W. B. *Philosopher's Banquet* (ed. 2) 45 The lightnesse and rarenesse of the substance. **1714** HALLEY in *Phil. Trans.* XXIX. 160 The extream Cold and Rareness of the Air in those upper Regions. **1857** R. TOMES *Amer. in Japan* xii. 287 The not infrequent rains.. give an occasional humidity and rareness to the atmosphere.

3. = RARITY 3.

1551 R. ROBINSON tr. *More's Utopia* II. vi. (1895) 174 Yf that the folly of men hadde not sette it in hygher estymacyon for the rarenes sake. **1620** VENNER *Via Recta* iv. 74 It may be.. doubted, whether it be so greatly esteemed for the rarenesse of it, or for the goodnesse of meate. **1721** R. KEITH tr. *à Kempis' Solil. Soul* xviii. 262, I rather accuse the Rareness than the Frequency of thy Approaches. **1884** *Contemp. Rev.* July 63 A noteworthy fact is the comparative rareness of ruined villages of the age of bronze.

4. = RARITY 4.

1577 B. GOOGE *Heresbach's Husb.* (1586) 167 This kind of Foule, both for their rareness, and also the greatnesse of their body, is at this daie kept in great flockes. **1575–85** ABP. SANDYS *Serm.* xviii. (1585) 308 Their prerogatiues.. were manifolde, and for the preciousnesse and rarenesse of them most wonderful. **1683** EVELYN *Mem.* (1857) II. 185 The greatest master both for invention and rareness of work, that the world ever had. **1866** GEO. ELIOT *F. Holt* xlv, That childhood to which common things have rareness.

ˈrare-ripe, *a.* and *sb. dial.* and *U.S.* [f. RARE *a.*[3] + RIPE.] **a.** *adj.* Rathe-ripe. **b.** *sb.* An early fruit or vegetable. Also *transf.* **c.** *attrib.* Of the colour of a peach called the *rare-ripe*.

1799 WASHINGTON *Writ.* (1893) XIV. 231 All that part.. is to be planted with rare-ripe corn. **1799** S. FREEMAN *Town Officer* 162 Onions for shipment in bunches shall weigh as follows, viz. rare-ripes two and a half lbs. **1860** O. W. HOLMES *Elsie V.* (1861) 75 Brunette, with a rareripe flush in her cheeks. **1890** LOWELL *Poems* II. 181 President Lincoln said of a precocious boy that 'he was a rareripe'.

Rarey (ˈrɛərɪ). The name of the horse-breaker J. S. *Rarey*, used *attrib.* and in the possessive to denote methods or equipment employed by him for the taming of horses. Hence **ˈRareying**, the action or fact of breaking in a horse by Rarey's methods. Cf. RAREYFY *v.*

[**1856** J. S. RAREY (*title*) The modern art of taming wild horses]. **1875** S. SIDNEY *Bk. of Horse* xxvi. 562 The Rarey principle consists in teaching the colt as much as possible without putting him in any pain, and without frightening him by any strange sight or sound. *Ibid.* 565 (*caption*) Horse, with Rarey fittings. *Ibid.* 567 The application of the Rarey straps in the following manner affords a better chance of success than the ordinary exhausting plans of old-fashioned colt-breakers and of circus-riders. **1896** M. H. HAYES *Illustr. Horse-Breaking* (ed. 2) iv. 124 Having 'picked up' the foot, we may secure it.. by Rarey's leg-strap, which is about 3 ft. long, and is furnished at one end with a buckle, below which a leather 'keeper' is placed on both sides. *Ibid.* 175 Mr. Norton Smith adopted.. a modification of Rarey's system. **1905** S. GALVAYNE *20th Century Bk. on Horse* 100 (*heading*) The Rarey system. *Ibid.*, It may not be uninteresting to the reader to briefly explain the method of 'Rareying' a horse. **1911** *Encycl. Brit.* XIII. 725/1 The method of subduing a colt by 'galvayning' is as good as any. It is a more humane system than 'rareying', which overcame by exhaustion under circumstances which were not fruitful of permanent results. **1942** Rareying [see GALVAYNE]. **1979** *Jrnl. R. Soc. Arts* Oct. 724/2 The 'Rarey' method of throwing a horse is explained.

Rareyfy (ˈrɛərɪfaɪ), *v. Obs.* Also rari-. [f. *Rarey* (see prec.) + -FY. Prob. suggested by RAREFY.] *trans.* To tame (animals, *esp.* horses) by the method of J. S. Rarey, the horse-breaker.

1858 O. W. HOLMES *Aut. Breakf.-t.* (1883) 198 If the Houyhnhnms.. send a man-tamer to Rareyfy me. **1892** *Sat. Rev.* 14 May 566/2 A handsome bay mare, which she has succeeded in 'Rarey-fying'.

†**raˈriety.** *Obs.* [f. RARE *a.*[1], on analogy of *variety*. Pretty frequent in early part of 17th c.] = RARITY (chiefly in senses 4 and 5).

1596 *Edward III*, II. ii. sig. D 4 The register of all rarieties Since Letherne Adam, till this youngest howre. **1611** HEYWOOD *Gold. Age* III. Wks. 1874 III. 52 Let all raryeties Showre downe from heauen a lardges. **1636** —— *Challenge for Beauty* IV. Wks. V. 52 If any clyme Could yeeld rarietie to equall ours. **1659** FULLER *App. Inj. Innoc.* I. 44 Give me leave to record the first Essays of this Pious Prince, especially they being unprinted rarieties.

rarifaction, -fy: see RAREFACTION, RAREFY.

rarin, obs. form (inf.) of ROAR *v.*

raring: see RARE *v.* 1 b.

‖**rariora** (rɛərɪˈɔərə, rærɪ-), *sb. pl.* [L., neut. pl. comparative of *rārus* rare.] Rare books. Cf. RARE *a.*[1] 5 e.

1863 *Macm. Mag.* VIII. 36 (*heading*) *Rariora* of old poetry. **1908** *Daily Report* 26 Aug. 8/3 Such books fetch far better prices in London and Paris than in New York, where the demand for such *rariora* is small. **1932** J. BUCHAN *Gap in Curtain* iv. 189 There was a fine set of Donne, two of the Shakespeare folios,.. besides a quantity of devotional and political *rariora*. **1964** D. COX in D. Daiches *Idea of New University* ix. 162 Where sufficient copies of not only European but of American *rariora* have been unavailable, microfacsimile has been called in.

ˈrarish, *a.* Also rare-ish. [f. RARE *a.*[1]] Somewhat rare.

1844 TUPPER *Heart* iv. 35 These instances are rarish too. **1875** BROWNING *Inn Album* III. 92 Would.. I winged were.. And so could straightway soar.. Back to my nest where broods whom I love best—The parson o'er his parish—garish—rarish—. **1959** N. MARSH *False Scent* (1960) i. 19 It's rare-ish. The frame's contemporary. I'm afraid it's twelve guineas.

‖**rarissima** (rɛəˈrɪsɪmə, raˈrɪ-), *sb. pl.* [L., neut. pl. superlative of *rārus* rare.] Extremely rare books. Also **raˈrissime** *a.* [lit. 'very rarely (*sc.* found)'], extremely rare.

1903 A. BENNETT *Truth about Author* iv. 56, I possessed a *rarissime* illustrated copy of *Manon Lescaut*. **1952** *Times Lit. Suppl.* 14 Nov. 752/3 The.. books.. of which Mr. Wing has been able to locate only a single copy.. are not as *rarissime* as one would infer. **1972** *Ibid.* 29 Sept. 1173/3 A few of the important *rarissima*, like Fust and Schoeffer's *Canon Missae* of 1458.

†**ˈraritive,** *a. nonce-wd.* [Irreg. f. RARE *a.*] Indicating rareness of occurrence.

1668 WILKINS *Real Char.* III. vii. 342 The opposite to each of these, viz. Desinative and Raritive [words].

rarity (ˈrɛərɪtɪ, ˈrærɪtɪ). Also 6–7 -itie, 7 -ietie, -iety, -yet-. [ad. L. *rāritās*, f. *rārus* RARE: see -ITY. Cf. F. *rareté* (15th c.), †*rarité* (16th c.). On the pron. see note to RAREFY.]

†**1. a.** Of a number of things or persons: The fact of being set at wide intervals. *Obs. rare.*

1598 BARRET *Theor. Warres* III. ii. 78 So will it be of no force to fight, by reason of their raritie & their standing.

†**b.** Of the pulse: Infrequency. *Obs. rare.*

1590 BARROUGH *Meth. Physick* 238 The pulses do keepe their naturall slownesse and raritie.

2. Of substances (now chiefly of air): Thinness of composition or texture. (Opposed to *density*.)

1644 H. HAMMOND *Pract. Catech.* v. iv. (1847) 335 Bodies.. spiritualized into a high agility, rarity, clarity. **1684** tr. *Bonet's Merc. Compit.* I. 8 Falling of the Hair, caused by rarity of the skin. **1794** G. ADAMS *Nat. & Exp. Philos.* II. xxi. 404 Though the transparency of bodies were explicable on the supposition of infinite strength and infinite rarity. **1834** MRS. SOMERVILLE *Connex. Phys. Sc.* §xvii. (1849) 164 The air, notwithstanding its rarity, is capable of transmitting its undulations. **1887** R. L. STEVENSON *Merry Men* v. ii. 224 An atmosphere of more than usual rarity.

3. Relative fewness in number; the fact of occurring seldom or in few instances.

1560–1 *First Bk. Discipl.* in Knox *Wks.* (1846) II. 194 The cheiffest remedy.. in all this raritie of trew ministeris, is fervent prayer unto God. **1604** R. CAWDREY *Table Alph.*, *Raritie*, fewnesse, scarseness. **1712** ADDISON *Spect.* No. 477 ¶ 1, I am so far from being fond of any particular one, by reason of its Rarity [etc.]. **1830** D'ISRAELI *Chas. I*, III. xi. 243 These libels, which enter into our national history, are of the greatest rarity. **1856** STANLEY *Sinai & Pal.* vii. (1858) 287 Confined to rare and remote occasions, the more remarkable from their very rarity.

4. Unusual or exceptional character, esp. in respect of excellence.

1601 R. CHESTER in *Shaks. Cent. Praise* 43 A Poeme enterlaced with much varietie and raritie. **1695** W. W. *New Lt. Chirurg. Put out* 30 His Method of Cure. Which hath several Pieces of Rarity in it. **1744** HARRIS *Three Treat.* I. (1765) 270 Some Sample of a Philosophy, which, from its Rarity perhaps, may possibly furnish some Amusement. **1873** SYMONDS *Grk. Poets* v. 130 Even Archilochus seems commonplace when compared with Sappho's exquisite rarity of phrase.

5. A rare or uncommon thing, or occurrence.

1592 DEE *Compend. Rehears.* (Chetham Soc.) 30 Of other rarities.. I will not make here any further rehearsall. **1635–56** COWLEY *Davideis* I. Note 54 But this was a Raritie; for Mallows are too soft to be proper for that use. **1673** RAY *Journ. Low C.* 27 A Museum well stored with natural and artificial Rarities. **1712–3** SWIFT *Jrnl. to Stella* lxi, It was a fine day, which is a rarity with us. **1796** H. HUNTER tr. *St.-Pierre's Stud. Nat.* (1799) II. 172 It had become such a rarity in his time as hardly any where to be seen. **1821** BYRON *Juan* IV. cxv, The virtues, even.. Charity, Are saving—vice spares nothing for a rarity. **1869** FREEMAN *Norm. Conq.* (1876) III. xii. 232 Milk was the chief diet of the people: bread was a rarity.

6. *Comb.*, as *rarity value*.

1962 *Listener* 30 Aug. 329/1 Shots.. came across with a breezy freshness that is only partly explained by their rarity value on television. **1978** P. MCCUTCHAN *Blackmail North* xiii. 138 The cave is *under* a layer of schist... Because of the rarity value the geologists play it down and hope to keep the tourists away.

Rarotongan (rærəˈtɒŋən), *sb.* and *a.* [f. *Rarotonga*, the name of the largest of the Cook Islands in the South Pacific + -AN.] **A.** *sb.* **a.** A native or inhabitant of Rarotonga. **b.** The language of Rarotonga: Cook Islands Maori, a member of the Polynesian group. **B.** *adj.* Of or pertaining to Rarotonga or its language.

1842 M. RUSSELL *Polynesia* vi. 226 The Rarotongans were a most ferocious class of men. **1851** G. BROWNE *Let.* 8 July in A. Buzacott *Mission Life Islands of Pacific* (1866) xiii. 188 It was resolved to request Miss Buzacott to accept.. a copy of the Bible in Rarotongan and English. **1854** A. BUZACOTT *Rarotongan & Eng. Gram.* 2/2 The Rarotongan alphabet has five soft letters. **1866** —— *Mission Life Islands of Pacific* xiv. 198 It is scarcely credible how strange it was to Mr. Buzacott to preach.. in the English language.. his mind being prone to think according to the habits and ideas of the Rarotongans. **1897** *Jrnl. Polynesian Soc.* VI. 10 The word *akono*.. appears from its use in the Rarotongan scriptures, to be.. akin to 'appointed'. **1910** F. W. CHRISTIAN *Eastern Pacific Lands* 193 The history of the Christianizing.. and progress of these Rarotongan Maori is the brightest chapter in the history of the South Seas. **1947** *Jrnl. Polynesian Soc.* LVI. 197, I wish to acknowledge assistance given to me by.. other Rarotongans. *Ibid.* 215 The manuscript.. requires translation into modern Rarotongan. **1966** J. E. BUSE in C. E. Bazell *In Memory of J.R. Firth* 52 Rarotongan Maori is spoken on the island of Rarotonga in the Southern Cooks. **1977** *Times* 2 Dec. 19/2 Rarotongans are almost wholly dependent on inflation-prone imported tinned goods.

rary-show, obs. f. RAREE-SHOW.

‖**ras** (rɑːs). [a. Amharic *rās* head, chief, from Arab.: cf. REIS[2], RAIS.] **1.** The title of a leading citizen. **a.** An Ethiopian king, prince, or feudal lord.

1682 tr. *H. Ludolf's New Hist. Ethiopia* II. xii. 213 To these succeeded another Chief Officer whom the Ethiopians call Ras, from the Arabic word which signifies a Head. **1710** B. TELLEZ *Trav. Jesuits in Ethiopia* x. 54 They constituted another call'd Raz, which signifies Head; because he who has that Employment is next the Emperor, Head of all the great Men in the Empire. **1735** JOHNSON tr. *Lobo & Le Grand's Voy. to Abyssinia* 262 There is now a Generalissimo established under the title of Ras, or Chief. [**1759** —— *Rasselas* i. 2 Rasselas was the fourth son of the mighty emperour, in whose dominions the Father of waters begins his course.] **1833** *Penny Cycl.* I. 58/1 Mr. Salt saw.. the Ras's wife. **1904** S. WALPOLE *Hist. Twenty-Five Yrs.* II. xi. 269 Practically, the power was in the hands of several ras, or chiefs—of whom Ras Ali was the foremost—who carried on a turbulent warfare among themselves. **1921** *Glasgow Herald* 14 Sept. 6/3 Most of the power lies in the hands of the important 'Rases', who correspond with the Dukes of mediæval Europe, and although nominally members of a vague State Council, are to a large extent independent rulers, with governors and chiefs in practically feudal subordination to them. **1926** *Ibid.* 27 Apr. 7 Mr Rey said that when he arrived in the capital of Abyssinia, Adis Ababa,.. he was most kindly received by the Empress and by the Regent, Ras Tafari, who was much interested in the expedition. The Ras not only gave the necessary permits, without which no one could move in Abyssinia, but supplied also some rifles for Mr Rey's men. *Ibid.*, He had an extraordinary welcome from the Governor, Ras Hailu, who was the last of the hereditary Provincial Governors in Abyssinia. The Ras exercised a feudal despotism in his government, and he maintained the old time hospitality. **1936** E. WAUGH *Waugh in Abyssinia* i. 38 The rases and officials copied the Emperor.

b. = REIS[2], RAIS 2.

1935 *Words* May 7/1 Legionaire Aurelius Philinus of ancient Palmyra set up in 251 A.D. an honorary statue to Septimius Hairan, illustrious senator and head man (*ras*) of Tadmor (Palmyra) accompanied by a bilingual inscription in Semitic and Greek.

2. *transf.* An Italian Fascist leader; a petty despot.

1923 *Glasgow Herald* 16 Oct. 6/4 The strength of the materialist group is to be found in the 'rases' or 'bosses' who have found in the revolution an excellent opportunity to establish themselves as the petty tyrants of their town or district. **1924** *Ibid.* 27 June 8/4 It [*sc.* a declaration] will compel the 'rases' and the physical force party generally to abandon their methods or to resist Mussolini's authority in the open. **1967** C. SETON-WATSON *Italy from Liberalism to Fascism* xiii. 594 The local fascist bosses were commonly known as *ras*, a title borrowed from the feudal nobility of Ethiopia. *Ibid.*, Mussolini hit back.., condemning the parochialism of the *ras* and the degeneration of Emilian fascism into the defence of sordid private interests. **1973** P. A. ALLUM *Politics & Society in Post-War Naples* ix. 301 The leadership of the party has been taken over by a solid conservative block.. that has as solid supporters that poor class of bosses (*ras*) of the various provincial centres. **1975** *Times Lit. Suppl.* 11 July 783/3 A biography of Roberto Farinacci, arguably the toughest and unquestionably the most uncouth of the Fascist 'ras'.

ras, obs. f. RACE *sb.*[1], RAISE *v.*, obs. pa. t. RISE.

ras, var. RASA[1], [2].

‖**rasa**[1] (ˈrasa). Also **ras.** [a. Skr. *rasa* juice; essence, character; sentiment.] Essence, character, sentiment.

1799 F. WILFORD in *Asiatick Researches* VI. 503 The Greeks supposed that mount Parnassus was the favorite abode of the Muses. The Hindus have not limited their residence to any particular spot... They are called Rasa in Sanscrit, in which language this word signifies juice in general, but is more particularly understood as the honied juice of flowers: it implies also any thing which we particularly delight in. *Ibid.* 505 The nine Rasas are represented as beautiful damsels. **1828** H. H. WILSON in *Ibid.* XVI. 118 The Bhakti of the followers of this division of the Hindu faith is supposed to comprehend five Rasas or Ratis, tastes or passions. **1926** in P. Hartog *On Relation of Poetry to Verse* 6 With them [*sc.* Sanskrit authors] what is essential in poetry is something incomprehensible, something which cannot be directly expressed, but only suggested—the aesthetic delectableness which they call *rasa*, a subjective condition of the reader's mind. **1967** [see NRITYA]. **1968** *Indian Music Jrnl.* V. 34 His life became lonely. Perhaps this accounts to some extent for his successful evocation of *Karuṇā* rasa. **1968** *Jrnl. Musical Acad. Madras* XXXIX. 8 In one sense there is only one Rasa, *Bhakti*, that runs through the songs of Tyagaraja... Thus *Bhakti Rasa* can wear different complexions... In these songs the melody is itself suggestive of the Rasa of the song. **1977** S. PANDIT *Approach to Indian Theory of Art & Aesthetics* ii. 32 An object which does not contain *rasa* cannot be classified in the category of an art work, and no experience without it can be called aesthetic.

‖**rasa**[2] (ˈrɑːsa). Also **ras**. [a. Skr. *rāsa* dance, sport.] A rustic Indian dance (commemorating that) performed by Krishna and the Gopis; a festival celebrating this.

1828 H. H. WILSON in *Asiatick Researches* XVI. 92 Another [festival] is the *Rás Yátra*, or annual commemoration of the dance of the frolicksome deity. *Ibid.* 93 The *Rás Yátra* is celebrated at the village of Sivapur. **1887** W. J. WILKINS *Mod. Hinduism* IV. iii. 233 *Rāsa Jātra.* This festival is held to commemorate the sports of Krishna with the milkmaids of Vrindāvana. **1912** *Encycl. Relig. & Ethics* V. 889/2 The *rāsa*, or sportive dance, performed by Kṛṣṇa's cowherds and cowherdesses. **1921** *Glasgow Herald* 29 Dec. 7 Graceful dancing women from Manipur.. went through their most famous diversion, the 'Ras' dance, in which 'Krishna', here played by a boy, is teased by his feminine playmates. **1933** S. SITWELL *Canons of Giant Art* 122 And now he pipes for them the pastoral rasa, The dance, the shepherds' dance, the Indian cordax. **1951** L. R. DAYAL *Manipuri Dances* p. ix, The main forms of dance are the Ras, which is performed in the months of Vaishak (May), Kartik (November), and Phalgoon (February). **1953** F. BOWERS *Dance in India* 130 Manipur's two most celebrated distinctions are polo and Ras Lila... Ras Lila is played according to season, and usually on mountain sides or in far-off temples. **1969** *Femina* (Bombay) 26 Dec. 27/1 Of all the seasonal delights of Winter that I've known, those of Gujarat remain the most clearly defined in my memory, especially the beautiful garba and ras dances, with their unforgettable rhythm and sheer vitality. **1972** N. HEIN *Miracle Plays of Mathurā* vi. 129 We have seen that the deeds of Vishṇu are *līlās*, 'sports'. Ras is the name of a particular one of these deeds, which was done by Vishnu in his Krishṇa incarnation. *Ibid.*, Krishṇa favored the gopis by dancing with them a circular dance, which the Vishṇu Puraṇa calls the rasa. *Ibid.* 130 The rāslīlā is a drama of which Braj claims the sole guardianship.

rasagoola, rasagulla, varr. RASGULLA.

rasalger, var. RESALGAR *Obs.*

‖**rasamala** (ræsəˈmɑːlə). [Malay (Javanese etc.) *ras-* or *rāsamāla*.] A tall East Indian tree (*Altingia excelsa* or *Liquidambar Altingia*) yielding an odoriferous resin. Also *attrib.*

1817 RAFFLES *Java* I. 43 Besides the *rásamala*, which is very limited as to its place of growth,.. few odoriferous resins are found. **1886** C. R. MARKHAM *Peruv. Bark* 77 Covered with rasamala trees of immense size.

rasant (ˈreɪzənt), *a. Mil.* Also **razant**. Now *rare*. [a. F. *rasant*, pres. pple. of *raser* to RASE *v.*[1]: see Littré. So also Pg. *rasante*.] In fortification: Sweeping, grazing. (Cf. quots.)

1696 PHILLIPS (ed. 5) s.v., Line of defence Rasant, so called, because the shot from thence only shaves but makes no Breach. **1706** *Accomplished Officer* iv. 36 In this Case you must suppose razant Fortifications. **1727–41** CHAMBERS *Cycl.* s.v., In fortification, rasant flank, or line, is that part of the curtin, or flank, whence the shot exploded rase or glance along the face of the opposite bastion. **1830** E. S. N. CAMPBELL *Dict. Milit.* s.v. *Razant.* **1944** S. PUTNAM tr. *E. da Cunha's Rebellion in Backlands* v. 256 Eight hundred rifles blazing, eight hundred rifles aimed in a rasant line down the drop of the hill.

rasaue, -awe, obs. Sc. ff. RECEIVE *v.*

rasberry, Rasboute, obs. ff. RASPBERRY, RAJPUT.

†**rascaˈbilia.** *Obs. rare*$^{-1}$. In 6 **rask-**. [Humorously f. RASCAL.] *collect.* Rascalry, rascals. Hence †**rascaˈbilian**, a rascal. *Obs.*$^{-1}$

1573 TUSSER *Husb.* (1878) 25 Beware raskabilia, slothfull to wurke. **1622** BRETON *Strange Newes* (1879) 6 Their names are often recorded in a Court of Correction, where the Register of Rogues makes no little gaine of Rascabilians.

So †**rascaˈbility**, rascality, rabble. *Obs.*$^{-1}$

a **1577** SIR T. SMITH *Commw. Eng.* (1612) 31 Such as be exempted out of the number of the rascability of the popular, be called and written Yeomen.

rascal (ˈrɑːskəl, -æ-), *sb.* and *a.* Forms: 4–5 **raskayl**, (4 **-kail(l)e, -kayle, -keyl**, 5 **-kell**), 5–7 **raskall**, 6–7 **-kal**, (7 **-kale**); 4–6 **rascaile**, (4 **rescail(l)e**, 4–5 **rascayl(e, -caille** (9), **-caly(e)**, 5–8 **rascall**, (6 **-kcal, -scal, -cald, -cold(e**, 6–7 **-chal**, 7 **-cole**, 9 *dial.* **rascat, -cot**), 5– **rascal**. [a. OF. *rascaille, -caile, rescaille* (12th c.; mod.F. *racaille*), of uncertain origin.]

A. *sb.* †**1.** *collect.* The rabble of an army or of the populace; common soldiers or camp-followers; persons of the lowest class. *Obs.* exc. *arch.*

c **1330** R. BRUNNE *Chron.* (1810) 276 Þe route of rascaile, Tille armes gan drawe, & dight þam to bataile. ? *a* **1400** *Morte Arth.* 2882 The raskaille was rade, and rane to þe grefes. **1415** HOCCLEVE *To Sir J. Oldcastle* 391 Yee broken meynee, yee wrecchid rascaille. **1523** LD. BERNERS *Froiss.* I. 703 It is nat convenyent that such raskall.. sholde be suffred to rule a countrey. **1553** BRENDE *Q. Curtius* F fiv, Such, as sometime were the rascal of al their citie, and then the refuse of al the outlawes. **1570** LEVINS *Manip.* 13/12 Y^e Rascall, *vulgus.* [**1819** SCOTT *Ivanhoe* xl, A score of such rascaille.. whom one good knight could drive before him.]

†**b.** A rabble or mob. *Obs. rare.*

c **1330** R. BRUNNE *Chron. Wace* (Rolls) 1536 Þat raskayl [*var.* rescaile] to þe schip al ȝod. *c* **1470** *Hors Shepe & G.* (Caxton 1479, Roxb. repr.) 32 A raskall of boyes. A rafull of knaues. **1532** MORE *Confut. Tindale* Wks. 412/1 Bothe Luther and he.. and all the rable of that rascaile, neuer cease to say this.

†**c.** Rubbish, refuse. (So F. *racaille*.) *Obs.*$^{-0}$

c **1440** *Promp. Parv.* 424/1 Rascaly, or refuse, where of hyt be,.. *caducum.*

†**2.** One belonging to the rabble or common herd; a man of low birth or station. *Obs.*

1461–83 *Househ. Ord.* (1790) 66 That the rascals and hangers upon thys courte be sought oute and avoyded from every offyce monethly. **1494** FABYAN *Chron.* VII. 326 The personys whiche entendyd this conspiracy, were but of the rascallys of the cytie. **1561** T. NORTON *Calvin's Inst.*, Table of Script. Quot., Hee.. made priests of the rascals of the people. **1592** WYRLEY *Armorie* 123 Mean conquest is it, base rascolds to subdue. **1674** BREVINT *Saul at Endor* 304 Catholics may look on us all, like so many poor Raskals, who have none of these Jewels.

†**b.** A camp-follower. *Obs. rare.*

1552 EDW. VI *Jrnl.* in *Lit. Rem.* (Roxb.) II. 420 About 20,000 footmen, and 8000 horsmen, wel appointed, besides rascalles. **1571** HANMER *Chron. Irel.* (1633) 28 They placed their rascals on their jades, nagges, and labouring garrons.

3. A low, mean, unprincipled or dishonest fellow; a rogue, knave, scamp.

1586 A. DAY *Eng. Secretary* (1625) 44 There was no rake-hell, no ruffian, no knaue, no villaine, no cogging raskall,.. but his hand was in with him. **1649** SIR E. NICHOLAS in *N. Papers* (Camden) I. 154 This rascall spake worse then they and more contemptuously of our late blessed king. **1688** R. HOLME *Armoury* III. 311/2 The Whip.. is a Punishment inflicted upon all Vagabonds, Wandering Beggars and Idle Rascals. **1709** HEARNE *Collect.* (O.H.S.) II. 197 That the 39 Articles.. is cut out of y^t Book by some Rascal. **1793** JEFFERSON *Writ.* (1859) IV. 20 The agents of the two people are either great bunglers or great rascals. **1859** W. COLLINS *Q. of Hearts* (1875) 58 Shifty Dick and the other rascal had been caught, and were in prison.

b. Used without serious implication of bad qualities, or as a mild term of reproof.

c **1610** COOKE *Greene's Tu Quoque* A 3 Sweet Rascal! if your love bee as earnest as your protestation, you will meete me this night at supper. **1698** FRYER *Acc. E. India & P.* 34 A set of these Rascals.. in a Week's time with this Load shall run down their choicest Horses. **1712** STEELE *Spect.* No. 493 ¶ 3, I live in Taverns; he is an orderly sober Rascal. **1899** W. E. NORRIS *Giles Ingilby* iv, You are a lucky rascal, and I wish.. I were in your shoes.

c. Applied to a woman or girl. *rare.*

1624 FLETCHER *Rule a Wife* v. iv, Why, how dar'st thou [Estifania] meet me again, thou rebel,.. thou rascal. **1899** H. CLIFFORD in *Blackw. Mag.* No. 1000. 319 What a clear colour that girl had.. What a lissom rascal it was!

†**4.** *collect.* The young, lean, or inferior deer of a herd, distinguished from the full-grown antlered bucks or stags. *Obs.*

1399 LANGL. *Rich. Redeles* II. 129 So whanne ȝoure hauntelere dere were all ytakyn, Was non of the rasskayle aredy ffull growe. *c* **1474** in *Christ Church Lett.* (Camden) 26 For lak of dier it [hunting] must be forboren unto the tyme that more Raskell may grow. **1575** TURBERV. *Venerie* 73 In Januarie they leave hearding with rascal and accompany themselves three or foure hartes together. **1607** J. NORDEN *Surv. Dial.* III. 114 What Deere hath the Lord of this Mannor in his Parke, red and fallow; how many of Antler, and how many rascall.

†**b.** A deer of this kind. *Obs.*

1522 *Warrant* in Jeayes *Catal. Berkeley Charters* (1892) 206 All the male dear and all other Rasscalls except the Hyndes. **1612** DRAYTON *Poly-olb.* xiii. 91 The Bucks and lusty Stags amongst the Rascalls strew'd.

fig. **1625** B. JONSON *Staple of N.* III. i, A new park is a-making there to sever Cuckolds of antler from the rascals.

c. Similarly applied to other animals.

1530 PALSGR. 260/2 Rascall, refuse beest, *refus.* **1576** FLEMING tr. *Caius' Dogs* 42 Some be called fine dogs, some course, other some mungrels or rascalls. **1577** B. GOOGE *Heresbach's Husb.* (1586) 126 b, When you perceiue y^t she is Horsing, away with the raskal, and put to your stallion. **1869** *Lonsdale Gloss.*, *Rascal*, a lean animal.

5. *Comb.*, as *rascal-like* adj.

1576 FLEMING *Panopl. Epist.* 383 His opprobrious speaches, and rascallike raylinges. **1591** SHAKS. *1 Hen. VI*, IV. ii. 49 If we be English Deere, be then in blood, Not Rascall-like to fall downe with a pinch.

B. *adj.* **1.** Belonging to, or forming, the rabble: cf. A. 1. (Common *c* 1530–1650, esp. in *rascal people* or *sort*.) Also *rarely*, rascally, knavish.

c **1430** *Life St. Kath.* (Gibbs MS.) 81 O how blessed schal I þan be whan þe folye of þe rascayl puple schal worschepe me. **1548** UDALL, etc. *Erasm. Par. Mark* i. 11 He that purifieth al thinges, came as one of the raskall sort. **1581** SAVILE *Tacitus, Hist.* I. xxx, Yet for your own interest prouide, that the raskallest sort be no Emperour-makers. **1667** POOLE *Dial. betw. Protest. & Papist* (1735) 93 Those Corporal Pains, which the Rascal-Herd must suffer without Bail or Main-prise. **1681** DRYDEN *Abs. & Achit.* 579 Nor shall the Rascal Rabble here have Peace. **1819** SCOTT *Ivanhoe* xxvii, We shall have need of their aid to-day before yon rascal rout disband. *Ibid.* Marshalling the farther troop of the rascaille yeomen. **1878** TENNYSON *Q. Mary* II. ii, To .. yield Full scope to persons rascal and forlorn.

†**b.** Common, private (soldiers). *Obs.*

1578 GOLDING *Justin* XIII. 74 Ptolomy, whome Alexander for his manhode and valiauntnesse had promoted from a raskal [1570 common] souldioure. **1581** MARBECK *Bk. of Notes* 169 Achab.. would not be knowne to be the king, but bee counted a rascall souldier.

c. Pertaining or appropriate to (†the rabble, or) rascals. = RASCALLY 3.

1566 T. STAPLETON *Ret. Untr. Jewel* III. 121 No sadde writinge, but a rascal wrangling. **1618** WITHER *Motto, Nec cares* in *Juvenilia* (1633) 531 The Rascall humours of the vaine And giddy multitude. **1867** HOWELLS *Ital. Journ.* 162 In the rascal streets in the neighborhood. **1894** F. S. ELLIS *Reynard Fox* 203 A holy life I'm always choosing, But rascal ways find more amusing.

†**2.** Wretched, mean, etc. = RASCALLY 4. *Obs.*

1585 GOLDING *Pomponius Mela* (1590) 54 It is but a rascall bancke all stonie. **1612** T. JAMES *Corrupt. Scripture* I. 55 Such rude, rascall and foolish stuffe, in steed of manie learned Treatises. *a* **1639** WOTTON in *Reliq.* (1685) 652 The streight and rascal Dyet of that Town in Lent. **1748** H. WALPOLE *Lett.* (1846) II. 211 On what rascal foundations were built all the pretences to virtue which were set up in opposition to him.

†**3.** Of deer: (see A. 4). Also *fig.* *Obs.*

1602 *2nd Pt. Return fr. Parnass.* II. v. 882, I causd the Keeper to seuer the rascall Deere, from the Buckes of the first head. **1653** WALTON *Angler* i. 15 How will a right Greyhound fix his eye on the best Buck in a herd.. and follow him and him only through a whole herd of rascal game. **1664** ETHEREDGE *Comical Revenge* V. iii, Lest some old woodman drop in by chance and discover thou art but a rascal deer.

†**b.** Similarly of other animals (cf. A. 4 c). *Obs.*

1576 FLEMING tr. *Caius' Dogs* 34 Curres of the Mungrell and Rascall sort. **1660** F. BROOKE tr. *Le Blanc's Trav.* 185 Laying some raschal sheep or goat for a bait.

†**c.** Applied to all beasts other than those of chase. *Obs. rare.* (Perh. intended as *sb.*)

1486 *Bk. St. Albans* E j, Other beestys all, Where so ye hem fynde Rascall ye shall hem call.

†**ˈrascal**, *v. Obs.* [f. the sb.] *trans.* To call (one) rascal.

1598 T. M. *Seruingmans Comf.* (1868) 162 What cares a Gentleman now adayes to knaue and rascall his Man at euery worde? **1683** T. HUNT *Def. Charter Lond.* 25 The Poet hath undertaken for their being kicked.. about the Stage to the Gallows, infamously rogued and rascalled.

rascaldom (ˈrɑːskəldəm, -æ-). [f. RASCAL *sb.*]

1. The world or body of rascals.

1837 CARLYLE *Diamond Necklace* viii, He has much the stature of Villette, denizen of Rascaldom. **1860** *Athenæum* 8 Sept. 313 The last Duke of Queensbury, whose death gave such regret to rascaldom.

2. Rascally conduct; a rascally act.

1862 THACKERAY *Philip* xi, He might be transported for forgery or some other rascaldom. **1879** TROLLOPE in *19th Cent.* Jan. 35, I will not say that Barry Lyndon's career has deterred many from rascaldom.

†**ˈrascaldry.** *Obs. rare.* Also 5 **rask-**. [f. *rascald* RASCAL *sb.* + -RY.] **a.** = RASCAL *sb.* 1. **b.** The character or condition of a rascal (in sense 2).

1470 HARDYNG *Chron.* Pref. p. iii, Knyghtes, squyers, and chosen yomanry, And archers fyne withouten Raskaldry. ? **1600** BRETON *Pasquil's Fooles-cappe* B iv b, So base a rascaldry As is too farre from thought of Chyualry.

†**ˈrascaless.** *nonce-wd.* A female rascal.

1748 RICHARDSON *Clarissa* (1811) I. xxxi. 221 Then shall I have all the rascals and rascalesses of the family come creeping to me.

ˈrascalism. [f. RASCAL *sb.* + -ISM.] The character or practices of a rascal.

1837 CARLYLE *Diamond Necklace* xiv, A tall handsome man.. with a look of troubled gaiety and rascalism. **1896** *Daily News* 23 Apr. 6/1 For unmitigated rascalism.. recommend us to Mr. Gordon.

rascality (rɑːˈskælɪtɪ, -æ-). Also 6–7 **rask-**. [f. RASCAL *sb.* + -ITY.]

1. The rabble; the class of rascals. = RASCAL *sb.* 1. (Common *c* 1600–1710.)

a **1577** SIR T. SMITH *Commw. Eng.* (1633) 6 The usurping of the rascalitie can never long endure. **1652–62** HEYLIN *Cosmogr.* II. (1682) 156 The Chief Heads of their Clans, with all the several Rascalities depending on them. **1705** VANBRUGH *Confederacy* I. iii, I love your men of rank, they have something in their air does so distinguish 'em from the rascality. **1791–1823** D'ISRAELI *Cur. Lit.* (1866) 409/1 That aversion the rascality had for the better sort of citizens. **1875** JOWETT *Plato* (ed. 2) I. 141 You would.. long to revisit the rascality of this part of the world.

2. Rascally character or conduct; a rascally act or practice.

1592 G. HARVEY *Four Lett.* 46 The thinges are paltry: and the very names sauour of rascallity. **1691** WOOD *Ath. Oxon.* II. 367 He was for that and other rascallities imprison'd at Coventry. **1825** COBBET *Rur. Rides* 30 It presents to us nothing of rascality, and roguishness of look. **1875** JOWETT *Plato* (ed. 2) III. 304 Frauds between man and man, and the other rascalities.

† **'rascaller.** *Obs. rare*$^{-1}$. One of the rabble.
c **1500** *Cocke Lorell's B.* 13 With this man was a lusty company, For all raskyllers fro them they dyde trye.

rascallion (rɑː'skæliən, -æ-). Also 8 -calion. [? f. RASCAL with fanciful ending; cf. *rampallion*. A later (now more usual) form is RAPSCALLION.] A low mean wretch or rascal.
1649 *Pol. Ballads* (ed. Wilkins, 1860) I. 82 To spend our dearest bloods to make rascallions flee. **1771** SMOLLETT *Humph. Cl.* 20 Apr. ii, I must desire you will wink hard at the practices of this rascallion. **1826** SCOTT *Woodst.* v, I saw two rascallions engaged in emptying a solemn stoup of strong water. **1885** LADY BRASSEY *The Trades* 300 Now, master rascallion of a wrecker [etc.].

rascally ('rɑːskəlɪ, -æ-), *a.* Also 6-7 rask-. [f. RASCAL *sb.* + -LY[1].]
†**1.** Forming one or part of the rabble or common sort. *Obs.* = RASCAL *a.* 1.
1642 J. EATON *Honey-c. Free Justif.* 47 Like rascally souldiers. **1661** PEPYS *Diary* 15 Sept., There was none of any quality, but poor and rascally people. **1687** A. LOVELL tr. *Thevenot's Trav.* III. 43 All the drudges and rascally People which Courts and Armies commonly draw after them.
†**b.** Poor, worthless. *Obs.* = RASCAL *a.* 2.
1600 SURFLET *Countrie Farme* III. xviii. 462 All the small and rascallie sort of fruit which you shall find vpon them.
2. Low, mean, or unprincipled in character or conduct; knavish.
1598 SHAKS. *Merry W.* II. ii. 276 At that time the iealious-rascally-knaue her husband will be forth. **1682** *Lond. Gaz.* No. 1688/4 Some rascally Boys (whom we call here Coal stealers). **1752** HUME *Pol. Disc.* x. 188 Our common soldiers are such a low rascally set of people. **1816** SCOTT *Antiq.*, I have so often warned you of the knavery of that rascally quack. **1887** *Spectator* 5 Nov. 1496 The mock-marriage effected with the connivance of a rascally valet.
3. Appropriate to a rascal or rascals.
1596 B. JONSON *Ev. Man in Hum.* I. iii, These same abominable, vile,.. rascally verses. *a* **1677** BARROW *Serm.* Wks. 1716 I. 276 As it is a raskally delight.. which men feel in wreaking spite. **1706** E. WARD *Wooden World Diss.* (1708) 20 By a rascally Recommendation to the Board, he endeavours to reward him at the publick Cost. **1818** SCOTT *Rob Roy* viii, A rascally calumny, which I was determined to probe to the bottom. **1862** MRS. H. WOOD *Mrs. Hallib. Troub.* I. xvii. 94 This is not the first time he has attempted a rascally action under cover of my name.
4. Wretched, miserable, mean.
1606 SHAKS. *Tr. & Cr.* v. iii. 101 A whorson rascally tisicke so troubles me.. that [etc.]. **1660** F. BROOKE tr. *Le Blanc's Trav.* 375 At the foot of these Mountains there are some rascally Innes. **1728** MORGAN *Hist. Algiers* I. Pref. 18, I am unpardonable in quoting noble Greek authors from rascally Translations. **1830** COBBETT *Rur. Rides* (1885) II. 337 A rascally heap of sand and rock, and swamp, called Prince Edward's Island. **1890** 'R. BOLDREWOOD' *Col. Reformer* (1891) 317 If we rescue the cattle we can be summoned.. all the way to that rascally hole of a township.
Comb. **1821** COBBETT *Rur. Rides* (1885) I. 21 A more rascally looking place I never set my eyes on.
So **'rascally** *adv.*, in a rascally manner.
1627 E. F. *Hist. Edw. II* (1680) 128 A garment.. tatter'd rascally. **1749** FIELDING *Tom Jones* VIII. iii, You have used me rascally, and I will not pay you a farthing. **1824** *Murder Mr. Weare* 225 They two have used me rascally.

'rascalment. *nonce-wd.* = RASCALRY.
1832 *Fraser's Mag.* V. 118 The pickpockets of Covent Garden,.. the blackguards of Barbican,.. or the rascalment in general.

rascalry ('rɑːskəlrɪ, -æ-). [f. RASCAL *sb.* + -RY. Cf. RASCALDRY.] = RASCALITY.
1832 SOUTHEY *Lett.* (1856) IV. 296 All the loose rabble from the surrounding towns and.. our own rascalry. **1868** DORAN *Saints & Sin.* I. 107 When Latimer was preaching before young Edward on rascalry in high places.

'rascalship. [f. RASCAL *sb.* + -SHIP.] The condition of being a rascal; used as a mock title.
1639 W. CARTWRIGHT *Royall Slave* I. i, What's thy Raskalship's pleasure. **1693** T. BROWN in Higden *Wary Widdow* a, I'll live to see your Rascalship interrd.

‖**rascasse** (raskas). [Fr.] A small Mediterranean scorpion-fish, *Scorpæna scrofa*, which has reddish skin and spiny fins which can cause painful wounds, and which is used esp. as an ingredient of bouillabaisse.
1921 W. J. LOCKE *Mountebank* xvi. 206 The wondrous dish [*sc.* bouillabaisse] was set before them.. *Rascasse, loup de mer*, mostelle, *langouste*—a studied helping of each. **1940** A. SIMON *Conc. Encycl. Gastron.* II. 81/1 Rascasse.. is caught in the Mediterranean only. **1950** E. DAVID *Bk. Mediterranean Food* 54 *Rascasse*.. is a red spiny fish. **1957** R. CAMPBELL *Portugal* iv. 67 The *rascasse*.. is the chief component of.. bouillabaisse. **1961** E. MCLEOD tr. *Colette's Break of Day* 36 A southern luncheon.. salads, stuffed *rascasse* and aubergine fritters. **1975** *Sat. Rev.* (U.S.) 29 Nov. 55/1 The ugly rascasse, without which, they say in Marseilles, a proper bouillabaisse cannot be made.

rasch(e, obs. forms of RASH.

Rasch-, Rasckolnik: see RASKOLNIK.

raschel ('ræʃəl). Also Raschel. [ad. G. *Raschelmaschine*, f. the name of the French actress *Rachel* (1820–58): cf. RACHEL.] **a.** A kind of knitting-machine (see quots. 1940, 1968). **b.** The coarse warp knitting produced by such a machine. Also *attrib.* Hence **'raschel** *v. trans.*, to knit with a raschel machine (in quot. pa. pple.).
1940 *Chambers's Techn. Dict.* 703/1 *Raschel* (Hosiery), the name for the two-bar warp loom, fitted with latch needles. **1957** M. B. PICKEN *Fashion Dict.* 195/1 *Raschel knitting*,.. type of warp knitting resembling tricot, but coarser. Done by machine in plain and Jacquard patterns, often with lacy effect. Used for underwear. **1968** J. IRONSIDE *Fashion Alphabet* 246 *Raschel*, a type of knitting-machine producing ribbed fabric. **1970** *Times* 12 May 11/6 The designer demonstrated the uses.. of the acrylic yarn in all its many shapes, in fabrics blended, bonded, Neospun, raschelled, knitted, woven, [etc.]. **1972** *Daily Tel.* 30 Oct. 12/6 Frank Usher will have this look, appropriately braid-edged, in a beautiful raschel knit of shaded brown and beige scallops on cream. **1974** *Ibid.* 7 Jan. 9/5 Acrylics, cotton bouclés and raschels, cotton mixed with linen or Vincel: all these give a crisper look to the stripes in your spring sweater than we've had for some time now. **1974** *Encycl. Brit. Macropædia* XVIII. 182/2 The two types of warp knitting are raschel, made with latch needles, and tricot, using bearded needles. *Ibid.*, In the Raschel machine, the needles move in a ground steel plate, called the trick plate.

Raschig ('rɑːʃɪg, -æ-). Also (*rare*) raschig. *Chem. Engin.* The name of Friedrich *Raschig* (1863–1928), German chemist, used *attrib.* (†or in the possessive), as **Raschig process**, a process developed by workers in Raschig's chemicals company in which phenol is produced by heating benzene vapour with hydrogen chloride and air over a copper-containing catalyst to yield chlorobenzene, which is then hydrolysed to form phenol; **Raschig ring**, a small cylindrical ring, introduced by Raschig, made of ceramic or other suitable material and used in bulk as a packing material in towers and columns for fractionation, solvent extraction, etc.
1920 *Chem. Abstr.* XIV. 2054 Attention is directed to the advantages attained by the use of Raschig's rings as a filling material for absorption towers in the manuf. of H_2SO_4, HNO_3, HCl, etc. **1926** *Ibid.* XX. 2214 Raschig rings have been used advantageously for clearing of liquids, the turbid liquor being run in at the bottom of a 80-cm. layer of rings, 15 × 15 mm. **1937** *Discovery* Sept. 282/2 Another form of acetifier contains raschig rings. **1940** *Chem. & Engin. News* 10 Nov. 921/1 The unit, which has been in continuous operation for four months.., employs the Raschig process, a catalytic vapor-phase system for the chlorination of benzene and the hydrolysis of the chlorobenzene produced. The process, invented by Prahl and Mathes of the Raschig organization, Ludwigshafen, Germany, produces a phenol purer than U.S.P. and does so with less than 0·1 per cent of by-product. **1947** KIRK & OTHMER *Encycl. Chem. Technol.* I. 16 Raschig rings have the greatest number of applications because they provide a large effective surface of contact between the gas and the liquid phases and they have a large free volume. They are available in sizes from ¼ to 6 in., and the usual design has a height equal to the diameter. **1959** R. J. HENGSTEBECK *Petroleum Processing* xi. 265 Modern furfural extraction columns contain about 40 to 50 ft of Raschig rings, with redistribution equipment at about 5-ft intervals. **1963** *Economist* 14 Dec. 1193/3 The ICI plant uses the Raschig process. **1972** *Materials & Technol.* IV. viii. 309 A modification of the Dow process is the Raschig process, in which benzene is chlorinated by Cl_2 generated by the catalytic oxidation of HCl with oxygen at 230° C, and HCl is recovered in the hydrolysis at 425° C, promoted by Cu catalyst without alkali.

rascle, variant of RASKLE *v. Obs.*

†**rase**, *sb.*[1] *Obs.* [f. RASE *v.*[1]]
1. The act of scraping or scratching; the fact of being scratched or cut.
1530 PALSGR. 261/1 Rase, a scrapyng, *rasure*. **1628** GAULE *Pract. The.* (1629) 266 The rase of whose skinne.. was more then the torment of their wretched Bodyes.
2. A scratch, cut, slit. = RACE *sb.*[3]
1579–80 NORTH *Plutarch* (1676) 739 Onely a little rase or scratch seen, as it were of a bodkin or penknife. **1601** HOLLAND *Pliny* II. 499 All the hacks, cuts, gashes, and rases all ouer the body. **1677** MOXON *Mech. Exerc.* No. 2. 17 Set the edge of it upon that Mark or Rase.

†**rase**, *sb.*[2] *Obs. rare*$^{-0}$. [a. OF. *rase* 'mesure rase' (see Godef.), fem. of *ras*, ad. L. *rāsus*: see next.] Struck measure.
1691 BLOUNT *Law Dict.* (ed. 2) s.v., Toll shall be taken by the Rase, and not by the Heap or Cantel.

rase (reɪz), *v.*[1] Also 5 *Sc.* rass-. [a. F. *raser* = Sp., Pg. *rasar*, It. *rādere*:—pop. L. **rāsāre*, f. *rās-* ppl. stem of *rādere* to scrape, etc. See also RACE *v.*[3], RAISE *v.*[2], RAZE *v.*]
†**1.** *trans.* To scratch or tear with something sharp; to cut, slit, or slash (esp. the skin or clothing). *Obs.* (Common *c* 1400–1700.)
c **1400** *Destr. Troy* 8519 Andromoca.. Rasit [*printed* rafit] þe red chekis roidly with hond. *c* **1440** *Partonope* 2108 Partanopes cote Was foule rasyd and eke I-rent. **1533** ELYOT *Cast. Helthe* IV. ii. (1541) 78 b, Yf the reume be sharp it raseth the inner skinne of the throte. **1583** STUBBES *Anat. Abus.* II. (1882) 37 They must be stitched finelie, pincked, cutte, karued, rased, nickt, and I cannot tell what. **1633** T. STAFFORD *Pac. Hib.* II. xxi. (1821) 420 Sir William Godolphin a little rased on the thigh with a Halbert. **1665–76** REA *Flora* 18 Rase or cut the bottoms of your roots. **1714** GAY *Trivia* II. 244 Wheels.. rase with whiten'd Tracks the slipp'ry tide.
†**b.** *intr.* To slash; to make way or penetrate; to make an incised mark. *Obs.*
1470–85 MALORY *Arthur* VII. iv, They rasshed to gyders lyke borys tracynge rasynge and foynynge. **1677** W. HUBBARD *Narrative* (1865) I. 117 Sorely wounded by a Bullet that rased to his Skull. **1677** MOXON *Mech. Exerc.* No. 2. 17 You mark the out-lines.. either with Chalk, or else rase upon the Plate with the corner of the Cold-Chissel.
c. *trans.* To incise (a mark or line).
1815 BURNEY *Falconer's Dict. Mar.* s.v. *Rasing-knife*, A small edged tool.. used for rasing particular marks on timber [etc.]. **1873** THEARLE *Naval Archit.* §39 This inside line is rased or scratched in.
2. To remove by scraping or rasping. Const. with advbs. as *away*, *forth*, *off*, *out*, or preps. as *from*, *off*, *out of*. Somewhat *rare* in literal sense.
1388 WYCLIF *Wisd.* xiii. 11 A carpenter, hewith doun.. a streiȝt tre, and rasith awei perfitli al the riynde therof. —— *Ezek.* xxvi. 41 Y schal rase the dust therof fro it. *c* **1420** *Pallad. on Husb.* XI. 236 Yf a tender tree Me kitte.. and with an yron se The mary rased out. *a* **1600** HOOKER *Eccl. Pol.* VII. xvi. §5 All standing superiority amongst persons ecclesiastical these men would rase off with the edge of his speech. **1869** GOULBURN *Purs. Holiness* ii. 13 Nothing which occurs in after-life can rase the seal off the bond of their Baptism.
b. *esp.* To remove (something written) in this way; to erase. Cf. 3. (Chiefly 16–17th c.)
1388 WYCLIF *Pref. Epist.* ix. 76/2 Whanne he scrapide or raside awey ony waast writyng. **1486** *Bk. St. Albans*, D ij b, The colouris be rasit owt as oon coloure in rasyng ware take away from an othir. **1523** SKELTON *Garl. Laurel* 72 Out of my bookis full sone I shulde hym rase. **1571** DIGGES *Pantom.* I. xxxv. I iij, Drawen with black lead,.. that you maye easely put oute or rase awaye. **1600** HOLLAND *Livy* VII. xli. 279 No soldiers name once entred into the muster-master his booke, should be rased out against his will. **1658** BRAMHALL *Consecr. Bps.* vi. 148 Unlesse you can rase these words.. out of the Statute. **1859** KINGSLEY *Misc.* (1860) I. 277 Let those too idolized names be rased henceforth from the Calendar.
c. *transf.* and *fig.* (chiefly from b).
1388 WYCLIF *Jer.* xi. 19 Sende we a tre in to the brede of hym, and rase we hym awei fro the lond of lyueris. **1560** tr. *Calvin's Foure Serm.* N viii, Thei which did swike it [the church] vtterly rased out and destroyed. **1581–2** in W. H. TURNER *Select Rec. Oxford* (1880) 419 Hopinge.. wth goode behavioure to rase owt of memorie this my.. discredite. **1606** G. W[OODCOCKE] *Hist. Ivstine* XXIII. 85 They had.. rast forth the record of their habitation in Italy. **1677** GALE *Crt. Gentiles* IV. 223 That which the most profligate men cannot rase out of their souls. **1726** DE FOE *Hist. Devil* I. x. (1840) 142 The Devil did not immediately rase out the notion of religion. **1748** SHENSTONE *Ode to Memory* 41 Oh from my breast that season rase. *a* **1822** SHELLEY *Fiordispina* 13 From the catalogue of sins Nature had rased their love.
3. (Without const.) To erase, obliterate (writing), orig. by scraping with a knife. (Freq. in 16–17th c., now *rare* or *Obs.*)
1390 GOWER *Conf.* II. 21 Lich to the bok in which is rased The lettre, and mai nothing be rad. **1508** FISHER 7 *Penit. Ps.* li. Wks. (1876) 101 In lyke maner as lettres be done awaye whan they be rased. **1669** MARVELL *Let. to Mayor of Hull* Wks. I. 135 To rase all records in their journals of that matter, that all memory thereof might be extinguisht. **1742** YOUNG *Nt. Th.* v. 514 As the tide rushing rases what is writ In yielding sands.
fig. **1401** *Pol. Poems* (Rolls) II. 92 He is callid an heretike that rasith oure bileve.
†**4.** To scrape (a thing) so as to remove something from its surface; also, to scrape down into small particles. *Obs.*
1388 WYCLIF *1 Kings* vii. 28 Thilke werk of foundementis was raside betwixe. *c* **1400** *Beryn* 2936 Hanybald.. be-held his contenaunce, & howe he was I-rasid. **1508** FISHER 7 *Penit. Ps.* li. Wks. (1876) 98 If a table be foule and fylthy of a longe contynuaunce, fyrst we rase it, after whan it is rased we wasshe it. **1561** HOLLYBUSH *Hom. Apoth.* 34 The small guttes are nearehande rased and gnawen through. **1572** BULLEYN *Def. agst. Sickness, Dial. Soarnes & Chir.* 45 Whyte Guaicum rased and put in a vessell. **1621** B. JONSON *Gipsies Metam.* II. 111 You are.. A table so smooth, and so newly ras'te. **1743** [see RASED *ppl. a.*].
†**b.** To alter (a writing) by erasure. *Obs.*
1429 *Sc. Acts Jas. I*, II. 17/2 Swa þat þai halde þe forme of the breif.. & be nocht rasit na blobit in suspect place. **1460** CAPGRAVE *Chron.* 86 He found it [the epistle] rased and amended. **1570** FOXE *A. & M.* 3000 He did find in many places.. the Book rased with a Pen by the said Wolsey. **1654** *Burton's Diary* (1828) I. 184 The same was, in divers places, rased, interlined, and half of one of the sheets cut off. **1697** *View Penal Laws* 308 Counterfeiting Rasing or Falsifying any Cocquet Certificate. **1703** [see RASED *ppl. a.*].
†**c.** To shave (a person). *Obs. rare.*
1580 LYLY *Euphues* (Arb.) 381 When a rasor cannot rase thee. **1674** CUNNINGHAM OF CRAIGENDS *Diary* 2 June (S.H.S.) 37 To a barber for rasing me.
5. To demolish, to level with the ground; to RAZE. Now *rare*. (†Also with *up*.)
1537 *Lett. Suppression Monasteries* (Camden) 165 As concerninge the rasing and takyn down the howse. **1560** DAUS tr. *Sleidane's Comm.* 288 That all suche Castells and fortes as he hath,.. he shall rase them down to the grounde. **1597** BEARD *Theatre God's Judgem.* (1612) 352 A certain Sirian.. pulled downe castles, rased vp townes, and destroyed euerïewhere. *a* **1680** BUTLER *Rem.* (1759) I. 302 They.. rased the noblest Structures in the Land, to sell the Materials. **1769** ROBERTSON *Chas. V*, XI. Wks. 1813 III. 286 Charles ordered not only the fortifications but the town to be rased. **1867** LADY HERBERT *Cradle L.* vi. 158 Ibrahim Pasha.. rased their houses to the ground.
transf. **1676** HALE *Contempl.* I. 255 A disease.. that will suddenly pull down thy Strength, and rase thy Beauty.
†**6.** To scrape in passing; to graze. *Obs.*
1609 HOLLAND *Amm. Marcell.* 33 Rhene.. rasing as it goes the high bankes.. entreth into a round and vast lake. **1786** tr. *Beckford's Vathek* (1868) 59 Sometimes his feet rased the surface of the water.
†**b.** So *intr.* Const. *on*, *upon*, *unto*. *Obs.*

1555 EDEN *Decades* 15 The keele of the shyps sumtyme rased on the sandes. *Ibid.* 58 The capitaynes of the brigantines who had rased nere vnto the coastes. 1753 CHAMBERS *Cycl. Supp.* s.v., To rase or glance upon the ground..is to gallop near the ground, as our English horses do.

†7. To strike off (corn, etc.) at the level of the measure. *Obs. rare*$^{-1}$.

1495 *Act 11 Hen. VII*, c. 4 §2 Be it also enacted, that ther be but only viij. busshelles rased and streken to the quarter of Corne.

†**rase**, *v.*[2] *Obs.* Also 5 ras(s, raase, 6 *Sc.* raise. [Variant of RACE *v.*[4], perh. influenced by prec.] *trans.* To pull or pluck.

1375 BARBOUR *Bruce* III. 134 Him gan he ras Fra be-hynd hym. 1422 tr. *Secreta Secret., Priv. Priv.* 164 Raase ham all out of rote, as the good gardyner dothe the nettylle. 1470–85 MALORY *Arthur* x. lxiv, Syr Palomydes..rassyd of his helme from his hede. *a*1533 LD. BERNERS *Huon* xliii. 145, I shall neuer haue ioy at my herte tyll I haue rased [1601, torne] his herte out of his body. 1594 SHAKS. *Rich. III*, III. ii. 11 He dreamt, the Bore had rased off his Helme.

†**rase**, *v.*[3] *Obs.* Also 6 raze. [= (M)Du. *razen*, (M)LG. *rasen* (hence G. *rasen*, Da. *rase*, Sw. *rasa*) to rage; also of dogs, to be rabid.] *intr.* To be furious, to rage; *esp.* of dogs, to growl or bark in rage.

13.. *Coer de L.* 3633 Saladyn began to rase for yre. *c*1440 *Promp. Parv.* 424/1 Rasyn, as hondys, *ringo*. 1513 DOUGLAS *Æneis* IX. ii. 69 [The wolf] Rasys in ire, for the wod hungris list. 1567 GOLDING *Ovid's Met.* XIV. (1593) 334 The stones did seeme To rore and bellow hoarse: and dogs to houle and raze extreeme.

†**rase**, *v.*[4] *Obs. rare.* [a. ON. *rasa* to rush headlong.] *intr.* To run quickly, to rush.

13.. *Gaw. & Gr. Knt.* 1461 Þen, brayn-wod for bate, on burnez he [the boar] rasez. 1390 GOWER *Conf.* II. 264 Thries sche began to rase Aboute Eson.

†**rase**, *v.*[5] *Obs. rare*$^{-1}$. [f. *rase* RACE *sb.*[5]] *intr.* To extend as a streak.

1686 *Lond. Gaz.* No. 2142/4 A black brown Nag,..a large Star in the Forehead rasing downwards.

rase, obs. f. RACE *sb.*, obs. f. RAISE *v.*, var. RESE, obs. pa. t. RISE *v.*

rased (reizd), *ppl. a.* [f. RASE *v.*[1] + -ED[1].] Cut, scraped, altered by erasure, demolished, etc.

1555 EDEN *Decades* 51 Rased or vnpaynted tables are apte to receaue what formes soo euer are fyrst drawen theron. 1603 KNOLLES *Hist. Turks* (1638) 125 The stones and rubbidge left of the rased city. 1703 *Lond. Gaz.* No. 3897/4 Having, by a Rased Note, defrauded the Bank of 80*l.* 1743 *Lond. & Country Brewer* III. (ed. 2) 230 An Ounce of rased Ginger.

†**b.** Of cloth: (cf. RAISED *ppl. a.*[2]). *Obs. rare*$^{-1}$.

The precise sense is not quite clear: the Du. original has *gheperst en ghefigureert Satijn*.

1598 W. PHILLIPS tr. *Linschoten's Voy.* I. xli. 75 Some.. haue all their bodies rased and seared with irons, and al figured like rased Sattin or Damaske.

†**rasedhead.** *Obs. rare*$^{-1}$. In 5 rasydhede. [? f. RASE *v.*[3]] Rage, fury.

*c*1440 *Jacob's Well* 207 Þey þat haue..in rasydhede, or malyce, or in wodehed, don harme or waste.

rasee, variant of RAZEE.

†'**rasely**, *adv.* *Obs. rare*$^{-1}$. [? f. RASE *v.*[3]] ? Fiercely, angrily.

*c*1440 *York Myst.* xlvi. 60 Þei rasid hym on rode als full rasely þei rugged hym.

†'**rasen.** *Obs.* Forms: 1 ræsn, 4, 7 rasen, 6 rai-, raysin, 8 raison. See also REASON *sb.*[2] [OE. *ræsn*, of obscure origin.] = RAISING-PIECE.

*a*1000 *Voc.* in Wr.-Wülcker 280/7 *Laquear*, ræsn. *c*1000 ÆLFRIC *Gram.* ix. (Z.) 43 *Asser*, ræsn. 1338 in Parker *Gloss. Archit.* (1850) I. 380 Item in vj peciis meremii emptis pro rasens ad eandem domum. 1577 HARRISON *England* II. x[ii]. in *Holinshed* 84 b, To vse no studdes at all, but onlie.. raysines,..groundselles,..transomes, and vpright principalles. 1674–91 RAY *N.C. Words* s.v. *Pan*, Pan..is that piece of wood that lies upon the top of the stone wall,.. to which the bottom of the spars are fastned: in timber buildings in the South it is called the *rasen*, or *resen*, or *resening*. 1703 T. N. *City & C. Purchaser* 30 Tennons are ..made on the Posts to go into the Raisons. *Ibid.* 31 The vacant space betwixt the Raison and the Roof.

rasen, obs. form of RAISE *v.*, RAISIN.

†'**raser**[1]. *Obs.* exc. *Hist.* Also 6 ras-, razier(e; 7- razer. [a. OF. (now dial.) *rasier*, *-ere* (13th c. in Godef.): see also RASURE[2].] A dry measure containing about four bushels.

1491 CAXTON *Vitas Patr.* (W. de W. 1495) I. cxiv. 137 b/2 One of the shyppes..he made be fylled wyth ten thousande rasers of whete. 1560 DAUS tr. *Sleidane's Comm.* 398 [To] offer as many rasers of Otes, as thei did before of wheate. 1583 STOCKER *Civ. Warres Lowe C.* III. 89 b, 70 last of corne, which are 1625 razieres. 1684 LD. STRATHMORE *Jrnl.* 6 Aug. in *Publ. Scottish Hist. Soc.* (1890) IX. 65, 19 Razers wheat sold at 8 lib 15 sh.s. 1915 C. A. MERCIER *Leper Houses* 40 During Lent each had a razer of wheat..and two razers of beans.

'**raser**[2]. *rare.* [f. RASE *v.*[1]] One who rases.

1581 NOWELL & DAY in *Confer.* I. (1584) D iij b, Master Campion, in his printed booke, hath charged vs as rasers, manglers and spoylers of the holy Scriptures.

raser, obs. form of RAZOR *sb.*

‖**rasgado, rasgueado** (ras'gado, rasge'ado). *Mus.* [a. Sp. *rasgado*, *rasgueado*, pa. ppl. of *rasgar*, *rasguear* to strum, to make a flourish.] The act of sweeping the strings of a guitar with the fingertips. Also, an arpeggio so produced.

1876 STAINER & BARRETT *Dict. Mus. Terms* 374/2 *Rasgado* .., to sweep the strings of a guitar with the thumb, for the purpose of producing a full chord, *arpeggio*. 1944 W. APEL *Harvard Dict. Music* 628/1 *Rasgado*,..in guitar playing, sweeping the strings with the thumb to produce an arpeggio. 1974 *Early Music* July 185/2 Guitar arrangements in the popular *rasgado* or strumming style. 1979 *Guardian* 29 Oct. 13/2 What he [*sc.* Segovia] didn't like was the *rasgeado*.. —the boastful chatter, the flourishes of strokes with the tips of the fingers.

‖**rasgulla** (ras'gu:la). Also rasgoola, rasgula, etc. [Hindi, f. *ras* juice + *gullā* ball.] An Indian sweet; balls of soft milk cheese soaked in syrup.

1936 E. P. VEERASWAMY *Indian Cookery* 207 Rasgollah... Drop these into a rose-flavoured syrup. 1944 M. R. ANAND *Barber's Trade Union* 72 A sweetmeat seller hawked: 'Gulab-jaman, rasgula, burfi, jalebi.' 1954 S. CHOWDHARY *Indian Cooking* 150 Rasgullas are served warm or cold. 1960 *Harper's Bazaar* July 76/2 Tables laden with curries, chutneys and rasgolas. 1961 B. SINGH *Indian Cookery* VII. 149 Rasgulla is a delicious Bengali sweet. The land of Bengal has long been famous for the preparation of exquisite sweets and in making rasgullas they have excelled themselves. 1962 HOSAIN & PASRICHA *Cooking Indian Way* 225 Rasagulla... They should be double their original size and floating on the surface of the syrup. 1968 P. LAL *Indian Recipes* 218 Rasogoolas... Drop the rasogoolas in the clean boiling syrup. 1969 *Femina* (Bombay) 26 Dec. 27/2 Our dinner however, in the midst of all this rusticity, was certainly no rustic fare;..and to top it all, delicious ice-cream and *rasagoolas*! 1975 R. H. CHRISTIE *Twenty-Two Authentic Banquets from India* xviii. 123 *Rasgullah*, (Milk Croquettes), six tumblers of milk, lemons sufficient in number. 1976 *Times* 18 Aug. 12/7 Try rasgoulas—balls of curd in syrup at 7p each.

rash, *sb.*[1] *Sc.* Also 5–6 (9) rasch, 6 rasche. [f. RASH *v.*[1]] **a.** A crash or clash. **b.** A plashing shower of rain.

*c*1470 *Gol. & Gaw.* 914 The rochis reirdit vith the rasch, quhen thai samyne rane. 1513 DOUGLAS *Æneis* IX. xii. 60 Of his huge wecht, fell wyth a rasche, The erd dyndlyt. *Ibid.* XII. xii. 74 For gret raschis all the hevynnis rang. 1808 JAMIESON, *Rasch* is still used for a sudden fall. 1824 MACTAGGART *Gallovid. Encycl.* s.v., *Rash* also means a fall of rain, attended with wind.

rash (ræʃ), *sb.*[2] Now only *Hist.* Also 6 rashe. [= Du. and LG. *ras*, G. *rasch*, Da. and Sw. *rask*; ad. F. *ras* (16th c.) = Sp., It. *raso*, silk, satin, or fine serge, sb. use of the adj. corresp. to L. *rāsus* scraped, shaven, smooth: see RASE *v.*[1]

The origin of the *-sh*, *-sch*, *-sk* in the Eng., Germ., and Scand. forms is not clear. There is no evidence of any connexion with It. *rascia* coarse woollen cloth (which Florio, app. in error, explains as 'rash') or with ARRAS, which has been suggested as the ultimate etym.]

A smooth textile fabric made of silk (*silk rash*), or worsted (*cloth rash*).

1578 *Richmond. Wills* (Surtees) 276, ix yeards of blacke rashe at ij^s. iiij^d. a yeard. 1590 *Acct. Bk. W. Wray* in *Antiquary* XXXII. 117, iiij yeardes silke rashe, xvj s. 1592 GREENE *Upst. Courtier* Wks. (Grosart) XI. 239 Quaintly attired in veluet and sattin, and a cloake of cloth rash. 1622 MABBE tr. *Aleman's Guzman d' Alf.* I. 158 Hee had a cloake, which (if I be not deceiued) was of Rash, or else of fine Cloth. 1674 JEAKE *Arith.* (1696) 65 In 1 Piece of Rashes, Flanders Serges, &c. 15 Yards. 1701 *Lond. Gaz.* No. 3701/4 All sorts of Mercery Goods, viz. Bristol Stuffs,..Russels, Rashes, Calamancas,..will be sold by Auction. 1721 C. KING *Brit. Merch.* I. 301 Cloth Rashes 209 Pieces. [1846 J. S. BURN *Hist. For. Prot. Refugees* 5 The Flemings taught the manufacturing of Wool into Broadcloth, Rashes, Flannel, and Perpetuanas.]

attrib. and *Comb.* 1590 *Lansdowne MS.* 66 fol. 55 b, His opinion towching ye suite of ye Rashe makers of Sowthampton. 1597 *Lanc. Wills* II. 229 My silke rash gowne. 1611 FLORIO, *Rasciere*, a Rash-maker or weauer.

rash (ræʃ), *sb.*[3] [Perh. a. OF. *rache*, *rasche* scurf, eruptive sores (Godef.; cf. It. *raschia* itch); but the late appearance of the word in Eng. is against this.] **1. a.** A superficial eruption or efflorescence of the skin in red spots or patches, as in measles, scarlet fever, etc.

1709 STEELE *Tatler* No. 38 ¶11 He understands..the Art of Medicine as far as to the Cure of a Pimple or a Rash. 1736 WESLEY *Wks.* (1872) I. 36 She had only the prickly heat, a sort of rash, very common here in the summer. 1840 LADY GRANVILLE *Lett.* (1894) II. 301, I have a cold and a rash on the tip of my nose. 1876 BRISTOWE *Th. & Pract. Med.* (1878) 153 Indications of the rash visible long after the actual rash has disappeared.

b. *attrib.* and *Comb.*, as ***rash-exanthem***, ***-fever***; ***rash-like***, ***-producing*** adjs.

1747 WESLEY *Prim. Physick* §101 A Rash Fever. 1753 N. TORRIANO *Gangr. Sore Throat* 117 Some rash-like Spots.. upon her Skin. 1822–34 *Good's Study Med.* (ed. 4) II. 341 The general complexion of the genus exanthesis, or rash-exanthem. *Ibid.* IV. 419 Rash fever or 'efflorescence springing from within'. 1899 *Allbutt's Syst. Med.* VIII. 936 Different specimens of serum vary greatly in their rash-producing capacity.

2. *transf.* and *fig.* A proliferation or spate; a sudden outbreak *of* something.

1820 J. HOGG *Winter Evening Tales* I. 312, I was workin' at the loom, wi' my leather apron on, an' a rash o' loom needles in my cuff. 1907 W. DE MORGAN *Alice-for-Short* xl. 427 There too appear more bells than Poe ever wrote about ..a rash of bells that makes you think before you ring. 1930 R. CAMPBELL *Adamastor* 67 A rash of stars upon the sky, A pox of flowers on the earth. 1933 *Times Lit. Suppl.* 16 Mar. 186/1 Her prose is marked by a rash of exclamation marks. 1956 J. M. MOGEY *Family & Neighbourhood* i. 8 By 1870 the pleasant meadow land..had disappeared beneath a rash of bricks and pavements. 1968 B. HINES *Kestrel for Knave* 30 Great rashes of buttercups spread across the fields. 1980 J. MCNEIL *Spy Game* xix. 189 A piece of open ground which has miraculously escaped the rash of building covering the rest of the site.

rash (ræʃ), *sb.*[4] [Echoic: cf. RAISH.] A rustling noise. So **rash-whish** (see quot.).

1668 DRYDEN *Even. Love* I. i, The whisking of a Silk-Gown, and the rash of a Tabby-Petticoat. 1899 CROCKETT *Kit Kennedy* 22 The strident rash-whish of the sharpening-strake on the scythe.

rash (ræʃ), *sb.*[5] *Coal Mining.* orig. *dial.* (esp. S. Wales) and *U.S.* [Prob. f. RASH *a.*] Usu. *pl.* = RASHING *vbl. sb.*[2]

1903 A. STRAHAN *Geol. S. Wales Coal-Field* IV. iii. 26 Black rashes, fireclay, and clift. *Ibid.* 27 Clift, rashes and rock. 1912 *Federal Reporter* (U.S.) CXCIII. 125 The appearance of rash in the eighth and ninth west entries and at the face of the slope justified the belief that the coal in that vicinity of the mine was inferior and unmerchantable. 1917 GIBSON & CANTRILL *Geol. S. Wales Coalfield* (ed. 2) IV. v. 70 Rashes and clod 1 ft. 3 in. 1964 [see RASHING *vbl. sb.*[2]]. 1964 WOODLAND & EVANS *Geol. S. Wales Coalfield* (ed. 3) IV. v. 126 At Western the section (from top): coal 7 in, rashes 2½ ft, coal 7 in, fireclay and rashes 5 ft.

rash, Sc. and north. form of RUSH (the plant).

rash, variant of RATCH *sb.*[1]

rash (ræʃ), *a.* and *adv.* Forms: 4 rasch, 5 rasshe, 6 rashe, *Sc.* rasche, 6– rash. [= (M)Du. *rasch*, OHG. *rasc* (G. *rasch*), ON. *rösk-r*, Sw. and Da. *rask*, active, vigorous, healthy; quick, hasty, etc.

The precise source of the Eng. word is not clear; in spite of its late appearance it may represent an OE. *ræsc. An adoption of the Scand. word would normally have given *rask*.]

A. *adj.* **1.** *Sc.* and *north. dial.* Active, fresh, vigorous; brisk, nimble, quick; eager.

13.. *E.E. Allit. P.* A. 1167 Of raas þaȝ I were rasch & ronk. 1804 ANDERSON *Cumberld. Ball.* 85 I's quite young and rash—eighty-five. 1808 JAMIESON s.v., *A rasch carle*, a man vigorous beyond his years. Loth. Tweedd. 1878- in northern glossaries (Chesh., Cumbld., Northumbld.).

2. a. Hasty, impetuous, reckless, acting without due consideration or regard for consequences.

1509 BARCLAY *Shyp of Folys* 154 Unwyse men rasshe, and mad of brayne Becomyth prestis onely for couetyse. 1530 PALSGR. 322/1 Rasshe rude or boystous of condycions, [*no French*]. 1560 DAUS tr. *Sleidane's Comm.* 55 A great occasion of this terrible Warre came by rashe and lewd preachers. 1638 JUNIUS *Paint. Ancients* 35 Rash and inconsiderate beginners fall to worke upon the first sight. 1671 MILTON *Samson* 907, I was a fool, too rash, and quite mistaken. 1715 N. ROWE tr. *Lucan's Pharsalia* IV. 462 The rash Petreians urge to Arms in vain. 1781 COWPER *Conversat.* 641 That fire ..which impels rash youth, Proud of his speed, to overshoot the truth. 1848 LEIGH HUNT *Jar of Honey* x. 135 Some rash persons were anxious to see the effect of lava upon a pool of water. 1865 TENNYSON *The Captain* 10 They hated his oppression, Stern he was and rash.

b. Of things: Operating quickly and strongly. *rare.*

1597 SHAKS. *2 Hen. IV*, IV. iv. 48 Though it doe worke as strong As Aconitum, or rash Gun-powder. 1611 —— *Wint. T.* I. ii. 319, I could doe this,..with no rash Potion, But with a lingring Dram. 1876 G. M. HOPKINS *Wreck of Deutschland* xix, in *Poems* (1967) 57 The rash smart sloggering brine Blinds her.

3. a. Of speech, actions, qualities, etc.: Characterized by, or proceeding from, undue haste and want of consideration.

1558 GOODMAN *How to Obey* 194 Yt is..no rashe or perelous doctrine. 1600 HOLLAND *Livy* XXVIII. xlii. 701 Rash aduentures speed not always best. 1651 HOBBES *Leviath.* I. xi. 49 Vain-glorious men..are enclined to rash engaging. 1710 STEELE *Tatler* No. 78 ¶7 An artful Way to disengage a Man from the Guilt of rash Words or Promises. 1814 CARY *Dante, Paradise* v. 65 Not bent, as Jephthah once, Blindly to execute a rash resolve. 1862 BURTON *Bk. Hunter* (1863) 96 There are often rash estimates made of the size of libraries.

†**b.** Urgent, pressing. *Obs. rare*$^{-1}$.

1606 SHAKS. *Tr. & Cr.* IV. ii. 62, I scarce haue leisure to salute you, My matter is so rash.

4. *dial.* (See quots.) Also *Comb.*

1674–91 RAY *N.C. Words*, *Rash*..is spoken of Corn in the Straw, that is so dry that it easily durses out, or falls out of the Straw with handling it. 1829 in BROCKETT. 1886 *S.W. Linc. Gloss.*, *Rash* or *Rash-ripe*, Said of grain in the ear, when it is over ripe and falls out easily.

5. *Comb.*, as ***rash-brain***, ***-brained***, ***-headed*** adjs.

1574 W. BOURNE *Regiment for Sea* Introd. (1577) 7 Hee ought..not to be light or rash headed. 1600 S. NICHOLSON *Acolastus* (1876) 35 Training my rash-braind thoughts in reasons waies. 1632 QUARLES *Div. Fancies* IV. xcvi. (1660) 171 Is rash-brain Mendax well advised then. 1841 JAMES *Brigand* xxvi, Young rash-headed boys run into these encounters for mere sport.

B. *adv.* †**1.** = RASHLY. *Obs.* (somewhat *rare.*)

*c*1420 *Liber Cocorum* (1862) 18 Wasshe þose herbes in water, þat rennes so rasshe. 1591 SPENSER *M. Hubberd* 1214 Unto the King so rash ye may not goe. 1604 SHAKS. *Oth.* III. iv. 79 Why do you speake so startingly and rash?

2. *Comb.*, as ***rash-conceived, -embraced, -levied, -running*** advbs.
1594 SHAKS. *Rich. III*, IV. iii. 50 Buckingham and his rash leuied Strength. **1596** —— *Merch. V.* III. ii. 109 Doubtfull thoughts, and rash imbrac'd despaire. **1611** SPEED *Hist. Gt. Brit.* VI. v. 57 His rashrunning head.. turned all to nothing. **1777** POTTER *Æschylus* 293 This was no hasty, rash-conceiv'd design.

rash, *v.*[1] Chiefly *Sc.* Now *rare* or *Obs.* Forms: 5 rassh-, 5–6 (9) rasch, 6– rash, (9 rashe). [Prob. onomatopœic (cf. *clash, crash, dash*, etc.); connexion with OE. *ræscan* to quiver or flash (found only once) seems unlikely.]

1. *intr.* To dash or rush hastily or violently.
?*a* **1400** *Morte Arth.* 2107 Thane riche stedes rependez, and rasches one armes. **1470–85** MALORY *Arthur* VII. iv, They rasshed to gyders lyke borys. *Ibid.* VII. vi, Ther with al he rasshyd in to the water. **1536** BELLENDEN *Cron. Scot.* I. ix. (1541) 8 b/1 The britonis fast raschand to harnes to resist this haisty effray. **1575** TURBERV. *Faulconrie* 265 By some other accident, as.. by rashing into bushes and thornes. **1616** ROLLOCKE *On Passion* 517 Young men yt haue health, habilitie & strength of body, to run & ride, rash here & there [etc.]. **1801** LEYDEN *Compl. Scot.* Gloss. s.v. *Rasche*, '*To rashe through a darg*', to perform a day's work hastily. **1824** MACTAGGART *Gallovid. Encycl.* s.v. *Rash* sb., 'Hear to the rain rashing', hear to it dashing.

†**2.** *trans.* To cast or pour *out* in a hurried or forcible manner. *Obs.*
a **1510** DOUGLAS *K. Hart* I. 10 Quhen at the sone so schene Out raschit had his bemis frome the sky. **1708** M. BRUCE *Lect.*, etc. 15 It is good that I hide my self, and not rash out all my Mind (like a Fool) and Testimony at once.

†**3.** To dash (things *together*, or one thing *against, in*, or *through* another). *Obs.*
1549 *Compl. Scot.* vi. 66 The rammis raschit there heydis to gyddir. **1567** *Gude & Godlie B.* (S.T.S.) 115 He that sall ..rasche thair harnis aganis a craig. **1605** SHAKS. *Lear* III. vii. 58, I would not see.. thy fierce Sister, In his Annointed flesh, sticke [*Qq.* rash] boarish phangs. **1666** W. SUTHERLAND *Declar.* in Wodrow *Hist.* (1721) I. App. xv. 102 If ye come one Foot further here, I shall rash my Pike through your Soul.

†**4.** To smash, break with violence. *Obs. rare*$^{-1}$.
1513 DOUGLAS *Æneis* XII. i. 19 Onabasytly raschand the schaft in sundir.

†**5.** *to rash up*: To put together hurriedly; to rush or run up. *Obs.*
Perh. associated with (or even derived from) RASH *a.*
1570 FOXE *A. & M.* 830/2 In my former edition of Actes and Monumentes, so hastely rashed vp at that present, in suche shortnes of time. **1650** W. D. tr. *Comenius' Gate Lat. Unl.* §622 Scaffolds (pageants) are frames of timber rasht up in haste.

†**rash**, *v.*[2] *Obs.* Also 5 rassh-. [Alteration of RACE *v.*[3] or RASE *v.*[1], perh. after prec. or next.]

1. *trans.* To cut, slash.
?*a* **1500** *Smyth & his Dame* 351 in Hazl. *E.P.P.* III. 214 The smyth ranne on reed blode, All to-rent and rasshed. **1596** SPENSER *F.Q.* IV. ii. 17 They.. shields did share, and mailes did rash, and helmes did hew. **1599** B. JONSON *Ev. Man out of Hum.* IV. vi, I.. rasht his doublet sleeue, ran him close by the left cheek.

2. To scrape out, erase.
1650 in Gardner *Hist. Dunwick* (1754) 160 Paid to John Prety for rashing out the King's Arms in our Church 1s.

†**rash**, *v.*[3] *Obs.* Forms: 4–5 (6 *Sc.*) rasch, 5–6 rassh(e, 6–7 rash. [Aphet. form of ARRACHE, perh. after OF. *racher, -ier*: cf. RACHE *v.*[2] and RACE *v.*[4]] **1.** *trans.* To pull, drag (*down, off, out*, etc.), to tear *away*. (Common in 16–17th c.)
1523 LD. BERNERS *Froiss.* I. cxlvii. 176 Ye newe towne.. was pulled downe, and the castell that stode on the hauyn rasshed downe. *c* **1530** —— *Arth. Lyt. Bryt.* (1814) 83 The seconde [knight] he toke in hys armes, and rasshed hym out of the sadell. *a* **1571** JEWEL *On 1 Thess.* (1611) 69 The tormentor.. taketh the Lawne by the other end, and rasheth it suddenly [etc.]. **1629** MAXWELL tr. *Herodian* (1635) 141 And rasht off all their clothes; leaving them starke naked. **1697** DRYDEN *Æneid* IX. 1094 His crest is rash'd away.

2. To draw hastily. *rare*$^{-1}$.
1675 TRAHERNE *Chr. Ethics* 326 A musician might rash his finger over all his strings in a moment; but melody is an effect of judgment and order.

Rashboote, obs. form of RAJPUT.

rash-bush, -buss: see RUSH-BUSH.

†**rashed**, *ppl. a. Obs. rare*$^{-1}$. (?)
1598 T. BASTARD *Chrestoleros* (1880) 15 Out of her fragrant sides she sendes.. The rashed primrose and the violet.

rashen, Sc. variant of RUSHEN *a.*

rasher[1] ('ræʃə(r)). [Of obscure origin; perh. f. RASH *v.*[2] 1, but Minsheu (1627) explains it as a piece 'rashly or hastily roasted'. Cf. '*Rashed*, burnt in cooking, by being too hastily dressed' (Halliwell).] A thin slice of bacon or ham, cooked (or intended to be cooked) by broiling or frying.
1592 NASHE *P. Penilesse* (ed. 2) 11 b, You may commaund his hart out of his belly to make you a rasher on the coales. **1647** R. STAPYLTON *Juvenal* 211 Broil'd rashers, that on wide gridirons lay. **1678** DRYDEN *All for Love* Prol. 34 Drink hearty draughts of ale.. And snatch the homely rasher from the coals. **1778** MAD. D'ARBLEY *Diary* 23 Aug., She would like an egg or two, and a few slices of ham, or a rasher. **1840** DICKENS *Barn. Rudge* xxi, Great rashers of broiled ham.. done to turn, and smoking hot. **1892** *Spectator* 23 Jan. 119 The curling of a rasher of bacon under similar stress of fire.
attrib. **1598** B. JONSON *Ev. Man in Hum.* I. iv, Why not the ghost of a herring-cob, as well as the ghost of rasher-bacon.

†**b.** A slice of some other eatable, intended for broiling. *Obs. rare*$^{-1}$.
1634 HEYWOOD *Maidenh. lost* III. Wks. IV. 142 We will haue a Cherry-Tart cut into Rashers and broyled.

†**c.** Anything acting as a provocative to drinking, or eaten as such. *Obs. rare.*
1613 BEAUM. & FL. *Captain* III. i, Give him but a rasher And you shall have him upon even terms Defy a hogshead. **1629** MASSINGER *Picture* IV. ii, For a rasher, To draw his liquor down, he hath got a pie Of marrowbones, potatoes, and eringos.

'**rasher**[2]. *U.S.* [ad. local Pg. *rasciera.*] A red-coloured rock-fish of California (*Sebastichthys miniatus*).
1882 JORDAN & GILBERT *Syn. Fishes N. Amer.* 663.

'**rashful**, *a. rare.* = RASH *a.*
1567 TURBERV. *Epit.*, etc. 59 With hastie doome and rashfull sentence. **1819** *Abeillard & Heloisa* 96 In others Love comes very bashful Though.. very rashful.

'**rashing**, *vbl. sb.*[1] [Echoic: cf. RASH *sb.*[1] and *sb.*[4]] A succession of harsh grating sounds.
1889 F. COWPER *Captain of Wight* 222 There was a slashing and rashing! The sparks flew like the sparks at the armourer's forge.

rashing ('ræʃɪŋ), *vbl. sb.*[2] *Coal Mining*. orig. *dial.* (esp. *S. Wales*) and *U.S.* [Prob. f. RASH *a.* + -ING[1].] Usu. *pl.* A loose brittle deposit of shale or poor coal (see quot. 1964). Cf. RASH *sb.*[5]
1883 W. S. GRESLEY *Gloss. Terms Coal Mining* 200 *Rashings* (S[outh] W[ales]), loose dirt or shaley beds of rock. **1903** A. STRAHAN *Geol. S. Wales Coal-Field* IV. iii. 10 Rashings 0 ft. 9 in. **1905** *Maryland Geol. Survey* V. 534 Immediately overlying the 'Big Vein' is a brittle slate inter-stratified with thin seams of coal known as the 'Wild Coal' or 'Rashings'. Upon exposure to the air the wild coal crumbles and falls. **1917** GIBSON & CANTRILL *Geol. S. Wales Coalfield* (ed. 2) IV. iv. 47 The Wet-and-Dry Coal is said to lie 14 yds. below the Lantern, and to consist of top coal, 2 ft. 8 ins. thick, bottom coal, 1 ft. 4 ins. to 1 ft. 6 ins. thick, with 6 ins. of soft rashings between. **1954** A. TRUEMAN *Coalfields Gt. Brit.* ii. 23 Black carbonaceous shales, containing abundant plant remains (the 'rashings' of some coalfields). **1964** WOODLAND & EVANS *Geol. S. Wales Coalfield* (ed. 3) IV. iv. 75 *Rashes* or *rashings, either* soft carbonaceous shale with streaks of coal *or* highly disturbed, slickensided, comminated shale or mudstone formed by movement parallel to the bedding and usually associated with the roof or dirt bands in coal seams. Normally 'rashes' should be retained for the former definition and 'rashings' for the latter. **1967** I. A. WILLIAMSON *Coal Mining Geol.* vii. 55 Batt and rashings are approximately synonymous for shale containing thin coal streaks.

rashleighite ('ræʃli:aɪt). *Min.* [See quot. 1948 and -ITE[1].] A hydrated basic phosphate of copper, aluminium, and iron, $Cu(Al,Fe)_6(PO_4)_4(OH)_8{\cdot}5H_2O$, found as crusts and friable masses of triclinic crystals.
1948 A. RUSSELL in *Mineral. Mag.* XXVIII. 353 The name rashleighite commemorates Philip Rashleigh, F.R.S., F.G.S., F.S.A., 1729–1811,.. one of the earliest Cornish mineralogists and famous for having amassed the finest collection of Cornish minerals ever made. **1971** *Country Life* 3 June 1382/2 Turquoise in the form of rashleighite occurs on St. Austell Moor, in Cornwall. **1972** *Amer. Mineralogist* LVII. 1681 Rashleighite.. can be described as a substitutional solid solution of turquois and chalcosiderite.

'**rashling**. *rare.* A rash person.
a **1618** SYLVESTER *Paradox* 1161 Wks. (Grosart) II. 65 What rashlings doe delight, that sober men despise. **1922** BARONESS ORCZY *Triumph of Scarlet Pimpernel* v. 57 The young Hotspur and his crowd of rashlings would ere now have been torn from their seats.

rashly ('ræʃlɪ), *adv.* [f. RASH *a.* + -LY[2].]

1. Quickly, rapidly, hastily. *Obs.* exc. *dial.*
a **1547** SURREY in *Tottell's Misc.* (Arb.) 17 With teares, for his redresse, I rashly to him ran. **1691** RAY *Creation* II. (1692) 102 As we see Fewel burns rashly in such weather. **1805** STAGG *Poems, Auld Lang Seyne* xvii, Rashly they scale the scattran swathe.

2. In a rash or inconsiderate manner.
1535 COVERDALE *Prov.* xxi. 29 An vngodly man goeth forth rashly. **1560** DAUS tr. *Sleidane's Comm.* 29 To the intente I.. do nothyng rashely,.. I require a time to take deliberation. **1631** GOUGE *God's Arrows* III. §43. 261 What is believed without a promise, is.. rashly and audaciously presumed. **1696** WHISTON *Th. Earth* (1722) 50 We ought not rashly to pass our Judgment on them. **1781** GIBBON *Decl. & F.* xxxi. III. 191 Honorius.. rashly disqualified many of his bravest and most skilful officers. **1861** GEO. ELIOT *Silas M.* 38 The butcher.. was not disposed to answer rashly.
ellipt. **1747** in *Col. Rec. Pennsylv.* V. 86 The Council of the Six Nations does not altogether like it, but think it too Rashly of the Mohocks.

†**3.** Without settled course. *Obs. rare*$^{-1}$.
1695 LD. PRESTON *Boeth.* IV. vi. 194 Those things which in their Nature are mutable and which would otherwise rashly and irregularly float about.

rashness ('ræʃnɪs). [f. as prec. + -NESS.] The quality of being rash; inconsiderate haste or boldness; an instance of this, a rash act.
1526 *Pilgr. Perf.* (W. de W. 1531) 131 All rasshnes or hastynes in spekynge. **1589** GREENE *Menaphon* (Arb.) 82 If I vanquish thee, thou shalt feele the burden of thy rashnesse. **1651** HOBBES *Leviath.* I. x. 45 Combatants, who engaged by rashnesse, are driven into the Lists to avoyd disgrace. **1741** RICHARDSON *Pamela* I. 173, I fear.. that your Disregard to me.. may throw you upon some Rashness. **1833** TENNYSON *Two Voices* 392 If I should do This rashness. **1852** GROTE *Greece* II. lxxi. IX. 201 Through rashness and bad management they first sustained several partial losses.

rasier(e, variants of RASER[1]. *Obs.*

rasin(e, obs. forms of RAISIN, RESIN.

rasing ('reɪzɪŋ), *vbl. sb.*[1] [f. RASE *v.*[1] + -ING[1].]

1. The action of the vb. in its various senses.
c **1440** *Promp. Parv.* 424/1 Rasynge, of scrapynge of bokys or other lyke, *abrasio, rasura.* **1508** FISHER *7 Penit. Ps.* xxxii. Wks. (1876) 24 By these.. we make a perfyte rasynge & clensynge of the soule from synnes. **1560** DAUS tr. *Sleidane's Comm.* 290 b, For the paiment of ye mony and rasing of his castels. **1624** CAPT. SMITH *Virginia* III. ix. 81 Having.. threatned their ruine, and the rasing of their houses. **1815** BURNEY *Falconer's Dict. Mar.*, *Rasing*, the act of marking, by the edges of moulds, any figure upon timber, &c. with a raising-knife. **1868** GLADSTONE *Juv. Mundi* v. (1870) 143 The rasing of that city by the Philistines.

b. *attrib.*, as ***rasing-iron, -knife*** (see quots.).
1815 BURNEY *Falconer's Dict. Mar.*, *Rasing-knife*, a small edged tool, fixed in a wooden handle, and used for rasing particular marks on timber, lead, tin, &c. **1846** A. YOUNG *Naut. Dict.* s.v. *Rasing.* **1867** SMYTH *Sailor's Word-bk.* 561 The rasing-knife.. has a peculiar blade hooked at its point, as well as a centre-pin to describe circles. *Ibid.*, *Rasing-Iron*, a tool for clearing the pitch and oakum out of the seams, previous to their being caulked afresh.

†**2.** *concr.* Shavings, scrapings. *Obs. rare.*
1544 PHAER *Regim. Life* (1553) I ij b, Take the rasyng of iuory, and the rasyng of an hartes horne [etc.].

†'**rasing**, *vbl. sb.*[2] [f. RASE *v.*[3]] Growling.
c **1440** *Promp. Parv.* 424/1 Rasynge, of hondys,.. *rictus.* **1552** in HULOET.

rasion ('reɪʒən). Now *rare* or *Obs.* [ad. L. *rāsiōn-em* (Cælius), n. of action f. *rādere* to scrape, RASE *v.*[1]] The action of scraping or shaving; division by scraping or filing.
1612 WOODALL *Surg. Mate* Wks. (1653) 273 Rasion is the scraping or paring of a thing. **1657** TOMLINSON *Renou's Disp.* 55 Which cannot be performed so much by Lotion as by Section, Rasion and Traction. **1678** in PHILLIPS.

†**rask**, *v. Obs. rare.* [var. RAX *v.*; cf. *ask* and *ax.*] *intr.* To stretch oneself; to yawn.
1303 R. BRUNNE *Handl. Synne* 4282 Þan begynneþ he [Sloth] to klawe and to raske, And ȝyueþ Terlyncel hys taske. He klawyþ, he shrubbyþ, wel at hys pay. *c* **1325** *Gloss. W. de Bibbesw.* in Wright *Voc.* 152 *Après dormer il ço espreche*, raskyt hym. *c* **1440** *Promp. Parv.* 424/1 Raskyn', *exalo.*
So †'**raskle** *v. intr.* = RAXLE *v. Obs.*
1393 LANGL. *P. Pl.* C. VIII. 7 He.. rascled and remed and routte at þe laste. **1570** LEVINS *Manip.* 35/26 To raskle, *pandiculari.*

raskaile, -kelt, obs. and dial. ff. RASCAL.

‖**raskol** (ræ'skɒl). Also rascol. [Russ.: see RASKOLNIK.] **1. a.** The schism in the Russian Church which resulted from the reforms of Patriarch Nikon, who excommunicated dissenters in 1667.
1887 A. F. HEARD *Russ. Church & Russ. Dissent* ix. 179 Both German Protestantism and Russian Raskol preserve the stamp of their similar religious origin, as issuing each from an established State Church. **1900** 'ODYSSEUS' *Turkey in Europe* vi. 288 This energetic and ambitious prelate [*sc.* Nikon].. provoked by his reforms the great schism (or *raskol*) from which spring the various sects of Old Believers. **1908** W. F. ADENEY *Greek & Eastern Churches* II. III. vii. 444 The Raskol obtained new vigour from another source —popular resistance to Peter the Great's Western innovations. **1963** N. V. RIASANOVSKY *Hist. Russia* xix. 221 The raskol constituted the only major schism in the history of the Orthodox Church in Russia. **1969** K. MINOGUE in Ionescu & Gellner *Populism* 203 The Russian *raskol* after 1654, although a religious phenomenon, has been taken as a peasant reaction to urban culture.

b. Dissent from an established orthodoxy.
1947 *Partisan Rev.* XIV. 396 Russian revisionism was a heterodoxy, a fanatic schism, a *raskol.*

2. *collect.* A body of dissenters under the raskol (sense 1 a).
1888 'STEPNIAK' *Russ. Peasantry* II. 441 The *Rascol* proper, the 'Old Believers'.

‖**Raskolnik** (ræ'skɒlnɪk). Also 9 Rasckolnick, Rascholnik. [Russ. *Raskól'nik* separatist, schismatic, f. *raskól* separation, schism.] A dissenter from the national Church in Russia.
1723 in tr. *F. C. Weber's Present State of Russia* I. 82 He was reported to be of the Sect of the Raskolniks, who have entirely separated from the Russian Church, a few Ceremonies excepted. **1799** W. TOOKE *View Russian Emp.* II. 220 The sectarists known by the name of raskolniks, distinguished themselves.. by their.. obedience. **1833** R. PINKERTON *Russia* 71 The ancient Russians, like the present Raskolniks or Dissenters, abstained from veal. **1897** *Daily News* 8 June 5/3 The Raskolnik who buried alive.. twenty-five of his fanatic co-religionists.

rasogoola, var. RASGULLA.

rason, obs. form of RAISIN.

rasophore ('ræzəʊfɔə(r)). Also **rasophor, rhasophore.** [ad. med. Gr. ῥασοφόρος, f. ῥάσον cassock + -φορος bearer.] The lowest grade of monk in the Greek Orthodox Church. Also ‖**rhasophoria**, the grade of a rasophore.

1887 A. RILEY *Athos* v. 68 The monks are divided into two classes, the *dokimos*.., or novice and the *caloyer*.., or professed monk. The caloyers, again, are divided into three grades—*rhasophoria*.., *the little habit*..and *the great habit*. **1934** WEBSTER, *Rhasophore*. **1960** P. SHERRARD *Athos* 63 The monk of the lowest grade is called a Rasophore, after the *rason* or tunic which he wears as part of his habit... He is.. more than a novice in the western sense. **1964** P. F. ANSON *Bishops at Large* i. 37 Almost any alien, provided that he.. calls himself an abuna,..pappas, rasophor, starets, synkellos,..vartapet..invariably finds a warm welcome in England.

†**'rasor.** *Obs. rare*$^{-1}$. [a. L. *rāsor*: see RASORES.] One who erases; = RASER².

1586 T. B. *La Primaud. Fr. Acad.* I. 173 Temperance is.. the preserver of good will, the rasor of evill thoughts.

rasor(e, obs. forms of RAZOR *sb.*

‖**Rasores** (rə'sɔəri:z). *Ornith.* [mod.L., pl. of *rāsor* agent-n. f. *rādĕre* to scrape, RASE *v.*¹] The name given by Illiger (1811) to his Fourth Order of birds, comprising those which obtain their food by scratching the ground.

1836 OWEN in Todd *Cycl. Anat.* I. 266/1 The third order corresponds with Nitzsch's *Aves terrestres*, and is denominated Rasores. **1841** *Penny Cycl.* XIX. 305/1 The *Rasores* of Illiger contained the following families and genera [etc.].

rasorial (rə'sɔərɪəl), *a. Ornith.* [f. *Rasor-es* (see prec.) + -IAL.] Scratching the ground for food; belonging to the order RASORES.

1836 TODD *Cycl. Anat.* I. 277/2 In the Rasorial birds the coronoid process is feebly developed. **1841** *Proc. Berw. Nat. Club* I. No. 9. 254 Of the Columbidæ belonging to the Rasorial order, we possess two..residents.

rasoun, obs. Sc. f. REASON.

rasour, var. RASURE² *Obs.*

rasour(e, obs. ff. RAZOR *sb.*

rasour: see also RÉSEAU.

rasp (rɑːsp, -æ-), *sb.*¹ Also 6–7 raspe; 6 *north.* respe, 6, 9 *Sc.* resp. [a. OF. *raspe* (F. *râpe*: see RAPE *sb.*³), f. *rasper* to RASP *v.*¹ Cf. med.L. *raspa* (1389 in Du Cange). Du., Da., Sw. *rasp*, G. *raspe*, are also of F. origin.]

1. a. A coarse kind of file, having separate teeth raised on its surface by means of a pointed punch; also, any similar tool or implement used for scraping or rubbing down.

1541 *Aberd. Reg.* (1844) I. 176 Item, ane resp, ane turcas, and four cuchin nailis of jrne. **1597** A. M. tr. *Guillemeau's Fr. Chirurg.* 14 b/1 The Raspes or Scrapers, called in Latine, *Radulæ*. **1611** COTGR., *Froyer*, a rubber; also, a raspe. **1677** MOXON *Mech. Exerc.* 54 Most Rasps have formerly been made of Iron and Case-hardned. **1698** T. FROGER *Voy.* 59 They are usually grated with Rasps made for that purpose. **1762–71** H. WALPOLE *Vertue's Anecd. Paint.* (1786) V. 138 A steel roller, cut with tools to make teeth like a file or rasp. **1846** HOLTZAPFFEL *Turning* II. 819 When the file is spoken of, a double-cut file is always implied, unless a single-cut file, or a rasp, is specifically named. **1881** YOUNG *Every Man his own Mechanic* §238. 86 Rasps generally speaking are used in carpentry for cutting away or smoothing wood.

b. In sugar making, a mechanical device for grating down beet-roots.

1839 URE *Dict. Arts* 1210 Blocks of wood, with which the workman pushes the beet-roots against the revolving rasp.

2. *transf.* **a.** A rough surface like that of a rasp.

1869 BLACKMORE *Lorna D.* lxix, The horses from the country..with the rasp of winter bristles rising through.. the soft summer-coat.

b. *Zool.* The radula of a mollusk, or one of the teeth on this.

1879 B. WATSON in *Jrnl. Linn. Soc., Zool.* XIV. 716 With several hooked or serrated central rasps. **1883** *Encycl. Brit.* (ed. 9) XVI. 639 Lingual ribbon, rasp, or radula.

c. A ribbed band or organ in some insects.

1826 KIRBY & SPENCE *Introd. Entomol.* III. xxx. 143 This animal..has on it a double series of rasps. **1871** DARWIN *Descent of Man* I. x. 378 The rasp generally consists of a narrow, slightly-raised surface, crossed by very fine, parallel ribs.

3. The act of rasping, or rubbing with something comparable to a rasp.

1875 J. GRANT *One of the '600'* iii. 30, I..angrily gave my hair a finishing rasp with a pair of huge..hair-brushes.

4. A rough sound as of a rasp.

a **1851** MOIR *Field of Pinkie* v, Hark to the rasp of Grey's fierce cavalry. **1878** GILDER *Poet & Master* 19 The grasshoppers' rasp, and rustle of sheaf. **1976** *National Observer* (U.S.) 25 Dec. 4/1 'Christ, can you believe that?' he cries in his staccato, Brooklyn-accented rasp that has been honed just enough so that his 'thats' don't come out 'dats'. **1977** *Rolling Stone* 30 June 113/1 Like many such groups, Detective centers around a guitarist (Michael Monarch, whose aggressive rasp distinguished the earliest Steppenwolf sides).

5. *attrib.* and *Comb.*, as ***rasp-cutter***, ***-maker*** (1885); ***rasp-cutting***, ***-like*** adjs.; **rasp-grass** (see quot.); **rasp-palm**, a Brazilian palm (*Iriartea exorhiza*), having exposed roots which are used by the natives as rasps; **rasp-pod**, an Australian tree (*Flindersia australis*), bearing woody capsules serving as rasps (Morris *Austral Eng.*); **rasp-punch**, a punch for raising the teeth of rasps (Knight 1875); **rasp-teeth**, teeth resembling those of a rasp.

1831 *Sutherland Farm Rep.* 67 in *Lib. Usef. Knowl. Husb.* III, The sheep find, on the peat of damper and deeper quality..rasp grass (*carex cæspitosa*). **1849–52** TODD *Cycl. Anat.* IV. 874/1 Conical teeth as close set and sharp pointed as the villiform teeth, but of larger size, are called 'rasp-teeth'. **1851–6** WOODWARD *Mollusca* 327 Shell..armed in front with rasp-like imbrications. **1875** KNIGHT *Dict. Mech.* 1881/2 The rasp-cutting machine resembles the file-cutting machine..in the striking and feeding parts. **1882** J. SMITH *Dict. Econ. Plants, Rasp-palm.*

rasp (rɑːsp, -æ-), *sb.*² Also 6 respe, 6–7 raspe. [Related to RASPIS², and perh. a back-formation from it. Now chiefly *north.* and *Sc.*]

1. = RASPBERRY 1.

1555 EDEN *Decades* 132 Bramble busshes bearynge blacke berries or wylde raspes. **1598** HAKLUYT *Voy.* I. 477 For kindes of fruites, they haue..rasps, strawberies, and hurtilberies. **1660** SHARROCK *Vegetables* 133 At Bristol he saw Raspes sold for four pence the quart at Michaelmas. **1731** ALBIN *Nat. Hist. Birds* 16 It feeds on Cherries.. Goosberries and Rasps, and other Fruit. **1871** *Routledge's Ev. Boy's Ann.* Aug. 507 Wild cranberries, strawberries, rasps, and other berries.

2. = RASPBERRY 2.

1573 TUSSER *Husb.* (1878) 32 Plant Respe and rose. **1626** BACON *Sylva* §487 Take Sorrell, and set it among Rasps. **1660** SHARROCK *Vegetables* 117 Rasps and Vines always bear upon a fresh sprout. **1796** C. MARSHALL *Garden.* iii. (1813) 39 The smooth wooded or cane rasp is to be preferred for a principal crop. **1853** G. JOHNSTON *Nat. Hist. E. Bord.* I. 71 The Rasp only ascends into the ravines and wooded deans.

rasp (rɑːsp, -æ-), *v.*¹ [App. a. OF. *rasper* (F. *râper*) = Sp., Pg. *raspar*, It. and med.L. *raspare*, perh. of Teut. origin: cf. OHG. *raspôn* to collect, scrape together. (MHG. *ûf raspen* occurs once; mod.Du. and G. *raspen* are app. from French). ME. *rospen* may also be related.]

†**1.** *trans.* To inscribe by scraping or scratching. *Obs. rare*$^{-1}$.

13.. *E.E. Allit. P.* B. 1545 Biholdand þe honde til hit hade al grauen, & rasped on þe roȝ woȝe runisch sauez.

2. a. To scrape or abrade with a rasp or other rough instrument.

13.. *E.E. Allit. P.* B. 1724 þe fyste..þat rasped renyschly þe woȝe with þe roȝ penne. **1686** PLOT *Staffordsh.* 384 He can turn 20 of these [twists], whilst one is cut or rasp't. **1694** *Phil. Trans.* XVIII. 278 The Root rasped affords a fine Flour or Powder. **1762** BORLASE *Ibid.* LII. 509 As if it had been rasped by a rough rounded file. **1811** *Self Instructor* 538 Logwood being rasped and shaved into small chips. **1859** F. A. GRIFFITHS *Artil. Man.* (1862) 90 The fuze must be rasped if necessary.

b. To scrape or rub in a rough manner.

1715 CHEYNE *Philos. Princ. Relig.* I. (ed. 2) 90 The Mercury in the Agitation of the Tube, rasping the Sides thereof. **1824** MISS FERRIER *Inher.* lxxxvii, He put his feet actually within the fender, and rasped and crunched the ashes. **1840** DICKENS *Old C. Shop* xxxviii, The pony.. evinced a strong desire to..rasp himself against the brick walls. **1878** HUXLEY *Physiogr.* 164 The ice played its part in rasping and grinding and polishing the surface of the land.

transf. **1868** J. G. HOLLAND *Kathrina* I. (1869) 20, I heard the harsh, reiterant katydids Rasp the mysterious silence.

c. *fig.* To grate upon, to irritate.

1810 *Sporting Mag.* XXXV. 80, I saw Flaherty, the deceased, and the two Jordans rasping each other. **1866** MRS. STOWE *Little Foxes* 14 The mistress is rasped, irritated, despairing. **1887** MISS CAREY *Uncle Max* xxxviii. 304 Her hard, metallic voice had rasped the invalid's nerves.

d. To grate (the hard crust) off (a roll); also *intr.* for *pass.*

1889 R. WELLS *Pastrycook & Confectioner's Guide* ii. 11 French rolls must always be rasped. **1892** —— *Mod. Pract. Bread Baker* 57 They must be well baked, or they will not rasp as all French rolls should. **1908** J. KIRKLAND *Mod. Baker* II. xxvi. 162 These rolls are occasionally baked with a very hard crust, which is afterwards rasped off.

3. To scrape *off* or *away*.

1789 *Trans. Soc. Arts* (ed. 2) II. 77, I began to rasp off the bark. **1862** TYNDALL *Mountaineer.* viii. 72 These rocks are known to have their angles rasped off, and to be fluted and scarred by the ice. **1863** KINGSLEY *Water-Bab.* viii. (1878) 329 The stream as it rushed up rasped away the sides of the hole.

4. To utter with a grating sound. Also *absol.*, *transf.* and with *out*.

1843 O. W. HOLMES *An After-Dinner Poem* 46 Grating songs..Rasped from the throats of bellowing amateurs. **1877** *Harper's Mag.* Oct. 664/1 A somewhat harsh clock rasped out the seconds. **1905** *Pall Mall Mag.* Sept. 276/1 Commander McTurk stiffened. 'Ah,' he rasped, 'that's news to me.' *Ibid.* Nov. 543/1 'Really, Bridget!' her brother rasped out, 'I wish you wouldn't interfere.' **1922** JOYCE *Ulysses* 442 A bunch of loiterers listen to a tale which their broken snouted gaffer rasps out. **1937** C. S. FORESTER *Happy Return* x. 124 'Hard-a-starboard,' he rasped at the quartermaster. **1962** [see HELL *sb.* 10 h]. **1976** W. GREATOREX *Crossover* 142 'I'm not thirsty,' Calder said. 'I've had enough for one night.' 'You're telling *me*,' the inspector rasped. **1977** *Time* 28 Nov. 50/3 Rasped an Agriculture official: 'That was a technically accurate statement. But it also was a god-damn lie.'

5. *intr.* or *absol.* **a.** To scrape or grate, *esp.* on a stringed instrument.

1808 S. W. RYLEY *Itinerant* I. iv. 91 A blind fiddler, mounted on a three footed stool, rasped away very *seriously* the black *Joke*. **1842** S. LOVER *Handy Andy* xviii. 155 Murphy, who presided in the cart full of fiddlers.., shouted ..'Rasp and lilt away boys'. **1870** A. STEINMETZ *Gaming Table* II. iv. 113 Sorrily rasping on an execrable fiddle.

fig. **1848** LOWELL *Vision Sir Launfal* i. 5 This man, so foul and bent of stature, Rasped harshly against his dainty nature. **1863** HOLLAND *Lett. Joneses* vi. 86 Your husband grew tired..with rasping against so much new domestic material.

b. To make a grating sound; to go *about* complaining in an irritating voice.

1868 M. H. SMITH *Sunsh. & Shad. N. York* 302 He has a loud, harsh, sharp tone, that rasps like a file. **1874** LISLE CARR *Jud. Gwynne* I. iii. 82 With a shrill voice ceaselessly echoing harshly-worded complaints..Mrs. Nosgood rasped about the place from morning till night.

c. With *on*: to grate upon or irritate.

1898 F. P. DUNNE *Mr. Dooley in Peace & War* 232 But wan day it happened that whole fam'ly begun to rasp on wan another. **1905** *Pall Mall Mag.* Dec. 674/2 Any reference to the Philippine campaign rasped on his nerves.

rasp (rɑːsp, -æ-), *v.*² Now *dial.* Also 9 **resp.** [? Imitative.] *intr.* and *trans.* To belch.

1626 BACON *Sylva* §123 All Eruptions of Aire..in Rasping, Sneezing, &c. **1627** BP. HALL *Heauen vpon Earth* §26. 96 The man of nice education..rasping since his last meale. **1640** W. STYLE *Antisco's Spanish Gallant* 9 [If] by reason of thy full feeding, or couldnesse of stomack, thou hast a provocation to rasp wind. *a* **1825** FORBY *E. Anglian Gloss., Rasp, Resp*, to belch.

raspass, variant of RASPIS². *Obs.*

raspatory ('rɑːspətərɪ, -æ-). [ad. med.L. *raspātōrium* (Du Cange), f. *raspāre* to RASP *v.*¹ Cf. obs. F. *raspatoire* (Godef.).]

1. A form of rasp used in surgery.

1562 BULLEYN *Def. agst. sickness, Dial. Searnes & Ch.* 44 Whiche thyng can not bee done with raspatorie. **1635** A. READ *Tumors & Ulcers* 244 The bone is to bee made even with the Raspatories, and smoothed. **1676** WISEMAN *Chirurg. Treat.* v. ix, You ought to be furnished with various sorts of Raspatories. **1804** *Med. Jrnl.* XII. 203 The different blades of the raspatory. **1879** BRYANT *Pract. Surgery* (ed. 3) I. 549 After detaching periosteum by means of the raspatory.

†**2.** 'A Butler's instrument, wherewith he chips bread' (Phillips 1658). *Obs. rare*$^{-0}$.

raspays, variant of RASPIS². *Obs.*

raspberry ('rɑːzbərɪ, -æ-). Forms: 7 res-, 7–8 ras-, 8– raspberry. [f. RASP *sb.*² + BERRY.]

1. The fruit of several plants of the genus *Rubus*, esp. *R. idæus*, consisting of many small juicy grains or drupes of a subacid flavour arranged on a conical receptacle, from which the ripe fruit is easily detached unbroken.

The common raspberry, both wild and cultivated, is of a red colour; white and yellow varieties also exist. The fruit is much used for making preserves, confections, liquors, etc.

1623 N. H. in Whitbourne *Newfoundland* 114 Cherries, Nuts, Resberries, Strawberries. **1664** EVELYN *Kal. Hort.* (1729) 207 Rasberries, Corinths, Strawberries. *a* **1756** MRS. HEYWOOD *New Present* (1771) 220 To preserve Rasberries. Let your rasberies be large. **1817** RAFFLES *Java* I. 36 The wild raspberry, which is found in the higher regions, is not destitute of flavour. **1891** MISS DOWIE *Girl in Karp.* 234 A ..handful of rasp, straw, and whortle berries.

2. The plant which produces the raspberry, or other plants of the genus *Rubus* resembling this.

The common species, *Rubus idæus*, has woody stems thickly covered with weak prickles, pinnate leaves which are white on the under-side, and whitish flowers.

flowering or ***Virginian raspberry***, the American species *Rubus odoratus*.

1733 MILLER *Gard. Dict.* s.v. *Rubus*, All the other Sorts are propagated from Suckers in the same Manner as the Garden Raspberries. **1741** *Compl. Fam.-Piece* II. iii. 380 There are several other Trees and Shrubs which are now in Flower, as..upright sweet Canada Rasberries. **1846** J. BAXTER *Libr. Pract. Agric.* (ed. 4) II. 229 The root of the raspberry is considered to be perennial.

3. Raspberry wine.

1768 GOLDSM. *Good-n. Man* v. i, A drop of as pretty raspberry as ever was tipt over tongue.

4. a. [App. an ellipt. use of *raspberry tart* (*b*) below.] A derisive sound; = *Bronx cheer* s.v. BRONX 2.

1890 in BARRÈRE & LELAND *Dict. Slang* (1890) II. 171/1 The tongue is inserted in the left cheek and forced through the lips, producing a peculiarly squashy noise that is extremely irritating. It is termed, I believe, a *raspberry*, and when not employed for the purpose of testing horseflesh, is regarded rather as an expression of contempt than of admiration. **1899** A. M. BINSTEAD *Gal's Gossip* 144 A loud and offensive noise, like the rending of glazed calico, made by obtruding the wet tongue between the closed lips, and by low cabmen and persons of that class, called a 'raspberry', came from the gallery. **1912** *Confessions of Dancing Girl* iv. 69 The custom of 'guying' a performer and giving him what is called a 'raspberry'. Not a few artistes have had 'raspberries' from the audiences in the Glasgow variety halls. **1932** A. J. WORRALL *Eng. Idioms* v. 33 As soon as the speaker rose the crowd gave him the raspberry. **1940** R. CHANDLER *Farewell, my Lovely* xxix. 211 The kind of bossy knock that makes you want to..emit the succulent raspberry. **1955** [see BRONX 2]. **1960** G. DURRELL *Zoo in my Luggage* vi. 157 To my complete astonishment Minnie responded by..giving a prolonged raspberry of the juiciest variety. **1975** *South Wales Echo* 30 Oct. 8/4 The only answer to that kind of nonsense is a long-drawn-out vintage raspberry.

b. *fig.* A refusal; a reprimand, disapproval; dismissal.

1920 WODEHOUSE *Damsel in Distress* vi. 71 Convict son totters up the steps of the old home and punches the bell!

What awaits him beyond? Forgiveness? Or the raspberry? **1923** —— *Inimitable Jeeves* ix. 89 He was given the respectful raspberry by Jeeves, and told to try again about three hours later. **1927** *Punch* 14 Dec. 649/2, I have embodied the above suggestions in a memo, and they are now on their way to the Army Council... They may even be on their way back, with a raspberry from Somebody Very Senior written across the top left-hand corner. **1942** *New Statesman* 1 Aug. 75/1 An ordinary reprimand is a *raspberry* (often referred to by other ranks as a *razzer*), which has been adopted from that form of civilian disapproval which one hears in the gallery of a theatre. **1947** [see ALL *adv.* 2 c]. **1960** O. MANNING *Great Fortune* I. 67 Miller made it! Nice scoop for Miller! And a raspberry for the rest of us. **1973** M. SPARK *Hothouse by East River* iv. 69 The security officer mutters all the way to the compound about what a raspberry the police are going to get because of this, a raspberry in these days being already an outdated expression meaning a reprimand. A man less set in his limited ways..would call it a rocket in this English spring of 1944. **1977** *Western Morning News* 1 Sept. 1/2 Controversial punk rock band Sex Pistols blew a raucous raspberry at the Establishment by sneaking into Plymouth to play an unannounced concert at Woods.

5. The colour of a raspberry, varying from pink to scarlet. Also *attrib.* or as *adj.*

1923 *Daily Mail* 19 Feb. 15 New tailor-mades of black or navy serge have shawl collars of mattelassé silk in a contrasting colour—raspberry, green, or kingfisher blue. **1935** *Times* 2 Oct. 17/4 A raspberry cellophane wrap has been shown over a white and gold lamé gown. **1941** [see HACKMANITE]. **1951** E. PAUL *Springtime in Paris* ii. 17 Two neon signs,..one..in a faint raspberry shade, and another ..in a luminous tone of white. **1969** 'H. PENTECOST' *Girl Watcher's Funeral* (1970), II. i. 88 The raspberry dress that clung to her lush figure. **1972** [see LIME *sb.*[2] 1 c]. **1978** J. KRANTZ *Scruples* ii. 24 The floor of the air-conditioned room was covered from one wall to another in thick raspberry carpet.

6. *attrib.* and *Comb.*, as ***raspberry bitters, brandy, bush, cream, drop, fool, jam, jelly, juice, noyau, pie, roll, seed, syrup, tart, tree, vinegar, wine***; ***raspberry-like, -scented*** adjs.; **raspberry apple**, an apple having the flavour of the raspberry; **raspberry beetle**, a beetle of the genus *Byturus*, esp. *B. tomentosus* (formerly *B. urbanus*), the larva of which attacks the fruit of raspberries and related plants: **raspberry fruitworm** = prec.; **raspberry jam (tree)**, an Australian tree, *Acacia acuminata*, so called from the smell of its wood; also, the wood itself; **raspberry kidney**, a kidney of a morbid granular structure resembling that of a raspberry; **raspberry lid**, an eye-lid having a morbid growth like a raspberry; **raspberry red**, the colour of the raspberry; also as *adj.*; **raspberry tart** *rhyming slang*, (*a*) the heart; (*b*) a breaking of wind or 'fart'.

1894 *Daily News* 5 Oct. 5/2 The *raspberry-apple, or pomme framboise, attracted the attention of gardeners, amateur and professional. **1884** E. A. ORMEROD *Observations Injurious Insects 1883* 65 A small brown Beetle..proved to be the '*Raspberry Beetle',..which was causing fearful havoc and entirely devouring the Raspberries. **1909** F. V. THEOBALD *Insects & Other Pests of Orchard, Bush & Hothouse Fruits* 420 There is no insect enemy so serious to raspberries as the Raspberry Beetle. **1959** E. F. LINSSEN *Beetles Brit. Isles* II. 23 This genus [sc. *Byturus*] includes a well-known pest of raspberries, loganberries and blackberries, commonly referred to as the Raspberry Beetle. **1849** THACKERAY *Pendennis* I. xv. 131 He..drank a glass of *raspberry bitters at the Clavering Arms. **1796** MORSE *Amer. Geog.* II. 503 They appeared to prefer cherry and *rasberry brandy. **1733** MILLER *Gard. Dict., Rubus*,..the Bramble or *Rasp-berry-bush. **1864** SOWERBY *Eng. Bot.* (ed. 3) III. 161 Raspberry bushes..bear the finest fruit in a light rich loamy soil. **1661** RABISHA *Body Cookery Diss.* 30 To make *Rasberry Cream. **1851** MAYHEW *Lond. Lab.* II. 46/2 Raspberry cream! Iced raspberry-cream, ha'penny a glass! **1897** 'S. GRAND' *Beth Book* iii. 19 Give me a ha'porth ..of *raspberry-drops. **1939–40** *Army & Navy Stores Catal.* 52/2 *Boiled sweets*..Raspberry drops. **1728** E. SMITH *Compl. Housew.* (ed. 2) 150 To make Strawberry or *Raspberry Fool. **1924** *Ann. Rep. Connecticut Agric. Exper. Station* 91 The *Raspberry Fruit Worm or Raspberry Beetle has long been known as a pest of red raspberries in the United States. **1945** L. PYENSON *Pest Control in Home Garden* vii. 122 The formula used in these two sprays controls the raspberry fruit worm. **1972** SWAN & PAPP *Common Insects N. Amer.* 396 The Western Raspberry Fruitworm..is a serious pest of raspberries and loganberries. **1747** *Raspberry jam [see JAM *sb.*[2] a]. **1769** MRS. RAFFALD *Eng. Housekpr.* (1778) 251 A quart of raspberries, or raspberry jam. **1846** [see *gooseberry jam* s.v. GOOSEBERRY 7 a]. **1846** STOKES *Disc. Australia* II. iv. 132 Raspberry Jam [Tree], Acacia..Sweet-scented—grows on good ground. **1847** LEICHHARDT *Jrnl.* x. 342 The raspberry-jam tree covered the approaches to the river. **1865** J. E. TENISON-WOODS *Hist. Discovery & Exploration Austral.* II. 68 The other trees beside the palm were known to the men by colonial appellations, such as the bloodwood and the raspberry-jam. **1896** *Australasian* 15 Feb. 313 The raspberry-jam-tree is so called on account of the strong aroma of raspberries given out when a portion is broken. **1948** F. H. TITMUSS *Conc. Encycl. World Timbers* 113 Raspberry Jam is rather a difficult timber to work. **1965** *Austral. Encyl.* VII. 389/1 Raspberry-jam, a popular name standardized in the timber trade for *Acacia acuminata* of Western Australia; the dark reddish-brown, durable, close-grained wood of this wattle has a distinct raspberry-like scent. **1861** MRS. BEETON *Bk. Househ. Managem.* 797 *Raspberry Jelly... To each pint of juice allow ¾ lb. of loaf sugar. **1661** RABISHA *Body Cookery Diss.* 216 A quarter of a pinte of *Raspberry-juice. **1897** *Allbutt's Syst. Med.* IV. 334 That condition known as red granular kidney, or *raspberry kidney, which occurs in middle-aged people. **1869** *Eng. Mech.* 3 Dec. 271/2 The lids are covered with hard granulations which are termed the '*raspberry lid'. **1894** *Daily News* 5 Oct. 5/2 It has a *raspberry-like taste. **1897** *Allbutt's Syst. Med.* II. 501 A chronic, specific and contagious disease, characterized by raspberry-like tubercles. **1913, 1963** *Raspberry noyau [see NOYAU 1 b]. **1828** E. LESLIE *Seventy-Five Receipts* 25 *Raspberry and apple-pies are much improved by..pouring in a little cream. **1864** *Harper's Mag.* Nov. 735/1 A green cheese, a dish of cucumbers, and two raspberry pies supplied a finish to the entertainment. **1974** J. GRIGSON *Eng. Food* 206 Raspberry Pie..Filling 1 lb raspberries About 4 oz sugar [etc.]. **1894** *Daily News* 7 July 6/6 Another party, who floated a *raspberry red flag on their boat. **1868** A. D. WHITNEY *Patience Strong's Outings* (1869) xii. 138, I..made her give up..the special *raspberry-roll for dinner. **1894** J. BROWN *Forester* II. 501 *Acacia acuminata*, 'Jam' or *Raspberry scented acacia. **1841** M. EDGEWORTH *Let.* 23 Mar. (1971) 590 Dr. Lindley..saw that they were *raspberry seeds and he put them in ground and they..have grown to real raspberry bushes. **1728** E. SMITH *Compl. Housewife* (ed. 2) 192 Two Ounces of Syrup of red Poppies, and as much of *Raspberry Syrup. **1965** *Savoy Cocktail Bk.* (ed. 3) 177 *Raspberry Lemonade Cocktail.* Put into tumbler juice of 1 Lemon..sugar..Raspberry Syrup..ice..water. **1723** J. NOTT *Cook's & Confectioner's Dict.* sig. Ff3 (*heading*) To make a *Raspberry Tart. **1848** [see HARD-BAKE]. **1859** *Household Encycl.* s.v., Raspberry Tart with cream. **1892** *Sporting Times* 29 Oct. 1/2 Then I sallied forth with a careless air, And contented raspberry tart. **1959** I. & P. OPIE *Lore & Lang. Schoolch.* i. 9 Breaking wind was, at one time, by the process of rhyming slang, known as a 'raspberry tart'. **1765** *Chron.* in *Ann. Reg.* 140/2 Some *raspberry trees in perfect leaf. **1713** SPRENGNELL in *Phil. Trans.* XXVIII. 139 Sprinkled with *Rasberry-Vinegar. **1841** *Penny Cycl.* XX. 215/2 Raspberry-vinegar is not only an agreeable beverage, but is said to act as a febrifuge. **1960** J. J. ROWLANDS *Spindrift* 55 That was the era of raspberry vinegar, lemonade, and homemade root beer. **1728** R. BRADLEY *Country Housewife* 115 To make *Rasberry Wine. **1841** *Penny Cycl.* XX. 215/2 Raspberry-wine is much used in Poland.

Hence **raspberri'ade, -berry'ette**, liquors made from, or flavoured with, raspberries.

1851 MAYHEW *Lond. Lab.* II. 46/1 Iced lemonade here! Iced raspberriade. **1883** *Pall Mall G.* 12 Oct. 12/1 Mixtures known as gingerette, raspberryette, and peppermint.

† **raspe** *a. Obs. rare*[−1]. [a. obs. F. *raspé*, now *râpé*: see RAPE *sb.*[6], and cf. RASPY *a.*[2]] ***raspe wine*** = RAPE *sb.*[6]

1600 SURFLET *Countrie Farme* VI. xxii. 787 Greene or raspe wine, in as much as it containeth more water then wine, nourisheth the body but a little.

So **rasped** *a. rare*[−1].

1823 COLEBROOKE in *St. Cape G. Hope* 363 They have added sweet wine, or boiled must, fermented for the purpose, like rasped wine in France [*note*, Vin rapé].

rasped (rɑːspt, -æ-), *ppl. a.* [f. RASP *v.*[1] + -ED[1].] Grated, scraped; rough as if rubbed with a rasp. Also *spec.* in *Book-binding* (see quot. 1890).

1599 A. M. tr. *Gabelhouer's Bk. Physicke* 302/2 Sodden Quince broth,..with rasped Hartes-horne. **1694** SALMON *Bates' Dispens.* (1713) 636/2 Gelly of Harts-horn and rasped Ivory. **1749** MRS. GLASSE *Cookery* 17 Garnish your Dish with rasp'd Bread, made into Figures. **1865** DICKENS *Mut. Fr.* I. xi, Chilled elbows, and a rasped surface of nose. **1890** ZÆHNSDORF *Bookbinding* Gloss., *Rasped*, the sharp edge taken off mill-boards.

rasper ('rɑːspə(r), -æ-). [f. RASP *v.*[1] + -ER[1].]

1. One who or that which rasps; a rasping-machine for beetroot, etc.

1725 *Lond. Gaz.* No. 6382/11 Richard Sill,..Harthorn-Rasper. **1865** J. T. F. TURNER *Slate Quarries* 17 The wages due to the sawyers, planers, and raspers. **1875** KNIGHT *Dict. Mech.* 1881/1 *Rasper*, a file for rasping the burnt surface from loaves of bread. **1882** *Spon's Encycl. Manuf.* 1824 The potatoes are introduced by the hopper, and are forced.. against the short saw-like teeth of the rasper.

2. *Hunting.* A high difficult fence.

1812 *Sporting Mag.* XXXIX. 232 Having to surmount in every field, what in sporting phrase is denominated a Rasper. **1841** J. T. HEWLETT *Parish Clerk* I. 79 Many raspers and bullfinches were cleared by the little Shetlands. **1929** H. A. VACHELL *Virgin* iii. 53 In front was a big solid fence, a rasper.

3. *slang.* A person or thing of sharp, harsh, or unpleasant character; also, anything remarkable or extraordinary in its own way.

1839 DICKENS *Nich. Nick.* lvii, He's what you may a-call a rasper, is Nickleby. **1844** *Spirit of Times* 19 Oct. 403/2 She promises to be a perfect 'rasper', and will have some 'tall' chronicling in the 'Spirit' before all of her yarn is spun. **1860** SIR T. MARTIN *Horace* 16 His bat at cricket was a rasper. **1886** *Field* 27 Feb. 256/3 Her course with Carsehill was such a rasper that there was little hope for her in the final. **1977** SCOLLINS & TITFORD *Ey up, mi Duck!* II. 52 *Rasper*, another expression of excellence; often describes a good goal in football.

raspes(se, variants of RASPIS[2] *Obs.*

'rasp-house. [ad. Du. *rasphuis* (G. *raspelhaus*), f. *raspen* RASP *v.*[1]] A house of correction formerly in use in Holland, Germany, etc., where prisoners were employed in rasping wood.

1641 EVELYN *Diary* 19 Aug., We went to see the Rasp-house, where the lusty knaves are compell'd to worke, and the rasping of Brasill and Logwood is very hard labour. **1670** R. HAINES *Meth. Govt.* (1679) 7 Another Officer was whipt and committed to the Rasp-house. **1756** NUGENT *Gr. Tour, Netherlands* I. 81 The Rasp-house, or house of correction, is ..very well worth a traveller's notice. **1865** *Daily Tel.* 28 Dec. 5/5 The judge..sent this rascal to the whipping-post, and that rogue to the rasp-house.

raspice, -ies, variants of RASPIS[1]. *Obs.*

rasping ('rɑːspɪŋ, -æ-), *vbl. sb.*[1] [f. RASP *v.*[1]]

1. The act of rubbing or scraping with or as with a rasp; a grating sound.

1597 A. M. tr. *Guillemeau's Fr. Chirurg.* 33 b/2 When we perceave, in raspinge, the bone to give bloode from it. **1641** [see RASP-HOUSE]. **1703** MOXON *Mech. Exerc.* 212 Either with Hewing, or as some Hard Woods and Ivory may require, with Rasping. **1889** DOYLE *Micah Clarke* 91 There was much creaking of locks and rasping of bolts.

2. *concr.* in *pl.* Small particles produced by rasping. In mod. usage, *spec.* breadcrumbs made from baked or stale bread.

1655 CULPEPPER, etc. *Riverius* I. i. 8 Take the shavings or raspings of a Skull that was never buried. **1736** BAILEY *Househ. Dict.* 343 Give him raspings of bread, which may be had of the London bakers for nine pence or 10 pence a strike. **1791** HAMILTON tr. *Berthollet's Art of Dyeing* I. I. I v. 101 Oak bark and raspings of heart of oak. **1846** *Jewish Manual Cookery* 47 Butter a mold, sprinkle it with raspings. **1875** H. C. WOOD *Therap.* (1879) 55 Quassia..is kept in the shops in billets and in raspings. **1945** *ABC of Cookery* (Ministry of Food) iii. 14 *Raspings*, very fine crumbs obtained by grating the crust of stale bread on a fine grater. Browned breadcrumbs are sometimes called raspings. **1951** *Good Housek. Home Encycl.* 629/1 Sprinkle raspings over the fat of cooked ham. **1976** M. PATTEN *Barbecue* 31/2 Cut the crusts from the loaf; these need not be wasted, but can be turned into crumbs (raspings) as described below.

3. *attrib.*, as ***rasping-machine, -mill.***

1655 MRQ. WORCESTER *Cent. Inv.* §83 A Rasping-Mill for Harts-horn. **1835** URE *Philos. Manuf.* 58 Rasping-mills for logwood. **1875** KNIGHT *Dict. Mech.* 1881/1 *Rasping-machine.*

rasping ('rɑːspɪŋ, -æ-), *ppl. a.*[1] [f. RASP *v.*[1] + -ING[2].] That rasps, in senses of the vb.

1656 RIDGLEY *Pract. Physick* 168 Scraped with rasping Instruments. **1735** W. SEWEL *Dutch Dict., Rasphuys boef*, a Rasping rascal, a Bridewel-rogue. **1856** MRS. CARLYLE *Lett.* II. 269 A cold, rasping, savage day; excruciating for sick nerves. **1873** MISS BROUGHTON *Nancy* II. 146 He, in his raspingest voice, is giving his [valet] a month's warning.

b. *Hunting.* Difficult to take. Cf. RASPER 2.

1829 *Sporting Mag.* XXIII. 372 Many ox-fences and two rasping brooks. **1837** T. HOOK *Jack Brag* i, We'll..pick out rasping fences.

c. Extremely or unpleasantly rapid.

1875 J. GRANT *One of the '600'* xi. 92 Away we went..at a rasping pace.

Hence **'raspingly** *adv.*, in a rasping manner.

1883 *Harper's Mag.* June 6/2 The wooden rattles with which..the people were raspingly summoned to public worship. **1887** F. WARDEN *Scheherazade* II. i. 17 'Try it!' said he raspingly.

† **'rasping,** *ppl. a.*[2] *Obs.*[−1] [f. RASP *v.*[2] + -ING[2].] Belching, emitting wind.

1629 T. ADAMS *England's Sickness* Wks. I. 328 Let them ..drink Cleopatra's draught..to ease their rasping stomacke.

† **'raspis**[1]. *Obs.* Forms: 5 **raspise, -ice, 6 raspays, -yce, 7 -is; 5 respice, 6 -yce.** [Of obscure origin.

Possibly connected with OF. *raspeit, -pei* (mod.F. *râpé*: see RAPE *sb.*[6]), It. *raspato* (rendered 'raspis wine' by Florio), med.L. *raspatum, -etum, -ecia*: in that case the ending *ice, -is* may be due to the med.L. form in *-ecia*. Boorde (quot. 1542) evidently supposed it to be raspberry-wine (cf. RASPIS WINE), but it seems unlikely, from the contexts in which it occurs, that this was the usual sense of the word.]

A kind of wine used in the 15th and 16th centuries.

c **1460** J. RUSSELL *Bk. Nurture* 118 in *Babees Bk.* 9 The namys of swete wynes..pyment, Raspise, Muscadelle of grew. ?*c* **1475** *Sqr. lowe Degre* 756 Mount rose and wyne of Greke, Both algrade, and respice eke. **1519** *Interl. Four Elem.* (Percy Soc.) 22 Ye shall han Spanyeshe wyne and Gascoyn,..Sak, raspyce, alycaunt, rumney. **1542** BOORDE *Dyetary* x. (1870) 254 All maner of wynes be made of grapes, excepte respyce, the whiche is made of a bery. **1584** COGAN *Haven Health* 218 Redde wine, if it be a deepe redde enclining to blacke as Raspis.

† **'raspis**[2]. *Obs.* Forms: α. 6 **raspyse, -ass, 6–7 raspes, -is, -ice, 7 raspies, -esse, -isse.** β. 6 **respis, -ies, -yce, 7 respas, -ass(e.** [Of obscure origin: perh. in some way related to prec.]

1. a. *collect.* Raspberries.

c **1532** DU WES *Introd. Fr.* in Palsgr. 912 Raspyse, *franboises.* **1565** GOLDING *Ovid's Met.* I. (1593) 4 Men..Did live by respis, heps, and haws. **1578** LYTE *Dodoens* 662 The fruite of this Bramble is called..in English Raspis or Framboys berries. **1658** EVELYN *French Gardiner* (1675) 256 Raspis are of two colours, the white and the red. **1688** R. HOLME *Armoury* III. 80/1 Preserves..as Pears, Plums,.. Grapes, Respass.

b. (With pl. in *-es.*) A raspberry.

1548 TURNER *Names Herbes* (E.D.S.) 68 Rubus ideus is called..in englishe raspeses or hyndberies. **1600** HAKLUYT *Voy.* III. 305 There are Raspasses, and a little berrie which we call among vs Blues. **1648** HERRICK *Hesperides* 168 The wine of cherries, and to these The cooling breath of Respasses. **1678** J. PHILLIPS tr. *Tavernier's Voy.* xix. 92 Of Strawberries and raspices there is great store.

2. The raspberry-plant.

1558 W. WARD tr. *Alexis' Secr.* I. I. 19 b, This..is taken of Ioannes Agricola to be the brier called Respis. **1573** TUSSER *Husb.* (1878) 72 Set Respis and Rose, yoong rootes of those. **1629** PARKINSON *Paradisus Terrestris* 557 The leaves of Raspis may be used..in gargles. **1682** GREW *Anat. Plants* v. 275 The Leavs of Rose-Tree, Raspis [etc.].

3. *attrib.*, as ***raspis-bush, juice, orchard, tree.***

c **1532** DU WES *Introd. Fr.* in Palsgr. 914 Raspis tre, *francboisier.* **1597** GERARDE *Herbal* III. 1089 The Raspis bush, or Hindberrie. **1622** WITHER *Philarete* (1633) 591 The shrubbie fields are Raspice Orchards there. *a* **1648** LD. HERBERT *Hen. VIII* (1683) 89 A Frambousier or Raspis-Bush. **1660** MAY *Accompl. Cook* (1665) 254 A quarter of a pint of raspas juyce.

† **raspis-berry.** *Obs.* [f. prec.] = RASPBERRY.
a **1548** HALL *Chron., Hen. VIII* (1809) 611 The Aubespine . . and the Framboister [*sic*] whiche is in English the Hathorne . . and the Raspis berry. **1600** HAKLUYT *Voy.* (1810) III. 192 The like plentie of raspis berries, which doe grow in euery place. **1623** WHITBOURNE *Newfoundland* 5 Faire Strawberries, red and white, and faire Respasse berries, and Gooseberries.

raspish (ˈrɑːspɪʃ, -æ-), *a. rare.* [f. RASP *v.*[1] + -ISH.] Irritating, irritable.
1854 P. B. ST. JOHN *Amy Moss* 77 Well, don't be so raspish. **1866** *Mattie, a Stray* II. 158 You were hot-headed, and I was ill-tempered and raspish, and so we quarrelled.

† **raspis wine.** *Obs.* Also 6 -ise, 7 respass.
a. = RASPIS[1]. **b.** ? Raspberry wine.
1562 TURNER *Herbal* II. 120 It were good to kepe some of the iuyce of the berries . . and to make of it as it were raspis wine. **1598** FLORIO, *Raspato*, . . Raspise wine. **1662** R. MATHEW *Unl. Alch.* §40. 40 A very good friend of mine . . was feasted . . with Venison and Respass wine.

raspite (ˈræspaɪt). *Min.* [ad. G. *raspit* (C. Hlawatsch 1897, in *Ann. des K.K. Naturhist. Hofmuseums* XII. 33), f. the name of Mr. *Rasp*, discoverer of the Broken Hill mines, New South Wales, where the first specimen was found: see -ITE[1].] A lead tungstate, $PbWO_4$, that is dimorphous with stolzite and occurs as brownish, yellow, or grey prismatic monoclinic crystals.
1898 *Mineral Mag.* XII. 47 Raspite, a new dimorphous form of lead tungstate, is found on some of the stolzite specimens as brownish or yellow monoclinic crystals with a strong adamantine lustre. **1931** J. W. MELLOR *Compreh. Treat. Inorg. & Theoret. Chem.* XI. lxii. 793 Stolzite occurs in tetragonal crystals, raspite in monoclinic crystals. **1956** *Mineral Abstr.* XIII. 30 Natural raspite transforms irreversibly to stolzite at about 400° C. **1968** I. KOSTOV *Mineralogy* II. viii. 486 Stolzite is uniaxial negative . .; raspite biaxial positive.

Rasputin (ræˈspjuːtɪn, ˈræspjuːtɪn). The acquired name (lit. 'debauchee') of Grigory Yefimovich Novykh (*c* 1872–1916), mystic and favourite at the court of the Russian Emperor Nicholas II, used allusively of one who resembles Rasputin in exercising an insidious or corrupting influence over another or (esp.) over members of the governing class. Also *attrib.*
1937 H. G. WELLS *Star Begotten* viii. 152 My professional gifts give me a kind of Rasputin hold on one or two exalted families. **1975** *Economist* 8 Feb. 35/2 Referred to in private . . as a Rasputin or a Svengali, her private secretary, Sr José López Rega, has enlarged his power. **1975** *Times* 23 May 2/2 Mr Wilson . . drove home the policy divisions on the Tory front bench by noting that Sir Keith Joseph—'Mrs Thatcher's . . mentor and Svengali' . . the right hon lady's Rasputin—had been kennelled up for the debate. **1978** G. MITCHELL *Wraiths & Changelings* xv. 149 He was becoming a sort of Rasputin where Mrs Crieff-Tweedle was concerned. . . I'm sure she was coming under . . a sinister influence.
So **Raˈsputinism**, the principles and practices held to be characteristic of Rasputin, chiefly with reference to his libertinism and his corrupting influence over government.
1918 *Pall Mall Gaz.* 26 Jan. 3/1 Some exceedingly fine shades of difference were explained, and some striking affinities pointed out. For instance, Bolshevism, in Mr. Wilton's opinion, is nothing but Rasputinism under another name. **1919** W. LE QUEUX *Rasputinism in London* xii. 160 London is surely vicious enough without the evil practices of Rasputinism! **1933** H. G. WELLS *Shape of Things to Come* II. iv. 169 It had a touch of Rasputinism, this revival of the ancient heresy that one must sin *thoroughly* before one can be saved. **1975** *Economist* 8 Feb. 35/3 But a new decree, signed by Sra Perón herself, has made it clear that he [*sc.* her private secretary] will have the last word about whom she sees and what she is told. This latest step towards the legitimisation of rasputinism (the latest word to be coined here [*sc.* in Argentina]) has aroused the armed forces.

raspy (ˈrɑːspɪ, -æ-), *a.*[1] [f. RASP *v.*[1] + -Y[1].]
1. Of a rasping nature; harsh, grating.
1838 CARLYLE *Varnhagen v. Ense, Misc.* (1857) IV. 197 Such a raspy, untamed voice as that of his I have hardly heard. **1882** BLACKMORE *Christowell* xxxvi, Ungainly, nubbly, fruit it was, . . raspy, to the teeth.
2. Easily exasperated; irritable.
1869 L. M. ALCOTT *Little Women* II. i. 20, I don't wish to get raspy, so let's change the subject. **1877** *Holderness Gloss.*, *Raspy*, short-tempered. **1893** *Harper's Mag.* 975/1 Her temper was . . certainly 'raspy'.
3. *Comb.*, as ***raspy-gaspy***.
1903 KIPLING in *Windsor Mag.* Sept. 363/2 She said it in a raspy-gaspy whisper that would have frightened a steam-cow.

† **ˈraspy,** *a.*[2] *Obs.* $rare^{-1}$. [Anglicized form of obs. F. *raspé*.] = RASPE *a.* (q.v.).
1703 *Art & Myst. Vintners* 20 They counterfeit Raspy wine, with Flower-de-luce Roots.

raspyce, -yse, variants of RASPIS. *Obs.*

rass (rɑːs), *sb.* (*a.*) and *v. Jamaica. coarse slang.* [f. ARSE *sb.* by metathesis and perh. partly also by metanalysis (of *your arse*).] **A.** *sb.* The buttocks, the arse. Also *transf.* as a term of contempt, and *attrib.* or as *adj.* **B.** *vb. trans.* = BUGGER *v.* 2; also *ellipt.* for 'shove it up your arse' used as an insult.
1790 J. B. MORETON *Manners & Customs in W. India Islands* 154 Then missess fum me wid long switch, And say him da for massa; My massa curse her, 'lying bitch!' And tell her 'buss my rassa!' *c* **1918** in CASSIDY & LE PAGE *Dict. Jamaican Eng.* (1967) 372/2 /raas/ as in 'Raas to you!'—common among schoolboys. **1952** *Caribbean Q.* II. iv. 27 Fred dropped his hoe and hit him hard. Big Joe was up roaring:—'Rass yah today!' **1959** A. SALKEY *Quality of Violence* vii. 101 You rass clothes going rip off. . . You, class-war rass hole, you! *Ibid.*, They believe they is superior and all that rass! **1965** I. FLEMING *Man with Golden Gun* xiii. 173 'Rass, man! Ah doan talk wid buckra.' The expression 'rass' is Jamaican for 'shove it'. **1976** BOOT & THOMAS *Jamaica* 88 If he gave them any *rass* they'd hit from all sides with a gale of maniacal rhetoric that would reduce the poor man to blubber.

rass, obs. f. RACE *sb.*[1] etc.; obs. pa. t. RISE *v.*

† **rassasy,** *v. Obs. rare.* [a. F. *rassasier* (13th c.), f. *re-* + OF. *assasier*, f. L. *ad-* + *satiāre*: see SATIATE *v.*] *trans.* To satisfy (a hungry person). Also const. *of*.
1483 CAXTON *G. de la Tour* I ij b, The brede of heuen wherof she was rassasyed and fylde. **1484** —— *Fables of Æsop* v. x, I must ete one of yow, to th'ende that I may be fylled and rassasyed of my grete honger.

rasse[1] (ˈræsə, ræs). [Javanese *rase*.] A kind of civet-cat (*Viverricula indica*, or Malacca Weasel) found in India, the Malay Peninsula, Java, China, etc., and frequently kept in captivity for the sake of the perfume obtained from it.
1817 RAFFLES *Java* I. 50 Musk, called *dedes*, is procured from the *rasé*. **1824** HORSFIELD *Zool. Researches in Java, Viverra Rasse*. . . The Rasse belongs to the division of strictly digitigrade Carnassiers. **1861** WOOD *Nat. Hist.* I. 232 The Rasse is spread over a large extent of country. **1896** R. LYDEKKER *Handbk. Carnivora* 216 While all the other civets are non-arboreal animals, the Rasse is said to be an expert climber. **1971** L. H. MATTHEWS *Life of Mammals* II. ix. 273 The rasse, *Viverricula indica*, widespread in India and southeast Asia, is smaller but similar [to the African civet] in diet and habits.

† **rasse**[2]. *Obs.* $rare^{-1}$. ? A peak, projection.
13.. *E.E. Allit. P.* B. 446 On a rasse of a rok, hit rest at þe laste.

† **rassed,** *ppl. a. Obs. rare.* [f. RACE *v.*[4] or RASE *v.*[2] + -ED[1].] Torn off; hence in *Her.* (of two colours) meeting in a jagged line. Cf. ERASED 2 a.
1513 in Glover *Hist. Derby* I. App. 61 An Asse hed goulls rassed and haltered. **1572** BOSSEWELL *Armorie* II. 27 b, These be called quartered Armes, rassed, for ye two colours be rassed, as though the one were rente from the other.

‖ **rassenschander** (ˈrasənˌʃandər). *rare.* [erron. f. G. *rassenschande*, f. *rasse* race + *schande* violation.] The violation of the purity of the ('Aryan') race by marriage to one of a different race.
1937 AUDEN in Auden & MacNeice *Lett. from Iceland* xiii. 201, I ought to be the prize, the living wonder, The really pure from any Rassenschander. . . The Nordic type, the too too truly Aryan.

rassh(e, obs. forms of RASH *a.* and *v.*

rassle, obs. form of *wrastle* WRESTLE *v.*

Rasspout, obs. form of RAJPUT.

‖ **rasta** (rasta), *sb.*[1] [Fr., abbrev. of RASTAQUOUÈRE.] = RASTAQUOUÈRE.
1905 *Truth* 18 May 1267/2 The *rasta*—for the word undergoes contraction—was twenty years ago apt to be unpleasant on account of his airs. **1929** J. BUCHAN *Courts of Morning* 25 One of his South American colleagues had taken him to dine at a restaurant much in vogue among the *rastas*. **1937** G. FRANKAU *More of Us* vii. 77 Doyen de Bouche, that celebrated rasta, Inventor of the coup de limonade.

Rasta (ˈræstə), *sb.*[2] Also **rasta.** [Shortened form of RASTAFARI or RASTAFARIAN(ISM).]
a. = RASTAFARIAN *sb.* **b.** = RASTAFARIANISM. Freq. *attrib.* and *Comb.* Hence **ˈRastaman,** a (male) Rastafarian.
1955 G. E. SIMPSON in *Social Forces* XXXIV. II. 167/1 The 'Rasta' people consider Marcus Garvey . . as the forerunner of their movement. **1960** M. G. SMITH et al. *Ras Tafari Movement in Kingston, Jamaica* 11 Those people who worshipped the Emperor and were locally known as 'Ras Tafaris' or 'Rastamen' came to describe themselves as 'Niyamen'. **1962** *Listener* 1 Feb. 209/1 There are other Rastas, fanatic and militant, whose ideology is a blend of myth, religion, anarchistic politics, and black nationalism. **1965** I. FLEMING *Man with Golden Gun* vi. 84 'You carry a gun?' 'Of course. You don't go after the Rastas without one.' **1966** [see LOCKSMAN[2]]. **1976** BOOT & THOMAS *Jamaica* 79/1 Rasta is not just some half-witted heretic sect selling space in the hereafter. *Ibid.* 93/1 Why should a Rastaman lift a finger to participate in a society that thinks he's just some poor dope-fiend with fried spinach for brains? **1976** *New Musical Express* 27 Mar. 19/6 Doris Day's son Terry Melcher and ex-Beach Boy Bruce Johnston scraping the bottom of the barrel with this well known primary school rasta chant. **1977** MCKNIGHT & TOBLER *Bob Marley* ii. 31 Remember the words of the song *Jah Live*, a Rasta-minded admonishment to all those who suggest that Selassie's physical and merely temporal death might represent the death of the living God. **1977** *Westindian World* 3–9 June 13/3 They are also reflections of Tosh's world view; a combination of Pan African nationalism and rasta mysticism.

Rastafari, Ras Tafari (ˌræstəˈfɑːrɪ; *locally also* ˌrastafaˈrai). Also **Rastafaria.** [f. the name *Ras Tafari* (cf. RAS), by which Emperor Haile Selassie of Ethiopia (1892–1975) was known from 1916 until his accession in 1930.] A Jamaican sect which believes that Blacks are the chosen people, that the late Emperor Haile Selassie is God Incarnate, and that he will secure their repatriation to their homeland in Africa. Also *pl.*, the members of this sect, and *attrib.* So **Rastaˈfarinism, Rastaˈfarism, Ras Taˈfarism; Rastaˈfarite,** a member of this sect.
1953 F. HENRIQUES *Family & Colour in Jamaica* iii. 62 The current expositors of black consciousness in Jamaica are a group of people who call themselves Ras Tafarites. **1955** G. E. SIMPSON in *Social & Econ. Stud.* (Kingston, Jamaica) IV. II. 133 The Ras Tafari movement began to take shape about 1930. *Ibid.* 137 Among the favourite chapters of the Ras Tafaris are: Isaiah 43. *Ibid.* 146 Ras Tafarism provides explanations of their plight to economically disadvantaged people. **1960** *Guardian* 12 Apr. 9/3 The 'Rastafari' cult, who have long, matted hair and beards and believe that the drug marihuana . . is ordained by the Bible for man's use. **1962** *Listener* 22 Feb. 345/1 The 'uppressors' . . go off into weirdness such as Rastafarinism. **1962** *Times Lit. Suppl.* 10 Aug. 578/4 The surcharge of an equally false nationalistic fantasy, at its most absurd and dangerous in the 'Rastafarism' of Jamaica with its worship of Haile Selassie and its slogan 'Death to the Whites'. **1965** I. FLEMING *Man with Golden Gun* iii. 41 He has groups of admirers (e.g. the Rastafari in Jamaica). **1973** *Caribbean Contact* Feb. 15/1 The Rastafaria brethren, too, who venerate Haile Selassie I and who keenly look foward to repatriation to their lost homeland of Africa, remain today faithful Garveyites. **1977** *Times Lit. Suppl.* 7 Jan. 9/5 Inadequate housing and insufficient jobs [in Kingston, Jamaica] . . also contributed to the rise of the Ras Tafari with their dreams of escape to Africa.

Rastafarian (ˌræstəˈfɑːrɪən, -ˈfɛərɪən), *a.* and *sb.* Also **Ras Tafarian.** [f. prec. + -AN.] **A.** *adj.* Of or pertaining to the Rastafari sect. **B.** *sb.* A member of this sect. Hence **ˌRastaˈfarianism.**
1955 G. E. SIMPSON in *Social & Econ. Stud.* (Kingston, Jamaica) IV. II. 134 Emphasis . . is placed on love and kindliness to fellow Ras Tafarians. **1960** *Guardian* 28 June 9/4 The bearded Marijuana-smoking Rastafarian sect. *Ibid.*, The Rastafarians run a campaign to get Jamaican negroes to return to Africa. **1963** *Times* 19 Apr. 9/1 Eight people were killed and others injured after members of the ganja-smoking Rastafarian cult went wild with guns and machetes. **1968** F. HENRIQUES *Family & Colour in Jamaica* (ed. 2) xiv. 181 The response of the University was to send a team of experts to investigate and report on Rastafarianism. **1976** *Peace News* 25 June 3/1 A group of Rastafarian West Indians wearing brightly-coloured woolly hats walking along the pavements alongside us, shaking their maracas. **1976** G. SIMS *End of Web* x. 69 A couple of Rastafarians whose thick matted tassels of hair hung down over their shoulders. **1977** *Vole* No. 4. 41/2 The cult of Rastafarianism, involving the deification of Haile Selassie, the promise of Ethiopia as their spiritual home, and above all, the rejection of . . white society.

Rastaman: see RASTA *sb.*[2]

‖ **rastaquouère** (rastakwɛr). Also **rastacouaire, rastaquère,** etc. [F. *rastaquouère, rastaquère*, ad. S. Amer. Sp. *rastacuero* upstart.] A social intruder or upstart of exaggerated manners or dress, esp. from a Mediterranean or S. Amer. country; a dashing but untrustworthy foreigner. Also *attrib.*
1883 M. E. BRADDON *Phantom Fortune* III. v. 110 He was the typical *rastaquouere*, a man of finished manners, and unknown antecedents. **1904** J. T. GREIN *Dramatic Crit.* 1902–1903 56 Even *rastaqouères* . . do not err in this direction. **1913** M. LARISCH *My Past* ix. 104, I rather liked the Baroness, although Count Larisch rudely termed the whole family *rastaquouères*. **1924** J. BUCHAN *Three Hostages* xiii. 199 The usual *rastaquouère* crowd of men and women drinking liqueurs and champagne. **1930** BELLOC *New Cautionary Tales* 28 Ambassadors and Papal Counts, And Rastaqouères from Palamerez. **1930** A. HUXLEY *Vulgarity in Literature* vi. 34 The *rastacouaire* might display the twin cabochon emeralds at his shirt cuffs and the platinum wrist watch. **1940** J. BUCHAN *Memory Hold-the-Door* vi. 128 There was a vulgar display of wealth, and a *rastaquouère* craze for luxury. **1975** *Times Lit. Suppl.* 19 Dec. 1511/2 The worst book ever written by an Old Etonian, even by a rather *rastaquouère* Old Etonian.

† **ˈrastel.** *Obs.* $rare^{-1}$. [a. OF. *rastel* (*ratel*, mod.F. *râteau*) rake, portcullis (see Godef.), etc.:—L. *rastellus*, dim. of *rastrum* rake.] A portcullis.
1598 BARRET *Theor. Warres* v. i. 127 The gate must haue . . his rastell or drawer of strong timber or iron.

† **ˈrasteling.** *Obs.* $rare^{-1}$. ? A tumult, uproar.
a **1400–50** *Alexander* 943 (Dubl. MS.) Alexander . . Herd suche a rastelyng in þe realm, & rydez þe faster. [*Ashm. MS.* Sees slike a rottilyng, etc.]

† **raster,** *sb.*[1] *Obs.* $rare^{-0}$. [? f. RASE *v.*[1] + -STER.] ? A barber. Only in ***raster-cloth, house*** (see quots.).
c **1440** *Promp. Parv.* 424/1 Rastyr howse, or schavyng howse (*S.* rasyr hows), *barbitondium*. **1483** *Cath. Angl.* 300/1

Raster clathe, *ralla*. *Ibid.* 300/2 Raster house (*A.* Raser howse), *barbitondium*. **1500** *Ortus*, *Ralla*, a raster cloth or a shauynge clothe.

raster (ˈræstə(r)), *sb.*[2] [a. G. *raster* screen, frame, f. L. *rastrum* rake, f. *rāsum*, supine of *rādĕre* to scrape.] **a.** A usu. rectangular pattern of parallel scanning lines forming or corresponding to the display on a cathode-ray tube; also more widely, with reference to other instruments and techniques involving systematic scanning movements or patterns without the use of a cathode-ray tube. Also ***raster pattern, scan***; ***raster-scan*** vb. trans., ***raster-scanning*** vbl. sb. and ppl. adj.

1934 Bedford & Puckle in *Jrnl. Inst. Electr. Engineers* LXXV. 64 The path of the spot must, so to speak, be mapped out beforehand into a suitable line *raster*, which is of such a size and shape as to allow the real image of the spot to explore the whole of one picture. [*Note*] This word, imported from the German, is used to mean a scanning field or grating. **1939** *Television & Short-Wave World Pract. Handbk.* No. 1. vi. 54/1 The production of the series of lines, or 'raster' as it is generally termed, is..purely a local function of the receiver and quite independent of any reception of signals. **1940** *Jrnl. R. Aeronaut. Soc.* XLIV. 103 It is claimed that the electron Raster microscope overcomes these difficulties. The principle of the microscope is as follows:—A thin electron beam is made to scan the object in a 'Raster' as in television. **1946** *Jrnl. Inst. Electr. Engineers* XCIII. IIIA. 1560/2 A raster approximately an inch square was then substituted for the noise pattern, obtained by applying the output from two saw-tooth oscillators, one of 50 c/s and the other of 10 kc/s, to the two pairs of plates of the tube. **1952** *Electronic Engin.* XXIV. 166/1 If a raster composed of horizontal scanning lines is further divided into the appropriate number of vertical lines, each line will become broken up into dots. **1966** [see interlace *v.* 6]. **1968** P. R. Thornton *Scanning Electron Microscopy* i. 8 Three years later [in 1938] v. Ardenne..built the first scanning electron microscope which used two magnetic lenses to provide a small electron spot at the specimen. Two sets of magnetic coils were used to scan the beam across the specimen in a television-like raster. **1969** Barton & Ward *Handbk. Radar Measurement* viii. 227 Raster-scanning pencil beams. These radars can be analyzed as search radars or sequential-processing trackers in both angular coordinates. **1970** *New Scientist* 4 June (Suppl.) 7/2 The screen can be 'raster-scanned' as on a TV screen (i.e. the light is deflected across the screen in a series of lines gradually moving to the bottom). **1973** *Sci. Amer.* Oct. 73/1 The spectroheliograms were made by holding the diffraction grating at one angle, so that only a single wavelength fell on the photomultiplier. The solar image was then scanned in a raster pattern to build up a picture of the sun in that one wavelength. **1973** *Physics Bull.* May 275/1 A flying spot performs a raster scan of the whole picture and with the help of a photodetector transforms the entire optical information—spots and all—into the memory of a large online computer. **1977** *Sci. Amer.* Oct. 84/2 In a circular-scan radar system the raster of the cathode-ray tube rotates synchronously with the antenna.

b. *Cinemat.* and *Photogr.* A fine grid, comprising wires, slits, or lenticular elements, placed in front of the projection screen in some stereoscopic cinematography systems, notably that invented by F. Savoye in 1942. Also ***raster screen***.

1952 E. F. Linssen *Stereo-Photogr. in Practice* xxi. 291 In 1945 B. T. Ivanov wrote on 'raster-stereoscopy in the cinema'. *Ibid.* 292 Savoye's Cyclostereoscopic system... The cone allows the two beams to pass through many slits.. with which it is provided, and these same slits (constituting a revolving grid or raster) also act as selectors for the spectators. **1957** K. C. M. Symons *Stereo Photogr.* 205 Another method depends on the provision of a grid or raster screen in front of the projection screen. This method, which has a certain affinity with the parallax stereogram..forms the basis of two methods of projection, one Russian, the other French. *Ibid.* 213 *Raster*, a term used to describe certain autostereoscopic methods which depend on the use of a screen for multiplying and selecting the images. **1958** *Newnes Compl. Amat. Photogr.* 235 An alternative method of projection is the Cyclosterscopic system... This system consists of a metal cone of fine grids or rasters which revolves around the screen and is not noticeable in motion. **1965** *Focal Encycl. Photogr.* (rev. ed.) II. 1207/1 Raster screens consist of an arrangement of vertical wires interposed between the screen surface and the audience... There are also patented screens in which the projection surface is composed of vertical lenticular prisms, or of spherical lenticular elements graduated in size.

Hence as *v. trans.*, to scan (an area) with a beam that goes over it in a raster pattern; **ˈrastered** *ppl. a.*, (of a beam) made to scan an area thus.

1975 *Nature* 9 Oct. 521/1 Methods by which the properties of inorganic materials may be measured quantitatively using the interaction of a rastered kilovolt electron beam with a solid. **1978** *Ibid.* 3 Aug. 457/2 Fig. 1 shows..two X-ray maps obtained (using electron microprobe X-ray fluorescence) by rastering the same region with a 30-kV electron beam and collecting in sequence the K Kα and Ca Kα rays.

†**rastilbow**. *Obs. rare*⁻⁰. [Corruptly ad. med.L. *resta bovis* or OF. *reste de beof* (mod.F. *arrête bœuf*), lit. 'stopping of the ox'.] The plant rest-harrow.

c **1440** *Promp. Parv.* 424/1 Rastylbow, wede, *resta bovis*.

rastle, obs. and dial. form of wrestle.

†**ˈraston**. *Obs. rare*⁻¹. [a. OF. *raston, raton*: see Godef., and cf. rattoon[1].] 'A fashion of round and high Tart, made of butter, egges, and cheese' (Cotgr.).

c **1430** *Two Cookery-bks.* 52 Rastons. Take fayre Flowre, & þe whyte of Eyroun, & þe ȝolke a lytel [etc.].

Rastus (ˈræstəs). *U.S.* [Prob. shortened form of the personal name *Erastus*.] A name applied joc. in a number of songs and moving picture films to a 'typical' Negro, subsequently used as an offensive term for a Black person.

1895 K. Mills *Rastus on Parade* (*song*) 5 No use in talking he's hot stuff, Is Rastus when on Parade. **1909** C. W. Hayes in *Lippincott's Mag.* May 636 (*title*) Rastus's baby. **1910** *Moving Picture World* 7 May 749/2 Rastus in Zululand.—Rastus is an odd-jobs man, that is he does odd jobs when he has to. **1932** F. DuBose *Episodes in Black & White* 1 Two little pickaninnies were sitting by the fire when in came Uncle Rastus with a pumpkin pie. **1932** E. V. White *Chocolate Drops from South* 13 Mandy: 'Rastus, yo' makes me think yo' got the equator on yo'.' Rastus: 'How cum, Mandy?' Mandy: 'Yo' got sech a hot line!' **1944** H. L. Mencken in *Amer. Speech* XIX. 172 In my boyhood *Cuffy* had disappeared and *Sambo* was being supplanted by *Rastus*. **1955** W. Moore *Bring Jubilee* vi. 59, I call him Sambo because it sounds nicer than Rastus. **1965** W. McCord *Mississippi: Long Hot Summer* vi. 163 Leaders like Medgar Evers..discovered in the armed forces a new sense of personal dignity... They returned to their state determined to play roles other than 'Sambo' and 'Rastus'. **1965** 'Malcolm X' *Autobiogr.* (1966) ii. 104 Wherever I showed my face..the audiences 'niggered' and 'cooned' me to death. Or called me 'Rastus'. **1978** J. Blackburn *Dead Man's Handle* vi. 73 On your way, Rastus. Me and Massa's buddies.

rasty, dial. var. reasty.

rasure[1] (ˈreɪzjʊə(r)). Now *rare*. Also 7–9 **raz-**. [a. F. *rasure* (1235 in Godef.), or ad. L. *rāsūra*: see rase *v.*[1] and -ure.]

†**1.** The act of scraping or shaving (also *fig.*); a scratch, mark, cut, slit. *Obs.*

1470–85 Malory *Arthur* xviii. xxv, Lyke as wynter rasure doth alway a rase and deface grene somer, soo..for a lytel blast of wynters rasure anone we shalle deface and lay a parte true loue. **1599** Hakluyt *Voy.* III. 674 They race some their faces, some their bodies,..the print of which rasure can neuer bee done away againe during life. **1611** Speed *Hist. Gt. Brit.* v. vi. (1632) 42 Carrying these rasures on their pictured limbes. **1721** Gibson *Farrier's Guide* ii. (1738) 250 Soaking Pledgits of clean Hurds in this Mixture, and laying them pretty warm on the Razures or Chinks.

†**b.** A particle, or the particles, scraped off.

c **1400** *Lanfranc's Cirurg.* 135, I leie on þe schauynge or ellis þe rasure of lynnen cloop. **1669** Evelyn *Sylva* (1776) 324 The wood should be cut about May and the Rasures well dried.

†**2.** The act of shaving (the head, hair, etc.); tonsure. *Obs.*

1483 Caxton *Gold. Leg.* 111/1 Saynt denys..sayth the rasure and cuttyng of of the heer signefyeth pure lyf. **1561** T. Norton *Calvin's Inst.* iv. xix. (1634) 726 *marg.*, The Popish rasure ministred unto Clerks at the first receit of their Cleargie. *a* **1603** T. Cartwright *Confut. Rhem. N.T.* (1618) 11 They had no razure commanded, onely it was prouided that they should not haue their haire long. **1737** Whiston *Josephus* (1755) IV. 333 Their heads were sooty: they had round rasures on them.

3. The act of scraping out something written; an erasure. (Freq. in 16–18th c.)

1508 Fisher *7 Penit. Ps.* xxxii. Wks. (1876) 24 We fyrste scrape the paper, and by that rasure or scraping sumwhat is taken awaye of the letters. **1602** Fulbecke *2nd Pt. Parall.* 28/1 Such writings obligatorie if they haue any razure in them in any materiall place are of no credit in law. *a* **1734** North *Lives Norths* (1742) I. 115 She had very credible information that there was a foul rasure in Sir John Cuts's will. **1791–1823** D'Israeli *Cur. Lit.* (1866) 208/2 A specimen of his continual corrections and critical rasures.

b. *transf.* Obliteration, effacement; cancelling.

1603 Shaks. *Meas. for M.* v. i. 13 A forted residence 'gainst the tooth of time And razure of obliuion. **1670** Marvell *Let. to W. Ramsden* Wks. (1875) I. 410 When we began to talk of the Lords, the King sent for us alone, and recommended a rasure of all proceedings. **1750** Johnson *Rambler* No. 41 Impressed upon the mind so as to defy all attempts of rasure or of change. **1761–2** Hume *Hist. Eng.* IV. lxv. (1806) 780 That a general razure should be made of all transactions with regard to that disputed question.

†**rasure**[2]. *Obs. rare.* Also 5 **-our**. [a. OF. *rasure* (Godef.); cf. Pg. *rasoura*.] = raser[1].

c **1489** Caxton *Sonnes of Aymon* viii. 187 The rasour of whete was solde for fourty shelynges and twenty pence. **1526** *Tolls* in Dillon *Calais & Pole* (1892) 89 Item, for evry Rasure of Lyme qr.

rasure, obs. f. razor *sb.*

rasydhede: see rasedhead.

rasyn(e, -ynge, obs. ff. raisin.

rasyst, obs. Sc. f. resist.

rat (ræt), *sb.*[1] Forms: 1 **ræt**, 4–6 **ratte**, 6 **ratt**, 5– **rat**. [OE. *ræt* (once) = Du. *rat*, MHG. *rat* (G. *ratz*), masc.; also OLG. *ratta*, OHG. *ratte* (G. *ratte, ratze*), fem., and OHG. *ratto* m.; = F. *rat* m., *rate* f., Sp., Pg. *rato*, obs. It. *ratto*, med.L. *ratus, rattus*.

The ultimate origin of the word is uncertain, but it seems probable that it was adopted first in the Teutonic languages when the animal came to be known in western Europe, and thence passed into the Romance tongues. Forms with *o* occur in the LG. and Scand. languages as well as in English: see rottan, rotte. The most usual form in ME. was *raton*, *-oun*, ratton.]

1. a. A rodent of some of the larger species of the genus *Rattus*, esp. *R. rattus*, the black rat (now almost extinct), and *R. norvegicus*, the common grey, brown, or Norway rat. (See also land-, musk-, water-rat.)

c **1000** Ælfric *Gloss.* in Wr.-Wülcker 118/41 *Fiber*.. befer. *Raturus*, ræt. *Lutria*, otor. **1377** Langl. *P. Pl.* B. Prol. 200 Had ȝe rattes ȝoure wille ȝe couthe nouȝt reule ȝoureselue. *c* **1450** Myrc *Par. Priest* 1897 ȝef hyt were eten wyth mows or rat, Dere þow moste a-bygge þat. **1561** Daus tr. *Bullinger on Apoc.* (1573) 119 They bewray themselues lyke a Ratte wyth theyr owne vtteraunce. **1596** Shaks. *Merch. V.* iv. i. 44 What if my house be troubled with a Rat. **1610** —— *Temp.* i. ii. 147 Nor tackle, sayle, nor mast, the very rats Instinctiuely haue quit it. **1625** Bacon *Ess.*, *Wisd. for Man's Self* (Arb.) 187 It is the Wisedome of Rats, that will be sure to leaue a House, somewhat before it fall. **1726** Gay *Fables* ii. viii. 87 Rats and mice purloin our grain. **1759** *Ann. Reg.* 123/1 A large Norway rat. **1774** Goldsm. *Nat. Hist.* (1776) IV. 66 The Great Rat... It is chiefly in the colour that this animal differs from the Black Rat, or the Common Rat, as it was once called, but now common no longer. **1820** Shelley *Œd. Tyr.* i. 183 Rats, when lean enough To crawl through such chinks. **1843** Dieffenbach *Trav. New Z.* II. 185 There exists a frugiferous native rat. **1862** Ansted *Channel Isl.* ii. ix. (ed. 2) 201 The black rat, so rare in England, is common in Alderney and Herm.

fig. **1855** Smedley *H. Coverdale* iii. 14 A pair of little hopping rats of ponies. **1875** Buckland *Log-Book* 204 Crabs are, in fact, the rats of the ocean. **1888** Kipling *Letters of Marque* (1891) xv. 111 Ram Baksh..headed his two thirteen-hand rats straight towards the morning sun. **1900** R. Barr *Unchanging East* 258 The Turkish Government has a little rat of a boat..which dare not venture out in a storm. **1907** J. Masefield *Tarpaulin Muster* 186 'I've been looking for truth,' he says; 'looking for truth in all these books... There's not a rat of truth in one of them. Not a solid rat, there isn't.' **1977** *Best of Austral. Angler* 12/2 Earlier, Col Noakes and myself had landed some 10 kg kings—comparative 'rats' that chased bait past all day.

b. *transf.* Applied to animals of other species resembling the rat, esp. the North American musk-rat, *Ondatra zibethica*, of the family Cricetidæ, an aquatic rodent hunted for its thick brown fur; also, the pelt of this animal or its flesh used as food.

†***rat of Inde***, the ichneumon. †***rat of Surinam***, the phalanger. ***marsupial rat***, an opossum. ***Pharaoh's rat***, the ichneumon (cf. OF. *rat de Fareon* in Marco Polo). ***Norway*** or ***Norwegian rat***, the lemming.

1584 R. Hakluyt *Discourse concerning Westerne Planting* in *Maine Hist. Soc. Coll.* (1877) II. 27 There is greate store of..bevers, squirrells, badgers, and ratts excedinge greate. **1598** Sylvester *Du Bartas* i. vi. 272 So Pharoah's Rat, yer he begin the fray 'Gainst the blinde Aspicke. **1601** Holland *Pliny* I. 303 Rats of Inde, called Ichneumones. **1753** Chambers *Cycl. Supp.*, *Leming*, the name of a creature of the rat kind, called by authors *mus Norwegicus*, the Norway rat. **1774** Goldsmith *Nat. Hist.* (1862) I. vii. i. 515 The Philanger..is about the size of a rat, and has, accordingly, by some, been called the Rat of Surinam. **1800** A. N. McLeod *Jrnl.* 18 Nov. in C. M. Gates *Five Fur Traders* (1933) 130 The first paid his Debt, the next gave 40 Ratts en present. **1824** S. Black *Jrnl. Voy. from Rocky Mountain Portage* (1955) 153 Saw no appearance of the Otter, Rat or Mink. **1863** H. W. Bates *Naturalist on R. Amazons* ix. (ed. 2) 260 A beautiful opossum:..this made the third species of marsupial rat I had so far obtained. **1882** *Edmonton Bull.* 18 Feb. 3/2 They are living principally on rats and jackfish from Buffalo Lake. **1886** *Riverside Nat. Hist.* V. 442 Pharaoh's Rat..feeds to a great extent upon the eggs of the crocodile. [**1886** *Pall Mall G.* 14 Sept. 1/1 On the suicidal principles of Norwegian ratdom.] **1944** J. Martin *Canad. Wilderness Trapping* 48 It is the food which makes the pelt ..and in the northwest we get the best rats. **1946** *Sun* (Baltimore) 15 Nov. 18/3 The 'rats' referred to are, of course, the musk-rats of the rich Dorchester marshes. **1953** *Jessen's Weekly* 19 Feb. 5/2. The trapping of Beaver and muskrat in the Huslia area does not show much promise as the ice is from three to six feet thick in the rivers and lakes. .. Many of the rats have been frozen in.

2. In phrases: **a.** ***to smell a rat***, to suspect something.

a **1550** *Image Hypocr.* i. 51 in *Skelton's Wks.* (1843) II. 414/2 Yf they smell a ratt, They grisely chide and chatt. **1602** *2nd Pt. Return fr. Parnass.* iii. ii. 1272 Ile say no more, gesse at my meaning, I smel a rat. **1660** Shirley *Androm.* ii. ii. 14, I smell a Rat sir, there's jugling in this business. **1736** [Chetwood] *Voy. Vaughan* I. 170, I ask'd her so many Questions, that, tho' a Woman ignorant enough, she began to smell a Rat. **1840** Lytton *Paul Clifford* xxxiv, Whew! I small a rat; this stolen child, then, was no other than Paul. **1894** Howells in *Harper's Mag.* Feb. 377 He'll be sure to smell a rat if I'm with you.

b. ***like*** (or ***as wet as***) ***a drowned rat***.

c **1500** [see drowned 1 b]. **1542** Udall *Erasm. Apoph.* 180 b, An hedde he had..Three heares on a side, like a drouned ratte. **1697** Dampier *Voy.* I. iv. 70 The Storm.. drencht us all like so many drowned Rats. **1771** Smollett *Humph. Cl.* III. 14 Oct. Let. iv, I was dragged out of a river like a drowned rat. **1880** [see drowned].

c. (***as***) ***drunk, poor***, †***rank***, or ***weak, as a rat***.

1538 Bale *Thre Lawes* 835 The monkes were fatte And ranke as a ratte. **1553** T. Wilson *Rhet.* (1580) 128 As if one had..kepte the Tauerne till he had been as dronke as a Ratte. **1661** *Merry Drollerie* i. 17 Drunk as a Rat, you'd hardly wot That drinking so he could trudge it. **1833** Marryat *P. Simple* xxxi, He's as poor as a rat. **1840** Col. Hawker *Diary* (1893) II. 186 Weak as a rat, and no appetite.

d. With reference to the alleged killing or expulsion of Irish rats by riming. Cf. rime *v.*

1600 Shaks. *A.Y.L.* iii. ii. 188, I was neuer so berim'd since..I was an Irish Rat. **1625** B. Jonson *Staple of News* 4th Interm., The fine Madrigall-man, in rime, to haue runne him o' the Countrey, like an Irish rat. **1660** (*title*) Rats Rhimed to Death, or, The Rump-Parliament Hang'd up in the Shambles. **1735** Pope *Donne Sat.* II. 22 Songs no longer move; No rat is rhym'd to death, nor maid to love.

e. *slang* (orig. *U.S.*). Used ironically in *pl.* to express incredulity: 'humbug', 'nonsense'. Also as a general expression of disgust, annoyance, etc.

1886 *Lantern* (New Orleans) 20 Oct. 5/2 What a rotten game. Rats! **1888** *Texas Siftings* 7 Jan. 5/2 Smaller Boy—'Let me shine 'em up, Sir; for I have to support a poor little sick brother at home who is lame and can't see.' Bigger Boy—'Rats! I'm that poor little sick brother myself.' **1890** *Spectator* Sept. 409/2 (quoting *Puck*) 'Why, what did he say when you told him of it?'—'Oh! just—"Rats!"' **1897** *Outing* (U.S.) XXX. 484/1 'A miss, by Jove'. 'Oh, rats', cries another onlooker. **1901** S. R. Crockett *Cinderella* xxvii. 188 'My cousin has lessons along with the younger children.' 'Rats!' declared Vic, smiling broadly; 'she sees that they do theirs—that's more like it.' **1914** G. B. Shaw *Misalliance* 23 *Mrs. Tarleton.* Dont boast, John. Dont tempt Providence. *Tarleton.* Rats! You dont understand Providence. Providence likes to be tempted. **1951** J. Cornish *Provincials* I. ii. 21 'I don't kiss girls,' I said hurriedly. 'I never kiss girls. Never.' 'Oh, rats!' **1976** *National Observer* (U.S.) 21 Feb. 9/2 About a day later another letter from the company turned up in my mailbox. Rats, I thought, they have discovered their mistake and are going to take all the fun out of my life. **1977** *New Yorker* 27 June 30/3 Rats, you sound like a sorority pledge at Sophie Newcomb College.

f. *to give* (a person) *rats*: to give (him) a hard time; to berate, rebuke. orig. *U.S.*

1863 *Sunday Herald* (Boston) 15 Feb. 4/1 Hooker is doing something in the way of giving the rebels 'rats'. **1869** 'Mark Twain' *Sk. New & Old* (1875) 48 You may write a blistering article on the police—give the Chief Inspector rats. **1940** F. D. Davison *Woman at Mill* III. 245 She was now going to give me rats, treat me as if I were personally responsible for the short-comings of the land of my birth.

g. *to get* (or *have*) *a rat* (or *rats*): to be eccentric or insane. *Austral.* and *N.Z. slang.*

[**1890** Barrère & Leland *Dict. Slang* II. 171/2 (American), 'to have *rats*', to have wild or eccentric fancies.] **1906** E. Dyson *Fact'ry 'Ands* vii. 84 The factory flat loudly asserted that Spats had 'got a rat'. **1908** H. Fletcher *Dads & Dan* 65 In a town a whole population gets rats together, an' though they's all clean daft at times, yet, 'cause they all thinks alike, they don't doubt they's sane. *c* **1926** 'Mixer' *Transport Workers' Song Bk.* 12 'Lend us a quid!' 'Lend you a what! Blime, have you got a rat?'

h. *rats and mice*: rhyming slang for 'dice'; a game of dice.

1932 P. P. *Rhyming Slang* 23 Rats and mice, dice. **1938** F. D. Sharpe *Sharpe of Flying Squad* xv. 170 We used to play dice with them... Rats and Mice the game was called.

3. a. Used as an opprobrious or familiar epithet.

1594 Shaks. *Rich. III*, v. iii. 331 These famish'd Beggers ..Who..For want of meanes (poore Rats) had hang'd themselues. **1629** Earle *Microcosm.* (Arb.) 98 One that nick-names Clergymen with all the termes of reproch, as Rat, Black-coate, and the like. *c* **1656** *Roxb. Ball.* (1886) VI. 106 No Female Rat shall me deceive, nor catch me by a crafty wild. **1830** Hood *Drop of Gin* iii, Hardly acknowledged by kith and kin, Because, poor rat! He has no cravat. **1888** Stevenson *Black Arrow* 29 Ha! Clipsby, are ye there, old rat! **1901** G. B. Shaw *Caesar & Cleopatra* IV. 188 Now, by great Jove, you filthy little Egyptian rat, that is the very word to make him walk out alone into the city. **1927**, **1928** [see *double-crosser* s.v. double-cross, double cross 1]. **1929** [see fink *sb.*[2]]. **1945** S. Lewis *Cass Timberlane* xliii. 324 The sort of male once described with relish as 'an agreeable scoundrel'..could now be referred to..as..a louse, a stinker, a rat, a twirp, a crumb, or a goon. **1959** [see fink *sb.*[2]]. **1976** *Western Mail* (Cardiff) 27 Nov., He turned to a group of policemen and said, 'I hope you are satisfied, you rats.' **1977** *Rolling Stone* 16 June 43/3 This is the terrible part of me, it's awful and I'm really a rat.

b. Preceded by a specifying sb., applied to one who is associated with or frequents the place specified (originally esp. a dock or riverside: in this context occas. without defining word); see also *rink-rat* (rink *sb.*[2] 5), *river rat* (river *sb.*[1] 5 e), *wharf-rat* (*b*) (wharf *sb.*[1] 3). Chiefly *U.S.*

1864 *Harper's Mag.* Feb. 341/1 At our swimming-place we were often much molested by the river-border citizens of the town, variously known as 'dock-rats' and 'townies'. **1870** *Scribner's Monthly* I. 41 Many of the inmates.., as 'dock-rats', house-thieves, peace-breakers, and horse-stealers, have grown preternaturally quick-witted. **1872** *Harper's Mag.* Oct. 673/2 Our business is with those smaller, but terribly annoying vermin, the 'dock rats', with the river thieves, and with the junk-shops. **1883** J. Greenwood *Tag, Rag, & Co.* 33 Then, again, there's the regler 'rats'. How many of them, sneaking about craft at anchor,..make a slip and get drowned? *Ibid.* 35 He was drowned, and carried away with the tide, and it wasn't till a week after that the 'rats'..fell in with the body and robbed it. **1890** [see extra C. *sb.* b]. **1928** H. Asbury *Gangs of New York* xi. 240 The police found him in company with a gang of notorious little dock rats. **1962** N. Maxwell *Witch-Doctor's Apprentice* iii. 25, I..gathered a lot of information on jungle medicine. I spent hours in bars buying *aguardiente* (local rum) for old jungle rats. **1967** *Boston Sunday Herald* 14 May (This Week Mag.) 2/2 As a kid, I was an airport rat. I rode my bike to the airport, 15 miles each way, and I would hang around and help. **1978** K. Bonfiglioli *All Tea in China* III. vi. 80 A gaggle of waterfront rats, wasters, the scum of the sea.

4. *spec.* †**a.** A pirate. *Obs.*

[**1596** Shaks. *Merch. V.* I. iii. 23.] **1673** Hobbes *Odyss.* xv. 371 Phaenician Merchants, Rats, then thither came. *Ibid.* xvi. 61 Thesprotian rats got him aboard their ship.

†**b.** (See quots.) *Obs.*

a **1700** B. E. *Dict. Cant. Crew, Rat*, a Drunken Man or Woman taken up by the Watch, and carried..to the Counter. **1781** R. King *Mod. Lond. Spy* 38 Men taken up for assaults or night-brawls were termed Rats.

c. In *Politics*: One who deserts his party.

(From the alleged fact that rats leave a house about to fall or a ship about to sink: see sense 1, quots. 1610, 1625.)

1792 Earl Malmesbury *Diaries & Corr.* II. 477 This would..pronounce..us..as having differed with him, and, of course, become rats and deserters. **1823** Bentham *Not Paul but Jesus* 199 In a word, in the language of modern party, Silas was a rat. **1888** H. D. Traill *Will. III*, i. (1892) 7 Charles transformed himself, with more than the celerity of the nimblest modern rat [etc.].

d. A workman who refuses to strike along with others, or takes a striker's place; also (esp. among printers), one who works for lower wages than the ordinary (or trade-union) rate. Chiefly *U.S.*

1824 [see *rat-printer*, sense 7 e below]. **1836** *Proc. Nat. Typogr. Convention, Washington* 4 Martin H. Andrews..has been recognised as being one of the individuals published on the *Rat List* of the Columbia Typographical Society. *Ibid.* 11 Men pronounced *Rats* by one society, shall be considered such by all others. **1851** *Proc. 1st Nat. Convention Journeymen Printers U.S., 1850* 11 The present system is prolific of 'rats'. Our trade should be purged of this vermin. **1868** *Oregon State Jrnl.* 17 Oct. 1/6 The President of the National Typographical Union has pronounced a general amnesty, by virtue of which all expelled members, 'rats', etc., will be admitted to the Unions. **1881** *American* No. 73. 181 The men who agree to go into the strike are always the more united and determined class. The rats who refuse suffer accordingly. **1892** *Nation* 11 Aug. 96/2 This orator declared..that 'rats' were still employed in the *Tribune* office. **1896** *Typographical Jrnl.* IX. 100 A force of rats were doubled up from the Evening Ledger to get out the paper. **1902** *Encycl. Brit.* XXXIII. 411/1 A strike occurred in Mr Weed's office in 1821 on account of the employment of a non-union man, who was then designated a 'rat'.

e. *U.S.* A new student or freshman, esp. a newly-recruited cadet.

1850 'M. Tensas' *Odd Leaves Life Louisiana 'Swamp Doctor'* 113 There were four or five brother 'Rats' besides myself residing in the hospital, all candidates for graduation, and..all desirous of obtaining sufficient medical lore. **1896** *Bomb* (Virginia Military Institution) 109 An unfortunate 'Rat' whose face was glum, As he often to himself did hum—Guard Duty. **1900** *Dialect Notes* I. 54 *Rat*, a new student. **1930** *Amer. Speech* VI. 129 The freshman class at this institution [*sc.* Alabama Polytechnic Institute] is known as 'The Rats', and any given member is a 'rat'. **1937** W. Couper in J. E. Johnston *Echoes of V.M.I.* 43 One of the recollections of every Rat is the comforter who goes through the barracks purring—'Mister, do you see that tree? Well, all the leaves have got to go, and all the leaves have got to come back, before you..' and you know the rest. **1939** W. Faulkner *Wild Palms* 35 'This is Rat,' she said. 'He is the senior living ex-freshman of the University of Alabama. That's why we still call him Rat.' **1951** *Time* 28 May 50/2 Of all the cadets, the 'rats' of the entering class have the roughest time.

f. A police informer; an informer in a prison. *slang.*

1902 Farmer & Henley *Slang* V. 376/1 *Rat*... 6. (thieves').—A police spy. **1917** *New Republic* 13 Jan. 294/1 In most cases they were 'rats', and the best tools the keepers had. **1929** [see heel *sb.*[2]]. **1970** G. Jackson *Let.* 22 Mar. in *Soledad Brother* (1971) 186 You see every time a rat does get put away, the prison authorities always release a different reason for the attack, never that he was an informer. **1977** *New Yorker* 24 Oct. 72/3 Like all prisons, Green Haven is run with the help of informers—'rats'... One way..of rewarding rats is with jobs.

5. Something resembling a rat in shape.

a. *U.S.* A hair-pad with tapering ends.

1869 Mrs. Whitney *We Girls* v. (1874) 98 She can't buy coils and braids and two-dollar rats. **1888** *Century Mag.* Sept. 769/1 The crescent shaped pillows on which it [hair] was put up, the startling names of which were 'rats' and 'mice'.

b. A plumber's tool.

1894 *Times* 27 Jan. 7/5 Some of the company's men..were using a red-hot plug or 'rat'.

6. [f. rat *v.*] The act of changing one's side.

1838 Lytton *Alice* v. ii, Political factions love converts... A man's rise in life generally dates from a well-timed rat.

7. *attrib.* and *Comb.* **a.** attributive, as *rat-cage*, *-fur*, *-haunt*, *-horde*, *kind*, *-land*, *-leather*, *pie*, *-plague*, *poison*, *-preserve*, *-season*, *-skin*, *-terrier*, *-warren*; (sense 4 e) *rat rule*.

1936 J. Steinbeck *In Dubious Battle* ii. 21, I did hate being in the *rat-cage. **1977** P. Dickinson *Walking Dead* I. i. 17 The neat rank of rat-cages in the animal room. **1907** *Daily Chron.* 24 Aug. 4/7 The hair was gathered up, chignon-fashion, and tied behind with strings made of *rat-fur. **1654** Gayton *Pleas. Notes* IV. v. 200 Mine Host wondred with himselfe, where the *Rat-haunt should be. *a* **1930** D. H. Lawrence *Last Poems* (1932) 189 In the moment of choice, the soul..utterly fails to recognize any more the grey *rat-hordes of classes and masses. **1753** Chambers *Cycl. Supp.*, *Leming*, the name of a creature of the *rat kind. **1955** J. R. R. Tolkien *Return of King* v. x. 166 Dwarf-coat, elf-cloak, blade of the downfallen West, and spy from the little *rat-land of the Shire. **1879** Goode *Catal. Anim. Resources & Fisheries U.S.* 214 *Rat leather, used for thumbs of kid gloves. **1812** Southey *Omniana* I. 25 *Rat pye would be as good as Rook pye. **1936** I. L. Idriess *Cattle King* (*caption facing p.* 50) These birds, in immense numbers, harry the '*rat plagues' which occur occasionally in portions of the interior. **1844** Stephens *Bk. Farm* III. 1296 A pot of..*rat poison. **1848** *Zoologist* VI. 2054 They were the lords of the *rat-preserve in the barn. **1933** *Sun* (Baltimore) 8 Nov. 20/3 The sophomore victory..meant that the freshmen would continue to wear little red caps and obey '*rat' rules. **1939** *Amer. Speech* XIV. 29 *Rat*, new cadet, recruit... *Rat rules*, .. see recruit regulations. **1921** *Beaver* May 14 *The rat season closes today. All the hunters are now in. **1812** Southey *Omniana* I. 26 *Rat-skin robes for the ladies would be beautiful. **1893** *Westm. Gaz.* 22 June 3/3 The length of the largest rat-skin, when dressed, is seven to eight inches. **1851** Mayhew *Lond. Lab.* II. 55 The cost of a bull-dog, or a bull-terrier or *rat-terrier. **1886** Miss Braddon *One Thing Needful* iv, Rooms that only serve as a *rat-warren.

b. Objective, and obj. genitive, as *rat-catching*, *-charmer*, *-hunting*, *-killer*, *-killing*, †*-taker*. See also rat-catcher.

1764 *Museum Rust.* I. 392 Those who professedly follow the art of *rat-catching. **1825** in Hone *Every-day Bk.* I. (1859) 291 My terriers—ratcatching Busy, Snap, and Nimbletoes. **1860** Marryat *Horace Jutland* II. 280 The *rat-charmer..must be sadly wanted in these parts. **1810** E. Weeton *Let.* 18 Jan. in *Jrnl. of Governess* (1969) I. 223, I set out on my *rat-hunting expedition. *a* **1817** Jane Austen *Persuasion* (1818) IV. x. 229 We had a famous set-to at rat-hunting all the morning. **1851** Mayhew *Lond. Lab.* II. 56/2 The main sport now..in which dogs are the agents is rat-hunting. **1966** *Beaver* Winter 54/1 All the different Indians started back to their own countries for rat [*sc.* muskrat] hunting. **1538** Elyot, *Muricidus*.., a *rat killer. **1851** Mayhew *Lond. Lab.* II. 56/2 As a rat-killer, a ferret is not to be compared to a dog. **1851–61** in Mayhew *Lond. Lab.* (1865) II. 491/1 Take the tax off *rat-killing dogs, and give a legality to rat-killing. *c* **1500** *Cocke Lorell's B.* 10 Mole sekers, and *ratte takers. **1538** *Arundel MS.* 97 in *Vicary's Anat.* (1888) App. II. 109 Iohn Willis, the Kingis rattaker.

c. Instrumental, as *rat-borne*, *-deserted*, *-eaten*, *-gnawn*, *-infested*, *-inhabited*, *-ridden*, *-riddled* adjs.

1928 *Moderna Språk* Sept. 187 Terms like..*mother-craft*, *rat-borne diseases, *wholemeal* bread. **1938** *Sun* (Baltimore) 1 Nov. 22/2 To protect the public health and to prevent the spread of rat-borne disease. **1859** Helps *Friends in Council* Ser. II. (ed. 2) I. 11 Sordid, window-broken, *rat-deserted ..houses. **1901** 'L. Malet' *Hist. R. Calmady* I. viii. 69 The fusty atmosphere of a cottage garret, right up under the *rat-eaten thatch. **1951** P. Abrahams *Wild Conquest* 49 He had a funny, rat-eaten beard. **1860** Wynter *Curiosities of Civilisation* 137 The *rat-gnawn ivory is selected by the turner as fitted for billiard balls. **1840** Dickens *Old C. Shop* iv, A small *rat-infested dreary yard. **1916** E. & O. Sitwell *20th Cent. Harlequinade* 23 On to that rat-infested maze. **1974** *Country Life* 14 Mar. 588/1 The pond was a rat-infested rubbish tip. **1832** Carlyle *Goethe's Wks.* Misc. (1840) IV. 198 Ancient rotten *rat-inhabited walls. **1870** Dickens *E. Drood* i, Some *rat-ridden doorkeeper. **1855** Browning *Hugues of Saxe-Gotha* xxix, Your rotten-planked *rat-riddled stairs.

d. Similative, as *rat-brained*, *-coloured*, *-eyed*, *-faced*, *-fat*, *-grey*, *-like*, *-poor*, *-shrewd*, *-souled*, *-swift*, *-toothed* adjs.

1971 B. Malamud *Tenants* 75 Those *rat-brained Jews. **1633** Massinger *Guardian* II. iv, Their *rat-coloured stockings. **1834** *Tait's Mag.* I. 518/2 Yellow or blue, Piebald or rat-coloured. **1866** J. Greenwood in *Evening Star* 19 Mar., A *rat-eyed, slim-limbed thief. **1862** H. Marryat *Year in Sweden* II. 45 *note*, This *rat-faced lady. **1930** E. Sitwell *Coll. Poems* 256 To show the same Of the *rat-fat soul to the grinning day. **1937** E. Muir *Coll. Poems* (1960) 71 The light was *rat-grey. **1846** Waterhouse *Nat. Hist. Mamm.* I. 225 Its *rat-like tail. **1857** Borrow *Romany Rye* (1858) II. 73 The rat-like eyes sparkled. **1952** J. Steinbeck *East of Eden* ii. 9 A man who might have been well-to-do on ten acres in Europe was *rat-poor on two thousand in California. **1960** S. Plath *Colossus* (1967) 63 *Rat-shrewd go her squint eyes. **1921** R. Graves *Pier-Glass* 49 Was Sisera then more ripe for the knife or nail Than *rat-soul'd Becker? **1969** G. Macbeth *War Quartet* 61 Air gushed in..*Rat-swift. **1930** S. Spender *Twenty Poems* 14 And older whores Skuttle *rat-toothed into the dark outdoors.

e. Special combs., as **rat-bat** *W. Indies* = bat *sb.*[1]; **rat-bean**, a species of caper (*Capparis frondosa*); **rat-bird**, the striated bush-babbler (*Chattarrhœa caudata*); **rat-bite fever**, either of two similar fevers of which the bacteria causing it are carried by rodents; **rat cheese** *U.S. colloq.* = mousetrap *sb.* 2; **rat-clam**, *dial.* a rat-trap; **rat-firm**, a firm which employs 'rats' or non-union workmen; **rat-fish**, a fish of the family Chimæridæ, characterized by a long tail, esp. *Hydrolagus colliei*, which is found off the Pacific coast of North America; **rat flea**, a flea infesting rats, esp. *Nosopsyllus fasciatus* or the tropical *Xenopsylla cheopis*, which are vectors of the bacillus causing plague; **rat-fucker** *coarse slang*, a base, despicable person (see also quot. 1967[1]); **rat-hare** = lagomys; **rat-house**, (*a*) a printing-house in which 'rats' are employed; (*b*) *Austral.* and *N.Z. slang*, a lunatic asylum; **rat-hunt**, a hunt for rats; also *fig.*; **rat-kangaroo** = kangaroo-rat, a very small kangaroo belonging to the subfamily Potoroinæ; **rat-labour** (see quot. and 4 d above); **rat-mole** = mole-rat; **rat-office** = *rat-house*; **rat pack** *slang* (orig. *U.S.*), a gang of disorderly young people; **rat-pill**, a pill used in rat-catching; **rat-pit**, a pit in which rats are confined to be worried by dogs; **rat-poison**, poison for destroying rats; also *spec.* (see quot. 1848); **rat-printer** = sense 4 d; **rat-proof** *a.*, able to keep out rats; hence **rat-proofing** *vbl. sb.*; **rat-run**, (one of) a maze-like series of small passages by which rats move about their territory; freq. *transf.* and *fig.* (usu. in derogatory sense); **rat-snake**, a snake which kills rats, esp. a colubrid snake of the South Asian genus *Ptyas*, particularly the Indian *P. mucosus*; = dhaman 1; **rat-tight** *a.* = *rat-proof* adj. See also rat-tail, -trap.

1851 P. H. Gosse *Naturalist's Sojourn in Jamaica* 163 All Bats are called by the negroes *Rat-bats, probably to distinguish them from Butterflies, to which they give the name of Bats. **1956** J. HEARNE *Stranger at Gate* xviii. 142 A cave full of rat-bat droppings. **1879** BARON EGGERS *Flora St. Croix* 25 *Rat-bean. **1883** E. H. A[ITKEN] *Tribes on My Frontier* 3 Down among the roots of the creeper..come a dozen dingy brown '*rat-birds'. **1910** *Q. Jrnl. Med.* III. 125 To the pathogeny of *rat-bite fever I am at present unable to offer any clue. **1910** *Lancet* 11 June 1618/1 The January issue of the Quarterly Journal of Medicine contains an interesting paper by Dr. T. J. Horder on three cases of irregularly periodic fever associated with the bite of a rat, and so alike in their other features as to cause him to group them together under the name of 'rat-bite fever'. **1917** *Jrnl. Exper. Med.* XXV. 42 The clinical symptoms of rat-bite fever are inflammation of the bitten parts, paroxysms of fever of the relapsing type, swelling of the lymph glands, and eruption of the skin. **1924** *Ann. Trop. Med. & Parasitol.* XVIII. 171 The correct name for the causal organism of rat-bite fever is *Spirillum minus*, Carter 1887. **1949** H. W. FLOREY et al. *Antibiotics* II. xxxi. 1030 In man the results of treating rat-bite fever due to Actino. muris [*sc. Streptobacillus moniliformis*] were from the first exceedingly good on very moderate doses of penicillin. **1970** *New Scientist* 27 Aug. 407/2 The mouse has been incriminated in the transmission of rat-bite fever (or soduku). **1939** *Sun* (Baltimore) 4 May 8/5 Guilty of saying, in regard to macaroni, that 'it is merely associated with a dish whose other component part is *rat cheese'. **1952** J. STEINBECK *East of Eden* xvii. 159 Their lunch of..bread and rat cheese. **1976** *Washington Post* 7 Nov. K1/5 We will try to recreate the atmosphere of a country store. Sardines, pickled pig's feet.. rat cheese. **1889** JEFFERIES *Field & Hedgerow* 86 The cat wandering about got caught in the *rat-clams—i.e. a gin. **1889** *Pall Mall G.* 18 Feb. 3/3 Is Mr. Morley sure that his books are not printed by '*rat firms'? **1882** JORDAN & GILBERT *Syn. Fishes N. Amer.* 54 *Chimæra*..*Rat-fishes.. Head somewhat compressed, the snout bluntish, protruding. *Ibid.* 55 *C. colliæi*—Rat-fish; Elephant-fish. **1905** D. S. JORDAN *Guide to Study of Fishes* I. xxxi. 564 The existing Chimæras are known also as spookfishes, ratfishes, and elephant-fishes. **1936** P. S. BARNHART *Marine Fishes California* 14 *Hydrolagus colliei*..Ratfish..San Diego to Alaska, in cold bottom waters. **1955** *Sci. News Let.* 19 Feb. 121/3 Liver oil from ratfish is the richest source of batyl alcohol. **1965** [see *holocephalian* sb. s.v. HOLO-]. **1974** *Daily Colonist* (Victoria, B.C.) 28 July 17/2 Kevin's prizes..were awarded for a two pound, 15 ounce ratfish, the heaviest landed. **1871** *Hardwicke's Science Gossip* May 99/2 The rat has two kinds of fleas, that is, the banded *Rat Flea..and the common Rat Flea. **1907** *Daily Mail* 19 Aug. 7/1 The Plague Commission has decided..that the vehicle of contagion is the rat-flea. **1929** H. E. EWING *Man. External Parasites* v. 170 The Common Rat Flea, *Ceratophyllus fasciatus* Bosc., is the flea most commonly found on rats in Europe and North America. **1953** L. F. HIRST *Conquest of Plague* xii. 335 Hygiene improvements must have greatly reduced the rat and rat-flea population of the old-fashioned cities. **1953** *New Biol.* XIV. 111 The species from which we have gained most of our knowledge are the tropical rat flea, *Xenopsylla cheopis*, and..the rat flea of temperate countries, *Nosopsyllus fasciatus*. **1977** RICHARDS & DAVIES *Imms's Gen. Textbk. Entomol.* (ed. 10) II. III. 941 In India the species mostly implicated [in the transmission of plague] is the rat flea. **1967** *Amer. Speech* XLII. 229 *Rat-fucker, a tool, usually made from a straight piece of metal coat hanger, approximately six to ten inches long, with a ninety degree bend two inches from each end, in such a manner that it ultimately has the shape of an old car crank handle. **1967** P. WELLES *Babyhip* vi. 61 'Scum,' John mumbled... 'Rat-fucker, prick,' George said. **1834** M'MURTRIE *Cuvier's Anim. Kingd.* 91 *Rat-Hares have moderate ears; legs nearly alike. **1891** *Pall Mall G.* 21 Nov. 2/3 The bills..are printed at what are commonly termed '*rat-houses'. **1913** A. J. REES *Merry Marauders* ii. 24 It was a rat-house—an asylum, to be perlite. **1922** A. WRIGHT *Colt from Country* 83 He'll be the long lost boy, instead of the guy that's missed and landed in the rat-house. **1946** F. SARGESON *That Summer* 108 Maybe they'd have to take me away to the rat-house. **1948** V. PALMER *Golconda* xxxiii. 278 Hadn't it been plain all along that there was a streak of madness in the old boy?.. He had done a spell in the rat-house and was only out on sufferance. **1957** I. CROSS *God Boy* (1958) ii. 17 You're heading for the rat house, the way you talk. Imagining things. **1825** G. SIMPSON *Jrnl.* 2 May in F. Merk *Fur Trade & Empire* (1931) 150 The *Rat hunts have likewise failed in consequence of the lowness of the Waters, but the returns in Beaver are very fair about 3,000. **1843** *Ainsworth's Mag.* III. 78 If my father's keepers invited me to a private rat-hunt, Tickle was sure to smell a rat. **1961** *Guardian* 1 Dec. 13/1 It is also to be doubted whether the OAS leaders, for all their deliberate use of murder and plastic bombs, want the 'rat hunts'. **1841** *Rat-kangaroo [see KANGAROO *sb.* 2]. **1846** G. R. WATERHOUSE *Nat. Hist. Mammalia* I. 196 The Rat-Kangaroo may be divided into three minor groups. **1894** R. LYDEKKER *Marsupialia* 63 The rat-kangaroo, often incorrectly spoken of as kangaroo-rats. **1926** LE SOUEF & BURRELL *Wild Animals of Australasia* 232 The rat-kangaroos for the most part live on the surface of the ground. **1944** F. CLUNE *Red Heart* 21 The two aboriginal guides ran tirelessly.., supplementing the larder by killing lizards, rat-kangaroos, and other small creatures. **1965** D. MORRIS *Mammals* 66 Rat-kangaroos differ from other members of the family in having well-developed canine teeth. **1978** D. OVINGTON *Austral. Endangered Species* 76/1 Also known as ..the burrowing rat kangaroo, the boodie is the only burrowing member of the kangaroo family. **1894** *Labour Commission, Gloss.* s.v., In the eyes of a trades unionist the terms **rat labour* and 'non-union' or 'free' labour are synonymous. By a unionist *rat labour* is defined as men who work for less than the established rate of wages. **1846** BUCHANAN, **Rat Mole*. **1810** *Sporting Mag.* XXXV. 7 The quantity of *rat-pills necessary for the great and important work. **1951** R. S. PRATHER *Bodies in Bedlam* ix. 65 It looked like three or four of L.A.'s juvenile moron gangs, sometimes called *rat packs, had taken turns going over the place. **1973** *Observer* 8 Apr. 48/4 Constance throws aside worldly success..and the ratpack to immerse herself in her first love —history. **1974** H. L. FOSTER *Ribbin'* iii. 91 More recently, gangs, fraternities, cliques, organizations, and 'rat packs' have again begun to be reported. **1977** *Time* 25 July 10/1 This summer Sweden has been hit by a small but ugly wave of racial incidents, three of which have been violent encounters between a rat pack of young Swedish ruffians and a community of Assyrian immigrants from the Middle East. **1851** MAYHEW *Lond. Lab.* II. 53 The terrier's education, as regards his prowess in a *rat-pit. **1848** CRAIG s.v. *Rat*, **Rat-poison*, the common name of the plant *Chailletia toxicaria*, a poisonous shrub, a native of Sierra Leone. **1824** *Microscope* (Albany, N.Y.) 6 Mar. 191/2 Loren ..Webster, chief ink-dauber in a *rat-printing office at the west. Ralph Walby, nothing at all but a rat-printer. **1931** T. S. STRIBLING *Forge* xviii. 159 The Lacefield barns were *rat proof. **1960** *Farmer & Stockbreeder* 26 Jan. 51/3 The virus is handled inside areas surrounded with a rat-proof fence. **1929** *Times* 2 Nov. 9/5 Surely it would be an economy to employ a man permanently for *rat proofing and rat catching at £150 per annum. **1870** *Gentl. Mag.* Sept. 497 The barracks are a mouldy *rat-run now. **1893** *Baily's Mag.* Oct. 253/1 The rat-runs had been stopped up, and he killed nearly..a hundred rats before he paused. **1924** GALSWORTHY *White Monkey* III. i. 223 Hurrying along the rat-runs of the Tube, she slipped her hand into his pocket. **1940** BLUNDEN *Poems 1930–1940* 202 In roofless barns, in rat-run saps. **1953** *Spectator* 13 Feb. 194/2 She will be able, through her own will and capacity, to escape from the rat-run of her environment. **1974** *Country Life* 24 Jan. 148/4 During weekday rush hours..a normally peaceful residential street can become a rat run. **1980** I. MURDOCH *Nuns & Soldiers* iii. 195 There were rat-runs of thought here into which Gertrude did not want to enter. **1860** TENNENT *Ceylon* I. 193 *note*, Wolf..mentions that *rat-snakes were often so domesticated by the natives as to feed at their table. **1882** C. C. HOPLEY *Snakes* iv. 85 The rat snake..and the *Clothonia* of India are 'said' to suck the teats of cows. **1907** *Country Life* July 328/3 The yellow rat snake or chicken snake is one of the most useful and is entirely harmless. **1927**, etc. [see DHAMAN 1]. **1958** R. CONANT *Field Guide Reptiles & Amphibians U.S.* 154 (*heading*) Rat Snakes: Genus *Elaphe*. *Ibid.* 155 All the Rat Snakes vibrate their tails rapidly when alarmed. **1969** A. BELLAIRS *Life Reptiles* I. vi. 242 In some genera such as the rat snakes (*Ptyas*), the viper *Echis* and most sea snakes it [*sc.* the right lung] stretches almost back to the cloaca. **1893** *Jrnl. Soc. Arts* 5 May 623/1 What is wanted is a mode of running the wires.. that shall not only be electric-tight, but shall also be water-tight, air-tight, oil-tight, fire-tight, and *rat-tight. **1908** *Installation News* II. 33/1 The union between two screw threads does not make a perfectly 'watertight, airtight, gastight, and rat-tight' joint, as the saying is.

rat (ræt), *sb.*[2] *Obs.* exc. *north. dial.* Forms: 3–4 **ratte**, 8–9 *dial.* **rat**. [Of obscure etym.] A rag, scrap.

a **1240** *Wohunge* in *Cott. Hom.* 277 Þu wunden was i rattes and i clutes. **13..** *S. Erkenwolde* 260 in Horstm. *Altengl. Leg.* (1881) 272 In cloutes, me thynkes, Hom burde haue rotid & bene rent in rattis longe sythene. *a* **1796** PEGGE *Derbicisms* s.v., All to rats, i.e. scraps. **1847** HALLIWELL, *Rats*, pieces, shreds, fragments. *North.*

†**rat**, *sb.*[3] *Obs.* Forms 5 **ratte**, 6 *Sc.* **ratt-**. [a. MDu., MLG. *rat* (*rad-*) or Da. *rat* (from LG.) = OFris. *rad*, *reth*, OS. *rath*, OHG. (mod.G.) *rad*, cognate with L. *rota*, OIr. *roth*, Lith. *rãtas* wheel, Skr. *rátha-s* (war) chariot.] The wheel which was formerly used in one method of executing criminals, and on which their dead bodies were afterwards exposed. Also in *pl.*

1481 CAXTON *Reynard* (Arb.) 12 It shal coste you your lyf he wyl hange yow or sette you on the ratte. **1508** DUNBAR *Flyting* 51 Evill farit and dryit, as Denseman on the rattis. **1560** ROLLAND *Seven Sages* 332 On the Rattis reuin, hangit, drawin, and quarterit.

rat, *sb.*[4] *Sc. rare.* [Of obscure origin.] A rut, furrow, mark, scratch.

1513 DOUGLAS *Æneis* VII. viii. 26 Hir forryt scoryt wyth runclys and mony rat. **1808** JAMIESON, 1. *Rat*, a scratch; as, *a rat with a prein*, a scratch with a pin... 3. The track of a wheel in a road.

†**rat**, *sb.*[5] *Sc. Obs.* In 7 **rate**, **ratt(e**. [Var. of ROT *sb.*[2], by Sc. substitution of *a* for *o*.] A file (of soldiers).

1646 LT. GEN. BAILLIE in *Baillie's Lett. & Jrnls.* (1841) II. 421, I found five ratt musqueteers, more than ane musquet-shott at randome before their bodie. **1653** BAILLIE *ibid.* III. 225 Cotterall besett the Church with some rattes of musqueteirs and a troup of horse. *a* **1670** SPALDING *Troub. Chas. I* (Spalding Club) II. 331 He directet also the Laird of Haddoche..to go to Torry, with a rate of mvskiteires.

†**rat**, *sb.*[6] *Obs. rare*$^{-1}$. = RAT-RIME.

1671 *True Non-Conformist* 254 If in hearty requests, we our selves can neither be confined..to a rat of words put in our mouth, nor relish the like practice from others [etc.].

†**rat**, *sb.*[7] *Obs.*$^{-0}$ [a. F. *rat*, obs. var. *ras*, *raz*: see RACE *sb.*[1] 6.] A strong or rapid current.

There is no evidence that the form has ever been in Eng. use. The latter part of quot. 1867 alludes to Pg. *rato* a sharp rock, which has no connexion with the Fr. word.

1753 CHAMBERS *Cycl. Supp.*, *Rat*, in the sea language, is used to express a part of the sea, where there are rapid and dangerous currents, or counter currents. **1867** SMYTH *Sailor's Word-bk.* 561 *Rat*,..a rapid stream or race, derived from sharp rocks beneath, which injure the cable.

rat (ræt), *v.*[1] [f. RAT *sb.*[1]]

1. *intr.* (chiefly *pres. pple.*) To catch or hunt rats.

1864 *Daily Tel.* 17 Dec., He wished to take it [a dog] ratting. **1871** M. LEGRAND *Cambr. Freshm.* 275, I believe the old pony would rat, too, if you put him in the pit.

2. *intr.* **a.** To desert one's party, side, or cause, *esp.* in politics; to go *over* as a deserter; to turn traitor. Also, in *Criminals' slang*, to inform.

1812 SOUTHEY *Let.* 18 May in *Life & Corr.* (1850) III. 341 W—— and C——, I doubt not, ratted upon the Catholic question because they expected the Prince upon that ground would eject Perceval. **1814** LD. BROUGHAM *Let.* 29 June in *Creevey Papers* (1903) I. ix. 195 The Whigs have just discovered old Sherry to be 'an old and valued friend and an ancient adherent of Fox'. They therefore support him. To be sure, he has ratted and left them—he kept them out of office twice—and he now openly stands on Yarmouth's influence and C[arlton] House. **1815** [cf. *re-rat*, RE- 5 a]. **1817** MAR. EDGEWORTH *Harrington* iii, If you have a mind to rat, rat *sans phrase*, and run over to the Jewish side. **1831** J. W. CROKER in *C. Papers* 1 Mar. (1884), Some of the steadiest old country gentlemen ratting over to Reform. **1888** SAINTSBURY in *Macm. Mag.* Sept. 349/2 Though Mackworth ratted to my own side, I fear it must be confessed that he did rat. **1910** *Blackw. Mag.* Aug. 256/2 Those who, in the slang of politics, are said to 'rat'. **1934** *Sun* (Baltimore) 20 Aug. 5/1 Misunas..has 'turned State's evidence'—'ratted' in gangland parlance. **1938** [see HOOLIGAN]. **1938** E. BOWEN *Death of Heart* III. iii. 371 The girl at the switchboard must have ratted. **1969** *Listener* 24 July 102/2 One's feeling for the Chamberlain government was one of such utter contempt that one felt they might very well rat once again. **1974** S. E. MORISON *European Discovery of Amer.: Southern Voyages* xx. 480 The captain of *San Gabriel* ratted..and sailed for Spain.

b. To act as a 'rat' (sense 4 d).

1847 WEBSTER cites T. F. ADAMS.

c. With *on*. To default on; to let (someone) down; to behave disloyally towards; (orig. *Criminals' slang*), to inform on.

1932 A. J. WORRALL *Eng. Idioms* 12 Of course I won't do that. Do you think I'd rat on a pal. **1938** E. AMBLER *Cause for Alarm* xviii. 311 The Italians may rat on that contract. **1938** E. BOWEN *Death of Heart* III. ii. 351 In a small way I have just ratted on Anna. **1938** *Sun* (Baltimore) 1 Sept. 4/2 This pair..have admitted the fatal attack on another prisoner for 'ratting on us'. **1948** *Richmond* (Va.) *Times-Dispatch* 13 Feb. 30/1 But of all persons to rat on the set up McKeever, the planner and perpetrator..should have been the last. **1957** C. MACINNES *City of Spades* II. xiv. 199 Why isn't Muriel here, anyway? She's ratted on him. **1973** *Times* 1 Dec. 9/6 If they were to rat on these policies he would become one of their strongest opponents and critics. **1974** *Socialist Worker* 2 Nov. 1/2 The Labour government has ratted on these men. **1977** *New Yorker* 24 Oct. 128/2 Finando and the two men he had ratted on..were all transferred to the same prison.

3. *trans.* To furnish with a 'rat' (sense 5 a).

1867 MRS. WHITNEY *L. Goldthwaite* x. 235 Next morning, at breakfast, Sin Saxon was as beautifully ruffled, ratted, and crimped..as ever.

4. To search (a person, his belongings, etc.) for things to steal; to pilfer. Chiefly *Austral.* and *N.Z.*

1919 DOWNING *Digger Dial.* 41 *Rat* (vb.), (1) Search a prisoner or dead body. (2) Pick a pocket. **1925** FRASER & GIBBONS *Soldier & Sailor Words* 236 *To rat*, to steal. To search a dead body. **1931** V. PALMER *Separate Lives* 267 'Look here, you slinking cur!' he began. 'You've been ratting other people's property for months.' **1937** J. A. LEE *Civilian into Soldier* 194 There must be a lot of dead Huns to rat. **1941** K. TENNANT *Battlers* i. 9 Some thieving (*adjective*) robber was 'ratting' his tucker-box. **1971** J. S. GUNN *Opal Terminol.* 38 *Rat*, to pilfer opal from a miner's hiding place or enter someone's mine and take out opal rock.

rat (ræt), *v.*[2] *vulgar.* [Substituted for ROT *v.*; cf. DRAT.] A form of imprecation, = DRAT.

1696 VANBRUGH *Relapse* I. iii, Rat my pocket-handerchief! have not I a page to carry it? **1747** DR. HOADLY *Suspicious Husband* II. i, Rat your inquisitive Eyes. **1792** CHARLOTTE SMITH *Desmond* I. 29 But, rat me, if I know why the plague we came. **1862** THACKERAY *Philip* xxxvi, Her very words were 'Rat that piano!' **1889** DOYLE *Micah Clarke* xxiii. 236 Rat me, if the scar is healed yet.

†**rat**, *v.*[3] *Obs. rare*$^{-1}$. [Related to RAT *sb.*[2]] *trans.* To break up, drive apart.

? *a* **1400** *Morte Arth.* 2235 Thane þe Romayns releuyde, þat are ware rebuykkyde, And alle to-rattys oure mene with theire riste horsses.

[**rat**, *v.*[4], error for RATTLE *v.* 2 b.

1723 PUCKLE *Club* (ed. 4) 84 Told us that an hart bellows, a buck groyns, a roe bells, a goat rats.]

rat, obs. f. 3rd pers. sing. pres. indic. READ *v.*

rata (ˈrɑːtə). Also 8 **ratta(h)**. [Maori.] **a.** An evergreen tree or woody climber belonging to one of several species of *Metrosideros*, of the family Myrtaceae, esp. a New Zealand species, the small *M. lucida* or the much larger *M. robusta*, both bearing terminal clusters of red flowers with long stamens; also, the fruit or the heavy reddish timber of a tree of this kind.

See Morris *Austral Eng.*, s.v.

[*a* **1771** S. PARKINSON *Jrnl. Voy. to South Seas* (1773) 40 E ratta, or e pooratta... This tree, or shrub, grows upon the Tooarao, or Lower-hills... The flowers are full of beautiful scarlet stamina.] **1792** W. BLIGH *Voy. to South Sea* xi. 139 The *rattah*, not much unlike a chestnut,..grows on a large tree. **1829** W. ELLIS *Polynesian Researches* I. xiii. 376 The wood of the rata has a fine straight grain. **1835** W. YATE *Acc. New Z.* 50 Rata.., this is a fine and useful tree, producing a heavy, close-grained, durable red-wood. **1843** DIEFFENBACH *Trav. New Z.* I. xiv. 224 The venerable rata, often measuring forty feet in circumference, and covered with scarlet flowers. **1847** [see NIKAU]. **1853** A. S. ATKINSON *Jrnl.* 7 Sept. in *Richmond-Atkinson Papers* (1960) I. 130 We found a beautiful little scorpion spider—it was under a rata log. **1889** T. KIRK *Forest Flora New Z.* 99 The southern rata is easily cultivated, and, although of slow growth, is of value for ornamental planting. *Ibid.* 263 The northern rata is one of the largest trees in the New Zealand flora. **1896** [see PAKIHI]. **1935** [see NIKAU]. **1949** F. SARGESON *I saw in my Dream* 127 Mr Anderson and Dave sat with their backs against the twisted barrel of a fallen rata. **1968** [see INANGA 2]. **1974** *Nat. Geographic* Aug. 195 The nightmare tree called rata, which begins as an innocent-seeming vine, and, in the end, strangles the tree to which it attaches itself.

b. *attrib.*, as ***rata-flower***, ***-root***, ***-tree***.

1835 W. YATE *Acc. New Z.* Index. Rata-tree. **1843** DIEFFENBACH *Trav. New Z.* I. xiv. 224 Of other parasitical plants, however, the rata-trees are very free. **1860** DONALDSON *Bush Lays* 37 The rata flowers whisper a message of death. **1872** DOMETT *Ranolf & Amohia* I. i. 1 Its butt against a rata-root.

ratable, etc.: see RATEABLE, etc.

ratafia (rætəˈfiːə). Also 8 **rattafia**, **-fee**, **ratifia**, **-fie**, **-fea**, **-fee**, 9 **ratafie**. [a. F. *ratafia* (17th c., Boileau), †*ratafiat*, of unknown origin (see Littré for conjectures).]

1. A cordial or liqueur flavoured with certain fruits or their kernels, usually almonds or peach-, apricot-, and cherry-kernels. Now applied esp. to a type of aperitif made from grape-juice and brandy.

1699 M. LISTER *Journ. to Paris* 164 All sorts of Strong Waters, particularly Ratafia's, which is a sort of Cherry Brandy made with Peach and Apricock Stones. **1719** D'URFEY *Pills* I. 6 Farewel Cold Tea, And Rattafee. **1737** DRURY *Rival Milliners* I. viii, If you refrain from Ratifea and Paint. **1810** CRABBE *Borough* xvi, She chose her comforts, ratafia and play; She loved the social game, the decent glass. **1852** THACKERAY *Esmond* III. viii, A half-dozen glasses of Ratafia made him forget all his woes and his losses. **1907** *Yesterday's Shopping* (1969) 18/1 Essences, for flavouring.. ratafia. **1946** A. L. SIMON *Conc. Encycl. Gastron.* VIII. 139/2 *Ratafia*, a generic name for a number of Cordials, usually home-made, always sweet and often of very highly alcoholic strength. Ratafia may be made with new wine or grape juice and sufficient spirit to stop its fermentation; being further flavoured with various fruits, herbs and spices; or else by the infusion of the same ingredients in brandy. **1959** W. JAMES *Word.-bk. Wine* 155 *Ratafias* were infusions of fruit or herbs in brandy, made by housewives in happier days when brandy was cheap... In the champagne country, ratafia is an aperitif, somewhat stronger than sherry or vermouth, made by mixing some unfermented champagne grape juice with brandy. **1964** *Harper's Bazaar* Nov. 146/2 *Ratafia*..bears no resemblance to our ratafia, which is a home-made liqueur, usually made with almonds. *Ratafia* is an aperitif made with local white wine and brandy. **1973** *Daily Tel.* 12 July 16, I was interested to learn..that Ratafia is an aperitif made in Champagne by mixing brandy with unfermented champagne grape juice. I have 'essence of Ratafia'..which..is made from bitter almonds.

attrib. *a*1711 E. Hamilton *Mordaunts* (1965) vi. 134 Rattefea biscakes, sugar puffs, chips. **1728** E. SMITH *Compl. Housewife* (ed. 2) 100 *A Ratafia Pudding*..Cream..Naples-bisket..Butter, some Sack, Nutmeg, and Salt..Almonds.. Eggs..bake... Scrape Sugar on it. *Ibid.* 142 (*heading*) To make Ratafia Cream. **1755** H. GLASSE *Art of Cookery* (ed. 5) xvi. 285 To make a Trifle. Cover the Bottom of your Dish ..with..Ratafia Cakes. **1769** MRS. RAFFALD *Eng. Housekpr.* (1778) 269 To make Ratafia Cakes. **1875** *Encycl. Brit.* I. 595/1 When bitter almonds are pounded in water a ratafia odour is produced.

2. A kind of cake or biscuit having the flavour of ratafia, or made to be eaten along with it.

1845 BREGION & MILLER *Pract. Cook.* 219 Put half a pound of ratafias in the mould. **1860** GEO. ELIOT *Mill on Floss* VI. i, Give him three ratafias soaked in a dessert-spoonful of cream. *c*1870 *Mirth* i. 12 The soles were worn to the thinness and brittle sponginess of ratafias.

3. A variety of cherry. (See quot.)

1835 *Trans. Hort. Soc.* Ser. II. I. 291 Ratafia..is so much allied to the Morello, that..it will be sufficient to state that its leaves are smaller and more tapering towards the base than those of the Morello.

ratal (ˈreɪtəl), *sb.* [f. RATE *sb.*[1] + -AL[1], prob. after *rental*.] The amount on which rates are assessed. Also *attrib.* (in some cases perh. taken as *adj.*).

1859 *Times* 21 Mar. 6/5 Lord John Russell was the author of the £5 and £6 ratal clause. **1866** *Pall Mall G.* 21 Feb. 7/1 Lord John was told that the £6 ratal was a shuffle. **1883** M. D. CHALMERS *Local Government* iii. 42 A ratal of £50 gives one vote. **1891** *Daily News* 4 Feb. 5/3 A Bill has been introduced into Parliament..seeking to abolish the ratal qualifications for members of vestries.

ratama, var. RETAMA.

ratan: see RATTAN.

ratanhia (rəˈtænɪə). Also 9 **ratinia**, **rhatania**. [Pg., = Sp. *ratania*, a. Quichuan *rataña* (Tschudi).] = RHATANY.

1804 CAPT. MOORE in *Naval Chron.* XII. 323, 32 chests of ratinia. **1805** *Med. Jrnl.* XIV. 129 The root, bark, and extract of the ratanhia. **1826** HENRY *Elem. Chem.* II. 383 The extract of rhatania, digested in hot water.

Comb. **1872** WATTS *Dict. Chem.* 1st Suppl. 992 Ratanhia-red..first obtained by Wittstein as a product of the decomposition of ratanhia-tannic acid.

Hence **ratanhine** (ˈrætənaɪn), *Chem.* a compound homologous with tyrosine, occurring in the extract of ratanhia.

1868 WATTS *Dict. Chem.* V. 77.

ratany: see RHATANY.

rataplan (rætəˈplæn), *sb.* [a. F. *rataplan*, of echoic origin.] A drumming or beating noise; a tattoo, rub-a-dub.

1847-8 G. A. A'BECKETT *Comic Hist. Eng.* VII. i, The sheriff..ordered the drums to strike up a *rataplan*. **1882** OUIDA *Under Two Flags* (1890) 345 She laughed and drummed the rataplan with her brass heel. **1897** *19th Cent.* June 936 The ceaseless rataplan of the bats of the washer-women.

Hence **rataˈplan** *v.* **a.** *trans.* To play (a march, etc.) by beating; **b.** *intr.* To beat *upon* (a drum).

1865 *Daily Tel.* 15 Dec. 5/2 An absurd drummer-boy rataplanning..some march adapted from the Rogue's own. **1889** *Daily News* 16 Dec. 3/6 A large white rabbit rataplans upon a big drum.

rat-a-tat (ˌrætəˈtæt). [Echoic.] = RAT-TAT. Also *attrib.* in **rat-a-tat ginger** (see quot. 1959).

1681 T. FLATMAN *Heraclitus Ridens* No. 28 (1713) I. 185 A Cooper was..busy, Rat-a-tat, Rat-a-tat, hooping Tubs. **1813** COLERIDGE *Lett.* (1895) II. 604 This bustle and endless rat-a-tat-tat at our door. **1895** Q. *Splendid Spur* 153 A wild rat-a-tat! on the street door. **1916** N. DOUGLAS *London Street Games* 64 Rat a tat tat, who is that? Only grandma's pussy-cat. What do you want? A pint of milk. **1959** I. & P. OPIE *Lore & Lang. Schoolch.* xviii. 381 Illegally knocking at doors... *Rat Tat Tat*. Abertillery and Newbridge in Monmouthshire, Barry in Glamorgan, Coventry. A variant in Lydney is *Rat-a-Tat Ginger*. *Rat-a-Tat-Tat*. Solihull, near Birmingham, and Grenoside, near Sheffield. **1961** *Times* 17 June 3/2 Any passing rat-a-tat of close volleying.

‖**ratatouille** (ratatuj, rɑːtɑːˈtuːɪ). [Fr.: the final element is app. f. *touiller* to stir up.] †**a.** A ragout. **b.** In full, ***ratatouille niçoise***: a dish, originating in Nice, consisting of aubergines, tomatoes, onions, peppers, and other ingredients stewed in olive oil.

1877 *Cassell's Dict. Cookery* 717/2 *Ratatouville* [*sic*]. This is a popular French method of making a savoury dish out of the remains of cold meat. **1946** F. M. FARMER *Boston Cooking-School Cook Bk.* (ed. 8) 472 Ratatouille Niçoise... Place in shallow baking dish, sprinkle with cheese and brown under the broiler. **1950** E. DAVID *Bk. Mediterranean Food* 125 Ratatouille is a Provençal ragoût of vegetables, usually pimentos, onions, tomatoes and aubergines, stewed very slowly in oil. **1956** L. MCINTOSH *Oxford Folly* 36 She prepared a *ratatouille* of aubergines, peppers, tomatoes, onions, and, of course, garlic. It was the only foreign dish she knew. **1960** E. DAVID *French Provincial Cooking* 242 Ratatouille Niçoise. Aubergines, tomatoes, onions and peppers stewed in oil. **1969** *Times Lit. Suppl.* 25 Dec. 1465/3 On the Riviera, the liberator's cause is seen as a distant grey dream, so easily dulled by ratatouille and red wine. **1973** R. LITTELL *Defection A. J. Lewinter* iv. 26, I have some cold *ratatouille* in the fridge.

ratbag (ˈrætbæg). *Austral.* and *N.Z. slang.* Also **rat-bag**. [f. RAT *sb.*[1] + BAG *sb.*] A stupid or eccentric person, a fool; an unpleasant person, a trouble-maker. Also *attrib.*, stupid, idiotic, uncouth.

1937 'W. HATFIELD' *I find Australia* 138 'You brought one rat-bag *in*,' said Evans to me, 'so now do me a favour by taking one off my hands.' **1948** V. PALMER *Golconda* xiv. 107 Why the hell, Donovan, are you backing that old ratbag, Christy Bangham? **1954** *Coast to Coast 1953–1954* 172 Or a ratbag watchman who'd run amuck if you breathed on a window. **1955** D. NILAND *Shiralee* 24 And what a ratbag situation, what a story. **1956** D. M. DAVIN *Sullen Bell* I. iii. 19 How did you ratbags get here, a highbrow joint like this? **1961** B. CRUMP *Hang on a Minute, Mate* 164 This'd be the best scrapper among you bunch of ratbags, wouldn't it? **1963** *Australasian Post* 14 Mar. 51/2 'He's not one of your ratbag mob, though, he—.' That cough again... 'He's a gentleman, you see.' **1965** W. DICK (*title*) A bunch of ratbags. **1967** H. HUNTER *Case for Punishment* ii. 37 Reading all about our little ratbags?.. A lot of kids from this school are involved. **1970** *N.Z. Listener* 12 Oct. 13/2 A bit late to find that out, you snobbish ratbag wowser. **1973** [see LEAD *sb.*[2] 1 f]. **1976** I. MURDOCH *Henry & Cato* I. 42 Well, it's just a game, you know me, scare a few ratbags, does no harm.

ˈrat-ˌcatcher. [f. RAT *sb.*[1]] **1. a.** One whose business it is to catch rats. Also *transf.* and *fig.*

1592 SHAKS. *Rom. & Jul.* III. i. 78 Tybalt, you Rat-catcher, will you walke? **1623** *Althorp MS.* in Simpkinson *Washingtons* (1860) App. 44 To the ratcatcher..for bating the house. **1668** DAVENANT *Man's the Master* III. ii, I rather fear 'tis the old rat-catcher, your master, that has caught us here in a trap. **1772** T. SIMPSON *Vermin-Killer* i, The nobility, farmers, &c...send for a man, known in the country by the name of a rat-catcher. **1814** CHALMERS in *Life* (1851) I. 399 The gains..from the calling of a rat-catcher. **1851** MAYHEW *Lond. Lab.* No. 45 The Rat-catchers of the Sewers.

b. Applied to animals.

1704 *Baldeus' Ceylon* lii, in Churchill *Voyages* III. 827/1 The Land-Serpents call'd *Ratcatchers* are..very large. **1856** KANE *Arct. Expl.* I. xxix. 395 He [a fox] had only one fault as a rat-catcher; he would never catch a second till he had eaten the first.

2. Unconventional hunting dress. Also *transf.* and *attrib.*

1910 KIPLING *Diversity of Creatures* (1917) 310 He came back to the bar, after he'd changed into those rat-catcher clothes. **1928** J. B. THOMAS *Hounds & Hunting* 254 *Rat-catcher*—referring to one informally dressed when hunting. **1930** *Field* 29 Nov. 764/1 The self-respecting beginner will want to be turned out properly, in the right 'rat-catcher style'. **1933** A. POWELL *From View to Death* viii. 200 Both sons were in ratcatcher and Torquil wore a canary-coloured waistcoat. **1963** M. MALIM *Pagoda Tree* xvi. 101 While one could exhibit oneself and did to the Cricket Club in rat-catcher, so to speak, one had to dress for presentation on the Thursday committee night at the Tulyar. **1976** *Horse & Hound* 3 Dec. 32/2 (Advt.), Moleskin ratcatcher trousers. Warm, tough, supple. Shirt-grip self-supporting waist... Slim leg style. **1977** 'E. CRISPIN' *Glimpses of Moon* xi. 205 Nor were they a very distinguished Hunt: the men mostly turned up in ratcatcher (Fen had that morning noted one.. who was wearing a hoicked-up caftan and prayer beads above his shining riding boots).

ratch (rætʃ), *sb.*[1] *Mech.* Also 7 *Sc.* **ratsche**, 8 **roch**, 8–9 **rash**. [Var. of RATCHET; the precise history of the form is not clear. Cf. G. *ratsche*, *rätsche*; also *ratschborer* ratchet-drill, *ratschscheibe* ratchet-wheel.]

†**1.** *Sc.* = FIRELOCK 1. *Obs. rare.*

1620 D. WEDDERBURN *Compl. Buik* (S.H.S.) 73, I have directit James to bring me hame a ratsche of a gun of fyve quarter lenth. **1657** COLVIL *Whigs Supplic.* (1751) 18 Some had guns with rusty ratches.

2. A ratchet.

1721 BAILEY, *Ratch* [in a Watch] are the small Teeth at the Bottom of the Barrel, which stop it in winding up. **1825** J. NICHOLSON *Operat. Mechanic* 502 The spring..must not be altered by the ratches' click. **1875** KNIGHT *Dict. Mech.* 1881/2 *Ratch*, a rack-bar with inclined angular teeth between which a pawl drops.

3. A ratchet-wheel; *spec.* in clock-work.

1721 BAILEY, *Ratch*, [in Clock-Work] a Sort of Wheel, which serves to lift up the Detents every Hour, and to make the Clock strike. **1741** ETTRICK in *Phil. Trans.* XLI. 563 The Roch, or snagged Wheel, being..accounted as Part of the great Wheel. **1780** *Encycl. Brit.* (ed. 2) IX. 6635/2 Ratch, or rash, in clock-work, a sort of wheel having twelve fangs [etc., as in Bailey]. **1875** KNIGHT *Dict. Mech.* 1881/2 A circular ratch is a ratchet-wheel.

b. So ***ratch-wheel***.

1741 ETTRICK in *Phil. Trans.* XLI. 567 The Roch-wheel to be cut with 48 Teeth. **1825** J. NICHOLSON *Operat. Mechanic* 314 The other end..by the motion of the arm *G*, is made to move the ratch-wheel.

†**ratch**, *sb.*[2] *Obs. rare*[−1]. ? = RACK *sb.*[1] 3.

1562 PHAER *Æneid* v. Oiv, Down sinck the surging waues..; from al the heauen the ratches flies.

ratch, *sb.*[3] *Naut.* [f. RATCH *v.*[1]] A reach.

1885 *Daily Tel.* 19 Aug. (quoted in *Cassell's Encycl. Dict.*).

ratch, hunting-dog: see RACHE[1].

ratch, white mark: see RACHE[2].

ratch, erron. form of ROTCH.

ratch (rætʃ), *v.*[1] *Obs.* exc. *dial.* Also 4–6 **rachche**, 5 **ratche**. [Back-form. from *raught*, pa. t. of REACH *v.*[1], on anal. of *caught*, *catch*.]

1. *intr.* †**a.** To proceed, go. *Obs. rare*[−1].

13.. *E.E. Allit. P.* B. 619 Resttez here on þis rote & I schal rachche after.

b. *Naut.* To sail on a tack, to 'reach'.

1881 CLARK RUSSELL *Sailor's Sweeth.* I. ii. 34 They ratched from shore to shore, slueing on their heels to run athwart the wind on another tack. **1897** *Outing* (U.S.) XXIX. 467/2 Getting our anchor we ratched around under mainsail and jib.

†**2.** *trans.* To reach, get hold of. *Obs. rare*[−0].

1530 PALSGR. 679/2, I ratche, I catche, I have raught. *Je attayns.* And I ratche the thou shalt bere me a blowe.

3. *trans.* To draw out, to stretch (hence *dial.* to exaggerate, to lie); to pull or tear asunder.

*a*1529 SKELTON *Agst. Garnesche* iii. 180 Thou xuldyst be rachchyd, If thow war metely machchyd. **1530** PALSGR. 679/2, I ratche, I stretche out a length. *Je estends.* If it be to shorte ratche it out. **1781** HUTTON *Tour to Caves* (ed. 2) Gloss., *Ratch*, to tear in pieces. **1829** in BROCKETT. **1847** in HALLIWELL. **1869-** in dial. glosses (Lancs., Yks., Linc., Hants, Dorset). **1904** HARDY *Dynasts* I. iii. 31 The thousands called..will ratch the lines Of English regiments ..To glorious length.

Hence **ratched** *ppl. a.*, stretched.

1835 URE *Philos. Manuf.* 179 He must take care not to stretch the cardings... If any fault is committed in this respect,..they are said to be 'ratched cardings'.

ratch, *v.*[2] *Mech.* [f. RATCH *sb.*[1]] *trans.* To cut into teeth like those of a ratch; to turn *round* in the process of doing this.

1777 RAMSDEN *Descr. Engine* (I.) 1 The Circumference of the Wheel is ratched or cut..into 2160 Teeth. *Ibid.* 10, I then ratched the wheel round continually in the same direction..and, in ratching the wheel about 300 times round, the teeth were finished. *Ibid.*, The screw in ratching had continually hold of several teeth at the same time. [**1846** HOLTZAPFFEL *Turning* II. 639 *note*, In ratching or cutting the wheel..the circle was divided with the greatest exactness.]

ratch (rætʃ), *v.*[3] *north. dial.* and *Sc.* [f. RACHE, RATCH *sb.*[1]] **a.** *intr.* To forage for food, to ferret *around*; to ramble or wander *about*. **b.** *trans.* To search thoroughly, ransack. Hence **ˈratching** *vbl. sb.*

1801 'BERWICKSHIRE SANDIE' *Poems* 73 Hens ratch'd through the house wi' greed. **1859** W. DICKINSON *Gloss. Words & Phrases Cumberland* (foreword), Yan wad ratch ivry neukk ov oald Cummerlan. *Ibid.* 91 *Ratch*, to ramble, to search vigorously. 'Ratchan about like a hungry hound.' **1869** A. C. GIBSON *Folk-Speech Cumberland* 96 Cook's house was ratch't through an' through. **1971** *Country Life* 9 Sept. 630/1 There's oalas an odd yan or two that'll leave their lambs an' ratch aboot. *Ibid.* 7 Oct. 900/1 Hill sheep can be very active, and when they feel like ratching it takes a very formidable fence to prevent them. **1973** *Guardian* 26 Feb. 10/2 The grass is poor, as yet, so some of the fell-sheep go foraging in and out of the woods..and into any fell-side garden with an open gate... 'Ratching' is part of their nature. **1976** *Jrnl. Lakeland Dial. Soc.* 21 Yan day t' auld Friesian bull gat oot, a' caved an' ratched aroond, Neabody durst gan near him as he rwoared an' scratted t' groond.

ratchel (ˈrætʃɪl). *techn.* or *dial.* Forms: 8–9 **ra(t)chill**, 9 **ratchil**, **-el(l**. [Of obscure etym.]

1. Fragments of loose shivery stone lying above the firm rock.

1747 Hooson *Miner's Dict.* I iv b, Under the Rachill.. where it is the most gankey, the chief Leader may be found. 1799 Kirwan *Geol. Ess.* 297 Decaying porphyry, which the miners call rotten stone;..fragments of stone they call ratchill. 1811 Farey in Hunt *Mining* (1884) 233 In many instances in alluvial mixtures the stones are..like the chippings of a stonemason's yard, and called Ratchel, Rumel, Keale, Skerry, or Rubble. 1884 R. Hunt *Brit. Mining* 912 *Rachill*, small loose stones that are usually found on the top of the rock forming as the depth increased into the nature of beds. 1888 in *Sheffield Gloss.*

2. (See quots.)

1807 Headrick *Arran* 250 Wacken Porphyry. Glomellaria. Scottish: Ratchell. 1808 Jamieson, *Ratchel*, a hard rocky crust below the soil; pan, till. 1865 J. T. F. Turner *Slate Quarries* 23 There are occasionally found, running east and west, walls of hardah, called 'ratchels'.

ratchet ('rætʃɪt), *sb.* Forms: α. 7–8 **rochet, -ett,** 8 **rotchet.** β. 8– **ratchet,** (9 **rachet**). [a. F. *rochet* (†*roquet*), a blunt form of lance-head, or lance having such a head (12–15th c.); a bobbin or spool; also, a ratchet or ratchet-wheel (16th c., in Paré XXIII. xii.) = It. *rocchetto* spool, ratchet, etc.: see ROCKET.

The development of the sense of 'ratchet' in F. and It. is not clear; it may have originated in the words being applied to spindles or barrels (in mechanism) provided with teeth.]

1. a. A set of angular or saw-like teeth on the edge of a bar or rim of a wheel, into which a cog, tooth, click, or the like may catch, usually for the purpose of preventing reversed motion; also, a bar or wheel (*ratchet-wheel*) provided with such teeth.

α. 1659 Leak *Waterwks.* 25 They make the peeces of Timber to come to the Saws by means of certain Toothed Wheels with a rochet. 1743 Freke in *Phil. Trans.* XLII. 558 A Wheel..notched round, which works as a Rotchet on a Spring Ketch. 1758 Fitzgerald *ibid.* L. 728 The outside rochet and outside wheel are fixed on the arbor.

β. 1729 Desaguliers in *Phil. Trans.* XXXVI. 204 To throw the Catch in again upon the Teeth of the Ratchet, and stop the whole Motion without Accidents. 1825 J. Nicholson *Operat. Mechanic* 501 The click attached to the great wheel is laid hold of by the teeth of the ratchet. 1881 Greener *Gun* 9 The ratchet is wound up by means of the lever and cogs.

b. *pl.* in same sense. *rare.*

1721 Bailey, *Ratchets*, [in a Watch], are the small Teeth at the Bottom of the Barrel, which stop it, in winding up. 1860 Maury *Phys. Geog. Sea* iii. §165 The cogs on this wheel are cut and regulated to the rachets on that.

2. A click or detent, catching into the teeth of a ratchet-wheel.

1846 Johnston tr. *Beckmann's Hist. Invent.*, etc. (ed. 4) I. 11 These two wheels are connected by a ratchet or pall.., the larger ratchet-wheel is held stationary by a ratchet. 1875 Knight *Dict. Mech.* 1881/2.

†**3.** (See quot.) *Obs. rare*⁻¹.

1763 W. Lewis *Phil. Comm. Arts* 56 From this the wire is wound off upon a smaller cylinder, called a Rochett, placed on the spindle of a spinning wheel.

4. = *ratchet-knife.*

1975 *Globe & Mail* (Toronto) 11 June 3/1 Walking with the road with a ratchet (knife) in your waist, Johnny you're too bad. 1976 *Daily Mirror* 2 Apr. 20/2 *Ratchet*, knife.

5. *attrib.* and *Comb.*, as ***ratchet-arbor, -bar, -brace, -catch, -drill, -jack, -lever, pinion, rifling, -ring, screwdriver, side, -stop, -tooth, -wheel***; **ratchet effect** (see quots. 1977); **ratchet knife**, a type of knife popular in Jamaica.

1849 Noad *Electricity* 383 A pinion on the *ratchet-arbor gives motion to other simple wheel-work. *a* 1824 A. Scott in *Trans. Highl. Soc.* (1824) VI. 34 So hinged that its lower end shall fall into the teeth of the same *ratchet-bar. 1849 Weale *Dict. Terms*, *Ratchet-brace. 1868 *Pall Mall G.* 17 May 3 Saws, files, ratchet-braces. *a* 1824 A. Scott in *Trans. Highl. Soc.* (1824) VI. 32 A ratchet-wheel of about 13 inches diameter, with *ratchet-catches. 1846 Holtzapffel *Turning* II. 561 The *ratchet-drill..is made by cutting ratchet teeth in the drill shaft. 1970 *Times* 13 Apr. 20/7 It appears that there has been a *ratchet effect in employment in the service industries. 1977 *New Society* 31 Mar. 643/2 One of the curiosities of political life is what you might call the 'ratchet effect'. This is the process by which one party makes the running over an issue, and gradually winds the other (or others) along after it. 1977 *Listener* 31 Mar. 397/2 It was Sir Keith Joseph who drew attention to the 'ratchet effect' in politics, whereby the right seems to have acquiesced in the changes the left brings about. Curiously, in broadcasting matters, the ratchet effect has worked the other way: the Conservatives broke the BBC's monopoly in the Fifties.., and it has been the left that has acquiesced. 1979 *Dædalus* Spring 122 These efforts are illustrated by the rediscovery of the 'ratchet effect' theory, which simply begins with the common wisdom that prices go up more freely than they go down. 1875 Knight *Dict. Mech.* 1882/2 *Ratchet-jack, etc. 1971 *Jrnl. Commonwealth Lit.* Dec. 140 The DJE..passed by such terms as..**ratchet-knife, trouble.* 1976 Boot & Thomas *Jamaica* 40/1 Just the sort of deft digital flourish you need to whip out the blade of a ratchet knife—which is a particular kind of nicely curved blade in a tapered handle, made in Germany for gutting fish. 1846 Holtzapffel *Turning* II. 561 The *ratchet-lever in part resembles the ratchet drill. 1779 in *Phil. Trans.* LXVIII. 979 We must..except the *ratchet pinions. 1881 Greener *Gun* 177 The *ratchet rifling we do not consider nearly so good as either of the other forms. 1779 Ramsden *Descr. Engine* (II.) 11 Till the piece (*j*) is brought under the stop on the *ratchet-ring. 1897 *Sears, Roebuck Catal.* 80/1 The old and well-known Gay's Double-Action *Ratchet Screw Driver. 1979 S. Brett in *Winter's Crimes 11* 12 A ratchet screwdriver... Just the job for putting up shelves. 1838 *Civil Eng. & Arch. Jrnl.* I. 192/1 The palls..are thrown into the *ratchet sides of the press. 1867 J. Hogg *Microsc.* I. iii. 204 The teeth answer the triple purpose of thumb-milling, *ratchet-stop, and graduation. 1735 in *Phil. Trans.* XXXIX. 89 Their Distance depends on the *Ratchet-Teeth ..in the Brass-Bottom. 1777 Ramsden *Descr. Engine* (I.) 11 A *ratchet-wheel, having 60 teeth. ? 1790 J. Imison *School of Arts* I. 17 It is requisite to have a ratchet-wheel on the end of the axle..with a catch to fall into its teeth. 1884 F. J. Britten *Watch & Clockm.* 220 A pawl or click is a necessary adjunct to a ratchet wheel.

Hence **'ratchetted** *a.*, provided with a ratchet; **'ratchety** *a.*, resembling the movement of a ratchet, jerky.

1892 *Star* 14 Dec. 3/2 The ratchetted arm of the derrick ..broke. 1885 *The Money-Makers* ix. 128 Raikes..poured out a ratchety but vehement panegyric.

'ratchet, *v.* [f. the *sb.*] **a.** *intr.* To move by means of a ratchet. Also *transf.* and *fig.*

1881 Young *Every Man his own Mechanic* §270. 103 The angular borer turning clear around without stopping to ratchet. 1977 *Time* 3 Jan. 44/3 The signal, according to some radio operators who have heard it ratcheting over their headsets, sounds like a 'buzzsaw' or 'the whirring of helicopter blades'. 1977 *Rolling Stone* 16 June 36/1 The movie director, age 34, spirals, ratchets, thrusts his chin like Mussolini.

b. *trans.* To move (something) *up* as by a ratchet. Cf. *ratchet effect* s.v. RATCHET *sb.* 5.

1977 R. Jenkins *Europe's Present Challenge & Future Opportunity* (Jean Monnet Lect.) 8 Floating exchange rates transmit violent and sudden inflationary impulses... Each new impulse ratchets up the inflationary process. 1979 *Daily Tel.* 9 Aug. 2/7 We are quite clear that the union movement has not been responsible for ratcheting up inflation.

ratchet, obs. f. ROCHET.

ratchetter, var. ROCHETER.

ratchil(l, varr. RATCHEL.

ratchit, obs. Sc. f. WRETCHED.

†**'ratchment.** *Obs. rare.* [Of obscure origin.] In a herse, 'a kind of flying buttresses which spring from the corner principals and meet against the central or chief principal' (Parker); also, (?) a sloping part of a wooden framework.

1557 in Bentley *Excerpta Historica* (1831) 306 It'm vj ratchementes with xiij^ne corsse lights a pece. 1558 *Funeral Q. Mary* in Leland *Coll.* V. (1774) 319 A very somptiouse Hersse..the viii Rochments hanged double with Vallence of Sarsenet. 1596 *Lanc. Wills* (1857) III. 3, v longe boardes upon stoopes withe three ratchmentes wth hookes to hange meat on.

rate (reɪt), *sb.*[1] Also 5–6 *Sc.* **rait,** 6 **ratte, rayt,** 7 **reat,** (9 *dial.* **raate**). [a. OF. *rate, (raite, ratte,* etc., see Godef.), ad. med.L. *rata* (from L. *pro ratā parte, portiōne,* also *pro ratā* PRO RATA), fem. of *ratus*, pa. pple. of *rērī* to think, judge: see RATIO *sb.*]

I. †1. a. The (total) computed or estimated quantity, amount, or sum *of* anything, usually as forming a basis for calculating other quantities or sums. *Obs.*

1472–3 *Rolls of Parlt.* VI. 49/2 Contributours to the costes and expenses..after the quantite and rate of the yerely value of the said rent. 1548 Udall *Erasm. Par. Luke* xix. 145 b, Accordyng to the quantite or rate of the fruict, which they haue brought into the lordes vineyard. 1574 tr. *Littleton's Tenures* 46 The escuage maye & shal bee apporcioned after the quantity and rate of the lande. 1597 Shaks. *2 Hen. IV*, IV. i. 22, I iudge their number Vpon, or neere, the rate of thirtie thousand.

†**b.** A fixed portion or quantity. *Obs. rare.*

1568 Bible (Bishops') *Exod.* xvi. 4 The people shall go out & gather a certaine rate euery day. 1611 Bible *2 Chron.* ix. 24 They brought euery man his present..a rate yeere by yeere. *c* 1611 Chapman *Iliad* IV. 275 Our inferior mates Drink even that mix'd wine measur'd out; thou drink'st, without those rates, Our old wine neat.

2. a. Estimated value or worth (of individual things or persons). †*for the rate*, in proportion to the value. † *beyond the rate*, too highly. Also in *pl.* (17th c.). Cf. sense 5.

1425 *Rolls of Parlt.* IV. 290/2 That everychon of home may holde residence for the rate opon yche of hire Benefice. 1560 Daus tr. *Sleidane's Comm.* 42 b, That Byshoppes and other spirituall parsons shoulde paye..after the rate of the benefice, and certeine summe of money. 1592 Shaks. *Rom. & Jul.* v. iii. 301 There shall no figure at the Rate be set, As that of True and Faithfull Iuliet. 1620 E. Blount *Horæ Subs.* 129 To esteeme life aboue the price, or to feare death beyond the rate, be alike euill. 1638 Suckling *Brennoralt* III. i, The world does set great rates upon you. *a* 1677 Hale *Contempl.* II. 91 They mightily prize them and set a great rate upon them. 1771 *Junius Lett.* lii. 267, I am a little offended at the low rate at which you seem to value my understanding.

†**b.** Estimation, consideration. *Obs.*

1610 Shaks. *Temp.* II. i. 109 My sonne is lost, and (in my rate) she too. 1651 Hobbes *Leviath.* (1839) 167 It is necessary that there be laws of honour, and a public rate of the worth of such men as have deserved..well of the commonwealth. 1727 De Foe *Syst. Magic* I. ii. (1840) 44 Wise Men were not..so high-prized as they had been, and grew daily less and less in the ordinary rate and esteem of the World.

†**c.** Valuation, rating. *Obs. rare*⁻¹.

1653 *Pub. Gen. Acts* 331 For want of sufficient time a just and perfect survey or rate of each parish..could not be made and returned.

3. a. Price, the sum paid or asked for a single thing. †Also *pl.* (17th c.)

Properly distinct from 6 b, in which *rate* implies that the same price or sum applies to a number of similar cases; but the two senses cannot always be clearly distinguished.

1590 Shaks. *Com. Err.* IV. iv. 14 *Ant. E.* Fiue Hundred Duckets villaine for a rope? *E. Dro.* Ile serue you sir fiue hundred at the rate. 1633 G. Herbert *Temple, Vanitie* 10 To purchase heaven for repenting, Is no hard rate. *a* 1660 Hammond *Serm.* xviii. Wks. 1684 IV. 599 The devil.. knows the price and value of a soul, and will pay any rate for it rather than lose his market. 1665 Boyle *Occas. Refl.* II. vi. (1848) 117 Giving great rates for neck-laces of true pearl. 1770 Earl Malmesbury *Diaries & Corr.* I. 66 His Catholic Majesty is inclined..to come to an accommodation with us at almost any rate. 1784 Cowper *Task* VI. 416 They prove too often at how dear a rate He sells protection.

†**b.** ***at the rate of***, at the cost of. *Obs.*

1665 Boyle *Occas. Refl.* v. iii. (1848) 305 The folly of gaining anything at the rate of losing their own Souls. 1709 Steele *Tatler* No. 58 ¶1 To purchase a..momentary Pleasure at the Rate of making an honest Man unhappy.

c. ***at an easy rate***, without great expense; also *transf.* without great loss or suffering. † ***of easy rate***, cheaply purchased. *Obs.*

1596 Drayton *Baron's Wars* (Roxb.) 340 O! hadst thou in thy glory thus beene slayne, All thy delights had beene of easie rate. 1665 Boyle *Occas. Refl.* II. xiv. (1848) 142 Having sadly Experienc'd..Sickness, I am thereby brought, though at no easie Rate, to set a high Value upon Health. 1726–31 Tindal tr. *Rapin's Hist. Eng.* (1743) II. XVII. 118 Thinking himself very happy in coming off at so easy a rate. 1819 Shelley *Cenci* I. ii. 73, I think to win thee at an easier rate.

II. 4. a. The amount or number of one thing which corresponds or has relation to a certain amount or number of some other thing. Chiefly in phr. ***at (†after) the rate of.***

The second number being commonly unity (esp. some unit of time) is sometimes omitted (cf. quot. 1860).

1497 *Naval Acc. Hen. VII* (1896) 147 Euery man takyng after the Rate of xij^d ob by the weke. 1538–9 *Lett. Suppress. Monast.* (Camden) 278 After the rate of xviij^s. the hundredd. 1596 Spenser *State Irel.* Wks. (Globe) 664/1 Six score acres, after the rate of 21 foote to every pearche of the sayd acre. 1630 *R. Johnson's Kingd. & Commw.* 148, I feare me, hee reckoneth after the Athenian rate, ten for one. 1660 *Act 12 Chas. II*, c. 20 §6 [Interest] after the rate of six pounds per cent. 1781 *Encycl. Brit.* (ed. 2) VII. 5163/2 They will contend who shall get the silver at the rate of 15 pounds for one of gold. 1807 *Europ. Mag.* LII. 112/1, I suppose we had gone at the rate of six miles an hour. 1860 Maury *Phys. Geog. Sea* xviii. §746 Although we were going at the rate of nine knots, the ship made no noise. 1879 Lubbock *Sci. Lect.* ii. 34 The ants brought in dead insects..at the rate of about twenty-eight a minute.

†**b.** Ratio, proportion. *Obs.*

1614 T. Bedwell *Nat. Geom. Numbers* i. 2 The Base and Height are said to be rational one to another, when as the rate or reason of both may be expressed by a number of the same measure given. 1659 Leak *Waterwks.* 4 There is the same rate of the Water D to the Water O, as there is of the length of the pipe N, to the length of the pipe M.

5. a. Value (of money, goods, etc.) as applicable to each individual piece or equal quantity.

Custom-house rates orig. belong to this sense, a standard value being assigned to each class of article, and duty paid in accordance with this. In 1657 the title of the 'book of rates' is 'Book of Values of Merchandize imported, according to which Excise is to be paid by the First Buyer'.

With reference to money, *rate* denotes the conventional or legal value of the metals or coins in relation to each other (cf. RATIO *sb.* 3).

1494 Fabyan *Chron.* v. cxxxvi. 122 After ye rate of money nowe currant, a quarter of whete was worth .ii. marks & a halfe. 1545 (*title*) The rates of the custome house bothe inwarde and outwarde. 1610 (*title*) Book of Rates. 1612 *Acc.-bk. W. Wray* in *Antiquary* XXXII. 214 Proclamation for the rate of goolde, as the angell, soueraigne and white royall at xis. a peece. *a* 1692 Pollexfen *Disc. Trade* (1697) 147 The Book of Rates by which the Prizes of all Goods are Regulated at the Custom-House for the Payment of Customs and Duties. 1758 J. Harris *Ess. Money & Coins* II. 53 The legal rate of an ounce of either of these metals in coin is called the mint price.

b. The basis of equivalence on which one form of currency is exchanged for another. (Cf. EXCHANGE 3 and 4.)

1727–41 Chambers *Cycl.* s.v. *Rate*, The rates of exchange, factorship, &c. 1779 *Encycl. Brit.* (ed. 2) IV. 2865/2 When the Flemish rate rises above par, Britain gains and Holland loses by the exchange. 1838 *Penny Cycl.* X. 109/1 The par, for the time being, would be brought to coincide with the actual rate. 1865 Phillips *Amer. Paper Curr.* II. 164 The only question was as to the rate at which they should be liquidated.

6. a. The amount *of* a charge or payment (such as interest, discount, wages, etc.) having relation to some other amount or basis of calculation.

1540 *Act 32 Hen. VIII*, c. 14 (*title*) An acte for maintenaunce of the nauy of England, and for certaine rates of frayctes. 1596 Shaks. *Merch. V.* I. iii. 46 He.. brings downe The rate of vsance here with vs in Venice. 1652 *Votes Parl. conc. Encouragem. Mariners*, That the Rates and Proportions of Pay..be allowed to the Officers of the several Ranks of ships. 1785 Paley *Mor. Philos.* Wks. 1825 IV. 107 The rate of interest has in most countries been regulated by law. 1833 Ht. Martineau *Manchester Strike* iii. 34 It is not on this that the rate of wages depends. 1885 *Manch. Exam.* 13 July 5/2 The rate of the income tax ought to vary with the means of the payers.

b. A fixed charge applicable to each individual case or instance; *esp.* the (*or* an) amount paid or demanded for a certain quantity of a commodity, material, work, etc.

In 17th c. freq. used of the prices of goods (cf. note to 3); in later use chiefly of charges for carriage.

1526 *Galway Arch.* in *10th Rep. Hist. MSS. Comm.* App. V. 402 Every man or woman which makith aquavitie.. to paye the accostomid ratte to the silver boxe. **1596** SPENSER *State Irel.* Wks. (Globe) 662/1 The rest.. should be placed in parte of the landes.. at such rate, or rather better then others. **1640** NABBES *The Bride* I. iv, I like the rates: may the wines please as well. **1663** GERBIER *Counsel* 56 The Rate of Bricklayers their work. Good London Brick-layers will work the Rod for forty shillings. **1687** A. LOVELL tr. *Thevenot's Trav.* I. 67 The set rate for the Blood of a Man is five hundred Piastres. **1709** STEELE *Tatler* No. 10 ¶ 11 Bread was sold at Paris for 6*d.* per Pound, and.. there was not half enough even at that Rate. **1727–41** CHAMBERS *Cycl.* s.v. *Coach*, Hackney-coaches.. exposed to hire.. at rates fixed by authority. **1795** J. PHILLIPS *Hist. Inland Navig.* Addenda 147 The company are authorised to take the following rates, viz. For clay, brick, or stones, one halfpenny per ton per mile. **1845** MCCULLOCH *Taxation* II. vii. (1852) 312 Letters containing one enclosure charged with two single rates. **1883** *Manch. Exam.* 29 Oct. 5/2 The high rates of the railway companies prevented the cheaper kinds of fish from being sent to the markets.

†**c.** Relative cost or expense (of living). *Obs.*

1633 BP. HALL *Occas. Medit.* §61 At how easie a rate doe these creatures live that are fed with rest! **1646** BOYLE *Let. to Marcombes* 22 Oct., Wks. 1772 I. p. xxxiii, I have been forced to live at a very high rate (considering the inconsiderableness of my income).

d. (Usually *pl.*) Amount of assessment on property for local purposes. (Cf. CHURCH-RATE, POOR-RATE.) Also *fig.*, the rate-collector.

1712 PRIDEAUX *Direct. Ch.-wardens* (ed. 4) 48 The Rates must be made with the consent of the major part of the Parish. **1807** CRABBE *Par. Reg.* III. Wks. 1823 I. 138 The rates are high; we have a-many poor. **1841** *Penny Cycl.* XIX. 307/1 If the parish fail to meet, the churchwardens may themselves impose a rate. **1881** GLADSTONE *Sp. at Leeds* 7 Oct., Rates have increased in towns with great rapidity. **1888** R. L. STEVENSON *Popular Authors* 11, Even the Rates and Taxes that besiege your door, have actually read your tales.

7. a. Degree of speed in moving from one place to another; the ratio between the distance covered and the time taken to traverse it. Chiefly in phr. (*to go* etc.) ***at a...rate***. Also const. *of* (travelling, etc.); ***at the rate of knots***: see KNOT *sb.*[1] 3 c.

1652 LOVEDAY tr. *Calprenede's Cassandra* I. 43 We travelled at a great rate, marching whole dayes without resting. **1697** CONGREVE *Mourning Bride* I. i, When my Lord beheld the ship pursuing, And saw her rate so far exceeding ours, He came to me. **1760–72** H. BROOKE *Fool of Qual.* (1809) I. 67 The coach drove on, at a round rate. **1834** PRINGLE *Afr. Sk.* ix. 292 The most rapid rate of ox-wagon travelling,.. about thirty miles a day. **1860** TYNDALL *Glac.* I. xiv. 99 The motion.. swiftly augmented to the rate of an avalanche. **1876** W. H. G. KINGSTON *On banks of Amazon* 119 The whole herd.. wheeling round, off they went at a rapid rate.

b. Relative speed of working, acting, etc.

1751 JOHNSON *Rambler* No. 165 ¶ 11 As workmen will not easily be hurried beyond their ordinary rate. **1858** HOMANS *Cyclop. Commerce* 1724/1 The operation has been since proceeding at a still greater rate. **1879** THOMSON & TAIT *Nat. Phil.* I. I. §268 The *actio agentis*.. is simply, in modern English phraseology, the rate at which the agent works. **1912** in C. B. SMITH *Testing Time* (1961) ii. 32 The rate of rising loaded as above has been tested up to 600 feet & found to be at the rate of 155 feet per minute. **1930** C. DIXON *Parachuting* ii. 21 Hampton descended very slowly.. landing after a most pleasant experience, such as the modern parachute gives, in thirteen minutes. This rate of descent worked out at 8 feet per second. The modern rate is about 21 feet per second. **1943** T. HORSLEY *Find, Fire & Strike* 21 Both pilots throttled back.. and used just sufficient engine to give them a rate of sink of 250 feet a minute. **1946** *Happy Landings* July 9/1 Your rate of climb indicator may show as much as 3,500 feet per minute up. **1963** B. FOZARD *Instrumentation Nuclear Reactors* xiii. 163 Reactivity must be released slowly by withdrawal of the control rods at a rate which is known to keep the rate of divergence within safe bounds.

c. Of time-pieces: Amount of gain or loss on the correct time during twenty-four hours.

1833 HERSCHEL *Astron.* iii. 139 Their clocks being regulated, and their errors and rates ascertained and applied.

8. a. Relative amount of variation, increase, decrease, etc.

1816 J. SMITH *Panorama Sc. & Art* II. 90 A set of glass bubbles, varying from each other in specific gravity at an equal rate. **1850** CARLYLE *Latter-d. Pamph.* iv. (1872) 133 Three millions of paupers.. increasing at a frightful rate per day. **1876** TAIT *Rec. Adv. Phys. Sc.* (1885) 357 Rate of change of velocity is called in Kinematics Acceleration. **1878** HUXLEY *Physiogr.* 200 The rate of augmentation being affected by the character of the rocks bored through.

b. *techn.* of the inclination in the thread of a screw.

1846 HOLTZAPFFEL *Turning* II. 637 In this comparatively inferior class of screws.. whether or not their pitches or rates have any exact relationship to the inch, is a matter of indifference.

c. Of a spring: a quantity relating the applied load to the compression or extension produced (see quots. 1959, 1961).

1957 E. B. JONES *Instrument Technol.* III. I. 6 For each value of the measured variable there will be a definite position of the feed-back bellows, and as the spring rate of the bellows and spring is fixed, this must mean a definite value of the transmitted pressure. **1959** *Motor Manual* (ed. 36) v. 123 This ratio can be expressed in terms of pounds weight required to produce a deflection of one inch.. and this figure is known as the spring rate. **1961** W. R. BERRY *Spring Design* i. 12 The rate *S* of the spring is equal to the load per unit of deflection. **1964** H. A. ROTHBART *Mech. Design & Systems Handbk.* xxxiii. 12 Some springs are such that their rate is constant over the entire usable range of deflection.

III. 9. a. Standard or measure in respect of quality or condition; hence, class, kind, sort, †rank. (See also FIRST-RATE A. 1.) † ***in rate of*** = as. † ***to the rate***, ? to the full.

1509 FISHER *Funeral Serm. C'tess Richm.* Wks. (1876) 291 She was of singuler wysedome ferre passynge the comyn rate of women. **1567** JEWEL *Def. Apol.* (1611) 45 Somewhat.. whereby it may be vnderstanded to be taken in rate of a vice. **1621** FLETCHER *Isl. Princess* IV. i, They had their sute, they landed, and too th' rate grew rich and powerfull. **1639** FULLER *Holy War* III. xxix. (1840) 170 He was very learned, according to the rate of that age. **1663** GERBIER *Counsel* C vij b, The several Materials.. are of the best Rate, as any can be. **1682** J. FLAVELL *Fear* 13 'Tis a great sin to love or fear any creature above the rate of a creature. **1703** MRS. CENTLIVRE *Beau's Duel* V. i, I look your coffers shou'd maintain me at my rate. **1711** STEELE *Spect.* No. 151 ¶ 7 The intemperate Meals and loud Jollities of the common Rate of Country Gentlemen. **1815** JANE AUSTEN *Emma* I. xi, Her brother's disposition to look down on the common rate of social intercourse.

b. *Naut.* Class of vessels, *esp.* war-vessels, according to their size or strength. (See also FIRST-, SECOND-RATE, etc.)

The old division of the British navy into six rates of vessels, according to the number of guns carried, is fully explained by Falconer (*Marine Dict.* s.v. *Rates*). The vessels of the U.S. navy are rated by tonnage.

1662 J. DAVIES tr. *Mandelslo's Trav.* 132 Frigots and Barks enter the River, and Vessels of a middle rate shelter under the Ilha da Naos. **1677** YARRANTON *Eng. Improv.* 40, I am very well satisfied that Ships of all Rates will be built at Wexford. **1691** T. H[ALE] *Acc. New Inventions* Ded. x, Fifteen Capital Ships for the Royal Navy, besides many more of the lesser Rate. **1702** *Lond. Gaz.* No. 3775/1 Any of Our Ships of the First, Second, Third, Fourth, Fifth or Sixth Rate, or Fire-Ships. **1742** YOUNG *Nt. Th.* VIII. 154 Of various rates they sail, Of ensigns various. **1802** *Naval Chron.* VIII. 3 A ship of so small a rate as the Trial. **1816** [see FIRST-RATE A 1].

c. *Naut.* = RATING *vbl. sb.*[1] 2.

1706 E. WARD *Wooden World Diss.* (1708) 18 View but his Muster-Books, and you'll, by their Rates, fancy his Men the stoutest Fellows in the Navy. **1963** *Amer. Speech* XXXVIII. 76 *Crow* (the embroidered eagle on the rating badge) was used to designate the insignia of rate for the petty officers of the Navy. **1977** *Navy News* Feb. 18/3 H.M.S. Tartar has no fewer than eight 'stripeys' among the junior rates on board. **1978** *Ibid.* Oct. 4/3 These numbers are calculated from the requirement, which is the number of ratings needed in each rate and branch to fill all sea and shore billets.

d. Class or sub-class of buildings, in respect of purpose or size.

Chiefly used with ref. to the construction and materials of the various classes of buildings, as regulated by Acts of Parliament.

1774 *Act 14 Geo. III*, c. 78 That the several Churches,.. Dwelling houses, and all other Buildings whatsoever.. shall be divided into the seven several Rates or classes of Building herein-after described. **1814** *Reg. Park* 51 As to the rates of houses, second and third rates would generally be most useful. **1845** *Act 7 & 8 Vict.* c. 84 §7 Any Building of whatever kind which is not hereby expressly assigned to any Class or Rate of a Class.

†**10. a.** Standard of conduct or action; hence, manner, mode, style. Chiefly with *after*. *Obs.*

c **1470** HENRYSON *Mor. Fab.* II. (*Town & C. Mouse*) viii, I keip the rait and custome of my dame. *a* **1529** SKELTON *Caudatos Anglos* 20 Skelton laureat After this rate Defendeth with his pen All Englysh men. **1596** SPENSER *F.Q.* IV. x. 52 Thus sate they all around in seemely rate. **1648** JENKYN *Blind Guide* i. 14 He speaking after the rate of the eldest sonne of Gogmagog; more like a Polyphemus than like a Paul. **1659** SHIRLEY *Hon. & Mam.* V. ii, I have not liv'd After the rate to fear another world. **1702** *Eng. Theophrast.* 77 They behaved themselves after another rate in private. **1792** COWPER *Let. to J. Johnson* 22 Oct., I proceed much after the old rate; rising cheerless.., and brightening a little as the day goes on.

†**b.** ***at a (certain) rate***: In a.. way or manner. So ***at this rate***, etc. *Obs.*

1654–66 EARL ORRERY *Parthen.* (1676) 782 He used me at a Rate, which might have assured me he would deny me nothing. **1692** R. L'ESTRANGE *Josephus, Antiq.* XIII. xviii. (1733) 351 Let them treat their King at never so coarse a Rate, the Multitude would be sure to side with them. **1707** WATTS *Hymns*, '*Come holy Spirit, heavenly Dove*' iv, Dear Lord! and shall we ever lie At this poor dying rate? **1722** DE FOE *Plague* (1756) 150 A grave and sober Man, and not pleased with their lying at this loose Rate the first Night.

11. Degree or extent of action, feeling, etc. Chiefly in phr. ***at a...rate*** (passing into 7 b and freq. not clearly distinct from 10 b).

1523 SKELTON *Garl. Laurel* 1130 Of your bounte the accustomable rate. *c* **1586** C'TESS PEMBROKE *Ps.* CXXXIX. xii, O Lord, thou know'st in highest rate I hate them all as foes to me. **1634** W. TIRWHYT tr. *Balzac's Lett.* (Vol. I) 304 If you feed all your flock at this rate [etc.]. **1666** BUNYAN *Grace Abound.* §26, I swore and curst at that most fearful Rate, that she was made to tremble to hear me. **1703** SHARP *Wks.* (1754) II. 105 It is very hard for flesh and blood to live after that rate of strictness. **1748** *Anson's Voy.* II. i. 122 The dogs.. laid themselves down, panting at a great rate.

IV. Phrases.

†**12. a.** ***after the rate***, on the same scale, in proportion. *Obs.*

1427 *Rolls of Parlt.* IV. 318/2 Ye inhabitantz.. pay to oure.. soverain Lord, 11*s.* And so above, aftre ye rate. **1505** *Berwick Reg.* (Hist. MSS. Comm.) *Varr. Collect.* I. 10 The gilde.. ordened.. the stone to wey xvj poundes.. and the halffstone after the rayt, and the quarter after the rayt. **1523** FITZHERB. *Husb.* §121 Let two of them be bores, and foure of them sowes, and so to contynue after the rate. **1589** PUTTENHAM *Eng. Poesie* III. v. (Arb.) 161 His manner of vtterance.. [is] more plaine, or busie and intricate, or otherwise affected after the rate.

†**b.** ***after one rate***, equally, to an equal extent; in the same manner. *Obs.*

1509 BARCLAY *Shyp of Folys* 158 The clargy both pore preste and prelate.. vse the same almost after one rate. **1561** DAUS tr. *Bullinger on Apoc.* (1573) 129 Therfore shall the world continue alwayes after one rate.

†**13. a.** ***of a rate***, on a par or equality, equal. *Obs.*

1542 UDALL *Erasm. Apoph.* 310 The cases of Pericles & Pompeius [were] muchewhat of a rate in all behalfes. **1642** FULLER *Holy & Prof. St.* V. xix. 438 This would.. make lazinesse and painfulnesse both of a rate, when beggary was the reward of both. **1663** BUTLER *Hud.* I. i. 629 Their Valours too were of a Rate.

†**b.** ***at a rate***, equally. Also, of equal cost, equally easy to attain. *Obs.*

a **1623** CAMDEN *Rem.* (1637) 184 He also graunted liberty of coyning to certaine Cities and Abbeies, allowing them one staple, and two puncheons at a rate, with certaine restrictions. **1642** FULLER *Holy & Prof. St.* III. vii. 166 Those that raise a new house from the ground are blameworthy if they make it not handsome, seeing to them Method and Confusion are both at a rate.

14. ***at any rate***. †**a.** At any price or cost; on any terms. *Obs.* †**b.** (With negatives.) On any account. *Obs.* **c.** Under any circumstances; in any or either case. **d.** At all events; at least. †**e.** By any means. *Obs.*

1619 FLETCHER *False One* I. i, I have no friend,.. or Country, but your favour, Which I'le preserve at any rate. **1634** SIR T. HERBERT *Trav.* A ij, The malice of such as carpe at any rate. **1693** EVELYN *De la Quint. Compl. Gard.* Pref., Some men.. seek in a few years after, to get rid of them at any rate. **1700** S. L. tr. *Fryke's Voy. E. Ind.* 95 People.. who go over to the Indies with no other design but to enrich themselves at any rate. **1730** A. GORDON *Maffei's Amphith.* 272 Those deserving Citizens have at any rate kept up the internal Part of a Fabrick. **1760–72** H. BROOKE *Fool of Qual.* (1809) IV. 58 We must not.. offend our Harry at any rate. **1818** JAS. MILL *Brit. India* II. V. iv. 442 He recommended, if not a dereliction, at any rate a suspension of the design. **1865** TROLLOPE *Belton Est.* xxix. 348 All would be well, or, at any rate, comfortable with her.

15. ***at all rates***. †**a.** At any cost or by any means. *Obs.* **b.** At all events = 14 d.

1704 *Gd. Expedient for Innocence & Peace* in *Harl. Misc.* (1746) VIII. 12/2 The vicious Man.. will boggle at nothing; but, at all Rates, will climb up to.. Posts of Advantage or Authority. **1745** A. BUTLER *Lives of Saints* (1836) II. 117 Let him at all rates make haste to find it, though for this he should sacrifice everything else. **1819** SCOTT *Br. Lamm.* xxxiv, Bucklaw's friends.. had previously insisted that he should, at all rates, be transported from the castle to the nearest of their houses. **1857** *Truths Cath. Relig.* (ed. 4) I. 291 They.. were determined at all rates that all should know that they could speak strange languages.

16. ***at that*** (or ***this***) ***rate***, in that case, things being so, under these circumstances. (Common in colloquial use.)

1781 *Encycl. Brit.* (ed. 2) VII. 4168/1 It may be asked, how, at this rate, any silver has remained in England? **1921** G. B. SHAW *Back to Methuselah* p. lx, But how, at this rate, did Darwin succeed with the capitalists too? **1930** —— *Apple Cart* I. 20 Oh for Heaven's sake dont contradict her, Joe. We shall never get anywhere at this rate.

17. a. *attrib.* and *Comb.* (chiefly sense 6 d), as ***rate-aid***, ***-aided*** adj., ***-collector***, ***-determining*** adj., ***-limiting*** adj., ***-making***, †***-master***, ***-payer***, ***-paying***, ***rebate***, ***-setting*** adj., ***-support***, ***-supported*** adj.; also **rate-buster** *slang*, a piece-worker whose high productivity causes or threatens to cause a reduction in piece-work rates; hence **rate-busting** *vbl. sb.*; **rate-capping**, the imposition of upper limits on the amount of money which a local authority can spend and also levy through rates, intended as a disincentive to excessive spending on local services, etc.; hence [as back-formation] **rate-cap** *v. trans.*, to subject to rate-capping; *intr.*, to impose rate-capping; also as *sb.*, an instance of rate-capping, and **rate-capped** *a.*; **rate-card**, a list of charges for advertising; **rate constant** *Physical Chem.*, a coefficient of proportionality relating the rate of a chemical reaction at a given temperature to the concentration of reactant (in a unimolecular reaction), or to the product of the concentrations of reactants (in a reaction of higher order); **rate-cutting**, a lowering of charges or of rates of pay; † **rate factor** *Biol.*, a biological factor which influences or determines the speed of a developmental process, and so may affect the phenotype of the mature organism; **rate-fixer**, one who fixes the rates at which piece-workers are paid; so **rate-fixing** *vbl. sb.*; † **rate gene** *Biol.*, a gene which acts as a rate factor; **ratemeter**, an instrument which displays or records the counting rate, usu. averaged over a time interval, of pulses in an electronic counter, esp. those resulting from incidence of ionizing radiation; † **rate tithe** (see quot.).

1894 *Ch. Times* 22 June 678/2 *Rate-aid, with its corollary of partially popular control. 1882 *Daily News* 20 Jan. 2/5 State-aided and *rate-aided schools. 1939 ROETHLISBERGER & DICKSON *Managem. & Worker* xxii. 522 You should not turn out too much work. If you do, you are a '*rate buster'. 1948 *Appl. Anthropol.* VII. 5/1 In every work group there is nearly always a very small minority of individuals who refuse to be held back and insist on making as much bonus as they like.. In current American industrial literature such workers are referred to as 'rate-busters'. 1972 M. ARGYLE *Social Psychol. of Work* vi. 113 A rate-buster may be given a raised eyebrow, a look of disapproval, a blow on the arm, or may simply be avoided. 1967 C. MARGERISON in Wills & Yearsley *Handbk. Managem. Technol.* 31 However, such practices as the prevention of *rate-busting are extremely logical and rational from the workers' point of view. 1983 *Daily Tel.* 28 Sept. 10/7 The Government's *rate-capping plan was 'yet another giant stride along the path of tight Whitehall control over life in Britain'. 1984 *Guardian* 25 July 2/8 Opposition cries of derision, as when the name of Portsmouth appeared among the rate-capped. 1985 *Economist* 26 Jan. 23/2 Will the government hit the target this time? At least it has the power to rate-cap. 1987 *Guardian* 14 Jan. 1/2 The rate cap takes no account of the effects of the outcome of the current negotiations on the teachers' pay settlement. 1987 *Library Assoc. Rec.* Feb. 60/1 The rate-capped authorities fell into two camps: those which apparently ignored rate-capping and continued to develop service provision and those.. which were faced with substantial closures. 1905 CALKINS & HOLDEN *Art of Mod. Advertising* 352 A *rate-card is a card or printed sheet giving the advertising rates in a given publication. 1962 *Rep. Comm. Broadcasting 1960* 69 in *Parl. Papers 1961–2* (Cmnd. 1753) IX. 259 These figures represent the cost, as shown in the programme companies' rate-cards, of booking the time taken for advertisements during the year. 1977 *Listener* 31 Mar. 399/2 The NBC and CBS affiliate stations.. are getting worried. Can they hold their advertising rate-cards when audiences are falling? 1888 MRS. H. WARD *R. Elsmere* v. xxxi, Imagine Mr. Langham interviewed by a *rate-collector or troubled about coals! 1927 *Jrnl. Amer. Chem. Soc.* XLIX. 1620 Let K_∞ be the fraction decomposed per second at high pressures, or the unimolecular *rate constant. 1950 W. J. MOORE *Physical Chem.* xvii. 516 The units of the rate constant depend on the order of the reaction. 1956 *Nature* 21 Jan. 127/1 The results allowed determination of the approximate values of the pseudo first-order hydrolytic rate-constants of the amide groups in these substances. 1972 R. A. JACKSON *Mechanism* iii. 28 If the equilibrium constant is known.., and the kinetic order and reaction rate constant is determined for the reverse reaction, the order and rate constant for the forward reaction can be calculated. 1888 *Scribner's Mag.* Oct. 485/2 Its percentage being fixed there is no motive for *rate-cutting. 1956 J. A. C. BROWN *Social Psychol. Industry* v. 145 The most frequent reasons given by the unorganized worker for such practices were rate-cutting, fear of unemployment, [etc.]. 1978 *Detroit Free Press* 16 Apr. 2A/1 Capitol Cartage and its owners deny that they have used shakedowns, payoffs, bribery, rate-cutting, intimidation and terror to eliminate competition. 1935 *Jrnl. Chem. Physics* III. 113 When the *rate determining step shifts to the collision process.. we again use well-known statistical methods. 1968 R. O. C. NORMAN *Princ. Org. Synthesis* xiv. 436 The rate-determining step in the reaction of neopentyl bromide is the formation of the high-energy primary carbonium ion. 1927 *Brit. Jrnl. Exper. Biol.* V. 121 (*heading*) Summary of families carrying accessory *rate-factors. 1931 E. B. FORD *Mendelism & Evolution* II. ii. 29 It is probable that such rate-factors controlling the speed and time of onset of processes in the body, are of very general occurrence. 1932 J. S. HUXLEY *Prob. Relative Growth* i. 4 Any genes controlling relative size of parts will have to exert their action by influencing the rates of processes, and so fall in line with the numerous other rate-factors whose importance has been summarized by Goldschmidt (1927) and by Ford and Huxley (1929). 1930 *Engineering* 30 May 696/2 In this office, the operations are made out on a master card and forwarded to the *rate fixers. The latter carefully estimate the cost of the work, and add the workmen's allowance of 33⅓ per cent. 1907 *Daily Chron.* 19 Mar 2/6 The operations of a specially-constituted *rate-fixing branch as regards piece work in the Royal Carriage Department. 1959 *Times* 14 Jan. 2/5 They [*sc.* candidates] must also be experienced in the running and organising of process planning, ratefixing. 1932 J. S. HUXLEY *Probl. Relative Growth* v. 230 (*caption*) Diagram to show effects of *rate-genes on eye pigmentation. 1938 R. GOLDSCHMIDT *Physiol. Genetics* II. iii. 52 Goldschmidt.. first drew attention to rate genes and their importance for an understanding of gene action. 1946 *Nature* 28 Sept. 448/2 A slow heterolysis of nitric acid cannot depend only on proton transfers, and therefore the *rate-limiting fission.. must occur in an NO-bond. 1974 M. C. GERALD *Pharmacol.* xii. 219 The rate at which this reaction occurs determines the speed at which alcohol is removed from the body, and hence this reaction is termed 'the rate-limiting step'. 1969 *Jane's Freight Containers 1968–69* 126/1 The formation of a Market Research Department to develop new methods of *rate-making. 1641 S. SMITH *Herring Buss Trade* 26 The *Rate-masters for their apprasement and visiting of each barrel of salt. 1949 *Nucleonics* Feb. 74/1 After the charge in the tank circuit of the *rate meter has reached equilibrium, the rate meter indicates the counting rate at a glance. 1962 G. A. T. BURDETT *Automatic Control Handbk.* ix. 33 The electronic system usually associated with nucleonic switches and gauges incorporating Geiger counters is known as a 'ratemeter'. This unit provides an indication of the rate at which the counter is detecting incident radiation and is usually provided with a variable integrating time control. 1974 *Physics Bull.* Aug. 349/1 The intensity of the x ray reflection is indicated by the frequency of clicks in a loud speaker, by the flashes of a GaP lamp and by the reading of a ratemeter. 1845 STEPHEN *Comm. Laws Eng.* (1874) I. 120 The election by the *rate payers of a certain number of vestrymen. 1898 G. B. SHAW *Let.* 12 Mar. (1972) II. 15 Ratepayers' Association in the evening. 1955 *Times* 27 June 9/3 No ratepayer can properly gauge the effect of revaluation until he knows what rate his local authority intends to levy in the new dispensation. 1976 *Daily Tel.* 30 June 2/6 Honest citizens and rate-payers alike. 1862 ANSTED *Channel Isl.* IV. xxiii. (ed. 2) 523 The *rate-paying constituency. 1857 TOULMIN SMITH *Parish* 473 Inhabitancy, not 'ratepaying', is the only right test of the Parish Roll. 1965 *Economist* 4 Dec. 1050/1 (*heading*) *Rate rebates. Helping the needy. *a*1974 R. CROSSMAN *Diaries* (1975) I. 303 The main issue was whether I should be allowed a special short Bill introducing rate rebates *before* the long-term reform of rating. 1963 *Economist* 7 Sept. 828/1 The foreign shipowners who dominate the *rate-setting consortiums. 1966 *Times* 21 Dec. 12/6 Mr. Greenwood, Minister of Housing and Local Government.., moved that the *Rate Support Grant Order, 1966, be approved. 1976 *Scotsman* 25 Nov. 9/4 They condemned the reduction in rate support for Scotland as mere transfer of existing expenditure from central government to the ratepayer. 1905 *Daily Chron.* 1 Feb. 6/1 A remission in rates should be made to companies which were the chief ratepayers in districts in which *rate-supported tramways run. 1922 JOYCE *Ulysses* 710 Ratesupported moribund lunatic pauper. 1961 T. LANDAU *Encycl. Librarianship* (ed. 2) 296/1 There is only one local authority area in the whole of the U.K. which has not a rate-supported public library. 1670 BLOUNT *Law Dict.*, **Rate Tythe* is where Sheep or other Cattel are kept in a Parish for less time than a year, the Owner must pay Tythe for them *pro rata* according to the Custom of the place.

b. *pl.* used *attrib.* in sense 6 d, as ***rates aid, man, rebate, reduction, tribunal.***

1966 *Times* 11 May 1/4 (*heading*) Rates aid to start next April. 1953 DYLAN THOMAS *Let.* 17 Mar. (1966) 397 Friendly Brown's can wait. These tradesmen and rates-men can't. 1966 *Times* 17 Aug. 8/6 Rates rebates in the first six months' operation of the Rating Act, 1966, are expected to total £6,850,000. 1971 *Reader's Digest Family Guide to Law* 90 (*heading*), How to apply for a rates reduction. 1935 *Economist* 23 Feb. 429/1 The task of the Railway Rates Tribunal will be unenviable when, next November, they are due to fix the rebates for the year 1935–36.

rate (reɪt), *sb.*[2] *Hunting.* [f. RATE *v.*[2]] A reproof to a dog.

1575 TURBERV. *Venerie* xiii. 30 With your wande you muste.. beate him a good while.. to the ende that another time he may know the rate. 1781 P. BECKFORD *Hunting* (1802) 95 As long as they will stop at a rate, they are not chastised. 1856 'STONEHENGE' *Brit. Sports* I. I. iii. §6 (ed. 2) 33 The dog.. should be brought back with the already-taught rate, 'Ware-chase'. 1976 *Shooting Times & Country Mag.* 18–24 Nov., Never fail to give a severe rate and a flick of your whip if any young hound gives a challenging voice to a bullock, cow, or a strange dog.

†**rate**, *sb.*[3] *Obs. rare.* [ad. L. *ratum* neut. of *ratus*: see RATE *sb.*[1]] Ratification.

*c*1611 CHAPMAN *Iliad* I. 509 Irrevocable; never fails; never without the rates Of all powers else.

†**rate**, *sb.*[4] *Obs. rare.* [a. F. *rate* (13th c.).] The spleen.

1486 *Bk. St. Albans* F iij, Than put owt the paunche, and from the paunche taas Away wightly the Rate sich as he haas. 1578 LYTE *Dodoens* III. lxv. 406 Greeues comming or proceeding from the Rate or Spleene. [1678 PHILLIPS (ed. 4) Suppl., *Rate of a Boar*, a word used by the old Venatory writers for the Spleen of a Boar.]

†**rate**, *a. Obs. rare.* [ad. L. *ratus*: see RATE *sb.*[3] Cf. OF. *rate* (1370 in Godef.).] Valid.

*c*1400 *Apol. Loll.* 70 Mariage mad in þrid & ferd degre, aȝen þe ordinaunce of þe kirk, is rate & stable. 1660 JER. TAYLOR *Duct. Dubit.* II. i. rule i. §56 The church of Rome.. hath pronounced some marriages void which by the rule of nature.. were rate and legal.

rate (reɪt), *v.*[1] [f. RATE *sb.*[1]]

†**1. a.** *trans.* To fix, assign, settle the amount of (a payment, fine, etc.). *Obs.*

1477 *Rolls of Parlt.* VI. 178/2 After the rate and afferant of the seid Rent, to be rated and affered with the seid Burgage. 1581 LAMBARDE *Eiren.* II. iv. (1588) 169 To rate the fine, according to the quantitie of their trespasse. *a*1623 CAMDEN *Rem.* (1637) 182 It was referred to the King to rate how much he should pay.

†**b.** To divide proportionally; to allot or apportion (*between* or *to* persons) as an amount or sum to be received or paid (quot. 1661); also, to give or assign (one) his share. *Obs.*

1491 *Act 7 Hen. VII*, c. 20 §6 The same DC. Marcs to be rated and apporcioned betwix the seid Mary and Elizabeth. 1530 PALSGR. 679/2, I rate one, I set one to his porcyon or stynte.. He wolde eate more than thre and he might be suffred, but I shall rate hym well ynoughe. 1548 UDALL *Erasm. Par. Luke* iii. 31 b, It is rated out vnto you by a plain rule, howe muche or litel ye ought to require of the people for any duetie. 1606 SHAKS. *Ant. & Cl.* III. vi. 25 We had not rated him His part o' th' Isle. 1661 MARVELL *Corr.* xxiv. Wks. 1872–5 II. 60 A Bill for inabling Church-wardens to rate such monys as are for the repare of churches.

2. To reckon, calculate, estimate the amount or sum of. Now *rare.*

1597 SHAKS. *2 Hen. IV*, I. iii. 44 When we see the figure of the house, Then must we rate the cost of the Erection. 1599 NASHE *Lenten Stuffe* (1871) 28 It hath lost by the Dunkirkers, a thousand pounds.. and other loses not rated. 1660 WILLSFORD *Scales Comm.* A ij b, Tis not Life, but Time, we ought to rate. 1799 CAMPBELL *Pleas. Hope* II. 173 There shall he pause with horrent brow, to rate What millions died—that Cæsar might be great! 1814 CARY tr. *Dante, Par.* XXIV. 19 They, by the measure paced.. Made me to rate the riches of their joy.

3. a. To estimate the (†nature) worth or value of; to appraise, value, †price.

1599 SIR J. DAVIES *Nosce Teipsum* Poems (Grosart) I. 76 When she rates things,.. The name of Reason she obtaines by this. 1626 SIR R. COTTON in Shaw *Monetary Tracts* (1896) 44 Being all either Mechanicks or Merchants, they can rate accordingly their labours or their wares.. to the present condition of their money in exchange. 1663 GERBIER *Counsel* 48 It were likewise better to agree with Painters, to have their work rated on running measure. 1710 SWIFT in *Tatler* No. 230 ⁋2 You may see them gilt and in Royal Paper of Five or Six Hundred Pages, and rated accordingly. 1751 JOHNSON *Rambler* No. 166 ⁋8 Instead of rating the man by his performance, we rate too frequently the performance by the man. 1798 FERRIAR *Illustr. Sterne* i. 14 Gold may be rated to its utmost grain. 1865 M. ARNOLD *Ess. Crit.* viii. (1875) 323 We English are capable of rating him far more correctly if we knew him better.

b. To value *at* a certain sum. Also with other preps. as *above*, *below*, or with advbs. as *high*(*ly*), *low*, etc.

1570–6 LAMBARDE *Peramb. Kent* (1826) 282 The Hospital of Saint Laurence.. rated at twenty poundes yeerely. *a*1660 HAMMOND *Serm.* xxv. Wks. 1684 IV. 651 They brought out their Books and burnt them..; which.. were rated at 50000 pieces of silver. 1672 PETTY *Pol. Anat.* (1691) 21 Slaves and Negroes are usually rated at about 15*l.* one with another. 1789 MRS. PIOZZI *Journ. France* II. 41 Human life is lower rated in all parts of Italy than with us. 1843 LYTTON *Last Bar.* III. v, A future age.. may rate high this poor invention. 1856 FROUDE *Hist. Eng.* (1858) I. iii. 191 Each offence against morality was rated at its specific money value. 1884 W. C. SMITH *Kildrostan* 57 You rate yourself too humbly.

c. To assign a certain value to (coin or metals) as, or in relation to, monetary standards. (Chiefly in *pass.*; also const. *to.*)

1758 J. HARRIS *Ess. Money & Coins* II. 60 Let us suppose that in England gold coins are rated five per cent. higher in proportion to silver. 1776 ADAM SMITH *W.N.* I. v. (1869) I. 44 Copper is rated very much above its real value. 1858 HOMANS *Cyclop. Commerce* 339/2 In England, copper pence and halfpence are rated at about 72 per cent. above their real value. 1893 LD. ALDENHAM *Colloquy on Currency* iv. (1900) 111 Silver was the standard; gold was rated to it.

d. *colloq.* To set a high value on, to think much of.

1973 *Times* 10 Feb. 7/7 You can never be sure of Brazil, of course, but I don't rate the South Americans next time. I believe 1974 will be dominated by the Europeans. 1973 *New Society* 12 Apr. 64/2 He would like to play cricket for Surrey, but he doesn't rate his chances. 1976 E. DUNPHY *Only a Game?* iv. 104 He's a good honest pro, but somehow Benny doesn't rate him. 1977 *World of Cricket Monthly* June 85/1, I must say we rated our chances going up to Headingley.

4. To reckon, esteem, consider, count. †Const. *to* with infin.

1565 JEWEL *Def. Apol.* (1611) 89 Thus God must be rated to gouerne aboue, and the Pope beneath. *a*1568 COVERDALE *Bk. Death* x. (1579) 291 Then should not he [Themistocles] afterward haue bene rated, as a betrayer of Greekeland. 1601 SHAKS. *All's Well* II. i. 182 All that life can rate Worth name of life, in thee hath estimate. 1713 STEELE *Guard.* No. 6 ⁋3 The Buildings would be rated as Lumber. 1776 JOHNSON *Let. to Mrs. Thrale* 11 May, Surely I may rate myself among their benefactors. 1847 TENNYSON *Princ.* I. 70 A king, Whom all men rate as kind and hospitable. 1871 B. TAYLOR *Faust* (1875) I. iv. 69 Consider well: my memory good is rated. 1932 *Sun* (Baltimore) 27 Apr. 15/2 Major General, avoiding interference going to the first turn, was rated in front until reaching the homestretch. 1950 *Amer. Jrnl. Psychol.* LXIII. 521 The *Ss*.. rated each pair on a scale of similarity. 1956 C. WILLOCK *Death at Flight* vi. 76, I still rate your type of scatter-gun old-fashioned. 1962 *Observer* 25 Feb. 21/4, I still rate him the tops. 1976 *Billings* (*Montana*) *Gaz.* 27 June 4-A/2 Gen. Antonio Ramalho Eanes, a dour disciplinarian pledged to restore law and order, was rated an overwhelming favorite Saturday to win the Portuguese presidency.

5. a. In *pass.* To be subjected or liable to payment of a certain rate; to be valued for purposes of assessment, taxation, or the like.

1580 *Act 23 Eliz.* c. 15 §27 The Inhabitants of the Parishe of S[t] Martyn.. shalbe assessed, rated and taxed [etc.]. *a*1692 POLLEXFEN *Disc. Trade* (1697) A iv, About 1400 sorts, or distinctions of Commodities, rated to pay Customs. 1726 SWIFT *Gulliver* III. vi, Constancy, chastity, good sense, and good nature, were not rated, because they would not bear the charge of collecting. 1809 BAWDWEN tr. *Domesday Bk.* 154 This is rated in the manor to which it belongs. 1860 DICKENS *Uncomm. Trav.* iii, One poor parish in this very Union is rated to the amount of five and sixpence in the pound. 1880 MCCARTHY *Own Times* IV. l. 68 Houses are generally rated at a value somewhat below the amount of the rent.

b. Const. *to* (the payment required).

1642 FULLER *Holy & Prof. St.* III. xxv. 230 Clergie-men are deeply rated to all payments. 1694 CROWNE *Regulus* I. 1 Were you not rated to the public charge? 1776 ADAM SMITH *W.N.* v. ii. (1869) II. 411 The estimation by which Great Britain is rated to the land-tax. 1845 STEPHEN *Comm. Laws Eng.* (1874) II. 356 The party shall have been rated to all poor rates.. made in respect of the premises.

c. *to rate up*, to impose a higher rate (of insurance).

1896 *Allbutt's Syst. Med.* I. 481 The habit of 'rating up' for tropical fever, ague, dysentery, &c... is also fully justified by experience.

6. a. Chiefly *Naut.* To place in a certain class or rank; to give rating to.

1706 E. WARD *Wooden World Diss.* (1708) 19 These.. are rated able on his Ship's Books. 1758 J. BLAKE *Plan. Mar. Syst.* 7 Each man.. shall have two months pay advanced him, according to the class in which he is rated. 1803 NELSON in Nicolas *Disp.* (1846) VII. p. ccxiv, Captain Hillyar has been so good as to say he would rate you Mid. 1885 *Hunt's Yachting Mag.* 383 As a ketch she should be rated as a B schooner. 1887 BESANT *The World went*, etc. i. 10 On board that ship I was rated as surgeon.

b. *intr.* To have a certain rating or position; to be rated *as*. Also quasi-*trans.* (quot. 1809). Hence, to be accorded a certain position; to be considered *as*, to count *as*.

1809 *Naval Chron.* XXII. 362 She rates 36 guns, and is to be named the Malacca. 1819 SHELLEY *Cenci* I. i. 24 The deed he saw could not have rated higher Than his most worthless life. 1854 H. MILLER *Sch. & Schm.* (1858) 174 My master was to be permitted to rate as a full journeyman. 1949 *Sun*

(Baltimore) 23 May 16/6 She will rate near the top of her class, which means that in racing she will have to give time to most of her competitors. **1959** A. FULLERTON *Yellow Ford* xiv. 186 I'm important to him, too, but I don't rate that high. **1961** *Observer* 12 Mar. 29 (Advt.), You can be an important person all the same. You'll certainly rate as one if you own a 'Retinette', the Kodak precision camera. **1965** *Listener* 16 Sept. 425/2 Although Madame de Beauvoir rates as an 'intellectual', her book is a narrative of doings and feelings rather than of ideas and reflections. **1966** J. PORTER *Sour Cream* viii. 104 The disappearance of Melkin didn't even rate as a nine-days' wonder. **1976** *National Observer* (U.S.) 18 Dec. 17/1 A show may rate as expected, may languish or may exceed expectations. **1977** *Ibid.* 1 Jan. 1/4 Toy poodles rate dumbest in a test you can give your dog too.

c. *trans.* To merit, to deserve; to be worthy to attain or obtain; to be treated as worthy of, be accorded.

1921 *Collier's* 3 July 22/1 Where does he rate that stuff?.. Where does he fit to grab off that Jane? **1928** *Amer. Speech* III. 220 *Rate, v.*, to obtain, or to be entitled to. 'Did you rate a bid to the Kappa party?' **1940** A. W. FEARN *My Days of Strength* xiv. 153 Fond as the Chinese are of weddings and funerals, only virgins in China rate weddings with all the trimmings. **1957** E. HYAMS *Into Dream* II. i. 93 His power of command barely rated his two stripes. **1959** *Listener* 4 June 992/3 Nor is one certain..whether C. W. Brodribb or Harold Child, nice men though they both were, really rate the *Dictionary of National Biography*. **1962** *New Statesman* 28 Dec. 935/1 Christmas cards don't even rate a mention in the *Encyclopaedia Britannica*. **1974** 'A. GILBERT' *Nice Little Killing* vi. 82 He got out his old second-hand car—the village bobby didn't rate a panda. **1974** *Howard Jrnl.* XIV. 95 Mannheim, Radzinowicz [etc.]..rate between them nine titles in the bibliography. **1976** *Times Lit. Suppl.* 16 Apr. 460/5 The work of A. Z. Steinberg, for instance, whose contribution to Dostoevsky studies is sadly undervalued, rates no more than a mention in a half-page summary. **1978** G. GREENE *Human Factor* v. i. 236, I rate a lifetime in jail. **1979** 'A. HAILEY' *Overload* III. xii. 257 The statement by the Governor of California in support of the project rated a brief paragraph near the end of the..report.

d. *intr.* To have some standing, to be of importance; to matter, 'count'; to be highly esteemed.

1928 *Amer. Speech* III. 220 Sometimes the word is used in another sense; 'Price is rating pretty high with Betty these days' means that he stands very high in her estimation. **1938** *Chatelaine* Feb. 44/1 Nowadays to really 'rate' you must have more than an attractive face and figure. **1951** M. MCLUHAN *Mech. Bride* (1967) 112/1 The eye is anxiously turned on the neighbor or friend with a 'How do I measure up?' 'Do I rate?' **1967** *Listener* 14 Sept. 350/3 As a rock group, then, the Kinks don't rate musically.

7. *trans.* **a.** To calculate or fix at a certain rate.

1845 MCCULLOCH *Taxation* I. iii. (1852) 91 From household servants being mostly paid by time, the generality of persons are most familiar with wages so rated. **1878** BOSW. SMITH *Carthage* 165 It was..the cost of their maintenance as rated by themselves which they threateningly demanded.

b. To ascertain the variation of (a chronometer) from true time.

1853 KANE *Grinnell Exp.* v. (1856) 36 The facilities which they offer for rating chronometers. **1875** BEDFORD *Sailor's Pocket Bk.* v. (ed. 2) 193 The watch used in rating chronometers, should..be carried in a box.

c. *U.S.* To convey at certain rates.

1881 *Chicago Times* 12 Mar., Large quantities of freight have been rated through to New York by..other lines.

d. To cause to proceed at a moderate pace, to regulate the pace of; *spec.* in horse-racing, to ride (a horse) at a moderate pace, conserving his energy for the finish. Also *intr.* for passive, of a horse: to be ridden in this way. orig. *U.S.*

1920 H. C. WITWER in *Collier's* 3 July 9/2 Ring generalship, that's what you're minus, and the only way you can get it is by experience. You gotta be rated along, not rushed... Many a promisin' kid has been ruined at the start by bein' overmatched. **1946** *Sun* (Baltimore) 28 June 9/2 Villa Nova, escaping the jam at the half-mile pole, was rated to head of stretch, then closed well through last eighth of a mile. **1961** J. S. SALAK *Dict. Amer. Sports* 354 *Rating* (harness racing), maintaining an even rate of speed and timing finishing rush. Harness horses are rated to a fraction of a second in miles. **1977** *N.Z. Herald* 5 Jan. 1-12/5 He rated Red Vesta perfectly in front, kicked clear in the straight and won comfortably. **1977** *Time* 20 June 51/2 But Turner's gentle methods have made Slew, a natural front runner, into a sound horse who 'rates kindly', or can tolerate another horse in front of him—at least for a while.

8. To assign a rating (sense 3) to (a piece of equipment, etc.). Const. *at* the value concerned. Usu. in *pass.*

1893 *Trans. Amer. Inst. Electr. Engineers* X. 255 Manufacturers cannot accurately rate their fuse-wire unless the length of the specimen to be used is specified. **1905** *Jrnl. Inst. Electr. Engineers* XXXV. 388 Fuses rated to blow with an excess current of 50 per cent of their normal carrying capacity get far too hot. **1940** *Amat. Radio Handbk.* (ed. 2) ii. 39/1 This valve..is rated at 25 watts dissipation at 500 volts. **1953** J. LISTON *Power Plants for Aircraft* i. 7 Nearly all aircraft power plants are capable of developing much more power than that at which they are rated. *Ibid.* iii. 104 By definition, iso-octane was given an octane number of 100 and normal heptane was rated at zero octane number. **1975** D. G. FINK *Electronics Engineers' Handbk.* VII. 6 Such resistors are rated from 5 to 20 kV, have a resistance range of 2,000 Ω to 1,000 MΩ, and are rated from 5 up to 20 W. **1977** *Offshore Engineer* Apr. 75/2 Average life of the new type thallium iodide bulb is rated by UMEL at approximately 500 hours.

rate (reɪt), *v.*[2] Also 6 rayt, rait. [Of obscure origin.

Langland has ARATE, of which *rate* may be an aphetic form. In the C-text (xiii. 35) two MSS. of the beginning of the 15th c. have the readings *rate* and *rehete*; with the latter cf. Udall's RAHATE.]

1. *trans.* To chide, scold, reprove vehemently or angrily. Const. *for*, †*of*. (In 16–17th c. freq. intensified by *all to.*) **a.** a person.

c **1386** CHAUCER *Miller's T.* 277 He shal be rated of his studiyng. **1392–3** *Complaint* in *Peasants' Rising* (1899) 50 The Maior did openlie rate the said ministers for that they had donne. **1470–85** MALORY *Arthur* X. xii, Sire Dagonet folowed after Kynge Mark cryenge and rateynge hym as a wood man. **1526** TINDALE *Col.* iii. 21 Fathers rate not youre children. **1534** [see ALL *adv.* 15]. **1587** HOLINSHED *Chron.* III. 1064/1 Hee rose vp and shut the doores, and..rated me for leauing them vnshut. **1605** CAMDEN *Rem.* 229 The Bishop being angrie, rated the fellow roughly. **1642** J. EATON *Honey-c. Free Justif.* 160 As if a father..should not be content to chide, beat, and all to rate him. **1724** DE FOE *Mem. Cavalier* I. 94 The King was in some Passion at his Men, and rated them for running away. **1832** HT. MARTINEAU *Hill & Valley* vi. 101 He..began to rate them soundly for their ingratitude. **1874** GREEN *Short Hist.* vii. §3. 363 [Elizabeth] rated great nobles as if they were schoolboys.

b. a dog. (Cf. RATE *sb.*[2])

1579 GOSSON *Apol. Sch. Abuse* (Arb.) 71 Hee rateth his dogge, for wallowing in carrion. *a* **1628** PRESTON *New Covt.* (1634) 124 The Shepheard sets his Dogge upon his Sheepe to bring them in, but when they are brought in, he rates his Dogge. **1781** P. BECKFORD *Hunting* (1802) 106 When hounds are rated and do not answer the rate, they should be coupled up immediately. **1845** YOUATT *Dog* (1858) 77 If he is immediately called in and rated, or perhaps corrected,.. he will learn his proper lesson.

†**2.** To drive *away*, *back*, *from* or *off*, by rating.

1575 TURBERV. *Venerie* 132 The Varlets of the kennel.. rate away the houndes. —— *Faulconrie* 183 Ryding..about hir on horsebacke, and rating backe your Spaniels. **1584** LYLY *Campaspe* v. iii, I am a dogge, and Phylosophy rates mee from carion. **1596** SHAKS. *1 Hen. IV*, IV. iii. 99 He.. Rated my Vnckle from the Councell-Boord. **1640** W. BRIDGE *True Sould. Convoy* 35 Afflictions shall be all rated of in due time, as the dog is when he falleth upon a friend. **1702** C. MATHER *Magn. Chr.* II. App. (1852) 228 All attempts of surviving malice..give me leave to rate off with indignation. **1872** A. C. STEELE *Broken Toys* II. xxv. 151 Ben Alymer..took up the butt-end of his gun and rated the pointer back.

3. *intr.* To utter strong or angry reproofs. Chiefly const. *at.*

1593 SHAKS. *2 Hen. VI*, III. i. 175 If those..Be thus vpbrayded, chid, and rated at. **1660** F. BROOKE tr. *Le Blanc's Trav.* 224 There were four Lions..under one mans charge, who never ceas'd raving and rating after them. **1741** RICHARDSON *Pamela* (1824) I. 98 Mrs. Jewkes..fell a rating at her most sadly. **1844** DISRAELI *Coningsby* I. vii. 31 Her step-mother..seemed seldom to address her but to rate and chide. **1872** TENNYSON *Gareth & Lynette* 1253 Such a one As all day long hath rated at her child.

†**rate**, *v.*[3] *Obs. rare.* [f. L. *ratus*: see RATE *sb.*[1] and *sb.*[3]] *trans.* To ratify.

c **1611** CHAPMAN *Iliad* III. 123 That they from thence might call King Priam,..to rate the truce they swore. *Ibid.* XIV. 230 That all the Gods..may to us be witnesses and rate What thou hast vow'd.

‖**raté** (rate), *a.* and *sb.* [Fr.] **A.** *adj.* Ineffective, miscarried; of a person, consistently unsuccessful. **B.** *sb.* A person who has failed in his vocation.

1905 R. FRY *Let.* 21 Jan. (1972) I. 233 His scheme being *raté* is a blow to his prestige. **1910** B. W. WELLS *Mod. French Lit.* xiii. 477 The mean spirit of D'Argenton, the poet, who, with his attendant group of *ratés*, the failures of literature and art, forms a sort of mutual admiration club. **1949** E. HYAMS *Not in our Stars* v. 47 A raté sensualist, he would willingly have enjoyed an 'affair' with Miriam. **1966** *New Statesman* 9 Sept. 369/1 Yves Montand..is too plump and groomed to make a creditable *raté*. *a* **1970** E. STARKIE in J. Richardson *Enid Starkie* (1973) iii. 58 The *raté*, the typical Paris figure. **1977** *Times* 7 Sept. 10/7 They are failures... They will all be *ratés* and hopeless when they are 30.

rate, variant of RET *v.*

ratea'bility. [f. next: see -ITY.] The quality of being rateable.

1849 PENFOLD *Princ. Rating Comp.* (ed. 2) 31 The general principle.., that..rent is to be taken to determine the amount of the rateability.

rateable ('reɪtəb(ə)l), *a.* Also 6– ratable. [f. RATE *v.*[1] + -ABLE.]

1. Capable of being rated, estimated, or calculated, esp. in accordance with some scale; proportional.

1503 *Rolls of Parlt.* VI. 533/1 Chargeable with lyke and egall Sommes, ratable at xxs of Freeholde. **1598** KITCHIN *Courts Leet* (1675) 420 He shall have the Writ to be discharged for a ratable proportion. **1611** SPEED *Hist. Gt. Brit.* IX. ix. §103. 624 A rateable distribution being made of their estates to the Kings well-deseruing friends. **1628** EARLE *Microcosm., Gallant* (Arb.) 40 He is..an ornament.. and is meerely ratable accordingly, fiftie or an hundred Pound. **1760–72** H. BROOKE *Fool of Qual.* (1809) II. 124 Men consented to fix certain rateable values upon money. **1827** HALLAM *Const. Hist.* (1842) I. 19 Requiring a rateable part, according to such declaration.

2. Liable to payment of rates. ***rateable value***, the value ascribed to a property for the purpose of assessing the rates to be levied on it.

1760 T. HUTCHINSON *Hist. Mass.* ii. (ed. 2) 231 English subjects, being free holders, rateable to a certain value. *Ibid.* 327 Protestants of 10*s.* rateable estate. **1818** BENTHAM *Ch. Eng., Catech. Exam.* 165 To paupers, as well as to rateable inhabitants. **1836** *Act 6 & 7 Will. IV* c. 96 Gross estimated Rental. Rateable Value. Rate at 6*d.* in the Pound. **1846** GROTE *Greece* I. xi. (1862) II. 319 The rateable property of the citizen. **1874** *Act 37 & 38 Vict.* c. 54 §4 The gross and rateable value of any land used for a plantation or a wood.. shall be estimated as follows. **1909** *Daily Chron.* 13 Aug. 4/3 Mr. Lloyd George is understood..to have promised favourable consideration to the plea of the London Members for some alteration in the 'rateable-value' basis. **1925** *Act 15 & 16 Geo. V* c. 90 §2 Every general rate shall be a rate at a uniform amount per pound on the rateable value of each hereditament. **1962** L. GOLDING *Dict. Local Govt.* 408 The net annual value is in most cases the rateable value. **1971** *Reader's Digest Family Guide to Law* 88/1 Ratepayers do not pay an amount equal to the full rateable value of their property each year. They pay a proportion of it—the rate in the £. **1976** *Evening Post* (Nottingham) 14 Dec. 4/7 The rateable values did not take into account the disadvantages of living in the city centre.

rateably ('reɪtəblɪ), *adv.* Also ratably. [f. prec. + -LY[2].] In a rateable manner; proportionately.

1490 *Act 7 Hen. VII*, c. 1 §2 Every Capteyn..shall..pay ..the Wages ratably as is allowed unto theym by the King. **1534** MORE *Treat. on Passion* Wks. 1288/1 We Christen people,..be ratabli bounden to the beliefe of moe thinges then were the Jewes. **1581** *Durham Wills & Inv.* (Surtees) 116 Payinge all chardges ratiblye for the same. **1596** BACON *Max. & Uses Com. Law* 35 A summe of mony ratably levyed according to the proportion of the lands. **1702** *Lond. Gaz.* No. 3835/4 Whoever discovers the said Goods, or Part, shall ..be Ratably rewarded. **1796** MORSE *Amer. Geog.* II. 126 The effectual mode of conducting canals, is by companies, subscribing rateably to the expense. **1852** GROTE *Greece* II. lxxii. IX. 256 A scheme of tribute..assessed rateably upon each city by Lysander. **1973** *N.Y. Law Jrnl.* 4 Sept. 17/1 The widow's elective share must be paid ratably by all beneficiaries under the will.

rate-book. [f. RATE *sb.*[1]]

1. A book of rates or prices.

1654 R. WHITLOCK *Zootomia* 240 When God maketh up his Jewells, it is thence Rate Books will be made. **1690** DRYDEN *Don Sebastian* Prol. 43 In no rate-book it was ever found That Pegasus was valued at five pound. **1876** VOYLE & STEVENSON *Milit. Dict.* 329/1 *Rate-book*, a priced vocabulary of government stores [etc.].

2. A book containing the valuations of properties for the purposes of local taxation.

1845 DISRAELI *Sybil* (Rtldg.) 300 They..burned rate-books in the market place. **1856** *Farmer's Mag.* Jan. 39 A list of the occupiers to whom they had delivered schedules..to be taken from the local rate-books.

rated ('reɪtɪd), *ppl. a.*[1] [f. RATE *v.*[1] + -ED[1].]

1. Reckoned, esteemed, classed; assessed, etc. Now usually, subject to rates.

1595 SHAKS. *John* v. iv. 37 Paying the fine of rated Treachery. **1596** —— *1 Hen. IV*, IV. iv. 17 [Q.] Owen Glendower's absence..Who with them was a rated sinew. **1758** BRAKENRIDGE in *Phil. Trans.* L. 467 The rated houses are to the cottages more than two to one. **1805** *Naval Chron.* XIII. 182 A rated Port Ship. **1812** J. SMYTH *Pract. of Customs* (1821) 225 If there be any quills found in the wings, they are chargeable with the rated duties thereon. **1883** J. CHAMBERLAIN in *Pall Mall G.* 26 Nov. 12/1 Additional burden on the rated occupiers.

2. Of a numerical characteristic or property: having the value that a device, apparatus, etc., is designed to operate at or attain under normal conditions, or at which other characteristics are evaluated.

1893 *Trans. Amer. Inst. Electr. Engineers* X. 260 Promptness of action requires that the temperature of fusion should not be too far removed from that attained when the wire is being worked at its rated capacity. **1916** [see RATING *vbl. sb.* 3]. **1931** R. N. LIPTROT in *Handbk. Aeronautics* (R. Aeronaut. Soc.) ii. 121 From ground level to the rated height the r.p.m. and horse-power progressively increase until at the rated height normal r.p.m. and horse-power are reached. **1942** I. GLEED *Arise to Conquer* ii. 16 One of my jobs was to test them [*sc.* Spitfires] at rated altitude, about 18,000 feet. **1945** G. V. WELBOURNE *Flight & Engines* xi. 135 The use of two separate jets is but one way of ensuring a sufficiently rich mixture at full rated power and take-off. **1975** D. G. FINK *Electronics Engineers' Handbk.* VII. 9 The surge voltage applicable to electrolytic capacitors is a voltage in excess of the rated voltage which the capacitor will withstand for a specified limited period at any temperature. **1978** *Nature* 6 Apr. 520/1 The wind speed data..were fed into simulated wind generators having the following characteristics: rotor diameter, 60 m; rated wind speed, 14 m s^{-1}; furling wind speed, 27 m s^{-1}.

rated ('reɪtɪd), *ppl. a.*[2] [f. RATE *v.*[2] + -ED[1].] Scolded, severely reproved.

1596 SPENSER *F.Q.* v. i. 29 As rated spaniell takes his burden up for feare. **1808** SCOTT *Marm.* IV. i, The rated horse-boy. **1825** —— *Talisman* iv, Couching like a rated hound. **1849** C. BRONTË *Shirley* xvi, He merely passed by sheepishly with a rated, scowling look.

rateen: see RATTEEN.

ratel[1] ('reɪtəl). Also 9 rattel. [a. Cape Du. *ratel*, of uncertain origin.

Kolbe identified the name with the Du. equivalent of RATTLE *sb.*[1] (see RATTLEMOUSE 2, and J. Platt in *Athenæum* 11 Apr. 1903, p. 466), but the reason he gives appears to be quite unfounded.]

The honey badger, *Mellivora capensis*, belonging to the family Mustelidæ, native to Africa and southern Asia, and distinguished by a coat that is light grey on the back and black elsewhere, powerful claws on the front feet, and a diet that includes honey, insects, reptiles, birds, and small mammals.

1777 tr. SPARRMAN in *Phil. Trans.* LXVII. 43 Not only the Dutch and Hottentots, but likewise a species of quadruped, which the Dutch name a Ratel [*note*, Probably a new species of badger], are frequently conducted to wild bee-hives by this bird. **1785** G. FORSTER tr. *Sparrman's Voy. Cape G. Hope* II. xiv. 179 The Ratel, so called in Africa both by the colonists and Hottentots. **1830** BENNETT *Menag. Zool. Soc.* i. 16 In size the Ratel is about equal to the Badger, to which it also bears a distant resemblance in form. **1862** C. ROSSETTI *Goblin M.* (1884) 3 One like a ratel tumbled hurry-skurry. *Ibid.* 13 Cat-like and rat-like, Ratel- and wombat-like. **1902** *Chambers's Jrnl.* Oct. 667/2 The camel and llama, the badger and ratel, all of which may be seen and compared at the Zoo. **1947** J. STEVENSON-HAMILTON *Wild Life S. Afr.* xxix. 242 The ratel does not hesitate to attack the most venomous species of snakes. **1961** L. VAN DER POST *Heart of Hunter* iv. 73 He gave me such a vivid picture of the ratel eating snakes that I saw it gobbling up tangles of serpents like spaghetti. **1969** B. SESHADRI *Twilight of India's Wild Life* v. 139 The ratel, or honey badger..has lived its life adapting it to many types of forest and plain. **1975** H. B. COTT *Looking at Animals* iii. 73 Ratels are said to trot unhurriedly with a long, swinging stride.

†**ratel**[2]. *Obs. rare*[−1]. Also 6 -yll. [a. OF. *ratelle* (Godef.), dim. of *rate* RATE *sb.*[4]; cf. F. *rateleux* splenetic.] The spleen.

1503 *Kal. of Shepherdes* I vj b, Cancer has lordshyp aboue ..the stomak..the ratel [**1506** ratyll] and the lyghttys.

ratel, -er, obs. forms of RATTLE, -LER.

'rateless, *a.* [f. RATE *sb.*[1] 6 d + -LESS.] Having no rates.

1889 HISSEY *Tour in Phaeton* 182, I would the town I lived in were rateless!

ratelier (rɑtəlje). [a. F. *râtelier* rack, stand, set of teeth, etc. f. *râtel* RATELL.]

†**1.** A stand for arms. *Obs. rare*[−1].

1640 tr. *Verdere's Romant of Rom.* III. 101 The rateliers were stored with Launces, the shields of these foure Princes were placed neere to the Barriers.

2. A set of teeth; a set of false teeth.

1839 THACKERAY in *Fraser's Mag.* June 746/1 In the large picture, everybody grins, and shows his whole *ratelier.* **1863** CROWN PRINCESS OF PRUSSIA *Let.* 1 Sept. in R. Fulford *Dearest Mama* (1968) 261 We are left to the care of a very funny old gentleman of the bedchamber who wears a 'ratelier' and is very tiresome besides. **1916** R. FRY *Let.* 8 Sept. (1972) II. 402, I dread the flashing *râtelier* of that Chicago girl. **1923** R. NEVILL *World of Fashion 1837–1922* iii. 62 When alone in his study he [*sc.* Labouchère] would take out his *ratelier* and lay it on the ground.

†**'ratelike,** *adv. Obs. rare*[−1]. = RATEABLY.

1579 FENTON *Guicciard.* XVII. (1599) 781 Taxing euerie towne ratelike with bands and numbers [of soldiers].

†**ratell.** *Obs. rare*[−1]. [ad. OF. *râtel* (F. *râteau*), *rastel*: see RASTEL.] A rake.

1489 CAXTON *Faytes of A.* I. xiv. 37 Ratellis, pycosis, sawis, axes, nayles.

ratell, obs. form of RATTLE *sb.*[1] and *v.*[1]

†**'rately,** *adv. Obs.* [f. RATE *sb.*[1] + -LY[2].] = RATEABLY.

1472–5 *Rolls of Parlt.* VI. 161/2 To receyve..such sommes of money,..rately as is aforeseid. **1512** in Willis & Clark *Cambridge* (1886) I. 608 Asmoche money as shall suffise to pay the Masons..rately after the numbre of workmen.

‖**ratemahatmaya** (ˌratema'hatmajaː). *Sri Lanka.* [Sinhalese, f. *ratē* of the district + *mahatmayā* gentleman.] A chief headman of a Kandyan district.

1821 J. DAVY *Acct. Interior of Ceylon* v. 147 The duties of Rate-mahatmeyas were similar to those of Dissaves; but their official rank was inferior. **1841** J. FORBES *Eleven Years in Ceylon* iv. 67 The authorities under the Kandian dynasty were thus arranged... The Rate Mahatmeás, chiefs of inferior districts. **1913** L. WOOLF *Village in Jungle* ii. 37 Disa Mahatmaya is the title used by villagers in referring to chief headmen or Ratemahatmayas. **1956** R. PIERIS *Sinhalese Social Organization* I. iv. 24 The *ratēmahatmayās*, as they were colloquially styled, bore the title *ratērāla* at court.

†**'ratement.** *Obs. rare.* [f. RATE *v.*[1] + -MENT.] Rating, valuation.

1613–8 DANIEL *Coll. Hist. Eng.* (1626) 41 A iust note of the quality and quantitie of euery mans ratement was taken. **1614** RALEIGH *Hist. World* IV. vii. (1634) 532 He first ordered ratements, subsidies, and valuations of the people's wealth.

rater[1] ('reɪtə(r)). [f. RATE *v.*[1] + -ER[1].]

1. One who (or a thing which) rates, estimates, measures, etc.

1611 COTGR., *Perequant*, an equall rater, taxer, assessor of others. **1654** R. WHITLOCK *Zootomia* 11 The wise Rater of things,..will obey the Powers over Him. **1697** *View Penal Laws* 292 A Clothier..shall not be a Rater of Wages of any Artificer. **1823** *Mechanics' Mag.* No. 4. 59 The Rater is to give the rate of a ship's sailing. **1957** D. T. HERMAN et al. in Saporta & Bastian *Psycholinguistics* (1961) 540/1 Two raters independently rated each of the reproductions. **1967** M. ARGYLE *Psychol. Interpersonal Behaviour* x. 182 The use of 'blind' ratings, where the raters do not know which of the individuals they are rating are being trained or belong to a control group. **1973** *Jrnl. Genetic Psychol.* Mar. 40 Raters had no knowledge of whether a given interview protocol was from the psychopathic or nonpsychopathic sample. **1977** RYAN & CARRANZA in H. Giles *Lang., Ethnicity & Intergroup Relations* ii. 70 Ethnicity of rater did not affect evaluation of the standard speakers. **1979** *Nature* 22 Mar. 357/2 The assessment on HRS was made by two independent raters who showed a satisfactory concordance.

2. A vessel, etc. of a specified rate.

In recent use with ref. to the tonnage of racing vessels.

1806–37 [see FIRST-RATER]. **1891** *Field* 7 Mar. 336/2 Three centre-board cutters..These include one 10-rater and two 2½-raters.

rater[2] ('reɪtə(r)). [f. RATE *v.*[2] + -ER[1].] One who reproves or scolds.

1863 COWDEN CLARKE *Shaks. Char.* ix. 218 Here was she already installed as rater of his conduct, instead of rendering him an account of hers. **1884** *Sat. Rev.* 8 Mar. 321/1 Far be it from us to say that the rating is generally undeserved. But ..the rater delivers it evidently from a purely personal point of view.

rat fink. *slang* (chiefly *U.S.*). Also **rat-fink, ratfink.** [f. RAT *sb.*[1] + FINK *sb.*[2]] One who is obnoxious or contemptible, esp. (*a*) an odiously pretentious person; (*b*) an informer, a traitor. Also *attrib.* or as *adj.* Hence as *v. trans.*, to inform *on.*

1964 *Guardian* 8 July 7/6 That's the hitcheroo, baby,.. this time when Cliff and Shirley dance on top of Everest it's a send up. That keeps the intellectual rat-finks happy, see. *Ibid.*, This is going to bring them all in: the dads and mums, the squares, the rat-fink intellectuals, and the teenagers. **1965** D. BOROFF *State of Nation* 212 In fitting American youth for its destiny in the free world of tomorrow, our schools may be virtually compelling them to become a bunch of ratfinks. **1965** P. DE VRIES *Let me count Ways* xx. 273 So cool and rat fink. What college did you go to? That made you so cultured and rat fink. **1966** *Listener* 9 June 838/1 The cool cats and the rat finks and the camp hips [in America]. **1969** C. BURKE *God is Beautiful, Man* 88 His name was Judas and he was a rat fink. So this dirty rat fink he says to the pres of the gang, Caiaphas, 'What's in it for me if I put the finger on him?' **1973** M. & G. GORDON *Informant* x. 46, I may be a rat fink but I'm not going to be a paid rat fink. **1973** *Houston Chron.* 21 Oct. 10/2 As for informing on an honor violator, the colonel said you didn't exactly rat fink on such a man, you usually confront that man with his conduct and expect him to do the honorable thing. **1975** A. PRICE *Our Man in Camelot* iii. 52 Gildas..was..denouncing the rulers of Britain as a bunch of rat-finks who were letting the country go to the dogs. **1976** L. DEIGHTON *Twinkle, twinkle, Little Spy* v. 30 It was Tony Nowak's rat-fink cousin Stefan who put the spaghetti in the piano. **1976** *Courier-Mail* (Brisbane) 19 Feb. 5/2, I still think you were a rat fink. **1977** *New Yorker* 26 Sept. 127 The hairy little hipster Go Go, a ratfink wearing a cross and a yarmulke.

rat-goose. *Ornith.* [Given by Willughby, app. as a local name.] A kind of wild-goose, supposed to be the brent-goose.

The statement of Pennant (*Zool.* II. 453) that 'the Danish and Norwegian names for this bird are *Radgaas* and *Raatgaas*' is app. erroneous.

a **1672** WILLUGHBY *Ornith.* (1676) 276 Rat-Goose or Road-Goose. *Brenthus fortasse.* **1753** CHAMBERS *Cycl. Supp.*, *Rat-goose*, in Zoology, the name of a small species of wild goose, common in some of the northern counties of England. **1768** PENNANT *British Zool.* II. 453 The Rat or Roadgoose of Mr. Willoughby agrees in so many respects with this kind [the brent goose], that we suppose it only to be a young bird not come to full feathers. **1824** LATHAM *Gen. Hist. Birds* X. 261 The Brent Goose is known in some parts of England by the name of Rat or Road Goose.

rath (rɑːθ, -æ-), *sb.*[1] [Ir. *rath*, now pron. (raː)] *Irish Antiq.* An enclosure (usually of a circular form) made by a strong earthen wall, and serving as a fort and place of residence for the chief of a tribe; a hill-fort. (Often incorrectly ascribed to the Danes.)

1596 SPENSER *State Irel.* Wks. (Globe) 642/2 There is a great use amongest the Irish to make greate assemblyes togither upon a rath or hill. *Ibid.*, They are called Dane-rathes, that is, hills of the Danes. **1617** MORYSON *Itin.* II. II. ii. 161 A ground of aduantage, being a strong Rath, between the towne and the Camp. **1700** E. LHWYD in *Phil. Trans.* XXVII. 525 Their round Entrenchments, commonly called Danes Rathes. **1807** SIR R. C. HOARE *Tour Irel.* 21 One of those raised earthen works, which the Irish writers call raths. **1845** E. WARBURTON *Crescent & Cross* II. 361 With the tombs of Hector and Achilles appearing like Irish raths. **1880** MCCARTHY *Own Times* IV. lvii. 231 The 'good people' still linger around the raths and glens.

Hence **rathed** *a.*, surrounded by an earthen wall.

1861 J. Y. SIMPSON *Archaeol.* 36 The true sites of the.. towns—or merely perhaps stockaded or rathed villages.

rath (rɑːθ, -æ-), *sb.*[2] A factitious word introduced by 'Lewis Carroll' (see quot. 1855[2]).

Quot. 1855[1] also occurs in the first verse of 'Jabberwocky' in *Through the Looking-Glass* (1871) i. 21.

1855 'L. CARROLL' *Rectory Umbrella & Mischmasch* (1932) 139 All mimsy were the borogoves; And the mome raths outgrabe. *Ibid.* 140 *Rath*, a species of land turtle. Head erect: mouth like a shark: the fore legs curved out so that the animal walked on its knees: smooth green body: lived on swallows and oysters.

rath, obs. form of RAITH; variant of RATHE.

rathare, obs. form of RATHER *adv.*

‖**Rathaus** ('raːthaʊs). Also **Rath-haus, Rathhaus.** [Ger., lit. council-house.] A German town hall.

1611 CORYAT *Crudities* 619, I..will make mention of their *Prætorium* or Senate house, which they commonly call the Rathausz [in Cologne]. **1855** GEO. ELIOT in *Fraser's Mag.* June 703/2 The Markt, a cheerful square [in Weimar], made smart by a new Rath-haus. **1864** C. M. YONGE *Bk. Golden Deeds* 208 The grim effigy..grins over the door of the Rathhaus [in Freiburg]. **1962** K. O'HARA *Double Cross Purposes* vii. 95, I did see two cars parked outside..the local Rathaus. **1975** *Times* 26 Apr. 10/5 The [Hamburg] Rathaus ..has a cellar restaurant of quite Gothic splendour.

rathe, obs. form of RAITH.

†**rathe,** *sb.*[1] *Obs.* In 3 raþ(e, rath. [a. ON. *ráð* = OE. *rǽd* REDE *sb.*] Counsel, advice; help.

c **1200** ORMIN 1414 Þatt te33 forr þe deofless raþ Drihhtiness raþ forrwurrpenn. *c* **1300** *Havelok* 75 To þe faderles was he rath, Wo so dede hem wrong or lath. *Ibid.* 2542.

rathe (reɪð), *sb.*[2] Now *dial.* Also 7 **raeth,** 8 **rath,** 8–9 **rade,** 9 **raithe.** See also RAER and RAVE *sb.*[2] [Of obscure origin; perh. the base of RADDLE *sb.*[1]]

1. A cart-rail = RAVE *sb.*[2] 1.

1497 *Naval Acc. Hen. VII* (1896) 102 Cart..without rathes. **1523** FITZHERB. *Husb.* §5 The bodye of the wayne of oke, the staues, the nether rathes, the ouer rathes [etc.]. **1705** *Lond Gaz.* No. 4112/4 With this Crest, a Cock upon a Rath. **1733** TULL *Horse-hoeing Husb.* 88 Three Waggons had each a Board..fix'd Cross the Middle of each Waggon by Iron Pins, to the Top of the Rades or Sides. **1875–** in dial. glossaries, in forms *rathe* (Chesh., Shropsh., Leic.) and *rade* (Som., Berks, Hants, Sussex). **1890** BUCKMAN *Darke's Sojourn* v. 34 Numerous waggons with hurdles tied along their rathes.

2. *Weaving.* = RAVE *sb.*[2] 3.

1564 *Inv.* in Noake *Worcestershire Relics* (1877) 13 In the weaving shoppe a rathe, a warpinge bore, a troughe. **1688** R. HOLME *Armoury* III. viii. 346/2 The Raeth is a thing like a Rake... The Raeth keeps the Yarn in Warping, that they shall not tangle or twist one with another. **1875** *Ure's Dict. Arts* (ed. 7) III. 1111 A comb or raithe..guides the threads with precision on to any length of beam. **1886** in *Cheshire Gloss.* Suppl.

rathe (reɪð), **rath** (rɑːθ, -æ-), *a.*[1] *poet.* and *dial.* Forms: 1 **hræð-,** *pl.* **hraðe,** 5 *Sc.*, 6–7, 9 **rath,** 7 **raith,** 4–7, 9 **rathe,** 9 *dial.* **rave.** [f. RATHE *adv.*; rare in OE. in place of *hræd* RAD *a.*[1], but common after *c* 1400. For the uses of the compar. and superl. see RATHER *a.*, RATHEST *a.*]

1. Quick in action, speedy, prompt; eager, earnest, vehement.

c **900** *Ags. Ps.* (Th.) xiii. 6 Heora fet beoð swiðe hraðe blod to aȝeotanne. *a* **1400** *Sir Perc.* 98 Was noȝte the rede Knyghte so rathe For to wayte hym with skathe. *c* **1450** *St. Cuthbert* (Surtees) 6442 To reule þaim wele he was full' rathe. **1575** GASCOIGNE *Dan Bartholomew* Wks. (1587) 66 In deede the rage which wrong him there was rathe. **1818** SCOTT *Rob Roy* vii, Art there, lad?—ay, youth's aye rathe —but look to thysell. **1949** E. POUND *Pisan Cantos* lxxxi. 113 Pull down thy vanity, Rathe to destroy, niggard in charity.

2. a. Done, occurring, coming, etc., before the usual or natural time; early.

Originally with *too*: cf. RATHE *adv.* 1 b.

c **1420** *Pallad. on Husb.* I. 247 Tilyng..Is not to rathe yf dayis thryis fyue Hit be preuent. **1584** COGAN *Haven Health* (1612) 249 Rathe marriage is the cause why men be now of lesse stature than they haue been before time. **1609** C. BUTLER *Fem. Mon.* v. (1623) I iij, Those swarmes..if they be rathe, will swarme againe unlesse they be ouer-hiued. **1670** RAY *Prov.* 22 The rath sower ne're borrows o' th' late. **1816** SCOTT *Antiq.* xxxix, Laying his head in a rath grave. **1833** H. COLERIDGE *Poems* I. 13 A rathe December blights my lagging May. **1886** *W. Som. Word-bk.* s.v. *Rathe*... The expression..a rave spring..is not uncommon.

b. esp. of fruits, flowers, etc., which grow, bloom, or ripen early in the year. (Cf. RATHE-RIPE.)

1572 MASCALL *Plant. & Graff.* (1592) 53 For to haue rath or timely Peares... For to haue them rath or soone, ye shall graffe them in the Pine Tree. **1600** E. B. in *Eng. Helicon* B iv b, And made the rathe and timely primrose grow. **1637** MILTON *Lycidas* 142. **1651** R. CHILD in *Hartlib's Legacy* (1655) 9 To sow Raith, (or early ripe) Pease. **1813** SCOTT *Rokeby* IV. ii, Where..the rathe primrose decks the mead. **1848** LOWELL *Fable for Critics* Poet. Wks. (1880) 357 A single anemone trembly and rathe. **1880** SWINBURNE *Songs of Springtides, On the Cliffs* 44 The labours, whence men reap Rathe fruit of hopes and fears.

3. Early in the day; belonging to the morning.

1596 DRAYTON *Legends* i. 8 The rathe Morning newly but awake. **1635** HAYWARD tr. *Biondi's Banish'd Virg.* 191 Intending to aske her what shee made there at so rathe an houre. *a* **1835** HOGG *Allan of Dale* 29 Beginning thy rath orisons here. **1877** SYMONDS *Renaiss. It., Fine Arts* (1897) III. iii. 110 The rathe tints of early dawn. **1914** C. MACKENZIE *Sinister Street* II. III. xiv. 787 Spring on these rathe mornings of wind and scudded blue sky was forward with her traceries.

4. Belonging to, or forming, the first part of some period of time.

1850 TENNYSON *In Mem.* cx, Thy converse drew us with delight, The men of rathe and riper years. **1898** CROCKETT *Standard Bearer* xxxi, The young ardour of spring and the rath summer-time.

†**rathe,** *a.*[2], obs. var. RARE *a.*[1] (Cf. next.)

1548 ELYOT s.v. *Rarus, Rarum inuentu*, harde and rathe to be found.

†**rathe, rath,** *a.*[3], var. of RARE *a.*[2] *Obs. rare.*

For the confusion of *th* and *r*, cf. *raer*, var. of RATHE *sb.*[2], RARE *a.*[3] and RATHE *a.*[2]

1684 LITTLETON *Lat. Dict.*, *Ovum sorbile*, a rathe egg, a poached or rath-roasted egg. **1706** PHILLIPS (ed. Kersey) s.v., A rath Egg. [See also RATHEREST.]

†**rathe**, *v. Obs.* Also 3 *inf.* **raþenn.** [a. ON. *ráða* = OE. *rǽdan* REDE *v.*] *trans.* and *intr.* To counsel, advise.

c **1200** ORMIN 2948 Godd himm sennde hiss enngell To raþenn himm þe bettste raþ. *Ibid.* 5514 Swa þatt te33 cunnenn raþenn rihht Hemm sellfenn & ec oþre. *c* **1300** *Havelok* 1335 Do nou als y wile rathe.

rathe (reɪð), *adv. poet.* and *dial.* Forms: 1 **(h)ræðe, hreðe, rað,** 1–2 **hraðe,** 1–3 **raðe,** 2 **reðe,** 2–4 **raþe,** 3 **ræðen, reaðe,** 3–7 **rath,** 4 **raþ,** 4–6 *Sc.* **raith,** 6, 9 *dial.* **rade,** 3–7, 9 **rathe.** [OE. *hraðe, hræðe* (*hreðe*) = OHG. *(h)rado, ratho* etc., the adv. corresponding to OE. *hræd* RAD *a.*[1]]

†**1.** Denoting rapidity in the performance or completion of an action: Quickly, rapidly, swiftly; *esp.* without delay, promptly, soon. *Obs.* (in common use down to 16th c.)

Beowulf (Z.) 224 þanon up hraðe wedera leode on wang stiʒon. *c* **825** *Vesp. Psalter* xxxvi. 2 Swe swe leaf wyrta hreðe fallað. *a* **900** CYNEWULF *Christ* 1525 [Hi] sceolon raðe feallan on grimme grund. *a* **1123** *O.E. Chron.* an. 1102 Þe he hine swa hraðe ʒewinnan ne mihte, he let þær toforan castelas ʒemakian. *a* **1200** *Moral Ode* 90 in *E.E.P.* (1862) 28 He scullen falle swiþe raþe in to helle grunde. *a* **1225** *Ancr. R.* 54 Þus wolde Eue inouh raðe habben i-onswered. *c* **1275** LAY. 25645 So rathe so hii mihten Vt of sipe hii rehten. *c* **1300** *Havelok* 2391 Cum to þe king, swiþe and raþe. **1375** BARBOUR *Bruce* v. 417 Gif he had haldin the casteill, It suld haue beyn assegit rath. **1480** CAXTON *Chron. Eng.* clxxxv. 162 He prayd hem that they shold make edward of Carrnariuan kyng of englond..as rathe as they myght. **1576** GASCOIGNE *Philomene* (Arb.) 96 Sende My daughter..And (since I counte al leasure long) Returne hir to me rathe. **1649** R. HODGES *Plain. Direct.* 36 Hee was wroth because she was ful of wrath so rath.

†**b.** With *too*: Too quickly, too soon; hence (passing into sense 2), too early; before the fitting, usual, or natural time. *Obs.*

c **888** K. ÆLFRED *Boeth.* iii. §1 Ic wat þæt þu hæfst þara wæpna to hraðe forʒiten. *c* **1205** LAY. 28362 Þer weore al þat fiht i-don ah þat niht to raðe com. *a* **1300** *Cursor M.* 8876 Al to rath he þat be-gan. **1330** R. BRUNNE *Chron.* (1810) 9 He regned fiftene ȝere, & died alle to rathe. *c* **1374** CHAUCER *Troylus* v. 937 He was slayn, allas..Vn-happyly at Thebes al to raþe. **1413** *Pilgr. Sowle* (Caxton 1483) IV. xx. 65, I songe to rathe, for I sange by the morowe. *a* **1541** WYATT in *Tottell's Misc.* (Arb.) 60 All to rathe alas the while, She built on such a ground.

†**2.** Denoting the point of time at which an action or occurrence takes place. *Obs.* (See also RARE *adv.*[2])

†**a.** ***as rathe as*** (***swa rathe swa***), as soon as, at the moment when. *Obs.*

c **1000** ÆLFRIC *Hom.* II. 526 He wæs Godes Bearn swa hraðe swa he mannes Bearn wearð. *c* **1175** *Lamb. Hom.* 97 Swa reðe swa he þes mannes heorte and his mod on lihte, hit iwendeð from ufele to gode. *c* **1425** *Eng. Conq. Irel.* 84 As rathe as thou hast I-sey these lettres, ne leue nat to come to socour vs.

†**b.** Early with respect to the proper or natural time. *Obs.*

1565 JEWEL *Repl. Harding* (1611) 8 It was verie rathe to haue Monasteries built in all S. Iames time. **1582** N. LICHEFIELD tr. *Castanheda's Conq. E. Ind.* 124b, For that it was somwhat rath for to returne, they went to the Iland of Cambalan. **1598** BARCKLEY *Felic. Man* III. (1603) 206 Though it was too rathe for those young yeeres to know the wickednesse of the world.

3. Early (in the morning or day). *poet.* and *dial.*

c **1386** CHAUCER *Shipman's T.* 1289 What eyleth yow so rathe for to ryse. **1575** TURBERV. *Venerie* 60, I am the hunte, whiche rathe and earely ryse. **1584** R. SCOT *Discov. Witchcr.* XII. xxi. (1886) 230 Upon some Sundaie morning rath, light it. **1612** DRAYTON *Poly-olb.* xii. 168 Commaunding him.. rathe as he could rise, to such a gate to goe. **1674–91** RAY *S. & E.C. Words* 75 Rathe in the morning, i.e. early in the morning. **1842** C. PULMAN *Rustic Sketches* 29 In th' marnin' up I gits, Za rathe as break o' day. **1859** TENNYSON *Elaine* 339 The face..held her from her sleep. Till rathe she rose.

†**b.** Early in the year. *Obs. rare*−[1].

1574 R. SCOT *Hop Gard.* (1578) 10 Where the Garden standeth bleake or the Hoppe springeth rath.

rathed, *a.*: see RATH *sb.*[1]

rathel, obs. form of RADDLE *v.*[1]

†'**ratheled,** *pa. pple. Obs. rare*−[1].

Perh. the same word as *ratheled* intertwined, cited under RADDLED *ppl. a.*[1]; but in that case the connexion of the various senses of RADDLE *sb.*[1] becomes doubtful.

13.. *Gaw. & Gr. Knt.* 2294 Gawayn..stode stylle as þe ston, oþer a stubbe auþer, þat raþeled is in roche grounde, with rotez a hundreth.

†'**rathely,** *adv. Obs.* Forms: 1 **hrædlice,** 3 **raðliche,** 4 **raþely, raþli,** 4–5 **rathly, ratheli,** 5–6 **rathely** (*Sc.* **raith-**). [f. RATHE *a.*[1] + -LY[2]. Cf. RADLY.] Quickly, etc. = RATHE *adv.* 1. (Common in 14–15th c.)

a **950** *Rit. Durham* (Surtees) 58/5 Angel driht[nes] ætʒistod..cvoedende 'aris hrædlice'. *a* **1225** *Ancr. R.* 422 Water þet ne stureð nout readliche [*Titus MS.* raðliche] stinkeð. *a* **1300** *Cursor M.* 23926 (Edinb.) If ik eft fal on ani wis Ratheli do me for to ris. *a* **1352** MINOT *Poems* vii. 91 Þe teres he lete ful rathly ren Out of his eghen. *c* **1400** *Rowland & O.* 292 Than sir Rowlande full rathely up he rase. *c* **1470** HENRY *Wallace* IX. 1805 Raithly he raid, and maid full mony wound. **1502** *Ord. Crysten Men* (W. de W. 1506) I. ii. 14 These ylles that we se come rathely.

'**ratheness.** *rare.* [f. RATHE *a.*[1] + -NESS.]

a. Earliness. **b.** Premature ending.

1635 HAYWARD tr. *Biondi's Banish'd Virg.* 220 God makes no difference betweene the ratheness and lateness of time. **1883** J. PAYNE *O.M.B.* xi. 4 If thy life's untimely ended story ..hold no room, For very ratheness [etc.].

'**rather,** *a. ? Obs.* Also 3–5 **raþ-, rathere,** 5 **raþ-, rathir.** [Comparative of RATHE *a.*[1]]

1. Earlier, preceding another or others in point of time, coming at an earlier hour, date, etc.

1388 WYCLIF *John* i. 30 Aftir me is comun a man, which was maad bifor me; for he was rather than Y. **1429** *Rolls of Parlt.* IV. 342/2 Atte a rather and nerre day. **1477** *Ibid.* VI. 194/1 For the rather execucion of his said false purpose. **1551** RECORDE *Cast. Knowl.* (1556) 131 Euery 15 degrees of distaunce estward, causeth the daye to be rather by one howers space. **1579** SPENSER *Sheph. Cal.* Feb. 83 The rather Lambes bene starved with cold. **1583** GOLDING *Calvin on Deut.* clvi. 966 But we see one winter longer, and another winter later, and an other rather. [**1620** SIR J. DAVIES *Eccl., To W. Browne*, What? been thy rather lamkins ill-apaid?]

†**b.** Antecedent, prior; of greater importance. *Obs. rare.*

1657 J. SERGEANT *Schism Dispach't* 278 A circumstance much encreasing the rather-probability of his greater Authority. *Ibid.* 297 The midle words importing his rather right to S. Paul's obedience. **1668** PEPYS *Diary* 10 Feb., A great blow either given to the King or Presbyters, or, which is the rather of the two, to the House itself.

†**2.** The earlier (of two persons or things); the former. *Obs.* (Common *c* 1375–1450.)

1297 R. GLOUC. (Rolls) 5809 Seint Edward þe martir.. was is sone Bi is raþere wiue. *c* **1374** CHAUCER *Boeth.* II. pr. i. 20 (Camb. MS.) Thow art defeted for desire and talent of thi rather fortune. *c* **1400** MAUNDEV. (1839) v. 46 The Sarazines maden another Cytee..and clepeden it the new Damyete. So that now no Man duellethe at the rathere Toun of Damyete. **1413** *Pilgr. Sowle* (Caxton) I. xvi. (1859) 17 In tyme of his rather lyf, he had space, and suffysaunt leyser ynow. **1484** *Will of Taylour* (Somerset Ho.), Wher as the body of Johanne my Rather wyf lieth enterid.

†**b.** The previous or preceding (day or year). *Obs.*

1387 TREVISA *Higden* (Rolls) III. 145 Þe trauail of þe raþer day oþer þe feste of þat day. *c* **1400** *Beryn* 26 As thouȝe he had I-knowe hir al the rathir yeer.

†**3.** Of earlier times. *Obs. rare*−[1].

1387 TREVISA *Higden* (Rolls) I. 177 Þat vertue keled..so þat þe raþer welles beeþ now but lakes oþer more vereyliche dreye chanels.

†**4.** More to be chosen, preferable. *Obs. rare.*

c **1430** *Hymns Virg.* 86 It is raþir to bileeue þe wageringe wijnde þan þe chaungeable world. *c* **1449** PECOCK *Repr.* III. xvii. 393 In such aventure it were rather to truste to the conscience and discrecion of him..than [etc.].

rather ('rɑːðə(r)), *adv.* Forms: 1 **hraðor, -ur, raðor,** 2–3 **raðer,** 3 **raþir, -ur,** 3–4 **rathere,** 3–5 **raþer,** (4 **-ere**), 4–5 **rathir,** (5 **-yr, -are,** 5, 6 *Sc.* **rether**), 4– **rather;** also 3 **rader,** 5 **radyr,** 9 *dial.* **raider, rayder.** [Compar. of RATHE *adv.*

The pron. with long vowel (ɑː) is now usual in England; the short sound ('ræðər, 'raðər) is common in Scotland (but not *dial.*) and America, and is given by Walker as the standard pron. in his time. The use of ('reɪðə(r)), preferred by Walker, is now confined to dialects.]

I. Denoting precedence in time.

†**1.** ***the rather***, (all) the more quickly, (all) the sooner. *Obs.*

In some instances not clearly distinguishable from sense 4.

c **850** *O.E. Martyrol.* 26 Dec., Hie him miclan þe reðran wæron & þe raðor hine oftorfod hæfdon. *a* **1123** *O.E. Chron.* (Laud MS.) an. 1009 [Hi] þa burh raðe ʒe-eodon, ʒif he þe raðor to him friðes to ne ʒirndon. *c* **1205** LAY. 21649 Ȝif Ardur neore þe rader icumen þenne weoren Houwel inumen. *c* **1330** *Sir Beues* (MS. A.) 431 Boute þow þe raþer hennes te, I schel þe greue! *c* **1420** *Chron. Vilod.* 796 Bot ȝyff Seynt Woltrud hurre þe rather holpe, he nys bot dedde. **1523** FITZHERB. *Husb.* §46 If thou put a lytel terre in his eye, he wil mende the rather. *a* **1536** TINDALE in Foxe *A. & M.* (1563) 159/2 The pilgrimage that now is vsed is..a good meane to come the rather to grace. **1605** SHAKS. *Macb.* I. vii. 62 When Duncan is asleepe (Whereto the rather shall his dayes hard Iourney Soundly inuite him).

2. a. Earlier, sooner; at an earlier time, season, day, hour, etc. Now *dial.* †***rather or later***, sooner or later.

c **1000** *Ags. Gosp.* John xx. 4 Se oðer leorning-cniht forarn Petrus forne & cum raðor to ðære byrʒenne. *a* **1300** *Cursor M.* 26516 Þan sal it helpe þe Vte o þi sin raþer to rise To crist. *c* **1330** R. BRUNNE *Chron. Wace* (Rolls) 5629 Raþer ne myghte [he] þider wende; Bote atte seue nyghtes ende He com. **1387** TREVISA *Higden* (Rolls) I. 167 Oþer þere was anoþer Dido, an elder þan sche; oþer Cartage was raþer i-founded. *c* **1475** *Partenay* 4011 This worle..goth vnto decline, Rather or later to an endly fine. **1566** *Pasquine in a Traunce* ii. b, I sawe the Heauen and the Starres..neither rather or later to rise or go downe. **1609** C. BUTLER *Fem. Mon.* (1634) 111 The continuance of hot and dry weather may cause them come somewhat rather. **17..** *Exmoor Courtship* (E.D.S.) 491 Why, tha Quesson es [= the question I] put a little rather. **1883–6** in dial. glossaries (Hants and Som.).

b. With *than. ? Obs.*

c **1330** *Sir Beues* (MS. A) 3537 He com raþer to þe tresore, Þ an hii be half and more. *c* **1391** CHAUCER *Astrol.* I. §21 Thilke sterres..arisen rather than the degree of hire longitude. **1454** *Paston Lett.* I. 301 Yn case he know of it rathyr then ye. **1519** HORMAN *Vulg.* 245b, The warke was finisshed rather than a man myght beleue. **1598** BARCKLEY *Felic. Man* III. (1603) 208 Rather then her yeares required, she was..chosen Abbesse. **1659** LEAK *Waterwks.* 32 As concerning the Vessel D it is necessary that it empty rather than E.

†**c.** (A specified time) earlier or sooner. *Obs.*

1455 *Paston Lett.* I. 338, I had lever ye were at London a weke the rather and tymelyer then a weke to late. *c* **1500** *Melusine* 233 Playsed god that ye were arryued two dayes rather, For thenne ye had found my fader on lyue.

3. a. At an earlier time or date than the one now present or in question; previously, formerly. *Obs.* exc. *dial.*

c **1275** LAY. 4650 He him ȝef þes womman; þat raþer was mi lemman. *c* **1305** *Land Cokayne* 120 Þe cristal turnip in to glasse, In state þat hit raþer wasse. **1387** TREVISA *Higden* (Rolls) I. 93 Perseus..made it a worþy lond þat was raþer vnworþy. *Ibid.* II. 357 Þe latter Hercules, anoþer þan we spak of raþer. **1559** *Mirr. Mag., Dk. York* xvi, An other hoast, wherof I spake not rather. **1886** W. BARNES *Dorset Gloss., Rather*, lately; just now.

†**b.** Previously, beforehand. *Obs. rare.*

c **1325** *Chron. Eng.* 675 in Ritson *Metr. Rom.* II. 298 The lordinges..the thef slowen anon, Ah rathere he woundede moni on. **1422** tr. *Secreta Secret., Priv. Priv.* 215 Oone man may not ouercome his enemys, but yf he haue radyr ouercome covardy.

II. Denoting priority in nature or reason.

4. a. ***the rather***, the more readily (on this account or for this reason); (all) the more.

c **888** K. ÆLFRED *Boeth.* xxxii. §2 Þeah þu nu hwæm fæʒer ðince, ne bið hit no þy hraðor swa. *c* **900** *Ags. Ps.* (Th.) iv. 5 Ne scule ʒe hit no þy hraðor þurhteon, þe læs ʒe synʒien. *a* **1225** *Ancr. R.* 190 Heie monnes messager, me schal heiliche underuongen,..& so muchel þe raðer, ȝif he is priue mid te kinge of heouene. ? **1447** *Lett. Marg. Anjou & Bp. Beckington* (Camden) 93 We shall the rather for our said chapellein sake have you in tendre remembrance. **1523** FITZHERB. *Husb.* §133 The weight of the bowes shall cause theym to be the rather cut downe. **1570–6** LAMBARDE *Peramb. Kent* (1826) 237 The true place of this conflict shoulde be Stouremouthe,..the rather for that it is derived of the mouth of the river Stoure. **1615** W. LAWSON *Country Housew. Gard.* (1626) 29 You shall finde them stirring in the morning or euening, and the rather in moist weather. **1710** *Tatler* No. 253 ¶8 A Case..which I the rather mention, because both Sexes are concerned in it. **1818** CRUISE *Digest* (ed. 2) II. 218 It ought not to be in the heir's power..to charge the lands..the rather because of the covenant [etc.]. **1885–94** R. BRIDGES *Eros & Psyche* Mar. xx, On earth he must maintain it as her son, The rather that his weapons were most fit.

†**b.** Without *the. Obs.*

1463 *Bury Wills* (Camden) 19 Þat it may be redde and knowe to exorte the pepill rathere to prey for me. **1654** BRAMHALL *Just Vindication* vii. (1661) 203 Why should not the Bull of Nicholas the second..be as advantageous..? why not much rather? **1660** BARROW *Euclid* I. xix, After the same manner $BC = AC$, wherefore rather $BC > AB$.

5. More truly or correctly; more properly speaking; with greater correspondence between the word or words and the fact.

a. With *than* (Sc. *nor*; also †***the rather***).

c **1380** WYCLIF *Wks.* (1880) 118 It were raþere almes to lordis to hire..þan to holde [etc.]. *c* **1400** *Beryn* 2908 Þe Romeyns were in poynt te pas; Til ther were a þowsand, rathir mo þen les, Men I-armyd cleen. *a* **1536** TINDALE *Doct. Treat.* 390 A thing begun rather than finished. **1560** DAUS tr. *Sleidane's Comm.* 110b, This demaunde of his..rather maketh them afrayde of a counsell, than provoketh them to it. **1567** *Reg. Privy Council Scot.* I. 578 Usurpand the rather the office of Princes nor liegis. **1657** R. LIGON *Barbadoes* (1673) 102 The Inhabitants..build their dwellings, rather like stoves then houses. **1711** STEELE *Spect.* No. 49 ¶3 Their Entertainments are derived rather from Reason than Imagination. **1816** J. WILSON *City of Plague* II. iii. 190 Her face..seem'd the face of sorrow Rather than of death. **1857** BUCKLE *Civiliz.* I. vii. 332 The new king, from levity rather than from reason, despised the disputes of theologians.

b. Without *than*, in opposition or contrast to a preceding statement.

c **1380** WYCLIF *Sel. Wks.* I. 409 We have litil mater for to laughe, but rather for to morne. *c* **1450** *Merlin* xxxiii. 690 'I pray yow that ye for-yeve it me that I haue mys-don'. 'So helpe me god', quod the damesell, 'rather shalt thou a-bye it full dere'. **1535** COVERDALE *Ezek.* xxxiii. 17 The children off thy people saye..the waye off the Lorde is not right, where as their owne waye is rather vnright. **1576** FLEMING *Panopl. Epist.* 227 *marg.*, Whether this were Lysistratus the Sicyonian..I doubt much: thinking rather it was some other priuate man. **1596** BACON *Max. & Uses Com. Law* Ep. Ded., An age wherein if science bee increased, conscience is rather decayed. **1768** GOLDSM. *Good-n. Man* I. i, Say rather, that he loves all the world. **1884** tr. *Lotze's Metaph.* 112 We are therefore not entitled to treat the validity of the law as an independently thinkable fact..Rather it is simply the observed or expected fulfilment itself.

c. ***or rather***, used to introduce a statement more correct than the one already made. †Also ***and rather*** (with comparatives).

1460 *Paston Lett.* I. 508 Myn autorite is as grete as theris, and rather more as I tolde you. **1545** UDALL *Erasm. Par. Luke* (1548) 86 Nere about the summe of twelue or fiftene poundes sterlynge or rather aboue. *c* **1645** HOWELL *Lett.* IV. 2 The Doctor by this Oversight (or Cunningness, rather) got a supply of Money. **1711** STEELE *Spect.* No. 4 ¶4 Thus my Want of, or rather Resignation of Speech, gives me all the Advantages of a dumb Man. **1836** J. H. NEWMAN *Par. Serm.* (1837) III. xxiv. 386 You will find there are few, or rather none at all. **1875** JOWETT *Plato* (ed. 2) I. 122 Last night, or rather very early this morning.

6. More (so) than not; more than anything else; hence, in a certain degree or measure; to some extent; somewhat, slightly.

a. With vbs. of thinking, fearing, etc.

1597 J. KING *On Jonas* (1618) 574 And surely I rather thinke, that they blessed Ionas in their hearts. **1611** A. STAFFORD *Niobe* 172, I put so great a difference betweene the ancient and modern papists, as that I resolue rather that the former are taken to mercy. **1709** E. WARD tr. *Cervantes* 55, I rather think I have worn the Mourning for you than for the dead Man. **1835** J. KENT *Private Corr.* II. 387, I rather guess I shall like it. **1875** JOWETT *Plato* (ed. 2) I. 10, I rather think that you know him.

b. With adjs., advbs., sbs., or phrases. (Sometimes implying slight excess = *rather too*.)

1662 PEPYS *Diary* 27 Dec., With the new Roxalana, which do [= does] it rather better in all respects,.. than the first Roxalana. **1713** HEARNE in *Rel. Hearnianæ* (1857) I. 282 These were rather later than the *campagi*. *a* **1766** MRS. F. SHERIDAN *Sidney Bidulph* IV. 65 It would be rather inconvenient to you at present to have your rent roll scrutinised. **1778** *Learning at a Loss* II. 163 His Appearance at the Baronet's must have been rather a silly one. **1788** M. CUTLER in *Life, Jrnls. & Corr.* (1888) I. 429 The town is situated, very injudiciously, in rather a valley. **1829** LANDOR *Imag. Conv.* Wks. 1853 I. 515/1 Our bed indeed is rather of the highest. **1850** SMEDLEY *Frank Fairlegh* xiii, Is it my trap you're talking about? rather the thing isn't it, eh? **1880** F. D. MATTHEW *Wyclif's Eng. Wks.* 114 If the tract be Wyclif's, we may date it rather before 1380.

†**c.** So *rather somewhat*. *Obs.*

1732 ARBUTHNOT *Rules of Diet* in *Aliments*, etc. I. 247 Apricocks, unless mellow, are rather somewhat styptick. **1768** *Woman of Honor* III. 233 A range of thirteen chests rather somewhat larger than the common size.

7. *colloq.* (formerly *vulgar*). Freq. with emphatic pronunc. (ˌrɑːˈðɜː(r)). Used as a strong affirmative in reply to a question: = 'I (should) rather think so'; very much so; very decidedly. Now, or until recently, common also in upper-class or affected speech.

1836–9 DICKENS *Sk. Boz.*, *Gt. Winglebury Duel*, 'Do you know the mayor's house?'.. 'Rather', replied the boots, significantly. **1856** ALB. SMITH *Adv. Mr. Ledbury* I. iv. 27 'Do you know the young lady?' 'Rather!' replied Johnson. **1885** A. EDWARDES *Girton Girl* I. xiv. 280 Rather proud of my own accent... But Arbuthnot puts me in the shade, ra-*ther*. **1905** H. VACHELL *Hill* i. 2 'You'll enjoy it—as I did —amazingly.' 'Ra-ther,' said John. **1928** C. A. NICHOLSON *Hell & Duchess* II. vi. 286 'May I give Audrey your blessing?' 'Ra-ther and my love.' **1933** J. BUCHAN *Prince of Captivity* II. i. 153 'You've heard Kenneth speak of him.' 'Rather. I want to meet him.' **1975** *Listener* 10 Apr. 472/2 The producer had.. prevented the willing son in the parable from saying 'Yes, ra-*ther*, Dad,' when asked to get on with the 'allotment'.

III. Denoting prior eligibility or choice.

8. a. Sooner (as a matter of fitness, expediency, etc.); with more propriety or advantage; with better reason or ground; more properly or justly. With *than*.

c **1200** *Trin. Coll. Hom.* 213 He sholde raðer helden hit ut, þene men þermide fordrenchen. *c* **1380** WYCLIF *Wks.* (1880) 376 Raþer þan þu schuldist be ocupied þerewiþ þu schalt renne awai þer-fro. *c* **1450** *Merlin* x. 148 Another ought rather to go on this massage than ye. **1573** L. LLOYD *Marrow of Hist.* (1653) 274 Therefore I rather deserve death than he. **1654** BRAMHALL *Just Vindication* ix. (1661) 263 Why they should rather submit themselves.. to that See.. then to any other Patriarchate. **1680** LOCKE *Govt.* I. xi. §127 'Tis rather to be thought, that an heir had no such Right by divine institution, than that God should give such a Right. *a* **1756** MRS. HEYWOOD *New Present* (1771) 256 Soft water should be used rather than hard.

†**b.** As against, to the exclusion of, the other. *Obs. rare*⁻¹.

1553 GRIMALDE tr. *Cicero's Offices* I. (1556) 34 b, Semblably fare they, who would striue together, whether of them should rather rule the common weale.

9. Sooner (as a matter of individual choice); more readily or willingly; with greater liking or good-will; with or in preference. **a.** Expressing choice between two courses of action, or preference of one event to another.

In sentences of this type *rather* is placed either before the vb. or clause expressing the action or event preferred, or immediately before *than*. For the use of *to* after *than*, see the latter word.

1297 R. GLOUC. (Rolls) 9419 Þe deserites gonne chese, Raþer þan to lese hor lond, hor lif þere to lese. **1440** in *Wars Eng. in France* (1864) II. 457 They.. wolde rather that the paix were letted thanne he shulde be delivered and come hoome. **1551** CROWLEY *Pleas. & Pain* 517 Rather let your leases go, Then they shoulde worke you endelesse woe. **1675** E. ESSEX *Lett.* (1770) 199, I will rather suffer myself to be made a pack-horse than bear other mens faults. **1711** ADDISON *Spect.* No. 261 ¶8 We love rather to dazzle the Multitude, than consult our proper Interests. **1788** MAD. D'ARBLAY *Diary* IV. 342 They would rather have died than refused. **1812** JEFFERSON *Writ.* (1830) IV. 175 A choice to fight two enemies at a time, rather than to take them by succession. **1885** *Manch. Exam.* 30 Dec. 5/3 Any man who resigns a great office in the State rather than act in opposition to the dictates of his judgment.

b. Expressing choice between two things, persons, qualities, conditions, etc. †Also *no rather* (1393), *more rather* (1560).

a **1300** *Fall & Passion* 27 in *E.E.P.* (1862) 13 Whi com he raþer to eue þan he com to adam. *c* **1380** WYCLIF *Sel. Wks.* III. 380 Þo blynde puple.. wil raþer gif to waste housis of freris þen to parische chirchis. **1393** LANGL. *P. Pl.* C. x. 123 He reuerenceþ hym ryght nouht, no raþer than anoþer. *c* **1450** tr. *De Imitatione* I. iii. 6 Þei chese raþer to be grete than meke. **1560** DAUS tr. *Sleidane's Comm.* 6 b, Nowe he would gratifie no man more rather than hym. **1611** BIBLE *Jer.* viii. 3 Death shall bee chosen rather then life. **1711** STEELE *Spect.* No. 6 ¶1 This unhappy Affectation of being Wise rather than Honest. **1856** RUSKIN *Mod. Paint.* IV. v. xix. §8 Painting cheeks with health rather than rouge.

c. Without *than*, in contrast to a preceding statement. Also rarely *the rather*.

c **1275** LAY. 3943 Raþir ich wolle þe slean mid mine spere. *c* **1290** *S. Eng. Leg.* 110/134 Heo nolde cristinedom a-fongue, heo seide heo wolde raþer tuyrne aȝen In-to hire owene londe. **1377** LANGL. *P. Pl.* B. IV. 5 But resoun rede me þer-to rather wil I deye. *a* **1480** *Lett. Marg. Anjou & Bp. Beckington* (Camden) 125 Ye.. wol not applie you.. unto the said marriage.. but rather induce yor said doghter to the contrarye. **1596** DANETT tr. *Comines* (1614) 331 There died Monsieur de Montpensier himselfe, some say of poyson, others of an ague, which I rather beleeue. **1633** BP. HALL *Occas. Medit.* §49, I would rather to see a plot less fair, and more yielding. **1703** ROWE *Fair Penitent* IV. i, I cou'd even wish we rather had been wreckt. **1819** SHELLEY *Cenci* I. i. 109 Which now delights me little. I the rather Look on such pangs as terror ill conceals. **1881** JOWETT *Thucyd.* I. 122, I do not now commiserate the parents of the dead who stand here; I would rather comfort them.

d. (One) *had rather* = (one) would rather. (See HAVE *v.* 22 c.) †Hence *to have rather*, to choose or prefer.. rather. (*rare.*)

The infin. after *had* is sometimes preceded by *to*.

c **1450** in *Rel. Antiq.* I. 72 Yett haid I rether dye, For his sake, ons agayne. **1478** [see HAVE *v.* 22]. **1523** LD. BERNERS *Froiss.* I. 157 He had rather they had bene taken prisoners. **1551** ROBINSON tr. *More's Utop.* (1895) 6 Bicause I had be good then wise rather. **1594** BEDINGFIELD tr. *Machiavelli's Flor. Hist.* (1595) 155 Which if we be not able to defend, then haue we rather to submit our selues to anie other Prince. **1667** EARL ORRERY *St. Lett.* (1743) II. 311, I had much rather to do it than say it. **1685** *Gracian's Courtier's Orac.* 18 To have rather be indifferent in a sublime employment, than excellent in an indifferent, is a desire rendred excusable by Generosity. **1719** DE FOE *Crusoe* II. v, Our men had much rather the weather had been calm. **1819** SHELLEY *Ess.*, etc. (1852) II. 155, I had rather err with Plato than be right with Horace. **1875** RUSKIN *Fors Clav.* lv. V. 189, I had rather come and draw the cart.

†**e.** (One) *would rather* = (one) would rather have or choose. *Obs.*

1557 NORTH *Gueuara's Diall. Pr.* 96, I woulde rather one onely day of lyfe then all the ryches of Roome. **1633** BP. HALL *Occas. Medit.* §49, I would rather never to have light, than not to have it always. **1675** R. BURTHOGGE *Causa Dei* 99 The Parent.. who would rather than the better part of his estate.. he could reclaim and turn him.

f. Ellipt. phr. *rather you than me* (or *I*): I would rather that you did or underwent something than I (used to convey admiration, commiseration, etc.).

1968 'C. AIRD' *Henrietta Who?* xv. 192 A proper mix-up, isn't it?.. Rather you than me. **1969** V. GIELGUD *Necessary End* xiii. 104 You're a brave fellow. Rather you than I. Good luck.

†**IV. 10.** Followed by *or*: see OR *adv.*¹ C 2.

1390 GOWER *Conf.* III. 45 For rathere er he scholde faile, With Nigromance he wole assaile To make his incantacioun. **1432** *Test. Ebor.* (Surtees) II. 20 To amend ye defawtes in ye said brigges.. rather or ye brygges forsayde falle. *c* **1440** *Gesta Rom.* xlvi. 185 Rathir shalle the sowle parte from my bodye or I lese hit. **1527** WAKFELDE *Let.* in *Kotser Codicis* (1528) P iv b, I had rather to dye a thousand tymes or suffer it.

rather (ˈræðə(r)), *sb. U.S. dial.* Also **ruther**. [f. the adv.] A choice, preference. Cf. DRUTHER and RUTHER *adv.*

1903 *Dialect Notes* II. 326 'I would stay at home if I *had my rather*.' Also pronounced *ruther*. **1913** H. KEPHART *Our Southern Highlanders* xiii. 283 'It matters not, so I've been told, Where the body goes when the heart grows cold; But,' she concluded, 'a person has a rather about where he'd be put.' **1930** W. FAULKNER *As I lay Dying* 106 And if I had my rathers, you wouldn't be here at all. **1935** Z. N. HURSTON *Mules & Men* I. ii. 49 Her tongue is all de weapon a woman got... She could have had mo' sense, but she told God no, she'd ruther take it out in hips. So God give her her ruthers. She got plenty hips, plenty mouf and no brains. *Ibid.* vii. 162 You didn't figger Ah was draggin' behind you when you was bringin' dat Sears and Roebuck catalogue over to my house and beggin' me to choose my ruthers. **1949** *Richmond* (Va.) *Times-Dispatch* 26 Dec. 6/5 In the Smokies,.. to take one's preference is to 'have your ruthers'. **1961** C. HIMES *Black on Black* (1973) 46 If I had my rathers I'd make up my own band.

ˈ**ratherest**, *adv.* (and *a.*) [f. RATHER *adv.* + -EST.]

†**1.** Soonest. *Obs. rare*⁻¹.

a **1425** *Cursor M.* 22129 (Trin.) Turne.. þei shul raþerest and siþen oþere at þe leest.

2. Most of all, most particularly. *Obs.* exc. *dial.*

c **1420** *Chron. Vilod.* 1014 þe best we shull ratherest byleve to. **1535** FISHER *Spir. Consolat.* Wks. (1876) 352 It shall anon lose the vertue & quicknesse in stirring & moving of your soule, when you wolde ratherest have it sturred. **1567** W. BARKER *Xenophon, Schole Cyrus* I. E iv b, When you haue most plentie, then ratherest prouide against wante. **1588** SHAKS. *L.L.L.* IV. ii. 19 His.. vntrained, or rather vnlettered, or ratherest vnconfirmed fashion. **1824** MACTAGGART *Gallovid. Encycl.* 66 Gin thou'lt no fancy her, And ratherest wad ha'e Meg.

3. *rather of the ratherest*, just a little too much or too little.

Grose assigns the phr. to Norfolk and explains it as 'meat underdone', and Forby says 'it is chiefly applied to the insufficient dressing of meat'. This appears to associate the origin of the expression with RATHE *a.*³

[**1787** in GROSE *Prov. Gloss.*] *a* **1825** in FORBY. **1865** MRS. H. WOOD *Mildred Arkell* II. iv. 68 The women would find it rather of the ratherest for heat.

rathe-ripe, rath-ripe (ˈreɪð-, ˈrɑːθ-, -æ-), *a.* and *sb.* Now *poet.* and *dial.* [f. RATHE *a.*¹ + RIPE *a.* (cf. OE. *rædrípe* and RARE-RIPE). With ref. to grain the usual spelling is *rath-*.]

A. *adj.* **1.** Of fruits, grain, etc.: Coming early to maturity; ripening early in the year.

Usually applied to special kinds or varieties, as *rathe-ripe barley*, *pease*, etc.

1578 LYTE *Dodoens* VI. xliii. 712 There be diuers sortes of Peares,.. whereof some be rathe ripe, some haue a later riping. **1620** VENNER *Via Recta* (1650) 184 Those hard Rathe-ripe Pease, which are brought to the Markets by the middle or end of May. **1677** *Phil. Trans.* XII. 876 A rath-ripe Barley, sow'd and return'd again into the Barn in two months time. **1745** tr. *Columella's Husb.* x. 615 Then from twice-bearing tree the rathe-ripe fig Descends. **1832** *Veg. Subst. Food of Man* 61 Spring Barley... Of this species farmers distinguish two sorts; the common, and.. the rath-ripe barley. **1840** BROWNING *Sordello* II. 313 Fruits like the fig-tree's, rathe-ripe, rotten-rich. **1879–** in dial. glossaries (Devon, Dorset, Hants, E. Anglia).

2. *fig.* Precocious, early developed in mind or body. Now *dial.*

1617 BP. HALL *Quo Vadis?* §4 These rathe-ripe wits preuent their owne perfection. **1691** WOOD *Ath. Oxon.* II. 217 Being extraordinary rath ripe [he].. was entred into his Accedence at five years of age. **1703** WHITBY *Comm. N.T.* I. 118 Quintilian saith of the rath-ripe wit, that it rarely comes to maturity. **1886** *W. Som. Word-bk.* s.v., A girl who developed into a woman at an early age would be called rathe-ripe by elderly educated people.

B. *sb.* Applied to various early fruits and vegetables, *esp.* peas and apples.

1677 PLOT *Oxfordsh.* 153 The small Rathe-ripes [Peas].. for poor and gravelly [Land]. **1825** BRITTON *Wiltsh. Words*, *Rathe-ripes* signifies early peas. **1874** T. HARDY *Far fr. Mad. Crowd* II. iii. 36 A Quarrington grafted on a Tom Putt, and a Rathe-ripe upon top o' that again. **1887** —— *Woodlanders* II. ix. 151 The mellow countenances of.. costards, stubbards, ratheripes.

ˈ**ratherish**, *adv. colloq.* [f. RATHER *adv.* 6 b + -ISH.] Somewhat, in a slight degree.

1862 in *New Yk. Tribune* (quoted in *Cent. Dict.*). **1887** *Library Mag.* (N.Y.) 12 Feb. 422 Longfellow, of whose poems Mr. Lang has a ratherish good opinion.

ˈ**ratherly**, *adv. Sc.* and *north. dial.* [f. RATHER *adv.* + -LY².] = RATHER *adv.*

1824 MACTAGGART *Gallovid. Encycl.* 162 He was ratherly what was called a jobber. **1830** J. WILSON in *Blackw. Mag.* XXVIII. 835 Whose looks gar you ratherly incline to the ither side. **1894** HALL CAINE *Manxman* II. i. 53 His deep voice that.. trembled ratherly.

†ˈ**rathermore**, *a. Obs. rare*⁻¹. [f. RATHER *a.* + -MORE.] Earlier, former.

1382 WYCLIF *Job* viii. 8 Aske the rathermor ieneracioun, and bisili enserche the mynde of the faders.

ˈ**rathest**, *a. Obs.* exc. *dial.* or *arch.* [Superl. of RATHE *a.*¹] †**a.** Quickest, soonest, most preferable, etc. *Obs.* **b.** Earliest.

c **888** K. ÆLFRED *Boeth.* xvi. §3 Swa hit is nu hraðost to secȝanne.. þæt nan wuht [etc.]. *a* **900** *O.E. Chron.* (Parker MS.) an. 755 þa þider urnon swa hwelc swa þonne ȝearo wearþ & raðost. *c* **1420** *Pallad. on Husb.* I. 753 Thyn assis donge is rathest forto dight A gardyn with; sheep donge is next of myght. **1556** LAUDER *Tractate* (1864) I Vnto quhose actionis, in speciall, suld Kyngis geue rathest attendence. **1611** CORYAT *Crudities* 68 Barley almost ripe to be cut, whereas in England they seldome cut the rathest before the beginning of August. **1633** W. VAUGHAN *Direct. Health* 55, I will begin with strawberies, as the first and rathest fruit in the beginning of summer. **1892** JANE BARLOW *Irish Idylls* 221 Blackberries.. in their rathest immaturity.

ˈ**rathest**, *adv.* [Superl. of RATHE *adv.*]

†**1.** Soonest, most readily. Also *the rathest*. *Obs.*

c **888** K. ÆLFRED *Boeth.* xxxiv. §10 þær hit ȝefret þæt hit hraðost weaxan mæȝ & latost wealowian. *c* **1000** ÆLFRIC *Hom.* I. 512 þone fisc ðe hine hraðost forswelhð, ȝeopena his muð. **1362** LANGL. *P. Pl.* A. v. 186 He that repenteth rathest schulde arysen aftur, and greten sir Gloten. *a* **1400–50** *Alexander* 726 The hyest thyng raþest heldes oþer while. **1437** in *Wars Eng. in France* (1864) II. Pref. 69, I beseech you.. to purvey some way how I shall mowe rathest neghe payment.. of the said somme. **1553** GRIMALDE *Cicero's Offices* I. (1558) 53 What race of life they would the rathest run. **1597** BACON *Coulers Gd. & Evill* i. (Arb.) 139 Whome next themselues they would rathest commend.

†**2.** Earliest. *Obs.*

1387–8 T. USK *Test. Love* I. v. (Skeat) I. 30 Nat the strongest; but he that rathest com and lengest abood. *c* **1420** *Pallad. on Husb.* III. 151 The rathest rypyng grapes.

3. Most of all, most particularly, 'chiefest'.

1549 CHALONER *Erasm. on Folly* I iij b, If any sainct amongs other, semeth rathest to be newfounde or poeticall [etc.]. *c* **1555** CAVENDISH *Wolsey* (1885) 162 God, whom I ought most rathest to have obeyed. **1619** W. SCLATER *Exp. 1 Thess.* (1630) 248 Both, perhaps, had place in this people; rathest the latter. **1644** HUME *Hist. Douglas* 28 The enemie .. not knowing which to pursue rathest, he might the better escape. *Ibid.* 248 He means rathest (as I think) George, now Lord Hume. **1884** B. POTTER *Jrnl.* 27 Oct. (1966) 107, I would rathest of all copy the raised plaques of Wedgwood.

rathir, -ur, -yr, obs. ff. RATHER.

rathite (ˈrɑːtaɪt, ˈræθaɪt). *Min.* [ad. G. *rathit* (H. Baumhauer 1896, in Zeitschr. f. Kryst. und Min. XXVI. 594), f. the name of G. vom *Rath* (1830–88), German mineralogist: see -ITE¹.] Any of a group of sulpharsenites of lead found in the Binnental in southern Switzerland.

1897 *Mineral. Mag.* XI. 225 Characteristic of rathite, but not invariably present, are parallel systems of very fine striæ .. on the crystal faces and on the fractured faces. **1905** [see HUTCHINSONITE]. **1953** *Amer. Mineralogist* XXXVIII. 330 Weissenberg and precession camera studies on baumhauerite, dufrenoysite and rathite, lead to the following new structural dara... Rathite-II is monoclinic. .. The unit cell dimensions do not agree with previous structural or morphological data on rathite, although they were obtained on a fragment of the original material. **1965** *Zeitschr. für Kristallogr.* CXXII. 434 Rathite-I, $(Pb,Tl)_3As_4(As,Ag)S_{10}$, is a mineral of a sulfosalt group, to which rathite-II, rathite-III, rathite-IV, dufrenoysite, baumhauerite and scleroclase belong. *Ibid.*, Rathite-I and -III form two modifications of a single species and should perhaps have a name different from rathite-II... In the Lengenbach quarry rathite-II is frequently found, whereas rathite-I occurs rarely, and then usually polysynthetically twinned. **1974** *Neues Jahrb. für Mineral.: Monatshefte* 530 Several kinds of minerals which belong to a group of lead sulfarsenites called 'rathite group' have been found in Lengenbach quarry (Ct. Wallis, Switzerland) and crystallographically investigated. The existence of two common periods of about 7·9 Å and 8·4 Å is a marked characteristic of them.

Rathke ('rɑːtkə). *Anat.* [The name of Martin Heinrich *Rathke* (1793–1860), German anatomist, who described the structure in 1838 (*Arch. für Anat., Physiol. und Wissenschaftl. Med.* 482).] ***Rathke's pouch*** or ***pocket*** (also ***pouch of Rathke***): a diverticulum of the oral cavity, which in developing vertebrates forms the anterior lobe of the pituitary body.

1889 A. MACALISTER *Textbk. Human Anat.* 620 The stomodæum joined the oral end of the mesenteron at about the fourteenth day and from its upper part is projected the hypophysial pouch of Rathke. **1892** E. L. MARK tr. *O. Hertwig's Textbk. Embryol.* xiv. 285 Even after the rupture of the pharyngeal membrane there is retained, in front of its attachment, a small pit, which constitutes Rathke's pocket. **1906, 1915** [see HYPOPHYSIS 3]. **1945** W. J. HAMILTON et al. *Human Embryol.* x. 153 An ectodermal diverticulum, Rathke's pouch, arises from the stomatodaeal roof. *Ibid.* xii. 253 Rathke's pouch loses its attachment to the pharyngeal roof..and develops into the various subdivisions of the anterior lobe of the definitive hypophysis. **1962** [see PARS INTERMEDIA]. **1973** F. BECK et al. *Human Embryol. & Genetics* xvii. 188 The thickening in the anterior wall of Rathke's pouch becomes the *pars anterior* of the adult pituitary gland.

rathoffite, erron. form of ROTHOFFITE.

'rat-hole, *sb.* [RAT *sb.*[1] 7.] **1.** A hole used by a rat for passage or abode. Also *fig.*, a cramped or squalid building, room, or the like; a refuge or hiding-place. Also *attrib.*

1812 H. & J. SMITH *Rej. Addr., Hampsh. Farmer's Addr.* (1833) 32 Who routed you from a rat-hole..to perch you in a palace? **1879** O. W. HOLMES *Motley* xviii. 129 The police set on the track of the writer to find his rathole if possible. **1879** [see *junk-shop* s.v. JUNK *sb.*[2] 5]. **1912** *Dialect Notes* III. 581 He wouldn't know enough to pound sand in a rat-hole; so don't get him. **1922** D. H. LAWRENCE *Let.* 30 Apr. (1962) II. 701 Yet I don't believe in Buddha—hate him in fact—his rat-hole temples and his rat-hole religion. **1941** M. U. SCHAPPES *Let.* 21 July in *Lett. from Tombs* (1941) 85 The rat-hole: a hotel where state's-witnesses are kept! *a***1944** K. DOUGLAS *Alamein to Zem Zem* (1946) 133 We stayed in our positions, like a terrier at a rat-hole. **1976** 'B. SHELBY' *Great Pebble Affair* 164 The warehouse is..a dummy warehouse designed to mask our rathole. **1976** N. THORNBURG *Cutter & Bone* iii. 80 Mo was not just frigid,..she was dead, a cadaver with a welded womb and a cunt like a rathole, full of dust and bits of straw and feathers from old nests.

2. *Oil industry.* **a.** A shallow hole drilled near a well hole to accommodate the kelly or a pipe joint when it is not in use. **b.** A hole of smaller diameter drilled at the bottom of a larger hole.

1921 W. H. JEFFERY *Deep Well Drilling* v. 209 Some rotary drillers drill a shallow well at a point midway and in front of the slush pumps, in which they rest the drill stem when not in use or when waiting to set in another joint of drill pipe. This is termed the 'rat hole'. **1939** D. HAGER *Fund. Petroleum Industry* ix. 210 When the kelly is deep enough for a joint of drill stem, the kelly and bit are pulled out. The kelly is set to one side, fitting in a hole (the 'rat-hole') cut in the floor of the derrick. **1972** L. M. HARRIS *Introd. Deepwater Floating Drilling Operations* xvi. 164 During and immediately following the unloading of the water cushion and the rathole mud, the surface pressure is determined by the amount of fluid to be unloaded. **1975** G. ANDERSON *Coring* v. 89 Most diamond coring is now done in the full diameter of the borehole. Whether coring is done this way or in a rat hole depends on the full gauge-keeping ability of the rock bits used prior to initiating the coring operation.

3. *N. Amer.* A seemingly bottomless hole; used *fig.* or allusively of something that demands excessive expenditure.

1961 in WEBSTER. **1975** D. LAMBRO *Federal Rathole* vi. 43 The contractor was refused..additional loan money because..it would be 'pouring money down a rathole'. **1976** *Globe & Mail* (Toronto) 21 Dec. 7/1 The committee will examine..Minaki Lodge, the rathole in northwestern Ontario down which increasing quantities of public money seem to be disappearing. **1977** *Time* 19 Dec. 13/2 Since the B-1 bomber will not be part of our military inventory, to build two more airplanes would simply amount to pouring half a billion dollars down a rathole.

'rat-hole, *v.* [f. prec.] **1.** *intr.* and *trans.* *Oil Industry.* To drill a hole of smaller diameter at the bottom of (one of larger diameter).

1922 L. C. SANDS in D. T. Day *Handbk. Petroleum Industry* 268 If the oil stratum should inadvertently be penetrated before the casing has been set and all water excluded from overlying formations, it will be expensive, if not impossible, to make a successful producer of the well. To forestall this danger it is common practice to 'rat-hole' ahead at intervals. **1939** D. HAGER *Fund. Petroleum Industry* ix. 228 If the sand is expected, the hole can be reduced and 'ratholed' ahead, a smaller hole being drilled.

2. To hide or store; not to invest or spend (money).

1948 *Amer. Speech* XXII. 220 Stashing was overt and frequently a co-operative enterprise, whereas to *rat-hole* implied that an individual was storing something of possibly public property for his own use. **1971** *Wall St. Jrnl.* 17 June 1/5 Everyone ratholed their money last year. Then they saw the (economic) situation hasn't changed so they decided if they're going to buy, now's the time to do it. **1977** *New Yorker* 4 July 55/1 Speaker said he was 'ratholing' the Jif jar. He was not ready to pay the Internal Revenue Service any portion of the gold's value (his privilege until it is sold).

Rathskeller, rathskeller ('rɑːtskɛlə(r)). Also **ratskeller**. [ad. G. *ratskeller* (formerly *rathskeller*), f. *rat* council as in RATHAUS + *-s* gen. ending + *keller* cellar.

The form *rathskeller* was preferred to avoid the phonetic association with RAT *sb.*[1] + CELLAR *sb.*]

a. A cellar in a German town hall in which beer or wine is sold. **b.** An underground beer-hall or restaurant. Also *transf.*

1900 ADE *More Fables* 159 Mr. Byrd..happened to be in a Rathskeller not far away. **1903** *Current Lit.* Apr. 495/2 The first rathskeller was established in New York in 1863 by Fred. Hollander. **1916** *Harper's Mag.* Dec. 18 He likes the religious cool of the rathskeller... He takes his ease in his inn. **1929** *Papers Mich. Acad. Sci., Arts & Lett.* X. 318/1 *Rathskeller*, a dugout. **1934** S. R. NELSON *All about Jazz* vi. 121 They used to work the *Rathskellers* or night-clubs of the lower grades. **1946** E. O'NEILL *Iceman Cometh* (1947) I. 27 It's the No Chance Saloon. It's Bedrock Bar, The End of the Line Café, The Bottom of the Sea Rathskeller! **1969** *Courier-Mail* (Brisbane) 30 June 3/4 The ratskeller will be a 'cellar, with barrels of wine and beer, where people will dine at leisure'. **1975** *Country Life* 11 Dec. 1676/1 The *Rathaus* or town hall..stands in the cobbled market square with the usual *Ratskeller* for refreshments.

ratian, obs. form of RATION *sb.*

raticide ('rætɪsaɪd). Also **ratticide**. [f. RAT *sb.*[1] + -I- + -CIDE.] **a.** One who, or that which, kills rats, esp. a chemical substance used as a rat poison. **b.** *rare.* The killing of rats.

1847 W. J. BRODERIP *Zool. Recreations* 319 The celebrated ratticide Billy has long since gone to that bourne whence neither rats, dogs, nor travellers ever return. **1908** W. R. BOELTER *Rat Problem* iv. 146 Raticide. This preparation.. is manufactured in the United States, where it is sold under the name of Azra. **1922** *Jrnl. R. Sanitary Inst.* XLII. 316 Practical experience..supports the view that the safety margin for Squills is greater than for any other practical raticide at present in use. **1936** *Times* 21 Aug. 11/5 The end of real research into effective raticides. **1941** *Nature* 1 Mar. 263/1 Guidance in production, research and application as relating to insecticides, fungicides, raticides and repellents for all purposes. **1976** *New Scientist* 26 Aug. 454/2 William Kotzwinkle's *Doctor Rat* is a comic triumph. About half is narrated by a mad laboratory rat, whose perceptions into the relationship between mass ratticide and grantsmanship do make delightful satire.

†'ratifactory, *a.* *Obs. rare*[−1]. [Irreg. f. RATIFY *v.* Cf. *ratificatory*.] Confirmatory.

1720 STRYPE *Stow's Surv.* (1754) I. I. xv. 76/1 This was a second instrument..ratifactory of his privileges as Constable of the Tower.

ratifia, -fie, obs. forms of RATAFIA.

ratification (rætɪfɪ'keɪʃən). [a. F. *ratification* (1358 in Godef. *Compl.*) or ad. med.L. *ratificātio* (1228 in Du Cange), n. of action f. *ratificāre* to RATIFY.] The action of ratifying or confirming; sanction, confirmation, approval. Also *attrib.*

ratification meeting (U.S.), a meeting held for the purpose of expressing approval of the nominations made by a political party.

1451 *Rolls of Parlt.* V. 221/1 Any Graunte or Grauntes, Ratifications or Confirmations, made by us. **1526** TAYLOR in Ellis *Orig. Lett.* Ser. II. I. 333 The Trety of Peace with ratificacion of the Kyngs oone hande. **1543–4** *Act 35 Hen. VIII*, c. 3 (*title*) An acte for the ratification of the Kinges maiesties style. **1612** T. TAYLOR *Comm. Titus* iii. 8 They stand not so much vpon ratifications and asseuerations. **1667** PEPYS *Diary* 16 Aug., Every body wonders that we have no news..of the ratification of the Peace. **1759** ROBERTSON *Hist. Scot.* I. II. 79 The day appointed for the ratification of the treaty with England. **1828** SCOTT *F.M. Perth* ix, Till such ratification, the contract was liable to be broken off. **1848** *Campaign* (Washington, D.C.) 21 June 64/2 A great democratic ratification meeting was held at New Orleans on the night of the 8th June. **1861** TRENCH *Comm. Ep. seven Ch.* (ed. 2) 17 God's own seal and ratification of his own word. **1864** *Daily Tel.* 12 July, Monday night they had a ratification meeting in this city. **1904** *N.Y. Even. Post* 23 June 2/6 The first Roosevelt ratification meeting..will be held this evening..when the Republican Club of the Thirty-first Assembly District will endorse the nominees of the Chicago convention.

ratifi'cationist. [f. RATIFICATION + -IST.] One who favours ratification (of a treaty, etc.).

1921 *Glasgow Herald* 23 Dec. 7/3 On the ratificationists' side it had been suggested that there should be a time limit to speeches.

†ratificatory, *a.* *Sc. Obs. rare*[−1]. [f. ppl. stem of med.L. *ratificāre* to RATIFY. Cf. obs. F. *ratificatoire* (1493 in Godef.).] = RATIFACTORY.

1639 in Aikman *Hist. Scot.* III. v. 531 Whereof those acts of Parliament were ratificatory.

ratified ('rætɪfaɪd), *ppl. a.* *rare.* [f. RATIFY *v.* + -ED[1].] Settled, confirmed.

1644 HAMMOND *Pract. Catech.* I. §3 Wks. 1684 I. 27 God ..consequently will accept the will for the deed, if it be a firm and ratified will.

Hence **†'ratifiedly** *adv.*, positively. *Obs.*

1593 NASHE *Christ's T.* Wks. (Grosart) IV. 179 Wilt thou ratifiedly affirm that God is no God because..thou canst not essentially see him?

ratifier ('rætɪfaɪə(r)). [f. next + -ER[1].] One who or that which ratifies.

1602 SHAKS. *Ham.* IV. v. 105 The Ratifiers and props of euery word. **1742** E. CARTER tr. *Algarotti on Newton's Theory* I. ii. 94 A chief Magistrate, who is only the Ratifier and Guardian of the Laws of Nature. **1832** in WEBSTER.

ratify ('rætɪfaɪ), *v.* Forms: 4–6 **ratefie**, (6 **-fye**); 5–6 **ratyfye**, (7 **-fie**); 4–7 **ratifie**, (5 *Sc.* **-fii**, 6 *Sc.* **-fe**; also 5 **radifie**, **ratiffye**, 6 **-ffie**), 5–6 **ratifye**, 6– **ratify**. [a. F. *ratifier* (1294 in Godef. *Compl.*), ad. med.L. *ratificāre* (1228 in Du Cange): see RATE *sb.*[1] and *a.*, and -FY.]

1. *trans.* To confirm or make valid (an act, compact, promise, etc.) by giving consent, approval, or formal sanction (esp. to what has been done or arranged for by another).

*c***1357** *Lay Folks Catech.* 569 (T.) Our fadir the ercebisshop..ratifies als-so that othir men gifes. **1439** *Rolls of Parlt.* V. 10/2 The whiche your seid Giftes and Grauntes, it hath liked you..to ratifie, conferme and appreve. **1469** in *Exch. Rolls Scotl.* VII. 618 We ratifii and approvis this charter in all poyntis. **1549** DUKE OF SOMERSET in Ellis *Orig. Lett.* Ser. I. II. 174 Their agreement and conclusion to be established and ratified by Parlyament. **1579** FENTON *Guicciard.* III. (1599) 107 To ratifie..the auncient friendship with a new peace. **1633** P. FLETCHER *Purple Isl.* I. iv, When the shepherd-lads with common voice Their first consent had firmly ratifi'd. **1667** PEPYS *Diary* 9 Aug., He tells me..it is supposed the peace is ratified at Bredah. **1774** PENNANT *Tour Scotl. in 1772*, 122 The endowment was ratified by the Pope's bull. **1840** THIRLWALL *Greece* lvi. VII. 125 The compact was ratified by a solemn reconciliation between the contending parties. **1879** GREEN *Read. Eng. Hist.* xviii. 90 The terms which he had come to ratify had been settled beforehand.

absol. **1838** THIRLWALL *Greece* xxxviii. V. 69 Asking whether the Thebans would permit the Bœotian towns to ratify for themselves.

†b. To confirm, to guarantee or ensure the fulfilment of (a purpose, hope, etc.). *Obs.*

1596 DRAYTON *Legends* iii. 551 The King suspending, should He not consent, To ratifie the Baronies intent. *c***1611** CHAPMAN *Iliad* XXIV. 270 Pray..that he will deine to vse His most lou'd bird, to ratifie thy hopes. **1649** BP. REYNOLDS *Hosea* vi. 91 God..onely can ratifie all our pious resolutions.

†c. To confirm the possession of. *Obs. rare*[−1].

1611 BIBLE *1 Macc.* xi. 34 We haue ratified vnto them the borders of Iudea.

2. To declare or confirm the truth or correctness of (a statement, etc.). Now *rare* or *Obs.*

*c***1400** MAUNDEV. (Roxb.) xxxiv. 156 Þe Pape hase ratified and confermed my buke in all poyntes. **1548–9** (Mar.) *Bk. Com. Prayer* Offices 9 They may then..with their owne mouth..ratifie and confesse the same. **1558** in *Vicary's Anat.* (1888) App. III. 139 The names..werre here red, ratefyed and allowyd. **1631** WEEVER *Anc. Funeral Mon.* 357 The prophesie..thus ratified by the euent. **1671** J. WEBSTER *Metallogr.* iii. 50 To ratifie this,..I shall relate what I my self have found. **1754** SHERLOCK *Disc.* (1759) I. i. 30 This Revelation..has been ratified by the blood of Christ and His Apostles. **1826** LAMB *Elia* Ser. II. *Sanity True Genius*, The transitions in this episode are..as violent as in the most extravagant dream, and yet the waking judgement ratifies them.

†3. To consummate, carry out, bring to fulfilment or completion. *Obs. rare.*

1561 in *Child-Marriages* (1896) 3 This deponent verilie belevis that the said matrimonie was neuer ratefied. **1562** *Ibid.* 76 The said Henrie Price did not ratifie the said matrymonie bie carnall copulacion. *c***1720** *Ship in a Storm* vii, Too soon the rolling Ruin came And ratify'd the Wreck.

†4. To confirm in faith or courage. *Obs. rare.*

1559 in Strype *Ann. Ref.* (1824) I. II. App. vi. 406 One chief pointe of spiritual government is to confirme his brethren, and ratifie them..by holsome doctryne. **1598–9** E. FORDE *Parismus* II. (1661) 227 Those that were also maimed and wounded..were..every one kindly ratified by Marcellus.

†5. To fix the rate or price of. *Obs. rare*[−1].

1511 *Galway Arch.* in *10th Rep. Hist. MSS. Comm.* App. V. 394 Corne or grayne that comith..to be sold in the market place shall be sold and ratiffied according the plentines of the yere.

Hence **'ratifying** *vbl. sb.* and *ppl. a.*

1555 W. WATREMAN *Fardle Facions* II. xii. 278 A confirming, a ratifieng,..of that went before. **1611** SPEED *Hist. Gt. Brit.* VI. xxxix. §4. 142 Vpon the ratifyings of his election by the Senate at Rome, hee hasted not thither. **1714** J. WYETH *Suppl. T. Ellwood's Life* (1765) 411 That which was the most ratifying of all His bodily Sufferings. **1829** SOUTHEY *All for Love* IX. xlii, Ye shall now in thunder hear Heaven's ratifying voice!

†ratihabit, *v.* *Sc. Obs.* [f. ppl. stem of med.L. *ratihabēre*: see RATIHABITION.] *trans.* To express approval or sanction of.

1678 SIR G. MACKENZIE *Crim. Law Scot.* II. viii. §7. 391 He had given orders to beat them, or ratihabited the beating of them. **1680** in Wodrow *Hist. Ch. Scot.* (1833) III. 227 That they treasonably owned the rebels at Bothwell..and ratihabited the same.

†ratihabitation. *Obs. rare.* [ad. med.L. *ratihabitatio*, irreg. var. *ratihabitio*.] = next.

1502 *Ord. Crysten Men* (W. de W. 1506) IV. vii. 187 Ratyhabytacyon..hath not power nor place in suche case. **1650** ELDERFIELD *Tythes* 80 Our next [gift] must be of ratihabitation or confirmation.

ratihabition (rætɪhə'bɪʃən). *Law.* [ad. late L. *ratihabitio* (Digesta), f. *ratum* confirmed (RATE *a.*[1]) + *habēre* to have, hold. Cf. obs. F. *ratihabition* (Godef.).] Approval, sanction.

1561 *Reg. Privy Council Scot.* I. 180 The said spulye wes committit of the causing, command, assistence, and ratihabitioun of the said Thomas. **1610** BP. HALL *Apol. Brownists* 20 Cannot the Ratihabition (as the Lawyers speake) bee drawne backe? **1672** H. STUBBE *Justif. Dutch War* 41 A ratihabition in deeds is more powerful, than a ratihabition in words. **1729** W. REEVE *Serm.* 234 Christ appearing to the Apostles..adds a promise of Ratihabition. **1810** LD. CAMPBELL in *Life* (1881) I. ix. 248, I make no doubt I shall still have your ratihabition of the step I have taken. **1875** STUBBS *Const. Hist.* III. xx. 425 They had letters of commission or of 'ratihabition', or powers of attorney.

ratil(le, obs. forms of RATTLE.

ratin(e, obs. forms of RATTEEN[1].

ratine (rə'ti:n). Also ‖**ratiné** (ratine). [Fr., pa. pple. of *ratiner* to frieze.] A clothing fabric of rough open texture.

1913–14 *T. Eaton & Co. Catal.* Fall & Winter 17 The materials for Suits are very beautiful..Whipcords, Corduroys, Boucle Tweeds, Ratines. **1922** *Daily Mail* 15 Nov. 1 (Advt.), All-silk ratine. For frocks, children's wear, furnishings. **1923** *Westm. Gaz.* 22 Mar. 9/2 Mrs. Almond's blue ratine looked as if it had just descended on her and had been made in heaven. **1934** WEBSTER, *Ratiné*... Also *ratine*. **1966** *Vogue* Dec. 71 White ratine tunic dress. **1967** *Times* 21 Feb. 9/1 Ratiné..was launched, or rather re-launched, at the French prêt-à-porter fair last year. **1969** N. W. PARSONS *Upon Sagebrush Harp* xi. 57 We noticed a long cobweb floating over our heads... Long silvery strands moving through the motionless air from west to east. Each was like a white ratiné string, fine as silk except for knots at irregular intervals.

rating ('reɪtɪŋ), *vbl. sb.*[1] [f. RATE *v.*[1] + -ING[1].]

1. a. The action of the vb., in various senses.

1534 *Act 26 Hen. VIII*, c. 3 §10 In the makinge and ratinge of the sayde yerely values. **1545** BRINKLOW *Complaynt* 15 b, By the parcyal act of ratyng of vytellys. **1596** SPENSER *State Irel.* Wks. (Globe) 663/2 What rating of rents meane you? **1764** BURN *Poor Laws* 129 Rating of the wages of servants, artificers, and labourers, is also..of very ancient date. **1858** BRIGHT *Sp., Reform* 21 Dec. (1876) 308 The system of rating forms the basis of the elective franchise. **1884** *B'ham Daily Post* 23 Dec. 3/5 Watch-jobber wanted; one who thoroughly understands the cleaning and rating of Chronometers.

b. The (*or* an) amount fixed as a rate.

1887 S. D. HORTON *Silver Pound* 77 A suggestion to change..the permitted rating of the Guinea in Government offices. **1896** *Allbutt's Syst. Med.* I. 481 The practice of applying an extra rating for residence in the tropics..has been found to work fairly on the whole.

attrib. **1866** BRIGHT *Sp., Reform* 13 Mar. (1876) 345 In Ireland they had a £12 rating franchise. **1893** *Times* 25 Apr. 5/5 Persons with a £20 rating qualification.

2. *Naut.* **a.** 'The station a person holds on the ship's books' (Smyth); also *transf.*, position, class, etc., in general.

1702 *Lond. Gaz.* No. 3815/3 The Names, Qualities or Ratings of the Company of such Man of War. **1840** MARRYAT *Poor Jack* ii, As he no longer did the duty of coxswain,..he was not entitled to the rating. **1853** DE QUINCEY *Autobiog. Sk.* Wks. I. 150 When my 'rating', or graduation in the school, was to be settled. **1891** *Daily News* 16 June 3/6 The third match was between yachts not exceeding a rating of twenty tons.

b. In *pl.* Men of a certain rating.

1893 *Westm. Gaz.* 2 Dec. 3/2 We certainly cannot build lieutenants in 3½ years! whilst in all engine-room ratings we are still more behindhand. **1906** *Ibid.* 6 June 6/2 The cruiser ..landed fourteen officers, 290 ratings, and eighty-five marines. **1925** *Nation* 26 Sept. 756/2 Numerous ground ratings are needed to handle airships in and out of the hangars in addition to a very considerable repair staff of specially skilled ratings. **1932** *Daily Express* 27 Jan. 1/2 Many of the ratings belong to Portsmouth, and some are married and have families. **1955** *Times* 12 May 7/5 Two naval ratings, both aged 19, were arrested on board H.M.S. Ark Royal. **1979** *Jrnl. R. Soc. Arts* CXXVII. 545/2 Six scholarships for deck ratings were awarded.

3. The value of a property which is claimed to be standard or limiting for a piece of equipment or a material, or to be necessary for its optimal or standard use; a rated value (RATED *ppl. a.*[1] 2).

Quot. 1893 repr. the action of RATE *v.*[1] 8 rather than the result.

1893 *Trans. Amer. Inst. Electr. Engineers* X. 260 This wire was quite uniform in diameter, and gave evidence of careful rating. The curve of rating should be of the same general equation as that of fusion, since both represent isothermal conditions. **1905** *Jrnl. Inst. Electr. Engineers* XXXV. 367 The 'normal carrying capacity' or 'rating' of a fuse wire may be defined as: The maximum current which the fuse is capable of carrying continuously without deterioration or undue heating. **1916** *Standardization Rules Amer. Inst. Electr. Engineers* 25 A transformer of given kv-a rating must be capable of delivering the rated output at rated secondary voltage. **1941** E. MOLLOY *Aero-Engine Pract.* 57 The rating of an aero-engine is prepared not with the mere hope that it may be suitable for some aircraft or other, but with the intention of fulfilling a definite specification, whether civil or military. **1967** G. ARNOLD *Re-Wiring House* 19 Cables used in house wiring usually operate at below their maximum current rating. **1967** M. CHANDLER *Ceramics in Mod. World* iv. 123 This enables the insulator to be operated at higher ratings than would otherwise be possible. **1968** MILLER & SAWERS *Techn. Devel. Mod. Aviation* iii. 94 The fuel used in the 1920's was no better than that sold for cars, with an octane rating of about 50. **1969** *Jane's Freight Containers 1968–69* 12/1 *Rating*, means the maximum gross weight and is the maximum permissible combined weight of the freight container and of its contents. **1974** *Homes & Gardens* Apr. 150/2 The fuse rating is given in the accompanying instruction book as well as being clearly marked on the appliance rating plate. **1978** *Amateur Photographer* 2 Aug. 131/1 It is important that the total current drawn from all sockets should not exceed the rating of the supply socket—13 or 15-amp.

4. a. An assessment or measure (of a person's achievement, behaviour, skill, status, etc.); a grade, category or standing.

1921 A. W. PROCTER *Princ. Public Personnel Admin.* viii. 162 A rating of individual efficiency is intended to be a measurement of the value of the services rendered throughout a given period of time by an individual employee. **1939** [see DATING *vbl. sb.* c]. **1948** B. G. M. GUNDKLER *Bantu Prophets S. Afr.* iv. 88 The farmer has certain definite rules for social rating. **1951** M. MCLUHAN *Mech. Bride* (1967) 58/2 Culture ratings à la Emily Post are not often made in accordance with the consumer mentality. *Ibid.* 59/2 Woe to the indigent intellectual who accidentally acquires a 'high' rating without the economic appendages. **1964** M. ARGYLE *Psychol. & Social Probl.* xi. 138 Suppose a firm selects personnel by interviewing applicants. We can find out how effective this is by comparing ratings (or the rank-order) of candidates made by the interviewer with their subsequent success at the job. **1968** *Listener* 6 June 748/2 There is to be a ballot during the interval to determine which of three works..should be repeated after the interval. One doesn't have to think very long to discover how invidious this could turn out to be. First performances are quite bad enough for the composers concerned without their having to worry about Instant Popularity Ratings as well. **1974** *Plain Dealer* (Cleveland, Ohio) 26 Oct. 4-D/4 Many sports publications may have underestimated the Cavaliers in the pre-season ratings.

b. *Broadcasting.* Usu. *pl.* orig. **Crossley rating** [from Archibald M. *Crossley* who in 1930 began the regular reports of the Cooperative Analysis of Broadcasting]: an estimate, based on statistical sampling, of the size of the audience of any particular radio or television programme; its popularity so assessed.

1939 *Business Week* 25 Feb. 36/2 You've heard some radio comedian crack, after getting off a poor gag, 'There goes my Crossley'. He is referring to his popularity rating with one of the services that measure..the size of radio listening audiences. **1940** *Time* 29 Jan. 50/2 In the radio business, 'Crossley ratings' are the official box-office count. Crossley's boss is the Cooperative Analysis of Broadcasting, instituted eleven years ago..and now subscribed to by 635 sponsors. **1941** G. MARX *Groucho Lett.* (1967) 47 The Tommy Riggs show, which I spurned, now has a Crosley rating of seventeen... This will give you an idea of how little I know about audiences and what they want. **1947** *Billboard* 1 Nov. 3 The majority of new shows on the air—so far at least—are failing to show evidence of any particular rating strength. This is especially true when ratings are related to talent budgets. **1952** H. V. GROHMANN *Advertising Terminol.* 64 *Rating*, the popularity test for a specific show. **1959** *Daily Mail* 11 Aug. 8/8 According to the ratings, the only court of public opinion that counts in these circles, Hylton shows are successful. **1962** *Times* 19 May 4/3 Public-service broadcasting, free from 'the tyranny of the ratings'. **1971** *Daily Tel.* 2 Aug. 7/4 Though the two BBC channels between them still share the ratings with ITV on a 50–50 basis, the trend is sufficiently strong to alarm the major companies. **1977** *Time* 7 Feb. 40/3 The hokiness of Hollywood fame got to him too. He would say, 'Even my friendships are related to ratings.'

5. *attrib.* and *Comb.*, as (sense 1) ***rating area, authority***; (sense 2) ***rating badge***; (sense 3) ***rating point, scale***; (sense 4 b) ***ratings battle, issue, terms, war***.

1928 *Britain's Industr. Future* (Liberal Industr. Inquiry) v. 408 Rating areas should be drastically revised with a view to a more equal distribution of the burden of rates. **1962** L. GOLDING *Dict. Local Govt.* 328 Rating authorities, i.e., the local authorities responsible for levying and collection of rates, are the councils of county boroughs and county districts. **1910** *Our Navy* (U.S.) Apr. 19/1 A following the sea Is plenty good enough for me, Since I've got a ratin' badge tacked on my arm. **1921** *Sea Bag* (U.S.S.S. Oklahoma) 22 June 2/1 How many men suddenly wake up to the fact that they haven't watch-marks on their jumpers or rating-badges on their sleeves? **1976** *Sun* (Baltimore) 16 May A12/4 Since it [*sc.* Washington] is a bigger TV market than Baltimore, it costs more for a political advertisement. The price in Washington is $90 a rating point. In Baltimore it is $50 a rating point. In Baltimore, a rating point represents about 7,500 homes. **1974** *Times* 15 Oct. 16/6 The silly ratings battle..claims about the number of viewers watching each channel. **1927** *Scribner's Mag.* Apr. 418/2 One institution, in its confidential rating scale to be filled out by the school principal,..and others.., asks..as to 'moral earnestness, loyalty,..modesty'. **1967** M. ARGYLE *Psychol. Interpersonal Behaviour* v. 102 Another method [of measuring competence] is to use ratings: a number of rating scales are devised covering various aspects of a task, and are filled in by special observers. **1958** *Wall St. Jrnl.* 28 Nov. 1/6 Behind the ratings issue is the bigger question of whether the big TV networks, including the Columbia Broadcasting system, National Broadcasting Co. and American Broadcasting Co., should come under Federal regulation. **1977** *TV Times* (Brisbane) 13 Aug. 11/1 Australian ratings terms have been revised to incorporate the introduction of colour TV and consequent multi-set use in many homes. **1980** *Times* 25 Jan. 19/6 The ratings war—the battle to win as many viewers as possible for a programme.

rating ('reɪtɪŋ), *vbl. sb.*[2] [f. RATE *v.*[2] + -ING[1].] The action of reproving, etc.; an instance of this.

1577 B. GOOGE *Heresbach's Husb.* (1586) 119 b, Least the stronger spoile the weaker, while hee dreadeth the rating and whipping. **1607** TOPSELL *Four-f. Beasts* (1658) 369 Horses and Dogs which live among men..do discern also their tearms of threatning, chiding and rating. **1667** PEPYS *Diary* (1877) V. 6, I was witness of a horrid rateing, which Mr. Ashburnham..did give him. **1854** MRS. GASKELL *North & S.* xxxi, I've helped old Mr. Leonards to give George a good rating. **1878** E. W. L. DAVIES *Mem. Rev. J. Russell* 299 A little rating and a few cracks of the whip, and their [hounds] heads are up.

'rating, *ppl. a.* [f. RATE *v.*[1]] Regulating.

1884 F. J. BRITTEN *Watch & Clockm.* 187 A screw..to receive the rating nut.

rating: see RETTING.

ratinia, obs. form of RATANHIA.

ratio ('reɪʃ(ɪ)əʊ), *sb.* [L., f. *rat-*, ppl. stem of *rērī* to think: see also RATION, REASON.]

1. a. Reason, rationale. *spec.* in *Law*, reason or rationale upon which a juridical decision is based; = *ratio decidendi* (see sense 1 b).

1636 MEDE *Reverence God's House* ii. Wks. (1672) 343 The true Ratio..of this Shecinah or Speciality of Divine Presence. **1752** WARBURTON *Serm.* i. Wks. 1811 IX. 16 Now, in this consists the ratio and essential ground of the Gospel-doctrine.

1964 G. ABRAHAMS *Police Questioning & Judges' Rules* i. 20 Therein, it is submitted, is the *ratio* of that decision against the admissibility of statements. **1971** *Mod. Law Rev.* XXXIV. vi. 691 The judge considered..that *Torquay Hotel Co.* v. *Cousins* was authority, 'that this tort of interference with contracts applies not only where there is interference with contracts already made but where there is interference with contracts to be made in accordance with a regular course of dealing.' Is this the *ratio* of the *Torquay* case? **1976** J. M. KELLY *Stud. Civil Judicature of Roman Republic* v. 112, I have, by negative implication, foreshadowed certain characteristics of the *unus iudex* inasmuch as the factors which form the *ratio* of the *centumviri* or *recuperatores* will not be present in his case. **1977** *Times* 23 Dec. 18/5 That restricted definition was unnecessary for the ratio of that decision.

b. In Lat. phrases, esp. *Philos.* and *Law*: **ratio cognoscendi**, that in virtue of which knowledge of something is possible; that in virtue of which something is known to exist; **ratio decidendi** (pl. **rationes decidendi**), rationale of judgment; a principle underlying and determining a judicial decision; **ratio essendi, existendi**, that in virtue of which something exists.

1830 W. HAMILTON in *Edin. Rev.* LII. 178 The existence of external things, which is given only *through* their intuition, it admits; the intuition itself, though the *ratio cognoscendi*, and *to us* therefore the *ratio essendi* of their reality, it rejects. **1862** in C. CLARK *House of Lords Cases* VIII. 392 The observations made by Members of the House, whether law Members or lay Members beyond the *ratio decidendi* which is propounded and acted upon in giving judgment, although they may be entitled to respect, are only to be followed in as far as they may be considered agreeable to sound reason and to prior authorities. **1865** S. H. HODGSON *Times & Space* vii. 488 Now both the cause, or ratio existendi, and the reason, or ratio cognoscendi, in every particular case must be given by actual experience. **1877** *Law Rep. Exchequer Division* II. 233 The ratio decidendi in these cases does not appear in the reports. **1890** W. JAMES *Princ. Psychol.* I. x. 337 But if the brand is the *ratio cognoscendi* of the belonging, the belonging, in the case of the herd, is in turn the *ratio existendi* of the brand. **1902** J. W. SALMOND *Jurisprudence* viii. 176 A precedent, therefore, is a judicial decision which contains in itself a principle. The underlying principle which thus forms its authoritative element is often termed the *ratio decidendi*. **1903** G. E. MOORE *Principia Ethica* iv. 127 Kant..admits that Freedom is the *ratio essendi* of the Moral Law, whereas the latter is only *ratio cognoscendi* of Freedom. **1923** C. D. BROAD *Sci. Thought* viii. 267 Sensa are..in some way the *ratio cognoscendi* of the physical world, whilst the physical world is..the *ratio essendi* of sensa. **1948** *Law Q. Rev.* LXIV. 463 The court is always at liberty to propound alternative rules of law, each of which it may elevate to the status of a ratio decidendi. **1970** *Internat. & Compar. Law Q.* XIX. i. 37 Which of these *rationes decidendi* possesses binding force? **1972** *Evangelical Q.* XLIV. 241 These activities compose the *ratio cognoscendi* of the pardoning grace of God; they make us aware of God's activity which is the *ratio essendi* that calls forth man's response. **1977** *Law Q. Rev.* XCIII. 378 The importance of the *ratio decidendi* is that it is the rule of law for which a case is authority.

2. a. *Math.* The relation between two similar magnitudes in respect of quantity, determined by the number of times one contains the other (integrally or fractionally).

This is sometimes distinguished as ***geometrical ratio*** (see GEOMETRICAL *a.* 1 b), in contrast to ***arithmetical ratio***, or the extent by which one magnitude exceeds another (now practically obs., though still mentioned in some text-books). For ***alternate, anharmonic, compound, duplicate*** (etc.) ***ratio***, see the adjectives.

1660 BARROW *Euclid* v. Def. 3 Ratio (or rate) is the mutual habitude or respect of two magnitudes of the same kind each to other, according to quantity. **1706** W. JONES *Syn. Palmar. Matheseos* 56 When two Ratio's are equal, the Terms that Compose them are said to be Geometrically Proportional. **1772** *Junius Lett.* lxviii. 356 The ratio..is exactly one to a hundred. **1854** BREWSTER *More Worlds* iv. 70 The matter of Jupiter is much lighter than the matter of our Earth, in the ratio of 24 to 100. **1884** tr. *Lotze's Logic* 114 Heat expands all bodies, but the ratios of the degree of expansion to an equal increase of temperature are different in different bodies.

b. The corresponding relationship between things not precisely measurable.

1808 SOUTHEY *Lett.* (1856) II. 66 Wishes to appropriate to himself the reputation which he had only a right to share, and that in no great ratio. **1820** LAMB *Elia* Ser. i. *South-Sea House*, Executorships..which excited his spleen or soothed his vanity in equal ratios. **1858** BUCKLE *Civiliz.* (1869) II. i. 103 The progress of knowledge bore the same ratio to the decline of ecclesiastical influence. **1872** LIDDON *Elem. Relig.* v. 174 The amount of will which we severally carry into the act of prayer is the ratio of its sincerity.

3. *spec.* In monetary science, the quantitative relation in which one metal stands to another in respect of their value as money or legal tender.

1879 E. CAZALET *Bimetallism* 26 Such a fixed ratio is eminently desirable for the welfare of all civilized nations. **1881** EVART in Horton *Silver Pound* (1887) 309 The adoption of the ratio of 15½ to 1, would accomplish the.. object with less disturbance in the monetary systems.. than any other ratio.

†**4.** = RATION *sb.* 3. *Obs.*

1760 STERNE *Tr. Shandy* III. xxxviii, A cow.. eat up two ratios and half of dried grass. **1806** A. DUNCAN *Nelson* 51 The Governor.. furnished the.. invaders with a ratio of biscuit and wine. **1824** LAMB *Elia* Ser. II. *Captain Jackson*, Sliding a slender ratio of Single Gloucester upon his wife's plate.

5. Special Comb.: **ratio detector** *Electronics*, an F.M. detector whose two output voltages are such that their sum is constant and their ratio, rather than their difference, is proportional to the ratio of the two applied frequency-dependent voltages, so that its insensitivity to changes in amplitude is not confined to the carrier frequency. Also RATIOMETER.

1947 *RCA Rev.* VIII. 201 A new circuit for f-m detection known as the ratio detector is coming into wide use. **1965** *Wireless World* July 8 (Advt.), Printed circuit for I.F. amplifiers and ratio detector. **1974** HARVEY & BOHLMAN *Stereo F.M. Radio Handbk.* v. 99 Normally, in a ratio detector of the balanced type, the centre-point of the load is earthed and the output signal is taken from the tertiary winding.

ratio ('reɪʃ(ɪ)əʊ), *v.* [f. the sb.] *trans.* To enlarge, amplify, or reduce by a certain ratio. So **'ratioed** *ppl. a.*, **'ratioing** *vbl. sb.*

1943 H. T. U. SMITH *Aerial Photographs* viii. 196 Each print which departs from the average scale or shows any apparent tilt is rectified and 'ratioed', or corrected for scale, by means of a projection printer. *Ibid.* 352 *Ratioed print*, a print prepared at a predetermined scale by photographic enlargement or reduction. **1970** J. A. HOWARD *Aerial Photo-Ecol.* ix. 105 Aerial photographs.. sometimes.. are enlarged or reduced in size for a special purpose. These photographs are then known as ratioed prints or ratioed photographs. **1978** *Nature* 9 Mar. 142/2 This ratioing operation reduces the effective amplitude fluctuations of the laser by more than 100-fold.

ratiocinable (ræʃɪ-, rætɪ'ɒsɪnəb(ə)l), *a. nonce-wd.* [f. RATIOCINATE *v.* + -ABLE.] Arrived at or deducible by reasoning.

1916 G. B. SHAW *Androcles & Lion* Pref. p. lxxxvii, An inveterate Roman Rationalist, always discarding the irrational real thing for the unreal but ratiocinable postulate.

†**rati'ocinant,** *a. nonce-wd.* [a. F. pr. pple. of *ratiociner* (see next), after scholastic L. *ratio ratiocinans.*] That reasons.

a **1693** *Urquhart's Rabelais* III. vi, I have not asked this question without cause causing, and reason truly very ratiocinant.

ratiocinate (ræʃɪ-, rætɪ'ɒsɪneɪt), *v.* [f. L. *ratiōcināt-*, ppl. stem of *ratiōcinārī* to calculate, deliberate, f. *ratio* RATIO *sb.* Cf. F. *ratiociner* (16th c. in Littré).] *intr.* To reason, to carry on a process of reasoning. Occas. *trans.* and *refl.* (Now *rare* in serious use.)

1643 DIGBY *Observ. Relig. Med.* (1644) 87 A Philosopher that should ratiocinate strictly and rigorously. **1678** CUDWORTH *Intell. Syst.* I. iii. §19 The Ax cuts for the sake of something, though it self does not ratiocinate. **1820** T. L. PEACOCK *Four Ages of Poetry* Wks. 1875 III. 333 Patriarchs.. who.. seemed to have ratiocinated in the following manner. **1887** R. L. STEVENSON *Merry Men* v. vi. 277 Don't ratiocinate with me—I cannot bear it. **1926** FOWLER *Mod. Eng. Usage* 483/2 *Ratiocinate* & its derivatives.. may fairly be pronounced rătĭ- rather than răshĭ-;.. the OED, however, gives only răshĭ-. **1934** C. P. SNOW *Search* II. iv. 180 Ratiocinating myself into honesty about my posturings.

Hence **rati'ocinating** *ppl. a.*; **rati'ocinated** *ppl. a.*

1694 MOTTEUX *Rabelais* v. xx. (1737) 89 My ratiocinating Faculty. **1896** *Daily News* 20 Jan. 7/1 All the ratiocinating.. character of the Germans showed itself. **1900** G. B. SHAW *Let.* 30 Dec. (1972) II. 214 The conventional, factitious, ratiocinated motives & conclusions of his characters.

ratiocination (ˌræʃɪ-, ˌrætɪɒsɪ'neɪʃən). Also 6 **raciocin-**, 7 **ratiotin-**. [ad. L. *ratiōcinātiōn-em*, n. of action f. *ratiōcinārī*: see prec. Cf. F. *ratiocination* (16th c. in Littré).]

1. The process of reasoning.

c **1530** L. COX *Rhet.* (1899) 78 Raciocinacion is, that cometh of hope of any commodity, or to eschewe any discommodity. **1603** HOLLAND *Plutarch's Mor.* 1344 Without any discourse of reason, or ratiocination. *a* **1677** HALE *Prim. Orig. Man.* I. i. 2 There are some truths so plain and evident, and open, that need not any process of ratiocination to evidence or evince them. **1758** JOHNSON *Idler* No. 31 ¶11 He has observed in many trades the effect of close thought and just ratiocination. **1798** EDGEWORTH *Pract. Educ.* (1811) II. 78 We resort to Geometry, as the most perfect, and the purest series of ratiocination which has been invented. **1879** FARRAR *St. Paul* I. 55 He had not arrived at any one of the truths of his special gospel by the road of ratiocination.

2. With *a* and *pl.* An instance of this; also, a conclusion arrived at by reasoning. (Common in 17th c.)

c **1620** A. HUME *Brit. Tongue* II. xii, The ratiocinative [conjunction] coples the partes of a ratiocination. **1644** MAXWELL *Prerog. Chr. Kings* 135 The Romanists must acknowledge [etc.].. or then they must foregoe these ratiocinations. **1759** JOHNSON *Rasselas* xxii, Other men may amuse themselves with subtle definitions, or intricate ratiocinations. **1818** JAS. MILL *Brit. India* Pref. 11, I have no apology, therefore, to make, for those inductions, or those ratiocinations. **1863** COWDEN CLARKE *Shaks. Char.* xx. 516 The one a cool, a frigid ratiocination; the other, an awful and terrible reality.

3. Power or habit of reasoning. *rare.*

1647 CLARENDON *Hist. Reb.* VII. §220 So infinite a Fancy, bound in by a most Logical ratiocination. *a* **1656** BP. HALL *Rem. Wks.* (1660) 285 For us, that have ratiocination.. we know [what] we have to do here. **1798** CHARLOTTE SMITH *Yng. Philos.* III. 94 A lady of prodigious ratiocination as well as of profound information.

ratiocinative (ræʃɪ-, rætɪ'ɒsɪnətɪv), *a.* [ad. L. *ratiōcinātīv-us*: see RATIOCINATE and -IVE. Cf. F. *ratiocinatif* (14th c., Oresme).] Characterized by, given to, or expressive of, ratiocination.

c **1620** A. HUME *Brit. Tongue* II. xii, Conjunction.. of it ther be tuoe sortes, the one enunciative, and the other ratiocinative. *a* **1625** BOYS *Wks.* (1629) 475 All the faculties of thy soule, vegitatiue, sensitiue, ratiocinatiue. *a* **1677** HALE *Prim. Orig. Man.* I. ii. 51 The conclusion is attained.. without any thing of ratiocinative process. **1817** COLERIDGE *Biog. Lit.* 82 The whole gamut of eloquence from the ratiocinative to the declamatory. **1884** *Manch. Exam.* 16 Oct. 4/7 The machinery of the ratiocinative logician.. has no place in his speeches.

ratiocinatively (ræʃɪ-, rætɪ'ɒsɪnətɪvlɪ), *adv.* [f. RATIOCINATIVE *a.* + -LY[2].] By the process of reasoning; by ratiocination.

1965 J. LAWLOR in J. Gibb *Light on C. S. Lewis* 68 Some of the inconsistencies we were after could be approached ratiocinatively, and examined for logical contradiction; but the deeper kinds of awareness were to be reached intuitively rather than through rationalizations.

rati'ocinator. [a. L. *ratiōcinātor* agent-n. f. *ratiōcinārī* to ratiocinate.] One who reasons.

1824 *Blackw. Mag.* XV. 51 The puzzlement of ratiocinators became profounder than ever. **1971** HEATH & PRENDERGAST tr. J. Kristeva in *Signs of Times* 4 His [*sc.* Leibniz's] attempt to construct a 'calculus ratiocinator'.

rati'ocinatory, *a.* = RATIOCINATIVE.

1810 BENTHAM *Packing* II. iii. (1821) 141 With ratiocinatory, or at least disceptatorial cunctation.

ratiometer (reɪʃɪ'ɒmɪtə(r)). [f. RATIO + -METER.] A device for measuring the ratio of two electrical quantities.

1925 R. O. KAPP *G. Kapp's Transformers* (ed. 3) ix. 220 The ratio of a transformer is tested by an apparatus known as a ratiometer. This is really an autotransformer of which the windings are so subdivided that any ratio within very fine limits is obtainable. **1942** *Jrnl. Sci. Instruments* XIX. 23/2 A suitable current ratiometer has been constructed.. consisting of two coils on the same spindle maintained in a non-uniform field by a torsionless suspension. **1976** *Physics Bull.* Nov. 509/1 It has two amplifiers, phase sensitive detection or 'lock-in' and a ratiometer in one unit.

ratiomorphic (ræʃɪəʊ'mɔːfɪk), *a. Psychol.* [f. RATIO + Gr. μορφ-ή + -IC.] (See quots. 1954 and 1966.) Hence **ratio'morphous** *a.*

1954 E. BRUNSWIK in *Acta Psychologica* XI. 109 Perception and thinking thus emerge as different forms of imperfect inferences regarding the environment, subsumable to a common behavior model patterned upon reasoning ('ratiomorphic' reduction, if this Latin-Greek hybrid be permitted). **1966** K. R. HAMMOND *Psychol. E. Brunswik* i. 38 By 1955, however, he [*sc.* Brunswik] had coined the term 'ratiomorphic' to represent the organism's process of coordinating uncertain data in order to make an inductive inference from them. Perception is a '.. ratiomorphic sub-system of cognition..'. The process is, in other words, 'reasoning-like'. **1971** R. MARTIN tr. *Lorenz's Stud. Animal & Human Behaviour* II. 302 All kinds of constancy apparatus are—in principle—'ratiomorphic' in the most rigorous sense of the term, since all incorporate processes analogous to those of both induction and deduction. **1977** R. TAYLOR tr. *Lorenz's Behind Mirror* vii. 119 Egon Brunswik coined the term 'ratiomorphous' to describe.. all these sensory and nervous processes [which] take place in areas of our nervous system which are completely inaccessible to our consciousness and our self-observation. *Ibid.* 162 These unconscious processes are what Egon Brunswik called 'ratiomorphous' computing mechanisms.

ration ('ræʃən, formerly 'reɪʃən), *sb.* Also 8 **ratian.** [a. F. *ration* (14th c. in Littré), or ad. L. *ratiōn-em* RATIO *sb.* The first pronunciation may be due to the adoption of the word in military use in sense 3 from Fr.]

†**1.** Reasoning. *Obs. rare*⁻¹.

1550 BP. HOOPER *Serm. Jonas* vi. 138b, We be not so addicte and geuen vnto humane ration, that we wyll beleue nothinge more than reason is able to accompt and geue answer for.

†**2.** = RATIO *sb.* 2 and 3. *Obs.*

1666 *Phil. Trans.* I. 272 What he saith here of Rations or Proportions. **1692** O. WALKER *Gr. & Rom. Hist. Illustr.* 6 That Ration of Gold to Silver was 12 to one. **1728** R. NORTH *Mem. Music* (1846) 24 The musick, and the rations of the intervals subtilized. **1815** J. C. HOBHOUSE *Substance Lett.* (1816) I. 347 Increasing in a reduplicating ration.

3. a. A fixed allowance or individual share of provisions; *spec.* in the army and navy, the daily amount of certain articles of food allotted to each officer and man. Also, esp. in *pl.*, simply = provisions, food.

1702–11 in *Milit. & Sea Dict.* **1720** OZELL *Vertot's Rom. Rep.* II. XIII. 276 The Corn that used to be measured out to them by Rations (or stinted Allowances) was given them with out Measure. **1776** J. HANCOCK in Sparks *Corr. Amer. Rev.* (1853) I. 236 The cost of a ration, as furnished by the Commissary-General. **1814** SCOTT *Wav.* xvii, Cutting with their dirks their rations from the carcasses which were there suspended. **1862** R. HENNING *Let.* 19 Oct. (1966) 110 Biddulph or Mr Hedgeland goes to the out-stations with provisions, or rations, as they call them. **1865** LIVINGSTONE *Zambesi* xx. 409 The fresh labour with diminished rations was too much for their strength. **1885** *Pall Mall G.* 1 July 3/2 A 'ration' in the literal military sense of the word means 1 lb. bread and ¾ lb. meat (bone included). **1917** A. G. EMPEY *Over Top* 305 *Rations*, various kinds of tasteless food issued by the Government to Tommy, to kid him into the fact that he is living in luxury, while the Germans are starving. **1919** W. H. DOWNING *Digger Dial.* 41 'Wet rations':.. Cooked foods etc... 'Dry rations':.. Uncooked food.. 'Iron rations':.. Emergency rations. **1922** C. E. MONTAGUE *Disenchantment* ii. 15 A little famished London cab-tout, a recruit, still rectilinear as a starved cat even after a month of army rations.

b. *Mil.* The daily allowance of forage or provender assigned to each horse or other animal.

1727–41 [see c]. **1802** JAMES *Milit. Dict.* s.v. *Forage*, This forage is divided into rations, one of which is a day's allowance for a horse. **1876** VOYLE & STEVENSON *Milit. Dict.* 143/1 The daily ration laid down for all horses is 12 lbs. of oats and 12 lbs. of hay.

c. An allowance, share, portion, *of* provisions or other supplies; *esp.* an officially limited allowance for civilians in time of war or shortage. Hence phr. *off (the) ration*, in addition to the allowance; unrestricted.

1727–41 CHAMBERS *Cycl.* s.v., The horse have rations of hay and oats, when they cannot go out to forage. **1823** SYD. SMITH *Wks.* (1859) II. 19/2 A sum of money.. in lieu of their regular ration of provisions. **1869** LECKY *Europ. Mor.* II. i. 78 Septimus Severus added to the corn, a ration of oil. **1879** A. FORBES in *Daily News* 25 June 6/1 He will be able to carry forward with him eighty thousand rations of fuel, consisting of coal. **1917** *Times* 28 Feb. 10/3 Captain Bathurst, replying to Mr. Faber, said the Food Controller, since the issue of voluntary rations, had been in communication with the War Office, and an Army Council instruction was issued last week limiting the sugar ration for civilian and combatant prisoners of war to 7 oz per week. **1919** E. H. STARLING *Feeding of Nations* vi. 127 Each individual can buy of it according to his desire and satisfy his Calorie needs above those supplied in the rations. **1922** H. W. CLEMESHA *Food Control in North-West Division* ii. 34 There must have been many families who were unable to afford the additional rations of meat which the cards of children would have enabled them to obtain. **1928** W. H. BEVERIDGE *Brit. Food Control* x. 230 The wealthy classes in particular suffered from the reduction of the meat ration. **1944** *Ourselves in Wartime* vii. 154/2 More often than not, they forfeited their personal sweet ration, which amounted to 3 ozs. of sweets or chocolate a week in 1943, for the sake of the children. **1948** *Ann. Reg. 1947* 246 Food shops were compelled to limit strictly the amount of 'off ration' foods which customers could buy at one time. **1950** N. STREATFEILD *Mothering Sunday* 31 She was the last person to look for extras off the ration. **1959** in I. & P. Opie *Lore & Lang. Schoolch.* vii. 105 We are three spivs of Trafalgar Square Flogging nylons tuppence a pair, All fully fashioned, all off the ration, Sold in Trafalgar Square. **1960** J. RAE *Custard Boys* I. iv. 41 A little shop.. where the old lady would sell us sweets and chocolate off the ration. **1975** S. BRIGGS *Keep Smiling Through* 150 Some articles off the ration could add an exotic touch to the menu. There was turbot in 1940 and whalemeat in 1942. *Ibid.* 161 'Off the ration' foods.. like salt cod were publicized as 'grand for children as well as grown-ups and what a bargain!'

d. *transf.*

1850 BROWNING *Christmas Eve* ii. 7 Still, as I say, though you've found salvation, If I should choose to cry—as now—'Shares!'—See if the best of you bars me my ration!

e. Mil. slang phr.: ***come up*** (or ***be given***) ***with the rations***, to be awarded automatically (used deprecatingly, of military medals and decorations, to imply that they have not been earned).

1925 *N. & Q.* 25 July 71/2 Came up with the rations. **1928** H. WILLIAMSON *Pathway* xvii. 378 'Did *you* get the Military Cross?' asked Mrs. Ogilvie. 'Yes, it came up with the rations.' 'Oh!' 'A soldier's joke, Mrs. Ogilvie.' **1937** J. A. LEE *Civilian into Soldier* 204 'Bit of decoration. Congratulations.' 'Came up with the rations.' He took the ribbon. But if he joked he was pleased in his soul. **1957** J. BRAINE *Room at Top* xviii. 162 Lampton has no decorations apart from those which all servicemen who served his length of time are given, as they say, with the rations. **1973** A. PRICE *October Men* xv. 210 The British Military Cross.. didn't come up with the rations.

4. *attrib.* and *Comb.*, as ***ration bag, beef, boot, -carrier, grievance, party, rum, scale, -sugar, -tea, warrant***, etc.; **ration book**, a book entitling its holder to a ration; **ration card, coupon**, a card or coupon entitling its holder to a ration; **ration sheep** *Austral.*, the sheep to be killed for food for the workers on a station; also ***ration-sheep paddock, ration paddock***; **ration strength**, the number of men in an armed force, estimated by the rations supplied to them; **ration ticket** = *ration card.*

1862 R. Henning *Let.* 5 Sept. (1966) 103 The 'ration bags' contained flour, sugar, tea, sardines, bacon, cheese, salt beef and salmon and jam. **1917** A. G. Empey *Over Top* 305 *Ration bag*, a small, very small bag for carrying rations. **1835** J. E. Alexander *Sketches in Portugal* iv. 101 Into an upper room marched two troopers, with a camp-kettle between them containing water, followed by two others with another kettle, containing a savoury mess of ration-beef, boiled with bread and onions. **1882** Mrs. B. M. Croker *Proper Pride* II. iii. 53 Dining heartily on ration beef and dry bread. **1918** *Times* 1 Nov. 3/2 The Ministry of Food wish to remind the public that persons registered with retailers for tea must renew their registration as soon as possible by depositing with the retailer the 'spare counterfoil 2' on leaf 7 of their new ration books. **1939** *New Statesman* 18 Nov. 700/1 The ration books.. have now been distributed. **1973** *Country Life* 20 Dec. 2120/1 As these notes are written, ration books are being issued and motorists seem anxious to use them. **1902** 'Coldstreamer' *Ballads of Boer War* vii. 70 If you find a time to suit, Just cop 'im with a ration boot. **1882** H. Vizetelly *Paris in Peril* II. vii. 35 At some establishments strangers were politely informed that dinners were only served to the regular clientèle, who had handed over their ration-cards to the proprietor. **1922** H. W. Clemesha *Food Control in North-West Division* ii. 39 When the ration cards and the vouchers had all been distributed they were lodged either with retailers or wholesalers. **1940** *Economist* 9 Mar. 415/1 A general census is to be taken preparatory to the issue of ration-cards [in France]. **1975** T. Allbeury *Special Collection* v. 32 The ration cards were no longer honoured. The food wasn't there any more. **1890** 'R. Boldrewood' *Col. Reformer* (1891) 115 The ration-carriers.. were always conveying provisions, water, wood, all things necessary to the shepherds. **1944** *Sun* (Baltimore) 12 Dec. 12/8 A 'red market' in meat—collection of ration coupons for point free cuts. **1890** *19th Cent.* Nov. 844 One more instance of a ration grievance, and we will pass on. **1935** G. L. Meredith *Adventuring in Maoriland* v. 41, I sometimes have to do the slaughtering. There is no 'ration paddock'. **1917** A. G. Empey *Over Top* 305 *Ration party*, men detailed to carry rations to the front line. **1928** Blunden *Undertones of War* xiii. 145 At the ration-party's rendezvous.., our hearty Quartermaster Swain.. was guarding.. our issue of rum. **1918** E. A. Mackintosh *War* 94 Punch concocted out of ration rum. **1897** P. Warung *Old Regime* 81 The daily ration-scale permitted him only 16 ozs. uncooked maize-meal. **1911** C. E. W. Bean *'Dreadnought' of Darling* xxxiv. 293 In some of the Western towns they find a convenient substitute even for ration sheep. **1914** H. B. Smith *Sheep & Wool Industry Australasia* vi. 34 On a station the first sheep that are usually shorn are the ration sheep. These are the sheep that are to be killed for household and shearers' use. **1946** F. Davison *Dusty* viii. 81 From then on he took him [the pup] out whenever he had to bring in the ration sheep for a killing. The ration sheep grazed in a small paddock near the homestead. *Ibid.* x. 105 The fence bounding the ration-sheep paddock. **1931** W. S. Churchill *World Crisis* VI. xxi. 323 Out of 425,000 men comprising the entire manhood of the country, borne on the ration-strength of the Serbian army at the beginning of October, over 100,000 had been killed or wounded. **1965** B. Sweet-Escott *Baker St. Irregular* vii. 201 The ration strength of A.F.H.Q. at this time was.. something like that of a fighting division. **1892** *Missing Friends* iii. 54 The most inferior goods in the market are called *ration-tea* and *ration-sugar*. **1938** N. MacOwan *Glorious Morning* II. ii. 59 There's food to get. Our ration tickets are only available today. **1830** E. S. N. Campbell *Milit. Dict.* s.v. *Ration*, The Commanding Officer has the power by the Ration Warrant of 14th July, 1827, of diminishing.. this allowance.

ration ('ræʃən, formerly also 'reɪʃən), *v.* [f. prec. sb.]

1. *trans.* To supply (persons) with rations; to provision; to put on a fixed allowance.

1859 *Times* 3 Mar. 7/6 The humane provision of rationing immigrants for the first 3 months. **1884** *Spectator* 4 Oct. 1286/1 He was able by rationing the townsmen as well as his troops to make this supply last to the present time.

2. To divide (food, etc.) into rations; to serve *out* in fixed quantities.

1870 *Daily News* 2 Nov., It will not be necessary to ration the bread until the 1st of January. **1873** A. L. Perry *Elem. Pol. Econ.* (ed. 8) 78 The crew of a boat abandoned at sea, among whom the last biscuit had been rationed out.

3. *intr.* (for *refl.*). To obtain a supply of food.

1859 R. F. Burton *Centr. Afr.* in *Jrnl. Geog. Soc.* XXIX. 303 In the sparse cultivation,.. they were rarely able to ration oftener than once a week.

Hence **'rationed** *ppl. a.*

1886 *Century Mag.* XXXII. 937 In preparation for the poorly rationed days.

†rationa'bility. *Obs. rare*⁻¹. [f. next + -ity. Cf. late L. *ratiōnābilitās* (once in Appuleius).] The faculty of being rational.

1656 Bramhall *Repl. Bp. Chalcedon* Wks. 1842 II. 24 Rationability, being but a faculty or specifical quality, is a substantial part of a man.

†'rationable, *a. Obs.* [ad. L. *ratiōnābilis*: see ration and -able. Cf. obs. F. *rationable*.]

1. Reasonable, just, right. (Chiefly *Sc.*)

1436 *Extr. Burgh Rec. Edinb.* (1869) I. 4 It is ordanit.. the alderman baillies and counsaile by this vitaile of rationable pryce as thai may. **1535** Stewart *Cron. Scot.* I. 38 Of that desyre content was euerie wicht, Tha thocht it wes rationabill and richt. **1570–80** in *14th Rep. Hist. MSS. Comm.* App. III. 44 Gyffand vs.. ane rationabyll drinksyluer. **1662** J. Chandler *Van Helmont's Oriat.* 19 Whatsoever is akin to truth, this reason judgeth rationable, and agreeable to Reason.

2. Rational; sensible.

1620 Melton *Astrolog.* 26 Astrologers or Astronomers,.. that thinke Starres rationable Creatures, are worthy to be accounted most unreasonable and senselesse themselves. **1649** Bulwer *Pathomyot.* II. ii. 131 Laughter.. is a passion of the Rationable part.

Hence **†'rationably** *adv.*, reasonably. *Obs.*

1646 J. Lilburne *Jonah's Cry* (1647) 4, I professe I would doe it, if I were rationably able to doe it to morrow. **1679** J. Smith *Narr. Popish Plot* 10 As they might very rationably believe.

rational ('ræʃənəl), *a.* (*adv.*) and *sb.*[1] Forms: 5 **racional**, (6 **-all, -elle**), 6 **racyonall**, 6– **rational**, (7 **-all**). [ad. L. *ratiōnāl-is*: see ratio *sb.*, ration, and -al[1]. Cf. obs. F. *rational* (16th c.), OF. *rationel* (12th c.), F. *rationnel*.]

A. *adj.* **1. a.** Having the faculty of reasoning; endowed with reason. (Freq. in ***rational being, creature***.)

1398 Trevisa *Barth. De P.R.* III. xiii. (1495) 56 The soule racional, in that he vsyth contemplacion, he hyghte *speculatiuus*. **1547** Boorde *Brev. Health* §321 The racionall sences consisteth in reason, the whiche doth make a man or woman a reasonable beaste. **1615** Crooke *Body of Man* 432 We determine that the Braine is the Pallace of the Rationall Soule. *a* **1641** Bp. Mountagu *Acts & Mon.* (1642) 409 Other bodies, not onely of rationall creatures, men and women, but also of irrational, birds and beasts. **1783** Cowper *Let.* 29 Sept., We are rational: but we are animal too. **1848** Dickens *Dombey* ii, If you're a rational being, don't make such ridiculous excuses. **1908** *Jrnl. Abnormal Psychol.* III. 166 Everyone feels that as a rational creature he must be able to give a connected.. account of himself. **1975** J. Plamenatz *K. Marx's Philos. Man* i. 17 He always speaks of man as a self-conscious, rational, active being who can make choices and can initiate change deliberately.

b. Exercising (or able to exercise) one's reason in a proper manner; having sound judgement; sensible, sane.

1632 B. Jonson *Magnetick Lady* III. v, You are one O' the deepest Politiques I ever met, And the most subtily rationall. **1641** H. L'Estrange *God's Sabbath* 34 Our most Rationall adversaries begin to reel towards us. **1712** E. Cooke *Voy. S. Sea* 239 They were told by a good rational Indian Woman [etc.]. **1791** Burke *App. Whigs* Wks. 1842 I. 535 Rational and experienced men tolerably well know,.. how to distinguish between true and false liberty. **1809** *Med. Jrnl.* XXI. 216 Frequent restlessness and delirium, yet at times he is rational and patient. **1835** Lytton *Rienzi* I. vii, Our rational and sober-minded islanders. **1856** C. Bronte *Professor* xix, The man of regular life and rational mind never despairs.

c. *Med.* Applied to an ancient class of physicians, who deduced their treatment of cases from general principles. (Opp. to empirical.) ***rational psychology, psychological science***: psychology, or the science of mind, as studied by deduction from general principles, and distinguished from an empirical approach. Now *Obs.*

1541 Copland *Galyen's Terap.* E iij b, Seynge that none Emperyke, nor racyonall hath so wryten before. **1654** R. Whitlock *Zootomia* 123 [They] are ready enough to slander the rationall Physitian. **1727–41** Chambers *Cycl.* s.v. *Physician*, The ancients distinguished their physicians into various classes, or sects:—as Rational Physicians [etc.]. **1817** Coleridge *Biog. Lit.* I. ix. 139 These delusions were such, as might be anticipated.. from his ignorance of rational psychology. **1837** Whewell *Hist. Induct. Sc.* IV. i. §5 That medical sect which was termed the Empirical, in contradistinction to the rational and methodical sects. **1849** L. P. Hickok *Rational Psychol.* 21 Those a priori conditions which give the necessary and universal laws to experience, and by which intelligence itself is alone made intelligible, are the elements for a higher Psychological Science which we term *Rational*. **1861** J. S. Mill *Let.* in A. Bain *John Stuart Mill* (1882) iv. 118 It will enable me.. to do the kind of service which I am capable of to rational psychology. **1892** W. James *Coll. Ess. & Rev.* (1920) xx. 321 We certainly need something more radical than the old division into 'rational' and 'empirical' psychology, both to be treated by the same writer between the covers of the same book.

d. ***Rational Christians***: Such as claim superior rationality for their own form of Christianity.

A sect was registered under this name in 1876.

1750 Masson *Contin. True Rationalist* xii. 155 This is.. what shews me how convincing your Reasons are to determine me for the Establishment of a Society of Rational Christians.

2. a. Of, pertaining or relating to, reason.

Chiefly in ***rational faculty, nature, power***, etc. Also †***rational philosophy***, mental philosophy.

a **1601** North *Plutarch* (1612) 1190 Morall Philosophie was his chiefest end: for the rationall, the naturall, and Mathematickes.. were but simple pastimes in comparison of the other. **1614** C. Brooke *Rich. III*, Poems (1872) 125 My aspick flatterie, That shed such venome in my rationall powre. **1675** Barclay *Apol. Quakers* IV. iii. 102 As he is a meer Man, he differs no otherwise from Beasts, than by the Rational Property. **1748** Chesterf. *Lett.* (1792) II. 61 Philosophy, rational logic, rhetoric [etc.]. **1788** Reid *Aristotle's Logic* vi. § 1. 126 Our rational faculty is the gift of God. *a* **1882** T. H. Green *Proleg. Ethics* §207 The consciousness of unfulfilled possibilities of the rational nature common to all men.

†b. Existing (only) in the mind. (Opposed to real.) *Obs.*

1628 T. Spencer *Logick* 104 Such things haue a being in our vnderstanding, and that is enough to make them rationall beings. **1677** Gale *Crt. Gentiles* IV. Proem. 6 These second Notions are not Real, but only Mental or Rational Beings, framed out of Real Beings.

3. a. Based on, derived from, reason or reasoning.

1531 Elyot *Gov.* III. xxvi, That parte of phisike called rationall, wherby is declared the faculties or powers of the body, the causis, accidentes, and tokens of sikenessis. **1649** Milton *Eikon.* vi. 56 He confesses a rational sovrantie of soule, and freedom of will in every man. **1701** Norris *Ideal World* I. iv. 218 Faith is a rational assent, or an assent founded on reason, tho' not the reason of the thing believed. **1785** Reid *Intell. Powers* 608 Of tastes that are natural, there are some that may be called rational, others that are merely animal. **1885** J. Martineau *Types Eth. Th.* (ed. 2) I. I. xi. §8. 212 Any.. instance of rational apprehension, e.g. our knowledge that the surface of a sphere is equal to the area of a circle of twice its diameter.

b. *spec.* in *Chem.* and *Med.* (see quots.).

1850 Daubeny *Atomic The.* ix. (ed. 2) 297 By rational, in contradistinction to empirical, formulæ, we mean expressions of the manner in which the respective atoms are combined or grouped together, and not merely of the number of atoms of each of the ingredients present. **1897** *Allbutt's Syst. Med.* IV. 275 Physical are more important than rational signs in establishing the diagnosis of cyst of the pancreas.

c. ***rational mechanics***: mechanics as deduced logically from first principles.

[**1687** Newton *Philosophiæ Naturalis Principia Mathematica* p. v, *Mechanicam* vero duplicem Veteres constituerunt: *Rationalem* quæ per Demonstrationes accurate procedit, & *Practicam*. *Ibid.*, Quo sensu *Mechanica rationalis* erit Scientia Motuum qui ex viribus quibuscunq; resultant, & virium quæ ad motus quoscunq; requiruntur, accurate proposita ac demonstrata. **1729** A. Motte tr. *Ibid.* I. p. vii, The ancients considered Mechanics in a twofold respect; as rational, which proceeds accurately by demonstration, and practical.] *Ibid.* p. ix, In this sense Rational Mechanics will be the science of motions resulting from any forces whatsoever and of the forces required to produce any motions, accurately proposed and demonstrated. **1902** J. W. Gibbs *Elem. Princ. Statistical Mech.* p. ix, Nothing will more conduce to the clear apprehension of the relation of thermodynamics to rational mechanics.. than the study of the fundamental notions and principles of that department of mechanics to which thermodynamics is especially related. **1928** R. De Villamil *Rational Mech.* p. vi, I have been asked: Why I call this a book on 'Rational Mechanics'? and Do I not consider all Mechanics as being 'Rational'? **1952** *Jrnl. Rational Mech. & Anal.* I. p. ii, The *Journal of Rational Mechanics & Analysis* nourishes mathematics with physical applications, aiming especially to close the rift between 'pure' and 'applied' mathematics and to foster the discipline of mechanics as a deductive, mathematical science in the classical tradition. **1958** *Science* 4 Apr. 729/1 In the United States.. rational mechanics is not a recognized science. Indeed, there are some who disbelieve in its existence. **1977** C. Truesdell *First Course Rational Continuum Mech.* i. 4 Rational Mechanics is the part of mathematics that provides and develops logical models for the enforced changes of position and shape which we see everyday things suffer.

4. a. Agreeable to reason; reasonable, sensible; not foolish, absurd, or extravagant.

1635 Pagitt *Christianogr.* I. iii. (1636) 123 We offer unto thee, this rationall and unbloody worship. **1654–66** Earl Orrery *Parthen.* (1676) 750 He might decline that Assistance, in which he had his Rationallest hopes. **1691** Locke *Money* Wks. 1727 II. 92 What Mr. Lowndes says about Gold Coins,.. appears to me highly rational. **1771** *Junius Lett.* lxiv. 325 [He] will.. concur in any rational plan that may provide for the liberty of the individual. **1804** Abernethy *Surg. Obs.* 176 On the following morning.. his answers were rational. **1879** Harlan *Eyesight* viii. 104 All the organs of the body are better for moderate and rational use.

b. ***rational dress***: A form of dress for women, proposed in the late 19th c. as more sensible than that in general use, usually denoting the use of knickerbockers in place of a skirt, esp. for cycling. (Also *attrib.*) So ***rational costume***, etc.

1883 *Catal. Rational Dress Exhib.* Pref., The Rational Dress Exhibition is intended to stimulate both the supply and the demand for good dress. **1888** *Rational Dress Society's Gaz.* No. 2 This is the time when rational dress principles will have more weight. **1899** *Cycl. Tour. Club Gaz.* Apr. 221 If.. senior churchwardens protest against rational costume.

5. a. *Math.* Applied to quantities or ratios which can be expressed without the use of radical signs. †***rational to*** (see quot. 1614). Also ***rational fraction*** (see quot. 1823).

1570 Billingsley *Euclid* v. def. iii, Such magnitudes or quantities, which may be expressed by numbre, are called rationall. **1614** T. Bedwell *Nat. Geom. Numbers* i. 2 The Base and Height are said to be rational one to another, when as the rate or reason of both may be expressed by a number of the same measure given. **1660** Barrow *Euclid* x. prop. lxi. 237 The square of a binomiall line ∴ applyed unto a rationall line. **1706** W. Jones *Syn. Palmar. Matheseos* 116 Rational Quantities may be reduced to the Form of any assign'd Root. **1798** Hutton *Course Math.* (1827) I. 82 The square root of 3 is a surd root; but the square root of 4 is a rational root, being equal to 2. **1823** J. Mitchell *Dict. Math. Sci.*, *Rational Fractions* is the term commonly used to express those fractions which may be decomposed into other fractions, the sum of which is equal to the given fraction. **1885** Watson & Burbury *Math. Th. Electr. & Magn.* I. 41 Y_i is a rational and integral function of cos θ. **1901** H. B. Fine *College Algebra* II. i. 86 An expression is called rational if it does not involve an indicated root of an expression in which a variable letter occurs. **1917** T. M. MacRobert *Functions of Complex Variable* v. 89 The ratio of two polynomials is called a Rational Function. **1930** C. C. MacDuffee *Introd. Abstract Algebra* iii. 82 A quadratic equation with rational coefficients which does not have a rational root. **1946** A. A. Albert *College Algebra* iv. 111 A rational function of several symbols is any algebraic expression obtainable by formally applying a finite number of the rational operations of addition, subtraction, multiplication, and division to the symbols and numbers. **1966** R. E. Johnson *University Algebra* i. 20 There exist consecutive integers n and $n + 1$, but there do not exist consecutive rational numbers.

b. ***rational horizon***: see horizon 3.

1625 N. Carpenter *Geog. Del.* I. vi. (1635) 149 The rationall Horizon diuides the whole spheare into two equall parts. **1642** Milton *Apol. Smect.* Wks. (1851) 310 The rationall horizon in heav'n is but one, and the sensible horizons on earth are innumerable. 1704 [see HORIZON 3]. 1833 HERSCHEL *Astron.* i. 52 If we suppose a spectator.. to have his view bounded by the rational horizon.

c. (With admixture of sense 4a.) *Physics.* The epithet given by O. Heaviside to electrical units and equations now described as RATIONALIZED.

1882 O. HEAVISIDE in *Nature* 24 Aug. 391/1 If.. electricity stands foremost amongst the exact sciences, it follows that its unit measures should be determined with the utmost accuracy. Yet, twenty years ago very little advance had been made toward the adoption of a rational system. 1892 *Ibid.* 28 July 293/1 If we let the rational practical units be the same multiples of the 'absolute' rational units as the present practical units are of *their* absolute progenitors, then [etc.]. 1905 *Proc. R. Soc.* A. LXXVI. 551 The calculations would have been the same if *e* had been measured in 'rational' electric units instead of those in common use, but we should then have had an experimental value equal to 4π times that mentioned above. 1905 [see GIORGI]. 1911 *Encycl. Brit.* XXVII. 744/2 If the filament is an endless or poleless iron filament magnetized uniformly by a resultant external magnetic force H, the flux density will be expressed in rational units by the equation B = I + H. 1925 W. H. TIMBIE *Elements of Electricity* (ed. 2) vi. 171 In order to have Ohm's Law hold with these units, the rational oersted must be equal to 1·26 C.G.S. units. 1942 *Phil. Mag.* XXXIII. 487 All the above formulæ, whether those of the rational system or of the ordinary system, are entirely independent of any choice of units.

†**6.** *Gram.* Of a conjunction: That indicates a reason. *Obs. rare.*

1678 GALE *Crt. Gentiles* IV. III. iii. 84 Those words.. are immediately subjoined to vers 16, and are connected therewith by the rational Particle γάρ, which points out the reason of that which next follows.

7. Descriptive of methods of analysis and planning that make use of calculation to bring about a projected result, esp. in economic or social organization.

1915 M. EPSTEIN tr. *Sombart's Quintessence of Capitalism* xii. 182 He is ever ready to adopt a newer method if it is more rational, whether in the sphere of organization, of production, or of calculation. 1926 E. GROSSMANN *Methods Econ. Rapprochement* 30 The most important economies will follow not from the simplification of the machinery of distribution but from a rational organization of production itself. 1930 T. PARSONS tr. *Weber's Protestant Ethic* 21 But in modern times the Occident has developed.. a very different form of capitalism which has appeared nowhere else: the rational capitalistic organization of (formally) free labour. *Ibid.*, Rational industrial organization, attuned to a regular market.. is not, however, the only peculiarity of Western capitalism. 1943 J. A. SCHUMPETER *Capitalism, Socialism & Democracy* xi. 122 The rational attitude presumably forced itself on the human mind primarily from economic necessity. *Ibid.*, When the habit of rational analysis of.. the daily tasks of life has gone far enough, it turns back upon the mass of collective ideas and criticizes.. them by way of such questions as why there should be kings.. or tithes or property. *Ibid.* 123 Capitalist practice turns the unit of money into a tool of rational cost-profit calculations, of which the towering monument is double-entry book-keeping. 1969 SIMON & STEDRY in Lindzey & Aronson *Handbk. Social Psychol.* (ed. 2) V. xl. 272 The classical economic theory of markets with rational agents and perfect competition is a deductive theory that requires almost no contact with empirical data.. to establish its propositions. 1977 A. GIDDENS *Stud. in Social & Polit. Theory* v. 206 Weber's characterization of modern capitalism as involving above all the 'rational' organization of resources geared to the accumulation of profit is unsatisfactory.

†**B.** *adv.* Rationally. *Obs. rare.*

1690 LOCKE *Hum. Und.* III. vi. §29 If Baalam's Ass had, all his life, discours'd as rational as he did once.

C. *sb.*[1] Absol. uses of the adj.

1. a. A rational being. Chiefly in *pl.* = human beings. Now *Obs.* or *rare.*

1606 WARNER *Alb. Eng.* XIV. lxxxii. (1612) 343 Beasts silent, that with Rationales was all a-mort suppose. 1663 GERBIER *Counsel* 6 b, Love to Art.. infers the party to be a true Rational. 1688 *Lond. Gaz.* No. 2357/1 We must deprive our selves of our selves, as Rationals, and become more stupid then Brutes. 1755 YOUNG *Centaur* 103 He is a Rational, dethroning Reason; and an Animal, transgressing Appetite. 1791 PAINE *Rights of Man* II. iii. (1792) 21, Kings succeed each other, not as rationals, but as animals. 1828 R. CRAIG in *Memorials* vi. (1862) 129 Something which might exercise the mind as well as limbs of the rationals assembled there.

b. An advocate of something 'rational'.

1756 in D'Israeli *Calam. Auth.* (1863) 65 He [Henley] called himself 'a Rationalist', and on his death-bed repeatedly cried out, 'Let my notorious enemies know I die a Rational'. 1896 *Westm. Gaz.* 28 Nov. 3/2 As a 'rational',.. she thought that members should be free to adopt any costume that they liked.

†**2.** *Gram.* A conjunction indicating a reason.

1612 BRINSLEY *Lud. Lit.* 97 Coniunctions, Copulatiues, Rationals, Aduersitiues,.. Expletiues, and certaine others.

3. *Math.* A rational quantity.

1685 J. WALLIS *Alg.* xcix. 373 A Fraction (in Rationals) less than the proposed (Irrational) *p.* 1797 STOKES in *Trans. Royal Irish Acad.* VI. 222 Four quadratics and a rational may be reduced at least with the same ease. 1958 D. E. LITTLEWOOD *University Algebra* (ed. 2) ix. 150 The set of integers *K* can be embedded in a field of quotients. This field of quotients is defined as the rationals. 1971 D. G. H. B. LLOYD *Mod. Syllabus Algebra* vi. 110 Between any two rationals a third rational can be inserted. In this respect the set of rationals differs completely from the set of naturals or the set of integers.

4. †**a.** The rational part of man. *Obs. rare*$^{-1}$. **b.** That which is rational or reasonable. **c.** A rational concept.

1698 FARQUHAR *Love & Bottle* II. ii, Your rational's reversed, carrying your understandings in your legs. 1874 H. SIDGWICK *Meth. Ethics* III. xiii. 362 This absolute end,.. can be nothing but Reason itself, or the Universe of Rationals. 1898 G. MEREDITH *Odes Fr. Hist.* 86 They not the less were mated, and proclaimed the rational their issue.

5. *pl.* 'Rational' dress; knickerbockers for women.

1889 *Pall Mall G.* 26 Dec. 6/2 Small shoes and latter-day 'rationals'. 1895 *Westm. Gaz.* 2 Sept. 8/1 A mild plot amongst lady cyclists to persuade her ladyship.. to adopt 'rationals'.

rational ('ræʃənəl), *sb.*[2] Forms: 4–5 racionale, (4 -al), 6 -all, 7 rationall, (-ale,) 9 rational. [ad. L. *ratiōnāle*, neut. of *ratiōnālis* adj. (see prec.); used in the Vulg. to translate Heb. *ḥōshen*, after the Sept. λογεῖον oracle, oracular instrument.]

†**1.** The breastplate worn by the Jewish high-priest. *Obs.*

1382 WYCLIF *Exod.* xxv. 7 The racionale, that is the clooth in the brest of the coope, and in the brest of the preest. 1413 *Pilgr. Sowle* (Caxton 1483) IV. xxxiii. 82 Aaron had a broche or a tatche fastned vnder his breste that was cleped racionale. 1526 *Pilgr. Perf.* (W. de W. 1531) 192 The adornament of Aaron, called his Racionall. 1646 SIR T. BROWNE *Pseud. Ep.* 93 The twelve stones in the Rationall or breast-plate of Aaron. [1662 H. MORE *Philos. Writ.* Pref. Gen. v, Philo writes of the Figure of the Rationale, or Sacerdotal Breast-plate.]

b. An ornament formerly worn on the breast by bishops during the celebration of mass.

The real nature of the rational has been the subject of much discussion: see Du Cange s.v. *Rationale*, Rock *Church* etc. I. 366, II. 159, and Macalister *Eccl. Vestments* (1896) 110.

1849 ROCK *Ch. of Fathers* I. 371 Bishop Giffard, who died A.D. 1301,.. is figured in a chasuble, having pinned upon his breast the rational. *Ibid.* II. 159 The real 'rational' has nothing to do with the 'pall'. 1884 A. J. BUTLER *Anc. Coptic Churches* II. 122 The rational.. is mentioned among the ancient ornaments of the Celtic bishops.

†**2.** = RATIONALE 2. *Obs. rare.*

1658 SIR T. BROWNE *Hydriot.* 34 To afford an account or rational of old Rites. 1676 MARVELL *Mr. Smirke* 17, I looked over the Canons, the Rational, the Ceremonial, the Rubrick, imagining the Exposing mention'd, must be some new part of our Ecclesiastical Discipline.

†'**rational**, *sb.*[3] *Obs. rare.* [ad. L. *ratiōnālis* (3rd c.), sb. use of *ratiōnālis* adj. RATIONAL.] *Rom. Antiq.* An accountant or auditor.

1610 HOLLAND *Camden's Brit.* I. 77 The Receiver of their Emperours Finances.. had under him in Britaine the Rationall or Auditor of the Summes and revenues of Britaine. 1683 *Brit. Spec.* 115 His Rational of Private State in Britain, to say nothing of other inferior Officers.

‖**rationale** (ræʃə'nɑːl(ɪ), -'neɪliː). [L., neut. of *ratiōnālis*: see RATIONAL *a.*]

1. A reasoned exposition of principles; an explanation or statement of reasons; †a set of reasoned rules or directions.

1657 BP. SPARROW (*title*) A Rationale upon the Book of Common Prayer of the Church of England. 1703 MAUNDRELL *Journ. Jerus.* (1721) 28 They could not give any manner of Rationale of their own divine Service. 1774 J. BRYANT *Mythol.* II. 396 The writings of all those, who have given a rationale of the Egyptian rites. 1846 MOZLEY *Ess.* (1878) I. 229 A rationale of heroism was not likely to tell much on English minds. 1876 C. M. DAVIES *Unorth. Lond.* (ed. 2) 99 Where these facts are admitted,.. the rationale usually appended is that their source is a diabolical one.

2. The fundamental reason, the logical or rational basis (*of* anything).

1688 BP. S. PARKER *Reas. Abrog. Test* 124 This gives us the true Rationale of the Mosaick Law. 1715 M. DAVIES *Athen. Brit.* I. 309 They laid down the Rationale and Ground-Work that the Judgment of the Assize was founded upon. 1791 PAINE *Rights of Man* (ed. 4) 161 He sees the rationale of the whole system, its origin and its operation. 1848 MILL *Pol. Econ.* III. xxv. §2 Such, I conceive, is the true theory or rationale of underselling. 1894 H. DRUMMOND *Ascent Man* 3 To discover the rationale of social progress is the ambition of this age.

rationalism ('ræʃənəlɪz(ə)m). [f. RATIONAL *a.* + -ISM. Cf. F. *rationalisme.*]

1. *Med.* The principles of the 'rational' school of physicians.

1800 *Med. Jrnl.* III. 283 A remark on medical empiricism and rationalism. 1803 *Edin. Rev.* I. 257 Acquainted with the divisions of empiricism and rationalism.

2. a. *Theol.* The practice of explaining in a manner agreeable to reason whatever is apparently supernatural in the records of sacred history. Also **b.** The principle of regarding reason as the chief or only guide in matters of religion, or of employing ordinary reasoning to criticize and interpret religious doctrines.

1827 C. H. SACK in Pusey *Hist. Enq.* (1828) p. xii, Common rationalism, which the theological faculty of Berlin has.. for more than fifteen years imparted to theological study. 1846 J. H. NEWMAN *Ess. Development* v. §3. 311 Its spirit was rationalizing, and had the qualities which go with rationalism. 1884 J. PARKER *Larger Ministry* 28 Rationalism does not more distinctly recognize human reason than it is recognised by evangelical philosophy.

c. The view that reason is the only guide leading to the improvement and progress of the human race and that adherence to religious or other 'non-rational' beliefs is out-dated.

1876 (*title*) Constructive rationalism. 1897 *Agnostic Ann.* I. 18 In my progress from Rome to Rationalism many other considerations have influenced me. 1923 J. S. HUXLEY *Ess. Biologist* 231 It is the task of Rationalism to see that religion, this fundamental and important activity of man, shall neither be allowed to continue in false or inadequate forms, nor be stifled or starved, but be made to help humanity in a vigorous growth that is based on truth and in constant contact with reality. 1968 A. J. AYER *Humanist Outlook* 3 A broader movement of Rationalism or Free Thought, which was not merely anti-clerical but hostile to any form of religious belief. 1973 C. CAMPBELL in *Rationalism in 1970s* 81 If the aim of rationalism is merely to attack and demolish the myths that we and others hold then there is more than enough work to keep us busy for a very long time. 1973 C. MACY (*title*) Rationalism and humanism in the new Europe.

3. *Metaph.* A theory (opposed to *empiricism* or *sensationalism*) which regards reason, rather than sense, as the foundation of certainty in knowledge.

1831 *Edin. Rev.* Sept. 247 The fundamental principles of Rationalism we take to be these:—That human reason, or the reasoning faculty, is the sole arbiter as to what is to be received as truth, and what is to be regarded as error, by the human mind; that facts recognized by sense or consciousness form the materials on which the reasoning faculty is to be exercised. 1857 FLEMING *Vocab. Philos.* 419 According to rationalism, reason furnishes certain elements, without which, experience is not possible. 1895 tr. *Falckenberg's Hist. Mod. Philos.* 81 Under [Wolff] rationalism stiffens into a scholastic dogmatism, soon to run out into a popular eclecticism. 1967 *Encycl. Philos.* VII. 69/1 The philosophical outlook.. which stresses the power of a priori reason to grasp substantial truths about the world and correspondingly tends to regard natural science as a basically a priori exercise... The spirit of rationalism in this sense is particularly associated with.. Descartes, Spinoza, and Leibnitz.

4. Used with reference to 'rational' dress.

1897 *Westm. Gaz.* 6 Sept. 1/3 The triumphs of Rationalism.. in the domain of dress.

5. The principle or practice of effecting assessment, planning, or organization in the economic or social sphere by rational (sense 7) methods.

1915 M. EPSTEIN tr. *Sombart's Quintessence of Capitalism* xii. 182 Absolute rationalism is the first [principle]. Economic activities are ruled by cold reason, by thought. *Ibid.* xxv. 325 Economic rationalism owes much of its growth to technical rationalism. 1930 R. H. TAWNEY in T. Parsons tr. *Weber's Protestant Ethic* 1 (e) The word 'rationalism' is used by Weber.. to describe an economic system based.. on the deliberate and systematic adjustment of economic means to the attainment of the objective of pecuniary profit. 1935 *Encycl. Social Sci.* XIII. 114/1 In social and historical life the power of rationalism derives from the confidence which individuals and societies place in reason. 1958 G. MYRDAL *Value in Social Theory* vii. 135 Basic to the eagerness in trying to drive valuations underground is the rationalism of our Western culture.

rationalist ('ræʃənəlɪst), *sb.* and *a.* [f. as prec. + -IST. Cf. F. *rationaliste* (1539).]

1. a. One who forms his opinions by pure or *a priori* reasoning; *spec.* a 'rational' physician.

a 1626 BACON *Apoph.* II. §21 The empirical philosophers are like to pismires... The rationalists are like the spiders. 1656 S. H. *Gold. Law* 79 It concerns the highest Governour, who is Judge of all,.. to be an absolute rationalist, for that reason is the intention of Law. 1801 SURR *Splendid Misery* II. 163 Whatever you may say, or all the Rationalists in the world may preach,.. there is such a thing as falling in love at first sight. 1876 tr. *Wagner's Gen. Pathol.* (ed. 6) 5 Those physicians are called rationalists who do not value the facts themselves so highly as their explanation.

b. One who applies scientific methods of reasoning or calculation to social and economic life.

1958 G. MYRDAL *Value in Social Theory* iii. 57 The American has.. started to measure, not only human intelligence,.. and personality traits, but moral leanings and the 'goodness' of communities. He is a rationalist. 1969 A. ETZIONI in Lindzey & Aronson *Handbk. Social Psychol.* (ed. 2) V. 547 In effect, the rationalists advocate an approach that maximises conflict and makes nuclear war more likely. 1977 T. PARSONS *Social Syst. & Evol. of Action Theory* i. 71 Phrasing it as 'the problem' I hope makes clear that I have not been a naïve rationalist.

2. a. *Theol.* One who rationalizes in matters of religion or sacred history; an adherent of rationalism. *gen.* One who believes that reliance upon human reason does away with the need for religion (cf. RATIONALISM 2 c).

1647 *Clarendon State Papers* II. App. p. xl, The Presbyterian and Independent agree well enough together. But there is a new sect sprung up among them, and these are the Rationalists. 1670 SANDERSON *Pref. Ussher's Power Princes*, A mere Rationalist (that is to say in plain English, an Atheist of the late Edition). 1747 [MASSON] (*title*) A Letter to the Author of an Address to all Rationalists in Great Britain. 1789 J. ERSKINE in *Life C. Nisbet* (1840) 197 He is half way over to the German Rationalists (as they call themselves). 1841 MYERS *Cath. Th.* III. §12. 45 The Rationalist.. makes the whole subject of Religion and Revelation.. a matter of sensible evidence or intellectual demonstration. 1876 *Constructive Rationalism* 5 The destruction of orthodox Christianity being accomplished, there remains for the Rationalist much more to do. He has to frame a code which shall rule in the place of the code of Moses and of Jesus. 1897 *Agnostic Ann.* I. 42 Why do eminent Rationalists, Freethinkers, and Agnostics stand aloof. 1908 [see ETHICIST]. 1942 E. T. KERR in *Why I am a Rationalist* 33 Few Rationalists.. owed to their schools.. any kind of.. approach to independent thinking. 1954 *Rationalist Ann.* 73, I cannot possibly make my probabilities into certainties, and this is what some Rationalists appear.. to do. 1973 C. CAMPBELL in *Rationalism in 1970s* 81 It is an important part of a rationalist's duty to clear himself of myths.. as well as to expose the myths of others.

b. *attrib.* or as *adj.* = RATIONALISTIC.

1828 PUSEY (*title*) An Historical Enquiry into the Probable Causes of the Rationalist Character. *a* **1857** R. A. VAUGHAN *Ess. & Rem.* I. 49 Rationalist criticism has always been content with the endeavour to destroy. **1873** L. STEPHEN *Ess. Freethinking* 319 The answer given by the rationalist divines. **1921** G. B. SHAW *Back to Methuselah* p. lxxiii, They banish the Bible from their houses, and sometimes put into the hands of their unfortunate children Ethical and Rationalist tracts of the deadliest dullness, compelling these wretched infants to sit out the discourses of Secularist lecturers. **1942** J. A. SCHUMPETER *Capitalism, Socialism & Democracy* (1943) xi. 122 There is however one more point about the concept of rationalist civilizations that I will mention here. *Ibid.*, The rationalist attitude may go to work with information and technique so inadequate that [etc.]. **1955** P. EDWARDS *Logic of Moral Discourse* ii. 52 The Rationalist view of causation. **1973** F. A. HAYEK *Law, Legislation & Liberty* i. 33 The desire to remodel society after the image of individual man.. since Hobbes has governed rationalist political theory. **1974** *New Humanist* May 16/1 Clerical pressure continued to be applied to booksellers, discouraging them from displaying Rationalist books. **1977** A. GIDDENS *Stud. Social & Pol. Theory* vii. 239 Durkheim replied by asserting the existence of a radical distinction between 'egoism' and 'rationalist individualism'.

3. One who adopts 'rational' dress.

1899 *Cycl. Tour. Club Gaz.* Apr. 222 The hotels, etc. at which Rationalists are welcome.

rationalistic (ˌræʃənəˈlɪstɪk), *a.* [f. prec.]

1. Characterized by rationalism.

1830 PUSEY *Hist. Enq.* II. 415 Against a rationalistic Christianity Rationalism may triumph. **1878** LECKY *Eng. in 18th C.* II. vii. 411 A rationalistic spirit which revolted against all formularies.

2. Given or inclined to rationalism.

1841 *Penny Cycl.* XIX. 311/1 The way being thus prepared, the number of rationalistic divines increased. **1883** WACE *Gospel & its Witnesses* i. 13 If we could be sure that a miracle was inconceivable, the method of rationalistic writers would.. be justified.

Hence **rationaˈlistical** *a.* (1847 in Webster); **rationaˈlistically** *adv.* (1847 *Ibid.*); **rationaˈlisticism**, rationalism.

1854 GEO. ELIOT tr. *Feuerbach's Essence Christianity* xxv. 245 Zwinglius only expressed.. rationalistically.. what the others declared mystically. **1865** R. DRUITT *Rep. Cheap Wines* 99 The contagion of rationalisticism. **1869** *Contemp. Rev.* XII. 77 He takes Homer into the account, but rationalistically. **1910** W. TEMPLE *Faith & Mod. Thought* iii. 79 Why rationalistically minded folk should suppose that in a moment of almost intolerable joy people are going to have an exact memory for dates and places I cannot conceive. **1934** A. C. EWING *Idealism* v. 258 The more rationalistically inclined philosophers have.. erred in putting forward extravagant claims to certainty.

rationality (ræʃəˈnælɪtɪ). [ad. late L. *ratiōnālitās* (Tertullian): see RATIONAL *a.* and -ITY. Cf. F. *rationalité*.]

1. The quality of possessing reason; the power of being able to exercise one's reason.

1628 T. SPENCER *Logick* 49 Rationalitie is the intrinsecall part of man. **1698** FARQUHAR *Love & Bottle* v. i, Thou hast impudence enough to draw thy rationality in question. **1726** BUTLER *Serm. Rolls Chap.* vii. 129 Some kind of brute Force within, prevails over the Principle of Rationality. **1777** M. MORGAN *Ess. Falstaff* 159 [Vice] is inconsistent with moral agency, nay, with rationality itself. **1830** GALT *Lawrie T.* I. ii. (1849) 5 She spoke with great rationality. **1870** J. H. NEWMAN *Gram. Assent* II. viii. 274 We call rationality the distinction of man, when compared with other animals.

2. a. The fact of being based on, or agreeable to, reason.

1651 BIGGS *New Disp.* ¶ 234 The ingenuity and rationality of it will prevail more then our slender performances. **1681** *Whole Duty Nations* 20 The Wisdom, and unquestionable Rationality of the Divine Ordination among the Jews. **1744** HARRIS *Three Treat.* III. I. (1765) 155 [To society] we owe.. the very Elegance and Rationality of our Existence. **1806** A. KNOX *Rem.* I. 29 To preserve the rationality of religion.. to secure it from the charge of enthusiasm. **1871** TYNDALL *Fragm. Sci.* (1879) II. ii. 21 A principle of belief, to which he flatly denies rationality.

b. A rational or reasonable view, practice, etc. Also *attrib.*

1660 JER. TAYLOR *Duct. Dubit.* II. ii. rule 6 §69 There are some little rationalities.. which are well, and decent and pretty. **1660** BURNEY *Κέρδ. Δῶρον* (1661) 57 The Court of Admiraltie, who depend upon that great head of Rationalities, Iustinian. **1835** F. W. FABER *Lett.* (1869) 21 Anticipating quite as much danger from the mysticisms of Newman as from the rationalities of Whately. **1865** LECKY *Ration.* (1878) II. 148 The rights of rationalities became a great question in Europe. **1908** *Jrnl. Abnormal Psychol.* III. 166 Any act.. is immediately justified by distorting the mental processes concerned and providing a false explanation that has a plausible ring of rationality. **1933** J. L. GILLIN *Social Path.* xxvi. 452 Capitalism is characterized by rationality. By that we mean a tendency to long range planning, careful consideration of the adaptation of means to ends, and cold and careful calculation of what measures will bring the greatest gain. **1961** H. M. JOHNSON *Sociol.* ix. 204 The expression 'economic rationality'.. is perhaps confusing, since purely technical rationality in production is also 'economic', although not necessarily economical. **1969** SIMON & STEDRY in Lindzey & Aronson *Handbk. Social Psychol.* (ed. 2) V. xl. 272 The first [principle] is the assumption of objective rationality, which permits strong predictions to be made about human behavior without the painful necessity of observing people. **1975** T. MCCARTHY tr. *Habermas's Legitimation Crisis* (1976) II. iii. 46 Output crises have the form of a rationality crisis in which the administrative system does not succeed in reconciling and fulfilling the imperatives received from the economic system. *Ibid.* v. 62 A rationality deficit can arise because contradictory steering imperatives.. are then operative within the administrative system. **1976** H. LEIBENSTEIN *Beyond Economic Man* v. 73 Suppose, but only for a moment, that rationality is interpreted as 'calculatedness'.

3. The tendency to regard everything from a purely rational point of view.

1791 BOSWELL *Johnson* an. 1784, 5 May, Even men of pretty dry rationality may believe that there was an intermediate interposition of Divine Providence. **1876** GEO. ELIOT *Dan. Der.* VIII. lviii, Phlegmatic rationality stares and shakes its head at these unaccountable prepossessions.

†**4.** *Math.* The quality of being rational (5 a). *Obs.*

1570 BILLINGSLEY *Euclid* x. prop. xviii. 247 These wordes in length and in power are neuer referred to rationalitie, or irrationalitie.

†**5.** = RATIONALE 2. *Obs. rare*$^{-1}$.

1646 SIR T. BROWNE *Pseud. Ep.* 373 Many well directed intentions, whose rationalities will never beare a rigid examination.

rationalizable (ˈræʃənəˌlaɪzəb(ə)l), *a.* [-ABLE.] That may be rationalized. Hence ˌ**rationalizaˈbility**.

1896 *Contemp. Rev.* Aug. 175 This adaptation justifies us in treating reality as everywhere rationalisable. **1936** WIRTH & SHILS tr. *Mannheim's Ideology & Utopia* iii. 124 The intuitional approach.. conceives of knowledge and rationalizability as somewhat uncertain.

rationalization (ˌræʃənəlaɪˈzeɪʃən). [-ATION.]

1. a. The act of making rational or intelligible, or the result of this.

1846 RUSKIN *Mod. Paint.* (1851) I. II. I. vii. §42 The two Carthages are mere rationalizations of Claude. **1888** *Encycl. Brit.* XXIV. 556 The rationalization which explains the legend.

b. *Psychol.* The justification of behaviour to make it appear rational or socially acceptable by (subconsciously) ignoring, concealing, or glossing its real motive; an act of making such a justification.

1908 *Jrnl. Abnormal Psychol.* III. 166 Two different groups of false explanations can be distinguished.. according as they are formed mainly for private or mainly for public consumption. The former of these I would term 'evasions', the latter 'rationalisations'. **1924** J. RIVIERE tr. *Freud's Coll. Papers* I. 341 His [*sc.* Adler's] theory does what all patients do and what our waking thought in general does —namely, makes use of a rationalization, as Jones has called it, in order to conceal unconscious motives. **1947** E. F. FRAZIER in *Amer. Sociol. Rev.* XII. 271 A dynamic sociological theory of race relations which will discard all the rationalizations of race prejudice. **1953** R. F. C. HULL tr. *Jung's Coll. Wks.* VII. 214 My patient clung to his intellectual world and defended himself with rationalizations against what he regarded as his illness. **1961** H. BONNER *Psychol. of Personality* ix. 281 The term 'rationalization' has become a household word. It is essentially a method of self-justification. It is motivated by the fear of criticism and disapproval by others. **1977** F. J. BRUNO *Human Adjustment* ii. 67 The defense mechanism called rationalization is used when the real motive for one's behavior is unacceptable to the ego.

2. a. *Math.* The process of clearing from irrational quantities. (See RATIONAL *a.* 5 a.)

1853 CAYLEY in *Camb. & Dubl. Math. Jrnl.* VIII. 97 (*title*) On the Rationalisation of certain algebraical Equations.

b. *Physics.* The reformulation of the equations and definitions of electromagnetism so that the factor 4π is removed from those relating to systems without spherical symmetry.

1891 O. HEAVISIDE in *Electrician* 16 Oct. 656/2 When.. the real advantages of the rational system become widely recognized and thoroughly assimilated, then will come a demand for the rationalisation of the practical units. **1942** *Phil. Mag.* XXXIII. 486 The simplification of formulæ due to rationalization can be illustrated by considering a parallel plate condenser. **1951** *Electr. Engin.* LXX. 332/2 Note that, in effect, a 4π was inserted in the denominator of the classical expression for force between parallel wires to accomplish rationalization, and that the elimination of 4π from the magnetomotive force relation followed without any additional arbitrary insertion of 4π. **1969** L. YOUNG *Systems of Units Electr. & Magn.* 197 The appearance or disappearance of 4π's in the equations of electromagnetism upon rationalization can be interpreted in two ways... Just as our point of view has been described as 'rationalization of units', so the other point of view has been called 'rationalization of quantities'.

c. *Econ.* and *Sociol.* The process of applying rational (sense 7) methods, esp. of standardization and simplification, to the planning and organization of economic enterprises or the administration of social groups in order to achieve a particular result such as maximum profit or efficiency; an example of this.

[**1905** M. WEBER in *Archiv f. Sozialwissenschaft u. Sozialpolitik* XX. 29 Alsdann nun wiederholte sich, was immer and überall die Folge eines solchen „Rationalisierungs"-Prozesses ist.] **1921** E. & C. PAUL tr. *Rathenau's In Days to Come* III. i. 125 The general wellbeing of the country is doubled or trebled by the setting of idle hands to work and by the rationalisation of production. **1926** D. HOUSTON *Memorandum on Rationalisation in U.S.* 3 The term rationalisation as used in Europe today includes, I take it, the three elements of stabilisation, standardisation and simplification of industry or of individual enterprises. **1934** P. & I. PETROFF *Secret of Hitler's Victory* iii. 38 The soullessness of modern labour, which had reached its climax in consequence of the rationalization, became the outstanding feature of the whole period. **1936** H. A. PHELPS *Princ. & Laws of Sociol.* xx. 424 A compensating general trend is the increasing rationalization of social life. **1939** H. HODGE *Cab, Sir?* 259 The would-be Napoleon.. puts his rationalisation schemes into the waste-paper basket. **1947** HENDERSON & PARSONS tr. *Weber's Theory Social & Econ. Organization* i. 112 One of the most important aspects of the process of 'rationalization' of action is the substitution for the unthinking acceptance of ancient custom, of deliberate adaptation to situations in terms of self-interest. **1959** *Listener* 31 Dec. 1147/2 A rationalization proposal [in the U.S.S.R.] is a technical improvement using known means which lacks the degree of originality demanded of a patentable invention. **1971** J. J. SHAPIRO tr. *Habermas's Toward Rational Society* vi. 99 Until then [*sc.* the 19th century] modern science did not contribute to the acceleration of technical development nor, consequently, to the pressure toward rationalization from below. **1972** W. J. MOMMSEN *Age of Bureaucracy* iv. 80 Another secular force of social change is found, namely rationalization.. by which tradition-bound or value-oriented forms of political and social organization are gradually replaced by purely instrumentally rational institutions. **1976** *Star* (Sheffield) 20 Nov., The company had announced 'rationalisation' plans meaning the closure of the Dronfield works.

rationalize (ˈræʃənəlaɪz), *v.* [f. RATIONAL *a.*]

1. a. *trans.* To render conformable to reason; to explain on a rational basis.

1803 *Lett. Miss Riversdale* II. 79 This interesting sentiment [*sc.* friendship].. secures the permanence of happiness, by rationalizing (if I may use such a word) its origin. **1817** COLERIDGE *Biog. Lit.* II. xviii. 89 The second Olympic composed for the.. purpose of rationalizing the Theban Eagle. **1846** GROTE *Greece* I. xvi. I. 533 The disposition of Herodotus to rationalise the miraculous narratives of the current mythes. **1883** H. SPENCER in *Contemp. Rev.* XLIII. 9 When life has been duly rationalized by science.. care of the body is imperative. **1935** *Encycl. Social Sci.* XIII. 116/1 The problem was to rationalize human social life on the basis of self-evident and universal principles. **1965** W. J. HARVEY in Geo. Eliot *Middlemarch* 11 Bulstrode.. who rationalizes his worldly success as an example of divine providence.

b. To clear *away* by reasoning.

1855 KINGSLEY *Sir W. Raleigh* Misc. (1859) I. 1 To rationalize away all the wonders, till we make them at last impossible, and give up caring to believe them.

c. *Psychol.* To give plausible reasons for (one's behaviour) that ignore, conceal, or gloss its real motive. Also *absol.* or *intr.*

1922 H. SOMERVILLE *Pract. Psycho-Anal.* i. 14 It is clear that patient is rationalising, and that as a matter of fact he is eaten up with jealousy. **1925** J. RIVIERE tr. *Freud's Coll. Papers* III. 330 The patient's consciousness naturally misunderstands them and puts forward a set of secondary motives to account for them—rationalizes them, in short. **1932** H. G. WELLS *Work, Wealth & Happiness of Mankind* vii. 279 To rationalize has one meaning in psychology, another meaning in the sociological writings of Max Weber, and quite another in the loose discussions of modern politicians and business men. **1966** *Word Study* Dec. 3/2, I think we all rationalize with the thought that the free democratic society which produced us.. had a right to be presented (*sic*) in such a fashion.

2. a. *Math.* To clear from irrational quantities.

1816 tr. *Lacroix's Diff. & Int. Calculus* 670 The differential function.. may be rationalized. **1888** C. SMITH *Algebra* (1893) 213 Find factors which will rationalize the following expressions.

b. *Physics.* To subject (the units or equations of electromagnetism) to rationalization (sense 2 b).

1892 *Nature* 28 July 292/2 It is.. very desirable that the practical units themselves should be rationalized. **1899** *Electrician* 29 Dec. 325/2 If we take the permeability of ether to be 4π units instead of unity, we rationalize at one stroke all our present units except the units of magnetic force and magnetic pole strength. **1973** J. YARWOOD *Electricity & Magnetism* ii. 32 In rationalising electrical units the object.. is to avoid the occurrence of 4π in systems without spherical symmetry and of 2π where cylindrical symmetry is absent.

c. To organize (economic production or the like) according to rational or scientific principles so as to achieve a desired or predictable result; esp. to reduce the number of (personnel, industrial plants, etc.) in such a way that the remainder are more efficiently deployed.

1926 E. GROSSMANN *Methods Econ. Rapprochement* 30 International cartels will be able to rationalise production in a way impossible in the present state of affairs. **1931** *Ann. Reg. 1930* II. 26 The Lancashire cotton industry. The steps taken to 'rationalise' the industry. **1953** J. B. CARROLL *Study of Lang.* iv. 127 A recent attempt to rationalize an artificial language by making maximal use of elements common to the most widely used natural languages is Interlingua. **1962** *Listener* 22 Mar. 509/2 Their numbers go down: they are 'rationalized'. In 1920 there were nine evening newspapers in London; now there are two. **1977** *R.A.F. News* 11–24 May 7/2, I am.. aware.. of the need to rationalise reporting systems to reduce paperwork.

3. To endow with reason. *rare.*

1896 [see RATIONALIZED *ppl. a.*].

4. *intr.* To employ reason or rationalism; to think rationally or in a rationalistic manner.

1835 J. H. NEWMAN *Lett.* (1891) II. 137 When we ask for reasons when we should not, we rationalise. **1868** BROWNING *Ring & Bk.* VIII. 1185 But subdue the bard And rationalize a little.

Hence ˈ**rationalizing** *vbl. sb.* and *ppl. a.*; ˈ**rationalizer**, one who rationalizes.

1834 T. KEIGHTLEY *Tales* vii. 250 Whittington's Cat has not escaped the *rationalisers. **1871** TYLOR *Prim. Cult.* I. 250 The fault of the rationalizer lay in taking allegory beyond its proper action. **1865** J. S. MILL *Auguste Comte* 54 The way to a complete *rationalizing of those sciences.. has been shown nowhere so successfully as there. **1873** M.

ARNOLD *Lit. & Dogma* (1876) 327 Partial and local rationalising of religion. **1927** A. HUXLEY *Let.* 25 Feb. (1969) 284, I can't see that there's anything to distinguish his rationalizings of religious emotions from those of anyone else. **1971** P. GRESSWELL *Environment* 105 Footpaths in some parishes need reorganising and rationalising for today's needs. **1841** GLADSTONE *State in Rel. with Ch.* x. (ed. 4) 367 The confession of faith of some *rationalising philosopher. *c* **1852** *Wylde's Circ. Sc.* I. 483/2 The rationalising multiplier here is 5 + √3. **1868** FREEMAN *Norm. Conq.* (1876) II. App. 543 Such rationalizing doubts are indignantly dismissed.

'rationalized, *ppl. a.* [f. RATIONALIZE *v.* + -ED[1].] **a.** That has been rendered rational.

1855 SIR G. C. LEWIS *Credib. Rom. Hist.* xi. I. 426 According to another, and probably a rationalized, version. **1896** *Spectator* 11 Apr. 519 Swift's grim conceptions of animalized man and rationalized animals.

b. *spec.* in *Physics*, applied to units, equations, and definitions in electromagnetism that are formulated so that the factor 4π appears only when a system with spherical symmetry is involved. Cf. RATIONAL *a.* 5 c.

1933 [see GIORGI]. **1951** *Electr. Engin.* LXX. 332/1 The MKS Rationalized system seems now to be replacing the others rapidly and may well come to be the accepted system for all theoretical work in electricity. **1969** L. YOUNG *Systems of Units Electr. & Magn.* vi. 78 The rationalized form of the CGS practical system is theoretically possible but is never used. **1973** J. YARWOOD *Electricity & Magnetism* xvi. 608 The rationalised mksA units in electricity form a part of the wider SI system of units.

rationally ('ræʃənəlɪ), *adv.* [f. RATIONAL *a.*]

1. In a rational manner; reasonably.

1612 WOODALL *Surg. Mate* Wks. (1653) 146 If he rationally follow the precedent method. **1659** BP. WALTON *Consid. Considered* 23 No such consectaries could be logically and rationally deduced from such premises. **1786** BURKE *Art. agst. Hastings* Wks. 1842 II. 174 The sum of money aforesaid, which in a time of such extreme distress.. could not be rationally given. **1844** H. H. WILSON *Brit. India* III. 387 The honest expression of opinions conscientiously and rationally entertained.

2. In respect of, by means of, reason. *rare.*

1620 T. GRANGER *Div. Logike* 150 Here are foure termes rationally distinguished, but three really, viz. Law, Magistrate, People. **1701** NORRIS *Ideal World* I. iv. 223 If.. the intelligible world be the more certain of the two, because rationally evident.

rationalness ('ræʃənəlnɪs). Now *rare.* [f. as prec.] The state or quality of being rational.

1659 *Gentl. Calling* viii. §15 He that would justifie the rationalness of any adventure, must prove the prize at least to equal the worth of that he hazards for it. **1664** H. MORE *Apology* 487 All that I averre is the Rationalness of this Position, not the Truth thereof. **1727** in BAILEY, vol. II. **1889** J. J. THOMAS *Froudacity* 215 The existence of a Deity and the rationalness of entreating him in prayer.

rationary ('ræʃənərɪ), *a. rare.* [ad. late L. *ratiōnārius*, or f. L. *ratiōn-em*: see RATIO *sb.* and -ARY[1].] †**a.** 'Of or belonging to account or reckoning' (Blount 1656). *Obs.* **b.** (See quot.)

a **1866** GROTE *Exam. Utilit. Philos.* (1870) xviii. 275 Ethics .. must be rationary (i.e. interested in the reasons of facts) as distinguished from positivist.

'rationate, *v. rare.* [f. late L. *ratiōnāt-*, ppl. stem of *ratiōnārī* to reason, f. *ratio* RATIO *sb.*] *intr.* To reason, to ratiocinate.

1644 DIGBY *Nat. Bodies* xxxviii. (1658) 419 When they will have beasts rationate and understand. **1819** *Blackw. Mag.* IV. 535 The doctor, therefore, rationated inconsequentially.

'rationative, *a. rare.* [f. as prec. + -IVE.] That gives or introduces a reason.

1650 WEEKES *Truth's Confl.* ii. 54 The first particular in the 11. Verse [For] which is a Rationative Particle. **1656** JEANES *Mixt. Schol. Div.* 5 An argumentative, or rationative description of the object of feare. *a* **1966** 'M. NA GOPALEEN' *Best of Myles* (1968) 195 An issue too imponderable for rationative evaluation.

'rationing, *vbl. sb.* [f. RATION *v.* + -ING[1].]

a. The action of the vb.

1865 *Englishman's Mag.* Oct. 312 The rationing of soldiers .. was much neglected. **1870** *Pall Mall G.* 10 Dec. 10 You have to dine at a restaurant until your rationing day comes round again.

b. *rationing by the purse*, raising the price of a commodity so as to restrict the number of people who can afford to buy it. Similarly *rationing by price*.

1917 *Times* 1 May 7/6 The German Government now knows all about rationing, but while it has been learning the German people has eaten up its supplies. **1924** E. M. H. LLOYD *Experiments in State Control* xxiii. 290 As for the argument that rationing increases consumption, this was not true of the articles most severely rationed in Great Britain. **1930** *Economist* 22 Mar. 637/1 In the last resort, a rationing of credit was the only expedient left to central banks. **1940** *Times* (Weekly ed.) 10 Jan. 9/3 Rationing may have to be used to a much greater extent than in the last war. **1947** PEOPLE 22 June 2, I find school lunches a great help with the rationing problems. *Ibid.*, It is the end of the rationing period. **1950** *Hansard Commons* 24 Apr. 617 Is this not a case of rationing by the purse? **1975** S. BRIGGS *Keep Smiling Through* 149 The great wartime invention, borrowed from the Germans, was points rationing. This widened choice as much as it could be widened within a rationing system. You could even.. choose where to shop without being tied to the grocer where you were registered for basic rations. **1979** W. SAFIRE in *N.Y. Times Mag.* 9 Sept. 16/1 *Rationing by price*, a system in which economic goods go to the people who are most willing to pay for them. This is the normal way of distributing goods in capitalist countries, and is increasingly used in Communist countries. Economists generally consider it an efficient system, but some politicians consider it immoral and prefer a system of rationing by political pull.

'rationless, *a. rare.* [-LESS.] Without rations.

1865 *Standard* 19 Apr., He might.. suddenly find himself and his army rationless and surrounded.

'rationment. *rare.* [f. RATION *v.* + -MENT, after F. *rationnement.*] The act of rationing.

1870 *Standard* 19 Nov., Very early in the siege.. the census was taken for the rationment of butchers' meat.

ratiotination, obs. form of RATIOCINATION.

‖**ratissage** (ratisaʒ). *Econ.* [Fr., lit. 'scraping, raking in of stakes'.] A device whereby the Bank of France calls in a portion of its country's commercial banks' foreign currency balances, and so temporarily improves its reserves of foreign exchange.

1957 *Economist* 28 Dec. 1144/1 The technique of *ratissage* dates from March of this year even though it is only now that it has been broadened to include dollars as well as EPU currencies. **1959** *Ibid.* 10 Jan. 155/2 A substantial part of the EPU deficit is ascribed to further *ratissage* by the Bank of France. **1959** *Times* 7 Apr. 17/1 The French recovery has now gone far enough for the French authorities to hope that their so-called 'ratissage' operations may be liquidated this month.

'ratitate, *a. rare*[−0]. [f. next, after *carinate.*] Ratite. (Ogilvie 1882.)

ratite ('rætaɪt), *a.* (and *sb.*) *Ornith.* [f. L. *ratis* raft + -ITE[2]. Cf. L. *ratītus* (of a coin) marked with the figure of a raft.] Of or belonging to the *Ratitæ*, a class of birds (so named by Merrem, 1812) having a keelless sternum, as the ostrich, emu, cassowary, etc. (Opposed to *carinate.*) Also as *sb.*, a bird belonging to this group.

1877 NEWTON in *Ann. Nat. Hist.* Ser. IV. XX. 500 *Megistanes* was used in 1816 by Vieillot.. for the whole group of Ratite Birds then known. **1885** —— in *Encycl. Brit.* XVIII. 19/2 The corresponding characters peculiar to the Ratite Division being the disconnected condition of the barbs of the feathers.., the non-existence of the furcula [etc.]. **1911** J. A. LEACH *Austral. Bird Bk.* 52 'Discontinuous distribution' as applied to land animals, e.g... ratite birds in South America.. implies a land connexion. **1939** J. FISHER *Birds as Animals* iii. 32 Sometimes.. it [*sc.* the hallux] is altogether absent, as it is in auks, bustards and ratite birds. *Ibid.* vi. 73 Ostriches flock, so do the other ratites. **1978** *Sci. Amer.* July 102/2 Among the other ratites are the ostrich, the emu and the extinct giant moa of New Zealand. **1979** *Nature* 14 June 633/2 The supposed presence of a ratite bird, a member of a group otherwise restricted to the Southern Hemisphere, in the Upper Cretaceous of Mongolia is very doubtful.

Hence **'ratitous** *a.*

1880 *Nature* XXI. 347 The avian, and indeed ratitous character of the animal.

ratle(r, obs. ff. RATTLE *sb.*[1] and *v.*[1], RATTLER.

ratlin(e, ratling ('rætlɪn, -lɪŋ). *Naut.* Forms: α. 5 **radelyng,** 5, 7– **ratling,** 7, 9 **rattling.** β. 8– **ratlin,** 9 **rattlin.** γ. 5 **rad(d)elyne,** 8– **ratline.** [Of obscure origin: perh. the same word as OF. *rael-, raalingue* (? from **rade-,* **ratelingue*), now *ralingue* small cordage employed to strengthen the edge of a sail.

There is no evidence that the ending *-line* is identical with LINE *sb.*[2]; cf. the synonymous Du. *weveling* with LG. *weveline*, G. *webeleine*.]

1. Thin line or rope such as is used for the ratlines (see 2); also *ratline stuff*, † *line*.

1481–90 *Howard Househ. Bks.* (Roxb.) 111 My Lord paid him for iij. hausers, a peir takkes, a ratling line for Chewdes, weing C. a quarter xiij. lb. xv. s. **1497** *Naval Acc. Hen. VII* (1896) 185 Raddelyne Marlyne & Sayletwyne. Also.. payed for DC weyght Radelyng.. liiij s. **1833** POE *MS. found in Bottle* in *Gift 1836* (1835) 80 A pile of ratlin-stuff and old sails. **1835** CONSTABLE in Leslie *Mem.* (1845) 268 A supply of rattlin for his hammock. **1883** *Man. Seamanship for Boys' Training Ships R. Navy* (Admiralty) (1886) 312 Hitch your rattling stuff round the third shroud from aft. **1899** F. T. BULLEN *Log of Sea-waif* 323 We had no new ratline stuff on board. **1954** BRADFORD & QUILL *Gloss. Sea Terms* 154/1 *Ratline stuff*, twelve- or fifteen-thread but usually eighteen-thread right-handed, tarred rope, used for ratlines, heavy lashings and heavy lines.

2. (Chiefly *pl.*) One of the small lines fastened horizontally on the shrouds of a vessel, and serving as steps by which to go up and down the rigging.

catch-ratlin(e: see latest quots. in β and γ.

α. **1611** COTGR., *Enflecheures*, the ratlings, the cordie steps whereby mariners climbe vp to the top of the mast. *a* **1685** OTWAY *Compl. Muse* xviii, With ill-furl'd Sails, and Rattlings loose. **1797** NELSON 23 June in Nicolas *Disp.* (1846) VII. p. cxliv, A brace, bowling, halyards, or any rope, even to a rattling. **1859** *All Year Round* No. 17. 399, I placed my hands on the shrouds.. and lightly touched with my feet the lower rattlings.

β. **1711** W. SUTHERLAND *Shipbuild. Assist.* 113 The Main Shrouds, and the Cross-lines, called Ratlins, serving as Steps to go into the Main-top. **1767** S. PATERSON *Another Trav.* II. 224 The seeming firm-set ladder to towering Fame, will become the rolling ratlins of lasting Infamy. **1816** SCOTT *Antiq.* viii, Make the chair fast with the rattlin —haul taught and belay! *c* **1860** H. STUART *Seaman's Catech.* 35 Every sixth ratlin will be a catch ratlin, that is, the end of the ratlin is seized to the after shroud.

γ. **1721** in BAILEY. **1773** *Gentl. Mag.* XLIII. 143 Up ladders and steps, and up ratlines and stairs, We pass'd. **1882** NARES *Seamanship* (ed. 6) 13 All the ratlines are seized to the after shroud but one, except every fifth ratline, which is seized to the after shroud, and is called a catch ratline.

Hence †**ratlin(e** *v., trans.* to furnish with ratlines. *Obs.* (Cf. RATTLE *v.*[2])

1495 *Naval Acc. Hen. VII* (1896) 277 DC Radelyne.. spent apon reparacion & Radelynyng of the Shrowdes. **1711** W. SUTHERLAND *Shipbuild. Assist.* 113 The main Swifter, a Part of the Shrowds, but not ratlin'd.

rat-line. *rare*[−0]. [Of obscure origin.] 'The rope or cord used for enclosing any spot or ground' (Voyle & Stevenson *Milit. Dict.* 1876).

'ratling. *rare.* [-LING.] A little rat.

1882 'BASIL' (R. A. KING) *Love the Debt* xlii, The cellar soon swarmed with rats and ratlings.

Rato ('reɪtəʊ). *Aeronaut.* Also **rato.** [f. the initial letters of *r*ocket-*a*ssisted *t*ake-*o*ff.] A jato in which the engine is a rocket engine.

1953 P. C. BERG *Dict. New Words* 134/2 *R.A.T.O., Rato*, rocket-assisted take-off. **1962** *Aeroplane* CIII. 26/1 Designed to carry outsize cargo, the Stratocruiser is to have an increased payload of 60,000 lb and RATO units will be used.

ratomorphic (ˌrætəʊˈmɔːfɪk), *a. rare.* [f. RAT *sb.*[1] + *-omorphic*, after ANTHROPOMORPHIC *a.*] (See quot. 1964.) Also **'ratomorph**, one who holds a ratomorphic view of human behaviour.

1964 KOESTLER in *Listener* 14 May 786/2 It refuses to attribute to man any mental processes which cannot be shown to occur in lower animals. In other words, for the anthropomorphic view of the rat, Behaviourism has substituted a ratomorphic view of man. **1967** *Economist* 21 Oct. 295/3 The author [*sc.* Koestler] presents a trenchant.. criticism of behaviourism and experimental 'ratomorphic' views of men. **1977** H. G. BURGER in B. Bernardi *Concept & Dynamics of Culture* 460 In trying to overlook symboling, those who oversimplify subhuman abilities are 'ratomorphs', and have overlooked two and a half million years of hominid evolution.

raton, ratoner: see RATTON, -ER.

ratoon (rəˈtuːn), *sb.* Also 8–9 **ratt-.** [ad. Sp. *retoño* a fresh shoot or sprout.] A new shoot or sprout springing up from the root of the sugar-cane after it has been cropped.

1779 *Phil. Trans.* LXVII. 232, I then took each rattoon apart, and found it fastened to a joint of these last canes. *a* **1818** M. G. LEWIS *Jrnl. W. Ind.* (1834) 88 After these original plants have been cut, their roots throw up suckers which in time become canes, and are called ratoons. **1887** *Century Mag.* Nov. 111 Next year the cane sprouts from the stubble, and is called first ratoons... The second year it sprouts again, and is called second ratoons.

transf. **1894** *Pop. Sci. Monthly* XLIV. 493 The Jamaican reference to a meal made off the remnants of a previous feast as 'eating the rattoons'.

attrib. **1777** ROBERTSON *Hist. Amer.* (1778) I. 459 On the banks of the Essequebo, thirty crops of ratoon canes have been raised successively. **1880** J. S. COOPER *Coral Lands* I. xviii. 213 When cut in March or April the ratoon canes are made to grow in cold dry weather.

ratoon (rəˈtuːn), *v.* [f. prec. or ad. Sp. *retoñar* to sprout again, f. *retoño.*] **a.** *intr.* Of plants, *esp.* the sugar-cane: To send up new shoots after being cut down or cropped. †Said also of the ground.

1756 P. BROWNE *Jamaica* 130 Where the ground is observed to produce a kind plant and to rattoon well. **1789** *Trans. Soc. Arts* I. 260 Some sorts of Cotton did not rattoon or stool so well as others. **1856** OLMSTED *Slave States* 666 In the West India plantations the cane is frequently allowed to ratoon for eight successive crops. **1880** J. S. COOPER *Coral Lands* I. xviii. 214 Such a cane must be hardy and healthy, grow rapidly, ratoon quickly and often.

b. *trans.* To cut down (plants) to induce them to send up new shoots.

1925 *Glasgow Herald* 23 Apr. 14/2 Reports indicate that ratooned cotton has suffered. Ratooned plants produce a much earlier crop than new plants and.. Zululand had ratooned a considerable quantity this year.

Hence **ra'tooned** *ppl. a.*, **ra'tooning** *vbl. sb.*

1790 *Phil. Trans.* LXXX. 357 He makes a greater revenue than the Grenada planter on the present mode of rattooning. **1882** *Spons' Encycl. Manuf.* V. 1868 By constant ratooning, the produce of sugar per acre.. yields [etc.]. **1925** Ratooned [see sense b of the vb.].

ratooner (rəˈtuːnə(r)). [f. prec. + -ER.] A plant that ratoons.

1922 *Chambers's Jrnl.* Dec. 800/2 A second crop can be obtained from the dwarfed stumps of the trees after the first crop has been picked, but the ochro is a bad ratooner.

ratorn, obs. Sc. form of RETURN *v.*

rat race. Also **rat-race.** [f. RAT *sb.*[1]]

†**1.** A dance. *U.S. slang. Obs.*

1937 *Amer. Speech* XII. 74/2 C.C.C. speech... Terms for recreations: *rat-race*, dance of low-grade nature. **1948** MENCKEN *Amer. Lang.* Suppl. II. 707 The vocabulary of the jazz addict... A dance is a *rat-race* or *cement-mixer*.

2. A fiercely competitive struggle or contest; a struggle to maintain one's position in work or life. orig. *U.S.*

1939 C. MORLEY *Kitty Foyle* xxvi. 261 Their own private life gets to be a rat-race. **1940** *Time* 16 Dec. 26/3 Veteran fliers blanched when they saw the hourly, crowded 'rat race' at Randolph—the close-packed stream of trainers, gliding in to land and take on fresh cadets and instructors. **1946** *War Report* (B.B.C.) 350 Our armour is now 'swanning' as they say in the British Army, or in American parlance, 'the rat race is on'. **1947** J. Steinbeck *Wayward Bus* 214 He was afraid of his friends and his friends were afraid of him. A rat race, she thought. **1954** Wodehouse & Bolton *Bring on Girls* 219 'Is anything the matter with you?' 'Just the rat-race. I don't quite know why I've been doing it.' **1956** R. Fuller *Image of Society* iii. 70 A boy's got to have guts to make his way in this rat race of a modern world. **1958** *Spectator* 19 Sept. 381/2 Modern economic life is more like a rat-race than a rational way of life. **1959** *Observer* 8 Mar. 17/7, I don't like this rat-race for promotion. **1959** *Spectator* 2 Oct. 435/2 A realism that encourages in its popular press a rat-race morality in the guise of room at the top. **1960** *Daily Tel.* 18 May 17/7 A spirited criticism of 'the daily rat race' to get to work in London. **1967** G. F. Fiennes *I tried to run Railway* iv. 31 It became a rat race to see who could get teams in first so as to improve recruitment. **1973** C. Bonington *Next Horizon* iv. 68 Another artist, who had abandoned the rat-race and settled in Coniston. **1976** F. Zweig *New Acquisitive Society* I. v. 52 The shedding of middle-class values and style of life in the younger generation..is an outright negation of middle-class existence, defined in such derogatory terms as 'rat race'. **1978** D. A. J. Seargent *UFO's* v. 111 A motor car—the prime symbol of our motorised, machine-oriented, rat-race society.

Hence as *v. trans.* and *intr.*, to take part in a 'rat race'; **'rat-racer, 'rat-racing** *vbl. sb.* and *ppl. a.*

1937 *Clarionette* (Univ. of Denver) (St. Patrick ed.) 18 Mar. 1/3 If you're off for a little body-swaying to music, you are..'rat-racing'. **1960** *Listener* 7 Jan. 41/2 A scarifying glimpse of rat racing in local government. **1962** *Guardian* 15 Oct. 7/2 A new modern figure—the new kind of ambitious rat-racer, the Snopes in the grey flannel suit. **1968** *Ibid.* 5 Oct. 6/5 Literary people in this country seem to have been ..rat-racing each other to the nearest vacant editor's chair. **1968** *New Scientist* 21 Nov. 418/3 Looking into an aquarium ..is just the medicine for a chap who has spent all day rat-racing against a computer. **1969** E. Lemarchand *Alibi for Corpse* ix. 116 I'm a damn sight saner than people who spend their lives rat-racing and jabbering their heads off. **1971** *New Scientist* 1 July 5/1 The belief among rat-racers that the physical exercise delays thrombosis. **1971** *Guardian* 3 July 8/6 Middle aged Frank who wants to be a drop-out from rat-racing society. **1977** D. Morris *Manwatching* 124 Eccentricity of dress and behaviour is commonplace for them and they enjoy social freedoms unknown to other rat-racing citizens.

†rat-rane. *Sc. Obs.* [rane *sb.*] = rat-rime.

1513 Douglas *Æneis* viii. Prol. 147 To reyd I begane The riotest ane ragment wyth mony rat rane.

ratret, obs. Sc. form of retreat.

'rat-rime. *Sc.* and *north.* Also 6 ratt-. [f. *rat*, prob. onomatopœic (cf. *rattle* vb.) + rime.] A piece of doggerel verse; a rigmarole.

1553 *Douglas' Æneis* viii. Prol. 147 The royetest ane ragment with mony ratt rime. *a* **1585** Polwart *Flyting w. Montgomerie* 146 Thy roustie ratrimes, made but mater. **1636** Row *Hist. Kirk* (1842) 404 What will a rat-ryme of words work upon an hard unrenewed heart? **1728** Ramsay *Last Sp. Miser* xix, With a lang rat-rhime of cant. **1818** Scott *Hrt. Midl.* viii, 'I cannot use a prayer like a rat-rhyme', answered the honest clergyman. **1894** in *Northumbld. Gloss.*

ratsbane ('rætsbeɪn). [f. rat *sb.*[1] + bane.]

1. Rat-poison; †*spec.* arsenic. (Now only *literary.*)

1523 *Churchw. Acc. St. Mary Hill, London* (Nichols 1797) 108 For milke and rattisbane for the rats in the church. **1597** J. Payne *Royal Exch.* 41 Men cover ratts bane vnder suger or hony. **1679** Dryden *Troilus & Cr.* Epil. 9 As we strew rat's-bane when we vermin fear. **1722** De Foe *Plague* (1884) 161 Endeavours were us'd..to destroy the Mice and Rats,.. by laying Rats-Bane. **1820** Shelley *Œd. Tyr.* i. 354 Black ratsbane, which That very Rat, who..Nurtures himself on poison, dare not touch. **1877** 'Mark Twain' in *Atlantic Monthly* Dec. 723/1 What was that cat's name that eat a keg of ratsbane by mistake over at Hooper's?

fig. **1593** Harvey *Pierce's Super.* Wks. (Grosart) II. 293 That peece of Alchimy, that can turne the Rattes-bane of Villany into the Balme of honesty. **1633** Prynne *1st Pt. Histrio-m.* iv. i. 140 Playes are Rats-bane to government of Commonweales. **1809** Malkin *Gil Blas* v. i. ¶15 Running in debt is ratsbane to him.

2. Applied to certain plants (see quots.).

1846 Lindley *Veget. Kingd.* 583 The fruit of *Chailletia toxicaria* is said to be poisonous, it is called Ratsbane in Sierra Leone. **1886** *W. Som. Word-bk., Rat's Bane*, chervil. A common wild umbelliferous plant, in appearance something like hemlock—probably mistaken for it.

Hence **'ratsbaned** *ppl. a.*, poisoned with ratsbane; also **'ratsbany** *a.*

1638 R. Junius (Younge) *Drunkards Character* 269 Which makes them like ratsband Rats, drinke and vent. **1937** Blunden *Elegy* 24 And sets pot to mouth And once again moistens his ratsbany drouth.

ratsche, obs. Sc. form of ratch *sb.*[1]

Ratspuche, obs. form of Rajput.

rat's-tail. [f. rat *sb.*[1] Cf. rat-tail.]

1. *pl.* in *Farriery*: †**a.** Chaps or cracks on the back of a horse's hind legs, also called cratches or scratches. *Obs.* **b.** Warty or suppurating excrescences on the same part. (See quots. and cf. rat-tail 1.)

1580 Blundeville *Horsemanship* iv. cxxxix. 61 Of the Cratches or Rats tailes, called of the Italians Crepaccie. This is a kind of long scabbie rifts growing right vp and downe in the hinder part from the fewterlock vp to the Curbe. **1639** T. de Grey *Compl. Horsem.* 314 They be all..one and the same disease, as mules, kibes, rats tayles, crepanches. **1687** *Lond. Gaz.* No. 2263/4 A brown Bay cropt Mare,..with two Rats Tails on each Leg behind. **1722** W. Gibson *Farrier's Guide* ii. 246 Of Warts, Scratches, Rats-Tails and other Excrescences on the Legs and Pasterns. *Ibid.* 247 Rats-tails ..generally creep from the Pasterns to the middle of the Shank. **1891** Dalziel *Dis. Horses* 101 Rats' Tails, excrescences discharging ichorous matter, extending from the middle of the shank to the fetlock.

2. Applied to various things resembling a rat's tail in shape: **a.** The tapering end of a rope (Smyth *Sailor's Word-bk.* 1867). **b.** A rat-tail file (*Ibid.*). **c.** A candle-end. **d.** A lank lock of hair. **e.** A tapering rib or tongue of metal. **f.** = *rat's-tail fescue* (see 3 below).

1810 J. Lambert *Trav. Lower Canada* I. ix. 162 The dress of the Habitant is simple, and homely;..His hair is tied in a thick long queue behind, with an eelskin; and on each side of his face a few strait locks hang down like, what are vulgarly called, 'rats' tails'. **1869** Blackmore *Lorna D.* i, The end of a candle of tallow, or 'rat's tail', as we called it. **1899** Besant *Orange Girl* ii. v. 174 Their hair hung about their shoulders loose and undressed: it was not unbecoming in the young, but in the older women it became what is called rats' tails. **1950** *N.Z. Jrnl. Agric.* Sept. 219/3 In a way the rapid ingress of ratstail into pastures during the 1930's was a good thing.

3. *attrib.* **rat's tail cactus** = *rat-tail cactus* s.v. rat-tail 5; **rat's tail crane** ?*Obs.* (see quot.); **rat's-tail fescue**, an annual grass, *Vulpia myuros.*

1957 *Dict. Gardening* (R. Hort. Soc.) I. 146/2 Rat's Tail Cactus. Stems weak, pendent, slender. **1958** S. H. Scott *Observer's Bk. Cacti* 61 *Aporocactus flagelliformis.* Usually referred to as the 'rat's tail cactus' because of its pendent method of growth. **1729** Desaguliers in *Phil. Trans.* XXXVI. 196 This Crane is of the Sort which is commonly call'd a Rat's Tail Crane,..moving round a strong Post like a Wind-mill, so that it may turn quite round with all its Load. **1858** G. Bentham *Handbk. Brit. Flora* 602 Rat's-tail Fescue... A tufted annual, usually about a foot high. **1917** S. F. Armstrong *Brit. Grasses* vii. 100 Rat's-tail Fescue... An annual, occurring chiefly in waste places. **1944** W. J. Stokoe *Caterpillars Brit. Butterflies* 224 Rat's-tail Fescue Grass... This small tufted grass grows mostly in dry pastures. **1954** C. E. Hubbard *Grasses* 137 (*heading*) Rat's-tail Fescue.

ratt, obs. form of rat.

ratta, obs. form of rata.

'rattage. *nonce-wd.* [f. rat *sb.*[1] or *v.*[1] + -age.] Percentage of people who 'rat'.

1807 in *Spirit Pub. Jrnls.* XI. 229 In the Scots Peers we find a Rattage of no less than ninety per cent.

rat-tail. [f. rat *sb.*[1] Cf. rat's-tail.]

1. *pl.* = rat's-tail 1.

1753 Chambers *Cycl. Supp.*, *Rat-tails*, or Arrests, in the manege, signify callous hard swellings upon the hinder legs under the hough, running along the sinew. **1831** Youatt *Horse* xiv. (1848) 275 On the back part of the leg, are sometimes excrescences, called by farriers Rat-Tails, from the appearance they give the hair.

2. A tail resembling that of a rat; *esp.* a horse's tail with little or no hair; also, a horse having a hairless tail, or the diseased condition which causes the hair of the tail to fall off.

1705 *Lond. Gaz.* No. 4086/4 A black Horse.., with a Rat Tail. **1787** 'G. Gambado' *Acad. Horsem.* (1809) 26 Buy a horse with a rat tail, if possible. **1897** *Outing* (U.S.) XXIX. 540/1, I like his [a pointer's] clean-cut appearance, his rat-tail, his style in the field.

3. a. *gen.* Something resembling a rat's tail. **b.** A rat-tailed spoon (see rat-tailed *a.* 2). **c.** = rat's-tail 2 d.

1871 Kingsley *At Last* xi. (1880) 266 Their rat-tails of small green flowers prove them to be peppers. **1974** *Country Life* 14 Nov. 1447/1 Spoons ranging from 1661 to 1718.. include..split-ended rat-tails or treffid spoons. **1977** J. Wainwright *Day of Peppercorn Kill* 121 The woman's hair was in sodden rat-tails... Her shoes squelched water.

4. A deep-water marine fish belonging to the family Coryphænoididæ, esp. one of the genus *Macrurus*, characterized by a long, tapering tail. Also *attrib.*

1882 Gilbert & Jordan *Syn. Fishes N. Amer.* 811. **1905** D. S. Jordan *Guide to Study of Fishes* I. xii. 209 In the deep-sea allies of the codfishes, the grenadiers or rat-tails (*Macrouridæ*), the numbers [of vertebrae] range from 65 to 80. **1928** Russell & Yonge *Seas* iv. 91 That curious fish of the cod family known as the Macrurus or rat-tail..spends the greater part of its life in the cold dark depths over the abyssal plain. **1936** P. S. Barnhart *Marine Fishes California* 24 Rat-tails. The fishes of this family are deep-water fishes, and are seldom seen or taken. **1956** J. L. B. Smith *Old Fourlegs* ix. 92 In this they [*sc.* seals] are like humans, who will not eat these perfectly wholesome but..unfortunately named 'Rat Tails'. **1975** *New Yorker* 19 May 32/1 There might be a few rattails (bottom feeders related to the shark family) near the ocean floor. **1975** *Sci. Amer.* Oct. 86/3 The bait was visited by only a few eelpouts, brotulids and rattail fish (grenadiers).

5. *attrib.* (Cf. rat-tailed.)

rat-tail cactus, a pendent or creeping cactus, *Aporocactus flagelliformis*, native to central America and having spiny stems bearing scarlet flowers. ***rat-tail comb***, a comb with a long tapering handle at one end. ***rat-tail file***, a fine round file used for enlarging holes in metal, etc. ***rat-tail grass***, a name given to two Australian grasses (*Ischæmum laxum* and *Sporobolus indicus*). ***rat-tail radish***, an East Indian radish (*Raphanus caudatus*); cf. rat-tailed *a.* 1 d.

1744 in *Maryland Hist. Mag.* (1926) XXI. 251, 6 Ratt Tale Files. **1793** [see rat-tailed 1 b, quot. 1768]. **1801** C. K. Sharpe *Corr.* 12 Jan. (1888) I. 103 The clowns with lank rat-tail hair. **1846** Holtzapffel *Turning* II. 824 Small taper round files are often called rat-tail files. **1866** *Harvard Memor. Biogr., S. Willet* I. 267 A rat-tail file..would render useless in a moment a superb piece of ordnance. **1867** *Gardeners' Chron.* 3 Aug. 807/1 (*heading*) Raphanus caudatus, or Rat-tail Radish. **1889** J. H. Maiden *Usef. Native Plants Austr.* 92 Rat-tail Grass. An upright, slender growing grass [etc.]. *Ibid.* 109 Rat-tail grass. A fine, open, pasture grass [etc.]. **1895** *Army & Navy Co-op. Soc. Price List* 754 (*caption*) Queen Anne or Rat-tail [spoons]. **1900** L. H. Bailey *Cycl. Amer. Hort.* I. 283/2 Rat-tail Cactus. Creeping or pendent, slender and very branching. **1904** *Daily Chron.* 20 July 5/6 The bride's father presented her with a superb tiara of diamonds and pearls, and a canteen of rat-tail silver. **1925** S. T. Warner *Espalier* 77 The rat-tail spoons, The china dishes. **1945** *Sun* (Baltimore) 30 Jan. 6-0/3 It was made in 1898 from a rat-tail file which had been used in a bicycle factory. **1946** M. Free *All about House Plants* xvii. 203 Rat-tail Cactus..has long flexible stems about ½ inch in diameter covered with bristly hairs. **1972** F. Perry *Flowers of World* 60/1 *Aporocactus flagelliformis*, the Rat-tail Cactus, is well named for the long flexible stems.. hang down all round the plant. They are covered with bristly hairs and carry masses of crimson flowers. **1978** *Chatelaine* (Canada) Dec. 67/1 Tuck ends in with a rat-tail comb.

'rat-tailed, *a.* [f. rat *sb.*[1] Cf. prec.]

1. a. Having a tail like that of a rat; *esp.* of horses, having a rat-tail.

1684 *Lond. Gaz.* No. 1950/4 A Black Nag,..Mareheaded, and Rat-tailed. **1753** Chambers *Cycl. Supp.*, *Rat-tailed*, a horse is thus called that has no hair upon his tail. **1828** *Sporting Mag.* XXII. 231 A lean, rat-tailed mare. **1845** Youatt *Dog* 31 He selected a bull-dog, one of the smooth rat-tailed species. **1890** *Pall Mall G.* 4 Jan. 6/2 The miserable little rat-tailed, greyhound beasts that furnish what is called mutton in this country.

b. of the larva of a drone-fly (*Eristalis*) having a long slender flexible respiratory organ resembling a tail. In full, ***rat-tailed maggot.***

1753 Chambers *Cycl. Supp.*, *Rat-tailed worms*, in natural history, a species of fly-worms, with long tails, resembling those of rats. **1768** Arscott in Pennant *Brit. Zool.* (1776) III. 335 Blowing flies and humble bees that come from the rat-tailed maggot. [In Polwhele's *Devon* (1793) I. 124 *note*, 'rat-tail maggot'.] **1836–9** *Todd's Cycl. Anat.* II. 874/1 The rat-tailed larva of *Eristalis tenax.* **1895** L. C. Miall *Nat. Hist. Aquatic Insects* ii. 198 The Rat-tailed Maggot, a common inhabitant of stagnant pools. **1935** *Discovery* July 212/1 The problem [of breathing under water] had been solved long before by the rat-tailed maggot, with its telescopic tube reaching to the surface. **1952** J. Clegg *Freshwater Life Brit. Isles* ii. 27 The larvae of one or two insects, such as the Rat-tailed Maggot,..are well adapted for living in the black mud at the bottom of these unwholesome waters. **1968** *Oxf. Bk. Insects* 130/2 They swim freely, breathing through their long tails, which can be extended to 6 inches to reach the water surface—hence their name Rat-tailed Maggots.

c. *spec.* in the names of certain animals.

rat-tailed kangaroo (see quot. 1846). ***rat-tailed serpent***, an American viper (*Bothrops lanceolatus*). ***rat-tailed shrew***, the musk-rat. ***rat-tailed snake***, the fer-de-lance.

1846 Waterhouse *Nat. Hist. Mamm.* I. 224 *Hypsiprymnus Murinus*, Rat-tailed Hypsiprymnus, or Rat-Kangaroo. *Ibid.*, Index, Rat-tailed Rat-Kangaroo. **1854** Davy *West Indies* 273 [St. Lucia] possesses besides several kinds of harmless snakes, one that is poisonous, the rat-tailed snake. **1871** Kingsley *At Last* ii, We were..anxious to obtain at St. Lucia specimens of that abominable reptile, the Fer-de-lance, or rat-tailed snake. **1884** *Cassell's Nat. Hist.* I. 378 The Rat-tailed Shrew.

d. In the names of certain plants, esp. ***rat-tailed radish***, an Asian radish, *Raphanus caudatus*, cultivated for its edible fruit. Cf. rat-tail 5.

1867 *Gardeners' Chron.* 3 Aug. 807/1, I shall continue to grow the Rat-tailed Radish. **1885** W. Robinson tr. *Vilmorin-Andrieux's Veg. Garden* 499 Rat-tailed Radish... The edible part of this Radish is not the root, but the silique or seed-vessel, which is gathered before it is fully grown. **1949** *Nat. Geogr. Mag.* Aug. 213/2 In India the rat-tailed radish..is grown for its fleshy, edible seed pods. **1969** *Oxf. Bk. Food Plants* 170/2 The Rat-tailed Radish..is grown in southern Asia. The part eaten is not the root but the fruit, which reaches a length of 8 to 10 inches.

2. a. Of a spoon: Having a tail-like prolongation of the handle along the back of the bowl.

1881 Miss Braddon *Asphodel* III. 21 The slender little rat-tailed spoons.

b. Of a comb: having a long, tapering, handle at one end. Cf. *rat-tail comb* s.v. rat-tail 5.

1973 *Daily Colonist* (Victoria, B.C.) 15 July 1/3 It turned out to be an ordinary, black rat-tailed comb.

rattan, ratan (rə'tæn), *sb.*[1] Also 7 rat(t)oon, 8 rat-tan. [var. rotan[1] a. Malay *rōtan*, app. for *rautan*, f. *rāut* to pare, trim, strip.]

1. a. One of several species of the genus *Calamus*, climbing palms growing chiefly in the East Indies, on the mainland and the islands, and to a small extent in Africa and Australia, and notable for their long thin jointed and pliable stems; also, a plant belonging to one of these species. **b.** = *ground rattan* (see ground *sb.* 18 c).

1681 R. Knox *Hist. Ceylon* 17 Rattans grow in great abundance upon this Island. **1777** Miller in *Phil. Trans.* LXVIII. 177 Precipices..so steep that we could only draw ourselves up..by a rattan. **1813** Sir H. Davy *Agric. Chem.*

(1814) 57 In the rattan, the Epidermis of which contains a sufficient quantity of flint to give light when struck by steel. **1860** GOSSE *Rom. Nat. Hist.* 129 These ratans form a tribe of plants..which, though they resemble grasses or reeds in their appearance, are true trees of the palm kind.

2. a. A portion of the stem of a rattan, used for various purposes (cf. quots.).

1681 R. KNOX *Hist. Ceylon* 86 Every thing..is tyed with rattans and other strings. **1698** FRYER *Acc. E. India & P.* 17 A shady Contrivance,..on the upper end of which sits the Master of the Family on a Bed of Rattans, a kind of Cane. **1796** tr. *Thunberg's C. of Good Hope* in *Pinkerton* (1814) XVI. 13 Small ratans..fastened together with cotton-thread, so as to form an arch or a vaulted roof over the tomb. **1817** RAFFLES *Java* I. 42 The rattans..of Java are on the whole inferior to those of Sumatra and Borneo. **1870** YEATS *Nat. Hist. Comm.* 252 These palms yield the canes or rattans of commerce.

b. *esp.* A switch or stick of rattan, used for beating a person or thing, or for carrying in the hand.

1660 PEPYS *Diary* 13 Sept., Mr. Hawley did give me a little black rattoon, painted and gilt. **1665** SIR T. HERBERT *Trav.* (1677) 90 He..was chabuck't upon the soles of his feet with rattans. **1761** *Ann. Reg.* 185 Striking him with a rattan, at grumbling to do his duty. **1786** *Lounger* (1787) II. 196 When I meet a gentleman I must..flourish my rattan, to show my shapes. **1806–7** J. BERESFORD *Miseries Hum. Life* (1826) XIX. xviii. 229 A clothes-horse with a great-coat stretched out upon it, just ready for the rattan. **1858** CARLYLE *Fredk. Gt.* VI. vi. (1872) II. 196 Fritz he often enough beats, gives a slap to with his rattan.

3. Without article, as a material.

1748 *Anson's Voy.* III. x. 415 Each mast has only two shrouds made of twisted rattan. **1779** FORREST *Voy. N. Guinea* 106 The bow is generally of bamboo, and the string of split ratan. **1884** *Sunday at Home* June 397/2 These huts..are built of bamboos..tied with rattan.

4. *attrib.*, as ***rattan bale, cable, cane, chair, furniture, mat, palm, rocker, rope, screen, stick, ware.***

1800 *Asiat. Ann. Reg., Misc. Tracts* 216/1 The nutmegs are..packed up in *rattan bales. **1779** FORREST *Voy. N. Guinea* 56 A wooden anchor, and *rattan cable, which by floating, made an excellent warp. **1681** tr. *Willis' Remg. Med. Wks.* Vocab. s.v. *Internodia*, the spaces in a *Ratoon Cane between the joynts or knots. **1704** *Lond. Gaz.* No. 4054/6, 143 Bundles of Rattan Canes. **1753** CHAMBERS *Cycl. Supp.* s.v. *Cane*, Canes make a considerable article in commerce. There are imported two sorts, viz. walking and rattan canes. **1870** KINGSLEY in *Gd. Words* June 389/1 'Calamus rotangi' from the East, of which rattan canes are made. **1879** *Harper's Mag.* July 211 In the large parlor..with *rattan chairs galore..presided Karl Whitaker. **1925** W. S. MAUGHAM *The Letter* I. 9 The room is..quite simply furnished with rattan chairs, in which are cushions. **1972** D. BLOODWORTH *Any Number can Play* xv. 140 Comfortable rattan chairs. **1895** *Montgomery Ward & Co. Catal.* Spring & Summer 617/3 (*heading*) *Rattan and reed furniture. **1966** D. FORBES *Heart of Malaya* ii. 31 The old kind, built on stilts like a Malay house, with wide verandahs and rattan furniture, is still the best. **1925** W. S. MAUGHAM *The Letter* I. 9 *Rattan mats on the floor. **1846** LINDLEY *Veget. Kingd.* 135 The *Rattan Palms..are described as inhabitants of dense forests. **1854** HOOKER *Himal. Jrnls.* I. vi. 145 Bound tightly together by strips of rattan palm stem. **1895** *Montgomery Ward & Co. Catal.* Spring & Summer 617/3 We show a larger assortment of *rattan rockers in our special Furniture Catalogue. **1900** W. W. SKEAT *Malay Magic* 172 Six or eight coils of *rattan rope..are placed on a triangle formed with three rice-pounders. **1902** CONRAD *Youth* 205 The straggling building of bricks,..resounded with the incessant flapping of *rattan screens. **1836** DICKENS *Pickw.* xix, A thick *rattan stick with a brass ferrule. **1971** K. HOPKINS *Hong Kong* 247 Industries in which collective agreements have been signed include..*rattan ware.

Hence **ra'ttan** *v.*, *trans.* to fit with rattans; †**ra'ttaner** *nonce-wd.*, one who wields a rattan; **ra'ttanning**, chastisement with rattan sticks.

1816 'QUIZ' *Grand Master* VII. 168 [He] then to teach him better manners, Converts the hammals to rattan-ers. **1847** H. MELVILLE *Omoo* xxix. 110 The ratanning of the young culprits..may also be considered as in some measure characteristic of the [French] nation. **1895** J. M. WALSH *Tea* 67 The chest..[is] nailed, clamped, matted and rattaned.

rattan (rə'tæn), *sb.*[2] Also 8 **ratan**. [Echoic.] = RATAPLAN.

1787 BURNS *Let. Dr. Moore* Wks. (Globe) 341, I did not know..why my pulse beat such a furious ratan. **1844** AINSWORTH *St. James* I. v. 136 Their ears were saluted with the loud rattan of a drum.

rattan, obs. form of RATTEN *v.*

rattany, variant of RHATANY.

†**rattar.** *Obs. rare.* A sieve used in gold-washing. Also ***rattar-work.***

1683 PETTUS *Fleta Min.* I. 104 There must..be made of Brass Wire a Rattar or Seeve as wide or narrow as the Work requireth... The bigness of the Rattar is to be seven spans long. *Ibid.* 107 The before described Rattar-work.

rattaree: see RAHDAREE.

rat-tat ('ræt'tæt), *sb.* [Echoic.] **a.** A sharp rapping sound, *esp.* of a knock at a door.

1774 T. HUTCHINSON *Diary* 3 Nov. I. 277 A violent rat-tat at the door made us jump. **1840–1** S. WARREN *Ten Thousand a Year* (ed. Warne) 87/2 A few moments before the postman's rat-tat was heard. **1870** MISS BRIDGMAN *R. Lynne* II. xi. 226 There came a soft little rat-tat at the street-door.

b. Used imitatively with vbs.

a **1845** HOOD *Double Knock* i, Rat-tat it went upon the lion's chin. *c* **1860** LOWELL *Pict. fr. Appledore* II, A breeze..playing rat-tat With the bow of the ribbon round your hat.

c. So **rat-tat-tat**, etc.; also freq. used to represent the noise of reports from fire-arms.

1779 MAD. D'ARBLAY *Diary* Jan. (1842) I. 183 A rat-tat-tat-tat ensued, and the Earl of Harcourt was announced. **1793** S. E. PHILLIPS *Let.* 6 May in F. Burney *Jrnls. & Lett.* (1972) II. 109 The dear Postman is just arrived... A loud *rattat tattoo* was heard at the door. **1811** *Sporting Mag.* XXXVII. 75 Coaches frequently drew up, with rat, tat, rat, tattere tat tat! **1843** DICKENS *Mart. Chuz.* xxv, A low melodious hammer, rat, tat, tat, tat. **1877** SPURGEON *Serm.* XXIII. 43 The man that can..give a good rat-tat-tat, and feel that he will be welcome. **1907** G. MANINGTON *Soldier of Legion* iii. 127 The sombre background was punctuated again and again..by lightning like red flashes. Rat! tat! tat! tat!... These were Winchesters. **1957** L. MACNEICE *Visitations* 42 Rat-tat-tat-tash of shields upon Ida. **1972** *Angling Times* 6 Apr. 14/5 It is only a matter of time before I get that tiny rat-tat-tat on the rod tip. **1974** M. BUTTERWORTH *Man in Sopwith Camel* i. 12 Rat-tat-tat-tat, his rear gunner was spraying a libation back on to Braithwaite's riddled body.

d. *Comb.*, as **rat-tat ginger** = *rat-a-tat ginger* s.v. RAT-A-TAT.

1962 M. DUFFY *That's how it Was* ii. 26 Rat-tat ginger, two door-knockers tied together and a piece of black cotton leading round the corner so I could knock on two doors at once.

Hence **rat-'tat(-tat**, etc.) *v. intr.* (and *trans.*), to (cause to) make a sharp rapping sound, to knock; also †**rattatattatory** *a.*; **rat-tattooing.**

1709 E. WARD tr. *Cervantes* p. viii, All the rattles in Bartholomew-Fair had been loudly conducing to the Rattatattatory Harmony. *c* **1852** THACKERAY *Yankee Volunteers* Misc. (1857) I. 50 Drummer making din..With thy rat-tattooing. **1910** *Daily Chron.* 14 Apr. 9/5 The lady rat-tat-tatted for half an hour. Then the housekeeper..sternly asked the visitor to be so good as to go away. **1916** H. S. WALPOLE *Dark Forest* I. vii. 188 A machine gun 'rat-tat-tat-tated' close to us. **1953** 'N. BLAKE' *Dreadful Hollow* 106 Nigel rat-tat-tatted an imaginary tommy-gun at them. **1966** A. CAVANAUGH *Children are Gone* II. vi. 49 'Well, g'night.' Her heels rat-tatted down the hall.

ratte, obs. form of RAT, RATE *sb.*[1]

†**'ratted**, *ppl. a.*[1] *Obs. rare*$^{-1}$. [f. RAT *sb.*[2] + -ED[2].] Ragged, torn.

13.. *E.E. Allit. P.* B. 144 How was þou hardy þis hous..[to] neȝe, In on so ratted a robe & rent at the sydez?

†**'ratted**, *ppl. a.*[2] *Obs. rare*$^{-1}$. [f. RAT *sb.*[3] or *vb.*[3] + -ED[2].] Exposed on a wheel.

1483 CAXTON *Gold. Leg.* 139/4 Al the bodyes that were dampned to dethe that he coude fynde in townes and citees hanged & ratted.

ratteen[1] (ræ'tiːn). Also 7–8 **ratine**, 8 **ratin**, 8–9 **rateen**. [ad. F. *ratine* (1642), of unknown origin.] A thick twilled woollen cloth, usually friezed or with a curled nap, but sometimes dressed; a frieze or drugget. Now only *Hist.*

1685 *Lond. Gaz.* No. 2042/4 A..Cloak Lined with a Scarlet Ratteen. **1721** SWIFT *Epilogue* Wks. 1755 III. II. 182 We'll rig in Meath-street Egypt's haughty queen, And Anthony shall court her in ratteen. **1721** C. KING *Brit. Merch.* II. 114 Cloths, Ratines, and Serges. **1785** G. A. BELLAMY *Apol.*, etc. III. 49, I recommended him to have a brown rateen, which at that time was much wore. **1809** MALKIN *Gil Blas* x. x. ¶12 A cushion of ratteen under my head, and a coverlet over me of the same stuff. **1850** W. IRVING *Goldsmith* xxv. 256 A half-dress suit of ratteen, lined with satin.

attrib. **1755** *Mem. Capt. P. Drake* I. vi. 42, I had a Ratteen Coat that I brought from Dublin.

b. A piece of ratteen.

1706 *Lond. Gaz.* No. 4218/3, 4 Ratteens, which make out 1028 Auns, and 5 Auns of Shalloon.

ratteen[2]. *rare*$^{-1}$. (See quot.)

1847 SMEATON *Builder's Man.* 84 There is another kind of mahogany, known by the name of Ratteen, which is often employed for panels, as its dimensions are large enough to prevent jointing.

rattel(l, obs. forms of RATTLE.

ratten ('ræt(ə)n), *v.* Also **ratton**, **-tan**. [Of obscure origin: connexion with *ratten* RATTON *sb.* has been suggested, but is not clear. The vbl. sb. is recorded earlier, and is more frequently used than the vb.] **a.** *trans.* To molest (a workman or employer) by rattening. **b.** *intr.* To practise rattening. Hence **'rattener**, one who rattens.

1867 *Morning Star* 15 July, I have heard of another [workman] who disposed of a rattener..and was never rattened afterwards. **1870** READE *Put yourself*, etc. II. 201 My cousin Godby, that has a waterwheel, was rattened, by his scythe-blades being flung in the dam. *Ibid.* 311 That sense of security which ratteners had enjoyed for many years.

ratten, variant of RATTON, rat.

ratten-, ratting-crook, varr. RACKAN-CROOK.

1665 BRATHWAIT *Two Tales Chaucer* 135 Having laid his Heel on the Ratting Crook, to pass the Winter-night away. **1785** HUTTON *Bran New Wark* (E.D.S.) 380 A seaty rattencreak hang dangling fra a black randle tree. **1866** E. L. LINTON *Lizzie Lorton of Greyrigg* I. xii. 268 Two large iron 'ratten-crooks' and several smaller ones, for cauldrons and kettles, hung from the 'rannel balk'. **1974** *Country Life* 17 Oct. 1149/2 A *ratten-crook* is a pot crane hanging from the *rannel-balk* which is the wooden beam across and above an open hearth.

'rattening, *vbl. sb.* [See RATTEN *v.*] The act or practice of abstracting tools, destroying machinery or appliances, etc., as a means of enforcing compliance with the rules of a trade-union, or of venting spite. (Chiefly associated with Sheffield.) Also *transf.*

1843 R. VAUGHAN *Age Grt. Cities* 292 The stone is made steady upon its iron spindle by means of wedges, and rattaning consists in driving in one of these wedges so far as slightly to crack the stone. **1870** READE *Put yourself*, etc. II. 201 You must not construe this that I was any way connected with the rattening. **1889** A. LANG *Lost Leaders* 204 If things go on as they are at present, perhaps we shall hear of literary rattening and picketing.

attrib. **1861** *Illustr. Lond. News* 7 Dec. 576/3 Another 'rattening' attempt was made in Sheffield. **1880** *Manch. Guard.* 30 Oct., The well known Sheffield rattening case.

ratter ('rætə(r)). [f. RAT *sb.*[1] and *v.*[1] + -ER[1].]

1. A rat-catcher; a dog, cat, or other animal which catches rats.

1857 S. H. HAMMOND *Wild Northern Scenes* xi. 121 There was an assemblage of all the cats in that part of the town... Off at the right was an old spotted ratter. **1858** LEWIS in Youatt *Dog* ii. 54 The little Dane is often a good ratter. **1887** *Century Mag.* Sept. 704/1 Against these ravages the company supply a special guardian in the person of the ratter. **1946** E. O'NEILL *Iceman Cometh* IV. 233 With that..line of bull, you ought to be able to sell skunks for good ratters! **1972** R. ADAMS *Watership Down* xxv. 190 The farm cat was bewildered by the speed and fury of Bigwig's charge. It was no weakling and a good ratter.

2. One who 'rats': **a.** One who deserts his party, a renegade. = RAT *sb.*[1] 4 c.

1834 MAR. EDGEWORTH *Helen* xxvii, In the famous old print of the minister rat-catcher..the ridicule on placemen ratters remains. **1885** E. A. ABBOTT *Bacon* 84 The *Essay on Faction* is..almost cynical in its suppression of resentment against ratters and traitors.

b. A workman who refuses to join a strike, etc. = RAT *sb.*[1] 4 d.

3. *Austral.* One who steals opal from another's mine.

1931 I. L. IDRIESS *Prospecting for Gold* xxvi. 239 Ratters are men, a gang as a rule, who work your opal out for you while you sleep. **1964** W. C. EYLES *Bk. of Opals* vii. 83 When the miners..went down the shaft, they found the ratters had cleaned the place out entirely. **1976** *Nat. Geographic* Oct. 564/2 The mine ratters (thieves) are here, but that's been going on since King Solomon's mines.

rattery ('rætəri). [f. RAT *sb.*[1] + -ERY.]

1. The qualities or conduct of a ratter; apostasy.

1822 SYD. SMITH *Lett.* ccvii. (1855) II. 226 The rattery and scoundrelism of public life. **1832** J. WILSON in *Blackw. Mag.* XXXII. 717, I can fancy him turning this rattery of your Lordship's to some account.

2. A place where rats are kept or abound.

a **1880** F. T. BUCKLAND *Notes & Jottings* (1882) 17 Our excellent friend..has set up a rattery.

ratticide, var. RATICIDE.

rattil(l, obs. forms of RATTLE.

'rattinet. ? *Obs.* [f. F. *ratine* RATTEEN + -ET[1].] A woollen stuff, somewhat thinner and lighter than ratteen.

1811 *Weekly Reg.* 21 Sept. 46/1 Rattinets..can only be made of wool long enough to be combed. **1836** H. MANWARING *Tailor's New Guide* 15 Velveteen Jacket, body and skirt, may be lined with rattinet. **1838** in WEBSTER.

ratting ('rætɪŋ), *vbl. sb.* [f. RAT *v.*[1] + -ING[1].]

1. Desertion of one's party or principles. Also with *over*.

1816 *Edin. Rev.* XXVI. 435 A minister of state suddenly changed sides..and the ratting..became general. **1827** CARLYLE in Froude *Life* (1882) I. 426 He characterises the papers as a splendid instance of literary ratting. **1839** *Times* 10 Apr., A general ratting over of the Cabinet. **1946** *Sun* (Baltimore) 17 June 18/3 His turning long-distance state's evidence, his ratting, so to speak, to the cops..strikes at the very core of the latest design to maintain 'power' in the hands of a people's government. **1948** *Richmond* (Va.) *Times-Dispatch* 13 Feb. 30/1 McKeever..performed the most odious job of 'ratting' college football has known.

attrib. **1818** MOORE *Fudge Fam. in Paris* vi. 105 This serves to nurse the ratting spirit; The less the bribe, the more the merit.

2. The catching or killing of rats.

1828 *Sporting Mag.* XXI. 399 Ratting, or any other school-boy's mischief. **1881** G. ALLEN *Evolut. at Large* xix, The most tempting solicitations to ratting and rabbiting.

attrib. **1832** *Boston Herald* 22 May 3/3 Committed for..maliciously stabbing..with a ratting spear.

3. *Comb.*, as **ratting canoe** *Canad.*, a small native boat designed for hunting muskrats in swamps and marshes.

1962 R. SLOBODIN *Band Organization of Peel River Kutchin* 14 A child armed with a .22 rifle, paddling or portaging the light, narrow ten-foot ratting canoe. **1968** R. M. PATTERSON *Finlay's River* 74 A—gave an initial display of his dexterity by upsetting a small ratting canoe with Butler and himself in it.

ratting-crook: see RATTEN-CROOK.

rattish ('rætɪʃ), *a.* [f. RAT *sb.*[1] + -ISH[1].]

1. Belonging to, resembling (that of) a rat; infested by rats.

1690 *Lond. Gaz.* No. 2571/4 A brown bay Gelding..with..a Rattish Tayl. **1822** W. IRVING in *Life & Lett.* (1864) II. 99 A huge old mansion, that..is now rather rattish. **1899** E.

PHILLPOTTS *Human Boy* 123 His thin white face had a rattish look sometimes.

2. Characteristic of a political 'rat'.

1840 *Fraser's Mag.* XXII. 636 Trimming, no doubt, and rattish thy career.

rattle ('rætəl), *sb.*[1] Also 6 **rattell** (*Sc.* **-ill**), **ratell**, **-ille**, 6–7 **ratle**, 7 **rat(t)el**. [f. RATTLE *v.* Cf. (in senses 1–3) Du. and LG. *ratel*, G. *rassel*.]

I. 1. An instrument used to make a rattling noise, as: **a.** A case of some hard material containing small bodies which rattle when the instrument is shaken. (Chiefly used as a child's toy.) **b.** An instrument having a vibrating tongue fixed in a frame, which slips over the teeth of a ratchet-wheel with a loud noise when the instrument is whirled round. (Formerly used by watchmen and others to give an alarm.)

1519 HORMAN *Vulg.* 147, I wyll bye a rattell to styll my baby for cryenge. **1548** PATTEN *Exped. Scotl.* K viij, Great rattels..coouered with old parchement or dooble papers, small stones put in them to make noys, and set vpon the ende of a staff. **1613** PURCHAS *Pilgrimage* VIII. vi. (1614) 764 All of them with Rattles in their hands making a great noise. **1711** STEELE *Spect.* No. 258 ¶4 An Entertainment very little above the Rattles of Children. **1792** WOLCOTT (P. Pindar) *Academic Ode* Wks. 1812 II. 509 That instrument the Rattle, That draws the hobbling brother-hood to battle. **1866** MRS. H. WOOD *St. Martin's Eve* xiv, His next movement was to..swing the watch round and round after the manner of a rattle.

transf. and *fig.* **1622** MABBE tr. *Aleman's Guzman d'Alf.* II. 18, I had..put into his head nothing but Hawkes-bells and Rattles: All that he tooke delight in were merry tales, idle jests, and the like vanities. **1665** GLANVILL *Scepsis* xxvii. 166 Opinions are the Rattles of immature intellects. **1758** H. WALPOLE *Lett. to Mann* 9 Sept. (1846) III. 388 A man at whom, in former days, I believe, Mr. Pitt has laughed for loving such rattles as drums and trumpets.

†**c.** A dice-box. *Obs.*

a **1732** GAY *Fables* II. xii. 39 When you the pilf'ring rattle shake, Is not your honour too at stake? **1796** in *Grose's Dict. Vulg. Tongue* (ed. 3).

2. a. A set of horny, loosely-connected rings forming the termination of the tail in the rattlesnake, by shaking which it produces a rattling noise. Also *pl.*

1624 CAPT. SMITH *Virginia* II. 30 Those Rattels..they take from the taile of a snake. *a* **1704** T. BROWNE *Martial* III. xliv. 151 Not snake in tail that carries rattle. **1774** GOLDSM. *Nat. Hist.* (1776) VII. 211 A rattle-snake..reared up, bit his hand, and shook his rattles. **1860** O. W. HOLMES *Elsie V.* xiii. (1891) 190 The long, loud, stinging whirr, as the huge ..reptile shook his many-jointed rattle.

†**b.** *pl.* Wattles. *Obs. rare*$^{-0}$.

1611 COTGR., *La barbe d'vn coq*, a Cockes rattles, or waddles.

3. Applied to certain plants having seeds which rattle in their cases when ripe: **a.** Yellow rattle, *Rhinanthus Crista-galli* = COCK'S-COMB 5 a. **b.** Red rattle, *Pedicularis sylvatica* = LOUSE-WORT.

So Du. *ratels*, G. *rassel*. OE. *hratele* (glossing L. *bubonica*, Wr.-Wülcker 296/2) and *hrætelwyrt* (gl. *hierobotanum* 301/3) have been compared; but the late appearance of the stem of *rattle* in Eng. and the cognate languages makes it probable that the resemblance is quite fortuitous.

1578 LYTE *Dodoens* IV. lvi. 516 Yellow Rattel. **1611** COTGR., *Creste au coq, ou, de coq*, the hearbe coxcombe, Penie-grasse, yellow and white Rattle. **1677** PLOT *Oxfordsh.* 255 Rattles they hand-weed as soon as in flower. **1748** SIR J. HILL *Brit. Herbal* 121 We confusedly call two genera in English by the name of rattle, distinguishing them only by epithets taken from the colour of the flower into red and yellow rattle. **1854** S. THOMSON *Wild Fl.* III. (ed. 4) 209 We must not overlook the yellow rattle.., for ere long its seeds will be rattling in its seed-vessel. **1880** JEFFERIES *Hodge & M.* II. 281 'Rattles' and similar plants destructive to the hay crop.

II. 4. a. A rapid succession of short sharp sounds, caused by the concussion of hard bodies. Fig. phr. ***with a rattle***: with sudden or unexpected rapidity (orig. *Horse-racing*). Also **rattle-rattle**.

1500–20 DUNBAR *Poems* xxvii. 74 His harnass brak and maid ane brattill, The sowtaris horss scart with the rattill. **1695** PRIOR *Ballad on Namur* 102 The rattle Of those confounded drums. **1790** BURNS *Ep. to R. Graham* xii, As Highland crags by thunder cleft..Hurl down with crashing rattle. *a* **1806** HORSLEY *Serm.* xxiii. II. 245 The sharp rattle of the whirling phaeton, and the graver rumble of the loaded waggon. **1823** J. BADCOCK *Dom. Amusem.* 32 The bottom one..makes a rattle when hit with the knuckle. **1860** TYNDALL *Glac.* I. vii. 48 Sent bounding down the slope with peal and rattle. **1888** *Daily Chron.* 10 Dec. 6/2 Bachelor came on with a rattle and won by a length and a half. **1909** in J. R. WARE *Passing Eng.* 206/2 The only approach to a sensation was caused by Warrington and Kettleholder, the former coming 'with a rattle' in the morning to the price taken about him in the excitement caused by his forward running in the Cesarewitch. **1926** E. BOWEN *Ann Lee's* 251 Only the rattle-rattle of my bicycle. **1928** D. H. LAWRENCE *Lady Chatterley's Lover* ii. 11 She heard the rattle-rattle of the screens at the pit. **1977** *Evening Gaz.* (Middlesbrough) 11 Jan. 13/5 The Merryweather crew came with a rattle to level at the penultimate end 15-15 [in Bowls].

b. *transf.* Racket, uproar, noisy gaiety, stir.

1691 T. H[ALE] *Acc. New Invent.* p. xxxiii, The great Controversie about Easter, that heretofore put all the World in a rattle. *a* **1700** B. E. *Dict. Cant. Crew* s.v. *Bustle*, What a Bustle you make! What a Hurry or Rattle you Cause! **1742** YOUNG *Nt. Th.* v. 639 Think you the soul, when this life's rattles cease, Has nothing of more manly to succeed? **1750** JOHNSON *Rambler* No. 74 ¶10 She cannot bear a place without some cheerfulness and rattle. **1874** KINGSLEY *Lett.* (1878) II. 424 New York was a great rattle, dining and speechifying and being received.

c. A rattling sound in the throat, caused by partial obstruction: see RÂLE, and *death-rattle* s.v. DEATH *sb.* 19. Also in *pl.* (spec. as a popular name for croup).

1752 BERKELEY *Th. Tar-water* Wks. III. 505 Persons have been recovered by tar-water after they had rattles in the throat. **1820** EARL DUDLEY *Lett.* 3 Apr. (1840) 244 The monarch is always immortal till the rattles are in his throat. **1848** LYTTON *Harold* v. v, Godwin..tried to speak, but his voice died in a convulsive rattle. **1898** *Allbutt's Syst. Med.* V. 142 The large coarse toneless rattles produced by mucus and air in the trachea and larger bronchi.

d. A 'rattling' breeze.

1896 *Daily News* 10 July 3/6 They came rushing along in a fine rattle of wind.

e. *N. Amer.* A succession of small, noisy waterfalls forming rapids; a fast-moving stream.

1776 G. CARTWRIGHT *Jrnl.* 14 Aug. (1779) 200 We fished in the stream below the rattle, and also in the lower pool, and killed seventy-eight fish. **1861** L. DE BOILIEU *Recoll. Labrador Life* xiii. 166 In the different bays are brooks, and in these brooks are 'rattles', as they are termed, or, more properly speaking, 'falls', though none are of any great magnitude. **1907** J. G. MILLAIS *Newfoundland* iii. 70 We had only to unload twice in passing 'rattles', as they called the strong rapids. **1925** *Dialect Notes* V. 339 *Rattle*,.. a swift brook. **1975** *Canad. Antiques Collector* Mar.–Apr. 23/1 From the sealhunt we have:..rattle, river rapids, and so on.

f. The rustling quality of a sheet of finished paper when handled, indicative of its hardness and density.

1900 CROSS & BEVAN *Paper-Making* (ed. 2) v. 137 As a consequence, it adds the quality of 'wetness' to the pulp, which again confers the quality of hardness and 'rattle' upon the finished paper. **1962** F. T. DAY *Introd. to Paper* ii. 24 Starch is added to paper furnishes and serves either as a sizing agent or to give the paper more substance and better handle for its use imparts stiffness and 'rattle' to the finished sheet.

g. *Hunting.* A particular note on the horn.

1908 L. C. F. CAMERON *Otters & Otter Hunting* 203 *Rattle*, the note sounded on the horn at the 'worry'. **1954** J. I. LLOYD *Beagling* 143 *Rattle*, an exciting, vibrant sounding of the horn. **1976** *Shooting Times & Country Mag.* 16–22 Dec. 25/2 A rattle on the horn had hounds racing to the spot.

5. a. *Sc.* and *north.* A rattling blow or shock.

1632 LITHGOW *Trav.* I. 33 The woman gaue the Frier such a rattle in the face. *Ibid.* IV. 154 Then hoysing him vp .., they let the rope flee loose, whence downe he falles, with a rattle. **1806** BLACK *Falls of Clyde* 200 I'd gi'e 'm a rattle, I'd break his collar-bane wi' a plough pattle.

†**b.** A sharp reproof. *Obs.*

c **1650** HEYLIN *Laud* (1668) 257 Receiving such a rattle for his former Contempt of the Bishop of London. **1679** *Hist. Jetzer* 17 At their return he gave them a round rattle, and spared none of his course Eloquence to tell them their own. **1711** *Brit. Apollo* IV. No. 3. 1/2 My Wife has given me such a Rattle, that another Peal will rattle all my Brains out of my Head. **1842** C. RIDLEY *Let.* in *Cecilia* (1958) ix. 111 Wells.. is tiresome again... I wish I had courage to give her a good rattle, but if I did I think she would not bear it.

6. a. A noisy flow of words.

1627 HAKEWILL *Apol.* (J.), All this ado about the golden age, is but an empty rattle and frivolous conceit. **1755** J. SHEBBEARE *Lydia* (1769) II. 193 What a rattle of words, without the least feeling or sentiment, does this letter contain.

b. Without article: Lively talk or chatter of a trivial kind.

1748 RICHARDSON *Clarissa* III. 127 Sir, said I, I see what a man I am with. Your rattle warns me of the snake. **1780** MAD. D'ARBLAY *Diary* May (1842) I. 374 And gay enough we were, for the careless rattle of Captain Bourchier [etc.]. **1813** J. ADAMS *Wks.* (1856) X. 86 If I am not weary of writing, I am sure you must be of reading such incoherent rattle. **1890** F. W. ROBINSON *Very Strange Fam.* 112 One is not called upon to repeat all the rattle and tattle that one hears.

7. A constant chatterer; one who talks incessantly in a lively or thoughtless fashion.

1716 D. RYDER *Diary* 17 May (1939) 235, I was vexed to see her so long entertained with such a rattle as he. **1744** ELIZA HEYWOOD *Female Spect.* No. 4 (1748) I. 167 Neither this old rattle..nor many others who act in the same manner, ever did a real hurt to any one. **1809** MALKIN *Gil Blas* x. x. ¶43, I paid so little attention to the talk of this rattle. **1859** JEPHSON *Brittany* ix. 147 My companion turned out to be a lively amusing rattle. **1969** *N.Y. Rev. Bks.* 2 Jan. 3/4 Editor of a biographical history of philosophy yet welcomed as a rattle and raconteur..Lewes stands in these pages like a wax effigy. **1971** E. MAVOR *Ladies of Llangollen* i. 33 Great confidante, greater rattle, she was ever recording ..what she was pleased to call 'boosey' whist parties beneath the Woodstock oaks.

8. *U.S.* Used as a mild expletive.

1790 R. TYLER *Contrast* v. i. (1887) 88 But what the rattle makes you look so tarnation glum?

†**9.** *slang.* A coach. = RATTLER 2 b. *Obs.*

1785 in GROSE *Dict. Vulg. Tongue.*

10. *Naut.* phr. ***in the rattle***: on the commander's report of defaulters; in confinement; in trouble.

1914 'BARTIMEUS' *Naval Occasions* ii. 10 'In the bloomin' rattle, I am,' explained the disturber of traffic. **1919** W. LANG *Sea-Lawyer's Log* xii. 152 Ordinary Seaman Oldroyd spent the first dog-watch last night..washing his undergarments, but, having done so, he hung the same up to dry in the fore ammunition lobby, where they were subsequently discovered by the Gunner, who promptly placed Oldroyd 'in the rattle', hence his appearance as a defaulter. **1942** *Penguin New Writing* XV. 13 He was taken off, bawled out, put in the rattle. **1951** H. HASTINGS in *Plays of Year 1950* IV. 72 You ain't gonna put him in the rattle on account of a bit of leg-pull? **1964** J. HALE *Grudge Fight* vi. 91 The Andrew, that had taken him round the world a few times, given him his good conduct stripes and removed them when he'd been in the rattle. **1973** 'B. MATHER' *Snowline* xviii. 212 The Old Man..let the others out, but.. your bloke is back in the rattle.

11. *attrib.* and *Comb.*, (in some cases perh. the verbal stem) as **rattle-baby**, a rattling doll, *fig.* a young child; **rattle-barrel**, a tumbling box for castings, to remove sand, etc. (Knight *Dict. Mech.* 1875); **rattle-bladder**, a bladder containing peas, pebbles, or the like, used as a rattle (in quot. *fig.*); **rattle-bones** = BONE *sb.* 5 b *pl.*; **rattle-box**, (*a*) a rattle in the form of a box or case; (*b*) = RATTLE 3; (*c*) a species of rattlewort (*Crotalaria sagittalis*); (*d*) *transf.*, applied to a conveyance or machine; **rattle-broom**, a species of rattlewort (see quot.); **rattle-bush**, a West Indian plant (*Crotalaria incana*); **rattle-clap**, a rattle; **rattle-free** *a.*, devoid of rattles; **rattle-gourd**, a primitive musical instrument (cf. *rattle-box* quot. 1884); **rattle-grass** = RATTLE 3; **rattle-jack**, (*a*) shaly coal; (*b*) = RATTLE 3 a; †**rattle-man**, a watchman provided with a rattle; †**rattle-noddled** *a.* = RATTLE-HEADED *a.*; **rattle-note**, a rattling note; **rattleproof** *a.*, capable of preventing rattling; hence ***rattleproofing*** *vbl. sb.*; **rattle-skull** *dial.* = RATTLE-HEAD; hence ***rattle-skulled*** adj.; †**rattle-watch** (see quot. for *rattle-man*); **rattle-weed**, (*a*) *U.S.*, the bugbane, *Cimicifuga racemosa*; (*b*) *dial.* Bladder Campion (*Wiltsh. Gloss.* 1893); (*c*) = LOCO[1]; (*d*) = *rattle-box*; **rattle-wing(s**, the Golden-eyed Duck, *Clangula glaucia*; **rattle-wort**, the genus *Crotalaria* (*Treas. Bot.* 1866). Also RATTLE-BAG, -BRAIN, -HEAD, etc.

1601 *2nd Pt. Return Parnass.* I. ii. 155 What new paper hobby horses, what *rattle babies are come out in your late May morrice daunce. **1636** HEYWOOD *Loves Mistress* I. Wks. 1874 V. 78 Fine little rattle-babies, scarce thus high, Are now call'd wives. **1548** PATTEN *Exped. Scotl.* Pref. c iiij, Our consciences, now quite vnclogd from the fear of his vaine terriculaments and *rattelbladders. **1809** W. IRVING *Knickerb.* (1861) 131 A full band of boys..performing on the popular instruments of *rattle-bones and clam-shells. **1780** JOHNSON in Croker's *Boswell* (1831) IV. 390 There certainly is no harm in a fellow's rattling a *rattle-box. **1817** A. EATON *Man. Bot.* 80 *Crotalaria..sagittalis*, (rattle-box) leaves lance-oblong. **1835** J. E. ALEXANDER *Sk. in Portugal* viii. 179 In May, the fleet of her Most Faithful Majesty consisted of the following ships:—..18, Audax,..Fine, stout brig, but very ugly. 16. Providenza,..Ditto, a perfect rattle-box. **1866** *Treas. Bot.* 961/1 *Rattle-box*, Rhinanthus Crista galli; also an American name for Crotalaria. **1884** F. CARPENTER *Round about Rio* iii. 33 A kind of a rattle-box produced by the clashing of a pint of beans within a dry gourd. **1884** [see LOCO *sb.*[1] a]. **1929** M. A. GILL *Underworld Slang*, *Rattle box*, machine gun. **1943** R. HOLT *George Washington Carver* 199 He would caution stockmen against the rattlebox (*Crotalaria*). **1972** G. BEINE *Land of Coyote* 90 These are rattleboxes, and there, some rabbitsfoot clover. **1973** 'H. HOWARD' *Highway to Murder* vii. 87 He was crowding ninety and so was his rattlebox. **1711** *Phil. Trans.* XXVII. 347 Lupine-leaved Malabar Crotolaria, or *Rattle-broom. **1750** HUGHES *Barbados* 212 The inclosed Peas, when ripe, make a Rattling Noise when shaken by the Wind. From hence they derive the Name of *Rattle-Bush, or Shake-Shake. **1879** BARON EGGERS *Flora St. Croix* 41 *Leguminosæ*..Rattle-bush. **1860** PIESSE *Lab. Chem. Wonders* p. viii, He may have been only a scarecrow or *rattle-clap. **1962** *Times* 3 May 19/4 It [*sc.* a car] is impressively quiet throughout..completely *rattle-free and draughtproof. **1791** W. BARTRAM *Carolina* 505 The tambour, *rattle-gourd, and a kind of flute. **1578** LYTE *Dodoens* IV. lvi. 515 *Rattel grasse..beareth redde flowers, and leaues finely iagged or snipt. **1753** CHAMBERS *Cycl. Supp.* App., *Rattlegrass*, a name sometimes used for a species of Pedicularis, or Louse-wort. **1877** *N.W. Linc. Gloss.*, **Rattle-jack*, a plant,..in some parts called cock's-comb, and yellow-rattle. **1883** GRESLEY *Gloss. Coal-mining* 200 *Rattle-Jack*, carbonaceous shale. **1885** *Daily Tel.* 21 Jan. 3/3 To burn in the fireplace some coke or rattlejacks. **1689** in *Ann. Albany* (1850) II. 110 Zacharias Sichells, *ratel man desyres he may have payment..due to him for his service as ratel watch. **1661** K. W. *Conf. Charact.*, *Informer* (1860) 47 Hees a..*rattlenodled, large-lugg'd eagle-ey'd hircocervus. **1851** G. MEREDITH *Love in the Valley* v, His *rattle-note unvaried,..spins the brown eve-jar. **1924** *Motor* 21 Oct. 626/1 Table utensils held in *rattleproof devices. **1976** *Norwich Mercury* 19 Nov. 8/5 (Advt.), But Ziebart is rustproofing and soundproofing..and squeakproofing and *rattleproofing. **1725** RAMSAY *Gentle Sheph.* I. ii, How can ye loe that *rattle-skull? **1788** SHIRREFS *Poems* (1790) 86 Some rattle-scull..like Geordy Will. **1887** *S. Chesh. Gloss.*, *Rattle-skull*, a talkative person; a chatter-box. **1805** SCOTT *Let. to Miss Seward* in *Lockhart*, A *rattle-skulled half lawyer, half sportsman. **1791** *Trans. Amer. Philos. Soc.* III. 114 American Bane-berry, Black Snake-root, *Rattle-weed. **1851** R. GLISAN *Jrnl. Army Life* (1874) vi. 70 The rattle-weed..derives its name from the fact that its pod is full of loose seed, and makes a rattling noise when dry. **1864** *Rep. Maine Board Agric.* 45 Last year nothing grew on the field where it had been applied but rattle-weed. **1883** *Harper's Mag.* Mar. 503/1 The loco, or rattle-weed, met with also in California, drives them raving crazy. **1931** W. N. CLUTE *Common Names Plants* 110 *Crotalaria sagitalis*..is frequently known as rattle-box or rattle-weed. **1843** YARRELL *Brit. Birds* III. 274 The boat-shooters [near Yarmouth]..are well acquainted with the Golden Eye, or *Rattle-wings, as they call it.

†**rattle**, *sb.*^{2} *Obs. rare*$^{-0}$. A kind of fishing-net. Also ***rattle-net***.

1753 CHAMBERS *Cycl. Supp.*, *Wolf-net*, a kind of net used in fishing..in rivers and ponds,..of the nature of the rattle, excepting only the wanting the four Wings. *Ibid.* App., *Rattle-net.*

†**rattle**, *a. Obs.*$^{-1}$ [App. f. RATTLE *sb.*^{1} or *v.*^{1}, but possibly an error for *racle* RACKLE *a.*] Rattling (in speech), voluble.

1541 HYRDE tr. *Vives' Instr. Chr. Wom.* II. v. 87 b, The cause why many women be ratle of tonge, is bycause they can nat rule their mindes.

rattle (ˈræt(ə)l), *v.*^{1} Forms: 4 ratellen, ratil-, ratyl, (5 -ylle), 4–5 ratel(en), 4–8 ratl-, (7 ratle); 5 rattyll(e, 6 rattell, -il, *Sc.* -ill, 6– rattle. [ME. *ratelen* = (M)Du., LG. *ratelen*, G. *rasseln*, prob. of echoic origin: cf. Gr. *κρόταλον* a clapper, *κροτεῖν* to rattle, *κρότος* rattling noise.

On OE. *hratele*, *hrætel*, see note to RATTLE *sb.*^{1} 3.]

I. *intr.* **1. a.** Of things: To give out a rapid succession of short sharp sounds, usually in consequence of rapid agitation and of striking against each other or against some hard dry body.

c **1330** *Arth. & Merl.* 7848 (Kölbing) þair gilt pensel wiþ þe winde Mirie ratled of cendel Ynde. *a* **1400** *Pol. Rel. & L. Poems* (E.E.T.S.) 250/6 þin teth ratilet, And þin hond quaket. *c* **1470** *Gol. & Gaw.* 691 Ryngis of rank steill rattillit. **1508** DUNBAR *Flyting* 180 Thy rigbane rattillis, and thy ribbis on raw. **1535** COVERDALE *Jer.* xlviii. 12 Hir tankerdes rattell, and shake to and fro. **1697** DRYDEN *Virg. Georg.* III. 342 The Forrest rattles, and the Rocks rebound. **1782** COWPER *J. Gilpin* 43 The stones did rattle underneath. *a* **1839** PRAED *Poems* (1864) II. 399 The canvas rattled on the mast. **1861** MISS PRATT *Flower. Pl.* III. 68 Its dead stalks rattle in the wind.

transf. **1682** DRYDEN *Abs. & Achit.* II. 420 He..faggoted his notions as they fell, And, if they rhymed and rattled, all was well.

b. Of sounds having this character.

1587 FLEMING *Contn. Holinshed* III. 1288/1 The acclamations and cries of the people..ratled so lowd. **1697** DRYDEN *Virg. Georg.* III. 408 Rowling Thunder rattl'd o'er his Head. **1719** DE FOE *Crusoe* II. iv, The echoes rattling from one side to another. **1801** *Med. Jrnl.* V. 491 Her respiration rattling like that of an apoplectic person. **1830** LYTTON *P. Clifford* i, Her voice..rattled indistinctly, and almost died within her. **1865** KINGSLEY *Herew.* xiii, With a blow which rattled over the fen.

c. Of places: To resound, be filled, with a noise of this kind.

1622 J. REYNOLDS *God's Revenge* II. ix. (1635) 163 The City..rattleth and resoundeth of this cruell and unnaturall Murther. *Ibid.* III. xii. 227 Millan ratleth with the newes of Baretano's bloody and vntimely end. **1855** KINGSLEY *Heroes, Theseus* II. 165 When he saw Theseus he rose, and laughed till the glens rattled.

d. Of an agent: To produce a succession of sharp sounds by striking or knocking on something, or by causing hard bodies to strike against each other.

1676 HOBBES *Iliad* (1677) 135 Then came his father rattling at his door. **1715** ADDISON *Drummer* I. i, He ratled so loud under the tiles. **1726–46** THOMSON *Winter* 93 The storm that blows Without, and rattles on his humble roof. **1781** COWPER *Hope* 77 Till half the world comes rattling at his door. **1852** MRS. STOWE *Uncle Tom's C.* xvi. 148 She rattled away with her needles.

e. *transf.* in *Shoe-making*: (see quot.).

1840 J. DEVLIN *Shoemaker* I. 51 So that the stitches..may rattle, as it is called, or distinctly shew themselves to the eye of the spectator.

2. a. To produce an involuntary sound of this kind, *esp.* in the throat; †to stutter.

1398 TREVISA *Barth. De P.R.* v. xxi. (Bodl. MS.) 11 b, Superfluyte of moisture is cause whiche somme men ratelep, þat mowe not soune alle letteres. **1483** *Cath. Angl.* 300/2 Ratylle, *travlare.* **1589** W. RIDER *Biblioth. Schol.* s.v., He that rattleth in the throate or cannot scarce vtter his words, *traulus.* **1619** R. BEST *Treat. Hawkes* (1890) 86 Vpon any bate she [the hawk] wil heaue and blow, and rattle in the throat. **1721** BAILEY, *To Rattle in the Sheath* [spoken of a Horse] is when he makes a Noise in the skinny Part of his Yard. **1753** N. TORRIANO *Gangr. Sore Throat* 5 Her Voice was much interrupted, and she rattled..in her Breath. *a* **1776** R. JAMES *Dissert. Fevers* (1778) 23 At this time he rattled in the throat.

†**b.** Of a goat: (see quot. 1678). *Obs.*

1575 TURBERV. *Venerie* 238 A Rowe belleth: a Gote rattleth. **1678** PHILLIPS (ed. 4), *To Ratle*, in Hunting, a Goat is said when she cries or makes a noise, through desire of copulation. **1688** R. HOLME *Armoury* II. 134/1 A Goat Rattleth, or Rotteleth. [*a* **1700** in *Dict. Cant. Crew.* **1721** in BAILEY.]

3. a. To talk rapidly in a thoughtless, noisy, or lively manner; to chatter. Also, to scold *at* (†rail *on*) in this manner.

1594 NASHE *Unfort. Trav.* Wks. (Grosart) V. 33 To the Enemie he went and offered his seruice, ratling egregiously on the king. **1715** J. CHAPPELOW *Rt. way to get Rich* (1717) 163 They shall not then roar and rattle in the taverns. **1806–7** J. BERESFORD *Miseries Hum. Life* (1826) XII. Concl. 313 The frothiest coxcomb that ever rattled in a ball-room. **1885** G. MEREDITH *Diana* xli, I rattled at her: and oh! dear me, she..defies me to prove. **1889** *Boy's Own Paper* 17 Aug. 730/2 How we chattered and rattled, and bandied the stalest chaff.

redupl. **1885** G. MEREDITH *Diana* xiv, Because a woman.. would rattle-rattle, as if the laughter of the company were her due.

b. So with advbs., as *on*, *away*, *along*.

1773 GOLDSM. *Stoops to Conquer* II. i, A resolution to break the ice, and rattle away at any rate. **1782** MAD. D'ARBLAY *Diary* 4 Nov., Dr. Johnson..went rattling on in a humorous sort of comparison he was drawing of himself. **1838** LYTTON *Alice* v. v, I rattle on thus to keep up your spirits. *Ibid.* VI. iv, Vargrave thus rattled away in order to give the good banker to understand [etc.]. **1887** HALL CAINE *Son of Hagar* II. xi, Paul Ritson rattled along with cheerful talk.

†**c.** *to rattle it out*, to declaim vigorously.

1709 SWIFT *Advancem. Relig.* Wks. 1755 II. I. 118 He rattles it out against popery and arbitrary power.

4. a. To move, fall, etc. rapidly and with a rattling noise. Usually with advbs. as *along*, *by*, *in*, *out*, or prep. phrases, and const. with †*it*. Also with *about*, *around*, esp. *transf.* and *fig.*, implying the occupation of an area or space larger than that which is comfortable, necessary, or desirable.

1555 [see RATTLING *vbl. sb*]. *c* **1610** COOKE *Green's Tu quoque* C iv, In silkes I'l rattle it of every colour. **1697** DRYDEN *Virg. Georg.* I. 161 Huge Torrents..ratling down the Rocks, large moisture yield. **1750** GRAY *Long Story* 60 Upstairs in a whirlwind rattle. **1795–7** SOUTHEY *Widow* iii, Fast o'er the heath a chariot rattled by her. **1816** BYRON *Ch. Har.* III. xxii, The car rattling o'er the stony street. **1830** LYTTON *P. Clifford* i, A violent gush of wind..rattling along the housetops. **1869** L. M. ALCOTT *Little Women* II. iii. 43, I saw you two girls rattling about in the what-you-call-it [*sc.* charabanc], like two little kernels in a very big nutshell. **1871** L. STEPHEN *Playgr. Eur.* (1894) vii. 159 A violent hailstorm rattled down. **1926** M. J. ATKINSON in J. F. Dobie *Rainbow in Morning* (1965) 81 He rattles around in his office like one pea in a pod. **1967** T. STOPPARD *Rosencrantz & Guildenstern are Dead* III. 95 We can move,..change direction, rattle about, but our movement is contained within a larger one that carries us along. **1973** *Washington Post* 13 Jan. A23/6, I don't want that kind of power rattling around inside the bureaucracy.

b. To drive in a rapid rattling fashion.

1838 STEPHEN *Trav. Greece* 32/1 The pope and his cardinals, with their gaudy equipages and multitudes of footmen rattling to the Vatican. **1840** THACKERAY *Catherine* iv, All..entered the coach, and rattled off. **1874** LADY BARKER *Station Life N. Zealand* iii. 20 We were soon rattling along the Sumner Road by the sea-shore.

c. *dial.* and *slang.* To make haste, to hurry *off*, to work briskly.

a **1700** B. E. *Dict. Cant. Crew, To Rattle*, to move off, or be gone. **1821** CLARE *Vill. Minstr.* I. 33 Milkmaids and clowns..rattle off, like hogs to London mart. **1877** *Holderness Gloss.*, *Rattle-away*, to hasten along; to go quickly. **1883** GRESLEY *Gloss. Coal-mining* 200 *Rattle*, to work (drive into or sink through) with great vigour and energy.

II. *trans.* **5. a.** To make (a thing or things) rattle.

1560 DAUS tr. *Sleidane's Comm.* 232 b, Whan a man doeth rattle or shake together a nomber of dead mens bones. **1593** G. HARVEY *New Lett.* Wks. (Grosart) I. 283 Yet I may chaunce rattle him, like a baby of pachment. **1785** BURNS *Jolly Beggars* Air ii, To rattle the thundering drum was his trade. **1828** CARLYLE *Misc.* (1857) I. 81 To rattle his chains by way of lullaby. **1881** RITA *My Lady Coquette* i, She begins with nervous haste to rattle the teacups and arrange the plates.

†**b.** To assail with a rattling noise. *rare*$^{-1}$.

1595 SHAKS. *John* v. ii. 172 Sound but another [drum] and another shall (As lowd as thine), rattle the Welkins eare.

c. To drive *away* or *out* with rattling. *rare.*

1622 BACON *Henry VII* 31 Hee should bee well enough able to..rattle away this Swarme of Bees, with their King. **1711** *Brit. Apollo* IV. No. 3. 1/2 Another Peal will rattle all my Brains out of my Head.

d. *Cricket.* To bowl *down* the opposing team's wickets speedily and cheaply; to skittle *out* batsmen in a similar manner.

a **1842** B. AISLABIE in P. Norman *Scores & Ann. W. Kent Cricket Club* (1897) 370 M was a Morgan, who rattled them down. **1862** *Baily's Mag.* Apr. 259 Caffyn and Bennett rattled down their wickets..for 20 runs. **1873** *Ibid.*, July 409 In the second innings the two fast bowlers..rattled out the Marylebone men in grand style. **1898** G. GIFFEN *With Bat & Ball* vii. 94 On the sticky wicket..Hearne and Poughet 'rattled' us out. **1926** H. S. ALTHAM *Hist. Cricket* xviii. 207 He..saw Kent rattled out by Painter and Roberts for 76.

6. a. To say or utter in a rapid or lively manner. Also with *off*, *out* advbs., *on* prep.

c **1380** WYCLIF *Wks.* (1880) 274 þerfore þei ratellen þat it is aȝenst charite to tellen opynly here cursed disceitis & synnes. **1401** *Pol. Poems* (Rolls) II. 64 Thou ratelist many thinges, bot grounde hast thou non. **1553** T. WILSON *Rhet.* (1580) 223 An other rattles his woordes. **1685** COTTON tr. *Montaigne* (1877) I. 75 It amuses me to rattle in their ears this word. **1785** BURNS *Death & Dr. Hornbook* xx, Their Latin names as fast he rattles As ABC. **1808** SOUTHEY *Let.* 20 May, Rhyme must be rattled upon rhyme, till the reader is half dizzy with the thundering echo. **1858** LYTTON *What will He do* II. xi, Lionel rattled out gay anecdotes of his schooldays. **1890** 'R. BOLDREWOOD' *Col. Reformer* (1891) 321 In his revulsion of feeling [he] rattled off these greetings.

†**b.** To give out (a rattling sound). *rare*$^{-1}$.

1582 STANYHURST *Æneis* II. (Arb.) 53 Thee towns men roared, thee trump taratantara ratled.

c. To play (music) in a rattling fashion. Also with *away*, *off*.

1848 THACKERAY *Van. Fair* xlviii, Sitting down to the piano, she rattled away a triumphant voluntary on the keys. **1852** MRS. STOWE *Uncle Tom's C.* xvi. 149 He sat down to the piano, and rattled a lively piece of music. **1852** DICKENS *Bleak Ho.* II. vii. 101 [She] sat down at a little jingling square piano, and really rattled off a quadrille.

d. To fire (bullets) rapidly; to carry off (a person) by firing.

1890 KIPLING in *Scots Observer* 12 July 200/2 If a beggar can't march, why, we [*sc.* machine-guns] kills 'im an' rattles 'im into 'is grave. **1916** 'BOYD CABLE' *Action Front* 198 He rattled off burst after burst of fire.

7. a. To scold, rate, or rail at, volubly.

Common *c* 1580–1730.

1542 N. UDALL *Erasmus's Apophthegmes* sig. K5, How Diogenes ratleed & shooke vp couetous persones. **1577** HANMER *Anc. Eccl. Hist.* (1619) 373 For which doctrine.. yet was he ratled of Sisimus the Novatian bishop. **1600** ABBOT *Exp. Jonah* 68 He so rebuketh Jonas, and ratleth him for his drowsiness. **1667** PEPYS *Diary* 9 Aug., I did soundly rattle him for neglecting her so much as he has done. **1710** S. PALMER *Proverbs* 70 A man's own friends will..reprove, catechise, and rattle him at so severe a rate. **1736** [CHETWOOD] *Voy. Vaughan* (1760) I. 132 My Uncle perceiving his Behaviour, rattled him, in his merry Way. **1931** S. W. RYDER *Blue Water Ventures* xvi. 217 He should have rattled his officer-of-the-watch for slackness.

†**b.** So with *up* or *off*. *Obs.*

1547 LATIMER in Foxe *A. & M.* (1563) 1349/2 Peraduenture ye wyll set penne to paper, and al to rattle me vp in a letter. **1560** DAUS tr. *Sleidane's Comm.* 202 b, The diuines of Collon assailed Bucer sore, and rattled hym vp with manye opprobrious wordes. *c* **1650** HEYLIN *Laud* (1668) 263 The King so rattled up the Bishop, that he was glad to make his peace. **1709** HEARNE *Collect.* 4 Apr. (O.H.S.) II. 182 He..rattled him off for Printing the Book. **1712** ARBUTHNOT *John Bull* III. viii, She, that would sometime rattle off her servants pretty sharply.

†**c.** With complement. *Obs.*

1624 MASSINGER *Parl. Love* II. ii, *Ser.* Madam, I rattled him, Rattled him home. *Le.* Rattle him hence, you rascal. **1669** PEPYS *Diary* 25 Mar., I did lay the law open to them, and rattle the master-attendants out of their wits almost. **1722** DE FOE *Relig. Courtsh.* I. iii. (1840) 89, I believe I rattled her out of it when I came away.

8. a. To stir *up*, rouse; to make lively.

1781 D. WILLIAMS tr. *Voltaire's Dram. Wks.* II. 119 Come, let us away, to hasten his scrawling redundancies, and rattle the old, plump gentlemen. **1879** MCCARTHY *Own Times* I. xvi. 397 A timely philippic rattling up an exhausted and disappointed House.

b. *Sporting.* To beat up or chase vigorously.

1829 *Sporting Mag.* XXIII. 303 A small covert close by the kennel, being well rattled, the varmint broke away in gallant style. **1860** WHYTE MELVILLE *Mkt. Harb.* 88 A fox well rattled, up to the first check, huntsmen tell us, is as good as half killed. **1878** E. W. L. DAVIES *Mem. Rev. J. Russell* xi. 259 To rattle..every stronghold visited by the foxes.

9. ***to rattle away***, to lose by dicing; ***to rattle off***, to dispose of in a rapid manner; also spec. *Cricket*: to score or 'knock off' with ease (the runs necessary for victory); ***to rattle up*** (chiefly *Cricket*): to score rapidly, within a certain time, or before enforced retirement.

1808 E. S. BARRETT *Miss-led General* 161 Another considerable estate, called Wheatlands, was rattled away in one night. **1822** *Blackw. Mag.* XII. 47 Currently rattled off at the Edinburgh book auctions. **1860** *Baily's Mag.* Sept. 427 Captain Bathurst, in the fine old family style, rattled up 10 and 21. **1875** *Ibid.* June 108 Ultimately the South were left with about 40 to get to win, and Mr. W. G. Grace and Jupp rattled off these without difficulty. **1896** G. B. SHAW *Let.* 15 Feb. (1965) I. 597, I do not make a third of the income expected by men who rattle off their copy at anything from 20/- to 40/- a thousand. **1926** H. S. ALTHAM *Hist. Cricket* xviii. 208 Jackson and Sellars rattled up 24 in a quarter of an hour. **1973** *Advocate-News* (Barbados) 20 Feb. 14/5 Such an 'uncertainty' would take the form of a dramatic batting collapse, giving the Australians enough time to rattle up a good second innings score. **1976** *0–10 Cricket Scene* (Austral.) 30/2 And to show he has lost none of his zest for runs, he rattled off scores of 171 not out, 12, 114 not out and 36 in the World Cup series in England.

10. To impel, drive, drag, bring, etc., in a rapid rattling manner. Freq. in recent use, esp. with advbs. or preps.

1825–8 CROKER *Fairy Legends* 342 As bold a rider as any Mallow boy that ever rattled a four-year-old upon Drumrue race course. **1840** J. DEVLIN *Shoemaker* 10 The sweep ascends to his task, rattles down the soot about our feet. **1867** J. MACGREGOR *Voy. Alone* (1868) 81 The anchor was rattled up in a minute. **1880** MCCARTHY *Own Times* III. 184 A Bill..was rattled, if we may use such an expression, through both Houses. **1977** J. LAKER *One-Day Cricket* 66 The Sri Lankans rattled the score along. **1977** *Sunday Times* 9 Jan. 28/6 They rattled their reply of 240 for four to the Bangladesh score of 266 for nine declared, at more than four runs an over.

11. orig. *U.S.* To shake the system of (a person), to agitate, frighten, scare. Also, to irritate, to 'nettle'.

1869 J. R. BROWNE *Adventures Apache Country* xxviii. 282, I think he was slightly rattled by the formidable appearance of our escort. **1887** *Sci. Amer.* 12 Feb. 106 Girls of good physique..are much less liable to irritation and impatience, much less liable to 'get rattled', than those who are weak and ill. **1895** *Outing* (U.S.) XXVI. 67/2 The previous long, uncertain stalk had rattled me, but things were now all right. **1897** W. D. HOWELLS *Landlord Lion's Head* 212, 'I wonder if you'd really have the courage'. 'I don't think I'm easily rattled'. 'You mean that I'm trying to rattle you'. **1904** F. LYNDE *Grafters* xxviii. 360 For once in a way the ex-district attorney was too nearly rattled to be fully alert to his surroundings. **1905** *Pall Mall Mag.* Nov. 546/1, I don't see you need be rattled. **1927** M. DE LA ROCHE *Jalna* xxii. 276 Don't be a duffer... The more Piers sees he can rattle you the more he'll do it. **1928** E. WALLACE *Double* iv. 52 Why the devil are they bothering me? There's something about this business that is rattling me. **1936** P. FLEMING *News from Tartary* 65 But I had the empty satisfaction of seeing that I had (slightly) rattled Pai. **1959** E. H. CLEMENTS *High Tension* v. 82 Trust a woman to put her oar in! That's got Alister nicely rattled! **1977** J. F. FIXX *Compl. Bk. Running* p. xviii, I was less easily rattled by unexpected frustrations.

rattle ('ræt(ə)l), *v.*² *Naut.* [Back-formation from *rattling* RATLIN(E, taken as a vbl. sb.] *trans.* To furnish with ratlines. Usually with *down.*

1729 CAPT. W. WRIGLESWORTH *MS. Log-bk. of the 'Lyell'* 1 Sept., Set up the Shrouds in order for Rattling, and Rattled the Mizon and part of the Fore Shrouds. **1829** MARRYAT *F. Mildmay* xvii, The men were ordered to rattle the rigging down. **1840** R. H. DANA *Bef. Mast* viii. 17 Everything was set up taut, the lower rigging rattled down, or rather rattled up, (according to the modern fashion).

'rattle-bag. [f. RATTLE *sb.*¹ or *v.*¹]

a. A rattle in the form of a bag. Also *transf.* **b.** *attrib.* or as *adj.* Rattling; reckless.

1583 GOLDING *Calvin on Deut.* xxiv. 140 Our dooings which are no better than rattlebagges to please babes withall. **1728** P. WALKER *Life Peden* 81 There comes the Devil's Rattle-bag, we do not want him here. **1824** SCOTT *Redgauntlet*, let. xi, The Bishop's summoner, that they called The Deil's Rattle-bag. **1886** ELWORTHY *W. Som. Word-bk., Rattle-Bag*, wild; harum-scarum; roystering; spendthrift. **1896** *Daily News* 4 May 5/6 Bicycles.. from the days of the old rattlebag 'bone-shaker'.

'rattle-brain. [f. RATTLE *sb.*¹ or *v.*¹]

1. An empty-headed noisy fellow.

1709 *Rumbling Fuddle-Caps* 8 Beholding the Rattle-brains, marry thought I, I have heard of a Puppy put into a Pye. **1823** DE QUINCEY *King of Hayti* Wks. 1859 XII. 46 He had taken down the conceit of the young rattle-brain. **1850** EMERSON *Repr. Men, Shaks.* Wks. (Bohn) I. 352 A poet is no rattlebrain, saying what comes uppermost.

2. Headlong noisy behaviour.

1838 HAWTHORNE *Amer. Note-bks.* (1883) 195 There is much exaggeration and rattle-brain about this fellow.

So **'rattle-brained** *a.*, characterized by foolish noisy levity of character or conduct.

1716 ADDISON *Freeholder* No. 9 ¶10 A story.. concerning a rattle-brained young fellow. **1866** J. TIMBS *Club Life* II. 172 The Golden Fleece Club, a rattle-brained society.

rattled ('ræt(ə)ld), *ppl. a.* [f. RATTLE *v.*¹ + -ED¹.] Agitated, confused, frightened. Also *Comb.* Cf. RATTLE *v.*¹ 11.

1910 *N.Y. Even. Post* 10 Feb. 8/1 The plight of Ohio's rattled Republicans is enough to win grimy tears from the stony basilisk. *a* **1974** R. CROSSMAN *Diaries* (1976) II. 413 'Oh God!' I thought, 'Harold's in such a rattled state, with Wigg on one side and poor Marcia and Gerald on the other.' **1977** W. M. SPACKMAN *Armful of Warm Girl* 62 It had seemed to her that he, rather, had been rattled-sounding.

rattled snake: see RATTLESNAKE *sb.*

†**rattle-gold.** *Sc. Obs.*⁻¹ [a. obs. Du. *ratelgoud* (Kil.), f. *ratelen* to rattle; cf. Du. *klatergoud*, G. *knitter-*, *rauschgold*, etc.] Gold-leaf or tinsel.

1508 *Accts. Ld. High Treasurer Scot.* (1902) IV. 113 Item, to Pieris the payntour, for glew, Rattil gold, Varneyis,.. for the chappell.

'rattle-head. ? *Obs.* **1.** = RATTLE-BRAIN 1.

1641 LAUD *Wks.* (1857) VI. 163 If this world go on, the dear sisters of these rattleheads will no longer keep silence in their churches or conventicles. *a* **1670** HACKET *Abp. Williams* I. (1692) 130 Many rattle-heads, as well as they, did bestir them to gain-stand this match. **1713** C'TESS WINCHELSEA *Misc. Poems* 126 No Cautions of a Matron, old and sage, Young Rattlehead to Prudence could engage. **1788** STEVENS *Adv. Speculist* II. 151 He was such a rattle-head, so inconstant and so unthinking, that he affronted his best friends.

†**2.** *spec.* A Cavalier (in contrast to a ROUND-HEAD). *Obs.*

Perh. orig. in the same sense as prec., but commonly used in reference to the long hair worn by the Cavaliers.

1641 *Dial. betw. Rattle-head & Round-head* 6 To speak my minde of Rattleheads, Roundheads, Loggerheads, etc. **1643** PRYNNE (*title*) A Gagge for Long Haired Rattle Heads who revile all civill Round Heads. **1649** *Roxbury Ch. Rec.* in Coffin *Hist. Newbury* (1845), Locks and long haire (now in England called rattle heads).

So **'rattle-headed** *a.* = RATTLE-BRAINED.

1647 *Parlt. Ladies* 3 The Rattle-headed Ladyes being Assembled at Kates in the Covent-Garden. **1705** ROWE *Biter* III. i, These Rattle-headed Young Fellows don't know how to value a discreet elderly Passion. **1864** T. NICHOLS *40 Yrs. Amer. Life* II. xiii. 224 As lively, sparkling, amiable, and rattle-headed as she knew how to be.

'rattle-mouse. [f. RATTLE *sb.*¹ or *v.*¹]

1. A bat. *Obs.* exc. *dial.*

1589 PUTTENHAM *Eng. Poesie* II. xiii. [xviii.] (Arb.) 147 The tale of the Rattlemouse who.. excused himselfe for that he was a foule and flew with winges. **1856** *Zoologist* Ser. I. XIV. 5216 Something alive was brought to me.. with the enquiry whether I wanted a 'rattle-mouse'. I found the mysterious stranger was a Serotine bat. **1960** M. BURTON *Wild Animals Brit. Isles* 48 In the Isle of Wight it [*sc.* the serotine bat] is known as rattle-mouse.

†**2.** = RATEL¹. *Obs.*

Called *Ratel-Maus* by Kolbe, though he adds that the Dutch name is simply *Ratel*; his account of the habits of the animal is very inaccurate.

1731 MEDLEY *Kolbe's Cape G. Hope* II. 124 There is a creature pretty often seen in the Cape colonies, and which the people there call a Rattle-Mouse... With its tail.. it makes now and then a rattling noise, and thence it is called the Rattle-mouse.

'rattle-pate. = RATTLE-HEAD 1.

1643 PRYNNE *Gag Long-haired Rattle-Heads* L ij, All Rattle-pates who 'gainst Round-heads declaime. *a* **1700** B. E. *Dict. Cant. Crew*, *Rattle-pate*, a Hot, Maggot-pated Fellow. **1829** in BROCKETT. **1857** KINGSLEY *Two Y. Ago* xi, Rattle-pate as I am, I forgot all about it.

So **'rattle-pated** = RATTLE-HEADED.

1633 PRYNNE *Histrio-m.* 993 The dissolutenesse of our lascivious, impudent, rattle-pated gadding females. **1779** *Sylph* I. 234 Your rattle-pated husband. **1814** SCOTT *Wav.* lxiii, The rattle-pated trick of a young Cantab. **1865** COLLINS *Armadale* II. xi, He is a rattle-pated young fool.

rattler ('rætlə(r)). [f. RATTLE *v.*¹ + -ER¹.]

1. †**a.** One who rattles *out.* †**b.** A stutterer. *Obs.* **c.** = RATTLE *sb.*¹ 7.

c **1449** PECOCK *Repr.* I. xvi. 88 He is a greet and thikke rateler out of textis of Holi Scripture. **1483** *Cath. Angl.* 300/2 Ratyller, *travlus.* **1709** W. KING *Useful Trans. Philos.* II. sig. A 2ᵛ, Nothing could be more useful than a full.. Inspection of Human Tongues... It is hop'd that if any Persons know themselves to be.. Tongue-Padds, Spokesmen, Rattlers, Bouncers, &c. they would.. bequeath their Tongues to be dissected. **1836** T. HOOK *G. Gurney* III. 50 The volatile, gay, agreeable rattler of other days. **1879** G. MEREDITH *Egoist* xxxix, We have only to sharpen our wits to trip your seductive rattler whenever.. we think proper. **1959** *She* May 21/3 *Rattler*, great talker.

2. a. A thing which rattles; †a rattle.

1594 GREENE & LODGE *Looking Gl.* G.'s Wks. (Grosart) XIV. 35 Her working-day words.. be ratlers like thunder, sir. **1648** GAGE *West Ind.* xxi. (1655) 202 The noise of Bels and ratlers to rouse up the drowsie Fryers. **1654** GAYTON *Pleas. Notes* III. xi. 146 The murmurer, (The silver rattler on the gravelly path). **1822** SCOTT *Pirate* viii, With slugs.. never gun shot closer... But.. the old rattler will never do you the service she has done me.

b. *slang.* A (rattling) coach. *gen.*, any (rattling) form of transport, esp. a train.

1630 J. TAYLOR (Water P.) [N.] If our hackney ratlers were so drawne, With cords, or ropes, or halters. *a* **1700** B. E. *Dict. Cant. Crew*, *Rattler*, a Coach. **1753** *Disc. John Poulter* (ed. 2) 34 Go three or four Miles out of Town to meet the Rattlers, that is Coaches. **1819** *Sporting Mag.* V. 123 The lads in their rattlers, heavy drags, and tumblers. **1825** [see HACKNEY *sb.* 6c]. **1829** P. EGAN *Boxiana* 2nd Ser. II. 674 Boscoe made his appearance in a rattler, with four prime prads. **1871** *Lakeside Monthly* Oct. 323/1, I am going on the rattlers tomorrow to nick a lot of flats and molls. **1903** A. M. BINSTEAD *Pitcher in Paradise* viii. 193 On the followin' Saturday afternoon I took the rattler down to Aldershot. **1904** 'No. 1500' *Life in Sing Sing* 252/1 *Rattler*, a car. **1922** R. PARRISH *Case & Girl* 333 We caught another rattler two hours later, and got off at Patacne. **1924** D. H. LAWRENCE *England, my England* 102 Miss Stokes had a puncture. 'Let me wheel the rattler,' said Albert. **1936** I. L. IDRIESS *Cattle King* xli. 348 'Well, sir, for last year you certainly paid your fare on the railways.' 'I've never jumped the 'rattler' in my life.' **1951** *Collier's* 17 Nov. 8/2 We're rolling across the country in a very luxurious rattler. **1966** 'L. LANE' *ABZ of Scouse* II. 88 *Rattler*, a tram or street-car. **1977** 'J. FRASER' *Hearts Ease* v. 38 'Where's the ambulance?' 'We sent it away... The first one was an old rattler. We've sent for the Daimler which has better springing.'

c. orig. *U.S.* A rattlesnake.

1827 J. F. COOPER *Prairie* I. xvii. 249 The snakes of the prairies are harmless, unless it be now and then an angered rattler. **1884** J. G. BOURKE *Snake Dance Moquis* xiii. 147 he was holding in his hand the biggest snake in the whole collection, a rattler not less than five feet long. **1909** *Chambers's Jrnl.* July 431/2 Many of the little snakes of the tropics are as poisonous as the dreaded rattler. **1918** W. CATHER *My Antonia* I. ii. 17 She had killed a good many rattlers. **1949** G. B. SHAW *Buoyant Billions* IV. 48 You cannot charm the rattlers and gaters as I can. **1956** L. M. KLAUBER *Rattlesnakes* I. i. 11 Some believe any snake that vibrates its tail when angry or alarmed to be a rattler. **1963** D. P. MANNIX *All Creatures Great & Small* xi. 190 A friend sent me a very fine Mexican green rattler nearly six feet long. **1978** P. THEROUX *Picture Palace* ii. 8, I was moving round the room, hunched like a cowboy that hears a rattler.

3. a. A sharp or severe blow, fall, storm, etc.

1812 *Sporting Mag.* XL. 66 Receiving a rattler in the neck. **1827** *Ibid.* (N.S.) XXI. 145 He got one rattler when I was in the country. **1835** T. POWER *Jrnl.* 25 Mar. in *Impressions Amer.* (1836) ii. 266 Our breeze freshened gradually all the evening, until by midnight it blew a rattler. **1858** ADM. HORNBY in *Autobiog.* (1896) 60 In the first watch we got a rattler, only got the fore- and mizzen-top sails in in time to save them. **1865** DICKENS *Mut. Fr.* I. viii, I should have given him a rattler for himself, if Mrs. Boffin hadn't thrown herself betwixt us.

b. A remarkably good horse. Also *gen.*, anyone or anything remarkably good or able, esp. with regard to speed.

1841 LYTTON *Night & Morning* II. viii, I want a good horse... Now then, out with your rattlers. **1853** F. GALE *Public School Matches* 13 The first ball is well pitched and comes in a rattler to the middle stump. **1860** WHYTE MELVILLE *Mkt. Harb.* 127 If he can only jump.. and get pretty quick over his fences, he ought to be a rattler. **1883** 'MARK TWAIN' *Life on Mississippi* xxiv. 271 That 'Cyclone' was a rattler to go, and the sweetest thing to steer that ever walked the waters. **1886** M. THOMPSON *Banker of Bankersville* ix. 134 Your partner is a whole team, hain't he? He's a rattler! **1894** 'MARK TWAIN' in *St. Nicholas* Mar. 395 It was a rattler, that caravan, and a mighty fine sight to look at. **1917** H. GARLAND *Son of Middle Border* xxiv. 290 You may consider yourself hired for as long as you please to stay. You're a rattler.

c. *dial.* An arrant lie. (Cf. RAPPER 3 a.)

1829 in BROCKETT. **1847-** in HALLIWELL, etc.

d. A long, resounding word.

1865 'MARK TWAIN' in *Californian* 18 Mar. 8/1 One of them rattlers with a clatter of syllables as long as a string of sluice boxes.

4. *techn.* **a.** A hard, brittle, jet-like coal, usually lying on the top of seams. Also *pl.*

1821 CURWEN in *Gill's Tech. Repository* (1822) I. 210 Rattler, which is a mixture of coal and schistus. *Ibid.*, Rattler does not fall, and is very light in comparison to its bulk. **1883** GRESLEY *Gloss. Coal-mining* 200.

b. A razor with a very thin blade. Also *attrib.*

1829 in BROCKETT. **1846** HOLTZAPFFEL *Turning* III. 1149 From the vibration to which they are liable when applied to a strong beard, they are called by the Sheffield cutlers, rattler razors.

5. *attrib.* and *Comb.*, as (sense 2c) ***rattler hatband***; **rattler-jumper**, one who jumps (JUMP *v.* 6b) a train; so **rattler-jumping** *vbl. sb.*

1978 *Detroit Free Press* 5 Mar. 23/1 'One day when we were in a local shop, the owner remarked that he would pay $10 for a rattler hatband.' That casual remark launched the couple into a business. **1934** *Bulletin* (Sydney) 7 Mar. 33/2 It looks as though the Queensland Government will have to run special trains to cope with 'rattler'-jumpers, who nowadays travel in packs. **1933** *Ibid.* 3 May 20/1 Of all vocations rattler-jumping is the least easy.

rattlesnake ('ræt(ə)lsneɪk), *sb.* Also 8 **rattled snake.** [f. RATTLE *sb.*¹ or *v.*¹ + SNAKE.]

1. a. A venomous American pit viper belonging to the genus *Sistrurus* or *Crotalus* of the family Crotalidæ, having a series of horny rings at the end of the tail which make a rattling noise when the tail is vibrated.

1630 CAPT. SMITH *Wks.* (Arb.) 955 Some [talk] of the danger of the rattell Snake. **1657** EVELYN *Diary* 19 Sept., I saw at Dr. Joyliffe's 2 Virginian rattle-snakes alive. **1748** WASHINGTON *Jrnl.* 12 Apr., Writ. 1889 I. 6 This day see a Rattled snake, ye first we had seen in all our journey. **1796** STEDMAN *Surinam* II. xxiv. 195 The rattle-snake of Surinam is sometimes eight or nine feet long. **1860** GOSSE *Rom. Nat. Hist.* 264 The bite of the American rattlesnake has been known to produce death in two minutes. **1932** W. FAULKNER *Light in August* ii. 29 He carried with him his own inescapable warning, like a flower its scent or a rattlesnake its rattle. **1956** L. M. KLAUBER *Rattlesnakes* I. i. 13 All rattlesnakes have rattles, and no other kind of snake has them. **1975** R. L. BEALS *Peasant Marketing System of Oaxaca, Mexico* iii. 31 The rattlesnake was associated with the rain cult.

fig. **1824** BYRON *Def. Transf.* I. ii. 290 There's a demon In that fierce rattlesnake thy tongue.

attrib. **1885** C. F. HOLDER *Marvels Anim. Life* 125 Rattlesnake oil, which is believed to possess wonderful curative powers. **1897** *Allbutt's Syst. Med.* II. 810 The poisonous properties of rattlesnake venom. **1910** *Encycl. Relig. & Ethics* III. 143/1 The rattlesnake-doctor, who cured or prevented the bite of the rattlesnake, was usually distinct from other medicine-men.

b. *Comb.* in names of American plants, as **rattlesnake fern**, a species of moonwort or grape-fern, *Botrychium virginianum*; **rattle-snake grass**, a kind of quaking-grass, *Glyceria canadensis*; **rattlesnake herb**, the Bane-berry, *Actæa rubra* or *alba*, and some other plants; **rattlesnake leaf** (see quots.); **rattlesnake('s) master**, the Button-snakeroot, *Liatris scariosa* or *squarrosa*, and other plants; **rattlesnake orchid**, an epiphytic orchid of the genus *Pholidota*, esp. *P. imbricata*, which is native to parts of south-east Asia and bears pendant racemes of light brown flowers; **rattlesnake plantain**, one of three species of *Goodyera*, esp. *G. pubescens*; **rattlesnake root**, (*a*) the root of a species of milkwort, *Polygala Senega* (see SENEGA); (*b*) one of several species of *Prenanthes*, esp. *P. serpentaria*; (*c*) one of several other plants believed to help cure the effect of rattlesnake bites; **rattlesnake weed**, (*a*) a species of *Eryngium*; (*b*) a species of hawk-weed, *Hieracium venosum*; (*c*) = *rattlesnake root* (*c*); **rattlesnake-wort** = *rattlesnake root* (*a*).

1814 F. PURSH *Flora Amer.* II. 656 *Botrychium virginianum*.. is known by the name of *Rattle Snake Fern. **1845-50** MRS. LINCOLN *Lect. Bot.* 82/2 Rattlesnake-fern. **1868** PAXTON *Bot. Dict.* 83/2 The largest of the American kinds.. is named the rattlesnake fern, on account of its generally being found where those reptiles abound. **1931** W. N. CLUTE *Common Names Plants* 109 The spore-cases of one of our ferns are borne in spikes that so strongly suggest the rattles of the rattlesnake that it is commonly known as the rattlesnake fern. **1814** J. BIGELOW *Florula Bostoniensis* 25 *Rattlesnake grass.. A large grass found in meadows and readily recognized by its swelling spikelets. **1878** J. B. KILLEBREW *Grasses of Tennessee* 232 Rattlesnake Grass.. resembles quaking grass very much. **1736** B. FRANKLIN *Poor Richard 1737* 3 (*caption*) *Rattle-Snake Herb. **1763** tr. *L. du Pratz's Hist. Louisiana* II. 43 The Rattle-snake-herb has a bulbous root like that of a tuberose, but twice as large. **1861** MISS PRATT *Flower. Pl.* I. 47 The tubers of an American species [of Actæa] are considered an efficacious remedy for the wound inflicted by the bite of the rattle-snake; hence that plant is one of several which are known in America as the Rattlesnake-Herb. **1822** A. EATON *Man. Bot.* (ed. 3) 294 *Goodyera pubescens*, *rattle-snake leaf, scrophula-weed. **1829** A. H. LINCOLN *Familiar Lect. Bot.* 288 *Goodyera pubescens*, rattle-snake leaf. **1806** *Farmer's Calendar* sig. D4, Notwithstanding a free use of sweet oil, plantane, hoarhound, *prenanthet alba*, called here *rattlesnake's master, &c. the swelling and pain progressed. **1836** M. HOLLEY *Texas* v. 103 A root called rattlesnake's master grows abundantly in the pine woods and is said to be an efficient remedy. **1843** F. MARRYAT *Narr. Trav. & Adv. M. Violet* II. vi. 134 Close to my feet I beheld five or six stems of the rattlesnake master weed. **1899** H. B. CUSHING *Hist. Choctaw Indians* 229 They [*sc.* the Choctaws] possessed an antidote for the bite and sting of snakes and insects, in the root of a plant called rattle snake's master. **1943** D. C. PEATTIE *Great Smokies* 189 Thus a little orchid, the rattlesnake plantain, with net-veined leaves, looks enough like a snakeskin to suggest that it may be 'rattlesnake master' or cure for snake bites. **1887** G. NICHOLSON *Illustr. Dict. Gardening* III. 105/1 *Pholidota*.. *Rattlesnake Orchid. **1903** H. J. CHAPMAN *Watson's Orchids* (ed. 2) 430 It [*sc. Pholidota*] is commonly known as the Rattlesnake Orchid. **1965** A. D. HAWKES *Encycl. Cultivated Orchids* 369/1 The persistent or deciduous, large, concave bracts which occur in most species—often almost hiding the blossoms—give the common name of 'Rattlesnake Orchid' to at least some of the cultivated Pholidotas. **1778** J. CARVER *Trav. Interior Parts N. Amer.* 482 The *Rattle Snake Plantain, an approved antidote to the poison of this creature. **1846–50** A. WOOD *Class-bk. Bot.* 536 Rattlesnake Plantain. **1898** L. H. BAILEY *Lessons with Plants* 223 Among the better known plants which are members of the Orchidaceæ are the..rattlesnake plantain, putty-root, and vanilla. **1943** [see *rattlesnake master*]. **1972** *Islander* (Victoria, B.C.) 16 Apr. 16/3 Rattlesnake plantain..is a denizen of the woods. **1682** T. A. *Carolina* 11 They have three sorts of the *Rattle-Snake Root which I have seen. **1760** J. LEE *Introd. Bot.* App. 324 Rattlesnake Root, Dr. Witts, *Prenanthes.* **1840** PEREIRA *Elem. Mat. Med.* II. 1257 Senega or seneka root.. sometimes called the seneka-snake-root, or the rattlesnake-root, is imported from the United States in bales. **1889** *Cent. Dict.* 786/3 Cancer-weed, the rattlesnake root, *Prenanthes alba*, of the United States, a milky-juiced composite having an intensely bitter root. **1941** R. S. WALKER *Lookout* 48 Among the wild plants once employed as antidotes for the bites of poisonous reptiles are..Virginia snakeroot, button snakeroot, and rattlesnake-root. **1760** J. LEE *Introd. Bot.* App. 324 *Rattlesnake Weed, *Eryngium.* **1861** N. A. WOODS *Tour Pr. Wales Canada* 298 It is the rattlesnake weed, always most plentiful where this deadly reptile abounds. **1885** *Outing* Nov. 180/1 A pretty thing sends a creeping feeling down our backs, because it is rattlesnake weed. **1936** G. A. REICHARD *Navajo Shepherd & Weaver* 45 A yellow-green commonly seen is made by brewing the leaves and stems of one of the goldenrods (Bigelovia) called by some Whites 'tall rattlesnake weed'. **1782** *Encycl. Brit.* (ed. 2) IX. 6392/1 The seeds of the *rattlesnake-wort seldom succeed.

2. *transf.* In full, ***rattlesnake cocktail, whisk(e)y.*** A potent alcoholic drink or cocktail.

1862 [see COBBLER 3]. **1867** T. C. BAKER *Hist. U.S. Secret Service* xix. 246 It is hardly worth the while to present to the Government a bill for a few decanters and rattlesnake whisky. **1903** A. M. BINSTEAD *Pitcher in Paradise* iv. 110 He went from bar to bar drinking 'rattlesnake cocktails'. **1930** *Savoy Cocktail Bk.* 132 Rattlesnake Cocktail... So called because it will either cure Rattlesnake bite, or kill Rattlesnakes, or make you see them. **1947** *Daily Progress* (Charlottesville, Va.) 3 Sept. 8/5 A bottle of 'rattlesnake whiskey' was seized in a recent Chinatown raid by the Federal Bureau of Narcotics, which offers this recipe for the concoction: Place a live rattlesnake in a large jar; add rice wine, dried toads, soy beans, sliced deer antlers and a handful of dried sea horses. Age six months. **1953** T. SHANE *Bar Guide* ii. 31 Rattlesnake. 2 dashes Pernod. 1 tsp. Lemon Juice. ½ tsp. Powdered Sugar. ½ Egg White. 1 oz. Rye. Shake with cracked ice and strain.

rattlesnake ('ræt(ə)lsneɪk), *v. rare.* [f. prec.]

1. *trans.* To deceive or trick, as with the cunning of a serpent.

1818 KEATS *Let.* 3 Feb. (1958) I. 223 We must cut this, and not be rattlesnaked into any more of the like.

2. *trans.* and *intr.* To snake (see SNAKE *v.*¹ 4) with a rattling sound; to travel like a rattlesnake.

1961 M. SPARK *Prime of Miss Jean Brodie* ii. 23 The evening paper rattle-snaked its way through the letter box. **1981** J. BARNETT *Firing Squad* II. 155 Messerschmitts came in at low level, rattlesnaking along the beaches.

'rattlesome, *a.* [f. RATTLE *v.*¹] Rattly.

1876 BLACKMORE *Cripps* xlix, The gate, which was quite shaky and rattlesome in its joints.

'rattletrap, *sb.* and *a.* [f. RATTLE *sb.*¹ or *v.*¹ + TRAP *sb.*]

A. *sb.* **1.** *pl.* Nick-nacks, trifles, odds and ends, curiosities, small or worthless articles. Also *sing.* of a single article of this kind.

1766 *Goody Two-Shoes* II. (1881) 27 She used to go round to teach the Children with these Rattle-traps in a Basket. **1785** in GROSE *Dict. Vulgar Tongue.* **1820** SCOTT *Abbot* xix, Your other rattle-trap yonder at Avenel, which Mistress Lilias bears about on her shoes in the guise of a pair of shoe-buckles. **1878** M. C. JACKSON *Chaperon's Cares* II. xi. 136 Rattletraps for the mantlepiece, gimcracks for the table.

2. A rattling, rickety coach or other vehicle.

1822 C'TESS BLESSINGTON *Magic Lantern* 22 The shabby rattle-trap is filled by a group that would require the pencil of Hogarth to paint. **1861** F. F. TUCKETT in *Peaks, Passes & Glac.* Ser. II. I. 304 At length..we tore ourselves away, and at eight entered our nondescript rattletrap.

3. Any rickety or shaky thing.

1833 M. SCOTT *Tom Cringle* xviii, A rickety rattletrap of a wooden ladder. **1857** TROLLOPE *Barchester T.* xxxv, He'd destroy himself and me too, if I attempted to ride him at such a rattle-trap as that. **1883** *Harper's Mag.* 884/1 The steamer was an old rattletrap.

4. *slang.* **a.** The mouth.

1824 SCOTT *Redgauntlet* ch. xv, Shut your rattle-trap. **1886–7** in Cheshire glossaries.

b. = RATTLE *sb.*¹ 7.

1880 *Life in Debtor's Prison* x, I see you're as great a rattletrap as ever.

B. *adj.* Rickety, shaky.

1834 SIR F. HEAD *Bubbles of Brunnen* 115, I ascended an old rattle-trap staircase. **1892** ANNIE RICHIE *Rec. Tennyson,* etc. III. ix. 225 We started almost the next day in a rattle-trap chaise.

rattlin, variant of RATLIN(E.

rattling ('rætlɪŋ), *vbl. sb.* [f. RATTLE *v.*¹ + -ING¹.] The action of the vb., in various senses.

1398 TREVISA *Barth. De P.R.* v. xxi. (Bodl. MS.), Rateling men beþ mosste ytake, for to moche moisture of suche men ..is cause of rateling. **1508** DUNBAR *Flyting* 230 Ffor rerd of the, and rattling of thy butis. **1555** W. WATREMAN *Fardle Facions* II. viii. 180 There is no glittering apparell, no rattelinge in sylkes, no rusteling in veluettes. **1656** *Artif. Handsom.* 126 What is this but like the ratling of haile upon tiles? *a* **1677** BARROW *Serm.* Wks. 1716 III. 32 The ratlings of clamorous obloquy. **1753** RICHARDSON *Grandison* (ed. 7) I. 2 My Grandmother Selby..is always pleased with his rattling. **1779** BURKE *Let. to Thomas Burgh* Wks. 1826 IX. 231 An obscure and feeble rattling in their throat. **1855** MACAULAY *Hist. Eng.* xxii. IV. 774 The rattling of dice.. never ceased during the whole night.

rattling ('rætlɪŋ), *ppl. a.* [f. as prec. + -ING².]

1. That rattles, or makes a rattle. †***rattling baby*** = rattle-baby (see RATTLE *sb.*¹ 11).

1398 [see RATTLING *vbl. sb.*]. *a* **1400–50** *Alexander* 4531 A ratland niȝt ravyn is him to rent ȝolden. *c* **1586** C'TESS PEMBROKE *Ps.* LXXVII. xi, Thy voices thundring crash..Did ..rattling horror rore. **1592** G. HARVEY *Foure Lett.* Wks. (Grosart) I. 225 Yet neuer childe so delighted in his rattling baby. **1646** SIR T. BROWNE *Pseud. Ep.* II. v. §9 Many sorts there are of this rattling Stone, beside the Geodes. **1667** MILTON *P.L.* VI. 546 Ratling storm of Arrows barbd with fire. **1784** COWPER *Task* IV. 144 No rattling wheels stop short before these gates. **1842** LEVER *J. Hinton* vi, The infantry poured in a rattling roar of small arms.

2. a. Characterized by a rapid flow of words or liveliness of manner.

1560 ROLLAND *Crt. Venus* III. 129 The ratland Rollis was red vnto the end. **1590** SHAKS. *Mids. N.* v. 102 The ratling tongue Of saucy and audacious eloquence. **1709** POPE *Ess. Crit.* 628 Rattling nonsense in full vollies breaks. **1774** MAD. D'ARBLAY *Early Diary* 29 Sept., I have returned to all my old original rattling spirits. **1883** F. M. CRAWFORD *Dr. Claudius* viii. 137 Glad of the rattling talk that delivered them from the burden of saying anything especial.

†**b.** Full of scolding or reproof. *Obs.*

a **1700** DRYDEN *Iliad* I. 724 Thus turbulent in rattling tone she spoke. **1874** GREEN *Short Hist.* vii. §2. 359 'Rattling letters' from the council roused the lagging prelates.

3. Of persons: Extremely lively in manners or speech.

1727 SWIFT *To a Young Lady,* A tribe of bold, swaggering, rattling ladies. **1780** MAD. D'ARBLAY *Diary* May (1842) I. 365 He seemed a mighty rattling, harem-scarem gentleman, but talked so fluently [etc.]. **1862** THACKERAY *Philip* xl, She gives excellent dinners which jolly fogeys, rattling bachelors ..frequent. **1880** MCCARTHY *Own Times* IV. xlviii. 21 A powerful speaker of the rattling declamatory kind.

4. a. Remarkably good, fine, fast, etc. (freq. with more or less suggestion of the literal sense).

1690 DRYDEN *Amphitryon* II. ii, If Jupiter ever let thee set foot in heaven, Juno will have a rattling second of thee. **1768** STERNE *Sent. Journ.* (1778) I. 131 *Postillion,* A good rattling gallop would have been of real service to me. **1831** TRELAWNY *Adv. Younger Son* II. 209 Running down with a rattling trade-wind. **1851** THACKERAY *Eng. Hum.* iii. (1876) 212 A gentleman of military appearance, who..has a rattling grey mare in the stables. **1874** LADY HERBERT tr. *Hübner's Ramble* II. ii. (1878) 258 Off we went at a rattling pace.

b. Extremely severe.

1861 WHYTE MELVILLE *Mkt. Harb.* 16 The limp..had been earned in a rattling fall over a turnpike-gate.

c. Adverbially with adjs. (esp. *good*): Remarkably, extremely. Also with vbs.: Extremely well.

1829 T. C. CROKER *Legends* (1862) 242 A rattling fine dinner we had of it. **1851** MAYHEW *Lond. Lab.* I. 223/2 We had a fine 'fake',..it sold rattling. **1877** BLACK *Green Past.* i. (1878) 6 A rattling good sort of a girl. **1885** *Punch* 4 July 4/1 You do see some rattling pretty, fresh faces. **1930** A. G. HAYS in W. E. Weeks *All in Racket* 13 This is a rattling good story. **1978** *Jrnl. R. Soc. Arts* CXXVI. 636/1 Herkomer's *The Last Muster* is a rattling good picture.

†**5.** *slang* or *Cant* (see quots.).

a **1700** B. E. *Dict. Cant. Crew, Rattling-cove,* a Coachman. *Rattling Mumpers,* such Beggars as Ply Coaches. [**1725** *New Cant. Dict.,* Such as run after, or ply Coaches.] **1754** *Scoundrel's Dict.* 21 The rattling mumper broke the rattling peeper [= 'coach-glass'].

6. *Comb.,* as ***rattling-boned*** adj.

1933 E. SITWELL *Eng. Eccentrics* ii. 42, I am afraid the ancient and rattling-boned gallant rather gloried in this fall from grace.

Hence **'rattlingly** *adv.*; **'rattlingness.**

1824 *Blackw. Mag.* XV. 101 [They] shake in skin as rattlingly as they ere shook the castor. **1855** WISEMAN *Fabiola* 220 The old capsararius, as he had had himself rattlingly called in his anteposthumous inscription. **1869** *Contemp. Rev.* XI. 18 The general rattlingness of the rhythmic movement.

rattling, variant of RATLIN(E.

rattly ('rætlɪ), *a.* [f. RATTLE *v.*¹ + -Y¹.] Of the nature of rattling; inclined to rattle.

1881 MRS. MOLESWORTH *Adv. Herr Baby* iv. 73 Baby was very pleased to get..out of rumbly, rattly noise. **1891** MISS DOWIE *Girl in Karp.* 21 Their little long wooden carts, light and rattly as possible.

ratton ('ræt(ə)n). Now *Sc.* and *north. dial.* Forms: 4–5 **ratoun,** 5 **ratone, -un,** 4–6 (9) **raton;** 6 *Sc.* **ratto(u)ne,** 7 **rattin,** 6 *Sc.*, 7– **ratton,** 8– **ratten,** 8–9 **rattan.** [a. OF. *raton,* f. *rat* RAT *sb.*¹ Cf. Sp. *raton,* med.L. *rato, ratōnis.*] A rat.

1300–20 in *Rel. Ant.* II. 78 Wessele, *reheite.* ratonz, *raz.* molde warpes, *taupaines.* **1377** LANGL. *P. Pl.* B. Prol. 146 Wiþ þat ran þere a route of ratones..And smale mys with hem. *c* **1400** MAUNDEV. (Roxb.) xiv. 64 Þai ete cattes and hundes, ratouns and myesse. **1486** *Bk. St. Albans* C j b, The fleshe of a kydde..and especiall Ratonys flesh. **1552** LYNDESAY *Monarche* 3985 Necessitie gart thame eit perforsse Dog, Catt and Rattone. **1601** HOLLAND *Pliny* VIII. xxxvi. 216 At the first, they [bear-whelps] seeme to be a lumpe of white flesh without all forme, little bigger than rattons. **1617** BRATHWAIT *Law of Drinking* 32 When I'm drunke as any Rattin, Then I rap out nought but Lattin. **1785** BURNS *Vision* I. iii, I..heard the restless rattons squeak About the riggin. **1849** C. BRONTE *Shirley* iii. 67 As much better..as a bull's bellow than a ratton's squeak. **1894** CROCKETT *Raiders* 59 A ratton's bite's poisonous.

fig. **1387** TREVISA *Higden* (Rolls) V. 119 Spadones..he clepede..ratouns of þe paleys. *a* **1585** MONTGOMERIE *Flyting w. Polwart* 288 Reavens rugand at that ratton [a child]. **1661** *Sir A. Haslerig's Last Will* Suppl. 6 The inraged Tygre no sooner furrowed his Front, then this feverish Ratoun let fall his Crest.

b. *attrib.*, as ***ratton bane, fell, man, poison***; **ratton-bread,** a poisoned paste for killing rats.

1544 PHAER *Pestilence* (1553) K vij, *Ratten bane, or other suche lyke kyndes of venymes. **1396** *Whitby Abbey Rolls* (Whitby Gl.), For Sperstane and *Ratonbrede, 1*s* 6*d.* **1876** *Whitby Gloss., Ratton-breead.* *c* **1400** *Turnam. Tottenham* 150 in Hazl. *E.P.P.* III. 89 Theire baner was ful bryȝt Off an olde *raton fell. **1481–90** *Howard Househ. Bks.* (Roxb.) 51 The xx. day of April, I..toke the *raten man iij. s. iiij. d. **1590** in Pitcairn *Crim. Trials* (Bann.) I. III. 195 To pas to Elgyne for bying *rattoun poysoune.

'rattoner. *Obs.* exc. *north. dial.* Also 4–5 **ratoner(e,** 5 **ratunner.** [f. prec. + -ER¹.] A rat-catcher.

1362 LANGL. *P. Pl.* A. v. 165 A ribibor, a ratoner, a rakere of Chepe. **14..** *Nom.* in Wr.-Wülcker 686/15 *Murida,* a ratunner. *c* **1440** *Promp. Parv.* 424/1 Ratonere, *soricus, soriceps, ratonarius.* **1876** *Whitby Gloss., Rattoner.*

†**rattoon**¹. *Obs. rare.* [ad. F. *raton,* earlier *raston, reston* (13th c.): see RASTON.] A kind of cheese-cake.

1656 MARNETTÈ *Perfect Cook* 148 You must..fill this your said Puff-paste with the same ingredients wherewithall you do make your Cheese Cakes, and accordingly you may cause your said Rattoon to be baked.

†**rattoon**². *Obs.* Also 7 **-ton.** [var. RACOON. Cf. F. *raton* in same sense.] A racoon.

1656 [H. MORE] *Second Lash Alaz.* 274 A fellow of a fit size to show the Lions and the Rattoon at the Tower. **1668** CHARLETON *Onomasticon* 14 *Vulpes Americana* Mapach *dicta, Anglicè* Ratton. **1704** W. COWPER in *Phil. Trans.* XXV. 1569 The Coati of Brasil and Virginia, or the Rackoon or Rattoon. **1706** PHILLIPS (ed. Kersey), *Rattoon,* a kind of Fox in the West Indies [etc.]. **1755** in JOHNSON (citing Bailey).

rattoon, obs. variant of RATTAN.

'rat-trap. [f. RAT *sb.*¹ + TRAP *sb.*]

1. a. A trap for catching rats. Also *fig.*, and *attrib.* in sense 'resembling a rat-trap'.

1469 *Churchw. Acc. St. Mich. Cornhill,* Payed for iij rat trappes for the churche, vj d. **1820** SCOTT *Monast.* xxx, Men peeping through their own bars like so many rats in a rat-trap. **1884** DK. ST. ALBANS in *Contemp. Rev.* Aug. 172 A Peer..finds himself in a rat-trap from which politically there is no escape except death. **1904** *Westm. Gaz.* 3 Mar. 1/3 A gaunt man with a rat-trap face. **1907** *Ibid.* 20 Sept. 4/2 His [*sc.* a pike's] rat-trap jaws. **1978** R. WESTALL *Devil on Road* xxii. 217 He had a rat-trap jaw and little deep-set eyes.

b. *transf.* A shabby or ramshackle building or dwelling. *colloq.*

1838 DE QUINCEY in *Blackw. Mag.* XLIII. 21/2 Ay; but mind you,—put case that he or that she should die in this rat trap before sentence is passed. **1876** H. T. WILLIAMS *Pacific Tourist* 205 The following are among the..oddities which have, through miners' freaks and fancies, been used to denote settlements and camps and diggings, small or large: ..Rat-Trap Slide. **1892** 'MARK TWAIN' *Amer. Claimant* iv. 56 It wouldn't have occurred to anybody else to name this poor old rat-trap Rossmore Towers. **1974** *Amer. Speech* 1971 XLVI. 77 *Shabby hotel,*..flop joint, joint, rat trap.

2. Applied (*attrib.* or *absol.*) to a cycle pedal consisting of two parallel iron plates with teeth cut in them, as in a common style of rat-trap.

1885 *Bazaar* 30 Mar. 1275/1 Balls to all bearings and pedals, which are rattrap. **1887** VISC. BURY & HILLIER *Cycling* 171 Pedals..should be preferably rat-traps which afford a good hold for the feet. **1931** H. W. BARTLEET *Bartleet's Bicycle Bk.* 33 Every practical cyclist who saw my pedals praised the scheme of rattrap and rubber in combination. **1974** *Sumter* (S. Carolina) *Daily Item* 24 Apr. (Western Auto Advts. Suppl.) 4 Chromed rat trap racing pedals! **1976** *Billings* (Montana) *Gaz.* 28 June 2-c (Advt.), Rat trap pedals... Big 'knobby' tread tires.

3. *Building.* Applied *attrib.* to a form of Flemish bond (BOND *sb.*¹ 13 a) in which the bricks are laid on edge and the 'headers' span the whole thickness of wall, dividing the wall cavity into square spaces.

1932 E. GUNN *Economy in House Design* ix. 31 Brickwork beneath the tile hanging should be built in rat trap bond. **1939** —— *Building Technique* 39/1 Rat-trap or box-bond... This form of walling, which may be briefly described as Flemish-bond with all bricks laid on edge, is well-recognised in Sussex and adjoining counties where tile-hung walls are common. **1974** *Bricks* (Brick Development Assoc.) 1. 33 (*heading*) Rat-trap bond.

ratty ('rætɪ), *a.* [f. RAT *sb.*¹ + -Y¹.]

1. a. Characteristic of a rat or rats.

1888 H. S. MERRIMAN *Young Mistley* II. vi. 78 Those delightful ratty odours that..assailed his sportive nostrils. **1895** SNAITH *Mistress Dorothy Marvin* vii, He puckered his ratty eyes till scarce aught was left of them.

b. Infested with rats.

1865 G. MEREDITH *Farina* 104 Your German dungeons are mortal shivering ratty places. **1891** H. S. MERRIMAN *Prisoners & Captives* I. ii. 36 No dog had rejoiced more thankfully in ratty sedges.

2. a. *slang.* Wretched, mean, miserable, nasty, etc.

1867 'MARK TWAIN' *Notebk.* (1935) viii. 99 Village of Bethany... It is fearfully ratty—some houses—mud. **1884** —— *Huck. Finn* ix. 78 We got..a ratty old bed-quilt off the bed. **1885** *Century Mag.* XXIX. 548/1 An old ratty deck of cards. **1900** *Blackw. Mag.* Nov. 670/1 Both were pretty 'ratty' from hardship and loneliness. **1962** J. D. MACDONALD *Girl* xii. 185 Pooty-Tat sat on a ratty couch. **1969** E. B. WHITE *Let.* 2 Nov. (1976) 586 When he received me, in a ratty apartment in the West Seventies or thereabouts, he was wearing toga and sandals. **1970** 'D. HALLIDAY' *Dolly & Cookie Bird* iv. 51 A ratty half-dozen people had spilled out of the bar-café.. A lot of money changed hands rather quickly. **1974** R. M. PIRSIG *Zen & Art of Motorcycle Maintenance* III. xxvi. 317 John always kept his BMW spic and span. It really did look nice, while mine's always a little ratty, it seems.

b. *colloq.* Ill-tempered, irritated, angry.

1909 M. B. SAUNDERS *Litany Lane* xvi. 215 Shut up. She's ratty. **1913** H. S. WALPOLE *Fortitude* I. iv. 53 All right, you needn't be ratty about it! **1929** W. P. RIDGE *Affect. Regards* 226 Have I ever got ratty with you, Elsie? **1976** T. HEALD *Let Sleeping Dogs Die* vi. 122 I'd simply have asked her what the hell she was so ratty about.

3. *Austral.* and *N.Z. colloq.* Mad, eccentric, silly. Phr. *to be ratty over*: to be infatuated with.

1900 H. LAWSON *On Track* 75 Trav'lers and strangers failed to see anything uncommonly ratty about him. **1906** E. DYSON *Fact'ry 'Ands* xiv. 184 Already the Beauties had decided that Connie was 'as ratty as rabbits'. **1922** A. WRIGHT *Colt from Country* 86 There was a rough-up in a pub; he got a knock, had a fit, and went real ratty, and that was the end of him. **1941** BAKER *Dict. Austral. Slang* 59 *Ratty*, stupid, silly. *Ratty over* (a person), infatuated with.

4. *Comb.*, as *ratty-looking* adj.

1884 'MARK TWAIN' *Huck. Finn* xix. 182 Both of them had big, fat, ratty-looking carpet-bags.

Hence **'rattily** *adv.*, ill-temperedly, irritably.

1977 T. HEALD *Just Desserts* vii. 169 'We're supposed to be buddies,' said Bognor, rattily. **1980** *Times Lit. Suppl.* 4 July 754/2 Compliments fly and are quoted in abundance in this symposium. One reads on, rattily, in the hope of meeting some unusual personal habit,..some outstanding trait of character or behaviour.

rattyll(e, obs. ff. RATTLE *v.*[1]

‖**ratu** (ra'tu). Also ratoo. [Indonesian.] The title of a petty monarch or native regional ruler in parts of Indonesia and in Fiji.

1798 S. H. WILCOCKE tr. *Stavorinus's Voy. E. Indies* I. II. i. 214, I..appoint the said *pangorang*, to be *pangorang ratoo*, or hereditary prince, and heir to the crown and the whole empire of Bantam. **1820** J. CRAWFURD *Hist. Indian Archipelago* III. VIII. i. 22 The genuine native term for king in Javanese is *Ratu*, which is the same word that is written *Datu* in some other languages. **1821** J. LEYDEN tr. *Malay Annals* 157 The toddy-man's son became ratu of Majapahit. **1880** *Encycl. Brit.* XIII. 607/2 Ratu Loro Kidul is princess of the southern sea, and has her seat among the caves and fiords of the southern coast. **1907** *Daily Chron.* 30 Nov. 4/6 They are captained by Ratu Kadavu Levu, the grandson of the last native monarch of Fiji, Thakombau. Ratu is Fijian for Prince. **1937** M. COVARRUBIAS *Island of Bali* (1972) viii. 250 Finally it is time for the prince, the *ratú*, to appear; the *patih* recites his praises and..begs him to enter. **1966** *Economist* 16 Apr. 232/1 General Suharto, Indonesia's strong man, has found a way of remaining loyal both to his guru..and to his ratu (king). **1977** *South China Morning Post* (Hong Kong) 14 Apr. (Business Suppl.) 11/3 Ratu Sir Kamisese Mara of Fiji, representing the developing countries, said in reply [etc.].

ratunner, obs. f. RATTONER.

‖**rature** (ratyr). *rare.* [Fr.] A scribal erasure or deletion.

1931 T. S. ELIOT *Charles Whibley* 5 He..composed rapidly..and made very few *ratures* or corrections.

raturn, obs. Sc. f. RETURN.

ratyl(le, obs. ff. RATEL[2], RATTLE *v.*[1]

rau, obs. f. RAW *a.*

rauasch-, obs. f. RAVISH.

rauascht, var. pa. t. REVEST *Obs.*

rauayn(e, obs. ff. RAVIN[1].

rauc, *a. rare*⁻¹. [a. L. *rauc-us.*] = RAUQUE.

1866 J. B. ROSE tr. *Ovid's Met.* 146 Rauc speech, and volubility of words.

'raucal, *a. rare*⁻¹. [f. L. *rauc-us.*] Raucous.

1839–47 *Todd's Cycl. Anat.* III. 124/1 In these cases there is..no raucal sound of voice.

†**rau'cedity.** *Obs. rare*⁻¹. [f. L. *raucēdo*, f. *raucus* hoarse + -ITY.] Hoarseness.

1599 A. M. tr. *Gabelhouer's Bk. Physicke* 100/1 Gargrise therwith your throte for the hoarsenes and raucedityе.

raucht, obs. Sc. pa. t. REACH *v.*[1]

rauchter, obs. Sc. form of RAFTER *sb.*[1]

‖**rauchwacke** ('raʊxvakə). *Geol.* [G., f. *rauch* smoke + *wacke*: cf. GRAU-, GREYWACKE.] A dolomitic limestone of the upper Permian or Zechstein group in Germany, corresponding to the Magnesian Limestone formation in England.

1831 SEDGWICK & MURCHISON *Struct. East. Alps* in *Geol. Trans.* Ser. II. III. (1835) 308 The *rauchwacké*, or magnesian limestone, associated with the new red sandstone. **1832** DE LA BECHE *Geol. Man.* (ed. 2) 397 The zechstein is represented as sometimes from twenty to thirty yards thick; the rauchwacke, when pure and compact, one yard thick.

'raucid, *a. rare*⁻¹. [f. L. *rauc-us* + -ID[1].] Raucous.

1831 LAMB *Elia* Ser. II. *Shade of Elliston*, Methinks I hear the old boatman,..with raucid voice, bawling 'Sculls'.

So **rau'cidity**, raucity. *rare*⁻¹.

1703 *Art & Myst. Vintners* 4 They degenerate also in Taste, and affect the palate with foulness, roughness, and raucidity very unpleasant.

raucity ('rɔːsɪtɪ). *rare.* [ad. L. *raucitās*, f. *raucus* hoarse: see RAUCOUS and -ITY, and cf. F. *raucité* (Littré).] Harshness, roughness, hoarseness (of the voice or other sounds).

1607 TOPSELL *Four-f. Beasts* (1658) 154 Aristotle calleth it Raucity, or hoarsness, like the low sound of a Trumpet. **1626** BACON *Sylva* §700 In the Raucity of a Trumpet. **1656** in BLOUNT. **1832** WEBSTER, *Raucity*,..among physicians, hoarseness of the human voice. **1860** in WORCESTER (citing HUNT).

rauc(k)le, Sc. variants of RACKLE *a.*

raucous ('rɔːkəs), *a.* [f. L. *rauc-us* hoarse + -OUS.] Hoarse, rough, harsh-sounding.

1769 PENNANT *British Zool.* III. 8 This raucous reptile [the toad]. **1793** tr. *Buffon's Hist. Birds* VI. 158 A raucous, thick tone, which is grating to the ear. **1847** EMERSON *Poems* (1857) 40 Where yon wedged line the Nestor leads, Steering north with raucous cry. **1879** SALA *Paris Herself Again* (1880) II. xxiii. 342 In a raucous strident voice, he sang the songs of divers epochs.

Hence **'raucously** *adv.*, in a raucous manner.

1852 *Blackw. Mag.* LXXII. 128 The pawkie proposal is straightway raucously ratified.

Raudive (rɔː'diːv). The name of Konstantin *Raudive* (1909–74), Latvian psychologist, used *attrib.* in connection with a phenomenon involving tape recordings of sounds said to represent voices of paranormal origin.

1971 *Psychic News* 20 Mar. 8/6 The Raudive story appears to have started when a Swede, Frederick Jurgenson wrote a book in 1969 describing how when he was in the woods recording birdsong, faint voices appeared on his tape. Some years later, Dr. Raudive contacted Jurgenson and discussed the phenomena. **1972** P. BANDER *Carry on Talking* vii. 85 It would require a fevered imagination to convert it to Raudive-type voices. **1973** *Times* 4 Dec. 17/7 There is nothing new in PK (psychokinesis) and telepathy, or even the seemingly incredible Raudive voices. **1974** C. F. PANATI *Supersenses* iv. 109 Professor..Dean..feels that the Raudive phenomenon is real enough and that the explanation is simple and straightforward. **1975** C. WILSON *Mysterious Powers* vi. 94 As a result of the publicity surrounding Dr. Raudive's work, voice phenomena have been dubbed 'Raudive voices'.

Raudixin (raʊ'dɪksɪn). *Pharm.* [f. RAU(WOLFIA + *-dixin.*] A proprietary name for a hypotensive preparation containing the dried root of *Rauvolfia serpentina* (RAUWOLFIA).

1953 *Trade Marks Jrnl.* 9 Sept. 811/1 *Raudixin*... Anti-hypertensive agents... E. R. Squibb and Sons Limited. **1953** *Official Gaz.* (U.S. Patent Office) 10 Nov. 317/1 Mathieson Chemical Corporation, New York..*Raudixin*... Claims use since May 4, 1953. **1954** *Jrnl. Amer. Med. Assoc.* 16 Oct. 736/1 About two months prior to the incident..he had received Raudixin (a whole rauwolfia root), 50 mg. twice a day. **1956** N. M. FERGUSON *Textbk. Pharmacognosy* viii. 207 There are several proprietaries on the market which contain rauwolfia or its constituents. Chief among these are Raudixin, Rauwiloid and Serpasil. **1967** [see RAUWILOID].

raueste, obs. variant of REVEST.

raueyner, -our, obs. forms of RAVENER.

raufter, -yng, obs. forms of RAFTER, -ING.

rauȝ, obs. form of RAW *a.*

†**raught**, *v. Obs. rare.* [f. *raught*, obs. pa. t. REACH *v.*[1]] *intr.* To reach, snatch *at* or *after*.

1571 GOLDING *Calvin on Ps.* xix. 9 Rawghting after the empty shadow of blissfull life. **1583** —— *Calvin on Deut.* xix. 113 To raught at euerie thing that we like off.

raught, obs. or archaic pa. t. and pa. pple. REACH *v.*, RECK *v.*

raughter, obs. form of RAFTER *sb.*[1]

†**'raughtish**, *a. Obs. rare*⁻¹. ? Harsh.

1567 GOLDING *Ovid's Met.* IX. 123 The temple doores did tremble like a reede And Rattels made a raughtish noyse.

†**'raughty**, var. RAFTY *a.*, raw, damp. Hence **'raughtiness.**

1674 N. FAIRFAX *Bulk & Selv.* 126 In coldish raughty weather. *Ibid.*, Feeding their earth and froath, with cold and raughtiness.

rauite. *Min.* [Erron. for *ranite*, f. ON. *Rán* the sea-goddess + -ITE.] A greyish-black mineral, a variety of hydronephilite.

Named by Paykull (as *rauit*) in 1874. Some recent Dicts. give the correct form *ranite*.

1875 in *Dana's Min.* (ed. 5) App. ii. **1881** WATTS *Dict. Chem.* 3rd Suppl. 1743 *Rauite*, a zeolite from the island of Lamö, near Brevig in Norway. It is related to thomsonite, and has probably been formed by decomposition of elæolite.

Raujepoot, variant of RAJPUT.

†**rauk**, *a. Sc. Obs.* Also 6 rawk. [ad. L. *rauc-us* (see RAUCOUS), or a. F. *rauque* (13th c.), RAUQUE.] Hoarse, raucous. Also *Comb.*

c **1470** HENRYSON *Mor. Fab.* XIII. (*Frog & Mouse*) ii, With voce full rauk scho said on this maneir. **1513** DOUGLAS *Æneis* XI. ix. 29 The rawk vocit swannis in a rabyll. **1533** BELLENDEN *Livy* I. x. (1901) 57 Þare Voce was rauk & þare sprete solist & dull.

raukie: see RAWKY *a.*[2]

raukle, Sc. variant of RACKLE *a.*

rauli ('raʊlɪ). [Amer. Sp., f. Mapuche *ruili.*] A deciduous tree resembling a beech, *Nothofagus procera*, belonging to the family Fagaceæ and native to temperate regions of Chile and Argentina; also, the reddish hardwood timber of this tree.

1908 ELWES & HENRY *Trees Gt. Brit. & Ireland* III. 555 *Nothofagus procera*, known as *Rauli*, is less common than *N. obliqua.* **1943** RECORD & HESS *Timbers of New World* 168/1 Rauli..has about the same range as Roble, but its timber is much more highly esteemed. **1955** *World Timbers* (Timber Devel. Assoc.) III. 97 Rauli works easily with both hand and machine tools. **1979** *Timbers of World* (Timber Res. & Devel. Assoc.) 214 Rauli occurs in pure stands on rich soil. *Ibid.*, There is also a tendency for rauli to show a pore ring on the tangential face.

raumpand, -aunt, obs. ff. RAMPANT.

raumpe, raumpp-, obs. ff. RAMP *sb.* and *v.*

raumso(u)n, obs. ff. RANSOM.

raun, var. RAWN.

raunce. *rare*⁻¹. [ad. F. *ronce.*] A bramble.

1840 BROWNING *Sordello* VI. 461 Alberic,..tied on to a wild horse, was trailed To death thro' raunce and bramble-bush.

raunce, obs. f. RANCE *sb.*[1]

raunceoun, -coun, obs. ff. RANSOM.

raunch (rɔːnʃ). *colloq.* (orig. *U.S.*). [Back-formation from next.] **a.** Shabbiness, grubbiness, dirtiness. **b.** Crudeness, vulgarity, licentiousness; boisterousness, earthiness.

1964 *Time* 21 Feb. 46/2 Presley made his pelvis central to his act, and the screams of his admirers were straight from the raunch. **1967** *Time* 18 Aug. 63 Calvin Coolidge High is an actual Manhattan school building, its rust and raunch unretouched for the camera. **1975** *Manch. Guardian Weekly* 2 Aug. 20 Bette Midler is..no Streisand, her material is blue and her songs are old. Yet she's been camped out at one of Broadway's biggest theatres for several months now, making raunch respectable in a sellout review called Clams on the Half Shell. **1976** *N.Y. Times* 9 July C19 There are bars that are all elegance, and bars that are all raunch, and bars that breathe both elegance and raunch and therefore are considered chic. **1978** *Maclean's Mag.* 4 Dec. 65/1 The result is a 200,000-word flop, in which raunch doesn't work and the highfalutin philosophy sinks without a trace. **1979** *Guardian* 14 Mar. 13/6 Her co-producer wanted to raise the raunch-quotient by having her perform in a garter belt.

raunch, var. RANCH *v.*[1], *v.*[2] *Obs.*

raunchy ('rɔːnʃɪ), *a. colloq.* (orig. *U.S.*) [Origin unknown: cf. RANCHY *a.*] **1.** Inept, incompetent, sloppy; unpleasant, contemptible, mean, disreputable; dirty, grubby.

1939 *Forum & Century* July 45/1 Depending on how good or how 'raunchy' we [*sc.* Air Force cadets] were, we drilled from one to three hours in the torrid heat. **1949** *Cavalier Daily* (Univ. of Va.) 22 Oct. 4/1 This situation could become embarrassing—if the writer in question happened to be well-known as a somewhat raunchy character in reality. **1953** BERREY & VAN DEN BARK *Amer. Thes. Slang* (1954) §759/2 *Raunchy flying*, clumsy flying technique. **1965** D. E. WESTLAKE *Fugitive Pigeon* 170, I suddenly felt raunchy. Still in the same slacks I'd been wearing when this thing started. **1968** *Amer. Speech 1967* XLII. 229 *Raunchy*,..a pejorative adjective used to modify anything which the speaker wishes to denigrate, with the general connotation of 'stinky, grubby, scabby, dirty, or cheap'. **1971** *Daily Colonist* (Victoria, B.C.) 30 Nov. 18/7 I'll bet..the girls would boycott guys with dirty, tangled hair, filthy jeans, raunchy sweat shirts and bare feet. **1979** *Now!* 14 Sept. 87/3 Millgarth police station, down the rough, raunchy end of Leeds's city centre.

2. Of persons, their actions, etc.: boisterous, earthy, sexually provocative, aggressively licentious, suggestive. Also in extended uses, esp. of language, humour, songs, etc.: bawdy, salacious, smutty; tending to excite sexual feeling.

1967 'E. QUEEN' *Face to Face* iv. 17, I fell in love with him. In a raunchy sort of way he's beautiful. **1969** *Sat. Rev.* (U.S.) 31 May 44/2 A blend of raunchy humor, unpleasant perversity, and..sickening brutality. **1970** *Melody Maker* 12 Sept. 7 Most of the songs were too twee, and the rest seemed to be too raunchy. **1971** *Sunday Australian* 7 Nov. 27/6 Russell now has two albums of his own on which to disport his raunchy rock compositions. **1973** *Daily Colonist* (Victoria, B.C.) 23 Nov. 23/1 A drunk at the next table was singing some raunchy songs. The songs kept getting dirtier and dirtier. **1974** T. P. WHITNEY tr. *Solzhenitsyn's Gulag Archipelago* I. I. i. 21 They had noticed two raunchy broads going to bathe. **1976** *Times* 4 Feb. 14/4 Jurors are asked to pronounce judgment on a particularly raunchy book, while lawyers make suggestive jokes. **1977** *Gay News* 7–20 Apr. 38/3 (Advt.), Interested in meeting guys in tight raunchy levis to show me around. **1977** D. ANTHONY *Stud Game*

xxiii. 145 If you mean *Couplings*, I liked it... I happen to like raunchy films.

Hence 'raunchily *adv.*, in a raunchy manner; 'raunchiness.

1972 *Time* 17 Apr. 66/3 They are a raunchily genteel exercise. **1975** *New Yorker* 20 Jan. 62/3 A shaggy-dog tale of a raunchiness Tolstoyan in scale, if not in tone, is related with single-minded, uninterruptible passion by one of the male guests. **1977** D. O'SULLIVAN in D. Marcus *Best Irish Short Stories* II. 96 No..customs and excise officer ever streaked from his intimations of mortality as raunchily as Emily Brontë from the stool. **1980** *Observer* 13 Jan. 36/2 The language is nearly devoid of metaphor, but doesn't shirk a beguiling raunchiness.

rauncour, obs. f. RANCOUR.

raundom, -don(e, -doun, obs. ff. RANDOM.

raundsom, obs. f. RANSOM.

raung(e, obs. ff. RANGE.

raunger, -ier, obs. ff. RANGER.

'rauning, *a.* [var. RAWLIN; but in Cornwall glossaries explained as 'ravening, ravenous', as if f. *raun*, 'to devour greedily'.] (See quot.)

1880 *E. Cornwall Gloss.* s.v., That voracious fish, *Merlangus Carbonarius*, is called the rauning pollack.

raunke, obs. f. RANK *a.*

raunp-, obs. f. RAMP *v.*

raunpick, dial. var. RAMPICK *a.*

raunpike, var. RAMPIKE.

rauns, obs. f. RANCE *sb.*[1]

raunsake, obs. f. RANSACK *v.*

raunscun', -som(e, -soun, etc., obs. ff. RANSOM *sb.*

raunsede, -sene: see RANSOM *v.*

rauntree, -try: see ROWAN-TREE.

rauon, obs. f. RAVEN *sb.*[1]

‖**raupo** ('raʊpɔː, 'raʊpəʊ). Also 9 **ra-poo.** [Maori.] A New Zealand bulrush (*Typha Muelleri*) used for building native houses, thatching roofs, etc. Also *attrib.*, and *ellipt.*, a hut built of raupo.

1832 A. EARLE 9 *Months' Resid. N. Zealand* 99 Another party was collecting rushes (which grow plentifully in the neighbourhood, and are called Ra-poo). **1835** W. YATE *Acc. N. Zealand* 205 To engage the natives to build raupo, that is, rush-houses. **1851** V. LUSH *Jrnl.* 25 Apr. (1971) 75 Reached the Lusks' *raupo* about 9. **1860** DONALDSON *Bush Lays* 5 Entangled in a foul morass A raupo swamp. **1863** 'PAKEHA MAORI' *Old N.Z.* vi. 79 My house was a good commodious *raupo* building. **1881** *Chequered Career* 104 My canteen was built of raupo, a reed something like the bulrush, that grows in the swamps. **1897** [see KORUPE]. **1905** W. BAUCKE *Where White Man Treads* 145 Here and there a patch of stunted raupo standing listless in its sour and stagnant ooze. **1920** J. MANDER *Story N.Z. River* xxvi. 317 There was suddenly a ghostly movement in the rapoo and the reeds. **1933** *Bulletin* (Sydney) 9 Aug. 21/2 The pollen and roots of the raupo.. were..regularly eaten. **1944** *Coast to Coast 1943* 96 They [*sc.* fleas] came from the dust under the raupo mats. **1960** *Guardian* 9 Dec. 6/3 It was five months on voyage and a tent or a raupo (rush) hut at the end of it. **1975** *Turangi* (N.Z.) *Chron.* 2 Apr. 1/1 Prior to the tailrace being established the area had been raupo swamp.

rauque (rɔːk), *a. rare.* [a. F. *rauque*, ad. L. *raucus*: cf. RAUC, RAUK.] Hoarse, harsh.

1848 LYTTON *K. Arthur* IX. lxxxvi, The deaf'ning, strident, rauque, Homeric roar. **1859** R. F. BURTON in *Jrnl. Geog. Soc.* XXIX. 214 The rauque bellow of the hippopotamus is heard on its banks.

raurekau (raʊ'reɪkaʊ). Also **raureka.** [Maori.] A small evergreen tree, *Coprosma australis*, belonging to the family Rubiaceæ, native to New Zealand, and bearing small white flowers and red berries. Also *attrib.*

1905 W. BAUCKE *Where White Man Treads* 254 Pork.. alternated with stacks of eels enclosed in wrappings of 'raurekau' leaves. **1928** COCKAYNE & TURNER *Trees N.Z.* 36 Raurekau. A low, bushy tree..or tall shrub, with dark-coloured bark. **1949** *Landfall* III. 31 He stumbled through a jungle of raureka and gorse. **1963** POOLE & ADAMS *Trees & Shrubs N.Z.* 173 Raurekau. Small tree reaching 7m... Flowers in fascicles.

rauriki ('raʊriki, 'rariki). Also **rariki.** [Maori.] = PUHA.

1944 *Mod. Jun. Dict.* (Whitcombe & Tombs) 331 Rauriki, raddiky..The Maori word for sowthistle. **1949** E. DE MAUNY *Huntsman in his Career* II. 122 Weeds grew in profusion, rariki and nettle. **1958** A. WALL *Queen's English* ix. 48 Sowthistle..is actually edible and much used by the Maoris as *rauriki*, corruptly 'raddiky'. **1966** *N.Z. Encycl.* II. 785/2 The juice of rauriki.., a latex, was also used.

‖**rauschpfeife** ('raʊʃpfaɪfə). *Mus.* Pl. **-n.** [Ger., = reed-pipe.] **1.** (See quot. 1964.)

1876 STAINER & BARRETT *Dict. Mus. Terms* 374/2 *Rauschpfeif* [*sic*],..a stop in old organs of two ranks of pipes, consisting of a twelfth and fifteenth, or a fifteenth and octave twelfth. **1964** S. MARCUSE *Mus. Instruments* 436/1 *Rauschpfeife*,..2..organ stop first mentioned by Arnold Schlick in 1511. It seems to have consisted originally of reed pipes with conical resonators; it became transformed in the course of the c. to a 2-rank stop of flue pipes. Since the mid-17th c. the stop was treated as a mixture, often 3-rank. .. In the 18th c. it was enlarged further... The original meaning of the word had long been forgotten: to Praetorius already it was a 'rustling' pipe (from [G.] *rauschen*, to rustle). **1976** D. MUNROW *Instruments Middle Ages & Renaissance* vii. 60/1 The 'manual', the main part of the instrument [*sc.* a Renaissance organ], with eleven registers, was composed of reeds and flue stops, including a *Zink, Regall*, and *Rauspfeiffen*.

2. A reed-cap shawm of the Renaissance period.

1939 A. CARSE *Mus. Wind Instruments* xi. 128 Two instruments of the shawm type figure in one of Burgkmair's famous series of woodcuts 'Kayser Maximilians I Triumph' (c. 1516) and are there named *rauschpfeiffen*. **1964** S. MARCUSE *Mus. Instruments* 436/1 *Rauschpfeife* (? MHGer. *Rusch*, rush), 1. family of Ger. Renaissance reed-cap shawms, with wide conical bore.., terminating in a bell, the double reed concealed in a wooden cap. **1968** *Observer* 19 May 40 David Munrow..has a collection of more than 100 historic woodwind instruments with engaging names like.. the rauschpfeife. **1976** D. MUNROW *Instruments Middle Ages & Renaissance* vi. 50/4 *Rauschpfeifen* and *schreierpfeifen*.. are reed-cap shawms... Of the two, rauschpfeifen seem to have been more common. **1978** *Early Music* Apr. 253/1 No rauschpfeifen..are preserved, and yet no one denies they existed.

raut, dial. var. ROWT *v.*

rauth, var. *raught*, obs. pa. t. REACH.

rauthe, obs. f. RUTH.

Rauwiloid ('raʊwɪlɔɪd). *Pharm.* [f. RAUW(OLFIA + *-iloid*.] A proprietary name for a hypotensive preparation containing a number of alkaloids extracted from *Rauvolfia serpentina* (RAUWOLFIA).

1953 *Trade Marks Jrnl.* 15 July 616/2 *Rauwiloid*... Medicinal tablets for the treatment of hypertension. Riker Laboratories Inc... City of Los Angeles. **1953** *Official Gaz.* (U.S. Patent Office) 13 Oct. 295/1 *Rauwiloid*... Claims use since Oct. 28, 1952. **1954** *Jrnl. Amer. Med. Assoc.* 17 July 1027/1 The treatment of hypertension of varying degrees of severity with alseroxylon (Rauwiloid). **1956** [see RAUDIXIN]. **1967** H. BECKMAN *Dilemmas in Drug Therapy* 175/1 Usual doses of the Rauwolfia preparations employed in treating hypertension are..alseroxylon (Rauwiloid), 2-4 mg. daily; ..rauwolfia (Raudixin, Rauserpa, Rauval), 200-400 mg. daily in divided doses.

rauwolfia (raʊ'wɒlfɪə, -vɒlfɪə). Also **rauvolfia** and with capital initial. [mod.L. (P. C. Plumier *Nova Plantarum Americanarum Genera* (1703) 19), f. the name of Leonhard *Rauwolf* (d. 1596), German physician, botanist, and traveller + -IA[1].] **1.** A tropical shrub or small tree of the genus so called, belonging to the family Apocynaceæ and bearing clusters of small white flowers and red or black berries; *esp.* a shrub of one of the several species cultivated for the medicinal drugs obtained from their roots.

1752 P. MILLER *Gardeners Dict.* (ed. 6) s.v. *Rauvolfia*, Four-leaved Rauvolfia, with narrow Leaves. **1823** *Curtis's Bot. Mag.* L. 2440 (*heading*) Three-leaved Rauwolfia. **1902** L. H. BAILEY *Cycl. Amer. Hort.* IV. 1503/2 The Rauwolfia flourishes with great luxuriance in the shade of other shrubs. **1955** *Sci. Amer.* Oct. 81/1 Reserpine is an alkaloid extract from the snakeroot plant (named Rauwolfia for a 16th-century German physician). **1962** N. MAXWELL *Witch-Doctor's Apprentice* i. 1 Many types of rauwolfia were employed by jungle shamans centuries before our medical men thought of tranquillizers. **1976** *Hortus Third* (L. H. Bailey Hortorium) 942/1 Rauvolfias are cultivated as ornamentals and for curiosity. **1976** W. A. R. THOMPSON *Herbs that Heal* ix. 148 This unleashed the flood-gates of the pharmaceutical industry, whose scouts started scouring the earth for rauwolfia.

2. *Pharm.* Also **rauwolfia serpentina.** The dried roots of *Rauvolfia serpentina* or related species, or an extract therefrom, containing a number of alkaloids (notably reserpine) and used medicinally, esp. to treat hypertension.

[**1949** *Brit. Heart Jrnl.* XI. 350/2 This overwhelming body of support in favour of regarding *R. Serpentina* as the remedy of choice. *Ibid.* 354/1 The hypotensive action of *R. Serpentina*.] **1952** *Ann. Internal Med.* XXXVII. 1149 In our clinic we have relied chiefly upon various combinations of hydrazinophthalazine, Rauwolfia and veratrum, principally because these drugs appear to be the safest..of any medicinal regimen we have tried. **1954** *Brit. Pharmaceutical Codex* 649 Rauwolfia has a depressant action on the central nervous system. **1957** H. W. YOUNGKEN in R. E. Woodson et al. *Rauwolfia* ii. 32 The drug Rauwolfia or Rauwolfia Serpentina consists of the dried root of *Rauwolfia serpentina*. .. The commercial sources of the drug..have been India, Pakistan, Ceylon, Burma, and Siam. **1966** *New Scientist* 27 Jan. 236/2 Physicians and pharmacists..are inclined to think that only a few vegetable drugs such as..digitalis, penicillin and rauwolfia are important in the present day *materia medica*. **1977** LEWIS & ELVIN-LEWIS *Med. Bot.* vii. 187/1 *Rauvolfia* acts synergistically with other hypotensive drugs, and in the more severe cases of hypertension it is used in combination with *Veratrum viride* or protoveratrines A and B.

3. *attrib.*, as ***rauwolfia alkaloid, berry.***

1942 *Biol. Abstr.* XVII. 117/2 The various effects suggest that the *Rauwolfia* alkaloids probably act on the vasomotor system and also directly on plain muscles of the blood vessels and intestines. **1977** S. LOEBL et al. *Nurse's Drug Handbk.* 252 The rauwolfia alkaloids decrease blood pressure and have a sedative effect accompanied by bradycardia. **1932** *Discovery* July 231/1 Three kinds of starlings come with the great blue pigeons to the Rauwolfia berries.

rav (rɒv). Also **rov.** [Yiddish.] A rabbi; freq. prefixed to personal names.

1892 I. ZANGWILL *Childr. Ghetto* I. I. xiv. 314 'Ah, you will become a Rav!'.. 'What's that about a Rav?.. Does he want me to become a Rabbi?' **1893** —— *Ghetto Tragedies* 4 The great Rav Rotchinsky from Brody was to deliver a sermon. **1962** 'E. MCBAIN' *Empty Hours* iii. 115 'I know who killed the *rov*.'.. 'She says she knows who killed the rabbi.' **1967** C. POTOK *Chosen* xiv. 238 From one to three we would have the actual Talmud session itself, the shiur, with Rav Gershenson. **1973** *Jewish Chron.* 19 Jan. 34/2 The daughters and family of the late Mrs B——. C——...wish to thank the Rav, rabbonim..and friends for their visits..and numerous letters of sympathy.

ravage ('rævɪdʒ), *sb.* [a. F. *ravage* (14th c.), f. *ravir* to RAVISH: see -AGE.]

†**1.** A flood, inundation. *Obs. rare*[−0].

1611 COTGR., *Ragats d'eau*, a great floud, inundation, rauage of waters.

2. The act or practice of ravaging, or the result of this; destruction, devastation, extensive damage, done by men or beasts.

1611 COTGR., *Ravage*, rauage, hauocke, spoyle. **1656** in BLOUNT *Glossogr.* **1684** *Scanderbeg Redivivus* vi. 154 They slew near one Hundred-Thousand; and having finisht their Ravage, took Bialogrod. **1691** RAY *Creation* I. (1692) 111 To secure their Eggs and Young from the ravage of Apes and Monkeys. **1751** JOHNSON *Rambler* No. 185 ¶3 What would so soon destroy all the order of society, and deform life with violence and ravage, as a permission to every one to judge his own cause. **1821** SHELLEY *Adonais* xlviii, 'Tis nought That ages, empires, and religions there Lie buried in the ravage they have wrought. **1872** TENNYSON *Gareth & Lynette* 429 Many another suppliant crying came With noise of ravage wrought by beast and man.

b. *pl.* Extensive depredations. †Also *sg.* with *a.*

1697 LUTTRELL *Brief Rel.* (1857) IV. 294, 60,000 Tartars are approaching to make a ravage in Poland. **1771** GOLDSM. *Hist. Eng.* II. 78 Unable to perceive any signs of an enemy, except from the ravages they had made. **1844** H. H. WILSON *Brit. India* III. 171 They..after a short interval, returned and renewed their ravages. **1853** J. H. NEWMAN *Hist. Sk.* (1873) II. I. i. 34 Six centuries have been unable to repair the ravages of four years.

c. *transf.*, esp. of the destructive action or effects of disease, time, storm, etc.

1704 F. FULLER *Med. Gymn.* (1711) 78 To what must we attribute the Ravage this Disease makes? **1745** J. MASON *Self-Knowl.* (1853) I. xiv. 99 The Torment of the Mind, under such an Insurrection and merciless Ravage of the Passions. **1786** BURNS *Author's Farewell* ii, The Autumn mourns her rip'ning corn By early Winter's ravage torn. **1801** *Lusignan* IV. 229 The ravage time and affliction had made on those features. **1868** TENNYSON *Lucret.* 176 Seeing with how great ease Nature can smile..At random ravage. *pl.* **1777** SHERIDAN *Sch. Scand.* II. ii, If Mrs. Evergreen does take some pains to repair the ravages of time. **1838** THIRLWALL *Greece* xxi. III. 169 The ravages of the pestilence continued..for two years. **1873** MAX MÜLLER *Sc. Rel.* 118 On rolls of papyrus which seem to defy the ravages of time.

3. *concr.* Plunder, spoil. *rare*[−1].

1809 MALKIN *Gil Blas* VI. i. ¶2 Three hundred pistoles, the lawful ravage of their pockets.

ravage ('rævɪdʒ), *v.* [ad. F. *ravager*, f. *ravage*: see prec.]

1. *trans.* To devastate, lay waste, despoil, plunder (a country). Also *transf.* or *fig.*

1611 COTGR., *Ravager*, to rauage, forray, spoyle, prey vpon. *a* **1704** T. BROWN *Satire Antients* Wks. 1730 I. 24 The barbarians who ravag'd Greece and Italy. **1758** JOHNSON *Idler* No. 8 ¶6 The Isle of Rhodes..was ravaged by a dragon. *Ibid.* No. 14 ¶4 Life is continually ravaged by invaders. **1838-43** ARNOLD *Hist. Rome* II. xxxvii. 481 Æmilius began to ravage their territory with fire and sword. **1848** THACKERAY *Van. Fair* xx, That sweet face so sadly ravaged by grief and despair.

2. *intr.* To commit ravages; to make havoc or destruction. Also *fig.*

1627 F. E. *Hist. Edw. II* (1680) 47 His wand'ring eyes now ravage through the confines of his great Court. **1659** HAMMOND *On Ps.* civ. 20, 21 Paraphr., Beasts of prey, which ..are inabled to ravage, and feed. **1769** GOLDSM. *Hist. Rome* (1786) II. 497 A dreadful enemy ravaging in the midst of their country. **1840** DICKENS *Barn. Rudge* iv, The locksmith who had..been ravaging among the eatables. **1874** GREEN *Short Hist.* ii. §7. 95 When the Danes were ravaging along Loire as they ravaged along Thames.

ravaged ('rævɪdʒd), *ppl. a.* [f. prec. + -ED[1].] Despoiled, devastated.

1728-46 THOMSON *Spring* 14 The shatter'd forest, and the ravag'd vale. **1799** KIRWAN *Geol. Ess.* 74 The more southern, ravaged or torn up continents. **1811** SCOTT *Don Roderick* I. ii, Each voice..That rings Mondego's ravaged shores around. **1821** SHELLEY *Hellas* 907 The weight which Crime..Leaves in his flight from ravaged heart to heart.

†**'ravagement.** *Obs. rare.* [a. F. *ravagement*: see RAVAGE *v.* and -MENT.] Ravage.

1723 *Briton* No. 20 (1724) 87 Success attended their Inroads and Ravagements. **1766** ENTICK *London* IV. 286 Houses within the ravagement of the flames.

ravager ('rævɪdʒə(r)). [f. RAVAGE *v.* + -ER[1].] One who or that which ravages.

1611 COTGR., *Ravageur*, a rauager, spoyler, forrayer. **1726** LEONI tr. *Alberti's Archit.* I. 39 They fall like so many Ravagers to demolishing..every thing before them. **1742** RICHARDSON *Pamela* III. 226 That very Innocence, which tempts some brutal Ravager to ruin it. **1815** *Monthly Mag.* XXXVIII. 500 He sees..in the torrent, now the fertilizer, now the ravager of districts. **1870** MORRIS *Earthly Par.* I. II. 670 The ravager of Rome his right hand slew.

ravaging (ˈrævɪdʒɪŋ), *vbl. sb.* [f. as prec. + -ING¹.] The action of the vb. RAVAGE.

1611 COTGR., *Sac*, a sacke,..pillage, depopulation, rauaging. **1710** PRIDEAUX *Orig. Tithes* iv. 176 We have seen ..the ravagings of our Wealth. **1753** N. TORRIANO *Gangr. Sore Throat* 48 A Witness of the ravaging of this Distemper. **1811** SCOTT *Don Roderick* I. viii, Where..shepherds sing.. Of feuds obscure, and Border ravaging. **1867** FREEMAN *Norm. Conq.* (1876) I. vi. 519 The ravaging of districts for treason.

ˈravaging, *ppl. a.* [-ING².] That ravages.

1886 W. J. TUCKER *E. Europe* 103 The ravaging hand of time. **1887** BOWEN *Virg. Æneid* I. 621 When Belus..with a ravaging horde, Swept over fruitful Cyprus.

†**raˈvalling,** *vbl. sb.* [? ad. F. *ravalement*, †*ravallement* (15th c.), f. *ravaler* to bring down, f. *re-* + *avaler* AVALE *v.*] Reduction, failure.

1609 [BP. W. BARLOW] *Answ. Nameless Cath.* 365 Raualling of a Confederacie, where affiance is placed in Number, is a tormenting discouragement.

ravanastron (ˌrɑːvəˈnɑːstrən). Also **ravanastra.** [Origin unknown: freq. associated with the legendary King Ravana (see quots.); cf. Skr. *rāvaṇahasra* a kind of stringed instrument.] An ancient Hindu stringed instrument played with a bow.

1864 C. ENGEL *Music of Most Anc. Nations* ii. 81 The Hindoos maintain that the *ravanastron*, one of their old instruments played with the bow, was invented about five thousand years ago by Ravanen, a mighty king in Ceylon. **1876** STAINER & BARRETT *Dict. Mus. Terms* 374/2 Ravanastron, a stringed instrument played with a bow in use among the Buddhists. **1896** H. SAINT-GEORGE *Bow* ii. 7 Of existing bowed instruments the Ravanastron..most certainly seems to be the oldest. **1903** R. HUGHES *Mus. Guide* I. 249/1 *Ravanastron*, a primitive violin with one or two strings... It is still used by the Buddhists. **1953** S. BECKETT *Watt* 71 A ravanastron hung, on the wall, from a nail, like a plover. **1965** S. KRISHNASWAMI *Mus. Instruments of India* 16 One of the earliest stringed instruments played with a bow was called the *ravanastra*. This instrument was associated with Ravana. **1969** N. DEANE tr. *Bachmann's Origins of Bowing* i. 8 The quest for rudimentary types of bowed instruments led to the Welsh crwth and the Indian *ravanastron*, both regarded as the ancestor of our violin.

ravar(e, obs. Sc. ff. RAVER.

ravary, dial. var. RAVERY.

ravayn(e, obs. ff. RAVIN¹.

†**rave,** *sb.*¹ *Obs. rare.* [a. F. *rave* (15th c.):—L. *rāpa* RAPE *sb.*⁵] A turnip.

c **1420** *Pallad. on Husb.* IV. 170 Armorace Or arborace that wilde raues are. *Ibid.* IX. 53 Rave as brasyk for vyne as ille is fonde. **1585** T. WASHINGTON tr. *Nicholay's Voy.* I. xviii. 21 Ther grow good Melons, Raues, and pateques.

rave (reɪv), *sb.*² [Var. of RATHE *sb.*²]

1. a. A rail of a cart; esp. *pl.* a framework of rails or boards (permanent or removable) added to the sides of a cart to enable a greater load to be carried. **b.** *U.S.* One of the vertical side-pieces in the body of a wagon or sleigh.

1530 PALSGR. 261/1 Ravys of a carte. **1575** TURBERV. *Venerie* 195 When the sayd cariage is loded, he forget not to cause his Cooke and Butler to hang good store of bags and bottels about the raues and pinnes thereof. **1623** J. TAYLOR (Water P.) *World runnes on Wheeles* Wks. (1630) II. 242/1 Of the bottome of an old Cart, one may make a fence to stop a gap; of the Raues one may make a Ladder for Hennes to goe to Roost. **1688** S. SEWALL *Diary* 18 Apr. (1878) I. 211 Jack ∴ dies..by the oversetting of the Cart, he (probably) sitting in it, the Rave fell on's neck and kill'd him. **1720** STRYPE *Stow's Surv.* (1754) II. v. xiv. 314/2 The Raves thereof shall be higher than the Raves of the street cars or carts to keep the fuel the safer from falling off. **1834** *Brit. Husb.* I. 163 The inside depth, below the raves, which are boarded, is 2 feet, and the projection of the raves 9 inches. **1847** *Rep. Comm. Patents 1846* (U.S.) 81 The raves are carried in front in such a form as to furnish a frame for the dash-board. **1851** J. S. SPRINGER *Forest Life* v. 106 It was astonishing to see how he [*sc.* a teamster] had gnawed the rave of the sled. **1865** *Jrnl. R. Agric. Soc.* Ser. II. I. II. 399 This cart has head and tail ladders, in place of raves. **1895** *Montgomery Ward Catal.* Spring & Summer 594/1 Bob Sleigh Gearing..Bob Knees ..Bob Raves..Bob Rollers.

attrib. **1884** *West Sussex Gaz.* 25 Sept., Rave cart, three dung carts. **1886** *Sci. Amer.* 27 Feb. 130/2 The rave bolts [in a bob sleigh] extend upward from the runners in front and rear of the knees, and the raves rest between their ends on the bottom of the recess.

†**2.** App. a rung of a ladder. *Obs. rare*⁻¹.

Cf. '*Rave*, bars or strips of wood across any opening' (Elworthy *W. Som. Word-bk.*).

1566 PARTRIDGE *Plasidas* C v b, The scaling lathers downe to throwe they haue their iron staues; They haue their hatchets for to cut in sunder all their raues.

3. *Weaving.* A bar fitted with teeth or pins, used to separate and guide the threads of the warp while it is being wound on the beam.

1886 ELWORTHY *W. Som. Word-bk.* s.v., The object of the rave is to keep the threads even, and to make them lie on the beam at the same width as the intended piece of cloth.

rave (reɪv), *sb.*³ [f. RAVE *v.*¹] **1.** The (*or* an) act of raving; frenzy, great excitement.

1598 YONG *Diana* 403 Like a sturdie rocke it standes Against the cruell raues..Of beating windes and waues. **1652** BENLOWES *Theoph.* X. xxxviii, So, have we rid out storms, when Eol's rave Plough'd up the ocean. **1765** J. BROWN *Chr. Jrnl.* (1814) 80 Whether I die in a rave or in extremity of pain. **1820** WIFFEN *Aonian Hours* (ed. 2) 27 Meanwhile the rave Of gusty winds spake loudly. **1896** MRS. C. CLARKE *My Long Life* 103 She concluded amid a rave of admiring plaudits.

2. *slang.* **a.** A passionate (and usu. transitory) liking for or infatuation with a person or thing; a sudden display of extreme enthusiasm or popularity, a 'craze'. Also, one who or that which excites feelings of this kind.

1902 FARMER & HENLEY *Slang* V. 380/2 *Rave*,..a strong liking; a craze: as 'X has a *rave* on Miss Z.' **1924** G. B. STERN *Tents of Israel* xvi. 240 Even if Jeanne-Marie had a rave on me, I'm not responsible. **1927** L. MAYER *Just between us Girls* xv. 91 He said I was simply a rave in these pajamas. **1941** L. EYLES *For my Enemy Daughter* vii. 161 That, too, is a bit schoolgirlish, isn't it? Getting a 'rave' on a woman I admire. **1949** N. MARSH *Swing, Brother, Swing* iii. 38 Carlisle remembered the confidences that Félicité had poured out in her convent days, concerning what she called her 'raves'. **1958** *People* 4 May 14/7 Kitza Kazacos, Greek singer, who became a rave on B.B.C. but was allowed to languish without follow-up dates, now tells me from New York that she is on three TV programmes. **1959** C. MACINNES *Absolute Beginners* 70 The newest of the teenage singing raves. **1962** L. DAVIDSON *Rose of Tibet* 8 T.L. had been having at the time one of his not uncommon raves; on this occasion for the mental-disciplinary benefits of a classical language.

b. A highly enthusiastic or laudatory review or notice of a book, play, film, etc. Also in extended use, a favourable opinion; a strong recommendation. Freq. *attrib.* (passing into *adj.*). orig. *U.S.*

No earlier definite example of this use has been traced in *Variety* (see quot. 1926).

1926 *Amer. Mercury* Dec. 464/2 One of the paper's [*sc. Variety's*] coinages should be officially embraced by the dictionary and bred into the language. It refers to a flattering, enthusiastic review by a sycophantic critic as a *rave*. **1935** E. E. CUMMINGS *Let.* 31 Jan. (1969) 135 Have been epistling with Pound, whom yessed in Paris for a full ½ hour under lurid misapprehension that his 'Douglas' rave intended 'South Wind'. **1936** *Amer. Speech* XI. 221 The producer waits for the early editions of the morning papers. He scans them avidly for the notices. They may be raves, in which case the critics have reviewed the show in glowing superlatives. **1942** *Melody Maker* 4 July 5/4 Raves coming thick and fast for George Auld's new powerhouse band now at the Arcadia Ballroom, N.Y. **1943** D. POWELL *Time to be Born* i. 6 The critical raves and the big sale. **1951** WODEHOUSE *Old Reliable* ix. 114 Of course he can open the safe. He's an expert. You should have read what the papers said of him at the time of the trial. He got rave notices. **1958** *Listener* 27 Nov. 898/1, I yield to none in my admiration for this pianist, whose first London notice I had the honour to write long before the war (a 'rave' in case you think I am always wrong). **1961** *John o' London's* 12 Oct. 423/1, I don't suppose *The Young Doctors*..will collect rave tributes. **1969** GISH & PINCHOT *Lillian Gish* xv. 222 Richard Barthelmess also received raves for his sensitive portrayal of Cheng. **1972** [see PAN *sb.*¹ 11]. **1974** *Publishers Weekly* 26 Aug. 299/2 The later work is distinctly finer than the earlier (though that was good enough to draw a rave foreword, here reprinted, from Ford Madox Ford). **1977** M. KENYON *Rapist* v. 50 His music..had opened to raves in New York. **1979** *Tucson Mag.* Apr. 68/3 These three-day bus tours..have received rave notices from all who have gone along. **1980** *Times Lit. Suppl.* 10 Oct. 1131/1 Enzensberger's rave review of the novel is reprinted.

c. A lively party; a rowdy gathering.

1960 *News Chron.* 16 Feb. 6, I wandered around to a rave I knew was going on in Covent Garden. **1963** *Sunday Times* 8 Sept. 29/3 A rave, blast or orgy—all synonyms for party. **1964** C. DALE *Other People* iv. 96 A man who..thought that parties—'raves'—ended at ten-thirty. **1965** G. MELLY *Owning-Up* vii. 75 We..organized all-night raves. **1968** *Listener* 7 Nov. 606/1 Have you heard, the Touch-Paceys are economising this year by combining their children's bonfire party with their annual fancy dress rave?

Hence **rave-in** (see -IN³), **rave-up** = sense 2 c above.

1967 *Melody Maker* 21 Jan. 10 Pop enthusiasts have been treated to rave-ups featuring such world-class stars as the Four Tops. **1967** *New Statesman* 17 Mar. 356/3 Last week police arrested scores of teenagers at a rave-in, and left-wing Catholics staged a pray-in. **1972** 'MISS READ' *Tyler's Row* vii. 88 'Well, let's have this rave-up of a meal now,' suggested Peter. **1973** H. MILLER *Open City* ix. 89 Phyllis McBain is invited to an old-style rave-up, knickers and husbands optional. **1974** R. RENDELL *Face of Trespass* ii. 29 Some Victorian pretence that a simple Westbourne Grove rave-up was really a conference. **1977** *Rolling Stone* 7 Apr. 20/1 (Advt.), When Argent, that legendary British band of so many hit songs and rave-up performances, began to wane, these three musicians stepped out of its shadow and into the fierce light of their own creative genius.

rave (reɪv), *v.*¹ Also 5 **rafe, raffe,** 6 *Sc.* **raif(f, rawe, reave.** [? a. OF. *raver*, app. a variant (of rare occurrence) of *rêver* to dream, be delirious, etc., of obscure origin: for conjectures, see Diez (s.v. *rêve*) and Körting (s.v. *rabia*).]

1. a. *intr.* To be mad, to show signs of madness or delirium (*obs.*); hence, to talk or declaim wildly or furiously in consequence of madness or some violent passion. Occas. (now only *dial.*), to talk loudly or boisterously, to shout or bawl.

c **1374** CHAUCER *Troylus* II. 116 (65) Ye ben so wylde it semeth þat ye raue. **1390** GOWER *Conf.* I. 282 Ech of hem.. wenen that I scholde rave For Anger that thei se me have. **1494** FABYAN *Chron.* VI. ccxiv. 231 Stigandus..sayde..yᵗ the Kynge raued, or ellys doted for age & sykenesse. **1508** DUNBAR *Tua Mariit Wemen* 481 Sum raiffis [*v.r.* raveis] furght rudly with riatus speche. **1552** LYNDESAY *Monarche* 5137 Thocht sum de Naturally, throuch aige, Fer mo deis raiffand in one raige. **1620** MIDDLETON *Chaste Maid* v. i. 13 He raves already; His senses are quite gone. **1727** SWIFT *Poisoning of E. Curll*, Mr. Curll raved aloud in this manner: 'If I survive this, I will be revenged on Tonson'. **1812** J. WILSON *Isle of Palms* III. 56 No more the pining Mariner In wild delirium raves. **1871** B. TAYLOR *Faust* (1875) I. vi. 110 She talks like one who raves in fever.

b. Const. with preps. as *about, against, at, of; for.*

1593 SHAKS. *Lucr.* 982 Let him have time against himself to rave. **1639** FULLER *Holy War* III. xx. (1647) 144 Those who when bemadded with anger, most rave and rage against them. **1707** E. SMITH *Phædra & Hipp.* I. i, Sometimes she raves for Musick, Light, and Air. **1733** SWIFT *Legion Club*, Let them rave at making laws. **1819** SHELLEY *Peter Bell 3rd* I. ix, Raved of God and sin and death, Blaspheming like an infidel. *a* **1822** —— *Tower of Fam.* 6 Whose dwellers rave for bread, and gold, and blood. **1884** *Chr. Commw.* 14 Feb. 416/2 The *Times* is already raving about our having reached 'a crisis'.

c. Of animals. *rare.*

1810 SCOTT *Lady of L.* I. viii, He heard the baffled dogs in vain Rave through the hollow pass amain. **1848** A. B. EVANS *Leicestersh. Words* s.v., That sow's always raving and revelling so.

2. *transf.* **a.** Of the sea, storms, etc.: To rage; to dash, rush, roar, etc., in a furious manner.

1559 *Mirr. Mag., Dk. Suffolk* xxii, The windy sourges whan they rave. **1590** SPENSER *F.Q.* II. xi. 32 Like as a fire, the which in hollow cave..With murmurous disdayne doth inly rave. **1629** MILTON *Nativity* 67 The milde Ocean, Who now hath quite forgot to rave. **1726–46** THOMSON *Winter* 186 The whirling tempest raves along the plain. **1767** SIR W. JONES *Seven Fountains* Poems (1777) 54 Where the dark sea with angry billows raves. **1811** SCOTT *Don Roderick* II. lix, When the pibroch bids the battle rave. **1856** LONGF. *Gold. Leg.* v. *Devil's Bridge*, The cataract, That raves and rages down the steep.

b. Of a disordered mental state. *rare.*

1611 SHAKS. *Cymb.* IV. ii. 135 Not Frenzie, Not absolute madnesse could so farre haue rau'd To bring him heere alone. **1638** SANDYS *Paraphr. Job* xi. 15 Shall these wild distempers of thy mind..thus rave, and find No opposition?

3. a. To talk or declaim with enthusiasm or poetic rapture. Also const. *about, of,* †*upon.*

a **1704** LOCKE *Conduct Und.* §24 This raving upon antiquity in matter of poetry, Horace has..exposed in one of his satires. **1725** RAMSAY *Gentle Sheph.* I. ii, How blythly can he sport and gently rave. **1781** COWPER *Retirement* 735 Solitude, however some may rave, Seeming a sanctuary, proves a grave. **1816** JANE AUSTEN *Emma* II. xv. 282, I quite rave about Jane Fairfax. **1838** LYTTON *Alice* IV. ix, How people can rave about Italy, I can't think. **1880** OUIDA *Moths* I. 56 It is not his singing that makes the great ladies rave of him. **1921** *Collier's* 16 Apr. 20/2 He began to 'rave', about the place he had built on Long Island for him and Delores. **1978** J. UPDIKE *Coup* iv. 150 So you're the young man my daughter has been raving about.

b. *slang.* To give oneself over to enjoyment; to 'live it up'; to depart rowdily or with the intention of having a good time. Cf. RAVE *sb.*³ 2 c.

1961 *New Statesman* 26 May 830/2 When we got there, most of the art-student element had raved off to some shindig. **1965** G. MELLY *Owning-Up* vii. 75 The word 'rave', meaning to live it up, was as far as I know a Mulligan-Godbolt invention. **1965** *Sunday Times* (Colour Suppl.) 19 Sept. 13/3 He started out by raving at weekends to Bridlington.

4. a. *trans.* To utter in a frenzied or enthusiastic manner. Also with *out.*

1602 MARSTON *Antonio's Rev.* IV. v, Like to some boy, that actes a tragedie,..and raves out passion. **1742** YOUNG *Nt. Th.* VII. 596 Pride, like the Delphic priestess, with a swell Rav'd nonsense. **1819** SHELLEY *Peter Bell 3rd* VI. xxxii, For he now raved enormous folly. **1887** G. MEREDITH *Ballads & P.* 95 Thus their prayer was raved, and ceased.

b. To lament frantically. *rare*⁻¹.

1810 *Splendid Follies* I. 16 It was then he wept—he raved the departure of Seraphina.

5. quasi-*trans.* with complement: To bring (into a specified state) by raving.

1812 BYRON *Ch. Har.* I. lxxxiii, But passion raves itself to rest, or flies. **1850** WHIPPLE *Ess. & Rev.* (ed. 3) I. 402 To rave men into some new heresy.

rave, *v.*² *north. dial.* and *Sc.* [App. of Scand. origin: cf. Icel. *ráfa* in same sense (not recorded in ON.).] *intr.* To wander, stray, rove, †err. (Now *rare* or *Obs.*)

13.. *E.E. Allit. P.* A. 665 Bot resoun, of ryȝt þat con not raue, Sauez euer more þe innossent. *c* **1400** *Rule St. Benet* 57/362 Hir awn sawle wele may sche saue, Al if hir schepe vnryght wyl raue. *c* **1440** *York Myst.* xxiv. 159 Allas! for ruthe, now may I raue, And febilly fare by frith and felde. **1596** DALRYMPLE tr. *Leslie's Hist. Scot.* I. 71 Quhen..he lang had rauet and wandirit, at last he arriuet in Numidie. *Ibid.* 85 Albeit sum of thame raue and declyne be the way [L. *alii aberrent*]. **1841** HAWKINS *Poems* v. 24 (E.D.D.) Wi' ither dogs I maunna rave.

Hence †**ˈraving** *ppl. a.*², straying. *Obs. rare*⁻¹.

c **1400** *Rule St. Benet* 56/292 Vnto no hird þai wil tak kepe, Bot raykes forth als raueand schep.

rave, *v.*³ *Obs.* exc. *dial.* [Of obscure origin: for the sense, cf. RIVE *v.*] *trans.* To tear, drag, pull. Usually with *up*: To drag or rake up.

c **1440** *Gesta Rom.* lx. 248 He Ranne to the false Emperes, and Ravid hir evin to the bone. **1486** *Nottingham Rec.* III. 247 Raving vp of gravell and leying hit on agayn. **1553** T. WILSON *Rhet.* (1580) 108 Whereas we should bee shorte in tellyng the matter..the best is to speake no more than needes we must, not rauyng it from the bottome. **1610** COOKE *Pope Joan* 63 He neuer purposed to raue vp all the filth which he found written of your Popes. **1877** *N.W. Linc. Gloss.*, *Rave up*, to take up, to pull up. (2) To repeat evil stories relating to by-past time.

b. To poke or pry *into*. (Cf. RAVEL *v.* 4.) *rare.*
1636 SANDERSON *Serm.* iv. Wks. 1854 I. 100 It can be little pleasure to us to rave into the infirmities of God's servants. **1856** THOMPSON *Boston* Gloss., *Rave up*, to repeat old stories; to search or rave into anything.

Hence **'raving**, *vbl. sb.*[2]
1553 T. WILSON *Rhet.* (1580) 9 Euermore the gladder the lesse rauyng there is, or stirryng in this matter.

†**rave**, *v.*[4] *Sc. Obs.* Also raif. [Perh. a. F. *ravir* to ravish, if not a mere variant of *reif*, *reve* REAVE *v.*] *trans.* To take away by force.
1549 *Compl. Scot.* viii. 73 My mortal enemeis purchessis to raif my liberte. **1552** LYNDESAY *Monarche* 6280 Deith.. rauis þame frome þare rent, ryches, and ringis. *a* **1598** ROLLOCK *Wks.* (1844) II. vii. 84 They would climb up to heaven and rave it from God.

Hence †**'raving** *vbl. sb.*[3] and *ppl. a.*[3] *Obs.*
1549 *Compl. Scot.* Ep. to Queen 2 The rauand sauuage volffis..that deuoris..scheip for ther pray. *a* **1578** LINDESAY (Pitscottie) *Chron. Scot.* (S.T.S.) II. 273 Thair was nathing bot rwgging and raveing of the puir laubouraris.

rave, obs. pa. t. RIVE *v.*

rave-hook. *Naut.* [? f. RAVE *v.*[3]] (See quot.)
1846 A. YOUNG *Naut. Dict.*, *Rave-hook*, an iron instrument used by caulkers to get the oakum thoroughly out of a vessel's seams, when a rasing-iron would not penetrate deep enough.

ravel ('ræv(ə)l), *sb.*[1] Also *Sc.* raivel, *dial.* revel. [f. the vb. Cf. Du. *rafel* a fraying out.]

1. A tangle, complication, entanglement; a cluster.
1634 JACKSON *Creed* VII. xxvi. §1 The thread which we are to unwind as far as possibly we can without knot or ravel. **1853** W. JERDAN *Autobiogr.* IV. 150 The act by which numerous political ravels seemed to be so happily disentangled. **1865** SWINBURNE *Poems & Ball.*, *At Eleusis* 185 She thought to thread this web's fine ravel out. **1913** D. H. LAWRENCE *Sons & Lovers* xiii. 380 There was a lovely yellow ravel of sunflowers in the garden.

2. A broken thread, a loose end. Also *fig.*
1832 CARLYLE in Froude *Life* (1882) II. 307 Great is self-denial... Life goes all to ravels and tatters, where that enters not. **1847** HALLIWELL, *Revels*, the broken threads cast away by women at their work.

'ravel, *sb.*[2] *Sc.* (and *north. dial.*) Also 7 reuele, ravell, 9 raivel. [Of obscure origin.]

1. A rail or railing.
1632 LITHGOW *Trav.* VI. 264 A foure squared stone; inclosed about with an yron Reuele, on which..the dead body of our Sauiour lay, and was imbalmed. [**1695** in *Hist. Brechin* (1867) v. 98 The east ravell is found to be very ruinous. In 1707 the whole ravell is directed to be amended.] **1792** *New Year's Morning* 12 (E.D.D.) A cellar, upo' the high street, But ony ravel, bare. **1821** GALT *Ayrsh. Legatees* v. let. xv, We then ran..up an old timber-stair with a rope ravel. **1892** N. DICKSON *Auld Scotch Min.* 115 An inside stair that had what was called a 'wooden ravel'.

2. 'The cross-beam to which the tops of cow-stakes are fastened' (Jam. 1825). Also ***ravel-stick***, ***-tree*** (Northumb. Gloss.; cf. *rail-tree* RAIL *sb.*[2] 6).

'ravel, *sb.*[3] Also *Sc.* raivel. [Synonymous with RADDLE *sb.*[1] 1 b and RAVE *sb.*[2] 3, but the mutual relationship of the words is not clear. Cf. prec. and RAVEL *v.*[1], which may have influenced the form.] *Weaving.* A separator (cf. quot. 1842).
1805 J. AUSTIN in *Trans. Soc. Arts* XXIII. 242 An universal ravel or sniffle, useful at the beaming of all kinds of webs. **1831** PORTER *Silk Manuf.* 220 The threads of the warp being separated and guided by means of the ravel. **1842** BISCHOFF *Woollen Manuf.* II. 412 In order that the warp may be laid evenly on the beam, an instrument is used similar to the reel... It is called a ravel or separator, and is composed of strips of cane fastened into a rail of wood [etc.].

†**'ravel**, *a.* *Obs.* *rare*[−1]. In 7 rauill. [Perh. related to RABBLE *v.*[1]] ? Loquacious, voluble.
a **1603** T. CARTWRIGHT *Confut. Rhem. N.T.* (1618) Pref. 35 Your Dirigie groats, and Trentall money, will make you lauish and rauill in your translation.

ravel ('ræv(ə)l), *v.*[1] Also 6–7 ravell, 7 ravill, ravle, 9 *dial.* raivel, reavel. [App. a. Du. *ravelen* (Kilian), *rafelen* to tangle, to fray out, to unweave; cf. LG. *reffeln*, *rebbeln* in same sense. A common dial. form is *raffle*: see RAFFLE *v.*[3]

In ordinary Eng. use *ravel* is synonymous with *unravel*. The more original sense of entangling or becoming tangled is still common in Sc. and dial.]

I. *intr.* **1.** To become entangled or confused. *rare* (exc. *dial.*).
a **1585** MONTGOMERIE *Flyting w. Polwart* 511 Litill tent to their time the toone leit them take, Bot ay..[they] raveld in their reeles. **1591** SHAKS. *Two Gent.* III. ii. 51 As you vnwinde her loue from him, Least it should rauell,..You must prouide to bottome it on me. **1671** MILTON *Samson* 305 By thir own perplexities involv'd They ravel more.

2. Of a fabric: To fray *out*, to suffer disintegration. (Also in fig. context.)
1611 COTGR., *Riuler*, to rauell out like silke. **1639** FULLER *Holy War* v. i. (1840) 242 To hem the end of our history that it ravel not out. **1688** R. HOLME *Armoury* III. 97/2 Ravell—when threads come out of the edges of the cloth. **1791** HAMILTON *Berthollet's Dyeing* I. I. II. i. 133 The stuff now participates of the nature of..felt..and it may be cut without being subject to ravel. **1860** H. WEDGWOOD in *Phil. Soc. Trans.* 32 The hem of a garment is that which binds it round, and prevents it from ravelling out.
fig. **1606** MARSTON *Fawne* II. i, Do's my Lord rauell out, do's he fret? *c* **1610** BEAUM. & FL. *Philaster* v. iv, Your royalty shall ravel. **1669** SHADWELL *Royal Shepherdess* II, How do men ravel back to childhood. **1956** *Essays in Crit.* III. 320 The discussion then ravels out into a note on such secondary Virgilian sources as the Saturnian prophecy. **1963** OGLESBY & HEWES *Highway Engin.* (ed. 2) xvii. 544 The roads raveled rapidly and in the worst instances became during a single season merely a pile of loose stones.

3. Of a clue or thread: To unwind; to come off the clue, reel, etc. *rare* (now *dial.*).
1649 G. DANIEL *Trinarch.*, *Rich. II*, lxxxvii, Shee gives the Clue: and if it can but ravel To the Thred's End, wee seeke no farther travel. **1653** WALTON *Angler* viii. 154 With such a nick..as may keep the line from any more of it ravelling from about the stick than so much of it as you intend. **1873** A. G. MURDOCH *Doric Lyre* 13 The threed in Tammie's shuttle Gaed raivelling aff the pirn.

†**4.** To examine or inquire *into* a thing. *Obs.* (freq. in 17th c.).
1618 SIR H. MAY in *Fortescue Papers* (Camden) 46 Being unwillinge to ravell into the memory of those offensive particulers. **1669** W. SIMPSON *Hydrol. Chym.* 34 We have already sufficiently ravell'd into the nature of both vitriol and iron. **1710** J. PALMER *Proverbs* 141 The malicious.. ravel into the conduct of a man of honour in the dark.

II. *trans.* **5. a.** To entangle, confuse, perplex.
1598 E. GUILPIN *Skial.* (1878) 51 Like Weavers shuttles which runne to and fro, Rau'ling their owne guts with their running so. *a* **1656** VINES *Lord's Supp.* (1677) 130 The words which are so ravelled and perplexed by contrary senses. **1706** DE FOE *Jure Divino* VIII. 188 Those wild, unhappy, self-defending Few, If not destroy'd in Time, will ravel all the Clew. **1727** BERKELEY *Let. to Prior* 27 June in *Wks.* 1871 IV. 145 My affairs were ravell'd by the death of his Majesty. **1845** P. FAIRBAIRN *Typol. Script.* (1857) I. I. iv. 133 It ravels and complicates the meaning of the prophecies.
absol. **1862** HISLOP *Prov. Scot.* 63 Fools ravel, and wise men redd.

†**b.** *transf.* To make (dust) rise in confusion.
1646 *J. Hall's Poems* To Authour, Summon thy lungs, and with an angry breath Ravell the curious dust. **1647** J. HALL *Poems* II. 100 Dust, ravel'd in the Aire will fly Up high.

6. a. To unwind or unweave; to unravel. †Also with *away*.
1607 TOURNEUR *Rev. Trag.* II. ii, You shall have one woman knit more in an hower than any man can rauel agen. **1650** W. BROUGH *Sacr. Princ.* (1659) 426 How then darest thou ravel away that pretious threed. **1726** POPE *Odyss.* XIX. 173 The night still ravell'd, what the day renew'd. **1809** MAR. EDGEWORTH *Manœuvring* ix, A fool, who ravels, as fast as one weaves, the web of her fortune. **1889** *Century Mag.* Apr. 841 A favorite gown had been woven by her maids, of cotton, striped with silk procured by raveling the general's discarded stockings.

b. *fig.* To take to pieces; to disentangle.
1582 STANYHURST *Æneis* To Rdr. (Arb.) 12 Many good verses would bee rauelde and dismembred. **1648** HEYLIN *Relat. & Observ.* I. 139 b, To rauell back all Governments, to the first principles of nature. *a* **1658** CLEVELAND *Hermaphrodite* 19 Ravel thy Body, and I find In every Limb a double kind. **1874** HOLLAND *Mistr. Manse* 161 A thousand chances of the feud She wove and raveled one by one.

7. a. ***to ravel out***: To draw or pull out by unwinding or unweaving.
1623–4 MIDDLETON & ROWLEY *Span. Gipsy* II. i. 161 A stitch in a man's stocking not taken up in time, ravels out all the rest. **1675** HOBBES *Odyssey* XIX. 139 All day I wove, but ere I went to bed, What I had wov'n, I ravel'd out agen. **1746** ARDERON in *Phil. Trans.* XLIV. 429 Whenever it ascended, it wound its Thread with its Feet into a sort of Coil, and when it descended only ravelled it out again. **1856** FROUDE *Hist. Eng.* vii. (1858) II. 164 We find a commission sitting at Lambeth..ravelling out the threads of a story.

b. To destroy, spoil, or waste, as by pulling a fabric into threads. ? *Obs.*
a **1616** BEAUM. & FL. *Wit at Sev. Weap.* v. i, Shelter, shelter, if you be seene All's ravell'd out agen. **1660** INGELO *Bentiv. & Ur.* I. (1682) 157 [They] slighted those mean Sports which ravel out the time of other people. *a* **1708** BEVERIDGE *Priv. Th.* I. (1730) 97 Why should I spend and ravel out my Thoughts upon that which will destroy my Soul.

c. To disentangle, make plain or clear.
1593 SHAKS. *Rich. II*, IV. i. 239 Must I rauell out My weau'd-vp follyes? **1602** —— *Ham.* III. iv. 186 Let him.. Make you to rauell all this matter out. *a* **1658** CLEVELAND *Wks.* (1687) 11 Then roll up, Muse, what thou hast ravel'd out. **1832** J. BREE *St. Herbert's Isle* 89 What there she did, took me full thrice as long To ravel out. **1870** MORRIS *Earthly Par.* III. IV. 195 Asking words from these To ravel out his tale for him.

†**8.** To turn or toss *over*. (? Cf. RABBLE *v.*[1] 2.)
a **1655** DIGBY (J.), They but ravel it over loosely, and pitch upon disputing against particular conclusions.

†**'ravel**, *v.*[2] *Obs.* *rare*[−1]. [Cf. RAFFLE *v.*[2]] *trans.* To ruffle or scratch.
1621 J. REYNOLDS *God's Revenge* I. ii. 62 A faire thrust.. which onely pierced his shirt, and ravelled his skinne.

†**'ravel**, *v.*[3] *Obs.* *rare*[−1]. [Perh. a back-formation from RAVELLED *a.*] *trans.* To sift.
1674 JEAKE *Arith.* (1696) 74 Houshold-Bread of the best Wheat unravelled, or ravelled through the coursest Boultel.

ravel, var. RABBLE *sb.*[2] or *v.*[3]

'ravel bread. *Obs.* exc. *dial.* [Of obscure origin: cf. RAVELLED *a.*] Bread made of whole meal, or of flour with the bran left in. Also *ravel loaf*.
1591 FLORIO *2nd Fruites* 51 Here is cheate bread, rauel bread, manchet bread, and houshold bread. **1608** T. COCKS *Diary* (1901) 37/4 Mr. Deanes boye, that brought me a ravell loafe. **1674** JEAKE *Arith.* (1696) 74 Bread made of the whole Wheat is sometime called Cribble or fine Ravel Bread. **1706** PHILLIPS (ed. Kersey), *Panis vocatus Black-whitlof*, bread of a middle sort, between White and Brown; such as in Kent is call'd Ravel-bread. **1887** in *Kentish Gloss.*

Ravelian (rə'vɛlɪən), *a.* Also **Ravellian.** [f. the name of Maurice *Ravel* (1875–1937), French composer.] Of, pertaining to, or characteristic of the works of Ravel. Also as *sb.*, an exponent of Ravel's music.
1933 M. D. CALVOCORESSI in *Listener* 22 Feb. 305/1 There is no mistaking the thoroughly 'Ravel-ian'—and therefore French—quality of the mind and imagination which is at work. **1937** *Times* 29 Dec. 12/3 The charm of the early quartet and septet will keep them fresh when some of the more purely Ravellian works have been discarded as too dry. **1946** *Penguin Music Mag.* Dec. 32 The progress of Walton from his early and somewhat Ravelian *Façade* to the Violin Concerto. **1952** B. ULANOV *Hist. Jazz in Amer.* (1958) xxii. 310 Johnny Richards' excursions into Debussyan and Ravelian pasture. **1965** *Listener* 28 Oct. 680/2 The two syllables '*Ma-man*', pronounced as a falling fourth (a characteristic Ravelian fingerprint), strike an almost sentimental note. **1970** L. DAVIES *Ravel Orchestral Music* 46 It culminates in a more virtuoso episode which leans too obviously on skimming Ravelian scales. **1981** *Times* 26 Feb. 13/6 Manuel Rosenthal, a Ravelian to his fingertips.

ravelin[1] ('rævlɪn). Also 6 rau-, reu-, revelin, rav'lin, 7 ravellin, (8 rablin); 6 rauelline, -yne, 7–8 raveline; 6–7 raveling, (7 -iling, 9 -elling). [a. F. *ravelin* (16th c., Rabelais), a. It. *rav-*, *revellino* (Florio), now *rivellino* = Sp. *rebellin*, Pg. *rebelim*; of unknown origin.] In fortification, an outwork consisting of two faces which form a salient angle, constructed beyond the main ditch and in front of the curtain.
1589 IVE *Fortif.* 35 There the defences would be placed without the counterscarfe..and being so placed they are tearmed to be rauelins of the Italyans and Frenchmen, and of vs they have been tearmed spurres. **1590** SIR J. SMYTH *Disc. Weapons* Ded. 10 The bulwarkes, platformes, and reuelins haue beene taken away. **1601** R. JOHNSON *Kingd. & Commw.* (1603) 85 It is indifferently well fortified with rauelings, bulwarkes and platteformes, besides a deepe ditch. **1665** MANLEY tr. *Grotius' Low C. Warres* 271 Finding the Bulwark too strong for the Cannon, though a great part of the Ravelin was beaten down. **1759** STERNE *Tr. Shandy* II. xii, Common men..confound the ravelin and the half-moon together,—tho' they are very different things. **1828** J. M. SPEARMAN *Brit. Gunner* (ed. 2) 204 The Ravelins are intended to cover the curtains and shoulders of the bastions, and to defend the ground in front of their saliants. **1834–47** J. S. MACAULAY *Field Fortif.* (1851) 23 Ravelins are seldom added to forts in the field, but almost always to fronts of permanent fortifications.
transf. and *fig.* **1629** B. JONSON in Sir J. Beaumont *Bosworth-Field*, This Booke will liue; It hath a Genius;.. Here needs no words expense In Bulwarkes, Rau'lins, Ramparts, for defense. **1852** NEWLAND *Lect. Tractar.* 133 The church..though protected by a strong ravelin of masonry from..the falling ice. **1856** R. A. VAUGHAN *Mystics* I. v. ii. 165 All the intellectual fortification of the time—the redoubts, ravelins..of dry stern logic.

†**ravelin**[2]. *Sc. Obs. rare.* [Cf. RAVEL *sb.*[2]] A railing, fence.
1626 *Burgh Rec. Aberdeen* III. 7 The councell grants licience..to big a dyick or ravelin of tymber, betwixt the chappell wall and the lard Forbes back dyke of his yaird.

†**'ravelled**, *a.* *Obs.* (See RAVEL BREAD.)
1577 HARRISON *England* II. vi. (1877) I. 154 The raueled is a kind of cheat bread also, but it reteineth more of the grosse, and less of the poore substance of the wheat. The raueled cheat..is generallie so made [etc.]. **1613** WITHER *Abuses* II. i, For bread, they can compare with Lord and Knight. They have both raveld manchet browne and white. [**1830** JAMES *Darnley* I. ix. 200 His pressed curds, his raveled bread, and his leathern bottle full of thin beer.]

ravelled ('ræv(ə)ld), *ppl. a.* [f. RAVEL *v.*[1]]

1. Tangled, confused, involved. (*lit.* and *fig.*)
1605 SHAKS. *Macb.* II. ii. 37 Sleepe that knits up the rauel'd Sleeue of Care. **1642** ROGERS *Naaman* 336 How to picke out an end out of the ravelled skeine. **1666** BAXTER *Call to Unconverted* 204 Because our ravelled wits cannot see them right together. **1725** RAMSAY *Gentle Sheph.* I. i, Ye.. have sae kind Redd up my ravel'd doubts, and clear'd my mind. **1835** SIR W. HAMILTON *Discuss.* (1852) 519 The difficult and ravelled problems touching the various collegiate foundations. **1883** ANNIE S. SWAN *Aldersyde* II. x, A higher hand holds the ravelled skein of life.

b. *Sc.* ***a ravelled hasp***: An intricate or involved matter.
1637 FLEMING in A. Whyte *Rutherford* (1894) xxiii. 201 My inward life is a ravelled hesp and I need guidance and direction. **1720** PENNECUIK *Helicon* (ed. 2) 26 Providence seems a ravel'd Hasp. **1822** SCOTT *Pirate* v, Speak her fair and canny, or we will have a ravelled hasp on the yarn-windles.

†**2.** Frayed out; with frayed edges; ragged. Also *transf.* *Obs.*
1599 NASHE *Lenten Stuffe* 47 The raueld buttonholes of her bleare eyes. **1613–16** W. BROWNE *Brit. Past.* II. iv, A ravell'd wound distain'd her purer brest.

'raveller. [f. RAVEL *v.*[1] + -ER[1].] One who ravels (Webster 1864).

ravellin(g, obs. forms of RAVELIN.

ravelling ('ræv(ə)lɪŋ), *vbl. sb.* [f. RAVEL *v.*[1]]

1. The action of the vb. in various senses.

1673 in *Essex Papers* (Camden) I. 79 Commissions issued out for ye searching and raveling into mens estates. **1688** *Col. Rec. Pennsylv.* I. 242 Tending to the ravelling into ye Resolutions of ye Last day's proceedings. **1830** GALT *Lawrie T.* II. xi. (1840) 78 All this breaking of banks and revalling [*sic*] of manufacturers.

2. *concr.* A thread from a woven fabric which is frayed or unravelled.

1658 A. FOX tr. *Wurtz' Surg.* II. ix. 83 Take the single threeds or ravellings of linnen, wet them in this Water, cleanse the Wounds with them. **1727** *Philip Quarll* (1816) 57 He.. with the ravelling of some of the sail made a string to the bow. **1792** SIR B. THOMPSON in *Phil. Trans.* LXXXII. 58 The ravelings of cloth, or cuttings of threads. **1870** LOWELL *Study Wind.* (1886) 14 The nest was.. woven and felted with ravellings of woollen carpet.

fig. **1778** *Love Feast* 21 Of Righteousness mere Rav'lings and vile Shreds. **1903** B. POTTER *Tailor of Gloucester* 22, I am worn to a ravelling.

'ravelly, *a. rare.* Somewhat ravelled.

1890 *Century Mag.* Jan. 444/1 *note*, A.. suit of clothes that looked seamed and ravelly.

ravelment ('ræv(ə)lmənt). [f. RAVEL *v.*[1] + -MENT.] Entanglement, confusion. Also with *a*.

1833 CARLYLE *Diderot* Misc. Ess. (1888) V. 28 A series of ravelments and squabbling grudges. **1837** —— *Fr. Rev.* III. II. ii, Mischievous deceitful persons cut the rope, and our Queue becomes a ravelment. **1870** *Daily News* 24 Sept., Heaps of Bavarian and French dead piled high in inextricable ravelment.

raven ('reɪv(ə)n), *sb.*[1] (*a.*) Forms: α. 1 hraebn, (h)ræfn, ræfen; 3 rauon, 4 ravoun; 3–6 rau-, ravin, -yn, (5 rawyn, -ine, ravyne), 4–5 rau-, ravene, 3–7 rauen, 4– raven. β. 1 (h)refn, 3 reafen, 3–4 reu-, reven, 3–5 reu-, revyn, (4 revon, 5 rewyn), 6 *Sc.* revin, 7 *Sc.* reavin. γ. 1 hremn, (h)remm, (h)ræm, 1–3 rem. [Comm. Teut.: OE. *hræfn* = MDu. *rāven* (Du. *raaf*), OHG. (*h*)*raban* (MHG. *raben*), ON. *hrafn* (MSw. *rafn*, Da. *ravn*), Goth. **hrabn-s* (cf. early ON. *Harabanaʀ* = *Hrabnaʀ*, the personal name *Hrafn*). A normal change of *fn* to *mn*, *m*(*m* gave also OE. *hræmn*, *hrem*(*m* = OHG. (*h*)*ram* (MHG. *ram*), MSw. *ramn*, (*rampn*,) *ram*(*m*.

A weak form of the stem appears in OHG. *rabo* (G. *rabe*, MLG. *rāve*): for the relationship of this to MHG. *rappe* raven (G. *rappe* a black horse) see Streitberg *Urgerm. Gramm.* 151.]

A. *sb.* **1. a.** A widely distributed corvine bird (*Corvus Corax*) of Europe and Asia, of large size, with black lustrous plumage and raucous voice, feeding chiefly on carrion or other flesh. The name has also been extended to birds belonging to various other species of *Corvus*, esp. the American Raven (*Corvus carnivorus*).

The common raven is easily tamed, but is mischievous and thievish, and has been popularly regarded as a bird of evil omen and mysterious character.

α. *a* **800** *Erfurt Gloss.* 285 Corax, hraebn. *c* **850** *O.E. Martyrol.* Jan. 10, þa.. fedde hine an hræfn sextiȝ geara. *c* **950** *Lindisf. Gosp.* Luke xii. 24 Behaldað ða ræfnas þætte ne sawæð ne hriopað. *c* **1220** *Bestiary* 408 Ðe rauen is swiðe redi.. & oðre fules hire fallen bi. *c* **1290** *S. Eng. Leg.* I. 312/452 Al þat oþur del with-Inne swiþe blak as a rauen it is. **13..** *E.E. Allit. P.* B. 455 Þe rauen so ronk þat rebel was euer. *c* **1400** MAUNDEV. (Roxb.) xxxiv. 153 Vowltures, egles, rauyns, and oþer fewlez of rauyne. *c* **1450** HOLLAND *Howlat* 215 The Ravyne, rolpand rudly in a roche ran. **1526** *Pilgr. Perf.* (W. de W. 1531) 63 The rauen wyll not gyue her blacke pennes for the pecockes paynted fethers. *c* **1592** MARLOWE *Jew of Malta* II. i, Like the sad-presaging raven, that tolls The sick man's passport in her hollow beak. **1656** S. HOLLAND *Zara* (1719) 130 Thou art always (like the Raven) croaking my infortunity and disgrace. **1688** R. HOLME *Armoury* III. 144/2 Pens made of Ravens Quills.. are to finish and shadow your draught. **1766** PENNANT *Brit. Zool.* (1768) I. 166 Ravens build in trees, and lay five or six eggs. *Ibid.* 167 The raven will pick out the eyes of young lambs when just dropped. **1822** SCOTT *Pirate* v, If the men of Thule have ceased.. to spread the banquet for the raven [etc.]. **1859** TENNYSON *Guinevere* 132 Till in the cold wind that foreruns the morn,.. the Raven, flying high, Croak'd.

β. *Beowulf* (Z.) 3025 Se wonna hrefn fus ofer fæȝum. *c* **825** *Vesp. Psalter* cxlvi. 9 Se seleð neatum mete heara & briddum hrefna. *c* **1000** *Ags. Gosp.* Luke xii. 24 Besceawiað þa hrefnas [*c* **1160** *Hatton MS.* refnes] þæt hiȝ ne sawað. *a* **1225** *Ancr. R.* 84 He.. mid his bile, roted stinkinde fleshs, as is reafnes kunde. *a* **1300** *Fragm. Pop. Sc.* (Wright) 63 Al that other del with-inne blac as a reven is. *c* **1475** *Pict. Voc.* in Wr.-Wülcker 761/33 *Hic cornix*, a rewyn. **1486** *Bk. St. Albans* D ij, That hawke that will slee a Roke or a Crow or a Reuyn. **1500–20** DUNBAR *Poems* xxvi. 117 Thae tarmegantis.. begowth to clatter, And rowp lyk revin and ruke. *c* **1630** SIR W. MURE *Ps.* cxlvii. 9 Of reavens who heares The yong ones, when they call.

γ. *c* **1000** ÆLFRIC *Gen.* viii. 7 Noe.. asende ut ænne hremn; se hremn fleah þa ut [etc.]. *c* **1000** —— *Saints' Lives* (Skeat) I. 492 Ðær fluȝon sona to hrocas and hremmas. *c* **1205** LAY. 30392 Habben bares heorte and remes brede.

†**b.** ***Indian raven***, the name given by Bontius to two East Indian birds (see quots. 1678). *Obs.*

1678 RAY *Willughby's Ornith.* II. vii. 126 Bontius his Indian Raven. There is a strange kind of Raven in the Molucca Islands.. which resembles our Country Raven in the bill. *Ibid.* viii. 127 The horned Indian Raven or Tapau, called the Rhinoceros Bird. **1752** SIR J. HILL *Hist. Anim.* 383 *Buceros niger*.. in shape somewhat resembles the crow kind, whence, and from it's size, it has been called the Indian Raven.

c. *fig.* A croaker.

1814 SIR R. WILSON *Priv. Diary* (1861) II. 301, I have done my duty honestly in my correspondence with government on this subject; but I am not sure that I shall not be voted an incorrigible raven.

2. a. The figure of a raven on the flag of the Danish vikings; also, the flag itself or the warlike power typified by this.

a **1100** *O.E. Chron.* (Laud MS.) an. 878 Þar wæs se guðfana ȝenumen þe hi ræfen heton. **1605** CAMDEN *Rem.*, *Armories* (1870) 228 The Danes [bore] in their Standard a Raven, as Asserius reporteth. *a* **1711** KEN *Edmund* Poet. Wks. 1721 II. 313 The mighty Hildebrand the Raven rears, A magick Flag. **1740** THOMSON & MALLET *Alfred* II. iii, Behold the warrior bright with Danish spoils!—The raven droops his wings. **1856** C. KNIGHT *Pop. Hist. Eng.* I. vii. 100 The banner of the White Horse floated triumphantly over the Danish raven.

b. *Her.* The figure of a raven as borne in arms.

1610 GUILLIM *Heraldry* III. xvii. 162 Hee beareth Or, a Raven proper, by the name of Corbet. **1780** EDMONDSON *Compl. Body Heraldry* II. *Gloss.*

†**3.** *Astron.* The southern constellation *Corvus*. = CROW 4. *Obs. rare.*

[*c* **1384** CHAUCER *H. Fame* II. 496 How goddes gonne stellifye Brid, fish, beste, or him or here, As the Raven, or either Bere.] **1551** RECORDE *Cast. Knowl.* (1556) 270 The Rauen standeth on the same Hydre,.. and it is formed of 7 starres.

4. *attrib.* (see also B.) and *Comb.*

a. Simple attrib., as ***raven kind***, ***quill***; similative, as ***raven-black***, ***-glossy***, ***-grey***, ***-like***, ***-shadowing*** adjs.; ***raven-wise*** adv.; parasynthetic, as ***raven-coloured***, ***-feathered***, ***-haired***, ***-plumed***, ***-toned*** adjs.; instrumental, as ***raven-covered***, ***-torn*** adjs.

c **1600** SHAKS. *Sonn.* cxxvii, My Mistersse [*sic*] eyes are *Rauen blacke. **1857** C. BRONTË *Professor* x, Raven-black hair, very dark eyes. **1588** SHAKS. *Tit. A.* II. iii. 83 Her *Rauen coloured loue. **1746** HERVEY *Medit.* (1818) 265 The raven-colored mantle of night. **1895** W. B. YEATS *Wanderings of Usheen* in *Poems* 7 We think on Oscar's pencilled urn, And on the heroes lying lain, On Gabhra's *raven-covered plain. **1798** SOTHEBY tr. *Wieland's Oberon* (1826) I. 8 The starless gloom of *raven-feather'd night. **1700** DRYDEN *Cymon & Iph.* 151 The snowy skin, the *raven-glossy hair. **1815** SCOTT *Guy M.* xix, Two suits of clothes, one black, and one *raven-grey. **1844** THACKERAY *May Gambols* Wks. 1900 XIII. 427 The dark-eyed and *raven-haired being. **1727–41** CHAMBERS *Cycl.*, *Corvus indicus*,.. a bird of the *raven kind. **1876** GEO. ELIOT *Dan. Der.* II. xxii. 82 Said Mrs. A—— in her most *raven-like tones. **1827** J. EVANS *Excurs. Windsor* 353 The *raven-plumed gulph of oblivion. **1776–96** WITHERING *Brit. Plants* (ed. 3) IV. 232 Stem solid.. 1½ inch high thick as a *raven quill. **1950** C. DAY LEWIS in *Penguin New Writing* XXXIX. 22 A driven heart, a *raven-shadowing mind Loom above all my pastorals. **1797** SOUTHEY in J. Cottle *Reminisc.* (1847) 210 The very voice.. will be enough to convict the *raven-toned criminal. **1860** RUSKIN *Mod. Paint.* V. IX. ii. §11. 211 The carcass of a ewe.. *raven-torn. **1891** ATKINSON *Last of Giant-killers* 61 Nests, built *raven-wise one a-top of the other.

b. Special combs., as **raven-bone** = *raven's bone* (see c); **raven-cockatoo**, a black cockatoo (of the genus *Calyptorhynchus*); **raven-crow** = RAVEN 1; **raven-duck** [ad. G. *rabentuch*], a kind of canvas (also *raven's duck*); **raven-fish** [tr. It. *coracino*], a black-coloured Mediterranean fish; †**raven-foot** (see quot.); †**raven messenger** = *corbie messenger* CORBIE 2; **raven standard**: cf. RAVEN 2 a; **raven-stone** [ad. G. *rabenstein*], the place of execution, the gallows or gibbet; **raven-tree**, a tree in which ravens build their nests.

1818 SCOTT *Br. Lamm.* ix, Disputing.. concerning nombles, briskets, flankards, and *raven-bones, then usual terms of the art of hunting. **1817** T. FORSTER *Nat. Hist. Swallow-tribe* 68 *Corvus corax*, the Raven, Great corbiecrow, or *Ravencrow. **1753** HANWAY *Trav.* (1762) I. II. xiv. 61 Sail-cloth, sheetings, *ravenducks and drillings. **1827** ROBERTS *Voy. Centr. Amer.* 36 In exchange we gave them ravenduck, osnaburg, [etc.]. **1755** T. H. CROKER *Orl. Fur.* VI. xxxvi, The salmon, mullet, *raven-fish. *c* **1265** *Voc. Names Plants* in Wr.-Wülcker 556/3 *Pollipodium, poliol*, *reuenfot. *a* **1300** *Cursor M.* 1892 (Gött.) þat messager.. þat duellis lang in his iornay, He may be cald, wid resun clere, An of the *rauyns messagere. **1822** SCOTT *Pirate* xv, To see our barks.. with the black *raven standard waving at the topmost. **1817** BYRON *Manfred* III. i. 74 The raven sits On the *raven-stone. **1871** B. TAYLOR *Faust* I. xxiv, What weave they there round the raven-stone? **1904** *Westm. Gaz.* 23 July 13/1 The '*raven tree' is all that remains.. to remind one of the former existence of these birds in those localities. **1908** *Chambers's Jrnl.* Apr. 284/1 Nearly every parish had its 'raven-tree'.

c. Combs. with *raven's*, as †**raven's bill**, a surgical instrument resembling the bill of a raven; †**raven's bone** (see quots., and cf. *corbin-bone* s.v. CORBIN b); **raven's book**, the list of the dead (*nonce-use*); **raven's duck** = *raven-duck* (Simmonds 1858); **raven's eye**, a species of toadstool; †**raven's morsel** = *corbel's fee* CORBEL *sb.* I.

1597 A. M. tr. *Guillemeau's Fr. Chirurg.* 14b/2, The *Ravens bille, in L. called Rostrum corvinum. **1575** TURBERV. *Venerie* xliii. 135 There is a litle gristle which is vpon the spoone of the brysket, which we cal the *Rauens bone, bycause it is cast vp to the Crowes or Rauens whiche attende hunters. **1637** B. JONSON *Sad Sheph.* I. ii, *Mar.* The brisket bone, upon the spoon Of which a little gristle grows; you call it—— *Rob.* The raven's bone. **1844** W. H. MAXWELL *Sports & Adv. Scotl.* iii. (1855) 53, I am fairly in the *raven's book. **1761** *Newport* (Rhode Island) *Mercury* 28 Apr. 4/3 Just Imported.. Russia and *ravens duck. **1775** in *New Hampsh. Hist. Soc. Coll.* (1863) VII. 4, 120 Tents, to be made of Raven's duck. **1868** G. G. CHANNING *Recoll. Newport* 200 A miller called one day at the store to purchase a piece of ravensduck, with which to make or to repair sails for his windmill. **1931** *Sun* (Baltimore) 12 Jan. 6/6 Hemp sails, known as raven's duck, were used, the cotton duck being unknown at that time. **1822–34** *Good's Study Med.* (ed. 4) I 181 Perhaps the plants that through such an error have been most frequently gathered are, the Medusa's head, the *raven's eye, the hemlock mushroom, and the *agaricus muscarius*. *c* **1500** *Wyl Bucke's Test.* A ij b, The *rauens morsell, sticke hit on a thorne faste. **1575** TURBERV. *Venerie* xlii. 129 The rauens morsell (which is the gryssell at the spoone of the brisket).

B. *attrib.* passing into *adj.* Of the colour of a raven; glossy black; intensely dark or gloomy.

1634 MILTON *Comus* 251 Smoothing the Raven doune Of darknes. **1727–46** THOMSON *Summer* 1088 Thus o'er the prostrate city black Despair Extends her raven wing. **1761** GRAY *Odin* 66 A wondrous boy.. Who ne'er shall comb his raven-hair. **1813** BYRON *Giaour* ix, Here loud his raven charger neigh'd. **1822** SCOTT *Pirate* iii, From her mother Minna inherited the.. dark eyes, the raven locks. **1850** TENNYSON *In Mem.* i, Let darkness keep her raven gloss.

Hence (*nonce-wds.*) **'ravendom**, the community of ravens; **'ravenhood**, the state of being a raven; **'ravenling**, a young raven.

1870 STEWART *Nether Lochaber* xix. 112 Permitted by the laws of ravendom. **1889** *Gd. Words* 483/2 That raven grew to the fullest stature of lusty ravenhood. **1896** E. J. HARDING *Slav Tales* 258 The old raven started off, and Niezginnek still held the ravenling.

raven, *sb.*[2]: see RAVIN[1].

Raven[3] ('reɪv(ə)n). The name of J. C. *Raven*, 20th-cent. psychologist, used *attrib.* and in the possessive with reference to non-verbal intelligence tests devised by him to measure Spearman's *g* factor in the ability to understand abstract relationships, solve problems, etc., and designed to be especially useful where language disadvantages exist; esp. ***Raven('s) Progressive Matrices*** (***Test***).

1948 *Psychometrika* XIII. 28 The results obtained by means of the Raven tests are indicative of the fact that these.. fulfill most of the requirements needed for testing normal and handicapped subjects. *Ibid.* 34 Apart from Raven B.. the remaining tests.. are not loaded in factor *L*. **1954** A. ANASTASI *Psychol. Testing* x. 270 The.. Raven Progressive Matrices Test provides a promising tool for this purpose. **1964** M. CRITCHLEY *Developmental Dyslexia* xiv. 82 On Raven's progressive matrices he scored 32 out of 60: his I.Q. was estimated to be 93. **1972** *Jrnl. Social Psychol.* LXXXVII. 69 Intelligence scores were available only for the controls, who had been administered the Raven's Progressive Matrices Test. **1973** B. B. WOLMAN *Introd. Gen. Psychol.* xxxii. 666/1 One of the most widely used nonverbal tests is the Raven Progressive Matrices Test. *Ibid.*, A vocabulary test is also available to accompany the Raven Matrices. **1976** H. M. PROSHANSKY et al. *Environmental Psychol.* (ed. 2) ix. 129/2 The.. tests of spatial skills were.. a short form (six items) of the Embedded Figures Test.. and the Ravens Matrices.

raven ('ræv(ə)n), *v.* Forms: 6 rau-, ravyne, 6–7 rau-, ravine, 7 rauin, -yn, 7, 9 ravin; 5–7 rau-, 6–7, 9 raven. [ad. OF. *raviner* to ravage:—L. **rapīnāre*, f. *rapīna*: see RAPINE, RAVIN[1].]

†**1.** *trans.* To take (goods) away by force; to seize or divide as spoil. *Obs.*

1494 FABYAN *Chron.* VII. ccxxxvii. 274 His mouable goodys were spoyled and rauenyd amonge y[e] kynges offycers. **1560** DAUS tr. *Sleidane's Comm.* 356 Ravening and destroying his goodes, they spoyled his wife and chyldren of all theyr apparell. **1593** Q. ELIZ. *Boeth.* I. pr. iii. 7 While they be busy to rauyne vnproffitable baggage.

†**b.** Const. *from* prep., *away* adv. *Obs.*

1602 CAREW *Cornwall* 3 The encroaching Sea hath rauined from it the whole Countrie of Lionnesse. **1621** HAKEWILL *David's Vow* 237 Hee.. sought to eat him up, and to raven all hee could get from him. **1657** G. THORNLEY *Daphnis & Chloe* 175 Nor had the Wolf raven'd away so much as one.

c. *absol.* or *intr.* To plunder; to seek *after*, to go *about*, with intent to plunder.

1603 DRAYTON *Bar. Wars* I. vii, [Blood-thirsting Warre] Transferd by fortune to the Scottish meare, To ransack that, as it had rauin'd heere. **1621** MOLLE *Camerar. Liv. Lib.* II. xvi. 125 He goes unto the wars to filch and rauen. **1670** COTTON *Espernon* III. ix. 442 That they might not be disturbed whilst busie ravening after Booty. **1865** CARLYLE *Fredk. Gt.* XX. iv. VI. 92 His Croats and loose hordes went openly ravening about.

2. To devour voraciously. Also *fig.*

1560 BIBLE (Geneva) *Ezek.* xxii. 25 Like a roaring lion rauening the pray. *a* **1571** JEWEL *On 1 Thess.* (1611) 91 The fishes belly destroieth those things which they rauine. **1615** BRATHWAIT *Strappado*, etc. (1878) 278 A Lion new returnde from rauening pray, Came to the fount, his blood to wash away. **1818** KEATS *Endym.* III. 510 Clusters of grapes, the which they raven'd quick. **1875** LOWELL *Poet. Wks.* (1879) 458/2 'Gainst Self's lean wolf that ravens word and deed.

b. So with *up*, *down*, *in*. Now *rare*.

1598 B. JONSON *Ev. Man in Hum.* III. ii, They rauen vp more butter then all the dayes of the weeke beside. **1603** KNOLLES *Hist. Turks* (1621) 833 Certain young men.. like greedie Harpies ravened it downe in a moment. **1607** TOPSELL *Four-f. Beasts* 303 If he rauen it in, as he wil do hauing much at a time. **1683** TRYON *Way to Health* 648

Saturn and Mars..with a fierce hunger destroy and raven up the friendly Properties and Preservatives of Life. **1814** CARY *Dante, Inf.* XXXII. 124 As bread Is raven'd up through hunger.

3. *intr.* or *absol.* To eat voraciously; to feed hungrily or greedily; to prey *on* or *upon*. Also *fig.*

1530 PALSGR. 679/2, I ravyne, I eate hastyly or gredyly. *Je briffe.* He is an horryble lurtcher, se how he ravyneth. **1575–85** ABP. SANDYS *Serm.* (1841) 128 For greedy cormorants to raven upon. **1603** H. CROSSE *Vertues Commw.* (1878) 56 The fish Polipus..doeth rauen vppon other fishes. **1667** *Decay Chr. Piety* ix. §1. 299 Those wild irregular flames which ravine and consume. **1811** JEFFERSON *Writ.* (1830) IV. 164 Our printers ravin on the agonies of their victims. **1862** S. LUCAS *Secularia* 376 They equally ravened on a smaller community.

b. To have a ravenous appetite or desire *for*.

1667 DRYDEN *Wild Gallant* IV. ii, She..ravens mightily for green fruit. **1687** —— *Hind & P.* III. 964 The more they fed, they ravened still for more. **1883** T. FOSTER in *Knowledge* 20 July 38/1 Beasts..ravening for blood and slaughter.

c. To have an intense longing for food. Also *fig.*

1858 BUSHNELL *Serm. New Life* 66 Those divine affinities in us that raven with immortal hunger. **1881** *Blackw. Mag.* CXXIX. 194 If I know anything of your constitution..you must have been ravening hours ago.

4. *intr.* To prowl ravenously; to go about in search of food.

1560 BIBLE (Geneva) *Gen.* xlix. 27 Beniamin shall rauine (as) a wolfe. **1577** B. GOOGE *Heresbach's Husb.* (1586) 155 b, Let them want no meate, for if they doe, they will for hunger rauen abroad. **1680** H. MORE *Apocal. Apoc.* 124 His feet..which are his strength and instrument of action to raven and prey with. **1877** M. M. GRANT *Sun-Maid* i, Fierce fiery lions went ravening to and fro.

fig. **1851** DIXON *W. Penn* xxvi. (1872) 236 Persecution had ravened through the land. **1857** RUSKIN *Pol. Econ. Art* 17 The unclean pestilence ravins in your streets.

Hence **'ravened** *ppl. a.*, ? glutted.

1605 SHAKS. *Macb.* IV. i. 24 Maw, and Gulfe Of the rauin'd salt Sea sharke.

†**'ravenage.** *Obs. rare*⁻¹. [f. RAVEN *v.* + -AGE.] Ravenousness.

1673 *Jackson's Creed* x. xxxvi. *Publisher's Notes*, The ravenage or voracity of dogs is such that..a diseased appetite in man is therefore denamed caninus appetitus.

ravene, obs. form of RAVEN *sb.*, RAVIN[1].

ravener ('ræv(ə)nə(r)). Forms: α. 4 rauaynour, 4–5 raueynour; 4 rauynour, (5 -or, -oure), 4–6 ravinour; 4–7 rauenour, -or, (5 -owre). β. 5 raveyner; 4–6 rau-, raviner, 5–6 ravyner; 4–6 rauener, 6 rauenar, rav'ner, 5– ravener. [a. OF. *ravineor, -our* (13th c. in Godef.):—L. *rapīnātōr-em*: see RAVEN *v.* and -OR, -ER. In common use from end of 14th to end of 17th c.; now *rare* or *Obs.*]

1. One who ravens or takes goods by force; a robber, plunderer, despoiler.

α. *c* **1374** CHAUCER *Boeth.* IV. pr. iii. 94 (Camb. MS.) Yif he ..be a rauaynour by vyolence of foreyne rychesse. *c* **1442** *Jacob's Well* (E.E.T.S.) 17 Alle þat comaundyn oþere to don raveyn & thefte, & alle raueynoures. **1539** TONSTALL *Serm. Palm Sund.* (1823) 67 To make this realme a praye to al venturers, al spoylers,..all rauenours of the worlde. **1610** HOLLAND *Camden's Brit.* I. 108 These shamelesse Irish ravenours returne home.

β. *c* **1375** *XI Pains Hell* 36 in *O.E. Misc.* 211 þese were proud men, raueners echon. **1393** LANGL. *P. Pl. C.* XVIII. 43 Men of holy churche Sholde..refuse reuerences and raueneres offrynges. *c* **1440** *Jacob's Well* (E.E.T.S.) 56 Alle opyn thevys, & alle false raveynerys, murdereres, nyȝt-thevys. *c* **1580** SIDNEY *Ps.* XVII. iv, Ledd by thy word, the rav'ners stepps I shun. **1632** LITHGOW *Trav.* III. 99 These ..Seas, are free from pestilent Raueners. **1697** C. LESLIE *Snake in Grass* (ed. 2) 96 Raveners from Christ, and his utter Enemies.

2. A deforcer, ravisher, destroyer, etc. *rare.*

1390 GOWER *Conf.* II. 312 Schrif thee hier, If thou hast ben a Raviner Of love. *Ibid.* 316 And so that tirant raviner, Whan that sche was in his pouer. **1594** CAREW *Tasso* (1881) 68 That murderer, Of my bloud royall cruell rauiner.

3. A ravenous or voracious animal or person; a glutton.

α. **1496** *Fysshynge w. Angle* (1883) 30 The ele is a quasy fysshe, a rauenour & a deuourer of the brode of fysshe. **1567** MAPLET *Gr. Forest* 94 The mouse..is for his bignes a verie rauenour or greedigut. **1591** LODGE *Catharos* D ij b, These two bold rauenors, seeking in the Summer euening for their ..Supper. **1601** HOLLAND *Pliny* I. 243 As for the sea Pontus, there enter into it few or no rauenours that haunt and deuoure fishes, vnlesse it be the Seales & little Dolphins.

β. **1520** WHITINTON *Vulg.* (1527) 13 He is great ravener, specyally if he come there as be good dysshes. **1577** tr. *Bullinger's Decades* (1592) 384 Of Birdes those are forbidden which are the greatest raueners. **1627** BP. HALL *Imprese of God* II. Wks. 456 This honie of the Church..is let downe and digested by these raueners. **1638** RAWLEY tr. *Bacon's Life & Death* (1650) 11 The Pike, amongst Fishes..is a Ravener.

b. With preps., as *after*, *for*, *of*.

1519 HORMAN *Vulg.* 71 Thou arte a rauenar of delicates and a francher. **1587** MASCALL *Govt. Cattle, Hogges* (1627) 255 The hog..is a great rauener for his meate. **1614** B. JONSON *Barth. Fair* I. i, He is such a ravener after fruit. **1692** R. L'ESTRANGE *Fables* II. clxxviii. (1699) 166 Well! says the Fox, and nobody will Tax me..for a Ravener of Roots and Apples.

raveness ('reɪvənɪs). [f. RAVEN *sb.* + -ESS.] A she-raven.

1623 WODROEPHE *Marrow Fr. Tongue* 321/2 The Rauen loues his Rauenesse, because he finds her most faire. **1870** STEWART *Nether Lochaber* xix. (1883) 112 Flirtations..with a neighbouring raveness.

ravening ('ræv(ə)nɪŋ), *vbl. sb.* [f. RAVEN *v.*]

1. The action of the vb. in its various senses.

1526 TINDALE *Luke* xi. 39 Youre inwarde parties are full of raveninge and wickednes. **1567** MAPLET *Gr. Forest* 49 b, The Wolfe, and all other beastes, those especially which liue by rauening. **1614** RALEIGH *Hist. World* III. (1634) 11 The art of ravening which is familiar to such as liue or border upon desarts. *a* **1713** ELLWOOD *Autobiog.* (1765) 154 To whom his Company was as offensive, as his Ravening was oppressive. **1854** MRS. GASKELL *North & S.* xxii, The dæmoniac desire of some terrible wild beast for the food that is withheld from his ravening. **1874** S. WILBERFORCE *Ess.* (1874) I. 285 An instance of selfish ravening for wealth.

†**2.** Madness, rabies. Also with *pl.*: A fit of madness. *Obs.* (? for RAVING *vbl. sb.*[1])

1607 TOPSELL *Four-f. Beasts* (1658) 568 The biting of a Weasel is reported..in his ravening or madnesse not to be lesse hurtfull then the bitings of mad Dogs. **1668** CULPEPPER & COLE *Barthol. Anat.* III. vi. 142 The overgreat and confused motion of these Idea's..makes ravenings, as in persons drunk, phrentick, [etc.].

ravening ('ræv(ə)nɪŋ), *ppl. a.* [f. RAVEN *v.*]

1. That ravens, in senses of the vb.; rapacious, voracious, etc. (In early use esp. of wolves.)

1526 *Pilgr. Perf.* (W. de W. 1531) 129 They wyll appere in terryble similitudes..as rauenynge wolves or rampynge lyons. **1548** UDALL, etc. *Erasm. Par. Matt.* v. 43 He hathe well cutte of his rauenyng ryght handle. **1601** R. JOHNSON *Kingd. & Commw.* 25 The Iland breedeth no woolues nor any other rauening beasts. **1670** MILTON *Hist. Eng.* III. Wks. (1851) 96 The ravening seizure of innumerable Thieves in Office. **1767** SIR W. JONES *Seven Fountains* Poems (1777) 50 A cave, where ravening monsters roar. **1822** SHELLEY *Hellas* 510 Some ships lay feeding The ravening fire. **1887** BOWEN *Virg. Æneid* II. 355 Wolves whom ravening hunger has driven all blind on the path.

†**2.** Rabid, mad. *Obs.* (? for RAVING *ppl. a.*[1])

1598 MARSTON *Sco. Villanie* I. iv. 190 To liue happily (I heare thee boast) from thy Philosophy, And from thy selfe, O rauening lunacy! **1607** TOPSELL *Four-f. Beasts* (1658) 584 A ravening Wolf by his biting bringeth the same danger, as a ravenous Dog. **1696** BP. PATRICK *Comm. Exodus* (1697) 175 In his ravening fit he called for Moses, as if he had been near him.

Hence †**'raveningly** *adv.*, ravenously. *Obs.*

1533 UDALL *Flowres* 100 b, Gredily and rauenninglye, or gluttonously to deuour veri moch. **1600** F. WALKER *Sp. Mandeville* 146 The Wolues..very raueningly with open mouth assayling them.

†**'ravenish,** *a. Obs. rare*⁻¹. [f. RAVEN *sb.*[1] + -ISH[1].] Blackish. (The quot. is burlesque.)

? *c* **1450** *Ballad Pleasant* in Stow's *Chaucer* (1561) 344/2 Her iyen been holow, and grene as any grasse And Rauinish yelowe is her sounitresse [? *read* sonni tresse].

†**'ravenize,** *v. Obs. rare*⁻¹. [f. *raven* RAVIN[1] + -IZE.] *intr.* To raven.

1677 W. HUGHES *Man of Sin* II. x. 189 That Great Beast of Prey, the Court of Rome, hath ravenized so, as to tear the flesh and break the bones together.

Ravenna (rə'vɛnə). The name of a town in northern Italy, used *absol.* or *attrib.* in *Ravenna grass* to designate *Erianthus ravennæ*, a large ornamental grass native to southern Europe and distinguished by greyish leaves and spikes of purplish-grey flowers.

1900 L. H. BAILEY *Cycl. Amer. Hort.* II. 540/1 Ravenna Grass. A tall, hardy grass, 4–7 ft. high, very ornamental. **1929** J. W. BEWS *World's Grasses* vi. 243 'Ravenna' is a Mediterranean species, extending as far north as upper Italy. **1976** G. S. THOMAS *Perennial Garden Plants* x. 308 Ravenna Grass. In hot summers this grass is a striking addition to the garden.

ravenous ('ræv(ə)nəs), *a.* Forms: 5 rav-, rauynous, ravenus, 5–7 rauenous, -ouse, (7 *Sc.* -ows), 5– ravenous; 6 rauynys, *Sc.* rawynnis. [a. OF. *ravineux, -os, -ous*, etc. (see Godef.) :—pop.L. **rapīnōsus*: see RAPINE, RAVIN[1], and -OUS.]

1. Addicted to plundering or taking by force; extremely rapacious. (Sometimes *transf.* from 2.)

1412–20 LYDG. *Chron. Troy* IV. xxxv, There is no degre Gredyer nor more rauynous Than priestes be. **1538** STARKEY *England* I. iv. 127 Spoylyd of the rauynys and pollyng offycerys. **1560** DAUS tr. *Sleidane's Comm.* 269 The hors-men of Hungary are commonly called Hussares, an exceadyng ravenous and cruell kynde of men. **1601** B. JONSON *Poetaster* v. i, Thus oft, the base and ravenous multitude Survive, to share the spoils of fortitude. **1725** DE FOE *Voy. round World* (1840) 183 Nations who were ravenous and mischievous, treacherous and fierce. **1855** MACAULAY *Hist. Eng.* xiv. III. 424 A crowd of negligent or ravenous functionaries..plundered, starved, and poisoned the armies and fleets of William.

2. Of animals: Given to seizing in order to devour; voracious, gluttonous. Hence of appetite, hunger, etc. (Freq. in fig. context.)

c **1430** LYDG. *Min. Poems* (Percy Soc.) 159 Thus by a maner of simylitude, Tirauntys [are] lyknyd to beestis ravynous. **1496** *Fysshynge w. Angle* (1883) 30 The menow..is a rauenous biter & an egre. **1522** MORE *De quat. Noviss.* Wks. 95 The rauenous appetite of dilicate meate & drink. **1590** SPENSER *F.Q.* I. xi. 12 Dead was it sure..What ever thing does touch his ravenous pawes. **1667** MILTON *P.L.* x. 991 Death shall..with us two Be forc'd to satisfie his Rav'nous Maw. **1719** DE FOE *Crusoe* I. xx. 353 The ravenous Creatures..were come down into the Forest and plain Country, press'd by Hunger to seek for Food. **1835** W. IRVING *Tour Prairies* 157 The black wolves, in their ravenous hunger and fury, took no notice of the distant group of horsemen. *a* **1859** MACAULAY *Hist. Eng.* xxiii. V. 21 He rushed with ravenous eagerness at every bait which was offered to his cupidity.

transf. **1598** SHAKS. *Merch. V.* IV. i. 138 Thy desires Are Woluish, bloody, steru'd, and rauenous. *c* **1614** SIR W. MURE *Dido & Æneas* I. 227 Let louse the winds, thy rav'nows postes imploy, Disperse their navie, and themselves destroy. *a* **1845** HOOD *Last Man* xxxii, Their jaws all white with foam Like the ravenous ocean brim.

b. Const. *of*.

a **1614** DONNE *Βιαθανατος* (1644) 65 For that age was growne so hungry and ravenous of it, that many were baptized onely because they would be burnt. **1856** KANE *Arct. Expl.* II. i. 13 They [dogs] are absolutely ravenous of every thing below the human grade. **1882** BLUNT *Ref. Ch. Eng.* II. 23 That full exercise of power of which he was ever so ravenous in all ecclesiastical matters.

3. Excessively hungry.

1719 DE FOE *Crusoe* II. viii. (1840) 184, I got up ravenous. **1877** BLACK *Green Past.* xlii. (1878) 337 Handsome girls who waited on the crowd of ravenous people.

†**4.** = RAVENING *ppl. a.* 2. *Obs. rare.*

1607 [see RAVENING *ppl. a.* 2]. **1624** QUARLES *Job* xviii. 73 Then how dare Thy ravenous lips thus, thus at randome runne, And counter-maund what I the Lord have done?

ravenously ('ræv(ə)nəslɪ), *adv.* [f. prec. + -LY[2].] In a ravenous manner.

1538 ELYOT, *Lurco*, to eate rauenously. **1611** COTGR., *Gloutement*, gluttonously, rauenously, greedily. *a* **1715** BURNET *Own Time* II. (1724) I. 245 She..lived at a vast expence, and was ravenously covetous. **1791** BOSWELL *Johnson* an. 1778, 15 Apr., Dr. Johnson..seemed to read it ravenously as if he devoured it. **1845** DARWIN *Voy. Nat.* ix. (1879) 184 It began ravenously to tear a piece of carrion. **1907** G. B. SHAW *Major Barbara* II. 217 Shirley (looking at it ravenously but not touching it..). *Ibid.*, (He turns to the table and attacks the meal ravenously). **1915** W. S. MAUGHAM *Of Human Bondage* xliv. 211 She could not have eaten more ravenously if she were starving. **1951** C. S. LEWIS *Prince Caspian* iii. 37 He would have made much more fuss about this if he had not by now been so ravenously hungry.

ravenousness ('ræv(ə)nəsnɪs). [f. as prec. + -NESS.] The quality or fact of being ravenous; rapacity, voracity.

1570 GOLDING *Justin* xxxviii. 157 b, The greedy rauenousnesse of their Proconsulles. **1600** SURFLET *Countrie Farme* I. xxiv. 147 The rauenousnes and greedie feeding of this beast. **1656** EARL MONM. tr. *Boccalini's Advts. fr. Parnass.* I. lxxvii. (1674) 101 To defend their own Estates from the ravenousness of these Harpies. *a* **1715** BURNET *Own Time* II. (1724) I. 224 [The treasure] was by the unpatient ravenousness of the English lost. **1829** J. L. KNAPP *Jrnl. Nat.* 304 There are natural causes which render these apparent asylums the field of ravenousness and death.

ravenry ('reɪv(ə)nrɪ). [f. RAVEN *sb.*[1] + -RY.] A place where ravens build their nests or are kept.

1888 *Nature* 26 Apr. 602/2 Nothing short of a reward given on the hatching-off of a ravenry..would insure protection.

Ravenscroft ('reɪvənzkrɒft). [The name of George *Ravenscroft* (1618–81), English glass-maker.] An article made of the flint-glass or lead-glass devised by George Ravenscroft. Also *attrib.* or as *adj.*

1929 W. A. THORPE *Hist. Eng. & Irish Glass* I. iv. 128 Threads of trailed glass applied on the surface..are evident in several marked Ravenscroft glasses. **1948** E. B. HAYNES *Glass through Ages* I. ix. 127 This..piece must be a Ravenscroft glass, perhaps the first example to be found with the plain seal. **1961** E. M. ELVILLE *Collector's Dict. Glass* 87/1 (*caption*) Ravenscroft roemer bearing the seal of the raven's head..circa 1677. **1970** G. SAVAGE *Dict. Antiques* 348/1 (*caption*) A rare Ravenscroft showing signs of criselling... Lead glass. 17th century. **1975** *Country Life* 2 Jan. 11/3 (*heading*) A Syllabub Jug in Ravenscroft Glass. *Ibid.*, This jug..is typical Ravenscroft of, I suppose, the late 1680s. **1976** *Times* 4 May 14/6 A documentary item of the beginning of English glass, a Ravenscroft silver-mounted and engraved decanter jug,..sold for £2,420.

†**'raveny.** *Obs.* Also 6 -any. [f. RAVEN *v.* + -Y[3].] Robbery, rapine.

1506 *Kalender of Sheph.* F iij, Thoughe thou loue rauany as dothe a roke, Goodes of this worlde maketh many one blynde. **1548** UDALL, etc. *Erasm. Par. Mark* i. 12 Nothing whose nature wurse agreeth with fighting and raueny. **1577** tr. *Bullinger's Decades* (1592) 749 The diuell..is full of greedie rauenie, and most cruell fiercenes.

raver ('reɪvə(r)). Forms: 5 rafar, ravare, 6 *Sc.* ravar, 6–7 rauer, 9 raver. [f. RAVE *v.*[1] + -ER[1].]

a. One who raves; a madman; an extravagant speaker.

c **1400** *Apol. Loll.* 96 Sum tyme men wen to see a þing wan þei see it not, as is schewid bi jogulors, dremers, & rafars. *c* **1440** *Promp. Parv.* 424/2 Ravare, *delirus, delirator.* *c* **1570** *Satir. Poems Reform.* xxxvii. 69 Rek not, þairfoir, how raschelie ravarris raill. **1632** SHERWOOD, A rauer, *resveur.* **1800** MOORE *Anacreon* liii. 19 He still can act the mellow raver, And play the fool as sweet as ever!

b. A passionate enthusiast for a particular thing, idea, or cause; a fanatic. Also, one who likes to 'live it up' or have a wild time esp. in sexual relationships (cf. RAVE *v.*[1] 3 b). *slang.*

1959 C. MacInnes *Absolute Beginners* 63, I did actually begin to be a raver for those weekly meetings. **1960** [see mod *sb.*[3] and *a.*]. **1961** *Guardian* 6 Mar. 3/4 The bearded ravers usually associated with the more esoteric ranges of HiFi. **1968** Busby & Holtham *Main Line Kill* v. 44 There's a bloke I know makes his own LSD. Some of the ravers are giving it a try. **1971** *Cape Herald* 15 May 7/4 She looks like a raver But I could never please her. **1976** P. Cave *High Flying Birds* iii. 31 She was neither attractive nor plain; not a raver or a ragbag. **1976** *Listener* 22 Jan. 84/2 Things hot up when a raver and his girl swoop in by motor-bike. **1978** *Sunday Mail* (Brisbane) 24 Sept. 34/4, I have never analysed why, but many pop musicians are ravers—people who like to live it up—with a strong self-destructive streak.

ravers (ˈreɪvəz), *pred. a. slang.* [f. rav(ing *ppl. a.*[1]; cf. crackers *pred. a.*] Raving mad, delirious. Also, in weakened sense, furious, angry.

1938 N. Marsh *Death in White Tie* xxii. 242 Bart has driven me stark ravers, he's been so awful. **1939** —— *Overture to Death* xvii. 189 In Henry's..opinion Miss Prentice is practically ravers. **1951** E. Hyams *Sylvester* xxviii. 150 'You said you wanted to meet Sylvester Green. Well, here I am.'.. 'Stark ravers. I served for two years with Green. This man isn't even much like him.' **1967** N. Marsh *Death at Dolphin* iv. 100 Jeremy..will probably go stark ravers if they're sold out of the country.

ravery (ˈreɪvərɪ). *Obs.* exc. *dial.* [? a. OF. *raverie*, rare var. of *rêverie* reverie: see rave *v.*[1]] Raging, raving, madness or delirium. Also with *a* and *pl.*, an instance of this; a fit of raving.

c **1400** *Laud Troy Bk.* (E.E.T.S.) 11365 How he sclow In his rauery The douȝti kyng Prothesaly! **1594** A. Hume *Hymns* To Rdr. (S.T.S.) 6 To rehearse some fabulos faits of Palmerine, Amadis, or other such like raueries. **1659** Macallo *Can. Physick* 8 Raving or Ravery designes the braine to be distempered. **1687** A. Lovell tr. *Thevenot's Trav.* ii. 105 If the King have sense enough not to give credit to all their raveries. **1721** Wodrow *Hist. Suff. Ch. Scot.* (1828) III. 348 The raveries and blasphemies emitted by John Gib. **1895** *E. Anglian Gloss.*, *Ravary*, a violent mad fit of passion, attended with loud vociferation.

ravestre, Sc. variant of revestry.

ravet (ˈrævɪt), variant of rabbet *sb.*[1] ? *Obs.*

1679 Rusden *Discov. Bees* 78 The two front doors to shut close against a ravet. **1794** W. Felton *Carriages* (1801) II. Suppl. 86 Rub the shutting edges, or ravets, with soap.

raveyn(e, obs. forms of ravin[1].

‖**ravigote** (ravigɔt). Also ravigotte. [Fr., f. *ravigoter* to invigorate.] (See quot. 1877.)

1830 R. Dolby *Cook's Dict.* 435/2 *Ravigote*, shred.. chervil, chives, pimpernel, and tarragon; this latter ought to predominate; (the mixture of these articles constitutes the *ravigote*); take some *velouté*,..add..butter and the *ravigote*; stir.., and serve. **1861** Mrs. Beeton *Bk. Househ. Managem.* 240 Ravigotte, a French Salad Sauce. **1877** E. S. Dallas *Kettner's Bk. of Table* 373 *Ravigote*, pick-me-up..from the French verb *ravigoter*, to cheer or strengthen... The French give the name of Ravigote to an assemblage of four herbs—tarragon, chervil, chives, burnet—minced small or used as a faggot, and supposed..to have a rare faculty of resuscitation. *Ibid.*, *Ravigote sauce* is simply the English butter sauce to which a ravigote is added. **1943** D. Powell *Time to be Born* x. 255 A dish of crab meat ravigote. **1951** *Good Housek. Home Encycl.* 594/1 Serve with a ravigote sauce flavoured with chopped chives, chervil and tarragon. **1964** A. Launay *Caviare & After* 142 *Ravigotte*, a highly-seasoned white sauce which is served either hot or cold. **1975** *Amer. Speech 1969* XLIV. 94 There is one instance of *ravigote*, but with two *t*'s, in *crabmeat ravigotte*..; it is 'a sauce or dressing coloured green with spinach purée and seasoned with vinegar and a mixture of herbs'.

raviling, obs. form of ravelin.

ravin[1] (ˈrævɪn), **raven**[2] (ˈræv(ə)n). Forms: α. 4–6 rau-, ravyn(e, 6 *Sc.* rawyne, 4–7 rauine, 6–7 -in, 4– ravine, 5– ravin. β. 4–5 rau-, raveyn, 4–6 rau-, raveyne, -ayn(e. γ. 4–7 rauen, 6 ravene, 4– raven. [a. F. *ravine* (†*rabine, raveine*, 12th c.):—L. *rapīna* rapine. The orig. sense of the word is now lost in Fr., see ravine *sb.*]

1. a. Robbery, rapine. (Sometimes *fig.* from 2.)

α. **1340** Hampole *Pr. Consc.* 3368 Thefte alswa and ravyn, Ilkan of þir es a dedly syn. *c* **1400** *Rom. Rose* 6813 Bailifs, bedels, provost, countours! These lyven wel nygh by ravyne. **1484** Caxton *Fables of Æsop* iii. vi, He that lyueth but of rauyn and robberye shal at the last be knowen and robbed. **1570–6** Lambarde *Peramb. Kent* (1826) 95 Oppressing the common people by insatiable rauine, extortion, and tyrannie. **1629** Maxwell tr. *Herodian* (1635) 103 Yet shall you want nothing which is..not clogged with violence and ravine. **1728–46** Thomson *Spring* 339 With hot ravine fir'd, ensanguin'd Man Is now become the lion of the plain. **1862** Rawlinson *Anc. Mon.* I. *Assyria* iii. 308 Blood, and ravin, and robbery are their characteristics.

β. *c* **1380** Wyclif *Serm.* Sel. Wks. I. 3 Sum men shal be dampnyd more felly for raveyne. *c* **1430** Lydg. *Min. Poems* (Percy Soc.) 210 To punysshe extorcioun, raveyne, and eche robbour. **1483** Caxton *Gold. Leg.* 88/1 He wold kepe hys people fro the Rauayne that they made. *c* **1520** *Treat. Galaunt* (1860) 21 Prelatis necligence, lordis rauayn, and marchauntis deceytes.

γ. **1502** Arnolde *Chron.* (1821) 240 Do thy besy deuor From my folke al rauen to disseuor. *c* **1510** More *Picus* Wks. 22 If thou withdrawe thine handes, and forbere The rauen of anything. **1617** Fletcher *Valentinian* v. iv, Why doe we like to feed the greedy Raven Of these blowne men? **1826** E. Irving *Babylon* II. viii. 303 A generation of raven and blood-thirstiness.

†**b.** With *a* and *pl.*: An act of rapine. *Obs.*

c **1374** Chaucer *Boeth.* i. pr. iv. 9 (Camb. MS.) Whan I say the fortunes..of poeple of þe prouinces ben harmyd.. by pryuey Raueynes [L. *privatis rapinis*]. **1475** *Bk. Noblesse* (Roxb.) 73 Suche oppressions and tirannyes, ravynes and crueltees. **1546** J. Heywood *Prov.* (1867) 77 Sens we were borne, Ruine of one rauine, was there none gretter. **1593** Q. Eliz. tr. *Boeth.* i. pr. iv. 9, I sorowed for the provinces misfortunes, wrackt by private ravins and publick taxes.

2. a. The act or practice of seizing and devouring prey or food; hence, voracity, gluttony.

c **1381** Chaucer *Parl. Foules* 336 þe goshauke that dothe pyne To bryddis for his outragious ravine. *c* **1440** Hylton *Scala Perf.* (W. de W. 1494) ii. xiv, Some men are torned into wulfes that lyuen by raueyn. **1578** *Chr. Prayers* A iv, Preserue me from..pride of eyes, rauine of the belly,.. hunger of richesse, [etc.]. **1609** Holland *Amm. Marcell.* xv. v. 57 As wild beasts, wont to liue of ravine and prey. **1691** Ray *Creation* (1714) 119 Exposed to the Ravine of any vermine that may find them. **1856** Ruskin *Mod. Paint.* IV. v. xviii. §26 Their pastured flocks..safe from the eagle's stoop and the wolf's ravin. **1935** W. Empson *Poems* 4 Nor heeds if the core be brown with maggots' raven.

b. *beast* (etc.) *of ravin*: beast of prey.

1340 Hampole *Pr. Consc.* 9448 Many hydus bestes of ravyn, Als wode wolfes, lyons and beres felle. *c* **1400** Maundev. (Roxb.) xxxiv. 153 Vowltures, egles, rauyns, and oþer fewlez of rauyne. **1503** Dunbar *Thistle & Rose* 125 And lat no fowll of rawyne do efferay. **1623** Lisle *Ælfric on O. & N. Test.* Ded. 32 To keepe Your flocks within, and beasts of ravine out. **1641** Milton *Animadv.* Wks. (1851) 233 The very garbage that drawes all the fowles of prey and ravin..to come, and gorge upon the Church. **1897** F. Thompson *New Poems* 143 All fair strong beasts of ravin.

†**c.** A beast of prey. *Obs. rare*$^{-1}$.

1623 Fletcher & Rowley *Maid in Mill* v. ii, Seiz'd on by a fierce and hungry Bear She was the Ravin's prey.

†**d.** Ravenous hunger. *Obs. rare*$^{-1}$.

1649 G. Daniel *Trinarch.*, *Hen. V*, cci, A Tiger, (whom lanke Ravin fires To sett vpon the Herds).

3. *concr.* That which is taken or seized; plunder, spoil; prey (of men or beasts).

a **1325** *Prose Psalter* lxi. 10 Ne wil ȝe nouȝt couaite rauyns. **1382** Wyclif *Nahum* ii. 12 The lyoun..fulfillede with praye her dennys, and his couche with rauyn [**1388** raueyn]. **1590** Spenser *F.Q.* i. xi. 12 His deepe devouring iawes Wyde gaped,..Through which into his darke abysse all ravin fell. **1667** Milton *P.L.* x. 599 There best, where most with ravin I may meet. **1836** *For. Q. Rev.* XVII. 163 There are others again which leap like tigers suddenly upon their ravin. **1860** Pusey *Min. Proph.* 238 Petra..was well suited to be the receptacle of ravin.

4. *attrib.* as *adj.* = ravenous.

1423 Jas. I. *Kingis Q.* clvii, The lesty beuer and the ravin bare. **1601** Shaks. *All's Well* iii. ii. 120, I met the rauine Lyon. **1615** Crooke *Body of Man* 165 The great abundance of meate deuoured by Rauen-stomackes and Trencher-friends.

†**'ravin**[2]. *Obs.* [a. F. *ravin* (1690), f. *raviner* to hollow out, to ravine.] = ravine *sb.* 3.

1760–72 tr. *Juan & Ulloa's Voy.* (ed. 3) I. 153 The inconveniences of the ravins are avoided. **1785** *Phil. Trans.* LXXV. 18, I found myself in the bottom of a narrow and deep ravin. **1813** Hobhouse *Journey* (ed. 2) 444 Uneven downs..terminating in heaths intersected by several ravins.

ravin, obs. f. raven *sb.*, var. raven *v.*

'ravinated, *ppl. a.* = ravined *ppl. a.*

1898 *Eclectic Mag.* LXVII. 646 The Urals..represent a wide expansion of ravinated plateaus.

ravine (rəˈviːn), *sb.* Also 5 ravayn, ravyne. [a. F. *ravine* a violent rush (now only of water), a ravine; identical with *ravine* ravin[1].]

†**1.** Impetus, violence, force. *Obs. rare.*

c **1450** *Merlin* 127 Bretell smote hym a-gein..with so grete ravayn that the spere ran thourgh his left sholder. *Ibid.* 324 Thei..spored theire horse and smote in-to the hoste with grete ravyne.

†**2.** A violent rush of water. *Obs. rare*$^{-0}$.

1611 Cotgr., *Ravine d'eau*, a great floud, a rauine, or inundation of water which ouerwhelmeth all things that come in it way.

3. A deep narrow hollow or gorge, a mountain cleft, properly one worn by a torrent. Also *fig.*

Cf. the earlier ravin[2], the stressing of which is sometimes found with the spelling *ravine* (see quot. 1807 here, and those for *ravine-pass, -rifted* in 4).

1781 G. Washington *Diary* 30 Sept. (1925) II. 263 We also began two inclosed works on the right of Pidgeon Hill —between that and the Ravine above Moves Hill. **1802** James *Milit. Dict.*, *Ravine*,..a deep hollow [etc.]. **1807** J. Barlow *Columb.* i. 267 Round each bluff base the sloping ravine bends. **1814** Scott *Ld. of Isles* iii. xiv, Each naked precipice, Sable ravine, and dark abyss. **1837** W. Irving *Capt. Bonneville* III. 189 Obliged to travel along the edges of frightful ravines, where a false step would have been fatal. **1853** Herschel *Pop. Lect. Sc.* i. §41 (1873) 31 The river had run in a ravine, 600 ft. deep and 200 broad. **1926** [see peak *sb.*[2] 5 c]. **1930** R. Campbell *Adamastor* 51 The phosphorescent whales..Bore through the gloom their long ravines of gold.

4. *attrib.* and *Comb.*, as ***ravine-gully, -pass***; ***ravine-like, -loving, -rifted, -wrinkled*** adjs.; **ravine-buck, -deer**, the Indian gazelle (*Gazella Bennettii*), which frequents ravines.

1877 J. H. Baldwin *Game Bengal*, etc. 202, I..informed my Commandant how I had disposed of one of the *ravine bucks. **1894** Phillips-Wolley *Big Game Shooting* II. xlix. 356 A ravine buck with a broken leg will give a good run to dogs. **1867** Jerdon *Mammals India* 280 *Ravine-deer of sportsmen in Bengal—Goat-antelope in Bombay and Madras. **1877** J. H. Baldwin *Game Bengal*, etc. 204 The little ravine deer is a regular bush-loving antelope, and much resembles a wild goat in its appearance and habits. *a* **1930** D. H. Lawrence *Etruscan Places* (1932) 22 A modest, Italian sort of *ravine-gully. **1885** H. O. Forbes *Nat. Wand. E. Archip.* 75 The parched surface of the ground broke up into *ravine-like cracks. **1861** R. F. Burton *City of Saints* 224 The *ravine-loving quaking-asp (*Populus tremuloides*). **1845** Mrs. Norton *Child of Islands* (1846) 93 Down *ravine-pass and mountain-gorge. **1832** J. Bree *St. Herbert's Isle* 68 To high Blencathra's *ravine-rifted head. **1950** C. Day Lewis in *Penguin New Writing* XXXIX. 20 Earth's face grew rapidly older, *ravine-wrinkled.

ra'vine, *v. rare.* [f. prec. sb. or a. F. *raviner* in same sense.] *trans.* **a.** To score with ravines. **b.** To hollow *out*.

1858 G. P. Scrope *Geol. Central France* (ed. 2) 167 Causes which have cut up and ravined to a great depth..Les Bouttieres. **1896** Howells *Impressions & Exp.* 258 A gulf ravined out of the bank for a street.

ravine, obs. form of raven *v.*

ravined (rəˈviːnd), *ppl. a.* [f. ravine *sb.* or *v.* + -ed.] Marked with ravines, furrowed.

1854 Ct. E. de Warren tr. *De Sauley's Journ. Dead Sea* II. 64 Between us and the sea, a large ravined plain extends. **1859** G. Meredith *R. Feverel* xxxiv, There hung Briareus with deep-indented trunk and ravined brows.

ravinement (rəˈviːnmənt). *Geol.* [a. F. *ravinement* gullying.] An unconformity in river or shallow marine sediments caused by interruption of deposition by erosion.

1921 L. D. Stamp in *Geol. Mag.* LVIII. 109 A 'ravinement' may be defined as an irregular junction which marks a break in sedimentation... Although one of the commonest of geological phenomena, there is no English word which expresses quite so aptly the relationship. *Ibid.*, The period between two successive 'ravinements' constitutes a 'cycle of sedimentation'. **1923** —— *Introd. Stratigr.* i. 17 When such an unconformity is traced laterally into a continuous series of marine deposits it is frequently found that, although the bedding of the upper series is parallel to that of the lower, there are signs that the sea, in depositing the upper series, has slightly eroded the top of the lower series. Such an erosion line is termed a 'ravinement'. **1969** Bennison & Wright *Geol. Hist. Brit. Isles* i. 8 In the field an unconformity can..be proved because the erosion surface or ravinement is conspicuous.

ravinere, obs. form of ravener.

raving (ˈreɪvɪŋ), *vbl. sb.*[1] [-ing[1].] The action of rave *v.*[1]; wild or delirious talk or declamation.

c **1440** *Promp. Parv.* 424/2 Ravynge, *deliracio*. **1530** Tindale *Answ. More* Wks. 285 That stoppyng of her throte, that rauyng, those greuous panges. **1624** Massinger *Renegado* iv. i, Our best hope for his recovery is that His raving leaves him. **1711** Addison *Spect.* No. 46 ¶1 There is nothing in them but Obscurity and Confusion, Raving and Inconsistency. **1803** Chalmers *Let.* in *Life* (1851) I. 480 In vain will you say that this is idle and declamatory raving.

attrib. **1749** Fielding *Tom Jones* xi. iv, Imagine the maddest woman in Bedlam in a raving fit.

b. With *a* and *pl.* An utterance of this kind; †a fit of madness.

c **1475** *Rauf Coilȝear* 895 Schir Rolland, I rek nocht of thy Rauingis. **1638** A. Read *Chirurg.* x. 75 A convulsion or raving, which ensueth after immoderate bleeding. **1798** Ferriar *Illustr. Sterne* etc. *Of Genius* 286 The ravings of lunatics have often been more regarded than the arguments of wise men. **1885** *Manch. Exam.* 7 Jan. 5/2 We hear ravings over here about 'one-sided' Free Trade.

raving, *vbl. sb.*[2] and [3]: see rave *v.*[3] and *v.*[4]

raving (ˈreɪvɪŋ), *ppl. a.*[1] [f. rave *v.*[1] + -ing[2].]

1. Delirious, frenzied; raging.

c **1475** *Rauf Coilȝear* 650 To his raifand word he gaue na rewaird. *a* **1585** Polwart *Flyting w. Montgomerie* 29 Thy ragged roundels, raueand royt. **1641** Milton *Reform.* ii. Wks. (1851) 71 To exercise a Raving and Bestiall Tyranny over them. *a* **1704** T. Brown *Sat. Quack* Wks. 1730 I. 64 All mankind the raving monster shun. **1781** Cowper *Conv.* 559 The raving storm and dashing wave. **1837** Dickens *Pickw.* xi, A settled gloom, which..finally terminated in raving madness.

b. quasi-*adv.* with adjs., esp. *mad*.

1786 Burns *Toothache* iii, Raving mad, I wish [etc.]. **1813** Shelley *Q. Mab* v. 113 When..religion Drives his wife raving mad. **1883** *Harper's Mag.* Mar. 503/1 The loco, or rattle-weed,..drives them raving crazy.

2. *U.S. slang.* That excites raving admiration; superlative.

1886 in *Cent. Dict.* **1892** F. M. Crawford *Three Fates* II. 102 You are such a raving success, as they call it.

raving, *ppl. a.*[2] and [3]: see rave *v.*[2] and *v.*[4]

†**raving fat.** *Obs. rare.* Also 6 ravin-. (Of obscure origin and meaning.) Also *attrib.*

1555 *Richmond Wills* (Surtees) 86 A paire of studles and ravinfat, a whealle and a gallan xiiij[d]. **1578** *Ibid.* 274 A pair of studills, quelis, cards, raving fatt gangs, and all other geare perteyning wooll worke.

ravingly (ˈreɪvɪŋlɪ), *adv.* [f. raving *ppl. a.*[1] + -ly[2].] In a raving manner.

a **1586** Sidney *Arcadia* (1622) 113 In this depth of muzes, and diuers sorts of discourses, would shee rauingly haue remained. **1650** A. B. *Mutat. Polemo* 3 These ravingly cursed their fortunes. **1728** Ramsay *Daft Bargain* 5 Quoth Rab (right ravingly) to Raff. **1793** J. Bowles *Ground War w. France* (ed. 5) 72 She..ravingly exults in the distempered idea. **1825** *Examiner* 721/1 Her 'Soldier tired'..was ravingly encored.

ravinour, obs. form of RAVENER.

†**'raviol.** *Obs. rare*⁻⁰. [a. It. *raviolo* (Florio), *raviuolo*, or obs. F. *raviole*.] = RAFIOL.

1611 FLORIO, *Rafioli*, a kind of little paste-meates in fashion of little pasties, rauiols.

ravioli (rævɪ'əʊlɪ), *sb. pl.* [It., pl. of *raviolo* in the same sense: see RAVIOL.] Small square pasta cases filled with meat or vegetables.

1841 THACKERAY in *Fraser's Mag.* June 721/2 For the same money, I might have had..a heap of macaroni, or ravioli. **1846** DICKENS *Pictures from Italy* 47 Real Genoese dishes, such as Tagliarini; Ravioli..with fresh green figs. **1898** L. MERRICK *Actor Manager* 66 Oliphant was duly introduced to ravioli. **1947** H. INNES *Lonely Skier* i. 23 'No need to try and catch their eyes,' Joe Wesson said through a mouthful of *ravioli*. **1956** A. WILSON *Anglo-Saxon Att.* II. iii. 363 *Ravioli* was in preparation for dinner. **1969** B. MALAMUD *Pictures Fidelman* 160 The deaf woman was up and down to supply the glass blower with ravioli, cheese, bread. **1972** H. C. RAE *Shooting Gallery* IV. 247 She cooked up a tin of Ravioli, spiced it with Parmesan and mixed herbs. **1975** J. GORES *Hammett* xvi. 110 Soup to start. Ravioli. Salad after.

†**ravisable**, *a. Obs.*⁻¹. [a. OF. *ravis(s)able* (Godef.), f. *raviss-*, *ravir* to seize.] Ravenous.

c **1400** *Rom. Rose* 7016 Outward lambren semen we..And inward we withouten fable Ben gredy wolues rauysable.

†**'ravish**, *sb. Obs. rare.* [f. RAVISH *v.*] An act of ravishing; ravishment, rapture.

c **1620** M. LOK in Hakluyt *Voy.* (1812) V. 408 After diuers complaints of those rauishes,..the Women brought from thence were apparelled [etc.]. *a* **1649** WINTHROP *New Eng.* (1853) I. 219 [They] had builded their comfort of salvation upon unsound grounds, viz., some upon dreams and ravishes of spirits by fits.

ravish ('rævɪʃ), *v.* Forms: α. 4-5 rav-, rauissch(e, -isch (also 6 *Sc.*), -ysch(e, -isshe, -esche, -es(s)he, -ych, (5 -ich), 4-6 rauysh(e, -yssch(e, (6 -yszsh), 4-7 -ishe, 5-6 ravissh, 4- ravish; 4 rewych, 5 revyssh. β. (Chiefly *north.* and *Sc.*) 4 raiuis-, rauice, ravese, 4-5 (6 *Sc.*) rauis, rauys; *Sc.* 5 rawis-, raves-, 6-7 ravis; 5 rewis, -ys, 6 reuis(s, reuys, reueis-, rewese, 6-7 revis. [a. F. *raviss-*, lengthened stem of *ravir* to seize, take away:—pop. L. **rapīre*, class. L. *rapĕre*. Cf. RAVIN¹.]

1. a. *trans.* To seize and carry off (a person); to take by violence, to tear or drag away *from* (a place or person). Now somewhat *rare*. †Also, to sweep or carry away; to drag off (*to* or *into* a place). *Obs.*

a **1300** *Cursor M.* 7680 His reners [saul] þeder send For to rauis dauid he wend. *a* **1340** HAMPOLE *Psalter* lxii. 8, I am thi bridde & if þou hill me not þe glede will ravishe me. **1422** tr. *Secreta Secret., Priv. Priv.* 174 The course of the ryuer so stronge and so styfe rane, that the knyght and his hors rauyshith, doune hym bare, and dreynte. **1585** T. WASHINGTON tr. *Nicholay's Voy.* III. i. 69 [They] by outragious force rauish these most deare infants..from..their fathers and mothers. **1603** B. JONSON *Sejanus* v. x, Now inhumanely ravish him to Prison! **1624** QUARLES *Sion's Elegies* iv. 20 Heaven's Anoynted, Their hands have crusht, and ravisht from his Throne. **1655** FULLER *Ch. Hist.* I. v. §20 The British are not so over-fond of St. Patrick, as to ravish him into their Country against his will, and the consent of Time. **1854** SUMNER *Speech* in Wks. 1895 III. 291 For the mother there is no assurance that her infant child will not be ravished from her breast.

fig. **1513** DOUGLAS *Æneis* VIII. i. 49 In mynd..Nou heyr, nou there, revist in syndry partis. **1560** DAUS tr. *Sleidane's Comm.* 464 b, Many men rauished & toste hither and thither with euery wynde of doctrine.

†**b.** In *pass.*: To be carried away *from* a belief, state, etc. *Obs.*

1362 LANGL. *P. Pl.* A. XI. 297 Arn none rathere yrauisshid fro the riȝt beleue Thanne arn thise grete clerkis. *a* **1400-50** *Alexander* 4424 þus fra þe rote of riȝtwisnes rauyst ere ȝe clene. *c* **1425** *Found. St. Bartholomew's* (E.E.T.S.) 45 In his slepe he was raueshid from his resonable wyttys. **1758** H. WALPOLE *Catal. Roy. Authors* (1759) I. 157 Ravished from all improvement and reflection at the age of seventeen.

†**c.** To draw forcibly *to* (or *into*) some condition, action, etc. *Obs.*

1398 TREVISA *Barth. De. P.R.* II. iv. (1495) b ij b/2 Aungels ben..rauysshed to the Innest contemplacion of the loue of god. **1450-1530** *Myrr. our Ladye* 329 That whyle we know god vysybly, by hym we mote be rauyshed in to the loue of inuysyble thynges. **1574** tr. *Marlorat's Apocalips* 23 Christes works..might rauish all men to haue them in wonderfull admiration. **1600** HOLLAND *Livy* x. xli. 382 The Romanes were ravished and carried on end to the battaile, with anger, hope, and heate of conflict.

2. a. To carry away (a woman) by force. (Sometimes implying subsequent violation.) Also said *fig.* of death. ? *Obs.*

a **1300** *Cursor M.* 7048 Alexandre, in þat siquar, þat paris hight, raiuist helayn. **1303** R. BRUNNE *Handl. Synne* 7422 þay rauys a mayden aȝens here wyl, And mennys wyuys þey lede awey þertyl. **1387** TREVISA *Higden* (Rolls) I. 171 Iupiter..rauisched Europa, Agenores douȝter. *c* **1477** CAXTON *Jason* 8 They rauisshed the fayr Ypodame out from alle the other ladyes. **1585** T. WASHINGTON tr. *Nicholay's Voy.* II. iii. 33 It was there..Paris after he had rauished Helene, tooke of her the first frutes of his loue. *c* **1665** MRS. HUTCHINSON *Mem. Col. Hutchinson* (1846) 49 Death quenched the flame and ravished the young lady from him.

b. To commit rape upon (a woman), to violate. Also *absol.*

1436 *Rolls of Parlt.* IV. 498/1 [He] fleshly knewe and ravysshed ye said Isabell. **1560** DAUS tr. *Sleidane's Comm.* 220 b, The women and maides that were fled thither for feare, they ravissh every one [L. *constuprant*]. **1642** FULLER *Holy & Prof. St.* v. xi. 397 Defiling virgins, or ravishing them rather, for consent onely defiles. **1756-7** tr. *Keysler's Trav.* (1760) II. 159 The Locis Turpitudinis, as it is called, where St. Agnes was in danger of being ravished by two soldiers. **1834** *Cycl. Pract. Med.* III. 583/1 Ravishing by force any woman-child..or any other woman. **1939** G. B. SHAW *Geneva* III. 70 Am I to allow him to kill me and ravish my wife and daughters? **1981** *Sunday Times* (Colour Suppl.) 8 Mar. 104 He ravished and pillaged...left sons to hate him, women to fight over his wealth.

fig. **1664** DRYDEN *Rival Ladies* II. i, Against her Will fair Julia to possess, Is not t'enjoy but ravish Happiness. **1782** COWPER *Table T.* 332 May no foes ravish thee [Liberty], and no false friend Betray thee, while professing to defend.

†**c.** To spoil, corrupt. *Obs. rare*⁻¹.

1593 SHAKS. *Lucr.* 778 O hateful, vaporous, and foggy Night..With rotten damps ravish the morning air.

3. a. To carry away or remove from earth (esp. to heaven) or from sight. Now *rare*.

a **1300** *Cursor M.* 18483 We sal be rauist forth a-wai, Sal na man se us fra þat dai. **1340** HAMPOLE *Pr. Consc.* 5050 We..Sal þan with þam in cloudes be ravyste Up in-to þe ayre. *c* **1375** *Sc. Leg. Saints* x. (*Matthew*) 210 It hapnyt þe kingis son be ded..þai tald þe kynge þat goddis had rawist hyme. *c* **1450** LYDG. & BURGH *Secrees* 97 He was Ravysshed Contemplatyff of desir Vp to the hevene lyk a dowe of ffyr. **1513** DOUGLAS *Æneis* I. i. 50 Ganimedes reveist abouе the sky. **1697** DRYDEN *Virg. Georg.* IV. 719 For ever I am ravish'd from thy sight. **1754** FIELDING *Jonathan Wild* IV. vii, A very thick mist ravished her from our eyes. **1885-94** R. BRIDGES *Eros & Psyche* Oct. xii, Ravisht to hell by fierce Agesilas, Thou soughtest her on earth and couldst not find.

b. To carry away (esp. to heaven) in mystical sense; to transport ***in spirit*** without bodily removal.

c **1330** *Arth. & Merl.* 8915 (Kölbing) This Naciens.. Whom seþþen þe holi godes gras Rauist in to þe þridde heuen, Where he herd angels steuen. *c* **1400** MAUNDEV. (Roxb.) xxvi. 124 þanne þei seyn þat he is ravissht in to anoþer world. **1482** *Monk of Evesham* (Arb.) 36 Y was rauyshte in spirite as y laye in the chaptur hows. **1552** LYNDESAY *Monarche* 6076 Quhen Paull wes reuyst, in the spreit, Tyll the thrid Heuin. **1615** G. SANDYS *Trav.* 56 They haue..naturall idiots, in high veneration; as men rauished in spirit, and taken from themselues, as it were, to the fellowship of Angels. **1644** EVELYN *Mem.* (1857) I. 117 It has some rare statues, as Paul ravished into the third heaven.

c. To transport with the strength of some feeling, to carry away with rapture; to fill with ecstasy or delight; to entrance. Also const. *from*.

13.. *E.E. Allit. P.* A. 1087 So was I rauyste wyth glymme pure. **1377** LANGL. *P. Pl.* B. II. 17 Hire arraye me rauysshed, succhе ricchesse saw I neuere. **1484** CAXTON *Fables of Alfonce* i, The medecyns..sayd that..he was rauysshed by loue. *a* **1533** LD. BERNERS *Huon* cxliv. 538 She had suche ioye that of a great spase she coude speke no word, she was so rauysshyd. **1586** A. DAY *Eng. Secretary* (1625) 23 Doth not the learned Cosmographie..rauish vs oftentimes and bring in contempt the pleasures of our owne soyle. **1695** BLACKMORE *Pr. Arth.* II. 316 Ambrosial Juices, sweet Nectarean Wine, Ravish'd their Tast. **1753** HOGARTH *Anal. Beauty* v. 28 Ravish the eye with the pleasure of the pursuit. **1826** E. IRVING *Babylon* II. VIII. 282, I have been wrapt in wonder, and ravished with delight, in the study of it. **1873** BROWNING *Red Cott. Nt.-cap* IV. 135 You ravish men away From puny aches and petty pains.

4. a. To seize and take away as plunder or spoil; to seize upon (a thing) by force or violence; to make a prey of. †Also with *away*.

c **1374** CHAUCER *Boeth.* IV. pr. v. 102 (Camb. MS.) Shrewes rauysshen medes of vertu and ben in honours and in gret estatis. **1382** WYCLIF *Nahum* ii. 9 Rauyshe ȝe syluer, rauyshe ȝe gold. **1483** CAXTON *Cato* B iij, To be wyllyng for to dyspoyle and rauysshe hys neyghbours goodes. **1535** COVERDALE *Gen.* xxxvii. 33 A rauyshinge beast hath rauyshed Ioseph. *a* **1661** FULLER *Worthies* (1840) II. 104 Some antiquaries are so jealous of their works, as if every hand which toucheth them would ravish them. **1731** MEDLEY *Kolben's Cape G. Hope* I. 66 The Free-booters had used to ravish away their lives and their cattle. **1794** BURKE *Sp. agst. W. Hastings* Wks. 1826 XV. 430 To steal an iniquitous judgment, which you dare not boldly ravish.

absol. **1712-14** POPE *Rape Lock* II. 32 He meditates the way, By force to ravish, or by fraud betray.

fig. *c* **1374** CHAUCER *Boeth.* III. pr. i. 50 (Camb. MS.) Whan þat thow ententyf and stylle rauysshedest my wordes.

†**b.** To carry, take, pull, or drag away or along in a violent manner without appropriation; to remove by force. Also with *away*, *down*. *Obs.*

c **1374** [see RAVISHING *ppl. a.* 1]. **1398** TREVISA *Barth. De P.R.* VIII. xxii. (Bodl. MS.) lf. 86/1 Aboute þe whiche axis alle þe swiftenes of þe firmament is rauessched and ymeued. **1460-4** *Paston Lett.* No. 434 II. 81 The gret fray..ravyched my witts and mad me ful hevyly dysposyd. **1535** COVERDALE *Prov.* i. 12 These are the ways of all soch as be couetous, that one wolde rauysh anothers life. **1620** MELTON *Astrolog.* 65 His minde was rauished downe the swift torrent of an insolent vanity. **1698** CROWNE *Caligula* III, Rivers he ravishes, and turns their courses!

c. Const. *from*, *out of*, †*into*, *to*.

1398 TREVISA *Barth. De P.R.* XVI. vii. (Bodl. MS.), ȝif þow doste þer on [on quicksilver] a scrupil of golde it rauesscheþ into it silfe þe liȝtnes þerof. *c* **1400** *Rom. Rose* 5198, I mene not that [love] which makith thee wood,..And ravysshith fro thee all thi witte. **1563** WINȜIT *Wks.* (1890) II. 16 We also..suld reuiss fra it, that mot proffet to the lyfe eternall. **1634** W. TIRWHYT tr. *Balzac's Lett.* (vol. I.) a ij, The onely thing hee supposed to possess..was ravished from him. **1722** DE FOE *Col. Jack* (1840) 175, I..am not..obliged to ravish my bread out of the mouths of others. **1748** RICHARDSON *Clarissa* (1811) II. xxxiii. 239 He even snatched..my struggling hand; and ravished it to his odious mouth. **1838** PRESCOTT *Ferd. & Is.* (1846) I. ii. 135 The crown was ravished from her posterity. **1871** R. ELLIS *Catullus* lxiv. 5 Fain from Colchian earth her fleece of glory to ravish.

†**d.** With double object. *Obs.*

c **1400** *Destr. Troy* 462 The sight of þat semely.. rauysshed hir radly þe rest of hir sawle. *a* **1500** *Sir Beues* 3917 (Pynson) Thou haste rauysshed my men theire liffe.

†**5. a.** To ravage, despoil, plunder. *Obs.*

1297 R. GLOUC. (Rolls) 4001 þou..rauissest france & oþer londes. *a* **1340** HAMPOLE *Psalter* ix. 32 He waites þat he rauysch þe pore. **1388** WYCLIF *Isa.* xlii. 22 Thilke puple was rauyschid and wasted. *c* **1619** BACON *Sp. concerning War w. Spain* Rem. (1734) 226 We ravished a principal City of wealth and strength.

†**b.** To despoil, rob, or deprive (one) *of* something. *Obs.*

1362 LANGL. *P. Pl.* A. IV. 34 And hou he rauischede Rose, Reynaldes lemmon, And Mergrete of hire maydenhod. **1560** DAUS tr. *Sleidane's Comm.* 29 b, I am not led rashely on like one that were ravished of his wittes. **1606** G. W[OODCOCKE] *Hist. Ivstine* VIII. 38 Assailing the brothers..[he] rauisht them both of their kingdomes. **1686** F. SPENCE tr. *Varilla's Ho. Medicis* 240 As he was..more methodick than Blondus, he ravish'd him of his reputation. *a* **1803** *Hughie Grame* xiv. in Child *Ballads* IV. 13 They may ravish me o' my life, But they canna banish me fro Heaven hie.

ravished ('rævɪʃt), *ppl. a.* [f. prec. + -ED².]

1. Carried away by force; violated; ravaged.

1513 DOUGLAS *Æneis* IV. v. 48 To Amon he was son, beget ..Apon the maid revist Garamantida. **1606** SHAKS. *Tr. & Cr.* Prol. 9 The rauish'd Helen, Menelaus Queene. **1692** RAY *Disc.* 35 When Sea, Earth, ravisht Heaven, the curious Frame Of this World's Mass should shrink in purging Flame. **1713** ADDISON *Cato* II. v, The spurious brood Of violated maids, of ravish'd Sabines. **1788** BURNS *'Fate gave the Word'*, The mother-linnet..Bewails her ravish'd young. *a* **1845** BARHAM *Cousin Nicholas* xxi, The porter..stretched out his hand to secure the ravished peruke.

2. Transported, entranced, enraptured.

1501 DOUGLAS *Pal. Hon.* I. ii, My rauist spreit in that desert terribill. **1549** COVERDALE, etc. *Erasm. Par. 1 Cor.* 38 Suche as are inspired with the holy gost are not theyr owne men, no more then we see rauished men to be. **1697** DRYDEN *Virg. Ecl.* v. 70 Thy Verse..So sweet, so charming to my ravish'd Ears. **1768** SIR W. JONES *Solima* Poems (1777) 5 Sooth'd with his lay, the ravish'd air was calm. *a* **1839** PRAED *Poems* (1864) II. 48 Before your ravished eyes New hopes appear. **1901** G. B. SHAW *Caesar & Cleopatra* I. 102 A man comes from the south with stealing steps, ravished by the mystery of the night. **1953** R. LEHMANN *Echoing Grove* 22 Ravished startled, they watched the apparition wave up and down,..with rapid wing beats, low above the terraces.

Hence †'**ravishedly** *adv. Obs.*

1593 NASHE *Christ's T.* (1613) 10 She breaketh violently from mee, to run rauishtly into his rugged armes. *Ibid.* 167 Which maketh them rauishtly melancholly.

ravisher ('rævɪʃə(r)). Also 4 rauissch-, 5 ravys(s)hour; 6 *Sc.* raviss-, reuesar. [f. RAVISH *v.* + -ER¹, in early use prob. after OF. *ravisserre*, *ravisseor*, *-eur*.] One who ravishes, in senses of the vb. (esp. 2 and 2 b).

c **1375** *XI Pains Hell* 78 in *O.E. Misc.* 225 To brenne.. Spous-brekers wiþ lechours, Rauisschers wiþ rauisschours. **1429** *Rolls of Parlt.* IV. 344/1 Ravyshours of Wymen ayens the lawe. **1552** ABP. HAMILTON *Catech.* (1884) 10 All adulteraris, deflouraris of virginis, ravissaris of women. **1588** SHAKS. *Tit. A.* v. ii. 104 Good Rapine, stab him, he is a rauisher. **1632** LITHGOW *Trav.* II. 74 Her matrones became a prey and prise to euery Rauisher. **1712-14** POPE *Rape Lock* IV. 103 Gods! shall the ravisher display your hair? **1750** JOHNSON *Rambler* No. 77 ¶14 The giddy libertine, or drunken ravisher. **1800** *Asiat. Ann. Reg., Poetry* 851 Without love I had stray'd, Till at length a sweet ravisher came. **1851** D. WILSON *Preh. Ann.* (1863) II. IV. iii. 259 Pure silver..found in the..tumulus by its unprincipled ravisher.

ravishing ('rævɪʃɪŋ), *vbl. sb.* [-ING¹.]

1. The action of taking or carrying away by force; plundering; violation, etc.

a **1300** *Cursor M.* 7080 And al þe chesun o þat strijf, Was for rauising of a wijf. **1398** TREVISA *Barth. De P.R.* VIII. xxii. (Bodl. MS.), Aboute þis lyne..þe firmament passeþ aboute wiþ eendeles rauessching. *c* **1430** LYDG. *Min. Poems* (Percy Soc.) 36 But be wel ware of feyned cosynage,..And lords lettres, and ravisshyng, and rage. **1535** COVERDALE *Nahum* iii. 1 Wo to that bloudthursty cite, which is all full of lyes and robbery, & wil not leaue of from rauyszshinge. **1580** HOLLYBAND *Treas. Fr. Tong, Rapt, ou ravissement*, rauishing or taking away by violence. **1603** KNOLLES *Hist. Turks* (1638) 272 The deflouring of our daughters, the rauishing of our wiues.

2. The action of transporting with ecstasy or delight. ? *Obs.*

1382 WYCLIF *Acts* xxii. 17 Forsoth it is don to me, turnynge aȝen into Jerusalem,..me for to be maad in rauyssching of soule. **1435** MISYN *Fire of Love* 86 Anoþer maner of rauischynge þer is þat is lyfting of mynde in-to god be contemplacion. **1482** *Monk of Evesham* (Arb.) 112 Yn the space of hys raueshyng, he was so fully helyd that he hym selfe meruelyd. **1526** *Pilgr. Perf.* (W. de W. 1531) 161 b, In suche hye eleuacyon or rauysshyng vp of the mynde. **1586** T. B. *La Primaud. Fr. Acad.* II. (1594) 294 This degree of loue may be rightly called rauishing, in which the louer is so rapt out of himselfe, that he forgetteth himselfe. **1622** WITHER in Farr *S.P. Jas. I* (1848) 216 He in his troubles eased the bodie's paines By measures raised to the soule's rauishing.

†**b.** An ecstasy, transport, rapture. *Obs.*

1435 MISYN *Fire of Love* 84 Of dobylle rauischyngis. *Ibid.* 86 And [als] well þis is cald a rauischynge als þe todyr. **1526** *Pilgr. Perf.* (W. de W. 1531) 272 The thyrde..is called a rapt or a rauysshynge of the soule. **1627-77** FELTHAM *Resolves* II. lxvi. 328 The ravishings that sometimes from aboue do shoot abroad in the inward man.

ravishing (ˈrævɪʃɪŋ), *ppl. a.* [-ING^{2}.] That ravishes, in senses of the vb.

†**1.** That carries along or away. *Obs. rare.*

c1374 CHAUCER *Boeth.* I. met. v. 13 (Camb. MS.) O Thou maker of the whel þat bereþ þe sterres which..tornest the heuene with a Rauessyng sweyh. *Ibid.* 14 Thow gouernour withdrawh and restryne thei rauesynge floodys.

†**2.** Seizing upon prey; ravenous. *Obs.*

a1340 HAMPOLE *Psalter* xxi. 12 þai oppynd on me þaire mouth as lyon rawysand and rumyand. c1400 MAUNDEV. (Roxb.) xxxii. 147 Diuerse maners of nedders and oþer rauyschand bestez. 1535 COVERDALE *Gen.* xxxvii. 33 A rauyshinge beast hath rauyshed Ioseph. 1605 SHAKS. *Macb.* II. i. 55 With his stealthy pace, With Tarquin's rauishing sides [*emend.* strides].

3. Exciting ecstasy or transports.

c1430 LYDG. *Reas. & Sens.* (E.E.T.S.) 3656 Whan they harpe pley, and synge, The noyse is so ravysshynge, That [etc.]. 1570 DEE *Math. Pref.* 3 O rauishing perswasion, to deale with a Science, whose Subiect is so Auncient. 1678 BUTLER *Hud.* III. i. 783 Those ravishing and charming Graces. a1703 BURKITT *On N.T., Matt.* xvii. 4 O what a ravishing comfort is the fellowship of the saints. 1840 BROWNING *Sordello* III. 351 Then, ravishingest lady, will you pass Or not each formidable group? 1873 HAMERTON *Intell. Life* I. iv. (1875) 24 His ears drank ravishing harmonies.

†**b.** as *adv.* Ravishingly. *Obs. rare.*

1616 BRETON *Goode & Badde* §8 The rauishing sweet in the musique of Honour. 1705 STANHOPE *Paraphr.* I. 57 Devotions..like a melodious Consort ravishing Sweet.

ˈ**ravishingly**, *adv.* [f. prec. + -LY^{2}.] In a ravishing manner, enchantingly.

1593 NASHE *Christ's T.* (1613) 96 [They] sing sweetly, glance piercingly, play on Lutes rauishingly. 1615 CHAPMAN *Odyss.* x. 151 To heare a voice so rauishingly rare. a1672 STERRY *Freed. Will* (1675) 105 An unbounded, equally-beautiful, ravishingly-harmonious variety. 1748 SMOLLETT *Rod. Rand.* xxxix, [Her] whole person was ravishingly delightful. 1848 THACKERAY *Lett.* 1 Nov., They have a full chorus of boys,..who sing quite ravishingly.

†**ravishmeal**, *adv. Obs. rare*$^{-1}$. [f. RAVISH *v.* + -MEAL.] In a 'ravishing' manner.

1382 WYCLIF *Job* vi. 15 My brethern passeden beside me, as a strem that raueshe melum [*v.rr.* rauyshe meel, raueshemeles; L. *raptim*] passeth in valeis.

ravishment (ˈrævɪʃmənt). Also 5–6 rauisshe-, 6 rauysshe-, rauishe-, etc. [ad. OF. *ravissement* (14th c.): see RAVISH *v.* and -MENT.]

†**1.** The act of carrying off a person; in ***ravishment of ward*** or ***de gard***, the taking away of a ward; also, the writ issued in consequence of this. *Obs.*

1530–1 *Act 22 Hen. VIII*, c. 15 And also excepted and forprised out of this pardon all rauysshementes of the Kynges wardes. c1640 J. SMYTH *Lives Berkeleys* (1883) II. 351 This lord Henry brought his Writ of ravishment de gard against Robert Hill. 1642 tr. *Perkins' Prof. Bk.* i. §30. 13 If Lord and Tenant be by Knights service and the Tenant die, his heire within age, and a stranger take him away, the Lord shall have a ravishment of ward. 1700 TYRRELL *Hist. Eng.* II. 1107 Penalties for Ravishment of a Ward from his Lord's Custody.

2. Forcible abduction or violation of a woman.

1529 S. FISH *Supplic. Beggers* (1871) 8 For the murdre of his auncestre, rauisshement of his wyfe, of his doughter. 1661 MORGAN *Sph. Gentry* III. ix. 101 Tatius King of the Sabines coming against him to revenge the ravishment of their women. 1712 STEELE *Spect.* No. 533 ¶2 Why should there be Accessaries in Ravishment any more than Murther? 1794 T. TAYLOR *Pausanias* I. 39 She was there informed, by Chrysanthis, of the ravishment of her daughter. c1850 *Arab. Nts.* (Rtldg.) 679 He begged the princess to acquaint him of what had passed from the time of her ravishment.
transf. 1647 N. BACON *Disc. Govt. Eng.* I. xliv. (1739) 72 For though he might have taken it by ravishment, yet he chose the way of wooing it by a kind of mutual agreement. a1671 LD. FAIRFAX *Mem.* (1699) 125 Even this I hope all impartial judges will interpret as force and ravishment of a good name, rather than a voluntary consent.

b. With *a* and *pl.*: = RAPE *sb.*^{2} 3 b.

1576 *Act 18 Eliz.* c. 7 §1 Felonious Rapes or Ravishements of Women Maydes Wieves and Damsells. 1686 *Lond. Gaz.* No. 2120/2 All Ravishments and wilful taking away or Marrying of any Maid. 1724 DE FOE *Mem. Cavalier* (1840) 188 Murders, ravishments, and barbarities. 1890 W. BOOTH *In Darkest Eng.* I. i. 13 Ravishments as horrible, as if we were in Central Africa.
fig. 1693 G. FIRMIN *Rev. Mr. Davis's Vind.* i. 9 Our coming to Christ, and union with him, is compared to Marriage,..but Dr. Crisp makes it a Ravishment.

3. Transport, rapture, ecstasy.

c1477 CAXTON *Jason* 67 b, In this rauisshement, him thought that the God mars saide to him, Appollo, Appollo. 1546 *Primer Hen. VIII* 146 In the mouth honie so mellifluous, In the heart ravishment celestious. 1627 W. SCLATER *Exp. 2 Thess.* (1629) 89 Cursed Moamed calls the dead fits of his falling Sicknesse, his Exstasie and rauishment at the appearance of the Angell Gabriel. 1718 *Entertainer* No. 21. 144 That Heavenly Bliss, which has absorb'd their Souls in Ravishment and Rapture. 1814 CARY *Dante, Par.* XIV. 115 A melody That, indistinctly heard, with ravishment Possess'd me. 1873 BROWNING *Red Cott. Nt.-cap* IV. 270 What folks nickname A lyre, those ancients played to ravishment.

b. With *a* and *pl.*

1581 MARBECK *Bk. of Notes* 655 Some of them haue visions, rauishments, & traunces. 1663 BP. PATRICK *Parab. Pilgr.* xvi, To make joy in heaven,..oh what a ravishment is it! 1744 J. PATERSON *Comm. Milton's P.L.* 266 Ravishments, exstacies, or transports of the mind for joy. 1841–4 EMERSON *Ess.* Ser. I. ix. (1876) 227 What was in the case of these remarkable persons [Fox, Swedenborg, etc.] a ravishment.

†**4.** An act of plundering or ravaging. *Obs.*

1570 LEVINS *Manip.* 68/6 A rauishmente, *rapina.* 1606 G. W[OODCOCKE] *Hist. Ivstine* II. 9 The foule rauishments they had offered them by the Athenians. 1650 B. *Discolliminium* 24 That Scotish Invasion and our English Defeat..was a very Ravishment.

ˈ**ravissant**, *a.* Also 3, 6 rauisaunt, -ant. [a. F. *ravissant*, pple. of *ravir*: see RAVISH.]

†**1.** Of beasts: Ravening. *Obs. rare.*

c1290 *MS. Laud* 108 lf. 11 þe wolf wilde and rauisaunt with þe schep ȝeode so milde so lomb. 1549 *Compl. Scot.* Prol. 2 Tha said rauisant volfis of ingland hes intendit ane oniust veyr.

b. *Her.* (See quot. 1780.) *rare*$^{-0}$.

The attitude of a 'wolf ravissant' corresponds to that of a 'lion salient'.
1727 in BAILEY (vol. II). 1780 EDMONDSON *Compl. Body Her.* II. Gloss., *Ravissant*, a term used by French Heralds to express the posture of a wolf, half raised, and just springing forward upon his prey.

2. Ravishing, delightful.

Now only as F. (ravisɑ̃), with fem. *ravissante* (-ɑ̃t).
1653 GAUDEN *Hierasp.* 254 The ravissant happiness of the blessed Angels. 1673 DRYDEN *Marr. à la Mode* I. i, O, 'tis the sweetest Prince! so obligeant, charmant, ravissant. 1848 THACKERAY *Van. Fair* li, The most *ravissante* little Marquise in the world. 1885 MABEL COLLINS *Prettiest Woman* ix, She is not *ravissante* like her sister.

ravissh-, obs. variant of REVEST *v.*

ravle, dial. form of RAVEL.

ravoun, obs. form of RAVEN *sb.*^{1}

ravyn(e, obs. forms of RAVEN, RAVIN^{1}.

ravyner, -ous, obs. forms of RAVENER, -OUS.

†**raw**, *sb.*^{1} *Obs. rare.* Some contrivance for catching fish.

1533–4 *Act 25 Hen. VIII*, c. 7 [No person shall take in any] crele, raw, web, lister, fier, or any other engine..the yonge frie..of any kinde of salmon. 1558 *Act 1 Eliz.* c. 17 §1 No Person..with any..Crele, Rawe, Fagnett, Trollnett, Trimmenet..shall take..Spawne, or Frye of Eeles, Salmon, Pyke or Pyckerell.

raw (rɔː), *a.* (*sb.*^{2}). Forms: α. 1 **hréaw, hræw,** (?**hréow**), 3 **ravȝ**, 4 **raughe**, 4–6 **rawe**, 4– **raw**. β. *north.* 5 **ra(e**, 8 **rey**, 9 **ray, reea**. [Comm. Teut.: OE. *hréaw* = Fris. *rä, ré*, OS. *hrâo (*hra-*, MDu. *raeu, rou, ro*, Du. *rauw*), MLG. *rô* (LG. *rau, râ, rô*), OHG. *râu-, rou-, rô* (MHG. *ráw-, rouw-, rô*, G. *roh*), ON. *hrá-r* (Sw. *rå*, Da. *raa*):—OTeut. *hrawa-z, pre-Teut. *krouo-z related to OIr. *crú*, Lat. *cruor*, Lith. *kraújas*, OSlav. *krŭvĭ* blood; Gr. κρέας, Skr. *kravíš* raw flesh.

The northern forms *ra, ray*, etc. are app. ad. ON. *hrá-r.*]

A. *adj.*

1. a. Uncooked, not prepared for use as food by the action of fire or heat. †Of water: Unboiled (*obs.*).

raw cream dial. (see quot. 1796). Also, ***raw milk.***

α. c1000 ÆLFRIC *Hom.* II. 264 Ne ete ȝe of ðam lambe nan ðing hreaw. c1000 *Sax. Leechd.* II. 102 Meng wið hreaw ægru. c1290 *S. Eng. Leg.* I. 304/152 þei heo hadde fisch and drinke, ȝe wuten wel it were ravȝ. 1387 TREVISA *Higden* (Rolls) V. 27 He ete nevere noþer drank his fulle, noþer ete rawe fruyte. c1420 *Liber Cocorum* (1862) 44 Take raw porke and hew hit smalle. c1511 *1st Eng. Bk. Amer.* (Arb.) Introd. 33/1 People the whiche ete none other than rawe fleshe. 1577 FRAMPTON *Joyfull Newes* II. (1596) 46 With the noughtie meates and drinking of the rawe waters,..the most parte of them fell into continuall Agues. 1613 PURCHAS *Pilgrimage* (1614) 693 If we killed a beast for our use, they would aske the inwards, and eat them raw. 1658 A. FOX *Wurtz' Surg.* II. xxiii. 139 The raw Water is better than if boyled. 1704 *Dict. Rust. et Urb.* s.v. *Appetite*, You must cause them to swallow raw Eggs. [1743 W. ELLIS *Mod. Husbandman* July x. 48 If we make raw Milk Cheese.] 1796 W. MARSHALL *W. England* Gloss. (E.D.S.), *Raw cream*, cream raised in the natural way, not scalded or clouted. 1861 FLOR. NIGHTINGALE *Nursing* 48 A patient should, if possible, not..even hear food talked about or see it in the raw state. 1871 *N. & Q.* 4th Ser. VIII. 415, I think that 'rammilk' is *rahm* milk—*i.e. cream* milk and not raw milk. 1950 *N.Z. Jrnl. Agric.* Mar. 221/2 Some doctors say raw milk is better for health than pasteurised milk, so who is to be believed? 1979 A. PARKER *Country Recipe Notebk.* viii. 103 Raw milk ('farm milk') is at present officially described as untreated milk.
β. c1400 MAUNDEV. (Roxb.) xxxii. 147 þai ete flesch and fisch rae. c1425 *Voc.* in Wr.-Wülcker 662/16 *Caro cruda*, ra flesche. 1740– in Lanc. and Yks. dial. (in forms *rey, ray, reea*).
transf. 1652 TATHAM *Pref. Verse* in Brome *Joviall Crew*, It is unhallowed heat, That boyles your Raw-brains.

†**b.** Applied to blood from a wound. *rare*$^{-1}$.

a1529 SKELTON *Ware Hauke* 58 The bloude ran downe raw Vpon the auter stone.

†**c.** Undigested. *Obs. rare.*

1533 ELYOT *Cast. Helthe* II. ix. [see CRUDE *a.* 3]. *Ibid.* II. xxix, In a cold stomake, the litell heate is suffocate with grosse meate, & the fine meate lefte rawe for lacke of concoction.

d. Unburnt, unbaked; not hardened or fused by fire. Cf. GREEN *a.* 9 d.

1698 FRYER *Acc. E. India & P.* 131 The Castle..was large, but rude, and the Wall of raw Brick. 1825 J. NICHOLSON *Operat. Mechanic* 472 Raw glazes are employed for the common pottery... They are generally composed of white-lead, Cornish-stone, and flint, ground by a hand-mill. 1882 [see GREEN *a.* 9 d]. 1885 *Encycl. Brit.* XIX. 638/2 The 'raw' vessels fresh from the wheel, which only require a moderate heat to prepare them for being glazed.

†**e.** Of fruit: Green, not preserved. *Obs.*

1686 tr. *Chardin's Trav. Persia* 391 They export from thence vast quantities of Fruit dry'd and raw.

f. Applied to the taste of tea: harsh, not mellow.

1881 *Tea Cycl.* III. 220/1 To obtain a raw, rasping and pungent flavor I am compelled to underferment, the indication of which is that the colour of infused leaves are of a greenish brown tint. 1892 J. M. WALSH *Tea, its Hist. & Myst.* vii. 170 Ceylon and Javas are either 'raw', 'uncooked'..or sour in flavour. 1933 C. R. HARLER *Culture & Marketing of Tea* xiv. 278 The infused leaf of tea made from under-withered leaf is generally *greenish.* The infusions from such leaf are usually *raw* and *rasping.* 1958 T. EDEN *Tea* xiv. 176 *Tea-Tasting Terms..Harsh, Raw, Rasping.* Bitter due to the presence of unfermented polyphenols; a common defect of non-wither teas.

g. ***raw humus***, vegetable matter not yet fully decomposed; incompletely formed humus.

1891 W. SCHLICH *Man. Forestry* II. i. 32 (*heading*) Accumulation of raw humus. 1926 TANSLEY & CHIPP *Study of Vegetation* vii. 117 In cold, moist soils poor in mineral salts and acid in reaction..the leaf litter and other plant debris remain on the surface very little changed and often form a thick layer which is called raw humus. *Ibid.* 132 The soil is covered with a thick layer of raw humus. 1935 *Forestry* IX. 43 Raw humus is characterized by its excessive accumulation (slow decomposition), expandibility, and frequently by the presence of some structural remains of plants... [It is] characterized also by an extremely low base content. 1952 S. A. WAKSMAN *Soil Microbiol.* v. 136 In evergreen forests, the largely organic surface layers are usually not mixed with the inorganic soil layers; the former are referred to as the 'raw humus' or 'duff'. *Ibid.* 144 The surface layer of the raw humus soil may undergo considerable leaching. 1975 *Soil Sci.* XX. 25/1 The raw humus..has been extracted successively with hexane, ether, and ethanol.

h. ***to come the raw prawn***: see PRAWN *sb.* 3 c.

2. In a natural or unwrought state; not yet subjected to any process of dressing or manufacture:

a. of the materials of textile fabrics; esp. ***raw silk***, silk simply drawn from the cocoons by the process of reeling; also, a fabric of spun silk. Also *fig.*

c1315 SHOREHAM *Poems* iii. 150 For wel to conne and nauȝ[t] to don Nys naþer rawe ne y-sponne. 13.. *E.E. Allit. P.* B. 790 Royl rollande fax to raw sylk lyke. 1463–4 *Rolls of Parlt.* V. 506/1 In rawe Silke allone unwrought. 1503 *Act 19 Hen. VII*, c. 21 All other maner of Sylkes,..rawe or unwrought. 1615 G. SANDYS *Trav.* IV. 245 Eight thousand bailes of raw silke are yearely made in the Iland. 1712 GAY *Story of Arachne* 27 Whether raw wool in its first orbs she wound. 1831 G. R. PORTER *Silk Manuf.* 207 The merely nominal duty of one penny per pound on raw silk. 1863 FAWCETT *Pol. Econ.* I. iv. 47 A tax on cotton goods would be far preferable to one on raw cotton. 1866 A. D. WHITNEY in *Our Young Folks* Feb. 104 Two pairs of bright brown raw silk stockings..completed the mountain outfit. 1953 M. MCCARTHY in *Harper's Mag.* Mar. 42/1, I was wearing a bright apple-green raw silk blouse. 1965 D. MACKENZIE *Lonely Side of River* i. 18 Raw-silk summer curtains rustled in the drawing room. 1978 *Observer* 29 Jan. 25/4 There are lots of clothes around made in what is loosely termed 'raw silk'. This is a misnomer as raw silk is actually the silk before it has been woven into fabric and what we call raw silk is actually a slub silk.

b. of cloth: Unfulled.

1381 in Bickley *Little Red Bk. Bristol* II. 7 Nule manere drap a foler qe home appele raucloth. 1467–8 *Rolls of Parlt.* V. 621/2 To bie Wollen Yarne..and also to bie rawe Clothes, untoked and unfulled. 1561 *Reg. Privy Council Scot.* I. 175 vj fardellis of raw claith allegit schippit in name of Petir de Randea. 1582 N.T. (Rhem.) *Matt.* ix. 16 No body putteth a peece of raw cloth to an old garment. 1723 RAMSAY *Monk & Miller's Wife* 140 Knaves..Whase kytes can streek out like raw plaiding. 1868 *Chambers's Encycl.* X. 265/2 When the cloth is taken from the loom, it has a bare look, and is called the raw thread. 1886 ELWORTHY *W. Som. Word-bk.* s.v., The room in which goods are placed when taken from the weaver is always the 'raw-piece shop'.

c. of leather or hides: Untanned, undressed. Cf. GREEN *a.* 9 c. Also ***rawhide***, a rope or whip of undressed hide; hence ***rawhiding***, a whipping; also *fig.*; ***rawhide*** vb. trans., to whip; also *fig.*

1489 CAXTON *Faytes of A.* II. xiv. 118 Covered wyth lamynes of yron or wyth rawe leder. 1585 T. WASHINGTON tr. *Nicholay's Voy.* IV. xxxiv. 156 b, Their headpeece was of a raw oxe hide. 1596 SPENSER *F.Q.* v. xii. 29 Her lips were, like raw lether, pale and blew. 1704 *Lond. Gaz.* No. 4004/3 A Parcel of Raw Hides. 1829 *Massachusetts Spy* 16 Sept. 2/4 She..took down a raw hide..and..kept the whip moving. 1847 GROTE *Greece* II. xlix. (1862) IV. 306 Hides, raw as well as dressed. 1848 *Knickerbocker* XVIII. 519 The editor, it was predicted, would catch a raw-hiding before sun-set. 1858 *Spirit of Times* 6 Feb. 356/3 One of our citizens was rawhided in the street..by a Mr. Huntington. 1890 L. C. D'OYLE *Notches* 174 He called to Peters and his companions to slacken the rawhide, and by this means they lowered him. 1935 W. FAULKNER *As I lay Dying* 109 Like as not you got to take a rawhiding for thinking they meant it. 1935 H. L. DAVIS *Honey in Horn* viii. 100 He had been rawhided into a hunt that showed up his lack of endurance. 1944 H. EVATT *Snow Owl's Secret* 85 The huskies do like the sound of the singing rawhide. 1949 *Sat. Even. Post* 7 May 103/1 Joe went along as packer, rawhiding a string of bony horses up into the brownie country. 1979 *Tucson Mag.* Apr. 28/2 Sometimes the whole door was of rawhide.
attrib. (also *fig.*) 1841 G. CATLIN *Lett. on N. Amer. Indians* I. x. 71 The raw-hide thong, with which it was tied to a stake. 1878 *Smithsonian Misc. Collect.* XIII. No. 6. 83 Split-leather, grain-leather, rawhide thongs. 1883 SWEET & KNOX *On Mexican Mustang through Texas* i. 18 I'm just pining away for a fight. I'm a rawhide Texan, *I* am. 1897 *Slocan* (B.C.) *Pioneer* 8 May 1/2 A rawhide and pack trail has been

constructed from the town of Brandon to the Two Friends mine. 1940 *Chambers's Techn. Dict.* 704/1 Rawhide hammer, a hammer the head of which consists of a close roll of hide projecting from a short steel tube; used by fitters to avoid injuring a finished surface. 1957 J. KEROUAC *On Road* (1958) iii. 21 Here came this rawhide old-timer Nebraska farmer. 1973 J. WAINWRIGHT *Devil you Don't* 14 The expensive, rawhide shirt. 1976 A. MURRAY *Stomping Blues* iv. 51 Down from the cloudlike realms of abstraction and fantasy to the bluesteel and rawhide textures of.. the everyday struggle for existence.

d. of other substances (or their qualities), e.g. undiluted (spirits), unrefined (oil), unmalted (grain), undistilled (water), etc. Also not filtered or otherwise treated; unrefined or partly refined (sugar), undeveloped (land) (*N. Amer.*), untreated (sewage).

1567 MAPLET *Gr. Forest* 3 b, [The beryl] is first found also raw and rude without eyther good looke or pleasant shewe. 1626 BACON *Sylva* §347 Distilled Waters will last longer than Raw waters. 1651 *Publ. Gen. Acts* 1336 Melting down Iron, Oare and Sinders into Raw Iron. 1787 WINTER *Syst. Husb.* 9 The application of raw dung unmixed with earth. 1797 Raw sugar [see SUGAR *sb.* 1 b]. 1830 M. DONOVAN *Dom. Econ.* I. 247 New spirit is stored in wooden vessels until the raw flavour is ameliorated. 1838 T. THOMSON *Chem. Org. Bodies* 1017 It existed, no doubt, in the raw grain, but underwent considerable modifications during the process of malting. 1839 URE *Dict. Manuf.* (1853) II. 75 The raw oil is converted into a drying oil of a pale straw colour. 1845 MCCULLOCH *Taxation* II. x. (1852) 361 Raw spirits could not be purchased.. for less than 4*s.* 6*d.* 1868 *Chem. News* 20 Nov. 248/2 Several accidents happened; one.. by which no less than 150,000 gallons of raw sewage were pumped into a tank holding 430,000 gallons of purified sewage. 1882 C. G. W. LOCK et al. *Sugar Growing & Refining* p. vii, Sugar-cane .. is extensively cultivated, and the manufactured product, under the name of 'raw sugar', forms the staple produce of many of our colonies. 1883 SWEET & KNOX *On Mexican Mustang through Texas* xxi. 282 [He] came to Atascoso County, Texas, and bought a piece of raw land. 1925 G. FAIRRIE *Sugar* vii. 151 At the commencement of the nineteenth century the methods of converting the juice of the cane into raw sugar and the process of refining the raw sugar were very different from what they are to-day. 1930 *Engineering* 25 July 121/1 The net quantity of raw water distilled and passed into the feed line as make-up amounts to 1,138 tonnes per day. 1939 *Sun* (Baltimore) 11 Apr. 3/2 His agency is not interested in the price paid for the 'raw land' on which such developments were built. *Ibid.* 28 Sept. 12/1 The work might be done in part by carrying raw sewage lines to Colgate creek. 1956 *Jrnl. Amer. Water Works Assoc.* XLVIII. 1281 (*heading*) Relation of treatment methods to limits for coliform organisms in raw waters. 1958 Raw sewage [see RECIRCULATE *v.*]. 1972 *Works Engineer* Nov./Dec. 32/1 Raw feed may contain domestic detergents, in which case, antifoaming agents must be added to the treated water. 1973 *Daily Colonist* (Victoria, B.C.) 7 July 3/1 Speculation in raw land is a major contributor to high housing costs.. according to Mayor Art Phillips. 1976 *Chem. in Brit.* XII. 375/3 A recent exercise which nicely illustrates the applications of radiotracers in large systems was carried out, in a raw-water reservoir of capacity 3.10^6 m^3. 1978 *Daily Tel.* 7 July 19/1 The slide in the daily price of raw sugar on the London futures market continued yesterday. 1978 *Oxford Times* 15 Dec. 4/6 Raw sewage has been bubbling up through manhole covers.

e. with general terms, as ***raw commodity, material, produce***, etc. (Freq. in 19th and 20th c.)

1738 BURKE *Rep. Aff. India* Wks. 1842 II. 28 This forced preference of traffick in a raw commodity. 1796 KIRWAN *Elem. Min.* (ed. 2) I. Pref. 8 The raw materials, or necessary instruments of all manufactures. 1825 MCCULLOCH *Pol. Econ.* III. v. 273 A farmer who rents a farm,.. employing upon it such a capital as will, at the existing prices of raw produce, enable him to pay his rent. 1846 —— *Acc. Brit. Empire* (1854) I. 109 The earths, the metals, and other substances.. sent abroad, either in a raw or manufactured shape. 1864 J. H. NEWMAN *Apologia* VII. 392 The raw material of human nature. 1868 FREEMAN *Norm. Conq.* (1876) II. App. 675 Here is quite raw material enough for a legend-maker. 1930 R. CAMPBELL *Poems* 12 Taking as raw material for his lays The good old English beer he loves to praise. 1971 I. G. GASS et al. *Understanding Earth* i. 26/2 The processes of erosion, which provide the raw materials of the sedimentary rocks.

f. Of measurements, data, or the like: not yet subjected to a process giving them significance; unadjusted; naïvely calculated.

1904 *Amer. Jrnl. Psychol.* XV. 263 Weight.. has a raw correlation of 0.34, after correction we eventually get 0.43. 1920 YOAKUM & YERKES *Mental Tests* iii. 78 The result of examination alpha is expressed in a total score which is the sum of the raw scores of the several tests. 1945 *Jrnl. Exper. Psychol.* XXXV. 46 Only the general problems involved in the evaluation of the raw data will be treated in this paper. 1950 *Sun* (Baltimore) 11 May 4/3 McCarthy's frequent statements that the proof of his charges of Communist infestation in the State Department lies.. in the 'raw files' of the FBI. 1954 A. ANASTASI *Psychol. Testing* ii. 24 The 'raw score' on the test.. may be expressed as number of correct items, time required to complete a task, number of errors, or some other objective measure appropriate to the content of the test. Such a raw score is meaningless until evaluated in terms of a suitable set of norms. 1971 *World Archaeol.* III. 120 Naroll's formula.. shows too much variation in raw numbers of population and square meters. 1974 *Nature* 1 Nov. 27/1 A raw spectrum was obtained by averaging the values for a given grating position weighted according to the reciprocal of their variances. 1975 *Ibid.* 31 Jan. 327/2 The raw magnetic field data are translated to a Jupiter centred spherical coordinate system. 1977 *Time* 4 Apr. 13/2 The console operators do not see a raw radar picture. The information is translated into digital bits and then filtered through complicated computer programming. 1978 *Daily Tel.* 16 Jan. 2/1 Sir Charles.. said he had been given warnings as far back as April about the deteriorating situation but had not been prepared to release what he felt were 'raw' forecasts about losses.

g. Of manufactured material: unused.

1917 BENNETT & HERON *Guide to Kinematogr.* i. 12 Raw stock is divided broadly into two classes, Ordinary and Non Flam. 1934 *Tit-Bits* 31 Mar. 12/2 Exposed film is 'stuff'; unexposed film is 'raw stock'. 1968 *Globe & Mail* (Toronto) 3 Feb. 27/3 She paints on the floor of her.. studio, beginning with raw canvas. 1971 W. G. SALM *Stereo in your Home* xii. 168 Prerecorded open-reel tape production line in Ampex plant records all four tracks simultaneously, taking raw tape from large blank pancake. 1973 *Center City Office Weekly* (Philadelphia) 9 Oct. 5 We could not shoot today. No money to buy the raw stock film. 1979 *N. & Q.* Aug. 348/2 Print-outs from the raw text tapes.

h. Of a glaze: (see quot. 1934).

1934 WEBSTER, *Raw glaze*, a glaze made from materials which need no preparation, but can be bought ready for use. 1964 H. HODGES *Artifacts* ii. 46 Any glaze in which the raw materials are simply ground up and applied in this way is called a raw glaze.

3. a. Crude, not brought to perfect composition, form or finish. (In mod. use chiefly of colouring.) ***raw sienna, umber***, sienna and umber which have not been calcined; also, the colours of these pigments; ***raw deal***: see DEAL *sb.*² 4 c; ***raw edge***, the unfinished edge of a cut piece of fabric; also *fig.*; (cf. *raw-edged*, sense 9); † ***to leave raw***, to leave unfinished (cf. RAWLY *adv.* 1).

1398 TREVISA *Barth. De P.R.* IV. ix. (1495) 94 His vryne is white and thycke, rawe and euyll coloured [L. *cruda et discolorata*]. 1526 SKELTON *Magnyf.* 71 Softe, my frende; herein your reason is but rawe. 1551 T. WILSON *Logike* 86 b, The Judges.. left the matter raw without judgement for that time. 1607 NORDEN *Surv. Dial.* III. 137 Some Surueyors ouer credulous, will take their raw reports for matter of record. *a* 1715 BURNET *Own Time* IV. (1724) I. 629 A raw rebellion would soon be crushed. 1720 WATERLAND *Farther Vind. Christ's Div.* viii. §7 To set his raw conceptions and fond reasonings about the meaning of a word, against such valuable authorities. 1762–71 H. WALPOLE *Vertue's Anecd. Paint.* (1786) III. 10 The colouring of the Saturn [was] too raw, and his figure too muscular. 1869 *Bradshaw's Railway Man.* XXI. 460/1 (Advt.), Raw Turk. Umb. 1871 L. STEPHEN *Hours in Library* (1892) I. v. 183 The.. scenery, so provokingly raw and deficient in harmony. 1876 E. JENKINS *Blot on Queen's Head* 13 That great raw pretentious building. 1886 H. C. STANDAGE *Artists' Man. Pigments* iv. 43 *Yellow ochres* (these include Jaune de Mars, Sienna, or Raw Sienna). *c* 1890 tr. *T. de Dillmont's Encycl. Needlework* 6 Rounded seam.—Back-stitch your two edges together.. then.. roll the outer one in, with the left thumb, till the raw edge is quite hidden, hemming as you roll. 1895 *Montgomery Ward Catal.* Spring & Summer 252/3 Artists tube oil colors... Prussian blue. Raw sienna. Raw umber. Roman ochre. 1906 R. FRY *Let.* 17 Apr. (1972) I. 263, I did the wood-work in one coat, pure raw umber and white over a burnt sienna stain. 1908 M. MORGAN *How to dress Doll* ii. 20 Overcasting is only used to keep raw edges on a seam.. from fraying. 1948 F. A. STAPLES *Watercolour Paintings* (1951) iv. 49 *Raw sienna.* Bright yellow with slight reddish tone. Transparent. 1951 R. MAYER *Artist's Handbk.* ii. 59 *Raw umber*... Its composition is similar to that of sienna but it contains no manganese. A dark brown, its tones vary from greenish or yellowish to violet-brown. 1978 *Detroit Free Press* 5 Mar. D9/1 Stitch a one-inch item on each side, turning under raw edge. 1979 A. V. BADGLEY *Rembrandt Decisions* (1980) viii. 108 Hot cups of coffee.. slowly salved the raw edges of Duncan Forbes' departure.

b. Uncultivated, uncivilized, brutal. *rare.*

1577 HARRISON *England* in Holinshed *Chron.* (1587) I. 2/2 Men, being as then but raw and void of all ciuilitie. 1847 TENNYSON *Princ.* II. 106 The man.. Raw from the prime, and crushing down his mate. 1865 BUSHNELL *Vicar. Sacr.* II. iii. (1868) 182 When raw force was everything.

c. *Psychol.* ***raw feel***, a term for the immediate impression evoked by a stimulus, prior to conscious evaluation.

1932 E. C. TOLMAN *Purposive Behavior in Animals & Men* 250 The dyed-in-the-wool mentalist will again protest. Such discrimination-box experiments.. will not and cannot convey what may be called the 'raw feel' of these discriminanda. *Ibid.* 452 *Raw feel*, a name for the peculiar *quale* of experience. 1950 *Mind* LIX. 174 What a psychology of discriminations leaves out.. he calls 'raw feels'. 1956 MEEHL & SELLARS in Feigl & Scriven *Minnesota Stud. Philos. Sci.* I. 249 To suppose that 'raw feels' as we shall call them, will be found to be emergent.. is to suppose that raw feels.. are the *a*'s and *b*'s in the *generalized* function. 1969 H. D. LEWIS *Elusive Mind* ix. 181 There seems, in short, to be some 'immediate data of first person experience .. (e.g. directly experienced sensations, thoughts, feelings.. etc.)'. These are also described in many places as 'raw feels', a somewhat inelegant but suggestive term made popular, I believe, by Professor R. W. Sellars.

†**4. a.** Unripe, immature. Chiefly *fig. Obs.*

1477 NORTON *Ord. Alch.* iv. in Ashm. (1652) 47 For foule and cleane by naturall lawe Hath greate discord, and soe hath ripe and rawe. 1495 *Trevisa's Barth. De P.R.* XVII. ii. (W. de W.) 596 The last frute rypeth nat, but abydeth rawe and grene. 1576 FLEMING *Panopl. Epist.* 357 Alowing one anothers weakenesse of wit, which, though it bee but rawe, yet in tracte of time.. it wil waxe riper. 1593 SHAKS. *Rich. II*, II. iii. 41, I tender you my seruice, Such as it is, being tender, raw, and young, Which elder dayes shall ripen. 1652 BP. PATRICK *Funeral Serm.* in *J. Smith's Sel. Disc.*, etc. 526 Holy and pious counsels for the teaching of rawer and greener heads.

†**b.** New, unfamiliar. *Obs. rare*⁻¹.

1447–8 SHILLINGFORD *Lett.* (Camden) 38 The ij^de Chif Justise.. to whom oure mater myche was rawe.

5. a. Of persons: Inexperienced, unskilled, untrained; quite new or fresh to anything.

1561 T. NORTON *Calvin's Inst.* IV. 23 They so framed them from their tender age, that they shoulde not come vnskilfull and rawe to the executyng of their office. 1652–62 HEYLIN *Cosmogr.* II. (1682) 33 The ill smells.. are ready to stifle and choak up the Spirits of raw Travellers. 1712 STEELE *Spect.* No. 288 ¶1 A raw, innocent, young Creature, who thinks all the World as sincere as herself. 1791 COWPER *Iliad* XI. 866 He supposed me raw As yet, and ignorant. 1826 DISRAELI *Viv. Grey* II. xvi, Surely, my Lords, you will not unnecessarily entrust this great business to a raw hand! 1867 TROLLOPE *Chron. Barset* I. xv. 122 It was remembered.. how raw a lad he had been when he first came there.

b. *esp.* of soldiers without training or experience in fighting.

1577 NORTHBROOKE *Dicing* (1843) 107 This is the cause why there are found so many rawe captaines and soldiers in Englande. 1685 LUTTRELL *Brief Rel.* (1857) I. 352 The horse (being most raw and badly mounted) never stood one shock. 1761–2 HUME *Hist. Eng.* (1806) IV. lvi. 302 Raw troops, conducted by unexperienced commanders. 1807 CRABBE *Par. Reg.* II. 195 Like raw recruits drawn forth for exercise. 1879 FROUDE *Cæsar* xxii. 394 With a raw and inexperienced army he engaged legions in perfect discipline.

c. Const. *at, in*, †*to*.

1548 UDALL, etc. *Erasm. Par. Mark* ii. 23 The disciples, who were as yet rawe in their profession. 1561 T. NORTON *Calvin's Inst.* II. 109 So that when they are called, they be not altogether rude and raw to discipline. *a* 1668 DAVENANT *Man's the Master* V. i, I have been a raw fellow at fighting. 1697 DRYDEN *Æneid* XI. 235 Young as thou wert in Dangers, raw to War. 1734 tr. *Rollin's Anc. Hist.* II. (1827) I. 398 So raw and unexperienced in naval affairs. 1790 WOLCOTT (P. Pindar) *Wks.* 1812 II. 259 Stiffer than Recruits so raw at drill. 1842 BARHAM *Ingol. Leg.* Ser. II. *Black Mousquetaire*, But painting's an art I confess I am raw in.

d. of things, qualities, actions, etc. *rare.*

1602 SHAKS. *Ham.* V. ii. 129 [Q.] The concernancy, Sir? why do we wrap the gentleman in our more rawer breath? 1672 OTWAY *Titus & Berenice* I. i, His Fancy does with wild Distraction rove, which thy raw Ignorance interprets Love. 1823 LAMB *Elia* Ser. II. *Old Margate Hoy*, The raw questions which we.. would be.. putting to them.

6. a. Having the skin removed, so that the flesh is exposed; excoriated. Also *transf.* of the eyes: Unprotected. ***raw side***, the flesh side of a skin. *Obs.*

14.. *Lat. & Eng. Voc.* in Wr.-Wülcker 589/25 *Incrudo*, to make rawe. *c* 1410 LYDG. *Lyfe Our Ladye* XXI. i. (Bodl. MS. 75) 25 Eyen raw may not abyde ffor to behold a3ens her bemyss bri3t. 1550 CROWLEY *Epigr.* 323 Sore legges, most lothsome to se; al rawe from the fote. 1576 FLEMING *Panopl. Epist.* 28 The woundes which.. haue beene healed vp and couered ouer with skinne, beginne a fresh to waxe rawe and greene. 1607 TOPSELL *Four-f. Beasts* (1658) 186 The man.. in Winter time, turneth the hairy side next to his body,.. and in Summer the raw side. 1719 YOUNG *Busiris* I. i, Felt him as the raw wound the burning steel. 1788 FALCONBRIDGE *Afr. Slave Tr.* 41 They were both flogged till their backs were raw. 1886 BURTON *Arab. Nts.* (abr. ed.) I. 70 She.. flogged him cruelly... Then she drew the cilice over his raw and bleeding skin.

fig. 1864 TREVELYAN *Compet. Wallah* (1866) 263 Always sore upon the question of the.. native, he now became positively raw and festering.

b. Painful, as when the raw flesh is exposed.

1590 SPENSER *F.Q.* I. x. 2 All his sinewes woxen weake and raw, Through long enprisonment, and hard constraint. 1898 *Allbutt's Syst. Med.* V. 11 It [the local pain in bronchitis] is variously described as 'sore', 'raw', or 'burning'.

c. Showing through the skin (*obs.*); raw-boned.

1596 SPENSER *F.Q.* IV. xii. 20 His wonted chearefull hew Gan fade,.. His cheeke-bones raw, and eie-pits hollow grew. 1849 E. B. EASTWICK *Dry Leaves* 75 They were.. miserably mounted on raw nags, that looked as if they had fed on sand for the last year.

†**d.** Affected with indigestion = CRUDE 3 b. *Obs.*

1574 *Homilies* II. *Sacrament* 412 Wholesome meate receiued into a rawe stomacke corrupteth and marreth all. 1591 [cf. *raw-stomached* in 9]. 1621 FLETCHER *Pilgrim* III. vi, *Gent.* Have you no fearfull dreams? *Schol.* Sometimes, as all have That go to bed with raw and windy stomacks.

e. Of a person: naked (esp. when sleeping). *colloq.*

1931 D. RUNYON in *Hearst's International* May 64/2 He puts her in the 'Vanities' and lets her walk around raw. 1952 M. R. RINEHART *Swimming Pool* xx. 185 Or maybe she sleeps raw. 1962 J. F. STRAKER *Coil of Rope* vii. 69 Did I shock you? I always sleep raw. 1974 H. WAUGH *Parrish for Defence* (1975) lxvii. 309 She didn't own any nightgowns. She slept raw.

7. Of the weather, etc.: Damp and chilly; bleak.

1546 *St. Papers Hen. VIII*, XI. 162 Mr. Wotton beyng so weake, and the wethur so rawe foule and fervent cold. 1601 ? MARSTON *Pasquil & Kath.* V. 70 The evening's raw and danke; I shall take cold. 1697 DRYDEN *Virg. Georg.* III. 673 When the raw Rain has pierc'd them to the quick. 1729 SAVAGE *Wanderer* I. 42 Raw clouds, that sadden all th' inverted year. 1773 GOLDSM. *Stoops to Conq.* I. i, You shan't venture out this raw evening. 1822 SCOTT *Pirate* xxix, The young ladies spend the night under cover from the raw evening air. 1876 J. R. HIND in *Chambers' Astron.* 197 The weather.. was raw and ungenial.

†**8.** Hoarse. (Perh. after obs. F. *rau.*) *Obs. rare.*

1474 CAXTON *Chesse* III. vi. (1883) 132 Luxurye.. blyndeth the syght, and maketh the woys hoors & rawe. 1480 —— *Ovid's Met.* XIV. xi, There was seen a fowle fleying & fyrst knowen, whyche hade a rawe voys.

9. *Comb.*, as ***raw-coloured, -devouring, -edged, -headed, -jawed, -looking, -mouthed, -nosed***, †***-reeked, -ribbed, -seamed, -skinned, -smelling***, †***stomached*** adjs.

1570–6 LAMBARDE *Peramb. Kent* (1826) p. vii, A *rawe coloured portraiture that lacketh licking. 1848 BUCKLEY *Iliad* 404 The *raw-devouring dogs whom I have nourished in my palaces. **1828** W. CARR *Dial. Craven* (ed. 2) II. 75 **Raw-edg'd*, not hemmed, without a selfedge. **1847** HALLIWELL, *Raw-edged*, not hemmed. **1876** MRS. WHITNEY *Sights & Ins.* viii. 92 A newness of oldness; there was nothing raw-edged; nothing unmellowed. **1920** E. SITWELL *Wooden Pegasus* 105 Where raw-edged shadows sting forlorn As dank dark nettles. **1972** *Ulster* (Sunday Times Insight Team) ix. 151 How raw-edged the relationship was ..was demonstrated by..the first Army 'victory' in Ulster. **1586** E. K. in *Spenser's Sheph. Cal.* Feb. (Emblem), The old man checketh the *raw-headed boy. **1932** *Flynn's* 24 Dec. 136/1 They..resort to what they call a 'cold-turkey' heel or a '*raw-jawed clout'... They refer to the act of going into a store and carrying out several articles without using any finesse at all. **1967** R. LOWELL *Near Ocean* 13 The chinook Salmon..Raw-jawed, weak-fleshed. **1827** SCOTT *Chron. Canongate* I. iv, A broad, *raw-looking, new-made road. **1508** DUNBAR *Flyting* 27 *Ramowd rebald. *Ibid.* 401 Raw-mowit ribald. **1679** *Lond. Gaz.* No. 1423/4 A white Gelding ..*raw-nosed, tender-footed. **1432** *Nottingham Rec.* II. 132 Dimidietatem unius quarterii brasii ordei *rawe reket. **1638** FORD *Lady's Trial* III. i, The *raw-ribb'd apothecary. **1922** BLUNDEN *Shepherd* 81 The young black heifer and the raw-ribbed mare. **1957** T. HUGHES *Hawk in Rain* 51 Suddenly he awoke and was running-raw In *raw-seamed hot khaki. **1922** JOYCE *Ulysses* 233 A *rawskinned crown, scantily haired. **1906** *Macmillan's Mag.* Apr. 476 Next morning I woke in the *raw-smelling dawn, feeling like a corpse. **1591** PERCIVALL *Sp. Dict., Ahitado*, *rawe stomacked, *crudus.*

B. Ellipt. or absol. uses passing into sb.

†**1.** An unfulled portion of a cloth. *Obs.*

1463-4 *Rolls of Parlt.* V. 501/2 In case that eny such diversite, or rawe, scawe, kokell or fagge happen to be in eny part of the seid Clothes.

2. a. ***the raw***, the exposed flesh. Chiefly in phrases ***to touch***, etc. (one) ***on the raw*** (usually *fig.*); ***in the raw*** (see quot. 1934); also, naked.

1823 BYRON *Juan* VIII. l, The veriest jade will wince whose harness wrings So much into the raw. **1837** MARRYAT *Dog-fiend* xxxvii, This was touching up Vanslyperken on the raw. **1866** W. E. FORSTER 31 Oct. in T. W. Reid *Life* (1888) I. x. 387 Obliging me to take any number of newspaper hits.. and these, too, on the raw. **1915** W. S. MAUGHAM *Of Human Bondage* 71 He had a knack of saying bitter things, which caught people on the raw. **1926** A. BENNETT *Lord Raingo* II. lxxiv. 341 What got 'im on the raw was Tommy Hogarth going against 'im in that business. **1934** WEBSTER s.v. Raw n., *In the raw*, in one's natural or crude state; hence, in one's or its true nature or character; in naked truth; as, to present life in the raw. **1941** B. SCHULBERG *What makes Sammy Run?* viii. 188 To go swimming in the raw. **1942** *R.A.F. Jrnl.* 27 June 24 There is a long tale of other victims of nature in the raw. **1944** E. WAUGH *Diary* 16 Apr. (1976) 561 Auberon surprised her in her bath and is thus one of the very few men who can claim to have seen his great-great-grandmother in the raw. **1959** *Times* 9 Nov. 6/7 That is an argument which gets me very much on the raw. **1961** NEW ENG. BIBLE *Acts* v. 33 This touched them on the raw, and they wanted to put them to death. **1970** V. CANNING *Great Affair* iv. 68 As Xavier's pyjamas were much too small for me I slept in the raw. **1972** L. P. DAVIES *What did I do Tomorrow?* vii. 93 My, my. Village life in the raw.

b. A raw place in the skin, a sore or sensitive spot. Freq. *fig.*

1825 SCOTT *Fam. Lett.* II. 235 Using the hackney coach-man's phrase of a raw. **1840** MRS. GORE in *New Monthly Mag.* LX. 470 Susceptibility on such points is an almost unfailing symptom of a raw. **1858** O. W. HOLMES *Aut. Breakf.-t.* (1883) 243 Parties of travellers have a morbid instinct for 'establishing raws' upon each other. **1883** V. STUART *Egypt* 12 Sundry awful raws which stood revealed now that their saddle cloths were removed.

c. ***the raws***, the bare fists. *slang.*

1899 C. ROOK *Hooligan Nights* ii. 27 The average Hooligan..has usually done a bit of fighting with the gloves. .. But he is better with the raws.

3. ***the raw***, applied to any raw article (esp. raw spirits) or quality. Also *transf.*

1844 J. BALLANTINE *Miller of Deanhaugh* v. 100 After swallowing a single glass of the 'raw'. **1864** CARLYLE *Fredk. Gt.* XV. xii. IV. 182 The raw of a September morning. **1928** *Daily Mail* 16 Aug. 19/3, I am not at all sure that here is not a star in the raw.

4. a. A raw person, article, product, etc.; *spec.* in *pl.* raw sugars, or raw oysters. Also *Comb.* in **raw bar** *U.S.*, a bar selling raw oysters.

1868 *Chamb. Jrnl.* 15 Feb. 110/2 Soft-going raws an' delicate boys with romantic heads. **1884** *New York Herald* 27 Oct. 6/2 Sugar—Raws steady but inactive. **1943** *Sun* (Baltimore) 5 Oct. 16/6 The boys at the raw bar in the end of Bill's place last night said the way oysters are this season a feller'll have to eat shells and all to get a mess. **1973** *Washington D.C. Yellow Pages* 1314 Chuck O'Brien's Riverboat. Featuring fine seafood and steaks. Informal raw bar. Cocktail lounge.

b. *U.S.* An untrained pony.

1895 *Outing* (U.S.) XXVI. 389/2 The animals are mostly from the Texan and New Mexican mustang herds. They pay for a 'raw' on an average fifty dollars.

raw (rɔː), *v.*[1] [f. RAW *a.*]

†**1.** *intr.* To become raw. *Obs. rare.*

1483 *Cath. Angl.* 301/1 Rawe as flesche, *crudere, crudescere.* **1765** *Compl. Maltster & Brewer* p. xxii, Acrospired malts..are not subject to raw nor rope.

2. *trans.* To make raw, to excoriate.

1593 NASHE *Christ's T.* (1613) 135 Some of them haue grated and rawed their smooth tender skinnes, with haire shirts and rough garments. **1613** HEYWOOD *Braz. Age* Wks. 1874 III. 250 Helpe me to teare this infernall shirt, Which rawes me where it cleaues. **1893** *Black & White* 4 Mar. 262/1 He..carries his head a little forward, just where the collar raws him. **1899** *Allbutt's Syst. Med.* VI. 646 The ends of the nerve being rawed and brought together by suture.

raw, obs. or dial. form of ROW.

Rawang (rəˈwæŋ). [Native name.] A Tibeto-Burman language.

1934 J. T. O. BARNARD *Handbk. of Răwang Dial. of Nung Lang.* p. v, This is the first book on the Nung language, which has many dialects, of which, however, Răwang may be taken as the one most commonly spoken. **1954** E. R. LEACH *Polit. Syst. Highland Burma* iii. 45 *Nung*—several distinct dialects. Rawang and Daru dialects said to be mutually unintelligible. **1964** E. A. NIDA *Toward Sci. Transl.* ix. 202 In Rawang, a language of Burma, a somewhat similar distinction between dead and alive is employed, but with special restrictions. **1976** *Sci. Amer.* Oct. 140/1 A translator has had to restate most of them, from the Japanese or the Xhosa or the Rawang ('just one of hundreds of Tibeto-Burman languages spoken').

†**raw-bone**, *a.* and *sb.* [f. RAW *a.* 6c.]

A. *adj.* = RAW-BONED.

1593 NASHE *Christ's T.* (1613) 65 So many men as were in Ierusalem, so many pale raw-bone ghosts you would haue thought you had seene. **1660** *Albert Durer Revived* 5 A thin slender wast, a raw-bone arm. **1686** *Lond. Gaz.* No. 2122/4 A slender raw-bone Man. **1704** N. N. tr. *Boccalini's Advts. fr. Parnass.* I. 235 Mounted on Sir Hudibrass's raw-bone Steed. **1772** BRYDGES *Homer Trav.* (1797) I. 10 His quiver ..Rattled against his raw-bone back.

B. *sb.* A very lean or gaunt person, a mere skeleton; *pl.* Death.

1638 BURTON *Anat. Mel.* III. ii. IV. i. (1651) 519 A long lean rawbone, a skeleton, a sneaker. **1784** *Unfortunate Sensibility* I. 116 Till old Raw-bones..strips them till they are, like himself, naked to the very bone.

ˈ**raw-boned**, *a.* [f. as prec.] Having projecting bones, barely covered with flesh; excessively lean or gaunt. Also *transf.*

1591 SHAKS. *1 Hen. VI*, I. ii. 35 Leane raw-bon'd Rascals, who would e're suppose, They had such courage and audacitie? **1638** JUNIUS *Paint. Ancients* 229 Those that are dry, raw-boned and bloudlesse. **1686** *Lond. Gaz.* No. 2127/4 Edward Woodcocke, a tall raw-boned Man, down lookt. **1762** FOOTE *Lyar* II. Wks. 1799 I. 305 A raw-bon'd, over-grown, clumsy cook-wench. **1802** C. WILMOT *Let.* 19 Oct. in T. V. Sadleir *Irish Peer* (1920) 102 A cold wild desolate country bare and rawboned. **1818** SCOTT *Heart Midl.* xxix, Dick turned again to the raw-boned steed which he was currying. **1861** HUGHES *Tom Brown at Oxf.* xxiii, An elderly raw-boned woman with a skin burnt..brown. **1886** W. MORRIS *Let.* 23 June in Mackail *Life Morris* (1899) II. xvi. 161 Stirling..a very raw-boned town.

rawcht, obs. Sc. pa. t. REACH *v.*[1]

rawchter, obs. Sc. form of RAFTER *sb.*[1]

†**rawed**, *a. Obs.* [Of obscure origin: the sense is that of RAYED *a.*, but connexion between the forms appears unlikely.] Striped.

1534 in *Eng. Ch. Furniture* (Peacock 1866) 205 The xth is of blak & Red velvett..& the other side of rawed satten of brigges. **1552-3** *Inv. Ch. Goods, Staffs.* in *Ann. Lichfield* IV. 73 One vestement off rawed saye, an albe to it. **1608** in *Best's Farm. Bks.* (Surtees) 162 *note*, Two dozen of fyne lynnen napkins, the one dozen is rawed with blewe. **1624** *Invent.* in *Archæologia* XLVIII. 136 A livery cubberd, a rawed-work cover on it. **1633** *Naworth Househ. Bks.* (Surtees) 325 For 29 yeardes dimid. of rawed stuffe for hanginges.

rawen, -eyne, obs. variants of ROWEN.

rawenge, rawess, obs. Sc. ff. REVENGE, REVEST.

†**raw-flesh.** *Obs. rare*$^{-0}$. = RAW-HEAD.

1598 FLORIO, *Caccianemico*, a bragging craking boaster, a bugbeare, a rawe-flesh and bloodie-bone.

rawght, obs. pa. t. REACH *v.*[1]

raw-head[1]. [f. RAW *a.* 6 + HEAD *sb.*[1]]

a. The name of a nursery bugbear, usually coupled with BLOODY-BONES. (Cf. RAW-FLESH and RAW NECK.)

c **1550** [? GASCOIGNE] *Wyll of Deuyll* C iij b, Written by our faithful Secretaryes, Hobgoblin, Rawhed, & Bloody-bone. **1659** *Leveller* 4 Most People are agast at them, like children at Raw-head and Bloody-bones. **1694** MOTTEUX *Rabelais* IV. lxvi. (1737) 271 Ruffians and Murtherers, worse than Raw-head and Bloody-bones. **1773** *Life N. Frowde* 19 Already I thought that I beheld Raw-head and Bloody-Bones stalking about my Garret. **1819** L. HUNT *Indicator* No. 11 (1822) I. 81 He was the Raw-head-and-bloody-bones of ancient fable. **1882-9** in Lanc. and Linc. glossaries.

attrib. **1823** SCOTT *St. Ronan's Well* II. vi. 110 Tell a raw-head-and-bloody-bone story about a footpad. **1828** SCOTT *Jrnl.* 1 Apr., They are very angry at the *Review* for telling a raw-head and bloody bones story. **1848** MRS. GASKELL *M. Barton* xx, A raw-head-and-bloody-bones picture of the suspected murderer. **1918** [see FUNK-HOLE].

b. In allusive or figurative use.

1678 BUTLER *Hud.* III. ii. 682 For Zeal's a dreadful Termagant,..Turns meek and sneaking Secret ones, To Raw-heads fierce and Bloody Bones. **1727** SWIFT *Art Polit. Lying* Wks. 1755 III. I. 119 Bringing out the raw-head and bloody bones upon every trifling occasion. **1849** D. J. BROWNE *Amer. Poultry Yd.* (1855) 70 They will welcome the little strangers by making raw head and bloody bones of them.

†**rawhead**[2]. *Obs.*$^{-0}$ [-HEAD.] Rawness.

c **1440** *Promp. Parv.* 424/2 Rawnesse, or rawhede, *cruditas.*

rawhide: see RAW *a.* 2c.

rawin (ˈreɪwɪn). *Meteorol.* [f. RA(DAR + WIN(D *sb.*[1]] A determination of the atmospheric wind speed and direction made by tracking a balloon-borne target with radar; also *transf.*, the instrument itself.

1946 *Bull. Amer. Meteorol. Soc.* XXVII. 371/1 A system of obtaining winds-aloft reports by electronic means known as rawins is now gaining great favor. **1948** T. A. BLAIR *Weather Elements* (ed. 3) iii. 70 By the use of radar methods developed during World War II, a balloon carrying a radar target (reflector) can be followed through and above the clouds, making possible the determination of upper-air wind direction and force in all kinds of weather... Such soundings are known as rawins. **1951** *Jrnl. Meteorol.* VIII. 126/1 Monthly resultant rawins for 24 United States stations were obtained for the layer surface to 10,000 ft and for the 10,000-ft level. **1967** R. W. FAIRBRIDGE *Encycl. Atmospheric Sci.* 581/1 It [*sc.* a radiosonde] consists of a small radio transmitter sent aloft by a helium or hydrogen-filled balloon which transmits the values of the meteorological elements in code to ground stations. If the instrument is tracked by radar to determine wind speed and direction aloft, it is called a rawin. If the two are combined in one, it is called a rawinsonde. **1979** C. KILIAN *Icequake* vi. 103 A few tractors and a collapsed rawin tower were all that was left of the station.

rawine, obs. Sc. form of RAVEN *sb.*[1]

rawing, dial. variant of *rowing* ROWEN.

rawinsonde (ˈreɪwɪnsɒnd). *Meteorol.* [f. RAWIN + SONDE.] A balloon-borne device comprising a radiosonde and a radar target which both transmits meteorological data to ground stations and permits rawin observations to be made, freq. applied to the balloon and instrument package combined.

1946 *Bull. Amer. Meteorol. Soc.* XXVII. 371/1 The recent trend in practice is to combine radiosonde observations and winds-aloft observations in one operation, a Rawinsonde. **1955** *Sci. News Let.* 24 Sept. 197/1 Equipment the Weather Bureau plans to purchase includes:..sixty-five new rawinsondes, to measure winds aloft, including the 200-mile-per-hour river of air known as the jet stream. **1959** *Jrnl. Geophysical Res.* LXIV. 1835 Because of the great altitude of the core of the 'polar-night' jet stream, only isolated rawinsonde observations have penetrated the core. **1970** *Jrnl. Atmospheric Sci.* XXVII. 420/1 Sufficient information content exists within the operational U.S. rawinsonde network to resolve the three-dimensional structure of frontal zones. **1975** *Q. Jrnl. R. Meteorol. Soc.* CI. 336 The rainfall patterns are interpreted within a framework provided by routine upper air data supplemented by long sequences of nominally 1-hourly rawinsondes.

rawish (ˈrɔːɪʃ), *a.* [f. RAW *a.* + -ISH[1].] Somewhat raw, in the various senses of the word.

1602 MARSTON *Antonio's Rev.* Prol., The rawish danke of clumzie winter [c]ramps The fluent summers vaine. **1667** POOLE *Dial. betw. Protest. & Papist* (1735) 194 Every Man that Eats rawish Meat may be said to drink the Blood which he eats in it. **1674** *Lond. Gaz.* No. 875/4 One white Pad Nag, with a rawish Nose. **1828** *Blackw. Mag.* XXIII. 494 The mouth of the drunkard..contracts a singularly sensitive appearance—seemingly red and rawish. **1858** HUGHES *Scour. White Horse* viii. 195 You'll find the night rawish.

Hence ˈ**rawishness**.

1628 VENNER *Baths of Bathe* in *Harl. Misc.* (Malh.) IV. 123 The water seems, by reason of the rawishness of the place, to be colder at its issuing forth, than it is otherwise. **1662** H. STUBBE *Ind. Nectar* iii. 25 It had also a rawishnesse in it, as if the fat required boiling.

rawk, vapour, fog: see ROKE.

rawk, variant of RAUK *a.*, hoarse. *Obs.*

†ˈ**rawky**, *a.*[1] *Obs. rare*$^{-1}$. [f. dial. *rawk* gum (of the eye), slime.] Slimy, gummy.

1509 BARCLAY *Shyp of Folys* (1570) 229 Their noses dropping,..Their eyne rawky, and all their face unpure.

ˈ**rawky**, *a.*[2] *rare.* Also 7 **raukie**. [f. *rawk* var. ROKE + -Y. Cf. ROKY *a.*[1]] Foggy, misty; raw.

1601 WEEVER *Mirr. Mart.* E iij, The gloomie morning.. Muffled in mists and raukie vapours rose. *a* **1864** CLARE *Rem.* (1873) 227 Nameless flowers..Culled in cold and rawky hours. **1869-82** in Lanc. glossaries. **1935** E. R. EDDISON *Mistress of Mistresses* x. 194 The air between the cliffs, ruffled in mists and rawky vapours. **1936** J. G. HORNE *Flooer o' Ling* 22 Or rawky day creeps up the sky.

rawlin pollack (see quot. *a* 1672 and RAUNING).

a **1672** WILLUGHBY *Hist. Piscium* (1686) 23 *Asellus niger*, the Cole-fish or Rawlin Pollack. **1674** RAY *Coll. Eng. Words* Fishes 100 The Ræwlin-Pollack. **1740** R. BROOKES *Art of Angling* 144. **1884** GOODE *Usef. Aquat. Anim.* 228.

Rawlplug (ˈrɔːlplʌg), *sb.* and *v.* Also **Rawl-plug**, and with small initial. [f. the name of J. J. and W. R. *Raw*lings, English electrical engineers, who introduced it + PLUG *sb.*] **A.** *sb.* A proprietary name for a kind of thin cylindrical plug, made of fibre or plastic, which can be inserted into a hole in masonry, etc., in order to hold a screw or nail. Also applied *loosely* to any plug of this type.

1912 *Trade Marks Jrnl.* 30 Oct. 1648 *Rawlplug*... A wall plug for electric wiring made of fibre. Rawlings Bros., Limited, 82, Gloucester Rd., London, S.W.; Electrical engineers. **1923** *Radio Times* 28 Sept. 35/1 For any job connected with Wireless where you use a screw..always use Rawlplugs. **1941** M. TREADGOLD *We couldn't leave Dinah* vii. 124 The shelf for brushes that Nick Lindsay had fixed up with rawl-plugs. **1947** 'G. ORWELL' in *Tribune* 7 Feb. 12/1 The amateur handyman, with his tack hammer and his pocketful of rawlplugs. **1960** WILLMOTT & YOUNG *Family & Class in London Suburb.* ii. 24 Her role is..to stand at the bottom of a ladder handing up his power-tool..or a box of Rawlplugs. **1962** H. THURSTON *Where is thy Sting?* iv. 55 A long panel of looking-glass which Philippa had fixed with rawlplugs on one side of the fireplace. **1972** D. HASTON *In High Places* i. 9 The climber drills a hole in the rock, hammers in an expansion bolt (something like the domestic Rawlplug), attaches a carabiner and proceeds in normal fashion.

Also **Rawl**, a proprietary term used *attrib.* or as a prefix in names of tools, screws, bolts, and related accessories.

1937 *Trade Marks Jrnl.* 29 Sept. 1151 *Rawl*... Cutlery and edge tools. The Rawlplug Company Limited. **1958** *Engineering* 14 Feb. 54 (Advt.), The holes are drilled with a Rawltool to the exact size, the Rawlbolts dropped in and after the machine has been positioned the bolts are tightened. **1971** C. BONINGTON *Annapurna South Face* 246 American rawl stud bolts for hard rock. **1976** *Shooting Mag.* Dec. 9/1 (Advt.), The cabinet has been designed for fixing to the wall by means of three Rawlbolts through strengthening bars.

B. *v. trans.* To attach by means of a Rawlplug or the like; to drill a hole in (a wall, etc.) and insert a Rawlplug. Hence **'rawlplugging** *vbl. sb.*

1960 'A. BURGESS' *Right to Answer* i. 5 He'd rawlplugged his pictures..deep into the walls. **1964** E. & M. A. RADFORD *Hungry Killer* xiv. 133 The bookcase, Rawlplugged to the wall. **1971** *Ideal Home* Apr. 52/1 Brass hooks rawlplugged to the wall hold it in place. **1972** R. QUILTY *Tenth Session* 92 You should have Rawl-plugged the wall. You're cracking the plaster. **1974** M. BUTTERWORTH *Man in Sopwith Camel* i. 17 Plastering, paperhanging, rawlplugging, joinering.

rawly ('rɔːlɪ), *adv.* [f. RAW *a.* + -LY^{2}. Common *c* 1570–1670, often in quasi-adjectival use.]

†**1.** With *to leave*: **a.** In an unfinished state. *Obs.*

1538 LELAND *Itin.* IV. 33 Eiton College, begon to be buildid by Henry the vj. but left very onperfect and rauly. **1580** LYLY *Euphues* (Arb.) 217 Nichomachus left Tindarides rawly, for feare of anger, not for want of Art. **1615** HIERON *Wks.* I. 599 If I left the matter so rawly, I might fall at vnawares into two extremities.

†**b.** At an immature age. *Obs.* $rare^{-1}$.

1599 SHAKS. *Hen. V*, IV. i. 147 Some swearing, some crying for a Surgean; some vpon their Wiues, left poore behind them;..some vpon their Children rawly left.

†**2.** Ignorantly; without sufficient knowledge or experience. *Obs.*

1565 JEWEL *Def. Apol.* (1611) 108 Had you well considered these things, M. Harding, ye would not so rawly haue thus concluded. **1593** R. HARVEY *Philad.* 13 To reject it, as this one Scot hath done very rawly and unadvisedly. **1612** BRINSLEY *Lud. Lit.* 309 How many euils doe come vpon the sending of schollars so rawly thither. **1680** BAXTER *Let.* in *Answ. Dodwell* 97 To tell you the truth, I entered so rawly, that..I remember not that I took that Oath.

†**3. a.** Crudely; imperfectly, in an insufficient or unsatisfactory manner. *Obs.*

1576 FOXE *A. & M.* 1895/2 The Story is but rawly and imperfectly touched before. **1581** MULCASTER *Positions* v. (1887) 32 Counterfeat the letter or some letterlike deuise first rawly and rudely. **1634** W. WOOD *New Eng. Prosp.* I. ii, The English comming over so rawly and uncomfortably provided. **1697** J. SERGEANT *Solid Philos.* 334 Were these Principles which I rawly and briefly touch on here, pursu'd by Learned Men [etc.].

†**b.** Barely, scarcely. *Obs. rare.*

1607 MIDDLETON *Michaelmas Term* IV. iv. 21 The world is very loath to praise me; 'Tis rawly friends with me. **1651** H. L'ESTRANGE *Answ. Mrq. Worcester* 65 Amongst the antients there is none at all, or very rawly any mention of Purgatory.

†**c.** With difficulty or annoyance. *Obs.* $rare^{-1}$.

1586 J. HOOKER *Hist. Irel.* in *Holinshed* II. 89/1 The archbishop of Dublin rawlie digesting the vicedeputie his long absence.

4. Immaturely (opposed to 'ripely').

1875 BROWNING *Aristoph. Apol.* 135 He who wrote Erechtheus may be rawly politic, At home where Kleophon is ripe. **1955** E. BLISHEN *Roaring Boys* II. 99 For..two years I had been rawly warring with my classes. **1979** *Chatelaine* Jan. 64/3 The secret realm in which their love flowered—so rawly, with such unanticipated greed!

5. So as to be bare or exposed.

1924 'L. MALET' *Dogs of Want* ix. 270 Every nerve of his body seeming rawly outside his skin instead of normally and decently covered by it.

rawmpe, obs. form of RAMP *v.*

rawn (rɔːn). *Sc.* and *north. dial.* Also 8 raan, 9 raun, (roan), ran. [Of Scand. origin, = Da. *ravn* roe; the relationship of this to Da. *rogn*, ON. *hrogn* (see ROE) is obscure.] The roe of a fish; a female fish. ***rawn-fleuk***, the turbot.

1483 *Cath. Angl.* 301/1 Rawne of a fysche, *lectis*. **1584** *Rec. Burgh Edinb.* (1882) 343 The heiring to be callour slayne.. having heid and taill with melt and rawne. **1585** JAS. I *Ess. Poesie* (Arb.) 78 Evin so of rawnis do mightie fishes breid. **1785** HUTTON *Bran New Wark* 85 An unshot codfish hes maar raans in its belly than thare be people on the face of the earth. **1810** NEILL *List of Fishes* 12 (Jam.) Turbot... This species is here commonly denominated the rawn-fleuk, from its being thought best for the table when in rawn or roe. **1824** SCOTT *Redgauntlet* let. vi, The water being in..rare trim for the saumon raun. **1877** *Holderness Gloss.* s.v., 'Melts an rauns', male and female fish.

Hence **rawned** *a.*, full of roe (Jam.); **'rawner**, a female salmon, *spec.* one which has not spawned at the proper time.

1808–25 JAMIESON. **1901** *Dundee Adv.* 26 Feb. 6 The fish was found to be unspawned, or what is known on the Tay as a 'rawner', and deemed an illegal fish to take.

rawn, dial. variant of ROWEN.

rawndoune, -down, obs. forms of RANDOM.

†**raw neck.** *Obs.* $rare^{-1}$. = RAW-HEAD.

1768–74 TUCKER *Lt. Nat.* (1834) II. 596 Boiled rabbits are trussed up to appear as frightful as possible, and made to resemble that terror of our childhood, raw neck and bloody bones.

rawness ('rɔːnɪs). [f. RAW *a.* + -NESS.]

1. The state of being raw or crude; *fig.* imperfection, incompleteness.

c **1440** *Promp. Parv.* 424/2 Rawnesse, or rawhede, *cruditas*. **1616** HIERON *Wks.* I. 586 The rawnesse and raggednesse and independance of that which is deliuered. **1646** P. BULKELEY *Gospel Covt.* To Rdr. 2 The rawnesse of the draught which I had written for the help of myself. *a* **1661** FULLER *Worthies* (1840) III. 108 His book, known by the name of 'Coriat's Crudities', nauseous to nice readers, for the rawness thereof. **1809** PINKNEY *Trav. France* 204 What we should call in wine, their rawness and their freshness.

fig. **1605** SHAKS. *Macb.* IV. iii. 26 Why in that rawnesse left you Wife, and Childe..Without leaue-taking?

2. Inexperience, ignorance.

1548 UDALL, etc. *Erasm. Par. Luke* xxii, Tempering his woordes to the rawnesse of his disciples, which rawenes he suffred..to remaine a long season in them. **1627** HAKEWILL *Apol.* (1630) 272 Considering the rawnesse of his seamen, and the manifold shipwracks which they sustained. **1710** HEARNE *Collect.* (O.H.S.) III. 94 The Bp. denied him Orders for his Rawness in Divinity. **1736** CARTE *Ormonde* II. 81 The inexpertness of..the Irish officers..and the rawness of their soldiers. **1861** DICKENS *Gt. Expect.* xxxvii, In my first rawness and ignorance.

3. Bareness of flesh, excoriation, soreness.

1607 MARKHAM *Caval.* III. (1617) 144 His nostrils wide and without rawnesse. **1659** HAMMOND *On Ps.* lviii. 9 Annot. 298 So shall rawness, so shall anger, or inflammation ..affright or perplex them. **1803** *Med. Jrnl.* IX. 525 Universal rawness and soreness in the trachea and chest. **1897** *Allbutt's Syst. Med.* III. 944 A sense of rawness and even actual tenderness in the abdomen.

†**b.** Indigestion. *Obs.*

1538 ELYOT, *Cruditas*, rawnes, or lack of digestion. **1587** GOLDING *De Mornay* xiv. 209 Our minde..for all that, neuer feeleth any rawness or lacke of digestion. **1671** H. M. tr. *Erasm. Colloq.* 61 He felt neither pain in his head, nor rawness in his stomach.

4. Chilly dampness, muggy cold.

1608 HEYWOOD *Lucrece* IV. ii, Hath not..the moist rawness of this humorous night, Impair'd your health? **1684** SOUTHERNE *Disappointment* III. i, I am to blame to call thee forth Into the rawness of a midnight air. **1818** MRS. SHELLEY *Frankenst.* let. iv, He is far too weak to sustain the rawness of the atmosphere.

rawng(e, obs. ff. RANGE.

rawnke, obs. f. RANK *a.*

rawnpiked, var. RAMPIKED.

rawnsake, -some, obs. ff. RANSACK, RANSOM.

rawranoke, rawthe, rawunson, rawyn, obs. ff. ROANOKE, RUTH, RANSOM, RAVEN.

rawyne, -ynnis, obs. Sc. ff. RAVIN^{1}, RAVENOUS.

rax, *sb.*^{1} *Sc.* [f. *racks*, pl. of RACK *sb.*^{2} 2.] A roasting-rack (see quot. 1808). Chiefly *pl.*

1697 *Inv. Furniture* in *Scott. N. & Q.* (1900) Dec. 90/2 A pair of raxes, two spits, a frying pann. **1717** RAMSAY *Elegy Lucky Wood* v, Rax, chandlers, tangs, and fire-shools. **1808** JAMIESON, *Raxes*, iron instruments consisting of various links, on which the spit is turned at the fire, andirons. **1824** SCOTT *Ep. Lockhart* 42 Speates and raxes..for a famishing guest, sir.

rax, *sb.*^{2} *Sc.* and *north. dial.* [f. RAX *v.*] A stretch, an act of stretching; a strain, wrench.

1790 D. MORISON *Poems* 118 To tak a turn an' gi'e my legs a rax, I'll through the land. **1819** W. TENNANT *Papistry Storm'd* (1827) 146 They grippit,..And, wi' enormous raxes, soucht T' unsaddle ane anither. **1855–** in northern glossaries (Northumbld., Yks.).

rax, *v. Sc.* and *north. dial.* Also 9 *Sc.* raux. [OE. *raxan*, of obscure formation. The word is rarely found in ME. (cf. also the variant RASK), but is common in older and modern Sc.]

I. *intr.* **1.** To stretch oneself after sleep. †*to rax up*, to start or waken up from a swoon.

a **1000** *Prose Life Guthlac* xii. (1848) 60 Swa he of hefeȝum slæpe raxende awoce. *a* **1300** *Cursor M.* 24351 (Gött.) Þat suime was of mi soru suage, Bot quen i raxed vp..I ne wist bot walaway. **1377** LANGL. *P. Pl.* B. v. 398 He roxed [*v.r.* raxed] and rored and rutte atte laste. **1715** RAMSAY *Christ's Kirk Gr.* III. i, Carles wha heard the cock had crawn, Begoud to rax and rift. **1805** A. SCOTT *Poems* (1808) 109 (E.D.D.) The drowsy queen Raise rauxing, gaunting rub'd her een.

2. To become longer by pulling, to stretch; †to be hanged.

1508 KENNEDIE *Flyting w. Dunbar* 368 Thou has a wedy teuch..about thy crag to rax. **1530** LYNDESAY *Test. Papyngo* 1165 The Rauin said: god, nor I rax in ane raipe. **1785** *Fergusson's Sc. Prov.* No. 730 Raw leather raxes. **1876–** in northern glossaries (Northumbld., Yks.).

b. To wax, grow, become. $rare^{-1}$.

a **1774** FERGUSSON *Farmer's Ingle* Poems (1845) 36 Wad they to labouring lend an eident hand, They'd rax fell strang upon the simplest fare.

c. *to rax out*: (see quot.).

1829 BROCKETT *N.C. Gloss.* (ed. 2), s.v., As applied to the weather, to *rax out* means to clear up, when the clouds begin to open, and expand themselves, so that the sky is seen.

3. To extend the hand, etc.; to reach out (*for*).

a **1585** MONTGOMERIE *Cherrie & Slae* 367 Then Dreid.. Forbad my minting anie mair, To raxe aboue my reiche. **1720** RAMSAY *Wealth* 10 Wha rax for riches or immortal fame. **1824** SCOTT *St. Ronan's* x, Ye..raxed ower the tether maybe a wee bit farther than ye had ony right to do. **1893** CROCKETT *Stickit Minister* 145 Raxing for a peat to light his pipe.

†**4.** To extend one's sphere or power; to have sway or rule; to prevail or have course. *Obs.* (15–16th c. Sc.)

c **1470** HENRYSON *Mor. Fab.* III. (*Cock & Fox*) xxi, He.. traistit ay to rax and sa to rin [etc.]. *Ibid.* v. (*Parl. Beasts*) xlvii, Than sall ressoun ryis, rax, and ring. **1535** STEWART *Cron. Scot.* I. 91 Mony theif and tratour in his tyme Raxit and rang. *Ibid.* II. 465 In Albione than wes gude peax and rest, Bot rycht schort quhile tha leit it rax or lest. *a* **1578** LINDESAY (Pitscottie) *Chron. Scot.* (S.T.S.) I. 346 He will not rax long nor ȝeit haue his realme in peace and rest.

II. *trans.* **5.** *refl.* To stretch or strain (oneself).

c **1325** *Gloss. W. de Bibbesw.* in *Rel. Ant.* II. 80/1 Raxes him, *se espreche*. *c* **1375** *Sc. Leg. Saints* xl. (*Ninian*) 703 Þat bysnyne..vaknit as of hewy slepe, & raxit hyme. **1513** DOUGLAS *Æneis* IV. xi. 93 Thrise scho hir self raxit vp for to rise. *Ibid.* VI. xiv. 45 Considdir Torquatus ȝondir doith hym rax. *a* **1670** SPALDING *Troub. Chas. I* (1829) 28 He should seem to rax himself, and shake loose off his arm. **1829** BROCKETT *N.C. Gloss.* (ed. 2), s.v., *To rax oneself*, is to extend the limbs, after sleep or long sitting. **1863** G. MACDONALD *D. Elginbrod* I. x, Tak' care an' nae rax yersel ower sair.

6. To stretch (a thing) by pulling.

1513 DOUGLAS *Æneis* XI. xvi. 61 Now hir handis raxit it euery stede. **1613** P. FORBES *Comm. Revelation* 229 He had a long chaine, which yet was further raxed. **1786** BURNS *Ordination* i, Ye wha leather rax an' draw. **1818** SCOTT *Hrt. Midl.* v, When ye gang to see a man..raxing a halter. **1861** RAMSAY *Remin.* Ser. II. 106 If I could win at him, I wud rax the banes o' him.

b. To strain (the eyes). *rare.*

1819 W. TENNANT *Papistry Storm'd* (1827) 94 A man mith rax his een in vain Ere he could spy..an idol.

7. To reach or hand (a thing) to one; to deal (a blow).

1711 RAMSAY *On Maggy Johnstoun* vii, Death wi' his rung rax'd her a yowff. **1792** A. WILSON *On a Man sawing Timber*, Rax me your haun. **1825** J. WILSON *Noct. Ambr.* i. Wks. 1855 I. 8 Rax me ower the loaf. **1894** A. ROBERTSON *Nuggets*, etc. 70 Rax me the brandy bottle, an' pit it doon beside me.

8. To stretch or hold *out* (the hand, etc.); to elongate (the neck).

1742 FORBES *Ajax* iii, Raxing out his gardies. **1788** PICKEN *Poems* 88 The darksome e'ening raxes Her wings owre day. **1810** COCK *Simple Strains* I. 89 (E.D.D.) Ye'll shortly see me rax my neck and craw. **1854** H. MILLER *Sch. & Schm.* vii. (1860) 76 Just rax out your han' and tak' in my snuffbox.

Hence **raxed** *ppl. a.*; **'raxing** *vbl. sb.* and *ppl. a.*

1637–50 ROW *Hist. Kirk* (1842) 323 The raxeing consciences of conforme men. **1785** BURNS *Ep. M'Math* iv, Their three-mile prayers,..Their raxin' conscience. **1822** SCOTT *Nigel* iii, That might have cost my craig a raxing. **1824** —— *Redgauntlet* ch. xi, Cloured crowns were plenty, and raxed necks came into fashion. **1876** C. C. ROBINSON *Gloss. Mid-Yorks.* 110/2 A person will tell of 'a nasty raxin' pain' he is subject to. **1893** R. L. STEVENSON *Catriona* I. xiii. 143 My craig'll have to thole a raxing. **1898** N. MUNRO *John Splendid* xv. 147 A raxed shoulder he had met with at Dumbarton. **1935** A. J. CRONIN *Stars look Down* I. ix. 67 What he did mind was the bother when a tub ran off; it nearly killed him, the raxing and straining to lift it back upon the line.

†**raxle**, *v. Obs.* Also raxhil, raxsil, raxill(e, -el. [Frequentative f. RAX *v.* Cf. RASKLE.] *intr.* and *trans.* To stretch, etc.: = RAX *v.*

c **1205** LAY. 25992 Seoððen he gon ræmien and raxlede swiðe. *a* **1300** *Cursor M.* 2209 (Cott.) Oueral he raxhild him wit rage. *Ibid.* 24447 (Gött.) Apon mi taas oft sith i stod, Roles raxland to þe rode. **13..** *E.E. Allit. P.* A. 1174 Þen wakned I..I raxled & fel in gret affray. *a* **1400–50** *Alexander* 4930 Þe renke within þe redell þan raxsils his armes. **1483** *Cath. Angl.* 301/1 Raxill(e, *alo* (*exalo* A.).

ray (reɪ), *sb.*^{1} Also 7 raie, raye; *pl.* 5, 7 rayes, (6 ? rayse), 6–7 raies. [a. OF. acc. *rai*, *ray* (nom. *rais*, *raiz*, etc., see Godef.; in mod.F. *rais*) = Prov. *rai*(*g*, *rait*, etc., Sp. and Pg. *rayo*, It. *raggio* (pl. *raggi*, *rai*):—L. *radium*, acc. of *radius* RADIUS *sb.*

Occasionally employed in Eng. from the 14th c. onwards, but not in common use until the 17th.]

I. 1. a. A single line or narrow beam of light.

In popular use applied to each of the lines in which light seems to stream from a distant glowing body or luminous point, and to similar lines, produced by the reflection of light from a polished surface, lens, etc.; also to a narrow line of light passing through a small opening. In early scientific use defined by Newton as the least portion of light which can be stopped alone or propagated alone; more recently as the motion of a simple particle of light, or the smallest conceivable line of light, and now usually regarded merely as the straight line in which the radiant energy capable of producing the sensation of light is propagated to any given point.

Ray is usually distinguished from *beam*, as indicating a smaller amount of light; in scientific use a beam is a collection of parallel rays. In ordinary language *ray* is the word usually employed when the reference is to the heat rather than the light of the sun (as in quot. 1698).

13.. *E.E. Allit. P.* A. 160, I sey..A crystal clyffe ful relusaunt; Mony ryal ray con fro hit rere. **1483** CAXTON *Cato* F ij, Lyke hym whyche is blynde of the rayes of the sonne. *c* **1586** C'TESS PEMBROKE *Ps.* CII. vii, The sunn of my life daies Inclines to west with falling raies. **1665** GLANVILL *Def.*

Van. Dogm. 34 'Tis as conceivable as how the Rays of Light should come in a direct line to the eye. **1698** FRYER *Acc. E. India & P.* 242 We had our skins flead off of those Parts exposed to the Solar Rays. *c* **1750** SHENSTONE *Progr. Taste* II. 116 The sheathless sword the guard displays, Which round emits its dazzling rays. *a* **1800** COWPER *Glow-worm* 6 Disputes have been, and still prevail, From whence his rays proceed. **1830** M. DONOVAN *Dom. Econ.* I. 59 If a ray of light is admitted, the vegetable grows with greater vigour. **1849** JAMES *Woodman* iii, The rays of the moon stole through the leafless branches and chequered the frosty turf.

fig. **1831** LYTTON *Godolphin* 4 A ray shot across his countenance as he uttered his last words.

transf. **1741** SHENSTONE *Judgm. Hercules* 202 Thy costly robe shall glow with Tyrian rays. **1830** TENNYSON *Arab. Nts.* 136 With argent-lidded eyes Amorous, and lashes like to rays Of darkness.

b. A representation of a ray (esp. *Her.*); a material thing representing or resembling a ray of light, a brilliant stretch (of something).

1729 SAVAGE *Wanderer* III. 84 O'er altars thus, impainted, we behold Half-circling glories shoot in rays of gold. **1780** EDMONDSON *Compl. Body Heraldry* II. Gloss., *Rays*, when depicted round the sun, should be sixteen in number, but, when round an etoile, six only. **1797** *Encycl. Brit.* (ed. 3) VIII. 457/1 Azure, one Ray of the Sun, bendways Gules, between six Beams of that Luminary Argent. **1835** LYTTON *Rienzi* v. i, Hung with silk of a blood-red, relieved by rays of white.

c. *fig.* of mental and moral influences, etc., comparable to light.

1634 MILTON *Comus* 425 The sacred rayes of Chastity. **1674** BOYLE *Excell. Theol.* I. ii. 75 Reason is such a ray of Divinity [etc.]. **1732** BERKELEY *Alciphr.* I. §2 A ray of truth may enlighten the whole world and extend to future ages. **1781** J. MOORE *View Soc. It.* (1790) I. vi. 63 This never fails to dart such a ray of comfort into my heart. **1838** THIRLWALL *Greece* III. xxiii. 265 Only one ray of hope broke the gloom of her prospects.

d. A trace of anything. (Chiefly with negatives.)

1773 EARL MALMESBURY *Diaries & Corr.* I. 97, I am resolved to push on in my career as long as I see a ray of the ladder, which is within my compass, to mount. **1847** DICKENS *Haunted M.* (C.D. ed.) 219 Isn't it enough that you were seven boys before, without a ray of gal. **1856** EMERSON *Eng. Traits, The 'Times'* Wks. (Bohn) II. 117 Rude health and spirits,.. and the habits of society are implied, but not a ray of genius.

e. Fig. phr. (*little*) ***ray of sunshine***, a person (freq. a young woman) who enlivens or cheers another; a happy or vivacious person. Cf. SUNSHINE *sb.* 2a.

1915 A. BENNETT *These Twain* (1916) xx. 485 You're a little ray of sunshine, and all that, and I'm the first to say so. **1929** J. B. PRIESTLEY *Good Companions* II. iv. 364 Why are you now our little ray of sunshine? **1959** M. SCOTT *White Elephant* v. 56 Are you two in this to make money or just to be little rays of sunshine? **1972** C. FREMLIN *Appointment with Yesterday* iv. 31 Milly rather fancied herself in the rôle of little ray of sunshine to brighten his declining years. **1978** 'M. M. KAYE' *Far Pavilions* xxxvii. 540 He hasn't exactly been a ray of sunshine up to now.

2. a. (Chiefly *poet.*) Light, radiance; (freq. also implying heat: see note to sense 1).

1592 DAVIES *Immort. Soul* Ded. vii, Where the Sun.. never doth retire his golden Ray. **1667** MILTON *P.L.* IV. 673 Earth, made.. apter to receive Perfection from the Suns more potent Ray. **1748** GRAY *Alliance* 66 Lamps, that shed at Ev'n a cheerful ray. **1770** GOLDSM. *Des. Vill.* 347 Those blazing suns that dart a downward ray. **1818** SHELLEY *Rev. Islam* VI. xxii, A mountain,.. whose crest.. in the ray Of the obscure stars gleamed. **1830** LYTTON *P. Clifford* xxviii, The ray of the lanterns glimmered on the blades of cutlasses.

fig. **1606** SHAKS. *Tr. & Cr.* I. iii. 47 In stormes of Fortune .. in her ray and brightnesse. **1635–56** COWLEY *Davideis* II. Wks. 1710 I. 346 Fair was the Promise of his dawning Ray. **1726–46** THOMSON *Winter* 465 Reared by his care, of softer ray appears Cimon sweet-souled. **1741** SHENSTONE *Judgm. Hercules* 77 Her air diffused a mild yet awful ray.

†**b.** *concr.* A star. *nonce-use. Obs.*

1700 PRIOR *Carm. Sec.* 398 Thou smiling see'st great Dorset's Worth confest, The Ray distinguishing the Patriot's Breast.

3. a. (Chiefly *poet.*) A beam or glance of the eye; †also, sight, power of vision (*obs.*).

1531 ELYOT *Gov.* II. xii, The rayes or beames issuinge from the eyen of her,.. hath thrilled throughout the middes of my hart. **1616** CHAPMAN *Homer's Hymn Hermes* 368 To me then declare, O old man,.. if thy grave ray Hath any man seen [etc.]. **1667** MILTON *P.L.* III. 619 The Aire, No where so cleer, sharp'nd his visual ray To objects distant farr. **1728** POPE *Dunc.* II. 7 All eyes direct their rays On him, and crowds grow foolish as they gaze.

b. A line of sight.

1700 MOXON *Math. Dict.* 177 The Visual Point.. is a Point in the Horizontal Line, wherein all the Ocular Rays unite. **1753** HOGARTH *Anal. Beauty* v. 25 A ray may be supposed to be drawn from the center of the eye to the letter it looks at first. **1842** GWILT *Encycl. Arch.* §2391 The visual rays upon every object may be compared to the legs of a pair of compasses.

†**4.** *Astrol.* = ASPECT *sb.* 4. *Obs. rare.*

1700 MOXON *Math. Dict.* 137 In Astronomy, a Radius or a Ray is taken for the Aspect or Configuration of two Stars: so we say Saturn beholds Venus with an Hostile Ray, &c. when she is square with him.

5. a. Used (on the analogy of sense 1) in reference to the emission or transmission of non-luminous physical energies propagated in radiating straight lines after the manner of light (in modern use *esp.* of heat: cf. RADIATION 2, X-RAYS *sb. pl.*).

Roentgen rays: see ROENTGEN.

1664 POWER *Exp. Philos.* III. 159 If the Magnetick rayes proceeded intrinsecally from the Stone. **1813** SIR H. DAVY *Agric. Chem.* (1814) 39 The beautiful experiments of Dr. Herschel have shewn that there are rays transmitted from the sun which do not illuminate. **1865** *Reader* 28 Jan. 105/1 The term dark, or invisible, or obscure rays, stimulates the imagination by its strangeness.

†**b.** A series (of atoms) moving in a straight line. *Obs. rare.*

1674 N. FAIRFAX *Bulk & Selv.* 196 Those rayes of other atoms that are shacking all over the worlds wasts.

c. Chiefly *Science Fiction.* A supposed destructive beam of energy emitted by a ray-gun or similar device. Cf. *death-ray* s.v. DEATH *sb.* 19.

1898 H. G. WELLS *War of Worlds* vi. 39 Only the fact that a hummock of heathery sand intercepted the lower part of the Heat-Ray saved them. **1919** G. B. SHAW *Heartbreak House* 39, I will discover a ray mighter than any X-ray: a mind ray that will explode the ammunition in the belt of my adversary before he can point his gun at me. **1926** G. HUNTING *Vicarion* xiii. 215 I'm glad they never perfected that ray they used to talk about for disposing of an enemy at a distance without betraying the disposer. **1940** GRAVES & HODGE *Long Week-End* vi. 93 An inventor.. claimed to have produced a ray that would set fire to anything inflammable. **1969** E. VON DANIKEN *Chariots of Gods?* ii. 25 They will hammer and chisel in the rock pictures of what they had once seen: Shapeless giants,.. staves from which rays are shot out as if from a sun.

II. 6. *Math.* **a.** = RADIUS *sb.* 3. Now *rare.*

1690 LEYBOURN *Curs. Math.* 735 If the Ray AC of the Concentrick ACEF be supposed to be equal to the Ray BD of the Eccentrick BDEF. **1704** C. HAYES *Treat. Fluxions* 45 The Arch of the Circle MQ, bounded at Q by the Ray FA. **1753** CHAMBERS *Cycl. Supp.*, *Ray of curvature*, in geometry, is used to signify the semi-diameter of the circle of curvature. **1825** J. NICHOLSON *Operat. Mechanic* 129 From each of these points draw a line to the opposite end of the base, as so many rays to a centre. **1835** LINDLEY *Introd. Bot.* (1848) I. 336 A corolla is said to be regular when its segments form equal rays of a circle.

b. Any one of the lines forming a pencil or set of straight lines passing through a point.

1879 *Encycl. Brit.* X. 389/2 Through every point in *p* one line in the pencil will pass, and every ray in Q will cut *p* in one point. **1885** LEUDESDORF *Cremona's Proj. Geom.* 73 The locus of the points of intersection of pairs of corresponding rays of the pencils.

7. One of any system of lines, parts, or things radially disposed.

1668 WILKINS *Real Char.* II. v. 131 A kind of Gelly,.. having several kinds of rays like legs, proceeding from the middle of it. **1672–3** GREW *Anat. Roots* I. iii. §7 These Parts, are like so many White Rays, streaming, by the Diameter of the Root, from the inward Edge toward the Circumference of the Barque. **1748** SIR J. HILL *Hist. Fossils* 654 Of these [Asteriæ] some have five angles, or rays, and others only four. **1849** NOAD *Electricity* (ed. 3) 350 The radii of the wheel must be so arranged that each ray shall touch the surface of the mercury, before the preceding ray shall have quitted it.

8. *Bot.* **a.** The marginal portion of a composite flower, consisting of ligulate florets arranged radially. = RADIUS *sb.* 2c (*a*).

1785 MARTYN *Rousseau's Bot.* vi. (1794) 65 Botanists have given the name of ray to the set of semiflorets which compose the circumference. **1837** *Penny Cycl.* VII. 422/1 Every head of flowers.. has a central part, or disk, and a circumference, or ray. **1872** OLIVER *Elem. Bot.* II. 195 In Daisy, the outside florets are irregular,.. and white, constituting the ray.

b. A pedicel or branch of an umbel. = RADIUS *sb.* 2c (*b*).

1785 MARTYN *Rousseau's Bot.* v. (1794) 51 The rays of the little umbels are no farther subdivided. **1776–96** WITHERING *Brit. Plants* (ed. 3) IV. 375 The Rays may be sometimes 3 or 5, but only accidentally. **1870** HOOKER *Stud. Flora* 155 Umbels lateral and terminal, subglobose; rays few or many, long or short.

c. = MEDULLARY *ray.*

1884 BOWER & SCOTT *De Bary's Phaner.* 458 With reference to their origin at the first commencement of the woody ring, the former have also received the name of the original primary rays. **1925** EAMES & MACDANIELS *Introd. Plant Anat.* vii. 176 The ray is more or less like a brick wall, the individual cells representing the bricks. **1953** K. ESAU *Plant Anat.* xi. 252 The dicotyledons typically contain only parenchyma cells in the rays.

9. *Zool.* **a.** = *fin-ray*, FIN *sb.*[1] 6.

1668 WILKINS *Real Char.* II. v. 142 Pike... Two finns; the hindermost of which is small, fleshy and without rays. **1769** PENNANT *Zool.* III. 166 The first ray of the first dorsal fin is very long. **1828** STARK *Elem. Nat. Hist.* I. 400 One great genus, characterized by the first dorsal fin with soft rays, followed by a second smaller one,.. not supported by rays. **1872** BAKER *Nile Tribut.* ix. 156 The back fin resembled that of a perch, with seven rays.

b. One of the radial divisions of a star-fish.

1753 CHAMBERS *Cycl. Supp.* s.v. *Star-fish*, There are many species of the star-fish,.. they have different numbers of rays, but the most common kind have five. **1834** MCMURTRIE *Cuvier's Anim. Kingd.* 466 There are also two ovaries in each ray. **1842** *Penny Cycl.* XXIII. 16/1 Specimens of star-fish with four large rays and a small one still growing.

10. *Astr.* Any of the long bright lines of pale material that can be seen to radiate from some lunar craters.

1838 J. P. NICHOL *Phenomena & Order Solar Syst.* II. vi. 171 The most remarkable circumstance connected with this variety in the Moon's shining power is those rays issuing chiefly from craters and extending over a large space. **1873** R. A. PROCTOR *Moon* iv. 253 The telescope.. has discovered numerous small craters of varying depth in the midst of many of the rays, and it reveals the fact, that these small craters.. do not penetrate through the matter we are examining, inasmuch as there comes from their bases always the same kind of light that characterizes the ray. **1895** T. G. ELGER *Moon* 27 The rays emanating from Tycho surpass in extent and interest any of the others. **1922** H. S. JONES *Gen. Astron.* iv. 102 From some of the craters, under favourable conditions of illumination, bright rays or streaks can be seen radiating radially in all directions. **1962** *Listener* 1 Feb. 223/2 The mysterious lunar rays issuing from Tycho, Copernicus, and other craters also fit better into an igneous theory. The rays cross mountains, walled formations, ridges, and seas without marked deviation.

11. *attrib.* and *Comb.* **a.** In sense 1, as ***ray-fringed, -gilt, -girt, -shorn, -strewn*** adjs.

1830 TENNYSON *To* —— 6 *Ray-fringed eyelids of the morn. **1773** J. ROSS *Fratricide* II. 54 (MS.) Those yet faithful, round his *ray-gilt throne Bask in their Maker's smile. **1797** T. PARK *Sonnets* 29 Glory's *ray-girt head. **1872** GEO. ELIOT *Middlem.* II. xxxvii. 265 The other great dread —of himself becoming dimmed and for ever *ray-shorn in her eyes. **1859** G. MEREDITH *R. Feverel* xxi, The dim *ray-strewn valley.

b. In sense 8a, as ***ray-corolla, -floret, -flower, -petal***; sense 8c, as ***ray cell, initial, tracheid.***

1907 D. P. PENHALLOW *Man. N. Amer. Gymnosperms* v. 83 Pits on the lateral walls of the *ray cells are an invariable feature of all investigated species of.. Coniferales. **1933** *Forestry* VII. 93 It is essential to study.. the development of the ray cells in the wood. **1870** HOOKER *Stud. Flora* 203 Artemisia.. *Ray-corollas dilated below. **1845** A. H. LINCOLN *Lect. Bot.* (1850) 185 Flowers without rays, or the *ray florets indistinct. **1877** DARWIN *Forms of Fl.* Introd. 5 The ray-florets of the Compositæ often differ remarkably from the others. **1852** GRAY in *Smithsonian Contrib. Knowl.* V. VI. 107 *Perityle aglossa*... This species is remarkable for the want of *ray-flowers. **1953** K. ESAU *Plant Anat.* vi. 126 The *ray initials give origin to the ray cells. **1975** *Sci. Amer.* July 102/2 Among the components of the cambium are what are called ray initials; the continuation of a ray initial down into the sapwood of a stem, a branch or a trunk is known as a wood ray. **1859** DARWIN *Orig. Spec.* v. (1872) 116 That the development of the *ray-petals by drawing nourishment from the reproductive organs causes their abortion. **1907** D. P. PENHALLOW *Man. N. Amer. Gymnosperms* vi. 88 In the higher Coniferæ the medullary ray is distinguished by the presence of an element which differs materially in its structure from the associated parenchyma cells. These elements have been designated as *ray tracheids. **1940** BROWN & PANSHIN *Comm. Timbers U.S.* vii. 128 Ray tracheids attain their best development in the genus *Pinus*. **1956** F. W. JANE *Structure of Wood* v. 91 Ray tracheids often form the marginal cells of the rays.

c. In sense 9a, ***ray-finned*** adj.; sense 9b, as ***ray-margin, -plate, -scale, -spine***, etc.

1841 E. FORBES *Brit. Starfishes* 28 The lateral ray-plates. *Ibid.* 50 Upper ray-scales transversely oblong. *Ibid.* 51 The ray-spines are long, slender, and sharp. *Ibid.* 133 The number of plates on each ray-margin. **1933** A. S. ROMER *Vertebr. Paleontol.* iv. 85 That [*sc.* the history] of the later ray-finned fishes has no such interest. **1968** [see *lung-fish* s.v. LUNG *sb.* 7]. **1970** R. M. BLACK *Elements Palaeont.* xvii. 249 The ray-finned fish have had an expansionist evolution.

d. ray blight, a fungus disease of chrysanthemums caused by *Ascochyta chrysanthemi*, which attacks the flowers, causing discoloration and shrivelling of the petals; **ray diagram**, a diagram showing the paths of light rays through an optical system; **ray-filter**, a means of separating the obscure from the luminous rays of electric light (see quot.); **ray-fin**, a fish belonging to the subclass Actinopterygii, to which most living bony fish belong and which includes those having thin fan-like fins with dermal rays; **ray fleck**, the marking caused by the exposure of a ray in sawn timber; **ray-fungus**, a fungus (*Actinomyces*) which enters the body and produces the disease *Actinomycosis*; **ray gun**, a hand-held device that can be made to emit rays, esp. (in *Science Fiction*) destructive or harmful ones; **ray therapy**, the treatment of disease with radiation; radio-therapy; **ray-tracing**, the calculation of the path taken by a ray of light through an optical system; **ray treatment** = *ray therapy*.

1907 F. S. STEVENS in *Bot. Gaz.* XLIV. 241 The Chrysanthemum Ray Blight... The common name chosen for the disease.. is taken from the most conspicuous symptom of the malady, a blighting of the corolla. **1961** *Amat. Gardening* 21 Oct. 6/2 Ray blight is much less common than the other two bloom diseases. **1965** NAKAJIMA & YOUNG *Art of Chrysanthemum* vii. 81 If the ray blight is not checked, it may continue on to destroy all blooms in the immediate area. **1980** J. W. HILL *Intermediate Physics* xii. 123 Draw two ray diagrams to show how a real and virtual image may be obtained of an object placed the same distance away from two different mirrors. **1871** TYNDALL *Fragm. Sci.* (1879) I. iii. 86 A substance.. has been discovered, by which these dark rays may be detached from the total emission of the electric lamp. This ray-filter is a liquid, black as pitch to the luminous, but bright as a diamond to the non-luminous, radiation. **1945** A. S. ROMER *Vertebr. Paleontol.* (ed. 2) v. 89 Most of the more characteristic Paleozoic ray-fins were once assigned to *Palaeoniscus*. **1963** P. H. GREENWOOD *Norman's Hist. Fishes* (ed. 2) xvii. 306 The Bony Fishes can be divided into three main groups or subclasses: Actinopterygii (ray-fins), Crossopterygii (fringe-fins) and Dipneusti (lung-fishes). **1934** BROWN & PANSHIN *Identification Comm. Timbers U.S.* 211 Ray fleck: a portion of a ray as it appears on the quarter surface. **1940** —— *Comm. Timbers U.S.* viii. 201 Some woods possess low, closely spaced, but relatively conspicuous ray flecks. **1968** *Canad. Antiques Collector* July 26/1 Quarter sawed figure is characterised by the annual growth rings appearing as parallel stripes and by the appearance of rays on the surface. In such woods as oak and chestnut these rays are called ray fleck or flake. **1897** *Syd. Soc. Lex.* s.v. *Ray-fungus*, The ray-fungus consists of a dense mycelium of interlacing hyphæ, with club-shaped extremities extending radially into the tissues. **1897** *Allbutt's Syst. Med.* III. 890 The livers contained a large focus of pus, in which colonies of the ray-fungus were found. **1931** *Amazing Stories* Dec. 804/1 The rayguns of the battlecraft, being of superior range, melted down the mortars of the fort at the magazine. **1951** A. C. CLARKE *Sands of Mars* iv. 40 It was a modified air pistol... 'If you say it's like a ray-gun I'll certify you.' **1957** [see BUG-EYED *a.*]. **1958** *Spectator* 19 Sept. 379/1 But as a space-veteran who once triggered a ray-gun with Flash Gordon, let me advise you to read on. **1967** *Autocar* 28 Dec. 29/3 As the car nears each set of lamps a patrolman.. points the ray gun at the cell situated between the two lamps. A beamed radio signal from the gun activates the fog warning lamp switch. **1977** W. MCILVANNEY *Laidlaw* xxvi. 116 It was a beautiful smile... It hit Harkness like a ray-gun and he felt his concentration atomise. **1928** *Daily Express* 20 Dec. 8/3 When the phrase 'ray-therapy' crept into one of the royal bulletins, I heard educated persons explaining that it meant treatment by wireless! **1943** *Gloss. Terms Electr. Engin.* (*B.S.I.*) 144 *Radio-therapy*, [deprecated synonym] *ray therapy*, the treatment of diseases by radiation. **1918** L. SILBERSTEIN *Simplified Method of tracing Rays* p. v, Our purpose is not to treat the whole subject of geometrical optics, but.. that part of it which is called by the short name of 'ray tracing'... Given the ray incident upon any system of lenses.. find the emergent ray. **1943** D. H. JACOBS *Fund. Optical Engin.* xxiv. 381 Ray-tracing equations are all derived from one *exact* law: Snell's law. **1974** W. T. WELFORD *Aberrations of Symmetrical Optical Syst.* iii. 41 This process of finding a ray path in terms of the numerical values of the incidence heights and convergence angles at each surface in turn is called raytracing. **1904** *Science Siftings* 12 Mar. 320/2 The Finsen light concentrates as much violet rays as can be found in a hundred square feet of sunlight. The same principle enters into all ray treatment. **1905** *Westm. Gaz.* 4 May 12/2 Six patients suffering from skin diseases.. died after the ray-treatment.

ray (reɪ), *sb.*[2] Also 4 rayȝe, 4–7 raye, 5 raie. [a. F. *raie* (13th c.) = Sp. and Pg. *raya*, It. *raja*:—L. *raia* RAIA.] A selachian fish of the family *Raiidæ*, having a broad flat body (sometimes of enormous size) and inferior gill-openings; *esp.* a skate.

1323–4 *Durham Acc. Rolls* (Surtees) 13 In.. vii Rayes et ix turbot emptis. *c* **1400** *R. Gloucester's Chron.* (Rolls) App. T., Folc þer was inne.. hengim on his cloþes fisch tayles of rayȝe [*v.r.* ray]. *c* **1450** *Two Cookery-bks.* 103 Ray boiled. Take a Ray, and draw him in þe bely [etc.]. **1565** COOPER *Thesaurus, Batis*.. the fishe called ray or skeate. **1588** HARIOT *Virginia* D iij, There are also Troutes: Porpoises: Rayes. **1623** COCKERAM III, *Pastorica*, a fish like a Raye, with strong pricks. **1726** SHELVOCKE *Voy. round World* 55 All their bays and creeks are well stock'd with mullets, large rays,.. and drum-fish. **1833** J. RENNIE *Alph. Angling* 11 In some fishes, such as the rays and the sharks, the nostril opens by a considerable chink into the mouth. **1862** ANSTED *Channel Isl.* II. ix. (ed. 2) 211 The ray is taken largely for bait, and is also sold for human food.

b. With defining adjs. (see quots.).

Also *eagle-*, *rock-*, *shark-*, *sting-*, *whip-ray*, etc.; see these words. For an enumeration of the various kinds of rays, see Couch *Brit. Fishes* (1862) I. 97–144.

1611 COTGR., *Raye estelée*, the starrie Skate, the rugged Ray. *Raye lize*, the smooth Raye... *Raye au long bec*, the spotted, long-snowted, or sharp-snowted Ray. **1753** CHAMBERS *Cycl. Supp.* s.v. *Raia*, Rays are generally divided by authors into the smooth and the prickly. The smooth are what we call skates and flairs; the prickly we call thornbacks. **1769** PENNANT *Zool.* III. 64 Sharp-nosed Ray..(*Raia oxyrinchus* Lin.). **1862** G. T. LLOYD *33 Yrs. Tasmania* iv. 51 The ray is termed in the colonies the 'stinging ray' from its possessing a barbed spear-bone. **1869** [see BEAKED 2 c.].

c. *attrib.* and *Comb.*, as *ray-fish*, *-mouthed* adj., *-tail*; **ray-dog**, ? the ray-mouthed dog-fish; **ray-maid**, **-oil** (see quots.).

1857 KINGSLEY *Two Y. Ago* I. 60 In the shallow muddy pools, lie.. some twenty non-exenterated *ray-dogs and picked dogs (*Anglice*, dog-fish). **1611** FLORIO, *Rhina*, the Skate-fish, a *Raye-fish. **1611** COTGR., *Coliart*, a kind of smooth, and straw-coloured Ray-fish. **1862** J. COUCH *Brit. Fishes* I. 99 Thornback Ray. *Ray-maid (Linn. *Raia clavata*). This is one of the commonest of the Rays, and the most valued. **1884** F. DAY *Fishes Gt. Brit.* II. 344 The young [of the Thornback ray] termed maids, maidens, or maiden-skates: ray-maids. **1875** *Trans. Devon. Assoc.* VII. 145 It [*Mustelus lævis*] is known in Plymouth and Cornwall as the '*ray-mouthed dog-fish'. **1881** *Spon's Encycl.* IV. 1376 *Ray-oils are very extensively procured from the livers of *Raja clavata*, *R. pastinaca*, and other species indigenous to Indian seas, and possess qualities like those of cod-liver-oil.

†**ray**, *sb.*[3] *Obs.* Also 4–6 raye, 6 raie (rey). [Aphetic form of ARRAY *sb.*, perh. a. ONF. **rei*, OF. *roi*: see ARRAY *v.*]

1. Order, arrangement, array, *esp.* of soldiers.

In 16–17th c. also freq. in the comb. *battle-ray*.

c **1470** HENRY *Wallace* v. 59 Butler be than had putt his men in ray. **1519** HORMAN *Vulg.* 274 Whan the ray of the hoste is all to scatered,.. and one byddeth sette in a newe raye. *a* **1553** UDALL *Royster D.* IV. vii. (Arb.) 71 Nowe sirs, keepe your ray, and see your heartes be stoute. **1609** HOLLAND *Amm. Marcell.* 119 Dispersed here and there out of ray. **1632** —— *Cyrupædia* 26 The setting of a battayle in ray was but a small part of the art.

fig. *a* **1529** SKELTON *Sp. Parrot* 415 Wylfulnes and braynles now rule all the raye. **1567** *Satir. Poems Reform.* iv. 43 Fra credite I crakit, Kyndnes brak ray.

2. A line or rank.

1481 CAXTON *Myrr.* I. xix. 57 She may.. passe only one ligne or Ray fro the place where she holdeth her in. **1542** UDALL *Erasm. Apoph.* 183 b, Takyng with hym thirteen rayes of horsemen, hymself flounced me into the floudde. **1587** *Mirr. Mag., Albanact* x, By Mars his force, their rayes and ranckes hee rent.

3. Dress. = ARRAY *sb.* 11.

1399 LANGL. *Rich. Redeles* III. 125 That [w]ho is riall of his ray, that light reede him ffolwith. **1426** LYDG. *De Guil. Pilgr.* 11503 Thogh thow holdest me nat wys, By cause my ray ys al to-rent. **1566** J. PARTRIDGE *Plasidas* 770 Thus fiftene yeares all desolate She liues in widdowes ray. **1637** B. JONSON *Sad Sheph.* II. i, Here he comes, new claithed,.. and helpes her forth! This is true court-ship, and becomes his ray. [*c* **1760** SMOLLETT *Burlesque Ode* 39, I am left behind.. To sing thy dirge in sad funereal ray.]

transf. **1596** SPENSER *F.Q.* v. ii. 50 As a ship, whom cruell tempest drives Upon a rocke.., spoyling all her geares and goodly ray.

ray (reɪ), *sb.*[4] (and *a.*) *Obs.* exc. *Hist.* Also 4 rai, 4–6 rey, raye, 6 raie. [a. OF. **raié*, **reié*, northern ff. *roié*, *roiet* (Godef.) f. *raie*, *roie* stripe, streak. (Cf. mod.F. *étoffe de raies*.)

In med.L. rendered by *radiatus*: see Du Cange.]

1. A kind of striped cloth.

The word was app. obsolete in the time of Cowel (1607), who says 'Ray seemeth to be a word attributed to cloth neuer coloured or died'. This explanation (adopted by some later lexicographers) was no doubt suggested by the separate mention of *drap de raye* and *drap de colour* in various Acts of Parliament.

13.. MICHAEL KILDARE in *Rel. Ant.* II. 192 Of fow no grai, no rede no rai, nastou bot a here. **1362** LANGL. *P. Pl.* A. v. 125 Among this riche rayes lernde I a lessun, Brochede hem with a pak-neelde [etc.]. **1426** LYDG. *De Guil. Pilgr.* 14082, I ffond vp fyrst devyses newe, Rayes off many sondry hewe. **1509** BARCLAY *Shyp of Folys* (1570) 8 The time hath bene.. When men with honest ray could holde them selfe content. **1552** in Money *Ch. Goods Berks* (1879) 18 A old vestymente of Raye. **1837** SIR F. PALGRAVE *Merch. & Friar* v. (1844) 188 Miniver and satin inspired as little respect as serge and ray.

b. So *cloth of ray*.

[**1328** *Act 2 Edw. III*, c. 14 La longure de chescun drap de Raye. **1388** *Act 12 Rich. II*, c. 14 En laeure come les draps de Ray.] **1587** HOLINSHED *Chron.* III. 802/2 Cloth, called vulgarlie cloth of raie. *c* **1640** J. SMYTH *Lives Berkeleys* (1883) I. 305 All the knights robes were of cloth of ray.

2. *attrib.* or as *adj.* (sometimes placed after the sb.). Striped; made of striped cloth.

1362 LANGL. *P. Pl.* A. III. 277 No ray robe with riche pelure. **1382** WYCLIF *Prov.* xxxi. 22 A rai cloth she made to hir. **1442** in Willis & Clark *Cambridge* (1886) I. 382 To euery of theym iij yerd of cloth Ray. **1494** FABYAN *Chron.* VII. 663 To be ladde aboute the towne wt raye hoodes vpon theyr heddes. **1533** WRIOTHESLEY *Chron.* (1875) I. 21 Their was a raye cloath, blew, spreed from the highe desses of the Kinges Benche unto the high alter of Westminster. **1611** SPEED *Hist. Gt. Brit.* IX. xix. §12 Himselfe and Queene vpon ray Cloth.. went into King Edwards shrine.

ray (reɪ), *sb.*[5] *rare.* [App. a. F. *raie* stripe, streak (see prec.), but in some cases perh. apprehended as a use of RAY *sb.*[1]]

†**1.** A stripe, streak, line. *Obs.*

a **1327** *Poem Time Edw. II* 283 in *Pol. Songs* (Camden) 336 A newe taille of squierie is nu in everi toun; The raie is turned overthvert that sholde stonde adoun. *a* **1500** *Chaucer's Dreme* 1824 A bird, all fedred blew and greene, With brighte rayes like gold betwene, As smalle thred over every joynt. **1573** BARET *Alvearie* s.v. *Ray*, Wrought with little rayes, streames, or streaks.

2. A groove in a rifle-barrel.

1802 JAMES *Milit. Dict.* s.v. *Rifled*, The rifled barrels in America, during the last war, contained from 10 to 16 rays or threads... Some persons have imagined, that those of 16 rays were the best.

†**ray**, *sb.*[6] *Obs.* Forms: 4 reye, 6 ray(e. [a. MHG. *reie* (*reige*), *rei*, *rê*, etc. (see Grimm: mod.G. *reihen*, *reigen*), or MLG. *rei*(*e*, Du. (late MDu.) *rei*, of obscure origin.] A kind of round dance.

c **1384** CHAUCER *H. Fame* III. 146 Pypers of the Duche tonge, To lerne love-daunces, springes, Reyes, and these straunge thinges. **1514** BARCLAY *Cyt. & Uplondyshm.* (Percy Soc.) 11, I can daunce the raye, I can both pipe & sing. *a* **1529** SKELTON *Replyc.* 169 Ye dawns all in a sute The heritykes ragged ray.

ray, *sb.*[7] *rare.* [Of obscure origin.]

†**1.** Darnel. *Obs.*

1398 TREVISA *Barth. De P.R.* XVII. lxv. (Bodl. MS.) lf. 206 Amonge þe beste wheete somtyme groweþ yuel wedes & venemos as Cocle & ray & oþer suche. **1578** LYTE *Dodoens* IV. xv. 469 In Englishe it is also called Iuraye, Darnell, and Raye. *Ibid.* xlv. 504 Wall Barley or Way Bennet.. may be called Red-Ray, or Darnell. **1597** [see IVRAY]. **1601** HOLLAND *Pliny* XVIII. xvii, As for the graine of Raie or Darnell, it is very small. **1617** in MINSHEU *Ductor.*

2. *ellipt.* = RAY-GRASS.

1805 R. W. DICKSON *Pract. Agric.* I. 351 Being laid down with fourteen pounds of white clover, and one peck of ray, the grass lets at twenty shillings.

†**ray**, *sb.*[8] *Obs. rare.* [a. ONF. *rei* = OF. *roi* ROY.] A king.

a **1400** *Sir Perc.* 178 Scho tuke hir leve and went hir waye, Bothe at barone and at raye. *c* **1460** *Emare* 430 Then sayde that ryche raye, I wyll have that fayr may, And wedde her to my quene.

b. Erroneously used for 'man', 'person'.

1513 DOUGLAS *Æneis* VIII. Prol. 157 Thir romanis ar bot rydlis, quod I to that ray.

†**ray**, *sb.*[9] *Obs.* [Of obscure origin; perh. a concrete application of RAY *sb.*[1]] A small piece of gold or gold-leaf; a spangle.

c **1450** *Durham Acc. Rolls* (Surtees) 633 Pro xxvj rayis pro garniamento.. senescalli d'ni Prioris, vjs. xjd. **1565** COOPER *Thesaurus, Bracteola*, a little leafe or raye of golde, silver or other metall. Also a thynne ray set under a precious stone in a ring. **1632** SHERWOOD, A raie of gold, or other mettall, *fueille d'or, ou d'aultre metal.* **1640** O. SEDGWICKE *Christs Counsell* 173 He carefully lookes upon every ray and dust of gold, and preserves it.

ray (reɪ), *sb.*[10] Now *dial.* [cf. RAY *v.*[2] 5 c.] Diarrhœa in sheep or cattle.

1577 B. GOOGE *Heresbach's Husb.* (1586) 133 The Flix, or the Laske, which in som places they call the Ray. **1741** *Compl. Fam.-Piece* III. 491 This Salve is very speedy.. in curing the Distempers called the Ray and the Scab in Sheep. **1869** *Lonsdale Gloss.*, *Ray*, a diarrhœa.

†**ray**, *sb.*[11] *Obs. rare*[−1]. App., chopped straw.

The Latin text has *cum desecto stramento*.

1656 W. D. tr. *Comenius' Gate Lat. Unl.* §440 A Driver.. winnoweth oats with a fan; being winnowed casteth them (together with Ray) unto the horses.

Ray (reɪ), *sb.*[12] The name of the English naturalist, John *Ray* (1627–1705), used in the possessive to designate **Ray's bream**, a deep-bodied, dark brown and silver, European, marine fish, *Brama brama* (formerly *B. raii*), of the family Bramidæ, which was named in his honour by M. E. Bloch (*Ichtyologie* (1797) VII. 75).

1836 W. YARRELL *Hist. Brit. Fishes* I. 117 Ray's Bream.. appears to have been less perfectly known to the older writers than might have been expected. **1925** J. T. JENKINS *Fishes Brit. Isles* 74 Ray's Bream is a fish of characteristic appearance, with a body elevated and compressed, and a very long dorsal fin. **1959** A. C. HARDY *Open Sea* II. x. 208 This species should not be confused with Ray's bream.. which has also been called the black sea-bream. **1969** A. WHEELER *Fishes Brit. Isles & N.-W. Europe* 339/2 Ray's bream has little commercial value in northern waters though its flesh is very palatable.

ray (reɪ), *v.*[1] [f. RAY *sb.*[1], or ad. F. *rayer*, OF. *raier*:—L. *radiāre* to emit beams, furnish with beams, f. RADIUS *sb.*]

1. *intr.* Of light: To issue from some point in the form of rays. Also with *beams*, etc. as subj. Const. *forth*, *off*, *out*.

1598 FLORIO, *Radiare*, to shine.., to radiate, to ray. **1635** QUARLES *Embl.* V. xiv. 302 The brighter beams, that from his eyeballs ray'd. **1698** NORRIS *Pract. Disc.* (1707) IV. 158 This excellent Glory that ray'd forth through our Saviour's Body at the Transfiguration. **1850** MRS. BROWNING *Poems* II. 87 A molten glory.. That rays off into the gloom. **1890** *Murray's Mag.* May 698 A glitter seeming to ray out from his cold, pale eyes.

b. *transf.* and *fig.*

1647 H. MORE *Song of Soul* III. II. xxviii, The soul.. when it raies out,.. Oretakes each outgone beam. **1710** R. WARD *Life More* 41 Early in the Morning he was wont to awake.. with all his Thoughts and Notions raying (as I may so speak) about him. **1797** BURKE *Regic. Peace* iii. Wks. 1808 VIII. 283 Philosophy, raying out from Europe, would have warmed.. the universe. **1865** MRS. WHITNEY *Gayworthys* xxiii. (1879) 213 On the side of God her soul lay open, and her thought rayed wide.

c. In indirect passive, with *upon*.

1656 TRAPP *Comm. Phil.* iv. 19 So they are rayed upon with a beam of divine love.

2. *intr.* Of luminous bodies or points: To emit light in rays. *rare.*

1647 H. MORE *Song of Soul* II. iii. II. xvi, In a moment Sol doth ray. **1655–87** —— *App. Antid.* iii. §2 What we fansy.. to befal light and colours, that any point of them will thus ray orbicularly.

3. *intr.* To radiate, extend in the form of radii.

1659 H. MORE *Immort. Soul* 196 That the Nerves.. may ray through the sides. **1873** MRS. H. KING *Disciples, Ugo Bassi* ii. (1877) 88 Gold-threaded hair that rayed from lips and brow. **1896** *Spectator* 12 Dec. 851/1 Iron roads raying out to the ends of the kingdom.

b. To move *in* to a centre along radial lines.

1876 MRS. WHITNEY *Sights & Ins.* xxxv. 332 Those in the far outskirts catching the impulse gradually, and raying in.

4. *trans.* To send *out* or *forth*, to emit (light) in rays. Also const. *into*.

1789 E. DARWIN *Bot. Gard.* II. (1791) 75 The star of Autumn rays his misty hair. **1850** BLACKIE *Æschylus* I. 26 The flaming pine Rayed out a golden glory like the sun. **1856** R. A. VAUGHAN *Mystics* (1860) I. 192 As the sun rays forth its natural light into the air. **1899** P. H. WICKSTEED tr. *Dante's Paradiso* 341 A point I saw which rayed forth light. **1922** E. R. EDDISON *Worm Ouroboros* xxx. 372 Yellow flames of candles.. on either side of the mirror rayed forth tresses of tinselling brightness.

b. *transf.* and *fig.*

1655 H. VAUGHAN *Silex Scint.*, *Isaac's Marriage* 8 Religion was Ray'd into thee as beames into a glasse. **1701** NORRIS *Ideal World* I. ii. 52 It being impossible.. that a figure that is not exactly round in itself should ray forth the image of a perfect circle. **1858** CARLYLE *Fredk. Gt.* V. ii. (1872) II. 74 He kept all Europe in perpetual travail;.. raying-out ambassadors, and less ostensible agents. **1863** COWDEN CLARKE *Shaks. Char.* xiii. 337 His presence rays life and manliness into every part of the drama.

5. a. To furnish *with* rays or radiating lines. **b.** To irradiate.

1750 G. HUGHES *Barbados* 199 It bears.. many yellow papilionaceous flowers, ray'd with purple veins. *Ibid.* 201 It is generally rayed with fine streaks of red. *a* **1835** HOGG *Grk. Pastoral Poet.* Wks. 1838–40 II. 148 Such a grace Ne'er ray'd a human virgin's face. **1871** B. TAYLOR *Faust* (1875) II. II. ii. 94 It rays the darkness with its lightning.

6. *trans.* To treat with, or examine by means of, X-rays or other invisible radiation.

1921 *Science* 23 Sept. 278/1 The total number of offspring by the pairs in which the females were rayed.. was 2460.

1933 *Discovery* Feb. 46/2 Tissues taken from an animal which had been rayed [with doses of Gamma rays]. **1955** *Proc. Nat. Acad. Sci.* XLI. 155 The *Tradescantia* microspore chromosomes react..as double threads when rayed at prophase.

Hence **raying** *vbl. sb.*[1] (also with *out*).

1856 R. A. VAUGHAN *Mystics* (1860) I. 65 There is a raying out of all orders of existence. **1921** *Science* 23 Sept. 278/1 Eggs which were laid during the first six days after raying and mating. **1933** *Discovery* Feb. 46/2 The dose of gamma rays needed to kill a culture at once..is enormous, and as the dose decreases the interval between the raying and the death of the culture becomes larger. **1955** *Proc. Nat. Acad. Sci.* XLI. 150 Accurate analysis of chromosomal aberrations could not be made until about 6 hours after raying.

ray (reɪ), *v.*[2] *Obs.* exc. *dial.* Also 4-7 **raie**, 5 **rai**, 6 **raiy**. [Aphetic f. ARRAY *v.* Cf. RAY *sb.*[3]]

†**1.** *trans.* To put (men) in order or array. *Obs.*

1387 TREVISA *Higden* (Rolls) III. 77 After long pees he rayed batailles, and overcom þe Albans. *a* **1450** *Le Morte Arth.* 2720 Ychone theyme rayed in alle ryghtis: Novther party thought to flee. *c* **1470** HENRY *Wallace* IV. 681 The rang in haist thai rayit sone agayne. *a* **1600** *Flodden F.* vii. (1664) 60 All ray'd in ranks, ready to fight. **1600** HOLLAND *Livy* XXIII. xxvii. 492 They encountered, thin and losely raied, with the enemies thicke and closely raunged together.

†**2.** To arrange, dispose, or deal with, in any fashion; also in *pass.*, to take oneself *away*. *Obs.*

c **1380** *Sir Ferumb.* 2295 Þe mete þat was ful richly raied in disches of golde fyn. *c* **1450** *St. Cuthbert* (Surtees) 7522 Þe saint be dreme him slepand flayde, And bade him sone away be rayde. *Ibid.* 7812 Raying þe cors in to þe bote þai led it to Jarow mynster. *c* **1475** *Partenay* 3090 The helme rent And foulle raide. **1509** HAWES *Past. Pleas.* XXXI. viii, Wyth him dismayde which you have rayed so.

†**3.** *refl.* To make ready, prepare, equip (oneself).

c **1380** *Sir Ferumb.* 270 Euere suþþe y haue me raid redely to þy seruyse. *c* **1400** *Arth. & Merl.* (D.) 436 (Kölbing) Þey raydyn [*v.r.* dighten] hem þanne to in hast, In to þat batayle for to wende. *c* **1440** *Promp. Parv.* 422/1 Rayd, or (a)rayde, or redy, *paratus*.

4. To dress (oneself or another). = ARRAY *v.* 8. Now *dial.* Also *absol.*

1399 LANGL. *Rich. Redeles* III. 120 Ffor ben they rayed arith they recchith no fforther. *c* **1400** *Beryn* 3812 Beryn rose, & rayd him, & to þe chirch went. *c* **1440** *Promp. Parv.* 422/1 Rayd, or arayd wyth clothynge, or other thynge of honeste, *ornatus*. **1509** BARCLAY *Shyp of Folys* (1570) 9 Both man and woman..Are rayde and clothed not after their degree. **1650** FULLER *Pisgah* IV. vi. 105 Their clothes were made large and loose,..so that they might run, and ray themselves. **1675** HOBBES *Odyssey* (1677) 169 If true, with coat and vest my news requite; If not, then not; although ill raid am I. **1886** in W. Som. and Dorset glossaries. **1898** T. HARDY *Wessex Poems* 118 She rose and rayed, and decked her head.

†**5.** To smear, bespatter, or soil *with* blood, dirt, etc.; to dirty or defile; to BERAY. Also const. *in*. *Obs.* (freq. in 16th c.).

1526 *Pilgr. Perf.* (W. de W. 1531) 257 All his precyous body wounded & rayed with blode. *a* **1535** MORE *Wks.* 614/1, I..shall shew you shortly how angrely he ryseth vp, and royally rayed in dyrte. **1618** BOLTON *Florus* II. xviii. (1636) 150 That those should bee rayed with durt, who would not be smeared with blood. **1663** MENNES & SMITH *Witt's Recreations* §469 His scarlet hose, and doublet very rich, With mud and mire all beastly raid.

†**b.** Without const. in same sense. *Obs.*

1533 J. HEYWOOD *Merry Play* (1830) 31, I burned my face, and rayde my clothes also. **1588** KYD *Househ. Phil.* Wks. (1901) 272 Soyled places which may spoile or ray her garments. **1596** SHAKS. *Tam. Shr.* IV. i. 3.

†**c.** *absol.* Of sheep: To become foul. *Obs.*[−1]

1523 FITZHERB. *Husb.* §41 If any shepe raye or be fyled with dounge about the tayle.

Hence †'**raying** *vbl. sb.*[2] *Obs.*

1552 ELYOT, *Basis*,..roundels made to set vnder wyne pottes for raiying of the table. **1591** PERCIVALL *Sp. Dict.*, *Encenagamiento*, raying with durt, *oblimatio*.

ray, var. RA[1] *Sc. Obs.*; var. REE *v.* to sift; obs. Sc. f. ROE.

raya, obs. form of RAJA(H.

‖**rayah** Now *Hist.* ('raɪə). Also **raiah**, **raya**. [a. Arab. *raᶜīyah* flock or herd, subjects, peasants, f. *raᶜā* to pasture or feed. Cf. next.] A non-Muslim subject of the Sultan of Turkey, subject to payment of the poll-tax (see KHARAJ).

1813 BYRON *Br. Abydos* II. xx, To snatch the Rayahs from their fate. **1863** KINGLAKE *Crimea* (1876) I. v. 77 They might rise against their Government and fall upon the Christian rayahs.

attrib. **1886** A. WEIR *Hist. Basis Mod. Europe* (1889) 298 The Greeks..possessed a..status to which other Rayah populations could lay no claim.

‖**rayat** ('raɪət). Also **rayet**, **rai(y)at**. [Indo-Pers. var. of prec.: see RYOT.] A cultivator of the soil; a peasant.

1818 in Gleig *Life Sir T. Munro* (1830) II. 278 Every rayet should be at liberty to cultivate as much or as little as he pleases. **1844** J. TOMLIN *Miss. Jrnls.* 99 A small dry patch of ground had just been cleared by the rayats. **1896** *Sat. Rev.* 18 Apr. 389/2 The murder of a raiyat was a matter of easy settlement.

raychter, obs. Sc. f. RAFTER *sb.*[1]

raycin, obs. f. RAISIN.

rayckin, **rayd**, obs. ff. RACKAN, RAID *sb.*

rayd(e, obs. Sc. pa. t. RIDE.

raye, var. RA[1], obs. f. RAY.

rayed (reɪd), *ppl. a.*[1] [f. RAY *sb.*[1] or *v.*[1]]

1. a. That has or consists of rays; arranged radially.

1853 KANE *Grinnell Exp.* xxxv. (1856) 322 The rayed prolongations stretched nearly across the sky. **1890** *Anthony's Photogr. Bull.* III. 31 Dark paper having some fine perforations, cross lines or a rayed star cut out of it.

b. Having rays of a specified number or kind.

1748 SIR J. HILL *Hist. Fossils* 654 Some have one of the rays bifid, so as to emulate the figure of a six-ray'd kind. **1825** *Greenhouse Comp.* I. 130 Of the barren-rayed [Dahlia], ..of the fertile-rayed species. **1870** HOOKER *Stud. Flora* 156 Umbels compound, few-rayed. *Ibid.* 158 Umbels rather irregular, many-rayed.

c. *Zool.* = RADIATE A. 1.

1841 *Penny Cycl.* XIX. 319/1 Rayed or Radiated Animals. **1851** RICHARDSON *Geol.* viii. (1855) 224 In the rayed families, the organs of locomotion are disposed around a central axis.

2. = IRRADIATED *ppl. a.* 1 c.

1921 *Science* 23 Sept. 277/2 Wild type (red-eyed) females ..were X-rayed... Sisters of the rayed females were used as controls. **1938** HEVESY & PANETH *Man. Radioactivity* xxiv. 245 The rayed rock-salt assumes a blue-violet colour.

†**rayed**, *ppl. a.*[2] *Obs.* [f. RAY *v.*[2] + -ED[1].] Drawn up, arranged, dressed, etc.

1382 WYCLIF *Esther* i. 6 Also goldene setis and siluerene, vp on the raied pament [1388 pawment arayede with] smaragd and pario stones, weren disposid. *c* **1470** HENRY *Wallace* IX. 535 Throu Gyan land in rayid battaill thai raid. **1513** DOUGLAS *Æneis* VI. xiv. 62 Pompey..With rayit hostis of the orient. *a* **1578** LINDESAY (Pitscottie) *Chron. Scot.* (S.T.S.) I. 271 The Earle of Huntlie and the lord of Home standand in ane rayit battell.

rayed, *ppl. a.*[3] *Obs.* exc. *arch.* or *poet.* [ad. OF. *raié* in same sense: see RAY *sb.*[4]] Striped, streaked.

c **1369** CHAUCER *Dethe Blaunche* 252, I woll yeue him a feather bed, Raied with gold. *c* **1400** MAUNDEV. (1839) xviii. 198 Theise Cocodrilles ben Serpentes, ȝalowe and rayed aboven, and han 4 Feet. **1481** CAXTON *Myrr.* II. vi. 78 Ther ben the basylicocks,..he is whyte rayed here and there. **1598** STOW *Surv.* (1603) 539 In the year 1516..it was agreed ..that the Shiriffes of London should..giue yearely Reyed Gownes, to the Recorder, Chamberlaine [etc.]. [**1866** ROGERS *Agric. & Prices* I. xxii. 578 The rayed, or variegated cloth being the cheaper.] **1905** W. H. HUNT *Pre-Raphaelitism* I. 163 From the depth of this rayed region we ascended to the further margin of the mist lake into the crystal air. **1918** W. STEVENS in *Others* Dec. 11 We hang like warty squashes, streaked and rayed.

rayeny, obs. f. RAINY *a.*

rayes, obs. f. REIS.

rayet, obs. f. RAYAT.

rayfart, **-ffert**, **-ffort**, varr. RAIFORT *Obs.*

rayge, obs. f. RAGE *sb.*

rayȝe, obs. form of RAY *sb.*[2]

raygn, var. RAIGN *v. Obs.*

raygne, obs. f. REIGN.

raygnes, var. RAINES *Obs.*

'**ray-grass**. Also 7 **rea**, 8 **rey-**. [f. RAY *sb.*[7]] = RYE-GRASS (now the usual form).

1677 *Lond. Gaz.* No. 1176/4 Pure and unmixt Trefoile Seed..freed and acquitted from all Rea, and other course Grass Seeds. **1677** PLOT *Oxfordsh.* 154 They have lately sown Ray-grass or the *Gramen Loliaceum*, by which they improve any cold, sour, clay-weeping ground. **1763** *Museum Rust.* I. 224 Saintfoin receives great benefit from this manure, and so does clover, ray-grass, and trefoil. **1831** *Sutherland Farm Rep.* 74 in *Lib. Usef. Kn.*, *Husb.* III, On soil of the second quality, one bushel and a half ray-grass. **1886** BRITTEN & HOLLAND *Plant-n.*, *Italian Ray Grass*,..a commercial name for *Lolium italicum*.

†'**rayie**, *a. Obs.*[−1] [f. RAY *sb.*[1]] Ray-like.

a **1687** COTTON *See, how the Twilight Slumber falls* Poems (1689) 353 See how Light..Beautifies The rayie fringe of her fair Eyes.

'**raying**, *ppl. a.* [f. RAY *v.*[1] + -ING[2].]

a. Moving in rays. **b.** Emitting rays; radiating.

1891 G. MEREDITH *One of our Conq.* III. vii. 131 Popular artists..have figured in scenes of battle the raying fragments of a man from impact of a cannon-ball on his person. **1905** *Westm. Gaz.* 25 Apr. 2/3 The day That crowns us royal with the raying sun.

rayis, obs. Sc. pa. t. RISE *v.*

rayk(e, **rayl(e**, obs. ff. RAKE, RAIL.

rayl (reɪl). *Acoustics.* [f. RAYL(EIGH.] A unit of specific acoustic impedance equal to one dyne-second/cm.[3] (in the C.G.S. system) or one newton-second/m.[3] (in the S.I.).

1954 L. L. BERANEK *Acoustics* i. 11 The specific acoustic impedance is the complex ratio of the effective sound pressure at a point of an acoustic medium or mechanical device to the effective particle velocity at that point. The unit is newton-sec/m[3], or the mks rayl. (In the cgs system the unit is dyne-sec/cm[3], or the rayl.) **1971** W. W. SETO *Schaum's Outl. Theory & Probl. Acoustics* ii. 40 At standard atmospheric pressure and 20°C..the characteristic impedance of air is..415 rayls.

Rayleigh ('reɪlɪ). *Physics.* [The title of J. W. Strutt, 3rd Lord *Rayleigh* (1842-1919), English physicist.] **1.** Used, usu. *attrib.*, to designate various concepts, devices, and phenomena he invented or investigated, as **Rayleigh('s) criterion**, the criterion by which adjacent lines or rings of equal intensity in a diffraction pattern are regarded as resolved when the central maximum of one coincides with the first minimum of the other; **Rayleigh disc**, a lightweight disc suspended by a fine thread so that when it is placed at an angle to incident sound waves their intensity can be calculated from the measured torque on the disc; **Rayleigh instability** (see quot. 1977); also called ***Rayleigh-Taylor instability*** [Sir Geoffrey *Taylor* (1886-1975), English mathematician]; **Rayleigh limit**, the upper limit of a quarter of a wavelength placed on the difference between the optical paths of the longest and shortest rays of those going to form an image in order that the definition shall be close to the ideal (which corresponds to no path difference); **Rayleigh number**, a dimensionless parameter that is a measure of the instability of a layer of fluid due to differences of temperature and density at the top and bottom (see quot. 1950); **Rayleigh scattering**, the scattering of light by particles small compared with its wavelength, the intensity of the scattered light being inversely proportional to the fourth power of the wavelength (and therefore much greater for blue light than for red); so **Rayleigh-scattered** *a.*; **Rayleigh wave**, a type of wave that travels over the surface of a solid with a speed independent of its wavelength, the motion of the particles being in ellipses so that the surface undulates.

1937 JENKINS & WHITE *Fund. Physical Optics* v. 123 Extending Rayleigh's criterion for the resolution of diffraction patterns..to the circular aperture, two patterns are said to be resolved when the central maximum of one falls on the first dark ring of the other. *Ibid.* vii. 159 The Rayleigh criterion for resolving of images. **1970** D. W. TENQUIST et al. *University Optics* II. v. 197 The chromatic resolving power of a prism, defined as $\lambda/\delta\lambda$ where $\delta\lambda$ is the smallest change of wavelength discernable [*sic*] in accordance with the Rayleigh criterion at a mean wavelength λ, is given by [etc.]. **1913** *Physical Rev.* I. 309 (*heading*) A method of producing known relative sound intensities and a test of the Rayleigh disk. **1972** J. M. TAYLOR tr. *Meyer & Neumann's Physical & Appl. Acoustics* vi. 209 The Rayleigh disk..is practically never used any more to determine particle velocity, which can be derived much more quickly and conveniently from electroacoustic sound pressure measuring devices. **1961** S. CHANDRASEKHER *Hydrodynamic & Hydromagnetic Stability* x. 428 An important special case..is that of two fluids of different densities superposed one over the other (or accelerated towards each other); the instability of the plane interface between the two fluids, when it occurs (particularly in the second context), is called Rayleigh-Taylor instability. **1971** I. G. GASS et al. *Understanding Earth* xix. 277/1 A Rayleigh instability..does not necessarily depend upon the existence of a density inversion... Where the depth of the fluid is very large, the fluid at the bottom is compressed by the overlying fluid and, in many cases, an instability develops before the temperature is high enough to produce a density inversion. **1977** *Sci. Amer.* Oct. 144/2 The instability at the interface between a denser fluid overlying a lighter fluid, when the interface is otherwise in hydrostatic equilibrium, is called a Rayleigh instability (or sometimes a Rayleigh-Taylor instability). **1923** GLAZEBROOK *Dict. Appl. Physics* IV. 216/1 The adoption of the Rayleigh limit thus makes it possible considerably to increase the aperture of a lens system of any given type and to come close to the full theoretical resolving power with systems which, judged geometrically, would appear hopelessly over- or under-corrected. **1976** *Sci. Amer.* Aug. 77/2 Ideally a lens should be at the Rayleigh limit for light of all wavelengths. **1950** O. G. SUTTON in *Proc. R. Soc.* A. CCIV. 298 The existence of a sustained convective regime depends upon the value of the non-dimensional quantity $Ra = -\beta gah^4/\kappa\nu$, which we shall call the Rayleigh number. **1980** *Sci. Amer.* July 82/2 Convection begins when the Rayleigh number exceeds a critical value. **1971** *Physics Bull.* July 387/1 More detailed studies of the linewidths of Rayleigh scattered lines can provide hitherto inaccessible information on the behaviour of fluids near their critical point or in the neighbourhood of phase transitions. **1937** JENKINS & WHITE *Fund. Physical Optics* xii. 280 The first quantitative study of the laws of scattering by small particles was made in 1871 by Lord Rayleigh, and such scattering is frequently called Rayleigh scattering. **1973** C. SAGAN *Cosmic Connection* (1975) xiii. 90 The beauty of the sunset, the sky, and distant landscapes are all due to Rayleigh scattering. **1920** A. E. H. LOVE *Treat. Math. Theory Elasticity* (ed. 3) xiii. 313 The waves travel over the surface with a velocity, which is independent of the wave-length $2\pi/f$, and slightly less than the velocity of equivoluminal waves propagated through the body. Waves of this kind are often called 'Rayleigh-waves'. **1956** J. C. JAEGER *Elasticity, Fracture & Flow* iii. 135 Rayleigh waves are not the only simple type of surface wave which can be predicted and identified. **1971** I. G. GASS et al.

Understanding Earth xxiv. 336/1 (*caption*) A Rayleigh wave from an earthquake in Columbia recorded in Montana.

2. *Astr.* Also **rayleigh**. A unit of luminous intensity equal to one million photons per square centimetre per second.

1956 D. M. HUNTER et al. in *Jrnl. Atmospheric & Terrestrial Physics* VIII. 345 We suggest that $4\pi B$ be given the unit of 'rayleigh' (symbol *R*), where *B* is in units of 10^6 quanta/cm^2 sec sterad. Hence $1R = 10^6$ quanta/cm^2 (column) sec. (The word 'column' is often inserted into these units to convey the concept of an emission-rate from a column of unspecified length). **1970** *Nature* 2 May 435/2 In the direction of maximum intensity the Lyman-α flux is 160 Rayleighs, which can be regarded as typical for the direction of the solar apex. **1974** *Science* 25 Jan. 317 A two-channel ultraviolet photometer aboard Pioneer 10 has made several observations of the ultraviolet glow in the wave-length range from 170 to 1400 angstroms in the vicinity of Jupiter. Preliminary results indicate a Jovian (1216 angstrom) glow with a brightness of about 1000 rayleighs and a helium (584 angstrom) glow with a brightness of about 10 to 20 rayleighs.

Rayleigh-Jeans (ˌreɪlɪˈdʒiːnz). *Physics.* The name RAYLEIGH and that of Sir James *Jeans* (1877–1946), English physicist and astronomer, used *attrib.* with reference to an approximation to Planck's law (see PLANCK) that is valid at long wavelengths, according to which the flux of radiant energy from a perfect radiator, at any particular wavelength, is proportional to its temperature divided by the fourth power of the wavelength.

1930 RUARK & UREY *Atoms, Molecules & Quanta* iii. 57 We obtain the radiation density, $\rho\lambda d\lambda = 8\pi kT\lambda^{-4}d\lambda$. This is called the Rayleigh-Jeans distribution law. *Ibid.* 59 Planck's law approaches the Rayleigh-Jeans law if *h* approaches zero. **1948** WORTHING & HALLIDAY *Heat* xiii. 445 Rayleigh erroneously included a factor of 8 in his evaluation of c_1. The error was pointed out by the English physicist James Jeans (1877–). For that reason, the law is often referred to as the Rayleigh-Jeans law. Just the reverse of what occurred in connection with the Wein law, the Rayleigh law predicts correct values in the long-wave-length region but fails elsewhere. **1970** G. K. WOODGATE *Elem. Atomic Struct.* iii. 36 The approximation corresponds, for thermal radiation, to..$\bar{n} \approx kT/h\nu \gg 1$, which in eq. (3.16) or (3.13) leads at once to the Rayleigh-Jeans approximation for the energy density per unit frequency range.

rayler, obs. f. RAILER.

rayless (ˈreɪlɪs), *a.* [f. RAY *sb.*[1] + -LESS.]

1. Devoid of, not illumined by, any ray of light; dark, gloomy.

1742 YOUNG *Nt. Th.* I. 20 Night.. In rayless majesty, now stretches forth Her leaden sceptre. **1820** SHELLEY *Orpheus* 10 Hid by a rayless night. **1850** BLACKIE *Æschylus* II. 68 The rayless homes Of gloomy Hades. **1875** L. MORRIS *At Last* v, Those dear souls, who sleep.. In rayless caverns dim.

fig. **1820** *Ellen Fitzarthur* 52 Ah rayless, joyless, lifeless state! **1845** JAMES *Smuggler* III. 94 Rayless, dull despair.

2. a. That sends out no rays; dull.

1832 *Fraser's Mag.* V. 123 The lamp of poesy was flickering and almost rayless. **1842** MOTLEY *Corr.* (1889) I. iv. 115 The sun.. round and rayless in the centre of its low arch. **1878** BROWNING *Poets Croisic* clii, Gold which comes up rude And rayless from the mine.

b. Of the eye (cf. RAY *sb.*[1] 3).

1834 H. AINSWORTH *Rookwood* IV. viii, Her eye gazed.. with a dying glare—then grew glassy, rayless, fixed. **1871** MACDUFF *Mem. Patmos* xviii. 241 That eye which once beamed affection now rayless.

c. *Physics.* Not accompanied by or emitting alpha, beta, or gamma rays. *Obs.*

1904 *Proc. R. Soc.* LXXIII. 493 The first change is a 'rayless' one, *i.e.*, the transformation is not accompanied by the appearance of α, β, or γ rays. **1906** [see ACTINIUM 2]. **1907** N. R. CAMPBELL *Mod. Electr. Theory* ix. 210 It appears that many changes which are usually classed as 'rayless' are accompanied by the emission of β rays without α rays, but the liberation of energy in such changes is so small compared to those in which α rays are emitted that it seems desirable to make the distinction implied by the term.

3. Excluding, dispensing with, rays of light.

1896 *Cosmopolitan* XX. 391/1 When they reached the tree, they sat down under the rayless boughs. **1898** *Daily News* 6 May 5/3 Revelations of what may be called Rayless Photography.

4. Having no ray-like parts.

1769 PENNANT *Zool.* III. 316 That they are not the young of smelts is as clear, because they want the.. rayless fin. **1837** *Penny Cycl.* VII. 422/2 The rayless Corymbiferæ.

Hence ˈ**raylessness**.

1843 POE *Premat. Burial* Wks. 1864 I. 336 The intense and utter raylessness of the Night that endureth for evermore.

raylet (ˈreɪlɪt). [f. as prec. + -LET.] A little ray.

1820 *Blackw. Mag.* VII. 603 Across the floor is sunny raylet shot. **1851** S. JUDD *Margaret* xvii. (1871) 144 A shower of fine tiny raylets of snow. **1878** HUXLEY *Physiogr.* 62 From the sides of these rays, secondary rays, or raylets, may be given off.

rayll(e, obs. ff. RAIL.

rayly, var. RAILLY *v. Obs.*

raym, rayment(e, raymson, obs. ff. RAME *v.*[1], RAIMENT, RANSOM.

raymonder (ˈreɪmɒndə(r)). *Cricket.* = RAMROD 2 a.

1870 [see RAMROD 2 a]. **1878** H. C. ADAMS *Wykehamica* xxiii. 431 *Raymonder*, a ball bowled underhand, in a series of hops along the ground, (traditionally said to be derived from one Raymond, who bowled after this fashion). Sometimes it was pronounced 'ramroder'.

rayn, var. RAIGN *v. Obs.*; obs. f. RAIN, REIGN, REIN.

raynard, rayndoun, obs. ff. REYNARD, RANDOM.

Raynaud (ˈreɪnəʊ). *Med.* [The name of Maurice *Raynaud* (1834–81), French physician, who described various cases displaying Raynaud's phenomenon in 1862 (*De l'Asphyxie Locale et de la Gangrène Symétrique des Extrémités*).] ***Raynaud's disease*** or ***syndrome***: an ill-defined disease or syndrome characterized by ***Raynaud's phenomenon***, in which spasm of the arteries of the digits (often due to low temperature or vibration) leads to pallor, pain, and numbness, and in severe cases to gangrene.

1883 *Trans. Clin. Soc.* XVI. 179, I have watched three cases which came within the category of Raynaud's disease. **1901** J. HUTCHINSON in *Med. Press & Circular* CXXIII. 403/1 The expression 'Raynaud's disease' would imply that there is some one malady complete in itself, and having all the symptoms the same in all cases which is suitably denominated by that name. That is not the case. *Ibid.*, I would rather speak of Raynaud's phenomena than of Raynaud's disease, for the former are things which we understand and are the same in all cases... What do we mean by Raynaud's phenomena?.. Local syncope, local asphyxia, symmetrical gangrene of the extremities are synonymous terms. **1925** Raynaud's disease [see GANGLIONECTOMY]. **1932** *Amer. Jrnl. Med. Sci.* CLXXXIII. 188 The increasing amount of literature attests to the tendency to utilize the terms 'Raynaud's disease' or 'Raynaud's syndrome' as a general depository for a heterogeneous group of cases far removed from the condition originally described by Raynaud. **1936** *Q. Jrnl. Med.* XXIX. 399 For more than sixty years the term 'Raynaud's disease' was used as a convenient label for case after case of obscure aetiology in which pallor, cyanosis, pain, or gangrene of hands, feet, nose, or ears, happened to be symptoms, prominent or otherwise. *Ibid.* 401 'Raynaud's Phenomenon' may, therefore, be defined as 'Intermittent pallor or cyanosis of the extremities, precipitated by exposure to cold, without clinical evidence of blockage of the large peripheral vessels and with nutritional lesions, if present at all, limited to the skin'. **1937** Raynaud's syndrome [see GANGLIONECTOMY]. **1946** E. V. ALLEN et al. *Peripheral Vascular Dis.* vii. 185 The predilection of Raynaud's disease for the female is one of the outstanding etiological factors. *Ibid.* viii. 206 Raynaud's phenomenon may occur primarily as in Raynaud's disease or it can occur secondarily in association with a number of conditions and diseases. **1973** *Times* 26 May 3/3 The name for the unusual affliction was Raynaud's Phenomenon, Mr Alan Lipfriend, Mr Lambert's counsel, told Mr Justice Mocatta. It was also known as vibratory white finger. The fingers went white, numb and stiff. **1975** *Daily Colonist* (Victoria, B.C.) 18 Nov. 2/1 My doctor says I have Raynaud's disease... It is just like I am allergic to cold... My hands and feet are affected and hurt.

†**rayne.** *Obs. rare.* (Meaning not clear.)

The rime-words are *slayne* and *Gawayne.*

a **1450** *Le Morte Arth.* 1980 Weilaway, the reufulle Rayne That euyr Launcelote was my fo. *Ibid.* 3223 The kynge gan woffully wepe and wake, And sayd, 'Allas, thys Rewffulle Rayne'.

rayne, obs. f. RAIN, RAINY, RANE *sb.*, REIGN, REIN; var. RAINES *Obs.*

raynecle: see RAYNOLL.

raynede(a)re, obs. ff. REINDEER.

raynes, -nez, varr. RAINES *Obs.*

rayney, -nie, obs. ff. RAINY *a.*

raynge, raynold, obs. ff. RANGE, REYNARD.

raynish, obs. f. RHENISH.

†**raynoll.** *Obs.* Also 5 ? raynecle. [Form and origin uncertain: cf. *raymolles* in Cotgr.] *pl.* Small cakes or balls made of pork with a large number of other ingredients.

c **1430** *Two Cookery-bks.* 42 Raynollez. Nym sode Porke & chese, & seþe y-fere [etc.]. *c* **1440** in *Househ. Ord.* (1790) 461 Put in therto the raynecles [*sic*], and when thai byn boyled take hom up.

rayny(e, obs. forms of RAINY *a.*

raynys, variant of RAINES *Obs.*

rayograph (ˈreɪəʊgrɑːf, -æ-). Also with capital initial. [f. the name of Man *Ray* (1890–1976), U.S. artist and photographer + -O + -GRAPH.] A type of photograph made without a camera by arranging objects on light-sensitive paper which is then exposed and developed. Cf. PHOTOGRAM 3. Also ˈ**rayogram**.

1932 *N.Y. Times* 17 Apr. VIII. 11/5 Julien Levy Gallery —Photographs by Man Ray. A fine retrospective, including a group of 'rayograms'. **1937** *Photography 1839–1937* (Museum of Mod. Art, N.Y.) 68 Man Ray refers to his shadowgraphs as 'rayographs' or 'rayogrammes'. **1942** P. GUGGENHEIM *Art of This Century* 106 Man Ray.. took up photography in 1917. Invented Rayograph technique, 1921, and explored other possibilities of photography, especially in making Dada and Surrealist compositions. **1951** J. I. H. BAUER *Revolution & Tradition Mod. Amer. Art* iii. 28 Dada attracted only one distinguished American follower, the painter and photographer Man Ray, much of whose life was spent in Paris where he produced without the use of a camera his extraordinary 'rayographs'. **1956** *Focal Encycl. Photogr.* 836/2 Further developments came about 1921 when Man Ray and L. Moholy-Nagy.. made their 'rayographs' and photograms, using not merely opaque flat objects but also three-dimensional and translucent ones. **1972** C. W. E. BIGSBY *Dada & Surrealism* ii. 19 The photomontage consisted of a collage of photographs. Like the Rayogram (a photographic process devised by Man Ray) it was a joke at the expense of realism. **1974** *Encycl. Brit. Macropædia* XIV. 320/2 Man Ray was supporting himself by making fashion photographs in 1922 when he accidentally set a glass funnel, a graduate, and a thermometer on a piece of photographic paper, thus producing 'Rayographs'. **1975** *New Yorker* 19 May 13/1 (Advt.), The prices are more out of the ordinary: $7,500 is asked for Ray's rayograph 'Egg-beater and Abstracted Segment of Living Space'.

rayon[1] (ˈreɪən, ˈreɪɒn, F. rɛjɔ̃). [a. F. *rayon* (1539), f. *rai* (mod. *rais*) RAY *sb.*[1]]

1. A ray of light. *rare.*

1591 SPENSER *Vis. Bellay* 21 Shining Christall, which.. a thousand rayons threw. *a* **1609** ALEX. HUME *Day Estivall* 177 The rayons of the Sunne we see, Diminish in their strength. **1859** SINGLETON *Virgil* II. 244 Here stood A cave, ..unreached by rayons of the Sun.

‖**2.** = RADIUS *sb.* 4.

1878 LADY HERBERT tr. *Hübner's Ramble* III. i. 459 Within a rayon of a certain number of miles. **1879** *Daily News* 26 May 5/6, I found myself within his rayon at Newcastle, which is one of his bases of supply.

3. a. Any of the class of fibres and filaments composed of or made from regenerated cellulose; also, fabric or cloth made from these. Formerly known as *artificial silk*.

1924 *Drapers' Record* 14 June 685/2 'Glos' having been killed by ridicule, the National Retail Dry Goods Association of America has made another effort to produce a suitable name for artificial silk. This time their choice has fallen on 'rayon'. **1925** *Glasgow Herald* 26 Mar. 15/1 The Viscose Company states that it will discontinue the use of wood pulp as a base for rayon when its wood pulp contracts expire. **1927** T. WOODHOUSE *Artificial Silk* 1 The sight of almost any article made from artificial silk (or Rayon, as it is also called) is sufficient to arouse admiration. **1951** *Good Housek. Home Encycl.* 230/2 Rayons are classified according to the highly technical processes by which they are manufactured. **1966** [see MAN-MADE *a.*]. **1969** *Encycl. Polymer Sci. & Technol.* XI. 844 High-tenacity rayons are consumed by industry as reinforcing cords for manufacturing all types of rubber tires, drive belts, high-pressure hoses, and straps and tapes. **1973** H. MCCLOY *Change of Heart* ii. 18 Her stockings were real silk, not flimsy nylon.. or coarse rayon.

b. *attrib.* and *Comb.*, as ***rayon damask, gabardine, jersey, satin, stocking, taffeta, yarn***; ***rayon-containing, -corded*** adjs.

1930 *Daily News Rec.* 17 Feb. 19/2 The manufacture of rayon-containing fabrics normally is a highly competitive business. **1964** *Economist* 26 Sept. 1254/1 The rayon-corded SP tyres. **1952** M. LASKI *Village* iv. 66 The rayon-damask couch of the three-piece suite. **1930** *Silk & Rayon Directory & Buyer's Guide of Gt. Brit.* 296/2 (*heading*) Gabardine, Rayon. **1947** *Sun* (Baltimore) 31 Oct. 3/7 (Advt.), Confident of its own good looks, this rayon gabardine wins your heart at once. **1965** *Which?* Mar. 94/2 *Rayon gaberdine*, a fabric with a diagonal rib effect. *Ibid.* 94/3 *Rayon jersey*, a soft stretch, knitted fabric. Drapes well. **1973** *Guardian* 19 June 15/1 Matte viscose rayon jersey, long evening dress. **1977** B. PYM *Quartet in Autumn* v. 51 The dressing gown was a jazzy rayon satin. **1929** *Rayon Record* III. 587/1 The lower temperature up to about 110° is utilized for silk or rayon stockings. **1948** 'J. TEY' *Franchise Affair* xi. 119 Fawn-grey rayon stockings. **1974** M. KELLY *That Girl in Alley* iv. 70 She was wearing.. beige rayon stockings. **1952** M. LASKI *Village* viii. 137 A counterpane of rayon taffeta machine-embroidered with flowers. **1929** *Rayon Record* III. 411/2 A few samples of yarns and fabrics illustrating the decorative value of rayon yarns.. have been received. **1947** *British Rayon Man.* x. 168 Much attention was given to the question of the best kind of package for rayon yarns.

‖**rayon**[2] (raˈjon). Also raion. [a. Russ. *raĭón.*] In the U.S.S.R., a small territorial division for administrative purposes.

1936 [see OBLAST]. **1948** J. TOWSTER *Polit. Power in U.S.S.R.* iv. 66 All the units are divided into districts (*raions*). **1959** *Economist* 14 Mar. 946/1 In at least two of Moscow's fifteen raions, the chaps at the local Agitpunkts seem to have been lying down on the job. **1964** S. P. DUNN tr. *Levin & Potapov's Peoples of Siberia* 9 The creation in 1931–1932 of nomadic and rural soviets, rayons and national okrugs on a territorial basis finally undermined the importance in the social structure of the peoples of the North, of their former clan and tribal organizations and of the social elements which headed them. **1976** [see OKRUG].

Rayonism, Rayonnism (ˈreɪənɪz(ə)m). Also rayon(n)ism, ‖rayonnisme. [ad. F. *Rayonnisme*, f. *rayon* RAYON[1] + *-isme* -ISM; cf. Russ. *luchízm*, f. *luch* ray.] A style of abstract painting developed *c* 1911 in Russia by M. Larionov (1881–1964) and N. Goncharova (1881–1962), in which projecting rays of colour are used to give the impression that the painting floats outside time and space. Hence ˈ**Rayon(n)ist** *a.*, of or pertaining to Rayonism; also as *sb.*; **Rayo**ˈ**nistic** *a.*

1922 *Encycl. Brit.* XXXII. 9/1 Gontcharova's setting for the 1914 production of the 'Coq d'Or' and Larionov's 'Les Contes Russes' of 1915 mark the invasion of the theatre by cubist ideas. The colour scheme was still that of Russian peasant art; but the design was based on abstract forms, and aimed at a rhythm in harmony with the music and the dances. To this development the name of *rayonnisme* has been given. **1956** B. S. MYERS *Encycl. Painting* 295 *Larionov, Michel* (1881–), Russian abstract painter who in 1909 developed a type of painting known as Rayonnism, a dynamic form of space penetration consisting of rays of light and suggesting in some ways the work of the Futurists. **1956** LAKE & MAILLARD *Dict. Mod. Painting* 241/1 *Rayonism*,.. launched by Michael Larionov in 1911–12... A Rayonist canvas must give the impression of gliding out of time. **1968** D. BARRAN tr. *Veronesi's Into Twenties* iii. 76 Larionov founded the rayonnist movement, loosely based on the concepts of the futurist movement. **1969** DENIS & DE VRIES *World's Art* II. xi. 224 Rayonism in Russia was of the same nature, (*Rayonistic Manifesto*, 1912, by Larionov). **1972** C. W. E. BIGSBY *Dada & Surrealism* ii. 10 In some ways it [*sc.* Dada] was a part of that artistic re-examination which spawned such schools as impressionism, cubism, futurism and, more exotically, suprematism, rayonism, plasticism, vorticism and synchronism. **1975** *Physics Bull.* Feb. 60/3 The art world was no less fertile with the cubists, the futurists, vorticists, rayonnists and the Blauer Reiter group all active. *Ibid.* 61/1 Rayonnism was a style of painting invented by Mikhail Larionov and used by him and Natalia Goncharova around 1912–14. **1977** *New Yorker* 2 May 31/3 What makes it unique is the inclusion of some dazzling experimental pictures from the early twentieth century—Cubist, Futurist, Rayonist, and Suprematist.

ˈrayonnance. *rare*⁻¹. [f. F. *rayonnant*: cf. RAYONNÉ *a.* and -ANCE.] Radiance.

1848 BAILEY *Festus* xix. 206 Some of a cold, pure bodily rayonnance As is the moon's of naked light.

‖**rayonnant** (rɛjɔnɑ̃), *a.* Also fem. **rayonnante** (-ɑ̃t); pl. **rayonnants.** [Fr.] Beaming, radiant. Also **rayonnant de joie,** radiant with joy.

The form with *-te* in quot. 1825 is erron.

1821 M. W. SHELLEY *Let.* 2 Apr. in P. B. Shelley *Lett.* (1964) II. 278 Yesterday he came *rayonnant de joie*—he had been ill for some days, but he forgot all his pains. **1825** H. WILSON *Mem.* II. 79 The next evening found us all quite rayonnante, waiting for our dinner. **1831** C. C. F. GREVILLE *Mem.* (1874) II. xiii. 111 The Ministers were *rayonnants.* **1965** LADY BIRKENHEAD *Illustrious Friends* ix. 92 Her ladyship was rayonnante... She sallied forth in a blue silk ball-dress and lively spirits.

‖**rayonné** (rɛjɔne), *a.* [F., pa. pple. of *rayonner*, f. *rayon* RAYON¹.]

†**1.** Of a kind of hood: Rayed. *Obs. rare*⁻¹.

1690 EVELYN *Mundus Muliebris* 7 Round which it does our ladies please To spread the Hood call'd Rayonnés. [*Ibid., Fop Dict.* 20 *Rayonné*, Upper Hood, pinn'd in Circle, like the Sunbeams.]

2. *Her.* Of a division between parts of the field: Having alternate pointed projections and depressions, whose sides are formed by wavy lines. (Cussans 1868.)

3. Of a person: radiant, effulgent.

1860 QUEEN VICTORIA *Let.* 20 June in R. Fulford *Dearest Child* (1964) 260 She is so embellié and rayonné as to look like a young girl.

‖**rayonnement** (rɛjɔnmɑ̃). [Fr.] Radiance, effulgence; influence (of culture, etc.).

1910 WYNDHAM LEWIS *Lett.* (1963) 45 The benevolence and rayonnement that is the sign and beauty of a fine nature shines on faults without hiding them. **1966** *Economist* 23 Apr. 340/2 Nor are the producers allowed to show the film outside France, because it might damage the reputation of 'communities' which contribute to the 'cultural and humanitarian *rayonnement* of France'.

Rayonnism, Rayonnist: see RAYONISM, RAYONNISM.

raype, obs. f. ROPE.

rayr, obs. f. REAR *v.*, ROAR *v.*

rays, obs. f. RACE *sb.*¹, RAISE *v.*; obs. pa. t. RISE *v.*

†**rayse,** *v. Obs. rare.* [Of obscure origin; perh. a special use of RAISE *v.*¹ or *v.*²] *trans.* (Meaning not clear.) Hence **raysed** *ppl. a.*; **ˈrayser; ˈraysing** *vbl. sb.*

1641 S. SMITH *Herring Buss Trade* 25 Of the choise, packing, and raysing of the Herrings. *Ibid.*, It is forbidden that no body may rayse or packe any Herrings but in the Lords street..and that with dores open. *Ibid.* 26 The Packer, Rayser, Cooper..that are imployed about the packing of the said Herring. *Ibid.* 27 The Coopers may not hoope any dryed or other raysed Herring barrell, with halfe barrell hoops.

rayse, obs. f. RAISE, RASE *v.*¹; obs. pa. t. RISE *v.*

raysen, obs. f. RAISIN.

raysin, obs. f. RAISIN; var. RASEN *Obs.*

†**ˈraysing.** *Obs. rare*⁻¹. [f. RAISE *v.*²] A cut.

1593 NASHE *Christ's T.* (1613) 146 As many iagges, blisters and scarres, shall Toades..make on your pure skinnes in the graue, as now you haue cuts, iagges or raysings, vpon your garments.

raysing, rayso(u)n, raysure, raysyn, obs. ff. RAISIN, REASON, RAZOR *sb.*

rayt, obs. f. RATE.

rayte, obs. f. *rait* RET *v.*

‖**Raza** (ˈrasa). [Mexican Sp., a. Sp. *raza* race.] Usu. in phr. *La Raza*, the race, designating the strong sense of racial and cultural identity held by Mexican-Americans.

1964 W. MADSEN *Mexican-Americans of S. Texas* iii. 15 The Mexican-American thinks of himself as both a citizen of the United States and a member of *La Raza* (The Race). **1968** *Economist* 8 June 54/1 The preservation of *La Raza* within the dominant American culture means that Mexican-American families observe the Roman Catholic faith, speak Spanish and yield to the male the authority associated with Mediterranean custom. **1969** *Time* 4 July 14/2 *La Raza*, the race, meaning all Mexicans and Mexican Americans, and derived from the mystical theory of the 19th century philosopher, José Vasconcelos, that people of mixed race will inherit the earth. At best, it is a rallying cry betokening a mild form of cultural nationalism; at worst, it connotes outright racism. **1973** *Black Panther* 7 Apr. 4/3 The Oakland Mexican-American 'Raza' community continues its boycott of public schools.

‖**Razakar** (ræzɑːˈkɑː(r)). Also **Razakhar.** [Urdu *razākār.*] A Muslim who voluntarily pledges to fight in defence of his religion; hence, a member of a fanatical semi-military faction with this end. Also *attrib.*

1948 *Keesing's Contemp. Archives* 31 July–7 Aug. 9421 Hyderabad's Moslems formed the Razakar (volunteer) movement which, in recent months, has in effect become the private army of the Moslem party in Hyderabad. **1957** P. GRIFFITHS *Mod. India* xii. 107 The Ittehad-ul-Muslimeen, with its semi-military organisation known as the Razakars, took a bitterly communal line. Each Razakar vowed to 'fight to the last to maintain the supremacy of the Muslim power in the Deccan'. **1968** H. GRAY in M. Weiner *State Politics in India* viii. 402 Kasim Razvi organized a voluntary group of fighters named 'Razakars', who provided protection to landowners and the government administration during a Communist-led uprising. **1970** R. WINGATE *Ismay* viii. 180 Attlee replied in a long personal letter [*c.* Sept.–Oct. 1948] pointing out that in fact the Nizam had not been a free agent, but in the hands of the 'Razakars' (the extreme Muslim party). **1971** *Guardian* 29 Oct. 13/1 They [*sc.* Pakistani army units] have left in the countryside a patchwork of police and Razakhar regimes. **1971** *Peace News* 29 Oct. 5/1 The mukti fouj attacked a radio station occupied by the Pakistani army and their civilian hirelings, the *razakars.* **1972** M. SHAKIR *Muslims in Free India* iv. 56 The emergence of the Razakars was a logical corollary of the Ittehad's political doctrine of collective Muslim sovereignty... It is the biggest exclusive Muslim Party in Hyderabad. **1974** *Encycl. Brit. Macropædia* IX. 76/1 Immediately after Indian independence a fanatical Muslim faction, the Razākārs, fomented tensions in the state and the city [*sc.* Hyderabad].

razamataz(z, varr. RAZZMATAZZ, RAZZAMATAZZ.

razant, variant of RASANT.

razbooche, obs. variant of RAJPUT.

†**raze,** *sb.*¹ *Obs.* [f. RAZE *v.* Cf. RASE *sb.*¹, RACE *sb.*³] A slash, scratch, cut, slit.

1610 MARKHAM *Masterp.* II. c. 383 If you make two razes on each side, it shall bee so much the better. **1656** SANDERSON *Serm.* (1689) 370 A man had better receive twenty wounds in his good Name, than but a single raze in his Conscience.

†**raze,** *sb.*² *Obs. rare*⁻¹. (See quot.)

a **1728** WOODWARD *Fossils* 54 The Tin-Veins..are either in Strata of Growan, or of that grey, Talky, Slaty Stone, that the Tinners call Killas, Raze, or Delvin.

raze (reɪz), *v.* [var. RASE *v.*¹ Cf. also RACE *v.*³]

†**1.** *trans.* To scratch, cut, slit, etc. = RASE *v.*¹ 1. *Obs.* (Common in 17th c.)

1587 TURBERV. *Trag. T.* (1837) 279 His death did raze hir harte. **1610** MARKHAM *Masterp.* II. c. 382 Then raze both the quarters of the hoofe with a drawing-knife,..so deepe that you may see the dew come foorth. **1684** R. WALLER *Nat. Exper.* 102 It appeared rough, as if it had been prettily razed with the point of a Diamond.

b. *esp.* (often with limiting word expressed): To cut or wound slightly, to graze (the skin, a part of the body, etc.).

a **1586** SIDNEY *Arcadia* III. (1629) 314 The point swirved and razed him but on the side. **1667** SOUTH *Serm., Chance* (1715) 317 Might not the Bullet, that perhaps razed his Cheek, have as easily gone into his Head? **1719** YOUNG *Busiris* v. i, I could not bear To raze thy skin to save the world from ruin. **1808** SCOTT *Marm.* III. xxiv, Yet did a splinter of his lance Through Alexander's visor glance, And razed the skin—a puny wound.

2. To remove by scraping; to scrape *off* or *out*; to cut or shave off. Now *rare.*

1567 TURBERV. *Epit.* etc. 33 Drowsie drouping Age.. With pensiue Plough will raze your hue. **1669** W. SIMPSON *Hydrol. Chym.* 361 Earths..which the..salt in the water razeth off from several rocks. *a* **1708** BEVERIDGE *Thes. Theol.* (1711) III. 347 Drunkenness..razeth out the image of God, and stampeth the image of beasts upon us. **1814** SCOTT *Ld. of Isles* VI. xxxii, An axe has razed his crest.

1871 PALGRAVE *Lyr. Poems* 14 Most men raze her stamp, and prove untrue.

3. *spec.* To erase or obliterate (writing, etc.) by scraping or otherwise. ? *Obs.*

1581 SAVILE *Tacitus, Hist.* III. xxxi. (1591) 132 The principall men..razed Vitellius name, and defaced his images. **1627** HAKEWILL *Apol.* (1630) 100 [They deserve] their writings to bee razed with sponges. **1646** J. HALL *Poems* I. 67 Now I will raze those Characters I wrote. **1709** *Col. Rec. Pennsylv.* II. 489 The clause formerly razed..is agreed to be kept in the bill.

b. Const. *out* adv.; *from, out of* preps.

1577 FENTON *Gold. Epist.* 74 He hath razed them out of the register of heauen. **1641** MILTON *Reform.* I. (1851) 20 Of those Books..who knows..what hath bin raz'd out, what hath bin inserted. **1693** WOOD *Life* (O.H.S.) IV. 19 Altered the aforesaid originall papers, by razing out many lines, sentences, and words. **1735** SWIFT *Corr.* Wks. 1841 II. 735 Having first razed out the writer's name, I have shown it to several gentlemen.

c. *transf.* and *fig.* (cf. RASE *v.*¹ 2 c.)

1576 FLEMING *Panopl. Epist.* 285 As for that which is euil, they raze it out of their memories. **1654** tr. *Scudery's Curia Pol.* 147 This base and ingrate person razed me out of her affection. **1702** ROWE *Tamerl.* I. i, The first feeble Blow I meet shall raze me From all Remembrance. **1720** MRS. MANLEY *Power of Love* (1741) I. 32 He became formidable enough to raze the very Name of Mendoza. **1877** GLADSTONE *Glean.* IV. xxii. 355 If we raze out all our earlier protests.

4. †**a.** To scrape (a writing) so as to erase something; to alter by erasure. *Obs.*

1594 MARLOWE & NASHE *Dido* III. ii, I will..raze th' eternal register of Time. **1602** FULBECKE *2nd Pt. Parall.* 31 A deede razed is not good in your Law. **1720** *Lond. Gaz.* No. 5825/2 The Decrees..were razed. **1724** BP. WILSON in Keble *Life* (1863) II. xviii. 609 Razing or adding to records being ever accounted..penal.

†**b.** To shave. *Obs.* Cf. RASE *v.*¹ 4 c.

1667 EVELYN *Public Employm.* Misc. Writ. (1805) 544 Trifling amongst barbers, razing and sprucing himself. **1732** *Hist. Litteraria* III. 421 Both had their Heads raz'd.

c. To scrape, or come close to, in passing.

1598 FLORIO, *Radere*,..Also to raze or go along the shore as a ship doth. **1885** M. BLIND *Tarantella* I. iii. 29 [The swallows] dive low, razing the grass, then soar aloft.

†**d.** *absol.* (see quot.) *Obs. rare*⁻⁰.

1753 CHAMBERS *Cycl. Supp.* s.v., A horse is said to have razed, whose corner teeth cease to be hollow; so that the cavity, where the black mark was, is filled up.

5. a. To sweep away, efface, or destroy (a building, town, etc.) completely. In later use esp. *to raze to the ground.*

a **1547** SURREY *Æneid* II. 707, I saw Troye fall..Neptunus town clene razed from the soil. **1582** STANYHURST *Æneis* II. (Arb.) 60 Now thee statelye pilers with gould of Barbarye fretted Are razde. **1633** G. HERBERT *Temple, Sacrifice* xvii, Some said, that I the Temple to the floore In three dayes raz'd. **1781** GIBBON *Decl. & F.* (1869) I. xxiv. 690 The fortifications were razed to the ground. **1843** PRESCOTT *Mexico* (1850) I. 354 If it were refused, the Aztecs would raze their cities to their foundations. **1870** BRYANT *Iliad* I. II. 40 Having razed Troy with her strong defences I should see my home again.

b. To take away, remove (*from* a place), in a thorough manner. (With various objects.)

1580 LYLY *Euphues* (Arb.) 360 That the heat of thy loue might clean be razed with ye coldnes of my letter. **1656** EARL MONM. tr. *Boccalini's Advts. fr. Parnass.* I. lxxvii. (1674) 102 [God] by sending universal Deluges of water, razed mankind..from off the World. **1874** H. R. REYNOLDS *John Bapt.* IV. i. 238 In Henoch, 'the Son of Man' is about to raze kings from their thrones.

Hence **razed, ˈrazing** *ppl. adjs.*

1582 STANYHURST *Æneis* II. (Arb.) 67, I ran too Priamus razd court. **1598** YONG *Diana* 60 His short cape cloke was ..lined with razed watchet satten. **1660** F. BROOKE tr. *Le Blanc's Trav.* 229 Amongst other things remarkable, there were three pages in raz'd tissue. **1715–20** POPE *Iliad* v. 419 Her snowy hand the razing steel profaned. **1813** SCOTT *Trierm.* II. xx, No striplings these, who succour need For a razed helm or falling steed. **1882** W. B. WEEDEN *Soc. Law Labor* 180 A razed table on which new classes build themselves.

raze, obs. form of RACE *sb.*⁶, RAISE *v.*¹

razee (rəˈziː), *sb.* Also 8 †**raze.** [ad. F. *rasé(e*, pa. pple. of *raser* to RASE *v.*¹: cf. RAZE *v.* and -EE¹.]

a. *Naut.* A war-ship or other vessel reduced in height by the removal of her upper deck or decks.

1794 R. F. GREVILLE *Diary* 14 Sept. (1930) 335 Two large Ships razes which are line of Battle Ships cut down & mounted with very heavy guns 24 Pdrs. **1803** SIR R. WILSON in *Life* (1862) I. iv. 216 The Captain of a twenty-four-razee. **1815** BURNEY *Falconer's Mar. Dict.* s.v., The Indefatigable, Majestic.., and Saturn have been cut down for Razees. **1844** HARWOOD *Irish Rebellion* 232 Two frigates and a sixty-gun razee bearing down upon him.

b. *transf.* and *fig.*

1829 MARRYAT *F. Mildmay* iv, This was the sole cause of my chest being converted into a razee. **1860** O. W. HOLMES *Elsie V.* xviii. (1891) 253 The hulks and the razees of enslaved or half-enslaved intelligences.

razee (rəˈziː), *v.* [f. RAZEE *sb.*]

1. *trans.* To cut down (a ship) to a lower size by reducing the number of decks.

1842 BRANDE *Dict. Mech.* s.v. *Razee*, By razeeing, the draught of water is diminished, while the centre of gravity is lowered, and the qualities of the vessel have generally..been improved. **1862** W. H. RUSSELL in *Times* 27 Mar., The Merrimac..has been razeed and iron-plated. **1894** C. N. ROBINSON *Brit. Fleet* 240 In 1793..old sixty-fours were cut down a deck, or 'razeed' (a term that now came into use) into forty-fours.

2. *fig.* To abridge, prune, dock.

1820 *Deb. Congress U.S.* 28 Jan. (1855) 1008 It would not follow that they should have power to *razee* a State..by depriving the admitted State of equal rights. **1837** MARRYAT *Dog-fiend* v, He was like a man *razéed* or cut down. **1882** BLUNT *Ref. Ch. Eng.* II. 77 They were razeed to the smallest possible dimensions as to numbers and endowment.

Hence **raˈzeed** *ppl. a.*

1847 *Knickerbocker* June 496 The 'Chicken Mauma' was persecuting the Cherokee advocate with her *razeed* (i.e., reduced,) offers in reference to the sale of the 'funny chickens'. **1867** *Harper's Mag.* Oct. 679/2 This 'mittimus' of the Squire's was a razeed, square-topped old chaise. **1884** *Daily News* 23 Sept. 3/1 The..Castles of Walmer, Deal, and razeed Sandown. *a* **1895** ADM. PAGET *Autobiog.* iii. (1896) 71 The command of the *Aigle*, razeed frigate.

razer, var. RASER[1].

‖**razet** (raze). *Bullfighting.* [Provençal *raset.*] In southern France: a contest in which teams of combatants compete to snatch a rosette from between the bull's horns.

1932 R. CAMPBELL *Taurine Provence* ii. 43 The finest thing in the French arena.. is the razet, or the course of the cocarde-bearing bulls. **1967** MCCORMICK & MASCAREÑAS *Compl. Aficionado* vi. 210 Confusion with Spanish toreo arises in the sport which the French call the *course de cocardes* (or *razet*), in which the athlete, unarmed with cape or muleta, attempts to snatch from between the bull's horns the rosette (*cocarde*), or divisa, of the owner.

‖**razeteur** (razɛtœr). [Provençal, f. prec.] A member of a bullfighting team which engages in a *razet.*

1932 R. CAMPBELL *Taurine Provence* ii. 43 They [*sc.* the bulls] know every habitual razeteur by sight. **1961** *Times* 8 July 10/6 There are two classes, a *tourneur* or decoy, whose function is to turn the bull in order to favour the chances of his partner, the *razateur* (sometimes *crocheteur*). **1963** E. & A. HEIMANN tr. *Droit's Camargue* iii. 28 The razéteurs... Called thus because they pass so close to the bull that they literally graze, or shave, by him. **1976** N. ROBERTS *Face of France* ix. 106 The *razeteurs*, the young men who get their name from the *razet*, or running half circle, which they describe in their efforts to snatch the [bull's] *cocarde.*

razie, obs. form of RACY *a.*

raziere, variant of RASER[1]. *Obs.*

razine, obs. form of RAISIN.

razing ('reɪzɪŋ), *vbl. sb.* [f. RAZE *v.* + -ING[1].] The action of cutting, erasing, levelling, etc.

1611 COTGR., *Rature*,.. a razing, or scraping out. *a* **1640** J. BALL *Answ. to Can* ii. (1642) 7 What hath beene their seeking from time to time? a razing of the communion booke! No. **1669** DRYDEN *Tyrannick Love* v. i, The rough razings of the pointed Steel. **1705** STANHOPE *Paraphr.* I. 126 The Messiah and his Messenger must have come, before the razing of that Temple. **1890** CHILD *Ballads* IV. 55/2 *note*, A letter of Arglye's.. would seem to show that he was not there in person during the razing and burning.

b. A scraping; a particle scraped off. *rare*[−1].

1669 W. SIMPSON *Hydrol. Chym.* 363 Particles.. as if they had been razings of crystals.

razmataz(z, varr. RAZZMATAZZ, RAZZAMATAZZ.

razom, obs. variant of RIZZOM *dial.*

razoo[1] (rə'zu:). *N. Amer. slang.* Also razzoo, razzooh. [Prob. alteration of RASPBERRY 4 (cf. RAZZBERRY, RAZZ *sb.*) with arbitrary suffix *-oo*, perh. after KAZOO.] Ridicule; the arousing of indignation or the like, provocation; a sound of contempt, a 'raspberry'. Also in phr. ***to give the razoo***: to ridicule. So as *v. trans.*, to arouse or provoke; to manhandle.

1890 *Grip* (Toronto) 18 Jan. 40/1 Shall I razoo old Mowat on the Separate School business? *Ibid.* 19 Apr. 265/1 What is all this racket about the Independence of Parliament?.. It is dependent on the presence of Members.. on the whips razoo round. **1908** H. GREEN *Maison de Shine* 208 Can't a man take a flat o' beer wit' out gittin' the razoo? **1926** *Flynn's* 16 Jan. 639/2 The ginny with th' poke gave th' fly th' razoo an' we split a bunch of nifty kale. **1939** R. CHANDLER *Big Sleep* xxvi. 235 My information is Apartment 301, but all I get there is the big razzoo. **1942** BERREY & VAN DEN BARK *Amer. Thes. Slang* §297/1 Ridicule; banter,.. *razoo. Ibid.* §297/4 (*Ripe*) *raspberry* or *razzberry, razoo*, a sound of contempt by vibrating the tongue between the lips, loosely any expression of derision or ridicule, hence ridicule. *Ibid.* §297/5 Ridicule; banter,.. *give the razz* or *the razoo.* **1944** H. WENTWORTH *Amer. Dial. Dict.* 496/1 *Razoo*, to manhandle, use roughly. **1959** *Washington Post* 22 Dec. C-18/5 Yesterday's hero, Fidel Castro, now gets the lustiest Bronx razzoohs since Adolf Hitler was flipping his wig for the cameras.

razoo[2] ('rɑ:zu:). *Austral.* and *N.Z. slang.* Also rahzoo, razhoo. [Origin uncertain.] A (non-existent) coin of trivial value, a 'farthing'. Also in phr. ***brass razoo.*** Used in neg. contexts only.

1930 *Bulletin* (Sydney) 5 Nov. 21/1 The useless graft on patch and flat! They never think a bloke has earned a darned razoo for that. **1931** W. HATFIELD *Sheepmates* xxx. 268 Richards never has a rahzoo. **1940** F. D. DAVISON *Woman at Mill* II. 151, I found myself on the streets again, without a brass razoo. **1943** *Coast to Coast 1942* 118 Up till the present he hadn't a brass razoo towards the seven and sixpence. **1947** J. MORRISON *Sailors belong Ships* 187, I wouldn't give you a razhoo for anything between there and Charmian Road. **1964** J. CLEARY *Flight of Chariots* viii. 361, I wouldn't give a brass razoo for his chances out there. **1968** R. CLAPPERTON *No News on Monday* vii. 80 He isn't rolling in the stuff—he hasn't got two brass razoos to rub together. **1976** *Sunday Mail* (Brisbane) 25 Apr. 16/7 Last week he signed a contract for the new $356,000 building and then cheerfully announced: 'I haven't a razoo.'

razor ('reɪzə(r)), *sb.* Forms: α. 3–4 rasor, 4–7 rasour, (5 -owre, -owyr, 5–6 -oure, 6 *Sc.* -iour, 6–7 ra(y)sor, 7 rasoir); 6– razor, (6–8 -our). β. 4–7 rasure, (6 ray-). γ. 5–6 raser, (5 -ere, 6 -ier, -ar), 6–7 razer. [a. OF. *rasor, -our, -ur* (12th c.), f. *raser* to RASE *v.*[1] Cf. OF. *rasoir* = It. *rasojo*:—late L. *rasōrium.*]

1. a. A sharp-edged instrument, specially used for shaving the beard or hair.

'In modern razors the blade has usually a slight curve backwards, and is of wedge-shaped section, or has the back much thicker than the edge; the sides are often made concave by grinding ('hollow-ground'). The blade is attached to the handle by a tang and rivet, so that it can be folded into this when not in use.' *N.E.D.*

α. *c* **1290** *S. Eng. Leg.* I. 98/222 Four ȝweles of Iren he let fullen with rasores, kene I-nowe. **1340** *Ayenb.* 66 þe tonge more keruinde þanne rasour. **1387** TREVISA *Higden* (Rolls) III. 325 For he dredde þe barbour to schave with rasoures ful soore. **1413** *Pilgr. Sowle* (Caxton 1483) III. i. 50, I wol be vpon a pyler fitched ful of sharp keruyng rasours. **1555** EDEN *Decades* 186 To annoynte the place with oyle and scrape it with a rasoure. **1655** CULPEPPER *Riverius* VI. vii. 144, I got ready my Raysor,.. and there I made a deep incision. **1700** DRYDEN *Pal. & Arc.* 1629 This length of hair.. Guiltless of steel and from the razour free. **1765** FOOTE *Commissary* I. Wks. 1799 II. 11 His little weezen face as sharp as a razor. **1856** EMERSON *Eng. Traits, Ability* Wks. (Bohn) II. 39 At.. Sheffield, where I was shown the process of making a razor and a penknife.

β. *a* **1340** HAMPOLE *Psalter* li. 2 As sharpe rasure þou did treson. **1486** *Bk. St. Albans* A iv, Thou most cutt it with a Rasure. **1534** WHITINTON *Tullyes Offices* II. (1540) 82 The eldre Dyonisius.. dreding Rasures dyd syndge his heere with a cole. **1570** LEVINS *Manip.* 192/29 A raysure, *nouacula.* **1576** NEWTON *Lemnie's Complex.* (1633) 240 He.. with a Barbers Rasure finely cut away the Nose.

γ. **1483** CAXTON *Cato* C iv b, Doo so moche that thys nyght ye haue a rasere and.. cutte the heeris of hys berde. **1585** T. WASHINGTON tr. *Nicholay's Voy.* III. xvii. 102 These.. cause their hayre and beard to be cut with a raser. **1599** *Ann. Barber-Surg. London* (1890) 192 Grindeinge of rasares.

b. *fig.* and in fig. context.

Occam's (also ***Ockham's***) ***razor***, the leading principle of the nominalism of William of Occam (see OCCAMISM), that for purposes of explanation things not known to exist should not, unless it is absolutely necessary, be postulated as existing; usually called the Law of Parcimony. ***on the razor's edge*** (after Gr. ἐπὶ ξυροῦ ἀκμῆς), in a precarious position (cf. *razor-edge* in 3 c).

c **1430** LYDG. *Min. Poems* (Percy Soc.) 198 Wyntris rasour doth al away arrace. **1594** WILLOBIE in *Shaks. C. Praise* 7 The sharpe rasor of a willing conceit. *c* **1611** CHAPMAN *Iliad* x. 150 Now on the eager razors edge, for life or death we stand. **1836–7** SIR W. HAMILTON *Metaph.* xxxix. (1859) II. 395 We are, therefore, entitled to apply Occam's razor to this theory of causality. **1879** BROWNING *Pheidippides* 86 Here am I back.. we stand no more on the razor's edge! **1901** T. C. ALLBUTT *Science & Medieval Thought* 57 Now this scientific economy, perhaps first formulated, or effectively used, by William Ockham, in the phrase 'entia non sunt multiplicanda'—known as 'Ockham's rasor'—is what is called now-a-days 'materialism'. **1907** LD. CURZON *Frontiers* 7 Frontiers are indeed the razor's edge on which hang suspended the modern issues of war or peace, of life or death to nations. **1936** J. BUCHAN *Island of Sheep* xii. 235 In the Norlands life had always been on a razor's edge. **1944** W. S. MAUGHAM (*title*) The razor's edge. **1960** A. HUXLEY *Let.* 17 July (1969) 894 Perhaps Ockham's razor isn't a valid scientific principle. Perhaps entities sometimes ought to be multiplied beyond the point of the simplest possible explanation. For the world is doubtless far odder and more complex than we ordinarily think. **1976** A. WHITE *Long Silence* vi. 49 He was living on a razor's edge. Sooner or later, the Germans were going to begin to suspect. **1977** M. GOULDER in J. Hick *Myth of God Incarnate* iii. 60 Natural explanations, where they are at all plausible, are surely to be preferred on the basis of Occam's razor.

†**c.** *transf.* The tusk of a boar (Phillips 1706).

2. †**a.** Applied to certain fishes: cf. RAZORFISH 2. *Obs. rare.*

c **1440** *Promp. Parv.* 424/1 Rasowre, fysche, *rasorius.* **1530** PALSGR. 261/1 Rasour a fysshe. **1601** HOLLAND *Pliny* II. 428 There is a fish called a Rasoir: looke whatsoever toucheth it, senteth presently of Yron.

b. = RAZOR-FISH 1, RAZOR-SHELL.

1610 GUILLIM *Heraldry* III. xxiii. (1611) 170 The rest of the crusted sort of fishes I will passe ouer viz. Crabs, Lobsters, Creuisses, Cuttles, Razers, Shrimpes &c. **1805** BARRY *Orkney Isl.* 287 The Razor.. or, as we name it, the spout-fish, is also found in sandy places. **1869** WOOD *Com. Shells* (ed. 3) 32 The common species, the Sabre Razor (*Solen ensis*).. another species the Pod Razor (*Solen siliqua*). *Ibid.* 34 It would scarcely be recognized as belonging to the Razors.

3. *attrib.* and *Comb.* **a.** With sbs., as ***razor blade, case, handle, hone, knife, -maker, mettle, -seller, sheath, strop, -stropping, wit.***

1846 HOLTZAPFFEL *Turning* III. 1051 The *razor blade is polished on a soft buff wheel fed with dry crocus. **1936** *Discovery* Aug. 255/1 Glass razor blades can be ground to powder under foot when used. **1945** 'G. ORWELL' *Animal Farm* viii. 64 Making cocks fight with splinters of razor-blade tied to their spurs. **1977** *Jersey Even. Post* 26 July 18/3 Also reported stolen is a silver razor-blade-shaped pendant. **1688** *Lond. Gaz.* No. 2410/4 A black Velvet embroidered *Rasor Case, with 3 or 4 Rasors. **1833** MACAULAY in Trevelyan *Life & Lett.* (1880) I. 323, I have bought a new ..razor-case. **1846** HOLTZAPFFEL *Turning* III. 1069 Two *razor handles or scales are.. held at the one end in a pair of clamps. *Ibid.* 1066 [The] German *Razor Hone.. is universally known throughout Europe. **1390** GOWER *Conf.* I. 187 In his hond a *rasour knif He bar, with which hire throte he cutte. **1865** LUBBOCK *Preh. Times* 20 A razor-knife said to have been found together with objects of the latter metal. **1677** MOXON *Mech. Exerc.* No. 3. 56 *Razor-makers generally clap a small Bar of Venice Steel between two small Bars of Flemish Steel. **1767** S. PATERSON *Another Trav.* I. 416 An infinite number of.. jack-smiths and razor-makers. **1679** J. GOODMAN *Penit. Pardoned* III. i. (1713) 264 Great wits and curious tempers are like *razor-mettle quickly turned. **1782** WOLCOTT (P. Pindar) (*title*) The *Razor Seller. **1812** W. DOOLEY in *Examiner* 31 Aug. 552/1 A *razor-sheath was found. **1759** *Newport* (Rhode Island) *Mercury* 26 June 4/3 Hones, *Razor-strops &c. **1822** *Gill's Techn. Repos.* III. 42 On Improved Razors and Razor-Strops. **1866** *Harper's Mag.* Nov. 788/2 Packwood, some fifty years ago, led the way in England of.. systematic advertising, by impressing his razor-strop indelibly on the mind of every bearded member of the kingdom. **1946** G. MILLAR *Horned Pigeon* i. 1, I only heard the noise of a man's razor strop. **1815** SIMOND *Tour Gt. Brit.* II. 278 He gave me a lesson of *razor-stropping. **1786** WOLCOTT (P. Pindar) *Ep. Boswell* Wks. 1816 I. 246 No *Razor-wit, for want of use, grows rusty.

b. With adjs., as ***razor-bladed, -bowed, -edged, -leaved, -shaped, -tongued, -weaponed; razor-keen, -sharp, -thin; razor-like.***

1765 *Ann. Reg.* 215 The two boys had found a *razor bladed clasp knife. **1885** *Royal River* xii. 338 The *razor bowed craft move slowly out. **1807–8** W. IRVING *Salmag.* (1824) 128 The *razor-edged zephyrs of our 'balmy spring'. **1831** J. W. CROKER in *C. Papers* (1884) II. xvi. 143 Warburton has given us razor-edged disquisitions, fine and false. **1972** K. BONFIGLIOLI *Don't point that Thing at Me* xiii. 98 Even the shadows, razor-edged, purple and green, were painful to look at. **1955** *Times* 11 May 14/6 Political interest is *razor keen. **1978** *Detroit Free Press* 5 Mar. (Parade Suppl.) 14D/1 (Advt.), With special Holder hands never come near razor-keen stainless steel blades. **1878** T. HARDY *Return of Native* II. iv, Urns.. used as flower-pots for two *razor-leaved cactuses. **1842** POE in *Gift* 148 The *razor-like crescent. **1977** *Rolling Stone* 19 May 93/2 The sultry title cut, with its razorlike clarion guitar lead. **1829** P. EGAN *Boxiana* 2nd Ser. II. 299 He had now not the slightest chance with Curtis, who.. drew streams of blood from his *razor-shaped nose, and knocked him down. **1897** MARY KINGSLEY *W. Africa* 236 Small black and white birds.. with heavy razor-shaped bills. **1921** R. HICHENS *Spirit of Time* v. 80 Something of it he must have seen—but what?.. The suggestion of a *razor-sharp silhouette? **1975** J. GRADY *Shadow of Condor* viii. 132 She carried.. a flat, thinly sheathed razor-sharp knife taped to her stomach. **1979** *N.Y. Rev. Bks.* 25 Oct. 48/1 (Advt.), A witty, razor-sharp satire on monogamy. **1971** C. BONINGTON *Annapurna South Face* viii. 95, I.. peered over the top, to see that the ridge was now *razor-thin and looked even more difficult beyond the point I had reached. **1973** P. EVANS *Bodyguard Man* viii. 64 He cut razor-thin slices through the most congested areas of traffic. **1873** O. W. HOLMES *Rhymes of an Hour* i, The saucy-aproned, *razor-tongued soubrette. **1828** SOUTHEY *Let. to A. Cunningham*, When at the looking-glass with lather'd chin, And *razor-weapon'd hand I sit.

c. Special combs., as **razor-bridge**, the bridge *Al Sirāt*, believed by Muslims to lead over hell; †**razor-chirurgeon**, a barber-surgeon; **razor clam** (U.S.) = razor-shell, RAZOR-FISH 1; **razor-cut** *v. trans.*, to cut (hair, etc.) with a razor; also *fig.*; hence as *sb.*, a haircut effected with a razor instead of scissors; also as *ppl. a.*; **razor-cutting** *vbl. sb.*; **razor-edge**, a keen edge, *fig.* a narrow foothold, a critical situation (cf. *razor's edge* in 1 b); also *attrib.*; **razor gang**, (*a*) a gang of thugs armed with razors; (*b*) *Railway slang* (see quots. 1966 and 1970); **razor-grass**, a West Indian sedge belonging to the genus *Scleria*, esp. *S. pterota*, which has sharp-edged leaves; **razor-man**, a thug armed with a razor; **razor-paper**, paper specially made for sharpening razors on (Knight 1875); **razor-paste**, a paste of emery- or crocus-powder for improving razor-strops; **razor plug, point**, a power-point for plugging in an electric razor; **razor-slasher**, one who slashes another (usu. across the face) with a razor; a member of a razor gang; hence **razor-slash** *v. trans.* [back-formation], to slash with a razor; also as *sb.*, the action of lacerating thus; a wound so made; **razor-slashing** *vbl. sb.*; **razor strop fungus**, the birch polypore, *Piptoporus betulinus*; **razor toe**, a pointed toe on a shoe; an (outmoded style of) shoe with a razor toe.

1812 SIR R. WILSON *Diary* in *Life* I. 380 The paths.. almost realize the perils of the *razor-bridge of Mahomet. **1624** GEE *Foot out of Snare* X 2 b, The *Razor-Chirurgions, very many of them Popish. **1882** SIMMONDS *Dict. Usef. Anim.*, *Razor Fish*, in America *Solen ensis* is called the *razor clam. **1935** J. C. LINCOLN *Cape Cod Yesterdays* 48 The dictionary.. even mentions the 'razor clam' among them. **1960** M. SHARCOTT *Place of Many Winds* ix. 162 Commercial crab fishermen often use clams, particularly razor clams, as bait. **1964** F. WARNER *Early Poems* 77 Cruelty *razor-cut my arteries. **1965** *Family Circle* Oct. 60 Hair as dark as this ideally goes into a sleek and sophisticated styling of the very short tapered razor cut. **1969** J. N. SMITH *Is he dead, Miss ffinch?* vi. 27 I'd had time for a hair-do.. a razor-cut, tapered down to the neck. **1971** R. FALKIRK *Chill Factor* vi. 57 His hair was razor-cut. **1974** R. B. PARKER *God save Child* (1975) iv. 33 He was dark-skinned with longish black hair carefully layered with a razor cut. **1976** SCOTT & KOSKI *Walk-In* (1977) xii. 66 Their hair was razor cut to just above the collar line. **1968** J. IRONSIDE *Fashion Alphabet* 197 *Razor cutting became popular in the 1950s, first in men's barber shops and later in women's hairdressers. The use of a razor means that the hair can be layered and thinned when wet and shaped more effectively. **1977** *Oxford Consumer* June 6/1 Razor cutting is now a rarity,.. and only 7 people had had a perm recently. **1687** DRYDEN *Hind & P.* III. 688 You have ground the persecuting knife And set it to a *razor edge on life. **1861** *Sat. Rev.* 7 Sept. 238 On the closest verge of destruction,.. on the very razor-edge of fate. **1877** E. CAIRD *Philos. Kant* II. xix. 664 Kant is solicitous to maintain himself on the exact razor-edge of critical orthodoxy. **1927** D. H. LAWRENCE *Mornings in Mexico* 61 The instant moment is forever keen with a razor-edge of oblivion. **1941** B. SCHULBERG *What makes Sammy Run?* iii. 49 With one razor-edge phrase he had cut me down to his level. **1962** H. O. BEECHENO *Introd. Business Stud.* i. 7 Ours is a razor-edge economy and maintaining our balance of payments.. becomes a matter of overriding importance. **1976** 'A. YORK' *Dark Passage* xiii. 152 His finances.. were in a razor edge state... He lived like a millionaire,.. but there was no cash around. **1957** *Essays in Criticism* VII. 311, I suppose that

Mr. Conquest would not consider deliverance from the caprice of motorists, or even of wide boys and *razor gangs, altogether undesirable for the free mind. **1966** H. Sheppard *Dict. Railway Slang* (ed. 2) 10 *Razor gang*, economy men from Headquarters. **1970** F. McKenna *Gloss. Railwaymen's Talk* 38 *Razor gang*, an investigating committee, searching rosters and rotas for 'unproductive time'. **1977** *Times* 4 May 10/6 There were razor gangs on our race-courses. **1864** A. H. R. Grisebach *Flora Brit. W. Indian Islands* 787 *Razor-grass: *Scleria scindens*. **1871** C. Kingsley *At Last* viii, Yonder beautiful green pest,..namely, a tangle of Razor-grass. **1879** Baron Eggers *Flora St. Croix* 109 Razor-grass. **1922** *Blackw. Mag.* July 11/1 The great sweep of razor-grass rustled golden. **1954** *Farmer's Guide* (Jamaica Agric. Soc.) 587 Razor-grass... At least nine different kinds of Scleria occur in Jamaica, and all of them can be unpleasant weeds due to the cutting edges of the leaves. **1969** S. M. Sadeek *Windswept & Other Stories* 29 The cart rolled on..into the savannah of..beezie-beezie reeds and razor-grass. **1958** *New Statesman* 5 Apr. 436/3 The *razor-men arrive at his door. **1977** E. W. Hildick *Loop* vii. 36 Noah..was..a 'painter' or razorman with some northern racetrack gang. **1851** Mayhew *Lond. Labour* I. 429/2 Of the Street-Sellers of..*Razor Paste. **1961** *Times* 26 May 9/6 Putting *razor plugs in the bathrooms. **1969** C. Hodder-Williams *98.4* i. 7 There was a *razor point so I went out to the car and fetched my shaver. **1978** *Cornish Guardian* 27 Apr. 15/1 (Advt.), 21 letting bedrooms (basins, razor points). **1958** M. Procter *Man in Ambush* xiv. 162 This girl had reason to be afraid. She had been *razor-slashed once. **1959** N. Mailer *Advts. for Myself* (1961) 292 In the worst of perversion, promiscuity, pimpery,..rape, razor-slash, bottle-break.., the Negro discovered a morality of the bottom. **1963** T. Tullett *Inside Interpol.* xi. 160 A razor-slash across the face. **1976** R. Hill *Another Death in Venice* I. iii. 55 Dunkerley the pimp, razor-slashing young prostitutes who wouldn't pay. **1980** P. Ableman *Shoestring's Finest Hour* ii. 30 The pimp..is called..Ted the Slash because he's got a razor slash on his cheek. **1951** S. Spender *World within World* iv. 213 Some of the recruits turned out to be a gang of Glasgow *razor-slashers. **1961** *John o'London's* 6 July 24/2 Greene's slum *Faust* was articulate in a way unlikely in the most intelligent razor-slasher. **1938** F. D. Sharpe *Sharpe of Flying Squad* xix. 204 Warfare between the gangs was confined to individual beatings-up and *razor-slashings. **1979** W. J. Fishman *Streets of E. London* 106/2 His face..resembling the cross lines of a railway complex as a result of razor slashing. **1923** J. Ramsbottom *Handbk. Larger Brit. Fungi* 129 The name '*razor-strop fungus' is often given to *P[olyporus] betulinus*, as up till the early part of last century it was used for making strops. **1966** F. H. Brightman *Oxf. Bk. Flowerless Plants* 116/2 *Piptoporus betulinus*..has also been recommended for stropping razors, and is sometimes referred to in books as the 'Razor Strop Fungus'. **1895** *Montgomery Ward Catal.* Spring & Summer 509/1 The *Razor Toe... This style shoe is becoming very popular on acount of the long narrow toe, and patent tip. **1897** C. T. Davis *Manuf. Leather* (ed. 2) xxii. 303 The pedestrian or runner avoids 'razor toes'.

razor ('reɪzə(r)), *v.* [f. prec.] **a.** *trans.* To shave as with a razor; to cut *down*. Also, to cut *out* (with a razor blade); to shave *away*, *off*.

1827 Pollok *Course T.* vii. (1860) 182 Upon the head that time had razored bare Rose bushy locks. **1872** De Morgan *Budget of Paradoxes* 337 He has announced his intention of bringing me..4159265..razored down to 25. **1974** *Globe & Mail* (Toronto) 24 July 5/1 Articles taken out of magazines in the libraries..'I'll just say they were razored out. Definitely.' **1975** M. Kenyon *Mr Big* xviii. 175 He..had razored off the moustache. **1977** D. Seaman *Committee* 42 A roughness on the chin each morning that had to be razored away.

b. To slash or assault with a razor.

1937 E. Ambler *Uncommon Danger* viii. 110 By the time I'd finished with the beggar he would have..razored his own father and mother if I'd told him to. **1954** 'N. Blake' *Whisper in Gloom* vii. 91 They might..terrorise a suspected informer—beat him up or razor him.

Hence **'razoring** *vbl. sb.*

1950 W. Sansom in *Penguin New Writing* XL. 44 It was not the kind of shop one would have expected of Sally—and perhaps this proved a key to the outcome of that night's razoring. **1963** *Times* 5 June 16/1 Mr. C. Lindsay, for the defence, said Osborne had been afraid of possible razoring by the barons over a debt of £1 and four or five ounces of tobacco.

†**'razorable**, *a.* *rare*$^{-1}$. [f. razor *sb.*] Capable of, or fit for, being shaved.

1610 Shaks. *Temp.* ii. i. 250 The man i'th Moone's too slow, till new-borne chinnes Be rough and Razor-able.

'razor-back, *sb.* and *a.* [f. razor *sb.*]

A. *sb.* **1.** The Razor-back whale or Rorqual.

1823 W. Scoresby *Jrnl. Voy. Northern Whale-Fishery* 143 Several razor-backs (Balaena physalis) had been seen, but no whales. **1832** Lyell *Princ. Geol.* II. 278 The other [whale]..mentioned by Sibbald..was probably a Razor-back. **1850** Scoresby *Cheever's Whalem. Adv.* vi. (1858) 77 The razor-back is sometimes met with one hundred and five feet long.

2. A pig having a sharp ridge-like back.

Now chiefly applied to a half-wild breed of hogs common in the southern United States; cf. *razor-backed*.

1849 J. Barrow *Facts Texas* iii. 57 Hogs are a very numerous family, but they are of very indifferent breed, and receive the appellation of 'razor backs', which is significant enough of their appearance. **1867** Hawker *Prose Wks.* (1893) 149 Prominent among them the old Cornish razor-back asserted his pre-eminence of height and bone. **1878** C. Hallock *Amer. Club List & Sportsman's Gloss.* p. ix, *Razorback*, a domestic hog which runs wild in the woods of the Southern States. **1901** *Munsey's Mag.* XXIV. 494/1 In the vernacular of the South, they were razor backs... Nevertheless, these two hogs had a value. **1941** *Arkansas: Guide to State* 99 Outside the imagination, a true razorback probably does not exist. **1976** N. Thornburg *Cutter & Bone* xiii. 302 It has come to him now, what it was about the razorback.

3. A narrow ridge-like back in cattle and horses.

1844 H. Stephens *Bk. of Farm* II. 164 A high narrow shoulder is frequently attended with a rigid back bone, and low-set narrow hooks, a form which gets the appropriate name of razor-back. **1908** *Animal Managem.* 25 The 'razor' back may..be due only to want of muscle which judicious rest, food, and work will produce. **1941** I. L. Idriess *Great Boomerang* vii. 51 Fine upstanding beasts... No 'razor-backs' going away with nothing behind. These were 'table-tops'; you could throw your blanket on any beast and camp on his back.

4. Chiefly *Austral.* and *N.Z.* A steep-sided, narrow ridge of land.

1874 W. M. Baines *Narr. E. Crewe* xi. 247 From a high 'razor-back', I had a magnificent view. **1889** *Trans. N.Z. Inst.* 110 Supposing the traveller to be standing on a narrow spur, or razorback, leading to the mountain-top. **1902** [see *cow-track* s.v. cow *sb.*[1] 7]. **1911** *Chambers's Jrnl.* Dec. 30/1 Twice the way led along a real 'razor-back'. On both sides the mountain sloped precipitously. **1957** P. White *Voss* vi. 153 Presently the path, which had reached a razorback.. wound suddenly..and plunged down.

5. *U.S. Circus slang.* A circus hand; *spec.* one who loads and unloads the wagons.

1904 *Everybody's Mag.* X. 658/1 That night it took the Old Man 'n Early Jim both to keep a razorback from carvin' up Ibree. **1909** *Youth's Compan.* LXXXIII. 289/4 There was too much worth seeing outside. The loaders—'razor-backs', in circus language—were putting the great clanking parade wagons on the flat cars. **1926** R. E. Sherwood *Here we are Again* 162 Canvasmen or 'razorbacks', as they are known in the slang of the circus, are rarely in funds. **1975** *New Yorker* 13 Oct. 38 Some people..were watching the roller coaster... I went up to the razorback who ran the controls.

B. *adj.* Having a very sharp back or ridge.

1836 *Uncle Philip's Convers. Whale Fishery* 34 The 'Razor-back whale'..is longer and stronger and swifter than any other sort. **1851** G. S. Cooper *Jrnl. Expedition Overland* 110 Gullies..ran down from each side of the razor-back ridge. **1859** Trollope *West Indies* iii. (1860) 50 Riding over some of these razorback crags. **1896** [see hump-backed *a.*]. **1899** B. Tarkington *Gentleman from Indiana* iv. 44 A squad of thin, 'razor-back' hogs. **1924** J. Masefield *Sard Harker* iii. 126 It was one of the half-wild razor-back hogs which the negroes allowed to stray in the woods there. **1976** N. Thornburg *Cutter & Bone* xiii. 302 As it fell open Bone was able to see his T-shirt underneath, and the emblem on it: a red Arkansas razorback hog, name and symbol of the state university's sports teams.

So **'razor-backed** *a.*

1829 *Sporting Mag.* XXIV. 116 A razor-backed yellow tit. **1846** Youatt *Pig* vi. (1847) 69 The old Cornish hog, a large ..razor-backed animal. **1885** *Times* (weekly ed.) 13 Feb. 1/3 A high ridge of razor-backed hills. **1894** *Outing* (U.S.) XXIV. 336/2 Their..razor-backed hogs climb the steep hills like goats. **1904** *Daily Chron.* 12 May 5/3 A fierce struggle ensued for the possession of two razor-backed ridges above which runs the main Peking road.

'razor-bill. [f. razor *sb.* + bill *sb.*[2]]

1. A name given to various birds.

a. A species of auk (*Alca torda*).

1674 Ray *Collect. Words, Water Fowl* 92 The Rasor-bill: Auk or Murre. **1768** Pennant *Zool.* II. 403 Razor-bill... These birds, in company with the Guillemot, appear in our seas the beginning of February. **1865** Gosse *Land & Sea* (1874) 40 The guillemots sitting in rows,..bolt upright, the manner of sitting common to the puffins and razor-bills.

b. *U.S.* The Cut-water or Skimmer. *rare*$^{-1}$.

1794 Morse *Amer. Geog.* (1796) I. 214 Shear Water or Razor Bill. **1832** in Webster.

c. 'The red-breasted merganser, *Mergus serrator*' (*Hants Gloss.* 1883).

2. *attrib.* Razor-billed.

1894 *Westm. Gaz.* 9 Aug. 4/2 A young razorbill puffin came alongside.

So **'razor-billed** *a.*, having a bill resembling a razor (applied *spec.* to certain birds: see quots.).

1748 Catesby *California* App. 103 The Razor-billed Black-bird of Jamaica. This Bird is somewhat less than our Jack-daw. **1824** Latham *Gen. Hist. Birds* X. 63 Razor-billed Auk.

†**'razored**, *a.* *rare*$^{-1}$. Sharp-edged.

1613 Heywood *Silver Age* iii. i, Be his teeth razored, and his talons keen,..Yet I ere night will case me in his skin.

'razor-fish. [f. razor *sb.*]

1. Any bivalve mollusc of the genus *Solen* or family *Solenidæ*, having a long narrow shell like the handle of a razor; esp. the European species *Solen ensis* or *siliqua*, common on sandy shores.

1602 Carew *Cornwall* i. 32 The Sheath, or Razor-fish, resembleth in length and bignesse a mans finger. **1632** T. Morton *New Eng. Canaan* ii. vii. (1838) 62 Raser-fishes there are. **1753** Chambers *Cycl. Supp.*, *Dactylus*,..a name used by many authors for the solen or razor-fish. **1802–3** tr. *Pallas's Trav.* (1812) II. 466, I have nowhere met with any rare sea-muscles; only the razor-fish, or Solen, of the Bosphorus. **1884** Goode *Usef. Aquatic Anim.* 707 The Californian Razor-fish (*Siliqua patula*) is also edible.

2. A Mediterranean labroid fish (*Xyrichthys novacula*); also, a related W. Indian fish (*X. lineatus*).

1753 Chambers *Cycl. Supp.*, *Novacula piscis*, the rasor-fish..the name of a sea-fish caught in the Mediterranean, and some other seas. [Description follows.]

'razor-,grinder. [f. razor *sb.*]

1. One who grinds or sharpens razors.

1789 *Boston Directory* 184 Fillis William, razor-grinder. **1798** D. Wordsworth *Jrnl.* 22 Feb. (1941) I. 9 Met a razor-grinder with..a boy to drag his wheel. **1833** *Boston Herald* 19 Mar. 4/3, I afterwards met a razor grinder and his wife. **1886** Besant *Childr. Gibeon* ii. ii, They are buhl cutters,.. razor grinders, glass bevellers.

2. A name given to various birds: **a.** The Australian Dishwasher or Restless Fly-catcher (*Seisura inquieta*). **b.** *dial.* The Night-jar. **c.** *dial.* The Grasshopper Warbler.

a. 1825 Vigors in *Trans. Linn. Soc.* XV. 250 A loud noise ..caused by a rasor-grinder when at work. **1848** R. Howitt *Australia* 332 The razor-grinder, fitly so called from making a grinding noise as it wavers in one position a foot or two from the ground.

b. 1895 P. H. Emerson *Birds*, etc. *Norfolk* 153 The night-hawk, or big razor-grinder, as he is more rarely called in the Broadlands.

c. 1895 P. H. Emerson *Birds*, etc. *Norfolk* 50 This shy, mysterious bird, the 'razor-grinder', as he is often called in the Broad district.

'razor-shell. [f. razor *sb.*: see quot. 1869.] The shell of a Razor-fish, or the mollusc together with its shell. Also *attrib.*

1752 Sir J. Hill *Hist. Anim.* 170 The large, brown, common Solen, called the Razor-shell and Sheath-shell. **1792** J. Belknap *Hist. New Hampshire* III. 183 The Razor-shell clam '*Solen ensis*'. **1794** *Collect. Mass. Hist. Soc.* (1810) III. 199 The shores and marshes afford large and small clams, quahaugs, razor-shells,..and cockles. **1869** Wood *Com. Shells* (ed. 3) 31 That curious family which are appropriately termed Razor-shells, because, when perfect, the shell looks something like the handle of a closed razor. *Ibid.* 32 All the Razor-shells are edible. **1901** E. Step *Shell Life* ix. 155 We now reach the Razor-shell family, characterised by having the valves of the shell of equal length. **1928** Russell & Yonge *Seas* ii. 38 The long razor-shells (*Solen*) may occasionally be dug at low tide. **1971** *Oxf. Bk. Invertebrates* 80 The razor shells, looking like the old-fashioned cut-throat razors, are among the most specialized of the burrowing bivalves.

razour, obs. form of rizzar. *Sc.*

razure, variant of rasure.

razy, obs. form of racy.

razz (ræz), *sb.* *slang* (orig. *U.S.*). [Short for razzberry.] = raspberry 4.

a **1919** C. Briggs *Oh Man!*, She'll prob'ly give me the razz for being out late last night! **1920** S. Lewis *Main Street* xxiii. 282 The Red Swede got the grand razz handed to him. **1921** *Collier's* 15 Jan. 20/1 The mob gave him the razz. **1926** N. V. Lindsay *Going-to-the-Stars* 52 Let us think of the Irish flute in the morn,..And forget our jazzes and our razzes and our hates. **1935** *Punch* 27 Feb. 248/2, I wasn't asked parties; I got no rise..; the girls gave me the razz—and all for the reason I'd no badge to show. **1960** E. W. Hildick *Jim Starling & Colonel* viii. 62 That band chap blew him the razz! **1961** *Punch* 18 Jan. 129 What say, honey?—let's give this communal living the razz and just go off somewhere, the two of us. **1961** *Spectator* 9 June 835/1 He selects one of them for punishment.., delivers a sonorous 'razz' and pretends to cane him. **1967** J. D. R. McConnell *Eton* 61 Offenders may be summoned to the Library for a 'razz'. **1977** *Times Lit. Suppl.* 29 Apr. 534/5 Even the peppiest, most two-fisted and up-and-coming borough librarian would get the razz for buying it.

razz (ræz), *v.* *slang* (orig. *U.S.*). [f. the sb.] *trans.* To hiss or deride; to make fun of (a person). Hence **'razzing** *vbl. sb.*

1921 *Collier's* 19 Feb. 5/3 It [*sc.* a crowd]..will razz its local favorite with as much enthusiasm as it will the visitin' boxer at the first sign of foul fightin'. **1921** *Sat. Even. Post* 18 June 65/2 I'd of rather took fifty socks on the jaw than the razzing the crowd give Bat. **1924** P. Marks *Plastic Age* 52 The fellows razzed the life out of me. *Ibid.* 60, I don't mind the razzing myself,..but I don't like the things they said to poor little Wilkins. **1932** J. Lawson *Man's Life* xvi. 161 The person who never could appreciate institutional life..is always with us... His chief hobby when at home has been razzing the wife, or his mother, because the bacon is too fat or too lean..and anyhow he doesn't like bacon at all. **1939** L. Jacobs *Rise Amer. Film* 378 He turned out a series of domestic comedies that caused him to be hailed for his 'razzing' of American foibles. **1941** J. McCormack in L. A. G. Strong *John McCormack* x. 168, I have seen a great deal of baseball in America, but I have never been able to reconcile myself to the continuous razzing of the pitcher. **1956** B. Holiday *Lady sings Blues* (1973) iii. 33 When I came to work the other girls used to razz me, call me 'Duchess' and say, 'Look at her, she thinks she's a lady.' **1968** *Punch* 24 July 129/2 Ilya Ilf, pooh-poohing purges, Razzed Red Russians with wry stories. **1975** A. Bergman *Hollywood & Le Vine* ii. 29, I continued on down the street. .. I anticipated the razzing of the Dead End Kids. **1977** *TV Times* (Austral.) 20 Aug. 29/1 My kids will get razzed about it at school the next day. No one knows more about my mistakes than I do.

razzamatazz, var. razzmatazz.

razzberry ('ræzbərɪ). *N. Amer. slang.* Also **razbery.** [Var. of raspberry.] = raspberry 4.

1922 *Collier's* 15 July 4/3 No matter if all the rest of the crowd gives me the razzberry, why they'll be at least two guys pulling for me. **1927** [see bird *sb.* 5 b]. **1928** C. Sandburg in *Woman's Home Compan.* Aug. 112/3 Hand 'em the razzberries. **1948** *Daily Ardmoreite* (Ardmore, Okla.) 27 May 8/3 Here in the home of the Bronx jeer it usually is rewarded with a noisy razberry. **1975** E. Iglauer *Denison's Ice Road* ii. 35, I sure got the razzberries from the boys.

‖**razzia** ('ræzɪə). [a. F. *razzia*, ad. Algerian Arab. *ghāzīah*, var. Arab. *ghazwah*, *ghazāh* war, battle, military expedition, raid against infidels,

f. *ghasw* to make war. Cf. Pg. *gazia*, *gaziva*, from the same source.

The initial *r* of the French form represents a pron. of the Ar. *ġ* approaching to a guttural *r* (*ghr*), also indicated in the form *ghrazzie* formerly used by some English writers:—**1821** CAPT. LYON *Trav. N. Africa* vi. 262 None but the Bedouins appear to approve of these ghrazzies. **1826** DENHAM *Trav.* 75 These people could lead 3000 men into action, for his ghrazzie was to consist of that number.

Some Dicts. give the pron. as ('rætsɪə) on the analogy of Italian words of similar form.]

a. A hostile incursion, foray or raid, for purposes of conquest, plunder, capture of slaves, etc., orig. as practised by the Muslim peoples in Africa; also *transf.* of similar raids by other nations.

1845 *Athenæum* 8 Feb. 144 If half those seized survive the atrocities of the razzia and the march, it is considered an excellent speculation. **1861** J. G. SHEPPARD *Fall Rome* ix. 515 The wars of Charlemagne..were something very different from the freebooting razzias of his Merovingian predecessors.

b. *fig.* = RAID 2 c.

1855 *Poultry Chron.* 4 Apr. 98/1 The owners of manors.. carried out a 'razzia' on the enemy's territory of Leadenhall market. **1859** GREEN *Lett.* (1901) 29 One of our maids has been making a razzia in my study. **1865** MERIVALE *Rom. Emp.* VIII. lxiii. 25 He executed what..we might call a *razzia* upon the remnant of the culprits. **1965** C. D. EBY *Siege of Alcázar* (1966) v. 100 Small bands had been stealing out of the fortress at night to scavenge in the houses near by. The purpose of these *razzias* was to bring back food for the infirmary.

So **'razzia** *v. intr.*, to maraud.

1846 R. FORD *Gatherings from Spain* iv. 34 The object of these border *guerrilla*-warfares was..to 'harry', to 'razzia'.

razzle (ræz(ə)l), *sb. slang.* [Short for RAZZLE-DAZZLE.] **a.** A 'good time', a spree; usu. in phr. ***on the razzle.***

1908 A. BENNETT *Old Wives' Tale* iv. i. 435 'What puzzles me most is what the devil you were doing in a place like that. According to your description, it must be a ——.' 'I went there because I was broke,' said Matthew. 'Razzle?' Matthew nodded. **1915** W. S. MAUGHAM *Of Human Bondage* 249 We won't 'alf go on the razzle. **1927** *Daily Express* 2 June 6/4 Its heroine..is a Frenchman's idea of a great English lady out on the razzle. **1930** J. B. PRIESTLEY *Angel Pavement* v. 213 And now we're going on the razzle. **1943** —— *Daylight on Saturday* xxvi. 201 I've got three [absentees]... One's off on a razzle. **1968** 'J. LE CARRÉ' *Small Town in Germany* 210 Your wife was in England, and you went on the razzle with Leo. **1978** 'L. BLACK' *Foursome* vii. 56 He loved making new friends, joining up with them for a razzle in the nightspots.

b. = RAZZLE-DAZZLE *sb.* b.

1969 *Wall St. Jrnl.* 30 Sept. 1/1 His specialty is 'Razzle', a game that in one form or another has entranced fair-goers since ancient times.

'razzle, *v. slang.* [f. the sb.] *intr.* To live a life of pleasure, to enjoy oneself; to go 'on the razzle'.

1908 G. B. SHAW *Lett. to Granville Barker* (1956) 120 He will probably put it to you whether, as a gentleman, you can ask for a salary when you have been doing nothing but razzling in America. **1951** E. BAGNOLD *Loved & Envied* iii. 39 We ought to be fairly flush... It's not an expensive island. We ought to be able to razzle a bit, if there's anywhere to razzle.

'razzle-'dazzle, *sb. slang.* **a.** A word, app. of U.S. coinage, used to express the ideas of bewilderment or confusion, rapid stir and bustle, riotous jollity or intoxication, etc. Also, deception, fraud; extravagant publicity.

1889 *Gallup* (New Mexico) *Gleaner* 18 Mar. 4/2 A Kansas paper..recently told of a 'regular old razooper, who, having got a skate on, indulged in a glorious razzle-dazzle'. **1890** GUNTER *Miss Nobody* xv (*heading*) Little Gussie's Razzle Dazzle. **1892** KIPLING & BALESTIER *Naulahka* 88 There isn't enough real downright rustle and razzle-dazzle..to run a milk-cart. **1898** G. B. SHAW *Mrs. Warren's Profession* I. 175, I don't bet much and I never go regularly on the razzle-dazzle as you did when you were my age. **1899** *Westm. Gaz.* 10 Mar. 3/1 Dick, who is still on the 'razzle dazzle'. **1928** *New Yorker* 15 Dec. 24/1 Suspecting some sort of razzle-dazzle, the wiser of the two men said he would buy the seats at their box-office value. **1938** *Sun* (Baltimore) 20 Jan. 3/2 With such razzle-dazzle financing the general practice, it is not surprising to find oil derricks sprouting up on the grounds of the State capitol. **1962** 'K. ORVIS' *Damned & Destroyed* vii. 51 The razzle-dazzle I had handed the two drug-ring musclemen. **1969** *New Yorker* 29 Nov. 47/1, I want models, I want a private plane, I want this, I want that, I want some razzle-dazzle. **1977** *Time* 19 Sept. 25/1 Lance ran for the Democratic gubernatorial nomination, using the financial razzle-dazzle that later was to become such a liability. **1978** *New York* 3 Apr. 17/3 It [*sc.* a musical] has pizzazz and razzle-dazzle, bursts of energy and invention, music and laughter.

b. (See quots.)

1891 *Daily News* 27 July 3/1 A new type of roundabout, called 'Razzle-Dazzle', which gives its occupants the pleasant (or otherwise) sensations of an excursion at sea. **1896** [see SWITCHBACK *a.*]. **1935** *Amer. Mercury* June 230/2 *Razzle-dazzle*, kelsy [i.e., a prostitute]; also used by the public in reference to carnival rides, although not so used by carnies themselves. **1968** D. BRAITHWAITE *Fairground Archit.* iii. 34 The steam swing and 'Razzle Dazzle' drew inspiration from mechanisms in the spinning frame, [etc.]. *Ibid.* 60 Four years before his death in 1897, Savage patented the 'Razzle Dazzle', otherwise known as 'Whirligig' or 'Aerial Novelty'.

c. *attrib.* or as *adj.* Of, pertaining to, or characterized by, razzle-dazzle; dazzling, spectactular.

1889 *Road* (Denver, Colorado) 28 Dec. 5/1 Clint Butterfield incloses us a razzle-dazzle card of some kind that has a very neat little design of a nightmare etched in blood red and India ink. **1946** *N.Y. Times Bk. Rev.* 4 Aug. 5/1 A great many people are reading Mr. Wakeman's razzle-dazzle novel these days. **1951** M. MCLUHAN *Mech. Bride* (1967) 10/2 The newsreel is provided with a razzle-dazzle accompaniment. **1965** *Economist* 22 May p. xxiv/1 A front page [of a newspaper] full of short items and a Gallic profusion of typefaces, alike in text and headlines—..what the Americans call 'circus' or 'razzledazzle' make-up. **1971** *Daily Tel.* 19 Oct. 19 Mr Thorley's chairmanship is, or was, intended to be an interregnum between the razzle-dazzle rule of Sir Derek Pritchard and the accession of the Showering dynasty. **1974** *Plain Dealer* (Cleveland) 13 Oct. c. 12/6 Freshman halfback Pat Healy scored three touchdowns, the last on a razzle-dazzle 32-yard pass from quarterback Bruce Basile. **1977** *Time* 13 June 39/1 Erdman comes to his subject with the sure hand of one who knows, from the inside, what lurks in the hearts of financial razzle-dazzle artists.

So **razzle-dazzle** *v. trans.*, to dazzle, daze, 'bamboozle', etc. **razzle-dazzler** (see quot.).

1890 GUNTER *Miss Nobody* xiv, I'm going to razzle-dazzle the boys..with my great lightning change act. **1897** *Daily News* 10 Aug. 5/2 Two dozen pair of plain socks and half a dozen pair of the sort known as 'razzle-dazzlers'. **1976** *Houston* (Texas) *Chron.* 22 Sept. 7-4/4 Lady Bird eats it in an orange print pants suit and that Texas smile that razzle-dazzles 'em.

razzmatazz, razzamatazz (ˌræzmə'tæz, ˌræzəmə'tæz). *colloq.* (orig. *U.S.*). Also **razamataz(z, razmataz(z, razz-ma-tazz,** etc. [Origin unknown; perh. alteration of RAZZLE-DAZZLE.] **a.** A type of rag-time or early jazz music; old-fashioned 'straight' jazz; sentimental, 'corny' jazz; hence anything old-fashioned; stuff, rubbish. **b.** Noisy, showy publicity; meretricious or extravagant display; an event surrounded by such publicity or display; fuss, commotion, garishness. Also *attrib.* or as *adj.*

In quot. 1899 the sense is uncertain but may be 'up-to-date, stylish' or 'cultured, superior'.

1899 G. ADE *Fables in Slang* 37 It would be a Big Help to the Poor and Uncultured to see what a Real Razmataz Lady was like. **1901** T. D. COLLINS (*title of piano music*) Raz-a-ma-taz. **1901** W. H. SMITH (*title of piano music*) Raz-ma-taz. **1936** *Amer. Mercury* XXXVIII. p. x/2 *Rooty-toot*,—unadulterated corn; razz-ma-tazz. **1937** *Amer. Speech* XII. 48/1 *Razmataz band*, a band which plays in an outmoded style. **1938** *Brit. Empire Mod. Eng. Illustr. Dict.* 1257/1 Razz-ma-tazz (*Am.*), old-fashioned jazz. **1942** BERREY & VAN DEN BARK *Amer. Thes. Slang* §579/2 'Straight Jazz.' (Old-fashioned jazz, which reproduces the score faithfully, as distinguished from 'swing'.)..*razzmatazz.* **1947** *Sat. Rev. Lit.* (U.S.) 25 Oct. 65/2 Expert horsing of the old razzmatazz style by an expert horsewoman. **1950** C. COBEN *Old Piano Roll Blues* (*song*), And while we kiss, kiss, kiss away all our cares, The player piano's playin' razzamatazz, I wanna hear it again. **1953** BERRY & VAN DEN BARK *Amer. Thes. Slang* (1954) (ed. 2) §233/5 Something old-fashioned, ..*razzmatazz.* **1958** *People* 4 May 8/2 She will, from next Friday when she flies to Cannes, be getting the full razza-ma-tazz, big-star build-up. **1958** *Spectator* 1 Aug. 174/3 Don't you remember *anything* about the Twenties but crime, booze, flappers, religious razzmatazz? **1959** J. WAIN *Travelling Woman* x. 148 The enormous selling bonanza that was going on about him, in its astonishing flood of genuine goodwill, even a grain here and there of genuine piety, with unscrupulous salesman's razzmatazz, heightened his sense of living in a dream. **1961** *Sunday Times* 26 Nov. 48/3 Barbara Murray, a girl who is entirely wasted on rats, retorts and all that razzmatazz. **1963** *The Beatles* 9 Though some of our material is a bit out of the way for a razzamatazz chap like him. **1965** G. MCINNES *Road to Gundagai* iv. 59 The great wide streets have an air of grandeur which even the razz-ma-tazz of neon cannot wholly mar. **1969** *Listener* 17 Apr. 544/1 *Oh! What a lovely war* (Paramount) is a razz-ma-tazz spectacular. **1970** *Times* 9 Mar. 13/1 He turned, as might have been expected, a fairly serious event into a razamataz. **1971** *Morning Star* 8 Mar. 4/7 Some of the hotels and centres can be a bit razzamataz and noisy, especially at night. **1972** *Daily Colonist* (Victoria, B.C.) 16 Feb. 32/1 There was no need to go through 'all this razzmatazz'. The replacing of white centre lines with yellow ones wasn't all that difficult to comprehend. **1973** *Daily Tel.* 8 Nov. 5 (Advt.), We thought the car good enough not to need any launch gimmicks or razmataz. **1973** *Daily Colonist* (Victoria, B.C.) 23 Nov. 22/3 Opening day Thursday had all the razzmatazz of a revival meeting. **1974** *Time Out* 27 Sept. 23/1 There is the host, resplendent in white satin, razmatazz shirt. **1977** *Listener* 20 Oct. 508/3 This programme included a razzmatazz of presentational devices which seemed better suited to a giveaway quiz show. **1979** *Guardian* 1 May 30/1 In keeping with the showbiz, razz-matazz side of the election, the most glamorous transport belongs to the media.

razzo ('ræzəʊ). *slang.* [Prob. alteration of RASPBERRY.] The nose.

1899 [see LOWER *v.* 1 e]. **1936** [see ACID *sb.* 3].

razzoo(h, varr. RAZOO[1].

R-boat. [Partial tr. G. *R-boot*, abbrev. of *räumboot* minesweeper.] In the war of 1939–45, a German minesweeper.

1942 *Times* 10 June 4/3 An R-boat is stated to be an armed motor minesweeper. **1945** P. SCOTT *Battle of Narrow Seas* ii. 5 Besides E boats there were flotillas of R boats (corresponding roughly to our M.Ls.), used for minesweeping and defensive patrolling along the occupied coasts. **1961** GRANVILLE & KELLY *Inshore Heroes* vii. 71 The Raumboot (R-boat) was a patrol vessel of between 85 and 115 feet, with a speed of about 20 knots. **1978** F. MACLEAN *Take Nine Spies* v. 183 A whole group of German R-boats was sent from Sicily to the Aegean.

RDX (ɑːdiː'ɛks). [f. *R*esearch *D*epartment (Woolwich, England) E*x*plosive.]

= CYCLONITE.

1941 *Newsweek* 8 Dec. 43/2 One [explosive], developed in cooperation with the British and identified with the stuff used in Britain's 'superbombs', is known as RDX and credited with 40 per cent more bursting power than TNT. **1947** *Times* 9 July 5/7 RDX, the main high explosive development of the war, was yet another chemical contribution to victory—opening up, incidentally, a new field of organic chemistry. **1974** *Encycl. Brit. Macropædia* VII. 89/1 The torpedo warhead torpex..is a cast mixture of RDX, TNT, and aluminum.

re (reɪ), *sb.*[1] Also 6 rey. [The first syllable of L. *resonāre*; see GAMUT.] **a.** The second note of Guido's hexachords, and of the octave in modern solmization. **b.** (As in Fr. and It.) The note D, the second of the natural scale of C major. (*rare.*)

c **1325** [see G-SOL-RE-UT]. *a* **1529** SKELTON *Bowge Courte* 258 A balade boke before me for to laye, And lerne me to synge, Re, my, fa, sol. *c* **1550** *Armonye of Byrdes* 185 in Hazl. *E.P.P.* III. 194 Chaungyng their key From ut to rey. **1596** SHAKS. *Tam. Shr.* III. i. 74 A re, to plead Hortensio's passion. *Ibid.* 77 D sol re, one Cliffe, two notes haue I. **1636** WALLER *To Mr. Henry Lawes*, Let those which only warble long,..Content themselves with Ut, Re, Mi. **1818** BUSBY *Gram. Music* 60 Whatever the key in which the octave is taken, *do* is the tonic, *re* the supertonic.

Hence †**re** *v.* (in nonce-use).

1592 SHAKS. *Rom. & Jul.* IV. v. 121, I will carie no Crochets, Ile Re you, Ile Fa you, do you note me?

‖**re** (riː), *sb.*[2] [Ablative of L. *rēs* thing, affair.] In the matter of, referring to. Cf. *in re* s.v. IN *Lat. prep.* 24 (*d*). Now freq. apprehended as a preposition, and used in weakened senses to mean 'about, concerning'.

re infecta, 'with the matter unfinished or unaccomplished', has also been freq. employed in Eng.

The use as a preposition has freq. been condemned: see Fowler *Mod. Eng. Usage* (1926) s.v. *illiteracies* and A. P. Herbert in quots.

1707 HEARNE *Collect.* 17 May (O.H.S.) II. 14 Amused by Charlett's trick *re* Tacitus. **1926** in H. W. Fowler *Mod. Eng. Usage* 484/1 Dear Sir,—I am glad to see that you have taken a strong line re the Irish railway situation. *Ibid.* 484/2 Reference had been made in a former issue to some alleged statements of mine re the use of the military during the recent railway dispute. **1935** A. P. HERBERT *What a Word!* iii. 80 We herewith enclose receipt for your cheque £4 on *a/c* *re* return of commission *re* Mr. Brown's cancelled agreement *re* No 50 Box Street top flat. **1939** [see INCLUSIVITY]. **1976** *Time* 27 Dec. 2/2 Re your article on legitimized gambling..and specifically state lotteries: the inefficiency of revenue collection is horrendous and the odds for winning are unconscionable. **1977** *Time* 7 Feb. 1/3 Re my archaeological explorations in Syria: it is not true that '..the Italian archaeologists have been slow to publicise their discoveries'. **1979** *Verbatim* Summer 5/2 G. Bocca's observations re public signs.

re, abbrev. of RUPEE.

1913 W. T. ROGERS *Dict. Abbrev.* 164/1 *Re.* (money), rupee. **1962** *Housewife* (Ceylon) Apr. 10 Twenties courses are practical, economical (Re. 1/- for 3 lessons). **1971** *Hindustan Times Weekly* (New Delhi) 4 Apr. 11/2 Gramdal was better by Re 1 on good offtake.

re, obs. sing. *rees* REIS (Portuguese money).

re, obs. Sc. form of ROE, deer.

re-, *prefix*, of Latin origin, with the general sense of 'back' or 'again', occurring in a large number of words directly or indirectly adopted from Latin, or of later Romanic origin, and on the model of these freely employed in English as a prefix to verbs, and to substantives or adjectives derived from these.

In earlier Latin *re-* was used before consonants, and *red-* before vowels or *h-*, as in *redīre*, *redimĕre*, *redhibēre* (rarely in other cases, as in *red-dĕre*). The latter form appears in Eng. only in a few words which are ultimately of Latin origin, as *redeem*, *redemption*, *redintegrate*. In later Latin the form with *d* was no longer in use, and *re-* was employed before vowels as well as consonants, as in *reædificāre*, *reagĕre*, *reexpectāre*, *reillūmināre*, etc.

In a few words adopted from French the prefix has so coalesced with the main part of the word that its real nature is obscured. In some cases this is due to the combination of *re-* with another prefix, as *ad-* (Fr. *a-*) or *in-* (Fr. *en-*). For examples of these types, see RANSOM, RALLY, RAMPART.

2. The original sense of *re-* in Latin is that of 'back' or 'backwards', but in the large number of words formed by its use, the prefix acquires various shades of meaning, of which the following are the most clearly marked. **a.** 'Back from a point reached', 'back to or towards the starting-point', as in *recēdĕre* to draw back, *recurrĕre* to run back, *redūcĕre* to lead back, *referre* to carry back, *refugĕre* to flee back, *remittĕre* to send back, *respicĕre* to look back, *retrahĕre* to pull back, *revocāre* to call back. Sometimes the sense of 'backwards' is also implied, as in *resilīre* to spring back or backwards. The return of light and sound is expressed in such verbs as *relūcēre* and *renīdēre* to shine or flash back, *reboāre* to bellow back, *resonāre* to echo, resound. In many cases the idea of force is present, as in *reflectĕre* to bend back, *repellĕre* to drive back, *reprimĕre* to force back, *rescindĕre* to cut back; hence arises the sense of resistance, as in *reluctārī* to struggle against, *repugnāre* to fight against, *reclāmāre* to cry out against, *recūsāre* to refuse. Occasionally the sense passes into that of 'away', as in *removēre* to move back or away, *revellĕre* to pull away or off. **b.** 'Back to the original place or position', as in *recondĕre, repōnĕre, restituĕre*, etc. to put back, replace; freq. implying 'back to one's hands or possession', as in *recipĕre* to take back, *redimĕre* to buy back, *rependĕre* to pay back, *resūmĕre* to take back. **c.** 'Again', 'anew', originally in cases implying restoration to a previous state or condition, and frequently occurring as a secondary sense in verbs of the two classes already mentioned; further examples are *recreāre* to create again, *reficĕre* to make again, *reformāre* to form again, *renovāre* to make new again, *refrīgēscĕre* to grow cold again, *revirēscĕre* to grow green again. This naturally passes into cases where the action itself is done a second time, as *recoquĕre* to cook or bake again, *refricāre* to rub again, *regenerāre* to produce again, *retractāre* to handle again, etc. This class of words is largely augmented in later Latin, as *reædificāre* to build again, *rebaptizāre* to baptize again, etc. Many of these later compounds have been adopted in English, and have chiefly supplied the models for the new formations illustrated in §5. **d.** In some cases *re-* has the same force as Eng. *un-*, implying an undoing of some previous action, as in *recingĕre* to ungird, *reclūdĕre* to unclose, to open, *refīgĕre* to unfix, *resignāre* to unseal, *revēlāre* to unveil. More rarely it expresses direct negation, as in *reprobāre* to disapprove of. **e.** 'Back in a place', i.e. 'from going forward', with verbs of keeping or holding, as *retinēre* to hold back, *religāre* to tie back or up, *refrēnāre* to rein back, *reprehendĕre* to (seize and) keep back; or 'without going on or forward' with verbs of rest, as *remanēre, residēre, restāre* to stay or stop behind, *requiēscĕre* to stay quiet, etc. Other shades of this sense appear in *relinquĕre* to leave behind, *reservāre* to keep back, store up.

Even in Latin the precise sense of *re-* is not always clear, and in many words the development of secondary meanings tends greatly to obscure its original force. This loss of distinct meaning is naturally increased in English, when the word has been adopted in a sense more or less remote from the strict etymological significance of the two elements which compose it. In many cases the simple word to which the prefix is attached is wanting in English; in others a change of sound or shifting of stress frequently assists in disguising its original sense.

In the Romance languages, as in later Latin, extensive use was made of *re-* as a prefix in verbs and verbal derivatives, and some of the words thus formed are among the earliest which were adopted in English, the immediate source being OF. To these and later adoptions from French belong many of the commonest words beginning with *re-*, as *rebate, rebound, rebuke, rebut, recoil, redress, refresh, regain, regard, regret, remark*, etc.

3. Words formed with the prefix *re-* first make their appearance in English about the year 1200. In the *Ancren Riwle*, the first text in which such forms are prominent, there occur *recluse, recoil, record, relief, religion, religious*, and *remission*. Towards the end of the century Robert of Gloucester uses *rebel, receit, release, relic, relief, remue, repent, restore, revest*. In the 14th c. the stock is largely increased, especially in the writings of Langland, Chaucer, Wyclif, and Trevisa, and by the year 1400 the number in common literary use is very considerable. During the 15th c. the additions are of less importance, but about the middle of the 16th an extensive adoption of Latin forms or types begins; the French element at this time is small in comparison, though it includes some important words. Towards the end of the 16th c. *re-* begins to rank as an ordinary English prefix, chiefly employed with words of Latin origin, but also freely prefixed to native verbs, a practice rare before this period, though Wyclif, Trevisa, and others have *renew* (after L. *renovāre*). Such formations, however, are common in Elizabethan writers: Shakespeare has *recall, regreet* (frequent), *relive, requicken, resend, respeak, restem, retell* (thrice), and *reword*, and many others occur in contemporary literature, as *rebuild, recast, refind, reflow, regather*, etc. Since 1600 the use of the prefix has been very extensive, though the number of individual formations appears to have been smaller in the 18th century than in the 17th and 19th.

The rapidly increasing use of *re-* in the early part of the 17th c. is strongly marked in the dictionaries of Florio and Cotgrave, both of whom freely invent forms with this prefix to render Italian or French words which begin with it. Many of these reappear at a later date, and most of them might be formed again at any time: the following may be quoted as specimens of those which have obtained little or no currency in later writers.

1598 FLORIO, *Rabbellimento*, a .. rebeauetifying. *Rimeritare*, to remerit or deserue againe. **1611** —— *Raccordare*,.. to reaccord. *Ricapricciare*, to re-affright. *Ricombattere*, to recombat or fight againe. *Ricompire*, to recomplish or end againe. *Riboccare*, to re-enbogue, to re-mouth. *Rimaledittione*, a remalediction. *Rimollire*,.. to remollifie, to resoften. *Risperso*, resprinckled. *Ristoppare*, to restop, to stop againe. **1611** COTGR., *Rabuser*, to re-abuse. *Reaffranchi*, reaffranchised. *Reblandir*, to re-blandish. *Redaigner*, to redaign. *Rabituer*, to .. reinure.

4. a. In English formations, whether on native or Latin bases, *re-* is almost exclusively employed in the sense of 'again'; the few exceptions to this have been directly suggested by existing Latin compounds, as *recall* after L. *revocāre*. In one or other application of this sense, *re-* may be prefixed to any English verb or verbal derivative, as *rearrange, rearranger, rearrangement*; *reignite, reignitible, reignition*; *resaddle, resaddling*; *resettlement*, etc. In all words of this type the prefix is pronounced with a clear *e* (riː), and frequently with a certain degree of stress, whereas in words of Latin or Romanic origin the vowel is usually obscured or shortened, as in *repair* (rɪˈpɛə(r)), *reparation* (rɛpəˈreɪʃən). In this way double forms arise, with difference of meaning, which in writing are usually distinguished by hyphening the prefix, as *recoil* and *re-coil*, *recover* and *re-cover*, *recreate* and *re-create*. The hyphen is also frequently employed even where there is no doublet, when emphasis is laid on the idea of repetition, as *bind and re-bind*, or when the main element begins with a vowel; before *e* it is usual to insert the hyphen, as *re-emerge, re-enter, re-estimate*, the use of the diæresis, as *reëmerge, reënter*, being much less frequent.

There is naturally a greater tendency to give full stress to the prefix when the simple word precedes the compound, as in *make and re-make, state and re-state*; this may also happen, but in a less degree, in cases where *re-* does not mean 'again', as *act and react*.

b. *Re-* is occasionally doubled or even trebled (usually with hyphens inserted) to express further repetition of an action, but this practice is rarely adopted in serious writing, although *re-* is readily prefixed to words of which it already forms the first element, as *re-recover, re-reform*.

1778 [W. MARSHALL] *Minutes Agric.* 3 April 1775 Re-re-re-tried the drill. Not yet compleat! **1838** MOORE *Mem.* (1856) VII. 218 A late publication (or rather re-re-publication of Bowles's). **1844** SOUTHEY *Life Andrew Bell* II. 483, I have read, re-read, and re-re-read your dedication. **1885** G. B. SHAW *Let.* 14 Dec. (1965) I. 146, I re-return the cheque, and if you re-re-return it I will re-re-re-return it again. **1922** JOYCE *Ulysses* 526, I rererepugnosed in rererepugnant. **1954** *New Biol.* XVI. 43 Under the title 'Vital Blarney'.. I reviewed, or to be pedantic I re-re-reviewed, Bernal's book *The Physical Basis of Life*.

5. The extent to which this prefix was employed in English during the 19th c., and especially during the latter half of it, makes it impossible to attempt a complete record of all the forms resulting from its use. The number of these is practically infinite, but they nearly all belong to one or other of three classes, which are illustrated by the quotations given below. The first of these is also abundantly represented in formations of the 17th and 18th centuries, which are entered in their alphabetical places.

a. Prefixed to ordinary verbs of action (chiefly transitive) and to derivatives from these, sometimes denoting that the action itself is performed a second time, and sometimes that its result is to reverse a previous action or process, or to restore a previous state of things (cf. 2 c), e.g. ***re-abolish*** vb., ***-alliance***, ***-apportion*** vb., ***-apportionment***, ***-bandage*** vb., ***-beam*** vb., ***-biff*** vb., ***-break*** vb., ***-cable*** vb., ***-calibrate*** vb., ***-calibration***, ***-canalization***, ***-canalize*** vb., ***-canvass*** vb., ***-carve*** vb., ***-centrifuge*** vb., ***-certification***, ***-certify*** vb., ***-chromatograph*** vb., ***chromatography***, ***-clean*** vb., ***-clone*** vb. (hence ***-cloning*** vbl. sb.), ***-codify*** vb., ***-conceptualization***, ***-conceptualize*** vb., ***-configure*** vb., ***-conscript*** vb., ***contamination***, ***-contrast*** vb., ***-cool*** vb. (hence ***-cooling*** vbl. sb.), ***-debit*** vb., ***-decontaminate*** vb., ***-decontamination***, ***-demarcation***, ***-differentiate*** vb., ***-differentiation***, ***-enrich*** vb., ***-enrichment***, ***-equilibrate*** vb., ***-equilibration***, ***-estimate*** vb. and sb., ***-evocation***, ***-exploration***, ***-explore*** vb., ***-expose*** vb., ***-fabricate*** vb., ***-feature*** vb., ***-fecundate*** vb., ***-flush*** vb., ***-foliate*** vb., ***-foliation***, ***-format*** vb., ***-forward*** vb. (hence ***-forwarding*** vbl. sb.), ***-incubate*** vb., ***-infarction***, ***-initialize*** vb., ***-input*** vb., ***-intensify*** vb., ***-isolate*** vb., ***-license*** vb., ***-list*** vb., ***-lubricate*** vb., ***-mapping*** vbl. sb., ***-nucleation***, ***-orchestrate*** vb., ***-orchestration***, ***-origination***, ***-originator***, ***-pattern*** vb. (hence ***-patterning*** vbl. sb.), ***-peg*** vb. (hence ***-pegging*** vbl. sb.), ***-phosphorylate*** vb., ***-pile*** vb., ***-postpone*** vb., ***-proportion*** vb., ***-proportioning*** vbl. sb., ***-punch*** vb., ***-punctuation***, ***-rat*** vb., ***-recovery***, ***-remember*** vb., ***-remembrance***, ***-riddle*** vb., ***-scrutinize*** vb., ***-scrutiny***, ***-sex*** vb., ***-sexing*** vbl. sb., ***-shade*** vb., ***-show*** vb. (hence ***-showing*** vbl. sb.), ***-stack*** vb., ***-stage*** vb., ***-structuration***, ***-suspend*** vb., ***-suspension***, ***-suture*** vb. and sb., ***-synthesis***, ***-synthesize*** vb., ***-tailor*** vb., ***-target*** vb., ***-tightening*** vbl. sb., ***-time*** vb., ***-triangulate***, vb., ***-triangulation***, ***-uptake***, ***-walk*** vb., ***-winded*** ppl. a., ***-zip*** vb.

With nouns of action the force of the prefix may frequently be rendered by 'second' or 'new', and on the analogy of these words it has sometimes been used in this sense with other sbs., as *re-charter, re-invoice*.

1870 ANDERSON *Missions Amer. Bd.* III. ix. 135 To induce him to *reabandon his original belief. **1963** AUDEN *Dyer's Hand* 461 The distinction between the things of God and the things of Caesar is *reabolished. **1879** *Temple Bar Mag.* Oct. 252 With a view to their *reacclimatisation in Switzerland. **1856** F. E. PAGET *Owlet Owlst.* 164 Mr. Page was too discreet to *readjudicate the matter. **1885** *Law Rep.* Weekly Notes 151/2 Each lot will be sold subject to *re-admeasurement. **1847** WEBSTER, *Realliance. **1973** *Jrnl. Genetic Psychol.* Mar. 137 Their [*sc.* neo-Freudians'] realliance will contribute something to the explanation of the latter theory. **1883** *Knowledge* 6 July 6/2 When the metal becomes dull, *reamalgamation is necessary. **1874** SULLY *Sensation & Intuition* 80, I regret having overlooked this *reannouncement of Mr. Bain's views. **1875** *N. Amer. Rev.* CXX. 103 To *reapportion the supply of labor. **1967** M. E. JEWELL *Legislative Representation in Contemp. South* v. 124 The Kentucky legislature was one of the first to reapportion both houses substantially on a population basis. **1971** C. A. AUERBACH in N. W. Polsby *Reapportionment in 1970s* ii. 90 All state legislatures will be reapportioned according to the principle of one vote, one value. **1884** *Fortn. Rev.* Nov. 707 The *reapportionment of electoral power. **1931** *Times Lit. Suppl.* 18 June 476/4 There should be a reapportionment of seats. **1974** *Anderson* (S. Carolina) *Independent* 19 Apr. 1 B/1 Members of the House-Senate conference committee asked .. for free conference power that would allow them to re-write district lines in the House reapportionment bill. **1853** KANE *Grinnell Exp.* xlii. (1856) 394 Acting as checks or wedges to prevent their *reapposition and cementation. **1821** W. TAYLOR in *Monthly Rev.* XCVI. 195 The reexamination and *reappreciation of the assertions. **1880** NICHOL *Byron* 84 His frequent resolutions, made, *re-asseverated, and broken. **1802–12** BENTHAM *Ration. Judic. Evid.* (1827) III. 285 The force of expansion and contraction (repulsion and *re-attraction). **1920** C. H. STAGG *High Speed* x. 180 Dan helped him *rebandage his hands. **1979** *Sunday Express* 28 Jan. 3/8 Within an hour of starting that wound had been stitched and rebandaged. **1826** DISRAELI *Viv. Grey* I. i, 'I won't have my hair curl', .. *rebawled the beauty. **1919** E. POUND *Quia pauper Amavi* 16 The infant beams at the parent, The parent *re-beams at its offspring. **1934** BLUNDEN *Choice or Chance* 53 Ye men of England, hear the clarion. If Inferior nations biff you, them *rebiff. **1869** *Eng. Mech.* 31 Dec. 389/3 The wax is then .. *re-bleached. **1881** *Sat. Rev.* 24 Sept. 375 A refurbishing and *rebrandishing of weapons. **1805** R. W. DICKSON *Pract. Agric.* II. 943 And when the weather is bad these cocks are never *re-broken out, being only lightened up to let the air pass through them more freely. **1877** LE CONTE *Elem. Geol.* (1879) 8 These .. are broken and rebroken until the rock is reduced to dust. **1905** *Daily Chron.* 31 July 4/7 The leg was badly set, and had to be re-broken. **1943** V. SACKVILLE-WEST *Eagle & Dove* I. xv. 89 Her left arm .. had had to be re-broken and re-set most painfully several times. **1877** MRS. OLIPHANT *Makers Flor.* iii. 74 The *re-bursting forth .. of the pacificated cities. **1908** *Daily Chron.* 7 Apr. 1/7 Chicago, Monday... This afternoon .. an alleged interview with Hackenschmidt is *re-cabled from a London newspaper. **1909** *Cent. Dict.* Suppl., *Recalibrate. **1971** *Nature* 6 Aug. 391/2 We are currently recalibrating our Dobson ozone spectrophotometers. **1978** *Sci. Amer.* Feb. 34/3 In the 1980's shuttle-recoverable instruments that can be recalibrated and still better instruments in high orbit may answer the questions. **1911** WEBSTER, *Recalibration. **1977** *Nature* 6 Jan. 18/1 Node markers .. can thus easily be reset by 93 yr periodic recalibration observations of maximum northerly midwinter full moonrise azimuth. **1961** R. D. BAKER *Essent. Path.* v. 82 New blood vessels form in the lumen (*recanalization). **1943** *Amer. Speech* XVIII. 222 General semantics .. is offered as a means of *recanalizing those responses .. that cause morbid over-excitation of the nervous system. **1962** *Punch* 12 Sept. 366/2 Water conservation .. to the extent of recanalising the water. **1925** T. DREISER *Amer. Trag.* II. III. xxvi. 329 The twelve men .. *re-canvassing for their own mental satisfaction the fine points made by Mason. **1880** E. OPPERT *Forbid. L.* iv. 110 Serious efforts for their recovery or *recaptivation. **1924** J. MASEFIELD *Sard Harker* 4 Men remembered this rhyme, and pled that it should be *recarven. **1878** NEWCOMB *Pop. Astron.* IV. i. 417 Tycho Brahe .. *re-catalogued the stars. **1956** *Nature* 7 Jan. 45/2 The homogeneous supernatant was *recentrifuged once or twice. **1976** *Ibid.* 15 Jan. 114/2 The supernatant was recentrifuged at 20,000*g* for 10 min. **1885** *Law Times* LXXIX. 217/2 The effect of *re-certificating a man who has been dishonest. **1976** P. R. WHITE *Planning for Public Transport* i. 20 Maintenance facilities may be very limited, problems of major overhaul and *recertification being handled by sale of a vehicle to a dealer who provides a reconditioned vehicle in part exchange. **1978** *Jrnl. R. Soc.*

Med. LXXI. 13 Such developments..could be more effective and acceptable than some form of periodic recertification in maintaining standards in practice. **1934** WEBSTER, *Recertify. **1976** *National Observer* (U.S.) 17 July 11/3 The Israelis were recertifying their credentials as a people of almost unbelievable resourcefulness and courage. **1977** *Proc. R. Soc. Medicine* LXX. 58/2 Only the American Board of Family Practice is putting the idea into practice by an MCQ recertifying exam from October 1976. **1863** *N. & Q.* 3rd Ser. III. 218 Jupiter..was *re-chiselled into St. Peter. **1945** *Rechromatograph [see *rechromatography*]. **1948** *Amer. Scientist* XXXVI. 511 If either of these two zones is cut out, eluted, and rechromatographed on a fresh column, it will form a single zone. **1971** *Nature* 16 Apr. 456/2 After 24 h dialysis against 0·01 M phosphate buffer.. the residual fibre was rechromatographed, the peak fractions were pooled and reduced to a final volume of 1 ml. **1945** *Jrnl. Biol. Chem.* CLVII. 327 *Rechromatography was usual, especially when two zones were bordering upon one another. In such instances they were cut out as one and rechromatographed. **1950** L. ZECHMEISTER *Progress in Chromatogr.* xii. 162 The peptides were characterized by the ratio, total nitrogen/amino nitrogen. Such ratios observed were not altered by rechromatography. **1978** *Nature* 14 Dec. 735/2 Rechromatography on Sephadex G-50 gave only a single peak. **1921** *Daily Colonist* (Victoria, B.C.) 29 Oct. 8/1 (Advt.), Fine *re-cleaned currants. **1960** *Farmer & Stockbreeder* 29 Mar. 5/1 The following are wholesale prices for recleaned seed per cwt ex-store unless otherwise stated. **1896** *Allbutt's Syst. Med.* I. 437 The catheter must be thoroughly *recleansed. **1971** *Nature* 30 July 313/2 Six clones were mixed (Gd^H/Gd^D), two of these were *recloned, and 106 out of 107 of these sub-clones showed either Gd^H or Gd^D while one was again mixed. **1962** *Cold Spring Harbor Symp. Quantitative Biol.* XXVII. 410 *Recloning of these clones gives rise to all converted clones. **1973** *Listener* 20 Dec. 846/3 We shall not avoid increasing dislocation.. unless we can *recodify large areas of international behaviour. **1961** WEBSTER, *Reconceptualization. **1973** *Sci. Amer.* Sept. 120/2 With a reconceptualization of the hospital as a therapeutic community.., many of the chronic inpatients were able to be returned to the community. **1977** FONTANA & VAN DE WATER in Douglas & Johnson *Existential Sociol.* iii. 126 Understanding the world in this manner demands a thorough-going reconceptualization of our usual notions of truth and progress in knowledge. **1961** WEBSTER, *Reconceptualize. **1977** A. GIDDENS *Stud. in Social & Polit. Theory* ii. 118 Let us at this juncture reconceptualize 'structure' as referring to *generative rules and resources* that are both applied in and constituted out of action. **1884** *Law Times* LXXVII. 331/2 The Divisional Courts have been *re-condemned. **1964** M. MCLUHAN *Understanding Media* II. xxxi. 313 The viewer of the TV mosaic, with technical control of the image, unconsciously *re-configures the dots into an abstract work of art. **1946** L. B. LYON *Rough Walk Home* 17 Only his singular, *re-conscripted breath Could fan to a purpose all that pyre his death. **1961** WEBSTER, *Recontamination. **1962** *Economist* 19 May 706/2 The gas must be protected against re-contamination through leaks. **1966** D. G. BRANDON *Mod. Techniques Metallogr.* 187 The gas used must be extremely pure if immediate re-contamination of the surface is to be avoided. **1957** R. N. C. HUNT *Guide to Communist Jargon* xlviii. 160 In connection with the Brest-Litovsk treaty [Lenin] *recontrasted those who were 'revolutionaries out of sentiment' with 'real revolutionaries'. **1934** WEBSTER, *Recool. **1969** *Gloss. Terms Water Cooling Towers* (*B.S.I.*) 5 *Recooled water temperature*, average temperature of the circulating water entering the basin. **1968** C. G. KUPER *Introd. Theory Superconductivity* v. 93 These nucleation centres are remarkably stable—they often survive the heating of the specimen to room temperature and subsequent *recooling. **1862** T. A. TROLLOPE *Marietta* II. xii. 205 Corrected and *recorrected sheets. **1860** FARRAR *Orig. Lang.* iii. 60 *Re-corrupted into a purely mechanical word. **1836** *Fraser's Mag.* XIII. 306 Will the recognition of the independence of Buenos Ayres..*recrowd its abandoned harbours? **1877** RAYMOND *Statist. Mines & Mining* 432 Sent back..to the first pair of rolls for *recrushing. **1934** S. W. ROWLAND *Hughes-Onslow's Lawyer's Man. Book-keeping* (ed. 3) i. 9 The bank, for its part and from its point of view, credited when the cheque was paid in. Consequently when the cheque is found to be worthless, it *redebits. **1968** *Lebende Sprachen* XIII. 87/2 The bank may redebit the account. **1827** SOUTHEY *Hist. Penins. War* II. 418 He consented to *re-decimate those on whom the lot had fallen. **1815** JANE AUSTEN *Emma* I. ix, He re-urged—she *re-declined. **1935** A. P. HERBERT *What a Word!* vi. 187, I do not think that she [*sc.* the Ship of State] was ever..'*redecontaminated'. *Ibid.* i. 21 The answer from high places was: 'A process of *redecontamination would be advisable.' **1969** *P.E.N.* IX. 48 He recalled that at the beginning of the 1939 War the use of the word 'contaminate' for a gas attack had seemed comic, particularly when it involved 'decontamination' and 'redecontamination' stations. **1938** *Times* 17 Jan. 11/5 The chief violations [of the Soviet constitution] have been the *redemarcation of internal frontiers and the formation of new territorial and administrative units. **1960** *Observer* 20 Mar. 1/4 The Ghana Government claimed that 14 people arrested last week..had conspired to conduct a campaign of violence and civil disturbance there to provoke 'foreign intervention' and the redemarcation of frontiers. **1876** BANCROFT *Hist. U.S.* VI. 572 He *redeserts, and offers to negotiate for return of colonies to allegiance. **1830** W. TAYLOR *Hist. Surv. Germ. Poetry* II. 76 [A panegyric which] has not been *redeserved by any subsequent poet. **1862** H. SPENCER *First Princ.* II. xv. §119 (1875) 335 Meanwhile each of these differentiated tissues is *re-differentiated. **1911** *Cornh. Mag.* Apr. 497 It is as if John Brown on his death-bed were to have his tissues pass into a state of flux, and then get simpler and simpler, until you would have to say, This is no longer a man, but merely a mass of man's protoplasm, and as if finally this mass were to redifferentiate up again. **1960** *New Biol.* XXXI. 90 A second possibility is that tissue cells undergo an apparent de-differentiation to form the young regenerate or the bud but, like cells in tissue culture, retain their tissue specificity and later re-differentiate into tissues of the same kind as those from which they came. **1970** *Jrnl. Gen. Psychol.* LXXXII. 182 He must again re-differentiate these boundaries. **1889** *Cent. Dict.*, *Redifferentiation. **1921** *Discovery* Feb. 28/2 Such a process, which we may style dedifferentiation followed by redifferentiation, is clear evidence of the possibility of reversing development. **1960** *New Biol.* XXXI. 89 Some cells..normally change their shapes and functions in the fulfilment of their proper roles in the organism's economy. Such reversible changes have been called 'modulations' by Weiss, and the distinction between them and more profound re-differentiations may seem rather arbitrary. **1875** BLACKMORE *Alice Lorraine* II. xxiii. 315 The British army,..sternly *redisciplined, was eager to bound forward. **1807** in *Spirit Pub. Jrnls.* XI. 353 The first expedition..was embarked, disembarked, re-embarked, *re-disembarked, about ten times in ten months. **1811–31** BENTHAM *Logic* Wks. 1843 VIII. 261 No counting, no collection, no *re-display, is necessary. **1856** *Q. Rev.* XCIX. 396 We are not going to *re-dissect the 'Essais'. **1882** *Rep. to Ho. Repr. Prec. Met. U.S.* 623 The gold has been *redissolved and reprecipitated. **1872** *4th Rep. Dep. Kpr. Irel.* 11 The *re-docketing and revival books. **1830** M. DONOVAN *Dom. Econ.* I. 87 Malt that has suffered injury.. will not be recovered by *redrying it. **1879** *Macm. Mag.* XL. 135 The opportunities of *re-earning a character. **1811–31** BENTHAM *Logic* Wks. 1843 VIII. 225 Recession out of or *re-emanation from it. **1858** BUSHNELL *Serm. New Life* 374 The torpid creatures..*re-empowered with life. **1815** *Zeluca* III. 212 Zeluca devoted all her attention to *re-engrossing him. **1823** BENTHAM *Not Paul* 376 Peter imprisoned, enlarged, recommitted, examined, and *reenlarged. **1951** *Sci. Amer.* Nov. 18/2 The gas is..cycled back into the reservoir several times to be *re-enriched. **1976** *Ibid.* Dec. 33/3 If the uranium is to be returned to the gaseous-diffusion plants for *reenrichment, it is converted into uranium hexafluoride. **1865** MASSON *Rec. Brit. Philos.* 65 Let us *re-enumerate them. **1971** I. G. GASS et al. *Understanding Earth* i. 27/1 Once an igneous rock has completely solidified, however, the absence of a fluid phase and the reduction of temperature make it very difficult for the minerals to *re-equilibrate to new assemblages which would be stable at lower temperatures. **1869** H. SPENCER *Princ. Psychol.* (1872) I. 283 The *re-equilibration of constitution and conditions. **1970** G. GERMANI in I. L. Horowitz *Masses in Lat. Amer.* xvi. 591 It satisfied their need for re-equilibration through the emphasis on 'order, discipline, hierarchy', and through the demobilization of the lower classes. **1971** I. G. GASS et al. *Understanding Earth* i. 33/1 The process of re-equilibration..is materially aided by the introduction of water in the environment of weathering. **1851** C. L. SMITH tr. *Tasso* II. lxxxix, His reasoning in these words he *re-essayed. **1934** WEBSTER, *Re-estimate, *v.t.* **1952** S. SPENDER *Shelley* 44 Not so much a *re-estimate, as a restoring of some sort of balance. **1964** K. G. LOCKYER *Introd. Critical Path Analysis* ix. 89 An alternative is to insert the actual (or re-estimated) times. **1924** S. JOYCE in J. Joyce *Lett.* (1966) III. 104 This *re-evocation and exaggeration of detail by detail and the spiritual dejection which accompanies them are purely in the spirit of the confessional. **1952** C. P. BLACKER *Eugenics* 138 The re-evocation of the repressed memory, though painful like an incision, cured the sufferer. **1812** J. HENRY *Camp. agst. Quebec* 195 It often *re-exhilarates my mind to remember the occurrences. **1804–6** SYD. SMITH *Mor. Philos.* (1850) 282 A writer has no such..power of *re-explaining them. **1977** *Proc. R. Soc. Med.* LXX. 385/2 One *re-exploration was done over the same period as 36 cholecystectomies overall. **1933** *Proc. R. Soc.* A. CXLII. 350 For this reason we have not *re-explored this region, since we could not hope to detect the presence of groups of such weak intensity. **1977** *Proc. R. Soc. Med.* LXX. 385/2 Over the same period another 22 patients were reexplored after operation elsewhere. **1946** *Nature* 28 Dec. 946/1 The slides are located in their former position and *re-exposed. **1950** F. E. ZEUNER *Dating Past* (ed. 2) 264 A Final wet phase, of a very minor character re-exposes by stream erosion the levels containing Middle Stone Age. **1831** T. HOPE *Ess. Origin Man* III. 301 The Portuguese..first made the power of Europe *re-extend over the realms of Asia. *a* **1942** B. MALINOWSKI *Sci. Theory of Culture* (1944) 164 In a small farcical form, such a charter has been *refabricated in the *Blut und Boden* doctrine of modern Naziism. **1976** *Dumfries & Galloway Standard* 25 Dec. 12/2 The policy favoured at present is to re-process all nuclear fuel in a few politically-stable countries, return the re-fabricated fuel to the country of origin, and retain the wastes for 'safe' storage. **1846** LANDOR *Hellenics* Wks. 1846 II. 485 With blood enough will I *re-fascinate The cursed incantation. **1922** JOYCE *Ulysses* 554 The face of Martin Cunningham, bearded, *refeatures Shakespeare's beardless face. **1957** L. DURRELL *Justine* III. 199 The resonance of this one phrase *refecundated his powers of feeling. **1898** *Mag. Art* Feb. 220 Firing and *re-firing the bronze with different acids. **1882** *St. James's Gaz.* 24 June 11/1 The same offender has..become liable to be *reflogged. **1880** 'MARK TWAIN' *Tramp Abroad* xlvii. 495 The tints remained during several minutes..paling almost away for a moment, then re-flushing,—a shifting, restless, unstable succession of soft opaline gleams. **1937** *Discovery* Aug. 246/2 Wintering, *refoliating, flowering, and seeding. **1963** *Times Lit. Suppl.* 22 Feb. 143/1 The Book of Durrow ..was taken to pieces,..rearranged, refoliated, repaired, reconditioned and..superbly rebound. **1956** *Nature* 31 Mar. 619/2 *Oidium heveae* is most prominent in Malaya at the time of *refoliation after 'wintering' of the trees. **1977** J. L. HARPER *Population Biol. Plants* xii. 398 Defoliation is often complete and is followed by refoliation. **1886** C. SCOTT *Sheep-Farming* 200 He quenches his thirst as he *re-fords the stream. **1967** E. R. LANNON in Cox & Grose *Organiz. Bibliogr. Rec. by Computer* IV. 88 The user may initially employ his own Preprocessor to edit and *reformat his data. **1973** *Computers & Humanities* VII. 214 The cards were built onto a disk file by a program that reformatted the material into fixed-length records. **1911** MRS. H. WARD *Case of Richard Meynell* xxiii. 484 Hester's telegram, sent originally to Upcote and *reforwarded, had reached Meynell in Paris. **1957** M. LOWRY *Let.* 29 Apr. (1967) 407 Your letter of March 12..Cape sent it back to Canada again, so that it had to get reforwarded again from B.C. before I received it. **1947** J. HILTON *So well Remembered* IV. 265 George's last two letters had never reached Charles... (They did arrive, eventually, after a series of fantastic *re-forwardings.) **1882** NARES *Seamanship* (ed. 6) 131 *Refurl the sails. **1812** J. SMYTH *Pract. of Customs* (1821) 411 The Warehouse-keeper..issues a Note for *re-gauging in the following form. **1884** *Athenæum* 9 Feb. 191/3 The *rehanging of the Turner pictures..is now completed. **1853** CLOUGH *Poems*, etc. (1869) I. 359 *note*, The word *spoom*.. seems hardly to deserve *re-impatriation. **1962** H. L. KERN et al. in A. Pirie *Lens Metabolism Rel. Cataract* 386 The lenses were subsequently removed, dipped in saline containing antibiotics, and *reincubated at 37°C. **1863** *Sat. Rev.* 10 Oct. 497 To *re-indorse old quotations in compliance with custom. **1961** *Lancet* 22 July 213/2 Absence of *reinfarction. **1972** *Computers & Humanities* VI. 282 As before, the user must establish output procedures and appropriate tests for upper and lower limits and *reinitialize counters. **1973** C. W. GEAR *Introd. Computer Sci.* vi. 246 It is very easy to make the mistake of transferring back to the start of the loop, forgetting to re-initialize variables when it is required. **1964** C. DENT *Quantity Surveying by Computer* vi. 88 The items are queried and *re-input, except for zero items, which will not be required to appear in the bill in any case. **1967** J. D. DEWS in Cox & Grose *Organiz. Bibliogr. Rec. by Computer* II. 24 The tape.. can then be corrected and re-input to correct the file. **1872** BUSHNELL *Serm. Living Subj.* 281 To be unsphered here and *reinsphered in a promised life. **1826** W. IRVING in *Life & Lett.* (1864) IV. 403, I have, as usual, intended and *reintended to write to you. **1963** *Daily Tel.* 1 Nov. 14/2 To these torments must be added that of *reintensified bombing. **1967** E. CHAMBERS *Photolitho-Offset* ix. 133 Reintensify if added contrast is required. **1868** LYELL *Princ. Geol.* II. III. xxxiv. 255 Nothing less than the *reintervention of the Deity was thought adequate. **1871** H. SPENCER *Princ. Psychol.* (1872) II. VII. iv. 356 The Space.. in which the *re-intuition or imagination of things occurs. **1946** *Nature* 14 Sept. 379/1 Leaf infection of onion seedlings was obtained by ascospore inoculation, and the fungus was *re-isolated from the lesions. **1977** J. L. HARPER *Population Biol. of Plants* xi. 348 The bacterial agent must be re-isolated from the experimentally infected plant. *Ibid.*, The re-isolated micro-organism and that originally inoculated must be tested for identity. **1934** WEBSTER, *Relicense. *a* **1974** R. CROSSMAN *Diaries* (1977) III. 870, I then said that we must break this relicensing operation into two stages. **1977** *Times* 11 Oct. 4/3 Dr Lemon..did not favour relicensing all pilots who had suffered heart attacks. **1963** *Times* 29 May 7/2 The practice of 'stop-listing', 'delisting', and then '*relisting' areas can be a powerful deterrent to industrialists. **1976** *Times* 25 Oct. 14/7 Save in cases of nullity, the jurisdiction to relist depended on the likelihood of an injustice having been done. **1967** KARCH & BUBER *Offset Processes* x. 474 Old grease should be removed and the gears *re-lubricated every one million impressions. **1882** *Knowledge* No. 16. 332 He..reduces the image..and then shows it by *re-magnification. **1965** G. J. WILLIAMS *Econ. Geol. N.Z.* viii. 99/1 A detailed *remapping of the area will reveal the importance of deep pre-Second Period weathering. **1878** F. S. WILLIAMS *Midl. Railw.* 359 Being *re-marshalled as empties for the down traffic. **1859** F. MILLS in *Athenæum* 9 July 49 Ere the shining valves *remeet. **1881** H. PHILLIPS tr. *Chamisso's Faust* 19 Thy empty sounds..*Re-mirror all the shadows of thy brain. **1861** LYTTON & FANE *Tannhäuser* 34 That..*Remultiplies the praise of what is good. **1863** LYTTON *Caxtoniana* I. 160 In proportion as he is always *renourishing his genius. **1933** H. G. WELLS *Shape of Things to Come* III. 261 The need for a planned '*renucleation' in the social magma that arose out of this dissolution. **1934** —— *Exper. Autobiogr.* II. vii. 481 Socialism, if it is anything more than a petty tinkering with economic relationships is a renucleation of society. **1881** *Athenæum* 18 June 824/3 A considerable portion of the work was *re-orchestrated. **1901** *Westm. Gaz.* 13 May 4/3 The 'Marseillaise' has just been reorchestrated by order of the Minister of War. **1975** *New Yorker* 19 May 85/1 It seems to me that the actual personalities and events of the Nez Perce war were possibly even more interesting..than were the respectfully created counterparts..reorchestrated for us today. **1940** L. MACNEICE *Poems* 251 Smuggling over the frontier Of fact a sense of value, Metabolism of death, *Re-orchestration of world. **1975** *New Yorker* 16 June 97/1 In the late sixties, the opera was quite often given..but always in an edition by Claudio Abbado marred by many cuts, by some reorchestration, and, most gravely, by the recasting of Romeo as a tenor. **1854** THOREAU *Walden* 163, I occasionally observed that he was thinking for himself and expressing his own opinion, a phenomenon so rare that I would any day walk ten miles to observe it, and it amounted to the *re-origination of many of the institutions of society. **1832** J. S. MILL *Let.* 22 Oct. in *Coll. Wks.* (1963) XII. 128 They were the *reoriginators of *any* belief among us. **1935** L. MACNEICE *Poems* 32 The basic facts *repatterned without pause. **1952** C. P. BLACKER *Eugenics* x. 246 The gene-complex has a holistic or integrative action of its own, a capacity to undergo changes, to adjust itself to a *re-patterning of its constituent elements. **1972** *Guardian* 28 Oct. 24 It is open to Mr Barber..to *repeg the pound at an exchange rate far above the level to which it has now fallen. **1978** *N.Y. Times* 30 Mar. D1/6 The yen..has actually been revalued upward by 38.43 percent since it was repegged at the Smithsonian rate of 308 to the dollar in December 1971. **1938** *Sun* (Baltimore) 12 July 14/5 Accompanied by rumors ..of a possible '*repegging' at its old ratio of between \$4.86 and \$4.87, the British pound sterling declined today..to its lowest point in more than a year. **1964** G. H. HAGGIS et al. *Introd. Molecular Biol.* vi. 182 (*caption*) An enzyme at the inner boundary *rephosphorylates the diglyceride to phosphatidic acid, in interaction with ATP. **1965** PHILLIPS & WILLIAMS *Inorg. Chem.* I. xvii. 638 The ADP is then rephosphorylated via various sugar-phosphates and the oxidation of glycogen. **1890** *Anthony's Photogr. Bull.* III. 400 *Re-photographing this positive and ruled screen together. **1877** *Nature* 27 Sept. 468/2 In *repiling and reheating this iron several times this defective appearance is gradually removed. **1947** *Penguin New Writing* XXX. 104 The lame boy stayed behind and helped me re-pile the tins. **1884** *St. Nicholas* XI. 379 They begin at once to *repitch their tent. **1823** in *Spirit Pub. Jrnls.* 112 The..monopolist slowly and blankly *repocket-booked his authorities. **1956** D. GASCOYNE *Night Thoughts* 37 To swell the roar that rises with each climax *repostponed. **1882** FLOYER *Unexpl. Baluchistan* 83 The wheat thus pounded was *re-pounded and sifted. **1828** *Lights & Shades* II. 87, I heard a shot..and saw a fellow with his gun *reprepared. **1813** T. BUSBY *Lucretius* II. IV. *Comm.* xxviii, Before the sound can be *re-propagated from that point. *a* **1878** SIR G. SCOTT *Recoll.* iii. (1879) 172 *Re-proportioning it with reference to its earlier form. **1967** KARCH & BUBER *Offset Processes* iv. 125 Modification is possible to condense, expand,.. reproportion height and width. **1969** P. L. BERGER *Rumor of Angels* v. 121 The openness and the *reproportioning this attitude entails have a moral significance, even a political significance, of no mean degree. **1857** TOULMIN SMITH *Parish* 136 Its adoption cannot be *re-proposed under a year's time. **1838** *Civil Eng. & Arch. Jrnl.* I. 194/2 At noon the *repuddling was completed. **1833** KEBLE in *Newman's Lett.* (1891) I. 453 Their continual puffing and *repuffing each other. **1963** *Rep. Comm. Inquiry Decimal Currency* xiv. 138 Ancillary machine costs:..*re-punching card and tape records. **1965** *Math. in Biol. & Med.* (Med. Res. Council) II. 48 A start has now been made on re-punching the British Columbia marriage records for 1946–55 in a form suitable for testing such a system. **1887** G. B. SHAW *Let.* 7 Feb. (1965) I. 162 The American printer..has taken upon himself the *repunctuation of 'Cashel Byron'. **1966** *Mod. Lang. Q.* Sept. 256, I was, I believe, responsible for most of the detailed examination of poems in *A Survey of Modernist Poetry*—for example showing the complex implications of Sonnet 129 before its eighteenth-century repunctuations. **1804** EUGENIA DE ACTON *Tale without Title* III. 87 'Then you think..that Mr. Conyers is to be married to-morrow!' *requestioned Mrs. Lambert. **1807** J. BARLOW *Columb.* VIII. 323 To tongue mute misery, and *re-rack the soul With crimes. **1815** MARY FRAMPTON *Jrnl.* (1885) 246 If [Talleyrand] has refused to *re-rat. **1975** D. W. S. HUNT *On Spot* iv. 54 As I heard him say over the lunch table once, 'to rat is difficult; to re-rat..' and he broke off as though to show that to find a description of a second change of party was beyond even his eloquence. **1860** CAPT. DENHAM in *Merc. Marine Mag.* VII. 263 [We] *re-rated chronometers. **1891** H. SPENCER *Justice* 54 This violent reaction will be followed by a *re-reaction. **1864** PUSEY *Lect. Daniel* iii. 136 Its provinces rebelled, and *re-rebelled. **1882** H. S. HOLLAND *Logic & Life* (ed. 3) 129 In token of his *re-recognised allegiance. **1938** *Times* 22 Jan. 5/1 The prospects of a *re-recovery in the United States. **1837** GEN. P. THOMPSON *Exerc.* (1842) IV. 248 We must have a *re-reformed one. **1810** SOUTHEY in *Q. Rev.* III. 451 No expression of regret escapes the *re-regenerated sinner. **1884** H. SPENCER in *Contemp. Rev.* July 30 A very reasonable rejoinder this seems until there comes the *re-rejoinder. **1922** JOYCE *Ulysses* 671 With greater difficulty remembered, forgot with ease, with misgiving *reremembered. **1923** D. H. LAWRENCE *Birds, Beasts & Flowers* 24 For we are on the brink of *re-remembrance. **1861** *Wheat & Tares* 284 He would repent and *re-repent, and die the same. **1891** H. SPENCER *Justice* 47 Such acts of revenge and *re-revenge. **1878** NEWCOMB *Pop. Astron.* III. ii. 268 We can even see the *re-reversal of the lines already reversed. **1922** JOYCE *Ulysses* 133 But my riddle! he said. What opera is like a railway?—Opera? Mr. O'Madden Burke's sphinx face *reriddled. **1875** RUSKIN *Fors Clav.* l. V. 29 Needlessly *re-rooting myself in the old [ground]. **1897** P. WARUNG *Tales Old Regime* 148 The Comptroller *re-scans the parchment and the application-form. **1973** *Nature* 6 Apr. 377/1 The role of postgraduate students may well be *rescrutinized. **1963** *Punch* 6 Feb. 182/3 The whole business..deserved *re-scrutiny. **1809** *Char.* in *Ann. Reg.* 734/1 An incessant succession of conscious sensations of *re-sensations. **1863** *Q. Rev.* Jan. 172 Only seventy-five..were *resentenced to the convict prisons. **1884** *Harper's Mag.* Aug. 431/1 Henry has..*resepulchred the Confessor's bones. **1869** BUSHNELL *Wom. Suffrage* v. 89 The *re-sexing of their sex, they knew to be impossible. **1955** AUDEN *Shield of Achilles* ii. 45 Re-sex the pronouns, add a few details. **1951** L. MACNEICE tr. *Goethe's Faust* I. 14 The little god of the world, one can't reshape, *reshade him. **1865** DICKENS *Mut. Fr.* I. ii, He *re-shakes hands with Twemlow. *a* **1849** J. C. MANGAN *Poems* (1859) 128 When spring *reshowers her beams on the plains. **1961** WEBSTER, Reshow. **1976** *Times Lit. Suppl.* 21 May 620/5 Pabst's maligned film, which is still frequently *reshown. **1977** *Listener* 24 Mar. 385/2 Most programmes are not re-shown. **1976** K. BENTON *Single Monstrous Act* iii. 17 Let's go and see that film at the local. It's a *re-showing of *The Godfather*. **1820** COLERIDGE *Lett.* (1895) II. 709 A horrid appetite of *re-skinning himself. **1873** BENNETT & 'CAVENDISH' *Billiards* 6 When the red was holed it was *re-spotted. **1822–34** *Good's Study Med.* (ed. 4) IV. 534 The superincumbent hairs falling off and never *resprouting. *a* **1849** POE *Man that was used-up* Wks. 1864 IV. 323 Presently *re-squeaked the nondescript. **1841** *Civil Engin. & Arch. Jrnl.* IV. 341/2 Scintling (removing and *restacking the bricks in the hacks). **1892** *Daily News* 26 Feb. 5/7 A patch of brickwork, six feet by three feet, had been taken out of the chimney to be re-stacked. **1923** *Daily Mail* 30 May 7 The combat will be *restaged at the forthcoming pageant. **1929** *Daily Express* 16 Jan. 6 A famous comedian..suddenly decided to alter his programme and not restage his old, worn-out material. **1854** J. SCOFFERN in *Orr's Circ. Sc.* Chem. 490 The copper leaves, by further *restratification, may be entirely converted into sub-carbonate. **1859** R. F. BURTON *Centr. Afr.* in *Jrnl. Geog. Soc.* XXIX. 112 The fields had been stripped and *restripped by every passing caravan. **1848** LYTTON *K. Arthur* II. lxxxv, He spreads it out.. Strokes and *restrokes it. **1962** M. COOK tr. *Dia's Afr. Nations & World Solidarity* ix. 97 It will be vain to hope for a profound change toward a progressive economy..without a bold *restructuration incompatible with an exaggerated desire to spare the former capitalist structures. **1970** B. BREWSTER tr. *Althusser & Balibar's Reading Capital* (1975) III. iii. 259 Reproduction appears to be the general form of permanence of the general conditions of production, which in the last analysis englobe the whole social structure, and therefore it is indeed essential that it should be the form of their change and restructuration, too. **1972** *Times* 26 June 12/4 The restructuration of a basic sector of European economy. **1895** G. MACDONALD *Lilith* xlii. 311 Rushing..to *resubmerge the orchard valley. *a* **1831** A. KNOX *Rem.* (1844) I. 62 *Re-submitting to the long dissolved chains. **1818** BENTHAM *Ch. Eng.* 236 The accession of Elizabeth, and the *re-substitution of the Protestant system. **1865** MRS. WHITNEY *Gayworthys* xxv, A certain quick spasm of keen *re-sufferance came over her. **1900** *Daily News* 27 Sept. 7 The Count..is hard at work directing the repairs to the airship, which has already been *resuspended. **1946** *Nature* 5 Oct. 486/2 The mixture is..re-suspended in saline to give a concentration of 2–5 per cent. **1976** *Nucl. Engin. Internat.* Nov. 37/2 Eventually the Pu settles to the ground and may be resuspended by being blown up by winds. **1884** *Pall Mall Gaz.* 16 Oct. 5/2 The Exchequer, however, is still in want of funds, and the *resuspension is expected before long. **1978** *Nature* 27 Apr. 754/2 The lack of response to fire in the pollen input could be due to..the resuspension and resedimentation which occurs in the lakes. **1884** *Practitioner* XXXIII. 289 (*heading*) *Resuturing of granulating wounds. **1901** *Brit. Med. Jrnl.* 2 Feb. 263/1 Should any difficulty be met with in replacing the bowel, the opening can be enlarged and then resutured without causing any weakening in the lower part of the abdominal wall. **1961** *Lancet* 19 Aug. 402/2 After *resuture of the wound the patient's general condition gradually improved. **1977** *Ibid.* 1 Jan. 28/1 One of these is abdominal wound disruption—a complication fatal at worst and a serious nuisance at best, for, should all go well directly after resuture, there is both a prolonged hospital stay and a much increased risk of incisional hernia. **1888** A. S. WILSON *Lyric of Hopeless Love* 171 My fancy's wings *Resweep Hellenic plains. **1862** *Macm. Mag.* Nov. 24 One kind of Anagram noticed by Mr. Wheatley..is that which arises not from the rearrangement or transposition of letters, but only from their redivision or *resyllabification. **1927** HALDANE & HUXLEY *Animal Biol.* v. 120 The actual process of contraction may have an efficiency of 90 to 100 per cent., but an amount of energy greater than the work done in contraction is wasted as heat during the *re-synthesis of the lactic and phosphoric acids, so that the whole process has an efficiency of only about 40 per cent. **1956** *Nature* 7 Jan. 22/2 There is little to support the notion that phospholipids act as intermediates in the resynthesis of triglycerides during fat absorption. **1978** *Ibid.* 12 Oct. p. ix/1 (Advt.), Components of cells in all living organisms undergo continual breakdown and resynthesis. **1928** A. B. CALLOW *Food & Health* 21 The fats are split up into their component parts, fatty acids and glycerol. These substances are absorbed by certain body-cells and again *resynthesized into fats. **1964** G. H. HAGGIS et al. *Introd. Molecular Biol.* v. 137 All cells require new proteins during growth and division, and are subsequently constantly resynthesizing their enzymes and other proteins. **1928** *Daily Express* 9 Aug. 14/1 (Advt.), O'coats turned and *retailored. **1949** M. MEAD *Male & Female* xii. 260 The reactionary and the cynic make common cause in suggesting that..laws and ideals should be re-tailored to recognize the deviations and discrepancies between ideal and practice. **1977** *Times* 27 Apr. 23/8 On the bonus side value-added tax machinery is retailored to harmonize with EEC directives. **1966** *Aviation Week & Space Technol.* 18 Apr. 31 This was the *retargeted date after the March 30 attempt. **1894** BARING-GOULD *Deserts S. France* I. 169 Grottoes..have been *retenanted. **1860** *Merc. Marine Mag.* VII. 141 Their being..*re-tested when returned into store. **1894** BARING-GOULD *Kitty Alone* III. 95 The pros and cons were thrashed and *re-thrashed. **1851** C. L. SMITH tr. *Tasso* XIX. xxvi, Then thrust his sword and *re-thrust. **1893** *Pall Mall Gaz.* 25 Jan. 7/1 The wedding of the Princess Sophie to the Crown Prince of Greece implied a further *re-tightening of the bonds of friendship between Copenhagen and Berlin. **1960** *Times* 1 June 18/7 But the production as a whole needs re-timing. **1967** KARCH & BUBER *Offset Processes* x. 468 The sheets should be ½ inch away from the guides at this point. If not, the feeder must be *retimed to the press. **1864** *Spectator* 440 That he only sent the reports back for the Inspectors to *re-tinker. **1852** R. S. SURTEES *Sponge's Sp. Tour* (1893) 59 He was toasted and *re-toasted, and toasted again. **1839–48** BAILEY *Festus* xxiii. (1848) 298, I now *retrack my course to earth. **1816** W. TAYLOR in *Monthly Mag.* XLI. 143 Echo *retrampling every gritty tread. **1977** *Dædalus* Summer 109 He persuaded the Survey of India to *retriangulate part of the region. **1927** *Blackw. Mag.* Feb. 256/1 It would mean the *retriangulation of the whole area, and endless delays and doubts as to the fixing of the position of soundings already taken off the coast. **1975** J. B. HARLEY *U.S. Maps* i. 7 Supplementary work on the retriangulation continues. **1879** MRS. A. E. JAMES *Ind. Househ. Managem.* 18 They can be more easily altered and *re-trimmed. **1833** J. RENNIE *Alph. Angling* 66 The hairs..must be *retwisted. **1882** DE WINDT *Equator* 126 To *re-undergo fresh sufferings. **1881** *Times* 5 Apr. 9/5 The *re-unification of Afghanistan. **1974** M. C. GERALD *Pharmacol.* v. 101 Norepinephrine is taken back into the presynaptic neurons (*re-uptake process), thus removing it from the receptor area. **1977** *Lancet* 21 May 1081/1 The amount of catecholamine entering the blood is dependent upon a complex process of neuronal release and reuptake into nerve terminals. **1885** SIR C. G. C. BOWEN in *Law Times Rep.* LII. 289/1 *Reventilating the question of domicile. *c* **1864** E. DICKINSON *Bolts of Melody* (1945) 246 One *rewalks a precipice. **1969** J. T. BURTCHAELL *Catholic Theories of Biblical Inspiration since 1810* vii. 303 The individual Christian can and certainly should rewalk the route from paganism to Christ. **1815** in J. Smyth *Pract. of Customs* (1821) 330 Returned Goods may be *re-warehoused. **1874** RAYMOND *Statist. Mines & Mining* 179 The *rewelding..costs on an average $10. **1877** G. M. HOPKINS *Poems* (1967) 68, I hear the lark ascend, His rash-fresh *re-winded new-skeinèd score In crisps of curl. **1970** 'D. HALLIDAY' *Dolly & Cookie Bird* xi. 168 He..pulled back a zipper..*re-zipped it. **1974** 'M. UNDERWOOD' *Pinch of Snuff* xi. 97 Brian watched him re-zip the bag.

b. Prefixed to verbs and sbs. which denote 'making (of a certain kind or quality)', 'turning or converting into ——', esp. those formed on adjs. by means of the suffix *-ize*, e.g. ***re-brighten*** vb., ***-catholicization***, ***-centralization***, ***-civilianization***, ***-civilianize*** vb., ***-institutionalization***, ***-institutionalize*** vb., ***-modernize*** vb., ***-phonemicization***, ***-phonologization***, ***-phonologize*** vb., ***popularize*** vb., ***-solemnize*** vb., ***-stabilization***, ***-Stalinization***, ***-Stalinize*** vb., ***-standardization***, ***-sterilization***, ***-sweeten*** vb., ***-vascularization***, ***-vascularize*** vb., ***-volatilization***.

1830 *Edin. Rev.* LI. 497 The required discipline of *re-Americanization. **1885** COUPLAND *Spirit Goethe's Faust* v. 107 Faust must perforce become *reanimalized. **1825** *New Monthly Mag.* XVI. 478 The church..*rebourbonized, and reconventualized. **1925** E. SITWELL *Poetry & Crit.* 23 Miss Stein..breaks down the predestined groups of words..; then she *re-brightens them,..and builds them into new and vital shapes. **1870** *Eng. Mech.* 11 Mar. 637/2, I know this to be a good receipt for *rebrowning gun barrels. **1852** *Meanderings of Memory* I. 21 O too *rebrutalized! oh too bereaved! **1885** COUPLAND *Spirit Goethe's Faust* v. 106 It is the aim of the Devil..to rebrutalize him. **1949** *Scottish Jrnl. Theol.* II. 241 The pressure for visible unity, for a *recatholicisation of the Churches, has..[come] from the 'evangelical' movements burdened with fulfilling the mission of the Gospel to the whole world. **1925** *Glasgow Herald* 5 Oct. 11 Only Scotland and the Northern (Newcastle) [administration] will continue to function, but the official policy is definitely *recentralisation because of the enormous fall in the volume of the work. **1957** C. P. MCVICKER *Titoism* p. x, Decentralization as Re-centralization. **1967** *Economist* 14 Oct. 149/2 There is not necessarily a contradiction between the drive for reform and the temporary re-centralisation of investment policy, plus a restrictive incomes policy. **1947** *Manch. Guardian* 18 July, Certain foreigners are eligible for '*recivilianisation'. **1962** S. E. FINER *Man on Horseback* xi. 190 How far it is possible for a military régime, starting with quasi-civilian institutions,..ultimately to *re-civilianize itself. *Ibid.* 197 Could the régime not pass..from a quasi-civilianized military régime..to a re-civilianized one? What would be the criteria of such re-civilianization? *Ibid.* 198 In both these cases it has taken a long time for the 're-civilianization' to take root. **1851** *Art Jrnl. Illustr. Catal., Science of Exhib.* III. p. x*/1 Pressing it in moulds..and *re-coking it with care. **1895** J. WINSOR *Mississ. Basin* 310 This journal..was..later *re-Englished by another hand. **1894** C. L. JOHNSTONE *Canada* 48 The duty of *refertilising the land. **1881** *Athenæum* 17 Sept. 363/3 The *re-Hellenization of the country by the Byzantine emperors. **1978** *Sci. Amer.* Feb. 50/2 Most patients are placed in nursing homes..., a process the Department of Health, Education, and Welfare has labeled '*reinstitutionalization', since most homes have more than 100 beds (and yet offer only custodial care). **1976** *Guardian Weekly* 14 Nov. 7/2 The first task of the Carter administration must be to *reinstitutionalise American foreign policy. **1890** EARLE *Eng. Prose* 421 They have been refashioned, respelt, *relatinized. *Ibid.*, '*Relatinization' provokes cavil. **1804** J. LARWOOD *No Gun Boats* 29 The uncassocked Prelate in his now *re-layman'd ministerial capacity. **1973** *Courier & Advertiser* (Dundee) 7 Aug. 1/3 (Advt.), *Remodernised 4-apartment house. **1976** *S. Wales Echo* 27 Nov. 9/4 (Advt.), Remodernised fur coats. **1892** HOWELLS in *Harper's Mag.* Mar. 641 To *reobjectivize the phenomenon of their recurrence. **1951** Z. S. HARRIS *Methods in Structural Linguistics* ix. 93 The following not infrequent situation is also a special case of resegmentation of a segment for purposes of *rephonemicization. **1972** R. JAKOBSON in A. R. Keiler *Reader in Hist. & Compar. Linguistics* 135 Within the framework of an isolated functional dialect, one cannot speak either of an increase or a reduction of a phonological system, but only of a restructuring, that is, of its *rephonologization. **1975** *Amer. Speech 1971* XLVI. 266 Change cannot be incorporated within Saussurian idealized homogeneity of structure; that does not change, it is merely *rephonologized. **1906** *Westm. Gaz.* 11 Aug. 12/2, I do not intend to *repopularize the stereoscope. **1959** I. & P. OPIE *Lore & Lang. Schoolch.* ii. 38 The following favourite accumulates on the principle of 'The House that Jack built'. It was repopularized by the American folk-singer Burl Ives in 1953, but had been current in Britain for anyway forty years before his visit. **1809** W. TAYLOR in Robberds *Mem.* II. 273 The army..will be *reroyalized. **1893** J. PULSFORD *Loyalty to Christ* II. 298 Selfish, until it becomes *reselfed in God. **1949** 'J. NELSON' *Backwoods Teacher* xvi. 173 There before an assemblage they wrote their names in the Bible and took each other for better or worse—the same to be *re-solemnized later when the preacher should come through. **1953** P. L. FERMOR *Violins of Saint-Jacques* 28 A phoenix's funeral that was resolemnised each evening. **1921** *Nineteenth Cent.* Feb. 231 A disastrous blow to the *restabilization of Europe. **1958** A. J. TOYNBEE *East to West* xxv. 75 The population started to increase at an accelerating rate (it is still increasing today, though re-stabilization is now in sight). **1956** *Washington Post* 19 Nov. A21/1 Even today, after the unspeakable horror of the blood bath in Hungary, the betting is still somewhat against a '*re-Stalinization'. **1974** R. J. OSBORN *Evolution Soviet Politics* v. 195 Just as with Khruschev's anti-Stalin campaign, Brezhnev's cautious but firm 're-Stalinization' has been a weapon for dealing with current problems. **1968** *Russian Rev.* XXVII. 309 All this evidence might appear to be leading to the conclusion that the party leadership is trying to *re-Stalinize, but is forced to proceed very gradually in the face of opposition. **1911** WEBSTER, *Restandardization. **1938** *Mind* XLVII. 103 It is to be urgently hoped that a similar restandardization will be attempted for the present scale. **1952** C. P. BLACKER *Eugenics* 204 The Pintner-Patterson scale (1917) and the Arthur Performance scale, the latter a restandardization of ten of the tests used in the former, are now in common use. **1899** *Pop. Sci. Monthly* Nov. 57 Unscrupulous manufacturers..*resterilize the cans with their contents. **1900** A. H. BUCK *Ref. Handbk. Med. Sci.* (ed. 2) I. 567/2 The best silk sponges are expensive so that *resterilization would be necessary. **1966** AUDEN *About House* 29 Shrines..Rose again *Resweetened the hirsute West. **1924** *Jrnl. Path. & Bacteriol.* XXVII. 205 *Revascularisation of the lobule takes place. **1954** MARTIN & HYNES *Clin. Endocrinol.* (ed. 2) i. 4 If the grafts were placed at a distance away from the portal trunks revascularization from other vessels was not followed by active function. **1963** *Lancet* 12 Jan. 89/2 Given sufficient time..dead bone can become *revascularized, and a case that starts off as a non-union with no callus can ultimately unite. **1971** *Nature* 23 July 279/2 The question of how skin grafts are revascularized is still not resolved. **1866** *Q. Jrnl. Geol. Soc.* XXII. 441 The volatile matters removed by distillation..have found a reception where no *revolatilization could occur. **1938** R. W. LAWSON tr. *Hevesy & Paneth's Man. Radioactivity* (ed. 2) xviii. 170 The condensation and revolatilization of bismuth hydride. **1882** *Athenæum* 18 Nov. 667/1 This deposit of the foreign metal may..be *revolatilized.

c. Prefixed to verbs and sbs. which denote fitting, furnishing, supplying, or treating with something, e.g. ***re-cane***, ***-fenestrate***, ***-lampshade***, ***-litter***, ***-mine***, ***-neck***, ***-pew***, ***-staff***, ***-washer*** vbs. (Frequent in technical use.)

1886 WILLIS & CLARK *Cambridge* I. 184 The interior of the Chapel was refitted in 1717 and its exterior *reashlared. **1871** *Figure-Training* 54 The staymaker should be directed to take out all the bones first and to *rebone them again afterwards. **1862** *Times* 22 Nov. *Advt.*, Lamps *rebronzed, regilt, and repaired. **1859** R. F. BURTON *Centr. Afr.* in *Jrnl.*

Geog. Soc. XXIX. 212 The central channel must be *rebridged with branching trees. **1971** *Islander* (Victoria, B.C.) 16 May 5/4 There was also a small chair that went with the set but he was having the seat *re-caned. **1879** F. W. Robinson *Coward Consc.* I. vi, *Re-chalking his cue. **1970** H. Braun *Parish Churches* xvii. 214 Few early churches escaped being at least in part *refenestrated during the High Gothic era. **1971** *Country Life* 3 June 1366/3 He did not make great changes.. other than to refenestrate the east and south sides. **1918** A. Bennett *Roll-Call* I. ii. 24 The lampshade craze increasing in virulence, they had between them *re-lampshaded the entire house. **1886** Willis & Clark *Cambridge* I. 513 The glazier.. was engaged to *relead them. **1884** R. F. Coffin *Old Sailor's Yarns* x. 105 To *releather the parral of the main royal-yard. **1884** *Manch. Exam.* 15 Oct. 5/4 Renaming and *relettering the streets of Paris with Republican signs. **1775** W. H. Marshall *Minutes Agric.* (1778) sig. D3, Shovelling the gangways, and *re-littering them with long dung. **1960** *Farmer & Stockbreeder* 16 Feb. 145/3 The whole place is then thoroughly cleaned,.. and rested a week before being re-littered. **1917** J. Masefield *Old Front Line* iii. 38 It was all mined, countermined, and *re-mined. **1967** *Guardian* 2 Mar. 6/6 A genuine theorbo, built as a lute in 1584 and *renecked in 1730. **1978** *Early Music* Oct. 531/2 It seems to have been cut down all round and re-necked in the 18th century to make a seven-string viol. **1857** Trollope *Barchester T.* (1861) 204 Should the bishop now be *repetticoated. **1839** F. Witts *Diary* 20 May (1978) 160 The church has been recently *repewed with deal. **1884** S. J. Reid *Life Syd. Smith* ii. 46 The Chapel has been repewed. **1865** Carlyle *Fredk. Gt.* IX. vii. (1872) III. 132, I *re-powdered her myself, and readjusted her dress a little. **1884** *Bee-keeping* 24, I *re-queened all my stocks.. with Ligurians. **1875** Bedford *Sailor's Pocket Bk.* v. (ed. 2) 151 The means of *re-quicksilvering its reflectors. **1852** Wiggins *Embanking* 113 The contractors had to strip the sod.. and *resoil and resod. **1893** Selous *Trav. S.E. Africa* 118, I had all the tools.. necessary for *re-spoking it. **1898** *Westm. Gaz.* 4 Apr. 7/2 The hospital committee accepted the resignation, and a special meeting has been called to consider the subject of *restaffing the institution. **1898** *Daily News* 16 Apr. 9/5 The Management Committee.. decided to close the Institution.. and restaff the place with as little delay as possible. **1884** *Manch. Exam.* 3 May 3/7 Venetian blinds can be *retaped and made equal to new. **1883** *Manch. Guard.* 12 Oct. 4/3 Putting yarn in a damp cellar.. and then *re-ticketing it. **1845** E. Warburton *Crescent & Cross* I. 166 Re-dressed, *re-turbaned, and re-seated on my carpet. **1960** *Times* 16 Sept. 13/5 Recently a tap over a wash hand basin in my office.. required *re-washering. *Ibid.*, The local water company re-washer water taps free of charge in order to save water. **1974** J. Wainwright *Evidence I shall Give* xx. 92 The handman who re-washers a tap.

're (-ə(r), -(r)), contraction of ARE, pl. pres. ind. of BE as *you're, they're*. Freq. used in the representation of speech (and for metrical reasons in verse). Cf. YARE, Y'ARE.

1591 Shaks. *Two Gent.* v. iv. 44 O, 'tis the curse in love, and still approv'd, When women cannot love where they're belov'd. **1676** G. Etherege *Man of Mode* IV. i. 56 The women indeed are little beholding to the young men of this age; they're generally only dull admirers of themselves. **1738** Swift *Polite Conv.* 2, I hope, you're never the worse. But where's your manners? **1836** Dickens *Pickw.* (1837) ii. 12 'They're beginning up stairs,' said the stranger—'hear the.. fiddles tuning.' **1978** J. Updike *Coup* (1979) i. 39 Whoever the hell you are, you're the best thing I've seen today.

rea, sing. of *reas* REIS (Portuguese money).

rea-, obs. form of RAY-GRASS.

†**reable**, *a.* *Sc. Obs. rare*$^{-1}$. [Cf. REABLE *v.*] Legitimate.

1581 N. Burne in *Cath. Tract.* (S.T.S.) 164/5 To persuade the people that he micht be reable air [= heir] to his father, ye preachit euer.. that promeiss of mariage vas lauchful mariage.

reable (rɪˈeɪb(ə)l), *v.* Also 6 -abill, -hable. [f. RE- + ABLE *v.*, prob. after F. *ra-*, *rhabiller*.]

†**1.** *trans.* To confirm, to legitimize. *Sc. Obs.*

1521 in Ellis *Orig. Lett.* Ser. II. I. 282 The Duc [of Albany] chalengethe the iiij[th] parte of her conjunctefee to be his enheritaunce.. and is reabled to the same by acte of parliament. **1536** Bellenden *Cron. Scot.* (1821) II. 452 That thay [the children] micht be lawchful and reabillit, be virtew of the matrimony subsequent. **1597** Skene *De Verb. Sign.* s.v. *Bastardus*, Ane bastard, legitimat and rehabled in his life-time. *a* **1682** Sempill *Picktooth for Pope* 395 Poems (1849), A bastards name doth duly them befit For they were never reabled as yet.

2. *Med.* To rehabilitate (a patient).

1945 *Lancet* 24 Mar. 387/2 For some year or two I have suggested to friends who write or teach that we should say 'reable' instead of 'rehabilitate'. It therefore gives me pleasure.. to read of 'reabling' and 'reablement' in your last three issues. **1947** E. Spriggs in I. Brown *Say Word* 101, I am glad to see that the words Reable and Reablement are now being frequently used in the *Lancet* and other journals.

Hence **re'ablement**, rehabilitation.

1945 *Lancet* 3 Mar. 275/2 The committee believe that a revised programme of reablement should be administered by a senior tuberculosis officer. **1945, 1947** [see 2 above]. **1955** *Brit. Jrnl. Physical Med.* XVIII. 119/1 Reablement is seen as an intricate problem which has to be considered from very various aspects. **1968** *Lancet* 2 Nov. 985/2 To be comprehensive and successful any reablement programme must be built on well-organised services for health, education, social work, and vocational training.

re-a'bridge, *v.* [RE- 5 a.] *trans.* To abridge a second time.

a **1631** Donne 6 *Serm.* ii. (1634) 27 God's abridgement of the whole world was man; re-abridge man into his least volume [etc.].

reab'sorb, *v.* [RE- 5 a. Cf. F. *réabsorber* (Littré).] **a.** *trans.* To absorb anew or again; to take in again by absorption.

1768–74 Tucker *Lt. Nat.* (1834) I. 465 Psyche becomes reabsorbed into the ocean from whence she sprung. **1837** Carlyle *Fr. Rev.* III. v. ii, Chaos has reabsorbed him; may it late or never bear his like again! **1882** J. H. Blunt *Ref. Ch. Eng.* II. 341 Some portions of the jurisdiction assumed by the Pope must.. be re-absorbed into the Crown.

b. *intr.* for *pass.* To be reabsorbed.

1916 Galsworthy in *Scribner's Mag.* Jan. 17/1 In one's heart rose an ecstasy of love for this.. earth which breeds us all, and into which we reabsorb.

reab'sorption. [RE- 5 a. Cf. prec. and F. *réabsorption* (Littré).] The action of reabsorbing, or fact of being reabsorbed: *spec.* in *Path.* = RESORPTION.

1755 Akenside in *Phil. Trans.* L. 328 The continual re-absorption of that moisture by the lymphatics is no less necessary. **1842** T. Griffith *Apostles' Creed* 141 The dream of re-absorption into the divine essence indulged by the Buddhists of Burmah. **1875** H. C. Wood *Therap.* (1879) 267 As reabsorption in the bladder is at least conceivable, the catheter should be used early.

reab'sorptive, *a.* [RE- 5 a.] Having the quality of reabsorbing.

1946 *Nature* 23 Nov. 730/1 The concept of competition for secretory and reabsorptive mechanisms in the renal tubules has proved very fruitful. **1975** *Ibid.* 27 Feb. 747/1 Mammalian bladder possesses, in addition to an exceptionally high electrical resistance, an aldosterone-stimulated Na^+ reabsorptive mechanism.

†**reac'cend**, *v.* *Obs.* [RE- 5 a; cf. late L. *reaccendĕre* (Jerome).] *trans.* To rekindle.

a **1645** Howell *Lett.* I. III. xxxiv. (1650) 96 To kindle and reaccend this tinder.

reac'cept, *v.* [RE- 5 a. Cf. med.L. *reaccipĕre* (14th c.).] *trans.* To accept again.

1623 Rowlandson *God's Blessing* 72 The comfortable assurance of his fathers love and relenting goodnesse to reaccept him. **1835** Lytton *Rienzi* IX. v, One caution before I re-accept your fealty. **1860** Froude *Hist. Eng.* V. 28 Henry VIII had insisted successfully that the Scotch should reaccept their engagements.

So **reac'ceptance.**

1633 Bp. Hall *Hard Texts O.T.* 374 Thou.. hast made thy selfe uncapable of my reacceptance by the law. *a* **1652** Brome *Damoiselle* I. ii, With reacceptance of this thousand pound. **1870** *Pall Mall G.* 17 Nov. 1 A formal reacceptance of the very disabilities she rebels against.

reaccess. [RE- 5 a.]

1. Return, renewed access.

1611 Florio, *Recessione*,.. a reaccesse or comming again. **1627** Hakewill *Apol.* II. i. §1 The withering of all things by the recesse, and their reviving and resurrection.. by the reaccesse of the Sunne. **1823** Chalmers *Serm.* I. 178 A Flaming Sword had to.. guard their reaccess to the bowers of Immortality.

†**2.** Reaccession (to the throne). *Obs. rare*$^{-1}$.

169. *Ad Populum Phaleræ* I. 54 When such Discourses fill the Town, what less Can be design'd than James's Re-access?

So **reac'cession.**

1825 Bentham *Offic. Apt. Maxim.*, *Indications* (1830) 26 Of the course of illegality begun under Lord Erskine, and pursued under Lord Eldon, the continuation commenced with his re-accession. *a* **1876** in Orton *Andes & Amazons* (ed. 3) 601 The exposure caused a re-accession of the fever.

rea'ccommodate, *v.* [RE- 5 a. Cf. F. *réaccommoder* (16th c. in Littré).] *trans.* To accommodate, adjust, †array, afresh or again.

1616 Capt. Smith *Descr. New Eng.* Wks. (Arb.) I. 221 Onely her spret saile remayned.., till we had reaccommodated her a Iury mast. **1639** N. N. tr. *Du Bosq's Compl. Woman* I. B2 He desired to reaccommodate what had been corrupted. **1641** Baker *Chron.* (1674) 125/1 King Edward.. instantly sends to charge that part, without giving them time to re-accommodate themselves. **1920** *Nineteenth Cent.* Oct. 629 It will take time before the Jews can again reaccommodate themselves to the local conditions.

So †**reacco'mmoderate** *v.* (Cf. COMMODERATE.)

1613–8 Daniel *Coll. Hist. Eng.* (1626) 200 [He] instantly sends to charge that part, without giuing them time to re-accommoderate themselues.

rea'ccompany, *v.* [RE- 5 a.] *trans.* To accompany again; †to escort back.

1611 Florio, *Raccompagnare*, to reaccompany. **1650** Howell *Giraffi's Rev. Naples* I. 114 Masaniello.. re-accompanied them to their Homes. **1673** O. Walker *Educ.* 219 If they will accompany further, many are wont to reaccompany them part of the way.

re-a'ccomplishment. [RE- 5 a.] A second accomplishment or fulfilling.

a **1656** Bp. Hall *Revelation Unrevealed* §1 A re-accomplishment [of prophecies] in these last times.

re-a'ccost, *v.* [RE- 5 a.] *trans.* To accost again.

1652 J. Wright tr. *Camus' Nat. Paradox* v. 105 Merinda.. was forced to joyn with them and re-accost Almeria.

rea'ccount, *v.* Also 6 -compt. [RE- 5 a.]

†**1.** *trans.* To recount, relate. *Obs. rare.*

Cf. RACCOUNT, and It. *raccontare*, F. *raconter*.

1561 Daus tr. *Bullinger on Apoc.* (1573) 55 Our Lord proceedeth in reaccomptyng much more ample rewardes. **1635** J. Hayward tr. *Biondi's Banish'd Virg.* 166 The King upon this.. reaccounted unto him openly Bramac's embassie with his answer.

2. To account again or anew.

1840 G. S. Faber *Prim. Doctr. Regen.* 44 Every Soul is accounted to be in Adam, until it is reaccounted to be in Christ.

re-a'ccrue, *v.* [RE- 5 a.] †*trans.* To gather up again (see ACCRUE 4). *Obs.*

1646 G. Daniel *Poems* Wks. 1878 I. 48, I will Assay My fancie.. and re-accrue My Thoughts into their Station.

rea'ccumulate, *v.* [RE- 5 a.] *intr.* To accumulate again.

1874 Lawson *Dis. Eye* 53 If.. the aqueous is found to have reaccumulated, the central point is again opened.

So **reaccumu'lation.**

1822–34 *Good's Study Med.* (ed. 4) IV. 320 The pressure will tend to prevent a re-accumulation [of dropsical effusion]. **1841** Calhoun *Wks.* IV. 7 There must be a great.. increase of expenditure.. or the reaccumulation of another surplus.

re-a'ccuse, *v.* [RE- 5 a.] *trans.* To accuse again.

1609 Daniel *Civ. Wars* I. lx, Who re-accus'd Norfolke for words of treason he had vs'd.

rea'ccustom, *v.* [RE- 5 a.] *trans.* To habituate again.

1611 Cotgr., *Rabituer*, to reaccustome, reinure. **1852** Hawthorne *Blithedale Rom.* xxiii. (1883) 541 Time long enough for my.. hands to reaccustom themselves to gloves.

reace, variant of RACE *v.*³ *Obs.*

reach (riːtʃ), *sb.*¹ Forms: 6 reche, reache, *Sc.* reiche, 6–7 reatch, 7 rech, 6– reach. See also RETCH *sb.*¹ [f. REACH *v.*¹]

I. An act of reaching.

1. a. An (*or* the) act of reaching out with the arm (*esp.* to take hold of something), or with something held in the hand. Also *transf.* and *fig.*

1570 Levins *Manip.* 205/10 Reache, *perretio* [read *porrectio*]. **1642** Rogers *Naaman* Ep. Ded. 2 A few good reaches and affections after holinesse are not enough for us. **1691** Norris *Pract. Disc.* 188 It must.. fan the Flame of our Affections, and make them tend upwards with importunate reaches towards Heavenly Objects. **1711** Steele *Spect.* No. 38 ¶1 Her Fan was to point to somewhat at a Distance, that in the Reach she may discover the Roundness of her Arm. **1825** Longf. *Sunrise on Hills* 22 The woods were bending with a silent reach. **1881** 'Mark Twain' *Prince & Pauper* xxii. 256 A brawny blacksmith.. made a reach for him.

b. With indication of, or reference to, the space or distance covered in the act of reaching.

1607 Topsell *Four-f. Beasts* (1658) 231 Making him fit to take longer reaches without doubling of his legs. *a* **1680** Charnock *Attrib. God* (1834) II. 41 Otherwise the reaches of a created.. fancy would be more extensive than the power of God. **1874** T. Hardy *Far fr. Mad. Crowd* xlix, You needn't take quite such long reaches with your rake. **1884** *St. James's Gaz.* 29 Mar. 5/2 Their pace then began to fall off, and the reach shortened all through the boat.

†**2.** *fig.* **a.** An attempt to attain or achieve something; a design or aim; a device, scheme, plan, contrivance. *Obs.* (very common *c* 1590–1700).

1590 Tarlton *News Purgat.* (1844) 84 Master Vickar had a reach in his head. **1621–3** Middleton & Rowley *Changeling* v. i, This is my reach: I'll set Some part a-fire of Diaphanta's chamber. **1678** Butler *Hudibras* III. ii. 1583 But Jesuits have deeper Reaches In all their Politick Far-fetches. *a* **1734** North *Exam.* I. ii. §6 (1740) 34 All which Matters.. could not be so done without some private Reach. **1785** Burke *Sp. Nabob Arcot* Wks. 1842 I. 329 In India this is a reach of deep policy.

†**b.** Without *a*: Scheming, policy. *Obs.*$^{-1}$

a **1635** Naunton *Fragm. Reg.* (Arb.) 36 A piece of reach and hazard beyond my apprehension.

3. *spec.* †**a.** A term in dice-playing. *Obs.*$^{-1}$

1600 Rowlands *Lett. Humours Blood* iii. 59 He calles for, Come on fiue; and there it is: Or else heele haue it with fiue and a reach.

b. *dial.* An addition to wages.

1851 *Jrnl. R. Agric. Soc.* XII. II. 404 Hay-mowing, corn-cutting, etc.,.. when the workmen.. generally obtain a small 'reach' in addition to their daily wages.

4. a. A single stretch or spell of movement, travel, flight, etc.

1652–62 Heylin *Cosmogr.* III. (1673) 4/1 Making two long reaches in his journey hither. **1682** N. O. *Boileau's Lutrin* III. 24 Then wafting at one Reach, they proudly Pearch On highest Pinnacle of the fatal Church! **1873** Tristram *Moab* xv. 290 There was a long reach and many a climb up and down before camp could be reached.

b. *Naut.* A run on one tack; a board. Also, a course that is approximately at right angles to the wind.

1830 J. F. Cooper *Water Witch* xv, 'Tis by many reaches that the leeward vessel gains upon the wind. *a* **1845** Hood *Pain in Pleasure-Boat* 21 Bill, give that sheet another haul—she'll fetch it up this reach. **1846** A. Young *Naut. Dict.* s.v., A vessel.. is said to be on a reach, when she is sailing by the wind upon any tack. **1884** *Sat. Rev.* 14 June 783/2 The race back.. was, save one little bit, but a run and a reach. **1949** *Sun* (Baltimore) 20 June 16/1 From the start to Sandy Point, the skippers had to face a headwind, the next leg.. was a reach, while the trip to Poole's Island Light resulted in another beat. **1976** *Oxf. Compan. Ships & Sea* 695/1 *Reach*, the point of sailing of a vessel which can point her course with the wind reasonably free and her sails full throughout. A broad reach is the same but with the wind abeam or from slightly abaft the beam. **1977** *Modern Boating* (Austral.) Jan. 14/1 Destiny II will go like a rocket on a reach or a run.

II. Power of, or capacity for, reaching.

5. a. The extent to which a person can stretch out the arm or hand, *esp.* so as to touch or grasp something (in early use freq. *pl.*); the distance to which an animal can extend a limb or other part, or to which any limb can be extended. *spec.* in *Cricket*, the extent to which a batsman can play forward without moving his back foot; in *Boxing* (see quot. 1958).

1579 LYLY *Euphues* (Arb.) 77 Kinges haue long armes, and rulers large reaches. **1655** FULLER *Hist. Camb.* (1840) 179 This horse, I may say, had a long-reach. **1667** MILTON *P.L.* IX. 591 High from ground the branches would require Thy utmost reach. **1851** *F. Lillywhite's Guide to Cricketers* 18 A good length ball depends entirely upon the size and reach of a batsman. **1866** *Routledge's Ev. Boy's Ann.* 327 Availing himself of his height, which..gave him a longer reach. **1897** *Century Mag.* 562/2 Their reach forward is prodigious, as I found..when my horse's hind hoof cut the heel clean off my boot. **1897** K. S. RANJITSINHJI *Jubilee Bk. Cricket* iii. 67 Batsmen vary greatly as to their 'reach'—that is, the distance they can safely play forward or advance the bat in making a drive. **1951** *Sport* 30 Mar.–5 Apr. 11/3 He quickly found that O'Hara, his opponent, was longer in the reach. **1958** F. C. AVIS *Boxing Ref. Dict.* s.v. *Reach*: the distance from the extremity of one hand to that of the other when the arms are fully held out sideways.

b. In prep. phrases, esp. ***within, above*** or ***out of*** (one's) ***reach***: freq. = Ability to obtain or procure something; power to affect or injure another.

a **1548** HALL *Chron., Henry VIII* 219 The bearer.. thought it..better for hym to bestowe it without the Kynges reche. **1557** *Tottell's Misc.* (Arb.) 129, I rowe not so farre past my reache. **1592** SHAKS. *Rom. & Jul.* III. v. 86 The Traitor liues..from the reach of these my hands. **1601** R. JOHNSON *Kingd. & Commw.* (1603) 196 They..made pray and spoile of whatsoeuer came into their reaches. **1698** FRYER *Acc. E. India & P.* 177 The Tigre seeing them out of his reach..falls a Roaring. **1712** J. JAMES tr. *Le Blond's Gard.* 197 Those..cost such vast Sums, that they seem to me above the Reach of the most wealthy private Gentleman. **1781** COWPER *Conv.* 586 Who..plucks the fruit placed more within his reach. **1871** ROSSETTI *Dante at Verona* lxxxii, How the Prince Sunned himself out of Dante's reach.

c. *transf.* of things, in various applications.

c **1586** C'TESS PEMBROKE *Ps.* XLVI. v, Our rock on Jacob's God we found, Above the reach of harmes. **1596** SHAKS. *Merch. V.* IV. i. 10 No lawful meanes can carrie me Out of his enuies reach. *a* **1656** BP. HALL *Rem. Wks.* (1660) 106 The Almighty is above all the reach of these unquiet perturbations. *a* **1687** PETTY *Pol. Arith.* (1690) 103 All of these ten Millions of People are obedient to their Sovereign, and within the reach of his power. **1827** HOOD *Hero & Leander* ci, Just past the reach Of foamy billows he lies cast. **1875** *Encycl. Brit.* I. 337/1 To plough deeply..places them [weeds] out of the reach of frost.

d. Power of reaching far.

1825 J. WILSON *Noct. Ambr.* Wks. 1855 I. 40 Although he has weight length and reach..yet has he lost every battle.

6. Capacity or power to perform or achieve some action, attain to some state or condition, etc. (Chiefly with preps., as in 5 b.)

a. of persons.

1576 FLEMING *Panopl. Epist.* 18 Whom to annoy is beyond my reache and abilitie. **1592** BABINGTON *Comf. Notes Gen.* l. §9 The mouing of others..to consider what wanteth to a multitude in this land, and to relieue them according to their reaches. **1711** HEARNE *Collect.* (O.H.S.) III. 176 His Learning was above yᵉ common Reach. **1784** COWPER *Task* III. 40 The fault is obstinate, and cure beyond our reach. **1820** W. IRVING *Sketch Bk.* I. 28 A picture of active yet simple virtues, which are within every man's reach. **1880** L. STEPHEN *Pope* vii. 163 Anything like sustained reasoning was beyond his reach.

b. of things.

1611 TOURNEUR *Ath. Trag.* II. iv, Any circumstance That stood within the reach of the designe Of persons. **1690** LOCKE *Hum. Und.* II. xxi. §21 In respect of Actions, within the reach of such a Power in him. **1711** W. KING tr. *Naude's Refined Politics* iii. 91 A very great design with a long reach, and contrived with much judgment. **1800–24** CAMPBELL *Margaret & Dora* ii, Dora's eyes of heavenly blue Pass all painting's reach. **1865** M. ARNOLD *Ess. Crit.* ii. (1875) 58 The highest reach of science is, one may say, an inventive power.

†**c.** Of the voice: Range, compass. *Obs.*

1597 MORLEY *Introd. Music* 7 That compasse was the reach of most voyces. **1674** EVELYN *Diary* (1827) II. 390 Mrs. Knight..who sang incomparably, and doubtleess has the greatest reach of any Englishwoman. *a* **1680** BUTLER *Rem.* (1759) II. 429 All he does is forced, like one that sings above the Reach of his Voice.

7. a. Capacity or power of comprehension; extent of knowledge or of the ability to acquire it; range of mind or thought.

1586 A. DAY *Eng. Secretary* I. (1625) iv, The ignorant.. hereof, whose reach hath not been so ample as others. **1601** HOLLAND *Pliny* I. 168 His high reach and deep wit, whereby he apprehended the knowledge of all things vnder the cope of heauen. **1667** MILTON *P.L.* x. 793 Let this appease The doubt, since humane reach no further knows. **1671** —— *Samson* 1380 How thou wilt here come off surmounts my reach. **1709** POPE *Ess. Crit.* 47 Be sure your self and your own reach to know, How far your genius, taste, and learning go. **1750** JOHNSON *Rambler* No. 79 ¶3 Has a long reach in detecting the projects of his acquaintance.

b. In prep. phrases, as ***above, beyond, out of*** (***one's***) ***reach***. (Cf. 5 b.)

1542 UDALL *Erasm. Apoph.* I. §23 This saiyng..whiche is fathered on Socrates.., What is aboue our reach, we haue naught to doe withall. **1572** H. MIDDLEMORE in Ellis *Orig. Lett.* Ser. II. III. 5, I sayd they were matters owt of my reache, and farre from myne acquayntawnce. **1613** PURCHAS *Pilgrimage* I. xii. (1614) 60 Many things they [Planets] foretold to Alexander..beyond the reach of men. **1671** MILTON *Samson* 62 Which herein Happ'ly had ends above my reach to know. **1711** ADDISON *Spect.* No. 58 ¶1 If my Readers meet with any Paper that in some Parts of it may be a little out of their Reach. **1842** MACAULAY *Fredk. Gt.* Ess. (1877) 663 Nothing beyond the reach of any man of good parts.

c. In phr. ***of*** (***a***) ***great*** (***deep***, etc.) ***reach***. (Very common *c* 1585–1710; in later use only without article.)

1586 J. HOOKER *Hist. Irel.* in *Holinshed* II. 143/1 In matters of policie he was verie prudent, and of a great reach. **1603** KNOLLES *Hist. Turks* (1621) 1128 A man of greater reach and courage. **1641** MILTON *Reform.* II. (1851) 54 Men more audacious, and precipitant, than of solid and deep reach. **1686** tr. *Chardin's Coronat. Solyman* 103 They that had a deeper reach, were not so positive in their judgments. **1710** STEELE *Tatler* No. 246 ¶8 Plumbeus acknowledges Levis a Man of a great Reach. **1763** J. BROWN *Poetry & Mus.* v. 54 If one..delivered his Stories in Verse, another of inferior Reach and Invention would naturally give them..in plain Prose. **1875** STEDMAN *Victorian Poets* 151 To claim that they have been overrated, and are not men of high reach.

8. a. Of the mind or mental powers: Range of efficiency in speculation, acquisition of knowledge, penetration, etc.

c **1580** SIDNEY *Ps.* XXXVI. iv, Pleasures past the reach of mind. **1597** HOOKER *Eccl. Pol.* v. lxiii. §1 The mysteries of our religion are above the reach of our understanding. **1662** STILLINGFL. *Orig. Sacr.* II. vi. §2 The events..must be such as do exceed the reach of any created intellect. **1725** WATTS *Logic* (1736) 271 Matters of Fact..which lye beyond the Reach of our own personal Notice. **1744** BERKELEY *Siris* §337 The most refined human intellect, exerted to its utmost reach.

b. With *a*. (Approximating to sense 12 c.)

1657 J. SERGEANT *Schism Dispatch't* 261 Hath not this Dr. of Divinity a strange reach of reason? **1707** *Curios. in Husb. & Gard.* 5 Those who have a sufficient Reach of Understanding to comprehend the..ordinary Course of Nature. **1773** *Life N. Frowde* 21 Perhaps no Child of my Years had ever more Cunning, or a readier Reach of Thought. **1875** JOWETT *Plato* (ed. 2) III. 186 The 'Utopia' of Sir Thomas More..shows a reach of thought far beyond his contemporaries.

9. Range; scope; extent of application, effect, influence, etc.

1546 J. HEYWOOD *Prov.* (1867) 2 Their sentenses include so large a reache. **1570** DEE *Math. Pref.* 37 These wordes.. the reach of their meaning, is farther, then you woulde lightly imagine. **1600** HEYWOOD *2nd Pt. Edw. IV*, Wks. 1874 I. 99 My simple wit Can never found a judgment of such reach. **1858** BUCKLE *Civiliz.* (1869) II. vii. 378 When we compare the shortness of his life with the reach and depth of his views. **1875** WHITNEY *Life Lang.* vi. 100 A process of wide reach and abundant results in English.

10. Range (of carrying or traversing).

a. of a gun, or shot.

1571–91 DIGGES *Pantom.* (1591) 179 The first parte of the violent course of Gunners, commonly termed the peeces pointe blanke reache. **1662** J. DAVIES tr. *Mandelslo's Trav.* 28 They could not go by, without coming within reach of our Muskets. **1698** T. FROGER *Voy.* 21 In order to level the shot within reach of the Place. **1748** *Anson's Voy.* II. v. 171 Captain Saunders alarmed them unexpectedly with a broadside, when they flattered themselves they were got out of his reach. **1805** in *19th Cent.* (1899) Nov. 725 We were now without any opponent within reach of our guns.

b. of the eye or sight.

1623 MILTON *Ps.* cxxxvi. 94 Above the reach of mortall ey. **1667** —— *P.L.* XI. 380 The Hemisphere of Earth..Stretcht out to amplest reach of prospect lay. **1709** ADDISON *Tatler* No. 119 ¶2 Those Heavenly Bodies which lie out of Reach of Humane Eyes. **1875** MANNING *Mission H. Ghost* xiii. 353 The capacity and the reach of the eye are developed by practice, and by experience.

c. of the voice.

1797 MRS. RADCLIFFE *Italian* xii, The travellers..were soon beyond the reach of the voices.

11. Power or possibility of getting to (or as far as) some place, person, or object; distance or limit from which some point may be reached. Only in prep. phrases, as in 5 b.

1784 COWPER *Task* VI. 263 That has..within his reach A scene so friendly to his favourite task. **1806–7** J. BERESFORD *Miseries Hum. Life* (1826) II. i, No knife in your pocket nor house within reach. **1833** HT. MARTINEAU *Briery Creek* ii. 23 Mrs. Temple had never been very happy while within reach of markets and shops. **1859** DICKENS *T. Two Cities* I. v, All the people within reach had suspended their business.

III. That which reaches or stretches.

12. A continuous stretch, course, or extent:

a. of some material thing or space.

1609 BIBLE (Douay) *Ezek.* xvii. 3 A great eagle with great winges, with a long reach of members. **1638** JUNIUS *Paint. Ancients* 68 Darksome night..dimming the spacious reach of heaven. **1674** N. FAIRFAX *Bulk & Selv.* Contents, The outmost reach of Body must needs be bounded. **1803** *Naval Chron.* IX. 440 Exposed to the whole reach of the Western Ocean. **1866** BLACKMORE *Cradock Nowell* x, The glades and reaches of gentle park and meadow.

b. of time.

1814 L. HUNT *Feast of Poets* 49 His look with the reach of past ages was wise. **1869** PHILLIPS *Vesuv.* xii. 323 Some mountains are now constantly active, and have been so in all the reach of history.

c. of immaterial things. (Cf. 8 b.)

1838–9 HALLAM *Hist. Lit.* II. III. ii. §66. 452 A prodigious reach of learning distinguishes the theologians of these fifty years. **1869** GOULBURN *Purs. Holiness* iv. 31 A reach of love, and wisdom, and power to which it is impossible to set bounds. **1955** *Times* 9 May 3/3 The action therefore slows almost to a standstill in the middle reaches of the play. **1971** J. B. CARROLL et al. *Word Frequency Bk.* p. xxxvi, *Hapax legomena*..come from almost anywhere in the lower reaches of the theoretical type distribution.

d. The space over which something extends or is distributed.

1850 H. MILLER *Footpr. Creat.* i. (1874) 9 The marine and fresh-water animals having each their own reaches.

13. *spec.* **a.** That portion of a river, channel, or lake which lies between two bends; as much as can be seen in one view. Also the portion of a canal between two locks, having a uniform level.

1536 in R. G. Marsden *Sel. Pl. Crt. Adm.* (1894) I. 58 The same catche beyng under sayle in the reche over agaynste Lymehowse callyd Limehowse Reche. **1562** PHAER *Æneid* VIII. X. iv, They pluckyng swift their Ores, that..tyre their lims, And reatches long they win. **1609** HOLLAND *Amm. Marcell.* 33 Rasing as it goes the high bankes with their curving reaches. **1724** DE FOE *Mem. Cavalier* (1840) 95 The king..examined every reach and turning of the river. **1792** A. YOUNG *Trav. France* 99 The river presents one reach, crossed by the bridge, and then dividing into two fine channels. **1880** HAUGHTON *Phys. Geog.* v. 242 Occasionally threading some narrow channel, to enter again some magnificent reach.

†**b.** A bay. *Obs.*

1526 TINDALE *Acts* xxvii. 39 They spied a certayne reache [Gr. κόλπος] with a banke. **1601** HOLLAND *Pliny* v. xxix. I. 108 All the coast thereof is very full of creekes and reaches. **1650** FULLER *Pisgah* v. vii. 156 The opposite shoar, on the same side of the Sea, but..over a reach, or bay. **1736** AINSWORTH *Eng.-Lat. Dict.*, A reach at sea, *duorum promontoriorum intervallum.*

c. A headland or promontory. *Obs.* exc. *U.S.* (local).

1562 PHAER *Æneid* I. A iij, On either side the reaches hie ..And vnder them the still sea lyeth. **1626** CAPT. SMITH *Accid. Yng. Seamen* 17 A headland, a furland, a reatch, a land marke. **1627** E. F. *Life Edw. II.* in *Select. fr. Harl. Misc.* (1793) 45 Twice had they gained St. Vincent's rock, but, from that reach, were hurried back, with sudden gusts and tempests. **1897** in *Cent. Dict.*

14. A bearing-shaft or coupling-pole.

1868 *Routledge's Ev. Boy's Ann.* 478 The Reach, or bearing-shaft [of a bicycle] is the most important portion. **1875** KNIGHT *Dict. Mech.* 1887/1 A reach for a certain description of city wagon is shown in Fig. 4190.

15. = RACHE *sb.*²

1897 M. H. HAYES *Points of Horse* xx. (ed. 2) 222 If it runs down the nose in the form of a line of no great width, it is known as a 'reach' or 'stripe'.

IV. 16. *attrib.* and *Comb.*, as (sense 13 a) ***reach land***; **reach rod**, a connecting rod for transmitting manual motion to a remote part of a mechanism.

1795 T. CHAPMAN *Jrnl.* 4 Nov. in *Hist. Mag. Amer.* (1869) V. 359 They appear contented and Happy, having Plenty of fine reach Land. **1909** *Cent Dict.* Suppl., *Reach-rod*, in a locomotive, a rod which connects the reverse-lever in the cab to the bell-crank on the reverse-shaft of the valve-gear. **1972** L. M. HARRIS *Introd. Deepwater Floating Drilling Operations* 238 Some compartments will have reach rods to bilge drainage valves.

17. Used *attrib.* to designate a fork-lift truck whose fork can be moved forward and backward as well as up and down.

1962 *Engineering* 2 Nov. 584/1 Until the reach truck appeared, the provision of two hydraulic functions in a fork truck was considered difficult. **1963** *Times Rev. Industry* May 91/3 Reach types—The fork carriage is movable in a horizontal plane, with forks reaching beyond the front wheels to withdraw the load to a position within the wheelbase.

†**reach**, *sb.*² *Obs. rare.* [f. REACH *v.*²] An act of clearing the throat, or of retching.

1575 LANEHAM *Let.* (1871) 41 [He] cleered his vois with a hem and a reach, and spat oout withal. **1736** AINSWORTH *Eng.-Lat. Dict.*, A reach, or reaching to vomit, *vomendi nisus.*

reach (riːtʃ), *v.*¹ Forms: *α. Infin.* 1 **rǽcan**, 3 **ræchen**, 2, 4 **rechen**, (5 **-yn**); 4–5 **reche**, (5 **ric(c)he**, 6 **rech**), 4–5 **reiche**, (5 **reyche**, 6 *Sc.* **reich**), 6 **reache**, (7 **reatch**), 6– **reach**. *Pa. t.* (*a*) 1 **rǽhte**, 3 **rehte**, 4 **reiȝte, reighte**; 1, 3 **ráhte**, 4 **raȝte**, 4–5 **raghte**; 4 **rauhte, rauȝte, -tte**, 5 **rawȝte**, 4–6 **raughte**, (6 **roughte**); (and *pa. pple.*) 4 **raht**, 4–5 **raȝt**, 4–6 **raght**, (4–5 **ragh**, 5 *Sc.* **racht**); 4–5 **rauht**, (4 **rahut**, 5 **rauth**), **rauȝt**, (4 **rauȝht**, 5 **rawȝt**), 5–9 **raught**, (5 **rawght, rought**, 6 *erron.* **wrought**), *Sc.* **raucht**, (6 **rawcht**); also *pa. pple.* 4 **i-rawt**. (*b*) 4–6 **reched**, (4 **recched**, 5 **rechid, reychid**), 6–7 **reach'd**, 7 **reachd, reacht**, 6– **reached**. *β.* 4, *Sc.* 5–6 **reke**, (4 **reque**, 5 *Sc.* **rek**), 5–6 (9) *Sc.* **reik**, (6 **reyk**), 8 *Sc.* **reek, ryke**, (9 **rike**). *Pa. t.* 4 **reked**, 6 *Sc.* **reikit**. [OE. *rǽcan* (also *ȝerǽcan*) = OFris. *reka, rets(i)a, resza*, MDu. (Du.) *reiken*, MLG. *reiken, reken*, OHG. (G.) *reichen*:—OTeut. **raikjan* of uncertain relationship.

The various parts of the verb exhibit considerable variety of form at different periods. In ME. the normal vowel *ē* of the infin. and pres. is sometimes replaced by *ă, ĕ*, or *ĭ*. The latter is unusual; the other two (see RATCH *v.*¹ and RETCH *v.*¹) have probably been developed by back-formation from the pa. t. *raught*, on the analogies of *catch, caught* and *stretch, straught*. Mod. dial. forms differing from the standard *reach* are *rei(t)ch, rey(t)ch* (Yks.), *raich, reighch* (Lanc.), *rache, raych* (Devon), etc., in addition to the northern forms with final *-k* (as in *streek* beside *stretch*), which are recorded from c 1400 and survive as *reek, ryke* (Sc.), *reak, raik* (Yks.), *reik, reyk* (Lanc.), etc.

The normal West Saxon form of the pa. t. was *rǽhte*, giving ME. *rehte, reihte* (rare). From the typically northern OE. *ráhte* came the usual ME. *raught(e*, which continued in general use down to c 1600, and was frequently employed for half a century later, but is now only archaic, or dialectal in the forms *raucht* (Sc.), *rought* (Lanc., Chesh., Staff.) and *raught* (West Midl.). The new preterite form *reached* (cf. northern *reekit*) appears about 1400, but is comparatively rare before 1600. For other modern dial. variants of the pa. t. and pa. pple. (mostly due to analogy) see the *Eng. Dial Dict.*

In addition to *rǽcan*, OE. had also the form *ȝerǽcan*, the use of which is naturally prominent in those senses in which stress is laid on the full completion of the action (see sense 4). In some senses (as 4 b, 4 c, and 5) the verb occurs chiefly or exclusively in the preterite form *raught*, which in later use was perhaps not clearly associated with *reach* in its other applications.]

I. Transitive senses.

1. a. To stretch out, extend, hold *out* or *forth* (one's hand, arm, etc.).

c 897 K. Ælfred *Gregory's Past. C.* xxxvi. 246 Ic ræhte mine hond to eow. a 900 Cynewulf *Christ* 1620 In þæt hate fyr..þær hy leomu ræcað..to bærnenne. c 1000 Ælfric *Gen.* xxxviii. 28 Se oðer ræhte forð his hand. a 1300 *Cursor M.* 19791 To saint petere sco raght hir hand. c 1400 tr. *Secreta Secret., Gov. Lordsh.* 83 Drynke he a syrupe of roses ..and after, reche out his armes a lityll. 1481 Caxton *Reynard* (Arb.) 54 He raught out his right foot and dubbed me in the necke. 1565 Jewel *Def. Apol.* (1611) 375 Iulius Cæsar raught out his foot for Pompeius Pœnus to kisse. 1662 J. Davies tr. *Olearius' Voy. Ambass.* 19 Some of us would have reach'd their arms over the Table, to take the Goblet. 1755 Ramsay *To Jas. Clerk* 48 [He] will at naithing stap or stand, That reeks him out a helping hand. 1850 Tennyson *In Mem.* lxxx, Unused example from the grave [shall] Reach out dead hands to comfort me.

b. Of a tree: To extend (its branches).

1613 Shaks. *Hen. VIII*, v. v. 54 He shall flourish, And like a Mountaine Cedar, reach his branches, To all the Plaines about him. 1667 Milton *P.L.* v. 213 Where any row Of Fruit-trees..reachd too far Thir pamperd boughes.

c. To thrust (a weapon) *forth* or *up* by stretching out the arm.

1596 Spenser *F.Q.* iv. iii. 33 At that instant reaching forth his sweard..He smote him. 1819 W. Tennant *Papistry Storm'd* (1827) 93 He raucht his halbert up, and brack An image that stood starin' out.

†**d.** To launch, direct, aim. *Obs.*$^{-1}$

1591 Spenser *M. Hubberd* 840 He would his impudent lewde speache Against Gods holie Ministers oft reach.

2. a. To hold out (a thing) and give (it) *to* a person; to hand *to* one. Also const. with *dat.*, and occas. with simple object.

α. a 1000 *Boeth. Metr.* xxix. 62 Hærfest to honda herbuendum ripa [bleda] receð. c 1000 *Ags. Gosp.* John xiii. 26 He ys se ðe ic ræce [*Hatton MS.* ræche] bedyppedne hlaf. a 1300 *Cursor M.* 3649 (Cott.) Quen it [mete] es dight þou it him reche [*Fairf.* salle þou hit reiche]. c 1369 Chaucer *Dethe Blaunche* 47, I..bade one reche me a booke. 1432–50 tr. *Higden* (Rolls) VII. 35 His stappemoder rechid to hym a pece that he myȝhte drynke. 1535 Coverdale *Ruth* iii. 15 Reach me the cloke yt thou hast on the, & holde it forth. 1581 in *Confer.* ii. (1584) M iij, The Greke testament being reached vnto him, he refused to reade it. 1613 Shaks. *Hen. VIII*, iv. ii. 4 Reach a Chaire, So now (me thinkes) I feele a little ease. 1655 Fuller *Ch. Hist.* i. i. §5 It pleased God with a strong hand and stretched-out Arme, to reach the Gospel unto them. 1760–72 H. Brooke *Fool of Qual.* (1809) II. 59 Taking out your picture.., I reached it to her. 1827 *Blackw. Mag.* Sept. 339/2, I reached him the letter.

absol. a 1300 *Cursor M.* 790 (Cott.) Quen sco þis frutte biheild, Sco..tok and ette and raght adam.

β. 1513 Douglas *Æneis* v. vii. 42 Reik to the man the price promist. 1567 *Satir. Poems Reform.* iii. 230 With that he rais and reikit me this bill. 1862 Hislop *Prov. Scot.* 129 [She] cried 'Reik me this, reik me that'.

b. With advbs., as *back, down, forth, out, round, up.* †Also *to reach up*, to surrender.

a 1400–50 *Alexander* 758 Oþire recouyre me þi rewme, or reche vp þe girdill. *Ibid.* 817 þis renke & his rounsy þai reche vp a croune. 1508 Dunbar *Tua Mariit Wemen* 148 Thai.. raucht the cop round about full off riche wynis. 1548 Udall, etc. *Erasm. Par. Luke* xxiv. 198 [He] brake it, and then raught it forth to theim. 1631 Weever *Anc. Funeral Mon.* 517, I caused some of the Nailes to be reached vp to me. 1642 Rogers *Naaman* 172 Beg of the Lord to reach you out the Lord Jesus. 1760–72 H. Brooke *Fool of Qual.* (1809) III. 5 The burdened trees reached forth fruits of irresistible temptation. 1865 Kingsley *Herew.* iv, The beaker I reach back More rich than I took it.

†**c.** With immaterial object: To give, yield, render; to grant, bestow, communicate, etc. *Obs.*

c 961 Æthelwold *Rule St. Benet* (Schröer 1885) 139 þara anra, þe for neode him þenunge æt þæs mynstres ingange ræcan scylon. a 1300 *Cursor M.* 5308, I sal þe to þe kinge beteche, And siþen þe mi blissing reche. 13.. *E.E. Allit. P.* B. 1369 Vche duk..Schulde com to his court..to reche hym reuerens. c 1470 Henryson *Mor. Fab.* iv. (*Fox's Confess.*) xvi, Heir I reik the [= thee] full remissioun. 1659 Hammond *On Ps.* cxv. 1 Unworthy of the least of all thy goodness, abundantly reached out unto us. a 1718 Rowe (J.), Through such hands The knowledge of the gods is reach'd to man.

3. a. To deal or strike (a blow); †to give (a wound). Const. *to, at,* or dat. Now *rare.*

1375 Barbour *Bruce* ii. 420 To philip sic rout he raucht, ..He gert him galay disyly. c 1400 *Sowdone Bab.* 1347 He raught a stroke to Ferumbras. c 1470 *Golagros & Gaw.* 630 Schir Rannald raught to the renk ane rout wes vnryde. a 1553 Udall *Royster D.* iv. iv. (Arb.) 66, I wish my distaffe will reache hym one rappe. 1577–87 Holinshed *Chron.* II. 57/2 Gegathus raught Haco such a wound, that the vpper part of his liuer appeared bare. 1666 Sancroft *Lex Ignea* 24 God hath reacht us now an Universal Stroke. 1760–72 H. Brooke *Fool of Qual.* (1809) II. 19 A sudden punch which he reached at the nose of his lordship. 1847 Chalmers *Romans* xxx. II. 82 Faith..reaches that exterminating blow whereby the body of sin is destroyed.

†**b.** To give (a kiss). *Obs. rare*$^{-1}$.

13.. *Gaw. & Gr. Knt.* 2351 þou kyssedes my clere wyf, þe cossez me raȝtez.

4. a. To succeed in touching or grasping with the outstretched hand (or with something held in it), or by any similar exertion.

971 *Blickl. Hom.* 207 Se hrof..wæs þæt man mid his handa nealice ȝeræcean mihte. a 1000 *Satan* 169 Eala..þæt ic mid handum ne mæȝ heofon ȝeræcan. a 1300 *Cursor M.* 24464 Me-thoght moght i..wit mi hand him ans reche..I suld ha ben all hale. 1377 Langl. *P. Pl.* B. xi. 353 Who tauȝte hem on trees to tymbre so heighe, There noither buirn ne beste may her briddes rechen. 1530 Palsgr. 680/2, I reche a thyng with my hande... I can nat reache it, myne arme is to shorte. 1591 Shaks. *Two Gent.* iii. i. 156 Wilt thou reach stars, because they shine on thee? a 1704 Locke (J.), Having let down his sounding-line, he reaches no bottom. 1747 Gray *Cat* 22 She stretch'd in vain to reach the prize. 1858 Kingsley *Poems* 113 If I could but reach that hand.

†**b.** To obtain by seizure or otherwise; to procure, gain, acquire, get possession of. *Obs.*

a 900 *O.E. Chron.* an. 885 þa metton hie xvi scipu wicenga & wiþ þa ȝefuhton, & þa scipo alle ȝeræhton, & þa men ofsloȝon. a 1000 *Ibid.* an. 918 Hie ne meahton nanne mete ȝeræcan. 11.. *Ibid.* (MS. C.) an. 1066 Hi ne micte þa brigge oferstiȝan, ne siȝe ȝerechen. a 1250 *Owl & Night.* 106 Tho hit bi-com that he haȝte, And of his eyre briddes y-raȝte. a 1300 *Cursor M.* 1912 þe beist[es] thoght selcutli god þat þai hade raght þair kindle fode. c 1394 *P. Pl. Crede* 733 After ..his rychesse is rauȝt he schal ben redy serued. a 1541 Wyatt *Poet. Wks.* (1861) 67 With hapless hand no man hath raught Such hap as I. 1603 Drayton *Bar. Wars* ii. xlv, Then had yee raught Fames richest Diadem. 1612 —— *Poly-olb.* ix. 290 All his diuelish wit, By which he raught the Wreath.

†**c.** To seize in the hand; to take or lay hold of; to carry off. *Obs.*

c 1330 R. Brunne *Chron.* (1810) 229 A trestille Edward rauht, þat heuy was of pais. c 1375 *Sc. Leg. Saints* xxi. (*Clement*) 453 He..hyre in armys racht & hyre embrasit. a 1400–50 *Alexander* 5284 Scho..raȝt him by þe riȝt hand & raikis to a chambre. c 1470 Harding *Chron.* cv. vi, Great people yt daye the death hath raught. a 1547 Surrey *Æneid* ii. 272 Then raught they hym..twise winding him about. 1591 R. Wilmot *Tancred & Gismunda* iii. iii, She raught the cane, And with her owne sweet hand she gaue it me. 1606 Shaks. *Ant. & Cl.* iv. ix. 30 The hand of death hath raught him. a 1626 Middleton *Mayor of Queenborough* iv. ii. 155, I was surprised by villains, and so raught.

absol. 1667 Milton *P.L.* xi. 94 Least..his now bolder hand Reach also of the Tree of Life, and eat.

transf. 1587 *Mirr. Mag., Porrex* vii, Can I complayne of this reuenge she raught? 1642 Fuller *Holy & Prof. St.* iv. xix. 338 Princes are not to reach, but to trample on recreations.

†**d.** To receive, catch, suffer. *Obs.*

c 1400 *Song Roland* 756 Of the hethyn hound no harm he reches. c 1410 *Sir Cleges* 193 As he knelyd on hys knee, ..He rawght a bowe on hys hede. c 1450 *Mirour Saluacioun* 3554 Of the Jewes cruwelle mykel persecucionne he raght.

†**e.** To fetch, heave (a sigh). *Obs. rare*$^{-1}$.

1582 Stanyhurst *Æneis* i. (Arb) 33 Groane sighs deepe reaching with tears his lyers ful he blubbred.

5. Const. with preps. and advbs. **a.** To take or snatch *from* a person or thing; to take *away, hence, out, up.* Now only *arch.*

a 1400–50 *Alexander* 799* þou must rewle all my realm qwen I am raght hyne. 14.. *Sir Beues* (MS. M) 837 Thes knyghtes, that Beues raught fro Bradmond. 1481 Caxton *Reynard* (Arb.) 22 Tybert..raught out his ryght colyon. 1563 *Mirr. Mag.* ii. *Rich. III*, xx, [The king] of kyngdome I bereft, His life also from him I raught away. 1587 Turberv. *Trag. T., First History*, He raught a truncheon from a pine by chaunce. 1593 Nashe *Christ's T.* (1613) 179 Many in their prime and best yeares are raught hence. 1634 Jackson *Creed* viii. xix. §12 Those bodies, which being alive shall be raught up into the air. 1718 Ramsay *Christ's Kirk Gr.* iii. xviii, They frae a barn a kabar raught. 1863 W. Lancaster *Praeterita* 51 Old confusions, which..Raught from my helm the garland of its praise.

b. To draw or bring towards oneself (esp. to take down) *from* a certain place or position; to lift *up*, take (†or pull) *down*, etc.

c 1450 *Merlin* 697 The damesell..raught hym vp be the honde. 1483 Caxton *Gold. Leg.* 61 b/1 He..ran and raught doun the Calf that they had made. 1545 Ascham *Toxoph.* i. (Arb.) 66 Ill fortune me that daye befell, Whan first my bowe fro the pynne I roughte. 1647 Crashaw *Steps to Temple* 67 Men of martyrdom, that could reach down With strong arms their triumphant crown. 1649 R. Hodges *Plain. Direct.* 17 He raught it from the shelf, when I wrought it with him. 1746 Collins *Ode to Fear* 33 [The Bard] reach'd from Virtue's hand the patriot's steel. 1830 Marryat *King's Own* xxiii, [He] reached down his hat. 1868 Holme Lee *B. Godfrey* viii. 43 She reached from the..shelf her..cup of ink.

†**c.** To take *in, to,* or *unto,* oneself. *Obs.*

1588 Kyd *Househ. Phil.* Wks. (1901) 253 First wold I that the parched earth did riue and raught me in. 1591 Spenser *M. Hubberd* 441 That same [rod] hath Iesus Christ now to him raught. 1660 Bloome *Archit.* C b, Calimachus.. reached unto himselfe the Basket.

6. a. To succeed in touching with a weapon or with the hand in delivering a blow (†hence, to strike or smite).

Beowulf 556 Ic aȝlæcan orde ȝeræhte. 13.. *Guy Warw.* (A.) 1477 Gii þat on wiþ his swerd rauȝt. c 1350 *Will. Palerne* 1193 What rink so he rauȝt he ros neuer after. c 1400 *Sowdone Bab.* 2923 Richard raught him with a barr of bras. c 1489 Caxton *Sonnes of Aymon* ii. 63 He..rought hym wyth soo grete a myghte, that sterke deed he ouerthrew hym. 1609 Heywood *Brit. Troy* xii. cvi, The inuincible Dardanian with one stroke, Raught Aiax Beauer and unplumed his hed. 1809 Roland *Fencing* 126 If you can conveniently reach your adversary upon the longe.

b. To succeed in affecting or influencing by some means; to impress, convince, win over, etc.

1667 Milton *P.L.* iv. 801 Assaying by his Devilish art to reach The Organs of her Fancie. a 1713 Ellwood *Autobiog.* (1714) 45 Being sensible that I was thoroughly reach'd; and the Work of God rightly begun in me. 1851 Dixon *W. Penn* x. (1872) 83 Men's opinions must be reached by reason, not by force. 1887 *Times* (weekly ed.) 14 Oct. 15/3 They [the merchants] know how Chinese are to be reached.

c. *U.S. slang.* To bribe.

1906 A. H. Lewis *Confessions of Detective* 72 I'd been squared; it was known that I could be reached. 1912 A. Train *Courts, Criminals & Camorra* III. ix. 234 In America, if the criminal can 'reach' the complaining witness or 'call him off' he has nothing to worry about. 1929 C. F. Coe *Hooch!* v. 105 You could reach the..Attorney without tippin' your hand to him at all. 1967 L. Katcher *Earl Warren* xvi. 124 It is impossible..to open a big, notorious gambling operation without buying off public officials... This does not necessarily mean a sheriff or a District Attorney or a chief of police is being reached. 1968 W. Safire *New Lang. Politics* 373/1 *Reached*, bought off; corrupted. A public official may be *approached* with no implication of commitment on his part; when he has been *spoken to*, the implication is that he is neutralized or partially persuaded pending a final decision; when he is *reached*, however, he has been bought and sold.

7. a. Of things (or of persons in respect of some part of the body): To come into contact with, to touch; to extend so far as to touch.

a 1225 *Juliana* 56 Hu hit grond in hwet so hit rahte. a 1300 *Cursor M.* 24390 It raght mi hert al thoru þe rote. c 1384 Chaucer *H. Fame* iii. 284 With hir feet she therthe reighte, And with hir heed she touched hevene. 1393 Langl. *P. Pl.* C. xx. 144 þe paume haþ power to..receuen þat þe fyngres rechen. 1667 Milton *P.L.* ii. 1029 A Bridge of wondrous length..reaching th' utmost Orbe Of this frail World. *Ibid.* iv. 988 His stature reacht the Skie. 1704 Pope *Windsor F.* 193 Now his shadow reach'd her as she run, His shadow lengthen'd by the setting sun.

b. Of immaterial things, in various applications derived from 7 a and 8, *esp.* to succeed in affecting or influencing.

c 1400 *Song Roland* 190 To help the, þat no harm þe reche. c 1489 Caxton *Sonnes of Aymon* x. 267 The stroke slided a syde & kyt a sondre all That it rought. 1613 Shaks. *Hen. VIII*, ii. ii. 89 Who can be angry now? What Enuy reach you? a 1625 Beaum. & Fl. *Bonduca* iv. iii, There is no mercy in mankind can reach me. 1675 H. More in R. Ward *Life* (1710) 347 Nor does that [conclusion] reach the present Controversie. 1712 Addison *Spect.* No. 287 ¶3 Liberty should reach every Individual of a People. 1761 Gray *Odin* 48 Pain can reach the Sons of Heav'n! 1786 Burns *Twa Dogs* 213 There's sic parade, sic pomp, an' art, The joy can scarcely reach the heart. 1844 Ld. Brougham *Brit. Const.* xvii. (1861) 259 Libels..which the ordinary process of the law reached, and would have been quite sufficient to punish.

8. a. To come to, arrive at (a place, object, or point in space), to get up to or as far as.

c 1330 R. Brunne *Chron. Wace* (Rolls) 1320 Two dayes þey sailled..lond ne hauene reche þey ne myght. 13.. *E.E. Allit. P.* B. 10 Reken with reverence þay rechen his auter. 1563 B. Googe *Eglogs*, etc. (Arb.) 109 Now was the Son got vp aloft, and raught the mydle Lyne. 1609 Holland *Amm. Marcell.* xxv. vi. 273 Sooner than a man would have thought [they] raught the banke on the further side. 1684 R. Waller *Nat. Exper.* 110 The point not onely again reacht the Line, but passed beyond it. 1709 Steele *Tatler* No. 107 ¶2 You may easily reach Harwich in a Day. 1808 Scott *Marm.* i. xi, The steps of stone, By which you reach the donjon gate. 1860 Tyndall *Glac.* i. xiv. 96 Brought him to rest before he had reached the bottom.

b. With personal object, in various applications. Now *esp.*, to communicate with (a person).

1706 E. Ward *Wooden World Diss.* (1708) 22 Those strong unexpected Turnadoes..sometimes reach him as far as Brasil and Jamaica. 1894 Hall Caine *Manxman* iii. xv. 177 Pete's letter had reached him. 1919 E. O'Neill *Moon of Caribbees* 113 Ut is only from your chance meetin' wid Harry..that I happen to know where to reach you. 1967 D. Francis *Blood Sport* v. 55 The two drivers, reached by telephone, met us by appointment. 1973 R. Ludlum *Matlock Paper* xiii. 122 I'm off the phone now. Would you like to try reaching Miss Ballantyne?

c. Of sounds: To come to (the ear, a person or place).

1649 G. Daniel *Trinarch., Hen. IV*, lxxx, Fame had before the escape of Richard told..wch raught her open Ears. 1671 Milton *Samson* 177, I hear the sound of words; thir sense the air Dissolves unjointed e're it reach my ear. 1727 Gay *Fables* i. xxxi. 11 My name, perhaps, hath reach'd your ear. 1784 Cowper *Task* ii. 5 Where rumour of oppression and deceit..Might never reach me more! 1828 Scott *F.M. Perth* xix, The alarm reached the royal residence. 1874 Micklethwaite *Mod. Par. Churches* 10 Every syllable should reach the ears of the auditors.

d. Of the eye, a gun, etc.: To carry to (a point).

1667 Milton *P.L.* xii. 556 Eternitie, whose end no eye can reach. 1669 Sturmy *Mariner's Mag.* v. xii. 72 What degree the Gun must be Mounted to, to reach the Mark. 1732 Pope *Ess. Man* i. 240 What no eye can see, No glass can reach.

9. To arrive at, to attain or come to (a point in time, a condition, quality, etc.): **a.** of persons.

1590 Spenser *F.Q.* i. vi. 29 Till ryper yeares he raught. 1604 Shaks. *Oth.* i. ii. 24 As proud a Fortune As this that I haue reach'd. 1647–8 Cotterell *Davila's Hist. Fr.* (1678) 2, I hope I shall be able to reach the proper order. 1709 Pope *Ess. Criticism* 145 Nameless graces which no methods teach, And which a master-hand alone can reach. 1727 Gay *Fables* i. xxxix. 35 He reach'd the height of power and place. 1789 *Trifler* No. 35. 448 Our poets..frequently reach the climax of absurdity. 1801 Strutt *Sports & Past.* ii. i. 60, I believe few, if any, of the modern archers in long shooting, reach four hundred yards. **1874** GREEN *Short Hist.* v. §3. 228 Wyclif..had already reached middle age.

b. of things.

1667 MILTON *P.L.* III. 197 Thy desire..leads to no excess That reaches blame. **1691** LOCKE *Lower. Interest* Wks. 1727 II. 7 But supposing the Law reach'd the Intention of the Promoters of it. **1724** A. COLLINS *Gr. Chr. Rel.* 215 The means..will not reach that end. **1784** COWPER *Task* I. 696 In the eye Of public note, they reach their perfect size. *Ibid.* IV. 662 His faculties..there only reach their proper use. **1888** BURGON *Lives 12 Gd. Men* x. II. 262 This little work reached a second edition.

10. a. To succeed in understanding or comprehending. ? *Obs.*

1605 B. JONSON *Volpone* IV. i, *Sir P.* I reach you not. *Lady P.* Right, sir, your policy May bear it through thus. *a* **1627** MIDDLETON *Wom. beware Wom.* v. i, But how her fawning partner fell I reach not. **1662** DRYDEN *Wild Gallant* IV. i, I do not reach your meaning, Sir. *a* **1715** BURNET *Hist. Ref.* III. Pref. 3 The Meaning of this dark Expression I do not reach. *a* **1822** SHELLEY *Tasso* 16 The words are twisted in some double sense That I reach not.

b. To succeed in acquiring or obtaining.

1638 JUNIUS *Paint. Ancients* 303 Zenodorus..could not reach the art of tempering the metalls as it was used by the ancients. *c* **1709** PRIOR *Charity* 4 Had I all knowledge..That thought can reach, or science can define. **1782** COWPER *Charity* 304 Knowledge such as..only sympathy like thine could reach. **1842** J. AITON *Domest. Econ.* (1857) 318 Paying a small sum yearly,..according as I could conveniently reach it.

11. To stretch; to draw or pull *out* †or *in*; †to extend (one's power). *Obs.* exc. *dial.* (Cf. RATCH *v.*[1] 3, RETCH *v.*[1])

971 *Blickl. Hom.* 191 Min heafod sceal beon on eorþan ȝecyrred, & mine fet to heofenum ȝereahte. *c* **1275** *Serving Christ* 5 in *O.E. Misc.* 90 Crist..on rode was rauht. **1297** R. GLOUC. (Rolls) 4829 Ȝoure fon ssolle hor poer among ow wide reche. *a* **1375** *Lay Folks Mass Bk.* App. iv. 348 He rauhte þe Rolle..Wiþ his teth. ? *a* **1400** *Morte Arth.* 2549 Than they raughte in the reyne and a-gayne rydes. *c* **1420** *Pallad. on Husb.* IV. 682 An huge breste, No litel wombe, and wel out raught the side. **1607** TOPSELL *Four-f. Beasts* (1658) 167 Whilest the members are reached and stretched with many strains and convulsions. **1648–60** HEXHAM *Dutch Dict.*, *Het leder Recken*, to Stretch or Reach out leather. **1823** MOOR *Suffolk Words* s.v. *Reech*, A pair of small shoes require to be reached.

II. Intransitive senses.

12. a. To make a stetch *with* the arm or hand; to extend the arm, hold out the hand. Also of the arm or hand: To stretch out.

Beowulf (Z.) 748 Ræhte onȝean feond mid folme. *a* **1225** *Ancr. R.* 338 Hwon God beot þe, recheð forð mid boðe honden. *c* **1305** *St. Andrew* 95 in *E.E.P.* (1862) 101 Here armes whan hi vpward reiȝte bicome as stif as treo. *c* **1400** N. LOVE *Bonavent. Mirr.* xxxix. (B.N.C.) lf. 92 The disciples seten..so þat þey alle myȝte reche into þe myddes and ete of one disshe. **1538** STARKEY *England* I. ii. 48 The ye to se,.. the fote to go, the hand to hold and rech. **1667** MILTON *P.L.* IX. 779 What hinders then To reach, and feed at once both Bodie and Mind? **1785** BURNS *Jolly Beggars* 5th Air, Let me ryke up to dight that tear.

b. Const. *to* or *unto* (a person or thing), usually with implication of catching (†or striking) at. Now only *dial.* (also *absol.*, to help oneself at table).

a **1000** *Satan* 437 Efe..ræhte þa mid handum to heofoncyninge. **13..** *Sir Beues* (A.) 2445 Þe lionesse seyȝe þat sight And rauȝt to B[eues], with out faile. *c* **1400** *Destr. Troy* 10882 Ho raght to hym radly, reft hym his sheld. **1586** J. HOOKER *Hist. Irel.* in *Holinshed* II. 7/1 But these two.. raught to their weapons. **1671** H. M. tr. *Erasm. Colloq.* 192 Reach to the Pompions, there's an end of the Lettices. **1674** BREVINT *Saul at Endor* 232 This Paiment, however, reacht to, is, they say, presented to God by the Pope. **1847** HALLIWELL, *Reach-to*, to reach out one's hand, so as to help oneself. **1890** AUSTIN CLARE *For Love of Lass* iii, Now do as the missus bids you, and reach to. Your father's son'll be always welcome at my table.

c. Const. *after*, *for* (a thing). ***to reach for the roof, sky***, etc. (orig. *U.S.*), of a person held at gunpoint: to raise the hands above the head; ***to reach for one's gun***, etc., used *fig.* for: to react with extreme hostility.

The statement in quot. 1953 is commonly attributed to the German Nazi leader H. Goering (1893–1946), but it has been traced (in a slightly different form) to the nationalistic play *Schlageter* (1933) by the German dramatist H. Johst (1890–1978): see *Oxf. Dict. Quotations* (ed. 3, 1980).

c **1386** CHAUCER *Prol.* 136 Whan she dronken hadde hir draughte, ffful semely after hir mete she raughte. **1571** CAMPION *Hist. Irel.* II. ix. (1633) 118 A Gentleman..raught in the morning for some paper. **1591** SPENSER *M. Hubberd* 1336 Rouzing up himselfe, for his rough hide He gan to reach. **1737** [S. BERINGTON] *G. de Lucca's Mem.* (1738) 33, I was..reaching for my Sword to defend myself to the last Gasp. **1904** L. TRACY *King of Diamonds* iii. 39 He reached over for the stone. **1910** W. M. RAINE *B. O'Connor* ii. 25 Now reach for the roof. **1927** *Ladies' Home Jrnl.* Dec. 6/3, I reached for the stars pronto, without even turning my head. **1931** W. JAMES *Sun Up* 42 'Stick em up,' I says... One of 'em flinches some but finally reaches for the sky. **1953** in *Oxf. Dict. Quotations* (ed. 2) 223/2 When I hear anyone talk of Culture, I reach for my revolver. **1959** *Spectator* 9 Oct. 480/2 Cherwell was not a cultured man; indeed he seems almost to have reached for his gun when 'culture' was in the air. **1967** *Guardian* 12 Oct. 9/6 This is the point at which Laing's critics reach for their guns. **1968** R. F. ADAMS *Western Words* (ed. 2) 245/2 *Reach for the sky!*, a gunman's command to raise the hands in the air. **1980** *Listener* 14 Aug. 200/1 Members of PRO Dogs..will..be reaching for their choke-chains because..criticism of..dogs is a treasonable activity.

d. To grasp or clutch *at.* (*lit.* and *fig.*)

1562 J. HEYWOOD *Prov. & Epigr.* (1867) 106 Master Sexten..Gredily raught at a goblet of wyne. **1593** SHAKS. *2 Hen. VI*, I. ii. 11 Put forth thy hand, reach at the glorious Gold. **1655** FULLER *Ch. Hist.* IX. Ded., The Third reached not at all at Honor. **1732** NEAL *Hist. Purit.* (1822) I. 66 Stretching the laws to reach at those whom they could not fairly come at an other way. **1818** KEATS *Endym.* III. 372 Wherefore reach At things which, but for thee,..Had been my dreary death?

e. *fig.* of mental striving.

1646 P. BULKELEY *Gospel Covt.* II. 131 The soule is of an intelligent nature, reaching after the knowledge of high and hidden things. **1845–6** TRENCH *Huls. Lect.* Ser. II. vii. 261 Some of old had been reaching out after this. **1870** J. H. NEWMAN *Gram. Assent* I. v. 109 His mind reaches forward with a strong presentiment to the thought of a Moral Governor. **1935** W. G. HARDY *Father Abraham* IV. i. 349 But Abraham strode along and snuffed the air and was tender to Sarai as he helped her on and felt his whole heart reaching out to her.

f. To make an unwarranted inference; to jump to a conclusion; to guess. orig. and chiefly *U.S.*

1960 'E. MCBAIN' *Give Boys Great Big Hand* x. 106 This may be reaching, but here it is anyway, for what it's worth. **1963** 'G. BAGBY' *Murder's Little Helper* xii. 149 Anderson moaned. 'Inspector,' he said, 'Isn't that reaching?' **1964** L. TREAT in H. Waugh *Merchants of Menace* (1969) 11 The way he saw things, the Lieutenant was sure reaching for it—far out. **1973** G. MOFFAT *Lady with Cool Eye* xi. 130 Dawson.. might very well be visiting Mrs Wolkoff..but no: as the Americans say, we're reaching. **1978** R. LUDLUM *Holcroft Covenant* xviii. 212 'Aren't you reaching, Miles?'.. 'I said it was a theory, but not without some support.'

13. a. To make a stretch of a certain length; to succeed in stretching one's arm, etc., so far.

a **1300** *Cursor M.* 1840 Na creatur in liue..moght to grund or reche or riue. *Ibid.* 11673 Þe frut hu sulde man reche vnto. **13..** *Sir Beues* (A) 1623 [Beues] knette þe rop þar while Ase hiȝ ase a miȝte reche. *c* **1402** LYDG. *Compl. Bl. Knt.* xvi, With myn hede unto the welle I raughte. *c* **1450** *Merlin* 344 He lifte vp his swerde..and he slytte the shelde as fer as that he raught. **1484** CAXTON *Fables of Æsop* II. xiii, He cowde not reche to the mete with his mouthe. **1535** COVERDALE *Eccl.* vii. 23 She wente..so depe that I might not reach vnto her. **1581** J. BELL *Haddon's Answ. Osor.* 471 By reaching beyond his reach, he reacheth nothing at all. **1590** SHAKS. *Mids. N.* III. ii. 289, I am not yet so low, But that my nailes can reach vnto thine eyes. **1667** MILTON *P.L.* VI. 140 With solitarie hand Reaching beyond all limit.

absol. **1667** MILTON *P.L.* IX. 593 All other Beasts.. envying stood, but could not reach.

b. *transf.* and *fig.* in various applications.

a **1300** *Cursor M.* 27332 Als ferre als he may reche, þe forme o scrift til him he teche. **1570–6** LAMBARDE *Peramb. Kent* (1826) 257 As farre as I can reache by coniecture. **1591** SHAKS. *Two Gent.* I. ii. 87 *Lu.* Melodious were it, would you sing it. *Ju.* And why not you? *Lu.* I cannot reach so high. **1611** BIBLE *Lev.* v. 7 *marg.*, His hand cannot reach to the sufficiencie of a lambe. **1633** BP. HALL *Hard Texts, N.T.* 51 This Woman hath herein reached beyond your conceit. **1653** H. MORE *Antid. Ath.* II. vii. §5, I might now reach out to Exotick Plants.

14. a. To stretch out (continuously), to extend; to project a certain distance (*above, beyond*, etc.).

α. *a* **1000** *Riddles* lxvii. 7 (Gr.) Ic eom mare þonne þes middanȝeard..wide ræce ofer engla eard. *a* **1000** *Cædmon's Gen.* 990 Ræhton wide ȝeond werþeoda wrohtes telȝan. *a* **1300** *Cursor M.* 2232 Do we wel and make a toure,..þat may reche heghur þan heuen. *Ibid.* 8080 (Gött.) Lang and side þair broues wern And recched al a-boute þair ern. ? *a* **1366** CHAUCER *Rom. Rose* 1022 Hir tresses yelowe..Unto hir helys down they raughten. *c* **1400** MAUNDEV. (Roxb.) iii. 9 Þe schadowe rechez vnto Lempny. **1526** *Pilgr. Perf.* (W. de W. 1531) 77 b, Saynt Austyn asketh a questyon: How hye recheth the hous of perfeccyon. **1623** GOUGE *Serm. Extent God's Provid.* §15 A partition..which reached up to the floore of the garret. **1687** A. LOVELL tr. *Thevenot's Trav.* I. 21 The Portico..reaches along the whole front of the Church. **1751** LABELYE *Westm. Br.* 28 These Frames reached about 2 Feet above the common High-water Mark. **1822** LATHAM *Gen. Hist. Birds* II. 63 The wings reach very little beyond the base. **1875** BRYCE *Holy Rom. Emp.* v. (ed. 5) 72 These vast domains, reaching from the Ebro to the Carpathian mountains.

β. *c* **1375** *Sc. Leg. Saints* xviii. (*Egipciane*) 1320 Þe sone cane fare bemys strek, þat fra þe hewine til erd can rek. **1462** *Extr. Burgh Rec. Peebles* (1872) 144 The sayde..akeris of land..on the northt half of the gat rekand to the Wenlaw. **1513** DOUGLAS *Æneis* III. ix. 12 His berd Rekand doun the lenth neir of a ȝerd. **1824** MACTAGGART *Gallovid. Encycl.* 191 He sought for through-ban's that wad rike.

b. Of immaterial things, in various applications.

a **1000** *Sal. & Sat.* 293 Yldo..ræceþ wide langre linan. **1340** HAMPOLE *Pr. Consc.* 6311 Þe mercy of God..reches over alle, bathe fer and nere. **1443** *Pol. Poems* (Rolls) II. 211 Hir contemplacioun rauht up to the hevene. **1535** COVERDALE *Dan.* iv. 22 Thy greatnesse increaseth, and reacheth vnto the heauen. *a* **1656** HALES *Gold. Rem.* (1688) 1 How far his intent and meaning reacht. **1718** *Freethinker* No. 2. 10 His Jurisdiction reaches even to the Councils of Princes. **1769** *Junius Lett.* i. 9 It reaches beyond the interest of individuals. **1871** FREEMAN *Norm. Conq.* (1876) IV. xviii. 131 The exclusion of Englishmen reached even to men of Norman descent born in England. **1935** B. MALINOWSKI in M. Black *Importance of Lang.* (1962) 90 A word rich in associations and reaching out in many directions.

c. Of a period of time, or with reference to duration of time.

1340 HAMPOLE *Pr. Consc.* 554 Þe tother part..reches fra þe begynnyng Of mans lyfe un-til þe endyng. **1535** COVERDALE *Lev.* xxvi. 5 The wyne haruest shal reache vnto the sowynge tyme. **1622** CALLIS *Stat. Sewers* (1647) 110 These things..do reach from the beginning of the Lease to the top of the Inheritance. **1711** ADDISON *Spect.* No. 159 ¶4 That Portion of Eternity which is called Time,..reaching from the Beginning of the World to its Consummation. **1951** M. MCLUHAN *Mech. Bride* (1967) 132/2 Some interesting assumptions that reach back more than two centuries.

d. To suffice, be adequate or sufficient *to* (also with *infin.*). Chiefly of money. ? *Obs.*

1377 LANGL. *P. Pl.* B. XIV. 230 His rentes ne wol nauȝte reche, no riche metes to bugge. **1456** SIR G. HAYE *Law Arms* (S.T.S.) 168 He aw till allow thai gudis as payment of his costis..in alsferr as thai mycht reke. **1642** ROGERS *Naaman* 159 Abilities will not reach to suffer for God, though they seeme to act for him. *a* **1657** BRADFORD *Plymouth Plant.* (1856) 215 Every one was to pay..what yᵉ profite of yᵉ trade would not reach too. **1733** TULL *Horse-Hoeing Husb.* xi. (Dubl.) 142 As much of the middle sort of Wheat as his Money would reach to purchase.

e. To amount *to.*

1596 SHAKS. *1 Hen. IV*, IV. i. 129 *Hotsp.* What may the Kings whole Battaile reach vnto? *Ver.* To thirty thousand. **1887** STUBBS *Mediæv. & Mod. Hist.* 360 Another sum of the same amount, reaching..to £120,000.

15. †**a.** To move, proceed, go, spread. *Obs.*

Some examples would also admit of being taken in sense 16, the history of which is somewhat obscure, in the absence of quotations for the 15th and 16th centuries.

a **1000** *Riddles* xvi. 27 (Gr.) Siþþan ic þurh hylles hrof ȝeræce. *c* **1205** LAY. 16265 Bruttes weoren balde & rehten ouer walde. *c* **1330** R. BRUNNE *Chron. Wace* (Rolls) 5003 Tydynges ronne, þat ouer al reches;..þat Romayns were aryue on land. *c* **1374** CHAUCER *Troylus* II. 447 Up he stert & on his way he raught. *a* **1400–50** *Alexander* 3852 Þus raȝt he fra þis reuer be many ruȝe waies.

†**b.** To go *on*, or proceed *to* (a place or point); to run *into*; to penetrate *to*. *Obs.*

a **1300** *Cursor M.* 15788 (Cott.) Ilk dint þat þai him gaf it reked to þe ban. *c* **1400** *Beryn* 168 To othir placis of holynes þey rauȝte. *a* **1400–50** *Alexander* 5510 [Alexander] Raȝt on to þe reede See & rerid þare his tentis. *c* **1425** WYNTOUN *Cron.* I. x. 554 Fra north on sowth the streme it strekys In tyll the Rede Se quhille it rekys.

c. *Naut.* To sail on a reach; (see also quot. 1867).

1832 MARRYAT *N. Forster* v, The sloop wearing round, reached in for the land. **1867** SMYTH *Sailor's Word-bk.*, *Reaching*, sometimes used for standing off and on... A vessel also reaches ahead of her adversary. **1884** *Hunt's Yachting Mag.* Apr. 150 A rattling breeze..got up..and she reached along like a schooner.

16. a. To attain or succeed in coming *to* a place, point, person, etc.; †to come *up* (to). Also *absol. spec.* in *Baseball*: to reach first base.

1632 J. HAYWARD tr. *Biondi's Eromena* 21 Posting on with such diligence that by darke night hee reached to Caleri. **1651** CROMWELL *Let.* 4 Aug. in Carlyle, To give the enemy some check, until we shall be able to reach up to him. **1719** DE FOE *Crusoe* I. xviii. (1840) 318 They could not reach back to the boat before it was dark. **1749** FIELDING *Tom Jones* III. vii, The public voice..seldom reaches to a brother or a husband, tho' it rings in the ears of all the neighbourhood. **1802** H. MARTIN *Helen of Glenross* III. 19 When we had reached to this stage of our proposed journey. **1891** *Young Man* Apr. 128/1, I sent letter upon letter after him, but they don't seem to reach. **1974** *Anderson* (S. Carolina) *Independent* 20 Apr. 6A/6 The Cavs tied it in their half of the inning as Duval White reached on an error, stole second, went to third on Dan Berstein's first of four hits and scored on Jonathan Williams' fly ball. **1976** *Billings* (Montana) *Gaz.* 6 July 1-C/3 Dan Fuchs reached on an error, Rich Popp singled to score Knudtson, and Mike Klunder brought Fuchs home on a sacrifice fly.

b. With other constructions. Also with specification of distance covered in attaining to a point.

1591 R. WILMOT *Tancred & Gismunda* I. ii, He neuer sought, with vast huge mounting towers To reach aloft, and ouer-view our raigne. **1622** DRAYTON *Poly-olb.* xxii. 1222 Hastings that before raught hither with his rear, And with King Edward join'd. **1627** SIR R. GRANVILLE in *Ld. Lansdowne's Wks.* (1732) II. 336 We had not raught a musket-shot out of the Town. **1760–72** H. BROOKE *Fool of Qual.* (1809) IV. 138 At length, reaching near the door. **1799** E. DU BOIS *Piece Family Biog.* III. 55 Continually receding until they have both reached as far as they can go.

c. Of the eye, a gun, etc.: To carry.

1632 HOLLAND *Cyrupædia* 166 They gave backe from thence foot by foot..so farre as a dart shot raught from the wall. **1698** FRYER *Acc. E. India & P.* 40 The Power of the English, who command as far as their Guns reach. **1885** G. ALLEN *Babylon* i, As far as the eye could reach in either direction.

17. a. To attain *to* an achievement, condition, etc. Now *rare* or *Obs.*

a **1300** *Cursor M.* 20026 A thusand year moght i noght reke..Til tend part of hir louing. **1303** R. BRUNNE *Handl. Synne* 1930 Alle þe penaunce þat þou mayst do Ne may nat reche here godenes to. *c* **1330** —— *Chron.* (1810) 195 In armes is þer none þat to þie renoun reches. **1594** SHAKS. *Rich. III*, I. i. 159 Another secret close intent, By marrying her, which I must reach vnto. **1603** OWEN *Pembrokeshire* vii. (1891) 55 Great aboundance of Wheat, barlie and other graine, not rechinge in finenes to Castlemartyn. **1633** BP. HALL *Hard Texts O.T.* 373 By no humane meanes which thou canst reach unto.

b. Const. with *infin.* Now *rare.*

a **1300** *Cursor M.* 11385 Elles moght not kinges thre Haf raght to ride sa ferr ewai. **1387** TREVISA *Higden* (Rolls) II. 217 And he may not reche for to greue oþere, þan he bycomeþ angry and cruel to hym self. **1871** FARRAR *Witn. Hist.* iv. 142 They could only reach to lay their garlands of admiration at his feet.

†**c.** To attain *to* (knowledge of). *Obs.*

1582 N. T. (Rhem.) *Mark* vi. 3 *note*, His countrie-folks.. not reaching to his godhead and divine generation did take offence or scandal of him. **1594** HOOKER *Eccl. Pol.* III. viii. §6 Festus..heard him, but could not reach unto that whereof he spake. **1653** H. MORE *Antid. Ath.* II. v. §5 To conclude there is no such thing as Reason and Demonstration because a natural Fool cannot reach unto it.

18. To undergo stretching. *rare*. Now only *dial.*

1362 LANGL. *P. Pl.* A. IV. 148 Bi him that rauhte on the roode. *c*1440 *Promp. Parv.* 425/1 Rechyn, as lethyr, *dilato, extendo*. 1570 LEVINS *Manip.* 88/32 To Reche, *distendi*. 1823 MOOR *Suffolk Words*, s.v. *Reech*, If your hat be too small it will 'reech i' the wearing'.

†**19.** To start up. *Obs.*⁻¹

*a*1450 *Le Morte Arth.* 3191 Hys chambyrlayns wakyd hym ther wt all, And woodely oute of hys slepe he raught.

reach (riːtʃ), *v.*[2] Now only *dial.* (cf. RETCH *v.*[2]). Also 5 areche, 6–7 reche. [OE. *hrǽcan*, = ON. *hrǽkja* to spit, f. OE. *hráca*, ON. *hráki* spittle, expectorated matter.

The apparent absence of the word in literature from the OE. period to the 15th c. is remarkable, but there can be no doubt of its continuity.]

†**1. a.** *intr.* To spit; also, to make an effort to clear the throat, to hawk. *Obs.*

*c*897 K. ÆLFRED *Gregory's Past. C.* v. 43 Ʒif he ðonne ðæt wif wille forsacan, ðonne hræce hio him on ðæt neb foran. *c*1000 *Sax. Leechd.* I. 148 Wið ʒeposu & wið þæt man hefelice hræce, ʒenim ðas wyrte [etc.]. [*c*1460 J. RUSSELL *Bk. Nurture* 290 Areche, ne spitt to ferre, ner be ye slow of herynge.] 1545 RAYNOLD *Byrth Mankynde* 58 Crieng or reching so loude as she can, so to stere her selfe. 1565 COOPER *Thesaurus*, *Screo*, to reache in spittyng.

†**b.** *trans.* To spit or bring *up* (blood or phlegm). *Obs.*

*c*1000 *Sax. Leechd.* I. 142 Ʒyf hwa blod swiþe hræce, ʒenime ðysse ylcan wyrte [etc.]. *c*1550 LLOYD *Treas. Health* (1585) L ij, Gume of a Peache tre geuen to hym that rechit or spitteth bloud, helpeth greatly. 1601 HOLLAND *Pliny* II. 59 For them that raught vp bloud at the mouth, he prescribeth to take Mints in a broth. 1606 —— *Sueton.* 189 Hee never durst once spit and reach up fleame.

2. *intr.* To make efforts to vomit; to retch.

In 18th c. freq. ***to reach to vomit*** (cf. REACHING *vbl. sb.*[2]).

1575 GASCOIGNE *Hearbes* Wks. 165, I poore soule which close in caban laye, And there had reacht til gaule was welneare burst. 1636 BRATHWAIT *Rom. Emp.* 47 As hee was reaching or striving to vomit. 1748 RICHARDSON *Clarissa* (1811) IV. xliii. 285, I shall reach confoundedly, and bring up some clotted blood. *a*1776 R. JAMES *Diss. Fevers* (1778) 51 She..reached to vomit very much.

reachable (ˈriːtʃəb(ə)l), *a.* [f. REACH *v.*[1]]

†**1.** Able to reach *to*. *Obs. rare*⁻¹.

1633 T. ADAMS *Exp. 2 Peter* ii. 10 A tower reachable to heaven!

2. a. That may be reached. Also, as *sb.*, one who may be reached (in quot. 1974, denoting a person who can be bribed).

1824 L. M. HAWKINS *Mem.* II. 5 *note*, My father..had strong oak shutters put on the outside of all the reachable windows in our house. 1873 W. S. MAYO *Never Again* xvii. 229 If through the sense of smell Her heart were reachable. 1914 R. & E. SHACKLETON *Four on Tour in Eng.* xviii. 186 Few visitors go to Runnimede [*sic*], because it has not been a readily reachable place by rail. 1974 *Publishers Weekly* 27 May 31 (Advt.), The secret deals behind the rip-off, put-down and sell-out of the American people..to Big Money interests..with the help of the reachables in office! 1978 *Detroit Free Press* 5 Mar. A4/1 Most buds and twigs and other reachable food are gone. If snow is deep enough, deer cannot escape.

b. *Math.* That may be reached (from a specified point) by passing along the lines of a graph.

1959 *Sociometry* XXII. 143 The matrix M contains all these paths and also a path of length l from each point to itself. Thus each point is reachable from itself. 1965 F. HARARY et al. *Structural Models* ii. 43 Point v is reachable from u in a digraph D if and only if there is a sequence from u to v. 1978 D. D. ŠILJAK *Large-Scale Dynamic Syst.* iii. 149 A reachable set $V_i(v_j)$ of a point v_j is a set of points v_i reachable from v_j.

Hence **reacha'bility** *Math.*, the possibility of reaching one point of a graph from another; freq. *attrib.*

1959 *Sociometry* XXII. 141 We present a logical sequence of theorems that characterize strengthening and weakening group members... We..find it convenient to introduce the concept of the 'reachability matrix' of a group. 1965 F. HARARY et al. *Structural Models* ii. 43 Reachability is reflexive since every point of V is reachable from itself by a path of length 0. *Ibid.* 45 The difference between reachability and joining is that in the latter instance we ignore the direction of the lines. *Ibid.* v. 117 The reachability matrix $R(D)$ whose entries are denoted r_{ij} and defined as follows: $r_{ij} = 1$ if v_j is reachable from v_i; otherwise $r_{ij} = 0$. 1978 D. D. ŠILJAK *Large-Scale Dynamic Syst.* iii. 149 The reachability concept of digraphs.

reache, variant of RECCHE *v. Obs.*

reached, *ppl. a. rare*⁻¹. [? f. REACH *v.*[1] 11.] ? Stretched, strained.

1650 WEEKES *Truth's Confl.* ii. 45 It doth arise from their own reached and unworthy carriages towards God.

reachelesse, obs. form of RECKLESS.

reacher (ˈriːtʃə(r)). [f. REACH *v.*[1] + -ER[1].]

1. a. One who or that which reaches.

1594 GREENE & LODGE *Looking Gl.* G.'s Wks. (Rtldg.) 120/1 Hold in your rapier; for though I have not a long reacher, I have a short hitter. 1598 FLORIO, *Recatore*, a bringer, a reacher. 1667 WOOD *Life* (O.H.S.) II. 111 [Prynne] spoke to Jennings the reacher of the records that he should let him have any record. 1819 BYRON *Juan* II. clxv, The highest reachers Of eloquence in piety and prose. 1899 *Daily News* 9 Oct. 6/2 Shamrock..has proved herself to be a good runner, a fine reacher.

†**b.** A certain type of beggar. *Obs.*⁻¹

1607 DEKKER *Jests to make you Merry* 35 There is a new company arising,..and these call themselues Reachers, they walke together Male and Female [etc.].

†**2.** An exaggerated statement, 'stretcher'. *Obs.*

1613 PURCHAS *Pilgrimage* II. x. (1614) 157 Adrian had a Vineyard eighteen miles square, which hee hedged with those slaine carkasses, as high as a man can reach (a reacher I thinke). *a*1661 FULLER *Worthies, Monmouth.* IV. (1662) 51, I can hardly believe that Reacher, which another writeth of him, that with the palms of his hands he could touch his knees, though he stood upright.

3. *Yachting.* (See quot. 1903.)

1903 *Outing* XLII. 646/2 Intermediate between the baby and the balloon are various jib-topsails called 'reachers' and numbered 1, 2, 3, according to the size. 1977 P. JOHNSON *Offshore Manual Internat.* 152 Under the rule 'jibs' includes all fore and after headsails such as genoas, staysails, big-boy/bloopers, reachers and drifters.

reaching (ˈriːtʃɪŋ), *vbl. sb.*[1] [f. as prec.]

1. a. The action of REACH *v.*[1], in its various senses. Also with *out*, *up*.

*c*950 *Lindisf. Gosp.* John *Intr.* 7/3 Mið ræcing [L. *porrectione*]. *Ibid.* 8/11 Mið racing honda [L. *extensione manuum*]. *c*1440 *Promp. Parv.* 425/2 Rechynge, or stretchynge, *extensio*. 1591 PERCIVALL *Sp. Dict.*, *Alcance*, ouertaking, obteining, pursuing, reaching. 1662 BETTY VERNEY 19 Apr. in *Mem. Verney Fam.* (1899) IV. 21 The reaching up of my armes. 1760 LAW *Spir. Prayer* I. 55 A natural..reaching after that eternal light. 1875 WHITNEY *Life Lang.* viii. 138 The reaching-out of the bodily organs. 1884 *Sat. Rev.* 14 June 783/2 According to all accepted tenets, mere running and reaching [in yacht-racing] is poor work.

b. With *a* and *pl.* An instance of this.

1785 BURKE *Sp. Nabob Arcot* Wks. 1842 I. 333 All the reachings and graspings of a vivacious mind. 1846 RUSKIN *Mod. Paint.* (1883) II. I. i, Reachings forward unto the things that are before. 1871 SPENCER *Princ. Psych.* II. §300. 82 All reasoning..is a reaching of the unknown through the known.

†**2.** A reach or stretch of country. *Obs.*⁻¹

1727 in M. A. Richardson *Hist. Table-bk. Leg. Div.* (1843) I. 401 There are many hills and reachings for many miles.

3. *Comb.* (in sense 15c of the vb.) ***reaching foresail, jib, sail, staysail***; **reaching-post** (see quot.).

1948 R. DE KERCHOVE *Internat. Maritime Dict.* (ed. 2) 581/2 *Reaching foresail*, a triangular sail which sets on the forestay... Also called Genoa foresail, Genoa jib. 1924 G. H. P. MUHLHAUSER *Cruise of Amaryllis* vii. 273 There is now rather more wind and we are carrying reaching jib and staysail. 1815 BURNEY *Falconer's Mar. Dict.*, *Reaching-Post*, in rope-making, a post..fixed in the ground at the lower-end of a rope-walk. It is used in stretching the yarn by means of a tackle. 1962 D. F. SOUTHERN in A. Garrett *Roving Commissions* 11 It was sunny, warm and most pleasant running under our large reaching sail. 1924 G. H. P. MUHLHAUSER *Cruise of Amaryllis* vii. 273 At sunset I changed to the working jib but left the reaching staysail.

'reaching, *vbl. sb.*[2] Now *dial.* [f. REACH *v.*[2]] The action of retching †or (in OE.) spitting. Also *pl.* (freq. in 18th c.).

*c*1000 *Sax. Leechd.* II. 174 Þis sint tacn adlies maʒan; ærest ʒelome spætunga oððe hræcunga. 1601 HOLLAND *Pliny* XXIV. iv, The said barke..is greatly commended for the reaching and spitting of blood. 1655 CULPEPPER *Riverius* I. vi. 24 Coughing, Yawning, Reaching, and Hiccoughs. 1719 DE FOE *Crusoe* (1858) 481 First hungry, then sick again, with reachings to vomit. 1777 G. FORSTER *Voy. round World* II. 238 They groaned most pitifully, had violent reachings. 1791 J. WOODFORDE *Diary* 7 June (1927) III. 275 She was..very much swelled in the face by reaching and very weak.

reaching (ˈriːtʃɪŋ), *ppl. a.* [f. REACH *v.*[1] + -ING[2].] That reaches, in senses of the vb.

1. Of the hand, etc.: Stretching out to or after something; able to reach far.

1593 SHAKS. *2 Hen. VI*, IV. vii. 86 Great men haue reaching hands. 1681 T. FLATMAN *Heraclitus Ridens* No. 31 (1713) I. 200 A sad Experiment I have made Of the long reaching Arm of Kings. 1817 KEATS *Sleep & Poetry* 362 Fauns and satyrs taking aim At swelling apples with a frisky leap And reaching fingers.

b. Characterized by reaching forward (with the legs. Cf. REACH *sb.* 5).

1866 BLACKMORE *Cradock Nowell* xxv, She broke from the long stride of her trot into a reaching canter.

2. Having great (mental) reach; far- or deep-reaching. (Freq. in 17th c. Now *rare.*)

a. of thoughts, views, plans, etc.

*c*1400 tr. *Secreta Secret., Gov. Lordsh.* 106 It ys nedfull ..[to] chese a sotell man, þat hauyn most stalworth tokenyng, and most rechand argument. *c*1592 MARLOWE *Jew of Malta* I. ii. 229 A reaching thought will search his deepest wits. 1674 BOYLE *Excell. Theol.* II. v. 207 To have so reaching and attentive a prospect of all things. *a*1718 PENN *Maxims* Wks. 1726 I. 840 St. James gives a short Draught of the Matter, but very full and reaching. 1836 BROWNING *Life of Strafford* (1891) 140 The views of the lord deputy, somewhat more reaching than their own, startled them.

b. of the mind, etc.; rarely of persons.

1582 STANYHURST *Æneis* Ep. Ded. (Arb.) 3 Such reaching wyts, as bend theyre endewours too thee vnfolding thereof. 1594 WILLOBIE *Avisa* 2 Then Pallas gaue a reaching head, With deepe conceites, and passing wit. 1664 POWER *Exp. Philos.* III. 161 The reaching soul of the renowned DesCartes. 1845 BP. WILBERFORCE *Let.* 27 May in A. R. Ashwell *Life* (1879) I. vii. 269 A very clever reaching mother.

3. Stretching; capable of stretching. *rare*⁻¹.

1651 N. BACON *Disc. Govt. Eng.* II. viii. (1739) 46 They saw that in such cases of Treason the King's honour was made of reaching Leather.

†**4.** ? Attractive, 'fetching'. *Obs.*⁻¹

1607 BEAUMONT *Woman Hater* v. i, My Book-strings are sutable, and of a reaching colour.

Hence '**reachingly** *adv.*

1664 H. MORE *Exp. 7 Epist.* iii. 31 Very reachingly and comprehensively Propheticall.

reachless (ˈriːtʃlɪs), *a.* [f. REACH *v.*[1] + -LESS.] That cannot be reached.

1628 SIR W. MURE *Doomesday* 318 What glorious lights Must beautifie those reachlesse hights. 1825 HONE *Everyday Bk.* I. 951 The hot little dog looking wistfully into the reachless warm water. 1863 LD. LYTTON *Ring Amasis* I. 121 Aloof upon her reachless rock, sat cold the Loreley.

Hence '**reachlessness**. *rare*⁻¹.

1861 LYTTON & FANE *Tannhäuser* 26 As one should love a star..who knows The distance of it, and the reachlessness.

reachless, obs. variant of RECKLESS.

reach-me-down, *a.* and *sb.* [REACH *v.*[1] 5 b.]

A. *adj.* **a.** Of clothes: Exposed for sale in a finished state, ready for wearing, ready-made; also, cast-off, second-hand.

1862 THACKERAY *Philip* xxiv, The most splendid reach-me-down dressing gowns. 1887 *Pall Mall G.* 22 Jan. 4/1 The reach-me-down finery of the East-end exquisite.

b. *transf.* and *fig.* Ready-made, stock; derivative, inferior.

1907 G. B. SHAW *Let.* 11 July (1972) II. 700 You are not ..one of these reach-me-down people. 1914 —— in *New Statesman* 14 Nov. 19/2 Europe has a stock of ready-made constitutions... It is therefore quite possible that a reach-me-down constitution proposed..by an international congress..might prove acceptable. 1932 V. WOOLF *Common Reader* 2nd Ser. 230 There are a dozen occasions on which a reach-me-down character will satisfy him well enough. 1951 C. DAY LEWIS *Lyrical Poetry of Thomas Hardy* in *Proc. Brit. Acad.* XXXVII. 158 Often..Hardy seems to lose all touch with his medium, and will dress up his subjects in the shoddiest, reach-me-down verse. 1962 *Times* 14 Jan. 12/5 The clergyman full of reach-me-down psychology. 1975 *Listener* 4 Dec. 760/1 The role he has chosen is that of a reach-me-down James Bond. 1976 *Glasgow Herald* 26 Nov. 5/5 Daniel Wayenberg's programme of works by Brahms, Bartok, Ravel and Mussorgsky proved an admirable one with not a reach-me-down sonata in sight.

B. *sb.* **1. a.** A ready-made or second-hand garment. Chiefly *pl.*

1862 F. SINNETT *Acct. Colony S. Australia* 53 Waxen dummies, in their model reach-me-downs. 1884 *World* 3 Dec. 13/1 The wide-awakes, billycocks, ulsters, and reach-me-downs. 1922 MRS. A. SIDGWICK *Victorian* i. 11 She has evidently bought a reach-me-down at one of the cheap shops, and as for her hat it's the limit. 1926 A. BENNETT *Lord Raingo* I. xxxv. 165 He had said stiffly that he would enter the House of Lords in no hired reach-me-down. 1928 D. BYRNE *Destiny Bay* i. 117 A small rat-faced man in a suit of reach-me-downs. 1931 R. CHURCH *High Summer* IV. vi. 322 'Buy a..ready-made suit'... 'Not even the prospect of saving Filosilk from irretrievable ruin could induce me to wear a reach-me-down.' 1981 *Times* 12 Mar. 10/8 The costumes..look..like tattered reach-me-downs from the Royal Shakespeare Company.

attrib. 1869 *Routledge's Ev. Boy's Ann.* 674 We preferred going to a reach-me-down store, as Prawle styled it.

b. *transf.* and *fig.*

1916 G. B. SHAW *Pygmalion* 191 The rest of the story.. would hardly need telling if our imaginations were not so enfeebled by their lazy dependence on the ready-mades and reach-me-downs of the ragshop in which Romance keeps its stock of 'happy endings' to misfit all stories. 1958 *Spectator* 31 Jan. 136/3 This second-hand reach-me-down of a musical comedy. 1963 *Times* 28 Jan. 6/3 Ministers realize.. that there would be acute political difficulties in dressing the shop window with the cast-off reach-me-downs of policy from years ago. 1977 *Gramophone* Dec. 1015/1 My particular ration of reviews usually spares me the necessity of sitting in judgement on the familiar reach-me-downs of the classical repertoire, and the past year has been no exception.

2. *pl.* Trousers.

1877 BESANT & RICE *Harp & Cr.* xv. 148 Two new pairs of second-hand machine-made reach-me-downs. 1905 *Westm. Gaz.* 20 Apr. 2/1 There is a gentleman in pegtop reach-me-downs (I believe this is the correct method in America of describing that portion of gentleman's attire which a lady is never supposed to notice). 1979 G. MITCHELL *Mudflats of Dead* ix. 96 Tatty old reach-me-downs..and a gosh-awful dirty sweater.

reachy (ˈriːtʃɪ), *a.* [f. REACH *sb.*[1] + -Y.] That has a long reach.

1888 *Poultry* 27 July 377 Game Cocks (four)—First (Plattin) a beautiful Black Red, very reachy, capital style. 1902 *Rep. Evolution Committee R. Soc.* I. 96 Though not so 'reachy' as a fine Indian Game, they never have the general appearance of Leghorn. 1952 A. W. HUNTER *Leighton's Compl. Bk. Dog* xvi. 227 *Neck* [of Kerry Blue Terrier]: Strong and reachy.

reack, obs. variant of RICK.

reack'nowledge, *v.* [RE- 5 a. In early use suggested by L. *recognoscĕre* or F. *reconnoître.*]

†**1.** *trans.* To recognize, confess, acknowledge.

1550 J. COKE *Eng. & Fr. Heralds* §225 (1877) 123 You, syr herald of Fraunce,..for ever herafter, shall reacknowledge your dutie, gevynge place to the heralde of Englande. 1555 HARPSFIELD in *Bonner's Homilies* 10 He teacheth vs in oure prayers, to reacknowledge oure selues synners.

†**2.** To reconnoitre, explore. *Obs. rare*⁻¹.

1622 F. Markham *Bk. War* v. ix. 196 To find out and reacknowledge the natures, dispositions and inclinations of all the Enemies Commaunders.

3. To acknowledge again or anew.

1640 Habington *Edw. IV* 70 King Henry set at libertie went..to Pauls Church, the Clergy, Nobility, and Commonalty reacknowledging all obedience to him. **1657** J. Sergeant *Schism Dispach't* 614 If then..they have broke in peeces his Church, and renounced the only-certain grounds of his law, they must..restore both to their former integrity by reacknowledging them. **1715** Pope *Lett.* (1735) I. 232 This puts me in mind of reacknowledging your continu'd Endeavours to enrich me.

Hence **reack'nowledgement, -ledging.**

1598 Florio, *Resipiscentia*,..a reacknowledging. **1611** *Ibid.*, *Riconoscenza*, reacknowledgement.

rea'cquaint, *v.* [re- 5 a.] *trans.* To make acquainted again; to bring back into acquaintance.

1647 H. More *Song of Soul* iii. i. xii, Tract of time at least all memory Will quite debarre, that reacquainten mought My self with mine own self. **1973** M. Amis *Rachel Papers* 20, I wondered if there were any important lies I had told her which it would be worth reacquainting myself with, but could think of none. **1977** *National Observer* (U.S.) 1 Jan. 6/5 One purpose of the tests is to give owners fun with their dogs and reacquaint them with their pets.

So **rea'cquaintance**, renewed knowledge.

1668 H. More *Div. Dial.* iii. ii. (1713) 183 Your reacquaintance of those many and most noble Truths that Philotheus recovered into your Mind.

rea'cquire, *v.* [re- 5 a. Cf. F. *réacquérir* (15th c. in Littré).] *trans.* To acquire anew.

a **1691** Boyle *Hist. Air* (1692) 225, I perceived one of them..that had almost quite lost its colour, to have re-acquired a very fair blew. *a* **1711** Ken *Hymnotheo* Poet. Wks. 1721 III. 361 Their penitential Tears..Had strove lost Heav'n and Love to re-acquire. **1805** W. Taylor in *Ann. Rev.* III. 291 The established interests..would, after the first novelty of an independant choice, shortly reacquire their natural ascendancy. **1884** Sir J. Pearson in *Law Times Rep.* L. 712/2 By losing an English domicil, he re-acquired a Scotch domicil, his domicil of origin.

Hence **rea'cquired** *ppl. a.* Also † **rea'cquist** *v. Obs. rare*$^{-1}$.

1635 J. Hayward tr. *Biondi's Banish'd Virg.* 166, I will endeavour to re-acquist you the kingdome or dye in the attempt. **1839** James *Louis XIV*, II. 299 To ensure durability to the reacquired power of the queen. **1880** C. & F. Darwin *Movem. Pl.* 524 This regeneration of the tips and reacquired sensitiveness.

reacqui'sition. [f. re- 5 a + acquisition.] The action of reacquiring; a thing which or a person who is reacquired.

1904 *Lancet* in *Westm. Gaz.* 30 Sept. 10/1 The man on his holiday..rises to the occasion by the reacquisition of powers which belong not to the town. **1959** *Times* 10 Jan. 8/5 He paid tribute to the Socratic wisdom which had rendered Mr. Forster so valuable a reacquisition to the college. **1977** *Word* 1972 XXVIII. 194 It looks as if we have a reacquisition here.

† **rea'cquite,** *v.* [re- 5 a.] *trans.* To requite.

1534 Cromwell in Merriman *Life & Lett.* (1902) I. 395, I shall accompt my self bounden to reaquite your gentilnes with semblable pleasures. *a* **1548** Hall *Chron.*, *Rich. III* (1809) 405 His bountyfulnes and liberalitie whiche they would God wyllynge shortly reacquyte. **1594** T. Bedingfield tr. *Machiavelli's Florentine Hist.* (1595) 166 So might he also hope in time to come, to be reacquited.

react (riː'ækt), *v.*[1] [See re- 2 a and act *v.* Cf. F. *réagir* (18th c.), late L. *reagĕre* (5th cent.).]

1. a. *intr.* To act in return, or in turn, *upon* some agent or influence. Also without const.

Sometimes used loosely when previous action is merely implied or possible.

1644 Digby *Nat. Bodies* xvi. 141 If fire doth heate water, the water reacteth againe..vpon the fire and cooleth it. **1724** Swift *Answer* Misc. (1735) V. 21 Because, the Soul her Power contracts, And on the Brother Limb re-acts. **1771** Wesley *Wks.* (1872) V. 233 God does not continue to act upon the Soul, unless the Soul re-acts upon God. **1831** Macaulay *Sp. in Ho. Comm.* 5 July, Government and society are cause and effect—they re-act on each other. **1880** McCarthy *Own Times* IV. l. 61 Applause reacts upon the orator.

b. *spec.* in *Chem.* of the action of reagents.

1797 *Encycl. Brit.* (ed. 3) IV. 415/1 The nitrous acid soon ..reacts on the other metals, and dissolves them. **1845** G. E. Day tr. *Simon's Anim. Chem.* I. 359 Chyle of different qualities may react with varying energy on the lymphatic glands.

c. *trans.* To cause to react chemically or immunologically *with* or *together*.

1944 [see adduct *sb.*]. **1949** [see oxo(-) 2 c]. **1962** J. C. Wright *Metallurgy in Nuclear Power Technol.* v. 91 In the Degussa process fine beryl is reacted with excess lime at 1,500°C. **1963** *Listener* 14 Mar. 459/2 A team of workers.. showed that xenon and fluorine could readily be reacted together to produce xenon-tetrafluoride. **1971** *Nature* 21 May 195/1 These, and several antisera previously made against Australasian marsupial sera, were reacted with a range of sera from Australasian and American marsupials in immunoelectrophoretic tests. **1972** *Sci. Amer.* Aug. 34/1 It is fairly easy to react unsaturated molecules with a variety of chemical reagents.

2. *intr.* To act, or display some form of energy, in response to a stimulus; to undergo a change under some influence. Const. *to* (in recent use). Also, of a person: to respond; to behave in response *to* an event, a statement, etc.

1656 tr. *Hobbes' Elem. Philos.* (1839) 393 Though all sense ..be made by reaction, nevertheless it is not necessary that every thing that reacteth should have sense. **1856** Kane *Arct. Expl.* II. v. 67 The less severe cases..are beginning to feel the influence of their new diet; but Wilson and Brooks do not react. **1882** Vines tr. *Sachs' Bot.* 895 The tendency to expand is increased by darkness..: light has the contrary effect, and the one half always reacts more powerfully than the other. **1891** F. Darwin in *Nature* 409 Plants may gain.. various aptitudes for reacting to light and gravitation. **1913** H. James *Small Boy & Others* xv. 212 What tenuity of spirit it argues that I should neither have enjoyed nor been aware of missing..a space wider than the schoolroom floor to react and knock about in. **1921** G. B. Shaw *Back to Methuselah* p. xlviii, The assumption that he may safely cross Oxford Street in a state of unconsciousness, trusting to his dodging reflexes to react automatically and promptly enough to the visual impression produced by a motor bus. **1928** E. O'Neill *Strange Interlude* i. 25 My heart pounding!.. seeing Nina again!..how sentimental..how she'd laugh if she knew! and quite rightly..absurd for me to react as if I loved..that way. **1931** —— *Haunted* ii, in *Mourning becomes Electra* (1932) 251 *Lavinia*... I have a right to love! *Orin* (reacting as his father had—his face grown livid—with a hoarse cry of fury grabs her by the throat). You—you whore! **1953** *Times* 13 May 3/5 Mr. Selwyn Lloyd said the Siamese Government..was reacting to this threat by taking precautionary measures on the north-eastern frontier. **1966** *Guardian* 11 Aug. 8/2 Pictures not only of the member addressing the House..but of other members reacting to his speech. **1979** *Economist* 28 Apr. 28/2 A firework lobbed by a demonstrator caused the police to react.

3. *intr.* To act in opposition to some force. Const. *against*.

1861 M. Arnold *Pop. Educ. France* p. xx, I know that some individuals react against the strongest impediments. **1871** *Daily News* 31 Jan., He..did all that lay in him to react against the cry, *à Berlin*.

4. *intr.* To move or tend in a reverse direction; to return towards a previous condition. *spec.* of share prices: to fall after rising.

1875 Tennyson *Queen Mary* iv. iii. 246 Heaven help that this re-action not re-act Yet fiercelier under Queen Elizabeth. **1893** *Westm. Gaz.* 29 Nov. 2/1 His father was a strong Wesleyan, and the son, as was natural, reacted towards the Church of England. **1896** *Daily News* 5 Nov. 7/4 Silver reacted 2½, but rallied 1⅜ on dealings. **1908** *Daily Chron.* 10 Jan. 1/7 In one or two directions Stock Markets were again heavy, and prices further reacted. **1927** *Daily Tel.* 22 Nov. 2 Cairn line reacted 9d and P. and O. fell 2. **1972** *Ibid.* 29 Apr. 17/6 The shares reacted to 222p before rallying to 228p, a net loss of 2.

† **5.** *trans.* **a.** To exercise in turn. **b.** To drive back, to reflect. *Obs.*

1646 Sir T. Browne *Pseud. Ep.* 386 The spirits of many ..meeting no assimilables wherein to react their natures, must certainely anticipate such naturall desolations. **1678** Cudworth *Intell. Syst.* i. v. 731 Every thing that suffered and reacted motion, especially polite bodies, as looking-glasses.

Hence **re'acting** *vbl. sb.* and *ppl. a.*

1611 Florio, *Reattióne*, a reacting, or reaction. **1685** J. Chamberlayne *Coffee, Tea, & Choc.* 60 The acting and reacting which they have one upon another. **1833** Chalmers *Const. Man* (1835) I. iv. 173 The actings and reactings that take place between man and man. **1871** Morley *Voltaire* (1886) 5 A kind of reacting sympathy. **1896** *Allbutt's Syst. Med.* I. 245 Some modification in the reacting tissue.

re-act (riː'ækt), *v.*[2] [f. re- 5 a + act *v.*] *trans.* To act, do, or perform a second time.

a **1656** Bp. Hall *Invisible World* iii. v, Encouraging a man, by the prosperous event of his sin, to re-act it. *a* **1711** Ken *Preparatives* Poet. Wks. 1721 IV. 18, But..I fear my treacherous Will Wou'd live re-acting the like Ill. **1755** Smollett *Quix.* iv. xv, The gay shepherdesses and gallant swains, who sought to renew and react the pastoral Arcadia. **1833** I. Taylor *Fanat.* vi. 144 They..wait only the leave or bidding of circumstances to re-act their part.

reactance (riː'æktəns). *Electr.* [ad. F. *réactance* (É. Hospitalier 1893, in *L'Industrie Électrique* 10 May 210/1), f. *réaction* reaction: see -ance and cf. Eng. *resistance*, *impedance*.]

1. a. The non-resistive component of impedance, arising from the effect of inductance or capacitance or both and causing the current to be out of phase with the e.m.f. causing it. Cf. impedance.

1893 *Trans. Amer. Inst. Electr. Engineers* X. 413 The term 'impedance' is suggested for the denominator..and for the quantity enclosed between the brackets, the term 'reactance' is proposed. **1896** F. Bedell *Princ. Transformer* iv. 68 The reactance is, accordingly, equal to the component of the impressed electromotive force at right angles to the current, divided by the current. Reactance is measured in ohms. **1902** W. G. Rhodes *Alternating Currents* 62 We propose to determine the equivalent resistance R, and the equivalent reactance S, of the combination. **1940** *Amateur Radio Handbk.* (ed. 2) i. 10/2 The reactance of a condenser increases as the frequency of alternating current decreases. .. The reactance of an inductance decreases as the frequency decreases, which is the opposite effect to that of a condenser. **1970** D. F. Shaw *Introd. Electronics* (ed. 2) ii. 33 The general definition of complex impedance is $Z = R + jX$, where R is the resistance and X is the reactance of the circuit. **1975** D. G. Fink *Electronics Engineers' Handbk.* vii. 8 The reactance of a capacitor is given by $X_c = 1/2\pi fC = 1/\omega C$ (ohms) where $f = \omega/2\pi$ is the frequency in hertz.

b. = reactor 2 a.

1923 *Mod. Wireless* I. 263 Try reversing the connections of the Armstrong inductance *or* reactance. **1947** R. Lee *Electronic Transformers & Circuits* vi. 150 To avoid introducing losses and attenuation in the transmission bands, reactances as nearly pure as practicable are used in the elements of a wave filter. **1961** [see reactor 2 a].

2. *Mech.* and *Acoustics.* The imaginary component of a mechanical or acoustic impedance, producing a phase difference between a driving force and the resulting motion but no dissipation of energy.

1925 *Physical Rev.* XXV. 91 In the acoustic filters the impedances were combinations of the reactances, $iM\omega$ and $i/C\omega$, ω being 2π times the frequency, M the inertance and C the capacitance. **1932** W. West *Acoustical Engin.* i. 3 Any impedance may be expressed as the vectorial sum of two components, a resistance and a reactance, whose phases differ by 90°. *Ibid.* iv. 54 The impedance comprises a resistance component, which depends on the rate of absorption of sound by the walls of the cavity..and an elastic reactance, in parallel, which depends on the volume of the cavity. **1950** Kinsler & Frey *Fund. Acoustics* viii. 202 The acoustic reactance x of a sound medium..is the component that results from the effective mass and stiffness of the medium. **1958** Condon & Odishaw *Handbk. Physics* ii. iii. 22/2 The reactance is the sum of the two contributions: $-ik/\omega$, the elastic reactance, and $i\omega m$, the inertial reactance. **1968** H. J. Pain *Physics of Vibrations & Waves* ii. 38 Mass, like inductance, produces a positive reactance, and the stiffness behaves in exactly the same way as the capacitance.

3. *Psychol.* A term sometimes used for the type of response aroused in a person who feels his freedom of choice is threatened or impeded.

1966 J. W. Brehm *Theory of Psychol. Reactance* i. 2 Since this hypothetical motivational state is in response to the reduction (or threatened reduction) of one's potential for acting, and conceptually may be considered a counterforce, it will be called 'psychological reactance'. **1970** *Jrnl. Personality & Social Psychol.* XIV. 18 If the communication arouses reactance, the individual will tend to reject its position in order to demonstrate his freedom to decide for himself. **1972** *Harvard Law Review* LXXXVI. 399 'Reactance' is conceived to be an aversive state created in the individual by a threatened loss of his freedom to act or choose.

4. *attrib.* and *Comb.*

1921 *Wireless World* IX. 187/1 Reactance coils are used in conjunction with valve sets. **1964** R. F. Ficchi *Electr. Interference* x. 203 A reactance-grounded system is one in which a reactance is inserted in the connection to ground. **1967** *Electronics* 6 Mar. 186/1 For slow scan applications, however, the reactance components would become excessively large and difficult to stabilize with temperature. **1972** L. S. Wrightsman *Social Psychol. in Seventies* x. 306 Reactance theory concerns itself with situations where one's freedom of choice is threatened. **1976** Tedeschi & Lindskold *Social Psychol.* viii. 360/1 Numerous experiments have shown reactance-like effects in the laboratory. *Ibid.* 361/1 Reactance studies in which subjects are told they are being evaluated for leadership.

reactant (riː'æktənt), *sb.* (*a.*) *Chem.* [f. react *v.*[1] + -ant[1].] A reacting substance or species. Also *attrib.* or as *adj.*

1928 *Chem. Rev.* V. 67 In hydrogenation there is an optimum ratio to the partial pressures of the reactants. **1936** T. J. Webb *Elem. Princ. Physical Chem.* viii. 253 In general the rate of a given reaction depends upon the instantaneous concentration of the reactants. **1948** *Ann. Rep. Progr. Chem.* XLV. 10 The immediate consequence of absorption of some of the energy of the incident radiation is the conversion of the absorbing reactant molecule into the product. **1950** *Sci. News* XV. 65 Once a layer of oxide has formed, subsequent reaction must take place by the reactants..diffusing through it. **1971** *Jrnl. Oil & Colour Chemists' Assoc.* LIV. 849 The necessary reactants, ammonia and sulphur dioxide, appeared to be absorbed from the atmosphere by droplets of water condensed on the paint surface. **1973** J. G. Tweeddale *Materials Technol.* II. ii. 23 With the majority of materials suitable for melting and freeze casting, gases such as oxygen, hydrogen and nitrogen..are much more soluble in, or reactant to, the liquid state of a material than they are to the solid state.

reaction (riː'ækʃən). [f. re- + action *sb.*; cf. react *v.*[1] and F. *réaction* (*a* 1610).]

Florio (1611) uses 'reaction' to render It. *reattione* (mod. *reazione*): see reacting *vbl. sb.*]

1. Repulsion or resistance exerted by a body in opposition to the impact or pressure of another body.

1644 Digby *Nat. Bodies* xvi. 139 Of reaction..in locall motion, that each agent must suffer in acting and acte in suffering. **1748** Hartley *Observ. Man* i. i. 47 It must be compressed in return, by the Re-action of the Skull. **1800** Vince *Hydrost.* i. (1806) 11 The reaction of the sides of the vessel against the fluid. **1881** *Encycl. Brit.* XII. 524/2 The reaction of the jets caused the rotation of the machine.

fig. **1643** Sir T. Browne *Relig. Med.* i. §5 It is the method of Charity to suffer without reaction. *a* **1660** Hammond *Serm.* xxi. Wks. 1684 IV. 687 In such a Soul as this, there is a perpetual re-action, an impatience of the presence of any thing which may trash, incumber or oppress it.

2. a. The influence which a thing, acted upon or affected by another, exercises in return upon the agent, or in turn upon something else.

1771 Wesley *Wks.* (1872) V. 232 A continual action of God upon the Soul, and a re-action of the Soul upon God. **1792** A. Young *Trav. France* 434 The effects of high or low prices on agriculture, and the re-action of culture on price. **1863** Tyndall *Heat* i. 2 Action and reaction have thus gone on from prehistoric ages to the present time. **1876** L. Stephen *Eng. Th. 18th C.* I. i. 12 Mr. Darwin's observations upon the breeds of pigeons have had a reaction on the structure of European Society.

b. *Chem.* (i) The action of one chemical agent on another, or the result of such action; also, any chemical change. Also extended to transformations of atomic nuclei and other particles.

1836 J. M. Gully *Magendie's Formul.* (ed. 2) 9 The great care that is requisite to prevent the re-action of this acid is an objection to its use. **1862** Miller *Elem. Chem.* (ed. 2) iii.

67 Owing to the feebler affinities of these elements, the reactions take place with less vehemence. *Ibid.* 435 The vegetable bases when in solution have generally a decidedly alkaline reaction upon test papers. **1926** H. G. RULE tr. *J. Schmidt's Text-bk. Org. Chem.* 131 The Hofmann method, in which bromine and potassium hydroxide are brought into reaction with acid amides. **1936** *Nature* 29 Feb. 344/1 The typical features of nuclear reactions are therefore perhaps most clearly shown by neutron impacts. **1950** N. V. SIDGWICK *Chem. Elements* I. 397 The reaction of boron trichloride with an alcohol is quite violent. **1956** A. H. COMPTON *Atomic Quest* i. 53 The amount of U-235 needed to bring about a chain reaction was many times smaller than earlier measurements had indicated. **1972** R. A. JACKSON *Mechanism* i. 5 Unimolecular reactions occur as a result of reorganization of the bonds within a molecule, with or without rupture into fragments. *Ibid.* 6 Bimolecular reactions take place during a collision of two molecules. **1977** J. NARLIKAR *Struct. Universe* ii. 36 The star's nuclear reactions generate energy which goes towards providing the necessary pressure to support the star against its tendency to contract with gravitation.

(ii) *spec.* (usu. with qualifying adj.) a reaction characteristic of acid or alkali; hence, acidity, neutrality or alkalinity.

1856 W. A. MILLER *Elem. Chem.* II. x. 710 A salt which affects neither the blue of litmus nor the yellow of turmeric is said to have a neutral reaction. **1899** *Jrnl. Physiol.* XXIV. 289 On the addition of acid a dispersion of the flakes of coagulum occurs with production of an opalescent fluid having an acid reaction. **1900** *Proc. R. Soc.* LXVI. 116 The effect of the acid or basic reaction of the salt on the hydrosol. **1938** *Jrnl. Inst. Brewing* XLIV. 466/1 The highest grade of asbestos is a completely insoluble material, neutral in reaction and tasteless. **1956** K. IMHOFF et al. *Disposal of Sewage* iv. 23 The 'Reaction' of aqueous wastes may be described as acid, neutral, or alkaline, depending on the concentration of hydrogen ions. Pure water is neutral in reaction. **1968** PASSMORE & ROBSON *Compan. Med. Stud.* I. vi. 2/2 It follows that the reaction of an aqueous solution may be expressed either in terms of $[H^+]$ or $[OH^-]$.

3. *Phys.* and *Path.* **a.** The supervention of an opposite physical condition, as the return of heat after cold, or of vitality after shock.

1805 W. SAUNDERS *Min. Waters* 498 If an intire immersion in cold water be employed, and the body be in a fit state to produce reaction, a full..perspiration will follow. **1842** ABDY *Water Cure* (1843) 165 The first impulse to the reaction of the heart has been found to have been given by these means. **1875** H. C. WOOD *Therap.* (1879) 652 The cold bath, when not followed by a healthy reaction, is anything but a tonic.

b. The response made by the system or an organ to an external stimulus.

reaction of degeneration, 'a gradual diminution and final loss of faradic excitability of both nerves and muscles, consequent on degeneration and atrophy of both' (*Syd. Soc. Lex.*). A variety of this is called ***reaction of exhaustion***.

1896 *Allbutt's Syst. Med.* I. 359 This condition is known as the reaction of degeneration, and is found in serious injury or disease in the motor nuclei of the anterior cornua. **1899** *Ibid.* VII. 347 The reaction to light was lost in both eyes.

c. *Psychol.* A response to a stimulus which can be observed, estimated, or measured.

1887 *Jrnl. Mental Sci.* XXXII. 604 The reaction is found to occupy less time in the insane than in the sane. **1943** C. L. HULL *Princ. Behav.* xviii. 326 Many reactions..approach the all-or-none type, which differs appreciably from the galvanic skin reaction,..etc. *Ibid.*, Reaction is a joint multiplicative function of habit strength and drive. **1968** R. F. C. HULL tr. *Jung's Analytical Psychol.: Tavistock Lectures* ii. 54 Other characteristic disturbances are:..reaction expressed by facial expression, laughing, movements of the hands or feet or body..insufficient reactions like 'yes' or 'no'.

d. In general use: a response (to an event, a statement, etc.); an action or feeling that expresses or constitutes a response.

1914 H. JAMES *Notes of Son & Brother* v. 117 His [*sc.* William James's] letters..mark the beginning of those vivacities and varieties of intellectual and moral reaction which were for the rest of his life to be the more immeasurably candid and vivid. **1922** JOYCE *Ulysses* 650 Did Bloom discover common factors of similarity between their respective like and unlike reactions to experience? **1932** KIPLING *Limits & Renewals* 134 Only the speed of my reactions saved me from bumping into Bunny when he pulled up without warning beside a lorry. **1946** E. O'NEILL *Iceman Cometh* I. 89 They all hoot him down in a chorus of amused jeering. Hugo is not offended. This is evidently their customary reaction. **1980** D. BRIERLEY *Blood Group O* 43 Reaction to the death of Desnos had set in.

e. *Radio.* A former name for positive feedback. Also *ellipt.*, a reaction coil.

1917 R. D. BANGAY *Elem. Princ. Wireless Telegr.* II. 205 We now come to the final and most efficient method of utilising the properties of the magnifying valve for the purposes of reception of spark signals. It is known as the reaction method. **1920** *Wireless World* 24 July 327/2 The reaction may cause some howling if it is not in phase with the frame. **1922** A. C. LESCARBOURA *Radio for Everybody* i. 32 This small coil is frequently called the 'tickler' or reaction. **1923** *Radio Times* 28 Sept. 22 Two-valve long range receiving set with anode tuning and reaction. **1933** *Boys' Mag.* XLVII. 117/2 To modernize an old set..swinging reaction can easily be altered to Reinartz reaction. **1943** C. L. BOLTZ *Basic Radio* xi. 184 Other names for positive feed-back are reaction and regeneration. *Ibid.* xiv. 222 Reaction in the hands of the inveterate knob twiddler is a curse to everybody.

4. a. A movement towards the reversal of an existing tendency or state of things, esp. in politics; a return, or desire to return, to a previous condition of affairs; a revulsion of feeling.

In 1816 referred to as a French use of the word (*Edinb. Rev.* XXVII. 480).

1792 A. YOUNG *Trav. France* I. 557 A most curious political combination, which seems to shew, that..where evils are of the most alarming tendency, there is a re-action, an under-current, that works against the apparent tide, and brings relief. **1801** HEL. M. WILLIAMS *Fr. Rep.* I. xii. 122 If I have delayed sending you the sketch of the re-action at Naples [etc.]. **1816** SCOTT *Old Mort.* xliv. *note*, That perpetuating of factious quarrels, which is called in modern times Reaction. **1836** HOR. SMITH *Tin Trump.* (1876) 161 Like every other excess, fanaticism provokes a reaction. **1875** JOWETT *Plato* (ed. 2) IV. 256 In the ancient as well as the modern world there were reactions from theory to experience. **1965** *New Statesman* 7 May 724/2 In spite of his achievements as a social reformer, he became a symbol of black reaction to organised labour. **1969** A. G. FRANK *Latin Amer.* (1970) xxii. 341 After eliminating popular leadership in labor, student, and other organizations..reaction settled back into comfort. **1974** tr. *Sniečkus's Soviet Lithuania* 29 Operating under conditions of extreme political reaction at home, the Communist Party of Lithuania skilfully combined legal and illegal forms of political activity.

b. *Econ.* A downward movement (of share prices, etc.) following an upward one.

1841 [see INFLATION 6]. **1925** *Scribner's Mag.* Sept. 338/1 The mercurial American..sees either a coming 'business boom' or a season of 'reaction', and he usually bases his belief on visible tendencies in trade and industry. **1930** *Daily Express* 8 Sept. 10/2 It is safer to buy on reactions than on the top of a rise.

5. *attrib.* and *Comb.*, as ***reaction drive, experiment, force, mechanism, period, potential, rate, speed, stage, threshold, time, velocity, vessel, word***; **reaction chamber**, (*a*) a vessel in which a chemical reaction occurs, esp. in an industrial process; (*b*) the combustion chamber of a rocket; **reaction circuit**, that part of the anode circuit of a thermionic valve which produces positive feedback in the grid circuit; **reaction coil**, an inductance coil included in the anode circuit of a thermionic valve so as to cause positive feedback in the grid circuit; **reaction engine** or **machine**, any engine in which motive power is derived from the reaction exerted by a jet of escaping fluid (usu. gas); **reaction formation**, a term originally used by Freud for the tendency of a repressed wish or feeling to be expressed in a contrasting or opposite form; **reaction index** *Broadcasting* (see quots.); **reaction jet**, a jet engine used to provide intermittent thrust for changing or correcting the velocity of a craft or the like; **reaction motor** = *reaction engine*; **reaction pattern**, an assumed pattern of behaviour or response established in the nervous system; **reaction process**, a method of treating galena, depending on the chemical reaction which follows upon roasting and fusing (Raymond 1881); **reaction propulsion**, any form of propulsion which utilizes the reaction exerted by escaping fluid as the source of motive power; *spec.* jet or rocket propulsion; **reaction rim** *Petrol.*, a zone of one mineral enclosing another and formed by reaction of the latter with its surroundings; **reaction shot** *Film* and *Television*, the photographing of a person responding to an event or to a statement made by another; **reaction time**, the time taken by a person (or any living organism) to respond to a stimulus; **reaction turbine**, a turbine which is driven by the pressure drop experienced by the working fluid in passing across or through the rotor; **reaction type**, a physical or personality type whose members are expected to react in specific ways; **reaction wheel**, a water-wheel impelled by the reaction of escaping water; **reaction wood**, modified wood that forms in branches and leaning trunks and tends to restore upward direction of growth.

1924 *Chem. Abstr.* XVIII. 2426 Liquid hydrocarbons are heated under pressures of 100–300 lbs. per sq. in. at temps of 350–550° and after partially cooling are passed through a series of vaporizing or *reaction chambers of successively diminishing pressure. **1952** E. BURGESS *Rocket Propulsion* iii. 61 The combustion chamber in which the burning takes place is sometimes known as the 'blast' or 'reaction' chamber. **1966** H. O. RUPPE *Introd. Astronautics* I. i. 10 Usually, an oxidizer and a fuel are stored in separate tanks, and transported by a feed system to the reaction chamber. **1969** H. T. EVANS tr. *G. Hägg's Gen. & Inorg. Chem.* xxi. 529 The nitrose is pumped up to a denitrating and concentrating tower..where it is combined with the chamber acid pumped up from the reaction chamber. **1919** *Sci. Abstr.* B. XXI. 291 The case of *reaction circuits is also dealt with, and conclusions are drawn as to the audion characteristics of importance in a particular arrangement. **1931** *Boys' Mag.* XLV. 125/1 A simple capacity coupled inductive reaction circuit, better known as 'swinging' reaction. **1917** R. D. BANGAY *Elem. Princ. Wireless Telegr.* II. 207 The amount of this extra E.M.F. induced in the grid coil by the *reaction coil can be controlled by adjusting the coupling between the two windings. **1943** C. L. BOLTZ *Basic Radio* xiv. 221 With telephones on head hold the reaction coil in the hand and move towards the aerial coil. **1957** 'T. STURGEON' *Thunder & Roses* 122 They fired up the *reaction drive and began to move toward the sun. **1868** *Model Steam Eng.* (1895) 82 *Reaction or resistance engines, described at pages 7 and 8. **1967** N. E. BORDEN *Jet-Engine Fundamentals* 9 All gas-turbine engines, together with pulsejets, ramjets, and rocket motors, belong to a class of power plants called reaction engines. **1893** *Amer. Jrnl. Psychol.* VI. 242 Is the sensorial-muscular difference entirely conditioned by the technique of the ordinary *reaction-experiment? **1933** J. C. FLUGEL *Hundred Years Psychol.* viii. 186 The reaction experiment was..a legacy both from the personal equation problems of the astronomers and from Helmholtz's measurement of the speed of the nervous impulse in the sensory nerves. **1965** C. N. VAN DEVENTER *Introd. Gen. Aeronaut.* ix. 201/2 The *reaction force, which is equal to the acceleration force, propels the balloon in the westerly direction shown. **1910** A. A. BRILL tr. *Freud's Three Contributions to the Theory of Sex* iii. 83 A sub-species of sublimation is the suppression through *reaction-formation, which..begins even in the latency period of infancy. **1924** [see *character-trait*]. **1934** *Mind* XLIII. 113 How rare is that love of virtue which does not bear the trace of neurotic reaction-formation. **1960** *Encounter* XV. v. 25 A 'reaction-formation' in the psycho-analytic sense. **1974** W. B. ARNDT *Theories of Personality* xvii. 349 Another common example of reaction formation is where repressed hostility for a person, say a mother's hostility toward her child, is converted by the ego into excessive concern for his well being. **1967** *Listener* 17 Aug. 195/3 The *reaction index? This is supposed to measure what the audience thought about the show. **1972** *Ibid.* 7 Sept. 295/3 If radio had existed in the mid-1820s, a series of late Beethoven quartets would have had..a 'Reaction Index' (that's the measure of appreciation) too low to be mentioned. **1972** P. MOORE *Can You speak Venusian?* xv. 153 Dr. Barber..proposes to fit large *reaction jets to the tops of mountains on opposite sides of the world... When the tilt begins, one simply switches on the jets. **1978** *Nature* 5 Oct. 378/2 Reaction jets are fired once or twice daily to reduce wheel momentum that accumulates due to disturbance torques on the spacecraft. **1863** GANOT *Physics* §380 In *reaction machines steam acts by a reactive force like water in the hydraulic tourniquet. **1972** D. G. SHEPHERD *Aerospace Propulsion* i. 4 It should also be recognized that the propeller operates by the same basic principle... Thus all propulsion systems are reaction machines, although this is often popularly attached only to jet engines. **1972** R. A. JACKSON *Mechanism* v. 80 Stereochemical studies allow us further insight into the details of a *reaction mechanism by providing information about the direction of approach of a reagent or of the movement of groups during a reaction. **1935** C. G. PHILP *Stratosphere & Rocket Flight* xi. 54 In its simplest terms the *reaction motor most favoured at present takes the form of a rocket. **1962** F. I. ORDWAY et al. *Basic Astronautics* ii. 13 Archytas devised a wooden pigeon propelled by a steam reaction motor. **1923** K. DUNLAP in *Psychol. Rev.* XXX. 94 A feeling is always a real stimulus pattern which is the beginning of a *reaction pattern. **1926** W. MCDOUGALL *Introd. Social Psychol.* (ed. 20) 417 Those who..imply that they can explain alleged instinctive behaviour by postulating in vague general terms a 'reaction pattern' in the nervous system corresponding to every movement and attitude displayed..have never succeeded in demonstrating the validity of such interpretation in any single case of instinctive behaviour. **1946** F. P. CHISHOLM in W. S. Knickerbocker *20th Cent. English* 177 Understanding the nature of language-situations is itself a very powerful developer of more mature reaction-patterns, and hence of more adequate 'command of the language'. **1959** *Times Lit. Suppl.* 27 Mar. 181/3 A psychic organism that..is bound up with instincts and emotions and is the source of innate reaction-patterns which go much farther to determine the behaviour of the individual than he cares to recognize. **1887** *Jrnl. Mental Sci.* XXXII. 604 Guicciardi and Tanzi have made a series of observations on the '*reaction period' in fourteen cases where there were hallucinations of hearing. **1897** *Syd. Soc. Lex.* s.v., *Reaction-period*, the period of reaction or return of vitality after a shock. **1952** C. L. HULL *Behavior System* i. 12 Absolute zero of *reaction potential. **1972** G. R. LEFRANCOIS *Psychol. Theories Human Learning* vi. 129 Reaction potential, sometimes called excitatory potential, is a measure of the potential that a stimulus has for eliciting a specific response. **1935** C. G. PHILP *Stratosphere & Rocket Flight* ii. 5 *Reaction propulsion may be said to date from 1919, in which year Professor Goddard..announced to the world the results of his researches made with rockets. **1962** F. I. ORDWAY et al. *Basic Astronautics* ii. 18 Konstantin Tsiolkovsky..seems to be the first scientist who realized that it is only possible to travel in space by means of reaction propulsion. **1971** P. J. MCMAHON *Aircraft Propulsion* iii. 80 Combining the thermodynamic and propulsion efficiencies gives the overall efficiency of the reaction propulsion engine. **1946** *Nature* 6 Apr. 439/1 This is strong evidence for the conclusion that the decrease in the bimolecular *reaction-rate as the reactive carbon atom changes from primary to secondary is due to an increase in steric hindrance. **1972** WESTON & SCHWARZ *Chem. Kinetics* i. 3 Experimental studies of reactions generally involve the determination of reaction rates as a function of several variables: chemical composition, temperature, pressure, or volume. [**1886** *Bull. U.S. Geol. Survey* No. 28. 52 Wherever it comes in contact with the olivine, the peculiar reactionary rims of amphibole described by Törnebohm..are finely developed.] **1892** *Amer. Jrnl. Sci.* CXLIII. 516 The attention of the writer was repeatedly attracted by a fibrous growth around olivine, that resembles..the *reaction rims that have been described as existing between garnet and serpentine. **1921** *Mineral. Mag.* XIX. 145 If the corona can be shown to be due to alteration or modification of the nucleus the term reaction rim is preferred. **1960** TURNER & VERHOOGEN *Igneous & Metamorphic Petrol.* (ed. 2) vi. 145 The very existence of solid-solution series in so many groups of igneous minerals, and the frequent development of reaction rims (coronas) of one mineral around central cores of another, are evidence of reaction. **1953** *Reaction shot [see OFF SCREEN, OFF-SCREEN *adv.* (*phr.*) and *a.*]. **1966** *Guardian* 11 Aug. 8/2 The Select Committee on televising the House of Commons..was understandably cautious about 'reaction shots', by which the committee meant pictures not only of the member addressing the House..but of other members reacting to his speech. **1930** G. R. DE BEER *Embryol. & Evolution* xv. 105 Atavism is..due to the reproduction of a set of conditions (a definite system of *reaction-speeds) which obtained in the ancestor. **1964** A. EDEL in I. L. Horowitz *New Sociology* xiv. 224 The comparable discovery of color blindness or different reaction-speed or influence of drugs or alcohol affects the concept of a reliable observer in other fields. **1899** *Allbutt's Syst. Med.* VI. 619 In the *reaction-stage of many cases of local asphyxia, there is distinct evidence of heat. **1970** W. SAHAKIAN *Psychol. Learning* xi. 230 The concept of the *reaction threshold is well established. **1879** *Reaction-time [see PSYCHOMETRY 2]. **1883** *Mind* Apr. 177 (*heading*) Reaction time and attention in the hypnotic state. **1893** *Outing* (U.S.) XXII. 152/2 It appears..that the reaction time varies with the loudness of the report. **1908** J. M. CATTELL in *Essays in Honor of W. James* 574 The incoming currents and the pre-existing structure of the centres cause the discharge, and the perception, in my opinion, usually follows the discharge in time. This time order I pointed out more than twenty years ago in the case of the reaction-time. **1923** R. A. KNOX *Memories of Future* v. 73, I went round to his house, where he looked at my tongue, X-rayed me, felt my pulse, took my reaction-times, and shook his head importantly. **1971** J. W. KLING et al. *Woodworth & Schlosberg's Exper. Psychol.* (1972) ix. 309/2 The simple reaction time of human subjects..is one form of latency measure. **1972** K. BONFIGLIOLI *Don't point that Thing at Me* xiii. 96 Another shot rang out, followed one fifth of a second later by the bang of the car door... There is still nothing wrong with the Mortdecai reaction-time. **1881** *Encycl. Brit.* XII. 524/1 Turbines in which part only of the available energy is converted into kinetic energy, before the water enters the turbine wheel, may be termed *Reaction Turbines. **1929** T. M. NAYLOR *Steam Turbines* i. 3 The only pure reaction turbines in use are of very small power, and are used for fluids other than steam, e.g. the garden sprinkler.., distributors on sewage filter beds, [etc.]. **1969** W. THOMSON *Thrust for Flight* 111 The reaction turbine is one in which the whole of the pressure drop and the velocity increase occur as the gas flows through the rotor blade passages. **1904** *Psychol. Bull.* I. 230 The chief directions in which Kraepelin has stimulated his associates to work psychologically, are a number of more biological than purely psychological *reaction-types, such as retardation and inhibition, flight of ideas, etc. **1917** C. E. LONG tr. *Jung's Analytical Psychol.* iii. 158 Relatives, and especially related women, have therefore on the average, resemblance in reaction-type. **1917** A. MEYER *Coll. Papers* (1951) II. 44 The organic reaction types. **1922** [see ECOPHENE]. **1934** E. B. STRAUSS tr. *Kretschmer's Text-bk. Med. Psychol.* xiii. 184 In our description of the various reaction-types we shall make use of psychopathological instead of normal material. **1953** H. READ *True Voice of Feeling* II. iii. 262 The artist..reveals an inward unity and concentration of personality in marked contrast with the extraneous dissipations and diversities of the average reaction-type. **1904** *Brit. Med. Jrnl.* 10 Sept. 564/2 The *reaction velocity of the chemical or physical processes that result in the agglutination of bacteria, is a very variable factor. **1926** *Jrnl. Inst. Petroleum Technologists* XII. 202A When the apparatus is shut down for cleaning, the *reaction vessel is opened and steam or water is pumped through the tubes. **1973** *Materials & Technol.* VI. viii. 504 The mixture is stirred in a reaction vessel and the monomer becomes suspended as an emulsion of tiny droplets. **1881** *Encycl. Brit.* XII. 524/2 The old *reaction wheel consisted of a vertical pipe balanced on a vertical axis, and supplied with water. **1949** H. P. BROWN et al. *Textbk. Wood Technol.* I. xii. 288 The existence of internal forces in living trees, independently of the presence of *reaction wood, has also been suggested. **1980** *Family Handyman* Sept. 70/3 The fruitwoods (cherry, apple) are more difficult [to dry out], depending upon the size of the log and the presence or absence of reaction wood. **1920** T. P. NUNN *Educ.* v. 44 The subject's memory does not throw up a number of suggestions from which a suitable *reaction-word is consciously selected.

Hence **re'actional** *a.*, characterized by reaction; **re'actionally** *adv.*

1856 J. GROTE in *Cambr. Ess.* 87 Under certain circumstances the mind may be likely to move reactionally. **1897** HUGHES *Medit. Fever* v. 207 This artificial reduction of temperature is followed by a slight reactional rise.

re'actionarily, *adv.* [f. REACTIONARY *a.* + -LY[2].] In a reactionary manner.

1966 *Economist* 23 July 329/1 Mr Wilson's Government is now following a right-wing policy of deflation more resolutely, more ruefully, more reactionarily..than any of its predecessors since the war. **1970** R. A. H. ROBINSON *Origins of Franco's Spain* 301 Prieto, leader of the Bilbao Socialists,..called the Statute reactionarily anti-liberal: 'Spain cannot tolerate that territory turning itself into a Vaticanist Gibraltar.'

re'actionariness. *rare.* [f. REACTIONARY *a.* + -NESS.] Reactionary character.

1923 U. L. SILBERRAD *Lett. Jean Armiter* vi. 149, I believe he felt almost kindly..towards me and my antiquated reactionariness.

reactionary (riː'ækʃənərɪ), *a.* and *sb.* [f. REACTION (chiefly in sense 4) + -ARY[1]. Cf. F. *réactionnaire* (19th c.).]

A. *adj.* **1.** Of, pertaining to, or characterized by, reaction.

1847 GROTE *Greece* II. xxxvi. IV. 497 The intensity of the subsequent displeasure would be aggravated by this reactionary sentiment. **1879** McCARTHY *Own Times* II. xviii. 40 The results of the year that followed were decidedly reactionary.

2. Inclined or favourable to reaction. Also, in Marxist use, unfavourably contrasted with *revolutionary*.

1840 J. S. MILL in *London & Westm. Rev.* Mar. 276 The philosophers of the reactionary school—of the school to which Coleridge belongs. **1858** FROUDE *Hist. Eng.* III. 161 The reactionary members of the council had suggested a call of parliament. **1875** JOWETT *Plato* (ed. 2) III. 174 The fixed ideas of a reactionary statesman. **1953** R. LEHMANN *Echoing Grove* iii. 156 The British Government's iniquitous non-intervention policy playing into the hands of Franco's abominable reactionary conspiracy. **1957** *Economist* 28 Dec. 1134/1 Hungarians are to have both the 'true freedom' and the bananas. Mr Kadar's masters were shrewd enough to realise that, in this reactionary country, the latter is appreciated more than the former. **1974** tr. *Sniečkus's Soviet Lithuania* 23 The bourgeois nationalists set up various kinds of reactionary armed organisations to combat the revolutionary movement. **1975** J. PLAMENATZ *K. Marx's Philos. of Man* xi. 299 Ideas and practices adopted by the bourgeois when they put themselves forward as the champions of society as a whole against irresponsible power and a reactionary nobility can become a nuisance to them once they are installed as the dominant class and their position comes to be challenged.

B. *sb.* One who favours or inclines to reaction. Also, in Marxist use, an opponent of communism.

1858 FROUDE *Hist. Eng.* IV. 485 The reactionaries.. watched for some change of fortune. **1908** *Nation* 1 Oct. 302/2 Part of Wall Street will vote for Taft because it believes him at heart a 'reactionary', or, at least, the less of two evils. **1921** G. B. SHAW *Back to Methuselah* II. 52, I can find you hundreds of the most sordid rascals, or the most densely stupid reactionaries, with all these qualifications. **1951** G. MIKES *Down with Everybody!* I. i. 15 'A reactionary and a foreign spy is a man who is not pleased when his wages are cut or when he is asked to work more for the same wages and who is not pleased to starve.' 'Very good, Comrade Barna, very good indeed.' **1967** tr. *Quotations from Chairman Mao Tsetung* (ed. 2) 75 The reactionaries in all countries are fools of this kind... Their persecution of the revolutionary people only serves to accelerate the people's revolutions. **1981** L. DEIGHTON *XPD* ii. 5 Literally *pogoni* means epaulette, but for a citizen of the USSR..it is a symbol of the hated reactionary.

re'actionaryism. Also reactionarism. [f. REACTIONARY *a.* and *sb.* + -ISM.] = REACTIONISM. Hence **re'actionarist.**

1911 GALSWORTHY *Patrician* I. i. 11 His common sense continually impelled him, against the sort of reactionaryism which his son Miltoun had so much, to that easier reactionaryism, which..makes what material capital it can out of its enemy, Progress. **1922** *Contemp. Rev.* Aug. 240 His party had previously been coloured by monarchism and reactionarism. **1924** *Glasgow Herald* 22 May 7 The advent of the Labour Government was heralded by the reactionarists as the end of all things. **1965** *Listener* 4 Nov. 723/1 Reactionaryism, whether in politics or art, is never pleasant to contemplate.

re'actionism. [f. REACTION + -ISM.] Reactionary principles or practice.

1891 J. M. ROBERTSON *Mod. Humanists* 91 For the Bentham group Burke finally represented sheer reactionism. **1930** A. I. NAZAROFF *Tolstoi* vi. 90 This lack of 'social sensibility' shocked them. They even mistook it for the mortal sin of 'reactionism'.

re'actionist, *sb.* and *a.* [f. as REACTIONARY *a.* and *sb.* + -IST.] **a.** A marked or professed reactionary. Also, a person who reacts *against* something.

1857 J. F. MAGUIRE *Rome: its Ruler & its Institutions* p. ix, I trust I have done sufficient to enable the reader..to estimate, at their right value, the accusations which have been made against him [*sc.* Pope Pius IX], as a reformer of the one day, and a reactionist of the next. **1861** *Q. Rev.* CIX. 294 The utter weariness of spirit which this unresting scepticism has bred in most minds of the highest order of thought; the deep study into which it has driven the noble reactionists who have arisen there..have entirely altered the whole tone of religious feeling amongst our Teutonic brethren. **1862** MERIVALE *Rom. Emp.* lii. (1865) VI. 266 As usual with reactionists in social life,..they mistook the cause of the disease. **1883** *Jrnl. Educ.* XVIII. 137 Nobody except the chronic reactionist and constitutional grumbler wants to keep back the colored people. **1900** *Dublin Rev.* Jan. 35 Reactionists..signatories to the Royal supremacy in 1559, who in 1579 appeared in prison as recusants. **1902** G. B. SHAW *Mrs. Warren's Profession* p. xxx, Clergymen's sons are often conspicuous reactionists against the restraints imposed on them in childhood. **1909** [see BABY *sb.* 1 e].

b. *attrib.* or as *adj.*

1858 FROUDE *Hist. Eng.* xiii. III. 177 To the clergy and the reactionist lords he would not yield a step. **1866** *Pall Mall G.* 21 Feb. 4/2 The Liberals..did not expect that the reactionist tendencies of the Government would be expressed so strongly.

reactivate (riː'æktɪveɪt), *v.* [RE- 5 a.] *trans.* To make active or operative again.

1903 *Med. Rec.* (N.Y.) 14 Feb. 251/2 The serum can be reactivated by a little fresh serum not only from a normal rabbit, but from the goat and the rat. **1949** M. MEAD *Male & Female* viii. 176 Menstruation..is itself believed to be reactivated by marriage. **1953** *Times* 13 May 3/5 The importance of maintaining the base there in such condition that it could be reactivated immediately in case of war. **1957** *Observer* 27 Oct. 12/2 An American recession may also cause trouble by reactivating the dollar problem. **1958** *Engineering* 14 Mar. 352/3 In this building humidity control is accomplished automatically by passing the air required for ventilation, plus a percentage of recirculated air, through desiccant driers automatically reactivated by gas. **1976** A. WHITE *Long Silence* xx. 179 Please reactivate the plan to surround the station. **1977** *Living with Tanker Surplus* (Shell Internat. Petroleum Co.) 6 A ship in lay-up cannot easily or quickly be reactivated.

Hence **reacti'vation**, the action or result of reactivating.

1903 *Med. Rec.* (N.Y.) 14 Feb. 251/1 It has been found that this 'reactivation' of the serum, as it has been called, can often be brought about by the serum of various animals. **1919** *Lancet* 26 Apr. 705/2 Professor Chauffard and M. L. Girard brought forward a new and striking proof of the tuberculous nature of erythema nodosum—the reactivation of the disease when nearly extinct by injection of tuberculin. **1926** *Glasgow Herald* 1 May 4 Very characteristic of spring is what may be called reawakening, if we may use the word to include reactivation from a rest that is deeper than sleep. **1957** *Times* 18 Nov. p. i/1 Sophisticated arguments about the 're-activation' of bank deposits or the velocity of circulation. **1970** H. TREVELYAN *Middle East in Revolution* 12 The Agreement provided for the reactivation of the Base for defence against the invasion of any Arab State or Turkey by a State other than Israel.

re'active (riː'æktɪv), *a.* and *sb.* [f. REACT *v.*[1] + -IVE. Cf. F. *réactif* (18th c.), It. *reattivo.*]

A. *adj.* †**1.** Repercussive, echoing. *Obs.*[−1]

1712 BLACKMORE *Creation* 357 Ye fish, assume a voice, with praises fill The hollow rock, and loud reactive hill.

2. Acting or operative in return.

1794 G. ADAMS *Nat. & Exp. Philos.* III. xxi. 103 Every body that acts, is at the same instant both active and re-active. **1851** H. SPENCER *Soc. Stat.* 318 We have to consider, not only what is done for the afflicted, but what is the reactive effect upon those who do it.

3. *Path.* **a.** Supervening on a previous opposite state; due to reaction. Also ***reactive formation*** = *reaction formation* s.v. REACTION 5; ***reactive inhibition***, the inhibiting effect of the supervention of fatigue or boredom on the response to a stimulus.

1822-34 *Good's Study Med.* (ed. 4) IV. 434 The patient.. was not rendered faint by the re-active glow that ensued upon his quitting the water. **1885-8** PYE-SMITH *Fagge's Princ. Med.* I. 51 Such patients..sometimes pass into a condition of reactive pyrexia. **1925** J. STRACHEY tr. *Freud's Case of Hysteria* in *Coll. Papers* III. 67 Repression is often achieved by means of an excessive reinforcement of the thought contrary to the one which is to be repressed. This process I call *reactive* reinforcement. *Ibid.* 68 The thought which asserts itself exaggeratedly in consciousness and (in the same way as a prejudice) cannot be removed I call a *reactive thought.* **1943** C. L. HULL *Princ. Behavior* xviii. 327 Uniform time intervals between reinforcements great enough to prevent the accumulation of appreciable amounts of reactive inhibition. **1968** *Globe & Mail* (Toronto) 3 Feb. 11/6 These young people can join 'negative identity' groups and become..therapeutically involved in extreme reactive kinds of activity. **1974** CHAPLIN & KRAWIEC *Systems & Theories of Psychol.* vii. 263 In and of itself fatigue will generate a form of inhibition which Hull calls reactive inhibition, and the animal will cease to respond. **1975** *Way* Suppl. No. 25. 67 Dynamic psychology might interpret this as evidence for reactive formation, which is a technical term suggesting that we control an unacceptable impulse by exaggerating the opposite tendency. **1977** G. H. SAGE *Introd. Motor Behav.* (ed. 2) xvi. 359 The first of these is an inhibition (reactive inhibition) caused by a reluctance to repeat a response.

b. Recuperative; responsive (*to* a stimulus); characterized by reaction to a stimulus.

1822-34 *Good's Study Med.* (ed. 4) I. 704 There is no longer any rallying or reactive power remaining. **1896** *Allbutt's Syst. Med.* I. 193 These granules are feebly reactive to light. *Ibid.* 293 Delicate children, with little reactive power. **1927** C. SPEARMAN *Abilities of Man* iv. 47 Stern's division of persons into the 'spontaneous' and the 'merely reactive'. **1952** M. K. WILSON tr. *Lorenz's King Solomon's Ring* xi. 171 A few birds—usually old, strongly reactive ones—take off, emitting 'Kiaw' cries and thereby provoking the whole flock to leave the ground with them.

c. *Psychol.* Of mental illness: thought to be caused by reaction to environmental stress; exogenous; so ***reactive schizophrenic***, a person with reactive schizophrenia (cf. *process schizophrenia* s.v. PROCESS *sb.* 13 a).

1924 A. A. BRILL *Bleuler's Textbk. Psychiatry* xii. 537 Reactive *depressions*, which become aggravated to a mental disease, are quite rare in the light of present views. **1955** McCARTHY & CORRIN *Med. Treatment of Mental Dis.* xix. 326 Reactive depressions are the mild, brief depressions, the result of situations depressing in themselves, and not out of proportion to circumstances. **1958** H. WEINER in L. Bellak *Schizophrenia* iv. 157 Whether such reactive psychoses actually imply a different series of etiologic contributing factors, i.e., 'non-organic', is highly speculative. **1962** *Lancet* 10 Jan. 105/1 Two were middle-aged men with anxiety states... The third was a middle-aged lady with a reactive depression. **1962** *Psychol. Bull.* LIX. 329/1 Reactive schizophrenia indicates a good prognosis..with notable stress precipitating the psychosis. *Ibid.* 332/1 If the Rorschach diagnosis is followed, then it appears that reactive schizophrenics are not psychotic. **1965** J. POLLITT *Depression & its Treatment* 95 The terms 'endogenous' and 'reactive'..differentiate types of depression on the basis of presence or absence of an external cause. **1966** I. B. WEINER *Psychodiagnosis in Schizophrenia* vi. 94 A group of process schizophrenics made no more frequent errors than the reactive schizophrenics. **1971** *Brit. Med. Bull.* XXVII. 77/2 One school of thought..allocates such cases to a special category of 'reactive psychoses'. **1974** M. C. GERALD *Pharmacol.* xvi. 310 When the cause of depression can be identified,..we term this reactive or exogenous depression. **1976** L. J. WEST et al. *Treatment of Schizophrenia* vi. 278 The good premorbid/bad premorbid, and process/reactive dimensions do seem to identify significant characteristics.

4. Characterized by reaction (sense 4).

1868 GLADSTONE *Juv. Mundi* i. (1870) 24 The reactive tendency to preserve the text by recurrence to a standard. **1890** *Harper's Mag.* June 77/1 He constantly inclined to reactive measures.

5. *Chem.* **a.** Readily susceptible to chemical reaction.

1888 *Nature* 22 Mar. 503/1 The unsaturated hydrocarbons..are..more reactive than the paraffins. **1942** G. WENDT *Chem.* vii. 179 As in the other families of elements we shall meet, the lightest of the group—in this case fluorine—is the most reactive. **1957** G. E. HUTCHINSON *Treat Limnol.* I. xi. 708 It is not clear, however, in what form this reactive iron is actually present in the lake water. **1972** R. A. JACKSON *Mechanism* iv. 78 A trapping or inhibiting agent may be insufficiently reactive towards a particular intermediate to divert it from its normal course of reaction, or the agent may react in such a way as to regenerate another reactive intermediate.

b. Of a process: involving chemical reaction.

1950 *Chem. Abstr.* XLIV. 8190 (*heading*) Reactive diffusion in metals. **1960** *Ibid.* LIV. 23646 The reactive diffusion in a system Nb-B is accomplished by diffusion of B atoms through the reaction products toward the metal. **1971** *New Scientist* 8 Apr. 96/1 Reactive evaporation.. is often used for depositing metal oxides. **1973** R. L. BURWELL in Basolo & Burwell *Catalysis* II. 72 Ethylene is adsorbed by reactive adsorption. Perhaps it first adsorbs as a π-complex and then reacts to monoadsorbed ethane. **1978** FELDER & ROUSSEAU *Elem. Princ. Chem. Processes* x. 384 In this chapter we show.. how calculated enthalpies of reaction are incorporated in energy balances on reactive processes.

c. Of a dye or other colouring material: designed to react chemically with the substrate, usu. in order to become fixed.

1957 *Jrnl. Soc. Dyers & Colourists* LXXIII. 238/2 The search for more practical methods of using reactive dyes has continued, and this work has now culminated in the production of a new range of dyes—the Procion (ICI) dyes—which are water-soluble but contain a reactive group capable of combining with cellulose under alkaline conditions. **1973** *Materials & Technol.* VI. iv. 310 The direct, basic, sulphur, vat, azoic and reactive dyes are all suitable for colouring the fibre [*sc.* rayon]. *a* **1977** *Harrison Mayer Ltd. Catal.* 39/1 *Reactive colours*, a new range of leadless colours for underglaze, on-glaze or in-glaze decoration... On firing, these colours react with the glaze to give interesting and variegated effects.

d. Of coke or coal: having a high reactivity (sense b).

1963 *Economist* 21 Dec. 1284/1 Reconciling the clean air policy with the British love of open fires means trying to produce enough smokeless fuel of the sort that can be burnt in the fireplaces of smokeless zones. But the Minister of Power now estimates that there will be a gap.. between the demand for such 'reactive' smokeless fuels and the supply. **1974** *Encycl. Brit. Macropædia* IV. 783/2 Coals of medium rank are used for low-temperature carbonization because they yield reactive cokes.

6. a. *Electr.* Possessing or pertaining to electrical reactance; *spec.* applied to the vector component of an alternating current (or voltage) which is 90° out of phase with respect to the associated voltage (or current), i.e. wattless; ***reactive power***, the product of the voltage and the reactive current, or of the current and the reactive voltage; ***reactive volt-ampere***, a unit of reactive power.

1892 J. A. FLEMING *Alternate Current Transformer* II. ii. 269 Reactive Coil or Dimmer.—This is a device used in alternating current work to serve the same ends as rheostats in direct current plants. **1892** S. P. THOMPSON *Dynamo-Electr. Machinery* (ed. 4) xxii. 628 We have here two electromotive-forces, the impressed O A and the reactive A E.. with their resultant the effective electromotive-force O E, with an angle E O A.. between them. **1914** J. H. MORECROFT *Continuous & Alternating Current Machinery* vi. 205 The component of voltage 90° out of phase with the current we shall call the reactive component of the voltage or reactive voltage. **1916** *Standardization Rules Amer. Inst. Electr. Engineers* 15 *Reactive volt-amperes*, the product of the reactive component of the voltage by the total current, or of the reactive component of the current by the total voltage. **1920** *Whittaker's Electr. Engineers' Pocket-Bk.* (ed. 4) 222 The reactive current changes from leading to lagging as the field excitation is reduced. **1951** W. SLUCKIN *Princ. Alternating Currents* ix. 225 In an induction motor, neglecting heating losses, the active component provides the useful mechanical power delivered by the motor, while the reactive component is associated with the production of the alternating magnetic field necessary for the operation of the motor. **1956** C. S. SISKIND *Electr. Circuits* xi. 265 The vertical component—the quadrature component—is *EI* sin θ. The latter, acting adversely to lessen the power factor, is expressed as the reactive volt-amperes, abbreviated R-va. **1961** *Listener* 9 Nov. 768/2 There is also the problem, with direct current lines, of providing what is called the reactive power—power where the current is out of step with the voltage—for the operation of converter equipment. **1970** J. EARL *Tuners & Amplifiers* iv. 83 The source itself can be mostly resistive or mostly reactive. **1978** *Gramophone* May 1958/1 It is claimed to have an output of 100 watts RMS working into an 8-ohm inductive or reactive load.

b. *Mech.* and *Acoustics.* Possessing or pertaining to mechanical or acoustic impedance.

1934 OLSON & MASSA *Applied Acoustics* ii. 32 (*caption*) Resistive and reactive air load per unit area on one side of a vibrating piston of radius R centimeters set in an infinite baffle. **1963** [see IMPEDANCE 2]. **1976** A. H. BENADE *Fund. of Musical Acoustics* xxi. 457/2 The other register hole on my special clarinet can be called a reactive register hole, i.e., an aperture in which the flow depends mainly on the inertia of the air moving through it.

7. *Gram.* (See quot.) *rare.*

1957 R. W. ZANDVOORT *Handbk. Eng. Gram.* v. ii. 224 To express the speaker's reaction to a previous statement by the person addressed which is repeated by the speaker (*reactive questions*)... You can't catch me.—I can't, can't I? said Philip.

B. *sb. Chem.* [ad. F. *réactif.*] A reagent. *rare.*

[**1790** *Monthly Rev.* III. 546 Chemical tests, or, as the French call them, *reactives.*] **1791** HAMILTON *Berthollet's Dyeing* I. I. II. iv. 192 A chemist should be employed for preparing a proper reactive. **1887** BROWNING *Parleyings, Ch. Avison* ix, Reviewing learnedly the list complete Of chemical reactives.

Hence **re'actively** *adv.*

1805 FOSTER *Ess.* I. ii. 30 The living world.. is re-actively throwing on him various moral influences and infections. **1860** A. L. WINDSOR *Ethica* v. 285 A very irritable temper, that bore him reactively into close relationship with a few.

So **re'activeness** (Webster 1847) = next.

reac'tivity. [f. REACTIVE *a.* + -ITY, after *activity.*] **a.** The state or power of being reactive.

1888 *Nature* 22 Mar. 503/1 The occurrence of colour.. is more frequently than not concomitant with a high degree of reactivity. **1896** *Allbutt's Syst. Med.* I. 558 Our knowledge.. of vital reactions and reactivity. **1907** *Chem. Abstr.* I. 1395 Transformation of open chains to cyclic compounds enhances their reactivity. **1934** *Jrnl. Theol. Stud.* XXXV. 402 The author would establish that religion consists in simultaneous reactivity of the affective, conative and cognitive elements of mentality. **1949** *Brit. Jrnl. Psychol.* Dec. 86 When the individual's P.G.R. [psychogalvanic reflex] scores are obtained for a given attitude they must be expressed for each person relative to his own general P.G.R. reactivity. **1950** *Sci. News* XV. 70 Consideration of the chemical reactivity of crystals will obviously be focussed primarily on the surfaces. **1956** *Nature* 10 Mar. 477/2 It is assumed that the reactivity of the anhydride is not increased by adsorption. **1972** DEPUY & CHAPMAN *Molec. Reactions & Photochem.* vii. 137 Electronic effects are more important than the steric effects in determining the relative reactivity of dienophiles.

b. The rate of reaction of a coke or coal with (orig.) carbon dioxide, or with oxygen, under specified conditions.

1926 *Rep. Fuel Res. Board 1925* (Dep. Sci. & Industr. Res.) 23 A method has been designed which gives an empirical figure for reactivity to carbon dioxide. **1930** *Engineering* 22 Aug. 251/4 A convenient distinction has been drawn between the combustibility of a coke, denoting the rate at which it burns in oxygen or air, and its reactivity, meaning the rate at which it reacts with carbon dioxide and produces the reducing atmosphere in which the metallic iron is extracted. **1947** G. W. HIMUS *Elem. Fuel Technol.* xv. 296 The 'Reactivity Value' of coke is defined by the Fuel Research Board as 'the number of millilitres of carbon monoxide formed from 100 millilitres of carbon dioxide' under certain definitely specified conditions. **1971** *Materials & Technol.* II. x. 601 Gas coke.. has a lower reactivity than most coals and is not suitable for use on open fires. *Ibid.* 604 The reactivity of coke with respect to oxygen is often measured by the Critical Air Blast (C.A.B.) method.

c. *Nuclear Physics.* A measure of the extent to which a reactor (or part of it) deviates from a steady critical condition (see quot. 1962).

Orig. in a broader sense.

1945 H. D. SMYTH *Atomic Energy* viii. 89 The reactivity of the pile was so far above expectations that it would have been beyond the capacity of the control rods to handle if the remainder of the heavy water had been added. **1947** *Physical Rev.* LXXII. 17/1 The reactivity of a chain-reacting pile depends critically on the balance of neutron production, absorption, and leakage. **1954** R. STEPHENSON *Introd. Nuclear Engin.* vii. 270 In order to operate at any appreciable power, some excess reactivity must be available to overcome the various factors which act to reduce the ability of the chain reactor to multiply neutrons. **1960** *Gloss. Atomic Terms* (U.K.A.E.A.) 44 At any steady state of operation the reactivity is zero. **1962** *Gloss. Terms Nuclear Sci.* (*B.S.I.*) 97 *Reactivity*, the value of the expression $(k_{eff} - 1)/k_{eff}$, which is a measure of the departure of a reactor from the critical condition... k_{eff} is the multiplication constant (effective). **1963** B. FOZARD *Instrumentation Nuclear Reactors* xii. 149 A sudden change in reactivity in either direction is liable to produce thermal shock in the fuel elements. **1974** *Encycl. Brit. Macropædia* XIII. 3142 The reactivity of the core increases when the rods.. are withdrawn.

reactor (ri:'æktə(r)). Also (*rare*) reacter. [f. REACT *v.*[1] + -OR.] **1.** A person, animal, or organism that reacts to a stimulus, esp. under test or experimental conditions; *spec.* one showing an immune response to a specific antigen.

1890 W. JAMES *Princ. Psychol.* I. xi. 433 One must bear in mind that in these experiments the reacter always knew in advance in a general way the *kind* of question which he was to receive. *Ibid.* xiii. 525 The reacter awaits the signal and reacts if it is of one sort, but omits to act if it is of another sort. **1895** E. B. TITCHENER in *Amer. Jrnl. Psychol.* VII. 83 *Reagent*, reagent or reactor. **1907** *Psychol. Rev.* (Monogr. Suppl.) VIII. III. 314 In Series III. the reaction consisted in stopping a vertical movement... The reactor moved the pencil up and down against this vertical guide. **1928** *Daily Tel.* 6 Nov. 7/7 Out of 835 animals.. 122 reacted to the double intradermal test, and 94 of these reactors proved tuberculous at autopsy. **1932** *Amer. Rev. Tuberc.* XXV. 367 In this case the reactor was the sanatorium chef, who has never had tuberculosis. **1932** [see *Schick-negative* adj.]. **1961** *Listener* 30 Nov. 933/1 There may be some value in recording people's reactions to events and also the appearance of the reactors at any given moment. **1969** MYERS & STEELE *Bovine Tuberculosis* vi. 351 Since 1961, the [N.Z.] Government has provided the funds to pay for the tuberculin testing costs, and compensation for reactors sent to slaughter. **1973** *Black Panther* 10 Nov. 3/4 They are not actors, but reactors, and not leaders, but followers. **1976** *Nature* 13 May 144/1 Among the other categories of patients tested, the percentage of negative reactors varied from 3 to 14%.

2. a. *Electr.* A coil or other piece of equipment which provides reactance in a circuit.

1915 H. B. DWIGHT *Constant-Voltage Transmission* iii. 14 The name 'synchronous condenser'.. is not quite so appropriate when the machine is used with a constant-voltage transmission line, because for a large share of the time the current in the machine is not leading, but lagging, and the machine at that time does not behave as a condenser, but would more accurately be called a 'synchronous reactor'. **1920** *Chem. Abstr.* XIV. 2756 The cast-in-concrete air-core reactor is recommended for furnace work. **1951** *Engineering* 9 Nov. 584/2 Each pair of ignitrons is capable of supplying a rectified current of 650 amperes at 600 volts, the 30 per cent ripple in which is reduced by the smoothing reactor. **1958** J. SHEPHERD et al. *Higher Electr. Engin.* xvi. 389 Current-limiting reactors may be connected in series with each generator, in series with each feeder, or between each bus-bar section. **1961** G. F. TAGG *Pract. Electr. Engin.* I. 33 One method of reducing short-circuit current is by the employment of reactances or inductance coils which, for large a.c. power systems, are known as reactors.

b. A vessel or apparatus in which substances are made to react chemically, esp. one in an industrial plant.

1935 *Industr. & Engin. Chem.* Sept. 1072/2 In the pyrolysis of ethane and propane best results were obtained when using a reactor consisting of a helical coil of KA2S tubing... This reactor was placed in a radiant-type electrically heated furnace. **1939** *World Petroleum* May 42/2 The plant consists essentially of an assembly of three polymerization reactors, debutanizer, rerunning column for separation of polymer into dimer.. and trimer.., with two nickel catalyst hydrogenation reactors for conversion of the dimer to finished iso-octane. **1974** *Daily Tel.* 17 July 19/4 The kettle he should have been watching was a three-ton reactor heating synthetic resin. The reactor.. was just two degrees under 100 degrees centigrade when it was seen and could have cracked.. or exploded. **1975** *Sci. Amer.* Nov. 107/1 Using air to remove the graphite from the diamond surface enables us to carry out both operations in a single reactor. **1978** *Nature* 22 June 582/1 The accident happened in a reactor used for the production of trichlorophenol.

c. = *nuclear reactor* s.v. NUCLEAR *a.* 4. Freq. *attrib.*

1945 [see *nuclear reactor*]. **1947** *Newsweek* 8 Sept. 76/3 The tight-lipped Atomic Energy Commission did not tell all it knows about the new 'reactor'. The active substance is plutonium. **1950** *Chemical Engin. Progress* XLVI. 110/1 It behoves this nation to keep in the forefront of reactor technology. *Ibid.*, The enormous cost of the reactor program. **1957** *Economist* 19 Oct. 256/1 A maximum limit of 20 per cent enrichment with uranium 235.. is usually imposed on uranium exports from the US, and the limit is exceeded only in such special cases as the fuel core for Harwell's Dido research reactor. **1963** B. FOZARD *Instrumentation Nuclear Reactors* xii. 144 Most of the neutrons in a reactor core.. are produced at the instant of fission as the products of a reaction of great violence. **1971** *Materials & Technol.* II. xii. 734 Reprocessing.. is essential if plutonium is to be utilized in a mixed national power system of fast and thermal reactors. **1975** *Nature* 16 Oct. 525/3 The air in the reactor room is maintained at a lower pressure than the air outside, so that if radioactivity were released from the reactor, it would not immediately be dispersed into the atmosphere.

re-'actuate, *v.* [RE- 5 b.] *trans.* To make actual again; to restore to actuality.

1810 COLERIDGE in *Lit. Rem.* (1838) III. 386 As far as the principle.. went to re-actuate the idea of the Church, as a co-ordinate and living Power.

reacuntar, obs. Sc. f. RECOUNTER.

read (ri:d), *sb.*[1] *Obs.* exc. *dial.* or *techn.* Also 4 (9 *dial.*) rede, 5, 9 *Sc.* reid, 8 red, 8–9 reed. [OE. *réada*, of obscure origin.] The stomach of an animal; in later use only *spec.* the fourth stomach of a ruminant.

It is probable that the special sense of the word is the original one, but the early examples are not sufficiently definite to establish this.

c **1000** ÆLFRIC *Gloss.* in Wr.-Wülcker 159/38 *Ilia*, smæle þearmas. *Tolia, uel porunula*, reada. *c* **1320** *Sir Tristr.* 489 He riȝt al þe rede, þe wombe oway he bare. *c* **1450** HOLLAND *Howlat* 839 He cryid: 'Allace.. revyn is my reid! I am vngraciously gorrit, baith guttis and gall!' **1601** HOLLAND *Pliny* I. 342 All creatures hauing a Stomack or Read, are not without a belly vnder it. **1666** J. SMITH *Old Age* (1676) 84 That is that which Anatomists call, *Omasum*, and our Butchers, the Read. **1701** GREW *Cosmol. Sacra* I. v. 29 Most of those [animals] which have no upper Teeth, or none at all; have Three Stomachs: As in Beasts, the Panch, the Read and the Feck. **1782** A. MONRO *Compar. Anat.* (ed. 3) 40 From this it passes into the fourth [stomach],.. or the red, which is the name it commonly has because of its colour. **1808** JAMIESON s.v., *A calf's reid*, the fourth stomach of a calf, used for runnet or earning. **1836–9** *Todd's Cycl. Anat.* II. 11/1 The food is finally deposited in the fourth stomach, the abomasum.. or reed. **1886** W. BARNES *Dorset Gloss.*, *Read.*

attrib. *a* **1756** MRS. HEYWOOD *New Present* (1771) 191 Get four pounds of reed tripe. **1895** *Daily News* 13 Dec. 8/1 Such technical particulars (to be understandable by butchers only) as 'weights of suet, caul, and reed fat'.

read (ri:d), *sb.*[2] [f. READ *v.*] An act of perusal; a spell of reading; also *Sc.*, a loan of a book, etc., for the purpose of reading it. *transf.*, something for reading, esp. with ref. to its value as entertainment or information (freq. with qualifying adj.).

1825 JAMIESON Suppl. s.v., Will ye gie me a read of that book? **1838** THACKERAY *Hist. Sam. Titmarsh* x, When I arrived and took.. my first read of the newspaper. **1862** DARWIN in *Life* (1887) II. 391, I have just finished, after several reads, your paper. **1870** LOWELL *Stud. Wind.* 39 A good solid read.. into the small hours. **1902** J. MILNE *Epistles Atkins* i. 8 The soldiers.. have 'another good read'. **1958** *Observer* 9 Feb. 15/3 A.G.'s usual solid, lively read. **1961** *John o' London's* 21 Sept. 327/3 *My Friend Sandy* can be hugely recommended.. as a pleasantly light, bright sophisticated read. **1963** T. PARKER *Unknown Citizen* v. 136 He'd come back to the prison, had his tea, and gone to bed to lie down and have a read. **1975** L. TRILLING in *Times Lit. Suppl.* (1976) 5 Mar. 250/4 Was she [*sc.* Jane Austen] perhaps to be thought of as nothing more than a good read? .. Now that we have before us that British locution, which Americans have lately taken to using, the question might be asked why the phrase should have come to express so much force of irony and condescension. **1977** J. I. M. STEWART *Madonna of Astrolabe* xviii. 256 *Tamburlaine* is a tolerable read... As a stage play it is pretty hopeless. **1981** *Times* 2 Mar. 12/6 The labels are informative to the point of saturation. If you do not like the wine, you might at least enjoy the read.

read (ri:d), *v.* Pa. t. and pa. pple. read (red). Forms: *Inf.* 1 rǽdan, (-on, ræddan, *north.* reda, reða), 3 ræden(n), raden, 2–4 reden, 5 redyn; (and *pres.*) 2, 4 rade, 3–6 rede, 5–6 reede, *Sc.* red, reid, 6 (8 *Sc.*) reed; (3) 6–7 reade, 6– read. (Also 3 *sing. pres.* 1 ræt, 2–4 ret, 3 red, 3–4 rat.) *Pa. t.* 1 *pl.* reordun; 1 rǽdde, 3–4, 6 radde, (4 rade), 4, 6 rad, (4 rat); 1 *pl.* red(d)on, 3, 6 (9) redd, 4 redde, 4–6 rede, 4–6 (7–8) red, 7– read. *Pa. pple.* 1 rǽden, 4 reddynn, 6 readen; 1 rǽded, 3–4 redd, 3–6 redde, (4 radde), 3–6 (7–8) red, 4 rede, 6 reed(e, 6– read; 1 ȝeredd, 3 ired, 3–4 irad, 4 iredde, yrade, 4–5 iradde. [Comm. Teut.: OE. *rǽdan* = OFris. *rêda*, OS. *râdan* (MLG. *raden*, MDu. and Du. *raden*), OHG. *râtan* (MHG. *râten*, G. *raten*, *rathen*), ON. *ráða* (Sw. *råda*, Da. *raade*), Goth. *-rêdan*:—OTeut. **rǣđan*, prob. related to OIr. *im-rádim* to deliberate, consider, OSl. *raditi* to take thought, attend to, Skr. *rādh-* to succeed, accomplish, etc.

The Comm. Teut. verb belonged to the reduplicating ablaut-class, with pa. t. **rerōđ* and pa. pple. **garǣđono-z*, whence Goth. *-rairôþ*, **-rêdans*, ON. *rếð*, *ráðinn*, OHG. *riat*, *girâtan* (G. *riet*, *geraten*), OS. *ried* or *rêd*, **girâdan* (Du. *ried*, *geraden*). The corresponding forms in OE. are *reord* and (*ȝe*)*rǽden*, but these are found only in a few instances in Anglian texts, the usual conjugation being *rǽdde*, *ȝerǽd*(*e*)*d*, on the analogy of weak verbs such as *lǽdan*: cf. MLG. *radde*, *redde*, Sw. *rådde*, and G. *rathete* (for usual *riet*), Da. *raadede*. The typical ME. forms are *redde* or *radde* in the pa. t., and (*i*)*red* or (*i*)*rad* in the pa. pple.; in the later language (from the 17th c.) all tenses of the verb have the same spelling, *read*, though in pronunication the vowel of the preterite forms differs from that of the present and infinitive. Individual writers have from time to time denoted this by writing *red* or *redd* for the pa. t. and pa. pple., but the practice has never been widely adopted.

The original senses of the Teut. verb are those of taking or giving counsel, taking care or charge of a thing, having or exercising control over something, etc. These are also prominent in OE., and the sense of 'advise' still survives as an archaism, usually distinguished from the prevailing sense of the word by the retention of the older spelling REDE. The sense of considering or explaining something obscure or mysterious is also common to the various languages, but the application of this to the interpretation of ordinary writing, and to the expression of this in speech, is confined to English and ON. (in the latter perhaps under Eng. influence).]

I. Transitive uses.

* *To consider, interpret, discern, etc.*

†**1. a.** To have an idea; to think or suppose *that*, etc. *Obs. rare.*

c **900** tr. *Bæda's Hist.* III. x, þa ongann he..þencean & rædan, þætte nan oðer intinga wære [etc.]. *c* **1400** *Destr. Troy* 3308 Tho truly þat are takon..Shalbe plesit with plenty..red ye non oþer. **1600** Breton *Pasquils Foolescappe* (1879) 22/1 Let him be sure that better wits doe reede Such Madhead fellowes are but Fooles indeede. **1768** Ross *Helenore* III. 122 Goodwife, I reed your tale is true. *Ibid.* 125, I reed 'twas they that me a dreaming set.

†**b.** To guess, to make out or tell by conjecture *what, who, why*, etc. *Obs.*

a **1000** *Riddles* lxii. 9 Ræd, hwæt ic mæne! *c* **1000** Ælfric *Hom.* II. 248 Iudei..heton hine rædan hwa hine hreopode. *a* **1300** *Cursor M.* 597 Þow mai ask..qui god him gaue sua mikel a nam; Parfay þat es bot eth to rede. **1530** Palsgr. 681/2 Rede who tolde it me and I wyll tell the trouthe. **1564** *Child-Marriages* 124 This deponent askid the said Margaret, who that shuld be; and the said Margaret bade this deponent reade if he cold. **1590** Spenser *F.Q.* II. xii. 70 Right hard it was for wight which did it heare To reade what manner musicke that mote bee.

†**c.** To take *for* something. *Obs. rare.*

1591 Spenser *Ruins of Time* 633, I saw a stately Bed,.. That might for anie Princes couche be red. [**1813** Scott *Rokeby* III. xvii, I read you for a blod Dragoon, That lists the tuck of drum.]

2. a. To make out or discover the meaning or significance of (a dream, riddle, etc.); to declare or expound this to another.

c **1000** Ælfric *Gram.* (Z.) 179 *Conicio*..ic ræde swefn. *a* **1300** *Cursor M.* 4553, I haf soght..At find a man mi drem to rede. *Ibid.* 7122 If þai cuth right þat redel rede. *c* **1380** Wyclif *Serm.* Sel. Wks. I. 69 Men þat can rede þes signes. *c* **1440** *Promp. Parv.* 426/2 Redyn or expownyn redellys, or parabol, and other privyteys, *idem quod* ondon'. **1593** Drayton *Ecl.* IV. iii, Let vs passe this wearie winters day In reading Riddles. **1768** Ross *Helenore* III. 124 I'm right, I'm right! My dream is read. **1810** Scott *Lady of L.* V. xiii, Then, by my word,..The riddle is already read. **1887** Ruskin *Præterita* II. 24 Neither he nor I were given to reading omens, or dreading them.

refl. **1865** Carlyle *Fredk. Gt.* XIV. vii. (1872) V. 239 The small riddle reads itself to him so.

b. To foresee, foretell, predict. Chiefly in ***to read one's fortune***.

In quot. 1647 passing into sense 10 c.

1591 Spenser *M. Hubberd* 698 For he mongst Ladies could their fortunes read. **1647** Cowley *Mistress, My fate* 19 You, who men's fortunes in their faces read. **1790** Shirrefs *Poems* 122 Like gospel, Sir, she credits a' ye said, And says, she's sure 'twill happen as ye read.

†**3.** To count, reckon, estimate. *Obs. rare.*

a **1225** *Juliana* 51 (Bodl. MS.) Ne mahte hit na mon rikenin ne reden [*v.r.* tellen]. *a* **1300** *Cursor M.* 2570 Þe barns þat o þe sal bred Namar sal þou þam cun rede, þan sterns on light and sand in see. **1340** Hampole *Pr. Consc.* 2484 Swa may we ay rekken and rede An hondreth syns agayne a gude dede. **1790** Grose *Prov. Gloss.*, *Read*, to judge of, guess. At what price do you Read this horse? *Glouc.*

†**4.** To see, discern, distinguish. *Obs. rare* (in Spenser only).

1590 Spenser *F.Q.* I. i. 21 Such vgly monstrous shapes elswhere may no man reed. *Ibid.* III. ix. 2 Good, by paragone Of evill, may more notably be rad. **1596** *Ibid.* V. xii. 39 Bit him behind, that long the marke was to be read.

** *To peruse, without uttering in speech.*

5. a. To inspect and interpret in thought (any signs which represent words or discourse); to look over or scan (something written, printed, etc.) with understanding of what is meant by the letters or signs; to peruse (a document, book, author, etc.); to understand (musical notation); *spec.* = *sight-read* s.v. SIGHT *sb.*[1] 17.

Formerly used in imperative (as in quot. 1563) in referring the reader to another book or author for information.

c **888** K. Ælfred *Boeth.* Proem., He halsað ælcne þara þe þas boc rædan lyste. *c* **950** *Lindisf. Gosp.* John xix. 20 Ðiosne ..taccon meniȝo redon [*Rushw.* reddon]. *c* **1200** Ormin Ded. 328 Þa Crisstene menn þatt herenn oþerr redenn þiss boc. *a* **1300** *Cursor M.* 8495 Þis writte wit fele was red and sene, Bot fa it wist quat it wald mene. **1375** Barbour *Bruce* I. 17 Auld storys that men redys, Representis to thaim the dedys Of stalwart folk. **1413** *Pilgr. Sowle* (Caxton) I. xxii. (1859) 23 He hath redde and knowen bothe wordes and werkes of the rather seyntes. **1532** More *Confut. Tindale* Wks. 684/2, I can proue that he red some commentours and holy doctours, that write exposicions vpon it. **1563** Shute *Archit.* B ij, The Pyramides..and manye other beautifull buildinges of that nacion. Reade Diado. Sic. li. I. 2. **1617** Moryson *Itin.* II. 230 Because I am not sure whether you can perfectly reade her Maiesties hand, I send you the same in a coppy. **1646** *Hamilton Papers* (Camden) 126 One word of it which I reade without my cipher. **1709** Pope *Ess. Crit.* 233 A perfect Judge will read each work of Wit, With the same spirit that its author writ. **1774** Mitford *Ess. Harmony Lang.* 16 What has been printed on both Sides is little red. **1792** H. Newdigate *Let.* Mar. in A. E. Newdigate-Newdegate *Cheverels* (1898) ix. 133 Her Voice was not strong but..they are quite astonish'd with her knowledge of Music & facility in reading it. **1864** Sir H. Taylor *Autobiog.* (1885) I. 198 My father, who had read the work.. in MS., rejoiced in it more and more when he came to read it in print. **1871** Smiles *Charac.* i. (1876) 23 He was always the most national of the Italian poets,..the most read. **1894** G. B. Shaw in *Fortn. Rev.* Feb. 258 To do half-a-dozen things much more difficult than reading music. **1918** —— in *Nation* 22 June 308/1 To wile away the time by reading at sight a bundle of band parts and vocal scores of a rather difficult opera. **1938** D. Baker *Young Man with Horn* I. v. 56 Jeff's band didn't play from music, though they could all read music. **1974** *Listener* 24 Jan. 106/3, I could read the music and be able to make it work right away with five minutes' rehearsal.

b. To peruse books, etc. written in (a certain language); *esp.* to have such knowledge of (a language) as to be able to understand works written in it. *spec.* to peruse books, newspapers, etc., for quotations suitable for inclusion as illustrative examples in a dictionary.

1530 Palsgr. 681/2, I rede latyn better nowe than I wene I shall do frenche hence of a yere. **1612** Brinsley *Lud. Lit.* iii. (1627) 22 Now they may goe thus forward..in reading English perfitly. **1692** Locke *Education* §163 When he can speak and read French well..he should proceed to Latin. **1779** Johnson *L.P.*, *Milton* (1868) 62 He read all the languages which are considered either as learned or polite. *a* **1862** Hogg in Dowden *Shelley* I. 73 He [Shelley] had in truth read more Greek than many an aged pedant. **1873** Hamerton *Intell. Life* III. vii. 109 By far the shortest way to learn to read a language is to begin by speaking it. **1876** J. A. H. Murray *Let.* 29 Nov. in K. M. E. Murray *Caught in Web of Words* (1977) vii. 146, I dont for words of that kind believe in the quotation test at all..because you know that not one millionth of current literature is read, & that it is the veriest chance or succession of chances which has caught *carriageless*..& missed a thousand others as good. **1961** R. W. Burchfield in *Essays & Studies* XIV. 39 A large number of literary sources..are being systematically read against an Oxford dictionary. **1977** K. M. E. Murray *Caught in Web of Words* xii. 235 Lowell's book of literary essays, *My Study Windows*, was one of those read for the Dictionary.

c. *transf.* and *fig.* in various applications.

1581 J. Hamilton in *Cath. Tract.* (S.T.S.) 87 Thou hes red (sayis he) the varkis of the varld. **1601** Shaks. *Twel. N.* V. i. 302 *Ol.* How now, art thou mad? *Clo.* No Madam, I do but reade madnesse. **1611** —— *Wint. T.* IV. iv. 172 Hee'l stand and reade, As 'twere, my daughters eyes. **1665** Glanvill *Scepsis Sci.* xxv. 154 [They] are the Alphabet of Science, and Nature cannot be read without them. **1741–2** Gray *Agrip.* 65 The dreadful powers That read futurity. **1782** Cowper *Charity* 333 He reads the skies. **1818** Shelley *Rev. Islam* IV. viii, All the ways of men among mankind he read. **1851** Mayne Reid *Scalp Hunt.* xxvi. 191 Indians can 'read' the smoke at a great distance. **1867** Craig *Palmistry* 42 One of the greatest of all difficulties in reading the hand. **1890** W. A. Wallace *Only a Sister?* 88 What's a man worth that cannot read his own watch? **1921** P. L. Haworth *Trailmakers of Northwest* 206 As Brennan had lost one eye and could not see any too well out of the other, he was glad to have one of us ride in his canoe and read water for him. **1932** L. Golding *Magnolia St.* II. ii. 300 In the little town in..Lancashire where she was born quite as many people read tea-leaves as read their ABC. **1951** E. Rickman *Come racing with Me* iii. 19 We are talking about 'reading' a race, which is the practice on the spectator's part of a comprehensive and discriminating view of a field of horses from start to finish, so that the performance of all or most of the runners, and their relative positions at various stages, are intelligently observed and memorised. **1965** Priestley & Wisdom *Good Driving* xi. 81 You get into the habit of registering mentally all the signs..which enable you to 'read' the road in front of you. **1967** *Boston Sunday Herald* 26 Mar. IV. 3/8 An optical scanner..may eliminate the sorting machines by 'reading' the zip code on the letter and dispatching it accordingly. **1967** Karch & Buber *Offset Processes* ii. 20 An optical system 'reads' the photograph, and a heated stylus is directed to penetrate the plate to be printed, producing halftone dots. **1969** R. Welsh *Beginner's Guide Curling* xvii. 120 The ability to read strange ice..and knowing exactly when to sweep are other qualities of a good skip. **1970** G. F. Newman *Sir, You Bastard* vi. 159 Ambition drowning the man was how she would read his promotion. **1971** *Sunday Express* (Johannesburg) 28 Mar. 17/1 You read a putt, stroke it properly along the line you have chosen, and then the ball breaks off in the opposite direction. **1972** *Daily Tel.* 5 May 3/3 A meter reader rang the bell and told my wife he wanted to read the meter in the garage. **1974** *Times* 19 Feb. 15/3 Most people are not used to 'reading' plans..and have only slightly less difficulty with architectural photographs. **1977** *Time* 14 Nov. 48/1 They broke down and then analyzed the RNA in the archaebacteria's ribosomes, the structures that 'read' the message of the master molecule DNA and produce the protein necessary for life. **1978** *Monitor* (McAllen, Texas) 12 Feb. 1-B/1 This generation of Gypsies..will wake up to modern life and give up many of the old customs... My job was supposed to be reading palms. **1979** *SLR Camera* Jan. 36/3 Like the now discontinued EF the AE-1 uses a silicon photocell to read the light.

d. *transf.* To make out the character or nature of (a person, the heart, etc.) by scrutiny or interpretation of outward signs.

1611 Shaks. *Wint. T.* III. iii. 73 Though I am not bookish yet I can reade Waiting-gentlewoman in the scape. **1647** N. Bacon *Disc. Govt. Eng.* I. Pref. (1739) 7 Historians..for the most part read Men. **1727** Swift *Letter on Eng. Tongue*, This they call knowing the world, and reading men and manners. **1838** Lytton *Alice* I. x, I wish you could read my heart at this moment. **1902** Edna Lyall *Hinderers* ix, We ordinary mortals are at the mercy of you artists... You read us like books.

e. To interpret (a design) in terms of the setting up needed to reproduce it on a loom. Also with *in*.

1839 Ure *Dict. Arts* 267 In both modes of manufacture, the piece is mounted by reading-in the warp for the different leaves of the heddles. **1895** T. F. Bell *Jacquard Weaving & Designing* i. 9 The straight-edge EE..will slide up and down in the frame, to mark the line on the design paper that is next to be read by the lasher. **1897** [see *reading-machine* s.v. READING *vbl. sb.* 10 b]. **1924** T. Woodhouse *Jacquards & Harness* iv. 107 Before describing the remaining parts of the machine, it will..be best to indicate how the design is read. **1958** A. Hindson *Designer's Drawloom* xi. 105 The weaver can tie up the pattern single-handed, but it can be done more easily and quickly if there is a helper to read the pattern draft.

f. To study (a subject, a 'school') at a university; to read for (a degree). Cf. sense 15 c.

1884 [see *Greats* s.v. GREAT C. 10]. **1955** *Times* 23 May 6/1 Agriculture is no longer a subject to be ashamed of; it produces no inferiority complex in those who read it. **1966** *Rep. Comm. Inquiry Univ. Oxf.* II. 49 Graduates reading first degrees. *Ibid.* 85 Women undergraduates reading arts. **1970** [see English *sb.* 3 d]. **1977** *Professional Careers Bull.* Autumn 1/1 Partially it has been due to an ever increasing demand from sixth formers to read law.

g. Phr. ***to read one's shirt*** (see quot. 1925). *slang.*

1918 *Nat. Geogr. Mag.* June 499 They..speak of 'reading their shirts'. **1925** Fraser & Gibbons *Soldier & Sailor Words* 237 *To read a shirt*, to search it for lice. **1931** 'D. Stiff' *Milk & Honey Route* xiii. 144 It is said, for instance, that the hobo spends a great deal of his time reading his shirt, seeking certain animals known as 'seam squirrels'.

h. *Computers.* To copy or extract data on or in (any storage medium or device); to copy, extract, or transfer (data). Also const. *into*, *out of*.

1940 W. J. Eckert *Punched Card Methods Scientific Computation* 4 The number are..read into the machines by ..electrical contacts made through the holes. **1945** *Jrnl. Franklin Inst.* CCXL. 277 When the punched tapes are ready, the problem is placed on the machine by automatic controls which 'read' the first tape and make the specified assembly. **1948** *Math. Tables & Other Aids to Computation* III. 123 The speeds at which words can be read (or written) by the machine will be much less than the speeds at which the machine can transfer words internally. *Ibid.* 124 When additional instructions are received they can be read into the machine from an instruction tape. **1950** *High-Speed Computing Devices* ix. 151 The tape reader automatically reads punched tape..and transcribes the data represented by the holes in the tape to a deck of cards. Other equipment can perform the reverse operation, reading the holes punched in the cards and producing a tape. **1959** E. M. McCormick *Digital Computer Primer* ix. 135 The tape is then connected into the computer system and the information read from it to the computer. **1964** F. L. Westwater *Electronic Computers* i. 2 The card or tape is then 'read'. This may be done by allowing the holes to pass under tiny wire brushes. *Ibid.* iv. 59 To read a word out of the store we have to open a gate at the end, and this permits pulses to escape. **1964** *Ann. N.Y. Acad. Sci.* CXV. 654 The length of time required to read information from or store information into one of the 1,024..12-bit memory locations. **1970** O. Dopping *Computers & Data Processing* xiv. 226 The computer time for file maintenance..is often mainly determined by the time for reading and writing magnetic tape. **1972** *Computer Jrnl.* XV. 201/1 The commonest way of reading a file into the system. **1972** *Guardian* 14 Aug. 10/3 Computers can already 'read' a high speed disc-store at around 500,000 characters a second. **1978** J. K. Atkin *Basic Computer Sci.* vii. 92 To read a bit from the memory it is necessary to interrogate a particular core by sending current pulses..along the appropriate x- and y-wires.

i. To receive and understand the words of (a person) by radio or telephone, to hear; to detect (an object) by sonar; *transf.*, to understand the words or intentions of (a person).

1956 *Amer. Speech* XXXI. 228 [U.S.A.F. slang] *Do you read me?* As in conversation by radio, this means 'Do you understand me?' The answer might be, 'Yes, *five by five*', meaning loud and clear. **1956** 'E. McBain' *Cop Hater*

(1958) ix. 85 'Are you stoned now, or can you read me?' 'I hear you,' Ordiz said. **1960** *Master Detective* July 83/1 Static-laced code crackle sounded from the speaker. 'Poelzell. I read you. Keep the Dodge in sight.' **1963** *Times* 25 May 10/7 'Does *anyone* read poor Philip?' A comforting voice from a glider, still airborne: 'Humphrey to Philip. Loud and clear.' **1967** R. J. SERLING *President's Plane is Missing* (1968) ix. 164 'Don't be so oversolicitous, Rod. It's as bad for a marriage as being too inconsiderate. Do you read me?' 'I read you, Nancy.' **1968** R. SEVERN *Game for Hawks* x. 120 'How d'you read her, Cass?' he asked, sourly. 'Could she be taking you for a ride?' **1970** B. KNOX *Children of Mist* v. 103 'If you can hear.. this is an emergency call.' .. Thane pressed the microphone button. 'Fenn, we read you.' **1972** J. PORTER *Meddler & her Murder* x. 131 The girl friend listening?.. Oh, I read you. Well, I'll make it short and sweet. **1974** L. DEIGHTON *Spy Story* xviii. 193 A couple of conventional subs steaming a parallel course... We read them on the sonar and ranged them. **1977** D. BENNETT *Jigsaw Man* xi. 203 As from the end of this call, this number will be discontinued. I am reading you back for the fast time.

6. With adverbs. **a.** To go *over* (a letter, book, etc.) in the act of perusal. Also *transf.*

c **1374** CHAUCER *Troylus* II. 1036 (1085) He.. radde it over, and gan the lettre folde. **1560** DAUS tr. *Sleidane's Comm.* 133 The Lantgrave readinge over their booke and their letters, noted what he thought blame worthy. **1594** LYLY *Moth. Bomb.* III. iii, Fooles.. Haue farre more knowledge To reade a woman ouer [etc.]. **1683** H. PRIDEAUX in *Lett. Lit. Men* (Camden) 185 Some booke or other.. which he will read over, and then bring me again. **1768** GRAY *Let.* 28 Oct., The first act of Caractacus is just arrived here, but I have not read it over.

b. *to read through* (†or *out*): to peruse from beginning to end. †Also *to read out*, to read to the end of, to finish the reading of. *Obs.*

1638 BAKER tr. *Balzac's Lett.* (vol. II.) 196, I may boldly say, I never yet read a Gazetta through. **1652** GATAKER *Antinom.* 21 Had this Autor but writ or red out the text he cites he had found somewhat more then faith in it. **1662** NEWCOME *Diary* 6 Sept. (Chetham Soc.) 120, I read out wt remained to be read in Rushworth. **1715** SWIFT *Let.* 28 June, Wks. 1841 II. 526/1, I borrowed your Homer from the bishop, and read it out in two evenings. **1747** MRS. S. FIELDING *Lett. David Simple* II. 151 The pretence of being eager to read out some new Book which I have borrowed. **1858** FROUDE *Hist. Eng.* vii. (1870) II. 113 He read it through, and replied that.. for himself it was impossible [to take the oath].

c. *to read off*: to note in definite form (the result of inspection, esp. of a graduated instrument).

Perh. originally used as in sense 11 d.

1816 J. SMITH *Panorama Sc. & Art* II. 69 Before the height of the mercury is read off. **1834** *Penny Cycl.* II. 525/2 The angle read off on the interior edge of the ecliptic is the longitude. **1899** *Allbutt's Syst. Med.* VII. 435 Passing the tip of the finger over the outlines of the letters and so reading off the result. **1956** E. H. HUTTEN *Lang. Mod. Physics* vi. 262 The empiricist prejudice.. is, indeed, very strong, but it is obviously not true that we simply read off our hypotheses from data.

d. To mark or impress *on* (a fabric).

1831 G. R. PORTER *Silk Manuf.* 258 The workman proceeds to read on the design.

e. *to read up*: to study (a subject, a topic, etc.) intensively and systematically; to familiarize oneself with (a subject) by reading.

1842 J. S. MILL *Let.* 22 Aug. in *Wks.* (1963) XIII. 542, I began to *read up* the subject. **1856** C. M. YONGE *Daisy Chain* II. xxvii. 657, I dread reading up all I must read presently. **1869** 'MARK TWAIN' *Innocents Abroad* xv. 147, I shall throttle down my emotions hereafter, about this sort of people, until I have read them up. **1894** 'R. ANDOM' *We Three & Troddles* xvii. 149 Those miserable, hollow shams who read up the cricket news.. in the evening papers. **1915** R. BROOKE *Coll. Poems* p. cxxxvii, I've been peacefully reading up the countryside all the morning. **1921** K. MACAULAY *Dangerous Ages* v. 103 You should read it up beforehand, and try if you can understand it. **1962** D. LESSING *Golden Notebk.* II. 280 Those Russians, they're pretty well up in my field, I read them up. **1977** F. BRANSTON *Up & Coming Man* xiv. 152 He would have covered his interests by reading up the minutes of all committees.

f. *Computers. to read out*, to extract (data); to transfer from internal storage; so *to read in.*

1946 *Ann. Computation Lab. Harvard Univ.* I. 62 The storage counter cams.. control the number impulses for reading out either from a switch or from a storage counter. Figure 26 shows the circuits for a read-out. *Ibid.* 159 The number of columns shifted is recorded in a counter and a predetermined number of significant digits and a power of ten are read out. **1957** [see OFF-LINE *a.* and *adv.* A. 2]. **1959** E. M. MCCORMICK *Digital Computer Primer* ii. 7 When the problem is completely solved.. the calculation is stopped, and the output, or answer, is read out. **1961** [see READ-OUT 1 a]. **1968** *Times* 10 Dec. 6/8 On each orbit the storage system reads out the information to a ground station. **1970** O. DOPPING *Computers & Data Processing* xiv. 222 When all the records have been read-in, all that is needed then is to print the contents of the 50 cells. **1971** *Physics Bull.* Mar. 158/3 It covers those devices in which information can be stored for a limited or controlled time and then read out leaving the device capable of repeated use.

7. a. To attach a certain meaning or interpretation to (what is read); to take in a particular way.

1624 BP. MOUNTAGU *Gagg* 201 Secondly, read it how you will, it is not to purpose. **1890** SIR N. LINDLEY in *Law Times Rep.* LXIII. 690/1, I think there are two methods of reading that order.

b. *transf.* To take a certain view of (a person, thing, event, etc.), to regard in a certain light. Also, to interpret or comprehend.

1847 HELPS *Friends in C.* (1851) I. 11 This is a matter which, as I read it, concerns only the higher natures. **1866** J. MARTINEAU *Ess.* I. 190 Every relative disability may be read two ways. **1962** *Listener* 22 Nov. 886/3 When East removed the double into One Spade, West read his partner for a psychic opening and bid Three No Trumps. **1967** *Ibid.* 28 Dec. 846/3 He.. wants.. the celebration of the Eucharist (so I read him) to take the form of a prayer meeting. **1970** *Sunday Tel.* 20 Dec. 21/7 Gleeson mesmerises batsmen unable to read him, not into error but into strokelessness.

8. Const. with preps. **a.** *refl.* To bring (oneself) *into* or *to* (a certain state) by reading.

1676 WYCHERLEY *Pl. Dealer* III. i, We shall have you read yourself into a Humour of rambling and fighting. **1873** BLACK *Pr. Thule* xxi. 345 Give me that book, that I may read myself into a nap.

b. To introduce (an additional idea or element) *into* what is being read or considered. (Freq. implying that the insertion is unwarranted or erroneous.) Also with *in.*

1879 H. SPENCER *Princ. Sociol.*, *Ceremonial Inst.* §346 Men read back developed ideas into undeveloped minds. **1882** AINGER *Lamb* 173 He reads something of himself into the composition he is reviewing. **1895** SIR A. KEKEWICH in *Law Times Rep.* LXXIII. 663/1 This is a sensible limitation which can easily be read into deed or will. **1903** *Westm. Gaz.* 13 Nov. 7/2 The learned counsel argued that his lordship must read in a negative... In a contract for personal service you must have in it a negative, express or implied. **1919** 'C. DANE' *Legends* 96 She said to me once that the critics had 'read in' things that she had never dreamed of—that it made her doubt her own motives. **1966** G. N. LEECH *Eng. in Advertising* xv. 141 In 'lovely, oveny biscuits', 'oveny' can only be made denotatively meaningful by reading in something extra. **1979** E. H. GOMBRICH *Sense of Order* iv. 99 Finding it difficult, if not impossible, to tell at any point where we see elements and where texture..; where we are reading and where we are 'reading in'.

9. a. To adopt, give, or exhibit as a reading in a particular passage.

1659 HAMMOND *Acts* xv. Annot., The Æthiopick and other interpreters retain.., *what you would not have done to your selves, do not ye to another*,.. for which other Jewish writers read, *doing as they would be done to.* **1697** BENTLEY *Phal.* 20, I cannot.. comprehend why the most learned Is. Casaubon will read σπεύδοντα in this passage, and not σπένδοντα. **1759** RUDDIMAN *Animadver. Vind. Buchanan* 60 Instead of.. *sexagesimo quinto*, we should read,.. *sexagesimo nono.* **1847** MADDEN *Layamon's Brut.* III. 346 For *Lovaine* some copies of Wace read *Alemaigne.*

b. To register, indicate.

1887 GUMMING *Electricity* 44 A rider reading thousands of an ounce on the beam of a grocer's balance.

c. To convey (a statement) when read; to say. Cf. sense 18 b below.

1894 [see IT *pron.* 3 f]. **1904** G. PARKER *Ladder of Swords* xvi. 229 A footman.. came to Angèle, bearing a note which read: 'Your friend is very ill, and asks for you.' **1916** G. B. SHAW *Androcles & Lion* p. lxvi, Your examination paper will read 'The time of Jesus was worth nothing... Dr. Crippen's time was worth, say, three hundred and fifty pounds a year. Criticize this arrangement.' **1946** BIBLE (Rev. Standard Version) *Mark* xv. 26 And the inscription of the charge against him read, 'The King of the Jews.' **1961** NEW ENGLISH BIBLE *Rom.* xii. 19 There is a text which reads, 'Justice is mine, says the Lord, I will repay.'

*** *To learn by perusal.*

10. a. To see or find (a statement) in a written or otherwise recorded form; to learn by perusal of a book or other document. (†Formerly sometimes const. with *obj.* and *inf.* or *pple.*)

c **975** *Rushw. Gosp.* Matt. xxi. 42 Hwæt.. ȝe næfre reordun in ȝewritum [etc.]. *c* **1000** *Ags. Gosp.* Matt. xii. 3 Ne rædde ȝe hwæt Dauid dyde þa hyne hingrede. *c* **1200** *Trin. Coll. Hom.* 11 We radeð on boc, þat elch man haueð to fere on engel of heuene. *a* **1225** *Ancr. R.* 170 Ase me ret in hire boc, heo was the kinge Assuer ouer alle icweme. *a* **1300** *Cursor M.* 1459 Cainan his sun, als it es redde, His lijf nine hundret yeir he ledd. **1387** TREVISA *Higden* (Rolls) VII. 77 So it is i-rad þat Ioseph dalf wiþ his fader moche tresour in þe erþe. *c* **1440** *Generydes* 1 In olde Romanns and storys as I rede, Of Inde somtyme ther was a nobyll kyng. **1555** HARPSFIELD *Divorce Hen. VIII* (Camden) 268 The terrible punishment .. the like whereof I never read sent to any. **1597** SHAKS. *2 Hen. IV*, I. ii. 133, I haue read the cause of his effects in Galen. **1621** W. SCLATER *Tythes* (1623) 76, I never read Christ speake so much of any Jewish Caeremonie as he did of Tythes. **1764** GRAY *Jemmy Twitcher* 27 The prophet of Bethel, we read, told a lie. **1839** LONGF. *Beleaguered City* i, I have read, in some old marvellous tale,.. That [etc.].

b. *transf.* or *fig.* in various applications.

1588 SHAKS. *L.L.L.* II. i. 109 Vouchsafe to read the purpose of my comming. **1604** —— *Oth.* III. iv. 57 She was a Charmer, and could almost read The thoughts of people. **1667** MILTON *P.L.* IV. 1011 For proof look up, And read thy Lot in yon celestial Sign. **1840** DICKENS *Old C. Shop* i, Her quick eye seemed to read my thoughts.

c. To discern or discover (something) *in* (or *on*) the face, look, etc., of a person.

1590 SHAKS. *Com. Err.* III. ii. 9 Muffle your false loue.. Let not my sister read it in your eye. **1638** JUNIUS *Paint. Ancients* 235 He might read in their eyes and countenance the severall faces of anger, love, feare [etc.]. **1713** *Guardian* No. 137 ¶4 You read his ancestry in his smile. **1768** *Woman of Honor* II. 15, I red in her looks a willingness to come to an explanation. **1818** SHELLEY *Rev. Islam* VIII. xvii, I cannot name All that I read of sorrow, toil, and shame, On your worn faces. **1860** TENNYSON *Sea Dreams* 163 My eyes.. Read rascal in the motions of his back.

**** *To peruse and utter in speech.*

11. a. To utter aloud (the words or sentences indicated by the writing, etc., under inspection); to render in speech (anything written, a book, etc.) according as the written or printed signs are apprehended by the mind. Also *reading* = being read.

to read aloud is frequently used to distinguish this sense of the vb. from 5.

c **900** tr. *Bæda's Hist.* v. xxi. §3 Mid ðy þæt ȝewrit ða wæs ræded beforan þam cyninge. **971** *Blickl. Hom.* 167 We ȝehyrdon, þa þa Esaias se witȝa ræden wæs [etc.]. *c* **1000** ÆLFRIC *Exod.* xxiv. 7 Moises.. rædde his boc þam folce. *c* **1175** *Lamb. Hom.* 125 Al þet me ret and singeð on þisse timan in halie chirche. *a* **1225** *Ancr. R.* 428 Ȝe ancren owen þis lutle laste stucchen reden to our wummen eueriche wike enes. *c* **1315** SHOREHAM I. 1292 Ine þe alde laȝe þe redere Rede þe prophessye By wokke. *c* **1412** HOCCLEVE *De Reg. Princ.* 2955 When þei [laws] weren byfore hem I-radde, þei made hem wondir wroth. **1542** UDALL *Erasm. Apoph.* 40 When he heard the dialogue of Plato entitleed Lysides, readen. **1601** SHAKS. *Jul. C.* III. ii. 152 Read the Will; wee'l heare it Antony. **1621** in *Crt. & Times Jas. I* (1848) I. 249 While the proclamation was reading [etc.]. **1662** J. DAVIES tr. *Olearius' Voy. Ambass.* 213 If we desired it, we might hear the Letter read. **1705** *Lond. Gaz.* No. 4152/2 The Dean and Prebendaries sat within the Rails,.. except such as Officiated in Reading Prayers. **1802–12** BENTHAM *Ration. Judic. Evid.* (1827) II. 285 Oftentimes have I observed them, while affidavits have been reading, looking about to their brethren on the bench. **1875** JOWETT *Plato* (ed. 2) IV. 160 Socrates requested that the first thesis.. might be read over again.

b. In phr. *to read a lesson* or *lecture*: (see these words). Freq. *fig.* To teach (one) something, to administer a reprimand or check (to one).

a **1225** *Ancr. R.* 66 Al þet lescun þet God hire hefde ilered [*MS. C.* ired hire]. *a* **1460** *Gregory's Chron.* in *Hist. Coll. Citizen Lond.* (Camden) 230 Doctor Ive.. radde many fulle nobylle lessonnys to preve that Cryste was lorde of all. **1593** SHAKS. *Rich. II*, IV. i. 232 Would it not shame thee, in so faire a troupe, To reade a Lecture of them? **1629** MASSINGER *Picture* III. ii, I'll be her tutor, And read her another lesson. *c* **1632** in *Athenæum* No. 2883. 121/3 Is this our Jurisdiction or'e the Sea To reade man Lectures of humanity? **1817** JAS. MILL *Brit. India* II. IV. iv. 157 Dreadful was the fate.. and important are the lessons which it reads. **1884** W. E. NORRIS *Thirlby Hall* viii, To read him a lesson which should prevent him from doing the same a second time.

c. Used of submitting a proposed measure to a legislative assembly by reading the whole or some part of it. Cf. READING *vbl. sb.* 2 c.

1647 CLARENDON *Hist. Reb.* III. §129 The bill was.. immediately read the first and the second time, and so committed. **1692** [H. SCOBELL] *Rules & Customs* 4 The first business in the House is ordinarily to read a Bill that was not passed in the last Parliament proceeding. **1783** *Hansard Parl. Hist.* (1814) XXIII. 1224 [Mr. Fox's East India Bill] was read for the first time, and ordered to be printed. **1863** H. COX *Instit.* I. ix. 166 A bill having been read a first time, is ordered to be read a second time on a future day.

d. With adverbs (cf. 6), esp. *to read out* (or *up*).

1588 SHAKS. *L.L.L.* IV. iii. 193 *Iaque.* I beseech your Grace let this Letter be read... *King.* Berowne, read it ouer. **1600** HOLLAND *Livy* XXIV. xxv. 526 Before it was all red out and published, it passed cleare. **1626** BRETON *Fantastickes* (1879) 15/1 The first course is served in,.. the dishes haue be red ouer. **1784** R. BAGE *Barham Downs* I. 224 Read it up, Timothy: I have not yet seen or heard a syllable of it. **1794** SOUTHEY *Wat Tyler* III. i, *Tom Miller.* Read it out—read it out. *Hob.* Ay, ay, let's hear the Charter. **1808** STOWER *Printers' Gram.* 395 That part of the copy.. should be carefully transcribed or read off. **1862** F. C. HUSENBETH *Life Milner* 173 After dinner the Secretary of the Catholic Board read up certain Resolutions. **1890** HALL CAINE *Bondman* I. v, The clerk and sexton read out the askings for the marriage.

e. Phr. *to take* (something) *as read*: to treat (a statement, a subject, etc.) as if it has been agreed, without having a discussion about it; to take for granted. Occas. with other introductory vbs.

1886 G. M. HOPKINS *Lett. to R. Bridges* (1955) 244 Objections on your part, if any, are now too late and will be 'taken as read'. **1928** D. L. SAYERS *Unpleasantness at Bellona Club* iii. 22 Don't let's harrow our feelings. Take it as read. **1930** E. M. BRENT-DYER *Chalet Girls in Camp* x. 151 'It's really I who ought to say 'sorry', you know.'.. 'We'll take it all as read,' put in Miss Wilson hastily. **1938** M. ALLINGHAM *Fashion in Shrouds* xxi. 397, I think we can almost take that as read, don't you? **1959** 'M. M. KAYE' *House of Shade* v. 59 I'll take it as read. **1973** H. MILLER *Open City* xvii. 187 You can regard your complaint of boorishness.. as read.

†**12. a.** To teach or impart (some art or branch of knowledge) *to* another by (or as by) reading aloud. Also const. *with*, and without const. *Obs.*

1560–1 *First Bk. Disc.* in *Knox's Wks.* (1848) II. 210 A Colledge, in whiche the Artis.. be read be sufficient Maisteris. *a* **1586** SIDNEY *Astr. & Stella* Sonn. xxviii, Loue onely reading unto me this arte. **1601** B. JONSON *Poetaster* I. i, We may read constancy and fortitude To other souls. **1637** —— *Sad Sheph.* II. ii, Are these the arts, Robin, you read your rude ones of the wood? **1662** J. DAVIES tr. *Olearius' Voy. Ambass.* 215 He understood Astrology, and read Euclid to some of his Disciples. **1885** A. EDWARDES *Girton Girl* I. iii. 68 Geoffrey Arbuthnot, B.A. Cantab., is willing to read classics and mathematics with Miss Bartrand. Terms, five shillings an hour.

†**b.** In *pass.* To be instructed, to become learned *in. Obs.* (Cf. READ *ppl. a.* 2.)

1458 *Paston Lett.* I. 431 William hath goon to scole.. to lern and to be red in poetre or els in Frensh.

13. a. *to read oneself in*: to enter upon office as incumbent of a benefice in the Church of England, by reading publicly the Thirty-nine Articles and making the Declaration of Assent. Also *transf.*

1857 TROLLOPE *Barchester T.* xxiii. *heading*, Mr. Arabin reads himself in at St. Ewolds. **1890** BARING-GOULD *Old Country Life* 136 The rector is said to have visited one of his livings twice only.. once to read himself in. **1977** F.

BRANSTON *Up & Coming Man* xiv. 152 What could be more natural than for a keen new councillor to read himself in on past decisions?

b. *to read out of*: to expel from (a body, party, etc.), properly by reading out the sentence of expulsion. Chiefly in *pass.*; also *refl.* *to read in*: to admit or induct formally; to make (a person) a member of an armed service, to conscript.

1836 W. DUNLAP *Thirty Years Ago* I. xxi. 201 By the death of his parents, he was left in possession of some property, which he dissipated even before he 'was read out of meeting'. **1841** *Congress. Globe* 30 June 133/2 Mr. Alford concluded by warning the 'tariff boys' of the South, that instead of their reading him out of church, if they did not mind he would read them out of church. **1865** HUNT *Pop. Rom. W. Eng.* Ser. I. 96 He left the 'people' that he mightn't be read out. **1875** WHITNEY *Life Lang.* xv. 301 It is high time that any one who takes the wrong view be read out of the ranks. **1890** *Harper's Mag.* Feb. 349/2 They said I wasn't no Christian; and so they got together and read me out o' the church. **1915** F. HOPWOOD *Let.* 20 May in M. Gilbert *Winston S. Churchill* (1972) III. Compan. II. 920 It is plain that a First Sea Lord remains in office until the new Patent appointing his successor is passed the Seal & he is 'read in' at the Board. **1938** C. S. FORESTER *Ship of Line* viii. 110 Excellent, Mr. Bush. Read 'em in. **1942** E. PAUL *Narrow St.* xxii. 186 Men..who may be read into the army and shot as traitors if they try to strike, are difficult material. **1976** *Time* 27 Dec. 14/2 Arafat also warned that any Palestinian group that rejected the idea..must read itself out of the P.L.O.

c. To bring or draw *down to*, by reading aloud.

1847 TENNYSON *Princ.* II. 235 Are you That Psyche, wont to..read My sickness down to happy dreams?

†**14. a.** To declare, as by reading aloud; to relate, tell, say. *Obs.*

a **1300** *Cursor M.* 10198 In almis dede hir lijf sco ledd, Als we find in the stori redd. *c* **1320** *Cast. Love* 1359 No tonge ne mihte reden Ne þou3t þenken his mihtful deden. **1393** LANGL. *P. Pl.* C. III. 14 Hure robe was ryccher þan ich rede couthe. *c* **1400** *Destr. Troy* 12579 Þan Palomydon..put was to dethe With the birre of his bow, as I aboue rede. *a* **1586** SIDNEY *Astr. & Stella* Sonn. lviii, Stella's sweet breath the same to me did reed. **1591** SPENSER *M. Hubberd* 604 But read, faire Sir, of grace, from whence come yee.

†**b.** To speak of or mention; to describe; to name or call. *Obs.*

1303 R. BRUNNE *Handl. Synne* 10801 3e men..þat haue herde me rede þys sacrament, How ouer alle þyng hyt haþ powere. *c* **1330** —— *Chron. Wace* (Rolls) 15099 In þat tyme, þat y now rede, þe date was [etc.]. *c* **1460** *Launfal* 299 May no man rede here atyre. **1590** SPENSER *F.Q.* I. vii. 46 Whose kingdomes seat Cleopolis is red. **1617** FLETCHER *Valentinian* III. i, Good men [will] raze thee For ever being read again, but vicious.

II. Intransitive or absolute uses.

* *In senses corresponding to* 5–10 *above.*

15. a. To apprehend mentally the meaning of written or other characters; to be engaged in doing this; to be occupied in perusing a book, etc.; to read (sense 5 a) music. Also with advbs. as *away*, *on*.

c **950** *Lindisf. Gosp.* Mark xiii. 14 Seðe redes oncnauað [*c* **1000** Ongyte se þe ræt]. *a* **1225** *Ancr. R.* 286 Ofte, leoue sustren, 3e schulen vren lesse uorte reden more. *c* **1320** *Cast. Love* 1241 Clerkes þat conne reden. *c* **1386** CHAUCER *Wife's Prol.* 791 Sodeynly three leves have I plight Out of his book, right as he radde. **1483** CAXTON *Cato* A ij b, He that redeth and no thynge understondeth. **1598** SHAKS. *Merry W.* II. i. 54 Heere; read, read: perceiue how I might bee knighted. **1671** MILTON *P.R.* IV. 322 Who reads Incessantly,.. Uncertain and unsettl'd still remains. **1757** MRS. GRIFFITH *Lett. Henry & Frances* (1767) I. p. vi, I used to take out a parcel from this collection..and so read away. **1794** MRS. RADCLIFFE *Myst. Udolpho* i, How often have I sat with my book in my hand, reading. **1865** MILL in *Evening Star* 10 July, Those persons who quoted this passage were not candid enough to read on. **1887** MISS BRADDON *Like & Unlike* i, She had read and thought much in those years. **1889** G. B. SHAW in *Star* 24 May 4/2 The few who are really able to read at sight. **1976** *Star* (Sheffield) 3 Dec. 16/7 (Advt.), Organist required for a 9-day period at Christmas. Must be able to read.

b. Coupled with *write*, usually with reference to education or instruction.

1490 CAXTON *Eneydos* xxii. 84 Cadynus inventour of the first lettres lerned the folke to rede and to write. **1567** *Gude & Godlie B.* (S.T.S.) 196 Preistis, reid and wryte, And 3our fals Cannowne law lat be. **1796** H. HUNTER tr. *St. Pierre's Stud. Nat.* (1799) III. 154, I applied myself night and day to the means of learning how to read and write. **1842** J. AITON *Domest. Econ.* (1857) 317 An English nursery governess,.. to learn them to read and write.

c. To occupy oneself seriously with reading, esp. with a view to examination; to study. Also *to read up*, to collect information by reading.

1823 M. WILMOT *Let.* 1 Oct. (1935) 202, I trust that Edw[d] may obtain the gold medal which he is reading for. **1826** DISRAELI *Viv. Grey* I. vi, Vivian..promised, protested, and finally sat down 'to read'. **1847** TENNYSON *Princ.* Prol. 175 We seven stay'd at Christmas up to read. **1859** FARRAR *J. Home* x, [He] was reading for honours. *Ibid.* xxxii, All three determined to read for Fellowships. **1863** MRS. GASKELL *Dark Night's Work* xv. 271 You knew him at Hamley, I suppose? I remember his reading there with Mr. Ness. **1874** J. CODMAN *Mormon Country* i. 2 They buy a big book..and, having read up thoroughly, fill the cavities of their minds with details from these to supply what they did not learn from their extended visit of half a day. **1889** *Harper's Mag.* Jan. 209/2 Men should..be compelled to 'read up' on questions of the time. **1890** C. M. YONGE *More Bywords* 129 The two sisters are reading up for the Oxford exam. **1911** J. LONDON *Let.* 17 Aug. (1966) 350, I should advise you..to read up on socialism. **1938** E. C. LODGE *Terms & Vacations* iv. 51 Those of us who read for University schools went to the different Colleges to lectures. **1962** [see LITTERÆ HUMANIORES]. **1976** 'M. ALBRAND' *Taste of Terror* xviii. 103 Why don't you read up on it in the *Britannica*?

d. To act as a publisher's reader.

1850 THACKERAY *Pendennis* II. iii. 27 Warrington artfully inspired the two gentlemen who 'read' for Messrs. Bacon and Bungay with the greatest curiosity regarding 'Walter Lorraine'. **1891** G. GISSING *New Grub Street* I. vi. 122 She ..liked to know who 'read' for the publishing-houses. **1956** P. SCOTT *Male Child* II. i. 112, I..asked her whether she had ever read for a publisher. **1978** S. HODGE *Gollancz* iii. 64 They went on reading for him.

e. To receive and understand a message by radio, telephone, etc.

1930 *Amer. Speech* V. 289 The receiving operator 'receives', 'copies' or 'reads'. **1962** J. GLENN in *Into Orbit* 213 *Schirra*: 'John, leave your retro-package on through your pass over Texas. Do you read?' *Glenn*: 'Roger'. **1963** *Times* 25 May 10/7 'Philip to Kitty—do you read?' No reply. **1966** D. FRANCIS *Flying Finish* ii. 26, I said, 'Port Ellen tower this is Golf Alpha Romeo Kilo November, do you read?'

16. a. *to read on*: to look on and read. Now *rare* or *Obs.*

c **1200** *Vices & Virtues* 141 Þanne we on boke radeð, ðanne spekeð godd wið us. *a* **1225** *Ancr. R.* 430 O þisse boc redeð eueriche deie hwon 3e beoð eise. *a* **1300** *Floriz & Bl.* 578 Alni3t heo set at hire boke And haþ þeron irad and loke. *c* **1375** *Sc. Leg. Saints* i. (*Peter*) 711 Angelis..brocht fra criste to hym a buk, and all þe wordis petir one rad. *a* **1450** *Arthur* 633 He þat wolle more loke, Reed on þe frensche boke. ? *a* **1550** *Freiris Berwik* 352 in *Dunbar's Poems* (1893) 297 Quhylis still he satt in studeing, And vthir quhylis vpoun his buk reding. **1642** MILTON *Apol. Smect.* Wks. 1738 I. 108 To take them nightly to read on and after make them his pillow. **1764** REID *Inquiry* vi. §16 Before the other eye was placed a printed book, at such a distance as that he could read upon it.

b. Similarly, *to read in*. Now *rare*. Also *transf.*

c **1470** HENRY *Wallace* VII. 902 As witnes weill in to the schort tretty Eftir the Bruce, quha redis in that story. **1485** CAXTON *Malory's Arthur* Pref. 3 Al noble lordes and ladyes ..that shal see and rede in this sayd book. **1530** TINDALE *Prol. Deuteron.* Wks. 21/2 This is a booke worthy to be read in, daye and night. **1593** SHAKS. *Rich. II*, IV. i. 276 Giue me that Glasse, and therein will I reade. **1820** SOUTHEY *Wesley* (ed. 2) II. 140 Neither had he read in any devotional book.

c. *fig.* in phrases. † *to read on one side of the leaf*: to regard or apprehend only one side of the question. *to read between the lines* (see LINE *sb.*[2] 23 a). *you wouldn't read about it*: exclamation used to express a mixture of incredulity and disgust (*Austral.* and *N.Z. colloq.*).

1456 SIR G. HAYE *Law Arms* (S.T.S.) 218 Syndry folk redis apon a syde of the lef and nocht on the tothir. **1866**, **1880** [see LINE *sb.*[2] 23 a.] **1886** *Manch. Exam.* 19 Jan. 5/4 People who have not the shrewdness to read a little between the lines..are grievously misled. **1950** J. CLEARY *Just let me Be* xiv. 135 Everything I backed ran like a no-hoper. Four certs I had, and the bludgers were so far back the ambulance nearly had to bring 'em home. You wouldn't read about it. **1962** D. CUSACK *Picnic Races* xxi. 249 He drew a deep breath. 'You wouldn't read about it.' **1973** H. WILLIAMS *My Love had Black Speed Stripe* x. 69 You wouldn't read about it. A bloke his missus reckons was a doctor of philosophy, whatever that was, and just about the biggest dill you could meet.

†**d.** *to read right*: to have or take a correct view; to be right in one's ideas or expectations. *Obs.*

Perh. originally related to senses 1 and 2.

c **1420** *Anturs of Arth.* 525, I shal rewarde þe þi route, if I cone rede righte. **1508** DUNBAR *Gold. Targe* 255 O reuerend Chaucere,..quho redis rycht, Thou beris of makaris the tryumph riall. *a* **1585** MONTGOMERIE *Cherrie & Slae* 1191 Gif 3e reid richt, it was not I.

17. To find mention or record *of* something by, or in the course of, reading.

[*c* **1000** ÆLFRIC *Hom.* II. 394 We rædað be sumon wife, þe wæs twelf 3ear 3euntrumod.] *a* **1225** *Ancr. R.* 244 Þe oðer deouel þet me redeð of þet he gredde lude to Seinte Bartholomeu. *c* **1400** *Apol. Loll.* 31 Þei were dekunis,..as Steuyn, & silk oþer þat is redd of in apostlis dedis. **1559** W. CUNNINGHAM *Cosmogr. Glasse* 80 Places towarde the south coast, of which neither I have heard of any credible person, nor yet red. **1595** SHAKS. *John* III. iv. 13 Who hath read, or heard Of any kindred action like to this? *c* **1645** HOWELL *Lett.* I. v. xxxvii, I have read of Caligula's Horse, that was made Consul. **1789** COWPER *Annus Mem.* 3, I read of bright embattled fields. **1850** TENNYSON *In Mem.* xcv, I read Of that glad year which once had been.

ellipt. **1611** SHAKS. *Wint. T.* I. ii. 424 Worse then the great'st Infection That ere was heard, or read.

18. a. To bear reading; to be readable.

1668 SHADWELL *Sullen Lovers* III, 'Tis a play that shall read and act with any play that ever was born. **1727** DE FOE *Hist. Appar.* (1840) 340 The book will read without it. **1887** A. BIRRELL *Obiter Dicta* 2nd Ser. viii. 260 When the dish is served, we only ask, Is it good?..when the book comes out, Does it read? **1931** *N. & Q.* 17 Oct. 287/2 The translation is oddly unequal. It is often conspicuously clear and vigorous; sometimes it is halting and dull; occasionally, it does not 'read'.

b. To turn out (well or ill), or have a specified character, when read; to produce a certain impression on the reader. Also, to convey a statement when read.

1731 *Gentl. Mag.* I. 21 Thy comedies excell..And read politely well. **1789** T. TWINING *Aristotle's Treat. Poetry* (1812) I. 254 Whose productions..read better than they act. **1805** W. TAYLOR in *Ann. Rev.* III. 231 This pamphlet is so pious as to read more like a sermon than a political address. **1828** *Examiner* 84/2 Nothing can read more free and easy than his present translation. **1878** BOSW. SMITH *Carthage* 371 The joke does not read to us like a very good one. **1891** F. H. WILLIAMS *Atman* v. 270 The letter reads as follows.

transf. **1863** JULIA KAVANAGH *Eng. Wom. Letters* vii. I. 187 There are lives that read like one long sorrow.

c. To admit of interpretation.

1866 J. MARTINEAU *Ess.* I. 28 This rule reads both ways.

d. Of a measuring instrument: to have a graduated scale of a specified kind.

1862 *Catal. Internat. Exhib., Industr. Dept., Brit. Div.* II. No. 2941, Standard barometer on Fortin's principle, reading from an ivory zero point in the cistern.

** *In senses corresponding to* 11–14 *above.*

19. a. To render or give forth in speech the words one is reading (in sense 5). Const. *to* (a person), *from* or *out of* (a book, etc.; †formerly *of*, *in*, *on*), and with advbs. as *away*, *on*, *out*.

c **950** *Lindisf. Gosp.* Luke iv. 16 [He] aras to redanne. *c* **1200** ORMIN 17286 E33whær þær mann rædeþþ þe Off hali3 wite3hunnge. *c* **1315** SHOREHAM I. 1306 He toke ysaies bok Ine þe synagoge, and radde. **1382** WYCLIF *Neh.* viii. 8 And thei radden in the boc of the lawe distinctli and apertli. —— *Jer.* xxxvi. 6 Go in therfore thou, and rede of the volum,.. herende the puple. *c* **1440** *York Myst.* xx. 144 Late se, sirs, in youre sawes Howe right þat 3e can rede. **1556** *Chron. Gr. Friars* (Camden) 56 Cardmaker, that rede in Powlles iij. tymes a weke. **1591** SHAKS. *Two Gent.* III. i. 329 That fault may be mended with a breakfast: read on. **1635** PAGITT *Christianogr.* 30 Comming on a Sunday into one of their Congregations..he found one sitting in the midst of them, ..reading on a Bible in the Chaldean tongue. **1718** *Freethinker* No. 7 (1733) I. 30 The Bridegroom..deposited one Moiety; and the Doctor read away. **1787** BURNS *Tam Samson's Elegy* i, Has..Robinson again grown weel, To preach an' read? **1844** LADY FULLERTON *E. Middleton* vi, Sir Edmund and Henry alternately read out loud to us. **1879** M. PATTISON *Milton* 150 Then he went up to his study to be read to till six.

†**b.** Coupled with *sing*, in ref. to church-services. *Obs.*

c **1250** *Hymn to God* I in *Trin. Coll. Hom.* App. 258 Hit bilimped forte speke to reden & to singe Of him. **1303** R. BRUNNE *Handl. Synne* 8018 Whyle y haue 3ow prestes þre Þat me mow rede ande synge. *c* **1420** *Anturs of Arth.* 704 Dame Gaynour garte besly wryte in to þe weste, To all manere of relygeous, to rede and to synge. **1500–20** DUNBAR *Poems* x. 29 All clergy do to him inclyne,..Ensence his altar, reid, and sing In haly kirk.

c. *to read in* = 13 a.

1828 J. H. NEWMAN *Lett.* (1891) I. 180, I read in—i.e. read the Thirty-nine Articles. **1863** CRIPPS *Law Church & Clergy* (1886) 481 *marg.*, Certificate of reading in should be obtained.

d. *Sc.* Of a minister: To read sermons, instead of preaching extempore or from memory.

1781 *Reading not preaching* II. 6 To read, and not preach, is to deny the Spirit his office. **1888** BARRIE *Auld Licht Idylls* iii, To follow a pastor who 'read' seemed to the Auld Lichts like claiming heaven on false pretences.

e. Of an actor: to audition *for*, to rehearse *for* a role. Also, *to read in for*, to take the part of (another actor) at a rehearsal.

1943 S. LEWIS *Gideon Planish* 71 'And will you read for it?' ..'You mean try and see if I can act one of the parts?' 'Professionally, we call it "read for a part".' **1966** A. E. LINDOP *I start Counting* ii. 44 She'd had a letter..asking her to report to the Jubilee Hall, where she was to read for the Amateur Dramatic Society. **1968** J. BINGHAM *I love, I Kill* iii. 32 Shirley, you read in for Sarah... You'll be understudying her anyway. **1970** E. BERCKMAN *She asked for It* ii. 18 'How's it done?' 'You ring your agent, and say you'll read for the part.' *Ibid.* 19, I stood over her, literally, till she'd rung and said she'd read for the producer. **1971** *Guardian* 10 Dec. 10/5 The [play] reading is on again... Somebody can read in for Graham.

†**20.** To give instruction by means of reading aloud; to lecture or discourse *upon* a subject. *Obs.*

c **1290** *S. Eng. Leg.* I. 446/521 3if þou me drifst out of þi lond..Ich can rede at parys..And þare-with winne me mete i-nov3. **1576** FLEMING *Panopl. Epist.* 341 In that College it was his happie lucke, to reade in the open schooles in Latine. **1596** SHAKS. *1 Hen. IV*, III. i. 46 Where is the Liuing.. Which calls me Pupill, or hath read to me. **1618** G. STRODE *Anat: Mortalitie* I The Statute which I haue chosen to reade vpon. *a* **1625** FLETCHER *Elder Brother* IV. iii, I shall dissect ye, And read upon your phlegmatic dull carcasses. **1691–2** WOOD *Life* 6 Jan. (O.H.S.) III, The Master of Pembroke College suffers him to read to Scholars of his house. **1700** COLLIER *2nd Def. Short View* (1738) 434 To read upon a putrified Carcass, and shew Nature, to the Affront of Religion.

†**21.** To rehearse, speak or tell *of*. *Obs.*

a **1300** *Cursor M.* 4327 Sua did þis wijf, i yow of redd, Sco folud ioseph ai þar he fledd. *c* **1330** R. BRUNNE *Chron. Wace* (Rolls) 10598 He wrot his dedes..& blamed boþe Gyldas & Bede Why þey wolde nought of hym rede. **1375** BARBOUR *Bruce* x. 276, I think of hym to reid And till schaw part of his gud deid. *c* **1425** WYNTOUN *Cron.* II. x. *heading*, Or I forthere nowe procede, Of the Genealogi will I rede. **1570** *Henry's Wallace* VI. 72 Heirof as now, I will na mair proceid ..Of vther thing my purpois is to reid.

III. 22. *Computers.* The infin. used *attrib.* and in *Comb.* with the sense 'reading'.

1953 A. D. & K. H. V. BOOTH *Automatic Digital Calculators* xii. 115 Mounted close to the drum are a series of read/record heads. **1960** *Proc. Inst. Electr. Engineers* (VII. B. 56) (*heading*) A digital computer store with very short read time. **1964** F. L. WESTWATER *Electronic Computers* iv. 77 The resulting change of flux as the core switches will cause an electromotive force in the read wire which we can recognise. **1965** *Wireless World* July 340/1 The read/write cycle time is 600 nsec. **1971** J. H. SMITH *Digital Logic* vi. 126 In practical core memories the *X* and *Y* co-ordinates are only used for identifying the core required and each core in the plane is threaded with additional 'read' and 'write' wires. **1979** J. E. ROWLEY *Mechanical In-House Information Syst.* I. 64 Read-write heads..give direct access to the opposite track, and then this track may be searched sequentially.

23. read-around ratio *Computers*, the number of times that a particular bit in an electrostatic store can be read without degrading bits stored nearby.

1953 *Math. Tables & Other Aids to Computation* VII. 112 The inherent coupling between adjacent storage locations on the face of any cathode ray tube places a limit on the number of times any point on the raster may be consulted before its neighbors are regenerated. For the Institute machine this number, called the 'read around' ratio, is in the neighborhood of 30. **1969** P. B. JORDAIN *Condensed Computer Encycl.* 415 A high read-around ratio means greater reliability.

read (rɛd), *ppl. a.* [f. READ *v.*]

1. That is read, *esp.* that is read out (in contrast to being expressed spontaneously or repeated from memory). ***read line*** (Sc.): see LINE *sb.*[2] 23 e.

1590 G. GYFFORD *Plain Declar.* Title-p., A Replie to Master Greenwood touching read prayer. **1642** S. RUTHERFURD *Peaceable Plea* 326 None by any Act of our Church..is obliged to a stinted or read prayer. **1781** *Reading not preaching* II. 9 Your read papers is a lame service. **1901** *Westm. Gaz.* 10 Dec. 11/1 The trouble of attending the meeting to hear a read speech. **1901** LAWSON *Remin. Dollar Acad.* 122, I have still a recollection of the read line being sung in that congregation.

2. In predicative use: Experienced, versed, or informed *in* a subject by reading. Also ***read up***.

Used simply and with adverbs (see also WELL-READ).

1586 A. DAY *Eng. Secretary* II. (1625) 127 He ought..to be well languaged, to be sufficiently read in Histories and Antiquities. **1631** MASSINGER *Emperor East* III. iv, You are read in story: call to your remembrance [etc.]. **1682** DRYDEN *Relig. Laici* Pref., Wks. (Globe) 187 Every man who is read in Church history. **1707** PRIOR *Epil. to Phaedra* 3 An Oxford Man, extreamly read in Greek. **1749** FIELDING *Tom Jones* III. iii, He was deeply read in the ancients. **1857** *Ecclesiologist* XVIII. 208 Chaucer, who was evidently quite as read in the Latin classics, as a well-educated person would be in the present day. **1873** 'MARK TWAIN' *Gilded Age* xi. 112, I *am* better read up in most sciences, maybe, than the general run of professional men. **1883** H. E. MANNING *Eternal Priesthood* xx. 277 He is a welcome visitor..a ready and amusing guest, read up in the newspapers, and full of the events of the day. **1897** *Pall Mall Mag.* Feb. 189 A man.., who was read in four Eastern languages.

3. (Chiefly predicative.) Informed by reading, acquainted with books or literature, learned.

Now only with adverbs (esp. WELL-READ).

1588 SHAKS. *Tit. A.* IV. i. 33 Thou art deeper read and better skild. **1607** TOURNEUR *Rev. Trag.* v. iii, You are read, my Lords. **1650** B. *Discolliminium* 43 If any read Gentleman or Divine will assoile these doubts, I shall be very much beholding to him. **1676** ETHEREDGE *Man of Mode* I. i, *Shoom.* Why shou'd not you Write your own Commentaries as well as Cæsar? *Med.* The Raskal's read, I perceive. **1709** POPE *Ess. Crit.* 612 The bookful block-head, ignorantly read, With loads of learned lumber in his head. **1824** JEFFERSON *Writ.* (1830) IV. 398, I might defy the best read lawyer to produce another scrap of authority for this judiciary forgery.

read, obs. f. RED *a.* and *sb.*[1], var. REDE *sb.*, obs. f. REED.

reada'bility. [f. next.] Readableness. Also in extended sense, the quality of, or capacity for, being read with pleasure or interest, considered as measured by certain assessable factors, as ease of comprehension, attractiveness of subject and style.

1843 S. COLERIDGE *Let.* July in *Mem. & Lett.* (1873) I. xi. 281 If bad arrangement in S.T.C. is injurious to readibility, in S.C. it will be destructive. **1860** TROLLOPE *Castle Richmond* I. 3 The readability of a story should depend..on its intrinsic merit rather than on the site of its adventures. **1886** *Spectator* 6 Feb. 205/1 Readability is the characteristic of his literary work. **1899** J. SOUTHWARD *Mod. Printing* II. i. 4 A book..is not a good book because it is a pretty one; readability is of far more importance than picturesqueness. **1935** GRAY & LEARY *What makes Book Readable* ii. 38 The weight of opinion of all judges is that an informal.., non-technical.., adult..vocabulary is an important contribution to readability, whereas a vocabulary limited to 1,000–1,500 words.., is not essential. **1948** R. FLESCH in *Jrnl. Appl. Psychol.* XXXII. 228 To measure the readability ('reading ease' and 'human interest') of a piece of writing, go through the following steps. **1953** *Journalism Q.* XXX. 417/1 One can think of cloze procedure as throwing all potential readability influences in a pot, letting them interact, then sampling the result. **1958** H. B. & A. C. ENGLISH *Dict. Psychol. & Psychoanal. Terms* 441 The criteria brought forward for determining readability suggest that it is not a single variable but a combination of at least three or four. **1963** R. MORRIS *Success & Failure in Learning to Read* iv. 97 The attempts that have been made to implement [E.L.] Thorndike's 'readability-control' programme have added considerably to the resources available to the teachers of reading today. **1975** *Language for Life* (Dept. Educ. & Sci.) xiv. 218 The writers would be able to refashion their stories to adjust readability levels. **1977** *N.Y. Rev. Bks.* 23 June 4 (Advt.), One might define a great essay as a short excursion which has infinite readability.

readable ('riːdəb(ə)l), *a.* (and *sb.*) [f. READ *v.*]

1. Capable of being read, legible.

1570 LEVINS *Manip.* 114 Both readable, and legible, signifie *legibilis*. **1874** M. BURROWS *Worthies of All Souls* 392 Hoveden and Codrington write good readable hands. **1890** 'R. BOLDREWOOD' *Col. Reformer* (1891) 232 Every one..will help the owner of a stray beast to get him, if his brand is readable.

2. a. Capable of being read with pleasure or interest. Usually of literary work: Easy or pleasant to read, agreeable or attractive in style.

1771 *Monthly Rev.* Dec. 493 The real Author of these Letters..chose to turn it to what literary advantage he might make of a couple of very *readable* volumes. *a* **1817** JANE AUSTEN *Northanger Abbey* (1818) I. vi. 74 Sir Charles Grandison! That is an amazing horrid book... I thought it had not been readable. **1826** DISRAELI *Viv. Grey* II. ii, Doubled up the sheet into a convenient readable form. **1832** MARRYAT *N. Forster* i, The second and third volumes are by far the most readable. **1895** J. H. ROUND in *Bookman* Oct. 25/2 This history..is..a straightforward, readable narrative.

b. As *sb.* in *pl.* Readable works.

1864 *Realm* 9 Mar. 8 Though the ingenuity of the story permits us to class this book among the readables. **1977** *New Yorker* 1 Aug. 13/3 Sales clerks..stacked giant displays of discounted readables.

3. Admitting of reading. *rare*$^{-1}$.

1819 McCRIE *Melville* I. iv. 217 The provost was bound to read lessons in Theology once a week—and the bachelor every readable day.

4. Enabling, making it possible, to read.

1859 H. T. ELLIS *Hong Kong to Manilla* 39 Only sufficiently transparent to admit what might be called a readable amount of light.

Hence **'readableness**, the quality of being readable or legible.

1844 S. R. MAITLAND *Dark Ages* 69 The correctness and readableness of our own edition of a father or a classic. **1861** SMILES *Engineers* Pref. 10 The interest and readableness of such narratives being often in an inverse ratio to their length. **1883** J. MILLINGTON *Are we to read backwards?* 48 Important factors..in the readableness of print.

rea'dapt, *v.* [RE- 5 a.] *a. trans.* To adapt anew.

1843 HOLTZAPFFEL *Turning* II. 663 To re-adapt it [the nut] to the lessened size of the screw. **1858** CARLYLE *Fredk. Gt.* I. i. (1872) I. 14 To readapt, in a purified state, the old eras.

b. *intr.* To become adapted anew.

1961 WEBSTER, *Readapt*.., to become adapted again. **1971** N. FREELING *Over High Side* III. 226 The little flat..had become 'working woman alone' instead of 'married couple'. ..'I'm glad to see you're re-adapting with no trouble.'

So **readapta'bility; readap'tation; rea'daptive** *a.*; **rea'daptiveness.**

1859 STOPFORD *Work & Counterwork* 29 This is but a readaptation..of the first faculty of reasoning. **1875** WHITNEY *Life Lang.* viii. 144 The adaptations and readaptations of articulate signs. **1889** *Pall Mall G.* 5 Jan. 3/3 The prodigal fund of ever fresh and readaptive humour. **1894** *Forum* (U.S.) Aug. 672 Evidence of their readaptability to society. *Ibid.* 673 Anti-social perversity or social readaptiveness.

rea'ddress, *v.* [RE- 5 a.]

1. *refl.* To address (oneself) anew.

1611 SPEED *Hist. Gt. Brit.* IX. v. §16. 471 King Stephen re-addressed himselfe for the North, to prosecute that which Thurstan had begunne. **1657** BOYLE *Martyrd. Theodora* vii. (1703) 102 Didymus..readdressed himself to her.

2. *trans.* To put a new address on (a letter, etc.). Hence **rea'ddressing** *vbl. sb.*

1884 *Daily News* 23 Oct. 2/1 The female staff to which the re-addressing is entrusted. **1889** *Ibid.* 3 Oct. 5/2 Why a letter from abroad should be readdressed in England without extra charge.

reade, obs. f. RED *a.* and *sb.*[1]

readeliche, var. REDELY *adv.*

readen, obs. f. REEDEN.

†**rea'dept**, *v. Obs.* [See RE- 5 a and ADEPT *a.*, ADEPTED *ppl. a.*] *trans.* To recover.

a **1548** HALL *Chron., Edw. IV* (1809) 285 King Henry the VI thus readepted..his Crowne and dignitie Royall. *Ibid.* 291 The which Duchie if he might by their meanes readept and recover [etc.]. **1577–87** HOLINSHED *Chron.* III. 869/1 In the said yeare..in which Henrie the sixt readepted the crowne of England.

So †**rea'deption**, recovery. *Obs.*

1471 in Rymer *Fœdera* (1710) XI. 693 Of the Readeption of our Roial Powerr the Furst Yere. **1750** CARTE *Hist. Eng.* II. 798 Upon her husband's re-adeption of the Crown.

reader ('riːdə(r)). Forms: 1 rǽdere, 3–6 redar(e, 4–6 reder(e, (6 *Sc.* reidar, ridar, reider), 5– reader. [f. READ *v.* + -ER[1].]

1. An expounder, interpreter (of dreams, etc.).

a **1100** *O.E. Glosses* (Napier) I. 4192 *A phitonibus*, wiccum, fram rædерum. *c* **1440** *Promp. Parv.* 426/2 Redare, or expownder of thyngys hard to vndyrstonde..*interpretator*.

2. a. One who reads or peruses.

c **1050** *Byrhtferth's Handboc* in *Anglia* VIII. 308 Þe þus ys awriten on þam bocfelle, ʒemun ðu la rædere [etc.]. *a* **1300** *Cursor M.* 26502 Vnderstand me wel, þou reder, quat birthyn mai þis wordes bere. **1423** Jas. I. *Kingis Q.* cxciv, Pray the reder to haue pacience Of thy defaute. *c* **1425** *Hampole's Psalter* Metr. Pref. 13 In þis boke is muche vertu, to reders wiþ deuocyown. **1526** *Pilgr. Perf.* (W. de W. 1531) 1 b, I trust it shall not be tedyous to the reders. **1611** BIBLE *Transl. Pref.* ¶ 14 Truly (good Christian Reader) wee neuer thought..that we should neede to make a new Translation. **1702** ADDISON *Dial. Medals* I. Wks. 1721 I. 449 All kinds of Readers find their Account in the old Poets. **1784** COWPER *Task* II. 581 My very gentle reader yet unborn. **1856** MRS. BROWNING *Aur. Leigh* III. 319, I wrote tales beside..To suit light readers. **1882** A. W. WARD *Dickens* i. 4 He was no great reader in the days of his authorship.

transf. **1784** COWPER *Task* III. 253 Sagacious reader of the works of God. **1838** LYTTON *Leila* II. i, He was a profound reader of men's characters. **1888** A. K. GREEN *Behind Closed Doors* iii, If I am any reader of countenances.

b. A proof-reader.

1808 STOWER *Printers' Grammar* 387 A careful and steady Reader must be indispensable in every printing-office. **1882** J. SOUTHWARD *Pract. Printing* (1884) 144 All corrections made by the reader are called 'marks' or readers' marks.

c. One employed by a publisher to read works offered for publication and to report on their merits. Also, one similarly employed by a theatre to read plays offered for production.

1829 H. FOOTE *Compan. Theatres* 146 Drury-Lane.—Season 1828–9. Lessee and Manager—B. Price, Esq... Reader of Plays—Mr. Frederick Reynolds. **1859** E. FITZBALL *Thirty-Five Years Dram. Author's Life* I. vii. 262, I have been dramatic reader myself, in the Theatre Royal, Covent Garden,..some years. **1871** in RINGWALT *Amer. Encycl. Printing*. **1891** G. GISSING *New Grub Street* II. xiii. 4 One of Mr Jedwood's 'readers'..was expressing a doubt whether Fadge himself was the author of the review. **1895** G. B. SHAW in *Sat. Rev.* 2 Mar. 280/2 The Lord Chamberlain's reader is not selected by examination either in literature or morals. **1924** J. GALSWORTHY *White Monkey* II. vi. 168 Here were manuscripts, of which the readers to Danby and Winter had already said: 'No Money in this.' **1956** P. SCOTT *Male Child* II. iv. 153 He told me..he'd get another reader..in your place. He thought your illness had impaired your judgment. **1976** M. GREEN *Children of Sun* v. 171 J. B. Priestley..became..a publisher's reader for John Lane.

d. One who reads designs in weaving (see READ *v.* 5 e).

1839 URE *Dict. Arts* 267 The weaving of imitation shawls is executed, as usual, by as many shuttles as there are colours in the designs, and which are thrown across the warp in the order established by the reader. **1932** L. HOOPER *New Draw-Loom* II. ix. 82 The reader, looking carefully at the line, No. 1 of the design at the side next to the numerals, must count the number of dark squares with which it begins ..and call 'Take 1'. **1970** *Classification of Occupations* (Office of Population Censuses & Surveys) 70/1 (Index), Reader: design; textile.

e. One who reads music; a sight-reader.

1947 G. B. SHAW in *Mus. Times* Jan. 10/1 It takes years of practice to train a group of good readers to sing in tune not only passably but exactly. **1977** *Grimsby Even. Tel.* 5 May 3/3 (Advt.), Pianist wanted also Trombonist by local rehearsal dance band. Must be readers.

3. a. One who reads aloud; *esp.* one who is appointed to read to others, and *spec.* one who reads the lessons or other parts of the service in a place of worship.

In the Roman Catholic Church the office of reader is the second of the minor orders (see LECTOR). After the Reformation, lay readers were appointed in the Churches of England and Scotland to read the lessons and perform some minor functions in parishes which had no regular incumbent or minister. In Scotland further appointments to the office were forbidden by an Act of the General Assembly in 1581; in England it remained in use till a much later period, and was partly revived in 1866.

c **961** ÆTHELWOLD *Rule St. Benet* xxxviii. (Schröer 1885) 62 Þæt nanes mannes stefn..ʒehyred ne sy, butan þæs ræderes anes. **10..** *Laws Ælfric* in Thorpe *Laws* II. 346 Lector is rædere, þe ræd on Godes cyrcan, and bið þærto ʒehadod þæt he bodiʒe Godes word. *c* **1290** *S. Eng. Leg.* I. 137/1070 Þis word þat ore louerd het is redare bi-fore him radde. *c* **1315** SHOREHAM I. 1291 Ine þe alde laȝe þe redere Rede þe prophessye By wokke; So schulle þe rederes now Hyrede. **1382** WYCLIF *1 Esdras* viii. 9 Esdras, prest, and redere of the lawe of the Lord. **1560–1** *First Bk. Discipl. Ch. Scot.* iv. in *Knox's Wks.* (1848) II. 196 In process of tyme he that is but ane Readar may atteane to the further degree, and ..may be permittit to minister the sacramentis. **1585** J. CARMICHAEL *Let.* in *Wodr. Soc. Misc.* (1844) 436 The readers are made ministers, and..every man hath gotten four kirks. **1661** PEPYS *Diary* 22 Dec., To Church in the morning, where the Reader made a boyish young sermon. **1733** [? WORSLEY] *Observ. Const. Middle Temple* (1896) 180 The Reader whose buisiness it is to read prayers twice every day. **1797** *Encycl. Brit.* (ed. 3) XVI. 18/2 The reader must be supposed..actually to personate the author. **1842** BRANDE *Dict. Sci.*, etc. s.v., There are..readers (priests) attached to various eleemosynary and other foundations. **1872** *Minutes S. Manch. Hebrew Congreg.* 29 Sept. in I. W. Goldberg *South Manch. Hebrew Congreg.: 80 Years of Progress* (1952) 8 That the Reverend H. D. Marks be elected Reader, Stipendiary Secretary and Minister to the Congregation. **1873** PHILLIMORE *Eccl. Law* (ed. 2) I. 451 Recently lay readers have been appointed by bishops in several dioceses to officiate with consent of the incumbent. **1973** *Jewish Chron.* 2 Feb. 43/1 A memorial service for Mr. Victor Schiller, honorary reader of the Lecton Synagogue.. was held at the synagogue.

b. reader-aloud, one who reads (a literary text, etc.) aloud, esp. to an audience. Also (*rare*) ***reader-alouder***. Cf. READ *v.* 11 a.

1938 *Times* 16 Sept. 13/4 Fountains are less trouble in bedrooms than readers-aloud or raconteurs. **1952** G. RAVERAT *Period Piece* viii. 145 Aunt Etty was the best reader-aloud I have ever known. **1952** *Sat. Rev.* (U.S.) 13 Sept. 6/3 Hemingway is a reader-alouder, it appears. **1977** *Listener* 10 Nov. 624/4 Lots of subordinate clauses can make life very difficult for the reader-aloud.

4. a. One who reads (and expounds) to pupils or students; a teacher, lecturer; *spec.* in some Universities as the title of certain instructors.

1519 HORMAN *Vulg.* viii. 88 b, He hath founded a reder in greke for a C. ducattes a yere. **1536** *Act 28 Hen. VIII*, c. 13 §2 Reders of diuinitie in the comon scholes of diuinitie. **1567** BUCHANAN *Wks.* (S.T.S.) 11 Ane Reidar in Medicine. **1630** *R. Johnson's Kingd. & Commw.* 50 Let his Lecture consist, more in questions and answers,..than in the Readers continued speech. **1667** *Decay Chr. Piety* xvi. ¶4 Have any of our idolized readers bought their interest in us so dear as Christ has done. **1703** T. N. *City & C. Purchaser* 91 Dr. Hook, Reader of Geometry in Gresham-colledge. **1846** McCULLOCH *Acc. Brit. Empire* (1854) II. 359 The University of Durham..consists of a warden, professors, tutors, readers, and lecturers. **1881** *Stat. Univ. Oxf.* (1882) 65 A Reader in Roman Law shall be appointed from time to time.

b. In the Inns of Court, a lecturer on law. (Now only as the title of an honorary office.)

On the nature of the office of reader in the various Inns see *Encycl. Brit.* (1881) XIII. 88/2, Douthwaite *Gray's Inn* (1886) 36, Worsley (?) *Observ. Const. Middle Temple* (repr. 1896) 57, *Black Books of Lincoln's Inn* (1897) III. p. xiv.

1517 *Black Bks. Lincoln's Inn* (1897) I. 182 Who so bryngith any repaster to the Redar's denar or sopar, except the Redar or any of the Benche, schall pay for the Repast, xij*d*. **1569** *Nottingham Rec.* IV. 133 Maister Recorder, then beyng Reder of Grey's Inne. *a* **1613** OVERBURY *A Wife*, etc. (1638) 121 He arrogates as much honour for being Reader to an Inne of Chancery. **1664-5** PEPYS *Diary* (1879) III. 124 Mrs. Turner..takes it mightily ill I did not come to dine with the Reader, her husband. **1733** [? WORSLEY] *Observ. Const. Middle Temple* (1896) 57 From the Benchers are chosen Readers who us'd to read law twice in the year, viz[t]: in the Lent, and Long Vacations.

5. Used as a title for books containing passages for instruction or exercise in reading.

1799 (*title*) The English Reader; or Pieces in Prose and Poetry selected from the best writers..by L. Murray. **1869** (*title*) The advanced reader: Lessons in literature and science. **1876** H. SWEET (*title*) An Anglo-Saxon Reader; in Prose and Verse.

6. a. *Thieves' cant.* A pocket-book.

1718 C. HITCHING *Regulator* 20 A reader, *alias* pocket-book. **1789** G. PARKER *Life's Painter Varieg. Char.* xv. 151 *Reader.* Is a pocket-book; a person cannot be too careful of this article, particularly if he should have..any rum screens in it, that is, bank notes. *a* **1790** in POTTER *New Dict. Cant.* **1819** J. H. VAUX *Mem.* I. xii. 140 He had that day turned out three readers, but without finding a shilling in either of them. **1834** H. AINSWORTH *Rookwood* III. v. (1878) 200 None [could] knap a reader like me.

b. *Gambling slang.* A marked card.

1894 MASKELYNE *Sharps & Flats* 27 Whatever method of marking may be adopted in the preparation of 'faked' cards or 'readers'. **1977** 'L. EGAN' *Blind Search* iv. 57 McAllister was a gambler... This is a deck of readers—marked cards.

c. *U.S. Criminals' slang.* (See quot. 1926.)

1926 *Clues* Nov. 162/1 *Reader*, a circular notifying police officers to arrest the party described thereon. **1955** *Publ. Amer. Dial. Soc.* xxiv. 150 Sometimes there is a 'detainer' issued for a thief... This is called a *reader* or a *dipsy*.

7. A device for obtaining data stored on tape, cards, or other media (usu. converting the data into coded electrical signals).

1946 *N.Y. Times* 15 Feb. 16/3 When the problem is punched on the cards they are dropped into a slot in a 'reader'. **1964** F. L. WESTWATER *Electronic Computers* iv. 80 Even with the faster types of card reader it is difficult to exceed 800 digits per second. **1968** *Brit. Med. Bull.* XXIV. 205/1 It may be possible to eliminate the stage of transfer onto punched cards by using an optical reader, for there is now a rapid development in this type of device. **1972** M. WOODHOUSE *Mama Doll* xi. 145 Some people at Admiralty ran the tape through a five-hole reader for us, and gave us back seven hundred and eighty-four groups of digits.

8. A machine for producing on a screen a magnified, readable image of any desired part of a microfilm or other microform.

1950 *Amer. Documentation* I. 141/2 A new reading machine just announced..holds much promise. This reader giving a clear, sharp image..is relatively inexpensive. **1962** A. GÜNTHER *Microphotogr. in Lib.* (Unesco) 7 Micro-opaque cards..may be readily filed. However, they need much more light for projection and, therefore, a more complicated and more expensive reader, which must be equipped with a blower for cooling. **1975** P. G. NEW *Reprography for Librarians* iv. 48 The librarian committed to exploiting micro materials must not only consider investing in a multitude of portable readers for loan, but must also ensure that his library is fully equipped with.. viewers for use on the premises.

9. *attrib.* and *Comb.*, as ***reader group, participation, response***; ***reader-contributor, -writer***; (sense 2c) ***reader's report***; **reader-printer**, a reading machine (sense (*b*) s.v. READING 10b) that can also produce enlarged, readable copies.

1946 *R.A.F. Jrnl.* May 146 The success of the new magazine will depend on the continuance of the excellent reader-contributor relationship which was fostered. **1951** M. MCLUHAN *Mech. Bride* (1967) 112/2 These magazines, carefully geared to both the purse and heart strings of their respective reader groups, feature houses and rooms in which almost nobody ever lives. *Ibid.* 5/2 This kind of newspaper invites reader participation in its triumphs. **1959** H. W. BALLOU *Guide to Microreproduction Equipment* 167 Thermo-Fax Brand Microfilm Reader-Printer... Special Features: Reader and Printer combined in one machine for automatic push-button copying or reading. **1971** *Ann. Rep. Curators Bodl. Libr. 1969–70* 47, 4,011 prints were made on the microfilm reader-printer. **1940** *Kenyon Rev.* II. 274 The reader-response has been altered through a lessening of the pleasure with which the utterance is received. **1979** *Maledicta* III. 83 Among those critics who use psychoanalytical theory there is little agreement over what one can say legitimately about 'reader response'. **1897** 'S. GRAND' *Beth Bk.* (1898) xlvii. 460 Mr. Kilroy took the manuscript himself to a publisher..who..accepted it... Beth.. heard the reader's report. **1978** E. TIDYMAN *Table Stakes* II. v. 241 Each morning a mailboy would arrive with a stack of scripts..Attached were the readers' reports. **1951** S. SPENDER *World within World* 310 Reader-writer walk together in a real-seeming dream-alliance leading into gardens inhabited by Stephen Daedalus and Marcel.

Hence **'readeress**, a female reader.

1864 *Realm* 16 Mar. 4 He paid only a just tribute to readeresses at the expense of readers.

readership ('riːdəʃɪp). [f. READER + -SHIP.]

1. The office of a reader (chiefly in sense 4).

1719 SWIFT *To Yng. Clergyman* Wks. 1755 II. II. 2 They ..first sollicit a readership, and..arrive in time to a curacy. **1840** *Act 3 & 4 Vict.* c. 86 § 2 The Term 'Preferment'..shall be construed to comprehend every Curacy, Lectureship, Readership [etc.]. **1883** *19th Cent.* May 833 A step in the ladder of promotion, first to a readership and ultimately to a professorship.

2. As a title: The personality of a reader.

1771 P. PARSONS *Newmarket* II. 186 An expectation which your readership cannot suppose I should..entertain. **1820** *Blackw. Mag.* VII. 477, I trust, O gentle reader,..that your readership will not [etc.].

3. The total number of (regular) readers of a periodical publication, as a newspaper or magazine; all, or a section, of such readers considered collectively. Also *attrib.* orig. *U.S.*

1923 O. G. VILLARD *Some Newspapers & Newspapermen* 189 The appeal of the *News* to the masses has been so successful that it now has a readership of some forty thousand. **1947** C. L. ALLEN (*title*) A readership study of 3 typical Wisconsin hometown dailies. **1951** *Sunday Times* 2 Dec. 1/3 Mr. Stephen's..experienced counsel and reflections [will] become available to the whole Sunday Times readership. **1958** *New Statesman* 30 Aug. 241/1 It holds its vast circulation..by grace of Mr. Gilbert Harding, whose weekly column (according to readership surveys) is the *People's* biggest pulling feature of all. **1963** *Guardian* 10 Apr. 7/2 Another variation, reflecting different readership, is the background of the characters. **1971** *Nature* 2 Apr. 310/3 In view of the intended readership the selection of topics seems reasonable enough. **1979** *London Rev. Bks.* 25 Oct. 2/3 The obvious difference will relate to the subjects generated by the nationality of the *London Review's* readership, and by that of its contributors.

readesmon, obs. form of REDESMAN.

readfoll, -full, variants of REDEFUL.

re-ad'here, *v.* [RE- 5a.] *intr.* To adhere again. So **re-ad'hesion**.

1813 J. THOMSON *Lect. Inflam.* 235 A tooth replaced in this manner not unfrequently re-adheres. *c* **1865** J. WYLDE in *Circ. Sc.* I. 4 The slightest film on the surfaces..will prevent their re-adhesion.

'readied, *ppl. a.* [f. READY *v.*] Made ready.

a **1773** R. FERGUSON *Farmer's Ingle*, The readied kail stands by the chimley cheeks.

readily ('rɛdɪlɪ), *adv.* Forms: 4-6 **redily**, (4 **redyli**), 5-6 (7) **redyly**, (5 **reddyly**), 6 *Sc.* **radilie**, 5- **readily**. [f. READY *a.* + -LY[2]. In early use sometimes difficult to distinguish from REDILY *adv.* Formerly compared *readilier, -liest* (16-17th c.).] In a ready manner.

1. Promptly, in respect of the voluntariness of the action; hence, with alacrity or willingness; willingly, cheerfully.

c **1320** *Sir Tristr.* 611 He..redily ȝaf him sa Of wel gode mone. *Ibid.* 1523 Þis tale he bi gan And redyli gan to say. *c* **1400** *Rom. Rose* 3293 Thyn herte was Ioly, but not sage, Whan thou were brought in sich a rage, To yelde thee so redily. *c* **1420** LYDG. *Assembly of Gods* 1291 That ye lyst to come to me soo reddyly. **1538** STARKEY *England* I. ii. 48 That they promptely and redyly may don that thyng wych ys requyryd. **1581** MULCASTER *Positions* xxxvii. (1887) 165 To whom the patrones would rediliest yield. **1626** GOUGE *Serm. Dignity Chivalry* §9 Such as..offer themselves readily and chearefully to this honourable service. **1658** EARL MONM. tr. *Paruta's Wars Cyprus* 98 Who shal contribute most, and readiliest, to the service of this his Country. **1777** MISS BURNEY *Evelina* xxvii, I accepted the offer very readily, and away we went. **1875** JOWETT *Plato* (ed. 2) I. 115 Hippocrates readily adopts the suggestion of Socrates.

2. Promptly, in respect of the time of action; quickly, without delay; also, without difficulty, with ease or facility.

1390 GOWER *Conf.* II. 137 This god, which herde of his grevance,..bad him go forth redily Unto a flod was faste by. **1526** *Pilgr. Perf.* (W. de W. 1531) 123 b, The more promptly or redily it discerneth & sheweth, what thynges we ought to byleue. **1585** T. WASHINGTON tr. *Nicholay's Voy.* Ep. Ded., To speake their language redily. **1631** J. DONE *Polydoron* 174 He sent his Sonne in Mans owne figure, to bee the Readilier Cogitated by Man. **1683** *Brit. Spec.* Pref. 9 The readilier to stir up against him the Animosity of the people. **1766** GOLDSM. *Vic. W.* iii, Her gratitude may be more readily imagined than described. **1846** J. E. RYLAND *Life Foster* II. 101 An allusion will readily be understood. **1873** HALE *In His Name* vi. 47 He did not mean to be readily overtaken.

b. *Sc.* As may easily happen; probably.

1643 R. BAILLIE *Lett. & Jrnls.* (1841) II. 71 Readilie it may cost him more time. **1883** ANNIE S. SWAN *Aldersyde* I. ii, Sandy Riddell wull hae been here the day readily?

†**3.** In a state of readiness. *Obs. rare*$^{-1}$.

c **1400** MAUNDEV. (Roxb.) xxv. 118 Þai schall fynd before þam redily puruayd all maner of thinges þat er necessary.

read-in ('riːdɪn). *Computers.* [f. vbl. phr. *to read in* (READ *v.* 6f).] The input of data to a computer or storage device.

1946 *Ann. Computation Lab. Harvard Univ.* I. 63 If a quantity is standing in the counter at the time of read-in so that addition must be performed, the carry circuits are utilized. **1952** [see MATRIX 6d]. **1959** E. M. MCCORMICK *Digital Computer Primer* ii. 8 When the storage..comprises relays and vacuum tubes,..special read-in equipment is required so that the information will be in a form the computer can use. **1970** *Computers & Humanities* IV. 166 Only the read-in statements of the program set would need to be changed to accommodate this programming.

readiness ('rɛdɪnɪs). Also 4-6 **redy-, redi-**, (6 **reddi-**, *Sc.* **radi-**, 7 **readdi-**), 6-7 **ready-**. [f. READY *a.* + -NESS. In early use not easily distinguished from REDINESS.] The quality, state or condition of being ready.

1. Promptness in voluntary action; prompt compliance, willingness, etc.

c **1400** *Beryn* 3088 He gan to tell his tale with grete redynes. **1509** FISHER *Funeral Serm.* Wks. (1876) 301 Consyderynge the redyness of mercy and pyte in our sauyour Ihesu. **1550** CROWLEY *Last Trumpet* 214 Refuse nothing that must be done, but do it wyth al redines. **1631** GOUGE *God's Arrows* III. §50. 278 That readinesse and forwardnesse that is in God to succour and support us. **1732** LEDIARD *Sethos* II. VIII. 206 The women..spoke less, but with greater readiness than the men. **1822** SCOTT 13 Sept. in *Fam. Lett.* (1894) II. xviii. 155 The readiness of all the country to take arms was very singular. **1875** JOWETT *Plato* (ed. 2) V. 291 There is no great inclination or readiness on the part of mankind to be made as good..as possible.

2. a. The quality of being prompt or quick in action, performance, expression, etc.

1390 GOWER *Conf.* II. 80 The worldes redinesse In bodi bothe and in corage. **1530** PALSGR. 261/2 Redynesse in doyng of a thyng, *practique*. **1576** FLEMING *Panopl. Epist.* 401 Beeing too too curious in imitations, [he] marreth the readinesse of his naturall inuention. **1615** W. LAWSON *Country Housew. Gard.* (1626) 27 Let your graffe haue three or foure eyes, for readinesse to put forth. **1718** *Freethinker* No. 72. 119 The Readiness and Faithfulness of the Memory is, likewise, very wonderful. **1742** FIELDING *J. Andrews* II. x, This fellow..had a readiness at improving any accident. **1863** GEO. ELIOT *Romola* xxii, His readiness in the French tongue, which he had spoken in his early youth.

b. The quickness or facility with which something is done.

1585 T. WASHINGTON tr. *Nicholay's Voy.* I. ix. 12 [He] caused with a marueilous readinesse a forte to be made. **1662** *Bk. Com. Prayer, Communion*, That he may with the more readiness and decency break the bread. **1781** COWPER *Expost.* 312 Thou canst not read with readiness and ease Providence adverse in events like these? **1805** *Med. Jrnl.* XIV. 247 The readiness with which the finger passed..is not to be conceived but by those who had an opportunity of examining.

3. A state of preparation: †**a.** With indef. article, in phr. *in* (rarely *on, into*) *a readiness*. (Common in 16-17th c., after *to be, get, have, put, set*, etc.) *Obs.*

1511 GUYLFORDE *Pilgr.* (Camden) 7 Alwaye in a redynesse to set forth whan they woll. **1523** LD. BERNERS *Froiss.* I. cclxxix. 419 The erle of Armynahe and the lorde Dalbre,.. made their people to be on a redynesse to kepe and defende their countreis. **1605** VERSTEGAN *Dec. Intell.* vi. (1628) 175 Caused his shipping to bee made in a readinesse at S. Valeries. **1647** MAY *Hist. Parl.* III. i. 14 That the Trayned Bands..should be put into a readinesse. **1723** BLACKMORE *Hist. Conspir. agst. K. William* 56 Captain Counter..said, they must be sure to be all in a readiness the next Morning.

b. So without article, in phr. *in readiness*.

1541 *Act 33 Hen. VIII*, c. 12 §12 The yoman of the chaundrie..shall..haue in rediness seared clothes, sufficient for the surgeon. **1612** WOODALL *Surg. Mate* Pref., Wks. (1653) 19 Such necessaries as by the ship Barbers are fit to be had in readinesse. **1644** VICARS *God in Mount* 186 That the trained-bands in and about London might be put in readinesse. **1726** *Adv. Capt. R. Boyle* 60 She would wait with some Impatience..and any Hour should find her in Readiness. **1820** KEATS *Isabel.* xxiv, He went in haste, to get in readiness. **1868** E. EDWARDS *Ralegh* I. xxvi. 654 He sent orders that she [the ship] should continue to lie in readiness for another night or two.

4. a. The condition or fact of being ready or fully prepared. *rare.*

1548 THOMAS *Ital. Dict.*, *Concio*, the dressyng, redinesse, or arraie. **1565** *Reg. Privy Council Scot.* I. 399 Anent the reddines of his hous at the King and Quenis Majesteis commandiment. **1612** BRINSLEY *Pos. Parts* (1669) 39 Is not a perfect readiness in the Verb *Sum*, as necessary as in any other of the Verbs? yes, and more also. **1638** BAILLIE *Lett. & Jrnls.* (1861) I. 200 We heard nought bot of all England's arming, at least of the readyness of six or seven thousand great horse.

b. *Psychol.* The stage of physiological or developmental maturity at which an organism is able to take in new learning with ease. Also *attrib.*

1948 E. R. HILGARD *Theories of Learning* ii. 22 There is another kind of readiness familiar to educators. This is illustrated by the use of such a term as 'reading readiness' to refer to the child's reaching a maturity level appropriate to the beginning of reading. **1956** H. C. LINDGREN *Educ. Psychol.* ix. 236 Many schools postpone the teaching of reading for first-graders who do not demonstrate 'reading readiness' on standardized tests. **1967** J. C. NUNNALLY *Psychometric Theory* iii. 77 In schools, predictive validity is at issue in measures of 'readiness'. **1976** *Woman's Day* (U.S.) Nov. 58/2 Clare Pederson..takes a particularly dim view of readiness tests... 'Why don't school systems take the money they waste on readiness tests and spend it on books instead?' **1977** P. R. AMMON in Hom & Robinson *Psychol. Processes in Early Educ.* vii. 184 The question of readiness pertains not only to *how* children can learn, but also to *what* they can learn.

†**5.** A thing or arrangement ready for use; ready use, convenience. *Obs. rare.*

1523 FITZHERB. *Surv.* xxiii. 42 The whiche shall be a great redynesse many yeres hereafter. *c* **1591** in *Lett. Lit. Men* (Camden) 77 Out of w[ch] booke for your Lordship's readines there is hereunto noted certen places offensive.

†**'reading**, *sb.*[1] *Obs. rare.* (See quot. 1688.)

1580 *Lanc. Wills* III. 36 Two payre of sheetes, th' one payre of canvas, th' other of redinge. **1688** R. HOLME *Armoury* III. 107/1 Readings is a course sort of Cloth.

Reading ('rɛdıŋ), *sb.*^{2} [The name of the county town of Berkshire.] **1.** ***Reading beds***, a set of beds of sand, clay, and gravel of fluviatile origin underneath the London clay in the London and Hampshire basins.

1817 *Trans. Geol. Soc.* IV. 283 In many parts of this great valley or trough of chalk [*sc.* the Thames valley] we recognized our Reading beds in their proper place, as the inferior strata of the plastic clay formation. **1854** *Q. Jrnl. Geol. Soc.* X. 164 The leaves preserved in the Reading beds. **1882** A. GEIKIE *Text-bk. Geol.* 844 The Woolwich and Reading Beds, or 'Plastic Clay' of the older geologists, consist of lenticular sheets of plastic clay, loam, sand, and pebble-beds. **1923** [see LANDENIAN *a.*]. **1969** BENNISON & WRIGHT *Geol. Hist. Brit. Isles* xv. 336 The Reading Beds facies is the most extensive of the three in the London Basin.

2. a. ***Reading onion***, a variety of onion developed by the firm of Sutton & Son (formerly of Reading). Also *absol.*

1845 E. ACTON *Mod. Cookery* (ed. 4) xxii. 508 The Reading onion is the proper kind for pickling. **1885** W. ROBINSON tr. *Vilmorin-Andrieux's Veg. Garden* 366 White Spanish, or Reading, Onion... Bulb quite flat, 3 to 4 inches in diameter. **1963** *Sutton's Seed Catal.* 66/1 Sutton's Improved Reading. A maincrop onion.

b. ***Reading sauce***, a sharp sauce flavoured with onions, spices, and herbs.

1861 MRS. BEETON *Bk. Househ. Managem.* 240 *Reading sauce*, .. walnut pickle .. shalots .. Indian soy .. bruised ginger [etc.]... *Seasonable.*—This sauce may be made at any time. **1862** 'L. CARROLL' in *College Rhymes* III. 114 There are epithets That suit with any word—As well as Harvey's Reading Sauce With fish, or flesh, or bird. **1878** M. JEWRY *Warne's Model Cookery* 46/1 A large spoonful of sauce, either Worcester or Reading. **1907** *Yesterday's Shopping* (1969) 33/2 *Sauces* (Other Makers')... Reading.

3. Designating the gypsy caravan of traditional design, supposedly first built in Reading (see quots.). Chiefly in ***Reading wagon***.

1940 F. G. HUTH in *Jrnl. Gypsy Lore Soc.* XIX. 117 The Reading Waggon, or old type of Gypsy *vardō*, with large wheels running outside the body of the van. **1951** *Archit. Rev.* CIX. 317 There are five distinct types of gypsy wagon in use on the roads today... Reading wagon. Originally built by the Dunton family at Reading, this is probably the oldest type of van and is generally accepted as the 'gypsy shape'. **1972** WARD-JACKSON & HARVEY *Eng. Gypsy Caravan* ii. 43 The Reading type of van had certainly been evolved by the 1860's. **1975** *Country Life* 2 Oct. 840/1 We thought we might buy an old gypsy wagon... I found the ruin of a 'Reading' or showman's wagon. **1976** *Horse & Hound* 3 Dec. 68/4 (Advt.), Gypsy Caravan of Reading style for sale.

reading ('ri:dıŋ), *vbl. sb.* [f. READ *v.* + -ING^1.] **1.** The action of perusing written or printed matter; the practice of occupying oneself in this way. Also with *up*, *off*.

c **897** K. ÆLFRED *Gregory's Past. C.* xxii. 169 Ðonne ic cume, ðonne beo ðu abisgad ymbe rædinge. *a* **1225** *Ancr. R.* 44 Redinge of Englichs, oðer of Freinchs, holi meditaciuns. *Ibid.* 286 Redunge is god bone. Redunge techeð hu & hwat me schal bidden. *c* **1460** *Emare* 550 As he stode yn redyng, Downe he fell yn sowenyng. **1534** STARKEY *Let. to Cromwell* in *England* (1878) p. ix, To trowbull you wyth the redyng of thys scrole. **1656** EARL MONM. tr. *Boccalini's Advts. fr. Parnass.* II. xiv. (1674) 154 Politick Salt, which makes the Reading of History very delightful. **1710** STEELE *Tatler* No. 147 ¶1 Reading is to the Mind, what Exercise is to the Body. **1771** *Junius Lett.* xlvii. 248 In the course of my reading this morning I met with the following passage. **1844** J. T. HEWLETT *Parsons & W.* xiii, A little reading-up would, he felt assured, qualify him for matriculation. **1894** BURN, etc. *Steam Eng. User* 55 The forms and the Reading off of Indicator Diagrams or Figures.

b. The extent to which one reads or has read; literary knowledge, scholarship. †Also *pl.*

1593 G. HARVEY *Pierce's Super.* III. 179 He is of no reading in comparison, that doth not acknowledge euery terme in those Letters to be autenticall English. *a* **1700** DRYDEN *Poems* (1822) I. 256 His knowledge more, his reading only less. *c* **1700** G. GREY *Life M. Robinson* (ed. Mayor) §25 He that had his writings had cause to question his great readings. **1724** SWIFT *Riddle*, Without my aid.. The scholar could not shew his reading. **1797** *Monthly Mag.* III. 93/2 That information which a man of some reading might, with ease, have imparted. **1865** M. ARNOLD *Ess. Crit.* i. (1875) 9 Shelley had plenty of reading; Coleridge had immense reading.

c. Ability to read; the art of reading.

reading made easy: the title of various reading-books for children formerly in use. Still freq. in *dial.*, usually in form *readimadeasy* (see *Eng. Dial. Dict.*).

1599 SHAKS. *Much Ado* III. iii. 20 For your writing and reading, let that appeare when there is no neede of such vanity. **1810** CRABBE *Borough* xxiv, Reading made easy, so the titles tell. **1827** SCOTT *Chron. Canongate* Ser. I. iv, A very responsible youth.. gied them lessons in Reediemadeasy. **1876** PREECE & SIVEWRIGHT *Telegraphy* 248 It.. becomes a matter of the highest importance that every telegraphist should thoroughly master acoustic reading.

d. A single or separate act or course of perusal; also *Sc.* = READ *sb.*

1757 HURD *Remarks on Hume's Essay* 5 The Remarks.. are such as occurred to him on a single reading of the Essay. **1786** WASHINGTON *Let. to Lafayette* 10 May, Some petitions .. could scarcely obtain a reading. **1825** J. WILSON *Noct. Amb.* i. Wks. 1855 I. 9 The beuk maun be a curious ane indeed, and you must gie me a reading o't. **1864** TENNYSON *Aylmer's F.* 553 Sir Aylmer watched them all, Yet bitterer from his readings.

e. *Computers.* The copying, extraction, or transfer of data. Also with *in*, *out*. Also *transf.* Freq. *attrib.* Cf. READ *v.* 5h, 6f.

1949 E. C. BERKELEY *Giant Brains* iv. 44 The reading of a hole in a column of a punch card is done by a brush of several strands of copper wire pressed against a metal roller. **1950** *High-Speed Computing Devices* ix. 155 The input to the Tabulator is from a single feed with reading stations examining the two most advanced cards simultaneously. **1964** F. L. WESTWATER *Electronic Computers* iv. 65 When the magnetised spot of wire passes under the reading head there will be a change of magnetic flux through the coils on the head. **1964** J. Z. YOUNG *Model of Brain* xiii. 217 We can thus say that the vertical lobe system is necessary for 'reading-out' of the memory as well as for 'reading-in'. **1970** O. DOPPING *Computers & Data Processing* viii. 122 After a few milliseconds, the beginning of the tape block reaches the reading head and the buffer register in the channel starts to be filled with information.

2. The action of uttering aloud the words of written or printed matter. (Also with ref. to the manner in which this is done.) Also with *aloud*, *out*.

c **961** ÆTHELWOLD *Rule St. Benet* xxxviii. (Schröer 1885) 62 ȝebroðra ȝereorde æt hyra mysum ne sceal beon butan haliȝre rædinge. *c* **1300** *Havelok* 2327 Harping and piping, .. Romanz reding on the bok. **1390** GOWER *Conf.* III. 31 Min Ere.. Is fedd of redinge of romance. **1583** *Leg. Bp. St. Androis* 103 Neather with preiching nor w^t reiding, Tuke he that faythless flock in feiding. **1779** G. KEATE *Sketches fr. Nat.* (ed. 2) II. 189 How frequently do we meet with men of great learning, whose reading gives one pain! **1828** SCOTT *F.M. Perth* vi, I wish to hear reading, and could listen to your sweet voice for ever. **1878** R. W. DALE *Lect. Preach.* viii. 228 It was genuine reading, not dramatic recitation. **1936** F. R. LEAVIS *Revaluation* ii. 44 Here, if this were a lecture, would come illustrative reading-out—say of the famous opening to Book 111. **1960** C. DAY LEWIS *Buried Day* iv. 64, I don't remember much reading-aloud, before I could read to myself.

b. The delivery in this manner of a specified portion of matter; a single act or spell of this; also, the portion so read at one time. Also with *aloud*.

c **961** ÆTHELWOLD *Rule St. Benet* ix. (Schröer 1885) 33 Man þreo rædinga ræde and þry ræpsas, and ealle þa ȝebroþra þa hwile sittan. *c* **1000** ÆLFRIC *Hom.* II. 384 Agustinus us onwreah þissere rædinge andȝit. *c* **1175** *Lamb. Hom.* 93 Ʒe iherden a lutel er on þisse redunge þat ðe halie gast [etc.]. *c* **1200** *Trin. Coll. Hom.* 163 On salmes, and on songes, and on redinges. **1382** WYCLIF *Acts* xiii. 15 Aftir the redinge of lawe and prophetis, the princes of the synagogue senten to hem. **1490** in *Somerset Medieval Wills* (1901) 290 In such place as the Mynisters of god may stand upon my body in the tyme of the Redyng of the gospellis. **1657** SPARROW *Bk. Com. Prayer* (1661) 112 Regard is had to the more solemn times by select and proper readings. **1673** *True Worship of God* 9 They had their weekly Readings of the Law of Moses. **1860** ELLICOTT *Life Our Lord* iv. 158 The reading of the prophets was to begin, and the reading of the season was from the old Evangelist Isaiah. **1864** *Sharpe's London Mag.* XXVI. 216 No reading should.. last longer than ten minutes. **1960** C. DAY LEWIS *Buried Day* vii. 149 These were H. R. K.'s incomparable readings-aloud from Jane Austen, Thackeray, Dickens or the poets. **1974** *Listener* 14 Mar. 347/2 The least we can ask from a reading-aloud of poetry we know is that it adds to our gain from private reading.

c. The formal recital of a bill (or some part of it) before a legislative assembly.

1647 CLARENDON *Hist. Reb.* III. §240 They called.. for the bill.. 'for the extirpation of episcopacy', and gave it a second reading. **1702–3** ATTERBURY *Let.* Misc. Wks. 1739 I. 164 The Bill about repairing Churches was thrown out by the Lords.. at the first reading. **1783** *Hansard Parl. Hist.* (1814) XXIII. 1224 That the Christmas recess should intervene before the second reading. **1858** J. BRIGHT *Sp. India* 24 June, Opposing the second reading of this Bill.

d. *Sc.* The act of reading a portion of Scripture to the members of a household, as a form of family worship.

1814 NICHOLSON *Poet. Wks.* (1897) 67 (E.D.D.) Breakfast done, and reading bye. **1889** BARRIE *Window in Thrums* 193 I'll sit up till the readin's ower.

e. A social or public entertainment at which the audience listens to a reader. Cf. *penny reading*.

1787 J. COBB *Eng. Readings* 5 But tell me, Kitty, how did this *rage* for English Readings reach a town so far from London? **1813** M. EDGEWORTH *Let.* 16 May (1971) 55 We have been to one of Mrs. Siddons readings—*Measure for Measure*... In settling with Sheridan she came short 10 or 12 thousand pounds and her Readings are to make up this defalcation. **1858** DICKENS *Lett.* 11 Sept. (1880) II. 71 After the reading last night we walked.. to the railway. **1869** *Nation* (U.S.) VI. 269/1 The intelligent classes in this country, who can read themselves, have little occasion for public readings. **1916** M. B. LOWNDES *Diary* 12 Apr. (1971) 71, I went to the most remarkable Poets' Reading I have ever attended... I was moved by Mr de la Mare reading five poems of great beauty. **1953** *Ann. Reg. 1952* CXCIV. 377 The Hell scene in Shaw's *Man and Superman* had been staged with elaborate simplicity as a 'reading'.

f. ***reading in*** (see READ *v.* 13a and 19c).

1858 DALE *Clergym. Legal Handbk.* (ed. 7) 35 *margin.* **1892** WHITEHEAD *Church Law* (ed. 2) 251 The church-wardens and some parishioners should certify that the reading in has been duly performed.

†**3. a.** The act of lecturing or commenting upon some subject, *esp.* a law text; also, the matter of such lecture or comment, a commentary or gloss. ***reading of the sentences***: (see SENTENCE). *Obs.*

1517 *Black Bks. Lincoln's Inn* (1897) I. 183 All such as be at the Bench and dwellyng in the town, schall come daily to the redynges. **1581** LAMBARDE *Eiren.* Proheme (1588) 1 The Office and Duetie of Iustices of the Peace, after M. Marrow (whose learned Reading in that behalfe.. is in many hands to be seene). **1598** MANWOOD *Lawes Forest* ii. (1615) 28/2 Both Master Hesket and M. Treherne in their reading of the lawes of the forest. **1656** EARL MONM. tr. *Boccalini's Advts. fr. Parnass.* I. xc. (1674) 121 The reading of good discipline in a famous University. **1727–41** CHAMBERS *Cycl.*, *Readings* are also used for a sort of commentary or gloss on a law text, passage, or the like, to shew the sense an author takes it in.

†**b.** Instruction by a tutor. *Obs. rare*$^{-1}$.

1630 *R. Johnson's Kingd. & Commw.* 54 Two Crownes a moneth his Fencing, as much for Dancing, and no lesse for his Reading.

4. The act of interpreting or expounding. *rare*$^{-0}$.

c **1440** *Promp. Parv.* 427/1 Redynge, or expownynge of rydellys, or oþer privyteys.. *interpretacio, edicio.*

†**5.** *a* or *in reading*: Being read. *Obs.*

1535 COVERDALE *1 Macc.* v. 14 Whyle these letters were yet a readinge,.. there came other messaungers. **1566** *Child-Marriages* 137 This respondent saieth, that the testament was written before this talk, and was then in readinge.

6. The form in which a given passage appears in any copy or edition of a text; the actual word or words used in a particular passage. ***various readings***: (see VARIOUS).

1557 N. T. (Genev.) *title-p.*, The Newe Testament.. With the arguments,.. also diuersities of readings. **1611** BIBLE *Transl. Pref.* ¶15 They.. had rather haue their iudgements at libertie in differences of readings. **1699** BENTLEY *Phal.* 281 If the Reading be not corrupted, this Oracle was given Olymp. lxxvi, 1. **1724** A. COLLINS *Gr. Chr. Relig.* 189 But this supposition.. will not prove the two readings genuine. **1823** BYRON *Juan* VII. viii, 'Fierce loves and faithless wars'—I am not sure If this be the right reading. **1868** FREEMAN *Norm. Conq.* (1876) II. App. 612 The readings of the manuscripts are so different that it is hard to tell their exact meaning.

7. a. Matter for reading, esp. with ref. to its quality or kind.

1706 SWIFT *To Peterborough*, Ne'er to be match'd in modern reading, But by his name-sake Charles of Sweden. **1809** [see LIGHT *a.*^{1} 19]. **1840** DE QUINCEY *Style* i. Wks. 1853 XI. 175 It is in newspapers that we must look for the main reading of this generation. **1851** MAYHEW *Lond. Labour* I. 415 The books sold at railways are nearly all of the class best known as 'light-reading', or what some account light reading. **1885** *Pall Mall Budget* 19 June 31/1 His account of the *America* is lively reading.

b. Printed or written characters; lettering.

1891 E. PEACOCK *N. Brendon* I. 163 You will observe the cover has no reading on it, but only seven stars.

c. An extract from a previously printed source; in *pl.* freq. denoting a particular selection of such extracts intended to be read at one time or as a unit.

1835 C. FRY (*title*) Daily readings. Passages of Scripture, selected for social reading. **1865** CTESS. OF CAWDOR (*title*) Short Sunday evening readings selected and abridged from various authors. **1908** ROBINSON & BEARD (*title*) Readings in modern European history. A collection of extracts from the sources. **1931** W. L. VALENTINE *Readings in Exper. Psychol.* p. xiv, The original purpose was to include as a single reading only a single experimental paper. **1947** *Mind* LVI. 278 This joint work is intended to be read in conjunction with a companion volume of 'readings' culled from the classics of ancient and modern philosophy. **1972** *Sci. Amer.* Feb. 117/1 *The Science of Matter* offers more than 160 samples, averaging a couple of pages each; *A History of Medicine*.. gives us a couple of dozen readings some 10 or 12 pages in length.

8. That which presents itself to be read; *spec.* the indication of a graduated instrument.

1833 HERSCHEL *Astron.* ii. 83 The division and fractional part thus noted.. is to be set down as the reading of the limb. **1838** DE QUINCEY *Charles Lamb* Wks. 1858 IX. 153 That pure light of benignity which was the predominant reading on his features. **1869** W. B. CARPENTER in *Scientific Opinion* 9 Jan. 174/1 *note*, Our third thermometer stood.. at 45°.. and its reading has not been taken into account.

b. So ***reading-off***.

1808 SAX in *Phil. Trans.* XCIX. 240 Taking a mean of the different readings-off for the true position of the wire. **1833** HERSCHEL *Astron.* §198 The same constant error of graduation, which depends on the initial and final readings off alone.

9. The interpretation or meaning one attaches to anything, or the view one takes of it; in recent use *esp.* the rendering given to a play or a character, a piece of music, etc., as expressing the actor's or performer's point of view.

1792 A. YOUNG *Trav. France* 37 There is a species of countenance here so horridly bad, that it is impossible to be mistaken in one's reading. **1814** *Morning Herald* 14 Mar. in J. Agate *These were Actors* (1943) 31 Mr. Kean thought fit to leave out the whole of the first line in this declaration... This, in the saucy jargon of the day, may be called 'a new reading'. **1858** J. MARTINEAU *Stud. Chr.* 151 Dogma.. is ever producing new readings of the history. **1860** READE *Cloister & H.* lviii, She gave him her reading of the matter. **1865** DICKENS *Mut. Friend* II. III. x. 94 By-the-by, that very word, Reading, in its critical use, always charms me. An actress's Reading of a chambermaid, a dancer's Reading of a hornpipe, a singer's Reading of a song, a marine-painter's Reading of the sea, the kettle-drum's Reading of an instrumental passage, are phrases ever youthful and delightful. **1882** P. FITZGERALD *Recreat. Lit. Man* (1883) 112 His reading of Balzac's Mercadet.. appeared somewhat airy and not tragic enough. **1929** A. CARSE *Orchestral Conducting* III. i. 96 The personality of a conductor, the individuality of his readings.. count for more than technical correctness. **1945** H. WOOD *About Conducting* 105 Every aspirant to a conductor's career should.. make himself acquainted with the traditional readings of the classical repertoire. **1969** *Listener* 13 Mar. 360/2 The structure of his film implies one reading of Isadora's life, while its content implies a quite contrary interpretation. **1977** M. ALLEN *Spence in Petal Park* iv. 16 Someone turned him over.. after death, I would say. The pathologist will tell us for sure, but that's my reading.

10. *attrib.* and *Comb.* **a.** Simple attrib., as ***reading-circle, -class, clinic, day, excursion, habit, hour, -lamp, light, list, material, matter, party, play, rate, -readiness, scheme, society, -stand, -table, time, tour.***

1871 Mrs. Stowe *Pink & White Tyranny* xi. 124 They would get up their *reading-circles, and he would set her to improving her mind. **1926** R. Macaulay *Crewe Train* ii. v. 118 A reading circle. You all study some book together, and meet and talk about it. **1838** Marg. Fuller *Wom. 19th C.* (1862) 347 The forwardness of their minds has induced me to take both into my *reading-class. **1963** R. I. McDavid *Mencken's Amer. Lang.* 320 Minton points out the spread of technical medical terminology to education, as *clinic* (yielding **reading clinic* and *speech clinic*). **1975** *Language for Life* (Dept. Educ. & Sci.) xxvi. 514 There should be a reading clinic or remedial centre in every L.E.A. *a* **1643** Cartwright *Ordinary* iii. v. *Song*, A *Reading-Day Frights French away, The Benchers dare speak Latin. **1654** Whitlock *Zootomia* 240 The Booke which in that grand reading day..will be Licensed or burnt. **1848** Thackeray *Van. Fair* lxii, Jaunty young Cambridgemen..going for a *reading excursion. **1940** R. S. Lambert *Ariel & all his Quality* v. 131 You could hear complaints..that broadcasting was undermining the *reading habit. **1963** D. Pryce-Jones in Sissons & French *Age of Austerity* 212 The war may have enlarged the reading habits of a great many people. **1975** *Language for Life* (Dept. Educ. & Sci.) xxi. 304 The reading habit should be established early. **1809** Campbell *Gert. Wyom.* ii. ix, A deep untrodden grot, Where oft the *reading hours sweet Gertrude wore. **1782** *Catal. Stock in Trade Benjamin Martin* 14 A *reading lamp, with magnifying glass and shade. **1861** Dickens *Gt. Expect.* xxxix, I took up my reading-lamp and went out. **1908** Mrs. H. Ward *Diana Mallory* ii. x. 212 She was bending over the fire..a reading-lamp beside her. **1960** T. Cooper *Winter's Day* ii. v. 134 Do..switch off the big light; this reading-lamp on the desk is ample. **1936** M. Allingham *Flowers for Judge* xix. 273 The green *reading light..shining down upon his papers. **1945** Wilson & Wright *Tomorrow's House* xi. 116/2 Getting a decent reading light is by no means a matter of setting a table lamp on the night table. **1981** L. Deighton *XPD* xli. 329 He had a small reading light by which to read the documentation. **1925** *Scribner's Mag.* July 61/1 Books on fishing..should, in my opinion, have a place on every *reading list. **1981** *Times Lit. Suppl.* 6 Feb. 136/4 The names of these daunting authors..make an occasional modest appearance on reading-lists. **1961** *Educ. in Scotland 1960* (HMSO) 44 A welcome increase in the provision of supplementary *reading material. **1975** *Language for Life* (Dept. Educ. & Sci.) xvii. 253 Her first task is to assess the attainment level of every child and provide each with reading material of the right level of readability. **1848** Thoreau in *Union Mag.* Aug. 79/2 An odd leaf of the Bible, ..Emerson's Address on West India Emancipation..an odd number of the Westminster Review... This was the readable, or *reading matter, in a lumberer's camp in the Maine woods. **1884** G. Allen *Philistia* III. 238 To supply the reading matter, the letterpress I think you call it. **1923** R. Macaulay *Told by Idiot* ii. i. 68 Wise men and women would derive such pleasure as they could from the writings of others, without putting themselves to the trouble of providing reading matter in their turn. **1972** 'E. Ferrars' *Breath of Suspicion* xi. 185 I'm leaving the choice of some reading-matter for you to Bernard. **1785** B. Sheridan *Jrnl.* (1960) i. 43 Yesterday evening we spent at Mr Vesey's—a sort of conversatione—and *reading party. **1860** Hughes *Tom Brown at Oxf.* xxvi, Others applied to know whether he would take a reading party in the long Vacation. **1930** J. S. Huxley *Bird-Watching & Bird Behaviour* iii. 61, I was spending some of the spring vacation with a reading-party on the coast of North Wales. **1980** D. Newsome *On Edge of Paradise* ii. 59 A meeting there with a reading-party was usually the prelude to some summer expedition abroad. **1729** Fielding *Author's Farce* i. vii, Your *reading play is of a different stamp, and must have wit and meaning in it. **1960** *Bookseller* 17 Dec. 2330/3 A '*reading-rate controller'..., an inverted T-square with the handle part moving down the page of a book,..is attached to a sloping desk... A ready reckoner shows the number of..[lines] read in a minute, and the pupil can set the speed of this and then try to read faster. **1975** *Broadcast* 28 July 11/3 Our videodisc player's reading rate is 30 million bits per second. **1948, 1956** *Reading-readiness [see readiness 4b]. **1964** M. Critchley *Developmental Dyslexia* iv. 15 Bound up with the problem of when a child should first receive formal instruction in reading is the notion of a state of 'reading-readiness'. **1976** *Woman's Day* (U.S.) Nov. 58/2 How can reading-readiness scores have meaning when reading experts are still debating what skills are needed for beginning reading? **1974** *Education & Community Relations* Jan. 3 Several multiracial primary schools foresaw a major change 'in the selection of *reading schemes and supplementary readers'. **1975** *Language for Life* (Dept. Educ. & Sci.) vii. 104 The reading scheme is at the centre of this material in most young children's early experience of reading. **1775** T. Campbell *Diary* 21 Mar. (1947) 58 Strolled into the Chapter Coffee-house..remarkable for a large collection of books, & a *reading Society &c—I subscribed a shilling for the right of a years reading. **1797** C. Toogood *Let.* in Polwhele *Trad. & Recoll.* II. 462 We meet now, in almost every town, with a reading-society. **1828** M. O'Brien *Jrnl.* 28 Oct. (1968) iii. 21, I hope we shall manage the reading society, though we can only muster three members at Present. **1890** G. B. Shaw in *Star* 28 Feb. 2/4, I repaired to the London Institution to see 'The Shakespeare Reading Society' recite 'Much Ado'. **1853** Dale tr. *Baldeschi's Ceremonial* 119 The Assistant Priest carries to the Altar the cushion, or *reading-stand, with the Missal. **1885** Mabel Collins *Prettiest Woman* xiii, Beside the bed was a reading-stand. **1794** T. Sheraton *Cabinet-Maker & Upholsterer's Drawing-Bk.* II. iii. Pl. 44 (*caption*) A *Reading & Writing Table. **1855** Trollope *Warden* ix. 134 A huge arm-chair fitted up with candlesticks, a reading table, a drawer, and other paraphernalia. **1875** *Carp. & Join.* 130, I will now describe a large elevating reading table. **1591** *Black Bks. Lincoln's Inn* (1898) II. 21 No Reader shall make anie dinner..but in the *Reading time. **1848** Thackeray *Bk. Snobs* (1881) 223 They are on a *reading tour for the Long Vacation.

b. Special combs.: **reading age**, reading ability expressed in terms of the age (during the period of development) for which a comparable ability is calculated as average; **reading-book**, †(*a*) a book of church-lessons (*obs.*); (*b*) a book containing passages for instruction in reading; **reading chair**, a chair designed to facilitate reading; *spec.* one equipped with a book-rest upon one arm; **reading-closet**, one of the small compartments in the reading-room of a printing-office; **reading-coat**, a coat to wear while reading (? *obs.*); **reading copy**, a copy of a book that is usable although in less than perfect condition; **reading-desk**, a desk for supporting a book while it is being read, *spec.* a lectern; **reading-glass**, (*a*) a large magnifying glass for use in reading; (*b*) in *pl.*, a pair of spectacles for use when reading; **reading-hook** (see quot.); **reading-machine**, (*a*) (see quot.); (*b*) a device for producing an enlarged, readable image from microform; (*c*) a device for automatically producing electrical signals corresponding to the characters of a text; **reading notice** *U.S.* (see quot. 1909); **reading-pew**, a pew from which the lessons are read in church; †**reading-psalms**, the prose psalms used for reading in church (*obs.*); **reading room**, a room devoted to reading, *esp.* one in the premises of a club or library, or intended for public use; also, the proof-readers' room in a printing-office (Jacobi 1888).

1921 C. Burt *Mental & Scholastic Tests* iii. iii. 271 Consequently, a score of sixty words indicates a mental age for reading at ten;..according to the formula:—*Reading Age = $(4 + \frac{\text{Words}}{10})$ years. *Ibid.*, The reading ages of four and five pretend to little more than a conventional significance. **1945** F. J. Schonell *Psychol. & Teaching of Reading* i. 21 There is always a great increase in eye movements as the reading material increases in difficulty for particular reading ages. **1952** Anderson & Dearborn *Psychol. of Teaching Reading* i. 10 If the reading age is appreciably below the mental age, the child is regarded as a reading problem. **1961** *Guardian* 28 Apr. 13/3 He looks a dissipated 20... His reading age is 8·2. **1975** *Language for Life* (Dept. Educ. & Sci.) ii. 11 There are at least a million adults with a reading age of below 9·0 who cannot read simple recipes. **10..** *Laws Ælfric* 21 in Thorpe *Laws* II. 350 Se mæsse-preost sceal habban..*rædingboc. **1050–73** *Charter* in Thorpe *Diplom.* 430, ii forealdode rædingbec. *c* **1315** Shoreham *Poems* i. 1311 Þe bisschop, wenne he ordreþ þes, Þe redyng bok hym takeþ. **1840** (*title*) The Church Scholar's reading book. **1803** T. Sheraton *Cabinet Dict.* 17 *Arm-chair* for a library, or a *reading chair... These are intended to make the exercise easy, and for the convenience of taking down a note or quotation... The reader places himself with his back to the front of the chair, and rests his arms on the top yoke. **1853** A. J. Downing *Architect. Country Houses* xii. 426 Fig. 218 is a reading-chair of a simple and good form,..having a desk for a book on one arm, and a stand for a candle on the other—both being..easily lifted out.., when not in use. **1951** E. Paul *Springtime in Paris* iii. 54 There was a long table, and ranged on both sides, good reading chairs. **1977** J. Hodgins *Invention of World* iii. 44 The tall green reading chair that had recipes..shoved under its cushion. **1886** *Referee* 10 Jan. 1/2, I was getting an honest..living in the composing-room or the *reading-closet. **1830** C. Wordsworth in Overton *Life* (1888) 51 Here I am, lying on my sofa, with my drab *reading-coat on. **1952** J. Carter *ABC for Book-Collectors* 164 *Reading copy, a usually apologetic, but occasionally slightly defiant, term meaning that the book is not in collector's condition. **1977** J. Wilson *Making Hate* iv. 52 The *Just So Stories*. I had an early edition, a torn reading copy, but quite clean. **1703** Maundrell *Journ. Jerus.* (1721) 8 A piece of plank supported by a Post, which we understood was the *Reading Desk. **1775** Johnson 10 Oct. in Boswell *Life* (1791) I. 502 In the reading-desk of the refectory lay the Lives of the Saints. **1838** Lytton *Alice* ii. iii, A huge armchair, with a small reading-desk beside it. **1670** Wood *Life* (O.H.S.) II. 200 Dr. Barlow gave me a *reading-glass, pretium 40s. **1747** Trembley in *Phil. Trans.* XLIV. 632 It would be..very inconvenient to hold it like a reading-glass in the hand. **1831** Brewster *Optics* xxxviii. 320 Spectacles and reading glasses are among the simplest and most useful of optical instruments. **1853** Dickens *Bleak House* xli. 405 The green lamp is lighted, his *reading-glasses lie upon the desk. **1972** G. Bill *Villains Galore* i. 1 Clara..needed reading glasses for all but the largest print. **1858** Simmonds *Dict. Trade*, **Reading-hook*, a book-marker, made of bone or ivory. **1897** *Sketch* 26 May 181/2 The pattern being read from the draft by the *reading-machine on to the Jacquard band or tape by the skilled designer or pantagrapher. **1937** M. L. Raney *Microphotogr. for Libraries* 76 There is today plenty of work for reading machines to do, since the entire contents of great libraries that have filming cameras lie open to order in so far as copyright allows. **1940** A. Huxley *Let.* 14 Oct. (1969) 461, I would like to have..micro-photographs suitable for reading by means of a reading machine. **1959** *Library Resources & Technical Services* III. 90 The average library user does not meet the microcopy until he has to use it on the reading machine. **1964** *Litho-Printer* Aug. 34/2 Even optical reading machines, which are now entering the field of practicability cannot quite dispense with human work: they need clean copy, at least re-typed from edited manuscripts. **1965** R. R. Karch *Graphic Arts Procedures* (ed. 3) xiii. 338 Specially-designed figures printed at the bottoms of bank checks are printed with ink capable of being magnetized and read by electronic reading machines for routing the checks to proper places. **1980** J. Drummond *Such a Nice Family* viii. 38 Would you like us to fix up a reading-machine for you?.. It'll throw up an enlargement of the text. **1909** Webster, **Reading-notice*, in a newspaper or periodical, a paid advertisement so set up as to have the appearance of regular news or editorial or contributed matter. **1970** R. K. Kent *Lang. Journalism* 109 *Reading notice*, an advertisement in a newspaper or magazine that is set in body type and in columns so as to appear the same as editorial matter. **1641** R. Brooke *Eng. Episc.* i. vii. 38 To wrangle downe a Sophister,..or acquaint themselves with a *Reading-Pue, in the Countrey. **1662** Pepys *Diary* 26 Oct., To church, and there saw for the first time Mr. Mills in a surplice; but it seemed absurd for him to pull it over his eares in the reading-pew. **1848** *Ecclesiologist* Oct. 144 An open reading-pew and lettern. **1706** A. Bedford *Temple Mus.* viii. 162 The like Order is observed in the Pointing of our *Reading Psalms. *a* **1707** Bp. Patrick *Autobiogr.* (1839) 150 The old translation of the reading Psalms. **1759** Gray *Lett.* 8 Aug. (1853) 186, I often pass four hours in the day in the stillness and solitude of the *reading room [at the British Museum]. **1817** Cobbett *Wks.* XXXII. 357 There are what are called Reading Rooms all over the kingdom. **1852** Rock *Ch. of Fathers* III. i. 298 Saint Edmund kept a figure of our Lady in his reading-room.

reading ('ri:dɪŋ), *ppl. a.* [f. read *v.* + -ing².]

1. †**a.** ***reading minister***, etc., one who merely reads the lessons or service, without preaching; also *Sc.*, one who reads his sermons (see read *v.* 19 d).

1583 Stubbes *Anat. Abus.* ii. (1882) 71 It were to be wished that all were preaching prelates, and not reading ministers only. **1650** in Hodgson *Northumberland* (1835) III. iii. p. lv, Those who formerly had the Rectory of Haltwistle did mainteyne a reading Minister. **1744** (*title*) Reading is not preaching, or a Letter to all reading Clergymen.

b. ***reading clerk***, the designation of one of the clerks to the House of Lords.

1788 Miss Rose in *G. Rose's Diaries* (1860) I. 96 My brother William, then reading Clerk, came to us as soon as the House adjourned. **1817** *Parl. Deb.* 16 The Lords were obliged to send this message by their Clerk-Assistant, and their Reading-Clerk. **1884** Yates *Recoll.* I. ii. 66 Slingsby, who is reading-clerk in the House of Lords.

c. ***reading boy***, a boy who reads copy aloud to the corrector of the press.

1808 Stower *Printers' Gram.* 392 The eye of the reader should not follow, but rather go before the voice of his reading-boy. **1888** *Encycl. Brit.* XXIII. 710/1 The reading department, sometimes called the closet, having for its occupants the reader and his reading-boy.

2. Given to reading; studious. Freq. in ***reading man***, applied *spec.* to a University student who makes reading his chief occupation; and ***reading public***.

1673 Dryden *Prol. Univ. of Oxford* 31 In London.. haughty dunces, whose unlearned pen Could ne'er spell grammar, would be reading men. **1759** *Hurd's Dial.* Pref. 6 The learned assemblies of reading divines. **1797** *Monthly Mag.* III. 266/1 During my residence at the university, and a constant intercourse with both reading and non-reading men [etc.]. **1831** *Blackw. Mag.* Jan. 94/2 The 'reading public', then, had little to do with the lower orders. **1837** Sir F. Palgrave *Merch. & Friar* Ded. (1844) 1 His attempts to be brought out into the reading world. **1877** M. W. Chapman in *Harriet Martineau's Autobiogr.* III. 99 The reading public..were longing to express their grateful acknowledgements. **1885** J. Martineau *Types Eth. Th.* II. ii. iii. §1. 517 Its..literary merits secured it immediate attention on the part of reading men. **1916** E. Pound *Let.* 17 Nov. (1971) 99 That many-eared monster with no sense, the reading public. *a* **1936** Kipling *Something of Myself* (1937) iii. 47 Our reading public..were..as well educated as fifty per cent of our 'staff'. **1962** M. McLuhan *Gutenberg Galaxy* 132 There was no reading public in our sense... Under manuscript conditions an author would..have no public. An advanced scientist today has no public. **1975** S. Schoenbaum *W. Shakespeare* xi. 120 A dramatist had least to say about..publication... He strove, after all, to please audiences in the theatre, not a reading public.

'readingdom. The aggregate of readers.

1832 Southey in C. C. Southey *Life* (1849) VI. 182 The commonwealth of Readingdom is divided into many independent circles.

†**readjoin**, *v.* [re- 5 a.] *trans.* To join again.

1646 Earl Monm. tr. *Biondi's Civil Warres* ix. 173 Readjoyning unto it whatsoever at sundry times has been dismembred from it.

rea'djourn, *v.* [re- 5 a. Cf. med.L. *readjornāre* (1240 in Du C.), F. *réajourner* (1531 in Godef.).] *trans.* and *intr.* To adjourn again.

1611 Cotgr., *Readjourner*, to readiourn. **1628** Wotton in *Reliq.* (1672) 443 The Parliament..was then re-adjourned by the Kings especial Command till Tuesday next. **1678** Marvell *Growth Popery* 41 He might have given Notice by Proclamation that upon this account, they should re-adjourn to a yet longer time.

Hence **rea'djournment** (Ogilvie 1882).

rea'djust, *v.* [re- 5 a. Cf. med.L. *readjustāre* (1236 in Du C.).] *trans.* To adjust again or afresh; to put in order again.

1742 Fielding *J. Andrews* iv. xi, The beau..taking out a pocket-glass..re-adjusted his hair. **1764** Maskelyne in *Phil. Trans.* LIV. 357 It is not always necessary to re-adjust the wires after each sett of observations. **1848** Mill *Pol. Econ.* iii. xvi. §1 The values and prices of the two things will ..readjust themselves. **1866** Felton *Anc. & Mod. Gr.* II. ii. i. 253 The early attempts to readjust the affairs of the East by the Great Powers.

absol. **1864** Pusey *Lect. Daniel* (1876) 214 It adjusts, re-adjusts, turns, re-turns, in every way it wills.

Hence **rea'djusted** *ppl. a.*; **rea'djusting** *vbl. sb.*

1776 Cavendish in *Phil. Trans.* LXVI. 385 It is not likely to want re-adjusting soon. **1863** *Q. Rev.* Jan. 283 He held out hopes of a readjusted and graduated income-tax.

rea'djuster. [f. prec.] One who readjusts.
1862 THORNBURY *Life Turner* II. 256 Turner was..a selector, reviser, a readjuster of Nature.
b. *U.S.* A member of a political party (formed in 1877–8) in Virginia, which advocated a legislative readjustment of the State debt.
1879 *Nation* (N.Y.) 13 Nov. 317/2 Further news from Virginia indicates that the Repudiators, or Readjusters, as they call themselves, have elected a majority of the General Assembly. **1883** M. D. CONWAY in *Glasgow Weekly Her.* 1 Sept. 3/2 The readjuster reminds the negro that he was a slave when this debt was formed..and should not be taxed for the interest.

rea'djustment. [f. as prec. + -MENT.]
1. The process of readjusting or of being readjusted.
1771 SMEATON in *Phil. Trans.* LXI. 208 After this re-adjustment they both agreed to 1°. **1793** WOLLASTON *ibid.* LXXXIII. 149 It is very steady; and rarely wants any re-adjustment at all. **1865** R. W. DALE *Jew. Temp.* xii. (1877) 129 Your theology needs alteration and readjustment. **1883** FROUDE in *Mrs. Carlyle's Lett.* I. 194 The house..requiring paint and other re-adjustments.
2. *Comb.*, as **readjustment rule** *Linguistics* (see quot. 1972).
1968 CHOMSKY & HALLE *Sound Pattern Eng.* I. i. 10 The 'readjustment rules' relating syntax to phonology make various other modifications in surface structures. **1972** R. A. PALMATIER *Gloss. Eng. Transformational Grammar* 141 *Readjustment rule*,..one of a set of special rules which prepare the syntactic surface structure of a sentence for inputting to the phonological component; one of the types of phonological rules..which determine admissible, or possible, and inadmissible, or impossible, classificatory matrices. **1977** *Canad. Jrnl. Linguistics 1976* XXI. II. 215 He also includes the suggestion, discussing Trager's similar analysis of short *a* in New Jersey English in 1940.., that such factors may be handled as a type of readjustment rule in the historical development of the phonology of a language.

†**readliche,** *adv.* *Obs.* Also 2–3 red-, 3 reaðliche. [Var. of ME. *radliche* RADLY.] Quickly, promptly.
c **1175** *Lamb. Hom.* 45 þa wes sancte paul swiðe wa and abeh him redliche to his lauerdes fet. *a* **1225** *Ancr. R.* 422 Water þet ne stureð nout readliche stinkeð. *a* **1240** *Sawles Warde* in *Cott. Hom.* 247 His hinen..swerieð somet reaðliche þat efter hire hit schal gan.

read'minister, *v.* [RE- 5 a.] *trans.* To administer again.
1597 HOOKER *Eccl. Pol.* v. lxii. § 12 That Baptisme is onely then to be readministred, when the first deliuerie thereof is void. **1762** R. GUY *Cancers* 44 The Hemlock was re-administered for some Weeks. **1897** *Columbia* (Ohio) *Disp.* 24 Mar. 1/2 The Democratic party..has regained power and readministered government.

†**re'admiral,** *v.* *Obs.*$^{-1}$ [RE- 5 b.] *trans.* To make (one) an admiral again.
1599 NASHE *Lenten Stuffe* 12 Peerebrowne did not only hold his office all the time of that King..but was againe readmirald by Edward the third.

read'mire, *v.* [RE- 5 a.] To admire again.
1782 ELIZ. BLOWER *Geo. Bateman* I. 202 The pleasure of having it re-admired by our friends. **1930** O. W. HOLMES *Let.* 12 May (1953) II. 1246, I finished it [*sc.* a book] a few days ago. I readmired the Rousseau and Machiavelli and believed without adequate knowledge what you say about foundations.

readmission (riːæd'mɪʃən). [RE- 5 a; cf. next and F. *réadmission* (Littré).] The action of admitting again.
1655 SIR E. NICHOLAS in *N. Papers* (Camden) II. 341 Twill proue a very difficult worke to make them allow of ye readmission of ye King. **1691** WOOD *Ath. Oxon.* II. 307 He ..preached at the readmission of a relapsed Christian into our Church. **1782** PRIESTLEY *Corrupt. Chr.* II. IX. 141 There was..re-admission to the privileges. **1879** *St. George's Hosp. Rep.* IX. 709 Within a week of their readmission, the disease appeared in nine other cottages.

readmit (riːæd'mɪt), *v.* [RE- 5 a. Cf. F. *réadmettre* (*readmis*, Cotgr. 1611).] *trans.* To admit again.
1611 COTGR., *Readmis*, readmitted. **1616** T. GODWYN *Moses & Aaron* I. (1641) 54 Sometimes they would re-admit such a one being brought neere unto death. **1665** MANLEY tr. *Grotius' Low C. Warres* 616 This was terrible..to them of Wesell, who were commanded to readmit the Roman Rites. **1742** YOUNG *Nt. Th.* IV. 670 Happy day! that..re-admits us..to our Father's throne. **1866** *Lond. Rev.* 6 Jan. 2/2 He would at once readmit the late rebel states to the full enjoyment of their rights.
absol. *c* **1659** THORNDIKE *Church's Power of Excomm.* § 36 Penance..readmits not but upon reasonable or legal presumption of sin first abolished.
Hence **read'mitting** *vbl. sb.*
1667 *Phil. Trans.* II. 583 The re-admitting of the Air.

read'mittance. [Cf. prec. and ADMITTANCE.] Readmission.
1669 *Ormonde MSS.* in *10th Rep. Hist. MSS. Comm.* App. V. 104 To order his readmittance and continuance in the..guard of halberdiers. *a* **1711** KEN *Urania* Poet. Wks. 1721 IV. 480 You give me..Re-admittance to the blissful Throne. **1845** LD. CAMPBELL *Chancellors* (1857) I. xxv. 357 The re-admittance of so great a prelate into your favour.

read-mostly (riːd'məʊstlɪ), *a.* *Computers.* [f. READ *v.* + MOSTLY *adv.*] Applied to a memory whose contents can be changed, though not by program instructions, but which is designed on the basis that such changes will be very infrequent compared with the number of occasions when the contents are read.
1971 *New Scientist* 1 Apr. 29/3 Initially, read-mostly memories will be used for semi-permanently stored computer instructions, such as in process control computers. **1977** *Sci. Amer.* Sept. 139/1 Another variation on the read-only memory is the read-mostly memory... Read-mostly memories have two forms. The commonest is the optically erasable read-only memory. *Ibid.*, An alternative form of read-mostly memory is the electrically alterable read-only memory.., which can be altered without the necessity of erasing the entire array.

read-only (riːd'əʊnlɪ), *a.* *Computers.* [f. READ *v.* + ONLY *adv.*] Applied to a memory whose contents cannot be changed by program instructions but which can usually be read at high speed; also *ellipt.* Abbrev. ROM s.v. R II. 2 a.
1961 H. R. FOGLIA et al. in *IBM Jrnl. Res. & Development* V. 67/1 Another form of memory can be used that may be read at these high speeds, with capability of being changed in a few minutes. Memories of this type, in which the fast-read cycle is of prime importance, may be called read only memories. **1969** P. B. JORDAIN *Condensed Computer Encycl.* 416 Read-only storage is used for rapid access to information of a permanent nature. *Ibid.*, Read-only stores are not to be confused with nondestructive read-out memories, memories that may be altered but can be repeatedly read without loss of data. **1970** O. DOPPING *Computers & Data Processing* x. 135 Read-only memories are sometimes used in the internal organization of a computer, but in some machines they are also used for the permanent storage of standard programs. **1977** *Engineering Materials & Design* Aug. 9/3 The function program for the device is held in a 16 kilobit read only memory. **1979** R. MUTCH *Gemstone* viii. 96 Probably only need one read-only.

rea'dopt, *v.* [RE- 5 a.] To adopt again.
1598 FLORIO, *Readottare*,..to readopt. **1611** COTGR., *Readopter*, to readopt. *a* **1711** KEN *Hymnotheo* Poet. Wks. 1721 III. 33, I come to save you..And God to re-adopt you to incline. **1742** YOUNG *Nt. Th.* IX. 1342 When shall my soul her incarnation quit, And, re-adopted to thy blest embrace, Obtain her apotheosis in thee? **1850** B. TAYLOR *Eldorado* I. xv. 103 The boundary which had first passed was re-adopted by a large vote.

rea'doption. [RE- 5 a; cf. prec.] Renewed adoption.
a **1562** G. CAVENDISH *Wolsey* (Ellis) 179 They feared hyme more after his fall.., doughtyng myche hys readopcion in to auctorytie. **1825** COLERIDGE *Aids Refl.* (1848) I. 243 John,..speaking of the re-adoption of the redeemed to be sons of God. **1878** BAYNE *Purit. Rev.* v. 162 The readoption of those religious doctrines and sentiments which..England had cast out.

rea'dorn, *v.* [RE- 5 a.] To adorn anew.
1598 FLORIO, *Rabbellire*, to rebeawtifie, to readorne againe. **1610** HOLLAND *Camden's Brit.* I. 299 King Henry the Fifth readourned it with new buildings. **1712** BLACKMORE *Creation* VI. 449 With Scarlet Honours re-adorn'd.
Hence **rea'dorning** *vbl. sb.*
1598 FLORIO, *Rabbellimento*, a readorning.

read-out ('riːdaʊt). Also readout. [f. vbl. phr. *to read out* (READ *v.* 6 f).] **1. a.** *Computers.* The extraction or transfer of data from a storage medium or device. Also *transf.*
1946 [see READ *v.* 6 f]. **1952** [see MATRIX 6 d]. **1961** *IBM Jrnl. Res. & Development* V. 67/1 During readout the voltage pulse will be applied to a selected conductor corresponding to the word to be read out. **1970** O. DOPPING *Computers & Data Processing* x. 151 Read-out is effected when a desired word passes through the pulse-shaping circuits. **1971** J. Z. YOUNG *Introd. Study Man* xxii. 302 This reprogramming of the read-out of the DNA may serve to bring into play a new complex of enzyme systems.
b. The display of data by an automatic device in an understandable form. Also *transf.*
1961 *Aeroplane & Astronautics* CI. 573/2 The range indicator displays have a six-figure readout correct to the nearest 25 m. **1965** *Wireless World* July 35 (Advt.), For rapid transistor measurements, it can be set up for direct meter readout. **1971** *Engineering* Apr. 44/2 (*caption*) The new Sangamo extensometer which offers direct readout plus great sensitivity. **1971** *Nature* 13 Aug. 443/3 Displays have been selected during evolution to provide an accurate 'read out' of an animal's internal state to another animal.
c. (See quot. 1966.)
1966 *Britannica Bk. of Year 1965* 807/2 *Readout*, the radio transmission of data or pictures from a space vehicle either immediately upon acquisition or later by means of playback of a tape recording. **1970** N. ARMSTRONG et al. *First on Moon* iii. 66 There was still work to do, starting with spacecraft-to-ground readouts.
2. A device for extracting or displaying data.
1954 *IRE Trans. Electronic Computers* Dec. 12 (*heading*) A radio-frequency nondestructive readout for magnetic core memories. *Ibid.* 15/1 It was possible to sense any core in this array plane using the rf readout. **1967** *Electronics* 6 Mar. 114/1 (Advt.), Our all-new NIXIE tube—the industry's lowest-cost electronic readout, and one sure to usher in a whole new generation of low-cost digital instrumentation. **1969** A. C. MARIN *Rise with Wind* i. 4 Any efforts..to create an identity for the Director always fell flat, killed by the ever-present awareness of the computerlike brain... You could almost sense the logic circuits working, the tapes running on the reels, the punch cards appearing on the read-out. **1972** *Physics Bull.* July 418/3 An easy to read 2½ digit LED readout reduces error when interpreting the measurements, particularly in low light conditions. **1976** M. MACHLIN *Pipeline* liii. 538 She was pleased to see that Schultheiss was alone in the control shack, which was a large building filled with a complicated set of flashing lights, meters, and digital readouts.
3. A record of its output produced by a computer or scientific instrument.
1967 *Economist* 11 Feb. 542/1 The computer read-out is fed into the draughting machine which should then draw the correct shape of the ship for the designer to check. **1970** H. HARRISON *Captive Universe* 142 Just look at these figures... These are from a machine, a readout. **1971** *Daily Colonist* (Victoria, B.C.) 11 Dec. 17/5 The echogram—the read-out of an electronic device that is useful in diagnosing such abnormalities as tumours. **1977** *Daily Tel.* 25 Jan. 15/3, I left behind at the institute about 100-yards of paper read-outs, my metabolic processes recorded in squiggly lines.
4. *attrib.*
1965 *Wireless World* July 352/3 The average readout time is two seconds but for maximum readout it is five seconds. **1966** *Times Rev. Industry* Oct. 52/1 The units in the range —sample injection systems, oven and temperature controllers, columns, detectors and read-out units—are of modular design. **1968** H. HARRIS *Nucleus & Cytoplasm* iv. 68 Our text-books are full of diagrams showing ribosomes rolling along a messenger tape and thus fulfilling their role as a 'read-out' mechanism. **1976** *Offshore Platforms & Pipelining* 57/1 Readout gauges on the control panel will display tension in each line. **1976** B. BOVA *Multiple Man* (1977) i. 16 The computer was humming to itself, lights flickering on its read-out console.

'read-through. Also readthrough, read through. [f. READ *v.*] **1.** An act of reading through; spec. *Theatr.*, an initial rehearsal at which actors read their parts from scripts.
1961 A. WILSON *Old Men at Zoo* ii. 95 She has to go to a read-through whatever that may be. **1963** E. HUMPHREYS *Gift* II. i. 209 He was late for the read through... Started talking loudly to the actress next to him and greeting everybody when we had already begun to read. **1966** 'O. NORTON' *School of Liars* vii. 113, I..came back for the first read-through, and the acting notes. **1971** *Guardian* 3 July 9/3 'This script is a mess..' said Adrienne Corri the other day at a read-through for my TV series. **1976** J. GRENFELL *Joyce Grenfell requests Pleasure* xvi. 230 Our spirits went up and down..after the usual enthusiastic read-through when the material seemed so original and imaginative.
2. *Biochem.* The continued transcription of genetic material by RNA polymerase that has overrun a termination sequence.
[**1970** GOFF & MINKLEY in L. Silvestri *RNA-Polymerase & Transcription* 134 One interesting interpretation of these results is that the largest RNA class is produced when rho fails to function at the first termination signal used *in vivo* and the polymerase reads through to a second 'stop signal'.] **1970** A. A. TRAVERS in *Nature* 14 Mar. 1011/2 (*caption*) Fig. 3. Readthrough by *E. coli* σ initiated RNA polymerase into sequences transcribed by σ^{T4} initiated polymerase. **1971** *Ibid.* 15 Dec. 207/2 These sequence data strongly suggest that the II*b* protein is a read-through product resulting from polypeptide chain elongation. **1978** *Ibid.* 30 Mar. 417/2 One of these..is the only oligonucleotide consistent with transcriptional 'read-through' of the termination site.

†**readunite,** *v.* *Obs.*$^{-1}$ [RE- 5 a; see ADUNITE and cf. late L. *readūnātio* (Tertullian), med.L. *readūnāre* (Du C.).] *trans.* To reunite.
a **1600** HOOKER *Eccl. Pol.* VIII. i. § 6 A man..is upon his repentance necessarily readunited into the one, but not of necessity into the other.

read'vance, *v.* [RE- 5 a.] To advance again.
a. In transitive senses of the vb.
1611 FLORIO, *Rinalzare*, to raise againe, to readuance. **1633** T. ADAMS *Exp. 2 Pet.* iii. 17 How able he is to re-advance the dejected. **1670** G. H. *Hist. Cardinals* II. II. 162 To re-advance all the Noble Families in Rome, that began to lessen and decay in their splendour. **1828** SOUTHEY in *Q. Rev.* XXXVIII. 574 It recedes from none of its claims, though it may wait the convenient season for re-advancing them. **1850** McCOSH *Div. Govt.* (1852) 266 *note*, We are swinging upon a hinge in advancing and re-advancing such maxims.
b. In intransitive senses.
1611 COTGR., *Remonter*,..to reascend; readuance. **1616** B. JONSON *Epigr.* I. lxxxv, Which if they misse, they yet should readvance To former height. **1655** FULLER *Hist. Camb.* (1840) 142 The Vice-Chancellor retreated to Trinity College... This done, he readvanceth to St. John's. **1813** SIR R. WILSON *Priv. Diary* (1861) II. 254 The Russians re-advanced to Peterswalde,..but were checked at Grossubel. **1848** MILL *Pol. Econ.* I. xiii. § 3 The tide which has receded, instantly begins to re-advance.
So **read'vancement; read'vancing** *vbl. sb.*
1611 SPEED *Hist. Gt. Brit.* IX. vii. § 1. 514 To the seruice of God, and re-aduancement of the Crosse of Christ. **1611** COTGR., *Rehaulsement*, a readuancing. **1647** CLARENDON *Hist. Reb.* VI. § 99 The re-advancing upon it and taking it.

read'vance, *sb.* Chiefly *Geol.* [f. the vb.] A renewed advance.
1879 *Geol. Mag.* Decade II. VI. 250 The recurring glacial conditions were too insignificant to cause a re-advance of the ice-sheet. **1927** PEAKE & FLEURE *Apes & Men* 29 With the re-advance of the temperate forest in Europe, as the climate improved, most of them [*sc.* the mammals] finally disappeared. **1975** J. G. EVANS *Environment Early Man Brit. Isles* ii. 45 In the north of the British Isles, three readvances during the general retreat of the ice are marked by 'moraines'.

†**read'vertency.** *Obs.*$^{-1}$ [RE- 5 a.] Renewed application (of the mind).
1692 NORRIS *Curs. Reflect.* 9 A Re-advertency or Re-application of mind to Ideas that are actually there.

readvertise, *v.* [RE- 5 a.] *trans.* To advertise again. Now *spec.* to give further notice of (a job vacancy). Hence **re'advertised** *ppl. a.*; **re'advertising** *vbl. sb.*; **read'vertisement**.

1669 WOODHEAD *St. Teresa* II. iii. 22 Who not giving me leave to go, our Lord often re-advertised me. **1934** WEBSTER, Readvertisement. **1963** *Times* 19 Apr. 7/1 The decision to readvertise the post of Chief Constable of Glamorgan was 'reluctantly' agreed to by the standing joint committee of the county council today. **1964** A. BATTERSBY *Network Analysis* x. 153 The table could obviously be extended to include reprinting, re-advertising, and later royalty payments. **1971** *Engineering* Apr. 124/2 Previous candidates for the second post (now re-advertised) will be reconsidered if they so indicate. **1977** *Times Educ. Suppl.* 21 Oct. 46/1 (Advt.), Headteachers; (1) Balderston Comprehensive Community School (readvertisement). **1978** *Nature* 9 Nov. 109/1 It would like to readvertise the head of technology post inviting both engineers and astronomers to apply.

read'vise, *v.* [RE- 5 a.]

1. *trans.* To advise again. Also *refl.*

1574 HELLOWES *Gueuara's Fam. Ep.* (1577) 116, I do aduise and readuise the man [etc.]. **1603** FLORIO *Montaigne* I. xxv. (1632) 73 The libertie for a man to repent and re-advise himselfe. **1748** RICHARDSON *Clarissa* (1811) VIII. 167, I was going to re-advise her to calm her spirits.

2. *intr.* To consider again; to take counsel afresh.

1598 FLORIO, *Rauisare*, to readuise, or marke againe. **1643** *Five Yrs. K. Jas.* 75 You may againe ruminate, and re-advise to make your defence. **1820** T. MITCHELL *Aristoph.* I. p. lxxxvii, To re-advise for the better security.

ready ('rɛdɪ), *a.*, *adv.*, and *sb.* Forms: 3 **rædi(ȝ)**; 3–5 **redi**, 3–6 **redie**, **redy** (7 *Sc.*), 4–5 **redye**, (6 **redey**, **reedy**; also *Sc.* 5–7 **reddy**, **reddie**, 6 **rady**, **radie**); 3, 6 **readi**, 6 **readye**, 6–7 **readie**, 6– **ready**. [Early ME. *rædi(ȝ)*, *readi*, *redi*, in southern texts also *ȝeredi*, *iredi*, etc. (see I-REDY), apparently formed on the analogy of other adjectives by the addition of *-iȝ*, -Y, to OE. *ræde* (?) or *ȝeræde* I-REDE, from the Teut. stem **raiđ-* to put in order, prepare: see I-RAD and GRAITH *sb.* and *a.*

The form *rædiȝ* is peculiar to ME., but synonymous words from the same base are common in the cognate languages, as MDu. *gereet*, *-reit* (Du. *gereed*), MLG. *gerêde*, MHG. *gereite*, *gereit*; OFris. *rêde*, *rêd* (mod. *ree*), Du. *reede*, *ree*, MLG. *rêde* (hence Da. *rede*, Sw. *reda*, *redo*, Icel. *reiðr*), OHG. *-reiti* (MHG. *reite*); MDu. *bereet*, *-reit* (Du. *bereid*), MLG. *berêde* (hence Da. *beredt*, Sw. *beredd*), OHG. *bireiti* (G. *bereit*). Mod.Sw. *redig* unentangled, clear, etc., is an independent formation from *reda* to disentangle.]

A. *adj.* **I. 1. a.** In a state of preparation, so as to be capable of immediately performing (or becoming the object of) such action as is implied or expressed in the context.

c **1205** LAY. 8651 Julius wes al rædi [*c* **1275** readi] alse he to wolde ræsen. *c* **1320** *Sir Tristr.* 259 [He] bad al schuld be boun..Redi to his somoun. **1382** WYCLIF *Matt.* xxv. 10 Tho that weren redy, entriden in with hym to the weddyngis. **1450** in *Wars Eng. in France* (Rolls) I. 511 Make oure sugites of youre cuntre to be arayyd and redy in thaire best maniere. **1568** GRAFTON *Chron.* II. 698 He wrote.. commaundyng all men..to be redie in harnesse. **1596** SHAKS. *Tam. Shr.* Induct. i. 59 Some one be readie with a costly suite. **1638** JUNIUS *Paint. Ancients* 22 Such kinde of Images, as might be ready at his call. **1697** DRYDEN *Virg. Georg.* II. 763 His Kine with swelling Udders ready stand. **1788** BURNS *Go, fetch to me* ii, The glittering spears are ranked ready. **1819** SHELLEY *Cenci* IV. iv. 169 As soon as you have taken some refreshment,..We shall be ready.

b. *spec.* Properly dressed or attired; having finished one's toilet.

As a special sense app. limited to the 16–17th c., earlier and later instances being merely contextual applications of the general sense.

c **1386** CHAUCER *Sqr.'s T.* 379 Vp riseth fresshe Canacee hir selue..Noon hyer was he [the sun] whan she redy was. **1523** FITZHERB. *Husb.* §146 Whan thou arte vp and redy, than first swepe thy house. *? a* **1642** ROWLEY *Thrac. Wonder* II. i. [Stage Direction] Enter Pheander, ready. **1653** DOROTHY OSBORNE *Lett. to Sir W. Temple* (1888) 100, I rise in the morning reasonably early, and before I am ready I go round the house. **1709** MRS. MANLEY *Secret Mem.* II. 234 Having permitted 'em time to get themselves ready, he enter'd the Chamber. **1856** THOMPSON *Boston* Gloss., *To get Ready*, to be dressed and prepared for a visit or journey.

†**c.** Used in replying to a call or summons. *Obs.*

1590 SHAKS. *Mids. N.* III. i. 165 Ready; and I,..and I, Where shall we go? **1596** —— *Merch. V.* IV. i. 2 *Duke* What, is Anthonio heere? *Ant.* Ready, so please your grace.

d. *Mil.* and *Naut.* as a word of command.

In military use shortened from *make ready* (see 15), the order to prepare the piece for firing. For the nautical uses, see quots. 1846, 1867.

1802 JAMES *Milit. Dict.* s.v. *Manual*, The officers, instead of giving the words *platoon*, *make ready*,..are to pronounce the words short, as for instance, *'toon*, *ready*. **1841** R. H. DANA *Seaman's Man.* 150 The master finds that the ship will not lay her course, and tells the chief mate to 'see all clear for stays', or 'ready about'. **1846** A. YOUNG *Naut. Dict.* s.v. *About*, Ready About! an order to the crew that all hands be at their stations, ready for tacking. **1867** SMYTH *Sailor's Word-bk.*, *Ready with the Lead*, a caution when the vessel is luffed up to deaden her way, followed by 'heave'.

e. *U.S. slang.* Excellent, first-rate; mature, fully competent. Chiefly of music or musicians.

c **1938** N. E. WILLIAMS *His Hi De Highness of Ho De Ho* 35/2 When an individual or a piece of music is high class or greatly admired, we indicate it by saying, 'He's ready!' or 'That's ready!' **1944** C. CALLOWAY *Hepsters Dict.*, *Ready*,.. 100 per cent in every way. Ex., 'That fried chicken was ready.' **1945** *Tomorrow* June 27/3 This time he was *ready*, so to speak, for it was on this second sojourn..that he began to impress his musical contemporaries. **1968** in R. Russell *Jazz Style in Kansas City* (1971) 183 When he came back, several months later, he was a new musician. *He was ready.*

f. ***ready room***, a room in an aircraft-carrier where pilots are briefed and await orders to fly. *U.S. Mil.*

1945 in WEBSTER Add. **1953** P. C. BERG *Dict. New Words* 134/2 *Ready room*,..the room of an aircraft-carrier where pilots ready for flight assemble to receive their briefing. **1971** W. H. CRACKNELL in *Profile Warship* III. 55/2 Below the flight deck..was the gallery deck. Here were a rudimentary combat intelligence centre, squadron ready rooms, and other air department offices. **1977** *Time* 2 May 1/1 Stamped indelibly inside my head is what used to be on Navy ready-room walls—'Flying itself is not inherently dangerous, but like the sea, it is unmercifully unforgiving of human error.'

2. a. Const. with infinitive: Prepared, or having all preparations made, *to* do something.

c **1200** ORMIN 11758 Þær wass efft te laþe gast rædiȝ forr himm to fandenn. *c* **1290** *S. Eng. Leg.* I. 106/176 Aungles þare weren redie I-nowe hire soule to heuene lede. **1375** BARBOUR *Bruce* XIX. 454 Than turnyt thai..And stude reddy to giff battale. **1478** W. PASTON in *P. Lett.* III. 238 And than I wol telle you when I schall be redy to come from Eton. **1568** GRAFTON *Chron.* II. 306 The king..sayd, howe he was not as then ready to geue them a playne aunswere. **1596** SHAKS. *Tam. Shr.* IV. iv. 104 To bid the Priest be readie to come against you come. **1662** STILLINGFL. *Orig. Sacr.* III. ii. §18 There are some more subtile particles of matter, which are ready to fill up those void spaces. **1719** DE FOE *Crusoe* II. i, My nephew was ready to sail. **1791** COWPER *Retired Cat* 20 Apparelled in exactest sort, And ready to be borne to court. **1860** TYNDALL *Glaciers* I. xvi. 115 We stood beside each other ready to march. **1884** CHURCH *Bacon* ix. 220 His incorrigible imaginativeness, ever ready to force itself in amid the driest details.

b. Willing; feeling or exhibiting no reluctance.

c **1200** ORMIN 12936 Godd iss rædiȝ tunnderrfon þatt follc þatt rihht himm follȝheþþ. *a* **1300** *Cursor M.* 26471 Iesus crist es redier to merci giue þan jugement. **1362** LANGL. *P. Pl.* A. IV. 155 'Icham Redi', quod Reson 'to Reste with þe euere'. *c* **1449** PECOCK *Repr.* III. x. 337 Redi in wil forto haue suffrid marterdom. **1550** CROWLEY *Way to Wealth* 512 How readi God is to take vengeaunce for the oppression of his people. **1648** MILTON *Ps.* lxxxvi. 54 Thou Lord art the God most mild Readiest thy grace to shew. **1786** COWPER *Gratitude* 43 To me ever ready to show Benignity, friendship, and truth. **1849** MACAULAY *Hist. Eng.* i. I. 137 The loyal gentry declared that they were still as ready as ever to risk their lives for the old government. **1875** JOWETT *Plato* (ed. 2) I. 142 There is no one to whom I am more ready to trust.

c. Inclined or disposed; apt.

1596 SPENSER *State Irel.* Wks. (Globe) 609/1 They are ready allwayes to impute the blame therof unto the heavens. **1656** G. COLLIER *Answ. 15 Quest.* 20 They were readier to suspect themselves than Judas. **1855** MACAULAY *Hist. Eng.* xiii. III. 273 He was but too ready to consider all who recommended prudence and charity as traitors to the cause of truth. **1875** JOWETT *Plato* (ed. 2) I. 298 You are too ready to speak evil of men.

d. Sufficiently angry or irritated to be on the point of (doing something violent). Cf. FIT *a.* 5 b.

1535 COVERDALE *Exod.* xvii. 4 What shal I do with this people? They are almost ready to stone me. **1596** DALRYMPLE tr. *Leslie's Hist. Scot.* VII. 12 Thay sune ar steirit up and radie to put hand in thair King. **1632** HAYWARD tr. *Biondi's Eromena* IV. 123 Murmuring in so open a manner, against the person of the Prince, as made him..ready to goe besides himselfe. **1722** DE FOE *Col. Jack* (1840) 28, I was ready to snatch the breeches out of her hands.

e. Used attributively (cf. 5) in preceding senses with *infin.* after the sb. Somewhat *rare.*

c **1200** ORMIN 13436 Swa þatt I muȝhe findenn ȝuw All rædiȝ follc to follȝhenn me. **1535** COVERDALE *2 Cor.* viii. 19 That like as there is a ready mynde to wil, there maye be a ready mynde also to perfourme the dede. **1607** SHAKS. *Timon* I. ii. 49 The fellow that sits next him..is the readiest man to kill him. **1660** WOOD *Life* (O.H.S.) I. 359 The most ready men to cring to and serve these times. **1706** E. WARD *Wooden World Diss.* (1708) 98 He's the readiest man living to make him sick with good Liquor.

3. Const. with infinitive: **a.** That has passed, or has been brought, into such a condition as to be immediately likely or liable (*to* do something). Also *ellipt.* in attributive use (quot. 1818).

c **1375** *Sc. Leg. Saints* vii. (*James less*) 300 Rycht as þe ȝerde suld tremyl al, & mak all werkis reddy to fall. **1500–20** DUNBAR *Poems* lxv. 5 All is bot tynt, or reddie for to tyne. **1526** TINDALE *Heb.* viii. 13 Nowe that which is disanulled and wexed olde, is redy to vanysshe a waye. **1593** SHAKS. *2 Hen. VI*, I. i. 229 Ready to sterue, and dare not touch his owne. **1662** J. DAVIES tr. *Olearius' Voy. Ambass.* 50 Drawing him from one side of it to the other, till he was ready to give up the ghost. **1710** PRIDEAUX *Orig. Tithes* iv. 172 Finding all things ready to run into confusion. **1748** RICHARDSON *Clarissa* (1868) III. 251 He has ordered her..only some little cordials to take when ready to faint. **1818** KEATS *Endym.* III. 1024 The hen-dove shall not hatch Her ready eggs, before I'll kissing snatch Thee into endless heaven. **1855** TENNYSON *Maud* I. vi. iii, A delicate spark..Ready to burst in a colour'd flame.

b. Hence (without reference to a previous process): Likely, liable; 'fit'.

1596 DALRYMPLE tr. *Leslie's Hist. Scot.* I. 59 Quha sailis frome thir Iles is verie radie to incur sik danger. **1633** EARL MANCH. *Al Mondo* (1636) 183 Our last thoughts are readiest to spend themselves upon somewhat that wee loved best while we lived. **1698** FRYER *Acc. E. India & P.* 295 The Sharp Winds are Serene Air..being ready to cut you through. **1817** JAS. MILL *Brit. India* II. v. viii. 635 At a moment..when every thing was ready to be reported, and every thing to be believed.

4. Const. with prepositions: †**a.** With *to* or *unto* (rarely *into*): Prepared, inclined, or willing to do, give, take, suffer, etc. (what is indicated by the sb.); also occasionally, prepared for (an act). *Obs.*

c **1200** *Trin. Coll. Hom.* 191 ȝif hie redie ben to golliche deden. *a* **1340** HAMPOLE *Psalter* xvi. 13 þai toke me as leoun redy til pray. **1382** WYCLIF *Ps.* xxxvii. 18 For I in to scourgis am redi [**1388** Y am redi to betyngis]. **1390** GOWER *Conf.* I. 275 He is redi to the feith. *Ibid.* 282 The more I am redy to wraththe. **1471** RIPLEY *Comp. Alch.* VII. v. in Ashm. (1652) 170 Lyke Wax yt wylbe redy unto Lyquacyon. **1558** GOODMAN *How to Obey* 103 The Lorde, who is redie to mercie and slowe to anger. *a* **1591** H. SMITH *Wks.* (1867) II. 313, I lament that the wisdom of the flesh should be readier to godly works than the wisdom of the spirit.

b. Prepared *for* (an event, action, state, etc.).

1591 SHAKS. *1 Hen. VI*, II. iv. 104 Thou shalt finde vs ready for thee still. **1603** —— *Meas. for M.* III. i. 107 Be readie, Claudio, for your death to morrow. **1789** BLAKE *Songs Innoc.*, *Echoing Green* iii, Many sisters and brothers.. Are ready for rest.

5. a. Having the quality of being prepared or willing to act when necessary; prompt, quick, expert, dexterous (in general, or in the special manner implied by the sb.). ***ready hand, man*** (see quots. 1840, 1851).

c **1320** *Sir Tristr.* 798 Rohand, þe riche kniȝt, Redy was he ay. **1535** COVERDALE *Ps.* xliv. 1 My tonge is yᵉ penne of a ready writer. **1552** ELYOT *Classiarius*,..a diligent persone, a ready felow. **1603** KNOLLES *Hist. Turks* (1621) 977 With these..was Amurath, upon a light and readie horse. *c* **1645** HOWELL *Lett.* (1650) II. 11 So I am Your most affectionate ready Servant, J. H. **1704** POPE *Windsor For.* 99 Before his lord the ready spaniel bounds. **1725** —— *Odyss.* III. 608 Bread and wine a ready handmaid brings. **1818** SHELLEY *Rev. Islam* XII. iv, A thousand torches..Borne by the ready slaves of ruthless law. **1840** J. DEVLIN *Shoemaker* I. 43 The quickest, or, as they are called in the trade, the readiest hands. **1851** MAYHEW *Lond. Labour* (1861) II. 333 He knew that he was a ready man (a quick workman).

b. Const. *at*, *in*, †*of*.

c **1375** *Cursor M.* 8404 (Fairf.) [Þ]of salamon þi sone be ȝonge, he [is] ful wise and redy of tonge. **1484** CAXTON *Fables of Alfonce* xii, And by cause that the yonge woman was redy in speche and malycious, she ansuerd forth with. **1508** KENNEDIE *Flyting w. Dunbar* 467 As thou was louse, and reddy of thy bune. **1611** SHAKS. *Cymb.* III. iv. 161 Ready in gybes, quicke-answered, sawcie. **1686** tr. *Chardin's Coronat. Solyman* 109 These Eunuchs are very ready at these kind of dark Contrivances. **1777** SHERIDAN *Sch. Scand.* I. i, 'Twould surprise you to hear how ready he is at all these sort of things. **1833** HT. MARTINEAU *Loom & Lugger* I. v. 67 Likely to be excellent Christians as they were very ready at the Bible. **1855** TENNYSON *Maud* I. v. i, Men ..in battle array, Ready in heart and ready in hand.

6. a. Of the mind or mental powers: Quick to devise, plan, comprehend, observe, etc.

a **1300** *Cursor M.* 17432 (Gött.) Nu es vs nede of redi thoght. **1390** GOWER *Conf.* II. 162 To every craft..He hadde a redi wit to helpe Thurgh naturel experience. **1413** *Pilgr. Sowle* (Caxton 1483) IV. xxxiv. 82 Suche as were of moost redy wyt couthe taken hede of alle. **1607** SHAKS. *Cor.* II. ii. 120 By and by the dinne of Warre gan pierce His readie sence. **1762** GOLDSM. *Cit. W.* lxii, Nature had furnished her not only with a ready but a solid turn of thought. **1830** D'ISRAELI *Chas. I*, III. v. 72 The intellect of Laud was.. earnest, ready, and practical above most minds.

b. Of persons, etc.: Prompt or quick in speech, discourse, or writing.

a **1300** *Cursor M.* 8404 He es wis and o redi tung. *Ibid.* 27566 Pride rises..for steuen suet, for rede tung. **1461** *Plumpton Corr.* (Camden) 2 Ye may nott faile to send hider all your bookes and some readie man for to answer unto him. **1531** ELYOT *Gov.* III. xxi, A man..shall,..with a littell refection,..haue his inuencyon quicker..his tonge redyar. **1597** BACON *Ess.*, *Studies* (Arb.) 10 Reading maketh a full man, conference a readye man. **1883** LD. R. GOWER *My Reminisc.* I. vi. 101 He had a..kind heart and a ready pen.

c. Proceeding from, delivered with, promptness of thought or expression.

1583 STUBBES *Anat. Abus.* I. (1877) 107 Til neuer a one can speak a redy woord. **1638** JUNIUS *Paint. Ancients* 31 The ready suggestions of our own naturall wit. **1816** SCOTT *Antiq.* i, Returning a ready answer. **1857** WILLMOTT *Pleas. Lit.* xxi. 124 A ready jest opens more intricacies of the true character than a siege or a battle.

d. *U.S. Blacks.* (See quots.)

1967 J. HORTON in *Trans-Action* Apr. 5/2 One either knows 'what's happening' on the street, or he is a 'lame', 'out of it', 'not ready' (lacks his diploma in street knowledge), a 'square'. **1970** C. MAJOR *Dict. Afro-Amer. Slang* 96 *Ready*, hip; receptive. **1973** T. KOCHMAN *Rappin' & Stylin' Out* 163 Another term such as 'ready' is descriptive of the person who 'has his diploma in street knowledge', which means knowing what's happening, taking advantage of opportunities, avoiding pitfalls, and being prepared to move where the action is.

7. a. Of action or capacity for action: Distinguished or characterized by promptness or quickness.

1390 GOWER *Conf.* III. 322 Leonin it herde telle,..And bad him gon a redy pas To fetten hire, and forth he wente. **1559** W. CUNNINGHAM *Cosmogr. Glasse* 13 For the redier conceiving..behold the figure insuing. **1601** CORNWALLIS *Ess.* II. xxx, Being soone off and soone on, of a readie, though not of a wise dispatche. **1754** SHERLOCK *Disc.* (1759) I. x. 292 Yeilding a ready, tho' unwilling Obedience. **1849** MACAULAY *Hist. Eng.* iv. I. 497 Gave him credit for..much readier elocution than he really possessed.

b. Characterized by alacrity or willingness in some respect. (In some cases passing into next.)

1548–9 (Mar.) *Bk. Com. Prayer*, *Communion* Collect, Defended by thy moste gracious and readye helpe. **1607** TOPSELL *Four-f. Beasts* 155 Beneuolence and ready minde toward their keepers and norishers. **1695** WOODWARD *Nat. Hist. Earth* III. i. (1723) 156 It finds the readyest Reception. **1742** YOUNG *Nt. Th.* I. 2 He, like the world, his ready visit pays Where fortune smiles. **1789** MAD. D'ARBLAY *Diary* Nov., I gave her my ready promise. **1813** BYRON *Br. Abydos* II. xx, Open speech, and ready hand. **1821** SCOTT *Kenilw.* xvii, Never was more anxious and ready way made for my Lord of Leicester. **1884** *Law Times* LXXVI. 331/2 This is one of those abstract principles which in the present day are pretty sure to find ready acceptance.

c. Taking place quickly or easily.

1730 *Col. Rec. Pennsylv.* III. 391 That when at Market they may find a readier sale. **1877** E. R. CONDER *Bas. Faith* v. 223 The..ready solubility [of sugar] in water.

II. 8. a. In the condition of having been prepared or put in order for some purpose. Const. *for*, †*to*, or with *infin.* (in some cases with suggestion of sense 2).

c **1200** ORMIN 6235 Heore leȝhe [= pay] birrþ hemm beon Rædiȝ, þann itt iss addledd. *a* **1300** *Cursor M.* 5270 þair mete to þam i rede [*v.r.* redi] broght. **1382** WYCLIF *Matt.* xxii. 4 My boles..ben slayn, and alle thingis redy. *Ibid.* 8 The weddyngis ben redy. *c* **1450** *Merlin* 362 A cheyer, that euer more sholde be redy for the knyght in to sitte. **1523** LD. BERNERS *Froiss.* I. lxxvii, Sir leaue your musyng and come into ye hall..yoʳ dyner is all redy. **1603** SHAKS. *Meas. for M.* IV. i. 56 This your companion..hath a storie readie for your eare. **1648** GAGE *West Ind.* 17 Our two Cock-Boates were ready to carry to shore such as..had clothes to wash. **1711** STEELE *Spect.* No. 132 ⁋1 His Horses were ready at the appointed Hour. **1732** BERKELEY *Alciphr.* IV. §15 A servant came to tell us the tea was ready. **1816** J. WILSON *City of Plague* II. v. 72 Here is a grave Just ready for thy body, Walsingham! **1878** BROWNING *La Saisiaz* 106 All awaits us ranged and ready.

b. Added to past participles (cf. 16).

1567 *Gude & Godlie B.* (S.T.S.) 96 The cruell men sall..haif thair bow bent reddy in thair hand. **1608** SHAKS. *Per.* III. i. 72 We have a chest beneath the hatches, caulked and bitumined ready.

c. In attributive use (passing into 5).

1559 *Mirr. Mag. Hen. VI*, xix, Our kingdomes are but cares,..Our riches redy snares. **1634** SIR T. HERBERT *Trav.* 147 They..when past the marke, with an other ready Arrow, can strike the rest looking backwards. **1725** POPE *Odyss.* II. 455 Along the strand The ready vessel rides. **1764** GOLDSM. *Trav.* 16 Bless'd that abode, where..ev'ry stranger finds a ready chair. **1820** KEATS *St. Agnes* xl, There were sleeping dragons..perhaps, with ready spears.

9. So placed or constituted as to be immediately available when required or wished for; close at hand; handy, convenient for use.

†a. In predicative use. *Obs.*

a **1240** *Wohunge* in *Cott. Hom.* 277, I þi childhad hafdes tu..þi moder readi hwen þu pappe ȝerndes. *a* **1375** *Joseph Arim.* 42 Whon þe lust speke with me, lift þe lide sone; þou schalt fynde me redi riȝt bi þi side. **1382** WYCLIF *John* vii. 6 My time cam not ȝit, but ȝoure tyme is euermore redy. *c* **1449** PECOCK *Repr.* III. x. 336 Persecucioun of tirantis was redier in tho daies. **1525** LD. BERNERS *Froiss.* II. ccii. 621 Bycause the langage of yrisshe is as redy to me as the Englysshe tong. **1577** B. GOOGE *Heresbach's Husb.* I. (1586) 11 b, I place fyrst by them selues, suche as are most in vse, that they may be the redier. **1656** H. PHILLIPS *Purch. Patt.* (1676) 155 The use of this Table is plain and ready. **1695** WOODWARD *Nat. Hist. Earth* I. (1723) 8 The next Cole-pit, or Mine..these are so ready and obvious in almost all Places.

b. Similarly in phrases ***ready to*** (one's) ***hand(s)***, ***ready at hand***. (See HAND *sb.* 2 and 25.)

c **1386** CHAUCER *Friar's T.* 21 He had a Somonour redy to his hond. **1530** PALSGR. 822/2 Redy at hande, *auant la mayn.* **1663** GERBIER *Counsel* f 3 The Grecians the readiest at hand had their choise. **1727–41** CHAMBERS *Cycl.* s.v. *Table*, Systems of numbers, calculated to be ready at hand for the expediting astronomical..and other observations. **1891** *Law Times* XC. 315/2 The chief guide which both courts found ready to their hands.

c. In attributive use.

In 16th c. app. only in Sc. use, especially of money, lands, goods, etc.

a **1425** *Cursor M.* 10890 (Trin.) þat goddes son calde shal ben I shewe þe redy token to sene. **1535** STEWART *Cron. Scot.* III. 48 At Ptolome ane reddie port tha fand. **1545** *Reg. Privy Council Scot.* I. 14 The reddiest money that may be gottin for the casualite. **1609** SKENE *Reg. Maj., Forme of Proces* 125 To..poynd, and distreinzie the reddiest cornes. **1659** HAMMOND *On Ps.* xcix. 8 This appears to be the full and ready importance of this passage. **1671** MILTON *P.R.* III. 128 The slightest, easiest, readiest recompence. **1796** H. HUNTER tr. *St. Pierre's Stud. Nat.* (1799) II. 432 Finding there readier means of subsistence, than in the other cities of the kingdom. **1816** SCOTT *Antiq.* ix, Rab..banged out o' bed, and till some of his readiest claes. **1874** GREEN *Short Hist.* ii. §5. 83 William found a more ready source of revenue in the settlement of Jewish traders.

10. a. Immediately available as currency; having the form of coin or money.

App. first in ***ready pennies*** or ***pence***: cf. Da. *rede penge*, Sw. *reda* (MSw. also *redo*) *penningar*, ON. *reiðupeningar*.

ready coin and ***ready gold*** are frequent in 16–17th c. See also *ready rhino* s.v. RHINO¹, and READY MONEY.

a **1300** *Cursor M.* 4835 [We have brought] Al redi penijs for to tell [*Gött. MS.* Redi penis we haue to tell]. **1303** R. BRUNNE *Handl. Synne* 6324 Ten mark of pens redy, And ten mark hys ouþer store. **1472** *Paston Lett.* III. 70 If ȝe shuld selle alle this wode togedyr for redy Sylver. **1550** CROWLEY *Epigr.* 1450 Thys lande he made sale, and toke readye golde. **1568** GRAFTON *Chron.* II. 42 Roger..left behinde him in readie coyne..fourtie thousand Markes. **1639** N. N. tr. *Du Bosq's Compl. Woman* II. 14 Procris..surrendred the place, as soon as she saw the ready chink. **1712** STEELE *Spect.* No. 450 ⁋4 What advantage might be made of the ready Cash I had. **1747** *Gentl. Mag.* 580/1 To turn their wrought bullion into ready sterling. **1826** SCOTT *Woodst.* ii, He had never known the ready-penny so hard to come by. **1885** [see CASH *sb.*¹ 2 b].

transf. *a* **1721** PRIOR *Chameleon* 5 The chameleon..struts as much in ready Light Which Credit gives him upon Sight [etc.].

†b. ***ready stock***: Surplus, amount on hand.

1661 COWLEY *Oliver Cromwell* Wks. 1710 II. 660 He found the Common-wealth..in a ready Stock of about 800,000*l.*

11. a. Of a way, path, etc.: Lying directly before one; straight, direct, near. ? *Obs.*

a **1300** *Cursor M.* 6252 þou sal see it cleue in tua, And giue yow redi wai to ga. **1375** BARBOUR *Bruce* XVII. 555 Thai ga Toward mytoune the reddy vay. *c* **1470** *Golagros & Gaw.* 310 The roy and his rout..To Rome tuke the reddy way. **1563** *Mirr. Mag., Hastings* xxii, The stearesman sekes a redier course to ronne. **1634** MILTON *Comus* 305 What readiest way would bring me to that place? **1667** — *P.L.* II. 976, I seek What readiest path leads where your gloomie bounds Confine with Heav'n. **1759** JOHNSON *Rasselas* xxxix, To the favour of the covetous there is a ready way.

b. Hence with *way* in the sense of 'method', 'means', etc.; and so ***ready means***.

1560 DAUS tr. *Sleidane's Comm.* 58 b, The rediest way to overthrow theyr authoritie. **1591** SPENSER *M. Hubberd* 127 Euerie thing that is begun with reason Will come by readie meanes unto his end. **1639** FULLER *Holy War* v. vi. (1840) 251 Teaching covetousness..a ready way to assault them. **1750** tr. *Leonardus' Mirr. Stones* 97 This is the readiest way of knowing it. **1883** *Law Times* 20 Oct. 409/2 If invention be required, the readiest way to secure it is to give proper remuneration to the inventor.

12. Of payment or pay: Made or given promptly; not delayed or deferred. ? *Obs.*

c **1375** *Cursor M.* 4835 (Fairf.) A party of siluer [we have] wiþ vs broȝt, redy payment for to telle. **1442** *Rolls of Parlt.* V. 63 Redy paiement in hand he hadde. **1545** *Reg. Privy Council Scot.* I. 15 To poynd and dystrenye for the said rest and mak reddy payment thairof. **1621** T. WILLIAMSON tr. *Goulart's Wise Vieillard* 84 His promise should passe for ready pay, and for money told on the nayle. **1697** LUTTRELL *Brief Rel.* (1857) IV. 267 The earl of Oxford's regiments and the foot guards haveing now ready pay, notice is given to their quarters not to trust them.

III. In phr. **to make ready.**

13. a. *refl.* To put (oneself) into a state of preparation; to prepare (oneself).

c **1330** R. BRUNNE *Chron.* (1810) 97 At Burgh in Schrobschire to werre [he] mad him redy. *c* **1380** WYCLIF *Serm.* Sel. Wks. I. 65 We shulden maken us redy to suffre. *c* **1470** HENRY *Wallace* IV. 425 He thaim commaunde to mak thaim redy fast. *a* **1548** HALL *Chron., Hen. VIII* 126 b, The garrison made them ready and bent their ordinaunce. **1610** SHAKS. *Temp.* I. i. 27 Make your selfe readie in your Cabine for the mischance of the houre. **1615** W. LAWSON *Country Housew. Gard.* (1626) 8 Trees cannot..make themselues ready to blossome [etc.]. **1859** TENNYSON *Elaine* 775 While she made her ready for her ride.

†b. *spec.* To array, attire or dress (oneself). *Obs.*

1511 GUYLFORDE *Pilgr.* (Camden) 24 Whiche [chapell] the freres kepe, and there they made theym redy in ornaments, and began there a very solempne procession. **1603** DEKKER, etc. *Patient Grissil* 164 Little girls that yesterday had scarce a hand to make them ready. *a* **1661** FULLER *Worthies* (1840) III. 181 Neatness he neglected into slovenliness; and..may be said not to have made himself ready for some seven years. [**1722** MRS. BRADSHAW in *Lett. C'tess Suffolk* (1824) I. 91 We repair to our own chambers and make ourselves ready; for it cannot be called dressing.]

14. *trans.* To prepare or put in order (a thing or things); †to dress (a person).

c **1375** *Sc. Leg. Saints* Prol. 95 Syne..lefit I nocht, til I had mad þaim redy. **1426** LYDG. *De Guil Pilgr.* 22918, I wente afforne..And made redy his passage. *a* **1533** LD. BERNERS *Huon* lxvi. 226 Theyr beddes were made redy. **1596** DANETT tr. *Comines* (1614) 157 Many a time haue I seene him made ready and vnready with great reuerence and solemnity. **1640** in *Ussher's Lett.* (1686) App. 27 There be great Preparations making ready against the Liturgy and Ceremonies of the Church of England. **1808** STOWER *Printers' Gram.* 345 Making ready a Form. **1842** TENNYSON *Gardener's Daughter* 268 Make thine heart ready with thine eyes. **1853** G. J. CAYLEY *Las Alforjas* I. 184 While our chocolate was being made ready.

15. a. *absol.* To make preparations. Const. *for* (†*to*), or with *inf.*; †formerly also common without const.

13.. *Seuyn Sag.* (W.) 3876 Thai spred clathes and salt on set, And made redy vnto the mete. **1375** BARBOUR *Bruce* XIX. 718 Thai turst harnas and maid reddy. **1382** WYCLIF *Mark* xiv. 15 There make ȝe redy to vs. **1473** WARKW. *Chron.* (Camden) 2 Wyth the whiche menne made redy, and beseged the same castelle[s]. **1526** TINDALE *Mark* xiv. 15 There make reddy for vs. **1603** SHAKS. *Meas. for M.* III. i. 172 To morrow you must die, goe to your knees, and make ready. **1669** STURMY *Mariner's Mag.* I. ii. 20 Make ready to board him. **1689** [see REAR *sb.*³ 7 a]. **1869** W. LONGMAN *Hist. Edw. III*, I. xvii. 319 His companions made ready to fight. **1890** T. F. TOUT *Hist. Eng. from 1689*, 29 Bolingbroke..made ready for a revolution.

b. *techn.* in *Printing* (see quots.).

1871 RINGWALT *Encycl. Amer. Print., Making Ready*—the act of getting a form ready to be printed;..Making ready may be said to form the chief portion of the pressman's duty. **1874** SOUTHWARD *Pract. Print.* xlv. (ed. 4) 413 Begin to 'make ready'—that is, get the impression equal and level over the whole forme.

IV. *Comb.* **16.** Placed before past participles to emphasize the completion of the process expressed by these (cf. 8 b): **a.** In predicative use. (Now frequently hyphened as in b.)

Additional examples are *ready beaten* (1617), *braced* (1596), *coined* (1603), *graithed* (1513), *grown* (1812), *mounted* (1596), *prepared* (1535), *shapen* (1571), *starched* (1602); see also READY MADE. With the early *ready boun*, which is frequent in the 15–16th c., compare ON. *reiðubúinn*, MSw. *redhoboin* etc. (Sw. *redebogen*, Da. *redebon*), which may conceivably have given the suggestion for the Eng. expression.

a **1300** *Cursor M.* 11595 Son was ioseph redi bun. *Ibid.* 12864 Quen he sagh iesu redi tift. **1390** GOWER *Conf.* I. 294 For evere his bowe is redi bent. *c* **1420** *Avow. Arth.* xxv, Mi rauunsun is alle redy boȝte. *a* **1425** *Cursor M.* 7452 (Trin.) Greet he was &..Al redy armed for to fiȝt. *c* **1435** *Torr. Portugal* 578 Be the gyant wase redy dyght, Torrent had slayne the dragon ryght. **1448–9** in Willis & Clark *Cambridge* (1886) II. 10 The seides howses shull accord with the other syde the wich is now redy framed next the Freres. **1535** COVERDALE *Josh.* iv. 13 Aboute a fortye thousande men ready harnessed to the warre. **1567** *Gude & Godlie B.* (S.T.S.) 235 Thairfoir leif weill, be reddy bowne. **1568** GRAFTON *Chron.* II. 2 The Duke..seeyng all the countrey ready set to hedge him in. **1613** PURCHAS *Pilgrimage* v. xvii. (1614) 542 Duckes, sometimes raw, and sometimes ready dressed. **1697** VANBRUGH *Prov. Wife* III. i, If woman had been ready created, the devil..had been married. **1727** POPE, etc. *Art of Sinking* 121 Old Troy is ready burnt to your hands. **1767** J. WOODFORDE *Diary* 24 July (1924) I. 64 My father sent me down a couple of fowls ready roasted. **1775** P. FRENEAU *Poems* (1902) I. 169 How could the wretches help but marching on, When at their backs your swords were ready drawn? **1796** J. WOODFORDE *Diary* 15 Oct. (1929) IV. 314 They have let their House ready furnished to a Revd. Mr. Beevor. **1809** MALKIN *Gil Blas* x. xii. ⁋29, I was the man of all others ready cut and dry for an intrigue. **1836** J. M. GULLY *Magendie's Formul.* (ed. 2) 161 His doctrine, that all the varied secretions of the body are ready formed in the blood. **1842** DICKENS *Amer. Notes* (1850) 57/1 Clothes ready-made, and meat ready-cooked. **1868** *E. Acton's Mod. Cookery* (rev. ed.) xxx. 590 Never purchase it [*sc.* coffee] ready ground unless compelled to do so. **1930** H. NICOLSON *Let.* 2 Jan. (1966) 40, I suppose that I shall get into the way of finding these paragraphs leaping ready-armed to the mind. **1952** J. B. OLDHAM *Eng. Blind-Stamped Bindings* 3 Sale of books ready-bound. **1960** *Farmer & Stockbreeder* 23 Feb. 123/3 Sold, ready-cooked in foil containers, the pies are in two sizes. **1976** *Glasgow Herald* 26 Nov. 16/3 Food can be bought ready prepared if not for the table at least for the oven or the saucepan.

b. In attributive use. ***ready-built, -carved, -cooked, -folded, -furnished, -ground, -prepared, -roasted, -sensitized, -shelled, -sliced, -traced, -trained, -written.*** (See also READY-MADE, READY-MIXED *a.*)

1827 SOUTHEY *Hist. Penins. War* II. 290 *note*, The Americans carried over ready-built houses for sale. **1803** M. WILMOT *Let.* 31 May in Londonderry & Hyde *Russian Jrnls.* (1934) I. 13 Then ready carved bouillé, ready carved fricasées etc. **1974** L. DEIGHTON *Spy Story* xi. 112 She put some ready-cooked pizzas into the oven. **1964** *McCall's Sewing* xiii. 234/2 *Ready-folded braid*, these braids are of a woven bias construction. **1766** SMOLLETT *Trav.* I. xii. 214 You will find no ready-furnished lodgings at Nice. **1960** *Farmer & Stockbreeder* 15 Mar. (Suppl.) 11/2 Put the almonds through a nut mill (neither minced nor ready-ground almonds will do.) **1802–12** BENTHAM *Ration. Judic. Evid.* (1827) II. 193 Ready-prepared and scientifically-planted ground. **1875** T. SEATON *Fret Cutting* vii. 71 The high price he has had to pay..for ready-prepared wood. **1959** *Times* 9 Mar. (Suppl.) p. vii/7 Ready-prepared vegetables and other fresh produce are now being offered in the supermarkets. **1754** RICHARDSON *Grandison* IV. xviii. 144 He makes her..become herself the cat's paw to help him to the ready-roasted chestnuts. **1892** WOODBURY *Encycl. Photogr., Ready-sensitised paper*..in sheets or in cut sizes. **1909** *Daily Chron.* 14 Dec. 6/3 Pound boxes of ready-shelled walnuts at 1s. 3d. **1958** *Times Lit. Suppl.* 23 May 281/2 Bud Floyd and his wife Debbie tortured in their antiseptic, ready-shelled, air-conditioned inferno. **1960** *Times* 11 Feb. 3/5 Every day on television one can see the new styles ingeniously used to advertise instant coffee and ready-sliced bread. **1977** J. WAINWRIGHT *Day of Peppercorn Kill* 17 Ready-sliced bread—because if she ever handled a bread-knife she'd cut her damn-fool fingers off. **1967** E. SHORT *Embroidery & Fabric Collage* iv. 94 As the firm also sold ready traced materials and supplied the threads for working them, Morris's influence was widespread. **1946** *Nature* 5 Oct. 491/1 Sir Reginald pointed out first that in research on the problems of an old traditional industry there are usually no ready-trained scientific workers. **1802–12** BENTHAM *Ration. Judic. Evid.* (1827) II. 62 A mass of ready-written evidence. **1977** *Belfast Tel.* 22 Feb. 4/1 (Advt.), With the full library of ready-written, ready-to-use application packages available in the U.K., the System Ten 220 Series can be quickly harnessed to your work.

†c. Used with *come, coming.* (Cf. B 2.) *Obs.*

1523 LD. BERNERS *Froiss.* I. cxxv. 150 At saynt Denyse were redy come the kynge of Behayne..and many other lordes. *a* **1548** HALL *Chron., Hen. VIII* 104 b, For redy comming is yᵉ lord talbot.., with a puissaunt army.

d. Const. with infin. or with *for* and following noun, and used as attrib. phrases expressing preparedness for the action indicated, as ***ready-to-eat, -use***, etc. (See also READY-TO-WEAR *a.* (and *sb.*).)

1887 G. M. HOPKINS *Let.* 12 May (1956) 379 Publishers 'tapped a stratum'..of almost untouched reading or ready-to-read public. **1897** *Sears, Roebuck Catal.* 294/3 (*heading*) Ready-to-use table cloths. **1907** *N.Y. Times* 14 Sept. 4 Through this store's efforts a new attitude toward ready-for-service clothing has been adopted by hundreds of men. **1909** H. N. CASSON *C. H. McCormick* 237 Certain ready-to-eat foods are now being made from wheat. *c* **1938** *Fortnum & Mason Price List* 72/1 'Ready to serve' dishes. **1959** *Times* 9 Mar. (Suppl.) p. vi/3 Preparing cartons of frozen ready-to-cook chickens. **1972** *Listener* 7 Sept. 292/3 A range of ready-to-serve fish dishes with shrimp and lobster sauces. **1976** N. ROBERTS *Face of France* v. 66 A civilisation of leisure will be raring for ready-to-eat pork products. *a* **1977** *Harrison Mayer Ltd. Catal.* 98/2, 1 of 0·28 litre pack of the following liquid, ready-to-use glazes.

e. With sbs. used attrib. in sense 7, as ***ready-reference, -use***.

1928 G. CAMPBELL *My Mystery Ships* xiv. 250 A lucky shot from her might 'touch off' any of the ready-use ammunition which was at the guns. **1955** 'N. SHUTE' *Requiem for Wren* iii. 69, I give her a coconut out of the ready-use locker. **1963** *Amer. N. & Q.* Jan. 77/1 The book

. . can be used as a ready reference tool to answer questions about nearly all basic biological research in modern times. **1971** *Engineering* Apr. 122/2 Here's the tough, expanding, ready-reference file.

17. a. In parasynthetic combs., as ***ready-handed***, ***-hearted***, ***-penned***, ***-winged***; also ***ready-smiling***; READY-WITTED.

1641 MILTON *Ch. Govt.* I. vii. Wks. (1847) 40/2 Two quick-sighted and ready handed virgins. **1771** T. HULL *Sir W. Harrington* (1797) IV. 77 You have no ready penn'd sister. **1876** GEO. ELIOT *Dan. Der.* lxiii, Ready-winged speech. **1881** BLACKIE *Lay Serm.* i. 37 Ready-handed interpretations of judgments. **1937** A. L. ROWSE *Sir Richard Grenville* ii. 31 So ready-hearted, so busy and generous about life's affairs. **1940** BLUNDEN *Poems 1930–40* 252 Bright-tressed, ready-smiling, April-eyed.

†**b.** Objective, as ***ready-making***. *Obs.*

1611 COTGR., *Appareillement*, a preparing, prouiding, readie-making.

B. *adv.* **1.** = READILY. (In later use chiefly, and now only, in compar. and superl.)

c **1250** *Gen. & Ex.* 998 And al ðat euere ðe louered bad, dede abraham redi and rad. *a* **1300** *Cursor M.* 19638 Sai me . . quat i sal do, þi will wil I do redi, lo! *c* **1485** *Digby Myst.* III. 136 Your arend it xall be don ful redy. **1557** *Order of the Hospitalls* F iiij, To thintent that all things in your Office may be the rediar answered. **1596** DALRYMPLE tr. *Leslie's Hist. Scot.* x. 319 He vnderstude al taknes perteineng to the flycht rady anuich. **1641** EARL MONM. tr. *Biondi's Civil Warres* III. 158 Giving him downe a ladder at the walles foote, that hee might the readier climb up. **1712** BLACKMORE *Creation* VI. 56 The Earth-born Race Could move, and walk, and ready change their Place. **1768–74** TUCKER *Lt. Nat.* (1834) II. 279 Thou . . canst seek, and readiest find, comforts in the distresses and uses in the evils thou beholdest. **1799** SOUTHEY *Eng. Ecl.* Poet. Wks. III. 20 There was not . . A child who . . answered readier through his Catechism.

†**2.** = ALREADY. *Obs. rare*⁻¹.

1450 *Rolls of Parlt.* V. 204/2 Bi the opressing of the peple . . he hath gretli enpovred and hurt the poure Ilond redy.

C. *sb.* **1.** Also **reddy**. *slang* or *colloq.* Ready money, cash (usually with *the*); in *pl.*, bank notes.

1688 SHADWELL *Sqr. Alsatia* I. i, Take up on the reversion; 'tis a lusty one, and Cheatly will help you to the ready. **1712** ARBUTHNOT *John Bull* I. iii, He was not flush in ready, either to go to law, or clear old debts. **1784** R. BAGE *Barham Downs* II. 136 Cherish your lovely spouse till you have got all her ready. **1822** SCOTT *Nigel* xxiii, An estate in the north, which changes masters for want of the redeeming ready. **1872** BESANT & RICE *Ready-money Mort.* iii, 'Some of the "ready",' he said . . 'Gold, father—gold!' **1937** PARTRIDGE *Dict. Slang* 690/2 *Readies*, money in bank . . notes. **1962** R. COOK *Crust on its Uppers* i. 24 Not enough reddy in it in my case. *Ibid.* iii. 39 'Loot!' . . 'In reddy?' *Ibid.* viii. 65 Reddies which should be sailing into her African kick. **1968** [see GREEN *sb.* 7 d]. **1974** D. FRANCIS *Knock Down* xiv. 157 He sort of winks at me and gives me a thousand quid in readies. **1977** *Private Eye* 4 Mar. 9/1 Send £50 to the address below, preferably in readies.

2. a. (Usually with *the*.) The position of a fire-arm when the person holding or carrying it is ready to raise it to the shoulder and aim or fire. Now usu. in phr. *at (the) ready*. Also *transf.*

1837 J. E. MURRAY *Summer in Pyrenees* I. 55, I . . found the guard with his musket at the 'ready'. **1875** RUGGLES *Perils of Scout-Life* 75 They brought their pieces to a ready, as if preparing to fire. **1897** *Outing* (U.S.) XXIX. 427/2, I approach, my gun thrown forward at ready. **1931** A. CURTAYNE *St. Anthony of Padua* viii. 78 Galloping full tilt with vizor down and lance couched at the ready. **1955** *Times* 22 July 10/5 Others were more cautious, with fur capes or dark coats over their frocks and umbrellas at the ready. **1978** J. CARROLL *Mortal Friends* I. iii. 30 The troops in the lorries were standing, rifles at ready.

b. *U.S. colloq.* The condition of being prepared to start (something). Freq. in phr. ***to get a good ready*** and varr., to assume a favourable stance or position for this. Also *transf.* Now *rare*.

[**1855** 'Q. K. PHILANDER DOESTICKS' *Doesticks; what he Says* xviii. 153 The music got 'good ready' for a fair start, and at the word 'go' they went.] **1872** 'MARK TWAIN' in *Buyers' Man. & Business Guide* 76, I could have ketched them cats if I had had on a good ready. **1878** B. F. TAYLOR *Between Gates* 71 A time hardly long enough for a century plant to get a good ready for blossoming. **1897** A. H. LEWIS *Wolfville* i. 2 So we begins to draw in our belts an' get a big ready.

3. *Rope-making.* A strand in a rope or cable.

1857 R. CHAPMAN *Treat. Ropemaking* 84 The only method to be obtained is to give one turn or twist to the strand or readie, while the machine draws it a certain length. **1883** *Man. Seamanship for Boys' Training Ships* (Admiralty) (1886) 125 You now commence to form the long-splice, by unlaying one strand, and filling up the space it leaves with the opposite strand next to it . . these strands being composed of three small strands, which are called readies. **1957** *Encycl. Brit.* XIX. 546/1 As the strand is twisted it is wound on a large reel and appears as a smooth, round strand composed of a number of individual yarns. This is known as the 'ready'.

4. ***ready-up***, a conspiracy or swindle; a case of fraudulent manipulation; a fake. Cf. READY *v.* 4 b. *Austral. slang.*

1924 *Truth* (Sydney) 27 Apr. 6 *Ready up*, a fake. **1926** J. DOONE *Timely Tips for New Australians* 7 *Ready-up*, a conspiracy. **1945** BAKER *Austral. Lang.* xv. 267 *Ready-up*, a case in which illegal methods are used to influence the outcome of a decision or an action. **1961** H. R. F. KEATING *Rush on Ultimate* v. 85, I don't accept all the pretences and ready-ups you people put out.

ready ('rɛdɪ), *v.* Forms: 4–5 **redy(e**, 4–6 **redi-**, 6 *Sc.* **reddy**, 7– **ready**. [f. READY *a.* Somewhat rare between the 15th and 19th c.]

1. a. *refl.* To make (oneself) ready in any way.

a **1350** *St. Laurence* 51 in Horstm. *Altengl. Leg.* (1881) 113 þarfore, lady, redy þe For here saltou noght ful lang be. *c* **1425** *Eng. Conq. Irel.* 26 He assembled hys hostes & redied hym to wend thedere. *c* **1475** *Rauf Coilȝear* 782 In Ryall array he reddyit him to ryde. **1864** MRS. LLOYD *Ladies of Polcarrow* 41 They readied and steadied themselves as best they might. **1892** BROOKE *Early Eng. Lit.* II. xvii. 105 One of his thegns sprang up and readied him for the journey.

b. *intr.* or *absol.* To make oneself ready or prepare in any way. *U.S.*

1967 *Wall St. Jrnl.* 12 Dec. 1 Machinists Union President Roy Siemiller, readying for aerospace bargaining, and Steelworkers chief I. W. Abel feel they must match the big rubber and auto settlements. **1972** *Time* 17 Apr. 22 (*caption*) In a cloud of catapult steam, a U.S. jet readies to attack Viet Nam.

†**2.** *trans.* and *refl.* **a.** To direct (one's way, oneself, or another); to guide. *Obs.*

c **1330** R. BRUNNE *Chron.* (1810) 315 To Scotlond now he fondes, to redy his viage. *c* **1400** MAUNDEV. (1839) xvii. 185 No man cowde redye him perfitely toward the parties that he cam fro, but ȝif it were be aventure and happ. *c* **1440** *Gesta Rom.* xxiv. 91 Eche good Cristen man . . owith to redy him toward the wey of heuen by praiers, fastyng [etc.].

†**b.** To instruct *in* (a matter). *Obs.*⁻¹

1600 HOLLAND *Livy* XXXIV. lxi. 886 He redied him in the names of all those persons with whom he was to talke.

3. *trans.* **a.** To make (a thing) ready; to prepare; put in order. Also const. *up*. Now chiefly *N. Amer.*

Perh. influenced in early use by REDD *v.*² 6, to put in order, make neat.

a **1340** HAMPOLE *Psalter* vii. 13 His bow he has bent and redid it. *c* **1380** WYCLIF *Sel. Wks.* III. 181 If þou doist away synne þou rediest Goddis weye. *c* **1400** *Destr. Troy* 5648 All the renkes to row redyn hor shippes. **1609** J. DOWLAND *Ornithop. Microl.* 23 This readied, set-to one string of wyre, strong, big, and stretched inough. **1633** T. ADAMS *Exp. 2 Pet.* ii. 5 When a great portion is readied for them, divers parents think they have done enough. *a* **1849** J. KEEGAN *Legends & Poems* (1907) 111 Hould your gob . . and go ready the room for the dacint boys to sit down. **1864** *Harper's Mag.* Apr. 616/1 The pot ought to be a-bilin' for dinner, and the Kitchen to be readied up. **1867** WAUGH *Owd Blanket* iii. 53 Come in, an' sit tho deawn while eawr lasses getten yon kitchen readied (made right) a bit. **1900** H. LAWSON *On Track* 73 Anyway, she'll have one readied up somehow. **1926** *Amer. Mercury* Dec. 464/2 The report that a certain man '*authored* the show, which will be *readied* next Fall, when it will be *hoked up* (from *hokum*)'. **1934** *Bulletin* (Sydney) 25 July 38/1 This has invited the All-Blacks to call in on their way back from their tour of Britain next year and get what is being readied up for them. **1937** V. MCNABB *God's Way of Mercy* xxi. 185 You have come apart from the world to ready your soul for the doings of that great week. **1958** *Observer* 2 Mar. 6/6 It can be readied in 15—in less if we have some warning—not in two hours. **1959** R. E. WATTERS *Check List Canad. Lit.* p. xiii, To the Editor, Miss Francess G. Halpenny, who readied the manuscript for the printers, . . I am heavily indebted. **1968** 'E. LATHEN' *Stitch in Time* xvi. 141 The tax people were readying an attack on Martin. **1969** *Sun* 22 July 3/8 American scientists are readying the first space station for lift-off into earth orbit in 1971. **1971** J. Z. YOUNG *Introd. Study Man* ii. 28 These ions are pumped back, readying the system for further signalling. **1978** J. A. MICHENER *Chesapeake* 303 She asked her slaves to ready the small shallop. **1979** *Arizona Daily Star* 5 Aug. A 10/2 An army of scientists and engineers readied a 2-mile floating defense line yesterday.

b. *Sc.* and *dial.* To make (food) ready for eating; to dress or cook.

1721 WODROW *Hist. Suff. Ch. Scot.* (1828) I. I. v. 393 His fuel to ready it with was sea-tangle. [**1765** J. BROWN *Chr. Jrnl.* (1814) 237 It is but coarse and ill-readied provision which I have for breakfast.] **1831** CARLYLE *Sart. Res.* I. v, Can a Tartar be said to cook when he only readies his steak by riding on it. **1881** *Isle of Wight Gloss.* s.v., That pork esn't readied enough.

c. Of a person. Also const. *up*. Now chiefly *N. Amer.*

1846 *Swell's Night Guide* 78 He's to be readied at any downey move, and knows how to work it. **1895** J. BARLOW *Strangers at Lisconnel* 303 Nothin' else 'ud suit them except gettin' all readied up for us to be slinkin' out in the evenin' late. **1900** H. LAWSON *Over Sliprails* 162 The girl's relations . . had a parson readied up, and they were married the same day. **1924** J. GALSWORTHY *White Monkey* II. ix. 198 I'll put you wise about our authors, and ready you up to go before Peter. **1940** *Sun* (Baltimore) 27 Feb. 13/2 Johnny Paycheck already has been matched with him. Lee Savold is being readied for a shot at him. **1968** *Globe & Mail* (Toronto) 17 Feb. 4 (Advt.), An exercycle . . to ready you for a party, or extra work.

4. *slang.* **a.** *Racing.* To prevent (one's horse) from winning, in order to secure a handicap in another race.

1887 BLACK *Sabina Zembra* 38 'Readying' a horse and running it out of form so as to scoop the big handicap. **1889** *Sat. Rev.* 2 Nov. 489/2 A handicap of 10,000*l.* will, indeed, be worth 'readying' a horse for. **1927** E. WALLACE *Mixer* iv. 58 He sat . . in his office . . deploring inwardly the tendency of owners to 'ready' their horses for Epsom.

b. *Australian.* With *up*: To prepare or manipulate in an improper way for some end.

1893 *Melbourne Age* 25 Nov. 13/2 (Morris) It has been said that a great deal has been 'readied up' for the jury by the present commissioners. **1933** *Bulletin* (Sydney) 15 Nov. 33/1 All readied-up, I thought, though not bad fun.

Hence '**readying** *vbl. sb.*

a **1340** HAMPOLE *Psalter* ix. 41 þe rediynge of þaire hert, þat is, þaire hert redy to serue þe. **1884** *St. James's Gaz.* 5 Dec. 5/2 Striking feats of dexterous 'readying' and 'passing' which his companion performed.

ready-made, *ppl. phr.*, *a.*, and *sb.* [f. READY *a.* 16 + MADE: orig. a participial phrase used only as a predicate, in later use regarded as a comb. and hyphened (even in predicative use).]

†**1.** Made ready, prepared. *Obs.*

c **1440** *Jacob's Well* 22, I se helle opyn, & my place redy made þere. **1547** BOORDE *Introd. Knowl.* (1870) 185 They haue euer . . tymber readye made to make a hondred gales or more. **1588** WHITEHORNE tr. *Machiauel's Art Warre* VII. 102 b, Yᵉ fortifications being readie made.

2. a. Of made or manufactured articles: In a finished state, immediately ready for use; now *spec.* of articles which are offered for sale in this state, in contrast to others of the same kind which are made to order.

[**1390** GOWER *Conf.* III. 312 Whanne he sih and redy fond This cofre mad.] **1535** COVERDALE *Ezek.* xxvii. 19 Dan, Iauan, and Meusal haue brought vnto thy markettes, yron redy made. **1568** GRAFTON *Chron.* II. 355 Neyther is there in Scotland . . leather to make harnesse for their horse, as Saddels, Bridels, &c. But they haue all these thinges readie made out of Flaundyrs. **1631** WEEVER *Anc. Funeral Mon.* 498 To each one, a Gowne and a hood ready made. **1687** A. LOVELL tr. *Thevenot's Trav.* I. 33 A Coffee-hane (so they call the place where they sell it [coffee] ready made). **1768–74** TUCKER *Lt. Nat.* (1834) II. 515 They expect to buy understanding and sentiments, as they do wares, ready made, at a shop. **1853** SIR H. DOUGLAS *Milit. Bridges* 337 To move the bridge, ready-made, to its place. **1860** MRS. CARLYLE *Lett.* III. 20, I fell to cutting out that jacket last Monday, . . better to have bought one ready-made. **1875** in Ruskin *Fors Clav.* lix. *notes* V. 321 Never buy cheap ready-made clothing of any kind whatsoever.

b. In phrases used attributively.

1844 ALB. SMITH *Adv. Mr. Ledbury* vi. (1886) 20 [He] repaired to a ready-made clothes establishment in the Palais Royal. **1874** BURNAND *My time* xviii. 151, I used . . [to] admire the garments in a ready-made clothes shop.

3. a. Hence applied to any thing or person which exists in a finished or complete form, either naturally or as the result of some process; freq. used with depreciatory force, in allusion to the inferiority of certain 'ready-made' articles of trade.

1738 SWIFT *Polite Conv.* 102 A good Wife must be bespoke, for there is none ready made. **1801** MOORE *To ——* Poems 88 You will be An angel ready-made for heaven! **1890** *Spectator* 7 June, We all nowadays . . elect our leaders instead of taking them ready-made.

b. In attributive use.

1777 P. THICKNESSE *Year's Journey* II. lii. 153 The principal manufacture of the city [*sc.* Paris]; i.e. *ready-made love.* **1797** BURKE *Regic. Peace* iv. Wks. IX. 44 A shop of ready-made Bankruptcy and Famine. **1813** SHELLEY *Q. Mab* III. 41 Some ready-made face Of hypocritical assent. **1869** J. MARTINEAU *Ess.* II. 64 He carries about with him certain ready-made formulas. **1871** FREEMAN *Norm. Conq.* (1876) IV. xvii. 64 Their own Richard's Castle was a ready-made outpost of the Norman King.

4. Pertaining to, dealing in, ready-made articles.

1809 MALKIN *Gil Blas* VI. i. ¶7 The ready-made warehouse, where I bought these dresses. **1853** LOWELL *Moosehead Jrnl.* Pr. Wks. 1890 I. 39 True enough, thought I, this is the Ready-made Age.

5. *sb.* **a.** A ready-made article; *esp.* a ready-made garment or suit of clothes. Also *transf.* and *fig.*

1831 M. EDGEWORTH *Let.* 29 Mar. (1971) 501 Then she is so fond of . . her own family. She seems as if she was a ready-made for Fanny. **1882** *Standard* 18 Dec. 8/3 Traveller wanted for the Ready-mades for the Midland Counties. **1898** *Daily News* 9 May 3/6 Stocks of cloths, especially ready-mades. **1905** *Daily Chron.* 22 Nov. 10/2 Wholesale manufacturers and confectioners rejoice greatly as they see their trade in Christmas 'ready mades' annually swelling. **1933** C. ST. J. SPRIGG *Fatality in Fleet St.* vii. 86 He looked like a film Cossack jammed into an East End ready-made. **1967** *Economist* 10 June 1142/1 The typical Italian clothing shop cannot afford to carry a big enough range to demonstrate the advantages of readymades.

b. The term introduced by Marcel Duchamp (1887–1967), French artist, to denote representatives of a dadaistic art-form created by him, in which simple manufactured objects are exhibited as works of art; the art-form itself.

[**1915** M. DUCHAMP in A. Schwarz *Marcel Duchamp* (1969) 54 Précises les 'Readymades'. En projetant pour un moment . . à venir . . '*d'inscrire* un readymade'.] **1935** D. GASCOYNE *Short Survey of Surrealism* ii. 28 Such was Marcel Duchamp's disgust for 'art' that he invented a new form of expression, which he called *Ready-Made*. A Ready-Made was any manufactured object that the artist liked to choose. **1958** *Times* 20 May 3/7 The 'ready-mades' in which Marcel Duchamp parodied the exhibition work of art, signing his name on such manufactured objects as a wash-basin or a snow shovel. **1968** *N. Y. City* (Michelin Guide) 17 Marcel Duchamp . . created his provocative 'ready-mades', which consist of simple . . objects, which the artist exhibits as works of art (having intervened only to give them names); thus, he displayed . . A Fountain, which was . . a can bought in a department store. **1972** C. W. E. BIGSBY *Dada & Surrealism* ii. 11 The ready-mades were simply objects which he [*sc.* Marcel Duchamp] himself had selected as being commonplace.

'**ready-mix**, *a.* (and *sb.*) orig. *U.S.* [f. READY *a.* + MIX *sb.*²] = READY-MIXED *a.* (and *sb.*). Also *fig.*

1950 M. MCCARTHY in *Reporter* 18 July 39/1 The ready-mix cake turns out 'terrific'. **1958** [see INSTANT *a.* 4 c]. **1963**

Punch 28 Aug. 322/3 A studio audience complete with ready-mix mirth and instant appreciation. **1966** *Guardian* 28 Apr. 4/2 Factory food, in the form of ready-mixes, was certainly better than that produced by 'the multitude of indifferent cooks..now wandering around the country'. **1976** E. WARD *Hanged Man* iii. 13 A ready-mix concrete truck marked Metro Concrete jolted along the access road. **1980** *Times Lit. Suppl.* 30 May 608/4 Germaine is the principal new ingredient in the Barthian narrative ready-mix.

ready-mixed, *a.* (and *sb.*) orig. *U.S.* [f. READY *a.* 16.] Of paints, concrete, and other artificial compound substances, having some or all of the constituents already mixed together. Also *ellipt.* as *sb.*

1895 *Montgomery Ward Catal.* Spring & Summer 254/2 Japanese Ready Mixed Paints and Enamels. **1908** *Sears, Roebuck Catal.* 71/1, 85 cents per gallon buys our guaranteed Seroco Ready Mixed House Paint. **1930** *Engineering* 16 May 631/3 The practice of selling ready-mixed concrete was introduced in the United States about ten years ago. **1960** *Farmer & Stockbreeder* 22 Mar. (Suppl.) 10/2 You can make up your own flooring compounds, but probably the simplest way is to buy a tin of ready-mixed material. **1973** M. TRUMAN *H. S. Truman* iii. 72 Mr. Pendergast owned the Ready-Mixed Concrete Company which in the past had been used almost exclusively by contractors paving Jackson County roads. In Judge Truman's 225-mile road-building program, only three-fourths of a mile were paved with Ready-Mixed. **1977** J. I. M. STEWART *Madonna of Astrolabe* iii. 51 To what extent should we be justified in pouring unexpected wealth, as if it were so much ready-mixed concrete, into shoring up a mere sense-of-beauty-occasioning object?

'ready 'money. [READY *a.* 10 a.] Coined money, cash, as being immediately available for use; also, immediate payment in coin for anything bought. (In common use from 15th c.)

c **1420** *Sir Amadace* (Camden) xii, A marchand of this cite, Hade..euiryche ȝere thre hundrythe pownde, Of redy monay, and of rowunde. **1503–4** *Act 19 Hen. VII*, c. 27 §7 The Capytayne..agreyd to have..the said thirde parte in redye money and nott in vitayles. **1613** PURCHAS *Pilgrimage* III. x. (1614) 295 Readie monie is their surest riches, because the Grande Signior is their surest Heire. **1712** STEELE *Spect.* No. 264 ⁋2 He had at this Time fifty Pounds in ready Money. **1787** BENTHAM *Def. Usury* iii. 19 No man..ever thinks of borrowing money to spend, so long as he has ready money of his own. **1885** *Law Rep. 29 Chanc. Div.* 468 The company was in great difficulties for ready money.

Prov. **1630** J. TAYLOR (Water P.) *Trav. Twelve Pence* Wks. I. 72/2 The Prouerbe true doth say That ready money euer will away.

Hence **'ready-,money** *attrib. phr.*

(*a*) Characterized by immediate payment in money for articles bought.

1712 STEELE *Spect.* No. 546 ⁋3 He cannot expose that to the hazard of giving credit, but enters into a ready-money trade. **1822** SCOTT *Pirate* xviii, Having been hitherto a ready-money trade. **1865** *Sat. Rev.* 21 Jan. 79/2 The transactions..require only ready-money dealing. **1898** J. B. WOLLOCOMBE *From Morn till Eve* x. 236 The landlord carried on a ready-money business.

(*b*) Paying ready money.

1796 NELSON in Nicolas *Disp.* (1845) II. 221, I think you will like to have these ready-money gentry come amongst you. **1895** *Pall Mall G.* 17 Oct. 3/1 Within handy reach of every ready-money housekeeper in the kingdom.

'ready-,moneyed, *a.* [f. prec.] **a.** Possessing ready money. **b.** Of the nature of ready money; (in quot. *fig.*).

1810 *Chron.* in *Ann. Reg.* 314/1 Mr. Elwes is, perhaps, the richest ready-moneyed commoner in England. *c* **1815** JANE AUSTEN *Northang. Abb.* (1833) II. xi. 175 Giving ready-monied, actual happiness for a draft on the future that may not be honoured.

'ready 'reckoner. [READY *a.*] A table, or collection of tables, showing at a glance the results of such arithmetical calculations as are most frequently required in ordinary business, housekeeping, etc.

1757 D. FENNING (*title*) The Ready Reckoner; or, Trade's most useful Assistant. **1811** S. SIMPSON (*title*) The Readiest Reckoner ever invented. **1838** DICKENS *Nich. Nick.* i, Abstract calculations of figures, or references to ready-reckoners. **1851** MAYHEW *Lond. Labour* I. 327/1 This book ..contains a diary.., an almanack, a ready-reckoner [etc.].

ready-to-wear, *a.* (and *sb.*) orig. *U.S.* Also **ready-for-wear**. [f. READY *a.* 16 d.]

1. Of clothing: = READY-MADE *a.* 2, 4.

1895 *Montgomery Ward Catal.* 276/1 (*heading*) Ready to wear clothing. **1905** *Daily Chron.* 27 Feb. 8/3 A more exclusive type of ready-to-wear hat is the..sailor turban, toque, or narrow boat shape. **1930** *Times* 17 Mar. 9/4 The ready-to-wear sections bring the new styles within the reach of modern purses... A new spring catalogue giving illustrations of their ready-for-wear clothes has been prepared. **1953** *Manch. Guardian Weekly* 30 July 7/1 They ..announced the premature birth of Neiman-Marcus as 'the South's finest and only exclusive women's ready-to-wear shop'. **1977** M. SOKOLINSKY tr. *R. Merle's Virility Factor* xvi. 315 She..had skillfully managed a ready-to-wear business. **1981** *Country Life* 12 Feb. 414/2 The ready-to-wear collections for spring and summer.

2. as *sb.* (An article of) ready-made clothing. Chiefly *pl.*

1923 *Blackw. Mag.* Apr. 503/2 There was a young person, looking quite the little man in a suit of ready-to-wears. **1973** 'J. ASHFORD' *Double Run* iii. 21 His clothes had the hangdog look of cheap ready-to-wears which had had a hard life. **1974** *Country Life* 3/10 Jan. 54/3 He has private clients, as well as selling ready-to-wear in boutiques. **1977** *South China Morning Post* (Hong Kong) 13 Apr. 14/8 A vice-president of Bloomingdales..commented that the ready-to-wear is wonderful for the film industry.

ready-witted, *a.* [READY *a.* 6 a.] Of a ready wit or intelligence; quick of apprehension.

1581 PETTIE tr. *Guazzo's Civ. Conv.* III. (1586) 127b, Manie grosse heads, by continuall studie become readie witted. **1784** BURNS *Ep. J. Rankine* i, O rough, rude ready-witted Rankine. **1821** SCOTT *Kenilw.* xvi, Varney was as bold-faced and ready-witted as he was cunning and unscrupulous. **1869** TROLLOPE *He Knew*, etc. xxxi. (1878) 175 Dorothy was not sufficiently ready-witted to see the danger of this position.

Hence **,ready-'wittedness**.

1884 *Spectator* 20 Dec. 1700/2 The ready-wittedness and power of observation, which makes in semi-civilized communities the successful doctor.

†**reaf.** *Obs.* Also 3 ræf, ræu-. [OE. *réaf*, usually regarded as a special sense of *réaf* spoil, booty (see REAVE *v.*), but the precise relationship is not quite certain.] A garment, mantle.

c **950** *Lindisf. Gosp.* Matt. xxii. 12 Ne hæfdes ðu wede *vel* reaf brydlic. *c* **1121** *O.E. Chron.* (Laud MS.) an. 1070 Mæsse hakeles & cantelcapas & reafes. *c* **1205** LAY. 23760 Warp he an his rugge a ræf swiðe deore. *Ibid.* 26636 Romanisce leoden mid ræue bihonged.

reaf(e, variants of REIF, plunder(ing).

reafen, obs. form of RAVEN *sb.*[1]

rea'ffect, *v.* **1.** [RE- 5 a.] *trans.* To affect (†aim at, have liking for, etc.) again or anew.

1599 SANDYS *Europæ Spec.* (1632) 174 The Germane.. will hardly..be brought ever in heart to re-affect the Papacie. **1652** J. WRIGHT tr. *Camus' Nat. Paradox* XII. 328 Iphigenes..seemed to re-affect the desire of Living. **1654** COKAINE *Dianea* II. 128 If I kill him, I can never hope to enjoy him, who living may become sensible of his errour, and re-affect me.

2. [RE- 2 a.] To affect in return.

1697 J. SERGEANT *Solid Philos.* 144 Those Phantasms.. which have already affected the said Seat of Knowledge.. and have been re-affected by it.

reafference (riːˈæfərəns). [ad. G. *reafferenz* (von Holst and Mittelstaedt 1950, in *Naturwissenschaften* XXXVII. 464). Cf. AFFERENT *a.*] Sensory stimulation in which the stimulus changes as a result of the individual's movements in response to it.

1965 *Sci. Amer.* Nov. 85/1 A key to its operation is the availability of 'reafference'. This word was coined by the German physiologists Erich von Holst and Horst Mittelstädt to describe neural excitation following sensory stimulation that is systematically dependent on movements initiated by the sensing animal. **1971** J. S. BRUNER *Beyond Information Given* (1974) xiv. 249 The crucial issue in the regulation of intentional action is the opportunity to compare what was intended with what in fact resulted, using the difference between the two as a basis of correction. It is immediately apparent that this is the concept of reafference as a source of regulation in behavior. **1973** R. MARTIN tr. *von Holst's Behav. Physiol. of Anim. & Men* I. iii. 141 Rather than asking about the relationship between a given afference and the evoked efference (i.e. about the reflex), we set out *in the opposite direction*..asking: What happens in the CNS with the afference (referred to as the 'reafference') which is evoked through the effectors and receptors by the efference? **1973** C. D. KERNIG *Marxism, Communism & Western Soc.* VII. 103/2 As early as 1935 Anokhin..had discovered a phenomenon corresponding to the reafference principle. **1979** S. COREN et al. *Sensation & Perception* xvi. 391/1 It has been suggested that reafference is necessary for the development of accurate visually guided spatial behavior.

re-'afferent, *a.* [f. RE- + AFFERENT *a.*] Of or pertaining to reafference.

1965 *Sci. Amer.* Nov. 87/1 This kind of movement, with its contingent reafferent stimulation, is the critical factor in compensating for displaced visual images. **1965** N. CHOMSKY *Aspects of Theory of Syntax* i. 34 Under certain circumstances reafferent stimulation (that is, stimulation resulting from voluntary activity) is a prerequisite to the development of a concept of visual space. **1971** R. MARTIN tr. *Lorenz's Stud. in Anim. & Hum. Behav.* II. 300 Such sensory signals directly produced by inherent movements of the organism are referred to as *reafferent signals*, and the signal relating to the outgoing motor command which is transmitted to the perceptual mechanism is the efferent signal copy. **1973** —— tr. *von Holst's Behav. Physiol. of Anim. & Men* I. iii. 149 There is absence of the reafferent 'stop'..which normally arrests the correcting movement. **1975** L. GANZ in A. H. Riesen *Developmental Neuropsychol. of Sensory Deprivation* vi. 198 They believe that the reafferent perception of a moving part of the body is essential for the development of coordination.

rea'ffirm, *v.* [RE- 5 a.]

†**1.** *trans.* To confirm anew. *Obs.*[−0]

1611 FLORIO, *Raffermare*, to re-affirme, to re-confirme.

2. To affirm or assert anew.

a **1842** CHANNING *Perfect Life* i. (1873) 25, I close with re-affirming the truth that I have aimed to impress. **1884** *Spectator* 4 Oct. 1289/2 The electors have since..reaffirmed and strengthened that decision.

Hence **rea'ffirmer**, one who reaffirms.

1892 BRUCE *Apologetics* II. v. 231 They were only re-affirmers with new emphasis of the ancient faith.

rea'ffirmance. [RE- 5 a.] = next.

1726 AYLIFFE *Parergon* 208 A persisting therein without Revocation of his Error, or a Re-affirmance thereof after such Revocation. **1790** BURKE *Fr. Rev.* 45 Nothing more than a re-affirmance of the still more ancient standing law of the kingdom. **1881** G. W. HERVEY *Manu. Revivals* vi. 45 At such a time the true Gospel may need a reaffirmance and defence.

reaffir'mation. [RE- 5 a.] Renewed affirmation; reassertion.

1857 P. FREEMAN *Princ. Div. Serv.* II. 100 The dogmatic re-affirmation of Eucharistic doctrine. **1885** *Athenæum* 14 Nov. 642/2 The..criticism..concludes with a reaffirmation of the great influence of the antique on Raphael.

rea'fforest, *v.* [RE- 5 a.]

†**1.** *trans.* To restore to the legal status of a forest. *Obs.*

1667–8 *Act 19 & 20 Chas. II*, c. 8 §5 All the other Waste Lands aforesaid shall be and are hereby reafforrested and shall from henceforth be governed by Forrest Law. [Hence in Manley (1706), Phillips (1706), and later Dicts.]

2. To replant with trees; to cover again with forest. Hence **rea'fforesting** *vbl. sb.*

1882 *Pall Mall G.* 10 Aug. 5/1 The great importance of reafforesting the denuded soil in over-cleared countries. **1890** W. MEYNELL *J. H. Newman* 2 His scheme for the reafforesting of England.

So **reaffore'station**.

1884 *Manch. Exam.* 28 Mar. 5/2 The question as to how the work of reafforestation is to be done.

†**rea'ffund**, *v.* *Obs.*[−1] [RE- 5 a.] *trans.* To pour on again.

1605 TIMME *Quersit.* I. xiii. 57 If..the oylely liquor of his proper sulphur..be drawen forth..and be reaffunded and distilled [etc.].

So †**rea'ffusion**. *Obs. rare.*

1657 G. STARKEY *Helmont's Vind.* 326 The spirit by re-affusion and powring off..will extract the whole tincture of the Vegetable. **1666** BOYLE *Orig. Formes & Qual.* II. vi. 371 By the Reaffusions of fresh Menstruum on the dry Calx of Gold.

reaflac: see REFLAC *Obs.*

Reaganism (ˈreɪgənɪz(ə)m). [f. the name of Ronald W. *Reagan* (b. 1911), American Republican politician, Governor of California 1967–75, and President of the United States 1981– + -ISM.] The policies and principles advocated by Ronald Reagan; adherence to or support of these. Also **'Reaganite**, a supporter of Reagan; also *attrib.* or as *adj.*

1966 *Punch* 7 Dec. 832/3 Reaganism is really rampant now. **1975** *Financial Times* 20 Nov. 5/8 Wits have suggested that 'Reaganism is extremism in defence of Fordism'. **1976** *Times* 21 Feb. 6/7 The Reaganites..have moved on... If organization was the key to success, Mr Ford would never stand a chance. **1977** *Time* 3 Jan. 22 (*caption*) Reaganite at G.O.P. convention. **1981** *Economist* 24 Jan. 13/2 The right way lies through greater scope for bodies like the International Monetary Fund..which lends its money tied to almost Reaganite advice. **1981** *Times* 31 Jan. 13/3 Mrs Thatcher approximates on occasions to the tones of Reaganism.

reagency (riːˈeɪdʒənsɪ). [RE- 2 a; cf. REACT *v.*[1]] Reactive power or operation.

1842 *Blackw. Mag.* LI. 284 Christianity..as a re-agency of destruction to all forms of idolatrous error. **1852** DE QUINCEY *Confess.* (1856) 12 The re-agency of these London sufferings did..enforce the use of opium.

reagent (riːˈeɪdʒənt). [RE- 2 a; cf. REACT *v.*[1]]

1. *Chem.* Orig., a substance employed as a test to determine the presence of some other substance by means of the *reaction* which is produced. Now, any substance employed in chemical reactions (cf. sense 2).

1797 HATCHETT in *Phil. Trans.* LXXXVIII. 115 The liquor..being examined by the re-agents commonly used, afforded no trace of matter in solution. **1812** SIR H. DAVY *Chem. Philos.* 27 Boyle..introduced the use of tests or reagents, active substances for detecting the presence of other bodies. **1880** DARWIN in *Life & Lett.* (1887) III. 346 Injecting various reagents into the tissues of leaves. **1904** L. W. RIGGS *Elem. Man. Chem. Laboratory* III. 82 Any positive ion..when separated from other cations..will exhibit with reagents certain phenomena characteristic of that ion. **1929** C. R. HAYWARD *Dict. Metall. Pract.* xxii. 487 Recarburizing ..may be accomplished by adding the reagents to the converter. **1948** CURRIER & ROSE *Gen. & Appl. Chem.* xix. 151 Nitric acid..is a very important substance: in the laboratory as an oxidizing reagent, and in industry for the manufacture of explosives. **1964** N. G. CLARK *Mod. Org. Chem.* v. 65 Traditional reagents and reaction conditions rarely affect the paraffins, but they exhibit useful reactivity at high temperatures. **1973** *Materials & Technol.* VI. viii. 545 To make a bonded joint, the PTFE is first etched with a reagent.

2. A reactive substance, force, etc. (Sometimes directly *transf.* from prec.)

1856 EMERSON *Eng. Traits, Race* 27 Civilization is a re-agent, and eats away the old traits. **1865** M. PATTISON *Serm.* 109 Mind is a reagent against society. **1880** W. MACCORMAC *Antis. Surgery* 113 The antiseptic method is not the mere employment of any single reagent.

3. *Comb.* **reagent grade**, a grade of commercial chemicals characterized by a high standard of purity; freq. *attrib.*; **reagent paper**, paper treated with a reagent for use in chemical tests.

1935 *Jrnl. Amer. Chem. Soc.* LVII. 408/2 Baker and Adamson $CuSO_4.5H_2O$, Reagent Grade, was recrystallized twice from distilled water. **1945** *Ibid.* LXVII. 1096/1 Reagent grade ammonium sulfate was heated at 75° for several days. **1966** A. S. PRASAD *Zinc Metabolism* xv. 275 Six of..[the patients] received reagent grade zinc sulfate 90 mg daily, and three received reagent grade ferrous sulfate 1 gm orally daily. **1973** *Jrnl. Amer. Chem. Soc.* XCV. 1913/1 All reagents and solvents used were reagent grade and, unless noted otherwise, were used without further purification. **1908** *Practitioner* Mar. 410 A pea-sized piece being rubbed up with 2 c.c. of water, and the reagent-paper dipped into this.

†**re'aggravate**, *v. Obs. rare.* [RE- 5a, after med.L. *reaggravāre* (1501 in Du C.), It. *raggravare* (Florio), F. *réaggraver* (15th c.): cf. next.] *trans.* To make still heavier.

1611 COTGR., *Rengraver*, to reaggrauate; reinforce, renew. **1626** C. POTTER tr. *Sarpi's Hist. Quarrels* 72 Reseruing to Himselfe and his successors power to aggrauate and reaggrauate the censures and penalties against them.

reaggra'vation. *Eccl.* [ad. med.L. *reaggravātio*; cf. obs. F. *réaggravation* (15th c.; the usual word is *réaggrave*). See prec. and AGGRAVATION 3.] The second warning given to a person before final excommunication.

1611 COTGR., *Reaggravation*, a reaggrauation; and (particularly) the last, and most direfull excommunication of offendors. **1727–41** CHAMBERS *Cycl.* s.v., Before they proceed to fulminate the last excommunication, they publish an aggravation, and a re-aggravation. **1864** [see AGGRAVATION 3].

re'aggregate, *v.* [RE- 5a.] **a.** *trans.* To collect or bring together again. **b.** *intr.* To come together again. Hence **re'aggregated** *ppl. a.*; **reaggre'gation**.

1849 MURCHISON *Siluria* xiv. 347 Simply a re-aggregated granite. **1862** G. P. SCROPE *Volcanos* 45 A proportionate diminution of temperature..reaggregates them in a solid mass. **1882** SPENCER *Princ. Sociol., Pol. Instit.* 243 The minglings of peoples and institutions, the breakings up and re-aggregations..destroy the continuity of normal processes. **1962** H. BLOEMENDAL et al. in A. Pirie *Lens Metabolism Rel. Cataract* 300 The subunits..reaggregate after removal of urea.

reagin (riː'eɪdʒɪn). *Immunol.* [a. G. *reagin*, f. *reag-ieren* to react + *-in* -INE[5].]

a. The complement-fixing substance in the blood of persons with syphilis which is responsible for the positive response to the Wassermann reaction.

1911 R. W. MATSON tr. *A. Wolff-Eisner's Clin. Immunity & Sero-Diagnosis* iii. 33 To avoid errors, it is..best to use the term 'reactive substances' (reagins) rather than 'antibodies', since the latter implies a neutralization in the sense of an antitoxin. **1915** J. E. R. MCDONAGH *Biol. & Treatm. Venereal Dis.* x. 71 Owing..to the fact that a positive Wassermann reaction may be obtained in conditions other than syphilitic ones, the reaction ceases to be a specific reaction. Therefore the third factor ought not to be called an antibody, since it is in no wise specific, hence it is best called reacting substance, or Reagin. **1937** H. EAGLE *Lab. Diagnosis Syphilis* i. 24 There is reason to believe that Wasserman's first theory was correct, and that the active component of syphilitic serum, so-called reagin, may well be an antibody to *Spirochaeta pallida* despite its reactivity with normal tissue lipoids. **1942** *Jrnl. Lab. & Clin. Med.* XXVII. 729 It seems controversial as to whether reagin is an antibody to lipid haptens of the host..or an antibody to the spirochete. **1976** A. E. WILKINSON in Catterall & Nicol *Sexually Transmitted Dis.* 215 Although the function of reagin is still uncertain, its level seems to be roughly related to the amount of tissue reaction by the host, rising rapidly with increasing numbers of treponemes in early syphilis and later falling as the number of organisms declines with developing immunity.

b. The antibody which is involved in allergic reactions, causing the release of histamine and similar agents when it combines with antigen in tissue and capable of producing sensitivity to the antigen when introduced into the skin of a normal individual.

1925 [see ATOPY]. **1963** *Advances in Immunol.* III. 181 Reagin still represents a nebulous concept to many immunologists, some doubting the legitimacy of its classification as an antibody. **1969** R. S. WEISER et al. *Fund. Immunol.* xv. 163 The antibodies responsible for P-K type sensitivities, the so-called 'reagins' or P-K antibodies, have long been a mystery. **1977** *Nature* 16 June 618/1 Allergic diseases such as hay fever, extrinsic asthma, drug hypersensitivities and some forms of urticaria are mediated by allergen-specific antibodies of the IgE class, known also as reagins.

Hence **rea'ginic** *a.*, of, pertaining to, or being (a) reagin.

1931 A. F. COCA *Asthma & Hay Fever in Theory & Pract.* I. xvii. 332 Bona fide reaginic reactions are indicative of past, present or potential sensitivities in the atopic individual. **1945** *Vet. Rec.* LVII. 339/2 (*heading*) Reaginic allergy in cattle. **1975** *Nature* 6 Feb. 475/1 In the rat, reaginic antibodies were reported and their possible significance in *S[chistosoma] mansoni* infection considered. **1977** A. M. DENMAN in Holborow & Reeves *Immunol. in Med.* x. 295 IgE constitutes the major class of reaginic antibody but it seems likely that some IgG..antibodies also contribute.

re'agitate, *v.* [RE- 5a.] To agitate again.

1813 T. BUSBY *Lucretius* II. IV. *Comm.* p. xxxiv, Certain minute moveable bones..provided to re-agitate the air.

†**reagnize**, *v. Obs.*$^{-1}$ [RE- 5a.] *trans.* To recognize.

1682 H. MORE *Annot. Glanvill's Lux Orient* 30 They will ..remember their former Paradisiacal state upon its recovery, and reagnize their ancient home.

†**reagree**, *v. Obs.*$^{-1}$ [f. RE- 5a + AGREE *v.* 4.] *trans.* To reconcile, make up again.

1609 DANIEL *Civ. Wars* VII. cxiv, Fain to see that glorious holiday Of union which this discord re-agreed.

reaisun, obs. f. REASON.

reak, (?) var. of RAKE *sb.*[3] and *v.*[1]

reak(e, obs. ff. REEK *sb.* and *v.*

reake, obs. f. RECK *v.*; (?) obs. var. of REACH *v.*

reaklesse, obs. var. of RECKLESS.

reakn-, obs. Sc. f. RECKON *v.*

†**reaks**, *sb. pl. Obs.* Also 6–7 **reakes**, 7 **reeks**, **reax**: and *sing.* 9 *Sc.* **reik**. [Of obscure origin: cf. FREAK. The precise relationship to REX is not clear; the evidence is not decisive for the view that *rex* is the original form.] Pranks, wanton or riotous tricks or practices. Chiefly in phr. ***to keep*** or ***play reaks*** (very common in 17th c.).

1575 GASCOIGNE *Flowers, Lookes of Louer forsaken* Wks. 15 Such reakes the rage of loue in thee had wrought. **1586** D. ROWLAND *Lazarillo* II. (1672) U i, The owner of the House, where these Reaks were Played. **1596** NASHE *Saffron Walden* 95 The olde reakes hee kept with the wenches in Queenes Colledge Lane. **1633** HEYWOOD *Eng. Trav.* II. Wks. 1874 IV. 25 They may be rather called Reakes then Reuells. **1692** R. L'ESTRANGE *Fables* (1694) 475 Throwing books at one another's heads and playing such Reaks as if Hell were broke loose. **1818** SCOTT *Rob Roy* xxvi, Mony a daft reik he has played.

Comb. **1611** COTGR., *Ribleur*, a disorderlie roauer,.. outragious reakes-player.

real ('riːəl, 'reɪəl), *sb.*[1] Also 7 **reall**. [Sp. *real*, sb. use of *real* adj., royal:—L. *rēgāl-em*: see REAL *a.*[1], and RIAL *sb.*]

1. A small silver coin and money of account formerly in use in Spain and Spanish-speaking countries. **a.** The old Spanish ***real de plata*** (largely circulated in the United States up to *c* 1850, and in Mexico until 1897) = an eighth of a dollar (6¼*d* *c* 1900). **b.** The former Spanish monetary unit, ***real (de) vellon*** (not current as a coin) = a quarter of a peseta..

The ***real of plate*** was formerly known in the northern U.S. by the name of *Mexican* or *Spanish shilling*, in the south by that of LEVY *sb.*[2] See also BIT *sb.*[1] 8b.

1611 COTGR., *Real*, a Reall, or Spanish sixpence. **1613** PURCHAS *Pilgrimage* VIII. x. (1614) 795 Euery Indian payeth tribute to the King [of Spain] twelue Reals of Plate. **1662** J. DAVIES tr. *Olearius' Voy. Ambass.* 97 The Muscovites.. carry them [Rixdollers] to the Mint, as they do also Spanish Reals. **1760** *Ann. Reg.* 89 All they owed to the crown.. which does not amount to less than sixty millions of reals. **1798** MALTHUS *Popul.* (1878) 359 The highest price is 48 reals vellon. **1850** B. TAYLOR *Eldorado* II. xiii. 84 The money..was paid to me in quarter-dollars, reals, and medios, which it took me more than an hour to count.

†**2.** ***real of eight*** = ***piece of eight*** (EIGHT 2d). *Obs.*

1612 SHELTON *Quix.* I. I. ii. 14 It being all one to me to be paid my Money in 8 single Reals, or to be paid the same in one Real of eight. **1628** DIGBY *Voy. Medit.* 38, 4 French vessels, whereof one..had still a hundred thousand reals of eight abord her. **1818** JAS. MILL *Brit. India* I. I. ii. 31 The prize money, which was estimated at 100,000*l.* and 240,000 reals of eight.

†**real**, *a.*[1] (and *sb.*[2]) *Obs.* Also 4–5 **reale**, 4, 6–7 **reall**; *pl.* 5 *Sc.* **reaws**. [a. OF. *real* (12th c.) = Prov. *real*, *reial*, Sp., Pg. *real*, It. *reale*:—L. *rēgāl-em* REGAL. As a variant of RIAL and ROYAL, the form chiefly occurs in MSS. written about 1400.]

A. *adj.* Royal, regal, kingly.

13.. *Guy Warw.* (A.) 3879 A real pauiloun he þer seye. *c* **1350** *Will. Palerne* 1597 Al þat real aray reken schold men neuer. **1397** *Rolls of Parlt.* III. 379/1, I amonges other restreyned my Lord of his fredom, and toke upon me.. Power Reall. *c* **1425** WYNTOUN *Cron.* III. iii. 560 Brute.. byggyd in his land a towne, Yhit realle [and] off gret renowne. **1460** CAPGRAVE *Chron.* (Rolls) 197 The qweena held a real Cristmasse aftir at Walingford. **1577** HELLOWES *Gueuara's Chron.* 109 He edified the reall palace named Neptunus. **1602** MARSTON *Ant. & Mel.* II. Wks. 1856 I. 23 Then whome I knowe not a more..pretious, reall, magnanimous, bountious.

B. *sb.*[2] A royal person. *rare.*

1399 LANGL. *Rich. Redeles* I. 91 Reffusynge the reule of realles kynde. *Ibid.* III. 301 Whanne realles remeveth,..And carieth ouere contre ther comunes dwelleth. *c* **1425** WYNTOUN *Cron.* VIII. i. 105 Gyve any male Of Reaws might fundyn be Worth to have that realté.

real ('riːəl), *a.*[2], *adv.*, and *sb.*[3] Also 5–7 **reall**. [a. OF. *real*, *reel* (13th c. in Godef.), or ad. late L. *reālis*, f. *rēs* thing, etc. + -AL[1].]

The precise sense is uncertain in the following early instances of the word:—*c* **1440** *Promp. Parv.* 424/2 Real, *realis.* **1570** LEVINS *Manip.* 13/31 Real, *realis.* **1598** MARSTON *Sco. Villanie* To iudic. Perusers 169 Some of his new-minted Epithets (as Reall, Intrinsecate, Delphicke).

A. *adj.* **I. 1. a.** Having an objective existence; actually existing as a thing.

1601 SHAKS. *All's Well* V. iii. 307 Is there no exorcist Beguiles the truer Office of mine eyes? Is't reall that I see? **1651** HOBBES *Leviath.* III. xxxiv. 210 That some such apparitions were not Imaginary, but Reall. **1667** MILTON *P.L.* VIII. 310 Whereat I wak'd, and found Before mine Eyes all real, as the dream Had lively shadowd. **1821** SHELLEY *Prometh. Unb.* I. 748 But from these create he can Forms more real than living man. **1859** PARKINSON *Optics* (1866) 130 A real visible object and its optical image differ in this respect.

b. In *Philosophy* applied to whatever is regarded as having an existence in fact and not merely in appearance, thought, or language, or as having an absolute and necessary, in contrast to a merely contingent, existence.

1701 NORRIS *Ideal World* I. iii. 150 An Hircocervus or any other Fictitious Being is true and real with respect to the Simple Essences or Natures. **1711** SHAFTESB. *Charac.* (1737) II. III. i. 369 Thought we own pre-eminent, and confess the reallest of Beings. **1797** *Encycl. Brit.* (ed. 3) XVIII. 79/1 Numberless absurdities, such as, that..forms or sensible qualities are real things independent of their subject and the sentient beings who perceive them. **1843** MILL *Logic* I. vi. §3 He [Locke] admitted real essences, or essences of individual objects, which he supposed to be the causes of the sensible properties of those objects. **1857** WHEWELL *Hist. Induct. Sc.* (ed. 3) I. 343 The perfections are unquestionably real existences. **1893** BRADLEY *Appearance & Reality* xxvii. (1897) 552 The more that anything is spiritual, so much the more is it veritably real.

c. ***real money***: (*a*) current coin or cash (esp. as opposed to imaginary money or money of account).

1685 PETTY *Will* p. v, An estate of about 1300*l.* in ready and real money. **1849** FREESE *Comm. Class-bk.* 71 Real monies are coins of any kind of metal, made current by the authority of the state.

(*b*) *colloq.* A large sum of money.

1918 R. W. LARDNER *Treat 'em Rough* 120, I could go out and pitch baseball and make real money. **1939** A. HUXLEY *After Many Summer* I. iv. 46, I did some business this morning... Might make a lot of money. *Real* money. **1964** L. DEIGHTON *Funeral in Berlin* iii. 21 'Whom do you feel like?' I liked that 'whom'—you've got to pay real money these days to get a secretary that could say that.

(*c*) *colloq.* The coinage or currency in which one habitually reckons, freq. as opp. to foreign currency.

1973 L. MEYNELL *Thirteen Trumpeters* iv. 50 So I'm paying one thousand seven hundred and ten lire for my Pimms?.. What's it mean in real money? **1977** *Vole* No. 2. 17/2 Just before the demise of real money and the introduction of decimal coinage, the officials of Gloucester Shoveha'penny League invested £10 in old-style halfpennies. **1977** *Zigzag* Mar. 7/1 They charged me three hundred francs. Well, that's..quite a lot in real money.

d. *Math.* Of quantities. (Opposed to IMAGINARY 1c, or IMPOSSIBLE 2.)

1727–41 CHAMBERS *Cycl.* s.v. *Root*, If the value of *x* be positive, *i.e.* if *x* be a positive quantity,..the root [of an equation] is called a real or true root. **1841** *Penny Cycl.* XX. 150/2 Here *a* and *b* are meant to be real algebraical quantities, that is, reducible to positive or negative whole numbers or fractions. **1875** *Encycl. Brit.* I. 544/2 Every quadratic equation has always two roots, real or imaginary. **1910** *Ibid.* I. 613/1 The development of the theory of equations leads to the amplification of real numbers, rational and irrational, positive and negative, by imaginary and complex numbers. **1952** S. C. KLEENE *Introd. Metamath.* i. 6 That there are infinite sets considered in mathematics which cannot be enumerated was shown by Cantor's famous 'diagonal method'. The set of the real numbers is non-enumerable. **1965** PATTERSON & RUTHERFORD *Elem. Abstract Algebra* iii. 85 The real number *a* is called the real part of the complex number (*a*, *b*) and the real number *b* is called the imaginary part. **1972** S. W. P. STEEN *Math. Logic* iii. 178 Having defined the integers we can then define rational numbers as triplets of integers, then real numbers as Dedekind Sections of rational numbers and lastly complex numbers as ordered pairs of real numbers.

e. *Optics.* (See quot.)

1859 PARKINSON *Optics* (1866) 130 If an image consist of points through which the light actually passes it is called real;—in other cases virtual. Hence a screen placed in the position of an image will receive illumination only when the image is real.

f. ***real time***, the actual time during which a process or event occurs, esp. one analysed by a computer, in contrast to time subsequent to it when computer processing may be done, a recording replayed, or the like.

1953 *Math. Tables & Other Aids to Computation* VII. 73 With the advent of large-scale high-speed digital computers, there arises the question of their possible use in the solution of problems in 'real time', i.e., in conjunction with instruments receiving and responding to stimuli from the external environment. The criteria for satisfactory operation in such real-time service are different from those generally encountered. **1964** *Listener* 19 Nov. 784/1 A higher speed in computers means that their complexity can increase very rapidly, too, and that they can more easily engage in activites in what we call 'real time'. That is to say, they can calculate at the actual speed of the events taking place. **1968** *Times* 10 Dec. 6/8 The data gathered by the telescopes are stored on board the satellite by magnetic tapes and discs... The Smithsonian experiment can also be used in real time, transmitting information as it gathers it. **1970** *Nature* 20 June 1110/2 The data are telemetered to ground-based stations which record the information on magnetic tape and provide a digital print-out in real time. **1973** *Sci. Amer.* May 115/2 It is wrong to detail a suspense plot, even though we all recall from real time how *Apollo 13* limped back safely. **1973** *Nature* 12 Oct. 294/1 As we are working in scientific 'real time', we have to ask at what stage the work will be when filming is in progress. **1979** R. HAWKEY *Side-Effect* xi. 83 The Real Time was three hundred milliseconds, but it was shot in slow motion.

attrib. **1953** [see above]. **1960** *N.Y. Times* 17 July 13/4 As an experiment, Air Force and Weather Bureau meteorologists attempted to use the pictures to make 'real time' forecasts of the weather—forecasts fresh enough to be useful. **1968** *Times* 1 Nov. 23/6 Computers have been slow to conquer the real-time control of industrial processes and traffic flows. **1970** O. Dopping *Computers & Data Processing* vi. 96 An example of a real-time process is a cheque account system in a bank where all transactions, e.g. withdrawals, are reported to the computer before they are finished. **1972** *Guardian* 9 Feb. 3/8 We do think we know how to develop a satellite with a near real-time (instantaneous) capability. **1975** *Offshore Engineer* Sept. 52/2 Sea & Storm is also..showing a wave data processing unit..which will give virtually realtime treatment of data from wave buoys. **1977** *Navy News* June 44 (Advt.), To undertake training of our customers' engineers/ programmers/technicians on all aspects of software applicable to real-time radar systems.

2. a. Actually existing or present as a state or quality of things; having a foundation in fact; actually occurring or happening. Phr. ***real life***, ***real world*** (passing into senses 3 and 4). Also *attrib.*

1597 Shaks. *Lover's Compl.* 114 His real habitude gave life and grace To appertainings and to ornament, Accomplished in himself, not in his case. **1662** Stillingfl. *Orig. Sacr.* iii. ii. §7 Time..denotes nothing real in its self existing..and so can argue nothing as to the real existence of things from all eternity. *c* **1689** Prior *To Chas. Montague* 4 He can imagin'd pleasures find, To combat against real cares. **1729** Butler *Serm. Hum. Nat.* ii. Wks. 1874 II. 18 Our inward feelings, and the perceptions we receive from our external senses, are equally real. **1771** T. Jefferson *Let.* 3 Aug. in Koch & Peden *Life & Selected Writings* (1944) viii. 358 Considering history as a moral exercise, her lessons would be too infrequent if confined to real life. **1794** Paley *Evid.* iii. ii. (1817) 288 The malady was real, the cure was real, whether the popular explication of the cause was well founded or not. **1801** M. Edgeworth *Belinda* I. iii. 70 Nothing is more unlike a novel than real life. **1816** J. Wilson *City of Plague* ii. iii. 122 More terrible These sights and sounds from the disastrous sky Than all the real terrors of the Plague. **1836** Dickens *Pickw.* (1837) v. 44 A curious manuscript..curious as a leaf from the romance of real life. **1838** J. S. Mill in *Westm. Rev.* XXXI. 28 The writers and readers..in France have..a thirst for something which shall address itself to their real-life feelings. **1852** Mrs. Jameson *Leg. Madonna* Introd. 36 The Caracci school..combined..the study of the antique with the observation of real life. **1876** C. M. Yonge *Womankind* v. 34 Insolence to a governess is an old stock complaint. In real life, I never heard of it from anyone by birth and breeding a lady. **1879** M. Arnold *Irish Cathol.* Ess. 115 From Christianity's being a real source of cure, for a real bondage and misery. **1884** tr. *Lotze's Logic* iii. ii. (1888) II. 208 We call..an event Real which occurs or has occurred, in contradistinction to that which does not occur. **1909** *Daily Chron.* 16 Apr. 3/5 Jocelyn Johnstone..showed ..humour in her sketches of..'real life' scenes. **1923** C. D. Broad *Sci. Thought* xiii. 536 Now, in real life, there are no examples of pure creation. **1937** 'G. Orwell' *Road to Wigan Pier* ix. 182 One could..give everything away, change one's name and start out with no money... But in real life nobody ever does that kind of thing. **1957** P. Suppes *Introd. Logic* xii. 286 Textbook problems (as opposed to real-life problems). **1963** *Amer. Speech* XXXVIII. 296 The instances in which its selection depends on real world context. **1966** *Listener* 19 May 727/1 The Vice Chancellor of Lancaster University strongly believes 'that the university must keep contact with the real world outside'. May I take this opportunity to ask..: (*a*) what is real about the real world? (*b*) why it is always outside? **1977** *National Observer* (U.S.) 15 Jan. 13/1 The roles each of us plays on the revolving stage of the real world have been well described. **1978** P. Marsh et al. *Rules of Disorder* ii. 33 In the perception of our non-academic pupils, school is..a waste of time..not..a part of their 'real' lives.

b. ***real presence***, the actual presence of Christ's body and blood in the sacrament of the Eucharist.

The precise sense attached to *real* depends on the belief held as to the nature or mode of the presence. In the Roman Catholic and Lutheran churches it implies the presence (by transubstantiation or consubstantiation) of the actual body and blood of Christ; by the Church of England it is held that the body and blood are present 'only after an heavenly and spiritual manner'.

1559 Feckman in Strype *Ann. Ref.* I. App. ix. (1709) 25 Doctor Cranmer..did most constantly affirme and defend the real Presence of Chryst's Bodye in the Holie Euchariste. **1563** [Latimer in] Foxe *A. & M.* 979/1 This same presence may be called moste fitly, a reall presence, that is a presence not fained, but a true and faythfull presence. **1655** Fuller *Ch. Hist.* ix. vii. §12 Confessing the reall presence, and that the manner thereof transcended his apprehension. **1687** Dryden *Hind & P.* ii. 32 And to explain what your forefathers meant By real presence in the Sacrament, After long fencing..Your salvo comes, that he's not there at all. **1797** *Encycl. Brit.* (ed. 3) XVIII. 78/1 This account of the Romish doctrine concerning the real presence. **1839** Keightley *Hist. Eng.* I. 322 Wickliffe..seems to have agreed with the present Church of England, in denying a bodily but acknowledging a real spiritual presence in the sacramental elements. **1882** M. Creighton *Hist. Papacy* I. ii. (1899) I. 124 Wyclif did not deny the real presence of Christ in the elements; he denied only the change of substance in the elements after consecration.

3. a. That is actually and truly such as its name implies; possessing the essential qualities denoted by its name; hence, genuine, undoubted.

1559 in Strype *Ann. Ref.* (1824) I. ii. App. vi. 401 Ecclesiasticall lawes made, cannot bynd the universall church of Christe, without the reall assent..of the sea apostolike. **1597** Hooker *Eccl. Pol.* v. lxvii. §2 That which alone is material, namely the real participation of Christ.. by means of this sacrament. **1667** Milton *P.L.* x. 413 Planets..real Eclips Then sufferd. **1712** Addison *Spect.* No. 275 ¶3 Homer tells us that the Blood of the Gods is not real Blood, but only something like it. **1790** Burke *Fr. Rev.* 51 Pressing down the whole by the weight of a real monarchy. **1836** Hor. Smith *Tin Trump.* I. 12 Dressing like a real, and driving like an amateur coachman. **1866** G. Macdonald *Ann. Q. Neighb.* iv. (1878) 52 It was evidently real and not affected doubt.

b. Natural, as opposed to artificial or depicted.

1718 Pope *Arachne* 158 A real bull seems in the piece to roar, And real billows breaking on the shore. **1827** Steuart *Planter's G.* Pref. (1828) 2 In removing Wood, for the purpose of creating Real Landscape, plants of a large size are necessarily employed.

c. *Mus.* (See quots.)

1869 Ouseley *Counterp.* xiv. 83 Counterpoint in more than four real parts, i.e. 'parts which proceed together, and yet have each a different melody'. *Ibid.* xix. 160 A fugue with a subject, the answer to which gives every interval by exact and simple transposition, is called a real fugue. **1889** Prout *Harmony* v. §139 If..the quality of the intervals is exactly the same in the imitations as in the pattern, the sequence will be real, i.e. exact... A real sequence is much rarer than a tonal one.

4. a. That is actually present or involved, as opposed to *apparent*, *ostensible*, etc.; *spec.* in *Econ.*, reckoned by purchasing power rather than monetary or nominal value.

1716 Pope *Let. to Lady M. W. Montagu* 18 Aug., Whatever I write will be the real thought of that hour. **1771** *Junius Lett.* lix. 307, I doubt not they delivered their real sentiments. **1775** Johnson *Journey to Western Islands* 368 Lesley..related so punctiliously, that a hundred hen eggs, new laid, were sold in the Islands for a peny... Posterity has since grown wiser; and having learned, that nominal and real value may differ, they now tell no such stories. **1776** Adam Smith *Wealth of Nations* I. i. v. 39 Labour, like commodities, may be said to have a real and a nominal price. Its real price may be said to consist in the quantity of the necessaries and conveniences of life which are given for it; its nominal price, in the quantity of money. **1802–12** Bentham *Ration. Judic. Evid.* (1827) IV. 644 *note*, There lurks the real reason at the bottom of the ostensible one. **1860** Tyndall *Glac.* ii. vii. 279 With regard to the real explanation of these effects, it may be shown [etc.]. **1870** Lowell *Study Wind.* 249 An imperturbable perception of the real relations of things. **1882** R. Bithell *Counting-House Dict.* 208 The nominal value of a coin is that value which is assigned to it by law, and often differs very materially from its *real* or *metallic* value. **1885** J. L. Joynes tr. *Marx's Wage-Labour & Capital* 10 The real wage expresses the price of labour in relation to the price of other commodities... Real wages may remain the same, or they may even rise, and yet the relative wages may none the less have fallen. **1929** *Soc. Sci. Abstracts* 23 The close similarity of the general price level.. substantiates its use as a measure of 'real income'. **1936** K. A. H. Egerton *Dict. Econ. Terms* (ed. 2) 131 Real wages at such times change at a very different rate, and sometimes in the opposite direction, from nominal or money wages; being based on the purchases a wage at any given time will make. **1964** Gould & Kolb *Dict. Soc. Sci.* 454/1 If a series of national product estimates for several years is divided by a price index, each year's national product being divided by the price index for that year, the resulting series is known as *deflated* or *real* national product, or national product in *real terms*. **1976** *Glasgow Herald* 26 Nov. 1/6 Real earnings have fallen in the past few years and there is no way we can agree to any further reduction in the purchasing power of our members. **1981** *Sunday Times* 26 Apr. 13/4 Despite an urgent maintenance and restoration programme, it [*sc.* the National Trust] is spending less in real terms on looking after its property than it was two years ago.

b. The actual (thing or person); that properly bears the name.

a **1631** Donne *Poems* (1650) 9 The Kings reall, or his stamped face. **1660** F. Brooke tr. *Le Blanc's Trav.* 10 One of them to his thinking favoured very much his companion, and as he was about to follow them, his reall companion called him to come back. **1704** [see horizon 3]. **1774** Goldsm. *Nat. Hist.* (1776) IV. 244 The bag..may rather be considered as a supplemental womb. In the real womb, the little animal is partly brought to perfection. **1813** *Sporting Mag.* XLI. 175 She went the real pace, having passed this extent of country in forty-five minutes. **1840** Macaulay *Ess., Clive*, It was absurd to regard him as the real master of Hindostan. **1869** Ruskin *Q. of Air* §5 From the real sun, rising and setting;—from the real atmosphere [etc.].

c. ***the real thing***: (*a*) The thing itself, as contrasted with imitations or counterfeits; hence *slang*, the 'genuine article'.

1818 Lady Morgan *Autobiog.* (1859) 15 He is the real thing, and no mistake. **1858** Hawthorne *Fr. & It. Notebks.* II. 37 Represented with the vividness of the real thing. **1846** *Punch* 20 June 272/2 You, who will not subscribe to the real thing; come, pull out your purse to the *name*:..although you know that you ask for the 'Ragged Schools',..beg subscriptions for the 'Youths of Limited Circumstances'. **1884** *Art Amateur* Dec. 23/1 Those persons who indulge in ..having..Japanese rooms in their houses, but have only a ludicrous imitation, will be interested in seeing here the real thing. **1902** T. W. H. Crosland *Outlook Odes* 31 My tobacco merchant, who sells me two ounces of the real thing every week. **1939** *War Illustr.* 2 Dec. 365 The 'stand-by' atmosphere of the first few weeks of war may be lost at any moment in the urgency of the 'real thing'. **1977** *Time* 22 Aug. 40/2 But the copied Coke may not work. India's soft-drink fanciers have learned to distinguish between ersatz Coke, which is peddled everywhere on the Indian market, and the Real Thing.

(*b*) *spec.* True love as distinct from infatuation, flirtation, etc.

1857 C. M. Yonge *Dynevor Terrace* I. xi. 173, I could not part with you where we were not sure the 'real thing' was felt for you. **1906** J. Galsworthy *Man of Property* iii. iii. 302 This was none of those affairs of a season that distract men and women about town... This was the real thing! **1919** Wodehouse *Damsel in Distress* v. 61 It had come at last. The Real Thing. George had never been in love before. Not really in love. **1931** J. Cannan *High Table* x. 152 He was afraid that she would think he was just flirting—that it wasn't the Real Thing. **1941** M. McCarthy in *Partisan Rev.* VIII. 327 All that conjugal tenderness had been a brightly packaged substitute for the Real Thing. **1955** E. Waugh *Officers & Gentlemen* ii. ii. 189, I thought of you at the last. Ever since we met I've known I had found the real thing. **1960** *Woman's Own* 19 Mar. 17/2 Once these phases are over, you should be ready for the Real Thing..the man who will be exactly right for *you*. **1973** G. Scott *Water Horse* (1974) xvi. 109 A girl..whom she knew to be looking for the Real Thing in Spain.

d. ***the real McCoy***: see McCoy.

e. ***real tennis*** = tennis *sb.* 1. Also *attrib.*

The usage distinguishes the original game from the modified form which became the more popular after 1874; see lawn-tennis and tennis *sb.* 2. Derivation from real *a.*[1] is a folk etymology.

1880 [see *jeu de paume* s.v. jeu d]. **1902** [see *royal tennis* s.v. royal *a.* 15 a]. **1954** A. S. C. Ross in *Neuphilol. Mitteilungen* LV. 22 The games of real tennis and piquet..are still perhaps marks of the upper class. **1966** *Oxford Mag.* Michaelmas, No. 8, p. 149 A splendid exhibition of real tennis was given at the Merton Street court on Sunday. **1972** *Daily Tel.* (Colour Suppl.) 14 Jan. 25/4 There are 17 Real Tennis courts in use in the country. **1975** *Country Life* 30 Jan. 258/1 Today tennis means to most people lawn tennis, while its..ancestor..has survived under the title 'real tennis'... Only one public school boasts a real tennis court... Canford in Dorset.

f. ***real ale***, a name sometimes applied to draught beer that has been brewed and stored in the traditional way, and which has undergone secondary fermentation of the yeast in the container from which it is dispensed; also called 'cask-conditioned' beer; ***real coffee***, coffee made directly from ground coffee beans, as opposed to 'instant' coffee.

1964 L. Deighton *Funeral in Berlin* iv. 281 Could you find us a little cup of real coffee? **1972** *What's Brewing* Oct., Mr A—— B——..is ripping out the keg taps and replacing them with real ale from wooden barrels. **1973** C. Hutt *Death of Eng. Pub* i. 25 The beer-drinker who feels strongly about the declining quality of his pint has two organisations he can turn to..—the long-established Society for the Preservation of Beers from the Wood, and the more recently formed, more militant CAMRA (Campaign for Real Ale). **1974** N. Freeling *Dressing of Diamond* 201 'Where's the patrol, Gilbert?' 'Be back any minute.' 'Then you might make us some real coffee.' **1974** *Good Beer Guide* (CAMRA) 2 The real ale we are talking about has to stand up to three tests; in the way it is brewed, the way it is stored and the way it is served. **1976** *Evening Standard* 29 Dec., The most popular of about a dozen real ales brought in from distant parts to a growing number of pubs in the capital. **1980** *Times* 23 Sept. 8/3 In the 1970s..the 'real ale' fashion took hold.

5. †**a.** Sincere, straightforward, honest. *Obs.* (freq. in 17th c.).

1597 Bacon *Ess., Ceremonies & Respects* (Arb.) 24 He that is only reall had need haue exceeding great parts of vertue. **1630** *R. Johnson's Kingd. & Commw.* 51 The Dutch hath an honest and reall manner of dealing. **1647** Clarendon *Hist. Reb.* i. §35 If his intentions were real. **1686** tr. *Chardin's Trav. Persia* 173 Supposing he should be real and sincere. **1709** Mrs. Centlivre *Gamester* i. i, If I could believe thee real, my joys would be compleat.

†**b.** True or loyal *to* another. *Obs.*

1642 Earl of Clanricarde in Carte *Ormonde* (1735) III. 79 To haue a person soe full of worth and honour to be firme and reall to me. **1690** *Secr. Hist. Chas. II & Jas. II*, 91 Which, had England been real to the confederate, might have been easily wrested again out of his hand.

c. Free from nonsense, affectation, or pretence; 'genuine'. Also *loosely*, aware of, or in touch with, real life.

1847 Tennyson *Princ.* Concl. 18 They hated banter, wish'd for something real. **1851** Hawthorne *Ho. Sev. Gables* ix, Phoebe's presence made a home about her... She was real! **1880** Mrs. Whitney *Odd or Even?* xxxvi, She had been so near real people who meant every bit of their lives. **1961** *Noble Savage* Fall 12 He [*sc.* Seymour Krim] alludes to something called 'direct writing', and he finds that criticism gets in the way of his 'truer, realer, imaginative bounce'. **1964** *Sunday Express* 1 Mar. 22/5 Most [actors]..are so insincere... Albie..is an exception... He's a real person. **1966** *New Statesman* 17 June 873/2 This was a realler America than I had known in the past, hitching on this or that bandwagon or presidential campaign. **1967** P. Welles *Babyhip* (1969) xxviii. 179 Sometimes I wish I were back in Paris. The people seemed realer. **1969** *Newsweek* 9 June 95 Why suffer all the bad hotels and rotten food and accountants and taxes if you waste the opportunity on stage to be real? **1973** *Scotsman* 7 Aug. 8/5, I notice..the editor-designate of the much discussed 'Scottish International' review telling us that Glasgow is a 'realler' city than Edinburgh. **1976** *New Yorker* 1 Mar. 35/1 'Ellen. Be real for once. I said we'd get together.' 'In your letter you said we'd have dinner.' **1977** *Time* 25 July 45/2 Billy is very sweet and very gentle and very real.

II. 6. *Law.* (Opposed to personal.)

a. Of actions, causes, etc.: Relating to things, or *spec.* to real property (see c).

In early use freq. placed after the sb., and with pl. in *-s*.

1448 *Shillingford's Lett.* (Camden) App. 139 Any action real personall and myxte apon any person or persons. **1535** *Act 27 Hen. VIII*, c. 26 §4 All actions realles, hereafter shalbe conueied, perpetrated, or sued for any landes. **1574** tr. *Littleton's Tenures* 41 If the villaine be demaundant in an accion reall, or plaintife in an action personal. **1603** Owen *Pembrokesh.* (1892) 155 Pleas reall and mixt for landes are and must be sued at home. **1652** Gaule *Magastrom.* 342 All matters or causes, criminall or reall. **1768** Blackstone *Comm.* III. 117 Real actions..which concern real property only. **1818** Cruise *Digest* (ed. 2) III. 491 After a real action was barred by length of time. **1863** H. Cox *Instit.* ii. ix. 512 Real actions, brought for the specific recovery of freeholds.

b. Connected in some way with things or real property: (see quots. and Wharton's *Law Lexicon*).

1467–8 *Rolls of Parlt.* V. 578/2 Lands, Tenementez and other Possessions..in demeane and reall possession. **1625** Burges *Pers. Tithes* 48 How much should bee due, where no Custome, Composition real, or other sufficient Priuiledges takes place. **1666–88** DALLAS *Stiles* (1697) 694 (*heading*) Real Rights. *Ibid.* 797 Disposition.. of certain Lands, Baronies, and others, in Real Warrandice of other Lands formerly Disponed. **1727–41** CHAMBERS *Cycl.* s.v., Customs are said to be real; that is, they determine all inheritances within their extent. **1766** BLACKSTONE *Comm.* II. iii. 28 A real composition is when an agreement is made between the owner of the lands, and the parson or vicar, .. that such lands shall for the future be discharged from payment of tithes, by reason of some land or other real recompence given to the parson, in lieu.. thereof. **1802–12** BENTHAM *Ration. Judic. Evid.* (1827) I. 53 Real evidence, that which is afforded by a being belonging, not to the class of persons, but to the class of things. **1832** AUSTIN *Jurispr.* (1879) I. 59 Real rights (property in things real or real property) are rights which are inheritable. **1837** tr. *Guizot's Hist. Civiliz.* iii. 89 Personal legislation, in contradistinction to real legislation, which is found upon territory.

c. Consisting of immovable property, as lands and houses; esp. ***real estate*** (see ESTATE *sb.* 11); also *attrib.*

1641 *Decay Trade* 2 The price and measure of all our other meanes both personall and reall. **1644** G. PLATTES in *Hartlib's Legacy* (1655) 209 A present estate, either real or personal. **1690** CHILD *Disc. Trade* (1694) 8 Securities of lands and houses [are] rendered, indeed such as we commonly call them, real securities. **1711** STEELE *Spect.* No. 97 ¶5 Their real Estate shall be immediately vested in the next Heir. **1756** [see ESTATE *sb.* 11]. **1827** JARMAN *Powell's Devises* II. 169 The word effects, without the word real, will not.. comprehend land. **1840** *Spirit of Times* 25 Jan. 562/1 A negro, the holder of a ticket in the grand real estate lottery.., came pushing into a lottery office in great excitement. **1843** *Niles' Nat. Reg.* 4 Mar. 5 Real estate bank. .. A committee of the legislature of Arkansas have reported the facts connected with the management of this institution. **1845** STEPHEN *Comm. Laws Eng.* (1874) II. 9 Things real comprise not only the land itself, but also such incorporeal rights as issue out of or are connected with it. **1849** *Knickerbocker* XXXIII. 174 His father had recently made some heavy real-estate purchases. **1854** H. D. THOREAU *Walden* 88 This experience entitled me to be regarded as a sort of real-estate broker by my friends. **1870** PINKERTON *Guide* 27 A sale of real estate by order of Orphans' Court.. must be public. **1880** *Harper's Mag.* Sept. 562 This region was.. seized upon by real-estate speculators. **1892** KIPLING *Lett. of Travel* (1920) 85 The packed real-estate offices; the real-estate agents themselves. **1903** *Westm. Gaz.* 11 Sept. 2/3 The law might almost be forgiven for making no provision for dealing with real-estate-owning paupers. **1965** H. T. ANSOFF *Corporate Strategy* (1968) vi. 104 A company which primarily buys and sells.. may be an investment trust, a pension fund, or a real estate syndicate. **1969** *Sydney Morning Herald* 24 May 30/1 (Advt.), The Real Estate Institute of New South Wales.. will commence the next evening course of lectures in Real Estate and Valuation Practice. **1972** *Accountant* 17 Aug. 193/2 The cannibalization of assets, particularly of real estate subsidiaries. **1978** S. BRILL *Teamsters* vi. 208 He sincerely believed that real-estate investments were the gold mines of the future.

d. ***chattels real***: (see CHATTEL 4 b).

7. †**a.** Consisting of actual things. *Obs. rare.*

1613 PURCHAS *Pilgrimage* VII. ix. (1614) 698 The ceremonies they used to them, were.. verball prayers, reall offerings. *Ibid.* IX. xiv. 912 The Colonie.. haue not onely sent verball, but reall commendations of the place.

b. Relating to, concerned with, things.

1593 G. HARVEY *Pierces Superer.* Wks. (Grosart) II. 162 The most endlesse altercations; being generally rather verbal, then reall, and more circumstantiall, then substantiall. **1620** T. GRANGER *Div. Logike* 143 Logicke is a Rationall, not reall art. **1681** RAY *Corr.* (1848) 130 Making your discoveries and observations public, for.. the advancement of real philosophy. **1697** tr. *Burgersdicius his Logic* II. xv. 64 A Real is when the Attribute of the Question is real; as, 'is a Place a Superficies?' or so. **1845** WHATELY *Logic* in *Encycl. Metrop.* I. 235/1 Those which are called real Definitions, viz. which unfold the nature of the thing. **1870** J. H. NEWMAN *Gram. Assent* I. i. 8 Propositions.. of which the terms stand for things external to us, unit and individual as.. 'the earth goes round the sun'..; these I call real propositions, and their apprehension real.

†**c.** Of written characters: Representing things instead of sounds. *Obs.*

1605 BACON *Adv. Learn.* II. xvi. §2 We understand further, that it is the use of China, and the kingdoms of the High Levant, to write in characters real, which express neither letters nor words in gross, but things or notions. **1668** WILKINS *Real Char.* I. iii. §5. 13 A Real universal Character, that should not signifie words, but things and notions. **1727–41** CHAMBERS *Cycl.* s.v. *Character*, The real character is no chimera; the Chinese and Japonese have already something like it.

d. Corresponding to actuality; true.

1657–83 EVELYN *Hist. Relig.* (1850) I. 87 But, though we can neither see God, nor our souls, we may and can have a real idea of both, without a sensible vision. **1690** LOCKE *Hum. Und.* II. xxx. §5 Ideas of substances are real, when they agree with the existence of things. **1862** H. SPENCER *First Princ.* I. ii. §11 (1875) 32 The impossibility of expanding our symbolic conception of self-creation into a real conception, remains as complete as ever. **1866** G. MACDONALD *Ann. Q. Neighb.* xiv. (1878) 287 Whether a story be real in fact or only real in meaning.

†**8.** Essential, important. *Obs.*⁻¹

1620 LD. HERBERT *Corr.* in *Life* (1886) 349 This being the reallest,.. I need not insist upon some less essential forms.

9. Attached, or pertaining, to scholastic Realism.

1528 TINDALE *Obed. Chr. Man* To Rdr., One holdeth this, an other that. One is reall, an other nominall. **1663** BUTLER *Hud.* I. i. 156 Profound in all the Nominal And Real ways beyond them all.

10. ***real school*** [tr. G. *realschule*: see REALSCHULE]. Applied to a class of schools in Germany which occupy themselves mainly with the sciences and modern languages, as subjects of practical utility. Hence ***real scholar***.

1833 SIR W. HAMILTON *Discuss.* (1852) 552 *Realschulen*, real schools.. because they are less occupied with the study of languages (Verbalia) than with the knowledge of things (Realia). **1836** *Ibid.* 269 The best of our former Real Scholars, when brought into collation with the Latin Scholars could, in general, hardly compete with the most middling of these. **1885** *Guardian* 6 May 697/3 Chapters on the State schools, whether.. real schools, or gymnasia.

III. 11. *Comb.*, as ***real-hearted***, ***-minded***, ***-seeming*** adjs.

a **1866** J. GROTE *Exam. Utilit. Phil.* ii. (1870) 37 The more real-minded the philosopher is, and the less he is the mere echo of others. **1884** J. PARKER *Apost. Life* III. 66 Would.. real-hearted men respect him now? **1948** E. BOWEN *Why do I Write?* 24 You and I, by writing a story, impose shape—on fictitious life, it's true, but on life that is real-seeming enough to be familiar and recognisable. **1951** S. SPENDER *World within World* 310 Reader-writer walk together in a real-seeming dream-alliance leading into gardens inhabited by Stephen Daedalus and Marcel.

B. *adv.* **1.** (Usually with adjs.) Really, genuinely. Also more loosely in later use (orig. *Sc.* and *U.S.*): Very, extremely.

In early use properly an adj. qualifying the phrase ('good turn', etc.) which follows, and only at a later period apprehended as an adv. qualifying the adj. ('good', etc.). Not common in standard use in southern England except to some extent in the orig. construction.

1658 *Whole Duty Man* xiii. §35 The reallest good turn that can be done from one man to another. **1718** J. FOX *Wanderer* No. 17. 116 An Opportunity of doing a real good Office. **1771** MRS. GRIFFITH *Hist. Lady Barton* II. 283 The burning of three real good and substantial houses in this town. **1827** R. H. FROUDE *Rem.* (1838) I. 448 Last Friday was a real fine day. **1885** G. ALLEN *Babylon* vi, It looks real nice. **1887** MABEL WETHERAL *Two N.-C. Maids* xxv. 174, I was real put out to think how [etc.]. **1939** *War Illustr.* 28 Oct. 219/1 If I had not been on fire I could easily have shot down two more. It was real bad luck, but my pals accounted for three besides the one I hit. **1943** K. TENNANT *Ride on Stranger* viii. 77 He's real clever. **1959** J. LUDWIG in *Tamarack Rev.* Summer 7 Some day she'd get real tough with her son Sidney. **1968** *Globe & Mail* (Toronto) 17 Feb. 50/3 (Advt.), Austin Healey Sprite black, radio, a real nice car. **1968** K. WEATHERLY *Roo Shooter* 111 It was real heavy going, and I must have dried the flamin' plugs and points twenty times. **1976** *Daily Mirror* 18 Mar. 24/4 I'm havin' a rest—I feel real listless.

2. (with advbs.) *colloq.* (chiefly *N. Amer.* and *Austral.*).

1893 H. A. SHANDS *Some Peculiarities of Speech in Mississippi* 52 Real down... Used by cultivated whites to mean *exceedingly* or *extremely*. A thing that is extremely nice is said to be *real down* nice. **1924** J. C. FRENCH *Writing* x. 290 Avoid: They live *good* in that camp (say live *well*), I *sure* will write *real* soon (say *surely* will, *really* soon). **1933** R. L. POOLEY in *Amer. Speech* VIII. 61/2 One such [grammarian], commenting on the sentence, 'I will write *real* soon,' corrects *real* to read *really*. This is utter nonsense. No one ever says *I will write really soon*... It simply isn't English. **1942** Z. N. HURSTON in A. Dundes *Mother Wit* (1973) 225/1 De man looked at me real hard for dat. **1947** K. TENNANT *Lost Haven* xix. 317 Everyone said she was lucky... Everything fell out 'real nice' for her. **1959** *Weekly Times* (Melbourne) 30 Sept. (Advt.), How about picking up your phone and asking your B.F.E. dealer to arrange a free demonstration of a '35' on your property real soon? **1967** G. JACKSON *Let.* 13 July in *Soledad Brother* (1971) 121, I felt real bad about that. **1975** D. LODGE *Changing Places* ii. 57 You and I must have lunch together real soon.

C. Absolute or as sb.

†**1.** = REALIST 2. *Obs.*

1519 HORMAN *Vulg.* 93 The wey of the nomynallys and reals is dyuers. **1604** T. WRIGHT *Passions* VI. 298 Those dissenting and contradicting Sectes of.. Realles and Nominalles. **1684** S. G. *Angl. Spec.* 801 W. Ockham headed the Nominals against the Reals, followers of Scotus.

2. a. A real thing; a thing having (or conceived as having) a real existence, either in the ordinary or in a metaphysical sense.

a **1626** BP. ANDREWES *Serm.* (1856) I. 142 The names of His imposing; there is no surer place in logic than from them. His nominals be reals. **1646** SIR T. BROWNE *Pseud. Ep.* 82 Hereunto we know not how to assent in the Generall, as having met with some whose Reals made good their representations. *c* **1810** COLERIDGE in *Lit. Rem.* (1838) III. 332 If we will confound actuals with reals. **1884** tr. *Lotze's Metaph.* 60 A material of reality, a Real pure and simple, which in itself is neither this nor that, but the principle of reality for everything.

†**b.** A piece of real property. *Obs. rare.*

1651 W. G. tr. *Cowel's Inst.* 26 And so of immoveables and realls if aliened by the Husband in his lifetime.

3. ***the real***: That which actually exists, contrasted (*a*) with a copy, counterfeit, etc., (*b*) with what is abstract or notional.

1818 COLERIDGE *On Poesy or Art*, For this does the artist for a time abandon the external real in order to return to it with a complete sympathy with its internal and actual. **1844** MRS. BROWNING *Dead Pan* xxxvi, And the Real is His song. **1852** MRS. STOWE *Uncle Tom's C.* xv, Thus ended.. the ideal of life for Augustine St. Clare. But the real remained. **1870** NEWMAN *Gram. Assent* I. v. 135 Religion has to do with the real, and the real is the particular.

4. *Math.* A real number.

1866 W. R. HAMILTON *Elem. Quaternions* I. i. 10 Such scalars are.. simply the reals (or real quantities) of Algebra. **1940** W. V. QUINE *Math. Logic* 273 The fact that every bounded class of reals has a least bound is the basic formal difference between the reals and the ratios. **1967** CONDON & ODISHAW *Handbk. Physics* (ed. 2) I. ii. 22/1 Apart from the reals and the complex numbers they are the only associative hypercomplex systems with real coefficients and no divisors of zero. **1979** *Proc. London Math. Soc.* XXXVIII. 367 Let x, h, Q denote large reals with $x \geqslant h > Q$.

D. In colloq. phr. ***for real*** (orig. *U.S.*). **a.** as *adj. phr.* Genuine, (in) earnest, true, sincere. Occas. *attrib.*

1954, etc. [see FOR *prep.* 19 g]. **1956** [see PICK *v.*¹ 21 r]. **1972** M. J. BOSSE *Incident at Naha* 55 Was that kid for real? I mean, he didn't look as if he could fight his way out of a paper bag. **1973** *Black Panther* 17 Mar. 8/1 This is no 'scare tactic', it is for real. **1973** W. FAIRCHILD *Swiss Arrangement* vii. 78, I told him I was staying with Mom and that's for real. **1977** B. RANDALL *Fan* 34 Dear Mr. Breen. Are you for real? .. Give us a rest.

b. *adv. phr.* Really, truly, actually; in reality.

1962 J. GLENN in *Into Orbit* 183 Everyone seemed to sense that we were going for real this time. **1964** M. MCLUHAN *Understanding Media* (1967) II. xxx. 320 It was Hitler who gave radio the Orson Welles treatment for real. **1970** E. BULLINS *Theme is Blackness* (1973) 179 Yeah! For real! Shoot me! That's what she says. **1972** J. E. FRANKLIN in W. King *Black Short Story Anthol.* 355 'We'll let her in on our team, see?' 'For real?' 'Not for real, just play-like.' **1977** *R. Air Force News* 22 June–5 July 11/2 Two pilots have in fact done the job 'for real'—both Sqn Ldr Marshall and Flt Lt Dave Fischer have put Harriers down on the deck of HMS Bulwark.

real, obs. form of REEL *sb.*

real estate: see REAL *a.*² 6 c.

realgar (riːˈælgə(r)). Also 8 **realgal**. [a. med.L. *realgar*, ultimately from Arab. *rehj al-ghār* 'powder of the cave': cf. Sp. *rejalgar*, F. *réalgar* (earlier *realgal*, *reagal*, *riagal*), It. *realgale*, and see RESALGAR.] The native or factitious disulphide of ARSENIC (1 b), also called *red*(*sulphide* or *sulphuret of*) *arsenic* and *red orpiment*, used as a pigment and in pyrotechnics.

c **1400** *Lanfranc's Cirurg.* 230 þou schalt in no maner leie þerto realgar, ne noon violent þingis. **1543** TRAHERON *Vigo's Chirurg., Interpr. Strange Wordes* s.v., Realgar is made of brymstone, vnsleked lyme, and orpigment. It kylleth rattes. **1685** BOYLE *Salubr. Air* 75 Divers native Orpimental Minerals, to say nothing of Realgar because it is a factitious combination of Orpiment and Sulphur. **1698** *Phil. Trans.* XX. 199 A Medicine made of red Arsenick, or Realgar Powdered. **1771** WOULFE *ibid.* LXI. 126 Arsenic forms a reddish mass like realgar. **1812** SIR H. DAVY *Chem. Philos.* 457 Sulphur and arsenic readily unite by fusion, and form a red vitreous semitransparent mass. The same substance is found native in different parts of Europe, and is called realgar. **1876** HARLEY *Mat. Med.* (ed. 6) 298 Realgar of Arsenic was in ancient times employed in Medicines, and still is in India.

reali, variant of REALLY *adv.*² *Obs.*

‖**realia** (reɪˈɑːlɪə, riːˈeɪlɪə). [neut. pl. of late L. *reālis* actual, real.] **1.** *Educ.* Objects which may be used as teaching aids but were not made for the purpose. *N. Amer.*

1950 J. S. KINDER *Audio-Visual Materials & Teaching Techniques* xiii. 333 Realia include such items as objects, specimens, samples, relics, artifacts, souvenirs, and even models and dioramas. **1962** *Library Jrnl.* LXXXVII. 819/1 They ignore the miniature models, facsimiles, mock-ups, and realia which one used in construction of exhibitions and bulletin boards. **1970** J. RIDDLE et al. *Non-Book Materials* (prelim. ed.) 44 Realia are entered under title. The title may be taken from the box or accompanying data. Where no title can be found, the catalogues will supply one, e.g. [Robin's egg] (Realia). **1975** *Ontario Libr. Rev.* LIX. 243 The study encompassed seventeen types of audio and visual materials; .. microforms, overhead projectors, sculpture replicas and realia, media kits and simulation games.

2. Real things, actual facts, esp. as distinct from theories about them.

1952 G. SARTON *Hist. Sci.* I. xiv. 362 The *realia*, we should always remember, cannot be learned in books but only in the practice of a scientific profession. *Ibid.* xix. 480 There is a real need of new translations.. fully explained by a scholar.. acquainted not only with philologic details but with all the realia expressed or implied. **1962** Y. MALKIEL in Householder & Saporta *Probl. Lexicogr.* 5 Attention is focused on.. strictly lexical data (at the expense of *realia*, proper names, and the like). **1975** *Times Lit. Suppl.* 25 Apr. 464/1 Takes Christian scholars to task for being too theological about Judaism, for ignoring its *realia*.

realie, obs. Sc. form of REALLY *adv.*¹

realign (riːəˈlaɪn), *v.* [f. RE- 5 a + ALIGN *v.*]

a. *intr.* for *refl.* To fall into line again; to return to previously aligned positions.

1923 *Glasgow Herald* 14 Aug. 7 If France does not meet us half way, enabling the Allied front to realign, there will be a separate reply to Germany.

b. *trans.* To align again or anew. Also *fig.*

1957 V. W. TURNER *Schism & Continuity in African Soc.* v. 131 Private intrigues provide means whereby individuals seek to realign the social structure in pursuit of their own advantage. **1967** COX & GROSE *Organization & Handling Bibl. Rec. by Computer* IV. 93 There is a Restructure program which realigns and copies the data base files. **1973** *Computers & Humanities* VII. 139 The texts are realigned at the place where the match was found.

reaˈlignment. orig. *U.S.* [RE- 5 a.] A new alignment.

1889 in *Public Opinion* 27 Apr., That the time has come for a partisan realignment on the vital economic concerns of to-day. **1896** *N. Amer. Rev.* CLXIII. 700 There need be no realignment of contemplated business plans. **1929** P. HUGHES *Catholic Question 1688–1829* III. ii. 197 A re-alignment in English political life suddenly brought uncertainty to an end. With that re-alignment the Catholic Question emerges. **1935** A. P. HERBERT *What a Word!* iv. 92 Comment in the Lobbies centred round the re-alignment of, etc., etc. **1957** *Times Lit. Suppl.* 20 Dec. 766/2 Clear and virtually immeasurable material benefits, widespread re-alignments of jobs, changes of thinking and attitudes, and alteration of ways of working. **1959** *Economist* 3 Jan. 11/2 The chance thus arose of the concerted realignment of European currencies. **1964** *Ann. Reg. 1963* 78 Externally, political realignments with the Pacific and South East Asia continued, a number of official visits being exchanged. **1979** *Time* 2 Apr. 10/2 In the scramble for realignment in the face of the impending treaty, Hussein has even reconciled with Yasser Arafat.. with whom he has been at bloody odds since 1970.

realism (ˈriːəlɪz(ə)m). [f. REAL *a.*[2] + -ISM; perh. after F. *réalisme* or G. *realismus.*]

1. *Philos.* **a.** The scholastic doctrine of the objective or absolute existence of universals, of which Thomas Aquinas was the chief exponent; (opposed to NOMINALISM and CONCEPTUALISM). Also in later use: The attribution of objective existence to a subjective conception.

1826 R. WHATELY *Logic* 299 Nothing, perhaps, has contributed more to the error of Realism than inattention to this ambiguity. *Ibid.* 300 All these absurdities are in fact but the extreme and ultimate point of Realism. **1828** J. S. MILL in *Westm. Rev.* IX. 155 Their [*sc.* Aristotelian logicians'] classification of names according to the *mode of their signification* (of which the doctrine of the Predicables forms a part) when purified from the taint of Realism which adheres to the expression but without infecting the substance, constitutes a prodigious step in the theory of naming. **1838–9** HALLAM *Hist. Lit.* I. I. iii. 187 Scotus and his disciples were the great maintainers of Realism. **1846** WRIGHT *Ess. Mid. Ages* I. vi. 236 The struggle between nominalism and realism, under different forms, has continued even to the present day. **1874** FISKE *Cosmic Philos.* II. 401 By a subtle realism, he projects the idea of himself out upon the field of phenomena, and deals with it henceforth as an objective reality. **1948** C. HARTSHORNE *Divine Relativity* iii. 122 Even if one takes the 'conceptualist' solution of the problem of nominalism and realism, one need not therefore deny that God may have something corresponding to concepts. **1970** N. WOLTERSTORFF *On Universals* vii. 170 Our position is that of realism and 'nominalism'. Is rapprochement between two such ancient armies possible?

b. (*a*) Belief in the real existence of matter as the object of perception (***natural realism***); also, the view that the physical world has independent reality, and is not ultimately reducible to universal mind or spirit. (Opposed to IDEALISM 1.)

1830 W. HAMILTON in *Edin. Rev.* LII. 169 If the veracity of consciousness be unconditionally admitted.. the doctrine is established which we would call the scheme of Natural Realism or Natural Dualism. *Ibid.* 180 The scheme of Natural Realism, which it is Reid's immortal honour to have been the first.. to embrace. **1836–7** SIR W. HAMILTON *Metaph.* xvi. (1859) I. 293, I would be inclined to denominate those who implicitly acquiesce in the primitive duality as given in consciousness, the Natural Realists or Natural Dualists, and their doctrine, Natural Realism or Natural Dualism. **1872** H. SPENCER *Princ. Psychol.* II. VII. xix. 491 It cannot.. construct its argument, without making many times over that assumption which Realism makes but once. **1881** R. ADAMSON *Fichte* 219 The opposition between Hegelianism on the one hand, and scientific naturalism or realism on the other.

(*b*) In the 20th century, applied to philosophical theories reacting against 19th-century idealism which, while they agree in affirming that external objects exist independently of the mind, differ in their accounts of appearance, perception, and illusion. More recently (opp. to VERIFICATIONISM), the theory that the world has a reality that transcends the mind's analytical capacity, and hence that propositions are to be assessed in terms of their truth to reality, rather than in terms of their verifiability. Cf. also *naïve realism* s.v. NAÏVE *a.* 1 b, NEW REALISM.

The quotations are chosen to give some idea of the range and diversity of views in modern theories of realism.

1906 *Mind* XV. 308 Some of the leading supporters of the new Realism (especially Mr. Moore and Mr. Russell) connect it with an extremely nominalistic type of Logic.. This Logic, however, seems to be quite capable of recognising types such as those of Plato. **1920** D. DRAKE et al. *Ess. Critical Realism* p. vi, Our realism is not a physically monistic realism, or a merely logical realism... To find an adjective that should connote the essential features of our brand of realism seemed chimerical, and we have contented ourselves with the vague, but accurate, phrase *critical realism.* **1920** J. LAIRD *Stud. in Realism* i. 13 Any realism of this kind, even if it defends common sense, defends a common sense which is very sophisticated indeed. **1938** G. D. HICKS *Critical Realism* p. xiii, Realism, as Professor Perry has defined it, stands for the principle that 'things may be, and are, directly experienced without owing either their being or their nature to that circumstance'. **1954** M. R. COHEN *Amer. Thought* ix. 271 The practical consequence of Peirce's realism is his sharp distinction between what is useful and what is true. **1963** J. MACQUARRIE *Twentieth-Cent. Relig. Thought* xvii. 259 In German realism, which stands rather apart from the Anglo-American brand, the influence of phenomenology is noticeable. **1967** *Encycl. Philos.* VII. 80/2 Representative realism also accounts for illusions, dreams, images, hallucinations, and the relativity of perception... [It] is the easiest inference from the scientific account of the causal processes up to the brain in all perceiving and fits other scientific evidence. **1969** L. W. FORGUSON in K. T. Fann *Symposium on J. L. Austin* III. 328 Austin's purpose with regard to both the sense-datum theory and philosophic realism was entirely negative... In his view, the problems.. either aren't problems at all or.. aren't philosophical.. but scientific problems. **1972** K. R. POPPER *Objective Knowl.* p. vii, While I am prepared to uphold to the last the essential truth of commonsense realism, I regard the commonsense theory of knowledge as a subjectivist blunder. **1973** M. DUMMETT *Frege: Philos. Lang.* xiii. 466 The fundamental tenet of realism is that any sentence on which a fully specific sense has been conferred has a determinate truth-value independently of our actual capacity to decide what truth-value is. **1979** *Sci. Amer.* Nov. 139/1 Realism can be stated formally as the belief that a mere description of data is not all that should be required of a theory.

2. a. Inclination or attachment to what is real; tendency to regard things as they really are; any view or system contrasted with IDEALISM 2.

1817 COLERIDGE *Biog. Lit.* 127 It is only so far idealism, as it is at the same time, and on that very account, the truest and most binding realism. **1851** CARLYLE *Sterling* III. ii. (1872) 180 Faithful assiduous studies.. of which, knowing my stubborn realism,.. he told me little. **1858** J. MARTINEAU *Stud. Chr.* 274 The realism of his mind makes him a better critic of the hard Judaical element. **1860** EMERSON *Cond. Life* vi. (1861) 126 Let us replace sentimentalism by realism, and dare to uncover those simple and terrible laws which, be they seen or unseen, pervade and govern.

b. The principle of giving practical subjects the chief place in education. (Cf. REAL *a.*[2] 10.)

1836 SIR W. HAMILTON *Discuss.* (1852) 270 One.. with a stronger bias to realism, in the higher instruction, than is of late.. easily to be found in Germany.

c. orig. *U.S.* (*a*) In legal theory, the doctrine that the law is to be discovered by studying actual legal decisions and procedures, rather than by recourse to enactments or statutes; (*b*) more loosely in political theory, the view that actual political power is the subject-matter of politics, as opp. to doctrine, law, rights, or justice.

1930 J. FRANK *Law & Modern Mind* v. 42 (*heading*) Legal realism. **1930** K. N. LLEWELLYN in *Columbia Law Rev.* XXX. 449 A sophisticated reversion to a sophisticated realism. Gone is the ancient assumption that law is because law is. *Ibid.* 461 (*heading*) Realism as to 'society'. **1951** J. H. HERZ *Polit. Realism & Polit. Idealism* ii. 24 Political Realism has at all times insisted that the nature of politics is fundamentally determined by the struggle for power. **1959** B. CRICK *Amer. Sci. of Polit.* v. 85 The popular character of pragmatic realism as reformism can be seen most vividly in the literature of the era. **1960** G. SCHUBERT *Public Interest* iv. 148 A second thread of Legislative Realism emphasizes the effect of each chamber.. in conditioning the behavior of the individual members. **1961** O. KIRCHHEIMER *Polit. Justice* v. 216 Through the psychological variant of legal realism we have become conscious of all the numerous factors in the judge's personality structure which might become determinative factors of judicial action. **1962** B. C. BORNING *Polit. & Soc. Thought C. A. Beard* ii. 19 The very spirit of science that stimulated Beard and others to aim at realism was closely related to the premise that man by using reason could not only understand but also control his environment. **1968** W. TWINING *Karl Llewellyn Papers* I. ii. 5 At Oxford, American Realism was just another Aunt Sally. **1977** M. CLANCHY in E. Attwooll *Perspectives in Jurisprudence* x. 176 Realism has been given a special meaning in jurisprudential thinking to distinguish between real rules of law and paper rules.

3. a. Close resemblance to what is real; fidelity of representation, rendering the precise details of the real thing or scene.

In reference to art and literature, sometimes used as a term of commendation, when precision and vividness of detail are regarded as a merit, and sometimes unfavourably contrasted with idealized description or representation. It has often been used with implication that the details are of an unpleasant or sordid character.

1856 RUSKIN *Mod. Paint.* IV. viii. §8 (1883) III. 103 To try by startling realism to enforce the monstrosity that has no terror in itself. **1863** D. G. MITCHELL *Sev. Stor., My Farm of Edgewood* 236 Let me illustrate by a little talk, which I think will have the twang of realism about it. **1878** GLADSTONE *Prim. Homer* 27 There is a curious realism in the difficulties which beset the re-establishment of Odusseus in his dominions. **1880** SWINBURNE *Stud. Shak.* 136 The one is a typical example of prosaic realism, the other of poetic reality. **1894** C. L. MORGAN *Psychol. for Teachers* ix. 203 Realism.. involves the introduction of such details as shall assimilate the representation to actual fact, and the incorporation of the results of generalisation in individual persons or concrete things. **1912** LARAN & GASTON-DREYFUS *Courbet* 51 Gautier was astonished at seeing Realism in a shed. **1924** [see EXPRESSIONISM]. **1937** H. READ *Art & Society* iv. 180 My underlying contention, that there is an inherent contradiction between art and vulgarism (or, to confine ourselves to æsthetic terms, between art and realism). *Ibid.* vii. 247 There are, in fact, only these three basic modes—realism, idealism and expressionism. **1957** B. S. MYERS *Art & Civilization* xxvi. 645 The late-nineteenth- and early-twentieth-century realism reappeared in the United States during the depression years after 1929 as a school of Social Realism. **1957** *Observer* 3 Nov. 14/2 Realism was Courbet's answer to the quarrelling schools of French Classicism (Ingres) and Romanticism (Delacroix). **1970** F. MARTI-IBAÑEZ *Adventure of Art* xii. 571/1 Some interpreters regard personal intimacy as the catalyst for Picasso's return to realism. **1977** T. NEVILLE *Challenge of Mod. Thought* xix. 117 It is precisely by means of this extreme realism that Kafka points the inadequacy of the known facts as a guide to ultimate truth.

b. A real fact or experience.

1858 CARLYLE *Fredk. Gt.* x. i. II. 558 A life-pilgrimage consisting.. of realisms oftenest contradictory enough.

realist (ˈriːəlɪst), *sb.* (and *a.*) [f. REAL *a.*[2] + -IST; cf. F. *réaliste.*]

†**1.** One who occupies himself with things rather than words. *Obs. rare.*

1605 CAMDEN *Rem.* (1637) 19 When as it is a greater glory now to be a Linguist, then a Realist. **1623** H. SYDENHAM *Serm. Sol. Occ.* (1637) 30 He that only sings unto God (the vocale professor) he doth but talk of his wondrous work, but he that psalmes it (the realist in Christianity) he glories in his holy name.

2. *Philos.* An adherent or advocate of Realism (as opposed either to NOMINALIST or to IDEALIST).

a **1695** WOOD *Hist. & Ann. Univ. Oxon.* an. 1340 (1792) I. I. 437 The faction now of the Nominalists and Realists being very rife and frequent in the University. **1725** WATTS *Logic* II. iii. §4 In the colleges of learning, some are for the nominals, and some for the realists. **1832** tr. *Sismondi's Ital. Rep.* vi. 130 He fancied himself, however, a philosopher, and took a part in the quarrel between realists and nominalists. **1836–7** [see REALISM 1 b]. **1864** BOWEN *Logic* x. 330 The Realist, who believes in the objective validity of our external perceptions. **1884** tr. *Lotze's Metaph.* I. vii. (1887) I. 217 While the Idealist conceives his one principle as a restlessly active Idea, the Realist conceives his as something objective.

3. a. One devoted to what is real, as opposed to what is fictitious or imaginary.

1847 EMERSON *Repr. Men, Napoleon* Wks. (Bohn) I. 370 He is a realist, terrific to all talkers, and confused truth-obscuring persons. **1889** *Spectator* 28 Sept., The multitude of protectionists do not dream. They are hard, if mistaken, realists.

b. An artist or writer addicted to realism.

1870 SWINBURNE *Ess. & Stud.* (1875) 337 No modern realist has excelled in quaint homeliness.. Piero's study of a Nativity. **1874** L. STEPHEN *Hours in Library* (1892) II. vi. 193 [Fielding] is, indeed, as hearty a realist as Hogarth.

c. One who adheres to or is influenced by principles of realism (sense 2 c).

1930 K. N. LLEWELLYN in *Columbia Law Rev.* XXX. 463 The problem calls for exploration, from the realist's angle, by cautious study of detail. **1954** M. R. COHEN *Amer. Thought* ii. 64 The realists insist that any theory of value that is not arbitrary must be based on actual experience. **1960** G. SCHUBERT *Public Interest* iv. 142 Political scientists generally.. appear to agree with those Realists who insist that there must be a general consensus to accept the decisions of public officials, if a democratic polity is to exist. **1971** CHAMBLISS & SEIDMAN *Law, Order & Power* i. 2 The American legal realists, who insisted that we must study the *law in action* as well as the *law in the books.* **1977** M. CLANCHY in E. Attwooll *Perspectives in Jurisprudence* x. 176 The historian of law will tend to be a realist.

4. *attrib.* or as *adj.* Pertaining to, characteristic of, realists.

1845 MAURICE *Mor. Philos.* in *Encycl. Metrop.* II. 644/1 It was this realist spirit.. which really held back the nominalism of the schools. **1871** KINGSLEY *At Last* ii, As long as the nominalist and the realist schools of thought keep up their controversy. **1874** R. TYRWHITT *Sketch Club* 1 They direct attention to good realist landscape. **1931** R. POUND in *Harvard Law Rev.* XLIV. 697, I approach the subject of the call for a realist jurisprudence.. with some humility. **1959** HART & HONORÉ *Causation in Law* iv. 92 The general scepticism as to the possibility of framing rules which developed into the 'Realist' movement of the 1930's. **1977** *Dædalus* Summer 58 We may discover that the realist paradigm, which stresses the primacy of foreign policy, has to be seriously amended, not only for the present but for the past.

realistic (riːəˈlɪstɪk), *a.* [f. prec. + -IC.]

1. a. Characterized by artistic or literary realism; representing things as they really are.

1829 H. C. ROBINSON *Diary* 13 Aug. (1967) 102 [Goethe] repeated the remark which is one of his fixed ideas that it is by.. facts that even a poetical view of nature is to be.. authenticated... It is this which had made Goethe a *realistic* poet, as opposed to the idealism of such poetry as Wordsworth's. **1856** EMERSON *Eng. Traits, Literature* Wks. (Bohn) II. 104 How realistic or materialistic in treatment of his subject is Swift. **1874** L. STEPHEN *Hours in Library* (1892) II. ii. 63 Crabbe, like all realistic writers, must be studied at full length. *Ibid.* vi. 193 His scenery is as realistic as a photograph. **1887** *Spectator* 26 Mar. 421/2 A woman in a realistic novel murders her child. **1943** *Ulster: Brit. Bridgehead* (H.M.S.O.) 6 (*caption*) This realistic picture shows British troops in training in Northern Ireland. **1971** *Hi-Fi Sound* Feb. 67/3 High fidelity stereo at its most successful is wide-ranging and realistic, analytical and rich in detail.

b. That conceives or imagines (a thing) as real.

1858 J. MARTINEAU *Stud. Chr.* 171 That realistic mode of conception in which alone a true atoning doctrine can rest in peace.

2. Concerned with, or characterized by, a practical view of life.

1862 'SHIRLEY' [J. Skelton] *Nugæ Crit.* x. 436 Carlyle's.. speculative genius (for his genius is speculative, however realistic it may appear in certain aspects). **1869** SEELEY *Ess. & Lect.* iii. 87 Could not be reconciled to life by any plain view of things, by any realistic calculations. **1936** *Sun* (Baltimore) 26 Feb. 1/5 Mr. Eden, although doubting his wisdom, wished Chamberlain success in his 'realistic' search for lasting peace. **1962** *Listener* 12 Apr. 626/2 Neither a minimum property qualification nor even a simple educational test.. would be realistic or just in the present situation of South Africa. **1963** *Observer* 3 Nov. 33/3 'Realistic' can vary from its theatre meaning of 'with damp washing' to its place at the top of the conjugation 'I am realistic, you have compromised, he has sold out'. **1973** *Howard Jrnl.* XIII. 321 Realistic payment of prisoners is a novel idea to students of the British penal system.

3. Of or pertaining to realists in philosophy; of the nature of philosophical realism.

1843 J. S. MILL *Logic* I. I. viii. 197 The philosophers who overthrew Realism.. retained long afterwards, in their own philosophy, numerous propositions which could only have a rational meaning as part of a Realistic system. **1874** J. FISKE *Cosmic Philos.* I. I. v. 122 The realistic tendency—the disposition to mistake words for things—is a vice inherent in all ordinary thinking. **1884** tr. *Lotze's Metaph.* 362 The

Realistic view inclines to treat general principles of this kind . . as designations of mere matters of fact, which might have occurred differently [etc.].

Hence **rea'listically** *adv.*, in a realistic manner, with realism. Also **rea'listicize** *v.*, *trans.* to make realistic.

1868 H. C. MERIVALE in *Fortn. Rev.* Nov. 476 Let us look a little more closely and 'realistically', as the phrase now runs, at the features of New World landscape. **1874** L. STEPHEN *Hours in Library* (1892) II. vii. 233 [He] painted the truth as realistically as Crabbe. **1900** H. D. TRAILL in *Contemp. Rev.* Feb. 200 (*heading*) Romance Realisticized.

reality (ri:'ælɪtɪ). Also 6 **realyte**, 7 **reallity**. [ad. med.L. *realitas* (1120 in Du Cange), or F. *réalité* (16th c.): see REAL *a.*² and -ITY.]

1. a. The quality of being real or having an actual existence.

1550 BALE *Eng. Votaries* II. 49 Sigebertus sayth, Realyte they ioyned to their sacramentall breade, to make the people beleue it to be Christes naturall body. **1620** MELTON *Astrolog.* 20 Your discourse . . hath no Realitie or Essence in it. **1651** HOBBES *Leviathan* III. xl. 250 The reality of his Conferences with God. **1711** ADDISON *Spect.* No. 110 ¶6 Lucretius . . makes no doubt of the Reality of Apparitions. **1790** PALEY *Horæ Paul.* i. 4 It proves the general reality of the circumstances. **1813** SHELLEY *Q. Mab* VII. 63 Fancy's thin creations to endow With manner, being, and reality. **1861** E. GARBETT *Boyle Lect.* 13 The presence or absence of faith . . no more affects the reality of the truths revealed, than sight creates the material objects of the natural world.

b. of feelings, etc. (with implication of sense 2).

1649 CROMWELL *Let.* 19 Oct. in *Carlyle*, By these you will see the reality of my intentions to save blood. **1686** tr. *Chardin's Trav. Persia* 36 The Port had never till then question'd the Truth and Reality of the Proposals. **1693** T. POWER in *Dryden's Juvenal* xii. Argt., He professes the reality of his Friendship, and the sincerity of his Intentions.

c. Correspondence to fact; truth. ? *Obs.*

1793 SMEATON *Edystone L.* §72 The reality of the assertion seemed however then incredible to Dr. Spry.

d. Suggestion of, resemblance to, what is real.

1856 STANLEY *Sinai & Pal.* xiii. (1858) 431 The simplicity and reality of a teaching which took its stand on the ordinary sights and sounds still seen and heard in the same land. **1896** *Harper's Mag.* Apr. 680/1 The showy girl and her showy accessories were reproduced on the canvas with almost startling reality.

†**2. a.** Sincere devotion or loyalty *to* a person; sincerity or honesty of character or purpose. *Obs.*

1652 FULLER *Holy & Prof. St.* (ed. 3) v. xviii. 466 We want not a will but wait a time, to express our reality to the Emperour. *a* **1657** R. LOVEDAY *Lett.* (1663) 126 A perfect confirmation of the opinion I ever cherished of your reality. **1665** MARVELL *Corr.* Wks. 1872–5 II. 187, I believe there is nothing but reality among the partys. **1677** W. HUBBARD *Narrative* 22 In token of the abovesaid Sachims reality in this Treaty. *a* **1761** LAW *Comf. Weary Pilg.* (1809) 54 If thy faith and desire does not seek and cry to Christ for them in the same reality as the lame asked to walk and the blind to see.

†**b.** A sincere expression of opinion or feeling.

a **1679** T. GOODWIN *Work of Holy Spirit* vii. Wks. 1704 V. 165 Will you take one of Paul's realities? (I must not term them complements).

3. a. Real existence; what is real; the aggregate of real things or existences; that which underlies and is the truth of appearances or phenomena.

1647 H. MORE *Song of Soul* I. *Psychoroia* Pref., God doth not fill the World with his Glory by words and sounds, but by Spirit, and Life, and Reality. **1663** COWLEY *College* Wks. 1710 II. 623 To carry it on from Discourse and Design to Reality and Effect. **1818** SHELLEY *Rev. Islam* VII. xvi, Like sweet reality among Dim visionary woes. **1864** SKEAT *Uhland's Poems* 16 What morning's dreams had promised, proved Reality when eve drew near. **1877** E. R. CONDER *Bas. Faith* iv. 178 The universe of Reality is built on Truth. **1884** tr. *Lotze's Metaph.* I. vii. (1887) I. 217 Limitations . . imposed by Reality on itself and within which it is.

b. *in reality*, really, actually, in fact. †Also *in reality of fact*.

1679 B. THOROGOOD *Succession* 5 Not by fiction of Law, but in reality. **1687** A. LOVELL tr. *Thevenot's Trav.* I. 229 In reality, the life of a Corsair is most wretched life. **1690** LOCKE *Hum. Und.* I. ii. §13 This Saying . . amounts, in reality of Fact, to no more but this. **1761** HUME *Hist. Eng.* III. lxi. 321 The military being now in appearance, as well as in reality, the sole power which prevailed in the nation. **1850** McCOSH *Div. Govt.* III. i. (1874) 321 Doubtless they intend thereby to benefit the cause of religion, but they are in reality doing it serious injury. **1869** J. MARTINEAU *Ess.* II. 166 In words, he does; in reality, he does not.

4. A real thing, fact, or state of things.

1646 SIR T. BROWNE *Pseud. Ep.* 113 Not to receive figures for realities. **1710** ADDISON *Tatler* No. 165 ¶1 To distinguish between Realities and Appearances. **1781** COWPER *Hope* 68 'Tis grave philosophy's absurdest dream, . . That . . earth has no reality but woe. **1860** TYNDALL *Glac.* II. i. 239 What effort of the imagination could transcend the realities here presented to us? **1884** F. TEMPLE *Relat. Relig. & Sci.* vii. (1885) 200 Their genuine success for a time has been enough to show that they rested on a reality.

5. a. The real nature or constitution *of* something; also without const., the real thing or state of things.

1690 LOCKE *Hum. Und.* II. xxx. §2 Our simple Ideas are all real, all agree to the Reality of things. **1756** WASHINGTON *Lett.* Writ. 1889 I. 404 You entertain notions very different from the reality of the case. **1875** JOWETT *Plato* (ed. 2) V. 130 He probably suspected . . that the appearance of the heavens did not agree with the reality.

b. That which constitutes the actual thing, as distinguished from what is merely apparent or external.

1840 MACAULAY *Ess., Clive*, A formal grant of the powers of which he already possessed the reality. **1861** M. PATTISON *Ess.* (1889) I. 45 Thick walls and turrets at the angles gave the whole the aspect and the reality of a fortress. **1878** J. P. HOPPS *Jesus* vii. 27 The reality and not the mere show of prayer.

6. *Law.* †**a.** = REALTY² 3. **b.** (See quot.)

1628 SIR E. COKE *Upon Littleton* II. xi. §177 Chattels . . Reall, because they concerne the realtie. **1706** PHILLIPS (ed. Kersey) s.v., In a Law-sense, Reality or Realty is oppos'd to Personalty. **1845–56** *Bouvier's Law Dict. U.S.* s.v. *Real*, *Reality of Laws*, those laws which govern property, whether real or personal, or things; the term is used in opposition to *Personality of laws*.

7. *attrib.* and *Comb.*, as ***reality content, control, -revealer, value***; ***reality-based, -centred*** adjs.; **reality principle**, the principle propounded by Freud that the actual conditions of living modify the pleasure-seeking activity of the libido; **reality-testing**, the testing of an emotion or thought in a real-life context; also *attrib.*; hence **reality-test** *sb.* and *v.*, **-tested** *ppl. a.*

1960 L. PINCUS *Marriage* I. 25 A challenge to move forward to fuller and more reality-based relations. **1962** *Listener* 19 Apr. 683/1 These concepts themselves keep the child's thinking 'reality-centred'. **1951** J. M. FRASER *Psychol.* x. 112 When we find someone in whose life . . phantasy achievements occupy a very large place, we are probably justified in thinking that the reality-content of his motivation is a little low. **1949** 'G. ORWELL' *Nineteen Eighty-Four* I. 37 Whatever was true now was true from everlasting to everlasting. . . All that was needed was an unending series of victories over your own memory. 'Reality control', they called it: in Newspeak, 'doublethink'. *Ibid.* 54 It's merely a question of self-discipline, reality-control. **1921** R. MACAULAY *Dangerous Ages* xii. 236 Your ego is at present in . . an impermanent stage in its struggle towards the adult level of the reality-principle. **1922** C. J. M. HUBBACK tr. *Freud's Beyond Pleasure Princ.* i. 5 Under the influence of the instinct of the ego for self-preservation it [*sc.* the pleasure-principle] is replaced by the 'reality-principle'. **1954** D. RIESMAN *Individualism Reconsidered* xxii. 345 By the reality principle alone, mankind could not be governed. **1957** N. FRYE *Anat. of Criticism* (1971) ii. 75 In literature, what entertains is prior to what instructs, . . the reality-principle is subordinate to the pleasure-principle. **1968** *Listener* 22 Feb. 244/1 The real world—where there are limits on what is possible . . where . . the reality principle operates. **1976** S. HYNES *Auden Generation* vi. 185 It is the existence of Europe, and not any political doctrine that is the reality principle here. **1962** A. HUXLEY *Island* ix. 136 Murugan calls it dope. . . We, on the contrary, give the stuff good names—the *moksha*-medicine, the reality-revealer, the truth-and-beauty pill. *Ibid.* 141 'Which is the easy way?' Will asked. 'Education and reality-revealers.' **1925** J. RIVIERE tr. *Freud's Papers on Metapsychol.* in *Coll. Papers* IV. 20 Their entire disregard of the reality-test. **1968** N. N. HOLLAND in Levine & Madden *Art Victorian Prose* 333 The more we reality-test a work of literature, the more we become aware of the reality of ourselves as separate beings. **1960** L. PINCUS *Marriage* I. 19 Some remnants of ego (reality-tested experience) may . . be repressed. **1925** J. RIVIERE tr. *Freud's Papers on Metapsychol.* in *Coll. Papers* IV. 16 One mode of thought-activity was split off; it was kept free from reality-testing and remained subordinated to the pleasure-principle alone. **1953** J. STRACHEY tr. *Freud's Interpretation of Dreams* II. in *Coll. Works* V. 566 In other words it becomes evident that there must be a means of 'reality-testing' (i.e. testing things to see whether they are real or not). **1955** M. LASEROWITZ *Struct. of Metaphysics* ii. 72 These then contribute their psychic charge, which both intensifies our feeling of disquietude and weakens our reality-testing abilities. **1960** L. PINCUS *Marriage* I. 20 The more healthy process of reality-testing and reassimilation. **1974** S. A. RENSHON *Psychol. Needs & Polit. Behav.* iv. 44 The principle of adequate reality testing allows us to come to grips with this problem. **1923** Reality-value [see IMAGE *sb.* 5 a]. **1961** *Listener* 23 Nov. 856/2 From the point of view of emancipation, as opposed that is to the point of view of truth or (as he called it) reality value, Freud was deeply affected by two considerations.

realizable ('ri:əlaɪzəb(ə)l), *a.* [f. REALIZE *v.*² + -ABLE.] That may be realized, in senses of the vb. (Common from *c* 1860.)

1848 *Tait's Mag.* XV. 254 He is establishing a property realisable only by his death. **1853** KANE *Grinnell Exp.* xli. (1856) 379 Warmth . . was realizable and apparent. **1881** G. ALLEN *Vignettes fr. Nature* ix. 88 A hopeful progress towards a . . realisable Paradise in the future.

Hence '**realizableness**, '**realizably** *adv.*; also ˌ**realiza'bility**.

1886 *Manch. Exam.* 10 Feb. 3/3 All the little details which give charm and realisableness to biography. **1885** *Ibid.* 18 Mar. 3/3 Its persons and its situations alike are well and realisably conceived. **1975** *Nature* 20 Mar. p. xiv (Advt.), The emphasis throughout is on the theoretical foundations of optimum source synthesis, including conditions for physical realizability and mathematical methods for satisfying them.

realization (ˌri:əlaɪ'zeɪʃən). [f. REALIZE *v.*² + -ATION.] The action or result of realizing.

1. a. The action of making real or investing with reality; the process of becoming or being made real; conversion into real fact.

1611 COTGR., *Realisation*, a realization, a realizing, a making real. **1799** W. TAYLOR in *Monthly Rev.* XXIX. 148 Conscious of the . . value of his lofty views, and desirous of dying for them . . to secure the trust of their realization. **1815** WRAXALL *Hist. Mem.* I. 243 No reflexions . . on the indecorum . . in the proceeding interposed to prevent its immediate realization. **1880** McCARTHY *Own Times* III. xxxvi. 132 There is as yet no sign of the realisation of the fears which he expressed.

b. A case or instance of this.

1837 HT. MARTINEAU *Soc. Amer.* III. 259 Such a realisation of high morals . . as the world has not yet beheld. **1853** KANE *Grinnell Exp.* v. (1856) 38 The rider seemed one with his craft, an amphibious realization of the centaur. **1966** *Guardian* 1 Sept. 7/3 Ralph Ortiz, American and destroyer of pianos . . doesn't call them happenings any more, he drawls them 'realisations'. **1976** *Southern Even. Echo* (Southampton) 6 Nov. 7/8 Another well-made film, John Huston's realisation of the Rudyard Kipling short story 'The Man Who Would Be King', is showing at the end of next week at the Palace, Bordon.

c. *Math.* An instance or embodiment of an abstract group as the set of symmetry operations or the like of some object or set.

1954 BEAUMONT & BALL *Introd. Mod. Algebra & Matrix Theory* iv. 135 Find a realization in geometry of the group consisting of the elements e, a, a^2, a^3, a^4, a^5 where $a^6 = e$, the identity of the group. **1965** PATTERSON & RUTHERFORD *Elem. Abstract Algebra* ii. 52 A particular member of an equivalence class is called a realisation . . of the corresponding abstract group. **1979** *Proc. London Math. Soc.* XXXVIII. 260 But this coequalizer, if computed in $\mathscr{T}$ (or in $\mathscr{F}$), would yield precisely the geometric realization $|K|$ of K . . so we have simply to prove that the coequalizer is preserved by the embedding $\mathscr{F} \rightarrow \mathscr{E}$.

d. *Statistics.* A particular series which might be generated by a specified random process.

1957 KENDALL & BUCKLAND *Dict. Stat. Terms* 242 A realisation of a stochastic process $\{x_t\}$ is one of the series of values $(. . x_{-2}, x_{-1}, x_0, x_1, . .)$ to which it may give rise. The realisation may be regarded as a 'member' of the process in the same way that an individual observation is regarded as the member of a population. **1965** COX & MILLER *Theory Stochastic Processes* i. 9 The realization illustrates well the very irregular behaviour of the system. **1975** D. R. BRILLINGER *Time Series* ii. 18 Once a θ has been generated (in accordance with its probability distribution), the function $X(t, \theta)$, with θ fixed, will be described as a realization, trajectory, or sample path of the time series.

2. a. The action of forming a clear and distinct concept, or the concept thus formed.

1828 PUSEY *Hist. Enq.* I. 157 His own views were rather dim . . conceptions than any full realization of the truths which flashed across rather than dwelt upon his mind. **1874** GREEN *Short Hist.* vi. §4. 299 His [Colet's] faith stood simply on a vivid realization of the person of Christ.

b. *Linguistics.* The phonetic, phonological, graphic, or syntactic manifestation of a linguistic unit, structure, or set of features. Also *attrib.*

1954 PEI & GAYNOR *Dict. Linguistics* 6 *Actualization*, the perceptible result of the articulation of the phonemic variants or of the archiphoneme. . . Also called *realization*. **1968** *Language* XLIV. 285 A transformation places an element in position, and a realization rule provides a spelling in terms of the alphabet of the neighboring component. **1971** R. FOWLER in *Archivum Linguisticum* II. 131 If I understand the implications of Chomsky's rule, it would seem that his presentation of deep structure has been misleadingly influenced by accidents of surface-structure realization. *Ibid.* 133 TG theory . . offers a pattern for what I call 'realization rules'—rules which effect the transition between combinations of feature sets and strings of morphemes. **1971** B. MAFENI in J. Spencer *Eng. Lang. W. Afr.* 102 The two words 'de' in 'de way' and in 'you de waste' are spelt alike, but they are actually two different lexical and grammatical items with different phonetic realisations. **1972** *Language* XLVIII. 384 All speakers clearly simplify to a certain extent the phonetic realization of words derived from their own languages, and yet pronounce them with their sound structures more intact than do non-native speakers. **1977** *Canad. Jrnl. Linguistics* 1976 XXI. II. 198 Important questions remain about Halliday's model, particularly as regards the precise relationship between meaning potential and its realization at the level of form and the nature and details of the realization rules which connect the two.

3. a. The action of converting (paper money, property, etc.) into a more available form; in later use chiefly applied to the sale of stock, or of a bankrupt's estate, in order to obtain the money value. **b.** The action of obtaining or acquiring (a sum of money, a fortune, etc.).

1796 MORSE *Amer. Geog.* II. 61 In 1777, a judicious realization of the paper took place; and silver, with national bank notes, form a sure medium. **1800** *Asiat. Ann. Reg., Proc. Parl.* 12/2 When the estimate . . was brought before the Committee, . . doubts were stated as to the realization of the net revenue. **1813** WELLINGTON in Gurw. *Desp.* X. 52 Some authority . . which should superintend the realization of the resources of the country. **1881** *Times* 11 Apr. 9/3 Bankruptcy legislation . . should intrust the creditors with the realization of the insolvent's estate. **1887** *Daily News* 10 Mar. 6/8 After a rise of nearly one in French Rentes some realisations were inevitable.

attrib. **1895** *Westm. Gaz.* 6 June 6/1 The new company was to be a realisation company, and not a trading concern. **1896** *Ibid.* 30 July 6/1 The price of the stock . . relapsed on some realisation sales.

4. *Mus.* The action of completing or enriching the texture of a piece of music left sparsely notated by a composer; also a piece of music so completed or enriched.

1911 E. NEWMAN tr. *Schweitzer's J. S. Bach* II. xxxv. 447 The only original instrument to be considered in connection with the realisation of the thorough-bass is the organ. **1946** *Penguin Mus. Mag.* Dec. 92 There is an atmosphere about these 'realisations' by Nadia Boulanger which is usually absent from our choral recordings. **1954** *Grove's Dict. Mus.* (ed. 5) VII. 69/1 *Realization*, a useful modern term for the setting forth of a thorough-bass in full harmony, with more or less elaborate textures, from a continuo part, either at sight in performance or in editing old music. **1958** *Listener* 4 Dec. 964/3 His [*sc.* Roman's] realization of Leo's *Dixit*, which he conducted in 1747, shows how far his predilection for the Italians went. **1959** *Collins Mus. Encycl.* 534/1

Realization, the act of completing the harmony of a 17th- or 18th-cent. work by providing a keyboard accompaniment based on the indications afforded by the figured bass. **1966** *Listener* 10 Mar. 364 Deryck Cooke's fine realization of Mahler's tenth symphony hardly received its due on Wednesday. **1980** *Early Music* Jan. 109/2 The continuo realization by Claire Caillard follows the principles of Saint Lambert.

Hence **reali'zational** *a.*

1965 LD. NORTHBOURNE tr. *Schuon's Light on Ancient Worlds* 66 The Biblical, mystical and 'realizational' character of Christianity. **1968** *Language* XLIV. 574 Working with Potawatomi, I found the rewrite format surprisingly easy to set up. The realizational format was rather more difficult. **1972** *Ibid.* XLVIII. 373 The realizational rule that, in his analysis, provides the input for the vowel-reduction rule by also converting *o* to *ö*.. would have to re-apply in order to convert *u* to *ü* again. *Ibid.* 408 The present article sets the frame for a wider study of suffixal *j* in Germanic by linking the realizational rules of underlying *j* in two Germanic dialects—Old English and Gothic. **1979** *Trans. Philol. Soc.* 203 Vowel-inventories are much less varied than those of the consonants, but there is one realizational difference which suggests interesting patterns of historical change.

† **'realize**, *v.*[1] *Obs.*—[0] [ad. obs. It. *realizzare*: see REAL *a.*[1] and -IZE.] (See quot.)

1611 FLORIO, *Realizzáre*, to reallize or make Kingly.

realize ('riːəlaɪz), *v.*[2] [f. REAL *a.*[2] + -IZE, perh. after F. *réaliser* (16th c. in Hatz.-Darm.).]

1. a. *trans.* To make real, to give reality to (something merely imagined, planned, etc.); to convert into real existence or fact; †to show the reality or truth of (a statement).

In common use from *c* 1750 with a variety of objects, as ideas or ideals, schemes, theories, hopes, fears, etc., and freq. in passive.

1611 COTGR., *Realiser*, to realize, to make of a reall condition, estate, or propertie; to make reall. **1661** GLANVILL *Van. Dogm.* 22 It will be as hard to apprehend, as that an empty wish should remove mountains; a supposition which, if realized, would releave Sisyphus. **1684** T. HOCKIN *God's Decrees* 322 We shall but make up the story of Icarus, and realize the fable. **1742** YOUNG *Nt. Th.* III. 517 Rich death, that realizes all my cares, Toils, virtues, hopes; without it a chimera! **1755** JOHNSON *Let. to Miss Boothby* 20 Dec., Designs are nothing in human eyes till they are realised by execution. **1763** J. BROWN *Poetry & Music* v. 46 In Support of the Truth of these Deductions, let us now endeavor to realize them; by shewing that such Consequences did in Fact arise in ancient Greece. **1812** WELLINGTON in *Sporting Mag.* XXXIX. 6 Nor has the experience of any officer realized the stories which all have read. **1845** MCCULLOCH *Taxation* III. ii. (1852) 441 These expectations were rarely realised. **1875** JOWETT *Plato* (ed. 2) III. 154 Ideals are none the worse because they cannot be realized in fact.

b. To make realistic or apparently real.

1769 A. FERGUSON *Inst. of Moral Philos.* VI. v. 257 Peevishness..tends to realize imaginary evils. **1779** SHERIDAN *Critic* II. ii, *Dangle.* Well, that will have a fine effect. *Puff.* I think so, and helps to realize the scene. **1865** *Strauss' Life Jesus* II. II. lxxxii. 299 The introduction of features that tend to realize and strengthen his account.

absol. **1859** LONGF. *Hyperion* II. viii, He [Goethe] does not so much idealize as realize. **1885** JANE HARRISON *Stud. Grk. Art* vii. 305 There the artist seemed well-nigh compelled to realism, and after all he has realized ideally.

c. To convert *into* by making real.

1872 LOWELL *Dante* Pr. Wks. 1890 IV. 207 His instinct as a poet..realized her into woman again.

d. *Mus.* To complete a piece of music left sparsely notated by a composer; to enrich the texture of a work, esp. by orchestrating music written for a single voice or instrument.

1911 E. NEWMAN tr. *Schweitzer's J. S. Bach* II. xxxv. 451 Our forces are different from those of Bach's day. Orchestra and choir are much larger..; if we realise the thorough-bass on the same scale it sounds too loud. **1947** A. EINSTEIN *Mus. in Romantic Era* ix. 98 To interpret the role of the piano in orchestral form, to 'realize' it—which means to coarsen it naturalistically. **1958** A. JACOBS *New Dict. Mus.* 304 *Realize*, to work out in full and artistically such music as was originally left by its composer in a sparsely-notated condition... Though lacking the advantage of being self-explanatory, 'realize' is superior to 'arrange' in this context since it avoids the implication of alteration. **1980** *Early Music* Jan. 111/2 Other reconstruction work has involved realizing short score into full score (as in parts of the Overture in D).

2. a. To make real as an object of thought; to present as real; to bring vividly or clearly before the mind.

1646 H. LAWRENCE *Comm. Angells* 146 A lively faith realizeth things, and makes them present. **1750** JOHNSON *Rambler* No. 60 ¶1 An Act of the Imagination, that realises the Event however fictitious, or approximates it however remote. **1798** *Geraldina* II. 235, In conjure up frightful forms which my imagination realizes. **1888** *Harper's Mag.* Apr. 806/1 To a certain degree the story realizes him.

b. Const. *to* (the mind, a person).

1682 FLAVEL *Fear* 37 It is the use..of faith to realize to the soul the invisible things. **1719** DE FOE *Crusoe* II. i, It was ..so realized to me, that..I could not be persuaded but that it was..true. **1870** EMERSON *Soc. & Solit., Domestic Life*, The child realizes to every man his own earliest remembrance.

c. Especially *to* (oneself or one's own mind).

1694 in C. Mather *Magn. Chr.* (1853) II. 369 Let us now realize unto ourselves that great and notable day of the Lord. **1778** A. HAMILTON *Wks.* (1886) VII. 538 Realize to yourself the consequence of having a congress despised at home and abroad. **1842** ARNOLD in *Life* (1844) II. 313 Strengthen my faith, that I may realize to my mind the things eternal. **1867** HOWELLS *Ital. Journ.* 170 They might thus realize to themselves something of the earnestness which animated the elder Christian artists.

3. a. To conceive, or think of, as real; to apprehend with the clearness or detail of reality; to understand or grasp clearly; to become aware of the presence of (a person).

In early use chiefly American, and frequently condemned as such by English writers about the middle of the 19th c.

1775 J. NEWTON *Cardiphonia* Let. to Nobleman No. 18 (1857) 96 Even these are much concerned to realize the brevity and uncertainty of their present state. **1781** P. SCHUYLER in Sparks *Corr. Amer. Rev.* (1853) III. 281 My heart realizes your feelings on the occasion, and cordially sympathizes with yours. **1820** W. IRVING *Sketch Bk.* I. 47 She cannot realize the change we must undergo. **1850** ROBERTSON *Serm.* Ser. III. ix. 115 He is compelled to realize at every moment the possibility of the extremes of life. **1891** E. PEACOCK *N. Brendon* I. xiv, When her mother died she was too young to realize the situation. **1916** H. S. WALPOLE *Dark Forest* II. iv. 269 The moment I realized him I felt afraid.

absol. **1896** 'M. FIELD' *Attila* II. 47 You realise—Torture and then the executioner..but torture first.

b. With subord. clause as obj.

1775 ABIGAIL ADAMS in *Fam. Lett.* (1876) 68 Can they realize what we suffer? **1817** B'NESS BUNSEN in Hare *Life* I. v. 117, I never could have realised that I should have borne the parting..so well. **1891** SWINBURNE *Stud. Prose & Poetry* (1894) 17 Scott..evidently failed to realize how far superior is Clara Mowbray to all his other heroines.

c. *U.S.* To have actual experience of.

1776 ABIGAIL ADAMS in *Fam. Lett.* (1876) 138 To-night we shall realize a more terrible scene still. **1791** WASHINGTON *Lett.* Writ. 1892 XII. 62 That you may find it [national happiness] in your nation, and realize it yourself.

4. a. To convert (securities, paper money, etc.) into cash, or (property of any kind) into money.

After F. *réaliser*, first used *c* 1719 in connexion with the speculations over Law's scheme, in the sense of converting securities into cash or permanently valuable property. Hence Johnson, perh. influenced by the phrase 'real property', gives as one sense of the word 'To convert money into land'; this, however, is unsupported by quotations.

1727–41 in CHAMBERS *Cycl.* **1768** *Woman of Honor* III. 225 Substantial securities..to be realised and converted into cash. **1799** E. DU BOIS *Piece Family Biog.* I. 25 One more voyage I must make, to realize the property I have in that quarter of the globe. **1848** MILL *Pol. Econ.* (1876) 3 When he retires from business it is into money that he converts the whole, and not until then does he deem himself to have realized his gains. **1894** H. NISBET *Bush Girl's Rom.* 21 Realizing what he could of his impoverished estates, and emigrating to Australia.

b. *absol.* To realize one's property; to sell out.

1781 BENTHAM *Wks.* (1843) X. 93 Caron de Beaumarchais has realized..to the tune of £30,000 or £40,000 a-year. **1849** THACKERAY *Pendennis* ii, He realised with great prudence while this mine was still at its full vogue. **1887** R. LODGE *Mod. Europe* xxii. §12 (1897) 510 On application the holder of one of these *assignats* could realise in land.

5. a. To obtain or amass (a sum of money, a fortune, etc.) by sale, trade, or similar means; to acquire for oneself or by one's own exertions; to make (so much) out of something.

1753 HANWAY *Trav.* (1762) I. VII. xc. 411 About four millions of dollars might be realised with great ease. **1775** S. J. PRATT *Liberal Opin.* lxxii. (1783) III. 46 You, sir, who have realized a fortune. **1802** MRS. E. PARSONS *Myst. Visit.* III. 166 Thus happily realizing a sum far beyond her expectations. **1845** MCCULLOCH *Taxation* I. ii. (1852) 71 The nett profits realised by those engaged in all departments of industry.

transf. **1847** MRS. CARLYLE *Let.* 6 Mar. in *New. Lett.* (1903) I. 224, I have been extremely lucky..in realizing so ..respectable a servant out of the great sink of London.

b. Of property or capital: To bring (a specified amount of money or interest) when sold or invested; to fetch (so much) as a price or return.

1845 MCCULLOCH *Taxation* (1852) 398 Have checked the transfer of capital from England to America, notwithstanding the high rate of profit it realises in the States. **1863** FAWCETT *Pol. Econ.* III. ii. 313 There would evidently be a much greater demand for them than if the same pictures realised a hundred guineas each. **1885** *Law Times Rep.* LII. 647/1 His duty was to see that the property realised its full value.

c. *intr.* With advb.: To turn out (well or ill) when sold.

1884 *Leeds Mercury* 27 Nov. 4/4 The liabilities are estimated at £130,000, and the assets will, it is assumed, realise well.

Hence **'realized** *ppl. a.*, spec. in phr. ***realized eschatology*** *Theol.* (see quot. 1946); also **'realizedness**.

1845 MCCULLOCH *Taxation* I. iv. (1852) 113 A tax on what is called realised property, that is, on lands, houses, the public funds, mortgages, and such-like securities. **1876** F. H. BRADLEY *Ethical Stud.* 119 Taking pleasure to be the feeling of the realizedness of the will or self. **1883** *Contemp. Rev.* XLIII. 268 The realized morals of a people find an expression in their usages and laws. **1936** C. H. DODD *Apostolic Preaching & its Devel.* iii. 156 This promise of a second coming is realized in the presence of the Paraclete.. in the life of the Church... The evangelist, therefore, is deliberately subordinating the 'futurist' element in the eschatology of the early Church to the 'realized eschatology' which..was from the first the distinctive and controlling factor in the *kerygma*. **1946** E. L. MASCALL *Christ, Christian, & Church* vi. 101 In recent years much stress has been laid upon the notion of 'realized eschatology',..the view that.. the last Day and the Final Judgment are actually present to Christians now. **1977** G. W. H. LAMPE *God as Spirit* i. 27 It has been argued convincingly that T. W. Manson, C. H. Dodd, and other exponents of 'realized eschatology' offered a one-sided interpretation of the evidence.

realizer ('riːəlaɪzə(r)). [f. REALIZE *v.*[2] + -ER[1].] One who or that which realizes.

1809–10 COLERIDGE *Friend* (1865) 74 Miserable was the delusion of the late mad realizer of mad dreams. **1839–40** W. IRVING *Wolfert's R.* (1855) 188 Sleek placemen—knowing realizers of present pay.

realizing ('riːəlaɪzɪŋ), *vbl. sb.* [f. as prec. + -ING[1].] The action of REALIZE *v.*[2]

1611 [see REALIZATION 1]. **1727** BOYER *Dict. Royal* I. s.v. *Realiser*, Misers call realizing, the hoarding up of Gold or Silver. **1785** BURKE *Nabob of Arcot* Wks. 1826 IV. 277 Suppose 1,200,000*l.* to be annually realised (of which we actually know no more than the realising of six hundred thousand). **1802** H. MARTIN *Helen of Glenross* I. 153 The realizing of one or two of your dismal reveries. **1818** JAS. MILL *Brit. India* II. IV. vi. 226 It has frequently been seen what difficulties attended the realizing of revenue.

attrib. **1895** *Boston Herald* 21 Mar. 5/7 Realizing sales caused irregularity and nervousness.

realizing ('riːəlaɪzɪŋ), *ppl. a.* [f. as prec. + -ING[2].] That realizes, in senses of the vb.; esp. ***a realizing sense*** (U.S.).

1768 WHITAKER *Two Serm.* II. 39 A realizing view and perception of the moral..glory of God. **1806** J. VAILL in *Memoir* (1839) 95, I have..a fixed and realizing sense of the truths contained in the word of God. **1816** J. SCOTT *Vis. Paris* (ed. 5) 243 The vivid Leonardo da Vinci, the grasping realizing Titian. **1838** H. BLUNT *Seven Ch. Asia* 75 A more realizing communion with God. **1897** HOWELLS *Landlord Lion's Head* 324, I ought to go, so that it can be brought home to me, and I can have a realising sense of what I am doing.

Hence **'realizingly** *adv.*, in a realizing manner.

a **1849** J. H. EVANS in Spurgeon *Treas. Dav.* Ps. cxix. 151 Then may I realizingly remember, that [etc.]. **1891** G. MEREDITH *One of our Conq.* I. xii. 232 Her subservience.. compelled her to think realizingly of any scheme he allowed her darkly to read.

reallich(e, obs. forms of REALLY *adv.*[1] and [2].

reallocate (riː'æləkeɪt), *v.* [f. RE- 5 a + ALLOCATE *v.* 1.] *trans.* To apportion or assign again.

1957 *Economist* 7 Sept. 863/1 When the French Government reallocates next month the oil prospecting rights over a 25,000 square mile tract of the Sahara Desert, several major British and American oil companies are likely to be committed to carry out intensive exploration in the area. **1964** A. BATTERSBY *Network Analysis* i. 9 It [*sc.* network analysis] reduces the examination of a large project to three stages:..(c) Re-allocating money or other resources to improve the schedule.

reallo'cation. [f. RE- 5 a + ALLOCATION.]

a. The action of apportioning or assigning again. **b.** A case or example of this.

1948 E. GOWERS *Plain Words* 48 We might find that, even though the Board of Trade could still not resist announcing that certain surplus government factories are now 'available for re-allocation', they would not leave it at that. 'In short,' they would add in a burst of confidence, 'they are to be relet.' **1960** *Farmer & Stockbreeder* 16 Feb. 122/3 Should there be any re-allocation of profitable pennies from corn, milk and sugar beet, the cattle producer is first in the queue. **1962** A. BATTERSBY *Guide to Stock Control* 108 No figure in the third column is less than any in the fourth column; this means any further re-allocation of orders must of necessity increase the total stock value. **1964** *Ann. Reg. 1963* 124 In 1963 this amounted to 81,563 tons, with sizeable additional reallocations. *a* **1974** R. CROSSMAN *Diaries* (1975) I. 626 We soon found that some of the 130 select authorities were not using up their allocation and we had some very nice re-allocations to do in order to make sure that our total didn't fall down.

re-a'llot, *v.* [RE- 5 a.] *trans.* To allot afresh.

1876 DIGBY *Real Prop.* i. §1. 6 The practice of re-alloting from time to time portions of the arable or meadow land is occasionally noticed in later times. **1885** SIR C. BOWEN in *Law Rep.* 29 *Chanc. Div.* 445 The conduct of the company in cancelling and re-allotting the shares.

Hence **re-a'llotment**.

1874 STUBBS *Const. Hist.* I. ii. 21 The annual re-allotment involves an equality of subdivisions.

† **re-a'lly**, *v. Obs.* Forms: 5 realy, (7 re-aly), 6 re-allie, 7 really, re-ally, re'ally, reallee. [a. obs. F. *realier*, *-yer*, *reallier*, var. *ralier*, *rallier* to RALLY *v.*[1]; see RE- 2 and ALLY *v.*]

1. *trans.* and *refl.* **a.** = RALLY *v.*[1] 1. Also with *up*.

1456 SIR G. HAYE *Law Arms* (S.T.S.) 59 Pompee..was discomfyte..and had agayn realyed his folk, and gevin thame bataill. *c* **1500** *Melusine* 144 The sawdan..realyed his folke about hym. **1614** RALEIGH *Hist. World* II. v. iii. §21. 495 Masanissa..not suffering them to re-ally themselues, draue them quite out of the field. **1645** SLINGSBY *Diary* (1836) 152 The enemy did not pursue, which gave us time to stop and really our men.

b. To connect, unite (again) *to* or *with*.

1603 FLORIO *Montaigne* III. xiii. (1632) 621 To acquaint and re-aly me with that people and condition of men that have most need of us. **1653** GAUDEN *Hierasp.* 32 The Ministers of this Church will never be able to stand..until ..they..re'ally themselves to that Primitive Harmony.

2. *intr.* (for *refl.*) = RALLY *v.*[1] 5.

1456 SIR G. HAYE *Law Arms* (S.T.S.) 47 Thai war discomfyte..bot efter that, thai realyd. **1596** Z. I. tr. *Lavardin's Hist. Scanderberg* I. 36 They reallied & assembled themselues together neare Alchria. **1647** WARD *Simp. Cobler* (1843) 66 That the Errors of State and Church, routed by these late stirs, may not re-allee hereafter.

3. *trans.* To form (plans) again. *rare*—[1].

a **1599** SPENSER *F.Q.* VII. vi. 23 Before they could new counsels re-allie.

† **'really**, *adv.*[1] *Obs.* Forms: 4 **reali, real(l)ich(e, realych**, 4–6 **real(l)y**, 6 *Sc.* **reallie**. [f. REAL *a.*[1] + -LY[2]. Cf. RIALLY.] Royally.

c **1350** *Will. Palerne* 1426 þe messageres riȝt realy were arayde, for soþe. **1387** TREVISA *Higden* (Rolls) III. 171 He hadde i-reigned nobliche and realliche þritty ȝere. *c* **1400** *Ywaine & Gaw.* 1569 Ful really thai rade about.. To justing and to turnament. *c* **1511** *1st Eng. Bk. Amer.* (Arb.) Introd. 36/1 Realy wrought with sterres lyke yf it were ye heuen. *a* **1578** LINDESAY (Pitscottie *Chron. Scot.* (S.T.S.) I. 93 He.. callit [him] to the supper and bankitit him werie reallie.

really ('riːəlɪ), *adv.*[2] Also 5 **rialliche**, 6 *Sc.* **realie**, 6–7 **reallie**. [f. REAL *a.*[2] + -LY[2].]

1. a. In a real manner; in reality; in point of, or as a matter of, fact; actually.

In later use commonly placed immediately in front of the word or phrase on which emphasis is laid.

c **1430** *Pilgr. Lyf Manhode* I. lxxxvii. (1869) 49 With inne this bred al the souereyn good is put;..bodiliche and rialliche, presentliche and verreyliche. **1528–37** *Lett. Suppress. Monast.* (Camden) 161 My dysfortune hathe byn ..not only with yntellectyon to have thought yt, but exteryally and really I have fulfyllyd the same. **1563** FOXE *A. & M.* 172/1 He held this opinion, that it was not the body of Christe really, the whiche was sacramentally vsed in the church. **1639** *Bury Wills* (Camden) 180, I will that twenty pounds..shalbe paid to the said ffeoffees when they shall really begin the said worke. **1662** STILLINGFL. *Orig. Sacr.* III. ii. §16 He imagined that which is said to be above as to us, was really the upper part of the world. **1692** E. WALKER tr. *Epictetus' Mor.* xxxvii, To have right Notions of the Deities; As that such Beings really are. **1712** ADDISON *Spect.* No. 315 ¶9 The Account of such things as have really happened. **1762** GOLDSM. *Nash* 21 Frequented only by such as really went for relief. **1798** FERRIAR *Illustr. Sterne*, etc. 287 The popular prophets of this country were all really or affectedly mad. **1820** SHELLEY *Witch Atl.* lxxiii, How the God Apis really was a bull, And nothing more. **1849** MACAULAY *Hist. Eng.* vi. II. 139 It soon appeared that the government was really directed, not at Dublin, but in London. **1886** LD. ESHER in *Law Rep.* 32 *Chanc. Div.* 26, I do not think that any of the cases that were cited did really prove that assertion.

b. Used to emphasize the truth or correctness of an epithet or statement; hence = positively, indeed.

a **1610** HEALEY *Cebes* (1636) 140 Hee..shall be really blessed, and lift up beyond the pitch of misery. **1687** A. LOVELL tr. *Thevenot's Trav.* I. 70 The Janizaries..seem to be sacred; and really I know no Order of Militia in the World, that is so much respected. **1722** DE FOE *Hist. Plague* (1754) 5 This last Bill was really frightful. **1772** *Test Filial Duty* II. 180 He was really very useful, perfectly commode. **1824** HOOD *Whims & Oddities, May-day* (1857) 308 A really pretty maiden, and worthy of the honour. **1834** R. H. FROUDE *Rem.* (1838) I. 378, I really think this illness is being a good thing for me. **1874** MICKLETHWAITE *Mod. Par. Churches* 207 It is really a pity that this is not true.

c. Coupled with *truly*. In adj. phr. **really truly** chiefly *N. Amer. Children's speech*, authentic, genuine.

1742 FIELDING *J. Andrews* II. xiii, The word really and truly signifies no more at this day. **1828** MOIR *Mansie Wauch* xx. 302 This was really and truly a terrible business. **1849** MACAULAY *Hist. Eng.* iv. I. 435 The king is really and truly a Catholic. **1852** DICKENS *Bleak Ho.* II. xv. 195 'Have you money for your lodgings?' 'Yes sir', she says, 'really and truly'.

1908 L. M. MONTGOMERY *Anne of Green Gables* xi. 114 They all had puffed sleeves..it was awfully hard there among the others who had really truly puffs. **1909** M. DIVER *Candles in Wind* xxxiii. 348 Such a really truly knight! **1911** G. STRATTON-PORTER *Harvester* xvi. 356 There are fairies! Really truly ones! They have found the remainder of the willow dishes. **1911** T. DREISER *Jennie Gerhardt* 249 She thinks you are her really truly uncle. **1942** *Post* (Morgantown, W. Va.) 2 May 5/7 The [family] have one of the prize sites with a really, truly beach.

2. Used without syntactical construction: **a.** As a term of asseveration or protest.

1602 SHAKS. *Ham.* v. ii. 132 Isn't not possible to understand in another tongue? You will do't, sir, really. **1728** GAY *Begg. Op.* III. viii, But really, Mistress Lucy [etc.]. **1819** KEATS *Let.* 22 Sept., How fine the air..Really, without joking, chaste weather. **1841** DE QUINCEY *Homer* Wks. 1853 VI. 338 Really no: a dyspeptic demigod it makes one dyspeptic to think of! **1875** JOWETT *Plato* (ed. 2) I. 61 Why really, I said, the truth is that I do not know.

b. Interrogatively.

c **1815** SIR D. WILKIE in Pinnington *Life*, etc. (1900) 75 Wilkie looked, smiled, and in the most unconscious manner said, 'Rea-al-ly!' **1893** *Scribner's Mag.* June 787/1 She exclaimed, 'Really? It is really true?'

†**3.** Sincerely, honestly, truly. *Obs.*[-1]

1650 T. B[AYLEY] *Worcester's Apoph.* 79, I protest my Lord, I speak, said Redman, really; he is coming.

†**4.** In the usual course of things, naturally.

1651 CULPEPPER *Astrol. Judgem. Dis.* (1658) 89 Diseases ..whether they come really, or by accident, as fractures.

†**5.** *Math.* Used with reference to an equation having real roots. *Obs.*

1706 W. JONES *Syn. Palmar. Math.* 128 In every Prepared Equation Really constituted, which has..all its Terms.

realm (rɛlm). Forms: α. 3–5 **reaume**, 4 **reeaum, reawme**. β. 4 **reome**, 4–5 **reem(e, regm(e**, 4–6 **rem(e, reame**, 5 **reyme, reiem, reamme**, *Sc.* **reime**, 6 **ream**. γ. 4–5 **reum(e**, 4–6 **rewm(e**. δ. 4–8 **realme**, 4– **realm**. [a. OF. *reaume, realme, reialme* = Prov. *re-, reyalme*, OSp. *rea(l)me*, It. *reame*:—pop.L. **rēgālimen*, f. L. *rēgālis* regal, royal: see also RIALM and ROYALME.

The earliest form adopted in Eng. was *reaume*, which subsequently appears also in the reduced forms *reame* or *reme* and *reume*. The more etymological spelling *realm* appears somewhat later, and did not finally become the standard form till about 1600.]

1. A kingdom. Now chiefly *rhet.*, and in such phrases as 'Statutes of the Realm'.

α. *c* **1290** *S. Eng. Leg.* I. 114/276 þare nas Man In engelond þat hadde so gret power Of þe reaume ase seint thomas. *c* **1350** *Will. Palerne* 135 þat he ne schuld wiȝtli in þis world neuer weld reaume. **1387** TREVISA *Higden* (Rolls) VIII. 87 þe kyng committed þe destourbance of þe reawme to þe bisshop of Durham. **1470–85** MALORY *Arthur* I. viii, It was a grete shame..to see suche a boye to haue a rule of soo noble a reaume.

β. *c* **1330** *Arth. & Merl.* 1642 (Kölbing) þou hast made flem þe riȝt aires out of þe rem. **1362** LANGL. *P. Pl.* A. IX. 99 To beo kyng..And rule þe reame. *c* **1430** LYDG. *Min. Poems* (Percy Soc.) 4 Sovereign lord and noble Kyng, ȝe be welcome oute of ȝoure reame of Fraunce, into this blissed reme of Englond. **1483** CAXTON *G. de la Tour* G iv, God.. sent to hym and to his reame many euyles. **1575** LANEHAM *Let.* (1871) 3 Born both indeed within the Ream heer, but yet of the race of Saxons. **1590** SPENSER *F.Q.* III. v. 53 And to your willes both royalties and reames Subdew.

γ. **1340** HAMPOLE *Pr. Consc.* 4033 Rewme ogayne rewme ..sal ryse. **1382** WYCLIF *Matt.* iv. 8 The deuel..shewide to hym alle the rewmys of the world. **1417** K. HENRY V in Ellis *Orig. Lett.* Ser. III. I. 62 How the said Duc Johan governeth him towardes us and oure Rewme of Englande. *c* **1475** *Partenay* 5552 That roiall rewine which in hand [ye] hold, And þat ye gouerne now. **1562** A. SCOTT *Poems* (S.T.S.) i. 147 So lairdis vpliftis mennis leifing ouir thy rewme.

δ. **1362** LANGL. *P. Pl.* A. I. 93 Kynges and knihtes scholde ..Rihtfuliche Raymen þe Realmes a-bouten. **1390** GOWER *Conf.* III. 86 Hou that a worthi king schal reule His Realme bothe in werre and pes. **1456** SIR G. HAYE *Law Arms* (S.T.S.) 11 His disciplis..convertit realmes and regionis. **1535** COVERDALE *Amos* ix. 8 The eyes of the Lorde are vpon the realme that synneth. **1591** SPENSER *M. Hubberd* 1185 Nobilitie,..The Realmes chiefe strength and girlond of the crowne. **1667** MILTON *P.L.* IV. 234 Wandring many a famous Realme And Country. **1705** HEARNE *Collect.* 22 Nov. (O.H.S.) I. 92 The Duke of Argyle is to be created a Peer of this Realme. **1765–9** BLACKSTONE *Comm.* (1793) 599 To the common law, and to their own by-laws, not contrary to the laws of the realm. **1818** CRUISE *Digest* (ed. 2) V. 247 Persons who are out of the realm at the time when a fine is levied. **1871** FREEMAN *Norm. Conq.* (1876) IV. xvii. 99 His work in his island realm, instead of being ended, was hardly begun.

transf. **1733** POPE *Ess. Man* III. 184 The ants Republic, and the Realm of bees.

2. *transf.* and *fig.* **a.** The kingdom of heaven, or of God.

a **1340** HAMPOLE *Psalter* xliv. 3 þe reum of þe whilke is nane endynge. **1380** *Lay Folks Catech.* (Lamb. MS.) 94 The Reme of þis fadyr ys callyd Holy chyrche. *c* **1450** tr. *De Imitatione* II. i. 39 þe reume of god is pes & ioy in þe holi goste. **1526** *Pilgr. Perf.* (W. de W. 1531) 7 In the whiche there be..many pleasures in many realmes, that we here shall neuer knowe. **1813** SHELLEY *Q. Mab* VI. 106 The avenging God! Who..sits High in heaven's realm.

b. Any sphere or region. (Sometimes with suggestion of a ruling power.)

c **1374** CHAUCER *Boethius* II. pr. ii. 24 (Camb. MS.) Thou þat art put in the comune Realme of alle, ne desire nat to lyuen by thin oonly propre ryht. **1596** SPENSER *F.Q.* IV. viii. 45 His soule descended downe into the Stygian reame. **1757** GRAY *Bard* 72 Proudly riding o'er the azure realm In gallant trim. **1784** COWPER *Task* VI. 579 He that hunts Or harms them there..Disturbs the economy of Nature's realm. **1816** J. WILSON *City of Plague* I. ii. 309 The realms of Hell are gleaming fiery bright. **1856** EMERSON *Eng. Traits, Personal* Wks. (Bohn) II. 132 New means were employed, and new realms added to the empire of the muse. **1899** *Allbutt's Syst. Med.* VI. 626 Loss of sensory and motor power in the realm of the nerve affected. **1924** W. B. SELBIE *Psychol. Relig.* 80 Though the term unconscious is used very loosely by Freudians it generally means a 'realm' where various emotions which have from time to time been repressed, lie hidden.

c. The sphere, domain, or province *of* some quality, state, or other abstract conception.

1667 MILTON *P.L.* II. 133 Thir Legions..Scout farr and wide into the Realm of night. **1682** DRYDEN *Mac-Fl.* 6 In prose and verse..Through all the realms of Nonsense absolute. **1725** YOUNG *Love Fame* VII. 62 A realm of death! and on this side the grave! **1781** COWPER *Hope* 651 The realms of Sin, where Riot reels. **1812** J. WILSON *Isle of Palms* I. 148 Lift thy queen-like diadem O'er these thy realms of rest. **1830** TENNYSON *Arab. Nts.* 101 Thro' the garden I was drawn—A realm of pleasance. **1873** HAMERTON *Intell. Life* x. ix. 385 The fairest realms of fancy.

d. A primary zoogeographical division of the earth's surface.

1876 WALLACE *Distrib. Anim.* I. 61 In an elaborate paper ..(Bulletin of Museum of Comparative Zoology, Cambridge, Massachusetts, vol. 2), Mr. J. A. Allen proposes a division of the earth..as follows: 1. Arctic realm..8. Australian realm. *Ibid.* 68 The following terms are proposed: realm, region, province, district..; the first being the highest, the last the lowest and smallest subdivision. **1895** BEDDARD *Zoogeogr.* 78 The fewness of the peculiar genera and their alliance with Australian forms seems to render it necessary to place the entire Polynesian realm within the Australian.

3. *attrib.* and *Comb.*, as †*realm raiker*, †*rape*; *realm-bounding, -destroying, -o'ershadowing, -sucking, -unpeopling* adjs.

1768–74 TUCKER *Lt. Nat.* (1834) I. 472 The wide-extended ocean, the *realm-bounding mountains. **1643** PRYNNE *Sov. Power Parl.* Ded. A iij, Their..*Realm-destroying, Church-subverting selfe-seeking. **1810** MONTGOMERY *West Indies* II. 60 The dun gloom of *realm-o'ershadowing trees. **1596** DALRYMPLE tr. *Leslie's Hist. Scot.* v. 307 All *Realme raikaris to put furth of the land. **1559** *Mirr. Mag., Dk. Clarence* xlix, For *realme rape spareth neither kin nor frend. **1633** *Costlie Whore* v. i. in Bullen *O. Pl.* IV, These *realme-sucking slaves, That build their pallace upon poor mens graves. **1777** POTTER *Æschylus* 495 He in *realm-unpeopling war Wasted not his subjects' blood.

Hence **'realmic** *a.*, of or belonging to a realm; **'realmist**, a supporter of the realm (in quot. *attrib.*); **'realmlet**, a little realm.

1865 *Intell. Observ.* No. 38. 149 Individual, realmic, and epicosmic. **1883** SWINBURNE *Les Casquettes* xi, As flowers on the sea are her small green realmlets. **1895** *Westm. Gaz.* 4 Mar. 3/2 When petty party politics shall have been forgotten in the rise of a great Realmist League.

realme, obs. (erron.) form of REAM *sb.*[3]

realmless ('rɛlmlɪs), *a.* [f. REALM + -LESS.] Destitute of a realm.

1820 KEATS *Hyperion* I. 19 His old right hand lay.. Unsceptred; and his realmless eyes were closed. **1843** LOWELL *Prometheus* Poet. Wks. (1879) 32/1 Realmless in soul, as tyrants ever are. **1863** LD. LYTTON *Ring Amasis* II. 282 Sethos the realmless prince, immoveable, before Amasis the usurper.

realness ('riːəlnɪs). [f. REAL *a.*[2] + -NESS.] The fact or quality of being real; reality, truth.

1642 ROGERS *Naaman* 181 It hath brought realnesse of comfort and peace into it. **1675** BROOKS *Gold. Key* Wks. 1867 V. 147 This expression is used..to note out the truth and realness of the thing. **1835** BROWNING *Paracelsus* III. Wks. 1896 I. 38/2 Demonstrate to itself The realness of the very joy it tastes. **1872** J. ROSS *Ministry Reconcil.* 53 A deep feeling of realness must pervade her spirit. **1885** *Science* 27 Nov. 472/2 There is such a freshness,..and such a realness to his narration that one is willing to overlook his many deficiencies in the art of expression.

‖**Realpolitik** (re,aːlpoli'tiːk). Also **realpolitik**. [Ger.] Practical politics; policy determined by practical, rather than moral or ideological, considerations. Also *transf.* Cf. *practical politics* s.v. PRACTICAL *a.* (*sb.*) 6.

1914 G. B. SHAW in *New Statesman* 14 Nov. (Suppl.) 5/2 He [*sc.* Friedrich von Bernhardi] prophesies that we, his great masters in *Realpolitik*, will do precisely what our Junkers have just made us do. **1915** E. B. HOLT *Freudian Wish & its Place in Ethics* iv. 151 This science is '*Realpolitik*', the Politics of Reality. **1920** *Times* 19 Jan. 13/2 An over-strong Russia..might not altogether suit the *Realpolitik* of this country. **1926** A. HUXLEY *Jesting Pilate* IV. 275 Freudism became the *realpolitik* of psychology and philosophy. **1928** C. H. DODD *Authority of Bible* xii. 266 In the last days of the monarchies Israel became involved to its cost in the large 'Realpolitik' of the time. **1931** *Times Lit. Suppl.* 4 June 433/2 The conflict between these two ideals —*Realpolitik* and a policy founded upon principles of justice and morality. **1948** R. ROBINSON tr. *Jaeger's Aristotle* II. v. 113 The letter that we possess is the solemn record of this peculiar pact between *Realpolitik* and theoretical schemes of reform. **1952** J. D. MACKIE *Earlier Tudors* x. 351 [Thomas Cromwell] had little belief in the omnipotence of the papacy and pinned his faith to *Realpolitik*. **1958** *New Statesman* 19 Apr. 494/2 But the bare-faced hypocrisy with which they have attempted to conceal their military *realpolitik*, and which has now been devastatingly exposed, is a serious tactical error. **1961** *Listener* 27 Apr. 731/2 Writing in the eighteen-fifties—the decade which saw the birth of the name and concept of *Realpolitik*—Mommsen was imbued with the sense of need for a strong man. **1970** G. GREER *Female Eunuch* 109 Even the best educated of them [*sc.* women] know that arguments with their men-folk are disguised real-politik. **1979** *N.Y. Rev. Bks.* 25 Oct. 49/2 Soviet policy may have sprung neither from revolutionary ideology nor from traditional *Realpolitik*.

Hence **realpo'litiker**, one who believes in, advocates, or practises *Realpolitik*.

1930 C. SFORZA in *Time & Tide* 4 Apr. 435/2 'The United States of Europe!' sneered..the *real-politikers*, whom, by a strange legerdemain, the defeat of Hohenzollern Germany has conjured up again in France. **1931** *Times Lit. Suppl.* 22 Jan. 53/1 Both [Cavour and Bismarck] were *Realpolitiker*, endowed with an extraordinary capacity for gauging the forces with which they had to deal. **1958** *Times* 14 June 8/5 In all this he [*sc.* Pierre Flandin] took the line of a French *Realpolitiker*. **1963** *Observer* 1 Dec. 21/4 He learned the lesson, and applied it in Laos—and not in the sentimentally tough way supposed by the *realpolitikers*. **1976** *Survey* Winter 16 Czechoslovakia may look even more remote than Angola..but its fate counts in the over-all balance, whatever the *Realpolitiker* may think.

‖**Realschule** (re'aːlˌʃuːlə). Also **realschule**. Pl. **Realschulen**. [Ger.] In Germany and Austria, a secondary school in which sciences and modern languages are taught. Cf. *real school* s.v. REAL *a.*[2] 10.

1833 SIR W. HAMILTON *Discuss.* (1852) 552 *Realschulen*, real schools..because they are less occupied with the study of languages (Verbalia) than with the knowledge of things (Realia). **1879** *Encycl. Brit.* X. 471/1 Of more recent growth is the system of *realschulen*, where Latin is the only ancient language taught, the other branches being modern languages, especially French and English, mathematics and natural philosophy, geography and modern history. **1949** R. K. MERTON *Social Theory & Social Structure* xiv. 343 Hecker, who first actually organized a *Realschule*. **1969** *Listener* 10 Apr. 480/2 Experimental step towards comprehensive education: class in a Realschule. **1980** *Jewish Chron.* 23 May 14/2, I later taught in the Realschule, founded by his grandfather, Rabbi Samson Raphael Hirsch.

re-'alter, *v.* [RE- 5 a.] *trans.* To alter again.

1816 SOUTHEY in *Q. Rev.* XIV. 347, I began to scribble, to alter, to read, and re-alter. **1824** MISS MITFORD *Village* Ser.

I. (1863) 6 He has a passion for bricks and mortar, and.. diverts himself with altering and re-altering.

Realtor ('ri:əltə(r)). *U.S.* Also realtor. [f. REALT(Y[2] + -OR.] A proprietary term in the U.S. for a real-estate agent or broker who belongs to the National Association of Realtors (formerly the National Association of Real Estate Boards). Also *gen.*, an estate agent.

1916 C. N. CHADBOURN in *Nat. Real Estate Jrnl.* 15 Mar. 111/2, I propose that the National Association adopt a professional title to be conferred upon its members which they shall use to distinguish them from outsiders. That this title be copyrighted and defended by the National Association against misuse... I therefore, propose that the National Association adopt and confer upon its members, dealers in realty, the title of *realtor* (accented on the first syllable). **1922** S. LEWIS *Babbitt* xiii. 157 We ought to insist that folks call us 'realtors' and not 'real-estate men'. Sounds more like a reg'lar profession. **1925** O. W. HOLMES *Let.* 17 Dec. in *Holmes-Laski Lett.* (1953) I. 807 These realtors, as they call themselves, I presume are influential. **1929** *Sun* (Baltimore) 8 Jan. 26/3 (*heading*) Realtors doubt plan for Fox Theater here. **1931** *Evening Standard* 25 Apr. 15/2 (*heading*) 'Realtor' recommends Surrey. **1934** E. POUND *Eleven New Cantos* xxxv. 23 His Wife now acts as his model and the Egeria Has, let us say, married a realtor. **1942** *Amer. Speech* XVII. 209/2 The ambitious realtor's favorites, the over-worked [street names] Grand, Broadway, and Inspiration. **1948** *Official Gaz.* (U.S. Patent Office) 14 Sept. 340/2 National Association of Real Estate Boards, Chicago, Ill... Service Mark. *Realtors.* For services in connection with the brokerage of real estate... Claims use since Mar. 31, 1916. **1962** R. BUCKMINSTER FULLER *Epic Poem on Industrialization* 139 The organized religions The world's premier realtors. **1969** *Parade* (N.Y.) 14 Dec. 18/2 The realtor who sold most of the property to the hippies has had her office windows smashed. **1970** *Globe & Mail* (Toronto) 25 Sept. 40/2 (Advt.), Metro wide established realtor with country wide referral contacts. **1973** R. C. DENNIS *Sweat of Fear* ix. 59 The realtor said... 'Let me point out some of the features of this lovely, lovely home.' **1979** *Tucson Mag.* Apr. 33/3 Included are.. bankers and lawyers; social and political activists; professors and artists, renovators and historians, journalists and realtors.

†'**realty**[1]. *Obs.* Forms: 4-5 realte, (4 -tee, reaulte), 7 realty, -tie; 4 reiate, reaute, *Sc.* reawte, (rewate). [a. OF. *reauté*, *realté*:—pop.L. **rēgālitāt-em* REGALITY: see also RIALTY and ROYALTY.]

1. Royalty; royal state, dignity, or power.

c **1350** *Will. Palerne* 5006 Alle þe clerkes vnder god couþe nouȝt descriue.. þe realte of þat day. **1377** LANGL. *P. Pl.* B. x. 335 Kynghod ne knyȝthod.. Helpeþ nouȝt to heueneward ..ne reaute of lordes. *c* **1400** MAUNDEV. (Roxb.) xxx. 134 Now will I speke of sum of þe principall iles of Prestre Iohn land, and of þe realtee of his state.

b. Used as a title.

1400 in *Royal & Hist. Lett. Hen. IV* (Rolls) 23 Likit yhour Realte to wit that I am gretly wrangit be the Duc of Rothesay.

2. *Sc.* **a.** A kingdom, realm.

1375 BARBOUR *Bruce* I. 593 Thiddir somownys he in hy The barownys of his reawte. *c* **1425** WYNTOUN *Cron.* VIII. i. 62 Na thare consent,.. Prejwdycyale suld [noucht] be Till off Scotland the realté.

b. A town or district under the immediate jurisdiction of the king; a regality.

1438 *Sc. Acts Jas. II* (1814) 32 Vyth help and supple of the lordis of the realteys geyff neyd be.

realty[2] ('ri:əltɪ). Also 5 realte, 7 -tie. [f. REAL *a.*[2] + -TY.]

†**1. a.** Reality. *Obs.*

c **1440** *Promp. Parv.* 424/2 Realte, *realitas.* **1627** W. SCLATER *Exp. 2 Thess.* (1629) 99 The man [leads into Error] through realty, or opinion of learning, or sanctity, or both. **1644** MAXWELL *Prerog. Chr. Kings* 47 He is King of kings.. truly so, kings upon earth are onely such.. more in resemblance, than realtie.

†**b.** A reality, a real thing. *Obs.*[−1]

1647 H. MORE *Song of Soul* I. II. xii, We may see The nearly couching of each Realtie.

†**2.** Sincerity, honesty. *Obs. rare.*

1619 in *Eng. & Germ.* (Camden) 170 He tould the Ambassador that he needed not doubt of his realty in observing such capitulations. **1667** MILTON *P.L.* VI. 115 That such resemblance of the Highest Should yet remain, where faith and realtie Remain not.

†**3.** A real possession; a right. *Obs. rare.*

1618 J. WILKINSON *Of Courts Baron* 120b, If any man hath fished, hawked, or hunted within this Lordship.. you must present them, for they are the Lords Realties. **1635** CHAPMAN & SHIRLEY *Chabot* I. ii, That kings do no [? *read* not] hazard infinitely In their free realties of rights and honours Where they leave much for favorites' powers to order!

4. *Law.* Real property or estate. (REAL *a.*[2] 6 c.) Also *attrib.*

1670 BLOUNT *Law Dict.*, *Realty*, is an abstract of real, and distinguished from Personalty. *a* **1683** SCROGGS *Courtsleet* (1714) 109 In Action of Debt which concerns the Realty. **1766** BLACKSTONE *Comm.* II. xxiv. 385 Our courts now regard a man's personalty in a light nearly, if not quite, equal to his realty. **1861** PEARSON *Early & Mid. Ages Eng.* 186 The realty of a man who died intestate, was divided equally among his sons. **1888** A. RANDALL-DIEHL *Two Thousand Words* 175 *Realty-man*, a dealer in real estate. **1908** E. WHARTON *Hermit & Wild Woman* 135, I chanced on a record of the transaction in the realty column of the morning paper. **1934** E. POUND *Eleven New Cantos* xi. 48 Beecher's church organized by realty agents. **1947** E. HODGINS *Mr Blandings* iii. 45 As a grizzled veteran of realty values, he would discuss his one time innocence with the real estate man. **1963** C. D. SIMAK *They walked like Men* viii. 47 People were storming realty offices in a mad attempt to find a place to live. **1968** *Globe & Mail* (Toronto) 17 Feb. 51 (Advt.), Lawyer to manage litigation, realty transactions by property development corporation. **1972** J. GORES *Dead Skip* (1973) xiv. 100 The tract home had been rented from the realty office by phone. **1975** *New Yorker* 1 Sept. 20/3 The realty company that is the agent for U.S. Steel gave us thirty days to get out.

realy, variant of REALLY *adv.*[1] *Obs.*

†**ream**, *sb.*[1] *Obs.* Forms: 1 hréam, 2-3 ream, 3 ræm, rem. [OE. *hréam*, of obscure origin; hence REME *v.*[1] The sb. is common in OE. and early ME., but is not found after *c* 1250.] Clamour, outcry, shouting.

c **897** K. ÆLFRED *Gregory's Past. C.* lv. 427 Ðætte swiðe wære ȝemanigfaldod Sodomwara hream & Gomorwara. *c* **1000** ÆLFRIC *Hom.* II. 336 Ðam halȝan were wæs ȝeþuht þæt þæs ȝefeohtes hream mihte beon ȝehyred ȝeond ealle eorðan. *c* **1205** LAY. 11280 Scottes huuen up muchelne ræm & Octaues folc nam flem.

b. *esp.* Noise of wailing or lamentation; hence, great sorrow, distress, or trouble.

Beowulf (Z.) 1303 Hream wearð in Heorote.. Ceara wæs ȝeniwod. *a* **900** CYNEWULF *Christ* 594 Swa mid Dryhten dream, swa mid deoflum hream. *c* **1200** ORMIN 8137 Þeȝȝre wop & teȝȝre ræm Comm full wel till hiss ære. *a* **1225** *Leg. Kath.* 2325 To arisen from ream to aa lestinde lahtre. *a* **1250** *Owl & Night.* 1213 Ʒef eni mon schal rem abide, Al ich hit wot ear hit i-tide.

c. With *a* and *pl.* A cry (of grief).

a **1225** *Leg. Kath.* 164 Swið feole ȝeinde.. wið reowfule reames. *c* **1250** *Gen. & Ex.* 1962 He missed Ioseph.. wende him slagen, set up an rem.

ream (ri:m), *sb.*[2] *Obs.* exc. *dial.* Forms: 1 réam, 4-5 rem, 5-6 reme, (6 *Sc.* reyme), 7 reame, 8- ream, (8-9 *dial.* reeam, reem, raim, etc.). [OE. *réam* = MDu. (Du.) *room*, MLG. *rôm(e*, MHG. *roum* (G. *rahm*, also dial. *raum*, *rohm*, etc.):—OTeut. **raumo-z*, of obscure origin: ON. *rjómi* (Norw. dial. *rjome*, *rome*, etc.) represents a different ablaut-grade with weak ending (**reumon-*).]

1. a. = CREAM *sb.*[2] 1. (In ME. occ. *milkes reme.*)

c **1000** *Sax. Leechd.* II. 314 Ʒenim god beren mela and hwit sealt, do on ream oððe gode flete. *c* **1330** *Arth. & Merl.* 1455 (Kölbing) On is white so milkes rem, þat oþer is red. **1483** *Cath. Angl.* 303/1 Reme, *quaccum.* **1549** *Compl. Scot.* vi. 43 Fresche buttir ande salt buttir, reyme, flot quhaye. **1728** RAMSAY *Betty & Kate* ii, Can dale dainties please Thee mair than moorland ream? **1788** SHIRREFS *Poems* (1790) 141, I laid upon the board Some cruds and ream. **1822** GALT *Sir A. Wylie* lxxxviii, A bonny wee china pourie, full o' thick ream. **1869-** in northern dial. glossaries (Yks., Lanc.). **1880** *E. Cornwall Gloss.* s.v., Cold cream is called 'raw ream'.

b. Used allusively (see quot. 1721).

1721 KELLY *Sc. Prov.* 136 He streaks Ream in my Teeth. .. Spoken when we think one only flattering us. **1722** RAMSAY *Three Bonnets* IV. 31 Rosie.. Rubs o'er his cheeks and gab wi' ream, Till he believes 't to be a dream.

†**2.** = CREAM *sb.*[1]

Perh. a mechanical alteration of *crem* in the original text.

13.. *Minor Poems fr. Vernon MS.* 624/435 Cristened we weore In Red[de] rem, Whon his bodi bledde on þe Beem.

3. *transf.* A scum or froth upon any liquid.

1460-70 *Bk. Quintessence* 2 Ʒe schal se as it were a liquor of oyle ascende vp, fletynge aboue in maner of a skyn or of a reme. **1594** T. B. *La Primaud. Fr. Acad.* II. 346 This liquor is called by the physicions chylus, which.. resembleth the reme of a ptisame. **1786** BURNS *Twa Dogs* 131 The nappy reeks wi' mantling ream. **1839** MOIR *Mansie Wauch* (ed. 2) xxiv. 306 The porter.. was in prime condition with a ream as yellow as a marigold.

4. (See quots.)

1962 *Gloss. Terms Glass Industry* (*B.S.I.*) 39 *Ream*, a non-homogeneous layer in flat glass. **1971** *Materials & Technol.* II. vi. 408 In the drawing of sheet the outer layers of glass may have come from the glass originally on the surface.. and may be somewhat deficient in alkali compared with the main glass... This results in a type of inhomogeneity known as 'ream', in which the inhomogeneity is in a direction at right angles to the plane of the glass.

ream (ri:m), *sb.*[3] Forms: *α.* 4 rem, 5-6 reme, (5 reeme, 7 rheme); 5-7 reame, 6 realme, 7-8 rheam, 6- ream. *β.* 5-6 rym, 6 rim. [ME. *rēm* and *rim* = Du. *riem* (16th c.), OF. *rayme*, *raime*, *reyme*, *remme* (1360-1489 in Godef.; mod.F. *rame*), and *riesme* (1492 ibid.), Sp. and Pg. *resma*, It. (and med.L.) *risma*, ad. Arab. *rizmah* bale or bundle (of clothes, paper, etc.).

The precise source of the ME. forms is not clear; the usual *reme* approximates to those which appear in OF., while the northern *rim* or *rym* has more resemblance to Du. *riem*. It. *risma* is app. the source of MHG. *ris*, *riz*, *rist* (G. *ries*, in 16th c. also *reisz*), whence Da. and Sw. *ris*.

The occasional 16th-c. spelling *realme* is due to the existence of *ream* as a variant of REALM.]

a. A quantity of paper, properly 20 quires or 480 sheets, but frequently 500 or more, to allow for waste; of paper for printing, 21½ quires or 516 sheets (a ***printers' ream***).

α. **1392-3** *Earl Derby's Exp.* (Camden) 154 Pro j rem papiri, viijs. **1411** *Close Roll 12 Hen. IV*, [Licence.. to export from England to Ireland, one] 'Reme de papiro'. **1481-90** *Howard Househ. Bks.* (Roxb.) 303, ij. lb. almondes, and half a reme paper. **1497** *Naval Acc. Hen. VII* (1896) 128 A reame of paper roiall, j reame & vij quires of small paper. **1545** *Rates of Customs* c iij, Paper the bale conteininge x. realme at xvid. the realme. **1549** J. CHEKE in *Lett. Lit. Men* (Camden) 8, I prai yow bi me a reme of paper at London. **1630** J. TAYLOR (Water P.) *Gt. Eater Kent* 9 Offring him, that for a wager he would deuoure 4. reame of his ballads; which in the totall are two thousand. **1689-90** WOOD *Life* 20 Mar. (O.H.S.) III. 328 Bought.. a reame of writing paper. **1766** C. LEADBETTER *Royal Gauger* II. xiv. (ed. 6) 371 Tied up into Reams or Bundles for Sale. *Note.* That 18 of the good Quires, and 2 of the broken go to each Ream. **1832** BABBAGE *Econ. Manuf.* ix. (ed. 3) 65 The hundred reams of paper were printed off. **1879** *Print. Trades Jrnl.* XXVI. 15 A hundred reams were actually made in Scotland and delivered in London in three days.

β. **1473-4** *Durham Acc. Rolls* (Surtees) 645 Pro di. rym et iij quaternis papiri empt., ijs. vijd. **1507-8** *Ibid.* 659 In ij Rymez papiri empt. **1568** *Wills & Inv. N.C.* (Surtees 1835) 293 Half a rim of paper.. Half a rim of dim paper.

b. Used to denote a large quantity of paper, without reference to the precise number of sheets.

1597 BP. HALL *Sat.* II. ii. 30 When ye have spent A thousand lamps, and thousand reams have rent Of needlesse papers. **1646** J. HALL *Poems* 1 Paper-tyrants reign, who presse Whole harmlesse reams to death. **1699** GARTH *Dispens.* IV. 46 Hither, rescu'd from the Grocers, come M—— Works entire, and endless Rheams of Bloom. **1781** COWPER *Progr. Err.* 311 Whose corresponding misses fill the ream With sentimental frippery and dream. **1814** SCOTT *Drama* (1874) 202 More fire than warms whole reams of modern plays. *a* **1839** PRAED *Poems* (1865) II. 14 Shield thee with a ream of rhyme.

c. With pun on *ream* REALM.

1589 *Pappe w. Hatchet* D ij, Let them but chafe my penne, and it shal sweat out a whole realme of paper, or make them odious to the whole Realme. *c* **1592** MARLOWE *Jew of Malta* IV. iv, Giue Me a Reame of paper, We'll haue a kingdome of gold for't.

d. *transf.* in *pl.* A large quantity.

1913 D. H. LAWRENCE *Love Poems & Others* 54 Eh, what a shame it seems As some should ha'e hardly a smite o' trouble An' others has reams. **1927** J. S. HUXLEY *Relig. without Revelation* iv. 113 This simple personal fact illustrates, better than could whole reams of argument, the extreme complexity of religion. **1976** *San Francisco Examiner* 30 May (This World Suppl.) 19/1 Spacecraft sent there in recent years have dispelled legends and added reams of sound, ordered data, yet the charisma of Mars remains.

ream, obs. variant of REALM.

ream, *v.*[1] *Obs.* exc. *dial.* Forms: 3 ræmien, 4-6 reme, 6- ream, 9 *dial.* ra(y)me, r(h)eem. [ME. *ræmien*, of obscure origin. Cf. REAM *v.*[3]

As the evidence for the word is chiefly south-western, it is doubtful whether the northern quots. in 1 b. belong here.]

1. *intr.* To stretch oneself after sleep or on rising; †to yawn.

c **1205** LAY. 25991 Seoððen he gan ræmien and raxlede swiþe. **1393** LANGL. *P. Pl.* C. VIII. 7 He.. hus brest knokede Rascled and remed and routte at þe laste. **14..** *Lat.-Eng. Voc.* in Wr.-Wülcker 563/9 *Alo*, to reme. **1591** PERCIVALL *Sp. Dict.*, *Enaspar el cuerpo*, to reame, to reach, *pandiculare, exporrigere se.* **1886** ELWORTHY *W. Som. Word-bk.*, *Ream*, to stretch oneself on awaking, or on getting up.

b. To stretch or reach after.

a **1225** *Ancr. R.* 72 Holde euerich his owene mester, & nout ne reame oðres. **1691** RAY *N.C. Words*, *Ream*, to stretch out the hand to take anything; to reach after. **1781** HUTTON *Tour to Caves* (ed. 2) Gloss., *Ream*, to reach with stretched out body and arms.

c. Of bread: (see quot.).

1778 *Exmoor Scolding* Gloss., Bread is said to ream, when ..if a Piece of it be broken into two Parts, the one draws out from the other a kind of String.. stretching from one Piece to the other.

2. *trans.* To draw out, to stretch, distend.

1398 TREVISA *Barth. De P.R.* VII. xlviii. (Bodl. MS.), Wombe ache comeþ.. of winde þat strecchiþ and remeþ. **1598** *Herrings Tayle* D i b, His pearching hornes are ream'd a yard beyond assise. **1880** *W. Cornwall Gloss.* s.v., Don't ream it out of shape. **1886** ELWORTHY *W. Som. Word-bk.* s.v., You can ream that there cloth [etc.].

b. To pull apart or to pieces; to tear open.

1587 *Mirr. Mag.*, *Irenglas* xxv, Which seeme.. to reme my hart, Before I come to open all my smart. **1746** *Exmoor Scolding* (E.D.S.) 18 Chell ream my Heart to tha avore Ise let tha lipped.

ream (ri:m), *v.*[2] Chiefly *Sc.* Also 5 remyn, 6 *Sc.* rem-. [f. REAM *sb.*[2]]

1. *intr.* To froth or foam. Also const. *over.* (Said of liquor, or the vessel containing it, and hence *transf.* or *fig.* in various applications.)

c **1440** *Promp. Parv.* 429/1 Remyn' as ale or other lycoure, *spumat.* **1513** [see REAMING *ppl. a.*[2]]. **1710** RUDDIMAN *Gloss. Douglas' Æneis* s.v. *Remand*, We say that ale reams, when it has a white foam above it. **1785** BURNS *Scotch Drink* ii, Or, richly brown, ream owre the brink In glorious faem. **1791** —— *Tam o' Shanter* 109 The swats sae ream'd in Tammie's noddle. **1814** SCOTT *Wav.* xi, A huge pewter measuring-pot ..which in the language of the hostess, 'reamed'.. with excellent claret. **1863** T. TAYLOR *Pict. in Words* xxiii, Where the white waters chafe and ream.

b. To become covered with cream.

a **1774** FERGUSSON *Farmer's Ingle* Poems (1845) 36 Wi buttered bannocks now the girdle reeks; I' the far nook the bowie briskly reams.

2. *trans.* To take the cream off; to skim. Also *intr.*, to be skimmed.

1768 ROSS *Helenore* II. 71 On skelfs.. the cogs were set, Ready to ream, an' for the cheese be het. **1899** J. COLVILLE *Scott. Vernacular* 15 (E.D.D.) When the milk was drawn in the cog it was.. reamed for the churn.

ream (ri:m), *v.*[3] *techn.* Also reem. [Of somewhat doubtful origin: perh. a survival in special sense of ME. *reme* to make room, open up.

The word is current in south-western dial., in which it is app. not regarded as distinct from REAM *v.*[1]; but the meaning, and the fact that *reamer* corresponds to a northern *rimer*, make it probable that the real source is ME. *reme, rime*:—OE. *rȳman*. The spelling *reem* is rare in the senses given here, but is usual in another application of the word, for which see REEMING *vbl. sb.*]

I. 1. *trans.* To enlarge or widen (a hole) with an instrument.

1815 [see REAMING *vbl. sb.* 1]. **1825** JENNINGS *Obs. Dial. W. Eng.*, *Ream*, to widen; to open. **1881** *Metal World* No. 1. 3 Bore the tang-hole with a gimlet, and slightly ream the hole with a taper reamer.

2. a. To enlarge the bore of (a gun) by the use of a special tool. Chiefly with *out*.

1867 in SMYTH *Sailor's Word-bk.* **1876** VOYLE & STEVENSON *Milit. Dict.* 330/1 The practice of reaming out guns, or boring them out, first took place in the British service in 1830. **1881** JEFFERSON DAVIS *Rise & Fall Confed. Govt.* I. 474 Iron guns which were reamed out to get a good bore.

b. To clear from lead.

1882 [see REAMING *vbl. sb.* 1]. **1886** J. M. CAULFEILD *Seamanship Notes* 7 *Reaming a shackle* is clearing the undercut portion of the lug of a shackle from any..lead which might remain after pin and pellet are knocked out.

3. With *out*: To remove (a defect) by reaming; to clear (something obstructed); to excavate. Also (*U.S.*) without *adv.*

1861 E. P. HALSTED *Let.* in *Times* 25 Oct., The interior of the gun itself was defective,..and the defect had been reamed out at Woolwich. **1967** 'T. WELLS' *Dead by Light of Moon* x. 99 The toilet..flowed over and Mr. Hawthorne had to come up and ream out the pipes. **1978** J. A. MICHENER *Chesapeake* 642 At the bottom of the Chesapeake..this primeval riverbed existed, sixty feet deeper than the shallow waters surrounding it, but as clearly defined as when first reamed out by tumbling boulders. **1978** J. UPDIKE *Coup* (1979) v. 200 The pipe came into even more elaborate play, the amber stem pointing this way and that as Craven knocked, blew into and rapidly reamed this little instrument of pleasure. **1980** *Nature* 19 June 532/3 As this plinian eruption column formed, it reamed out the volcanic conduit, forming a central crater more than 1·5 km in diameter.

II. *fig.* **4.** *U.S. slang.* To cheat, to swindle. Cf. RIM *v.*[3] 2.

1914 'HIGH JINKS, JR.' *Choice Slang* 17 *Ream one* (*to*), to swindle one. **1938** A. J. LIEBLING *Back where I came From* 84 He had invented a new technique for reaming the customers. **1942** BERREY & VAN DEN BARK *Amer. Thes. Slang* §314/8 Cheat; defraud,..*ream.* **1952** S. KAUFFMANN *Philanderer* (1953) xiii. 216 Yeah, I smell the rat. Joe Bass's new relatives. Well, palsy, they're liable to ream you yet.

5. Usu. with *out*. To reprimand. *U.S. colloq.*

1950 E. HEMINGWAY *Across River* xii. 117 You ream out people you respect, to make them do what is fairly impossible, but is ordered. **1972** R. BUSBY *Reasonable Man* xvi. 145 Banner's back—reamed you out as well, has he? **1973** J. RYDER *Trevayne* (1974) xi. 89 I'll get my ass chewed... I'll get reamed anyway for letting you make this tour. **1979** 'A. HAILEY' *Overload* IV. xvii. 380 A half-wit in my department has been sitting on the thing all morning. I'll ream her out later.

†ream, *v.*[4] *Obs.* Also ræm-, rem-. [Of obscure origin; found only in Layamon, usually along with *ræsen* RESE *v.*] *intr.* To rush, charge.

c **1205** LAY. 623 Ofte heo ræsden & ræmden togadere. *Ibid.* 9339 Heo ræsden to Romleoden & heo remden to flonne. *c* **1275** *Ibid.* 26813 Bruttus to ȝam reamde, and flowen Rom-leode.

ream, *a. Cant.* Genuine.

1851 MAYHEW *Lond. Labour* I. 313 Not one 'swell' in a score would view it in any other light than a 'ream' (genuine) concern. *Ibid.*, Petition with ream monekurs (genuine signatures).

re-a'mass, *v. rare.* [RE- 5 a.] *trans.* To bring or heap together again.

1611 FLORIO, *Ramassare*, to re-ammasse together. *a* **1631** DONNE *Serm.* (1640) lxxvi. 767 All that is written in our hearts..is reamassed, and reduced to the Ten Commandments, the Lords Prayer and to the Creed.

reame, obs. form of REALM, REAM *sb.*[2], *sb.*[3]

reamed (ri:md), *ppl. a.* [f. REAM *v.*[3] + ED[1].] Of a hole: enlarged by reaming.

1909 *Westm. Gaz.* 9 Nov. 5/1 Two bolts..engage in two carefully reamed holes in the pivot and lever, and are secured by castellated nuts and split pins.

re-a'mend, *v.* [RE- 5 a.] *trans.* To amend anew. So **re-a'mendment**.

1796 LAMB *Lett.* ii. To Coleridge 17 Take my sonnets, once for all, and do not propose any re-amendments. **1884** *Century Mag.* May 149 The Constitution might be re-amended.

reamer ('ri:mə(r)), *sb.* [f. REAM *v.*[3] + -ER[1]: see also RIMER.] An instrument used to enlarge a hole or boring.

1825 in JENNINGS *Obs. Dial. W. Eng.* *a* **1864** GESNER *Coal, Petrol.*, etc. (1865) 28 The Reamer is used to enlarge the hole made by the Bit. **1883** CRANE *Smithy & Forge* 167 This 'half round' reamer is justly a favourite with experienced workmen.

reamer ('ri:mə(r)), *v.* [f. the sb.] *trans.* To use a reamer on; to clear *out* with a reamer.

1934 WEBSTER, *Reamer*,..v.t., to cut with a reamer, as in enlarging diamond dies. **1935** tr. *H. Mignet's Flying Flea* (Air League Brit. Empire) xiii. 237 It may happen..that the platinum points..have seized up... Reamer this out, a very little, with a metal rod covered with a strip of emery cloth. **1938** J. HEALEY *Metal Aircraft for Mechanic* ii. 14 Tubular rivets are a reamer fit, so having reamered the hole to size, radius the edge of the metal slightly.

'reaming, *vbl. sb.* [f. REAM *v.*[3] + -ING[1].]

1. (See the vb. and quots.)

1815 BURNEY *Falconer's Mar. Dict.*, *Reaming*, in block-making, the act of increasing the size of a hole with a large instrument. **1882** NARES *Seamanship* (ed. 6) 156 The lead that remains in the groove must be extracted—this is called reaming.

2. *fig.* A reprimand. *colloq.*

1973 M. WOODHOUSE *Blue Bone* xi. 111 One major stink... Massive reamings are being handed out. **1976** 'J. CHARLTON' *Remington Set* xxiii. 119 You're bloody cheerful ..for a bloke that's headed for a number one reaming from the CO.

'reaming, *ppl. a.*[1] *rare.* [f. REAM *v.*[1]] Stretching out in threads; ropy; forming masses of filaments.

1495 *Trevisa's Barth. De P.R.* v. xxii. (W. de W.), Moche grete spityll & thycke, gleymy & reamyng. **1647** HERRICK *Noble Numbers, Widow's Teares* v, Farewell the Flax and Reaming wooll, With which thy house was plentifull.

'reaming, *ppl. a.*[2] Chiefly *Sc.* [f. REAM *v.*[2]] Frothing, foaming. Also in phr. ***reaming full***.

1513 DOUGLAS *Æneis* I. xi. 89 He merely ressauis the remand tais, All out he drank. **1717** RAMSAY *Elegy Lucky Wood* vi, Reaming swats. **1721** —— *Prospect of Plenty* 196 With reaming quaff. *a* **1774** FERGUSSON *Poems* (1845) 5 Come and gie's the tither blaw O' reaming ale. **1824** SCOTT *Redgauntlet* ch. ii, It's a sore thing to see a..cow kick down the pail when it's reaming fou. **1842** J. AITON *Domest. Econ.* (1857) 201 They give a reaming handful of rich milk. **1894** CROCKETT *Lilac Sunbonnet* 23 The reaming white which filled the blanket tub.

reaming, variant of REEMING *vbl. sb.*

reamme, obs. form of REALM.

†re-a'mount, *v. Obs.* [RE- 5 a.] To remount.

1621 QUARLES *Argalus & P.* (1678) 64 All rites perform'd, he re-amounts his Steed.

reamy ('ri:mɪ), *a.* [f. REAM *sb.*[2] + -Y[1].] Creamy, frothy; made with cream.

1831 J. WILSON in *Blackw. Mag.* XXIX. 553 A reamy richness, unknown to any other malt. **1868** G. MACDONALD *R. Falconer* vi, A bit o' reamy cakes.

rean (ri:n). *Obs.* exc. *dial.* Forms: 6 reian, 6–7, 9 reane, 7, 9 reean, 9 rean(n, reen(e, etc. [App. a var. of RAIN *sb.*[2], but the difference in vowel over the northern area is difficult to explain. In the west perhaps associated with *reen* RHINE.]

1. A water-furrow; = RAIN *sb.*[2] 2.

? *a* **1500** *Chester Pl.* ii. 478 Cornes fayre and cleane that groweth on ridges out of the reane. **1523** FITZHERB. *Husb.* §21 He taketh up the wede, and casteth it in the reane. *Ibid.* §33 It wolde be water-forowed bytwene the landes, there-as the reane shulde be. **1688** R. HOLME *Armoury* III. iii. 73 A Reean, is the distance between two Buts. **1859** *Jrnl. R. Agric. Soc.* XX. I. 221 The work being thus all 'cops' and 'reanes', not only was there a waste of ground from such a redundance of water-furrows, but there was a great loss of time in ploughing. **1879-** in dial. glossaries (Northumb., Lanc., Chesh., Shropsh., Glouc.).

†b. A streamlet; = RAIN *sb.*[2] 2 b. *Obs.*[−1]

1611 COTGR., *Ruisselet*, a small brooke or gullet; a reane, or gutter of running water.

2. A balk, ridge, terraced strip, etc.; = RAIN *sb.*[2] 1.

1781 HUTTON *Tour to Caves* (ed. 2) Gloss., *Rean*, a dale, or rig in a field. **1869-** in northern glossaries (Cumb., Northumb., Durh., Yks., Derby). **1883** SEEBOHM *Eng. Village Comm.* x. 381 Similar terraces in the Dales of Yorkshire..are still called by the Dalesmen 'reeans' or 'reins'.

rean, obs. form of REIN *sb.*

re-'analyse, *v.* [RE- 5 a.] *trans.* To analyse again.

1934 in WEBSTER. **1946** *Nature* 17 Aug. 243/2 As commercial penicillins recently have contained much more penicillin *K* than was formerly the case, the statistics of the Johns Hopkins Hospital were re-analysed as regards the time factor. **1964** K. G. LOCKYER *Introd. Critical Path Anal.* ix. 88 By taking the original network and inserting into it the *actual* times..it is simple to re-analyse the network. **1973** J. J. MCKELVEY *Man against Tsetse* iii. 200 Ehrlich rushed to Liverpool, confirmed the results of Thomas and Breinl, returned to Germany, and with his colleague Alfred Bertheim reanalyzed atoxyl. **1977** *Word 1972* XXVIII. 93 Yet, because of changes elsewhere in the adjective system, they must be reanalyzed synchronically as NPs.

rea'nalysis. [Cf. prec. and ANALYSIS.] A second, or further, analysis.

1934 in WEBSTER. **1962** H. A. GLEASON in Householder & Saporta *Probl. Lexicogr.* ii. 92 In some cases no kind of analysis or reanalysis can force the material into the sort of model that descriptive linguistics find appropriate to grammatical statements. **1968** CHOMSKY & HALLE *Sound Pattern Eng.* I. i. 10 If the syntactic component were to be connected to an orthographic rather than a phonetic output system, the reanalysis into phonological phrases would be unnecessary. **1977** *Times* 19 Nov. 14/4 The Bancroft Library..decided to submit the plate to detailed re-analysis.

re-'anchor, *v.* [RE- 5 a.] *trans.* and *intr.* To anchor again.

a **1711** KEN *Hymnarium* Poet. Wks. 1721 II. 27 Soon as she re-anchor'd in my heart, She thus began her Cargo to impart. **1897** MARY KINGSLEY *W. Africa* xviii. 418 The Lafayette having dragged her anchor..must be rescued and re-anchored.

reane, obs. form of RANE *sb.* and REAN.

re'animate, *a. rare.* [Cf. next and ANIMATE *a.*] Reanimated, revived, etc.

1810 SOUTHEY *Kehama* XIV. x, With other life re-animate, She saw the dead arise. **1885** in Schaff & Gilman *Libr. Relig. Poetry* 567, I would..with reanimate and quickened step.. go on my way.

reanimate (ri:'ænɪmeɪt), *v.* [f. RE- 5 a + ANIMATE *v.*, prob. after med.L. *reanimāre* or F. *réanimer*, (†*r'animer*) *ranimer* (16th c.).]

1. *trans.* To animate with new life, to make alive again, to restore to life or consciousness. Also *fig.*

1611 COTGR., *Ranimer*, to reanimate, reincourage, reuiue [etc.]. **1714** *Spect.* No. 578 ¶8 The Power of re-animating a dead Body, by flinging my own Soul into it. **1786** tr. *Beckford's Vathek* (1868) 14 The wakeful lark hailed the rising light that reanimates the whole creation. **1812** BYRON *Ch. Har.* I. xliv, Fame that will scare re-animate their clay. **1865** DICKENS *Mut. Fr.* III. iii, Doctor examines the dank carcase, and pronounces..that it is worth while trying to reanimate the same. **1886** RUSKIN *Præterita* I. 271 Byron.. reanimated for me the real people whose feet had worn the marble I trod on.

2. a. To give fresh heart or courage to (a person); to stimulate anew. Also const. *with*.

1706 PHILLIPS (ed. Kersey), *To Re-animate*,..to put in heart again. **1792** *Anecd. W. Pitt* II. xxiii. 57 His late Majesty could not re-animate the Dutch with the love of liberty. **1870** DISRAELI *Lothair* xxxii, Your presence always reanimates me.

b. To impart fresh vigour, energy, or activity to (a thing).

1762 FOOTE *Orators* I. Wks. 1799 I. 204 He reanimates their slackened nerves with the mystic picture of an apple-tree. **1785** BURKE *Wks.* (1826) IV. 267 To reanimate the powers of the unproductive parts. **1823** DE QUINCEY *Dice* Wks. 1862 X. 314 The picture..called up and re-animated in his memory..all his honourable plans. **1872** YEATS *Growth Comm.* 250 He reanimated the textile manufactures.

3. *intr.* To recover life or spirit.

1645 SYMONDS *Diary* (Camden) 244 All ours re-animated, and expected to follow Pointz to the North. **1782** MISS BURNEY *Cecilia* IX. v, 'There spoke Miss Beverley!' cried Delvile, re-animating at this little apology. **1796** JANE AUSTEN *Sense & Sens.* xvii, His affections seemed to re-animate towards them all. **1841** J. CURTIS in *Jrnl. R. Agric. Soc.* II. II. 207 They reanimate as they are dried by the sun.

Hence **re'animated, -'animating,** *ppl. adjs.*

1661 GLANVILL *Van. Dogm.* 138 We are our re-animated Ancestours and antedate their Resurrection. **1746** HERVEY *Medit.* (1818) 157 The resurrection of the just, and the state of their re-animated bodies! **1817** J. SNART (*title*) Thesaurus of Horror, or the Charnel-House Explored, showing the re-animating power of earth in cases of Syncope. **1871** SMILES *Charac.* iii. (1876) 84 Gazing on them with reanimated eye.

reanimation (ˌri:ænɪ'meɪʃən). [f. prec.: see -ATION.]

1. a. The action of restoring to life. Also *fig.*

1797 *Encycl. Brit.* (ed. 3) XVI. 26/1 Reanimation means the reviving or restoring to life those who are apparently dead. **1858** SEARS *Athan.* II. xi. 237 The reanimation of the corpse. **1889** RUSKIN *Præterita* III. 147 The first two of his great poems..are the re-animation of Border legends.

b. The fact, or process, of returning to life.

1816 W. TAYLOR in *Monthly Mag.* XLI. 502 Canonized on the express ground of a miraculous reanimation. **1838** POE *A. G. Pym* Wks. 1864 IV. 31, I experienced..a giddy and overpowering sense of deliverance and reanimation.

2. Renewal of vigour or liveliness.

1815 JANE AUSTEN *Emma* II. v, A most delightful re-animation of exhausted spirits. **1833** SIR F. B. HEAD *Bubbles fr. Brunnen* 4, I felt a reanimation of mind.

reanneal (ri:ə'ni:l), *v.* [RE- 5 a.] *trans.* To anneal again; in *Biochem.*, to change (single-stranded nucleic acid) back into a double-stranded form; also *intr.*, to change from a single-stranded to a double-stranded form. Hence **rea'nnealing** *vbl. sb.*

1963 J. OSBORNE *Dental Mech.* (ed. 5) x. 212 If a considerable amount of bending and re-bending has to be done the wire must be re-annealed from time to time. **1971** *Nature* 25 June 503/1 Mouse satellite DNA..consists of highly repetitive nucleotide sequences which therefore reanneal relatively rapidly after denaturation with alkali. **1980** *Sci. Amer.* Apr. 77/3 The first step of this process is called denaturation, the second step reannealing. *Ibid.*, When the DNA is denatured and reannealed to radioactive RNA, only the remains of those colonies that contained a plasmid whose sequence matches the messenger become radioactive.

reannex (ri:ə'nɛks), *v.* [a. OF. *reannexer* (1476 in Godef. *Compl.*): see RE- and ANNEX *v.*] *trans.* To annex again.

1495 *Rolls of Parlt.* VI. 469/2 That the same Manours.. be reuiued and reannexed to the said Duchie of Cornwall. **1622** BACON *Hen. VII* 40 King Charles was not a little inflamed with an ambition to repurchase, and reannex that Duchie. **1642** C. VERNON *Consid. Exch.* 58 The said Court of Wards and Liveries..might.. escape from being re-annexed to the Exchequer. **1750** CARTE *Hist. Eng.* II. 284 Declaring the feif forfeited, re-annexed it to the domaine of the Crown. **1808** W. TAYLOR in Robberds *Mem.* II. 223, I believe I shall be re-annexed to the Critical Review if it go on. **1896** LELY *Stat. of Pract. Utility* 8 *note*, The 9th.. section..reannexed to Lower Canada certain parts of Labrador and the adjacent islands.

Hence **rea'nnexing** *vbl. sb.*

1622 BACON *Hen. VII* 45 The French Ambassadors were dismissed; the King auoiding to vnderstand any thing touching the reannexing of Britaine.

reannexation (ˌriːænɪk'seɪʃən). [Cf. prec. and ANNEXATION.] The action of reannexing; the fact or process of being reannexed.

1860 MOTLEY *Netherl.* (1875) I. 360 One general scheme; the main features of which were the reannexation of Holland [etc.]. **1866** *Macm. Mag.* Feb. 280 Adjusting the terms of reannexation to Rome.

reanoint (riːə'nɔɪnt), *v.* [RE- 5 a.] *trans.* To anoint again.

1611 FLORIO, *Riungere*, to reanoint. **1626** BACON *Sylva* §998 The Party Hurt, hath been in great Rage of Paine, till the Weapon was Reannointed. **1627** DRAYTON *Agincourt* 99 Edward..re-annoynted mounts th' Imperiall Chaire.

reanson, obs. form of RANSOM *sb.*

†**re'answer**, *sb. Obs.*$^{-1}$ [Cf. next.] Reply.

1599 *Sir Clyom.* in Peele's Wks. (Rtldg.) 531/1 Who art thou, or what's thy name? re-answer quickly make.

†**re'answer**, *v.*[1] *Obs.* [f. RE- + ANSWER *v.*, prob. after *respond*, *reply*, *rejoin*, etc.]

1. *trans.* **a.** To answer; to give answer to.

1523 MORE in *State Papers* (1830) I. 143 Which [commendation] I can never otherwise reanswere than with my pore prayoure. *c* **1594** CAPT. WYATT *R. Dudley's Voy. W. Ind.* (Hakl. Soc.) 3 Our great ordenance..was re-answeared by the Queenes ordenance out of Callshott Castle. **1599** *Sir Clyom.* in Peele's Wks. (Rtldg.) 511/1 In case you will re-answer me my question to absolve.

b. To meet, be sufficient for, or equivalent to.

1598 BARRET *Theor. Warres* IV. i. 97 If..your enemy [be] very strong in horse, and you few horse or none to re-answere them. **1599** SHAKS. *Hen. V*, III. vi. 136 The losses we haue borne..which in weight to re-answer, his pettinesse would bow vnder. **1630** *R. Johnson's Kingd. & Commw.* 513 Rewards of their abstinence and vertues, as also to re-answer their benefactors confidence.

c. To make good. *rare*$^{-1}$.

1591 GREENE *2nd Pt. Conny-Catching* Wks. (Grosart) X. 109 If a purse bee drawen..they take vp all the Nips and Foists abovte the cittie, and let them lie there [in Newgate] while the money be reanswered vnto the party.

2. *intr.* To make an answer or return.

1526 *Pilgr. Perf.* (W. de W. 1531) 21 b, He commeth to vs helpyng..vs: and we reanswere to his grace.

re'answer, *v.*[2] *rare.* [RE- 5 a.] *trans.* To answer a second time.

1608 HIERON *Defence* II. 179 Lyraes distinction betwene the facte and the zeale is before answered, and by and by shal be reanswered. **1933** J. CLAYTON *Sir Thomas More* v. 87 From the time of S. Anselm..the most profound and subtle philosophical questions had been raised and answered, and again reconsidered and reanswered. **1977** *Word 1972* XXVIII. 78, I am grateful for her patience in answering and reanswering countless questions and either producing or approving almost all the sentences included in this article.

re-'anvil, *v.* [RE- 5 a.] *trans.* To put on the anvil again; to forge afresh.

1716 M. DAVIES *Athen. Brit.* III. 61 Of which Arian forgeries some were re-anvill'd again by..Turrianus.

reap (riːp), *sb.*[1] Forms: 1 reopa, rypa, 4-5 reepe, 4-6 repe, 7- reap. [OE. *reopa*, *rypa*, prob. for **ripa*, related to *ripan* or *rīpan* REAP *v.*[1]] A bundle or handful of grain or any similar crop; a sheaf, or the quantity sufficient to make a sheaf. (Cf. RIP *sb.*)

c **825** *Vesp. Psalter* cxxv. 6 Cumað..berende reopan heara. *Ibid.* cxxviii. 7 Se ðe reopan somnað. *a* **1340** HAMPOLE *Psalter* cxxv. 8 Þai sall cum with gladnes: berand þaire repis. **1388** WYCLIF *Judith* viii. 3 Men byndynge togidere reepis in the feeld. *c* **1420** *Pallad. on Husb.* VII. 247 Barly..vppon repes bounde And in a oone ybake. *c* **1460** *Towneley Myst.* ii. 235 As mych as oone reepe. **1523** FITZHERB. *Husb.* §29 In some places they lay them [beans and peas] on repes,..and neuer bynde them. **1613** MARKHAM *Eng. Husbandman* xviii. (1635) 116 You may put twentie reapes together, and thereof make a cocke. **1764** *Museum Rust.* II. 81 Though the bottom of the reaps will be a little greenish, they must not be turned to weather the under side. **1805** R. W. DICKSON *Pract. Agric.* II. 706 They are usually reaped with the sickle, and laid in thin grips or reaps. **1829** in BROCKETT (ed. 2). **1876-** in dial. glossaries (Cumb., Northumb., Yks.; Glouc., Som.).

reap (riːp), *sb.*[2] Forms: α. 1 hríp(p-, hrip(p-, 1, 4 rip, ryp, 4 ripe, rype, rijp; ripp, ryppe, rep. β. 6 reape, 7, 9 reap. [OE. *rip* or *rīp* related to *rīpan* or *ripan* REAP *v.*[1]; on the relationship and history of the forms cf. the note to the vb. Sense 2 is perh. directly from the vb.]

†**1.** Harvest, reaping. *Obs.*

α. *c* **950** *Lindisf. Gosp.* Matt. xiii. 30 Forletas eʒðer ʒewæxe við to hrípe..& in tid hrípes [etc.; *Rushw.* ripe(s)]. *c* **1000** *Ags. Gosp.* Matt. ix. 37-8 Micel rip ys..Biddaþ ðæs ripes hlaford þæt he sende wyrhtan to his ripe. **1382** WYCLIF *Gen.* viii. 22 All the daies of the erthe, seed and ripe..shulen not rest. —— *2 Sam.* xxi. 9 In the dais of the fyrst rijp [**1388** the firste rep *or* ripp]. **1387** TREVISA *Higden* (Rolls) VIII. 185 Þou hast no leve to sette þyn hook in oþer men ripe [*v.r.* ryppe, rip, ryp(e)].

β. **1542** BECON *David's Harp* Pref., We had nede therefore to pray vnto the Lord of the haruest, to sende out labourers into his reape. **1600** W. WATSON *Decacordon* (1602) 239 Your plants are blasted in the bud: your corne shaken before the reape. **1679** BLOUNT *Anc. Tenures* 21 He was..to come to the Lords Reap with all his houshold.

2. A set of reapers.

1826 in Hone *Every-day Bk.* II. 1167 The lord of the harvest is accompanied by his lady (the person is so called who goes second in the reap).

3. *Judo.* (See quot. 1968.) Cf. next, B. 2 e.

1968 K. SMITH *Judo Dict.* 167 *Reap*, an action of the leg or foot to sweep away the legs or feet of an opponent in execution of a throw. **1975** R. BUTLER *Where All Girls are Sweeter* ii. 8, I..locked his arm and gave him what the judo boys call a 'reap' and his arm cracked loudly as he went down on his back.

reap (riːp), *v.*[1] Forms: see below. [OE. *rīpan* or *ripan* (North. *rioppa* etc.), *rypan*, *reopan*, not represented in the cognate languages: the relationship of the various forms and their subsequent history in ME. is to some extent obscure.

The quantity of the vowel in WS. is not certain, but the pl. pa. t. *ripon* (*rypon*) would normally correspond to an infin. *rīpan* (conjugated like *rīdan* ride.) For Anglian and North. dial., however, a short vowel is proved by the forms with umlaut (*reop-*, *riop-*), and by the spelling with double *p*; how these forms were conjugated does not appear. Whether an OE. **repan* can also be inferred from the late pl. pa. t. *rǽpon*, and early ME. *reopen*, is doubtful.

In ME. the infin. types are *rīpe(n* and *rēpe(n*, the former of which might represent either OE. *rīpan* or *ripan*, and the latter OE. *ripan* or **repan*. The strong conj. of *rēpe(n* is that of verbs of the fourth and fifth classes, with pa. t. *rap*, and pa. pple. *repe(n* or *rope(n*. The rare pa. t. *rope* (pl. *ropen*) may either be a relic of the old conj. of *rīpan*, or a new formation on analogy of the pa. pple. From the 15th c. the conj. has usually been weak, though some strong forms have been retained (or re-formed) in dialect use. The infin. *rip*, found in some 16th c. writers, is also common in mod. dial., and may partly represent the old northern forms with double *p*.]

A. Illustration of forms.

1. *Inf.* (and *Pres.*) α. 1 ripan, rypan, *north.* hriopa, 3 ripen, ripe, 4 rype.

The normal forms of the present tense in OE. are 1. *ripe*, 2. *ripst*, 3. *ripð*, or *ripeð*; pl. *ripað*.

c **825** *Vesp. Psalter* cxxviii. 7 Of ðæm ne ʒefylleð hond his se ripeð. *c* **950** *Lindisf. Gosp.* Matt. xxv. 24 Ðu hripes ðer ðu ne sawes. *c* **975** *Rushw. Gosp.* ibid. 26 Ic ripe [*c* **1000** ripe, rype] þær ic ne seow. *c* **1000** ÆLFRIC *Gen.* xlv. 6 Man ne mæʒ naðer erian ne ripan. *c* **1200** *Moral Ode* 22 (Trin. Coll. MS.) Alle men sulle ripen þat hie ar sewen. *c* **1290** ripe [see B. 2 b]. **1387** TREVISA *Higden* (Rolls) I. 11 Ʒif ȝe [= she] wole wiþ ȝow rype, forbedeþ hir nouȝt.

β. 1 reopa, 3 reopen; 2- 4 repen, 4-6 repe, 5-6 reepe, 6-8 reape, (6 *Sc.* raipe), 6- reap.

c **825** *Vesp. Psalter* cxxv. 5 Ða sawað in tearum, in ʒefian hie reopað. *a* **1200-25** repen, reopen [see B. 2 b]. *a* **1300** *E.E. Psalter* cxxv. 6 In mikel gladschip repe sal þai. *a* **1325** *Prose Psalter* cxxviii. 6 Of which he þat shal repen, ne fild nouȝt his honde. **1393** LANGL. *P. Pl.* C. VI. 15 Canstow..Repe. *c* **1420** LYDG. *Assembly of Gods* 1245 Suche as ye haue sowe Must ye nedes reepe. **1530** PALSGR. 686/2, I repe corne with a syckell. **1535** COVERDALE *Matt.* xxv. 26, I reape where I sowed not. —— *Rev.* xiv. 15 Thruste in thy sycle and reepe. **1588** A. KING tr. *Canisius' Catech.* 185 Quhat so euer a man saues, the same sal he raipe. **1591** SPENSER *M. Hubberd* 263 To plough, to plant, to reap. **1707** in Hearne *Collect.* 9 Aug. (O.H.S.) II. 32, I should not reape one peny advantage. **1833** TENNYSON *Lotos Eaters* 166 Sow the seed, and reap the harvest.

γ. 1 *north.* hrioppa, hripp-, 6-7 rippe, 6 rip.

c **950** *Lindisf. Gosp.* Matt. vi. 26 Fuglas heofnes ne settas ..ne rioppas. *Ibid.* xxv. 26 Ic hrippo ðer ne seawu ic. **1533-4** *Act 25 Hen. VIII* in Bolton *Stat. Irel.* (1621) 75 Their wages to rippe or binde corne. **1565** COOPER *Thesaurus* s.v. *Demeto*, to rippe or cut downe with a sickle.

2. a. *Str. pa. t.* 1 *pl.* ripon, -rypon, ræpon; 4 rap, rope (*pl.* ropen); *dial.* 8-9 rope, 9 rep.

c **893**-*a* **1122** [see B. 2]. **1377** LANGL. *P. Pl.* B. XIII. 374 If I rope [I wolde] ouer-reche, or ȝaf hem red that ropen [etc.]. **1388** WYCLIF *Ruth* ii. 23 So longe sche rap with hem.

b. *Str. pa. pple.* α. 4 ropen, ropun, -yn, 4-5 rope.

β. 4 repe, 4-5 repen, -yne, (9 reapen).

1382 WYCLIF *Gen.* xlv. 6 It may not be eerid, ne ropun. **1388** —— *Song Sol.* v. 1, Y haue rope [*v.r.* repe] my myrre. *c* **1385** ropen, -yn, repyne [see B. 2 b]. *c* **1420** repe [see B. 2]. **1874** OUIDA *Two little wooden Shoes* 256 The wheat was reapen in the fields.

3. a. *Weak pa. t.* 4 repide, 6 rieped, 7-8 reapt, 8- reaped.

1382 repiden [see B. 3]. **1542** rieped [see B. 4]. **1613** PURCHAS *Pilgrimage* IX. ix. (1614) 876 That which they reapt on the land. **1724** DE FOE *Mem. Cavalier* (1840) 183 The king reaped the fruits of the victory.

b. *Weak pa. pple.* 5-6 reped, 6 reeped, 6- reaped, 7- reap'd; 6 reapt, rept; ripped.

1489 reped [see B. 4]. **1535** COVERDALE *Rev.* xiv. 16 The earth was reeped. *a* **1547** SURREY *Æneid* IV. (1557) F 2 b, Springyng herbes reapt vp with brasen sithes. **1566** PAINTER *Pal. Pleas.* I. 72 When the wheate was ready to be ripped. **1573** TUSSER *Husb.* (1878) 45 Much profit is rept, by sloes well kept. **1611** BIBLE *Rev.* xiv. 16 The earth was reaped. **1653** MILTON *Hirelings* Wks. (1851) 365 From him wherfore should be reap'd?

B. Signification.

1. *intr.* To perform the action of cutting grain (or any similar crop) with the hook or sickle. Also freq. *fig.* or in fig. context.

c **825** [see A. 1 α and β]. *c* **897** K. ÆLFRED *Gregory's Past. C.* xxxix. 284 Se þe him ælc wolcn ondræt, ne ripð se næfre. *c* **950**- [see A. 1 α]. *c* **1000** ÆLFRIC *Hom.* II. 462 Behealdað þas fleoʒendan fuʒelas, ðe ne sawað ne ne ripað. *c* **1250** *Moral Ode* 11 in *E.E.P.* (1862) 23 Hy mowen sculen & rien þer þe hi ær seowen. *c* **1290** *S. Eng. Leg.* I. 303/126 He ne þurte carie of non oþur weork, noþur to ripe ne mowe. **1382** WYCLIF *Rev.* xiv. 15 Sende thi sikel, and repe. *c* **1450** *Mirour Saluacioun* 4203 The Austere juge wille repe in place where he noght sewe. **1526** *Pilgr. Perf.* (W. de W. 1531) 11 b, They dyd sowe, & we do repe. **1600** SHAKS. *A.Y.L.* III. ii. 113 They that reap must sheafe and binde. *a* **1822** SHELLEY *Men of Eng.* vi, Sow seed,—but let no tyrant reap. **1842** TENNYSON *Dora* 76 The reapers reap'd, And the sun fell, and all the land was dark.

2. a. *trans.* To cut (grain, etc.) with the sickle, esp. in harvest; hence, to gather or obtain as a crop (usually of grain) by this or some other process.

c **893** K. ÆLFRED *Oros.* IV. viii. §7 þæt folc him ʒeþuhte þa hie heora corn ripon..þæt ealle þa ear wæron blodeʒe. *a* **900** *O.E. Chron.* (Parker MS.) an. 896 On hærfæste..þa hwile þe hie hira corn ʒerypon. *a* **1122** *Ibid.* (Laud MS.) an. 1089 Maniʒ men ræpon heora corn onbutan Martines mæssan. **13..** *Propr. Sanct.* (Vernon MS.) in *Archiv Stud. neu. Spr.* LXXXI. 83/22 [The wheat] is ropen and leid ful lowe. **1382** WYCLIF *Deut.* xxiv. 19 Whanne thou repist corn in thi feeld. *c* **1420** *Pallad. on Husb.* X. 127 Now in sum stede is panyk rope and mylde. **1495** *Trevisa's Barth. De P.R.* XVII. clvii. 707 Repers haue repen the corn with hokys and gadred it home. **1523** FITZHERB. *Husb.* §29 Pees and benes be moste commonly laste reped or mowen. **1585** HIGGINS tr. *Junius' Nomenclator* 107 The strawe, stubble..remaining in the grounde after the corne is rept. **1667** MILTON *P.L.* XII. 18 Labouring the soile, and reaping plenteous crop. **1717** PRIOR *Alma* I. 156 No man ever reapt his Corn, Or from the Oven drew his Bread. **1784** COWPER *Task* V. 203 They ploughed and sowed, And reaped their plenty without grudge or strife. **1812** SIR J. SINCLAIR *Syst. Husb. Scot.* I. 268 Many have reaped more than 60 bolls [of potatoes] from one acre. **1825** COBBETT *Rur. Rides* 239, I am told they give twelve shillings an acre for reaping wheat. **1850** TENNYSON *In Mem.* lxiv, Who ploughs with pain his native lea And reaps the labour of his hands.

b. In fig. context.

c **1000** ÆLFRIC *Hom.* II. 534 ʒif we eow þa gastlican sæd sawaþ, hwonlic biþ þæt we eowere flæsclican þing ripon. *a* **1200** *Moral Ode* 20 Ʒe mawen sculen & repen þet ho er sowen. *a* **1225** *Juliana* 74 (Bodl. MS.) Ʒe schulen..reopen ripe of þat sed þat ȝe her seowen. *c* **1385** CHAUCER *L.G.W.* Prol. 74 Well I wote that ye haue here byforn Of makyng ropyn [*v.r.* ropen, repyne] and lad a-wey the corn. *c* **1420** LYDG. *Assembly of Gods* 1245 Suche as ye haue sowe Must ye nedes reepe. **1590** SPENSER *F.Q.* I. iv. 47, I hop'd to reape the crop of all my care. **1667** MILTON *P.L.* III. 67 Reaping immortal fruits of joy and love. **1718** LADY M. W. MONTAGU *Let. to Abbé Conti* 19 May, We die or grow old before we can reap the fruit of our labours. **1842** TENNYSON *Locksley Hall* 139 What is that to him that reaps not harvest of his youthful joys? **1853** SIR H. DOUGLAS *Milit. Bridges* 147 To reap the fullest fruits of a victory.

c. With *down* adv., *off* adv. and prep.

1563 GOLDING *Cæsar* IV. (1565) 104 In all other quarters ye corn was reaped down, & none standing any where saue in thys one place. **1592** *Knaresborough Wills* (Surtees) I. 187 When the same [barley] shalbe reapte of the feilde. **1649** BLITHE *Eng. Improv. Impr.* (1653) 75 I'll..begin to enter upon it as soon as the Crop is reaped off.

d. *transf.* To cut (plants, flowers, etc.) after the fashion of reaping. Also in fig. context.

1721 MORTIMER *Husbandry* II. 123 It will repair the hurt you have done to the Plants in reaping their Shoots. **1781** COWPER *Retirement* 753 We reap with bleeding hands Flowers of rank odour upon thorny lands. **1784** —— *Task* VI. 939 Compared with which The laurels that a Cæsar reaps are weeds. **1820** KEATS *Lamia* I. 318 Baskets heap'd Of amorous herbs and flowers, newly reap'd Late on that eve.

e. *Judo.* To sweep (one leg or both legs) from under one's opponent.

1950 E. J. HARRISON *Judo* iii. 56 When reaping your opponent's leg..you should turn your head..and gaze upwards at the ceiling. **1954** E. DOMINY *Teach Yourself Judo* vii. 73 Now bring your right hip past his right and reap his leg away as already described. **1956** K. TOMIKI *Judo* iii. 74 Making a sickle of your leg, apply the back of your right knee to that of *uke's* left knee, crosswise. Sharply reap his left leg toward your right oblique back corner.

3. a. *fig.* To get in return; to obtain or procure (esp. some profit or advantage) for oneself; to gain, acquire.

c **1300** *S. Cecilia* 155 (Ashm. MS.) We schulleþ uor our trauail, þi blisse repe atenende. **1382** WYCLIF *Hosea* x. 13 Ʒe han sowe vnpite, ȝe repiden [**1388** han rope *or* repe] wickidnesse. **1560** DAUS tr. *Sleidane's Comm.* Pref. 2 Men may reape frute and commodity. **1573** TUSSER *Husb.* (1878) 46 By malt ill kept, small profit is rept. **1630** PRYNNE *Anti-Armin.* 159 They can reape nothing but discomfort from it. **1671** MILTON *Samson* 966 Why do I..suing For peace, reap nothing but repulse and hate? **1711** STEELE *Spect.* No. 262 ¶6 Those Advantages, which the Publick may reap from this Paper. **1752** HUME *Ess. & Treat.* (1777) I. 182 He reaps no satisfaction but from low and sensual objects. **1833** LAMB *Elia* Ser. II. Pref., He sowed doubtful speeches, and reaped plain, unequivocal hatred. **1863** BRIGHT *Sp. Amer.* 26 Mar. (1876) 126 Where labour..has reaped its greatest reward. **1875** JOWETT *Plato* (ed. 2) III. 197 The greatest blessing which you have reaped from wealth.

†**b.** With material object. *Obs. rare.*

1601 SHAKS. *Twel. N.* III. i. 144 When wit and youth is come to haruest, Your wife is like to reape a proper man. **1630** *R. Johnson's Kingd. & Commw.* 69 The hils swarme with cattell and sheepe, from whence they reape plenty of butter, cheese, and milke.

c. To take away by force. *rare*$^{-1}$.

1634 SIR T. HERBERT *Trav.* 50 The Bramini..vnresisted reaps her Virgin honour.

4. To cut down or harvest the crop or produce of (a field, etc.). Also with *down*.

1382 WYCLIF *Jas.* v. 4 The hijre of ȝoure werkmen, that repiden ȝoure cuntrees. **1489** CAXTON *Faytes of A.* II. ix. 108 Theyre landes were almost ripe for to be reped. **1526** TINDALE *Jas.* v. 4 The labourers which haue reped doune youre feldes. **1542** UDALL *Erasm. Apoph.* 210 b, He rieped Asia and had all the eres, and I dooe but gather the stalkes.

1697 DRYDEN *Virg. Georg.* III. 279 With thy Sickle reap the rankest Land. **1784** COWPER *Task* v. 755 Ye may fill your garners, ye that reap The loaded soil. **1827** G. S. FABER *Sacr. Calend. Prophecy* (1844) III. 217 If a king shall behold a country reaping or reaped..he shall quickly hear of the slaughter of his people.

transf. **1596** SHAKS. *1 Hen. IV*, I. iii. 34 His Chin new reapt, Shew'd like a stubble Land at Haruest home.

Hence **reaped, 'reapen, 'reaping** *ppl. adjs.*

1765 *Museum Rust.* III. 193 At market I sold the reaped wheat at one pound per comb. **1819** KEATS *Fancy* 41 Thou shalt hear..Rustle of the reaped corn. **1844** H. STEPHENS *Bk. Farm* III. 1069 In reaped sheaves..the straws are straight and hard pressed. **1865** SWINBURNE *Poems & Ball., Garden of Proserpine* 6 For reaping folk and sowing. **1874** OUIDA *Two little wooden Shoes* 206 The purple brow of the just reapen lands. **1887** R. L. STEVENSON *Merry Men* III. 131 Scythes for the reaping angel of Death.

reap (riːp), *v.*[2] Now only *dial.* [Var. of RIP, due to the existence of *rip* as var. of REAP *v.*[1]] *trans.* To rip *up* (a matter).

1580 LYLY *Euphues* Wks. 1902 II. 143 The rages of friendes, reaping vp al the hidden malices, or suspicions, or follyes that lay lurking in the minde. **1698** FRYER *Acc. E. India & P.* 374 The Courtiers are shy of her Company, because of reaping up their old Sins. **1862** MRS. H. WOOD *Channings* III. 52, I am sorry you should have reaped up this matter. **1873-** in many dial. (esp. northern and western) glossaries.

reapable ('riːpəb(ə)l), *a. rare.* [f. REAP *v.*[1] + -ABLE.] That can be reaped; fit for reaping.

1570 LEVINS *Manip.* 2/30 Reapable, *messibilis*. **1858** CARLYLE *Fredk. Gt.* IX. i. II. 390 A strange sowing of dragon's teeth, and the first harvest reapable from it a world of armed men.

reape, obs. var. RIPE *v.*[1]; dial. var. ROPE *sb.*

reaper ('riːpə(r)). Forms: 1 ripere, 4–6 reper, (5 repare, 6 repar), 6– reaper. [f. REAP *v.*[1]]

1. a. One who reaps.

c **1000** *Ags. Gosp.* Matt. xiii. 39 þæt rip is worulde endung, þa riperas synt englas. **1382** WYCLIF *Ruth* ii. 3 She..gedride eeris after the backis of reperis. **1387–8** T. USK *Test. Love* Prol. (Skeat) l. 105 These noble repers, as good work-men and worthy their hier han al draw and bounde vp in the sheues. *c* **1440** *Promp. Parv.* 430/1 Repare, hervyst-manne, *messor*. **1495** *Act 11 Hen. VII*, c. 22 §3 A Reper and Carter ..iijd. by the day. **1523** FITZHERB. *Husb.* §29 Loke that your sherers, repers, or mowers geld not your beanes. **1576** FLEMING *Panopl. Epist.* 228 Keeping company with the labouring reapers. **1667** MILTON *P.L.* XI. 434 Thither anon A sweatie Reaper from his Tillage brought First Fruits. **1740** SOMERVILLE *Hobbinol* II. 21 The ripen'd Grain, whose bending Ears Invite the Reaper's Hand. **1845** FORD *Handbk. Spain* I. 69 Reapers..could never stand the sun's fire without this cooling acetous diet.

attrib. **1715–20** POPE *Iliad* XVIII. 638 With bended sickles stand the reaper train. **1730–46** THOMSON *Autumn* 225 He.. chanced beside his reaper-train To walk.

b. fig. *the (Great, Grim, Old) Reaper*: Death personified.

The expression arises from the iconographic portrayal of Death wielding a scythe: cf. SCYTHE *sb.* 2.

1839 LONGFELLOW in *Baltimore Lit. Monument* May 17/1 O, not in cruelty, not in wrath, The reaper came that day. **1931** *N. & Q.* 5 Sept. 180/2 One is startled by the inroads which the great reaper has made in the ranks of the Knights since the 15th Edition. **1940** A. UPFIELD *Bushranger of Skies* xiv. 161 That he happened to be the seventh son of a seventh son..was said..to account for his escapes from The Reaper. **1976** R. LEWIS *Witness my Death* v. 182 The old house had been silent, waiting with him for the Old Reaper to come again. **1977** *New Statesman* 2 Sept. 304/1 The Grim Reaper has been rather too vigorously at work among us... At least ten of the best have gone.

2. a. A mechanical device for cutting grain without manual labour, the more modern types having also a device for binding the sheaves.

1844 *Let.* 8 Nov. in *Ohio Cultivator* (1845) 15 Mar. 47, I intended..to have written you immediately after harvest, respecting the performance of your Reaper. **1845** *Ohio Cultivator* 1 Jan. 8/3 (*heading*) McCormick's Virginia Reaper. This is another valuable invention for wheat growers. **1847** *Monthly Jrnl. Agric.* June 583 In what consists the difference between their [*sc.* Hussey's and McCormick's] Reapers we are not exactly advised. **1862** *Times* 12 June 6/1 In addition to the agricultural machines ..there are a variety of reapers and mowers. **1868** *Iowa State Agric. Soc. Rep. 1867* 237 By the folding arrangement the driver can fold the reaper-bar..rendering it perfectly portable. **1871** LOWELL *Study Wind.* (1886) 76 Our pianos and patent reapers have won medals. **1883** *Stubbs' Mercantile Circular* 26 Sept. 862/2 English reapers suit well in some parts of South Russia, but self-binders are not understood. **1923** R. HERRICK *Homely Lilla* xvi. 238 But there are tractors and reapers and sprayers. **1981** *Country Life* 7 May 1266/1 Meadows were mown by horse-drawn reaper.

attrib. **1887** *Pall Mall G.* 23 Aug. 10/2 He fell off his seat and became entangled in the reaper knives.

b. reaper-(and-)binder = SELF-BINDER.

1895 C. D. WARNER *Golden House* ix. 116 He's got no more feeling in business than a reaper-and-binder. **1901** G. B. SHAW *Three Plays for Puritans* p. xxxii, Fools who go laboriously through all the motions of the reaper and binder in an empty field. **1915** C. MACKENZIE *Guy & Pauline* 238 Close at hand was the hum of a reaper-and-binder. **1953** E. HYAMS *Gentian Violet* 54 A reaper-binder was cutting oats.

'reap-hook. [f. REAP *v.*[1]] A reaping-hook.

1591 PERCIVALL *Sp. Dict.*, *Hocino*, a reape hooke. **1761** *Brit. Mag.* II. 447 One of them struck at him with the reap-hook, and cut his arm almost off. **1820** *Blackw. Mag.* VIII. 143 The reap-hook had been busy among the ripened corn. **1896** BRUCE *Econ. Hist. Virginia* I. 464 In harvesting wheat, both the reap-hook and the sickle were used.

reaping ('riːpɪŋ), *vbl. sb.* [f. REAP *v.*[1]]

1. a. The action of the vb. REAP, in *lit.* or *fig.* uses; also, the amount reaped.

c **1380** WYCLIF *Serm.* Sel. Wks. I. 97 Tyme of þis repinge is clepid þe day of dome. *c* **1440** *Promp. Parv.* 430/1 Repynge, of corne, *messura*. **1548** UDALL, etc. *Erasm. Par. John* iv, There is more pain and labour about the tilling and sowing, then in the haruest and reaping. **1576** FLEMING *Panopl. Epist.* 179 To the readie reaping of your comoditie. **1693** EVELYN *De la Quint. Compl. Gard.* I. 32 Those which ..require some help in order to a good Reaping. **1765** *Museum Rust.* III. 136 Let the wheat stand ever so well, yet reaping is preferable to mowing. **1812** SIR J. SINCLAIR *Syst. Husb. Scot.* I. 270 An acre of potatoes gives 120 days reaping (shearing). **1844** H. STEPHENS *Bk. Farm* III. 1053 Calculating every day's reaping of those who are hired by the day. **1881** *Athenæum* 5 Nov. 603/2 That blueness which proves thousands of reapings by a razor.

b. *Judo.* The action of reaping (REAP *v.*[1] 2 e) the leg or legs of one's opponent.

1954 E. DOMINY *Teach Yourself Judo* vii. 70 The Major Outer Reaping. This is one of the most effective and popular throws in judo. **1956** K. TOMIKI *Judo* iii. 68 *O-soto-gari* (Major Outer Reaping Leg Throw). **1976** *Oxf. Compan. Sports & Games* 547/2 The most successful throws have proved to be..*o-soto-gari* (major outer reaping throw), [etc.].

2. *attrib.* and *Comb.*, as ***reaping-fork, -hook, -scythe, -sickle, -time***; **reaping-machine** = REAPER 2.

1805 R. W. DICKSON *Pract. Agric.* II. 793 A *reaping fork is sometimes made use of for collecting it into sheaves. *a* **1700** DRYDEN (J.), It looks Most plainly done by thieves with *reaping-hooks. **1765** *Museum Rust.* III. 134 They must imagine..that the new-fashioned scythes are much better for use than the old-fashioned reaping-hooks. **1805** R. W. DICKSON *Pract. Agric.* II. 794 The sickle with teeth should be employed in preference to the reaping-hook with a cutting blade. **1842** MACAULAY *Horatius* xiv, Sun-burned husbandmen With reaping-hooks and staves. **1812** SIR J. SINCLAIR *Syst. Husb. Scot.* I. 328 No *reaping machine has yet been invented, that will answer the object they had in view. **1844** H. STEPHENS *Bk. Farm* III. 1076 The first reaping-machine that came before the public with any claim to efficiency was that of Mr. Smeath of Deanston, about the year 1814–15. *Ibid.* 1081 Of this form of mounting a *reaping-scythe there are many varieties. **1611** COTGR. s.v. *Moissonnier*, a *reaping sickle. **1388** WYCLIF *Matt.* xiii. 30 Suffre ȝe hem bothe wexe..in to *repyng tyme. **1611** COTGR., *Moisson*,..reaping time.

†**reap-man.** *Obs.* Forms: 1 hrip(p)emonn, 2 ripman, 4 ripeman, 4–5 repman, 5–6 repeman. [OE. *rip(p)e-, ripmann*, f. *ripp-, rip* REAP *sb.*[2]] A reaper.

c **950** *Lindisf. Gosp.* Matt. xiii. 30 In tid hripes ic willo cuoeða ðæm hrippe-monnum [etc.]. *Ibid.* 39 Ða hripemenn soðlice engles sindon. *c* **1160** *Hatton Gosp.* Matt. ix. 37 Witodlice mycel rip ys, & feawe ripmen. **1387** TREVISA *Higden* (Rolls) I. 11 Ruth..lase vp þe eeres after his ripe-men. *c* **1400** *Solomon's Bk. Wisd.* 246 Repmen forto bere mete sone he hym þider sent. **1426** LYDG. *De Guil. Pilgr.* 10420 Thow semyst..A repman, for thyn vnkouth guyse. *c* **1449** PECOCK *Repr.* III. xvi. 383 Whanne money is paied to a repe man for his dai labour in the haruest feeld. **1566** WITHALS *Dict.* 17 b, A repe man or he that repeth the corne.

reappaise, variant of REAPPEASE *v. Obs.*

re-a'pparel, *v.* [RE- 5 a.] *trans.* To apparel again. Hence **re-a'pparelling** *vbl. sb.*

1624 DONNE *Devotions* 358 (T.), Then we shall all be invested, reapparelled in our own bodies. **1901** *Edin. Rev.* Oct. 416 Ideas must re-apparel themselves in modern dress. *Ibid.*, All such re-apparelling is of secondary import when [etc.].

re-a'pparent, *a.* [RE- 5 a.] Of a star: Reappearing periodically.

1794 G. ADAMS *Nat. & Exp. Philos.* IV. xliv. 190 Three changeable or re-apparent stars have been discovered in.. the Swan.

reappa'rition. [RE- 5 a.] A reappearance.

1599 SANDYS *Europæ Spec.* (1632) 15 With many other re-apparitions and delectable strange accidents. **1634** BP. HALL *Contempl., N.T.* IV. xii, Remember thy glorious re-apparition with thy Saviour. **1766** MATY in *Phil. Trans.* LVI. 65 Sufficient to render the reapparition of the comet uncertain. **1883** A. WINCHELL *World-Life* 281 (Cent. Dict.), Colonies, reapparitions, and other faunal dislocations in the vertical and horizontal distribution of fossil remains.

rea'ppeal, *v.* Also 5 -appell. [f. RE- + APPEAL *v.* In early use after obs. F. *reappeller* var. *rappeler* RAPPEL *v.*; cf. med.L. *reappellare* (1330).] *trans.* and *intr.* †**a.** To call back; to recall. *Obs.* **b.** To appeal again. Hence **rea'ppealing** *vbl. sb.*

1480 CAXTON *Ovid's Met.* XIII. iv, Ayax..sholde have mayntened the warre ayenst the Troyans, and have re-appelled and called them agayn to the stour. **1579** FENTON *Guicciard.* II. 89 Almost all the kingdom expected..an occasion to reappeale the Aragons. **1598** FLORIO, *Rappellare*, to reapeale..or call againe. **1611** *Ibid.*, *Rappello*, a reappealing vnto. **1748** RICHARDSON *Clarissa* (1811) V. 133 May I not re-appeal this to your own breast?

So **rea'ppeal** *sb.*, †(*a*) a recall (*obs.*); (*b*) a second appeal.

1611 FLORIO, *Rappellatione*, a reappeale, a reuoking. **1899** *Westm. Gaz.* 11 Sept. 5/2 Peace cannot be reached by a vista of endless retrials and re-appeals.

reappear (riːə'pɪə(r)), *v.* [f. RE- 5 a + APPEAR *v.*] *intr.* To appear again.

1611 COTGR., *Reparoistre*, to reappeare. **1728** POPE *Dunc.* III. 322 The dull stars roll round and reappear. **1792** MURPHY *Ess. Johnson* 20 [The Nile waters] continue hidden in the grass and weeds for about a quarter of a league, when they re-appear amongst a quantity of rocks. **1821** SHELLEY *Adonais* xviii, The ants, the bees, the swallows, reappear. **1863** *Sat. Rev.* 16 May 638 That which was 'motion'..re-appears as heat. **1900** G. C. BRODRICK *Mem. & Imp.* 92, I never felt quite sure for years afterwards that he might not reappear in my rooms.

Hence **rea'ppearing** *vbl. sb.* and *ppl. a.*

1816 SOUTHEY *Lay of Laureate* lviii, In re-appearing light confess'd, There stood another Minister of bliss. **1884** *Harper's Mag.* Mar. 607/2 The next afternoon went by without his re-appearing. **1891** *Daily News* 11 Sept. 3/3 One or two [cottages] that have become shelters for the reappearing small holders.

rea'ppearance. [RE- 5 a.] The act of appearing again; a second or fresh appearance.

1664 POWER *Exp. Philos.* I. 35 All my little Animals made their re-appearance. **1753** N. TORRIANO *Gangr. Sore Throat* 29 We bled her again..on account of a Re-appearance of bleeding at the Nose. **1828** LANDOR *Imag. Conv.* Wks. 1853 I. 341/1 The most favourite word with her ever since her re-appearance among us. **1856** KANE *Arct. Expl.* II. xiii. 131 About a month after the reappearance of the sun.

†**reappease**, *v. Obs. rare.* Also 6 **reappaise.** [RE- 5 a.] *trans.* To pacify or appease again.

1579 FENTON *Guicciard.* I. (1599) 44 To be aduertised, afore he entered the Citie: whether the tumult of the people were in any sort reappaised. **1598** FLORIO, *Rachetare*, to reapease, to quiet. **1611** in COTGR., s.v. *reblandir*.

reappell, obs. form of REAPPEAL.

reap-penny. *rare*[−1]. = REAP-SILVER.

1843 CARLYLE *Past & Pr.* II. v, [What difficulty..has our Cellerarius to collect the repselver, 'reaping silver', or penny. *Ibid.*] Wise Lord Abbots..did in time abolish or commute the reap-penny.

re-appli'cation. [RE- 5 a; cf. next.] A fresh application.

1692 NORRIS *Curs. Reflect.* 9 A Re-advertency or Re-application of mind to Ideas that are actually there. **1823** J. BADCOCK *Dom. Amusem.* 27 The simple re-application of fire produces nearly the same result. **1897** *Daily News* 12 Mar. 3/3 Racing licences should hold good from year to year without re-application.

re-a'pply, *v.* [RE- 5 a.] To apply again.

1723 HOUSTOUN in *Phil. Trans.* XXXII. 388 She went chearfully Abroad, and re-apply'd herself to Business. **1805** R. W. DICKSON *Pract. Agric.* I. 388 Mixing them [slices of soil] into composts with lime, and re-applying them. **1873** M. ARNOLD *Lit. & Dogma* (1876) 88 By giving a fuller idea of righteousness, to reapply emotion to it.

Hence **re-a'pplier**, one who reapplies.

1884 CRAFTS *Sabbath for Man* (1894) 384 Knox seems to have been..the re-applier of the term 'Sabbath' to it.

rea'ppoint, *v.* [RE- 5 a.] *trans.* To appoint again. Hence **rea'ppointed** *ppl. a.*

1611 COTGR., *Redeleguer*, to redelegate, reappoint, giue a new commission vnto. **1815** *Zeluca* III. 58 Before the re-appointed day. **1855** MACAULAY *Hist. Eng.* xvii. IV. 46 The convert had..been reappointed Master of the Temple. **1884** *Manch. Exam.* 13 Sept. 5/2 A member may be reappointed for five years.

So **rea'ppointment**, a second appointment.

1800 *Asiat. Ann. Reg., Proc. E. Ind. Ho.* 72/2 The court postpone the re-appointment of a committee of patronage. **1900** *Westm. Gaz.* 6 Dec. 2/1 The sooner, therefore, [he] is withdrawn, or his reappointment prevented, the better.

†**reapport**, *sb. Obs. rare.* [var. RAPPORT or REPORT *sb.*, as if f. RE- + APPORT *sb.*] A report.

1579 FENTON *Guicciard.* I. (1599) 18 Ferdinand and Isabell..Princes in those times of great reapport and name for gouernment and wisedome. *Ibid.* II. 86 The reapport of his ouerthrow in Calabria.

So †**reapport**, *v.*, *trans.* to report. *Obs.*[−1]

1587 HOLINSHED *Chron.* III. 885/1 The losse of the battell was no sooner reapported at Millaine, than [etc.].

†**reappose**, *v. Obs.* [var. REPOSE *v.*, as if f. RE- + APPOSE *v.*] *intr.* and *trans.* To repose.

1579 FENTON *Guicciard.* I. (1599) 2 To reappose almost an absolute faith and credit in his councels. *Ibid.* 11 Lodowyke ..reapposed much in the friendship and familiarity which [etc.]. **1587** HOLINSHED *Chron.* III. 896/2 Such as reapposed in the confidence of their faction.

rea'ppraisal. [RE- 5 a: cf. next.] A second appraisal; a reassessment (of something) esp. in the light of new facts.

1911 in WEBSTER. **1953** [see *agonizing reappraisal* s.v. AGONIZING *ppl. a.* 1 b]. **1959** *Listener* 17 Dec. 1063/1 The Government of Signor Segni has found it necessary to make a reappraisal of the Vanoni plan. **1971** C. M. KERNAN *Lang. Behavior in Black Urban Community* i. 2 It promotes an informed reappraisal of the linguistic abilities of Black students. **1976** *Morecambe Guardian* 7 Dec. 15/4 Local government was reorganised by them without any reappraisal of the whole basis of local government finance.

rea'ppraise, *v.* [RE- 5 a.] *trans.* To make a fresh valuation of, to revalue; to reassess, freq. in the light of new facts. Hence **rea'ppraised** *ppl. a.*, **rea'ppraisement, rea'ppraiser.**

1895 *U.S. Customs Guide* 124 As I consider the appraisement made by the United States appraisers too high ..I have to request that the same may be reappraised..with as little delay as your convenience will permit. *Ibid.* 125 Reappraisement should take place immediately. **1903** *Daily Chron.* 3 Nov. 5/3 Mr. Low..arranged to have the rental reappraised every twenty-five years. **1906** *Westm. Gaz.* 1 Sept. 2/1 The August circular issued by the United States Government, and dealing with 'Reappraisements of

Merchandise by U.S. General Appraisers'. *Ibid.*, Autograph bats specially selected, entered at 15*s.* 6*d.*, reappraised at 21*s.* per each... Entered value is net. Reappraised value less 20 per cent. and 5 per cent. *Ibid.*, The appraisers put a higher value upon them; the reappraisers decide that the true value is 21*s.*, less 20 per cent. and 5 per cent. **1961** *Lancet* 22 July 213/1 There is singularly little evidence that sufficient thought has been devoted to the problem of reappraising the treatment. **1976** *New Yorker* 8 Mar. 127/1 His subject—finding appropriate uses for technology, and reappraising the engineer's role in society—is important.

re-a'pproach, *v.* [RE- 5 a.]
1. *trans.* To approach again.
1652 LOVEDAY tr. *Calprenede's Cassandra* III. 198 Re-approaching him, and raising him by the Arme. **1755** SMOLLETT *Quix.* (1803) IV. 151 Re-approaching the hole, he ..surveyed the depth of the cave. **1854** P. B. ST. JOHN *Amy Moss* 90 He then rose,..re-approached the fire, and sat down upon a log.
†**2.** To bring together again. *Obs.*
1663 BOYLE *Exp. Hist. Colours* III. Exp. xiv, Severing or reapproaching the edges of the two irises.

rea'ppropriate, *v.* [RE- 5 a.] *trans.* †**a.** To restore. *Obs.* **b.** To take back to oneself.
1653 MILTON *Hirelings* Wks. (1851) 372 What shall be found hertofore given by Kings or Princes out of the publick, may justly by the Magistrate be recall'd and reappropriated to the Civil Revenue. **1863** *Sat. Rev.* 3 Jan. 19/1 That forest which has reappropriated the conquests made from it. **1864** W. HANNA *Earlier Years Our Lord's Life* 112 St. Matthew should revive, reappropriate and reapply that image.

†**reap-reeve.** *Obs.*$^{-1}$ [f. REAP *sb.*² + REEVE.] A harvest overseer.
1393 LANGL. *P. Pl.* C. VI. 15 Canstow..Repe oþer be a repereyue [*v.r.* rip(p)-, rype-] and a-ryse erliche?

reap-silver. *Obs.* exc. *Hist.* [f. as prec. + SILVER.] The sum paid by a tenant to a superior, in commutation of his services in harvest-time.
12.. *Chron. Joc. de Brakelonda* (Camden) 73 Solebant homines de singulis domibus dare celerario unum denarium in principio Augusti, ad metendum segetes nostras, qui census dicebatur rep-selver. **1299** *Muniment. Magd. Coll. Oxf.* (1882) 145 Ripsulwer. **1843** CARLYLE *Past & Present* II. x. 123 The Lakenheath eels cease to breed squabbles between human beings; the penny of reap-silver to explode into the streets of the Female Chartism of St. Edmundsbury. **1929** F. M. POWICKE in *Cambr. Med. Hist.* VI. vii. 229 The definition of the competence in jurisdiction of the monastic cellarer and the borough reeve, the wrangles about reapsilver and other dues.

†**reap-time.** *Obs. rare.* [f. as prec. + TIME.] Harvest-time.
c **1000** *Ags. Gosp.* Matt. xiii. 30 Lætað æȝþer weaxan oð rip-timan & on þam rip-timan ic secge þam riperum. **1382** WYCLIF *Prov.* xxvi. 1 What maner snoȝ in somer, and reyn in rep time, so vnsemende is to the fool glorie.

reaquite, variant of REACQUITE *v. Obs.*

†**rear**, *sb.*¹ *Obs.*$^{-1}$ [variant of REERE.] A crash, peal.
1584 HUDSON *Du Bartas' Judith* II. in *Sylvester's Du Bartas* II. (1621) 702 At this Hebrew's prayer such a reare Of thunder fell that brought them all in feare.

†**rear**, *sb.*² *Obs. rare.* [f. REAR *v.*¹] That which is reared or got (from cattle).
a **1618** RALEIGH *Anc. Tenures* Wks. 1829 VIII. 608 Fructus not only comprehends cattle, with their wool and milk, but the rear, and that which cometh from them. *Ibid.* 615 The wool, or milk, or rear of them.

rear (rɪə(r)), *sb.*³ (and *a.*¹) Also 7 reer, reare, (9) rere. [Aphetic form of ARREAR *sb.*, prob. originating in *the rear* for *th' arrear*, or under the influence of *rear-guard*, *rear-ward*.
The form became current in the 17th c.; an app. instance in R. Brunne's *Chron.* (1810) 204 is no doubt to be taken as elliptical for *rereward*.]
I. 1. a. *Mil.* (and *Naval*). The hindmost portion of an army (or fleet); that division of a force which is placed, or moves, last in order. (In later use tending to pass into sense 2.)
1606 SHAKS. *Tr. & Cr.* III. iii. 162 Like a gallant Horse falne in first ranke, Lie there for pavement to the abject reare [*conj. for* neere]. **1629** DONNE *Devotions* Expost. xvi. 380 When an Army marches, the vaunt may lodge to night, where the Reare comes not till to morrow. **1667** MILTON *P.L.* II. 78 When the fierce Foe hung on our brok'n Rear Insulting. **1684** *Scanderbeg Rediv.* vi. 137 One great Detachment following the Imperial Army fell upon their Reer. **1732** LEDIARD *Sethos* II. x. 372 The cavalry..soon overtook the enemy's rear. **1769** FALCONER *Dict. Marine* (1780), *Rear*, a name given to the last division of a squadron, or the last squadron of a fleet. **1790** BEATSON *Nav. & Mil. Mem.* I. 190 Expecting that the van of the enemy would necessarily come to the assistance of their rear. **1802** JAMES *Milit. Dict.*, *Rear of an Army*,..Generally the third component part of a large body of forces, which consists of an advanced guard, a main body and a rear guard. **1876** VOYLE & STEVENSON *Milit. Dict.* 330/1 A detachment of troops which brings up and protects the rear of an army.
b. *fig.* and in fig. context.
1629 DONNE *Devotions* Expost. xvi. 381 That [bell] which rung to day was to bring him in his reare, in his body, to the Church. **1632** MILTON *L'Allegro* 50 While the Cock.. Scatters the rear of darkness. **1671** —— *Samson* 1577 The first-born bloom of spring Nipt with the lagging rear of winters frost. **1821** SHELLEY *Hellas* 339 That shattered flag of fiery cloud Which leads the rear of the departing day.

2. a. The back (as opposed to the front) of an army, camp, or person; also, the space behind or at the back; the position at or towards the back.
1600 EDMONDS *Obs. Cæsar's Comm.*, *Mod. Training*, When the whole Battalion being in their close order shoulde turne about and make the Rere the Front. **1651** N. BACON *Disc. Govt. Eng.* II. i. 4 The King was advised to give place, ..till he had tryed masteries with Scotland, and thereby secured his Rere. **1663** BUTLER *Hud.* I. iii. 76 His rear was suddenly inclos'd, And no room left him for retreat. **1735** SOMERVILLE *Chase* III. 536 He stands at Bay against yon knotty Trunk That covers well his Rear. **1796** *Instr. & Reg. Cavalry* (1813) 93 The Divisions marching through each other from Rear to Front. **1838** THIRLWALL *Greece* IV. xxxiv. 334 The rear, as the post of danger, he claimed for Timasion and himself. **1847** *Infantry Man.* (1854) 40 They will carry their right foot..diagonally to their right rear. **1888** P. H. SHERIDAN *Personal Mem.* II. 37 Crook.. conducted his command south in two parallel columns until he gained the rear of the enemy's works.
b. The buttocks or backside. *colloq.*
1796 *True Briton* 26 Oct. 3/3 Lord Camelford can boast of a power which rivals that of the First Lord of the Admiralty. He has made Captain Couver a *yellow rear*. **1851** H. MELVILLE *Moby Dick* I. xxi. 159 He put his hand upon the sleeper's rear. **1876** 'MARK TWAIN' *Adv. Tom Sawyer* ii. 28 In another moment he was flying down the street with his pail and a tingling rear.., and Aunt Polly was retiring from the field with a slipper in her hand. **1949** N. R. NASH *Young & Fair* I. ii. 16 Just once is enough, Baby. (*She slaps her on the rear*) Come on—get to work. **1965** H. GOLD *Man who was not with It* vi. 49 You used to have some fat, some curves there. Quite a rear you used to have—quite a rear.
3. a. In general use: The back, or back part, of anything; *spec.* the back part of a motor vehicle.
1641 J. JACKSON *True Evang. T.* III. 191 The front, and the reare, the beginning, middle, and end of our salvation. **1667** MILTON *P.L.* IX. 497 Not with indented wave, Prone on the ground,..but on his reare, Circular base of rising foulds. **1679** MOXON *Mech. Exerc.* ix. 152 By the width I mean the sides that range with the Front and Rear of the Building. **1864** TENNYSON *En. Ard.* 729 The ruddy square of comfortable light, Far-blazing from the rear of Philip's house, Allured him. **1966** *Publ. Amer. Dial. Soc.* **1964** XLII. 8 *Rear*,..the aft suspension of a car; the differential of a car; the entire aft of an automobile. **1976** *Evening Post* (Nottingham) 16 Dec. 8/2 The 38-ton Bedford TM costs £16,887 for the tractor business end and trailers or huge van-type rears are £1,100 to £1,700 extra.
b. A (public or communal) water-closet, lavatory, or latrine. Also *pl.* (const. as *sing.*). orig. *School* and *University slang.*
1902 FARMER & HENLEY *Slang* VI. 4/2 *Rear* ..(University), a jakes. **1907** H. NICOLSON *Let.* 31 Apr. in J. Lees-Milne *Harold Nicolson* (1980) I. ii. 29 The usual bad rears with its hook and eye lock. **1940** [see LAT³]. **1946** B. MARSHALL *George Brown's Schooldays* xliii. 170 And now let's raid the rears and rout out any of the other new swine that are hiding there. **1969** VISCT. BUCKMASTER *Roundabout* ii. 30 We also had to know a Latin description of the rear, which we called Foricas.
4. In adverbial and prepositional phrases:
a. ***in the rear*** (less freq. ***in rear***), in the hindmost part (of an army, etc.); hence, at or from the back, behind.
1600 EDMONDS *Obs. Cæsar's Comm.*, *Mod. Training*, Another meanes to preuent the enemy his assaulting vs in the reare or flanke. **1614** RALEIGH *Hist. World* III. (1634) 126 The horsemen..were placed on the flanks, only a troupe of the Eleans were in reare. **1689** *Perfect. Milit. Discipl.* (1691) 20 Fall back with your right Arm and Leg, keep the Spear in the Rear. **1722** WOLLASTON *Relig. Nat.* ix. 216 Followed many times by sharp reflections and bitter penances in the rear. **1782** COWPER *Gilpin* 235 With postboy scampering in the rear, They raised the hue and cry. **1844** [see FRONT *sb.* 5 c]. **1852** MRS. STOWE *Uncle Tom's C.* xvii. 165 The women ..saw, far in the rear,..a party of men looming up. **1857** YOUNGHUSBAND *Handbk. Field Service* 208 If possible to take any enemy in rear, it should be done.
b. ***in*** (or ***on***) ***one's rear***, at one's back, behind one.
1639 R. BAILLIE *Lett. & Jrnls.* (1861) I. 212 To..march forward, leist his unkannie trewesmen should light on to call [= drive] them up in their rear. **1653** HOLCROFT *Procopius* I. 34 They began on both sides.., Vitigis and Belisarius incouraging their men in their Reares. **1745** *De Foe's Eng. Tradesman* vi. (1841) I. 39 His payments may come in on his front as fast as they go out in his rear. **1827** SOUTHEY *Hist. Penins. War* II. 303 A plan which was impossible, unless Soult should..allow the enemy to get in his rear. **1862** STANLEY *Jewish Ch.* (1877) I. v. 108 The huge mountain range which rose on their rear, and cut off their return.
c. ***in*** (†or ***within***) ***the rear of***, at the back of, behind. Also in later use with *at*, and occas. without *the*.
1602 SHAKS. *Ham.* I. iii. 34 Feare it Ophelia,..And keepe within the reare of your Affection. **1643** R. M. *Schoole of Warre* A 3 b, Half of the Muskettiers to be in the Reare of the Pikes. **1699** BENTLEY *Phal.* 194 In his own time, in the Rear of so many Poets. **1815** W. H. IRELAND *Scribbleomania* 13 Slush from the ditch that's in rear of the mountain. **1852** MRS. STOWE *Uncle Tom's C.* xv. 141 Miss Ophelia disappeared in the rear of Mammy. **1886** *Law Times* LXXXI. 59/2 The houses were built in 1877. At the rear of them was a 9-inch sewer.
5. a. In verbal phrases: ***to bring up*** (or ***close***) ***the rear***, to come last in order. † ***to get the rear of***, to get behind. ***to hang on one's rear***, to follow closely, in order to attack when opportunity offers.
1643 SIR T. BROWNE *Relig. Med.* I. §58 My desires onely are..to be but the last man, and bring up the Rere in Heaven. **1653** HOLCROFT *Procopius* II. 61 Whom he directed ..to get the Reare of them, and to follow at their backs. **1667** [see 1]. **1717** LADY M. W. MONTAGU *Let. to Abbé Conti* 17 May, The rear was closed by the volunteers. **1728** POPE *Dunc.* I. 308 Let Bawdry, Billingsgate..Support his front, and Oaths bring up the rear. **1759** ROBERTSON *Hist. Scot.* III. (1817) I. 209 A body of the enemy hung upon their rear. **1860** TYNDALL *Glac.* I. xiv. 98 Lauener was in front,..while I brought up the rear. **1884** *Graphic* 6 Aug. 159/1 A Lancashire army of quite as great dimensions would be able to hang on his rear.
b. In phr. ***front and rear*** used in loose construction.
1689 *Perfect. Milit. Discip.* (1691) 28 Upon marching from your Arms, step Front and Rear together with the left Feet. **1692** HICKERINGILL *Good Old Cause* Wks. 1716 II. 512 His Army stood in battalia, ready to fight the Enemy that had beset them Front and Rear. **1808** SCOTT *Marmion* VI. xxxiv, Front, flank, and rear, the squadrons sweep. **1816** —— *Antiq.* xxvii, Keep thegither, front and rear.
6. One who stands in the rear of another. *rare*$^{-1}$.
1851 MAYNE REID *Scalp Hunt.* li. 387 The heads of the front-rank men rested between the feet of their respective 'rears'.
II. *attrib.* and *Comb.*
7. *attrib.* passing into adj. Placed or situated at the back; hindmost, last.
a. In *Mil.* (and *Naval*) use of divisions of troops, etc., as ***rear-brigade***, ***company***, ***division***, †***forlorn***, †(***lorne***) ***hope***, ***-line***, ***-link***, ***rank***, etc.
1600 DYMMOK *Ireland* (1843) 32 In the head of the reare lorne hope. **1623** BINGHAM *Xenophon* 114, I will goe and take some of the Reare Companies. **1650** CROMWELL *Let.* 4 Sept. in *Carlyle*, The Enemy..had like to have engaged our rear-brigade of horse with their whole Army. **1689** *Perfect. Milit. Discipl.* (1691) 59 The Rear half Files are to March exceeding slow. *Ibid.* 91 The Rear Ranks of Musketiers make Ready. **1727–41** CHAMBERS *Cycl.*, *Rear-Line*, of an army encamped, is the second line; it lies about four or five hundred yards distant from the first line, or front. **1769** FALCONER *Dict. Marine* (1780), *Arriere-garde*, the rear-division of a squadron of vessels of war. **1796** *Instr. & Reg. Cavalry* (1813) 95 If on a rear division. That division will be placed... The change will then be made as on a front division. **1802** JAMES *Milit. Dict.* s.v. *Rear front*, The rear-rank-men stand where the front-rank-men ought to be. **1861** MAY *Const. Hist.* (1863) II. viii. 83 The halting rear-rank of their own Tory followers. **1971** C. BONINGTON *Annapurna South Face* iii. 40 Lieutenant Bishnuparsad, our rear-link wireless operator, was already installed there. *Ibid.*, He was to stay here at the pension paying-post throughout the expedition, acting as rear link and also handling all our mail. **1974** T. P. WHITNEY tr. *Solzhenitsyn's Gulag Archipelago* I. iv. 167 They were vehement in their rear-line wrath (the most intense patriotism always flourishes in the rear).
b. In *Mil.* or general use, of things.
1667 PRIMATT *City & C. Build.* 72 Front and rear walls in the first Story to be two Bricks and a half thick. *c* **1860** H. STUART *Seaman's Catech.* (1862) 12 Why are the rear trucks taken off?.. To give the gun more elevation. **1862** *Patents, Abridg. Velocipedes* (1886) I. 11 Bicycle steered by small rear wheel. **1884** *Mil. Engineering* (ed. 3) I. II. 45 Choose the best men for diggers in the gun-spaces and rear-trench. The diggers in the front ditch have easier work. **1920** Rear pocket [see *custard pie* s.v. CUSTARD 2 b]. **1920** *T. Eaton & Co. Catal.* Spring & Summer 395/3 Rear Tire Carrier suitable for all models of Ford touring cars. **1925** F. SCOTT FITZGERALD *Great Gatsby* i. 10 Then there was a boom as Tom Buchanan shut the rear windows and the caught wind died out about the room. *Ibid.* 12 All the cars have the left rear wheel painted black as a mourning wreath. **1931** E. S. GARDNER in *Detective Fiction Weekly* 7 Mar. 325/1 One of the officers..ensconced himself in the rear seat. **1951** *Catal. Exhibits, Festival of Britain* p. xxix, This new Foden rear-engine chassis has revolutionised normal design practice. **1952** V. CANNING *House of Seven Flies* 5 A second sailor opened the rear door of the car for him. **1964** V. J. CHAPMAN *Coastal Vegetation* vi. 170 Whether one is investigating fore-, mid- or rear-dunes, it will be found that the water is fresh. **1966** 'A. HALL' *9th Directive* xx. 184 The car..was gathering speed..when I..got the rear door open and lurched inside. **1968** *Listener* 26 Dec. 868/3 Following the coffee-table book comes the rear-window book: the huge unread, unreadable volume that lies on the shelf behind the back seat. **1969** B. KNOX *Tallyman* vi. 120 Rear-wheel skids should be steered into, said the rule-book. **1973** *Country Life* 1 Mar. 540/2 Rear-seat passengers are not too badly off for leg room. **1975** *Ibid.* 2 Jan. 32/2 A real omission here is a heated rear window... Rear wipers are likewise unknown. **1976** P. R. WHITE *Planning for Public Transport* iii. 56 The rear-engine layout was also adopted for single-deckers. **1978** *Dumfries Courier* 20 Oct. 22/1 (Advt.), All are quality cars with spacious reclining seats, fitted carpets,..heated rearscreen, radial tyres, etc.
8. With adverbial force: **a.** Towards the rear, as ***rear-directed***, ***-facing***. **b.** From the rear, as ***rear-driven*** (so ***-drive***, ***-driving***), ***-lit***, ***-steering***; ***rear-illuminate***, ***-project*** vbs.
1855 SINGLETON *Virgil* I. 147 Trusting in flight and rear-directed shafts. **1887** VISC. BURY & G. L. HILLIER *Cycling* 159 (Badm. Libr.) The rear-driving safety bicycle. *Ibid.* 162 The old class of single-driving rear-steering tricycles. **1888** *Encycl. Brit.* XXIII. 559/2 The evil of rear-steering is only reduced, not removed. **1904** *N.E.D.*, *rear-driven*. **1961** *Twentieth Century* Feb. 124 Rear-lit cloths become more common [in the theatre]. **1970** *Nature* 19 Dec. 1217/1 A number of test-areas in the form of circular holes in a metal plate are uniformly rear-illuminated to a supra-threshold luminance. **1972** *Country Life* 26 Oct. 1060/3 The rack and pinion steering is responsive yet without quite the feel of a rear-drive car. **1973** *Jrnl. Genetic Psychol.* June 255 The stimuli..were rear-projected onto a 27·9 cm² opaque glass screen. **1977** *Lancashire Life* Jan. 79/1 No rear drive Citroen has been made since the 1930s. **1978** *Cornish Guardian* 27 Apr. 24/5 (Advt.), 1973 Volvo 145 D/L Estate... Rear-facing child seats.
c. At the rear, as ***rear-engined***, ***mounted***.
1933 *Motor* 10 Oct. 524/1 The rear-engined Trojan. **1957** *Sci. News Let.* 23 Mar. 190/1 Rear-engined cars are here to

stay. **1960** *Farmer & Stockbreeder* 19 Jan. 90/1 In this country the accepted method of handling silage has been by means of a rear-mounted buckrake. **1975** *Drive* New Year 102/2 The protesting chatter from the air-cooled rear-mounted engine is more a symptom of asthma than mechanical stress. **1976** P. R. WHITE *Planning for Public Transport* iii. 56 The higher maintenance costs and poorer availability of the rear-engined models.

9. Special combs., as **rear-crew** *U.S.*, the party of men who attend to the rear of a 'drive' of logs; **rear-cut**, applied attributively to a mower having the cutting-bar in the rear of the carriage (Knight 1884); **rear driver**, a cycle driven by means of the rear wheel; **rear echelon** *U.S. Mil.*, that section of an army concerned with administrative and supply duties; also *transf.*; **rear end**, (*a*) the back part or section (of anything, esp. a vehicle); (*b*) *slang*, the backside or buttocks (of a person); hence as *v. trans.* (N. Amer.), to collide, or cause (one's vehicle) to collide, with the rear end of another vehicle; **rear-ender**, a rear-end collision; **rear front**, †? a covering for the wall at the back of an altar (cf. FRONT 9 b); †the back of a building (*obs.*); *Mil.* (see quot. 1802); **rear gunner**, a member of the crew of a military aircraft who operates a gun from a compartment or turret at the rear of the aircraft; **rear-lamp, -light**, a (usu. red) lamp at the rear of a vehicle which can be switched on to serve as a warning light in the dark; **rear man**, *Naut.* (see quots.); **rear mirror**, a rear-view mirror (see *rear-view* attrib.); **rear pillar** (see quot. 1930); **rear projection** = *back projection* s.v. BACK- B; **rearsight**, a part of a camera viewfinder, situated at the back, to which the eye is applied; **rear-steerer**, a tricycle steered from the back; **rear-view** *attrib.*, giving a view to the rear; *spec.* of a mirror inside a motor vehicle in front of the driver.

1893 *Scribner's Mag.* June 715/1 Behind them follows the *'rear crew', the name indicating the work they do. **1934** WEBSTER, *Rear echelon. **1947** *Amer. Speech* XXII. 55 *Rear echelon commando*, a soldier assigned to the rear. **1967** *Boston Sunday Herald* 7 May III. 14/2 The number [of servicewomen] in Vietnam will remain small, chiefly because there is no large 'rear echelon' setup of the kind maintained in Europe in World War II. **1977** P. JOHNSON *Enemies of Society* xii. 165 This shaky argument, of the type which convinced the rear echelons of the Gadarene swine, carried the day. **1868** *Rep. to Govt. U.S. Munitions War* 97 The metallic *rear-end of the cartridge. **1926** *Daily Colonist* (Victoria, B.C.) 19 Jan. 5/3 Two passengers were killed and fifty injured today in a rear-end collision of..two subway trains. **1937** J. WEIDMAN *I can get it for you Wholesale* xxviii. 268 She's a pain in the rear end. **1961** *Amer. Speech* XXXVI. 273 *Rear end*,..the differentials of a tractor. **1967** G. KELLY in *Coast to Coast 1965–6* 95 Blokes my age are sitting on their rear-ends ordering the rest..around. **1976** *Islander* (Victoria, B.C.) 1 Aug. 3/4 A driver came to an abrupt stop in front of me. I slithered all over the wet road but did I *rearend her? Of course not. **1978** *Detroit Free Press* 2 Apr. 3A/1 The men, who were on a chartered city bus traveling to a football game in 1972 when it was rear-ended by another bus, rejected a settlement of $500 apiece and took their case to the jury. **1932** *Erie Railroad Mag.* Apr. 46/1 With all his fast running I never knew of him piling them up, of any but a few derailments and never a *rear-ender. **1483** in *Somerset Medieval Wills* (1901) 144 [Also one white chalice, one] 'frount' [and] '*rerefrount' [of] 'Grenetarteryn'. **1703** MOXON *Mech. Exerc.* 265 A Building, which is 25 Feet, both in the Front and Reer Front. **1802** JAMES *Milit. Dict.* s.v., When a battalion, troop, or company is faced about, and stands in that position, it is then said to be rear front. **1920** *Flight* XII. 11/1 A central passage leads through to what in the military machine was the *rear gunner's cockpit, which is now occupied by the 'postman'. **1944** 'N. SHUTE' *Pastoral* i. 3 He had developed into a very good rear-gunner in the Wimpey. **1977** *R.A.F. News* 27 Apr.–10 May 8/2 The aircraft was hit again and again and the rear gunner was wounded. **1907** *Westm. Gaz.* 17 Sept. 4/2 When the compulsory carrying of *rear-lamps has been suggested the proposal has always been violently resisted. **1937** *East London Rubber Co. Ltd. Motor Catal.* 154/2 Top covers for rear lamps. **1918** A. QUILLER-COUCH *Foe-Farrell* iii. 54 The car purred and glided away... We watched the *rearlight turn the corner. **1967** N. FREELING *Strike out where not Applicable* 159 There is nothing that looks so like the rear lights of a car as the rear lights of another car. **1968** *Rear mirror [see *G.T.* s.v. G III. f]. **1859** F. A. GRIFFITHS *Artil. Man.* (1862) 227 The two men whose numbers place them farthest from the ship's side [in working a gun] are to be termed right, and left *rear-men. *c* **1860** H. STUART *Seaman's Catech.* 12 Who places the inclined planes? The rear-man. **1930** *Motor Body Building* LI. 105/1 **Rear pillar*, a vertical frame member at the back corner of the body. **1977** Rear pillar [see PILLAR *sb.* 2 c]. **1960** *Practical Wireless* XXXVI. 316/2 A team of demonstrators who operated the sequence of exhibit animations, *rear projection films and synchronised sound and provided a live commentary. **1976** BOTHAM & DONNELLY *Valentino* xii. 93 Working behind the screen, with rear-projection to help them follow the story. **1971** *Amateur Photogr.* 13 Jan. 50/3 The *rearsight is quite large, has a permanently attached rubber eye-cup and is adjustable between +1 to −4 dioptres to suit individual eyesight. **1978** *Ibid.* 2 Aug. 79/2 Accessories included: carrying strap, body cap, rearsight rubber eyecup, etc. **1883** BROWNING in *Knowledge* 18 May 289/2, I prefer a *rear-steerer with ratchets for easy riding. **1887** VISC. BURY & G. L. HILLIER *Cycling* 374 (Badm. Libr.) The old bath-chair.. front-steering tricycle is fast following the old rear-steerer into obscurity. **1926** *Rear-view [see DRIVING *vbl. sb.* 3 a]. **1959** H. NIELSEN *Fifth Caller* xiii. 195 His face had been in the rearview mirror. **1969** G. MACBETH *War Quartet* 17 For the moment they were framed In rear-view mirrors. **1974** V. NABOKOV *Look at Harlequins* (1975) IV. iv. 173, I see today ..the rearview reflection of that sweet wild past.

rear (rɪə(r)), *a.*[2] *Obs.* exc. *dial.* Forms: 1 hrer, 4–7 (9 *dial.*) rere, 6 reere, 6–7 (9 *dial.*) reer, 6–7 reare, 6–8, 9 *dial.* rear. See also RARE *a.*[1] [OE. *hrér*, of uncertain origin.] Slightly or imperfectly cooked, underdone. In early use only of eggs.

c **1000** *Sax. Leechd.* II. 272 Nim scamoniam..& hrer henne æᵹ swiðe sealt. [Cf. *Ibid.* III. 294 On an hreren-bræden æᵹ.] *c* **1400** *Lanfranc's Cirurg.* 58 Þe broþis of fleisch,..& rere eyren, & smale fischis. *a* **1450** *Knt. de la Tour* (1868) 27 Thei had atte her dyner rere eggis. **1532** MORE *Confut. Tindale* Wks. 667/2 Supping of a rere roten egge. **1584** COGAN *Haven Health* cxciii. (1636) 174 Rere egges,..that is to say little more than through hot. **1655** CULPEPPER, etc. *Riverius* IV. vii. 121 Let the Patient abstain ..from Wine, Flesh, and Rear Eggs. **1731** MEDLEY *Kolben's Cape G. Hope* I. 201 The Hottentots,..love their victuals, whether roasted or boil'd, should be very rear. *a* **1796** PEGGE *Derbicisms* Ser. II, *Rear*, meat underdone. *a* **1825** in FORBY *Voc. E. Anglia.* **1865–** in dial. glossaries (Cumbld., Durham, Lancs., Yks., Lincs., Shropsh., Dorset, Hants, etc.).

transf. or *fig.* **1620** MIDDLETON & ROWLEY *World Tost* Wks. (Dyce) V. 192 I'll have thee ramm'd Into a culverin else, and thy rear flesh Shot all into poach'd eggs. **1625** MIDDLETON *Game at Chess* IV. ii, Can a soft rear, poor poach'd iniquity So ride vpon thy conscience?

b. As complement with verbs.

1542 BOORDE *Dyetary* xii. (1870) 264 Let the egge be newe, and roste hym reare. **1700** DRYDEN *Ovid's Met., Baucis & Phil.* 98 New laid Eggs, which Baucis busie Care Turn'd by a gentle Fire, and roasted rear.

c. *Comb.* (cf. quot. *c* 1000 above), as ***rear-boiled, -dressed, -poached, -roasted***.

1548 ELYOT s.v. *Ouum, Sorbile ouum*, a reere rosted egge. **1576** BAKER *Jewell of Health* 55 The hearbe [Eyebright].. eaten euerie day in a reare potched Egge. **1586** BRIGHT *Melanch.* xxxix. 253 Eggs..reare dressed somewhat. **1626** BACON *Sylva* §53 Eggs (so they be Potched, or Reare boyled). **1656** HEYLIN *Surv. France* 260 A dish of Egges, rear-roasted by the flame.

rear (rɪə(r)), *v.*[1] Forms: 1 rǽran, 3 ræren, 3, 4 reren, 5 reryn; 4–6 rere, 5, 6 reere, (3) 6 reare, 7– rear; (6–7 rair, 9 *dial.* rare). [OE. *rǽran* (:—OTeut. **raizjan*) = Goth. *-raisjan*, ON. *reisa*, to RAISE. OE. had also *árǽran* AREAR (in use down to the 17th c.).

The main senses of *rear* run parallel with those of the Scandinavian equivalent RAISE, but the adopted word has been much more extensively employed than the native, and has developed many special senses which are rarely or never expressed by *rear*. Hence, on the one hand, *rear* has in many applications been almost or altogether supplanted by *raise*, a process which is clearly seen in the usage of the Wyclif Bible (see note to RAISE; in the version of 1611 *rear* is found only in *1 Esdr.* v. 62, while *raise* is freely employed). On the other hand, it is probable that *rear* has sometimes, esp. in poetry, been used as a more rhetorical substitute for *raise*, without independent development of the sense involved. As in the case of *raise* there is some overlapping of the senses, and occasional uncertainty as to the precise development or meaning of transferred uses.]

I. To set up on end; to make to stand up.

1. a. *trans.* To bring (a thing) to or towards a vertical position; to set up, or upright. = RAISE 1.

Frequently with suggestion of senses 8 or 11, and now usually implying a considerable height in the thing when raised.

a **1000** *Cædmon's Gen.* 1675 (Gr.) Ceastre worhton & to heofonum up hlædræ rærdon. *c* **1205** LAY. 1100 Heo rærden heora mastes. *Ibid.* 17458 Mærlin heom [the stones] gon ræren [*c* **1275** reare] alse heo stoden ærer. **1387** TREVISA *Higden* (Rolls) V. 455 Þe place þere Oswaldus knelede and rerede a crosse. *c* **1400** *Sowdone Bab.* 2658 Thai rered the Galowes in haste. **1530** PALSGR. 687/2 It is a great deale longer than one wolde have thought it afore it was reared up. **1571** DIGGES *Pantom.* I. xxix. I j b, Fixing on the dimetient thereof two sightes perpendicularly reared. **1631** WEEVER *Anc. Funeral Mon.* 637 A broken peece of a faire marble stone, reared to the side of a pillar. **1688** PRIOR *Ode Exodus iii* 108 That Ladder which old Jacob rear'd. **1725** POPE *Odyss.* XI. 3 At once the mast we rear, at once unbind The spacious sheet. **1822** W. IRVING *Braceb. Hall* xxvi. 225 The May-pole was reared on the green. **1847** TENNYSON *Princ.* v. 404 Your very armour hallow'd, and your statues Rear'd.

refl. **1596** DRAYTON *Legends* IV. 933 The Corne..being once downe, it selfe can never reare.

b. *spec.* of setting up the crust of a pie. Now *dial.* = RAISE 1 c.

c **1420** *Liber Cocorum* (1862) 34 Take floure and rere the cofyns fyne, Wele stondande withouten stine. **1588** SHAKS. *Tit. A.* V. ii. 189 Of the Paste a Coffen I will reare. **1879–** in dial. glossaries (Chesh., Shropsh., Warw.).

2. a. To lift (a person or animal) to or towards an erect or standing posture; usually, to set (one) on one's feet, assist to rise. Now chiefly *dial.*

1590 SPENSER *F.Q.* I. viii. 40 He found the meanes that Prisoner vp to reare, Whose feeble thighes..him scarse to light could beare. *Ibid.* x. 35 She held him fast, and firmely did upbeare; As carefull nourse her child from falling oft does reare. **1667** MILTON *P.L.* XI. 758 Till gently reard By th' Angel, on thy feet thou stood'st at last. **1667** N. FAIRFAX in *Phil. Trans.* II. 457 Nor could she lie flat, but rear'd up with pillows. **1769** SIR W. JONES *Pal. Fort.* in *Poems* (1777) 30 The Matron with surprize her daughter rears.

b. *refl.* To get up on one's feet, to rise up (*rare*); also of animals, to rear (sense 15 b).

c **1580** SIDNEY *Ps.* III. iii, I laid me downe and slept,..And safe from sleepe I rear'd me. **1591** SPENSER *M. Hubberd* 237 Eftsoones the Ape himselfe gan up to reare. **1749** FIELDING *Tom Jones* IV. xiii, The unruly beast presently reared himself an end on his hind-legs. **1856** KANE *Arct. Expl.* II. xv. 164 He [a bear] will rear himself upon his hind-legs.

c. So with *body*, etc. as object. Chiefly *refl.*

1593 SHAKS 2 *Hen. VI*, III. ii. 34 Helpe Lords, the King is dead. *Som.* Rere vp his Body, wring him by the Nose. **1610** WILLET *Hexapla Daniel* 137 Whereas before he went groueling..now he reareth vp his bodie. **1667** MILTON *P.L.* I. 221 Forthwith upright he rears from off the Pool His mighty Stature. **1810** SHELLEY *St. Irvyne* III. xvi, Her skeleton form the dead Nun rear'd. **1815** —— *Alastor* 182 He reared his shuddering limbs.

d. To cause (a horse) to rear. *rare*⁻¹.

1814 SOUTHEY *Roderick* xxv, He raised his hand, and rear'd and back'd the steed.

†**3. a.** To raise from the dead. *Obs.* = RAISE 3.

c **1320** *Sir Beues* (MS. A) 2839 Lord, þat rerede þe Lazaroun. **1387** TREVISA *Higden* (Rolls) IV. 461 Iulianus.. rered þre men fro deth to lyve. **1572** R. H. tr. *Lavaterus' Ghostes* (1596) 177 [Saule] sought helpe of a witch to reare Samuel from the dead.

refl. *c* **1450** LONELICH *Grail* xlix. 201 ȝif that to lyve he rere him Ageyn thanne ben they myhty [gods].

†**b.** To raise (a person) *to, out of*, or *from* a certain condition. *Obs.*

Connexion with sense 17 is also possible. Cf. RAISE 19.

c **1450** tr. *De Imitatione* III. lxii. 145, I am it þat rere to helth hem þat morneþ. *c* **1580** SIDNEY *Ps.* XXXIV. ix, God shall him to safety reare, When most he seemes opprest. **1590** SPENSER *F.Q.* III. i. 64 Their Ladye..they reard out of her frosen swownd. **1624** QUARLES *Div. Poems, Job* (1717) 187 Then doubt not, but he'll rear thee from thy sorrow.

4. To cause to rise: **a.** To rouse from bed or sleep. *Obs.* exc. *dial.* = RAISE 4 a.

a **1000** *Riddles* iv. 73 (Gr.) Saᵹa hwæt ic hatte oþþe hwa mec rære, þonne ic restan ne mot. *c* **1200** *Trin. Coll. Hom.* 77 [To pray] þat he..weche us of ure heuie slape and rere us of ure fule lust bedde. **13..** *E.E. Allit. P.* C. 188 Þer ragnel in his rakentes hym rere of his dremes. **1382** WYCLIF *Jer.* xxxi. 26 Therfore as fro slep I am rered. *c* **1440** *Promp. Parv.* 430/2 Reryn, or revyn of slepe, *infra in* wakyn', *excito*. **1886** ELWORTHY *W. Som. Word-bk.*, *Rear*, to rouse; to disturb.

†**b.** To rouse or dislodge (a beast of chase, *spec.* a boar) from covert. *Obs.* = RAISE 4 b.

1486 *Bk. St. Albans* E iv, Whiche beestes shall be reride with the lymer. **1575** TURBERV. *Venerie* xl. 115 Beating and following vntill they haue reared and found the Harte againe. **1582** STANYHURST *Æneis* I. (Arb.) 28 Rearing with shoutcry soom boare. **1685** DRYDEN tr. *Horace Epode* ii, Into the naked Woods he goes And seeks the tusky Boar to rear. *a* **1700** B. E. *Dict. Cant. Crew, Rear the Boar*, dislodge him. **1774** GOLDSM. *Nat. Hist.* (1776) III. 174 When the boar is rear'd, as is the expression for driving him from his covert. **1846** YOUATT *Pig* iv. (1847) 37 When first the animal was '*reared*', he contented himself with slowly going away.

5. To rouse up for common action. *Obs.* exc. *dial.* = RAISE 5.

c **1400** *Beryn* 2905 [He] made an hidouse Cry,..& rerid vp al þe town. **1460** *Paston Lett.* I. 506 The kyng cometh to London ward, and..rereth the pepyll as he come. **1464** *Ibid.* II. 148 That..he rere the contre and take hem and bryng hem to the Kyng. **1593** SHAKS. *Rich. II*, IV. i. 145 If you reare this House against this House. **1864** BARNES *Dorset Gloss.*, *Rear*,..to rouse; to excite. **1878** *Cumbld. Gloss.*, *Rear*,..rally, bring up. **1891** T. HARDY *Tess* (1900) 143/1 There are sixteen of us on the Plain, and the whole country is reared.

†**6.** To arouse, animate, stimulate. *Obs.* = RAISE 6.

1526 *Pilgr. Perf.* (W. de W. 1531) 97 b, Therfore rere vp thy courage & shewe thy manhode. **1621** BURTON *Anat. Mel.* II. ii. VI. iii. (1651) 299 A roaring-meg against Melancholy, to rear and revive the languishing soul. **1647** H. MORE *Song of Soul* II. i. II. ii, New strength my vitals doth invade And rear again, that earst began to fade.

II. To build up, create, bring into existence.

7. a. To construct by building up. = RAISE 8.

It is not clear whether the common OE. phrase *Godes* (or *dryhtnes*) *lof rǽran* is a fig. use of this sense, or is to be associated with branch III.

a **900** tr. *Bæda's Hist.* III. ii[i]. (1890) 158 He Cristes cirican in his rice ᵹeornlice timbrede & rærde. *a* **1000** *Cædmon's Gen.* 1880 (Gr.) Ongunnon him þa bytlian & heora burh ræran. *c* **1205** LAY. 15459 Ich faren wulle to þan munte of Reir & ræren þer castel. **1297** R. GLOUC. (Rolls) 5408 Abbeys he rerde monion In mony studes. **1382** WYCLIF *Gen.* xxxiii. 20 And there, an auter reryd, he.. clepide vpon the..God of Israel. **1479** *Nottingham Rec.* II. 390 That the seid howse be fenysshit, reryd and made upp. *a* **1548** HALL *Chron., Hen. VIII* 73 A tower..rered by great crafte. **1590** SPENSER *F.Q.* III. x. 52 Amongst the hives to reare An hony combe. **1634** MILTON *Comus* 798 Till all thy magick structures rear'd so high, Were shatter'd into heaps. **1697** DRYDEN *Virg. Ecl.* II. 30 When summon'd Stones the Theban Turrets rear'd. **1779** J. MOORE *View Soc. Fr.* (1789) I. xlviii. 408 He had reared a building greatly larger. **1849** MACAULAY *Hist. Eng.* V. I. 629 Her family reared a sumptuous mausoleum over her remains. **1874** GREEN *Short Hist.* iii. §4. 129 The canons..reared the church which still exists as the diocesan cathedral.

fig. **1772** MACKENZIE *Man World* I. ii. (1803) 421 The fall of those hopes we had been vainly diligent to rear. **1781** COWPER *Table-t.* 532 From him who rears a poem lank and long, To him who strains his all into a song. **1812** MISS MITFORD in L'Estrange *Life* (1870) I. vi. 193 How weak the fame the lowly songstress rears.

†**b.** To bring into existence; to cause to arise or appear. *Obs.* = RAISE 9, 11.

In the Wyclif Bible (up to the end of Jeremiah) *rere* is regularly employed to render L. *suscitāre* in the above senses: it is not quite clear whether the underlying idea belongs here or to branch I.

1382 WYCLIF *Gen.* xxxviii. 8 Go yn to the wijf of thi brother..that thou rere seed to thi brother. —— *1 Sam.* ii. 35, I shal rere to me a trewe preest. **1591** SHAKS. *1 Hen. VI*, IV. vii. 92 From their ashes shall be reard A Phœnix.

†**8. a.** To originate, bring about, set going (a state or condition of things, *esp.* one which

causes trouble or annoyance); to commence and carry on (some action, *esp.* war). *Obs.* = RAISE 12, 14.

a **900** CYNEWULF *Christ* 689 God..sibbe ræreþ ece to ealdre engla & monna. *a* **1023** WULFSTAN *Hom.* xxxiii. (1883) 156 Dæghwamlice man ihte yfel æfter oðrum, and unriht rærde. *c* **1052** *O.E. Chron.* (MS. C.) an. 1052 Ealle Frencisce men þe ær unlaȝe rærdon. **12..** *Moral Ode* 172 (Egerton MS.) þo scullen habben hardne dom..þa þe euele heolden wreche men & vuele laȝes rerde. **1297** R. GLOUC. (Rolls) 8987 Erl thebaud..bigan to rere worre vpe þe king of france. *c* **1330** *Florice & Bl.* (1857) 685 We han irerd this schame and schonde. **1382** WYCLIF 2 *Sam.* xii. 11, I shal rere vpon thee yuel of thin hows. *a* **1450** MYRC 1243 Hast þow reret any debate. **1494** FABYAN *Chron.* VII. 454 Which tempest, after ye oppynyon of some wryters, was reryd by ye negromauncers of ye Frenshe Kynge. *a* **1548** HALL *Chron., Hen. IV* 10 If any persones would presume to rere warre or congregate a multitude. **1577** NORTHBROOKE *Dicing* (1843) 25 Rearing vp slanders vpon the preachers of the worde of God. **1590** SPENSER *F.Q.* II. vi. 21 Her mery fitt she freshly gan to reare. *Ibid.* xii. 22 Unweeting what such horrour straunge did reare.

b. To make (a noise) by shouting; to utter (a cry); to begin to sing. *rare.* = RAISE 13. *Obs.*

Also associated with (or originating in) branch III.

13.. *E.E. Allit. P.* B. 873 þenne þe rebaudez so ronk rered such a noyse. *c* **1330** *Arth. & Merl.* 6417 (Kölbing) þe paiens..gun rere a wel foule crie. **1382** WYCLIF *Isa.* xv. 5 The cri of contricioun thei shul rere [L. *levabunt*]. *c* **1500** in Arnolde *Chron.* (1811) 94 Ye shall rere vp hue and crye and ..folowe theym fro strete to strete. **1784** COWPER *Task* VI. 662 The simple clerk..did rear right merrily, two staves, Sung to the praise and glory of King George.

9. a. To bring (animals) to maturity or to a certain stage of growth by giving proper nourishment and attention; *esp.* to attend to the breeding and growth of (cattle, etc.) as an occupation. = RAISE 9 b, 10 b.

c **1420** *Pallad. on Husb.* I. 610 The pocok me may rere vp [L. *nutrire*] esely If beestes wilde or theuys hem ne greue. **1523** FITZHERB. *Husb.* §8 That countrey is not for men to kepe husbandry vppon, but for to rere and brede catell or shepe. *Ibid.* §66 Yet is it better to the housbande, to sell those calues, than to rere them, bycause of the cost. [**1697** DRYDEN *Virg. Georg.* III. 668 Thoughtless of his Eggs, [the snake] forgets to rear The hopes of Poison, for the following Year.] **1759** BROWN *Compl. Farmer* 49 It is a common saying, the worst housewife will rear the best pigs. **1774** GOLDSM. *Nat. Hist.* (1776) II. 248 Those persons whose employment it is to rear up pigeons of different colours, can breed them..to a feather. **1805** R. W. DICKSON *Pract. Agric.* II. 985 Calves reared in this manner are to be enticed to eat hay as early as possible. **1844** H. STEPHENS *Bk. Farm* III. 845 No man rears a stallion for the use of his own mares only. **1863** *Sat. Rev.* 11 July 49 Man devotes his energies to the..employment of rearing pigs.

b. To bring up (a person), to foster, nourish, educate. = RAISE 10.

1590 SHAKS. *Mids. N.* II. i. 136 For her sake I doe reare vp her boy. **1605** SYLVESTER *Du Bartas* II. iii. III. *Lawe* 180 She takes him up and rears him royall-like. **1671** MILTON *Samson* 555 God with these forbid'n made choice to rear His mighty Champion. **1784** COWPER *Task* VI. 38 We loved, but not enough, the gentle hand That reared us. **1803** J. DAVIS *Trav. U.S.* 215 This gentleman..is not only a Latin, but a Greek Scholar. He was reared at Cambridge. **1879** M. PATTISON *Milton* 179 When Milton was being reared, Calvinism was not old and effete.

absol. **1850** TENNYSON *In Mem.* xl, Her office there to rear, and teach.

c. To attend to, promote, or cause the growth of (plants); to grow (grain, etc.). = RAISE 10 c. Also const. *into.*

1581 W. STAFFORD *Exam. Compl.* i. (1876) 19 Breade Corne, and Malte corne ynough, besides, reared alltogether vpon the same lande. **1728** YOUNG *Love Fame* v. 230 In distant wilds..She rears her flow'rs. **1784** COWPER *Task* VI. 753 Happy to rove among poetic flowers, Though poor in skill to rear them. **1810** SCOTT *Lady of L.* v. vii, While on yon plain The Saxon rears one shock of grain. **1834** H. MILLER *Scenes & Leg.* v. (1857) 61 In those times it was quite as customary for farmers to rear the flax which supplied them with clothing. **1871** R. ELLIS tr. *Catullus* lxii. 50 A flower.. rear'd by the showers. **1871** BROWNING *Prince Hohenstiel-Schwangau* 52 To play at horticulture, rear some rose Or poppy into perfect leaf and bloom.

transf. **1728–46** THOMSON *Spring* 1148 Delightful task! to rear the tender thought, To teach the young idea how to shoot. **1770** BURKE *Pres. Discont.* Wks. II. 340 It is therefore our business..to rear to the most perfect vigour and maturity, every sort of generous and honest feeling. **1781** COWPER *Hope* 295 Hopes of every sort, whatever sect Esteem them, sow them, rear them, and protect.

d. To raise or grow (meat or food).

1799 J. ROBERTSON *Agric. Perth* 345 In the highlands every man rears, on his own farm, what butcher meat his family requires.

III. To lift from a lower to a higher position.

10. a. To lift up or upwards as a whole. = RAISE 17.

Sometimes also with implication of sense 1, esp. in *to rear the head.*

971 *Blickl. Hom.* 187 Rære up þin heafod & ȝeseoh þis þæt Simon deþ. *c* **1320** *Sir Tristr.* 1391 þai rered goinfay-noun. **1382** WYCLIF *Exod.* x. 13 A brennynge wynd reride vp locustes. —— *Matt.* xi. 23 And thou, Caphernaum, whether til in to heuen thou shalt be rerid vp? *c* **1450** *Bk. Curtasye* 754 in *Babees Bk.*, Who so euer he takes þat mete to bere Schalle not so hardy þo couertoure rere. *c* **1485** *Digby Myst.* III. 1878 Rere vp þe seyll In all þe hast, as well as þou can. **1571** DIGGES *Pantom.* I. xvii. E iij b, The nature of water is such, as by pipes it may be rered aboue the fountaine hed. **1610** SHAKS. *Temp.* II. i. 295 When I reare my hand, do you the like To fall it on Gonzalo. **1668** CULPEPPER & COLE *Barthol. Anat.* IV. vii. 165 Its Use is to rear up the Chest. **1726** POPE *Odyss.* XXII. 14 High in his hands he rear'd the golden bowl. **1827** HOOD *Mids. Fairies* xviii, Upon a mast rear'd far aloft, He bore a very bright and crescent blade. **1864** TENNYSON *En. Ard.* 752 The babe, who rear'd his creasy arms.

refl. **1398** TREVISA *Barth. De P.R.* XII. i. (Bodl. MS.), þe more brides haueþ of holownes of pennes..þe more eselich þei rereþ þemsilf and fleeþ vpward.

b. To have, hold, or sustain (some part) in an elevated or lofty position. (Also quasi-*refl.*) *fig.* phr. ***to rear its (ugly) head,*** and varr. = *to raise its (ugly) head* s.v. RAISE *v.*^{1} 17 e.

1667 MILTON *P.L.* IV. 699 Each beauteous flour..Rear'd high thir flourisht heads between, and wrought Mosaic. **1671** —— *P.R.* IV. 546 Higher yet the glorious Temple rear'd Her pile. **1757** GRAY *Bard* 112 Sublime their starry fronts they rear. **1781** J. MOORE *View Soc. It.* (1790) I. xxxv. 381 The ancient Mistress of the World rears her head in melancholy majesty. **1823** BYRON *Island* IV. ii, A black rock rears its bosom o'er the spray. **1857** TROLLOPE *Barchester T.* II. viii. 124 Rebellion had already reared her hideous head within the [bishop's] palace. **1872** JENKINSON *Guide Eng. Lakes* (1879) 150 Honister Crag, the grandest in the district, rears its front on the left. **1946** K. TENNANT *Lost Haven* (1947) vii. 96 Another problem reared its ugly head. **1966** B. KIMENYE *Kalasanda Revisited* 21 Scandal of even the mildest type failed to rear its head. **1971** *Daily Tel.* 5 July 1 The problem of broken rails is rearing its ugly head again in the current spate of railway accidents. **1976** *0–10 Cricket Scene* (Austral.) 21/1 They crumbled as their inexperience reared its ugly head.

c. *refl.* To rise up to a height, to tower.

1774 GOLDSM. *Nat. Hist.* (1862) I. ii. 10 The ground.. rears itself..in lofty mountains and inaccessible cliffs. **1839** J. H. NEWMAN *Par. Serm.* (1842) IV. xvii. 298 The stately tree rears itself aloft. **1860** TYNDALL *Glac.* I. ix. 63 A steep slope of snow..reared itself against the mountain wall.

†**d.** *absol.* or with *it.* To raise anchor. *Obs.*

14.. *Sailing Directions* (Hakluyt Soc. 1889) 13 Yif ye Ride in the Doowns and will go into Sandwiche haven, Rere it by turnyng wynde at an est south of the moone. *Ibid.* 15 A man that ridith in the way of odierene at an ankre, he may begyn to rere at an est southest moone for to turne.

11. To lift up, raise, elevate, exalt, in various fig. applications (sometimes with suggestion of other senses of *rear* or *raise*). Now *rare* or *Obs.*

1382 WYCLIF *Jer.* li. 1 Babilon and..his dwelleris, that ther herte rereden aȝen me. *c* **1450** tr. *De Imitatione* I. xxiii. 32 Kepe þin herte fre & rere it up to þy god. **1586** MARLOWE *1st Pt. Tamburl.* III. ii, And higher would I rear my estimate Than Iuno. **1611** SHAKS. *Wint. T.* I. ii. 314 His Cup-bearer, whom I from meaner forme Haue bench'd, and rear'd to Worship. **1637** R. ASHLEY tr. *Malvezzi's David Persecuted* 5 The same action which at one time hath reared up a Prince, should..sink him. **1655** JER. TAYLOR *Guide Devot.* (1719) 154 Thy Goodness may hereafter rear Our Souls unto thy Glory.

12. To turn or direct (*esp.* the eyes) upwards.

1596 SPENSER *F.Q.* VI. ii. 42 The Ladie..Gan reare her eyes as to the chearefull light. **1621** QUARLES *Div. Poems, Esther* (1717) 14 Jonah (humbly rearing up his eyes). **1671** MILTON *P.R.* III. 285 Up to a hill anon his steps he rear'd. **1712–14** POPE *Rape Lock* I. 126 To that she bends, to that her eyes she rears. **1807** J. BARLOW *Columb.* IV. 135 O'er the dark world Erasmus rears his eye.

13. To cause to rise: **a.** *Naut.* = RAISE 23 a.

1555 EDEN *Decades* 351 In .xv. degrees we dyde reere the crossiers. **1559** W. CUNNINGHAM *Cosmogr. Glasse* 49 We reared the north starre in short space .xij. degr. and at length, 30. deg. **1867** SMYTH *Sailor's Word-bk.* s.v., To *rear* an object in view, is to *rise* or approach it.

†**b.** To raise (a fiend). *Obs.*

1567 GOLDING *Ovid's Met.* VI. (1593) 148 The tyrant with a hideous noise away the table shooves, And reares the fiends from hell.

c. To make (the voice) heard. = RAISE 21.

1817 SCOTT *Harold* VI. xiii, When his voice he rear'd,.. The powerful accents roll'd along. **1818** SHELLEY *Rev. Islam* XI. xx, His voice then did the stranger rear.

†**14. a.** To levy, raise, gather, collect (fines, rents, etc.). *Obs.* = RAISE 25. Also const. *upon.*

c **1420** *Sir Amadace* (Camden) xii, A marchand of this cite, Hade riche rentus to rere. **1449** *Rolls of Parlt.* V. 144/2 A Subsidie to be take and rereyd of al manere Prests seculers. **1475** *Bk. Noblesse* (Roxb.) 30 Oppressid..by over gret taskis and tailis rered uppon them. **1574** *Galway Arch.* in *10th Rep. Hist. MSS. Comm.* App. V. 423, xxti pound sterlinge current mony of England to be rered and levied to the commone use. **1599** HAKLUYT *Voy.* II. II. 60 Which rent is reared onely in goats skinnes.

†**b.** To levy, raise (an army). *Obs.*$^{-1}$

a **1400–50** *Alexander* 81 Artaxenses is at hand & has ane ost rerd, And resyn vp with all his rewme.

†**c.** To take away *from* one. *Obs.*$^{-1}$

1596 SPENSER *F.Q.* IV. vi. 6 He, in an open Turney lately held, Fro me the honour of that game did reare.

IV. 15. a. *intr.* To rise up (towards a vertical position or into the air); to rise high, to tower.

Spec. in *Husb.* of a furrow-slice: see quots. 1523 and 1790.

13.. *E.E. Allit. P.* B. 366 þe mukel lauande loghe to þe lyfte rered. *Ibid.* 423 Ofte hit roled on-rounde & rered on ende. **1523** FITZHERB. *Husb.* §16 Lette the husbande..plowe a brode forowe and a depe..and lay it flat, that it rere not on the edge. **1790** W. MARSHALL *Mid. Counties* (1796) II. Gloss. (E.D.S.) *Rear,* to rise up before the plow, as the furrows sometimes do in plowing. **1840** DICKENS *Old C. Shop* xxxviii, The loftiest steeple that now rears proudly up from the midst of guilt. **1881** *Scribner's Mag.* Aug. 532/2 If a wind on the beam is so strong as to make her either slide or 'rear up' too much.

b. *intr.* Of a quadruped, *esp.* a horse: To rise on the hind feet. Also with *it.*

1375 BARBOUR *Bruce* XIV. 69 Hobynis, that war stekit thar, Rerit and flang. **1592** SHAKS. *Ven. & Ad.* 279 Sometimes he trots,..Anon he reres vpright, curuets, and leaps. **1611** COTGR., *Cabrer,* to reare, or stand vpright on the hinder feet; ..as a Goat, or Kid that brouses on a tree. **1761** STERNE *Tr. Shandy* III. xxxvi, Let me beg of you, like an unback'd filly ..to jump it, to rear it, to bound it. **1800** COLERIDGE *Wallenstein* IV. iv, His charger, by a halbert bored, rear'd up. **1870** EMERSON *Soc. & Solit.* x. 207 When he began to rear, they were so frightened that they could not see the horse.

fig. **1629** GAULE *Holy Madn.* 92 How he reares in the Necke. *a* **1761** JOHNSON in *Boswell* an. 1780 Johnson.. professed that he could bring him out into conversation, and used this illusive expression, 'Sir, I can make him *rear*'. **1899** *Scribner's Mag.* Jan. 98/1 [He] is a brave man and has been known to rear on occasions.

c. *trans.* To throw *off* by rearing. *nonce-use.*

1852 BAILEY *Festus* xxii. (ed. 3) 395 Earth rear off her cities As a horse his rider.

16. *intr.* To turn out (well or ill) in course of, or after, rearing (in sense 9).

1894 *Daily News* 2 Oct. 6/6 In the counties mentioned pheasants have reared well.

rear (rɪə(r)), *v.*^{2} *Obs.* exc. *arch.* Also 5–6 **rere.** [Of obscure origin.] *trans.* To cut up or carve (a fowl, *spec.* a goose).

c **1470** in *Hors, Shepe & G.* (Caxton 1479, Roxb. repr.) 33 A dere broken, a ghoos rerid, a swan lyfte..a heron dismembrid. *c* **1500** *For to serve a Lord* in *Babees Bk.* 374 To lose or untache a bitorn: kitte his nekke,..rere hym legge and whynge, as the heron. *a* **1756** MRS. HEYWOOD *New Present* (1771) 269 To rear a Goose. **1804** FARLEY *London Art Cookery* (ed. 10) 293 To rear a goose, cut off both legs in the manner of shoulder of lamb. **1840** H. AINSWORTH *Tower of London* (1864) 412 In the old terms of his art, he leached the brawn, reared the goose.

†**rear,** *v.*^{3} *Obs. rare.* [f. REAR *sb.*^{3}]

1. *trans.* To attack or assail in the rear.

1670 EACHARD *Cont. Clergy* 48 He falls a fighting with his text, and makes a pitch'd battel of it,..he rears it, flanks it, entrenches it, storms it. **1682** BUNYAN *Holy War* xv, Then the captains fell on, and began roundly to front and flank and rear Diabolus' camp.

2. To strengthen in the rear.

1680 J. SCOTT *Serm. bef. Artillery Comp.* Wks. 1718 II. 24 We cannot talk in Rank and File, Flank and Rear our Discourses with Military Allusions.

†**rear,** *v.*^{4} *Obs.*$^{-1}$ *Naut.* (Of obscure origin and meaning.)

1599 HAKLUYT *Voy.* II. II. 40, I tooke our skiffe and went to them to know why they lost vs,..and Iohn Kire made me answere that his ship would neither reare nor steere.

†**rear,** *adv.*^{1} *Obs.*$^{-1}$ = ARREAR *adv.*

The sense of the passage is not clear; the phrase may mean simply 'not at all'.

c **1412** HOCCLEVE *De Reg. Princ.* 1247 Sone, as for me, nouthir avaunte ne rere.

†**rear,** *adv.*^{2} *Obs. rare.* = RARE *adv.*^{2} Early.

1714 GAY *Sheph. Week* I. 6 O'er yonder Hill does scant the Dawn appear, Then why does Cuddy leave his Cott so rear? *Ibid.* 11 This rising rear betokeneth well thy mind.

rear, dial. variant of ROAR *v.*

rear-, comb. form, partly of OF. or AF. origin, as in *rear-ward, -guard, rearsupper* (and hence by analogy in *rear-admiral, -feast, -freight*), partly ad. F. *arrière-,* as in *rear-vassal, -vault,* and partly (from *c* 1600) an attributive use of REAR *sb.*^{3} In recent use the older spelling **rere-** has sometimes been adopted, esp. in archaic or architectural terms (see *rear-arch, -vault*).

Rear-'Admiral. [f. REAR-.]

1. A flag-officer in the navy, the next in rank below a vice-admiral. (See ADMIRAL 3.)

In the U.S. navy formerly the highest rank granted except in special circumstances.

1589 [T. CATES] *Sir F. Drake's W. Ind. Voy.* 2 Captaine Francis Knolles, Rieradmirall in the Gallion Leicester. *a* **1642** SIR W. MONSON *Naval Tracts* III. (1704) 332/1 The use of a Rear-Admiral is but a late invention, and is allow'd but the ordinary Pay of a Captain. **1702** *Lond. Gaz.* No. 3829/3 Sir John Munden, Rear-Admiral of the Red, hoisted his Flag this day on the Mizen-top-mast of her Majesty's Ship the Victory. **1769** FALCONER *Dict. Marine* s.v. *Admiral,* There are at present in England..four rear admirals of the red, four of the white, and five of the blue squadron. **1802** JAMES *Milit. Dict.* s.v. *Rank,* Admirals..rank with generals of horse and foot; rear-admirals, as major-generals. **1867** SMYTH *Sailor's Word-bk., Rear-Admiral,* the officer in command of the third division of a fleet, whose flag is at the mizen.

†**b.** Formerly used in the designation ***Rear Admiral of England*** or ***Great Britain.*** Now *Obs.*

1684 *Lond. Gaz.* No. 1901/3 His Majesty has been graciously pleased to constitute Arthur Herbert Esq. Rear Admiral of England. **1705** *Ibid.* No. 4086/3 The Lord High Admiral has been pleased to appoint Sir Cloudesly Shovell ..to be Rear-Admiral of England. **1707** *Ibid.* No. 4397/3 He was at the Time of his Death Rear-Admiral of Great Britain. **1799** *Naval Chron.* I. 368 *note,* In August 1771 [Sir George Rodney] was made Rear Admiral of Great Britain.

†**2.** A ship carrying a rear-admiral's flag. *Obs.*

1587 R. LENG *True Descr. Voy. Sir F. Drake* (Camden) 14 We all put out to sea..: videlicet..the Golden Lyon, vize-admirall; the Dreadnaughte, reare admirall [etc.]. **1628** DIGBY *Voy. Medit.* (1868) 28 The newes of my Rere-admirall fighting the day before with the Venetian shippe. **1690** *Lond. Gaz.* No. 2541/3 Their Majesties Ship the Coronation, being a second Rate, and Rear-Admiral of the Red.

rear-arch. *Arch.* Also **rere-.** [f. REAR- + ARCH.] The inner arch of a window- or door-opening, when differing in size or form from the external arch. (Cf. REAR-VAULT.) Also *attrib.*

1849 FREEMAN *Archit.* 343 By these two means the splay and the distinct rear-arch are abolished. **1860** G. E. STREET in *Archæol. Cant.* III. 116 From these a richly-moulded rear-arch springs. **1878** SIR G. SCOTT *Lect. Archit.* I. 280 Taking all styles together, the rear, or rere arch, or in earlier works the wider internal splay, is greatly more frequent, probably because less costly than the other form, the 'through arch'. *Ibid.* 282 The two systems may be distinguished as rere-arch windows and through arch windows.

rear-banquet: see RERE-BANQUET.

reard, variant of RERD, noise.

reardemain, variant of REREDEMAIN *Obs.*

reardors, obs. variant of REREDOS.

reared (rɪəd), *ppl. a.* [f. REAR *v.*¹ + -ED².]
 1. Raised, elevated, exalted.

1382 WYCLIF *Isa.* xxx. 25 Vp on alle rered hil. **1595** BARNFIELD *Cassandra* (1841) 32 Stately Ilion (whose provd reared walls Seem'd to controule the cloudes). **1606** SHAKS. *Ant. & Cl.* v. ii. 82 His rear'd arme Crested the world. **1638** KILLIGREW *Conspiracy* Epil., From your reared and exalted Throne. **1726** LEONI tr. *Alberti's Archit.* II. 59/1 On the rear'd Column be my Story wrote.

 2. Brought up to a certain stage of growth.

1889 *Pall Mall G.* 27 Dec. 1/2 Freely giving the millions of reared fish away.

rearer ('rɪərə(r)). [f. REAR *v.*¹ + -ER¹.]
 1. One who rears (in transitive senses, esp. sense 9).

1382 WYCLIF *Judith* xiv. 9 That not of the rereres, but of the noise makeris Olofernes shulde waken. **1611** COTGR., *Esleveur*, a rearer, breeder. **1767** LEWIS *Statius* x. 323 The Rearer of the Steed, When the kind Spring renews his gen'rous Breed [etc.]. **1841–3** ANTHON *Class. Dict.* 579 She ..is, by the appointment of Jupiter, the rearer of children. **1880** *Daily News* 23 Oct. 2/1 The demand of the English rearer of store cattle for Irish lean cattle.

 2. A horse that rears, or has a habit of rearing.

1829 *Sporting Mag.* XXIV. 89 In nine cases out of ten I have found that confirmed rearers are tender mouthed. **1882** *Daily News* 1 June 3/1 He was a respectable rearer, and a hearty horse at a kick.

 3. *Slang.* (See quot.)

1827 *Sporting Mag.* XXI. 131 We were favoured with.. what is technically called 'a rearer', that is to say, the near side wheels went into a ditch deep enough to have turned us keel upwards.

 4. *Coal-mining.* An edge-seam (see EDGE *sb.* 12, and cf. REARING *ppl. a.* 1, quot. 1686).

1883 GRESLEY *Gloss. Coal-mining* 200.

†**rear-feast.** *Obs.*⁻¹ [f. REAR- + FEAST.] The latter meal, supper.

1615 CHAPMAN *Odyss.* IV. 286 But let us not forget our rear feast thus.

†**rear-freight.** *Obs.*⁻¹ [Alteration of REFREIT, after REAR- and FREIGHT.] Refrain, burden.

c **1557** ABP. PARKER *Ps.* 309 The reare freyt of the Psalme.

rear-guard¹ ('rɪəgɑːd). *Mil.* Forms: 5 rier-, ryere-, 5–6 reregarde; 5 rere-, 6 *Sc.* rearegard; 6 *Sc.* reir-, 7 rere-, 7 rearguard. [a. OF. *rereguarde*, AF. *reregard*, *rergarde* (*c* 1307): see note to ARREAR-GUARD and cf. REARWARD *sb.*¹

Variously written *rearguard*, *rear-guard*, and *rear guard*.]

 †**1.** The rear portion of an army or armed force drawn up for action. *Obs.* = REAR *sb.*³ 1, REARWARD *sb.*¹ 1.

1481 CAXTON *Godfrey* xlv. 85 He kepte alwey the rier garde with grete plente of his peple. *c* **1500** *Melusine* 191 The two bretheren..them self toke & conduyted the gret baytayll... And of the reregarde were captayns the two knightes of poytou. **1598** BARRET *Theor. Warres* 57, 1400 armed men, the which are to arme the front and reregard of the battell. **1636** E. DACRES tr. *Machiavel's Disc. Livy* II. 335 Though they have made their Armie tripartite, terming the one the Vauntguard, the other the Battell, and the last the Rereguard.

 2. a. A body of troops detached from the main force to bring up and protect the rear, *esp.* in the case of a retreat.

1659 RUSHW. *Hist. Coll.* I. 417 The King of Denmark.. endeavored to make his retreat; but Tilly followed so close his Rear-guard, that he kept them in continual action. **1777** A. ST. CLAIR in Sparks *Corr. Amer. Rev.* (1853) I. 404 The rear-guard..wasted so much time in the morning, that they were overtaken and surprised. **1811** WELLINGTON *Let.* 30 Mar. in Gurw. *Desp.* (1838) VII. 412 The enemy went off towards Setubal, the rear guard in admirable order. **1876** VOYLE & STEVENSON *Milit. Dict.* 330/2 Under such circumstances, seldom more than a fifth or sixth of the total force forms the rear guard.

fig. **1837** HT. MARTINEAU *Soc. Amer.* III. 283 If the clergy of America follow the example of other rear-guards of society. **1860** TYNDALL *Glac.* I. xxv. 185 The storm, too, had left a rear-guard behind it.

 b. *rear-guard action*, a defensive stand by the rear-guard of a retreating army; also *fig.*

1898 *Westm. Gaz.* 6 Jan. 4/3 The worst of all battles to fight—a rearguard action. **1946** *Ess. & Stud.* XXXI. 46 Yet this scene is a magnificent rear-guard action by Cleopatra. **1954** F. C. AVIS *Boxing Ref. Dict.* 93 *Rearguard action*, defensive boxing. **1977** *World of Cricket Monthly* June 29/1 It was left to Murray and Roberts to provide a defiant rearguard action which postponed the end.

rear-guard². [f. REAR *sb.*³] The guard at the rear of a railway train; or the van he occupies.

1897 *Daily News* 17 Mar. 8/7 The rear-guard of the Hounslow train.

reargue (riːˈɑːgjuː), *v.* [RE- 5 a.] *trans.* To argue (*spec.* a case in law) a second time; to debate over again. Also *absol.* or *intr.*

1776 BURROW *Rep.* IV. 2320 The Court ordered the Cause to be re-argued. **1863** *Sat. Rev.* 6 June 724 The case does not need or admit of re-arguing now. **1884** *Law Times Rep.* XLIX. 584/2 The Court..desired that the point should be reargued before a full Court of Appeal. **1972** *N.Y. Law Jrnl.* 31 Oct. 15/5 The informal motion to reargue is granted. **1973** *Ibid.* 31 Aug. 2/5 A letter from counsel for South Wall Associates, which shall be deemed a motion to reargue.

 So **'reargument.**

1884 LD. FITZGERALD in *Law Times Rep.* LII. 200/1 The Lord Chancellor directed a re-argument of the Case.

rear-horse. *Entom.* [f. REAR *v.*¹ 15 b.] A mantis.

1869 *Rep. U.S. Comm. Agric. 1868* 308 The *Mantes* or 'rear-horses' prey upon other insects. **1884** *Stand. Nat. Hist.* II. 173 The Mantidæ have become popularly known under a variety of names, such as Rear-horses, Race-horses, ..from the peculiar positions assumed by them at different times. **1900** *Everybody's Mag.* July 21 Most people are acquainted with the praying mantis—otherwise known as the 'rearhorse'. **1935** H. T. FERNALD *Appl. Entomology* (ed. 3) xvi. 87 They [*sc.* mantids] are often called rearhorses, devil-horses,..or mule killers.

rearing ('rɪərɪŋ), *vbl. sb.* [f. REAR *v.*¹] The action of the vb. in various senses.

 1. The action of lifting up, raising, elevating, †increasing, etc.

c **1440** CAPGRAVE *Life St. Kath.* v. 1232 If ye deye in this same errour, youre reryngе ageyn shal cause you grete dolour. **1526** *Pilgr. Perf.* (W. de W. 1531) 260 b, In the whiche reryngе doutlesse his handes & fete dyd rent & teare. **1549** LATIMER *Serm. bef. Edw. VI*, i. (Arb.) 41 Al the enhansinge and rearing goth to your priuate commoditie and wealth. *Ibid.* vi. 168 [The deuil] sturres men up to outragious rearyng of rentes.

 2. The action of erecting, building up, etc.

In various dialects *spec.* the erection of the roof-timbers, putting on the roof, of a house; hence *rearing-feast*, *-supper* (or simply *rearing*), a supper given to the workmen on this occasion. (See Rochd., Lonsd., Chesh., Linc., and Hants glossaries.)

1387 TREVISA *Higden* (Rolls) IV. 99 Scipio..fforbeed þe reryngе of þe theatre in þe citee of Rome. **1535** COVERDALE 1 *Esdras* v. 62 In the rearinge vp of the house of the Lorde. **1542** UDALL *Erasm. Apoph.* 232 Buyldyng an hous euen from the foundacion vnto the vttermost raftreyng and reirynge of the roofe. **1639** *MS. Acc. St. John's Hosp., Canterb.*, The rareinge of our house in Ruttinton Lane. **1867** FREEMAN *Norm. Conq.* (1876) I. App. 682 In the minster of the Holy Trinity of his own rearing.

 3. The action (practice or occupation) of bringing up to or towards maturity.

1398 TREVISA *Barth. De P.R.* XVIII. i. (Bodl. MS.), Bestes ..haue redines of wytte in bredynge and reringe of here brode. **1611** COTGR., *Eslevement*, a rearing, breeding, or bringing up. **1681** DRYDEN *Prol. to Saunders' Tamerlane* 23 He's a young plant,..But his friend swears he will be worth the rearing. **1776** ADAM SMITH *W.N.* I. viii. (1869) I. 83 Poverty..is extremely unfavourable to the rearing of children. **1796** MORSE *Amer. Geog.* I. 770 The soil..is thin, and better adapted to the rearing of cotton than sugar. **1797** BEWICK *Brit. Birds* i. 263 The breeding and rearing of these charming birds. **1886** *Paul's Fish Culture* Sept. 67 They aim at the stocking of waters rather than the rearing of fish for the table.

 4. †**a.** The fact of rising up. *Obs.*⁻¹

1398 TREVISA *Barth. De P.R.* XIV. xlvi. (Bodl. MS.), Valeis ben ischadowed bi reringe & hiȝenes of hilles.

 b. The action of rising on the hind legs.

1831 YOUATT *Horse* xix. 337 Then rearing may be immediately and permanently cured by using a snaffle-bridle alone. **1892** E. REEVES *Homeward Bound* 262 In the frantic rearing of the horse..both horse and rider turned a somersault.

 5. *attrib.* **a.** Of animals: Being reared, intended for rearing.

1599 *Nottingham Rec.* IV. 251, viij. olde swyne and twelve rearinge pigges. **1778** [W. MARSHALL] *Minutes Agric.* 29 Aug. 1774 This is the same [cow] which suckled the two rearing calves. **1887** in *S. Chesh. Gloss.* s.v., Promising well-bred rearing heifer calf.

 b. Of appliances or places used in or for the rearing of animals (*esp.* fowls or fishes), as *rearing box*, *coop*, *glass*, *ground*, *jar*, *pond*, *tank*.

1854 *Zoologist* XII. 4189 For rearing-glasses [for insects], I have used confectioners' show-glasses of various sizes. **1884** *Pall Mall G.* 4 Apr. 4/2 Building hatching-houses and boxes, constructing rearing-coops and runs. **1886** *Paul's Fish Culture* Sept. 71 Rearing grounds similar to those which are found on the coast of France. **1891** *Chambers' Encycl.* VIII. 198/1 Rearing ponds situated near the sea. **1967** K. M. SMITH *Insect Virol.* x. 184 The hot medium is poured into rearing jars.

 6. *Comb.*: **rearing-bit**, a bit employed to prevent a horse from lifting the head while rearing (Knight *Dict. Mech.* 1875); **rearing-house**, a building in which young chickens are kept.

1824 J. H. BARLOW *Hatching Poultry by Steam* 15 The Rearing House is of the same size and dimensions as the Hatching House, in which Fowls are kept until they are three weeks or a month old. **1948** L. ROBINSON *Mod. Poultry Husbandry* xi. 227 When growing stock are first placed in arks or other types of range rearing-house, a temporary run of wire netting should be erected. **1962** D. DE SAULLES *Pictorial Poultry Keeping* (ed. 2) This pullet is just about ready to be taken from the rearing house and put into laying quarters. **1975** T. ALLBEURY *Special Collection* xxiii. 168 The lights were on in the rearing house... He could hear the shrill noise of eight thousand week-old chicks.

rearing ('rɪərɪŋ), *ppl. a.* [f. REAR *v.*¹]
 1. That rears or rises up.

With the first quot. cf. REARER 4.

1686 PLOT *Staffordsh.* 147 If it be a rearing mine or edg-coal as some call it, cutting the superficies of the earth at right angles. **1816** L. HUNT *Hero & Leander* II. 65 Surmounted like a god the rearing tide. **1851** J. M. WILSON *Rural Cycl.* IV. 29 A viciously rearing horse..is sometimes dealt with by being pulled over backward by a rider.

 2. That rears or brings up. (Cf. prec. 5 b.)

1884 *Health Exhib. Catal.* 119/1 A Rearing Mother for the artificial rearing of the chickens.

 3. = *raring* adj. s.v. RARE *v.* 1 b.

1926 G. FRANKAU *My Unsentimental Journey* viii. 104 A good many of the eight hundred other diners were 'raring' (Anglicé—rearing) 'to go'. **1947** H. WALSH *Fourth Point of Star* 34, I am rearing to talk this business over with her. **1963** *Listener* 28 Feb. 393/3 Inside most liberal Lincolnographers there seems to be a Lincolnolater rearing to genuflect.

rearing-bone, -piece. (See quots.)

1736 BAILEY *Househ. Dict.* 349 Take two buttock pieces or as they are also call'd two rearing pieces of pork (these are the lean that is cut off the gammon on the inside of the flitch). **1883** *Hants. Gloss.*, *Rearing-bone*, the hip-bone of a pig.

rearing crew. *N. Amer.* [app. f. REAR *sb.*³] = *rear-crew* s.v. REAR *sb.*³ 9.

1963 R. D. SYMONS *Many Trails* xviii. 184 The last men ..will form the nucleus of the 'rearing crew'—that is, the crew which will bring up the rear of the drive, taking care to roll into the water any logs left stranded on the banks. **1971** *Daily Progress* (Charlottesville, Va.) 6 May 7-D/5 Freeing stranded logs is the job of a 32-man 'rearing crew', which works seven days a week with power boats, winches and occasionally a stick of dynamite.

rearise (riːəˈraɪz), *v.* [RE- 5 a.] *intr.* To arise again.

1865 SWINBURNE *Poems & Ball.*, *Hesperia* 31 As a ghost rearisen. **1887** BOWEN *Virg. Æneid* IV. 129 Morn, meanwhile rearising, has left dark Ocean.

'rearling. *rare*⁻¹. [f. REAR *v.*¹] A fosterling.

1884 J. PAYNE *Tales fr. Arabic* II. 100 This youth is my rearling, and he was born of one of my slave-girls.

†**'rearly,** *adv.* *Obs. rare.* [f. REAR *a.*² + -LY².] Early.

1612 *Two Noble K.* IV. i, I'll bring it tomorrow. *Daughter.* Do very rearly; I must be abroad else. **1714** GAY *Sheph. Week* IV. 39, I rearly rose just at the break of day.

rearm (riːˈɑːm), *v.* *Mil.* [RE- 5 a.] *trans.* To arm again; *esp.* to arm afresh with more modern weapons. Hence **re'arming** *vbl. sb.*

1871 *Pall Mall G.* 6 Mar. 7 At this moment the effort of the Government is to ream as many soldiers of the line as possible. **1898** *Daily News* 31 Aug. 5/4 The recent re-arming of the German artillery with a new weapon.

 So **re'armament.**

1870 *Observer* 13 Nov., The revictualment of Paris is more important than the rearmament of France. **1905** *Daily Chron.* 14 Mar. 1/7 The artillery rearmament scheme accounts for £1,213,000. **1935** *Hansard Commons* 22 May 363 Re-armament that could not fail to cause all lovers of peace considerable anxiety. **1938** *Encycl. Brit. Bk. of Year* 60/2 In Great Britain the economic consequences of rearmament are..rather intangible and remote. **1938**, etc. [see *Moral Rearmament* s.v. MORAL *a.* 7 f]. **1961** *Daily Worker* 25 May 2 Without Britain's tolerance German rearmament in the air would be jeopardised.

rearmost ('rɪəməʊst), *a.* [f. REAR *a.*¹ + -MOST.] Farthest in the rear, coming last of all.

1718 ROWE tr. *Lucan* II. 1110 The rest pursue their Course ..These of the Rear-most only left behind. **1790** BEATSON *Nav. & Mil. Mem.* II. 193 The rearmost ship of the enemy's line. **1851** MAYNE REID *Scalp Hunt.* xli. 322 The Indians halted until those who were rearmost should close up. **1880** *Nature* XXI. 357 The rearmost end of this fragment.

rearmouse, reremouse ('rɪəmaʊs). Now only *arch.* or *dial.* Forms: α. 1 hrere-, hryremus, (2 reremus), 4–5 reremous, -mows(e, 6–7, 9 reremouse, (7 reere-, 7, 9 *dial.* reer-). β. 6–7 reare-, 7– rearmouse, (9 *dial.* rare-). γ. 6–7 *pl.* remice, -mise, 9 *dial.* ry(e)-, ray-, raa-, rawmouse. [OE. *hreremús*, f. *mús* MOUSE.

The first element may represent the stem of OE. *hréran* to move, but the length of the vowel is not certain. It is also possible that the form is an alteration (by phonetic corruption or popular etymology) of the older *hréaðemús*, found in the earliest glosses and some later texts, and perh. represented by some of the existing dialect forms.]

 = BAT *sb.*¹ (Cf. *flicker-*, *flinder-*, *flitter-mouse.*)

α. *a* **1100** *Voc.* in Wr.-Wülcker 318/27 *Uespertilio*, hreremus. **1382** WYCLIF *Lev.* xi. 19 A lapwynk and a reremous. **1382** —— *Baruch* vi. 21 Aboue the hed of hem backis, or reremijse, and swalewis fleeȝen. **1399** LANGL. *Rich. Redeles* III. 272 Not to rewle as reremys, and reste on the daies. **1552** HULOET, Backe or Reremouse which flieth in the darke, *nicteris.* **1590** SHAKS. *Mids. N.* II. ii. 4 Some warre with Reremise for their leathern wings. **1634** SIR T. HERBERT *Trav.* 212 Reer-mice, or Bats so large as Gos-hawkes. **1686** J. DUNTON *Lett. fr. New-Eng.* (1867) 24 One of the Seamen affirm'd that he had seen Flying Fishes, and that they had wings like a Rere-Mouse. **1863** WISE *New Forest* 192 The bat is here called rere-mouse. **1864-** in dial. glossaries (Dorset, Som., Glouc., Hants). **1886** R. F. BURTON *Arab. Nts.* (abr. ed.) I. Foreword 8 The rere-mouse flitted overhead with his tiny shriek.

β. **1581** J. BELL *Haddon's Answ. Osor.* 504 We shall wander and straggle blindely.. as wantes and rearemyce at the bright beames of the cleare Sunne. **1668** DRYDEN *Even. Love* v. i, Some flying, and some sticking upon the Walls like Rear-mice. **1728** MORGAN *Algiers* I. iv. 129 These Brutes, whose language resembled the screeching of Bats, or Rear-Mice. **1835** BROWNING *Paracelsus* III. 391 Do the rear-mice still Hang like a fretwork on the gate? **1892** EARL LYTTON *King Poppy* Epil. 163 The rear-mice flit In the hard furrow.

γ. **1565** GOLDING *Ovid's Met.* IV. (1593) 92 We in English language bats or remice call the same. **1603** KNOLLES *Hist. Turks* (1621) 544 Their lights are oftentimes put out with the.. swarmes of remise flying about their eares. **1825** BRITTON *Beauties Wilts* III. Prov., *Rymouse*, a bat. **1851**, **1893** in Glouc. and Wilts glossaries (*rye-, raa-, rawmouse*).

†**b.** *transf.* (See quot.) *Obs.*⁻¹

1611 COTGR. *Rondole*, the sea Bat, or Rearemouse of the sea; a flying fish.

rea'rousal. [f. RE-AROUSE *v.*] A second or further arousal.

1934 in WEBSTER. **1949** M. MEAD *Male & Female* IV. xiv. 293 The demon to be avoided.. is lack of potency, defined in a number of quantitative ways—frequency, time, interval before rearousal.

re-a'rouse, *v.* [RE- 5 a.] To arouse again.

1830 LYTTON *P. Clifford* xix, The witness, re-aroused into anger,.. said in a low voice [etc.]. **1860** EARL LYTTON *Lucile* II. iv. §6. 37 The heart of a man re-aroused to the use Of the conscience God gave him.

re-a'rrange, *v.* [RE- 5 a.] To arrange anew.

1824 DE QUINCEY in *London Mag.* Jan. 5/2, I have therefore abstracted, re-arranged, and in some respects.. have improved, the German work on this subject. **1860** TYNDALL *Glac.* 4 Is it meant that these particles, each taken as a whole, were re-arranged after deposition? **1863** A. C. RAMSAY *Phys. Geog.* 13 On cooling, the constituents re-arranged themselves.

So **re-a'rrangeable** *a.*; **re-a'rrangement.**

1867 H. SPENCER *First Princ.* II. xiii. §102. 297 Its parts are no longer appreciably re-arrangeable by any save violent actions. **1863** *Sat. Rev.* 6 June 719 It will repay the trouble of rearrangement and fresh elaboration.

re-a'rray, *v.* [RE- 5 a.] To array again.

a **1711** KEN *Hymns Festiv.* Poet. Wks. 1721 I. 249 In wonted Splendor re-array'd, He strait invisible retir'd. *c* **1858** ELIZ. WATTS *Poultry Yard* 112 This bird.. was presented.. on a large dish, re-arrayed in its glorious plumage.

re-a'rrest, *v.* [RE- 5 a.] To arrest again.

1655 FULLER *Hist. Camb.* (1840) 186 As for the duke.. he was re-arrested of high treason. **1889** *Daily News* 12 July 5/5 If he escapes this time, it is almost certain that he will be rearrested.

So **re-a'rrest** *sb.*

1864 *Morn. Star* 29 Dec., The issue of new warrants.. for the re-arrest of the raiders.

rear-rib: see REAR-VAULT (quot. 1844).

re-a'rrive, *v.* [RE- 5 a.] To arrive again.

1598 SYLVESTER *Panaretus* 1423 [They,] re-arrived in their own camp, their prize Unto their prince present. **1637** WOTTON in *Reliq.* (1672) 74 The Arch-bishop of Spalato being then re-arrived from England.

So **re-a'rrival.**

1891 MISS DOWIE *Girl in Karp.* 262 The village soon got wind of my re-arrival.

rear-shaft: see REAR-VAULT (quot. 1844).

rear-supper, variant of RERE-SUPPER *Obs.*

re-ar'ticulate, *v.* [RE- 5 a.] To articulate for a second or further time. So **re-ar'ticulated** *ppl. a.*

1963 *Economist* 21 Sept. 987/2 A wholly rearticulated Office of External Relations. **1964** *Language* XL. 78 Verbs with rearticulated root vowel often appear in apocopated form in rapid speech. **1964** E. PALMER tr. *Martinet's Elem. General Linguistics* ii. 45 The necessity.. of re-articulating a foreign mode of experience to conform to the model which is familiar to us. **1973** MATIAS & WILLEMEN tr. M. Cegarra in *Screen* Spring/Summer 177 It is clearly the whole notion of film rhetoric which needs to be re-articulated.

rear-vassal. *Hist.* Also rere-. [f. REAR- + VASSAL, after F. *arrière-vassal*, 'an vnder-vassall, a vassall vnto a vassall' (Cotgr.).] A sub-vassal; one who does not hold directly of the sovereign.

1761 GIBBON *Misc. Wks.* (1814) III. 215 His own immediate vassals were bound to follow him into the field against a prince of whom they were themselves the rear-vassals. **1832** AUSTIN *Jurispr.* (1879) II. lii. 875 This.. is the case with freehold land.. where the tenant in fee simple is properly a rere vassal. **1844** LD. BROUGHAM *Brit. Const.* xiii. (1862) 183 *note*, Mr. Hume erroneously thinks that the statute 7 Hen. IV. gave rear-vassals their right of election.

rear-vault. *Arch.* Also rere-. [f. REAR-, after F. *arrière-voussure.*] The vaulted space connecting an arched window- or door-head with the arch in the inner face of the wall.

1844 WILLIS *Archit. Nomencl.* §81 We may therefore call the said vault, rib, and shaft, the rear-vault, rear-rib, and rear shaft of the window or door. **1861** BERESF. HOPE *Eng. Cathedr. 19th C.* ii. 46 These window groups being internally set back into a single recessed panel, and surmounted by a single rear-vault.

rearward ('rɪəwɔːd), *sb.*¹ Forms: 4-5 rer-, 4-9 rere-, 5 *Sc.* reir-, 6-7 reare-, 7 reer-, 6 rearward; also 4-7 -warde. [a. AF. *rerewarde* (*c* 1307): see note to ARREAR-WARD.]

1. *Mil.* (and *Naval*). That part of an army (or fleet) which is stationed behind the main body; the third division in a force drawn up for battle. Cf. REAR-GUARD 1. *Obs.* exc. *arch.*

13.. *Coer de L.* 3147 Alle the rerewarde Was i-slayn with Kyng Rychard. **1375** BARBOUR *Bruce* VIII. 71 Quhen the reirward saw thaim swa Discumfit.. Thai fled on fer. *a* **1430** *Syr Gener.* (Roxb.) 9024 Thei without folowed hard, And slogh many of the rereward. **1450-1530** *Myrr. our Ladye* 119 An hooste in batayle is departed in thre, that ys to saye, the forwarde, the mydel warde, and the rerewarde. **1585** T. WASHINGTON tr. *Nicholay's Voy.* I. xvii. 19 At thys Cape.. were foure Galliots of the rearewarde of the Turkes armie. **1609** HOLLAND *Amm. Marcell.* 119 The souldiors of our rereward, who kept the upper part of the hill. **1654** EARL MONM. tr. *Bentivoglio's Warrs Flanders* 322 The third Squadron of the Rereward got almost all safe off. **1828-40** TYTLER *Hist. Scot.* (1864) II. 41 He himself followed with the rearward, composed of the main strength of his army. *fig.* **1592** SHAKS. *Rom. & Jul.* III. ii. 121 [Q. 2] But with a rereward following Tybalts death Romeo is banished [etc.].

b. *transf.* in various applications.

c **1586** C'TESS PEMBROKE *Ps.* LXVIII. ix, The rereward lowd on instruments did play. **1611** BIBLE *Num.* x. 25 The campe of the children of Dan.. which was the rere-ward of all the campes throughout their hostes. —— *Isa.* lviii. 8 Thy righteousnesse shall go before thee, the glory of the Lord shall be thy rereward. **1665** BUNYAN *Holy Citie* 174 As he is to be the Captain and Leader of his People, so he is to be the Rere-ward and Bringer-up of his People. **1860** WARTER *Seaboard* II. 27 God went before them, and was their rereward also.

†**2.** In verbal phrases: ***to have, keep, make the rearward*** (in early use said of the leaders, later of the troops). ***to close the rearward***, to bring up the rear. *Obs.*

13.. *K. Alis.* 7788 Antioche hadde the former-warde, And Tolome the reirwarde. **1375** BARBOUR *Bruce* XVI. 58 Schir Eduard.. Befor in the avaward raid. The Kyng him-self the reirward maid. *c* **1380** *Sir Ferumb.* 2712 Y me-self and Olyuer.. Wolleþ come be-hynde her; & kepe þe rereward. *c* **1400** *Laud Troy Bk.* 14662 (E.E.T.S.) Ho schal haue the vaunwarde, Who the myddel, and ho the rerewarde? *c* **1430** *Syr Gener.* (Roxb.) 3757 Aufreus of Tharse.. The rereward he kept ful wiselie. **1583** in Grosart *Spenser's Wks.* I. 484 The examinate.. appointed the souldieres to keepe the rere-warde. **1613** HAYWARD *Norm. Kings* 9 The lances and men at Armes cloased the Rereward. **1614** RALEIGH *Hist. World* II. (1634) 248 These had the Rereward and moved last.

3. In prepositional phrases (cf. *sb.*²):

a. ***in*** (or ***at***) ***the rearward***, in the rear.

14.. [see 4]. **1487** *Barbour's Bruce* XIV. 60 (Camb. MS.) The vaward had the erll thomas, And in the rereward schir eduard was. **1600** HOLLAND *Livy* XXXIX. xlix. 1054 Whiles he came himselfe behind in the rereward.. his horse fell and cast him at once. **1601** DOLMAN *La Primaud. Fr. Acad.* (1618) III. 759 Cranes come from the farthest orientall seas of India.. Euery troup hath a captaine who is alwaies at the rereward. **1866** NEALE *Sequences & Hymns* 67 Some in the van Thou call'st to do.. And in the rearward not a few Thou only bidd'st to bear.

b. ***in*** (or ***on***) ***the rearward of***, in the rear of.

1597 SHAKS. *2 Hen. IV*, III. ii. 339 Hee was the very Genius of Famine: he came euer in the rere-ward of the Fashion. **1599** —— *Much Ado* IV. i. 128 [Q.] My selfe would on the rere-ward of reproches Strike at thy life. **1603** DEKKER *Wonderfull Yeare* A iv b, There stands in the Rere-ward of this Booke a Troope of straunge Discourses. **1808** SCOTT *Marm.* VI. xxvi, Lord Dacre with his horsemen light, Shall be in rear-ward of the fight. **1841** *Blackw. Mag.* XLIX. 152 It would occupy its right position.. in the advance, not in the rearward of the times.

4. *transf.* The hinder parts, posteriors.

14.. *Tourn. Tottenham* in Hazl. *E.P.P.* III. 86 He gurde so fast his gray mare That she lete a fowkyn fare At the rerewarde. *c* **1557** ABP. PARKER *Ps.* lxxviii. 227 Hys foes rearwardes even down he felde. **1855** MARTIN & AYTOUN *Bon Gaultier Ball.* 238 Already in his rearward Felt he Jove's tremendous toes.

rearward ('rɪəwəd), *a.* [f. REAR- + -WARD.]

1. Situated in the rear.

1598 BARRET *Theor. Warres* 54, 6 rankes at 2 men per ranke in the reareward angles. **1813** SCOTT *Rokeby* II. vi, As champions, when their band is broke, Stand forth to guard the rearward post. **1876** 'MARK TWAIN' *Tom Sawyer* vi, His coat.. had the rearward buttons far down the back.

2. Directed towards the rear; backward.

1861 *Sat. Rev.* 7 Dec. 585/1 If the execution of a rapid rear-ward movement be required. **1872** JENKINSON *Guide Eng. Lakes* (1879) 28 A rearward view discloses a fine grouping of the hills which have been passed.

rearward ('rɪəwəd), *adv.* (*sb.*²) [f. as prec.]

1. a. Towards the rear; backward.

1625 MARKHAM *Souldiers Accid.* 18 Open your Rankes, from the front rereward. **1818** SOUTHEY in *Q. Rev.* XVIII. 33 The heavy weapon reached me in the rear, And rearward I returned a long loud sigh. **1868** *Rep. to Govt. U.S. Munitions War* 53 The head of the locking bolt.. causes this block to move obliquely rearward.

b. At the back *of.*

1880 L. WALLACE *Ben-Hur* IV. x, Rearward of the structure which graced the entrance-way.

c. *Comb.*, as ***rearward-facing***, ***-hinged*** adjs.

1955 *Times* 23 June 4/4 It had been decided in Australia to have rearward-facing seats. **1959** *Economist* 13 June 1042/1 The engine drives a ducted fan, which supplies compressed air to two concentric rings of jet openings facing downward.. while rearward-facing jets propel it. **1967** *Jane's Surface Skimmer Systems 1967-68* 25/1 There is a rearward-hinged car-type door on each side of the cabin.

2. As *sb.* in phr. ***in the rearward***, in the rear.

1832 G. DOWNES *Lett. Cont. Countries* I. 55 The view in the rearward now became agreeably diversified by the mountains we had lately traversed.

So **'rearwardly** *adv.*; **'rearwards** *adv.*

1856 OLMSTED *Slave States* 91 A room that extended out, rearwardly, from the house. **1888** *Engineer* 4 May 374/3 Having a handle.. extending rearwardly beyond the suction tube. **1897** *Daily News* 25 May 8/1 The unfit were gradually weeded out and sent rearwards. **1934** *Canad. Patent Office Rec.* 30 Oct. 2464/1 Beams extending.. rearwardly of the rear axle. **1946** A. W. JUDGE *Mod. Petrol Engines* vi. 237 The cooling air.. leaves the engine cowling through a rearwardly inclined exit. **1973** *Times* 30 Oct. 17/8 A reasonable proportion of the water is thrown rearwardly.

rearwardness ('rɪəwədnɪs). *rare.* [f. REARWARD *a.* + -NESS.] The state of being in the rear or in arrears.

1903 *T.P.'s Weekly* 16 Oct. 621/2 It is advantageous to keep oneself quite a year behind contemporary literature; this rearwardness saves both time and money.

reas, variant of REIS (Pg. money).

reascend (riːə'sɛnd), *v.* [RE- 5 a.] To ascend again: **a.** *intr.* (Cf. ASCEND 1-4, 7-10.)

c **1450** *Mirour Saluacioun* 4088 Crist descendid to helle.. so to heven is he reascendit. **1594** SPENSER *Amoretti* lxxxvi, I wish that day would shortly reascend. **1621** T. WILLIAMSON tr. *Goulart's Wise Vieillard* 166, I reascend to the nintith one Epistle, from whence I will deduce that which followes. *a* **1691** BOYLE *Hist. Air* (1692) 134 The mercury re-ascended to its first stations. **1760-72** H. BROOKE *Fool of Qual.* (1809) IV. 14 How shall he.. be able to re-ascend in the state of his weakness? **1814** SIR R. WILSON *Priv. Diary* II. 355 How many degraded sovereigns have re-ascended from a dungeon to a throne? **1850** DE QUINCEY in 'H. A. Page' *Life* II. xvii. 67 Up from the river banks you behold it reascending.

b. *trans.* (Cf. ASCEND 5-6.)

1615 CHAPMAN *Odyss.* XX. 86 The Goddesse.. re-ascended the Olympian skies. **1624** MASSINGER *Renegado* III. v, To re-ascend that glorious height we fell from. *a* **1711** KEN *Hymnotheo* Poet. Wks. 1721 III. 120 Till they the Lunar Mountains re-ascend. **1781** COWPER *Truth* 395 She.. As soon shall rise and reascend the throne. **1891** T. HARDY *Tess* lvi, She heard Tess re-ascend the stairs to the first floor.

Hence **rea'scending** *vbl. sb.* and *ppl. a.*

1611 FLORIO, *Risalita*, a reascending or getting vp againe. **1664** POWER *Exp. Philos.* II. 92 The re-ascending Quick-silver will never totally.. fill the Tube. **1818** BYRON *Ch. Har.* IV. clxxiv, 'Arms and the Man', whose reascending star Rose o'er an empire.

So **rea'scendant, -ent** *a.*, **rea'scendancy, -ency, rea'scension.**

1668 MILTON *P.L.* VII. Argument, The Angels celebrate.. his reascention into Heaven. **1808** BENTHAM *Let. to Ld. Holland* Wks. 1843 X. 440 Since the reascension of this thinking.. great court has, in my absence, been paid to him. **1868** MILMAN *St. Paul's* 237 St. Paul's witnessed the triumph of reascendant Roman Catholicism. **1875** LIGHTFOOT *Comm. Col.* (1886) 110 He described this re-ascension of the Christ as a return 'to His own pleroma'. **1885** *Cornh. Mag.* Mar. 267 The eventual reascendency of Brahmanism.

re-a'scended, *ppl. a.* [f. REASCEND *v.* + -ED¹.] That has ascended again.

a **1838** R. GRANT *Sacred Poems* (1839) 8 Oh! from earth to heav'n restor'd, Mighty re-ascended Lord. **1906** *Westm. Gaz.* 14 Apr. 6/2 Rise, O saints.. Round your re-ascended Sun circling soar!

reascent (riːə'sɛnt). [f. RE- 5 a + ASCENT.]

1. The act of reascending.

a **1711** KEN *Hymnotheo* Poet. Wks. 1721 III. 87 The Heav'nly Standard then shall wave in Air, And the bright Hosts for Re-ascent prepare. **1733** TULL *Horse-hoeing Husb.* xvi. 247 To prevent the Re-ascent of what that brings down. **1808** BENTHAM *Sc. Reform* 43 Where the descent has not been occasional, alternating with re-ascent. **1851** C. L. SMITH tr. *Tasso* XV. xxxiii, The sun.. shone behind them on its re-ascent.

2. The way by which one reascends.

1784 COWPER *Task* I. 327 Hence the declivity is sharp and short, And such the reascent. **1855** BAILEY *Mystic* 6 They.. Move ever up the reascent to light.

3. The distance to which one reascends.

1807 WORDSW. *White Doe* VII. 297 Dire overthrow, and yet how high The re-ascent in sanctity.

rease, obs. f. RAISE *v.*¹, var. RESE *Obs.*, obs. Sc. pa. t. RISE *v.*, Sc. dial. var. of ROOSE *v.*

reased, variant of REESED *a.*, rancid.

†**reasemblance.** *Obs.*⁻¹ [Perh. for *resemblance*, but cf. ASSEMBLANCE².] Resemblance.

1638 R. BAKER tr. *Balzac's Lett.* (vol. II.) 212, I can make you a reasemblance at least of the good Cheere of Paris.

reasen, reasin, obs. forms of RAISIN.

reasiness: see REASY *a.*

re-'ask, *v.* [RE- 5 a.] To ask again.

1611 FLORIO, *Radimandare*, to redemaund, to re-aske. **1803** J. WHITAKER in Polwhele *Trad. & Recoll.* (1826) II. 547 'Why then should we fear?' she re-asked. **1856** LEVER *Martins of Cro' M.* 602 The few questions to which I will ask your answers, now,.. may, very probably, be re-asked of you under more solemn circumstances.

reasnable, obs. form of REASONABLE.

reason ('ri:z(ə)n), *sb.*[1] Forms: α. 3 reisun, 4 -oun, (5 reissoun), 3–5 reyson, (5 -one), 4–5 reison; 3 reaisun, 4–6 rayson, (4 -oun), 6 raisson, rasone, *Sc.* rasoun. β. 3–5 resun, (4 -une), 3–6 resoun, (4–5 -oune, 4 -owne), 3–7 reson, (4–6 -one); 4 reesoun, 5 -on; 5–6 ressoun, (7 *Sc.* -oune), resson, (6 -one); 7 *Sc.* reassoune, 4– reason. [a. OF. *reisun, -on, raisun, -on, reson*, etc. (mod.F. *raison*):—L. *ratiōn-em* reckoning, account, relation, understanding, motive, cause, etc., vbl. sb. f. *rat-*, ppl. stem of *rērī* to think, reckon: see RATIO *sb.* and RATION.]

I. 1. a. A statement of some fact (real or alleged) employed as an argument to justify or condemn some act, prove or disprove some assertion, idea, or belief.

In common use down to *c* 1600; after that date somewhat rare, except as elliptical for sense 5.

a **1225** *Ancr. R.* 164 Ihereð nu reisuns hwui me ouh for to fleon þene world: eihte reisuns et te leste. *c* **1305** *St. Katherine* 31 in *E.E.P.* (1862) 90 Mid oþer reisouns of clergie þat maide preouede also þat here godes noþing nere. **1362** LANGL. *P. Pl.* A. XI. 41 Þei..Bryngeþ forth Ballede Resouns..And puyteþ forþ presumpcion to preue þe soþe. *c* **1440** CAPGRAVE *Life St. Kath.* II. 704 Ȝe may..New wordes reherse & new resones speke, Whech wer rehersyd & haue her answers eke. **1533** BELLENDEN *Livy* V. xxv, It is said camillus movit þe Romanis fra migration to veos be mony ressonis. **1563** FOXE *A. & M.* 1369/2 Cirillus..prouing to the Jewes that Christ was come, vseth this reason. **1585** T. WASHINGTON tr. *Nicholay's Voy.* III. xxii. 112 b, They would not depart without hauing of me some present, alleadging by their reasons that they had done me great honour in comming. **1600** E. BLOUNT tr. *Conestaggio* 15 Strengthning their reasons with many examples. **1638** R. BAILLIE *Lett. & Jrnls.* (1841) I. 90 Ye have here also some Reasons against the Service in print. **1810** CRABBE *Borough* xxi, They proved (so thought I then) with reasons strong That no man's feelings ever lead him wrong.

b. ***a woman's*** (or ***the ladies'***) ***reason***: (see quots.).

1591 SHAKS. *Two Gent.* I. ii. 22, I haue no other but a womans reason: I thinke him so, because I thinke him so. *a* **1641** BP. MOUNTAGU *Acts & Mon.* (1642) 106 They were, scilicet, because they were; which is more foolish then a womans reason. **1768–74** TUCKER *Lt. Nat.* (1834) I. 287 A pretty way of proving the point, being no better than the ladies' reason, it is divisible because it is. **1792** MARY WOLLSTONECR. *Rights Wom.* v. 254 This mode of arguing, if arguing it may be called, reminds me of what is vulgarly termed 'a woman's reason'; for women sometimes declare that they love or believe certain things 'because' they love or believe them.

c. *Logic.* One of the premises in an argument; *esp.* the minor premise when placed after the conclusion.

1826 WHATELY *Logic* i. §2 A premiss placed after its conclusion is called the Reason of it, and is introduced by one of those conjunctions which are called causal. [*Note.* The Major-premiss is often called the Principle: and the word Reason is then confined to the Minor.] **1864** BOWEN *Logic* vii. 211 To deny the Consequent is also to deny the Reason.

2. a. ***to give, yield*** or ***render*** (***a***) ***reason***: to give an account (of one's acts or conduct). Now *arch.*

a **1225** *Ancr. R.* 82 Of swuche speche..schal euerich word beon irikened, & iȝiuen reisun, hwi þe on hit seide [etc.]. *a* **1225** *Leg. Kath.* 2248 Ich am her..mid alle mine hirdmen to ȝelden reisun [*v.r.* reaisun] for ham. **1340** HAMPOLE *Pr. Consc.* 5966 Þus sal men þan yhelde resons sere Of alle þair lyf, als writen es here. **1382** WYCLIF *Matt.* xii. 36 Of euery ydel word that men speken, thei shul ȝelde resoun therof in the day of dome. *c* **1400** *Rule St. Benet* 42 Þe abbes..salle vmbeþinke hir..þat sho sal yelde resun of alle. **1818** SCOTT *Hrt. Midl.* xxxiv, Ye have an undoubted right to ask your ain son to render a reason of his conduct.

†**b.** ***to do, put,*** or ***set to reason*** (tr. OF. *mettre a raison*): to bring or call to account. *Obs.*

a **1300** *Cursor M.* 3881 Þan did he laban to resun: 'Qui has þou don me sli tresum?' **1340** HAMPOLE *Pr. Consc.* 5791 It semes þat þe kyng had grete encheson To sette hym for þat kepyng to reson. **1425** *Rolls of Parlt.* IV. 296/2 To putte ye said parties to reson.

†**c.** Monetary reckoning; *pl.* accounts, moneys. *Obs.*

1382 WYCLIF *1 Macc.* x. 40, I shal ȝeue in eche ȝeris fiftene thousandis of siclis of syluer, of the kyngis resyons, that perteynen to me. **1382** —— *Matt.* xviii. 23 A man kyng, that wolde putte resoun with his seruauntis.

†**3. a.** A statement, narrative, or speech; a saying, observation, or remark; an account or explanation *of*, or answer *to*, something. Also, without article, talk or discourse.

In common use throughout the 14th c. after OF. *raison*; in later examples perh. a fresh development of sense 1.

a **1300** *Cursor M.* 219 Þe last resun of alle þis ron Sal be of hir concepcion. *Ibid.* 1632 Drightin of heuen spak til him þan, And þus his resun he began. *Ibid.* 12211 Of ilk letter for to ask Resun of ilkan be nam. **13..** *Coer de L.* 117 The kyng ham tolde, in hys resoun, It com hym thorugh a vysyoun. *c* **1374** CHAUCER *Boeth.* IV. pr. vi. 111 (Camb. MS.) But I se now that þou art..weerey with the lengthe of my reson. *c* **1400** MAUNDEV. (1839) xv. 165 And so seyn thei, that maken here resounes, of othere Planetes; and of the Fuyr also. **1460** *Lybeaus Disc.* 109 Wiþ oute more resoun Duk, erl and baroun Wesch and ȝede to mete. **1481** CAXTON *Myrr.* II. xxix. 122 Of the wyndes may men enquyre reson of them that vse the sees. **1588** SHAKS. *L.L.L.* v. i. 2 Your reasons at dinner haue beene sharpe and sententious. *a* **1635** NAUNTON *Fragm. Reg.* (1641) 35 The Queene..began to be taken with his election, and loved to heare his reasons to her demands.

†**b.** A fact, event, or incident, as a subject of discourse. *Obs. rare.*

13.. *Cursor M.* 5456 (Gött.) Mani resunes he þaim tald, Bath þat þai suld ouer bide, And in þair last dais bitide. *a* **1375** *Joseph Arim.* 76 Þat tyme þat Augustus Cesar was Emperour..þis reson bi-gon þat I schal now rikenen.

†**c.** ***part of reason***: a part of speech. *Obs. rare.*

1481 CAXTON *Myrr.* I. v. 16 Vnneth..knowe they their partes of reson whiche is the first book of grammaire. **1530** PALSGR. Introd. 24 Partes of reason..they have thryse III, for, besydes the VIII parts of speche commen betwene them and the latines..they have also a nynth part of reason whiche I call article.

†**4. a.** A sentence. *Obs.*

1388 PURVEY *Prol. Bible* xv. 57 Whanne oo word is oonis set in a reesoun, it mai be set forth as ofte as it is vndurstonden. **1450–1530** *Myrr. our Ladye* 7 There is also many wordes that haue dyverse vnderstondynges,..and som tyme they may be taken in dyuerse wyse in one reson or clause. **1530** PALSGR. Introd. 24 Of these letters, lyke as it is in all tonges, be made syllables, of syllables wordes, of wordes sentences or reasons.

†**b.** A motto, posy. *Obs.*

1434 *E.E. Wills* (1882) 96 A ryng of golde with a ston, & a reson '*sans departir*'. **1463** *Bury Wills* (Camden) 18 My armys and my reson therto, *Grace me gouerne*. *a* **1548** HALL *Chron., Hen. VIII* 80 Gounes..enbrodred with reasons of golde that sayd, *adieu Iunesse*, farewell youth.

II. 5. a. A fact or circumstance forming, or alleged as forming, a ground or motive leading, or sufficient to lead, a person to adopt or reject some course of action or procedure, belief, etc. Const. *why, wherefore, that*; *of, for* preps.; *to* with inf.

a **1225** *Ancr. R.* 78 Þis is nu þe reisun of þe veiunge hwi Isaie ueieð hope & silence. **1297** R. GLOUC. (Rolls) 9304 An oþer reson..meueþ more me þer to, þat þe king..Mid vnriȝt halt þis kinedom. **13..** *E.E. Allit. P.* C. 191 [He] Arayned hym..what raysoun he hade In such slaȝtes of sorȝe to slepe so faste. *a* **1450** *Knt. de la Tour* (1868) 122 She shewed so mani good resounes vnto the kynge her husbonde, that he forgaue Absolon. **1533** BELLENDEN tr. *Livy* III. xxxv, He couth fynd na resson quhy he aucht nocht to helpe þe romane pepill to recovir þe land. **1588** SHAKS. *L.L.L.* v. ii. 715 *Brag.* Sweet bloods I both may, and will [deny]. *Ber.* What reason haue you for't? **1633** BP. HALL *Hard Texts, O.T.* 560 Is there any reason in you..why I sh[d] respect you any more than the very Ethiopians? **1662** J. DAVIES tr. *Olearius' Voy. Ambass.* 202 The Ambassador Brugman would by no means accept of the horse, for no other reason, doubtlesse, than this, that his was not so good as his Collegue's. **1711** ADDISON *Spect.* No. 101 ¶7 He made a Voyage to Grand Cairo for no other Reason, but to take the Measure of a Pyramid. **1763** C. JONES *Hoyle's Games Impr., Backgammon* (1778) 181 For the same Reason avoid hitting any Blots which your Adversary makes. **1843** MILL *Logic* I. iii. §7 Should we not have as much reason to believe that it still existed as we now have. **1875** JOWETT *Plato* (ed. 2) V. 7 There is no reason..to imagine that this melancholy tone is attributable to disappointment.

b. ***reason of state***, a purely political ground of action on the part of a ruler or government, esp. as involving some departure from strict justice, honesty, or open dealing. Freq. without article, as a principle of political action. So † ***public reason***.

A rendering of F. *raison d'état* or It. *ragione di stato*, the latter used or cited by Scarlett *Estate Eng. Fugitives* (1595) R iij, Ben Jonson *Cynthia's Rev.* (1599) I. i, *Volpone* (1605) IV. i, and Bacon *Adv. Learn.* (1605) I. ii. §3.

1611 FLORIO, *Ragione di stato*, the law, reason, or policie of State. **1622** BACON *Hen. VII* 3 As if the King..were become effeminate and lesse sensible of Honour, and Reason of State, then was fit for a King. **1660** R. COKE *Power & Subj.* 116 King Charles had not the same Reason of State to indulge the House of Commons. **1667** MILTON *P.L.* IV. 389 Public reason just..compels me now To do what else..I should abhorre. **1735** BOLINGBROKE *Stud. Hist.* ii. (1752) 39 The notion of attaching men to the new government..was a reason of state to some. **1756** BURKE *Vind. Nat. Soc.* Wks. 1842 I. 34 The whole of this mystery of iniquity is called the reason of state. It is a reason which I own I cannot penetrate. **1897** MORLEY *Machiavelli* 40 The most imposing of all incarnations of the doctrine that reason of State covers all, is Napoleon.

c. Phr. ***for reasons best known to oneself***, for seemingly perverse reasons.

1638 W. CHILLINGWORTH *Relig. Protestants* 84 Yet it hath pleased God (for Reasons best known to himselfe) not to allow us this convenience. **1743** FIELDING *Jonathan Wild* IV. xiii. 383 Indeed those, who have unluckily missed it, seem all their Days to have laboured in vain to attain an End, which Fortune, for Reasons only known to herself, hath thought proper to deny them. **1847** A. BRONTË *Agnes Grey* xiii. 191 If they chose to 'take' me, I went; if, for reasons best known to themselves, they chose to go alone, I took my seat in the carriage. **1894** SOMERVILLE & 'ROSS' *Real Charlotte* III. xli. 133 Removing his pipe and the hat which, for reasons best known to himself, he wore while at work. **1938** G. GRAHAM *Swiss Sonata* vi. 250 She tried very hard to adopt me, but my father, for reasons best known to himself, wouldn't give me up.

6. A ground or cause of, or for, something:

a. of a fact, procedure, or state of things, in some way dependent upon human action or feeling.

a **1300** *Cursor M.* 551 For þis resun þat ȝee haue hard, Man is clepid þe lesse werld. *c* **1450** HOLLAND *Howlat* 544 Throw this ressonis ald, The bludy hart it is cald. **1592** SHAKS. *Rom. & Jul.* IV. i. 15 Now doe you know the reason of this hast? **1659** PEARSON *Creed* IX. 697 This reason did the ancient Fathers render why the Church was called Catholick. **1698** ASGILL *Argument* 9 Custom it self, without a reason for it, is an argument only to fools. **1797** *Encycl. Brit.* (ed. 3) XI. 477/1 This holds equally in metaphor and allegory; and the reason is the same in all. **1841** LANE *Arab. Nts.* I. 105 Respecting this palace, and the reason of thy being alone in it.

b. of a fact, event, or thing not dependent on human agency.

c **1374** CHAUCER *Boeth.* IV. pr. vi. 104 (Camb. MS.) To vnwrappen the hyd causes of thinges and to discouere me the resouns couered with dyrknesses. **1484** CAXTON *Fables of Æsop* V. xii, The wulf on a daye came to the dogge and demaunded of hym the rayson why he was soo lene. **1601** SHAKS. *Jul. C.* I. iii. 30 When these Prodigies Doe so conioyntly meet, let not men say, These are their Reasons, they are Naturall. **1656** tr. *Hobbes' Elem. Philos.* (1839) 484, I should think comets were made in the same manner... For I could very well from hence give a reason both of their hair, and of their motions. **1690** LOCKE *Hum. Und.* III. vi. §9 We know not their Make; and can give no Reason of the different Qualities we find in them. **1826** WHATELY *Logic* (1840) App. Ambig. Terms xix, The Reason of an eclipse of the sun is, that the moon is interposed between it and the earth. This should strictly be called the cause. **1879** LUBBOCK *Sci. Lect.* ii. 67 There is not a hair or a line, not a spot or a color, for which there is not a reason.

†**c.** In phr. ***by the reason of*** or ***that***. (Cf. 7.)

1422 tr. *Secreta Secret., Priv. Priv.* 244 Hit nedyth a man do more abstynence in that tyme..by the reyson that [*text* than] in colde tyme the colde chasyth the naturall hete. **1530** in W. H. Turner *Select. Rec. Oxford* (1880) 88 Ther is a corporacyon made..amongst fischmongers.., by the reason wherof all maner of fische is sold derar. **1538** STARKEY *England* I. i. 9 You se..what glotony..ys had in cytes and townys, by the reson of thys socyety and company of men togydur.

7. (Without article.) **a.** ***by*** (†or ***for***) ***reason of***, on account of.

Very common in the Bible of 1611.

a **1300** *Cursor M.* 16372 A prisun ar yee wont at hafe, for resun o þe dai. **1393** LANGL. *P. Pl.* C. XVII. 49 The ryche is yreuerenced by reson of his richesse. **1432–50** tr. *Higden, Harl. Contin.* (Rolls) VIII. 471 John Holand, broþer to the kynge by reason of his moder. **1496** *Rolls of Parlt.* VI. 512/2 [Lands] whiche came..to youre handes of possession, by reason and force of the same Acte. **1568** GRAFTON *Chron.* II. 39 In the night [they] had quarrelled among themselves, by reason whereof they ranne vpon a rock. **1665** MANLEY *Grotius' Low C. Warres* 391 The Commanders being unserviceable, by reason of their wounds, quickly abated their Courage. **1750** tr. *Leonardus' Mirr. Stones* 137 By reason of its softness, it is turned and cut. **1840** HERSCHEL *Ess.* (1857) 76 Their labours are highly deserving of notice by reason of their having attempted to execute this task systematically. **1885** *Academy* 6 June 397 Irritating by reason of its deficiency in organisation.

b. ***by reason*** (***that***), for the reason that, because. (Freq. *c* 1560 to 1720; now *rare.*)

1534 *Lett. Suppress. Monast.* (Camden) 42 The cause of their dissent..was by reason that that article was clerely agaynst their professyon. **1537** *Ibid.* 165, I ame myndet to let it staunde to the sprynge of the yere, by reason the days ar now so short. **1582** N. LICHEFIELD tr. *Castanheda's Conq. E. Ind.* 8 b, They doe not flye, by reason they have no feathers in their wings. **1662** STILLINGFL. *Orig. Sacr.* I. vi. §1 By reason that their Moneths must of necessity by degrees change their place. **1745** P. THOMAS *Jrnl. Anson's Voy.* 52 There were several Murmurings..by reason the Prize-Money was not immediately divided. **1829** LANDOR *Imag. Conv., Mary & Eliz.* Wks. 1853 II. 91/2 By reason that she is adorned with every grace and virtue.

8. (Without article, and sometimes with adj., as *good, great, little, small.*)

a. ***there is*** (***was***, etc.) ***reason***. Also with omission of verb (sometimes not clearly distinct from 14).

1588 SHAKS. *L.L.L.* v. ii. 28 You care not for me. *Ros.* Great reason: for past care, is still past cure. **1593** —— *2 Hen. VI*, I. i. 155 There's reason he should be displeased at it. **1667** MILTON *P.L.* VIII. 443 Whose fellowship..Good reason was thou freely shouldst dislike. **1671** —— *P.R.* IV. 526 Good reason then if I [etc.]. **1849** C. BRONTE *Shirley* xviii, I have rather a leaning to the agricultural interest too; as good reason is [etc.]. **1892** *Law Times* XCIII. 414/2 If the defendant was let out of prison before these things were done, there was reason to believe that they would never be done at all.

b. ***to have reason for***, or ***to*** do, something. Also *ellipt.* without construction (cf. 17).

1590 SHAKS. *Mids. N.* III. i. 146 Me thinkes..you should haue little reason for that. **1597** J. KING *On Jonas* (1618) 177 Hee had reason to exclame as he did. **1605** SHAKS. *Macb.* III. v. 2 Why how now Hecat, you looke angrily? *Hec.* Haue I not reason. **1663** BUTLER *Hud.* I. iii. 272 Noble Orsin, th' hast Great reason to do as thou say'st. **1776** *Trial of Nundocomar* 66/1, I have reason to remember it. I was, after the battle, flung into confinement. **1824** SCOTT *Redgauntlet* ch. xviii, 'I applaud your caution', said Darsie. 'You have reason', replied his sister. **1859** F. E. PAGET *Curate Cumberworth* 353, I had good reason to hope that I was being of use at Roost.

c. ***to see reason*** (***to*** do something).

1596 SHAKS. *1 Hen. IV*, I. ii. 207 If he fight longer then he sees reason, Ile forswear Armes. **1740** J. CLARKE *Educ. Youth* (ed. 3) 154, I never yet saw Reason..to believe [etc.]. **1833** HT. MARTINEAU *Brooke Farm* v. 62, I began this winter by admiring Sir Henry's benevolence..more than I saw reason to do afterwards.

d. ***with*** or ***without reason***.

1601 DOLMAN *La Primaud. Fr. Acad.* (1618) III. 837 Yet hath not God giuen their beeing without good and iust reason. **1667** MILTON *P.L.* II. 431 With reason hath deep silence and demurr Seis'd us. **1781** COWPER *Hope* 316 Could he with reason murmur at his case, Himself sole author of his own disgrace? **1833** HT. MARTINEAU *Brooke Farm* iii. 30 It is very wrong in you to make your neighbours discontented without reason.

†**9.** Rationale, fundamental principle, basis. *Obs.*

1585 GREENE *Planetom.* Wks. (Grosart) V. 19 The Egiptians..found out the reason of Diuination, increasing the Science greatly. **1607** TOPSELL *Four-f. Beasts* (1658) 181 The reason of the Latin word *Hircus*, is derived of *Hirtus* (signifying rough). **1668** MOXON *Mech. Dyalling* 4 Geometry, and the Projecting of the Sphere.. are only useful to those that would know the reason of Dyalling. **1678** GALE *Crt. Gentiles* III. 7 The formal reason or nature of Sin consists in its being a deordination or transgression of the Divine law.

III. 10. a. That intellectual power or faculty (usually regarded as characteristic of mankind, but sometimes also attributed in a certain degree to the lower animals) which is ordinarily employed in adapting thought or action to some end; the guiding principle of the human mind in the process of thinking. (Freq. more or less personified.)

a **1225** *Ancr. R.* 272 Wummon is þe reisun, þet is, wittes skile. *a* **1300** *Fall & Passion* 19 in *E.E.P.* (1862) 13 Skil, resun, an eke miȝt he ȝef adam in his mode. *c* **1315** SHOREHAM *Poems* i. 515 Þat alle þyng his ase he seiþ þy resoun wole þe rede. **1340** HAMPOLE *Pr. Consc.* 62 Þan aght man.. noght to be of wers condicion, þan þe creatours withouten reson. **1362** LANGL. *P. Pl.* A. I. 52 For rihtfoliche resoun schulde rulen ou alle. **1406** HOCCLEVE *La Male Regle* 105 Reson me bad.. To ete and drynke in tyme attemprely. **1450–80** tr. *Secreta Secret.* 38 Of his wijsdome and resoun he refreyneth him silff from these vicis that nature shewith in him. **1538** STARKEY *England* I. i. 4 Seyng the perfectyon of man restyth in the mynd and in the chefe and puryst parte therof, wych ys reson and intellygence. **1590** SHAKS. *Mids. N.* II. ii. 115 The will of man is by his reason sway'd: And reason saies you are the worthier Maide. *c* **1665** MRS. HUTCHINSON *Mem. Col. Hutchinson* (1846) 26 In matters of faith his reason always submitted to the Word of God. **1693** DRYDEN *Persius* v. (1697) 478 Reason still is whisp'ring in your Ear, Where you are sure to fail, th'Attempt forbear. **1785** REID *Intell. Powers* 530 It is absurd to conceive that there can be any opposition between reason and common sense. **1859** DICKENS *T. Two Cities* I. ii, Some brute animals are endued with Reason. **1871** DARWIN *Desc. Man* I. ii. 46 Of all the faculties of the human mind, it will, I presume, be admitted that Reason stands at the summit.

b. So (†*good* or) *right reason*. Now *rare*.

Perhaps sometimes understood as in sense 11.

a **1300**–*c* **1400** [see 13 a, 13 e, 13 g, and 14]. **1508** KENNEDIE *Flyting w. Dunbar* 305 It war aganis bayth natur and gud ressoun, That Dewlbeiris bairnis were trew to God or man. **1538** STARKEY *England* II. i. 147 Yf man wold folow euer ryght reson and the jugement therof. **1611** BIBLE *Transl. Pref.* ¶1 That the Church be sufficiently prouided for is so agreeable to good reason and conscience. **1647** H. MORE *Song of Soul* II. i. II. xvii, The Dog, the Horse.. Will all.. claim their share in use of right reason. **1709** POPE *Ess. Crit.* 212 If once right reason drives that cloud away, Truth breaks upon us with resistless day. **1809–10** COLERIDGE *Friend* (1865) 27 The clue of right reason, which we are bound to follow in the communication of truth. **1887** BROWNING *Parleyings, G. B. Dodington* i, Right reason being judge.

c. In the Kantian transcendental philosophy: The power (*Vernunft*) by which first principles are grasped *a priori*, as distinguished from UNDERSTANDING (*Verstand*).

1809–10 COLERIDGE *Friend* (1850) I. 240 *note*, By the pure 'reason' I mean the power by which we become possessed of principles. **1827** CARLYLE *St. Germ. Lit.* Misc. (1840) I. 102 Reason, the Kantists say, is of a higher nature than Understanding; it works by more subtle methods, on higher objects.

d. In various mystic or transcendental uses: (see quots.).

1702 tr. *Le Clerc's Prim. Fathers* 86 The Son is called Reason as well as the Paternal Reason. *Ibid.* 87 Cerinthus held the Preexistence of the Reason which he called the Christ. **1841** *Penny Cycl.* XIX. 323/2 Schelling defines reason to be the identity of the subjective and the objective. .. God and reason are essentially of the same nature; they are identical. **1870** EMERSON *Soc. & Solit., Art* Wks. (Bohn) III. 20 There is but one Reason. The mind that made the world is not one mind, but *the* mind. **1874** SIDGWICK *Meth. Ethics* III. xiii. 362 This absolute end.. can be nothing but Reason itself, or the Universe of Rationals.

e. ***the age of reason***, (*a*) (freq. with capital initials) the late seventeenth and eighteenth centuries in Western Europe, during which cultural life was characterized by faith in human reason; the Enlightenment (cf. ENLIGHTENMENT 2); (*b*) *R.C. Ch.*, the age at which a child is capable of discerning right from wrong and can be held responsible for his or her actions; also *loosely*.

(*a*) **1794** T. PAINE (*title*) The age of reason; being an investigation of true and fabulous theology. **1902** CHESTERTON *Twelve Types* 129 Carlyle.. denied every one of the postulates upon which the age of reason based itself. **1926** R. H. TAWNEY *Relig. & Rise of Capitalism* i. 61 The sanguine optimists of the Age of Reason. **1971** R. J. WHITE *Second-Hand Tomb* xviii. 200 You medieval scholars suffer from a double dose of spiritual pride where the Age of Reason is concerned.

(*b*) **1884** ADDIS & ARNOLD *Cath. Dict.* 17/1 The age of reason is generally supposed to begin about the seventh year... At that time a child becomes capable of mortal sin. **1947** E. SUTTON tr. *Sartre's Age of Reason* viii. 126 You have .. reached the age of reason, my poor Mathieu.. but you try to dodge that fact too, you try to pretend you're younger than you are. *Ibid.* xviii. 360 He yawned again as he repeated to himself: 'It's true, it's absolutely true: I have attained the age of reason.' **1955** tr. *Maupassant's Compl. Short Stories* 1237, I am seven years old today. As it is the age of reason, I want to thank you for having brought me into this world. **1974** *Oxf. Dict. Chr. Ch.* (ed. 2) 24/1 The attainment of the age of reason is commonly marked by a child's First Communion.

11. a. The ordinary thinking faculty of the human mind in a sound condition; sanity.

c **1380** WYCLIF *De Ecclesia* Sel. Wks. III. 342 Þat man is out of resoun þat trowiþ þat Clement in Petris tyme was more þan Joon evaungelist. **1602** SHAKS. *Ham.* II. ii. 214 A happinesse, That often Madnesse hits on, which Reason and Sanitie could not so prosperously be deliuer'd of. **1611** BIBLE *Dan.* iv. 36 At the same time my reason returned vnto me. **1765** BLACKSTONE *Comm.* I. xiv. 351 A fourth incapacity is want of reason. **1818** SHELLEY *Rev. Islam* VII. xxv, So now my reason was restored to me. **1863** *Spectator* 25 July 2295 We are fully convinced that any attempt to show Hamlet's reason to be shaken is utterly hopeless.

b. A reasonable or sensible view of a matter; chiefly in phr. ***to bring to reason***.

a **1300** *Cursor M.* 12759 To here of his sermon þat maniman broght to resun. **1525** LD. BERNERS *Froiss.* II. ccii. 621 The kyng.. commaunded me.. to gouerne and bringe them to reason. *a* **1548** HALL *Chron., Hen. VIII* 150 b, Whiche thynges if he deny to dooe, then the confederates certifie hym, that thei shall neuer cease till he be brought to reason. **1647** CLARENDON *Hist. Reb.* IV. §279 He would sit still till they who were over-active would come to reason. **1703** FARQUHAR *Inconstant* Dram. Pers., Oriana.. would bring him to reason. **1870** BURTON *Hist. Scot.* VI. lxvi. 332 They had failed to bring a recusant clergyman to reason.

12. In verbal phrases denoting the conformity of something to the dictates of reason: †**a.** ***reason will*** or ***would***. *Obs.*

a **1300** *Cursor M.* 11663 'Ioseph', sco said, 'fain wald i rest' .. 'Gladli', said he, 'þat wil resun'. **1377** LANGL. *P. Pl.* B. x. 112 Whi shulde we [etc.]?.. resoun wolde it neuere. **1423** *Rolls of Parlt.* IV. 257/2 Hit semeth resoun wolde he shuld have the disavaille therof, and not the Marchant. **1433** *Ibid.* 424/2 To be as reson will, Chief þereof. **1526** TINDALE *Acts* xviii. 14 Yf it were a matter of wronge,.. reason wolde that I shuld heare you. [So COVERDALE & **1611**.] **1597** SHAKS. *2 Hen. IV*, IV. i. 157 Our Cause [is] the best; Then Reason will, our hearts should be as good.

b. ***it stands*** (†***with*** or) ***to reason***.

1528 PAYNEL *Salerne's Regim.* B iij, Considerynge then that mans eies be colde of nature: hit standeth with reason they shulde be washed with colde water and not with hotte. **1612** SHELTON *Quix.* I. i. I. 6 For it stood greatly with reason, seeing his Lord and Master changed his estate and vocation, that he should alter likewise his denomination. **1632** HOLLAND *Cyrupædia* 149 It standeth to good reason, that they who repose mutuall trust one in another, will joyntly sticke to it. **1698** C. BOYLE, etc. *Ep. Phalaris Exam.* 137 It stands to reason, that he thought the Expression common enough; or else he would not have us'd it. **1873** BLACK *Pr. Thule* xxiv, Of course it stands to reason that the rich never have justice done them in plays and stories: for the people who write are poor.

13. In prepositional phrases (chiefly *Obs.*), denoting agreement with, or opposition to, what reason directs or indicates:

†**a.** ***by reason*** (= OF. *par raison*). Also rarely ***by good*** (or ***right***) ***reason***, ***by no reason***. *Obs.*

a **1300** *Cursor M.* 14742 Mi hus agh be, [be] right resun Hus o praier and of orisoun. **13..** *K. Alis.* 3937 The kyng .. n'olde him sle, bote by resoun. *c* **1400** MAUNDEV. (1839) x. 120 Seynt Petre the Apostle, and thei that camen aftre him, han ordeynd to make here Confessioun to man; and be gode Resoun: for [etc.]. *a* **1425** *Cursor M.* 10535 (Trin.) Shal no mon bi no resoun Aȝeyn hir haue no wicke chesoun. *a* **1450** *Knt. de la Tour* (1868) 53 Thei that seethe the good and takithe the evelle, by reson they shulle repent hem. **1523** LD. BERNERS *Froiss.* I. xviii. 26 He delyuered them sufficient by reason, to pay all their small charges. **1563** *Mirr. Mag., Collingbourne* 145 b, The gylty alwayes are suspicious, And dread the ruyne that must sewe by reason.

b. ***in reason***. Also *in all* or *any reason*; † *upon reason*.

a **1400–50** *Alexander* 1670 Aske it at Alexander quat þou will apon reson, And I sall grant. **1597** SHAKS. *2 Hen. IV*, II. ii. 53 Keeping such vild company as thou art, hath in reason taken from me, all ostentation of sorrow. **1598** —— *Merry W.* I. i. 249 In any reason. **1603** —— *Meas. for M.* III. i. 250 In all reason. **1650** T. B[AYLEY] *Worcester's Apoph.* 97 The Law could not in reason take notice of any such thing. **1678** BUNYAN *Pilgr.* I. (1862) 68 Had he had a thousand souls, they had in reason been cast away. **1712** BUDGELL *Spect.* No. 277 ¶12, I am willing to do anything in reason for the Service of my Country-women. **1823** KEBLE *Serm.* iii. (1848) 65 To.. consider fairly, what effect, in all reason, their believing it ought to have on themselves. **1898** G. B. SHAW *Plays* I. (*Unpleasant*) 186 If you want a cheque for yourself.. you can name any figure you like—in reason.

†**c.** ***of reason***. Also with *all*, *good*. *Obs.*

1413 *Pilgr. Sowle* (Caxton 1483) IV. xxx. 78 They shall.. brynge hit in to good couenable fourme as to suche a lord bilongeth of reson. **1449** in *Wars Eng. in France* (Rolls) I. 493 Purveaunce shalbe made for you in such wise as of reasone ye shal holde you wel contente. **1523** FITZHERB. *Husb.* §12 In some places they sowe bothe pees and beanes vnderforowe: and those of reson must be sowen betyme. **1533** BELLENDEN tr. *Livy* v. ii, May it nocht be said to him of gude resoun: 'Thow has ȝerelie wagis, suffir þareof ȝerelie laubouris?' **1664** H. MORE *Antid. Idolatry* ix. 103 The Council of Trent.. must of all reason be conceived to mean these very Circumstances.

†**d.** ***out of reason***. *Obs.*

c **1400** *Destr. Troy* 2222 We may boldy vs byld with bostis out of Reason. **1480** CAXTON *Chron. Eng.* ccxix. 209 Mortimer disgised him with wonder riche clothes out of al maner reson. **1576** FLEMING *Panopl. Epist.* 385 You sell the same.. to your Brother too deere and out of reason.

†**e.** ***through*** (***good*** or ***right***) ***reason***. *Obs.*

13.. *Sir Beues* (MS. A.) 48 Man, whan he falleþ in to elde, Feble a wexeþ.. þourȝ riȝt resoun. *c* **1325** *Chron. Eng.* 842 in Ritson *Metr. Rom.* II. 305 And so thourh god resoun He yeld hem heore tresoun. *c* **1330** R. BRUNNE *Chron. Wace* (Rolls) 3628 After Belyn, Gurgoint his sone Hadde þe heritage þorow resone.

†**f.** ***with*** (or *to*) ***reason***. Also with *no*. *Obs.*

c **1290** *S. Eng. Leg.* I. 44/359 Seint Ieme ne miȝhte habbe þe soule.. with no resun ne riȝhte. *a* **1300** *Cursor M.* 14705 Þe werckes þat i werc in his nam, Quat man þan mai wit resun blam. *c* **1330** *Amis & Amil.* 874 Then seyd thai al with resoun, Sir Amis schuld ben in prisoun. **14..** *Sir Beues* (MS. M.) 179 Syr Guy answered hym with reason And sayd: 'Alas, for here is treason!' *c* **1489** CAXTON *Sonnes of Aymon* vii. 159 As ye knowe, I wolde be reformed with rayson to the sayenge of his barons. **1556** HOBY tr. *Castiglione's Courtyer* Epist. A iij b, Because you may see him confirme with reason the Courtly facions. **1615** T. ADAMS *White Devill* 37 These ride in the open streetes, whiles the other lurke in close woods—and to reason, for [etc.].

†**g.** ***without*** (***right***) ***reason***. *Obs.*

a **1300** *Cursor M.* 16296 Qui smites þou me wit-vten right resun. *c* **1330** R. BRUNNE *Chron.* (1810) 150 Men mad tille him grete mone, it was without reson. **1390** GOWER *Conf.* III. 42 Delicacie in loves cas Withoute reson is and was. **1484** CAXTON *Life of Æsop* 2 b, He.. went in without rayson and hath eten al the fygges. **1568** GRAFTON *Chron.* II. 629 This multitude.. spoyled, robbed and rifled, without reason or measure.

14. a. A matter, act, proceeding, etc., agreeable to reason; in phrases ***it is reason*** or ***reason is*** (also with ***good***, ***great***), ***it is no*** (or ***not***) ***reason***, ***to think*** (***it***) ***reason***, etc. Freq. *c* 1400–1650; now *rare*.

So OF. *il est raison, c'est (bien) raison, c'est raison et droit*, etc.

c **1320** *Cast. Love* 1096 'Þat is skile', quaþ Jhesu, 'and good reson'. **1340** HAMPOLE *Pr. Consc.* 6891 Þarfor it es reson and ryght, þat þai ay se þat grysely syght. **1423** *Rolls of Parlt.* IV. 257 Hit is no reson that the Maister take his worship of another mannes harme. **1454** *Ibid.* V. 248/1 In suche wyse as it can be thought reason unto our Tresorer. **1523** LD. BERNERS *Froiss.* I. 348 It is reason that it shulde so be. *a* **1533** —— *Gold. Bk. M. Aurel.* D d vi, Reason is, that I succour thy povertee with moneie. **1577** B. GOOGE *Heresbach's Husb.* I. (1586) 25 b, It is good reason to sowe timely in wette groundes. **1625** BACON *Ess., Marriage* (Arb.) 264 It were great Reason, that those that haue Children, should haue greatest care of future times. **1676** HOBBES *Iliad* I. 129, I thought it reason th' Argives should collect. **1686** tr. *Chardin's Coronat. Solyman* 100 It was not reason to punish the innocent with the Guilty. **1809** MALKIN *Gil Blas* VI. ii. ¶2 It is but reason that you should distrust our purity. **1818** T. L. PEACOCK *Nightmare Abbey* iv, 'Do you know, sir, that Marionetta has no fortune?' 'It is the more reason, sir, that her husband should have one'. **1864** MANNING *Let. to Pusey* 28 It is, however, but reason that I should rejoice.

†**b.** In parenthetic phrases, ***as reason is*** (or ***was***), ***as*** (***it***) ***is reason***, etc. *Obs.*

c **1386** CHAUCER *Prol.* 847 Telle he moste his tale as was reson, By foreward and by Composicion. **1535** COVERDALE *Baruch* ii. 6 We with oure fathers (as reason is) are brought to open shame. **1596** DANETT tr. *Comines* (1614) 198 To which his commandement I obeyed as reason was. **1604** E. G[RIMSTONE] *D'Acosta's Hist. Indies* I. xxii. 74 If we shall give that respect to the authoritie of Plato (as it is reason), we must [etc.]. **1671** MILTON *Samson* 1641 What your commands impos'd I have perform'd, as reason was, obeying.

†**c.** ***and reason***, placed after a statement. *Obs.*

1563 MAN *Musculus Commonpl.* 279 They do sufficiently confesse.. that the sacrament is not the very grace itselfe, and reason. *c* **1592** MARLOWE *Jew of Malta* IV. i, *Barabas.* I'd cut thy throat, if I did. *Ithamore.* And reason too. **1671** MILTON *P.R.* III. 122 To whom our Saviour fervently reply'd. 'And reason; since his word all things produc'd'.

†**d.** Similarly ***and good reason***, and (rarely ***as***) ***reason good***. *Obs.* (Cf. 8 a.)

1593 SHAKS. *2 Hen. VI*, IV. ii. 171 Wee'l haue the Lord Sayes head... *Cade.* And good reason. **1657** W. RAND tr. *Gassendi's Life Peiresc* I. 75 He wrote most frequently (and good reason) to his Father and Uncle. **1714** MRS. MANLEY *Adv. Rivella* 60 Lord Crafty, as Reason good, immediately assumed the Management of his Lady's Affairs. **1757** MRS. GRIFFITH *Lett. Henry & Frances* (1767) I. 115 True love.. never attacks us but once, and reason good, because it lasts us for life.

†**15. a.** That treatment which may with reason be expected by, or required from, a person; justice; satisfaction; chiefly in phr. ***to do*** (one) ***reason*** (tr. F. *faire raison*). *Obs.*

c **1400** MAUNDEV. (Roxb.) xxxi. 141 Þai do resoun and trewth till ilke man, als wele to pouer as to riche. *c* **1420** *Anturs of Arth.* xxviii, Welecome, worthyly wyghte! Thou sall hafe resone and ryghte. *c* **1477** CAXTON *Jason* 72 b, To holde them in pees reson and justice. *a* **1533** LD. BERNERS *Huon* x. 30, I shal do hym reason yf it be founde that I haue done any wronge. **1588** SHAKS. *Tit. A.* I. ii. 278, I.. [am] resolu'd withall To doe my selfe this reason, and this right. **1638** R. BAILLIE *Lett. & Jrnls.* (1841) I. 94 If they gett reason, it is thought they are both undone. *Ibid.* 132 The Thesaurer.. required that his Grace would see justice done upon him... The Commissioner promised him reason. **1651** tr. *De-las-Coveras' Don Fenise* 301 The more I endeavoured by faire meanes to oblige him to doe me reason, the more I excited him to derision.

b. With reference to drinking. *Obs.* exc. *arch.*

1594 PLAT *Jewell-ho.* III. 62 Quaffing companions.. wil require reason at their hands as they terme it. **1663** DRYDEN *Wild Gallant* I. i, First I'll drink to you, Sir; upon my faith I'll do you reason, Sir. **1698** FRYER *Acc. E. India & P.* 279 After.. every one's Health has reason done it, they take off the Table-Cloth. **1819** SCOTT *Ivanhoe* xlii, I pray you.. to do me reason in a cup of wine. **1826** —— *Woodst.* xix, Nor was his follower slow in doing reason to the royal pledge.

†**c.** Satisfaction by a duel. *Obs.*[−1]

1619 in *Crt. & Times Jas. I* (1849) II. 120 Sir Edward Villiers told him himself was the man. 'I hope', said the other, 'you will do me reason'. Thereupon a challenge was made and accepted.

†**16. a.** A reasonable quantity, amount, or degree. Also *spec.* the measure by which a miller took his toll. *Obs.*

1426 LYDG. *De Guil. Pilgr.* 10614 As touchyng off the melle, Thow myghtest ther..be-holden A mesure Wych (by folkys oppynyoun,) Bereth the name off 'Resoun'. *c* **1430** *Pilgr. Lyf Manhode* II. xv. (1869) 80 At the mille perauenture ye haue seen a mesure that is cleped resoun. *Ibid.* III. xvii. 144 Millewardes also that filleth here resoun, with oute clepinge of resoun. **1591** SPENSER *M. Hubberd* 887 In case his paines were recompenst with reason. **1598** GRENEWEY *Tacitus, Ann.* VI. vi. (1622) 130 Agrippina not contented with reason, and greedy of rule. **1599** SHAKS. *Much Ado* V. iv. 74 *Bene.* Doo not you loue me? *Beat.* Why no, no more than reason. **1675** EARL ESSEX [A. CAPEL] *Lett.* (1770) 15, I have not yet heard precisely what terms mr. Thinne stands upon, but in case he will take reason..it would be a great convenience to me to be provided of a dwelling in town.

†**b.** Moderation. *Obs.*^−1

1615 LATHAM *Falconry* (1633) 93 When she hath cast them againe, giue her her breakefast of good meat, with reason in the quantity.

†**17.** *to have reason* (tr. F. *avoir raison*): to be right (esp. in making a statement). *Obs.* (Cf. 8 b.)

1557 NORTH *Gueuara's Diall Pr.* I. x. (1568) 13 b, This if they had demaunded of the true God, they should haue had reason. **1594** CAREW *Huarte's Exam. Wits* 8 Aristotle excepteth naturall Philosophie, saying, a yoong man is not of fit disposition for this kind of doctrine, wherein it semeth he hath reason. **1624** BEDELL *Lett.* vi. 95 The King him-selfe said aloud, that both sides had reason. **1667** DRYDEN & DK. NEWCASTLE *Sir M. Mar-all* III. i, *Sir Mart.* You have reason, sir. *Mood.* There he is again too; the town phrase. **1704** SWIFT *Mech. Operat. Spir.* Misc. (1711) 285 The Objectors have Reason, and their Assertions may be allowed. **1771** *Junius Lett.* xliii. (1804) II. 181 Louis XIV had reason when he said 'the Pyrenees are removed'.

18. a. The fact or quality of being agreeable to the reason; such a (†procedure or) view of things as the reason can approve of.

c **1470** *Golagros & Gaw.* 331 Ressaue him reuerendly, as resoun in lyis. **1599** SHAKS. *Hen. V*, V. ii. 358 Wee haue consented to all tearmes of reason. **1601** —— *Jul. C.* III. ii. 113 Me thinkes there is much reason in his sayings. **1653** WALTON *Angler* ii. 47 This is reason put into Verse, and worthy the consideration of a wise man. **1667** MILTON *P.L.* IX. 738 His perswasive words, impregn'd With Reason, to her seeming, and with Truth. **1732** BERKELEY *Alciphr.* II. §4 There is reason in what you say. **1819** SHELLEY *Cenci* II. ii. 17 Nay, there is reason in your plea; 'twere hard. **1880** T. HARDY *Wessex Tales, Fellow-Townsmen* iii. (1896) 124 There was reason in Mrs. Downe's fear—that he owned.

b. In phrases ***to hear, listen to,*** or ***speak reason.***

1535 STEWART *Cron. Scot.* I. 596 For na counsall that tyme wald he heir ressoun. **1545** ELYOT s.v. *Ius, Ius dicis*, thou speakest reason. **1599** SHAKS. *Much Ado* I. iii. 5 You should heare reason. *Ibid.* V. i. 41 There thou speak'st reason. **1664** J. WILSON *A. Commenius* V. iii, Troth he speaks reason. **1719** DE FOE *Crusoe* II. iii, The rogues were now more capable to hear reason than to act reason. **1768** GOLDSM. *Good-n. Man* I, When I'm determined I always listen to reason, because it can then do no harm. **1832** HT. MARTINEAU *Hill & Valley* vi. 101 The people were now in a condition to hear reason. **1880** T. HARDY *Wessex Tales, Fellow-Townsmen* iii. (1896) 124 Her impression is that your wife will listen to reason.

IV. †**19.** The exercise of reason; the act of reasoning or argumentation. *Obs.*

c **1330** *King of Tars* 276 The doughter dude overcome hem bothe Beo riht reson and evene. *c* **1440** *York Myst.* xxxvii. 255, I schall þe proue be right resoune. **1542** RECORDE *Gr. Artes* (1575) 8 Reson is the expressing of a iust matter with witty persuasions, furnished with lerned knowledge. **1565** JEWEL *Repl. Harding* (1611) 361 Wee may not argue by reason in this sort [etc.]. **1620** T. GRANGER *Div. Logike* 8 That part of euery proposition that goeth afore in reason, howsoeuer the words be placed, is the Theme there handled. **1647** H. MORE *Poems* Interpr. Gen. 433, I understand by Reason, the deduction of one thing from another.

†**20.** Consideration, regard, respect. *Obs.*

c **1385** CHAUCER *L.G.W.* 728 *Thisbe*, And certeyn as by reson of hir age Ther myght haue ben bitwixe hem mariage. **1398** TREVISA *Barth. De P.R.* XVIII. liii. (Bodl. MS.), Amptes..take grete charge of heyr comyn profite and haue þereof reson and mynde. **1533** BELLENDEN tr. *Livy* III. xxiv, More respect suld haue bene had to ressoun of þe senatouris þan to ony ressoun of þare vassalege or meritis.

†**21. a.** Way, manner, method; *spec.* the method of a science. *Obs.*

c **1380** WYCLIF *Serm.* Sel. Wks. I. 15 ȝif men avysiden hem on þis resoun, noone shulde juge bi mannis lawe. **1530** PALSGR. 889 And by lyke reason forme they *tintouin, chariuaris*, and suche lyke. **1551** RECORDE *Pathw. Knowl.* Argts., The fourth booke teacheth the right order of measuringe all platte formes, and bodies also, by reson Geometricall. **1643** in Clarendon *Hist. Reb.* VI. §353 We cannot believe the intermixture of the present ecclesiastical government with the civil state to be other than a very good reason.

†**b.** Possibility of action or occurrence. Const. *but. Obs. rare.*

1591 SHAKS. *Two Gent.* II. iv. 212 When I looke on her perfections, There is no reason, but I shall be blinde. *c* **1592** MARLOWE *Jew of Malta* V. ii, Since things are in thy power, I see no reason but of Malta's Wrack. **1596** SHAKS. *Tam. Shr.* II. i. 409, I see no reason but suppos'd Lucentio Must get a father.

†**22.** *Math.* = RATIO *sb.* 2. *Obs.*

c **1374** CHAUCER *Boeth.* II. pr. vii. 44 (Camb. MS.) Al the enuyronynge of the erthe abowte ne halt but the resoun of a prikke at regard of the gretnesse of heuene. *c* **1400** tr. *Secreta Secret., Gov. Lordsh.* 86 If it be yn tokenynge ffleumetyke, a lityll [medicine] after þe qualyte & resoun of þe tokenynge. **1570** BILLINGSLEY *Euclid* XI. def. i. 312 There are..three reasons or meanes of measuring, which are called commonly dimensions. **1587** GOLDING *De Mornay* xiv. 212 There is the same reason in the proportion of eight vnto six that is of fower vnto three. **1614** T. BEDWELL *Nat. Geom. Numbers* i. 8 Like-plaines haue a doubled reason of their correspondent sides. **1678** COCKER *Arithm.* vi. 60 A third [number], which shall have such reason to the one, as the other hath to unite. **1713** BERKELEY *Hylas & Phil.* iii. Wks. 1871 I. 337 The moments or quantities of motion in bodies are in a direct compounded reason of the velocities and quantities of Matter contained in them.

V. 23. *attrib.* and *Comb.* (chiefly objective and obj. gen.), as ***reason-monger, -plating*** (after *armour-plating*), ***-poisoning, -renderer, -scanner, -worship***; ***reason-contained, -derived, -giving, -proof, -wrought*** adjs.; **reason-ring**, a ring bearing a 'reason' or motto.

1973 *Art Internat.* Mar. 75/2 The frost of the passage, its chill, *reason-contained fire is even more remarkable. **1874** W. WALLACE *Hegel's Logic* §36. 61 A *reason-derived knowledge of God is the highest problem of philosophy. **1855** BAGEHOT in *Nat. Rev.* July 36 The strong analytic, comprehensive, *reason-giving powers..were utterly foreign to his mind. **1933** DELL & BAYNES tr. *Jung's Mod. Man in Search of Soul* viii. 186 In works of art of this nature ..we cannot doubt that the vision is a genuine, primordial experience, regardless of what *reason-mongers may say. **1870** *Spectator* 24 Dec. 1536/1 If his heavy artillery could not penetrate the thick *reason-plating of the states-men, it was passion-proof. **1888** F. M. CRAWFORD *With the Immortals* I. 69 Doctor Saul Ascher, who died an abstract death from *reason-poisoning. **1829** *Westm. Rev.* Oct. 442 A man who on this topic..is pretty nearly *reason proof. **1589** PUTTENHAM *Eng. Poesie* III. xix. (Arb.) 236 This assignation of cause the Greekes called Etiologia...We also call him the *reason-rendrer. **1877** W. JONES *Finger-ring* 416 Among the motto or '*reason' rings, as they were termed, is an example..found in 1823, at Thetford. **1591** SYLVESTER *Du Bartas* I. iii. 970 *Reason-scanners have resolved all, That heavie things, hang'd in the Aire must fall. **1893** G. A. DENISON in *Ch. Times* 24 Mar. 325 *Reason-worship, the parent of all heresies. **1906** HARDY *Dynasts* II. I. ii. 152 Here, then, ends My hope for Europe's *reason-wrought repose!

reason ('riːz(ə)n), *sb.*[2] Forms: 6 resun, 7 resen, 8 reson, *dial.* **rezen,** 7– **reason.** [var. RASEN, q.v.] = RAISING-PIECE. Also *attrib.* with *piece.*

a **1548** [see RAISING-PIECE]. **1611** COTGR., *Architrave*,.. the reason peece, or master beame (in buildings of timber). **1674–91** [see RASEN]. **1703** T. N. *City & C. Purchaser* 183 Betwixt them and the Sell, or Reson. **1736** PEGGE *Kenticisms* (E.D.S.), *Rezen*, the raising; 'tis much the same as the wall-plate. **1875** KNIGHT *Dict. Mech.* 1899/1 *Reason-piece*, a timber which lies under the beams on the brick or timber in the side of a house.

reason ('riːz(ə)n), *v.* Forms: 4 **resun,** 5 **resoune,** 5–7 **reson,** 6 **rai-, rayson, reazon,** *Sc.* **resson,** 5– **reason.** [ad. OF. *raisoner* (F. *raisonner*):—late L. *ratiōnāre* to discourse, f. *ratiōn-em*: see REASON *sb.*[1] In sense 1 perh. aphet. for AREASON.]

†**1.** *trans.* To question (a person); to call (one) to account. = AREASON *v. Obs. rare.*

13.. *Cursor M.* 8676 (Gött.), I knew wel.. Of þis tresun scho had me don. I hir resuned þan al-sua son. *c* **1430** *Syr Gener.* (Roxb.) 2809 Generides thoo he [Anazaree] gan reason Whi the Sowdon did him in prison. *a* **1578** LINDESAY (Pitscottie) *Chron. Scot.* (S.T.S.) I. 33 Quhen he had pansit in this maner wp and doun and ressonit himself for his slouthfulnes.

2. †**a.** *intr.* To hold argument, discussion, discourse or talk *with* another. *Obs.*

The precise sense depends greatly on the context.

1483 CAXTON *G. de la Tour* L vj, Yf one begynne to resone and talke with yow of suche mater, lete hym alone. *c* **1489** —— *Sonnes of Aymon* i. 32 Thenne he resoned wyth his prynces and barons. **1530** PALSGR. 680/1 By that time that I have reasonned a lytell with hym I shall soone fele his mynde. **1568** GRAFTON *Chron.* II. 127 He sent for the Maior and Shirifes of London, with whome he reasoned greuously for the escape of one called John Gate. **1596** SHAKS. *Merch. V.* II. viii. 27, I reason'd with a Frenchman yesterday, who told me [etc.]. **1611** BIBLE *1 Sam.* xii. 7 Now therefore stand still, that I may reason with you before the Lord. **1671** MILTON *P.R.* IV. 233 How wilt thou reason with them, how refute Thir Idolisms, Traditions, Paradoxes?

†**b.** (Without const.) To argue, discourse, converse, talk. *Obs.*

1526 *Pilgr. Perf.* (W. de W. 1531) 99 Glotony commeth in full subtylly, & reasoneth full craftely, sayenge [etc.]. **1551** ROBINSON tr. *More's Utop.* II. (1895) 271 That no man shalbe blamed for reasonynge in the mayntenaunce of his owne religion. **1594** SHAKS. *Rich. III*, IV. iv. 537 Away towards Salsbury, while we reason here, A Royall battell might be wonne and lost. **1611** BIBLE *Matt.* xvi. 7 And they reasoned among themselues, saying, It is because we haue taken no bread.

†**c.** Const. *about, against, of, on* (a matter). *Obs.*

1551 ROBINSON tr. *More's Utop.* II. (1895) 270 He, as sone as he was baptised, began..to reason of Christes religion. **1588** SHAKS. *L.L.L.* I. i. 95 How well hee's read, to reason against reading. **1599** —— *Hen. V*, III. vii. 38 My Horse ..'tis a subiect for a Soueraigne to reason on. **1667** MILTON *P.L.* II. 558 Others apart sat on a Hill retir'd,..and reason'd high Of Providence, Foreknowledge, Will, and Fate.

d. To employ reasoning or argument *with* a person, in order to influence his conduct or opinions.

1847 MARRYAT *Childr. N. Forest* iv, All he could do was.. to reason with him. **1875** JOWETT *Plato* (ed. 2) V. 72 Mankind must be reasoned with before they are punished.

3. a. *intr.* To think in a connected, sensible, or logical manner; to employ the faculty of reason in forming conclusions (in general, or in a particular instance).

In early use not clearly distinguished from 2 b.

1593 SHAKS. *Rich. II*, I. iii. 277 [Q. 1] Teach thy necessity to reason thus,—There is no vertue like necessity. **1620** T. GRANGER *Div. Logike* 2 God doth not reason, or discourse. **1651** HOBBES *Leviath.* II. xxix. 168 Kings deny themselves some such necessary Power..: wherein they reason not well. **1667** MILTON *P.L.* IX. 765 Hee hath eat'n and lives, And knows, and speaks, and reasons, and discernes, Irrational till then. **1713** ADDISON *Cato* V. i, It must be so—Plato, thou reason'st well. **1782** COWPER *Doves* i, Reasoning at every step he treads, Man yet mistakes his way. **1810** CRABBE *Borough* xix, Temptation came; I reason'd, and I fell. **1846** RUSKIN *Mod. Paint.* II. III. I. xiv. §5 Though we cannot, while we feel deeply, reason shrewdly.

b. Const. *from* (premises or data); *about, of, upon* (a subject).

1651 HOBBES *Leviath.* III. xlii. 280 By Reasoning from the already received Scripture. **1695** BLACKMORE *Pr. Arth.* I. 398 He reason'd deep of Heav'ns mysterious Ends. **1785** PALEY *Mor. Philos.* I. vii, To reason about his duty. **1812** SIR H. DAVY *Chem. Philos.* 3 If the phenomena are reasoned upon,..the enquirer is guided by analogy. **1822** SHELLEY *Faust* II. 341 Oh! He is far above us all in his conceit: Whilst we enjoy, he reasons of enjoyment. **1844** H. H. WILSON *Brit. India* II. xi. II. 489 Reasoning from experience of the past abuses..they anticipated a like result from the present.

4. With object-clause:

a. To question, discuss *what, why*, etc.

1529 BRIGHTWELL [Frith] *Ep. to Christian Rdr.* 111 b, If thou woldist reason why God doth thus. **1594** SHAKS. *Rich. III*, I. iv. 94, I will not reason what is meant heereby, Because I will be guiltlesse from the meaning. **1596** —— *1 Hen. IV*, II. iii. 107, I must not haue you henceforth, question me, Whether I go: nor reason where-about. **1855** TENNYSON *Lt. Brigade* 14 Their's not to reason why. **1864–8** BROWNING *J. Lee's Wife* IV. i, I will be quiet and talk with you, And reason why you are wrong.

b. To argue, conclude, infer *that*, etc.

1527 R. THORNE in Hakluyt *Voy.* (1589) 257, I reason, that as some sicknesses are hereditarious,..so this inclination or desire of this discouerie I inherited of my father. **1727** POPE & GAY *What passed in London* Swift's Wks. 1751 VI. 262 She reasoning, that it would be time enough..after the Comet had made its appearance.

c. To say by way of argument. *nonce-use.*

1840 DICKENS *Barn. Rudge* i, 'What have I done', reasoned poor Joe.

5. *trans.* **a.** To discuss or argue (a matter). Now *rare.*

1526 *Pilgr. Perf.* (W. de W. 1531) 187 b, They wyll reason yͤ mysteryes of our fayth, whiche be aboue reason. **1560** DAUS tr. *Sleidane's Comm.* 175 b, Ther should be chosen two divines to reason the matter. **1625** BURGES *Pers. Tithes* 26 Thence a tender conscience may iustly thus reason the case. **1660** *Trial Regic.* 116 [He] was pleased to do me, and several other Gentlemen..the favour to reason the Law with us. **1802** MAR. EDGEWORTH *Moral T.* (1816) I. 205, I am in no humour to reason that point.

b. To explain, support, infer, deal with, by (or as by) reasoning. *nonce-uses.*

1605 SHAKS. *Lear* I. ii. 114 Though the wisedome of Nature can reason it thus, and thus, yet Nature finds it selfe scourg'd by the sequent effects. **1607** —— *Cor.* V. iii. 176 This Boy, that cannot tell what he would haue, Doe's reason our Petition with more strength, Than thou hast to deny't. **1732** POPE *Ess. Man* I. 18 Say first, of God above, or Man below, What can we reason, but from what we know? **1821** SHELLEY *Prometh. Unb.* III. iv. 22 It saw much, Yet idly reasoned what it saw.

6. a. To bring (a person) *into, out of* (a state of mind, etc.) by reasoning.

1599 SHAKS. *Hen. V*, V. ii. 165 These fellowes of infinit tongue, that can ryme themselues into Ladyes fauours, they doe alwayes reason themselues out again. **1653** H. MORE *Conject. Cabbal.* 233 Men commonly reason themselves into an allowance of sin, by pretending humane infirmities or natural frailties. **1749** FIELDING *Tom Jones* XV. ii, You know us better than to talk of reasoning a woman out of her inclinations. **1785** PALEY *Mor. Philos.* I. vii, A man, who has to reason about his duty, when the temptation to transgress it is upon him, is almost sure to reason himself into an error. **1893** FORBES-MITCHELL *Remin. Gt. Mutiny* 289 David tried to reason him out of his fears.

b. To put *down* by reasoning.

1686 GOAD *Celest. Bodies* II. i. 155 This..is the grand popular objection, which Cries, not reasons us down. **1713** ADDISON *Cato* I. i, Love is not to be reason'd down, or lost In high ambition. **1900** *Outrageous Fortune* x. 117 There is little need now to recapitulate those arguments with which I reasoned down the dictates of my better nature.

c. To drive *away* or *off* by reasoning.

1839 E. A. POE in *Burton's Gentleman's Mag.* (Philadelphia) Sept. 150, I struggled to reason off the nervousness which had dominion over me. **1854** M. L. CHARLESWORTH *Ministering Children* ix. 139 Let the sinner then beware how he reasons away and rejects the awful Word of God. **1866** M. C. HARRIS *Christine* xiv. 74 It was very natural, the doctor said to himself, trying to reason away the pain he felt.

7. To think *out*, to arrange the thought of, in a logical manner.

1736 BUTLER *Anal.* I. vi. Wks. 1874 I. 124 There is no hint or intimation in history, that this system was first reasoned out. **1851** THACKERAY *Eng. Hum., Swift* (1858) 34 They are reasoned logically enough. **1874** CARPENTER *Ment. Phys.* I. ix. (1879) 414 By thus reasoning-out the probable consequences of an action, motives..may lose more or less of their force.

8. To provide with reason; to accompany with a reason. *nonce-uses.*

1562 J. HEYWOOD *Prov. & Epigr.* (1867) 161 Which.. Shewth thy nose better sesond than thy hed resond. **1796** BURKE *Reg. Peace* i. Wks. 1826 VIII. 129 This offer so reasoned plainly implies, that [etc.].

reason, obs. form of RAISIN.

ˌreasonaˈbility. *rare.* [f. as next + -ITY.] Reasonableness.
1897 *Advance* (Chicago) 22 July 105/1 The reasonability of man, and the reasonability of the contention of God with his sinful creature. **1973** *Atlantic Monthly* June 58/2 In those early days of knowing him, I still believed in reasonability.

reasonable (ˈriːz(ə)nəb(ə)l), *a.*, *adv.*, and *sb.* Forms: 4 raison-, reison-, 4–5 resoun-, (5 resun-), 4–7 reson-, 5–6 resson-, 6 rezon-, 5– reasonable (also 4–6 -abil, -abyll, etc.; 5 resenable, 6 reasnable). [a. OF. *raison(n)able*, *reson(n)able*, etc. (mod.F. *raisonnable*), f. *raison*, *reson*, etc. REASON, after L. *ratiōnābilis* RATIONABLE. The 15th c. form *resenable* may represent the earlier *resnable* RENABLE, q.v.]

A. *adj.* **1.** Endowed with reason. = RATIONAL *a.* 1. Now *rare.* **a.** of persons or living things, esp. ***reasonable creature*** (†or ***beast***).
c**1374** CHAUCER *Boeth.* v. pr. iv. 128 (Camb. MS.) Man is a resonable two foted beest. *Ibid.* pr. vi. 133 The commune Iugement of alle creaturis resonablis..is this þat god is eterne. **1456** SIR G. HAYE *Law Arms* (S.T.S.) 64 Or lang tyme be gane, thare sall men that ar callit resonable do mare bestly dedis. **1502** *Ord. Crysten Men* (W. de W. 1506) Prol. 2 Every creature resonable unto whome god hathe gyuen mynde and understandynge. **1588** KYD *Househ. Phil.* Wks. (1901) 251 Man, a reasonable creature whose dignity doth come so neere the Angels. **1650** JER. TAYLOR *Holy Living & Dying* (1870) 7 Let your employment be such as may become a reasonable person. **1725** WATTS *Logic* III. ii. §5 If every Creature be reasonable, every Brute is reasonable. **1791** BURKE *App. Whigs* Wks. 1826 VI. 218 For man is by nature reasonable.

b. of the soul or intellectual powers.
1390 GOWER *Conf.* III. 378 Thilke intelligence In mannys soule resonable Hath schape to be perdurable. c**1425** *Found. St. Bartholomew's* (E.E.T.S.) 45 In his slepe he was raueshid from his resonable wyttys. **1538** STARKEY *England* I. ii. 40 Some sayd that man was no thyng els but hys resonabul soule. **1595** SHAKS. *John* III. iv. 54 My reasonable part produces reason How I may be deliuer'd of these woes. **1648** *Shorter Catech.* §22 Christ..became man by taking to Himself a true body and reasonable soul. **1736** CHANDLER *Hist. Persec.* Introd. 2 Every Man is bound..to make the best use he can of his reasonable powers. **1838–9** HALLAM *Hist. Lit.* II. II. iii. §6. 102 The reasonable soul of mankind is not numerically one.
fig. **1610** SHAKS. *Temp.* v. i. 81 Their vnderstanding Begins to swell, and the approching tide Will shortly fill the reasonable shore.

2. a. Having sound judgement; sensible, sane. = RATIONAL *a.* 1 b. Also, not asking for too much.
13.. *E.E. Allit. P.* B. 724 Fyfty fyn frendez..þat..reȝtful wern & resounable & redy þe to serue. c**1386** CHAUCER *Wife's Prol.* 441 Sith a man is moore resonable Than womman is, ye moste been suffrable. **1573** G. HARVEY *Letter-bk.* (Camden) 10 He is able to satisfi ani reasnable natural philosopher in that point. **1638** JUNIUS *Paint. Ancients* 39 Reasonable and judicious Readers will not dislike the same digression. **1669** STURMY *Mariner's Mag.* II. 46 To give any reasonable Man an answer to any useful Question in the Art of Gunnery. **1751** SMOLLETT *Per. Pic.* xxxix, Those polite, candid, reasonable watermen demanded a Louis d'or for that service. **1769** *Junius Lett.* i. 10 We are governed by counsels from which a reasonable man can expect no remedy but poison. **1802** GOUV. MORRIS in Sparks *Life & Writ.* (1832) III. 369 If mankind were reasonable they would want no government. **1883** ANNA K. GREEN (Mrs. Rohlfs) *Hand & Ring* iii, 'Ferris is a reasonable man', said the coroner.

b. Requiring the use of reason. *nonce-use.*
1611 SHAKS. *Wint. T.* IV. iv. 409 Is not your Father growne incapable Of reasonable affayres.

†**3. a.** Able to discourse or discuss matters; ready of tongue or speech. Also const. *of*. *Obs.*
c**1369** CHAUCER *Dethe Blaunche* 534 Loo how goodely spake thys knyghte..I..fonde him so tretable Ryght wonder skylful and resonable. **1387** TREVISA *Higden* (Rolls) VIII. 25 He was..resonabel of speche, and wel i-lettred. c**1400** *Rom. Rose* 2214 Wherfore be..Goodly of word, and resonable Bothe to lesse and eek to mar.

†**b.** Of language: Marked by reasoning. *Obs.*
1387 TREVISA *Higden* (Rolls) I. 11 After so noble spekers þat sownede at þe beste; and of hem faire facounde and resonable speche, folowed and streynede all her lyf tyme. **1390** GOWER *Conf.* III. 136 Rethorique the science Appropred to the reverence Of wordes that ben resonable.

4. a. Agreeable to reason; not irrational, absurd or ridiculous.
a**1300** *Cursor M.* 26767 Stedfast and stabil Sal scrift be, þat es resonabil, And noght als neus þat er tan. c**1340** HAMPOLE *Prose Tr.* 24 Charite..lith both ine loue of God and of thyne evyne cristene, and þere fore itt is resounable that he that hath cherite vse both. **1390** GOWER *Conf.* III. 210 Pite..Makth that the god is merciable, If ther be cause resonable. **1411** *Rolls of Parlt.* III. 650/2 Atte such resonable tyme as it likyth the forsaid Lord..to assigne. **1494** FABYAN *Chron.* VI. clxxxv. 184 This pylgryme..layde for hym many resonable excuses, as well for his age as otherwyse. **1573** G. HARVEY *Letter-bk.* (Camden) 1 Uppon a reasnable vew of the matter. **1594** SHAKS. *Rich. III*, I. ii. 136 It is a quarrell iust and reasonable, To be reueng'd on him that kill'd my Husband. **1655** STANLEY *Hist. Philos.* III. (1701) 78/1 That God, not chance, made the World and all Creatures, is demonstrable from the reasonable disposition of their parts. **1725** DE FOE *Voy. round World* (1840) 154 Something which it was much more reasonable to worship. **1796** BP. WATSON *Apol. Bible* 232 So far from this genealogy being a solemn truth, it is not even a reasonable lie. **1858** GREENER *Gunnery* 359 The reasonable assumption would be that this bullet would range a greater distance if projected at the same velocity. **1877** E. R. CONDER *Bas. Faith* i. 3 The conviction would be reasonable, for it would be based upon universal experience.

†**b.** That may reasonably be used. *Obs.*$^{-1}$
1465–6 *Act 5 Edw. IV* in Bolton *Stat. Irel.* (1621) 37 The Bowes [to be] of Ewe, Wych-hassell, Ashe, Awburne, or any other reasonable tree.

5. Not going beyond the limit assigned by reason; not extravagant or excessive; moderate.
a. of requests, desires, wishes, expectations, etc.
?a**1366** CHAUCER *Rom. Rose* 1499 This prayer was but resonable, Therefor god held it ferme and stable. c**1399** *Pol. Poems* (Rolls) II. 5 Axe of thi God, so schalt thou noght be werned Of no reqwest, which is resonable. **1561** WINȜET *Cert. Tractates* Wks. (S.T.S.) I. 4 Our ressonable desyris being knawin. **1581** J. HAMILTON in *Cath. Tract.* (S.T.S.) 76 This demand appeiret ressonabill to sum, that thay could not reiect the same. **1832** HT. MARTINEAU *Life in Wilds* iv. 55 The reasonable wishes of the whole people. **1882** A. W. WARD *Dickens* iv. 91 He never had a reasonable want which he could not and did not satisfy.

b. of amount, size, number, etc., or of things in respect of these properties.
13.. *E.E. Allit. P.* A. 523 What resonabele hyre be naȝt be runne, I yow pay in dede and þoȝte. c**1380** WYCLIF *Sel. Wks.* III. 200 Men and wymmen schulden lyven in..resonable abstynence of mete. **1477** *Rolls of Parlt.* VI. 178/2 Suche resonable costs and expenses, as shall happen to be done. **1504** *Bury Wills* (Camden) 98, I wyll that J. P. shall by my house..for xl li...to be payd in resonablyl yeerys as he can agre wt myn executors. **1573** TUSSER *Husb.* (1878) 20 Rent corne to be paid, for a reasonable rent. **1632** LITHGOW *Trav.* VI. 256 Nothing will sinke into it, of any reasonable weight. **1653** WALTON *Angler* ii. 41, I long to be doing; no reasonable hedge or ditch shall hold me. **1755** COLMAN & THORNTON *Connoisseur* No. 68 ¶9 The old lady had the hardiness to squint at the sum total, and declared 'it was pretty reasonable, considering'. **1849** MACAULAY *Hist. Eng.* ii. I. 206 Doing a great service on reasonable terms to the Church of which he was a member. **1895** *Bookman* Oct. 25/2 A straightforward, readable narrative in a very reasonable compass.

c. Moderate in price; inexpensive.
1667 COLLINS in Rigaud *Corr. Sci. Men* (1841) II. 471 Mr. Stephens..will undertake it when paper is more reasonable. **1805** W. IRVING in *Life & Lett.* (1864) I. 148 This part of Paris is tranquil and reasonable. **1885** *Field* 3 Oct. 502/2 Feeding materials..are unusually reasonable just now.

†**d.** *Law.* ***reasonable aid***: (see quot.). *Obs.*
1607 COWELL *Interpr.*, *Reasonable ayde*, is a duty that the Lord of the Fee claimeth holding by Knights seruice or in soccage to marie his daughter, or to make his sonne Knight.

6. a. Of such an amount, size, number, etc., as is judged to be appropriate or suitable to the circumstances or purpose.
1436 *E.E. Wills* (1882) 104 Beyng yn Resonable helth of body. **1523** FITZHERB. *Husb.* §62 If the beaste be fatte, and any reasonable meate vpon hym. **1560** DAUS tr. *Sleidane's Comm.* 251 We trust surely, that moste men..wil be content for reasonable [L. *tolerabilis*] wages rather to followe oure campe, than theirs. **1614** LATHAM *Falconry* (1633) 116 Put it into a pipkin or posnet with some reasonable store of faire water. **1755** FRANKLIN *Autobiog.* Wks. 1887 I. 252 All..forage..is to be taken for the use of the army and a reasonable price paid for the same. **1784** COWPER *Task* II. 623 A man o' the town dines late, but soon enough, With reasonable forecast and dispatch, To ensure a side-box station at half-price. **1849** MACAULAY *Hist. Eng.* v. I. 656 They were determined to prosecute..unless a reasonable sum were forthcoming, and..by a reasonable sum was meant seven thousand pounds.

†**b.** Of a fair, average, or considerable amount, size, etc. *Obs.* (Freq. c1590–1650.)
1588 PARKE tr. *Mendoza's Hist. China* 317 There are many prouinces..that euery one of them is as bigge as a reasonable kingdome. *Ibid.* 337 They saw two reasonable riuers, vppon whose bankes there were many vines. **1597** MORLEY *Introd. Mus.* 69, I haue a Brother..a reasonable musition for singing. **1612** WOODALL *Surg. Mate* Wks. (1653) 9 My self have had reasonable experience in piercing wounds. **1653** GREAVES *Seraglio* 154 A Customer, who receiveth custom of the buyers and sellers of slaves, which amounteth to a reasonable sum in a year, for the toll is very great. **1726** SWIFT *Gulliver* I. vi, A barrel of their liquor a reasonable draught.

†**7.** Proportionate. Also const. *to*. *Obs. rare.*
c**1460** FORTESCUE *Abs. & Lim. Mon.* x. (1885) 132 Also moche salte as by thair coniecture ys ressnable to the nombre off þe men, women, and childeren. **1546** *Reg. Privy Council Scot.* I. 51 The said Dame Marioun to haue ane ressonable terce of Eglintoun. **1766** BLACKSTONE *Comm.* II. 492 The shares of the wife and children was called their reasonable parts, and the writ *de rationabili parte bonorum* was given to recover it.

8. *Comb.*, as ***reasonable-bladed***, ***-minded***, ***-sized*** adjs.
1764 *Museum Rust.* III. 373 You cannot possibly hurt the gut,..which no reasonable-bladed pen-knife can touch. **1895** *Outing* (U.S.) XXVII. 226/2 Enough for any reasonable minded person. **1965** E. JUTIKKALA in Glass & Eversley *Population in Hist.* xxiii. 554 The only reasonable-sized city in Finland, Turku,..must be discussed separately from the surrounding province.

B. *adv.* Reasonably. **a.** With adjs. and advbs.
1470–85 MALORY *Arthur* x. lxxvi, I helde hym resonable hote though ye had not holpen me. **1523** LD. BERNERS *Froiss.* I. ccclvi. 574 The first day the wynde was reasonable good for them. **1583** STOCKER *Civ. Warres Lowe C.* I. 16b, The minister..made a reasonable long exhortation. **1603** KNOLLES *Hist. Turks* (1638) 185 The common people began to like reasonable well of the Turks. **1698** FRYER *Acc. E. India & P.* 66 There is also a reasonable handsome Buzzar. **1835–40** HALIBURTON *Clockm.* (1862) 180 Reasonable well, I give you thanks, sir, said he.

b. With verbs. *rare*$^{-1}$.
c**1550** *Disc. Common Weal Eng.* (1893) 326 Thincke youe that..he did not speake..reasonable.

C. *absol.* as *sb.* †**a.** A reasonable being. *Obs.*
c**1400** *Rom. Rose* 6760 In al this caas and in semblables If that ther ben mo resonables He may begge as I telle you here. **1620** T. GRANGER *Div. Logike* I. xxvi. 57 A mixt action in reasonables is voluntarie, because there is some consent of will, or self-motion. **1633** BP. HALL *Occas. Medit.* §24 That woeful hostility, which is exercised betwixt us reasonables.

b. A reasonable person. *rare*$^{-1}$.
a**1814** *Savoyard* I. i. in *New Brit. Theatre* IV. 360 What, fool, are you one of the reasonables too?

reasonableness (ˈriːz(ə)nəb(ə)lnɪs). [f. prec.]
1. †**a.** The quality of being reasonable or rational; rationality. *Obs.*
c**1511** *1st Eng. Bk. Amer.* (Arb.) Introd. 27 These folke lyuen lyke bestes without any resonablenes. **1620** T. GRANGER *Div. Logike* II. vi. 231* Reasonablenesse is in man vniuersally. a**1677** HALE *Prim. Orig. Man.* I. i. 16 Porphiry..and some others have been bold to make reasonableness not the specifical difference of the Humane Nature.

b. The fact or quality of being amenable to reason, or of acting or thinking in a sensible manner.
1533 UDALL *Floures* 168b, Lette your goodnes or resonablenes be som refuge or succour vnto my folyshnes. **1576** FOXE *A. & M.* (ed. 3) II. 1884/1, I haue heard you talke this houre and a halfe, and can heare no reasonablenes in hym. **1736** BUTLER *Anal.* I. v. 134 A settled moderation and reasonableness of temper. **1850** KINGSLEY *Alt. Locke* Pref. (1879) 105 The self-restraint, the reasonableness, the chivalrous honour of the men. **1873** M. ARNOLD *Lit. & Dogma* 379 For the right inculcation of the method and secret of Jesus, we need the *epieikeia*, the sweet reasonableness, of Jesus.

2. Of actions, opinions, words, etc.: The fact of being based on, or agreeable to, reason.
1568 Q. ELIZ. in H. Campbell *Love-lett. Mary Q. Scots* (1824) App. 10 They shall..judge thereby the reasonableness of the things propounded. **1581** SIDNEY *Apol. Poetrie* (Arb.) 23 May I not presume a little further, to shew the reasonablenes of this worde *Vates*? **1641** SMECTYMNUUS *Vind. Answ.* ii. 44 The reasonablenesse or unreasonablenesse of this we determine not. **1712** *Spectator* No. 524 ¶2 A serious Reflection on the Reasonableness of Virtue, and great Folly of Vice. **1751** SMOLLETT *Per. Pic.* xli, He saw the reasonableness of her fear. **1825** MCCULLOCH *Pol. Econ.* II. ii. 74 All have been impressed with the reasonableness of the maxim which teaches that those who sow ought to be permitted to reap. **1860** TYNDALL *Glac.* I. viii. 60 To acknowledge the reasonableness of my remarks.

b. Moderateness, cheapness. *rare.*
1742 FIELDING *J. Andrews* II. xiii, They had no objection to the reasonableness of the bill, but many to the probability of paying it. **1813** *Guide Watering Places* 289 The reasonableness of this place, joined to the beauty of its situation, draws to it a considerable number..during the season.

reasonably (ˈriːz(ə)nəblɪ), *adv.* [f. as prec.]
1. According to reason, with good reason, justly, properly.
1377 LANGL. *P. Pl.* B. XIV. 102 Ricchesse riȝtfulliche ywonne and resonablelich yspended. **1456** SIR G. HAYE *Law Arms* (S.T.S.) 66 He gave to man wit and resoun, knaulage and discrecioun to governe him resonably. a**1533** LD. BERNERS *Huon* cxlix. 563 He wolde gyue hym as moche golde & syluer as he could resonably demaunde. **1585** T. WASHINGTON tr. *Nicholay's Voy.* III. iii. 74 Reasonably to consider aswel the time past, present, and too come. **1651** HOBBES *Leviath.* II. xxvi. 150 One may very reasonably distinguish Laws in that manner. **1718** *Freethinker* No. 87 ¶9 He can reasonably blame only Himself. **1830** MISS MITFORD in L'Estrange *Life* (1870) II. xiii. 302 The French Revolution is most happily over; never was anything French so reasonably conducted. **1879** LUBBOCK *Addr. Pol. & Educ.* iii. 49 The results which we might reasonably expect from a more enlightened system of education.

2. At a reasonable rate; †to a reasonable extent.
?a**1400** *Morte Arth.* 1508 Raunsone me resonabillye, as I may over reche, Aftyre my renttez in Rome may redyly forthire. **1422** tr. *Secreta Secret., Priv. Priv.* 191, xije causes enduceth a man to loue his wif reissonnabli and tempora[t]li. **1600** SURFLET *Countrie Farme* II. li. 351 When you see that all the water is consumed..boile them altogither reasonablie.

3. a. Sufficiently, suitably, fairly.
c**1502** *Joseph Arim.* (E.E.T.S.) 47 Verely she was heled, and lefte her styltes thore, And on her fete wente home resonably well. **1589** PUTTENHAM *Eng. Poesie* III. xxiii. (Arb.) 278 The Earle..could reasonably well speake French. **1638** JUNIUS *Paint. Ancients* 15 The helpe of a reasonably good wit. **1665** MANLEY *Grotius' Low C. Warres* 720 A town..reasonably well fortified, having therein a strong garrison. **1791** MRS. RADCLIFFE *Rom. Forest* ii, Their distress was reasonably great. **1861** DICKENS *Gt. Expect.* v, There was a reasonably good path now.

†**b.** With vbs.: Fairly or pretty well. *Obs.*
1586 A. DAY *Eng. Secretary* I. (1625) 76 It is reported..that you are groune prettely skilled in Instruments whereon you play reasonably. **1613** PURCHAS *Pilgrimage* VI. ii. (1614) 566 To which also the computation of Herodotus dothe agree reasonably in the time.

†**4.** Normally, naturally. *Obs.*$^{-1}$
1615 CROOKE *Body of Man* 335 The Infant borne the seuenth month is reasonably borne and liueth.

5. *Comb.*, as ***reasonably-priced***, ***-sized*** adjs.
1902 *Daily Chron.* 22 June 3/3 See that reasonably-priced meals are provided. **1960** *Farmer & Stockbreeder* 8 Mar. 77/3 A reasonably-priced flowmeter was necessary. **1968** FOX & MAYERS *Computing Methods for Scientists & Engineers* v. 76 That is if the elements of the inverse matrix A^{-1} are large for reasonably-sized A.

†**'reasonal**, *sb.* and *a. Obs. rare.* [f. REASON *sb.*[1] + -AL[1], after RATIONAL *sb.* and *a.*] **a.** *sb.* = RATIONAL *sb.*[2] 2. **b.** *adj.* = RATIONAL *a.* 2.

1577 *Test. 12 Patriarchs* (1706) 46 Put on the stool of priesthood, the crown of righteousness, the reasonal of understanding. **1594** CAREW *Huarte's Exam. Wits* (1616) 286 [They] make their children defectiue, as well in the powers reasonall, as in the naturall.

†**reasonate**, *v. Obs.*$^{-1}$ (? error for *resonate*, to resound, shout.)

1631 R. H. *Arraignm. Whole Creature* xii. §4. 127 He cryes out of a suddaine..like that passionate Orator, that reasonates; Oh tempora? Oh mores?

†**'reasoned**, *a. Obs.*$^{-1}$ [f. REASON *sb.*[1]] Provided with reason or reasoning power.

1521 FISHER *Serm. agst. Luther* Wks. (1876) 345 These heretykes all be it they..were fell wytted men and depely resoned..yet were they disceyued.

reasoned ('ri:z(ə)nd), *ppl. a.* [f. REASON *v.* + -ED[1].] **a.** Characterized by or based on reasoning, carefully studied. Also with *out*.

1684 T. BURNET *Th. Earth* I. II. x. 297, I do generally distinguish of two sorts of opinions in all men, Inclination-opinions, and Reason'd-opinions. **1815** J. C. HOBHOUSE *Substance Lett.* (1816) I. 304 The official letter of Lord Clancarty..which is a sort of renewed and reasoned declaration. **1862** H. SPENCER *First Princ.* II. vi. §61 (1875) 192 All reasoned-out conclusions whatever must rest on some postulate. **1874** L. STEPHEN *Hours in Library* (1892) II. vi. 200 He prefers nature to law, instinct to reasoned action. **1904** E. F. BENSON *Challoners* vii. 146 He would sooner have mated her with a thief or an adulterer..than with a reasoned atheist.

b. ***reasoned amendment***, an amendment to a bill in Parliament that seeks to prevent a further reading by proposing reasons for the alteration or rejection of the bill.

1909 *Times* 9 Nov. 10/3 Such an amendment would.. have obvious advantages over the longer form which is known as a reasoned amendment. **1975** *Daily Tel.* 23 July 1 The Conservative 'reasoned amendment'..supported the Government's belated commitment to reduce the disastrous rate of inflation.

c. ***reasoned bibliography*** [cf. CATALOGUE RAISONNÉ], a descriptive survey of relevant books and articles appended to an essay or the like.

1958 *Listener* 11 Sept. 392/3 The fourth essay..which.. is accompanied by a reasoned bibliography of formidable fullness. **1969** *Archiv* CCV. 490 Her reasoned bibliography ranges as far afield as Calcutta and Hiroshima.

Hence **'reasonedly** *adv.*

1836 A. WALKER *Beauty in Woman* 281 The Greeks, either intuitively or reasonedly, distinguished the three species of beauty as to the Figure.

reasoner ('ri:z(ə)nə(r)). [f. as prec. + -ER[1].]

1. One who reasons.

1548 ELYOT, *Ratiocinator*,..a disputer, a reasoner. **1551** T. WILSON *Logike* X vj, Vpon such matters as are necessary ..for the godlye reasoner to teache. **1639** ROUSE *Heav. Univ.* Advt. (1702) 3 By too many of the great Reasoners of the age. **1741** WARBURTON *Div. Legat.* II. 642 Our Reasoner has here mistaken the very question. **1769** *Junius Lett.* xix. 82 A correspondent..censures him for a bad reasoner. **1864** BOWEN *Logic* ix. 271 The ambiguities of language which.. originally led the reasoner astray.

†**2.** A keeper of accounts. *Obs.*$^{-1}$

1509 *Plumpton Corr.* (Camden) 205 John Wythers, his Surveyor & generall Reasonner.

†**'reasonfully**, *adv. Obs.*$^{-1}$ [f. REASON *sb.*[1] + -FUL + -LY[2].] Reasonably.

1387-8 T. USK *Test. Love* III. i. (Skeat) I. 136 Reasonfulli maye he sey, y^t mercy both right and lawe passeth.

reasoning ('ri:z(ə)nɪŋ), *vbl. sb.* [f. REASON *v.* + -ING[1].] The action of the vb. REASON, *esp.* the process by which one judgement is deduced from another or others which are given.

c **1374** CHAUCER *Troylus* IV. 1046 (1018), I may wel maken ..My resoninge of goddes purveyaunce. —— *Boeth.* v. pr. v. 131 (Camb. MS.) Yif þat wit and ymaginacion stryuen ayein resonynge. **1494** FABYAN *Chron.* IV. lxix. 47 For resonyng and profe of this was after assygned vii. score Iewes. **1538** STARKEY *England* I. iv. 137 Hyt ys a commyn faute in resonyng, to lay a faute ther as non ys. **1587** GOLDING *De Mornay* i, There is no reazoning against those which denie the Principles. **1643** MILTON *Divorce* Introd. (1851) 4 Who..make it their chief designe to envie and cry-down the industry of free reasoning. **1725** DE FOE *Voy. round World* (1840) 313 A little reasoning with them brought some of the men to their senses. **1781** COWPER *Table-t.* 53 Such reasoning falls like an inverted cone, Wanting its proper base to stand upon. **1866** GEO. ELIOT *F. Holt* (1868) 29 The Rector was helped to this chain of reasoning by Harold's remarks.

b. With *a* and *pl.* An instance of this.

1552 EDW. VI *Jrnl.*, etc. (Roxb.) 457 The reasonings be in my deske. **1611** BIBLE *Luke* ix. 46 There arose a reasoning among them, which of them should be greatest. **1651** HOBBES *Govt. & Soc.* ix. §1. 135 Socrates is a man, and therefore a living creature, is a right reasoning, and that most evident. *a* **1720** SEWEL *Hist. Quakers* (1795) I. ii. 101 Several people accompanied him, and he had great reasonings with them. **1812** L. HUNT in *Examiner* 14 Dec. 785/2 He would not enter into a reasoning on the subject. **1880** L. STEPHEN *Pope* vii. 163 The reasonings in the Essay are confused, contradictory, and often childish.

c. *attrib.*, as ***reasoning faculty, ground, power, thread.***

1728 POPE *Dunc.* I. 179 Or quite unravel all the reas'ning thread. **1775** HARRIS *Philos. Arrangem.* Wks. (1841) 325 Of all the animals we see around us, man alone possesses the reasoning faculty. **1781** COWPER *Conversat.* 431 The reasoning power vouchsafed of course inferred The power to clothe that reason with his word. **1875** E. WHITE *Life in Christ* I. i. 14 Such contradictory arguments as these, the reasoning-grounds..of two opposing schools.

reasoning ('ri:z(ə)nɪŋ), *ppl. a.* [f. as prec. + -ING[2].] That reasons, in senses of the vb.

1665 GLANVILL *Def. Van. Dogm.* 80 Thus was the reasoning World despoil'd of that Freedom which is the priviledge of Humane Nature. **1737** POPE *Hor. Epist.* I. i. 185 That reas'ning, high, immortal Thing, Just less than Jove. **1781** COWPER *Hope* 143 Then praise is heard instead of reasoning pride. **1821-2** SHELLEY *Chas. I*, II. 158 All that makes the age of reasoning man More memorable than a beast's. **1870** J. H. NEWMAN *Gram. Assent* I. iv. 91 After all, man is not a reasoning animal.

Hence **'reasoningly** *adv.*

1886 H. JAMES *Bostonians* III. III. xxxvi. 111 'That's not the way,' Verena went on, reasoningly.

†**'reasonist.** *Obs. rare.* [f. REASON *sb.*[1] or *v.* + -IST.] A professed reasoner.

1610 HEALEY *St. Aug. Citie of God* (1620) 843 But what say our great Reasonists unto those ordinary things which are so common? *a* **1740** WATERLAND *Chr. Vind. agst. Infid.* Wks. 1823 VIII. 67 Such persons are now commonly called reasonists and rationalists, to distinguish them from true reasoners and rational inquirers.

reasonless ('ri:z(ə)nlɪs), *a.* (and *adv.*) [f. REASON *sb.*[1] + -LESS.]

1. Not endowed with reason. = IRRATIONAL *a.* 1.

1398 TREVISA *Barth. De P.R.* XVIII. lii. (Bodl. MS.) 273/1 [The ant is] a litel beste wiþoute prince and resonles. *c* **1412** HOCCLEVE *De Reg. Princ.* 3659 If he tho weies take wolde That beestes resonles vsen and holde. **1581** PETTIE *Guazzo's Civ. Conv.* II. (1586) 80 b, Nature..giuing a very long life to many reasonlesse creatures. **1604** T. WRIGHT *Passions* v. §4. 201 Beasts, though reasonlesse, yet in loue follow this generall instinct and inclination of reason. **1633** W. STRUTHER *True Happines* 14 Three instances prove the same: The first is from reasonlesse creatures. **1877** BLACKIE *Wise Men* 250 So great a gap Betwixt the reasonless and the reasoning life A favouring God hath set.

b. Of natural forces or their results: Acting or produced without the aid of reason.

1867 H. MACMILLAN *Bible Teach.* ii. (1870) 36 The forces of nature.. are not reasonless, merciless forces. **1895** *Q. Rev.* Apr. 492 A purely reasonless concourse of atoms.

2. Devoid of ordinary reason; senseless.

1421 HOCCLEVE *Complaint* 222 Yet homly reason know I nevartheles; not hope I founden be so resonles as men demen. **1592** GREENE *Groatsw. Wit* (1617) 24 Reasonlesse Roberts, that hauing but a Brokers place, asked a Lenders reward. **1628** WITHER *Brit. Rememb.* III. 626 Now, most thou need'st it, be not reasonlesse. **1671** F. PHILLIPS *Reg. Necess.* Ep. Ded. 1 These unhappy times have brought forth a sort of reasonless men, whose humors and phancies.. makes them unwilling to submit to Laws. **1868** BROWNING *Ring & Bk.* IV. 11 This rabble's-brabble of dolts and fools Who make up reasonless unreasoning Rome.

3. Not grounded upon reason or reasons; not supported by any reason.

1553 GRIMALDE *Cicero's Bk. Offices* III. (1558) 124 That is reasonlesse that some say [etc.]. **1591** SHAKS. *1 Hen. VI*, v. iv. 137 This proffer is absurd, and reasonlesse. **1658** T. WALL *Charact. Enemies Ch.* 23 Casting a fraudulent shew of reason upon those things which are indeed reasonless. **1794** ANNA SEWARD *Lett.* (1811) IV. 34 The shallow, reasonless oratory, which is so perpetually shifting its ground. **1874** T. N. HARPER *Peace through Truth* Ser. II. I. p. xx, The feelings of the great body of the people, even though reasonless, ought to be respected.

†**b.** of a reason. (Common *c* 1600–50.) *Obs.*

a **1603** T. CARTWRIGHT *Confut. Rhem. N.T.* (1618) Pref. 26 To affirme that a substantiall reason..should be iudged reasonlesse. **1634** CANNE *Necess. of Separ.* (1849) 210 It is likely he saw that there was no help for him there, and therefore only makes use of this reasonless reason. **1670** G. H. *Hist. Cardinals* I. I. 20 The good Father..made me a long discourse.., alleging reasonless reasons.

†**4.** *adv.* Without reason. *Obs. rare*$^{-1}$.

1632 BROME *Crt. Beggar* IV. iii, Since reasonlesse you layd those wrongs upon me.

Hence **'reasonlessly** *adv.*, **'reasonlessness.**

1889 *Harper's Mag.* Apr. 721/2 Reasonlessly, silently, all her anger against him vanished. **1891** MAX MÜLLER *Pres. Addr. Brit. Assoc.* in *Nature* 3 Sept., He saw..that there is no possible transition from reasonlessness to reason.

reasoune, obs. form of REASON *sb.*[1]

re-a'spire, *v.* [RE- 5 a.] To aspire again.

1621 S. WARD *Life of Faith* 2 It would pittie one to see how lamely and blindly hee re-aspires thereunto. **1646** E. F[ISHER] *Mod. Divinity* (ed. 2) 222 The soule is thereby made to re-aspire towards..that chief good, even God. **1936** R. CAMPBELL *Mithraic Emblems* 17 From the sacred flames they feast In hymns of incense re-aspire To praise His throne of silver fire.

rea'ssail, *v.* [RE- 5 a.] To assail again.

1579 FENTON *Guicciard.* II. (1599) 67 The king complayned..that he did not eftsoones reassayle with a new supply [of vessels] the rocke of Yschia. **1665** GLANVILL *Def. Van. Dogm.* 75 And possibly could with an humor brisk enough have reassailed the spirit of proud and unreasonable presumption. **1851** C. L. SMITH tr. *Tasso* III. xxxi, Then showed her front and re-assailed the foe.

rea'ssault, *sb.* [RE- 5 a.] A renewed or repeated assault.

1611 FLORIO, *Riassalto*, a re-assault. **1631** R. BYFIELD *Doctr. Sabb.* 3 Never so subtle or serpentine in malice to a re-assault. *a* **1711** KEN *Urania* Poet. Wks. 1721 IV. 471 The Chaste..By Watching, Prayr, Fasts, Alms, Lust's Fury quell, and all its reassaults repell.

rea'ssault, *v.* [RE- 5 a.] *trans.* To assault or attack again.

1654 H. L'ESTRANGE *Chas. I* (1655) 24 One Turner a Doctor of Physick, reassaults it in these six Queries. **1674** T. FLATMAN *Agst. Thoughts* Poems 102 Then they throng again, And reassault me with a trebled pain. *a* **1711** KEN *Hymnotheo* Poet. Wks. 1721 III. 220 Soon as this lower World becomes our own, We with success may reassault the Throne. **1851** C. L. SMITH tr. *Tasso* III. xxiii, She covered her fair head..And re-assaulted him.

rea'ssay, *v.* [RE- 5 a.] **a.** *intr.* To make a fresh attempt. **b.** *trans.* To test the purity of (metals) again. Hence **rea'ssaying** *vbl. sb.*

1598 FLORIO, *Rattentare*, to reattempt, to reassaie. **1665** BRATHWAIT *Comment Two Tales* 140 In this sort she re-assaies to course him before she leave him. **1677** *Touchstone* in Rigland *Assay Gold & Silver W.* 71 Four grains out of every twelve ounces that is marked, is..to be detained and kept for a reassaying. **1898** *Daily News* 2 May 6/7 They require hall-marked silver to be re-assayed.

†**reassecure**, *v. Obs. rare*$^{-1}$. [RE- 5 a.] *trans.* To make secure again.

1654 EARL MONM. tr. *Bentivoglio's Warrs Flanders* 384 Thinking that it was sufficient for them to reassecure their Neutralities which had been violated.

rea'ssemblage. [RE- 5 a.] A collecting, meeting, or gathering together again.

1744 HARRIS *Three Treat.* I. *notes* (1765) 264 New Beings arise from the Re-assemblage of the scattered Parts. **1792** *Ann. Reg., Chron.* 49 A reassemblage of the mob was apprehended. **1815** SOUTHEY in *Q. Rev.* XIII. 482 It will not now be doubted that Buonaparte had this reassemblage in view. **1890** WEISSMANN in *Nature* 6 Feb. 319 The giving off, circulation, and reassemblage of gemmules.

reassemble (ri:ə'sɛmb(ə)l), *v.* [RE- 5 a. Cf. F. *rassembler*, †*reassembler* (14th c.).]

1. *trans.* To bring together again, to collect anew.

1494 FABYAN *Chron.* VII. ccxlvi. 289 Kynge Phylyp reassembled his Knyghtes, and sped hym towarde the countrey of Poytoys. *c* **1520** BARCLAY *Jugurth* xxxi. 43 b, Whan Metellus (as sayd is) had reassembled them againe: he began in fewe wordes to pray and exhort them. **1667** MILTON *P.L.* I. 186 Reassembling our afflicted Powers, Consult how we may henceforth most offend Our Enemy. **1751** JOHNSON *Rambler* No. 157 ¶ 12, I was reassembling my scattered sentiments. **1762-71** H. WALPOLE *Vertue's Anecd. Paint.* (1786) V. 267 King Charles's collection, which his royal highness wished as far as possible to re-assemble. **1863** COWDEN CLARKE *Shaks. Char.* vii. 173 Her old father pathetically endeavours to reassemble his wandering ideas.

refl. **1818** SCOTT *Rob Roy* viii, Morris, whose scattered wits had hardly yet reassembled themselves.

2. *intr.* To meet, come together, again. Also *fig.*

1611 COTGR., *Reconvenir*, to reassemble, reunite. *c* **1645** HOWELL *Lett.* I. II. xix. (1890) I. 133 At the dissolution of the last Assembly at Lodun, where he solemnly gave his word, to permit them to re-assemble when they would six months after. **1677** COLES *Eng.-Lat. Dict.*, To Reassemble, *rursum convenire*. **1821** SHELLEY *Hellas* 1003 If Greece must be A wreck, yet shall its fragments re-assemble. **1882** J. HAWTHORNE *Fort. Fool* I. xviii, They would reassemble in London once more. **1945** P. LARKIN *North Ship* 9 The meadows are bright With the coldest dew; The dawn reassembles.

Hence **rea'ssembled** *ppl. a.*, **rea'ssembling** *ppl. a.* and *vbl. sb.*

1611 COTGR., *Ralliement*, a rallying, reassembling, reuniting. **1817** *Parl. Deb.* 247 Mr. Hunt's parliament at Spa-fields was prorogued, and at the re-assembling received a royal message. **1863** H. COX *Instit.* I. vi. 32 This rule.. applies as well to the original meeting of a Parliament as to its reassembling after prorogation. **1904** *Westm. Gaz.* 21 Oct. 2/3 The first sitting of the reassembled Chambers. **1906** *Macmillan's Mag.* Apr. 438 To my reassembling senses ..came the realisation of a greater tragedy. **1977** W. M. SPACKMAN *Armful of Warm Girl* 88 Nicolas collected his wits enough to follow, with a re-assembled smile.

rea'ssembly. [RE- 5 a. Cf. obs. F. *réassemblée* (1606–9 in Godef.)] = REASSEMBLAGE.

1611 FLORIO, *Radunanza*, a re-assemblie. **1632** H. SEILE *Augustus* xlviii. 157 The Soldiers..he dispersed..all about Italy, in 32. Colonios:..for their more speedy reassembly, if need should require. **1779-81** JOHNSON *L.P.*, *Young* Wks. IV. 278 The re-assembly of the atoms that compose the human body. **1896** *Daily Chron.* 25 Aug. 3/5.

reassert (ri:ə'sɜ:t), *v.* [RE- 5 a.]

1. *trans.* To assert (a statement, claim, etc.) again.

a **1665** J. GOODWIN *Filled w. the Spirit* (1867) 162 We might re-assert our former argument for the divinity of the Holy Ghost. **1726** POPE *Odyss.* XVII. 147 With equal fury, and with equal fame, Shall great Ulysses re-assert his claim. **1771** *Junius Lett.* lvi. 293 You replied with abuse, and re-asserted your charge. **1835** LYTTON *Rienzi* v. v, I re-asserted each right, and proved it. **1879** FROUDE *Cæsar* xxii. 368 They had an opportunity of reasserting their independence.

refl. **1840** MILL *Diss. & Disc.* (1875) I. 417 The natural tendency..reasserted itself. **1854** KINGSLEY *Alexandria* Pref. 10 These laws will..reassert themselves.

†**2.** To reassign (a person) *to* a condition. *Obs.*$^{-1}$

1675 SOUTH *Serm.* (1823) I. 297 Gross ingratitude in the person..made free, forfeits his freedom, and re-asserts him to his former conditions of slavery.

3. To claim (a thing) again. *rare.*

1725 POPE *Odyss.* I. 52 To warn the wretch, that young Orestes grown To manly years shou'd re-assert the throne. **1853** KANE *Grinnell Exp.* xxv. (1856) 202 Both of these documents reassert the name of Albert Land for the large tract of high lands.

Hence **rea'sserting** *vbl. sb.*

1697 C. LESLIE *Snake in Grass* (ed. 2) 233 A fair occasion ..towards the Re-asserting of the Good Old Cause.

rea'ssertion. [RE- 5 a.] A repeated assertion, a reaffirmation.

1843 MILL *Logic* I. II. i. 221 That cannot be called reasoning or inference which is a mere reassertion in different words of what had been asserted before. **1848** R. I. WILBERFORCE *Doctr. Incarnation* xii. (1852) 327 The glowing words in which Scripture describes the privileges of Christians, are regarded..as a re-assertion of the claims of nature. **1880** E. WHITE *Cert. Relig.* 106 A resolute reassertion by scholars of the Baconian laws of scientific interpretation.

So **rea'ssertor**, one who asserts again.

1859 SMILES *Self-Help* iii. (1860) 48 A recent reassertor of the power of perseverance.

re-a'ssess, *v.* [RE- 5 a.] *trans.* To assess anew.

1803 W. TAYLOR in *Ann. Rev.* I. 427 Whatever taxes are laid on the rent of land, must be re-assessed by the grower of corn on the produce. **1813** —— in *Monthly Mag.* XXXVI. 7 This..will be re-assessed with a profit on the poor. **1884** *Law Times Rep.* L. 142/1 The rateable value of certain property having been re-assessed at a much higher sum.

So **re-a'ssessment.**

1777 BURROW *Rep.* IV. 2291 Personal Estate is not generally rated to the Poor, throughout the Kingdom; and very seldom to the Land Tax, unless upon a Re-assessment. **1886** *Pall Mall G.* 10 Aug. 8/2 There had been lately in London a quinquennial reassessment.

†reassiege, *v. Obs. rare*⁻¹. [RE- 5 a.] *trans.* To lay siege to anew.

1577 HOLINSHED *Hist. Scot.* 412/1 Which occasioned the castell of Edenborough to be reasseeged and inuironed both by sea and land.

rea'ssign, *v.* [RE- 5 a.] To assign anew.

1611 COTGR., *Reconsigner*, to reconsigne, reassigne, reappoint. **1721** in BAILEY [hence in later Dicts]. **1893** *Voice* (N.Y.) 8 June, Generally on the occasion of a new sovereign all lands were reassigned.

So **reassig'nation** (Bailey 1721); **rea'ssignment** (Worcester 1850).

1884 *Law Times* LXXVI. 333/2 If the assignor paid his debt he would be entitled to re-assignment. **1960** *Amer. Speech* XXXV. 216 Hoenigswald recognizes the following types of sound change:..split from reassignment of noncontrasting phones. **1976** *National Observer* (U.S.) 18 Dec. 2/4 The Appeals Court..ordered reassignment of 20,000 to 30,000 students—up to half the student total—to achieve racial balance. **1978** *N.Y. Times* 29 Mar. B4/4 Sent ..Sam Perlozzo, second baseman, to minor leagues for reassignment.

rea'ssimilate, *v.* [RE- 5 a.] To assimilate anew. So **reassimi'lation.**

1828 in WEBSTER. **1876** DOUSE *Grimm's L.* 111 A partial, but now arrested reassimilation. **1952** G. SARTON *Hist. Sci.* I. xvi. 395 Another result of the long wars was the existence of a relatively large body of veterans who..could not be easily reassimilated.

rea'ssociate, *v. rare.* [RE- 5 a.] *refl.* and *intr.* To come together again.

1494 FABYAN *Chron.* VII. 552 Some euyll dysposyd.. reassociat them, and sayde and cryed that [etc.]. **1809** A. HENRY *Trav.* 124 The Indian families..separate in the winter season,..and re-associate in the spring and summer. **1964** G. H. HAGGIS et al. *Introd. Molecular Biol.* xi. 293 When the pH is brought back to neutrality the α and β pairs reassociate into the four-unit molecule.

Hence **,reassoci'ation.**

1923 J. S. HUXLEY *Essays of Biologist* iv. 152 Dissociation in most cases is not complete;..now and again re-association of the parts [of the mind] occurs. **1953** HINSIE & CAMPBELL *Psychiatric Dict.* (ed. 2) 738/2 *Reassociation*, a process of renewed or refreshed association occurring in hypno-analysis of the war neurosis, during which the patient relives the traumatic event with emotional vividness. Such forgotten experiences will then become a part of his normal personality and consciousness. **1977** *Proc. R. Soc. Med.* LXX. 560/1 Nucleic acid reassociation experiments indicate that at least a proportion of tumour cells carry virus genetic material.

rea'ssort, *v.* [RE- 5 a.] *trans.* To assort again. So **rea'ssortment.**

1779 FORREST *Voy. N. Guinea* 294 He took care to provide ..reassortments of stock, which he safely deposited in his warehouse. **1870** ORTON *Andes & Amazons* II. xxxii. (1876) 438 Wool is generally taken to that city..to be re-assorted and repacked. **1872** W. S. SYMONDS *Rec. Rocks* vi. 193 The whole mass has evidently been reassorted by water. **1959** B. WOOTTON *Social Sci. & Social Path.* xi. 330 He may break down under the stress of the eleven-plus reassortment. **1971** D. J. COVE *Genetics* i. 8 The formation of a zygote by the gametes of the two different strains, followed by the production of ascospores must provide an opportunity for the shuffling or reassortment of genetic information affecting different characters.

†reassort, obs. variant of RESORT *v.*

1535 in *Lett. Suppress. Monasteries* (Camden) 85 There was here suche frequence of women commyng and reassorting to this monastery.

reassoune, obs. Sc. form of REASON *sb.*[1]

reassume (riːə'sjuːm), *v.* [f. RE- 5 a + ASSUME *v.* Cf. Sp. *reasumir*, Pg. *reassumir*, It. *riassumere*. See also RESUME *v.*, with which this word formerly coincided in many of its senses.]

1. *trans.* To take, or take up, again (a material thing laid down or handed to another).

1494 FABYAN *Chron.* VII. 319 Pandulph toke yᵉ Crowne of the Kynge,..yᵉ Kynge reassumyd the Crowne of Pandulph. **1628** FELTHAM *Resolves* II. xxi. 70 Beware him, as an Enemie, apt to re-assume his Armes. **1679** *New Advice* in *Roxb. Ball.* (1883) IV. 548 Painter, once more thy Pencil reassume. *a* **1766** MRS. F. SHERIDAN *Sidney Bidulph* V. 44, I shall break off here, and shall re-assume my pen in the evening. **1848** C. C. CLIFFORD tr. *Aristophanes, Frogs* 18 No nonsense, Xanthias; reassume your pack.

b. To revoke, take back (a grant, gift, etc.).

1609 DANIEL *Civ. Wars* III. lxxxix, His successour..did reuocate And re-assume his liberalities. **1675** H. NEVILE *Machiavelli's Prince* vii. Wks. 209 Lest the next Pope should ..reassume all that Alexander had given him. **1726** POPE *Odyss.* XVI. 476 She waves her golden wand, and reassumes From ev'ry feature every grace that blooms. **1792** CHARLOTTE SMITH *Desmond* I. 129 What then should prevent a nation from re-assuming grants? **1816** SCOTT *Antiq.* xviii, His lands..lay waste till they were re-assumed by the emperor as a lapsed fief.

†c. To rescind, recall (a vote). *Obs.*

1685 S. SEWALL *Diary* 22 Oct., Deputies reassume their vote as to the treasurer, and consent with the magistrates. **1716** B. CHURCH *Hist. Philip's War* (1867) II. 128 The Lieut. Governour..told them except they did Re-assume that Vote..they should sit there till the next Spring.

2. a. To take back (a person) into close relationship with oneself.

1610 DONNE *Pseudo-martyr* 13 The seuerity which the Church vsed towards them,..and her bitternesse and auersenes, from re-assuming them, euen after long penances, into her bosome. **1647** N. BACON *Disc. Govt. Eng.* I. xlvi. (1739) 76 He reseized and reassumed the English, in partnership with the Norman in their ancient right of Government. **1667** MILTON *P.L.* X. 225 Into his blissful bosom reassum'd In glory as of old.

b. To take back (a thing) as a constituent part.

1692 RAY *Disc.* II. ii. (1732) 74 Carried off by the rivers and reassumed by the sea. **1741** MONRO *Anat.* (ed. 3) 22 The Marrow..is reassumed into the Mass of Blood. **1883** *Cath. Dict.* (1897) 744/1 St. Thomas says..that all the particles of blood which Christ shed in his Passion were reassumed by him in His resurrection.

3. To take again upon oneself:

a. a shape or form, a garb or something worn.

1624 HEYWOOD *Gunaik.* I. 31 By the bankes of Nilus reassumed her humane shape. **1660** F. BROOKE tr. *Le Blanc's Trav.* 221 The..Steward of houshold..caused him to reassume his apparell. **1719** J. T. PHILIPPS tr. *Thirty-four Confer.* 283 At the great Day of Accompts the Souls shall reassume their former Bodies. **1771** MRS. GRIFFITH *Hist. Lady Barton* II. 271, I could again be weak enough..to reassume those rosy fetters. **1855** LONGF. *Hiaw.* XII. 304 Then the birds, again transfigured, Reassumed the shape of mortals. **1873** B. STEWART *Conserv. Force* §157 The heat thus spent reassumes the form of molecular motion.

b. a charge, office, exercise of power, etc.

1632 SIR T. HAWKINS tr. *Mathieu's Unhappy Prosp.* I. 24 Hee should re-assume the charge [which] had beene taken from him. **1670** MILTON *Hist. Eng.* I. Wks. (1851) 25 Elidure now in his own behalf re-assumes the Government. **1726** AYLIFFE *Parergon* 162 After Henry the VIIIth had re-assum'd the Supremacy. **1774** tr. *Helvetius' Child Nat.* II. 245 At last, reason reassumed her empire. **1821** SHELLEY *Prometh. Unb.* III. i. 58 The tyranny of heaven none may retain, Or reassume, or hold. **1885** M. ARNOLD in *Pall Mall G.* 3 Nov. 3/2 To reassume an office at sixty-two is not the same thing as to assume it at thirty-two.

c. a character, attribute, quality, feeling, etc.

1632 MASSINGER *Maid of Hon.* V. ii, I conjure you To re-assume your order [of knighthood]. **1655** tr. *Com. Hist. Francion* XII. 23 Little and little he began to reassume his Spirits. **1671** MRS. BEHN *Forc'd Marriage* I. iii, Go, re-assume your beauty; dry your eyes. **1712** STEELE *Spect.* No. 432 ¶4 These little Republicks reassume their National Hatred to each other. **1785** G. A. BELLAMY *Apol.* IV. 37 Upon rejoining the company, he reassumed his good humour and politeness. **1810** SOUTHEY *Kehama* XXIV. iv, Then did the Man-God re-assume His unity. **1899** *Allbutt's Syst. Med.* VIII. 482 The quality of reassuming turgescence on excitement.

d. a right, title, name, etc.

1660 T. M. *Hist. Independ.* IV. 101 The Lords (who had now reassumed their Native right by taking their places in the higher House). **1761** GRAY *Odin* 92 Night Has reassum'd her ancient right. **1813** EUSTACE *Class. Tour* (1821) IV. 328 Whether Italy be destined to re-assume her honors. **1830** LYTTON *P. Clifford* xxxiii, He had re-assumed his hereditary name. **1847** MRS. A. KERR tr. *Ranke's Hist. Servia* vi. 114 They re-assumed the title of Dahi.

e. *refl.* To return to one's natural character.

1682 N. O. *Boileau's Lutrin* I. 149 Then Reassume yourself, forbear to Doat. **1811** *Henry & Isabella* I. 168 She instantly combated what she considered an ungenerous suspicion, and reassumed herself.

f. *absol.* To take office again. *Obs. rare.*

1716 B. CHURCH *Hist. Philip's War* (1867) II. 3 Soon after this was the Revolution, and the other Government Re-assumed.

4. To take, resume (one's place) again.

1640 in Rushw. *Hist. Coll.* III. (1692) I. 45 Mr. Solicitor ..reassumed the Chair again. **1670** DRYDEN *Conq. Granada* I. ii, But now my Reason re-assumes its Throne. *a* **1711** KEN *Hymnotheo* Poet. Wks. 1721 III. 84 The scatter'd Atoms of each humane Mold..Shall..re-assume in Men their pristine site. **1789** CHARLOTTE SMITH *Ethelinde* (1814) IV. 131 Again reassuming his place at the breakfast-table. **1821** SHELLEY *Ess. & Lett.* (1852) II. 255 We could easily reassume our station with the spring at Pugnano or the baths. **1841** CLOUGH *Poems* (1862) 8 The day may come I yet may re-assume My place.

5. To recommence, take up again, resume:

†a. speech, discourse, thought, a subject, etc. Very common in the 17th and 18th centuries.

1608 WILLET *Hexapla Exod.* 818 After the Iewes had made answere..the Lord presently reassumeth that speech. **1660** INGELO *Bentiv. & Ur.* II. (1682) 102 They might afterwards re-assume their delightful conversation. **1682** VERNON *Life Heylin* 183 He again re-assumes the Argument and confutes all that Bellarmin and others produce for it. **1715–6** *Town Talk* No. 4 Mr. Arthur reassumed the discourse. **1755** B. MARTIN *Mag. Arts & Sc.* I. 11 We will re-assume the Subject of the Ptolomaic System.

b. a practice, action, occupation, etc. Common in the 17th and 18th centuries.

1624 BP. MOUNTAGU *Gagg* 244 A thing prohibited in the councell of Laodicea, but re-assumed, and long time frequented in the Church. *a* **1641** —— *Acts & Mon.* (1642) 144 They re-assumed the work upon warrant of Cyrus his former Edict. **1702** ECHARD *Eccl. Hist.* (1710) 492 Those kind of Spectacles were already over, and not to be reassumed the same day. **1756** TOLDERVY *Hist. 2 Orphans* III. 12 Our company reassumed their march; and..arrived in good time. **1791** CHARLOTTE SMITH *Celestina* (ed. 2) I. 220 To quiet the perturbation of her mind by re-assuming her usual occupations. **1824** in *Spirit Pub. Jrnls.* (1825) 508 Mary Stuart having brought some superb diamonds into France, the ladies of the Court re-assumed the wear of them.

†c. With *inf. Obs. rare.*

1646 FULLER *Wounded Consc.* (1841) 313, I re-assume to personate a wounded conscience.

†d. *intr.* To resume, continue speaking, after a pause. *Obs.*

1719 J. T. PHILIPPS tr. *Thirty-four Confer.* 32 Then they re-assumed and said. **1768** STERNE *Sent. Journ.* II. 110 *Case of Conscience*, I own it is necessary, re-assumed the master of the hotel, that [etc.]. **1796** CHARLOTTE SMITH *Marchmont* I. 60 'Ah, my dear love!' reassumed this admirable woman, after a short pause.

†6. To repeat. *Obs. rare.*

1631 R. BYFIELD *Doctr. Sabb.* 17, I re-assume that your exposition is meerely a dreame. **1684** T. HOCKIN *God's Decrees* 353 Here give me leave to re-assume that great Apostolical caution.

Hence **rea'ssuming** *vbl. sb.*

1633 BP. HALL *Hard Texts, N.T.* 120 The voluntary resigning and the reassuming of my life. **1656** EARL MONM. tr. *Boccalini's Advts. fr. Parnass.* I. v. (1674) 5 In the Venetian Common-wealth, those reformations of Government, those re-assumings of State were never seen.

†rea'ssumpt, *v. Obs. rare*⁻¹. [RE- 5 a.] = REASSUME *v.* (Only in *pa. pple.*)

1561 DAUS tr. *Bullinger on Apoc.* (1573) 273 b, S. Iohn speaketh not of the bodyes reassumpted, chaunged, or raysed agayne at the last iudgement.

rea'ssumption. [RE- 5 a.] The act of reassuming.

1611 FLORIO, *Reassuntióne*, a reassumption. **1695** J. EDWARDS *Perfect. Script.* 469 Ver. 11..is but a repetition or reassumption of this. **1701** DE FOE *Trueborn Eng.* I. 145 He did not send his Dutchmen home again. No Re-assumptions in his Reign were known. **1815** SOUTHEY in *Q. Rev.* XIII. 55 The return from Elba and the reassumption of the throne.

reassurance (riːə'ʃʊərəns). [RE- 5 a. Cf. F. *rassurance* and, in sense 3, *réassurance* (1681).]

1. Renewed or repeated assurance; repetition of assuring statements.

1611 FLORIO, *Rassicuránza*, a re-assurance. **1643** PRYNNE *Sov. Power Parl.* III. 25 He hastily dispatcheth messengers to him with great summes of Money, and a re-assurance of his tributary Subjection. **1863** J. C. JEAFFRESON *Sir Everard's Dau.* 186 So wrought upon by the re-assurances of his physician. **1873** BROWNING *Red Cott. Nt.-cap* I. 403 By reassurance of that promise old.

2. Renewed or restored confidence.

1875 CHURCH *Pascal*, etc. xvi. (1895) 272 We have learned from facts a reassurance which some only can find in the most self-consistent theories.

3. Reinsurance.

1745–6 *Act 19 Geo. II*, c. 37 §4 It shall not be lawful to make Re-assurance, unless the Assurer shall be insolvent, become Bankrupt, or die. **1826–30** KENT *Comm.* v. xlviii. (1858) III. 368 The contract of reassurance is totally distinct from, and unconnected with, the primitive insurance.

reassure (riːə'ʃʊə(r)), *v.* [f. RE- 5 a + ASSURE *v.* Cf. F. *rassurer* (Of. *rasseurer*), and, in sense 3, *réassurer* (1681 in Littré).]

†1. *trans.* To re-establish, confirm (a thing). Also const. *to* (a person). **b.** To confirm (one) again in (an honour). *Obs.*

1613 SIR R. BOYLE in *Lismore Papers* (1886) I. 28, I.. reassured the said land to him by my lease for xxi yeares. **1637** SALTONSTALL *Eusebius' Constantine* 36 [They] were restored to their former dignities, and reassured their former honours. *a* **1711** KEN *Anodynes* Poet. Wks. 1721 III. 422 They long sharp Penances endur'd, Till ghostly Health was reassur'd. **1764** CHURCHILL *Gotham* III. Poems 1772 III. 153 Ere 'tis too late wish'd Health to re-assure.

2. To restore (a person, the mind, etc.) to confidence. †Also const. *from* (a fear), and with inf.

1598 DALLINGTON *Meth. Trav.* M iij, By this meanes hee should reassure other Cities that then stoode wauering. **1687** A. LOVELL tr. *Thevenot's Trav.* II. 184, I endeavoured to reassure him and the rest from the fear which made him speak so. **1697** DRYDEN *Æneid* VIII. 146 They rose with Fear,..Till dauntless Pallas reassur'd the rest, To pay the Rites. **1728** ELIZA HEYWOOD tr. *Mad. de Gomez's Belle A.* (1732) II. 289 The Air with which I spoke these Words something re-assuring him. **1806** SURR *Winter in Lond.* III. 34 With a calmness of manner that reassured me, as it demonstrated that he had no suspicion of me. **1879**

McCarthy *Own Times* II. xxviii. 333 This was a sort of explanation more likely to alarm than to reassure the public.

b. To confirm again in an opinion or impression. Const. *of*.

1811 Syd. Smith *Lett.* lxxvi, There is great happiness in the country, but it requires a visit to London every year to reassure yourself of this truth. **1821** Byron *Juan* III. xxxvii, And long he paused to reassure his eyes.

3. To reinsure.

1826–30 Kent *Comm.* v. xlviii. (1858) III. 368 The insurer may have the entire sum he hath insured, reassured to him by some other insurer. **1828** Webster, *Reassure*, to insure a second time against loss..; to insure against loss that may be incurred by taking a risk.

Hence **rea'ssured** *ppl. a.*; **rea'ssurement; rea'ssurer; rea'ssuring** *ppl. a.*; **rea'ssuringly** *adv.*

1896 *Westm. Gaz.* 28 Dec. 5/2 One of the two Johannesburg deputies..sent off a *reassured and reassuring telegram. **1891** E. & D. Gerard *Sensit. Plants* II. II. xii. 124 This was meant as a *reassurement, but his words startled Janet further. **1787** J. A. Park *Marine Insurances* xv. 315 Reassurance..may be said to be a contract, which the first insurer enters into, in order to relieve himself from those risks which he has incautiously undertaken, by throwing them upon other underwriters, who are called *re-assurers. **1828** Webster, *Reassurer*, one who insures the first underwriter. **1897** *Allbutt's Syst. Med.* II. 273 In this matter the profession should take the part of the reassurer and not of the alarmist. **1861** Trench *Ep. 7 Churches Asia* 114 This may not sound, at the first hearing, a *reassuring word. **1884** *Athenæum* 14 June 754/3 If there be any fears of severance from old associations,..such works as the present may have a reassuring effect. **1872** Geo. Eliot *Middlem.* xxxii, 'I shall take a mere mouthful of ham and a glass of ale,' he said, *reassuringly.

rea'ssuring, *vbl. sb.* [f. reassure *v.* + -ing[1].] The action of the verb reassure.

1865 in Webster. **1902** 'Mark Twain' in *Harper's Weekly* 6 Dec. 5/2 Alfred..did what he could..to respond with some show of heart to the Major's kindly pettings and reassurings.

reast, var. reest *v.*, obs. f. rest *v.*

reasty ('ri:stɪ), *a.* Chiefly *dial.* Also 7, 9 **reisty**, 9 **reesty, reeasty, raisty**, etc. [Later form of resty *a.*; cf. reesed *a.*]

1. Rancid. Cf. reasy 1.

1573 Tusser *Husb.* (1878) 53 Through follie too beastlie much bacon is reastie. **1632** Sherwood, Reasie (or reastie), *ranci, relant.* **1639** Horn & Rob. *Gate Lang. Unl.* xxvi. §329 Musty,..tainted, sappy, rotten, reisty things such as bacon and grease is wont to be. **1688** R. Holme *Armoury* III. 269/1 Much Bacon and long kept, groweth reasty. **1821** A. Welby *Visit N. Amer.* 113 For six months the food..was only some reasty bacon and Indian corn. **1848** A. B. Evans *Leicestersh. Words* s.v., 'That ere oil's as raisty, as raisty.' **1855–** in many dial. glossaries. **1914** C. Mackenzie *Sinister Street* II. IV. ii. 859 A luxurious mournfulness was in the view, and he leaned out over the sill scenting the reasty London air. **1959** *Listener* 10 Dec. 1035/2, I paid for all mistakes with drops of sweat Strained from the reasty gammon of my pain. **1964** J. Hale *Grudge Fight* v. 76 What you'll do is shut your trap and get back to your reasty pit. **1974** P. Wright *Lang. Brit. Industry* xvii. 166 In some homes..bacon with a strong nasty taste is not rancid but *reasty*. **1978** *Jrnl. Lancs. Dial. Soc.* XXVII. 13 Please, Looard, send summat good to eyt; Not reeasty bacon or fatty meyt.

transf. **1593** G. Harvey *Pierce's Super.* III. 147 Martins Vnbrideled stile, and Pap-hatchets reastie eloquence.

†**2.** = reasy 2 (q.v.).

'reasy, *a. Obs.* exc. *dial.* Also 8 **reesy**, 9 **reezy**. [Obscurely related to prec.; cf. reese *v.*]

1. Rancid, 'reasty'.

1611 Cotgr., *Ranci*, musty, fusty, reasie, resti, tainted. **1736** Bailey *Househ. Dict.* 140 The butter-milk in fresh butter must not by any means be wash'd out with water;..for water will make it rusty or reesy. **1848** A. B. Evans *Leicestersh. Words, Reasy* or *Reezy*, rancid: said of bacon.

†**2.** Idle, lazy. *Obs. rare*$^{-0}$.

1679 Coles *Eng.-Lat. Dict.* (ed. 2), Reasy, reasty, *reses, deses*. To be reasie, *resideo, stupeo, torpeo*.

Hence †**'reasiness.** *Obs. rare*$^{-0}$.

1611 Cotgr., *Rancissure*, mustinesse, fustinesse, reasinesse. **1679** Coles *Eng.-Lat. Dict.* (ed. 2) Reasiness, *desidia, pigritia*.

reasynge, obs. form of raisin.

†**reat**, *sb. Sc. Obs. rare*$^{-1}$. [ad. L. *reāt-us*, f. *reus* accused.] Offence, wrong-doing.

1535 Stewart *Cron. Scot.* II. 667 Of thi reat this tyme full soir I rew; In tyme to cum so that thow wilbe trew, Heir I forgif the all faltis bygone.

†**reat**, *v.* (*pa. t.*) *Obs. rare.*

Of doubtful origin and meaning; the intransitive example may belong to *ruten* to dart, rush: see rout *v.*

a **1225** *Juliana* 54 þe edie meiden..reat him mitte raketehe unrudeliche swiðe & warp him forð efter þet from hire. *Ibid.* 58 So þer lihtinde com an engel of heouene & reat to þat hweol swa þat hit al to refde.

reat, obs. f. rate *sb.*[1]

reata: see riata.

reatch, obs. form of reach *sb.*[1] and *v.*[1]

reatchlessness, obs. var. recklessness.

reate (ri:t). *Obs.* exc. *arch.* [Of obscure origin: cf. reit.] A species of water-crowfoot, *Ranunculus fluitans*.

1661 Walton *Angler* (ed. 3) xx. 242 To kill the water-weeds, as Water-lillies, Candocks, Reate and Bullrushes. **1840** Browning *Sordello* VI. 81 Pure, loquacious pearl the soft tree-tent Guards, with its face of reate and sedge.

reath, obs. form of raith.

reaðe, obs. form of rathe *adv.*

reattach (ri:ə'tætʃ), *v.* [re- 5 a. Cf. F. *rattacher* (15th c.); OF. *rattachier*.]

†**1.** *trans. Law.* To seize (a person) by authority of a writ of reattachment. Const. *for. Obs.*

1607 Cowell *Interpr.* s.v. *Reattachment*, Reattachment general seemeth to be, where a man is reattached for his appearance vpon all writs of Assise lying against him.

2. To attach again. Const. *to*.

1814 Sir R. Wilson *Priv. Diary* (1862) II. 489 His lordship..suggests that marshal Bellegarde should re-attach to his own army the division Göber. **1841–4** Emerson *Ess.* Ser. II. i. (1876) 22 The poet, who reattaches things to nature and the Whole. **1921** O. E. Inglis *Burchard's Textbk. Dental Path. & Therapeutics* (ed. 6) VI. xxviii. 777 The first indication [of when a tooth has been forced out by accident] has ever been acted upon by parents who have quickly pressed teeth into their places where they became reattached. **1952** W. H. Archer *Manual of Oral Surg.* i. 41/2 The tooth became re-attached, and circulation into the pulp tissue was re-established. **1957** G. Ryle in C. A. Mace *Brit. Philos. in Mid-Century* 254 The notion of meaning had been ..partly detached from the notion of naming and re-attached to the notion of saying.

refl. **1813** W. Taylor in *Monthly Rev.* LXXII. 424 The church separated from the aristocracy, and re-attached itself to the regal order. **1860** Tyndall *Glac.* II. xxii. 347 The ice was crushed, but the crushed fragments soon re-attached themselves. **1953** I. Glickman *Clin. Periodontol.* xxxvii. 609 The problem hinges upon the question of whether the periodontal tissues reattach themselves to tooth surface previously denuded by disease..or whether they are attached at the level of the pre-existent pocket. **1980** D. Williams *Murder for Treasure* v. 45 The guard..had re-attached himself to Treasure's entourage.

Hence **rea'ttached** *ppl. a.*

1928 H. K. Box *Treatm. Periodontal Pocket* III. 117 The arrangement of the reattached tissues on the curetted cemental surface.

rea'ttachment. [re- 5 a.] **a.** A fresh attachment, esp. in *Law*.

1574 tr. *Littleton's Tenures* 42 The demaundante or pleintife..may have a resummons or a reattachment uppon his original. **1607** Cowell *Interpr., Reattachment*, a second Attachment of him, that was formerly attached. **1634** *Irish Act 10 Chas. I*, Sess. II. c. 14 To prosecute and sue re-summons, re-attachments,..or other such like processe. **1860** Tyndall *Glac.* II. xxx. 405 Some of them have yielded along a plane passing through them,..but the re-attachment is very strong.

b. *Dentistry*. The re-establishment of the connections between a tooth and the jaw.

1908 O. E. Inglis *Burchard's Textbk. Dental Path. & Therapeutics* (ed. 3) IV. xv. 410 Kirk records a case of immediate replantation in early life, followed in old age by root resorption. The tooth when extracted contained secondary dentine, which could only have formed as the result of a reattachment of the pulp. **1928** H. K. Box *Treatm. Periodontal Pocket* III. 103 Gentle digital pressure ..appeared to be the only precaution taken to insure reattachment. **1953** I. Glickman *Clin. Periodontol.* xxxvii. 609 The term 'reattachment' is to be used here to connote the restoration of gingival contour effected by the re-embedding of the periodontal membrane into newly formed cementum, and attachment of gingival epithelium to tooth surface denuded by periodontal disease. **1962** Blake & Trott *Periodontol.* x. 96 By combined cementum and soft tissue curettage, it is possible to obtain a degree of attachment of soft tissue to cementum with a consequent real reduction in pocket depth... This is..called 'reattachment'.

rea'ttack, *v.* [re- 5 a.] To attack again.

a **1711** Ken *Psyche* Poet. Wks. 1721 IV. 195 And if I chance my Watch to slack, My Soul they re-attack. **1795** Nelson 7 Feb. in Nicolas *Disp.* (1845) II. 6, I was the cause of re-attacking Bastia, after our Generals gave it over, from not knowing the force. **1894** *Westm. Gaz.* 16 Oct. 5/1 The Kaffirs are re-attacking Lorenzo Marquez.

rea'ttain, *v.* [re- 5 a.] To attain again.

1609 Daniel *Civ. Wars* v. lv, And got and lost, and reattaines (againe) That which again was lost.

So **rea'ttainment.**

1853 Mill *Diss. & Disc., Grote's Greece* (1859) II. 513 The resurrection of Athens, and her reattainment..of something like imperial dignity.

rea'ttempt, *sb.* [re- 5 a.] A second trial.

1598 Florio, *Ritento*, a reattempt, reassaying. **1662** Hickeringill *Jamaica* 56 Being so often refrustrated in their reattempts.

rea'ttempt, *v.* [re- 5 a.] *trans.* To attempt anew. Hence **rea'ttempting** *vbl. sb.*

1583 Hayes *Voy. Sir H. Gilbert* in Hakluyt *Voy.* (1600) III. 158 Also laying downe his determination in the Spring following, for disposing of his voyage then to be reattempted. **1598** Florio, *Rattentare*, to reattempt, to reassaie. *Ibid., Rattento*, a reattempting, a reassaying. **1646** Sir T. Browne *Pseud. Ep.* 319 It was first attempted by Sersostris,..but was long after re-attempted, and in some manner effected by Philadelphus. **1669** Woodhead *St. Teresa* II. ii. 8, I should..discourse no more of it, till the season came for re-attempting the business. **1861** M. Arnold *On Translating Homer* iii. 102, I think that the task of translating Homer into English verse both will be re-attempted, and may be re-attempted successfully. **1895** Hardy *Jude the Obscure* III. vi. 198 He had begun to sit in his parlour during the dark winter nights and re-attempt some of his old studies.

†**rea'ttend**, *v. Obs.* [re- 5 a.] *trans.* To attend to again; to give renewed attention to (a thing).

1642 Quarles *Div. Poems, Jonah* (ed. 2) 22 With prayers, and pains, re-utter'd, re-attended; They try'd new ways, despairing of the old. *a* **1711** Ken *Christophil* Poet. Wks. 1721 I. 429 We Thoughts on Things extraneous spend, And Heav'n can hardly re-attend.

reaue, obs. form of reave, reeve.

reaulte, variant of realty[1] *Obs.*

reaume, obs. form of realm.

Réaumur (reomyr). [See def.] The name of a French physicist, René-Antoine Ferchault de *Réaumur* (1683–1757): **a.** used *ellipt.* to denote the thermometer or thermometric scale introduced by him about 1730, in which the freezing point of water is 0° and the boiling point 80°.

In English works the accent on the *e* is usually omitted.

1782 Jefferson *Notes on Virginia* (1787) 132 In rooms heated to 140° of Reaumur, equal to 347° of Farenheit. **1799** Malthus *Jrnl.* 30 May (1966) 39 In the summer of 1793 the therm was 25 Reaumur. **1814** tr. *Klaproth's Trav.* 271 The water..commonly has a temperature of more than 55° Reaumur. **1832** S. Austin tr. *H. Pückler-Muskau's Tour in Germany, Holland & England* III. 196 The room..is regularly heated to a temperature of fourteen degrees Reaumur. **1855** *Englishwoman in Russia* 5 There were but 18° of Reaumur; the sky was beautifully blue. **1950** 'G. Orwell' *Shooting Elephant* 18, I had been unequal to translating Réaumur into Fahrenheit, but I know that my temperature was round about 103.

b. Used in the possessive and *attrib.* to designate various processes, materials, and concepts developed by him, as **Réaumur malleable iron**, a name for white-heart malleable cast iron; **Réaumur's porcelain**, a devitrified form of glass produced by prolonged exposure to heat near but below the fusion temperature, formerly used for chemical vessels; **Réaumur process**, a process for annealing iron leading to the production of white-heart malleable iron, first published by Réaumur in 1722; **Réaumur('s) scale**, his temperature scale.

1912 W. H. Hatfield *Cast Iron* xiii. 195 Sample J..was a..sample of English Réaumur malleable cast iron. It consisted mainly of well-laminated pearlite, in which was immersed the remaining annealing carbon, with a skin of well-developed ferrite. **1832** G. R. Porter *Porcelain & Glass* xvi. 317 M. Reaumur,..in..1739, communicated the result of these to the Royal Academy of Sciences in Paris. The subject becoming by this means more generally known, glass, when thus converted, obtained, and has since kept the name, of Reaumur's porcelain, a designation which it owes to its appearance rather than to its real properties. *Ibid.* 325 Glass has been converted into Reaumur's porcelain during volcanic eruptions, by being enveloped in burning lava. **1868** C. L. Eastlake *Hints Househ. Taste* x. 219 In the production of what is called Réaumur's porcelain, the formation of crystals may be determined by the application of heat lower than that necessary to effect the perfect fusion of the glass. **1918** P. Marson *Glass* iii. 17 'Réaumur's Porcelain' is a glass in a devitrified state, and is used for pestles and mortars, devitrified glass being less brittle than ordinary glass and similar to vitrified porcelain. **1911** B. Stoughton *Metall. of Iron & Steel* (ed. 2) xiii. 356 In the original Réaumur process the castings are packed in iron oxide during the anneal, and this operation is carried on at a temperature of about 800 to 875°C..for a period of four or five days. **1949** J. E. Garside *Process & Physical Metall.* xxi. 374 Malleable cast-irons are made by two methods—..(2) The Whiteheart process, also known as the European or Réaumur process. **1795** W. Nicholson *Dict. Chem.* II. 935 In Reaumur's scale, the number of degrees between these two points is 80. **1863** E. Atkinson tr. *Ganot's Elementary Treatise on Physics* VI. i. 194 Besides the centigrade scale two others are frequently used—Fahrenheit's scale and Réaumur's scale. **1958** S. Petterssen *Introd. Meteorol.* (ed. 2) ii. 20 The Reaumur scale was much used in Central Europe until the beginning of this century but has since gone out of use.

reaunceoune, obs. form of ransom *sb.*

reaute, variant of realty[1] *Obs.*

reauthenti'cation. [re- 5 a.] A renewed authentication.

1802–12 Bentham *Ration. Judic. Evid.* (1827) IV. 634 Until the authenticity of the supposed transcript can be put out of doubt (for example, by being sent to the original for reauthentication..).

re'authorize, *v.* [re- 5 a.] To authorize anew.

1646 Trapp *Comm. John* xxi. 17 To confirm him..and to re-authorize him in his apostleship.

reave (ri:v, reɪv), *sb. Archæol.* [Origin unknown: perh. f. OE. *rǣw* rew *sb.*[1]] A long low bank or wall found on Dartmoor.

1848 J. H. Mason in S. Rowe *Perambulation of Dartmoor* 130 In tracing the northernmost *reave* from Hamildon..we lost it in a tin-work. **1976** *Current Archaeol.* V. 250/2 Four major walls on the moor... The walls were known as reaves in local dialect (pronounced 'raves'). *Ibid.* 252/1 The lynchets seem to show that the reaves..were built by a people who already had fields laid out in parallel strips. **1978** *Antiquity* Mar. 16/1 Dartmoor reaves..(the word derives from the Old English *raew*, meaning a row) are long, low banks, constructed mainly of stone, and often covered in vegetation. These may run for any distance up to 15 km, and they may reach 0·5 m or more in height.

reave (riːv), *v.*[1] Now only *arch.* or *poet.* Forms: *Infin.* 1 **réafian**, 2 **ræuen**, 2–3 **reauen**, 3 **ræfenn, reafen**, 3–5 **refe(n**, 3–6 **reu-, reve(n**, 5 **revyn**; (? 4 **reyue**), 5–6 *Sc.* **reif(f)e**, **rewe**, 6 *Sc.* **reff-**, 6 (8–9 *Sc.*) **reeve**, 6–7 **reaue**, 6– **reave**, (*Sc.* **reive**, 9 **rieve**). *Pa. t.* α. 1 **réafode**, 2–3 **ræuede, reuede**, 3 **rewede, ræfde, refde**, 4 **revede**; (and *pa. pple.*) 4–5 **reu-, reued**, (**-id, -yd**, 5 **refyd, reuet**, *Sc.* **rewyt**, etc.), 6–7 **reaued**, 6– **reaved**, 9 **rieved**. β. 3–6 **reft(e**, 5 **raffte**; 3–5 **refte**, 4 **reeft**, 5 **refft**, 3– **reft**. Also *pa. pple.* 3 **ræfedd, refd**, 4 **yreued, -raft**, 7 **reauen**. (See also RIVE *v.*) [Comm. Teut.: OE. *réafian* = OFris. *râvia, râva*, OS. *rôbôn* (MLG. *rôven*, MDu. *roven*, Du. *rooven*), OHG. *roubôn* (MHG. *rouben*, G. *rauben*), Goth. (*bi*)*raubôn*:—OTeut. **raubôjan*, f. **raubo*ᵐ (OE. *réaf*: see REIF), from the *o*-grade of a pre-Teut. ablaut series **reup-, roup-, rup-*, widely represented in the cognate languages; the original sense is app. that of breaking, as in OE. *réofan*, ON. *rjúfa, raufa*, Lat. *rup-, rumpĕre*.

In the sense of robbing or plundering the word is wanting in ON. The later Icel. *reyfa* (from about 1400) is ad. Da. *röve* (MDa. *röffue*, etc.), which like Sw. *röfva* (MSw. *röffua, röwa*, etc.) is from MLG. *rôven*: cf. note to REAVER.

The spelling *reive* (or *rieve*), originally Sc., is sometimes employed when the reference is to the taking of goods or cattle by force (cf. *reiver, reiving*); in other senses the normal Eng. spelling is retained, as in the comb. BEREAVE.]

1. *intr.* To commit spoliation or robbery; to plunder, pillage. Const. *from*. (In later use chiefly *Sc.*, sometimes written *reive, rieve*.)

c **950** *Lindisf. Gosp.* Matt. Contents xv, Ne ðæm sloegende ne ðæm reafende..wiðstonda. *a* **1023** WULFSTAN *Hom.* xxxiii. (Napier) 163 Hy herʒiað..rypað and reafiað and to scipe lædað. *c* **1175** *Lamb. Hom.* 31 Bluðeliche þe mon wile gan to scrifte & segge þe preoste þet he haueð ireaueð & istolen. *c* **1205** LAY. 10584 Heo rupten, heo ræfden [*v.r.* refden], noht heo ne bi-læfden. *a* **1300** *Cursor M.* 6477 Lok þat þou ne reue ne stele. **1375** BARBOUR *Bruce* XVI. 551 Thai ..Tuk land, and fast begouth to reif. *c* **1450** *St. Cuthbert* (Surtees) 4898 þai slew, þai brent, þai robbed, þai reued. *c* **1520** BARCLAY *Jugurth* xxvii. 37 Euery man..robbyng and reauynge without measure, from the commen wele. **1607** R. C[AREW] tr. *Estienne's World of Wonders* 48 The Church from liue and dead doth reaue. **1783** BURNS *Unco Mournfu' Tale* 37 To slink thro' slaps, an' reave an' steal, At stacks o' pease. **1851** LOWELL *Poems, Anti-Apis*, Thor the strong could reave and steal. **1864** BURTON *Scot Abr.* I. ii. 62 A troop of bare-legged ruffians, who rieved and ravaged far and near.

†**2.** *trans.* **a.** To despoil or rob (a person); to deprive (one) of something by force. *Obs.*

Beowulf 2986 þenden reafode rinc oðerne, nam on Ongenðio irenbyrnan. **971** *Blickl. Hom.* 63 Sume myccle swiþor rihtaþ Godes folc þonne hie reafian earme & unscyldigan. *c* **1154** *O.E. Chron.* (Laud MS.) an. 1135 Æuric man sone ræuede oþer þe mihte. *a* **1225** *Ancr. R.* 286 Hwo so euer on him sulf nimeð ouðer of þeos two, he robbeð God & reaueð. **13..** *Cursor M.* 6149 (Gött.) Godd, þat grace to his folk gaue,..For to reue þat folk vn-sele. **1456** SIR G. HAYE *Law Arms* (S.T.S.) 91 Gif a knycht be reft doand his princis charge. *Ibid.* 92 A revare that set to reve him be the way. **1567** *Gude & Godlie B.* (S.T.S.) 9 Commit na thift, na man thow reif.

†**b.** To spoil, rob, or plunder (a place or district).

c **950** *Lindisf. Gosp.* Mark iii. 27 Nymðe ærist ðone stronga [he] ʒebinde, & ðonne hus his reafað. *c* **1122** *O.E. Chron.* (Laud MS.) an. 1087 [Hi] woldan þa ðæne port bærnen & þæt mynster reafian. *c* **1154** *Ibid.* an. 1137 þa ræueden hi & brendon alle the tunes. *c* **1250** *Gen. & Ex.* 2802 Ge sulen cumen..And reuen egipte ðat is nu prud. *c* **1465** in *Three 15th Cent. Chron.* (Camden) 23 The Kynge off Scottes.. robbed and revid the contre about Derham.

3. To despoil, rob, or forcibly deprive (usually a person) *of* something. (In mod. use chiefly in pa. pple. *reft*.)

c **1275** LAY. 8799 He wolde me vt driue and refe me of þan lifue. *c* **1300** *Harrow. Hell* 119 3ef þou reuest me of myne Y shal reue þe of þyne. *c* **1375** *Sc. Leg. Saints* xix. (*Christopher*) 658 Ane arow..rewyt þe king of ane ee-sycht. *c* **1470** HARDING *Chron.* LXVIII. x, So shall wee reue theim sonest of their life. **1559** SACKVILLE *Induct. Mirr. Mag.* liii, Pale death Enthryllyng it to reue her of her breath. **1567** GOLDING *Ovid's Met.* XII. (1593) 283 Amycus..began To reeve and rob the bridehouse of his furniture. **1610** G. FLETCHER *Christ's Vict.* I. lxviii, Though of present sight her sense were reauen, Yet shee could see the things could not be seen. **1757** GRAY *Bard* 79 Reft of a crown, he yet may share the feast. **1813** SCOTT *Trierm.* III. Introd. i, A wild resemblance we can trace, Though reft of every softer grace. **1884** TENNYSON *Becket* I. iii. 364 We fear that he may reave thee of thine own [eyes].

4. With double object: To take (a thing or person) from (one) by, or as by, robbery or violence; to deprive (one) of (a possession, quality, etc.). ? *Obs.*

The personal object prob. represents an original dative, and in early use is retained when the construction is passive.

c **1200** ORMIN 4470 3iff þu ræfesst me min þing þu ræfesst Godd tin sawle. *Ibid.* 8238 Himm wass þa þe kinedom Forr hise gilltess ræfedd. *c* **1300** *Havelok* 2590 He moun vs..thral maken, and do ful wo Or elles reue us ure liues. *c* **1320** *Sir Tristr.* 1220 þai raft me fowe & griis. *Ibid.* 3304 Mi leman fair and swete A kniʒt haþ reued me. *c* **1374** CHAUCER *Boeth.* IV. met. vii. 147 (Add. MS.) He slouʒ þe lyoun and rafte hym hys skyn. *c* **1440** *Partonope* 3204 A wyne I dranke..Thorwe whiche my wyt was me rafte. **1450–80** tr. *Secreta Secret.* 38 If thou maiste not reve hem her watir..envenyme it. **1561** NORTON & SACK. *Gorboduc* II. i, I meruaile muche what reason leade the kynge..to reue me halfe ye kingdome. **1591** SYLVESTER *Du Bartas* I. i. 723 He reaves him [Job] all his Cattel. **1594** CAREW *Huarte's Exam. Wits* xv. (1596) 274 To say that Eue for her offence was reft that knowledge which she wanted cannot be auouched.

5. To take forcible possession of (something belonging to another); to take away from another for oneself.

c **825** *Vesp. Psalter* lxviii. 5 Ða ic ne reafade, ða ic onlesde. *c* **888** K. ÆLFRED *Boeth.* xiii, Se ðe hit [gold] gaderað & on oðrum reafað. *c* **1000** ÆLFRIC *Hom.* I. 130 Swa hwæt swa he ær on unriht..reafode. *a* **1225** *Ancr. R.* 396 þi luue..is forto sullen, oðer heo is forto reauen & to nimen mid strencðe. *a* **1300** *Cursor M.* 1962 Ete..O nakin worme þat es made, Na o fouxul þat refes his liuelade. *c* **1350** *Will. Palerne* 1824 Bred oþer drinke..redeli i wol it reue & come a ʒein swiþe. *c* **1400** *Ywaine & Gaw.* 2253 My landes haves he robbed and reft, Noght bot this kastel es me left. *c* **1470** HENRY *Wallace* IV. 59 The hors thai reft quhilk suld your harnes ber. **1587** TURBERV. *Trag. T.* (1837) 83 It were a worthie deede..To murther him, and reave his realme. **1609** SKENE *Reg. Maj.* 14 The cattell, or anie other thing thifteouslie stollen or reft. **1768–73** W. COLE in Willis & Clark *Cambridge* (1886) II. 40, I observed all the Brass of Dr. Stokes's Monument reaved, ..except a small Peice. **1808** SCOTT *Marm.* III. Introd. 69 The last, the bitterest pang..For princedoms reft, and scutcheons riven. **1866** SKEAT *Ludlow Castle* I. iii, Crafty foemen long to..reave or spoil The herdsman's care, the peasant's toil.

b. To take away (life, rest, sight, etc.).

c **1330** *Arth. & Merl.* 9088 (Kölbing) þai hem þrewe wiþ spere & kniif & oþer armes to reuen her liif. **1375** BARBOUR *Bruce* III. 715 The wawys reft thar sycht of land. *c* **1440** *Partonope* 239 Let no such thoughtes reve youre rest. **1559** *Mirr. Mag.* (1563) X ij, Who reft my wyts? or howe do I thus lye? **1590** SPENSER *F.Q.* II. i. 17 Sith that false traytour did my honour reave. **1591** —— *M. Hubberd* 34 Talke, that might unquiet fancies reave. *a* **1771** GRAY *Dante* 79 For then Hunger had reft my Eye-sight. **1872** BLACKIE *Lays Highl.* 82 They shot..And reaved his purple life.

c. Const. *from* (a person, etc.), †*of*, *out of* (a place, etc.).

Usually conveying the idea of deprivation (as in a and b), but sometimes merely expressing removal or separation.

c **1200** *Vices & Virtues* 11 An oðer senne, ðe reaueð godes luue of mannes hierte. *a* **1300** *Cursor M.* 28791 To reue a-noþer his right him fra. *c* **1330** *Arth. & Merl.* 4967 (Kölbing) For to haue anon yreued His bodi fram his gentil heued. *c* **1386** CHAUCER *Monk's T.* 111 He golden Apples refte of the dragoun. *c* **1400** *Destr. Troy* 7680 He..The right arme, with a rappe, reft fro þe shuldurs. *c* **1470** HENRY *Wallace* x. 484, I mycht reiff..Fra the thi crowne off this regioun. **1513** DOUGLAS *Æneis* III. iii. 95 The rane and roik reft fra we sicht of hevin. **1590** SPENSER *F.Q.* I. i. 24 From her body..He raft her hatefull heade without remorse. **1606** G. W[OODCOCKE] *Hist. Ivstine* XXXIX. 125 Hauing giuen commaundement to haue the Image of Iupiter reft out of the Temple also. *a* **1638** MEDE *Wks.* (1672) 311 The wicked shall be condemned at the last day, not for reaving the meat from the hungry, but for not feeding their poor brethren. **1825** SCOTT *Talism.* viii, His soul should not have been reft from his body. **1884** TENNYSON *Becket* I. iii, There be among you those that hold Lands reft from Canterbury.

d. With *away*.

1382 WYCLIF *Jer.* I. 11 3ee ful out ioʒen, and grete thingus speken, reuende awei myn eritage. *c* **1400** *Rowland & O.* 561 His schelde a waye it reuede. *c* **1450** *St. Cuthbert* (Surtees) 2648 All his webb þat he weues, A puft of wynde away reues. **1768** BEATTIE *Minstr.* I. xxxvi, Fell chanticleer! who oft hast reft away My fancied good. *a* **1839** PRAED *Poems* (1864) II. 290 The daily labour, and the nightly lamp, Have reft away ..from him The liquid accent and the buoyant limb.

6. To take or carry away (a person) *from* another, *from* earth, *to* heaven, etc.; also *ellipt.* to carry off to heaven; to take *away* from earth or this life. (Also with *soul* as object.)

c **1200** ORMIN 19825 Herodian Filippess wif..þatt fra Filippe ræfedd was..& gifenn till Herode. *a* **1300** *Cursor M.* 17551 He þam said he was be-nummen, 'Reft awai forsoth es he'. **1340** *Ayenb.* 143 [The soul] huanne hi is y-reaued þanne to heuene, hi lokeþ oþe þe erþe uram uer. *c* **1375** *Sc. Leg. Saints* vi. (*Thomas*) 464 þane cumys ded vnwenandly & rewis þame a-wa in hy. *c* **1450** *St. Cuthbert* (Surtees) 6463 þat he was fra þe erde reuyd And in thoght to heuyn heuyd. **1563** *Mirr. Mag.* II. *Compl. Henry Dk. Buckhm.* 126 When the fates had reft that royal prince Edward the fowrth. **1590** GREENE *Orl. Fur.* Wks. (Rtldg.) 106/2 A Fury, sure, worse than Megæra was That reft her son from trusty Pylades. **1637** MILTON *Lycidas* 107 Who hath reft (quoth he) my dearest pledge? **1721** RAMSAY *I'll never leave thee* i, Tho'.. honour should reave me To fields where cannons rair. **1818** SHELLEY *Rev. Islam* VIII. xxiv, We are wretched slaves, Who from their..native land Are reft. *a* **1873** LYTTON *Pausanias* II. iv, Wouldst thou see my daughter reft from me by force.

†**b.** To deliver or rescue by carrying off. *Obs.* (Also with double object, as in 4.)

a **1225** *Juliana* 68 Bihald me ant help me ant of þisse reade leye ref me [and] arude me. *a* **1340** HAMPOLE *Psalter* xvii. 20 He reft me out fra my faes stalworthest. *c* **1400** *Destr. Troy* 6838 Let vs reskew the Renke, refe hym his fos! **1550** *Reg. Privy Council Scot.* I. 97 The said Capitane Skenestoun.. reft the said Schir Robert fra thaim efter that thai had takin him. *a* **1649** DRUMM. OF HAWTH. *James III* Wks. (1711) 56 If found guilty, they should not be reft from justice by strong hand.

†**c.** To take away, remove, *from* some condition, activity, etc. *Obs.*

c **1340** HAMPOLE *Prose Tr.* 40 It reuys the fra þi slepe on nyghtys. **1377** LANGL. *P. Pl.* B. XIV. 132 Allas! þat ricchesse shal reue and robbe mannes soule Fram þe loue of owre lorde. *c* **1381** CHAUCER *Parl. Foules* 86 The derke nyʒt That revith bestis from here besynesse. **1621** BRATHWAIT *Nat. Embassie*, etc. (1877) 188 How hard it was from error to be reau'd. **1665** DRYDEN & HOWARD *Ind. Queen* V. i, 'Till fit for arms, I reaved you from your sport, To train your youth in the Peruvian court.

†**d.** *Sc.* To snatch or lift *up* (in *lit.* and *fig.* senses). *Obs.*

1561 WINȜET *Cert. Tract.* Wks. (S.T.S.) I. 8 Gospellaris and cunning in Scripture..reft vp in hie curiositie of questionis. **1715** RAMSAY *Christ's Kirk Gr.* I. xii, The wyves cam furth, and up they reft him, And fand lyfe in the loune.

reave, *v.*[2] Now *dial.* or *arch.* Forms: *Inf.* 4 **reue**, 6 **reve**, 6–7 **reave**, 7, 9 **reive**, 9 **reeve**. *Pa. t.* 3 **reafde, refde**, 4 **raft**, 5 *Sc.* **reft**. *Pa. pple.* 6 **refte**, 9 **reft**. [App. a confusion of prec. with RIVE *v.* In mod. literary use only in the preterite form *reft*.]

†**1.** *intr.* To break in pieces; to burst. *Obs.*

a **1225** *Juliana* 58 An engel..reat to þat hweol swa þat hit al to refde [*Bodl. Ms.* to reafde]. *c* **1560** *Disobed. Child* (Percy Soc.) 6 Though ye crye tyll ye reve asunder I wyll not meddle with such a matter.

2. *trans.* To tear; to split, cleave.

a **1300** *Cursor M.* 4490 A mikel rauen mi basket hent, Aboute mi heued he raft and rent. *c* **1375** *Sc. Leg. Saints* xxvii. (*Machor*) 251 Scho..with hyr newis reft hir brest. **1393** LANGL. *P. Pl.* C. IV. 203 Religion hue al to-reueþ and out of ruele to lybbe. **1578** T. PROCTOR *Gorg. Gallery* in *Heliconia* (1815) I. 70 My sighes from sobbing harte Doth reaue my brest in twayne. **1590** R. PAYNE *Descr. Irel.* (1841) 6 Timber..so good to reaue, that a simple workeman with a Brake axe will cleaue a greate Oke. **1660** STANLEY *Hist. Philos.* IX. (1701) 369/1 Finding a great Tree with Wedges in it, he set his Hands and Feet to it, trying to reive it asunder. **1814** SCOTT *Ld. of Isles* III. xxvii, The patriot's burning thought..Of England's roses reft and torn. **1887** *Pall Mall G.* 11 Nov. 7/1 The rock was reft asunder.

absol. **1895** CROCKETT *Men of Moss-Hags* xxxii. 235 [A dog] ruggin' an' reevin' at the hinderlands o' him.

†**3.** To pluck or pull *up*. *Obs.*

a **1400–50** *Alexander* 409 þis diuinour..3ede him furthe ..herbis to seche, Reft þam vp be þe rotes. **1558** PHAER *Æneid* II. C i b, Against them Troians down the towres and tops of houses rold, And rafters vp they reaue.

†**reave**, *v.*[3] *Obs. rare.* ? var. of RAVE *v.*[3]

1615 SIR G. HELWYS in *Buccleuch MSS.* (Hist. MSS. Comm.) I. 161 Whether..I had got any inkling of this foresaid foul act or not, and if I had, whether he could perceive any desire in me to have it reaved into or not. **1643** HORN & ROB. *Gate Lang. Unl.* xlvi. §504 Sometimes also hee rips the seams, and reaveth [ravelleth out] the threds.

reave, obs. Sc. f. RAVE *v.*[1], var. REEVE *v.*

reavel, obs. form of RAVEL.

†**reavel-ravel.** *Sc. Obs.*⁻¹ A rigmarole.

a **1689** W. CLELAND *Poems* (1697) 107 Like some Lawyers making Speeches, He..Half singing vents this Reavel Ravel.

reaven, obs. Sc. form of RAVEN *sb.*[1]

reaver, reiver (ˈriːvə(r)). Forms: α. 1 **réafere**, (**hréaf-, réof-**), 2–3 **ræuere**, (3 **-are**), 2–4 **reuere**, 4–5 **reuour**, 4–6 **reu-, rever**, 5–6 *Sc.* **reu-, revar(e**, 6–7 **reauer**, 6– **reaver**. Also 4 **refar**, 5 *Sc.* **reffayr**. β. 4 **reyuour**, 6 **reyvar**. γ. *Sc.* 5–6 **reiffar**, 6 **reifar**, 7 **reivar**, 6, 9 **reiver**, 9 **riever**. [OE. *réafere*, agent-n. f. *réafian* to REAVE *v.*[1] = OFris. *râvere*, MDu. *rover* (Du. *roover*), MLG. *rôver*, OHG. *roubari* (MHG. *roubære, rouber*, G. *räuber*, †*rauber*). MSw. *rövare* (Sw. *röfvare*), MDa. *rövere* (Da. *röver*), and Icel. *raufari* (13th c.), *reyfari* (*c* 1400) are from MLG. *rôver*: see note to REAVE *v.*[1], and cf. Eng. ROVER.

In mod. use the normal Eng. spelling *reaver* is less usual than the Sc. *reiver* (or *riever*), brought into literary use by Scott.]

1. A robber or plunderer; a marauder, raider. Occas. with *of*. Also *transf.* or *fig.*

α. *c* **888** K. ÆLFRED *Boeth.* xxxvii. §4 ʒif þu on hwilcum men onʒitst þæt he bið ʒitsere & reafere. *c* **950** *Lindisf. Gosp.* Luke xxii. 52 Suæ to hreafere [*Rushw.* reofere] ʒie cuomon mið suordum. *c* **1000** ÆLFRIC *Hom.* II. 330 Sceaðan & reaferas, oððe reðe manslaʒan. *c* **1154** *O.E. Chron.* (Laud MS.) an. 1137 Al þe tunscipe fluʒæn for heom, wenden ðæt hi wæron ræueres. *c* **1230** *Hali Meid.* 29 þeoues hit stelen ham, reaueres hit robbeð. *a* **1300** *Cursor M.* 2205 þer wit was he [Nimrod]..Reuer and man-queller gret. *c* **1400** *Apol. Loll.* 77 Clerkis now are fals witnes aȝen þer lawis, & þefis, & refars, & fals intrewsars. *c* **1440** *Gesta Rom.* lxix. 386 (Add. MS.) The prophete seith, wo shall be Robbers and revers of pore mennes goodes. **1559** SACKVILLE *Induct. Mirr. Mag.* xlii, [Sleep] Reuer of sight, and yet in whom we see Thinges oft that tide. **1583** STOCKER *Civ. Warres Lowe C.* I. 6 b, The reauers and robbers of all churches and images. **1615** JACKSON *Creed* IV. viii. §2 [Bodies politic] the one hath reavers the other only plain thieves. **1721** KELLY *Scot. Prov.* 284 Reavers should not be Ruers. **1846** SIR W. HAMILTON *Diss.* in *Reid's Wks.* 890 *note*, This paper is remarkable for the sagacity which tracks the footsteps of the literary reaver.

β. *c* **1380** *Sir Ferumb.* 1798 For þov mayntenest þef reyuours,..To gon aboute & robby ous. **1525** LD. BERNERS *Froiss.* II. xxiii, There is nother Englyshe, nor French, nor robbers, nor reyvars, yᵗ dothe them any hurte.

γ. **1479** *Barbour's Bruce* XIV. 441 (Edin. MS.) The fyscher ..said, 'Reiffar, thow mon her out'. **1553** *Reg. Privy Council Scot.* I. 148 The said Capitane of Norame reiffar of the said fyscheing. *a* **1578** LINDESAY (Pitscottie) *Chron. Scot.* (S.T.S.) I. 66 To theif and reiver he was ane sicker targe. *a* **1615** *Brieue Cron. Erlis Ross* (1850) 11 Scap-thriftis, alias reivars and sorneris. **1725** RAMSAY *Gentle Sheph.* IV. ii, Carried by some reiver's hand, Far frae his wishes. **1824** SCOTT *Redgauntlet* ch. xi, Harry was none of your bold-speaking, ranting reivers. **1880** McCARTHY *Own Times* III. xxxii. 62 The chiefs of Oudh were reivers and bandits; the king was the head reiver and bandit.

attrib. **1864** J. C. ATKINSON *Stanton Grange* 292 A gun might warn the reiver crow to be less audacious.

†**2.** A pirate, sea-robber (cf. *sea-reaver*). *Obs.*

c **1375** *Sc. Leg. Saints* xxi. (*Clement*) 305 þare come in þe sithtware Reueris sayland. **1436** *Pol. Poems* (Rolls) II. 164 The commodytes of Pety Brytayne, wyth here revers on the see. *c* **1470** HENRY *Wallace* IX. 87 The best wer man in se is ws beforn, .. The Rede Reffayr thai call him.

†**'reavery.** *Obs.* Forms: 3-5 reu-, revery(e, 5 *Sc.* reuere. [f. REAVE *v.*^{1} + -ERY. Cf. MDu. *roverij* (Du. *rooverij*), MLG. *rôverîe*, G. *raub-*, *räuberei*, MSw. *rov-*, *röveri* (Sw. *röfveri*), Da. *röveri*, obs. Icel. *reyfari* (1453).] Robbery.

1297 R. GLOUC. (Rolls) 4000 þou .. mid þi reuerye Rauissest france & oþer londes. *c* **1330** R. BRUNNE *Chron. Wace* (Rolls) 5827 Longe dured þat reuery [*v.r.* robberie]. **1456** SIR G. HAYE *Law Arms* (S.T.S.) 3 Weris discensiouns thiftis and reveryis. *c* **1490** *Plumpton Corr.* (Camden) 81 Such other as .. have made revery and withdrawen goods, contrayrie to the Kings lawes.

reaving, reiving ('riːvɪŋ), *vbl. sb.* [f. as prec. + -ING^{1}.] The action of REAVE *v.*^{1}

In recent use chiefly in Sc. form *reiving*.

c **1122** *O.E. Chron.* (Laud MS.) an. 1116 Wurdon manega unrada & ræfunga. *c* **1205** LAY. 2647 þes wes þe aereste king, þe ferde vt to ræuing [*v.r.* reuing], þat ouer sæ wende. *a* **1300** *Cursor M.* 28797 Vr lauerd .. wil na gift of oker, reuing, ne o thift. **1387** TREVISA *Higden* (Rolls) VII. 495 Al þe ȝere was in þe lond robbynge and manslauȝter, and revynge. *c* **1440** *Promp. Parv.* 432/1 Revynge of reste, *inquietacio*. **1567** TURBERV. *Epit.* etc. 101 For it a Friendly hart .. In value doe not passe The Ring, you may reprooue The reauing of the same. **1596** DALRYMPLE tr. *Leslie's Hist. Scot.* III. 187 Trubling the west seyes in thift, ruging and reiueng. **1851** SIR F. PALGRAVE *Norm. & Eng.* I. viii. 684 They must help themselves .. by robbing and reiving.

reaving, reiving ('riːvɪŋ), *ppl. a.* [f. as prec. + -ING^{2}.] That robs or reaves.

c **1000** ÆLFRIC *Saints' Lives* I. 328 Hi synd wiþ-innan reafiȝende wulfas. **1500-20** DUNBAR *Poems* lix. 2 A refying sone of rakyng Muris. **1816** SCOTT *Old Mort.* iv, The twa reiving loons drave the cow frae the gudewife. **1828** —— *F.M. Perth* viii, A party of reiving night-walkers. **1858-61** J. BROWN *Horæ Subs.* (1882) III. 417 His ancestors were of the sturdy border stock, reiving pastoral lairds.

re-a'vouch, *v.* [RE- 5 a.] To avouch again.

1645 MILTON *Tetrach.* 70 (*1 Cor. vii.*) That this heer spoken by Paul .. cannot be a command, these reavouch.

re-a'vow, *v.* [RE- 5 a.] *trans.* To avow again.

1654 H. L'ESTRANGE *K. Chas. I* (1655) 118 Upon the evidence formerly given in by the Countesse, and re-avowed then by her, .. [they] were found guilty.

rea'wake, *v.* [RE- 5 a.] *intr.* and *trans.* To awake again.

1831 T. HOPE *Ess. Origin Man* I. 11 When from the sleep of death .. I again reawake to a new life. **1863** W. PHILLIPS *Speeches* iii. 53 Prophets .. to .. reawake the people to the great ideas that are constantly fading out of our minds. *a* **1873** S. WILBERFORCE *Ess.* (1874) II. 186 The great questions .. seem .. to have suddenly reawoke amongst us.

Hence **rea'waking** *ppl. a.*

1848 LYTTON *Harold* XI. viii, William's re-awaking and ready intellect.

rea'waken, *v.* [RE- 5 a.] *trans.* and *intr.* To awaken again.

1846-55 [see below]. **1860** PUSEY *Min. Proph.* 35 By God .. alone the longing for Himself is kept alive or reawakened in His creature. **1899** *Pop. Sci. Monthly* LV. 62 The consciousness of the truth .. reawakens.

Hence **rea'wakened** *ppl. a.*; **rea'wakening** *vbl. sb.* and *ppl. a.*; **rea'wakenment**.

1846 BP. BLOMFIELD in *Life* (1863) I. ix. 247 We cannot afford to wait for the re-awakened liberality of the legislature. **1855** MILMAN *Lat. Chr.* XIV. iii. (1864) IX. 152 A sign of the reawakening life of the human mind. **1862** *Q. Rev.* Oct. 465 Some extreme views which have disfigured the great reawakening of the Church of England. **1886** *Gd. Words* 602 The overthrow of Darius at Marathon is not unnaturally marked by a reawakenment of piety.

reawe, obs. f. ROW.

reawme, obs. f. REALM.

reaws: see REAL *sb.*^{2}

reawte, obs. f. REALTY^{1}.

reazed, variant of REESED *a.*, rancid.

reb^{1}. Chiefly *U.S.* Abbreviation of REBEL *sb.*^{1} 1 e; cf. *Johnny Reb* s.v. JOHNNY, JOHNNIE 3. Also *attrib.*

1862 in Post *Soldier's Lett.* II. xxxii. 90 As soon as the rebs saw our red breeches (the Zouaves) coming through the woods they skedaddled. **1886** *Century Mag.* June 316/1 You will ride right into the Rebs. **1897** KIPLING *Captains Courageous* iii. 62 Earnin' my bread on the deep waters, an' dodgin' Reb privateers. **1904** —— *Traffics & Discoveries* 31 Then we got into the Colony [*sc.* Orange Free State], and the rebs—ministers mostly and schoolmasters—came round the cars with fruit and sympathy and texts. **1909** 'O. HENRY' *Options* (1916) 81 The alleged aristocratic superiority of a 'reb' ought to be visible to him at once. **1916** 'TAFFRAIL' *Pincher Martin* v. 73 They wanted me to order the rebs. to shove off. **1928** S. V. BENÉT *John Brown's Body* 181 'Hello, Charley,' he said, 'Where you been?' .. 'Out hearing the Rebs,' he said. **1938** J. DANIELS *Southerner Discovers South* xxxv. 346 The boy .. insisted in the hospital that he was the best alligator catcher on the coast of Georgia. Perhaps he was. Maybe still one Reb can beat ten Yankees. **1947** *Sierra Club Bull.* May 80 The stars and stripes, the flag of our now united country raised in honor of our visit, and I, an old battle-scarred and weather-worn Reb. **1963** *Amer. Speech* XXXVIII. 45 *Reb*, a Southern driver or a Southern trucking firm. **1979** S. SHEPPARD *Four Hundred* i. 4 A certain scheme for separating some of the Rebs from their money.

reb^{2} (rɛb). Also **rebb** and with capital initial. [Yiddish, *abbrev.* of *rebbe* REBBE.] A traditional Jewish courtesy title prefixed to a man's first name or surname.

1882 [see KEHILLA]. **1892** I. ZANGWILL *Childr. Ghetto* I. 147 'Well, how goes it, Reb Moshé?' said Reb Shemuel .., noticing Moses loitering. He called him 'Reb' out of courtesy and in acknowledgement of his piety. The real 'Reb' was a fine figure of a man. **1932** L. GOLDING *Magnolia Street* I. v. 84 The beard of Reb Berel, the beadle, was in attendance. **1967** C. POTOK *Chosen* i. 15 Reb Saunders ordered them never to lose because it would shame their yeshiva. **1975** *Publishers Weekly* 3 Feb. 75/3 A ragged stranger stands by the door of the synagogue... The boy whispers to the woman that the stranger, reb Naftoli, is a *badchen*, a merrymaker, who speaks in rhymes. **1978** I. B. SINGER *Shosha* ix. 170 We had a preacher in our family—Reb Zekele Preacher, they called him.

reb, obs. Sc. and north. form of RIB.

rebab (rɪ'bæb). Also **rabab(a, rabap, rebaba, rubabah,** etc. [a. colloq. Arab. *rebāb*, classical Arab. *rabāb* in the same sense: cf. RIBIBE *sb.*] A plucked or bowed stringed instrument of Arabian origin, now in use in North Africa and the Middle East, and among the Islamic populations of the Indian sub-continent, Malaysia, and Indonesia.

1738 [see OUD]. **1802** *Jrnl. F. Horneman's Trav.* iii. 72 The song of these Fezzan girls is Soudanic. Their musical instrument is called *rhababe*. **1836** E. W. LANE *Acct. Manners & Customs Mod. Egyptians* II. v. 73 A curious kind of viol, called rabab, is much used by poor singers, as an accompaniment to the voice. **1856** R. F. BURTON *Personal Narr. Pilgrimage to El-Medinah* III. ii. 76 They have the one-stringed Rubabah, or guitar. **1925** *Blackw. Mag.* Feb. 217/2 Zakka Khel the *Subedar* played cunningly, on the rebab, an instrument like a mandoline. **1929** F. STARK *Let.* 22 Dec. (1974) I. 226 Mahmud .. got his *rebaba*, played with the fingers and a bow on one string, and they [*sc.* Bedouin tribesmen in Iraq] showed us the four different modes of their music. **1937** M. COVARRUBIAS *Island of Bali* (1972) viii. 213 There are other instruments, such as .. the two-string violin (*rebab*), which are used mainly as a lead for the melody. **1958** O. CAROE *Pathans* xix. 309 There were performers who chanted to the *rabap*. **1960** G. E. EVANS *Horse in Furrow* xiii. 177 In Arabia the poet singer to the 'rebab' (lute with one string and a bow) is a recognised authority who dare not for his life deviate by a word from the known facts. **1967** I. DIQS *Bedouin Boyhood* xi. 104 Long minutes later I heard some broken tunes sent up by the *rababa*. **1972** M. SHEPPARD *Taman Indera* iii. 57 (*caption*) A [Malay] maker of musical instruments, working on a *rebab*. **1976** *Listener* 17 June 784/2 A musician in eastern Afghanistan who played a rebab, a bowed string instrument he had made out of a biscuit tin and a broom handle.

reback (riː'bæk), *v.* [f. RE- 5 a + BACK *v.* 2.] *trans.* To replace the damaged spine of (a binding or book). So **re'backed** *ppl. a.*, **re'backing** *vbl. sb.*

1901 D. COCKERELL *Bookbinding* xxii. 305 Re-backing. Bindings that have broken joints may be re-backed. **1952** J. CARTER *ABC for Book-Collectors* 150 Re-backed. This means that the binding of the book has been given a new backstrip or spine. **1970** *Bodl. Libr. Rec.* VIII. 192 Although it [*sc.* an eighteenth-century New Testament] has been rebacked and repaired .. it is now very worn. **1981** *Sotheby's Catal. Printed Bks.* 16 Mar. 34, 179 Lambarde (W.), Dictionarium Angliae Topographicum & Historicum, portrait, calf, rebacked, 1730.

rebaik, variant of REBALK *v. Obs.*

†**rebail,** *v. Obs.*$^{-1}$ [a. OF. *rebailler*, f. *re-* RE- + *bailler* BAIL *v.*^{1}] *trans.* To hand over again.

1601 F. TATE *Househ. Ord. Edw. II* §66 (1876) 48 If it happen the same wines, or any parte of them, be not spent before the kinge departe .. then let them be rebailed, redelivered to the chief purveiour to carry or keep them.

re'bait, *v.* [RE- 5 a.] *trans.* To bait (a fishhook or line) again. Also *absol.*

1848 *Life Normandy* (1863) I. 164 During the night tide, when they have to rebait their lines. **1893** *Outing* (U.S.) XXII. 96/1 Quickly disengaging our respective hooks .., we rebaited and cast out again.

rebait, obs. form of REBATE *v.*

rebak, variant of REBALK *v. Obs.*

re'bake, *v.* [RE- 5 a.] *trans.* To bake again.

1727 BRADLEY *Fam. Dict.* s.v. *Sallet*, Re-bake 'em a second time, till they are Stone hard. **1834** G. BENNETT *Wanderings* II. 212 It is then resifted at another bench and rebaked.

rebald(e, obs. Sc. (and north.) ff. RIBALD; obs. f. REBEL *a.*

rebaldaill: see RIBALDAIL.

rebaldrie, obs. Sc. form of RIBALDRY.

†**rebalk,** *v. Sc. Obs.* Also 6 **rebak, -baik.** [Of obscure etym.] *trans.* To assail with abuse or reproaches.

c **1450** HOLLAND *Howlat* 915 All birdis he rebalkit that wald him nocht bowe. **1535** STEWART *Cron. Scot.* II. 85 The Britis all richt bitterlie and bald Rebalkit him .. Of tha wordis that he said. *a* **1578** LINDESAY (Pitscottie) *Chron. Scot.* (S.T.S.) II. 83 Everie ane of thame rebakit ane wther witht ewill dispossit wordis. **1596** DALRYMPLE tr. *Leslie's Hist. Scot.* II. 139 Silius quha befor sa vncourteouslie had rebaikit Reuther wᵗ sa rude, rasche, and rouch wordes.

reban (riː'bæn). [RE- 5 a.] A second or additional ban.

1845 S. AUSTIN *Ranke's Hist. Ref.* II. 185 He forbade the assembly, on pain of being found guilty of high treason, and incurring sentence of ban and reban. **1873-4** DIXON *Two Queens* II. VIII. v. 82 He .. has commanded that ban and reban be proclaimed within his countries.

reban, obs. Sc. form of RIBBON.

†**re'band,** *v. Obs. rare.* [f. RE- + BAND *v.*^{2}, or ad. F. *rebander* (Cotgr.) in same sense.] *trans.* To throw back, retort.

1588 SIR W. STANLEY *Brief Disc. Dr. Allen's Sedit. Drifts* 95 Slanderous defamations .. most truely and iustlye refuted, and rebanded vpon himselfe and his partie. **1600** W. WATSON *Decacordon* (1602) 348 [The Jesuits] reband this surmised assertion with the speeches which some great persons should vse.

re'bandy, *v. rare*$^{-1}$. [RE- 2 b.] *trans.* To bandy or toss back again.

1650 R. STAPYLTON *Strada's Low-C. Warres* VI. 2 From thence being rebandied to his country .. he bounded againe into the Belgick Tumults.

re'banish, *v.* [RE- 5 a; cf. F. *rebannir* (Cotgr.).] *trans.* To banish again. Hence **re'banished** *ppl. a.*

1611 FLORIO, *Ribandito*, rebanished or proclaimed againe. **1617** BP. HALL *Quo Vadis?* §15 No bulwarke of lawes .. can keepe our rebanished fugitiues from returning.

rebant, obs. form of RIBBON.

rebaptisant. *rare*$^{-0}$. [a. F. *rebaptisant* (18th c.).] = REBAPTIST.

1727-41 CHAMBERS *Cycl.* s.v., The Anabaptists are re-baptisants, inasmuch as they baptize those at maturity, who had been before baptized in childhood.

rebaptism (riː'bæptɪz(ə)m). [RE- 5 a; cf. REBAPTIZE *v.*] A second baptism; rebaptizing.

1795 BURKE *Lett., to Dr. Hussey* (1844) IV. 284 Re-baptism you won't allow, but truly it would not be amiss for the Christian world to be re-christened. **1850** J. E. MIDDLETON *Lect. Eccl. Hist.* 44 Disputes respecting the rebaptism of those who had been baptized by heretics.

Hence **rebap'tismal** *a.*

1892 *Daily News* 3 Aug. 5/2 In the re-baptismal certificate he was called the son of George Large.

†**re'baptist.** *Obs.* [RE- 5 a.] One who baptizes again, or advocates a second baptism; *spec.* an Anabaptist.

1651 C. CARTWRIGHT *Cert. Relig.* I. 49 Cyprian [was] a rebaptist. **1673** T. JOLLY *Note-bk.* (Chetham Soc.) 13 Shee was cast out of the church of Duckenfeild long since, and then fell in with the Rebaptists. **1738** [G. SMITH] *Cur. Relat.* I. ii. 138 Several of the Re-baptists were apprehended.

†**rebapti'zation.** *Obs.* [a. late L. *rebaptizātio* (4th c.): cf. REBAPTIZE *v.*] The act or practice of baptizing again.

Very common *c* 1570-1700, esp. with ref. to the view, held by St. Cyprian and opposed by Pope Stephen I, that those baptized by heretics ought to be baptized again before being admitted to the Church.

1570 FOXE *A. & M.* (ed. 2) 98/2 Agrippinus, which also was yᵉ fyrst author of rebaptization. **1593** BELL *Motives conc. Romish Faith* (1605) 49 Pope Stephanus .. defined flatlie against rebaptization. **1680** BAXTER *Answ. Stillingfl.* 7 It must be acknowledg'd .. that Re-ordination is an uncouth thing ..; and put usually into the same predicament .. with Re-baptization. **1780** in Kippis *Biog. Brit.* II. 315 *note*, This extraordinary Baptism of theirs [laymen] was counted valid, without any need of Re-baptization.

transf. **1617** DONNE *Serm.* cxlvii. VI. 10 Tears which should be thy Souls Rebaptization for thy Sins. **1623** BARGRAVE *Serm. bef. Ho. Comm.* (1624) 14 This Bathe of Mary Magdalens repentance .. is a kind of Rebaptization, giuing strength and effect to the first washing.

rebaptize (riːbæp'taɪz), *v.* [a. late L. *rebaptizāre*: cf. F. *rebaptiser* (14th c.).]

1. *trans.* To baptize again or anew.

Common *c* 1550-1650: see note to prec.

1460 CAPGRAVE *Chron.* 77 The Donatistes sey that .. thoo that schuld come to her secte must be rebaptized. **1540** *Act 32 Hen. VIII*, If they [infants] be baptysed that they ought to be rebaptised when they come to lawful age. **1635** PAGITT *Christianogr.* I. iii. (1636) 165 They are accused of rebaptizing themselves yeerely. **1699** BURNET *39 Art.* xxiii. (1700) 261 We do not Annul such Baptisms, nor Rebaptise Persons so Baptised. **1736** CHANDLER *Hist. Persec.* 332 Whosoever was discovered to re-baptize any person, should forfeit twenty dollars. **1817** BYRON *Beppo* xcviii, His wife received, the patriarch re-baptized him. **1865** PUSEY *Truth Eng. Ch.* 34 The question of rebaptizing heretics was settled by the Council of Arles.

absol. **1597** HOOKER *Eccl. Pol.* v. lxii. §6 The Bishop .. yet durst not aduenture to rebaptize. **1678** *Lively Orac.* vi. §11 You say 'tis lawful to rebaptize, we say 'tis not lawful.

b. *transf.* and *fig.*

1635 QUARLES *Embl.* III. i. 125 You whose better thoughts are newly born, And (rebaptiz'd with holy fire) can [etc.]. *a***1711** KEN *Hymnotheo* Poet. Wks. 1721 III. 34 While he rebaptiz'd himself in Tears. **1742** YOUNG *Nt. Th.* IV. 738 Reason rebaptiz'd me when adult. **1818** BYRON *Mazeppa* xiv, With a temporary strength My stiffen'd limbs were re-baptized. **1878** B. TAYLOR *Deukalion* I. iii. 29 They consent to see Themselves in sacred marble rebaptized.

2. To give a new name to; to name afresh.

1596 RALEIGH *Discov. Gviana* 24 Baraquan farther down is also rebaptized by the name of Orenoque. **1646** SIR T. BROWNE *Pseud. Ep.* 101 What is practised by many is.. relinquishing their proper appellations, to re-baptise them [herbs] by the names of Saints [etc.]. **1670** MILTON *Hist. Eng.* III. Wks. (1851) 106 Of any Paganism.. we read not, or that Pelagianism was rebaptiz'd. **1828** *Lights & Shades* II. 142 Every misnamed 'gentleman' who reads this proposal for re-baptizing him. **1852** THACKERAY *Esmond* II. xiii, That name, with which sorrow had rebaptized her.

Hence **rebap'tized** *ppl. a.*

1620 QUARLES *Div. Poems, Jonah* (1638) 34 The voice of heavens high Commander.. Came downe.. to Jonah new-born Man, To re-baptized Jonah. **1657** AUSTEN *Fruit Trees* II. 192 Some are for the Episcopal way,.. some for the Rebaptized way.

rebap'tizer. Also 6 rebaptisour. [f. prec. + -ER: cf. F. *rebaptiseur* (1532).] One who rebaptizes; a rebaptist, Anabaptist.

1552 HULOET, *Anabaptistes*.. signifieth rebaptisoures. *c***1645** HOWELL *Lett.* IV. xxix, There were Adamites in former times and rebaptizers. **1651** BAXTER *Inf. Bapt.* 148 This man continued a most zealous re-baptizer many years. **1721** in BAILEY. **1823** CRABB *Technol. Dict.* s.v. *Anabaptists*, They are called Anabaptists, that is 'Rebaptizers'.

rebap'tizing, *vbl. sb.* [f. as prec. + -ING[1].] The action of the vb. REBAPTIZE.

1579 FULKE *Heskins' Parl.* 414 The matter of rebaptising. *a***1631** DONNE *Let. to C'tess Bedford*, From need of tears he will defend your soul Or make a rebaptizing of one tear. **1684** BAXTER *Answ. Theol. Dial.* 2 What if Rebaptizing prove a Sin? **1860** FROUDE *Hist. Eng.* V. 298 He would have no conventicles, no rebaptisings [etc.].

re-bar ('riːbɑː(r)). *U.S.* [f. RE(INFORCING *ppl. a.* + BAR *sb.*[1]] A steel reinforcing rod in concrete.

1961 *Publ. Amer. Dial. Soc.* XXXVI. 29 *Re-bar*,.. abbreviated term for reinforcing steel, which is used to strengthen nearly all concrete structures. **1974** *Spartanburg* (S. Carolina) *Herald* 24 Apr. A1/6 Reinforcing steel bars, known in the industry as re-bars, are used to reinforce concrete in the construction of highways, bridges, buildings and other structures. **1979** *Civil Engineering* Nov. 39/2 A rebar bolt has exponential load transfer characteristics.

re,barbari'zation. [f. next + -ATION.] The fact or condition of being rebarbarized.

1840 MILMAN *Hist. Chr.* I. 130 The comparative rebarbarisation of the human race. **1949** WELLEK & WARREN *Theory of Lit.* 340 For the 'rebarbarization' of literature, cf. the brilliant article, 'Literature' by Max Lerner and Edwin Mims.

rebarbarize (riː'bɑːbəraɪz), *v.* [RE- 5 b.] *trans.* To reduce again to barbarism. Also *absol.*

1798 W. TAYLOR in *Monthly Rev.* XXV. 567 A love of military achievement, which tends to rebarbarize. **1807** SOUTHEY *Espriella's Lett.* (1808) II. 109 Nations can never take too many precautions against the possibility of being rebarbarized. **1842** BISCHOFF *Woollen Manuf.* II. 104 If the object was to rebarbarise the country, the proposition.. would be well calculated to attain that end.

Hence **re'barbarizing** *vbl. sb.* and *ppl. a.*

1804 W. TAYLOR in *Ann. Rev.* II. 692 Destructive and re-barbarizing actions. **1807** HAZLITT *Pol. Ess.* (1819) 406 The re-barbarising and the re-enslaving the country.

re'barbative, *a.* [a. F. *rébarbatif, -ive* (14th c.), f. *barbe* beard.] Repellent, forbidding; unattractive, dull; unpleasant, objectionable.

1892 *Sat. Rev.* 12 Nov. 571/1 It is not very clear why Sir Robert Coke.. bestows so much trouble and time on this very rebarbative lady. **1927** *Observer* 1 May 20 The small minority that is not put off by the dry and rebarbative quality of the tuition. **1946** BEERBOHM *Mainly on Air* 67 Even A. B. Walkley.. found Ibsen rather rebarbative. **1958** I. MURDOCH *Bell* iv. 48 Still, everyone appeared to be extremely nice, except that that Dr. Greenfield man was a trifle rebarbative. (This was a word which Toby had recently learnt at school and could not now conceive of doing without.) **1958** J. PRESS *Chequer'd Shade* i. 12 Unless he commands sufficient poetic authority to compel the general acceptance of his minted coinage his work will inevitably be judged rebarbative and obscure. **1963** *Listener* 7 Mar. 436/1 Some rebarbative club member does seem to have opened one or two windows in the smoking-room. **1971** P. D. JAMES *Shroud for Nightingale* iii. 63 Her face matched her personality, rebarbative and defensive. **1976** *Gramophone* Aug. 266/1 An accessible musical language can be equally deceptive and pose as many (though of course different) problems as an entirely novel and rebarbative idiom.

Hence **re'barbatively** *adv.*; **re'barbativeness**; **rebarba'tivity.**

1947 I. BROWN *Say Word* 102 Is Max our only dealer in rebarbativity? **1966** *Punch* 16 Nov. 754/3 A veritable drummer boy, all knobbly North Country rebarbativeness and almost incomprehensible obsolete dialect. **1968** I. MURDOCH *Nice & Good* vii. 57 Beyond Uncle Theo were some alien holiday-makers,.. of whom this part of the beach happily attracted few, because of its rebarbatively stony nature. **1975** M. AMIS *Dead Babies* lvii. 214 During the Americans' twenty-minute absence from the sitting-room Celia joined in her husband's wholly successful attempt.. to moderate Roxeanne's rebarbativeness to the odd aside. **1976** *Listener* 22 Apr. 495/1 A rejection of formal logic and with it of a rebarbatively technical foundation and medium for philosophical thinking.

rebarbere, obs. form of RHUBARB *sb.*

†**rebarri'cado,** *v. Obs.* In 7 -oe. [RE- 5 a.] *trans.* To barricade anew.

1655 tr. *Com. Hist. Francion* I. 15 The cowardly Clownes.. going all away, gave the besieged time enough to re-barricadoe their Avenues.

†**re'barter,** *v. Obs.*[−1] [RE- 5 a.] *trans.* To give in return or exchange.

1616 J. LANE *Cont. Sqr's. T.* viii. 220 All quarters.. chaungd wordes for bloes, and thrustes for thrustes rebarters.

†**rebash,** *v. Obs.*[−1] In 5 -bassh. [a. F. *rabaisser* to bring or come down (13th c. in Littré): see RE- and ABASH *v.*] *intr.* To descend.

1481 CAXTON *Myrr.* III. viii. 147 Whan he [the sun] re-basshith and declyneth he maketh the wynter to bygynne.

†**rebat.** *Sc. Obs.* [ad. F. *rabat*: cf. RABAT *sb.*[2]] A collar.

1657 *Sp. Fife Laird* in J. Watson *Coll. Scots Poems* (1706) I. 30 Rebats, Ribands, Bands, and Ruffs, Lapbends, Shag-bands, Cuffs and Muffs.

rebat, obs. form of REBATE *v.*, RYBAT.

rebat(e, varr. RABAT *v.*

rebata, variant of REBATO. *Obs.*

rebate ('riːbeɪt, rɪ'beɪt), *sb.*[1] [ad. F. *rabat*, sb. f. *rabattre* REBATE *v.*[1]] A deduction from a sum of money to be paid, a discount; also, a repayment, drawback.

1656 H. PHILLIPS *Purch. Patt.* (1676) 103 What is the rebate out of 500 pound due 6 months hence, to be paid at present? **1694** LUTTRELL *Brief Rel.* (1857) III. 332 Such as subscribe before Sunday will be allowed 50*s.* per cent. rebate. **1727–41** CHAMBERS *Cycl.*, *Rebate, Rebatement*, in commerce, a term much used at Amsterdam for a discount or abatement in the price of certain commodities. **1882** *Contemp. Rev.* Aug. 234 The company gives the settler a rebate, or payment back, of 5*s.* for every acre of land so improved. **1891** *Law Times* XCII. 94/1 The company.. had made payments in advance under its agreement without receiving any discount or rebate. **1955** *Times* 10 May 15/3 An interesting feature of German price lists for the outside world is the appearance of rebates to shipbuilders—rebates for indirect exports, which recall the cartel. **1957** CLARK & GOTTFRIED *University Dict. Business & Finance* 292 In current usage, a rebate is distinguished from a discount in that the former is not taken out or deducted in advance, but is handed back after payment of the full amount. **1965** H. K. COMPTON *Gloss. Purchasing & Supplies Managem. Terms* 115 *Rebate*, an allowance (or discount) on price, usually given after the completion of the contract, and most frequently based on some relationship with the business turnover. **1965** *McGraw-Hill Dict. Mod. Econ.* 426 Rebates to large and more favored shippers were used extensively in the U.S. railroad industry in the nineteenth century as a form of price discrimination.

attrib. and *Comb.* **1869** *Bradshaw's Railway Man.* XXI. 448 Rebate account.. £1,348. **1894** *Daily News* 4 Dec. 7/1 Returning the amount in the form of a 'rebate' coupon entitling the possessor to a ten per cent. reduction on the prices of.. articles. **1907** *Daily Chron.* 9 Dec. 4/3 They cannot dislodge the Welsh makers [of tin-plates] from their hold of the rebate trade. **1908** *Times* 1 Feb. 5/2 The rebate-taker, the franchise-trafficker, the manipulator of securities.. and the man-killer all alike work at the same web of corruption. **1908** *Daily Chron.* 1 Feb. 5/3 The President [*sc.* Roosevelt] attacks by name.. the Atchison and Santa Fé Railway.. for its rebate practices and intervention in the money market. **1976** *Milton Keynes Express* 2 July 21/2 The decision to ban rebate tenants at Fishermead was revealed in this month's issue of the magazine 'City Limits'.

rebate (rɪ'beɪt), *sb.*[2] [Respelling of RABBET *sb.*, on analogy of prec. and REBATE *v.*[1]] A rabbet.

The pron. (rɪ'beɪt) is given in all Dicts. from 1845 onwards, but in technical use the word is commonly pronounced as if written *rabbet.*

1674 GOULDMAN *Eng.-Lat. Dict.*, A rebate, rebating or chamfering, *strix.* **1731** BAILEY, Vol. II. (ed. 2), *Rebáte* (with Architects), chamfering or fluting. **1785** PEACOCK in *Phil. Trans.* LXXV. 370 Fix the.. groove.. in the rebate. **1823** P. NICHOLSON *Pract. Build.* 421 Cottage and some kinds of church windows are glazed in squares, or other figures, in leaden rebates. **1894** BOTTONE *Elect. Instr. Making* (ed. 6) 201 The movable back fits into a rebate in the bottom of this box.

b. *attrib.*, as ***rebate-joint, -plane.***

1797 *Trans. Soc. Arts* XV. 261 The sort of planes I have used are what, by the joiners, are called the levelled rebate plane, and small rounds. **1825** J. NICHOLSON *Operat. Mechanic* 582 A third sort of rebate-planes, called a fillister, is used for sinking or cutting away the edge of a piece of wood, to form the rebate. **1875** *Carpentry & Join.* 27 The rebate plane is.. made as follows. **1886** LOCKWOOD *Dict. Terms, Rebate-Joint*, a joint which is made by the overlapping of the edges of material.

rebate, *sb.*[3] *rare*[−0]. [App. for *rabbet*, ad. F. *rabot*: cf. RABAT *sb.*] **a.** = RABBIT *sb.*[3], RAB[1]. **b.** 'An iron tool sharpened something like a chisel, and employed in dressing and polishing wood, etc.'

1826 ELMES *Dict. Fine Arts.* Hence in Webster (1847) and later Dicts.

rebate, *sb.*[4] *rare*[−0]. [Of obscure origin.] 'A kind of hard freestone used in the formation of pavements' (Elmes 1826).

rebate (rɪ'beɪt), *v.*[1] Also 5 **rabat,** 6 **rabb-, rabate,** 6–7 **rebait,** 7 **rebayte.** [ad. OF. *rabattre*, f. *re-* RE- + *abattre* ABATE *v.*[1] (cf. BATE *v.*[2]).]

†**1.** *trans.* **a.** *Falconry.* To bring back (a 'bating' hawk to the fist). Also *intr.* of the hawk: To settle down. *Obs.*

Cf. BATE *v.*[1] 2, and OF. *rebat* sb. in Godef. VI. 636.

1486 *Bk. St. Albans* A vj, The secunde [term] is rebate youre hawke to yowre fyst, & thatt is whan yowre hawke batith the leest meuyng that ye can make with yowre fyst she will rebate ayen vppon yowre fyst. **1632** [see RABATE *v.*]. **1677** COLES *Eng.-Lat. Dict.*, To Rebait a hawk, *accipitrem relicere.*

†**b.** Of a horse: (cf. ABATE *v.*[1] 19). *rare*[−0].

1611 COTGR., *Rabatre*,.. also, a horse to rebate his curuet. **1727** BOYER *Dict. Royal* I. s.v. *Rabattre*, A Horse that rebates his Curvets very handsomely.

2. †**a.** To deduct (a certain amount from a sum); to subtract (one quantity or number from another). *Obs.*

1427 *Rolls of Parlt.* IV. 257/2 Yf [Silver] be as good in alay as the old Sterlyng, to take it wythoute gruchyng.., and yif it be wars, to rebate truly the disavaill therof, after the feblenesse of the alay. **1472–3** *Ibid.* VI. 4/2 The Rentes and Services goyng oute of the seid Londes.. therof oonly to be deducte and rebated. **1542** RECORDE *Gr. Artes* E iij b, Than do I rebate 6 out of 8, & there resteth 2. **1633** T. STAFFORD *Pac. Hib.* II. iv. (1821) 275 Detaining only, and rebating to her Highnesse use, twelue pence sterling upon every twentie shillings. **1675** GREGORY in Rigaud *Corr. Sci. Men* (1841) II. 273 Ye say ye are owing me 44*s.*, but ye are not owing so much. You have to rebate the price of the Archimedes [etc.].

absol. **1440** in *Wars Eng. in France* (Rolls) II. 587 The king may rebate yerely of the said som as shalbe thoughte resonable. **1542** RECORDE *Gr. Artes* E iij, If you shoulde go aboute to rebate, you muste haue two sundry summes proposed. **1586** WARNER *Alb. Eng.* III. xix. (1589) 81 God.. with a Plague did crosse The Brutons, that had els at least rebated from their losse.

†**b.** To reduce or diminish (a sum or amount). *Obs.* (Cf. 3.)

1538 STARKEY *England* II. i. 175 Al such rentys as be inhaunsyd by memory of man schold be rebatyd, and set to the old stynt. **1599** HAKLUYT *Voy.* II. II. 43 We began.. to rebate our allowance of drinke, to make it indure the longer. *transf.* **1627–77** FELTHAM *Resolves* II. x, If I be able to do a Courtesie, I rebate it by remembring it.

†**c.** To give or allow a reduction to (a person).

1523 LD. BERNERS *Froiss.* I. cccxliv. 543 Therle was set to his raunsome to pay sixscore M. frankes, so that whan he had maryed the lady Maude, than to be rebated threscore thousande, and the other threscore thousande to pay. **1656** H. PHILLIPS *Purch. Patt.* (1676) 19 All the money the Landlord receives for the Fines of those Leases, he rebates his Tenant for it. **1669–70** MARVELL *Corr.* cxxxvii. Wks. 1872–5 II. 303 The merchant paying down the duty in ready money is to be rebated blank per cent.

d. To pay back (a sum of money) as a rebate; to give a rebate on.

1957 CLARK & GOTTFRIED *University Dict. Business & Finance* 292/2 Under customs regulations.. import duties paid on goods which are later re-exported may be rebated in part or in full. **1977** *Time* 21 Feb. 49/1 Much of the energy tax would have to be rebated in some form to the poor to help them meet higher living expenses.

3. a. To reduce, lessen, diminish (a condition, quality, feeling, activity, etc.). Now *rare.*

Common *c* 1575–1725, with a large variety of objects.

*c***1450** *Cov. Myst.* viii. (Shaks. Soc.) 76, I xal sey here the same here sorwys to rebate. **1495** *Trevisa's Barth. De P.R.* XVII. cxxxii. 689 Pulegium hath the vertue.. to rebate [1398 abate] ventosyte. **1562** LEIGH *Armorie* 123 b, Who so killeth his prisoner.. with hys owne hande, rebateth his honor. **1593** MUNDAY *Def. Contraries* 98 Dearth of victuals.. rebateth the pride of the highest mounted. **1624** CAPT. SMITH *Virginia* IV. 128 Their fury was not onely rebated, but their hastinesse intercepted. **1686** GOAD *Celest. Bodies* II. xii. 322 Warmth it self, when dull'd and rebated by the Affluence of the contrary, is not wholly bound up. **1748** RICHARDSON *Clarissa* (1811) V. xxxvi. 349 To pacify her, or, at least, to rebate her first violence. **1759** MARTIN *Nat. Hist. Eng.* II. 182 The Sulphur has so sufficiently rebated the Acidity. **1897** F. THOMPSON *New Poems* 144 Thou dost rebate thy rigid purposes.

b. To reduce the effect or force of (physical agencies, a blow, stroke, etc.). Now *rare.*

1579 TOMSON *Calvin's Serm. Tim.* 278/2 This fire will be put out, or so rebated that we shall burne no more as we were woont to do. **1586** BRIGHT *Melanch.* xi. 53 The poysons, being maistred or at least rebated by.. remedies. **1609** HEYWOOD *Brit. Troy* VI. xlviii. 124 To yeeld way, rebates the greatest stroke. **1663** in *Boyle's Wks.* (1772) VI. 371 The flesh of the viper rebateth the poison of the viper. **1713** C'TESS WINCHELSEA *Misc. Poems* 93 When the Coquette.. Assumes a soft, a melancholy Air, And of her Eyes rebates the wand'ring Fires. **1814** SOUTHEY *Roderick* xxv. 493 Many a foin and thrust Aim'd and rebated.

†**c.** To lessen the vigour or activity of (the mind, etc.); to repress, stop (a person or action).

1581 SAVILE *Tacitus, Hist.* IV. lxvii. (1591) 220 The success of the Sequani rebated and stayed the course of the warre. **1597** BEARD *Theatre God's Judgem.* (1612) 34 His malicious and bloudthirstie mind was somewhat rebated and repressed from doing that which he pretended. *Ibid.* 472 He.. was cut short and rebated by a small and base creature, and constrained to leaue this life. **1645** *King's Cabinet Open.* in *Select. fr. Harl. Misc.* (1793) 356 Digby's sanguine complexion, not to be rebated from sending good news. *a***1683** OLDHAM *Wks.* (1686) 42 Let no defeat Your sprightly Courage, and Attempts rebate. **1788** *Trifler* No. 30. 384 Where universal torpidity rebates the animal spirits.

4. To make dull, to blunt: **a.** the edge or point of a weapon, or *fig.* of a feeling, action, person, etc. Now *rare.*

Common *c* 1590–1720 in both lit. and fig. contexts.

1565 COOPER *Thesaurus, Gladiorum aciem praestringit*, it rebateth or dulleth. *c* **1586** C'TESS PEMBROKE *Ps.* LXXXIX. xiv, Takes he his weapon? thou the edge rebatest. **1601** R. JOHNSON *Kingd. & Commw.* (1603) 193 The footemen try it out at sword and buckler with point and edge rebated. **1686** HORNECK *Crucif. Jesus* xx. 577 When the very tools whereby the soul is to work, are blunt, and their edge rebated. **1715–20** POPE *Iliad* XI. 304 The broad belt,.. The point rebated, and repell'd the wound. **1801** STRUTT *Sports & Past.* III. i. 123 Armed with a pointless sword, having the edges rebated.

fig. *a* **1586** SIDNEY *Arcadia* (1622) 251 Compassion so rebated the edge of Choler. *c* **1611** CHAPMAN *Iliad* XXIV. 585 So long would I rebate Mine own edge set to sack your town. **1630** LENNARD tr. *Charron's Wisd.* II. iii. (1670) 249, I will here adde a word or two.. to rebate and blunt the point of detraction. **1700** DRYDEN *Pal. & Arc.* III. 502 The keener edge of battel to rebate. **1773** J. ALLEN *Serm. St. Mary's, Oxf.* 16 To.. rebate the edge of Erastian insolence.

b. a weapon, or something compared to one.

1574 HELLOWES *Gueuara's Fam. Ep.* (1584) 210 His rule commaunded, that they shoulde not torney more than thirtie with thirty, and with swords rebated. *a* **1625** FLETCHER *Faithf. Friends* III. iii, This shirt of mail worn near my skin Rebated their sharp steel. **1676** MARVELL *Mr. Smirke* 48 He forthwith relented, he rebated the Sword of the Executioner. **1708** OZELL tr. *Boileau's Lutrin* 101 My Front rebates your soft Artillery. **1814** SOUTHEY *Carmina Aulica* VI. i, Of arrows and of spears they told Which fell rebated from his mortal mould. **1863** W. THORNBURY *True as Steel* (1868) I. 136 To see that the horses were well shoed and the spear-heads properly 'rebated' or blunted.

fig. **1649** G. DANIEL *Trinarch., Hen. V*, cvii, Nature will not, (haveing forg'd him vp To Life, and Edge) rebate him, in her Shoppe. **1681** DRYDEN *Abs. & Achit.* To Rdr., By rebating the satire, where justice would allow it, from carrying too sharp an edge.

5. a. *Her.* To diminish (a charge) by removal of a portion, esp. a point or projection. Cf. REBATEMENT 3. **b.** To remove (a point, etc.) from a charge.

1562 LEIGH *Armorie* 122 b, When the father is dead, it may please yᵉ prince to adde agayne to the sonne that, that was rebated from the father. *Ibid.* 127 b, The fielde is Geules, three Escocheons Argent, one rebated on the Sinister chiefe point. **1610** GUILLIM *Heraldry* III. ii. 87 To shew that the Canton doth not rebate the Starre in the Dexter point. **1637** HEYWOOD *Dial.* iv. Wks. 1874 VI. 163 Some of the raies are broke, others rebated. **1868** CUSSANS *Her.* iv. 60 A Cross Moline, with its eight points rebated, or cut off.

†**6.** To repulse, drive back. *Obs.*

1590 LODGE *Rosalind* L, Hee was not onely rebatted, but sore wounded. **1590** GREENE *Orl. Fur.* Wks. 1831 I. 34 This is the city of great Babylon, Where proud Darius was rebated from. **1633** W. STRUTHER *True Happines* 46 Hatred, Feare.., and Sorrow.. which serve to rebate and keep us in Separation from it.

†**7.** *intr.* **a.** To diminish, lessen, abate. *Obs.*

1545 RAYNOLD *Byrth Mankynde* 133 When the infant falleth away, and the flesshe rebateth remaynyng nothynge but as it ware skynne and bone. **1557** GRIMALDE *Cicero's Death* in *Tottell's Misc.* (Arb.) 124 Rage rebated, when They his bare neck beheld, and his hore heyres. **1597** BEARD *Theatre Gods' Judgem.* (1612) 170 He had scarce ended these speeches, but the Christians battell and courage began to rebate.

†**b.** To grow blunt. *Obs.*

1587 GOLDING *De Mornay* xvi. (1617) 280 The edge of vnderstanding rebateth at the outside of the least things that are. **1614** C. BROOKE *Rich. III* Poems (1872) 141 But soone my archers slack their strongest bent, My souldiers' steel rebated.

†**c.** To depart, fall away *from* a thing. *Obs.*⁻¹

1570 FOXE *A. & M.* (ed. 2) 1951/2 In king Edwardes dayes, he began a litle to rebate from certeine poynts of Popery, and somewhat to smell of the gospell.

†**8.** (Meaning not clear: cf. REBATING *vbl. sb.*¹)

1502 ARNOLDE *Chron.* (1811) 110, ix. tonne of good Ciuill oyle, vessels fylled, the gauge payde and rebated. *Ibid.* 113 Which tonne wyne wele rebatid ful and gawge J. Alman byndith him.. to delyuer.

Hence **rebatable** (rɪˈbeɪtəb(ə)l, ˈriːˌbeɪtəb(ə)l) *a.*

1972 *Daily Tel.* 15 Feb. 17 The CBI's two main recommendations are a 2½ p.c. cut in corporation tax.. and a halving of the rebatable heavy oil duty.

rebate, *v.*² [Later spelling of RABBET *v.*, on analogy of prec. For pron. see REBATE *sb.*²]

1. *trans.* To make a rebate or rabbet in.

1674 GOULDMAN *Eng.-Lat. Dict.*, To rebate or make rebates, *strio.* **1706** PHILLIPS (ed. Kersey), *To rebate*, to channel or chamfer. **1785** PEACOCK in *Phil. Trans.* LXXV. 368 The edges of the said board are to be rebated. **1825** J. NICHOLSON *Operat. Mechanic* 583 This kind of plane is usually employed to rebate narrow pieces of wood, such as are used in sashes. **1863** WYNTER *Subtle Brains & Lissom Fingers* 275 Another machine rebated and bearded the keel.

2. To join *together* with a rebate.

1838 *London's Arch. Mag.* V. 579 It will be seen that the headers and stretchers are rebated together. **1847** SMEATON *Builder's Man.* 90 A lap dovetail, which, when put together, shows only a joint, as if the pieces were rebated together.

reˈbated, *ppl. a.*¹ [f. REBATE *v.*¹ + -ED¹.] Blunted; dulled.

1587 HOLINSHED *Chron.* III. 1297/2 Six gentlemen on either side with rebated swords. **1616** SURFL. & MARKH. *Country Farme* 66 Make them cleane.. with a rebated knife made of purpose, such a one as will not cut. *a* **1661** FULLER *Worthies, Northants* II. (1662) 292 During his reign.. a shrude thrust was made at all Abbies, not with a Rebated point, but with sharps indeed.

fig. **1589** NASHE *Pref. Greene's Menaphon* (Arb.) 8 Recreate their rebated witts.

rebated, *ppl. a.*² [f. REBATE *v.*²] Having a rebate or rabbet.

1785 PEACOCK in *Phil. Trans.* LXXV. 370 The stock.. is to slide in a rebated or dove-tail groove. **1837** *Civil Eng. & Arch. Jrnl.* I. 70 A letter.. on Hitch's 'Patent Rebated Brickwork'. **1875** *Carpentry & Join.* 104 The moulded, bevelled, or rebated strips can be set on edge in these.

reˈbatement. ? *Obs.* [a. OF. *rebatement* (1290 in Godef.): see REBATE *v.*¹ and -MENT.]

1. A sum to be deducted from another; a discount.

1542 RECORDE *Gr. Artes* E iij, The rebatemente or summe to bee withdrawen.. muste be sette vnder the fyrste [sum]. **1635** R. DAFFORNE *Merch. Mirr.* title-p., The Ready mony.. that we are to Receive or Pay upon Rebatement. **1687** *Addr. from Chichester* in *Lond. Gaz.* 2270/4 We having no rebatements to make, are totally thankful. **1727–41** CHAMBERS *Cycl.* s.v. *Rebate*, The merchants having not always wherewithal to pay for their goods in hand, by means of the rebatement, such as have, will find their account in it.

2. Diminution in amount, force, etc.

1598 STOW *Surv.* xxxviii. (1603) 373 The rebatement of Bishops liuings. **1663** T. TULLY in *Lett. & Poems* (1676) 95 Mine I fear may look like Injury and Rebatement to their Worth. **1701** BEVERLEY *Glory of Grace* 37 The Law hath its full Course, it is pointed still against Them, without Rebatement.

3. *Heraldry.* = ABATEMENT 4.

1562 LEIGH *Armorie* 127 This is a rebatement,.. but is rebated onely for dought of challenge. **1586** FERNE *Blaz. Gentrie* 97, I haue heard of these nine vices before: and also of certaine rebatements of armes appointed to them. **1661** MORGAN *Sph. Gentry* I. vii. 101 There are notes of infamy as well as of honour, which in Arms are called Rebatements. **1727–41** in CHAMBERS *Cycl.* and later Dicts.

†**4.** A narrowing (of a wall). Cf. RABATE *sb.* *Obs.*

1611 BIBLE *1 Kings* vi. 6 In the wall of the house hee made narrowed rests [*margin*, narrowings, or, rebatements] round about, that the beames should not bee fastened in the walles of the house.

rebater (rɪˈbeɪtə(r)). [f. REBATE *v.*¹ + -ER¹.] One who or that which rebates.

1601 DENT *Pathw. Heaven* (1603) 37 God, in his great mercy sent him a cooler, and a rebater: to wit, a pricke in the flesh. **1893** *Independent* (N.Y.) 19 Oct. 32/2 What is to be done with rebaters? There is a law.. [in] many of the states providing a penalty for its practice.

rebater, variant of REBATO *Obs.*

rebating (rɪˈbeɪtɪŋ), *vbl. sb.*¹ [f. REBATE *v.*¹]

1. The action of the vb., in various senses.

a **1483** *Liber Niger Edw. IV* in *Househ. Ord.* (1790) 74 All other crafte for the rackinge, coynynge, rebatinge, and other salvation of wynes. **1561** in Froude *Hist. Eng.* (1881) VI. 486 Punishing of massmongers for the rebating of their humours. **1598** R. HAYDOCKE tr. *Lomazzo* II. 138 How the Lights, Reflexions and naturall rebating of the lights doe vary. **1632** SHERWOOD, A rebating, or rebatement, *rabais.* **1889** *Times* 6 June 5/1 Both houses of the Cape Parliament have passed the convention tariff, which confers similar powers of rebating on the Government.

†**2.** = REBATEMENT 3. *Obs.*

1562 LEIGH *Armorie* 122 There are nyne rebating[s] of armes,.. for nyne sondry vngentilmanly dedes done.

rebating, *vbl. sb.*² [f. REBATE *v.*²] The making of a rebate or rabbet.

1823 P. NICHOLSON *Pract. Build.* 159 Grooving and Rebating consist in taking or abstracting a part which is every where of a rectangular section. **1861** WYNTER *Soc. Bees* 144 As there is no window-framing, planing, mortising, or rebating required, the cost is very inconsiderable.

attrib. **1812–16** J. SMITH *Panorama Sc. & Art* I. 111 Rebating-planes without a fence have the iron the whole breadth of the sole. **1842** GWILT *Archit.* §2104 Of the sinking rebating planes there are two sorts.

†**reˈbating,** *a.* *Obs.*⁻¹ [Prob. f. *rebat-er*, var. of next.] Supporting the ruff.

1596 GOSSON *Quips Upst. Gentlew.* 80 (Percy Soc.) 6 This starch, and these rebating props, as though ruffes were some rotten house.

†**reˈbato.** *Obs.* Also 6 rebatu, 6–7 rabato, rebater, 7 rebata, -oe. [f. F. *rabat* collar, etc., on anal. of Italian words in *-ato*, or ad. obs. F. *rabateau*, recorded in 16–17th c. in some of the senses of *rabat* (see Godef.).] A kind of stiff collar worn by both sexes from about 1590 to 1630.

1591 HARINGTON *Orl. Fur.* 410 You fayre Ladies, that spend so many houres in looking and prying in a glasse to see if this shadow sit handsomlie, if your rebatoes be well set. **1593** NASHE *Christ's T.* (1613) 161, I see Gentlewomen.. burning out many pounds of Candle in pinning their treble rebaters. **1598** MARSTON *Sco. Villanie* II. vii. 208 Alas, her soule struts round about her neck, Her seate of sense is her rebato set. **1609** HEYWOOD *Brit. Troy* XII. xvi, His smooth Rebata from his Neck he fals. **1630** J. TAYLOR (Water P.) *Wks.* II. 254 The Tires, the Periwigs, and the Rebatoes, Are made t'adorne ilshap'd Inamoratoes.

fig. **1601** BP. W. BARLOW *Defence* 162 The men who haue made scarfes, and veiles, and rebaters for sinnes.

b. A collar of this kind used to support a ruff, or a frame of wire serving the same purpose. Also *fig.*

1592 NASHE *P. Penilesse* (ed. 2) 11 b, Their Lords authoritie is as a rebater to beare vp the Peacockes taile of their boasting. **1601** DENT *Pathw. Heaven* (1831) 36 These great ruffs, which are borne up with supporters and rebatoes, as it were with post and rail. **1617** MORYSON *Itin.* III. IV. i. 166 In Prussia I obserued them to weare long ruffes, with rebatoes of wire to beare them up, such as our women vse. **1634** PEACHAM *Gentl. Exerc.* I. xvii. 56 King Salomon sitting in his throne with a deepe laced Gentlewomans Ruffe, and a Rebatoe about his necke.

c. *attrib.*, as *rebato-pinner*, *-wire*.

1601 *Jack Drum's Entertainm.* IV, Peace! you Rebato-pinner, Poting-stick. **1607** HEYWOOD *Wom. Killed w. Kindn.* (1617) H iij, A Bodkin or a Cuffe, A Bracelet, Necklace, or Rebato wier. **1612** in *Naworth Househ. Bks.* (Surtees) 10 A rebatoe wyer for Mrs Mary.

rebaude, rebaudry, obs. ff. RIBALD, RIBALDRY.

rebawde, rebawdous, obs. ff. RIBALD, RIBALDOUS.

rebayn, obs. f. RIBBON.

rebb, var. REB².

rebbe (ˈrɛbə). Also with capital initial. [Yiddish, f. Heb. *rabbī* RABBI *sb.*] A rabbi; *spec.* a Chasidic religious leader.

1881 *Encycl. Brit.* XIII. 681/2 The Zaddikim (or 'righteous') and Rebbés, as their leaders are called, live in magnificence upon the contributions of the most ignorant of the people. **1882** [see CHEDAR]. **1965** J. A. MICHENER *Source* (1966) 45 Two others prayed in loud voices on a line of their own, while the old rebbe, incredibly ancient, Cullinane thought, mumbled prayers that no one else could have heard. **1967** *N.Y. Times* 22 Mar. 29 (Advt.), The Lubavitcher Rebbe, Rabbi.. Schneerson, has issued his annual call to world Jewry to observe the Purim festival. **1978** I. B. SINGER *Shosha* xiv. 243 To me.. you are my rebbe. Your every word is filled with wisdom and love of God as well.

rebbec, obs. f. REBECK.

†**rebbit,** obs. variant of RABBET *sb.*

1675 J. GEDDE *Meth. Bee-Houses* 3 At the top of the Box there is a crease or rebbit all round it, about half an inch in depth on the outside.

rebbitzin (ˈrɛbɪtsɪn). Also **rebbetzin, rebbitzen** and with capital initial. [Yiddish, fem. of REBBE.] The wife of a rabbi.

1892 I. ZANGWILL *Childr. Ghetto* I. iv. 110 'His third wife was Kitty Green..,' persisted the Rebbitzin. **1926** S. ASH *Kiddush Ha-Shem* II. ii. 109 She was standing in the next room together with her mother, the *rebbetzin.* **1965** J. A. MICHENER *Source* (1966) 670 For the next ten years Leah, the young rebbetzin of Eliezer bar Zadok, knew only the Judenstrasse. **1966** H. KEMELMAN *Saturday Rabbi went Hungry* (1967) xxxvii. 236, I just called the hospital and they told me the rebbitzen had a boy. **1972** —— *Monday Rabbi took Off* v. 43 Believe me, the *rebbitzin* is real class, a Wellesley graduate. **1978** I. B. SINGER *Shosha* xii. 212 Mother's old-fashioned clothes brought a condescending expression from the rebbitzen.

†**reˈbeat,** *v.*¹ *Obs.* [f. RE- back + BEAT, prob. after F. *rebattre* REBATE *v.*¹] *trans.* To beat *back* again; to force or drive back, to repel. Hence †**reˈbeating** *vbl. sb.*

In last quot. perhaps 'to blunt': cf. REBATE *v.*¹ 4.

1595 DANIEL *Civ. Wars* III. cix, An equall fury thrusts to stay And rebeat backe that force. **1611** FLORIO, *Rabbattimento*, a rebeating backe or downe. *a* **1634** RANDOLPH *Muses Looking-gl.* II. ii, An undaunted rock, whose constant hardnesse Rebeats the fury of the raging Sea. *a* **1634** —— *Poems* (1652) 14 Am I invulnerable? is the Dart Rebeaten which thou levelst at my heart?

re-ˈbeat, *v.*² [RE- 5 a.] *trans.* To beat again.

1654 GAYTON *Pleas. Notes* IV. xvii. 259 Beaten and re-beaten by the Carriers. **1825** J. NICHOLSON *Operat. Mechanic* 532 The mortar.. should be kept covered up, and when wanted be re-beaten.

re-beautify, -fying: see READORN (1598).

rebec (ˈriːbɛk). Chiefly *Hist.* Forms: 6–7 rebecke, (7 -beke), 6–9 rebeck, (7 rebbeck); 8– rebec, (8 rebbec). [a. F. *rebec* (†*rabec*, 15th c.) = med.L. *rebeca* (*c* 1400), It. *ribeca*, Pg. *rebeca*, *rabeca*, app. variants of the forms cited under RIBIBE, but the alteration in the final consonant has not been clearly explained.] **a.** A mediæval instrument of music, having three strings and played with a bow; an early form of the fiddle. (Also personified, in quot. 1509.)

1509 HAWES *Past. Pleas.* XVI. (Percy Soc.) 61 There sat dame Musyke, with all her mynstrasy;.. Rebeckes, clarycordes, eche in theyr degre, Dyd sytte aboute theyr ladyes mageste. *c* **1530** LD. BERNERS *Arth. Lyt. Bryt.* (1814) 232 Than began.. taboures, and rebeckes, and other instrumentes. **1598** YONG *Diana* 50 Syrenus did these verses sing, And on his Rebecke sweetely play. **1632** MILTON *L'Allegro* 94 When.. the jocond rebecks sound To many a youth, and many a maid. **1644** —— *Areop.* (Arb.) 50 The bag-pipe and the rebbeck. **1755** SMOLLETT *Don Quix.* II. iii. 56 [A] young fellow.. who.. can read and write, and play upon the rebec. **1811** SCOTT *Don Roderick* II. xxv, Far to Asturian hills the war-sounds pass, And in their stead rebeck or timbrel rings. **1870** MORRIS *Earthly Par.* III. IV. 188 While round about the rebecks played. **1915** A. DOLMETSCH *Interpretat. Mus. 17th & 18th Cent.* vii. 463 A little band consisting of a bass-viol, a tenor viol, a violin or rebec.. and a flute. **1932** R. DONINGTON *Work & Ideas A. Dolmetsch* 15 It is probably the rebecs that are the nearest relatives of the violins... A number of fine rebecs have recently been finished... Now that the difficulties of the preliminary research work have been overcome.. the rebecs are not difficult or costly to make. **1955** *Times* 20 May 3/5 A concert for children will consist of recorder and harpsichord pieces.. and 'French brawls' for rebec and tambourin. **1980**

Early Music Jan. 87/3 Progress Instruments, by applying modern plastics to make the backs of rebecs and plucked stringed instruments, are seeking to bring them within everyone's purse without sacrificing their authenticity of tone.

†**b.** *ellipt.* Applied to the player. *Obs.*

1540 *Arundel MS.* 97 lf. 122 b in *Vicary's Anat.* (1888) App. xii. 241 Item, for Thomas Evans, Rebeke, wagis xxs. viijd. **1647** HAWARD *Crown Rev.* 25, Musicians and Players, ..Rebeck: [£]28. 6. 8.

Rebecca (rɪˈbɛkə). **a.** The name given (in allusion to Gen. xxiv. 60) to the leader in woman's attire of those rioters who demolished toll-gates in South Wales in 1843–4. Also *attrib.*

1843 *Times* 10 Jan. 6/3 There has been..a mob of lawless depredators..who assembled nightly for the purpose of destroying the turnpike gates... These ruffians are headed by a very tall man, dressed for disguise as a female who goes by the name of Rebecca, and, as many of his associates are likewise dressed as females, the whole gang have been christened 'Rebecca and her daughters'. *Ibid.* 8 May 4/2 Rebecca and her Daughters. The counties of Carmarthen and Cardigan appear to be in a most fearful state from these daring depredators. *Ibid.* 22 June 5/5 *(heading)* Rebecca riots. **1846** *Times* 17 June 7/6 Rebecca wanted in Glocestershire. **1879** MCCARTHY *Own Times* xiii, An odd feature of the time was the outbreak of what were called the Rebecca riots in Wales.

b. *transf.* A salmon-poacher.

1881 *19th Cent.* Apr. 692 The poor emaciated salmon..is transfixed by the unerring aim of 'Rebecca'.

c. Var. REBEKAH.

Hence **Re'becca** *v. trans.*, to demolish or remove (a gate). **Re'beccaism**, the practices and principles of the Rebeccaites. **Re'beccaite**, a follower of 'Rebecca'; also *transf.* and *attrib.*

1843 A. SEDGWICK *Let.* 23 June in *Life* (1890) II. i. 56 Dress me like one of the Welsh Rebeccites [*sic*], and call me a water-nymph. **1878** F. KILVERT *Diary* 25 Nov. (1940) III. 434 A large party of Rebaccaites being out spearing salmon below Rhayader Bridge. **1879** *Rebecca Riots in Radnorshire* 1 The outrages the 'Rebeccaites' committed did not.. appear to originate in political causes. *Ibid.* 7 In dealing.. with the Rebeccaite question. **1881** *Daily News* 8 June 6 The report of Mr. Walpole and Professor Huxley..as to the cause and existence of Rebeccaism was issued yesterday. **1890** *Sat. Rev.* 14 June 719/2 The desire of the County Council to 'Rebecca' certain of the Duke of Bedford's gates.

†**re'beck**, *sb.* *Obs.*$^{-1}$ [Of obscure origin: connexion with next is doubtful, but cf. RIBIBE.] A term of abuse applied to a woman.

c **1386** CHAUCER *Friar's T.* 275 Brother, quod he, heere woneth an old rebekke That hadde almoost as lief to lese hire nekke As for to yeue a peny of hir good.

†**re'beck**, *sb.*^{3} *Obs.*$^{-1}$ [f. F. *rebéquer* to resist or oppose saucily.] Resistance.

1609 [BP. W. BARLOW] *Answ. Nameless Cath.* 199 Generous mindes yeeld where they find a relenting passage; rebecke by opposition prouokes to wrath.

†**re'beck**, *v.* *Obs.*$^{-1}$ [f. RE- back + BECK *v.* 2.] *trans.* To beckon back, to recall, reclaim.

1607 HEYWOOD *Wom. Killed w. Kindn.* Wks. 1874 II. 99 Now she hath seis'd the Fowle, and 'gins to plume her, Rebecke her not; rather stand still and checke her.

rebeck, var. REBEC.

re-be'come, *v.* [RE- 5 a.] *intr.* (with *compl.*) To become again.

1590 C'TESS PEMBROKE *Antonie* I. 100 Thy loue with such things nourished..stealingly Retakes his force and rebecomes more great. **1599** R. LINCHE *Fount Anc. Fict.* K ij, The Ægyptians..held that Serpents..by despoiling and vncasing them of their vpper skins..instantly againe rebecome youthfull. **1611** COTGR., *Redevenir*, to returne, rebecome, or become againe. **1719** T. GORDON *Cordial Low Spirits* I. 100 They abandoned the Gospel and their Wives, and re-became orthodox Catholics. **1788** EARL MALMESBURY *Diaries & Corr.* II. 415 If we mean..to prevent this country..from re-becoming a French province. **1861** R. F. BURTON *City of Saints* 569 Snow still lay,..but in the fine clear sunny day..the lowest levels re-became green. **1920** A. HUXLEY in E. Sitwell *Wheels* (Fifth Cycle) 35 And the stretched gargoyles re-become Women and men! **1938** L. MACNEICE *I crossed Minch* II. ix. 131 It is useless to ask you..to re-become your ancestor the Irish peasant.

re-be'get, *v.* [RE- 5 a.] *trans.* To beget again or a second time. Hence **re-be'getting** *vbl. sb.*; **re-be'gotten** *ppl. a.*

1587 GOLDING *De Mornay* xxxiv. 638 Palingenesian, that is to say, a Regeneration, Rebeegetting, or New Birth. *a* **1631** DONNE *St. Lucy's Day* ii, He ruined me, and I am re-begot Of Absence Darkness Death. **1645** WITHER *Vox Pacif.* 136 Themselves to re-beget Into a perfect bodie. **1839–48** BAILEY *Festus* x. 105 All being shall be rebegotten. *Ibid.* xx. 254 The rebegotten world is born again. **1935** W. EMPSON *Poems* 19 Searching the cave gallery of your face My torch meets fresco after fresco ravishes Rebegets me.

re-be'gin, *v.* [RE- 5 a.] *trans.* To begin again or anew. Hence **re-be'ginning** *vbl. sb.*

1598 FLORIO, *Ripigliare*,..to rebegin a speech. *Ibid.*, *Raccomminciamento*, a rebeginning. **1632** J. HAYWARD tr. *Biondi's Eromena* 150 Having landed the fresh forces..they re-began the fight. **1778** [W. MARSHALL] *Minutes Agric.* 29 Nov. 1774 Re-began to stir the fallow. **1893** in Barrows *Parlt. Relig.* I. 636 A re-beginning, and another fall. **1930** AUDEN *Poems* 44 And love's worn circuit re-begun.

re-be'guile, *v.* [RE- 5 a.] To beguile again.

a **1711** KEN *Urania* Poet. Wks. 1721 IV. 484 The Question startled me awhile, But I myself would re-beguile.

re-be'hold, *v.* [RE- 5 a.] *trans.* To behold, or look upon, again.

1605 SYLVESTER *Du Bartas* II. iii. III. *Law* 808 When the Sun..doth haste his Race To re-behold the beauty, number, order..Of th' awfull Hoast. **1812** CARY *Dante, Purg.* XVII. 8 So thy nimble thought May image, how at first I re-beheld The sun. **1830** LYTTON *P. Clifford* xxvi, One.. whom in such a scene it will..wound thee to re-behold.

Rebekah (rɪˈbɛkə). *U.S.* Also **Rebecca.** [The form, in the Authorized Version of the Bible, of the name *Rebecca*, used in allusion to Gen. xxiv. 60.] A member of a society or 'order' of women, founded in Indiana in 1851 as a complementary organization to that of the Odd Fellows. Also *attrib.*

1860 C. E. DE LONG *Jrnl.* 27 July in *Calif. Hist. Soc. Q.* (1931) X. 252 Met in the Lodge Room. Rebeccas & Brothers & had a free & easy. **1913** *Chicago Record-Herald* 16 Mar. v. 6/5 The staff of Maple Leaf Rebekah Lodge, No. 369, will confer the Rebekah degree on a large class of candidates. **1930** *Randolph Enterprise* (Elkins, W. Va.) 16 Jan. 5/4 They sure have a fine bunch of Odd Fellows and Rebekahs down there. **1949** *Milwaukie* (Oregon) *Rev.* 28 July 6/3 Mrs. Wanda Million and Mrs. Esther Lineagar were initiated into the Milwaukie Rebekah lodge at last week's meeting in the city hall. **1972** *Fairbanks* (Alaska) *Daily News-Miner* 3 Nov. 7/2 *(caption)* Rebekahs—Members of the Rebekahs are interested in forming an Independent Order of the Odd Fellows in Fairbanks.

rebel (ˈrɛbəl), *a.* and *sb.*^{1} Also 4–6 **rebele**, 4–7 **rebell(e**, 6 **rebald.** [a. F. *rebelle* adj. (12th c.) and sb., ad. L. *rebellis* rebellious, f. *re-* RE- + *bellum* war.]

A. *adj.* (Formerly common in predicative use, freq. with const. *against* or *to*; now only attributive, and sometimes capable of being taken as an *attrib.* use of the *sb.*)

1. a. Refusing obedience or allegiance, or offering armed opposition, to the rightful or actual ruler or ruling power of the country.

pred. **1297** R. GLOUC. (Rolls) 1625 Adrian..temprede hom vol wel, & made hom sone milde ynou, þo hii were rebel. *c* **1330** R. BRUNNE *Chron.* (1810) 222 þe flemed ageyn þe kyng ros eft full rebelle. *c* **1385** CHAUCER *L.G.W.* 591 *Cleopatra*, Rebel un-to the toun of rome is he. *c* **1400** tr. *Secreta Secret., Gov. Lordsh.* 108 þe hertys of þi subgitz sall be rebell to þy gouernaill. **1494** FABYAN *Chron.* VII. ccxxii. 246 Whyle Kyng William was thus occupyed in Normandy, the Northumbers waxte sterne & rebell. *a* **1548** HALL *Chron., Hen. VIII* 88 b, And where as the duke of Geldre is subiect to the Emperor, is he not yet at this day..rebell? *attrib.* **1382** WYCLIF *Isa.* xli. 12 Thi rebel men thei shul ben as thoȝ thei ben not. —— *1 Macc.* iii. 20 Thei cummen to us in rebelle multitude. **1616** J. LANE *Cont. Sqr.'s T.* xi. 40 His ffather now heere sendes to her her conquerd rebell sonn, bound prisoner. **1667** MILTON *P.L.* I. 484 The Rebel King Doubl'd that sin in Bethel and in Dan. *Ibid.* VI. 647 Amaze..and terrour seis'd the rebel Host. **1726** POPE *Odyss.* XXIV. 611 Now by the sword and now the jav'lin fall The rebel-race. **1812** BYRON *Ch. Har.* II. lxxvii, Wahab's rebel brood, who dared divest The prophet's tomb of all its pious spoil. **1861** LOWELL *Pickens-and-Stealin's Rebell.* Pr. Wks. 1890 V. 82 To acknowledge the independence of the Rebel States. **1944** H. FAST *Freedom Road* 167 It was not essentially a problem of reconstruction, not even a problem of readmission of the rebel states into the Union. **1963** *Times* 11 May 11/5 Dubbed the Rebel City for espousing the cause of Perkin Warbeck in 1492, Cork has always maintained a fighting reputation.

b. Consisting of, belonging or falling to, in command of, rebels.

1682 DRYDEN & LEE *Duke of Guise* II. ii, He was the author of the rebel-league. **1776** GIBBON *Decl. & F.* vi. (1869) I. 119 The rebel ranks were broken. **1821** SHELLEY *Hellas* 529 If the rebel fleet Had anchored in the port. *Ibid.* 1020 Now shall..British skill..Thunder-strike rebel victory. **1825** J. NEAL *Bro. Jonathan* III. 138 The seamen, having the same fear of the rebel chief..stuck to the shipping. **1861** O. W. NORTON *Army Lett., 1861–65* (1903) 24 The rebel camps are within two miles of us. **1937** *Granta* 3 Feb. 219/1 Seeing the contrast between the military efficiency of the rebel army and the unpreparedness of the people for war [at the time of the Spanish Civil War 1936–39]. **1980** *Times* 3 Jan. 1/7 The sources said..that the Russians were using sophisticated M124 helicopter gunships against rebel strongholds.

2. a. Disobedient to a superior or to some higher power; contumacious, refractory. †Also const. *of*, and with *infin.*

a **1300** *Cursor M.* 28094 Gayn haly kyrk was i rebell. **1340** *Ayenb.* 69 To þe rede of oure lhorde ofte hi byeþ rebel. **1389** *Eng. Gilds* 95 Qwo-so be rebele of his tonge aȝein þe aldirman. *c* **1430** LYDG. *Min. Poems* (Percy Soc.) 145 [He] Deyed accursyd, rebel to paye his dymes. **1496** *Dives & Paup.* (W. de W.) v. x. 376/2 Yf he be ouer proude & to rebell to his mayster. **1523** LD. BERNERS *Froiss.* I. ccxxix. 307 He was rude and rebell agaynst the commaundementes of holy churche. **1667** MILTON *P.L.* x. 83 The third best absent is condemn'd, Convict by flight, and Rebel to all Law. **1685** DRYDEN *Misc.* II. 454 Sinai..where was receiv'd the Law, That ought to keep the Rebel World in aw. **1742** YOUNG *Nt. Th.* IV. 328 A rebel universe!..not one exempt! **1821** SHELLEY *Hellas* 301 To speak in thunder to the rebel world. **1931** *Ann. Reg. 1930* II. 49 The Prime Minister's speech, as was to be expected, was considered unsatisfactory by the 'rebel' group in the Labour Party. **1976** *Southern Even. Echo* (Southampton) 18 Nov. 17/5 Action would now be concentrated on Albert Johnson quay where most of the rebel dockers worked.

†**b.** Said of animals. *Obs. rare.*

13.. *E.E. Allit. P.* B. 455 þe rauen so ronk þat rebel was euer. *c* **1420** *Pallad. on Husb.* IV. 776 Yf they be rebel, so let hem stonde ffastyng oon day and nyght in yokis bonde.

c. *transf.* of things.

1340 *Ayenb.* 68 þe herte þet is rebel and hard. *c* **1386** CHAUCER *Pars. T.* ¶ 192 Right as reson is rebel to god right so is..sensualitee rebel to reson. **1593** SHAKS. *Lucr.* 625 From a pure heart command thy rebell will. **1647** TRAPP *Comm. Matt.* vi. 16 [It] subdues rebell-flesh, which with fullnesse of bread will wax wanton. **1702** ROWE *Tamerlane* IV. i. 1752 All my Rebel-blood assists the Fair. **1885–94** R. BRIDGES *Eros & Psyche* July xv, She set the lamp beneath a chair, and cloked..its rebel lustre from the eye.

†**d.** Of ulcers: = REBELLIOUS 3. *Obs.*$^{-1}$

1541 R. COPLAND *Galyen's Terap.* 2 D iv, The curacyon of vlceres, nat inueterate, but contumaced and rebell.

3. Of words, actions, etc.: Characterized by rebelliousness; characteristic of a rebel or rebels.

c **1393** CHAUCER *Scogan* 23 þe ilke rebel word that thou hast spoken. **1700** CONGREVE *Way of World* v. vii, Must I live to be confiscated at this rebel-rate? **1715–20** POPE *Iliad* xv. 248 Desists at length his rebel-war to wage. **1755** H. WALPOLE *Corr.* (1837) I. 296 However rebel this may sound at your Court my Gothic spirit is hurt. **1812** H. & J. SMITH *Rej. Addr., Living Lustres* viii, Unaccustom'd to rebel commotion.

B. *sb.* **1. a.** One who resists, or rises in arms against, the established governing power; one who refuses or renounces allegiance or obedience to his sovereign or the government of his country.

c **1400** *Destr. Troy* 1466 He [Priam] was faryn to fight in a fer londe, To riche hym of Rebelles þat of þe rewme held. *c* **1460** FORTESCUE *Abs. & Lim. Mon.* ix. (1885) 129 When such a rebell hath more riches than his soueryane lorde. **1560** DAUS tr. *Sleidane's Comm.* 56 The rebelles had encamped them on a Hill. **1612** DAVIES *Why Ireland*, etc. (1747) 113 We find the degenerat and disobedient English called Rebelles, but the Irish which were not in the King's peace are called Enemies. **1719** DE FOE *Crusoe* I. x, I could ..give Liberty, and take it away, and no Rebels among all my Subjects. **1778** GOUV. MORRIS in Sparks *Life & Writ.* (1832) I. 158, I know that for such sentiments I am called a rebel. **1902** KIPLING *Traffics & Discoveries* (1904) 32, I shot my Bible full of bullets after Bloemfontein went... Take it and pray over it before we Federals help the British knock hell out of you rebels. **1966** *BBC Handbk. 1966* 97 Stanleyville radio was in the hands of the rebels in the Congo (Leopoldville) Republic. **1976** *Daily Tel.* 20 July 4/2 Armed men, believed to be Moslem rebels, ambushed a bus in the southern Philippines on Sunday.

†**b.** In collect. sense (cf. *enemy*). *Obs.*$^{-1}$

1600 DYMMOK *Ireland* (1843) 33 The small losse we susteyned in this place was multiplied upon the rebell by our quarter and skoutmasters.

c. *Law.* One who resists or disobeys a legal command or summons. Now only *spec.* in *Sc. Law*: A debtor who disobeys a charge on letters of horning.

1592 *Sc. Act 12 Jas. VI* § 129 (1597) 119 Quhen-ever onie persones, that hes fund sovertie to vnderly the Law, compeiris not at the day appoynted, and their-throw are decerned to be denunced rebelles, as fugitiues fra the law. **1607** COWELL *Interpr.* s.v. *Rebellion*, Rebell is sometime attributed to him that wilfully breaketh a lawe.., sometime to a villein disobeying his Lord. **1609** SKENE *Reg. Maj.* 86 The lands and tenements of felonis (of rebelles at the horne) quhilk are escheit induring their lyftime. *Ibid., Burrow Lawes* 140 b, The rebelles (disobedient) and perturbers within the burgh. **1666–88** DALLAS *Stiles* (1697) 289 Being ..orderly denunced Rebel and put to the Horn, by vertue of Letters of Horning raised, used and execute against him. **1752** A. MCDOUALL *Inst. Laws Scot.* III. iii. II. 260 It was for his not surrendering his person, (in default of payment) which was in his power, that he was pronounced rebel. *a* **1768** ERSKINE *Inst. Law Scot.* II. v. § 56 If the debtor obey not the will of the letters within the days mentioned in them, the messenger may immediately after publish the diligence by denouncing the debtor rebel. **1882** WATSON *Bell's Dict. Law Scot.* s.v.

d. A supporter of the American cause during the War of Independence (1775–83).

1775 *Massachusetts Spy* 3 May 3/1 The commanding officer accosted the militia in words to this effect, 'Disperse you damn'd rebels!' **1788** *Ann. Reg. 1776* I. 181 Gen. Clinton, with two brigades of British..were sent to make an attempt upon Rhode Island... The rebels having abandoned the island at their approach, they took possession of it without the loss of a man. **1847** *Knickerbocker* XXIX. 54 Mrs. Mowatt is..a great granddaughter of one of those old 'rebels' who signed the Declaration of Independence.

e. A supporter of the Southern, or Confederate, cause during the American Civil War (1861–5); hence, by extension, used colloq. for SOUTHERNER 2. Chiefly *U.S.*

1861 E. COWELL *Diary* 15 Apr. in *Cowells in Amer.* (1934) 290 [The] proceeding caused the necessary diversion of 'the rebels'' course. **1864** LOWELL *Gen. McClellan's Report* Pr. Wks. 1890 V. 107 General McClellan, by the admission of the Rebels themselves, had Richmond at his mercy. **1895** W. H. CHAMBLISS *Diary* 305 The malignant epithets, 'Yankee' and 'Rebels',..were invented by fanatics and foreigners to aggravate our interstate quarrel. **1905** A. C. RICE *Sandy* 123 'Was he a rebel?'..'He was a Confederate, sir! I never knew a rebel.' **1929** *Amer. Speech* IV. 344 *Rebel*, a Southerner. **1938** *Oklahoma Supreme Ct. Rep.* CLXXXIII. A. 509/2 The Northern man is often referred to as 'Yankee' and the Southern man as 'Rebel'. **1959** W. PETERS *Southern Temper* xiii. 211 [The] publisher of the Augusta *Courier*..exudes pleasantness and good will, even when his caller is a Northern newspaperman or writer. 'Well,' he said to one such not long ago, 'I guess you've come down here to give us rebels hell.'

2. a. One who, or that which, resists authority or control of any kind.

1340 *Ayenb.* 69 Þos hy byeþ rebels to þe heste of oure lhorde. *a* **1400** *Vernon MS.* in *Hampole's Wks.* (1896) II. 345 To chastise the rebel.. beo wiþ-drawyng.. þe occasion of his sunne. **1484** CAXTON *Fables of Auian* xxi, The cursyd & rebelles whiche doo no thynge but playe with dees and cardes. **1567** *Gude & Godlie B.* (S.T.S.) 104 God,.. Ceis not to send thy Sanctis sune support,.. For thay Rebellis with rage do resort. **1606** SHAKS. *Ant. & Cl.* IV. ix. 14 That Life, a very Rebell to my will, May hang no longer on me. **1665** GLANVILL *Scepsis Sci.* xiii. 76 'Tis Imagination is the Rebel, Reason contradicts its impious suggestions. **1738** WESLEY *Dryden's 'Creator Spirit, by whose Aid'* iv, Create all new, our Wills controul; Subdue the Rebel in our Soul. **1822** BYRON *Werner* IV. i, You are not jealous Of me, I trust, my pretty rebel! **1955** *N.Y. Times* 27 Oct. 28/2 Mr. Dean.. is a mixed-up rebel because his father lacks decisiveness and strength.

b. ***rebel without a cause***: the title of a cinematographic film released in the U.S. in 1955, applied to a (young) person whose aggressive behaviour is attributed to feelings of frustration or insecurity rather than to loyalty to a particular cause.

[**1955** *N.Y. Times* 27 Oct. 28/2 It is a violent, brutal and disturbing picture of modern teenagers that Warner Brothers presents in its new melodrama.. 'Rebel Without a Cause'. Young people neglected by their parents or given no understanding and moral support by fathers and mothers who are themselves unable to achieve balance and security in their homes are the bristling heroes and heroines.] **1963** *Times* 30 May 15/6 It is a story of a rebel-without-a-cause.. and of the gradual disillusioning of a younger man.. with the romantic image that at first glance he presents.

3. *Comb.*, as ***rebel-high, -like*** advbs.; ***rebel-hearted, -held*** adjs.; **rebel yell**, a characteristic shout or battle-cry uttered by Confederate soldiers during the American Civil War; also *transf.*

1926 C. DAY-LEWIS in *Oxford Poetry* 19 What sense Have they the pioneer-minded, the rebel-hearted, If man's fulfilment rest on no 'perhaps' Outside him? **1966** *BBC Handbk. 1966* 98 The Service's East African Unit.. became.. the only source of news from rebel-held territory [in the Congo Republic]. **1719** YOUNG *Brothers* III. Wks. 1757 II. 240 Demetrius borrows those [wings], To mount full rebel-high. **1605** SHAKS. *Lear* IV. iii. 16 (Q. 1) It seemed, she was a queene Ouer her passion, Who most rebell-like, sought to be King ore her. *a* **1661** HOLYDAY *Juvenal* (1673) 73 How he seems arm'd for resistance, rebel like! **1863** A. J. L. FREMANTLE *Jrnl.* 2 July in *Three Months in Southern States* 265 The Southern troops, when charging, or to express their delight, always yell in a manner peculiar to themselves... The Confederate officers declare that the rebel yell has a particular merit, and always produces a salutary and useful effect upon their adversaries. A corps is sometimes spoken of as a 'good yelling regiment'. **1868** *Harper's Mag.* Sept. 488/1 A tall woman.. uttered a long, piercing cry, which Humphreys afterward described as 'a rebel yell', and Alec as 'a keen whoop'. **1936** M. MITCHELL *Gone with Wind* vi. 121 Stuart Tarleton's voice rose, in an exultant shout, 'Yee-aay-ee!' as if he were on the hunting field. And she heard for the first time.. the Rebel yell. **1945** S. LEWIS *Cass Timberlane* (1946) xxix. 193 No dance at the Heather Country Club was canonical without the presence of Jay Laverick, emitting the rebel yell. **1974** P. RUELL *Death takes Low Road* x. 126 For God's sake, lassie, can you no' keep your voice down to less than a rebel yell?

† **rebel**, *sb.*[2] *Obs.* [f. REBEL *v.* (perh. on analogy of prec.) or ad. med.L. *rebellum, -ium* (Du Cange).] Rebellion.

c **1400** *Rule St. Benet* 46 Lauerd for his merci giue vs sua obediens and mekenes at halde, and rebel at fle, þat [etc.]. **1444** *Rolls of Parlt.* V. 104/1 The secunde rebell of the seid Walssh men, the which arosen with Owen of Glan-doure. *c* **1470** HARDING *Chron.* XXX. viii, His subiect, or another wight, That with rebell vnlawful kill hym might. **1581** J. BELL *Haddon's Answ. Osor.* 75 In my opinion it is a manifest rebell agaynst the holy Scriptures. **1618** RALEIGH in *Four C. Eng. Lett.* (1880) 38 If I had resisted.. the rebells and spoils which my companyes would have made.

rebel (rɪˈbɛl), *v.* Also 4–8 rebell, (4–6 -e). [ad. F. *rebeller* (14th c.), ad. L. *rebellāre* to make war again, to revolt, f. *re-* RE- 2 c + *bellāre* to fight, make war, f. *bellum* war.]

1. a. *intr.* To rise in opposition or armed resistance against the rightful or established ruler or government of one's country. Const. *against*, †*from*, *to*.

1375 BARBOUR *Bruce* IX. 649 He duelt furth in-to the land, Thame that rebelland war warrand. **1390** GOWER *Conf.* II. 196 The king of Puile, which was tho, Thoghte ayein Rome to rebelle. *c* **1460** FORTESCUE *Abs. & Lim. Mon.* iii. (1885) 114 Bi cause the commons.. haue not rebelled or beth hardy to rebelle. **1523** LD. BERNERS *Froiss.* I. cii. 122 The kyng ordayned therle of Salisbury.. into the northe parties,.. for the Scottes had rebelled agayne to hym. **1560** WHITEHORNE *Ord. Souldiours* (1588) 35 b, The same towne beeing rebelled from the French men,.. the Venetians.. had laid the streete full of artillerie. **1651** HOBBES *Leviath.* III. xxxviii. 240 They rebelled, and would have a mortall man for their King. **1718** *Free-thinker* No. 56 ¶9 It is astonishing.. the People should ever rebell for Slavery. **1767** *Junius Lett.* xxxv. 163 You would not be the first prince.. against whom they have rebelled. **1863** W. PHILLIPS *Speeches* xix. 446 The government.. deserves to be rebelled against.

b. To resist, oppose, or be disobedient to, some one having authority or rule.

1340 *Ayenb.* 28 Þo rebeleþ þe enuyous uor to ssende and to destrue be his miȝte. **1382** WYCLIF *Numb.* xxvi. 9 In the dissencyoun of Chore, whanne aȝens the Lord thei rebelden. **1495** *Trevisa's Barth. De P.R.* (W. de W.) VI. xiv. 199 The faders herte is sore greuyd yf his chyldren rebell ayenst hym. **1526** *Pilgr. Perf.* (W. de W. 1531) 17 Rebellyng agaynst theyr prelates & curates. **1566** *Pasquine in a Traunce* 50 b, Howe wilt thou that they should be honest, if in their cursed othe, they rebel from Christe. **1631** GOUGE *God's Arrows* III. §69. 309 To take vengeance of such as obstinately rebell against his will. **1667** MILTON *P.L.* VI. 179 This is servitude, To serve th' unwise, or him who hath rebelld Against his worthier. **1817** SHELLEY *Rev. Islam* IV. xx, They.. bend beneath the spell Of that young maiden's speech, and to their chiefs rebel.

c. *transf.* or *fig.* in various contexts: To offer resistance, exhibit opposition, to feel or manifest repugnance, etc.

c **1386** CHAUCER *Sqr.'s Prol.* 5, I wol nat rebelle Agayn youre lust; a tale wol I telle. **1597** SHAKS. *2 Hen. IV*, II. iv. 379 His Grace sayes that, which his flesh rebells against. **1634** HEYWOOD *Maidenhead lost* IV. Wks. 1874 IV. 151 My blood rebells against my reason. **1738** JOHNSON *London* 1, Tho' grief and fondness in my breast rebel, When injur'd Thales bids the town farewell. **1781** COWPER *Retirement* 16 Thus Conscience pleads her cause.. Though long rebelled against, not yet suppressed. **1859** TENNYSON *Elaine* 648 Amorous adulation, till the maid Rebell'd against it. **1874** GREEN *Short Hist.* vii. §2. 354 The temper of the whole people rebelled against so lawless a usurpation.

†**d.** *refl.*, and with *it.* *Obs. rare.*

1456 SIR G. HAYE *Law Arms* (S.T.S.) 125 Quhen ever a baroun rebellis to mak were on his king, or rebell him in ony thing to cum agaynis him, he fallis in the crime of lese mageste. **1656** S. H. *Gold. Law* 68 Yet it kill'd Achan, and infinite Innocents enough.. to have rebell'd it.

2. *trans.* To oppose rebelliously. *rare.*

c **1450** HOLLAND *Howlat* 562 Quhen they rebellit the crovne, and couth the kyng deir. **1908** A. S. M. HUTCHINSON *Once aboard Lugger* IV. ii. 219 To-day the empress sway of conventionality is rarely rebelled.

Hence † **re·belled** *ppl. a.*, in active sense; in quot. *absol.* *Obs.*

1667 MILTON *P.L.* VI. 737, I.. shall soon, Armed with thy might, rid Heav'n of these rebell'd.

rebeldom (ˈrɛbəldəm). [f. REBEL *sb.* + -DOM.]

1. The domain of rebels. Chiefly applied by their opponents to the Confederate States during the American Civil War.

1862 GRAY *Lett.* (1893) 480 As to Rebeldom, there is now hardly any State that we have not got some foothold in. **1866** VISCT. STRANGFORD *Selection* (1869) II. 198 Its neighbours call it Yaghistan, the land of revolt, rebeldom. **1887** J. D. BILLINGS *Hardtack & Coffee* 280 Afterwards [soldiers] went by thousands into other sections of Rebeldom. **1893** [see CHINCAPIN].

2. Rebellious behaviour.

1859 THACKERAY *Virgin.* li, Never mind his rebeldom of the other day.

† **rebelism** (ˈrɛbəlɪz(ə)m). *U.S. Obs.* [f. REBEL *sb.*[1] + -ISM.] Adherence to the principles or practice of the Confederates during the American Civil War (1861–5).

1862 *Constitution* (Middletown, Conn.) 26 Mar. 4/1 There is a good deal of rebelism in the *Old Bailie*. **1864** *Harper's Mag.* July 271/1 He.. is silent or pretends to rebelism when his mistress.. is by. **1867** *Congress. Globe* 10 Dec. 103/3 The action of Congress can have no other effect than to embarass the work of reconstruction,.. to feed the spirit of rebelism and incite insubordination.

† **re·bellant**, *a.* and *sb.* *Obs. rare.* [a. OF. *rebellant*, pr. pple. of *rebeller* to REBEL, used as adj. and sb. in 14–16th c. (see Godef.).] **a.** *adj.* Rebellious. Const. *to.* **b.** *sb.* A rebel. Const. *to.*

1432–50 tr. *Higden* (Rolls) II. 217 That other infortuny is exterialle, that man scholde haue his inferior rebellante to hym. **1586** WARNER *Alb. Eng.* III. xviii. (1597) 86 Rebellants to a common good, and sinning without awe. **1641** SIR E. DERING *Sp. Relig.* xi. 38 Although my.. reason be rebellant to your conclusions.

rebeller (rɪˈbɛlə(r)). Now *rare.* Forms: 5 (6 *Sc.*) rebellour, (5 -e), 5 rebellar, (6 *Sc.* -e), 6–7 rebellior, 5– rebeller. [f. REBEL *v.* + -ER[1]: see also -IOUR and -OUR.] A rebel, one who rebels.

1422 tr. *Secreta Secret., Priv. Priv.* 206 Sooner Is graciously hardyn oone Prayere of the obedient, than ten thowsante of oon rebelloure. **1495** *Paston Lett.* III. 388 The shippes with the Kynges rebellars. **1548** UDALL *Erasm. Par. Luke* xxi. 166 A continuall rebeller against God. *c* **1640** J. SMYTH *Lives Berkeleys* (1883) I. 290 The same kinge affirmed the same Maurice to bee his enemy and his rebellior. *a* **1787** J. BROWN *Sel. Rem.* (1807) 165 A robber of and rebeller against God. **1837** CARLYLE *Fr. Rev.* I. VI. i, Who is it that especially for rebellers and abolishers can make a Consitution?

rebelling (rɪˈbɛlɪŋ), *vbl. sb.* [f. as prec. + -ING[1].] The action of the vb. REBEL.

a **1340** HAMPOLE *Psalter* xvii. 41 Til þat þai faile and wite awey and leue þaire rebellynge. *c* **1386** CHAUCER *Knt.'s T.* 1601 Myn is.. The murmure, and the cherles rebellyng. **1560** A. L. tr. *Calvin's Foure Serm. Songe Ezech.* i, He tormenteth.. with a rebelling uncomely for a servant of God. **1661** HEYLIN *Hist. Ref.* II. 68 After Absalom's rebelling was suppressed, and the kingdom setled.

rebelling (rɪˈbɛlɪŋ), *ppl. a.* [f. as prec. + -ING[2].] That rebels; rebellious.

1575 GASCOIGNE *Flowers* Wks. 77, I thinke the Goddesse of reuenge deuisde So to bee wreackt on my rebelling wyll. **1611** SHAKS. *Cymb.* V. iv. 96 The Thunderer, whose Bolt.. Sky-planted, batters all rebelling Coasts. *a* **1677** MANTON *Serm. Ps. cxix*, cxv. Wks. 1872 VIII. 91 An unconstant and rebelling heart. **1847** J. KIRK *Cloud Dispelled* ii. 44 Sin is the intrusion.. of a free and rebelling creature on the plans.. of a holy God.

rebellion[1] (rɪˈbɛljən). Forms: 4–5 rebellyoun, 4–6 -ioun; 5 rebylione, -billion, -belyone, 5–6 rebellyon(e, 4– rebellion. [a. F. *rébellion* (14th c.), ad. L. *rebelliōn-em* a renewal of war, revolt, rebellion, f. *rebell-is* REBEL *a.*]

1. Organized armed resistance to the ruler or government of one's country; insurrection, revolt.

c **1440** *Promp. Parv.* 425/1 Rebellyone, or vnbuxumnesse, *rebellio*. *c* **1460** FORTESCUE *Abs. & Lim. Mon.* iii. (1885) 114 He wolde not sett any such charges.. vppon the nobles for fere of rebillion. **1542–5** BRINKLOW *Lament.* (1874) 107 They teache sedycyon, & cause rebellyon agaynst the hygher powers. **1593** SHAKS. *Rich. II*, II. iii. 109 In grosse Rebellion, and detested Treason. **1667** MILTON *P.L.* XII. 36 He.. from Rebellion shall derive his name, Though of Rebellion others he accuse. **1788** GIBBON *Decl. & F.* xlvi. (1869) II. 717 Every province of the empire was ripe for rebellion. **1857** BUCKLE *Civiliz.* I. xii. 686 There can be no doubt that rebellion is the last remedy against tyranny.

b. With *a* and *pl.* An instance of this.

the Great Rebellion, the civil war of 1642–9 and the Commonwealth government of 1649–60. In Sc. Hist. the name of Rebellion is spec. applied to the risings of 1715 and 1745, and in U.S. Hist. to the Civil War of 1861–5.

1382 WYCLIF *1 Kings* xi. 27 The cause of the rebellioun aȝens hym. **1460** CAPGRAVE *Chron.* 62 He was sent be Nero to Palestyn, for to withstand the rebellion of Iewis. **1511–2** *Act 3 Hen. VIII*, c. 17 §2 As.. yf the same treasones rebellyones & oder mysdedes.. hadde never be doone. **1602** SHAKS. *Ham.* IV. v. 121 What is the cause.. That thy Rebellion lookes so Gyant-like? **1647** CLARENDON *Hist. Reb.* I. §1 To present to the world a full and clear narration of the grounds, circumstances, and artifices of this Rebellion. **1746** *Ascanus* 273 The Duke of Perth.. had for some Time been suspected by the Government before the Rebellion broke out. **1838** THIRLWALL *Greece* xiv. II. 198 His meditated expedition had been delayed by a rebellion which broke out at Babylon. **1861** LONGF. in *Life* (1891) II. 418 John Bull is not behaving well about this Rebellion.

c. *Law* (now only *Sc. Law*). Disobedience to a legal summons or command; also *ellipt.*, the fact of being regarded as a rebel on account of such disobedience.

1550 *Reg. Privy Council Scot.* I. 102 Under the pane of rebellioun. **1607** COWELL *Interpr.* s.v., *Commission of rebellion*.. is otherwise called a writte of rebellion.., and it hath vse, when a man after proclamation.. to present himselfe to the court by a certaine day, appeareth not. **1666–88** DALLAS *Stiles* (1697) 289 All Goods, Gear,.. that shall happen to fall.. to him in any time coming during his Rebellion. **1720** T. WOOD *Instit. Laws Eng.* IV. i. (1722) 463 If a *Non est Inventus* is Return'd, then an Attachment with Proclamation of Rebellion Goes against Him; and if He stands further out in Contempt, then a Commission of Rebellion may be issued. *a* **1768** ERSKINE *Inst. Law Scot.* II. v. §61 All moveables belonging to the rebel [at] the time of his rebellion.. fall under his single escheat, whether the rebellion proceeds on denunciation, or on conviction in a criminal trial. **1882** WATSON *Bell's Dict. Law Scot.* s.v.

2. Open or determined defiance of, or resistance to, any authority or controlling power.

a **1340** HAMPOLE *Psalter* ix. 6 Þe swerdis of oure enmy ere þe rebellions of þe deuel. *c* **1430** LYDG. *Min. Poems* (Percy Soc.) 141 He was bounde by lawe.. To pay his dymes, and for rebellioun I cursyd hym. **1552** ABP. HAMILTON *Catech.* (1884) 43 Without ony murmur rebellioun or contradictioun. **1595** SHAKS. *John* III. i. 289 Thy later vows, against thy first, Is in thy selfe rebellion to thy selfe. **1715** DE FOE *Fam. Instruct.* I. iv. (1841) I. 92 Contempt of God, and rebellion against your parents. **1781** COWPER *Hope* 565 His aim was mischief,.. His speech rebellion against common sense. **1885** E. GARRETT (Mrs. Mayo) *At any Cost* xiii. 235 Perhaps some rebellion against his destiny accounts for his atheism.

†**b.** Of ulcers: Obstinacy. *Obs.*[−1]

1541 R. COPLAND *Galyen's Terap.* 2 D iv, It happeneth that some vlceres and diseases are contumacy and rebellyon [*sic*] to heale. Howbeit indicacyon curatyfe is nat taken of this contumacy and rebellyon.

†**c.** Opposition, variance. *Obs. rare.*

1456 SIR G. HAYE *Law Arms* (S.T.S.) 78 Now spere I.. gif man suld have this rebellioun and contrarietee, ane agaynis ane othir, quhen thai ar of divers complexiouns?

† **re·bellion**[2]. *Obs.* [ad. late Lat. *rebelliōn-em*, f. as prec.] A rebel.

1461 *Paston Lett.* II. 27 The seyd Stapylton, &c., makyn gret gaderyngs of the Kyngs rebelyones, lying in wayte to morder me. **1543** GRAFTON *Contn. Harding* 437 Anye manne beyng a traytoure or rebellion hertofore to hys grace.

rebellior, obs. form of REBELLER.

rebellious (rɪˈbɛljəs), *a.* Also 5 rebellous(e. [ad. L. type **rebellōsus* or **rebelliōsus*, f. *rebellis* REBEL *a.*, or *rebellio* REBELLION. Cf. obs. F. *rebelleux* (Godef.).]

1. Insubordinate, defying lawful authority; belonging to a party of rebels. Const. *against*, *to*.

rebellious assembly, in Cowell (1607) and later Dicts., is defined in accordance with the act cited in quot. 1553.

1432–50 tr. *Higden* (Rolls) II. 449 Men of Peloponense beynge rebellous ageyne men of Athenes. *c* **1450** *St. Cuthbert* (Surtees) 4812 To ilk man he was rebellouse. **1535** COVERDALE *Esther* xiii. 7 They which of olde (and now also) haue euer bene rebellious. **1553** *Act 1 Mary* II. c. xii, An Acte againste unlawfull and rebellyous Assembles. **1611** BIBLE *Transl. Pref.* 3 A Pandect of profitable lawes against rebellious spirits. **1641** THORNDIKE *Prim. Govt. Ch.* Ep. Ded., It is a Child rebellious to the Fathers intentions. **1738** WESLEY *Hymn, 'Father, how wide thy glory shines'* iv, When we view thy strange Design To save rebellious Worms. **1795** SOUTHEY *Joan of Arc* V. 61 My weak heart.. Will beat, rebellious to its own resolves. **1871** R. ELLIS tr. *Catullus* lxiii. 13 Lost sheep that err rebellious to the lady

Dindymene. **1888** MISS BRADDON *Fatal Three* I. i, A horrid rebellious girl who has been expelled from a school.

absol. **1462** *Pol. Poems* (Rolls) II. 270 Alle rebellyous undyr he schal hem brynge. **1611** BIBLE *Ps.* lxvi. 7 Let not the rebellious exalt themselues. **1667** MILTON *P.L.* VI. 414 On th' other part Satan with his rebellious disappeerd.

b. *transf.* of the hand, head, a weapon, etc.

c **1580** SIDNEY *Ps.* XVII. vi, Thou by faithfull men wilt stand, And save them from rebellious hand. **1605** SHAKS. *Macb.* I. ii. 56 Point against Point, rebellious Arme 'gainst Arme. **1667** MILTON *P.L.* III. 86 Revenge, that shall redound Upon his own rebellious head. **1810** SCOTT *Lady of L.* II. xxxii, Douglas ne'er Will level a rebellious spear. **1848** LYTTON *Harold* II. ii, When Mangor..let loose his rebellious tongue.

c. *transf.* of intoxicating liquor. *rare*$^{-1}$.

1600 SHAKS. *A.Y.L.* II. iii. 49 In my youth I neuer did apply Hot and rebellious liquors in my bloud.

2. Of actions, etc.: Characteristic of a rebel or of rebels; marked by rebellion.

1492 *Rolls of Parlt.* VI. 447/1 Joyed in rumour and rebellious novelries. **1544** BALE *Sir J. Oldcastle* 20 Vpon youre rebellyouse contumacye ye were both excommunicated. **1667** MILTON *P.L.* VI. 786 His hapless Foes,..to rebellious fight rallied thir Powers. *a* **1704** T. BROWN *On Dk. Ormond's Recov.* Wks. 1730 I. 50 Cæsar to aid, and end rebellious strife. **1862** LONGF. *Wayside Inn* Prel. 113 The sword his grandsire bore In the rebellious days of yore.

3. Of things: Offering resistance to manipulation or treatment; refractory. **a.** Of diseases, sores, etc.

1578 LYTE *Dodoens* I. xv. 24 Very good against.. rebellious old sores. **1600** SURFLET *Countrie Farme* III. liv. 557 They..vse the oyle for rebellious ringwormes. **1698** FRYER *Acc. E. India & P.* 229 It [a tumour] is rebellious to all common Medicines. **1899** *Allbutt's Syst. Med.* VIII. 800 Few skin lesions have proved more rebellious [than lupus].

b. Of material things.

1594 GREENE & LODGE *Looking Gl.* G.'s Wks. (Rtldg.) 120/1 If his mane grow out of order, and he have any rebellious hairs. **1828** SCOTT *F. M. Perth* xvii, 'Bring forward', he said, 'our key..and apply it to this rebellious gate'. **1882** *Rep. to Ho. Repr. Prec. Met. U.S.* 609 The new processes for the treatment of rebellious gold ores.

rebelliously (rɪˈbɛljəslɪ), *adv.* [f. prec. + -LY².] In a rebellious manner.

1551–2 *Act 5 & 6 Edw. VI*, c. xi. §3 If any person.. rebelliouslye doe.. withholde from our saide Soveraigne Lorde..Castles [etc.]. *a* **1661** HOLYDAY *Juvenal* (1673) 73 The beast is forraign and behaves himself rebelliously. **1729** BUTLER *Serm. Hum. Nat.* ii. Wks. 1874 II. 28 Men violate [conscience] and rebelliously refuse to submit to it. **1884** FREEMAN in *Manch. Guard.* 22 Sept. 5/6 The body which thus disloyally, almost rebelliously, flouted the crown.

rebelliousness (rɪˈbɛljəsnɪs). [f. as prec. + -NESS.] The state of being rebellious.

1583 FOXE *A. & M.* (1596) 299/2 The king..perceiuing the waiwardnesse of his owne clergie, or rather rebelliousnesse. **1649** ROBERTS *Clavis Bibl.* 374 Teaching us submission, and bridling all undutifulness and rebelliousness. **1681** H. MORE *Exp. Dan.* Pref. 90 Our Schismaticalness and Rebelliousness. **1873** HELPS *Anim. & Mast.* i. (1875) 29 The singular rebelliousness of young people.

rebellour(e, obs. forms of REBELLER.

rebellow (riːˈbɛləʊ), *v.* [f. RE- + BELLOW *v.*, after L. *reboāre* (see RE- 2 a).]

1. *intr.* Of cattle: To bellow in reply or in turn. Also *transf.* of the wind.

1596 SPENSER *F.Q.* IV. x. 46 The raging buls rebellow through the wood. [**1700** DRYDEN *Pal. & Arc.* III. 140 For thee the bulls rebellow through the groves.] **1776** MICKLE tr. *Camoens' Lusiad* 240 The blast rebellows o'er the ocean wide. *a* **1790** WARTON *Poet. Wks.* (1802) II. 179 Rebellows to the roar the staggering ox.

b. Of places or material objects: To re-echo loudly (*to* or *with* a sound; also rarely *to* the agent producing the sound). Freq. in 18th c.

1590 SPENSER *F.Q.* I. viii. 11 He loudly brayd with beastly yelling sownd, That all the fields rebellowed againe. **1697** DRYDEN *Virg. Georg.* I. 686 Here the Rhine rebellows with Alarms. **1715–20** POPE *Iliad* V. 1057 Earth and heaven rebellow to the sound. **1791** COWPER *Iliad* II. 566 The earth Rebellow'd to the feet of steeds and men. **1837** CARLYLE *Fr. Rev.* I. VII. i, The Palais Royal rebellows with Veto.

c. Of sounds: To re-echo loudly. *lit.* and *fig.*

a **1806** K. WHITE *Gondol.* lxxii, Hollow peals of laughter loud Again rebellow'd round. **1867** GOLDW. SMITH *Three Eng. Statesmen* (1882) 198 A storm of denunciation, which still rebellows in the histories.

2. *trans.* To return or repeat (a sound) in a bellowing tone.

1765 *Meretriciad* (ed. 6) 51 Panders, Boys, and Men, In cadence hoarse, re-bellow out—Amen. **1800** W. TAYLOR in *Monthly Mag.* X. 425 Echo hears, and aloud more wildly rebellows the bellow. **1807** J. ADAMS *Wks.* (1854) IX. 592 The English, the Scotch, the tories, and hyperfederalists will rebellow their execrations against me.

Hence **reˈbellowing** *ppl. a.*

1712 BLACKMORE *Creation* 260 And strike rebellowing caves on either side. **1789** E. DARWIN *Bot. Gard.* II. (1791) 60 With loud acclaim, A present God! they cried. A present God, rebellowing shores reply'd.

rebelly (ˈrɛbəlɪ), *a.* [f. REBEL *sb.* + -Y¹.] Inclined to rebellion; marked by rebelliousness.

1827 LADY MORGAN *O'Briens & O'Flahertys* II. 328 Did you not give me your word..that you knew nothing of that rebelly thief? **1849** *Fraser's Mag.* XXXIX. 490 Laudations of such persons as Hugh O'Neill, and the Red O'Donnell and others (*vide* the recent rebelly literature *passim*). **1936** 'F. O'CONNOR' *Bones of Contention* 179 The child and grandchild of rebelly men. **1959** *Manch. Guardian* 2 July 5/4 Finsbury..seems always to have been a fairly rebelly quarter.

†**rebelly**, *adv.* *Obs.*$^{-1}$ [f. REBEL *a.* + -LY².] Rebelliously.

c **1400** *Master of Game* (MS. Digby 182) xxxv, If þei drawe fer fro hym rebellyche, he shulde sey to hem in þat caas as when he seketh for þe hare.

†**ˈrebelness.** *Obs.* [f. REBEL *a.* + -NESS.] Rebelliousness.

c **1380** *Antecrist* in Todd *Three Treat. Wyclif* (1851) 145 To putte out of chirche for rebelnesse to hem. *c* **1450** *St. Cuthbert* (Surtees) 3376 þaim self of rebelnes þai blamed. **1480** CAXTON *Chron. Eng.* ccvi. 187 With hem that were outlawed oute of England for hyr rebelnesse.

re-beˈlove, *v.* *trans.* ? *Obs.* [RE-.] To love in return. (Only in *pass.*)

1592 WARNER *Alb. Eng.* VII. xxxvi. 175 Erickmon languisht all this while not re-beloued long. **1649** EARL MONM. tr. *Senault's Use Passions* (1671) 238 He loves without hope of being re-beloved.

†**rebel rout**, var. RABBLE ROUT, by confusion with REBEL *sb.*¹

a **1700** B. E. *Dict. Cant. Crew*, *Rebel-rout*, the Rabble, running Riot.

ˈrebelry. *nonce-wd.* [f. REBEL *sb.*¹ + -RY. Cf. *revelry*.] The behaviour characteristic of rebels.

1893 LELAND *Mem.* II. 110, I..joined in the dreadful rebelry and returned unharmed.

†**rebelty.** *Obs.* [ad. OF. *rebelleté* (Godef.): see REBEL *a.* and -TY.] Rebellion.

c **1380** WYCLIF *Wks.* (1880) 75 Not for rebelte aȝenst god ne his lawe. **1388** —— *1 Kings* xi. 27 This was cause of rebelte aȝens the kyng.

re-beˈmire, *v.* [RE- 5 a.] To bemire again.

1608 SYLVESTER *Du Bartas* II. iv. IV. *Decay* 786 But Israel back to his vomit turns, Him rebemires.

reˈbend, *v.* [RE- 5 a.] *trans.* To bend again or in a new direction (in various senses of the word).

1601 SIR W. CORNWALLIS *Ess.* II. xxvii. P 4 Custome is a mettal that stands which way so euer it is bent & is not to be rebent without the danger of breaking. **1611** FLORIO, *Reclinatorio*, rebending or inclining againe. *c* **1828** BERRY *Encycl. Her.* s.v., *Rebending*, is the same as bowed embowed, bent first one way and then another like the letter S. **1832** MARRYAT *N. Forster* xi, Her topsail-sheet was..soon rebent. **1897** KIPLING *Captains Courageous* 48 These hooks are made of soft metal to be rebent after use.

So **rebend** *sb.*, a bend following another.

1893 H. M. DOUGHTY *Our Wherry in Wendish Lands* 63 We..unravelled the bends and rebends and surrebends of the Geeste.

†**re-beneˈdiction.** *Obs.* [RE- 5 a.] A second or renewed benediction.

1611 FLORIO, *Ribenedittione*, a rebenediction. **1656** EARL MONM. tr. *Boccalini's Pol. Touchstone* (1674) 289 The re-benediction of the most Christian King, Henry the Fourth.

re-beˈsiege, *v.* [RE- 5 a.] To besiege again.

a **1661** FULLER *Worthies, Lincoln* II. (1662) 159 Tyrons credit now lay a bleeding, when to stanch it, he rebesieged Blackwater.

†**rebesk**, *a.* *Obs.*$^{-0}$ [Aphetic f. *arabesque*; cf. It. *rabesco* (Florio).] = ARABESQUE *a.* I.

1611 COTGR., *Arabesque*, Rebeske worke; a small and curious flourishing. **1656** in BLOUNT (hence in Phillips, etc.).

re-beˈstow, *v.* [RE- 5 a.] *trans.* To bestow again. So **rebeˈstowal.**

1835 LYTTON *Rienzi* VII. ix, A fair name vindicated, and rightful honours re-bestowed. **1896** *Daily News* 11 Dec. 2/6 His formal placing of his office in the hands of the Academicians, and their equally formal rebestowal of it.

†**rebet**, *v.* *Sc.* *Obs.*$^{-1}$ [App. ad. F. (*se*) *rebattre* to turn, take a new course = REBATE *v.*¹] *intr.* To return.

c **1470** HENRY *Wallace* x. 802 Gret harm it war at he suld be ourset; With new power thai will on him rebet.

re-beˈtake, *v.* [RE- 5 a.] *refl.* To betake (oneself) again *to* a place, etc.

1635 QUARLES *Embl.* IV. xii. (1818) 242 At length..She re-betakes her to her lonely bed. **1642** FULLER *Holy & Prof. St.* II. xix. 128 He rebetakes himself to his former calling.

rebeuc, obs. form of REBUKE *sb.*

re-beˈwail, *v.* [RE- 5 a.] To bewail anew.

a **1711** KEN *Psyche* Poet. Wks. 1721 IV. 166 They re-bewail'd their own, and publick crimes.

rebid (riːˈbɪd, ˈriːbɪd), *v.* *Bridge.* [RE- 5 a.] *trans.* and *intr.* To bid (BID *v.* 3 c) again. Hence **ˈrebid** *sb.*; **reˈbiddable** *a.*

1923 *Daily Mail* 6 Oct. 6/4 Z has called '3 clubs'. A bids '2 spades'. Y or Z may point out the insufficiency or may in turn re-bid 3 clubs. **1927** M. C. WORK *Contract Bridge* iii. 27 It is not the one-bids, or the ones jumped to twos, which produce the heavy sets in Contract; it is the game-going jumps and the rebids to reach game-going declarations that do the damage. **1929** —— *Compl. Contract Bridge* iv. 25 One of them being strong enough to bid two of a major, and East not being able to rebid. **1945** PHILLIPS & REESE *How to play Bridge* vi. 45 If your hand is weak, but your suit is rebiddable, you should bid Three of it. **1958** *Listener* 9 Oct. 572/3 The Diamonds are not rebiddable. **1971** *Daily Tel.* 21 Aug. 8/3 East contested the part score with 3 diamonds, judging that his two honours would be adequate support opposite the rebid suit. **1975** *Times* 11 Jan. 7/5 By rebidding his suit he imagined that he was asking his partner to choose between Hearts and Spades. **1976** *Cumberland News* 26 Nov., In many respects rebids are more important than opening bids or first responses for very rarely do these bids give precise information about the hands.

rebillion, obs. form of REBELLION.

rebind (riːˈbaɪnd), *v.* [RE- 5 a.] *trans.* To bind again, in senses of the vb.; *esp.* to give a new binding to (a book). Hence **reˈbinding** *vbl. sb.*

1820 *Rep. Comm. Public Rec. 1800–1819* 525 The total sum of £1,000 per Annum..to the Purposes of maintaining ..and..occasionally re-binding..the Public Records. *Ibid.* 527 Many different Series of Records..have been carefully repaired and suitably rebound. **1850** KINGSLEY *Alt. Locke* xxv, He had numbers of his books rebound in plain covers. **1857** D. LAING *Penni Worth of Witte* p. iii, It must have suffered in the rebinding, by being rather unsparingly cut in the edges. **1865** *Spectator* 4 Feb. 120/2 A great victory might still rebind the fetters upon its serfs. **1886** *Athenæum* 30 Oct. 566/2 Why these old covers were not restored to the volume on its rebinding it is hard to say. **1901** D. COCKERELL *Bookbinding* i. 18 Nearly all librarians complain that they have to be continually rebinding books. *Ibid.* xxii. 306 When the sewing cords or threads of a book have perished it should be re-bound. **1931** A. ESDAILE *Student's Man. Bibliogr.* vi. 178 Most bibliographers are aware of the great mass of important knowledge which has been destroyed by careless re-binding. **1946** H. J. PLENDERLEITH *Preservation of Leather Bookbindings* 10 Some [volumes of a catalogue] have actually had to be rebound. **1963** B. C. MIDDLETON *Hist. Eng. Craft Bookbinding Technique* ii. 8 Thousands of old books..were rebound in modern morocco.

rebirth (riːˈbɜːθ). [RE- 5 a; cf. REBORN.] A second birth (physical or spiritual); also *fig.* of things.

In common use from *c* 1850, now especially with reference to the reincarnation of the soul in new forms.

1837 tr. *Guizot's Hist. Civiliz.* vi. 196 This re-birth of the spirit of free inquiry. **1855** BAILEY *Mystic*, etc. 22 The destruction and re-birth of things He saw. **1866** J. MARTINEAU *Ess.* I. 14 The rebirth of his heart was indispensable. **1871** ALABASTER *Wheel of Law* p. xlv, The request to a living Buddha to reward an offering by some particular rebirth.

†**reˈbite**, *v.*¹ *Obs.*$^{-1}$ *trans.* To bite in return.

1594 T. B. *La Primaud. Fr. Acad.* II. 325 When the heart is wounded with griefe by any one, it desireth..to rebite him of whome it is bitten.

rebite (riːˈbaɪt), *v.*² [RE- 5 a.] *trans.* To bite again (in sense 11 of the vb.). Hence **reˈbiting** *vbl. sb.*

1816 J. SMITH *Panorama Sc. & Art* II. 768 When any part of the plate is materially too faint, it may be rebitten. **1822** IMISON *Sc. & Art* II. 429 This second biting in the same lines is called re-biting. **1875** KNIGHT *Dict. Mech.* 1899/1 The parts which do not require rebiting.

reˈbless, *v.* [RE- 5 a.] *trans.* To bless again.

1599 SANDYS *Europæ Spec.* (1632) 181 The Popes refusall to reblesse the King upon his sodaine reconversion. **1614** C. BROOKE *Eclogue* Poems (1872) 159 Take thy pleasant reed, And with thy melody reblesse mine eare. **1630** J. TAYLOR (Water P.) *Wks.* II. 303/1 At last the Pope was pleased, and I reblest.

‖**reblochon** (rəblɔʃɔ̃). [Fr.] The name of a soft French cheese made originally and chiefly in Savoy.

1908 DOANE & LAWSON *Varieties of Cheese* 43 *Reblochon.* This is a soft French cheese weighing 1 to 2 pounds. It is made from fresh whole milk which is curdled with rennet at a temperature of 80 °F. or above, the time allowed being about thirty minutes. **1931** F. COLCHESTER-WEMYSS *Pleasures of Table* vii. 70 Reblochon is a delightful cheese, and not at all awkward as regards keeping. **1935** O. BURDETT *Little Book of Cheese* iv. 59 Though not often to be had in England, and, perhaps, not very often beyond the borders of Savoy, *Reblochons* must be mentioned. It makes a convenient postscript to Brie, for it is a smallish round, flat cheese, very creamy and rich in flavour. **1967** *House & Garden* Apr. 96/3 Fertilizers mask the taste of grass... Reblochon is losing its hint of gentian. **1971** *Sunday Times* 28 Mar. (Colour Suppl.) 34/4 *Reblochon*, the most distinguished of the cheeses of the Haute Savoie. Made with the yield of the second milking of the fawn Tarentais cow (*rebloche* in the local patois means 'second milking'). **1973** J. M. WHITE *Garden Game* 44 He cut off a sliver of *reblochon* and sampled it... He waved the cheese-knife.

rebloom (riːˈbluːm), *v.* [RE- 5 a.] *intr.* To bloom again.

1605 SYLVESTER *Du Bartas* II. iii. III. *Law* 1236 His oft-quickned Rod, Which dead, re-buds, re-blooms, and Almonds bears. **1793** SOUTHEY *Lines 1st December* xi, Nature soon..Shall..Expand the bursting bud again, And bid the flower re-bloom. **1812** CRABBE *Tales* 59 Faded beauty with new grace re-bloom'd. **1864** TENNYSON *Aylmer's F.* 142 They..Gather'd the blossom that rebloom'd.

reblossom (riːˈblɒsəm), *v.* [RE- 5 a.] *intr.* To blossom again.

1611 FLORIO, *Rigermogliante*, budding or burgeoning againe, reblossoming. **1747** *Gentl. Mag.* 339 Your charms reblossom in a female face. **1768** STERNE *Sent. Journ.* (1778) II. 55 (*The Sword*) The little tree his pride and affection wish'd to see re-blossom. **1863** LYTTON *Caxtoniana* I. 115 Mere dandies are but cut flowers in a bouquet—once faded, they never can reblossom.

re-'blue, *v. rare.* [RE- 5 a.] *trans.* To make (the sky) blue again.

1598 SYLVESTER *Du Bartas* II. i. IV. *Handie-crafts* 13 Fair Goddesse that renew'st Th' old golden age, & brightly now re-blew'st Our cloudy sky.

reboant ('rɛbəʊənt), *a.* Chiefly *poet.* [a. L. *reboant-*, ppl. stem of *reboāre*, f. *re-* RE- 2 a + *boāre* to bellow: cf. REBOATION.] Rebellowing, re-echoing loudly.

1830 TENNYSON *Conf. Sensit. Mind* 97 Unpiloted i' the echoing dance Of reboant whirlwinds. **1844** MRS. BROWNING *Vis. Poets* 13 Spiritual thunders.. Crushing their echoes reboant With their own wheels.

rebo'antic, *a.* Chiefly *poet.* [f. REBOANT *a.* + -IC.] = REBOANT *a.*

1903 KIPLING *Five Nations* 124 When the Conchimarian horns Of the reboantic Norns Usher gentlemen and ladies With new lights on Heaven and Hades. **1907** *Academy* 23 Mar. 298/1 Even then the Norns couldn't be reboantic, supposing that word to be correctly derived from *reboo* = to bellow back.

re'board, *v.* [RE-.] *trans.* To board (a vessel) again or in return. Also *absol.*

c **1594** CAPT. WYATT *R. Dudley's Voy. W. Ind.* (Hakluyt) 11 After great bordinge and rebordinge each other, one the morrow wee solemnlie feasted one another. *Ibid.* 19. **1906** *Westm. Gaz.* 24 Mar. 10/2 Her bulwarks kept her afloat, and the crew reboarded her and brought her safely to Milford Haven. **1977** *R.A.F. News* 5–18 Jan. 3/2 He was winched to safety and later put down on the tanker to.. reboard the catamaran. **1977** *Western Living* (Vancouver) Apr. 33/2 The conductor ordered all to reboard.

†**reboation.** *Obs. rare.* [f. L. *reboāre*: see REBOANT and -ATION.] A rebellowing echo.

1654 R. CODRINGTON tr. *Iustine* xxiv. 337 The sound is heard more multiplyed by the reboation. **1659** BP. PATRICK *Div. Arith.* 2, I imagine that I should hear the reboation of an universal groan. [**1736** in BAILEY; hence in Johnson and later Dicts.]

re'body, *v. trans.*

†**1.** = RE-EMBODY *v. Obs.*⁻¹

1622 H. SYDENHAM *Serm. Sol. Occ.* II. (1637) 174 Man.. is.. rebodied with the soule, to the honour of a Resurrection.

2. *trans.* To furnish (a motor vehicle, etc.) with a new body. Hence **re'bodied** *ppl. a.*

1963 *Times* 19 Jan. 3/6 His car had to be rebodied. **1977** *Custom Car* Nov. 30/3 Their Rio was slated by the press, who saw it as nothing more than a rebodied Dolomite.

†**reboil**, *sb. Obs.*⁻¹ [f. next.] Wine which has fermented a second time.

c **1460** J. RUSSELL *Bk. Nurture* 115 The reboyle to Rakke to þe lies of þe rose þat shalle be his amendynge.

†**re'boil**, *v.*¹ *Obs.* Forms: 5 reboille, 5–7 -boyle, 6–7 -boile. [a. OF. *rebouillir* (13th c. in Littré):—L. *rebullī-re* to bubble up: see BOIL *v.* and EBULLITION.]

1. *intr.* Of wine: To ferment a second time.

1444 *Rolls of Parlt.* V. 114/1 Neither Clusters of Grapes, ne hole Grapes.. yat myght cause yat Wyne after that to reboille or myscare. *c* **1460** J. RUSSELL *Bk. Nurture* 110 Take good hede to þe wynes.. þat þey not reboyle nor lete. **1594** PLAT *Jewell-ho.* III. 63 If anie sweete Wines happen to reboile in the hot part of the Summer. **1601** HOLLAND *Pliny* I. 417 New wine.. must be suffered to work: and afterwards to reboile and work againe.. the Summer following.

2. *intr.* To boil up or over (in *fig.* uses).

1477 SIR J. PASTON in *P. Lett.* III. 174 It semythe that the worlde is alle qwaveryng; it will reboyle somwher. **1531** ELYOT *Gov.* II. vii, Some of his companyons therat reboyleth, infamynge hym to be a man without charitie. **1556** PHAER *Æneid* IV. Liij b, Fixed vnderneth her brest her wound reboyleth fast. **1601** F. GODWIN *Bps. of Eng.* 501 The auncient hatred he bore vnto the king.. now reboiled in his stomacke.

b. *trans.* To cause to boil up (*fig.*).

a **1529** SKELTON *Replyc.* Wks. 1843 I. 209 These demy diuines.. feruently reboyled with the infatuate flames of their rechelesse youthe.

Hence †**reboiled** *ppl. a.*; †**reboiling** *vbl. sb.*

1432 *Rolls of Parlt.* IV. 405/2 After thei have lyen a little while, thanne for reboylyng.. because of the saide falsnesse they wer all noght. *a* **1483** *Liber Niger* in *Househ. Ord.* (1790) 73 If any wynes be corrupted, reboyled, or unwholsome for mannys body. **1513** W. DE WORDE *Bk. Keruynge* in *Babees Bk.* 267 Drawe the reboyled wyne to yᵉ lyes, & it shal helpe it. **1598** FLORIO, *Ribollimento*, a reboyling, a heating, or skalding.

reboil (riː'bɔɪl), *v.*² [RE- 5 a.] *trans.* To boil again (*lit.* and *fig.*). Hence **re'boiling** *vbl. sb.*

1615 CROOKE *Body of Man* 267 [The vein] powreth the blood into the right ventricle.., there it is reboyled and attenuated. **1628** tr. *Mathieu's Powerfull Favorite* 120 Tiberius hauing boyled and reboyled his project in his heart. **1806** A. HUNTER *Culina* (ed. 3) 247 Let them [eggs] be reboiled for the same space of time as at first. **1875** MISS BIRD *Sandwich Isl.* (1880) 76 This reboiling of the drainings is repeated two or three times.

reboiler (riː'bɔɪlə(r)), *v.* [RE- 5 c.] *trans.* To fit with a new boiler.

1889 *Daily Chron.* 30 June 7/1 What has been the total cost of re-boilering H.M.S. Salamander? **1908** *Westm. Gaz.* 25 Apr. 2/3 The Banter Line decided to reboiler the *Caesar* and go for the Atlantic record. **1961** *Guardian* 5 June 10/6 One of the two original engines.. was.. reboilered just a year before the line closed.

reboiler (riː'bɔɪlə(r)), *sb.* [f. REBOIL *v.*² + -ER¹.] A heater for vaporizing the liquid at the bottom of a fractionating column.

1956 MCCABE & SMITH *Unit Operations of Chem. Engin.* xii. 685 The liquid feed flows down the column to the still, which in this type of plant is called the 'reboiler', and is subjected to rectification by the vapor rising from the reboiler. **1966** *McGraw-Hill Encycl. Sci. & Technol.* XIII. 185/2 Many [stripping] processes employ a combination of all three; that is, after absorption at elevated pressure, the solvent is flashed to atmospheric pressure, heated, and admitted into a stripping column which is provided with a bottom heater (reboiler). **1977** F. G. SHINSKEY *Distillation Control* ix. 273 Multiple reboilers are generally used in severe fouling service, so that they may be individually cleaned without interrupting operation of the column.

reboise (rɪ'bɔɪz), *v. rare.* [ad. F. *reboiser*, f. *re-* RE- + *bois* wood.] *trans.* To reafforest, reforest.

1891 in *Cent. Dict.*

reboisement (rɪ'bɔɪzmənt). [a. F. *reboisement*, f. *reboiser*: see prec.] Reafforestation.

1882 *Pall Mall G.* 10 Aug. 5/1 By reboisement of much waste land wholly unfit for the plough. **1893** R. KIPLING *Many Invent.* 189 The reboisement of all India is in its hand.

†**re'boke**, *v. Obs.* [f. RE- + *boke*, var. BOLK *v.*] *intr.* To belch, eructate.

1509 BARCLAY *Shyp of Folys* (1570) 229 He is king of dronkardes and of dronkennes Reputed of them.. As grunting and drinking, reboking up agayne. **1514** —— *Cyt. & Uplondyshm.* (Percy Soc.) 47 Sometime thy felowe reboketh in thy face. *a* **1529** SKELTON *Bouge of Court* 180 His stomak stuffed ofte tymes did reboke.

re'bolt, *v.* [RE- 5 a.]

1. *trans.* To bolt (a door) again.

1877 *Sunday Mag.* 113/1 John came back, rebolted the scullery door, looked to his other fastenings [etc.].

2. To cut up again into bolts or lathes. Hence ***rebolting-machine*** (see quot.).

1875 KNIGHT *Dict. Mech.* 1899/1 *Rebolting-machine*, a species of sawing-machine for rebolting large blocks of timber without quite separating smaller bolts from each other. [Description follows.]

rebon, obs. variant of REBOUND *sb.*

re-'book, *v.* [RE- 5 a.] *trans.* and *intr.* To book again (see BOOK *v.* 4 b).

1864 *Railw. Time Table*, Passengers cannot be re-booked at any Intermediate Station by the Train in which they are travelling. **1885** *Law Rep.* 14 *Q.B.D.* 228 At Stockport the plaintiff re-booked to Ashton-under-Lyne. **1898** G. GISSING *Let.* 27 Jan. in R. A. Gettman *G. Gissing & H. G. Wells* (1961) 85 The trunk.. will have to be.. re-booked to Rome. **1906** *Westm. Gaz.* 6 Sept. 8/3 Such a bylaw.. compels a passenger to get out and rebook, even though he miss his train. But he would still have to rebook if going by a later train. **1978** 'S. WOODS' *Exit Murderer* 55 I've re-booked your room for you.

reboot, obs. Sc. form of REBUT *v.*

rebop: see BEBOP.

rebore ('riːbɔə(r)), *sb.* [f. the vb.] A re-boring of one or more cylinders of an internal-combustion engine; also, an engine which has had its cylinders re-bored.

1954 'TORRENS' *Motor Cyclist's Workshop* (ed. 6) xx. 126 When your piston is 'worn out', your cylinder is sorely in need of a rebore or.. regrinding. **1967** J. MILLS *Low-Cost Car Repairs* iii. 75 The check is to determine whether a recon-set can be used or whether a rebore is needed. **1970** K. BALL *Fiat 600, 600D Autobook* i. 13 A rebore will require new pistons and rings a size larger than the original and these will usually be supplied by the garage.. undertaking the rebore. **1977** *S. Wales Echo* 18 Jan. (Advt.), Exchange crankshafts, camshafts, short engines, rebores, pistons.

re-'bore, *v.* [RE- 5 a.] *trans.* To bore (a gun-barrel, wheel, etc.) again.

1821 COL. HAWKER *Diary* (1893) I. 239 Weight of gun since reboring.. 83 lb. **1884** F. J. BRITTEN *Watch & Clockm.* 152 If the wheel is out of truth it must be re-bored.

reborn (riː'bɔːn), *pa. pple.* and *ppl. a.* [RE- 5 a.] Born again (physically or spiritually).

1598 FLORIO, *Rinato*, reborne or sprung vp againe. **1614** H. GREENWOOD *Jayle Deliv.* 476 O better for these never to have been borne, then not to be reborne. **1652** BENLOWES *Theoph.* IV. iv, The New-man is By th' quickning Spirit of the High'st reborn. **1842** PUSEY *Crisis Eng. Ch.* 12 Through her we were reborn, within her have we been trained. **1871** ALABASTER *Wheel of Law* p. xxxix, According to them, it is not the soul or self which is reborn, but the quality.

b. *transf.* of things.

1824 MISS MITFORD *Village* Ser. I. (1863) 17 The road is alive again. Noise is re-born. **1864** PUSEY *Lect. Daniel* iii. 105 Noah at the head of the newly cleansed and as it were reborn world.

reborrow (riː'bɒrəʊ), *v.* [RE- 5 a.] *trans.* To borrow back again; to borrow anew. Also *absol.*

1631 BP. H. KING *On Death Dr. Donne*, Nor is't fit Thou, who didst lend our age such summes of wit, Shoulds't now reborrow from her Bankrupt Mine That Ore to bury thee, which once was thine. **1806** W. TAYLOR in Robberds *Mem.* (1843) II. 135 For your specimens I will re-borrow and transcribe an ode or two of Stevens. **1863** GLADSTONE *Financ. Statem.* 393 We shall ask the House to intrust us with power to reborrow that money. **1885** *Law Times Rep.* LII. 800/1 One of the powers of the company is to borrow and reborrow for the purposes of the company.

reborrowing (riː'bɒrəʊɪŋ), *vbl. sb.* [f. REBORROW *v.* + -ING¹.] The action of the vb. REBORROW (esp. in *Philol.*); also, that which is reborrowed.

1869 *Bradshaw's Railway Man.* XXI. 221 Pay off and create in lieu of reborrowing. **1933** L. BLOOMFIELD *Language* xxv. 452 The same re-borrowing of this last word appears in Old English. **1953** K. JACKSON *Lang. & Hist. Early Brit.* II. 332 Förster notes that the AS. form of Nene is spelt five times in Peterborough documents as *Nyn*, and regards this as a re-borrowing. **1979** *Amer. Speech* LIV. 29 Of the 6 pure reborrowings, 4 are from *cent*: Indonesian *sen*, Samoan *sene*, Tongan *seniti*, and Swahili *senti*.

rebosa, reboso: see REBOZO.

re'bottle, *v.* [RE- 5 a.] To bottle again.

1807 SOUTHEY in Robberds *Mem. W. Taylor* (1843) II. 198 To rebottle water which he has distilled till it has lost all its life and freshness. **1888** J. ELLIS *New Christianity* vi. 137 The clear portion of the wine must be carefully removed.. and then heated and rebottled and corked while hot.

rebouk, obs. form of REBUKE *v.*

re'bounce, *v.* [RE-.] To bounce back or again.

1616 J. LANE *Cont. Sqr.'s T.* VII. 245[The fight] More and more encreasinge, hotter grew,.. bowncing, rebowncinge, new noise immitatinge.

rebound (rɪ'baʊnd, now usu. 'riːbaʊnd), *sb.* Also 5 **rebon**, 6 **rebowne**. [f. the vb. Cf. F. *rebond* (16th c.). The early forms without *d* are prob. a. AF. *reboun* (Gower).]

†**1.** ? Noise, din. *Obs.*⁻¹

c **1485** *Digby Myst.* III. 1465 Who made the so hardy to make swych rebon?

†**2.** A violent blow. *Obs.*⁻¹

Cf. mod.Sc. 'He got a great rebound for his carelessness', i.e. a severe rebuke or reprimand.

a **1500** *Sir Beues* (Pynson) 3515 Than rode.. syr Terry To the kynges broder.. And gaue to hym suche a rebowne That both he and his hors fel downe.

3. The act of bounding back after striking; resilience, return, recoil.

a. of material things; *spec.* in *Basketball*, *Football*, etc., the return of a ball from the backboard, goal-post, etc., after an unsuccessful shot; a ball that rebounds in this manner; (also *attrib.*).

1530 PALSGR. 261/1 Rebounde of a ball, *bond.* **1596** RALEIGH *Discov. Gviana* 67 The rebound of water made it seeme, as if it had beene all couered ouer with a great shower of rayne. **1698** FRYER *Acc. E. India & P.* 398 They play Balls with Rackets, bringing their Steeds to observe the Rebound. **1732** LEDIARD *Sethos* II. VII. 55 His head.. made three rebounds upon the scaffold. **1814** BYRON *Ode Napoleon* vi, He who of old would rend the oak, Dream'd not of the rebound. **1876** T. HARDY *Ethelberta* (1890) 344 The water began to thunder into these [caverns] with a leap that was only topped by the rebound seaward again. **1922** W. E. MEANWELL *Basket Ball for Men* vi. 61 The opposing attack is following in hard for the rebound. *Ibid.*, The hook pass.. permits the guard to reverse and present his back to the oncoming rebound man. **1948** *Sun* (Baltimore) 7 Jan. 11/1 Jimmy Kirby.. tapped in four field goals when taking rebounds. **1954** *Basketball* ('Know the Game' Series) 35 When a shot is missed obtaining the rebound is vital... Although defensive players usually start with the best position for the rebound offensive, players must make every effort to beat the defender to the best rebound positions. **1955** *Sun* (Baltimore) 4 Feb. 15/1 He is an outstanding rebound man and the team's third leading scorer. **1969** *Eugene* (Oregon) *Register-Guard* 3 Dec. 1D/3 'It was the board play that killed us,' continued Belko, pointing to Wichita's 62–43 edge in rebounds. **1971** *N.Y. Times Guide Spectator Sports* iii. 78 A man much taller than the rest.. had the best chance to retrieve the 'rebound' over the heads of smaller players. **1976** *Western Mail* (Cardiff) 22 Nov. 16/3 Preece was on hand to fire home the rebound from close range. **1978** *Dumfries Courier* 13 Oct. 4/6 Milligan levelled the scores for Girvan connecting with a rebound after a shot had been blocked in the goalmouth.

b. of sound and light.

1594 T. B. *La Primaud. Fr. Acad.* II. 81 The soundes woulde not be conueyed in so well, as they are in places that bend and giue backewarde, where they haue rebounds. **1603** HOLLAND *Plutarch's Mor.* 1217 The stroks.. be heard a farre off,.. by reason of the resonance and rebound. **1689** BURNET *Tracts* I. 93 The Rebound of the Sun-beams from the Mountains doth so increase the heats here. **1810** SOUTHEY *Kehama* I. iv, With quick rebound of sound, All in accordance cry.

c. *transf.* or *fig.* in various applications. Now freq. *attrib.*

1562 J. HEYWOOD *Prov. & Epigr.* (1867) 135 Throw no gyft againe at the gyuers hed: If thou do the rebounde may be so red, That the red bloud may run downe in thy necke. **1589** PUTTENHAM *Eng. Poesie* III. xix. (Arb.) 216 Ye haue another figure which by his nature we may call the Rebound. **1606** SHAKS. *Ant. & Cl.* V. ii. 104, I do feele By the rebounde of yours, a grief that suites [*emend.* shoots] My very heart at roote. *a* **1658** CLEVELAND *Cl. Vindic.* (1677) 169 She had return'd your Summons without perusal. Which rebound of your Letter.. is the most compendious Answer to what you propound. *a* **1708** BEVERIDGE *Wks.* (1846) VIII. 654 The report.. I heard, by a second rebound from the prints which go about the country. **1763** EARL MARCH 21 June in Jesse *G. Selwyn* (1843) I. 235 My dinner is a rebound of one we had at Eglinton's. **1782** MISS BURNEY *Cecilia* IX. iii, Nature herself.. is not more elastic in her rebound. **1853** MAURICE *Proph. & Kings* xvii. 292 The feeling would be all the stronger because it was a rebound from a state of depression and shame. **1951** *Jrnl. Clin. Endocrinol.* XI. 235 (*heading*) Spermatogenic rebound phenomenon after administration of testosterone propionate. **1954** *Jrnl. Nerv. & Mental Dis.* CXX. 46 (*heading*) Abstention [from addictive drugs], rebound, and readjustment. **1974** M. C. GERALD *Pharmacol.*

vi. 115 The relief produced by the shrinkage of swollen nasal membranes is merely temporary and is followed by rebound congestion. *Ibid.* xv. 288 More often death has been attributed to secondary causes such as.. suicides arising from rebound depression during periods of drug withdrawal or abstinence. **1977** *Lancet* 9 Apr. 774/1 Thrombocytopenia caused by alcohol is reversible after alcohol withdrawal, and is followed by rebound thrombocytosis. **1978** M. G. HARMATZ *Abnormal Psychol.* vii. 162/1 Patients felt even more deeply depressed when drug action wore off than before they had treatment (a rebound effect). Modern anti-depressants.. avoid these side effects.

d. *fig.* †(*a*) in phrases ***to take at*** (***a*** or ***the***), ***by***, ***from***, or ***upon rebound***; also, ***to accept***, ***catch***, etc., ***at rebound***. *Obs.* (Freq. in 17th c.) (*b*) (†***in*** or) ***on the rebound***: during a period of reaction following an emotionally disturbing experience, esp. a broken engagement or a refusal of marriage. Also used without *prep.*

1577 STANYHURST *Descr. Irel.* in *Holinshed* VI. 5 Here percase some snappish carper will take me at rebound. **1639** FULLER *Holy War* III. xix. (1840) 150 St. Bernard, taking it rather from the rebound than first rise chargeth them therewith. **1660** *Trial of Regic.* 118 If he doth but write them by the command of another, by speaking them after another, taking them upon rebound, that is not treason. **1675** COCKER *Morals* 2 Accept a Courtesie at first Rebound. **1739** MELMOTH *Fitzosb. Lett.* (1763) 361 Either to seize upon their conclusions at once, or to take them by rebound from others. **1853** MRS. GASKELL *Ruth* III. iv. 129 His first rebound to Jemima. **1859** *Harper's Mag.* Aug. 341/1 Ellen Bond caught his heart 'in the rebound', as somebody says. **1861** C. M. YONGE *Young Step-Mother* xxi. 295 We may steer her safely through, above all, if one of the six cousins will but catch him in the rebound. **1864** G. J. WHYTE-MELVILLE *Queen's Maries* II. xxxviii. 234 It is an old saying that 'many a heart is caught on the rebound'. *a* **1899** V. S. LEAN *Collectanea* (1904) IV. 41 Many a heart is caught in the rebound, *i.e.* after a repulse by another. **1921** GALSWORTHY *To Let* III. x. 290 Ah! it was strange—this marriage. The young man, Mont, had caught her on the rebound, of course, in the reckless mood of one whose ship has just gone down. **1931** H. S. WALPOLE *Judith Paris* III. i. 428 She has but accepted him on the rebound from her trouble with Beaminster. **1969** A. GLYN *Dragon Variation* ix. 283 Maybe the girl had had a fight with Carl, and had turned to Jeff on the rebound. **1977** A. MORICE *Murder in Mimicry* I. ix. 91 Her passion for Gilbert was already on the wane... The rebound was in full swing. **1978** *Lancashire Life* Sept. 47/2 Perhaps it was on the rebound from this disappointment that he contracted his disastrous first marriage.

rebound (rɪˈbaʊnd), *v.* Also 6 rebowne, reboune. [ad. OF. *rebonder*, *-bondir*, *-bundir* (mod.F. *rebondir*) to resound, bound back: see RE- and BOUND *v.*[2] In ME. and early mod.E. freq. confused with REDOUND *v.*; see 1 b–1 d and 3 c.]

1. a. *intr.* To spring back from force of impact, to bound back.

1398 TREVISA *Barth. De P.R.* VIII. xxviii. (Bodl. MS.) Þat besschynyng þat reboundeþ aȝen is icleped *lumen refluxum*. *c* **1450** *Merlin* 245 He droff hem a-wey discounfited, and made hem to rebounde vpon the warde of ffalsabres and vpon the warde of Pyngnoras. **1530** PALSGR. 680/1, I never sawe gonne stone skyppe on that facyon, it rebounded thrise one after an other. **1559** W. CUNNINGHAM *Cosmogr. Glasse* 42 The Sonne beames rebounding from th' earth. **1634** PEACHAM *Gentl. Exerc.* I. x. 33 A ball being strucken hard downe with your hand, reboundeth backe in the same line. **1692** BENTLEY *Boyle Lect.* vii. 235 Those few [atoms] that should happen to clash might rebound after the collision. **1751** SMOLLETT *Per. Pic.* xxxvi, My shot rebounded from his face like a wad of spun-yarn from the walls of a ship. **1816** BYRON *Ch. Har.* III. lviii, When shell and ball Rebounding idly on her strength did light. **1855** MACAULAY *Hist. Eng.* xii. III. 236 The shock was such that the Mountjoy rebounded, and stuck in the mud.

b. *transf.* or *fig.* of immaterial things (common in 15–17th c.).

In early use prob. confused with REDOUND *v.*; cf. 3 c.

?*c* **1400** LYDG. *Æsop's Fab.* v. 164 Where frawde is vsed, frawde mote rebounde. **1412–20** —— *Chron. Troy* II. xii, The shame.. doth rebounde Upon vs all. *a* **1533** LD. BERNERS *Gold. Bk. M. Aurel.* (1546) I, That benefite rebounded onely to the myserable prysoners. **1581** J. BELL *Haddon's Answ. Osor.* 186 The question reboundeth backe agayne from whence it came first. **1647** COWLEY *Mistr.* XXVIII. iv, When it does Hardness meet and Pride, My Love does then rebound t'another side. **1707** NORRIS *Treat. Humility* vi. 246 The respect that is shewn to those below us, rebounds upwards. **1788** BURKE *Sp. agst. W. Hastings* Wks. XIII. 16 An evil example, that would rebound back on themselves. **1852** ROBERTSON *Serm.* Ser. III. xiv. 170 Through the medium of reaction rebounding from extremes which produce contrary extremes. **1955** *Times* 9 Aug. 12/2 Equities rebounded sharply yesterday after their reaction last week although they did not always fully hold their gains. **1979** *Arizona Daily Star* 1 Apr. D2/3 Coal prices just don't seem to want to rebound.

†**c.** To redound *to* one's shame, honour, etc. *Obs.*

1412–20 LYDG. *Chron. Troy* II. xvi, Reprefe to their name That iustly might rebounde to their shame. *c* **1460** G. ASHBY *Dicta Philos.* 76 So it shal rebounde to youre honour. **1528** ROY *Rede me* (Arb.) 36 Unto oure dishonowre all doeth rebowne Seyinge that gone is the masse.

¶**d.** Used by Wyclif to render L. *redundāre*.

1382 WYCLIF *Prov.* iii. 10 Thi bernes shul ben fulfild with fulnesse, and with win thi presses shul rebounden. —— *Esther* vii. 4 Our enemy.. whos cruelte reboundeth in to the king. *Ibid.* x. 6 A litil welle, that grew into a flod,.. and in to manye watris reboundide.

e. *Basketball.* To catch a rebound (REBOUND *sb.* 3 a).

1954 *Sun* (Baltimore) 20 Dec. B18/2 Pollard is the best balanced basketball player I have ever seen;.. he can rebound with the best big men in the business. **1974** *State* (Columbia, S. Carolina) 3 Mar. 1-D/1 Kelley went to the line for a one-and-one at 1:04 and missed. Stewart rebounded and McCurdy failed to connect twice.

2. To re-echo, reverberate, resound. Now *rare* or *Obs.* **a.** of sounds.

c **1440** *Promp. Parv.* 425/1 Rebowndyn', or sowndyn aȝene', *reboo.* ?*a* **1500** *Knt. of Curtesy* 347 The noise of gonnes did rebounde. **1530** RASTELL *Bk. Purgat.* I. xvi, Every man hereth the hole voyce, sown, or worde, & it reboundyth hole in every mannes erys. **1582** STANYHURST *Æneis* III. (Arb.) 71 With playnts most pitiful to oure ears thus sadlye rebounding. **1646** CRASHAW *Sospetto d'Herode* xxxviii, A gen'ral hiss, from the whole tire of snakes Rebounding, through hell's inmost caverns came. *a* **1711** KEN *Preparatives* Poet. Wks. 1721 IV. 51 More surprising Sound Will through the hollow Graves rebound. **1781** COWPER *Hope* 346 From stuccoed walls smart arguments rebound. *a* **1822** SHELLEY *Homer's Hymn Merc.* lxxxvii, Far and wide rebounded The echo of his pipings.

b. of places. Const. *of*, *with*, *to*, and *absol.*

1555 EDEN *Decades* To Rdr. (Arb.) 49 Hauens with echo seuen tymes reboundynge. **1579–80** NORTH *Plutarch* (1612) 430 Made the mountaines.. to rebound againe of the sound and eccho of their cries. **1697** DRYDEN *Virg. Georg.* IV. 100 With hoarse allarms the hollow Camp rebounds. **1725** POPE *Odyss.* VIII. 16 With tumultuous sounds Of thronging multitudes the shore rebounds. **1788** WARTON *On his Majesty's Birthday* ii, Where the long roofs rebounded to the din Of spectre chiefs, who feasted far within.

3. a. To bound or leap, esp. in return or response to some force or stimulus. Now *rare* or *Obs.*

13.. *E.E. Allit. P.* B. 422 [The ark] flote forthe with þe flyt of þe felle wyndez; Wheder-warde so þe water wafte, hit rebounde. *c* **1420** *Avow. Arth.* xi, Als sone as he come thare, A-ȝaynus him rebowndet the bare. **1513** DOUGLAS *Æneis* VII. vii. 91 [The top] smyttin wyth the tawis dois rebound. **1634** SIR T. HERBERT *Trav.* 7 Sometimes the surges or Sea-flashes doe rebound top-gallant height. **1653** H. COGAN tr. *Pinto's Trav.* xxiii. 86 By means of a bellows.. the water rebounded up so high, that.. it fell as small as dew. **1667** MILTON *P.L.* I. 788 At once with joy and fear his heart rebounds. **1725** POPE *Odyss.* xv. 162 Along the court the fiery steeds rebound. **1791** COWPER *Iliad* XIII. 741 The heart Rebounded of Pisander, full of hope.

b. To bound back (without impact).

1513 DOUGLAS *Æneis* VII. Prol. 112, I.. slepit sownd Quhill the orizont upwart gan rebound. **1856** FROUDE *Hist. Eng.* II. 213 The stone which had been laboriously rolled to the summit of the hill was trembling on the brink, and in a moment might rebound into the plain.

†**c.** To result, arise *from* a source. *Obs.*[−1]

Prob. confused with REDOUND: cf. 1 b.

a **1471** FORTESCUE *Wks.* (1869) 485 Thou knowest nat what spiritual wynnyng reboundeth from theis temporal hurts. **1662** J. CHANDLER *Van Helmont's Oriat.* Pref., As soon as any one shall come to be fined, let the money rebounding from hence, be laid aside for the use of suppressing the Enemies.

4. a. *trans.* To cause to bound back; to cast or throw back, to return. Now *rare*.

c **1560** in *Œcon. Rokebiorum* in *Richmond Wills* (Surtees) 200 *note*, Christofer Rokeby, being assaulted.. was able soe to have rebounded the blowes given him [etc.]. **1596** *Edw. III*, I. i, Defiance, Frenchman? we rebound it back. **1657** J. SMITH *Myst. Rhet.* 126 When Anthony charged Cicero,.. Cicero rebounded the same accusation again to Antony. **1658** GURNALL *Chr. in Arm.* verse 14. xi. §3 (1669) 99/1 Now to rebound his love in thankfulness, she bestirs her self [etc.]. **1713** STEELE *Spect.* No. 423 ¶6 They have the whole Woman between them, and can occasionally rebound her Love and Hatred from one to the other. **1803** JANE PORTER *Thaddeus* xxvi. (1831) 231 His dignified composure rebounded their darts upon his insulters. **1865** S. FERGUSON *Forging of Anchor* ii, The leathern mail rebounds the hail.

†**b.** To reflect (light). *Obs.*

1398 TREVISA *Barth. De P.R.* VIII. xxix. (Bodl. MS.), A merroure.. and oþer glistering bodies reboundeþ aȝen þe schynynge that he fongeþ. **1599** DAVIES *Hymns Astræa* xv, Rebound vpon thy selfe thy light. **1653** MORE *Antid. Ath.* II. xii. §3 The rays falling upon the Retina.. being rebounded thence upon the Uvea.

5. a. To re-echo, return (a sound). Now *rare*.

1555 EDEN *Decades* 96 The wooddes and montaynes.. rebounded the noyse of the horryble crye. **1591** SPENSER *Tears of Muses* 22 The hollow hills.. Were wont redoubled Echoes to rebound. **1655** FULLER *Ch. Hist.* I. v. §10 They reckoned their Foes by the increase of the Noise rebounded unto them. **1703** POPE *Thebais* I. 163 The dreadful signal all the rocks rebound. **1751** LAVINGTON *Enthus. Meth. & Papists* III. (1754) Pref., I have little more Honour than that of being an Echo, rebounding your own Words. **1813** T. BUSBY *Lucretius* I. II. 370 Loud to the neighbouring hills the clamours rise, The neighbouring hills rebound them to the skies.

†**b.** To send *out*, exalt, celebrate, by a re-echoing sound. *Obs.*

c **1557** ABP. PARKER *Ps.* lxxxi. 235 Open.. the mouthes of us thy suppliants to rebounde out the prayse of thy glorious majesty. **1598** YONG *Diana* 444 They shall rebound His famous name.. Vnto the highest spheares. **1647** J. HALL *Poems* II. 101 His throne,.. whom your plumy pipes rebound.

Hence **reˈboundable** *a.*; **reˈbounded** *ppl. a.*

1659 *Gentl. Calling* 78 Everie degree of unmercifulness they shew to others, reverts with a rebounded force upon themselves. **1685** COTTON tr. *Montaigne* III. 244 Our reasons.., our arguments and controversies are reboundable.

reboundant (rɪˈbaʊndənt), *a. Her. Obs.* (exc. *Hist.*). [f. REBOUND *v.* + -ANT[1].] = REVERBERANT *a.* 1.

1688 [see REVERBERANT *a.* 1]. **1828** W. BERRY *Encycl. Heraldica* I., *Reboundant, or Rebounding*, a term sometimes used, in ancient heraldry, for the tail of a lion, when turned up like the letter S, the end of the tail being outwards, which was called *reverberant*, *beaten back*, or *reboundant*, as if the animal had beaten it to his back and it had rebounded; the usual way of turning the end of the tail, in ancient times, being inwards; but it is now seldom borne otherwise than outwards, and, therefore, not noticed in the blazon. **1878** B. BURKE *General Armory* p. xliv, *Reboundant*, an ancient term for the tail of a lion when turned up and bent in the form of a letter S with the point outwards, the ancient way of depicting the tail was usually with the point turned towards the back, unless blazoned reboundant. **1910** W. A. COPINGER *Heraldry Simplified* 368/1 *Reboundant*, or Rebounding, formerly applied to the tail of a lion when turned up like the letter S.

rebounder. [f. REBOUND *v.*]

a. A device in a gun-lock by which the hammer is thrown back after it has struck the cap (Knight *Dict. Mech.* 1875).

b. *Basketball.* A player who is skilled in catching rebounds (REBOUND *sb.* 3 a).

1949 *Sun* (Baltimore) 28 Dec. 14/6 Dolhou goes on the injured list with.. a growing reputation as an adept floorman, rebounder and set shot. **1954** *Ibid.* 20 Dec. B18/3 What more do you want.. shooter, playmaker, rebounder, durability. **1974** *Spartanburg* (S. Carolina) *Herald-Jrnl.* 21 Apr. B1/1 He started on the basketball team.. playing the point position as playmaker and still being one of the leading rebounders for Coach Bill Hinson's Viking team. **1979** *N.Y. Times* 25 Nov. v. 10/3 In winning the Southeastern Conference regular-season title and posting a 23–8 mark, Dale Brown had size, quickness, shooters, ballhandlers, rebounders and experience.

rebounding (rɪˈbaʊndɪŋ), *vbl. sb.* [f. REBOUND *v.* + -ING[1].] The action of the vb. REBOUND, in various senses; an instance of this. Also *attrib.*

1382 WYCLIF *Wisd.* xvii. 18 The aȝeen sounende rebounding of sound fro the heȝest hillis maden them failende for drede. *c* **1440** *Partonope* 4212 This hors.. was euer neyng And ther to so gretly reboundyng Hit made. **1526** *Pilgr. Perf.* (W. de W. 1531) 30 By reason of the great refleccyon or rebownynge of the sayd beame it causeth an hete. **1582** STANYHURST *Æneis*, etc. (Arb.) 138 Now doe they rayse gastly lyghtnings, now grislye reboundings Of ruffe raffe roaring. *a* **1635** SIBBES *Confer. Christ & Mary* (1656) 88 This reflection, this return, this rebounding back to God. **1698** CAPT. LANGFORD in *Phil. Trans.* XX. 414 The Reverse or Rebounding back of the Wind.

b. *spec.* in *Basketball*, the action of catching a rebound (REBOUND *sb.* 3 a). Also *attrib.*

1954 *Basketball* ('Know the Game' Series) 35 (*heading*) Rebounding. **1957** *Encycl. Brit.* III. 181 *Rebounding*,.. the fundamental ability to get proper position, time the jump and properly retrieve rebounds is a vital part of the game. **1969** *Eugene* (Oregon) *Register-Guard* 3 Dec. 1D/4 The rebounding was that close only because the hosts had trouble getting going on the backboards. **1972** *N.Y. Times* 4 June 7/4 Bill Moore, who holds most of Susquehanna University's rebounding records, has been appointed assistant basketball coach at the university. **1976** *Springfield* (Mass.) *Daily News* 22 Apr. 39/1 We lost this game chiefly for two reasons: offensive rebounding (16–10 Celts with Cowens pulling nine) and turnovers (the Braves coughing up 30 to 17).

rebounding (rɪˈbaʊndɪŋ), *ppl. a.* [-ING[2].] That rebounds, in various senses of the vb.

1382 WYCLIF *Prov.* xviii. 4 The reboundende [L. *redundans*] welle of wisdam. **1555** EDEN *Decades* 134 The reboundyng noyse of a horseman comminge. **1635** SWAN *Spec. M.* vii. §3 (1643) 348 The harmlesse choristers of the rebounding woods. **1667** MILTON *P.L.* x. 417 Chaos.. with rebounding surge the barrs assaild. **1790** A. WILSON *Poems, Thunder Storm*, Trembling he stops,.. When bursting, harsh, rebounding thunders roll! **1822** GOOD *Study Med.* II. 26 The dicrotic, coturnising, and inciduous [pulses].. as mere subvarieties of the rebounding, or redoubling.

b. ***rebounding lock***, a gun-lock fitted with a 'rebounder'.

1871 GREENER *Mod. Breech-loaders* 32 We consider that sufficient striking power cannot be imparted to the rebounding lock to insure certainty of ignition with the cartridges as now made. **1881** —— *Gun* 259.

rebours, *a.* and *sb.* Forms: 4 rebürs, rebours(e, robours, 5 *Sc.* rebowris. [a. F. *rebours* rough, perverse, etc. (as sb., the wrong side of a fabric):—pop. L. *rebürs-um*, L. *reburrum* rough-haired, bristly.]

†**A.** *adj.* Perverse, froward. *Obs. rare*[−1].

1340 *Ayenb.* 68 Wyþstondynge is a zinne þet comþ of þe herte þet is rebel and hard and rebours and dyuers.

B. *sb.* in phr. ‖***à rebours*** (a rəbur) (formerly (*Sc.*) †***at rebours***), in the wrong way, perversely; through perversity.

c **1330** R. BRUNNE *Chron. Wace* (Rolls) 5165 Androcheus .. answered hym al at rebürs [*v.r.* robours]. *Ibid.* 12652. *c* **1375** *Sc. Leg. Saints* l. (*Katherine*) 860 Þir quhelis.. twa aganis twa Sall alwais turne in contrare cours As thingis beand at rebourse. *c* **1425** WYNTOUN *Cron.* IX. viii. 48 Schyre Willame persaywyd then His myschef, and hym send succowris, Ellis had all gane at rebowris. **1906** W. JAMES *Let.* 3 Apr. in R. B. Perry *Thought & Character W. James* (1935) II. 393 How lamely I, for one, must have expressed myself to be taken so *à rebours*. **1939** T. S. ELIOT *Idea Christ. Society* i. 19 It [*sc.* a dislike of everything maintained by Germany or Russia] may.. lead us to be mere imitators *à rebours*, in making us adopt uncritically almost any attitude which a foreign nation rejects. **1949** I. DEUTSCHER *Stalin* iv. 96 In making a fetish of the underground, in shying away from the broader opportunities for action, they tended to reduce the resolution to impotence. They were liquidators *à rebours*. **1951** M. LOWRY *Let.* 25 Aug. (1967) 262 While he took no human action at all.. some principle of tyrannic yet thwarted force in his feeling has worked against him, *à* *rebours*: now he does take action..mysteriously the thing begins to work for him.

†**rebous.** *Sc. Obs. rare.* ? Din, disturbance.
Etym. and precise meaning not clear: connexion with OF. *rebous* var. of *rebours* (see prec.) is perh. possible.
1535 STEWART *Chron. Scot.* II. 212 The schawis schuik and trimlet all the erd With sic rebous reboundand fra the bruke. *Ibid.* 647 His wyfe that tyme, but bargane or rebous, Rycht reuerentlie to him gaif ouir the hous.

rebout-, obs. form of REBUT *v.*

rebowne, obs. form of REBOUND *sb.* and *v.*

rebowris, Sc. var. REBOURS *Obs.*

rebowt-, obs. form of REBUT *v.*

reboyle, obs. form of REBOIL *v.*[1]

reboyt-, obs. Sc. form of REBUT *v.*

‖**rebozo, reboso** (re'boθo, -'bozo). Also **rebosa**, **ribosa**. [Sp. *rebozo*.] A shawl or long scarf used by Spanish-American women as a covering for the head and shoulders.
1807 J. PINKERTON *Mod. Geogr.* (rev. ed.) III. 185 The Mexican ladies..when they are at home, or go out in a carriage,..wear what is called the *rebozo*, or muffler, like the shawls now used at Madrid. **1844** J. GREGG *Commerce of Prairies* I. 216 A Mexican female is scarcely ever seen without her rebozo or shawl. **1850** B. TAYLOR *Eldorado* II. ix. 52 The men in their white shirts, and the women in their bewitching rebosas. **1851** MAYNE REID *Scalp Hunt.* ix. 70 Swarthy ill-favoured faces appear behind the folds of dingy rebozos. **1888** *Literary World* (Boston) 18 Aug. 262/1 The women move shyly, covered to the eyes in the long blue scarf, or reboso, which is part of the national costume. **1927** W. CATHER *Death comes for Archbishop* I. ii. 25 She was dressed in black, with a white apron, and a black reboso over her head, like a Mexican woman of the poor. **1947** J. STEINBECK *Wayward Bus* 235 The little modest dark girls in blue *rebozos*. **1956** R. BRADBURY *October Country* 19 Behind him came women in black rebozos. **1977** *Guider* July 310/3 The dancers wear white dresses with coloured belts and rebozos tied from hand to hand.

rebrace (riː'breɪs), *v.* [RE- 5 a.] *trans.* To brace again. Hence **re'bracing** *vbl. sb.*
1741–2 GRAY *Agrippina* 138 A cause To arm the hand of childhood and rebrace The slackened sinews of time-wearied age. **1797** MRS. RADCLIFFE *Italian* vii, Vivaldi's nerves were instantly rebraced, and he sprang to the door. **1826** SOUTHEY *Lett.* (1856) III. 540 The rebracing of a bodily frame. **1848** LYTTON *Harold* XI. viii, Rebraced to its purpose by Lanfranc's cheering assurances, the resolute, indomitable soul of William now applied itself [etc.].

rebranch (riː'brɑːnʃ, -æ-), *v.* [f. RE- 5 a.] *intr.* To ramify; to branch again. Hence **re'branching** *vbl. sb.*
1888 J. LE CONTE *Evolution* I. i. 14 A growing tree branches and again branches in all directions... Even so the tree of life, by the law of differentiation, branches and rebranches continually. **1895** W. H. HUDSON *Introd. Philos. H. Spencer* i. 19 That doctrine of the gradual branching and rebranching of species..went somewhat vaguely by the name of the development hypothesis. **1935** HUXLEY & HADDON *We Europeans* v. 161 Evolutionary branches may.. unite again after they have diverged and then either rebranch or remain united.

rebreathe (riː'briːð), *v.* [RE- 5 a.] *trans.* To breathe (air) again. Hence **re'breathed** *ppl. a.*; **re'breathing** *vbl. sb.* (freq. *attrib.*).
1606 HEYWOOD *Challenge for Beauty* IV. i, Have hope to bee redeemd;..Hope to re-breathe that ayre you tasted first. *c* **1865** J. WYLDE in *Circ. Sc.* I. 427/1 He must..re-breathe these..exhalations. **1896** *Allbutt's Syst. Med.* I. 310 The consequence is that patients have to inhale rebreathed air. **1897** W. MARCET *Contrib. Hist. Respiration in Man* 109 Curves were taken showing the effects produced by the rebreathing of six litres of air during two minutes. **1935** *Sun* (Baltimore) 17 May 5/2 Their faces are covered with four layers of gauze, muffling nose, mouth, eyes and ears. One purpose of the gauze is to increase slightly the rebreathing of exhaled carbon dioxide. **1960** *Brit. Jrnl. Anaesthesia* XXXII. 256 (*heading*) A rebreathing technique for the determination of arterial P_{CO_2} in the apnoeic patient. **1976** H. MACINNES *Death Reel* xxiii. 184 He was pulled in..by a diver using re-breathing apparatus.

re'breed, *v. rare*[−1]. [RE- 5 a.] To breed again.
1608 SYLVESTER *Du Bartas* II. iv. III. *Schisme* 788 My Childe returns, re-breeding in my Womb.

re'brew, *v.* [RE- 5 a.] *trans.* To brew again.
1761 ARMSTRONG *A Day* 219 Brewed and rebrewed, a double, treble curse.

re'bribe, *v.* [RE- 5 a.] *trans.* To bribe a second time.
1602 *2nd Pt. Return fr. Parnass.* IV. ii. 1646 It is vsuall with them..to be bribed and rebribed on the one side, then to be feed and refeed of the other. **1849** DE QUINCEY *Eng. Mail Coach* Wks. 1862 IV. 294 This whole corporation was constantly bribed, rebribed and often sur-rebribed.

re'bring, *v.* [RE-.] *trans.* To bring back. Also with *back*.
1595 DANIEL *Civ. Wars* I. xxiv, Now this great succeeder all repaires, And rebrings-backe that discontinued good. **1616** J. LANE *Cont. Sqr.'s T.* viii. 112 But then afreshe.. rebringes these canons foorth that back weare run. **1839–52** BAILEY *Festus* 557 Lo! ye are all restored,..rebrought To Heaven by Him who cast ye forth.
Hence **re'bringer**; **re'bringing** *vbl. sb.*
1598 FLORIO, *Rapportatore*,..a rebringer. *Ibid.*, *Rapporto*,..a rebringing.

rebroadcast (riː-), *v.* [RE- 5 a.] *trans.* To broadcast again; *spec.* to broadcast (a programme received from another station).
1923 *Daily Mail* 14 Aug. 5/3 A special orchestral concert ..will be relayed to all the broadcasting stations in Britain, and thence be re-broadcast by them on their own particular wave-lengths. **1939** *Sun* (Baltimore) 9 Feb. 1/2 Several hours after the vessel's first distress call, she rebroadcast her SOS appeal. **1948** *John o' London's Weekly* 10 Dec. 598/3 The difficulty in receiving the Scottish station makes it unlikely that more than a handful of Scott's English admirers will be able to judge how *Waverley* sounds on the air, but perhaps the serial will be re-broadcast later on another wavelength. **1951** A. C. CLARKE *Sands of Mars* viii. 94 It was a live programme, beamed to Mars..picked up and rebroadcast. **1965** *Economist* 9 Oct. 152/3 Plays supplied by the networks to their provincial affiliates, and already censored in Madrid, must be recensored before being rebroadcast. **1974** P. GZOWSKI *This Country* 12/2 What I said live to the Maritimes was recorded in Toronto and rebroadcast an hour later, then recorded in Winnipeg and so on.
Hence **re'broadcast** *ppl. a.*, **re'broadcasting** *vbl. sb.*; also **re'broadcaster**, a station that rebroadcasts material received from elsewhere.
1956 *Nature* 10 Mar. 451/2 There are fuller accounts of the External Services and of the re-broadcasting of the B.B.C. programmes throughout the world. **1957** *BBC Handbk.* 38 Programmes of this kind may be conveyed to the rebroadcaster either by short-wave transmission or as recordings by sea or airmail. **1962** *Ibid.* 102 The local station may record the BBC transmission for rebroadcasting later. **1969** *Listener* 17 July 91/3 The rebroadcast *Morals and Medicine* debate on abortion was a sterilised, factual affair by comparison. **1973** *Ibid.* 13 Sept. 348/3 No one could tell which programmes might one day be required..for rebroadcasting. **1974** *BBC Handbk.* 273/1 Every programme chosen for distribution to re-broadcasters is of the highest quality.

re'broadcast (riː-), *sb.* [f. the vb.] A repeat broadcast, esp. one of a programme received from another station; also, the action of broadcasting again.
1927 *Observer* 24 July 4/5 Rebroadcasts can be made on both sides of the Atlantic and..though they are interesting the quality is usually painful and always bad. **1939** *Sun* (Baltimore) 9 May 2/4 Thousands of British subjects heard the message as broadcast by the French stations or picked up through the short-wave rebroadcast from the United States. **1940** *Ibid.* 23 Feb. 1/4 Explaining the experiment, involving receipt of National Broadcasting Company programs from New York city by a receiver 130 miles distant, and simultaneous rebroadcast by Station W2XB, Dr. Baker said [etc.]. **1943** R. CHANDLER *High Window* x. 79 This ball game is a studio re-broadcast. **1963** *Guardian* 19 Apr. 12/2 The National Aeronautics and Space Administration had promised to allow some broadcasts direct from the capsule as well as the rebroadcast of television tapes. **1965** *Economist* 9 Oct. 152/2 Even [Spanish] commercials taped for rebroadcast day after day must be vetted daily. **1974** *Radio Times* 14 Mar. 30/3 Re-broadcasts of programmes from a fortnightly series on the arts.

rebstone, obs. form of RUBSTONE.

re'bubble, *v.* [RE-.] To bubble up again.
1823 BYRON *Island* IV. iv, They watch'd awhile to see him float again, But not a trace rebubbled from the main.

rebuck, obs. form of REBUKE *v.*

re'buckle, *v.* [RE- 5 a.] *trans.* To buckle again. Hence **re'buckling** *vbl. sb.*
1611 FLORIO, *Raffibbiare*, to buckle againe, to rebuckle. *Raffibbiatura*, a rebuckling. **1845** BROWNING *How they brought the good News* ii, I..Rebuckled the cheek-strap, chained slacker the bit.

rebucous: see REBUKOUS.

re'bud, *v.* [RE- 5 a.] *intr.* To bud again. Hence **re'budding** *vbl. sb.*
1605 SYLVESTER *Du Bartas* II. iii. III. *Law* 1236 His oft-quickned Rod, Which dead, re-buds, re-blooms, and Almonds bears. **1611** FLORIO, *Ripampinare*, to rebud or reburgeon out a new as a Vine doth. *a* **1618** SYLVESTER *Job Triumph.* 888 It will revive, and, as a Plant, re-bud. **1814** *Sporting Mag.* XLIV. 95 When earth rebuds with kindly rain. **1871** *Daily News* 7 Mar., The rebudding of the wand of peace.

rebuff (rɪ'bʌf), *sb.* [a. obs. F. *rebuffe* (16th c.; mod.F. *rebuffade*), ad. It. *ribuffo* (also *rabbuffo*), f. *ri-* RE- + *buffo* puff.]
1. A peremptory check given to one who makes an advance of any kind; a blunt refusal of a request or offer; a snub. Also without article (quot. 1847).
1611 FLORIO, *Ribuffo*,..a chiding, a taunt, a rebuffe. **1685** WOOD *Life* 25 Oct. (O.H.S.) III. 168 In Mr. Paynter's chamber, [I received] a rebuff from Dr. Ll...a pedagog. **1736** *Swift's Lett.* (1766) II. 229 Perhaps, if I seek it too much, I might meet with a rebuff. **1784** COWPER *Task* IV. 411 The rugged frowns and insolent rebuffs Of knaves in office. **1833** J. H. NEWMAN *Hist. Sk.* (1873) II. I. i. 8 Great men love to be courted, and little men must not mind rebuffs. **1847** C. BRONTË *J. Eyre* xviii, All eyes met her with a glance of eager curiosity, and she met all eyes with one of rebuff and coldness. **1880** L. STEPHEN *Pope* ii. 53 Pope undoubtedly must have been bitterly vexed at this implied rebuff.
b. A check to further action or progress, due to circumstances.
1672 MARVELL *Reh. Transp.* I. 208 Too glorious an Enterprize to be abandoned at the first rebuffe. **1759** STERNE *Tr. Shandy* II. i, These perplexing rebuffs gave my uncle Toby Shandy more perturbations than you would imagine. **1853** KANE *Grinnell Exp.* (1856) 544 Bontschitscheff met the same rebuff at the same height thirty degrees further west.
2. A repelling puff or blast. *rare.*
1667 MILTON *P.L.* II. 936 The strong rebuff of som tumultuous cloud Instinct with Fire and Nitre. **1812** H. & J. SMITH *Rej. Addr.*, *Archit. Atoms* 52 Æolian Monarch! Emperor of Puffs! We modern sailors dread not thy rebuffs.

rebuff (rɪ'bʌf), *v.*[1] [ad. obs. F. *rebuffer* (*rabuffer*), ad. It. *ribuffare* (also *rabbuffare*), f. *ribuffo*: see prec.]
1. *trans.* To repel bluntly or ungraciously; to give a rude check or repulse to (one).
a **1586** SIDNEY *Arcadia* III. (1655) 319 Marvelling, that hee, who had never heard such speeches from any knight, should be thus rebuffed by a woman. **1611** FLORIO, *Ribuffare*, to rebuke..to rebuffe. **1697** DRYDEN *Æneid* III. 319 At length rebuff'd, they leave their mangled Prey. **1774** MAD. D'ARBLAY *Early Diary* 30 Mar., I answered.., that I could not possibly comply: he would not be rebuffed. **1827** SCOTT *Surg. Dau.* vi, He could not find any proper mode of rebuffing, or resenting it. **1869** TROLLOPE *He knew*, etc. xxiv. (1878) 137 She had certainly not intended to rebuff him.
2. To blow or drive back. *rare.*
1747 [see REBUFFING *ppl. a.* below]. **1798** LANDOR *Gebir* Wks. (1846) II. 493 The fierce element..earths adamantine arch rebuft.
Hence **rebuffed** (rɪ'bʌft), **re'buffing** *ppl. adjs.*
1747 HALES in *Phil. Trans.* XLIV. 582 Those tempestuous, rebuffing, whirling Hurricanes, which bear down all before them. **1788** H. WALPOLE *Reminisc.* viii. 66 The rebuffing spite of the princess dowager. **1792** MARY WOLLSTONECR. *Rights Wom.* vi. 265 His manners..are rebuffing, and his conversation cold and dull. **1886** *Pall Mall G.* 17 Apr. 4/1 Some of the rebuffed ones seat themselves.

rebuff (riː'bʌf), *v.*[2] *rare.* [f. RE- 5 c + BUFF *a.* or BUFF *v.*[3] 2.] *trans.* To restore to a buff colour.
1924 GALSWORTHY *White Monkey* III. x. 281 On both sides flat houses, recently re-buffed.

rebuffer (rɪ'bʌfə(r)). *rare.* [f. REBUFF *v.*[1] + -ER[1].] One who rebuffs others.
1950 O. NASH *Family Reunion* (1951) 109 The medica tyrant, the social rebuffer.

re'buffet, *v.* [RE-.] *trans.* To reject or return with a buffet.
1672 EACHARD *Lett.* 64 Mandringo's Pismires rebuffetted. **1697** C. LESLIE *Snake in Grass* (ed. 2) 251 This was soon Re-buffeted back again upon them, by the Quakers in the West of England.

rebuik, obs. Sc. form of REBUKE *sb.*

rebuild (riː'bɪld), *v.* [RE- 5 a.] **a.** *trans.* To build again; to reconstruct.
1611 COTGR., *Rebastir*, to reedifie, rebuild. **1612** DRAYTON *Poly-olb.* viii. 159 In whose..name Great London still shall live, (by him rebuilded). **1655** H. VAUGHAN *Silex Scint.*, *Ascension Hymn* vii, Hee alone..can Bring bone to bone And rebuild man. **1743** BULKELEY & CUMMINS *Voy. S. Seas* 1 The Ships were all in prime Order, all lately rebuilt. **1790** BURKE *Fr. Rev.* Wks. V. 163 We have rebuilt Newgate, and tenanted the mansion. **1840** MILL *Diss. & Disc.* (1875) I. 423 When society requires to be rebuilt, there is no use attempting to rebuild it on the old plan. **1875** STUBBS *Const. Hist.* I. xii. 458 Farmhouses and palaces had alike been re-built. **1927** *Scribner's Mag.* Apr. 356/1 Another boy..wore a black silk handkerchief across his face because he had no nose then and his face was to be rebuilt... They rebuilt his face, but..they could never get the nose exactly straight. **1961** M. BEADLE *These Ruins are Inhabited* (1963) ii. 19 The fire..had gone out... While George rebuilt it, I set about frying bacon and eggs.
absol. **1818** CRUISE *Digest* (ed. 2) IV. 88 Where a remainder-man..suffers the lessee or assignee to rebuild. **1861** M. PATTISON *Ess.* (1889) I. 44 When the Company proceeded to rebuild, they no longer did so in the massive and imposing style of the fourteenth century.
b. *rebuilding* = being rebuilt. Cf. BUILD *v.* 7.
1668 H. DUKE *Londons-Nonsuch* title-p., That most stately and magnificent structure now re-building. **1745** *Observ. Conc. Navy* 33 She is re-building. **1776** G. SEMPLE *Building in Water* 30 The Bridge at that Time rebuilding at Orleans.
Hence **'rebuild** *sb.*, an operation of rebuilding, a thing rebuilt; **re'builded** *ppl. a.* (*poet.*); **re'built** *ppl. a.*
1692 *Lond. Gaz.* No. 2761/3 Two rebuilt Ships, the Prince,..and the Dunkirk. **1856** P. FAIRBAIRN *Prophecy* II. ii. 268 A restoration to the Land of Canaan, and a rebuilt Jerusalem. **1878** F. S. WILLIAMS *Midl. Railw.* 646 We enter the erecting shops,..one for 'rebuilds', renewals, and new engines. **1924** R. CAMPBELL *Flaming Terrapin* iii. 48 Sodom, rebuilded, scorns the wilting power. **1934** WEBSTER, *Rebuilt* .., of factory products, as typewriters, disassembled, reconstructed with new parts replacing those that are worn, and refinished. **1959** J. THURBER *Years with Ross* vii. 124 A rebuilt typewriter I had been using. **1960** K. M. KENYON *Archæol. in Holy Land* iv. 106 Sometimes the collapsed wall survived in the shape of an inverted **U**, and the rebuild consisted of a capping which might have foundations on the same level as the original wall. **1972** *World of Wild Wheels* (Custom Car) 10/1 As the moulding drops off they tend to leave it off. It's less work in the re-build. **1973** *Country Life* 1 Mar. (Suppl.) 11 Modern house being a rebuild of the original manor house. **1976** *Evening Post* (Bristol) 23 Apr. (Advt.), Bodywork, resprays, engine re-build, reasonable prices. **1978** *Gramophone* July 173/3 The Canterbury organ was ailing and unfit (in fact a rebuild is about to begin).

rebuilder (riːˈbɪldə(r)). [f. REBUILD *v.* + -ER[1].] One who rebuilds or reconstructs.

1686 PLOT *Staffordsh.* 295 The Founder or rebuilder of this Church. **1831** CARLYLE *Sart. Res.* III. vii, An English Radical, who..it is to be hoped, will become an English Rebuilder. **1856** FROUDE *Hist. Eng.* I. 116 He saw himself, in imagination, the rebuilder of the Catholic faith.

rebuilding (riːˈbɪldɪŋ), *vbl. sb.* [f. as prec. + -ING[1].] The action of the vb. REBUILD. Also *pl.*

1601 HOLLAND *Pliny* XVI. xl, Brought with other timber for the rebuilding of the foresaid bridge. **1691** T. H[ALE] *Acc. New Invent.* p. lxi, The Fire and Rebuilding of London. **1772** *Ann. Reg.* 222 The buildings, re-buildings, and repairs of ships of war in his Majesty's yards. **1867** FREEMAN *Norm. Conq.* (ed. 3) I. v. 399 All the rebuildings of that wonderful pile. **1886** WILLIS & CLARK *Cambridge* III. 254 The rebuilding of the entire college on a new site was undertaken.

rebuit, variant of REBUTE *Sc.*

rebukable: see REBUKEABLE.

reˈbukative, *a. rare.* [f. REBUK(E *v.* + -ATIVE.] Disapproving, rebuking. So **reˈbukatively** *adv.*

1924 'O. DOUGLAS' *Pink Sugar* iii. 30 Miss Dickson.. asked if we had called yet.. and added, rather rebukatively, that Mr. M'Clandish had called at once. **1950** —— *Farewell to Priorsford* 219 Do you suppose she meant gangsters or only what Jane Austen called 'less worthy females'? No, Janet, I'm not backbiting, so don't look so rebukative.

rebuke (rɪˈbjuːk), *sb.* Also 5 rebeuc, 6 rebuk, *Sc.* rebuik. [f. the vb.]

†**1.** A shameful or disgraceful check; a shame or disgrace. *Obs.* (Common in 15th c., esp. in phr. *to put to a rebuke.*)

c **1430** LYDG. *Min. Poems* (Percy Soc.) 258 Behold the rebukys that do me so menace. *c* **1470** GREGORY *Chron.* (Camden) 197 That yere the Pope put that hethyn hounde ..to a grete rebuke. **1470–85** MALORY *Arthur* IX. iv, The rebukes that sir Launcelot dyd vnto many knyghtes causeth them that be men of prowesse to beware.

†**b.** Without *a* or *pl.*: Shame, disgrace, reproach. *Obs.* (Common in 16th c.)

1495 *Act 11 Hen. VII*, c. 19 To the grete rebuke and disclaunder of the seid Crafte. *a* **1533** LD. BERNERS *Huon* xlvii. 160 We shall do hym all the shame and rebuke that we can. **1542** UDALL *Erasm. Apoph.* 174 He dyd not stayne ne putte to lacke or rebuke hys royall autoritie. **1590** SPENSER *F.Q.* III. i. 55 For great rebuke it is love to despise.

2. Reproof, reprimand.

c **1430** LYDG. *Min. Poems* (Percy Soc.) 127 Scorne and rebuke cast in his visage, He.. sayde nothyng therto. *c* **1515** *Cocke Lorell's B.* 8 On your owne sleue to wype your nose Without rebuke takynge. **1596** SHAKS. *1 Hen. IV*, v. i. 111 If he will not yeeld, Rebuke and dread correction waite on vs. **1611** BIBLE *Prov.* xiii. 1 A wise sonne heareth his fathers instruction: but a scorner heareth not rebuke. **1671** MILTON *P.R.* I. 468 Sharply thou hast insisted on rebuke. **1781** COWPER *Expost.* 397 Hast thou.. Despising all rebuke, still persevered. **1844** MRS. BROWNING *Drama of Exile* Poems 1850 I. 48 God hath rebuked us, who is over us, To give rebuke or death.

b. With *a* and *pl.* (the commonest use): A reproof, a reprimand.

1514 BARCLAY *Cyt. & Uplondyshm.* (Percy Soc.) 47 Thou shalt at the least way rebukes soure abide. **1560** DAUS tr. *Sleidane's Comm.* 424 b, It is incredible, with what rebukes and railinges y[e] people received hym. **1611** SHAKS. *Cymb.* III. v. 48 Shee's a Lady So tender of rebukes, that words are stroke[s]. **1667** MILTON *P.L.* IV. 844 So spake the Cherube, and his grave rebuke..added grace Invincible. **1784** COWPER *Task* II. 720 His gentle eye Grew stern, and darted a severe rebuke. **1837** W. IRVING *Capt. Bonneville* III. 66 The only punishment this desperado met with, was a rebuke from the leader of the party. **1877** SPARROW *Serm.* xx. 272 The very existence of these forms in our Prayer Book is a standing rebuke of the selfish ingratitude of those who [etc.].

†**3. a.** A check, stop. **b.** A severe blow. **c.** Reproof or correction by a blow. *Obs. rare.*

1615 W. LAWSON *Country Housew. Gard.* (1626) 27 The sap in graffing receiues a rebuke, and cannot worke so strongly. **1692** R. L'ESTRANGE *Fables* I. xxxvii. 36 [The horse] gave him so Terrible a Rebuke upon the Forehead with his Heel, that he laid him at his Length. **1712** STEELE *Spect.* No. 436 ¶9 Miller's Heat laid him open to the Rebuke of the calm Buck, by a large Cut in the Forehead.

rebuke (rɪˈbjuːk), *v.* Also 4 rebuk(k, -bouk, -buyk, -bukie, 5 rebuck. [a. AF. (Langtoft) and ONF. *rebuker* = OF. *rebuch(i)er* (Godef.), f. *re-* RE- + *bucher* to beat, strike. (Connexion with ONF. *rebouquer*, F. *reboucher*, to blunt, is doubtful.)]

†**1.** *trans.* To beat down or force back; to repress or check (a person); to repulse. *Obs.*

c **1330** R. BRUNNE *Chron.* (1810) 180, I am now comen here, þise Sarazins to rebuke [F. *destrure*], & slo at my powere. *Ibid.* 194 Rebuke [F. *rebuke(z)*] him for þat ilk of þat auauntrie. **1380** *Sir Ferumb.* 4692 þ[e] frensche to þam shute & caste, & rebuked hem foule with-ynne. **1422** tr. *Secreta Secret., Priv. Priv.* 204 Anoone..he rebukid the forsayden breenys and bourkeyns..and ham to Pees reformed. *c* **1500** *Melusine* 252 Two of his knightes..proudly rebuckyd Claudes men with theire speres. **1599** SHAKS. *Hen. V*, III. vi. 128 Wee could haue rebuk'd him at Harflewe. **1605** —— *Macb.* III. i. 56 Vnder him My Genius is rebuk'd, as it is said Mark Anthonies was by Cæsar.

†**b.** To check, repress (a quality, action, etc.).

1450–1530 *Myrr. our Ladye* 28 The holynes of the chyrche & deuoute prayers made therin..rebuketh the boldnes of the fende. **1584** COGAN *Haven Health* ccxv. (1636) 232 The drinke being cold, it rebuketh naturall heat that is working. **1595** SHAKS. *John* II. i. 9 Hether is he come..to rebuke the vsurpation Of thy vnnatural Vncle, English John.

†**c.** To beat, buffet. *Obs. rare.*

1611 BEAUM. & FL. *King & No King* IV. iii, A head rebuked With pots of all size, daggers, stools, and bed-staves.

2. To reprove, reprimand, chide severely. Sometimes const. *for*, †*of* (a fault).

c **1325** *Lai le Freine* 75 The knight..was sore agramed, And rebouked his leuedy. **1377** LANGL. *P. Pl.* B. v. 371 Repentance riȝte so rebuked hym þat tyme. **1413** *Pilgr. Sowle* (Caxton) II. lviii. (1859) 56 Why shold the ashes be blamed, or rebuked for theyr vnthryftynesse? **1486** *Bk. St. Albans* B iij b, Iff ye haue a chastised hounde that will be rebuket. *c* **1500** MEDWALL *Nature* (Brandl) 517 These .ii. folk..euer enbesyeth theym to rebuke you of syn. **1574** tr. *Marlorat's Apocalips* 13 To rebuke al such as are vngodly for al the works which they haue done wickedly. **1608** SHAKS. *Per.* III. i. 1 Thou god of this great vast, rebuke these surges. **1611** BIBLE *Luke* iv. 39 He stood ouer her, and rebuked the feuer, & it left her. **1676** HOBBES *Iliad* I. 510 And angry him rebuk't with Language keen. **1738** WESLEY *Ps.* LXXXVIII. ii, Rebuke these Storms, and set me safe on Land. **1791** COWPER *Iliad* v. 514 Him thus the Archer of the skies rebuked. **1834** LYTTON *Pompeii* I. ii, 'Thy heart rebukes thee while thou speakest', said the Egyptian. **1883** FROUDE *Short Stud.* IV. I. vi. 70 He rebuked them for their cowardice and want of faith.

absol. **1535** COVERDALE *Ps.* lxxiii[i]. 18 Remembre this.. how the enemie rebuketh. **1611** BIBLE *Amos* v. 10 They hate him that rebuketh in the gate.

b. To express blame or reprehension of (a quality, action, etc.) by reproof or reprimand addressed to persons.

1529 MORE *Supplic. Soulys* Wks. 335/2 Albeit we cannot well..rebuke or blame this negligence and forgeatfulnes in you. **1550** CROWLEY *Langland's P. Pl.* To Reader, There is no maner of vice..whiche this wryter hath not godly, learnedlye, and wittilye rebuked. **1590** SPENSER *F.Q.* II. xii. 69 The Palmer..much rebukt those wandring eyes of his. **1632** QUARLES *Div. Fancies* II. vi. 49 His indulgent tongue Compounded rather than rebuk'd the wrong. **1784** COWPER *Task* VI. 655 The Muse perhaps..rebukes a deed Less impious than absurd. **1821** SHELLEY *Hellas* 928, I must rebuke This drunkenness of triumph ere it die. **1875** JOWETT *Plato* (ed. 2) IV. 131 Parmenides rebukes this want of consistency in Socrates.

c. *transf.* or *fig.* of things.

1611 SHAKS. *Wint. T.* v. iii. 37 Do's not the Stone rebuke me, For being more Stone then it? **1728** YOUNG *Love Fame* III. 76 Impatient art rebukes the sun's delay. **1859** WHITTIER *My Psalm* iv, The manna dropping from God's hand Rebukes my painful care. **1876** J. PARKER *Paracl.* I. viii. 134 Holy and unblamable lives, whereby ungodly men are silently rebuked and instructed.

†**3.** To treat lightly, despise. *Obs. rare.*

c **1330** R. BRUNNE *Chron.* (1810) 246 þis Reseamiraduk, als fole & onwise, His letter gan rebuk, sette it at light prise. **1485** CAXTON *Paris & V.* (1868) 14, I wyl be lothe to see the beaulte of my lady vyenne to be rebuked.

†**4.** To put to shame, bring into contempt. *Obs.*[−1]

1529 MORE *Dyaloge* III. Wks. 228/1 The order is rebuked by the priestes begging and lewde liuing.

†**5.** *Falconry.* To check (a hawk). *Obs.*

1575 TURBERV. *Faulconrie* 121 Take heede that you caste not your lewre into the water, least she shoulde thereby be rebuked. *Ibid.* 134, 141, etc.

rebuke, obs. Sc. form of ROEBUCK.

rebukeable (rɪˈbjuːkəb(ə)l), *a.* Now *rare.* [f. REBUKE *v.* + -ABLE.] That may be rebuked; deserving of rebuke. (Freq. in 16th c.)

1550 BALE *Eng. Votaries* II. 91 Nothynge [is] more rebukeable, if ye respect fame. **1576** FLEMING *Panopl. Epist.* 343 Frowardnesse, and suche lyke rebukeable conditions. *c* **1660** *To All Friends & People in Christendom* 25 These were rebukeable, that were not to be numbered among the Christians. **1882** SWINBURNE *Tristram of Lyonesse* 108 Yet am I not rebukable by thee.

rebukeful (rɪˈbjuːkfʊl), *a.* [f. REBUKE *sb.*]

1. a. Of words: Of a rebuking character.

1523 [COVERDALE] *Old God & New* (1534) D iij, The chefe preestes..fell to opprobrious and rebukefull wordes. **1570** FOXE *A. & M.* (ed. 2) 269/1 Becket..replyeth agayne, expostulating and checking them with rebukefull wordes. **1623** COCKERAM I, *Opprobation*, rebukefull, spightfull. **1887** *Illustr. Lond. News* 17 Dec. 700/1 This retort..evoked some very rebukeful language.

b. Of persons: Full of, given to, rebuke.

1868 HEAVYSEGE *Jezebel* II. 81 She turned away Rebukeful. **1869** BLACKMORE *Lorna D.* xxi, Not that he is rough with them, or querulous, or rebukeful.

†**2.** Deserving of rebuke; disgraceful, shameful. *Obs.*

1530 PALSGR. 322/1 Rebukefull,..*culpable*. *a* **1535** FISHER *Wks.* (E.E.T.S.) II. 429 It shalbe moche rebukefull and moche worthy punishement. **1548** UDALL, etc. *Erasm. Par. John* i. 13 He toke vpon him the rebukefull miserie of our mortalitie. **1570** LEVINS *Manip.* 187/21 Rebukeful, *culpandus*.

Hence **reˈbukefully** *adv.*, **reˈbukefulness**.

1531 ELYOT *Gov.* III. xxviii, He wyl gyue to the a fayned thanke, & after reporte rebukefully of the. **1552** HULOET, Speakinge despitefullye, rebukefullye, or reprochfullye, *Opprobatio*. **1888** *Cornh. Mag.* May 475, 'I hope not often', said Sir Lucas, rebukefully. **1891** L. KEITH *Lost Illusion* I. ix. 225 Said Oliver, with cold rebukefulness.

rebuker (rɪˈbjuːkə(r)). [f. REBUKE *v.* + -ER[1].] One who rebukes.

c **1420** LYDG. *Assembly of Gods* 901 Rebukers of synne & myschefes odyous. **1532** MORE *Confut. Tindale* Wks. 651/2 These rebukers of our liuyng, liue themselfe at the leaste wyse as euill as we. **1579** GOSSON *Sch. Abuse* (Arb.) 53 Euery rebuker shoulde place a hatch before the doore. **1670** MILTON *Hist. Eng.* III. Wks. (1851) 97 These great Rebukers of Nonresidence. **1741** in *Lett. C'tess Suffolk* (1824) II. 182 You should, for Miss Hobart's sake, begin your office of rebuker with her. **1867** SWINBURNE *Ess. & Stud.* (1875) 146 They can turn round upon their rebukers, and say [etc.].

rebuking (rɪˈbjuːkɪŋ), *vbl. sb.* [f. as prec. + -ING[1].] The action of the vb. REBUKE. Also with *a* and *pl.*: An instance of this.

c **1400** *Master of Game* (MS. Digby 182) xxxiii, þei ought to holde þe abay as longe as þei may withouten rebukynge of þe houndes. *c* **1430** LYDG. *Reason & Sens.* 580 To thy name Hyt is rebukyng and gret shame. **1526** *Pilgr. Perf.* (W. de W. 1531) 241 b, Without ony exprobracyon or rebukyng [I] admyt the to my grace. **1561** T. NORTON *Calvin's Inst.* II. v. (1634) 142 Exhortations and rebukings much availe..to enflame the desire of goodnesse. **1611** BIBLE *2 Sam.* xxii. 16 The channels of the Sea appeared..at the rebuking of the Lord. **1821** CLARE *Vill. Minstr.* I. 103 Her worst rebukings wore a smile.

reˈbuking, *ppl. a.* [f. as prec. + -ING[2].] That rebukes.

1611 COTGR., *Satyric*, satyricall,..sharpe, rebuking, reprouing. **1829** S. TURNER *Mod. Hist. Eng.* IV. II. xxxi. 336 Her..rebuking sense of the atrocious transaction.

Hence **reˈbukingly** *adv.*

1582 BENTLEY *Mon. Matrones* ii. 13 The liuelie voice of God rebukinglie tooke me vp. **1652** GAULE *Magastrom.* 29 That art or power which the Holy Ghost thus rebukingly derides. **1829** LYTTON *Disowned* xi, 'Have not I prayed, and besought you, many and many a time', said the lady, rebukingly, [etc.]. **1896** MRS. CAFFYN *Quaker Grandmother* 2 She glanced rebukingly at the ceiling.

†**reˈbukous**, *a. Obs.*[−1] In 5 rebucous. [f. REBUKE *sb.* + -OUS.] = REBUKEFUL *a.* 1.

1494 FABYAN *Chron.* VII. 557 She gaue vnto hym many rebucous wordys.

†**reˈbulliency.** *Obs.*[−1] [ad. L. type **rebullientia*, f. *rebullīre*: cf. next.] A tendency to boil up. In quot. *fig.*

1681 RYCAUT tr. *Gracian's Critick* 15 Suppressing with what power I could the strong rebulliency of my Passions.

†**rebuˈllition.** *Obs.*[−1] [Noun of action (cf. *ebullition*), f. L. *rebullīre*: see REBOIL *v.*[1]] A boiling up again. In quot. *fig.*

a **1639** WOTTON in *Reliq.* (1685) 582 The Scotish gentlemen, who have been lately sent to that King, found (as they say) but a brusk welcome; which makes all fear that there may be a rebullition in that business.

reˈbunch, *v. U.S.* [RE- 5 a.] *trans.* To arrange in new groups. Also *absol.* Hence **reˈbunching** *vbl. sb.*

1881 *Harper's Mag.* Oct. 723 A sure though gradual re-bunching of the small farms into large estates. **1888** in Bryce *Amer. Commw.* II. III. lxvi. 500 They can destroy, rebunch, fail to distribute, and what not as they please.

rebunk (riːˈbʌŋk), *v.* [f. RE- 5 a + BUNK *sb.*[4], after DEBUNK *v.*] *trans.* To restore the reputation of or regard for (a person who has been debunked). So **reˈbunking** *vbl. sb.*

1960 *Times Lit. Suppl.* 6 May 291/4 We live in an age of rebunking, when it has become fashionable once more to take the Victorians almost as solemnly as they took themselves. **1962** *Ibid.* 11 May 341/1 Mr. Swanberg sets out neither to debunk nor to rebunk 'the Chief', but to describe him..as a social and political phenomenon.

rebunker (riːˈbʌŋkə(r)), *v.* [f. RE- 5 a + BUNKER *v.* 1 b.] *intr.* To take in a further supply of coal or oil for consumption on a voyage.

1899 C. J. C. HYNE *Further Adv. Capt. Kettle* iii. 60 But wood, as compared with coal, is bulky stuff to carry, and as the stowage capacity of these stern wheelers is small, they have to make frequent calls to rebunker. **1929** *Daily Express* 14 Jan. 11/1 The Wimpole rebunkered and provisioned here and sailed for Grimsby on the midday tide.

rebuoy (riːˈbɔɪ), *v.* [RE- 5 a, 5 c.] *trans.* **a.** To buoy up once more. In quot. *fig.* **b.** To furnish with a new set or arrangement of buoys.

1818 BYRON *Ch. Har.* IV. xxii, Some, with hope replenish'd and rebuoy'd, Return to whence they came. **1860** *Merc. Marine Mag.* VII. 94 The entrance to Frazer River has been re-buoyed.

So **reˈbuoyage**, the act of rebuoying.

1890 *Chamb. Jrnl.* 12 July 433/1 The ever-shifting bars and sandbanks of our river estuaries necessitate frequent soundings and rebuoyage.

reˈburden, *v.* [RE- 5 a.] *trans.* **a.** To lay a new burden on. †**b.** To make more burdensome. *Obs.* Hence **reˈburdening** *vbl. sb.*

1611 FLORIO, *Ricarcatura*, a recharge, a reburthening. *Ricaricare*, to recharge, reburthen. **1631** BRATHWAIT *Whimzies, Jayler* 49 He redoubles his wards, reburdens his irons.

So †**reˈburden** *sb.*, a new burden. *Obs.*[−0]

1611 FLORIO, *Ricarica*, a recharge, a reburthen.

†**reˈburgeon**, *v. Obs. rare.* [a. OF. *rebourgeonner*: see RE- and BURGEON *v.*] **a.** *trans.* To cause to bud or sprout again. **b.** *intr.* To bud or sprout anew.

c **1400** tr. *Secreta Secret., Gov. Lordsh.* 59 He by rayne what þing þat is makys whik, dede þinges reburgones, and he geuys hys benysoun in alle vertuz. **1611** FLORIO, *Ripampinare*, to rebud or reburgeon out a new as a Vine doth.

re'burgeoning, *vbl. sb.* [f. REBURGEON *v.* + -ING[1].] A renewed budding or sprouting (in quot. *fig.*).

1929 'M. B. ELDERSHAW' *House is Built* ix. 210 The reburgeoning of life throughout the country did not leave this household quite untouched.

re'burial. [RE- 5 a.] A second interment (of a corpse).

1922 Z. GREY *To Last Man* viii. 185 It struck Jean as singular that neither Esther Isbel nor Mrs. Jacobs suggested a reburial of their husbands. **1980** J. BARNETT *Palm-Print* v. 50 I've arranged for a re-burial service by the Reverend Solomon.

†**re'burse**, *v. Obs.* [f. RE- + *-burse*, as in *disburse*, *imburse*.] *trans.* To reimburse (a person).

(In B. Jonson *Tale Tub* III. i., prob. intended as an error for *de-* or *disburse*.)

1587 *Sc. Acts Jas. VI* (1814) III. 508/2 And [the strangers] alsua salbe rebursit and payit of þair expense and passage.

rebury (riː'bɛrɪ), *v.* [RE- 5 a.] *trans.* To bury again.

1584 [R. PARSONS] *Leycesters Commw.* (1641) 36 My good Lord..would needs have her taken up againe and re-buried. **1611** SPEED *Hist. Gt. Brit.* IX. xv. §86. 649/2 Her Coffin..hath euer since so remained, and neuer reburied. *a* **1711** KEN *Hymnotheo* Poet. Wks. 1721 III. 86 Some [shall] wish themselves re-buried in the Grave. **1837** CARLYLE *Fr. Rev.* II. III. vii, Reburied hastily at dead of night. **1862** LYTTON *Str. Story* xli, No one..could suppose that some third person had..forced open the casket to abstract its contents and then rebury it.

rebus ('riːbəs), *sb.* [a. F. *rebus* (1512 in Hatz.-Darm.), or L. *rēbus*, abl. pl. of *rēs* thing.

The precise origin of this application of the Latin word is doubtful. It is variously explained as denoting 'by things', from the representation being *non verbis sed rebus*, and (in Ménage) as taken from satirical pieces composed by clerks in Picardy for the annual carnival, which dealt with current topics, and were therefore entitled *de rebus quæ geruntur* 'about things which are going on'.]

a. An enigmatical representation of a name, word, or phrase by figures, pictures, arrangement of letters, etc., which suggest the syllables of which it is made up. **b.** In later use also applied to puzzles in which a punning application of each syllable of a word is given, without pictorial representation.

1605 CAMDEN *Rem.* (1634) 146 They which lackt wit to expresse their conceit in speech, did vse to depaint it out (as it were) in pictures, which they called Rebus. **1630** B. JONSON *New Inn* I. i, I will maintain the rebus against all humours, And all complexions in the body of man. *a* **1661** FULLER *Worthies, Somerset* III. (1662) 23 He gave for his Rebus (in allusion to his Name [Beckinton]) a burning Beacon. **1713** BIRCH *Guard.* No. 36 ¶14 If this meets with encouragement, I shall write a vindication of the Rebus, and do justice to the Conundrum. **1777** SHERIDAN *Sch. Scand.* I. i, I back him at a rebus or a charade against the best rhymer in the kingdom. **1854** E. A. FREEMAN in *Ecclesiologist* XV. 318 A certain John Chapman was a benefactor to the building, and carved a chapman with a dog, as a rebus on his name. **1882** F. HARRISON *Choice Bks.* (1886) 305 Many an ingenious picture is nothing but a painted rebus.

attrib. **1744** WARBURTON *Occas. Refl.* 23 Mistaking, for Egyptian, a ridiculous Kind of rebus-writing. **1765** BP. LOWTH *Lett. Warburton* 13 From Egyptian Hieroglyphics to modern Rebus-writing. **1864** *Reader* 14 May 614 The rebus addresses..that postmen sometimes get. **1928** O. JESPERSEN *Internat. Lang.* II. 170 The number of roots admitted in primitive Esperanto was extremely small, and a good deal of ingenuity was used to express as much as possible by means of compounds and derivatives... The great number of these rebus-words..has deterred many intelligent people from Esp. **1969** A. PARPOLA et al. *Decipherment of Proto-Dravidian Inscriptions of Indus Civilization* ii. 8 It now appears that it [*sc.* the Indus script] is a purely logographic script, based on the so-called rebus principle. This means that each sign represents a whole word, which may comprise one or more syllables, and that a given word is expressed by a clearly recognizable picture of a quite different thing, which has, however, the same phonetic value.

Hence **'rebus** *v. trans.*, to mark or inscribe with a rebus or rebuses.

In quot. 1864 substituted for *berebus* used by Fuller, *Worthies, Essex* (1662) 330.

1655 FULLER *Ch. Hist.* IV. xv. §35 John Morton..had a fair library (rebussd with More in text and Tun under it). **1864** *Athenæum* No. 1932. 595/1 A fine cenotaph..rebused with hawks.

re-bush (riː'bʊʃ), *v.* [f. RE- 5 c + BUSH *v.*[3]] *trans.* To provide with a replacement bush. Hence **re-'bushing** *vbl. sb.*

1885 C. G. W. LOCK *Workshop Receipts* 4th Ser. 331/2 It is important..that enough metal is left round these holes to admit of their being re-bushed if necessary. **1970** K. BALL *Fiat 600, 600D Autobook* ix. 110/2 If this clearance is exceeded, replace either the roller shaft or rebush the shaft bore. *Ibid.* 112/1 Rebushing must be followed by reaming to a uniform internal diameter of ·867 inch ± ·0004 inch.

‖**rebus sic stantibus** ('reɪbəs sɪk 'stæntɪbəs), *phr.* [mod.L.] Things standing thus; provided that conditions have not changed; *spec.* in *International Law* the principle that a treaty lapses when conditions are substantially different from those which obtained when it was concluded; ***clausula rebus sic stantibus*** [CLAUSULA], a clause to this effect.

[**1598** A. GENTILI *De Iure Belli Libri Tres* III. xiv. 599 Et tandem facto, ac silentio hîc quoque, vt in priuatis, dices ratificari foedus... Item excipitur de rerum statu immutatio. Si mutatio nequit praeuideri. Etiam & adiecto iureiurando subintelligi clausula, *Rebus sic stantibus*. **1760** tr. *de Vattel's Law of Nations* I. II. xvii. 230 The only state of things, on account of which the promise is made, is essential to it, and the change of that state alone can lawfully hinder or suspend the effect of that promise. This is the sense which ought to be given to that maxim of the civilians, *Conventio omnis intelligitur rebus sic stantibus*.] **1849** R. WILDMAN *Institutes Internat. Law* I. iv. 175 The doctrine, that every treaty implies a condition of defeasance on any material change of circumstances, which is usually called the rule de rebus sic stantibus, is rejected by Grotius and Bynkershoek as calculated to destroy the obligation of all compacts. **1883** *Wharton's Law-Lex.* 693/2 *Rebus sic stantibus*, at this point of affairs. **1927** *Amer. Jrnl. Internat. Law* XXI. 509 The principle of *rebus sic stantibus* was invoked by Austria-Hungary in 1908 as a justification..for the annexation of Bosnia and Herzegovina. **1939** E. H. CARR *Twenty Years' Crisis* xi. 233 International lawyers evolved the doctrine that a so-called *clausula rebus sic stantibus* was implicit in every treaty, i.e. that the obligations of a treaty were binding in international law so long as the conditions prevailing at the time of the conclusion of the treaty continued, and no longer. **1973** I. M. SINCLAIR *Vienna Convention on Law of Treaties* iv. 105 All international lawyers are aware of the pitfalls surrounding the application of the *clausula rebus sic stantibus* and the controversies which have raged as to its admissibility as a ground for the unilateral denunciation or termination of a treaty. **1975** D. FISICHELLA in S. E. Finer *Adversary Politics & Electoral Reform* III. 264 It seems probable that the second ballot would create '*rebus sic stantibus*' further incentives to manipulation from outside and therefore increased factionalization.

rebut (rɪ'bʌt), *v.* Forms: α. 3-4 (6 *Sc.*) **rebute**, 4 **rebuyt**; *Sc.* 5 **reboyt**, **rabut**, 5-6 **raboyt**, 6 **reboot**. β. 4-5 **rebout(e**, 5 **rebowte**. γ. 5-7 **rebutte**, 7 **rebutt**, 6- **rebut**. [a. AF. *reboter* (1302-7), OF. *reboter*, *rebuter*, *rebouter*, etc., f. *re-* RE- + *boter*, *buter*, *bouter* to BUTT *v.*[1]]

†**1.** *trans.* To assail (a person) with violent language; to revile, rebuke, reproach. *Obs.*

a **1300** *Cursor M.* 29520 For-þi es fele rebuted [*v.r.* reuyled] here þat forwit crist self es dere. **1330** *Arth. & Merl.* 3000 (Kölbing) King & erls, wiþ outen dout, Þer gun him anon rebout For to prouen his maner. *c* **1375** *Sc. Leg. Saints* xii. (*Mathias*) 174 Rubene..fand hyme sa takand his froyte. quhare-for he cane hyme faste reboyte; & he hyme with wordis fell answerte. *c* **1470** HENRY *Wallace* x. 595 'Wallace', said Bruce, 'rabut me now no mar'.

†**2.** To repel, repulse, drive back (a person, or an attack). *Obs.*

1375 BARBOUR *Bruce* VII. 617 Fiften hundreth men & ma Wyth fewar war rebutit swa, That thai vith-drew thaim schamfully. *c* **1400** *Melayne* 743 Was neuer kynge that werede a crown So foule rebuytede. *c* **1470** HENRY *Wallace* VI. 754 Raboytit ewill, on to thar king thai rid. **1480** CAXTON *Ovid's Met.* XIV. xiv, Romulus & his peple..made them to retorne and flee abacke & rebowted them alle out of Rome. **1513** DOUGLAS *Æneis* XI. viii. 38 Quha can that say..That I rebutit was or dung abak? **1568** GRAFTON *Chron.* II. 542 The Englishe Capteynes..rebutted and draue away the Frenchmen. **1590** SPENSER *F.Q.* II. ii. 23 But he..Their sharp assault right boldly did rebut.

b. *transf.* in various uses. Also const. *from*.

1536 BELLENDEN *Cron. Scot.* (1821) I. 24 The Scottis and Pichtis, more insolent efter this victory than afore, rebutit the Britonis, and denyit peace. **1570-6** LAMBARDE *Peramb. Kent* (1826) 495 The Eldest Sonne onely shall be rebutted, or barred, by the warrantie of the auncestour. **1593** NASHE *Christ's T.* 66 Our Atheist,..with nothing but humaine reasons will bee rebutted. **1661** COWLEY *O. Cromwell* Wks. 1710 II. 660 The other Design..from which he was rebutted by the universal Outcry of the Divines. **1848** *Fraser's Mag.* XXXVII. 510 This demand upon the exercise of the imagination will rebut the mere novel reader.

†**c.** To foil or deprive *of* (a thing) by repulse.

1508 DUNBAR *Gold. Targe* 180 Syne [they] went abak reboytit of thair pray. **1535** STEWART *Cron. Scot.* III. 466 He had far leuer sterue,..Of his honour or he rebutit be.

3. To force or turn back (a thing, now usually something abstract); to give a check to.

1490 CAXTON *Eneydos* x. 40 The lyghte of the daye rebouted and putte a backe the shadowe of the nyghte. **1596** SPENSER *Hymn Heav. Beaut.* 125 Their points rebutted backe againe Are duld. **1601** WEEVER *Mirr. Mart.* B v b, A naked piller, Whose force rebutts the streame which runneth after. **1633** P. FLETCHER *Pisc. Ecl.* I. iii, Rebutting Phœbus parching fervencie. *a* **1720** SHEFFIELD (Dk. Buckhm.) *Wks.* (1753) II. 157 Rowing in the Gallies is nothing to the toil of popularity; but ambition is rebutted with nothing. **1814** SOUTHEY *Roderick* XVI. 66 [The stream] here, from the rock Rebutted, curls and eddies. **1859** I. TAYLOR *Logic in Theol.* 24 Fatalism..has been rebutted in its attempt to interfere with the energies of the day.

†**b.** To repel, reject (a thing offered). *Obs.*

1562 A. SCOTT *Poems* (S.T.S.) i. 108 As waspis ressauis of þe same bot soure, So reprobatis Christis buke dois rebute.

4. *Law.* To repel by counter-proof, refute (evidence, a charge, etc.). Hence in general use: To refute, disprove (any statement, theory, etc.).

1817 W. SELWYN *Law Nisi Prius* (ed. 4) II. 709 The presumption of legitimacy..may be rebutted by circumstances inducing a contrary presumption. **1830** D'ISRAELI *Chas. I*, III. v. 70 This faculty..enabled him to rebut the minute and harassing charges brought against him. *a* **1862** BUCKLE *Civiliz.* (1873) III. v. 327 This antiquated notion is further rebutted by the fact that wages are always higher in summer than in winter. **1869** ROGERS *Pref. Adam Smith's W.N.* I. 26 He rebuts their strange doctrine.

5. *intr.* or *absol.* †**a.** To draw back, retire, retreat, recoil. *Obs.*

1422 tr. *Secreta Secret., Priv. Priv.* 139 Company..makyth the honnoure of lordshupp rebutte in dyspite. *Ibid.* 246 The grete colde..makyth the naturall hette reboute and retourne to the stomake. **1481** CAXTON *Myrr.* II. xxi. 111 As the sabboth day approcheth he [a river] rebouteth and goth into therthe agayn. **1590** SPENSER *F.Q.* I. ii. 15 Themselves..Doe backe rebutte, and ech to other yealdeth land. **1624** QUARLES *Div. Poems, Sion's Elegies* ii. 5 As the Pilot..striving to 'scape The danger of deepe-mouth'd Carybdis rape, Rebutts on Scylla.

b. *Law.* To bring forward a rebutter. ? *Obs.*

1602 FULBECKE *2nd Pt. Parall.* 67 If the prouiso had beene that he should neyther vouche nor rebutte, the prouiso had beene void. **1628** COKE *On Litt.* 365 The action of the heire by the Warrantie of his Ancestor..is called to Rebut or repell. **1768** BLACKSTONE *Comm.* III. xx. 310 The plaintiff may answer the rejoinder by a sur-rejoinder; upon which the defendant may rebut.

c. *Curling.* To play a random shot with great force towards the close of a game, in the hope of gaining some advantage for one's own side.

1831 [see REBUTTING *vbl. sb.*]. **1890** KERR *Curling* 404 To rebut..and to cannon.., were two favourite points by which the ancient curlers were wont to win distinction.

rebute (rɪ'bøt). *Sc.* (and *north.*) ? *Obs.* Forms: 5 *north*, **rebuyte**, *Sc.* 5 **rabut**, 6 **rebuit**, 6, 8 **rebute**. [f. *rebute*, obs. form of REBUT *v.* Cf. obs. F. *rebout*.] †**a.** Rebuke, reproach. *Obs.* **b.** Repulse.

c **1450** *St. Cuthbert* (Surtees) 4531 Restyng place to our refuyte ȝit haue we nane bot beres rebuyte. *c* **1470** HENRY *Wallace* IX. 860 Allace, how [may] this be; And do nor harm? Our gret rabut haiff we. **1513** DOUGLAS *Æneis* XII. v. 166 Drevin abak Wyth a schamefull rebute and mekill lak. *c* **1585** MONTGOMERIE *Misc. Poems* xlvi. 14 My hairt hes biddin sik rebute. **1794** BURNS '*O steer her up*' ii, Ne'er break your heart for ae rebute.

rebutment (rɪ'bʌtmənt). [a. obs. F. *rebuttement* (also *reboutte-*, *reboute-*): see REBUT *v.* and -MENT.] The act of rebutting; the fact of being rebutted. Now only as = REBUTTAL.

1593 NASHE *Christ's T.* (1613) 40 Iustled head-long downe..and breaking their backes with their stumbling rebutment. **1623** COCKERAM, *Rebutments*, iustlings. **1824-6** LANDOR *Imag. Conv.* Wks. 1846 I. 204 In fact, 'will I' can only be used in the rebutment of a question. **1871** *Daily News* 11 Mar., In rebutment of the presumption of law.

rebuttable (rɪ'bʌtəb(ə)l), *a.* [f. REBUT *v.* + -ABLE.] That may be rebutted.

1879 *Smith's Leading Cases* (ed. 8) II. 883 Payment of rent..was held not to be a conclusive admission of title..but rebuttable by showing that he never had any title. **1908** *Westm. Gaz.* 28 Jan. 8/3 Will you state when you think it is rebuttable and when you think it is irrebuttable? **1971** *Daily Tel.* 25 May 3/3 If the gift is substantial..there should be a rebuttable presumption that the witness exercised undue influence on the testator.

rebuttal (rɪ'bʌtəl). [f. as prec. + -AL[1].] Refutation, contradiction; *spec.* in *Law* (cf. REBUT *v.* 4). Also *attrib.*

1830 S. WARREN *Diary Physic.* I. xiv. 302 There is generally preserved an amazing consistency in the delusion, in spite of the incessant rebuttals of sensation. **1881** *Times* 20 June 6/1 To hear the defendant's evidence first,..reserving his right..to call evidence in rebuttal thereof. **1925** *North Western Reporter* CCII. 898/2 Rebuttal evidence properly is that which explains away, contradicts, or otherwise refutes the defendant's evidence 'by any process which consists merely in diminishing or negativing the force of' it. **1971** *N.Y. Law Jrnl.* 23 Nov. 18/3 Petitioner's rebuttal affidavit..was received by the court after the court's decision had been published. **1976** *Billings* (Montana) *Gaz.* 17 June 3-H/8 Smith's attorney..presented John L. Agro..as a rebuttal witness. **1976** *Southern Even. Echo* (Southampton) 11 Nov. 4/4 So bitter was the resentment in Southampton of the criticism contained in the late Sir John Hodsoll's report, that the Public Records Office took the unique step of including rebuttal evidence in the State Archives.

rebutter (rɪ'bʌtə(r)), *sb.* [In sense 1, a. AF. *rebuter* (see REBUT *v.* and -ER[4]); in 2, partly f. REBUT *v.* + -ER[1].]

1. *Law.* **a.** An answer made by a defendant to a plaintiff's surrejoinder.

1540 *Act 32 Hen. VIII*, c. 30 §1 Replycacyons, reioynders, rebutters,..and other pleadynges. **1588** FRAUNCE *Lawiers Log.* I. iv. 25 Formal precidents of..rejoynders, surrejoynders, rebutters, issues. *a* **1734** NORTH *Exam.* III. viii. §61 (1740) 630 Of all the several Pleas,..Rebutters, Sur-rebutters &c. the Public were made Judges by the Favour of the Press. **1770** FOOTE *Lame Lover* II. Wks. 1799 II. 71 Rebutters, sur-rebutters, replications.., and imparlance. **1875** POSTE *Gaius* IV. §129.

transf. **1599** *Broughton's Lett.* v. 17 It had been too much for any such..to haue aduanced a Rebutter against his Grace. **1613** CHAPMAN *Rev. Bussy D'Ambois* Wks. 1873 II. 176 Ioyne in mee all your rages, and rebutters.

†**b.** (See quots.) *Obs.*

1607 COWELL *Interpr.* s.v., The Donnee..repelleth the heire, because though the land were intailed to him: yet he is heire to the warranty likewise; and this is called a Rebutter. *a* **1625** SIR H. FINCH *Law* (1636) 378 If the sonne bring an action to recouer the land, he shall be barred by the warrantie made by his father, and this is called a Rebutter. **1658** PHILLIPS, *Rebutter*, a Term in Law, is, when the Donnee by virtue of a Warranty made by the Donour repelleth the Heir.

†**c.** (See quot.) *Obs.*

1607 COWELL *Interpr.* s.v., If I graunt to my tenent to hould *sine impetitione vasti*, and afterward I impede him for waste made, he may debarre me of this action, by shewing my graunt, and this is likewise a Rebutter.

2. That which rebuts, repels, refutes, etc.; a refutation.

1794 GODWIN *Cal. Williams* 170 Surely, it is no sufficient rebutter of a criminal charge [etc.]. 1829 GEN. P. THOMPSON *Exerc.* (1842) I. 181 If they have received a rebutter for their pains, they must ascribe it to the fatality which prompted them to folly. 1868 *Daily News* 3 Aug., The constitutional course which the Queen has adopted..is a sufficient rebutter of the suspicion.

Hence †**re'butter** *v. intr.*, to make a rebutter *to* (a statement); to reply.

1715 M. DAVIES *Athen. Brit.* I. Pref. 30 An English Fryar.., writ a Pamphlet, which he call'd, The Case Re-stated; which was presently reply'd to..in a Pamphlet, styl'd, The Case truly stated; which has been again rebutter'd to, by another Missioner.

rebutting (rɪˈbʌtɪŋ), *vbl. sb.* [f. as prec. + -ING[1].] The action of the vb. REBUT, in various senses; *spec.* in *Curling* (see quot. 1831).

1375 BARBOUR *Bruce* XII. 339 Thai haf tald thair reboyting, Thai of the vaward. *a*1548 HALL *Chron., Rich. III* 25 b, Yᵗ his aduersaries in no wise should haue any place apte or oportune easely to take lande withoute defence or rebuttynge back. 1695 *Colbatch's New Lt. Chirurg. put out* 39 Sounding the Wound with his Probe, and being alarmed with the rebutting of it by the Systole and Diastole of the Heart. 1831 J. WILSON in *Blackw. Mag.* XXX. 971 Rebutting, is towards the end of the game, when the ice is blocked up, and the aspect of the game hopeless or desperate, to run the gauntlet through the same.

So **re'butting** *ppl. a.*, that rebuts.

1871 *Daily News* 11 Mar., The rebutting evidence..was exceedingly strong. 1901 *N. Amer. Rev.* Feb. 248 The medical member of the commission practically testified as a rebutting expert.

re'button, *v.* [RE- 5 a.]

1. *trans.* To button (a garment, etc.) again.

1852 R. S. SURTEES *Sponge's Sp. Tour* (1893) 278 Then he commenced to rebutton the easy, brown great-coat. 1882 ANSTEY *Vice Versâ* (ed. 19) 120 The boys began..to unbutton and rebutton their gloves with great care.

2. To furnish (a garment) with new buttons.

1867 A. GRANT *Mr. Sec. Pepys*, An old seedy black coat, re-buttoned, sponged, and 'goosed up'.

re'buy, *v.* [RE- 2 b and 5 a.]

1. *trans.* To buy back.

1611 COTGR., *Retraict Lignagier*, a power, giuen by custome vnto the neerest kinsman of one that sells land, to rebuy it within a certaine time. 1693 LUTTRELL *Brief Rel.* (1857) III. 118 Prince Lewis had taken some horses, mules, with part of D'Lorges baggage; who sent to the prince to rebuy their horses, but was refused. 1886 *Law Times* LXXX. 206/1 To sell and to rebuy the same amount of stock at a future day at the same price.

2. To buy a second time.

1866 NEALE *Sequences & Hymns* 186, I bought them; and I will rebuy them.

rebuyk-, obs. form of REBUKE *v.*

rebuyt-, obs. form of REBUT *v.*

rebuyte, variant of REBUTE. *Sc.*

rebylione, obs. form of REBELLION.

rebylle rable, obs. f. RIBBLE-RABBLE.

rec, rec. (rɛk), colloq. abbrev. of RECREATION[1]. Also *attrib.* and *ellipt.* (= *recreation ground*).

1929 'R. CROMPTON' *William* iv. 86 Somehow or other the Outlaws got through the lessons before 'rec'. 1931 E. RAYMOND *Mary Leith* v. 170 You saw the mounted specials clear the Rec. 1948 PARTRIDGE *Dict. Forces' Slang* 153 *Rec space*, the ratings' recreation spaces on board ship. 1950 P. TEMPEST *Lag's Lex.* 176 *Rec*, used in some prisons instead of the word 'association'. The prisoners' recreation time. 1960 J. R. ACKERLEY *We think the World of You* 46 The only open space, besides the Rec., in the neighbourhood. 1962 W. GRANVILLE *Dict. Sailors' Slang* 94/2 *Rec room*, recreation *room* at Osborne, now closed. 1967 *Boston Sunday Globe* 23 Apr. B 41/1 (*heading*) A rec hall for patients. 1972 *Sat. Rev.* (U.S.) 24 June 18/3 The dance was held in the games room of the rec center. 1975 'E. LATHEN' *By Hook or by Crook* xiii. 129 The wedding presents were supposed to go on the Ping-Pong table in the rec room. 1977 J. SAVAGE *Nemesis Club* vi. 75 He often goes to the rec. after school.

†**re'cadency.** *Obs.*[−1] [f. med.L. *recad-ĕre* to fall back + -ENCY: cf. CADENCY.] A falling back, recidivation, backsliding.

1648 W. MOUNTAGUE *Devout Ess.*, Addr. to Court a 4 One pattern of relapse and retrogradation..is apt to render many sincere progressions in the first fervor, suspected of unsoundness and recadency.

‖**recado** (reˈkado). Also 7 **recaudo, recarder.** [a. Sp. or Pg. *recado* (also *recaudo*) a message or errand, a gift, equipment or furnishings, etc.; of uncertain origin (see Diez and Körting).]

†1. A present; a message of compliment. *Obs.*

1615 R. COCKS *Diary* (Hakluyt Soc.) I. 26 Our hostis.. sent her sonne to me with a present of 2 barilles wine and other *recado*. *c*1645 HOWELL *Lett.* I. v. ix. 205 Yours of the 2 of July came to safe hand, and I did all those particulars recaudos, you enjoyned me to do to som of your friends here. 1698 FRYER *Acc. E. India & P.* 71 The Padre-Superior, whose Mandate whereever we came caused them to send his Recarders (a Term of Congratulation, as we say, Our Service).

2. A South American saddle. Also, a saddle-cloth.

1826 SIR F. HEAD *Pampas* 246 (Stanf.), I was standing in despair, gazing at the recado which had formed my bed. 1845 DARWIN *Voy. Nat.* iii. (1873) 44 The complicated gear of the recado or saddle used in the Pampas. 1961 G. DURRELL *Whispering Land* vii. 180 Using our saddles and the woolly sheepskin saddle-cloth, called a *recado*, as back-rests.

recal, variant of RECALL *sb.*[1], *v.*[1]

†**re'calcate**, *v. Obs.*[−0] [ad. L. *recalcāre.*] 'To tread under foot' (Cockeram 1623).

recalcination (riːkælsɪˈneɪʃən). [RE- 5 a.] The action of recalcining; a second calcination.

1768 *Elaboratory laid open* 149 The recalcination of the ashes..is wholly unnecessary. 1802 SMITHSON in *Phil. Trans.* XCIII. 26 Disoxidation of the zinc calx,..its sublimation in a metallic state, and instantaneous recalcination.

re-calcine (riːkælˈsaɪn), *v.* [RE- 5 a.] *trans.* To calcine again. Also *fig.*

1635 QUARLES *Embl.* II. xv. (1818) 129 So, now the soul's sublim'd; her sour desires Are re-calcin'd in Heaven's well-temper'd fires. 1662 MERRETT tr. *Neri's Art of Glass* I. xxv, Powder it [brass] again, serce it fine, and re-calcine it. 1758 REID tr. *Macquer's Chym.* I. 376 As it would have been too tedious to re-calcine them all separately, he made four parcels of the whole. 1860 TOMLINSON *Arts & Manuf.* Ser. II. *Sugar* 28 It [charcoal] is then taken to the retort-house and re-calcined, a process which restores all its valuable properties.

recalcitrance (rɪˈkælsɪtrəns). [See next and -ANCE. Cf. mod.F. *récalcitrance.*] Recalcitrant temper or conduct.

1856 FROUDE *Hist. Eng.* (1858) I. iii. 279 Armed with this letter, the heads of houses subdued the recalcitrance of the overhasty 'youth'. 1882 FARRAR *Early Chr.* I. 32 The Senate showed signs of indignant recalcitrance against her attacks on those whose power she feared.

So **re'calcitrancy.**

1869 *Daily News* 15 Apr., This judgment is not at all unlikely to strengthen them in their recalcitrancy.

recalcitrant (rɪˈkælsɪtrənt), *a.* and *sb.* [a. F. *récalcitrant* (17–18th c.), or L. *recalcitrānt-*, pres. pple. of *recalcitrāre* to RECALCITRATE.]

A. *adj.* 1. 'Kicking' against constraint or restriction; obstinately disobedient or refractory. (Said of person or animals, and *transf.* of things.) Also const. *to*.

1843 THACKERAY *Fitzboodle's Confess., Mr. & Mrs. F. Berry* 361 In oaths both French and English [he] called upon the recalcitrant Anatole. 1861 *Sat. Rev.* 7 Sept. 240/2 If you are recalcitrant to the rules of his art. 1866 *Cornh. Mag.* Sept. 339 A recalcitrant pin falling from its rightful place. 1874 GREEN *Short Hist.* vii. §3. 371 For a time it was necessary to suspend the more recalcitrant ministers.

absol. 1865 MAFFEI *Brigand Life* II. 50 The number of the recalcitrant was exceedingly small.

2. Characterized by refractoriness.

1865 MILL *Comte* 25 A single Deity..keeping in recalcitrant subjection an army of devils. 1876 FOX BOURNE *Locke* I. vi. 284 Parliament met..to be again prorogued, on account of its recalcitrant temper.

B. *sb.* A recalcitrant person. Also *transf.*

1865 *Pall Mall G.* 30 May 10 All recalcitrants were treated as rebels and traitors. 1881 *Times* 4 July 11/2 The Registrar ..will take legal proceedings against the recalcitrants. 1918 *Oxf. Mag.* 21 June 343/2 The American Universities have generally adopted the 'Elective System'... There is, however, a distinguished recalcitrant in the University of Princeton.

Hence **re'calcitrantly** *adv.*; also **re'calcitrary** *a.*

1862 F. WILFORD *Maiden of our own day* 505 If this troublesome landlord is still recalcitrary,..I have another plan to propose. 1976 *Gramophone* Apr. 1603/1 A dialogue between God and a recalcitrantly sinful soul.

recalcitrate (rɪˈkælsɪtreɪt), *v.* [f. ppl. stem of L. *recalcitrāre* to kick out (Horace), to be refractory (Vulgate): see RE- and CALCITRATE *v.*]

1. *intr.* To kick out, kick backwards. *rare.* (Now only with *fig.* connotation, as in b.)

1623 COCKERAM, *Recalcitrate*, to kicke with the heele. 1656 in BLOUNT *Glossogr.* 1852 W. WICKENDEN *Hunchback's Chest* 258 Another was recalcitrating like a kicking horse. 1852 *Fraser's Mag.* XLV. 176 We recalcitrate with all our heels against the conclusion.

b. To 'kick out' *against* or *at* a thing; to show strong objection or repugnance; to manifest vigorous opposition or resistance; to be obstinately disobedient or refractory.

1767 STERNE *Tr. Shandy* IX. xxxiii, Why then did the delicacy of Diogenes and Plato so recalcitrate against it? 1824 *Blackw. Mag.* XV. 563 Many good fellows..have recalcitrated against every proposal. 1852 LANDOR *Wks.* (1876) II. 126 Those who..recalcitrate at their caresses, they threaten with Tartarus. 1862 GOULBURN *Pers. Relig.* II. i. (1873) 42 Slothfulness always recalcitrates against an effort of mind.

2. *trans.* To kick back. *rare.*

1832 *Blackw. Mag.* XXXII. 745 When this man..was stopping the rock with his feet, to recalcitrate it upon the enemy. *a*1859 DE QUINCEY (Ogilvie), The more heartily did one disdain his disdain, and recalcitrate his tricks.

Hence **re'calcitrating** *vbl. sb.* and *ppl. a.*

1837 CARLYLE *Fr. Rev.* I. III. vi, There is nothing but rebellious debating and recalcitrating. 1870 J. H. NEWMAN *Gram. Assent* I. v. 129 Seeming to force, and to exult in forcing, a mystery upon recalcitrating minds.

recalcitration (rɪˌkælsɪˈtreɪʃən). [See prec. and -ATION.] The action of recalcitrating, or 'kicking' against something.

1658 PHILLIPS, *Recalcitration*, a striking back with the heel. 1678 J. J[ONES] *Brit. Church* 364 With unevangelical revenge, and recalcitration, after fair eviction. 1818 SCOTT *Hrt. Midl.* xl, These symptoms of recalcitration. 1861 J. G. SHEPPARD *Fall Rome* viii. 415 The hard battle which they had daily to maintain with the recalcitration of the proprietor and the extortion of the treasury. 1880 L. STEPHEN *Pope* ii. 46 One cannot read Addison's praises without a certain recalcitration.

recalculate (riːˈkælkjʊleɪt), *v.* [RE- 5 a. Cf. F. *récalculer.*] *trans.* To calculate afresh; to recount. Also *absol.*

1611 COTGR., *Recalculer*, to recalculate, or make a new computation of. 1652 BROME *Damoiselle* II. i, Whilst I recalculate The miseries of a distressed man. 1669 FLAMSTEED in Rigaud *Corr. Sci. Men* (1841) II. 77 These occultations..I recalculated from the exactest tables. 1856 DOVE *Logic Chr. Faith* VI. §1. 334 If you have made an error in your process, then you must recalculate. 1885 *Athenæum* 3 Jan. 18/3 Dr. Hurter..has recalculated the tables for English weights and measures.

recalcu'lation. [f. RECALCULATE *v.*: see -ATION.] The action of recalculating.

1848 M. SOMERVILLE *Phys. Geogr.* (1849) App. II. 425 The height here assigned to the Peak of Aconcagua differs 700 feet from that given by Captain Fitzroy. A re-calculation..of his elements has led us to adopt a much greater elevation for the giant of the Chilian Andes. 1872 H. WRAY *Some Applic. of Theory to Practice of Construction* 150 This gives a weight rather less than was provided for, but the difference is not enough to render recalculation necessary.

†**re'calefy**, *v. Obs.* [RE- 5 a. Cf. L. *recalefacĕre.*] *trans.* To heat again.

1599 A. M. tr. *Gabelhouer's Bk. Physicke* 80/2 When it is coulde, then recalefy the same agayne. 1657 TOMLINSON *Renou's Disp.* 548 They coct them to the consistence of an Electuary, then they recalifie them.

recalescence. [ad. L. *recalēscĕre*: see RE- 2 c and CALESCENT.] The temporary generation of heat associated with a change in crystal structure when a solid is cooled through a transformation temperature (sometimes sufficient to produce a brief rise in temperature). So **reca'lesce** *v. intr.*; **reca'lescent** *a.*

1873 W. F. BARRETT in *Phil. Mag.* XLVI. 477 Wherever the momentary expansion of the wire is feeble or absent, there likewise this recalescence, as it might be termed, is also feeble or absent. 1887 *Nature* 15 Dec. 165 If an iron bar.. be heated to a white heat and allowed to cool, the brightness at first diminishes, and then reglows (recalesces) for a short interval. 1887 TOMLINSON *Recalescence of Iron* in *Proc. Physical Soc.* (1888) Apr. 107 The metal, to all appearances, receives a sudden accession of heat, and reglows. This phenomenon was discovered by Professor Barrett, and is frequently designated the 'recalescence' of iron. 1899 W. F. BARRETT in *Nature* 22 June 173 In this paper, the phenomenon, for which I suggested the name recalescence, was first described. 1912, 1916 [see DECALESCENCE]. 1973 J. G. TWEEDDALE *Materials Technol.* II. ii. 15 Once nucleation is really started solidification may proceed quite quickly and is then likely to be associated with release of thermal energy as recalescence.

recall (rɪˈkɔːl, also with orig. U.S. pronunc. ˈriːkɔːl), *sb.*[1] Also 8–9 **recal.** [f. RE- + CALL *sb.*, after the vb.]

1. a. The act of calling back; an invitation or summons to return to or from a place.

In recent use *spec.* the calling back of an actor, singer, or other performer to the stage or platform; an encore.

1611 FLORIO, *Riapello*, a recall, a reappeale. 1616 J. LANE *Cont. Sqr.'s T.* 195 Canac, on knees, did too Cambuscan fall, With begging pleasure for Algarsifes recall. 1759 J. G. COOPER tr. *Gresset's Ver Vert.* IV. 191 There the blest day of his recall Is annually a festival. 1794 *Ld. Auckland's Corr.* (1862) III. 201, I shall..wait at Brussels for my letters of recall, and for orders. 1806 A. DUNCAN *Nelson* 86 The admiral..gave the signal of recal. 1849 MACAULAY *Hist. Eng.* vi. II. 139 About three quarters of a year elapsed between the recall of Ormond and the arrival of Clarendon at Dublin. 1869 *Sphinx* 27 Nov. 274/2 Even the gods forgot to applaud—about the highest compliment which could be paid to the actor, and worth fifty recalls. 1884 MRS. H. WARD *Miss Bretherton* vii, He..escaped behind the scenes as soon as Miss Bretherton's last recall was over. 1964 *Financial Times* 3 Mar. 13/1 Several hundred were called back yesterday, and the recall will continue this week and next. The final assembly tracks for bicycles..are being restarted. 1969 T. PARKER *Twisting Lane* 197 What's more I did a Borstal recall as well; that's like an extension of it. 1972 *Sat. Rev.* (U.S.) 17 June 6/3 The previous December, General Motors had announced the biggest recall ever—6·7 million Chevys were called in for breaking engine mounts. 1976 *Globe & Mail* (Toronto) 15 Dec. 5/1 More glass has been found in Coca-Cola bottles and..he expects the soft drink company will have to issue another recall.

fig. 1748 RICHARDSON *Clarissa* Lett. LXXV. iii. 352 A poor girl..having no recalls from education.

b. *Naut.* A signal flag used to call back a boat to a ship, or a vessel to a squadron.

1832 MARRYAT *N. Forster* xli, The recall is up on board of the commodore. 1833 —— *P. Simple* (1863) 117 The Sea-horse, who saw the recall up, did not repeat it, and our captain was determined not to see it.

c. Any sound made as a signal to return; esp. *Mil.* a signal sounded on a musical instrument to call soldiers back to rank or camp.

1835 J. E. ALEXANDER *Sketches in Portugal* vii. 160 The bugle sounds the recal for the skirmishers. **1855** KINGSLEY *Westward Ho!* ix, The trumpets blow a recall, and the sailors drop back again by twos and threes. **1880** J. H. SHORTHOUSE *John Inglesant* xxii. 283 The horn below sounding the recall.

2. The act of recalling to the mind. In *Psychol.*, the act of calling to mind something previously learned or experienced, esp. in memory tests, usu. distinguished from recognition; also *attrib.*; ***total recall***, the ability to call to mind every detail that caught the attention.

1651 tr. *De-las-Coveras' Don Fenise* 243 A history I will tell you, at the recall whereof this Cavalier.. will understand [etc.]. **1887** BAIN in *Mind* Apr. 161 The recall, resuscitation, or reproduction of ideas already formed. **1894** M. W. CALKINS in *Psychol. Rev.* I. 480 The likelihood of recall increases, therefore, by the recency of the position. **1901** *Ibid.* VIII. 363 A somewhat similar feeling had that day been generated by wholly different content..and..there had been direct emotional recall through emotion. **1932** F. C. BARTLETT *Remembering* xv. 256 The matter of recall is mainly a question of interest, while the manner of recall is chiefly one of temperament and character. **1934** R. MACAULAY *Going Abroad* xvii. 134 Total Recall is always subject to the gaps in one's memory. **1953** *Columbia-Viking Desk Encycl.* 805/2 His complicated style seeks by total recall to recapture the minutest psychological and sensory detail. **1953** MILLER & SELFRIDGE in Saporta & Bastian *Psycholinguistics* (1961) 203/1 The same data are replotted to show the relation of the recall-score to the length of the list. **1963** J. D. SALINGER *Seymour: an Introduction* 238, I was not ..the least bit intoxicated by my own powers..of almost total recall. **1970** *Jrnl. Gen. Psychol.* Oct. 236 Part-whole learning interferes with motor recall just as it does with verbal recall. **1971** *Ibid.* Oct. 215 Recall-memory tests call for reproduction of previous input-output events. **1976** GHATALA & LEVIN in Levin & Allen *Cognitive Learning in Children* iii. 62 The possibility has been raised that the processes and/or types of stored information utilized in recognition decisions differ from those utilized in recall. **1977** M. W. EYSENCK *Human Memory* ii. 35 On a subsequent, unexpected recall test, semantically processed material was much better recalled than phonemically or structurally processed material. **1977** *Lancashire Life* Feb. 70/3 Clara's memory may be less than the total recall she would have wished.

3. a. The act or possibility of recalling, revoking, or annulling something done or past. Chiefly in phrases ***beyond, past,*** or ***without recall.***

1667 MILTON *P.L.* v. 885 Other Decrees Against thee are gon forth without recall. **1680** DRYDEN *Span. Friar* III. ii, 'Tis done, and since 'tis done, 'tis past recall. **1790** in Dallas *Amer. Law Rep.* I. 143 After foreclosure, the land is in the mortgagee without any possibility of recal. **1833** HT. MARTINEAU *Fr. Wines & Pol.* i. 15 Since the bargain is.. beyond recall it is no longer my affair. **1864** BROWNING *Rabbi Ben Ezra* xxvii, All that is, at all, Lasts ever, past recall. **1884** *Law Times* LXXVII. 25/2 The Chancery Division may possess power to order the recall of probate.

b. A claim to rescind a bargain.

1894 *Daily News* 14 Apr. 2/7 If you buy that stone you buy it on your own entire judgment, and you have no 'recall' upon me.

c. *U.S.* Removal of an elected government official from office by a system of petition and vote; this method of terminating a period of office. So ***recall election.***

1902 *Arena* XXVIII. 470 If the Recall was in force in any locality, whenever a petition signed by any number over one-half of the registered voters of that locality for the recall of any officer of that locality was filed, that office would become vacant. **1911** *Ann. Amer. Acad. Pol. & Soc. Sci.* XXXVIII. 163 (*heading*) Popular control under the recall. **1970** *Internat. & Compar. Law Q.* 4th Ser. XIX. II. 188 Electoral laws..or the right of recall, or the right to be elected to public office. **1976** *Billings* (Montana) *Gaz.* 16 June 3-B/1 *Philadelphia* (AP)—Critics of Mayor Frank L. Rizzo..filed petitions Tuesday asking for his recall. **1978** *Detroit Free Press* 16 Apr. 8A/4 Five suburban politicians have lost their jobs because they supported a MSHDA-backed housing program, and three more are facing a recall election in Birmingham next month. **1979** *Tucson* (Arizona) *Citizen* 3 Oct. 5A/1 A near-loss in a bitter recall election.

4. *attrib.* and *Comb.*, as ***recall clause, coverage, signal, telegram.***

1976 *Sunday Times* 30 May 8/3 If by June 15 they can collect 145,448 signatures..then Rizzo has 10 days to resign or face a referendum... Hence, the procedure is known as the 'recall clause'. **1971** *Wall St. Jrnl.* 11 Aug. 28/1 Practically every week now brings news that a potentially faulty or dangerous product is being recalled... Many manufacturers are increasingly interested in..product recall coverage. **1904** *Daily Chron.* 11 June 5/4 The eight blocking ships saw the recall signal right enough, but.. disregarded it. **1916** H. G. WELLS *Mr. Britling sees it Through* I. i. 27 He wished he knew of somebody who could send a recall telegram from London.

recall (riːˈkɔːl), *sb.*[2] [RE- 5 a.] A repeated call or demand.

1823 W. TAYLOR in *Monthly Rev.* CI. 254 He makes frequent calls and recalls on our attention.

recall (rɪˈkɔːl), *v.*[1] Also 7–9 **recal.** [f. RE- + CALL *v.*, prob. after F. *rappeler* or L. *revocāre.*]

1. a. *trans.* To call back, to summon (a person, or *fig.* a thing) to return to or from a place.

1591 SHAKS. *Two Gent.* v. iv. 155 Let them be recall'd from their Exile. **1632** LITHGOW *Trav.* I. 38 These..were all re-cald home to their fathers Pallaces. **1670** MARVELL *Corr.* Wks. 1872–5 II. 314 About the same time the King had resolved to recal the Lord Roberts back. **1759** ROBERTSON *Hist. Scot.* (1817) 209 To recal those legions which guarded the frontier provinces. **1816** SHELLEY *Mont Blanc* 48 Some phantom, some faint image; till the breast From which they fled recalls them. **1874** GREEN *Short Hist.* iv. §1. 162 His father's death recalled him home.

b. To bring back by (or as by) calling upon.

1582 T. WATSON *Centurie of Love* To Rdr., Nothing is more easlie let flowne,..nothing later recalled backe againe, then the bitter blast of an euill spoaken man. **1632** BROME *Northern Lass* I. iii, There's no recalling time. **1667** MILTON *P.L.* IX. 926 But past who can recall, or don undoe? **1766** tr. *Beccaria's Ess. Crimes* xii. (1793) 47 Can the groans of a tortured wretch recal the time past, or reverse the crime he has committed? **1817** SHELLEY *Rev. Islam* XII. xxviii, Ye who must lament The death of those that made this world so fair, Cannot recall them now. **1834** MRS. SOMERVILLE *Connex. Phys. Sc.* ix. (1849) 78 The attraction of the earth would have recalled the greatest axis to the direction of the line joining the centres of the moon and earth.

c. To summon or bring back (the attention, mind, etc.) *to* a subject. Also without const.

1667 MILTON *P.L.* XI. 422 But him the gentle Angel by the hand Soon rais'd, and his attention thus recall'd. **1790** BURKE *Fr. Rev.* 21 We must recall their erring fancies to the acts of the Revolution. **1820** SHELLEY *Let. Maria Gisb.* 253, I recal My thoughts and bid you look upon the night. **1848** W. H. KELLY tr. *L. Blanc's Hist. Ten Y.* I. 430 Whether it was that the king wished to recall to his own person the too long diverted attention of the public [etc.].

2. a. To call or bring back *to* (or *from*) a certain state, occupation, etc.

1591 SHAKS. *1 Hen. VI*, I. i. 66 If Henry were recall'd to life againe, These news would cause him once more yeeld the Ghost. **1621** T. WILLIAMSON tr. *Goulart's Wise Vieillard* 103, I will not bee recalled from my last end, to my first state and condition. **1667** MILTON *P.L.* XI. 330 Recall'd To life prolongd and promisd Race, I now Gladly behold [etc.]. **1766** GRAY in *Corr. w. Nicholls* (1843) 63 He..by such afflictions recalls us from our wandering thoughts and idle merriment..to serious reflection. **1798** FERRIAR *Illustr. Sterne*, etc. ii. 36 We are so constantly recalled to right and severe reason. **1821** BYRON *Cain* III. i, May his soft spirit.. recall thee To peace and holiness! **1871** R. W. DALE *Commandm.* Introd. 9 The Commandments recall us to the better faith of earlier times.

refl. **1575–85** ABP. SANDYS *Serm.* (Parker Soc.) 69 That all heretics not recalling themselves by admonition should be avoided. **1638** JUNIUS *Paint. Ancients* 58 Polemo, forced by the weightinesse of his speech, could not but recall himselfe by little and little.

b. To bring back or down, to reduce, *to* a certain number. *rare*[−1].

1836–7 HAMILTON *Metaph.* xxxi. (1859) II. 231 Aristotle recalled the laws of this connection to four, or rather to three.

3. a. To call or bring back (a circumstance, person, etc.) *to* the mind, memory, thoughts, etc.

1611 BIBLE *Lam.* iii. 21 This I recall to my mind, therefore haue I hope. **1671** MILTON *P.R.* II. 106 Mary pondering oft, and oft to mind Recalling what remarkably had pass'd. **1779** J. MOORE *View Soc. Fr.* II. xcv. 423 Any statue of the Virgin would serve as effectually as that to recal her to the memory. **1796** H. HUNTER tr. *St.-Pierre's Stud. Nat.* (1799) III. 303, I tried to recal myself to him by the image of Arcadia. **1817** SHELLEY *Rev. Islam* v. xxxvii, The sleepless silence did recal Laone to my thoughts. **1875** JOWETT *Plato* (ed. 2) I. 46 The name does not recall any one to me.

b. To bring back to the mind; to cause one to remember.

1651 HOBBES *Leviath.* I. iv. 13 Wheras a Proper Name bringeth to mind one thing onely; Universals recall any one of those many. **1819** SHELLEY *Julian* 557 In towns, with little to recal Regret for the green country. **1875** JOWETT *Plato* (ed. 2) IV. 225 The expectation of his death recalls the promise of his youth.

c. To recollect, remember. †Also with *over.*

1671 LOCKE *Essay Draft B* (1931) 264 The mind can repeat..those ideas..by the power it has of recalling and bringing in view any of its own ideas. **1690** LOCKE *Hum. Und.* I. i. §17 'Tis strange that the Soul should never..recall over any of its pure native Thoughts. **1729** BUTLER *Serm. Love of God* Wks. 1874 II. 194 Recall what was before observed concerning the affection to moral characters. **1798** FERRIAR *Illustr. Sterne*, etc. 247 We now begin to recall the Gothic labours of our ancestors. **1822** DE QUINCEY *Confess.* 23, I cannot yet recal, without smiling, an incident which occurred at that time. **1888** BURGON *Lives 12 Gd. Men* II. v. 1 It would be easy to recall the names of men who eclipsed him by their achievements.

4. To bring back, restore, revive, resuscitate (a feeling, quality, or state).

1593 SHAKS. *2 Hen. VI*, III. ii. 61 Might liquid teares.. recall his Life; I would be blinde with weeping, sicke with grones. **1667** MILTON *P.L.* IV. 95 How soon Would highth recal high thoughts. **1727** GAY *Begg. Op.* III. xiii, Their Eyes, their Lips, their Busses, Recall my Love. **1819** SHELLEY *Cenci* III. ii. 54 Once gone, You cannot now recall your sister's peace. **1850** TENNYSON *In Mem.* lxxxv, Autumn..Recalls, in change of light or gloom, My old affection of the tomb.

5. a. To revoke, undo, annul (a deed, sentence, decree, etc.).

1588 GREENE *Pandosto* (1607) 18, I haue committed such a bloodie fact, as repent I may: but recall I cannot. **1590** SHAKS. *Com. Err.* I. i. 148 Passed sentence may not be recal'd. **1659** H. THORNDIKE *Wks.* (1846) II. 505 A man of so much knowledge as to think himself fit to recall the laws of his country. **1686** tr. *Chardin's Coronat. Solyman* 45 You have not kept your word with him,..he recalls his own. **1788** GIBBON *Decl. & F.* xl. (1869) II. 497 They recalled the hasty decree. **1828** D'ISRAELI *Chas. I*, II. iii. 84 Charles instantly recalled the new duties on merchandize, which he had imposed. **1885** *Manch. Exam.* 27 Feb. 5/2 They have no more right..than a chess player who finds out that he has made a bad move has to recall it.

b. To revoke, take back (a gift).

1608 SHAKS. *Per.* III. i. 25 We here below Recall not what we give. **1850** TENNYSON *Tithonus* 49 The Gods themselves cannot recall their gifts.

†**c.** *absol.* To retract. *Obs. rare*[−1].

1598 MARSTON *Sco. Villanie* II. vi. 201, When I..heard him sweare I was a Pythian, Yet straight recald, and sweares I did but quote Out of Xilinum.., I scarce could hold.

Hence **reˈcalled** *ppl. a.*; **reˈcaller.**

1640 R. BAILLIE *Canterb. Self-convict.* Pref. 10 Would not ..all of you who shall remaine in life, bee most earnest recallers..of your owne Countrie men. **1895** *Westm. Gaz.* 1 Oct. 7/1 The recalled Governor of Indo-China.

recall (riːˈkɔːl), *v.*[2] [RE- 5 a.] *intr.* and *trans.* To call again, call a second time.

1794 BURNS *She says she lo'es me*, etc. iii, While falling, recalling, The amorous thrush concludes his sang. **1863** *Times* 19 Mar. 13/1 He then proceeded to recall the names in a regular way.

recallable (rɪˈkɔːləb(ə)l), *a.* [f. RECALL *v.*[1] + -ABLE.] That can be recalled.

1657 TRAPP *Comm. Ps.* cxix. 176, I am recallable, and ready to hear thy voice. **1830** JAMES *Darnley* vi, An office given and recallable at pleasure. **1869** H. SPENCER *Princ. Psychol.* §99 The glow of a gorgeous sunset continues to be recallable long after faintly coloured scenes of the same date have been forgotten.

recalling (rɪˈkɔːlɪŋ), *vbl. sb.* [f. as prec. + -ING[1].] The action of the vb. in various senses.

1611 COTGR., *Revocation*,..a countermaund, recalling, recantation. **1646** *Hamilton Papers* (Camden) 115 The recalling of the copy of the letter then ready to be sent. **1696** T. BRAY *Lect.* I. xvii. 195 The Mischief and Poyson of such Temptations do fly beyond his Recalling. **1835** BROWNING *Paracelsus* I. 85 Recall With all the said recallings, times when [etc.]. **1836** J. H. NEWMAN in *Lyra Apost.* (1849) 155 Who knows but myriads owe their endless rest To thy recalling?

recallment (rɪˈkɔːlmənt). [f. as prec. + -MENT.] = RECALL *sb.*[1]

1650 T. BAYLY *Herba parietis* 115 Now the time is come for her recallment. **1678** SHADWELL *Timon* II. ii, If he sollicites his recallment with you. **1753** W. SMITH *Thucydides* Disc. iii. (1805) I. 106 A change of government is judged a necessary measure to bring about his recalment. **1845** BROWNING *The Glove* 122, I followed after, And asked ..If she wished not the rash deed's recalment?

†**reˈcamara, -era.** *Obs. rare.* [a. Sp. *recamara*, It. *recamera* (Florio): see RE- and CAMERA.] A back chamber, retiring room, closet.

1622 MABBE tr. *Aleman's Guzman d'Alf.* I. I. viii. 92 They made ready their Recamara, and all fitting provision for such a businesse. **1625** BACON *Ess., Building* (Arb.) 552 An Infirmary..with Chambers, Bed-chamber, Anticamera, and Recamera, ioyning to it.

recambole, obs. form of ROCAMBOLE.

†**reˈcamby.** *Sc. Obs. rare*[−1]. [ad. med.L. **recambium* (cf. Sp. **recambio**, It. *ricambio*), f. RE- + CAMBIUM.] = RECHANGE *sb.* I.

1489 *Acta Dom. Conc. Scotl.* 129 The payment of þe soume of twa hundreth fourti ducatis... And of þe Recamby ilke foure moneth..of ilke x ducate a ducate.

Récamier (reɪˈkæmjeɪ, ‖rekamje). [Name of Jeanne Françoise Julie Adélaïde *Récamier* (1777–1849), French hostess.] **a.** (Also ***Madame Récamier*** and with small initial.) Used *attrib.* and *absol.* to designate a *chaise-longue* of the type on which Madame Récamier is portrayed reclining in a painting by David. **b.** Used *attrib.* and *Comb.* to designate a reclining position similar to that in which Madame Récamier is portrayed.

1924 M. J. MURRY *Voyage* ix. 168 Mrs. Tancred got up from her Récamier and stretched out both hands to him. **1936** H. NICOLSON *Let.* 19 Feb. (1966) 244 Draped curtains and Madame Récamier sofas and wall-paintings. **1938** E. BOWEN *Death of Heart* I. iii. 66 Anna, on the sofa in a Récamier attitude. **1944** 'P. QUENTIN' *Puzzle for Puppets* i. 9 A Madame Récamier couch and a huge mirror. **1964** H. GRISEWOOD *Last Cab on Rank* i. 7 A charming récamier sofa. **1966** J. AIKEN *Trouble with Product X* v. 88 She herself was disposed, Recamier-fashion, on one of the twin beds, against a pile of pillows. **1971** M. SMITH *Gypsy in Amber* vii. 53, I don't understand..how a man of your obvious good taste could put a récamier in this room. **1972** J. AIKEN *Butterfly Picnic* x. 180, I had adopted a sort of Récamier posture, reclining on my elbows. **1974** H. MCCLOY *Sleepwalker* iv. 49 She..sat on a Récamier couch. **1979** *N.Y. Times Mag.* 16 Dec. 142/3 The smaller studio at the north end of the space is more formal, primarily because of the major furnishings —a matching pair of *récamiers* (Empire-style lounges).

recanˈdescence. [RE- 5 a. Cf. L. *recandēscĕre.*] The process of becoming brilliant again.

1861 BUMSTEAD *Ven. Dis.* (1879) 483 If mercury be given for the primary sore, it may somewhat diminish for a time, but commonly undergoes a recandescence upon the evolution of secondary symptoms.

recant (rɪˈkænt), *v.*[1] [ad. L. *recant-āre* to recall, revoke (Horace), f. *re-* RE- 2 d + *cantāre* to sing, chant: cf. Gr. παλινῳδεῖν.]

1. *trans.* To withdraw, retract, or renounce (a statement, opinion, belief, etc.) as erroneous, and *esp.* with formal or public confession of error in matters of religion.

1535 LYNDESAY *Satyre* 1136, I will recant nathing that I haue said nathing bot the veritie. **1542–3** *Act 34 & 35 Hen. VIII*, c. 1 Suche offendour..shalbe for the first time admitted to recante and renounce his said errours. **1560** DAUS tr. *Sleidane's Comm.* 200b, He was enforced to recant suche thynges as he had taught before. **1601** F. GODWIN *Bps. of Eng.* 246 He was content to recant his opinions at Paules crosse. **1636** FEATLY *Serm.* in *Strict. Lyndom.* (1638) II. 219 They recanted the Protestant Religion, and were reconciled to the Roman Church. **1719** WATERLAND *Def. Queries* v, Can you deny it without recanting all that you had said before? **1817** MOORE *Lalla R.* (1824) 344 His criticisms were all..recanted instantly. **1853** KANE *Grinnell Exp.* xxxvii. (1856) 338, I was forced to recant in a measure my convictions as to the force of the opposing floes.

†**b.** To renounce, abjure (a course of life or conduct) as wrong or mistaken. *Obs.*

1576 WHETSTONE *Rocke of Regard* IV. 99 Before the world, I here recant my life, I do renounce both lingring loue and lust. **1579** LYLY *Euphues* (Arb.) 101 Musing to renue his ill fortune, or recant his olde follyes. **1605** *Play of Stucley* in Simpson *Sch. Shaks.* (1878) I. 227 Let it suffice If with his tongue he do recant his fault. **1701** C. WOLLEY *Jrnl. New York* (1860) 55, I cannot say I observed any swearing or quarrelling, but what was easily reconciled and recanted by a mild rebuke.

2. a. To withdraw, retract (a promise, vow, etc.). Now *rare.*

1596 SHAKS. *Merch. V.* IV. i. 391 He shall doe this, or else I doe recant The pardon that I late pronounced heere. **1600** FAIRFAX *Tasso* V. lxix, The Captaine sage the damsell faire assured, His word was past, and should not be recanted. **1667** MILTON *P.L.* IV. 96 Ease would recant Vows made in pain, as violent and void. **1855** MILMAN *Lat. Chr.* IX. ii. V. 230 Recanting all his promises and struggling out of his vows.

b. To renounce, give up (a design or purpose).

1652 J. WRIGHT tr. *Camus' Nat. Paradox* x. 232 Lest.. compassion..should have made mee..recant the Design which I had resolved to execute upon him. *a* **1814** *Word of Honor* II. i. in *New Brit. Theatre* I. 361 *Edw.* Then Thomas lied? *Car.* But I recant my purpose.

3. *intr.* To retract, renounce, or disavow a former opinion or belief; *esp.* to make a formal or public confession of error.

1553 M. WOOD [? Bale] tr. *Gardiner's True Obed.* To Rdr. A vj, How these incarnate deuils could..say yea than, & so impudentli..recant and say nay now. **1633** P. FLETCHER *Poet. Misc.* 78 Here I recant, and of those words repent me. **1645** PAGITT *Heresiogr.* (1601) 44 Of a Congregation of Dutch Anabaptists..four recanted at Pauls Cross. **1768** H. WALPOLE *Hist. Doubts* 88 Not one of the sufferers is pretended to have recanted. **1830** D'ISRAELI *Chas. I*, III. xiv. 306 To induce him to recant, they attempted to confute his principles. **1876** MOZLEY *Univ. Serm.* i. 21 The earth must roll back on its axis again before the moral sense of society recants on these questions.

†**b.** To go back on, resile from, an agreement; to refuse to fulfil a contract. *Obs. rare.*

1660 F. BROOKE tr. *Le Blanc's Trav.* 316 We agreed for threescore and odd pistols, which I laid down; but he recanting and demanding more, I withdrew my money. **1755** MAGENS *Insurances* I. 403 Should the Giver of the Premium not approve of the Contractor, he may very justly recant.

†**4.** *refl.* To make retractation (*of* something).

c **1590** GREENE *Fr. Bacon* vi, Recant thee, Lacy, thou art put in trust. **1646** GAULE *Sel. Cases Consc.* 199, I will conceive, withall, that witches have as great cause as may be to recant them of their bargaine.

Hence **re'canted** *ppl. a.*, **re'canting** *vbl. sb.*

1538 ELYOT *Palinodia*.., nowe of some men called a recantynge. **1580** HOLLYBAND *Treas. Fr. Tong, Abjurement*, a recanting. **1671** GLANVILL *Disc. M. Stubbe* 8 Some, you phancy, may think, that you writ against the Errors of that recanted Book.

†**recant**, *v.*^{2} *Obs. rare.* [ad. L. *recant-āre*: see prec. and RE- 2 a, 2 c.]

1. To sing again; to repeat in singing.

1603 HOLLAND *Plutarch's Mor.* 704 (R.) They were wont ever after in their wedding songs to recant and resound this name—Thalassius. **1611** FLORIO, *Ricantare*, to recant or sing againe. **1656** BLOUNT, *Recant*, to sing after another.

2. To relate, recount, rehearse.

1603 HOLLAND *Plutarch's Mor.* 137 If one that sits by him ..recant of some processe of law or action commenced. **1611** FLORIO, *Ridetto*, said, repeated, or recanted againe.

recant (rɪ'kænt), *v.*^{3} *rare*$^{-1}$. [f. RE- + CANT *v.*^{2}] *intr.* To cant or tilt *back.*

1793 *Trans. Soc. Arts* XI. 199 Wheel Cranes, by their recanting back, when overpowered by the weight.

recantation^{1} (riːkæn'teɪʃən). [f. RECANT *v.*^{1} + -ATION.] The action of recanting; an instance of this.

1545 JOYE *Exp. Dan.* v. 94 The kyng with publyke rescript and open recantacion confessinge his synne. **1616** R. C. *Times' Whistle* VI. 2413 Turn convertite, and make true recantation. **1667** PEPYS *Diary* (1879) IV. 261 Two papist women lately converted, whereof one wrote her recantation. **1771** *Junius Lett.* xliv. 232 My offences are not to be redeemed by recantation or repentance. **1814** D'ISRAELI *Quarrels Auth.* (1867) 453 Recantations usually prove the force of authority, rather than the force of conviction. **1846** GROTE *Greece* I. xv. (1862) I. 257 His poem of recantation (the famous palinode now unfortunately lost).

attrib. **1619** R. JONES *Two Serm.*, The Recantation Sermon. **1690** LUTTRELL *Brief Rel.* (1857) II. 109 Mr. Sheapherd..has preacht a recantation sermon in Pinners hall.

†**recantation**^{2}. *Obs. rare*$^{-0}$. [Cf. RECANT *v.*^{2}] (See quot.)

1611 FLORIO, *Ricantatione*, a recantation or singing againe.

recanter^{1} (rɪ'kæntə(r)). [f. RECANT *v.*^{1} + -ER^{1}.] One who recants or retracts.

1589 J. RIDER *Biblioth. Schol.* s.v. *Recant*, A recanter, or he that recanteth, *palinodicus.* **1607** SHAKS. *Timon* v. i. 149 The publike Body, which doth sildome Play the re-canter. **1689** HICKERINGILL *Modest Inq.* IV. 29 Heaven is fill'd with no glorified Saints, except Recanters. **1826** W. E. ANDREWS *Rev. Foxe's Bk. Mart.* II. 52 A recanter, a prevaricator, and frontless liar.

†**recanter**^{2}. *Obs. rare*$^{-1}$. [f. RECANT *v.*^{2}] (See quot.)

a **1661** FULLER *Worthies* (1840) III. 428 To recant;..to say over the same again (in which sense the cuckoo, of all birds, is properly called the recanter).

recanting (rɪ'kæntɪŋ), *ppl. a.* [f. RECANT *v.*^{1} + -ING^{2}.] That recants or retracts.

1593 SHAKS. *Rich. II*, I. i. 193 My teeth shall teare The slauish motiue of recanting feare. **1607** —— *Timon* I. ii. 17 Recanting goodnesse, sorry ere 'tis showne. **1648** MILTON *Tenure Kings* Wks. 1738 I. 320 Have..not..their now recanting Ministers preach'd against him?

Hence **re'cantingly** *adv.*

1593 NASHE *Christ's T.* (1613) 119 Iulian..recantingly cryed out, *Vicisti, Galilæe, vicisti.*

recap ('riːkæp), *sb.*^{1} orig. *U.S.* [f. RECAP *v.*] A pneumatic tyre that has been recapped.

1939 in WEBSTER Add. **1940** in *Amer. Speech* (1944) XIX. 63/2 In recapping it is necessary to make a distinction between a full recap and a top-cap. **1943** *Sun* (Baltimore) 28 Apr. 7/1 The 'recaps for all' announcement had given the public the impression we are over the hump in the rubber situation. **1968** *Wanganui* (N.Z.) *Chron.* 15 Nov. 10/6 (Advt.), If it's tyres or Recaps you need, then try our 10-minute exchange service. **1969** *Truth* (Melbourne) 12 July 31/7 (Advt.), Guaranteed recaps from only $6.50.

recap ('riːkæp), *sb.*^{2} Colloq. abbrev. RECAPITULATION^{1} I.

1950 in WEBSTER Add. **1955** POHL & KORNBLUTH *Space Merchants* ii. 22 A brief recap of the extensive plans his lecture agent had made. **1959** *Times Lit. Suppl.* 2 Oct. 561/1 Comments and 'recaps', hints of tragedies to come or to be overcome, helped to give to oral narrative both atmosphere and shape. **1969** *Morning Star* 1 Nov. 3/8 Three films by John Lennon and Yoko Ono were shown to the Press this week—a recap of a recent New Cinema programme and a foretaste of two new John-Yoko programmes. **1973** *Times* 13 July (Motor Racing Suppl.) p. vi/1 A quick recap on my instructor's words. **1977** *N.Y. Rev. Bks.* 24 Nov. 42/4 Instant observation, like sports' reporting, is seldom more than re-cap, resumé, or the usual proclamation of personal preference.

recap (riː'kæp), *v.*^{1} [RE- 5 a.]

1. *trans.* To put a (*or* the) cap on (a thing) again; *esp.* to provide (a cartridge) with a new cap. Also *absol.*

1856 'STONEHENGE' *Brit. Sports* I. ii. 21 The cases may easily be recapped, and used many times. **1870** GREENER *Mod. Breech-Loaders* 235 The principal advantage of this cartridge is, that it can be recapped and fired a great number of times. *Ibid.* 246 *advt.*, It both extracts and re-caps at the same time. **1890** *Anthony's Photogr. Bull.* III. 27, I..blow the magnesium powder through the flame, and then recap the lens. **1967** KARCH & BUBER *Offset Processes* ix. 375 Fill the fountain bottle with the fountain solution and re-cap it.

2. *trans.* To renew (a worn pneumatic tyre) by cementing, moulding, and vulcanizing a strip of camel-back on the tread. orig. *U.S.*

1939 in WEBSTER Add. **1943** *Sun* (Baltimore) 28 Apr. 7/1 Any civilian can get his tires recapped. **1946** W. H. GROUSE *Automotive Mechanics* xxvii. 579 Worn tires that have good casings without separated plies or broken or damaged cord can be recapped so that they will have considerably longer life.

Hence **re'cappable** *a.*, that can be recapped; **re'capped** *ppl. a.*; **re'capper**, (*a*) a tool for recapping shells or cartridges; (*b*) one who recaps tyres; **re'capping** *vbl. sb.*; also ***recapping-machine.***

1870 GREENER *Mod. Breech-Loaders* 112 A re-capped cartridge-case should not be trusted when in pursuit of dangerous game. *Ibid.* 246 *advt.*, Improved Central-fire Cap Extractor and Re-capper. **1885** *Bazaar* 30 Mar. 1274/1 Loading, turning-over, and re-capping machines. **1939** WEBSTER Add., Recappable. **1940** Recapping [see RECAP *sb.*^{1}]. **1942** *Sun* (Baltimore) 9 Apr. 26/5 Camelback would be released to retreaders and recappers for passenger tires. **1959** L. E. ONEACRE in M. Morton *Rubber Technol.* iv. 104 The main advantage of an electric mold is that the recapper does not have to install a steam boiler to supply heat that would be needed for steam molds. **1967** H. J. STERN *Rubber* (ed. 2) ix. 401 Many of the tyres produced are retreaded when worn. Sometimes the process is described as recapping, or remoulding, according to the external area which is renewed. **1973** *Black Panther* 24 Nov. 11/3 Rebozo was the largest tire re-capper in Florida. **1976** *Billings* (Montana) *Gaz.* 30 June 7-E/4 (Advt.), Plus ·32 to ·58 federal excise tax each and recappable tire.

recap ('riːkæp), *v.*^{2} Colloq. abbrev. RECAPITULATE *v.* 1. Also *absol.*

1950 in WEBSTER Add. **1958** 'N. BLAKE' *Penknife in my Heart* ii. 36 Let me recap. the situation. **1959** H. HOBSON *Mission House Murder* xviii. 183 Let us recap, Mr. Ford, and assess your position. **1971** *New Scientist* 1 July 44/1 The computer résumé they use when she recaps the results to the other scientists. **1976** 'A. HALL' *Kobra Manifesto* ix. 129 'Want to recap anything?' 'No, I've got it.'

reca'pacitate, *v.* [RE- 5 a.]

1. *trans.* and *refl.* To make (legally) capable again. (Cf. CAPACITATE *v.* 2.) *rare.*

1702–3 ATTERBURY *Let. Misc. Wks.* 1739 I. 166 There was another [amendment], which provided, that persons, recapacitating themselves by taking the oaths, should not come into the places out of which they were turned, if full. **1703** *Lond. Gaz.* No. 3892/1 An Act for Enlarging the Time for taking the Oath of Abjuration, and also for Recapacitating and Indempnifying such Persons as have not taken the same by the Time limited.

2. *trans. Physiol.* To restore potency to (a spermatozoon). Cf. CAPACITATE *v.*, CAPACITATION.

1959 M. C. CHANG in C. W. Lloyd *Rec. Progress Endocrinol. & Reproduction* 153 Decapacitated rabbit sperms can be recapacitated again. *Ibid.* 161 The capacitated sperms can be decapacitated by treatment with seminal plasma..but can be recapacitated if they remain longer in the female tract. **1969** *New Scientist* 31 July 234/1 Such sperm were said to have suffered decapacitation, and could regain fertilizing ability (be 'recapacitated') by spending a second period in the female tract.

Hence **,recapaci'tation.**

1970 [see DECAPACITATED *ppl. a.*]. **1974** *Jrnl. Reproduction & Fertility* XLI. 243 It was possible to demonstrate sperm recapacitation.

re'capitalize, *v.* [RE- 5 b.] *trans.* and *intr.* To capitalize (shares, etc.) again. Also *fig.* So **,recapitali'zation; re'capitalized** *ppl. a.*

1927 *Sunday Express* 11 Sept. 1/1 The 'recapitalisation' bubble..is still crowding northern Bankruptcy courts with failures affecting thousands of people. **1928** *Observer* 15 July 20/3 Does anybody suppose that the recapitalised mills are paying their shareholders any such return? **1945** *Richmond* (Va.) *News-Leader* 1 Aug. 13/2 Thomas E. Wilson, chairman of the Board of Directors of Wilson & Co., Inc., today announced plans to recapitalize the company's 274,085 outstanding shares of $6 preferred stock. **1947** J. HAYWARD *Prose Lit. since 1939* 25 The break with the pre-war period was irreparable, and..a reorientation of intelligence and sensibility, a recapitalisation of experience, was inevitable. **1979** *Beautiful British Columbia* Spring 16/1 Bishop declared bankruptcy, re-capitalized, and Secrets of Chinatown was released the following year.

†**re'capitate**, *v. Obs.*$^{-1}$ [ad. It. *ricapitare* in same sense.] *trans.* To send, to forward.

1592 WOTTON in *Reliq.* (1685) 700 Being yesterday from my Friend advertis'd that your Honour resided still in Padoa, and that my last [letters] were recapitated thither; I now proceed to effectuate your Will.

†**re'capitle**, *v. Obs.* Also 6 -capytele. [ad. obs. F. *recapitler*, var. *récapituler*; see RECAPITULE *v.*] *trans.* To recapitulate.

1430–40 LYDG. *Bochas* IV. Prol. (1554) 99b, He..doth recapitle agayn The fal of many that sate in hye stages. **1502** *Ord. Crysten Men* (W. de W. 1506) II. xv. 121 For to understonde y^{e} better & retayne these thynges before sayd they ben recapyteled. **1529** MORE *Dyaloge* I. Wks. 175/2 The author in this chapiter doth briefely recapitle certaine of the principall pointes that he before proued.

recapitulant (riːkə'pɪtjʊlənt), *a. rare.* [f. RECAPITULATE *v.*: see -ANT^{1}.] = RECAPITULATORY *a.*

1929 W. FAULKNER *Sound & Fury* 378 He repeated his story, harshly recapitulant. **1932** —— *Light in August* xii. 269 The boys' diction was slow now, recapitulant. **1939** —— *Wild Palms* 244 You expressed gratitude almost tediously recapitulant.

reca'pitulary, *a. rare*$^{-1}$. = RECAPITULATORY.

1830 *Westm. Rev.* Oct. 437 Re-inquiry, or call it repetitional or recapitulary hearing.

recapitulate (riːkə'pɪtjʊleɪt), *v.* [f. ppl. stem of late L. *recapitulāre*: see RE- and CAPITULATE *v.*]

1. a. *trans.* To go over or repeat again, properly in a more concise manner; to give the heads or substance of (what has been already said); to summarize, restate briefly.

1570 FOXE *A. & M.* (ed. 2) 7/1 Wherof as mention is touched before, so breeflye to recapitulate the same. **1607** T. ROGERS *39 Art.* Pref. 14 These and many more (too many here to be recapitulate)..this first subscription brought first to light. **1642** FULLER *Holy & Prof. St.* IV. viii. 275 Judge Markham in a grave speech did recapitulate select and collate the materiall points on either side. **1699** BENTLEY *Phal.* 108, I would summ up the Particulars of this Second Head, if the Examiner's Performance could bear recapitulating. **1768** H. WALPOLE *Hist. Doubts* 121, I will recapitulate the most material arguments that tend to disprove what has been asserted. **1783** BURKE *Sp. E. Ind. Bill* Wks. 1826 IV. 27 It only remains..for me just to recapitulate some heads. **1861** BERESF. HOPE *Eng. Cathedr. 19th C.* 205 All that I feel bound to do is to recapitulate the alternative possibilities. **1875** JOWETT *Plato* (ed. 2) I. 404 Socrates recapitulates the argument of Cebes.

absol. **1821** CRAIG *Lect. Drawing*, etc. viii. 428 My object being now merely to recapitulate, I give you the rules without the reasoning. **1875** JOWETT *Plato* (ed. 2) I. 485 Let me recapitulate—for there is no harm in repetition.

b. *transf.* in *Biol.* of young animals: (see RECAPITULATION 1 b). Also *absol.*

1879 E. R. LANKESTER *Advancem. Sc.* i. (1890) 43 Suppose ..that the Barnacles..instead of recapitulating in their early life, were to develope directly from the egg to the adult form. **1879** *Athenæum* 19 July 83/2 The fact that in their early development young animals recapitulate their ancestral history.

c. *Mus.* To restate, usu. in similar but distinct form, a musical theme which has been developed in an intervening section. Cf. RECAPITULATION[1] 1 c.

1959 D. COOKE *Lang. Music* v. 250 The second subject of the finale picks up the six-note chromatic scale..; when it is recapitulated, the same notes are used in the bass.

2. a. To bring together again; to sum up or unite in one. *rare.* Also *refl.*

1607 BP. ANDREWES *Serm. Nativity* iii. (1631) 21 That this Mysterie is..the fulfilling of all Prophecies; That all Moses veiles, and all the Prophets' visions, are recapitulate in it. **1629** DONNE *Serm.* Wks. 1839 V. 436 Truly even this first work,..to recapitulate ourselves, to assemble and muster ourselves [etc.]. **1870** W. GRAHAM *Lect. Ephes.* i. 46 Jesus Christ is the Head in whom all things are to be recapitulated. **1874** H. R. REYNOLDS *John Bapt.* iii. §3. 197 The two offices were alike recapitulated in the person of Him who is at once our Prophet and our Priest.

†**b.** *intr.* To come together into one. *Obs.*$^{-1}$

1623 BP. ANDREWES *Serm. Nativity* xvi. (1631) 152 The Head is (as it were) the Summe of all sense; motion, speech, understanding, all recapitulate into the Head.

Hence **reca'pitulating** *ppl. a.*

1845 A. SYMINGTON in *Ess. Chr. Union* viii. 467 The Redeemer in heaven is the grand recapitulating Head in which redeemed and holy creatures..are to be united.

recapitulation[1] (ˌriːkəpɪtjʊ'leɪʃən). [a. F. *recapitulacion* (13–14th c.), or ad. late L. *recapitulātiōn-em*: see prec. and -ATION.]

1. a. The action of recapitulating; a summing up or brief repetition.

1388 PURVEY *Prol. Bible* xii. 48 The vi. reule is of recapitulacoun, either rehersing a thing don bifore. *Ibid.*, This is seid by recapitulacoun. *c* **1410** LYDG. *Lyfe Our Ladye* xviii. *heading* (MS. Ashm.), A recapitulacion of þe wordes of gabriell to oure lady. **1526** *Pilgr. Perf.* (W. de W. 1531) 7 A shorte recapitulacion or rehersal of all yt is sayd. **1579** FENTON *Guicciard.* I. (1599) 13 It is a time vainely spent to stand long vpon the recapitulation of these reasons. **1628** VENNER *Baths of Bathe* (1650) 363 Take this short hint or recapitulation for all. **1752** JOHNSON *Rambler* No. 194 ¶1, I shall therefore continue my narrative without preface or recapitulation. **1812** BYRON *Ch. Har.* II. i. *note*, The reflections suggested by such objects are too trite to require recapitulation. **1869** FARRAR *Fam. Speech* iii. (1873) 85, I will content myself with a mere recapitulation of the elements which we possess for the decision.

transf. **1673** tr. *Harvey's Anat. Exerc.* 28 Nature in death making as it were a recapitulation, returns upon her self with a retrograde motion.

b. *Biol.* The repetition of evolutionary stages in the growth of a young animal. Also *attrib.*

1875 DYER in *Encycl. Brit.* III. 692/2 In the animal kingdom the 'recapitulation theory' steps in. **1880** E. R. LANKESTER *Degener.* 21 In some animals this recapitulation is more, in others it is less complete. **1904** G. S. HALL *Adolescence* I. p. viii, Realizing the limitations and qualifications of the recapitulation theory in the biologic field, I am now convinced that its psychogenetic applications have a method of their own. **1919** J. B. WATSON *Psychol.* vii. 266 The recapitulation theory..holds..that ontogeny repeats phylogeny—that the developing child must pass through all the stages the race has passed through. **1924** R. M. OGDEN tr. *Koffka's Growth of Mind* ii. 48 He can dismiss both the recapitulation- and the utility-theories. **1957** P. HALMOS *Towards Measure of Man* i. 19 Today, the theory of recapitulation is, on the whole, discredited.

c. *Mus.* The section of a composition or movement (esp. one in sonata form) in which some or all of the themes presented in the exposition are repeated, usu. in a modified form. Also *attrib.*

1879 GROVE *Dict. Music* I. 551/1 In the recapitulation of his [*sc.* Beethoven's] subjects,..there is a growing tendency to avoid the apparent platitude of repeating them exactly as at first. **1898** G. B. SHAW *Perfect Wagnerite* 3 In classical music there are, as the analytic programs tell us, first subjects and second subjects, free fantasias, recapitulations, and codas. **1934** C. LAMBERT *Music Ho!* II. 127 His [*sc.* Satie's] unusual employment of what might be called interrupted and overlapping recapitulations. **1947** A. EINSTEIN *Music in Romantic Era* vii. 70 Beethoven had been criticized for having held too fast to the sonata form in his third *Leonore* Overture, or—more precisely—that he had not foregone the recapitulation. **1947** *Penguin Music Mag.* Dec. 29 After the climax Mendelssohn duly modulates to his 'recapitulation-section'. **1959** *Collins Music Encycl.* 613/2 The procedures denoted by the names of its [*sc.* sonata form's] three sections—Exposition (*i.e.* presentation), Development (*i.e.* discursive treatment), and Recapitulation (*i.e.* return)—were present in earlier music. *Ibid.* 614/1 The Recapitulation may differ from the Exposition in details, *e.g.* in orchestration and in the use of new accompaniments to themes. **1959** *Listener* 23 July 152/1 The first theme of the sonata-form opening movement, expounded in three-four time, is transformed in the abbreviated recapitulation to four-four. **1979** C. DEXTER *Service of all the Dead* iii. 22 He had sedulously drilled the set works into them—their themes, their developments and recapitulations.

2. A gathering together into one. *Theol.*

a **1635** SIBBES *Confer. Christ & Mary* (1656) 3 There is a recapitulation, a gathering of all things in heaven and earth. **1913** E. GRUBB *Doctrine of Person of Christ* iv. 28 This idea of 'recapitulation'..is one of the deepest and most pregnant thoughts contributed by Irenæus. **1957** *Oxf. Dict. Chr. Ch.* 1142/1 The conception of recapitulation was elaborated esp. by St. Irenaeus, who interpreted it as both the restoration of fallen humanity to communion with God through the obedience of Christ and as the summing-up of the previous revelations of God in past ages in the Incarnation. **1969** J. ATKINSON in *Dict. Chr. Theol.* 285/2 The recapitulation in Christ connotes the total work of God for man's redemption.

Hence **recapitu'lationist**, an adherent of the theory of recapitulation in biology.

1897 MIALL in *Nature* 26 Aug. 408/2 If I had time to discuss the Recapitulation Theory, I should begin by granting much that the Recapitulationist demands.

recapitu'lation[2]. *rare*$^{-1}$. [RE- 5 a.] A second capitulation or surrender.

1641 EARL MONM. tr. *Biondi's Civil Warres* v. 100 Being blockt up on all sides, this their retreate served onely for their recapitulation.

recapitulative (riːkə'pɪtjʊlətɪv), *a.* [f. RECAPITULATE: see -ATIVE.] Characterized by (biological) recapitulation.

1875 DYER in *Encycl. Brit.* III. 692 The economy of nutrition [in plants] has probably generally led to the suppression of recapitulative structural details. **1879** E. R. LANKESTER *Advancem. Sc.* i. (1890) 19 The tadpole is a recapitulative phase of development.

reca'pitulator. *rare.* [f. as prec.: see -OR.] One who or that which recapitulates.

1382 WYCLIF *Bible* Pref. Ep. Jerome vii. 72 Perlipomynon, that is, the book of the olde instrument, recapitulatour, word bregger. **1589** PUTTENHAM *Eng. Poesie* III. xix. (Arb.) 244 Ye may geue him more properly the name of the collectour or recapitulatour.

recapitulatory (riːkə'pɪtjʊlətərɪ), *a.* [f. as prec. + -ORY.] Of the nature of, characterized by, recapitulation.

1669 BARROW *Expos. Decalogue* Wks. 1716 I. 516 This law is comprehensive and recapitulatory (as it were) of the rest concerning our neighbour. **1685** R. LUCAS *Happiness* (1692) I. 66 *marg.*, A recapitulatory conclusion. **1781** WARTON *Hist. Eng. Poetry* xxxviii. III. 358 Illustrating it by recapitulatory moral reflections. **1829** BENTHAM *Justice & Cod. Petit.* 180 A fresh hearing, termed a recapitulatory hearing, or say a new trial. **1881** FITCH *Lect. Teaching* 153 A most effective form of recapitulatory lesson.

b. *Biol.* = RECAPITULATIVE.

1890 *Nature* 11 Sept. 468/1 Sudden changes of this kind ..cannot possibly be recapitulatory.

†**recapitule**, *v. Obs.*$^{-1}$ [ad. F. *récapituler* (14th c.), ad. L. *recapitulāre*. Cf. RECAPITLE *v.*] *trans.* To recapitulate. Hence †**reca'pituler**.

1489 CAXTON *Faytes of A.* I. xxix. 86 To recapytule shortly almost all the substance. *a* **1533** LD. BERNERS *Gold. Bk. M. Aurel.* xii. 140 b, Colliodrus recapituler of the antyke lawes, that was banyshed by Nero the cruell. **1623** COCKERAM, *Recapituler*, which briefly rehearseth.

recapped, -capper, -capping: see RECAP *v.*[1]

recaption (rɪ-, riː'kæpʃən). [f. RE- + CAPTION *sb.*]

1. *Law.* **a.** A second distress (see quots.).

1607 COWELL *Interpr.* s.v., Recaption..signifieth a second distresse of one formerly distreined for the selfe same cause, and that during the plea grounded upon the former distres. **1641** *Termes de la Ley* 20 If a man be convict before the sherife in the County of a Recaption, he shall be but amerced. **1753** in CHAMBERS *Cycl. Supp.* **1841** *Penny Cycl.* XIX. 402/2 If after goods have been replevied, and before the suit has been decided, the defendant makes another distress for the same cause, such second distress is called a recaption.

b. (Also ***writ of recaption.***) A writ issued in favour of one who has been distrained twice.

1607 COWELL *Interpr.* s.v., Recaption..likewise signifieth a writ lying for the party thus destreined. *a* **1625** SIR H. FINCH *Law* (1636) 447 Recaption is for him whose goods being distreined before for rent or seruices,..are distreyned again for the same thing. **1768** BLACKSTONE *Comm.* III. 150 If, pending a replevin for a former distress, a man distreins again for the same rent or service, then the party is not driven to his action of replevin, but shall have a writ of recaption. **1841** *Penny Cycl.* XIX. 402/2 If the landlord.., finding the goods of B upon the land,..distrains them for the same rent, no writ of recaption lies.

2. *Law.* The peaceful seizure without legal process of one's own property wrongfully taken or withheld.

1768 BLACKSTONE *Comm.* III. 22 Though I may retake my goods if I have a fair and peaceable opportunity, this power of recaption does not debar me from my action of trover or detinue. **1769** *Ibid.* IV. 336 Reception is unlawful, if it be done with intention to smother or compound the larciny; it then becoming the heinous offence of theft-bote.

†**3.** = RECAPTURE I. *Obs. rare*$^{-1}$.

1766 *Chron.* in *Ann. Reg.* 76/2 The king and the magistrates of that city have offered a reward of 100*l.* each for her re-caption.

recaptor (riː'kæptə(r)). [f. RE- + CAPTOR.]

1. One who retakes by capture; *esp.* one who makes a recapture at sea.

1752 BEAWES *Lex Mercat.* 280 She and her cargo were sold, to pay the salvage due to the recaptors. **1804** LD. ELLENBOROUGH in *Best's Rep.* V. 320 Lyde in that case accepted the goods from the recaptors, and not from the master. **1848** ARNOULD *Law Mar. Insur.* (1866) II. III. viii. 969 A perishable cargo having, after capture of ship, been brought by recaptors into a foreign port.

2. *Law.* One who takes goods by a reception or second distraint.

1841 *Penny Cycl.* XIX. 402/2 The course is to sue out a special writ for the restoration of the goods and for the punishment of the recaptor.

recapture (riː'kæptjʊə(r)), *sb.* [f. RE- + CAPTURE.]

1. The fact of taking, or being taken, a second time; recovery or retaking by capture.

1752 BEAWES *Lex Mercat.* 280 There is no room to claim a loss in cases of a recapture. **1787** R. MACKENZIE *Strict. Tarleton's 'Campaigns 1780–1'* title-p., The Recapture of the Islands of New Providence. **1856** KANE *Arct. Expl.* II. x. 111, I learned too that Godfrey was playing the great man at Etah, defying recapture. **1873** SYMONDS *Grk. Poets* vii. 209 The simplicity of Giotto was gone beyond recapture.

2. That which is captured again.

1861 HUGHES *Tom Brown at Oxf.* xxiii, After carrying his re-capture safely home, and erecting the hive on a three-legged stand,..he hastened to rejoin Simon.

recapture (riː'kæptjʊə(r)), *v.* [RE- 5 a.] *trans.* To capture again; to recover by capture.

1799 *Hull Advertiser* 6 Oct. 3/2 She..had been in possession of the French a day or two only prior to her being re-captured. **1834** SIR F. B. HEAD *Bubbles fr. Brunnen* 284 They had nowhere to run but to their own homes, where they would instantly have been recaptured. **1899** W. E. NORRIS *Giles Ingilby* viii, Something which every writer loses, as time goes on, and never can recapture.

Hence **re'captured** *ppl. a.*; **re'capturer**.

1804 *Naval Chron.* XI. 413 A recaptured brig of the convoy. **1889** STEVENSON *Master of B.* 296 The master.. thanked his recapturers as for a service.

re'carbon, *v.* [f. RE- 5 c + CARBON *sb.*] *trans.* To fit (an arc-lamp) with new carbon electrodes. So **re'carboning** *vbl. sb.*

1902 W. J. DIBDIN *Public Lighting* 445 There are two pairs of carbons in each lamp, such being necessary to allow of the lamp burning throughout the whole of a winter night without being re-carboned. **1902** *Encycl. Brit.* XXVIII. 86/2 The cost of carbons and the labour of recarboning. **1917** C. N. BENNETT *Guide to Kinematogr.* xi. 185 If someone will..kindly re-carbon the arc for us and turn on the electric current we shall be ready to start showing.

recarbonate (riː'kɑːbəneɪt), *v.* [f. RE- 5 c + CARBONATE *v.*[1]] To charge (water) with carbon dioxide after softening. Hence **re'carbonated** *ppl. a.*; ˌ**recarbo'nation**.

1907 CROSS & BEVAN *Paper-Making* (ed. 3) xv. 356 In order to retain this carbonate in a more permanently soluble form the Archbutt-Deely plant is provided with means for re-carbonating the softened water by the injection of carbon dioxide. **1926** *5th Ann. Rep. Ohio Conf. Water Purification* 60 (*heading*) Methods of recarbonation of lime-soda softened water. **1936** E. S. HOPKINS *Water Purification Control* ix. 163 The lime-softened water may be satisfactorily stabilized at low cost by recarbonating it with carbon dioxide gas. **1969** *Civil Engin.* (N.Y.) June 40/1 The recarbonated water then flows through two ballast ponds in series. **1978** R. WALKER *Water Supply, Treatment & Distribution* xv. 183 The recarbonation chamber must be sized and baffled to provide between 15 and 30 minutes retention time.

recarburization (riːˌkɑːbjʊəraɪ'zeɪʃən). *Steel-making.* [RE- 5 c.] Addition of carbon (in the form of coke, anthracite or a carbon-rich alloy such as pig iron) to steel to produce the desired composition after refining.

1888 *Jrnl. Iron & Steel Inst.* 331 The recarburisation of the bath of iron gives rise, in the case of basic or neutral open hearth furnaces, to a very considerable loss of metal. **1924** E. L. RHEAD *Metallurgy* (ed. 3) xi. 222 Recarburisation is now often effected by the use of anthracite. This is put at the bottom of the ladle or thrown into the stream of metal as it runs from the furnace. **1940** SIMONS & GREGORY *Steel Manuf. simply Explained* xv. 105 Anthracite coal is used if the recarburization is carried out in the ladle.

Also **re'carburize** *v. trans.*; **re'carburizing** *vbl. sb.*

1888 *Jrnl. Iron & Steel Inst.* 332 This recarburising material consisted in the case of the first charge of 0·145 ton of ferro-manganese and 0·030 ton of ferro-silicon. **1929** C. R. HAYWARD *Outl. Metall. Pract.* xxii. 475 Deoxidize and recarburize the bath. **1950** *Engineering* 30 June 738/3 When making high-carbon steels..it was formerly common practice to run the carbon down in the furnace and then to recarburise to the composition required by the addition of coke or anthracite to the ladle. **1974** *Encycl. Brit. Macropædia* XVII. 645/1 For a long time, high-carbon steels such as rails were made by recarburizing the steel with hot metal. **1974** D. M. CONSIDINE *Chem. & Process Technol. Encycl.* 654/1 Deoxidizing, recarburizing, or alloying additions are made to the ladle during steel tapping from the furnace to adjust the final composition of the steel to the desired specification.

recarder, obs. form of RECADO.

†**re'carga(i)son.** *Obs. rare*$^{-0}$. [a. obs. F. *recargaison* (Cotgr.), or f. RE + CARGASON.] The cargo of a ship for the homeward voyage.

1661 in BLOUNT *Glossogr.* (from Cotgr.). **1677** COLES *Eng.-Lat. Dict.*, A Recargason, *sarcina navis domum rediture.*

re'carnify, *v. rare*$^{-1}$. [RE- 5 a.] *trans.* To convert into flesh again.

c **1645** HOWELL *Lett.* II. li. 65 The flesh which is daily dish'd upon our Tables is but concocted gras, which is re-carnified in our stomacks.

recarriage (riː'kærɪdʒ). Also 6 **recariage**. [f. RE- + CARRIAGE: cf. next.] The act of carrying or conveying back again, *esp.* conveyance back of merchandize; also, the fact of being carried back.

1541 *Act 33 Hen. VIII*, c. 6 For the cariage & recariage of them. *a* **1603** T. CARTWRIGHT *Confut. Rhem. N.T.* (1618) 16 This story of his carriage and re-carriage to and fro the Wildernesse. **1633** MUNDAY *Stow's Surv.* I. iv. 18/1 Three thousand poore Watermen are maintained, through the carriage and recarriage of suche persons as passe and repasse ..upon the [river]. **1889** *Pall Mall G.* 15 June 7/1 The return or recarriage of goods broken or damaged in transit.

recarry (riːˈkærɪ), *v.* [f. RE- + CARRY *v.*; cf. F. *rapporter*, L. *reportāre*.]

1. *trans.* To carry, bear, or convey, back or again. (Common in 16–17th c., esp. in ***carry and recarry***.)

1429 *Rolls of Parlt.* IV. 345/1 Which Rever is comone to alle yowr poeple..for to carye, recarye and lede..in botes..alle maner of Marchaundise. **1494** FABYAN *Chron.* II. li. b, The body..was recaryed vnto saynte Denys of Fraunce. **1533–4** *Act 25 Hen. VIII*, c. 17 If the said owner of the said lodging cause the bringer thereof to take and recarie awaie the saide crossebowe. **1609** BIBLE (Douay) *Gen.* xliii. 12 Duble money also carie with you: and recarie that you found in your sackes. **1637** J. TAYLOR (Water P.) *Carrier's Cosmogr.* C iv b, Great Boats that doe carry and Recarry Passengers..to and fro. **1745** *De Foe's Eng. Tradesman* xxxiv. (1841) II. 687 Thousands of men and horses are employed in the carrying and recarrying to and from London the growth of England. **1855** SINGLETON *Virgil* I. 82 So all things..gliding gradually, are re-carried back.

absol. **1578** FLORIO *1st Fruites* 15 b, They cary and recary, no body saith any thing to them. **1622** MABBE tr. *Aleman's Guzman d'Alf.* II. 31 Moyling and toyling in the world..carrying and re-carrying home, and out againe. **1673** T. JORDAN *London in Splendor* in Heath *Grocer's Comp.* (1869) 514 The..Inhabitants are very actively imployed, some in working and planting, others carrying and recarrying.

2. To carry again by storm.

1839 ALISON *Europe* (1850) XIV. xciv. §21. 24 Planchenoil was recarried; Bulow was driven back into the wood.

Hence **re'carrier**; **re'carrying** *vbl. sb.*

1563 FOXE *A. & M.* 890/2 A matter not of taking, but of gasing,..carying, recariyng [etc.]. **1610** HEALEY *St. Aug. Citie of God* (1620) 667 Mercury..feigned to be the carier and recarier of soules to and from hell. **1677** YARRANTON *Eng. Improv.* 31 For carrying and recarrying of Wood, Coles, Corn, and all other Commodities to and fro. **1711** *Lond. Gaz.* No. 4866/1 The..Carrying, Recarrying, or Delivering of any Letter.

re'cart, *v.* [RE-.] To cart off or back again.

1820 SYD. SMITH *Wks.* (1850) 291/1 No sooner have the poor wretches become a little familiarised to their new parish, than the order is appealed against, and they are re-carted with the same precipitate indecency.

re-'case, *v.* [RE- 5 c.] *trans.* To furnish with a new case; to case again; *spec.* to rebind (a book) using its original case or a new one. Hence **re'cased** *ppl. a.*; **re'casing** *vbl. sb.*

1853–8 HAWTHORNE *Eng. Note-bks.* II. 340 The body of the church has been almost entirely recased with stone. **1920** T. J. WISE *Bibliogr. Writings J. Conrad* I. 4 It is clear that ex-library copies of *Almayer's Folly*..have recently been made attractive and marketable by the apparently simple process of re-casing them in cloth. *Ibid.*, when the binding looks very green and new..the book is probably a re-cased one. **1952** J. CARTER *ABC for Book-Collectors* 150 A book which, being shaken or loose, has been taken out of its covers and re-settled in them more firmly is said to be re-cased. *Ibid*, Most re-casing is not hard to detect. **1977** *Shotton's* (Durham) *Catal.* Oct., Recased into orig. cloth.

re'cash, *v.* [RE-.] *intr.* To make repayment.

1843 MARRYAT *M. Violet* xxvii, The poor fellow was condemned to recash and pay expenses.

re'casket, *v.* [RE-.] To enclose again in a casket.

1853 C. BRONTË *Villette* xxvi, I had hardly time to re-casket my treasures and lock them up.

recast (riːˈkɑːst, -kæst), *sb.* [RE- 5 a. Cf. next and CAST *sb.* VIII.] An act or instance of recasting; the new thing or form produced by recasting.

1840 DE QUINCEY *Homer* v. Wks. 1857 VI. 386 Popular feeling called for a *diaskeué*, or thorough recast. **1862** MERIVALE *Rom. Emp.* (1865) III. xxx. 402 In the second recast of the imperial drama, Agrippa might seem to play the part of Brutus. **1868** M. PATTISON *Academ. Org.* 229 Not merely a revision, but an entire re-cast of the Statute.

recast (riːˈkɑːst, -kæst), *v.* [RE- 5 a.]

1. *trans.* To cast or throw again.

1603 FLORIO *Montaigne* I. xlviii. 155 In the middest of their running-race, [they] would cast and recast themselves from one to another horse. **1894** E. FAWCETT *New Nero* 17 He recast a sudden look upon Fanshawe and his face drearily brightened. **1899** P. H. WICKSTEED tr. *Dante's Paradiso* ii. 21 Now thou wilt urge that the ray here is darkened rather than in other parts, because here it is recast from further back.

2. a. To cast or found (metal) again. Also *fig.*

1768–74 TUCKER *Lt. Nat.* I. vi. §9 Taking their terms from the common language,..recasting them in a mould of their own. **1809–10** COLERIDGE *Friend* (1865) 156 They..would melt the bullion anew in order to recast it in the original mould. **1846** ELLIS *Elgin Marbles* II. 146 Recasting some articles of gold and silver. **1863** *Q. Rev.* Jan. 275 To no purpose has the taxation..been recast in the moulds of their narrow philosophy.

b. To refashion, remodel, reconstruct (a thing, *esp.* a literary work, a sentence, etc.); to invest with new form or character. (Freq. in 19th c.)

1790 BP. T. BURGESS *Serm. Div. of Christ* 28 The advocates of free inquiry have recast the annals of Christian antiquity. **1817** MALTHUS *Popul.* (ed. 5) I. p. xiii, I have recast and rewritten the chapters. **1828** WHATELY *Rhetoric* in *Encycl. Metrop.* (1847) I. 287/1 Young writers..should always attempt to recast a sentence which does not please. **1840** *Fraser's Mag.* XXII. 63 Buonaparte recast the art of war. **1852** GROTE *Greece* II. lxxii. IX. 255 He sent Eteonikus to Thrace for the purpose of thus recasting the governments every where.

absol. **1820** BYRON *Let. to Murray* 23 Apr., I can neither recast nor replace.

c. *Theatr.* To assign (an actor) to another part; to cast (a role, etc.) again. Also *fig.* Cf. CAST *v.* 48.

1951 N. MARSH *Opening Night* vii. 163 A lively and almost cosy discussion about recasting had developed. **1962** L. PAYNE *Too Small for his Shoes* viii. 162 I'll have to recast the part and re-shoot every sequence he was in. **1979** A. SCHOLEFIELD *Point of Honour* 80 My father was recast as a hero..saviour of lives in the face of the enemy. **1981** N. J. CRISP *Festival* vi. 143 Should the play..justify..a possible transfer to the West End, it will..have to be recast.

3. To compute over again, recalculate.

1865 NEALE *Hymns on Paradise* 48 Now the years of their affliction In their memory they recast.

Hence **re'cast** *ppl. a.*; **re'caster**, one who recasts; **re'casting** *vbl. sb.* (also *attrib.*).

1687 in Harwood *Lichfield* (1806) 68 Towards the re-casting of the bells. **1857** GLADSTONE *Oxf. Ess.* 27 All the recasting processes which have yet been tried. **1869** J. MARTINEAU *Ess.* II. 139 No re-casting..can adapt it to our psychological methods. **1884** *Athenæum* 5 July 7/2 The original and the recast Carolingian poems and romances. **1888** *Edin. Rev.* Apr. 510 These are only additions by the recaster of the narrative.

re'catch, *v.* [RE- 5 a.] To catch again.

1824 in *Spirit Pub. Jrnls.* (1825) 294 As to recatching the Speaker! as soon They might hope to have caught Mr. Graham's Balloon. **1871** *Daily News* 19 Jan., French officers..recaught by the Germans. **1895** *Chamb. Jrnl.* 5 Oct. 634/2 Of 337 dabs marked and liberated, 11 were recaught.

recategorize (riːˈkætɪgəraɪz), *v.* [RE- 5 a.] *trans.* To assign to another category; to reclassify. So **recategori'zation**; **re'categorizing** *vbl. sb.*

1949 M. MEAD in M. Fortes *Social Structure* 32 We may find..a recategorizing of cultural experience into such characteristic American forms as fraternities. **1957** PARTRIDGE *English gone Wrong* i. 12 Those..horrifics, *recategorize* and *recategorization*, have..fascinated the combatant services and the Civil Service. **1970** *Jrnl. Gen. Psychol.* Apr. 151 The meaning properties tend to be exhausted rather rapidly by the recategorization instructions. **1977** *Guardian Weekly* 19 Sept. 6/3 He claims there are no political detainees in Chile. (Those left in gaol have been recategorised as common criminals.)

†**re'catholize**, *v. Obs. rare*[−1]. [RE- 5 a.] *trans.* To make Catholic again.

1599 SANDYS *Europæ Spec.* (1632) 101 To have her re-catholized and absolved.

recaudo, obs. form of RECADO.

recaulescence (riːkɒˈlɛsəns). [RE- 5 a: see CAULESCENT *a.*] *Bot.* The adhesion throughout its whole length of a bract or leaf to its stem.

1880 GRAY *Struct. Bot.* (ed. 6) 158 *note*, Bracts or leaves may be for a good distance adnate to sympodial shoots, whether peduncles or leafy flowerless branches. This (named recaulescence by Schimper) is of most frequent occurrence in Solanaceæ.

recaulk (riːˈkɔːk), *v.* [RE- 5 a.] *trans.* To caulk again.

1860 *Merc. Marine Mag.* VII. 242 If a vessel requires to be..re-caulked. **1885** LADY BRASSEY *The Trades* 6 Her decks..had not been recaulked after her last voyage.

recawnt, obs. variant of *reckan* RACKAN.

recce (ˈrɛkiː), *sb.* orig. *Mil. slang.* Also reccy. Shortened form of RECONNAISSANCE. Freq. *attrib.* Cf. RECCO.

1941 *Illustr. London News* CXCVIII. 802 (*caption*) A motor-cycle 'reccy' unit (special reconnaissance troops of armoured force). **1942** E. WAUGH *Put out more Flags* 151 The C.O. has just gone forward with his recce group to make his recce. **1944** *R.A.F. Jrnl.* Aug. 260 We aren't likely to do any serious fighting unless..we are faced by recce patrols by the enemy. **1951** R. CAMPBELL *Light on Dark Horse* iv. 71 My lads became truly proficient in practical recce-work. **1958** G. USHER *Death in Bag* vi. 56, I did a bit of a recce. **1961** W. VAUGHAN-THOMAS *Anzio* iii. 45 No recce plane tried a quick dash to capture a tell-tale photograph. **1968** *Listener* 19 Dec. 812/1 In a side-street we stopped. 'I'll just do a bit of a recce,' the Fiddler said. **1974** *Observer* (Colour Suppl.) 28 Apr. 25/4 We were interrupted by a knock at the door of the mews flat in Belgravia, where Deighton had set up temporary headquarters during his London recce. **1977** 'E. CRISPIN' *Glimpses of Moon* xii. 235 He had had it off all right, thanks..to making careful reccys. **1979** 'A. HAILEY' *Overload* I. xvii. 102, I sometimes think about two guys in Korea, close buddies of mine. We were on a recce patrol near the Yalu river.

recce, *v.* orig. *Mil. slang.* Also reccy. [Shortened f. RECONNOITRE *v.*] *trans.* and *intr.* To reconnoitre (a place, etc.).

1943 J. H. FULLARTON *Troop Target* xxiv. 175 We're even reccying alternative positions twenty miles back to withdraw to. **1944** M. STANDING in *War Report* (B.B.C.) (1946) II. iv. 106 Do not unload until waders have recce'd the water in front of your door. **1945** *Comment from Italy* (Three Arts Club) 48 So I find four bottles and start out across the fields to recce for a farmhouse. **1945** E. WAUGH *Brideshead Revisited* 299 I'm going out myself with the adjutant to recce training areas. **1958** P. SCOTT *Mark of Warrior* I. 59 I'll know better to-day when I've recced it. **1959** 'J. CHRISTOPHER' *Scent of White Poppies* x. 156 These two recce'd up here, and found them gone. **1968** *Listener* 11 July 40/3 He was..recce-ing the new tourist 'firsts' like the Canadian North-West Passage. **1972** *Shooting Times & Country Mag.* 4 Mar. 21/2 'Lofters'..come over to recce the food situation in the more populated areas. **1976** *Listener* 8 Apr. 438/1 Neither of us had seen any of his architecture in Virginia, so I set off to recce Richmond and Charlottesville.

†**recche, reche**, *v. Obs.* Forms: 1 reccan, reccean, 3 ræcchen, recchen, rechen, 4 rachen; 3 reache, 3–4 recche, 4 richche, 4–5 reche. *Pa. t.* 1 reahte, 1, 3 rehte, 3 ræhte. *Pa. pple.* 1 ȝereaht, 2 ireht, 3 iraht. [Comm. Teut.: OE. *recc(e)an* = OS. *rekkian* (MDu. *recken*, Du. *rekken*), MLG. *recken* (hence Da. *række*, Sw. *räcka*), OHG. *recchan* (G. *recken*), ON. *rekja*, Goth. *rakjan* (in comb. *ufrakjan*):—OTeut. **rakjan*, prob. related to Gr. ὀρέγειν, L. *regĕre*, *por-rigĕre*.

The original sense of the word, retained in Du. *rekken*, G. *recken* to stretch, reach, is not prominent in OE.; how far it existed in ME. is not quite clear, as the pa. t. and pa. pple. of *recche, reche* cannot well be distinguished from those of REACH, but it is possible that RATCH *v.* and RETCH *v.* may partly represent both *recche* and *reach*.]

1. *trans.* To tell, narrate, say. **a.** with simple object.

Beowulf (Z.) 91 Se þe cuþe frum-sceaft fira feorran reccan. *c***1000** *Ags. Gosp.* Matt. xiii. 31 He rehte him þa ȝyt oþer biȝspel. *c***1205** LAY. 25131 þa spac Howel þe hende..and his quides ræhte. *c***1430** *Freemasonry* (ed. Halliw. 1840) 550 An angele smot hem so with dyveres speche, That never won wyste what other schuld reche.

b. with dependent clause.

Beowulf (Gr.) 2093 To lang ys to reccenne hu ic þam leodsceaðan yfla ȝehwylces ondlean forȝeald. *c***888** K. ÆLFRED *Boeth.* xxxii. §2 Forðæm ic þe recce eall þæt ic þe ær reahte. *c***1000** *Ags. Gosp.* Mark v. 16 Hi rehton him..hu hit ȝedon wæs. *c***1205** LAY. 10842 Nu ich habbe þe iraht hu he hauede þene nome icaht. *a***1250** *Owl & Night.* 1447 Ich reache heom bi mine songe, That swucch luve ne lest noȝt longe.

2. To explain, expound, interpret (a dream, etc.).

*c***1000** ÆLFRIC *Gen.* xl. 16 Hu gleawlice he þæt swefen rehte. *c***1250** *Gen. & Ex.* 2122 Ðe king him bad ben hardi & bold If he can rechen ðis dremes wold. *a***1400–50** *Alexander* 521 þus he vndid him ilka dele & him þe dome reched. *Ibid.* 1354 þe kyng callis him a clerke..to reche [*v.r.* rachen] him his sweuyn.

3. *intr.* To go, proceed, make one's way.

*c***897** K. ÆLFRED *Gregory's Past. C.* xi. 65 He nat hwider he recð mid ðæm stæpum his weorca. *c***1205** LAY. 25646 Swa sone swa heo mihten ut of scipe heo rehten. *a***1225** *Ancr. R.* 164 Seint Peter seið þat þe helle liun rengeð & recheð euer abuten. *a***1300** *Vox & Wolf* 268 in Hazl. *E.P.P.* I. 67 On frere..hem shulde awecche Wen hoe shulden thidere recche. **13..** *Gaw. & Gr. Knt.* 1898 Renaud com richchande þurȝ a roȝe greue.

b. *trans.* To pursue (one's course). *rare*[−1].

*a***1225** *S. Marherete* 9 þe sunne reccheð hire rune euch buten reste.

Hence †**'recching** *vbl. sb.*, interpretation. *Obs.*[−1]

*c***1250** *Gen. & Ex.* 2058 Tel me ðin drem..Queðer-so it wurðe softe or strong ðe reching wurð on god bilong.

recche, obs. f. RECK *v.*, RETCH *v.*

reccheles, -lesly, -lesnes, obs. ff. RECKLESS, -LESSLY, -LESSNESS.

reccleslaic: see RECKLESSLAIK.

reccless, var. REKELS, incense.

reccnenn, obs. inf. of RECKON *v.*

recco (ˈrɛkəʊ). *Mil. slang.* Abbrev. of RECONNAISSANCE. Also *attrib.* Cf. RECCE *sb.*

1917 A. G. LEE *Let.* 24 May in *No Parachute* (1968) 19 They were still flying two-seater Nieuports, doing..reccos and photography. **1934** *Flight* 18 Jan. 51/1 A shorter 'recco' is also done to the north, if trouble is brewing. **1942** in Forbes & Allen *Ten Fighter Boys* 60 Green section were detailed to..proceed to Chatham, where a recco-machine was hanging around. *Ibid.* 155 My next trip was a scramble to intercept some Hun Machines on recco off Dungeness. **1942** W. SIMPSON *One of our Pilots is Safe* ii. 19 That was the last 'recco.' flight we made, and for months we had to content ourselves with mock air battles. **1943** *Life* 9 Aug. 100/2 (*caption*) Armed recco over Rabaul. **1966** P. DERRIG *Pride of Green Berets* 61 Civil Guard recco units.

reccy, var. RECCE *sb.* or *v.*

recd. Also rec'd. Abbrev. of *received* pa. t. and pa. pple. of RECEIVE *v.*

1599 J. DAY in P. Henslowe *Henslowe's Diary* (1904) I. 57 Rec[d] of m[r] Hinchloe more in ernest of The Tragedy of Thomas Merrye 20[s] Joh. Day. W Haughton. **1775** D. GARRICK *Let.* 1 Nov. (1963) III. 1044 In the middle of the play last night I rec[d] your very extraordinary Note. **1851** J. CHAPMAN *Diary* 23 Apr. in G. S. Haight *Geo. Eliot & J. Chapman* (1940) 158 Rec[d] a letter from Susanna giving a better account of Beatrice. **1876** W. WHITMAN *Daybks. & Notebks.* 12 Mar. (1978) I. 6 Sent & recd. **1934** E. POUND *Eleven New Cantos* xxxiv. 17 And on his return was recd. by Gouverneur Morris and Mr Astor with a pubk. dinner at Tammany Hall. **1965** H. GOLD *Man who was not with It* xi. 86 It had cost me to go back to Pittsburgh, although I had rec'd value.

receande, var. RESEANT *Obs.*

†**re'cede**, *sb. Obs.*[−1] [f. next.] Withdrawal.

1658 SLINGSBY *Diary* (1836) 202, I shall now take occasion to make my recede from the world.

recede (rɪˈsiːd), *v.*[1] Also 5 reysede, 6 recead, 7 receed. [ad. L. *recēdĕre*, f. *re-* RE- 2 a + *cēdere* to go, CEDE. Cf. obs. F. *recéder* (Godef.).]

1. *intr.* To go back or further off; to remove to or towards a more distant position.

a. of persons. Usually = to retreat, retire.

1660 F. BROOKE tr. *Le Blanc's Trav.* 93 You must recede and keep at distance, when you meet women. **1725** POPE *Odyss.* VI. 263 But, nymphs, recede! sage chastity denies To raise the blush. **1799–1805** S. TURNER *Anglo-Sax.* (1836) I. III. iii. 168 Of the events of the battle, he only says, that Arthur did not recede. **1822** LAMB *Elia* Ser. I. *Dream Children*, While I stood gazing, both the children gradually grew fainter to my view, receding, and still receding. **1848** LYTTON *Harold* III. iii, The Earl ceased and receded behind his children.

b. of things. (Said also of things from which one is moving away.)

1662 GLANVILL *Lux Orient.* xiii. 140 As the sun recedes, the moon and stars discover themselues. *a* **1763** SHENSTONE *Elegies* vii. 73 When proud Fortune's ebbing tide recedes. *c* **1790** IMISON *Sch. Arts* I. 66 If it be charged positively.. the balls will recede still further asunder. **1818** SHELLEY *Eugan. Hills* 21 The dim low line.. Of a dark and a distant shore Still recedes. **1860** MAURY *Phys. Geog. Sea* (Low) i. §13 When the two [waves] receded, there was not a house.. left standing in the village.

c. Const. *from*. Also in *fig.* context.

1605 BACON *Adv. Learn.* II. xxv. §12 It is plain that the more you recede from your grounds, the weaker do you conclude. **1653** H. MORE *Antid. Ath.* II. ii. 44 The resistance.. could no more keep down the above-said bullet from receding from the earth [etc.]. **1759** JOHNSON *Rasselas* xxviii [xxix], Those conditions.. are so constituted, that, as we approach one, we recede from another. **1860** TYNDALL *Glac.* I. xi. 73 We receded from him into the solitudes. **1868** Q. VICTORIA *Life Highl.* 26 As the fair shores of Scotland receded more and more from our view.

d. To become more distant; to lie further back or away; to slope backwards.

1777 MASON *Eng. Garden* II. 86 Oft let the turf recede, and oft approach, With varied breadth. **1784** COWPER *Task* I. 65 Not with easy slope Receding wide, they pressed against the ribs. **1815** SHELLEY *Alastor* 404 Where the embowering trees recede and leave A little space of green expanse. **1877** A. B. EDWARDS *Up Nile* vii. 167 The mountains here recede so far as to be almost out of sight.

e. Of a colour: to appear to be more distant from the eye than another in the same plane; = RETIRE *v.* 3 b. Cf. ADVANCE *v.* 2 b.

1935 A. H. RUTT *Home Furnishing* iv. 35 Advancing and receding qualities in colors are a reality, as psychologists have proved. The warm hues seem to advance and the cool ones to recede. **1951** *Good Housek. Home Encycl.* 152/1 The cool tints.. tend to 'recede' and will give a feeling of space.

2. a. To depart *from* some usual or natural state, an authority, standard, principle, etc. ? *Obs.* (Common 1650–1700.)

1480 CAXTON *Chron. Eng.* III. (1520) 19/1 It is mervayle that suche men so excedynge in wyt.. receded from the knowlege of the very god. **1651** HOBBES *Leviath.* I. xi. 50 Receding from custome when their interest requires it. **1665** GLANVILL *Def. Van. Dogm.* 60 By the instances alleg'd, he recedes from his Master Aristotle. **1702** STUBBS *For God or Baal* 17 The Brute.. recedes not from the Directions of Instinct. **1796** H. HUNTER tr. *St.-Pierre's Stud. Nat.* (1799) I. 194 We recede very widely from the intentions of Nature.

b. Of things: To depart, differ, or vary *from* something else. Now *rare*.

1576 FOXE *A. & M.* (ed. 3) 3/1 If they held any thyng whiche receded from the doctrine and rule of Christ. **1605** BACON *Adv. Learn.* I. i. §3, I sawe well that knowledge recedeth as farre from ignorance as light doth from darknesse. **1659** HAMMOND *On Ps.* lxxxvi. 2 Another possible notion of the word, and which recedes very little from this. **1724** A. COLLINS *Gr. Chr. Relig.* 171 The Septuagint, which greatly receded from the Hebrew text, by its additions [etc.]. **1834** MRS. SOMERVILLE *Connex. Phys. Sc.* iii. 12 In paths now approaching to, now receding from, the elliptical form.

3. †**a.** To fall away (in allegiance or adherence) *from* a person. *Obs. rare*.

1480 CAXTON *Chron. Eng.* IV. (1520) 33/1 Many kyngdoms, the whiche receded from all other Emperoures, wylfully to this man torned agayne. **1568** GRAFTON *Chron.* II. 75 That neither he nor his sonne, should recede or disseuer from Pope Alexander, or from his Catholique successors.

b. To draw back *from* a bargain, promise, etc. Also without const.

1648 DK. HAMILTON in *H. Papers* (Camden) 154 They ar so far from receding from anie engagement to you. **1651** G. W. tr. *Cowel's Inst.* 184 If.. the Buyer repents of his Bargain, so that he desires to recede, he shall loose what he gave. **1759** ROBERTSON *Hist. Scot.* v. Wks. 1813 I. 357 By receding from the offer which she made. **1792** *Anecd. W. Pitt* III. xxxix. 51 How could I recede from such an engagement? **1802** MAR. EDGEWORTH *Moral T.* (1816) I. 220 A. felt no inclination to recede from the agreement, into which he had entered. **1885** *Law Rep. 29 Chanc. Div.* 437 There was a concluded contract from which neither party could recede.

c. To withdraw *from* a position, proposal, undertaking, opinion, etc. Also without const.

1716 *Lond. Gaz.* No. 5447/2 The Deputies.. thought fit to recede from the Objections. **1738** *Col. Rec. Pennsylv.* IV. 324 They hope the Governour would recede from this part of the Amendment. **1844** THIRLWALL *Greece* lxiii. VIII. 233 Chilon, whose hopes were dashed by this failure, now only persevered because it was too late to recede. **1863** H. COX *Instit.* III. ii. 602 From this opinion some of the judges subsequently receded.

4. a. To go away, depart, retire (*from* or *to* a place or scene). *rare*.

c **1485** *E.E. Misc.* (Warton Club) 29 The grettyst payn.. Was when my sole dyde from me reysede. **1679** WOOD *Life* (O.H.S.) II. 446 About the same time that the Treasurer went away, 'twas reported that the dutchess of Portsmouth receeded also. **1691** —— *Ath. Oxon.* I. 5 Afterwards receeding to his Native Country, he wrot in his own Language. **1818–20** E. THOMPSON *Cullen's Nosol. Method.* (ed. 3) 201 Inflammation of the joints suddenly receding. [**1842** BRANDE *Dict. Sci.* etc., s.v. *Recess of the Empire*, They are thought to have been so termed from being pronounced at the time when the diet was about to 'recede', or separate. **1892** KIRK *Abingdon Acc.* p. xxviii, Two monks had 'receded', one to Colne.]

†**b.** To retire *from* an occupation. *Obs.*[−1]

1666 *Ormonde MSS.* in *10th Rep. Hist. MSS. Comm.* App. V. 20 Bankes thinks to recede from those imployments to follow his owne.

†**c.** To have recourse *to* one. *Obs.*[−1]

1681–6 J. SCOTT *Chr. Life* (1747) III. 368 This Power is subordinate to the Civil Legislation.. and.. stands obliged to recede to the Civil Sovereign.

5. a. To go back or away in time.

1788 E. SHERIDAN *Let.* 27 July in *Betsy Sheridan's Jrnl.* (1960) iv. 107 And now to *recede*—I had just sent off my letter yesterday when Mrs Angelo call'd, as usual all life and spirits and full of news. **1831** *Blackw. Mag.* XXX. 660 From Green and Bewick.. let us recede (in a chronological sense) to Hogarth. **1834** CALHOUN *Wks.* (1864) II. 392, I shall endeavor to recede, in imagination, a century from the present time.

b. To go or fall back, to decline, in character or value.

1828 HALLAM *Mid. Ages* I. ix. (1869) 585 A nation that ceases to produce original and inventive minds.. will recede from step to step. **1883** *Daily News* 7 Nov. 4/7 American prices were firm, but foreign Government stocks receded fractionally.

6. *trans.* †**a.** To retract, withdraw. *Obs.*[−1]

1654 H. L'ESTRANGE *Chas. I* (1655) 57 Rather willing to submit to the hazard of Lewes his breach of Faith, then to the blame of receding his own from pollicitation.

b. To remove back or away.

1819 in Picton *L'pool Munic. Rec.* (1886) II. 364 The widening of Dale Street by taking down and receding of the houses. **1823** J. BADCOCK *Dom. Amusem.* 51 Introducing two lenses.. and approaching or receding these by means of the slider.

Hence **re'ceded** *ppl. a.*; **re'ceder**; **re'ceding** *vbl. sb.*

1605 BACON *Adv. Learn.* II. xxv. §24 When there is once a receding from the word of God. **1748** RICHARDSON *Clarissa* (1768) IV. xxxv. 214 'Do I what, Madam?' 'And why vile man?'.. O the sweet receder! **1909** M. B. SAUNDERS *Litany Lane* I. vi. 69 Her attendant lady.., Augusta of the receded fringe.

recede (riː'siːd), *v.*[2] [f. RE- 5 a + CEDE *v.*] *trans.* To cede again, give up to a former owner.

1771 J. BAILEY in F. Chase *Hist. Dartmouth Coll.* (1891) I. 435 The lands on the west side Connecticut river might be receded back to New Hampshire. **1805** M. CUTLER in *Life, Jrnls. & Corr.* (1888) II. 185 The first step was to re-cede Alexandria to Virginia.

recedence (rɪ'siːdəns). [f. RECEDE *v.*[1] + -ENCE: cf. *precedence*.] = RECESSION.

1859 J. TOMES *Dental Surg.* 494 The gradual waste of the alveolar processes, accompanied by a corresponding recedence of the gums. **1883** *New Eng. Jrnl. Educ.* XVII. 329 An age approximating the recedence of the flood.

recedent (rɪ'siːdənt), *a. Med.* [f. as prec. + -ENT: cf. *precedent*.] = RETROCEDENT.

1822 GOOD *Study Med.* II. 505 Retrograde; recedent; misplaced gout. **1830** *Fraser's Mag.* II. 381 Persons subject to gout.. particularly in that form of the disease which the learned call recedent.

receding (rɪ'siːdɪŋ), *ppl. a.* [f. as prec. + -ING[2].] That recedes.

1781 COWPER *Charity* 147 The sable warrior.. Loses in tears the far receding shore. **1805** EMILY CLARK *Banks of Douro* III. 299 Embittering the receding moments of existence. **1866** HUXLEY *Preh. Rem. Caithn.* 98 The forehead is smooth and not receding. **1878** —— *Physiogr.* 141 The muddy bank left by the receding tide. **1895** A. W. PINERO *Second Mrs. Tanqueray* III. 103 A man.. with a low forehead, a receding chin, a vacuous expression. **1956** *Jrnl. Theol. Stud.* VII. 18 The incidence of the gradually receding preposition παρά supports the impression. **1958** [see ADVANCE *v.* 2 b]. **1977** *Transatlantic Rev.* LX. 183 If I have learned anything it is that the past is not a receding dream but an ever burgeoning presence at our backs that sustains us.

recedure (rɪ'siːdjuə(r)). *Arch.* [f. as prec. + -URE.] A recess or ledge on the inner side of a chimney stalk.

1839 URE *Dict. Arts* 280 To facilitate the erection.. of an insulated stalk of this kind, it is built with three or more successive plinths, or recedures.

receipt (rɪ'siːt), *sb.* Forms: α. 4–6 receyt, (5–6 -e, 6 receeyte), 4–7 receite, 5–8 receit, (8 reciet); 4–5 resceyte, 5 (7) resceyt, 5, 7 (8) resceit, (5–6 -e); 4 resseit, 4–5 reseit, (6 -e), 5 resseyt(e, -ayt, 5–6 resayte, -eyt, 6 -ayt, 6 (7 *Sc.*) ressait, (6 reseight); 5 recyt(e; 6 receate, 7 -eat. β. 4–7 receipte, 5 resceipte, 5–6 receypte, 6– receipt. [ME. *receite, receit*, a. AF. (ONF.) *receite, receyte* (1304–5) = OF. *reçoite*, var. of *recete* = Sp. *receta*, Pg. *receita*, It. *ricetta*:—L. *recepta*, fem. pa. pple. of *recipĕre* to RECEIVE.

The vowel of OF. *receite, reçoite* is app. due to the influence of such verbal forms as *receit, reçoit*. The normal OF. form is *recete*, the more usual *recepte* (whence mod.F. *recette*) being a learned reversion to the Latin form (cf. RECEPT *sb.*[1]). In Eng., the spelling *receipt* (with *p* from Latin, as in OF. *reçoipte*) has prevailed in this word, in contrast to the related CONCEIT and DECEIT.]

I. 1. a. A formula or prescription, a statement of the ingredients (and mode of procedure) necessary for the making of some preparation, esp. in *Med.* (now *rare*) and *Cookery*; a RECIPE.

c **1386** CHAUCER *Can. Yeom. Prol. & T.* 800 What schal this receyt coste? telleth now. *c* **1400** tr. *Secreta Secret., Gov. Lordsh.* 84 Off þe Receytes off Medicynes. **1530** PALSGR. 261/1 Receyte of dyvers thynges in a medycine, *drogges, recepte*. **1595** *Widowes Treasure* B iv b, A notable receite to make Ipocras. **1632** J. HAYWARD tr. *Biondi's Eromena* IV. 125 The severall antidotes by mee taken, whereof I shewed them the receipts. **1703** J. TIPPER in *Lett. Lit. Men* (Camden) 307 Medecinal and Cookery receipts collected from the best authors. **1791** HAMILTON *Berthollet's Dyeing* I. Pref. 5 A few books of receipts [for dyeing] taken from Hellot. **1828** SCOTT *F.M. Perth* vi, The thin soft cakes, made of flour and honey according to the family receipt. **1859** W. COLLINS *Q. of Hearts* (1875) 24 She spent hours in the kitchen, learning to make puddings and pies, and trying all sorts of receipts.

fig. **1647** COWLEY *Mistr.* Wks. 1710 I. 113 I'll teach him a Receipt to make Words that weep, and Tears that speak. **1709** POPE *Ess. Crit.* 115 Some.. Write dull receipts how poems may be made. **1742** YOUNG *Nt. Th.* v. 94 Till the destin'd youth Stept in, with his receipt for making smiles.

b. The formula or description of a remedy *for* a disease, etc.; also *absol.*, a remedy, means of cure.

1586 T. B. *La Primaud. Fr. Acad.* (1589) 143 As surgeons do to cut off and to burne.. when there is no way to finde or use any other receit. **1612** BACON *Ess., Studies* (Arb.) 13 Euery defect of the mind may haue a speciall receit. *a* **1656** BP. HALL *Soliloquies* 29 Dark rooms, and cords, and hellebore are meet receipts for these mental distempers. **1693** DRYDEN *Juvenal* Ded. (1697) 75 The Patients, who have open before them a Book of admirable Receipts for their Diseases. **1711** STEELE *Spect.* No. 52 ⁋3 The most approved Receipt now extant for the Fever of the Spirits. **1809** MALKIN *Gil Blas* XII. iv. ⁋5 There is not a receipt in the whole extent of chemistry which I have not tried.

fig. **1628** tr. *Mathieu's Powerfull Favorite* 108 Death is the onely receit for their euils, and they keepe her by force from it. **1646** GATAKER *Mistake Removed* 39 [They have] made up all their receipts for distempered souls of so much Law and so much Gospel.

c. The formula of a preparation, or an account of the means, by which some effect may be produced; hence, the means to be adopted *for* attaining some end.

1621 T. WILLIAMSON tr. *Goulart's Wise Vieillard* 22 That hee had a receipt would preserue a man from growing old. **1646** SIR T. BROWNE *Pseud. Ep.* I. vi. 23 From the knowledge of simples shee had a receipt to make white haire black. **1707** *Curios. in Husb. & Gard.* 276 These Receipts for the Vegetation of Plants. **1827** POLLOK *Course T.* VII, [He] sought Receipts for health from all he met.

fig. **1691** HARTCLIFFE *Virtues* 166 The best Receipt, both for the amending our Manners, and the managing our Business, is the Admonition of a Friend. **1777** SHERIDAN *Sch. Scand.* IV. iii, Well certainly this is.. the newest receipt for avoiding calumny. *a* **1868** BROUGHAM (Ogilvie), A more certain receipt for producing misgovernment of every kind.. it would be difficult to devise.

†**2. a.** A drug or other mixture compounded in accordance with a receipt. *Obs.*

1398 TREVISA *Barth. De P.R.* XVII. viii. (Bodl. MS.), In alle good receites and medicynes Amomum is ofte ido. *c* **1430** LYDG. *Min. Poems* (Percy Soc.) 69 This ressayt is bought of no poticarye,.. To al indifferent, richest diatorye. *c* **1500** *Sloane MS.* 2491 lf. 73 A Booke.. teachinge the waye of making diuerse good and excellent Receiptez. **1560** WHITEHORNE *Ord. Souldiours* (1588) 40 b, Fill the bottels halfe full of this foresaide receipt. **1605** BACON *Adv. Learn.* II. viii. §3 It can be done with the vse of a fewe drops or scruples of a liquor or receite. *a* **1631** R. BOLTON *Comf. Affl. Consc.* 64 He throwes the glasse against the Wall, spills that precious Receipt, and drives the Physition out of doores. **1773** GOLDSM. *Stoops to Conq.* II. i, Did not I prescribe for you ever day, and weep while the receipt was operating?

transf. and *fig.* *c* **1430** LYDG. *Min. Poems* (Percy Soc.) 50 My lord may al my sorowe recure, With a receyte of plate and of coyngnage. **1576** FLEMING *Panopl. Epist.* 27 Their noblenesse.. quite quenched their calamitie, with preseruatiue receiptes of comforte.

†**b.** *pl.* Ingredients of a mixture. *Obs.*

1669 STURMY *Mariner's Mag.* v. xii. 65 Gun-powder of a.. Russet colour is very good, and it may be judged to have all its Receipts well wrought.

II. 3. That which is received; the amount, sum, or quantity received. **a.** of money.

a **1400** *Minor Poems fr. Vernon MS.* 225/145 Þenk also.. Þat longe hast lyued and muche reseiued,.. hou þou hast spendet þat reseit. *c* **1483** CAXTON *Dialogues* 3/9 Your recyte and your gayne goute Brynge it all in somme. **1570** *Act 13 Eliz.* c. 4 §8 Any Treasorer.. whose whole Receipt from the begyning of his Charge, is not.. above the Summe of Three Hundred Poundes. **1648** BP. HALL *Breathings of Devout Soul* §38 None of the approved servants.. brought in an increase of less value than the receit. **1800** *Asiat. Ann. Reg., Proc. Parl.* 16/2 The Tanjore subsidy is stated at something more than the receipt last year. *Ibid.*, The deficient receipt in 1797–8. **1849** MACAULAY *Hist. Eng.* vi. II. 102 The Commissioners of the Customs reported to the King that.. the receipt in the port of the Thames had fallen off by some thousands of pounds.

pl. **1422** tr. *Secreta Secret., Priv. Priv.* 134 Whan the Myses & the exspensis.. ouer-Passyth.. the receitis, than moste the kynge of his Peple har goodis take. **1535** *Act 27 Hen. VIII*, c. 27 The said chauncellour shall.. take reconisances of euery particular receiuour.. for the sure paiement of his receites. **1589** WARNER *Alb. Eng.* VI. xxxi. (1612) 153, I spake of great accompts, Receites [etc.]. **1691** HARTCLIFFE *Virtues* 87 Liberality.. is designed to be a Virtue moderating our Receipts, as well as our Gifts. **1805** W. COOKE *Mem. Foote* I. 96 His own pieces, and Macklin's *Love-a-la-Mode*, brought great receipts to Crow-street theatre. **1863** *Sat. Rev.* 6 June 714 That a possible margin should be left for an excess of actual revenue over estimated receipts.

transf. and *fig.* **1612** T. TAYLOR *Comm. Titus* ii. 12 The end of all thy receits is Gods glory in the seruice of the

Church. **1692** RAY *Disc.* II. ii. (1732) 78 In the Mediterranean the Receipts from the rivers fall short of the expence in Vapour.

†**b.** of other things. *Obs. rare.*

1593 SHAKS. *Lucr.* 704 Drunken Desire must vomite his receipt, Ere he can see his owne abhomination. **1607** —— *Cor.* I. i. 116 The belly..taintingly replyed To th' discontented Members,..That enuied his receite. **1623** LISLE *Test. Antiq. Anc. Faith Ch. Eng.* 13 He which will receive that housell, shall..take with chastitie that holy receit.

III. 4. a. The act of receiving something given or handed to one; the fact of being received.

1399 LANGL. *Rich. Redeles* II. 98 Whedir the grounde of ȝifte were good other ille,..reson hath rehersid the resceyte of all. **1439** *Rolls of Parlt.* V. 16/2 After the date and receit of the saide Writte. **1442** *Ibid.* 57/1 To see the bookes of receyte. **1494** FABYAN *Chron.* IV. lxix. 47 After the receyte of thyse letters, he wrote answer to his moder. **1588** J. MELLIS *Briefe Instr.* F vij b, Whan you pay money to another, cause the day of receite to be written in your booke of recorde. *a* **1617** BAYNE *On Eph.* (1658) 20 The receit of benefits, is the foundation of thankfulness. **1661** MARVELL *Corr.* Wks. 1872–5 II. 61 We thought it would be a good answer to giue you account of the receit of your letter. **1774** JEFFERSON *Autobiog.* Wks. 1859 I. 133 On receipt of such a sum as the Governor shall think it reasonable for them to spend. **1831** T. HOPE *Ess. Origin Man* III. 341 The receipt of the radiance that..proceeds to us as its common centre and focus. **1848** MILL *Pol. Econ.* I. vii. §5 (1876) 69 Fit to be entrusted with the receipt and expenditure of large sums of money.

†**b.** *bill* or *ticket of receipt* = next. *Obs.*

1509–10 *Act 1 Hen. VIII*, c. 3 §1 All Acquittaunces and Billes of Receyte heretofore made by the seid John Heyron. **1551** *Reg. Privy Council Scot.* I. 114 Conforme to the tekat of ressait maid betuix the saidis parteis thairupoun.

c. A written acknowledgement of money or goods received into possession or custody.

1602 in *Maitl. Cl. Misc.* (1840) I. 23 Certane buikis.. gevin to Mr. Adam Newtoun for the Prince his use, as the said Mr. Adamis ressait thairof producit testifeis. **1651** MARIUS *Bills of Exchange* 13 Make a receit for the same on the backside of the said Bill. **1721–41** CHAMBERS *Cycl.* s.v., Where the receipt is on the back of a bill, &c., it is usually called an indorsement. **1838** *Murray's Hand-Bk. N. Germ.* 190 The fare must be paid beforehand, and a receipt is always given for it.

fig. **1781** COWPER *Conv.* 202 Then each might..carry in contusions of his skull A satisfactory receipt in full.

5. The act or practice of receiving (stolen goods); reset. ? *Obs.*

1413 *Pilgr. Sowle* (Caxton 1483) III. v. 54 Had not be youre redy receyt, they had not be at al tymes so redy to stele. **1596** SPENSER *State Irel.* Wks. (Globe) 620/1 The stollen goodes are convayed to some husbandman or gentellman, which..liveth most by the receit of such goodes stoln.

6. a. The act of receiving or taking in; admittance (of things) to a place or receptacle. ? *Obs.*

c **1400** tr. *Secreta Secret., Gov. Lordsh.* 96 Þe wirkynge of þis last..ys yn þe receyte of þe seed in þe mariz. *Ibid.* 101 As þe see waxis by þe receyt of fflodes and waters. **1561** T. NORTON *Calvin's Inst.* I. 53 Fiue senses..whereby al objectes are poured into common sense, as into a place of receite. *a* **1600** in Hakluyt *Voy.* (1810–12) III. 141 Shipping used among us either for warre or receit. **1615** G. SANDYS *Trav.* 22 Ample cisternes for the receit of raine. **1651** *Raleigh's Ghost* 200 It [the ark] was sufficient for the receite ..of all living Creatures.

†**b.** The act of taking in (food, medicine, etc.) by the mouth or otherwise. *Obs.*

c **1400** tr. *Secreta Secret., Gov. Lordsh.* 82 Drynkes of swete wyn, and ressayt of hony moyst. **1522** MORE *De Quat. Noviss.* Wks. 74/2 The pleasure that men may finde by the receeyte of this medicine. **1567** MAPLET *Gr. Forest* 26 b, [Plants] by their more hid receit of necessaries..have given great causes of doubting. **1599** B. JONSON *Every Man out of Hum.* III. i. (Rtldg.) 49/1 He shall receive the first, second, and third whiffe [of tobacco-smoke].., and, upon the receipt [etc.].

†**c.** An act of taking; a definite amount taken.

1390 GOWER *Conf.* III. 11 If I myhte..Of such a drinke ..have o receite. **1601** HOLLAND *Pliny* II. 36 A greater receit than one Obulus, killeth him or her that taketh it.

†**d.** The act of receiving the sacrament. *Obs.*

1500–20 DUNBAR *Poems* ix. 92 Of ressait sinffull of The my Saluiour,..I cry The mercy. **1552** R. HUTCHINSON *3rd Serm.* (1560) G vi. A manifest deniall of the transubstantiation, and of all corporall, reall, and naturall receit.

†**7. a.** The act of receiving or admitting (a person) to a place, shelter, accommodation, assistance, etc.; the fact of being so received; reception. *Obs.* (Common *c* 1600–50.)

1557 *Order of Hospitalls* F viij b, Against Easter yow shall prepare a Booke for the receipt home of the children. *a* **1586** SIDNEY *Arcadia* III. (1598) 338 Come, death, and lend Receipt to me, within thy bosome darke. **1615** G. SANDYS *Trav.* 10 When all the earth at the intreatie of Juno, had abjured the receipt of Latona. *a* **1641** BP. MOUNTAGU *Acts & Mon.* (1642) 539 Speciall lodgings for receit of women dedicated to God. **1676** HALE *Contempl.* I. 528, I have A little room,..not that I think it fit For thy Receit or Majesty, but yet It is the best I have.

†**b.** The ordinary or habitual reception of strangers or travellers; esp. in *place of receipt*. *Obs.*

1608 HEYWOOD *Lucrece* Wks. 1874 V. 183 There is no newes there but at the Ale-house, ther's the most receit. **1634** SIR T. HERBERT *Trav.* 154 Noble places of Receipt or Carrauans-rawes for Trauellors to rest in. **1642** ROGERS *Naaman* 846 Inne-Keepers who stand at their doors or gates of receit..to welcome and lodge travellers. **1650** FULLER *Pisgah* II. ix. §25 The greatest place of receipt in Samaria.

†**c.** Receptiveness, welcome. Also with *a*: A (good or bad) reception. *Obs. rare.*

1596 in Nichols *Progr. Q. Eliz.* (1823) III. 384 This Master Dorstetell came and made his speach in Latin, full of receit, love and curtesie. **1664** PEPYS *Diary* 26 Feb., I had a kind receipt from both Lord and Lady as I could wish.

†**d.** *Law.* The admission of a third person to plead in a case between two others in which he is interested. Also, admittance of a plea in a court of justice. *Obs.*

1607 COWELL *Interpr.* s.v. *Resceyt.* **1628** COKE *On Litt.* II. iii. §96 As there may be a demurrer upon counts and pleas, so there may be of Aide prior, Voucher, Receite, waging of Law, and the like. **1658** in PHILLIPS.

†**8.** Acceptance of a person or thing. *Obs. rare.*

c **1460** G. ASHBY *Dicta Philos.* 852 For kynge they wolde haue hym in Receite, Howe be it that they haue hym not in love. **1607** COWELL *Interpr.*, *Resceyt of homage*, is a relatiue to doing homage, for as the Tenent, who oweth homage, doth it at his admission to the land: so the Lord receiueth it. **1621** BP. MOUNTAGU *Diatribæ* 569 Not so generall, euery where in vse, and receit, because not so obuious euery where vnto the vnderstanding.

9. The fact of receiving (a blow, wound). ? *Obs.*

a **1533** LD. BERNERS *Huon* lv. 186 They had neuer sene before so grete a stroke nor a goodlyer reseyt therof without fallynge to the erthe. **1615** G. SANDYS *Trav.* 28 Hearing his brother cry out at the receipt of a blow. **1651** *Life Father Sarpi* (1676) 62 The day after the receipt of his wounds [etc.]. *a* **1676** WISEMAN *Chirurg. Treat.* (J.).

†**10.** *to stand at receipt*: to stand ready to receive. *Obs.*

Perh. originally a hunting term; cf. sense 14.

1546 HEYWOOD *Prov.* II. v. (1867) 59 If ye can hunt, and stand at receite. *a* **1569** KINGESMYLL *Man's Est.* x. (1580) 62 Happie it was that there stoode some at receipte to receive the precious seede sowen by our Saviour. **1587** GREENE *Euphues his Censure* Wks. (Grosart) VI. 245 Yet hee would alwaies gyue the onset, saying that souldiers which stood at receipt, and felt the furious attempt of the enemy, were halfe discomfitted. *c* **1611** CHAPMAN *Iliad* VI. 375 Helen stood at receipt, And took up all great Hector's pow'rs t' attend her heavy words.

IV. 11. a. The chief place or office at which moneys are received on behalf of the Crown or government; the public revenue-office. Also in Eng. use, ***Receipt of the* (*King's*) *Exchequer***. Now only *Hist.*

1442 *Rolls of Parlt.* V. 62/2 Certayn Tailles reysid at the resceyt of your Escheker. **1450** *Ibid.* 176/1 If Shirrefs, Eschetours, or eny other persones shall..paie eny sommes of money therof att Kynges receite at Westm. **1485** *Naval Acc. Hen. VII* (1896) 7 Thomas Roger hath receyved at the Receypt of the Kinges Exchequier..ccli. **1596** DANETT tr. *Comines* (1614) 242 One other also being of the receit was a furtherer thereof till his heart failed him. **1603** KNOLLES *Hist. Turks* (1621) 1277 The Magistrates in the publicke receipt. **1620** WILKINSON *Coroners & Sherifes* 75 To levie the Kings debts, and to pay them into the receit duely and orderly. **1691** LOCKE *Lower. Interest* Wks. 1727 II. 93 Who will not receive clipp'd Money,..whilst he sees the great Receipt of the Exchequer admits it. **1765** *Act 5 Geo. III*, c. 26 Preamble, A fine of £101. 15*s.* 11*d.*, paid into the receipt of his said Majesty's Exchequer. **1863** H. COX *Instit.* III. vii. 683 The officer..was to reside at the Receipt of Exchequer.

fig. **1684** T. BURNET *Th. Earth* II. 75 Thousands of lesser [rivers] that pay their tribute at the same time into the great receit of the ocean.

b. The receiving-place *of* custom. Hence *fig.*

1539 BIBLE (Great) *Matt.* ix. 9 He sawe a man (named Mathew) syttyng at the receate of custome. **1847** L. HUNT *Men, Women & B.* II. vii. 96 The bird sat at the receipt of victory. *a* **1859** —— *Bk. Sonnet* (1867) I. 87 Lamb..sat at the receipt of impressions, rather than commanded them.

†**12. a.** A place for the reception of things; a receptacle. *Obs.*

1388 WYCLIF *Exod.* xxxviii. 3 He made redi of bras dyuerse vessels, caudruns, tongis,..and resseittis of firis. *c* **1400** MAUNDEV. (1839) x. 112 Men han made a litylle Resceyt, besyde a Pylere of that Chirche, for to resceyve the Offrynges of Pilgrymes. *c* **1430** LYDG. *Compl. Bl. Knt.* xxxiii, The thought [is] resseyt of woo and of compleynt. **1593** NASHE *Christ's T.* 33 b, Hauing her receipt of disgestion almost closed vp with fasting. **1601** HOLLAND *Pliny* I. 340 [The heart] contains within it certaine ventricles and hollow receits, as the chiefe lodgings of the life, and bloud. **1605** SHAKS. *Macb.* I. vii. 66 Memorie..Shall be a Fume, and the Receit of Reason A Lymbeck onely.

†**b.** *esp.* A receptacle for water; a basin or other part of a fountain; a reservoir. *Obs.*

c **1450** *Plan Charterhouse Waterwks.* in *Archæologia* LVIII. (1902) 303 Seint John receyte undir þe hegge. *c* **1512** *Ibid.* *a* **1548** HALL *Chron., Hen. VIII* 166 The second receit of this fountaine was enuironed with wynged serpentes all of golde. **1575** LANEHAM *Let.* (1871) 52 Sundrye fine pipez did liuely distill continuall streamz intoo the receyt of the Fountayn. **1601** HOLLAND *Pliny* II. 411 The least leuell for to carry and command water vp hill from the receit, is one hundred foot. **1625** BACON *Ess., Gardens* (Arb.) 561 Fountaines I intend to be of two Natures: The One that, Sprinckleth or Spouteth Water; The Other a Faire Receipt of Water. **1646** J. GREGORY *Notes & Obs.* (1650) 114 The dry land appeared..recompensed with an exuberancy of Hils and Mountaines for the Receipts into which he had sunk the waters.

†**c.** A recess in a wall. *Obs.*$^{-1}$

1560 WHITEHORNE *Arte Warre* (1588) 94 To make the walles crooked, and full of tourninges, and of receiptes.

†**13. a.** A place of reception or accommodation for persons; a place of refuge. *Obs.*

1390 GOWER *Conf.* III. 118 Aries..is the receipte and the hous Of myhty Mars. **1430–40** LYDG. *Bochas* VII. viii. (1554) 172 b, His tonne to hym [Diogenes] was receite and housholde. **1495** *Act 11 Hen. VII*, c. 5 Preamble, The grettest haven succour and receite..for marchauntes and shippes. **1579–80** NORTH *Plutarch* (1895) III. 423 His house was a common receite for all them that came from Greece to Rome. *a* **1603** T. CARTWRIGHT *Confut. Rhem. N.T.* (1618) 655 Their Munkeries are Receits of children starting from their fathers. **1625** MARKHAM *Bk. Hon.* III. v. §4 His House became as it were an Hospitall or Receit for all that wanted.

†**b.** A chamber, apartment. *Obs. rare.*

1593 NASHE *Christ's T.* 28 In the inner receipt of the Temple, was hearde one stately stalking vp and downe. **1615** CHAPMAN *Odyss.* IV. 413 Atrides, and his..spouse,..In a retired receit, together lay.

†**14.** *Hunting.* (Cf. 10.) A position taken up to await driven game with fresh hounds; a relay of men or dogs placed for this purpose. *Obs.*

1575 TURBERV. *Venerie* 244 They use their greyhounds only to set backsets or receytes for deare wolfe foxe or such like. **1580** LYLY *Euphues* (Arb.) 419 In hunting I had as liefe stand at the receite, as at the loosing. **1622** BACON *Hen. VII* (1876) 154 The lords that were appointed to circle the hill, had some days before planted themselves, as at the receit, in places convenient. **1688** HOLME *Armoury* III. 187/1.

V. †**15. a.** Capability of receiving, accommodating, or containing; capacity, size. *Obs.* (Common in 17th c., esp. of houses or other buildings.)

1563 GOLDING *Cæsar* V. (1565) 108 Newe shippes to be buylded.., and the olde to be mended, declaring of what receite and fasshyon he wold haue them made. **1592** *Nobody & Somebody* C ij b, To purchase me a name, Take a large house of infinite receipt. **1615** G. SANDYS *Trav.* 5 One only harbor..of a conuenient receit for ships, respect we either their number or burthen. **1652** COTTERELL *Cassandra* VI. (1676) 567 The Palace which was of receipt sufficient to lodge them all commodiously. **1657** R. LIGON *Barbadoes* (1673) 90 After much keeling, they take it..and put it into ladles that are of greater receipt. **1703** T. N. *City & C. Purchaser* 12 He that designs..the Building,.. must have respect to its due Situation, Contrivance, Receipt, Strength [etc.].

fig. **1642** FULLER *Holy & Prof. St.* V. xix. §11. 438 His popular manner was of such receipt that he had room to lodge all comers.

†**b.** Mental capacity; power of apprehension.

c **1400** tr. *Secreta Secret., Gov. Lordsh.* 114 Many heres in þe brest..bytokyns..lessenynge of þe resceyt. **1605** BACON *Adv. Learn.* I. i. §3 If then such be the capacitie and receit of the mind of man [etc.]. **1607** HIERON *Wks.* I. 262 The heart of man is of great receit and able to containe many things. **1628** BP. HALL *Old Relig.* (1686) 31 This justice being wrought in us by the holy Spirit according to the modell of our weak receit.

†**16.** Accommodation or space provided. *Obs.*

1615 T. ADAMS *Leaven* 114 Do not..thrust it into a narrow corner in your conscience, while you give spatious receat to lust and sin. **1627** CAPT. SMITH *Seaman's Gram.* x. 49 To make roome and receit for the Sea.

VI. 17. *attrib.*, as ***receipt duty, form, side, stamp, tax***; **receipt-book**, (*a*) a book of medical or cooking receipts (also *fig.*); (*b*) a book containing receipts for payments made.

1654 WHITLOCK *Zootomia* 50 One Remedy shall serve.. severall Diseases, and distempers..; Their *Receipt-Book is as universally indifferent, as a Church-Booke. **1797** *Encycl. Brit.* (ed. 3) III. 391/2 Receipt book. In this book a merchant takes receipts of the payments he makes. **1808** HAN. MORE *Cœlebs* II. xlvii. 446, I now found her grand receipt-book was the Bible. **1873** MISS BROUGHTON *Nancy* I. 6 Keep stirring always!..say I, closing the receipt-book. **1878** JEVONS *Prim. Pol. Econ.* 130 The penny *receipt duty ..is..a good tax. **1898** *Engineering Mag.* XVI. 46 Further below is the *receipt form: Rec'd [etc.]. **1800** *Asiat. Ann. Reg., Proc. Parl.* 41/2 The most prominent article on the *receipt side is that of the sale of goods. **1879** *Chambers' Encycl.* s.v., A penny *receipt stamp. **1787** DUKE OF DORSET in O. Browning *Despatches from Paris* (1909) I. 217 It is fear'd that the Duty is intended to include Stamp-receipts after the plan of the *Receipt-Tax in England. **1795** PITT in *G. Rose's Diaries* (1860) I. 203 Funds on the Receipt Tax.

†**re'ceipt**, *v.*^{1} *Obs.* Forms: 4–6 receit-, 7–8 *Sc.* receipt. [a. OF. *receiter*, var. *receter* to RESET: cf. prec. and RECEPT *v.*]

1. *trans.* To receive, harbour (a person, esp. a criminal).

c **1300** *Beket* 1242 That thu ne suffri noȝt that he beo Receited in thi londe. **1483** *Rolls of Parlt.* VI. 251/1 The said Water..falsly and traiterously receited, herboured, comforted and ayded the same Sr John. **1600** O. E. *Repl. Libel* I. viii. 207 They would not haue abetted traytors to rebell, nor receited rebelles, that are fled out of the realme. *a* **1670** SPALDING *Troub. Chas. I* (1828) I. 3 Letters of intercommoning against the Clanchattan..that none should receipt, supply or intertain any of them. *a* **1733** *Shetland Acts 4* in *Proc. Soc. Ant. Scot.* (1892) XXVI. 196 That none receipt them [beggars] in their houses, nor give them hospitality or service.

2. To reset (a thing stolen). *rare*$^{-1}$.

1714 R. SMITH *Poems of Controversy* (1869) 21 Invercall would not receipt A thing that's got by stealth or cheat.

receipt (rɪˈsiːt), *v.*^{2} [f. RECEIPT *sb.* 4 c.]

1. *trans. U.S.* To acknowledge in writing the receipt of (a sum of money, etc.).

1787 M. CUTLER in *Life, Jrnls. & Corr.* (1888) I. 376, I.. have delivered him one hundred and ten dollars.., which he has receipted to me as received on the account of the Ohio Company. **1798** I. ALLEN *Hist. Vermont* 233 Forty prisoners were returned... Major Fay, as Commissary of prisoners, receipted them. **1828–32** WEBSTER, *Receipt*, to give a receit for; as to receipt goods delivered by a sheriff.

2. To mark (an account) as paid. Also *fig.*

1844 DICKENS *Mart. Chuz.* xlvi, If you will have the goodness to send us a note of the expense, receipted, we shall be happy to pay it. **1876** SAUNDERS *Lion in Path* vi, He pays promptly, for the account has been receipted at the time of purchase. **1938** E. Bowen *Death of Heart* III. i. 327 She receipted Portia's remark with an upward jerk of the chin.

3. *intr. U.S.* To give a receipt *for* (a sum of money, etc.).

1832 *Sen. Doc. 23rd U.S. Congress I Sess.* No. 512 (1835) II. 829 [Stock] will be delivered.. to an issuing officer,.. who will receipt therefor. **1862** O. L. Jackson *Colonel's Diary* (1922) v. 96 Major Lyford.. receipted to me for the safe delivery of the cargo. **1880–6** in Webster. **1889** *Scribner's Mag.* Aug. 216/1 The supplies.. are there weighed or measured and receipted for. **1913** J. London *Valley of Moon* 503 These two assistants had.. been receipted for by the local deputy sheriff.

Hence **re'ceipted** *ppl. a.*

1848 Thackeray *Van. Fair* xix, The destruction of every written document (except receipted tradesmen's bills). **1979** *Daily Tel.* 21 Nov. 3/3 Drivers would need to present full log sheets of receipted bills to support their case for relief.

receiptable, *a.* [f. receipt *v.*[2] + -able.] That may be receipted (Ogilvie 1882).

†**receipter.** *Obs.* Forms: 4 resceitour, 5 receytour, 5–7 receitor, 6 reyceter, 7 receipter. [a. AF. **receitour*, var. OF. *receteur* resetter. Cf. receipt *v.*[1]] One who receives or harbours criminals or stolen goods.

c **1380** Wyclif *Sel. Wks.* III. 294 þei maken holy Chirche a bande of here synne, and resceitour of here raveyn. **1487** *Act 3 Hen. VII*, c. 11 §11 That such mysdoers.. procurators to the same and receytours.. be hensforth reputed and juged as principall felons. **1537** in Froude *Hist. Eng.* (1858) III. 418 An old man, who with his two sons, being arrant thieves, were the receitors. **1579–80** North *Plutarch* (1895) III. 360 Such as the pyrates and sea rovers had hidden being parte of their spoyles and bestowed with their receitors. **1626** Jackson *Creed* VIII. vi. §4 Shee alone.. committed the robbery in taking the forbidden fruit from off the tree, her husband was the receipter onely.

re'ceiptless, *a.* [f. receipt *sb.* 4 c + -less.] Not receipted.

1873 Miss Broughton *Nancy* III. 74 Gnashing his teeth .. at his exasperated creditors and receiptless bills.

receiptor (rɪ'siːtə(r)). [f. receipt *v.*[2] + -or.] *U.S.* A person who receipts property attached by a sheriff; a bailee.

1814 *Mass. Supreme Court Rep.* XI. 319 The receiptors are precluded, by their own act, from calling in question the validity of the attachment. **1839** J. Story *Law of Bailments* §125 Upon bailments of this sort it may not be without use to consider.. what are the rights and duties of the bailee, commonly called the receiptor. **1847** in Webster. **1864** in Wharton *Law Lex.* (ed. 3). **1914** F. Rawle *Bouvier's Law Dict.* III. 2824/2 The officer taking the goods often.. delivers them to some third person, termed the 'receiptor', who gives his receipt for them.

receit(e, obs. forms of receipt *sb.* and *v.*[1]

receitor: see receipter.

receivable (rɪ'siːvəb(ə)l), *a.* and *sb. pl.* [Orig. a. AF. *receivable* (1304), var. OF. *recevable*; in later use f. receive *v.* + -able.]

A. *adj.* **1. a.** Capable of being received.

1382 Wyclif *Ecclus.* ii. 5 Men.. resceyuable [L. *receptibiles*] in the chymne of mecnesse. **1646** Sir T. Browne *Pseud. Ep.* 87 There will remaine a quantity of water not receiveable. **1669** Woodhead *St. Teresa* I. Pref. 31 Without considering.. the benefits receivable by it. **1777** Wesley *Wks.* (1872) XI. 382 This is spoken of as receivable by mere faith. **1836** *Penny Cycl.* V. 163/1 Bills.. receivable or payable. **1865** M. Arnold *Ess. Crit.* viii. (1875) 326 His doctrine was more intelligible than Coleridge's, more receivable.

b. Of indictments, excuses, evidence, etc.

1581 Lambarde *Eiren.* IV. v. (1588) 503 Now let us.. consider what enditements be receivable by the Iustices of Peace. **1621** Molle *Camerar. Liv. Libr.* II. ix. 103 A fresh testimonie.. which may seeme receiuable. **1662** J. Davies tr. *Mandelslo's Trav.* 231 If they can alledge any receivable excuse, they are shut up again. **1880** Ld. Blackburn in *Law Times Rep.* XLIII. 213/2 The general rule of English law is, that hearsay evidence is not receivable. **1884** Ld. Coleridge *ibid.* L. 277/1 Does that make the husband a receivable witness against his wife?

c. Of certificates, paper money, etc.: That is to be received as legal tender.

1790 Hamilton *Wks.* (1886) VII. 50 The certificates.. shall also be receivable in all payments whatsoever for land. **1856** *Tait's Mag.* XXIII. 648 Government paper.. receivable in payment of taxes. **1889** *Spectator* 7 Dec., These certificates are to be receivable in all State Treasuries for all purposes, and may be redeemed whenever the holder chooses.

d. Of a broadcast signal or a broadcasting station.

1962 *Rep. Comm. Broadcasting 1960* 196 in *Parl. Papers 1961–2* (Cmnd. 1753) IX. 259 Both the BBC and the ITA.. accept it as their duty to see that their present services are as nearly as possible available to everybody in the country. Not only should they be receivable; they must also be technically acceptable.

2. Capable of receiving; †receptive *of.* Now *rare.*

c **1530** tr. *Erasmus' Serm. Ch. Jesus* (1901) 11 He formed [vs] to his owne lykenes; that is to wyte, receyuable of the highe ioy. **1548** Udall, etc. *Erasm. Par. Mark* ii. 15 b, The feastes of the Iewes bee small, and receiuable but of fewe persones. *Ibid.* viii. 50 b, Crying ofte.. that his audience is not receyuable of so high misteries. **1887** Mary Burt *Browning's Women* 198 The susceptible, receivable, teachable quality in woman or in man.

B. *sb. pl. Comm.* Debts owed to a business, esp. regarded as assets. Cf. payables *sb. pl.*

1863 'E. Kirke' *My Southern Friends* xxii. 231 When I went home.. we had only nineteen thousand in bank. I had exhausted all our receivables. **1947** *Sun* (Baltimore) 30 Sept. 19/1 A move to.. take care of a steadily expanding volume of receivables acquired. **1955** *Times* 10 May 17/2 Long-term receivables have been separated from current receivables, and a new item, short-term borrowings, appears under current liabilities. **1978** *Daily Tel.* 21 Mar. 3 (Advt.), The HP 3000 will run your payroll, process invoices, print out receivables and take care of general ledger work.

Hence **receiva'bility, re'ceivableness.**

1580 Hollyband *Treas. Fr. Tong, Capacité*, capacitie or receyuablenesse. **1654** Whitlock *Zootomia* 352 Exuberances of Fancy, or Desires, [which] various Reading might imprint on such waxy Molds, or tender Receivablenesse. **1813** Jefferson *Writ.* (1830) IV. 200 These bills would make their way.. by their receivability for customs and taxes.

receival (rɪ'siːvəl). Now *rare.* [f. receive *v.* + -al[1].] The act of receiving, receipt, reception.

1637 Earl Monm. tr. *Malvezzi's Romulus & Tarquin* 40 Witnessing the receivall of them. **1656** —— tr. *Boccalini's Advts. fr. Parnass.* II. xxviii. (1674) 177 This Edict caused great commotion.. [and no] threats were able to make those of Marca give way to the receival thereof. **1792** A. Wilson in *Poems & Lit. Prose* (1876) I. 56, I hope, on receival of this, you will oblige me. **1823** Southey *Hist. Penins. War* I. 152 On the receival of the dispatches. **1871** B. Taylor *Faust* (1875) II. I. iii. 30 Graceful be in your receival. **1895** *Funk's Stand. Dict., Receival*,.. in railway use, the receipt of a car by one road from another.

†**receivant.** *Obs.*$^{-1}$ [ad. F. *recevant*, pr. pple. of *recevoir* to receive: see -ant.] One who receives.

1623 tr. *Favine's Theat. Hon.* IX. vi. 394 The Receiuant causing him to rise, speaketh thus to him.

receive (rɪ'siːv), *v.* Forms: α. 4 receyf-, 4–6 receyve, 4, 6– receive, (? 4 *Imper.* receiuf); 4 resceyve, rescheyve, 4–5 resceive, resseyve, 5–6 reseyve; 4 receve, 4–6 reseve, 5 resceve, 5 *Sc.* resseve, 5 rescewe; 6–7 receave, 6 *Sc.* receawe; 7 recieve. β. 4 (9 *Ir. dial.*) resaive, 4–5 ressayve, 4–6 resayve, 4 (6–7 *Sc.*) ressaive, 5 resaywe; 4 *Sc.* resaiff, 4 *north.*, 6 *Sc.* resaif, 5 resayfe, ressayf, 5–6 *Sc.* ressaif, 6 *north.* resayff, 6 *Sc.* rassaif; 4 rescaive, -ayve, 5 reschayfe; 4–6 (9 *Ir. dial.*) resave, 4 *Sc.* reschave, 4 (5–7 *Sc.*) ressave, (? 6 recave); 4 *Sc.* resaf, ressawe, 4, 6 *Sc.* resawe, rasawe. γ. 4–6 recive, 4 reycive, rescyve, 6 recyve, (? 5 reciffe). *Pa. pple.* 6 *Sc.* rassave. [ad. ONF. *receivre*, *receyvre* = OF. *reçoivre*:—L. *recipĕre* (f. *re-* re- + *capĕre* to take); or OF. *receveir*, *recevoir*:—pop. L. **recipēre*: cf. conceive and deceive.]

The leading distinction between the senses of *receive* in Eng. is that between the more active senses included in branches I and II, and the almost passive ones placed under III. This distinction, however, is not always perfectly clear in actual use, and it is often difficult or impossible to determine which aspect of the word is meant to be prominent in particular instances. Owing to the very extensive use of the vb. from the 14th c. onwards, there is also much overlapping of its various applications, and in many examples it is uncertain whether a specific or merely general sense is intended.

I. 1. a. *trans.* To take in one's hand, or into one's possession (something held out or offered by another); to take delivery of (a thing) from another, either for oneself or for a third party.

a **1300** *Cursor M.* 7746 Nou her I leue þe kinges glaiue, Yee send a man at it receiue. *c* **1350** *Will. Palerne* 1260 þanne william.. receyued of þat riche duk realy his swerde. *c* **1420** *Chron. Vilod.* st. 557 þe lytulle childus honde he streyȝte forthe þo To resayve þat tapre wyth þe lyȝt. *c* **1470** *Golagros & Gaw.* 195 This kyth and this castell, Firth, forest and fell,.. Ressaue as your awin. **1539** Bible (Great) *Matt.* xvii. 24 They that vse to receaue tribute-money cam to Peter. **1591** Shaks. *Two Gent.* I. ii. 40 He would haue giuen it you, but I being in the way, Did in your name receiue it. *c* **1620** Sir W. Mure *Misc. Poems* ii. 39 Receaue, in sing that thou hes won the field, Ye bow, ye schafts [etc.]. *c* **1738** Pope *To Lady F. Shirley* 10 Aw'd, on my bended knees I fell, Receiv'd the weapons of the sky. **1819** Shelley *Cyclops* 411 He.. Received it, and at one draught drank it off. **1859** Tennyson *Elaine* 1196 In one cold passive hand Received at once and laid aside the gems.

b. Of God: To take (one's soul, spirit, etc.) to Himself. (Perh. partly in sense 2.)

a **1300** *Cursor M.* 19472 To þe iesu Yeild i mi gast, receiuf it nu! **1382** Wyclif *Acts* vii. 58 Thei stoonyden Steuene.. seyinge, Lord Ihesu, receyue my spirit. **1423** Jas. I *Kingis Q.* cxxiii, Ressaue I sall ȝour saulis of my grace. **1594** ? Greene *Selimus* 2180 Thou God of Christians, Receive my dying soul into thy hands. **1827** Keble *Chr. Y., St. Stephen's Day* v, Jesu, do Thou my soul receive.

c. To reset (stolen goods).

1583 Stubbes *Anat. Abus.* II. (1882) 39 If they would not haue receiued our stollen goods, we woulde neuer haue stollen them. *a* **1625** Fletcher *Love's Cure* V. iii, You must restore all stolen goods you receiv'd. **1727–41** Chambers *Cycl.* s.v. *Receiver*, Such as knowingly receive stolen goods from thieves and conceal them. **1898** Besant *Orange Girl* II. xv, Guilty of receiving stolen goods.

d. To take from another by hearing or listening; to attend, listen, or give heed to.

1388 Wyclif *Prov.* ii. 1 Mi sone, if thou resseyuest my wordis, and hidist myn heestis anentis thee. **1489–90** *Plumpton Corr.* (Camden) 91, I have a *dedimus potestatem* out of the Escheker.. derected to Sir Guy Fayrfax, to resayve your hothes and my ladyes. **1535** Coverdale *Prov.* x. 8 A wyse man wil receaue warnynge. **1566** Painter *Pal. Pleas.* I. (1569) 232 Madame sith it pleaseth you to receiue mine aduise [etc.]. **1601** Shaks. *All's Well* II. i. 22 Our hearts receiue your warnings. **1841** Lane *Arab. Nts.* I. 80 Receive news, O fisherman. **1874** Green *Short Hist.* ix. §6 (1895) 663 A priest named Huddleston.. received his confession. **1896** W. H. Hutton *Philip Augustus* ii. 51 He.. charged the archbishop of Rheims and others to receive the oath of fealty from his new vassals.

†**e.** *Med.* = recipe A. *Obs.*$^{-1}$ (In quot. *fig.*)

1588 Greene *Perimedes* 5 Receiue twenty ounces of merrie conceipts, pounded in the mortar of a quiet resolution.

2. a. To accept (something offered or presented).

In some cases, esp. in negative clauses, this use is not clearly distinguishable from sense 1.

a **1300** *Cursor M.* 28794 (Cott.) Vr lauerd.. receues.. right nan Almus þat o wrang es tan. **13..** *Ibid.* 10276 (Gött.) Quen þu has barntem in lande, Gladly sal we rescyue þi offrand. **1375** Barbour *Bruce* I. 419 [I pray you] That ȝe resaue her his homage, And grantis him his heritage. **1422** tr. *Secreta Secret., Priv. Priv.* 162 [A man] the whyche.. the grace that fortune hym yewyth nel resceive. **1513** Douglas *Æneis* V. ii. 35 Beseik.. That my fadir wald eftir this ressave This sacrifice. **1561** Winȝet *Cert. Tractates* i. Wks. (S.T.S.) I. 7 Na man.. wald resaue the office of ane pastour, quhil he wes almaist compellit thairto. **1601** Shaks. *All's Well* I. iii. 243 But thinke you.. If you should tender your supposed aide, He would receiue it? **1647** *Portland Papers* VI. (Hist. MSS. Comm.) 55 The Commissioners refusing to receave my Answer sealed, I.. read and delivered it open to them. **1776** *Trial of Nundocomar* 16/1 The books must be produced, as we cannot receive parole evidence of their contents. **1836** Calhoun *Wks.* (1864) II. 472 He who votes for receiving this petition.. votes that Congress is bound to take jurisdiction of the question.

†**b.** To accept the surrender of (a person or place). *Obs.*

1375 Barbour *Bruce* XIII. 530 'Till ȝow her I ȝeld me, at ȝour will to be'. 'And I resaiff the, schir' saide he. *c* **1470** *Gregory's Chron.* (Camden) 120 Noo captayne.. shalle nought ressayvynne, nor suffer to ressayvynne.. the captayne ther of. **1470–85** Malory *Arthur* V. xii, Knelyng bifore kynge Arthur [they] requyred hym for the loue of god to receyue the cyte, & not to take it by assaulte.

†**c.** To listen to, or hear, with acceptation. *Obs.*

1388 Wyclif *Ps.* vi. 9 [10] The Lord hath herd my bisechyng; the Lord hath resseyued my preier. [Also in Coverdale and 1611.]

3. a. To become the support of (something superimposed).

1432–50 tr. *Higden* (Rolls) V. 163 The grownde was elevate in maner of a hepe to receyve Hillarius. **1736** Gray *Statius* i. 19 Ye Argive flower,.. Receive a worthier load. **1842** Tennyson *Morte d' Arthur* 164 Make broad thy shoulders to receive my weight, And bear me to the margin.

b. To catch (a person or thing falling or descending) in the arms or otherwise.

1470–85 Malory *Arthur* I. ix, His four knyghtes receyued hym and set hym an horsback. *c* **1485** *Digby Myst.* (1882) IV. 442 Stonde ner, Nichodemus! resaue hym softlye! Mawdleyn, hold ye his fete! **1594** ? Greene *Selimus* 1272 A band of armed soldiers Received him falling on their spears' sharp points. **1671** Milton *P.R.* IV. 583 A fiery Globe Of Angels.. on their plumy Vans receiv'd him soft From his uneasie station.

c. To catch or intercept (a missile, blow, etc.); to encounter or stand the force or effect of.

1560 Daus tr. *Sleidane's Comm.* 56 b, All the pellettes yᵗ they shall shoute, I will receave them with my cote. **1606** Shaks. *Tr. & Cr.* III. iii. 122 Like a gate of steele, Fronting the Sunne, receiues and renders backe His figure, and his heate. **1632** J. Hayward *Biondi's Eromena* III. 79 By this time had the horse (issued from their side) received the charge, after the foote were cut all to pieces. **1704** Swift *Batt. Bks.* Wks. 1751 I. 213 Paracelsus.. darted his Javelin with a mighty force, which the brave Antient received upon his Shield. **1751** Smollett *Per. Pic.* xxxv, The son interposing, received the first discharge of her fury. **1814** Southey *Roderick* xxv. 489 The Goth objects His shield, and on its rim received the edge. **1855** Brewster *Life of Newton* I. iii. 46 The rays reflected by the speculum were received upon a plane metallic speculum.

d. To catch (a sound) by the sense of hearing.

c **1385** Chaucer *L.G.W.* 752 *Thisbe*, Vpon the o syde of the walle stood he, And on that other syde stood Tesbe, The swoote sovne of other to receyve. **1599** Shaks. *Hen. V*, IV. Prol. 6 The fixt Centinels almost receiue The secret Whispers of each others Watch. **1773–83** Hoole *Orl. Fur.* VIII. 528 A lamb.. strays With tender bleats,.. Till from afar the wolf the sound receives.

4. a. To permit oneself to be the object of (some action, etc.); to allow (something) to be done to, or (some quality, etc.) to be conferred on, oneself; to submit to, endure.

a **1300** *Cursor M.* 18714 All þat wald tru fra þat time, And siþen wald receiue baptime. **1382** Wyclif *John* v. 44 How mown ȝe bileue, that receyuen glorie ech of other. *c* **1386** Chaucer *Pard. T.* 598 Com forth anon, and kneleth heere adoun And mekely receyueth my pardoun. **1535** Coverdale *Jer.* vii. 28 This is the people, that nether heareth the voyce of the Lorde.. ner receaueth his correction. **1556** Robinson tr. *More's Utop.* II. (Arb.) 108 *marg.*, The religiously disposed person.. ought pacientlye to receaue and suffer them [griefs]. **1601** Holland *Pliny* XV. iii, If the barke of an Olive tree be slit and cut, it will receive the rellice and smell of any medicinable spice. **1818** T. L. Peacock *Nightmare Abbey* i, Family interests compelled Mr. Glowry to receive occasional visits from Mr. and Mrs. Hilary. **1861** D. G. Rossetti tr. *Dante's Vita Nuova* 299 The sonnet has two parts... It might well receive other divisions also.

b. To admit (an impression, etc.) by yielding or by adaptation of surface. Also *fig.*

c 1391 Chaucer *Astrol.* II. §40, I..wexed my label in Maner of a peyre tables to resceyue distynctly the prikkes of my compas. **1533** Bellenden *Livy* IV. xxiii, Quhat place was left hail in all þare bodyis to ressaue ony new woundis. **1592** Shaks. *Ven. & Ad.* 353 His tendrer cheeke receiues her soft hands print. **1655** Stanley *Hist. Philos.* III. (1701) 88/2 They being eager in prosecution of their design, and he prepared by want, and malice, to receive their impression. **1759** Sterne *Tr. Shandy* II. ii, The wax is over hardened, it will not receive the mark of her thimble. **1785** Cowper *Poplar Field* 4 The winds play no longer and sing in the leaves, Nor Ouse on his bosom their image receives. **1898** Maxwell Gray *House of Hid. Treas.* III. iii, Chip's brain..was more calculated to retain than to receive impressions.

c. To allow (something) to be applied to, or placed on, oneself.

1549 *Compl. Scot.* iv. 31 It is said generelye tyl al them that hes resauit the ȝoilk ande the confessione of crist. **1713** Addison *Cato* II. i, Egypt has since Received his yoke, and the whole Nile is Cæsar's. **1784** Cowper *Task* IV. 329 Earth receives Gladly the thickening mantle. **1788** —— *Negro's Compl.* 42 By our blood in Afric wasted, Ere our necks received the chain. **1820** Shelley *Œd. Tyr.* II. i. 109 To receive upon her chaste white body Dews of Apotheosis. **1898** Maxwell Gray *House of Hid. Treas.* II. iii, Barling Harbour received the crimsoning light on its still levels and held it faithfully.

d. Of recording instruments, radio and television sets, etc.: To be affected, or operated on, by (the thing transmitted).

1862 *Catal. Internat. Exhib.* II. xiii. 12/2 The apparatus..for receiving and indicating the signals. **1884** *Telegraphist* June 88/2 Chemically prepared paper..receives the record of signals sent over the lines. **1957** *Encycl. Brit.* XXI. 912I/2 The television signal is received on a short wave antenna and carried by a transmission line to the receiver.

e. Of a radio or television set: to reproduce the sound or picture transmitted by (a station or a person). Also *transf.*, of the user, and *absol.*

1908 *Rep. Brit. Assoc. Adv. Sci.* 1907 621 In this way it is possible to receive at Hythe from Elmers End. **1930** *Morn. Post* 18 Aug. 3/4 In order to receive foreign stations consistently it is necessary to employ a powerful receiver. **1969** M. Pugit *Last Place Left* xxv. 187 Get what I mean, now? You receiving me, strength four? **1970** J. Earl *Tuners & Amplifiers* iii. 75 If you are proposing to try receiving distant stations..you will need a tuner of the best possible selectivity.

5. a. To take in; to admit as to a receptacle or containing space; to allow to enter or penetrate.

a 1300 *Cursor M.* 1135 [The] erth..þat reseued þi broþer blode, Wit pine it sal þe ȝeild þi fode. **c 1380** Wyclif *Wks.* (1880) 97 Swolwis of þe see and helle, þat resceyuen al þat þei may & ȝelden not aȝen. **c 1400** Maundev. (Roxb.) xiv. 61 Þare es a vessell of marble vnder þe table to ressayue þe oel. **1422** tr. *Secreta Secret., Priv. Priv.* 243 The stomake shal be nuet to resceue more charge than hit was wonyt. **1541** Copland *Guydon's Quest. Chirurg.* Gijb, A concauyte wherin is receyued the ende of the addicyon. **a 1548** Hall *Chron., Hen. VIII* 73b, Doores and enteryinges into the chambers..to receiue light and aire at pleasure. **1588** Shaks. *Tit. A.* v. ii. 184 The Bason that receiues your guilty blood. **1615** W. Lawson *Country Housew. Gard.* (1626) 4 Some for this purpose digge the soyle of their Orchard to receiue moisture. **1667** Milton *P.L.* vi. 55 The Gulf Of Tartarus, which ready opens wide His fiery Chaos to receave thir fall. **1712–4** Pope *Rape Lock* III. 110 From silver spouts the grateful liquors glide, While China's earth receives the smoking tide. **1784** Cowper *Task* I. 562 A kettle, slung Between two poles..Receives the morsel. **1814** Southey *Roderick* xxv. 351 Let One grave with Christian rites receive them both.

transf. **1388** Wyclif *Ecclus.* xxxvi. 21 An vnwise herte resseyueth false wordis. **1533** Bellenden *Livy* v. ii, We differ nocht þe batall bot ressauis It within þe bosum of oure landis. **1780** Cowper *Progr. Err.* 431 Learning itself, received into a mind By nature weak.

b. Of a place or building: To admit (a person); to give accommodation or shelter to.

a 1300 *Cursor M.* 17982 'Helle', he seide, 'make þe redy To receyue iesu hastily'. **1382** Wyclif *Acts* iii. 21 Jhesu Crist, whom sotheli it bihoueth heuene for to resceyue. **c 1400** Maundev. (1839) xxii. 243 Innes ordeyned..to resceyve bothe Man and Hors. **c 1475** *Partenay* 160 Som receit nye the wodes lynde, Wher we mow thys tym receyued to be. **a 1625** Beaum. & Fl. *Knt. of Malta* IV. i, This cave, fashion'd..To be a den for beasts, alone receives me. **1667** Milton *P.L.* I. 252 Hail Infernal world, and thou profoundest Hell Receive thy new Possessor. **1784** Cowper *Task* I. 354 We tread the Wilderness..The Grove receives us next. **1819** Scott *Leg. Montrose* x. motto, More doubtful show'd The mansion which received them from the road. **1898** Maxwell Gray *House of Hid. Treas.* Prol. ii, It was a long time since the Old House had received a child-guest.

c. To afford proper room or space to; to hold or contain conveniently.

c 1440 *Generydes* 1972 All ther hoole puysaunce, Whiche was so grete..The Cite myght resseyue them day ne night. **1549** T. Some *Ded. to Latimer's Serm. bef. Edw. VI* (Arb.) 19 As it is vnpossyble that a litel ryuer should receiue ye recourse of ye mayne sea with in his brymmes. **1585** T. Washington tr. *Nicholay's Voy.* IV. xxiii. 139 A port..able to receiue a 100. Gallies. **1611** Bible *1 Kings* viii. 64 The brasen Altar..was too little to receiue the burnt offerings. **1697** Dryden *Æneid* Ded. in *Ess.* (1900) II. 228 The scantiness of our heroic verse is not capable of receiving more than one. **1856** 'Stonehenge' *Brit. Rur. Sports* 474/1 The well [of a rowing-boat]..is long enough to receive two men instead of one.

6. a. To take in by the mouth; to swallow. (In later examples prob. a contextual use of other senses.) ? *Obs.*

c 1400 tr. *Secreta Secret., Gov. Lordsh.* 77 A mouth-full of hoot water, ilk morwe twyes ressayued. **1484** Caxton *Fables of Poge* x, He gaf to hym the sayd pylles & badde hym to receyue and take them. **1574** Hellowes *Gueuara's Fam. Ep.* (1577) 242 The patient that doth determine to receiue a litle Rheubarb. **1599** B. Jonson *Every Man out of Hum.* III. i. (Rtldg.) 46/2 The Cuban..whiff, which he shall receive or take in here at London, and evaporate at Uxbridge. **1608** Shaks. *Per.* I. ii. 69 Thou..minister'st a potion unto me That thou wouldst tremble to receive thyself. **1742** Pope *Dunc.* IV. 383 Down his own throat he risk'd the Grecian gold, Receiv'd each Demi-God,..Deep in his Entrails. **1840** Browning *Sordello* v. 447 If lies are true, The Caliph's wheel-work man of brass receives A meal.

b. To participate in, take (the sacrament or sacred elements). See also 23.

1303 R. Brunne *Handl. Synne* 10199 Þe folk þat to þe preste went For to receyue þe sacrament. **c 1375** *XI Pains of Hell* 188 in *O.E. Misc.* 216 Þese beleuid not..in cristis carnacione..And neuer resayuyd cristis body. **c 1420** *Chron. Vilod.* st. 468 Þe mayden kneled at þe auters ȝende..& abode þere to resaue hurre saueour. **1500–20** Dunbar *Poems* xxxiv. 8 Ane preist sweirit be God verey Quhilk at the alter ressauit he. **1594** Shaks. *Rich. III*, I. iv. 208 Thou did'st receiue the Sacrament, to fight In quarrell of the House of Lancaster. **1686** [H. More] *Brief Disc. Real Presence* 52 We really though spiritually..eat or receive the real Body and Blood of Christ. **1791** Burke in *Hansard Parl. Hist.* (1814) XXIX. 397 The priest, from whom they had received the sacrament, had not submitted to the test. **1874** Green *Short Hist.* viii. §4 (1895) 510 The habit of receiving the communion in a sitting posture.

7. To take into the mind; to apprehend mentally; to understand; to learn.

1603 Shaks. *Meas. for M.* II. iv. 82 But marke me, To be receiued plaine, Ile speake more grosse. **1660** Stanley *Hist. Philos.* III. I. 37 He made him presently fit to receave his doctrine. **1667** Milton *P.L.* vii. 179 The Acts of God..to human ears Cannot without process of speech be told, So told as earthly notion can receave. **1733** Pope *Ess. Man.* III. 175 Thy arts of building from the bee receive. **1892** Westcott *Gospel of Life* 191 Man is fitted by his essential constitution to receive a knowledge of God.

II. 8. a. To admit (a person) into some relation with oneself, esp. to familiar or social intercourse; to treat in a familiar or friendly manner.

a 1300 *Cursor M.* 4939, I receiud þam, and warnd ham noght Of alle thing þai me be-soght. **1320–30** *Horn Ch.* in Ritson *Metr. Rom.* III. 291 Houlac king was wel hende, Ressaived hem nighen. **c 1384** Chaucer *H. Fame* I. 339 Anon as we han yeu receyued Certenly we ben deceyuyd. **1484** Caxton *Fables of Poge* viii, Two wymmen..came to a curteyzan,..whome he receyued [etc.]. **1568** Grafton *Chron.* II. 303 The other prisoners..went to see the king at their pleasure, and were receyued onely vpon their faythes. **1611** Bible *2 Cor.* xi. 16 Let no man thinke mee a foole; if otherwise, yet as a foole receiue me. **1703** Steele *Tend. Husb.* I. i, He is a Gentleman so Receiv'd, so Courted, and so Trusted. **1784** Cowper *Task* III. 81 A waif, Desirous to return, and not received. **1885** Mabel Collins *Prettiest Woman* ii, 'She shall be received at my house' said Prince Sucha.

b. In religious use, with reference to the acceptation of man by God, or of Christ by man.

1303 R. Brunne *Handl. Synne* 236 Þouȝe he to-day fro hys god weyue, To-morwe hys god wyl hym receyue. **1382** Wyclif *John* i. 11 He cam in to his owne thingis, and hise receyueden not him. *Ibid.* xiii. 20 He that receyueth me, receyueth him that sente me. **1535** Coverdale *Ps.* xlviii. [xlix.] 15 God shal deliuer my soule from the power of hell, when he receaueth me. **1567** *Gude & Godlie B.* (S.T.S.) 87 Aduert till Goddis word and Discipline, Ressaif his Sone. **1852** Tennyson *Wellington* 281 God accept him, Christ receive him.

†**c.** *Astrol.* (Cf. reception 2 a.) *Obs.*

c 1386 Chaucer *Man of Law's T.* 209 O fieble Moone,..Thou knyttest thee ther thou art nat receyued. **c 1391** —— *Astrol.* II. §4 The lord of the assendent..where-as he is in his dignite & conforted with frendly aspectys of planetes & [wel] resceued.

9. a. To meet (a person) with signs of welcome or salutation; to pay attention or respect to (one who comes to a place); to greet or acknowledge upon arrival or entrance. (See also 10.)

a 1300 *Cursor M.* 15059 Þe receiues þin aun folk and welcums þe hame. **c 1430** Lydg. *Min. Poems* (Percy Soc.) 3 Alle of assent..Ther noble Kyng were glad to resseyve. **1480** Caxton *Chron. Eng.* ccxliii. 287 The dukes sone of Barre with a fayre meyny resseyued this worthy lady. **1585** T. Washington tr. *Nicholay's Voy.* I. vi. 4b, Ther came with him.. captaines and Ianissaries to receiue the Ambassadour. **1647** Clarendon *Hist. Reb.* IV. §78 The city of London made great preparations to receive the King. **1850** Tennyson *In Mem.* lxxxv, The great Intelligences fair That range above our mortal state..Received and gave him welcome there. **1883** Howells in *Harper's Mag.* Dec. 81/1 You stay here and receive him, Nettie.

b. To admit *to* one's presence. *rare.*

1687 A. Lovell tr. *Thevenot's Trav.* I. 85 The Grand Signior..is willing first to see what he hath brought, before he receive him to Audience.

10. a. To meet, welcome or greet (a person) in a specified manner.

c 1330 *Arth. & Merl.* 3376 (Kölbing) Al, þat euer wald þider gon, Curteyseliche were ressaiued anon. **1375** Barbour *Bruce* II. 163 He resawyt him in gret daynte. *Ibid.* III. 661 The king rycht weill resawyt he. **c 1400** *Destr. Troy* 8311 Ho receyuit hym with Reuerence. **1480** Caxton *Chron. Eng.* ccxliii (1482) 287 Our kynge with al his lordes goodly and worshipfully hym resceyued and welcomed hym. **1516** Wriothesley *Chron.* (1875) I. 10 The Queene of Scottes..was richly receaved, and rode thorowe London. **1560** Daus tr. *Sleidane's Comm.* 18 He was royally received of kynge Henry the eight. **1656** Earl Monm. tr. *Boccalini's Pol. Touchstone* (1674) 268 This Duke visited..Prospero Colonna, of whom he was received with all sorts of Honour. **1702** Addison *Dial. Medals* Wks. 1721 I. 484 Well received among the Prætorian guards, and afterwards declared their Emperor. **1849** Macaulay *Hist. Eng.* vi. II. 101 The lord mayor came to quell the tumult, but was received with cries of 'No wooden gods'. *Ibid.* xv. II. 598 Mulgrave was received not ungraciously at Saint James's. **1853** J. H. Newman *Hist. Sk.* (1873) II. I. i. 30 Attila..had received the Roman ambassadors, as a barbarian indeed, but as a king.

b. *Mil.* To meet with resistance (an enemy, his attack, etc.).

1375 Barbour *Bruce* XIII. 16 Thair fais resauit thame weill, I hycht, With swerdis, speris, and with macys. **c 1477** Caxton *Jason* 15b, [They] broched their horses with their spores and receyuid them..with the might of their speris. **1650** Cromwell *Let.* 4 Sept. in *Carlyle*, The Enemy being in a very good posture to receive them. **1749** Fielding *Tom Jones* v. xi, Our friend received the enemy's attack with intrepidity. **1892** *Chamb. Jrnl.* 24 Sept. 610/2 There was no time to get into square formation to 'receive' the charging horsemen.

11. a. To admit (a person) to a place; *esp.* to give accommodation or shelter to; to harbour.

1390 Gower *Conf.* III. 318 To his In, Wher he whilom sojourned in, He goth him straght and was resceived. **c 1400** Maundev. (1839) vi. 66 Men resceyved there alle manere of Fugityfes of other places, for here evyl Dedis. **1533** Bellenden *Livy* IV. xxiii, It was betrasit be ane servand, quhilk ressauit þame at ane secrete place. **1565** Cooper *Thesaurus* s.v. *Occultator*, A place meete to receyue and hide theeues in. **1597** Shaks. *2 Hen. IV*, II. iv. 101 Take heede what Guests You receiue: Receiue (says he) no swaggering Companions. **1640–1** *Kirkcudbr. War-Comm. Min. Bk.* (1855) 53 Nae hostler, heritor or yeoman..shall ressaive any such masterless or idle man. **1704** Addison *Italy* 8 It..drove out the Spanish Garrison and receiv'd a French one. **1846** *Penny Cycl.* Supp. II. 165/2 A married woman also shall not be liable to conviction for receiving her husband. **1859** Tennyson *Guinevere* 140 O peaceful Sisterhood, Receive, and yield me sanctuary.

b. Const. *into* or *within* (a house, city, one's arms, etc.).

c 1380 Wyclif *Serm.* Sel. Wks. I. 22 Oþir tenauntis of þe lord shall resceyve me into þere housis. **c 1400** Maundev. (1839) vi. 67 Of tho same resceyved Abraham the Aungeles in to his Hous. **1526** Tindale *John* vi. 21 Then wolde they have receaved hym into the shippe. **1560** Daus tr. *Sleidane's Comm.* 354 The Senate refused to make surrender or to receive a power into the citie. **1617** Moryson *Itin.* I. 20 Another gate..by which passengers are receiued into the City by night. **1713** Addison *Cato* I. ii. To-morrow should we thus express our friendship, Each might receive a slave into his arms. **1805** Scott *Last Minstr.* IV. xxiv, Either receive within thy towers Two hundred of my master's powers, Or [etc.]. **1874** Green *Short Hist.* ix. §4 (1895) 650 Titus Oates..had been received into Jesuit houses at Valladolid and St. Omer.

c. With other than personal object.

1545 *Reg. Privy Council Scot.* I. 10 The said pryse of Portingal takin be the saidis Franchemen may be ressavit in this realm. **1551** Robinson tr. *More's Utop.* II. (1895) 116 A large and wyde sea, which..receaueth in shyppes towardes euery parte of the lande. **1896** W. H. Hutton *Philip Augustus* v. 116 The bishop of Limoges did homage..and his see was received into the king's direct domain.

12. a. To admit (a person or thing) *to, into* (†*in*) a state, condition, privilege, occupation, etc.

c 1366 Chaucer *A.B.C.* 35 Ful ofte..Hast þou to misericorde resceyued me. **1375** Barbour *Bruce* IX. 523 The chiftanis in hy can ta Thair way to Bothwell, for till be Resauit in-to gude savite. *Ibid.* x. 127 He resauit him till his pes. **1382** Wyclif *Mark* v. 37 He resceyuede not ony man to sue him, no but Petre, and James [etc.]. **c 1400** *Rule St. Benet* 141 This is þe furme how A Nouice sall be made & resaiuid to religiun. **1535** Coverdale *Ps.* lxxii[i]. 24 Thou ledest me with thy councel, and afterwarde receauest me vnto glory. **1596** Dalrymple tr. *Leslie's Hist. Scot.* VI. 314 The king forgyues him, and receaues him in his fauour. **a 1648** Ld. Herbert *Hen. VIII* (1683) 436 We..do crave to be received and adopted into the same Laws and Privileges which your other Subjects enjoy. **1662** Stillingfl. *Orig. Sacr.* Ded., The greatest ambition of the Author of it, is, to have it received into your Patronage and Protection. **1784** Johnson in *Boswell*, Receive me, at my death, to everlasting happiness. **1864** Miss Braddon *Henry Dunbar* II. 211 A lady whom she used to receive to music lessons.

b. To admit to membership of a society or class or to partnership in work; to take in *among* other persons or things. Also const. *into*.

1389 in *Eng. Gilds* (1870) 6 Whan a brother or a suster schal be receyued, þat þey schul be swore vpon a book to þe brotherhede. **c 1400** *Rule St. Benet* 110/2201 Fro time þai resauyd be, All salbe sarued in o degre. **1533** Bellenden *Livy* IV. ii, Haue we nocht ressauit sindri of the house of Claudius..amang þe nowmer of patricianis? **1549** Latimer *5th Serm. bef. Edw. VI* (Arb.) 136 They that wyl not for the offyce sake receyue other, regarde more the flese than the flocke. **1724** Waterland *Athan. Creed* vi. Wks. 1823 IV. 230 One may..infer, that this Creed was not received into the Roman Offices so early as the year 809. **1843** *Baptist Reporter* Jan. 48 Forty-five persons have been received by immersion into the church. **1894** Forsyth *Forms of Service Ch. Scot.* 42 Your brethren in office will receive you into the Kirk-Session by giving you the right hand of fellowship.

13. a. To take or accept (a person) in some capacity. Const. *as, for,* †*to,* †*to be,* or with simple predicate. Also in phr. ***to receive in marriage*** = ***to take in marriage*** s.v. take *v.* 14 b.

a 1400–50 *Alexander* 3478 Alexander..Resayued to his riche quene Rosan his doȝtir. **c 1400** *Rule St. Benet* 133 Al strangers or ghestes arn to be receyued..as god. **1513** Douglas *Æneis* XIII. vii. 79, I the ressaue..As son in law and successour to me. **1533** Bellenden *Livy* IV. ii, Oure progenitouris contempnit nocht strangearis, bot ressauit þame to be kingis. **1582** N. Lichefield tr. *Castanheda's Conq. E. Ind.* I. vii. 16b, One of the Moores, which was receiued for Pilot. **1644** *Shetland Witch Trial* in Hibbert *Shetland Isl.* (1822) 602 The Assyze being recavit, sworn and admittit. **1654** tr. *Scudery's Curia Pol.* 79 He was chearfully received Generall to that victorious Army. **1671** Milton *Samson* 883 Why then Didst thou at first receive me for thy husband? **1835** O. Pratt in *Utah Gen. & Hist. Mag.* (1938) XXIX. 34, I baptized Sarah Marinda Bates, near

Sacketts Harbor, whom I received in marriage upwards of one year after.

b. To admit (a person) to plead or give evidence.

1607 Cowell *Interpr.* s.v. *Resceyt*, He in the reuersion commeth in, and prayeth to be receiued to defend the land, and to plead with the Demandant. **1647** Clarendon *Hist. Reb.* iv. §130 The law was clear that less than two witnesses ought not [to] be received in case of treason.

14. a. To take, accept, regard, hear, etc. (anything offered or presented, or to which attention is given) in a specified manner or with a specified expression of feeling.

1390 Gower *Conf.* III. 163 Thessamplerie Of Arisippe is wel received And thilke of Diogene is weyved. **1422** tr. *Secreta Secret., Priv. Priv.* 172 He toke not to hevynesse the damagis that hym befell, but..ham rescewyth lyghtly. **1560** Daus tr. *Sleidane's Comm.* 16 His bokes are joyfullye received and red of good and well learned men. **1602** Shaks. *Ham.* ii. ii. 129 But how hath she receiu'd his Loue? **1605** —— *Lear* ii. ii. 155 My Sister may recieue it much more worss. **1647** Clarendon *Hist. Reb.* iv. §166 This, though a known truth to any one who knew anything of the law, was received with noise and clamour. **1667** Milton *P.L.* xii. 503 Thus they win Great numbers of each Nation to receave With joy the tidings brought from Heav'n. **1874** Green *Short Hist.* ii. §8. 105 The brutal murder was received with a thrill of horror throughout Christendom.

b. To take *for*, regard *as*, etc. (Cf. 13.)

1377 Langl. *P. Pl.* B. xv. 502 Now is routhe to rede how ..þe Rode [is] receyued for þe worthier þan crystes crosse. **1500–20** Dunbar *Poems* xlvi. 76 Man may tak in his lady sic delyt,..[as] for his hevin rassaif hir cullour quhyt. **1596** Dalrymple tr. *Leslie's Hist. Scot.* ix. 259 This he for a takne ressaiuet and sygne, that the end of his lyfe was at hande. **1613** Shaks. *Hen. VIII*, ii. i. 125 This from a dying man receiue as certaine. **1671** Milton *Samson* 473 These words I as a Prophecy receive. *a* **1817** Jane Austen *Persuasion* (1818) III. iv. 58 He thought it a very degrading alliance; and Lady Russell..received it as a most unfortunate one.

15. a. To accept as an authority, rule, or practice; to admit the truth or validity of; to make use of.

1382 Wyclif *Prol. Bible* i. 2 Holy chirche resceyueth not siche bookis. —— *Acts* xvi. 21 These men..schewen a custom, the which it is not leueful to vs for to receyue. **1482** Caxton *Trevisa's Higden* v. xiv. 250 b, But he plesyd her and other that had resseyued his lawe in this maner [etc.]. **1513** Douglas *Æneis* v. x. 99 And mychty Rome syne eftir mony ane day Sik ois rasavit has. **1589** Puttenham *Eng. Poesie* iii. xxii. (Arb.) 260 This word *egar* is as much to say as to wander or stray out of the way, which in our English is not receiued. **1626** Bacon *Sylva* §104 This Computation of Eight, is a thing rather receiued, than any true Computation. **1652** Needham tr. *Selden's Mare Cl.* 21 This appear's plain in the Imperial Law; nor do wee know of any Nation where it is not received. **1709** Berkeley *Th. Vision* §131 An axiom universally received. **1790** Paley *Horæ Paul.* Wks. 1825 III. 263 These books were not only received from the beginning, but received with the greatest respect. **1884** D. Hunter tr. *Reuss' Hist. Canon* xvii. 349 The duty of approving and receiving Scripture.

b. To give credit to; to believe. Also *absol.*

1382 Wyclif *Matt.* xi. 14 Ʒif ʒe wolen resseyuen, he is Ely that is to cume. **1601** Shaks. *Twel. N.* iii. iv. 212, I will.. driue the Gentleman (as I know his youth will aptly receive it) into a most hideous opinion [etc.]. **1605** —— *Macb.* i. vii. 74, 77 *Macb.* Will it not be receiu'd,..That they haue don't? *Lady.* Who dares receiue it other? **1784** Cowper *Task* v. 855 They..speak in ears That hear not or receive not their report. **1868** Browning *Ring & Bk.* vi. 2055 This stupid lie, Its liar never dared propound in Rome, He gets Arezzo to receive.

†**c.** To give assent to, to pass (a law). *Obs.*

1538 Starkey *England* i. i. 15 Lawys..receyuyd and stablyschyd for the mayntenaunce..of vertue. **1647** Clarendon *Hist. Reb.* iv. §138 The greatest invitation to the House of Commons so irregularly to receive that bill to remove the bishops.

III. 16. a. To have (a thing) given or handed to oneself; to get from another or others. Also *receiving* = being received.

a **1300** *Cursor M.* 16470 Wit his penis forth he lepe he had resaueid are. *c* **1330** R. Brunne *Chron.* (1810) 24 He resceyued þe coroune, after his broþer dede. *c* **1375** *Sc. Leg. Saints* xxiv. (*Alexis*) 128 Scho suld..þare-of rasawe gret med In hewine. **1484** Caxton *Fables of Poge* viii, The sellar ..delyuerd the hors and receyued the xv. ducattes. **1556** *Aurelio & Isab.* (1608) C vi, Sins that I haue of yowre hignesse..so muche goode resavede. **1583** *Leg. Bp. St. Androis* 383 Ane William Symsone,..Whome fra scho hes resavit a buike. **1584** Hudson *Du Bartas' Judith* v. (1608) 74 in *Sylvester's Du Bartas*, Come all to Court, and there ye shall resaue A thousand gaines. **1667** Milton *P.L.* v. 423 The Sun that light imparts to all, receives From all his alimental recompence In humid exhalations. **1689** *Answ. Lords & Commons Sp.* 34 The very Money that is now receiving, was asked with Two Armies on Foot. **1788** Gibbon *Decl. & F.* xlix. V. 133 The conquerors of the West would receive their crown from the successors of St. Peter. **1818** Cruise *Digest* (ed. 2) III. 369 His mother..residing in one of them..and receiving rent for the others. **1891** Rosebery *Pitt* ix. 149 The essential point..is to receive in return the services for which the payment is made.

b. To get (a letter, etc.) brought to oneself or delivered into one's hands.

c **1400** tr. *Secreta Secret., Gov. Lordsh.* 48 Þis Epistel ressayued, Alexander did after his consaill. **1478** W. Paston in *P. Lett.* III. 237, I have resevyd of Alwedyr a lettyr. **1530** Palsgr. 680/2, I receyved but one letter from my father sythe he went in to the countraye. **1594** Shaks. *Rich. III*, v. ii. 5 Heere receiue we from our Father Stanley Lines of faire comfort. **1647** Clarendon *Hist. Reb.* ii. §44 Arundel and Holland gave another kind of reception to the letters they received. **1798** Jefferson *Writ.* (1859) IV. 208 A letter is certainly received here by an individual from Talleyrand. **1888** Mrs. H. Ward *R. Elsmere* xxxvii, Elsmere received a characteristic letter from him.

c. To get by communication from another; to learn, ascertain, etc., in this way.

1526 Tindale *1 Cor.* xi. 23 That which I gave vnto you I receaved off the lorde. **1596** Shaks. *Merch. V.* i. i. 164 Sometimes from her eyes I did receiue faire speechlesse messages. **1608** —— *Per.* i. i. 1 Young prince of Tyre, you have at large received The danger of the task you undertake. **1647** Clarendon *Hist. Reb.* ii. §10 To enjoin that no presbyter should reveal any thing he should receive in confession. **1674** Ray *Collect. Words, Allom Work at Whitby* 139 The process of making Allom, as we partly saw, and partly received from the workmen. **1748** *Anson's Voy.* ii. iv. 169 On Mr. Anson's receiving any other intelligence. **1893** *Weekly Notes* 68/2 The date at which he received notice of the receiving order.

17. a. To get (a person) into one's custody, control, vicinity, society, etc. Now *rare* or *Obs.*

a **1300** *Cursor M.* 22077 Þe deuil sal..vmbelai hir al bidene, Al in his weild hir to receiue. **1382** Wyclif *Luke* xv. 27 Thi brodir is comen, and thi fadir hath slayn a fat calf, for he receyuede him saf. **1500–20** Dunbar *Poems* xxxiv. 23 The Feind ressaif me gif I le. **1513** Douglas *Æneis* i. v. 81 Romulus sall the peple ressaue and weild. **1596** Dalrymple tr. *Leslie's Hist. Scot.* iv. 219 Conran receaueng in mariage Ada, the sister of Ambrose. **1611** Bible *Ps.* lxxv. 2 When I shall receiue the congregation, I will iudge vprightly.

b. To get, or come into, possession of (a town, country, etc.). *rare.*

1568 Grafton *Chron.* II. 739 He..besieged a towne.., which when he had receyued,..he caused all the inhabitants cruelly to be put to death. **1596** Dalrymple tr. *Leslie's Hist. Scot.* ii. 139 His countrey and kingdome, quhilke..he receiuet sair oppressit be his nychtbouris.

c. To get or acquire (some feature).

1789 *Ann. Reg.* 132/2 About ten years ago she received a new set of teeth. **1874** Green *Short Hist.* ii. §8. 112 The three distinct courts..which by the time of Edward the First received distinct judges. **1880** T. Hardy *Wessex Tales, Fellow-Townsmen* iv. (1896) 126 A window-niche which had as yet received no frame.

18. a. To have (some quality, attribute, or property) given, bestowed, conferred or impressed.

c **1320** *Cast. Love* 1661 Comyth..And receyvyth the blysfull joy anon. **1382** Wyclif *Acts* ix. 12 He sy3 a man.. puttinge to hym hondis, that he receyue siȝt. *c* **1400** tr. *Secreta Secret., Gov. Lordsh.* 58 Al þe body ressayues strynght. **1422** *Ibid., Priv. Priv.* 243 Al the Erthe rescewyth his anournement and his beute. *c* **1450** *Merlin* 109 Worthier men and wise, that were better worthi to resceyve that dignyte, than a boy. **1552** Abp. Hamilton *Catech.* (1884) 5 Quhilk hes ressavit the office of teching. **1651** Hobbes *Leviath.* ii. xxvi. 138 They promise obedience, that they may receive life. **1666** G. Harvey *Morb. Angl.* xxvi. (1672) 62 The place is, where the acrimonious humours..receive the form of humours. **1708** Swift *Sentiments Ch.-Eng. Man* Wks. 1751 IV. 76 Those who receive orders must have some Vices to leave behind them when they enter into the Church. **1754** Richardson *Grandison* IV. v. 45 If your mind.. should then have received alteration. **1813** *Edin. Rev.* Oct. 174 Such collections of stony fragments..receive the name of Moraines. **1883** *Catholic Dict.* s.v. *Reception*, In many countries..bishops receive power as delegates of the Holy See..to absolve from the censure.

b. In religious use, of the reception of spiritual influences.

a **1300** *Cursor M.* 19544 Þai praid for þam..þai suld receue þe haligast. **1382** Wyclif *Acts* viii. 17 Thanne thei puttiden hondis on hem, and thei receyueden the Hooly Gost. **1597** Hooker *Eccl. Pol.* v. lvii. §6 We receive Christ Jesus in baptism once as the first beginner..of our life.

19. a. To be the object of (some action); to experience or meet with (some treatment).

c **1330** *King of Tars* 850 In to the watur he con gon, And reseyvede the baptise. **1382** Wyclif *Acts* x. 43 For to receyue remyscioun of synnes by his name. **1460–70** *Bk. Quintessence* 3 þe knees..þat resseyuen a synguler influence of þe sterris of Capricorn. **1535** Coverdale *Ps.* xxiii[i]. 5 He shal receaue the blessinge from the Lord, and mercy from God his sauioure. **1596** Dalrymple tr. *Leslie's Hist. Scot.* iv. 216 He had beine vnthankful of al benifite and gude deid ressauet. **1662** J. Davies tr. *Olearius' Voy. Ambass.* 6 The honour he had receiv'd in our Court, during his Exile. **1697** Dryden *Virg. Georg.* iv. 704 A Fault which easie Pardon might receive, Were Lovers Judges. **1781** Cowper *Retirem.* 302 This [malady]..Claims most compassion, and receives the least. **1859** Stopford *Work & Counterwork* 88 The pleasure of receiving unwonted sympathy. **1891** *Law Times* XCI. 2/2 The proposal..deserves more attention than it is likely at present to receive.

b. To suffer, undergo, be subjected to (something hurtful or unpleasant).

1375 Barbour *Bruce* iv. 273 Throu hir feill the ded resauit. **1390** Gower *Conf.* I. 9 For every lond..of desese his part receyveth. *Ibid.* 82 He schal noght faile to receive His peine. *c* **1450** *Merlin* 32 He hadde resceyved deth thourgh me. **1484** Caxton *Fables of Æsop* ii. x, Men ought to presume ouer hym by whome they receyue somme dommage. **1535** Coverdale *Hos.* x. 6 Ephraim shal receaue full punishment. **1570–6** Lambarde *Peramb. Kent* (1826) 125 King Canutus.., after that he had received the woorse in a fight in Lincolne shyre. **1604** E. G[rimstone] *D'Acosta's Hist. Indies.* iii. xxvi. 200 The Townes and Provinces..receive sometimes great losses by these Earthquakes. **1656** Earl Monm. tr. *Boccalini's Advts. fr. Parnass.* i. lxxxvii. (1674) 117 The ruines, plunderings.., and other utter desolations which she had received from the Goths. **1745** *Col. Rec. Pennsylv.* V. 4 That the House might not receive any delay. **1796** H. Hunter tr. *St.-Pierre's Stud. Nat.* (1799) II. 293, I have received..calumny only as the reward of all my services. **1840** Dickens *Old C. Shop* xxxii, Mrs. Jarley..recounted, word for word, the affronts she had received. **1887** Lecky *Hist. Eng. 18th C.* (1892) VII. xx. 167 France..had undoubtedly received much real provocation.

c. To be exposed to (heat, light, etc.).

c **1400** tr. *Secreta Secret., Gov. Lordsh.* 71 Þe mete of þe myddāy resceyueth þe hete of þe day. **1697** Dryden *Virg. Georg.* ii. 411 Nor plant it to receive the setting Sun.

20. a. To have (a blow, wound, mark, etc.) inflicted or made upon one or *in* some part; to get (a specified injury).

13.. *Gaw. & Gr. Knt.* 2076 Þat schulde teche hym to tourne to þat tene place, þer þe ruful race he schulde resayue. **1382** Wyclif *2 Cor.* xi. 24, I resceyuede of the Jewis fyue sythis fourty strokis oon lesse. **1526** Tindale *Rev.* xiii. 16 He made all..to receave a marke in their right hondes. *a* **1548** Hall *Chron., Hen. IV* 28 b, The earle received such a wound in his head that he departed out of this world. **1597** A. M. tr. *Guillemeau's Fr. Chirurg.* 8 b/1 Hippocrates reciteth to have cured a personage which had receaved a shot with an arrowe. *a* **1671** Ld. Fairfax *Mem.* (1699) 54 Here I received a shot in the wrist of my arm, which made the bridle fall out of my hand. **1687** A. Lovell tr. *Thevenot's Trav.* i. 162 This Kiaya..after a long fight, received a thrust with a Pike in the Belly. **1759** Sterne *Tr. Shandy* I. xxv, The wound in my uncle Toby's groin, which he received at the siege of Namur. **1797** *Encycl. Brit.* (ed. 3) XI. 282/1 Excision will be of use a considerable time after the bite is received. **1860** Tennyson *Sea-Dreams* 157, I stood like one that had received a blow. **1898** *Daily News* 25 Feb. 3/2 One man's thigh was broken, another received a broken jaw.

†**b.** Of a ship: To spring (a leak). *Obs.*

1595 *Drake's Voy.* (Hakl. Soc.) 25 The Hope received a leake and was forced to go from the fleete, to an iland.

c. To come in the way of and suffer from (a missile, gun, etc.).

1715–20 Pope *Iliad* v. 712 His bended arm received the falling stone. **1805** Duncan *British Trident* IV. 227 The boats..(after having beat the launch.., and receiving several guns and small arms from the frigate) boarded. **1844** Dickens *Mart. Chuz.* lii, Mr. Pecksniff started back as if he had received the charge of an electric battery.

21. To have (a law, etc.) imposed or laid on one; to get as a charge.

1382 Wyclif *2 John* 4 As we receyueden maundement of the fadir. **1535** Coverdale *2 Esdras* ix. 36 We y^t haue receaued the lawe, perish in synne, and oure hert also which receaued the lawe. **1585** Jas. I *Ess. Poesie* (Arb.) 17 Two champions braue, With armies huge approching to resaue Thy will. **1593** Shaks. *2 Hen. VI*, ii. iii. 3 Receiue the Sentence of the Law for sinne. **1604** E. G[rimstone] *D'Acosta's Hist. Indies* v. xxv. 398 They received penaunce, yea sometimes very sharpely. **1647** Clarendon *Hist. Reb.* iv. §358 Four lords and eight commoners,..who were always to receive instructions from themselves. **1667** Milton *P.L.* ii. 240 With what eyes could we Stand in his presence humble, and receive Strict Laws impos'd. **1784** Cowper *Task* vi. 200 The infant elements received a law From which they swerve not since. *Ibid.* 335 The total herd [of cattle] receiving..a summons to be gay. **1839** Keightley *Hist. Eng.* II. 25 He reported the case and received directions from the prelate. **1875** Jowett *Plato* (ed. 2) V. 82 No man likes to receive laws when they are first imposed.

IV. Absolute uses.

22. a. To take, accept, or get, in various senses; to be or become a recipient; to take in, admit, etc.

1382 Wyclif *Acts* xx. 35 It is more blessid for to ȝyue, more than for to receyue. **1422** tr. *Secreta Secret., Priv. Priv.* 173 The Prynces in olde tyme..more gladly they yawyn than rescevet. ? *a* **1500** *Wycket* (1828) 1 He that seketh fyndeth, and that axeth receyueth. **1541** R. Copland *Guydon's Quest. Chirurg* D ij b, Some [bones] are enbossed for to entre, and other haue vacuytes that receyueth. **1596** Shaks. *Merch. V.* iii. ii. 141, I come by note to giue, and to receiue. **1667** Milton *P.L.* ix. 109 Thou Centring receav'st from all those Orbs. **1797** *Encycl. Brit.* (ed. 3) III. 391/2 The receipt..must be signed by the person receiving. **1817** Byron *Beppo* xxxiv, His heart was..Wax to receive, and marble to retain. **1869** Skeat *Langland's P. Pl.* B. xvii. 177 *marg.*, The palm..receives from the fingers.

b. Const. *of.*

1382 Wyclif *Mark* xii. 2 [He sent] a seruaunt, that he schulde receyue of the fruyt. —— *Rev.* xviii. 4 Ʒe schulen not receyue of the plagis of it. **1526** Tindale *John* xix. 30 As sone as Iesus had receaved of the venegre. **1535** Coverdale *Deut.* xxxiii. 3 They shall set them selues downe at thy fete, and receaue of thy wordes. **1684** Bunyan *Pilgr.* ii. 4 He.. receiveth of the smiles and favours of him that is Judge of all. **1833** Tennyson *Lotos-Eaters* 30 Whoso did receive of them, And taste.

23. To take the sacrament; to communicate.

1560 Daus tr. *Sleidane's Comm.* 19 b, They receyved under bothe kyndes. **1584** Fenner *Def. Ministers* (1587) 88 The priuate Masse of the Papistes, where the Priestes and his Clearke onely doe receyue. **1653** Baxter *Chr. Concord* 89 Our Objectors will never prove that they Received standing. **1686** Wood *Life* 5 Jan. (O.H.S.) III. 176 Mr Boys and Mr Deane were in the outer Chapel, but did not come in to receive. **1874** G. A. Denison *Let.* 18 Aug. in *50 Yrs. at East Brent* (1902) 157, I do not understand worshipping where I cannot receive if I desire to receive.

24. To hold receptions; to receive visitors.

1854 J. S. C. Abbott *Napoleon* xxviii. (1855) 445 He declared, that she should be crowned with him, and that she should receive at his side. **1877** *World* VII. No. 180. 4 He goes into society, or, what is still more agreeable to him, receives at home. **1902** H. James *Wings of Dove* ix. xxxii. 499 'I'm commissioned to ask you from her to go and see her.'.. He was..bewildered. 'Then she can receive—?'

25. The infin. used, usu. *attrib.*, to designate the receiving mode, controls, etc., of a radio or telecommunication system.

1920 *Wireless World* 7 Aug. 356/1 A send-receive switch. **1966** 'A. Hall' *9th Directive* xiii. 121 Loman was buzzing for me so I switched the radio to 'receive'. 'Do you hear me, Quiller?' **1970** *New Scientist* 24 Dec. 554/3 The Applications Technology Satellite 3..provided two transmit and two receive voice channels.

received (rɪˈsiːvd), *ppl. a.* [f. prec. + -ed[1].]

1. a. Generally adopted, accepted, approved as true or good. Chiefly of opinions, customs, etc.;

received idea = *idée reçue* s.v. IDÉE. Cf. also *received text* s.v. TEXT *sb.*[1] 1 d.

c **1440** *Promp. Parv.* 425/1 Receyvyd, *receptus, acceptus.* **1542** RECORDE *Gr. Artes* 130 b, Procedynge by no grounded reason, but onely by a receaued fourme. **1597** MORLEY *Introd. Mus.* Annot., I am loth to breake a receiued custome. **1608** E. TOPSELL *Serpents* 219 Suidas followeth the common received opinion, that the Salamander quencheth the fire. **1652** NEEDHAM tr. *Selden's Mare Cl.* 69 Very many things.. clearly prove it to have been a most received opinion. **1710** STEELE *Tatler* No. 164 ¶4 That Pride and Vanity which naturally arise in the Mind of a received Author. **1838–9** HALLAM *Hist. Lit.* IV. IV. i. 15 He defended the received chronology. **1867** FREEMAN *Norm. Conq.* (1876) I. App. 613 Divisions.. for which there were no received geographical names. **1959** *Times Lit. Suppl.* 20 Feb. 94/4 The error he has discovered in the received reference books.. deserves special note from all those concerned with the period. *Ibid.* 20 Mar. 159/1 Her neat and tidy balance sheets are summaries of received ideas into which she ventures to inject no new thought. **1960** J. BAYLEY *Characters of Love* ii. 52 The appearance of Courtly Love.. has left an immense legacy of received ideas about sex and society. **1973** *Howard Jrnl.* XIII. 330 In former days, the received view was accepted more readily and unquestioningly. **1973** *Times* 13 Dec. 13/4 It is a received idea that television is the most powerful medium ever devised. The proposition is hardly ever questioned. **1976** E. MACLAREN *Nature of Belief* iv. 39 His formal education may help him to be critical or sceptical about quite a lot of 'received opinion'.

b. Of language or pronunciation: ***received pronunciation***, the pronunciation of that variety of British English widely considered to be least regional, being originally that used by educated speakers in southern England; also, the 'accepted', standard pronunciation of any specified area, Received Standard; ***Received Standard (English)***, the spoken language of a linguistic area (usu. Britain) in its traditionally most correct and acceptable form. Hence in other derived uses.

[**1818** *Trans. Amer. Philos. Soc.* I. 259 According to its most generally received pronunciation, it is more properly a diphthong.] **1869** A. J. ELLIS *On Early Eng. Pronunc.* I. 13 The alphabet required for writing the theoretically received pronunciation of literary English. **1874** —— *Ibid.* IV. 1095/1 The tip of the tongue for received English is not so advanced towards the teeth or gums, as for the continental sound. **1882** —— in *Trans. Philol. Soc.* 21 We say they are dialectal forms of the received *down.* **1889** [see *RP* s.v. *R II. 2 a]. **1890** *Dialect Notes* I. 26 For the study of pronunciation the received spelling is very ill adapted. **1913** H. C. WYLD in *Mod. Lang. Teaching* IX. 261/2 When he speaks of *Standard English*, he is, I believe, referring to what I now call *Received Standard.* **1914** M. MONTGOMERY in *Ibid.* X. 11/2 Yet in that country [*sc.* Germany], as time goes on, a process of assimilation towards a single 'Received Standard' is said to be growing more, rather than less, marked. **1932** D. JONES *Outl. Eng.* xviii. 148 In Received English there are six affricates which may be represented phonetically by.. diagraphs. **1932** *S.P.E. Tract* XXXVII. 542 These authors.. define the 'Received Pronunciation' as that of 'the great public schools, the Universities, and the learned professions'. **1936** *Trans. Philol. Soc.* 80 My own recollection of this opposition to Received Speech is that the dialect speaker acquires a consciousness of 'correctness' in speech accompanied by a powerful objection to being caught.. 'talking fine'. **1937** D. JONES in *Le Maître Phonétique* Apr.–June (Suppl.), I take the view that foreigners learning English should be free to choose whatever pronunciation they prefer. Many naturally choose what has been termed 'received' pronunciation (R.P.), as being a widely understood type of English. **1940** J. H. JAGGER *Eng. in Future* i. 15 The influence of the various forms of Modified Standard—to accept Professor Wyld's terms—upon each other and upon Received Standard. **1962** A. C. GIMSON in R. Quirk *Use of Eng.* 281 *Received Pronunciation*, or RP, suggesting.. the result of a collective social judgment rather than of a conscious, prescriptive agreement. **1964** C. BARBER *Ling. Change Present-Day Eng.* ii. 20 The influence of the mass-media and of mass-education.. does not necessarily produce speakers of Received Standard English. **1969** S. POTTER *Changing Eng.* i. 14 Other cities, notably Edinburgh and Dublin, have their received pronunciations, and so have other regions of the English-speaking world. **1973** G. W. TURNER *Stylistics* v. 147 Even now 'received pronunciation' will help its user to obtain credit when ordering goods by telephone. **1974** J. I. M. STEWART *Gaudy* x. 179 There is no such thing as an Oxford accent, since what phoneticians call Received Standard English came into existence without the university's playing any very identifiable part in the process.

2. a. In other senses of RECEIVE *v.*

1575 PAINTER *Pal. Pleas.* II. xxxv. (1890) III. 429 The memorye of a receyued good turne. **1707** NORRIS *Treat. Humility* viii. 345 Health, beauty, strength, &c. are no reasons why we should be proud, as being received endowments. **1895** *Daily News* 19 Dec. 5 The cost of having their received telegrams telephoned.. to their offices.

b. *Entom.* Admitted between other parts.

1826 KIRBY & SP. *Entomol.* IV. 332 An insect having a visible Scutellum... *a.* Rejected... *b.* Received (Receptum). When it intervenes between the elytra at their base.

Hence **re'ceivedness.**

a **1691** BOYLE (J.), Others will, upon account of the receivedness of the proposed opinion, think it rather worth to be examined, than acquiesced in.

receiver[1] (rɪ'siːvə(r)). Forms: see RECEIVE and -ER[1] (-OR); also 5 **ryssavour.** [Orig. a. AF. *receivere* or *receivour, receyvour* = OF. *recevere* (*-erre, -eire*) and *recevour* (mod.F. *receveur*), agent-n. f. *receivre, recevoir* to RECEIVE. In later use also directly f. the verb + -ER[1].]

1. a. One who receives, in various senses of the vb.

a **1340** HAMPOLE *Psalter* lxxxviii[i]. 26 My fadire ert þou, my God and reseyuere of my hele. *c* **1380** WYCLIF *Sel. Wks.* III. 279 Boþe þe ȝevere and resceyvere of ordris in þis caas schulden be degradid. **1472–5** *Rolls of Parlt.* VI. 157/2 Yevers, takers, and receyvers of Lyveres and Signees. **1526** *Pilgr. Perf.* (W. de W. 1531) 294 b, Therfore this ioye is perfyte, and the receyuer therof is perfytly mortifyed. **1579** FULKE *Ref. Rastel* 727 An other miracle of an vnworthie receiuer, in whose hand the Sacrament was turned into ashes. **1656** COWLEY *Pindar. Odes* I. xi, In this thankless world the Givers Are envi'ed ev'n by the Receivers. **1705** STANHOPE *Paraphr.* II. 312 The Condition of the Receiver is.. a great deal worse than if he had not received it at all. **1809** PINKNEY *Trav. France* 11 Though they cost little to the giver, [they] are not the less valuable to the receiver. **1883** *Law Rep. 9 App. Cases* 80 If the Crown paid income tax it would be at once payer and receiver.

†**b.** *Hunting.* The huntsman who with his dog intercepts and brings down the hunted deer. *Obs. rare*[−1].

c **1400** *Master of Game* (MS. Digby 182) xxxv, And as of feutreres if þei ben sette, þe firste teysoure and þe resceyuour that draweth hym doune shull parte þe skynne.

c. (*a*) *Amer. Football*, an offensive player eligible to catch a pass; also, a defender designated to receive a kick-off or punt, a safety man (cf. *wide receiver* s.v. WIDE *a.*); (*b*) *U.S. Baseball*, a catcher.

1897 *Encycl. Sport* I. 421/2 The direction of a pass must depend upon where the prospective receiver is. **1908** *Baseball Mag.* Aug. 16/1 Flint was a wonderful catcher and the amount of work he could stand would make some of the receivers of today take notice. **1921** *Outing* Jan. 156/3 (*caption*) Crangle of Illinois was.. a sure receiver of the forward pass. **1935** L. LITTLE *How to watch Football* vii. 140 The passer.. would be helpless without the receiver who is able to get into position. **1940** D. HILL *Football through Years* 64/2 The accompanying illustrations.. show what a split second can mean to the receiver of the ball in fast brilliant play. **1957** *Encycl. Brit.* IX. 474/2 Eligible receivers were the players at the end of the line of scrimmage. **1967** *Ebony* June 128/3 Battey has been Howard's chief rival as the American League's premier receiver. **1972** J. MOSEDALE *Football* i. 7 A great receiver like Paul Warfield.. loafs through his pass patterns until the defender relaxes. **1981** *Sports Illustr.* 12 Feb. 28 The Irish set up one touchdown by Walker when their kickoff receivers got their signals crossed.

2. One who receives on behalf of others:

a. An official, officer, or servant appointed to receive money due; a treasurer, collector. Also ***general receiver***: see RECEIVER-GENERAL.

In ordinary use down to *c* 1700; now chiefly *Hist.*, or in reference to foreign countries.

c **1330** R. BRUNNE *Chron.* (1810) 287 A lord of grete honoure, þat was þe tresorere, of Flandres resceyuoure. **1432** *Rolls of Parlt.* IV. 396/2 Be the handes of the Receyvour of Cornewayll for the tyme beyng. *c* **1500** *Melusine* 356 Duryng that long space of tym he asked of his receyuours none acomptes. **1534** *Act 26 Hen. VIII*, c. 3 §10 All fees for stewardes, receiuers, bailliffes, and auditours. **1600** J. PORY tr. *Leo's Africa* IV. 221 Fiue great gates.. at euery one of which there is placed a garde of soldiers, and certaine receiuers of the Kings custome. **1693** LUTTRELL *Brief Rel.* (1857) III. 102 The jury this day gave in a verdict at the court of exchequer in the cause between the kings receiver of Worcestershire and the county of Bucks. **1781** GIBBON *Decl. & F.* xvii. II. 55 Twenty-nine provincial receivers, of whom eighteen were honoured with the title of count, corresponded with the treasurer. **1855** MACAULAY *Hist. Eng.* xv. III. 534 Their receivers were appointed receivers for the Crown, and continued to collect the revenues of the vacant sees. **1874** DASENT *Half a Life* I. 72, I was sorry to see.. that the Receiver's house—for Gell was the Chapter Receiver [at Westminster]—was being pulled down.

fig. **1705** STANHOPE *Paraphr.* II. 304 He hath declared the Poor his Receivers. *a* **1711** KEN *Hymnarium* Poet. Wks. 1721 II. 55 Love my Receiver best can know The mighty Debts I owe. **1869** SPURGEON *Treas. Dav.* Ps. xvi. 3 Poor believers are God's receivers, and have a warrant from the Crown to receive the revenue of our offerings in the King's name.

b. A person appointed by a court to administer the property of a bankrupt, or property which is the subject of litigation, pending the suit. In recent use also ***official receiver.***

1793 F. VESEY Jr. *Chancery Repts.* I. 139 The security given by a receiver here does not relate to the faithful management. **1841** *Penny Cycl.* XIX. 325/1 The cases in which a receiver is appointed are those in which there is great danger of property being wasted or lost. **1886** *Pall Mall G.* 26 Oct. 11/1 The official receiver is the outward and visible sign of the new departure in bankruptcy legislation.

c. (See quots.)

1607 COWELL *Interpr.* s.v. *Receiver*, There is also an officer called the Reiceiuer of Fynes, who receueth the mony of all such as compound with the King.. for the buying of any lands, or tenements houlden in *Capite.* **1863** H. COX *Instit.* I. xi. 260 To distinguish between those petitions which were properly within the cognizance of Parliament and those which were not, certain 'Receivers and Triers' were appointed. **1867** SMYTH *Sailor's Word-bk.* 564 *Receivers of Droits of Admiralty,.. Receivers of Wreck*, persons specially charged with wrecked property for the benefit of the shipping interests. **1977** *N.Z. Herald* 8 Jan. 1–3/10 Meanwhile, the Nelson receiver of wreck, Mr R. K. Watson, said no legal action would be taken against the three men who boarded the boat and claimed salvage rights.

d. An official of the Metropolitan Police Force (see quot. 1966).

1829 *Act 10 Geo. IV.* c. 44 §10 It shall be lawful for His Majesty to appoint a proper Person to receive all Sums of Money applicable to the Purposes of this Act, who shall be called 'The Receiver for the Metropolitan Police District'. **1902** *Encycl. Brit.* XXXI. 818/1 The county council of any county within the Metropolitan Police District has to transfer to the receiver of police a sum bearing.. proportion to the police rate. **1928** *Daily Mail* 7 Aug. 17/2 The Receiver is concerned with equipment and so forth.. of.. the Metropolitan Police. **1966** J. D. DEVLIN *Police Procedure, Administration & Organisation* iii. 20 The police authority of the Metropolitan Police Force is the Home Secretary, and the official responsible for police property, buildings and finance is the Receiver for the Metropolitan Police.., who is appointed by the Crown. *Ibid.*, In provincial forces, the duties and functions of the Receiver fall on the police authority.

3. One who knowingly receives stolen goods or harbours offenders; a resetter.

c **1330** R. BRUNNE *Chron.* (1810) 255 þe robbed he alle held, as a resceyuour. **1532** MORE *Debell. Salem* Wks. 996/1 Murderers & theues and such as are theues receiuours. **1544** BALE *Sir J. Oldcastle* 39 b, Receyuers, defenders.., ayders, and maynteners of condemned heretyques. **1655** tr. *Com. Hist. Francion* II. 33 Perretta.. became their Receiver, and concealed the Goods they stole. **1715** LEONI *Palladio's Archit.* (1742) II. 78 For apprehending Incendiaries, Thieves, or their Receivers. **1828** P. CUNNINGHAM *N.S. Wales* (ed. 3) II. 194 Decided receivers ought indeed to be worked in irons during the whole of their sentence. **1877** A. B. EDWARDS *Up Nile* xxi. 653 An organised band, not only of robbers, but of receivers, who lived by depredations.

4. a. That which receives; a receptacle.

1398 TREVISA *Barth. De P.R.* v. xxxix. (Bodl. MS.), What is fleting and watry.. turneth into flewme and þe resceyuoure þereof is þe lunges. **1541** R. COPLAND *Guydon's Quest. Chirurg.* I iv, The bladder.. is a receyuer of ayguous superfluytees of the kydnees. **1609** C. BUTLER *Fem. Mon.* v. (1623) K iij, Having first parted the new Combs and the old with a long knife, take off the upper Hiue or Receiuer. **1751** HARRIS *Hermes* Wks. (1841) 131 The ship.. being so eminently a receiver and container of various things. **1780** *New Newgate Cal.* V. 126 The screws of the receiver of the bolt [had been] forced out of the wood.

b. A tank or reservoir; a vessel to hold anything.

1538 LELAND *Itin.* III. 88 Much Ground therabout is playne and low, and as a Pan or Receyver of most parte of the Water of Wyleshire. **1677** PLOT *Oxfordsh.* 239 Behind that [are] the Receivers of water to supply the Pipes. **1725** DE FOE *Voy. round World* (1840) 280 Channels of the water, which might easily be formed into proper receivers. **1839** URE *Dict. Arts* 136 After the superfluous alkaline ley had been drained from them, they were arranged on a grating in a receiver. *a* **1864** GESNER *Coal, Petrol.*, etc. (1865) 147 The receivers are vessels in which the crude oil pumped from the retort vat is settled.

c. A mould to receive molten metal.

1846 GREENER *Sci. Gunnery* 112 Any person may case-harden a few pounds weight of stubs, and afterwards melt them in a crucible, and run them into a receiver.

d. (See quot. 1970.)

1938 M. LANGLEY *Refuelling in Flight* 18, I insisted that the tanker (giver) should formate on the liner or bomber (receiver). **1970** *Gloss. Aeronaut. & Astronaut. Terms* (*B.S.I.*) x. 17 *Receiver aircraft*, an aircraft which is being refuelled in the air.

5. As the name of certain parts of apparatus or machinery, intended to receive and contain something.

a. *Chem.* A vessel for receiving and condensing the product of distillation. **b.** The bell glass of an air-pump. **c.** The receptacle for mercury in a barometer. **d.** An airtight vessel for receiving and containing gases. **e.** *Engin.* A chamber to receive steam and water alternately, used in old forms of water-raising steam-engines. **f.** (see quots.).

a. 1576 BAKER *Jewell of Health* IV. 256 The Retort then set into ashes, fixing a large receiuer to it. **1605** TIMME *Quersit.* I. v. 21 Those saltes, being put into a retort,.. with a receiver, stilleth forth a volatile salt. **1662** R. MATHEW *Unl. Alch.* 152 Lay to it a receiver as big as the retort. **1758** REID tr. *Macquer's Chym.* I. 226 Set the retort in a reverberatory furnace: fit thereto a large glass receiver. **1800** tr. *Lagrange's Chem.* I. 299 When the heat is very strong, it assumes the form of an oil, which falls into the water of the receiver. **1899** CAGNEY tr. *Jaksch's Clin. Diagn.* vii. (ed. 4) 393 The dark brown oily fluid in the receiver is freed from æther by evaporation.

b. 1660 BOYLE *New Exp. Phys. Mech.* Proem 6 The Receiver, or Glass to be empty'd, consisting of one entire and uninterrupted Globe and Neck of Glass. *Ibid.* 9 Which we, with the Glass-men, shall often call a Receiver, for its affinity to the large Vessels of that name, used by Chymists. **1705** W. DERHAM in *Lett. Lit. Men* (Camden) 317, I tryed it divers hours and divers times in the Receiver, unexhausted and exhausted. **1816** J. SMITH *Panorama Sc. & Art* II. 6 When the operation of pumping the air out of the receiver must cease.

attrib. **1797** *Encycl. Brit.* (ed. 3) XV. 110/1 The hole in the receiver-plate [being] shut up, the pump was made to exhaust as far as it could.

fig. **1878** T. SINCLAIR *The Mount* 296 The 'religion of humanity' is an exhausted receiver.

c. 1682 LOCKE in Boyle *Hist. Air* (1692) 128 That new fitting my Barometer, here the Mercury was raised by Addition of more in the receiver.

d. 1817 *Conversat. on Chem.* I. vi. 193 We shall introduce a small lighted taper under this glass receiver. **1871** B. STEWART *Heat* §134 This generator is connected with an equally strong iron vessel called the receiver.

e. 1702 SAVERY *Miner's Friend*, Fill the Vessels called Receivers with Steam strong enough. **1797** *Encycl. Brit.* (ed. 3) XVII. 745/2 The entry of the steam into the receiver merely allowed the water to run out of it by a large valve. **1824** R. STUART *Hist. Steam Engine* 43 The pipe.. is sixteen feet long, from the surface of the water to the stage on which the receiver.. is placed.

f. 1882 SENNETT *Marine Steam Engine* IV. xix. 328 By the term receiver is to be understood the whole of the space between the high-pressure piston and the back of the low-pressure slide-valve or valves. **1887** *Encycl. Brit.* XXII. 494. **1900** J. ROSE *Key to Engines* 200 A Receiver.. acts as a reservoir of steam for the low pressure or intermediate cylinder, as the case may be.

6. a. *Med.* A piece of flannel in which a newly-born infant is placed.

1688 *Lond. Gaz.* 22 Oct. 3 This Deponent opened the Receivor, and saw it was a Son. **1797** *Encycl. Brit.* (ed. 3) XI. 781/1 The infant must be wrapped in a warm receiver. **1896** *Allbutt's Syst. Med.* I. 451 Linen thread, ligatures, flannel receiver, antiseptic lubricant.

b. *Surg.* A surgical basin.

1767 GOOCH *Treat. Wounds* I. 450 Towels and receivers for the Viscera, when they are to be taken out of their cavities. **1896** *Allbutt's Syst. Med.* I. 425 In washing or syringing a wound a receiver must always be placed to collect the water or lotion that has touched the sore.

7. a. A device or instrument which receives an electric current or a telegraphic message.

1873 J. C. MAXWELL *Electr. & Magn.* §213 During this cycle the positive receiver has lost a charge *a V* and gained a charge *B'V'*. **1876** PREECE & SIVEWRIGHT *Telegraphy* 119 The Receiver is a Morse direct inkwriter, of a novel and sensitive character. **1894** *Times* 30 Apr. 3/4 The recording instrument known as Kelvin's syphon receiver.

b. An apparatus which receives and reproduces sounds transmitted from another part of an electric circuit; that part of a telephone which is applied to the ear. Also occas. applied loosely to the complete telephone receiving-unit.

1877 *Nature* XVI. 403/2 The apparatus at each end.. becomes alternately transmitter and receiver, first being put to the mouth to receive sounds, and then to the ear to impart them. **1889** PREECE & MAIER *Telephone* vi. 49 These intense vibrations produce powerful induced currents, which give rise in the receiver to corresponding vibrations, and thus create a considerable noise. **1897** *Sears, Roebuck Catal.* 472/2 (Advt.), The improved long distance battery telephone of the regular Bell telephone style with.. compound pole receiver. **1918** S. LEACOCK *Frenzied Fiction* iv. 52 'Great-grandfather,' I said, as I hung up the receiver in disgust, 'you are a Mutt!' **1936** DYLAN THOMAS in *New Verse* Dec. 17 The parting of hat from hair, Pursed lips from the receiver. **1971** *Daily Tel.* 11 June 32/6 The amount of telephoning which has to be done does not justify two receivers at the charity's office. **1980** A. N. WILSON *Healing Art* xvi. 195 He had a telephone receiver to his ear.

c. An apparatus for receiving radio or other signals transmitted as electromagnetic waves; now *spec.* a combined tuner and amplifier (without a loud-speaker).

1891 *Rep. Brit. Assoc. Adv. Sci. 1890* 757 To calculate the force between two neighbouring Hertzian receivers. **1912** *Chambers's Jrnl.* Jan. 60/2, I had got our receiver into 'tune' with the transmitter on board a steamer some miles away. **1927** *Radio Assoc. Official Handbk.* 50 The ultimate Television receiver will be a simple piece of apparatus. **1930** *Morning Post* 18 Aug. 3/4 With any good receiver.. several foreign stations may be regularly well received. **1933** [see LOOKER *sb.* 1 d]. **1955** *Radio Times* 22 Apr. 3/2 The F.M. receiver is designed to take advantage of the full frequency range transmitted. **1966** *McGraw-Hill Encycl. Sci. & Technol.* XI. 200/1 In most pulse-radar systems a single antenna serves for both transmission and reception... The duplexer protects the sensitive receiver by disconnecting it from the antenna during the presence of the powerful transmitter pulse. **1973** *Daily Tel.* (Colour Suppl.) 12 Oct. 31/4 Other products not listed include radio tuners and tuner/amplifiers (known now as 'receivers'). **1976** A. WHITE *Long Silence* 31 By the time Dick was thirteen, he'd built his own radio receiver and transmitter. **1978** *Gramophone* May 1958/1 Trio (B. H. Morris) plan to demonstrate several new amplifiers, tuners, receivers and turntables.

d. A detector of sound or other compressional waves.

1920 *Physical Rev.* XV. 178 A pair of receivers mounted on a horizontal rod which may be rotated.. is an efficient device for getting the direction of a source of sound. **1931** STEWART & LINDSAY *Acoustics* x. 261 The earliest type of acoustic receiver was the so-called Broca tube, consisting.. of a sphere or nipple *C* of rubber or sheet metal attached to the end of a listening tube *T*. **1957** NOLTINGK & TERRY in E. G. Richardson *Technical Aspects of Sound* II. ii. 111 Magnetostrictive and piezoelectric receivers may be designed. **1973** *Nature* 30 Nov. 297/1 This communication describes the results of a reversed seismic refraction line carried out with explosives and seabed receivers in the median valley of the Mid-Atlantic Ridge.

†**re'ceiver²**. *Obs.*⁻¹. [f. RECEIVE *v.*, app. on anal. of words ending in -ER⁴.] A bow made in acknowledgement of something received.

1620 SHELTON *Quix.* IV. xiii. II. 158, I kissed the Cross, and took up the Money.. and we all together made our Receivers.

receiver-general.

1. A chief receiver, esp. of public revenues. (Also † ***general receiver***.)

In Great Britain now only as the title of an official of the Duchy of Lancaster. In some of the United States of America an additional title of the State Treasurer.

1439 *Rolls of Parlt.* V. 7/2 Delivered bi the Receyvours Generall of the saide Duchies. **1460** *Ibid.* 383/1 In and of all our said Duchie [of Lancaster], ther hath been.. oon general Receyvour. **1509–10** *Act 1 Hen. VIII*, c. 3 The Kyng.. entendythe that divers Revenues & Duetys dewe.. to hys Highnes shalbe payde to.. his generall Receyvor. **1540** *Act 32 Hen. VIII*, c. 46 §31 To make payment to the kinges receyvour generall. **1607** in COWELL *Interpr.* **1630** *R. Johnson's Kingd. & Commw.* 167 Treasurer of the Exchequer, instituted in Francis the first his time, in place of the Receiver generall. **1656** *Pub. Gen. Acts* 217 The Receivers-General for this whole Six Moneths Assessment shall.. Receive from the Receivers-General of the respective Counties, Cities, and Places,.. the Sums of Money.. to be Taxed. **1702** *Lond. Gaz.* No. 3825/3 Receiver-General of the Rights and Perquisites of the Admiralty. **1705** *Ibid.* No. 4104/3 The Receiver-General for Prizes. **1709** *Ibid.* No. 4535/3 Late Receiver-General for the County of Suffolk. **1839** ALISON *Hist. Europe* (1849–50) VII. xlii. §16. 99 The receivers-general of the service were invited to deposit the sums they had drawn. **1876** BANCROFT *Hist. U.S.* IV. xiv. 413 Having voted to pay no more money to the royal collector, they chose a receiver-general of their own, and instituted a system of provincial taxation.

fig. **1809** MALKIN *Gil Blas* VII. iii. ⁋3, I mean to make you the receiver-general of all my inmost ruminations.

†**2.** *transf.* **a.** *slang.* A prostitute. *Obs.* **b.** *Pugilists' slang.* (See quot. 1903.) *Obs.*

1811 *Lexicon Balatronicum*, *Receiver General*, a prostitute. **1821** P. EGAN *Boxiana* III. 356 It was evident M'Dermot was doomed to be a Receiver-General; although he had nobbed Purcell over the right eye.. Purcell had the best of it. **1829** *Ibid.* 2nd Ser. II. 180 Dick was now a receiver-general, and his mug was severely bruised. **1903** FARMER & HENLEY *Slang* VI. 5/1 *Receiver-general*.. (pugilists'), a boxer giving nothing for what he gets.

Hence **receiver-generalship**.

1874 *Daily News* 2 June 5/5 A Minister of Finance's patronage comprised receiver-generalships [etc.].

receivership (rɪˈsiːvəʃɪp). [f. RECEIVER¹.]

1. The office of a receiver (in senses 2 a and 2 b). Also in extended use.

1485 *Rolls of Parlt.* VI. 361/1 The Receyvourshipp of the Honour of Leycestre. **1535** *Act 27 Hen. VIII*, c. 26 §39 The office of receiuorship of the said lordshippe of Bealth. **1590** SWINBURNE *Testaments* 233 Accountable of their stewardship, receiuership, and their other offices. **1617** in *Fortescue Papers* (Camden) 42 My Recevorship of the Lycences of wynes. **1791** PITT in *G. Rose's Diaries* (1860) I. 112 A letter applying for the Receivership of Kent. **1850** SMEDLEY *F. Fairlegh* li, Are you in earnest about the receivership? **1885** *Act 48 & 49 Vict.* c. 40 Preamble, It was ordered that.. Beisley should be discharged from the said receivership, and that a fresh receiver should be appointed. **1934** H. G. WELLS *Exper. Autobiogr.* II. ix. 732 Lenin's reconstructed Communist Party was a much more effective step towards an organized receivership.

2. The condition of being in the hands of a receiver.

1884 *Q. Rev.* July 79 [The railway] had gone through the lingering diseases of receivership and reorganisation. **1929** *Times* 30 Oct. 14/2 After the close of the market it became known that the receivership in the Cuba Cane Sugar Company had been made permanent. **1967** R. STEIN *Great Cars* 222/2 Other troubles piled up. In 1921, Lincoln was forced into receivership, and Ford bought the company. **1976** F. ZWEIG *New Acquisitive Society* II. v. 113 The sinking enterprise finally ends up in receivership.

receiving (rɪˈsiːvɪŋ), *vbl. sb.* [-ING¹.]

1. The action of the verb RECEIVE, in various senses. Also *pl.*, what is received.

c **1380** WYCLIF *Wks.* (1880) 377 Criste.. dampned þe ressauyng of þe lordeschip þe whiche siluestre toke of constantyne. *c* **1450** LYDG. & BURGH *Secrees* 1824 Of metys & drynkes [to] knowe dyuersite, With proporcioun and tyme of Receyvyng. **1472–3** *Rolls of Parlt.* VI. 55/1 By Indentures to be made of all such retayndres, receyvyngs and perceyvynges. **1526** *Pilgr. Perf.* (W. de W. 1531) 10 Yf any mortall synne be forgoten, by the receyuynge of this sacrament it is forgyuen. **1568** GRAFTON *Chron.* II. 836 He caused all his brothers daughters to be conueyed into his palace with solempne receauing. **1642** W. MOUNTAGU in *Buccleuch MSS.* (Hist. MSS. Comm.) I. 306 The petition of the Houses concerning the receiving of the Yorkshire petition. **1685** BAXTER *Paraphr. N.T.*, *Matt.* xx. 13 Thou shouldst be glad of thy Brother's receivings. **1931** *Writer's Digest* Oct. 28 (*To*) *fall for receiving*, to be convicted to having stolen property in one's possession... 'He caught me with the rocks, so I fell for receiving.' **1956** E. GRIERSON *Second Man* ii. 37 He was also in trouble again with the police: a little receiving. **1979** *Tucson* (Arizona) *Citizen* 20 Sept. 11D/7 Paul Jones of Cal, who caught 10 passes against Arizona last Saturday, leads in receiving with 13.

2. *attrib.* **a.** Of the nature of, pertaining or relating to, receiving.

1681 FLAVEL *Meth. Grace* vi. 115 This receiving act.. is that upon which both our righteousness and eternal happiness do depend. **1827** FARADAY *Chem. Manip.* xv. 352 Bladders and bags.. are very useful in many receiving or transferring operations. **1883** *Act 46 & 47 Vict.* c. 52 §5 (*Bankruptcy Act*) The Court may.. make an order, in this act called a receiving order, for the protection of the estate. **1930** *Daily Express* 30 July 2/7 Receiving Orders are announced in the 'London Gazette'. **1977** *Private Eye* 1 Apr. 4/1 Harry Alan's financial affairs last attracted attention in 1973 when Air Express Travel obtained a receiving order against him for £700.

b. Of places: Intended or serving for the receipt or reception of things, persons, etc., as ***receiving country***, ***depot***, ***home***, ***-house***, ***-office***, ***pen***, ***-room***, ***-ship***, ***-station***, ***-yard***.

In some cases the sense approaches that of the *ppl. a.*

1938 *Washington Post* 21 Dec. 6/1 Refugees would be allowed to leave Germany for a '*receiving country'. **1958** J. J. SPENGLER in B. Thomas *Economics of Internat. Migration* ii. 17 (*title*) Effects produced in receiving countries by pre-1939 immigration. **1970** *Soviet Weekly* 13 June 11 Our laundry has 32 *receiving depots and washes for 150,000 people. **1967** *U.S. Supreme Court Reports* CCCLXXXVII. 27 The fact of the matter is that, however euphemistic the title, a '*receiving home'.. for juveniles is an institution for confinement. **1973** *Washington Post* 13 Jan. A5/2 Under the plan children in 'predisposition status' and under Receiving Home authority will be transferred into one of five categories. **1824** E. WEETON *Jrnl.* May (1969) II. 280, I wished to see the General Post Office, so.. I took that letter all the way there, instead of putting it into one of the *receiving Houses nearer at hand. **1832** MISS MITFORD *Village* Ser. v. 47 A receiving-house for letters and parcels. **1854** E. E. HALE *Kanzas & Nebraska* ix. 224 A boarding-house or receiving-house, in which three hundred persons may receive temporary accommodation on their arrival. **1900** S. A. NELSON *ABC of Wall St.* 157 *Receiving houses*, houses which make a business of receiving and selling cash grain. **1908** *Daily Chron.* 21 Apr. 1/6 He should.. see that the receiving house clause was given the very fullest effect to. *c* **1865** in R. Whitehouse *London Album* (1980) Pl. 70, Midland Railway, *Receiving Office. **1885** *List of Subscribers, Classified* (United Telephone Co.) 2 The Midland Railway Company will also receive Goods at the following Receiving Offices. **1972** *Classification of Occupations* (Dept. Employment) II. 366/2 *Receiving office assistant*, receives from customers articles requiring service and returns finished articles at a receiving office. **1931** *Receiving pen [see CRUSH *sb.* 4 c]. **1830** LYTTON *P. Clifford* viii, As it was rather late in the day when Paul made his first *entrée* at Bridewell, he passed that night in the '*receiving-room'. **1846** G. DODD *Brit. Manuf.* VI. 184 [The] sail-cloth is taken to a 'receiving-room', where it is examined, freed from lumps and irregularities, measured, and weighed. **1899** *Allbutt's Syst. Med.* VIII. 618 The patient walks into the receiving room of the hospital for a diagnosis. **1978** M. PUZO *Fools Die* v. xxix. 333, I noticed that most of the men threw their car keys on the table in the first receiving room. **1830** MARRYAT *King's Own* xl, A guard-ship is a *receiving-ship for officers and men, until they are enabled to join.. their.. ships. **1846** A. YOUNG *Naut. Dict.*, *Receiving-ship*, a vessel employed at any port to receive supernumeraries, or pressed, or entered men for the Royal Navy. **1901** *Daily Colonist* (Victoria, B.C.) 3 Nov. 2/3 A third class ensign on the receiving ship Columbia lying at the New York Navy Yard. **1978** K. BONFIGLIONI *All Tea in China* IV. xiii. 180 The only other vessels in the anchorage were the receiving ships. **1895** *Daily News* 19 Dec. 5 There is only one branch telegraph *receiving-station besides the Central. **1939** *War Illustr.* 28 Oct. 219/1 From his bed in an R.A.F. medical receiving station hidden away in the woods 'somewhere in France'. **1890** 'R. BOLDREWOOD' *Col. Reformer* (1891) 217 These.. animals he managed.. to impel into the large *receiving yards. **1923** Receiving yard [see FORCING *vbl. sb.* 3 a].

c. Of things: designed for the reception of radio signals or the like, as ***receiving aerial***, ***apparatus***, ***circuit***, ***set*** (also *fig.*), ***station***.

1923 E. W. MARCHANT *Radio Telegr. & Teleph.* iii. 24 The exact arrangement of the receiving aerial may be varied within fairly wide limits. **1962** A. NISBETT *Technique Sound Studio* 267 This highly inefficient transformer action is improved if the receiving aerial is so constructed as to resonate at the desired frequencies of reception. **1908** Receiving apparatus [see PICK *v.*¹ 21 i]. **1925** *Times* 28 May 20/4 Such a standard must obviously be based upon a consideration of two factors—namely, the limitations of the present transmitting and receiving apparatus; and, secondly, the æsthetic element. **1923** E. W. MARCHANT *Radio Telegr. & Teleph* iv. 38 When the coherer was first used in connection with receiving circuits, it was connected between the aerial and the ground. **1955** *Radio Times* 22 Apr. 3/2 A special type of receiving circuit is necessary for F.M. **1916** *Lit. Digest* (N.Y.) 1 Jan. 13/2 His outfit comprised only a cheap home made receiving set! But it did the work, just the same. **1937** *Discovery* Nov. 334/2 His [*sc.* the shrew's] bewhiskered snout is a receiving-set fitted to pick up any broadcast interesting to a shrew. **1953** A. HUXLEY *Let.* 9 Aug. (1969) 682 Receiving sets grafted into the tissues of animals, so as to make them robots responsive to the radioed will of their masters. **1975** *Listener* 4 Dec. 738/2 A fee required of each owner of a receiving set. **1923** E. W. MARCHANT *Radio Telegr. & Teleph.* iii. 23 A number of vertical wires are attached to a suspended horizontal wire and brought down in a fan-shape to the receiving station. **1977** G. W. H. LAMPE *God as Spirit* ii. 54 Divine communications at the subconscious level, for which the actual recipients had acted simply as passive receiving stations.

3. Special combinations. **receiving barn** *U.S.*, a stable in which horses are placed before a race to prevent tampering; **receiving blanket** *N. Amer.*, a soft blanket in which to wrap a baby (cf. RECEIVER¹ 6 a); **receiving line** orig. *U.S.*, a row of persons by whom guests are greeted in turn on arrival.

1946 *Sun* (Baltimore) 26 Oct. 8/4 Refusal of George D. Widener to allow his equine star, Lucky Draw, to compete in the Pimlico Special simply because of the receiving barn is to be regretted. **1949** *Ibid.* 29 Apr. 18/4 There has been no doping case since the rules governing the receiving barn were revised last fall. **1974** TILLEY & PLOWDEN *This is Horse Racing* 181 *Receiving barn*, facility where horses are isolated for certain period before post time, to minimize chances of tampering. **1926** *Infants' Dept.* Oct. 5028/1 *Layette*... 1 Receiving blanket. **1944** K. HARDY *Sewing for Baby* viii. 214 You will need two cotton receiving blankets. **1970** *Globe & Mail* (Toronto) 26 Sept. 12/8 (Advt.), Since mid-summer we have paid out Four Hundred and Twenty-one Dollars for the basic essentials in layettes; shirts, diapers, gowns, and receiving blankets. **1933** H. L. ICKES *Diary* 17 Nov. (1955) I. 125 He told Anna in the receiving line last night that he was going to order me down there. **1971** M. LEE *Dying for Fun* xl. 189 Millie Panhard Geltzer went to the Woman of the Year Luncheon... She shook hands with the receiving line.

receiving (rɪˈsiːvɪŋ), *ppl. a.* [f. as prec. + -ING².]

1. That receives, in senses of the vb.

In some cases not clearly distinct from prec. 2 b.

1599 SHAKS. *Hen. V* Prol. 27 Horses.. Printing their prowd Hoofes i' th' receiuing Earth. **1634** SIR T. HERBERT *Trav.* 149 [Persian] women when they goe abroad, wrap themselues in a large receiuing sheet. **1712** J. JAMES tr. *Le Blond's Gardening* 191 Water-Engines.. raise it.. into receiving Cisterns. **1804** LARWOOD *No Gun Boats* 14 Masts .. nicely and accurately appropriated to the receiving boat. **1840** *Cottager's Manual* 22 in *Lib. Usef. Kn., Husb.* III, The receiving tank.. has another pipe from the inside with a funnel. **1883** GRESLEY *Gloss. Coal-mining*, *Receiving Rods*, auxiliary cage guides at insets and at pit tops. **1897** *Allbutt's Syst. Med.* III. 819 The outermost of the three layers is known as.. the sheath or the receiving layer.

2. *receiving end*, the position that receives a transmitted signal or discharged object. Usu. *fig.*, used loosely in colloq. phr. ***to be on*** (or ***at***) ***the receiving end***, to be the (unfortunate) recipient of some action, event, etc.; to bear the brunt, to suffer.

1933 [see INVERT *v.* 2g]. **1937** H. L. ICKES *Diary* 2 Oct. (1955) II. 219, I shall refuse to be at the receiving end of any more brickbats. **1942** BERREY & VAN DEN BARK *Amer. Thes. Slang* §674 *Catcher's position*, receiving end. **1946** B. PEMBERTON in S. H. Adams *Alexander Woollcott* xiv. 142 But it [*sc.* the nature of Woollcott's criticism] was hell for those on the receiving end. **1949** J. SZIGETI *With Strings Attached* xxxiii. 302 It cannot be the love of music pure and simple, for we share this with multitudes who either are on the receiving end alone or, not content with this, also aspire to the satisfaction of making music themselves. **1955** W. C. GAULT *Ring around Rosa* vi. 78 Jan had just brought a right hand from right field and the wrestler had been on the receiving end. **1958** P. KEMP *No Colours or Crest* viii. 151 His experience of guerrilla warfare had been, as it were, on the receiving end; for he had served before the war on the North-West Frontier and in Palestine. **1962** A. NISBETT *Technique Sound Studio* x. 176 Dialling is rather more of a performance than being on the receiving end of a phone call. **1968** G. JONES *Hist. Vikings* III. ii. 202 As in Scandinavia, so at the receiving end in Europe the times were favourable to the art and practice of *viking*. **1976** J. SNOW *Cricket Rebel* 134 The wrist had been on the receiving end of a Dennis Lillee bouncer.

re-'celebrate, *v.* [RE- 5a.] *trans.* To celebrate or commemorate again.

1598 BARCKLEY *Felic. Man* I. (1631) 12 They..place him [a prisoner] in a house of some man that was lately slaine in the warres, as it were to re-celebrate his funerall. **1629** B. JONSON *Underwoods, To Edw. Filmer*, Who..with their chained dance, Recelebrates the joyful Match with France.

re-ce'ment, *v.* [RE- 5a.] *trans.* To join together again with, or as with, cement; to unite firmly or closely.

1647 WARD *Simp. Cobler* 64 They are..determined to re-cement you to your Body. **1850** HOLTZAPFFEL *Turning* III. 1327 The stone..is detached from the stick, and re-cemented with the front outwards. **1863** *Sat. Rev.* 23 May 659/2 Some anxiety, lest a partial re-opening of the river to trade should re-cement the waning loyalty of the Western States.

So **re-cemen'tation; re-cemented** *ppl. a.*

1848 HERSCHEL *Ess.* (1857) 331 Rocks constructed by the re-cementation of fragments and pulverized matter. **1946** *Nature* 13 July 58/1 The lower part of the profile consists, according to the district, either of re-cemented chalk or compact sand, both of which are very water-retentive. **1965** G. J. WILLIAMS *Econ. Geol. N.Z.* iii. 26/2 Re-cemented brecciated quartz is occasionally seen.

recen, obs. form of RECKON *v.*

recency ('riːsənsɪ). [f. RECENT: see -ENCY. Cf. med.L. *recentia* (Du Cange).] **a.** The state or quality of being recent. (Common in 19th c.)

1612 WOODALL *Surg. Mate* Wks. (1653) 303 Such wounds, in their recency..resemble Vlcers. **1657** TOMLINSON *Renou's Disp.* 41 A peculiar antiquity or recency consists in several medicaments. **1751** SMOLLETT *Per. Pic.* cvi, She objected the recency of her kinswoman's death. **1800** COLERIDGE *Lett.* (1895) 330 If I am not deceived by the recency of their date. **1875** MAINE *Hist. Inst.* xiii. 398 The comparative recency of legislative activity in Germany. **1882** C. E. DUTTON *Tertiary Hist. Grand Cañon District* v. 83 Even here where historic antiquity merges into geologic recency the one gives us no measure of the other. **1948** H. NICOLSON *Diary* 23 Sept. (1968) 149 Frank Pakenham tells me that I was on the list for peerages last December... I might have come up again had it not been for the recency of Croydon. **1964** *Language* XL. 204 The recency and taxonomic character of paralinguistics and kinesics are not sufficient cause for overlooking them. **1976** *Nature* 5 Feb. 395/2 Genetic similarity may serve as direct measure of the recency of the cladistic event which separated the two compared lines of descent.

b. *Psychol.* The fact of being recent as it affects the facility with which learned material or an experience is recalled; freq. *attrib.* Cf. PRIMACY 1 b.

1894 M. W. CALKINS in *Psychol. Rev.* I. 482 The influence of recency, too, can be studied. **1916** J. B. WATSON in *Psychol. Bull.* XIII. 77 Other investigators hold that the stamping in of a successful act depends upon the principles of *recency* and *frequency* and is not dependent upon the pleasantness or unpleasantness resulting from the activity. **1929** K. S. LASHLEY in C. Murchison *Found. Exper. Psychol.* xiv. 555 It seems probable that primacy and recency are effective only when they increase the intensity or stimulating value of the situations. **1938** R. S. WOODWORTH *Exper. Psychol.* ii. 38 The wrong name recalled acquires recency value and blocks the correct name. **1948** E. R. HILGARD *Theories of Learning* vii. 183 As it applies to memory, the law of proximity becomes a law of recency. **1964** W. K. ESTES in A. W. Melton *Categories of Hum. Learning* 98 The suggestion has been put forward..that the negative recency function results largely from response tendencies the *S*s bring with them to the experiment. **1971** *Sci. Amer.* Aug. 85/1 There is considerable evidence that the recency effect is due to retrieval from short-term storage.

recense (rɪ'sɛns), *v.* [ad. L. *recensēre* (f. *re-* RE- + *censēre* CENSE *v.*²) or F. *recenser* (14th c.).] *trans.* To survey, review, revise (now *spec.* a text: see RECENSION).

1597 A. M. tr. *Guillemeau's Fr. Chirurg.* 52 b/2 Nether may we heere omitt to recense and speake of the feare wherewith cowardes are oftentimes taken. **1613** CAWDREY *Table Alph.*, *Recensed*, repeated, rehearsed, named. **1716** BENTLEY *Corr.* (1842) 506 Pope Sixtus and Clemens..had an assembly of learned divines, to recense and adjust the Latin Vulgate. **1902** J. S. PHILLIMORE *Sophocles* Introd. 78 Alexander Aetolus, who recensed the Dramatists for the Museum Library.

So †**re'censeate,** to go over, enumerate. *Obs.*$^{-1}$

1657 TOMLINSON *Renou's Disp.* 296 Twenty two..varieties, which to recenseate, were superfluous.

recension (rɪ'sɛnʃən). [ad. L. *recensiōn-em*, n. of action f. *recensēre*: see prec. and cf. mod.F. *récension*.]

1. An enumeration, survey, review. Now *rare*. (Freq. in 17th c., esp. in Evelyn's works.)

a **1638** MEDE *Wks.* (1672) 276 Their number cannot be known, because Moses does not make a recension of all the Families or Heads of families. *a* **1677** BARROW *Pope's Suprem.* (1687) 90 In the recensions of the Roman Bishops, sometimes the Apostles are reckoned in, sometimes excluded. **1819** HOPE *Anastasius* II. 228 Intent upon tempting Providence by the daily recension of his growing riches.

b. A review (of a book). *rare*$^{-1}$.

1872 GEO. ELIOT *Middlem.* xxix, Bitterly convinced that his old acquaintance Carp had been the writer of that depreciatory recension.

2. The revision of a text, esp. in a careful or critical manner; a particular form or version of a text resulting from such revision.

1818–28 HALLAM *Mid. Ages* (1872) I. 279 The Burgundian law, though earlier than either of these in their recensions, displays a far more advanced state of manners. **1860** WESTCOTT *Introd. Study Gosp.* iii. (ed. 5) 205 The Gospels of St. Matthew and St. Luke represent the two great types of recension to which it may be supposed that the simple narrative was subjected. **1894** J. T. FOWLER *Adamnan* Pref. 8 There are two recensions of the text.

b. *transf.* A revised or distinct form of anything.

1835 I. TAYLOR *Spir. Despot.* IX. 388 We are the creatures of that recension of Christianity which happens to be current in our times. **1859** —— *Logic in Theol.* 331 There is no new recension of the worship of the ancient Church.

Hence **re'censionist,** one who makes a recension. Also **re'censor.**

1876 SPURGEON *Commenting* 17 The laborious recensor of the various MSS. *c* **1904** Recensionist [in recent Dicts.] **1962** *Listener* 29 Nov. 920/1 Mr Edel is a recensionist, reconstructing the life of his hero from a myriad documents.

re-'censure, *v.* [RE- 5a.] *trans.* To censure again. So **re-'censure** *sb.*, a censure in return.

1645 *King's Cabinet Opened* in *Select. fr. Harl. Misc.* (1793) 343 Out of fear, that Hamilton might return to a capacity of re-censuring me. **1829** CARLYLE *Misc.* (1857) II. 43 That censure of Shakspeare which elicited a re-censure in England.

recent ('riːsənt), *a.* [ad. L. *recent-*, *recens*, or a. F. *récent* (16th c.). App. first in Sc. use.]

1. Lately done or made; that has lately happened or taken place, etc.

1533 BELLENDEN *Livy* I. Prol. (S.T.S.) 8, I dout nocht bot the beginnyng of Romanis..sall be of les pleser to þe redaris þan recent historyis, becaus þai will haisty þame self to here þir novellis and recent dedis done in our dais. **1572** *Reg. Privy Council Scot.* Ser. I. II. 131 The persoun being apprehendit in the recent deid salbe deliverit in the handis of the Provest Marschell. **1574–5** *Ibid.* 437 For na recent crymes committit be thame. **1661** BOYLE *Style of Script.* (1675) 161 Recent translations I have seen of it in French. **1748** *Anson's Voy.* I. v. 51 The discovery of these valuable stones is much more recent than that of gold. **1821** J. Q. ADAMS in C. Davies *Metr. Syst.* III. (1871) 150 The recent coinage of dimes..alluded to in our public journals. **1837** LYTTON *E. Maltrav.* I. viii, The bright drops of a recent shower sparkled upon the buds of the lilac. **1966** *Listener* 29 Sept. 479/2 Gerhard's Op. 1..its beauty [is] marred only by a lack of variety and a tendency to go on too long. Nearly fifty years more recent, the *Duo Concertante* for violin and piano shows neither quality. **1976** *Encounter* June 72/2 Professor Daiches' method, then, consists partly of summarising the results of recent research on the ancient Near East, and partly of commentary on the Pentateuch. **1976** *Daily Tel.* 20 July 1/1 The four countries had agreed on the ban during their recent economic summit in Puerto Rico.

2. a. Lately formed, created, originated, or begun; †new-born.

a **1676** WISEMAN *Chirurg. Treat.* 117 How dangerous it is to neglect the consulting the..Chirurgeon while the Disease is recent. **1678** CUDWORTH *Intell. Syst.* I. v. 776 We have made it unquestionably Evident, that this Opinion..is no Novel or Recent thing. *c* **1709** PRIOR *1st Hymn Callimachus* 22 She sought a neighbouring spring To wash the recent babe. **1748** THOMSON *Cast. Indol.* II. xxvii, Gay plains extend where marshes slept before; O'er recent meads th' exulting streamlets fly. **1788** GIBBON *Decl. & F.* xlix. V. 147 Lorraine and Arles, two recent and transitory kingdoms. **1816** SINGER *Hist. Cards* 217 Erasmus..seems to have had the then recent system of Murner in his eye. **1899** *Allbutt's Syst. Med.* VII. 502 We found recent lymph becoming organised.

b. Fresh; not yet affected by decay, decomposition, or loss of moisture.

1632 MASSINGER & FIELD *Fatal Dowry* II. i, The old man's virtues [are] So recent in him as the world may swear Nought but a fair tree could such fair fruit bear. **1759** B. STILLINGFLEET tr. *Improv. Physic* in *Misc. Tracts* (1762) 221 The recent root of the rose-wort is vastly superior to the dry in head-achs. **1808** BARCLAY *Muscular Motions* 477 A cursory inspection of a recent eye is sufficient at any time to prove the contrary. **1839** URE *Dict. Arts* 903 The odour [of essential oils] is seldom as pleasant as that of the recent plant. **1877** *Encycl. Brit.* VI. 134/2 If not set when either moist or recent, they [*sc.* beetles' legs] may be softened by being placed for a night in any small vessel containing a layer of wet sand.

c. *poet.* Lately or freshly come or arrived *from* a place.

1715–20 POPE *Iliad* XIV. 382 Shall I not think that..All heav'n beholds me recent from thy arms? **1759** GIBBON *Autobiog.* (1896) 207 Recent from Paris, I assisted with pleasure at the representation of several tragedies. **1820** WIFFEN *Aonian Hours* (ed. 2) 73 Here Caesar, recent from barbaric wars, Leads Rome in chains. **1864** SWINBURNE *Atalanta* 1260 Recent from the roar of foreign foam.

3. a. Belonging to a (past) period of time comparatively near to the present. (Opposed to *ancient* †or *antique*.)

1622 BACON *Hen. VII*, 35 Though it be an action of so recent memorie. **1666** BOYLE *Orig. Formes & Qual.* To Rdr., Upon perusal of several Scholastick Writers, (especially the recenter). **1699** BENTLEY *Phal.* 400 The Sense of some of them occurs there, but express'd in a more recent way. **1730** MARTIN in *Phil. Trans.* XXXVI. 453 Garangeot..who is one of the recentest Writers. **1829** LANDOR *Imag. Conv.*, *Emp. China & Tsing-Ti* Wks. 1853 II. 148/1 The older creation of the nobility..is more ill-constructed and ill-favoured than the recenter. **1876** BIRCH *Rede Lect. Egypt* 12 The Egyptian belongs after all to the more recent race of men.

b. *Geol.* Of or pertaining to the present geological epoch. (Cf. 4 b.)

1830 LYELL *Princ. Geol.* I. 95 Murex cornutus, fossil at Asti, is now only known recent in warmer latitudes. **1833** *Ibid.* III. 60 In the Pliocene we find an intermixture of extinct and recent species of quadrupeds. **1877** J. A. ALLEN *Amer. Bison* 457 These remains differ in no appreciable respect..from those of the recent bison of the Plains.

4. a. Of a point or period of time: Not much earlier than the present; not long past.

1823 *Edin. Rev.* Oct. 109 Up to a very recent period. **1841** ELPHINSTONE *Hist. India* I. 425 The celebrity of the Marattas was reserved for recent times. **1856** KANE *Arct. Expl.* II. xii. 120 Of such a character as to indicate for them a tolerably recent date.

b. *Geol.* (With capital initial.) Applied to the later portion of the Quaternary or Post-Pliocene period. Also = HOLOCENE *a.*

1833 LYELL *Princ. Geol.* III. 343 During the newer Pliocene epoch, partly, perhaps, in the Recent. **1882** A. GEIKIE *Text-bk. Geol.* 883 Above them [*sc.* glacial deposits] lie younger accumulations such as river-alluvia, peat-mosses, lake-bottoms,..raised lacustrine and marine terraces, which, merging insensibly into those of the present day, are termed Recent or Prehistoric. **1927** [see HOLOCENE *a.*]. **1959** J. D. CLARK *Prehist. Southern Afr.* ii. 49 A..method of correlating the succession of events in Africa with those in Europe during the Pleistocene and early Recent times. **1975** *Nature* 20 Mar. 209/2 Sterols..have been identified in Recent and ancient sediments.

recent, obs. form of RESENT *v.*

†**re'centity.** *Obs.*$^{-1}$ [f. RECENT *a.* + -ITY.] Recency, newness.

1631 W. SALTONSTALL *Pict. Loquent.* D iv b, Hee gaynes most by the recentity of freshmen, unto whom he sticks as close as a Horseleech.

recently ('riːsəntlɪ), *adv.* [f. RECENT *a.* + -LY².]

a. At a recent date; not long before or ago; lately, newly.

1533 BELLENDEN *Livy* II. ii. (S.T.S.) I. 133 The commoun liberte sa recentlie Recouerit was nere loist be falset and tressoun. *Ibid.* 135 þis tressoun recentlie ymaginate. *a* **1548** HALL *Chron.*, *Rich. III* (1550) 25 Sodeinly he herde newes that fyer was spronge out of the smoke, and the ware recently begonne. **1611** COTGR., *Recentement*, recently, freshly, newly, lately. *a* **1735** ARBUTHNOT (J.), Those tubes, which are most recently made of fluids, are most flexible and most easily lengthened. **1788** GIBBON *Decl. & F.* xlix. V. 142 The people of Hesse and Thuringia were recently incorporated with the victors. **1849** MACAULAY *Hist. Eng.* vii. II. 221 James did not pretend to have been recently convinced. **1864** BRYCE *Holy Rom. Emp.* ix. (1875) 151 Its prelates and nobles..retained till recently the style and title of Princes of the Holy Empire.

b. With pples. or adjs. used attributively.

1794 GODWIN *Caleb Williams* xiii, A recently conceived purpose. **1848** BUCKLEY *Iliad* 243 The blood flowed from his recently-wounded hand. **1856** KANE *Arct. Expl.* I. xxx. 410 A small space of recently-open water that was glazed over with..ice. **1887** MOLONEY *Forestry W. Afr.* 28 One of the recently-acquired German Protectorates. **1922** JOYCE *Ulysses* 123 What is it?..—A recently discovered fragment of Cicero's. **1937** *Granta* 3 Feb. 219/1 He was off with the five survivors of our English group to join the recently formed English Battalion. **1960** *Farmer & Stockbreeder* 19 Jan. 102/3 Females changed hands at prices ranging to 130 gs, paid for a recently-calved C.M. cow. **1979** *Tucson (Arizona) Citizen* 20 Sept. 3C/6 It already has been replaced by the recently-completed 254-bed West Wing.

c. Const. *after*, *from*. *rare*.

1791 BOSWELL *Johnson* an. 1752, The situation in which he found him recently after his wife's death. **1858** HAWTHORNE *Fr. & It. Note-bks.* I. 251 We saw the Clitumnus, so recently from its source.., that it was still as pure as a child's heart.

recentment, obs. form of RESENTMENT.

recentness ('riːsəntnɪs). [f. RECENT *a.*] The state or quality of being recent; recency.

a **1677** HALE *Prim. Orig. Man.* II. v. 167 This Inference of the Recentness of Mankind from the Recentness of these Apotheoses [etc.]. **1823** LAMB *Guy Faux* Misc. Wks. (1871) 373 Men's minds were still shuddering from the recentness of the escape. **1872** PROCTOR *Ess. Astron.* xviii. 210 A value founded rather on their recentness than on their specific importance.

re-'centre, *v.* [RE- 5 a.] *trans.* To centre again. Hence **re-'centring** *ppl. a.*

1796 COLERIDGE *Ode Departing Year* ix, Now I recentre my immortal mind In the deep sabbath of meek self-content. **1843** HOLTZAPFFEL *Turning* II. 549 Making the drill with a cylindrical lump, so as to fill the hole; this is called the re-centering drill.

recep. (rɪ'sɛp). **1.** Abbrev. of ***reception room(s)*** s.v. RECEPTION 10. (Freq. used in advertisements.)

1920 *Evening News* 2 Mar. 7/2 (Advt.), Exchange tenancy houses, . . 4 bed. 2 recep. bath. **1926** [see BED *sb.* 1 f]. **1950** *Evening Standard* 21 Mar. 12/3 (Advt.), At Harrow... Charm. mod. hse... 2 recep., kit. **1976** 'Z. STONE' *Modigliani Scandal* I. iv. 41 The house . . was small—three bedrooms, two recep. and a study.

2. *Theatr.* = RECEPTION 5 c.

1936 W. H. LANE CRAUFURD *Murder to Music* vii. 104 'Did you hear my little recep.!' he cried ecstatically.

† **re'cept,** *sb.*[1] *Obs.* [a. OF. *recept*, ad. L. *recept-um*, or refashioning of *recet* RESET *sb.* under influence of the L. spelling; in later use prob. directly associated with the L. form.] = RECEIPT *sb.*, in various senses. (Chiefly in 16th c.)

1422 tr. *Secreta Secret., Priv. Priv.* 246 Bestis that no recepte haue tremblyth . . for the colde. **1503** *Rolls of Parlt.* VI. 524/2 Of all suche receptes, reteynders and perceyvyng. **1541** R. COPLAND *Guydon's Quest. Chirurg.* G iij, These two coniunctions of bones be called the recepte of the hande. **1571–2** *Reg. Privy Council Scot.* Ser. I. II. 108 [At] the tyme of thair recept in the universitie. **1576** FLEMING *Panopl. Epist.* 246 Thirst which requireth moyst recepts. **1631** *Strathbogie Presbytery Bk.* (1843) 5 Thomas Murray, . . summondit for recept and consulting with witches.

recept ('riːsɛpt), *sb.*[2] [ad. L. *recept-um* (see RECEIPT), after *concept*, *percept*.] A term suggested by Romanes to express a 'compound idea' formed by the repetition of similar percepts.

1888 ROMANES *Mental Evol. Man* ii. 36 In addition, then, to the terms Percept and Concept, I coin the word Recept. . . A recept is that which is taken again, or a re-cognition of things previously cognized. *Ibid.* 37 Recepts, then, are spontaneous associations, formed unintentionally as what may be termed unperceived abstractions. **1889** MIVART *Orig. Hum. Reason* 217 The relation between the highest recept of a brute and the lowest concept of a man.

† **re'cept,** *v. Obs.* [var. RECEIPT *v.*[1]; cf. RECEPT *sb.*[1] and OF. *recepter*.] *trans.* To harbour, reset. = RECEIPT *v.*[1]

1472 *Surtees Misc.* (1888) 25 Robert Broun . . receptes Scottes and othir suspect peple. **1542** in *Add. MS.* 32,646 (B.M.) lf. 197 b, The Names of certain of the most notable and arrant traitours recepted in Scotland. *c* **1670** in G. Hickes *Spirit of Popery* (1680) 44 And further, That I, nor they shall Recept, Supply, or Commune with forfeited Persons. **1687** in Burnet *Six Papers* 54 It is declared High Treason . . to Recept, Supply or Intercomon with declared . . Traitors.

† **re'ceptable.** *Obs.* [a. obs. F. *receptable* (Godef.), alteration of *réceptacle*.] A receptacle.

1615 G. SANDYS *Trav.* 256 [Naples] being first the receptable of Philosophie, then of Muses, and lastly of the souldiery. **1634** SIR T. HERBERT *Trav.* 45 But that his bones want sence and expression, they would tell you the earth is not worthy his receptable.

receptable, variant of RECEPTIBLE *a.*

receptacle (rɪ'sɛptək(ə)l). [ad. L. *receptāculum*, f. ppl. stem of *recipĕre* to RECEIVE. Cf. F. *réceptacle* (14th c.).]

1. That which receives and holds a thing; something into which another thing may be put; a containing vessel, place, or space; a repository.

c **1420** *Pallad. on Husb.* I. 497 But clene, Thyn oiles receptaclis thow demene. **1527** ANDREW *Brunswyke's Distyll. Waters* B iv/1 Ye shal set a receptacle or vyole so that the pype of the alembyke hange within it. **1555** EDEN *Decades* 85 They may be the receptacles of the water passing through the landes. **1607** TOPSELL *Four-f. Beasts* (1658) 153 In this receiveth he his meat, having no other receptacle for it. **1675** tr. *Camden's Hist. Eliz.* II. (1688) 249 He fired a rich Receptacle or Store-house of Merchandise. **1783** COWPER *Let. to J. Hill* 23 Nov., His receptacle of my squibs is the Public Advertiser. **1834** LYTTON *Pompeii* III. i, His belt, or girdle, contained a small receptacle for ink. **1878** HUXLEY *Physiogr.* 117 The river becomes the common receptacle for all the soluble matter delivered by its tributary streams.

b. *fig.* in ref. to qualities, feelings, etc.

1412–20 LYDG. *Chron. Troy* IV. xxxv, They be in theyr entente Of couetyse very receptacle. **1559** W. CUNNINGHAM *Cosmogr. Glasse* 43 The receptakle of heauenly influence. **1597** HOOKER *Eccl. Pol.* v. lxvii. §2 The soule of man is the receptacle of Christ's presence. *a* **1625** FLETCHER *Nice Valour* v. i, Away, receptacle Of luxury and dishonour! **1664** POWER *Exp. Philos.* I. 2 One would wonder at the great strength lodged in so small a Receptacle. **1709** ATTERBURY *Serm.* (1726) II. vii. 221 Some of these Publick Funds and Receptacles of Charity. **1827** LYTTON *Falkland* I. 37, I have descended into the receptacles of vice. **1863** GOULBURN *Pers. Relig.* I. iii. (ed. 2) 26 His glorified humanity is the appointed receptacle of Grace.

2. Any place into which persons (ships, animals, etc.) are received or retire, esp. for shelter or security; †a room or apartment in a building.

1412–20 LYDG. *Chron. Troy* II. xxi, From storme and rayne them selfe for to saue They deuysed other habytacles Tiguryes and smalle receptacles. *a* **1548** HALL *Chron., Edw. IV* (1550) 35 Lest his neighbors countrey might be an harborough, or receptacle of his foes and aduersaries. **1599** HAKLUYT *Voy.* I. 127 An Hauen . . which is a commodious and safe receptacle for all ships directing their course for the same. **1615** G. SANDYS *Trav.* Ded., Those rich lands . . remaine waste and ouergrowne with bushes, receptacles of wild beasts. **1634** SIR T. HERBERT *Trav.* 59 A third Chamber . . was a receptacle for the Queene and Ladies. **1672** PETTY *Pol. Anat.* xii. in *Tracts* (1769) 364 Holy-wells, rocks and caves, which have been the reputed cells and receptacles of men reputed saints. **1751** JOHNSON *Rambler* No. 91 ¶ 11 They entered this general receptacle [the Hall of Expectation] with ardour. **1809** PINKNEY *Trav. France* 196 It was a standing receptacle for all vagabonds and beggars. **1868** FREEMAN *Norm. Conq.* (1876) II. viii. 224 Now applied to the degrading purposes of a receptacle of French cavalry.

† **b.** Without article: Receipt, admittance. *Obs.*

1656 EARL MONM. tr. *Boccalini's Advts. fr. Parnass.* I. lxxxix. (1674) 119 Whosoever durst give receptacle to so pernicious a man in his Library.

3. *spec.* in scientific use. (The L. form *receptaculum* is also used in the same senses.)

a. *Anat.* and *Bot.* An organ or space which receives a secretion, esp. ***receptacle of chyle*** (the dilated lower portion of the thoracic duct), ***of secretion*** (in plants).

1543 TRAHERON tr. *Vigo's Chirurg.* VIII. xii. 205 b/1 By oppilation of the pores . . as by stronge bynding and replecyon of the receptacles. **1722** QUINCY *Physical Dict.* s.v. *Lacteal Veins*, The Receptacle of the Chyle is easily found in live Bodies... The Receptacle receives all the second order of Lacteals. **1819** *Pantologia* s.v. *Receptaculum*, In brute animals the receptacle of the chyle is situated on the dorsal vertebræ where the lacteals all meet. **1832** LINDLEY *Introd. Bot.* I. i. 27 The receptacles . . in the leaves of the Orange and of all Myrtaceæ . . are called . . receptacles of oil. *Ibid.*, Although the receptacles of secretion have no proper coat, yet they are so surrounded by cellular tissue that a lining or wall is formed. **1882** VINES tr. *Sachs' Bot.* 93 The canal-like Receptacles for Secretions are formed, in many plants, by cells, . . separating from one another and leaving an intercellular space.

b. *Bot.* The common base which supports the floral organs, the torus or thalamus (***floral receptacle***). Also, the axis or rachis of a head, spike, or other cluster (***receptacle of inflorescence***).

proper receptacle, the apex of the peduncle or pedicel supporting a single flower. ***common receptacle***, the support of the florets in a composite flower-head; the clinanthium; also = receptacle of inflorescence.

1753 CHAMBERS *Cycl. Supp.* s.v. *Receptaculum*, The disk of the receptacle is of various shapes in the various plants. **1777** W. CURTIS *Flora Lond.* I. 58 Receptacle [of Dandelion] naked and full of little holes. **1830** LINDLEY *Nat. Syst. Bot.* 198 Flowers . . collected in dense heads upon a common receptacle. **1870** HOOKER *Stud. Flora* 254 Nutlets . . attached by the edge to an elevated receptacle.

c. *Bot.* In Ferns, Mosses, Algæ, and Fungi, the support of the fructification or reproductive organs; an apothecium, pycnidium, sporophore, etc.

1842 in BRANDE *Dict. Sci.*, etc. **1852** HENSLOW *Dict. Bot. Terms* s.v., Receptacle . . is also applied to various forms of support to the fructification of cryptogamous plants. **1874** COOKE *Fungi* 59 There is manifestly a succession in formation and maturity of the asci in a receptacle. **1882** VINES tr. *Sachs' Bot.* 370 The receptacle of Mosses either terminates the growth of a primary axis, . . or the axis is indeterminate, and the receptacle is placed at the end of an axis of the second or third order.

receptacu'laceous, *a. Bot.* [f. as next + -ACEOUS.] = next. ? *Obs.*

1760 J. LEE *Introd. Bot.* I. xii. (1765) 30 *Receptaculaceous Nectaria*, such as join to the Receptacle. **1853** in MACDONALD & ALLEN *Botanist's Word-bk.*

receptacular (rɛsɛp'tækjʊlə(r)), *a.* [f. L. *receptacul-um* receptacle + -AR. Cf. F. *réceptaculaire*.]

1. *Bot.* Pertaining to the receptacle of a flower.

1847 in WEBSTER.

2. Of the nature of, serving as, a receptacle.

1848 OWEN in *Times* 14 Nov. 8/7 Being an air-breathing animal, with long vesicular and receptacular lungs.

† **re'ceptance.** *Obs.*$^{-1}$ [f. L. *recept-*, *recipĕre*, or *receptāre*, after *acceptance*.] Reception.

1681 LUTTRELL *Brief Rel.* (1857) I. 128 A solemn speech . . which mett with a gracious receptance from his majestie.

So **re'ceptant** *a.*, receiving. *rare*$^{-1}$.

1872 RUSKIN *Munera P.* 32 The holder of wealth, in such temper, may be regarded . . as a money-chest with a slit in it, not only receptant but suctional.

† **re'ceptary,** *sb.* and *a. Obs. rare.* [f. as prec. + -ARY. In sense 1, ad. obs. F. *receptaire* (16th c.).]

1. A book or collection of receipts.

1611 COTGR., *Receptaire*, a receptarie, a note of Phisicall receipts. **1656** in BLOUNT *Glossogr.*

2. a. *sb.* A received or accepted notion or belief. **b.** *adj.* Merely received or accepted as true, without proof.

1646 SIR T. BROWNE *Pseud. Ep.* Pref., Our sober enquiries in the doubtfull appertinancies of Arts, and Receptaries of Philosophy. *Ibid.* 34 Baptista Porta, in whose workes, although there be contained many excellent things, and verified upon his own experience, yet are there many also receptary, and such as will not indure the test.

receptation. *Obs. rare.* [ad. med.L. *receptātio*, f. L. *receptāre* to receive: cf. *acceptation*.] The fact of being received into a place.

1574 *Reg. Privy Council Scot.* Ser. I. II. 400 Ony crymes that it salhappin the saidis transgressouris . . to commit the tyme of thair returning and receptatioun. **1576** *Ibid.* II. 550.

† **re'ceptative,** *a. Obs.*$^{-1}$ [f. as prec.: see -ATIVE.] Receptive.

1509 HAWES *Past. Pleas.* xxiv. ix, Thus comyn wytte worketh wonderly, Upon the v. gates whyche are receptatyve Of every thynge for to take inwardly.

recepte, var. *recet* received: see RESET *v.*

re,cepti'bility. Also 9 **-ability.** [f. next.]

1. The quality or state of being receptible.

1676 *Doctrine of Devils* 50 There is one Doctrine of his, would spoil all the receptibility of the whole System of Religion promulgated in his Gospel. **1757** tr. *Henckel's Pyritologia* 114 Some inequality in this receptibility. **1820** L. HUNT *Indicator* No. 55 (1822) II. 20 Without at all diminishing his receptability among the said circles.

† **2.** Capacity for receiving. *Obs.*$^{-1}$

1661 GLANVILL *Van. Dogm.* xvi. 153 The Peripatetick matter is a pure unactuated Power, and this conceited Vacuum a meer Receptibility. [*Cf. ibid.* The imaginary space is receptive of any body.]

receptible (rɪ'sɛptɪb(ə)l), *a.* Now *rare.* Also 7 **-able.** [ad. late L. *receptibilis*: see -IBLE and cf. obs. F. *receptible* (Godef.).]

1. That may be received, receivable.

1574 NEWTON *Health Mag.* G, Hoate bread he vtterlie discommendeth . . because it is not (as he there affirmeth) receptible of nature. **1652** GAULE *Magastrom.* 60 Whether it be a clear and receptable distinction of magick. **1886** C. A. WARD in *Temple Bar Mag.* LXXVII. 542 A bright idea is lost on the masses, and the smoke of verbosity is required to make it receptible by their understanding.

2. Capable of receiving. Const. *of.*

1656 STANLEY *Hist. Philos.* v. (1701) 201/1 Water, continually flowing, easily receptable of any Form. **1793** HOLCROFT tr. *Lavater's Physiog.* xxxiv. 175 All their organs are tender, yielding, easily wounded, sensible and receptible. **1894** *Emanuel Swedenborg* v. 113 Not a conception of life but only of the first and purest forms receptible of life.

recepticious: see RECEPTITIOUS.

reception (rɪ'sɛpʃən). Also 5 **recepcion.** [a. F. *reception* (12–13th c.), or ad. L. *receptiōn-em*, n. of action f. *recipĕre* to RECEIVE.]

1. The action or fact of receiving or getting.

c **1489** CAXTON *Blanchardyn* 82 The Ioye that blanchardyn had made at the recepcion of the present that she had sent vnto hym. **1689** *Col. Rec. Pennsylv.* I. 256 Upon yᵉ Reception thereof, I informed the said David Lloyd, and delivered it to him. **1709** BERKELEY *Th. Vision* §128 A Man Born Blind wou'd not, at first reception of his Sight, think the things he saw were of the same Nature with the Objects of Touch. **1789** GIBBON *Let. to Ld. Sheffield* Misc. Wks. 1814 I. 297 Within an hour after the reception of your last, I drew my pen for the purpose of a reply. **1834** HT. MARTINEAU *Moral* I. 5 The prospect of the wealth which awaits man's reception.

† **b.** *pl.* Receipts, sums received. *Obs. rare*$^{-1}$.

1514 *Churchw. Acc., Pilton* (Som. Rec. Soc.) 67 The wyche nobyll ys caste yn ye cownte of the recepco[n]is.

2. a. *Astrol.* The fact of each of two planets being received into the other's house, exaltation, or other dignity.

1390 GOWER *Conf.* III. 67 He loketh the conjunccions, He loketh the recepcions, His signe, his house, his ascendent. **1632** MASSINGER *City Madam* II. ii, Venus . . and Mars . . in mutual reception of each other . . assure a fortunate combination to Hymen. **1679** MOXON *Math. Dict.* 128 The first is a Reception by House (which is the best and strongest). The second is a Reception by Triplicity. **1686** GOAD *Celest. Bodies* I. xv. 98.

b. The action of receiving (esp. persons), or fact of being received, into a place, company, state, etc.

1650 CROMWELL *Let.* 13 Dec. in *Carlyle*, Making way for the reception of professed Malignants, both in their Parliament and Army. **1671** MILTON *P.R.* III. 205 All hope is lost Of my reception into grace. **1725** POPE *Odyss.* x. 14 This happy port affords our wand'ring fleet, A month's reception. **1794** MRS. RADCLIFFE *Myst. Udolpho* xliv, The Count gave orders for the north apartments to be . . prepared for the reception of Ludovico. **1863** GEO. ELIOT *Romola* xxi, The great palace . . had been prepared for the reception of another tenant.

c. The action of receiving, or fact of being received, in a formal or ceremonious manner.

1662 J. DAVIES tr. *Olearius' Voy. Ambass.* 6 We stayed above six weeks, in expectation of the Great Duke's orders for our reception. **1681** PRIDEAUX *Lett.* (Camden) 99 This day is appointed for his comeing to town, and great preparations are makeing for his reception. **1702** ADDISON *Dial. Medals* Wks. 1721 I. 484 His reception is here recorded on a Medal, in which one of the Ensigns presents him his hand. **1841** ELPHINSTONE *Hist. India* II. 411 Abdullah Sháh was preparing an entertainment for his reception, when he suddenly advanced as an enemy. **1886** *Manch. Exam.* 14 Jan. 4/7 Lord Salisbury has fixed Tuesday next for the reception of a deputation from the Irish Defence Union.

d. An occasion of ceremonious receiving; an assemblage of persons for this purpose. Now usu. a party at which guests are formally greeted, esp. after a wedding.

1865 LD. BROUGHTON *Recoll. Long Life* (1911) VI. ix. 54 On March 5 [1842] I dined at Lord Palmerston's... Lady

Palmerston had a reception afterwards. **1882** M. ARNOLD *Irish Ess.* 113 In a short time there will be held in Paris a reception, as it is called, of.. M. Renan at the French Academy. **1906** *Mrs. Beeton's Bk. Househ. Managem.* 1680 The orthodox wedding breakfast seems likely to become a thing of the past, so much has it been superseded by the tea and reception which usually follow afternoon weddings. **1907** *St. Nicholas* Oct. 1119/1 The 'happy couple'.. will hurry back to Red Feather's house to the reception. **1928** J. SYKES *M. A. Disraeli* 3 Lord Broughton ('Recollections of a Long Life') says it was in Lady Palmerston's day that an evening party at a Minister's house began to be called a reception. **1944** J. LEES-MILNE *Prophesying Peace* (1977) 72 We went together to the Dorchester reception given by the bride's mother. **1965** *Proc. Classical Assoc.* LXII. 35 During the Reception a gavel was presented for the use of the Association by Miss D. J. Wood, Joint Hon. Secretary of the Manchester and District Branch. **1977** *Times* 14 July 16/6 *Receptions...* Lord Grey of Naunton, accompanied by Lady Grey, entertained members of the Royal Over-Seas League at a reception in the House of Lords last night.

e. A place where guests register on arriving at a hotel, etc., or where an organization's clients, etc., are received. Usu. without article and with capital initial.

1917 E. FENWICK *Diary* 13 Nov. in *Elsie Fenwick in Flanders* (1981) 183 The reception was a regular Hades of women and children and men.. all terribly wounded. **1930** E. WAUGH *Vile Bodies* x. 169 'Bless you,' said the woman at the counter marked 'Reception', 'all our rooms have been booked for the last six months.' **1958** 'CASTLE' & 'HAILEY' *Flight into Danger* viii. 107 Those cars.. were promptly waved.. to parking spaces well clear of the entrance to Reception. **1969** D. CLARK *Nobody's Perfect* iii. 110 Not one gets past me or Bert. We hold them in reception, phone up the one they want to see, and make them wait till they're fetched. **1970** G. F. NEWMAN *Sir, You Bastard* v. 148 A sister met him in the reception of the decaying building. **1975** M. DRABBLE *Realms of Gold* IV. 246 Frances had a call from Reception telling her that it would take at least two hours to put a call through to London.

f. Shortened f. ***reception room*** s.v. RECEPTION 10. Cf. RECEP. 1.

1929 *Daily News* 13 Sept. 11/5 Semi-detached Houses... Attractive Elevations... Large hall, 2 reception, 3 bedrooms. **1977** *Evening Post* (Nottingham) 27 Jan. 14/3 (Advt.), An extremely good two double bedroomed semi-detached house with garage, two receptions, kitchen, bathroom, gardens. **1980** *Daily Tel.* 29 July 1/8 The 18th century house has four receptions, nine bedrooms and eight bathrooms.

3. The action of receiving, or taking in, physically or spatially. Also *transf.*

1432–50 tr. *Higden* (Rolls) II. 425 Apuleus rehersethe.. that same thynge to haue happede to hym thro the recepcion of suche venome. **1651** BAXTER *Inf. Bapt.* 319 Some Divines say—That Faith is Physically a Passive Reception of Christ himself. **1659** PEARSON *Creed* (1839) 192 By that connexion of his operations, showing the reception of his essence. **1837** DICKENS *Pickw.* ii, Ready for the reception of any discoveries worthy of being noted down. **1868** FREEMAN *Norm. Conq.* (1876) II. x. 515 Two smaller towers for the reception of the bells were designed.

b. The action of receiving mentally.

1850 MAURICE *Mor. & Met. Philos.* (ed. 2) 180 The absence of a faculty of reception. **1867** SWINBURNE *Ess. & Stud.* (1875) 176 Culture, sanity, power of grasp and reception [etc.].

4. The action of accepting or admitting; acceptance, admittance, approbation.

1660 R. COKE *Justice Vind.* 15 If they had not been the word of God before the Church received them.. their reception and tradition could never have made them so. **1669** CLARENDON *Ess.* Tracts (1727) 97 A virtuous mind appearing with more lustre in the rejection than in the reception of good turns. **1718** ATTERBURY *Serm.* (1734) I. vii. 186 God never intended to compell, but only to persuade us into a Reception of Divine Truth. **1765** BLACKSTONE *Comm.* I. 15 In those of our English courts wherein a reception has been allowed to the civil and canon laws. **1788** PRIESTLEY *Lect. Hist.* II. xii. 101 If.. I shall thus contribute to the more general reception of the great outlines of this system. **1867** FROUDE *Short Stud., Spinoza* (1878) I. 351 We refuse to submit to the demonstrations by which it thrusts itself on our reception.

†**b.** An idea received or accepted without evidence of its truth. *Obs.*

1646 SIR T. BROWNE *Pseud. Ep.* I. vii. 26 Our mature and secondary enquiries are forced to quit those receptions. **1691** SIR T. P. BLOUNT *Ess.* iii. 62 Most Men.. obstinately adhere to those unexamined Receptions.

5. The action of receiving, or fact of being received, in a certain manner; kind or manner of reception. (Usually with qualifying adj.)

a. of persons.

1649 CROMWELL *Let.* 26 Feb. in *Carlyle*, An account of the kind reception, and the many civilities afforded them. **1666** PEPYS *Diary* 20 May, My wife much pleased with the reception she had. **1702** *Lond. Gaz.* No. 3808/7 The Imperial Forces were in so good a Posture, that the French would meet with a warm Reception. **1795** BURKE *Abr. Eng. Hist.* Wks. 1842 II. 537 Baldwin, earl of Flanders, gave him a very kind reception. **1828** SCOTT *F.M. Perth* viii, The discourse turned on the reception which they were to expect from their Provost. **1858** FROUDE *Hist. Eng.* III. xiv. 205 He found in the Netherlands a scarcely more cordial reception than in France.

b. of ideas, proposals, etc.

1647 CLARENDON *Hist. Reb.* III. §149 When it was brought into the House [the bill] found a better reception than was expected. **1718** *Freethinker* No. 17 ¶4 New Opinions at first meet with a cold Reception. **1745** *Col. Rec. Pennsylv.* V. 7 Whatever shall be laid before me for the Welfare of this Province, will meet with a favorable Reception. **1803** *Edin. Rev.* Apr. 236 They only have an interest in.. procuring a good reception for his name. **1849** MACAULAY *Hist. Eng.* iii. I. 372 His inventions, therefore, found no favourable reception.

c. *Theatr.* An ovation granted a popular actor on taking the stage. Cf. RECEP. 2.

1847 F. A. KEMBLE *Let.* 15 Feb. in *Records Later Life* (1882) III. 160, I wish I could avoid my 'reception', as it is called, because any loud sound shakes me from head to foot.

d. The receiving of broadcast signals; the efficiency with which this is done, as regards audibility, picture quality, freedom from interference, etc.

1907 *Rep. Sel. Comm. Radiotelegr. Convention* 129/2 in *Parl. Papers* VIII. 1 Receivers tuned for the reception of waves of such lengths.. can be rendered quite immune from influence by.. longer and more powerful waves. **1923** E. W. MARCHANT *Radio Telegr. & Teleph.* ix. 104 For the long wave-lengths the change in the spacing produces less effect on the efficiency of reception than it does for shorter wave-lengths. **1943** C. L. BOLTZ *Basic Radio* xiii. 203 We are here concerned with the reception of C.W., I.C.W., and amplitude-modulated carriers. **1949** *Radio Times* 15 July 6/3, I expected the television to be perfection, but.. the same excuses everywhere—'Of course, reception isn't so good here because of the electrical appliances in the district.' **1962** [see RECEIVING *vbl. sb.* 2c]. **1968** A. MARIN *Clash of Distant Thunder* (1969) ix. 63 We can get the Television Français... The reception is not very good. **1972** *Times* 21 Sept. (Ireland Suppl.) p. ii, At that time television was only just getting off the ground.. and many areas still did not have reception.

6. The action of receiving or taking, in various applications of the vb.

1863 H. COX *Instit.* I. viii. 123 The parties.. produce evidence, the reception of which is.. regulated by the rules of law. **1898** BESANT *Orange Girl* II. xiv, It is proper to show that you were not an accomplice of the removal and the reception [of the stolen goods] in your house. **1976** *Billings* (Montana) *Gaz.* 16 June 5-c/3 Bell is expected to have a chance at several receptions, with two top passing quarterbacks on hand.

†**7.** Capacity for receiving. *Obs.*

1667 MILTON *P.L.* x. 807 Natures Law, By which all Causes.. To the reception of thir matter act. **1670–98** LASSELS *Voy. Italy* II. 167 This Hospital.. is of great reception. It maintains two thousand sick and decrepid in it.

†**8.** A receptacle, a place of reception. *Obs.*

1646 SIR T. BROWNE *Pseud. Ep.* 172 Ascending first into a capsulary reception of the breast bone. **1696** STANHOPE *Chr. Pattern* (1711) 324 Make me room in thy heart, and let it be a clean and fit reception for so pure a guest.

†**9.** Recovery, recapture. *Obs.*$^{-1}$

1622 BACON *Hen. VII* 44 Hee was right glad of the French Kings reception of those Townes from Maximilian.

10. *Comb.*, as (sense 2 c) ***reception area, camp, -clerk, committee, counter, day, desk, evening, hall, night, room, town***; **reception centre**, a centre for the reception of newcomers or visitors; *spec.* a hostel providing temporary accommodation for the destitute; **reception class**, the lowest class in an infant school, into which children going to school for the first time are admitted; **reception order**, an order authorizing the reception and detention of a person in a lunatic asylum; **reception statute** *U.S. Law*, a statute passed by an American state after Independence providing that the common law of England be received as binding in that state, subject to repeal and local interpretation.

1939 *Times* 2 Nov. 8/7 While anxiety was expressed about the effects of breaking up home life, tributes were paid to householders and others in the *reception areas for their friendly helpfulness. **1971** F. FINLAY *Boy in Prison* vi. 79, I was handed over to one of the Grendon officers, who greeted me pleasantly and took me down an open pathway to the reception area. **1979** *Tucson Mag.* June 40/1 There was.. a wedding performed in an airplane followed by a sky dive to the reception area. **1918** W. OWEN *Let.* 13 Sept. (1967) 576 Write to the 2nd Man., not this *Recep. Camp as I'll be joining about Sunday. **1954** *Encounter* Feb. 39/2 It is when the fugitive succeeds in moving to the reception camps of Western Germany, and.. back into civil life, that his enthusiasm turns to disgust. **1942** *Nation* 27 Apr. 41 Men passing the 'screening test' will be ordered promptly to *reception centers for final examination and induction. **1948** *Act 11 & 12 Geo. VI.* c. 29 §17 It shall be the duty of the [National Assistance] Board to make provision whereby persons without a settled way of living may be influenced to lead a more settled life, and the Board shall provide and maintain centres, to be known as reception centres, for the provision of temporary board and lodging for such persons. **1957** H. ROOSENBURG *Walls came tumbling Down* ix. 199 We were waiting for a truck to take us to a DP reception centre. **1978** C. A. BERRY *Gentleman of Road* ix. 69 Normal folk who live on the other side of the soup enjoy reception centres close to their doors as little as they favour Salvation Army hostels or prisons. **1972** *Where* Jan. 10/1 If a few children in each *reception class could already read well, teachers would be forced to make more flexible arrangements. **1980** *Guardian* 24 June 11/2 Children with problems are very often referred as priority cases to.. reception classes in infants schools. **1934** T. F. TWEED *Blind Mouths* ii. 11 The *reception-clerk, who had been placidly reading his newspaper, dropped it and became suddenly alert. **1981** L. DEIGHTON *XPD* xxvii. 220 [He] walked quickly across to.. the lift... The reception clerk looked up. **1851** W. K. NORTHALL *Before & Behind Curtain* 89 We believe Mr. Marks consulted some members of the *reception-committee. **1920** [see EXTREMIST]. **1960** C. MACINNES *Mr. Love & Justice* 96 If you've got any ideas of seeing a lawyer, or having any sort of reception committee for me, that's up to you. **1978** *Navy News* Oct. 2/1 Among the 'reception committee' were the mayor and treasurer of the town of Ajax, Ontario. **1975** N. LUARD *Robespierre Serial* xv. 133 The hotel manager was behind the *reception counter. **1853** E. TWISLETON *Let.* 16 Jan. (1928) iv. 67 It was Mrs. Crawford's *reception day, and I was struck with her excellent, easy manners. **1884** G. MEREDITH *Let.* 30 May (1970) II. 738, I.. hope to present my respects on one of her reception days. **1896** *Harper's Mag.* Apr. 680/1 By this time Duncan and his friends were frequenting all Madame de Champbaron's reception days. **1936** 'J. TEY' *Shilling for Candles* xxiv. 263 He shot into the darkness of the great lounge and across it to the green light of the *reception desk. **1940** E. GILL *Autobiogr.* vi. 180, I went to the hotel and managed to make myself understood at the Reception Desk. **1978** S. SHELDON *Bloodline* xliii. 363 Alec followed the waiter out of the large dining room into the small office behind the reception desk. **1846** J. K. POLK *Diary of President* (1929) 70 These informal *reception evenings are very pleasant. **1938** D. DU MAURIER *Rebecca* iii. 17 A certain sofa.. midway between the *reception hall and the passage to the restaurant. **1976** *Washington Post* 19 Apr. C17/6 (Advt.), First floor has a very large reception hall, spacious living room [etc.]. **1848** S. THORNE *Jrnl. Boy's Trip* (1936) 30 To night being *reception night I went to see the President and his lady again. **1890** *Act 53 Vict.* c. 5 §4 Received and detained as a lunatic.. under a *reception order made by the judicial authority. **1899** *Allbutt's Syst. Med.* VIII. 430 The Reception Order of a justice is sufficient authority to take the patient to, and to receive him in an asylum, or to detain him there if he has already been removed on an Urgency Order. **1829** LYTTON *Devereux* II. v, Such was the *reception-room of Beau Fielding. **1846** S. S. MAGOFFIN *Diary* 7 Aug. in S. M. Drumm *Down Santa Fé Trail* (1926) 70 My dirt-floored chamber, dining-room, parlour, reception room &c. &c. *is* quite dessolate. **1880** G. MEREDITH *Tragic Com.* (1881) 8 He was in her father's reception-room when she reached home. **1906** C. H. B. QUENNELL *Mod. Suburban Houses* p. vii, The accommodation generally required is the three usual reception rooms—sometimes Drawing and Dining Rooms will suffice with what is known to the House Agent as the Sitting Hall in addition. **1961** *Times* 18 Oct. 20/2 More often than not, reception-room heating is inadequate. **1931** *Columbia Law Rev.* XXXI. 416 The so-called *reception statutes vary in form, in the date chosen as a deadline, and as to the implications of the extent of reception. **1956** E. H. POLLACK *Fundamentals of Legal Research* i. 10 The 'reception' statutes, enacted by most American states in the eighteenth and nineteenth centuries, gave special recognition to the English common law and statutes.. as of 1607, the date of the earliest English settlement at Jamestown. **1976** J. K. LIEBERMAN *Milestones!* i. 19 Reception statutes did not freeze into place the particulars of the common law of England... What was received.. was the *process* of the common law.. not the particular results that English judges had reached. **1958** *Times Rev. Industry* Feb. 24/1 Some 70,000 people are to be 'overspilled' from Glasgow City over the next 10 to 15 years into the new towns.. and other *reception towns.

Hence **re'ceptionism** (see quot. 1900); **re'ceptionist**, (*a*) a believer in receptionism; (*b*) a person employed by a hotel, medical surgery, or other organization, to receive clients, etc. (cf. RECEPTION 2 e.)

1867 COBB *Kiss of Peace* 4 We must.. give this opinion a name. Let us call it the 'Theory of Reception', and its professors 'Receptionists'. **1900** D. STONE *Outl. Chr. Dogma* xi. 191 Receptionism is the view that the bread and wine remain only bread and wine after consecration; but that, together with them, the faithful communicant really receives the body and blood of Christ. **1901** *Girl's Own Paper* 12 Jan. 234/1 She answered an advertisement of a Kensington photographer who needed a 'receptionist' and saleswoman—shop-woman in fact. **1927** *Daily Express* 19 Feb. 2/4 An operation which she underwent.. for the purpose of advertising the [plastic surgery] business, and on condition that she would continue to be employed as secretary and receptionist. **1932** D. L. SAYERS *Have his Carcase* iii. 41 'Ai'm afraid,' said the receptionist.. 'that all our rooms are engaged.' **1956** *Times* 21 Jan. 7/5 Such a qualification would ensure that the secretary.. could, in her employer's absence, conduct responsible interviews on his behalf, as opposed to receptionist duties. **1960** M. SPARK *Bachelors* vii. 99 Dr Lyte sat in his consulting room after the last of the evening surgery had departed and his receptionist had locked up and gone home. **1976** B. BOVA *Multiple Man* (1977) vi. 66 The reception lobby was equally quiet... A curved desk with all the paraphernalia of a busy receptionist... But no people.

receptitious (riːsɛpˈtɪʃəs), *a.* Also 9 -icious. [ad. L. *receptitius* or *-icius*: see RECEIPT and -ITIOUS[1].] *Roman Law.* (See quots.)

1656 BLOUNT *Glossogr.*, *Receptitious*, that is received, kept, or reserved to ones use from another. **1727–41** CHAMBERS *Cycl.* s.v. *Goods*, Receptitious goods were those which the wife might reserve the full property of to herself, and enjoy them independently of her husband. **1880** MUIRHEAD *Ulpian* vi. §5 An adventicious dowry always remains with the husband, unless the person who gave it have expressly stipulated that it shall be returned to him; such a dowry is called specifically recepticious.

receptive (rɪˈsɛptɪv), *a.* [ad. med.L. *receptīvus*: see RECEIPT and -IVE, and cf. obs. F. *receptif*.]

1. Having the quality of, or capacity for, receiving; able to receive; pertaining to, of the nature of, reception. (Common in 17th and 19th c.; in later use esp. of the mind, or of persons in respect of it, or of sensory processes in an organism.)

1547 BOORDE *Brev. Health* Pref. 4 Chierurgyons must knowe.. what synges.. be receptyve [*printed* recentyve], what signes be expulcive. **1594** HOOKER *Eccl. Pol.* I. xi. §3 The soul.. shall, as it is receptive, be.. perfected with those supernatural passions of joy, peace, and delight. **1656** BRAMHALL *Replic.* iv. 160 That receptive Power.. to admit or not admit such new Laws. *a* **1677** HALE *Prim. Orig. Man.* I. iii. 89 The Earth and Sun..; the one active, piercing,.. the other passive, receptive. **1817** COLERIDGE *Biog. Lit.* I. v. 95 The passive sense, or what the school-men call the merely receptive. **1836–41** BRANDE *Chem.* (ed. 5) 210 The receptive and transmitting powers of bodies in regard to radiant heat. **1875** WHITNEY *Life Lang.* ii. 30 The passive receptive work of the mind. **1906** C. S. SHERRINGTON *Integrative Action of Nerv. Syst.* iii. 90 The flexion-reflex has a 'receptive skin-field' which though extensive is characteristic for it. **1934** A. FORBES in C. Murchison *Handbk. Exper. Psychol.* iii. 175 When the receptive substance is excitatory the combination causes contraction of the muscle cell. **1975** M. & N. SAMUELS *Seeing with Mind's Eye* xi. 152 Receptive visualization provides us with the means for getting in touch with images from our inner center.

b. Const. *of*.

1641 'SMECTYMNUUS' *Answ.* xviii. (1653) 74 A heaven that hath a broad way leading thither, and is receptive of Drunkards. **1727** DE FOE *Syst. Magic.* II. i. (1840) 234 The heart of man became receptive of wickedness. **1825** COLERIDGE *Aids Refl.* (1848) I. 90 We are to answer every one that inquires a reason..which supposes something receptive of it. **1875** JOWETT *Plato* (ed. 2) V. 291, I should wish the citizens to be as receptive of virtue as possible.

c. *Med.* and *Psychol.* Affecting or relating to the comprehension of speech or writing, esp. as impaired by a brain disorder.

1926 H. HEAD *Aphasia* I. II. iii. 204 Closer observation showed that the 'receptive' aspect of her use of language had not in reality escaped. *Ibid.* 207 These defects..are entirely inexplicable on any theory..of separate loss of the 'emissive' and 'receptive', 'motor' and 'sensory' functions, which are supposed to accompany speech. **1955** R. JAKOBSON in Saporta & Bastian *Psycholinguistics* (1961) 423/2 The classical distinction between the so-called emissive (or expressive) aphasia on the one hand, and the receptive (or sensory) aphasia on the other. **1963** OSGOOD & MIRON *Approaches to Study of Aphasia* iii. 60 Patients displaying breakdown..in the comprehension of speech and word meanings, but without impairment of hearing per se (i.e., the classical 'sensory' or 'receptive' aphasia), are most likely to have lesions in the left temporal zone. **1961** R. BRAIN *Speech Disorders* vii. 93 Central aphasia is characterized by both receptive and expressive disturbance. **1973** J. W. BROWN *Pick's Aphasia* p. xi, With regard to 'receptive' disturbances, Pick assumed a complementary mental structure underlying the transition of heard sound to thought. **1977** W. H. PERKINS *Speech Path.* (rev. ed.) v. 132/2 By the same token, receptive aphasia, sensory aphasia, posterior aphasia, and fluent aphasia identify essentially the same language disorder as Wernicke's aphasia, or pragmatic aphasia. *Ibid.* xv. 341 The North-western Syntax Screening Test..of receptive and expressive grammatical ability has become available.

2. *spec.* †**a.** ***receptive measures***, measures of capacity. *Obs.*

1680 MORDEN *Geog. Rect., Coin* (1685) 281 Receptive Measures are two-fold. First of liquid or moist things; Secondly of dry things. **1727** W. MATHER *Yng. Man's Comp.* 197 Of Receptive Measure, that is, Things Measured inwardly.

b. ***receptive spot***, the spot in an oosphere at which the male gamete is admitted.

1875 BENNETT & DYER tr. *Sachs' Bot.* 344 The entrance takes place at a lighter spot of the oosphere facing the neck, which is termed the Receptive Spot.

Hence **re'ceptively** *adv.*

1881 W. SPOTTISWOODE in *Nature* No. 624. 570 We can cause the discharge to be from one terminal only, the other terminal acting merely receptively.

receptiveness (rɪˈsɛptɪvnɪs). [f. prec. + -NESS.] Receptivity. (Common in recent use.)

1681 FLAVEL *Meth. Grace* v. 104 There is found in us a capacity, aptness, or receptiveness, of this principle of life. **1701** NORRIS *Ideal World* I. i. 79 From the receptiveness of first matter he concludes the real and actual existence of it. **1858** GLADSTONE *Homer* II. 8 The retentiveness of that people equalled its receptiveness. **1874** BLACKIE *Self-Cult.* 85 A young man..with a reverential receptiveness and a delicate sensibility.

receptivity (riːsɛpˈtɪvɪtɪ). [f. as prec. + -ITY.] The quality of being receptive; ability or readiness to receive or take in. (Common in 19th c., esp. with ref. to the mind.) Also, in the philosophy of Kant, a passive quality contrasted with spontaneity or activity.

a **1619** FOTHERBY *Atheom.* II. i. §6 (1622) 181 Hee cannot worke any where beyond the possibilitie or receptiuitie of his matter. **1686** GOAD *Celest. Bodies* I. iii. 11 The Air being of a thin Body..is of an easie receptivity for all sorts of Impressions. **1796** F. A. NITSCH *View of Kant's Princ.* 74 That a given variety can occur in our perceptions, knowledge, &c. supposes a..Receptivity which is totally Passive. *Ibid.* 75 The Receptivity, as far as it receives varieties of the first description, may be called external sense, and as far as it receives varieties of the second description, internal sense. **1798** W. TAYLOR in *Monthly Rev.* XXV. 585 His receptivity for aesthetic gratification [is] not delicate. **1837** *Fraser's Mag.* XV. 728 They are here receptivities, or moulds of matter. **1886** G. ALLEN *Darwin* x. 175 He had the sympathetic receptivity of all truly great minds. **1950** M. PEAKE *Gormenghast* xxiv. 159 This poem..shall be addressed to as many as are here present in all the variance of their receptivity, status and acumen. **1956** C. MORRIS *Var. of Human Nature* i. 17 Receptivity should be the keynote of life. *Ibid.* ix. 191 In Factor D receptivity is directed toward nature, toward the man-cosmos relation, or to the needs of other persons. **1958** B. BERNSTEIN in J. A. Fishman *Readings in Sociol. of Lang.* (1968) 234 It is now necessary to show how this mode of perceiving and the attendant structuring of receptivity conflicts with and induces a resistance to formal education. **1973** CHURCHILL & AMERIKS tr. *Husserl's Experience & Judgment* I. i. 79 This phenomenologically necessary concept of receptivity is in no way exclusively opposed to that of the activity of the ego. **1974** A. E. BLUMBERG tr. *Schlick's Gen. Theory of Knowl.* iii. §40. 371 The introduction of the antithesis between spontaneity and receptivity—in modern terms, between activity and passivity—is entirely inappropriate at this point.

†**re'ceptment.** *Obs.*$^{-1}$ [= AF. *receptment*, var. *recettement* RESETMENT.] The act or practice of harbouring criminals.

1620 J. WILKINSON *Coroners & Sherifes* 28 Men have used ..to outlaw the people appealed of commandement, force, aide, and receptment.

receptor (rɪˈsɛptə(r)). Also 5–6 -our(e. [a. OF. *receptour*, *-eur*, or L. *receptor*, agent-n. f. *recipĕre* to RECEIVE.]

†**1.** = RECEIPTER 1, RESETTER. *Obs.*

c **1440** *Jacob's Well* 30 Ony heretykes..or here receptourys, defenderys, or fauouerrys. **1472** *Surtees Misc.* (1888) 25 Robert Mascald..is a receptour of suspect persones. **1585** FLEETWOOD in Ellis *Orig. Lett.* Ser. I. II. 297 The searching out of sundrye that were receptors of ffelons. **1609** [BP. W. BARLOW] *Answ. Nameless Cath.* 13 The kind Receptors of the Fugitiues after the Detection. **1660** *Virginia Stat.* (1823) I. 538 Against pyrats, their assistors or abettors,..or receptors.

2. A telephonic receiver.

1898 *Westm. Gaz.* 17 Feb. 1/3 In the hospital..each Roman Catholic patient has a receptor connected with the cathedral at the head of his bed on Sunday.

3. a. *Med.* The region of an antibody molecule which shows specific recognition of an antigen. Also *attrib.* and *Comb.*, as ***receptor group***; ***receptor-destroying*** adj. [The sense is due to P. Ehrlich, who coined the G. *receptor* (*Berlin klin. Wochenschr.* (1900) 21 May 453/2).]

Ehrlich's theory of receptors originally took a broader form than that in which it is now accepted; hence in the first part of this century there was some overlap between this sense and sense c below.

1900 *Lancet* 18 Aug. 528/1 The fixation..of the Toxin molecule in the protoplasm was accomplished by means of certain lateral chains which the latter possessed and which were termed 'receptors'. **1903** J. COATS *Man. Path.* (ed. 5) 151 By careful and increasing dosage the protoplasm of the cell may be gradually stimulated to form more and more receptor groups. **1935** F. P. GAY *Agents of Dis. & Host Resistance* xix. 377 The entire receptor hypothesis of Ehrlich rests on a purely imaginary misconception... There is no particular objection in referring to this absorption as due to certain chemical units that one may call the 'receptors' of the susceptible cell... It is another matter to assume..that the hypothetical receptors.., when injured or destroyed, are reproduced in excess and poured into the blood stream as specific antibodies to those foreign incitants that have engendered their production. **1941** KOLMER & TUFT *Clin. Immunol. Biotherapy & Chemotherapy* iii. 63 This [*sc.* Ehrlich's side-chain theory] is now regarded as untenable because of the physiologic improbability that there can exist a sufficient number of specific receptors for an innumerable number of antigens. **1951** WHITBY & HYNES *Med. Bacteriol.* (ed. 5) xii. 221 The enzyme is best known..as the receptor-destroying enzyme (RDE) which has helped to elucidate the phenomenon of hæmagglutination by viruses of the mumps—influenza group. **1967** *Cold Spring Harbor Symp. Quantitative Biol.* XXXII. 431/1 We assume first that nothing except antibody recognizes antigen, and we must therefore assume that the receptor for antigen is antibody already present at a site, in or on the cell, prior to exposure to antigen. **1970** FENNER & WHITE *Med. Virol.* iii. 45 The importance of glycoprotein receptors for the attachment of influenza virus has been demonstrated in experiments in which they have been destroyed by bacterial neuraminidase ('receptor-destroying enzyme'). **1973** *Sci. Amer.* June 82/3 The essential initial step in the immune response is the contact of an antigen—a foreign substance—with receptors on the surfaces of lymphocytes derived from the bone marrow, the so-called *B*-lymphocytes.

b. *Biol.* Any organ or structure which on receiving stimuli of a certain kind from its environment generates nerve impulses that convey information about that aspect of the environment. Freq. *attrib.*

1906, etc. [see EFFECTOR 2]. **1906** C. S. SHERRINGTON *Integrative Action Nerv. Syst.* i. 13 Electrical stimuli applied to receptor organs are..efficient excitors of reflexes. *Ibid.* ix. 309 The branching at the receptive end places it in communication not with one but with several receptor cells. **1919** W. M. BAYLISS *Introd. Gen. Physiol.* ix. 112 The eye may be said to be the most accurately adjusted of all our receptor organs. **1920** T. P. NUNN *Education* xiii. 170 To pick out and distinguish the different elements and qualities of which the world is composed..is more possible for higher animals by the enormous development of the receptor-system. **1934** *Nature* 22 Sept. 445/1 Normal vision may be due to a receptor which gives rise to a red sensation, one which gives rise to a blue sensation and one which gives rise to a not blue, not red sensation which, of course, corresponds to a green sensation. **1962** *Listener* 8 Nov. 779/2 The use of the eye instead of the ear as the principal receptor for information probably has produced some consistent concomitant psychological changes. **1971** *Jrnl. Gen. Psychol.* LXXXV. 87 Reason..has proposed that susceptible persons are more highly receptive to incoming stimuli, and that this receptivity is global rather than being confined to one receptor system alone. **1974** D. & M. WEBSTER *Compar. Vertebr. Morphol.* x. 197 A blow on the head mechanically stimulates the eye's receptor cells. **1975** *Sci. Amer.* July 108/2 There are other receptors on the antennae of mosquitoes that respond to chemical stimuli.

c. *Physiol.* A region of a neurone or other tissue which specifically recognizes and responds to a neurotransmitter, hormone, or other substance. Freq. *attrib.*

1912 E. H. STARLING *Princ. Human Physiol.* vi. 312 The existence of..a 'receptor' substance, as he calls it, has been furnished by Langley. *Ibid.* 314 Receptor substances may act as intermediaries in every case of propagation of an impluse across a synapse of whatever description. **1939** M. A. GOLDZIEHER *Endocrine Glands* ii. 7 The organotropic hormones of the pituitary..are supposed to act upon the cells of the individual endocrine glands which constitute their receptor organs. **1955** *Biochim. & Biophys. Acta* XVI. 268 The picture which has emerged, assumes that acetycholine is stored in an inactive bound form. Stimulation releases the ester which combines with a receptor protein. **1961** R. D. BAKER *Essent. Path.* iii. 38 Materials from the infarct stimulate the bone marrow and cause leukocytosis, and their influence on central nervous system receptors may cause fever. **1973** *Nature* 20 Apr. 497/2 Receptors can be defined as components of a tissue which specifically react with a drug or hormone. *Ibid.*, The meaning of 'receptor' is becoming very diffuse and a clearer definition of the word is necessary. **1975** *N.Y. Times* 27 Mar. 9/1 The test shows whether the tumor cells contain receptors, or 'landing sites', for estrogen molecules, which are then taken into the cells and stimulate their growth.

†**re'ceptory,** *sb. Obs.* [ad. late L. *receptōrium*, neut. of *receptōrius*: see next, and cf. obs. F. *receptoire*.] A receptacle.

1533 ELYOT *Cast. Helthe* (1541) 51 b, The humours.. fylleth and extendeth the receptories of the bodye, as the stomacke, the vaynes, and bowelles. **1563** T. GALE *Antidot.* II. 68 Put these in a Glasse styll wyth his receptorye well luted. **1601** HOLLAND *Pliny* II. 222 A paile or trey made of kids or goats leather for a receptory. **1678** *Phil. Trans.* XII. 1053 A Current that turneth the Liquor into a Receptory, from whence it is pumped into another Pit or Mine. **1727** A. HAMILTON *New Acc. E. Ind.* I. xxiii. 282 Those three Rivers ..disembogue at one Mouth into the common Receptory of Rivers.

†**re'ceptory,** *a.* [ad. late L. *receptōri-us*: see RECEIPT and -ORY, and cf. F. *receptoire* (16th c.).] Pertaining to reception; receptive.

1633 T. ADAMS *Exp. 2 Peter* i. 17 You see, the form of the words is receptory, He received. **1651** BIGGS *New Disp.* ℙ 170 Dam up the receptory vessels.

receptual (rɪˈsɛptjuːəl), *a.* [f. L. *receptu-s* + -AL[1]; in mod. use after *conceptual*.]

†**1.** Capable of receiving or taking in other substances. *Obs.*$^{-1}$

1477 NORTON *Ord. Alch.* xxxii. in Ashm. (1652) 198 And soe after the Colour of that Erth ys Sulphuri and receptuall, Some men do say ys engendered every Mettall.

2. Of the nature of, pertaining to, a (mental) recept or recepts. Hence **re'ceptually** *adv.*

1888 ROMANES *Mental Evol. Man* ii. 41 *note*, The term apperception as used by some German psychologists is also inclusive of what I mean by receptual ideation. *Ibid.* iii. 58 The animal is able to distinguish receptually between the numbers 1, 2, 3, 4, 5.

‖**recercelé(e** (rɪsəsəˈleɪ, ‖rəsɛrsle). *Her.* [a. OF. *recercelé*, *-lée* circular, curled, pa. pple. of *recerceler*, f. *re-* RE- + *cercel* a circle.] Of a cross: Having the ends of the arms curling into divergent spirals.

1766 PORNY *Heraldry* (1777) Dict., *Recercelée*..is said of a Cross that circles or curls at the ends, very much resembling a Rams horn. **1864** BOUTELL *Her. Hist. & Pop.* xv. (ed. 3) 218 A chesuble charged with his *cross recercelée*. **1868** CUSSANS *Her.* (1893) 62 The Cross Recercelé resembles a Cross Moline with its floriations more expanded.

recerve, obs. form of RESERVE.

recess (rɪˈsɛs, ˈriːsɛs), *sb.* [ad. L. *recess-us*, f. *recēdĕre* to RECEDE; cf. It. *recesso* (Florio).]

†**1.** The act of retiring, withdrawing, or departing (from or to a place); withdrawal, departure. *Obs.* (Common in 16–17th c., freq. in phr. ***access and recess***.)

1531 *St. Papers Hen. VIII*, IV. 576 Ye write unto Us of the recesse ande departing of our and your Commissioners. **1538** CROMWELL *Let.* 13 July in Merriman *Life & Lett.* (1902) II. 147 He may haue free accesse and recesse from tyme to tyme. **1608** TOPSELL *Serpents* (1658) 782 They have easie accesse and recesse to and fro to their beguiling nets. **1660** BOYLE *New Exp. Phys. Mech.* xxviii. 216 The sudden recess of the Air made the bubbles..appear..numerous. **1692** WAGSTAFFE *Vind. Carol.* v. 58 Not only Petition the King,..but upon his recess from Whitehall, send him a Peremptory Petition.

transf. **1536** in Burnet *Hist. Ref., Coll. Records* No. 52 Hen. VIII, His Recesse from the Church, ye proffe not otherwise, than by the..Comon Opinion of those Parts.

†**2. a.** The (*or* an) act of retirement from public life or into privacy; the fact of living retired or in a private manner; a period of retirement. *Obs.*

1645 EVEYLN *Diary* 31 Jan., Famous for the debauched recesses of Tiberius. **1654** H. L'ESTRANGE *Chas. I* (1655) 135 Long lived he in that retirement..yet was not his re-cesse in-glorious. **1700** DRYDEN *Fables* Ded. 163 The soft recesses of your hours improve The three fair pledges of your happy love. **1762** *Ann. Reg.* II. 2 His indispositions and other reasons made him determine entirely to quit the court: During his recess, however he lost nothing of his..respect for the king.

†**b.** Without article: Retirement, seclusion, privacy. *Obs.*

1645 EVELYN *Diary* 6 May, Faire Parks or Gardens.. being onely places of recesse and pleasure. **1709** PRIOR *Chloe Hunting* 16 Ev'ry neighbouring Grove Sacred to soft Recess and gentle Love. **1768** *Woman of Honor* II. 208, I had chosen..my Aunt Clifford's..there to remain in recess for some time.

3. a. The act of retiring for a time from some occupation; a period of cessation from usual work or employment. Chiefly *N. Amer.* exc. in Parliamentary use.

In early use chiefly of Parliament, later also of schools.

1620 *Jrnls. House of Lords* 22 Mar. 61/1 They [*sc.* the Commons] humbly desire to know the Time of the Recess of this Parliament, and of the Access again, as they may accordingly depart and meet again at the same Time their Lord-ships shall. **1642** Sir E. Dering *Sp. on Relig.* x. 35 Since the late Recesse, some endeavours of mine have been reported more distastive then before. *a* **1671** Ld. Fairfax *Mem.* (1699) 22 In this recess of action, we had several treaties about prisoners. **1706** *Royal Sp.* 16 Feb. in *Lond. Gaz.* No. 4202/1 It will be convenient to make a Recess in some short Time. **1797** Mrs. A. M. Bennett *Beggar Girl* (1813) I. 210 Every recess of the school they passed at Mushroom Place. **1851** K. Quentin *Reisebilder & Studien* II. 58 Um 12 Uhr verliess ich mit den Kindern die Schule. Sie haben eine Pause (Recess) von einer Stunde. **1860** O. W. Holmes *Elsie V.* xxvi. (1891) 394 In the recess, as it was called, or interval of suspended studies in the middle of the forenoon. *c* **1860** E. Dickinson *Poems* (1955) I. 117 Whose Beryl Egg, what School Boys hunt In 'Recess'—Overhead! **1881** Gladstone in *Times* 8 Oct. 6/3 We are in a Parliamentary recess, but the leaders of the Tories do not appear to have had any recess at all. **1913** A. Huxley *Let.* 3 Feb. (1969) 47, I had a very good vacation, or do you call it Ree-cess?, as one (female) American asked me. **1942** *Amer. Mercury* July 91 Must be a recess in Heaven—pretty angel like that out on the ground. **1951** E. Paul *Springtime in Paris* ii. 27, I could not possibly hope to reach the cage before the bank closed at 12 o'clock noon, for the two-hour lunch recess. **1975** *Weekend Mag.* (Montreal) 1 Nov. 22/1, I watched him carefully as he won game after game at recess one day.

†**b.** Without article: Cessation from work, relaxation, leisure. *Obs.*

1711 Shaftesb. *Charac.* (1737) II. ii. ii. ii. 159 A Love of moderate Recess and Rest from Action. **1781** Cowper *Retirem.* 215 His hours of leisure and recess employs In drawing pictures of forbidden joys.

†**4.** Delay; respite. *Obs. rare.*

1622 J. Reynolds *God's Revenge* ii. vi. 4 After the protraction and recesse of a yeeres time, Victoryna consenteth to Sypontus to be his wife. **1706** De Foe *Jure Div.* x. 229 The small Recess the weary Land obtain'd So little Breath to rising Freedom gave.

5. a. A place of retirement, a remote and secluded spot, a secret or private place.

1636 G. Sandys *Paraphr. Ps.* cxxxiv. (1648) 205 Your hands devoutly raise To his divine Recesse. **1698** Fryer *Acc. E. India & P.* 199 Airy and cool Choultries, private Recesses for their Women. **1784** R. Bage *Barham Downs* II. 250 A woman..who had been housekeeper at Lord Winterbottom's recess. **1831** Lamb *Elia* Ser. ii. *Ellistoniana*, The last retreat, and recess, of his every-day waning grandeur.

†**b.** A dark resource, a secret. *Obs. rare.*

1646 J. Gregory *Notes & Obs.* (1650) 6 To cast out Devills (by a knowne Recesse of the blacke Art) through him that is the Prince. **1649** Jer. Taylor *Gt. Exemp.* Ad. Sect. iv. 52 Magnifying the recesses of his Counsell and Wisdome and Predestination.

6. a. The act of receding, of going back or away, from a certain point. (Used chiefly of the motion of things, and *esp.* of water, the sea, or the heavenly bodies.)

1607 J. Norden *Surv. Dial.* i. 19 Alwayes at the waters recesse, euery man could finde out his owne land by the plot. **1653** Gataker *Vind. Annot. Jer.* 157 The accesse or recesse of the Sun unto and from several parts of the world. **1728** Pemberton *Newton's Philos.* 202 As the earth in its recess from the sun recovers by degrees its former power. **1756** Burke *Subl. & B.* iv. xvi, As we recede from light..the pupil is enlarged by the retiring of the iris, in proportion to our recess. **1818** G. S. Faber *Horæ Mosaicæ* I. 266 It is at present dry, in consequence of the gradual recess of the waters. **1834** Mrs. Somerville *Connex. Phys. Sc.* iii. (1849) 19 An alternate recess and advance of the apsides.

b. *transf.* or *fig.* of immaterial things.

1620 T. Granger *Div. Logike* 109 It is the defect, and recesse of the opposite facultie. **1646** Earl Monm. tr. *Biondi's Civil Warres* vi. 60 Leaving her in the recesse of her Fortune. **1722** De Foe *Hist. Plague* (1756) 235 The principal Recess of this Infection..was from February to April. **1782** Jefferson *Notes on Virginia* (1787) 132 The access of frost in the autumn, and its recess in the spring. **1843** J. Martineau *Chr. Life* xliii. (1876) 506 Painting the access and recess of his thought.

7. *transf.* or *fig.* (from senses 1 and 6).

†**a.** A dislike or disgust *to* a thing. *Obs.*⁻¹

1567 Maplet *Gr. Forest* 26 It becommeth to haue an appitite to that which it holdeth good and pleasant, and a recesse or lothsomnesse to yᵗ which maketh against it.

†**b.** A drawing back (*from* a promise). *Obs.*

1601 J. Wheeler *Treat. Comm.* 96 Queene Marie by the way of Recesse..reuoked this Decree, and restored the Hanses to their former priuiledges. **1628** Feltham *Resolves* ii. xlii. 125 Some..admit of an absolute recesse from a word already passed.

†**c.** A departure *from* some state or standard. *Obs.* (Common in 17th c.)

1605 Bacon *Adv. Learn.* ii. vii. §5 Men..have made too untimely a departure, and too remote a recess from particulars. **1661** Lovell *Hist. Anim. & Min.* 430 Recesses of the parts of mans body, from the natural state. **1692** Beverly *Disc. Dr. Crisp* 7 Every Sin..is a Recess from the Holiness of God.

†**d.** A falling back; decline. *Obs.*

a **1635** Naunton *Fragm. Reg.* (Arb.) 55 Others,..when he was in the right course of recovery, and setling to moderation, would not suffer a recesse in him. **1659** J. Harrington *Lawgiving* iii. iv. (1700) 456 This Standard in a well founded Monarchy, must bar recess; and in a well founded Commonwealth must bar increase.

8. a. A retired or inner place or part; one of the remotest or innermost parts or corners of anything.

1616 Bullokar *Eng. Expos.*, *Recesse*, a bye-place. **1673** Ray *Journ. Low C.* 224 Gentlemens houses..having more in the recess than they promise in the front. **1697** Dryden *Virg. Georg.* iv. 604 Within a Mountain's hollow Womb, there lyes A large Recess, conceal'd from Human Eyes. **1797** Mrs. Radcliffe *Italian* vi, To carry torches into every recess of the ruin. **1801** Strutt *Sports & Past.* Introd. 4 A pursuit..only requisite in the gloomy recesses of the cloister. **1871** L. Stephen *Playgr. Eur.* (1894) iv. 89 The little village..lies..deep in the recesses of the Pennine chain.

b. *fig.* especially of the soul or heart.

1688 South *Serm.* (1727) II. 301 Sorrow..must force, and make its way into the very inmost Corners, and Recesses of the Soul. **1715–20** Pope *Iliad* i. 711 The thoughts that roll Deep in the close recesses of my soul. **1814** Cary *Dante, Inf.* i. 18 The fear, That in my heart's recesses deep had lain. **1840** Mill *Diss. & Disc.* (1875) I. 408 The question lies..in the recesses of psychology.

9. a. A receding part or indentation in the line of some natural feature or object, as a coast, range of hills, etc.

1697 Dryden *Æneid* i. 228 Within a long Recess there lies a Bay. **1781** Cowper *Truth* 79 His dwelling a recess in some rude rock. **1838** *Murray's Hand-bk. N. Germ.* 273 Every projection on the one side of it [a valley] corresponds with a bay or recess on the other. **1846** McCulloch *Acc. Brit. Empire* (1854) I. 242 The recesses between the hills are mostly filled with gentlemen's seats.

b. *spec.* A receding part or space breaking the continuity of a wall; a niche or alcove.

1774 *Act 14 Geo. III*, c. 78 §28 It shall also be lawful to cut perpendicular Recesses into any Party-wall. **1826** Scott *Woodst.* iii, The recesses within them [oriel windows] were raised a step or two from the wall. **1840** Dickens *Barn. Rudge* xlviii, They sat down in one of the recesses on the bridge, to rest. **1875** Mrs. Ritchie *Miss Angel* x. 90 The gallery was evidently used as a..sitting room. There was a spinnet in a recess.

c. Any small depression or indentation; also *Anat.* a sinus or fold in an organ or part.

1839 Lindley *Introd. Bot.* i. ii. (ed. 3) 135 Leaves..divided more or less deeply into lobes, which leave void spaces between them, which we call recesses (*sinus*). **1897** *Syd. Soc. Lex.* s.v. *Recessus*, A recess or fold between the duodenum and jejunum. **1902** Marshall *Metal Tools* 49 The cutting edges..on either side of the pin produce the required recess as the drill is fed down.

†**d.** A cesspool. *Obs.*⁻¹

1764 *Museum Rust.* II. 73, I..have in my yard, what you usually see in most farmers yards, two recesses or pools, as reservoirs of dung and water.

e. *Criminals' slang.* The lavatory in a prison. Usu. *pl.*

1950 P. Tempest *Lag's Lexicon* 177 *Recess*, the lavatory and urinal, which are generally situated in a recess (two cells knocked into one). **1958** F. Norman *Bang to Rights* iii. 103 The recesses are give [*sic*] a good clean out. **1974** *Observer* (Colour Suppl.) 10 Feb. 17/1 Locked in their cells [*sc.* in Winson Green Prison, Birmingham] at 5.30., with one opening later to go to the recesses (lavatories) and to have a hot drink.

f. = *recess printing* below.

1971 D. Potter *Brit. Eliz. Stamps* iii. 36 This different-size stamp, printed by recess, interrupted the unity of the set.

10. †**a.** ? An agreement or convention. *Obs.*⁻¹

1516 *Inv. R. Wardr.* (1815) 22 Efter the forme and tenor of the recesse maid be ambaxiatouris of this realme, and procuratouris and commissionaris of Ingland thairapoun.

b. *Hist.* A resolution, decree, or act of the Imperial Diet of Germany or of the Diet of the Hanseatic League.

After med.L. *recessus* (see Du Cange); so F. *recez*.

1706 tr. *Dupin's Eccl. Hist. 16th C.* II. iii. xi. 149 The Recess was published: It contained the following Articles. [*note.* What we call an Act of Parliament in England is called a Recess in Germany.] **1779** *Hist. Mod. Europe* II. lix. 254 The famous Recess of Augsburgh, which is the basis of religious peace in Germany. **1882–3** Schaff *Encycl. Relig. Knowl.* I. 638 When the three colleges [of a diet] agreed, the decree, or recess as it was called, was submitted to the imperial sanction.

†**c.** (See quot.) *Obs. rare.*

1726 Ayliffe *Parergon* 275 In the Imperial Chamber the Prætors have half a Florin..for every substantial Recess, as they call it. *Ibid.*, The substantial Recesses are the Introduction of the Cause, the exhibiting of the Libel [etc.].

11. *attrib.* and *Comb.*, as (sense 3) *recess time*; (sense 9 b, 9 c) *recess decoration, plate, shop*; **recess printing**, a method of printing used in the production of postage stamps (see quot. 1951); hence **recess-print** *v.* (usu. as pa. pple.).

1851 Ruskin *Stones Ven.* I. xxiv. §11 *Recess decoration by leaf mouldings. **1874** Thearle *Naval Archit.* 88 The armour shelf or *recess plate is a part of the longitudinal framing of the ship. **1930** *Times Educ. Suppl.* 26 July p. iv/1 All [stamps] are *recess-printed in designs appropriate to the occasion. **1976** *Times* 30 Aug. 6/7 The first issue, containing a finely drawn head of Queen Victoria..and recess printed by Bradbury Wilkinson. **1914** A. B. Creeke *Stamp-Collecting* iii. 66 **Recess-printing.* The design is cut into the plate, and the ink stands up slightly on the stamp. **1951** R. J. Sutton *Stamp Collector's Encycl.* 190 Recess Printing: Strictly speaking, any process where the inked image is below the plane surface of the plate, cliché, block or cylinder; but in modern philatelic parlance refers to the present-day machine-printed, photo-mechanically engraved plate method of reproduction, which in its essentials is similar to the line-engraving by which most of the first and early stamps were printed. A 'recess' printed stamp has a distinct raised image. **1828** *Lights & Shades* II. 170 We hurried into one of the little *recess shops [on Brighton Pier] to avoid them. **1869** Mrs. Stowe *Oldtown Folks* xxxiii. 431 At *recess-time she strolled out with me into the pine woods back of the school-house. **1885** Miss S. O. Jewett *Marsh Island* xii, The boarder had..treated the children to apples at recess-time. **1946** G. Wilson *Fidelity Folks* iii. 84 A half dozen biscuits soaked in it ought to keep starvation away until recess time.

†**re'cess**, *v.*¹ *Obs.*⁻¹ [f. L. *recess-um*, pa. pple. of *recēdĕre* recede.] To recede.

1581 Dee *Diary* (Camden) 13 Roger Cook..thowght that he was utterly recest from intended goodnes toward him.

recess (rɪ'sɛs, 'riːsɛs), *v.*² [f. recess *sb.*]

1. a. *trans.* To place in a recess or in retirement; to set back or away.

1809 Mar. Edgeworth *Manœuvring* vii, Behind the screen of his prodigious elbow you will be comfortably recessed from curious impertinents. **1820** *Examiner* No. 620. 132/2 The writ was then served in the expectation of recessing me in the Fleet during the long vacation. **1874** T. Hardy *Far fr. Mad. Crowd* I. xviii. 199 His house stood recessed from the road.

b. *spec.* To set (part of a wall or other structure) in a recess. Also *refl.*

1845 Petrie *Eccl. Archit. Irel.* 180 The arches, of which there are two, one recessed within the other. **1853** Kane *Grinnell Exp.* vi. (1856) 44 Little man-of-war port-holes recessed into its wooden sides. **1865** Mrs. Whitney *Gayworthys* ix, The window recessed itself into the wall.

2. To make a recess or recesses in; to cut away, so as to form a recess.

1876 J. Rose *Pract. Machinist* ix. 162 Providing that the cutter is not recessed and does not cut on both sides. **1882** *Bazaar* 15 Feb. 174 The inner..hubs are recessed, within them being placed stout steel rings.

3. a. *intr.* Chiefly *U.S.* To take a recess or interval.

1893 *Columbus* (Ohio) *Disp.* 14 Apr., The Senate recessed five minutes yesterday afternoon. **1933** W. J. Abbot *Watching World go By* xvii. 316 The convention was thrown into confusion. It recessed almost in a riot. **1943** *Sun* (Baltimore) 12 Feb. 17/1 Tomorrow's holiday on which the country's major securities and commodities exchanges will recess. **1970** *Daily Tel.* 6 July 9 The French Parliament recessed for its three-month summer holiday last week. **1977** *Ibid.* 4 May 19/1 A Turin court trying 53 Leftist 'Red Brigade' guerillas recessed indefinitely yesterday for lack of citizens willing to serve on the jury. **1977** *New Society* 7 July 23/2 The inquiry recessed earlier this month so that the contending parties would have a chance to wade through transcripts. **1977** *Time* 26 Dec. 22/1 Congress recessed last week for a month-long holiday without enacting his energy bill.

b. *trans.* Chiefly *U.S.* To put (a meeting, etc.) into recess; to adjourn, suspend.

1954 W. Faulkner *Fable* 80 It takes more ammunition to recess a war for ten minutes than to stop a mere offensive. **1967** *Guardian* 12 June 8/4 Hans Tabor recessed the meeting and told them to 'stand by' for any urgent call. **1970** W. Wager *Sledgehammer* xxv. 213 When Gillis recessed the proceedings..not a single juror had been picked. **1978** *Detroit Free Press* 2 Apr. 10A/5 Exhausted negotiators agreed to recess formal talks for the weekend and meet in private.

Hence **recessed** (rɪ'sɛst) *ppl. a.*, set in a recess; **re'cessing** *vbl. sb.*

recessed arch, an arch set within another arch. *recessing-bit*, a bit for enlarging the ends of screw-holes, etc.

1809–12 Mar. Edgeworth *Ennui* x, Lady Geraldine and Cecil Devereux..were in a recessed window. **1867** Lady Herbert *Cradle L.* iii. 90 Underneath this basilica is a little recessed chapel. **1873** Shelley *Workshop Appliances* 223 The first [pin-drill], with three cutting edges,..being sometimes called a recessing-bitt. **1874** Parker *Goth. Archit.* i. iv. 114 In many of the earlier examples the square profile of the recessed Norman arch is retained.

†**re'cessful**, *a. Obs.*⁻¹ [f. recess *sb.* + -ful.] To which recess or recourse may be had. Also **re'cessfully** *adv.* (cf. recess *sb.* 5 b).

1646 J. Gregory *Notes & Obs.* 33 It was disposed of in some eminent or recessefull place of the City. *Ibid.* To Rdr., Who recessefully and impertinently pretend to a Spirit of Interpretation.

recession (rɪ'sɛʃən), *sb.*¹ [ad. L. *recessiōn-em* (Vitruvius), n. of action f. *recēdĕre* to recede. Cf. mod.F. *récession*, It. *recessione* (Florio).]

1. a. The action of receding from a place or point; withdrawal, retirement.

†*recession of the equinoxes*: see precession.

a **1652** J. Smith *Sel. Disc.* ix. vi. (1660) 419 Neither were it a Happiness worth the having, for a Mind,..by a recession into it self, to spend an Eternity in self-converse. **1691** Ray *Creation* i. (1692) 185 The Sun..plying them always alike without any annual Recession or intermission. **1704** J. Harris *Lex. Techn.*, *Recession of the Equinoxes* is the going back of the Equinoctial Points every Year about 50 Seconds. **1789** E. Darwin *Bot. Gard.* i. (1791) Notes 15 Particles mutually recede from and approach each other reciprocally; at the times of their recession from each other [etc.]. **1853** C. Bronte *Villette* xxvi, She seemed to recede. I drew nearer: her recession, still silent, became swift. **1879** Proctor *Pleas. Ways Sc.* iv. 99 The method shows no signs of approach or recession in the moon's case.

b. Used with ref. to receding or distant parts of surfaces or outlines. (See also recessor.)

1753 Hogarth *Anal. Beauty* xii. 101 Planes or flat surfaces..have their appearances of recession perfected by the first species of retiring shades. **1821** Craig *Lect. Drawing*, etc. i. 44 Those degrees of light and dark which arise from difference of local colour, or from recession in distance. **1870** Ruskin *Lect. Art* v. 126 The solid forms of an object, that is to say, the projections or recessions of its surface within the outline.

c. A setting or going back in time. *rare.*

1646 Sir T. Browne *Pseud. Ep.* 317 They must..endure anticipation and recession from the moveable condition of their causes. *a* **1876** M. Collins *Th. in Garden* (1880) II.

290 Has there really been a recession of the seasons, so that summer comes later every year?

d. *Philol.* The transference of accentuation towards or on to the first syllable of a word.

1886 *Amer. Jrnl. Philol.* VII. II. 246 A tendency existed to recession from the end of the word. **1929** *S.P.E. Tract* XXXII. 388 This condition, which lightens the syllable, allows and even invites loss and recession of accent.

2. The action of receding, retiring, or departing, in various *transf.* or *fig.* senses. Const. *from*.

Common in 17th c. (esp. in Jer. Taylor's works) of departure from a principle, state or condition.

1647 JER. TAYLOR *Lib. Proph.* viii. 152 It is a plaine recession from Antiquity. **1659** W. BROUGH *Schism* 524 There is no sin nor schism in our recession from them. *a* **1716** SOUTH *Serm.* X. 301 (T.) His [Christ's] whole life went in a constant recession from his own rights. **1758** JOHNSON *Idler* No. 32 ¶13 All this is a temporary recession from the realities of life to airy fictions. **1859** J. CUMMING *Ruth* iii. 41 He may leave us..to taste the bitterness of our recession so far and so criminally from Him.

3. The departure *of* a quality or property from that in which it exists.

1659 PEARSON *Creed* iv. (1839) 301 Death is nothing else but the privation or recession of life. **1836** TODD *Cycl. Anat.* I. 801/2 The recession of heat from the limbs was noticed by Hippocrates. **1899** *Allbutt's Syst. Med.* VIII. 304 There is little wonder that in some cases the recession of mental function is not on physiological lines.

4. *Econ.* A temporary decline or setback in economic activity or prosperity.

1929 *Economist* 2 Nov. 806/1 The material prosperity of the United States is too firmly based, in our opinion, for a revival in industrial activity—even if we have to face an immediate recession of some magnitude—to be long delayed. **1930** *Engineering* 3 Jan. 21/2 The paramount problem is now whether this recession is yet at an end. **1938** E. AMBLER *Cause for Alarm* i. 16 'Trade recession' they called it... As far as I could see there wasn't a great deal of difference between a trade recession and a good old-fashioned slump. **1958** *Spectator* 30 May 676/2 This is partly due to the continued inability of the United States to pull itself out of recession. **1976** F. ZWEIG *New Acquisitive Society* II. iii. 99 The private sector, particularly in the throes of recession, is limited in its ability to pay by the discipline of the market system. **1981** *Times* 11 Mar. 19/4 The economy is now in deep recession.

recession (riːˈsɛʃən), *sb.*[2] [f. RE- 5 a + CESSION: cf. RECEDE *v.*[2]] The action of ceding back.

1890 *Century Mag.* Jan. 475/2 A bill for the recession [of the Yosemite Valley] to the United States.

recessional (rɪˈsɛʃənəl), *a.* and *sb.* [f. RECESSION *sb.*[1] + -AL[1].]

A. *adj.* **1.** *Eccl.* Belonging to the recession or retirement of the clergy and choir from the chancel to the vestry at the close of the service; esp. ***recessional hymn***, a hymn sung while this retirement is taking place.

1867 *Ch. Opinion* 13 Apr. 15 The service concluded with a recessional hymn. **1882** *Homilet. Monthly* Apr. 410 The ritualist..orders his processional and recessional movements with toll of bell and thunder of organ. **1932** CHESTERTON *Coll. Poems* (1933) 45 We fancied heaven preferring much Your rowdiest song..to such Very recessional repentance. **1973** *Times* 15 Nov. 6/6 Timothy Farrell, sub organist of Westminster Abbey, thundered recessional music.

2. Belonging to a recess (of Parliament).

1895 *Westm. Gaz.* 24 Aug. 2/2 The Government.. continues to pile up work for the Recess and next Session. The recessional work promised by the Home Secretary [etc.].

3. ***recessional moraine*** (Geol.), a form of moraine which is deposited during a temporary halt or minor readvance of a receding glacier or ice sheet, similar in appearance to a terminal moraine.

[**1897** *Jrnl. Geol.* V. 427 To account for the moraines of recession by any scheme of ups and downs of the solid earth.] **1907** R. D. SALISBURY *Physiogr.* v. 277 As the edge of the ice was melted back, it sometimes halted for a time far back from the position of its maximum advance. Beneath the edge in such positions, terminal moraines were made. Such terminal moraines are sometimes called recessional moraines. **1925** W. J. MILLER *Introd. Physical Geol.* viii. 255 Recessional moraines, forming a great succession of curving ridges, are wonderfully displayed to the south of Lakes Michigan and Erie. **1957** G. E. HUTCHINSON *Treat. Limnol.* I. i. 82 The terminal or recessional moraines of valley glaciers may persist, in certain circumstances, in a sufficiently well-preserved state that they can dam the stream that replaces the glacier. **1976** C. L. MATSCH *N. Amer. & Great Ice Age* vii. 84 Recessional moraines are valuable aids to the glacial geologist because their spacing might allow the calculation of rates of melting if appropriate materials are available for radiocarbon dating.

B. *sb.* A recessional hymn.

1867 in *Life Jas. Skinner* xiii. (1884) 253 To crown all, we had 'O Paradise!' as a recessional.

recessionary (riːˈsɛʃənərɪ), *a.* [f. RECESSION *sb.*[1] + -ARY[1].] Of, pertaining to, or characterized by (economic) recession.

1958 *Times* 24 Nov. 15/2 Moreover, there are several factors that have so far provided a cushion against recessionary forces. **1970** *Times* 22 May 8 He admits himself baffled by the combination of high inflationary symptoms in prices and interest rates with recessionary symptoms in output. **1974** *Daily Tel.* 19 July 19 The outlook is clearly recessionary, but it is still doubtful if the Chancellor could afford to put back more than £500 million into the economy. **1979** *Nat. Westm. Bank Q. Rev.* Aug. 4 The desire to keep the economy at a high level of activity in general world wide recessionary conditions.

reˈcessive, *a.* and *sb.* [f. L. *recess-*, ppl. stem of *recēdĕre* to RECEDE + -IVE.] **A.** *adj.* **1. a.** Tending to recede. Also (*rare*) of persons, retiring, reserved.

1672-3 GREW *Veget. Roots* §38 They will also be more Pliable and recessive from the Centre. **1721** J. CLARKE *Moral Evil* 23 That the constituent particles of it should be induced with particular impulsive or recessive forces. **1925** T. DREISER *Amer. Tragedy* I. I. xiii. 95 She, for her part, felt recessive and thence evasive.

b. *Philol.* ***recessive accent***, stress transferred towards or on to the first syllable of a word.

1879 W. W. GOODWIN *Elem. Gr. Gram.* (ed. 2) I. 19 When a word throws its accent as far back as possible..it is said to have *recessive* accent. **1926** FOWLER *Mod. Eng. Usage* 168/1 He [*sc.* the latinist] has still to reckon with the recessive-accent tendency, which has as good a right to a voice in the matter as his erudition. **1955** *Sci. Amer.* Aug. 82/3 Add to these specimens the 'recessive accent'—stressing of the first syllable of a word which has previously been accented on the second or third syllable. **1973** A. H. SOMMERSTEIN *Sound Pattern Anc. Gr.* v. 171 *Action* nouns..have recessive accent if masculine but final accent if feminine.

c. *Philol.* That tends to recede from use or fall into desuetude.

1935 *Univ. Mich. Publ. Lang. & Lit.* XIII. 14 Inasmuch as the *-eth* plural was a recessive characteristic, we naturally find the *-e(n)* form as well as the *-eth* form occurring south of this line. **1962** *Amer. Speech* XXXVII. 172 Possibly *coal hod* is a recessive form on the Banks. **1972** M. L. SAMUELS *Linguistic Evol.* vi. 92 The isogloss for a given feature may or may not shift. If it does shift, there may be complete levelling resulting in the elimination of the recessive form.

2. *Biol.* [tr. G. *recessiv* (Mendel, *Versuche über Pflanzenhybriden*, in *Verh. d. Naturforsch. Ver., Brünn* (1865) IV. 10).] Applied to a hereditary trait which is not perceptibly expressed in heterozygotes, being masked by a dominant allele of the gene that determines it; hence applied also to an allele which can affect the phenotype only in the absence of some other, dominant, allele. Const. *to* the dominant allele.

1900, etc. [see DOMINANT *a.* 7]. **1920** *Glasgow Herald* 21 Aug. 4 The characters of tallness and dwarfness were thus separating out again. One of them, dwarfness, had temporarily disappeared in the first filial generation, and for that reason was called by Mendel the recessive character. **1930** R. A. FISHER *Genet. Theory Nat. Selection* iii. 52 The pronounced tendency of the mutant gene to be recessive, to the gene of wild type from which it arises, calls for explanation. **1950** *Science News* XV. 124 The research worker may find blood group inheritance a convenient field for study... Recessive characters, even in the presence of dominant ones, are quite easily recognised, for the heterozygotes can be distinguished from the homozygotes by using the appropriate antibodies. **1964** M. ARGYLE *Psychol. & Social Probl.* vi. 78 A single recessive gene produces the phenomenon of skipping generations and of carriers who do not show the condition themselves; certain kinds of mental deficiency are like this. Schizophrenia is thought by some to be inherited by two or more recessive genes. **1971** D. J. COVE *Genetics* ii. 14 If a heterozygous strain..resembles the strain homozygous for the *A* allele.., thus the *A* allele is said to be dominant to the *a* allele, or conversely the *a* allele is said to be recessive to the *A* allele.

B. *sb.* *Biol.* **a.** An individual in which a particular recessive allele is expressed. **b.** A recessive allele or character.

1900 W. BATESON in *Jrnl. R. Hort. Soc.* XXV. 58 Mendel discovered that in this generation the numerical proportion of dominants to recessives is approximately constant, being in fact as three to one. **1902** *Rep. Evolution Committee R. Soc.* I. 8 The recessives are thenceforth not only apparently but *actually pure*, and if allowed to fertilise themselves give rise to recessives only, for any number of generations. **1905** R. C. PUNNETT *Mendelism* 15 This condition behaves as a single recessive to the normal state. **1916** W. BATESON *Probl. Genetics* iv. 91 We find that..a diversity of recessives may appear within a moderately short period. **1931** E. B. FORD *Mendelism & Evolution* II. iii. 47 The first gene to be discovered in *Drosophila simulans* was that for yellow body-colour. It is a sex-linked recessive. **1949** W. C. ALLEE et al. *Princ. Animal Ecol.* xxxiv. 655/1 Deleterious autosomal recessives are strikingly abundant in certain wild populations of *Drosophila*. **1972** J. MURRAY *Genetic Diversity & Natural Selection* ii. 5 The lowered fitness is the result of the unmasking of deleterious recessives.

Hence **reˈcessively** *adv.*, in a receding manner.

1886 *Edin. Rev.* Oct. 494 As she [Greece] passes recessively from the grand Attic period to the Spartan, the Theban, the Macedonian, and the Asiatic.

recessiveness (rɪˈsɛsɪvnɪs). *Biol.* [f. prec. + -NESS.] The state or property of being recessive. Opp. DOMINANCE 2.

1909 W. BATESON *Mendel's Princ. Heredity* 71 Basing his procedure on a knowledge of the dominance or recessiveness of each character the breeder may thus guide his operations with certainty. **1938** L. RIDE *Genetics & Clinician* ii. 17 In the case of the red and white four o'clocks, the dominance of 'red' is but 50% as is also the recessiveness of white, i.e., neither character is definitely dominant nor recessive. *Ibid.*, The dominance of some characters in the echinoderm may be changed to recessiveness by altering the chemical nature of the sea-water. **1975** J. B. JENKINS *Genetics* iii. 83 Bateson ..proposed his presence-and-absence hypothesis..which stated that dominance is due to the presence of a particular gene and that recessiveness results from the loss of that gene.

recessor. (? Misprint for *recession*.)

a **1637** B. JONSON *Discov.* (1640) 112 From the opticks it [painting]..tooke shadowes, recessor, light, and heightnings.

recet, -cett(e, obs. ff. RESET *sb.* and *v.*

recetter, -or, obs. ff. RESETTER.

receve, obs. f. RECEIVE.

recewle, var. of RECUEIL.

receypte, receyt(e, receytour, receyve, obs. ff. RECEIPT, RECEIPTER, RECEIVE.

rech, obs. f. REACH *sb.*[1] and *v.*[1], RICH *v.*

Rechabite (ˈrɛkəbaɪt). [ad. biblical L. *Rechabīta*, used in pl. to render Heb. *Rēkābīm*, f. the personal name *Rēkāb*: see *Jer.* xxxv. 2–19.] One of a Jewish family descended from Jonadab, son of Rechab, which refused to drink wine or live in houses. Hence (*a*) one who abstains from intoxicating liquors; now *spec.* a member of the Independent Order of Rechabites, a benefit society founded in 1835; (*b*) a dweller in tents.

1382 WYCLIF *Jer.* xxxv. 3 Jeconye..and alle his sonus, and al the hous of Rechabitis. **1535** COVERDALE *ibid.*, The whole housholde off the Rechabites. *c* **1681** (*title*) The English Rechabite, or a Defyance to Bacchus and all his Works. *c* **1720** PRIOR *Wandering Pilgrim* 9 A Rechabite poor Will must live, And drink of Adam's ale. **1860** RUSSELL *Diary India* II. xviii. 345 Cone after cone of canvas offers brief shelter to the Rechabite.

Hence **ˈRechabitism**, the practice of abstaining from intoxicating liquors; the principles or practice of the friendly society of Rechabites.

1870 *Rechabite & Temperance Mag.* Jan. 8 To extend the blessings of Rechabitism throughout..the land.

†**rechace.** *Obs. rare*[−1]. [ad. OF. *rachas* nom. of *rachat* f. *re-* RE- + *achat* ACHATE *sb.*[2]] The act of buying back or redeeming.

c **1460** SIR R. ROS *La Belle Dame*, etc. 324 He þat ones to loue dothe his omage, Full often tyme, der boght is the rechace.

rechace, variant of RECHASE *sb.* and *v.*

†**rechafe**, *sb.* [RE- 5 a.] A repeated chafing.

1581 J. BELL *Haddon's Answ. Osor.* 307 b, Archbyshoppes, and monckes..roonning to Rome in their often chafe and rechafe, sweating and turmoyling.

rechafe, *v.* [RE- 5 a. Cf. RECHAUFE *v.*] *trans.* To chafe again.

1583 GOLDING *Calvin on Deut.* Pref. 3 Although they haue been oftentimes chafed and rechafed yet are they so starke and stiffe for colde that they haue no force nor might.

So †**reˈchafement.** *Obs.*[−1]

1609 [BP. W. BARLOW] *Answ. Nameless Cath.* 364 They take order to keep out and cut off the originall nourishing inflamers, which minister the rechaffment to these disloyal attempts.

reˈchain, *v.* [RE- 5 a.] *trans.* To chain again.

a **1711** KEN *Hymns Evang.* Poet. Wks. 1721 I. 171 He their malicious Tyranny restrain'd, And orders gave they shou'd be all rechain'd.

rechange (riːˈtʃeɪndʒ), *sb.* Also 5 *Sc.* **recheng(e**, 5–6 **rechaunge**, 6 **rechaynge**. [f. RE- 5 a + CHANGE *sb.*]

†**1.** The RE-EXCHANGE on a bill. *Obs.*

So F. *rechange* (1680 in Hatz.-Darm.). See also RECAMBY.

1489 *Sc. Acta Dom. Conc.* 130/1 þe recheng interess dampnage & expensis sustenit be þe said reuerent faider extending..to þe soume of xij[xx] of ross noblis. **1492** in Arnolde *Chron.* (1502) Hiv, Alle maner costis lossis and damagis whiche shall happen too falle for lac of payment at the daye aforesayde of the principall somme aboue sayde be it bee exchaunge rechaunge or other wyse. **1538** in R. G. Marsden *Sel. Pl. Crt. Adm.* (1894) I. 72 To pay change and rechaunge after the use and custum of merchants. **1682** SCARLETT *Exchanges* 294 By Re-change here and else-where, is meant, the whole Bill which is advanced with the Re-change, Provisions and Charges, &c...and not the bare Re-change only, which is the Monyes that exceeds the Value of the first Bill.

†**2.** The act of re-exchanging (money or goods).

1487 *Rolls of Parlt.* VI. 403/1 An Act against Exchange and Rechange, without the Kings License. **1503** *Ibid.* 525/1 Money in Golde or Silver, whiche..cannot come to the proffete of the Kyngs Realme..without exchaynge or rechaynge made in the Landes beyond the See. **1570** DEE *Math. Pref.* *ij, Certaine and generall Rules for Exchaunge of money, and Rechaunge. **1622** MALYNES *Anc. Law-Merch.* 371 The benefit or profit of exchange is never known directly but by the rechange thereof. **1625** in Rymer *Foedera* XVIII. 146 With sufficient Meanes for the Re-change of the Tokens to be uttered to the Citizens.

3. The act of changing or altering again.

a **1550** *Image Hypocr.* I. 192 in *Skelton's Wks.* (1843) II. 416/1 Which [? *read* with] chaunge and rechaunge Of fastinges and of feestes. *a* **1586** SIDNEY *Arcadia* (1622) 232 Neuer the Muses more tired then now with changes & rechanges of his deuises. **1642** SPELMAN *View Printed Bk.* 36 With in the space of 500 yeares..how many changes [*printed* thinges] and rechanges had they of their Gouernment. **1890** LOWELL *Inscr. Bust Fielding*, He..saw the Sphinx, now bestial, now divine, In change and rechange.

rechange (riːˈtʃeɪndʒ), *v.* Also 6 **rechaung(e**. [f. RE- 5 a + CHANGE *v.*, perh. after F. *rechanger*.]

1. To change or alter again. **a.** *intr.* or *absol.*

1579 LYLY *Euphues* (Arb.) 98 Helen of Greece.. chaunged and rechaunged at hir pleasure, I graunt. **1594** T. B. *La Primaud. Fr. Acad.* II. 155 It..addeth thereunto or diminisheth, changeth and rechangeth. **1682** BUNYAN *Holy War* 129 How often hast thou changed and rechanged. **1811** W. TAYLOR in *Monthly Rev.* LXV. 141 The eye soon sickens of identical furniture, and unvarying imagery... Let us change and rechange.

b. *trans.*

1592 KYD *Sol. & Pers.* I. i. 22 Did not I change long loue to sudden hate; And then rechange their hatred into loue? **1644** FEATLY *Roma Ruens* 7 The whole world shall be changed into a second chaos, and that chaos shall be re-changed into a new world. *a* **1774** GOLDSM. *Hist. Greece* I. 170 By this changing and rechanging the order of battle, nothing farther was done for that day. **1896** *Daily News* 19 Nov. 6/5 Recusancy, or the crime of not being able to change, and even re-change, one's religion at the command of the Privy Council, figures conspicuously.

†**2.** *trans.* (and *absol.*) To re-exchange (goods or money). *Obs.*

1551 EDW. VI *Jrnl.* in *Lit. Rem.* (Roxb.) II. 406 Liberty was gevin to the marchauntis to exchaung and rechaung money for money. **1622** MABBE tr. *Aleman's Guzman d' Alf.* II. 239 There is no negociating now adayes, but with it [honesty] and with money; changing and rechanging as the market goes.

Hence **re'changing** *vbl. sb.*

1611 FLORIO, *Rimuta*, a remoouing or rechanging. **1612** BREREWOOD *Lang. & Relig.* 47 Nothing is found of any rechanging of those languages from the Roman, into the state wherein now they are.

re'chant, *v.* [f. RE- + CHANT *v.*, perh. after F. *rechanter* (1288) or L. *recantāre*: cf. RECANT *v.*[2]] *intr.* and *trans.* To chant again or in reply; to repeat in chanting. Hence **re'chanted, re'chanting** *ppl. adjs.*

1598 SYLVESTER *Du Bartas* II. i. IV. *Handie-crafts* 31 Hark, hark, the cheerfull and re-chanting cries Of old and young; singing this joyfull Ditty. **1633** PRYNNE *1st Pt. Histrio-m.* 532b, Whiles they chaunt and rechaunt this. **1641** R. BAILLIE *Canterb. Self-convict.* Large Suppl. Postscr. 1 To parallel the Scottish Covenanters with Jesuites is the old and oft rechanted son[g] of your fellows.

re'chaos, *v. rare.* [RE- 5 a.] *trans.* To reduce again to chaos.

1611 J. DAVIES *Scourge of Folly* Wks. (Grosart) II. 53 Shee shall Preserue thy name till she re-chaos'd go To purging-flames. **1616** —— *Sir T. Overbury* Ibid. 16 So shall thy stay, when states re-chaosed lie, Make thee great Steward to Eternitie.

recharge (riː'tʃɑːdʒ, 'riː-), *sb.* [f. RE- + CHARGE *sb.*, prob. after F. *recharge* (1433).]

1. A fresh charge or load. *spec.* in *Hydrology*, the replenishment of the water content of an aquifer as a result of the absorption of water into the zone of saturation (freq. induced artificially by sinking wells into the aquifer); the water so added. Also (*rare*), the action of recharging a battery.

1611 FLORIO, *Ricarica*, a recharge, a reburthen. **1727–41** CHAMBERS *Cycl.* s.v., The recharge should never be so deep as the first charge, lest the piece..should burst. **1928** M. ARENDT *Storage Batteries* vii. 146 This is a common feature of all high rate recharges, as the more dense electrolyte formed by the electrolytic action within plate pores and at plate surfaces does not have time to diffuse throughout the electrolyte during the earlier part of the recharge period. **1931** *Trans. Amer. Geophysical Union* XII. 208 At eight of the plats some recharge was indicated, but some of these had been irrigated in the previous summer. **1942** O. E. MEINZER *Hydrol.* x. 404 The recharge is increased if the intake area receives not only the local precipitation but also the surface flow of a tributary catchment area. **1965** R. G. KAZMANN *Mod. Hydrol.* v. 139 When the supply of soil moisture in a given place is fully replenished, any additional water received from the surface is carried downward under the influence of gravity, either directly to the water table or to the intermediate belt of the zone of aeration: this phenomenon is termed the 'recharge' of an aquifer. **1976** J. D. BREDEHOEFT et al. in J. C. Rodda *Facets of Hydrol.* ix. 241/2 Variations in recharge change the inflow as well as the saturated thickness of the aquifers to the west of Barstow.

†**2.** The act of accusing in return. *Obs.*[−1]

1637 C. DOW *Answ. H. Barton* 127 His brave retort and recharge of sedition upon them.

3. a. A renewed or return charge in battle.

1603 HOLLAND *Plutarch's Mor.* 675 That buffetting representeth the charging of the enemie, and the avoiding of his recharge. *a* **1656** USSHER *Ann.* (1658) 749 Caesars ships being..ready for any needs of service, either for charge or recharges, or to turn about. **1802** JAMES *Milit. Dict.*, *Recharge*, a renewal of the charge or attack.

†**b.** *fig.* A renewed attack *of* something. *Obs.*[−1]

1620 J. PYPER tr. *Hist. Astrea* I. VII. 234 This recharge of griefe surprized me so forcibly.

4. Special Comb. in *Hydrology*: **recharge area**, an area of ground surface through which is absorbed the water that will percolate into a zone of saturation in one or more aquifers; **recharge basin**, an artificially constructed basin, freq. in sandy material, used to collect water for artificial recharge of an aquifer; **recharge well**, a well used to inject water into an aquifer by artificial recharge.

1951 H. E. THOMAS *Conservation of Ground Water* ii. 29 The ground-water phase of the hydrologic cycle is one of movement from the places where water enters the aquifer—the '*recharge' areas—to the place where the water is discharged from the ground. **1978** BETSON & ARDIS in M. J. Kirkby *Hillslope Hydrol.* viii. 308 The impact upon stream-flow of paving over a thin-soil primary source area..would be far less than a similar amount of paving over a primary recharge area. **1951** H. E. THOMAS *Conservation of Ground Water* iii. 143 The city has *recharge basins totaling 65 acres which permit infiltration of up to a million gallons a day into the ground. **1970** *Daily Tel.* 18 Sept. 5/2 Long Island is combating the threat [of drought] by constructing 'recharge basins' capable of retaining about 10 per cent. of the water now being lost to the sea. **1951** H. E. THOMAS *Conservation of Ground Water* iii. 125 Permits were issued with the proviso that water used for cooling and air conditioning be returned to the same aquifer through *recharge wells. **1976** RAUDKIVI & CALLANDER *Analysis of Groundwater Flow* iii. 58 Water is pumped through the aquifer from the recharge well to the well.

recharge (riː'tʃɑːdʒ), *v.* [f. RE- + CHARGE *v.*, perh. after F. *recharger* (13th c.).]

1. *trans.* †**a.** To reload (a vessel). Also *refl.* and *absol.* *Obs.*

1432 *Rolls of Parlt.* IV. 417/2 They [ships] have atte all tymes be discharged and recharged. **1497** *Naval Acc. Hen. VII* (1896) 250 The seid veassayle..saylyng..vnto Portesmouth & ther dyscharged then frome thens to Southampton & ther Recharged with the cordage. **1600** HAKLUYT *Voy.* III. 863 They bee there all the winter in the ports, to discharge their loding and recharge backe againe. **1615** tr. *De Monfart's Surv. E. Indies* 35 The Portugalls mutually come to discharge and recharge themselues.

b. To put a fresh charge in; to refill, reload. *spec.* to replenish the water content of (an aquifer).

1839 URE *Dict. Arts* 167 As soon as the melting-pot is emptied, it is immediately re-charged. **1942** A. C. SWINNERTON in O. E. Meinzer *Hydrol.* xiv. 698 It is possible to recharge basalt by running water down drilled wells. **1966** DAVIS & DE WIEST *Hydrogeol.* xii. 425 Where infiltration is most vigorous, underlying aquifers may be recharged. **1976** RAUDKIVI & CALLANDER *Analysis of Groundwater Flow* v. 108 If the well is at the centre of an island,..the aquifer is recharged from the lake surrounding the island.

2. †**a.** To charge or accuse in return. *Obs.*

1594 HOOKER *Eccl. Pol.* III. xi. §13 Whereupon they re-charge vs, as if in these things we gaue the Church a libertie which hath no limits or bounds. **1697** G. KEITH *2nd Narr. Proc. Turner's Hall* 33 Whereas I charged T. Elw. with perverting the Apostles Creed, he recharges me, and lays the whole Ground of his Charge upon a Quibble.

b. To make a new charge against.

1895 *Daily News* 4 June 2/5 The magistrate..then directed that she should be re-charged for the assault on the assistant gaoler.

c. *intr.* To repeat a charge or accusation. *Obs.*[−1]

1595 DANIEL *Civ. Wars* I. lxi, Norfolke denies them peremptorily. Herford recharg'd.

3. To lay or impose again as a charge. *rare.*

1611 COTGR., *Reimposer*, to reimpose, to recharge. **1665** WITHER *Lord's Prayer* 2 [He] shall have all his suits rejected, and his sins..recharged upon him. *a* **1734** NORTH *Lives* (1826) II. 111 The unfair traders, and runners, and such as come in before the duties are recharged.

4. *intr.* To charge (in battle) again or in return.

1598 BARRET *Theor. Warres* III. i. 43 Then recharging aduisedly to be ready to come vp. **1616** J. LANE *Cont. Sqr.'s T.* IX. 90 With valient secondes, placd to recharge after. **1666** DRYDEN *Ann. Mirab.* lxvii, They charge, re-charge, and all along the Sea They drive and squander the huge Belgian Fleet.

5. a. *trans.* To restore an electric charge to (a battery). **b.** *intr.* Of a battery: to acquire an electric charge again, to become recharged.

1876 PREECE & SIVEWRIGHT *Telegraphy* 21 In recharging the battery the liquid drawn off from the zinc cells is again employed in them. **1893** J. T. NIBLETT *Portative Electricity* III. 188 As a rule the user of a secondary battery knows..at what rate his battery is intended to be recharged. **1928** M. ARENDT *Storage Batteries* vii. 143 A partial charge..may be given to recharge a battery sufficiently to meet some special demand. **1960** *Farmer & Stockbreeder* 22 Mar. (Suppl.) 8/2 The battery runs for 2¼ hours on a single charge and is recharged for a few pence with a trickle charger. **1974** *Sci. Amer.* Nov. 134/2 The fully discharged battery would recharge..in about 40 hours. **1976** *Country Life* 22 Jan. 200/3 Batteries for a lawnmower..have been recharged.

c. In *fig.* phr. ***to recharge one's*** or (***the***) ***batteries***, to restore fitness and mental composure by means of changed circumstances, esp. rest; also *absol.*

1921 W. S. CHURCHILL *Let.* 9 Feb. in M. Soames *Clementine Churchill* (1979) xiii. 194 Subordinate everything in yr life to regathering yr nervous energy, and recharging yr batteries. **1971** A. PRICE *Alamut Ambush* x. 127 His London existence had been frenetic, and Firle was where he recharged his batteries. **1976** J. SNOW *Cricket Rebel* 83, I felt that I was at the halfway stage of my career and needed the rest to recharge the batteries. **1976** G. MOFFAT *Short Time to Live* xii. 136 London's..overwhelming... You come home to recharge, and go back.

Hence **re'chargeable** *a.*, that may be recharged; **re'charging** *vbl. sb.*

1892 *Daily News* 3 June 7/3 The recharging occupies six hours. **1893** J. T. NIBLETT *Portative Electricity* III. 187 Nearly all cases of failure of secondary batteries are due to lack of sufficient knowledge on the part of the user for properly conducting the operation of recharging. *Ibid.* 188 The rate at which a secondary battery receives the recharging current may be allowed to vary considerably without fear of damage to any of its parts. **1897** R. KEARTON *Nature & Camera* 358 The recharging of dark slides. **1926** C. CONNOLLY *Let.* 8 June in *Romantic Friendship* (1975) 139, I need recharging. I expect we both do. **1942** PARTRIDGE *Usage & Abusage* 170/2 The invention of either new words or new senses (i.e., the re-charging of old words). **1949** *Econ. Geol.* XLIV. 523 In considering sites for water storage, the hydrologic engineer and the economic geologist should not overlook rechargeable aquifers. **1964** T. L. KINSEY *Audio-Typing & Electric Typewriters* iii. 16 The batteries, like accumulators, are rechargeable. **1972** *New Scientist* 11 May 321/1 These newcomers have provided..new electrical devices—such as..a rechargeable battery with an energy-to-weight ratio some 10 times higher than that of the familiar lead and sulphuric acid system. **1977** *Sci. Amer.* May 27/2 More expensive techniques are to build infiltration pits..and recharging wells, by means of which water is pumped into the ground rather than drawn from it. **1978** *Nature* 15 June p. xv/1 The recorders are..supplied with rechargeable fibre tipped pens.

recharter (riː'tʃɑːtə(r)), *sb.* [RE- 5 a.] The renewal of a charter; a new or second charter.

1847 in WEBSTER. **1852** J. M. LUDLOW *Hist. U.S.* 159 In 1832..Webster led the new Whig party in support of its re-charter. **1878** F. A. WALKER *Money* xx. 457 In 1832 occurred the Recharter, when the Bank directors showed a still further change of views.

recharter (riː'tʃɑːtə(r)), *v.* [RE- 5 a.] *trans.* To charter again; to give a new charter to. Hence **re'chartering** *vbl. sb.*

1847 in WEBSTER. **1876** BANCROFT *Hist. U.S.* III. vi. 373 He prepared to recharter the bank of England. **1884** *19th Cent.* Dec. 1005 The Vice-President..was found to be opposed to the rechartering of a United States Bank.

†**rechase,** *sb. Obs.* Also 5 rechas, -chayse, 5, (7) -chace. [Perh. ad. OF. **rachas*, nom. of **rachat* RECHEAT *sb.*] = RECHEAT *sb.* (but in later quots. possibly associated with RECHASE *v.*[1] 2 a).

c **1420** *Venery de Tuety* in *Rel. Ant.* I. 152 Than shall yͤ blowe on this maner a mote, and aftirward the rechace upon my houndys that be past the boundys. *c* **1420** *Anturs of Arth.* 58 The huntes þei halowe, in hurstes and huwes, And bluwe rechas ryally. ? *c* **1475** *Sqr. lowe Degre* 772 To here the bugles there yblow,..And sevenscore raches at his rechase. **1634** *Malory's Arthur* II. cxxxviii, All the blasts that long to all manner of games;..to the rechace [*Caxton* rechate] to the flight [etc.].

re'chase, *v.*[1] *Obs.* exc. *dial.* Also 5 **rechasse,** 5–6 **rechace.** [a. F. *rechasser* (13th c.; OF. also *rechacier*, etc.): see RE- and CHASE *v.*]

†**1.** *trans.* To chase or drive back (an assailant); to chase in turn. *Obs.*

c **1477** CAXTON *Jason* 18 After..the worthy Jason had re-chaced his enmyes unto nyghe by the ooste. **1523** LD. BERNERS *Froiss.* I. cccv. 458 These fortresses..made dyuers yssues and assautes on their neighbours, Somtyme chasyng and somtyme rechased agayne. **1614** SYLVESTER *Bethulia's Rescue* v. 358 One-while the Syrians by the Medes are chas't; Anon the Medes by Syrians are rechas't.

absol. **1609** DANIEL *Civ. Wars* IV. xlvii, Then these assaile, then those rechase again.

†**b.** To drive or force back (a thing). *Obs.*[−1]

a **1533** LD. BERNERS *Gold. Bk. M. Aurel.* (1546) Q vij, There is nothyng that more rechaceth the balle of the thought.

2. †**a.** *Hunting.* To chase (a deer) back into the forest. *Obs.*

c **1369** CHAUCER *Dethe Blaunche* 39 Withynne a while the herte founde ys I-halowed and rechased faste Longe tyme. **1678** PHILLIPS (ed. 4), *To Rechace*,..among Hunts-men is to make homewards, to drive back towards the place where the game was rouzed or started. **1727–41** CHAMBERS *Cycl.* s.v. *Rechacing*, The keeping of running dogs to rechace the deer into the forests.

b. To drive back (cattle or sheep) from one pasture to another.

1618 J. WILKINSON *Courts Baron* (1620) 147 If any tenant ..doth vse in the Summer time or open time of the yeere,.. to bring Cattell from his other Farme into his farme within this Manor,..this is called chasing and rechasing. **1720** T. WOOD *Instit. Eng. Law* IV. i. 490 The Homage may also Enquire..Of Chasing Cattle into the Manor, and Re-chasing them. **1851** *Dorset Gloss., Chase and re-chase*, to drive sheep at particular times from one pasture to another.

†**c.** To drive or course (horses) back over the same ground. *Obs.*

1607 MARKHAM *Caval.* I. (1617) 54 Albe some Authors giue aduice to chase and rechase your Mares vp and downe the ground. *Ibid.* III. 9 The best mettald Horses, if they be chaste and rechaste without..some incouragement, will by degrees growe worse and worse.

†**3.** *intr.* ? To be engaged in rechasing. *Obs.*[−1]

Perh. a transferred use of 2 a, suggested by the hunting sense of *quest*; but the correct reading may be *theire chase is*.

c **1485** *Digby Myst.* v. 723 The queste of holborn come into this places, a-geyne the right euer thei rechases.

Hence †**re'chaser**; †**re'chasing** *vbl. sb.*[1]

1611 FLORIO, *Riccacciamenti*, rechasings. **1727–41** CHAMBERS *Cycl.* s.v. *Rechacing*, Antiently there were offices of rechacers of the deers bestowed by the king on gentlemen, or old hunters.

†**re'chase,** *v.*[2] *Obs. rare.* Also 5 -chace. [var. of *rechate* RECHEAT *v.*, after RECHASE *sb.*] *intr.* To recheat. Hence †**re'chasing** *vbl. sb.*[2]

c **1450** *Master of Game* (MS. Douce 335) xxxiii. lf. 60 He sholde rechace with oute long mote; for the mote shold neuer be blowe before this rechasyng.

re'chasten, *v.* [RE- 5 a.] To chasten again.

1817 MOORE *Lalla R.*, *Proph. Khor.* II, To see Those virtuous eyes for ever turn'd on me; And in their light re-chasten'd silently..Grow pure by being purely shone upon.

rechat(e: see RECHEAT *sb.* and *v.*

‖**réchaud** (reʃo). [Fr., f. stem of *réchauffer* RÉCHAUFFER *v.*] A receptacle in which food is warmed or kept warm.

1925 B. RACKHAM tr. *E. Hannover's Pottery & Porcelain* III. viii. 185 The factory hardly created much in the way of new forms..beyond a series of '*Réchauds*' (foodwarmers). **1955** H. NEWMAN in *Apollo* Feb. 35 The pedestal of a food-warmer (*réchaud*) is usually cylindrical or slightly conical, and is of greater diameter than that of a tea-warmer. **1958** R. GODDEN *Greengage Summer* ix. 106 The rose-coloured wine, the réchaud flame, the lights were reflected in the windows over and over again.

re'chauffe, *v. rare.* Also †rechaufe. [a. F. *réchauffer*: see next.] *trans.* To warm (again). Also *fig.* Cf. RÉCHAUFFER *v.*

a **1521** R. COPLAND *Knt. of the Swanne* ix, After that the good hermit had done his possibilitie to susteine and rechaufe the .vii. litle chyldren. **1579** BAKER *Guydon's Quest. Chirurg.* 27 It is ordeyned for to rechaufe the partes next thereto, as Galen sayth. **1836** DISRAELI in Monypenny & Buckle *Life Disraeli* (1910) I. App. B. 387 Canning irritated by Copley's rechauffing in a speech Philpotts'..pamphlet. **1931** R. CAMPBELL *Georgiad* I. 18 His melancholy recipès [*sic*] For 'happiness'... How to 'rechauffe' the stock-pot of desire.

‖**réchauffé** (reʃofe), *sb.* and *adj.* Also **rechauffe, réchauffée.** [F., pa. pple. of *réchauffer* to warm up again, f. *re-* + *échauffer*: see RE- and CHAFE *v.*]

A. *sb.* A warmed-up dish; hence *fig.* something old served up or presented again, esp. a rehash of literary matter.

1805 *Edin. Rev.* Apr. 133 It is really wasting time to confute this *réchauffé* of a theory. **1851** E. WARD *Jrnl.* 5 Feb. (1951) 123 Took tea with the Godleys, met the Russells, and had a *rechauffe* both of the ball supper and the ball gossip. **1864** *Q. Rev.* July 83 A *réchauffé* of the forgotten criticisms of one of our old English deists. **1870** MISS BROUGHTON *Red as Rose* I. xiii. 272 A *réchauffé* of one's own stale speeches is not an appetising dish. **1976** *Times Lit. Suppl.* 26 Mar. 337/2 The main objection to the book is that it is a *réchauffé*... Stevenson's contribution now bears a family resemblance to his piece then. **1977** *Times* 3 Sept. 10/5 Cru de Meynas..is a useful bottle for casual meals of cold game or réchauffées.

B. *adj.* Of food: reheated. Also *fig.*, rehashed.

1909 WEBSTER, *Réchauffé*..p.a. masc., *réchauffée*..p.a. fem... Warmed over;—of a dish food. Also fig. **1921** *Sat. Westm. Gaz.* 17 Sept. 14/1 Professor Wendell..frequently inserts what the dust-cover or jacket of the English edition denominates his 'humanity' between a hackneyed quotation and a platitude tastefully rechauffé. **1977** *Gramophone* Feb. 1307/1 These, then, are humdrum, *rechauffé* performances full of gestures by rote. **1977** *Broadcast* 19 Dec. 16/2 Canned laughter: Artificial sauce used to season rechauffe mirth.

Hence **rechauffeed** *ppl. a.* = sense B above.

1883 E. W. HAMILTON *Diary* 3 Feb. (1972) II. 395 The programme, to which he leans in addition to the unexciting non-contentious, *rechauffeed* bills, is Metropolitan Government and Local Government for Ireland.

‖**réchauffer** (reʃofe), *v.* [Fr.: see RÉCHAUFFÉ.] Usu. as *infin.*, to warm up again; *fig.*, to rehash. Hence ‖**réchauffage** (-aʒ) [Fr. suff. *-age*: cf. -AGE], a rehash.

1965 *Punch* 31 Mar. 473/3 This plan to store up the dead at minus two hundred degrees C. and then *rechauffer* them to life when medical science has learned how to put right whatever it was they died of. **1967** *Punch* 28 June 961/3 In telling the story of her career Lady Summerskill has fallen into the Politician's Pitfall of believing that it is possible to *réchauffer* old Parliamentary speeches. **1972** E. LUCIE-SMITH in Cox & Dyson *20th-Cent. Mind* III. xvi. 466 Most of what they produced was a mere *réchauffage* of pre-war ideas.

re-chaw, *v.* [RE- 5 a.] *trans.* To chaw again.

1616 J. LANE *Cont. Sqr.'s T.* VII. 102 Which soddaine motion so entind his blood, as causd him aye rechawe his moodie cudd.

rechayse, variant of RECHASE *sb. Obs.*

rechche, reche, obs. forms of RECK *v.*

†**reche**, *v. Obs.*⁻¹ [Of obscure origin: cf. RACHE *v.*²] *trans.* To tear, rend.

c **1400** *Destr. Troy* 13939 He wan vpo fote, All-to rechit his robis & his ronke here; Fowle frusshet his face with his felle nailes.

reche, obs. form of REACH, RETCH.

recheat (rɪ'tʃiːt), †**rechate**, *sb. Obs.* exc. *arch.* Also 8 ra-. [Prob. ad. OF. *rachat, vbl. sb. from *rachater* RECHEAT *v.*] †**a.** The act of calling together the hounds to begin or continue the chase of a stag, or at the close of the hunt. *Obs. rare.* **b.** The series of notes sounded on a horn for one or other of these purposes.

1470–85 MALORY *Arthur* x. lii, Fyrste to the vncoupelynge, to the sekynge, to the rechate, to the flyghte. **1575** TURBERV. *Venerie* xl. 111 They may come in nearer towardes their houndes & blowe a Rechate to their houndes to comforte them. **1590** COCKAINE *Treat. Hunting* D iv, The Rechate, with three winds, The first, one long and fiue short. The second one long and one short. The third, one long and sixe short. **1602** *2nd Pt. Return fr. Parnass.* II. v. 853 As you sounded the recheat before, so now you must sound the releefe three times. **1651** DAVENANT *Gondibert* II. xxxvii, Now winde they a Recheat, the rous'd Dear's knell. **1741** *Compl. Fam.-Piece* II. i. 292 He that gives the fatal Blow, ought to sound a Racheat, to assemble together the rest of the Company, as also the Dogs. **1862** *Luck of Ladysmede* II. 343, I did not think there was one amongst ye who could sound a recheat so like mine own.

fig. **1599** SHAKS. *Much Ado* I. i. 242 That I will haue a rechate winded in my forehead..all women shall pardon me.

†**recheat, rechate**, *v. Obs.* Also 6 **rechat.** [ad. OF. *rachater, racheter* to reassemble, rally (Godef.).] *intr.* To blow a recheat. Also with *in.*

13.. *Gaw. & Gr. Knt.* 1911 Huntes hyȝed hem þeder, with hornez ful mony, Ay rechatande aryȝt til þay þe renk seȝen. *Ibid.* 1446. *c* **1400** *Master of Game* (MS. Digby 182) xxxiii, He shulde rechate..and blowe after þat a moote. *Ibid.* xxxv, þei shull blowe a moot and rechate and relaye and go forth þer with awaye rechatynge amonge. **1526** SKELTON *Magnyf.* 2177 Yonder is a horson for me doth rechate: Adewe, syrs, for I thynke leyst that I come to late. **1575** TURBERV. *Venerie* xl. 114 If they finde that he hunteth the chaffed Deare, they shall rechate in for the rest of the houndes. **1602** *2nd Pt. Return fr. Parnass.* II. v. 850 Then must you sound 3 notes, with 3 windes, and recheat..vpon the same with 3 windes. **1612** DRAYTON *Poly-olb.* xiii. 127 Rechating with his horn, which then the hunter chears.

Hence **re'cheating** *vbl. sb.*

c **1400** *Master of Game* (MS. Digby 182) xxxiii, þe moot shulde neuer be blowe byfore þe rechatynge.

'recheck, *sb.* [f. the vb.] A renewed or second examination or investigation.

1926 *Amer. Jrnl. Med. Sci.* CLXXI. 851 A recheck showed that no fermentation test had been done on the urine, which vitiated the value of the result. **1972** T. ARDIES *This Suitcase is going to Explode* xii. 190 Those rechecks on the refugee scientists were *supposed* to be thorough. **1977** J. M. JOHNSON in Douglas & Johnson *Existential Sociol.* viii. 243 Upon receiving the reports and memo, the supervisor of Unit Two did not return the forms to the workers for a recheck.

re'check, *v.* [RE- 5 a.] *trans.* and *intr.* To check again. Hence **re'checking** *vbl. sb.*

1902 'MARK TWAIN' in *Harper's Weekly* 6 Dec. 4/2 Your luggage..rechecked, fare-ticket and sleeper changed. **1957** J. S. HUXLEY *Relig. without Revelation* iii. 51 Constant checking and rechecking against fact. **1962** L. DEIGHTON *Ipcress File* xi. 71, I decided to recheck his security clearance. **1967** KARCH & BUBER *Offset Processes* x. 469 Retighten the sprocket and recheck by running sheets. **1977** 'E. TREVOR' *Theta Syndrome* ii. 27 A young intern rechecked the patient. **1977** P. G. WINSLOW *Witch Hill Murder* II. 215 All that's left to us is to check and re-check on every aspect of the case.

†**reched.** *Obs.*⁻¹ (Meaning unknown.)

?*a* **1400** *Morte Arth.* 3264 The rowelle whas rede golde with ryalle stonys, Raylide with reched and rubyes inewe.

recheer (riː'tʃɪə(r)), *v.* [RE- 5 a.]

1. *trans.* To cheer or encourage again.

1614 SYLVESTER *Bethulia's Rescue* IV. 392 Untill..The courteous General's words re-cheer her. *a* **1618** —— *Job* III. 63 Re-comfort them shalt Thou, And thus re-cheer them. *a* **1711** KEN *Hymnarium* Poet. Wks. 1721 II. 142 In short time the Light Recheers their Sight. **1773** J. ROSS *Fratricide* III. 545 (MS.) Eternal clemency will hear thy suit, Absolve the error and thy soul recheer.

2. To salute again with a cheer or cheers.

1880 *Standard* 20 May 3 The vessels sail one by one out of the Sound, cheered and re-cheered by women and children.

†**'rechelen**, *v. Obs.*⁻¹ [f. *rechel-s* REKELS: cf. OE. *recelsian.*] *trans.* To smoke with incense.

c **1200** *Trin. Coll. Hom.* 133 Zacharie þo þe he gede in þe temple mid his rechel fat to rechelende þe alter.

recheles, var. of REKELS, incense. *Obs.*

recheles, -leshed(e, -lesliche, -lesnes(se, obs. ff. RECKLESS *a.*, RECKLESSHEAD, etc.

†**recheles-ship.** *Obs.* In 4 -shepe, -schipe, 5 rechelaschepe. [f. ME. *recheles* RECKLESS + -SHIP.] Recklessness, carelessness.

1303 R. BRUNNE *Handl. Synne* 2559 Wyllyng, certys, y dyd hyt noght, But for rechelesshepe of þoght. **13..** *Prick of Love* 355 in *Min. Poems fr. Vernon MS.* 277 Rechelesschipe is the thridde [sin]—þou takest no kep what men þe bidde. *c* **1430** *Freemasonry* (1840) 191 Suche a mon, throȝe rechelaschepe, Myȝth do the craft schert worschepe.

†**rechelest, -lust.** *Obs. rare.* [OE. *recceliest*, f. *recceléas* RECKLESS.] Carelessness, negligence.

c **888** K. ÆLFRED *Boeth.* xviii. §3 Hi..for recceleste forleton unwriten þara monna ðeawas. *c* **1200** *Trin. Coll. Hom.* 45 þurh mannes gemeleste and þurh mannes recheleste. *Ibid.* 63 þurh uniweald oðer recheluste.

rechel-fat, var. of REKEL-FAT, censer. *Obs.*

rechelis, var. REKELS, incense. *Obs.*

‖**recherché** (rəʃɛrʃe), *a.* [F., pa. pple. of *rechercher*, f. *re-* RE- + *chercher* to seek, SEARCH.] Carefully sought out; hence, extremely choice or rare. (Common in 19th c., esp. of meals, articles of food or drink, and dress.)

1722 RICHARDSON *Statues Italy* 121 This Excuse may be thought too partial, and *Recherché*. **1776** H. WALPOLE *Corr.* (1857) VI. 310 Sly as Montesquieu without being so *recherché*. **1823** BYRON *Juan* XIII. xxviii, At Henry's mansion, then,..Was Juan a *recherché*, welcome guest. **1838** LONGF. in *Life* (1891) I. 298 A quiet *recherché* dinner at the Albion. **1883** *Century Mag.* Aug. 608/1 A tasteful and *recherché* stock of frames and feathers and ribbons. **1939** JOYCE *Finnegans Wake* (1964) 149 The fiery goodmother Miss Fortune (who the lost time we had the pleasure we have had our little *recherché* brush with, what, Schott?). **1946** A. CHRISTIE *Come, tell me how you Live* viii. 148 We have a very delicious and recherché lunch with the French Commandant. **1955** *Times* 16 May 11/4 The more recherché of whose oratorios ought to be remembered for future eighteenth-century festivals. **1970** I. MURDOCH *Fairly Honourable Defeat* I. v. 55 The smell..was fresh and bitter and at the same time nauseating. Hilda wondered if it were not caused by some extremely recherché form of dry rot. **1978** *Dædalus* Fall 4 Our perception of a lifetime has become increasingly recherché.

‖**recherche du temps perdu** (rəʃɛrʃ dy tɑ̃ pɛrdy). [ad. F. *à la recherche du temps perdu* (also used), lit. 'in search of the lost time', used by Marcel Proust (1871–1922) as the title of a reminiscent novel (1913–27).]

The remembrance of things past; the narration or evocation of one's early life.

1946 L. P. HARTLEY *Sixth Heaven* xi. 233 A feeble poor-spirited attempt to revive the joys of childhood, a journey à la recherche du temps perdu. **1952** *Spectator* 19 Dec. 854/2 Like so many sensitive novels by contemporary women novelists, it is a *recherche du temps perdu*. **1966** M. STEEN *Looking Glass* x. 217, I..listened to the two old friends sharing their *recherche du temps perdu*. **1975** *Broadcast* 3 Nov. 14/3 Old Times by Harold Pinter..is, of course, a play about *recherche du temps perdu*.

reches, obs. form of RICHES.

rechew (riː'tʃuː), *v.* [RE- 5 a.] To chew again.

1609 J. DAVIES *Holy Rood* G iij b, Nor could He (as some Beasts rechew their meat..) Rechew this Bread. **1713** C'TESS WINCHELSEA *Misc. Poems* 292 When..unmolested Kine rechew the Cud. **1856** J. CUMMING *Script. Readings, Deut. xiv.* 228 The animal that rechews its food as the sheep.

re'child, *v.* [RE- 5 a.] To become a child again.

1606 SYLVESTER *Du Bartas* II. iv. II. *Magnificence* 526 When he (re-childing) sought With childish sport to still thy cryes.

rechless(e, -les(s)ly, -lesness, obs. ff. RECKLESS *a.*, RECKLESSLY, -NESS.

rechoose (riː'tʃuːz), *v.* [RE- 5 a.] *trans.* To choose again.

1690 CHILD *Disc. Trade* (1694) 149 All the twelve to be rechosen. **1795** W. TAYLOR in *Monthly Rev.* XVI. 524 The liberty of rechoosing the members of the..assembly. **1885** *North Star* 1 July 3/2 The old-time ceremony of re-choosing a representative.

rechristen (riː'krɪs(ə)n), *v.* [RE- 5 a.] *trans.* To christen anew; to rename.

1796 LAMB *Let. to Coleridge* 10 June, Now it is rechristened from a Sonnet to an Effusion. **1822** T. L. PEACOCK *Maid Marian* 221 He was rechristened without a priest. **1861** J. G. SHEPPARD *Fall Rome* vi. 334 It was deemed advisable to re-christen the district with the old imperial name.

re'christianize, *v.* [RE- 5 a.] *trans.* To christianize again or afresh.

1792 *Gentl. Mag.* LXII. I. 147 His assertion, that the world wants to be re-christianized. **1851** C. WORDSWORTH *Occas. Serm.* Ser. II. 25 His more proper task of re-christianizing the multitudes of his own Italy.

recht, Sc. form of RIGHT *a.* and *adv.*

‖**Rechtsstaat** ('rɛçtsʃtaːt). Also (*erron.*) **Rechtstaat.** [Ger., f. *rechts* gen. of *recht* RIGHT *sb.*¹ + *staat* STATE *sb.*] A country in which the rule of law prevails.

1935 J. D. LEWIS *Genossenschaft-Theory of Otto von Gierke* vi. 69 Being a *Rechtstaat*, the modern state, the German state for example, stands within law and recognizes legal limitations upon its own sovereign will. **1944** F. A. HAYEK *Road to Serfdom* vi. 54 The early nineteenth-century discussions in Germany about the nature of the *Rechtsstaat*. **1948** [see *kulturstaat* s.v. KULTUR]. **1963** *Economist* 5 Oct. 5/1 In a *Rechtsstaat* (state based on law) only the judgements of a competent court are valid and binding. **1977** *Times Lit. Suppl.* 1 July 809/2 Try as the lawyers might..to make Franco Spain a *Rechtsstaat*.

rechy, variant of REECHY *a.*

‖**recibiendo** (reθi'vjɛndo). *Bullfighting.* [Sp., lit. 'receiving', f. *recibir* (see next).] A method of killing the bull by which the bullfighter receives the charging bull on the point of his sword. Also as quasi-*adv.*

1902 *Encycl. Brit.* XXVI. 460/1 If the *matador* remains without moving, or rather moving only his body to avoid the stroke of the horns, the thrust is known as *recibiendo*. **1932** E. HEMINGWAY *Death in Afternoon* ix. 88 He did kill several times recibiendo, receiving the bull on the sword in the old manner. **1976** E. P. BENSON *Bulls of Ronda* iv. 30 'He's going to receive the bull. What they call a *recibiendo*.'..The bull ..propelled itself against the waiting man... The sword plunged deep into the entrails of the bull.

‖**recibir** (reθi'vir). *Bullfighting.* [Sp., lit. 'to receive'.] The action on the part of a bullfighter of receiving a charging bull while remaining stationary.

1838 *Q. Rev.* LXII. 411 The picador, holding his lance under his right arm, pushes to the right, and pulls his horse to the left; the bull is thus turned from his plunge, and passes on to the next horseman. This is called 'recibir', 'hoc habet'. **1932** R. CAMPBELL *Taurine Provence* iii. 76 There are several forms of estocada... Some..are attacks on stationary bulls, others, as in the Recibir, are performed by the stationary man on the charging bull.

†**re'cide**, *v. Obs.* Also 7 reside. [ad. L. *recidĕre*, f. *re-* RE- + *cadĕre* to fall. Cf. INCIDE *v.*[2]]

1. *intr.* To fall back, relapse.

1628 FELTHAM *Resolves* II. xcvii. 284 All good things,.. without perpetuall vigilancie,.. will reside [*ed.* 1677, recide], and fall away. **1643** *Plain English* 21 People conceive the Parliament recide from their principles and votes.

2. [For *reside.*] To subside, go down.

1634 T. JOHNSON *Parey's Chirurg.* VIII. xiii. (1678) 205 The tumor..will recide without noise, either by the pressure of your fingers, or [etc.].

recide, recidence, obs. ff. RESIDE, etc.

†**recidivate,** *pa. pple.* and *v. Obs. rare.* Also 6 res-. [f. ppl. stem med.L. *recidīvāre*, f. *recidīvus* RECIDIVE.] **a.** *pa. pple.* Fallen back. **b.** *v. intr.* To fall back, relapse.

1528 in W. H. Turner *Select. Rec. Oxford* (1880) 59 Y[e].. Mayor..being residivate into the saide interdiction. **1611** COTGR., *Recidiver*, to recidiuate, relapse, fall backe, or againe. *a* **1626** BP. ANDREWES *Opuscula* (1629) 79 (L.) Thus then to recidivate, and to go against her own act and promise [etc.]. **1677** COLES *Eng.-Lat. Dict.*, To Recidivate, *recido, relabor.*

†**recidivation.** *Obs.* Also 5 resydyuacion, 5–6 -iuation, 6 -evatyon; 6–7 resid-, recydiuation (-acion, etc.). [a. F. *récidivation* (15th c.), or ad. med.L. *recidīvātiōn-em*, n. of action f. *recidīvāre*: see prec.]

1. Relapse into sin, error, crime, etc.; backsliding, apostasy. (Very common in 17th c.)

c **1420** LYDG. *Assembly of Gods* 1856 As for Resydiuacion ys no more to sey But aftyr confession turnyng ayene to syn. **1513** BRADSHAW *St. Werburge* II. 452 The faith of holy churche dyd ever there endure Without recidiuacion and infection sure. **1609** BIBLE (Douay) *Ecclus.* xxxiv. *comm.*, Recidivation into sinne maketh the former repentance frustrate. **1693** in Hickes & Nelson *J. Kettlewell* III. lxxii. (1718) 382, I promise a great Watchfulness..against all Temptations to any Degrees, or Instances,..of Recidivation till I am called to lay aside my Business here.

2. A relapse in a sickness or disease. (Common in 16–17th c.)

1513 MORE *Rich. III* (1883) 34 There is as phisicians saye ..double the perill in the recidiuacion that was in the first sicknes. **1525** *St. Papers Hen. VIII* (1849) VI. 509 The Frenche King was..sore syke agayne, fallon in to a newe recidivation. **1610** DONNE *Pseudo-martyr* 138 As all recidiuations and relapses, are worse then the disease. **1697** R. PEIRCE *Bath Mem.* I. v. 85 Drinking the Waters, to prevent the Return of his Chollick (for he had had some Threatnings of a Recidivation). **1706** in PHILLIPS.

3. The fact of falling again under an interdict.

1528 in W. H. Turner *Select. Rec. Oxford* (1880) 59 Uppon payne of residivation into y[e] same interdiction.

recidive ('rɛsɪdɪv), *a.* and *sb. rare.* [ad. L. *recidīv-us*, f. *recidĕre*: see RECIDE and -IVE. In sense B. a. = F. *récidive*, med.L. *recidīva.*]

†**A.** *adj.* Falling back, relapsing. *Obs.*

1537 CROMWELL *Let.* 6 June in Merriman *Life & Lett.* (1902) II. 60 But seing their cankred recidive hert [etc.]. **1659** MACALLO *Can. Physick* 75 The evil humours remaining after a Crise, are wont to make one recidive or relapsing.

B. *sb.* †**a.** = RECIDIVATION 2. *Obs.*

1600 HOLLAND *Livy* XXIV. xxix. 529 It might soone after by relapse fall backe, as it were, into a recidive, and a worse disease and more daungerous than the other.

b. = RECIDIVIST.

1854 J. B. DALGAIRNS *Devot. Heart of Jesus* (ed. 2) 32 The feeble penance of such a recidive as Anne de Rohan.

†**recidive,** *v. Obs.*[-1] [ad. med.L. *recidīvāre* or F. *récidiver* (1517): see prec.] = RECIDIVATE *v.*

1548 UDALL, etc. *Erasm. Par. Mark* x. 73 Ofte tymes recidiuing, and falling into the same disease.

recidivism (rɪ'sɪdɪvɪz(ə)m). [f. as next + -ISM.] The habit of relapsing into crime.

1886 *Pall Mall G.* 24 May 3/2 Recidivism is largely represented by the low foreheads, the scowling brows and cunning eyes. **1895** tr. *Ferri's Crim. Sociol.* 256 The great importance of statistics of recidivism. **1971** *Sci. Amer.* May 51/1 There is no strong evidence..that recidivism increases with leniency of sentence. **1977** *Listener* 15 Dec. 803/2 But though the problem of recidivism and rehabilitation still remains, it can hardly be the chief cause of today's overcrowded prisons.

recidivist (rɪ'sɪdɪvɪst). [ad. mod.F. *récidiviste*, f. *récidiver*: see RECIDIVE *v.* and -IST.] **a.** One who relapses; *esp.* one who habitually relapses into crime.

1880 COBBOLD in *Lond. Med. Record* May 172 Of the 82 males, 61 were cases of relapse; of the 28 women, 10 were recidivists. **1882** *Pall Mall G.* 16 Dec. 3 The convicts..are to be transported to Madagascar and their places taken by the recidivists of France. **1895** tr. *Ferri's Crim. Sociol.* 255 The hardened recidivists, who ought to be considered as degenerate criminals, or criminals by profession. **1931** *Sun* (Baltimore) 20 Jan. 10/2 This creates a body of recidivists who are being constantly released and as constantly returned. **1964** *Listener* 26 Mar. 507/1 The Reader in criminology at Oxford has given me the following definition of a recidivist: A recidivist is the offender who neither mends his ways spontaneously nor learns to avoid detection, and who is neither deterred by the experience of conviction nor reformed by any of the methods in the courts' repertoire. **1981** W. EBERSOHN *Divide Night* ii. 26 Old recidivists who felt at home only in jail and would be back again and again.
fig. **1896** *Life A. J. Gordon* 302 The human heart is, in his opinion, an incorrigible recidivist.

b. *attrib.* or as *adj.*

1920 *Contemp. Rev.* Nov. 684 It is the source of depraved, unchastened, even of recidivist, tendencies, as well as of those which point towards a wider and more perfect life. **1931** J. S. HUXLEY *What dare I Think?* iii. 88 Sterilization has been suggested, but this seems disproportionate save in recidivist cases of philoprogenitiveness which seem otherwise incurable. **1950** *Chambers's Jrnl.* 230/1 Often..he had the opportunity of seeing the overcrowded masses of recidivist (frequent offender) prisoners, many of them unprepossessing and hardened-looking roughs, with whom he was glad he had not to mix. **1962** *Lancet* 15 Dec. 1278/1 My work as a probation officer among recidivist alcoholics in Pentonville Prison.

reci'divity. *rare.* [f. as prec. + -ITY.] Tending to relapse (*Syd. Soc. Lex.* 1897).

1937 G. FRANKAU *More of Us* xii. 123 Man asks you..not to nag him for his recidivities.

recidivous (rɪ'sɪdɪvəs), *a.* [f. L. *recidīv-us* + -OUS.] Liable to fall back or relapse.

1658 PHILLIPS, *Recidivous*, falling, or sliding back to the same passe as it was before. [Hence in Bailey, Johnson, and later Dicts.] **1890** *Times* 24 Oct. 3/5 The establishment of agricultural colonies for recidivous criminals.

†**recidu'ity.** *Obs. rare*[-1]. [f. L. type **recidu-us* (cf. *dēciduus*) + -ITY.] = RECIDIVATION 2.

1597 A. M. tr. *Guillemeau's Fr. Chirurg.* 19/1 Wherethroughe the whole curatione consisteth without reciduitye.

reciet, recieve, reciffe, obs. ff. RECEIPT *sb.*, RECEIVE.

†**recinct.** *Obs. rare*[-1]. [f. as next, or ad. It. *recinto, ricinto*: cf. *precinct.*] Compass, circumference, encircling line.

1665 J. WEBB *Stone-Heng* (1725) 7 He calls Cronets those that lie upon the Pylasters of the outward Circle, in relation to the Form of a Crown, as making the Recinct thereof.

†**recinct,** *v. Obs. rare*[-1]. [f. L. *recinct-*, ppl. stem of *recingĕre*: see RE- 2 and CINCT.] *trans.* To surround, enclose.

1597 A. M. tr. *Guillemeau's Fr. Chirurg.* 31 b/1 They with wett cloutes..recincted and defended them.

†**recine'ration.** *Obs. rare*[-1]. [RE- 5 a.] A second reduction to ashes.

1657–83 EVELYN *Hist. Relig.* (1850) I. 199 Things visible are made invisible, and visible again by the art of fermentation,..cribration, and even recineration.

recipe ('rɛsɪpiː), *v. imper.* and *sb.* [L. *recipe* take (2nd sing. imper. of *recipĕre* to RECEIVE), used by physicians (abbreviated R, ℞) to head prescriptions, and hence applied to these and similar formulae. So F. *récipé* (15th c.).]

†**A.** *v. imper.* = 'Take'. *Obs.*

c **1400** *Lanfranc's Cirurg.* 81 Recipe litargium as myche as þou wolt. *a* **1500** *Harl. MS.* 5401 in *Babees Bk.* 53 Recipe brede gratyd, & eggis. **1543** TRAHERON *Vigo's Chirurg.* 52 b/1 Recipe of syrupe de besantiis, of syrupe of roses. *a* **1652** BLOOMFIELD *Blossoms* xiii. in Ashm. (1652) 308 Some ..unto thee shall say, Recipe this, and that, with a thousand things more.

B. *sb.* **1.** *Med.* A formula for a medical prescription; a prescription, or the remedy prepared in accordance with this.

1584 R. PARSONS *Leicester's Commw.* (1641) 23 Hee died in the way of an extreame Flux, caused by an Italian Recipe. **1622** MABBE tr. *Aleman's Guzman d' Alf.* I. 31 Hee would thrust his hand into his Satchell,..and then would hee take forth one of his recipe's. **1697** TUTCHIN *Search Honesty* ix, They, with their Recipes, Corrupt our Blood. **1742** BLAIR *Grave* 333 Where are thy recipes and cordials now? **1801** WOLCOTT (P. Pindar) *Tears & Smiles* Wks. 1812 V. 50 To bring her back to health again Of recipes a score. **1899** *Allbutt's Syst. Med.* VIII. 579 It would be useless to try to enumerate all the..drugs, and recipes for their application, which have been tried.

transf. *a* **1679** T. GOODWIN *Unregen. Man's Guilt.* XIII. viii. Wks. 1865 X. 546 Those two known cordial recipes.. commonly taken by most Christians in their distresses. **1865** CARLYLE *Fredk. Gt.* IX. x. (1872) III. 151 But Friedrich Wilhelm steps in with a healing recipe: 'Let there be Four Reich's-Feldmarschalls'.

attrib. **1674** R. GODFREY *Inj. & Ab. Physic* Pref., Many of those Recipe-Medicines..do more harm than good. **1781** J. RIPLEY *Sel. Orig. Lett.* 113 Every author (before..Dr. Brachin) appears to me only recipe men, and smatterers in farriery.

2. A statement of the ingredients and procedure necessary for the making or compounding of some preparation, esp. of a dish in cookery; a receipt. Also *fig.*

1716 T. CAVE *Let.* 5 Oct. in M. M. Verney *Verney Lett. 18th Cent.* (1930) II. xxii. 45 Sister Lovett and I greatly admire the Ink you wrote last with,..but dare not wish for the Recipe it being no doubt a Secrett. **1743** H. WALPOLE *Let.* 12 Oct., Recipes for pastry ware. **1775** R. CHANDLER *Trav. Asia Minor* lvii. 195 The epicure will not lament that the entire recipe has not reached us. **1846** GREENER *Sci. Gunnery* 177 The best method of staining barrels is by the following recipe;..1 oz. Muriate Tincture of Steel [etc.]. **1853** SOYER *Pantroph.* 289 Two thousand years have elapsed since Cato wrote the recipe for his somewhat heavy tart. **1947** [see PROMOTING *vbl. sb.* 3]. **1969** *Times* 12 May 16/3 The D.N.A. molecules in the cells of normal people contain a chemical recipe for manufacturing ordinary haemoglobin. **1981** *Times* 9 Apr. 9/7 Another recipe made especially for Easter is fritters of soft ricotta cheese.

3. *transf.* A means (actual or suggested) for attaining or effecting some end.

a **1643** SUCKLING *Let.* Wks. (1646) 69 To marry is the best Recipe for living honest. **1675** *Art Contentm.* x. §11 (1684) 234 When those are precluded, for all the rest St. Pauls recipe is a catholicon, 'Be careful for nothing'. **1789** H. WALPOLE *Let.* 14 Aug., Easy as I call this recipe, you, I believe, would find it..difficult to execute. **1820** SCOTT *Abbot* xxvi, We have the Plague proposing us a visit, the best of all recipes for thinning a land. **1876** MOZLEY *Univ. Serm.* i. 23 This Corporation has one recipe against all difficulties —organisation.

4. *Comb.*, as **recipe-book**, a book containing recipes, a cookery-book; also *fig.*

1872 *Young Englishwoman* Dec. 662 Recipes of practical utility will appear..to be neatly copied into their recipe-books. **1952** M. LASKI *Village* iii. 62 To have read the recipe-books and produced appetising meals for her family would have meant, to her, willing acceptance of..servitude. **1964** P. STREVENS in D. Abercrombie et al. *Daniel Jones* 125 Teaching grammars in the future..will be superior..to those of the past which have simply been grammar-teaching recipe-books. **1976** L. DEIGHTON *Twinkle, twinkle, Little Spy* xiv. 140 Bessie Mann was asking me how many kids we were going to have, and I found myself looking at recipe books and baby carriages.

re'cipher, *v.* Also recypher. [RE- 5 a.] *trans.* To encipher again (a message that is already in cipher). Hence **re'cipher** *sb.*; **re'ciphering** *vbl. sb.*

1961 in WEBSTER. **1963** *Times* 21 May 7/3 He said the purpose of such a table would be to convert plain language letters or punctuation into figures which could then be subsequently reciphered on a reciphering pad. **1975** C. MOTT-RADCLYFFE *Foreign Body in Eye* ii. 28, I remember one telegram, all in re-cypher, beginning, 'I saw the Minister of Foreign Affairs on return from leave yesterday. His Excellency remarked how sunburnt I was looking after my recent holiday in Ireland.'

recipiangle (rɪ'sɪpɪæŋg(ə)l). [a. F. *récipiangle*, f. stem of L. *recipĕre*: see RECEIVE and ANGLE.] An instrument formerly used (chiefly in France) for measuring and laying off angles, esp. in fortification. (See first quot.)

The description in Chambers is based on the article in Trevoux *Dict. Univ.* (1721).

1727–41 CHAMBERS *Cycl.* s.v., The recipiangle..is usually very simple, in form of a square or rather a bevel; consisting of two arms or branches rivetted together and yet moveable like a sector on the centre or rivet. **1802** JAMES *Milit. Dict.* **1875** KNIGHT *Dict. Mech.* 1900/1. **1939** *Nature* 22 Apr. 673/2 The seventy objects which comprise Mr. Court's most recent benefaction include an Italian recipiangle of about 1600. This is an instrument used for measuring angles in surveying, and it is also marked with lines and scales which can be used for making calculations.

recipience (rɪ'sɪpɪəns). *rare.* [f. as next: see -ENCE.] **a.** The act or process of receiving.

1882 in OGILVIE. **1891** *Harper's Mag.* Dec. 156/2 They went and came in rapid processions of renunciation and recipience.

b. Recipient state or condition.

1902 in WEBSTER. **1906** S. S. LAURIE *Synthetica* I. 7 The subject-reality..appears to be a mere potency of recipience and reaction. **1923** *Times Lit. Suppl.* 29 Nov. 801/2 Their [*sc.* the neo-realists'] insistence on the independent reality of the physical world and the passive recipience of the mind in knowing it.

recipiency (rɪ'sɪpɪənsɪ). [f. RECIPIENT: see -ENCY.] Receptivity; reception.

1822 LAMB *Elia* Ser. I. *Dist. Corresp.*, The fine slimes of Nilus..whose maternal recipiency is as necessary as the 'sol pater.' **1850** R. I. WILBERFORCE *Holy Baptism* 52 Their powers of recipiency are yet imperfect. **1855** BROWNING *Cleon* 246 We struggle, fain to enlarge Our bounded physical recipiency.

recipiendary (rɪ'sɪpɪəndərɪ). *rare.* [f. L. *recipiend-*, gerundial stem of *recipĕre* to RECEIVE + -ARY[1], perh. after F. *récipiendaire.*]

1. One about to be received into a society.

1662 J. DAVIES tr. *Olearius' Voy. Ambass.* 43 Enjoyning.. the Bishop of the Province..to examine, not onely the Recipiendaries, but also the Pastors themselves. **1833** CARLYLE *Ct. Cagliostro* Misc. (1872) V. 95 The apt Recipiendary is rapidly promoted through the three grades of Apprentice, Companion, Master.

2. ? A receptacle.

1834 BECKFORD *Italy* II. 76 The old Marialva's delights are centered between his two silver recipiendaries.

recipient (rɪ'sɪpɪənt), *a.* and *sb.* [ad. L. *recipient-em*, pres. pple. of *recipĕre* to RECEIVE: cf. F. *récipient* (16th c.).]

A. *adj.* That receives or is capable of receiving; receptive.

1610 HEALEY *St. Aug. Citie of God* 372 The ponderative judgement of reason, consisting of two intellects, the Recipient and the Agent. **1694** R. BURTHOGGE *Reason & Nat. Spir.* 130 There mention is made..of the Abyss of Waters wrought upon, as the first Recipient Subject. **1872** H. SPENCER *Princ. Pyschol.* (ed. 2) I. II. iv. 220 A difference in feelings, according as the organization is or is not highly recipient. **1893** SIR R. BALL *Story of Sun* 253 Waves which produce the sensation of heat whenever they fall on properly recipient nerves.

B. *sb.* **1.** One who or that which receives, in senses of the vb.

1615 E. HOWES *Stow's Ann.* 939/2 Turning and winding to come from the head to the great Recipient. **1675** TRAHERNE *Chr. Ethics* 351 That they might be fit recipients for the infinite bounty and goodness of God. ? *c* **1730** WATERLAND *Rem. Clarke's Exp. Ch. Catech.* iv, When the recipient is fitly qualified..there is a salutary life-giving virtue annexed to the sacrament. 1794 G. ADAMS *Nat. & Exp. Philos.* III. xxv. 55 This invisible and formless being, the universal recipient of all forms. 1877 FROUDE *Short Stud.* IV. I. xi. (1883) 134 The recipient of the gift expressed his gratitude by corresponding presents.

2. a. *Chem.* A receiver; a (glass) vessel for receiving or holding a liquid. ? *Obs.*

1558 WARDE tr. *Alexis' Secr.* I. I. (1580) 6 Powre the water out of the Recipiente. 1610 B. JONSON *Alch.* II. v, Take away the recipient, And rectifie your menstrue, from the phlegma. 1658 R. WHITE tr. *Digby's Powd. Symp.* (1660) 78 The mercury in the limbick will gather there, and nothing will passe into the recipient. 1707 *Curios. in Husb. & Gard.* 289 The Moisture..filtrates it self to drop into the little Recipients. 1794 G. ADAMS *Nat. & Exp. Philos.* III. xxxiv. 382 Whatever fluid is to be weighed, let it be put into the glass recipient.

b. The receiver of an air-pump. ? *Obs.*

1672 *Phil. Trans.* VII. 5029 He suspended them in the Recipient of his Engin, and exhausted it of Air. 1709 F. HAUKSBEE *Phys.-Mech. Exper.* (1719) 3 Upon the plate of the [air] Pump is always laid a wet Leather, on which the Recipients are placed. 1815 SIMOND *Tour Gt. Brit.* I. 378 A cup of pure water, under the recipient of the pneumatic machine, became a mass of ice.

3. A re-entrant angle.

1811 PINKERTON *Petral.* II. 306 The remarkable articulations..strengthened by projecting angles and recipients.

4. *Linguistics.* The indirect object of a verb or the complement of an adjective.

1937 O. JESPERSEN *Analytic Syntax* xxxviii. 156 In conventional grammar the term *object* is further used for what is governed by an adjective. Here, too, I have avoided the term object..and have adopted instead the term *Recipient*, abbreviated R... R is seen to be chiefly used where Latin, German, etc. have a dative which is not governed by a transitive verb. 1972 R. QUIRK et al. *Gram. Contemp. Eng.* vii. 350 The most typical function of the indirect object is that of *recipient* (or 'dative' participant); *ie* of animate being passively implicated by the happening or state: I've found *you* a place. *Ibid.* 353 The subject may also have a recipient (or 'dative') role with verbs such as *have*, *own*, [etc.]..., as is indicated by the following relation: Mr Smith has bought/given/sold his son a radio→So now his son has/owns/possesses the radio.

re'cipio,motor, *a. rare.* [f. *recipio-* as comb. form of L. *recipĕre* + MOTOR.] Receiving, or connected with the reception of, motor impulses.

1868 H. SPENCER *Princ. Psychol.* I. I. iii. §18 (1872) 49 We shall be..helped by thinking of the afferent nerves as *recipio-motor* and the efferent nerves as *dirigo-motor*.

re'ciprocable, *a. rare*⁻¹. [f. as next + -ABLE.] Capable of reciprocating.

1788 T. TAYLOR *Proclus' Comm.* I. Diss. 44 The superior genera and differences..among which no equal predicate can be assigned reciprocable with man.

reciprocal (rɪ'sɪprəkəl), *a.* and *sb.* Also 6-7 **-all.** [f. L. *reciproc-us* RECIPROQUE + -AL[1].]

A. *adj.*

†**1. a.** Having, or of the nature of, an alternate backward and forward motion. (Said *esp.* of tides.) *Obs.*

Used by Chapman *Iliad* XVIII. 355 to render Gr. ἀψόρροος. 1601 HOLLAND *Pliny* II. 400 Amid the reciprocall tides of the sea, ebbing and flowing in their alternatiue turnes. 1631 MILTON *Epit. Hobson* ii. 30 Obedient to the Moon he spent his date In cours reciprocal. 1662 HOBBES *Seven Prob.* Wks. 1845 VII. 26 The reciprocal and contrary motions of the two pieces of wood. 1726 tr. *Gregory's Elem. Astron.* VI. 843 The reciprocal Tide arising from the four moons [of Jupiter]..is various and uncertain.

†**b.** Of actions: Alternate, alternating. *Obs.*

1667 HOOKE in *Phil. Trans.* II. 539 The Dog being kept alive by the Reciprocal blowing up of his Lungs with Bellowes, and they suffered to subside. 1758 BORLASE *Nat. Hist. Cornwall* 283 The pigeon (whose reciprocal contraction and dilation in those parts is well known).

†**c.** (See quot.) *Obs.*⁻⁰

1727-41 CHAMBERS *Cycl.* s.v., Reciprocal, in poetry, is applied to verses which run the same both backwards and forwards; called also *recurrents*.

2. a. Of the nature of, pertaining to, a return made for something; given, felt, shown, etc., in return; correspondent.

1596 DRAYTON *Legends* iv. 523 And shew in how reciprocall a sort My thankes did with his Courtesie agree. 1647 N. BACON *Disc. Govt. Eng.* I. lviii. (1739) 107 After that Royalty sprung up, the influence thereof upon them exhaled ..a reciprocal interest back again. 1711 HARLEY in Ellis *Orig. Lett.* Ser. II. IV. 266 This the Queen has done without any reciprocal obligation or promise from her Majesty to France. 1770 *Junius' Lett.* xxxviii. 187 He had a right to expect from them a reciprocal demonstration of firmness. 1883 H. DRUMMOND *Nat. Law in Spir. W.* Pref. (1884) 22 No science contributes to another without receiving a reciprocal benefit.

b. Existing on both sides; felt or shared by both parties; mutual. (Cf. 4 a.)

reciprocal defence, in Fortification, a form of flanking defence (Voyle & Stevenson *Milit. Dict.* 1876).

1579 LYLY *Euphues* (Arb.) 130 If the Mother nourysh the childe, and the childe sucke the Mother, that there be as it were a relation and reciprocall order of affection. 1607 J. NORDEN *Surv. Dial.* I. 37, I know there is a kind of reciprocall bond of duty each to the other, and may be broken of either side. 1652 EARL MONM. tr. *Bentivoglio's Hist. Relat.* 66 Spain and..Flanders..may be said to joyn in one common and reciprocall Government. 1751 JOHNSON *Rambler* No. 166 ¶7 Kindness is generally reciprocal. 1785 TRUSLER *Mod. Times* III. 106 We were as happy as matrimony, reciprocal affection, and good circumstances could render us. 1804 WELLINGTON in Gurw. *Desp.* III. 157 This treaty of general defensive alliance, for the reciprocal protection of their respective territories. 1879 FARRAR *St. Paul* (1883) 636 A reciprocal recognition of honest convictions.

3. a. Inversely correspondent or related; correlative, complementary; †opposed. Now chiefly *Math.* (cf. 4 d).

1570 BILLINGSLEY *Euclid* XI. xxxiv. 347 In equall Parallelipipedons the bases are reciprokall to their altitudes. 1632 LITHGOW *Trav.* x. 488 With shrew'd Acerbious speech, you Anathematize My will Reciprocall to yours. 1690 LOCKE *Hum. Und.* II. xxv. §2 Relative Terms that have others answering them with a reciprocal Intimation, as Father and Son,..Cause and Effect. 1852 MULCAHY *Princ. Mod. Geom.* 39 This is the required reciprocal theorem. 1860 TYNDALL *Glac.* I. xv. 103, I first thought it [a chamois] was a man... It evidently made the reciprocal mistake to my own. 1861 FERRERS *Trilinear Co-ordinates* vi. 108 Hence, if the Conic..be a parabola, the point (a, b, c) must lie in the reciprocal Conic.

b. *Math.* Based upon an inverse relationship. ***reciprocal equation, proportion, ratio*** (see quots.). ***reciprocal spiral***, a spiral in which the radius vector varies inversely as the angle through which it is turned.

1823 MITCHELL *Dict. Math. & Phys. Sci.* 411 *Reciprocal equations are those which contain several pairs of roots, which are the reciprocal of each other. 1656 tr. *Hobbes' Elem. Philos.* (1839) 171 If there be three continual proportionals, and again, three other continual proportions, which have the same middle term, their extremes will be in *reciprocal proportion. 1709 J. WARD *Introd. Math.* I. vii. §2 If More require Less, or Less require More..then the Terms will be in Reciprocal Proportion. 1823 MITCHELL *Dict. Math. & Phys. Sci.* 412 *Reciprocal proportion* is when the reciprocals of the two last terms have the same ratio as the quantities of the first terms. *Ibid.*, **Reciprocal ratio* is the ratio of the reciprocals of two quantities. 1743 EMERSON *Fluxions* ii. 144 To draw a Tangent to the *reciprocal spiral. 1886 CARR *Synopsis Math.* I. II. 725 The Hyperbolic or Reciprocal Spiral.

c. ***reciprocal innervation*** or ***inhibition*** (Physiol.): an arrangement of nerve stimulation as a result of which contraction of one muscle or group of muscles to produce movement is accompanied by simultaneous inhibition of an antagonistic muscle or group of muscles, whose contraction would tend to produce the opposite movement.

1897 C. S. SHERRINGTON in *Jrnl. Physiol.* XXII. 327 It has revealed to me an almost unexpectedly significant number of examples of depressor effect generally, perhaps always, in combination with pressor effects, that is to say, in the form of reciprocal innervations. 1906 —— *Integrative Action Nervous Syst.* iii. 83 (*heading*) Reciprocal inhibition. 1942 JOHNSTON & WHILLIS *Gray's Anat.* (ed. 28) 942 Experimental evidence shows that all the fundamental reflexes of posture.., the reciprocal innervation of antagonists, and the elementary combination of synergists, can still occur without the cerebellum. 1960 W. B. CROW *Synopsis of Biol.* lxv. 445 Neurons connect up two or more efferent paths so that two or more muscles come into action together, or one is inhibited when another comes into operation (reciprocal innervation). 1971 *Sci. Amer.* Aug. 75/1 One principle Sherrington discovered was 'reciprocal innervation'. 1977 G. H. SAGE *Introd. Motor Behav.* (ed. 2) viii. 157 The flexion reflex consists of a contraction of the flexor muscles while reciprocal connections with the antagonistic extensor muscles cause reciprocal inhibition.

d. *Genetics.* Of each of a pair of crosses: complementary to another in that the male parent in each is of the same kind as the female parent in the other.

1902 W. BATESON *Rep. Evolution Comm. R. Soc.* I. 21 Reciprocal crosses..showed clearly that of the two pairs of antagonistic characters, the violet colour is dominant. 1909 —— *Mendel's Princ. Heredity* xi. 203 When the cross is in the form pure single ♀ × double-throwing ♂, all the F_1 plants give a mixture of doubles and singles in F_2; but when the reciprocal cross is made, namely double-thrower used as ♀ × pure single used as ♂, it is found that the F_1 plants are of two kinds. 1948 H. P. RILEY *Genetics & Cytogenetics* vi. 88 The cross curved × wild type is known technically as the reciprocal of the cross wild type × curved. *Ibid.* vii. 96 When genes are in autosomes reciprocal crosses normally give identical results, but when genes located in the X chromosome are dealt with, the results of reciprocal crosses are different. 1971 D. J. COVE *Genetics* viii. 111 If some genetical information is also carried in the cytoplasm, the unequal contribution of cytoplasm to the zygote by the two gametes should provide a way of detecting it. The technique used for this is the reciprocal cross.

e. *Physics.* In the names of quantities defined as reciprocals of standard physical units, as ***reciprocal centimetre, ohm, second*** (see quots.).

1934 H. E. WHITE *Introd. Atomic Spectra* i. 6 Wave numbers..are units with the dimensions of reciprocal centimeters, abbreviated cm^{-1}. 1960 BRAND & SPEAKMAN *Molecular Struct.* i. 8 The passage of energy between matter and radiation occurs in quanta of magnitude ΔE, where $\Delta E = h\nu$. When ΔE is expressed in terms of the erg and ν as reciprocal seconds, Planck's constant, h, has the value 6.6256×10^{-27} erg sec. 1960 A. D. CROSS *Introd. Pract. Infra-Red Spectroscopy* I. 2 Band positions are quoted in units of wave number (ν) which are expressed in reciprocal centimetres (cm^{-1})... However, the true unit of frequency (ν) is given in reciprocal seconds (sec^{-1}). 1978 *Sci. Amer.* Dec. 66/1 The maximum conductivity is somewhat greater than 2,000 reciprocal ohms per centimeter (equivalent to a resistivity of less than .0005 ohm per centimeter).

f. ***reciprocal course***: a path followed by a person or craft which is opposite in direction to one with which it stands in relation, e.g., to the one desired or the one which was followed immediately before.

1946 *Happy Landings* (Air Ministry) July 5/3 The immediate action is to turn on the reciprocal course. 1958 'N. SHUTE' *Rainbow & Rose* ii. 57, I..flew out to sea..on the reciprocal course, and then turned in again and flew towards the coast on 110°. 1961 B. FERGUSSON *Watery Maze* ii. 49 All these craft had lately been 'degaussed'..with unexpected effects on their compasses, and some of the shoreward-bound parties were steering on a reciprocal course.

4. Corresponding or answering to each other, as being either similar or complementary.

a. of acts, feelings, duties, etc. (Cf. 2 b.)

1605 SHAKS. *Lear* IV. vi. 267 Let our reciprocall vowes be remembred. 1632 LITHGOW *Trav.* IX. 405 Leauing our reciprocall loues behind vs, wee diuided our bodies East and West. 1741 RICHARDSON *Pamela* (1824) I. 210 The highest civilities..and reciprocal good wishes all around. 1781 GIBBON *Decl. & F.* xix. II. 134 After so many reciprocal injuries, Gallus had reason to fear and to distrust. 1856 FROUDE *Hist. Eng.* (1858) II. vii. 138 Their relations were already embittered by many reciprocal acts of hostility. 1872 YEATS *Growth Comm.* 160 Barcelona and Cadiz..also entered into like alliances for reciprocal privileges.

†**b.** of things or persons sent by one party to another. *Obs.*

1633 PRYNNE *1st Pt. Histrio-m.* 20 Pagans, who Consecrated this day,..and sent reciprocall Newyeeres-gifts to their friends vpon it. 1641 EARL MONM. tr. *Biondi's Civil Warres* III. 142 Reciprocall Embassadors..had already accorded all differences with the Dolphin. 1716 M. DAVIES *Athen. Brit.* II. 30 Some of King Henry the 8th's and Queen Anne Bolen's reciprocal letters were printed. 1783 *Prelim. Art. Peace w. Spain* viii. 21 The necessary orders shall be sent by each of the high Contracting parties, with reciprocal passports for the Ships.

c. of things in themselves. Somewhat *rare*.

1661 BOYLE *Style of Script.* (1675) 75 The Books of Scripture illustrate and expound each other: Genesis and the Apocalypse are in some things reciprocal commentaries. 1718 *Freethinker* No. 40 ¶5 Allegiance and Protection are reciprocal in all Countries. 1839-48 BAILEY *Festus* xxv. 312 The world and man are just reciprocal Yet contrary. 1884 tr. *Lotze's Metaph.* 27 Each will continue to exercise influences on others or to be affected by their influence. These reciprocal agencies [etc.].

d. *Math.* in ***reciprocal curves, figures, polars, quantities, triangles***, etc. (Cf. quots.)

1570 BILLINGSLEY *Euclid* VI. def. ii. 153 b, Reciprocall figures are those, when the termes of proportion are both antecedentes and consequentes in either figure. 1797 *Encycl. Brit.* (ed. 3) XVI. 29/1 Reciprocal, in mathematics, is applied to quantities which multiplied together produce unity. 1848 *Solutions Camb. Senate-Ho. Problems* (1851) 119 This theorem may also be proved by the method of Reciprocal Polars. 1852 MULCAHY *Princ. Mod. Geom.* 145 The theory of reciprocal curves on the sphere. 1857 CAYLEY in *Q. Jrnl. Math.* 7 On a Theorem relating to Reciprocal Triangles.

†**5. a.** Convertible, synonymous, equivalent in meaning or force. *Obs.*

1621 BURTON *Anat. Mel.* To Rdr. (1676) 26 Aristotle, in his Ethicks, holds..to be wise and happy are reciprocal termes. 1681 R. L'ESTRANGE *Tully's Offices* 139 Make Profit and Honesty Reciprocal. 1733 SHAW tr. *Bacon's De Sapientia, Sphinx* (1803) 61 *note*, Knowledge and power are reciprocal.

†**b.** *Logic.* = CONVERTIBLE *a.* 1 b. *Obs.*

1697 tr. *Burgersdicius his Logic* I. xxxi. 123 Terms are said to be Reciprocal, when there may be a Conversion of the Predicate into the Place of the Subject, and on the contrary. 1725 WATTS *Logic* II. ii. §3 These are the Propositions which are properly convertible, and they are called reciprocal Propositions. 1727-41 CHAMBERS *Cycl.* s.v. *Theorem*, Reciprocal Theorem is one whose converse is true.

6. *Gram.* Of pronouns and verbs, or their signification: **a.** Reflexive.

1611 FLORIO *Rules Ital. Tongue* in *Dict.* 631 It [*si*] makes the Verbe to which it is affixed to be sometimes directly Actiue..and other times Passiue or Reciprocall. 1727 BOYER *Dict. Royal* II. s.v., A Pronoun or a Verb reciprocal. 1766 DEL PINO *New Span. Gram.* 27 The two first serve for the Active, Neuter, and Reciprocal Verbs. *Ibid.* 171 *Estarse*, reciprocal, signifies *to stay long*. 1797 *Encycl. Brit.* (ed. 3) VIII. 50/2 The word *self* subjoined to a personal pronoun forms also the reciprocal pronoun. 1837 G. PHILLIPS *Syriac Gram.* 41 The Demonstrative pronouns..become reciprocal by being joined to the personal pronouns. *Ibid.* 114 The ordinary method of expressing a reciprocal or reflexive sense. 1879 LEWIS & SHORT *Lat. Dict.* s.v. *Reciprocus*, A reciprocal pronoun, as *sibi, se*.

b. Expressing mutual action or relationship.

[1727-41 CHAMBERS *Cycl.* s.v., The abbé de Dangeau defines *reciprocal verbs* to be those whose nominative is plural, and denotes persons acting mutually on one another.] 1844 LATHAM in *Proc. Philolog. Soc.* I. 232 (*heading*) On the Reciprocal Pronouns, and on the Reciprocal Power of the Reflective Verb. *Ibid.*, Too often the terms Reciprocal and Reflective have been made synonymous. 1872 MORRIS *Eng. Accidence* 150 *One another, each other*, are sometimes called reciprocal pronouns.

7. Phonetics. ***reciprocal assimilation*** (see quot. 1972).

1915 G. NOËL-ARMFIELD *General Phonetics* ix. 32 If the adjacent sounds act upon each other more or less equally the influence may be called reciprocal. *Ibid.* 33 Reciprocal assimilation is common in diphthongs. 1939 L. H. GRAY *Foundations Lang.* iii. 68 It [*sc.* assimilation] may be reciprocal, when the modification is mutual. 1972 HARTMANN & STORK *Dict. Lang. & Linguistics* 21/2 If two sounds influence each other mutually the term *reciprocal assimilation* (alternative term: *coalescent assimilation*) is used, e.g. English *seven* pronounced as [sebm̩] where the labio-dental [v] has become bilabial [b] which in turn influences the alveolar nasal [n] changing it to the bilabial nasal [m].

B. *sb.* †**1.** One who is sent back. *Obs. rare*⁻¹.

1616 CHAPMAN *Homer's Hymn Apollo* 734 No more Yee must be made, your own Reciprocalls To your lou'd Cittie.

2. A thing corresponding in some way to another; a return, equivalent, counterpart, etc.
1570 in Digges *Compl. Ambass.* (1655) 12 Offering to deliver unto her the reciprocal of our part under our Great Seal. **1622** BACON *Hen. VII* (1876) 205 After he had received the King of Castile into the fraternity of the Garter, and for a reciprocal had his son the prince admitted to the order of the Golden Fleece. **1626** —— *Sylva* §329 Corruption is a Reciprocall to Generation. **1750** CHESTERF. *Lett.* (1792) III. 42 Pleasure is a necessary reciprocal; no one feels who does not at the same time give it. **1852** MULCAHY *Princ. Mod. Geom.* 37 By means of the theory of polars, every Proposition.. leads immediately to another, called its reciprocal. **1885** J. MARTINEAU *Types Eth. Th.* (1886) II. I. i. 31 The two cognitions are, therefore, independent reciprocals.

3. *Gram.* †**a.** A reflexive verb. *Obs.*
1659 HAMMOND *On Ps.* lxxvi. 5 The reciprocal from [*ṡll*] prædatus est. **1766** DEL PINO *New Span. Gram.* 177 Verbs Passive, and the greatest part of the Reciprocals, require the Ablative.

b. A noun, pronoun, or verb that expresses mutual action or relationship.
1961 R. B. LONG *Sentence & its Parts* xvi. 357 Reciprocals can refer only to plural nouns, pronouns, or nounal units; reflexives can refer to singulars as well. **1965** *Canad. Jrnl. Linguistics* Spring 175 Especially reflexives, reciprocals, iteratives, passives, and the Eyak progressive almost always take the vocalic forms.

4. *Math.* **a.** A function or expression so related to another that their product is unity; the inverse.
1782 HUTTON in *Phil. Trans.* LXXIV. 33 The reciprocal of the cosine will be the secant. **1797** *Encycl. Brit.* (ed. 3) XVI. 29/1 Likewise $\frac{1}{x}$ is said to be the reciprocal of *x*, which is again the reciprocal of $\frac{1}{x}$. **1831** BREWSTER *Optics* xvii. 151 The radius O a of the ellipse will be what is called the reciprocal of the index of refraction at a. **1882** MINCHIN *Unipl. Kinemat.* 185 Their combined resistance is found from the fact that its reciprocal is equal to the sum of the reciprocals of their separate resistances.

b. *polar reciprocal*: (see quot. 1885).
1852 MULCAHY *Princ. Mod. Geom.* 38 The two figures are, therefore, properly called polar reciprocals. **1885** LEUDESDORF *Cremona's Proj. Geom.* 240 Two curves.. such that each is the locus of the poles of the tangents of the other, and at the same time also the envelope of the polars of the points of the other, are said to be polar reciprocals one of the other with respect to the auxiliary conic.

reciprocality (rɪsɪprəˈkælɪtɪ). [f. prec. + -ITY. Cf. RECIPROCALTY.] = RECIPROCITY.
1736 BAILEY (folio) App. to Pref., *Reciprocality*, reciprocalness. **1748** RICHARDSON *Clarissa* (1811) III. xxxi. 188 An acknowledged reciprocality in love sanctifies every little freedom. **1786** *Hist. Eur.* in *Ann. Reg.* 172/1 Similar concessions were made by France,.. reciprocality.. being the ground-work of all these arrangements. **1827** SCOTT *Napoleon* xxxvi. Wks. 1870 XII. 275 The reciprocalities of love and duty. **1873** tr. *Swedenborg's True Chr. Rel.* 591 There cannot possibly be conjunction without reciprocality.

reˈciprocalize, *v. rare*$^{-1}$. [f. as prec. + -IZE.] *trans.* To make reciprocal.
1802–12 BENTHAM *Ration. Judic. Evid.* III. xv. (1827) II. 401 Which consists of the effect of the equity bill reciprocalized, and in that way doubled.

reciprocally (rɪˈsɪprəkəlɪ), *adv.* [-LY².]
†**1.** Backwards and forwards. *Obs. rare*$^{-1}$.
1632 LITHGOW *Trav.* IX. 395 Euen as the Turkes.. are tossed.., hanging betweene two high trees, reciprocally wauing in the ayre.
†**b.** Alternately. *Obs. rare*$^{-1}$.
1621 BURTON *Anat. Mel.* I. i. II. viii. 39 The Lungs, which dilating themselues as a paire of bellowes reciprocally fetch it [the air] in and send it out.

2. In turn, in return.
1601 HOLLAND *Pliny* XXXVII. v. 611 As they ever send out their owne raies by little and little, so they entertaine reciprocally the visuall beames of our eyes. **1654** BRAMHALL *Just. Vind.* v. (1661) 92 Churches from whence.. their neighbours did fetch sound doctrine, and reciprocally paid to them due respect. **1756** *Monitor* No. 35 I. 327 As the mind affects the body, the body reciprocally affects the mind. **1864** BURTON *Scot. Abr.* II. ii. 150 Gustavus.. confided.. in the valour.. of the Scottish nation and they reciprocally in the gallantry.. of him.

3. Mutually.
1577 tr. *Bullinger's Decades* (1592) 579 The Apostle.. vseth this worde ἀλλήλους which signifieth mutually, one another,.. and as it were reciprocallie. **1642** PR. CHARLES in Ellis *Orig. Lett.* Ser. II. IV. 2 *note*, Although a while dissevered we may reciprocally understand of each other's welfare. **1692** BENTLEY *Boyle Lect.* vii. (1724) 278 The sun, moon, and all the planets do reciprocally gravitate one toward another. **1759** SARAH FIELDING *C'tess of Dellwyn* I. 142 A lively.. Capacity rendered them reciprocally agreeable to each other. **1822** SCOTT *Pirate* xxix, The two sisters.. sat with their arms reciprocally passed over each other's shoulder. **1876** BANCROFT *Hist. U.S.* III. iii. 7 The existence of our kind is continuous, and its ages are reciprocally dependent.

4. *Math.* Inversely.
1570 BILLINGSLEY *Euclid* VI. Addit. prop. iv. 182 The sections of the one to the sections of the other shall be reciprokally proportionall. **1656** tr. *Hobbes' Elem. Philos.* (1839) 163 From hence the cause is evident why two equal products have their efficients reciprocally proportional. **1696** WHISTON *Th. Earth* IV. (1722) 363 The Heat of the Sun is.. reciprocally as the Squares of the Earth's distance from him. **1743** EMERSON *Fluxions* 113 The Square of the Velocity is reciprocally as the Weight of the Body. **1823** MITCHELL *Dict. Math. & Phys. Sci.* 412 In bodies of the same weight, the density is reciprocally as the magnitude; viz. the greater the magnitude the less is the density. **1853** SIR H. DOUGLAS *Milit. Bridges* 320 Agreeably to a principle in hydrodynamics, the velocity of the current in different sections is reciprocally as those sections.

5. Conversely.
a **1628** PRESTON *New Covt.* (1629) iii. 561 You must vnderstand it reciprocally, the battel is not alwayes to the strong, therefore it is sometimes to the weake. **1641** WILKINS *Math. Magick* I. iv. (1648) 21 As the weight is to an equivalent power, so is the distance betwixt the weight and the center, unto the distance betwixt the center and the power, and so reciprocally. **1715** DESAGULIERS *Fires Impr.* 118 What opens the passage for hot Air to go into the Room, may shut out the cold Air, and so reciprocally. **1744** HARRIS *Three Treat.* Wks. (1841) 15 If it be true that all art implies such principle, is it reciprocally true that every such principle should imply art? **1881** *Nature* XXIV. 419/1 Substances capable of exerting great force by their combination are those which can undergo a great diminution of the velocity of their internal motions, and reciprocally.

†**b.** Convertibly, by way of equivalence. *Obs.*
1658 BRAMHALL *Consecr. Bps.* xi. 223 There is nothing either in our forme or theirs which doth distinctly and reciprocally expresse Episcopall power and Authority.

†**reˈciprocalness.** *Obs. rare.* [f. as prec. + -NESS.] Reciprocity.
1667 *Decay Chr. Piety* xiv. ¶3 The reciprocalness of the injury ought to allay the displeasure at it. **1731** BAILEY vol. II, *Reciprocalness*, interchangeableness.
So †**reciprocalty.** *Obs. rare*$^{-1}$.
1621 BURTON *Anat. Mel.* I. i. I. v, He knowes not the condition of it, where with a reciprocalltye, pleasure and pain are still vnited.

reˈciprocant. *Math.* [ad. L. *reciprocant-em*, pres. pple. of *reciprocāre* to RECIPROCATE.] A differential invariant.
1885 SYLVESTER in *Amer. Jrnl. Math.* VIII. 199 We are.. led.. by prosecuting this inquiry to lay the foundations of the theory of Reciprocation or Reciprocants.
Hence **reˈciprocantive** *a.*, pertaining to a reciprocant (*Cent. Dict.* 1891).

reˈciprocate, *a. rare.* [ad. L. *reciprocāt-us*, pa. pple. of *reciprocāre*: see next.]
†**1.** Complementary; closely connected. *Obs.*
1619 SIR J. SEMPIL *Sacrilege Handled* 28 They are of Nature, Reciprocate; that is, the one cannot be without the other. **1653** *Consid. Dissolv. Crt. Chancery* 30 Principles.. so interwoven and radicated in the very Being of Parliaments, so inseparable from it, and so reciprocate to it.
2. = RECIPROCAL *a.* 2 b.
1833 *Fraser's Mag.* VIII. 343 The congenial and reciprocate stupidity and ignorance of the majority of actors and the majority in audiences.

reciprocate (rɪˈsɪprəkeɪt), *v.* [f. L. *reciprocāt-*, ppl. stem of *reciprocāre*, f. *reciproc-us* RECIPROQUE.]
1. *intr.* †**a.** To go back, return; to have a backward direction. *Obs.*
1623 COCKERAM, *Reciprocate*, to returne from whence one came. **1629** JACKSON *Creed* VI. II. xi. §4 Our thankfulness would reciprocate upon the fountain from which they flow. **1661** LOVELL *Hist. Anim. & Min.* Introd., The gula, to which the intestine is joyned, which is single, and reciprocating towards the head.
b. To move backwards and forwards (now only *Mech.*); †to go up and down, to vary (*obs.*).
1678 CUDWORTH *Intell. Syst.* I. iv. §13. 221 Whereby things reciprocate forwards and backwards, as when a Bow is successively Intended and Remitted. **1730** *Phil. Trans.* XXXVI. 254 Always in a Morning it reciprocated between 80 Deg. and 100 Deg. **1843** HOLTZAPFFEL *Turning* II. 740 The saw blade is strained in a rectangular frame, which both reciprocates and descends in a vertical plane.
c. *trans.* To alternate the direction of; to cause to move backwards and forwards.
1653 HARVEY *Anat. Exerc.* (1673) 46 [The blood] like Euripus reciprocating its motion again and again, hither and hither. *a* **1677** BARROW *Serm.* xxix. Wks. 1700 I. 359 Vainly reciprocating the saw of endless contention. **1875** KNIGHT *Dict. Mech.* 1900/2 The propeller is reciprocated by a horizontal engine.

2. *trans.* **a.** To give and receive in return or mutually; to interchange; †to have in common.
1611 COTGR., *Reciproquer*, to reciprocate, interchange, returne one for another. **1645** EVELYN *Diary* 7 Feb. (Baiæ), The waters reciprocating their tides with the neighbouring sea. **1654** H. L'ESTRANGE *Chas. I* (1655) 6 Affectionate adieus, reciprocated and interchanged between the King and herself. **1719** J. T. PHILIPPS tr. *Thirty-four Confer.* 34 We are not come here to reciprocate Questions and Answers out of this or that System of borrow'd Principles. **1837** J. PHILLIPS *Geology* 24 The sources of variation which are daily in action may not exactly reciprocate their influence. **1866** HOWELLS *Venet. Life* iii. 34 At night men crowd the close little *caffès*, where they reciprocate smoke, respiration, and animal heat.
b. To return, requite; to do, feel, etc., in or by way of return.
1820 W. IRVING *Sketch Bk.* I. 68, I verily believe he reciprocated the sentiment with all his heart. **1855** PRESCOTT *Philip II*, I. II. ii. 21 He took some pains to reciprocate the civilities he had received by entertaining his hosts in return. **1903** G. B. SHAW *Man & Superman* III. 97 He.. is peevish and sensitive when his advances are not reciprocated. **1922** JOYCE *Ulysses* 717 Hospitality extended and received in kind, reciprocated and reappropriated in person. **1924** C. MACKENZIE *Old Men of Sea* viii. 131, I was rather disappointed to hear that she was unlikely to reciprocate Dick Duffy's affection.

3. a. *intr.* To make a return or interchange *with* (another or others). Now *rare* or *Obs.*
1626 R. HARRIS *Hezekiah's Recov.* 4 In manners wee must reciprocate with men, much more with God. *a* **1662** HEYLIN *Laud* I. (1671) 52 She so far reciprocated with him in the like affection.. that some assurances past between them of a future Marriage. **1781** COWPER *Charity* 119 'Tis thus reciprocating each with each Alternately the nations learn and teach.
b. *spec.* To make a return or exchange of good wishes. Also *gen.*, to return love or liking.
1779 JOHNSON in *Boswell* 12 Oct., Then when the two glasses of water were brought,.. he said, 'Madam, let us reciprocate'. **1874** LISLE CARR *Jud. Gwynne* I. viii. 258 Oh! yes, thanks; quite right again. And I reciprocate by hoping that you have got over that horrible fire. **1883** 'MARK TWAIN' *Life on Mississippi* iv. 542 He had loved one 'too fair for earth', and she had reciprocated. **1916** G. B. SHAW *Androcles & Lion* p. xxx, Unless you love your neighbor as yourself and he reciprocates you will both be the worse for it. **1922** JOYCE *Ulysses* 679 In what manners did she reciprocate? She remembered... She provided... She admired. **1936** L. C. DOUGLAS *White Banners* xi. 235 Hannah liked her, and felt that the girl heartily reciprocated.

4. a. *trans.* To make correspondent or convertible *with*; to convert. ? *Obs.*
1620 T. GRANGER *Div. Logike* 47 End is adequate which is euened or reciprocated with the whole thing. **1640** J. STOUGHTON *Def. & Distrib. Divinity* i. 38 It is more aptly resembled to a Rule or Canon, as it respects faith and things to be beleeved, with which it is every way reciprocated. **1788** REID *Aristotle's Logic* v. §2. 111 If the attribute cannot be reciprocated, it must be something contained in the definition or not.
b. *intr.* To be correspondent or in agreement (*with* something); to be equivalent or convertible.
1683 O. U. *Parish Churches No Conventicles* 7 Logicians will tell [him].. that every Definition must reciprocate with the Thing defin'd. **1746** SARAH FIELDING *Fashion* in *David Simple* (1747) II. 290 Truth and Falshood can never reciprocate, but are immutably distinct thro' all Eternity. **1788** T. TAYLOR *Proclus' Comm.* I. Diss. 44 Risibility.. mutually reciprocates with its subject; since every man is risible, and whatever is risible is man. *a* **1806** BP. HORSLEY *Serm.* (1812) I. ix. 175 This atonement was the end of the incarnation: And the two articles reciprocate.

5. *Math.* **a.** *trans.* To find the reciprocal to (a curve).
1861 FERRERS *Trilinear Co-ordinates* vi. 100 The process of generating E from L, or L from E, is called reciprocating L or E. *Ibid.* 103 If one conic be reciprocated with respect to another, the reciprocal curve will be an ellipse, parabola, or hyperbola, according as [etc.].
b. *intr.* To pass *into* by reciprocating.
1861 FERRERS *Trilinear Co-ordinates* vi. 103 The asymptotes.. reciprocate into the points of contact of the tangents drawn to the reciprocal curve from the centre of the auxiliary conic. **1885** SYLVESTER *Theory of Reciprocants* iii.
Hence **reˈciprocated** *ppl. a.*
1782 COWPER *Friendship* 48 'Tis a union that bespeaks Reciprocated duties. **1858** W. ARNOT *Laws fr. Heaven for Life on Earth* Ser. II. xiv. 123 The heart of the man Christ Jesus yearns for the reciprocated love of saved men.

†**reˈciprocately,** *adv.* *Obs. rare*$^{-1}$. [f. RECIPROCATE *a.* + -LY².] Convertibly.
1666 G. HARVEY *Morb. Angl.* xxvi. (1672) 71 Whether there be any other sort of true, perfect, exquisite, or proper (for those terms are reciprocately used by Authors) Consumptions, besides a Pulmonique Consumption?

reˈciprocating, *ppl. a.* [f. RECIPROCATE *v.*]
†**1.** Back-flowing. *Obs. rare*$^{-1}$.
1632 LITHGOW *Trav.* III. 99 Those that got to land, were pulled backe by the reciprocating waues.
2. a. Moving backwards and forwards; characterized by alternation in movement or action.
1697 DRYDEN *Virg. Georg.* IV. 249 One brawny Smith the puffing Bellows plyes; And draws, and blows reciprocating Air. **1759** B. MARTIN *Nat. Hist. Eng.* I. 26 From Waters gathered in the subterraneous Basons in this Hill, proceeds this wonderful reciprocating Fountain. *a* **1766** S. CHANDLER *Life David* II. ii. 9 *marg.*, The reciprocating motion of the buckets of a well, one descending as the other rises, and *vice versa*. **1830** KATER & LARDNER *Mech.* xviii. 247 Reciprocating circular motion is seen in the pendulum of a clock. **1892** *Pall Mall G.* 2 Mar. 3/2 This tool is provided with a reciprocating plunger, located and moving within.. two coils of insulated copper wire.
b. *Mech.* Of machines, etc.: Having a reciprocating part or parts. Applied *spec.* to engines in which the working fluid drives an oscillating piston.
1822 J. ROBISON *Syst. Mech. Philos.* II. 577 When water is to be driven along a main by the strokes of a reciprocating engine, it should be forced into an air-box. **1825** J. NICHOLSON *Operat. Mechanic* 441 Reciprocating saw-mills, for cutting timber,.. do not exhibit much variety in their construction. **1843** HOLTZAPFFEL *Turning* II. 739 Rectilinear, or reciprocating, saw machines. **1873** J. RICHARDS *Wood-working Factories* 153 For the lighter class of work.. the reciprocating machine is best. **1901** *Trans. Inst. Engineers & Shipbuilders in Scotland* XLV. I. 25 An ordinary reciprocating engine performs one complete cycle of operations.. in two strokes of the piston. **1911** *Encycl. Brit.* XXV. 824/1 The rapid development of the marine steam turbine makes it probable that it will displace the reciprocating engine in all large and fast ships. **1948** *Daily Tel.* 9 Apr. 4/4 The aircraft developed in recent years in America were.. of conventional design. Their engines were reciprocating engines, and they were designed to fly at normal speeds. **1973** *Times* 13 Dec. 35/2 The Wankel still relies on petrol and unfortunately uses rather more of it than a comparable reciprocating engine.
3. That reciprocate(s), in other senses of the vb.

1827 R. Craig in *Mem.* (1862) 93 A false religion cannot exist without its [Despotism's] reciprocating support. **1858** W. Arnot *Laws fr. Heaven for Life on Earth* Ser. II. xxiii. 193 Sellers and buyers alike would be ashamed.. to begin, in this form, the reciprocating series of deceit. **1864** Bowen *Logic* iv. 93 Reciprocating, Convertible or Coextensive Concepts are those which have precisely the same Extension.

reciprocation (rɪsɪprəˈkeɪʃən). [ad. L. *reciprocātiōn-em*, n. of action f. *reciprocāre*, to reciprocate. Cf. F. *réciprocation* (16th c.).]

†**1. a.** Reflexive action; a reflexive mode of expression. *Obs.* (Cf. reciprocal *a.* 6.)

1530 Palsgr. Introd. 35 They double the pronowne, and in the thyrde parsones use reciprocation, as *Je me maruaille*, ..*il se maruaille*. **1631** Gouge *God's Arrows* III. §42. 256 The Hebrew word..intimated both a reciprocation, and also a continuance of the action.

†**b.** Backward motion. *Obs.*$^{-0}$

1623 Cockeram, *Reciprocation*, a going backe.

2. Motion backwards and forwards. Now only *Mech.* (Common in 17th c., esp. of the tides.)

1646 Sir T. Browne *Pseud. Ep.* 363 Aristotle drowned himself in Euripus as despairing to resolve the cause of its reciprocation, or ebbe and flow seven times a day. **1685** Boyle *Enq. Notion Nat.* 306 The Box will, after some Reciprocations, return to its Horizontal Situation. **1843** Holtzapffel *Turning* II. 919 The machine..makes two reciprocations for every revolution of the shaft. **1847** T. Milner *Gallery of Nature* (1855) 268 The reciprocations of the spring are easily observed by this contrivance.

b. Alternate action or operation. *rare.*

1656 tr. *Hobbes' Elem. Philos.* (1839) 459 Such motion is the reciprocation of pressure, sometimes one way, sometimes the other. **1802** Paley *Nat. Theol.* xi. §2 (1819) 170 Distending and contracting their many thousand vesicles, by a reciprocation which cannot cease for a minute. **1844** H. Stephens *Bk. Farm* II. 306 A few repetitions of such reciprocation would so fill the condenser as to render it ineffective.

†**c.** Alternation; alternate change or succession; vicissitude. *Obs.*

1610 Healey *St. Aug. Citie of God* 909 How delightfull is the dayes reciprocation with night! **1659** H. More *Immort. Soul* I. xi. (1713) 41 That we may not think this Reciprocation into Motion and Rest belongs onely to Terrestrial particles. *a* **1766** S. Chandler *Life David* II. ii. 9 *marg.*, The verb is here applied..to point out the various reciprocations and changes of David's fortunes. **1794** in Polwhele *Trad. & Recoll.* (1826) II. 397 A man who has been an author so long as you have must have experienced a reciprocation of praises and censures.

†**d.** Alternate singing or chanting. *Obs.*$^{-1}$

1641 R. B. K. *Parall. Liturgy w. Mass-Bk.* 11 The answering of the people was the invention of the Italians, as the Reciprocations and Antiphonies was the invention of the Greeks.

3. The action of making a return, or doing something in return; *esp.* a mutual return or exchange of acts, feelings, etc.

1561 T. Norton *Calvin's Inst.* III. 202 Hys worde is in greke *allelous*, mutually, enterchangeably, by turnes, or (if they so like best to terme it) by way of reciprocation one to an other. **1605** Timme *Quersit.* I. iv. 14 These simple elements..do render to the elements and beginnings mutual reciprocation of love. **1698** Norris *Pract. Disc.* (1707) IV. 56 The Union between Soul and Body..is only a mutual Reciprocation of Action and Passion between Soul and Body. **1788** Mme. D'Arblay *Diary* 29 Sept., The birthdays ..are made extremely interesting..by the reciprocation of presents and congratulations. **1841** Dickens *Lett.* (1880) I. 41 With a sincere reciprocation of all your kindly feeling. **1853** Kane *Grinnell Exp.* iv. (1856) 33 We showed our colors, but the little craft declined a reciprocation.

4. The state of being in a reciprocal or harmonious relation; correspondence.

1605 L. Hutten *Aunswere* 64 These..differ only as relatiues, whose difference is, their naturall reciprocation. **1677** Plot *Oxfordsh.* 288 Our common principle of the Reciprocation of strength and time. **1803** Beddoes *Hygeia* IX. 73 The nice reciprocation in the contractions and dilatations in the several sets, concerned in every kind of motion.

†**b.** *Logic.* The conversion of terms or propositions, or the relation involved by this. *Obs.*

1588 Fraunce *Lawiers Log.* I. xiii. 56b, In distribution and definition there is a most necessary reciprocation or conversion. **1613** Bp. Andrewes *Serm.* (1841) IV. 291 That reciprocation I touched before; that seeing they reign by Him, He may reign by them. **1677** Gale *Crt. Gentiles* II. IV. 249 Platos plain naked mind is that the First being and One admit of reciprocation, i.e. God the First Being is the prime Unitie.

†**c.** Equivalence; meaning. *Obs.*$^{-1}$

a **1661** Fuller *Worthies* I. (1662) 79 A Corrollary about the Reciprocation of Alumnus: The word Alumnus is effectually directive of us..to the Nativities of Eminent persons.

d. *Math.* The process of converting a proposition, quantity, or curve, to its reciprocal.

1852 Mulcahy *Princ. Mod. Geom.* 37 The process by which one Proposition is thus deduced from another, is called reciprocation. **1885** [see reciprocant].

re'ciprocative, *a. rare.* [f. reciprocate *v.*] Characterized by, inclined to, reciprocation.

1888 *Pop. Sci. Monthly* (U.S.) XXXIV. 111 Our four-handed cousins apparently credit their biped kinsmen with reciprocative tendencies.

reciprocator (rɪˈsɪprəkeɪtə(r)). [Agent-n. on L. types, f. reciprocate *v.*] **a.** One who, or that which, reciprocates.

1850 *Tait's Mag.* XVII. 167/2 The recipient and reciprocator of her deepest feelings. **1874** Sylvester in *Proc. R. Instit.* VII. 184 The numbers denoting the two were always inverse or reciprocal to each other... Hence a Peaucellier's cell may be conveniently termed a Reciprocator or Inverter.

b. A reciprocating engine forming part of a composite power plant.

1907 *Westm. Gaz.* 16 Sept. 4/1 Not an ounce of steam will be wasted, the principle being to carry the exhaust steam from the high-pressure reciprocators to the low-pressure turbines. **1931** *Times* 24 Jan. (Trade & Engin. Suppl.) p. iv/3 Another alternative, in which the exhaust steam from the reciprocator is led to a turbo generator which delivers its current to a motor on the propeller shafting, has been applied to the existing 'City' ships of the Ellerman Line. **1952** Fox & McBirnie *Marine Steam Engines & Turbines* xi. 197 Only the reciprocator is used while entering or leaving port.

reciprocatory (rɪˈsɪprəkətərɪ), *a.* [f. as reciprocate *v.* + -ory.] = reciprocating *ppl. a.* 1.

1857 Smiles *Life Stephenson* viii. 64 The reciprocatory action being turned into a rotatory one by toothed wheels and a sun and planet motion. **1882** Dredge *Elect. Illumination* I. 388 A rotatory movement could be combined with the reciprocatory one.

ˌreciproci'tarian. [f. next, after *Trinitarian* etc.] One who advocates reciprocity in trade. Also *attrib.* or as *adj.*

1881 *Times* 16 July 13/2 The new reciprocitarians or advocates of free trade. **1891** *Pall Mall G.* 5 Feb. 1/2 The dictionary has been ransacked..for epithets to fling at the reciprocitarians. **1906** *Athenæum* 3 Feb. 134 To these he appeals on reciprocitarian lines by offering a reduction of our wine duties. **1932** *Times Lit. Suppl.* 1 Dec. 909/4 Dilke asserts that he [*sc.* Joseph Chamberlain] was a strong 'Reciprocitarian' and had already the notion of a 'British Zollverein'.

reciprocity (rɛsɪˈprɒsɪtɪ). [ad. F. *réciprocité* (1729), or L. type **reciprocitāt-em*, f. *reciproc-us* reciproque.]

1. a. The state or condition of being reciprocal; a state or relationship in which there is mutual action, influence, giving and taking, correspondence, etc., between two parties or things; *spec.* in *Social Science* (see quots. 1960, 1972).

1766 Blackstone *Comm.* II. 445 Any degree of reciprocity will prevent the pact from being nude. **1791** Paine *Rights of Man* (ed. 4) 121 A Declaration of Rights is, by reciprocity, a Declaration of Duties also. **1835** I. Taylor *Spir. Despot.* II. 75 People and priest ought to be connected by some sort of effective reciprocity. **1867** Freeman *Norm. Conq.* (1876) I. App. 623 Reciprocity of a certain kind was the essence of the feudal relation. **1904** W. T. Mills *Struggle for Existence* xx. 262 Reciprocity is a new word in politics, but it expresses an old fact in real life. **1952** T. M. Newcomb *Social Psychol.* ix. 308 The last stage in acquiring roles involves recognizing reciprocity between oneself and others. **1960** G. W. Allport *Personality & Soc. Encounter* xi. 175 The child understands that members of other countries are as attached to their own lands as he is to his; this is the principle of reciprocity. **1967** E. A. Hoebel in P. Bohannan *Law & Warfare* II. 187 In Comanche society reciprocity is not developed to an exaggerated degree. **1971** E. Ardener *Soc. Anthrop. & Lang.* p. lv, Maussian systems of exchange and reciprocity are analogous to systems of communication, of which language is also one. **1972** *Jrnl. Social Psychol.* LXXXVII. 89 Gouldner has postulated the existence of a universal norm of reciprocity which stipulates that..people should help those who help them.

b. A reprisal. *rare*$^{-1}$.

1865 Carlyle *Fredk. Gt.* xx. vi. (1872) IX. 114 Touched by these horrors of war, and by the reciprocities evidently liable to follow.

2. *spec.* **a.** Mutual or correspondent concession of advantages or privileges, as forming a basis for the commercial relations between two countries.

1782 *Prelim. Art. Peace w. U.S.* (1783) 25 It is agreed to form the Articles of the proposed Treaty on such principles of liberal equity and reciprocity, as that..a beneficial and satisfactory intercourse between the two countries may be established. **1783** *Prelim. Art. Peace w. France* xviii. 10 To agree upon new arrangements of trade, on the footing of reciprocity and mutual convenience. **1868** G. Duff *Pol. Surv.* 24 The Danish Government passed two new..laws granting freedom from remeasurement in Danish ports to all foreigners according reciprocity. **1880** A. J. Wilson (*title*) Reciprocity, Bimetallism and Land Tenure Reform.

attrib. **1876** *Encycl. Brit.* IV. 766/2 The Reciprocity Treaty was negotiated by the late Earl of Elgin. **1887** Morley in *Daily News* 16 May 2/5 Protectionists and Reciprocity men. **1893** *Ibid.* 13 Mar. 2/6 A report to the British Foreign Office, dated Washington, February 2, on the reciprocity clause, is now published.

b. In the Kantian philosophy: Mutual action and reaction.

1838 F. Haywood tr. *Kant's Critick Pure Reason* I. II. ix. 76 Both the Judgments, the relationship of which forms the hypothetical judgment.., in whose reciprocity likewise the disjunctive consists. **1883** A. Barratt *Phys. Metempiric* 232 We can think of Things-in-themselves..only under the categories of substance, causality and reciprocity.

3. *attrib.* and *Comb.*, as ***reciprocity-monger***, ***technique***, ***treaty***; **reciprocity failure** *Photogr.*, departure from adherence to the reciprocity law, found with all emulsions, in which greater exposure than that predicted by the law is required at both very low and very high light intensities; **reciprocity law** *Photogr.*, the statement that the degree of blackening of an ideal emulsion is constant for a given incident energy, i.e., for a given product of light intensity and exposure time; **reciprocity theorem** *Physics*, a theorem which states that the response of a given physical system is unchanged under interchange of the locations of a constant excitation and of the measured response; also called the Onsager principle; *spec.* (*a*) *Electr.* (see quot. 1957); (*b*) *Nucl. Physics*, the statement that time-reversal leaves the transition rate for a nuclear reaction unchanged.

1923 *Jrnl. Optical Soc. Amer.* VII. 1110 In order to show in a different way the magnitude of the *reciprocity failure, the values of sensitivity have been computed. **1966** D. G. Brandon *Mod. Techniques Metallogr.* 13 Emulsions produced specifically for metallography are designed to retain their speed for long periods, that is, to have a low reciprocity failure, while emulsions for astronomical applications, involving exposure times of several hours, show almost no reciprocity failure at all. **1973** *Sci. Amer.* Dec. 122/3 Lowering the temperature of the emulsion tends to suppress the recombination of the ions and hence to suppress reciprocity failure. **1979** *SLR Camera* May 11/1 Unless the meter takes into account reciprocity failure then the film cannot be correctly exposed. [**1900** *Astrophysical Jrnl.* XI. 89 Scheiner, in 1891, proved that the increase in the number of fainter stars on prolonging the exposure fell far below what would be expected according to the law of reciprocity.] **1907** Sheppard & Mees *Investigations Theory of Photogr. Process* II. vi. 214 A reversing action of the released bromine may..be deduced from the failures of the Bunsen and Roscoe '*reciprocity law'. **1942** C. E. K. Mees *Theory of Photogr. Process* vi. 236 Bunsen and Roscoe laid down a general law for photochemical reactions which states that the product of a photochemical reaction is dependent simply on the total energy employed... From the reciprocal relation between time and intensity in the Bunsen–Roscoe expression, it was called the reciprocity law. **1974** Dainty & Shaw *Image Sci.* ii. 35 For very long or very short exposure times the process of latent image formation is less efficient, and this is known as reciprocity law failure. **1885** A. Crump *Formation Polit. Opin.* 198 The declamations of the Fair Traders and the *reciprocity-mongers..fail to disturb the convictions of the sound thinkers in the country. **1973** *Times* 18 Oct. (Brazil Suppl.) p. ii/4 There is a dependence on imported technology and design, as well as insufficient use of *reciprocity techniques. [**1876** *Proc. R. Soc.* XXV. 118 Although the principle of reciprocity appears to be firmly grounded on the theoretical side, instances are not uncommon in which a sound generated in the open air at a point A is heard at a distant point B, when an equal or even more powerful sound at B fails to make itself heard at A.] **1938** G. P. Harnwell *Princ. Electricity & Electromagnetism* xiii. 451 The *reciprocity theorem is a consequence of the symmetry of the determinant and is generally stated in a limited form involving the current in one branch and the emf. in another. **1952** Blatt & Weisskopf *Theoret. Nucl. Physics* x. 529 We obtain the reciprocity of theorem... This theorem states that the probability for a transition proceeding one way in time is equal to the probability for the same transition but with the sense of time reversed. **1957** B. I. & B. Bleaney *Electr. & Magnetism* iii. 69 We have the Reciprocity Theorem, which states that a given e.m.f. in the *p*th branch will produce the same current in the *q*th branch of a circuit as the same e.m.f. in the *q*th branch would produce in the *p*th branch. **1968** [see Onsager]. **1970** I. E. McCarthy *Nuclear Reactions* ii. 31 The reciprocity theorem or time-reversal invariance is an essential property of nuclear systems. **1847** H. Clay in *Whig Almanac 1848* 22/1 Out of these acts have sprung a class..of treaties,.. commonly called *Reciprocity Treaties.

reciprock(e, variant of reciproque.

recipro'cornous, *a. rare*$^{-0}$. [ad. L. *reciprocicornis* (Laberius), f. *reciproc-us* reciproque *a.* + *cornu* horn.] 'Having horns that turn backwards and forwards like those of a ram' (Ash 1775; hence in recent Dicts.).

†**re'ciprocous**, *a. Obs. rare.* [f. L. *reciproc-us* reciproque + -ous.] = reciprocal *a.*

1567 *Reg. Privy Council Scot.* I. 536 The band and contract to be mutuall and reciprocous. **1721** Strype *Eccl. Mem.* I. I. v. 67 Letters of Instruction and Commission, authorizing the French Ambassador to conclude on Obligation reciprocous.

Hence †**re'ciprocously** *adv. Obs.*$^{-1}$

1683 E. Hooker *Pref. Pordage's Mystic Div.* 94 Reciprocously ratified by these Testimonies.

†**re'ciprocy**, obs. var. reciprocity.

1803 *Censor* 1 Sept. 92 If so, there is a reciprocy of affection, and he need not use any words or ink.

†**reciproque**, *a.* and *sb. Obs.* Also reciprock(e, -procq(ue, -prok(e, recyproque. [a. F. *réciproque* (14–15th c.), or ad. L. *reciproc-us*, app. f. *re-* back and *pro* forward.]

A. *adj.* = reciprocal *a.* (Chiefly in senses 2b and 4a; common *c* 1570–1620.)

c **1532** Du Wes *Introd. Fr.* in Palsgr. 1049 Suche love is nat reciprocque or retorning. **1594** T. Bedingfield tr. *Machiavelli's Florentine Hist.* (1595) To Rdr., Succession.. planteth a certaine reciproke loue betweene the Prince and the people. **1603** Sir R. Cecil in Ellis *Orig. Lett.* Ser. II. III. 207 The King receaved it with reciprocq generall kindness. **1619** Sir J. Sempil *Sacrilege Handled* 69 Giuing and Taking then, are on both sides, mutuall and reciprock.

B. *sb.* **1.** A return or equivalent. = RECIPROCAL *sb.* 2. Also with *the*: The natural return, the like.
1538 HEN. VIII *Let. to Wyatt* 17 May in *Wyatt's Wks.* (1816) 492 We would be content upon convenient reciproque that [etc.]. **1542** SIR W. PAGET in Burnet *Hist. Ref.* (1865) VI. 256 Ask reasonably for the dote, and make a reciproque for the rest. **1552** *Ibid.* V. 115 The king is bound by the treaty; and if he will be helped by that treaty, he must do the reciproque. **1612** BACON *Ess., Love* (Arb.) 446 It is a true rule that loue is euer rewarded either with the reciproque or with an inward and secret contempt. *a* **1648** LD. HERBERT *Hen. VIII* (1683) 442 That they should give King Henry no Reciproke, as lying at that distance.

2. A reflexive pronoun. *rare*$^{-1}$.
1681 W. ROBERTSON *Phraseol. Gen.* (1693) 730 A Relative is sometimes used for the Reciproque *sui*.

Hence †**reciproquely** *adv. Obs.*
1558 *Sc. Acts Mary* (1814) 505/1 To be ratifeit and apprevit and consentit vnto Receproquilie be his maiestie and my lord daulphin his sone. **1592** G. HARVEY *Four Lett.*, etc. Sonn. xvi, Each one with Cordiall indulgence forbeare And Bondes of Love reciproquely enseale.

re'circle, *v. rare.* [RE- 5 a.] To circle again.
1611 FLORIO, *Recirculare*, to recircle or compasse about againe. *a* **1711** KEN *Hymns Evang.* Poet. Wks. 1721 I. 173 His Blood re-circling made his Pulses beat.

recirculate, *v.* [RE- 5 a.] To circulate again. **a.** *trans.* To make available for reuse. **b.** *intr.* Of material: to take part in recirculation.
1916 HARDING & WILLARD *Mech. Equipment Buildings* I. xv. 349 The air is simply re-circulated, no fresh air being taken into the heating system from the outside. **1934** W. TRINKS *Industrial Furnaces* (ed. 3) I. vi. 392 In several designs of fuel-fired furnaces, burned gases are drawn from the heating chamber by a fan and recirculated, mixing with the fresh combustion gases. **1958** *Jrnl. Amer. Water Wks. Assoc.* L. 1025/2 Treated sewage can be recirculated from the bottom of the final tank to the wet well where it is mixed with the incoming raw sewage. **1959** *Motor Manual* (ed. 36) v. 107 The balls recirculate (thereby reducing the rate of wear) and their use reduces friction in the mechanism to a minimum. **1964** *Proc. R. Soc.* B. CLIX. 262 The few large lymphocytes which re-circulate from the blood to the lymph do so for only a brief period. **1967** E. CHAMBERS *Photolitho-Offset* ix. 127 The machine has a unique roller-jet agitation ..allowing for the developer to be recirculated. **1977** *Jrnl. Neuropath. & Exper. Neurol.* XXXVI. 471 Microglial cells are continually replaced by circulating mononuclear cells and may, themselves, also recirculate.

Hence **re'circulated** *ppl. a.*, **re'circulating** *vbl. sb.*
1916 HARDING & WILLARD *Mech. Equipment Buildings* I. xvi. 442 This apparatus is designed for use where maximum cooling of the air by evaporation in addition to air cleansing is desired with recirculated spray water. **1947** T. N. ADLAM *Radiant Heating* 5 It can be arranged to discontinue recirculating and admit all fresh air after the correct room temperature has been attained. **1967** *Punch* 5 July 22/2 Once he has overcome in training the psychological objection to drinking recirculated fluids, the astronaut will not be bothered by such trivialities.

re'circulating, *ppl. a.* [f. prec. + -ING^2.]
1. Circulating again or continuously, in senses of the vb.
1916 HARDING & WILLARD *Mech. Equipment Buildings* I. xiv. 337 The use of recirculating ducts, through which part or all of the air delivered to the rooms is returned to the furnace to be reheated, will greatly reduce the cost of operation. **1954** G. M. FAIR et al. *Water Supply & Waste-Water Disposal* xxx. 908 The recirculating system generally includes pumps, hair-catchers, chemical feeds.., filters, disinfecting equipment.., and heaters. **1964** *Proc. R. Soc.* B. CLIX. 262 Some of the large lymphocytes in thoracic duct lymph divide..but..the number of new small lymphocytes which they contribute to the total re-circulating pool is extremely small. **1975** *Offshore* Aug. 3/1 (Advt.), Even the initial lead slurry, when you use our patented recirculating mixer, will be to the desired weight.
2. *recirculating ball*, a ball-bearing running in a closed ball race; usu. *attrib.* with reference to a form of automotive steering mechanism in which a half-nut containing an eccentrically mounted ball race can be made to move along a helical cam by rotation of the cam.
1946 W. H. CROUSE *Automotive Mech.* xxiii. 494 The recirculating ball-and-nut type of steering-gear mechanism that uses a grooved ball nut, ball bearings, and a gear sector. **1956** E. MOLLOY *Automobile Engineer's Ref. Bk.* xv. 37 Screw-and-nut gears incorporating balls between the screw and nut, and known as recirculating ball steering gears, are widely used on all classes of vehicles above the 12-h.p. range. **1960** *Farmer & Stockbreeder* 23 Feb. 45/2 Light, responsive, re-circulating ball type steering. **1970** *A.A. Bk. of Car* 151/4 (*caption*) Recirculating balls are used to reduce friction between a rotating worm and a nut moving along it. **1980** *Times* 9 May 26/2 Instead of rack and pinion Toyota has decided to stick with recirculating ball steering.

recirculation (stress variable). [RE- 5 a; cf. RECIRCLE *v.*] A renewed or fresh circulation, *esp.* the process of making available for reuse waste products or other material.
1611 FLORIO, *Recirculatione*, a recirculation. **1812** J. J. HENRY *Camp. agst. Quebec* 111 Rubbing with my hands.. soon caused a recirculation of the blood. **1899** *Star* 5 July 3/4 Putting the old stamps into recirculation. **1916** HARDING & WILLARD *Mech. Equipment Buildings* I. xiv. 330 All of the air is brought in from the outside to warm the building, and no recirculation is allowed. **1934** W. TRINKS *Industr. Furnaces* (ed. 3) vi. 394 (*caption*) Furnace designed for recirculation of products of combustion. **1954** G. M. FAIR et al. *Water Supply & Waste-Water Disposal* xxx. 905 Modern swimming pools are designed for the recirculation of pool water and its continuous repurification, reheating, and redisinfection. **1964** *Proc. R. Soc.* B. CLIX. 280 It seems likely that a re-circulation through the lymph nodes is a feature of the life-history of small lymphocytes among mammals generally. **1975** *Nature* 20 Mar. 175/2 Recirculation of metal and other wastes could save an increasing proportion of the total energy used in Sweden.

recirculatory (rɪ'sɜːkjuːlətərɪ, ˌriːsɜːkju'leɪtərɪ), *a.* [RE- 5 a.] Involving recirculation; recirculating.
1951 *Engineering* 23 Nov. 664/1 The steering gear is of the recirculatory-ball pattern. **1959** *Motor* 23 Sept. 179/2 Available as an extra is a recirculatory interior heater.

recision (rɪ'sɪʒən). Now *rare.* [ad. L. *recīsiōn-em*, n. of action f. *recīdĕre* to cut back. In early use also ad. F. *recision*, obs. var. *rescision* RESCISSION.] **a.** The action of cutting back or pruning. †**b.** The action of rescinding. *Obs.*
1611 COTGR., *Recision*, a recision, cancelling, or cutting off. **1656** J. HARRINGTON *Oceana* (1658) 111 A solemn and annual Feast call'd the Sisacthia, or Recision. **1664** EVELYN *Sylva* (1776) 371 If they present us their blushing double flowers for the pains of recision and well pruning. **1706** tr. *Dupin's Eccl. Hist. 16th C.* II. IV. ix. 433 Unless His Majesty rather chose to grant a Recision of the Contracts. **1706** in PHILLIPS (ed. Kersey); and hence in Bailey, Johnson, and later Dicts.). **1881** SWINBURNE *Misc.* (1886) 256 The rearrangement and recision and reissue of a single verse.

recission, -ory, erron. ff. RESCISSION, -ORY.

‖**récit** (resi). [Fr.] **1.** *Mus.* (See quots.)
1884 F. NIECKS *Conc. Dict. Mus. Terms* 201 *Récit* (Fr.), (1) what is performed by one singer or one instrumentalist, a vocal or instrumental *solo*. (2) The principal part in a piece of concerted music. (3) One of the manuals and corresponding stops of the organ, the Swell Organ. **1924** L. J. DE BEKKER *Black's Dict. Mus. & Musicians* 538/1 *Recit*, Fr. solo part; principal of several parts. **1954** *Grove's Dict. Mus.* (ed. 5) VII. 72/1 *Récit*.., a 17th-century term for a declamatory melody supported by simple accompaniment, ..but also, by analogy, an instrumental piece, such as an organ piece with the tune played on a solo stop. **1968** A. NILAND *Introd. to Organ* 109 Cavaillé-Coll never really took to the swell box, being content to enclose only the récit expressif, even in a five manual organ. **1975** *New Yorker* 28 Apr. 133/2 The *Récit* [*sc.* a rank of organ pipes] is in mysterious darkness, behind the louvres of the box that encloses it.
2. *Lit.* Narrative, account (freq. opposed to dialogue); a relating of events. Also, a book or passage consisting largely of narrative.
1944 'G. ORWELL' in *Horizon* X. 237 The whole book, *récit* as well as dialogue, is written in the American language. **1959** *Times Lit. Suppl.* 27 Mar. 173/1 The *récit*..studies always to keep an uncluttered foreground where only one or two characters are permitted to disport themselves; for the most part it sticks to narrative and reported speech. **1960** *Ibid.* 18 Nov. 737/3 The four *récits* which compose his latest work are set as far apart as Ethiopia, Spain, Italy and the Midi. **1964** *New Statesman* 17 Apr. 610/2 Its form is French: a flowery *récit* by an ageing recluse describing his attempts to make life and thought converge. **1978** *Observer* 26 May 30/1 The rhythms of his *récit*—his dialogue is a different matter—are terribly unvarious.

recital (rɪ'saɪtəl). Forms: 6 recyghtall, 6–7 recitall, (6 resyt-, recyt-), 6– recital. [f. RECITE *v.* + -AL^1 5.]
1. a. A rehearsal, account, or description *of* some thing, fact, or incident; also (esp. in early use), an enumeration or detailed account *of* a number of things, facts, etc.; a relation of the particulars or details *of* something.
c **1550** J. MARDELEY (*title*) A short Resytall of certeine holy Doctours [etc.]. **1586** W. WEBBE *Eng. Poetrie* (Arb.) 43 A laciuious disposed personne, whom the recitall of sins..wyll not staie. **1651** BAXTER *Inf. Bapt.* 300 The Antecedent is undeniable, as might be manifested by a recital of the particular Texts. **1691** WOOD *Ath. Oxon.* I. 110, I shall not make a recital of it now. **1781** COWPER *Conversat.* 313 Some men..give us in recitals of disease A doctor's trouble, but without the fees. **1838** LYTTON *Alice* II. v, Caroline's lively recital of their adventures was received with much interest. **1876** LOWELL *Among my Bks.* Ser. II. 322 At the recital of a noble action..they would suffuse with tears.
b. A discourse, account, relation, narrative.
a **1565** J. HEYWOOD *Wit & Folly* (Percy Soc.) 5 The sotts pleaseure in this last aquyghtall Cownterwayleth his payne, in yowr fyrst recyghtall. **1577** tr. *Bullinger's Decades* (1592) 841 Who is able to recite all..the studies of the Church, in a verie large discourse, much lesse in this short recitall? **1692** DRYDEN *St. Euremont's Ess.* 163 In their Narrations they engage us to follow them by the insensible bond of an agreeable and natural recital. **1732** LEDIARD *Sethos* II. VIII. 168 This recital struck our..auditors with astonishment. **1791** COWPER *Iliad* IX. 742 That dread recital roused him. **1860** TYNDALL *Glac.* I. xxvii. 219, I cannot finish this recital without saying one word about my men.
c. Without article: Narration. *rare.*
1771 MACKENZIE *Man Feel.* xl, Peter came one morning into his master's room with a meaning face of recital. **1772** —— *Man World* II. xi, Those short letters of recital, which I was obliged to write to Sir Thomas.
d. An occasion of narrating or rehearsing.
1842 J. WILSON *Chr. North* II. 287 Some old tragic event that gathered a deeper interest from every recital.
2. *spec.* The rehearsal or statement in a formal or legal document of some fact or facts closely connected with the matter or purpose of the document itself; the part containing this statement.
1512 *Act 4 Hen. VIII*, c. 13 Any recytall or other matter in thys Acte..notwithstandyng. **1614** SELDEN *Titles Hon.* 354 Neither do the Patents..proue that by the Patent they were made, but the recitall do of the Creation. **1687** *Assur. Abb. Lands* 44 In this Bull are the fullest Recitals of the Pope's dispensing Power, that I have yet met with. **1774** BURKE *Sp. Amer. Tax.* Wks. 1842 I. 156 All you suffer is the purging the statute-book of the opprobrium of an empty, absurd, and false recital. **1810** BENTHAM *Packing* (1821) 168 The particular recital prefixed, by way of preamble, to this very clause. **1891** *Law Times* XCII. 107/1 The titles and recitals of both the [Acts]..show them to be Real Property Acts.
Comb. **1834** T. MARTIN (*title*) The Conveyancer's Recital-book.
3. a. An (*or* the) act of (†reading or) reciting.
1612 T. WILSON *Chr. Dict.* s.v. *Read*, Reading is nothing else, but such a recitall and speaking forth the letters and sillibles. **1724** WATERLAND *Athan. Creed* vi. Wks. 1823 IV. 231 From this time..I presume, the Athanasian Creed has been honoured with a public recital. **1863** *Sat. Rev.* 11 July 58 The recital of the poems revealed an entirely new talent. **1875** JOWETT *Plato* (ed. 2) IV. 121 [A] dialogue, combining with the mere recital of the words spoken, the observations of the reciter.
b. *Music.* A musical (esp. only instrumental) performance given by one person. Also, a concert consisting of selections from one composer, and in wider sense, a performance of instrumental music or of music and songs, freq. from the works of several composers. *opera recital*, a performance of the music and words of an opera without appropriate costume or acting.
The use of the word in quots. 1840, to which its present currency is due, is attributed to Mr. F. Beale. The term is now applied to the whole performance, not to the rendering of each separate piece.
1811 BUSBY *Dict. Mus.* (ed. 3), *Recital*, formerly the general name for any performance with a single voice. But at present only applied to recitative. **1840** *John Bull* 31 May 1 Liszt's Pianoforte Recitals. M. Liszt will give at Two o'clock on Tuesday morning, June 9, Recitals on the Pianoforte. *Ibid.* 7 June 3 On Wednesday evening..M. Liszt will also give a recital of one of his great fantasias. **1867** *Musical Times* 1 June 74/1 Mr. Walter Macfarren gave the first of a series of three Pianoforte recitals..on the 18th ult. **1929** *Radio Times* 8 Nov. 417/2 A Recital of Gramophone Records. **1962** *Amer. Speech* XXXVII. 19 New York City boasts of many fine museums, art galleries, and recital halls. **1981** *Early Music News* Mar. 2 Gillian Weir..will give a joint harpsichord and organ recital, conceived as a salute to Couperin and Bach.
4. A repetition; a quotation. *rare*$^{-1}$.
1790 PALEY *Horæ Paul.* i. 4 If it should be objected that this was a mere recital from the Gospel [etc.].

Hence **re'citalist**, one who gives musical recitals.
1889 *Pall Mall G.* 22 May 6/1 Our 'vocalists' seem as chary as our 'recitalists' are prodigal of their talents. **1897** *Scotsman* 31 Mar. 8/7 Mr. Benda..is not altogether unknown as a recitalist in Edinburgh.

†**re'citally,** *adv. Obs.*$^{-1}$ [f. RECITE *v.* + -AL^1 + -LY^2.] By way of citation.
a **1641** BP. MOUNTAGU *Acts & Mon.* (1642) 389 So much Hierome, not recitally delivering other mens opinions, but positively putting down his own.

recitant ('rɛsɪtənt). [f. pres. ppl. stem of L. *recitāre* to RECITE.] One who recites or repeats.
1888 *Ch. Times* XXVI. 472/3 In the private recitation of Matins and Evensong, the recitant can omit the exhortation and the absolution, but should say all else.

†**'recitate,** *v. Obs.*$^{-1}$ [f. pa. ppl. stem of L. *recitāre*.] *trans.* To recite, deliver in recitative.
1774 tr. *Helvetius' Child of Nature* II. 187 They will soon oblige the composers to substitute notes to words, and have them recitated, or sung, by the performers of the opera.

recitation (rɛsɪ'teɪʃən). Also 5 recytacion. [ad. L. *recitātiōn-em*, n. of action f. *recitāre* to RECITE; or a. F. *récitation* (14–15th c.).]
1. a. The action of rehearsing, detailing, †or enumerating; recital.
1484 CAXTON *Fables of Poge* v, The v fable is of the recytacion of somme monstres. **1648** JENKYN *Blind Guide* i. 15 Though indeed the recitation of such cheape and poore stuffe, be a sufficient refutation of them among intelligent Readers. **1685** BAXTER *Paraphr. N.T., Matt.* i. 14, I reduce them to fourteen in the recitation, for memory-sake.
b. An instance of this; an account, narrative.
1641 MILTON *Ch. Govt.* II. Wks. (1851) 148 Wise and artfull recitations sweetned with eloquent and gracefull inticements. **1654** HAMMOND *Fundam.* xv. §7 The recitations and descriptions of God's decreed wrath.
2. a. The action of reciting (†or reading aloud); the repetition of something got by heart.
1623 COCKERAM, *Recitation*, a reading with a loude voice. **1659** PEARSON *Creed* (1839) 18 The recitation of the Creed at the first initiation into the Church by baptism. **1828** WHATELY *Rhet.* in *Encycl. Metrop.* (1847) I. 302/1 Let all studied recitation therefore..be carefully avoided. **1841** BORROW *Zincali* II. ii. III. 60 From the recitation of this individual we wrote down the..Deluge. **1879** GROVE *Dict. Mus.* I. 626 The note on which the recitation is made in each Psalm or Canticle tone.
b. An instance of this; an act of reciting.
1841 LANE *Arab. Nts.* I. 15 Thus, on the first night of the thousand and one, Shahrazād commenced her recitations. **1847** GROTE *Greece* II. xxviii. (1862) III. 60 There were recitations and lectures in a spacious council-room. **1858** RUSKIN *Arrows of Chace* (1880) II. 264, I heard your daughter's recitations in London last Autumn.
3. *U.S.* The repetition of a prepared lesson or exercise; an examination on something previously learned or explained.

1770 P. Fithian *Let.* 30 Nov. in *Jrnl. & Lett.* (1900) 8 At nine the Bell rings for Recitation, after which we study till one, when the Bell rings for Dinner. **1780** E. Parkman *Diary* 9 Feb. (1899) 208 He has been absent from ye Recitations so long, that he ought to be one of ye first that returns at this Term. **1824** W. N. Blaus *Excursion* 364 The 'recitations' mentioned, are examinations on the subject of the lecture of the preceding day. *a* **1882** J. Quincy *Figures of Past* (1884) 4 He took up his Livy to prepare for the last recitation that he could hope to attend.

4. *attrib.*, as (sense 3) ***recitation-bench, -method, -room***; (sense 2) ***recitation-music, -note***.

1887 *Lippincott's Mag.* Aug. 293 A Freshman..never tires of inscribing his class numerals on *recitation-benches. **1949** 'J. Nelson' *Backwoods Teacher* 48 Likely-looking ones I placed on the table..beside the four, long, recitation benches. **1899** W. James *Talks to Teachers* i. 4 Traditions of instruction..evolved from the older American *recitation-method. **1927** *Grove's Dict. Mus.* (ed. 3) III. 371/2 A long series of '*Recitation Music', *i.e.* compositions for piano intended to accompany the declamation of various well-known poems, was written by Stanley Hawley. **1844** W. B. Heathcote *Canticles* p. iii, The first half of the verse is said on the *recitation-note G. **1850** Helmore *Man. Plain Song* 6 This is set for G,..as the recitation-note of the Priest. **1827** *Harvard Reg.* Sept. 202 We hurry to the Chapel, and then crowd to the *recitation room. **1844** Emerson *New Eng. Reformers* Wks. (Bohn) I. 261 Shut up in schools, and colleges, and recitation-rooms for ten or fifteen years. **1899** W. James *Talks to Teachers* xiv. 161 The flowing life of the mind is sorted into parcels suitable for presentation in the recitation-room.

Hence **reci'tationalism**, the characteristics of the usual style of recitation; **reci'tationist**, one who gives recitations.

1885 E. C. Stedman in *Century Mag.* Feb. 512/1 The youth, who has heard this last of the recitationists deliver one of his poems [etc.]. **1890** *Pall Mall G.* 18 Aug. 3/1 His delivery was admirable..without a taint of rant or recitationalism.

recitative (ˌrɛsɪtə'tiːv), *a.*[1] and *sb. Mus.* [ad. It. *recitativo* RECITATIVO; cf. F. *récitatif* sb.

Johnson (1755) gives the stressing as *'recitative*, and Webster (1828) as *re'citative* (defending it in a note): see also quots. 1655 in A. 1 and 1821 in B. 1.]

A. *adj.* **1.** Of the nature of, in the style of, recitative (see B).

1645 Evelyn *Diary* June (Venice), We went to the Opera where Comedies and other plays are represented in recitative Musiq. **1655** [J. Phillips] *Satyr agst. Hypoc.* (1674) 6 Then out he whines the rest like some sad ditty, In a most doleful recitative style. **1711** Addison *Spect.* No. 29 ¶2 The Transition from an Air to Recitative Musick being more natural, than the passing from a Song to plain and ordinary Speaking. **1892** E. Reeves *Homeward Bound* 40 The oratorio..is a peculiar and difficult work of the dramatic recitative order.

†**2.** Employing a recitative style. *Obs.*$^{-1}$

1660 Jer. Taylor *Duct. Dubit.* iii. iv. rule 20 §11 Musicians..are not so recitative, they do not sing and express the words so plainly that they which hear do understand.

B. *sb.* **1. a.** A style of musical declamation, intermediate between singing and ordinary speech, commonly employed in the dialogue and narrative parts of operas and oratorios.

1656 Blount *Glossogr.* s.v. *Opera*, A Tragedy..performed by Voyces in that way, which the Italians term *Recitative.* **1685** Evelyn *Diary* 27 Jan., His singing was after the Venetian recitative, as masterly as could be. **1706** in Phillips. **1780** Harris *Philol. Enq.* Wks. (1841) 428 The ancient choruses between the acts were probably sung, and perhaps the rest was delivered in a species of recitative. **1821** Byron *Juan* iv. lxxxvii, To hear him you'd believe An ass was practising recitative. **1882** Farrar *Early Chr.* II. 552 Maimonides carefully preserves..the reason why the name was pronounced in an almost inaudible recitative.

†**b.** The tone or rhythm peculiar to any language. *Obs.*

1771 Smollett *Humph. Cl.* 13 July, Because every language had its peculiar recitative. **1791** Boswell *Johnson* xxvi. an. 1772, I could name some gentlemen of Ireland, to whom a slight proportion of the accent and recitative of that country is an advantage.

2. Words or passages intended to be delivered in recitative.

1716 Rowe *Let. to Hughes* 22 Oct. in *Sotheran's Catal.* No. 12. (1899) 46 Three or four Airs with some little Recitative between is what the composer will be glad of. **1727** Gay *Begg. Op.* Introd., I have not made my Opera throughout unnatural, like those in vogue; for I have no Recitative. **1845** E. Holmes *Mozart* 171 The libretto..still wanted alterations and abbreviations of the recitative.

3. a. A part rendered in recitative, or a piece of music intended for such a part.

1754 Richardson *Grandison* (1781) IV. xii. 95 How will the dear Harriet bear these abominable recitatives? **1762** Kames *Elem. Crit.* xviii. (1833) 290 The melody of a recitative approaches sometimes to that of a song. **1874** Lady Herbert tr. *Hübner's Ramble* ii. ii. (1878) 249 The flute begins playing a recitative evidently of great antiquity.

b. A performance in recitative. Also *fig.*

1873 Tristram *Moab* ii. 28 A capital 'fantasia' or Arab dance and recitative round our camp fire. **1957** M. Spark *Comforters* iii. 42 It said: On the whole she did not think there would be any difficulty with Helena... There seemed, then, to have been more than one voice: it was a recitative, a chanting in unison.

4. *Comb.*, as ***recitative-like*** adj.

1947 A. Einstein *Mus. in Romantic Era* xi. 143 Characteristically Lisztian recitative-like interjections. **1963** *Times* 28 Feb. 16/3 It was especially in his perfect shaping of the recitative-like passages that Mr. Frank demonstrated his cultivated musicianship.

Hence †**recitatively** *adv. Obs.*$^{-1}$

1702 *Lett. on Q. Anne's Going to St. Paul's* (T.), The jubilee was sung in the same manner, after which the office was performed only recitatively; no organs made use of.

recitative ('rɛsɪteɪtɪv, rɪ'saɪtətɪv), *a.*[2] *rare.* [f. RECITE *v.* + -ATIVE, perh. suggested by prec.] Of the nature of a recital or repetition.

1860 Westcott *Introd. Stud. Gosp.* iii. (ed. 5) 193 Of verbal coincidences,..one-fifth occur in the narrative, and four-fifths in the recitative parts. **1896** C. Johnson in *Cal. Petit. to Pope* I. Pref. 6 Although in other respects the recitative portion of the bull is usually full.

recitative (ˌrɛsɪtə'tiːv), *v.* [f. RECITATIVE *a.*[1]]

1. *trans.* To render or deliver in recitative.

1806 R. Cumberland *Mem.* 59 Mrs. Cibber..sung or rather recitatived Rowe's harmonious strain. **1833** *Q. Rev.* XLIX. 353 The elder verse—the Homeric and Hesiodic—was sung, or..recitatived.

2. *intr.* To declaim in recitative.

1832 Southey *Hist. Penins. War* III. 598 Sundry..Lusitanian worthies recitatived in praise of Lord Wellington. **1932** [see PRELUDINGLY *adv.*].

recita'tivical, *a. rare*$^{-1}$. [f. RECITATIVE *sb.* + -ICAL.] Of the nature of recitative.

1791–1823 D'Israeli *Cur. Lit.* (1866) 145/2 It approaches to the former by recitativical declamation.

recitativo (ˌrɛsɪtə'tiːvəʊ, ‖retʃita'tivo). [It., f. ppl. stem of *recitare* to RECITE + *-ivo* -IVE. Cf. med.L. *recitative* adv. (Du Cange).]

1. = RECITATIVE *sb.* 1.

[**1617** B. Jonson *Masques* (1641) II. 10 The whole Maske was sung (after the Italian manner) Stylo Recitativo. **1678** T. Jordan *Triumphs Lond.* (Percy Soc.) 169 The performance of a song of three parts, *in stilo recitativo*.]

1645 Evelyn *Diary* 10 Oct., She presented me afterwards with two recitativos of hers, both words and musiq. **1667** Pepys *Diary* 12 Feb., All in the recitativo very fine. **1711** Addison *Spect.* No. 29 ¶1 There is nothing that [has] more startled our English Audience, than the Italian Recitativo at its first Entrance upon the Stage. **1748** Richardson *Clarissa* (1811) IV. lii. 351 Charming matrimonial recitativoes! **1819** T. Hope *Anastasius* (1820) III. xii. 323 He soon discovered in my recitativos and arias a mystic sense. **1864** Engel *Mus. Anc. Nat.* 231 They sang in recitativo, as they sing in Italy the ritornello.

attrib. **1780** *Ann. Reg.* ii. 21 He repeated stanzas from Ariosto in a pompous recitativo cadence, peculiar to the natives of Italy. **1812** *Religionism* 41 Recitativo preaching call we this. **1813** *Edin. Rev.* XXII. 143 The habit of using somewhat of *recitativo* intonation.

‖**2.** Used in certain Italian phrases designating varieties of recitative, as **recitativo accompagnato** (akkompaɲ'ɲato): in which the vocalist is accompanied by an orchestra; **recitativo secco** ('sekko) [lit. 'dry recitative']: in which the vocalist has little or no musical accompaniment; **recitativo stromentato** (stromen'tato) [lit. 'accompanied recitative'] = *recitativo accompagnato* above.

[**1771** C. Burney *Present State of Mus. France & Italy* 285 Signor Rinaldo di Capua has at Rome the reputation of being the inventor of accompanied recitatives. **1801** T. Busby *Dict. Mus., Recitative accompanied*, a *recitative* is said to be *accompanied* when besides the bass there are parts for other instruments.] **1866** [see *recitativo stromentato* below]. **1947** A. Einstein *Mus. in Romantic Era* ix. 96 The genuine melodrama, in which the spoken word, usually an emotional monologue, was given an orchestral background in the manner of a *recitativo accompagnato*. **1963** *Listener* 14 Feb. 313/1 *Recitativo accompagnato* began to encroach more and more on the traditional *secco*. **1828** T. Busby *Mus. Man.* 144 *Recitativo secco*, (Ital.) unaccompanied recitative. **1876**, **1883** [see SECCO *a.*]. **1891** G. B. Shaw in *World* 13 May 27/2 Start on the *recitativo secco* by entirely expunging the first two lengths after the duel. **1955** E. Dent in H. Van Thal *Fanfare for E. Newman* 105 It is practically a reversion to *recitativo secco* in a more pretentious form. **1963** Auden *Dyer's Hand* 524 Ariel is song; when he is truly himself, he sings. The effect when he speaks is similar to that of *recitativo secco* in opera. **1977** *Listener* 26 May 692/1 The vocal line is written in the customary *recitativo secco* style. [**1828** T. Busby *Mus. Man.* 144 *Recitativo istromento*, (Ital.) accompanied recitative.] **1837** J. A. Hamilton *Dict. Two Thousand Italian, French, German, Eng. & Other Mus. Terms* 58 *Recitativo stromentato* (Italian) recitative accompanied by the orchestra. **1866** *Chambers's Encycl.* VIII. 140/2 It is termed *recitativo accompagnato*, *strumentato*, or *obbligato*. **1905** E. J. Dent *Alessandro Scarlatti* ii. 45 Here we have an unmistakable *recitativo stromentato*, the earliest (1686) that I have been able to find.

'recitator. *rare*$^{-1}$. [ad. L. *recitātor*, agent-n. f. *recitāre* to RECITE; cf. F. *récitateur*.] One who recites; a recitant.

1880 J. Ross *Hist. Corea* x. 334 The recitators then step before the incense table.

recite (rɪ'saɪt), *sb. rare.* [f. the vb., or ad. F. *récit*.] A recital.

1685 Temple *Ess., Health* Wks. 1731 I. 277 All the former Recites or Observations, either of long-lived Races or Persons in any Age or Country. **1886** R. F. Burton *Arab. Nts.* (abr. ed.) I. 331 Small birds on branches sang with melodious recite.

recite (rɪ'saɪt), *v.* Forms: 5–7 **resite**, 6 **resyte**, **-syght**, **-zyt**, 6–7 **resight**; 5–6 **recyte**, (6 **-ceite**, *Sc.* **-ceat**), 6– **recite**. [a. F. *réciter* (12th c.), or ad. L. *recitāre*, f. *re-* RE- + *citāre* to CITE.]

1. a. *trans.* To repeat or utter aloud (something previously composed, heard, or learned by heart); now *spec.* to repeat to an audience (a piece of verse or other composition) from memory and in an appropriate manner. Also, to read out or aloud (now *rare*).

1481 Caxton *Myrr.* iii. x. 153 The Orysons that ben sayd and recyted euery day in the chirches. **1530** Palsgr. 681/1 He hath a syngular memorie, he recyted al our hole comunycacion and myssed nat a worde. **1589** Puttenham *Eng. Poesie* i. xv. (Arb.) 50 All other kinde of poems..were onely recited by mouth. *a* **1660** Hammond *Serm.* xxii. (1850) ii. 481 Moral precepts [young men] cannot be said to believe,..they now recite them only, and shall then understand them, when they come of age. **1709** Steele *Tatler* No. 47 ¶3, I recited some Heroick Lines of my own. **1789** Burney *Hist. Mus.* IV. 18 The dialogue was neither sung in measure, nor declaimed without Music, but recited in simple musical tones. **1816** J. Wilson *City of Plague* ii. ii. 151 Methinks I hear his voice while he recites Some fragment of a poem. **1884** Horner *Florence* (ed. 2) II. xxxi. 421 Strozzi..endowed the Church in 1589 on condition of masses being recited for his soul.

†**b.** To read out the name of (a person); to call on by name. *Obs.*$^{-1}$

1572 R. H. tr. *Lauaterus' Ghostes* (1596) 107 After this, the question is to be moved, eache man there present being recited whether he would answere unto this or that man.

c. To read out the charges on (a shield).

1859 Thackeray *Virgin.* xxxii, 'I make', cries Charley, reciting the shield, 'three merions [? morions] on a field *or*, with an earl's coronet'.

2. a. To relate, rehearse, narrate, tell, declare; to give an account of; to describe in detail. ? *Obs.*

1483 Caxton *Cato* E vij b, Alle that thyn eyen seen thou oughtest not to recyte ne telle but..kepe hit secrete. **1538** Starkey *England* i. iv. 128 As touchyng thys poynt, yf I schold recyte al that I know [etc.]. **1585** T. Washington tr. *Nicholay's Voy.* i. xv, In his treaty..of the warres of Malta, [he] doth recyte a history no lesse lamentable. **1599** Massinger, etc. *Old Law* i. i, It is thought fit..that they be put to death as is before recited. **1653** H. Cogan tr. *Pinto's Trav.* xix. 68 Antonio..recited unto them his unhappy voyage. **1725** Pope *Odyss.* i. 221 Sincere, from whence began thy course, recite.

b. *Law.* To rehearse or state in a deed or other document (some fact bearing closely upon the matter in hand).

1430–1 *Rolls of Parlt.* IV. 376/1 A remembrance..resityng ye issue yat is joyned..and certefying [etc.]. **1473–4** *Ibid.* VI. 33/2 Recityng by the same among other that where, among certeyn liberties and privileges [etc.]. **1532** *Test. Ebor.* (Surtees) VI. 31 Reciting that by a deed bipartite he had enfeoffed [etc.]. **1682** [see RECITING *ppl. a.*]. **1766** Blackstone *Comm.* II. xxi. 358 The subsequent proceedings are made up into a record or recovery roll, in which the writ and complaint of the defendant are first recited. **1818** Cruise *Digest* (ed. 2) VI. 450 John Ivy, reciting that he had made a former will in the life of his wife [etc.]. **1859** C. Barker *Assoc. Princ.* i. 13 The preamble..recites that many visitations had been made in the 200 years preceding.

†**3.** To compose; to write *down*. *Obs. rare.*

1523 Ld. Berners *Froiss.* I. i. 2, I toke on me..to wryte and recite the sayd boke, and bare yᵉ same compyled into Ingland. **1611** Bible *Ecclus.* xliv. 5 Such as found out musical tunes, and recited verses in writing. **1654** Fuller *Two Serm.* 52 Wherefore he [God] reciteth downe mens Actions, not out of any necessitie to helpe himself to remember them; but partly out of State.

4. a. To go through or over in detail; to make separate mention of (a number of things); to enumerate, give a list of. Now *rare*.

a **1533** Ld. Berners *Huon* lxviii. 234 Yf and I sholde resyte all the ryches that they had there, it shold be to longe to be rehersed. **1578** T. N. tr. *Conq. W. India* 200 All the things recited, and many others which I speake not of, are sold in every market of Mexico. **1613** Purchas *Pilgrimage* v. vii. (1614) 508 What should I heere recite their Camphora, Mirrhe, Frankincense,..and a world of others? **1641** Wilkins *Math. Magick* i. v. (1648) 36 Divers other naturall problemes..which I forbear to recite. **1695** Woodward *Nat. Hist. Earth* i. (1723) 18 They were Minerals as the Belemnites and the others recited, are. **1787** J. Wesley *Serm.* II. xliii. 26 In many cases, by reciting the sins of their neighbours, men indulge their own foolish..desires. **1818–28** Hallam *Mid. Ages* (1841) I. iv. 386 We find only bishops and magnates recited as present.

†**b.** To mention, speak of (a single thing). *Obs.*

1552 *Bury Wills* (Camden) 143 To make vpp yᵉ full of xxˡⁱ wᵗʰin this wyll resytted. **1573** L. Lloyd *Marrow of Hist.* (1653) 126 What should I recite Arganthonius, who was threescore years before he came unto his Kingdome? *a* **1645** Habington *Surv. Worcs.* in *Worcs. Hist. Soc. Proc.* ii. 321 Lendewyke..in the Charter of Kynges Kenred and Offa, recyted next to Evesham.

†**5. a.** To cite, quote. *Obs.*

1542 Udall *Erasm. Apoph.* 290 Allegeyng and recityng certain lawes many yeres afore graunted vnto them. **1570** Foxe *A. & M.* (1596) 78/2 After that, he reciteth the decree which he himselfe made against them. **1621** Burton *Anat. Mel.* i. ii. i. ii, Some few I will recite in this kinde out of most approoued Phisitians. **1653** H. More *Antid. Ath.* iii. ii. §1 (1712) 89, I will briefly recite some few of those many Miraculous passages. **1710** Prideaux *Orig. Tithes* iv. 165 The passage of Mathew Paris above recited. **1793** Beddoes *Math. Evid.* 14, I might recite the opinions of a considerable number of writers.

†**b.** To cite or mention, to quote from (a book).

a **1568** Ascham *Scholem.* ii. (Arb.) 153 Which booke is oft recited, and moch praysed, in the fragmentes of Nonius. **1672** Sir T. Browne *Pseud. Ep.* i. viii. (ed. 3) 22 His Books are often recited (*ed.* 1 cited) by ancient Writers. **1807** G. Chalmers *Caledonia* I. ii. vi. 302 The Chronicon of Dunblane..is recited by Innes, in his MS. Collections.

†**6. a.** *intr.* (or without direct object.) To relate, rehearse, etc. *Obs.* (Cf. sense 2.)

1484 CAXTON *Fables of Æsop* III. xiv, He that gyueth ayde and help to his enemy is cause of his dethe, as recyteth this fable. **1541** R. COPLAND *Galyen's Terap.* 2 E iv, Where they haue estemed that it shulde be superflue to recyte, they haue obmysed and left some. **1554-9** T. WATERTOUNE in *Songs & Ball.* (1860) 11 Thus Esaye the prophet pleanly dothe resyght.

†**b.** Const. *of*, or *to* with inf. *Obs.*

1485 CAXTON *Paris & V.* (1868) 16 Now it sholde be ouerlonge to recyte of the barons. *c* **1531** *Hye way to Spyttel Hous* 36 in Hazl. *E.P.P.* IV. 24 Of suche ryche men recyteth the gospell, . . Saying [etc.]. **1597** A. M. tr. *Guillemeau's Fr. Chirurg.* 8 b/1 Hippocrates reciteth to have cured a personage which had receaved a shot with an arrowe.

7. *intr.* To repeat something from memory; *U.S.* to repeat a lesson, or be examined on one.

1742 E. A. HOLYOKE *Diary* 22 Aug. (1911) 32 This day began to recite to Mr Flynt & Mr Appleton in Tully and virgill & Greek testament. **1759** S. GARDNER *Jrnl.* 21 Mar. in *Essex Inst. Hist. Coll.* (1913) XLIX. 6 Finished reciting, the Dr. gave us good advice. **1815** *Niles' Weekly Reg.* IX. 18/1 Those not immediately engaged in reciting to some one or other of the professors, remain in their own chambers. **1828** WEBSTER, *Recite*, to rehearse a lesson. The class will recite at 11 o'clock. **1847** TENNYSON *Princ.* II. 430 There One walk'd reciting by herself. *a* **1882** J. QUINCY *Figures of Past* (1884) 14 From each of these books we were required to recite once a week.

recited (rɪˈsaɪtɪd), *ppl. a.* [f. RECITE *v.* + -ED[1].] Repeated, related, mentioned, etc.

Also freq. in 17th c. in *above-*, *afore-*, *last-recited*.

1630 PRYNNE *Anti-Armin.* 173 All these recited Fathers . . haue approued. **1650** BULWER *Anthropomet.* 111 The bored lips, so shamefully worn by some of the recited Nations. *a* **1691** BOYLE *Hist. Air* (1692) 194 A part of the Alpes, less high than that where the recited observation was made. **1786** BURKE *Art. agst. W. Hastings* Wks. 1842 II. 112/2 Called to answer for the said recited irregularities.

†**reˈcitement.** *Obs.* [a. F. *récitement* (1611 Cotgr.): see RECITE *v.* and -MENT.] Recital.

1646 SIR T. BROWNE *Pseud. Ep.* 75 These conceits are of that monstrosity that they refute themselves in their recitements. **1686** GOAD *Celest. Bodies* III. iii. 463, I delight not in the Raven-Notes that do befal Recitements at large of those Subjects. **1766** ENTICK *London* I. 350 The laws, recitements, and statutes of holy King Edward.

reciter (rɪˈsaɪtə(r)). Also 6 -our, -or. [f. RECITE *v.* + -ER[1].] One who recites.

1572 HULOET, Recitour, *recitator*. **1598** FLORIO, *Recitante*, a rehearser, a recitor, or reader. **1624** BURTON *Anat. Mel.* II. ii. IV. (ed. 2) 229 Solemne Declamations of certaine select yong Gentlemen in Florence (like those Reciters in old Rome). **1712** STEELE *Spect.* No. 521 ¶4 The others repeat only what they hear from others . . and are called Reciters. **1796** WASHINGTON *Let.* Writ. 1892 XIII. 215 If the persons through whom it has passed to the reciter are not mistaken in their details. **1821** SCOTT *Kenilw.* xvii, The graceful form and animated countenance of the young reciter. **1893** FORBES MITCHELL *Remin. Gt. Mutiny* 76 An excellent vocalist and reciter.

b. Used as the title of books containing passages for recitation.

1829 (*title*) The Universal Reciter, and Cabinet of Comicalities; an elegant collection of . . recitations. **1867** (*title*) Routledge's Comic Reciter.

reˈciting, *vbl. sb.* [f. as prec. + -ING[1].] The action of the vb. RECITE.

1530 PALSGR. 261/1 Recityng of a matter, *recitation*. **1580** HOLLYBAND *Treas. Fr. Tong*, *Recit*, a reciting, a declaration. **1660** R. COKE *Power & Subj.* 136 In the reciting of these laws, I do not affirm [etc.].

b. *reciting note* (see quots.).

1876 STAINER & BARRETT *Dict. Mus. Terms* s.v. *Chant*, The opening chord of a chant, and also the first chord after each double bar, may be sustained at will, to accommodate the number of syllables contained in each part of the verse. These chords are called *reciting notes*. **1881** GROVE *Dict. Mus.* IV. 86 *Reciting-note*, a name sometimes given to that important note, in a Gregorian Tone, on which the greater portion of every Verse of a Psalm, or Canticle, is continuously recited.

So **reˈciting** *ppl. a.*, that recites.

1682 W. MOUNTAGU in *Buccleuch MSS.* (Hist. MSS. Comm.) I. 338 The warrant . . is not altered in a word, only some . . addition . . inserted in the reciting part. **1858** GLADSTONE *Homer* III. 552 To Homer, a reciting poet, the Catalogue was a great effort of memory.

recive, obs. form of RECEIVE.

recivili'zation. [RE- 5 a.] The action of recivilizing.

1816 W. TAYLOR in *Monthly Rev.* LXXIX. 463 An amalgamation . . that might be favourable to the re-civilization of an important corner of Africa. **1837** CARLYLE *Fr. Rev.* III. VII. iv, The Thermidor effulgence of recivilisation.

reˈcivilize, *v.* [RE- 5 a.] *trans.* To civilize again. Hence **reˈcivilized** *ppl. a.*

1813 G. EDWARDS *Meas. True Pol.* 25 France and Great Britain . . would readily recivilize the ancient World. **1837** CARLYLE *Fr. Rev.* III. VII. ii, Fair Cabarus, . . struggling to recivilise mankind. **1899** MACKAIL *Life W. Morris* I. 6 In the restored and recivilized England of a distant future.

reck (rɛk), *sb.*[1] *Obs.* exc. *poet.* Forms: 6 recke, reake, *Sc.* **rak**, **rack(e**, 6, 8–9 **reck**. [f. RECK *v.*]

1. Care, heed, consideration, regard.

1568 *Jacob & Esau* I. ii. in Hazl. *Dodsley* II. 196 One that hath no recke ne care what way he walke. **1594** CAREW *Huarte's Exam. Wits* xv. (1596) 268 The vulgar make little reake thereof. **1866** H. C. LEA tr. *Audefroid-le-Batard* in *Superst. & Force* I. (1878) 63 Your love [is] another's, and of mine, You have nor reck nor care.

2. *Sc.* In phr. ***what reck?*** What matters it?

1535 LYNDESAY *Satyre* 210 Quhat rak of ȝour prosperitie Gif ȝe want Sensualitie! *c* **1600** MONTGOMERIE *Cherrie & Slae* 1359 Thoch it be cummersom, quhat reck? **1792** BURNS *The Tither Morn* i, When I, what reck, did least expect To see my lad sae near me.

†**reck,** *sb.*[2] obs. variant of RACK *sb.*[2] 5 d.

1671 *Phil. Trans.* VI. 2111 A Reck . . is a frame made of boards about three foot and an half broad, and six long, which turns upon two iron pegs fastened in both ends, and the whole placed upon two posts.

reck, obs. variant of RICK, WREAK *sb.*

reck (rɛk), *v.* Forms: (*a*) *Inf.* *α.* 1 recan, recc(e)an, 2–5 recchen, (recthen), (and *Pres.*) 3 ræcche, rechche, 4–5 retche; 2–5 reche(n, 4 reiche, reyche. *β.* 3–6 rekke(n, 4–7 reck(e, 4–6 rek, 6– reck, (7 wrecke); 4–6 reke, 6–7 (w)reak(e; *north.* and *Sc.* 4–6 **rak(k**, 7–8 **rack**, 9 *Sc.* **raik**. (*b*) *Pa. t.* *α.* 1–3 róhte, 3–5 roȝt(e, 4–6 roght(e, 4 roht; 3–5 rouht(e, rouȝt(e, rowght, 4–7 rought(e, 5 rowȝte, rough, rowth, 6 *Sc.* roucht; 4–6 raught(e, 5 *Sc.* racht. *β.* 5 recched, retched, -yd; 6 wreaked, *Sc.* rakit; 7– recked. (*c*) *Pa. pple.* *α.* 4 roght, 5–6 rought(e, 6 wrought; 5 raught. *β.* 5 reckid, 6– recked. [Comm. Teut.: OE. *reccan* (? *récan*) = OS. *rôkjan* (MDu. *roeken*), OHG. *ruoh(h)en* (MHG. *ruochen*), ON. *rœkja* (mod.Norw. dial. *rökja*):—OTeut. **rōkjan*, the base of which does not appear in the cognate languages.

The reason of the double consonant in OE. *reccan* (for the normal *récan*) is not clear; it may have been due to association with *reccan* RECCHE. In ME. there is considerable variation of form, arising from differences both in vowel and consonant; the typical forms with short vowel are *recche* or *retche*, *recke* and *rack*, contrasted with *rēche* or *rēke*, later *reak*. The latter is common in the 16th c., but from about 1600 the usual literary form has been *reck*.

The OE. pa. t. *róhte* gives the usual ME. pret. forms *roȝt(e*, *rought(e*, etc.; the occasional *raught* may be due to the influence of the pa. t. of REACH. The new formations in *-ed*, as *recched*, *recked*, are app. not older than the 15th c.]

From its earliest appearance in Eng., *reck* is almost exclusively employed in negative or interrogative clauses. In the former the simple negative may be replaced by *nought*, *nothing*, *little*, *not much*, etc.; in the latter the pron. *what* is most usual. There are comparatively few examples of the word during the 17th and 18th c., but in the 19th it again becomes common in rhetorical and poetic language.

1. *intr.* Const. with *of*: **a.** To take care, heed, or thought *of* some thing (or person), with inclination, desire or favour towards it, interest in it, or the like; to think (much, etc.) *of*.

c **888** K. ÆLFRED *Boeth.* xxv, Þeah heora lareowas him þonne biodan þa ilcan mettas . . ðonne ne reccað hi þara metta. *c* **1000** ÆLFRIC *Hom.* I. 224 He ne rohte þæs eorðlican reafes syððan he of deaðe aras. *c* **1205** LAY. 17051 Ne recche ich noht his londes his seoluer ne his goldes. *a* **1250** *Owl & Night.* 1404 Þe gost . . lutel rekþ of milce and ore. *a* **1300** *Cursor M.* 15776 'Iudas, quilum was', he said, 'þat mikel o þe i roght'. *c* **1375** *Sc. Leg. Saints* xliii. (*Cecilia*) 394 A murtherere . . þat racht noþire of mensk na honoure. *c* **1440** CAPGRAVE *Life St. Kath.* III. 1370 3e neuyr mech rowth [*v.r.* rought] Of no wordly . . plesauns. **1481** CAXTON *Reynard* (Arb.) 48 Ye retche not of brede of flesshe ne suche maner mete. **1579** SPENSER *Sheph. Cal.* July 34 Syker, thous but a laesie loord, And rekes much of thy swinck [*gloss* counts much of thy paynes]. **1616** R. C. *Times' Whistle* v. 1928 He would not wrecke Of all celestiall ioyes. **1810** SCOTT *Lady of L.* IV. xix, What from a prince can I demand, Who neither reck of state nor land? *a* **1845** BARHAM *Ingol. Leg.* Ser. III. *Jerry Jarvis*, Little recked he of flowers—save cauliflowers. **1887** BOWEN *Virg. Æneid* v. 400 Of gifts I reck but lightly.

b. To take heed or have a care *of* some thing (or person), so as to be alarmed or troubled thereby, or to modify one's conduct or purpose on that account.

Beowulf (Z.) 434 Se æglæca . . wæpna ne recceð. *a* **900** CYNEWULF *Crist* 1440 Fylgdon me mid firenum; fæh þe ne rohtun. *c* **1200** ORMIN 16165 Nan mann ne þurrfte off himm Ne nimenn gom, ne rekkenn. **1297** R. GLOUC. (Rolls) 4419 So gret was is herte þat of deþ he ne roȝte no þing. *c* **1375** *Sc. Leg. Saints* xlii. (*Agatha*) 154 Do one as þu has thocht, for of þi panys rak I nocht. *c* **1450** tr. *De Imitatione* III. v. 68 If troup e delyuere þe, þou shalt . . not recche of mennes veyn wordes. **1578** T. PROCTOR *Gorg. Gallery Gallant Inuent.*, *Pure Consc.*, A Conscience pure . . That . . Of slaunders lothsome reketh not. **1579** SPENSER *Sheph. Cal.* Oct. 29 What wreaked I of wintrye ages waste. **1667** MILTON *P.L.* II. 50 Of God, or Hell, or worse He reckd not. **1775** SHERIDAN *Duenna* III. i, Then it was, old Father Care, Little reck'd I of thy frown. **1810** SCOTT *Lady of L.* v. xvi, He . . Received, but reck'd not of a wound. **1876** BLACK *Madcap V.* v. 47 What recked she of the mad course she was pursuing.

c. To know, be aware, or think *of*.

1813 BYRON *Corsair* III. v, Ah! little reck'd that chief of womanhood—Which frowns ne'er quell'd, nor menaces subdued. **1835** LYTTON *Rienzi* IV. i, If this last, I shall have done better for my charge than I recked of. **1865** DICKENS *Mut. Fr.* II. v, Little recked Mr. Podsnap of the traps and toils besetting his Young Person.

2. With other preps. To set store or account *by*; to care *for*; †to think or have pity *on*; †to be troubled or distressed *at*.

With *by* and *for* the sense may be either as in 1 a or 1 b.

c **1000** *Ags. Gosp.* Mark xii. 14 We witon þæt . . þu ne recst be ænegum menn. *c* **1275** LAY. 2789 Alle his riche eorles . . nolde for þan kinges bode noþing . . reche. **1423** JAS. I *Kingis Q.* xxvii, Was non that myght, that on my peynes rought. **1490** CAXTON *Eneydos* v. 21 The wymmen . . were to fore the sayd aulter . . wythoute retchynge ought by theym selfe. **1530** PALSGR. 681/1 He is the moste neglygent folowe that ever I sawe, he recketh for nothynge. **1566** DRANT *Wail. Hierim.* K vi b, And lende his cheeke unto the stroke, nor recke at wordes of spite. **1615** BRATHWAIT *Strappado* (1878) 131 Ane, we raught on meanely. ? **1788** BURNS *Song*, Louis, what reck I by thee, Or Geordie on his ocean? **1853** KINGSLEY *Hypatia* xxv, [The gods] recked nothing for the weal or woe of earth.

3. With *inf.* **a.** To care, desire, be willing or anxious *to* do something.

a **900** *Laws of Ælfred* Introd. c. 40 in Schmid *Gesetze* (1858) 62 Leases monnes word ne rece þu no þæs toȝehieranne. *a* **1200** *Moral Ode* 221 Neure in helle hi com, ne þer ne come reche. *c* **1386** CHAUCER *Knt.'s T.* 1377, I recche nat, . . To haue victorie of hem, or they of me. *c* **1450** *St. Cuthbert* (Surtees) 6557 In þe chapiter twenty and sex he may se, to knawe wha rex. **1481** CAXTON *Godfrey* xliii. 83 Tancre his neuew . . retched not for to see Themperour ne to speke to hym. **1574** HELLOWES *Gueuara's Fam. Ep.* (1577) 290 Such as be of good gouernment, and reck not to follow physick. **1600** SHAKS. *A.Y.L.* II. iv. 81 My master . . little wreakes to finde the way to heauen By doing deeds of hospitalitie. **1873** SYMONDS *Grk. Poets* iii. 72 Old eyes forlorn Scarce reck the very sunshine to behold.

b. To care, to be troubled, distressed, or reluctant; to feel aversion or repugnance *to*, etc.

c **1300** *Becket* (Percy Soc.) 405 Lute hi wolde recche to loose here ordre so. *a* **1340** HAMPOLE *Psalter* xxi. 13 Þai roght na mare to sla me þan to spill watere. **1430–40** LYDG. *Bochas* I. i. (1554) 3 Ye retche not by sin To slea your soule. **1485** CAXTON *Chas. Gt.* 214 The cristen men . . raught not for to deye for þe crysten fayth. **1610** BOYS *Expos. Ep. & Gosp.* Wks. (1629) 507 Schismatikes . . reake not to be condemned of the learned for ignorant; so they may be commended of the ignorant for learned.

4. With dependent clause: To care, be troubled, concern oneself, *if*, *that*, *though*; *how*, *when*, *whether*; *who*, *what*, etc.

c **888** K. ÆLFRED *Boeth.* xviii. §4 ȝe ne reccað ðeah hweðer ȝe auht to gode don. *c* **950** *Lindisf. Gosp.* Mark iv. 38 Ne reces ðu þæt [*Rushw.* ðah] we deado sie. *c* **1000** ÆLFRIC *Colloq.* in Wr.-Wülcker 89/14 Hwæt rece we hwæt we sprecan. *a* **1122** *O.E. Chron.* (Laud MS.) an. 1086 Se cyng . . ne rohte na hu swiðe synlice þa ȝerefan hit beȝeatan of earme mannon. *c* **1205** LAY. 18042 Ne þurfen ȝe nauere rehchen, þah ȝe slæn þa wrecchen. *a* **1225** *Juliana* 19 Cristene womman icham iwis; I ne reche ho it wite. *a* **1300** *Cursor M.* 5446 Nou rek i neuer quen i dei. *c* **1380** WYCLIF *Wks.* (1880) 44 [Let friars] recke not þat [*v.r.* þ o] þei ben vnkunnynge to lerne letteris. *a* **1450** *Knt. de la Tour* (1868) 60 There be many women that rechin neuer what fallithe of her counsayle. **1485** CAXTON *Chas. Gt.* 196, I retche not though he be put to dethe. **1532** MORE *Confut. Tindale* Wks. 530/1 As though he roughte not whether they dydde good or ill. *c* **1570** *Satir. Poems Reform.* xxxvii. 69 Rek not . . how raschelie ravarris raill. **1606** SHAKS. *Tr. & Cr.* v. vi. 26, I wreake not, though thou end my life to day. **1641** MILTON *Animadv.* i. Wks. (1851) 187 They wreck not whether you . . know them or not. **1813** SCOTT *Rokeby* I. xix, Whether false the news, or true, Oswald, I reck as light as you. **1825** —— *Talism.* xii, Sir Kenneth little recked, that [etc.]. **1845** HIRST *Com. Mammoth*, etc. 15 We recked not what our fates might be.

5. Without const. (usually *ellipt.* for one or other of prec. uses): To care, heed, mind, etc.

c **1000** *Sax. Leechd.* III. 254 Hi habbað þurh þæt cornes swa fela swa hi mæst recceað. *a* **1122** *O.E. Chron.* (Laud MS.) an. 1070 þa munecas . . beaden heom grið, ac hi na rohten na þing. *c* **1205** LAY. 16179 To þan castle heo brohten swa muchel swa heo rohten. *c* **1320** *Cast. Love* 341 They . . lyed to him therof, and lytelle rowghton. *c* **1386** CHAUCER *Nun's Pr. Prol.* 48 If he wol serve thee, rekke not a bene. *c* **1430** *Chev. Assigne* 177 She rawȝte hit hym aȝeyne & seyde she ne rowȝte. **1483** CAXTON *Gold. Leg.* 198/2 There were many fayr myracles whyche by neglygence . . and not retchyng were not wryton. *a* **1548** HALL *Chron., Rich. III* 31 b, In faith, quod he, I neither wote ne recke, so I were once hence. *a* **1591** H. SMITH *Wks.* (1867) II. 485 Who little recks, much good foregoes. **1667** MILTON *P.L.* IX. 173 Revenge . . back on itself recoiles; Let it; I reck not. **1746** W. THOMPSON *Hymn to May* xxx, Who hears them cry, ne recks. **1791** COWPER *Iliad* XI. 97 The eternal father reck'd not. **1813** SCOTT *Rokeby* III. ii, I reck not. In a war to strive, . . Suits ill my mood.

6. *trans.* To heed, regard, care for, etc. (either as in sense 1 a or 1 b).

c **1205** LAY. 28851 Mucchel scome heom þuhte þat wepmen heom ne rohte. **1390** GOWER *Conf.* III. 186 The king his oghne astat ne roghte. *c* **1449** PECOCK *Repr.* II. viii. 182 If thei be not remembrid, thei schulen not be reckid. **1513** DOUGLAS *Æneis* XIII. v. 81 O haitfull deid . . Quhilk gret and small doun thringis, and nane rakkis. **1591** R. WILMOT *Tancred & Gismunda* IV. iii, Not that she recks this life. **1602** SHAKS. *Ham.* I. iii. 51 Himself . . reaks not his owne reade. **1637** G. DANIEL *Genius of this Isle* 631 Eagles doe not recke the Wren's weake flight. **1786** BURNS *Ep. Young Friend* xi, May ye better reck the rede Than ever did th' Adviser! **1839** KEIGHTLEY *Hist. Eng.* I. 102 He was so stern, that he recked not all their hatred. **1871** R. ELLIS tr. *Catullus* xlv. 22 Septimius . . Recks not Syria, recks not any Britain.

b. To reckon, consider, think. Now only *Sc.* †Also const. *in*.

1599 T. M[OUFET] *Silkwormes* 52 Which kings themselues in highest prize do reake. **1639** G. DANIEL *Ecclus.* xiii. 6 Doe not recke Thy selfe the wiser, to b' Associate With those who are beyond thee in Estate. **1791** LEARMONT *Poems* 114, I ne'er thought . . [she] Coud e'er harbour a thought o' distrust Or reck her shepherd unkind. **1892** LUMSDEN *Sheephead* 91 Ye wha reck our Scottish name Fit wi' the warld's first to ally.

†**7.** *refl.* To trouble or concern (oneself). *Obs.*

a **1250** *Owl & Night.* 533 Of none winters ich me recche. **13..** *Guy Warw.* (A.) 593 Henne forward ne reche y me Of mi liif. *c* **1450** *Merlin* 93 Of that ne recche the nothinge for to enquere. **1489** CAXTON *Faytes of A.* I. i. 2 Retche the not what they saye. **1674** RAY *N.C. Words* 38 Never Rack you; i.e. Take you no thought or care.

8. In impersonal use: To concern or trouble (one); to interest. (With various const., as in senses 1–4 above.)

a **1225** *Ancr. R.* 104 ȝif heo beoð feor, me ne reccheð. *c* **1290** *Beket* 449 in *S. Eng. Leg.* I. 119 Luyte heom wolde rechche to leosen heore ordre so. *a* **1300** *Cursor M.* 1834 Littel roght þam of his manance. *c* **1385** CHAUCER *L.G.W.* 605 *Cleopatra*, Hym roughte nat in armys for to sterve. *c* **1460** *Towneley Myst.* i. 129 Now, therof a leke what rekys vs? *a* **1592** GREENE *George a Greene* Wks. (Rtldg.) 264/1 What recks it us, though George-a-Greene be stout. **1634** MILTON *Comus* 404 Of night, or loneliness it recks me not. **1637** —— *Lycidas* 122 What recks it them? What need they? **1869** BLACKMORE *Lorna D.* ii, Little it recked us and helped them less that they were our founder's citizens.

b. *absol.* To matter; to be of importance or interest.

a **1225** *Ancr. R.* 188 ȝe schulen lihtlie iseon hu lutel hit reccheð. *c* **1374** CHAUCER *Boeth.* (E.E.T.S.) 38 þerfore what wenist þou þar recche [L. *quid igitur referre putas*] yif þou forlete hir in deynge or ellys þat she.. forlete þe? **1483** *Cath. Angl.* 299/2 It Rakkes, *refert.* *a* **1547** SURREY *Æneid* II. 499 Craft, or manhod, with foes what reckes it which? *a* **1600** MONTGOMERIE *Misc. Poems* xxviii. 44 Quhat reks then of the reid? Or of the trees what reks? *a* **1771** GRAY *Dante* 17 It rekes not That I advise thee. *a* **1774** FERGUSSON *On J. Hogg* Wks. (1800) 156 What recks tho' ye ken mood and tense? **1825** SCOTT *Talism.* iii, 'But what recks it', said stout Sir Kenneth.

Hence '**recking** *vbl. sb. rare.*

1886 R. F. BURTON *Arab. Nts.* (abr. ed.) I. 14 [He] thanked him, saying, 'Right is thy recking'.

reckan(d, varr. RACKAN.

reckelæs, obs. f. RECKLESS.

recken, -in, obs. ff. RECKON *v.*, RACKAN.

reckevere, obs. f. RECOVER.

Reckitt ('rɛkɪt). Also *erron.* **Reckett.** [See quot. 1877.] Used in the possessive as the proprietary name of a blue (BLUE *sb.* 2 c) for laundry use; also as the name of the colour of this substance, a clear cobalt blue, esp. *transf.* Hence **Reckitt's bluebag**, the bag in which this product is marketed.

1877 *Trade Marks Jrnl.* 19 Feb. 471 Reckitt's Blue in squares will be found far more beautiful & much more economical than any other... Francis Reckitt, of Hull, Yorkshire, on behalf of self and partner, James Reckitt, trading as I. Reckitt and Sons, at..London, and as Isaac Reckitt and Sons, at Hull, Yorkshire; starch manufacturers. **1893** S. R. CROCKETT *Stickit Minister* 46 The book..was bound in a peculiarly deadly blue, of a rectified Reckitt tint, which gave you dazzles in the eye. **1898** G. B. SHAW *Let.* 25 Apr. (1972) II. 37 Mud & fog are not so fatal as siroccos [*sic*]..& Reckitt's blue. **1920** E. SITWELL *Wooden Pegasus* 83 Then (Recketts' blue) a puff of wind. **1925** 'H. H. RICHARDSON' *Way Home* II. i. 113 As for the sky, Mahony declared it made him think of a Reckitt's bluebag. **1930** E. V. LUCAS *Down Sky* 138 A bunch of yellow-haired girls lying on marble slabs looking at a sea of Reckitts. **1969** R. HARRIS *Nat. Hist. Collecting* 49 Some sponges are brightly coloured. One is called the Reckitt's blue, not without reason. **1971** *Guardian* 6 Feb. 3/3 The flies zoom between the Reckitt's Blue walls. **1976** *Trade Marks Jrnl.* 1 Dec. 2497/2 Reckitt's Bag Blue. Ready for use... Laundry blue for sale in the United Kingdom and for export to the Irish Republic. Reckitt & Colman Products Limited, trading as Reckitt & Colman,..Hull, Yorkshire; manufacturers and merchants.

†**reckle**, var. *rackle*, RAKYL, chain. *Sc. Obs.*

c **1603** *Lindesay's (Pitscottie) Cron. Scot.* (1814) 190 Ane faire blowing horne, in ane reckle of gold borne and tipped with fyne gold at both the endis.

reckless ('rɛklɪs), *a.* Forms: α. 1 recci-, recceléas, 4 recchelees, rechcheles, 4–6 **retche-**, 4–7 **retchless**, (7 **wretch-**); 1 receléas, 2–6 recheles, (6–7 -lesse, 6 rechelles), 6–7 **reachless**; 6 rache-, riche-; 3 rechyles, 5 rechilesse, richilees. β. 3 reckelæs, 4–6 **rekke-**, 6–7 **reckeless**; 4 rec(c)-, 4–6 rek-, 6– **reckless**, (9 **wreck-**); 4–6 **reke-**, 6 **reak**, 6–7 **wreak(e)less**. *north.* and *Sc.* 4–6 **rakless**, (4–5 -lese), 6–8 **rackless**; 4–5 **rakelese.** [OE. *recceléas* (early *recciléas*) and *réceléas* = MDu. (and Du.) *roekeloos*, MLG. *rôkelôs*, OHG. *ruachalôs* (MHG. *ruochelôs*, G. *ruchlos*), f. OE. **recce*, **rēce* = OHG. *ruacha, rocha* care (see RECK *v.*) + *-léas* -LESS.

The α-forms are very common from *c* 1375 to 1650; those with *k* are originally northern, and are rarely found in southern writers before the second half of the 16th c.]

1. Of persons: Careless, heedless. **a.** Careless in respect of (†one's conduct, reputation, or) the consequences of one's actions; lacking in prudence or caution.

α. *c* **725** *Corpus Gloss.* 1646 *Præfaricator*, reccileas. *c* **888** K. ÆLFRED *Boeth.* v. § 3 Đu wendest ðætte stiorlease men & recelease wæren ȝesælie. *c* **1290** *S. Eng. Leg.* I. 47/17 Wylde Men ne louede he nouȝt, þat rechelese weren of þouȝte. **1377** LANGL. *P. Pl.* B. XVIII. 2 Wolleward and wete-shoed went I ..As a reccheles [*v.r.* recheles] renke, that of no wo reccheth. *c* **1420** *Chron. Vilod.* st. 670 Ever after forsothe a parfyt lever was he, þe whyche hadde be a ful rechelesse womon byfore. **1480** CAXTON *Chron. Eng.* ccxlvi. 311 In his yougthe he had ben wyld and recheles. **1538** STARKEY *England* I. iv. 113 Thys intaylyng..makyth many rechles heyrys. **1592** NASHE *P. Penilesse* (ed. 2) 25 Of him that is an idle glutton at home, or a retchlesse vnthrift abroad. **1666** BP. S. PARKER *Free & Impart. Censure* (1667) 183 To reform a debauch'd and wretchlesse child.

β. *c* **1400** *Cursor M.* 27772 (Cott. Galba) He es rekles in word and dede, in tyme when he of both has nede. *c* **1400** *Rule St. Benet* 6/14 þa þat ere fraward and recles, hede þaim þe straiter. **14..** *Battle of Otterbourn* 53 The roo full rekeless ther sche runnes, To make the game and gle. **1500–20** DUNBAR *Poems* xc. 58 [When one] is rekless in his governance,..That man is abill to fall ane gret mischance. *a* **1585** MONTGOMERIE *Cherrie & Slae* 595 They are bot rakles, ȝoung and rasche. **1613** R. CAWDREY *Table Alph.*, *Recklesse*, rash, carelesse. *a* **1667** COWLEY (J.), Next this was drawn the reckless cities flame When a strange hell pour'd down from heaven there came. **1812** H. & J. SMITH *Rej. Addr., Cui Bono?* ii, Ye reckless dupes, who hither wend your way. **1829** LYTTON *Disowned* iii, I became bold, reckless and adventurous. **1879** DIXON *Windsor* II. vi. 63 A rough and reckless soldier, caring for nothing but a fight.

†**b.** Careless in respect of some duty or task; negligent, inattentive. *Obs.*

α. *a* **900** tr. *Bæda's Hist.* III. xi[ii]. (1890) 190 Ymb þa ȝemænne his ecre hælo [he] wæs to sæne & to receleas. *c* **1200** *Trin. Coll. Hom.* 39 He..hloneð and slepeð and syneȝeð on gemeleste alse he þat is recheles. *a* **1240** *Sawles Warde* in *Cott. Hom.* 245 Alle hit [*v.r.* ha] beoð untohene & rechelese hinen, bute ȝef he ham rihte. **1387** TREVISA *Higden* (Rolls) IV. 361 He was recheles a morwe, and wolde nouȝt come or he hadde i-ete. *c* **1449** PECOCK *Repr.* III. v. 307 Thei ouȝten not be ouer myche recheles in lesing her godis. **1523** FITZHERB. *Husb.* § 7 He that wyll..be slouthefull, recheles, and not diligent. **1573** TUSSER *Husb.* (1878) 21 A retcheles [*v.r.* reachelesse] seruant, a mistres that scowles. **1657** R. LIGON *Barbadoes* 45 The carelessness and slothfulness of retchless servants. **1681** W. ROBERTSON *Phraseol. Gen.* (1693) 1048 Reachless or careless.

β. *c* **1200** ORMIN 932 ȝiff þat he wære reckelæs To ringen hise belless. *a* **1300** *Cursor M.* 28269 Mi childer als and my menȝe a reckeles leder þai fand me. **1340** HAMPOLE *Pr. Consc.* 5802 Whaswa es rekles and kepes it ille, He sal be aresoned. *c* **1375** *Sc. Leg. Saints* xviii. (*Mary Egypt*) 1281 Repentand hyme..he had (bene) þane sa raklase þat hyre name nocht had he speryt. *c* **1440** *Promp. Parv.* 428/2 Rekkeles, *necgligens, incurius.* **1483** *Cath. Angl.* 299/2 Rakles (*A.* Rakelese), *ignavius, necligens, & cetera, vbi* slawe. **1593** SHAKS. *3 Hen. VI*, v. vi. 7 So flies the wreaklesse shepherd from yᵉ Wolfe.

†**c.** Having no care or consideration for oneself or another. *Obs. rare.*

?*a* **1366** CHAUCER *Rom. Rose* 340 To sorowe was she ful ententyf, That woful recchelesse caityf. **1591** SHAKS. *Two Gent.* v. ii. 52 More to be reueng'd on Eglamoure, Then for the loue of reck-lesse Siluia. **1717** RAMSAY *Elegy Lucky Wood* ii, Rackless Death, wha came unsenn To Lucky Wood.

2. Heedless or careless *of* something.

a **1023** WULFSTAN *Hom.* xlix. (1883) 258 *note*, To hwam wurde þu swa receleas þæra ȝyfena (ðe ic ðe ȝeaf). *c* **1375** *Sc. Leg. Saints* xvi. (*Magdalene*) 290 Gyf scho ware mare rakles of It,..scho suld rew it farly sare. *a* **1547** SURREY in *Tottell's Misc.* (Arb.) 17 Retchlesse of his life, he gan both sighe and grone. **1631** *Celestina* II. 33 The cause of your growing carelesse and wretchlesse both of your body, soule, and goods. **1700** DRYDEN *Pal. & Arc.* III. 1074 Retchless of laws, affects to rule alone. **1791** COWPER *Odyss.* VI. 356 Reckless of her parents' will. **1805** WORDSW. *Prelude* v. 118 He hurried on Reckless of me. **1849** GROTE *Greece* (1862) III. xlii. 521 This unfortunate man had become reckless of life. **1887** R. LODGE *Mod. Europe* xxii. § 16 (1897) 517 The king's brothers..were utterly reckless of the dangers to which their conduct exposed Louis XVI.

transf. **1879** GEO. ELIOT *Theo. Such* ii. 41 Hedgerows reckless of utility.

3. Of actions, conduct, things, etc.: Characterized or distinguished by (†negligent carelessness or) heedless rashness.

α. **1529** MORE *Dyaloge* III. Wks. 207/1 The good meane maner betwene scrupulouse superstition and rechlesse negligence. **1559** SACKVILLE *Induct. Mirr. Mag.* xlvi, Death ..With retcheles hande in grave doth couer it. **1581** MULCASTER *Positions* xxxiii. (1887) 119 Being full of excrementes by reason of their reacheles diet. **1633** PRYNNE *1st Pt. Histrio-m.* 157 Too deare a price for so fruitlesse, so wretchlesse a purchase. *a* **1640** JACKSON *Creed* x. xxxv. § 6 A retchless temper or neglective content in living from hand to mouth.

β. *a* **1300** *Cursor M.* 12315 O barns an..Brak þe pott..wit wil or wit recles dint. *c* **1400** *Rule St. Benet* 69/857 Of slike rekles warkes Sais haly writ [etc.]. *c* **1470** HENRY *Wallace* v. 455, I haiff tynt men throw my (our) rakless deid. **1500–20** DUNBAR *Poems* xv. 34 Asking wald haif convenient place.. But hairt abasit, but toung rekless. **1581** T. HOWELL *Deuises* (1879) 236 A troubled wyt, a reakelesse hande, a wrathfull hart to spill. **1596** DALRYMPLE tr. *Leslie's Hist. Scot.* I. 109 Rekles negligence in preicheng the worde of God. **1721** KELLY *Sc. Proverbs* 284 Rackless Youth makes rueful Age. **1827** SCOTT *Chron. Canongate* Introd. 3 He had lost..all the reckless play of raillery which gave vivacity to his original acting. **1863** FAWCETT *Pol. Econ.* II. vi. 216 A system of small landed properties..is supposed to encourage a reckless increase of population.

4. Quasi-*adv.* Recklessly. Also *Comb.*

c **1430** *Hymns Virg.* 62 Quod leccherie, 'pi seed richelees þou schake, And make no force of no mariage'. *c* **1470** HENRY *Wallace* VIII. 270 Than ane Mawthland rakless betwixt thaim past. **1548** UDALL, etc. *Erasm. Par. Acts* i. vi b, What daunger it wer for vs negligently and recheles to execute thoffice, whiche we take in hande. **1591** SPENSER *M. Hubberd* 950 Through the forest rechlesse they did goe. **1866** BLACKIE *Homer & Iliad* I. 163 The hurly-burly of reckless-shifting war.

†'**reckless**, *v. Obs.* Also 6 *Sc.* **rakles.** [OE. *receléasian* (= OHG. *ruahha-, ruachalôsôn*), f. *réceléas* RECKLESS *a.* In later use only Sc., and perh. formed anew from the adj.] *trans.* To neglect; to be negligent or heedless of (a thing). Also *refl.* and *absol.*

a **1023** WULFSTAN *Hom.* xlix. (1883) 258 To hwon receleasedest þu þære ȝife, þe ic þe ȝeaf. *c* **1560** A. SCOTT *Poems* (S.T.S.) iii. 26 Rekles nocht ȝour eirand for the rane. **1567** Q. MARY in Keith *Hist. Scot.* (1734) I. 391 Albeit he [Bothwell] hes in some Pointis or Ceremoneis raklest himself. *a* **1600** MONTGOMERIE *Misc. Poems* xxiii. 31 Quhair I haif recklest, I recant.

†'**recklesshead.** *Obs.* Forms: re(c)che-, retche-, rekleshed(e, -heed. [f. RECKLESS *a.* + -HEAD. Cf. (M)Du. *roekeloosheid.*] Recklessness.

α. **1430–1** *Rolls of Parlt.* IV. 378/1 Of recheleshed addyng or levyng more or lesse than nedeth. **1496** *Dives & Paup.* (W. de W.) II. xx. 132/1 Yf they by retcheleshede of speche or of dede ben cause of brekynge of peas.

β. **1412–20** LYDG. *Chron. Troy* I. vi, For rekleshed she sawe it all to late. **1447** BOKENHAM *Seyntys* (Roxb.) 71 This errour..Wher in throgh rekleshеed thou art falle.

So †**recklesshood, -laik.** *Obs. rare.*

a **1300** *Cursor M.* 27772 O suernes cums..reccles-laic in mede and ded. **1833** COLLIER *Hist. Eng. Dram. P.* II. 290 They are called Recklesshood, Idleness, Surfeit [etc.].

recklessly ('rɛklɪslɪ), *adv.* Forms: see RECKLESS *a.* [f. RECKLESS *a.* + -LY².]

1. In a reckless manner: †**a.** Carelessly, negligently. *Obs.*

α. *c* **897** K. ÆLFRED *Gregory's Past. C.* lvii. 439 Nis us nawht recceleaslice to ȝehiranne ðætte he nemde ða undiorestan wyrta [etc.]. *c* **1000** *Ags. Hom.* (ed. Assmann) xiv. 121 Se þe hit þonne receleæslice..wyrceð, he bið awyrȝed into helle. **1377** LANGL. *P. Pl.* B. XI. 125 He may.. as a reneyed caityf recchelesly gon aboute. **1413** *Pilgr. Sowle* (Caxton 1483) IV. xxvii. 73 Thou haste thy body rechelesly gouerned and blamest hyt for thy gylt. **1496** *Dives & Paup.* (W. de W.) II. ii. 111/1 People kepe not theyr vowes..but breke them retchelesly or wylfully. **1548** UDALL, etc. *Erasm. Par. Luke* viii, Because he so rechelessely kept the euangelicall treasure. **1612** DRAYTON *Poly-olb.* x. 271 When of ages past we look in books to read, We retchlesly discharge our memory of those.

β. *a* **1300** *Cursor M.* 28279 Quare i was scheperd had sauls to kepe, to reckelesly i geit my schepe. **1340** HAMPOLE *Pr. Consc.* 3907 Penance..done Parchaunce over reklesly and over sone. *c* **1470** HENRY *Wallace* IV. 227 The lauboreris latt rakleslye went in.

b. Without regard to consequences, rashly.

c **1400** *Rule St. Benet* 58/367 And þai wil not þair mys amend, Bott reklisly hir rede refuse. **1513** DOUGLAS *Æneis* IX. vi. 48 Thre of his seruandis, that fast by hym lay, Full raklesly he kyllyt. **1571** GOLDING *Calvin on Ps.* lxxiii. 19 They rechelesly despyse all daungers as if they were out of all gonneshot. **1629** EARLE *Microcosm.*, *Drunkard* (Arb.) 82 Nothing..makes him more retchlesly carelesse, what becomes of all. **1843** BETHUNE *Sc. Fireside Stor.* 60 Mr. M'Quiddit drank recklessly and deep. **1871** H. AINSWORTH *Tower Hill* II. iv, He had turned a deaf ear to their supplications, and hurried them recklessly to the scaffold.

†**2.** *Sc.* Through carelessness; accidentally. *Obs.*

c **1375** *Sc. Leg. Saints* xxii. (*Laurence*) 609 Rek[l]asly he let It fall, and brak quhyt in pecis smal. *c* **1425** WYNTOUN *Cron.* II. Prol. 11 Thre thousand ȝhere..Neyr forȝet were reklesly [by historians]. *c* **1470** HENRY *Wallace* v. 158 Thus raklesly this gud knycht [haiff] thai tynt. **1552** LYNDESAY *Monarche* 1157 [To tell] quhow blynd Lameth raikleslye Did slay Cayn vnhappelye. *a* **1578** LINDESAY (Pitscottie) *Chron. Scot.* (S.T.S.) I. 148 How he was slaine..be ane of his awin gunis that brak rackleslie in hir schutting. **1609** SKENE *Reg. Maj.*, *Crimes* 159 Gif ane stranger, or traveller burnes ane other mans house rakleslie, he sall be arreisted. *a* **1670** SPALDING *Troub. Chas. I* (1829) 92 There was a sudden fray among them occasioned by a shot racklesly let go in the same house.

recklessness ('rɛklɪsnɪs). Forms: see RECKLESS *a.* [f. RECKLESS *a.* + -NESS.] The quality of being reckless.

α. *a* **975** *K. Edgar's Canons* in Thorpe *Laws* (1840) II. 262 Ic andette mines modes morðor..receleasnessa Godes beboda. *a* **1023** WULFSTAN *Hom.* vii. (1883) 53 Onȝean þam wislican ræde..se wiðerræda deofol sæwð receleasnesse. *c* **1380** WYCLIF *Wks.* (1880) 392 If eny siche lordeschips be ..take fro hem by rechelesnes of her predecessouris. *c* **1449** PECOCK *Repr.* III. xi. 344 Forto forsake God in a liȝtnes and in a rechelesnes. **1502** ATKYNSON tr. *De Imitatione* III. v. 199 How many good thinges thou hast lefte vndon of rechelesnes. **1581** J. BELL *Haddon's Answ. Osor.* 206 b, Neyther can any such retchlesnes agree with the gracious mercifulnes of God. *a* **1656** HALES *Gold. Rem.* (1688) 147 Through the wrechlessness of our first Parents. **1676** MARVELL *Mr. Smirke* Wks. 1875 IV. 15 A retchlessness and mockery ill becoming his character.

β. **1340** HAMPOLE *Pr. Consc.* 3909 Penance þat enioynt es And es forgeten thurgh reklesnes. **1439** *Rolls of Parlt.* V. 29/2 By rekelesnesse..of suche Maistres and Mariners. *c* **1470** HENRY *Wallace* x. 173 The gret trespace that [he], throw raklesnace, Had gert him mak. **1560** DAUS tr. *Sleidane's Comm.* 37 b, Throughe a certeine negligence, and racklesnes of suche as shoulde have redressed it in tyme. *a* **1586** SIDNEY *Arcadia* I. vi. (1891) 26 That ouer-many good fortunes began to breed a proude recklesnesse in them. **1828** SCOTT *F.M. Perth* xxiv, Hardly listening to them, in the pride and recklessness of his nature. **1873** SYMONDS *Grk. Poets* vii. 195 Oedipus, in his youthful recklessness,..kills his father and weds his mother.

b. Neglect or disregard *of* something.

1387 TREVISA *Higden* (Rolls) II. 173 Englisshe men.. woneþ hem to..rechelesnesse of Goddes hous. **1586** T. B. *La Primaud. Fr. Acad.* I. (1594) 184 For his retchlesnes of feats of armes. **1587** FLEMING *Contn. Holinshed* III. 1999/2 For his owne priuat lucre and retchlesnesse of that noble realme. **1837** HT. MARTINEAU *Soc. Amer.* II. 348 A society where recklessness of life is treated with leniency. **1868** FREEMAN *Norm. Conq.* (1876) II. ix. 348 In their insular recklessness of canonical niceties.

'reckling. Also wreck-. [Of obscure formation; variant dial. forms are *(w)rack-*, *rick-*, *ruck-*, *rig-*, *wreg-*, and *ritlin(g*, and forms without the ending also occur, as *wrig*, *rit*, *rut*.] The smallest and weakest animal of a litter; the youngest or smallest child in a family.

In general use in northern and midland counties.

1781 HUTTON *Tour to Caves* (ed. 2) Gloss., *Wrecklin*, the least animal in a brood or litter. **1859** TENNYSON *Vivien* 559 On returning found Not two but three [babes]; there lay the reckling, one But one hour old! **1863** HOLME LEE *Annie Warleigh* I. 3 John was Rachel's elder by ten years; he was the first-born of his mother, and she was her little reckling.

attrib. **1834** SIR H. TAYLOR *2nd Pt. Artevelde* v. iii, A mother dotes upon the reckling child, More than the strong.

Recklinghausen's disease, var. VON RECKLINGHAUSEN'S DISEASE.

†**'reckly**, *a. Obs. rare*⁻¹. [Perh. for Sc. *rickly*, f. RICKLE *sb.*] ? Rickety, tumble-down.

1715 in Ellis *Orig. Lett.* Ser. I. III. 361 The.. Highlanders ..will be..left to make the best of their way to their own reckly cells in the Braes of Athol.

reckon ('rɛk(ə)n), *v.* Forms: α. 1 -recenian, 3-4 rekeni, 4-5 rekeny; 3-4 rekene, 4-6 reken, (4 recen), rekin, (4 -ine), 5-6 rekyn; 4 rekoun, 5-6 rekon, recon(e, 6 rekan-, *Sc.* reakn-, 7 (9 *dial.*) reacon. β. 3 rikeni(e)n, 3-4 rikenen, 4 rikene, ryken(e, 5 riken; 9 *dial.* ricken, -on. γ. 3 reccnenn, 4-5 rekne(n, 5 -nyn; 4-5 rekken(e, 4-6 rekkin, (6 *Sc.* -ine), reckin, 6 recken, 6- reckon. δ. 4 raken, -ine; *Sc.* 5 rakyn, 6 -in, racken, -in, rakkin, 7 raikn-; *dial.* 9 rackan, -en, -on, rakkon. [OE. *(ȝe)recenian* (found only once) = OFris. *rek(e)nia*, MLG. and MDu. *rekenen*, OHG. *rechenôn*, *-inôn* (MHG. *rechenen*, G. *rechnen*) :—OTeut. **rekenôjan*, perh. f. **reken-* REKEN *a.* and ultimately from the root *rek-* found in OE. *reccan* RECCHE. The Scand. forms, late ON. *reikna*, Norw. *rekna*, Sw. *räkna*, Da. *regne*, are early adoptions from LG.]

I. *trans.* †**1. a.** To enumerate serially or separately; to name or mention one after another or in due order; to go over or through (a series) in this manner. *Obs.*

c **1200** ORMIN 11217 He biginneþþ Cristess kinn To reccnenn & to rimenn Att Abraham, & reccneþþ aȝȝ Dunnwarrd fra mann to manne. *a* **1225** *Ancr. R.* 210 Alle sunnen sunderliche, bi hore owune nomeliche nomen, ne muhte no mon rikenen. *a* **1300** *Cursor M.* 18992 He tald þam mani takens sere, þat es na nede all recken here. **1377** LANGL. *P. Pl.* B. I. 22 Nempne hem I thinke, And rekne hem bi resoun, reherce thow hem after. *c* **1470** *Golagros & Gaw.* 743 Now wil I rekkin the renkis of the Round Tabill. **1533** GAU *Richt Vay* 3 Thay reknit mony foul and abhominabil sinnis..the quhilk mony guyd men..kneu neuer of befor.

b. So with *up*, rarely *over*.

13.. *E.E. Allit. P.* B. 2 Clannesse who-so kyndly cowþe comende, & rekken vp alle þe resounz þat ho by riȝt askez. *c* **1450** *Pol. Poems* (Rolls) II. 228 Pite for to here the people complayne, And riken up the ragmanne of the hole rowte. **1576** FLEMING *Panopl. Epist.* 336 [He] reckoneth vpp by name diuerse Gentlemen, with whome he was in fauour. **1638** JUNIUS *Paint. Ancients* 105, I shall reckon up only such authors whose records..are lost and gone. **1694** W. WOTTON *Anc. & Mod. Learn.* (1697) 410 France could reckon up Des Cartes, Mersennus, Fermat, and Gassendi. **1846** H. W. TORRENS *Rem. Milit. Hist.* 355 In 1585, a pamphlet was addressed to..[the] Mayor of London, reckoning over the advantages of a marching watch for the city. **1884** tr. *Lotze's Metaph.* 477 It would be mere trifling to reckon up reactions of a third and fourth order.

†**c.** To recount, relate, narrate, tell. *Obs.*

a **1000** *Cædmon's Exod.* 525 (Gr.) Run bið ȝerecenod, ræd forð gæð. *c* **1350** *Will. Palerne* 3179 Sche..rapli gan away renne, to reken þe soþe. *a* **1375** *Joseph Arim.* 76 Þat tyme ..þis reson bi-gon þat I schal now rikenen. *a* **1400-50** *Alexander* 4124 Þen ferd þai furth..Euyn to þe heued of Eumaure, as I first rekend. **1530** PALSGR. 684/1, I wyll reken all the mater to hym as it vas. **1586** A. DAY *Eng. Secretary* I. (1625) 45 To reckon to you since, how he came into the country here,..why should I clog myself?

†**d.** To repeat, recite, utter. *Obs. rare.*

a **1400-50** *Alexander* 4931 The renke..rekind þir wordis: 'Haile Alexander'. **1533** GAU *Richt Vay* 31 That is noth aneucht that ony reid the creid or rekin ye articulis contenit in it x or xii timis apone ye day. **1621** *Gude & Godlie B.* (S.T.S.) 174 Sum mumlit Auies, sum raknit [**1567** craknit] Creidis.

†**e.** To mention; to allege. *Obs. rare.*

1513 DOUGLAS *Æneis* VI. ix. 143 Quhat suld I rekin [L. *quid memorem*] thai peple of Thessaly, That Lapithas ar hait ..? **1532** MORE *Confut. Tindale* Wks. 352/2 Belieue me not if any man can reken a place where euer he founde it otherwyse. **1596** SPENSER *F.Q.* IV. x. 15 Cast into sundry shapes by wondrous skill, That like on earth no where I recken may.

2. a. To count, so as to ascertain the number or amount of; to ascertain or arrive at (a number, quantity, etc.) by counting or calculating; to compute. Also with *out*.

Now usually implying some process of calculation, as distinguished from the mere counting of individual things.

a **1225** *Ancr. R.* 214 Þe ȝiscare..makeð þerinne figures of augrim, ase þeos rikenares doð þet habbeð muchel uorto rikenen. **1340** HAMPOLE *Pr. Consc.* 2484 Swa may we ay rekken and rede An hondreth syns agayne a gude dede. *c* **1386** CHAUCER *Shipman's T.* 216 How longe tyme wol ye rekene and caste Youre sommes and youre bookes and youre thynges? ? *a* **1400** *Arthur* 410 Fowre hundred þowsand An hunderd and foure & twenty,—Thus herawdes dude ham rekeny. **1530** PALSGR. 684/1, I shall reken it syxe tymes by aulgorisme, or you can caste it ones by counters. **1602** SHAKS. *Ham.* II. ii. 121 O deere Ophelia, I am ill at these Numbers; I haue not Art to reckon my grones. **1633** T. ADAMS *Exp. 2 Peter* iii. 10. 1307 A woman reckons out her nine moneths, and can guesse neare to the day of her comming. **1687** A. LOVELL tr. *Thevenot's Trav.* I. 36 They Divine with Beans, which they put together without reckoning them. **1833** HT. MARTINEAU *Brooke Farm* iv. 46 But I can't reckon it; will you?—Eleven pounds and sixpence, is it? **1845** LEVER *The O'Donoughoe* xliv. (1858) 324 Mark..pointed straight out to sea, where now seven sail could be reckoned.

b. With subordinate clause as obj.

1390 GOWER *Conf.* I. 281 Whan I beginne To rekne with miself withinne How many yeres ben agon [etc.]. *c* **1400** MAUNDEV. (1839) xix. 213 Now may men wel rekene, how moche that it amountethe. **1568** GRAFTON *Chron.* II. 289 He is now looking on your crownes..to recken if he haue his whole some or no. **1667** FLAVEL *Saint Indeed* (1754) 44 Antigonus over-heard his soldiers reckoning how many their enemies were.

c. To count or calculate *from*; to calculate or keep count of, in relation to some starting-point or base. Also with *over*.

1540 in *Vicary's Anat.* (1888) App. xii. 239 The same half yere accompted and reconned fromme Michaelmas last paste. **1651** HOBBES *Leviath.* III. xxxviii. 240 Death is reckoned from the Condemnation of Adam. **1774** ABIGAIL ADAMS in *Fam. Lett.* (1876) 24, I shall reckon over every week as they pass, and rejoice at every Saturday evening. **1868** LOCKYER *Elem. Astron.* vii. §43 (1879) 264 Declination is reckoned N. or S. of the plane of the earth's equator.

†**d.** To count out, to pay. Also with *out*. *Obs.*

c **1200** ORMIN 3540 Illc mann shollde cumenn ham..Forr þær to reccnenn till þe King An peninng for himm sellfenn. *Ibid.* 3561. **1713** STEELE *Guard.* No. 17 ¶7 There is an honest Man..who has often said he would marry her with Two Hundred Pounds. The Knight ordered his Man to reckon out that Sum.

e. To count *up*; also, to sum *up*, to estimate the character of (a person).

1836 MARRYAT *Japhet* viii, To reckon up their means—that is, to count the money which they may have in their pockets. **1852** DICKENS *Bleak Ho.* liv, The deceased Mr. Tulkinghorn employed me to reckon up her Ladyship—if you'll excuse my making use of the term we commonly employ—and I reckoned her up, so far, completely.

3. a. To include in a (*or the*) reckoning; hence, to place or class. Const. *among(st)*, *for*, *in*, *with* preps.; *in* adv.

1387 TREVISA *Higden* (Rolls) VI. 171 Þe þridde Leo..is nouȝt i-rekened in þe ordre of bisshopes. *c* **1400** MAUNDEV. (1839) xviii. 186 Also these Yles of Ynde..beth noght reckned in the Climates. **1526** *Pilgr. Perf.* (W. de W. 1531) 248 b, Fyrst the matyns..is rekened for one of the vij. **1583** *Leg. Bp. St. Androis* 613 Gude Robert Melwene..I shuld not racken in with thea. **1630** *R. Johnson's Kingd. & Commw.* 231 The number of souldiers..amount to eight thousand, not reckoning any man of sort, nor Mariners. **1711** ADDISON *Spect.* No. 40 ¶4 There is also another Particular, which may be reckoned among the Blemishes.. of our English Tragedy. **1774** GOLDSM. *Nat. Hist.* (1776) II. 230 In this class we may reckon the Georgians, Circassians, and Mingrelians. **1868** HAWTHORNE *Amer. Note-bks.* (1879) I. 52 Among other languages spoken hereabouts must be reckoned the wild Irish.

b. To accept or state as a total.

1563 MAN *Musculus' Commonpl.* 273 b, Wherein he reconneth but two sacramentes only, giuen by the Lorde himselfe. **1671** J. WEBSTER *Metallogr.* vii. 115 He reckons four of a silver colour, that hold no metal, nor yield any fire. **1848** W. H. BARTLETT *Egypt to Pal.* iii. (1879) 52 Lepsius reckons about sixty, including some very small ones.

4. †**a.** To calculate, work out, decide the nature or value of. *Obs. rare.*

? *a* **1400** *Morte Arth.* 1275 Thane salle we rekkene fulle rathe, whatt ryghte that he claymes. *a* **1400-50** *Alexander* 41 He was wyse enoȝe wirdis to reken, When he þe heuyn beheld, of ledes opon lyfe. **1567** *Satir. Poems Reform.* viii. 9 War 30ʳ richt reknit to þe croun It myᵗ be laid with litill menss.

†**b.** To estimate, value. *Obs.*

a **1533** LD. BERNERS *Huon* li. 173, I wold reken all the sorow that I haue enduryd at no thynge. **1601** SHAKS. *All's Well* v. iii. 90, I haue seene her weare it, and she reckon'd it At her liues rate. **1642** ROGERS *Naaman* 136 Never harkening what God will answer..but reckoning her worke for a price. **1667** PEPYS *Diary* (1879) IV. 360 The world sees it, and reckons my interest accordingly.

†**c.** To take into consideration, to consider. *Obs. rare.*

1613 PURCHAS *Pilgrimage* v. viii. (1614) 486 If a man doe any thing worth reckoning, presently his Captaine imparteth this honour to him. **1686** PARR *Life Usher* 94 Which [treatises] being not set down in my Lord Primates own Words..cannot be reckoned, being much enlarged by the Dr., as himself confesseth.

5. a. To consider, judge, or estimate by, or as the result of, calculation. (Const. as in b.)

1555 EDEN *Decades* 351 We sette owre course east,.. rekenynge owre selues .xxxvi. leagues from the coast of Guinea. **1632** LITHGOW *Trav.* x. 456 [This] I reckon to be foure hundred and fifty English miles. **1745** P. THOMAS *Jrnl. Anson's Voy.* 343 They reckon that this..Work will be finish'd in about fifty Years. **1781** COWPER *Let.* 4 Oct., I reckon my volume will consist of about eight thousand lines. **1848** W. H. BARTLETT *Egypt to Pal.* xiv. (1879) 315 We reckoned the distance about sixteen miles and back.

b. To set down, to hold, consider, or regard, as being of a specified character, importance or value, or (rarely) as being in a certain condition. Const. *for*, *as*, *to be*, or with appositive complement.

1340 *Ayenb.* 214 Al þane time þet þou ne þengst naht a god, þou hise sselt rekeni uor naȝt. ? *a* **1400** *Morte Arth.* 2334 To rekkene theis Romaynes recreaunt and ȝoldene. *c* **1450** *Sc. Cuthbert* (Surtees) 4360 Þis I rekyn bot schort aray. *a* **1533** LD. BERNERS *Huon* vii. 16, I reken our wyage to be a daungerous passage. **1561** T. NORTON *Calvin's Inst.* III. 192 He reckeneth repentance and fayth as two diuerse thinges. **1603** OWEN *Pembrokeshire* (1891) 244 This is reconned for a strange and rare thinge. **1687** A. LOVELL tr. *Thevenot's Trav.* I. 39 They reckon Women with big black Eyes, and red Cheeks, to be the greatest Beauties. **1712** STEELE *Spect.* No. 422 ¶6 Fortius would have been reckoned a Wit, if there had never been a Fool in the World. **1748** H. WALPOLE *Let.* 18 May, The Princess of Wales has got a confirmed jaundice, but they reckon her much better. **1764** GIBBON *Misc. Wks.* (1814) IV. 354, I reckon for nothing the researches of a Coyer. **1833** L. RITCHIE *Wand. by Loire* 117 Here..we reckon the women to be among the prettiest in France. *c* **1850** *Arab. Nts.* (Rtldg.) 181 He was reckoned one of the richest merchants in the city. **1870** YEATS *Nat. Hist. Comm.* 108 Quite a fourth of the soil is reckoned as unproductive.

c. With *inf.* To regard as doing something.

1513 MORE in Grafton *Chron.* (1568) II. 760 Yee see their youth, of which I rekon the onely suretie to rest in your concord. **1732** ARBUTHNOT *Rules of Diet* in *Aliments*, etc. I. 249 It is reckoned to increase milk. **1852** MRS. STOWE *Uncle Tom's C.* i. 5, I believe I'm reckoned to bring in about the finest droves of niggers that is brought in.

d. *colloq.* To rate highly, to esteem. Usu. in negative phrases.

1957 *Evening News* 12 Nov. 6/4 If..an East Ender wants to say that he does not consider the character of another to be worth while he says 'I don't reckon him'. **1977** *Sunday Times* 52/3, I don't reckon the chances of *Young Scientists of the Year*..against *Just William*.

6. a. To consider, think, suppose, be of opinion, etc., *that*. Also with omission of *that*. Now usu. *colloq.*, esp. in the U.S. (formerly chiefly in southern States).

1513 MORE in Grafton *Chron.* (1568) II. 803 Men woulde not recon that hee coulde haue right to the realme. **1530** WRIOTHESLEY *Chron.* (1875) I. 16 Some recken he killed himselfe with purgations. **1611** BIBLE *Isa.* xxxviii. 13, I reckoned till morning, that as a Lyon so will hee breake all my bones. **1668** GLANVILL *Plus Ultra* Pref., Whether his reply be publique or not, I reckon he will blow the dust upon me. **1712** SWIFT *Jrnl. to Stella* xlviii, I reckon the queen will go to Windsor in three..weeks. **1796** BURNEY *Mem. Metastasio* II. 78, I reckon that I shall have a humpback. **1810** M. DWIGHT *Jrnl.* 9 Nov. in *Journey to Ohio in 1810* (1912) 37 The people here talk curiously, they all reckon instead of expect. **1860** MRS. GASKELL *Sylvia's Lovers* v, 'A reckon it's a bargain', said Harry. **1863** *Congress. Globe* 7 Feb. 783/3 If you can take this property by compact, I reckon you cannot take it against the consent of the owners. **1875** JOWETT *Plato* (ed. 2) I. 443, I reckon, said Socrates, that no one..could accuse me of idle talking. **1893** H. A. SHANDS *Some Peculiarities of Speech in Mississippi* 53 *Reckon*,..this word is almost always used in the ordinary conversation of our best educated people for *think* or *suppose*, and corresponds to a like use of *guess* in the Northern States. **1900** *Cosmopolitan* Feb. 389/1 She met Sam on the way out, and says she: 'Sam, what do you reckon? My quilt took the premium.' **1963** *Social Problems* Spring 367/1, I reckon it'll always be lucky. **1977** I. SHAW *Beggarman, Thief* III. ii. 193, I don't reckon I've had a fare there for more than ten years.

b. ***I reckon***, used parenthetically or finally.

Formerly in literary Eng. use; still common in Eng. dialects, and current in the southern States of America in place of the northern *I guess*.

1603 SIR R. CECIL in Harington *Nugæ Ant.* (1804) I. 345 He is, I reckon, no wise man that looketh this waye to heaven. **1748** RICHARDSON *Clarissa* Wks. 1883 VII. 144, I shall have a good deal of trouble, I reckon,..to be decent on the expected occasion. **1776** FOOTE *Capuchin* I. Wks. 1799 II. 389 All your family..come over to be polish'd, I reckon. **1827** J. F. COOPER *Prairie* I. vii. 107 Neither of us, I reckon, has ever had much to do with [etc.]. **1883** STEVENSON *Treas. Isl.* IV. xx, You would just as soon save your lives, I reckon.

†**7.** To account, assign, or attribute *to* (a person or thing). *Obs.* (In quots. only *pass.*)

1526 TINDALE *Rom.* iv. 9 We saye verely how that fayth was rekened to Abraham for rightewesnes. **1641** J. SHUTE *Sarah & Hagar* (1649) 142 The Ishmaelites..are reckoned unto Hagar, not unto Abraham; and therefore called Hagareans. **1688** COLLIER *Several Disc.* (1725) 285 The last Sermon de Sanctis..is mistakenly reckon'd to this Father. **1719** WATERLAND *Vind. Christ's Div.* 25 As if the Ray were not to be reckon'd to the Sun, as included in it.

II. *intr.* †**8. a.** To place or name things in order. *Obs. rare.*

c **1290** *S. Eng. Leg.* I. 312/440 Of þe Mone, Monen-day [is named], ȝif ȝe wel rikeni konne. **1390** GOWER *Conf.* III. 122 After Virgo to reknen evene Libra sit in the nombre of sevene. *c* **1470** *Golagros & Gaw.* 403 He is the riallest roy.. Of all the rentaris to ryme or rekin on raw. **1535** STEWART *Cron. Scot.* II. 708 Mony mo than I will heir report, To reckin heir becaus the tyme is schort.

†**b.** To speak or discourse *of* something. *Obs.*⁻¹

a **1400-50** *Alexander* 150 Slik care kindils in his curte..þat it ware tere any tonge of þar tene to reken.

†**c.** ***to reckon right***: to judge correctly, to take a correct view of things. *Obs.*

c **1400** *Rom. Rose* 3032 Ther was a womman eke, that hight Shame, that, who can reken right, Trespasse was hir fadir name. **1535** LYNDESAY *Satyre* 1308, I traist, gif I can reckon richt, Scho schaips to ludge with him all nicht. **1556** LAUDER *Tractate* 63 Nothing, at all,—to rekin rycht,— Different, in-to Goddis sycht. **1667** MILTON *P.L.* VIII. 71 This to attain, whether Heav'n move or Earth, Imports not, if thou reck'n right.

9. To count, to make a calculation; to cast up an account or sum.

to reckon without one's host: see HOST *sb.*² 2 b.

a **1300** *Cursor M.* 9228 Four thusand yeir and sex hundreth, Qua reckens right to tell es eth. *c* **1369** CHAUCER *Dethe Blaunche* 436 Thogh Argus the noble covnter Sete to rekene.. Yet shulde he fayle to rekene evene The wondres me mette. **1530** PALSGR. 684/1, I holde you a grote you have reckened false. **1599** SHAKS. *Hen. V*, IV. i. 241 Wee haue French Quarrels enow, if you could tell how to reckon. **1669** STURMY *Mariner's Mag.* II. ix. 74 The North Point of the Nocturnal is the first Point you reckon from,.. and so reckon forward North and by East. **1697** POTTER *Antiq. Greece* I. i. (1715) 3 Meursius reckons to the number of forty Plantations peopled by Athenians.

†**10. a.** To render or give an account (*of* one's conduct, etc., or *for* something received). *Obs.*

12.. *Prayer to Our Lady* 44 in *O.E. Misc.* 193 Hwan ich hier-of rekeni schal, wel sore me mei drede. **1340** HAMPOLE *Pr. Consc.* 5984 Fadirs and modirs sal rekken þat tyde, Of þair sons and þair doghtirs unchastide. **1362** LANGL. *P. Pl.* A. II. 96 ȝe schule abygge it bothe.. At oo ȝeris ende whan ȝe reken schul. **1450–1530** *Myrr. our Ladye* 89 We muste haue as they had and worse for we haue receyued more to reken for. **1575–85** ABP. SANDYS *Serm.* xx. 345 Christ is comming in the cloudes, All fleshe shall rise and recken.

†**b.** To account *for*, explain. *Obs.*−1

1674 N. FAIRFAX *Bulk & Selv.* 153 We can give no reason why a Fool should rise more Mathematically from a seat, than the wisest man can fully reckon for.

11. a. To go over or settle accounts (in *lit.* or *fig.* sense) *with* one, or *together*.

1297 R. GLOUC. (Rolls) 6575 Bi þe fey ich owe to god, icholle rekeni mitte. *c* **1380** WYCLIF *Wks.* (1880) 425 þis lord wole rikene wiþ þes seruauntis fully. *c* **1400** *Melayne* 1517 That there no sarazene solde come owte, To þay had rekkenede with þat rowte. *c* **1470** HENRY *Wallace* IX. 1154 Erar he wald bid chalans off his king, Than with Wallace to rakyn for sic a thing. **1552** *Bk. Com. Prayer, Communion*, Euery Parishioner shal reken with his Person, Vicare, or Curate. **1572** HULOET, To recken together, or to come to reckening, *conferre rationes*. **1605** SHAKS. *Macb.* v. vii. 108 We shall not spend a large expence of time, Before we reckon with your seuerall loues. **1784** COWPER *Task* VI. 606 God.. Will reckon with us roundly for the abuse. **1825** SCOTT *Talism.* ix, The blame rests not with thee, but with those with whom.. I hope to reckon roundly.

b. *to reckon with*: to take into account or consideration; to be prepared for.

1885 *Manch. Exam.* 16 June 4/6 A Ministerial crisis.. is always a contingency to be reckoned with. **1896** W. H. HUTTON *Philip Augustus* vi. 182 It might seem.. as if the Jews were the only dissenters with whom the king and the church had to reckon. **1902** KIPLING *Five Nations* (1903) 63 We reckon not with those Whom the mere Fates ordain. **1945** T. S. ELIOT *What is a Classic?* 8 We may say confidently that it [*sc.* the definition] must be one which will expressly reckon with him.

12. a. To calculate, design, or expect *to* do something. Now only *dial.*

c **1550** BALE *K. Johan* (Camden) 44 The Cystean monkes are in soche perplexyte That owt of Englond they reken all to flee. **1568** GRAFTON *Chron.* II. 737 They departed to.. Saint Malo.. where they reckned to haue taken shippyng. **1601** R. JOHNSON *Kingd. & Commw.* (1603) 160 He neither defendeth himselfe, nor intreatethe for mercie, as reckoning straight to die. **1770** JOHNSON *Let. to Mrs. Thrale* 7 July, I reckon to go next week to Ashbourne. **1872** HARTLEY *Yorksh. Ditt.* Ser. II. 44 Ov a Thursday aw reckon to brew.

b. To look *for* something. *rare.*

1848 J. H. NEWMAN *Loss & Gain* III. v. 330 You may have more to bear than you reckon for, when you find yourself with men of rude minds and vulgar manners.

13. a. Const. *of*: To account or think (much, etc.) of; to take account of, think highly of, approve of. Now *rare* exc. *dial.*

1594 R. ASHLEY tr. *Loys le Roy* 47 Traitours.. were most reckoned of in Court. **1601** SIR W. CORNWALLIS *Disc. Seneca* (1631) 40 Wee reckon of Physitians because the end of them is health. **1653** H. COGAN tr. *Scarlet Gown* 109 He is not much reckoned of in the Court, but is reuerenced in the sacred Colledge. **1803** tr. *P. Le Brun's Mons. Botte* II. 208 He reckoned a good deal of the pleasures of the table. **1878** *Cumb. Gloss.* (E.D.S.) 117.

†**b.** To regard in a certain light. *Obs. rare.*

1600 W. WATSON *Decacordon* (1602) 95 He was to be reckned of for an inurious calumniator. **1625** BP. MOUNTAGU *App. Cæsar* 151 So he was esteemed and held.. during life, and so is he reckoned of by his followers at this day.

†**c.** To reck of, take heed of. *Obs. rare.*

1622 R. HAWKINS *Voy. S. Sea* (1847) 115 They reckon not of a musket shot, a sword pierceth not their skinne. **1634** *Malory's Arthur* II. xxx, Like as it had beene a man.. which reckoned not of himselfe.

14. To count, depend, or rely *on* or *upon*.

1632 LITHGOW *Trav.* v. 173 No man could reckon vpon felicity so long as he liued. **1665** BOYLE *Occas. Refl.* 205 His reward would be much less than he reckons upon. **1796** H. HUNTER tr. *St.-Pierre's Stud. Nat.* (1799) I. p. lxx, I reckon on the indulgence of the really intelligent. **1836** *Backwoods of Canada* 22, I was reckoning much on seeing the falls of Montmorenci. **1874** GREEN *Short Hist.* ii. §4. 74 He could reckon on no support within England itself.

15. a. To number, amount to.

1877 MISS YONGE *Cameos* Ser. III. xxx. 301 He marched [them] into the camp before his own troop, which did not reckon nearly so many.

b. To count, have a place or value.

1879 MCCARTHY *Own Times* II. xxii. 159 Such discretion .. would in the long run reckon to his credit and his advantage. **1898** BESANT *Orange Girl* I. i, After the fashion .. of the sailors, with whom strength of arm reckons before style.

Hence as *sb.*, an act of consideration; a 'think' (*colloq.*). Also **'reckonable** *a.*, capable of being reckoned; admissible for the purposes of reckoning; **reckona'bility**, the quality of being reckonable; **'reckoned** *ppl. a.*

1658 CROMWELL *Sp.* 25 Jan. in *Carlyle*, A thing far from reckonable as a suggestion to any ill end. **1812** WOODHOUSE *Astron.* xxxviii. (1823) 756 The difference of actual or absolute time, which depends on the reckoned time at each place of observation. **1859** BRIGHT in *Times* 18 Aug. 9/6 [The Government] having no reckonable majority in the House of Commons. **1905** *Daily Chron.* 21 July 4/4 Its only drawback is that it is called 'Hardy's country' by those fiction-enthusiasts who now form so reckonable a section of Weymouth guests. **1949** F. SARGESON *I saw in my Dream* vii. 57 He reckons he's going to... Then he'd better go and have another reckon, the girl said. **1967** *Encycl. Philos.* VII. 94/1 (*heading*) Reckonability. **1971** *Daily Tel.* 15 Sept. 6/8 This means that for every £1,000 of reckonable earnings the pension offered must amount to at least £10 for each year of service. **1973** *Times* 29 Nov. 16/3 There were bound to be practical difficulties and problems of definition in reopening at this late stage the question of reckonable service of teachers who joined the profession immediately after the war.

reckon(-crook), var. RACKAN(-CROOK).

reckoner ('rɛk(ə)nə(r)). Also 3 **rikenare**, 5 **reknare**, 6 **reck(e)ner**. [f. RECKON *v.* + -ER[1].]

1. One who reckons, in senses of the verb.

a **1225** *Ancr. R.* 214 þeos rikenares.. þat habbeð muchel uorto rikenen. *c* **1440** *Promp. Parv.* 428/2 Reknare, *computator*. **1546** J. HEYWOOD *Prov.* (1867) 16 Reckners without their host must recken twyce. **1611** COTGR., *Compteur*, a reckoner. **1745** WARBURTON *Occas. Refl.* II. xiii, Retrospects with bad Reckoners are troublesome Things. **1823** MRS. HEMANS *Vespers of Palermo* v. ii, We shall have Stern reckoners to account with. **1875** WHITNEY *Life Lang.* ii. 20 Fingers are the most ready and natural of aids to an unready reckoner.

2. An aid to reckoning. (Cf. READY RECKONER.)

1827 G. HIGGINS *Celtic Druids* 7 His fingers would be his first reckoners.

reckoning ('rɛk(ə)nɪŋ), *vbl. sb.* Forms: see RECKON *v.* (also 3 **recnig**, 5 *Sc.* **rek-**, **raknyne**, 5–6 **rekning**, **rakning**, 6 **reckning**, **-yng**, etc.). [f. RECKON *v.* + -ING[1]. Cf. Du. *rekening*, MLG. *rekeninge* (whence late ON. *reikningr*, Sw. *räkning*, Da. *regning*), OHG. *rechenunga* (MHG. *-unge*, G. *rechnung*).]

1. a. The action of the vb. RECKON; enumeration, calculation, computation.

a **1300** *Cursor M.* 1566 Reckining cuth þai nan o right. *c* **1375** *Sc. Leg. Saints* xii. (*Mathias*) 266 Of thre hundir þe teynd leyly,.. cumys be raknyne to thretty. *c* **1440** *Promp. Parv.* 428/2 Reknynge, *computacio*. **1500–20** DUNBAR *Poems* lxxix. 6 For rekkyning of my rentis and roumes, ȝe neid nocht for to tyre ȝour thowmes. **1588** SHAKS. *L.L.L.* v. ii. 498 *Ber.* I alwaies tooke three threes for nine. *Clow.* O Lord sir, it were pittie you should get your liuing by reckning sir. **1651** HOBBES *Leviath.* I. iv. 14 Without words, there is no possibility of reckoning of Numbers. **1869** E. A. PARKES *Pract. Hygiene* (ed. 3) 2 The usual mode of reckoning is to divide the total daily supply in gallons by the total population.

b. Manner or mode of computing or numbering.

c **1375** *Sc. Leg. Saints* xxxi. (*Eugenia*) 943 Be þe reknyne of rome.. twa hundir ȝere sex & fyfty. ?*c* **1540** *Hye wey to Spyttel Hous* 919 in Hazl. *E.P.P.* IV. 64 That is but lytell used in this lande,.. For Englysshe men knowe not of suche rekenynges. *a* **1727** NEWTON *Chronol. Amended* Introd. (1728) 2 The reckoning by Olympiads was not yet in use. **1849** MACAULAY *Hist. Eng.* ix. II. 475 On the sixteenth of October, according to the English reckoning.

2. a. An instance of enumerating or counting, or the result of this; an enumeration, calculation, or account. Also with *up*.

a **1300** *Cursor M.* 12713 O þis reckining na mar her nu, Bot o Iohn baptist and o iesu. *c* **1391** CHAUCER *Astrol.* II. §22 Understond wel this Reknyng. *c* **1440** *Promp. Parv.* 428/2 Rekenynge, or a counte,.. *compotus*. **1561** DAUS tr. *Bullinger on Apoc.* (1573) 149 Let vs thinke, that our Lord God kepeth a rekoning of all the dayes of our calamitie. **1674** N. FAIRFAX *Bulk & Selv.* 188 There is not a full reckoning up of those attributes of his that have to do in the work. **1719** DE FOE *Crusoe* I. xvii, As for an exact Reckoning of Days, after I had once lost it, I could never recover it again. **1864** D. G. MITCHELL *Sev. Stor.* 284, I tried to keep some reckoning of the streets through which I passed.

b. The process or result of (one's) counting, etc. Freq. in phrases, as *to be out in* or *of*, *to leave out of*, *to lose*, *one's reckoning*.

1585 Q. ELIZ. in *Four C. Eng. Lett.* (1880) 29 If I mad not my rekening the bettar of the moneths. **1668** CULPEPPER & COLE *Barthol. Anat.* I. xiv. 34 According to his reckoning, there will be two Ligaments, not one only. **1699** BENTLEY *Phal.* Pref. 12 A plain argument, that the Examiner is quite out in his reckoning. **1719** DE FOE *Crusoe* I. iv, I should lose my reckoning of time. **1783** COWPER *Let.* 13 Oct., It is ever the way of those who rule the earth to leave out of their reckoning Him who rules the universe. **1809** MALKIN *Gil Blas* VII. xii. ¶ 1 He was short in his reckoning by an arm and a leg.

c. *spec.* The calculated period of pregnancy.

1638 G. SANDYS *Paraphr. Job* xxxix, Can'st thou their Recknings keepe, the time compute. **1751** SMOLLETT *Per. Pic.* lxxxi, The time of my reckoning was nearly expired. **1844** H. STEPHENS *Bk. Farm* II. 599 A shepherd that has attentively.. marked the reckoning of every ewe.

d. *Naut.* The estimate made of a ship's position by calculation from the log, the course steered, observation of the sun, etc. See also DEAD RECKONING.

1669 STURMY *Mariner's Mag.* IV. i. 138, [I] took our Reckoning from Lundy, in the Mouth of Severn. *Ibid.* 139 Currents is a means of great mistake in keeping of a Reckoning. **1727–41** CHAMBERS *Cycl.* s.v. *Log*, Log-Board is a table divided into four or five columns, whereon are marked the reckonings of every day. **1769** FALCONER *Dict. Marine* (1780) s.v. *Dead-reckoning*, This reckoning.. is always to be corrected, as often as any good observation of the sun can be obtained. **1840** R. H. DANA *Bef. Mast* xxx. 108 Having gone by reckoning over thirteen hundred miles in seven days.

fig. **1706** E. WARD *Wooden World Diss.* (1708) 14 Sometimes he comes many Leagues short of his Reckoning, for through loss of Hands to work her the Ship is lost. **1884** PAE *Eustace* 91 You have got out of your reckoning.

3. a. A computation or account of the sum owing by, or due to, one; a statement of a charge or charges; a bill, *esp.* at an inn or tavern. †Also without article, in phr. ***upon reckoning*** (quot. 1617).

c **1386** CHAUCER *Prol.* 760 After soper.. Whan that we hadde maad our rekenynges. *c* **1481** *Plumpton Corr.* (Camden) 41 Henry Fox bad me send my rakning at Ripon, & I should be answered to my money. **1533** [see HOST *sb.*[2] 2 b]. **1590** *Wills & Inv. N.C.* (Surtees 1860) 198 He owes me the rest of a reckening for c quarters of barley. **1617** MORYSON *Itin.* I. 165, I paid each night foure bolinei for my bed, and eating vpon reckoning, I spent lesse then two giulij by the day. **1650** FULLER *Pisgah* II. x. 215 They liked the wine, but not the reckoning which was to be paid for it. **1749** FIELDING *Tom Jones* VII. xi, Having now pretty well satisfied their Thirst, nothing remained but to pay the Reckoning. **1818** SCOTT *Rob Roy* iv, He called for a reckoning for the wine. **1874** T. TAYLOR *Leic. Sq.* vii. 154 Reckonings were called and paid.

transf. and *fig.* **1635–56** COWLEY *Davideis* IV. 584 Our watchful Prince by bending sav'd the Wound, But Death in other coyn his reck'ning found. **1784** COWPER *Task* v. 278 He deems a thousand.. lives, Spent in the purchase of renown for him, An easy reckoning.

b. *a Dutch reckoning*: (see quots.).

a **1700** [see DUTCH *a.* 4]. **1724** SWIFT *Drapier's Lett.* Wks. 1755 V. II. 78 A Dutch reckoning, wherein if you dispute the unreasonableness and exorbitance of the bill, the land lord shall bring it up every time with new additions. *a* **1814** *Forgery* II. ii. in *New Brit. Theatre* I. 449 Come, we'll have a Dutch reckoning to-night, for we will share the dust, or see them shopp'd [= put in prison].

4. a. The action of rendering an account of property etc., entrusted to one's charge; an account so rendered. Chiefly in phrases, as *to **give*** or ***yield***, ***to hear***, ***hold*** or ***make***, ***to bring*** or ***call to***, ***reckoning***; sometimes also ***count and reckoning***. Now only in legal use.

1340 *Ayenb.* 18 His lhordes guodes huer-of him behoueþ straitliche yelde rekeninge and scele. **1377** LANGL. *P. Pl.* B. v. 427, I can holde louedayes and here a reues rekenynge. **1413** *Pilgr. Sowle* (Caxton 1483) IV. xxxiv. 83 Of al reuenues that to the kynge bylongen in his Countre the Shirreue muste yeue rekkenynge. **1568** GRAFTON *Chron.* II. 58 The king.. began to call him [Becket] to reconynges, and to burthen him with paymentes. **1596** DALRYMPLE tr. *Leslie's Hist. Scot.* x. 264 The keiperis of the Thesaurhous.. he bringis to compte and rekning. **1611** BIBLE *2 Kings* xxii. 7 Howbeit, there was no reckoning made with them, of the money that was deliuered into their hand. **1869** *Act 32 & 33 Vict.* c. 116 §7 The grantee being always bound, upon payment of the price, to hold count and reckoning with the grantor for the same.

transf. **1568** GRAFTON *Chron.* II. 683 As for the towne of Calice.. the sayde Monsire de Vawclere promised thereof to make him a good reconyng.

b. The action of rendering to another an account of one's self or one's conduct.

c **1450** LONELICH *Merlin* 1300 (Kölbing) Respyt gonnen they take.. xv dayes thanne next sewenge Hire forto bringen to rekenenge. **1530–1** *Act 22 Hen. VIII*, c. 12 If any man.. be vagrant, and can gyue no rekenynge howe he dothe lefullye get his lyuynge. **1599** SHAKS. *Much Ado* v. iv. 9 Being.. enforc'd To call young Claudio to a reckoning for it. **1706** E. WARD *Wooden World Diss.* (1708) 18 A servile Constraint being much more resented by a generous Soul than a deep Reckoning. **1828** SCOTT *F.M. Perth* vi, I have also a reckoning to hold with you.

c. *spec.* with ref. to rendering an account of one's life or conduct to God at death or judgement.

a **1300** *Sarmun* xxiii. in *E.E.P.* (1862) 3 Hit nis no doute he sal be dede to ȝelde recning at þe dome. **1340** *Ayenb.* 214 God will acsi rekeninge ate daye of dome. *c* **1375** *Sc. Leg. Saints* xxiv. (*Alexis*) 133 We sal.. gyf reknyne þat Iuge til of al dedis, gud & Il. **1434** *E.E. Wills* 97 As myne executoures wyl answere at the laste rekenyng. *c* **1500** *Lancelot* 1358 Wharof that god a raknyng sal craf At the, and a sore Raknyng sal hafe. **1599** SHAKS. *Hen. V*, IV. i. 141 If the Cause be not good, the King himselfe hath a heauie Reckoning to make. **1641** HINDE *J. Bruen* xxxiv. 108 The reckoning and account of a true Professor and sound Christian is not to seeke, nor to make at the houre of their death. **1784** COWPER *Task* III. 179 He will judge the earth, and call the fool To a sharp reckoning that has lived in vain.

d. In phr. *day of reckoning*. (See also 9.)

1838 DICKENS *Nich. Nick.* xx, There will be a day of reckoning sooner or later. **1861** BUCKLE *Civiliz.* (1873) III. iii. 132 The patience of the country was well nigh exhausted, and the day of reckoning was at hand.

†**e.** An account, statement *of* something. *Obs.*

a **1375** *Joseph Arim.* 444 Whon þat þou comest aȝeyn.. þou miht haue more redi roume my rikenyng to here. **1543** [T. COTTESFORD] (*title*) The Rekening and declaracion of the faith and beleif of Huldrik Zwingly.

5. The settlement of accounts or differences between parties.

c **1470** *Golagros & Gaw.* 850 Rude reknyng raise thair renkis betuene. **1546** J. HEYWOOD *Prov.* (1867) 53 Euen recknyng maketh longe friendis,.. For alwaie owne is owne, at the recknyngis eend. **1776** PAINE *Com. Sense* (1791) 62 A firm bargain and a right reckoning make long friends.

6. a. The action of calculating or estimating chances or contingencies; (an) anticipation, or expectation.

1568 Grafton *Chron.* II. 689 Makyng sure reconyng to haue had theyr pray and pryse. **1588** Parke tr. *Mendoza's Hist. China* 144 It went not with Limahon and his foure hundred souldiers according as he did make reckoning. **1686** tr. *Chardin's Coronat. Solyman* 25 The General of the Slaves expected the Precedency as his due... However he missed of his reckoning. **1871** Freeman *Norm. Conq.* (1876) IV. xviii. 113 Most likely the reckonings of the men of Kent did not go so far afield.

†**b.** Thought, idea. *Obs.*⁻¹

1574 Hellowes *Gueuara's Fam. Ep.* (1584) 231 After I.. read againe your letter, I fell in the reckoning that it was of Mosen Rubin my neighbour.

†**7. a.** Mode of regarding a matter. *Obs.*

1390 Gower *Conf.* I. 356 As to the worldes rekeninge Ther schal he finde no winnynge. **1522** More *De quat. Noviss.* Wks. 79/2 With this reckening shal thei loke vpon death muche nerer hande. **1596** Shaks. *Tam. Shr.* iv. i. 87 By this reckning he is more shrew than she. **1649** Milton *Eikon.* ix. 86 By this reckning his consent and his denials come all to one pass.

†**b.** *to make reckoning of*: to hold or account of, to take heed of. *Obs.* (Common *c* 1580–1680.)

1581 Pettie tr. *Guazzo's Civ. Conv.* i. (1586) 7 b, A man must not make reconing or account of the multitude of people. **1613** Purchas *Pilgrimage* ii. xix. (1614) 217 That Iew.. is accounted a Traytor, and neuer made reckoning of after. **1686** tr. *Chardin's Coronat. Solyman* 99 The General at that time made little reck'ning of what he said.

†**c.** *to be,* or *come to, one reckoning*: to be of the same value, to be equivalent. *Obs.*

1599 Shaks. *Hen. V*, iv. vii. 18 The great, or the mighty, or the huge.. are all one reckonings. **1674** N. Fairfax *Bulk & Selv.* 93 To take away place, or to take away the body plac'd, comes all to a reckoning.

†**8.** Estimation, consideration, distinction. (Used with adjs., as *good, little, mean*, etc., and absolutely.) *Obs.*

1582 Stanyhurst *Æ neis* ii. (Arb.) 46 Whilst counsel auayled, Then we were of reckning. **1586** A. Day *Eng. Secretary* i. (1625) 5 A woman of very meane reckoning. **1598** Manwood *Lawes Forest* xx. §10 (1615) 179/2 Such beasts.. are.. not meete for any man of reckoning to eate. **1602** Carew *Cornwall* 6 For Windowes, Domes, and Chimnies, Moore stone carrieth chiefest reckoning. **1653** H. Cogan tr. *Pinto's Trav.* xlvii. 271 He found that some fifty thousand were missing, all men of little reckoning.

9. *attrib.*, as ***reckoning book, chamber, day, tablet.***

1548 Elyot *Rationarius codex*,.. a reckenyng booke. **1613** R. Cawdrey *Table Alph.* (ed. 3), *Register*, kalender, a reckoning booke. **1647** Hexham s.v., A reckoning chamber, or a chamber of accounts, *een reecken-kamer.* **1765** Johnson (ed. 2), *Reckoning book*, a book in which money received and expended is set down. **1812** Byron *Ch. Har.* i. lii, Ah! Spain! how sad will be thy reckoning-day. **1851** Mayne Reid *Scalp Hunt.* xvii. 120, I may yet find a reckoning day for him. **1930** T. S. Eliot tr. *St.-J. Perse's Anabasis* 67 He who has spread on the ground his reckoning tablets.

†**reckonmaster.** *Obs. rare*⁻¹. In 6 recken-. [f. reckon *v.*; cf. Du. *rekenmeester*, G. *rechenmeister.*] A professional reckoner, an arithmetician.

1570 Dee *Math. Pref.* *ij, The common Logist, Reckenmaster, or Arithmeticien.. imagineth lesse partes: and calleth them Fractions.

recks, variant of rex, pranks.

reclaim (rɪˈkleɪm), *sb.*¹ Forms: see claim *sb.* (also 5 **racleyme**). [a. OF. *reclaim*, sb. from *reclaimer*, *reclamer* to reclaim.]

I. Now *rare.* †**1. a.** The act of recalling a hawk; esp. *to come to reclaim*, to return when called. *Obs.*

1398 Trevisa *Barth. De P.R.* xii. ii. (Tollem. MS.), He wexeþ ramaioue oþer slowe, and dedeyneþ not to come to reclayme. **1486** *Bk. St. Albans* B ij, And or she come to the reclame make her that she sowre not.

†**b.** The recall or bringing back of a person.

c **1430** Lydg. *Min. Poems* (Percy Soc.) 77 Defye false fortune, And al recleymes of hyr double luyne. **1533** Bellenden tr. *Livy* i. xii. (S.T.S.) I. 70 Þe Sabinis complanit þat þare rebellis.. war þare Intertenyit but ony reclame or punycioun eftir following. **1590** Spenser *F.Q.* iii. x. 16 The loving couple.. leasure had.. to frame Their purpost flight, free from all mens reclame.

†**c.** Revocation (of an edict). *Obs. rare*⁻¹.

1604 T. Wright *Passions* v. §4. 234 Ester.. procured the death of Hamman, and the reclaime of that bloody edict.

2. a. The act of recalling, or state of being recalled, to right conduct.

In early examples prob. *transf.* from sense 1.

a **1300** *Cursor M.* 1578 Wimmen þai forced a-mang þaim, Was nan þam moght bring to reclaim. **1494** Fabyan *Chron.* vii. 395 He.. buylded newe the cytie & castell of Beau Maryse, and broughte the vnsteadfast Walshman to newe reclayme. **1582** N. T. (Rhem.) Pref. 11 For the better preseruation or reclaime of many good souls endangered thereby. **1598** B. Jonson *Ev. Man in Hum.* i. i, I see you are e'en past hope Of all reclaim. *a* **1656** Hales *Gold. Rem.* i. (1673) 96 Let him examine his own conscience, and impartially sift all the manner of his reclaim. **1891** J. Aitchison *Signa Christi* vi. 225 [Christ is] the real Originator of societies for reclaim of the fallen.

b. The reclamation of land.

1799 J. Robertson *Agric. Perth* 421 While the country underwent the work of reclaim.

†**3.** A challenge, protest. *Obs. rare.*

c **1440** *Promp. Parv.* 425/2 Recleyme, or chalange, *clameum, vendicacio. c* **1449** Pecock *Repr.* iii. xvi. 386 He him silf mai it lette bi the reclaime.. which he mai make.

†**4.** The act of claiming back. *Obs. rare.*

1560 Daus tr. *Sleidane's Comm.* 417 b, Fridericke maketh reclaime to hys landes. **1609** Bible (Douay) *Judg.* xi. 26 Wherfore have you so long attempted nothing for reclaime?

II. 5. = *reclaimed rubber.*

1935 Dawson & Porritt *Rubber* 208/2 Although reclaim as compared with new rubber definitely leads to inferior mechanical properties in vulcanisates,.. it has important applications in rubbers where mechanical strength and abrasion resistance are of secondary significance. **1954** H. J. Stern *Rubber* vi. 200 Small differences in temperature from one part of the rubber to the other greatly affect the uniformity of the reclaims. **1971** R. Singleton in C. M. Blow *Rubber Technol. & Manufacture* vi. 207 First-quality reclaim made from whole tyres contains about 45% rubber hydrocarbon by weight. The remaining 55% consists of valuable carbon black, a little mineral filler, and softeners.

re-ˈclaim, *sb.*² [re- 5 a.] A fresh claim.

1890 *Pall Mall G.* 18 Aug. 2/3 The overseers.. have.. exposed a very large number of the electors to the chance of being struck off on objection, if re-claims are not made.

reclaim (rɪˈkleɪm), *v.* Forms: see claim *v.* [ad. OF. *reclamer*, †*reclaimer* (12th c.):—L. *reclāmāre* to cry out against, contradict, also to re-echo: see re- and claim *v.*]

I. *trans.* †**1. a.** *Falconry.* To call back (a hawk which has been let fly). *Obs.*

In some cases not easily distinguished from sense 3.

a **1300** *Cursor M.* 3530 Hauk es eth, als i here say, To reclaym þat has tint his pray. **1390** Gower *Conf.* II. 285 Fulofte he faileth of his game That wol with ydel hand reclame His hauk. *c* **1477** Caxton *Jason* 126 The kyng.. came into this gardyne for to reclayme a sperhawke of his. **1600** Surflet *Countrie Farme* vii. xliii. 872 To reclaime and bring them to the lure. **1727-41** Chambers *Cycl.* s.v., The spar-hawk, gos-hawk, &c. are reclaimed with the voice, the falcon only by shaking the lure.

transf. c **1330** R. Brunne *Chron.* (1810) 72 Morkar recleymed es [F. *est reclamé*], as es þe faukon fre. *c* **1386** Chaucer *Manciple's Prol.* 72 Another day he wole.. Reclayme thee, and brynge thee to lure. *c* **1460** Sir R. Ros *La Belle Dame* 634 Þaire bysy hertes passen to and fro, þai be so wele reclaymed to the lure.

†**b.** To call back; to recall. *Obs.*

1596 Spenser *F.Q.* v. xii. 9 Willed him for to reclayme with speed His scattred people, ere they all were slaine. **1597** Beard *Theatre God's Judgem.* (1612) 223 When.. he oppressed the people with exactions, and was reclaimed home. *a* **1700** Dryden (J.), The head-strong horses hurried Octavius.. along, and were deaf to his reclaiming them. **1727-41** Chambers *Cycl.* s.v., The partridge is also said to reclaim her young ones, when she calls them together upon their scattering too much from her.

fig. **1590** Greene *Mourn. Garm.* (1616) B iv, Knowing young wits were wandring, he began to reclaime him thus.

†**c.** To restrain, check, hold back. *Obs.*

a **1529** Skelton *Agst. Garnesche* iv. 105 Auaunt, rybawde, thi tung reclame! **1596** Danett tr. *Comines* (1614) 319 Then the Duke vsed to reclaime vs, saying ho, one to one. **1633** T. Stafford *Pac. Hib.* i. iii. (1810) 51 They would reclaime themselves and their followers from committing any outrage. **1700** Prior *Carmen Sec.* 292 Is her tow'ring Flight reclaim'd By Seas from Icarus' Downfall nam'd?

†**d.** To recall, withdraw (a statement); to revoke. *Obs. rare.*

1615 T. Adams *Two Sonnes* Wks. (1630) 425 Let vs reclaime our impudent and refractory renegations. **1639** Drumm. of Hawth. *Memorials of State* Wks. (1711) 129 If Henry VI.. would.. have reclaimed the approbation.. of Richard duke of York. **1670** W. Simpson *Hydrol. Ess.* 76 What I have said.. I find no reason to reclaim.

2. a. To recall, bring back (a person or animal) *from* a wrong course of action, etc., *to* a proper state. †Also const. *of.*

The first quot. may rather belong to sense 3.

1390 Gower *Conf.* III. 277 Adam and Eve.. hem aschamed, Til that nature hath hem reclamed To love. *c* **1450** *St. Cuthbert* (Surtees) 2368 Cuthbert wayued his hand on þaim, Fra ryuyng of thak þaim to reclaym. **1565** Jewel *Def. Apol.* (1611) 362 Luther.. did write maruellous vehemently and sharply against them, and reclaimed them home to peace and obedience. **1581** Mulcaster *Positions* xxxv. (1887) 126 If the soule it selfe be reclaymed from follie. **1633** P. Fletcher *Purple Isl.* i. xlix, Being one soon into two he framed it, And now made two, to one again reclaimed it. **1681-6** J. Scott *Chr. Life* (1747) III. 2 A Man.. may upon due Consideration.. reclaim himself to a very pious and virtuous Life. **1686** Blome *Gentl. Recreat.* II. 38 In a little time this will Reclaim her of that Roaveing Kytishtrick. **1768** Ferriar *Illustr. Sterne*, etc. vi. 165 A young man, who was reclaimed from a very dissolute course of life. **1841** Lane *Arab. Nts.* I. 74 So was he reclaimed to a sense of his duty. **1849** Macaulay *Hist. Eng.* v. I. 624 Henrietta had reclaimed him from a life of vice.

b. To call back from wrong-doing or error; to bring back to the right way; to reform.

1577 Northbrooke *Dicing* (1843) 77, I am glad to heare this of you, that you are so reclaimed. **1610** Willet *Hexapla Dan.* 361 Such an one was Saul, that would by no meanes be reclaymed. *a* **1680** Butler *Rem.* (1759) I. 70 Like the Plagues of Ægypt, meant a Curse, Not to reclaim us, but to make us worse. **1742-3** *Johnson's Parl. Deb.* (1811) II. 360 We shall give those, who have accustomed themselves to this liquor, time to reclaim their appetites. **1779-81** Johnson *L.P.*, *Addison* (1868) 234 Addison.. had very diligently endeavoured to reclaim him. **1819** T. B. Johnson *Shooter's Comp.* 85 [Young dogs] if they are suffered to acquire any bad habits.. will be with great difficulty reclaimed. **1831** Miss Ferrier *Destiny* v, Employing the industrious,.. or reclaiming the wicked.

refl. **1586** A. Day *Eng. Secretary* i. (1625) 54 As a yong man I went astray I grant, but.. I reclaimed my selfe ere I fell. **1609** T. Morton *Answ. Higgins* 26 Do you not also see how he reclaimeth himselfe, and accordeth vnto the common opinion?

absol. **1667** Milton *P.L.* vi. 791 They hard'nd more by what might most reclame,.. at the sight Took envie.

c. To win back, win over (again). Also with *inf. rare.*

1587 Turberv. *Trag. T.* 35 No loue deuise, no iewels fet from farre, Could so reclaime this noble Ladies minde. **1622** Bacon *Hen. VII* 11 Fit also to reclaime them to know him for their King, whom they had so lately talked of as an Enimie. **1853** C. Bronte *Villette* xx, Once alienated, [I doubt] whether he were ever to be reclaimed.

d. To put right, to remedy, correct, amend (something wrong, an error, fault, etc.). *rare.*

1596 Bacon *Max. & Uses Com. Law* Pref., In deciding of doubts, and.. in reclaiming vulgar errors. **1622** —— *Hen. VII* 17 By his presence.. to reclayme and rectifie those humours. **1742-3** *Johnson's Parl. Deb.* (1811) II. 398 The same provisions by which the vices of our own people are to be reclaimed. **1849** Alison *Hist. Europe* I. iii. §74. 332 In these abuses, which we have a right to reclaim, will be found a mine of riches.

3. a. To reduce to obedience, tame, subdue (an animal, *esp.* a hawk, also rarely a person).

The legal term for reducing animals *feræ naturæ* to domestication (see quot. 1766).

1390 Gower *Conf.* III. 366, I thoghte thanne how love is swete, Which hath so wise men reclamed. *c* **1440** *Promp. Parv.* 425/2 Recleymyn', or make tame, *domo.* **1486** *Bk. St. Albans*, a iij, The same nyght after the fedyng, wake her all nyght.., then shee will be preui Inowgh to be reclamed. **1530** Palsgr. 681/1 He was the stoburnest boye that ever I sawe, but I have reclaymed hym. **1579** Lyly *Euphues* (Arb.) 41 Though the Fawlcon be reclaimed to the fist, she retyreth to hir haggardnesse. **1607** Markham *Caval.* ii. ix. 102 This course of reclaiming a horse by gentlenesse.. I have found much to auaile. **1632** Massinger *Maid of Hon.* ii. ii, *Camiola.* I am still myself, and will be. *Fulgentio.* A proud haggard, And not to be reclaimed! **1737** Stackhouse *Hist. Bible* ii. i. (1752) I. 150/2 Such Creatures as are immorigerous, we have found out Expedients to reclaim. **1766** Blackstone *Comm.* II. xxv. 391 A qualified property may subsist in animals *feræ naturæ, per industriam hominis*; by a man's reclaiming and making them tame by art, industry, and education. **1852** R. F. Burton *Falconry in Valley Indus* vi. 71 Allowing a week or ten days for reclaiming the bird.

†**b.** To keep the growth of (wood or trees) within bounds. *Obs.*

1601 Holland *Pliny* xvii. xxii, By this means also the wood is reclaimed and repressed from running out in length beyond all measure. **1697** Dryden *Virg. Georg.* ii. 86 Much labour is requir'd in Trees, to tame Their wild disorder, and in ranks reclaim.

c. To remove (rude qualities) by means of instruction or culture; to bring (savage people) to a state of civilization.

1760 Goldsm. *Cit. W.* lxxv, Savage rusticity is reclaimed by oral admonition alone. **1844** Lingard *Anglo-Sax. Ch.* (1858) I. Pref. 6 By religion they were reclaimed from savage life. **1865** *Reader* 12 Aug. 180/1 A fair field,.. with no aborigines to be protected or reclaimed.

d. To bring (waste land, or land formerly covered by water) under, or into a fit state for, cultivation.

1764 *Museum Rust.* I. 370 The plain reason, why potatoes are an excellent crop for reclaiming land. **1808** J. Walker *Hist. Hebrides* I. 162 There has.. been more wild land in Scotland, reclaimed by means of lime, than by any other manure. **1874** Green *Short Hist.* viii. §5. 503 A great scheme was set on foot for reclaiming the Fens. **1903** G. B. Shaw *Man & Superman* p. xi, Far beyond mere lovemaking into politics, high art, schemes for reclaiming new continents from the ocean. **1922** Joyce *Ulysses* 68 Reclaim the whole place. Grow peas in that corner there. **1943** J. S. Huxley *TVA* vi. 30 Gullied and badly eroding land reclaimed in the Valley. **1966** *Listener* 26 May 751/2 You could take advantage of this fact by reclaiming a large area of the Wash itself.

e. To recover (rubber) for reuse by freeing it from impurities and rendering it plastic again; more widely, to make (re)usable (what has been used or rendered unusable.) Also *absol.*

1895 *Sci. Amer.* 26 Oct. 267/1 Methods of reclaiming rubber. **1898** *India-Rubber & Gutta-Percha & Electr. Trades' Jrnl.* XVI. 184/1 Prior to that time [*sc.* 1870] the use of rubber reclaimed from fibrous wastes had been confined practically to one large factory in Boston and one near New York. **1937** H. Barron *Mod. Rubber Chem.* xxi. 254 Miller carried out four cycles of reclaiming starting from a reclaim. That is, he vulcanised, reclaimed, added sulphur, revulcanized, reclaimed, etc. **1937** *Iron Age* 5 Aug. 38/3 Many new parts of Monel rendered unserviceable as a result of being turned undersize or bored oversize in the process of manufacture are readily reclaimed by spraying. **1962** A. Nisbett *Technique Sound Studio* vi. 113 The tape is finally wiped and reclaimed. **1970** [see reclamation 2 d]. **1972** P. W. Allen *Natural Rubber & Synthetics* v. 121 About 90 per cent of the world's supply of new rubbers is not reclaimed but ends up as unwanted waste products. **1976** *Conservation News* Nov./Dec. 18/2 It cost twice as much to reclaim bottles as it did to buy new ones. **1977** *Lancashire Life* Dec. 92/4 It is particularly annoying to see stones from old property bulldozed aside instead of being reclaimed for future use.

4. †**a.** *Sc.* To make a claim against (one), to sue at law. *Obs. rare.*

1456 Sir G. Haye *Law Arms* (S.T.S.) 92 Quhethir.. he may lefully recover apon him be were his thing, gif he may reclame him in jugement. *Ibid.* 168 Thai quite clamand him in time tocum, to nocht reclame him of thai gudis.

b. To claim the restoration of, to demand or take back (a person or thing).

In later use properly a new formation on re- 5 a and claim *v.* with distinct pron. of the prefix (riː).

1530 in W. H. Turner *Select. Rec. Oxford* (1880) 91 Hys Mʳ..desyred to have hym reclaymed of the Maire. **1590** SPENSER *F.Q.* III. iii. 48 So shall the Briton blood their crowne agayn reclame. **1701** *Lond. Gaz.* No. 3758/7 Captain Arena,..being reclaimed by the Imperial Ambassador, was set at Liberty. **1760–72** H. BROOKE *Fool of Qual.* (1809) III. 94 Reclaiming the bar,..he threw it to a length..judged to exceed my cast. **1835** MARRYAT *Pacha Many T.* iii, To make a note of any particular marks upon the children by which they might be eventually reclaimed. **1872** SWINBURNE *Ess. & Stud.* (1875) 27 In vain he reclaimed for Paris, in the face of Versailles, the right of municipal self-government.

fig. **1875** BLACKMORE *Alice Lorraine* III. vi. 94 This cold resistless flood calmly reclaimed its ancient channel.

†**5. a.** To call repeatedly upon. (In Caxton only.)

1481 CAXTON *Myrr.* III. xii. 159 Thise thre bountees reclayme alle crysten men. **1491** —— *Vitas Patr.* I. xxxvi. (1495) 37 a/1 The name of god was reclamed and named in al townes and cytees.

†**b.** To proclaim. *Obs. rare.*

a **1529** SKELTON *Bk. 3 Foles* Wks. 1843 I. 202 If that I am beloued of dyuers persons which reclaymeth mee good and vertuous. **1565** KNOX *Serm.* Wks. 1864 VI. 265 Stil to reclayme Him to be our God..is the greatest victorie of faith.

†**c.** To re-echo, return (a sound). *Obs.*⁻¹

1590 GREENE *Mourn. Garm.* (1616) E ij, Melt to teares, poure out thy plaints, let Eccho reclame them.

†**6.** To cry out, or protest, against (a thing or person); to gainsay, reject. *Obs.*

1634 CANNE *Necess. Separ.* (1849) 94 Your consciences reclaimeth not the wearing of such garments: but many thousand both godly and learned are otherwise persuaded. **1650** FULLER *Pisgah* II. viii. §3 Herod..in stead of reclaiming what they exclaimed, imbraced and hug'd their praises as proper to himself.

II. *intr.* **7. a.** To exclaim, protest. Now *rare.*

c **1440** *Promp. Parv.* 425/2 Recleymyn', or wythe seyn, ..*reclamo.* *a* **1471** FORTESCUE *Title of House of York* Wks. (1869) 500 Kinge Henry..was annoynted and crouned.., no man reclaiminge. **1549** COVERDALE, etc. *Erasm. Par. Heb.* xi. 20 She gave no eare to nature reclaming and harking to the contrarie. **1579** FULKE *Confut. Sanders* 680 All the Bishops..subscribed and allowed all that had bene saide.., and no man reclamed. **1719** WATERLAND *Vind. Christ's Div.* viii, Scripture reclaims; and the whole Catholick Church reclaims; and Christian Ears would not bear it. **1869** BROWNING *Ring & Bk.* VIII. 354 We could reclaim,—..But no,—we'll take it as spontaneously Confessed.

b. Const. *against*, †*at*, †*to*.

c **1449** PECOCK *Repr.* III. xvii. 398 That y..am stille in not reclaymyng aȝens the trust neither aȝens the ȝifte. **1534** CRANMER *Let. to Cromwell* in *Misc. Writ.* (Parker Soc.) II. 286, I think there is not one..that would once reclaim against it. **1565** KNOX *Serm.* Wks. 1864 VI. 262 Began to call [it] in doubte..bicause that naturall judgement..reclaymed thereto. **1604** HUBBOCKE *Orat. Grat. K. James* 9 Every one acclaming to it, no man reclaiming at it. **1699** BENTLEY *Phal.* 60 The whole Context in Dionysius reclaims against this Emendation. **1769** BLACKSTONE *Comm.* IV. xiii. 164 In Northern countries, the very nature of the climate seems to reclaim against it. **1818** JEFFERSON *Writ.* (1830) IV. 308 He wrote to reclaim against an expression of Mr. Wirt's. **1875** ULLATHORNE *Gladstone's Expost. Unrav.* 70 Against which act..we..loudly reclaim, in like manner as, on other occasions, we have protested against like attempts.

c. With obj. clause. To declare or say in protest.

c **1449** PECOCK *Repr.* III. xviii. 398 If y theraȝens reclame or proteste for me and hem, that y..wole be fre. **1714** EUSDEN *To Ld. Halifax* in Steele *Poet. Misc.* 192 Where are the Flights, (true Criticks may reclaim) The Heat, the Force, and Fancy..? **1846** W. H. MILL *Five Serm.* (1848) 26 Will not experience bitterly reclaim, that from this consideration..the gloomiest answer only can follow.

d. *Sc. Law.* To appeal; now *spec.* from a judgement of the Lord Ordinary to the Inner House of the Court of Session.

1578–9 *Reg. Privy Council Scot.* Ser. I. III. 109 The said decreet..fra the quhilk the said Dame Grissell hes reclamit. **1666–88** DALLAS *Syst. Stiles* (1697) 455 By the saids Acts, their is a Provision and Salvo for the Defender to Reclaim and make Application to the Lords in case of unjustice of the Judge. **1709** *Act Sederunt* 9 July, Act anent Interloquitors in the Outter-house, and Bills reclaiming against them. **1752** MᶜDOUALL *Inst. Laws Scot.* IV. xxxvi. II. 676 Parties are presumed to acquiesce to the judgments of the ordinary, when they do not reclaim to the lords. **1884** *Law Times* LXXVI. 333/1 The trustees have reclaimed against the recent interlocutor of Lord Fraser.

†**8.** To call out, cry loudly. *Obs. rare.*

1647 W. BROWNE *Polexander* IV. iv. 297 The voice flying into aire, I call'd a long time to intreat it to instruct me... But I re-claim'd in vain. *a* **1700** DRYDEN *Iliad* I. 294 One whisper'd soft, and one aloud reclaim'd.

†**9. a.** To draw back; to recant. *Obs. rare.*

1596 SPENSER *F.Q.* VI. iii. 43 Yet would he not perswaded be for ought, Ne from his currish will a whit reclame. **1604** T. WRIGHT *Passions* (1620) 310 Why may they not as well reclayme again, as they did before?

†**b.** To reform. *Obs.*

1625 B. SPENSER *Vox Civitatis* 2, I wish you to reclaime, repent, beleeue. **1742** RICHARDSON *Pamela* III. 47 If he was in earnest to reclaim. **1757** MRS. GRIFFITH *Lett. Henry & Frances* (1767) I. 242 Few of such creatures ever reclaim of themselves; but..die without repentance.

reclaimable (rɪˈkleɪməb(ə)l), *a.* [f. prec. + -ABLE.] That may be reclaimed.

a **1677** HALE *Prim. Orig. Man.* IV. viii. 371 He..hath power to reclaim those that are reclaimable..; as Horses, Elephants, Camels. *c* **1720** J. COCKBURN *Rem. Burnet's Hist. Own Times* 41 He said, that he was young, and so reclaimable; that this was his first Fault. **1765** BLACKSTONE *Comm.* I. viii. 288 Any beast may be an estray, that is by nature tame or reclaimable. *a* **1814** *Masquerade* IV. iv. in *New Brit. Theatre* I. 261 If you have resolution to do that, I shall begin to think you reclaimable. **1848** W. H. BARTLETT *Egypt to Pal.* vi. (1879) 145 The valley appeared as though it might be reclaimable by Nile water.

Hence **reˈclaimableness**, **reˈclaimably** *adv.*

1695 J. SAGE *Article* Wks. 1844 I. 70 Such as are in a state of reclaimableness. **1882** OGILVIE, *Reclaimably.*

reclaimant (rɪˈkleɪmənt). ? *Obs.* [f. RECLAIM *v.* as CLAIMANT. Cf. F. *réclamant* (*c* 1800 in Littré).] One who reclaims.

17.. in Richardson s.v. *Reclaim*, The famous council..of 318 bishops, very unanimous in their resolutions, excepting a few reclaimants. **1755** MAGENS *Insurances* I. 325 Capt. John Hunt's Lawsuit Charges, which the Reclaimants engaged to satisfy. **1778** *Sketches for Tabernacle Frames* 15 Acting..the mild Reclaimant's Part.

reclaimed (rɪˈkleɪmd), *ppl. a.* [f. RECLAIM *v.* + -ED¹.] **1.** Tamed, reformed, brought under cultivation, †protested against.

c **1440** *Promp. Parv.* 425/2 Recleymyd, or chalangyd, *reclamatus.* *Ibid.*, Recleymyd, as hawkys, *redomitus.* **1481** CAXTON *Myrr.* II. xvi. 102 The goshawke and sperhawk.. that ben tame and reclaymed brynge that they take to theyr lord. **1592** GREENE *Disput.* 35 The gentleman..found her afterward a reclaimed woman. **1600** SURFLET *Countrie Farme* VII. viii. 813 The chiefe and principall furtherance.. that can be giuen to trees, either reclaimed or wilde. **1686** BLOME *Gentl. Recreat.* II. 36/2 He that hath once experienced a well Reclaimed Sparrow-Hawk will hardly be without one. **1769** G. WHITE *Selborne* xxii, What you mention with respect to reclaimed toads raises my curiosity. **1840** BUEL *Farm. Comp.* 47 The crops best calculated for reclaimed swamps. **1881** *Macm. Mag.* XLV. 40 Here is a 'reclaimed' hawk: he can be..recovered as soon as his owner pleases. **1961** D. M. DISNEY *Mrs. Meeker's Money* vii. 77 A reclaimed island of land-scaped brick and glass on the fringe of the business district. **1974** W. J. BURLEY *Death in Stanley St.* ix. 164 The new waste-disposal unit, pride of the city, had been built on a promontory of reclaimed land.

2. Rendered reusable; ***reclaimed rubber***, rubber obtained from used vulcanized rubber by treating it to remove free sulphur and foreign substances and to render it plastic, chiefly used mixed with crude rubber in low-grade rubber goods.

1897 *Sci. Amer.* 25 Sept. 196/2 The reclaimed rubber of commerce is obtained by steaming or devulcanizing old rubber waste, generally shoes, freed more or less perfectly from fiber. **1913** B. D. PORRITT *Chem. Rubber* v. 66 The consumption of reclaimed rubber..is probably equal to the world's production of raw rubber. **1942** *Time* 2 Feb. 63/3 Reclaimed rubber, ordinarily bypassed by manufacturers because it wears out faster than natural rubber. **1958** *Jrnl. Amer. Water Works Assoc.* L. 1021 (*heading*) Emergency use of reclaimed water for potable supply at Chanute, Kan. **1971** R. SINGLETON in C. M. Blow *Rubber Technol. & Manufacture* vi. 203 Reclaimed rubber has become widely accepted as a raw material which possesses processing and economic characteristics that are of great value in the compounding of natural and synthetic rubber stocks. **1976** *Lancs. Evening Post* 7 Dec. 13/5 (Advt.), Demolition materials. Reclaimed timber (cut to your requirements)... Reclaimed stone.

reclaimer¹ (rɪˈkleɪmə(r)). [f. as prec. + -ER¹.] One who reclaims.

1676 *Rep. French Capers* 4 Aug. in Marvell *Growth Popery* (1678) 58 That all Privateers and Reclaimers know it. **1721** C. KING *Brit. Merch.* I. 103 A Suit being commenced between the Captors of Prizes on one part, and the Reclaimers of the same on the other. **1742** RICHARDSON *Pamela* III. 143 The whole Country round you..owe great Obligations to your fair Reclaimer. **1861** SMILES *Engineers* I. 22 The first reclaimers of the Fen lands seem to have been the religious recluses. **1868** *Act 31 & 32 Vict.* c. 100 §52 After a reclaiming note has been present, the reclaimer shall not be at liberty to withdraw it.

†**reˈclaimer²**. *Obs. rare.* [App. ad. AF. *reclaimer*: see -ER⁴.] Reclamation, reform.

1650 H. BROOKE *Conserv. Health* 230 We ought even in our Angers to give some manifest of a desire of good to the Person we are angry withall, as of Reclaimer, of his amendment and altering his Course. **1667** WATERHOUS *Fire London* 40 Obstinacy and opposition to, and despight of the meanes and motions of reclaimer.

reclaiming (rɪˈkleɪmɪŋ), *vbl. sb.* [-ING¹.] **a.** The action of the vb. RECLAIM, in various senses.

c **1385** CHAUCER *L.G.W.* 1371 *Hypsipyle*, Thow madist thyn recleymyng and thy lures To ladyis. *c* **1440** *Promp. Parv.* 425/2 Recleymynge, of wyldenesse, *redomitacio.* **1575** TURBERV. *Faulconrie* Cont., The reclayming, imping,..and fleyng both the fielde and riuer of the same Haukes. **1580** HOLLYBAND *Treas. Fr. Tong*, *Criement*.., a reclaming, a crying againste. **1601** *2nd Pt. Return fr. Parnass.* II. v. 913 Through good reclaiming my faulty hounds found their game againe. **1641** HINDE *J. Bruen* xxxi. 97 For their better information in the way of God, and more effectuall reclaiming of themselves. **1755** MAGENS *Insurances* I. 345 We made it..an express Condition to be entirely free of all Charges of Detention and Reclaiming. **1776** G. SEMPLE *Building in Water* 118 The reclaiming of Ground. **1852** R. F. BURTON *Falconry in Valley Indus* iv. 44 Their reclaiming commences with being broken to the hood. **1892** *Sci. Amer.* 7 May 293/3 These [*sc.* old boots and shoes] are sorted roughly, put up in bales, and shipped to the companies who make a business of reclaiming. **1913** B. D. PORRITT *Chem. Rubber* v. 60 'Reclaiming' at the present time is an industry by itself, several large works being exclusively engaged on this work. **1971** R. SINGLETON in C. M. Blow *Rubber Technol. & Manufacture* vi. 203 The raw material for reclaiming is scrap rubber in a wide variety of forms, but tyres..form the major quantity.

b. *attrib.*, as **reclaiming bill, days, note, petition** (see RECLAIM *v.* 7 d).

1709 *Act Sederunt* 9 July, Ordain the clerk of the proces carefully to compare reclaiming bills with the minutes. **1747** *Ibid.* 27 Jan., Resolution of the Lords of Council and Session, anent reclaiming Petitions. **1765** *Ibid.* 27 Feb., The Lords declare, that no marking of the clerks..shall hereafter keep the reclaiming days open till next Session. **1831** MISS FERRIER *Destiny* xliii, Not a decreet, or reclaiming petition. **1868** [see RECLAIMER¹]. **1888** *Law Rep. Ho. Lords* XIII. 404 The appellants reclaimed, and the respondents took advantage of that reclaiming note, to ask [etc.]. **1895** *Sci. Amer.* 26 Oct. 267/1 Rubber reclaiming factories. **1954** H. J. STERN *Rubber* vi. 200 Peptising agents accelerate the reclaiming process and are useful with both natural and synthetic rubbers. **1957** *Times* 20 Dec. 17/6 In our reclaiming plant overtime working was in force from October.

So **reˈclaiming** *ppl. a.*, that reclaims.

1560 in Strype *Ann. Ref.* (1709) I. xviii. 214 They should ..procure to their reclaiming consciences the biting worm that never dies. **1813** SHELLEY *Q. Mab* IX. 145 A pathless wilderness remains, Yet unsubdued by man's reclaiming hand. **1843** CANDLISH in *Life* (1880) 273 We could abstain from intruding ministers upon a reclaiming congregation.

reˈclaimless, *a.* *rare*⁻¹. [f. RECLAIM *sb.*¹ + -LESS.] That cannot be reclaimed.

1682 DRYDEN & LEE *Dk. Guise* II. i, A Resolution to preserve his Life, And look on Guise, as a reclaimless Rebel.

reclaimment (rɪˈkleɪmmənt). *rare.* [f. RECLAIM *v.* + -MENT.] Reclamation.

1861 SMILES *Engineers* I. 26 These attempts at reclaimment, however, made comparatively small impression on..the great Fen Level.

reclamation (rɛkləˈmeɪʃən). Also 8 reclaim-. [a. F. *réclamation* (1549 in Hatz.-Darm.), or ad. L. *reclāmātion-em*, n. of action f. *reclāmāre* to RECLAIM.]

1. a. The action of protesting; a protest.

1533 BELLENDEN tr. *Livy* III. ix. (S.T.S.) I. 281 Nochtwithstanding ony reclamacioun of tribunis, twa strang armyis belive war rasit. **1631** R. BOLTON *Comf. Affl. Consc.* 26 The many secret grumblings..and stinging reclamations of a gauled conscience against its present guilty courses. **1650** BULWER *Anthropomet.* 131 An act..done against the reclamation of the Law of Nature. **1793** PAINE in Sparks *Life & Writ. Morris* (1832) I. 417 A reply is necessary, were it only to continue the reclamation. **1829** LANDOR *Imag. Conv.*, *Emp. China & Tsing-Ti* Wks. 1853 II. 135/2 That two of the perpetrators might be kept on their thrones, against the reclamation of their subjects. **1872** PROCTOR *Ess. Astron.* iv. 60 My reclamation was not well received.

†**b.** *Sc.* An appeal at law. *Obs.*

1563–4 *Reg. Privy Council Scot.* Ser. I. I. 264 Quhilk decrete..thai..sall abide.., but ony appellatioun, reclamatioun, or agane calling quhatsumevir. **1579** *Ibid.* III. 169 To obey thair declaratioun and jugement, without reclamatioun, appellatioun, or contradictioun.

2. a. The action of calling or bringing back from wrong-doing, reformation.

1633 T. ADAMS *Exp. 2 Peter* iii. 17 To them that wilfully continue in a state of sin, there is a monument of reclamation, the lake of Sodom. **1640** BP. HALL *Episc.* Ep. Ded. 4 The fervent desire of whose reclamation..hath put my pen upon this..taske. **1709** *Tatler* No. 71 ¶5 These out of many such irregular Practices, I write for his Reclaimation. **1849** ROBERTSON *Serm.* Ser. IV. xxii. (1876) 266 It is meet that God should be glad on the reclamation of a sinner. **1867** HOWELLS *Ital. Journ.* 141 There were altogether some hundred boys in the first stages of reclamation.

b. The action of reclaiming *from* barbarism.

1868 ROGERS *Pol. Econ.* xviii. (1876) 245 The reclamation of nations..from barbarous customs, is gained from experience as to the humanising influences of honest trade.

c. The making (of land) fit for cultivation. Also *attrib.* Cf. also *land reclamation* s.v. LAND *sb.*¹ 10 a.

1848 J. S. MILL *Let.* 3 Feb. in W. Ward *Aubrey de Vere* (1904) iv. 132, I look much more than you do to reclamation of waste lands. **1861** SMILES *Engineers* II. 156 The reclamation of these unhealthy wastes became quite a hobby with him. **1884** KNIGHT *Dict. Mech.* Suppl. 745/2 *Reclamation Plow*, a plow for breaking new land. **1886** *Manch. Exam.* 22 Feb. 6/1 There have been reclamations of fresh land by means of the enclosure of commons. **1890** J. NEWMAN *Earthwork Slips* (title-p.), The Construction or Maintenance of..Reclamation Embankments, Drainage Works, &c. **1955** *Times* 24 May 8/3 The United Nations Relief and Works Agency is soon to present..a report on the feasibility of an ambitious reclamation scheme known as the Sinai strip. **1970** *New Yorker* 15 Aug. 32/1 The Dutch.. knew..how difficult and dirty any sort of reclamation work could be.

d. The action or process of reclaiming used or unusable objects or materials.

1937 *Iron Age* 5 Aug. 36/2 This..has been largely responsible for the extended use of the spray process in applying this metal both for the protection of new parts and for the reclamation of worn or unserviceable items. **1954** *Publ. Calif. State Water Pollution Control Board* No. 9. i. 13 Implicit in the study of waste water reclamation and utilization is the idea that eventually it will be of economic value as a water source. **1962** A. NISBETT *Technique Sound Studio* vii. 133 In BBC practice reclamation also includes not only checking through the tape to remove spacers, trailers, etc...but also removing all temporary joints and replacing them by cemented joints. **1970** *New Society* 5 Mar. 387/3 The reclamation industry reckons it saves Britain £1,000 million by reclaiming otherwise imported material.

†**3.** Revocation. *Obs.*

1577 HANMER *Anc. Eccl. Hist.* VII. x. (1636) 129 The suffering of reclamations, perils, persecutions,..and sundry tribulations which happened..under Decius. **1611** FLORIO, *Richiamo*, a reclamation, a reuokeing.

†**4.** An echoing shout. *Obs.*⁻¹

a **1639** WOTTON *Disparity* in *Reliq.* (1651) 48 So many thousand Citizens..made within the reach of his own ears large reclamations in his praise.

5. The action of claiming the return of something taken away; a claim *for* something.

1787 JEFFERSON *Writ.* (1859) II. 114 It was a silent reclamation and acknowledgment of fraternity, between two religions of the same family. **1846** LANDOR *Imag. Conv., Penn & Peterb.* Wks. I. 534/1 [Popes never] pardon a reclamation made on any side for redress. **1873** BROWNING *Red Cott. Nt.-cap* II. 649 They quarrelled..from reclamation of her rights To wifely independence.

6. Special *Comb.*: **reclamation disease** [tr. G. *urbarmachungskrankheit* (B. Sjollema 1933, in *Biochem. Zeitschr.* CCLXVII. 151)], a disease affecting crops, esp. cereals, grown on reclaimed land, caused by a deficiency of copper and distinguished by discoloured leaves and the failure of affected plants to produce seed.

1937 F. T. HEALD *Introd. Plant Pathol.* xviii. 365 The curative value of boron has also been demonstrated for the 'reclamation or bog disease', a trouble characteristic of swampy heath soils in European countries. **1949** BUTLER & JONES *Plant Pathol.* ix. 312 Among the group of crop disorders..owing to the active measures taken during modern times to reclaim peat moor, swamp, and polder soils, that which eventually became widely termed 'reclamation disease' is one of the most important. **1961** W. STILES *Trace Elements in Plants* (ed. 3) iii. 99 Reclamation disease..affects oats and other cereals.

‖**réclame** (reklam). [Fr., f. *réclamer*: see RECLAIM *v.*] The attainment of notoriety by 'puff' or advertisement. Also, popular acclaim, notoriety, glory, fame.

In quot. 1870 the sense seems to be 'an advertisement'.

1870 O. LOGAN *Before Footlights & behind Scenes* xxii. 255 Perhaps you think I mean this as a *reclame* for the Sherman House. **1883** MISS BRADDON *Gold. Calf* III. vi. 195 Byron was an adept in the art of *réclame*. **1896** A. BEARDSLEY *Three Music.* iii. in *Savoy* Jan. 65 A slim gracious boy..dies for *réclame* and recall. **1906** R. FRY *Let.* 16 Mar. (1972) I. 257 Pictures..which he offered at ridiculous prices for the *réclame* of getting into the Museum. **1945** R. HARGREAVES *Enemy at Gate* 105 The effulgent *réclame* of the conqueror of Wurmser and the Archduke Charles. **1977** *Times Lit. Suppl.* 25 Feb. 200/2 The author of a novel..which the serious papers denounced as prurient, so adding both to the number of copies sold and to his réclame among his colleagues.

reclang (riːˈklæŋ), *v.* [RE-, as in *re-echo.*] *intr.* To clang in return.

1848 LYTTON *K. Arthur* II. xci, The floors reclang'd with armour as he walk'd.

reclasp (riːˈklɑːsp, -æ-), *v.* [RE- 5 a.] *trans.* and *intr.* To clasp anew.

1802 PALEY *Nat. Theol.* xii. 234 When two laminæ, which have been separated by accident or force, are brought together again, they immediately reclasp.

reclassify (riːˈklæsɪfaɪ), *v.* [RE- 5 a.] *trans.* To classify again; to alter the classification of.

1920 in WEBSTER. **1928** *Daily Tel.* 27 Nov. 8/2 They will have an opportunity of reclassifying their institutions. **1946** *Nature* 28 Sept. 439/1 Existing roads should be reclassified and the design of new roads should not be attempted before their purpose was clearly determined. **1953** *Times* 8 June 7/4 Whether the Government will consider the advisability of reclassifying crash helmets as motor-cycle accessories. **1972** W. MCGIVERN *Caprifoil* iii. 47 'Those files aren't available.' 'They've been reclassified?' **1977** *Evening Post* (Nottingham) 27 Jan. 2/8 Re-classify their status—they are part retired, but certainly not wholly unemployed.

Hence **reclassifiˈcation**.

1885 *Manch. Exam.* 17 Jan. 5/5 Bills deposited by the principal railway companies for the re-classification of their rates.

reclear (riːˈklɪə(r)), *v.* [RE- 5 a.]

1. *trans.* To make clear again.

1605 SYLVESTER *Du Bartas* II. iii. III. *Law* 469 He.. Recleers the Floods, and sends the frogs away. **1670** G. H. *Hist. Cardinals* I. II. 57 Re-clearing the Foundations, and re-establishing the Church. **1880** *Times* 16 Oct. 12/3 The old forest of Genquoich was only re-cleared of sheep some six years ago.

2. *intr.* To become clear again. *rare*⁻¹.

a **1618** SYLVESTER *Mem. Mortality* II. lxxxvii, Thick streams reclear, when storms and stirring cease.

recle-fatt, variant of REKEL-FAT, censer. *Obs.*

recles(s, variants of REKELS, incense. *Obs.*

recleslaike: see RECKLESSLAIK.

reclimb (riːˈklaɪm), *v.* [RE- 5 a.] *trans.* To climb again.

1744 ELIZA HEYWOOD *Female Spect.* No. 8 (1748) II. 94 A kind of precipice, which, when once leaped, there is no possibility of reclimbing. **1817** MOORE *Lalla R., Fire-Worshippers* Wks. (1897) 260/2 He..reclimb'd the steep And gain'd the Shrine. **1886** HISSEY *On Box Seat* 272 We reclimbed the cliffs,..and found our way back to our little inn.

reˈclinable, *a.* [f. RECLINE *v.* + -ABLE.] Capable of being reclined.

1894 *Pop. Sci. Monthly* Nov. 75 His fangs are always partially or wholly erect, and not in the true sense of the word reclinable. **1957** *Archit. Rev.* CXXII. 351 (*caption*) In both, seats are reclinable and the windows are double-glazed.

reclinant (rɪˈklaɪnənt), *a.* [a. F. *réclinant*, pr. pple. of *récliner* to RECLINE.] *Her.* Bending or bowed.

1850 in OGILVIE.

reclinate (ˈrɛklɪneɪt), *a.* [ad. L. *reclīnātus*, pa. pple. of *reclīnāre* to RECLINE.] Bending downward; esp. *Bot.* of stems, branches, leaves, etc.

1753 CHAMBERS *Cycl. Supp.* s.v. *Leaf*, *Reclinate* or *reflex Leaf*, one which has its summit lower than its base. *Ibid.* s.v. *Stalk*, *Reclinate stalk*, that which stoops towards the ground. **1861** BENTLEY *Man. Bot.* 144 The upper half of the leaf may be bent upon the lower, so that the apex approaches the base, it is then said to be reclinate or inflexed. *Ibid.* 329 In some plants..the ovule is suspended from the end of a long funiculus..; such an ovule is frequently termed reclinate.

So **ˈreclinated** *a. rare.*

1797 *Encycl. Brit.* (ed. 3) XVI. 231/2 The reclinatum or reclinated broad-leaved gooseberry-bush rises with a low shrubby stem and reclinated somewhat prickly branches.

reclination (rɛklɪˈneɪʃən). [ad. late L. *reclīnātiōn-em* (4th c. in Quicherat), n. of action f. *reclīnāre* to RECLINE. Cf. F. *réclinaison* (Littré).]

1. The action, posture, or practice of reclining. Now *rare.*

1578 BANISTER *Hist. Man* I. 19 How hapneth yᵉ inclination and reclination of the head. **1619** LUSHINGTON *Repetition Serm.* (1659) 65 It signifies rather the reclination or posture of one asleep, than the affection of sleep it self. **1657** THORNLEY tr. *Longus' Daphnis & Chloe* 133 She lifted him up from the reclination on his side. **1822–34** *Good's Study Med.* (ed. 4) III. 249 Rest, reclination, general tonics ..constitute the best plan of treatment.

b. The action of resting or relying upon one.

1822 COLERIDGE *Lett., Conv.*, etc. 25 Jan. II. 79 With unwrinkled confidence and inmost reclination.

2. *Dialling.* The angle made by the plane of the dial with a vertical plane intersecting it. ? *Obs.*

1593 FALE *Dialling* 4 The degrees of the Reclination are found out thus. **1669** STURMY *Mariner's Mag.* VII. vi. 11 The Reclination is the distance of his Poles from the Zenith and Nadir of your place. **1727–41** CHAMBERS *Cycl.* s.v., The reclination is easily found, by means of a ruler, and a quadrant. **1797** *Encycl. Brit.* (ed. 3) V. 788/1 It cannot be a gnomon..when the reclination is equal to the co-latitude.

†**3.** The action of drawing back; aversion. *Obs.*⁻¹

1678 MRS. BEHN *Sir Patient Fancy* V. i, I saw with pleasure, Sir, your reclination from my addresses.

4. *Surg.* An operation formerly used for cataract (cf. quots.).

1820 TRAVERS *Dis. Eye* III. iii. §1 The lens may be depressed vertically or horizontally. The term 'reclination' has been applied to the latter method. **1825** GOOD *Study Med.* (ed. 2) IV. 229 Upon the ordinary operation of depression M. Willburg seems to have made a considerable improvement,..to this mode of operation is given the name of reclination. **1875** H. WALTON *Dis. Eye* 807 'Reclination' disposes of the cataract by tilting it backwards.

†**reclinatory.** *Obs.* Also 5 reclyn-. [ad. late L. *reclīnātōrium* the back of a couch (7th c.), the seat of a chariot (Vulg.), f. *reclīnāre* to RECLINE. Cf. OF. *reclinatoire* (Godef.).] Something on which to recline; a couch.

1412–20 LYDG. *Chron. Troy* II. xi, Costly tabernacles Vauted aboue lyke to reclynatoryes. **1430–40** —— *Bochas* I. xii. (1554) 25 Fortune in her reclinatorie. **1502** *Ord. Cristen Men* (W. de W. 1506) V. vi. 409 His trone and his reclinatorye. *a* **1633** AUSTIN *Medit.* (1635) 48 His Couches (or Reclinatories) were but meane ones.

b. *spec.* A seat for the use of a priest while hearing confession.

1637 POCKLINGTON *Altare Chr.* 24 To the Chancels belong the Vestry..and Reclinatories for hearing Confessions. **1640** R. BAILLIE *Canterb. Self-convict.* 76 A publik penitentiarie, who..might in the Kirk sit in his reclinatorie.

recline (rɪˈklaɪn), *sb. rare.* [f. the vb.] A recumbent or reclining posture.

1753 HOGARTH *Anal. Beauty* xvii. 229 Holding the head erect is but occasionally right; a proper recline of it may be as graceful. **1773** J. ROSS *Fratricide* v. 529 (MS.) From recline erecting her fine front. **1882** CABLE *Dr. Sevier* x. (1884) I. 69 He drew partly up from his half recline.

†**reˈcline**, *a. Obs.*⁻¹ [ad. L. *reclīnis* reclining, f. *reclīnāre* to RECLINE.] Recumbent, reclining.

1667 MILTON *P.L.* IV. 333 Fruits which the compliant boughs Yeilded them, side-long as they sat recline On the soft downie Bank.

recline (rɪˈklaɪn), *v.* Also 5 reclyne. [ad. OF. *recliner* (13th c. in Godef.), or L. *reclīnāre*, f. *re-* RE- + *-clīnāre*: see DECLINE *v.*]

1. a. *trans.* To lay down, or make to lie down (properly on the back); to cause to incline (backwards); to place in a recumbent or leaning position; to rest (the head, etc.) in this way.

Properly distinguished from *incline* (as in quot. 1578), but the distinction is not always clearly preserved.

c **1420** *Pallad. on Husb.* IV. 142 Her seed yf me reclyne In baume, or narde, or opi daies thre. *Ibid.* XII. 402 The Grekish sheep..on bored plankis they reclyne. *c* **1440** *Gesta Rom.* xlvii. 204 (Harl. MS.) The sonne of man haþe not wer he may reclyne or enbowe his hede. **1578** BANISTER *Hist. Man* I. 19 By meanes of which Articulation, the Head is now inclined, and now reclined. *a* **1667** COWLEY *Horace, Ep.* ii. 25 With how much Joy does he..His careless Head on the fresh Green recline. **1682** DRYDEN *Medal* 322 Our wild labours wearied into Rest Reclin'd us on a rightful Monarch's Breast. **1762** CHURCHILL *Night* 114 The homely bed, Where virtue, self-approv'd, reclines her head. **1792** *Bar. Munchausen's Trav.* xxix. 133 Both the warring champions..'neath their feet reclined their weapons. **1822** T. TAYLOR *Apuleius* 243 She easily reclined me on the bed. **1972** *Daily Tel.* (Colour Suppl.) 25 Aug. 19/2 A back-row, next-to-bulkhead seat is often fixed, i.e. the backrest cannot be reclined.

refl. **1774** J. BRYANT *Mythol.* II. 182 Reclining himself under the shade of an oak. **1813** SCOTT *Rokeby* II. ii, Each huge trunk that..Reclines him o'er the darksome tide.

b. In *pa. pple.* denoting position or posture.

1697 DRYDEN *Virg. Georg.* III. 134 On his right Shoulder his thick Mane reclin'd, Ruffles at speed. **1726** SWIFT *Gulliver* III. ii, Their heads were all reclined either to the right or the left. **1784** COWPER *Task* IV. 302 Thus oft, reclined at ease, I lose an hour At evening. **1818** SHELLEY *Rev. Islam* XII. xviii, Cythna sate reclined Beside me. **1841** *Penny Cycl.* XIX. 496/1 The branches are so much reclined that..the flowers will not be well seen. **1885** *Mag. Art* Sept. 443/1 The great god Pan reclined on moss-covered stones And fluting to the attentive Dryads.

†**c.** To incline (one's ear). *Obs.*⁻¹

1566 PAINTER *Pal. Pleas.* I. 113 b, The Lorde which reclined his eare to every trifling report and credited the wordes of every whistling pickethanke.

†**d.** To turn (a person) *from* something. *Obs.*⁻¹

a **1614** DONNE *Βιαθανατος* (1644) 215 To make it of more use, they would utterly recline and avert our nature from it.

†**e.** ? To turn aside, divert. *Obs.*⁻¹

1613 DAY *Festivals* viii. (1615) 233 The Authoritie of a Father, commanding that which is not to bee done, must rather bee reclined, then resisted.

2. *intr.* Of a dial: To have a backward inclination, to lie away back from the vertical. ? *Obs.*

1593 FALE *Dialling* 4 If the plat standeth not upright, but maketh an obtuse or blunt angle with the Horizon, it is said to recline. **1668** MOXON *Mech. Dial.* 18 It is not upright, but Inclines or Reclines... If you find the Plane Reclines, apply the side AD to it. **1690** LEYBOURN *Curs. Math.* 706 Suppose a direct West Plain, should recline from the Zenith towards the Horizon 35 deg. **1797** *Encycl. Brit.* (ed. 3) V. 788/1 If the plane..be made to incline, or recline, any given number of degrees, the hour-circles of the sphere will still cut the edge of the plane [etc.].

3. a. Of persons or parts of the body: To rest in a recumbent or inclined position, lean or repose *on* or *upon* something.

1697 DRYDEN *Æneid* IX. 581 His snowy Neck reclines upon his Breast. **1742** POPE *Dunc.* IV. 20 Soft on her lap her Laureate son reclines. **1797** SOUTHEY *Lett. Journ. Spain* 89 When there reclining on this grassy slope, I bore thee, Relic of my Love! away. **1815** SHELLEY *Alastor* 635 Upon an ivied stone Reclined his languid head. **1841** MYERS *Cath. Th.* III. §43. 164 It can matter little to him to know whether the Jews ate sitting or reclining.

transf. **1807** WORDSW. *White Doe* IV. 153 Not forbidden to recline With hope upon the Will divine.

b. Of inanimate things. Const. *over, to.*

1793 WORDSW. *Descr. Sketches* 278 The wood-crowned cliffs that o'er the lake recline. **1849** H. MILLER *Footpr. Creat.* x. 186 The stream to which they [fossil trees] reclined, must have flowed from nearly north-east to south-west.

c. *Mil.* Of one extremity of an army: To rest *upon* a place. *rare.*

1850 MERIVALE *Rom. Emp.* (1865) I. vii. 283 His rear reclined upon the river.

d. Of a seat: to admit of mechanical inclination of the back to a reclining or recumbent position.

1972 *N.Y. Law Jrnl.* 24 Oct. 3/2 The company is engaged in the manufacture and sale of upholstered furniture, principally medium priced chairs that recline. **1974** *Trafford's Catal.* 963/3 Multiposition metal reclining chair. .. Can recline to many positions.

†**4.** To incline, have a tendency, to return *to* a certain condition, physical or mental. *Obs. rare.*

c **1450** *Cov. Myst.* (Shaks. Soc.) 141 It wyl turne to watyr ageyn..For snow onto watyr dothe evyr more reclyne. **1706** DE FOE *Jure Divino* Introd. 5 She still reclines to the first State she Loves.

†**5.** To fall backwards or down. *Obs.*⁻¹

1764 GOLDSM. *Captivity* iii, See yonder tower just nodding to the fall:..And now behold the battlements recline.

reclined (rɪˈklaɪnd), *ppl. a.* [f. prec. + -ED¹.] Placed in a reclining or recumbent position; characterized by recumbency.

1669 STURMY *Mariner's Mag.* VII. xvii. 28 The Pole of the Reclined Plane FLE. **1779** J. DUCHE *Disc.* (1790) II. xix. 403 Who is yonder pensive mourner, whose reclined head and sad dejected countenance speak more than common anguish? **1822–34** *Good's Study Med.* (ed. 4) III. 384 During the paroxysm, perfect rest and a reclined position will be always found necessary. **1853** MACDONALD & ALLAN *Botanist's Word-bk.*, *Reclined*,..applied to leaves which are bent backwards, so that their apex is lower than the base.

recliner (rɪˈklaɪnə(r)). [f. as prec. + -ER¹.]

1. One who or that which reclines; *spec.* a reclining dial or plane.

1668 MOXON *Mech. Dial.* 28 If your Plane be an East Incliner, or a West Recliner. **1669** STURMY *Mariner's Mag.* VII. xiv. 23 Now we will proceed to draw the Hour-lines in a North Recliner. **1727–41** CHAMBERS *Cycl.* s.v., *Declining Recliner*,..is a dial which neither stands perpendicularly, nor opposite to one of the cardinal points. **1867** C. B. CAYLEY in *Fortn. Rev.* Nov. 590 While from thy lip is hung the breath drawn by the recliner.

2. A chair in which one may comfortably recline; a reclining chair or seat. Also *Comb.*, as **recliner chair, seat.** orig. *U.S.*

1928 E. O'Neill *Strange Interlude* ix. 275 There is a stone bench at center, a recliner at right. **1948** Partridge *Dict. Forces' Slang* 153 *Recliners*, Navy 'issue' armchairs. (Wardroom.) **1970** *Globe & Mail* (Toronto) 25 Sept. 31/2 (Advt.), The comfort of hushed travel in recliner seats. **1977** E. Leonard *Unknown Man No. 89* xx. 192 Jay Walk, in his desk-chair recliner, had his shoes off. **1978** *Lancashire Life* Oct. 115/2 Buoyant Upholstery have just introduced the Wellbeck Chameleon range of fourteen interchangeable items, made up of Chesterfields, unit pieces, settees, recliner chair, wing chair, [etc.].

reclining (rɪ'klaɪnɪŋ), *ppl. a.* [f. as prec. + -ing².] That reclines, in senses of the vb.

reclining dial, plane (see quots. 1668–9, 1797).

1668 Moxon *Mech. Dial.* 7 Direct Reclining Planes, which lean from you. **1669** Sturmy *Mariner's Mag.* vii. xiii. 21 Reclining..Planes have their Bases or Horizontal Diameters lying in the Horizontal Diameter of some Azimuth. **1726** Leoni tr. *Alberti's Archit.* II. 81/1 This Window..must either be higher than it is broad, or else on the contrary broader than it is high, which last sort is called a reclining window. **1748** Thomson *Cast. Indol.* i. xxxvi, Reclining lovers, in the lonely dale, Pour'd forth at large the sweetly-tortur'd heart. **1797** *Encycl. Brit.* (ed. 3) V. 787/1 Those dials..are called inclining or reclining dials, according as their planes make acute or obtuse angles with the horizon. **1807** J. E. Smith *Phys. Bot.* 118 *Reclinatus*, reclining, curved towards the ground, as in *Ficus*, the Fig. **1883** L. M. Mitchell *Hist. Anc. Sculpture* xix. 354 By a recent correction in the placing of the reclining figure..lines of unexpected beauty in the composition of Pheidias have been revealed to us. **1966** D. Hall *Henry Moore* iv. 72 He exploited his stone-carving breakthrough in a series of female figures: upright busts, reclining figures.

So **re'clining** *vbl. sb. attrib.* in **reclining-board,** = back-board 4 (Ogilvie 1882); **reclining-chair,** a chair whose back can be adjusted to any required angle (Knight *Dict. Mech.* 1875); **reclining seat,** a seat which may be adjusted to a reclining position, esp. in a motor vehicle or aeroplane.

These combinations can equally be seen as examples of the *ppl. a.*

1863 Geo. Eliot *Let.* 26 Dec. (1956) IV. 124 Another munificent friend has given me the most splendid *reclining chair conceivable. **1907** *Yesterday's Shopping* (1969) 276/2 Improved portable suspensory Reclining Chair, with leg rest in canvas. **1976** B. Bova *Multiple Man* (1977) xiv. 148 We sat side by side in the most luxurious reclining chairs I'd ever flown in. **1943** S. C. Menefee *Assignment: U.S.A.* i. v. 117 She settled her ample proportions into the *reclining seat next to me. **1974** 'D. Craig' *Dead Liberty* xix. 108 Boxanford arranged..to change his car... He wanted reclining seats.

reclis, variant of rekels, incense. *Obs.*

reclivate ('rɛklɪveɪt), *a. Entom. rare.* [f. late L. *reclīv-is* or *recliv-us* bending backwards + -ate.] Forming a double or sigmoid curve.

1825 Say in *Wks.* (1859) II. 245 Spot on the vertex..and reclivate line on the hemelytra. *Ibid.* 246 A rufous, somewhat reclivate line.

†reclose, *v.*¹ *Obs.*⁻¹ [ad. L. *reclūs-* (see recluse *v.*), after *close*.] *trans.* To shut up, confine.

1382 Wyclif *Wisd.* xvii. 15 Theraftir if any of hem hadde falle doun, he was kept in prisoun, with oute iren, reclosid.

reclose (riː'kləʊz), *v.*² [re- 5 a.] To close again.

a. *intr.*

1541 R. Copland *Guydon's Quest. Chirurg.* Mj, To kepe the lyppes of woundes open..that the rottennes reclose nat but come out. **1846** Lytton *New Timon* (ed. 3) 203 The winds leap forth, the cloven deeps reclose. **1894** A. Webster *Mother & Dau.* (1895) 19 The broad blue lightnings flamed the sky;..And sudden dark re-closed when it went by.

b. *trans.*

1661 Hickeringill *Jamaica* 41 Arguments, that perswaded the Spaniard to reclose and dam up a rich Silver Vein. *a* **1711** Ken *Sion* Poet. Wks. 1721 IV. 402 My broken Heart Love fill'd, and Love reclos'd. **1725** Pope *Odyss.* i. 552 The silver ring she pull'd, the door reclosed. **1822** Byron *Werner* iii. iv, You reclosed the panel? **1885** *Truth* 28 May 844/1 The receiver of it reclosed the envelope.

reclothe (riː'kləʊð), *v.* [re- 5 a.] *trans.* To clothe again; to provide again with clothing.

1632 Lithgow *Trav.* x. 467 They recloathing my..cold trembling body. **1826** Miss Mitford *Village* Ser. ii. (1863) 364 Not sufficient to reclothe herself and her half-naked children. **1865** *Pall Mall G.* 4 Aug. 10/1 The other tramps had carried off all their clothes, and the workhouse authorities had no choice but to reclothe them.

transf. and *fig.* **1822** Lamb *Elia* Ser. ii. *Th. on Bks. & Reading*, A tithe of that good leather would comfortably reclothe my shivering folios. **1842** Tennyson *Day-Dream, Sleeping Pal.* i, The varying year with blade and sheaf Clothes and re-clothes the happy plains. **1872** Whittier *Brew. of Soma* xii, Reclothe us in our rightful mind.

Hence **re'clothing** *vbl. sb.*

1846 Trench *Mirac.* xxxi. (1862) 447 The image of the reclothing of the bare and withered fig-tree with leaf and bud. **1887** Moloney *Forestry W. Afr.* 242 Judicious reclothing with vegetation.

reluce, obs. form of recluse *a.*

†re'clude, *v. Obs.* [ad. L. *reclūdĕre* to open; later, to shut up: see re- and close *v.*]

1. *trans.* To open (a gate, etc.).

c **1420** *Pallad. on Husb.* i. 1069 Hem, softe enclude, And towarde nyght her yatis thou reclude. **1665** G. Harvey *Disc. Plague* xiv. (1673) 145 The Ingredients..reclude oppilations, mundifie the blood.

2. a. To shut up (a thing or person); to close.

1576 Baker *Jewell of Health* 169 Let it be recluded in the pitte of a penitent breast. **1578** Banister *Hist. Man* i. 22 Neyther doth Os sacrum obscurely reclude, but playne and largely open and discouer the passages. **1651** *Raleigh's Ghost* 243 The meanes for the wicked to their salvation should be recluded and shut up. [*a* **1843** Southey *Comm.-pl. Bk.* (1850) III. 401 A King and Queen recluded.]

b. To shut (a person) off *from* a thing. Also *refl.*

1598 in *Archpriest Controv.* (Camden) I. 51 You are not recluded from the world to disquiett the world. **1600** W. Watson *Decacordon* (1602) 87 The party..is recluded from the speech of any body but the sayd father for a certaine time. **1657** W. Morice *Coena quasi Κοινή* Def. xv. 208 Eastern people..think it conduceth to the Majesty of their Kings to be recluded and shut up from publick intercourse. **1911** M. Beerbohm *Zuleika Dobson* ii. 22 No woman who knows that of herself can be rightly censured for not recluding herself from the world.

3. To shut out (a thing). *rare*⁻¹.

1634 W. Tirwhyt tr. *Balzac's Lett.* (vol. I.) 359 To small purpose had they recluded the power of strangers.

Hence **†re'cluded** *ppl. a. Obs.*⁻¹

1597 A. M. tr. *Guillemeau's Fr. Chirurg.* 15 b/2 The recluded Parrates Bille.

†re'cludent, *a. Obs.*⁻¹ [ad. L. *reclūdent-em*, pr. pple. of *reclūdĕre*: see prec.] Of a muscle: That opens (the eye).

1684 tr. *Bonet's Merc. Compit.* xiv. 466/1 A Wound inflicted from the Eye-brows downwards hinders..not the opening of the Eyes: for by such a Wound the Fibres of the Recludent or Elevating Muscle..are not cut asunder.

reclus, obs. form of recluse *a.*

reclusage. *rare.* [a. OF. *reclusage* (Godef.): see recluse *a.* + -age.] **†1.** A hermitage, place of seclusion. (Only in Caxton.) *Obs.*

1480 Caxton *Ovid's Met.* xii. viii, Ulixes bethought hym ..that Achylles was in some reclusage. **1483** —— *Gold. Leg.* 111 b/1 He fledde the world and entred into a reclusage.

2. Retirement, reclusion.

1960 *Times Lit. Suppl.* 18 Nov. 742/3 For more than half a lifetime..he had enjoyed a voluntary reclusage on the Riviera di Levante.

recluse (rɪ'kluːs), *a.* and *sb.* Also 3–4 reclus, 6 reluce. [ad. F. *reclus, recluse*, pa. pple. of *reclure*:—L. *reclūdĕre* to shut up, reclude.]

A. *adj.* 1. Of persons: Shut up, secluded from society, esp. as a religious discipline.

a. In predicative use, or placed after the sb.

a **1225** *Ancr. R.* 378 Nes he him sulf reclus iðe meidenes wombe? **1387** Trevisa *Higden* (Rolls) VII. 81 He lerned of a man recluse þat in Wlcanes potte..þe soules of dede men were tormented. **1390** Gower *Conf.* I. 254 An holy clerk reclus, Which full was of gostli vertus. *c* **1491** *Chast. Goddes Chyld.* 22 Some tyme thei wylle goo on pylgremage, somtyme they wyll be recluse. **1581** Mulcaster *Positions* iv. (1887) 15 As most beseeming him, which must liue among many and neuer be recluse. *c* **1610** Beaum. & Fl. *Philaster* i. i, A virtuous court: to which your great ones may..retire, and live recluse. **1662** Pepys *Diary* 24 May, How recluse the Queene hath ever been, and all the voyage never come upon the deck. **1698** Fryer *Acc. E. India & P.* 156 The Women, both White and Black, are kept recluse. **1751** Johnson *Rambler* No. 89 ¶3 It..frequently happens that the most recluse are not the most vigorous prosecutors of study. **1781** Cowper *Conversat.* 801, I have lived recluse in rural shades. **1868** Masson *Mem.* in *Goldsm.'s Wks.* (Globe) p. xxxvii, Young was dying; Gray was recluse and indolent.

b. In attributive use (usually denoting attachment to seclusion or retirement).

1634 Habington *Castara* i. (Arb.) 18 The Vowes of recluse Nuns, and th' An'thrits prayer. **1710** Steele *Tatler* No. 139 ¶4 Falling into the Error which recluse Men are very subject to. **1769** Robertson *Chas. V*, xi. III. 340 He acquired..the qualities and passions of a recluse ecclesiastick. **1865** Merivale *Rom. Emp.* lxiv. VIII. 114 The fashion set by princes has more influence..than the example of recluse philosophers. **1891** E. Peacock *N. Brendon* l. 315, I care much more now for our recluse friend than I did before.

absol. **1726** Leoni tr. *Alberti's Archit.* I. 85/1 To disorder, or pollute the minds of the Recluse. *Ibid.*, Those Recluse who to Religion join the study of the liberal Arts.

†c. Shut off, retired *from* company, etc. *Obs.*

1708 J. Philips *Cyder* i. 23, I all the live-long Day Consume in Meditation deep, recluse From human Converse. **1789** *Triumphs Fortitude* I. 159, I resolved to keep myself as recluse from company as I could during my short stay.

2. Of one's life, condition, etc.: Characterized by seclusion or close retirement.

c **1645** Howell *Lett.* (1688) II. 376 One who by this recluse passive Condition hath his share of this hideous Storm. **1673** *Lady's Call.* i. v. §28 Devotion in a Cloister is as recluse as the Votary. **1709** *Tatler* No. 32 ¶4 A Lady who had writ a fine Book concerning the Recluse Life. **1797** Holcroft tr. *Stolberg's Trav.* (ed. 2) II. xl. 51 Their mode of living is exceedingly recluse and severe. **1849** Grote *Greece* ii. xlvi. (1862) IV. 109 His private habits were sober and recluse. **1867** Barry *Sir C. Barry* x. 329 Few men had less of a recluse character.

3. a. Of places: Secluded, hidden from observation, solitary. Now *rare*.

1652 J. Wright tr. *Camus' Nat. Paradox* vii. 158 You might rather wonder how the news..should penetrate my Ears in that recluse Mansion. **1708** *Brit. Apollo* No. 26. 3/2 Those Limpid Streams retrieve their Heats, From Earth's recluse Sulphureous Seats. **1782** *Contin. Sterne's Sent. Journ., Tuileries* (1784) 234 The most recluse retreats..are constantly chosen for these oblations. **1825** Cobbett *Rur. Rides* (1885) II. 1, I never saw any inhabited places more recluse than these. **1825–9** Mrs. Sherwood *Lady of Manor* III. xxii. 332 Though it lay quite as deep in the clay as Stanbrook Court, it was, in reality, less recluse.

†b. Of things, actions, etc.: Hidden, secret, private. *Obs.*

1660 Ingelo *Bentiv. & Ur.* ii. vi. (1682) 138 Having made their more recluse Mysteries the exercise of all Unnatural Lust. **1673** *Phil. Trans.* VIII. 6132 Of the Sensible Natures of Vegetables, as also of their more recluse Faculties and Powers. **1713** Derham *Phys.-Theol.* iv. iii. 129 These recluse Parts..ministring to this Sense of Hearing. **1773–83** Hoole *Orl. Fur.* xliii. 60 When a husband, with too curious eye, Into his wife's recluser deeds would pry.

†c. Of words or ideas: Recondite. *Obs. rare.*

1748 Hartley *Observ. Man* i. i. 39 This is a mere Supposition, and that of a very recluse Nature. *a* **1770** Akenside *Let.* Wks. (1867) p. lxxxiv, Systems [is] too recluse and subtle a word.

B. *sb.* 1. a. A person shut up from the world for the purpose of religious meditation; a monk, hermit, anchorite or anchoress, *spec.* one who remains perpetually shut up in a cell under a vow of strict seclusion. b. One who lives a retired life, one who mixes little with society.

a **1225** *Ancr. R.* 10 þe latere dole of his sawe limpeð to recluses. **1395** *E.E. Wills* 7, I bequethe to the Reclus frere Thomas..xl. s. *c* **1425** *St. Christina* xxvi. in *Anglia* VIII. 129/25 She dwellid nyne ȝeere with a womman recluse.. Of þe whiche recluse I hadde many thinges þat I haue writen. **1470–85** Malory *Arthur* xiii. xvii, This Iustes was done to fore the hermytage where a recluse dwelled. **1574** tr. *Littleton's Tenures* 92 If there be a recluse that he may not because of his order go out of his house. **1632** Massinger & Field *Fatal Dowry* iii. i, I will not consent to have you live Like to a recluse in a cloister. **1703** Maundrell *Journ. Jerus.* (1732) 71 The dayly employment of these Recluses is to trim the lamps. **1750–1** Mrs. Delany *Autobiog. & Corr.* (1861) III. 22 He is..a plain young man, a recluse in his nature, and very ignorant of the world. **1837** Emerson *Addr., Amer. Schol.* Wks. (Bohn) II. 180 There goes in the world a notion, that the scholar should be a recluse, a valetudinarian. **1874** H. R. Reynolds *John Bapt.* iii. §2. 152 He was clothed with the rough hairy garment worn by the recluse and the prophet.

transf. **1746–7** Hervey *Medit.* (1748) II. 59 The sprightly Morning, which awakens other Animals into Joy, administers no Pleasure to this gloomy Recluse [the owl].

c. *Comb.*, as **recluse-like** adj.

1946 E. Blunden *Shelley* xvii. 213 The fashionable round ..did not prevent her from falling under the spell of the recluse-like Shelley.

†2. What is shut up; contents, store. *Obs. rare.*

c **1420** *Pallad. on Husb.* xii. 308 Baskettis of seggis me may vse, So they be thykke, and saue ther recluse. *c* **1430** Lydg. *Min. Poems* (Percy Soc.) 51 Of crosse nor pile there is no recluse, Prynte nor impressioun in all thy seyntwarye.

†3. a. A place of seclusion. *Obs.*

1621 Brathwait *Nat. Embassie* (1877) 88 Hast thou..no Refuge nor no Recluse for thy hope? **1630** —— *Eng. Gentlem.* (1641) 156 Let our bosome (the recluse of secrets) be like the Lions den in the Apologue. **1658** Slingsby *Diary* (1836) 208 Privacy,..the only recluse of safety,..may become as dangerous as a place of agency. **1772** J. Wise *Churches' Quarrel Espoused* 65 It is certain, that the church of Christ is the..sacred recluse and peculiar assilum of religion.

†b. A reservoir for water. *Obs.*⁻¹

Cf. med.L. *reclausa* in the same sense (Du Cange).

1593 Nashe *Christ's T.* 23 b, Heere ebbe the spring-tide of my Teares, Eyes from this present, prepare your selues to be recluses.

†4. Reclusion; retirement. *Obs.*⁻¹

1665 Wither *Lord's Prayer* Preamble, This made me desirous to spend those days of recluse..in what might glorifie God.

†re'cluse, *v. Obs.* [f. L. *reclūs-*, ppl. stem of *reclūdĕre*: see prec.] *trans.* To shut up, seclude.

1382 Wyclif *Lev.* xiii. 4 The preest shal recluse hym seuen daies. **1393** Langl. *P. Pl.* C. v. 116 Til..religious out-ryders [be] reclused in here cloistres. **1450** *Rolls of Parlt.* V. 195/2 The Priours or Convent of the Howses and places.., in which eny Nonnes are reclused. **1526** *Pilgr. Perf.* (W. de W. 1531) 99 b, Beynge reclused or shut vp in a derke prison. *a* **1631** Donne *Annunciation & Passion* Poems (1654) 333 She sees..the Virgin mother stay Reclus'd at home. **1657** Trapp *Comm. Neh.* vi. 10 A house he had in the Temple: and there he had reclused and shut up himself. **1713** C'tess Winchelsea *Misc. Poems* 95 To Desarts banish'd, or in Cells reclus'd.

†re'clused, *ppl. a.*¹ *Obs.* [f. prec. + -ed¹.] Shut up, secluded, retired.

1613 Donne *Eclogue* 48 So reclus'd hermits oftentimes do know More of heaven's glory, than a worldling can. **1627** E. F. *Hist. Edw. II* (1680) 8 This kind of reclus'd behaviour makes him unpleasant. **1653** A. Wilson *Jas. I* 231 The fained and cousening Miracles of reclused holiness.

Hence **†re'clusedness.** *Obs. rare*⁻¹.

1653 A. Wilson *Jas. I* 72 His health was impaired, which he imputed to his reclusednesse, and want of Air.

†reclused, *ppl. a.*² *Obs.*⁻⁰ [f. L. *reclūs-us*, pa. pple. of *reclūdĕre* to open + -ed¹.] (See quot.)

1623 Cockeram ii, Opened, *reclused*.

reclusely (rɪ'kluːslɪ), *adv.* Now *rare.* [f. recluse *a.* + -ly².] In a recluse manner.

1673 R. Head *Canting Acad.* 182 If you jest and mean loosly, Though ne'r so reclusely. **1748** H. Walpole *Let.* 3 Sept., From a melancholy turn, from living reclusely,..he [Gray] never converses easily. **1794** W. Taylor in *Monthly Rev.* XV. 22 Ida, reclusely brought up by a most worthy man. *a* **1806** H. K. White *Clifton Gr.* 251 In yon hamlet's solitary shade, Reclusely dwelt the far-famed Clifton maid.

recluseness (rɪˈkluːsnɪs). [f. RECLUSE *a.* + -NESS.] The state of being recluse; reclusion.
1654–66 EARL ORRERY *Parthen.* (1676) 375 Why did he impose on himself so strict a penance as a three years recluseness? **1698** FRYER *Acc. E. India & P.* 394 The Recluseness of their Condition is such [etc.]. **1809** PINKNEY *Trav. France* 190 [A road] which by its recluseness and solitude seemed to lead us into the recesses of the country. **1881** MASSON *De Quincey* iv. 36 This recluseness was not owing to the extreme necessity of economy.

reˈclusery. [f. RECLUSE *sb.* + -ERY. Cf. *nunnery*.] A residence for recluses.
1881 T. E. BRIDGETT *Hist. Holy Eucharist* II. 194 The more common ankerhold or reclusery was a small house of one or two cells.

reclusion (rɪˈkluːʒən). Also 5 recluc-. [ad. L. *reclūsiōn-em*, n. of action f. *reclūdere* to RECLUDE. Cf. F. *reclusion* (17th c. in Hatz.-Darm.).]
1. a. The action of shutting up, or fact of being shut up, in seclusion; a state of retirement.
c **1400** LOVE *Bonavent. Mirr.* v. (Brasenose MS.) þis one benefece of so longe reclucioun for oure sake. **1600** W. WATSON *Decacordon* (1602) 87 Vpon his first reclusion the father .. giueth him a meditation to study vpon. **1670** G. H. *Hist. Cardinals* III. II. 275 Thus Gregory the 14th. was chosen, after .. two whole months reclusion of the Conclave. **1727–41** CHAMBERS *Cycl.* s.v., The bishop having harangued the people in praise of the new recluse, .. conducted her processionally to her reclusion. **1824** SOUTHEY *Bk. of Ch.* (1841) 194 Reclusion for the purpose of religious meditation, was the object of the earlier religious orders. **1908** E. WHARTON *Hermit & Wild Woman* 33 In a life of penance and reclusion her eyes might be opened to her iniquity. **1971** T. MERTON *Contemplation in World of Action* II. v. 300 It must not be imagined that these problems of order rose exclusively from a lack of legislation and from a too-free development of 'charisms' of pilgrimage, hermit-solitude or reclusion.
b. The fact of being shut up as a prisoner, esp. in solitary confinement. (Usu. after F. *reclusion.*)
1872 *Daily News* 13 Aug., A promise that the five years' 'reclusion' shall be changed to five years' simple imprisonment. **1886** STEVENSON *Kidnapped* 290 We could no doubt find some men of the *Covenant* who would swear to your reclusion.
2. A place of religious retreat or seclusion.
1797 SOUTHEY *Lett. Journ. Spain* (1808) I. 116 He was obliged to establish Convents and Reclusions, as they were called, in other parts.

reclusive (rɪˈkluːsɪv), *a.* [f. as RECLUSE *v.* + -IVE.] Marked by reclusion or retirement. Now freq. of persons.
1599 SHAKS. *Much Ado* IV. i. 244 You may conceale her .. In some reclusiue and religious life, Out of all eyes. **1661** R. DAVENPORT *City-Nightcap* IV. 45 You shall unto the Monasterie of Matrons, And spend your daies reclusive. **1850** O. WINSLOW *Inner Life* 207 The gospel of Jesus is not reclusive or selfish. **1965** *Listener* 16 Sept. 426/2 A reclusive New Englander who wrote but did not flourish in the literary climate of Transcendentalism. **1971** *Wall St. Jrnl.* 13 Aug. 1/6 Esquire .. ran a cover showing the reclusive Howard Hughes. **1979** *Daily Tel.* 1 Sept. 21/3 Equal partnership deals are not common in the business career of the reclusive Mr Ludwig.
Hence **reˈclusively** *adv.*, in the manner of a recluse; **reˈclusiveness.**
1895 TH. WATTS in *19th Cent.* Feb. 235 Her reclusiveness shut her in and away from many people. **1925** C. CONNOLLY *Let.* 25 Jan. in *Romantic Friendship* (1975) 56 The last week of Minehead .. left me with an intense reclusiveness. **1963** *Punch* 13 Feb. 249/1 His life was spent uneventfully, reclusively almost. **1976** *National Observer* (U.S.) 14 Feb. 15/2 My symptom was reclusiveness. **1979** *N. & Q.* June 240/2 W. S. W. was both a Scholar and subsequent Fellow of Trinity College, Cambridge, where he lived reclusively.

reclusory (rɪˈkluːsərɪ). [ad. med.L. *reclūsōrium* (Du Cange), f. *reclūdere* to RECLUDE.] The cell of a recluse. (Cf. RECLUSERY.)
1821 BAYLEY *Tower Lond.* 129 [The cell] .. was inhabited by a recluse... In one place it is noticed as the reclusory, or hermitage of St. Peter.

reclyne, obs. form of RECLINE *v.*

recoaguˈlation. *rare*⁻¹. [RE- 5 a.] A second coagulation.
1661 BOYLE *Phys. Ess., Hist. Firmness* Wks. 1772 I. 423 This salt we speak of, being .. dissolved in a convenient quantity of water, does upon its re-coagulation so dispose of the aqueous particles among its own saline ones, that [etc.].

recoal (riːˈkəʊl), *v.* [RE- 5 a.] **a.** *trans.* To supply with fresh coal. **b.** *intr.* Of a steamship: To take in a fresh supply of coal.
1884 *Pall Mall G.* 13 Nov. 5/1 The necessity for frequent recoaling seriously reduces her speed. **1887** PROCTOR *Chance & Luck* 212 My fire, which in the meantime must very nearly have gone out, had been recoaled. **1895** *N. Amer. Rev.* Mar. 375 Such vessels can accomplish about 6,000 miles without recoaling.

reˈcoast, *v. trans.* [RE- 5 a.] To coast again.
1775 R. CHANDLER *Trav. Asia M.* (1825) I. 55 We left this lively scene with regret, and re-coasting the rough European shore, landed not far from the town.

recoat (riːˈkəʊt), *v.* [RE- 5 a.] *trans.* To coat afresh (with paint or the like).
1876 'MARK TWAIN' *Tom Sawyer* iii, She found the entire fence .. not only whitewashed but elaborately coated and recoated. **1882** *Pall Mall G.* 26 June 8/1 She will be placed in the vacated dock .. for slight recoating.

recock (riːˈkɒk), *v.* [RE- 5 a.] *trans.* To cock (a firearm) again. Also *absol.*
1797 *Encycl. Brit.* (ed. 3) I. 337/2 By re-cocking the piece, another discharge may be made. **1851** MAYNE REID *Rifle Rangers* ii. 27, I drew a pistol .. and fired... His comrade, hearing me re-cock, took to his heels. **1868** *Rep. to Govt. U.S. Munitions War* 54 The pulling out of the trigger-guard will then re-cock the piece.

recoct (rɪˈkɒkt), *v.* [f. L. *recoct-*, ppl. stem of *recoquĕre*: see RE- and COOK *v.*] *trans.* To boil or cook a second time; also *fig.* to vamp or furbish up anew. Hence **reˈcocted** *ppl. a.*
1562 BULLEYN *Bk. Simples* 85 b, Recocted or two times sodden whay, is the best whay. **1605** L. HUTTEN *Aunswere* 126 Your olde Crambe of *Religionis ergo*, so often recocted. **1657** TOMLINSON *Renou's Disp.* 542 If it yet appear too fluid, recoct it. **1687** A. LOVELL tr. *Bergerac's Com. Hist.* 64 So that the Sun recocted it once more. **1836** LANDOR *Peric. & Asp.* xlviii. Wks. 1853 II. 373/2 He picked up all the arrows that were shot against him, recocted all the venom of every point [etc.].
So **reˈcoction.** (Cf. *decoction.*)
1749 *Phil. Trans.* XLVI. 185 Its Recoction or Annealing deprives it of this Brittleness. **1847** in WEBSTER, and in recent Dicts.

recode (riːˈkəʊd), *v.* [RE- 5 a.] *trans.* To put into another or different code; *spec.* in *Psychol.*, to rearrange mentally (information presented by a problem, situation, or test).
1951 [implied in RECODING *vbl. sb.*]. **1957** J. S. BRUNER *Contemp. Approaches in Psychol.* 59 All the measurements can be recoded into a simple rule. **1964** M. MCLUHAN *Understanding Media* (1967) viii. 90 The human ear can be compared to a radio receiver that is able to decode electro-magnetic waves and recode them as sound. **1971** *Jrnl. Gen. Psychol.* LXXXV. 213 There are often possibilities for *S* to encode the information in one of the languages not intended or to recode the information in a second language. **1977** J. M. SCANDURA *Problem Solving* vii. 301 In order to recover the original elements .. they must be recoded. *Ibid.* 309 Extraneous processes may reduce memory load .. where two digits are recoded .. as one unit.
So **reˈcoding** *vbl. sb.*
1951 G. A. MILLER *Lang. & Communication* xi. 233 The task also illustrates something we can call recoding, and in many problems it can be shown that the restructuring process is, in whole or in part, a matter of coding the information in a new form. **1957** J. S. BRUNER *Contemp. Approaches to Cognition* 60 Once a system of recoding has been worked out whereby information is condensed into more generic codes, the problem of mastery becomes one of mastering the recoding system. **1964** J. Z. YOUNG *Model of Brain* ii. 21 The conversion from one sort of physical system to another is called re-coding (e.g. speech into writing). Information is thus that feature of the system that remains invariant under re-coding. **1970** B. MILNER in Pribram & Broadbent *Biol. of Memory* 42 This maze has 28 choice-points, so that, even with recoding, the sequence of turns to be remembered cannot be encompassed within the span of immediate memory. **1977** J. M. SCANDURA *Problem Solving* vii. 304 Even on simple tests of memory span, recoding and rehearsal processes tend to be highly dependent on individual preference.

recoeure, obs. form of RECOVER *v.*¹

reˈcogitate, *v. rare.* [f. ppl. stem of L. *recōgitāre* to think over (med.L., to change one's mind), or f. RE- + COGITATE *v.*] †**a.** *intr.* To reconsider, change one's mind. *Obs.* **b.** To think over again.
1651 C. CARTWRIGHT *Cert. Relig.* II. 29 He cites Origen saying, that Christ did in those words recall his desire, and as it were recogitate. **1656** BLOUNT *Glossogr.*, *Recogitate*, to weigh and consider in minde earnestly, to think and think again upon some thing. **1920** in WEBSTER. **1932** H. CRANE *Let.* ? Feb. (1965) 401, I had to spend the rest of the day and evening cogitating and recogitating.
So **recogiˈtation** [L. *recōgitātio*]. ? *Obs.*
1615 JACKSON *Creed* IV. viii. §3 So deeply did the recogitation of what he had .. heard sink into this true patriot's heart. **1624** GATAKER *Transubst.* 218 A recogitation or a serious consideration and faithfull meditation.

recogneis, -nis, obs. Sc. ff. RECOGNIZE *v.*¹

recognition (rɛkəgˈnɪʃən). Also 6 -ni(s)cyon. [ad. L. *recognitiōn-em*, n. of action f. *recognit-*, *recognōscĕre* to RECOGNOSCE. Cf. F. *récognition* (15th c.).] The act of recognizing.
†**1.** *Sc. Law.* The resumption of lands by a feudal superior for any reason, in later use *spec.* on account of unwarranted alienation by the vassal. *Obs.*
1473 *Acc. Ld. High Treas. Scot.* (1877) I. 47 Lettres vndir the priue sele for the recognicione of the Bischop of Sanctandros temporalite. **1578** *Reg. Privy Council Scot.* Ser. I. II. 693 All recognicionis, dispositionis of landis falling be forfaltour or last air. **1597** SKENE *De Verb. Sign.* s.v., Recognition of landes is commonly vsed in the law, and practicque of this realme. **1666–88** DALLAS *Syst. Stiles* (1697) 253 Whilks Lands .. fell and became in Our Hands, .. as Superior and Over-lord, by reason of Recognition. **1747** *Act 20 Geo. II*, c. 50 §1 The Tenure of Lands in .. Scotland, by Ward Holding, and the consequences of the same, being the Casualties of Ward Marriage and Recognition. *a* **1765** ERSKINE *Inst. Law Scot.* II. v. §10 Recognition, though ranked by some writers among the casualties of superiority, was indeed a total forfeiture of the fee.
†**2. a.** The action of reviewing or revising; revision, recension. *Obs.*
1568 ABP. PARKER *Corr.* (Parker Soc.) 338, I trust by comparison of divers translations .. will appear .. the circumspection of all such as have travailed in the recognition. [**1862** *Quaritch's Catal.* Dec., By Edmund Becke after Taverner's recognition, with prologues to the New Testament by William Tindale.]
b. *Hist.* The form of inquest by jury in use in England under the early Norman kings.
The chief source for the use of the term is Glanvil *De Legibus Angliæ* (II. vii, etc.), from which the earliest quot. is ultimately derived.
1609 SKENE *Reg. Maj.* 58 It rests that we speik of divers recognitions. 3. Some recognition is called of mortancestrie. **1628** COKE *On Litt.* 158 b, Recognition is a serious acknowledgement or opinion upon such matters of fact as the jurors shall have in charge. **1863** H. COX *Instit.* II. iii. 346 The new method of inquiry, which was called a recognition of assize. **1876** FREEMAN *Norm. Conq.* V. xxiv. 453 The greatest step made at any one time in the developement of the Jury system was when the practice of recognition was organised by the great Assize of Henry the Second.
†**3.** Knowledge or consciousness. *Obs.*
1526 *Pilgr. Perf.* (W. de W. 1531) 167 b, Euer hauyng recognicyon or remembraunce of his owne vnworthynesse. **1547** BOORDE *Brev. Health* 73 b, Sensualitie, the whiche can neuer be subdued without the recognition and knowledge of a mannes selfe.
4. a. The action of acknowledging as true, valid, or entitled to consideration; formal acknowledgement as conveying approval or sanction of something; hence, notice or attention accorded to a thing or person.
1597 HOOKER *Eccl. Pol.* V. xx. §9 A fourth kind of publick reading, whereby the lives of such saints had, at the time of their yearly memorials, solemn recognition in the church of God. **1622** BACON *Hen. VII* 11 He did not presse to haue the Act penned by way of Declaration or Recognition of right. **1766** BLACKSTONE *Comm.* II. xxvi. 407 Much may be also collected from the several legislative recognitions of copyrights. **1788** GIBBON *Decl. & F.* xlix. V. 99 Even this title was a recognition of the six preceding assemblies. **1853** KANE *Grinnell Exp.* xxii. (1856) 170 He was told that his nephew's claim to the service had received a recognition. **1876** MOZLEY *Univ. Serm.* v. 111 The Christian recognition of the right of war was contained in Christianity's original recognition of nations.
b. The formal acknowledgement by subjects of (the title of) a sovereign or other ruler (†*esp.* of James I as King of England); *spec.* as the name of a part of the Coronation ceremony (see quot. 1902).
1558–9 *Act 1 Eliz.* c. 3 (*title*) An Acte of Recognition of the Quenes Highnes Title to the Imperyall Crowne of this Realme. **1603** *Act 1 Jas. I*, c. 1 (*title*) A moste joyfull and juste Recognition of the immediate lawfull and undoubted Succession Descent and Righte of the Crowne. **1655** CROMWELL in Stainer *Speeches* (1901) 177 From your entering into the House upon the Recognition to this very day. **1685** *Coronation Order of Jas. II* in Wickham Legge *Coronation Rec.* (1901) 293 The Recognition... The People signify their Willingness, and Joy, by loud and repeated Acclamations; crying out, God save King James. **1702** *Lond. Gaz.* No. 3804/1 The Archbishop of Canterbury .. began with the Recognition. **1727–41** CHAMBERS *Cycl.*, *Recognition* .. is particularly used in our law-books for the title of the first chapter of the Stat. i. Jac. I. **1902** EELES *Eng. Coronat. Service* 31 First comes the Recognition: the Sovereign is presented to the people by the Archbishop, and is received as such by them.
c. In international law: (see quot. 1824).
1824 MACKINTOSH *Sp. S. Amer.* Wks. 1846 III. 441 The true and legitimate sense of the word 'recognition', as a technical term of international law, is that in which it denotes the explicit acknowledgment of the independence of a country by a state which formerly exercised sovereignty over it. **1863** F. W. GIBBS *Recognition* 5.
5. The acknowledgement or admission of a kindness, service, obligation, or merit, or the expression of this in some way. Now chiefly in phr. ***in recognition of***.
1570 MARG. ASCHAM *Ded. Ascham's Scholem.* (Arb.) 16 Besechyng you .. to accept the thankefull recognition of me and my poore children. **1635** F. WHITE *Sabbath* (ed. 2) 86 All Christians are redeemed by Christ .. and all observe the Lord's-day in recognition of this gracious benefit. **1658** JER. TAYLOR *Let.* in *12th Rep. Hist. MSS. Comm.* App. V. 5, I find .. nothing but recognitions and acknowledgment of your greatest tendernesse, wisdome and affections to her. **1675** TRAHERNE *Chr. Ethics* 417 The great part of our eternal happiness will consist in a grateful recognition .. of benefits already received. **1880** C. R. MARKHAM *Peruv. Bark* 279, I made an urgent appeal for some small grant in recognition of Weir's excellent and faithful services.
†**6.** A formal declaration, admission, or confession (of some fact). *Obs.*
1523 FITZHERB. *Surv.* 15 b, A recogniscyon of a tenaunt what he holdeth of the lorde. **1580** *Act 23 Eliz.* c. 1 §7 [He] shall uppon his Recognicion of such Submission in open Assises or Sessions .. be discharged of all .. the said Offences. **1631** *Star Chamber Cases* (Camden) 57 Sʳ Arthur Savage was this day brought to the barre .. to make his recognition of wrong donne to my Lord Falkland.
7. a. The action or fact of perceiving that some thing, person, etc., is the same as one previously known; the mental process of identifying what has been known before; the fact of being thus known or identified.
1798 WORDSW. *Tintern Abbey* 59 With many recognitions dim and faint .. The picture of the mind revives again. **1833** HT. MARTINEAU *Loom & Lugger* II. iii. 57 One of them turned .. and an immediate recognition took place. **1860** TYNDALL *Glac.* I. xxii. 157 The brown crags seemed to look at me with a kind of friendly recognition. **1866** G.

MACDONALD *Ann. Q. Neighb.* xiii. (1878) 267, I could not escape recognition. **1878** HOLBROOK *Hyg. Brain* 25 Taking recognition of Sound.

b. The action or fact of apprehending a thing under a particular category, or as having a certain character.

1881 FROUDE *Short Stud.* (1883) IV. II. vi. 249 The recognition that certain things were not true was the first step. **1884** tr. *Lotze's Metaph.* 164 They would thus only satisfy him who could content himself with the mere recognition of a state of things as unconditional matter of fact.

c. *Psychol.* In the study of thinking and memory, the mental process whereby things are identified as having been previously apprehended or as belonging to a particular known category, usu. distinguished from the process of recall.

1894 CREIGHTON & TITCHENER tr. *Wundt's Hum. & Anim. Psychol.* xx. 297 The simplest case of assimilation is the cognition of an object; the simplest case of successive association, its recognition. **1894** *Psychol. Rev.* I. 608 There were some incidental illustrations of false recognition. **1923** C. SPEARMAN *Nature of Intell.* xix. 313 Recognition..is often traceable to nothing more than an awareness of similarity. **1951** G. A. MILLER *Lang. & Communication* vi. 121 It is a general rule of verbal learning that recognition is easier than recall. **1965** E. E. HARRIS *Foundation of Metaphys.* in *Sci.* xix. 380 There are two kinds of problems ..in attacking which the cybernetic approach has been used. .. The second are problems of transmission and of recognition. **1965** K. M. SAYRE *(title)* Recognition: a study in the philosophy of artificial intelligence. *Ibid.* i. 33 The task of achieving mechanical recognition of letter-patterns brings up problems of both sorts. **1973** A. J. POMERANS tr. *Piaget & Inhelder's Memory & Intelligence* 1 It is difficult to decide whether his [*sc.* the subject's] recognition is based on the remembrance or conservation of perceptive schemata.. or whether it reflects the organization of the sense data by these schemata.

d. ***out of*** (or ***beyond***) ***recognition***, to such a degree as to be unrecognizable.

1901 G. B. SHAW *Three Plays for Puritans* 202 The world, instead of having been improved in 67 generations out of all recognition, presents, on the whole, a rather less dignified appearance. **1916** —— *Androcles & Lion* p. xli, Jesus is refined and softened almost out of recognition. **1964** M. DRABBLE *Garrick Year* ii. 33 After she was born,..things improved out of all recognition. **1977** *Rolling Stone* 5 May 30/5 Futuristic explorers..returning to their own world to find it changed beyond recognition.

8. *attrib.*, as (sense 7 a) ***recognition-call, scene***; (sense 7 c) ***recognition habit, learning, memory, schema, test, vocabulary, word***; **recognition colour, mark(ing**, a colour or marking on an animal or bird, supposed to serve as a means of recognition to others of the same species; also *transf.* in *Mil.* use; **recognition grammar** *Linguistics*, a grammar based on the analysis of given sentences in a corpus (opp. generative grammar); **recognition mark(ing** = *recognition colour* above; **recognition picketing** *U.S.*, the picketing of an employer to obtain union recognition; **recognition-service**, a church service held for the purpose of introducing a new pastor to his congregation; **recognition signal** *Mil.* (see quot. 1963).

1911 J. A. THOMSON *Biol. Seasons* II. 155 Love-calls and song probably had their roots in the simple *recognition-call or characteristic signal of the species. **1891** A. R. WALLACE *Tropical Nat.* 367 *note*, For numerous examples of *recognition-colours in birds, see *Darwinism*, pp. 217–226. **1944** *Return to Attack* (Army Board, N.Z.) 32/2 Three tanks, displaying British recognition colours, climbed the hill. **1966** A. F. R. BROWN in *Automatic Transl. of Lang.* (NATO Summer School, Venice 1962) 49 A *recognition grammar will turn out to be a thousand times more complicated than a conventional descriptive grammar. **1968** J. LYONS *Introd. Theoret. Ling.* vi. 230 We have put the categorial system in the form of a 'recognition' grammar and the 'rewrite' system in the form of a 'production' grammar. **1920** T. P. NUNN *Educ.* xiii. 169 Learning to read involves, in fact, building up *recognition-habits. **1970** M. R. AMATO *Experim. Psychol.* xii. 550 The simplest case of *recognition learning is verbal discrimination in which an arbitrarily selected 'correct' item is to be identified from an accompanying, but in-correct, item. **1896** A. R. WALLACE *Studies* (1900) I. xviii. 382 These '*recognition marks', as I have termed them, are of great use even to existing well-defined species. **1906** M. C. DICKERSON *Frog Bk.* 26 These brilliant colours..may act as recognition marks for others of the same species. **1939** A. S. PEARSE *Anim. Ecol.* (ed. 2) iii. 31 He [*sc.* E. S. Poulton] cites the conspicuous white tails of the rabbit and antelope as examples of recognition marks. **1960** M. BURTON *Wild Animals Brit. Isles* 121 A patch of white around the short tail [of the red deer] furnishes a 'recognition mark', common to most of the deer family. **1977** T. I. STORER et al. *Elements Zool.* (ed. 4) xiii. 220/2 Recognition marks and other signals are often important in intraspecific communication. **1889** A. R. WALLACE *Darwinism* viii. 220 An inspection of the figures of antelopes ..in..illustrated works will give a better idea of the peculiarities of *recognition markings than any amount of description. **1940** in *Brit. Aviation Colours of World War Two* (R.A.F. Museum Series) (1976) III. 9 *(heading)* Aircraft colouring and recognition markings. **1975** GANDER & CHAMBERLAIN *German Tanks of World War 2* vi. 53/2 Perhaps the most universally applied markings used on German tanks was the tactical national recognition marking. This was usually a black cross outlined in white. **1955** H. E. GARRETT *Gen. Psychol.* x. 396 Students do not always distinguish between those facts which should be learned for recall and those for which *recognition memory is sufficient. **1973** J. G. GREENO in B. B. Wolman *Handbk. Gen. Psychol.* viii. 150/2 The agreement between the data and the theory demonstrates that it is appropriate to analyze recognition memory in terms of a concept of trace strength. **1960** *U.S. Statutes at Large 1959* LXXIII. 542 *(heading)* Boycotts and *recognition picketing. **1962** N. S. FALCONE *Labor Law* xi. 345 Recognition picketing is generally defined as picketing an employer's establishment to force the employer to recognize and bargain with the union. **1932** T. S. ELIOT *Selected Ess.* 194 The *Recognition Scene, so important in Shakespeare's later plays. **1971** *Jrnl. Gen. Psychol.* Jan. 166 *Recognition schema operating on coded features are entirely possible. **1897** *Westm. Gaz.* 9 Nov. 9/3 The Baptist Church..where his *recognition service was held last night. **1958** P. SCOTT *Mark of Warrior* II. 149, I want you to set up your *recognition signals on the D[ropping]. Z[one]. itself. **1963** *Dict. U.S. Mil. Terms* (U.S. Dept. Defense) 180 *Recognition signal*, any prearranged signal by which individuals or units may identify each other. **1978** R. V. JONES *Most Secret War* v. 48 You have to shoot your opponent out of the ocean..if he does not make the right recognition signal. **1923** P. B. BALLARD *New Examiner* vii. 81 The third and last test was a *Recognition Test... The candidate..had to underline the one word or phrase which would make each statement true. **1966** J. M. BROWN et al. *Applied Psychol.* xii. 418 Recognition tests..were used to evaluate the memorability of advertising messages. **1966** J. DERRICK *Teaching Eng. to Immigrants* ii. 99 Most stories will contain far more material than the pupils are expected to reproduce themselves (i.e. relying on and helping to build up their 'passive' or *recognition vocabulary). **1977** P. STREVENS *New Orientations Teaching Eng.* v. 62 Recognition vocabulary..can lie outside the confines of controlled vocabulary, grammar, etc., as long as the learner understands it when he meets it. **1957** PARTRIDGE *Eng. gone Wrong* II. 44 *Monolithic*, especially perhaps in *monolithic unity*, is a *recognition-word, a keyword, a badge.

recognitive (rɪˈkɒgnɪtɪv), *a.* [ad. L. type **recognitīv-us*: see prec. and COGNITIVE.] Of or pertaining to recognition; that recognizes.

1884 TRAILL *Coleridge* ix. 165 Deeply as his criticism penetrates, it is yet loyally recognitive of the opacity of millstones. **1884** H. JENNINGS *Phallicism* Introd. 11 The Americans..wrote and published in recognitive quarters. **1930** *New Statesman* 16 Aug. 593/1 Its function appears to be mainly critical and recognitive. **1977** *Maledicta* Summer 33 The relatively passive attitude of acceptance of good or evil we call *recognitive*.

recognitor (rɪˈkɒgnɪtə(r)). Now only *Hist.* Also 6 -our. [a. med.L. *recognitor* (Bracton), agent-n. f. *recognit-*, *recognōscĕre* to RECOGNOSCE.] A member of a jury impanelled on an assize or inquest (cf. RECOGNITION 2 b).

1574 tr. *Littleton's Tenures* 78 The recognitours of the assise may say and yelde to the justices their verdite at large uppon all the matter. **1628** COKE *On Litt.* I. 253 So may he shew the Recognitors in an Assise, the view of lands in another County. **1768** BLACKSTONE *Comm.* III. xx. 297 In assises of land, where also there is..merely a question of right stated for the determination of the recognitors or jury, the tenant makes no such defence. **1819** *Edin. Rev.* XXXII. 10 Bok-land was held by the oaths of seven recognitors. **1876** FREEMAN *Norm. Conq.* V. xxiv. 452 The recognitors are not judges but witnesses, witnesses declaring their verdict from their personal knowledge.

recognitory (rɪˈkɒgnɪtərɪ), *a.* [ad. L. type **recognitōri-us*: see prec. and -ORY².] Of or pertaining to recognition or acknowledgement. Now *rare*.

1822 LAMB *Elia* Ser. I. *Dist. Corresp.*, A pun and its recognitory laugh must be co-instantaneous. **1849** KEMBLE *Saxons in Eng.* II. II. vii. (1876) 329 *note*, Probably a recognitory rent for land held under the burh or city. **1897** C. DIXON *(title)* Curiosities of Bird Life, an Account of the ..Protective and Recognitory Colours..of Birds. **1964** R. PERRY *World of Tiger* iii. 42 It is difficult to think of any recognitory purpose this marking could serve.

recogniza'bility. [f. next: see -ITY.] The quality of being recognizable.

1873 *Contemp. Rev.* XXI. 191 Starting..with this postulate, the existence and recognisability of God. **1938** [see EXTRUDER 2]. **1979** *Sci. Amer.* June 42/2 The transformation of an embryo into a fetus..is a transformation from external recognizability only as human to increasing recognizability as an emergent person.

recognizable (ˈrɛkəgnaɪzəb(ə)l), *a.* [f. RECOGNIZE *v.*¹ + -ABLE.] Capable of being recognized; that admits of recognition.

1799 WRAXALL *Mem. Crt. Berlin* II. 301 So disfigured her features, that they are no longer recognizable. **1838** POE *A. G. Pym* Wks. 1864 IV. 73 It was of singular form and character, and easily recognizable. **1861** THACKERAY *Four Georges* iv. (1862) 184, I could at this very desk perform a recognizable likeness of him. **1880** GEIKIE *Phys. Geog.* iv. 239 In many springs the proportion of dissolved gas is so small as to be hardly recognisable.

recognizably (ˈrɛkəgnaɪzəblɪ), *adv.* [f. prec. + -LY².] In a recognizable manner, perceptibly.

1840 CARLYLE *Heroes* iii. (1858) 261 No thought, word or act of man, but..works sooner or later, recognisably or irrecognisably, on all men! **1875** WHITNEY *Life Lang.* ii. 16 There is, recognizably and traceably, a time when..many of our words came into use.

recognizance (rɪˈkɒgnɪzəns, rɪˈkɒn-), *sb.* Forms: *α.* 4 reconnissaunce, 4–5 reconisaunce, -ys(s)aunce, 5–6 -isance, 6–7 -usance, (6 requynesaunce). *β.* 5–6 recognysa(u)nce, 6 -isaunce, -usance, 7 -issance, 4– recognizance, -isance. [a. OF. *recon(u)issance*, (*requenoysance*), *recognussance*, etc. (see Godef.; mod.F. *reconnaissance*), f. *recon(o)iss-ant*, pres. p. of *reconoistre* + ANCE: see RECOGNIZE *v.*¹ On the spelling and pron. cf. the note to COGNIZANCE.]

1. *Law.* A bond or obligation, entered into and recorded before a court or magistrate, by which a person engages himself to perform some act or observe some condition (as to appear when called on, to pay a debt, or to keep the peace); also, a sum of money pledged as a surety for such performance and rendered forfeit by neglect of it.

c **1386** CHAUCER *Shipman's T.* 330 He was bounden in a reconyssaunce, To paye twenty thousand sheeld anon. **1436** *Rolls of Parlt.* IV. 499/2 Bounde by a reconysaunce in youre Chauncellerye, to paye to you at certain dayes in the same recognisance specified. **1459** *Ibid.* V. 369/1 That every of the seid persones, fynde to youre Highnes sufficient suerte, by reconisauns in youre Chauncerie, of his good beryng. *c* **1500** in Arnolde *Chron.* (1811) 89 Vpon payne of forfeytour of his requynesaunce to bee payd..to yᵉ chambre of London. **1561** DAUS tr. *Bullinger on Apoc.* (1573) 193 b, They..do binde them selues to the Pope and Sea of Rome, as it were by recognisance. **1602** FULBECKE *2nd Pt. Parall.* 65 If the defendant did make a reconusance vpon statute marchant such a daie at Canterburie to the plaintife. **1660** *Trial Regic.* 35 And all those bound by Recognizance to appear, let them come forth, and give their Evidence, or else to forfeit their Recognizance. **1749** FIELDING *Tom Jones* VIII. xi, He committed him to prison, and bound Frank in a recognizance, I think they call it. **1792** BURKE *On Negro Code* Wks. IX. 296 The said Trader or Factor shall be deemed to have forfeited his recognizance. **1849** MACAULAY *Hist. Eng.* v. I. 521 Three of the peers who were thus under recognisances were Roman Catholics.

transf. **1609** J. DAVIES *Holy Roode* Wks. (Grosart) 13 Then, by Recognizance Wee'l aye be bound to praise Thee, for our parts. **1696** SOUTHERNE *Oroonoko* IV. ii, An oath is a recognisance to Heav'n, Binding us over in the courts above To plead to the indictment of our crimes.

2. Recognition or acknowledgement (of a person as holding a certain position, of a fact, duty, right, service, etc.). Now *rare*.

14.. in *Tundale's Vis.* (1843) 110 They broght hym gold ..And gaff hym..Hooly of al her hart for a reconysaunce. *a* **1450** *Knt. de la Tour* (1868) 5 Eueri tyme he awakithe, he ought to yeve God reconisaunce,..that he is his lorde, creatour, and maker. **1538** STARKEY *England* II. iii. 199 And so for the recognysance of thys superyoryte, I wold that our reame schold pay thys Peter pens. **1593** G. HARVEY *Pierce's Super.* III. 109 Some-body oweth the three-shapen Geryon a greater duty, in recognisance of his often-promised curtesies. **1659** H. L'ESTRANGE *Alliance Div. Off.* 212 The Antient form of thanksgiving, that by which special recognisance was made to God as the Creator. **1685** *Lond. Gaz.* No. 2009/3 In recognisance of your just Right and Title. **1787** ANNA SEWARD *Lett.* (1811) I. 269 His even affectionate recognizance of our youthful acquaintance. **1791** NEWTE *Tour Eng. & Scot.* 132 A recognizance of the prescriptive rights of the antient tacksmen. **1830** HERSCHEL *Stud. Nat. Phil.* 303 The recognisance of the important distinctions which appear to divide these great classes of bodies from each other. **1845** A. DUNCAN *Disc.* 175 Let us endeavour to honour it by a dutiful recognizance..of his goodness.

b. Recognition (of a person) as the same, or as having a known character. Now *rare*.

c **1489** CAXTON *Blanchardyn* 149 After their teeris and pytuable reconyssaunce were past..they taryed the space of a moneth wyth in the cyte. **1575–85** ABP. SANDYS *Serm.* (Parker Soc.) 68 Some such badge of recognisance. **1597** HOOKER *Eccl. Pol.* v. xlii. §10 They chose it to serve as their special mark of recognizance, and gave it secretly..a sinister construction. **1801** tr. *Gabrielli's Myst. Husb.* I. 164 Having waved his helmet in token of recognizance, he endeavoured by signs to convince them how much he regretted their absence. **1831** *Fraser's Mag.* III. 53 From known faces she stole away, to avoid recognizance.

3. A token, badge, emblem; a cognizance. Now only *arch.*

c **1477** CAXTON *Jason* 57 b, Fyfty thousand women.. garnisshed with pennons and recognysaunces. **1563** FOXE *A. & M.* 30/2 A girdle..hauyng vii. keies, wyth vii. seales hanging there vpon, for a recognisance or token, of his seuenfold power. **1604** SHAKS. *Oth.* v. ii. 214 That Recognizance and pledge of Loue Which I first gaue her. **1890** Æ. PRINCE *Of Joyous Gard* iv. 724 His choicest troop of barons, harnessed black, With black recognisances.

†**4. a.** Cognizance: (*a*) knowledge; (*b*) notice.

c **1450** LYDG. *Secrees* 235 Ther of to have Cleer entendement, And of scryptures Just Reconysaunce. **1716** M. DAVIES *Athen. Brit.* II. 245 As for his being the Son, either Begotten or Unbegotten, the Sabellian Hypothesis took no Recognizance of it.

†**b.** *Law.* = RECOGNITION 2 b. *Obs.*

1607 COWELL *Interpr.* s.v., If any man be attainted of disseisin..by Recognisance of Assize of nouel disseisin, the iudgement shall etc. **1706** in PHILLIPS. **1727–41** CHAMBERS *Cycl.*, *Recognizance* is also used, in our antient statutes for the verdict of the twelve jurors impanelled upon an assize.

Hence †**re'cognizance** *v.*, to recognize. *Obs.*⁻¹

1657 HEYLIN *Ecclesia Vind.* 11 The submission of the Clergy, to the said King Henry, whom they had recognizanced for their supream Head.

recognizant (rɪˈkɒgnɪzənt), *a.* [f. RECOGNIZE: cf. COGNIZANT.] That recognizes, affords recognition or acknowledgement; perceptive.

1867 E. YATES *Forlorn Hope* iii, His..stately wife might have been..a little more recognisant of the girl's charms. **1881** G. MACDONALD *Mary Marston* II. v. 69 He..went through a series of bows and smiles recognizant of favour.

†**recognizate**, *v.* *Obs. rare*⁻¹. [f. RECOGNIZE *v.*¹ + -ATE.] *trans.* = RECOGNIZE *v.*¹

1799 in *Spirit Pub. Jrnls.* III. 312 Who could have thought, he would..have deigned to demand in full assembly to be matriculated and recognizated as he has been.

So †**recognization**, recognition. *Obs. rare*$^{-1}$.
1560 in Strype *Ann. Ref.* (1709) I. xvii. 208 Against the day of ordering.., to give open recognizations to all men.

recognize ('rɛkəgnaɪz), *v.*^{1} Forms: 5 *Sc.* **racwnnis, racunnys, recognis,** (6 **-eis**); 6 **recognish(e, -yse, -yce,** 6– **recognise, -ize.** [a. OF. *reconuiss-*, *recognoiss-* etc., stem of *reconoistre* (mod.F. *reconnaître*):—L. *recognōscĕre* to RECOGNOSCE. The ending was early assimilated to that of verbs in *-ise*, *-ize*: cf. note to COGNIZE.]

†**1.** *trans. Sc. Law.* = RECOGNOSCE *v.* 4. *Obs.*
1456 *Burgh. Rec. Peebles* (1872) 117 The balyeis has racwnnis the wast land in the North Gat for faut of the Kyngis burroumallis. *c* **1470** HENRY *Wallace* III. 276 His wncle Schir Ranald may mak this band. Gyff he will nocht, racunnys all his land. **1488** *Acta Dom. Concil.* (1839) 103/1 The landis of breþirtoune.. recognist bi þe said William erle merschell for alienacioune wᵗout consent of the owrlord. **1609** SKENE *Reg. Maj.* 52 (Act Robt. III, c. 2 §3) Provyding that he doe his diligence to repledge his lands, quhilks are recognised fra his overlord.

†**2. a.** To look over again; to revise, correct, amend. *Obs.*
1534 CRANMER, etc. *Inst. Chr. Man* Pref., We do moste humbly submytte it [this treatise] to.. your maiestie, to be recognised, ouersene, and corrected. **1539** (*title*) The most sacred Bible,.. translated into English, and newly recognised with great diligence.. by Rycharde Taverner. **1570** FOXE (*title*) A Sermon of Christ crucified... Newly recognished by the Author. **1605** *Willet's Hexapla Gen.* Printer to Rdr., The author.. was absent and could not recognize what was printed. **1631** HEYLIN *St. George* 95 Being corrected first by Pope Pius Quintus, and after recognised by Clement. **1656** —— in *Extraneus Vapulans* 238 Not only to alter their opinions,.. but retract and recognize.. what they said before. **1715** M. DAVIES *Athen. Brit.* I. 25 Several times printed.. recogniz'd and amended by Joachim Camerarius,.. 1591.

†**b.** To reconnoitre. Also *absol. Obs. rare.*
1637 MONRO *Exped.* I. 9 In quartering either in village, field or Citie, he ought himselfe to recognize all avenues. **1814** SCOTT *Wav.* lxv, Neither, as he observed, was he without sentries for the purpose of recognizing.

†**c.** To go over again, to expound. *Obs.*$^{-1}$
1676 TOWERSON *Decalogue* 199 One taketh the book and readeth; another.. recogniseth that which is least understood, that is, expoundeth it.

†**3. a.** To acknowledge by admission, confession, or avowal; to admit (to oneself or another). *Obs.*
1531–2 *Act 23 Hen. VIII*, c. 6 §1 Euery obligacion.. shal be sealed with the seale of the partie.. that shall recognise or knowledge the same. **1535** in *Lett. Suppress. Monast.* (Camden) 27, I thought it expedient for you to write unto his highnes, and to recognise your offence and desire his pardon. **1570** MARG. ASCHAM *Ded. Ascham's Scholem.* (Arb.) 15 How gladly.. he vsed in hys lyfe to recognise and report your goodnesse toward hym. **1633** PRYNNE *1st Pt. Histrio-m.* 628 That the minde.. might be.. occupied in the service of God, in recognizing his benefits. *a* **1641** BP. MOUNTAGU *Acts & Mon.* (1642) 204 In honour of God, to avow his dominion paramount over all, to recognize their hold from him, their subsisting by him.

†**b.** Const. *that* or with *inf.*, expressing the fact acknowledged. *Obs.* (common in 16th c.).
1533 HENRY VIII in *St. Papers* (1830) I. II. 392 Ye duely recognysyng, that it becomethe youe not.. to enterprise any parte of your saide office. **1535** in *Lett. Suppress. Monast.* (Camden) 86 For somuche as your sayd maistership.. counselled me to recognishe the kynges highnes to be our patrone and ffounder. **1587** HOLINSHED *Chron., Irel.* II. 61/2 Some adde, that he gaue awaie his kingdoms to the see of Rome for him and his successors, recognising to hold the same of the popes in fee. **1603** DEKKER & CHETTLE *Grissil* (1893) 37, I must recognize and confesse very generouslie.. the welsh knight, making a very desperate thrust at my bosome,.. fairely mist my imbroydered Ierkin.

†**c.** Const. *for. Obs.*$^{-1}$
1550 BALE *Image Both Ch.* I. v. E v, They worshypped him.. and recognysed him for theyr mercyfull Lorde.

4. a. To acknowledge by special notice, approval or sanction; to treat as valid, as having existence or as entitled to consideration; to take notice of (a thing or person) in some way. †Also const. *to*. Also *absol.*
1548–9 (Mar.) *Bk. Com. Prayer, Private Baptism*, Whosoeuer shal confesse the, o lorde; recognise him also in thy kingdome. **1581** SAVILE *Tacitus, Hist.* (1598) 217 Liuing in some equalitie of alliance, and yet recognizing a superiority. **1705** ADDISON *Italy* 21 There are Canons Regular,.. that will by no means allow it to be the Body of the Saint, nor is it yet recognis'd by the Pope. **1771** *Junius Lett.* lxii. 291 They have been frequently recognised and admitted by parliament. **1792** *Anecd. W. Pitt* III. xlii. 125 As an Englishman.. I recognize to the Americans their supreme unalienable right in their property. **1818** JAS. MILL *Brit. India* II. v. v. 499 The majority of the Council however recognised the suspension. **1849** MACAULAY *Hist. Eng.* iii. I. 290 The only army which the law recognised was the militia. **1891** *Law Times* XCI. 225/1 A contract by a foreigner with a rebel State which has not been internationally recognised. **1974** M. PENDYRE *Breach of Security* xxiii. 132 Our customary criteria for recognition are that the government should control the whole country... But.. those raving Afro-Asian countries have recognized already. **1977** D. BEATY *Excellency* v. 66 The State Department isn't going to recognize until they *do* have the details.

b. *spec.* in *U.S.* (see quot.).
1888 BRYCE *Amer. Commw.* I. I. xiii. 187 A recent Speaker,.. universally condemned because he had usually 'recognized' (*i.e.* called on in debate) his own friends only.

c. To admit to consideration, or to a status, *as* being something.
1858 MILL *Liberty* ii. (1865) 22/2 This discipline recognises a knowledge of the enemy's case as beneficial to the teachers. **1874** GREEN *Short Hist.* v. §3. 228 Wyclif.. was.. recognized as first among the school-men of his day.

5. a. To know again; to perceive to be identical with something previously known.
1533 [see RECOGNOSCE *v.* 1]. **1656** BLOUNT *Glossogr.*, *Recognize*, to call or bring into remembrance,.. to know again. **1784** COWPER *Task* II. 454 The better hand.. aids the indebted eye With opera-glass to.. recognise the slow-retiring fair. **1801** MRS. CROFTS *Salvador* II. 228 The voice of Dermandoft was recognized by him calling his name. **1855** H. SPENCER *Princ. Psychol.* II. viii. 180 We know the object as one previously perceived.. we recognize it. **1878** BROWNING *La Saisiaz* 159 Can I.. sharpen ear to recognize Sound o'er league and league of silence?

b. To know by means of some distinctive feature; to identify from knowledge of appearance or character.
1725 POPE *Odyss.* I. 415 Then first he recognis'd the Æthereal guest. *a* **1822** SHELLEY *Triumph Life* 283 He pointed to a company, Midst whom I quickly recognised the heirs Of Cæsar's crime. **1855** BAIN *Senses & Int.* II. ii. §2 (1864) 166 The Spice Islands of the Indian Archipelago are recognised far out at sea. **1876** MOZLEY *Univ. Serm.* xiii. 240 Without being able to express accurately all we mean by love, we recognise it when we meet it.

c. To perceive clearly, realize.
1865 R. W. DALE *Disc. Spec. Occ.* (1866) vii. 241 Linnell has made us recognise a new beauty in the heather. **1879** HARLAN *Eyesight* iii. 31 Kepler first recognized the fact that the eye is a camera.

†**6.** [Cf. *v.*^{2}] **a.** To know again or further. *Obs.*$^{-1}$
1563 MAN *Musculus Commonpl.* 374 b, Wee doe defyne, that God is fyrst to be knowen by nature, Secondly to be recognised by doctrine.

†**b.** To mark or distinguish again. *Obs.*$^{-1}$
1639 FULLER *Holy War* IV. xi. (1647) 187 He required the Crosse should be restored to him again and vowed to eat no bread until he was recognized with the Pilgrims badge.

7. *Law.* **a.** *U.S. refl.* and *intr.* To enter into a recognizance. **b.** *trans.* To bind over by a recognizance. ? *Obs.*
1699 *Col. Rec. Pennsylv.* I. 563 The said Edward Robinson recognized himself in 300*l.* **1783** *Hist. Pelham* (Mass.) (1898) 250 Samuel Sampson as principal in behalf of said John recognizes to the Commonwealth in the sum of fifty pounds with sureties. **1809** TYLER *Rep.* I. 148 Mallery was recognised by Justice Seaton to appear in this court.

'**recognize** (riːkɒg'naɪz), *v.*^{2} *rare.* [RE- 5 a.] *trans.* To cognize again.
1875 LEWES *Probl. Life & Mind* Ser. I. II. III. v. 193 By the aid of Reasoning we are guided in our search, and by it re-cognize known relations under somewhat different attendant circumstances.

recognized ('rɛkəgnaɪzd), *ppl. a.* [f. RECOGNIZE *v.*^{1} + -ED^1.] Acknowledged, admitted; known.
1826 DISRAELI *Viv. Grey* III. viii, The nice etiquette, which was observed between recognised states, and non-recognised states, was really excessively amusing. **1841** W. SPALDING *Italy & It. Isl.* I. 93 The three centuries and a half during which classical paganism was the recognised religion of the empire. **1867** FREEMAN *Norm. Conq.* (1876) I. App. 547 The real and only recognized name of the united nation. **1945** *Guide to Educ. System Eng. & Wales* (Min. of Educ.) 60 *Recognised Efficient School*, independent school inspected by H.M.I.s and regarded as efficient by the Ministry. **1966** *Rep. Comm. Inquiry Univ. Oxf.* I. i. 47 We recommend that the existing university category of 'Recognized Student' should be revised. **1974** G. HUBBARD *Quaker by Convincement* IV. i. 180 Until recently we were a Recognized Meeting, part of the Preparative Meeting of Kingston upon Thames, some three miles away.

Hence '**recognizedly** *adv.*
1861 BERESF. HOPE *Eng. Cathedr. 19th C.* vi. 238 An honest adaptation of materials recognisedly in use to purposes in which their real nature was not disguised. **1875** RUSKIN *Fors Clav.* xlix. 7 The consequences of recognizedly vicious conduct.

recognizee. *Law.* ? *Obs.* Also 6 **-isee**, 7 **reconusee.** [f. as RECOGNIZE *v.*^{1} + -EE^1.] The person to whom one is bound in a recognizance.
1592 WEST *1st Pt. Symbol.* §41 G, When the moietie of the Recognisours landes bee delyuered to the Recognisee. **1602** FULBECKE *2nd Pt. Parall.* 65 So in an auoydance of a statute merchant it is a good plea to saie that part of the land is purchased by the reconusee. **1634** *Ir. Act 10 Chas. I*, Sess. III. c. 7 The said recoverers, obligees and recognizees, have been.. without remedy. **1706** in PHILLIPS (ed. Kersey; hence in later Dicts.).

recognizer ('rɛkəgnaɪzə(r)). [f. RECOGNIZE *v.*^{1} + -ER^1.] **1.** One who recognizes; †a reviser.
1608 S. WARD in *Ussher's Lett.* (1686) 25 The Recognisers of Gratian in their Annotations. **1711** SHAFTESB. *Charac.* (1737) II. III. i. 353, I find no warrant for our being such earnest Recognizers of a controverted Title. **1851** CARLYLE *Sterling* III. vii, A Poet after his sort, or recogniser and delineator of the Beautiful. **1887** BROWNING *Parleyings, Ch. Avison* viii, With form enough to know and name it by For any recognizer sure of ken And sharp of ear.

2. A device which can interpret speech by identifying the sounds and assigning them the correct meaning.
1952 *Jrnl. Acoustical Soc. Amer.* XXIV. 637 The recognizer discussed will automatically recognize telephone-quality digits spoken at normal speech rates by a single individual, with an accuracy varying between 97 and 99 percent. **1958** *Listener* 11 Dec. 984/2 One aspect of this work.. is that of Drs. Ahmed and Fatehchand.. on the direct recognition of the spoken word [by a computer]... It is safe to predict that a recognizer of 95 per cent. accuracy could be built within five years. **1973** *Physics Bull.* May 281/1 Ideally the recognizer should perform this action irrespective of the speaker and the acoustic environment in which he is speaking. This means that the machine not only has to recognize the speech sounds it receives, but it also has to ignore those facets of the signal that convey information irrelevant to the task of recognizing the speech. **1976** W. A. AINSWORTH *Mechanisms of Speech Recognition* x. 104 An automatic speech recognizer may be defined as any mechanism, other than the human auditory system, which decodes the acoustic signal produced by the human voice into a sequence of linguistic units which contain the message that the speaker wishes to convey. *Ibid.* 111 If the world of discourse of the speech recognizer is sufficiently restricted it is sometimes possible to employ semantic information to choose between words or phrases which seem equally likely on phonetic, syntactic or other grounds.

recognizing ('rɛkəgnaɪzɪŋ), *vbl. sb.* [f. as prec. + -ING^1.] The action of the vb. RECOGNIZE^1.
1611 COTGR., *Recognoissance*, a recognizing,.. acknowledgement. **1651** BAXTER *Inf. Bapt.* 115 The latter is the actuall recognizing of the Covenant. **1682** BURNET *Rights Princes* v. 187 A Recognizing of the Customs and Liberties of the King's Ancestors.

'**recognizingly**, *adv.* [f. pres. pple. of RECOGNIZE *v.*^{1} + -LY^2.] With recognition.
1854 CARLYLE in Froude *Life Lond.* (1884) I. xxii. 158, I know not if among all his 'friends' he has left one who feels more recognizingly what he was.. than I.

†**recognizon.** *Obs. rare.* [var. of RECOGNITION, after AF. sbs. in *-ison*.] Acknowledgement.
1596 BACON *Max. & Uses Com. Law* (1630) 37 The fourth Institution was that for Recognizon of the Kings bounty by euery heire succeeding his ancestor in those Knights seruice lands, the King should haue *Primer seisin* of the lands.

recognizor. *Law.* ? *Obs.* Also 6–7 **-isor**, (6 **-isour**), 7 **reconusor.** [f. as RECOGNIZE *v.*^{1} + -OR.] One who enters into a recognizance.
1531–2 *Act 23 Hen. VIII*, c. 6 §3 Everi person.. shall haue.. ayenste the said recognisour.. like processe.. & advauntage. **1602** FULBECKE *2nd Pt. Parall.* 41 The Shirife returned an Extent of the lands of the reconusor in this maner. **1628** COKE *On Litt.* 290 Neither in that case can he haue a *Scire fac'* vpon this Statute against the first Debtor or Recognizor. **1706** in PHILLIPS (ed. Kersey; hence in later Dicts.).

†**recognosce**, *v. Obs.* Chiefly *Sc.* Also 6 **-os(s.** [ad. L. *recognōscĕre*: see RE- and COGNOSCE.]
1. *trans.* To recognize, identify. *rare*$^{-1}$.
1533 BELLENDEN tr. *Livy* v. vi, Two dayis lasere war gevin to Ilk man to recognos [*v.r.* recognis] his awne gere [L. *ad recognoscendas res*].

2. To recognize or acknowledge.
1555 *Sc. Arts Mary* (1814) 506 Wᵗ quhat zele and affectioun hir subiectis ar myndit To obserue and recognoss hir said spous. **1570** BUCHANAN *Admonit.* (S.T.S.) 36 Refuse not ȝe help send to ȝow be god bot recognosce thankfullie his fauour towardis ȝow. **1644** MAXWELL *Prerog. Chr. Kings* 21 The possessour.. recognosceth or acknowledgeth.. no superiour but Almightie God. **1671** *True Nonconf.* 437 That.. the Emperour [is] Liege-lord, and all the Princes feudataires recognoscing him.

3. a. To revise, amend. *rare*$^{-1}$.
1563 WINȜET *Wks.* (S.T.S.) II. 83 In the buke of iiiixxiii quæst. sum places explanit or recognoscit.

b. To reconnoitre. *rare.* Also *absol.*
1637 MUNRO *Pract. Obs.* in *Exped.* II. 202 We must recognosce on horse or foot, according to the exployt we have before us. *Ibid.* 204 You are to recognosce both his strength and order.

4. *Sc. Law.* Of a feudal superior: To resume possession of (lands). See RECOGNITION 1 and RECOGNIZE *v.* 1.
1597 SKENE *De Verb. Sign.* s.v. *Recognition*, The superiour hes entresse and regresse to the propertie of the landes, and may recognosce the samin. **1609** —— *Reg. Maj.* 114 That Lord may not knaw, nor recognosce that land to him be law. *a* **1765** ERSKINE *Inst. Law Scot.* II. v. §10 The overlord was said to recognosce the lands by the falling of the vassal's escheat, or by the nonentity of the heir.

b. *intr.* Of lands: To return to the superior by recognition.
1752 MᶜDOUALL *Inst. Laws Scot.* II. xi. II. 155 If the vassal neglect payment of the feu-duty.., the feu becomes void by statute, and recognosces and returns to the superior. **1754** ERSKINE *Princ. Sc. Law* v. (1809) 155 By the feudal customs it was only the part aliened which recognosced.

Hence †**recog'noscence**, recognition. *Obs.*$^{-1}$
1594 LYLY *Moth. Bomb.* IV. ii, Your eloquence passes my recognoscence.

re-cohabi'tation. [RE- 5 a.] Renewed co-habitation.
1858 LD. ST. LEONARDS *Handy Bk. Prop. Law* xii. 74 In case of re-cohabitation, the property will continue to be her separate estate.

recoil (rɪ'kɔɪl, 'riː-), *sb.* Forms: 6 **recule**, 6–7 **recoyle**, (6 **requoyle**), 7 **recoyl, -coile**, 4, 7– **recoil.** [f. next; in common use only from the latter part of the 16th c. Cf. F. *recul* (16th c. in Hatz.-Darm.).]
1. The act of retreating, retiring, or going back. Now *rare*.
c **1330** *Arth. & Merl.* 9182 (Kölbing) Þer was swiche cark & swiche defoil, Þat al Leodeganes folk made recoil To Denebleise vnder þe wal. **1536** in *Hexham Priory* (Surtees) I. App. cxxix, The comissioners.. all togeders reculed back to Corbrigg, after the recule of the said Lyonell and Robert.

1577 STANYHURST *Hist. Irel.* 80/2 Hauing knowledge of Omore his recule, he pursued him. **1643** TUCKNEY *Balme of G.* 39 Especially since of late after our recoiles backwards towards Egypt, he hath been about to leade us the second time in a more direct and full way Canaan-ward. **1808** SCOTT *Marm.* VI. xxv, Life and death were in the shout, Recoil and rally, charge and rout.

fig. **1686** tr. *Chardin's Trav. Persia* 110 The Recoyl of my Fortune. **1716** M. DAVIES *Athen. Brit.* II. 214 A more retir'd recoyle and recess of their..Devotionary Calls.

2. a. The act of bounding or springing back, esp. through impact or elasticity; resilience.

1613 W. BROWNE *Brit. Past.* I. ii. 40 [The river] against a mountaine dashes, And in recoile, makes Meadowes standing plashes. **1677** HALE *Contempl.* II. Lord's Pr. 201 The reflection of thine own Glory, a recoyl of that Beam that came from thy Sun. **1831** J. HOLLAND *Manuf. Metal* I. 324 It gives a recoil to the hammer, and permits the workman to modify or shorten the stroke. **1855** H. SPENCER *Princ. Psychol.* II. xvi. 271 We strain a bow and let its recoil propel the arrow. **1877** *Encycl. Brit.* VI. 17/2 The pallet B will drive the wheel back a little, and produce what is called the recoil.

fig. **1848** MILL *Pol. Econ.* III. xii. §3 The recoil of prices after they have been raised by a spirit of speculation.

b. *fig.* of feelings; *esp.* with ref. to shrinking *from* something.

1643 MILTON *Divorce* I. x. Wks. (1851) 47 A powerfull reluctance and recoile of nature. **1801** COLERIDGE *Christabel* II. Concl., A sweet recoil of love and pity. **1833** CHALMERS *Constit. Man* (1835) I. iv. 186 With the recoil of delicacy and self-respect. **1886** RUSKIN *Præterita* I. 269 Reverent love of beauty, and indignant recoil from ugliness.

3. a. *spec.* The rebound or 'kick' of a gun or firearm when discharged.

1575 GASCOIGNE *Weedes* Wks. 183 A peece which shot so well,..It neyther bruzed with recule, nor wroong with ouer-weight. **1589** IVE *Fortif.* 23 Draw a lyne..vnto the parapet in the flanke for the requoyle of the artillery. **1669** BOYLE *Contn. New Exp.* I. 19 The Recoyl [of guns] seems to depend upon the Dilatation and Impulse of the Powder. **1781** THOMPSON in *Phil. Trans.* LXXI. 258 The recoil of great guns is much more violent after the second or third discharge than it is at first. **1832** BABBAGE *Econ. Manuf.* ii. (ed. 3) 23 Amongst different kinds of shot, that which is the smallest, causes the greatest recoil against the shoulder. **1879** SLADEN *Gunnery* 17 The velocity of recoil is generally taken as the velocity imparted to the gun and carriage by the discharge of the piece.

b. *ellipt.* A recoil-check.

1882 *Daily News* 10 Feb. 6/1 A..duck gun, mounted ready for action in a punt. It is fitted with Booth's recoil.

4. *Nucl. Physics.* The result of a collision between two sub-atomic particles, or of spontaneous decay of a single particle, in which the two resulting particles move in opposite directions with speeds determined by conservation of momentum.

1909 *Nature* 24 June 490/1 Rutherford..suggests the possibility of the phenomenon being due to a recoil effect rather than to a volatility possessed by the product radium B. **1912** *Phil. Mag.* XXIV. 622 It is well known..that the emission of α particles from radioactive substances is accompanied by a vigorous recoil of the residual atoms. **1933** *Discovery* Apr. 107/2 The energy of recoil is greatest when it [*sc.* a neutron] strikes a hydrogen nucleus, and the recoiling atom may travel 30 c.m. or more in air before it is brought to rest. **1964** J. B. HASTED *Physics of Atomic Collisions* iii. 107 Since the angle of recoil is related to the velocity, a suitable positioning of slits should serve to select atoms of a certain velocity.

5. *attrib.* or *Comb.* **a.** In names of devices intended to diminish or absorb the recoil of a firearm or piece of ordnance, as ***recoil box, -breeching, -check, pad, -plate, reducer, -spring, -toggle***; also, names of devices used to measure the force or energy of the recoil of a firearm, as ***recoil gauge, machine, recorder***; also ***recoil action***.

1908 *Westm. Gaz.* 13 Feb. 4/2 The *recoil action of the spring..closes these valves. **1892** W. W. GREENER *Gun & its Development* (ed. 5) 480 Recoil breeching of rope is..the simplest gear for taking the recoil. Others in use are..the indiarubber breeching, or the *recoil box of Mr. E. T. Booth. **1881** GREENER *Gun* 460 (Plate) Greener-Field Punt Gun, with India-rubber *Recoil-breeching. **1876** in *Smithsonian Misc. Collect.* VIII. No. 6. 30 Accessories of loading... *Recoil-checks. **1890** *Field* LXXVI. 461/1 Ascertaining, by chronograph and *recoil-gauge, what the forward velocity of the shot and the backward movement of the gun respectively amount to. **1896** W. W. GREENER *Gun & its Development* (ed. 6) xii. 316 (*caption*) New mechanical gun-rest and recoil-gauge. **1900** G. T. TEASDALE-BUCKELL *Experts on Guns & Shooting* xii. 138 We cannot follow Mr. Toms..in his remarks about the recoil gauge. **1896** *Field* 28 Mar. 457/1 There would thus be an increase of the back-thrust registered on the *recoil machine. **1931** G. BURRARD *Mod. Shotgun* I. vi. 145 A *recoil pad can be a great boon to those who are at all sensitive to recoil or to almost anyone who uses a gun in a hot climate where one frequently has to shoot in nothing but a thin shirt. **1974** R. DUNLAP *Gun Owner's Bk. of Care, Repair & Improvement* xiii. 207 We have the obvious changes in original wood fittings for firearms: fitting recoil pads to shotguns and rifles, which more or less combines with the desire for shortening or lengthening buttstocks. **1976** *Shooting Times & Country Mag.* 18–24 Nov. (Advt.), Beavertail fore-end in walnut, pistol grip stock with recoil pad. **1868** *Rep. to Govt. U.S. Munitions War* 281 A small space is left between the tenon on the rear of this block, and the front surface of the breech-block,..to admit of a slight rocking motion of the *recoil-plate. **1906** H. SHARP *Mod. Sporting Gunnery* v. 123 The sportsman does not appear to have attached very much importance to these *recoil recorders, possibly for the reason that machines devised on the above lines tell only the weight of recoil. **1942** *R.A.F. Jrnl.* 3 Oct. 29 The compensator or *recoil reducer was very effective. **1975** G. T. GARWOOD *Shotguns & Cartridges for Game & Clays* (ed. 3) xvi. 155 In the USA various proprietary 'recoil reducers' are advertised, the best known being the Edwards. This is a sealed device, and the working principle is not disclosed. **1859** H. C. FOLKARD *Wild-Fowler* xxii. 126 The best plan of all is Colonel Hawker's invention of a steel spiral *recoil-spring. **1882** 'MARKSMAN' *Dead Shot* (ed. 5) 331, I have recently seen several attached to heavy breech-loaders, in which the recoil-spring and fittings were so short and cramped, as to be only twelve or fourteen inches in length. **1971** G. T. GARWOOD *Gough Thomas's Second Gun Bk.* xi. 211 If it were not for the friction device and the recoil spring, the parts of the gun with which the shooter makes contact.. would not commence to recoil at all. **1881** GREENER *Gun* 531 It is immaterial to which end of the breeching the '*recoil toggle' is affixed.

b. In *Nucl. Physics.* (cf. sense 4 above), as ***recoil atom, electron, energy, momentum, nucleus, proton, ray, track.***

1912 *Phil. Mag.* XXIV. 622 *Recoil atoms produce a strong ionization in the gas they traverse. **1942** POLLARD & DAVIDSON *Appl. Nucl. Physics* iii. 40 A cloud chamber for observation of alpha particles, protons, and heavy recoil atoms is not hard to construct. **1923** *Physical Rev.* XXI. 483 The velocity of secondary β-rays excited in light elements by γ-rays agrees with the suggestion that they are *recoil electrons. **1966** S. E. LIVERHANT *Outl. Atomic Physics* iv. 111 In an experimental arrangement designed to measure the coincidences between the scattered photon and the recoil electron in Compton scattering, the detectors are to be placed symmetrically about the direction of the incident X-ray beam. **1949** FRIEDLANDER & KENNEDY *Introd. Radiochem.* xi. 253 Neutron capture is always followed by γ-ray emission, and the nucleus receives some *recoil energy in this process. **1963** *Radiochem. Man.* (Radiochemical Centre) II. ii. 5 When an atom in a chemical compound captures a neutron, by an (n, γ) reaction, the atom recoils with an energy usually greater than that of the chemical binding forces: recoil energies are usually in the range of a few MeV whilst chemical bond energies are usually only a few eV. **1950** D. HALLIDAY *Introd. Nucl. Physics* iii. 106 The *recoil momentum of a disintegrating nucleus will be influenced in magnitude and direction by the presence of a neutrino. **1962** SEMAT & ALBRIGHT *Introd. to Atomic & Nuclear Physics* (ed. 4) xiv. 470 The mass to which the recoil momentum is transferred can be considered infinite in comparison with that of an atom, so that the velocity of recoil is zero. This phenomenon is sometimes called recoilless emission of radiation. **1934** *Proc. Cambr. Philos. Soc.* XXX. 99 The ionisation due to *recoil nuclei of the energies here concerned is almost entirely primary. **1949** O. OLDENBERG *Introd. Atomic & Nuclear Physics* xxi. 237 The two tracks so produced, that of the original alpha particle deflected by the collision and that of the 'recoil nucleus', are both well defined. **1942** POLLARD & DAVIDSON *Appl. Nucl. Physics* iii. 41 The *recoil protons caused by neutrons in a gas containing hydrogen can..be detected with such equipment. **1949** O. OLDENBERG *Introd. Atomic Physics* xix. 195 When the cloud chamber is filled with CH_4 and subjected to neutron bombardment, the short, straight tracks of recoil protons show up. **1913** E. RUTHERFORD *Radioactive Substances* iv. 178 By observing the deflections of a pencil of *recoil rays, both in a magnetic and electric field, the velocity and value of e/m of the recoil atoms can be deduced. **1926** R. W. LAWSON tr. *Hevesy's Man. Radioactivity* vi. 59 In consequence of their smaller velocity, the phenomenon of scattering occurs in a much more marked degree with recoil rays than with α-particles. **1927** *Proc. R. Soc.* A. CXVI. 664 This paper describes the measurement of the mobility of a single atom of actinium A immediately after it reaches the end of its *recoil track. **1930** E. RUTHERFORD et al. *Radiations from Radioactive Substances* vi. 155 At ordinary pressure, the recoil track is shown by a knob at the end of the track. As the pressure is reduced, the recoil track becomes longer and often shows evidence of a marked scattering.

c. recoil escapement, an ordinary form of escapement in clocks and watches, in which the teeth of the crown- or balance-wheel act on the pallets by recoil; **recoil gear** *Mil.* (see quot. 1940); **recoil pallet**, a pallet in a recoil escapement; **recoil starter**, a device for starting a small internal-combustion engine in which a cord, wound round a pulley, is rewound by a spring after being pulled for the starting cycle; **recoil wave**, a dicrotic wave.

1838 *Penny Cycl.* XII. 299/1 [This] motion is called the recoil, and this escapement is thence called the recoil escapement. **1850** DENISON (Sir E. Beckett) *Clocks & Watches* (Weale) 71 The recoil escapement, which is still used in all the common clocks in the world, though it has long been abandoned in all that make any pretension to a great accuracy. **1883** *Ibid.* (ed. 7) 79 Recoil pallets—and dead ones too—should only just clear the teeth. **1884** F. J. BRITTEN *Watch & Clockm.* 7 The Recoil Escapement (invented by Dr. Hooke about 1675) is the one most generally applied to the ordinary run of dials and house clocks. **1904–5** *Jrnl. R. Artillery* XXXI. 303 Recoil gear. **1911** H. A. BETHELL *Mod. Artillery in Field* i. 26 (*heading*) Hydropneumatic recoil gear. **1940** *Chambers's Techn. Dict.* 706/2 *Recoil gear* (Artillery), The whole recoil mechanism, embracing both buffer and recuperator. **1960** *Farmer & Stockbreeder* 16 Feb. 106/2 (Advt.), Petrol-engine model with..two-stroke engine;..automatic recoil-starter eliminating the use of loose starting rope. **1972** P. DEMPSEY *How to repair Small Petrol Engines* vii. 235 Rewind starters. Sometimes called recoil starters, these devices are found on outboards, lawnmowers, go-karts.

recoil (rɪ'kɔɪl), *v.*[1] Forms: α. 4 (6 *Sc.*) reculle, 5 recuyel(l)e, recuyll-, 6–7 recuile, (7 recool), 4–7 (9 *Sc.*) recule. β. 3–4, 7 recoile(n, 6–7 recoyl(e, (7 requoyle), 6– recoil. [ad. OF. *reculer* (12th c.), f. *re-* RE- + *cul* CUL, CULE:—L. *cūlus* the posteriors: cf. Sp. *recular*, Pg. *recuar*, It. *rinculare*, med.L. (14–15th c.) *recul(l)are*. For the change of *u* to *oi* cf. DEFOIL *v.*, FOIL *v.*[1], FOIST *sb.*[1]; *recule* is the usual form in the 15–16th c.]

†**1.** *trans.* To beat, drive, or force back (also with *back* or *aback*); to cause to retreat or retire.

a **1225** *Ancr. R.* 294 þu..ȝiuest þe ueonde inȝong..so þet tu ne meiht recoilen him aȝanward. *c* **1330** *Arth. & Merl.* 6693 (Kölbing) .v. forlong he dede hem recoile & vnder hors fete defoile. *c* **1380** *Sir Ferumb.* 4585 þay wyþ-stode hem al wyþ strengþe, And reculede hem þar an acres lengþe. *c* **1489** CAXTON *Blanchardyn* 58 He..reculed his enemyes abacke tyll within the barreys of the towne. *a* **1547** SURREY *Æneid* II. 560 With this from thense I was recuiled back. **1590** SPENSER *F.Q.* II. xii. 19 Neither toyle nor traveill might her back recoyle. **1667** *Obs. Burn. Lond.* 33 When it found any let or hinderance that did recoil it back, it blew equally both to the right and to the left. **1713** SWIFT *Cadenus & Vanessa*, The darts were..often blunted and recoil'd.

fig. **1628** tr. *Mathieu's Powerfull Favorite* 104 He was author of my Vnckles death, who recoiled his hopes. **1645** *City Alarum* 10 Our passionate desire of an end recoyles us from the end. **1650** GENTILIS *Considerations* 164 How behove-full would it be to recule and set by unfortunate men ere they were scarce known.

†**b.** *refl.* To draw back, retire. *Obs. rare.*

c **1489** CAXTON *Blanchardyn* 106 They..lepte and reculed hem self abake six passes or moo. **1579** TOMSON *Calvin's Serm. Tim.* 33/2 Whosoeuer will order himselfe according to Gods rule, must learne to recule & withdraw himselfe.

†**c.** To take or carry *back*. *Obs.*[−1] (Cf. 3 c.)

1603 FLORIO *Montaigne* I. ix. (1632) 16 Who recoile their narration so farre-backe, and stuff it with so many vaine circumstances, that..they smoother the goodnesse of it.

†**d.** To return or retort (a thing) *upon* one. *Obs.*

1626 W. FENNER *Hid. Manna* Ep. Ded., I say, this [argument] may be recoyled back upon them. **1662** GURNALL *Chr. in Arm.* III. verse 18 xlv[i]. §1 (1669) 404/1 She reverseth the unjust judgement past upon the life of her people, and recoyls it upon the life of him that laid the plot.

2. *intr.* To retreat, retire, go or draw *back* (or *aback*) before an enemy or opposing force.

Very common (in form *recule*) from *c* 1490–1610.

α. *c* **1380** *Sir Ferumb.* 971 þe frensche men þai made reculle wel an akers lengþe. **1470–85** MALORY *Arthur* v. xii, The knyghtes..made them to recuyelle & flee. *a* **1533** LD. BERNERS *Huon* ci. 335 When Huon sawe them he sayd to his men 'syrs, it is good that we recule to our cyte'. **1550** J. COKE *Eng. & Fr. Heralds* §70 (1877) 80 Charles..secretly reculed home with suche Hungariens as escaped. **1610** HOLLAND *Camden's Brit.* (1637) 35 The Britans being troubled with the strange forme of those gallies..reculed. **1640** tr. *Verdere's Romant of Rom.* I. 13 Doest thou not know that worthy Knights must never recuile for any consideration of danger whatsoever.

β. **1511** GUYLFORDE *Pilgr.* (Camden) 59 We were with vyolence and rage of the sayde tempest constreyned to recoyle and turn backwardes. **1570** LEVINS *Manip.* 215/11 To Recoyle, *recedere*. **1637** R. HUMPHREY tr. *St. Ambrose* I. 11 Skilfull darters who by recoyling are wont to gaine the day. **1644** VICARS *God in Mount* 118 They were forced swiftly to recoyle and flie backe. **1807** J. BARLOW *Columb.* v. 209 The French recoiling half their victory yield. **1865** KINGSLEY *Herew.* vi, The peasants swarmed like flies but they soon recoiled.

transf. **1598** DRAYTON *Heroic. Ep.* vi. 156 At first our Troubles easily recul'd But now growne head-strong, hardly to be rul'd. **1623** MILTON *Ps.* cxiv. 9 Jordans clear streams recoil, As a faint host that hath receiv'd the foil.

b. To stagger back, from the effects of a blow.

a **1533** LD. BERNERS *Huon* xvi. 42 Huon..gaue þe erle such a stroke þat he..reculyd backe more than .ii. pases. *c* **1650** *Don Bellianis* 58 Arsileos horse with the strong stroke recoyled back three or four paces. **1667** MILTON *P.L.* VI. 194 Ten paces huge He back recoild.

†**3.** To go back (or backwards); to recede, retire, retreat, return. *Obs.*

1483 CAXTON *Gold. Leg.* 317/1 The shyppe recuyeled backward in to the Water soo that he fylle doune in to the deppest of the flood. **1489** —— *Faytes of A.* II. xxxv. 146 As a ramme..whan he reculeth a bak for to hurte with hys hornes. **1548** UDALL, etc. *Erasm. Par. Luke* xxi. 5 Whom soeuer of theim, this extreme distresse shall soodainly take in any forein countreyes..: leat not suche recule into Jewrie. **1601** HOLLAND *Pliny* II. 370 It goeth as it were reculing backward. **1601** DOLMAN *La Primaud. Fr. Acad.* (1618) III. 718 According as the sunne doth approch neere, or recule from vs,..so haue we the daies longer or shorter. **1651** tr. *De-las-Coveras' Don Fenise* 199 They perceived the earth to fall upon them, which terrified them very much, not knowing whether they should advance or recule.

fig. **1641** in Carte *Ormonde* (1735) III. 36 This gentleman will acquaint your Lordship how the affaires stand here, which rather recoyle than advance to his Majestie's service. **1642** ROGERS *Naaman* 157 Then Self will most recoile, and selfe-deniall will most appeare.

†**b.** To fall back or away (from some state or condition), to degenerate. *Obs. rare.*

1601 WEEVER *Mirr. Mart.* C v, Orleance Saw that his Souldiers courage gan recoile. **1605** SHAKS. *Macb.* IV. iii. 22 A good and vertuous Nature may recoyle, In an Imperiale charge. **1611** —— *Cymb.* I. vi. 128 Be reueng'd, Or she that bore you was no Queene, and you Recoyle from your great Stocke.

†**c.** To go back in memory or in a narrative. *Obs. rare.* (Cf. 1 c.)

1611 SHAKS. *Wint. T.* I. ii. 154 Looking on the Lynes Of my Boyes face, me thoughts I did requoyle Twentie three yeeres. **1655** FULLER *Ch. Hist.* VII. i. §34 Now followed the fatall tragedy of the Duke of Somerset, and we must recoile a little, to fetch forward the cause thereof.

†**d.** To lie back or away *from*. *Obs.*[−1]

1579 FENTON *Guicciard.* (1618) 37 A place betweene the walls of the same towne, and a ditch which reculeth about a thousand paces from the towne.

†**4.** To retire, withdraw oneself *to* a place. *Obs.*

1548 UDALL, etc. *Erasm. Par. Mark* v. 38 The Lorde.. reculed unto the water syde and toke shippe. **1590** SPENSER

F.Q. I. x. 17 A whyle I read you rest, and to your bowres recoyle. **1591** —— *M. Hubberd* 754 When this Courtly Gentleman with toyle Himselfe hath wearied, he doth recoyle Unto his rest. **1627** DRAYTON *Agincourt*, etc. (1631) 13 The Lawyer to his chamber doth recule For he hath now no bus'nesse at the barre.

†**b.** *fig.* To draw back *from* an act or course of action, a promise, etc. Also without const. *Obs.*

1481 CAXTON *Myrr.* I. v. 24 They that ought wnderstande vertues and to teche other.. they ben they that recule and withdrawe fro it. **1483** —— *Gold. Leg.* 271 b/1 The Appostle recuylled not but.. wente forth Joyeng. *c* **1510** BARCLAY *Mirr. Gd. Manners* (1570) C vj, Submitting him selfe to death.. Rather then to recule from the defence of right. **1586** T. B. *La Primaud. Fr. Acad.* I. (1594) 57 If I recule now and draw backe, the reputation thereof will be diminished. *a* **1632** T. TAYLOR *God's Judgem.* I. I. xvi. (1642) 49 So filthily recoyling from the Truth.. that he became a setter up of false Idols. **1761** HUME *Hist. Eng.* (1806) III. xxxix. 294 He again renewed his consent; but in a few days he began anew to recoil.

5. To start or spring back in fear, horror, disgust, or the like.

1513 DOUGLAS *Æneis* IX. xiii. 38 He full fers.. Seand the scharp poyntis, recullis backwart. **1577** STANYHURST *Descr. Irel.* 5/1 A toad.. indeuoring to haue skipt ouer it, suddenlie reculed backe, as though it had beene rapt in the head. **1601** HOLLAND *Pliny* II. 176 If a Vine stand neare vnto it, a man shall sensibly perceiue the same to shrinke away and recule backward from it. **1667** MILTON *P.L.* II. 759 Back they recoild affraid At first, and call'd me Sin. **1746** COLLINS *Passions* 20 Fear.. back recoil'd he knew not why, Even at the sound himself had made. **1865** BARING-GOULD *Werewolves* vii. 88 The little girls recoiled, and the youngest took refuge behind Jeanne.

b. *fig.* of persons, in respect of the mind or feelings.

1644 H. PARKER *Jus Pop.* 47 The ten Tribes, recoyling from the pressures under Rehoboam. **1662** BP. HOPKINS *Fun. Serm.* (1685) 64 Yet even he, as man, recoiles at that death, which, as God, he was assured to conquer. **1792** COWPER *On Bill Mortality* v, Why deem we Death a foe? Recoil from weary life's best hour, And covet longer woe? **1838** LYTTON *Alice* I. x, I recoil from the idea of marrying him. **1874** GREEN *Short Hist.* ii. §7. 96 The age.. recoiled from the cool cynicism of his crimes.

c. *fig.* of the mind, heart, etc.

1605 SHAKS. *Macb.* v. ii. 23 Who then shall blame His pester'd senses to recoyle and start. **1680** OTWAY *Orphan* v. ix, At each word that my Distraction utter'd My heart recoyl'd. **1764** REID *Inquiry* v. §7 Something within me that recoils against it. **1836** J. GILBERT *Chr. Atonem.* ix. (1852) 262 The mind naturally recoils against the position. **1871** L. STEPHEN *Playgr. Eur.* (1894) ii. 68 The imagination fairly recoils from the prospect in horror.

6. a. To rebound, to spring or fly back through force of impact.

1581 SAVILE *Tacitus, Hist.* I. lxxxvi. (1591) 49 Tiber.. by the ruines of it beeing dammed, reculing againe, ouerflowed. **1613** PURCHAS *Pilgrimage* IX. i. (1614) 820 He [the Orenoque].. with his vomited abundance maketh the salt waters to recoyle. **1660** BOYLE *New Exp. Phys. Mech.* i. 35 They must press upon the surface of the Earth, and, as it were recoyling thence [etc.]. **1784** COWPER *Task* VI. 874 He gleans the blunted shafts that have recoiled. **1811** SHELLEY *Marg. Nicholson, Spec. Horsem.* 41 The meteors of midnight recoil from his figure. **1871** TYNDALL *Fragm. Sci.* (1879) II. v. 63 They [two balls] clash together, but, by virtue of their elasticity, they quickly recoil.

b. Of firearms or artillery: To spring back by the force of the discharge.

1530 PALSGR. 681/2 Se howe yonder gonne reculeth or ever she lowse. *a* **1658** CLEVELAND *Wks.* (1687) 25 The Bullet flying makes the Gun recoil. **1660** W. SECKER *Nonsuch Prof.* 141 A peece ill charged instead of hitting the mark, does but recoil on him that shoots it. **1727–41** CHAMBERS *Cycl.* s.v., The ball, when the gun had liberty to recoil, was always thrown to the right. **1797** *Encycl. Brit.* (ed. 3) VIII. 246/2 A barrel mounted upon a very straight stock will recoil more than one that is considerably bent. **1876** VOYLE & STEVENSON *Milit. Dict.* 331/1 The shot it is believed has left the piece before the gun commences to recoil.

fig. **1640** SIR E. DERING *Sp. on Relig.* 14 Dec. 13 They have charged their Canons at us to the full, and never fearing that ever they would recoyle back into a Parliament, they have ramm'd a prodigious, ungodly Oath into them.

c. To spring back to the original position.

1768–74 TUCKER *Lt. Nat.* (1834) II. 571 Habit.. is more tough and stubborn; when you think you have quite weakened its spring, it will recoil again with wonted vigour.

7. To rebound, spring *back*, or return, to the starting-point or source. Const. *against, to, on, upon.* Chiefly *fig.* (now with *on*).

1599 *Broughton's Lett.* iii. 13 They are like.. arrowes shot vp against the Sunne, these reculing to their hurt that shot them. **1632** SIR T. HAWKINS tr. *Mathieu's Unhappy Prosperitie* I. 49 *marg.*, There is nothing so deformed as an injury which reculeth backe against him who spake it. **1664** POWER *Exp. Philos.* III. 156 Electrical fluors do presently recoyl by short streight lines to their Bodies again. **1682** FLAVEL *Fear* 3 All their councels and cruelties recoyl upon themselves. **1749** FIELDING *Tom Jones* XIV. vii, The good or evil we confer on others, very often.. recoils on ourselves. **1855** MACAULAY *Hist. Eng.* xv. III. 513 That evidence missed the mark at which it was aimed, and recoiled on him from whom it proceeded. **1882** J. H. BLUNT *Ref. Ch. Eng.* II. 185 Their treason recoiled on their own heads.

Hence **re'coiled** *ppl. a.*

1599 NASHE *Lenten Stuffe* 61 By the honor of his house, and his neuer reculed sword. **1611** COTGR., *Reculé*, recoiled, repulsed.

†**recoil**, *v.*[2] *Obs. rare.* In 7 -coile, -coyle. [ad. It. *raccogliere* (see RACCOLTA) or F. *recueillir* (OF. *recoiller*): see RECUEIL *v.* and COIL *v.*[1]] *trans.* To collect, gather, obtain.

1632 LITHGOW *Trav.* II. 58 Fertile soyle, And trees from whence all times they fruit recoyle. *Ibid.* VI. 275 A contribution is granted.. and also recoiled. *Ibid.* VII. 329 Some Bay, or Creeke.. Whence Ancorage, and safety ships recoile.

recoil (riː'kɔɪl), *v.*[3] [f. RE- 5 a + COIL *v.*[3]] *trans.* To coil again.

1865 TYLOR *Early Hist. Man.* ix. 245 Uncoiling the string, and recoiling it as before.

recoiler (rɪ'kɔɪlə(r)). [f. RECOIL *v.*[1] + -ER[1].] One who recoils.

a **1670** HACKET *Abp. Williams* I. (1692) 98 He became an humble Suppliant to his Majesty, that he might have his Leave to return for Italy.. As if this recoiler had told him no news, he spake but little, and dismissed him. **1813** *Memoir Sir J. E. Smith* (1832) II. 351 Shall the Patriot e'er prove a recoiler? **1840** BROWNING *Sordello* IV. 758 Recoil? That's nought; if the recoiler leaves His name for me to fight with, no one grieves.

recoiling (rɪ'kɔɪlɪŋ), *vbl. sb.* [f. as prec. + -ING[1].] The action of the vb. in various senses.

c **1380** *Sir Ferumb.* 2771 In þe reculynge þat þay made an hundred of hem wer sleyn. **1523** LD. BERNERS *Froiss.* I. l. 72 On the see ther is no reculyng nor fleyng, ther is no remedy but to fight. **1590** SIR J. SMYTH *Disc. Weapons* 18 b, They either put their peeces in hazard of breaking, or els themselues to bee ouerthrowne with the reculing of them. **1617** HIERON *Wks.* II. 308 That recoyling, which Dauid prescribed to Ioab, could not bee with the death of Vriah only. *a* **1715** BURNET *Own Time* (1724) I. 50 The recoiling of cruel counsels on the authors of them never appeared more eminently. **1829** R. STORY *Mem. Isabella Campbell* xii. 474 Thoughts of death seemed to have lost all power for a season to excite the recoilings of nature. **1892** *Athenæum* 26 Nov. 737/1 After sundry self-searchings and recoilings.. she marries Dering.

recoiling (rɪ'kɔɪlɪŋ), *ppl. a.* [f. as prec. + -ING[2].] That recoils. *recoiling escapement, pallet* (see RECOIL *sb.* 5 c).

1632 LITHGOW *Trav.* III. 100 The recoiling waues brought vs backe from the Shelfes. **1642** ROGERS *Naaman* 14 A rebelling and recoyling spirit against God. *Ibid.* 538 In shooting off his recoyling gun. **1776** G. SEMPLE *Building in Water* 150 The remaining Part of its recoiling Force.. will be quite swallowed up in that Depth of Water. **1825** J. NICHOLSON *Operat. Mechanic* 516 The motion of the wheel is hobbling and unequal, by which this escapement has received the appellation of the recoiling 'scapement. **1842** *Encycl. Brit.* (ed. 7) VI. 769/1 It is sometimes called the recoiling scapement or the recoiling pallets. *Ibid.* 773/2 No rule can be given for the angle which the recoiling arch should make with the concentric one. **1911** *Ann. Rep. Progress of Chem.* VII. 272 A coating of silver 20$\mu\mu$ in thickness stopped the recoil completely, while 10$\mu\mu$ allowed some 60 per cent of the recoiling atoms to pass through. **1950** D. HALLIDAY *Introd. Nucl. Physics* iii. 107 Allen tried to detect recoiling Li^7 ions formed during the disintegration by *K*-capture of Be^7. **1963** BOWEN & GIBBONS *Radioactivation Analysis* vii. 109 The recoiling atom travels for a short distance before it gives up all its excess energy, and may undergo various chemical reactions in the process.

Hence **re'coilingly** *adv.* (Webster 1847).

recoilless (rɪ'kɔɪllɪs, 'riː-), *a.* Also recoil-less. [f. RECOIL *sb.* + -LESS.] Having no recoil.

a. *Mil.* Applied to a firearm in which recoil is reduced or eliminated by deflection of much of the combustion gas to the rear.

1948 *Jrnl. British Interplanetary Soc.* July 163 There were two types [of rocket-firing guns] scheduled for development, one static.., the other a portable 'recoilless' model on a wheeled chassis. **1953** *Times* 28 May 5/4 Both the United States and the French armies have produced admirable recoilless guns since 1946. **1957** *Economist* 7 Sept. 855/1 Recoilless anti-tank rifles could knock out any tank built in the Soviet Union. **1972** M. KENYON *Shooting of Dan McGrew* i. 9 You'll be wanting a recoil-less rifle to defend your honour. **1975** *Times* 10 Apr. 8/7 Mortar and recoilless rifle fire has been used against the international airport.

b. *Nucl. Physics.* Applied to transitions occurring in an atomic nucleus bound in a crystal lattice in which a photon is emitted from the nucleus without recoil (the Mössbauer effect: see MÖSSBAUER).

1960 *Physical Rev.* CXX. 1093/1 Mössbauer's observation rests on the fact that in the case of a nucleus bound in a crystal, a γ ray can be emitted or absorbed without any energy transfer to and from the lattice. The probability of such a recoilless transition is, in most cases, small. **1962** [see *recoil momentum* s.v. RECOIL *sb.* 5 b]. **1971** GREENWOOD & GIBB *Mössbauer Spectrosc.* i. 11 Mössbauer experiments usually utilise the recoilless emission of γ-rays by a radioactive source followed by their subsequent resonant recoilless reabsorption by a non-active absorber. **1974** *Nature* 19 Apr. 638/2 The 13·3-keV transition to the ground state has long been one of the most attractive candidates for high resolution experiments because.. the low energy of the γ photon assures that a high probability of recoil-less transitions will result even at room temperature.

re'coilment. Now *rare* or *Obs.* Also 7 recuil-, recule-. [f. RECOIL *v.*[1] + -MENT.]

†**1.** The act of removing or sending away; dismissal. *Obs. rare.*

a **1608** SIR F. VERE *Comm.* (1657) 46 Though I was sensible as became me, who saw no cause in myself, of this recuilment and disgrace. *Ibid.* 67 When notwithstanding I had discouered.. in my recuilment his Lordships coldnesse of affection to me.

2. The act of recoiling or springing back.

1651 *Fuller's Abel Rediv.* Wks. 1867 I. 118 A man might easily perceive the recoilments of his own natural and exorbitant proclivities. **1684** FELL *Life Hammond* in *H.'s Wks.* (1684) I. 49 The recuilment of serous moisture into the habit of the body and insertions of the Nerves. **1766** G. CANNING *Anti-Lucretius* IV. 314 Such feign'd recoilment never could exist. **1847** in WEBSTER.

recoin (riː'kɔɪn), *v.* [RE- 5 a.] *trans.* To coin over again, to pass again through the mint.

1685 in *15th Rep. Hist. MSS. Comm.* App. VIII. 131 The remedy.. is to recoyne the forreign money to our standard. *a* **1727** NEWTON *Chronol. Amended* (1728) 40 Darius the Mede recoins the Lydian money. **1797** *Encycl. Brit.* (ed. 3) XII. 229/1 It may be found convenient.. to recoin such denominations altogether. **1879** H. PHILLIPS *Notes Coins* 6 These pieces, upon their arrival at Rome, by reason of their.. fineness of quality, were at once recoined.

fig. **1836** E. FITZGERALD *Lett.* (1889) I. 34, I wish with you that people would.. recoin some of the everyday compliments into a simpler form.

Hence **re'coining** *vbl. sb.*; also **re'coiner**, one who recoins (Ogilvie 1882).

1691 LOCKE *Lower. Interest* Wks. 1727 II. 90 It will enforce the recoining of all our Money, both old and new. **1740** W. DOUGLASS *Disc. Curr. Brit. Plant. Amer.* 32 In France their recoinings.. did rise the Price of Goods. **1882** *Rep. to Ho. Repr. Prec. Met. U.S.* 547 An annual consumption of gold in England.. for use in the arts, for abrasion and for recoining.

recoinage (riː'kɔɪnɪdʒ). [f. RE- 5 a + COINAGE.] The act or process of recoining money.

1622 BACON *Hen. VII* 216 The Recoinage of Groats and Halfe-groats, now Twelue-pences and Six-pences. **1707** *Lond. Gaz.* No. 4366/2 After the Recoinage, each Piece of Money is to receive a Denomination much above the.. Value it bears at present. **1776** ADAM SMITH *W.N.* I. xi. III. (1869) I. 206 Before the late re-coinage the gold coin was a good deal defaced. **1864** H. AINSWORTH *John Law* IV. ii, A diminution of nearly fifty per cent. on the money already reduced in value by a previous recoinage.

attrib. **1884** *St. James's Gaz.* 29 Apr. 7/2 The dislike of Mr. Childers's recoinage scheme.

†**recolage.** *Obs.* Also 4 ricol-, rycol-, rigol-, rekelage. [ad. OF. *rigolage*, f. *rigoler* to be merry or riotous.] Wanton or riotous conduct.

a **1300** *Cursor M.* 49 In riot and in rigolage [*v.rr.* ricolage, rekelage], Of all þere lijf spent þai þe stage. **1303** R. BRUNNE *Handl. Synne* 7273 Þan wyl þey.. sytte vp þare wyþ recolage And ȝyt do moche more outrage. *c* **1375** *Cursor M.* 1952 (Fairf.) Fle recolage and thefe as dede.

†**recolation.** *Obs.*—[0] [n. of action f. L. *recōlāre*: see RE- and COLATION.] (See quot.)

1753 CHAMBERS *Cycl. Supp.*, *Recolation*, a method of fining the decoctions of vegetables, etc. by repeated percolation, or straining them several times successively through a linnen or woollen bag.

recolet, obs. form of RECOLLET.

recoll, obs. Sc. variant of RECUEIL.

reco'llate, *v.* [RE- 5 a.] To collate again. Hence **reco'llating** *vbl. sb.* (in quot. *attrib.*).

1853 'L. N. R.' *Book & its Story* II. ii. (1857) 214 After the Bibles are sewn, they are again taken to the re-collating-room to be examined. **1881** *Athenæum* 12 Feb. 236/1 The volume will also contain a number of old Irish fragments.., which have all been recollated by Dr. Zimmer. **1881** P. FITZGERALD *World behind Scenes* III. 177 This [painting] represents Farren & Farley, but the recollating with Zoffary's work makes this picture comparatively feeble.

So **reco'llation**, the action of recollating.

1816 *2nd Rep. Comm. Public Rec.* App. ¶1, The many Omissions discovered on Re-collation. **1881** *Academy* 19 Feb. 139/2 The MS... has been missing.. since June last, so that recollation is for the present impracticable.

Recollect ('rɛkəlɛkt), *sb.* [ad. L. *recollect-us* or F. *récollet* RECOLLET, q.v.] A member of an Observantine branch of the Franciscan order, which originated in Spain in the end of the 15th c., and was so named 'from the detachment from creatures and recollection in God which the founders aimed at' (*Catholic Dict.*).

1631 WEEVER *Anc. Funeral Mon.* 139 Many other reformations haue beene from time to time of the Franciscans, as by the Minims, Recollects, Penitentiaries, Capuchins, &c. **1683** *Lond. Gaz.* No. 1806/4 The Council of State.. forbid the Cordeliers, the Recollects, and other Religious, of the Order of St. Francis, to obey their General, who is a Spaniard. **1746** in *Acc. French Settlem. N. Amer.* 21 Opposite to it is the convent of the Recollects. **1767** S. PATERSON *Another Trav.* I. 115, I met with a pious soul of a Recollect in the barge. **1883** *Catholic Dict.* s.v., The Recollects were uninfected by Jansenism.

b. *attrib.* and *appos.* Belonging to the order of the Recollects.

1655 FULLER *Ch. Hist.* VI. vii. *Douay*, Some report this erected.. by the charity of English Catholicks for recollect Fryers of the Order of S. Francis. **1710** *Lond. Gaz.* No. 4650/3 The Body.. was interred.. in the Church of the Recollect Friars. **1897** *Catholic Dict.* (ed. 5) s.v., There appear to be at present six Recollect houses in Great Britain.

c. *transf.* The cedar-bird or Carolina chatterer.

1783 LATHAM *Gen. Syn. Birds* II. I. 94 At Quebec it is called the Recollect [*note*, Perhaps from the similarity of the crest or plumage to the habit of this order of friers].

recollect (riːkə'lɛkt), *v.*[1] [Orig. ad. L. *recollect-*, ppl. stem of *recolligĕre*, f. *re-* + *colligĕre*, but in later use apprehended as an Eng. formation from RE- 5a + COLLECT *v.*, and consequently sometimes written *re-collect*. The earlier pron. was prob. as in *v.*[2], from which it is now distinguished by the vowel of the prefix.

In some senses the distinction between this and *v.*[2] is not clearly maintained, and the pron. may vary accordingly.]

†**1.** *trans.* To collect, gather. *Obs.*

1513 DOUGLAS *Æneis* I. Prol. 99 A lord sa gentle and kynd, ..Quhilk..Bukis to recollect, to reid and se, Hes greit delite als euir hed Ptolome. **1608** SHAKS. *Per.* II. i. 54 How..These Fishers..from their watry empire recollect All that may men approue, or men detect! **1628** tr. *Mathieu's Powerfull Favorite* 133 Neither the Consuls nor the Prætor gaue their vote at all, but recollected those of the others. **1645** QUARLES *Sol. Recant.* iii. 6 There is a time to recollect and lay Thy treasure up; a time to cast away. **1670** DUMARESQUE in *Evelyn's Mem.* (1857) III. 227 It was no wonder if planting was not so much in fashion before you were pleased to recollect that art in a body.

†**b.** To collect *again*. (Cf. 2.) *Obs.*

1607 TOPSELL *Four-f. Beasts* 152 The drops disperse the scent of the Hare and the drye weather recollecteth it againe. **1613** W. BROWNE *Brit. Past.* I. i, Call backe thy spirits, and recollect againe Thy vagrant wits. **1693** *Mem. Cnt. Teckely* III. 32 To recollect once again the Friends he still retained in Hungary.

2. To collect, gather, or bring together (things or persons) again.

In 17th c. examples it is often difficult to decide whether this or sense 1 is intended.

1615 G. SANDYS *Trav.* 168 When broken by the Saracens, the peeces were recollected. **1655** SPURSTOWE *Wels of Salvation* 54 How dust scattered and blown up and down should be recollected, was altogether beyond the line of their reason. **1768** H. WALPOLE *Hist. Doubts* Pref. 9 Our empire was but forming itself or re-collecting its divided members. **1800** W. TAYLOR in *Monthly Mag.* X. 6 When Zerubbabel ..was already returned to Jerusalem, to re-collect its scattered inhabitants. **1870** *Standard* 16 Nov., Since the Crimean war..Russia has been carefully engaged in recruiting her strength and in re-collecting her resources. *fig.* **1615** DANIEL *Queen's Arcadia* Wks. (1717) 224 Therefore let us recollect our selves, Dispers'd into these strange confused Ills. **1650** FULLER *Pisgah* II. 67 So Reuben could never after recollect his lost credit, to recover the full favour of his Father.

refl. **1642** LORD W. ST. LEGER in *Lismore Papers* Ser. II. (1888) V. 43 That..Army..now will aske some tyme to recollect it self after this vnexpected Discomfiture. **1671** SALMON *Syn. Med.* I. xxxvii. 86 Flegm, as it is speedily dissipated, so it as speedily recollects it self. **1770** LANGHORNE *Plutarch* (1879) I. 408/2 The Achæan cavalry recollecting themselves after their flight, found that Philopœmen was not with them.

b. *intr.* To come together again. *rare.*

a **1631** DONNE *Lett., to Lady Bedford* (1651) 174 Of this all though many parts decay, The pure, which elemented them, ..Shall recollect, and in one all unite. **1855** MRS. GATTY *Parables fr. Nat.* Ser. I. (1869) 27 The first thing they attempted, when they had re-collected to consult.

3. To collect (one's spirits, thoughts, mind, etc.).

1614 RALEIGH *Hist. World* v. ii. 329 The enemies..not hauing recollected their Spirits to make it good. **1649** I. AMBROSE *Media* ii. 36 When we call in all our thoughts and affections, and recollect them together. **1705** STANHOPE *Paraphr.* III. 361 As oft as He says Let us pray; They should recollect their wandering Thoughts. **1759** JOHNSON *Rasselas* xlv[i], He was timorous and bashful; but, when the talk became regular, he recollected his powers. **1800** *Asiat. Ann. Reg., Misc. Tr.* 12/2 Upon recollecting his spirits,..he found his affairs very far from being as yet in a desperate condition.

†**b.** With impersonal subject. ? *Obs.*

1611 J. DAVIES *Scourge Folly* Wks. (Grosart) 56 The heauenly charme that..recollects the mind that cares distract. **1627** E. F. *Hist. Edw. II* (1680) 16 The injustice of the quarrel which might in time have recollected his senses. **1703** ATTERBURY *Serm.* (1737) IV. 112 Darkness and solitude which recollect the thoughts and turn the mind inward.

4. To gather or summon up (strength, courage, etc.); to rally; to recover by an effort.

1655 tr. *Com. Hist. Francion* v. 1 He determined to keep his Bed for that day, the better to recollect his strength. **1667** MILTON *P.L.* IX. 471 Then soon Fierce hate he recollects, and all his thoughts Of mischief..thus excites. **1760–72** H. BROOKE *Fool of Qual.* (1809) I. 98 Recollecting all my force, and drawing my sword. **1791** MRS. RADCLIFFE *Rom. Forest* (1806) III. xxiii. 279 She..re-collected sufficient resolution to submit. **1886** STEVENSON *Dr. Jekyll* 71 Mr. Utterson's nerves..gave a jerk that nearly threw him from his balance; but he re-collected his courage.

b. *refl.* To nerve or brace (oneself).

1652 BP. HALL *Invis. World* III. §11 When thou hast recollected thyself to a resolution of defiance and unwearieable resistance, cast thine eye upon the deplorable condition of those Damned Souls.

†**5.** To bring back again *to* or *from* some position or state; to withdraw (oneself) *from*. *Obs.*

1620 T. GRANGER *Div. Logike* 204 Daily experience.. shewes it [Category] to be the most obuious..way to amplifie a..particular sentence..by retracting, or recollecting it to his generall head or fountaine. **1621** DONNE *Serm.* xv. 150, I who can do that, can also recollect you from yr present desperation. **1643** MILTON *Divorce* II. xxi. Wks. (1847) 155/2 Recollecting himself from an unmeet help which was never meant. **1655** *Theophania* 32 He recollected himself from that profound trance.

†**b.** *refl.* To bring (oneself) back to a reconsideration or better view of something. *Obs.*

1641 J. SHUTE *Sarah & Hagar* (1649) 118 It may be she had in part recollected herself, and did repent of her foolish carriage. **1670** G. H. *Hist. Cardinals* II. I. 118 That Pope recollected himself, discover'd his errour. **1696** PHILLIPS (ed. 5), *To Recollect a Man's self*, to change a Mans mind upon better Consideration.

6. *refl.* To bring (oneself) back to a state of composure; to compose, recover (oneself). Also const. *from*. Now *rare*.

1639 FULLER *Holy War* III. xxix. (1840) 170 Nor were his thoughts ever so scattered with any sudden accident, but he could instantly recollect himself. **1653** H. COGAN tr. *Pinto's Trav.* viii. 23, I was not able to utter a word; howbeit at length recollecting myself a little, I signified [etc.]. **1748** SMOLLETT *Rod. Rand.* xxxi, They..allowed the Spaniards to recollect themselves from the terror occasioned by the approach of an English fleet. **1798** *Geraldina* I. 124, I recollected myself after a little, and assumed sufficient composure to finish my dress. **1802** MAR. EDGEWORTH *Moral T.* (1816) I. xviii. 148 His heart beat violently, and he ..stopped, to recollect himself.

absol. **1740** RICHARDSON *Pamela* (1824) I. 200 Till I can recollect, I am not pleased with you.

b. In *pass.* without expressed agent. ? *Obs.*

1629 SHIRLEY *Gratef. Serv.* I. i, The duke is re-collected; where's the prince? *a* **1689** MRS. BEHN *Lucky Mistake* Novels 1871 II. 266 She gave a great shriek, which frighted Vernole; so both stood, for a while, staring on each other, till both were recollected. **1759** JOHNSON *Rasselas* xlii[i], The princess was recollected, and the favourite was abashed.

†**7.** To retrace (one's steps). *Obs.*−[1]

1698 FRYER *E. India & P.* 37 The Sand was scalding hot, which made me recollect my steps, and hasten to the Fort.

Hence **reco'llecting** *vbl. sb.*[1]

1613 DAY *Dyall* (1614) vii. 150 A recollecting and gathering of the same matter, whereof our body was first composed. **1880** C. R. MARKHAM *Peruv. Bark* 255 Besides the first gatherings..there has since been three 'recollectings'.

recollect (rɛkə'lɛkt), *v.*[2] [Of the same origin as prec., but now distinguished by the pronunciation (see *v.*[1]). In sense 4 prob after F. *récolliger*.]

1. *trans.* To call or bring back (something) to one's mind; to recall the knowledge of (a thing, person, etc.); to remember.

Recollect, when distinguished from *remember*, implies a conscious or express effort of memory to recall something which does not spontaneously rise in the mind.

1559 in Strype *Ann. Ref.* (1709) I. xi. 141 To move her Majesty that she would seriously recollect to memory her Gracious Sister's zeal unto the holy see. **1647** CLARENDON *Hist. Reb.* I. §114 The Treasurer quickly recollected the ground of his perturbation. **1712** ADDISON *Spect.* No. 293 ¶7 A famous Grecian General, whose Name I cannot at present recollect. **1781** COWPER *Truth* 153 Conscious of age, she recollects her youth. **1868** TENNYSON *Lucretius* 35 Perchance We do but recollect the dreams that come Just ere the waking.

absol. **1863** DRAPER *Intell. Devel. Europe* (1875) II. x. 364 Animals remember, man alone recollects.

b. With obj. clause, infin., etc.

1776 *Trial of Nundocomar* 26/1 Do you recollect being at Mr. Driver's house some time ago? **1784** COWPER *Task* v. 335 Recollecting still that he is man, We trust him not too far. **1835** LYTTON *Rienzi* I. v, Recollectest thou not how the noble Boniface himself..was kept in thraldom..? **1860** WARTER *Sea-board* II. 458, I recollect to have read somewhere of Sir Thos. More, how [etc.].

c. To say upon recollecting. *nonce-use.*

1748 RICHARDSON *Clarissa* VII. 247 But come, recollected she, how do I know but all is for the best..?

d. *intr.* To have a recollection *of* something.

1837 HENDERSON in *Proc. Berw. Nat. Club* I. No. 5. 151, I recollect of being shewn..a quagmire.

†**2. a.** To reflect *with* (oneself). *Obs.*

1697 POTTER *Antiq. Greece* II. vi. (1715) 257 Glaucus.. promis'd to recollect with himself, and if he found anything due, to pay it. **1675** EARL ESSEX *Lett.* (1770) 271, I humbly beseech your lordship to recollect with yourself who should insinuate any such matter. **1719** WATERLAND *Vind. Christ's Div.* xvii. Wks. 1823 I. II. 181 Recollect with yourself, that he is sometimes distinctly and personally invocated.

b. *refl.* To recall (oneself) to something temporarily forgotten.

1828 SCOTT *F.M. Perth* xi, 'Well, but that was not what I wished of thee just now', said the Prince, recollecting himself.

†**3.** To recall (a thing) *to* a person. *Obs.*

1673 *Lady's Call.* I. v. §37 When the apostle recollects to the Ephesians the wretchedness of their gentile state. **1724** WELTON *Chr. Faith & Pract.* 364 My chief design..has been to recollect to your minds some instances.

†**b.** To go over again. *Obs. rare*−[1].

1741 WATTS *Improv. Mind* I. vi. §5 The learner..should always recollect and review his lectures, read over some author..upon the same subject.

4. To concentrate or absorb (the mind, oneself, etc.) in contemplation; *spec.* in mystical religious use (cf. RECOLLECTION[2] 1, RECOLLECTED *ppl. a.*[2] 1).

1671 WOODHEAD *St. Teresa* I. xxxiv. 241, I took a.. Rosarie,..procuring not to recollect my Understanding, though, for my exteriour, I was sufficiently recollected. *Ibid.* II. xi. 91 Any kind of vertuous Exercise so recollected them, that they were presently out of themselves. **1862** GOULBURN *Pers. Relig.* II. xi. (1870) 144 It is wonderfully refreshing thus to recollect the mind.

Hence **reco'llecting** *vbl. sb.*[2]

1669 WOODHEAD *St. Teresa* I. xiv. 85 This is a kind of recollecting, and as it were, a shutting up of the powers of the soul within herself.

reco'llectable, *a. rare.* [f. prec. + -ABLE.] That may be recollected.

1778 [W. MARSHALL] *Minutes Agric.* 18 July 1776 This adduces to the mind the whole chain of recollectable facts and words incident to the subject. **1801** COLERIDGE *Lett.* (1895) 357 His deepest and most recollectable delights have been in solitude. **1891** *Harper's Mag.* Sept. 542/1 It was more 'recollectable' than all my real adventures.

recollected (riːkə'lɛktɪd), *ppl. a.*[1] [f. RECOLLECT *v.*[1] + -ED[1].]

1. (Meaning uncertain.)

Variously taken by commentators as 'gathered with pains, not spontaneous', 'picked, refined', 'studied', 'recalled, repeated', etc.

1601 SHAKS. *Twel. N.* II. iv. 5 Light ayres, and recollected termes Of these most briske and giddy-paced times.

2. Of things: Collected or brought together again.

1628 in Rushw. *Hist. Coll.* (1659) I. 570, I shall not peradventure follow the Method of your Lordships recollected Reasons in my answering to them. **1659** T. PHILIPOTT *Vill. Cant.* A, The Roman Eagles..breaking in again with a recolected and multiplied Strength. **1735** H. BROOKE *Univ. Beauty* IV. 136 Here rallies last the recollected blood. **1784** COWPER *Task* IV. 305 Till at length the freezing blast.. summons home The recollected powers.

3. Restored to composure or confidence.

1799 MRS. J. WEST *Tale of Times* III. 238 Whence this cruel distrust of your adopted brother? returned the recollected dissembler.

recollected (rɛkə'lɛktɪd), *ppl. a.*[2] [f. RECOLLECT *v.*[1] (sense 6) and *v.*[2]]

1. Collected, composed, calm; also, in religious use, given up to, or absorbed in, contemplation.

a. In attributive use.

1627 E. F. *Hist. Edw. II* (1680) 129 To see such a Monster so monstrously used, no question pleased the giddy Multitude..: the recollected Judgment that beheld it,— censur'd it was at best too great and deep a blemish to suit a Queen. **1650** JER. TAYLOR *Holy Living* (1727) 239 A sober fixed and recollected spirit. **1707** NORRIS *Treat. Humility* viii. 333 A waking and recollected state of the soul. **1860** T. T. CARTER *Imit. Christ* vi. 79 One such essential point is a recollected spirit, the constant remembrance of the awful Presence that dwells within us. **1889** *Tablet* 14 Dec. 954, 5,000 men of all classes, who formed a recollected procession to Our Lord in the Eucharist.

b. In predicative use.

1633 EARL MANCH. *Al Mondo* (1636) 45 That death was best, which was well recollected, quietly suffering what it could not possibly prevent. **1671** WOODHEAD *St. Teresa* I. xxxiv. 241 Though..I was sufficiently recollected. **1737** WATERLAND *Eucharist* 591 Some particular chosen Days, when a Man might be most recollected, and best prepared. **1792** COWPER *Let. to Mrs. Courtenay* 12 Aug., I am not sufficiently recollected to compose even a bagatelle at present. **1854** FABER *Growth in Holiness* iii. (1872) 44 We were recollected without feeling it.

2. Recalled to memory.

1742 RICHARDSON *Pamela* III. 301, I would have stood up; but quite abashed at my recollected Behaviour before so many Witnesses,..my Feet were unwilling to support me. **1805** WORDSW. *Prelude* I. 631 If the song be loth to quit Those recollected hours. **1859** MASSON *Brit. Novelists* iii. 182 As far as my recollected acquaintance..entitles me to judge. **1873** MISS BROUGHTON *Nancy* II. 25 Looking down at me with a smile of recollected entertainment.

Hence **reco'llectedly** *adv.*, in a composed manner, with self-control.

1789 P. SMYTH tr. *Aldrich's Archit.* (1818) 74 Unable to speak, recollectedly, of their intercourse with him. **1860** S. WILBERFORCE *Addr. Cand. Ordination* 32 To do all our acts sensibly and recollectedly, as in the sight of our Lord.

recollectedness (rɛkə'lɛktɪdnɪs). [-NESS.]

1. The state of being concentrated or absorbed in religious meditation.

a **1699** BONNELL in W. Hamilton *Life* 11 (1703) 111 In such intentness and recollectedness of Thought, that we are hardly sensible ourselves, that we are at our Devotions. **1862** GOULBURN *Pers. Relig.* 130 That the mind should ever and anon..be called home for a second or two to the Presence of God..: this is the meaning of recollectedness of spirit. **1891** *Month* LXXIII. 36 During the Adorable Sacrifice..a most profound recollectedness was observed.

2. Collectedness or clearness of thought.

1857 S. WILBERFORCE in *Life* (1881) II. x. 339, I spoke with recollectedness and power. **1876** MISS YONGE *Womankind* xxviii. 245 How many negligences have not also been committed in the flurry which prevents all recollectedness.

3. The quality of having been recalled to memory.

1802–12 BENTHAM *Ration. Judic. Evid.* (1827) I. 295 In every instance there exists a point of time down to which recollectedness and suggestedness are qualities of which no man's testimony can be deprived.

recollection[1] (riːkə'lɛkʃən). [a. F. *récollection*, or ad. med.L. *recollectiōn-em*, n. of action f. *recolligĕre* RECOLLECT *v.*[1] Now taken as f. RE- 5a + COLLECTION.]

1. A gathering together again.

1598 MANWOOD *Forest Lawes* To Rdr., The residue of his paines bestowed on his said first collection, and not set forth in his said recollection. **1633** EARL MANCH. *Al Mondo* (1636) 93 The incineration and dissipation of this dust shall haue a recollection in the day of Resurrection. **1673** MARVELL *Reh. Transp.* II. 37 He has diffused his poyson so publickly..that it might be beyond his own recollection. **1728** EARBERY tr. *Burnet's St. Dead* I. 230 We may ask in what Manner this Recollection of Parts..from indefinite distances is made. **1868** KINGSLEY *Hermits* 127 Without habitual collection and re-collection of our own selves from time to time no great purpose is carried out.

†**2.** A recapitulation. *Obs.*

1649 ROBERTS *Clavis Bibl.* Introd. iii. 43 Hereby also you shall have a summary Recapitulation, or Recollection of the

..subject-matter of every book. **1659** PEARSON *Creed* To Rdr., Lastly, by a recollection of all, briefly to deliver the sum of every particular truth.

recollection² (rɛkəˈlɛkʃən). [The same word as prec. in special senses: cf. RECOLLECT *v.*² In sense 1 after F. *récollection.*]

1. Religious or serious concentration of thought; †conduct regulated by such concentration.

1642 R. CARPENTER *Experience* I. viii. 26 An excellent Sanctity, and a spotlesse Recollection of life, in their Orders of Religion. **1669** WOODHEAD *St. Teresa* I. Relat. v. 308 An Internal Recollection, which is perceived in the Soul. **1764** FLETCHER *Let.* Wks. 1795 VII. 127 Recollection is a dwelling within ourselves; a being abstracted from the creature and turned towards God. *a* **1773** A. BUTLER *Trav. France & Italy* (1803) 221 He..performs the sacred office with great recollection and devotion. **1869** F. B. A. WILBERFORCE *Lives Domin. Mission. Japan* 158 The modesty of his exterior was the sign of his interior recollection.

2. Composure, calmness of mind, self-possession.

1757 BORLASE in *Phil. Trans.* L. 505, I do not hear of any person in those parts, who..had recollection enough to attend to the motion of the waters. **1788** *Disinterested Love* II. 110 He was nearly as much agitated as myself, but sooner came to his recollection.

3. The act of recalling to the memory; the mental operation by which objects or ideas are revived in the mind; also, an instance of this.

Sometimes contrasted with *remembrance*: see quot. 1690.

1683 MOXON *Mech. Exerc., Printing* xiii. ¶1 Upon every one of these Wooden Patterns I use to write..the number of Punches to be Forged of that Size, lest afterwards I might be troubled with Recollections. **1690** LOCKE *Hum. Und.* II. xix. §1 The same Idea, when it again recurs without the Operation of the like Object on the external Sensory, is Remembrance; if it be sought after by the Mind, and with Pain and Endeavour found, and brought again in view, it is Recollection. **1784** COWPER *Tiroc.* 311 The pleasing spectacle at once excites Such recollection of our own delights. **1875** JOWETT *Plato* (ed. 2) IV. 275 The power of recollection seems to depend on the intensity or largeness of the perception.

attrib. **1802–12** BENTHAM *Ration. Judic. Evid.* (1827) II. 247 The principal circumstances on which the demand for recollection-time is apt to depend.

b. The power of recalling to the mind; the sphere or period over which such power extends; the memory.

1732 POPE *Ep. Cobham* 47 As the last image..(Tho' past the recollection of the thought,) Becomes the stuff of which our dream is wrought. **1776** *Trial of Nundocomar* 66/2 Did you ever, to the best of your recollection, see Meer Hussud Alli before yesterday? **1828** SCOTT *F.M. Perth* xix, The scene of the preceding night ran in his recollection. **1860** TYNDALL *Glac.* II. xx. 336 The extraordinary coldness of the weather..is in the recollection of everybody. **1878** GLADSTONE *Prim. Homer* 41 It is likely that modern recollection has been weakened by habitual reliance upon..manuscript and print.

4. A thing or fact recalled to the mind; the memory *of* something.

1781 COWPER *Conversat.* 515 The recollection, like a vein of ore, The farther traced, enrich'd them still the more. **1815** SCOTT *Guy M.* l, I have an indistinct remembrance..; but it is an imperfect and confused recollection. **1856** STANLEY *Sinai & Pal.* xiv. (1858) 473 Nor can the Church of the Holy Sepulchre ever cease to be bound up with the recollections of the Crusades. **1883** MAINE *Early Law & Custom* ix. 292 A recollection or a fresh tradition.

5. *pl.* A message expressing recollection of, or a desire to be recollected by, another.

1816 LADY MORGAN *Autobiog.* (1859) 109 Our compliments to Sir Arthur and Clarke; most particular remembrances to Mrs. Fletcher... Recollections to the Doyles.

recollective (rɛkəˈlɛktɪv), *a.* [f. RECOLLECT *v.*² + -IVE. Cf. *collective.*]

1. Relating to, characterized by, concerned with, recollection.

1789 MME. D'ARBLAY *Let.* 27 Oct., A sort of recollective melancholy. **1802** MRS. E. PARSONS *Myst. Visit* III. 86 After a recollective silence of some minutes. **1852** LYNCH *Lett. to Scattered*, etc. (1872) 255 For this purpose, we must often cast a recollective glance over our history.

2. Given to, distinguished by (the power of), occupied with, recollection.

1813 MAR. EDGEWORTH *Patronage* (1833) II. xxii. 23 He possessed..an uncommonly recollective memory. **1824** MISS MITFORD *Village* Ser. I. (1863) 151 Then she was fanciful, recollective, new. **1838** WHEWELL in Todhunter *Acc. Writ.* (1876) II. 271 Live recollective of us.

Hence **recoˈllectively** *adv.*, **recoˈllectiveness**.

1820 *Examiner* No. 658. 744/1 The sullen din of the recent storm still murmurs recollectively in our ears. **1824** *Ibid.* 323/2 The pensive recollectiveness of the daughter.

‖**recollet** (rekɔle). Also 8 recolet. [F. *récollet* = Sp., Pg. *recoleto*, It. *recolletto*, ad. L. *recollect-us*: see RECOLLECT *v.*² 4 and cf. RECOLLECTION² 1.] = RECOLLECT *sb.*

1760 *Ann. Reg.* I. 227 If..the jesuits and the recolets [in Canada] chuse to go to France, passage shall be granted them in his Britannic majesty's ships. **1766** SMOLLETT *Trav.* 115 Here I found a young Irish recollet, on his way from Rome to his own country. **1801** CHARLOTTE SMITH *Lett. Solit. Wand.* II. 283 He..knocked softly at a door..which was opened by an old recollet. **1889** J. G. ALGER *Englishm. Fr. Rev.* 350 One of the Irish recollets at Boulay.

b. *attrib.* and *appos.* Cf. RECOLLECT *sb.* b.

1695 MOTTEUX *St. Olon's Morocco* 13 Towards the maintaining of a little Hospital, and two Spanish Recollet Monks. **1748** *Earthquake Peru* i. 75 That they call del Prado ..was for the Recolet Augustines. **1876** *Encycl. Brit.* IV. 765/1 A cathedral was erected..at Quebec, on the site of the old Recollet church.

reˈcollocate, *v. rare*⁻¹. [RE- 5 a.] *trans.* To put in place again. (In quot. app. *refl.*)

1597 A. M. tr. *Guillemeau's Fr. Chirurg.* 14 b/2 The Crochet or hoocke, which descendinge, elevateth it selfe, and recollocateth as much as is needfulle.

reˈcolonize, *v.* [RE- 5 a.] **1.** *trans.* To colonize (a place) anew. Hence **reˈcolonizing** *ppl. a.*

1598 SYLVESTER *Du Bartas* II. ii. I. *Ark* 60 Now while the World's re-colonizing Boat Doth on the waters over Mountains float. **1797** W. TAYLOR in *Monthly Mag.* IV. 335 After this devastation, the Persian court..were desirous of recolonizing the town. **1849** GROTE *Greece* II. xlii. V. 284 He planted in it new inhabitants, of Dorian and Messenian race, recolonizing it under the name of Messene. **1976** *Listener* 18 Mar. 329/2 The Europeans are back, recolonising Africa.

2. *Ecol.* Of a plant, animal, or other organism: to return to (a former habitat of the species or group concerned).

1943 J. S. HUXLEY in *Discovery* Jan. 9/1 Mountain regions ..have become re-colonized since the retreat of the ice. **1954** *New Biol.* XVII. 18 The best that can be done is to allow the elephant-grass, *Pennisetum*, to recolonize a fallow plot. **1958** *Ibid.* XXVII. 47 The appropriate cells..then find their way into the damaged tissue to recolonize it. **1961** *Times* 19 Apr. 14/7 The hares have recolonized the fields. **1963** *Lancet* 19 Jan. 133/1 This pattern suggested that the patients' skin had been recolonised by normal commensal organisms. **1967** *Oceanogr. & Marine Biol.* V. 320 It [*sc.* a sea-urchin]..became extinct during the glacial periods, though surviving in Australia, and recolonizing New Zealand in interglacial periods.

So **recoloniˈzation**.

1822 W. TAYLOR in *Monthly Mag.* LIII. 401 The protection shown by him to the re-colonization of Jerusalem under Nehemiah. **1884** J. T. BENT in *Macm. Mag.* Oct. 430/1 There were many projects afloat for the re-colonisation of different parts of Hellas. **1923** *Jrnl. Ecol.* XI. 242 In places re-colonisation by *Saxifraga oppositifolia* of such 'blow-outs' was observed. **1956** *Nature* 11 Feb. 282/1 By recolonization, the yield of a sprayed plot may be diminished. **1958** *New Biol.* XXVII. 47 The 'homing' instinct of the injected cells is so remarkable that the recolonization hypothesis was not at first accepted. **1973** *Nature* 3 Aug. 254/2 Factors inhibiting the recolonization by plants of colliery spoil..were reviewed by American and British workers.

recolour (riːˈkʌlə(r)), *v.* [RE- 5 a.]

1. *intr.* Of a thing: To resume its colour. *rare.*

1814 BYRON *Lara* I. xiii, The swarthy blush recolours in his cheeks, His lip resumes its red.

2. *trans.* To colour (a thing) anew.

1839 ARNOLD in Stanley *Life* (1844) II. ix. 162 That they must recolour all their geological maps. **1887** D. A. LOW *Machine Draw.* (1892) 3 If it is necessary to recolour any part, let the first coating dry before beginning.

recolta, variant of RACCOLTA. *Obs.*

‖**récolte** (rekɔlt). Also 8 recolt. [Fr.] A harvest or crop. (Chiefly in France.)

1788 *Antiq.* in *Ann. Reg.* 121 The face..has a calathus, or recolt basket, on the top of its head. **1865** M. EYRE *Lady's Walks* xxix. 311 Chesnuts are also a *récolte*, they are.. commonly sold ready roasted and stripped of the husk in the markets. **1971** *Country Life* 2 Dec. 1557/2 Much of this surplus..has now been re-classified to help the meagre *récolte* in 1971.

recomand(e, -aund(e, varr. RECOMMAND *v.*¹

recomˈbinable, *a.* [f. as next + -ABLE.] Capable of recombining or being recombined.

1964 D. MICHIE in G. H. Haggis *Introd. Molecular Biol.* x. 272 The most important conclusion from this work concerns the attempt to relate the size of the recombinable units, as measured genetically, to the dimensions of the DNA molecule. **1970** J. S. BRUNER in K. Connolly *Mechanisms Motor Skill Development* 79 It is in the altered nature of failure that one sees most vividly the differentiation of a gross act into a set of recombinable constituents.

recombinant (rɪˈkɒmbɪnænt), *a.* and *sb. Genetics.* [f. RECOMBIN(E *v.* + -ANT¹.]

A. *adj.* Formed by recombination.

1942 *Jrnl. Genetics* XLIII. 320 Double and higher recombinant types were neglected. **1960** *New Biol.* XXXI. 71 A daughter chromosome might be formed by copying first the ab fragment and then the C portion of the original chromosome so that we now have a recombinant chromosome, abC. **1971** D. J. COVE *Genetics* iii. 21 If a yellow-conidiospored strain is crossed to a strain requiring the vitamin biotin, it is found that a considerable excess of parental types over recombinant types is obtained. **1975** *Nature* 18 Dec. 562/3 The hazards associated with cloning recombinant DNA molecules can only be speculated about, since there is no experimental evidence to prove or deny that they exist. **1977** *Time* 7 Mar. 51/1 Should Harvard and M.I.T. be permitted to go ahead with experiments in so-called recombinant DNA-experiments involving the implantation, in cells of a common bacterium, of alien DNA-borne genes? **1978** *Daedalus* Spring 39 Much of the discussion about recombinant DNA research has centred on whether the work is likely to create hazardous organisms.

B. *sb.* A recombinant organism or cell.

1951 *Jrnl. Gen. Microbiol.* V. 59 Produce a double infection and..obtain in the population of virus units resulting a proportion of recombinants. *Ibid.*, The existence of recombinants can..only be demonstrated if conditions can be so arranged as to favour their selective proliferation. **1969** A. M. CAMPBELL *Episomes* ix. 124 Crosses between lambda and 434 fail to produce any recombinants that generate one immunity and respond to another. **1976** *Nature* 1 July 2/3 Foreign genes are inserted into the bacterium by splicing them into a plasmid..and reintroducing the recombinant into the bacterium.

recombinase (riːˈkɒmbɪneɪz). *Biochem.* [f. RECOMBIN(ATION + -ASE.] An enzyme or enzyme system which promotes genetic recombination.

1964 A. W. & P. B. KOZINSKI in *Proc. Nat. Acad. Sci.* LII. 211 We postulated..that recombination between T4DNA molecules requires a specific enzyme, 'recombinase'. **1969** A. M. CAMPBELL *Episomes* ii. 18 These two proteins seem to function in a recombinase system. **1970** *Austral. Jrnl. Biol. Sci.* XXIII. 1237 The product of *rec-w*⁺ could be a regulator specifically controlling the recombinase which initiates recombination at the *cog* locus.

recombiˈnation. [RE- 5 a.] **1.** The action or an instance of recombining.

1828 in WEBSTER. **1847** A. DE MORGAN *Formal Logic* xi. 218 It is good against those who confound analysis and recombination of existing materials with introduction of them. **1850** GROTE *Greece* II. lxvii. (1862) VI. 45 Was it a decomposition and recombination of elements still continuing? **1873** SYMONDS *Grk. Poets* xi. 344 A complete revision and recombination of all pre-existing anthologies.

2. *Physics.* The recombining of ions and electrons to form neutral atoms. Freq. *attrib.*

1897 *Phil. Mag.* XLIV. 424 When a gas is acted on by the Röntgen rays a steady state is reached when the rate of production of the ions by the rays is equal to their rate of recombination. **1942** J. D. STRANATHAN *'Particles' Mod. Physics* i. 8 Let us suppose that there are n pairs of ions present per cc. at any time, n positive ions and n negative ions... The number of recombinations R per cc. per second is then given by $R = an^2$ where a is a constant called the coefficient of recombination. **1962** *Guardian* 10 July 9/5 Atoms in the atmosphere would be broken up in extremely large numbers, so that this recombination light would be visible even to the naked human eye. **1969** J. J. SPARKES *Transistor Switching* i. 13 It will first have to supply the recombination current for any charge already present. **1974** *Encycl. Brit. Macropædia* XIV. 506/2 Other forms of radiation met with in plasma physics include line and recombination radiation.

3. *Genetics.* **a.** The formation by a sexual process of genotypes that differ from both the parental genotypes.

1903 *Proc. Cambr. Philos. Soc.* XII. 53 Since the resolution of a compound character may be spoken of as an analysis leading to a distribution of the components among the gametes, the term synthesis should surely be reserved for a recombination that has taken place in such a way that the gametes become bearers of the compound character again, as they were in the pure compound form. **1909** W. BATESON *Mendel's Princ. Heredity* iii. 71 These cases of novelties resulting through a re-combination of the factors brought in by the original pure types are striking because it is not at first sight evident how the novelty has been produced. **1941** J. S. HUXLEY *Uniqueness of Man* iv. 107 Recombination—*i.e.*..reshuffling of old genes in new constellations owing to independent assortment after a cross. This accounts for most of the differences observed between brothers and sisters in the same family. **1976** *Times Lit. Suppl.* 6 Aug. 985/2 Recombination was an idea that Darwin had lacked in his attempt to explain how natural selection and breeding were connected.

b. The formation by crossing-over of chromosomes that differ from both the chromosomes from which they derive. Also *attrib.*

1923 BRIDGES & MORGAN *Third-Chromosome Group of Mutant Characters of Drosophila Melanogaster* i. 9 If Dichæte is crossed to pink, and the F_1 female is back-crossed to a pink male, most of the flies are of the two original types, Dichæte or pink; but a small number of the offspring are both Dichæte and pink or neither (i.e., wild-type). These two latter classes are called 'recombination classes' and the 'percentage of recombination' may be found... The use of the term 'recombination' in this technical sense is a shortening of the full term 'recombination of linked characters'. **1939** C. D. DARLINGTON *Evolution of Genetic Systems* xiv. 77 This recombination we now see is more profound than Weismann imagined. It extends beyond the chromosomes to the genes. The number of units capable of recombination is not five or even fifty, but five thousand or fifty thousand. *Ibid.*, Taking the sum of the haploid number of chromosomes and of the average chiasma frequency of all the chromosomes in a meiotic cell as a recombination index. **1940** *Jrnl. Genetics* XL. 429 Let x be the recombination frequency. **1943** *Biol. Rev.* XVIII. 50 In one set of individuals AB and ab may be more favoured than Ab and aB, the reverse may be true elsewhere and, as recombination is the only means short of mutation of changing the arrangement, this inconstancy of advantage must favour some degree of recombination. **1955** *Jrnl. Gen. Microbiol.* XIII. 346 Genetic recombination has now been demonstrated amongst several viruses. **1965** *Proc. Nat. Acad. Sci.* LIII. 457 The term 'recombination' when used in the context of bacterial genetics connotes to many either the process of DNA transmission known as conjugation or the formation by conjugation of any progeny which inherit phenotypic traits derived from both parents. It can, however, be used more strictly to denote the series of physical and chemical events which serve to link genes derived from one parental DNA with those derived from another parental DNA. **1976** *National Observer* (U.S.) 5 July 6/1 The object of these guidelines is to ensure that experimental DNA recombination will have no ill effects on those engaged in the work, on the general public, or on the environment. **1977** A. W. F. EDWARDS *Foundations Math. Genetics* viii. 94 Linkage is not complete, and its magnitude is measured by the recombination fraction, r, between the two loci.

recombi'national, *a. Genetics.* [f. prec. + -AL.] Of or pertaining to recombination.
1959 *Nature* 14 Nov. 1593/1 (*heading*) Recombinational lethals in a polymorphic population. *Ibid.* 1594/1 A recessive lethal can be produced by recombinational instead of mutational change. **1969** *Genetics* LXI. 298 The problem of recipient culture variability during recombinational analyses. **1977** *Jrnl. Protozool.* XXIV. 27/2 The duplex forms could have arisen as a consequence of a prior mutational or recombinational event.
Hence **recombi'nationally** *adv.*, by or as a result of recombination.
1969 W. D. STANSFIELD *Theory & Probl. Genetics* ix. 184 Recombinationally separable forms of a gene within a cistron are referred to as heteroalleles.

recombi'nationless, *a. Genetics.* [f. as prec. + -LESS.] That does not show recombination.
1969 L. LEVINE *Biol. of Gene* v. 101/2 They were able to isolate two recombinationless (Rec) mutants in an F strain of *Escherichia coli* K12. **1974** *Nature* 4 Jan. 44/1 Recombinationless bacterial mutants are highly sensitive to near-ultraviolet, suggesting that DNA may be an indirect target of the action of near-ultraviolet.

recombine (riːkəm'baɪn), *v.* [RE- 5 a.]
1. *trans.* To combine (things) anew.
a **1639** T. CAREW *Poems, On Marriage of T.K. & C.C.*, Which [hands] when to-day the Priest shall recombine [etc.]. **1832** BABBAGE *Econ. Manuf.* xxv. 210 The idea of separating these letters, and of recombining them into other words. **1865** GROTE *Plato* I. i. 54 *note*, Ingredients might be disengaged and re-combined in countless ways.
absol. **1846** GROTE *Greece* I. xvi. I. 543 He left out, altered, recombined, and supplied new connecting principles.
2. *intr.* To enter into a fresh combination.
1859 MILL *Liberty* ii. 85 With what a salutary shock did the paradoxes of Rousseau explode like bombshells in the midst..of onesided opinion..forcing its elements to recombine in a better form. **1881** FLOWER in *Nature* XXIV. 436 They cannot recombine, and so give rise to new forms. **1910** W. M. WHEELER *Ants* viii. 131 These characters..are relatively stable in particular races or varieties and have a tendency to combine and recombine in endless permutation. **1942** J. D. STRANATHAN *'Particles' Mod. Physics* i. 27 Ions formed in a gas have a tendency to recombine. **1974** *Encycl. Brit. Macropædia* IX. 811/2 Nitrogen ions may recombine similarly.

recombinogenic (riːˌkɒmbɪnəʊ'dʒenɪk), *a. Biol.* [f. RECOMBIN(ATION + -O + -GENIC.] Tending to cause genetic recombination.
1965 *Genetics* LII. 107 (*heading*) The recombinogenic effect of thymidylate starvation in *Escherichia coli* merodiploids. **1971** *Nature* 12 Nov. 71/3 It is not unreasonable to assume that the protein plays an important part in some facet of meiosis, and in view of the T4 evidence, neither is it unreasonable to suppose that it has some recombinogenic activity.

recomende, obs. form of RECOMMEND *v.*[1]

†**recomfort**, *sb. Obs.* Also 5 recoum-. [ad. F. *reconfort* (13th c.): see RE- and COMFORT *sb.*] Comfort, support, consolation.
c **1420** LYDG. *Hist. Thebes* II. 580 He shall be relessed of his peine, Through recomfort of some high mariage. **1474** CAXTON *Chesse* III. ii. (1860) Fj, And wyth this ought the maronners..to be of good recomforte. *c* **1555** ABP. PARKER *Ps.* xlii. 121 When this..came soone to hart, I yet therein recomfort felt. **1588** N. YONGE *Mus. Transalp.* xxxi. Div, He..so great a fire had framed, As were enough to burne mee, Without recomfort. **1605** CAMDEN *Rem.* (1637) 403, I will..for his [the reader's] recomfort end this part with a few..laughing Epitaphes.

recomfort (riː'kʌmfət), *v. Obs.* exc. *arch.* Forms: see COMFORT *v.* [ad. F. *reconforter* (11th c.): see RE- and COMFORT *v.*]
1. *trans.* †**a.** To strengthen or inspire with fresh courage; to put heart or spirit in again. *Obs.*
1375 BARBOUR *Bruce* IX. 97 He..To perellis him abawndonys ay For to reconfort his menȝe. **1442** T. BECKINGTON *Corr.* (Rolls) II. 188 By our commyng and arriveng al your cite was gretly recomforted. *c* **1477** CAXTON *Jason* 17 Whan the noble Jason felte hym self so aduironned on alle sydes by hys enemyes he was more reconforted than tofore. **1525** LD. BERNERS *Froiss.* II. xlv. 152 There myght well haue ben sene good ordre of batayle, and people well recomforted. **1533** MORE *Apol.* 3 b, Agaynste all thys feare this one thynge recomforted me, that [etc.]. **1600** FAIRFAX *Tasso* VI. i, But better hopes had them recomforted That lay besieged in the sacred towne. *Ibid.* IX. xciv, At last they went and to recomfort thought, And stay theire troopes from flight. **1667** MILTON *P.L.* IX. 918 As one from sad dismay Re-comforted.
b. To soothe, console, or relieve in distress or trouble. Const. *from*, †*of*. Now *rare* (common *c* 1375–1650).
c **1374** CHAUCER *Troylus* II. 1623 (1672) Hym with al hire wit to reconfort, As sche best coude, sche gan him disport. *c* **1402** LYDG. *Compl. Bl. Knt.* ii, Hertys hevy for to recomforte From dreriheed of hevy nightes sorowe. **1470–85** MALORY *Arthur* VII. xxxiv, Syr Gareth recomforted his moder in suche wyse that she recouerd and made good chere. *c* **1530** LD. BERNERS *Arth. Lyt. Bryt.* (1814) 297 In especyall Florence was ryght sorowful, for there was none yᵗ could recomfort her. **1597** HOOKER *Eccl. Pol.* v. lxxv. §3 Others,..bringing their Ancestors vnto the graue with weeping eyes, haue notwithstanding meanes wherewith to be recomforted. **1626** G. SANDYS *Ovid's Met.* I. 7 The King of Gods re-comforts their despaire. **1647** H. MORE *Song of Soul* II. i. III. iii, I grew sick of the worlds vanity Ne ought recomfort could my sunken spright. **1822** DE QUINCEY *Confess.* (1853) 67 Recomforted by this promise.., I returned in a Windsor coach to London. **1890** S. EVANS *Graal* I. 150 This doth recomfort me, that the Best Knight gat blame in like manner as I.
†**c.** *refl.* and *absol.* To take courage or heart again; to recover one's spirits. *Obs.*
c **1386** CHAUCER *Knt.'s T.* 1994 Ful wisely to enhorte The peple that they sholde hem reconforte. **1475** *Bk. Noblesse* (Roxb.) 64 The Romayns..recomforting hem foughten so vigorouslie ayenst theire adversaries that they hadde the victorie. **1525** LD. BERNERS *Froiss.* II. 499 Therwith they reconforted & toke corage. **1625** K. LONG tr. *Barclay's Argenis* v. x. 362 At these words Hyanisbe recomforted herselfe, insomuch as shee could hardly conceale her joy. **1654** GAYTON *Pleas. Notes* IV. vi–vii. 204 He recomforted himselfe, calling to mind that the artifice was all his friends, unto which he had scarce concurr'd.
2. (Usu. of things): To strengthen or invigorate physically; to refresh. Also *absol.* Now *rare*.
c **1430** LYDG. *Min. Poems* (Percy Soc.) 15 The pome-cedre corageos to recomfort. *c* **1470** HENRY *Wallace* II. 275 The womannys mylk recomford him full swyth. **1481** CAXTON *Myrr.* II. vii. 79 The Emerawde..recomforteth alle the sight of hym that beholdeth it. **1575** TURBERV. *Venerie* 21 That oyntment..recomfortes the skynne and the synewes of dogges. **1596** BARROUGH *Meth. Physick* III. xxx. (1639) 152 You must be much diligent..to give him a diet that recomforteth and refresheth strength. **1626** BACON *Sylva* §403 It is usuall to help the Ground with Muck; And likewise to Recomfort it sometimes with Muck put to the Roots. **1814** CARY *Dante, Inf.* I. 27 My weary frame After short pause recomforted, again I journey'd.
†**b.** *refl.* of persons (and animals): To refresh or recreate (oneself). *Obs.*
1511 GUYLFORDE *Pilgr.* (Camden) 61 We rested vs and refresshed vs..and so recomforted our self after the greate scarsnesse that we hadde susteyned. **1513** BRADSHAW *St. Werburge* I. 1061 This harte sore strayned ranne..To a well, with water..Hym to reconforte and the more fressher be. **1591** SPENSER *M. Hubberd* 758 With Loves, and Ladies gentle sports, The ioy of youth, himselfe he recomforts.
Hence †**re'comfortable** *a.*, comfortable, consoling; †**recomfor'tation**, consolation; †**re'comforted** *ppl. a.* (also *absol.*). *Obs.*
1581 J. BELL *Haddon's Answ. Osor.* 392 A certayn never interrupted course of recomfortable refreshyng in Christ. **1585** HATTON in Ld. Campbell *Chancellors* (1857) II. xlv. 273, I most humbly thank your sacred Majesty for your two late recomfortations. *a* **1586** SIDNEY *Arcadia* III. Wks. 1724 II. 623 The now fully recomforted Dorus. **1607** SHAKS. *Cor.* v. iv. 51 Ne're through an Arch so hurried the blowne Tide, As the recomforted through th'gates.

†**re'comforting**, *vbl. sb. Obs.* [f. prec. + -ING[1].] Encouragement, consolation.
1375 BARBOUR *Bruce* XI. 499 Apon this wiss the nobill king Gaf all his men reconforting. **1423** JAS. I *Kingis Q.* clxxvi, Gif ȝe goddis..Haue schewit this for my reconforting. *a* **1550** *O Lusty Flour* 31 in *Dunbar's Poems* (1893) 327, I sall my pen address Sangis to mak for thy recomforting. **1611** COTGR., *Refocillation*, a refreshing,..recomforting.

†**re'comfortless**, *a. Obs.*$^{-1}$ [f. RECOMFORT *sb.* + -LESS.] Without comfort.
1596 SPENSER *F.Q.* v. vi. 24 There all that night remained Britomart, Restless, recomfortlesse.

†**re'comforture.** *Obs.*$^{-1}$ [f. RECOMFORT *v.* + -URE.] Consolation, comfort.
1594 SHAKS. *Rich. III*, IV. iv. 425 They will breed Selues of themselues, to your recomforture.

†**reco'mmand**, *v.*[1] *Obs.* Forms: 4–5 recoma(u)nde, 4–6 recommaunde, 5 recoma(u)nd, recumaunde, etc. [ad. F. *recommander* (12th c.), f. *re-* RE- + *commander* to command or commend: on the relationship to RECOMMEND *v.*[1], see the etym. notes to the vbs. COMMAND and COMMEND.]
1. = RECOMMEND *v.*[1] I.
c **1380** *Sir Ferumb.* 256 He lifte vp ys hond & blessed him þan & recomandedem to god almiȝte. **1490** CAXTON *How to Die* 9, [I] recommaunde at thys tyme my spyryte in to thy handes. *a* **1533** LD. BERNERS *Huon* l. 169, I recommaunde thee to yᵉ kepinge of our lorde god. *Ibid.* lxii. 218 Therfore, syr, I recommaunde you to our lord god.
b. = RECOMMEND *v.*[1] I b.
c **1374** CHAUCER *Troylus* II. 1021 (1070) In ful humble wyse..He gan hym recommaunde unto her grace. **1390** GOWER *Conf.* Prol. 29 *So ferforth I me recomande To him which al me may comande. *c* **1400** MAUNDEV. (Roxb.) ix. 33 þai take lefe at þe mounkes and recomaundes þam specially to þer praiers.
c. *ellipt.* To commend to the prayers of the people. *rare*$^{-1}$.
1389 *Eng. Gilds* 31 þe comoun belleman schal..recomandyn al þe brethere soules and systeres of þe gilde be name, and alle crystene soules.
d. = RECOMMEND *v.*[1] I c.
1390 GOWER *Conf.* III. 33 To youre avis, Min holi fader, ..I recomande myn astat. *c* **1400** *Master of Game* (MS. Digby 182) Prol., I..am me auntred to make this litel symple booke, which I recommaunde and submytte to youre noble and wyse correccioun. *c* **1500** *Melusine* 191 To these two knightes Raymondyn & Melusyne had recommanded the estate of theire two sones.
2. *refl.* and *absol.* To commend (oneself) to the kindly remembrance or regard of another. (Used in letters.)
a **1413** PRINCE HENRY *Let.* in *Nat. MSS.* I. 36, I recomande me to yowr good & gracieux lordship. **1425** *Paston Lett.* I. 21 Right worthy and worshepeful Sir, I recomaunde to yow preyeng yow to wite [etc.]. **1455** *Rolls of Parlt.* V. 280/2 We recommaunde us unto you.
b. To speak of or mention (a person) *to* another, with a view to exciting kindly remembrance or regard. Freq. used in messages.
c **1374** CHAUCER *Troylus* I. 1000 (1056) 'This in special', Quod Troilus, 'that thou me recomaunde To hir that to the deeth me may comaunde'. *c* **1430** LYDG. *Min. Poems* (Percy Soc.) 163 Go litel bille..And of hool herte recomaund me, ..To alle tho folk which lyst to have pité. **1470–85** MALORY *Arthur* IV. viii, Accolon..said, recommaunde me vnto my lady Quene and telle her all shal be done that I haue promysed her. *a* **1533** LD. BERNERS *Huon* cxlvi. 547 When he saw that I wold depart thence to come into this countre, he humbly prayed me to recommaunde hym to you.
absol. *a* **1440** *Sir Degrev.* 877 Recumaunde, for God's pyne To my lady and thinne.

reco'mmand, *v.*[2] [RE- 5 a.] *trans.* To command again.
1509 HAWES *Past. Pleas.* XVI. xix, She commaunded her mynstrelles right anone to play..She me recommaunded..To daunce true mesures. **1622** WITHER *Mistr. Philar.* Wks. (1633) 731 For as much as doubt you make To re-command me: of mine own accord Another Strain, I freely will afford. **1653** J. HALL *Paradoxes* 82 So can wee no more recommand them then call back yesterday. **1864** *Reader* 18 June, The great *bravura* duet..was, of course, recommanded by an irresistible encore.

recommence (riːkə'mɛns), *v.* [ad. F. *recommencer* (11th c.): see RE- and COMMENCE *v.*]
1. *intr.* To begin again.
1481 CAXTON *Godfrey* clxiv. 242 Thenne recommenced and began agayn the playnte and the clamour. **1603** HOLLAND *Plutarch's Mor.* 1140 Violence That never ends, but aie doth recommence. *c* **1645** HOWELL *Lett.* I. xxxii. 276 If any odd thoughts intervene and grow upon me, I check my self, and recommence. **1812** SOUTHEY *Omniana* II. 238 Shortly afterwards that war recommenced. **1860** TYNDALL *Glac.* I. xii. 87 The sound..ceased, but it soon recommenced.
b. With complement. (See COMMENCE *v.* 3 b.)
1778–81 JOHNSON *L.P.*, *Swift* Wks. III. 396 He seems desirous enough of recommencing courtier. **1791** BENTHAM *Wks.* (1843) X. 266, I am recommenced wild beast.
2. *trans.* To cause to begin again; to renew.
1494 FABYAN *Chron.* VII. 313 The Frenshe Kynge had recommencyd his warre. **1585** T. WASHINGTON tr. *Nicholay's Voy.* II. xiii. 48 [He] caused to be recommenced the works of Calcedon. *a* **1648** LD. HERBERT *Hen. VIII* (1683) 178 Whensoeuer the said Duke shall re-commence his former suit. **1784** KING *Cook's 3rd Voy.* VI. ii. III. 210 We..told him, that we purposed recommencing our voyage about the 5th of June. **1829** SOUTHEY *Sir T. More* I. 250 Well will it be if the present age should not see its ravages recommenced. **1875** JOWETT *Plato* (ed. 2) I. 185 The two brothers recommence their exhortation to virtue.
Hence **reco'mmencing** *ppl. a.*
1830 J. DOUGLAS *Truths Relig.* (1832) II. 114 The fancy of the recommencing series of existences is realised.

reco'mmencement. [RE- 5 a.] A fresh commencement.
1778–81 JOHNSON *L.P.*, *Addison* Wks. III. 64 The Spectator, from its recommencement, was published only three times a week. **1823** LAMB *Elia* Ser. II. *Poor Relations*, The recommencement..of actual hostilities. **1885** *Manch. Even. News* 6 July 2/2 The reassembling of Parliament, and the recommencement of actual work.

reco'mmencer. [f. RECOMMENCE *v.* + -ER[1].] One who begins again.
1803 W. TAYLOR in *Ann. Rev.* I. 257 The recommencers of hostile practises. **1854** EMERSON *Lett. & Soc. Aims* i. (1875) 30 He is a true re-commencer, or Adam in the garden again.

recommend (rɛkə'mɛnd), *sb. colloq.* (orig. *U.S.*). [f. the vb.] A recommendation.
1806 L. DOW *Travels* I. iv. 110 This morning, I went on shore, having no proper recommends with me. **1832** J. J. STRANG *Diary* 19 Feb. in M. M. Quaife *Kingdom of St. James* (1930) 202 There is no complaint against me and they offer me a good recommend. **1892** B. POTTER *Jrnl.* (1966) 227 Miss Emmet..wedged in a recommend of farmhouse lodgings of her cousins. **1894** *Harper's Mag.* Feb. 351/1, I think he would give it an autograph recommend. **1897** R. KIPLING *Capt. Cour.* 227 I'm glad to have a recommend from that quarter. **1908** *Practitioner* Nov. 731 The Committee pays for out-patient 'recommends' at the rate of one guinea for six. **1924** J. GALSWORTHY *White Monkey* I. viii. 65 They'll give you a good recommend, won't they? **1967** [see *book-society* s.v. BOOK *sb.* 19]. **1977** *Listener* 30 June 867/4 William McIlvanney's *Laidlaw* comes with a recommend from Ross Macdonald.

recommend (rɛkə'mɛnd), *v.*[1] Also 4–5 recomende. [ad. med.L. *recommendāre* (1216 in Du Cange), f. *re-* RE- + *commendāre* to COMMEND. Cf. obs. F. *recommender*, an occasional variant of *recommander* to RECOMMAND *v.*[1] (q.v.).]
1. a. To commend or commit (oneself or another, one's soul or spirit) *to* God, his keeping, etc. Also (rarely) without const. (Cf. COMMEND *v.* I.)
c **1400** MAUNDEV. (1839) xvi. 177 Seyenge his Orysounes, recommendynge him to his God. **1418** in *E.E. Wills* (1882) 30, I recommend my saule to almyghty god. **1572** HULOET s.v., To recommende him selfe to God. **1611** BIBLE *Acts* xiv. 26 And thence sailed to Antioch, from whence they had been recommended to the grace of God. **1676** RAY *Corr.* (1848) 124, I recommend you to the Divine protection. **1711** ADDISON *Spect.* No. 7 ¶6 When I lay me down to Sleep, I recommend myself to his Care. **1760–72** H. BROOKE *Fool of Qual.* (1809) IV. 106, I recommended my spirit in a short

ejaculation. **1791** Mrs. Radcliffe *Rom. Forest* ix, I silently recommended myself to God. **1883** Stevenson *Treas. Isl.* v. xxiii, I..devoutly recommended my spirit to its Maker.

absol. *c* **1489** Caxton *Sonnes of Aymon* xxviii. 576 He made the signe of the crosse vpon him and recomended to our lorde.

b. (Chiefly *refl.*) To commit (oneself or another) *to* a person (or thing), or *to* some one's care, prayers, etc.

In some cases perh. with implication of sense 4 c.

c **1386** Chaucer *2nd Nun's T.* 544, I axed this at hevene king, To han respyt..To recomende to yow er that I go Thise soules. *c* **1400** Maundev. (1839) vi. 63 Than wil thei take leve of the Monkes and recommenden hem to here Preyeres. *a* **1533** Ld. Berners *Gold. Bk. M. Aurel.* xlvii. 91 b, My sonne I recommend to the Helia thy stepmother. *a* **1649** Drumm. of Hawth. *Hist. Jas. V* Wks (1711) 92 He ..recommended himself to the sea in the spring time. **1713** Steele *Guard.* No. 17 ¶8 He led her to a relation's house, to whose care he recommended her for that night. **1844** Lingard *Anglo-Sax. Ch.* (1858) I. vii. 310 [They] recommended themselves to the prayers of those who were distinguished by the austerity and sanctity of their lives.

†**c.** To give in charge, consign, commit, submit (a thing) *to* a person or thing. *Obs.*

c **1586** C'tess Pembroke *Ps.* lxvi. viii, What I to praiers recommended, Was gratiously by him attended. **1590** *Art. agst. Cartwright* §25 in Fuller *Ch. Hist.* ix. vii. §27 After it was perused by others..he recommended the same to the censures, and judgements of moe brethren. **1601** Shaks. *Twel. N.* v. i. 94 [He] denide me mine owne purse, Which I had recommended to his vse, Not halfe an houre before.

†**d.** To communicate or report (a thing) *to* a person. Also without const., to mention. *Obs.*

c **1586** C'tess Pembroke *Ps.* lxxviii. ii, The thinges our fathers did to us commend, The same are they I recommend to you. **1599** *Warn. Faire Wom.* ii. 77 I'll leave you, sir, to recommend my thanks Unto your kind respective wife. **1600** Holland *Livy* xxxix. l. 1055 Some of them have recommended to posteritie..that in this one yeere there dyed three renowned captaines. *a* **1641** Bp. Mountagu *Acts & Mon.* (1642) 119 Concerning him so to come, and to be incarnate, two things are recommended in this Prophecie.

†**e.** To inform (a person). *Obs. rare*$^{-1}$.

1604 Shaks. *Oth.* i. iii. 41 Signior Montano.. recommends you thus, And prayes you to beleeue him.

†**2. a.** = recommand *v.*[1] 2. *Obs.*

1444 *Paston Lett.* I. 55 Your sonys and..your brother arn heyle and mery, and recommend hem to yow. **1449** *Ibid.* 78, I recomend me hertily, thankyng yow for the tydings. **1529** More *Dyaloge* i. Wks. 107/1 As hartelye as I possible can, I recommende me to you. **1572** Huloet s.v., He recommendes him hartely to thee.

†**b.** = recommand *v.*[1] 2 b. *Obs.*

1539 Cromwell in Merriman *Life & Lett.* (1902) II. 201 The same Bernard..desired the said Christophor to aduertise your grace thereof and have hym recommended most humbly. **1773** Johnson *Let. to Mrs. Thrale* 24 May, Recommend me to the poor dear lady.

†**3.** To praise, commend: **a.** a person. *Obs.*

1377 Langl. *P. Pl.* B. xv. 228 Riche men he recomendeth ..That with-outen wyles leden her lyues. *c* **1400** *Sowdone Bab.* 919 He recomendide the olde Knightes That þat daye hade the victorye. *c* **1477** Caxton *Jason* 6 Seeyng that Jason was somoche recommended of euery man. **1523** Ld. Berners *Froiss.* I. xi. 6 b/2 The fyrste..was a good knyght, & greatly recommended. *a* **1703** Burkitt *On N.T., Matt.* xxiii. 33 They continued in their own wickedness, and yet recommended the saints departed.

†**b.** a thing. (Cf. 5 b.) *Obs.*

1705 Stanhope *Paraph.* II. 278 This glorious Testimony when Jesus had recommended as a Truth inspired from Heaven [etc.]. **1738** *Pref. J. Keill's Anim. Oecon.* 43 [They] have generally recommended and extolled those Parts which they best understood themselves.

4. †**a.** To commend to favour. *Obs. rare*$^{-1}$.

a **1601** North *Plutarch* (1610) 1177 Nonius Asprenas, one of his greatest friends, was accused by Cassius Severus... Augustus did not recommend him, but let the Senatours alone, who banished Cassius.

b. To name or speak of (one) as fit or worthy to hold some position or employment.

1641 *Nicholas Papers* (Camden) 48 The King did many dayes since intimate who they were he would recommend, but none were declared untill this morning. **1784** Cowper *Tiroc.* 417 A king, that would, might recommend his horse. **1802** James *Milit. Dict.* s.v., It is a regulation, that none under the rank of field officer in the regulars, can recommend a person so circumstanced.

c. To present or bring forward (a person) as worthy of notice, favour, care, etc. Const. *to* (a person, etc.), *for* (the thing desired).

1687 A. Lovell tr. *Thevenot's Trav.* i. 39 They [Turks].. invocate their Saints, as being able to recommend them to God. **1703** Steele *Tender Husb.* iii. ii, Madam, may I.. recommend Mr. Gubbin..to your Ladyships Notice? **1734** Swift *Lett.* (1766) II. 271 The trouble I gave in recommending a gentleman to your protection. **1830** D'Israeli *Chas. I*, III. viii. 162 [He] had been earnestly recommended by the Earl of Strafford to Charles. **1850** Mrs. Jameson *Leg. Monast. Ord.* 65 Whom the abbess thought qualified for orders, she recommended to the bishop who ordained them. **1853** Dearsly *Crim. Process* 73 If..the offender is a fit subject to be recommended for the royal mercy.

5. a. To mention or introduce (a thing) with approbation or commendation *to* a person, in order to induce acceptance or trial.

1581 Mulcaster *Positions* xxxix. (1887) 196, I must recommend vnto them exercise of the bodie. **1647** Clarendon *Hist. Reb.* ii. §1 He would both recommend and enjoin the practice and use of both to that of his native kingdom. **1687** A. Lovell tr. *Thevenot's Trav.* i. 96 [Biscuits] which were recommended to me, as an excellent thing to drink a mornings draught with. **1728** Veneer *Sinc. Penit.* Pref. 7 Tho' I do not care to say much in order to recommend my book..to such as are in the very gall of bitterness. **1781** Cowper *Retirem.* 541 O grant a poet leave to recommend..Her slighted works to your admiring view. **1826** Disraeli *Viv. Grey* v. xv, Let me recommend you a little of this pike! **1863** *Sat. Rev.* 16 May 640 We will conclude by recommending his work to our readers.

b. Without personal const. (Cf. 3 b.)

1714 Pope *Epil. Jane Shore* 34 He'd recommend her as a special breeder. **1725** De Foe *Voy. round World* (1840) 355, I take the liberty to recommend that part of America as the best and most advantageous part of the globe. **1781** Cowper *Retirem.* 388 For once I can approve the patriot's voice, And make the course he recommends my choice. **1820** Shelley *Œd. Tyr.* ii. ii. 22 Allow me now to recommend this dish. **1876** Mozley *Univ. Serm.* x. 231 Christianity and worldly wisdom..both recommending the same course.

6. To make (a person or thing) acceptable. Also const. *to.* (Chiefly of qualities, circumstances, or things.)

1665 Boyle *Occas. Refl.* vi. vi. (1848) 360 Roses..retain.. divers useful Qualities, and Virtues, that..recommend them all the Year. **1712** Addison *Spect.* No. 418 ¶3 There is yet another Circumstance which recommends a Description more than all the rest. **1782** Priestley *Corrupt. Chr.* I. i. 101 It was chiefly a wish to recommend their religion to others. **1832** Lewis *Use & Ab. Pol. Terms* iii. 21 A claim recommended by the practice..of the constitution. **1863** Cowden Clarke *Shaks. Char.* x. 268 That man has little enough to recommend him whom women dislike.

refl. **1605** Shaks. *Macb.* i. vi. 2 The ayre nimbly and sweetly recommends it selfe Vnto our gentle sences. **1651** Hobbes *Leviath.* ii. xxx. 185 To recommend themselves to his favour. **1758** S. Hayward *Serm.* xvii. 535 A person of eminent rank greatly recommends himself to the esteem of his fellow-creatures when he appears affable and friendly. **1859** Mill *Liberty* i. 12 This view of things, recommending itself equally to the intelligence of thinkers [etc.].

7. To counsel, advise. **a.** Const. *to* a person, usually with *it* as obj. (cf. 5) and appositive infin.

1746 *Col. Rec. Pennsylv.* V. 38 His Majesty has order'd me to recommend it to you..to proceed immediately [etc.]. **1749** Fielding *Tom Jones* xvi. viii, He..recommended to her ladyship to do him the honour. **1818** Cruise *Digest* (ed. 2) VI. 203 She recommended it to him to do justice to B. and her children.

b. Without personal const. (Cf. 5 b.)

1733 Pope *Hor. Sat.* ii. ii. 43 Let me extol a Cat, on oysters fed,..Or ev'n to crack live Crawfish recommend. **1818** Jas. Mill *Brit. India* I. iii. iv. 606 [He] recommended, what was probably wise, to gain Nizam al Mulk by resigning to him Deccan. **1829** W. Irving *Granada* I. x. 85 He recommended, that the whole disposition of the camp should be changed.

c. With personal obj., and infin.

1813 Jane Austen *Pride & Prej.* I. xviii. 217 Let me recommend you, however, as a friend, not to give implicit confidence to all his assertions. **1856** W. Collins *After Dark, Yellow Mask* II. 247, I recommend you to control your temper, and to treat me with common courtesy. **1877** Froude *Short Stud.* (1883) IV. i. ix. 103 He recommended the guardians to consult the king.

recommend, *v.*[2] *rare*$^{-1}$. [re- 5 a.] *trans.* To commend again.

1576 Fleming *Panopl. Epist.* 140, I am constrained of courtesie, to commend, and recommend the same L. Oppius ..to your patronage and defence.

recommendable (rɛkə'mɛndəb(ə)l), *a.* [f. recommend *v.*[1] + -able.] That may be recommended, worthy of praise. Also const. *to.*

1477 Earl Rivers (Caxton) *Dictes* 19 A Right recommendable thing in heuen and in erthe is a true tunge. **1602** T. Fitzherbert *Apol.* 6 The honorable cours of lyf he hath led..doth make him no lesse recomendable for true Christian pietie and vertue then for wisdome and valour. **1652** J. Wright tr. *Camus' Nat. Paradox* i. 12 All the recommendable qualities and exercise requisite for a Gentlewoman of such Extraction. *a* **1734** North *Lives* (1826) II. 217 The matchless pattern of his most recommendable character and successes. **1768–74** Tucker *Lt. Nat.* (1834) II. 662 There is a work..recommendable as well to those who have, as those who have not done any good work before. **1832** Carlyle in *Fraser's Mag.* V. 407 The Wise had found such Loyalty still practicable, and recommendable. **1888** H. S. Merriman *Phantom Fut.* II. x. 146 This method is scarcely recommendable to young men of impressionable hearts.

Hence **recommenda'bility, reco'mmendableness, reco'mmendably** *adv.*

1611 Cotgr., *Recommendablement*, recommendably,.. praise-worthily. **1660** H. More *Myst. Godl.* x. iii. §4 The fourth and last Rule or Measure of opinions is, The Recommendableness of our Religion to those which are without. **1796** Ld. St. Helens in *Bentham's Wks.* (1843) X. 319 Whether your quality of French citizen, instead of adding to your recommendability [etc.].

recommendation (ˌrɛkəmən'deɪʃən). [a. OF. *recommendation* (F. *recommand-*), or med.L. *recommendatiōn-em* (1270 in Du Cange), n. of action f. *recommendāre* to recommend.]

†**1.** The action of recommending oneself to another's remembrance; a message of this nature. *Obs.*

1450 *Paston Lett.* I. 135 After al due recomendacion, I recomaund me to yow. **1478** in *Surtees Misc.* (1888) 37 We ..sendes gretyng..& recommendaccin unto whome it seruys. *c* **1532** Du Wes *Introd. Fr.* in Palsgr. 1025, I you pray to do my most humble recommendations to the good grace of the Kyng. **1634** *Malory's Arthur* ii. cxlv, The letter..said thus..I send to all Knights arraunt recommendation.

attrib. **1552** Huloet s.v., Recommendation brynger, *salutifer.*

†**2.** The action of recommending or committing to another's care; hence, care, protection. *Obs.*

1483 Caxton *Gold. Leg.* 100/2 The fourth [privilege] is the recomendacion of the moder of god. *a* **1533** Ld. Berners *Gold. Bk. M. Aurel.* 91 b, Remembre she is..thy mother adoptife..wherfore I leue her vnder thy recommendation. **1557** Mrs. Basset tr. *More's Treat. Passion* M.'s Wks. 1400/1 At hys recommendacion [he] tooke hir from thencefoorth as hys owne [mother].

†**3.** Commendation, favour, repute, esteem. *Obs.*

1474 Caxton *Chesse* (ed. 2) A ij, It is a werke of ryght special recomendacion. **1481** —— *Myrr.* iii. xiii. 164 They that gladly myssaye of peple of recommendacion. **1523** Ld. Berners *Froiss.* I. ccxxxi. 314 They..were..well receyued, ..bycause they were lordes and knightes of great recommendacion. **1585** T. Washington tr. *Nicholay's Voy.* iii. xvii. 102 b, The Turkes haue aboue all thinges charitie in greate recommendacion.

4. a. The action of recommending a person or thing as worthy or desirable. Also, that which is recommended; a proposal or suggestion.

1578 *Reg. Privy Council Scot.* III. 25 [He must proceed by himself] uncareing langer for thair recommendatioun of ony [person]. **1585** T. Washington tr. *Nicholay's Voy.* iii. iii. 74 It is not..that either fauour or recommendation shal stand them in steed for the aduancing of them to any higher degree. **1651** Hobbes *Leviath.* iii. xlii. 296 Kings..may receive Schoolmasters for their Subjects from the recommendation of a stranger. **1709** Steele *Tatler* No. 94 ¶5 Buying at his Shop upon my Recommendation. **1778** Foote *Trip Calais* ii. Wks. 1799 II. 354 You have a notion that I should bring a..fortune to this spouse of your recommendation? **1841** Elphinstone *Hist. Ind.* II. ix. iii. 323 He had no..restrictions about food, except a recommendation of abstinence, as tending to exalt the mind. **1911** G. B. Shaw *Doctor's Dilemma* 299 How this was effected may be gathered from the recommendations finally agreed on. **1929** *Star* 21 Aug. 19/1 It is interesting to record that some of our recommendations have duly improved in capital value. **1976** *Daily Tel.* 20 July 2/3 A report following a public enquiry into the disaster made a number of observations and recommendations.

b. *letter of recommendation*, a letter recommending a person; in later use, a letter of introduction. Cf. recommendatory *a.* 1 b. Also *fig.*

1494 Fabyan *Chron.* v. cxv. 89 He..sent to hym a great summe of golde, with letters of recommendacion, exortynge hym [etc.]. **1548** Elyot, *Commendatitiæ literæ*, letters of recommendacion. *c* **1645** Howell *Lett.* (1650) II. 48 An honest, ingenious look is a good letter of recommendation, of itself. **1662** J. Davies tr. *Olearius' Voy. Ambass.* 130 The Duke of Holstein..gave him Letters of Recommendation to the Great Duke of Muscovy. **1725** De Foe *Voy. round World* (1840) 31 The Dutch captain would..give us a letter of recommendation to the governor. **1810** J. Adams *Wks.* (1854) IX. 626 His conduct to our President..is not, however, a letter of recommendation of his temper, policy, or discretion. **1870** Burton *Hist. Scot.* VI. lx. 55 *note*, They complained that the ambassador had only a letter of recommendation in place of a letter of credit.

c. A letter or certificate of recommendation.

1645 Evelyn *Diary* May (Bologna), I enquired out a priest and Dr. Montalbano, to whom I brought recom'endations from Rome. **1802** James *Milit. Dict.*, *Recommendation*, in a military sense, a certificate, stating an individual to be properly qualified for a situation in the army.

5. That which procures a favourable reception or acceptance.

1647 Clarendon *Hist. Reb.* i. §14 Upon no other advantage or recommendation, than of the Beauty..of his Person. **1794** Mrs. Radcliffe *Myst. Udolpho* xii, 'That is no recommendation at all', replied her aunt. **1858** Froude *Hist. Eng.* IV. xviii. 101 His recommendation had been his connexion with a powerful native family.

6. Exhortation, advice.

1585 Earl Leicester in Motley *Netherl.* (1860) I. v. 280, I would he were in Fort Rammekyns..with a recommendation from me to Russell to look well to him.

reco'mmendative, *a.* and *sb. rare.* ? *Obs.* [f. recommend *v.*[1] + -ative. Cf. OF. *recommandatif* (1521 in Godef.).] **a.** *adj.* That recommends. **b.** *sb.* That which recommends.

1611 Cotgr., *Recommandatif*, recommendatiue, recommending. **1727** *Art Speaking in Public* Introd. (ed. 2) 15 The Rules and Laws of Speaking and Action, the Ornament and Recommendative of all Discourse.

recommendator. *rare*$^{-1}$. [f. recommend *v.*[1]; cf. commendator.] One who recommends.

1818 *Quarles' Embl.* 4 Notwithstanding that some of his evangelical recommendators, 'leave to better judges' to pronounce 'what share of merit is due to the poet'.

recommendatory (rɛkə'mɛndətərɪ), *a.* [f. recommend *v.*[1] after commendatory *a.* Cf. OF. *recommandatoire* (1533 in Godef.).]

1. Having the attribute of recommending; expressing or conveying a recommendation.

1611 Cotgr., *Recommandatoire*, commendatorie, recommendatorie. **1705** Hearne *Collect.* 28 July (O.H.S.) I. 18 There are several Recommendatory Verses before it. **1712** Addison *Spect.* No. 458 ¶3 How many Men..give Recommendatory Characters of Men whom they are not acquainted with..? **1796** Washington *Let.* Writ. 1892 XIII. 269 Let me pray you therefore to introduce a section in..the address..recommendatory of the measure. **1859** Sala *Tw. round Clock* (1861) 290 At which confession the chaplain..puts him down in the front rank for his next recommendatory report to the visiting magistrates.

b. *recommendatory letter*: (see COMMENDATORY *a.* 1 b, and cf. RECOMMENDATION 4 b).

1618 *Demeanour of Sir W. Raleigh* 59 His Letters recommendatory for his safe conduct and reception. **1683** CAVE *Ecclesiastici, Athanasius* 153 Having procur'd the Recommendatory Letters of George Bishop of Laodicea. **1766** GOLDSM. *Vic. W.* xx, My first care was to carry his recommendatory letter to his uncle. **1812** D'ISRAELI *Calam. Auth.* (1867) 61 He..came to the metropolis with thirty recommendatory letters. **1885** *Manch. Exam.* 5 Nov. 5/3 Mr. Spencely has the advantage of a letter recommendatory from Mr. Chamberlain.

c. *recommendatory prayer*: (see COMMENDATORY *a.* 1 c and RECOMMEND *v.*[1] 1).

1718 *Freethinker* No. 6 ¶12 He has left us the best Recommendatory Prayer in the Hour of Death.

2. Of a quality, feature, etc.: That recommends its possessor.

1709 STEELE *Tatler* No. 50 ¶1 To none of these Recommendatory Advantages was his Title so undoubted as that of his Beauty. **1741** RICHARDSON *Pamela* (1824) I. lxxxiv. 446 The only recommendatory point in Mr. H—— is, that he dresses exceedingly smart. **1818** BYRON *Ch. Har.* IV. clxxiv. *note*, The gentlemanly spirit, so recommendatory either in an author or his productions. **1868** *Morn. Star* 2 June, Park horses, ladies' horses, and ponies were trotted out to display their respective recommendatory points.

3. Of a resolution, appointment, etc.: In the form of a recommendation, without binding force.

1690 *Col. Rec. Pennsylv.* I. 329 This following Recommenditary order was ordered by y[e] board. **1798** in Dallas *Amer. Law Rep.* II. 169 If the resolve of Congress had been absolute and imperative, instead of being barely recommendatory. **1853** GROTE *Greece* II. lxxxix. XI. 538 The resolution of the synod (noway binding upon the Athenian people, but merely recommendatory).

†**b.** Applied to a person recommended for appointment to a position. *Obs.*[−1]

1691 LUTTRELL *Brief Rel.* (1857) II. 250 The lord mayor ..drunk to sir Wm. Ashurst, as a recommendatory sherif for the ensuing year, if approv'd by the common hall.

reco'mmended, *ppl. a.* [f. RECOMMEND *v.*[1] + -ED[1].] Praised, commended. Also, advised, prescribed.

1481 CAXTON *Myrr.* III. xv. 168 Plato whiche was a puissaunt and a recommended maistre of Athenes. *c* **1532** DU WES *Introd. Fr.* in Palsgr. 896 Decessed of noble and recomended memory the prince Arthur. **1663** BOYLE *Usef. Exp. Nat. Philos.* II. v. xvi. 267 What if a recommended Specifick..seem unable to produce the promised Effect? **1968** *Globe & Mail* (Toronto) 3 Feb. 10/7 Sulphur dioxide levels in the smelter were 40 times the recommended safe level. **1977** *Sniffin' Glue* July 17 Recommended reading: Anything by Colin Wilson.

recommender (rɛkə'mɛndə(r)). Also 7 -or. [f. as prec. + -ER[1].] One who recommends.

1579 J. STUBBES *Gaping Gulf* D vij, Some..do sclaunder those religious princes as recommenders to vs of thys mariage. **1611** COTGR., *Recommandeur*, a recommendor, commendor, praiser. **1663** BOYLE *Usef. Exp. Nat. Philos.* I. i. 7 That severe Teacher, and perswasive Recommender of the strictest Virtue, Seneca. **1748** RICHARDSON *Clarissa* (1811) I. xxvii. 190 Is not this a plain indication that even his own recommenders think him a mean creature? **1836** KEBLE *Serm.* viii. Postscr. (1848) 349 This is the very chiefest advantage which the warmest recommenders of Tradition in our Church expect from it. **1873** M. ARNOLD *Lit. & Dogma* (1876) 240 It is obvious how well this notion of faith suits the recommenders of such doctrine.

recommending (rɛkə'mɛndɪŋ), *ppl. a.* [f. as prec. + -ING[2].] That recommends.

1611 COTGR., *Recommendatif*, recommendatiue, recommending. **1693** DRYDEN *Juvenal* xvi. (1697) 383 One happy Hour is to a Souldier better, Than Mother Juno's Recommending Letter. **1769** *Junius Lett.* xv. 67 The.. purity of your manners..and a thousand other recommending circumstances. **1872** GEO. ELIOT in Cross *Life* (1885) III. 172 The outside is not, I think, quite equally recommendable and recommending.

So **reco'mmending** *vbl. sb.*, recommendation.

1470–85 MALORY *Arthur* x. lix, I send vnto alle knyghtes erraunt recommaundynge. **1591** PERCIVALL *Sp. Dict.*, *Encomienda*, recommending, commendations.

†**recommends.** *Obs. rare.* [f. the vb. For the form cf. COMMEND *sb.* 2 b.] A recommendation.

1623 WEBSTER *Devil's Law-Case* II. 1, That I might take my leave, sir, and withal Entreat from you a private recommends To a friend in Malta. **1665** J. SERGEANT *Sure Footing* 90 The greater the Recommends of any Truth is, the greater is the obligation not to bely our selves and it.

†**reco'mmendum.** *Obs.*[−1] [irreg. f. RECOMMEND *v.*[1]] ? Praise, commendation.

1599 NASHE *Lenten Stuffe* 74 Euen those that attend vppon the pitch-kettle, will bee druncke to my good fortunes, and recommendums.

†**recommiss, -mise,** *v. Obs. rare.* [f. med.L. *recommiss-us* (1278 in Du Cange), pa. pple. of *recommittĕre* to RECOMMIT; or f. RE- 5 a + COMMISE *v.*] *trans.* (in *pa. pple.* only) To recommend.

1427 *Rolls of Parlt.* IV. 322/2 We beseeche youre Hieghnesse..to..yeve in special commandement to youre Ambassatours..to have ye saide Archebisshop, and oure Moder his Cherche of Canterbury speciali recommissed. **1454–5** *Ibid.* V. 450/2 The Bisshop of Ely..shold be recommised to..the Pope, for to be promoted to th' archiebisshopricke.

reco'mmission, *v.* [RE- 5 a.] **a.** *trans.* To commission (a person, ship, etc.) anew.

1858 *Times* 24 Nov. 9/5 Paying off a fleet in 1857 and re-commissioning the same fleet in 1858. **1888** *Ibid.* 22 Nov. 5/1 They will be recommissioned with the grades which they held in the Russian army.

b. *intr.* for *pass.* Of a ship. Hence **reco'mmissioning** *vbl. sb.*

[**1909** *Army & Navy Gaz.* 1 May 431/2 Fleet Surg. H. B. Marriott to Doris on recommis.] **1922** *Daily Mail* 3 Nov. 12/5 Naval Appointments..to Emperor of India on recommissioning. **1928** *Observer* 15 July 12/4 It was intended that she should return home at the end of the present cruise to re-commission. **1977** *Navy News* June 15/1 The Arethusa recommissioned at Portsmouth in April.

†**recommit,** *v.*[1] *Obs. rare.* [ad. med.L. *recommittĕre* to recommend: cf. RECOMMISS.] *trans.* To commit or commend *to* a person, etc.

1521 FISHER *Serm. agst. Luther* iv. Wks. (1876) 344 All the soules that by his false doctryne he sleeth and murdereth, he recommytteth them vnto almyghty god. **1570** FOXE *A. & M.* (ed. 2) 618/1 Beseching the court aforesayd, that they wyll receaue fauorably the sayd Wylliam vnto them thus recommitted. **1658** EARL MONM. tr. *Paruta's Wars Cyprus* 199 We ought not to recommit the total of our Fortune..to the uncertain event of Battel.

recommit (ri:kə'mɪt), *v.*[2] [RE- 5 a.]

1. *trans.* To send or refer (a bill, etc.) back to a committee.

1621 ELSING *Debates Ho. Lds.* (Camden) 85 The House to debate the doubte,..and if the major part doubt, yt may be recommitted. **1729** *Votes & Proc. Pennsylv. Ho. Repr.* (1754) III. 72 Ordered, That the said Act be re-committed for several Amendments. **1790** BEATSON *Nav. & Mil. Mem.* I. 37 The House..agreed to the address; but when a motion was made for its being recommitted [etc.]. **1863** H. COX *Instit.* I. ix. 168 A bill may be re-committed generally, or on amendments proposed on the consideration of the report.

b. To entrust (a person or thing) again *to* a person.

1783 BURKE *Sp. E. Ind. Bill* Wks. 1826 IV. 111 It is to recommit the government of India to the court of directors. **1870** ANDERSON *Missions Amer. Bd.* II. xvii. 136 The code was then recommitted to the graduate, with instructions to supply certain deficiencies.

2. To commit (a person) again *to* (a court, prison, etc.). Also without const.

1647 CLARENDON *Hist. Reb.* IV. §312 The House of Commons..caused them immediately again to be recommitted to the Tower. **1863** *Times* 11 Feb., Criminals, who are recommitted, after having been convicted of former offences.

3. To commit or do (an action) again.

1647 HERRICK *Noble Numb.*, *To God*, God..Will add a power to keep me innocent; That I shall ne're that trespasse recommit. **1677** GILPIN *Demonol.* (1867) 84 The inclinations that are begot in us by any act of sin to recommit it. **1795** tr. *Mercier's Fragm. Pol. & Hist.* II. 467 When you wish to recommit a sin, you must there pay double.

reco'mmitment. [RE- 5 a.] A renewed commitment or committal.

1779 *Hansard Parl. Hist.* (1814) XX. 1003 The question of re-commitment, which the House has rejected. **1817** COLERIDGE *Biog. Lit.* xxi, No re-commitment (for new trial) of juvenile performances. **1861** MAY *Const. Hist.* (1863) I. iii. 146 Lord Halifax..moved the recommitment of the bill.

reco'mmittal. [RE- 5 a.] Recommitment.

1837 *Second Rep. Inspectors of Prisons* I. 90 in *Parl. Papers* XXXII. 1 Judging from the immense number of recommittals, it would almost seem that the effect produced by imprisonment..is not such as materially to deter from the commission of crime. **1863** H. COX *Instit.* I. ix. 168 There may be several recommittals of the same bill. **1884** *Contemp. Rev.* July 86 In the local jails..75 per cent. of the inmates are constantly entering on very short re-committals.

†**reco'mmixture.** *Obs.*[−1] [RE- 5 a.] A renewed commixture.

1652 *News fr. Lowe-Countr.* 1 To those four segregated forms Whose recommixture now informs.

reco'mmunicate, *v.* [RE- 5 a.] To communicate anew. Hence **reco'mmunicated** *ppl. a.*

1611 FLORIO, *Raccomunicare*, to recommunicate. **1751** JOHNSON *Rambler* No. 97 ¶9 What additional charms has devotion given to her recommunicated features!

†**recom'pack,** *v. Obs.*[−1] = RECOMPACT *v.*

1602 WARNER *Alb. Eng.* XIII. lxxviii. (1612) 321 Beginner of beginnings..Who, were not aught of all, his word the world could recompack.

recom'pact, *pa. pple.* [See next and COMPACT *ppl. a.*[1]] Recompacted, put together again.

1868 LYNCH *Rivulet* CLXVII. iv, Then, like a broken city recompact, My heart shall fortress be and home desired.

recompact (ri:kəm'pækt), *v.* [RE- 5 a.] *trans.* To join or fit together again.

1626 DONNE *Serm.* xxi. 206 God shall re-compact and re-compile those atomes and graines of dust into that Body which was before. **1813** COLERIDGE *Remorse* v. i. 170 Curse on remorse! Can it give up the dead, or recompact A mangled body? **1860** TYNDALL *Glac.* I. ii. 12 The crushed ice being recompacted into a solid mass.

Hence **recom'pacting** *vbl. sb.*

1630 DONNE *Serm.* xiii. 129 His dissections are so many re-compactings, so many resurrections.

recompanse, obs. Sc. f. RECOMPENSE *v.*

recom'pare, *v.* [RE- 5 a.] *trans.* To compare again. So **recom'parison.**

1814 W. TAYLOR in *Monthly Rev.* LXXIII. 496 He has re-compared the texts with the manuscripts whence it was derived. **1875** *Chamb. Jrnl.* Jan. 7/1 These instruments are returned to the office..for recomparison with standards.

re'compass, *v. rare.* [RE- 5 a.] *trans.* To compass (obtain, go round) again.

? *c* **1600** *Distracted Emp.* v. iv. in Bullen *O. Pl.* III. 260 At her deathe had I recompast it, I had beene kynge of Fraunce. **1654** COKAINE *Dianea* I. 33 Having compassed and recompassed much ground to no purpose,..I laid me downe to rest me.

recom'pel, *v.* [RE-.] *trans.* To force back.

1624 QUARLES *Job* sec. xi, You'l say, perchance, Wee'l recompell your word.

recompence, var. RECOMPENSE *sb.* and *v.*

'**recom,pensable,** *a. rare.* Also 5 -pensible, 6–7 -penceable. [f. RECOMPENSE *v.* + -ABLE; cf. obs. F. *recompensable* (Godef.).] †**a.** That may serve as a recompense. †**b.** Willing to make a return. *Obs.* **c.** That may be recompensed.

1454 in *E.E. Wills* (1882) 133 Y can not assigne no thyng of my good recompensible to his good brotherhede. **1576** FLEMING *Panopl. Epist.* 329 Hee promisseth to shewe himselfe recompenceable to his power, though not with like recourse of benefits, yet with giuing thankes. **1648** HEXHAM, *Loonbaer*, rewardable, or recompenceable. **1875** H. JAMES *R. Hudson* xii. 437 Rowland's fancy hovered about the idea that it was recompensable.

recompensation (rɪ,kɒmpən'seɪʃən). [a. OF. *recompensacion* (13th c.):—late L. *recompensātiōn-em* (6–7th c.), n. of action f. *recompensāre* to RECOMPENSE. Cf. COMPENSATION.]

†**1.** = RECOMPENSE *sb.* in various senses. *Obs.* (Common in 15th c.)

c **1374** CHAUCER *Boeth.* IV. pr. iv. 101 (Camb. MS.) For the recompensacyon [L. *compensatio*] for to geten hem bownte and prowesse which þat they han lost. ? **1450–4** *Lett. Marg. Anjou & Bp. Beckington* (Camden) 119 Ye will ordeine and see unto the recompensacion of the same oure cousyn. **1494** FABYAN *Chron.* VII. ccxxxvi. 274 He..dyd to the sayd Henry recompensacion, in yeldynge vnto hym ye cytie of Carlell. **1581** MARBECK *Bk. of Notes* 353 It is not that reward,..but is all one, as if it shuld be called a recompensation. **1651** *Raleigh's Ghost* 300 The which remunerations and recompensations, seeing they are not ever payed in this life, ..are to be reserved for the life to come. **1715** M. DAVIES *Athen. Brit.* I. Pref. 61 The Court..order'd old Mugnoz to be kept close Prisoner..till he made full Restitution or Recompensation to his..Son.

†**b.** In phr. *in* (*some*, etc.) *recompensation of.*

c **1384** CHAUCER *H. Fame* II. 157 In somme recompensacion Of labour and deuocion That thou hast had. **1426** LYDG. *De Guil. Pilgr.* 16901 In Recompensacion off the grete benefetys which thow hast Receyved ffor Synnerys. **1533** BELLENDEN *Livy* I. xxii. (S.T.S.) I. 128 He was slane in recompensacion of þe grete murdir and slauchter made be him afore. **1562** *Wills & Inv. N.C.* (Surtees 1835) 200 To my doughter..xxx[l] in full recompensacion off her childes porcion. *c* **1578** LINDESAY (Pitscottie) *Chron. Scot.* (S.T.S.) I. 114 His son..in recompensatioun thairof was maid Earle of Caitnes.

2. *Sc. Law.* In actions for debt, a counter-plea of compensation raised by a pursuer to meet the defender's plea of compensation.

1681 STAIR *Institutes* I. xviii. §6 Compensation is sometimes elided by recompensation, which doth but seldom occur, and hath not been distinctly determined as to the several cases in which it may occur. *a* **1768** ERSKINE *Inst. Law Scot.* III iv. §19 A pursuer..may if the defender should plead any ground of compensation, elide his defence by pleading recompensation upon that separate debt. **1838** W. BELL *Dict. Law Scot.* **1855** *Scots Law Rep.* XVII. D. 739 The judicial factor in obtaining authority from the surviving partner was entitled to plead recompensation against the counter claims of the defenders.

recompense ('rɛkəmpɛns), *sb.* Also -pence. [a. OF. *recompense* (13–14th c. in Hatz.-Darm.), f. *recompenser* to RECOMPENSE. The spelling -*ence* is more frequent than the etymological -*ense* (cf. the vb.) until the 19th c.]

1. Reparation or restitution made to another for some wrong done to him; atonement or satisfaction for some misdeed or offence.

c **1420** LYDG. *Assembly of Gods* 97 Tyll he haue made full seethe and recompence For hurt of my name thorough thys gret offence. **1494** FABYAN *Chron.* II. cxcv. 200 Fall nat to lyke offence, Leste for thy faute thou make lyke recompence. **1535** COVERDALE *Prov.* vi. 31 A thefe..maketh recompence with all the good of his house. **1568** GRAFTON *Chron.* II. 36 And also make recompence and restitution unto him for the hurtes and harmes that his Normanes had done. **1651** HOBBES *Leviath.* III. xxxviii. 248 Sin cannot be taken away by recompence. **1697** POTTER *Antiq. Greece* II. xx. (1715) 371 This Festival is said to have been first instituted by Theseus, as a recompence of his Ingratitude to her.

2. Compensation (received or desired) for some loss or injury sustained.

1508 DUNBAR *Tua Mariit Wemen* 136 Thoght his pen purly me payis..His purse pays richely in recompense efter. **1600** J. PORY tr. *Leo's Africa* II. 51 There is some recompence due unto me, sithens ten of my people haue beene slaine, and but eight of this my neighbours. **1667** MILTON *P.L.* II. 981 No mean recompence it brings To your behoof, if I that Region lost. **1770** *Junius Lett.* xxxvi. 171 Have you secured no recompense for such a waste of honour? **1841** ELPHINSTONE *Hist. Ind.* II. XI. ii. 475 He may, perhaps, have looked to some recompence for the temporary sacrifice of his pride.

b. Compensation for some defect or imperfection. *rare*⁻¹.

1690 Locke *Hum. Und.* iii. xi. §15 The signification of their Names cannot be made known.. by any shewing; but in recompence thereof, may be.. exactly defin'd.

3. Return or repayment for something given or received.

1473 *Rolls of Parlt.* VI. 73/1 So that the thyng soo graunted, restored, [etc.] passed not from the Kyng undre any of his Seales, afore the seid eschaunge, sale or recompense. **1526** Tindale *Luke* xiv. 12 When thou makest a diner or a supper: call not thy frendes.. lest they bidde the agayne, and make the recompence. **1601** Shaks. *Twel. N.* v. i. 7 This is to giue a dogge, and in recompence desire my dogge againe. **1667** Milton *P.L.* v. 424 The Sun that light imparts to all, receives From all his alimental recompence In humid exhalations. **1783** Cruise *Common Recoveries* 116 In the preceding modes of barring estates tail.. the recompense in value.. was a real and *bona fide* recompence. **1818** —— *Digest* (ed. 2) V. 432 Seven of the petitions were by fathers upon the marriage of their sons, and an equal recompence given.

†**b.** In phr. ***in recompense of***, in payment of, as an equivalent for. *Obs.*

1463 *Bury Wills* (Camden) 15, I beqwethe vnto the high awter of the seid chyrche, in recompense of my dewtees to holy chirche not payed dewly, xxs. **1542** *Test. Ebor.* (Surtees) VI. 157 In full recompence of certen landes in Methley. **1581** *Knaresbor. Wills* (Surtees) I. 142 To my doghter.. vs, in recompence of her childes porcion.

4. Compensation or return for trouble, exertion, services or merit.

1500–20 Dunbar *Poems* xliii. 42 Alhaill almoist, Thay mak the coist, With sobir recompens. **1590** Spenser *F.Q.* i. iii. 30 His lovely words her seem'd due recompence Of all her passed paines. **1638** R. Baker tr. *Balzac's Lett.* (vol. II) 45 This long continued state of youth is no doubt the recompence of her extraordinary vertue. **1730** Franklin *Ess.* Wks. 1840 II. 62 Renown and applause have always been the recompense of true merit. **1777** Robertson *Hist. Amer.* I. i. 55 In recompence of his labours and perseverance, he at last descried that lofty promontory. **1853** J. H. Newman *Hist. Sk.* (1873) I. i. ii. 81 The riches which he amassed.. were a recompense amply sufficient.

5. Retribution for some injury or offence.

1538 Elyot, *Talio*, an equall peyne in recompence of a hurte. **1585** T. Washington tr. *Nicholay's Voy.* i. xix. 23 b, If they would not.. consent.., for theyr recompence, all they within the Castle should continue slaues. **1611** Bible *Ecclus.* xvii. 23 Afterward he will rise vp and reward them, and render their recompence vpon their heads. **1653** H. Cogan tr. *Pinto's Trav.* v. 13 To dissemble what she had executed against him, for which he would one day return her a recompence according to her merit. **1821** Shelley *Prometh. Unb.* i. 388 Such is the tyrant's recompense: 'tis just: He who is evil can receive no good.

recompense (ˈrɛkəmpɛns), *v.* Also -pence, 6 *Sc.* -panse. [ad. OF. *recompenser* (1322 in Godef.), ad. late L. *recompensāre* (6–7th c.), f. L. *re-* re- + *compensāre* to compensate.]

1. *trans.* To reward, requite, repay (a person) for something done or given. Const. *for*, †*of* (the thing done) and *by*, *with* (the return made).

1422 T. Hostel in Ellis *Orig. Lett.* Ser. ii. I. 96 Being for his said service never yit recompensed ne rewarded. **1484** Caxton *Fables of Æsop* iii. i, He wold thenne haue recompensed hym of the good whiche he had done to hym. **1555** Eden *Decades* 160 They recompensed owre men with many rewardes. **1602** Marston *Ant. & Mel.* iii. Wks. 1856 I. 31 Wee vowe.. to recompence any man that bringeth his head. **1666** Dryden *Ann. Mirab.* cclxiv, Thou who hast taught me to forgive the ill, And recompense as friends the good misled. **1718** *Freethinker* No. 87 ¶2 Will the Student's Labour recompence him with large Possessions? **1719** De Foe *Crusoe* i. xix, The first Thing I did, was to recompense my original Benefactor. **1841** Lane *Arab. Nts.* I. 82 Thus he who acted kindly to the undeserving is recompensed in the same manner as the aider of Umm A'mir.

absol. **1814** Cary *Dante, Purg.* iv. 118 Be his To recompense, who sees and can reward thee.

b. To compensate, give compensation to (a person) *for* some loss or injury sustained. Also *refl.*, and †const. *of* (expense).

1477 Earl Rivers (Caxton) *Dictes* 19 A man.. ought to holde him self recompensed whan his aduerse partie required of him pardon. **1560** Daus tr. *Sleidane's Comm.* 224 b, [He] sendeth worde to the Cities.. that they shoulde recompence hym for the injuryes done. *a* **1578** Lindesay (Pitscottie) *Chron. Scot.* (S.T.S.) II. 18 To recompense him of his expenssis.. in comming to Scotland. **1653** Holcroft *Procopius* i. 4 If I be devoured be it your part, Sir, to recompence my children for their fathers death. **1709** Lady M. W. Montagu *Let. to Anne Wortley* 5 Sept., The kindness of your last recompenses me for the injustice of your former letter. **1726** Swift *Gulliver* i. vi, Out of his Goods or Lands the innocent Person is quadruply recompensed for the Loss of his Time. **1803** J. Bristed *Pedestr. Tour* II. 328 We, therefore, now recompensed ourselves for the four banyan, or fasting, days which we had undergone.

2. a. To make up for, to make or give compensation for (some loss, injury, defect, etc.); †to take the place of.

1430–40 Lydg. *Bochas* vii. v. (1554) 169 Nero.. Lete bylde an house.. To recompence that other that was olde. **1456** Sir G. Haye *Law Arms* (S.T.S.) 135 Quhethir harnes lent, and tynt in weris, suld be restorit, and recompensit agayne to the lennaris of it. **1558** Goodman *How to Obey* 222 Whatsoeuer you lose in this world.. it shall be here recompenced with double. **1639** Fuller *Holy War* iv. iv. (1840) 181 The length of the journey will be recompensed by the goodness of the way. **1684** *Contempl. St. Man* i. vii. (1699) 79 Another [ship] may arrive loaden with such Riches as may recompence the loss of the former. **1772** Johnson *Let. to Mrs. Thrale* 3 Dec., I found two letters here, to recompense my disappointment at Ashbourne. **1871** Morley *Voltaire* (1886) 2 A gracious, benevolent, and all-powerful being, who would one day redress all wrongs and recompense all pain.

b. To make compensation or atonement for (a misdeed, wrong, etc.).

1450–1530 *Myrr. our Ladye* 11 To recompense suche neglygence; seuen tymes on the day we do seruice to God. **1588** A. King tr. *Canisius' Catech.* 95 b, Worthy fruicts of penance, quhairbe we recompense.. the faults and sinnes of our former lyf. **1611** Bible *Num.* v. 8 If the man haue no kinsman to recompense the trespasse vnto, let the trespasse be recompensed vnto the Lord. **1671** Milton *Samson* 746 In some part to recompense My rash but more unfortunate misdeed. **1837** Browning *Strafford* iv. iii, We have done Less gallantly by Strafford: well! the future Must recompense the past.

c. To make a return or requital for (something done or given).

1530 Palsgr. 681/1, I recompence ones servyce or a good tourne doone to me. *c* **1586** C'tess Pembroke *Ps.* ciii. v, He doth not.. recompence Unto us each offence With due revenge. **1605** Verstegan *Dec. Intell.* v. (1628) 129 His death was recompensed with the slaughter of Categerne. **1754** Edwards *Freed. Will* iii. i. (1762) 139 It is our Duty to recompense God's Goodness, and render again according to Benefits received. **1816** Shelley *Alastor* 4 Natural piety to feel Your love, and recompense the boon with mine.

†**3.** To give as a recompense or return; to mete out in requital. *Obs.*

1473 *Rolls of Parlt.* VI. 73/1 Grauntes made by the Kyng, of any of the premisses eschaunged, sold or recompensed by the Kyng. **1526** Tindale *Rom.* xii. 17 Recompence to no man evyll for evyll. —— *2 Thess.* i. 6 It is verely a rightewes thynge with god to recompence tribulacion to them thet trouble you.

4. *intr.* To make repayment, return, or amends.

1432–50 tr. *Higden* (Rolls) VIII. 201 [The archbishop] spende so grete goodes in that solennite that unnethe the iiij^the successoure to hym recompen[se]de for the dettes. **1535** Coverdale *2 Chron.* xxxii. 25 But Ezechias recompensed not accordinge as was geuen vnto him. **1555** W. Watreman *Fardle Facions* ii. xi. 256 He that endamageth any manne: as the losse or hinderaunce shalbe valewed, so muste he of force recompence. **1668** Hale *Pref. Rolle's Abridgem.* a ij, This, though it.. takes up longer time for their study, yet it recompenceth with great advantages. **1838** W. Bell *Dict. Law Scot.* 822 The Court found generally, that he might re-compense on any other debts.

†**recompensement.** *Obs. rare*⁻¹. [a. OF. *recompensement* (1358 in Godef.), f. *recompenser* to recompense.] Recompense, return.

1494 Fabyan *Chron.* v. cxxxv. 121 Edfryde had great summes of money in recompencement of his brothers deth.

ˈrecompenser. *rare.* [f. recompense *v.* + -er¹.] One who or that which recompenses; †also *spec.* (see quot. 1589).

1563 Foxe *A. & M.* 56/1 A thankful recompenser of the benefites receiued at hys hande. **1589** Puttenham *Eng. Poesie* iii. xix. (Arb.) 224 *marg.*, Antenagoge, or the Recompencer. *Ibid.*, We have another manner of speech much like to the repentant... It is called by the originall name in both languages, the Recompencer. **1611** Cotgr., *Recompenseur*, a recompencer.

recompensing (ˈrɛkəmpɛnsɪŋ), *vbl. sb.* [f. as prec. + -ing¹.] The action of the vb. recompense.

1450 *Rolls of Parlt.* V. 188/2 Whom we have in recompensyng therof made Squier. **1535** Coverdale *Hos.* ix. 7 The tyme of visitacion is come, the dayes of recompencinge are at honde. **1561** T. Norton *Calvin's Inst.* iii. 210 They.. that go about to appease God with their owne recompencinges. **1625** tr. *Gonsalvio's Sp. Inquis.* 144 His reward for his paines, if we respect mans recompencing, was [etc.].

So **ˈrecompensing** *ppl. a.*, That recompenses.

1676 Dryden *Aurengz.* ii. i. 729 A kind of recompensing ease. **1851** Trench *Poems* 150 Vengeance, and the recompensing years.

recompensive, *a. rare.* [f. as prec. + -ive; cf. med.L. *recompensīvus* (1327 in Du Cange).] That recompenses.

1643 Sir T. Browne *Relig. Med.* i. §47 This is the day that must.. reduce those seeming inequalities.. in this world, to an equality and recompensive Justice in the next. **1924** *Brit. Weekly* 21 Aug. 443/2, I am glad to tell that I am having recompensive explorations here.

recompile (riːkəmˈpaɪl), *v.* [re- 5 a. Cf. It. *recompilare* (Florio), Sp. *recopilar.*] *trans.* To compile again. Hence **recomˈpiling** *vbl. sb.*

1611 Florio, *Recompilatione*, a recompiling. **1616** Bacon *Compil. & Amendm. Laws* Wks. 1730 IV. 1 The reducing and recompiling of the laws of England. *c* **1617** —— *Digest of Laws* Wks. 1826 V. 357 There was such a race of wit and authority, between the commentaries and decisions of the lawyers, and the edicts of the emperors... Whereupon Justinian.. recompiled both. **1626** [see recompact *v.*].

So **recomˈpilement**, a new compilation.

1629 Bacon *Advt. touching Holy War* Ep. Ded., Although ..I had a purpose to make a particular digest or recompilement of the laws..; yet.. I have laid it aside.

recomˈplain, *v.* [re- 5 a.] *intr.* To complain again.

1616 J. Lane *Contn. Sqr.'s T.* vii. 68 Of his litle virtue whiche remaines Hee to his inmost reason recomplaines.

recomˈplete, *v.* [re- 5 a.] *trans.* To complete again. So **recomˈpletion.**

1655 tr. *Com. Hist. Francion* iii. 55, I had no sooner put them in their places, but the Head and the Arms came of their own accords, to recompleat the whole. **1865** Carlyle *Fredk. Gt.* xxi. ii. (1872) IX. 260 Regiment Schenkendorf got, every year, for recompletion, what recruits were wanted. **1874** Dana *Text-bk. Geol.* (ed. 3) 33 By successive destructions and re-completions.

reˈcomplicate, *v.* [re- 5 a.] *trans.* To complicate again. So **recompliˈcation.**

1874 T. H. Green *Introd. Hume* (1890) 41 Why make them over again by abstraction and recomplication? **1882** H. Spencer *Princ. Sociol., Pol. Inst.* 242 The complicated processes of development are frequently re-complicated by changes in the sets of factors. **1889** Mivart in *Nature* 14 Nov. 40 Simplification, and possible recomplication, of the germ-plasm itself.

recompose (riːkəmˈpəʊz), *v.* [re- 5 a. Cf. F. *recomposer* (1549), L. *recompōnĕre.*]

1. *trans.* To put together again; to recombine; to form again by composition. Chiefly in antithesis to *decompose*.

1611 Cotgr., *Recomposer*, to recompose, to frame anew. **1649** J. H. *Motion to Parl. Adv. Learn.* 6 These.. industries that endeavour to gather them up, and.. recompose them. **1663** Boyle *Exp. Hist. Colours* iii. xiv. Wks. 1772 I. 738 We were able to produce a lovely purple, which we can destroy or recompose at pleasure. **1748** Hartley *Observ. Man* i. iii. 337 To take to Pieces, recompose, and ascertain our Evidences. **1777** Priestley *Matt. & Spir.* (1782) I. xvii. 200 Whatever is decomposed may be recomposed by the being who first composed it. **1836–7** Sir W. Hamilton *Metaph.* vi. (1859) I. 97 The far greater number of the objects presented to our observation can only be decomposed, but not actually recomposed.

absol. **1861** Buckle *Civiliz.* (1869) III. v. 389 Fire and water.. can really destroy nothing, but can only decompose and recompose.

b. To compose again in writing. *rare*⁻¹.

1656 Earl Monm. tr. *Boccalini's Advts. fr. Parnass.* i. lxxxiv. (1674) 111 [They] desire.. that Tacitus may re-compose those Books of his.. which are lost.

2. To put together again in a new form or manner; to rearrange.

1816 *2nd Rep. Comm. Public Rec.* App. ¶5 The old Titles have in most Cases been re-composed. **1849** Macaulay *Hist. Eng.* vi. II. 144 The change was not confined to the officers alone. The ranks were completely broken up and recomposed. **1861** J. Pycroft *Ways & Words* 21 He [Simeon] once told Mr. Carns that he had recomposed the plan of one discourse nearly thirty times.

b. *absol.* To make new (artistic) compositions.

1861 Thornbury *Turner* (1862) II. 326 Turner never imitated Salvator Rosa—because he had rocks and torrents of his own to go and copy and recompose from.

3. To restore to composure. Also *refl.*

1649 Jer. Taylor *Gt. Exemp.* i. iv. 124 He called for a minstrell, who by his harmony might recompose his disunited and troubled spirit. **1655** *Theophania* 92 * When we had recomposed our selves.. we sate in the Cabin descanting thereon. **1700** Congreve *Way of World* iii. v, I shall never recompose my features to receive Sir Rowland with any Œconomy of face. **1749** Fielding *Tom Jones* Wks. 1775 III. 86 Our spirits, when disordered, are not to be re-composed in a moment.

4. To restore to harmony.

1856 Froude *Hist. Eng.* II. 332 A man who.. was the most likely to recompose the quarrels in the church.

Hence **recomˈposed** *ppl. a.*, **recomˈposing** *vbl. sb.* and *ppl. a.*

1659 Gauden *Tears Ch.* iv. xviii. 527 The recomposing of this Church to any Ecclesiasticall Uniformity. **1700** Congreve *Way of World* iv. i, It.. furnishes with blushes, and re-composing airs beyond comparison. **1753** Chambers *Cycl. Supp.* s.v. *Recomposition*, The recomposed body shall not be distinguishable by the senses from that which never had been separated by the fire. **1862** Ansted *Channel Isl.* ii. xi. (ed. 2) 293 Boulders formed out of a recomposed rock.

recomˈposer. *rare*⁻¹. [f. prec. + -er.] One who or that which recomposes.

1653 H. More *Conject. Cabbal.* 33 It meets with a proper corrector and recomposer of its motions.

recomposition (riːkɒmpəˈzɪʃən). [re- 5 a.]

a. The action or process of recomposing, in senses of the vb.

1690 Leybourn *Curs. Math.* 340 Which is the Root of the Cube..; which may be proved by re-composition. **1753** Chambers *Cycl. Supp.*, *Recomposition*, in Chemistry, the compounding of bodies from their separated parts, or principles, so as to compose the original whole again. **1788** Priestley in *Phil. Trans.* LXXIX. 17 The formation, the decomposition, and recomposition of water. **1871** *Daily News* 9 Feb., He gives us, instead of a mere translation, an English recomposition. **1897** *Ibid.* 2 Feb. 2/1 To omit or insert even a comma.. requires the re-composition and re-casting of the entire line.

b. *Linguistics.* (See quots.)

[**1933** J. Marouzeau *Lexique Terminol. Linguistique* 158 *Recomposition*.. Procédé par lequel on restitue à l'un des éléments d'un composé la forme qu'il avait à l'état autonome; ainsi quand on donne à lat. *recludo* la forme *reclaudo* d'après le simple *claudo*.] **1935** T. Hudson-Williams *Short Introd. Study Compar. Gram.* 8 *Recomposition* is a species of analogy; the form of a compound verb is affected by that of the simple verb; the simple form is restored or, occasionally, retained consciously in the compound; e.g. *sē* + *paro* should give ..*sēpero*; but the literary dialect reformed it to *sēparo*... *Decomposition* is the opposite process, the simple verb being affected by the compound. **1964** A. Martinet *Elements of General Linguistics* iv. 126 An element like *tele-*.. which today combines freely with monemes and syntagms that exist outside the combinations in question..behaves in fact like an affix... Perhaps in the case where a new syntagm is formed we might speak of 'recomposition' from elements which are extracted by analysis. **1972** HARTMANN & STORK *Dict. Lang. & Linguistics* 192/2 *Recomposition*, the process or result of using a borrowed element as an affix to form new words, e.g. *tele* in *telecast, teleview, teleprinter*.

So †**recom'posure**. *Obs. rare*$^{-1}$.

1651 CHARLETON *Ephes. & Cimm. Matrons* (1668) 19 The re-composure of her disordered mind.

recompound (riːkəm'paʊnd), *v.* [RE- 5 a.] *trans.* To compound again. Hence **recom'pounded** *ppl. a.*, **recom'pounding** *vbl. sb.*

1683 TRYON *Way to Health* 536 All their Regiments of Compounded, Recompounded, Decompounded and Surrecompounded Medicines. **1816** BENTHAM *Chrestom.* 122 Methods of compounding, decompounding, and recompounding the matter. **1825–34** B. MONTAGU tr. *Bacon's Wisd. Anc.* B.'s Mor. & Hist. Wks. (Bohn) 249 Of all things in the universe, man is the most compounded and recompounded body. **1843** MILL *Logic* III. x. §4 Many substances, though they can be analysed, cannot by any known artificial means be recompounded. **1872** H. SPENCER in *Contemp. Rev.* June 143 The compounding and re-compounding of ultimate homogeneous units.

recompress (riːkəm'prɛs), *v.* [RE- 5 a.] *trans.* To compress again; to increase again the pressure of air or other gas in (a vessel) or acting on (a person); *esp.* to subject (an aircraft pilot, diver, etc.) to increased pressure again.

1945 *Jrnl. Gen. Physiol.* XXVIII. 220 The frogs..were recompressed within 30 seconds. **1950** *Ibid.* III. 255 The chamber was recompressed at free-fall rate. **1951** A. R. BEHNKE in J. F. Fulton et al. *Decompression Sickness* iii. 87 Should symptoms recur.., recompress the diver to a depth giving relief. **1967** P. D. GRIFFITHS in R. I. McCallum *Decompression of Compressed Air Workers* 230 The patient must be observed constantly and recompressed at once should symptoms return, preferably to the minimum effective pressure. **1969** HAXTON & WHYTE in Bennett & Elliott *Physiol. & Med. of Diving* i. 12 It is sometimes necessary to recompress a patient to a pressure slightly higher than that at which he has been working.

recompression (ˌriːkəm'prɛʃən). [RE- 5 a.]

1. a. The state of being compressed again. **b.** The action of compressing again, *esp.* by exposure to increasing air pressure (e.g. during descent from a high-altitude flight without pressurization or following decompression after a dive).

1939 *Jrnl. R. Aeronaut. Soc.* XLIII. 822 After the shock the speed again becomes subsonic, so that the consequent divergence of the streamlines on the back part of the upper surface generates a recompression. **1943** M. A. & F. A. HITCHCOCK tr. *Bert's Barometric Pressure* I. II. iv. 501 M. Bucquoy mentions..the cure of muscular swellings by recompression. **1951** FERRIS & ENGEL in J. F. Fulton et al. *Decompression Sickness* ii. 23 The pain of bends is immediately relieved by recompression of 3000- to 6000-foot equivalents and recurs upon reascent to the original altitude. **1969** A. R. BEHNKE in Bennett & Elliott *Physiol. & Med. of Diving* xi. 227 Hoppe-Seyler (1857) described blockage of pulmonary vessels by nascent bubbles and the inability of the heart to propel blood under these conditions. He proposed recompression to absorb the liberated gas and re-establish circulation. **1973** *Nature* 21–28 Dec. 523/1 These did not occur at maximum altitude, but during the recompression. The other runs gave clear heart signals throughout. **1977** *Hongkong Standard* 14 Apr. 16/3 Mr Ng was later sent to Queen Mary Hospital, after the specialists were satisfied there was no need for further recompression.

2. recompression chamber or **lock**, a chamber in which a person can be subjected to an air pressure above that of the atmosphere.

1951 A. R. BEHNKE in J. F. Fulton et al. *Decompression Sickness* iii. 87 Individuals believed to be 'cured'..have been rushed to the recompression chamber in a state of collapse. **1967** P. D. GRIFFITHS in R. I. McCallum *Decompression of Compressed Air Workers* 229 An important factor is that medical recompression locks often have a safe working pressure..of only 45–50 p.s.i.g. **1976** *Daily Tel.* 27 Jan. 15/1 A 14-year-old boy, critically ill with carbon monoxide poisoning, recovered consciousness yesterday in the Royal Navy's recompression chamber at Rosyth dockyard. **1977** *Proc. R. Soc. Med.* LXX. 503/2 This involves being able to carry out a detailed examination of the patient, and to put up infusions, give injections or insert catheters in the confined, noisy and pressurized space of a recompression chamber.

recompt, obs. variant of RECOUNT *v.*[1]

recompute (riːkəm'pjuːt), *v.* [RE- 5 a.] *trans.* To compute again, recalculate.

1767 HORSLEY in *Phil. Trans.* LVII. 184 To satisfy myself more fully of the accuracy of my work, I this day re-computed the whole. **1806** HUTTON *Course Math.* (ed. 2) I. p. iv, Re-computing the examples, and rendering them more correct in the numbers. **1880** HAUGHTON *Phys. Geog.* iv. 198 *note*, I have recomputed the areas of the rain-basins of the Ganges..and of the Brahmapûtra.

So **recompu'tation**.

1867 CHAMBERS *Astron.* I. i. 4 The recomputation of all numerical quantities involving the Sun's distance as a unit.

re'con, *v.*[1] [RE- 5 a.] *trans.* To con again. Hence **re'conning** *vbl. sb.*

1651 HOBBES *Leviath.* I. iii. 10 As he that foresees what wil become of a Criminal, re-cons what he has seen follow on the like Crime before. *Ibid.*, This we call Remembrance, or calling to mind: the Latines call it *Reminiscentia*, as it were a Re-conning of our former actions.

recon (rɪ'kɒn), *v.*[2] *U.S. Mil. slang. trans.* and *intr.* Abbrev. of RECONNOITRE *v.*

1966 *National Observer* (U.S.) 26 Dec. 1/4 We launched a small operation and while reconning the area, saw a bunch of color near a tree line. **1969** I. KEMP *Brit. G.I. in Vietnam* v. 96 Our orders are to recon only, and avoid all contact with the enemy whatsoever.

recon (rɪ'kɒn), *sb.*[1] *U.S. Mil. slang.* Abbrev. of RECONNAISSANCE; a reconnaissance unit. Freq. *attrib.*, as ***recon company, unit*** (etc.). Cf. RECCE *sb.*

1918 E. M. ROBERTS *Flying Fighter* 337 *Long Recon*, a trip of from 20 to 80 miles behind the Hun lines to gather information. **1942** *Yank* 25 Nov. 21 He was temporarily with the recon. **1943** J. GOODELL *They sent me to Iceland* ii. 31 Convoyed by jeeps and recon cars we sped through the town. **1946** *Sun* (Baltimore) 27 July 12/1 (*heading*) Ex-Patton recon unit to parade in Cumberland. **1948** N. MAILER *Naked & Dead* I. ii. 20 The men in recon looked small and lost in comparison to the other platoons. **1950** 'D. DIVINE' *King of Fassarai* xiv. 108 Should have the recon reports by now. Get through to Air Command again. **1968** *Globe & Mail* (Toronto) 13 Feb. 4/1 It is recon's bad luck to live in an area bordered by an ammunition dump, a flightline loading area and the 26th Marine Regiment's command post. *Ibid.* 4/3 The survivors of the recon company are frightened but uncowed. **1975** A. PRICE *Our Man in Camelot* v. 93 'He was a pilot in recon.'.. 'Photographic reconnaissance,' he explained. **1977** 'E. McBAIN' *Long Time no See* xiii. 208 Our recon patrol found an enemy base camp.

recon ('riːkɒn), *sb.*[2] *Biol.* [f. REC(OMBINATION + -ON[1].] A piece of genetic material which can be exchanged but not divided by genetic recombination; thus the shortest piece which can be so exchanged.

1957 S. BENZER in McElroy & Glass *Symposium on Chem. Basis of Heredity* 71 The unit of recombination will be defined as the smallest element in the one-dimensional array that is interchangeable..by genetic recombination. One such element will be referred to as a 'recon'. **1969** A. M. CAMPBELL *Episomes* iii. 38 The 'unit factor' of the classical geneticist is replaceable by the muton, the recon, the cistron, or even a collection of linked cistrons, each in the appropriate operational context. **1978** N. JARDINE in Hookway & Pettit *Action & Interpretation* 122 The operons, cistrons, recons and mutons of the molecular geneticist.

reconceal, obs. Sc. form of RECONCILE *v.*

†**re-conceit**. *Obs.*$^{-1}$. [RE- 5 a.] (See quot.)

1603 BRETON *Packet Mad Lett.* I. xxviii, Re-conceit is a kinde of dizzinesse which worse tormented then with idlenes is troubled with too strong a madness.

recon'ceive, *v.* [RE- 5 a.] *trans.* To conceive again or in a new way.

1865 MASSON *Rec. Brit. Philos.* 113 Reconceive if you can my cosmological conception. **1889** *Literary World* (Boston) 2 Feb. 39/1 Both [books] attempt to reconceive Jesus.

reconcele, variant of RECOUNSEL *v.*, *Obs.*

reconcentrate (riː'kɒnsəntreɪt), *v.* [f. RE- + CONCENTRATE, partly (sense a) after Sp. *reconcentrar*.] **a.** *trans.* To bring together, concentrate, now *spec.* for military reasons. **b.** *trans.* and *intr.* To concentrate again. Also *refl.*

1622 MABBE tr. *Aleman's Guzman d' Alf.* II. 284 The visiue beames in both, reconcentrating themselues, in this encounter..strucke home vpon our soules. **1877** RAYMOND *Statist. Mines & Mining* 432 The concentrated ore, with some gangue with it, flows to the concentrators on the basement-floor, where it is reconcentrated to remove all the gangue. *Ibid.*, This system of reconcentrating renders good concentration easy. **1884** A. FORBES *Chinese Gordon* ii. 103 He abandoned further attempts on Kintang, and on the 24th had reconcentrated at Liyang.

So **reconcen'tration**.

1898 *Westm. Gaz.* 6 Apr. 7/1 Starvation of thousands of non-combatants [in Cuba] through reconcentration. **1956** *Nature* 21 Jan. 126/2 Kunkel and Tiselius were not able to demonstrate the heterogeneity of serum albumin by their method, and the ability of the method here described to do this may also be due to this reduction of diffusion by reconcentration. **1972** *Times* 26 June 12/3 Biological reconcentration of filter feeding organisms..invalidates the dilution hypothesis.

†**recon'centre**. *Obs. rare*$^{-1}$. [Cf. prec.] *trans.* To concentrate on the same point.

1634 SIR T. HAWKINS *Pol. Observ.* 9 His eyes reconcentred with his imaginations, manifested in their wannesse what anxieties tormented him.

recon'ception. [RE- 5 a.] A renewed or new conception; something reconceived.

1760–72 H. BROOKE *Fool of Qual.* (1809) III. 31 A small embryon or reconception of that lately forfeited image, which..had borne the perfect likeness of the Creator. **1779** J. DUCHÉ *Disc.* (1790) I. xi. 207 Thou hast within thee a Seed of Eternal Life, a Birth of the Triune God,..a reconception of the Light and Love of God.

recon'cession. [RE- 5 a.] The action of conceding again.

1777 BURKE *Corr.* (1844) II. 149 The minister gave, he retracted, and he gave again, with a sure majority to vote for his concession, retraction, or reconcession.

ˌreconcila'bility. Also -cilea-. [f. next + -ITY.] The fact or quality of being reconcilable.

1865 MASSON *Rec. Brit. Philos.* 367 The reconcileability of Mr. Mill's Cogitationism with the mind's knowledge of a world pre-existing itself. **1894** *Liberal* 17 Nov. 10/1 His.. attitude of reconcilability to the present order of things.

reconcilable ('rɛkənsaɪləb(ə)l), *a.* Also -cileable. [f. RECONCILE *v.* + -ABLE.]

1. Of statements, opinions, facts, etc.: Capable of being mutually reconciled, or brought into agreement or coexistence with each other.

1612 SELDEN *Illustr. Drayton's Poly-olb.* ix. 206 But howsoever these things might be reconcileable, I think clearly [etc.]. **1705** ARBUTHNOT *Coins*, etc. (1727) 259 The different accounts that are given of the Numbers of Ships on both Sides by several Authors are reconcileable, by supposing that [etc.]. **1781** GIBBON *Decl. & F.* xviii. II. 77 The opposite yet reconcileable vices of rapaciousness and prodigality. **1818** JAS. MILL *Brit. India* I. II. iv. 147 *note*, When there are two sacred texts, apparently inconsistent, both are held to be law, for both are pronounced by the wise to be valid and reconcileable. *a* **1873** MACREADY *Remin.* (1875) I. xiv. 227 To render his [Hamlet's] seeming inconsistencies reconcilable and intelligible, is the artist's study.

b. *Math.* (See quot. and IRRECONCILABLE 3.)

1873 MAXWELL *Electr. & Magn.* I. 19 If two curves are such that one of them may be transformed into the other by continuous motion without at any time passing through any part of space for which the condition of having a potential is not fulfilled, these two curves are called Reconcileable curves.

2. Capable of being reconciled *with* something.

1640 HAMMOND *Serm.* xii. Wks. 1684 IV. 549 Before we could scarce allow it reconcileable with his infinite justice. **1698** FRYER *Acc. E. India & P.* III. i. 92 The Habits and Customs of this Place are reconcileable with them in the Kingdom of Gulconda. **1736** BUTLER *Anal.* I. i. Wks. 1874 I. 33 That we are to live hereafter, is just as reconcileable with the scheme of atheism. **1818** BYRON *Ch. Har.* IV. lxiii. *note*, The account in Polybius is not so easily reconcileable with present appearances as that in Livy. **1882** A. W. WARD *Dickens* vii. 199 The irony of Smollett is drier than was reconcileable with Dickens' nature.

b. Const. *to*. Now *rare*.

1691 HARTCLIFFE *Virtues* 209 Thus to represent Religion, as a thing reconcileable to Evil, is the greatest Scandal to it. **1748** HARTLEY *Observ. Man* I. ii. 158 The Action of acrid Poisons is very reconcileable to the Doctrine. **1818** BENTHAM *Ch. Eng. Catech. Exam.* 56 The language is here reconcileable to the rules of common sense.

†**c.** *ellipt.* without const. *Obs. rare.*

1646 SIR T. BROWNE *Pseud. Ep.* 108 But with more difficulty, or hardly at all is that reconcilable which is delivered by our Countreyman. **1719** WATERLAND *Vind. Christ's Div.* 375 Are you well assured that you understand whatever is intelligible or reconcilable?

3. Of persons, their natures, etc.: Easily conciliated or reconciled. Now *rare*.

1621 T. WILLIAMSON tr. *Goulart's Wise Vieillard* 78 When we see the minde of man..to abandon hatred, and to be of a peaceable and reconcilable inclination, it is a signe that it is in an excellent state of rest and tranquilitie. **1641** J. JACKSON *True Evang. T.* III. 172 It is a disposition and temper truly Euangelicall, and savouring of Christ, to be peaceable, and reconcileable. *a* **1711** KEN *Div. Love* Wks. (1838) 291 Let thy love, thou God of love, make me peaceful and reconcileable, always ready to return good for evil, to repay injuries with kindness.

4. a. Admitting of reconciliation. *rare*$^{-1}$.

1643 MILTON *Divorce* II. xvii. Wks. (1851) 107 Christ.. declares that no accidental, temporary, or reconcileable offence except fornication, can justifie a divorce.

†**b.** Capable of being made acceptable or agreeable. Const. *to* (a person). *Obs. rare.*

1790 HAN. MORE *Relig. Fash. World* (1791) 252 The dark veil..is reconcileable to him who..trusts confidently that the catastrophe will set all to rights. **1799** WASHINGTON *Lett.* Writ. 1893 XIV. 165, I do not think it will be a very reconcilable matter to Gentlemen of more respectable ages ..to have a young man..placed over their heads.

Hence **'reconcilably** *adv.*

1688 COLLIER *Several Disc.* (1725) 197 Except we are kindly and reconcileably disposed towards our Neighbour.

'reconcilableness. Now *rare*. [f. prec. + -NESS.] Reconcilability.

1654 HAMMOND *Fundam.* xvi. §33 Thirdly, that this [cylinder] cannot be a fit resemblance to shew the reconcileableness of fate with choice. **1685** BOYLE (*title*) Of the Reconcileableness of Specifick Medicines to the Corpuscular Philosophy. **1757** EDWARDS *Orig. Sin* IV. iv. (1837) 278 Which the apostle signifies are testimonies to Gods reconcilableness to sinful men. **1882** *Blackw. Mag.* July 90 There never lived a man that had less malice and revenge nor more reconcilableness and kindness and generosity in his nature than he.

reconcile ('rɛkənsaɪl), *v.* Forms: 4–6 **reconsile**, (5 **-syle**, 6 **-cyle**), 4– **reconcile** (also 4–5 **recounsile**, **-syle**, **-cile**, 7 *Sc.* **-ceal**). [ad. F. *réconcilier* (12th c.) or L. *reconciliāre*, f. *re-* RE- + *conciliāre* to CONCILIATE. See also RECOUNSEL *v.*]

I. 1. a. *trans.* To bring (a person) again into friendly relations *to* or *with* (oneself or another) after an estrangement.

13.. *Propr. Sanct.* (Vernon MS.) in *Archiv Stud. neu. Spr.* LXXXI. 315/133 þis ilke holi chirche..þat god in his sone..To him-self Reconciled, hit was clene vndefuiled. **1382** WYCLIF *2 Cor.* v. 19 God was in Crist, reconcilynge to him the world. **1450–1530** *Myrr. our Ladye* 191 Oure lady delyuer vs from all our wyckednesses, reconsylynge vs to thy moste pyteous sonne. **1560** DAUS tr. *Sleidane's Comm.* 426 b, They..reconcile hym to Marques Albert. **1593** SHAKS. *2 Hen. VI*, IV. viii. 72 Follow me souldiers, wee'l deuise a meane, To reconcile you all vnto the King. **1879** DIXON *Windsor* II. x. 105 The king's desire to reconcile his cousin with his friend.

transf. **1849** De Quincey *Mail-Coach* Wks. 1897 XIII. 324 Battle-fields that, long since, nature had healed and reconciled to herself with the sweet oblivion of flowers.

b. *refl.*

1535 Coverdale *Tobit* viii. 4 These thre nightes wil we reconcyle oure selues with God. **1582** N. Lichefield tr. *Castanheda's Conq. E. Ind.* i. lxviii. 139 They returned to the king of Coching, with whom they reconcyled themselues. **1675** H. Nevile tr. *Machiavelli's Prince* Wks. 207 The Ursini reconciled themselves to him, by the mediation of Seignor Paulo. **1819** Shelley *Cenci* i. i. 36 Thou mightst.. reconcile thyself with thine own heart And with thy God, and with the offended world.

c. In *pass.*, without specified agent.

c **1380** Wyclif *Serm.* Sel. Wks. I. 17 It suffiseth þat þou go out of ire and be recounsilid in herte wiþ him. **1460** Capgrave *Chron.* (Rolls) 247 Dreding that if the duke were reconciled onto the Kyng, it wold bring him onto grete schame. **1550** Coverdale *Spir. Perle* iv. (1560) 31 God is reconciled, and at one with al Christian men, through his sonne. **1611** Bible *1 Esdras* iv. 31 If she tooke any displeasure at him, the King was faine to flatter, that she might be reconciled to him againe. **1715** De Foe *Fam. Instruct.* i. i. (1841) I. 20 [He] is reconciled to them, as though they had not sinned against him. **1876** Miss Braddon *J. Haggard's Dau.* I. 8 When this father died, reconciled to his only son at the last [etc.].

transf. *a* **1652** J. Smith *Sel. Disc.* (1821) 492 Light and darkness.. can never.. be reconciled one to the other. **1671** Milton *P.R.* iv. 413 Fierce rain with lightning mixt, water with fire In ruine reconcil'd. **1688** Miége *Gt. Fr. Dict.* ii. s.v., He cannot be reconciled with Tobacco (he cannot endure it).

†**d.** To recommend, make agreeable. *Obs. rare.*

1647 Clarendon *Hist. Reb.* i. §98 His courtesy and affability.. marvellously reconciled [him] to all men. *Ibid.* §105 The Treasurer's talent in removing prejudice and reconciling himself to wavering and doubtful affections.

2. a. To win over (a person) again to friendship with oneself or another.

1387 Trevisa *Higden* (Rolls) II. 405 Iason reconsilede and took aȝen his wif Medea wiþ his stepsone Medus. **1494** Fabyan *Chron.* v. cxxvii. 108 Wherfore by fayre and easy meanes he called home his sone and recouncilid hym, and forgaue all trespace. *a* **1547** Surrey in *Tottel's Misc.* (Arb.) 29 An eye.. Frendes to allure, and foes to reconcile. **1592** Shaks. *Rom. & Jul.* iii. iii. 151 Till we can finde a time To .. reconcile your Friends, Beg pardon of thy Prince, and call thee backe. *a* **1700** Dryden *Iliad* i. 430 To reconcile the shooter God, Within her hollow Sides the sacrifice he stow'd. **1712** Lady M. W. Montagu *Let. to W. Montagu* 9–11 Dec., Lord Halifax.. says.. he.. will take pains to reconcile my F[ather]. **1813** Scott *Rokeby* iv. xxi, He came in secret to inquire Her state and reconcile her sire. **1833** Tennyson *Lotos Eaters* 126 Let what is broken so remain. The Gods are hard to reconcile.

b. In *pass.*, without specified agent.

c **1386** Chaucer *Melib.* ¶216 Thou shalt eschue the conseillyng of thyne olde enemys that been reconsiled. **1494** Fabyan *Chron.* vi. cxcvii. 203 Elfricus.. fled as a false traytour, and after that reconsyled, fled the seconde tyme to the Danys. **1667** Milton *P.L.* xi. 39 Let him live Before thee reconcil'd. **1847** Tennyson *Princ.* vii. 73 Nor did her father cease to press my claim, Nor did mine own now reconciled.

3. To set (estranged persons or parties) at one again; to bring back into concord, to reunite (persons or things) in harmony.

1429 *Pol. Poems* (Rolls) II. 145 Eschew flatery.., Folkes reconsile that stonde desolate. **1495** *Trevisa's Barth. De P.R.* x. iii. (W. de W.) 373 Though the elementes ben neuer so contrary eueryche to other yet by influence of heuen and vertue of planetes they ben reconsyled in theyr dooynges and broughte to acorde. **1588** Shaks. *Tit. A.* i. i. 467 Let it be mine honour.. That I haue reconcil'd your friends and you. **1681** T. Jordan *London's Joy* 8 Till an Invasion make them Friends too late, And Reconcile in Ruine. *a* **1727** Newton *Chronol. Amended* ii. (1728) 227 An embassador who reconciled two contending nations. **1782** Cowper *Lily & Rose* 25 Thus sooth'd and reconciled, each seeks The fairest British fair. **1877** Froude *Short Stud.* (1883) IV. i. vii. 80 Lewis and Henry were reconciled amidst general satisfaction and enthusiasm.

†**4.** To bring (a person) back *to*, *into* peace, favour, etc. Also *refl.* *Obs.*

1382 Wyclif *1 Esdras* iv. 31 If she were wroth to hym, he glosith, to the time that he be recounsilid in to grace. *c* **1386** Chaucer *Melib.* ¶39 Somme of hise olde enemys reconsiled .. to his loue and in to his grace. **1526** *Pilgr. Perf.* (W. de W. 1531) 261 For them.. whiche.. be at discorde & debate, to reconsyle them to peace & concorde. **1577–87** Holinshed *Chron.* III. 7/1 Earle Walteof, who had.. slaine manie Normans with his owne hands, was reconciled into the kings fauour. **1594** Shaks. *Rich. III*, ii. i. 59, I desire To reconcile me to his Friendly peace.

†**5. a.** To bring back, restore, or readmit to the Church, *spec.* the Church of Rome. (In later use also with const. *from*). *Obs.*

1387 Trevisa *Higden* (Rolls) V. 317 Þe pope Iustinus reconcilede þe bisshoppes þat Anastacius hadde exciled. *c* **1400** *Apol. Loll.* 93 If þei mend by þe penaunce of þe kirk [they may] be recounsilid. **1494** Fabyan *Chron.* vii. (1533) II. 47b/1 The albygensis.. had ben effected with dyuers poyntes of herysy, and many tymes reconcyled by the kynges of Fraunce. ? **1567** Norton *Bull granted to Harding* Bj, The Pope.. hath graunted to Doctor Harding.. a certain authoritie.. to reconcile Englishmen to the bosome of the Romane Chirch. **1607** *Drewrie's Arraignm.* in *Harl. Misc.* (1745) III. 39/1 Being made Priest by Authority deriued from the Pope.. to reconcile, seduce, and alienate loyall Subiects Harts from Loue.. and Dutie to their Soueraigne. *a* **1625** Sir H. Finch *Law* (1636) 223 To put in vre any bull, or instrument of absolution, or reconciliation from Rome, or to take vpon one.. to absolue or reconcile any person.

†**b.** *pass.* and *refl.* To become united *to* a church. *Obs.*

Perh. sometimes associated with sense 1 or 8.

1639 Drumm. of Hawth. *Conv. w. B. Jonson* Wks. (1711) 224 Ben Johnson.. was 12 years a papist; but after this he was reconciled to the church of England. **1689** Luttrell *Brief Rel.* (1857) I. 597 The house of commons have thought fitt to committ Sir Edward Hales and Obadiah Walker for high treason in reconcileing themselves to the church of Rome. **1700** *Ibid.* IV. 662 The countesse of Jersey, who was a Roman catholick, is said to be reconciled to the church of England. **1769** Blackstone *Comm.* IV. 555 Where a person is reconciled to the see of Rome, or procures others to be reconciled, the offence amounts to high Treason. **1840** *Act 3 & 4 Vict.* c. 52 §6 If.. Prince Albert shall.. be reconciled to or shall hold Communion with the See or Church of Rome.

c. *refl.* [After It. *riconciliarsi.*] To confess (oneself). *rare*$^{-1}$.

1869 Browning *Ring & Bk.* xii. 181 He turned to the confessor, crossed And reconciled himself, with decency.

6. *Eccl.* **a.** To purify (a church, etc.) by a special service after profanation.

c **1386** Chaucer *Pars. T.* ¶891 (Ch. Ch. MS.) If the chirche be halewed.. the chirche is entredited til it be reconsiled by the bysshope. *c* **1440** *Jacob's Well* 130 Whanne þou dost violens in halwyd place.. þanne þou diffoulyst þe place, þat it nedyth to be reconsyled aȝen. **1535** Coverdale *Lev.* xvi. 20 Whan he hath made an ende of reconcylinge the Sanctuary. *a* **1656** Bp. Hall *Rem. Wks.* (1660) 257 Upon the burial of an heretick within the precincts the Church must be reconciled. **1727–41** Chambers *Cycl.* s.v. *Reconciliari*, A church is said *reconciliari*, to be *reconciled*, when it is consecrated afresh, after having been polluted or profaned; as by the possession of pagans, heretics, etc. **1884** *Catholic Dict.* s.v. *Desecration*, If any of the cases cited above have occurred,.. the church or cemetery cannot be used till it has been purified or reconciled by the bishop.

†**b.** To restore to purity, to absolve or cleanse.

c **1430** Lydg. *Min. Poems* (Percy Soc.) 102 The sacrament is justly consecrate,.. Reconsilyng us when we trespas or erre. **1535** Coverdale *Ps.* l[i]. 7 O reconcile me with Isope, and I shal be clene: wash thou me, and I shalbe whyter than snow.

†**c.** To expiate, atone for. *Obs.*

1535 Coverdale *1 Sam.* iii. 14 This wickednes of yᵉ house of Eli shall not be reconcyled.. with sacrifice. —— *Ecclus.* xxvii. 21 As for woundes they maye be bounde vp agayne, and an euell worde maye be reconcyled. **1575** *Brieff Disc. Troub. Franckford* 180 As water quencheth burninge fire, so dothe mercie reconcile synnes.

†**d.** *absol.* To make atonement. *Obs. rare*$^{-1}$.

1539 Bible (Great) *Lev.* vi. 30 And no synne offrynge.. brought into the tabernacle of witnesse to reconcyle with all in the holy place, shal be eaten.

†**7.** To conciliate, recover (a person's favour, etc.); to gain (credit). *Obs.*

1390 Gower *Conf.* v. 1742 a, His Sone.. haþ his grace reconciled ffro which þe man was ferst exiled. **1590** Spenser *F.Q.* ii. ii. 33 To rest themselves, and grace to reconcile. **1609** Hume *Admonit.* in *Wodrow Soc. Misc.* (1844) 585 That .. the Prince's.. unfainzed favour [might be] reconcealed. **1665** Glanvill *Def. Van. Dogm.* 80 That they might reconcile credit to their writings upon him.

8. a. To bring into a state of acquiescence (†*with*) or submission *to* a thing. Also *refl.* and with *inf.*

1606 Shaks. *Ant. & Cl.* ii. vii. 8 Hee cries out, no more; reconciles them to his entreatie, and himselfe to th' drinke. **1677** Miége *Fr. Dict.* ii. s.v., He could not reconcile himself to do it. **1694** Locke *Hum. Und.* ii. xxi. (ed. 2) §69 Trials often reconcile us to that, which at a distance we looked on with aversion. **1722** De Foe *Hist. Plague* (1756) 202 People who had been used to join with the Church, were reconcil'd at this Time with the admitting the Dissenters to preach to them. **1753** Hogarth *Anal. Beauty* 7 How gradually does the eye grow reconciled even to a disagreeable dress. **1838** Lytton *Alice* i. x, He contrived to reconcile himself to the intended visit. **1879** Froude *Cæsar* xx. 335 Not subdued only, but reconciled to subjugation.

absol. **1795** *Montford Castle* II. 155 Launcelot.. felt quite reconciled at not following our hero.

b. *refl.* To settle into position.

c **1857** Adm. Mends in *Life* xxii. (1899) 310 A cheer on deck announced the ship afloat, and by the time I reached the deck she was just reconciling herself between the bowers.

II. 9. a. To adjust, settle, bring to agreement (a controversy, quarrel, etc.).

1390 Gower *Conf.* III. 138 The word this worldes cause entriketh And reconsileth whan him liketh. **1560** Daus tr. *Sleidane's Comm.* 37 He wil have such continual warre with the, as shall never be reconciled. **1617** Moryson *Itin.* i. 161 There is no more hope that wee should meete to reconcile this quarrell. **1699** Luttrell *Brief Rel.* (1857) IV. 481 The lords.. reconciled a difference between the earls of Peterborough and Orford about the army. **1749** Fielding *Tom Jones* v. ix, The quarrel was.. reconciled. **1863** E. V. Neale *Anal. Th. & Nat.* 117 Some independent principle, through which to reconcile the opposition of subject and object in the individual.

†**b.** To smooth over (an inequality). *Obs.*$^{-1}$.

1712 J. James tr. *Le Blond's Gardening* 64 Grass-plots.. that serve to reconcile the Inequality of two Pieces of Ground.

10. a. To make (discordant facts, statements, etc.) consistent, accordant, or compatible with each other.

1560 Daus tr. *Sleidane's Comm.* 180 b, They.. have reconcyled dyverse and weyghty articles of doctryne. **1605** Shaks. *Macb.* iv. iii. 139 Such welcome, and vnwelcom things at once, 'Tis hard to reconcile. **1697** Collier *Ess. Mor. Subj.* ii. (1703) 145 Conscience and covetousness are never to be reconciled: like fire and water, they always destroy each other. **1759** Sterne *Tr. Shandy* I. xxii, Two contrary motions are introduced, and reconciled which were thought to be at variance with each other. **1835** Thirlwall *Greece* I. 57 In this respect, as in others, they present two aspects, which it is not easy to reconcile, and neither of which can be shown to be absolutely false. **1868** Freeman *Norm. Conq.* (1876) II. App. 530 The only means of reconciling the different accounts.

absol. **1675** Baxter *Cath. Theol.* ii. i. 88 Let me hear what your own conceptions are of the matter, if they tend to elucidate or reconcile.

b. *Accountancy.* To establish the consistency of (one account) *with* another, esp. by allowing for transactions made or begun but not yet fully recorded (as when a cheque has been issued but not yet presented for payment). Cf. reconciliation 4 b.

1900 W. W. Snailum *Fifteen Studies in Book-Keeping* xi. 122 At the end of each financial period it will be necessary to 'reconcile' the bank account... This is effected by means of a 'reconciliation statement'. **1930** A. Palmer *Munro's Book-Keeping & Accountancy* (ed. 10) 26 The Bank Pass Book.. would show a balance at the credit of £174, which would be reconciled as follows. **1947** [See reconciliation 4 b]. **1970** R. W. Wallis *Accounting* v. 66 Reconciliations may also establish the accuracy of the different parts of the accounting system within an organization, for example by reconciling the debtor's control account in the ledger with the total of the individual accounts in the sales (debtors) ledger.

11. a. To make (an action, condition, quality, etc.) compatible or consistent in fact or in one's mind *with* another; to regard as consistent *with*. Also const. *to*.

1624 Bp. H. King *Epit. Ld. Dorset*, A soul.. That reconciled the sword unto the pen, Using both well. **1649** Jer. Taylor *Gt. Exemp.* i. iv. §4. 46 But God hath pleased to reconcile his glory with our eternal benefit. **1769** *Junius Lett.* ix. 40 It was hardly possible for you to reconcile your political interest with your duty. **1809** Malkin *Gil Blas* viii. i. ¶2 There was no reconciling such a frosty reception with the glowing portrait ascribed to this paragon. **1874** Green *Short Hist.* vii. §6 Every day made it harder for a Catholic to reconcile Catholicism with loyalty to his Queen.

b. To make (a theory, statement, author, etc.) agree *with* another or with a fact; to show to be in agreement *with*. Also const. *to*.

1613 Purchas *Pilgrimage* i. xiii. 60 It breedes much difficultie, to reconcile the ancient historie of the Babylonian .. Empire, with the kingdomes and Kings in that Chapter. **1662** Stillingfl. *Orig. Sacr.* i. v. §2 Thus we see.. that it is possible to reconcile some of the Ægyptian extravagant accounts to some probability and consistency with truth. **1729** Butler *Serm. Compassion* Wks. 1874 II. 54 *note*, A plain matter of fact, which men cannot reconcile with the general account they think fit to give of things. **1748** Richardson *Clarissa* (1811) VII. 260 It is impossible.. to reconcile those contents to the facts I have to communicate. **1884** tr. *Lotze's Metaph.* 201 To show by what general line of thought my view of space might be reconciled with the particular facts of Nature.

c. *ellipt.* without const.

1656 Bramhall *Replic.* i. 1 Yet there is one thing which I cannot reconcile [etc.]. *a* **1658** Cleveland *Wks.* (1687) 182 Who reconcil'd the Covenant's doubtful sence. **1761** Foote *Liar* ii. Wks. 1799 I. 302 But suppose, Sir, there should be an unsurmountable objection? *O. Wild.* Oh, leave the reconciling that to me; I am an excellent casuist.

d. To bring (a thing) *to* form etc. *rare.*

1709 Pope *Ess. Crit.* i. 174 Some figures monstrous and mis-shap'd appear, Consider'd singly, or beheld too near, Which.. Due distance reconciles to form and grace.

12. To make even or smooth, or fit together so as to present a uniform surface.

a **1687** [see reconciled *ppl. a.* b]. **1793** [see reconciling *ppl. a.* b]. *c* **1850** *Rudim. Navig.* (Weale) 140 *To reconcile*, to make one piece of work answer fair with the moulding or shape of the adjoining piece; and, more particularly, in the reversion of curves. **1875** [see reconciling *vbl. sb.* b].

†**III. 13.** *intr.* To become reconciled. *Obs.*

1666 Abp. Sancroft *Occas. Serm.* 104 Your Thoughts though much startled at first, by degrees reconcile to it. **1683** Crowne *City Politiques* iv. i, For shame, reconcile, pray reconcile. **1756** H. Walpole *Let. to Mann* 19 Sept., He.. abuses Count Bruhl with so much contempt, that one reconciles to him very fast.

Hence ˌ**reconci'lee**, one who is reconciled; '**reconˌcileless** *a.*, that cannot be reconciled.

1876 Egan tr. *Heine's Atta Troll*, etc. 38 Be the mortal foe of all such Fierce oppressors, reconcileless. **1894** Lloyd *Wealth agst. Commw.* 67 The 'reconciler' to enforce the provisions that the 'reconcilees' should not engage in business elsewhere, extended a system of espionage over them.

reconciled ('rɛkənsaɪld), *ppl. a.* [f. prec. + -ed¹.] Restored to friendship, harmony, etc.

? *c* **1470** G. Ashby *Active Policy* 755 He endith not wele that vngodly ment, Withoute a reconsiled amendment. *a* **1548** Hall *Chron., Hen. VIII* 170 The Frenche kyng, his newe reconsiled frende. **1598** Dallington *Meth. Trav.* F iij b, A man must neuer trust a reconciled enemy, especially his King. **1677** W. Hubbard *Narrative* 102 Capt. Church.. with but thirty English-men, and twenty reconciled Indians, took twenty three of the Enemy. **1732** Pope *Ep. Bathurst* 166 Thro' reconcil'd extremes of drought and rain. **1820** Scott *Monast.* v, The look of a confessor who resigns a reconciled penitent, not to earth, but to heaven. **1860** Motley *Netherl.* viii. I. 504 No language could describe the misery of the reconciled Provinces.

absol. **1628** T. Spencer *Logick* 115 If Christs death reconciled an enemie, then his life will saue the reconciled.

†**b.** Made to run evenly with each other. *Obs.*

a **1687** Petty *Nav. Philos.* in T. H[ale] *Acc. New Invent.* (1691) 124 The forementioned Incurvations are to be trimmed and repaired by reconciled lines.

reconcilement ('rɛkənsaɪlmənt). [-ment.]

1. The fact of reconciling or being reconciled to another or to each other. Cf. reconciliation 1.

1549 *Form Consecr. Bps.* in Lindsay *Vind. Ch. Eng.* (1734) p. xxv, Grant..suche grace that he maie euermore be ready to sprede abrod thy Gospell, and glad tidynges of reconcilement to God. **1611** SPEED *Hist. Gt. Brit.* IX. viii. (1623) 551 The Generall..seriously perswaded his Lord to reconcilement with his vncle. **1667** MILTON *P.L.* IV. 98 Never can true reconcilement grow Where wounds of deadly hate have peirc'd so deep. **1760–72** H. BROOKE *Fool of Qual.* (1809) I. 157 [He] was fain to plead and sue for reconcilement. **1847** TENNYSON *Princ.* VI. 268 Make reconcilement sure With one that cannot keep her mind an hour.

b. With *a* and *pl.* An instance of this.

1560 DAUS tr. *Sleidane's Comm.* 263 He ought..to forget al displeasure, though no reconcilement had bene made. **1595** DANIEL *Civ. Wars* I. xxxiv, A reconcilement made, although not meant. **1692** SOUTH *12 Serm.* (1697) I. 418 Hector and Ajax..ended that combat in a reconcilement. **1761** HUME *Hist. Eng.* I. iv. 123 The interposition of the queen, and other common friends, brought about a reconcilement. **1831** SCOTT *Ct. Robt.* ix, Four weeks.. marked by quarrels and reconcilements between the crusaders and the Grecians of the empire.

†**2.** The fact of restoring or reuniting to the Church, *spec.* to the Church of Rome. *Obs.* = RECONCILIATION 2.

?**1567** NORTON (*title*) A Bull graunted by the Pope to Doctor Harding.., by reconcilement and assoyling of English Papistes, to vndermyne faith and allegeance to the Quene. **1600** W. WATSON *Decacordon* (1602) 266 Such straite lawes..for comming into England of Seminarie priests,..reconcilement, perswasions to the catholike faith, and the like.

3. The act of settling or bringing to an agreement; a harmonizing or bringing into concord.

1560 DAUS tr. *Sleidane's Comm.* 92 George Truckesse, and Vehus..had deuysed a reconcilement touchyng the Masse and Vowes. **1624** WOTTON *Archit.* in *Reliq.* (1651) 218 Two opposite affectations, Uniformity and Variety, which yet will very well suffer a good reconcilement. **1649** ROBERTS *Clavis Bibl.* 105 The reconcilement of this seeming discord. **1817** MOORE *Lalla R.* 293 The reconcilement of a sort of lover's quarrel. **1877** MRS. OLIPHANT *Makers Flor.* iii. 74 The arbitrary settlement of her affairs and reconcilement of her difficulties.

†**4.** The act of appeasing. *Obs. rare*$^{-1}$.

1581 J. BELL *Haddon's Answ. Osor.* 453 b, The Sacrifice of the body and bloud of Christ offred for the reconcilement of Gods wrath and displeasure.

5. The fact or condition of being (or becoming) reconciled *to* or *with* a thing.

1805 WORDSW. *Prelude* v. 517 The time of trial, ere we learn to live In reconcilement with our stinted powers. **1832** HT. MARTINEAU *Homes Abroad* i. 17 This assisted his reconcilement to the emigration plan. **1876** BANCROFT *Hist. U.S.* V. i. 335 The illusion of a reconcilement to the dominion of Britain.

reconciler ('rɛkənsaɪlə(r)). Also 6 -or, -our. [f. as prec. + -ER^1.]

1. One who reconciles. Cf. RECONCILIATOR.

1586 T. B. *La Primaud. Fr. Acad.* I. (1594) 102 Sent from heaven to be a common reformer, governor, and reconcilour of the whole world. **1665** MANLEY *Grotius' Low C. Warres* 457 He accepted of him to be a Moderator and Reconciler of Differences in Religion. **1768–74** TUCKER *Lt. Nat.* (1834) II. 381 In order to maintain the character I have assumed in this volume of a reconciler between religion and reason. **1836** HOR. SMITH *Tin Trump.* (1876) 265 The reconciler of all misgivings. **1884** COURTHOPE *Addison* ix. 163 He is to be regarded as the reconciler of parties, and founder of public opinion.

b. *spec.* applied to Christ.

1563 FOXE *A. & M.* 1035/1 Christ, our only and sufficient mediatour, reconcilor, priest and sacrifice. **1616** HAYWARD *Sanct. Troub. Soul* I. vi. (1620) 99 O Reconciler! whom wilt thou reconcile to thy Father..? **1690** NORRIS *Beatitudes* (1692) 3 Blessing became the mouth of him, who was the Reconciler of God and Man. **1875** LIGHTFOOT *Comm. Col.* (ed. 2) 180 The conception of the person of Christ as..the true and only reconciler of heaven and earth.

2. That which reconciles; †*spec.* a reconciling argument or statement.

1588 FRAUNCE *Lawiers Log.* I. ii. 7 That which they call *Medium*, a third argument, is, as it were, an *Arbiter honorarius*, a determiner, a reconciler. **1615** CROOKE *Body of Man* 921 If it be obiected out of Galen..We answere with the Reconciler; that Galen then speaketh of membranous and broade ligaments which issue from the bones. **1654** FULLER (*title*) A Triple Reconciler, stating the Controversies [etc.]. **1830** LYTTON *P. Clifford* xxvi, The universal reconciler—custom. **1860** WARTER *Sea-board* II. 453 Many a hard grip of the hand..was a sure Reconciler.

attrib. *a***1700** DRYDEN *Iliad* I. 613 The Reconciler Bowl, went round the Board.

b. *Shipbuilding.* (See quots.)

1849 [see RECONCILING *ppl. a.* b]. *c***1850** *Rudim. Navig.* (Weale) 140 Reconciler or reconciling sweep. A curve which reconciles the floor and lower breadth sweeps together, and thus the shape of the body is formed below the breadth.

So **'reconciless**, a female reconciler.

1865 PUSEY *Truth Eng. Ch.* 179 Being..the most powerful mediatress and reconciless (conciliatrix) of the whole world with her only-begotten Son.

recon'ciliable, *a.* *rare*$^{-1}$. [f. L. *reconcili-āre*; cf. CONCILIABLE *a.* and obs. F. *reconciliable*.] Reconcilable. Hence **ˌreconcilia'bility**.

1856 OLMSTED *Slave States* 500 This ruling intellect tries to make practicably reconciliable the social system of the State with the Constitution of the Confederacy. *a***1861** CUNNINGHAM *Hist. Theol.* (1864) II. xxiv. 322 Not properly reconciliation, but rather what has been called reconciliability, or a capacity of being reconciled.

†**reconciliage.** *Obs.* *rare*$^{-1}$. [f. as prec. + -AGE.] Reconciliation, reconciling.

1626 LD. HERBERT *Let.* in *Life* (1886) 258 After the reconciliage of the distracted affections of this..people.

†**reconciliate**, *sb.* *Obs.* *rare*$^{-1}$. In 7 -at. [ad. L. *reconciliātus*, pa. pple. of *reconciliāre* to RECONCILE.] One who is reconciled.

1611 SPEED *Hist. Gt. Brit.* IX. viii. §7. 485 But Heauens were not so propitious to these Reconciliats, as so to hold them long.

recon'ciliate, *v.* ? *Obs. rare.* [See prec.] *trans.* To conciliate again, reconcile. Hence **recon'ciliating** *ppl. a.*

1723 *Briton* No. 11 (1724) 51 One..who possesses such calm reconciliating Principles. **1748** LD. CRAWFURD in *Lett. Lady Jane Stewart* 16, I have also engaged my Lord Horne, who is gone down to Lord Mark Kerr's to reconciliate him. **1791** E. CLARKE *Sword* I. 132 Let me request that you will ..repair to your Father's Tent, where the Princess now is, and..endeavour to reconciliate her Affections. **1922** *Glasgow Herald* 26 Apr. 11/5 The question of reconciliating the two wings of the army.

reconciliation (ˌrɛkənsɪlɪ'eɪʃən). [a. F. *reconciliation* (14th c. in Littré), or ad. L. *reconciliātiōn-em*, n. of action f. *reconciliāre* to RECONCILE.]

1. a. The action of reconciling persons, or the result of this; the fact of being reconciled.

*c***1386** CHAUCER *Melib.* ¶724 If I hadde seyd that ye sholde han purchaced the pees and the reconsiliacion I ne hadde nat muchel mystaken me. **1473** *Rolls of Parlt.* VI. 66/1 By the reconsiliation of the merchauntes of the said Hanze. **1494** FABYAN *Chron.* I. xvii. 16 And after certayne message sent to hym of reconcilyacion. **1569** *Reg. Privy Council Scot.* Ser. I. II. 10 [They] sall entir in reconsiliatioun freindschip and amytie ilkane with utheris. **1603** HOLLAND *Plutarch's Mor.* 38 Nestor, contrariwise, intending to make a motion as touching the reconciliation and pacifying of Achilles. **1693** CONGREVE *Old Bach.* III. ii, I..have fram'd a Letter, that makes her sue for Reconciliation first. **1741** RICHARDSON *Pamela* (1824) I. 67 Well, come, I will forgive you for this time; and so kissed me as a mark of reconciliation. **1841** ELPHINSTONE *Hist. Ind.* II. x. i. 371 Messages passed between Sháh Jehán and the emperor, but with..little effect in producing a reconciliation. **1874** MAHAFFY *Soc. Life Greece* viii. 254 To live in reconciliation with political foes.

b. *spec.* in religious use, of God and man.

13.. *Propr. Sanct.* (Vernon MS.) in *Archiv neu. Spr.* LXXXI. 315/148 þe goode world..þat holi chirche we calle moun, Is falle to Reconsiliacioun. *c***1420** LYDG. *Assembly of Gods* 1753 For then came the Tyme of Reconsylyacion of man to God. **1526** *Pilgr. Perf.* (W. de W. 1531) 244 b, One act of adoracyon of hym had ben sufficyent for our reconsiliacyon to his eternall father. **1582** N. T. (Rhem.) *2 Cor.* v. 18 **1641** HINDE *J. Bruen* xxvii. 83 Ambassadors of peace, preaching unto the the glad tydings of the Gospell, by the word of reconciliation. **1884** J. TAIT *Mind in Matter* (1892) 330 He presents Himself as at once the Reconciliation and the Reconciler.

†**c.** Restoration *to* favour. *Obs. rare*$^{-1}$.

1536 CROMWELL in Merriman *Life & Lett.* (1902) II. 41 Two letteres writen..for their restitucion and reconsiliacion to the king of Scottes fauour.

2. Reunion of a person to a church.

1625 tr. *Gonsalvio's Sp. Inquis.* 110 Another sort of sentences there are that haue a shew of more mercie, which they call reconciliations. **1639** DRUMM. OF HAWTH. *Conv. w. B. Jonson* Wks. (1711) 224 At his first communion, in token of his true reconciliation, he drunk out the full cup of wine. **1753** CHAMBERS *Cycl. Supp.*, *Reconciliation* of penitents, in church history. **1884** in *Catholic Dict.*

3. The purification, or restoration to sacred uses, of a church, etc., after desecration or pollution.

1533 BELLENDEN *Livy* v. (1822) 476 Eftir the reconsiliacioun of the templis, confederacioun and alliance of amite wes made betwix the Romanis and pepil, namit Ceretes. **1554** *Churchw. Acc. St. Margaret's, Westminster* (Nichols 1797) 14 Paid for iii Capons for the Bishop's dinner at the reconciliacion of the Church. **1846** MASKELL *Mon. Rit.* I. p. cclvi, At the laying of the first stone of a church: at its consecration and reconciliation. **1889** *Ch. Times* 23 Aug. 759 Reconciliation of a Font.

4. a. The action of bringing to agreement, concord, or harmony.

1560 DAUS tr. *Sleidane's Comm.* 89 b, If they went about the reconsiliation of Religion. *a***1729** J. ROGERS *19 Serm.* (1735) i. 8 These Distinctions..give us a clear and easy Reconciliation of those seeming Inconsistencies of Scripture, with Respect to this Affection. **1758** JOHNSON *Idler* No. 4 ¶13 The spirit of charity can only be continued by a reconciliation of these ridiculous feuds. **1847** EMERSON *Repr. Men, Montaigne* Wks. (Bohn) I. 348 The absence of any appearance of reconciliation between the theory and practice of life. **1875** JOWETT *Plato* (ed. 2) IV. 11 Without any reconciliation..he speaks at one time of God or Gods, and at another time of the good.

b. *Accountancy.* The action or practice of rendering one account consistent with another by balancing apparent discrepancies; ***reconciliation statement***, a statement of account whereby such discrepancies are adjusted.

1895 J. THORNTON *Man. Bookkeeping* xi. 187 See that all Banker's charges..are duly entered in your own books, or you will have difficulty with your Reconciliation. **1929** L. C. CROPPER *Book-Keeping & Accounts* iv. 46 In order to explain this divergence it is necessary to construct a statement, known as a 'Reconciliation Statement'... A specimen example is appended showing how this 'reconciliation' is arrived at. **1947** F. H. JONES *Jordan's Mod. Book-Keeping* I. iii. 33 In order to reconcile the Cash Book balance with the statement of Account balance a Bank Reconciliation Statement is compiled. **1957** W. W. BIGG *Cost Accounts* xiii. 231 Assuming that it is desired to keep the Cost and Financial Accounts entirely distinct it is still imperative that they be rendered capable of reconciliation one with the other. **1973** A. & E. E. FIELDHOUSE *Elem. Book-Keeping* 80 If the balances of the two books should disagree a Reconciliation Statement should be made out.

reconciliative (rɛkən'sɪlɪətɪv), *a.* *rare.* [ad. L. type **reconciliātīv-us*, f. ppl. stem of *reconciliāre* to RECONCILE: see -ATIVE.] Reconciliatory.

1773 J. ROSS *Fratricide* v. 101 (MS.) Eve's sweet maternity And earnest reconciliative will. **1855** LYNCH *Lett. to Scattered* vi. 89 On those who believe, his [God's] reconciliative Love exerts Power to produce moral union with Him.

reconciliator (rɛkən'sɪlɪeɪtə(r)). [a. L. *reconciliātor*, agent-n. f. *reconciliāre* to RECONCILE. Cf. F. *reconciliateur* (16th c. in Littré).] A reconciler.

1577 tr. *Bullinger's Decades* (1592) 662 He that is an intercessour, must also be a reconciliatour or an attonement maker. **1820** *Blackw. Mag.* VII. 667 A good dinner is the *facillime princeps* of reconciliators. **1882–3** SCHAFF *Encycl. Relig. Knowl.* I. 73 Ammonius Saccas, the pagan eclectic, the reconciliator of Plato and Aristotle.

So **reconciliatrix.** *rare*$^{-0}$.

1611 COTGR., *Conciliatrice*, a conciliatrix, reconciliatrix.

reconciliatory (rɛkən'sɪlɪətərɪ), *a.* [ad. L. type **reconciliātōrius*: see prec. and -ORY. Cf. F. *reconciliatoire* (16th c. in Littré).] Of words, actions, etc.: Tending to reconciliation.

1586 A. DAY *Eng. Secretary* I. (1625) 87 An example Reconciliatorie, from one friend to another. **1613–18** DANIEL *Coll. Hist. Eng.* (1626) 105 Deceiuing both the world, and themselues with shewe of couenants reconciliatory. **1657** HEYLIN *Ecclesia Vind.* 345 After the said Commination there are some certain reconciliatorie Psalms, or Prayers, that follow after. **1748** RICHARDSON *Clarissa* (1811) V. 226 All blessed the reconciliatory scheme. **1784** J. BROWN *Hist. Brit. Ch.* (1820) I. vi. 144 Reconciliatory letters passed between them. **1865** tr. *Strauss' Life Jesus* I. II. x. 74 His statements are sometimes reconciliatory.

reconciling ('rɛkənsaɪlɪŋ), *vbl. sb.* [f. RECONCILE *v.* + -ING^1.] The action of the vb. RECONCILE; reconciliation.

1382 WYCLIF *Isa.* lx. 10 In my recounsiling I hadde reuthe of thee. *c***1386** CHAUCER *Melib.* ¶725 The dissension bigynneth by another man, and the reconsilyng by-gynneth by thy self. **1535** COVERDALE *2 Macc.* xii. 46 He thought it to be good & honorable for a reconcylinge, to do the same for those which were slayne. **1667** W. MOUNTAGU in *Buccleuch MSS.* (Hist. MSS. Comm.) I. 316 His business was to desire the completing of your Lordship's reconciling to him, ..he desiring so much your reconciling.

b. The action of smoothing or planing; removal of roughnesses (see RECONCILE *v.* 12).

1875 LASLETT *Timber* 297 Kauri Pine is also employed for the decks of yachts..and does not require the reconciling or planing over, which is frequently found necessary if other woods are worked.

reconciling ('rɛkənsaɪlɪŋ), *ppl. a.* [f. as prec. + -ING^2.] That reconciles.

1594 ? GREENE *Selimus* 1545 Friend, let me see thy letter once again, That I may read these reconciling lines. **1658–9** *Burton's Diary* (1828) IV. 204 That is agreed to be a very reconciling motion, and may heal all the heats and differences about it. **1717** POPE *Eloïsa* 145 Thy eyes diffused a reconciling ray. **1801** SOUTHEY in Robberds *Mem. W. Taylor* (1843) I. 378 A man of gentle and reconciling manners. **1878** SEELEY *Stein* II. 475 The peaceful and reconciling revolution to which Stein had shown the way.

b. *spec.* Applied to curves or moulds which accommodate lines or surfaces to each other.

1793 SMEATON *Edystone L.* §81 By reconciling Curves, I could adapt every part of the base upon the rock to the regularly turned tapering body. **1849** WEALE *Dict. Terms*, *Reconciler*, a mould sometimes used to form the hollow in the topside, which is called the reconciling mould.

'reconcilist, *a.* *rare.* [f. as prec. + -IST.] That inclines to reconciliation.

1898 *Speaker* 10 Dec. 695/2 In his early works..he posed as orthodox and reconcilist.

†**reconcinnate**, *v.* *Obs.* *rare*$^{-0}$. [f. ppl. stem of L. *reconcinnāre*: see RE- and CONCINNATE *v.*] 'To mend or make fit' (Cockeram 1623).

recon'coct, *v.* [RE- 5 a.] To concoct again.

1630 LENNARD tr. *Charron's Wisd.* I. xiv. (1670) 51 The repetition and action of ruminating, reconcocting, trying by the whetstone of reason.

reconcyle, obs. form of RECONCILE *v.*

†**recond**, *v.* *Obs.* *rare.* [ad. L. *recondĕre*: see RECONDITE *a.*]

1. *trans.* ? To put off, dispense with.

1464 *Paston Lett.* II. 145 As touchyng Rysyng, he hath his day Utas Purificationis, but I have that weye that his presence is recondet for al this terme.

2. To put away, to set apart.

1658 tr. *Porta's Nat. Magic* IV. xiii. 139 Figs..put in an Oven, and whil'st hot imposed in their own leaves and reconded in a pot. **1693** *Phil. Trans.* XVII. 657 A Ferment ..somewhere reconded out of the Road of the circulating Blood, and there gradually maturated.

reconden'sation. [RE- 5 a.] A fresh condensation.
1860 MAURY *Phys. Geog.* (Low) iv. 100 During the conversion..of liquids into vapours, heat is absorbed, which is again given out on their recondensation.

recon'dense, *v.* [RE- 5 a. Cf. F. *recondenser* (Godef.).] *trans.* and *intr.* To condense again.
trans. **1660** BOYLE *New Exp. Phys. Mech.* xxii. 176 Such vapors are even by a very little cold recondensed into Water. **1664** POWER *Exp. Philos.* II. 117 The Ayr is recondensed again into its natural and ordinary Consistence. **1871** TYNDALL *Fragm. Sci.* (1879) II. xiv. 343 Vapour, which rises in the air and is recondensed on mountain heights. *intr.* **1658** R. WHITE tr. *Digby's Powd. Symp.* (1660) 77 As it cools, it recondenseth there into water. **1879** *Chambers' Encycl.* (U.S. repr.) VI. 269 Removing the vapor which would otherwise recondense on the descent of the piston.

reconde'scension. [RE-.] Condescension (sense 3) shown in return *for* something.
1679 PULLER *Moder. Ch. Eng.* (1843) 240 What re-condescension hath been made by them for all the indulgences of his Majesty from first to last?

recondite ('rɛkəndaɪt), *a.* Also 7 -dit. [ad. L. *recondit-us*, pa. pple. of *recondĕre* to put away, hide, f. *re-* RE- + *condĕre*: see CONDITE *a.*[2] Cf. It., Sp., Pg. *recondito*, obs. F. *recondit* (Cotgr.).
The pronunciations (rɪ'kɒndaɪt, ri:'kɒndɪt) are also recognized by some recent Dicts. By Bailey (1731) and Sheridan (1789) the stressing is given as *recon'dite*, by Johnson as *re'condite*. See also Walker's note, s.v.]
1. Of things: Removed or hidden from view; kept out of sight. Now *rare*.
1649 BULWER *Pathomyot.* II. ii. 108 The Eye is somewhat recondit betweene its Orbite. **1684** tr. *Bonet's Merc. Compit.* XIX. 848 The more recondite Seeds of Diseases, are seldom extirpated without Vomitories. **1796** COLERIDGE *Lett.* I. 209 My recondite eye sits distent quaintly behind the flesh-hill, and looks as little as a tomtit's. **1818** T. L. PEACOCK *Maid Marian* xiv, The husband produced some recondite flasks of wine. **1821** LAMB *Elia* Ser. I. *Old Benchers Inner Temple*, The young urchins,..not being able to guess at its recondite machinery, were almost tempted to hail the wondrous work as magic.
b. *spec.* in *Bot.* and *Entom.*
1826 KIRBY & SP. *Entomol.* IV. 306 *Recondite*,..when the head is wholly covered and sheltered by the shield of the thorax. **1866** *Treas. Bot.* 962/1.
c. Retired, avoiding notice.
1881 *Cassell's Nat. Hist.* V. 316 The Pselaphidæ..bear a certain analogy to the Paussidæ, being, like them of recondite habits.
2. Removed from ordinary apprehension, understanding, or knowledge; deep, profound, abstruse.
a **1652** J. SMITH *Sel. Disc.* vi. 200 That so his sublime and recondite doctrine might be the better hid up therein. **1672** *Mede's Wks.* Pref., In the more abstruse and recondite parts of Knowledge. **1706** PHILLIPS (ed. Kersey), *Recondite*, secret, hidden; as Recondite Mysteries. **1772** MACKENZIE *Man World* II. ii, The recondite principles of philosophy. **1796** BP. WATSON *Apol. Bible* (ed. 2) 376 The origin of arts, or the recondite depths of science. **1850** MCCOSH *Div. Govt.* II. ii. (1874) 191 In some cases the cause is obvious, and in others more recondite. **1875** HELPS *Soc. Press.* xxv. 392 This is all too recondite for me and the examples given are almost impossible ones for me to imagine.
b. Of learning, investigation, discussion, etc.: Consisting in, relating to, uncommon or profound knowledge.
1654 H. L'ESTRANGE *Chas. I* (1655) 4 A king, (for recondite learning, and abstruse knowledge) so near a match to Solomon. **1665** GLANVILL *Def. Van. Dogm.* 40 A close and recondite Search into the Seminalities of Plants. **1711** FELTON *Dissert. Classics* (1718) 65 Men of more recondite Studies and what they call deep learning. **1822** HAZLITT *Table-t.* Ser. II. i. (1869) 7 A dispute, the most learned and recondite that ever took place. **1862** H. SPENCER *First Princ.* I. i. §5 The office of the most recondite and abstract inquiries of Science.
c. Of writers, sources, etc.: Obscure, little known.
1817 COLERIDGE *Biog. Lit.* I. iii. 65, I look in vain for any writer who has conveyed so much information [as Southey], from so many and such recondite sources. **1841** D'ISRAELI *Amen. Lit.* (1867) 662 His knowledge..in the recondite literature of the middle ages. **1865** *Sat. Rev.* 15 July 76/1 The traditional edition of a recondite classical author.
3. Of persons: Writing in an obscure fashion.
1788 V. KNOX *Winter Even.* II. v. i. 109 They afford a lesson to the modern metaphysical and recondite writers not to overvalue their works. **1817** COLERIDGE *Biog. Lit.* xxii. II. 172 In the play of fancy, Wordsworth, to my feelings, is not always graceful and sometimes recondite.
Hence **'reconditely** *adv.*
1854 GILFILLAN *Life Blair* in *B.'s Wks.* 127 We could have conceived of him treating the subject more reconditely.

†**recondite,** *v.* *Obs.* *rare*[−1]. [f. as prec. Cf. RECOND *v.*] *trans.* To hide, cover up.
1578 BANISTER *Hist. Man* I. 32 Tendons recondited, and hidde in their Muscle, as if they were in a purse imposed.

reconditeness ('rɛkəndaɪtnɪs). [f. RECONDITE *a.* + -NESS.] The quality of being recondite.
1835 CHALMERS *Nat. Theol.* I. III. i. 300 The sense we have of the reconditeness of his wisdom. **1876** LOWELL *Among my Bks.* Ser. II. 45 In spite of the reconditeness and complexity of allusion.

recon'dition, *v.* [RE- 5 a.] *trans.* **1.** To restore to a proper, habitable, or usable condition; to repair or rehabilitate.
1920 *Glasgow Herald* 29 Apr. 7/1 The Agamemnon..is being reconditioned at the Brooklyn Navy Yard. **1922** *Flight* XIV. 366/1 In the name of economy, the R.A.F. has had to be content with machines built during the War and 'reconditioned', or, at best, with designs got out during the War. **1930** S. RUNCIMAN *Hist. First Bulgarian Empire* II. i. 53 A strong line of Imperial fortresses..had probably been reconditioned by Constantine Copronymus. **1935** *Punch* 27 Mar. 346/2, I see with shame that H.M. Gov. propose in a White Paper to 'recondition' the Navy. But I see with delight and surprise that for once the *Shorter O.E.D.* does not acknowledge the existence of the filthy verb. **1966** J. S. COX *Illustr. Dict. Hairdressing* 125/2 *Recondition* (Hair),..to restore hair by means of suitable substances and/or treatments to its normal condition.
2. *Forestry.* To reduce warping and collapse in (timber) by heating in a steam-filled atmosphere for several hours.
1932 *Rep. Forest Products Res. Board 1930* iv. 42 Experiments have been made during the year to ascertain the possibility of reconditioning or restoring collapsed Tasmanian oak. **1938** H. E. DESCH *Timber* x. 127 Timber that is badly warped or cupped, without showing any visible signs of collapse, may also be successfully re-conditioned. **1979** J. G. WILKINSON *Industr. Timber Preservation* vii. 198 Conventional kilns can also be used to: 1. Recondition timber which has collapsed. 2. Destroy fungal growth and insect infestations.
3. *Psychol.* To alter the responses of (a person) by means of conditioning techniques; to replace (existing reponses) in this manner.
1935 [implied in RECONDITIONING *vbl. sb.* 3]. **1942** *Sun* (Baltimore) 4 Nov. 9/5 The army has been consistently uninterested in taking the rejects into conditioning battalions and reconditioning them. **1957** W. SARGANT *Battle for Mind* x. 220 It is very difficult indeed to condition or recondition such persons [*sc.* psychopaths], some of whom are criminals, until later in life when their brainwave patterns become much more normal. **1967** J. A. HADFIELD *Introd. Psychotherapy* xiv. 88 The objection then to treatment by re-conditioning the symptoms alone is..that we are not dealing with the real illness.
Hence **recon'ditioned** *ppl. a.*
1932 KIPLING *Limits & Renewals* 374 Our pernicious system of employing reconditioned souls on such delicate duties. **1933** *Sun* (Baltimore) 21 Apr. 19/3 (Advt.), Guaranteed reconditioned cars. **1944** AUDEN *For Time Being* (1945) 52, I moved the vices out of the city into a chain of re-conditioned lighthouses. **1957** L. F. R. WILLIAMS *State of Israel* ix. 155 Israel's first elected Parliament, which met in a reconditioned cinema. **1977** *Western Mail* (Cardiff) 5 Mar. 14/3 (Advt.), Massey Ferguson 35, 4-cylinder Tractor. Reconditioned engine.

recon'ditioning, *vbl. sb.* [f. prec. + -ING[1].] The action or process of the vb. **1.** Restoring to proper or adequate condition; rehabilitation, repair. Also, conversion or modernization (of houses, etc.).
1920 *Sphere* 27 Mar. 339 (*heading*) *Reconditioning.* A present striking phase of the great British shipping industry. *Ibid.* (*caption*) The word at the top of this page—'Reconditioning'—may be unfamiliar to the general public, but it is to-day well known to all the shipping world. **1926** *Manch. Guardian Weekly* Feb. 104/2 Measures are being considered for the improvement and reconditioning of existing rural cottages. **1936** *Discovery* Apr. 117/1 Systematic re-conditioning of working-class houses throughout the country. **1944** M. LASKI *Love on Supertax* x. 95 You really ought to let me give your hair a thorough re-conditioning.
2. *Forestry.* The steaming of timber to reduce warping and collapse (se RECONDITION *v.* 2).
1932 *Rep. Forest Products Res. Board 1931* ii. 11 The treatment, which has been called re-conditioning, consisted essentially of warming the timber, which was first dried to a moisture content of 15 per cent.,..to 210 °F in saturated air. **1948** *New Biol.* IV. 89 The kiln load is given a stress-relieving or reconditioning treatment. **1979** J. G. WILKINSON *Industr. Timber Preservation* vii. 198 Reconditioning typically involves heating defective boards for between four and eight hours at 100 °C in a steam-filled atmosphere.
3. *Psychol.* The replacement through conditioning of one conditioned response by another; the re-establishing of a conditioned response after its extinction.
1935 J. E. WALLIN *Personality Maladjustments* xi. 461 Such bonds must be loosened or dissipated by substituting other emotional bonds that are more potent by a process of emotional reconditioning. **1940** HILGARD & MARQUIS *Conditioning & Learning* 349/1 *Reconditioning*, the re-establishment of a conditioned response after it has been diminished by extinction or forgetfulness. **1957** W. SARGANT *Battle for Mind* x. 221 The need to vary methods of conditioning and reconditioning according to the different temperaments is clearly shown by a study of the way prison sentences affect various types. **1967** J. A. HADFIELD *Introd. Psychotherapy* xiv. 88 One could not deal with this guilt by re-conditioning because neither she nor we knew of its existence. **1972** J. W. KLING et al. *Woodworth & Schlosberg's Exper. Psychol.* xiv. 570/2 Reconditioning: if extinction trials are followed by a single presentation of the CS-US combination much or all of the effects of extinction will be overcome.

†**re'conditory.** *Obs.* [ad. late L. *reconditōrium* a repository for documents, relics, etc. (816 in Du Cange): see RECONDITE *a.* and -ORY[1].] A store-house, repository, treasury.
1633 T. ADAMS *Exp. 2 Peter* iii. 10 Good workes are such a Treasure, fit for the reconditory of Heaven. **1639** LD. DIGBY *Lett. conc. Relig.* (1651) 47 In Scripture..the perfect reconditory of all necessary Doctrines. **1685** *Phil. Trans.* XV. 924 The manifold Variety of exhalations prepared in..the vast Magazines, and severall reconditories below.

†**re'conditure.** *Obs.* *rare*[−1]. [RE- 5 a.] A renewed process of conserving.
1657 TOMLINSON *Renou's Disp.* II. xxix. 87 Fruits..after conditure and Reconditure may be preserved with a sirup.

re'condity. *rare.* [irreg. f. RECOND(ITE) + -ITY.] Reconditeness.
1856 *Titan Mag.* Dec. 496 A fruitful butt for the shafts of the university wits is the Examination papers..their ridiculous recondity contrasted with the often slender attainments of the students.

re-con'dole, *v.* [RE-.] *intr.* To condole in return. Hence **re-con'doling** *ppl. a.*
a **1711** KEN *Hymns Evang.* Poet. Wks. 1721 I. 159 With re-condoling Love and melting Eyes.

reconduct (ri:kən'dʌkt), *v.* [f. L. *reconduct-*, ppl. stem of *recondūcĕre*, to hire anew, also to lead back: see RE- 2 and CONDUCT *v.* Cf. F. *reconduire* (14th c. in Littré *Suppl.*).] *trans.* To lead back.
1611 COTGR., *Reconduire*, to reconduct, bring backe. **1653** H. COGAN tr. *Pinto's Trav.* x. 31 Well, replied the Mahomedan, I am contented to redeem, and reconduct thee to Malaca. **1760–72** H. BROOKE *Fool of Qual.* (1809) IV. 97, I suffered myself to be reconducted to the..palace. **1825** J. NICHOLSON *Operat. Mechanic* 106 The canal, which re-conducts the water from the course of discharge to the river. **1868** BROWNING *Ring & Bk.* II. 877 Three successive times, Had he to reconduct her by main-force..Back to the husband and the house she fled.
So **recon'ductor.** *rare*[−1].
1611 COTGR., *Reconduiseur*, a reconductor; a leader.

reconduction. [a. F. *réconduction*, a. L. type **reconductiōn-em*, f. *recondūcĕre*: see prec.] *Civil Law.* The renewal of a lease.
1876 in WILL *Wharton's Law Lex.*

recon'fer, *v.* [RE- 5 a. Cf. obs. F. *reconferer* (Cotgr.).] *trans.* and *intr.* To confer again.
1611 COTGR., *Reconferer*, to reconferre, or talke of the matter againe. *a* **1661** FULLER *Worthies, Kent* II. (1662) 67 The Lord waited Stafflesse almost a day..before the same was reconferred upon him. **1871** ALABASTER *Wheel of Law* 180 The new king..re-conferred all upon him.

recon'fine, *v.* [RE- 5 a. Cf. F. *reconfiner* (Cotgr.).] *trans.* To confine again; †to define or limit the sense of (a word).
1611 COTGR., *Reconfiner*, to reconfine, or banish anew. *a* **1661** FULLER *Worthies, Shropshire* III. (1662) 3 Confessors:—This County afforded none, as the word is reconfined in our Preface. But if it be a little enlarged [etc.]. *a* **1711** KEN *Anodynes* Poet. Wks. 1721 III. 446 My Conscience with thy Voice conspires, To reconfine my loose Desires.

reconfirm (ri:kən'fɜ:m), *v.* [RE- 5 a. Cf. late L. *reconfirmāre* (6th c.), F. *reconfirmer* (13th c.).]
1. *trans.* To confirm, ratify, or establish anew.
1611 COTGR., *Reconfermer*, to reconfirme, reinforce, reassure. **1644** QUARLES *Sheph. Orac.* iv. 47 Flowing cups of wine Shall reconfirme thy brotherhood and mine. **1679** OATES *Myst. Iniq.* 26 They would re-confirm the same Priviledge for Five Years more. **1821** LAMB *Elia* Ser. I. *Mackery End*, The scene soon re-confirmed itself in her affections. **1861** WILSON & GEIKIE *Mem. E. Forbes* i. 17 He was reconfirmed in his rights and privileges.
†**2.** To confirm again in courage, or in an opinion.
1653 H. COGAN tr. *Pinto's Trav.* xxiv. 89 Being thus reconfirmed by Similaus speeches, and certified of this new course we were to take. *a* **1674** CLARENDON *Life* (1759) III. 835 And so being reconfirmed..He sent Secretary Morrice ..to require and receive the Great Seal.
Hence **recon'firming** *vbl. sb.*
1611 COTGR., *Restablissement*, a..reconfirming.
So **reconfir'mation.** [Also in Fr. (16th c.).]
1611 FLORIO, *Racconfermatione*, a reconfirmation. **1647** JER. TAYLOR *Lib. Proph.* v. 89 Why should not Divines doe in the Question of reconfirmation as in that of rebaptization? **1897** *Daily News* 6 Sept. 5/2 A reconfirmation of the vitality of the Triple Alliance.

re'confiscate, *v.* *rare*[−0]. [RE- 5 a. Cf. F. *reconfisquer* (Cotgr.).] *trans.* To confiscate again. So **reconfi'scation.**
1611 COTGR., *Reconfisquer*, to reconfiscate, or make a new seisure vnto the Princes, or publike, vse. **1839** *Times* 5 Jan., Longing desires for a reconfiscation of lands transferred from defeated rebels.

recon'geal, *v.* [RE- 5 a.] *trans.* To congeal again. Hence **recon'gealed** *ppl. a.*
1832 *Hand-bk. Nat. Philos.* II. *Thermom. & Pyrom.* i. §1. 4 (U.K.S.), Thawed and recongealed oil of aniseeds. **1860** TYNDALL *Glac.* I. xx. 138 They shone..as if their surfaces had been melted and recongealed to frosted mirrors.
So **reconge'lation.**
1860 MAURY *Phys. Geog.* (Low) xv. 354 The melting of the polar ices..and their recongelation.

reconjoin (ri:kən'dʒɔɪn), *v.* [RE- 5 a. Cf. It. *ricongiungere* (Florio).] To join together again.
1603 FLORIO *Montaigne* II. xii. (1632) 307 Alwayes reconjoyning and entermingling themselves unto that Universall matter. **1694** SALMON *Bate's Dispens.* (1713) 412/2 And being thus divided in its essential Parts it may be reconjoyned with new and perfect Sulphur.

Hence **recon'joining** *vbl. sb.*

1598 FLORIO, *Ricongiungimento*, a reconioyning together.

recon'junction. [RE- 5 a.] The action of reconjoining; a fresh conjunction.

1598 FLORIO, *Ricongiuntione*, a reconiunction. **1669** GALE *Crt. Gentiles* I. III. vii. (ed. 2) 82 Among many [nations] there were reliques of its [the soul's] reconjunction with the bodie, which we cal the Resurrection. **1673** NEWTON in Rigaud *Corr. Sci. Men* (1841) II. 349 By trying the effects of reconjoining two or more, or all of those, and lastly, by separating them again to examine what changes reconjunction had wrought in them.

re'conjure, *v.* [RE- 5 a; cf. F. *reconjurer* (Cotgr.).] *trans.* To conjure again; to reconstruct in imagination; to recall.

1611 COTGRAVE *Dict., Reconjurer*, to reconiure, to coniure againe. **1904** *Edin. Rev.* Jan. 53 Nor can the antiquarian reconjure their image in the past from their ruins of today. **1915** C. MACKENZIE *Guy & Pauline* i. 57 There was neither passion nor sentiment in the music..yet in solitude when Guy reconjured the sound afterward, it returned to his memory like fire.

reconnaissance (rɪˈkɒnəsəns). [Fr., f. *reconnaiss-*, stem of *reconnaître* to RECONNOITRE. See also RECONNOISSANCE.]

1. *Mil.* **a.** An examination or survey of a tract of country, made with a view to ascertain the position or strength of an enemy, or to discover the nature of the ground or resources of the district before making an advance. Also *Naval*, a survey of a coast, etc. made for similar purposes.

reconnaissance in force, an advance made with a considerable body of troops to discover the position of the enemy.

1810 WELLINGTON in Gurw. *Desp.* VI. 93 When I went to Setuval, it was a dark and foggy day, and the reconnaissance which I was able to make of the place was very imperfect. **1860** GEN. P. THOMPSON *Audi Alt.* III. cxxxviii. 112 The force..is to be sent to make a reconnaissance on the road to Paris. **1875** CLERY *Minor Tactics* iii. (1877) 44 With what are usually termed reconnaissances in force we are not here concerned. **1944** *Return to Attack* (Army Board, N.Z.) ii. 7 When he [*sc.* Rommel] attacked, Maryland bombers of the RAF caught his tanks... He withdrew, calling his attack a 'reconnaissance in force', a phrase which he was to use again. *attrib.* **1898** *Daily News* 25 June 5/4 A small reconnaissance party of about forty men. **1899** *U. Serv. Mag.* XIX. 668 The Zeiss range-finder is a good reconnaissance-glass. **1950** 'D. DIVINE' *King of Fassarai* vii. 46 One of the big four-engined aeroplanes that came past them occasionally on reconnaissance flights. **1966** *Daily Tel.* 19 Apr. 32/5 A multi-million-pound order for a British EMI 'reconnaissance pod'. **1976** H. TRACY *Death in Reserve* xxi. 167 They should have a light aircraft going to take reconnaissance photographs.

b. A body of troops sent to reconnoitre.

1811 WELLINGTON in Gurw. *Desp.* VIII. 304 The enemy sent a reconnaissance of cavalry..consisting of about fourteen squadrons..of the Imperial Guard.

2. *transf.* **a.** A survey of a district made for practical or scientific purposes.

1838 *Civil Eng. & Arch. Jrnl.* I. 94/2 A reconnaissance, or examination of the country between the two points to be connected by the line [of road, canal, etc.]. **1877** RAYMOND *Statist. Mines & Mining* 109 Some rapid reconnaissances were made by Professor Whitney and his assistants..of the most prominent points of Plumas County.

b. A survey, inspection, etc., made in order to gain information of any kind.

1824 DIBDIN *Libr. Comp.* 504 After completing his reconnaissances, Mr. Harding dispatched artists in all directions. **1885** R. BUCHANAN *Annan Water* xiv, In your absence I took the liberty of making a reconnaissance.

3. Without article: Reconnoitring, surveying.

1887 *Encycl. Brit.* XXII. 712 If hills are numerous..a large area may be covered..by reconnaissance.

†reconnaitre, *v. Obs. rare.* [a. F. *reconnaître*: cf. prec.] = RECONNOITRE *v.*

1800 WELLINGTON in Gurw. *Desp.* I. 142 Yesterday I sent a patrol to Arnee to reconnaitre the place, meaning to attack it this day. **1813** *Ibid.* X. 512 It was necessary to reconnaitre each of them very closely before they were attacked.

reco'nnect, *v.* [RE- 5 a.] To connect again.

1825 LYTTON *Falkland* I. ii, To reconnect it with the present. **1858** FROUDE *Hist. Eng.* III. 273 The alliance.. would be a link reconnecting England with the Empire.

reconnoissance (rɪˈkɒnɪsəns). [Fr., older spelling of RECONNAISSANCE. In sense 1 by substitution for *recognizance.*

This form, in the military sense, though less usual than *reconnaissance*, appears earlier than it in Dictionaries, being given by Webster in 1847 with a reference to the *Penny Cycl.* (1841, article on *reconnoissance* in vol. XIX. 329).]

†1. = RECOGNIZANCE I. *Obs. rare*$^{-1}$.

1672 MARVELL *Reh. Transp.* I. 199 By dying at the time prefixed, they have saved their Reconnoissances.

†2. = RECOGNITION. *Obs. rare.*

a **1734** NORTH *Exam.* I. iii. §58 (1740) 159, I must confess it is very hard to give a due Character of, and I think nothing, less than its pure self, will be its just Reconnoisance. **1779** in Jesse *Selwyn & Contemp.* (1844) IV. 15 In a note of great respect and *reconnoissance*, [I].. wrote as follows.

3. = RECONNAISSANCE I.

1813 WELLINGTON in Gurw. *Desp.* X. 512 My time so much occupied by reconnoissances. **1833** MARRYAT *P. Simple* (1863) 329 It was agreed that if the boats did go away, it should be for a reconnoissance. **1834** J. S. MACAULAY *Field Fortif.* 228 (*heading*) Military Reconnoissance. *Ibid.* 235 The reconnoissance of the road from Truxilla to Merida, made on the 1st May, 1809. **1884** *Times* (weekly ed.) 7 Mar. 5/1, I have just returned from a reconnoissance ..under Colonel Stewart.

b. = RECONNAISSANCE I b.

1884 *Times* (weekly ed.) 7 Mar. 5/1 Another reconnoissance which leaves here to morrow, will have the best effect.

4. = RECONNAISSANCE 2.

1833 *Edin. Rev.* Oct. 172 The first chapter is devoted..To a sort of *reconnoissance* of the outworks of the science. **1856** KANE *Arct. Expl.* I. ix. 101, I determined to seek some high headland beyond the cape, and make it my final point of reconnoissance. **1877** E. G. SQUIER *Peru* 258 Should the reconnoissance prove satisfactory, it will resume an erect position.

reco'nnoitre, *sb.* [f. next.] An act of reconnoitring; a reconnaissance.

1799 WASHINGTON *Lett.* Writ. 1893 XIV. 167 Your Reconnoitre of the seaboard to St. Mary's..will be made to the Department of War. **1863** LD. LYTTON *Ring Amasis* II. 232 All his senses were sentinels... He was making his great reconnoitre. **1891** T. HARDY *Tess* lii, As she returned from a reconnoitre of the church and graveyard.

reconnoitre (rɛkəˈnɔɪtə(r)), *v.* Also *U.S.* reconnoiter. [a. F. *reconnoître* (now *reconnaître*), OF. *reconnoistre*:—L. *recognōscĕre* to look over, inspect: cf. RECOGNIZE.]

1. *trans.* **a.** *Mil.* (and *Naval*). To make an inspection or take observations of (an enemy, his strength, position, etc.).

1707 SIR C. SHOVEL in Tindal *Contin. Rapin* (1745) IV. II. 27/1 *note*, Colonel Pheffercorn..having been killed the day before, as he went to reconnoitre the enemy. **1711** ADDISON *Spect.* No. 165. **1765** R. ROGERS *Jrnls.* (1769) 1, I embarked ..to reconnoitre the strength of the enemy. **1828** D'ISRAELI *Chas. I*, II. ii. 67 The veteran officer..was unfortunately shot in reconnoitring the enemy. **1867** LADY HERBERT *Cradle L.* v. 153 The guides advised a halt, while they reconnoitred the force and dispositions of the enemy.

b. *transf.* To make an inspection, examination or survey of (persons).

1742 YOUNG *Nt. Th.* II. 265 She reconnoitres Fancy's airy band. **1755** SMOLLETT *Quix.* (1803) IV. 201 One of the gang, who was placed centinel on the road to reconnoitre travellers and bring intelligence. **1824** W. IRVING *T. Trav.* II. 27 Amusing ourselves with reconnoitring this group. **1845** DARWIN *Voy. Nat.* iii. (1879) 48 The deer frequently, out of curiosity, approach to reconnoitre him.

2. a. *Mil.* To inspect, examine, or survey (a district or tract of ground) in order to discover the presence or position of an enemy, or to find out the resources or military features of the country.

1726 CAVALLIER *Mem.* IV. 317 For fear of Accidents I went to Reconnoitre [the] Wood, with a Peasant of the Place. **1781** SIMES *Milit. Guide* (ed. 3) 11 The Quarter-master-general,..with an able engineer, should sufficiently reconnoitre the country. **1876** VOYLE & STEVENSON *Milit. Dict.* 332/1 Making a rapid examination of the country or object he is ordered to reconnoitre. *Ibid.* 333/2 In reconnoitring a fortified post or village [etc.]. **1948** N. MAILER *Naked & Dead* III. v. 523 He could not reconnoiter the pass.

b. *transf.* To survey or explore (a district, etc.) in order to learn its character, geography, etc.

1754 RICHARDSON *Grandison* (1781) VII. viii. 40 The gentlemen are all rid out..to *reconnoitre* the country, as my Uncle calls it. **1791** W. BARTRAM *Carolina* 107 Whilst my fellow travellers were..fixing our camp, I improved the opportunity, in reconnoitring our ground. **1820** W. IRVING *Sketch Bk.* I. 19 As we sailed up the Mersey, I reconnoitred the shores with a telescope. **1860** MAURY *Phys. Geog.* (Low) xx. §811 Some one..of the fleets that are out reconnoitring the seas for us, returns with additional facts for our storehouse of knowledge.

c. *transf.* To examine, inspect, look into (a thing or matter).

1753 HOGARTH *Anal. Beauty* 8 The least motion we make to reconnoitre any other side of the object. **1825** JEFFERSON *Autobiog.* Wks. 1859 I. 76 The Duke of Brunswick..sent some of his officers to Givet, to reconnoitre the state of things there, and report them to him. **1850** L. HUNT *Autobiog.* II. x. 29 Matthew..proceeded towards the window, to reconnoitre the state of the weather.

3. *absol.* or *intr.* To make a reconnaissance.

1712 STEELE *Spect.* No. 326 ¶2, I shall every now and then have a saucy Rascal ride by reconnoitring (as I think you call it) under my windows. **1777** WATSON *Philip II* (1839) 213 They perceived a hundred of the enemy's horse that had been sent before to reconnoitre. **1784** BELKNAP *Tour to White Mts.* (1876) 12 Here we sat down and dined, while our pilot went back to reconnoitre. **1856** KANE *Arct. Expl.* I. xvii. 211 Reconnoitring stealthily beyond Sylvia Head, we discovered a train of sledges.

†4. *trans.* To recollect, remember, recognize.

1748 HARTLEY *Observ. Man* I. i. 58 The Readiness with which we reconnoitre Sensations of Feeling, Taste, and Smell, that have been often impressed. **1768** H. WALPOLE *Hist. Doubts* Pref. 3 Whether, if the dead of past ages could revive, they would be able to reconnoitre the events of their own times, as transmitted to us. **1787** *Minor* II. xi. 103 Sir Cadwallader's son with difficulty reconnoitred [*printed* reconnotred] me.

Hence **reco'nnoitrer**, one who reconnoitres.

1860 C. M. YONGE *Hopes & Fears* III. xiii. 254 Tearfully she thanked the trusty reconnoitrer. **1865** J. SHAW *Country Schoolm.* ii. (1899) 122 Some nooks and corners..which had not been profaned by the reconnoiterer or the opera-glass. **1875** CLERY *Minor Tactics* iii. (1877) 45 Before entering a village, defile, or wood, it should be carefully examined by the reconnoitrers in front.

reco'nnoitring, *vbl. sb.* [f. prec. + -ING[1].] The action of the vb. RECONNOITRE.

1778 M. CUTLER in *Life*, etc. (1888) I. 68 The Light-horse advanced on the right for reconnoitering. **1851** GALLENGA *Italy* 247 His attempts against Peschiera and Mantua, which had no other object than mere reconnoitering. *attrib.* **1840** W. B. LEIGH (*title*) Reconnoitering Voyages and Travels, with Adventures in the New Colonies of South Australia, etc. **1870** *Daily News* 1 Dec., The various skirmishes had only a reconnoitring end.

reco'nnoitring, *ppl. a.* [f. as prec. + -ING[2].] That reconnoitres.

1759 LD. G. SACKVILLE *Let.* 16 June in *Rep. MSS. Mrs. Stopford-Sackville* 307 in *Parl. Papers 1904* (Cd. 1892) XLVII. 1 Prince Ferdinand's and Marshal Contades' reconnoitering partys met this morning. **1799** WELLINGTON in Gurw. *Desp.* I. 27 They keep clear of our picquets, and are most probably a reconnoitring party. **1834-47** J. S. MACAULAY *Field Fortif.* (1851) 251 The reconnoitring officer. **1877** *Field Exerc. Infantry* 324 Reconnoitring and visiting patrols must avoid firing.

Hence **reco'nnoitringly** *adv.*, in a reconnoitring manner. *rare.*

1924 A. D. SEDGWICK *Little French Girl* IV. iii. 324 Giles could almost see him nibbling reconnoitringly at the edge of the stained oak mantelpiece.

reconquer (riːˈkɒŋkə(r)), *v.* [RE- 5 a; cf. F. *reconquérir*, OF. *reconquerre* (12th c. in Godef.).] *trans.* To conquer again; to recover by conquest.

1584 HERLE *Let.* in Motley *Netherl.* (1860) I. iii. 76 To expulse the enemy and to reconquer their towns and country lost. **1602** WARNER *Alb. Eng.* Epit. (1612) 386 France by degrees..reconquered there more than our former conquests. **1611** COTGR., *Reconquerir*, to resubdue, reconquer. **1755** in JOHNSON [quoting DAVIES]. **1809** PINKNEY *Trav. France* 8 Can the Continent be reconquered at sea? **1830** LYTTON *P. Clifford* iv, This idea, though conquered and reconquered, gradually swelled and increased at his heart. **1880** PARKMAN *France & Eng. N. Amer.* p. viii, Rome, ranging the earth to reconquer abroad what she had lost at home.

Hence **re'conquering** *vbl. sb.*; **re'conqueror.**

1654 COKAINE *Dianea* I. 30, I resolved to intreat the aide of his Maiesty for the reconquering of my kingdome. **1864** KINGSLEY *Rom. & Teut.* 53 Our own conquerors and reconquerors of Hindostan have shewn enough that [etc.].

re'conquest (riː-), *sb.* [RE- 5 a; perh. after obs. F. *reconqueste* (16th c. in Godef.).] The (*or* an) act of conquering again; recovery by conquest.

a **1548** HALL *Chron., Hen. VI* 164 There was no doubte of the regayning or reconquest. **1598** BACON *Lett. to Essex conc. Tyrone* Wks. 1879 II. 17/1 A full re-conquest of those parts of the country. **1668** DRYDEN *Even. Love* I. i, Look on those grave plodding fellows, that pass by us, as though they were meditating the re-conquest of Flanders. **1746** H. WALPOLE *Lett.* (1846) II. 172 All the letters by last post make it a re-conquest. **1828-40** TYTLER *Hist. Scot.* (1864) I. 48 In the reconquest of his native country. **1884** *Manch. Exam.* 6 Oct. 4/7 The present expedition was not for the reconquest of the Soudan.

†reconquest, *v. Obs. rare.* [f. RE- + CONQUEST *v.*: cf. obs. F. *reconquester* (1582 in Godef.).] *trans.* = RECONQUER. Also const. *to.*

1456 SIR G. HAYE *Law Arms* (S.T.S.) 106 Sum gracious persone that may have grace and poware, to reconquest it and bring it to the kynde airis. **1560** DAUS tr. *Sleidane's Comm.* 417 b, Many excellente parsonages are condemned in Englande, beinge wholy reconquested to the Pope.

reconsaille, -sale, varr. RECOUNSEL *v. Obs.*

re'consecrate (riː-), *v.* [RE- 5 a. Cf. F. *reconsacrer* (16th c. in Littré *Suppl.*).] *trans.* To consecrate again or anew.

1611 COTGR., *Resacrer*, to reconsecrate. *a* **1711** KEN *Sion* Poet. Wks. 1721 IV. 326 Should we to God re-consecrate the mind [etc.]. **1733** NEAL *Hist. Purit.* II. 221 He interdicted the church and shut up the doors, till it should be reconsecrated. **1795-1814** WORDSW. *Excurs.* IV. 909 This scheme..would re-consecrate our wells To good Saint Fillan and to fair Saint Anne. **1864** J. H. NEWMAN *Apologia* 386 Your passions, and your affections,..must all be bathed in a new element, and reconsecrated to your Maker.

So **reconse'cration.**

1763 BURN *Eccl. Law* I. 237 A church, once consecrated, may not be consecrated again..unless they be polluted by the shedding of blood; and in that case the canon supposes a reconsecration. **1847** MASKELL *Mon. Rit.* III. p. cxlviii, There were some difficulties in deciding whether, if the altar was destroyed or removed, a reconsecration of the church would be required.

reconsele, -seyl, varr. RECOUNSEL *v. Obs.*

reconsider (riːkənˈsɪdə(r)), *v.* [RE- 5 a. Cf. F. *reconsidérer* (16th c.).]

1. *trans.* To consider (a matter or thing) again.

1571 GOLDING *Calvin on Ps.* iv. 5 Then doo they consider and reconsider, whither they have cast themselves. *a* **1711** KEN *Edmund* Poet. Wks. 1721 II. 80 Even Priests too oft, who to consider teach, Themselves scarce re-consider what they preach. **1782** MISS BURNEY *Cecilia* v. vii, She would fain have been left quietly to re-consider her plans. **1849** MACAULAY *Hist. Eng.* ix. II. 467 If his majesty would re-consider the points in dispute between the Churches of Rome and England. **1876** GEO. ELIOT *Dan. Der.* III. xxiv, He had set himself..to reconsider his worn suits of clothes.

b. To consider (a decision, etc.) a second time, with a view to changing or amending it if now disapproved of; to rescind, alter.

1849 MACAULAY *Hist. Eng.* vi. II. 43 If James could even now be induced to reconsider his course, to let the Houses reassemble, and to comply with their wishes, all might yet be well. **1881** JOWETT *Thucyd.* I. 189 The majority of the citizens were anxious to have an opportunity given them of reconsidering their decision.

absol. *a***1856** CUSHING *Man. Parl. Pract.* §1270 The motion to reconsider, though relating to the same subject already considered, is, in a parliamentary sense, a new one, distinct both from a motion to rescind the former vote, and from the subject of it. **1865** in Hart *Amer. Hist.* (1901) IV. 466 The House vote to reconsider.

2. *refl.* To reflect on one's conduct, with a view to repentance or amendment. *rare.*

1855 KINGSLEY *Westw. Ho!* v, To bring him home again, and make him at least to reconsider himself. **1863** —— *Water-Bab.* vi, Did she..set him on a cold stone to reconsider himself, and so forth?

So **reconside'ration**.

1783 JOHNSON *Let. to Barry* 12 Apr. in *Boswell*, I repeat my request that you will propose the re-consideration of Mr. Lowe's case. **1800** *Asiat. Ann. Reg., Proc. E. Ind. Ho.* 82/1 He would..finally make up his mind after consideration and reconsideration of the subject. *a***1856** CUSHING *Elem. Law & Pract. Legis. Assemblies U.S.* §1264 The inconvenience.. has led to the introduction into the parliamentary practice.. of the motion for reconsideration.

recon'sign, *v.* [RE- 5 a. Cf. F. *reconsigner* (Cotgr.).] *trans.* To consign again.

1611 COTGR., *Reconsigner*, to reconsigne, reassigne. **1798** *Invasion* II. xxv. 243 From the moment when I was reconsigned to captivity [etc.]. **1881** *Daily News* 8 Feb. 5/1 He spoke with..considerate regard for the circumstances under which Davitt has been reconsigned to prison.

So **recon'signment**.

1852 DICKENS *Bleak Ho.* xix, On pain of instant reconsignment to her patron saint.

reconsile, obs. f. RECONCILE *v.*

†**reconsolate,** *v. Obs. rare*⁻¹. [RE- 5 a.] *trans.* = RECONSOLE.

1626 WOTTON in *Reliq.* (1672) 439 It is that only God who can reconsolate us both.

So **reconso'lation**. [Cf. F. *reconsolation* (16th c.).]

1526 *Pilgr. Perf.* (W. de W. 1531) 299 b, O moost meke lambe of god, offred in sacrifyce for our reconsolacyon.

recon'sole, *v.* [RE- 5 a.] To console anew.

In quot., by readmission to the sect of the Cathari. Cf. Du Cange s.vv. *Consolamentum, Consolare, Consolatio.*

1832 S. R. MAITLAND *Facts & Docum.* 384 It is the faith of all the heretics, that no one who after receiving the *consolamentum* eats meat..can be saved, unless he receives penance from them and is re-consoled.

reconsolidate (riːkən'sɒlɪdeɪt), *v.* [RE- 5 a. Cf. F. *reconsolider* (1417 in Godef.).] *trans.* and *intr.* To consolidate anew.

a. *trans.* **1541** R. COPLAND *Guydon's Quest. Chirurg.* Cj, To regenerate the substaunce of the sanguyne membre lost, and for to reconsolidate and knyt it agayne. **1611** COTGR., *Reconsolidé*, reconsolidated, closed vp againe. **1654** H. L'ESTRANGE *Chas. I* (1655) 74 Such obliging..compliance, as might re-consolidate them by continuity of affection. **1794** SULLIVAN *View Nat.* I. 485 A petrifying fluid, with which a broken stone will be reconsolidated like a broken limb. **1876** DOUSE *Grimm's L.* 78 Various causes of social and political compression, which reconsolidate the diverging sections of people.

b. *intr.* **1541** [see RECONSOLIDATION]. **1659** H. L'ESTRANGE *Alliance Div. Off.* 317 The whole structure..requireth no few daies to knit and reconsolidate.

reconsoli'dation. [RE- 5 a.] A renewed consolidation.

1541 R. COPLAND *Guydon's Quest. Chirurg.* Cj, For these causes and reasons they do nat reconsolydate with trewe reconsolydacyon after the desolucion of their seperatyng. **1628** DONNE *Serm.* lxxv. 762 The re-consolidation of a scattered conscience. **1802** PLAYFAIR *Illustr. Hutton Th.* 503 At the same time subject to waste above the surface of the sea, and re-consolidation under it. **1864** BURTON *Scot Abr.* I. i. 44 The late reconsolidation of Italy.

recon'stituent, *a.* and *sb.* [See RE- and CONSTITUENT *a.* and *sb.* Cf. F. *reconstituant* (Littré).] **a.** *adj.* That builds up anew; *spec.* in *Med.* of a remedy. **b.** *sb. Med.* A remedy that builds up the body after wasting by disease.

1876 BARTHOLOW *Mat. Med.* (1879) 121 In the same group, however, are remedies which, while they are tonic and reconstituent, do not enter into the composition of the body. *Ibid.* 94 As a reconstituent, cod-liver oil is a very useful remedy in certain chronic affections of the brain.

reconstitute (riː'kɒnstɪtjuːt), *v.* [RE- 5 a. Cf. F. *reconstituer* (Littré).] **1.** *trans.* **a.** To constitute anew.

1812 SIR H. DAVY *Chem. Philos.* 232 A quantity of oxygene, that, added to the residual elastic substance, will reconstitute common air. **1868** M. PATTISON *Academ. Org.* v. 183 Sir W. Hamilton lived to see the history of Rome reconstituted by a German professor. **1944** J. LEES-MILNE *Prophesying Peace* (1977) 68 Thurstan wants to pull down some Georgian dwellings of little intrinsic worth, and to reconstitute some medieval overhangs and fronts. **1977** *Church Times* 5 Aug. 16/3 Bishop Runcie said he thought that, if the Orthodox were dissatisfied with the reactions of the Conference, the dialogue might have to be reconstituted.

b. *spec.* to restore the previous constitution of (dehydrated food) by the addition of liquid.

1917 *Nat. Food Jrnl.* 24 Oct. 59/1 The total amount of dried milk (full cream) that may be available equals approximately 2,200 tons, and would represent nearly 4,000,000 gallons of whole milk when reconstituted. **1945** *ABC of Cookery* (Min. of Food) vii. 22 It is not always necessary to reconstitute dried eggs before use. **1951** L. NICHOLLS *Trop. Nutrition & Dietetics* (ed. 3) x. 202 Vegetables, fish or meat dried by this method are easily reconstituted with good retention of flavour and colour. **1960** *Times Rev. Industry* July 18/1 Fruits..stored..in the dried state and..reconstituted..by soaking in water and cooking. **1972** *Homes & Gardens* Aug. 98 Ice cream powders ..can be reconstituted with water, or with milk and cream.

2. *intr.* To undergo or take part in reconstitution.

1974 *Sci. Amer.* June 77/3 Both sodium and potassium reconstitute into feldspars during metamorphism or igneous melting.

re'constituted, *ppl. a.* [f. RECONSTITUTE *v.* + -ED¹.] That has been constituted or formed anew; applied *spec.* to food which has been dehydrated and subsequently made ready for use by adding liquid. ***reconstituted stone*** = *reconstructed stone* s.v. RECONSTRUCTED *ppl. a.* a.

1850 H. MARTINEAU *Hist. Peace* II. IV. xii. 157 The first act of the reconstituted government was to carry a new Coercion Bill. **1925** *Chem. Abstr.* XIX. 545 Acidity of the reconstituted milk was a little lower than that of raw milk. **1928** *Daily Mail* 30 July 13/3 Reconstituted and synthetic cream. **1946** *Daily Tel.* 30 Jan. 2/1 Dark fruit cake... 6 oz fruit, 2 reconstituted eggs, [etc.]. **1951** *Good Housek. Home Encycl.* 348/2 Reconstituted dried egg may be used in making batter. **1966** D. FRANCIS *Flying Finish* vi. 77 The floors were some sort of reconstituted stone heated from underneath. **1969** *Guardian* 20 Sept. 9/7 Mother and father eating fish fingers and reconstituted potatoes in gloomy silence. **1976** A. DAVIS *Television* ii. 32 The BBC converter ..works by storing the signals relating to each line of the picture and releasing them at the right moment to take their place in a reconstituted picture at the new standard. **1977** A. HALLAM *Planet Earth* 159/3 Reconstituted stone, where the natural material is crushed and recast in blocks simulating the original in color and texture, with the advantage that the blocks are of uniform size.

reconsti'tution. [RE- 5 a. Cf. F. *reconstitution* (Littré).] **1. a.** A fresh constitution.

1848 E. A. POE *Eureka* 141 The regathering of..Matter and Spirit will be but the re-constitution of..God. **1853** MILL *Diss. & Disc., Grote's Greece* (1859) II. 542 Demanding a reconstitution of society from its foundations, and a complete renovation of the human mind. **1884** in *Littell's Living Age* CLXI. 62 On the re-constitution of the Abbey as a collegiate church.

b. In French criminal procedure, the action of going over the supposed details of a crime at the place where it was committed.

1897 *Daily News* 13 Dec. 5/6 The two prisoners..were taken to the scene of the murder for the 'reconstitution' of the crime.

2. The restoration of dehydrated food to its original constitution by the addition of liquid.

1920 *Nat. Food Jrnl.* II. 595/1 The Clauses..prohibiting the addition to milk of colouring matter or water, the reconstitution of milk [etc.]..will remain in force. **1945** *ABC of Cookery* (Min. of Food) xvii. 59 If dried eggs are used they may be added dry with the other dry ingredients and the water needed for reconstitution added with the mixing liquid.

reconstruct (riːkən'strʌkt), *v.* [RE- 5 a. Cf. F. *reconstruire* (1549).]

1. *trans.* To construct anew.

1768 TUCKER *Lt. Nat.* II. III. xxxi. 492 It seemed no blameable attempt to reconstruct the whole afresh from the very ground. **1849** MACAULAY *Hist. Eng.* i. I. 117 He saw that it was necessary to reconstruct the army of the Parliament. **1861** SMILES *Engineers* II. 31 Having made up his mind that the lighthouse could only be reconstructed of wood. **1881** FROUDE *Short Stud.* (1883) IV. II. i. 173 Each [party] in its way supposed that it had a mission to reconstruct society.

2. To construct anew in the mind; to restore (something past) mentally; *spec.* in *Philol.*, to reform hypothetically (part of) a protolanguage by deduction from (later) recorded languages.

1862 MERIVALE *Rom. Emp.* (1865) VII. lv. 1 It may not be impossible..to reconstruct the true character of Tiberius. **1862** TYNDALL *Mountaineer.* ii. 11 He must regard the facts, discern their connection, and out of them reconstruct the world gone by. **1917** *Science Progr.* XI. 682 Not only is the past retrieved in fragments; in some museums and exhibitions, and to a certain extent in historical plays, it is actually reconstructed. **1930** *Language* VI. 164 It is a well-known fact that it is impossible to reconstruct a complete paradigm of Indo-European personal pronouns. **1965** *Ibid.* XLI. 19 The younger protolanguages which we can reconstruct within the Indo-European family..cannot be placed in an indentical frame of reference with Proto-Indo-European. **1976** E. MACLAREN *Nature of Belief* ii. 11 We can reconstruct how the process must have gone on.

Hence **recon'structable, -ible** *adjs.*, capable of being reconstructed.

1961 WEBSTER, Reconstructible. **1965** *Language* XLI. 19 [Proto-Indo-European] is reconstructible only on the basis of internal evidence. **1978** *Ibid.* LIV. 285 Morphology is harder to recapture, and syntax is even more slippery—if indeed it is reconstructable at all beyond a rather shallow level. **1978** *Nature* 13 Apr. 605/2 By using chronologies recording different elements of climate a greater range of climatic variables will be reconstructable.

recon'structed, *ppl. a.* [f. prec. + -ED¹.]

a. That has been reconstructed. ***reconstructed stone*** (see quot. 1950).

1865–6 H. PHILLIPS *Amer. Paper Curr.* II. 97 Choice was made of persons to fill the offices of the reconstructed treasury department. **1888** *Encycl. Brit.* XXIII. 781/1 The legislatures of the reconstructed States. **1909** W. G. RENWICK *Marble & Marble Working* xv. 175 Reconstructed Sicilian marble was selected for lining the walls of the operating-rooms at the Manchester Royal Infirmary, opened last year. *Ibid.* 176 (*caption*) The first building to be erected in Reconstructed Portland Stone. **1933** BLOOMFIELD *Language* 302 Students of the Romance languages reconstruct a Primitive Romance ('Vulgar Latin') form before they turn to the written records of Latin, and they interpret these records in the light of the reconstructed form. **1935** *Specification* XXXVII. 245/1 Reconstructed stone is natural stone—reconstructed, and is to be distinguished from artificial stone, which may be described as high-grade concrete. **1950** *Ibid.* LII. 343/1 Reconstructed stone is natural stone crushed and moulded into the required shape after it has been formed into a plastic mass by the addition of cement and water. **1951** E. E. EVANS-PRITCHARD *Social Anthrop.* iii. 43 The reaction against the attempt to explain social institutions by their reconstructed past..came at the end of last century. **1957** *Gloss. Terms Stone in Building (B.S.I.)* 30 *Reconstructed stone*, a building material manufactured from cement and natural aggregate for use in a manner similar to and for the same purpose as natural building stone. **1959** *Language* XXXV. 425 We.. agree on the essential artificiality of Reconstructed Proto-Indo-European.

b. *U.S.* Converted from (a form of) Communism.

1966 *New Statesman* 14 Oct. 549/1 (Vietnam) As reconstructed peasants sleep Upon their AID-assisted beds. [**1973** R. HAYES *Hungarian Game* viii. 63 All 10 seem to be unreconstructed Stalinists, somewhat to the fanatical left of both Rákosi and Gerö.]

reconstruction (riːkən'strʌkʃən). [RE- 5 a. Cf. F. *reconstruction* (Littré).]

1. a. The action or process of reconstructing.

1791 MACKINTOSH *Vindic. Gall.* Wks. 1846 III. 30 It was theirs to decide..whether, from its ruins, fragments were to be collected for re-construction of the political edifice. **1848** GALLENGA *Italy* II. iii. 7 It was mainly with these views that Manzoni laboured at the reconstruction of his country's creed. **1878** HUXLEY *Physiogr.* xvi. 268 The process of reconstruction of solids is not permanent.

b. *U.S. Hist.* Usu. with capital initial. The process by which after the Civil War the States which had seceded were restored to the rights and privileges of the Union; the period during which this process occurred. Also *attrib.*

A fuller treatment of this sense (also in derivative forms) may be found in M. M. Mathews *Dict. Americanisms* (1951).

1865 SCHURZ in Hart *Amer. Hist.* (1901) IV. 454 As to what is commonly termed 'reconstruction', it is..the whole organism of southern society that must be reconstructed. **1880** 'E. KIRKE' *Garfield* 34 After the war was over, and reconstruction completed, this same Southern political hierarchy came back into power in Washington. **1888** *Encycl. Brit.* XXIII. 781/1 The Reconstruction Acts divided the seceding States into military districts. **1890** C. L. NORTON *Political Americanisms* 93 *Reconstruction.* After the Civil War the question of restoring the lately seceded States..became the leading civil problem of the time. The measures introduced into Congress were popularly known as Reconstruction Bills. **1949** D. S. FREEMAN in B. A. Botkin *Treas. S. Folklore* p. x, The existing general pattern of Southern folklore probably was set in late 'slave days' and during the Reconstruction. **1967** *Freedomways* VII. 133 In history the horrors of slavery are watered down and sketchily covered so as not to enrage the complacent black student, while the period following Reconstruction is covered as if the Negro had strangely disappeared from the face of the earth. **1978** *Names* Mar. 106 In much of the South it [*sc.* the township] is an artifact of Reconstruction governments after The War.

c. The rebuilding of an area devastated by war. Also, the restoration of economic stability to such an area.

1925 A. J. TOYNBEE *Survey of Internat. Affairs 1920–23* 1.39 Austrian reconstruction (scheme drafted; protocols signed). *Ibid.* 40 Hungarian reconstruction (collaboration decided on). **1933** *Radio Times* 14 Apr. 75/1 Several grandiloquently named new departments of State, such as the Ministry of Supply and the extremely short-lived Ministry of Reconstruction. **1940** *Economist* 31 Aug. 280/1 Those who did not find work before August 1st were assembled in reconstruction camps. **1946** *R.A.F. Jrnl.* May 172 All the women were free to return to their interrupted training, to resume their pre-war occupation or to help with the gigantic task of reconstruction. **1953** P. C. BERG *Dict. New Words* 135/1 *Reconstruction area*, an area which has to be redeveloped as a whole, on account of war damage. **1974** tr. *Sniečkus's Soviet Lithuania* 51 As soon as the nazis had been expelled, the working people plunged into the task of reconstruction.

2. An instance or example of reconstructing; a thing reconstructed.

1795 BELSHAM *Reign Geo. III*, II. 247 A few of the largest [vessels] were re-constructions, having been first framed and sent over from Great Britain. **1798** W. TAYLOR in *Monthly Rev.* XXVI. 245 The cloaca maxima is suspected to be a reconstruction of the original common sewer of Rome. **1930** *Language* VI. 185 The scarcity of material for dual forms to substantiate the I[ndo-]E[uropean] reconstruction is not surprising. **1937** 'M. INNES' *Hamlet, Revenge!* II. vi. 166 You must do that reconstruction all over again. **1959** *Language* XXXV. 423 No reputable linguist pretends that Proto-Indo-European reconstructions represent a reality. **1977** M. GOULDER in J. Hick *Myth of God Incarnate* iv. 65 As with the account I have given of Jesus, we are forming a reconstruction of history, and such reconstructions can never be more than probable.

Hence **recon'structional** *a.*, of or pertaining to reconstruction; reconstructionary; **recon'structionary** *a.* (*U.S.*), of or relating to reconstruction; **recon'structionist,** (*a*) (*U.S.*), one who favours reconstruction; (*b*) one who reconstructs the past mentally (see RECONSTRUCT *v.* 2); also *attrib.* or as *adj.*

1864 M. H. THROOP *Future* 119 The act of secession extinguished the Union party as soon as it was adopted, except as a *reconstructionist* party. **1879** TOURGEE *Fool's Err.* xxiv. 148 The interest of the Southern leading classes will compel them to accept and carry out in good faith your reconstructionary idea. **1888** J. C. HARRIS in *Harper's Mag.* Apr. 703/2 The Republican 'reconstructionists'..barred the way. **1920** G. S. GORDON *Let.* 21 Jan. (1943) 133 Now—in this reconstructional mood—Professors are no longer Scholars or Professors, but 'Heads of Depts.'. **1925** E. F. NORTON *Fight for Everest: 1924* vi. 131 These were undoubted signs of reconstructional work. **1949** WELLEK & WARREN *Theory of Lit.* iv. 32 We must, these literary reconstructionists argue, enter into the mind and attitudes of past periods. **1958** *Archivum Linguisticum* X. I. 8 The..prism of literature..may twist the actual sequence of events, as the reconstructionist is tempted to envision it. **1966** M. SCRIVEN in W. H. Dray *Philos. Analysis & Hist.* 255 The difference between this analysis and the reconstructionist approach. **1978** *Language* LIV. 470 The reconstructional changes he suggested have withstood the test of time. **1979** *Jrnl. R. Soc. Arts* Apr. 262/2 Rationality, objectivity, universalism and abstract analysis are features of the reconstructionist approach.

recon'structive, *a.* and *sb.* [RE- 5 a.]

A. *adj.* Relating to, concerned or occupied with, reconstruction. *rare.*

1862 MERIVALE *Rom. Emp.* (1865) III. xxx. 413 The antiquated forms of the republic were incapable of any reconstructive effort. **1880** EARLE *Philol. Eng. Tongue* (ed. 3) §286 The..reconstructive eye of modern Philology. **1927** *Daily Express* 24 Nov. 5 (Advt.), The prescribed reconstructive which creates the good red blood in which *no* germ can obtain a footing.

B. *sb.* That which reconstructs, a reconstituent.

1890 *Science* XV. 219/2 Oysters, on the other hand, are extremely useful as nerve reconstructives.

Hence **recon'structiveness**.

1843 J. CAIRNS in *Life* (1895) 140 Tholuck..has..more original reconstructiveness in his Commentary than Stuart.

recon'structor. [RE- 5 a.] One who reconstructs.

1871 *Daily News* 25 Sept., Perhaps the reconstructors of the statue in 1821 were led away by these signs of portraiture. **1882** G. MATHESON in *Expositor* Aug. 137 He was no innovator on the national faith; he was rather the reconstructor and restorer of that faith.

recon'sult, *v.* [RE- 5 a. Cf. F. *reconsulter* (1595).] *trans.* and *intr.* To consult anew.

1611 COTGR., *Reconsulter*, to reconsult of, take new aduise on. **1627** in Rushw. *Hist. Coll.* (1659) I. 481 That by your gracious Command the House may reconsult, and settle their better thoughts on some more worthy their Election. **1652** J. WRIGHT tr. *Camus' Nat. Paradox* XI. 279 This long reply having given Iphigenes some leisure to..re-consult his Judgement. **1806** W. TAYLOR in *Ann. Rev.* IV. 219 His sources must all be reconsulted.

So **reconsul'tation**.

1624 DONNE *Devotions* (ed. 2) 214 Take me then, O blessed, and glorious Trinity, into a Reconsultation, and prescribe me any phisicke.

reconsyle, obs. form of RECONCILE *v.*

†**re'conter**, *v. Sc. Obs.* [var. RECOUNTER *v.*, with vowel as in F. *rencontrer*: cf. RECONTRE.] *trans.* To encounter.

1513 DOUGLAS *Æneis* IX. vii. *heading*, Quhow capitane Volscens..Recontrit Nysus and hys fallow. **1536** BELLENDEN *Cron. Scot.* (1821) I. 46 [He] gatherit haistely ane army to reconter his ennimes. **1549** *Compl. Scot.* xiv. 114 The hors men of the romans..met and recontrit the cartagiens.

recon'test, *v.* [RE- 5 a; cf. F. *recontester* (Cotgr.).] *trans.* To contest again.

1611 COTGRAVE *Dict.*, *Recontester*, to recontest; make new protestation of, or complaint vnto. **1897** W. J. LOCKE *Derelicts* xviii. 239 The old man vaunting the ancients and Joyce defending the moderns, until a veritable Battle of the Books was recontested. **1922** *Glasgow Herald* 11 Nov. 9 Both are recontesting the seats they have occupied in Parliament.

†**recontinual**, *a. Obs. rare*$^{-1}$. [RE- 5 a.] That continues again.

1735 H. BROOKE *Univ. Beauty* IV. 143 The..Stream, Which salient, thro' the Heart's contractile Force, Expulsive springs its recontinual Course.

†**recontinuance.** *Obs.* [RE- 5 a: cf. next.] The act of recontinuing; resumption.

1540 *Act 32 Hen. VIII*, c. 31 Those persons..haue..ben driuen to their actions for the recontinuance and obteynyng of the sayd landes. **1589** PUTTENHAM *Eng. Poesie* I. xxvi. (Arb.) 66 Encoraging them to the recontinuance of the same entertainments. *a* **1631** DONNE *Lett.* (1651) 25 By the continuance of my acquaintance with you, by Letters, you may perceive how much I desire..the recontinuance of our acquaintance, by conversation.

recon'tinue, *v.* ? *Obs.* [ad. obs. F. *recontinuer* (13th c. in Littré): see RE- and CONTINUE *v.* In common use *c* 1570–1640.] *trans.* To go on again with (an action, occupation, state, etc., which has been discontinued).

c **1420** LYDG. *Assembly of Gods* 1112 Rescu yondyr knyghtes & recontynu fyght. **1536** ELYOT *Let. to Cromwell* in *Gov.* (1883) I. p. cxxxi, As for my first sute, I shall at your lordshippes better laysour recontynue it, trusting allso in your lordshippes favor therein. **1570–6** LAMBARDE *Peramb. Kent* (1826) 423 He was..annointed king, and so re-continued the right of the house of Yorke. **1647** N. BACON *Disc. Govt. Eng.* I. xlvii. (1739) 79 He re-continued the Liberty of publick Consultations. **1802** MARY CHARLTON tr. *La Fontaine's Reprobate* I. 106 He had resumed the care of his flowers, and my father had recontinued his journal.

Hence **recon'tinued** *ppl. a.*; **recon'tinuing** *vbl. sb.*

1535–6 *Act 27 Hen. VIII*, c. 24 (*title*) An Acte for re-contynuyng of certayn liberties. **1587** T. HUGHES *Misfort. Arthur* III. i, Where men with reconciled mindes Renew their loue with recontinued grace.

recontr-: see RECONTER *v.*

recontract, *sb. rare*$^{-1}$. [RE- 5 a.] A fresh contract.

a **1610** PARSONS *Leicester's Ghost* (1641) 18 It was pure love which made mee undertake This haplesse recontract with thee to make.

recon'tract, *v.* [RE- 5 a. Cf. F. *recontracter* (Cotgr.).] To contract again, in senses of that vb.

1597 BEARD *Theatre God's Judgem.* (1612) 415 [He] sent him..a dispensation to put away his wife..and to recontract Anne of Bretaigne, the widow of Charles the eight lately deceased. **1622** J. REYNOLDS *God's Revenge* II. ix. 160 My soule hath made my peace with God, and my heart desires to recontract it both with thyselfe and her. **1647** N. BACON *Disc. Govt. Eng.* I. Sum. Concl. (1739) 201 For the sense of State once contracted into a Privy Council, is soon recontracted into a Cabinet-Council, and last of all into a Favourite or two.

So **recon'traction**.

1861 BUMSTEAD *Ven. Dis.* (1879) 297 Continuous dilatation is likely to be attended with untoward symptoms and is always followed by a strong tendency to recontraction.

†**re'contre.** *Sc. Obs. rare*$^{-1}$. [var. of RECOUNTER *sb.* Cf. RENCONTRE.] An encounter.

1570 BUCHANAN *Chamæleon* Wks. (S.T.S.) 50 [The Queen had] to wryte to hir lieutenentis to mak ye regent be put sauf in Scotland, and so he wes without any recontre.

reconva'lesce, *v.* [RE- 5 a. Cf. late L. *reconvalēre* (Du Cange).]

intr. To become convalescent again. So **reconva'lescence** [cf. med.L. *reconvalescentia* (1341)]; **reconva'lescent** *a.*

1767 *Douglas Trial* 57 The proof brought of Lady Jane's reconvalescence. **1790** BEATSON *Nav. & Mil. Mem.* II. 261 They once more got to sea, where the troops were joined by their reconvalesced men from the isle of Wight. **1824** SCOTT *St. Ronan's* xvi, His reconvalescence was attended with..debility, it seemed both of mind and body. **1871** *Standard* 14 Jan., The glowing patriotism of the reconvalescent soldiers has perhaps not abated.

†**reconvalidation.** *Obs. rare*$^{-1}$. [RE- 5 a.] A renewed confirmation.

1525 BP. J. CLERK *Let. to Wolsey* (MS. Cott. Vit. B. vii. lf. 126), The Venetians, who hathe made stykyng hetherto to agre withe the Emperor..for the reconvalidation off the ligge by them brokyn.

recon'vene, *v.* [RE- 5 a. Cf. med.L. *reconvenīre* (13th c.), F. *reconvenir* (1347 in Godef.).] *trans.* and *intr.* To convene again. Hence **recon'vening** *vbl. sb.*, a renewed convening.

1647 CLARENDON *Hist. Reb.* IV. §24 There was a worse accident than all these which fell out..about the time of the two Houses reconvening. **1676** HALE *Contempl.* I. 101 He is..then sent into the high Priest's Hall; then re-convened before the Council. **1903** *Westm. Gaz.* 20 June 7/1 A prominent delegate..urges the reconvening of the Joint High Commission. **1906** *Ibid.* 11 Apr. 5/1 The anthracite operators..made a counter-proposal—namely, to re-convene the Coal Commission. **1972** *Maclean's Mag.* Sept. 10/2 The Select Committee..which he reconvened. **1977** *Time* 17 Jan. 12/2 To break the deadlock when and if the talks reconvene..Richard last week made firm Britain's readiness to accept a major role in the transition period from white to black rule.

†**reconvent**, *v. Obs.* [RE- 5 a.] *trans.* To reassemble. Hence **reconventing** *vbl. sb.*

1589 WARNER *Alb. Eng.* V. 571 He reconuenting armes therefore,..Died to his countrie's friends a friend. **1611** FLORIO, *Reconuentione*, a reconuenting.

reconvention (riːkən'vɛnʃən). [a. F. *reconvention* (13th c. in Littré). Cf. med.L. *reconventio* (14th c.). See RE- and CONVENTION.]

†**1.** An agreement made in return. *Obs.*

c **1449** PECOCK *Repr.* III. xviii. 397 As bi boond and withoute eny reconvencioun or couenant of bond expressid or priueli understonde forto ȝeue aȝen.

2. *Law.* A counter-charge; a counter-action brought against the plaintiff by the defendant in a suit. †Also *transf.* in general use.

1538 *Extr. Aberd. Burgh Rec.* (1844) 158 My lord prowest..humely menis, schawis, and, be the way of reconuentioune, complenis [etc.]. **1629** MABBE tr. *Fonseca's Dev. Contempl.* 423 Hee vnderstood by sinne in that place, the sinne of adulterie, for otherwise..the reconuention had not beene so strong and forcible. **1633** AMES *Agst. Cerem.* II. 303 In vie of those grounds, laid by the Repl. against humane significant Ceremonies, out of the second Commandement, the Rej. by way of Reconvention faineth two grounds to the contrary. **1726** AYLIFFE *Parergon* 83 An Appeal in a cause of Convention does not impeach and hinder the Execution of a Sentence in a Cause of Re-convention. **1760–5** BURN *Eccl. Law* (1797) II. 137 But in these cases of re-convention, the parties must proceed together in the contesting of suit. **1838** W. BELL *Dict. Law Scot.* 823 Where an action is brought in Scotland by a foreigner,..his adversary in the suit is entitled, by reconvention, to sue the foreigner on a counter-claim. **1884** *Law Rep.* 9 *App. Cases* 582 A claim in reconvention is in substance nothing else than a cross action brought by the defendant against the plaintiff.

†**3.** The reassembling (of Parliament, etc.). *Obs.*

1641 SIR E. DERING in Rushw. *Hist. Coll.* III. (1692) I. 393 My humble motion therefore is this, I beseech you to declare, That upon this our Reconvention, your Order of the 8th. of September is out of date. **1664** EVELYN *Diary* 24 Nov., The heads of the speech he made at the re-convention of the Parliament, which now began to meet.

recon'verge, *v. rare.* [RE- 5 a.] *intr.* To converge again.

1847 DE QUINCEY *Secret Societies* Wks. 1857 VII. 289 Armies of brave men,..by the clapping of hands, in a moment have reconverged in battle array.

reconversion (riːkən'vɜːʃən). [RE- 5 a.] Conversion back to a previous state. **a.** Of persons, *spec.* in religious sense.

1599 SANDYS *Europæ Spec.* (1632) 181 The Popes refusall to reblesse the King upon his sodaine reconversion. *a* **1628** F. GREVIL *Sidney* (1652) 237 Those cob-webs of re-conversion in Queen Maryes dayes, I had no intent to meddle with. **1655** FULLER *Ch. Hist.* III. Ded., He could recount his Re-conversion, after his foul Offences of Adulterie and Murder. **1778** JOHNSON in *Boswell* 30 Mar., How often are the primary motives of our greatest actions as small as Sibbald's, for his re-conversion. **1817** COLERIDGE *Biog. Lit.* (Bohn) 97, I cannot doubt, that the difference of my metaphysical notions from those of Unitarians in general contributed to my final re-conversion to the whole truth in Christ. **1867** FREEMAN *Norm. Conq.* (1876) I. App. 680 The Danish Chroniclers assert a repentance and reconversion.

b. Of things; *spec.* alteration (of industry, etc.) to peacetime requirements after war; in recent use, conversion by adaptation of function, modernization; also, an object so converted.

1783 PRIESTLEY in *Phil. Trans.* LXXIII. 426 The re-conversion of air into water, by decomposing it in conjunction with inflammable air. **1830** LYELL *Princ. Geol.* I. 83 The reconversion of the sedimentary into the crystalline by subterranean fire. **1881** ARMSTRONG in *Nature* XXIV. 449/1 Internal as well as external work may be reconverted into heat, but until the reconversion takes place, the heat which did the work does not exist as heat. **1944** *Sun* (Baltimore) 21 Jan. 7/2 'Reconversion' in the foreign field.., like the reconversion of domestic industry from war to peace production, is one of our major problems. **1946** *News Chron.* 2 Mar. 2/2 The difficulties of demobilisation and of industrial re-conversion. **1956** *Planning* XXII. 239 Reconversion in industry is an essential consequence of the introduction of the common market... Reconversion as defined in the [Spaak] report means modernisation or rationalisation of production methods to cope with increased competition. **1976** *National Observer* (U.S.) 28 Aug. 14-B/4 (Advt.), He covers reconversions as well as new buildings.

re'convert, *sb.* [RE- 5 a.] One converted a second time.

1843 GLADSTONE *Glean.* (1879) V. 34 She has made (we refer to the latter part of the sixteenth century) converts and reconverts by thousands—nay, even by millions.

reconvert (riːkən'vɜːt), *v.* [RE- 5 a. Cf. med.L. *reconvertĕre* (Du Cange), F. *reconvertir* (1591 in Godef.), It. *reconvertire* (Florio).]

1. *trans.* To convert back to a previous state: **a.** persons, *spec.* in religious sense.

1611 COTGR., *Reconvertir*, to reconuert. **1649** *Alcoran* 278 We..sent him to preach to more then an hundred thousand persons, that we reconverted. **1670** MILTON *Hist. Eng.* IV. Wks. (1847) 520/2 About this time the East Saxons, who..had..renounc'd the Faith, were by the means of Oswi thus reconverted. **1737** WESLEY *Wks.* (1872) I. 50, I myself having known many Papists..reconverted. **1849** MACAULAY *Hist. Eng.* x. II. 647 In December ambition had converted him into a rebel. In January disappointment reconverted him into a royalist. **1882** SAINTSBURY *Short Hist. Fr. Lit.* III. vii, He soon distinguished himself by reconverting a considerable number of persons to the Roman form of faith.

b. things.

1662 PETTY *Taxes* 17 Money; which being paid to the King, is again reconverted into corn. **1762** MILLS *System Pract. Husb.* I. 160 There will be no danger of it's re-converting the soil into a bog. **1783** PRIESTLEY in *Phil. Trans.* LXXIII. 427 The result was such as to afford a strong presumption that the air was re-converted into water. **1862** ANSTED *Channel Isl.* IV. xx. (ed. 2) 474 The islanders in Jersey replaced much of their arable land by orchards. These have since..been re-converted.

2. *Logic.* To transpose again the subject and predicate of (a proposition). Cf. CONVERT *v.* 4 b.

1864 BOWEN *Logic* vi. 161 It is evident that, by reconverting the Converse, we ought to regain the Convertend. *Ibid.*, This is reconverted simply into 'Some men are mortals'.

3. *Law.* To change back again into something of equivalent value. Cf. CONVERT *v.* 15.

1884 SIR E. E. KAY in *Law Times Rep.* L. 56/2 It does not decide that if the court or a trustee sell more than is necessary there is any equity to reconvert the surplus for the benefit of the heir-at-law.

Hence **recon'verted** *ppl. a.*; **recon'vertible** *a.*, capable of being reconverted.

1738 WESLEY *Ps.* LXXX. xxiii, King of a re-converted Land. **1886** *American* XII. 251 That these waves are reconvertible into heat.

reconvey (riːkən'veɪ), *v.* [RE- 5 a.]

1. *trans.* To convey (†or escort) back to a previous place or position; to convey in a reverse direction. Now *rare.*

1506 in *Mem. Hen. VII* (Rolls) 286 After the King had showed him his chamber and would he should take no further pains the King would have somewhat reconveyed him. **1636** *Destr. Troy* 10 Then, that we should our Sacriledge restore And reconveigh their gods from Argos shore, Chalcas perswades. **1707** *Curios. in Husb. & Gard.* 77 There are Vehicles in Plants, to reconvey towards the Roots, the Juices that were mounted up into the Stem. **1766** *Phil. Trans.* LVII. 125 The nerves may..become incapable of conveying the commands of the will, and yet remain sufficiently capable of re-conveying sensible perceptions. **1846** McCulloch *Acc. Brit. Empire* (1854) I. 25 The water that thus overspread the country would be reconveyed to the sea at ebb tide.

2. *Law.* To make over again or restore to a former owner.

1665 Brathwait *Comment Two Tales* 64 She repents her of her Gift. Gladly would she have him re-convey it to her. **1682** Dryden *Satyr* 78 He buys the Purchase, with design t'improve; And like some prudent Kinsman reconvey What the wild Heir hath vainly thrown away. **1734** *Act 7 Geo. II*, c. 16 §2 For redisponing or reconveying the said Lands and Estate in any Manner of Way. **1818** Cruise *Digest* (ed. 2) II. 91 If the mortgagor pays the money borrowed on a certain day, the mortgagee will reconvey the lands. **1881** *Act 44 & 45 Vict.* c. 41 (Conveyancing Act), Then B. and C...will at the request and cost of A...re-convey the premises to A. *absol.* **1838** W. Bell *Dict. Law Scotl.* 67 When he [*sc.* the assignee] reconveys to the cedent, it [*sc.* the deed] is called a *retrocession.* **1858** Ld. St. Leonards *Handy Bk. Prop. Law* xiv. 94 If a mortgagee will not re-convey upon payment of the principal and interest, and costs, and the right to redeem is still open, the mortgagor may..compel a redemption.

recon'veyance. [RE- 5 a.] The act of reconveying; *spec.* in *Law*, restoration to a previous owner.

1767 S. Paterson *Another Trav.* I. 84 The conveyance was almost as astonishing as the re-conveyance. **1768** Blackstone *Comm.* III. xxvii. 439 As by setting aside fraudulent deeds, decreeing re-conveyances, or directing an absolute conveyance merely to stand as a security. **1804** Eugenia de Acton *Tale without Title* I. 154 Soon after its reconveyance to its owners, Lady Laura was again very ill. **1858** Ld. St. Leonards *Handy Bk. Prop. Law* xiv. 89 His prior disposition will..still remain good, nor will a re-conveyance to him upon paying off the money affect the validity of the will.

recon'vict, *v.* [RE- 5 a.] *trans.* To convict again. Hence **recon'victed** *ppl. a.*

1884 *Contemp. Rev.* July 73 *note*, An old offender was re-convicted for a violent assault upon a woman. **1891** H. Matthews in *Law Times* XCII. 96/2 The earning of marks ..will extend to reconvicted licence-holders serving the remanets of former sentences.

So **recon'viction.**

1892 *Daily News* 2 Dec. 6/6 Were it the rule..that a longer sentence was to be expected at each reconviction, crime would at once largely diminish. **1909** *Rep. Commissioners of Prisons* I. 15 in *Parl. Papers* (Cd. 4847) XLV. 133 The highest proportion of re-convictions is in this class no less than 40 per cent. **1968** *Economist* 3 Feb. 16/2 Reconvictions bring those under suspended sentences into prison after all. **1976** *Howard Jrnl.* XV. I. 7 Striking variations in reconviction rates.

recon'voke, *v.* [RE- 5 a. Cf. F. *reconvoquer* (Cotgr.).] *trans.* To convoke again.

1837 Carlyle *Fr. Rev.* I. VII. viii, To reconvoke his Assembly Members by sound of drum. **1872** *Echo* 23 Aug. 5 The French Cardinals have requested his Holiness to re-convoke the Council to some French city.

recool-, obs. Sc. var. *recule* RECOIL *v.*

†**re'cooper.** *Obs. rare.* [app. irreg. f. L. *recuper-āre* to RECUPERATE.] Recovery.

1652-60 in Gilbert *Contemp. Hist. Irel.* (1879) I. I. 1 All men desirous of honor, must trie theire fortune, in the recooper therof, but none escaped. *Ibid.* III. I. 49 Either the destruction of a whole nation or the recooper of a kingdome.

†**recope.** *Obs.*$^{-1}$ [app. a. OF. *recope* (not recorded in this sense), f. *recoper* (*-couper*) to sound (a bell).] A hunting-note on the horn.

c **1400** *Master of Game* (MS. Digby 182) xxxiii, And after þe iiij mote euen forthwith þei shulde blowe ij recopes, as þus: trut, trut, trorororowte.

†**recopilation.** *Obs. rare.* [ad. Sp. *recopilacion*, f. *re-* RE- + *copilacion*, n. of action f. *copilar*:—L. *compīlāre* to COMPILE.] = RECOMPILATION.

1622 Mabbe tr. *Aleman's Guzman d'Alf.* I. iii. 197 Besides these Ordinances, they had many other... So that it might be said of them, that they were another new Recopilation, or gathering together of those of Castile. **1656** in Blount *Glossogr.* (citing Selden).

re-'copper, *v.* [RE- 5 c.] *trans.* To sheathe (a vessel) again with copper.

1857 *Merc. Marine Mag.* (1858) V. 12 The ship has to be hove down and re-coppered. **1897** *Mission. Herald* (Boston) June 219 These repairs, including the recoppering of the vessel.

re'copy, *v.* [RE- 5 a.] *trans.* To copy again.

1710 Shaftesb. *Adv. to Author* III. ii. 146, I have a very fair Hand offer'd, which may save me the trouble of re-copying. *a* **1779** Tweddell *Rem.* xxxix. (1798) 200 If I have time to recopy, also, my remarks upon the Crimea,..I will send one copy home. **1895** *Forum* (N.Y.) Nov. 354 Paul Verlaine recopied here his Saturnian poems on the paper of the administration.

record ('rɛkɔːd), *sb.* Also 4-6 recorde, 5 *Sc.* racord. [a. OF. *record* (*recort*, *recor-s*, etc.), f. *recorder* to RECORD. Cf. Sp. *recuerdo*, It. *ricordo*. The original stressing (rɪ'kɔːd) is found in verse as late as the 19th c.]

I. 1. *Law.* **a.** The fact or attribute of being, or of having been, committed to writing as authentic evidence of a matter having legal importance, *spec.* as evidence of the proceedings or verdict of a court of justice; evidence which is thus preserved, and may be appealed to in case of dispute. Chiefly in phrases *of* (common in 15-16th c.), † *in, by, on,* or *upon record.*

a **1300** *Cursor M.* 9711 Ne dom agh haf right na record, Ar we ben all at an a-cord. **1423** *Rolls of Parlt.* IV. 201/2 þair namys also, to be entred of record, what and how thei determyne. **1455** *Paston Lett.* I. 364 As it apperith pleynlye by accompt made of the sayd office of Constabulrye, remaynyng in the Kyngs Cheker at Westminster of record. **1523** Fitzherb. *Surv.* 20 Whan a mater..is past by verdyt.. and entred in the kynges recordes there it resteth of recorde, and also yf a dede or a patent be inrolled there it remeyneth of recorde in lyke maner. **1596** Bacon *Max. & Uses Com. Law* (1630) 50 These Estates are created by word, by writing, or by record. *Ibid.* 81 So that he for-see that he pay Debts vpon Record, first debts to the King, then vpon Iudgements. **1603** Shaks. *Meas. for M.* II. ii. 40 To fine the faults, whose fine stands in record, And let goe by the Actor. *a* **1677** Hale *Prim. Orig. Man.* II. x. 235 Which was accordingly done, and remains of Record in the Exchequer. **1700** Tyrrell *Hist. Eng.* II. 837 These Letters..remain upon Record in the Tower on the Clause Roll of this Year. **1766** Blackstone *Comm.* II. 119 All estates-tail are rendered liable to be charged for payment of debts due to the king by record of special contract. **1818** Cruise *Digest* (ed. 2) V. 55 The manor..was let at a greater rent, or appeared upon record to be of a greater value. **1870** 'Mark Twain' in *Galaxy* Oct. 575/1 That verdict is of record, and holds good to this day.

fig. **1709** Hearne *Collect.* 12 Jan. (O.H.S.) II. 163 An Ass upon Record cried up for a man of..learning.

b. In phr. *matter* (*thing, debt,* etc.) *of record.* Also *debt by record.*

1433 *Rolls of Parlt.* IV. 424/1 Thay to abide enacted as þinges of recorde. **1472-3** *Ibid.* VI. 52/2 Any relesse, arbetrament, or any other plee, not matier of Recorde. **1596** Bacon *Max. & Uses Com. Law* (1630) 62 This Fine is called a Feofment of Record, because that it includeth all that the Feofment doth. **1642** tr. *Perkins' Prof. Bk.* x. §655. 283 If it were by Matter of Record it should be good without attornment. **1766** Blackstone *Comm.* II. xxx. 464 A debt of record is a sum of money, which appears to be due by the evidence of a court of record. **1827** Hallam *Const. Hist.* (1876) I. i. 15 It then became a matter of record, and could not be impeached. **1842** Stephen *Comm. Laws Eng.* II. II. II. v. 187 Another species of debt by record is that upon adjudgment; which is, where any sum is adjudged to be due from one party to the other, in an action in a court of record.

c. *court of record*: a court whose proceedings are formally enrolled and valid as evidence of fact, being also a court of the sovereign, and having authority to fine or imprison. So †*judge of record.*

[**1419** *Liber Albus* in Riley *Munim. Gildh.* (Rolls) I. III. I. 217 Si issint soit qe mesme le defendaunt veigne en court de recorde, etc.] **1451** *Rolls of Parlt.* V. 219/1 Your Officers in youre Courtes of Record. **1581** Lambarde *Eiren.* I. xiii. (1602) 59 It maketh not a little..for the credit of the Iustices [of the Peace].., that they are numbered amongst the Iudges of Record. **1607** Cowell *Interpr.* s.v., Queene Elizabeth.. made the Consistory Court of the University of Cambridge a Court of Record. **1641, 1765** [see COURT *sb.*[1] 11]. **1768** Blackstone *Comm.* III. iii. 25 That the very erection of a new jurisdiction with power of fine and imprisonment makes it instantly a court of record. **1844** Stephen *Comm. Laws Eng.* III. v. vi. 442 The Commissioners [of Sewers] are a court of record and may fine and imprison for contempts. **1865** F. M. Nichols *Britton* I. 136 *note*, It was decided in later times, that the county court, though sitting by virtue of the King's writ..., had not the powers of a court of record. **1888** [see COURT *sb.*[1] 11].

†**d.** *to have record*: to be entitled to have one's judicial acts and decisions enrolled. *Obs.*

1581 Lambarde *Eiren.* I. xiii. (1602) 60 Bracton..writing of a speciall case, where the Sherife in his Countie hath Record. [**1865** F. M. Nichols *Britton* I. 136 *note*, The sheriff..is treated by our Author as the King's Justiciary, and as having the power of record incident to that office.]

2. The fact or condition of being preserved as knowledge, *esp.* by being put into writing; knowledge or information preserved or handed down in this way. Freq. in phrases († *of,*) *on* or *upon record.* Also (orig. *U.S.*), *to go on record*: to give oneself a place on a formal record, to be recorded (*as* favouring a given course of action, etc.); to express one's opinion; similarly (orig. *U.S.*) *to be on record, to put* (oneself, etc.) *on record.*

c **1386** Chaucer *Sompn. T.* 409 Syn Ennok was or Elise Han freres been, that fynde I of record. **1390** Gower *Conf.* III. 166 For this I finde ek of record, Which the Cronique hath auctorized. **1470-85** Malory *Arthur* I. ii, By all record he was dede or euer kynge Vther came. **1570-6** Lambarde *Peramb. Kent* (1826) 177, I finde on Recorde that the Priory at Bylsington was first advaunced by John Maunsell. **1588** J. Mellis *Briefe Instr.* F vij b, Yee must haue a seuerall booke of record, wherein you shall record the copy of letters of charge. **1606** Shaks. *Tr. & Cr.* I. iii. 14 Euery action that hath gone before, Whereof we haue Record. **1628** Wither *Brit. Rememb.* 7 The glorioust things, That stand upon record of mortall Kings. *a* **1720** Sewel *Hist. Quakers* (1722) I. Let. to King, Remarkable Cases, which I thought worthy to be kept upon Record, and not buried in Oblivion. **1815** Shelley *Alastor* 25 In charnels and on coffins, where black death Keeps record of the trophies won from thee. **1884** *Times* 2 Dec. 10 Having beaten the highest break on record. **1900** *Congress. Rec.* 11 Jan. 785/1, I would be perfectly contented if Senators would put their vote on record. **1920** H. G. Wells *Outl. Hist.* 169/1 Greece had suddenly begun to produce literature, and put itself upon record as no other nation had ever done hitherto. **1930** E. M. Brent-Dyer *Chalet School & Jo* v. 64 It is on record that seventeen people had to go and remake theirs [*sc.* beds]. **1930** *Daily Express* 8 Sept. 10/4 President Parsons of Woolworths has also gone on record with the statement that [etc.]. **1940** *Publishers' Weekly* 1 May 3007/1 The Association has previously been on record against legislation of this kind. **1967** *N.Y. Times* (Internat. Ed.) 11-12 Feb. 1/1 West German Vice Chancellor Willy Brandt put the Bonn Government on record today as being willing to bar any nuclear explosions. **1975** J. Grady *Shadow of Condor* vii. 116 I've hardly heard anything of what's being done..and I would like to go on record right now to that effect. **1978** *Lancashire Life* July 43/2 It is on record that soldiers from the 6th Manchester Regiment in Egypt provided enough eager players to hold a Lancs. v Cheshire match shortly before going on to Gallipoli.

†**3. a.** Attestation or testimony of a fact; witness, evidence, proof. In early use chiefly in phrases *by record of, to take record* (*at*). *Obs.*

13.. *E.E. Allit. P.* A. 830 Lombe was taken þere, By trw recorde of ayþer prophete. **1377** Langl. *P. Pl.* B. xv. 85 ȝe ..louten to þis lordes..Aȝeine ȝowre reule and Religion, I take record at Ihesus. **1417** in *E.E. Wills* (1882) 39 ȝyf þer be eny man or woman þat wil say þat I howght hem eny goud, and swere vppon a boke by record of goud men, y wyl þat dey be payd. **1465** *Paston Lett.* II. 223 The qwych peticion I made diverse tyme to fore moche recorde. **1533** More *Debell. Salem* Wks. 1011/1 Where one is openly and notably suspected of heresye, and sufficient recorde and witnesse agaynste hym. **1547** Hancock in Strype *Eccl. Mem.* (1721) II. I. ix. 115, I answered that he spake those words betwyxt him and me, but yf I had record of them he would not speak them. **1646** H. Lawrence *Comm. Angells* 90 Of which I could give you account enough upon as good record as story can give us of any thing.

†**b.** *to bear record*: to bear witness. *Obs.*

Tr. AF. *porter record* (Britton): cf. BEAR *v.* 2 c.

13.. *Coer de L.* 4591 With Kyng Richardes armes pourtrayed In sygne to bere record That Kyng Richard was her ovyr-lord. **1390** Gower *Conf.* I. 70 Forto bere hierof record He sende ous hider bothe tuo. **1413** *Pilgr. Sowle* (Caxton) I. xii. (1859) 9 Of this wyl I bere hym good record, that he has clerely kepte hys byleue in to this last ende. **1526** Tindale *John* i. 34 And I sawe yt, and have borne recorde, that thys ys the sonne off God. **1542-5** Brinklow *Lament.* (1874) 107 All that reade their workes maye beare recorde with them agaynst your lyes. **1611** Bible [in a number of passages, after earlier versions].

†**c.** *to take* or *call to record*: to call to witness. *Obs.* (Cf. CALL *v.* 20 c.)

1390 Gower *Conf.* I. 7 That I take to record..The comun vois, which mai noght lie. **1494** Fabyan *Chron.* I. xiv. 14 Gonorilla..callynge her goddes to recorde, sayd, she loued hym more than her owne soule. **1526** Tindale *Acts* xx. 26, I take you to recorde this same daye that I am pure from the bloud of all men. **1535** Coverdale *Deut.* xxx. 19, I take [**1611** call] heauen and earth this daye to recorde ouer you. **1591** Sylvester *Du Bartas* I. vi. 344, I call to record that same Roman Thrall Who..Fled through the desart.

†**d.** A witness. *Obs.* (In later use only in Biblical language.)

1526 Tindale *Acts* v. 32 We are his recordes as concernynge these thynges. **1568** *Wills & Inv. N.C.* (Surtees 1835) 291 Recordes hereof thomas Barker..and Thomas Slogen wth others. **1593** Shaks. *Rich. II*, I. i. 30 Heauen be the record to my speech. **1768** Sterne *Sent. Journ.* I. 33 (*In the Desobligeant*) God is my record,..that I do not speak it vauntingly.

II. 4. a. *Law.* An authentic or official report of the proceedings in any cause coming before a court of record, together with the judgement given thereon, entered upon the rolls of court and affording indisputable evidence of the matter in question.

The reference in Cowell (quot. 1607) is to Sir R. Brooke *La Graunde Abridgement* (1573) II. 192.

1455 *Rolls of Parlt.* V. 341/1 Fynes, obligacions, reconysaunces, and othir recordes upon the same. **1472** *Ibid.* VI. 63/1 And therupon Juggement ayenst him yeven: as in the Record therof, wherof the Copie hereto is annexed, more playnly it is conteyned. **1568** Grafton *Chron.* II. 856 All attaynders..were adnichilated, and the recorde of the same adiudged to be defaced. **1597** Skene *De Verb. Sign.* s.v. *Recordum*, Ilk lauchfull court..hes thair awin recordes in all sik actiones as are..decided before them. **1607** Cowell *Interpr.* s.v., That caveat of Brooke..that an act committed to writing in any of the King's Courts during the terme wherein it is written is alterable & no record; but that terme once ended and the said Act duly enrolled, it is a record. **1628** Coke *On Litt.* 260 The Rolles being the Records or memorialls of the Judges of the Courts of Record..admit no auerment, plea, or proofe to the contrarie. And if such a Record be alleaged, and it be pleaded, That there is no such Record, it shall be tried only by it selfe. **1765** Blackstone *Comm.* I. Introd. 69 The judgment itself, and all the proceedings previous thereto, are carefully registered and preserved, under the name of records, in public repositories set apart for that particular purpose. **1825** *Act 6 Geo. IV*, c. 86 §11 All the said Judgments and Verdicts shall be deemed to be and shall become Records of the said Sheriff to all Intents and Purposes whatsoever. **1838** W. Bell *Dict. Law Scot.* 1025 It is then transferred to the record and read aloud to the jury, who are asked, 'Is this your verdict?'

b. *Law.* A copy of the material points, pleadings, and issue between defendant and plaintiff on a matter of law, constituting the case to be decided by the court; hence, a case so constituted or presented.

1627 POWELL *Attornies Almanacke* Title-p., Such as shall have occasion to remoue any Person, Cause, or Record from any inferiour Court to any the higher Courts at Westminster. **1768** BLACKSTONE *Comm.* III. 317 The record is a history of the most material proceedings in the cause, entered on a parchment roll, . . in which must be stated the original writ and summons, all the pleadings [etc.]. **1817** W. SELWYN *Law Nisi Prius* (ed. 4) II. 1087 A person having a bare authority, and not being a party to the record, is not prevented from being a witness. **1824** J. MARSHALL *Const. Opin.* (1839) 329 In cases where a state is a party on the record the question of jurisdiction is decided by inspection. **1827** HALLAM *Const. Hist.* (1876) III. xiii. 19 No record was ever removed thither [to the Star chamber] upon assignment of errors in an inferior court. **1885** *Encycl. Brit.* XIX. 219/1 Since the Judicature Acts (1873) there has been no record properly so called, in civil cases, though it has not been expressly abolished.

c. Phr. ***to travel out of the record*** (see quot. 1770). Also *transf.*, to go off the subject. So ***to keep to the record.***

1770 CHATHAM *Sp.* 11 Dec. in *Junius Lett.* (1772) I. Pref. 18 *note*, The court . . are so far confined to the record, that they cannot take notice of any thing that does not appear on the face of it; in the legal phrase, they cannot travel out of the record. **1772** *Junius Lett.* I. Pref. 18 If I stated the merits of my letter to the King, I should imitate Lord Mansfield, and travel out of the record. **1840** W. L. GARRISON in *Life* II. 430 [He] will speak to a point that is pertinent, and not travel out of the record. **1861** DICKENS *Gt. Expect.* xviii, Never mind what you longed for. Keep to the record.

d. *Sc. Law.* A minute, subscribed by the counsel on both sides and by the judge (in the Court of Session by the Lord Ordinary), by which the parties to a suit mutually agree to hold certain pleadings as a full and final statement of the facts and pleas on which their case rests.

The record when finally adjusted and authenticated by the Lord Ordinary or the inferior judge is said to be *closed*. For details of the practice, which dates from the Act of 1825, see Bell's *Dict. Law Scot.* s.v.

1825–6 *Act 6 Geo. IV*, c. 120 §10 The Record so made up and authenticated shall be held as foreclosing the parties from the statement of any new averments in point of fact. **1850** *Act 13 & 14 Vict.* c. 36 §2 Where Defences are lodged, and unless the Record shall be closed upon the Summons and Defences, the Record shall be made by Revisal.

5. a. An account of some fact or event preserved in writing or other permanent form; a document, monument, etc., on which such an account is inscribed; also, *transf.* any thing or person serving to indicate or give evidence of, or preserve the memory of, a fact or event; a memorial. Freq. in *pl.*, a collection of such accounts, documents, etc. Also, in recent use, a tracing or series of marks, made by a recording instrument.

1611 BIBLE *Ezra* vi. 2 There was found . . a rolle, and therein was a record thus written. **1655** H. VAUGHAN *Silex Scint.*, *Agreement*, I wrote it down. But one that saw And envyed that Record [etc.]. **1790** COWPER *In Mem. Thornton* 48 Thy bounties all were Christian, and I make This record of thee for the Gospel's sake. **1822** SHELLEY tr. *Calderon* II. 163 In my wisdom are the orbs of Heaven Written as in a record. **1841** *Penny Cycl.* XIX. 332/2 The journal stamp on a letter is a record that it has passed through the post-office. **1876** *Nature* XV. 101/2 Thus a permanent record is made of every signal that is sent. **1881** I. TAYLOR *Alphabet* I. 16 The very earliest record which we possess of any actual event is the scene depicted on a fragment of an antler [etc.].

transf. **1594** SHAKS. *Rich. III*, IV. iv. 28 [Thou] breefe abstract and record of tedious dayes. *c* **1600** —— *Sonn.* lv, The living record of your memory. **1790** COWPER *Receipt Mother's Pict.* 54 The record fair That memory keeps, of all thy kindness there. **1797** WORDSW. *Old Cumbld. Beggar* 89 The villagers in him Behold a record. **1842** TENNYSON *Gardener's Dau.* 173 Shaping faithful record of the glance That graced the giving.

pl. **1581** SAVILE *Tacitus, Hist.* IV. xl. (1591) 199 To communicate a copie to the Senate of the Princes recordes and papers. **1615** BEDWELL *Arab. Trudg.* Talby, This I translated for the office of the Records in the Towre well neare thirtie yeares since. **1697** DRYDEN *Virg. Past.* IX. 63 Why, Daphnis, dost thou search in old Records, To know the Seasons when the Stars arise? **1751** JOHNSON *Rambler* No. 143 ¶8 That no records were so durable as poems. **1781** COWPER *Conversat.* 615 Who . . Could fetch from records of an earlier age, . . His rich materials. **1819** SHELLEY *Cenci* IV. i. 58 My parchments and all records of my wealth. **1841** *Penny Cycl.* XIX. 336/2 The Victoria Tower . . has been named as a likely repository for the public records. **1875** HELPS *Soc. Press.* iii. 50 No historical records remain of this great transaction.

transf. *a* **1610** PARSONS *Leicester's Ghost* (1641) 28 Can this injurious World so quickly blot A name so great out of records of fame. **1662** BP. HOPKINS *Funeral Serm.* (1685) 13 The records of the grave. **1759** MASON *Caractacus* Wks. 1811 II. 97 That black hour, (May Memory ever raze it from her records). **1843** MILL *Logic* I. i. §5 Either in the records of our own experience or in the discourse of others.

b. An account or reckoning of past time. *rare.*

1611 BIBLE *Transl. Pref.* ¶3 For conseruing the record of time in true supputation. **1711** POPE *Temp. Fame* 112 Who measured earth . . And traced the long records of lunar years.

c. The leading facts in the life or career of a person, *esp.* of a public man; the sum of what one has done or achieved.

App. of American origin, but now in common Eng. use.

1856 H. GREELEY *Sp., on Lincoln* 20 Mar. 133 A candidate must have a slim record in these times. **1879** TOURGEE *Fool's Err.* xi. 49 Contending so hotly over each other's records during and before the war. **1888** *Century Mag.* May 3 My literary record—so far as I had made a record.

d. A performance or occurrence remarkable among, or going beyond, others of the same kind; *spec.* the best recorded achievement in any competitive sport. Freq. in phr. ***to beat*** or ***break the record***: to surpass all previous performances.

1883 W. WILSON *Swim. Instructor* 137 The following records are given. **1884** *Longm. Mag.* Feb. 483 This performance, which beat all previous records was considered a very fine one. **1887** M. SHEARMAN *Athletics & Football* v. 143 T. G. Little and J. H. T. Roupell . . tied at 5ft. 9in., a height which remained the 'record' for the next five years. **1924** C. MACKENZIE *Heavenly Ladder* xxiii. 286 The various 'records' we've broken . . were not of our own seeking. **1955** N. & R. MCWHIRTER (*title*) Guinness book of records. **1975** *Oxf. Compan. Sports & Games* 734/1 Thin air, a handicap in the endurance events, contributed to the shattering of world records in 11 track and field events with a premium on explosive effort.

e. (i) A disc or, formerly, a cylinder from which recorded sound or television pictures can be reproduced. Occas. also, a recording made on magnetic tape.

1878 *Design & Work* 19 Jan. 72/2 The vibrations resulting when a voice . . utters certain words or other sounds, instead of being caused to transmit corresponding vibrations to a distance, are caused to produce a material record. . . The record can also be multiplied precisely as a photographic portrait can be multiplied. **1878** *Cassell's Family Mag.* June 443/1 Mr. Edison is now engaged in devising a finished instrument capable of storing up speeches and music of all kinds, and of allowing the records to be sent by post. **1892** W. GILLET *Phonograph* ii. 11 Previous to taking a record the cylinder has a sheet of tinfoil carefully wrapped round it. *Ibid.*, The record being finished, to reproduce it we have but to bring the cylinder back to the point of starting, and again rotate it. **1897** *Sears, Roebuck Catal.* 485/2 One graphophone talking machine. . . 12 Musical and Talking Records, your own selection. **1919** H. L. WILSON *Ma Pettengill* i. 20 With a . . hired help to bring him his breakfast in bed and put on another record and minister to his lightest whim. **1919** WODEHOUSE *Damsel in Distress* xxiii. 278 I've been dancing to your music for years! I've got about fifty of your records on the Victrola at home. **1949** FRAYNE & WOLFE *Elem. Sound Recording* xxix. 601 The making of very high-quality magnetic records has become possible commercially. **1966** *Listener* 3 Nov. 646/1 Musicians' Union . . objects to any new broadcast popular music programmes relying mainly on records. **1975** G. J. KING *Audio Handbk.* vii. 154 Although there are still a few mono releases, the basic record is cut for two-channel stereo. **1976** *National Observer* 13 Nov. 8/2 Video-disc players, which attach to your television and broadcast shows from records, are being developed by several major manufacturers. **1978** *Gramophone* June 136/3 The programme is recorded digitally using the well proved PCM (pulse code modulation) encoding system. . . Philips are forecasting that players and disc records will be available in the early 1980s.

(ii) *fig.* (See quots.)

1926 MAINES & GRANT *Wise-Crack Dict.* 12/2 *Put on a new record*, change the subject. **1976** W. GOLDMAN *Magic* III. xii. 207 'There's something crazy here . . and I care.' 'Oh Jesus, I'm sick of that record.' **1977** PARTRIDGE *Dict. Catch Phr.* 177/2 *Put another record on! and change the record!* . . Addressed to . . anyone . . 'going on about something'.

f. An account of a person's conduct in a particular sphere, preserved for reference; *spec.* a record (or history) of criminal convictions or prison sentences. orig. *U.S.*

1901 *Land of Sunshine* Apr. 234 In that crowded hall were many men with 'records'. *a* **1911** [see PEDIGREE *sb.* 2 d]. **1918** A. WOODS *Crime Prevention* vii. 87 The convict has a hard enough row to hoe when he gets out to overcome his record, even if he is mechanically capable. **1938** [see ARM *sb.*[1] 2 b]. **1952** M. ALLINGHAM *Tiger in Smoke* x. 168 Not one of you has got a real record . . and you don't want to spoil it, eh? **1954** *Manch. Guardian Weekly* 18 Mar. 3 McCarthy had described her as a 'code clerk' whose 'Communist record' was known to the country. **1969** [see MODERATE *sb.* a]. **1973** 'E. FERRARS' *Foot in Grave* viii. 144 'You didn't know . . that he'd got a record.' 'A police record?' 'Yes.'

g. In various phrases: ***off the record*** (orig. *U.S.*): unofficially, confidentially; also as adj. phr.; also, ***for, on the record***, for the sake of having the facts recorded or known; also, ***to put*** (***set***, etc.) ***the record straight***: to achieve a proper record of the facts; to correct a misapprehension.

1933 H. L. ICKES *Secret Diary* 24 Mar. (1953) I. 9 He met and answered every question, although in some instances his answers were off the record. **1935** *Time* 2 Sept. 16/2 Only a very few Canadian tycoons took a calmer off-the-record view. **1939** *Time* 16 Oct. 101/1 By such slightly off-the-record stunts as burglarizing the plane factory . . the Major sleuths out a sabotage gang. **1943** M. ASQUITH *Off Record* 10 If it is an Americanism, all the better. They are our allies, and if no one else understands the meaning of 'Off the Record', they will. **1949** *Manch. Guardian Weekly* 31 Mar. 2/3 Professor Schuman, who is a tidy-minded man, wanted to keep the record straight. **1949** R. CHANDLER *Little Sister* xxxi. 226 Off the record—we were always sure. We just didn't have a thing on him. **1951** *N.Y. Times Book Rev.* 22 Apr. 35/4 (*heading*) For the record. **1953** A. C. CLARKE *Prelude to Space* viii. 43, I thought you might like to come along. For the record, you can be one of our legal advisers. **1965** A. NICOL *Truly Married Woman* 34 Look here, Olu, do you chaps hate us? . . Of course, this is all off the record. We are speaking as man to man. **1967** N. FREELING *Strike out where not Applicable* 30, I said we'd get the gendarmerie to look at things, just to get the record straight, what? **1971** *Daily Tel.* 24 Apr. 9/6 Our Saxon forebears . . [regarded] all smithy conversations as off-the-record and therefore not slanderous at law. **1972** *N.Y. Times* 3 Nov. 35/1 Sir Rudolf is a spirited and independent man who feels he is obligated to put the record straight. **1973** D. WESTHEIMER *Going Public* i. 15, I wouldn't . . advise you to lower your standards. I'll say for the record I'm not advising that. **1973** *Times* 17 Dec. 14/4 An unattributable criticism of the oil companies by one minister was followed next day by an on-the-record reversal. **1976** J. SNOW *Cricket Rebel* 76, I was impressed by the fact that he had bothered to get in touch with me to put the record straight. **1977** *Oxford Consumer* Mar. 5/1 Mr. Shergold made further investigations and sent us the following letter which should help to set the record straight. **1978** *Church Times* 1 Sept. 10 I'd be surprised if they didn't get down to some pretty forthright talking about women priests—not necessarily on the record, but among themselves. **1978** R. V. JONES *Most Secret War* iv. 41 Our discussion, which he had assured me was 'off the record', was reported back to the Air Ministry.

h. *pl.* Used *absol.* and *attrib.* (with capital initial) to designate a place where official records are kept; *spec.* a criminal records office or department (cf. sense 5 f).

1934 *Discovery* Nov. 319/2 The buildings under observation were the Great Temple, the Records Office and the Police Barracks. **1937** M. ALLINGHAM *Dancers in Mourning* xxvi. 314 Yeo had become a new man since the message from the [Police] Records Department. **1958** 'J. BYROM' *Or be he Dead* iii. 52 'I'll send you a copy . . so that you can bring your files up to date.' . . 'I'm sure Records will be much indebted to you.' **1973** 'C. AIRD' *His Burial Too* iv. 38, I did a person check with Records before I left the Station. . . Criminal Records Office have no knowledge of him.

i. *Computers.* A number of related items of information which are handled as a unit.

1957 *Proc. Western Joint Computer Conf.* 215/1 A record might be defined as all of the individual items of information (or words) about a given file unit. **1963** *Communications* (Assoc. Computing Machinery) VI. 267/1 Suppose each record of an input tape contains up to 50 fields . . , some of which may be missing in any given input record. **1964** T. W. MCRAE *Impact of Computers on Accounting* vi. 189 A tape reel holds a certain number of records just as a ledger holds a certain number of accounts. **1966** C. J. SIPPL *Computer Dict. & Handbk.* 265/1 The most basic subdivision of a record is called a field. **1970** O. DOPPING *Computers & Data Processing* i. 14 We know that the first word in this record is always the last name of the subscriber, the second one is his first name, etc. **1973** C. W. GEAR *Introd. Computer Sci.* i. 13 To avoid confusion we will refer to the set of information on each card (name and phone number) as a record.

III. †**6.** Reputation, repute, account. *Obs.*

c **1386** CHAUCER *Sompn. T.* 341 Dronkenesse is eek a foul record Of any man and namely in a lord. **1390** GOWER *Conf.* II. 230 Protheus of his record Which was an Astronomien. *Ibid.* III. 326 Sche was a womman of record And al is lieved that sche seith. *c* **1470** HENRY *Wallace* IX. 1133 Off him he maid bot lycht record.

†**7.** Memory, remembrance, recollection. *Obs.*

13.. *Minor Poems fr. Vernon MS.* xlix. 61 Long record of þat malice. *c* **1400** tr. *Secreta Secret., Gov. Lordsh.* 106 It fallys þat þou chese of wyse men & of Skreueyns . . of sotyll record. **1577–82** BRETON *Flourish upon Fancy* (1879) 55/1 When that in minde I feede upon the freshe recorde of thee. **1601** SHAKS. *Twel. N.* v. i. 253 O that record is liuely in my soule.

†**8.** *Sc.* Reply; tale, statement. *Obs.*

c **1470** HENRY *Wallace* VII. 1260 Schir Jhon Menteth . . Till Wallace come, and maid a playne record. *Ibid.* x. 1145 To that langage Cumyn maid na record. *c* **1475** *Rauf Coilȝear* 729 The king fell in carping, and tauld his Intent To mony gracious Grome he maid his record.

†**9.** Accord, reconcilement. *Obs. rare*$^{-1}$.

c **1400** *Rule St. Benet* 65/654 For our enmes sal we pray, Til a recorde be redy ay.

†**10.** A musical note. *Obs. rare*$^{-1}$.

1582 T. WATSON *Centurie of Love* xi, O Goulden bird . . Whose sweete records and more then earthly voice . . did then my griefe asswage.

†**11.** = RECORDER[2]. *Obs. rare.*

?*c* **1475** *Sqr. lowe Degre* 1075 With sytolphe and with sautry songe With fydle, recorde, and dowcemere. **1589** PUTTENHAM *Eng. Poesie* II. i. (Arb.) 79 Melodious instruments, as Lutes, Harpes, Regals, Records, and such like.

†**12.** = RECORDER[1]. *Obs. rare.*

a **1550** *Vox populi* 702 in Hazl. *E.P.P.* III. 292 The laweare and the landelorde, The greate reave and the recorde, The recorde I mean is he That hath office or els ffee.

IV. 13. *attrib.* and *Comb.* **a.** objective and objective genitive, as (sense 5 a) ***record bearer, bearing, keeper, -keeping, -maker, -making***; (sense 5 d) ***record-breaker, -breaking, -holder, -setting, -smasher, -smashing***; (sense 5 e) ***record-buying, -collecting, collector.***

1549 COVERDALE, etc. *Erasm. Par. 2 Thess.* i. 9 b, You, which trusted in Christ at our *recorde bearing. —— *Erasm. Par. 2 John* 54 Thys is the true doctrine, whiche you haue receaued of true *recorde bearours from the begynnyng. **1581** MARBECK *Bk. of Notes* 216 Those faithfull christen men, that heard and sawe Christ, and were his record bearers. **1894** *Rep. Vermont Board Agric.* XIV. 93 Raising trotters for sporting men . . has been done with the one idea of producing a *record breaker, regardless of every other qualification. **1929** A. HUXLEY *Do what you Will* 145 Modern record-breakers have been ready to undergo . . hardships for the sake of money. **1976** *Liverpool Echo* 7 Dec. 7/3 A Birkenhead company is making a name for itself as record breakers in the shipping world. **1886** *Pall Mall G.* 10 July 6/1 This Henley Regatta has been a *record-breaking one. **1929** A. HUXLEY *Do what you Will* 147 The record-breaking was to have a numerous audience. **1937** C. ISHERWOOD *Sally Bowles* 66 Huge contracts for Sally, record-breaking sales for the novels I should one day write. **1950** *Sport* 22–28 Sept. 20/4 Not satisfied with his record-breaking average of 23 m.p.h., Joy rode again last weekend in vain hope of lowering his hundred mile time. **1949** L. FEATHER *Inside Be-Bop* i. 5 Lester's introduction to the *record-buying jazz public. **1970** *Guardian* 7 Aug. 8/2 The two orchestras . . are . . little known . . by the record-buying public. **1956** M. STEARNS *Story of Jazz* (1957) xvii. 216 To the *record-collecting converts known as 'moldy figs', however, this was not 'authentic' jazz. **1932** *New Yorker* 14

May 57/1 Mme. Ljungberg, hitherto accessible to *record-collectors principally in opera albums, introduces herself as a singer of Strauss. **1946** *Penguin Music Mag.* Dec. 91 The record collector, who has built up his library.., really gets to know the music to which he listens. **1934** *Discovery* Dec. 352/1 The *record holders of the fastest time between England and Australia. **1963** *Times* 30 Jan. 4/3 That graceful and intelligent runner, Johnson, is still the United Kingdom recordholder over 800 metres. **1977** *Whitaker's Almanack 1978* 584/2 Terry Paine,..the Football League's appearance record-holder, played his..final League match against Southampton. **1715** Willis *Notitia Parl.* I. Pref. 3 Deputy *Record Keeper of the Tower. **1965** D. E. C. Eversley in Eversley & Glass *Population in Hist.* I. 34 Where central legislation..enforces *record-keeping, the change tends to be abrupt. **1977** J. M. Johnson in Douglas & Johnson *Existential Sociol.* viii. 246 Those typifications of the daily work of intake workers that did not result in an official 'case' for record-keeping purposes. **1884** *Longm. Mag.* Feb. 480 Some severe strictures on the '*record-makers' [in cycling]. *Ibid.*, Whilst I am writing in familiar style of 'records' and '*record-making'. **1969** *Jane's Freight Containers 1968–69* 112/2 Time required to unload a trailer has been reduced from 10 minutes to a *record-setting 90 seconds. **1972** J. Mosedale *Football* ii. 21 The Eagles won 14–0, a record-setting two playoff shutouts in a row. **1928** *Daily Sketch* 7 Aug. 22/3 Arne Borg, the *record-smasher at all distances in the swimming world, was at work again yesterday. **1889** *Puck* (N.Y.) 7 Aug. 399/2 We will soon have as many *record-smashing ocean-steamers as we now have champion pugilists.

b. *attrib.* in senses 4 and 5, as ***record book***, ***-bottle***, ***card***, ***commission***, ***committee***, ***-cross***, ***-office***, ***-room***, ***-stone***; (sense 5 e) ***record cabinet***, ***case***, ***company***, ***deck*** (DECK *sb.*^{1} 3 f), ***groove***, ***label*** (LABEL *sb.*^{1} 7 c), ***library***, ***needle***, ***rack***, ***shop***, ***storage***, ***store***.

1961 *Evening Standard* 6 Feb. 22/3 A further step toward deathless *record-book fame in its dreariest form. **1976** *0–10 Cricket Scene* (Austral.) 5/1 That was the start of the climb ..which was to re-write the record books and lift Australia to the peak of performance. **1853** Kane *Grinnell Exp.* xxv. (1856) 203 Planting a flagstaff, with..a *record-bottle below it. **1967** H. Pinter *Basement* 70 *Law* goes to the *record cabinet. He examines record after record. **1934** *Burlington Mag.* Sept. 142/1 Prolonged study of the data which *record-cards may provide. **1960** M. Spark *Bachelors* i. 6 The specialist himself would possibly remember only the gist, and then only with the aid of his record cards. **1977** *News of World* 17 Apr. 7/2 Details..noted down by teachers on their pupils' record cards. **1908** *Sears, Roebuck Catal.* 201/1 Disc *Record Cases..made from wood covered with black seal grain imitation leather... No. 1 holds 50 7-inch disc records. **1949** D. Smith *I capture Castle* xiii. 245 A wireless and a gramophone combined..[and] a record case to match. **1811** *First Ann. Rep. Rec. Ireland* App., The Statutes..which have been published under the English *Record Commission. **1841** *Penny Cycl.* XIX. 336/1 The Record Commission was renewed six several times between the years 1800 and 1831. **1801** *Ann. Rep. Comm. Public Rec.* §2 The *Record Committee of the House of Commons. **1938** D. Baker *Young Man with Horn* IV. vii. 278 The *record company went broke before any of their records were issued. **1978** *Lancashire Life* Apr. 29/3 Life after death is a tall order, but this month a record company comes near to meeting it by supplying the next best thing. **1838** Miss Pardoe *River & Desert* II. 17 The hand..which had planted the *record-cross, and the tributary wreath. **1976** A. Hope *Hi-Fi Handbk.* 116 If you intend giving your *record deck a fairly hard working life [etc.]. **1946** E. Hodgins *Mr. Blandings* i. 9 He lowered the rusty tone arm, complete with needle, on to the *record groove. **1976** M. Maguire *Scratchproof* xi. 172 'The *record labels too, I suppose.' 'Steaming off and switching?' **1977** *Listener* 25 Aug. 247/2 Elvis had been doing it..already, on a little Tennessee record label. **1961** *Times-Picayune* (New Orleans) 19 June III. 11/3 A stereo series called 'Adventures in Music', which is an instructional *record library for elementary schools. **1974** E. Ambler *Dr. Frigo* I. 50 On shelving built along the inner wall was..hi-fi equipment and a record library. **1918–19** *T. Eaton & Co. Catal.* Fall & Winter 369/2 *Record Needles, 100 for 15c. **1800** *First Rep. Public Rec.* 18 Upon Inquiry into the *Record Offices of the Sheriffs [etc.]. **1855** Singleton *Virgil* I. 141 Nor people's record-offices beheld. **1904** G. B. Shaw *Let.* 23 Nov. (1972) II. 467, I was startled to hear that Edith Livia was getting..twenty-five shillings a week for work at the Record Office. **1973** A. Roy *Sable Night* ii. 22 The bookcase and *record-rack yielded nothing. **1975** R. Butler *Where All Girls are Sweeter* ii. 17, I looked through his record racks... There was a nice mixture from Bach to Vivaldi. **1800** *First Rep. Public Rec.* App. Pl. i, *Record Room for Principal Clerks of Session. **1812** *Sporting Mag.* XXXIX. 152 Convicted by the magistrates at the record-room, Northampton. **1960** *Twentieth Cent.* Apr. 341 *Record-shops..have mushroomed all over Britain in the last five years. **1975** *Guardian* 22 Jan. 14/5 The top 40 singles are based on local record shop returns. **1836** J. H. Newman in *Lyra Apost.* (1849) 53 So, let the cliffs and seas of this fair place Be named man's tomb and splendid *record-stone. **1939–40** *Army & Navy Stores Catal.* 838/2 Radiogramophone.. with five record albums and..extra *record storage. **1974** *Times* 8 Apr. 13/3 A record storage cabinet in a Queen Anne style. **1949** *Billboard* 2 Apr. 34 Albums listed are those classical and semi-classical albums selling best in the nation's retail *record stores. **1977** D. Westlake *Nobody's Perfect* (1978) 107 A branch of a major department store.. the record stores, the shoe stores, the ladies' clothing stores.

c. *attrib.* in sense 5 d, passing into *adj.*

1893 Lydekker *Horns & Hoofs* 135 The 'record' dimensions are..a length of $13\frac{1}{2}$ in., with a girth..of $6\frac{1}{2}$ in. **1895** *Times* 2 Jan. 13/1 Record prices have been made. **1912** Chesterton *Manalive* II. i. 194 Smith was one of the University's record men for shooting. **1922** *Brit. Med. Jrnl.* 2 Sept. 412/1 During 1919,..3,420 new students were registered, being 1,105 greater than the 'record' entry of 1891. **1937** *Discovery* Sept. 264 His 'dash'..was accomplished in record time. **1948** 'J. Tey' *Franchise Affair* viii. 86 If you could have seen your face when I introduced you to her... It cured me of her in record time. **1960** *Farmer & Stockbreeder* 16 Feb. 83/1, 27,000 gn record-priced bull. **1978** *Lancashire Life* Apr. 69/2 Visitors numbered a record 114,000 in 1977, and it is hoped that this trend will continue.

14. Special combinations. **record album**, †(*a*) a holder for gramophone records, *obs.*; (*b*) = ALBUM^1 6; **record changer**, a device for automatically placing another record on the turntable of a gramophone when the preceding record has ended; also **record-changing** *a.*; **record club**, a society which enables members to purchase selected gramophone records at reduced prices; **record hop** *slang*, a dance at which the music is provided by gramophone records; a place where such entertainment is held; **record jockey** *U.S. slang* (immediately supplanted by *disc jockey*: see DISC 8 f); **record linkage**, the process of combining items of information or sets of data relating to the same subject; **record player**, orig. a turntable and pick-up unit designed to be plugged into and played through a radio; now usu. a gramophone; **record sleeve**, a stiff envelope in which a gramophone record may be stored (cf. SLEEVE *sb.* 7); **record token**, a voucher exchangeable in a shop for a gramophone record or records; **record type**, a type-face including special sorts reproducing the contractions or particular letter forms found in mediæval manuscripts.

1925–6 *T. Eaton & Co. Catal.* Fall & Winter 391/1 These *Record Albums are made with strong cardboard covers... Each album will hold 12 records. **1945** *Billboard* 24 Mar. 18/2 (*heading*) Best-selling record albums by classical artists. **1955** Keepnews & Grauer *Pictorial Hist. Jazz* viii. 87/2 When people got around to..dissecting it [*sc.* a variety of jazz] in books and record-album notes,.. it became known as 'Chicago style'. **1931** *N.Y. Times* 12 July 4/8 The Capehart 400 series..has several novel features... The *record changer is equipped with a special constant-speed electric motor which operates both the turn-table and the record-shifting mechanism. **1947** *Gramophone* Nov. 88/1 The amplifier and record changer are contained in a small chair-side consol. **1977** *Times* 18 Apr. (Gramophone Suppl.) p. i/2 A radio-gramophone, with automatic record changer, was installed in our living room. **1931** *Wireless World* 23 Sept. 349/3 H.M.V.'s ace set is the model 531, being a nine-valve superheterodyne with automatic *record-changing radio-gramophone. **1943** *Gramophone* Dec. 107/1 The spindle and turntable move left and down, which leaves the area free for the first record to drop upon the 'floor' of the record-changing unit. **1958** *Manch. Guardian* 21 Jan. 6/6 If anything the *record club is likely to spread an interest in records of serious music rather than reduce the profits of the big companies. **1961** G. Smith *Business of Loving* xi. 229 We started as a record club... The first discs..were fifteen shillings. **1960** *Punch* 9 Mar. 345/1 Akin to the juke-box joints are the *record-hops. **1966** *Wall St. Jrnl.* 25 July 1 'Record hops'..are dances often organized by a disc jockey and plugged by him over the air, as a means of supplementing his income. **1940** *Variety* 3 Apr. 39/3 [Quoting J. Kapp] The name bands are come on for the *record jockeys who ride herd over not only Decca records but all the others. **1946** H. L. Dunn in *Amer. Jrnl. Public Health* XXXVI. 1412/2 In the process of *record linkage the uniting of the fact-of-death with the fact-of-birth has been given a special name, 'death clearance'. **1959** *Science* 16 Oct. 954/1 The term record linkage has been used to indicate the bringing together of two or more separately recorded pieces of information concerning a particular individual or family. **1968** *Brit. Med. Bull.* XXIV. 208/2 If birth and marriage records are included in the system, it is possible to use record linkage to assemble sibships, parent-offspring groups and eventually pedigrees. **1934** *Wireless World* 5 Jan. 10/3 (*caption*) The Collaro *record player incorporated in a radio-gramophone cabinet. **1939** *New Regal-Zono Records* Feb. 4 (Advt.), The thousands already sold of the Columbia electric record-player prove conclusively how many fully appreciate the facility of playing their records through their radio sets. **1958** *Sunday Times* 3 Aug. 3/6 Now that the station has bought a new record-player and gets all its music in prerecorded tapes, the personal touch is all but gone. **1960** *Practical Wireless* XXXVI. 377 (Advt.), Turns any gramophone into a first-class tape-recorder and back into a record-player in a moment. **1973** M. Amis *Rachel Papers* 68 You mean to tell me that it's only made in stereo?.. What about the people who don't own stereo record-players? **1977** *Gramophone* July 241/1 The humble record player of earlier years could still be found in a few places. **1954** *Gramophone Record Rev.* July 415 On the *record sleeve, the user is extolled to play the record at full room volume. **1963** L. Deighton *Horse under Water* xviii. 74 The brightly coloured record sleeves that are the folk art of the new world. **1978** P. Porter *Cost of Seriousness* 47 An old woman, So the record sleeve denotes, Is singing of death In a young world. **1958** M. Kelly *Christmas Egg* II. 76 The envelope that had held his brother's *record token. **1977** *Radio Times* 26 Nov.–2 Dec. 56/1 EMI Record Tokens..can be exchanged at over 5,000 leading record shops. **1886** F. W. Maitland *Let.* 24 Apr. (1965) 19 As regards mode of printing:—The use of '*record type' seems undesirable. **1934** V. H. Galbraith *Introd. Use of Public Records* v. 77 A century ago the Record Commission in its publications tried by means of 'record type' virtually to reproduce the document, with all its abbreviations. **1972** C. R. Cheney in A. Campbell *Charters of Rochester* p. vi, Originals and early copies are reproduced as faithfully as is possible, without going to the extreme of using 'record type'.

record (rɪˈkɔːd), *v.*^{1} Also 5 *Sc.* **racord**, 6 **record.** [ad. OF. *recorder* (in most senses of the Eng. word) = Sp. *recordar*, It. *ricordare*:—L. *recordāre* (classical *recordārī*), f. *re-* RE- + *cord-*, *cor* heart: cf. *accord*, *discord*, etc.]

I. †**1.** *trans.* **a.** To get by heart, to commit to memory, to go over in one's mind. **b.** To repeat or say over as a lesson, to recite. *Obs.*

a **1225** *Ancr. R.* 256, & makie so þeo þet bereð þet word recorden hit ofte biuoren hire, er heo go ut. *c* **1330** R. Brunne *Chron.* (1810) 172 Better him wer..þe seruise of his song recorded & lered. *c* **1374** Chaucer *Troylus* III. 2 (51) Lay al this mene while Troilus Recordyng his lesson in this manere. *c* **1477** Caxton *Jason* 37 If ye will recorde the lessons and epistles of loue by the space of ten yere. **1542** Udall *Erasm. Apoph.* 250 b, Anon the crowe recorded also the other woordes whiche she had so often heard. **1579** Spenser *Sheph. Kal.* Apr. 30 If hys ditties bene so trimly dight, I pray thee, Hobbinoll, recorde some one. *a* **1656** Hales *Gold. Rem.* I. (1673) 142 The Gardiner whilst he prunes his Vines and Arbours, may record some one of David's sonnets.

†**c.** To take to heart, give heed to. *Obs.*$^{-1}$

1390 Gower *Conf.* II. 250 He tolde him many a dredful sawe Bot Jason wolde it noght recorde.

2. a. To practise (a song, tune, etc.). In later use only of birds (cf. 3); †freq. (*c* 1580–1620) = to sing or warble (a tune, etc.).

1413 *Pilgr. Sowle* (Caxton 1483) v. viii. 99 When they hadde these instrumentes they recorded songes besyly tylle that they were..parfyte ynowe in al maner musike. **1580** Lyly *Euphues* (Arb.) 278 Where vnder a sweete Arbour of Eglentine, be byrdes recording theyr sweete notes [etc.]. **1601** Dolman *La Primaud. Fr. Acad.* (1618) III. 760 The young little nightingales harken to the old, and do record by themselues apart, the songs which they heard. *a* **1654** Selden *Table-t.* (Arb.) 95 You see a Bird by often whistling to learn a tune, and a Month after record it to her self. **1834** E. Jesse *Glean. Nat. Hist.* Ser. II. 84 This tune..I could distinctly hear it inwardly whistle, or, in the language of bird-fanciers, record it.

†**b.** To sing of or about (something); to render in song. *Obs.*

1576 Gascoigne *Philomene* (Arb.) 110 Then Phylomene records the rewth Which craueth iust remorse. **1597** Lyly *Wom. in Moon* III. i. 79 Let vs go walke the woods, Where warbling birds recorde our happines. **1591** Shaks. *Two Gent.* v. iv. 6 Here can I..to the Nightingales complaining Notes Tune my distresses, and record my woes.

3. a. *intr.* Of birds (rarely of persons): To practise or sing a tune in an undertone; to go over it quietly or silently. Now only *techn.*

c **1510** Barclay *Mirr. Gd. Manners* (1570) E vj, Therfore first recorde thou, as birde within a cage,..thy tunes tempring longe, And then..forth with thy pleasaunt songe. **1530** Palsgr. 681/2 This byrde recordeth all redy, she wyll synge within a whyle. *a* **1592** H. Smith *Serm.* (1637) 429 Like a bird that is taught to record, when he had sung it he sang it again. **1619** Fletcher *M. Thomas* III. iii, Ye may record a little, or ye may whistle, As time shall minister; but, for main singing, Pray ye satisfy yourselves. **1727–41** Chambers *Cycl.* s.v., The cock thrush is distinguished from the hen in recording, the first being more loud and frequent in it than the second. **1773** Barrington in *Phil. Trans.* LXIII. 250, I have known instances of birds beginning to record when they were not a month old. **1871** Darwin *Desc. Man* I. I. ii. 55 The young males [birds] continue practising, or, as the bird-catchers say, recording, for ten or eleven months.

†**b.** To sing or warble. *Obs.*

1590 Lodge *Rosalind* (Hunter. Cl.) 27 Partlie to heare the melodie of the sweete birdes which recorded. **1592** Kyd *Sp. Trag.* II. iv. 28 Harke, Madame, how the birds record by night. **1613–6** W. Browne *Brit. Past.* II. iv, While the nymph did earnestly contest Whether the birds or she recorded best.

II. †**4.** *trans.* To call to mind, to recall, recollect, remember. *Obs.*

1303 R. Brunne *Handl. Synne* 4191 Treytur! recorde what þou hast herde Seyde and sunge yn al þe werlde. **1340** *Ayenb.* 142 Huanne he recordeþ þet lif of iesu crist and his holy passioun. *c* **1400** *Rule St. Benet* 11 Þat ye be noght forgetil,..And tat ye recorde wel þe cumantemens of god. **1480** Caxton *Chron. Eng.* lxxxv, Do we so..that men mowe recorde the worthynesse of knyght hode. **1530** Palsgr. 681/2 When I recorde the gentyll wordes he hath had unto me, it maketh my herte full sorye for hym. **1599** T. M[oufet] *Silkwormes* 65 For they recording what they were of late Dare not yet mount aboue their former state. *a* **1656** Hales *Gold. Rem.* III. (1673) 4 Do you already know your duty? it serves to commemorate, and to make you record it. **1789** Cowper *Annus Mem.* 34 An era..Which joyful I will oft record, And thankful, at my frugal board.

absol. *c* **1440** *Jacob's Well* 181, I haue seyd my synne in herte recordynge. *c* **1460** *Launfal* 831 The Kyng recordede tho, And bad hym bryng hys lef yn syght.

†**5.** To meditate, ponder (something) *with* oneself. *Obs.*

c **1374** Chaucer *Boeth* I. pr. i. 2 (Camb. MS.) While þat I stille recordede thise thinges with myself. **1583** Stocker *Civ. Warres Lowe C.* II. 46 Certaine dayes of deliberation are giuen to the prisoner to record with himselfe, who or what his enemies be. **1586** A. Day *Eng. Secretary* I. (1625) 86 We shall record with our selues, in what league, amity or duty, we haue before-time stood charged.

†**6.** *intr.* **a.** To have mind or recollection *of* a person or thing. *Obs.*

1382 Wyclif *Gen.* viii. 1 The Lord forsothe recordide of Noe. —— *Isa.* lxiii. 11 He recordide of the daȝes of the world. **1509** Hawes *Past. Pleas.* I. (Percy Soc.) 9 Recorde of Saturne, the first kyng of Crete. **1567** *Triall Treas.* (1850) 28 Recorde of Dionisius, a king of much fame.

†**b.** To think or meditate *on* a thing or person. Also with *in*. *Obs.*

c **1374** Chaucer *Troylus* III. 1130 (1179) Evermore on this night ye recorde, And beth wel ware ye do no more amys. *c* **1430** Lydg. *Min. Poems* (Percy Soc.) 125 Recorde on Fraunce and Parys the fayre citee. **1430–40** —— *Bochas* VIII. i. (1558) 3 Recorde on Cyrus, and many other mo. **1532**

Tindale *Expos. Matt.* vi. 34 (*c* 1550) 82 b, To kepe the couenaunt of the Lorde thy God, and to recorde therin daye and night. **1560** Becon *New Catech.* Wks. I. 488 Let not the boke of this lawe departe out of thy mouth, but recorde therein daye and nyght. *a* **1604** R. Hall *Life Bp. Fisher* xxii. (ed. Baily, 1655) 206 Himselfe praying all the way, and recording upon the words which he before had read.

†**7. a.** To remind (one) of (a thing). *Obs. rare*$^{-1}$.

c **1386** Chaucer *Prol.* 829 Ye woot youre foreward and I it yow recorde.

†**b.** *refl.* To remember. Also const. *of*. *Obs.*

1413 *Pilgr. Sowle* (Caxton 1483) I. xv. 9 Ful wel I me record, of this mater ne touchyd I no word. **1422** tr. *Secreta Secret., Priv. Priv.* 150 A man sholde hym recorde of thynges that afore hath bene.

III. †**8. a.** *trans.* To relate in words; to tell or narrate orally. Also *intr.* in ***to hear record***, to hear tell (*of* a person). *Obs.* (in later use only as *transf.* from 9).

13.. *Cursor M.* 19112 (Gött.) Bi his fadir sitt he sall, Till he record haf vs all, þat he spac feirst wid prophecis. **1340** *Ayenb.* 59 Þet is þe zenne of þan þet zuo bliþeliche recordeþ hare dedes and hare prowesses. **1390** Gower *Conf.* I. 36 In this wise, as I recorde, The man is cause of alle wo. *a* **1450** *Knt. de la Tour* (1868) 52 Beting hem self [and] recordyng her synne tofore the pepille. **1500–20** Dunbar *Poems* lix. 13 Quhois crewall sclander seruis deid, And in my name all leis recordis. **1550** Lyndesay *Sqr. Meldrum* 1520 Thair dwelt in Fyfe ane aged Lord That of this Squyer hard record. **1738** Wesley *Hymn*, '*To Thee, O Father of Mankind*' ii, Who in th' Assembly of the Just Will still record thy Praise.

†**b.** Const. *to* or *unto* (a person). *Obs.*

1375 Barbour *Bruce* I. 72 Thai all concordyt, That all thar spek suld be recordyt Till Schyr Eduuard. **1390** Gower *Conf.* III. 49 Somwhat of his aventures, To thee, mi Sone, I wol recorde. *c* **1470** Henry *Wallace* x. 542 The Bruce than in his mynd remordyt Thai wordis suth that Wallace had him recordyt. *c* **1500** *Melusine* 102 The erle..demanded of Raymondin where he had be so long, and he recorded to hym alle his auenture.

†**c.** To declare as one's verdict. *Obs.*

1377 Langl. *P. Pl.* B. xviii. 197, I, Riȝtwisnesse, recorde thus with treuth, That her peyne be perpetuel. **1393** *Ibid.* C. iv. 474 After the dede that ys ydo, the dome shal recorde, Mercy other no mercy. *a* **1400** *Pistill of Susan* 60 Riȝtwys Jugement recordet þei none.

9. a. To relate in writing; to narrate or mention in a written account; to put or set down in writing; to put on record. Also, in recent use, of telegraphic and other instruments: To set down (a message, etc.) in some permanent form.

In later use the sense of setting down in a written or permanent form becomes the prominent one; early examples are more closely connected with sense 8.

13.. *E.E. Allit. P.* B. 25 Me mynez on one amonge oþer, as Maþew recordez. *c* **1375** *Sc. Leg. Saints* xxxi. (*Eugenia*) 239 It nedis nocht to recorde here þe dole. *c* **1430** Lydg. *Min. Poems* (Percy Soc.) 47 Clerkys recorde, by gret auctoryte, Hornes wer yove to bestys for dyffence. **1554–9** in *Songs & Ball.* (1860) 2 Yet God made hyme promys, as Scrypture dothe reccord. **1579** E. K. *Gloss. Spenser's Sheph. Cal.* May 54 Which story is first recorded of Plutarch, in his booke of the ceasing of oracles. **1601** Dolman *La Primaud. Fr. Acad.* (1618) III. 828 Plinie recordeth many other wonders concerning these beasts. **1662** Stillingfl. *Orig. Sacr.* II. iii. §1 After he hath recorded those faults, he seeks not to extenuate them. **1696** Whiston *Th. Earth* III. (1722) 253 Their Numbers were exactly taken, and are as exactly Recorded. **1771** *Junius Lett.* I. 259 The services you have done the nation..have been faithfully recorded. **1820** W. Irving *Sketch Bk.* II. 265 The last words of his that are recorded, are worthy the greatness of his soul. **1860** Tyndall *Glac.* II. xxi. 343, I have recorded certain winter measurements made on the Mer de Glace. **1873** F. Jenkin *Electr. & Magn.* xxii. §5 Sometimes the Morse signals are indicated to the ear or eye without being recorded. **1895** [see recorder[1] 4].

fig. **1601** Daniel *To C'tess Cumbld.* xvi, This note (Madam) of your Worthiness Remaines recorded in so many Hearts. **1647** H. More *Song of Soul* I. I. i, What so under eye Doth fall, or is record in memorie. **1726** Pope *Odyss.* xvii. 580 Just and unjust recording in their mind. **1781** Cowper *Truth* 161 In faithful memory she records the crimes, Or real or fictitious, of the times.

absol. *c* **1425** Wyntoun *Cron.* II. Prol. 30 Wiþe Orosius we wil discorde In til our dat qwhen we racorde Befor or fra þe byrtht of God.

refl. **1818** Scott *Ivanhoe* ix, By this name the stranger had recorded himself in the books of the tourney.

b. To have (a gift, etc.) properly recorded; to give (a verdict or vote).

1596 Shaks. *Merch. V.* IV. i. 388 That he doe record a gift Heere in the Court of all he dies possest Vnto his sonne [etc.]. *a* **1856** Cushing *Law & Pract. Legisl. Assemblies U.S.* VI. iii. 708 If they do not apply until afterwards, they can only be permitted to record their votes by leave of the house. **1884** *Manch. Exam.* 10 May 5/4 There is only one verdict which those who disapprove of it can record.

c. To convert (sound or visual scenes, esp. television pictures) into a permanent form from which they can afterwards be reproduced by machine. Also *absol.*

1892 W. Gilbert *Phonograph* II. 31 The instrument is now ready to register any sound... While the handle is steadily turned.., speak slowly and distinctly the words you wish to be recorded. **1902** *Encycl. Brit.* XXXI. 680/2 When the phonograph records the sound of an orchestra, it does not record the tones of each instrument. **1935** H. C. Bryson *Gramophone Record* iv. 70 A good modern recorder is designed to record frequencies between 250 and 5,000 without discrimination. **1960** *How TV Works* 37/1 A video-tape machine recording the opening of Parliament. **1967** S. Beckett *Eh Joe* 15 Joe's opening movements followed by camera at constant remove... No need to record room as a whole. **1972** *Daily Tel.* 29 Jan. 3 The full proceedings of an inquest were recorded for broadcasting for the first time yesterday. **1978** *Radio Times* 9–15 Dec. 81/4 Most people who record and play back BBC television programmes using videocassette equipment do not realise they infringe copyright. **1980** S. Brett *Dead Side of Mike* xiii. 145 I'd better go. We're about to record.

d. *intr.* Of a performer or instrument: to be suited to sound recording.

1923 O. Mitchell *Talking Machine Industry* viii. 88 It has been complained by some that, in technical phrase, she does not record well. **1925** P. A. Scholes *Second Bk. Gramoph. Rec.* p. xviii, The Piano, as an instrument, records less well than other instruments.

e. *trans.* and *intr.* Of a performer: to give a performance, or a performance of (a work), that is recorded.

1927 *Daily Tel.* 12 Feb. 7 She has recorded the Ave Maria from 'Otello'..as if she had recorded all her life! **1928** *Melody Maker* Feb. 155/3 The band..has recently jumped into prominence, having already recorded for Edison Bell. **1966** *Listener* 10 Mar. 345/1 Mostly they recorded at the end of their careers, and violinists seem to deteriorate much earlier than pianists.

†**10. a.** To bear witness to (a fact, etc.); to attest, confirm. Also *absol.*, to testify. *Obs.*

1377 Langland *P. Pl.* B. IV. 157 Alle riȝtful recorded þat resoun treuthe tolde. **1387** Trevisa *Higden* (Rolls) VIII. 348 Þese were i-sent to the popes court for to have þese covenauntes recorded by þe popes billes. *c* **1440** *Promp. Parv.* 426/1 Recordyn', or bere wytnesse, *testificor*. **1476** in *Surtees Misc.* (1888) 35 Thys wyll we recorde and bere wittenesse be thys lettre of record sealed with our seales. **1514** Barclay *Cyt. & Uplondyshm.* (Percy Soc.) p. xlvi, That can Amintas record and testify. **1570** Levins *Manip.* 171/21 To Recorde, *contestari*. **1607** Shaks. *Timon* IV. ii. 4 Let me be recorded by the righteous Gods, I am as poore as you.

absol. **1393** Langl. *P. Pl.* C. v. 29 To take red at Reson, that recorde sholde By-fore the kyng and Conscience. *c* **1460** *Towneley Myst.* xii. 327 It was a mery gle, sich hard I never none, I recorde.

†**b.** To call to witness. *Obs. rare*$^{-1}$.

1586 Marlowe *1st Pt. Tamburl.* v. ii, For all blot of foul inchastity, I record Heaven, her heavenly self is clear.

†**IV. 11.** To pertain or belong *to* (one). *Obs. rare*$^{-1}$.

c **1500** *Lancelot* 606 Hyme lakid nocht that to a lord recordith.

V. 12. The infin. used in the sense 'recording'.

a. *attrib.* (often as a name of a part), as ***record button, head***; also ***record-reproduce*** adj.

1950 Godfrey & Amos *Sound Recording & Reproduction* (1952) vi. 162 When the *Record button is depressed, current is fed to the wiping head. **1973** *Times* 28 Nov. 6/7 Miss Woods..pressed the 'record' button (it was next to the 'stop' button). **1975** P. G. Winslow *Death of Angel* ix. 186 He pushed the record button. But the heads of his machine were too old. They didn't erase the music. **1946** *Trans. Amer. Inst. Electr. Engineers* LXV. 216/2 The playback head is located a few feet along the wire from the *record head so that in listening tests it is possible to get a quick comparison between a few bars of music as recorded and played back. **1950** G. A. Briggs *Sound Reproduction* (ed. 2) xix. 135 For reproduction, the erase and record heads are switched off and the play-back head is brought into use. **1976** I. R. Sinclair *Master Stereo Cassette Recording* i. 9 Though some high quality reel-to-reel machines use separate record and replay heads,..it is usual on cassette recorders to have only one head used for both recording and for replay. **1951** *Bell Syst. Technical Jrnl.* XXX. 1146 The ring-type *record-reproduce head. *Ibid.*, The process was repeated..for several record-reproduce speeds.

b. Not *attrib.*

1950 G. A. Briggs *Sound Reproduction* (ed. 2) xix. 136 By suitable switching of output circuits, one amplifier may be arranged to function for both record and replay. **1968** C. N. G. Matthews *Tape Recording* iv. 36 During record or reproduce it [*sc.* the tape] is kept in close contact with the heads by pressure pads or by its own tension. *Ibid.* 38 Equalization is switched automatically as the machine is switched from record to playback. **1971** *Hi-Fi Sound* Feb. 49/2 (Advt.), 4 track stereo record and replay using popular Compact Cassettes. **1976** K. Bonfiglioli *Something Nasty in Woodshed* x. 119 Even on virgin tape I still got the gentle muttering if it was played through on 'record'..at a nil recording level.

re-cord (riː'kɔːd), *v.*[2] [f. re- 5 a + cord *v.*[1]] *trans.* To cord again, in senses of that vb.

1797 *Term Rep.* VII. 182 All that they had done was to measure the wood and re-cord a very small part of it. **1869** *1st Rep. Dep. Kpr. Irel.* 14 The document sought is usually found in a few minutes, and the piece re-corded and returned to its place.

recordable (rɪ'kɔːdəb(ə)l), *a.* [f. record *v.* + -able.] Capable of being recorded, admitting of record. Also, worthy of record, memorable.

1483 Caxton *Gold. Leg.* 258/2 Thou that arte called to the lyf perdurable..to refection not recordable. **1815** Jane Austen *Emma* xxxviii, Of very important, very recordable events. **1858** Carlyle *Fredk. Gt.* IX. xi. II. 541 Prince Lichtenstein..does nothing else recordable in Berlin. **1917** *Wireless World* May 87 It might prove useful when signals of recordable strength are obtainable. **1971** *Jrnl. Gen. Psychol.* Jan. 168 Psychologists sometimes deal with body process in either recordable terms or in hypothetical body-process terms. **1974** 'M. Innes' *Appleby's Other Story* viii. 62 Everything recordable about this room had been recorded.

Recordak (rɪ'kɔːdæk). Also with small initial. The proprietary name of an apparatus manufactured by Kodak Ltd. for producing a photographic record of a series of documents, as bank cheques, etc.

1929 *Encycl. Brit.* XVII. 805/1 G. L. McCarthy..has designed a camera intended to photograph upon a strip of motion picture film all the checks passing through a bank. This camera, which is known as the 'Recordak', provides a permanent record which greatly diminishes the risk of fraud. **1937** *Trade Marks Jrnl.* 31 Mar. 360/2 Recordak... Photographic apparatus and parts thereof,..and films prepared for exhibition. Kodak Limited,..London,..; manufacturers. **1942** *R.A.F. Jrnl.* 2 May 11 The Recordak machine has replaced the clumsy methods of the Tours' post office. The airgraph service is now established. **1948** E. L. Irey *Tax Dodgers* xiii. 251 It was the only bank in Atlantic City which used a recordak. **1967** Cox & Grose *Organization & Handling Bibl. Rec. by Computer* 185 In 1956 we installed a 'magnetic tape to microfilm' device..and decentralized the whole file, using about forty Recordak readers, each containing all of the 160 million names.

re'cordal. *rare*$^{-1}$. [-al[1].] = record *sb.*

1859 T. S. Henderson *Mem. E. Henderson* i. 13 Boyish escapades which are not worth recordal.

†**re'cordance.** *Obs. rare.* [a. OF. *recordance* (13th c.) = It. *ricordanza*: or f. record *v.*[1] and -ance.] Remembrance.

1490 Caxton *Eneydos* xvi. 61 Hauynge noo mynde ne recordaunce for to goo conquere the cytees. *Ibid.* xxv. 90 For often commeth in mynde, to theym of good recordaunce [etc.]. **1592** Wyrley *Armorie* 145 Recordaunce make with griefe and dolefulnes. **1630** J. Taylor (Water P.) *Verbum Sempiternum* Wks. III. 131/2 This Booke againe, againe, Recordance brings.

So †**re'cordancy.** *Obs. rare*$^{-1}$.

1654 Cokaine *Dianea* IV. 364, I know the Recordancie of thy vertues have no need of Commiserations.

re'cordant, *a. rare.* [f. as prec. + -ant.] Containing a record, reminiscent.

1813 in *Parr's Wks.* (1828) VIII. 656 Monument or memorial recordant of the virtues..of man. **1877** Ruskin *St. Mark's Rest* II. iv. 42 They are merely shapes of amphora..usefully recordant of different ages of the wine.

recordar, obs. Sc. form of recorder[2].

re'cordate, *v. rare*$^{-1}$. [f. ppl. stem of L. *recordārī* to record.] *trans.* To remember, recollect.

1830–2 Carleton *Traits* (1843) I. 131 When Rose recovered, she seemed as if trying to recordate what had happened.

recordation (rɛkɔ'deɪʃən). [a. OF. *recordation* (14–16th c.), or ad. L. *recordātiōn-em* (hence also Sp. *recordacion*, It. *ricordazione*), n. of action f. *recordārī* to record.]

†**1.** The faculty of remembering or recollecting.

1398 Trevisa *Barth. De P.R.* v. iii. (Bodl. MS.), In the hyndermeste [cell of the brain is] recordacioun and mynde. **1594** T. B. *La Primaud. Fr. Acad.* II. 163 For this cause some Philosophers attribute vnto man beside memorie both recordation and remembrance. **1666** J. Smith *Old Age* (ed. 2) 46 Another receptacle for the intelligible species, which they call Reminiscency or Recordation.

†**2.** Remembrance or recollection *of* something.

c **1450** tr. *De Imitatione* III. xxiv. 94 Of þe recordacion of þe manyfolde benefetes of god. **1475** *Bk. Noblesse* (Roxb.) 3 The recordacion of actis and dedis in armes of so many famous..Kingis. *a* **1540** Barnes *Wks.* (1573) 351/2 They doe..pray vnto them in remembraunce and recordation of the first fruits. **1579** Fenton *Guicciard.* (1618) 147 Ioyning to that new offence a recordation of old iniuries done against him. **1609** [Bp. W. Barlow] *Answ. Nameless Cath.* 159 It strooke a..recordation of their former disloyaltie into our first parents. **1657** W. Morice *Coena quasi Κοινὴ* Diat. v. 244 The recordation thereof, and external acknowledgment of Christ to be the Redeemer [etc.]. **1881** Meredith *Tragic Comedians* I. iii. 40 She was prepared to express her recordation of the circumstance in her diary.

attrib. **1748** Richardson *Clarissa* (1811) III. x. 71 Let me call myself back to my recordation-subject. Thou needest not remind me of my Rosebud.

†**3.** An act of commemorating or making mention; a commemorative account. *Obs.*

1598 Yong *Diana* Pref., Discurring most of those townes and places in it with a pleasant recordation of my pen. **1609** [Bp. W. Barlow] *Answ. Nameless Cath.* 69 A short, but pithy and worthy recordation of Her Clement gouernment. **1670** Walton *Life Donne* 63 Methinks they be persons that seem to challenge a recordation in this place.

4. The action or process of recording or committing to writing.

1802–12 Bentham *Ration. Judic. Evid.* (1827) I. 279 Notation: or say recordation, registration, scription, note taking. **1831** *Examiner* 723/2 An accurate recordation or representation of the transactions of an individual. **1877** Burroughs *Taxation* 326 It is difficult to perceive upon what principle recordation is necessary. **1924** G. W. Thompson *Commentaries on Mod. Law of Real Property* VIII. liv. 274 The majority rule holds to the tenet that the recordation of an instrument void on its face is not of itself constructive notice. **1938** *U.S. Statutes at Large* LII. 1006 Recordation of Aircraft Ownership. *Ibid.*, Every such conveyance so recorded..shall be valid as to all persons without further recordation. **1948** *Columbia Law Rev.* Dec. 1248 Recordation of title to chattels is normally governed by local laws. **1962** *Iowa Law Rev.* Winter 227 Was his recordation at that time at such place in the records that it should be concluded [etc.]?

attrib. **1802–12** Bentham *Ration. Judic. Evid.* (1827) II. 94 Every cause is recordation-worthy, unless in so far as some special reason can be shewn to the contrary. **1976** *Washington Post* 19 Apr. c 10/4 All costs incident to settlement and conveyancing, including..recordation costs and taxes..will be at the cost of the purchaser.

recordative (rɪ'kɔːdətɪv), *a.* [a. obs. F. *recordatif* (16th c.) or ad. late L. *recordātīv-us* (once): see RECORDATE *v.* and -IVE.] Commemorative.

1551 GARDINER in Foxe *A. & M.* (1563) 795/1 A sacrifice recordatiue of that only sacrifice of the crosse. **1607** *Schol. Disc. agst. Antichr.* I. i. 32 There be Papists that tollerate Images only for their signification and as they are recordatiue. **1811–31** BENTHAM *Ess. Lang.* Wks. 1843 VIII. 297 Recordative of the matter of thought. **1898** *Month* June 646 In the few sentences recordative of his teaching.

Hence **re'cordatively** *adv.*

1633 AMES *Agst. Cerem.* II. 291 If we admitte of significant Images, as religious Ceremonies, I would fain know how we in England can condemne, those that worship..them commemoratively or recordatively.

†**recordator.** *Obs.*$^{-1}$ [a. med.L. *recordātor*, f. *recordārī* to RECORD.] = RECORDER[1].

1691 WOOD *Ath. Oxon.* I. 246 Dav. Middleton of Gwenock, Recordator of North-Wales.

recorded (rɪ'kɔːdɪd), *ppl. a.* [f. RECORD *v.*[1] + -ED[1].] **1.** †**a.** Tuned or musically rendered. *Obs.* **b.** Put on record, preserved in writing. ***recorded delivery***, a Post Office service whereby the safe delivery of an item of mail is recorded in a register signed by the recipient; also *ellipt.*, a letter or package sent by recorded delivery.

1568 T. HOWELL *Arb. Amitie* (1879) 83 With ioyes the Nightingal gan rayse, hir right recorded song. **1603** SHAKS. *Meas. for M.* II. iv. 61, I (now the voyce of the recorded Law) Pronounce a sentence. **1606** —— *Macb.* V. v. 21 To the last Syllable of Recorded time. **1871** FREEMAN *Hist. Ess.* Ser. I. i. 27 An age of recorded history for one nation, is an age before recorded history for another. **1877** *Nature* XVI. 446/2 The recorded ascents to the height of 21,000 feet are extremely few. **1961** *Use Recorded Delivery* (G.P.O. Leaflet P.L. 140) 2 Recorded delivery is designed for the customer who wants to be able to prove, if necessary, that a letter or packet has been delivered. **1968** R. PETRIE *MacLurg goes West* I. iv. 31 There was this package, see. Registered. No. I'm wrong there; it was that other thing. Recorded delivery, with a little orange sticker on the top. **1969** W. J. BURLEY *Death in Willow Pattern* i. 8 The post—two recorded deliveries among the rest. **1977** 'E. CRISPIN' *Glimpses of Moon* xii. 256 A letter marked in one place 'Special Delivery', and in another, 'Recorded Delivery'.

2. a. Of sounds or images: converted into a durable form (e.g. on disc, tape, or film) from which the original can be reproduced by suitable apparatus.

1932 *Radio Times* 29 July 242/1 The B.B.C...[has] decided to supplement with recorded programmes the proposed broadcasting service from the new Empire short-wave transmitter at Daventry. **1949** *Ibid.* 15 July 13/1 Stand Easy... (Wednesday's recorded broadcast). **1958** M. KELLY *Christmas Egg* III. 106 He was addicted to the collection of recorded music. **1962** A. NISBETT *Technique Sound Studio* 167 Recorded effects consist principally of those which cannot conveniently be created in the studio: cars, aircraft, birdsong,..and so on. **1975** *Sci. Amer.* May 45/1 A 'videodisc' system that presents recorded pictures and sound on a standard television set will be put on the home-appliance market next year.

b. Of a recording medium: bearing a recording.

1962 A. NISBETT *Technique Sound Studio* 243 A little of the bias signal can still be heard if recorded tape is pulled slowly over the reproducing head.

Hence **re'cordedly** *adv.*

1893 *Temple Bar* Apr. 511 Mrs. Charles Kemble, an actress, recordedly, and a character.

recorder[1] (rɪ'kɔːdə(r)). Also 4–5 **recordour.** [Orig. a. AF. *recordour*, OF. *recordeour*, *-eur* (14th c.); in later use partly f. RECORD *v.*[1] + -ER[1].]

1. a. Formerly, a certain magistrate or judge having criminal and civil jurisdiction in a city or borough. Now, in England and Wales, a barrister or solicitor appointed as a part-time judge presiding esp. over certain Crown Courts (see quot. 1971).

The Recorder was originally a person with legal knowledge appointed by the mayor and aldermen to 'record' or keep in mind the proceedings of their courts and the customs of the city, his oral statement of these being taken as the highest evidence of fact. (See Riley *Munimenta Gildhallæ* I. 42–3.) The Recorder of London, to whom most of the early evidence refers, is still appointed by the court of aldermen; elsewhere the appointment is made by the crown, the duties of the office being regulated by the Municipal Corporations Act of 5 and 6 William IV and subsequent enactments.

[*c* **1325** in Riley *Munim. Gildh.* (Rolls) II. I. 151 Solonc le record des Recordours de la Gilhale. **1347** *Rolls of Parlt.* II. 186/1 Au Mair & au Recordour & as Aldermannes de mesme la Citee. **1419** *Liber Albus* in Riley *Munim. Gildh.* (Rolls) I. III. I. 182 Et si les parties pleident a jugement, le jugement serra done par bouche de loure Recordoure. *Ibid.* I. 308 Sacramentum Recordatoris. Vous jurrez, qe vous serrez foialx et loialx..a la citee de Loundres, en loffice du Recordour.]

1426 in *Surtees Misc.* (1888) 8 [At York] Richard Russell, Thomas Bracebryg, aldermen, Gui Rouclyff, recordour. **1463–4** *Rolls of Parlt.* V. 504/2 Aldermen or Recorders of the same Cite [London]. *a* **1548** HALL *Chron., Hen. VIII* 142 b, Whatsoeuer was saied by the Recorder, in his excuse, was taken as..a dissimulacion or a mocke. **1594** SHAKS. *Rich. III*, III. vii. 30 His answer was, the people were not vsed To be spoke to, but by the Recorder. **1607** COWELL *Interpr.* **1630** *Galway Arch.* in *10th Rep. Hist. MSS. Comm.* App. V. 476 The Recorder of this towne..shall have per annum tenn poundes sterling. **1642** CALTHROP *Liberties London* 23 That the Recorder shall or may *ore-tenus*,..record and certifie the Customs being traversed. And his certificate shall be as strong in the Law as the verdict of 22 men. **1709** STEELE *Tatler* No. 39 ¶4 [He] has, by Advice of the Recorder of Oxford, brought this Action. **1765** BLACKSTONE *Comm.* I. 76 The customs of London differ from all others in point of trial: for, if the existence of the custom be brought in question, it shall not be tried by a jury, but by certificate from the lord mayor and aldermen by the mouth of their recorder. **1850** HT. MARTINEAU *Hist. Peace* V. iii. II. 244 Boroughs having a Recorder have separate Courts of Quarter-Sessions of the peace. **1886** *Encycl. Brit.* XX. 160/1 The recorders of Dublin and Cork are judges of the civil bill courts in those cities. **1955** *Times* 3 May 6/3 At the first trial before the Recorder (Sir Gerald Dodson) earlier in the session the jury had failed to agree. **1965** *Modern Law Rev.* XXVIII. v. 563 The Recorder of Manchester..interrupted a case..to address us on the iniquitous way in which his court was being used. **1971** *Act 19 & 20 Eliz. II.* c. 23 §. 21 Her Majesty may from time to time appoint qualified persons, to be known as Recorders, to act as part-time judges of the Crown Court and to carry out such other judicial functions as may be conferred on them under this or any other enactment... Every appointment of a person to be a Recorder shall be of a person recommended to Her Majesty by the Lord Chancellor, and no person shall be qualified to be appointed a Recorder unless he is a barrister or solicitor of at least ten years' standing. **1972** *Daily Mail* 2 Aug. 6/4 Judges' itineraries can be changed, solicitors can sit as recorders. **1979** T. SKYRME *Changing Image Magistracy* 219 New-style Recorders differed from their predecessors in that they were not affiliated to any borough, or to any other local government area, but might be required to sit in any part of the Circuit. They were also required before appointment to undertake to sit on not less than twenty days a year.

transf. **1593** DONNE *To C'tess Huntingdon* xvii, I but your Recorder am in this..A ministerial notary.

†**b.** The chief justice of an East Indian settlement. *Obs.*

1800 *Asiatic Ann. Reg., St. Papers* 5/2 So much of the charter..for erecting the Courts of Recorder at Madras and Bombay, as relates to the appointment of Recorder.

†**2.** A witness. *Obs.*

c **1440** *Promp. Parv.* 426/1 Recordowre, wytnesse berer, *testis.* **1522** *Knaresborough Wills* (Surtees) I. 14 Also I wyll John Wylkes..and Richard Roundell to be recorders with other moo. **1556** *Richmond Wills* (Surtees) 87 Recorders hereof, Lawranse Robinson..withe other mo. **1607** COWELL *Interpr.* s.v., I find not that wee in our Courts (especially in the Kings Courts) stand much upon the number of recorders or witnesses for the strength of the testimonie which the record maketh.

3. One who records or sets down in writing.

Recorder of the Great Roll, a former officer of the Scottish Court of Exchequer, also called *Clerk of the Pipe*.

1537 BIBLE (Matthew) *1 Kings* iv. 3 Jeosaphath the sonne of Ahilud the recorder. **1640** BP. HALL *Episc.* II. xix. 198 Faithfull recorders of all occurrences that befell the Church. **1771** LUCKOMBE *Hist. Print.* 10 He had got Corsellis into his hands, as the recorder imports, so many years before. **1830** D'ISRAELI *Chas. I*, III. xvii. 370 The faithful recorder of our once country-customs. **1834** *Act 4 & 5 Will. IV*, c. 16 (*title*) An Act to abolish the Office of Recorder of the Great Roll or Clerk of the Pipe in the Exchequer in Scotland. **1871** BLACKIE *Four Phases* i. 3 A faithful..recorder of what he heard and saw.

4. A recording apparatus; *Telegr.*, a device in a telegraphic instrument for recording the signals received. Also, †the recording part of an early gramophone or phonograph. Now *spec.* a tape-recorder. (See also *siphon recorder*.)

1873 F. JENKIN *Electr. & Magn.* xxiii. §6 Keeping..the glass tube end of the recorder within a very narrow strip of paper. **1876** *Nature* XV. 102/1 The Recorder consists of a powerful electro-magnet [etc.]. **1895** *Daily News* 29 Jan. 6/5 The Thompson and Marsden Patent Recorder..is a machine to be attached to the indicator posts of steam vessels for recording..every order as it is given by the master from the bridge to the engineer below. **1899** *T. Eaton & Co. Catal.* Spring & Summer 191/2 A Columbia Graphophone, with clockwork motor, recorder, reproducer, hearing tube, speaking tube and horn. *Ibid.* 191/3 Recorder, with sapphire point, $5.00. Reproducer, with sapphire point, $5.00. **1902** *Encycl. Brit.* XXXI. 680/1 The recorder describes a series of spirals diminishing from the circumference to the centre of the disc. **1908** *Sears, Roebuck Catal.* 201/3 Recorder, for..our special home graphophone. **1914** *Cassier's Engineering* XLV. 414/2 Typical thermoelectric recorders were..described. **1935** *Discovery* Nov. 324/1 The necessary constancy of motion of cinematographic film in recorders, reproducers, printers, and associated apparatus. **1948**, etc. [see *flight recorder* s.v. FLIGHT *sb.*[1] 15]. **1957** *Times* 13 Dec. 18/2 The Minifon pocket recorder is..regarded as an essential item for every-day use in the office. **1959** W. S. SHARPS *Dict. Cinemat.* 109/1 A magnetic recorder is equipment incorporating an electromagnetic transducer..for recording electric signals as magnetic variations in the medium. **1971** *Engineering* Apr. 105/1 (Advt.), One of Bell & Howell's portable, multi-channel recorders is the answer. **1973** A. BROINOWSKI *Take One Ambassador* iii. 32 She cocked an eyebrow over her mini-cassette recorder.

5. *attrib.* and *Comb.*, as ***recorder-reproducer***.

1937 *Jrnl. Soc. Motion Picture Engineers* XXIX. 217 (*caption*) Magnetic recorder-reproducer. **1970** *Proc. IEEE* LVIII. 886 (*heading*) Signal recorder-reproducer using a coherent light source and a photographic film record.

re'corder[2]. Forms: 5–6 recordre, 5 *Sc.* -our, 6 *Sc.* -ar, (5 recourder), 5– recorder. [app. f. RECORD *v.*[1] (senses 2 and 3) + -ER[1].] **a.** A wind instrument of the flute or flageolet kind (see quot. 1626).

The popularity of the instrument spread in the twentieth century after its revival by Arnold Dolmetsch in 1919.

1430–40 LYDG. *Bochas* II. xv. (1554) 54 b, Pan..Of recorders fond fyrst the melodies. *c* **1450** HOLLAND *Howlat* 759 The rote, and the recordour,..The trumpe, and the talburn. **1542** UDALL *Erasm. Apoph.* 5 b, Yf a manne would fayn bee reputed a good player on the recordres. **1598** YONG *Diana* 475 One of them plaied on a Lute; another on a Harpe; another made a maruellous sweet countertenour vpon a Recorder. **1626** BACON *Sylva* §221 The Figure of Recorders, and Flutes, and Pipes are straight; But the Recorder hath a less Bore and a greater; Above, and below. **1683** TRYON *Way to Health* 655 Flutes or Recorders are a brave noble Instrument, being skilfully handled. **1719** D'URFEY *Pills* (1872) IV. 94 All maids that make trial of a Lute or a Viol,..If you like not this Order, come try my Recorder. **1773** BARRINGTON in *Phil. Trans.* LXIII. 250 A musical instrument, formerly used in England, called a recorder. **1791** COWPER *Iliad* x. 14 Pipes, and recorders, and the hum of war. **1920** *Glasgow Herald* 10 Aug. 6 One was able to understand why the Greeks went into battle to the soft strains of solemn music rendered on flutes and recorders. **1932** R. DONINGTON *Work & Ideas A. Dolmetsch* 16 The first group of early instruments to regain something of its original popularity has been the family of recorders, or English flutes. Many hundreds of Dolmetsch recorders are already in use. **1958** M. DOLMETSCH *Personal Recoll. A. Dolmetsch* viii. 88 Our broken consorts now, for the first time, included the recorder, the instrument employed being, of course, the ancient boxwood and ivory recorder which Arnold had brought over from England. It was played by his first recorder pupil, namely the Harvard Professor Peabody. **1962** E. HUNT *Recorder & its Music* 7 The present-day meteoric return to popularity of the recorder—whose seductive tone charmed the ears of Henry VIII, Shakespeare and Pepys—is a development unparalleled in the history of any other musical instrument. **1976** D. MUNROW *Instr. Middle Ages & Renaissance* i. 14/1 The essential features of the recorder are its beak-shaped mouthpiece and the number of its finger-holes: seven finger-holes plus a thumb-hole.

†**b.** One of the pipes of an organ. Also *transf.*

1613 *Organ Specif. Worcester Cathedral*, The particulars of the great organ..1 recorder of mettal, a stopt pipe. **1650** BULWER *Anthropomet.* 92 In the curious Machin of speech, the Nose is added as a Recorder, to advance the melodious eccho of the sound.

†**c.** *transf.* One who plays a recorder. *Obs.*$^{-1}$

1630 J. TAYLOR (Water P.) *Gt. Eater Kent* 5 Such are poets, trumpetters, cornets, recorders, pipers, bag-pipers.

recordership (rɪ'kɔːdəʃɪp). [f. RECORDER[1] + -SHIP.] The office, or term of office, of a recorder.

1553 *Shrewsbury MSS.* in *15th Rep. Hist. MSS. Comm.* App. X. 13 It ys supposed to be incident to his office of recordarshipp. **1678** LADY CHAWORTH in *12th Rep. Hist. MSS. Comm.* App. V. 45 To confirme your Lordship's election to the Recordership of Grantham. **1689** J. BENT *Bloody Assizes* 13 To whose influence..he attributed his dismission from the Recordership. **1835** *Fraser's Mag.* XII. 64 The fees of registration and recordership. **1884** *Law Times* LXXVII. 248/1 County Court judges could retain their recorderships after their appointment. **1975** *Daily Tel.* 5 Nov. 12/5 (*heading*) Recordership for woman solicitor.

recording (rɪ'kɔːdɪŋ), *vbl. sb.* [-ING[1].] The action of the vb. RECORD in various senses.

†**1.** Remembrance, recollection; meditation. *Obs.*

1340 *Ayenb.* 55 Þe blisse þet hi habbeþ ine þe recordinge. **1382** WYCLIF *2 Tim.* i. 5 Takinge recordinge [*gloss* or mynde] of that feith, that is in thee. **1483** CAXTON *G. de la Tour* N iv b, They whiche kepe them self fro recordynge of ony wordes. **1519** HORMAN *Vulg.* 277 Huntyng is a playn recordyng of warre. **1559** *Homilies* I. *Exhort. Holy Script.* Bj, Continual readyng and recordyng of Gods worde.

2. The practising or singing of birds.

1530 PALSGR. 261/1 Recordyng of byrdes, *patois.* **1611** COTGR., *Resonnance*,..a recording, as of birds. **1681** W. ROBERTSON *Phraseol. Gen.* (1693) 1053 The recording of birds, *modulatio avium alterna.* **1773** BARRINGTON in *Phil. Trans.* LXIII. 250 The next stage in the notes of a bird is termed, by the bird-catchers, recording. **1852** MISS PRATT *Nat. Songst.* 49 This practising is by bird fanciers called recording.

3. a. The action of setting down or putting on record. Also *attrib.*

1662 STILLINGFL. *Orig. Sacr.* IV. i. §1 So certain a recording of them, as may be least liable to any suspicion of imposture or deceit. **1684** I. MATHER (*title*) An Essay for the recording of Illustrious Providences. **1838** W. BELL *Dict. Law Scot.* 827 This recording is necessary, in order that the deed may have the benefit of the statute.

b. The action or process of recording sound or television pictures.

1904 S. R. BOTTONE *Talking Machines & Records* 67 Male voices generally come out more true to the singer's timbre than ladies', the delicate overtones of these latter being more altered in recording. **1923** O. MITCHELL *Talking Machine Industry* ii. 15 Mr. Fenby,..in 1863, took out a patent for the electrical recording and reproducing of sound. **1935** *Discovery* Oct. 309/1 The air plant has to be shut off for a few minutes during an actual recording, on account of the noise of the air being forced through the ventilators. **1976** I. R. SINCLAIR *Master Stereo Cassette Recording* i. 5 Magnetic recording..is almost as old in concept as disc recording, but has had to wait for modern technology to be developed to the stage at which it could be used successfully.

4. A representation of sounds or pictures in a form from which the original can be reproduced by suitable apparatus.

1932 *New Yorker* 11 June 46/3 Accepting the recordings as accurate, I venture that Mme. Leider is a musicianly performer with a fine sense of text. **1949** *Radio Times* 15 July 13/1 Sandy Macpherson takes you to 'The Chapel in the Valley' (BBC recording). **1958** J. MOIR *High Quality Sound Reproduction* vii. 130 The standards adopted for 78-r.p.m. recordings have proved unnecessarily robust for electrical reproducers. **1968** *Listener* 18 July 91/1 The

Seekers, lugubriously watching a recording of themselves singing 'The Carnival is Over'. **1977** *Times* 24 Aug. 14/4 The basis of the library will be its gradual acquisition of recordings by poets of their verse at the time of its publication.

5. *attrib.* and *Comb.*, as (sense 3 a) ***recording fee***; (sense 3 b) ***recording deck*** (DECK *sb.*[1] 3 f), ***right, room, session, studio, tape, van***; **recording amplifier**, one provided to amplify the signals supplied to the cutter (in disc recording) or to the recording head (in tape recording); **recording channel**, a circuit or set of equipment used for sound or video recording; **recording engineer**, an engineer responsible for the technical aspects of recording when a sound or video recording is made; **recording head**, a head (HEAD *sb.* 11 g) for recording on to magnetic tape or wire; **recording level**, a measure of the average strength of a recorded signal.

In some cases not clearly distinguishable from the ppl. adj.

1934 *Wireless World* 5 Jan. 9/3 The *recording amplifier is specially designed to amplify the currents delivered by the microphone or 'A' amplifier to a degree suitable for the electrical conditions as determined by the recording head. **1964** A. A. McWilliams *Tape Recording & Reproduction* ix. 185 The purpose of the recording amplifier is to deliver sufficient current to the record head to magnetize the tape correctly over the working frequency range. **1975** G. J. King *Audio Handbk.* vii. 160 The difference signals are finally mixed with the sum signals and pass with the latter through the RIAA equaliser and hence to the cutter head, via the recording amplifier. **1938** *Motion Pict. Sound Engin.* (Acad. Motion Pict. Arts & Sci.) v. 69 A stage *recording channel uses one or more transmitters on the stage to initiate the electrical energy necessary for recording either on film or on disc. **1949** Frayne & Wolfe *Elem. Sound Recording* xi. 184 A complete recording system is known as a recording channel. **1975** G. J. King *Audio Handbk.* x. 237 The controlled amplifier in the recording channel is adjusted in gain by rectified signal from a control amplifier fed from the recording amplifier. **1977** *Times* 24 Aug. 14/2 Three superior *recording decks would cost £8,000. **1962** A. Nisbett *Technique Sound Studio* 268 **Recording engineer* (BBC), professional engineer whose job includes the technical recording of sound and the editing of tape, but not microphone balance and control. **1977** *Gramophone* Mar. 1453/1 It is indifferently balanced, with the recording engineer conspicuously experimenting with his levels. **1898** *Daily News* 15 Aug. 7/1 *Recording fees are regulated solely by the miners themselves. **1934** *Wireless World* 5 Jan. 9/2 The '*recording' and 'reproducing' heads are each provided with a micrometer adjustment for controlling the separation of the pole pieces. **1971** *Physics Bull.* June 359/1 Magnetic tapes of the kind used in computers or as video-tapes in television vary in abrasiveness so that some tapes cause excessive wear of expensive recording heads. **1934** *Wireless World* 5 Jan. 10/2 Provided that the maximum *recording level of 10 dbs. below 1 milliwatt is not seriously exceeded when recording, the distortion due to non-linear magnetic effects is hardly noticeable aurally. **1975** G. J. King *Audio Handbk.* vii. 157 Recording level may be given in terms of amplitude or velocity. **1962** *Recording right [see GEAR *v.* 4 a]. **1907** *Westm. Gaz.* 12 Dec. 9/4 Employees..assisted many of the frightened girls to cross from the blazing building to the Gramophone *recording-rooms. **1975** *Language for Life* (Dept. Educ. & Sci.) xxv. 425 Almost a quarter of the schools had a projection room and 14 per cent a recording room. **1927** *Melody Maker* Sept. 923/1 All their days..appear to be occupied with *recording sessions. **1962** *Times* 5 July 15/4 The raw product of a recording session is a magnetized length of tape. **1928** *Gramophone* Apr. 451 (*heading*) Round the *recording studios. **1958** [see CUT *v.* 23 d]. **1977** *Times* 18 Apr. (Gramophone Suppl.) p. iv/2 Contemporary popular music is to a large extent a child of the recording studio. **1960** *Guardian* 9 Nov. 11/2 The biggest manufacturer of *recording tape in Europe. **1977** *Times* 24 Aug. 14/1 Imagine 10 shelves..holding 380 reels of 10½ in polystyrene recording tape. **1940** P. Fleming *Flying Visit* i. 17 Wires..poured into the streamlined flanks of a..lightly armoured *recording van.

recording (rɪ'kɔːdɪŋ), *ppl. a.* [-ING[2].] **a.** That records, freq. in phr. ***recording angel***.

In some cases not clearly distinguishable from the vbl. sb. used *attrib.* (see prec., sense 5).

1761 Sterne *Tr. Shandy* V. viii, The recording angel, as he wrote it down, dropp'd a tear upon the word. **1781** Cowper *Conversat.* 551 Marble and recording brass decay. **1781** —— *Table-t.* 21 When recording History displays Feats of renown. **1841** Lane *Arab. Nts.* I. 30 Every believer is attended by two guardian and recording angels. **1870** Burton *Hist. Scot* lxv. (1873) VI. 2 Had the Romans been a recording people like the Normans [etc.]. **1892** W. Gilbert *Phonograph* III. 82 Adjust the screw on the guide rod until the recording stylus makes a slight groove on the revolving wax cylinder. **1937** 'M. Innes' *Hamlet, Revenge!* III. iii. 249 Phonetic nicety apart..the machine..combined recording and reproducing units in an unusually compact way. **1949** *Radio Times* 15 July 14 Richard Dimbleby, with the BBC Mobile Recording Unit. **1962** A. Nisbett *Technique Sound Studio* 260 The Peak programme meter (PPM) is used by the BBC and most recording companies.

b. Of measuring instruments: able to produce a record of readings obtained.

1873 F. Jenkin *Electr. & Magn.* xxii. §7 The electro-magnet of the recording instrument. **1904** R. M. Walmsley *Electr. in Service of Man* I. ix. 357 A recording wattmeter, which would record the number of watts at every instant, so that..the total energy could be measured up or calculated. **1930** C. J. Stewart *Aircraft Instruments* viii. 146 It is sometimes necessary to record the temperature of the air during flight, and for this purpose recording thermometers are used. **1961** R. Rawlinson in G. F. Tagg *Pract. Electr. Engin.* III. 363 Situations demanding the use of a recording ammeter are fortunately not common.

recordist (rɪ'kɔːdɪst). [f. RECORD *v.*[1] + -IST.] One who records or makes recordings.

1931 L. Cowan *Recording Sound for Motion Pictures* 384 *Recordist*, person engaged in recording sound. **1938** *Nature* 5 Feb. 226/2 That highly skilled, imaginative, ingenious, agile and patient collaborator in film-making who bears the regrettable though comprehensible title of 'recordist'. **1956** *B.B.C. Handbk.* 1957 65 The Corporation has made steady progress in securing world-wide sources of news in pictures. .. It maintains a staff of newsreel film cameramen and recordists in this country. **1958** *Times* 2 Dec. 3/2 (Advt.), Electro-Encephalography Recordist (single-handed) required. **1960** *Guardian* 9 Nov. 11/1 The federation issued a policy statement for the guidance of amateur recordists. **1966** V. C. Lewis *Bird Recognition* III. 3/1 The recordist of the 'songs' and 'calls' illustrated herewith is of the opinion that the use of sound concentrators..tends to detract from 'naturalness' of the recorded sounds. **1978** *Daily Tel.* 23 Sept. 1/3 All BBC television programme production is threatened from today by an unofficial overtime ban by cameramen and sound recordists.

Recordite ('rɛkɔːdaɪt), *sb.* (and *a.*) *Obs.* exc. *Hist.* [f. the name of the *Record* newspaper + -ITE[1].] One who subscribes to views represented by the evangelical Church of England newspaper, the *Record* (1828–1949). Also *attrib.* or as *adj.*

1853 W. J. Conybeare in *Edin. Rev.* XCVIII. 284 This exaggeration of Evangelicanism, sometimes called the Puritan, sometimes, from its chief organ, the Recordite party, we shall now endeavour to describe. *Ibid.*, Thus from *justification by faith* the Recordite infers the worthlessness of morality. **1875** F. Arnold *Our Bishops & Deans* I. i. 11 We suspect we may supply the ellipse by the words 'Protestants' or 'Recordites'. **1965** W. R. Ward *Victorian Oxford* x. 224 Gladstone arranged with Vice-Chancellor Jeune to delay the by-election till the last possible moment, but his legal adviser Phillimore was still on tenterhooks that 'some *Recordite* would be put up to poll two or three votes and claim to be returned before a committee'.

'recordless, *a.* [f. RECORD *sb.* + -LESS.] Having no record or records; unrecorded.

1854 'G. Greenwood' *Haps & Mishaps* 116 That old, old city of a forgotten and recordless past. **1892** A. E. Lee *Hist. Columb.* (Ohio) I. 62 The line which separates the extinct and recordless races from the races known to history.

recordour, -dre, obs. ff. RECORDER[2].

re-cork (riː'kɔːk), *v.* [RE- 5 a.] *trans.* To cork again; to provide with new corks. Also *fig.*

1843 *Penny Cycl.* XXVII. 464/1 Such also are most liable to the aggressions of insects, and must frequently be re-corked. **1884** *Graphic* 23 Aug. 207/2, I ordered the..bottles to be refilled, recorked, and served a second time. **1906** *Daily Chron.* 3 Apr. 7/4 While he was recorking the bottle Dunstan picked up the glass. **1922** Joyce *Ulysses* 523 (He uncorks himself behind: then, contorting his features, farts loudly.) Take that! (He recorks himself.) **1969** E. Penning-Rowsell *Wines of Bordeaux* xviii. 271 The leading châteaux re-cork their reserves of old wines roughly every twenty-five years.

†recorporification. *Obs.*$^{-1}$ [RE- 5 a.] A making or becoming corporeal again.

1666 Boyle *Orig. Formes & Qual.* 216 This Factitious Vitriol may not be barely a new Production, but partly a Recorporification.

So **†recorporify** *v.*; **recorporize** *v.*

1694 Salmon *Bate's Dispens.* (1713) 490/2 The recorporified Spirits have a greater Sphere of Activity.. than the Substances purely natural. **1781** *Westm. Mag.* IX. 74 Spirits re-corporised render the water colder than the salts do, out of which they were drawn.

‖recorte (re'korte). *Bull-fighting.* [Sp., lit. 'cutting, trimming'.] A pass by which the torero cuts short the bull's charge.

1925 E. Hemingway in *This Quarter* I. II. 217 A series of acceptable veronicas ending in a very Belmontistic recorte. **1932** —— *Death in Afternoon* vii. 67 A recorte is any pass with the cape that..stops him brusquely. **1932** R. Campbell *Taurine Provence* iii. 71 The cape, the use of which varies from the vulgar vuelta and recorte to the most perfect designs. **1967** McCormick & Mascareñas *Compl. Aficionado* ii. 54 The banderillero..performs a rough *recorte* to fix the toro gently before he disappears behind a burladero.

†recotising, *vbl. sb. Her. Obs.*$^{-1}$ [RE- 5 a.] A second cotising.

1586 Ferne *Blaz. Gentrie* ii. 69 The Fret is as it were a recotizing of the feeld: but in Armes bended or cotized, the cullors conteined be equally deuided with the feeld.

re'couch, *v. rare*$^{-1}$. [RE- 5 a.] *intr.* To couch again, to retire again to rest.

a **1639** Wotton *Poems, civ Psalm* vii, Then savage Beasts creep from the silent Wood,.. Who when at Morn they All recouch again, [etc.].

recouer(e, -ir, obs. ff. RECOVER *sb.* and *v.*

recouncile, obs. form of RECONCILE *v.*

†re'counsel, *v. Obs.* Forms: α. 4 **reconseyle**, 4 (6 *Sc.*) **-sale**, 5 **-saille**; 4 **reconcele, -sele**, 6 *Sc.* **-sel(l**. β. 4 **recounseil**, 5 **-seille**, 5–6 **-seyll**, 4–5 **-sail**, 6 *Sc.* **-saill, -sale**; 4–5 (6 *Sc.*) **recounsel**, 5 **-selle**, 6 *Sc.* **-sell, -cel(l**. [a. OF. *reconseiller*, ad. L. *reconciliāre* after *conseiller* to COUNSEL. The forms in Eng. follow those of the simple vb.]

1. *trans.* = RECONCILE *v.* 1 and 2.

13.. *Propr. Sanct.* (Vernon MS.) in *Archiv neu. Spr.* LXXXI. 308/55 Crist forsoþe was in heuene þe goode worlde Reconseylinge To him-self. **1382** Wyclif *Matt.* v. 24 Go first for to be recounseilid to thi brother. *c* **1450** *Mirour Saluacioun* 2370 And with his blode vs to godde his fadere to reconsaille. **1482** Caxton *Trevisa's Higden* II. xxiii. 98 b, Jason recounseylled and toke ayene his wyfe media. **1533** Gau *Richt Vay* (S.T.S.) 42 We war inimis with god bot now we ar reconsalit be the deid of his sone.

2. *Sc.* = RECONCILE *v.* 4.

1501 Douglas *Pal. Hon.* Prol. 94 O Nature Quene, and O ȝe lustie May,.. Recounsell me out of this greit affray. **1533** Bellenden *Livy* I. xi. (S.T.S.) I. 63 He kest him to recounsell him agane to the favoure of his pepill. **1563** Winȝet *Wks.* (S.T.S.) II. 4 He apperis weil to hef bene recouncelit vnto his fauour.

3. = RECONCILE *v.* 5 a and b. Also, to bring back, or admit again, to allegiance.

1375 Barbour *Bruce* IX. 740 Thou has a quhill renyit thi fay; Bot thou reconsalit now mon be. **1496** *Dives & Paup.* (W. de W.) VII. xviii. 305/2 Yf ony curate..recounseyll hym that wyll not amende hym..he doth symonye. **1572** *Sc. Acts Jas. VI* (1814) III. 72/1 Quhill thay haue recounsallit tham selfis to the trew Kirk submittand þame selfis to the Discipline thairof. *a* **1578** Lindesay (Pitscottie) *Chron. Scot.* (S.T.S.) II. 76 Mr. George [Wishart] ansuerit..he wald..be recounsellit in ony thing his conscience movet him.

4. = RECONCILE *v.* 6.

c **1450** *St. Cuthbert* (Surtees) 7147 þe new kirke was recounsailde Solemply, and reparailde. **1496** *Dives & Paup.* (W. de W.) I. lxiv. 108/2 Yf it [pollution] myght be preued, ther sholde noo preeste synge ne saye noo masse therin, ne bodye be buryed tyll it [the churchyard] were recounseylled ayen by the bysshop. **1533** Bellenden *Livy* v. xxiii, þat þe templis of þe goddis (quhilkis war pollutit & violet be Inemyis) suld be recounseld, renewit, & purifyit.

5. To recover, regain. *rare*$^{-1}$.

c **1400** Maundev. (Roxb.) Pref. 2, I trowe wele þat within a lytill tyme oure riȝt heritage..schuld be recounsailed and putte in to þe handes of þe right heyers of Ihesu Criste.

Hence **†re'counseller; re'counselling** *vbl. sb.*

a **1340** Hampole *Psalter* xliv. 3 þe warld resayued grace of reconcelynge. **1388** Wyclif *Deut.* v. 5 Y was reconcelere and mediatour bitwixe God and ȝou in that tyme. —— *Isa.* lx. 10 In my recounselyng Y had merci on thee. **1483** *Cath. Angl.* 301/2 A Recounsillynge, *reconsiliacio*.

recounsile, -syle, obs. ff. RECONCILE *v.*

re'count, *sb.*[1] *rare.* [f. RECOUNT *v.*[1], in early use perh. after OF. *raconte* (Godef.).] Account, narrative, narration.

c **1489** Caxton *Blanchardyn* liii. 204 And for the recounte of their aduenture, they chased Subyon [etc.]. **1582** T. Watson *Centurie of Love* lx, No Night with sleepe shall close mine eyes at all, Before I make recount of such a debt. *a* **1635** Naunton *Fragm. Reg.* (Arb.) 34 In recount of whom I proceed with Sir Philip Sidney. **1905** *Daily Chron.* 20 July 3/1 We..are not bored by the intolerable recount of flukey rounds.

recount ('riːkaʊnt, riː'kaʊnt), *sb.*[2] [RE- 5 a; cf. RECOUNT *v.*[2]] A new count; a second or subsequent enumeration (*esp.* of votes in an election).

1884 *Pall Mall G.* 22 Nov. 7/2 In reply to the Conservative application for a re-count. **1890** *Times* 21 Oct. 5/4 The Government Census Bureau has refused to make a recount of the population of New York.

recount (rɪ'kaʊnt), *v.*[1] Also β. 5–6 **recompte**, 6 **-coumpte**. [a. ONF. and AF. *reconter, recunter* (12th c.) f. *re-* RE- + *conter* to COUNT. Cf. also F. *raconter*.]

1. *trans.* To relate or narrate; to tell in detail; to give a full or detailed account of (some fact, event, etc.). Also const. *to* (a person).

α. **1456** Sir G. Haye *Law Arms* (S.T.S.) 7 As is re-countit be Sanct Gregore the haly doctour. **1483** Caxton *G. de la Tour* K iij b, Gladde to here telle and recounte the goodness of them. *a* **1533** Ld. Berners *Huon* lxxxiii. 262, I am ashamyd to recounte it. **1599** Nashe *Lenten Stuffe* 41 To recount *ab ouo*..howe the Herring first came to be a fish. **1617** Moryson *Itin.* I. 186 He ceased not to bewaile my misery, and to recount my Tragedy. **1653** H. Cogan tr. *Pinto's Trav.* ix. 28 He recounted unto me, that he had in all but six thousand men. **1782** Miss Burney *Cecilia* IX. v, Mrs. Hill wept for joy in recounting how well she succeeded. **1809** Malkin *Gil Blas* VII. ii. ¶2, I recounted..all that had passed..without garbling the facts in any particular. **1858** Doran *Crt. Fools* 269 The two..fell to recounting to each other many a good story.

β. *c* **1477** Caxton *Jason* 45 b, I shal recompte to yow my lyf and all myn astate. **1568** Grafton *Chron.* II. 803 With yᵉ which aunswere John Greene returned, recompting the same to king Richarde. **1575** Turberv. *Venerie* i. 3, I have thought good to recoumpte this historie.

b. (With plural object.) To relate in order; to enumerate by particulars.

α. **1483** Caxton *Gold. Leg.* 428 b/1 Who that coude re-counte alle the myracles doon by hym. *a* **1533** Ld. Berners *Huon* xxi. 60 Yf I sholde recounte all the aduentures,..it sholde be to longe a processe to show it. **1584** R. Scot *Discov. Witchcr.* x. ii. (1886) 143 Macrobius recounteth five differences of images. **1667** Milton *P.L.* VII. 112 To recount Almightie works What words or tongue of Seraph can suffice? **1745** Fielding *True Patriot* Wks. 1775 IX. 304 To enumerate all those vices which I have already declined recounting. **1816** J. Scott *Vis. Paris* (ed. 5) 267 These are advantages and gratifications which it makes one almost feverish to recount. **1870** M. D. Conway *Earthw. Pilgr.* viii. 113 Rites and prayers, recounting to God the items of his magnificence.

β. **1561** Daus tr. *Bullinger on Apoc.* Pref. (1573) 3 He recompteth most plentifully..all the dolefull destinies of the Church. **1601** Bp. W. Barlow *Defence* 171 In the articles which the auncient fathers doe recompt.

†**2.** To consider or reflect on; to debate or weigh (*with* or *within* oneself). *Obs.*

1526 *Pilgr. Perf.* (W. de W. 1531) 34 They begyn to recount with them selfe what they haue done. **1582** Stanyhurst *Æneis* I. (Arb.) 18 This Iuno fearing, and old broyls bluddye recounting. *a* **1619** Fotherby *Atheom.* Pref. (1622) 18 To perpend and to recompte within it selfe, that God hath made all his seuerall Creatures. *a* **1656** Ussher *Ann.* (1658) 106 Cambyses in a rage..nor re-counting with himself, that [etc.].

†**b.** To go over, examine. *Obs.*$^{-1}$

1526 *Pilgr. Perf.* (W. de W. 1531) 214 Saynt Crisostom counseyleth the ofte to recount thy conscyence, and to remember..thy..synnes.

†**3.** To regard, consider, or account (a person or thing) as possessing a certain character or quality. Const. *as, for, to be*, or with simple complement. *Obs.*

1526 *Pilgr. Perf.* (W. de W. 1531) 61 b, Than moost of all recount thy selfe but a wretche and a synner. *c* **1550** R. Bieston *Bayte Fortune* A iv b, Thy wordes as Iapes ought wel to be recompted. **1577** Hanmer *Anc. Eccl. Hist.* (1619) 145 There were some..recounted for sacrificers. **1581** J. Bell *Haddon's Answ. Osor.* 330 Recomptyng murther to be a more tollerable offence. **1609** Bible (Douay) *Dan.* Comm., Recounting him also the most renowmed of his time for wisdom. *a* **1661** Fuller *Worthies* (1840) II. 467 Sir William Pæston..is justly recounted a public benefactor.

†**b.** To reckon or mention *among* or *in* (a class). *Obs.*

1560 Becon *New Catech.* v. Wks. I. 433 b, So many as..desired to be recompted among the Christians. **1577** B. Googe *Heresbach's Husb.* II. 94 b, Among Nuttes, is also to be recounted the Hasel Nuttes. *a* **1648** Ld. Herbert *Hen. VIII* (1683) 450 Learned men, in which number Hugh Latimer..and Nicholas Saxton..are recounted.

†**4.** *intr.* and *trans.* To reckon, count *up*. *Obs.*

1547 Boorde *Introd. Knowl.* i. (1870) 124 Whan they haue recounted to a hondred, they saye *Kans.* And if they nomber to a thousand, than they saye *Myle.* *a* **1641** Bp. Mountagu *Acts & Mon.* (1642) 256 Iosephus, recounting up his [Herod's] many wives..hath this excuse for it. **1647** Trapp *Comm. 1 Pet.* v. 9 He will recount from the bloud of righteous Abel..to the bloud of mean Ignatius.

Hence **re'counting** *vbl. sb.*[1]

a **1529** Skelton *Col. Cloute* 1104 But my recountyng is of them that do amys. **1581** Mulcaster *Positions* iii. (1887) 13 If controversie arise, and be worth the recounting, the matter shall not sleepe. *a* **1610** Healey *Epictetus* (1636) 73 The re-counting of thy fortunes is nothing so pleasing unto others.

recount (riː'kaʊnt), *v.*[2] [re- 5 a.] *trans.* To count or reckon over again.

1764 Goldsm. *Trav.* 52 As some lone miser..Bends at his treasure, counts, recounts it o'er. **1838** Dickens *O. Twist* xxvii, Mr. Bumble had re-counted the tea-spoons, re-weighed the sugar-tongs, [etc.]. **1877** Lowell *Night-Watches* 2 While the slow clock, as they were miser's gold, Counts and re-counts the mornward steps of Time.

Hence **re'counting** *vbl. sb.*[2]

1892 *Daily News* 23 Mar. 2/1 The vote being taken first by show of hands and afterwards by a recounting of members standing up.

†**recount**, *v.*[3] Freq. in Caxton for recounter.

c **1489** Caxton *Sonnes of Aymon* i. 52 There they recounted the duke Beues. *Ibid.* 344 etc. **1490** —— *Eneydos* 29 b, Thus rennynge aboute she recounted Eneas.

re'countable, *a. rare.* [f. recount *v.*[1] + -able.] That may be recounted; that admits of being related.

1483 Caxton *Gold. Leg.* 256/2 Laudes and praysynges of the cherubyns and..not recountable Songes of the Seraphyns. **1855** Bagehot *Lit. Stud.* (1895) I. 123 The dinner..only recountable in blank verse.

recountal (rɪ'kaʊntəl). [f. as prec. + -al[1].] The act of recounting, recital.

1861 J. Pycroft *Ways & Words* 270 Hear the poor author's pathetic recountal. **1874** J. Caird in *Gd. Words* Nov. 792 The great deeds of history at the recountal of which our hearts thrill with involuntary admiration.

recounter, *sb.*[1] *rare.* [f. as prec. + -er[1].] One who relates or recounts.

1576 Fleming *Panopl. Epist.* 158 Wise counselers and recounters of honestie and vertue. **1591** Percivall *Sp. Dict.*, *Relator*, a recounter, a teller. **1598** Florio, *Raccontatore*, a reporter, a recounter. **1953** Partridge *Shaggy Dog Story* ii. 17 But not even the most cavalier of casual recounters may omit two extremely significant and pertinent literary examples.

†**recounter**, *sb.*[2] *Obs.* Also 5–6 -tre, 6 *Sc.* reacuntar. [f. the vb. Cf. rencounter *sb.*]

1. A meeting, *esp.* a hostile one; an encounter.

1471 *Paston Lett.* II. 422 Entendyng fro thence to goo foorth..to the recountr of the said enemyes. **1494** Fabyan *Chron.* vii. 372 Many a Cristen man was slayne at that recounter. **1545** Raynold *Byrth Mankynde* 41 In there recountre and metyng, they produce always bygger and bygger vaines and artires. **1599** Hakluyt *Voy.* II. i. 68 He departed towards London, with a good conduct..for feare of any recounters.

b. A blow, stroke. *rare*$^{-1}$.

a **1533** Ld. Berners *Huon* cxx. 431 The Gryffon resyd vp his fete and spredde..his wyngis, and gaue Huon suche a recountre that the noble knyghte was stryken to the erthe.

2. *Sc. Law.* A counter-pledge or security.

1429 *Sc. Acts Jas. I*, c. 7 (1814) 18 [He] sal remayn in ane vnlaw of the courte ande tyne the accioun of the quhilk þe borgh & þe recounter was fundyn. **1471** *Sc. Acts Jas. III* (1814) 101 And þar be excepciouns ane or ma proponit & þaruppone borowis & Recounteris fundin [etc.].

†**re'counter**, *v. Obs.* [f. re- + counter *v.*[1] prob. after F. *rencontrer*: cf. rencounter *v.*]

1. *trans.* To encounter in battle or combat. Also *absol.*, to encounter each other.

c **1425** Wyntoun *Cron.* ix. xxvii. 3224 The awaward..To recountir the first perile, First than entrit in the pres. **1455** *Rolls of Parlt.* V. 279/1 It must hastely be purveid, that they [the king's enemies] mowe..be recountred and resisted. **1485** Caxton *Paris & V.* (1868) 9 [They] recountred eche other so vygorously þat they breke bothe there speres. **1503** *Rolls of Parlt.* VI. 544/2 They were recountred, vanquesshed,..overcome and dyvers put to deth. **1533** Bellenden *Livy* ii. ix. (S.T.S.) I. 162 The romanis..with new curage recounterit þare Inemyis. *a* **1578** Lindesay (Pitscottie) *Chron. Scot.* (S.T.S.) I. 234 Quhilk efterwart gat new speiris and recounterit freischelie agane.

b. To encounter, withstand, resist (a feeling or action).

1470 *Reb. Linc.* (Camden) 17 If they wold have biden, to have recountred theire malice. *a* **1598** Rollock *Lect. Passion* ii. (1616) 24 This taking recounters and meetes our taking by the deuill, and death. **1702** Mrs. Behn *Forc'd Marriage* ii. ii, I must either resolve never to provoke His jealousie, or be able to re-counter [**1671** re'ncounter] his..valour.

2. To encounter or meet by chance; to come upon or fall in with.

1456 Sir G. Haye *Law Arms* (S.T.S.) 227 He passis fra his company..and sa is recounterit be a knycht of Fraunce. **1490** Caxton *Eneydos* xvi. 62 With this rodde fleeynge he..departed the troublouse clowdes that he recountred in hys waye. **1549** *Compl. Scot.* Ded. 7 Ane pure man of perse, quha be chance recountrit kyng darius. **1600** *Gowrie Conspir.* A 2 b, There by accident [he] affirmed to haue recountred a baselike fellow, vnknowne to him.

b. *intr.* To meet or fall in *with* one. *rare*$^{-1}$.

1583 Foxe *A. & M.* (ed. 4) 756/1 Making toward the Turkes, and recountring with the Tartarians.

3. To meet (a person) on arrival. *rare*$^{-1}$.

c **1500** *Melusine* 348 Thus they rode thrugh the toun into the Castel... There were the six bretheren recountred of two noble ladyes.

4. *Sc. Law.* To oppose (the giving of a pledge).

1429 *Sc. Acts Jas. I*, c. 7 (1814) 18 Quhare twa partiis apperis at þe bar and þe tane strek a borgh apone a weir of law þe toþer party sal haf leif to be avisit..quheþir he wil recounter it or nocht... Ande gif he recounteris þe borgh, & strenthis it with resounis [etc.].

5. *Sc.* 'To turn the contrary way, to reverse, to invert; a technical term among tradesmen' (Jamieson 1825).

Hence †**re'countering** *vbl. sb. Obs.*

c **1477** Caxton *Jason* 6 They mette wyth no knightes in recountring..but that they bare hem out of their arsonnes. *c* **1500** *Melusine* 132 [In] that recountryng were many one slayn & wounded. **1533** Bellenden *Livy* ii. x. (S.T.S.) I. 165 But ony recountering or debate, þai gaif..plegeis for peace. **1536** —— *Cron. Scot.* (1821) I. 14 Ilk ane of thame slew othir at thair recountering.

†**re'countermand.** *Obs.*$^{-1}$ [re-.] A recalling or revocation of a decree.

1570 Foxe *A. & M.* (ed. 2) 121/2 The generall recountermaunde sent forth by hym, for the persecution againe of the Christians.

recountless (rɪ'kaʊntlɪs), *a.* [f. recount *sb.*[1] + -less.] Incapable of being recounted.

1601 *Song of Mary* in Farr *S.P. Eliz.* (Parker Soc.) II. 424 Sinne with recountlesse shapes afflicts him. *c* **1650** *Don Bellianis* 68 To whom I render recountless thanks. **1837** R. Wilson *Pleas. Piety* ii. 27 Spring..evolving in recountless forms The leaves of many-tinted green.

†**re'countment.** *Obs.*$^{-1}$ [f. recount *v.*[1] + -ment.] Relation, recital.

1600 Shaks. *A.Y.L.* iv. iii. 141 When..betwixt vs two, Teares our recountments had most kindely bath'd.

recoup (rɪ'kuːp), *sb. Law.* [f. next.] (See quots. and cf. recoupe b.) Also *attrib.*

1860 *Wharton's Law Lex.*, *Recoup*, the keeping back or stopping something which is due; discount; recompense. **1869** [see recoupment]. **1904** H. G. Turner *Hist. Colony Victoria* II. ix. 276 The too general use of the recoup system under which public works were authorised to be paid for out of future loans. **1966** *Public Administration* XLIV. 411 If the recoup mechanism is to do its job.

recoup (rɪ'kuːp), *v.* Also 5, 7 recoupe. [ad. F. *recouper* (12th c.), to cut back, etc., f. *re-* re- + *couper* to cut: see coup *v.*[2] and *sb.*[3]]

†**1.** *trans.* To cut short, interrupt. *Obs. rare*$^{-1}$.

Cf. Cotgrave's rendering of F. *recouper*.

c **1430** *Pilgr. Lyf Manhode* ii. cxvi. (1869) 118 Swich a fool..seith þat he wot wel and vnderstant what folk wolden seye, and recoupeth here woordes, and holt hem as fooles.

2. *Law.* To deduct; to take off or keep back. Also *absol.*, to make a deduction.

1628 Coke *On Litt.* 39 The demandant..shall recoupe the third part of the profits. **1642** tr. *Perkins' Prof. Bk.* xi. §809. 363 This land shall be extended, and the common shall be recouped and deducted. **1672** Manley *Cowell's Interpr.*, *Recoupe*,..to defalke or discount. As if a man hath ten pounds issuing out of certain Lands, and he disseises the Tenant of the Land in an Assise brought by the Disseisee, the Disseisor shall Recoupe the Rent in the Damages. **1869** Waterman *Law of Set-off & Recoupment* 152 *note*, The defendant might recoup for the damages resulting from the plaintiff's want of skill. *Ibid.*, The defendant might recoup damages for a breach of warranty for the thing sold.

3. a. (With double object.) To recompense (a person) for (some loss or outlay); to make up or make good (loss, etc.) to (a person).

1664 in *New England Co.* (1896) 6 A man who hath as little estate to recoupe us the wrongs done us, as he made scruple to doe the same. **1860** Reade *8th Commandm.* 107 So my partner..had run us into fresh expenses, which he was entitled to be recouped. **1870** *Observer* 13 Nov., The amounts returned in sale of land..will tend to recoup the Metropolitan Board a considerable amount of their outlay.

b. To recompense, repay (a person). Also const. *for* (the loss or expense). Freq. *refl.*, to recover what one has expended or lost. Also *absol.* or *intr.*

1862 M. Hopkins *Hawaii* 94 They made reprisals, in the way of pilfering, to recoup themselves for their forced gratuities. **1863** Fawcett *Pol. Econ.* x. vii. (1876) 627 The home trader, when rates increase, will only be able partly to recoup himself by a rise in prices. **1906** L. J. Vance *Terence O'Rourke* i. iii. 19 Each..had seemed to be broken in fortune, and..ready to seize upon any chance to recoup. **1976** C. Bermant *Coming Home* ii. vii. 218, I had..acquired so many debts that if I didn't return to England to recoup, we might have to run for it.

c. *intr.* To regain lost health, vitality, etc.; to recuperate.

Prob. arising from confusion with *recuperate*.

1939 M. Spring Rice *Working-Class Wives* iv. 79 We have sent her away for two years running to help her to recoup. **1955** W. Gaddis *Recognitions* i. ii. 66 The Society recouped: found its own Marguerite.

4. a. To make up for, compensate for, make good.

1860 Reade *8th Commandm.* 107, I offered in Court to recoup these expenses incurred. **1880** *Standard* 11 Dec., How to recoup the loss occasioned to the State revenue by the abolition of the salt tax.

b. To yield in return, make up (an amount).

1868 *Sat. Rev.* 1 Aug. 151/1 Securing to the shareholders dividends that in three or four years would recoup their whole capital. **1870** *Echo* 7 Nov., It is estimated that the aggregate cost of the whole..will be £150,000, and that the amount realised by the sale of land, &c.,..will recoup about £50,000 or £60,000.

Hence **re'coupable**, deductible; **re'couper**, one who recoups or keeps back. (In recent Dicts.)

1885 *Law Rep. 14 Q.B.D.* 491 The dead rent to be recoupable out of royalties during the first sixteen years.

re'coupe, *sb. rare*$^{-0}$. [f. recoup *v.*; cf. F. *recoupe* cuttings, waste.] (See quots.)

The first sense is a mistake based on Manley (1672).

a. 1704 J. Harris *Lex. Techn.* I, *Recoupe*, in Law, is a quick and sharp reply to a peremptory Demand. [Hence in Bailey (1721) and later Dicts.]

b. 1810 Tomlins *Law Dict.*, *Recoupe*, the keeping back or stopping something which is due.

recouped, *a. Her. rare*$^{-0}$. [f. recoup *v.*, or ad. F. *recoupé*.] = couped.

c **1828** Berry *Encycl. Her.*, *Recopyd* or *Recouped*, old English terms for *Couped*.

recouperation (rɪkuːpə'reɪʃən). *nonce-word.* [App. blend of recoup *v.* and recuperation.] = recoupment.

1904 G. B. Shaw *Let.* 23 Nov. (1972) II. 466 It seems to me that unless you were living quite madly beyond your income in the old days, the economies of the last few years ought by this time to have produced some degree of recouperation.

re'couple, *v. rare*$^{-1}$. [re- 5 a.] *trans.* To couple again, reunite. Hence **re'coupling** *vbl. sb.*, a repeated joining in pairs or linking.

1607 Hieron *Wks.* I. 396 In the last day their bodies be raised out of the dust and recoupled to their soules. **1890** W. James *Princ. Psychol.* I. ii. 76 The multiplicity of emotional and instinctive reactions in man, together with his extensive associative power, permit of extensive recouplings of the original sensory and motor partners.

re'coupment. [f. recoup *v.* + -ment.] The act of recouping or recompensing; the fact of being recouped for loss or expense.

Formerly common with ref. to schemes of municipal improvement, which aimed at recouping the community for part of the expense incurred.

1839 *N.Y. State Supreme Court Rep.* (Wendell XXII, 1840) 156 The offer came under the third category, *recoupment.* **1869** Waterman *Law of Set-off & Recoupment* 468 It is evident that recoup or recoupment, in its original sense, was a mere right of reduction from the amount of the plaintiff's recovery. **1880** *Edin. Rev.* Apr. 357 A claim for the recoupment of a fee of which he had not executed the conditions. **1888** *Act 51 & 52 Vict.* c. 20 §5 The amount paid towards such recoupment shall be dealt with as purchase money of the land under this Act. **1905** *Daily Chron.* 18 July 5/5 The full effect of 'recoupment' and 'betterment' would reduce it [*sc.* net cost]. **1953** *Words & Phrases* (St. Paul, Minn.) XXXIX. 28/2 A 'recoupment' is a counterclaim arising out of the contract sued upon, whereas a 'set-off' is a counterclaim arising from an independent transaction. **1977** *Times Educ. Suppl.* 21 Oct. 3/1 A nationwide recoupment scheme to equalize the burden of financing advanced further education.

†**re'cour**, *sb. Obs.* Also 5 -owre. [var. of recover *sb.* Cf. recure *sb.*] Recovery, support, help, resource.

c **1330** *Arth. & Merl.* 4452 (Kölbing) Of þat castel hadde socour þe Sarrazins & gret recour. **1375** Barbour *Bruce* ii.

543 [Thai] entryt and destroyit the tour, And slew the pupill but recour. **1387-8** T. USK *Test. Love* I. iv. (Skeat) I. 14 By no maner of semblaunt..thou lyste not to haue any recour. *c* **1450** LONELICH *Merlin* 204 Thanne was he ryht a sorweful man, For that non recowre ne knew he than.

So †**re'cour** *v. trans.*, to recover. *Obs. rare.* (The form *recoured*, occas. found early in the 17th c., is probably to be taken as = *recov'red.*)

1596 SPENSER *F.Q.* IV. ix. 25 For sometimes Paridell and Blandamour The better had, and bet the others backe; Eftsoones the others did the field recoure [etc.].

†**re'courage.** *Obs.*⁻¹ [RE- 5 a.] Renewal of courage.

1556 J. HEYWOOD *Spider & F.* lxi. 11 The spiders tale he did treate, And what recoorage that did the spiders win.

recouraie, obs. Sc. form of RECOVERY.

†**re'courbled,** *ppl. a. Obs. rare*⁻¹. [ad. OF. *recourbelé, recorbelé*, pa. pple. of *recorbeler*, f. *re-* RE- + *courber* to curve.] Bent back, recurved.

1491 CAXTON *Vitas Patr.* (W. de W. 1495) I. lxii. 113 b/1 Our lorde hadde in his feet and his hondes holes percyd by force of grete naylles recourbled and blont.

recourcy, *Her.*: see RACCOURCY.

recourder, obs. form of RECORDER².

recourere, variant of RECOVERER *Obs.*

†**re'coursary,** *a. Obs.*⁻¹ [f. next + -ARY¹.] Of the nature of a recourse or return.

1662 J. CHANDLER *Van Helmont's Oriat.* 334 Therefore the thought or cogitation reacheth the Young..onely by a reciprocal or recoursary action of government.

recourse (rɪ'kɔəs), *sb.*¹ Also 4-6 recours. [a. F. *recours* (13th c.):—L. *recurs-um*, f. *re-* RE- + *currĕre* to run: see COURSE *sb.*]

†**1. a.** A running, coming, or flowing back, a return (in *lit.* or *fig.* uses), refluence; also, opportunity or passage to return. *Obs.*

c **1386** CHAUCER *Sqr.'s T.* 67, I wol nat taryen yow, for it is pryme,..Vn to my firste I wol haue my recours. **1413** *Pilgr. Sowle* (Caxton 1483) v. xiii. 104 These ben thre glorious recours of the sonne. *c* **1483** SKELTON *Death Edw. IV* 16 What ordeyned God to be terestryall, Without recours to the erth of nature? **1555** BONNER *Necess. Doctr.* C, The Excourse of hym is even unto the helles, and the recourse of him is unto the seate of God. **1591** R. WILMOT *Tancred & Gism.* II. i, How time once past, may neuer haue recourse. **1644** BULWER *Chiron.* 31 The Hand directed towards the Auditours..maintaining its gravity with a swift recourse. **1668** CULPEPPER & COLE *Barthol. Anat.* Man. I. i. 302 The recourse of the Blood into the Heart is hindred.

†**b.** Freq. in phr. ***course and recourse.*** *Obs.*

1461 *Petit. Citizens Exeter* in *West. Morn. News* (1884) 15 Aug. 8/4 To have course and recourse with their boates. **1547** BOORDE *Brev. Health* cclxxi. 90 b, Opilacion or stoppynge of the bloude which hath not his true course nor recourse. **1610** HOLLAND *Camden's Brit.* I. 71 In their courses and recourses [they] observe a warlike kind of motion round. **1653** GATAKER *Vind. Annot. Jer.* 169 [He] delivered the set time of the Suns course and recourse from tropik to tropik.

†**c.** A coming back or round in due season; a periodical recurrence. *Obs.*

1584 R. SCOT *Discov. Witchcr.* VIII. i. (1886) 125 Some Siloah..whereinto at certeine ordinarie recourses of times sicke folke maie plunge themselves. **1653** MILTON *Hirelings* 61 The seaventh day is..a convenient recourse of worship in fit season. *a* **1677** BARROW *Serm.* vii. Wks. 1687 I. 92 The constant rising of the Sun upon us,..the recourse of temperate seasons.

†**2. a.** Course, movement, or flow in some direction; a course, passage, or path *to* or *into* something. *Obs.*

c **1374** CHAUCER *Boeth.* I. met. ii. 4 (Camb. MS.) Which sterre in heuene vseth wandrynge recourses [L. *vagos recursus*]. *c* **1540** BOORDE *Boke for to Lerne* A iv b, That some freshe spryng haue a recourse to noryshe and to refreshe the sayd standynge waters. **1555** EDEN *Decades* 83, I doo not vnderstande howe soo many and soo great ryuers may haue recourse into this north sea. **1620** MARKHAM *Farew. Husb.* II. xviii. (1668) 92 The second dryed up by the air which hath free recourse into it. **1653** HARVEY *Anat. Exerc.* (1673) 61 You shall quickly see the distance betwixt the heart and the ligature emptied, so that you must needs affirm the recourse of blood.

transf. **1566** DRANT *Horace, Sat.* II. vi. H vij b, Thus I spende my dayes, in muche recourse of care. **1576** FLEMING *Panopl. Epist.* 41 All times are..replenished with recourse of fresh calamities.

†**b.** The ebb and flow of the tide. *Obs.*

1592 BRETON *C'tess Pembrokes Loue* (1879) 24/1 Thou makest the tides to take their due recourse. **1622** CALLIS *Stat. Sewers* (1647) 27 Not accounted grounds left or gained from the sea, because the sea hath daily her recourse thereon.

†**c.** A gathering or collection (of matter). *Obs.*⁻¹

1559 MORWYNG *Evonym.* 83 Aqua vitæ simple and alone ..breaketh an impostume or recours of matter.

3. a. Resort or application *to* some person or thing for assistance, help, or safety.

c **1374** CHAUCER *Troylus* II. 1303 (1352) To pandarus was alwey his recours, And pitousli gan ay to him pleyne. **1529** MORE *Dyaloge* IV. Wks. 270/1 It minished the necessitie of mannes recourse vnto god, for calling helpe of his grace. **1568** GRAFTON *Chron.* II. 761 Being farre of from the lawe and recourse to justice. *a* **1639** WOTTON *Life Dk. Buckhm.* in *Reliq.* (1651) 118 Thus died this great Peer..in a time of great recourse unto him and dependance upon him. **1734** tr. *Rollin's Anc. Hist.* (1827) I. Pref. 23 This perpetual recourse to the Deity is one of the principal foundations of religion. **1775** FLETCHER *Last Check* § 3 Wks. 1795 VI. 38 A heart-felt ceaseless recourse to the righteousness of Christ. **1871** NAPHEYS *Prev. & Cure Dis.* I. v. 151 Our first recourse is to the windows.

b. Freq. in phr. ***to have*** (†***one's*** or ***a***) ***recourse to***: to apply or betake oneself to (a person, etc.) for help, advice, or information.

c **1386** CHAUCER *Melib.* ¶476 If ye wol thanne take vengeance of youre enemys, ye shul retourne or haue youre recours to the Iuge that hath the Iurisdiccion vp-on hem. **1484** CAXTON *Chivalry* 31 The feble and lasse haue recours to the grete. **1502** ATKYNSON tr. *De Imitatione* III. xliii. 232 Moyses euer had a recours to the tabernacle of god for doubtis & questyons. **1611** BIBLE *Transl. Pref.* ¶11 They had recourse at the last, to this shift. **1650** FULLER *Pisgah* II. xi. 229 In this straight he hath his recourse by prayer to God. **1707** *Curios. in Husb. & Gard.* 22 They who have a liking to that sort of Compositions, may have recourse to Dornavius in his *Amphitheatrum Sapientiæ.* **1776** GIBBON *Decl. & F.* xvi. (1869) I. 400 If threats and persuasions proved ineffectual, he had often recourse to violence. **1865** TYLOR *Early Hist. Man.* ii. 18 Those who cannot speak, and must therefore have recourse to other means of communication.

†**c.** Similarly, ***to take*** or ***make recourse to.*** *Obs.*

1432-50 tr. *Higden* (Rolls) VI. 265 If eny man desire to see moore of the story of kynge Charls, y cownsayle that he take recourse to the wrytenges of Alcuinus his maister. **1623** tr. *Favine's Theat. Hon.* VI. ix. 151 Pedro the Cruell, made recourse with his Treasures to the English. **1637** R. ASHLEY tr. *Malvezzi's David Persecuted* 218 When hee could have no answer, [he] makes recourse to the Devill.

4. a. The thing, means, or person applied or resorted to for help, etc.; †a supply, relay.

c **1440** *York Myst.* xxvii. 141 Ye nedis non othir recours to craue. **1544** *Exhort. vnto Praier* A ij, Forasmoche as Prayer is the verye true mean..wherby..we may..haue a recourse and a refuge for helpe. **1612** DRAYTON *Poly-olb.* x. 47 Cluyd doth quickly call Her great recourse, to come and gard her. **1654-66** EARL ORRERY *Parthen.* (1676) 533, I have so many fresh recourses of Men, that [etc.]. **1700** DRYDEN *Sigism. & Guisc.* 415 Thy little care to mend my widow'd nights Has forc'd me to recourse of marriage rites. **1774** J. BRYANT *Mythol.* II. 142 This is their usual recourse, when they are hard pressed by inconsistencies. **1855** MILMAN *Lat. Chr.* VI. ii. (1864) III. 403 The Greeks in despair of maintaining their ground..had vainly sought recourse in craft.

b. *Law* (chiefly *Sc.*). The right to demand pecuniary compensation from some one; *esp.* the right which the holder of a bill of exchange has to come back upon the drawer and indorsers if the acceptor fails to meet it.

1747 *Sc. Acts Sederunt* 401 The question..whether a bill of Exchange..must be protested upon the..last day of grace..in order to afford recourse against the drawer. **1751** MᶜDOUALL *Laws Scot.* I. xiii. I. 360 They [bills] must be protested..otherwise recourse against the drawer will be denied. *Ibid.* 368 The correspondent who furnishes the goods loses his action of recourse against the writer [of a letter of credit]. *a* **1768** ERSKINE *Inst. Law Scot.* III. ii. § 34 The possessor of a bill who has not used exact diligence, should lose his recourse against the drawer. **1838** W. BELL *Dict. Law Scot.* 827 *Recourse* is the right competent to an assignee or disponee, under the warrandice of the transaction, to recur on the vender or cedent for relief, in case of eviction or of defects inferring warrandice. **1879** *Times* 12 Dec., Holders of 'agency' bills would have no recourse. **1885** SIR E. FRY in *Law Rep.* 29 *Chanc. Div.* 264 A property or fund against which Russell had a right of recourse.

c. *Law.* Phr. ***without recourse***, used to indicate that the endorser of a bill, etc., shall not be held liable for its non-payment.

1800 *U.S. Supreme Ct. Rep.* (1816) VII. 160 Pay the within to James Welch, on order, without any recourse whatever. **1805** *Ibid.* (1807) III. 203 The words *without recourse* do not imply *without value.* **1839** J. BOUVIER *Law Dict.* I. 499/1 The words commonly used are *sans recours*, without recourse. **1878** M. D. CHALMERS *Digest of Law of Bills of Exchange* iv. 97 It is held in America that an indorser 'without recourse' is responsible..*e.g.*, where the bill is a forgery. **1948** D. RICHARDSON *Simple Guide Bills of Exchange Acts* II. 56 When a party adds to his signature the words *sans recours* (*i.e.*, without recourse to me)..he means that, should the bill be dishonoured, the holder cannot look to him for repayment.

†**5. a.** Usual or habitual going or resorting to a particular place. *Obs.*

1523 LD. BERNERS *Froiss.* I. ccxxix. 306 All their chefe recours was in France, for they called the realme of Fraunce their chambre. **1553** EDEN *Treat. Newe Ind.* (Arb.) 25 Whether the marchauntes and straungers haue their continual recourse as to ye burse or strete. **1603** KNOLLES *Hist. Turks* (1621) 212 It yeelded them a great profit by the recourse of devout Christians travelling thither. **1623** GOUGE *Serm. Extent God's Provid.* § 15 This withdrawing chamber was next to his bed-chamber. He had oft recourse thither. **1658** W. BURTON *Itin. Anton.* 70 They had their place of recourse or rendevouz. **1705** in W. S. Perry *Hist. Coll. Amer. Col. Ch.* (1870) I. 165 There is such a recourse of the Clergy to Govʳ Nicholson's Lodgings.

†**b.** Gathering or concourse (of people) at a particular time. *Obs.*

1516 *Life Bridget* in *Myrr. our Ladye* p. lvii, In suche grete recourse of the people the Body was caryed to the monastery of Seynt Laurence. **1544** BALE *Chron. Sir J. Oldcastell* 39 b, That ye cause this condemnacyon..to be publyshed..by youre curates and paryshe Priestes, soche tyme as they shall haue most recourse of people. **1599** *Warn. Faire Wom.* I. 448 Beside, Recourse of servants and of passengers Might have been jealous of our conference. **1656** DUCHESS NEWCASTLE *True Relat.* Life (1886) 285 Their customs were..to ride in their coaches about the streets to see the concourse and recourse of people.

†**c.** The act of retiring (to rest). *Obs. rare*⁻¹.

1590 SPENSER *F.Q.* III. ix. 26 Her crased helth, her late recourse to rest.

†**d.** An occasion of going, a visit. *Obs. rare*⁻¹.

1632 LITHGOW *Trav.* VIII. 369 The chiefe Mosque too in which..[he] and I had three sundry recourses accompanied with our Moorish hoste.

†**6. a.** Opportunity of resorting *to* a person; access, admission. *Obs.*

1540-1 ELYOT *Image Gov.* (1556) 40 This familiar and secrete recourse, that he had to the emperour. **1591** SHAKS. *Two Gent.* III. i. 112, I, but the doores be lockt,..That no man hath recourse to her by night. **1594** —— *Rich. III*, III. v. 109 To giue order, that no manner person Haue any time recourse vnto the Princes.

†**b.** A going backwards and forwards between persons; intercourse of this nature. *Obs.*

1677 W. HUBBARD *Narrative* 125 We feared we should be discovered by reason of the frequent recourse between them by certain Squaws (who have mutual recourse). **1719** *Col. Rec. Pennsylv.* III. 86 That they expected to have free recourse for the peple amongst the English Plantations.

†**re'course,** *sb.*² *Sc. Obs.* [var. RESCOURSE *sb.*; cf. F. *recousse*, var. *rescousse.*] Rescue.

1533 BELLENDEN *Livy* III. xx. (S.T.S.) II. 29 To bring agane the residew of þare armye to þare recours. **1616** *Barbour's Bruce* (ed. Hart) 40 [iii. 76] When the King theim made recourse, Duke Betyse tooke on hym the flight.

recourse (rɪ'kɔəs), *v.*¹ [f. RECOURSE *sb.*¹]

†**1.** *intr.* To run back, return (*to* a place). *Obs.*

c **1500** *Lancelot* 1798 Out of this world when þow sal pas the cours, Fair well, I-wys! þow neuer shall Recours. **1513** BRADSHAW *St. Werburge* I. 1127 The harte to the forest recoursed certayne. **1570** FOXE *A. & M.* (ed. 2) 1152/1 The flame departyng and recoursing thrise ere the woode tooke strength..to consume him. **1632** LITHGOW *Trav.* IX. 422, I recoursed backe in a Flemish Pink to Stockhollem.

†**b.** *transf.* To recur *to* the mind; to go back *to* an earlier point. *Obs.*

1561 ABP. PARKER *Corr.* (Parker Soc.) 158 St Hierome's rhetoric recourseth to my mind. **1590** SPENSER *F.Q.* Auth. Let., A Poet thrusteth into the middest..and there recoursing to the thinges forepaste [etc.].

†**2.** To resort or flow *into. Obs. rare*⁻¹.

1576 NEWTON *Lemnie's Complex.* (1633) 34 [Man] hath also..externall spirits recoursing into his body and minde.

3. Const. *to.* To have recourse to, to fall back on. Now *rare* or *Obs.*

1586 J. HOOKER *Hist. Irel.* in *Holinshed* II. 51/1 Recoursing deuoutlie to the onlie refuge of humane saluation. **1605** SYLVESTER *Du Bartas* II. iii. III. *Lawe* 431 The Court recourst to Lakes, to Springs, and Brooks. **1668** HALE *Pref. Rolle's Abridgm.* 9 He will be able upon any occasion suddenly to find any thing he hath read, without recoursing to Tables, or other Repertories. *a* **1670** HACKET *Abp. Williams* II. (1692) 201 These dogmatists dare not recourse to Scripture. **1804** *Something Odd* II. 209 One or other of your personages are for ever recoursing to tears.

Hence **re'coursing** *ppl. a.*, returning.

1632 LITHGOW *Trav.* II. 49 The wandring night was chased..by the recoursing day.

†**re'course,** *v.*² *Sc. Obs.* [var. of RESCOURSE *v.*] *trans.* To rescue.

1533 BELLENDEN *Livy* II. ix. (S.T.S.) I. 161 Manilius was haistelie recoursit be ane weyng of latynis. *Ibid.* xxii. 221 He was nocht fer distant.., and mycht haue recoursit þe samyn [garrison] gif he had plesit.

†**re'courseful,** *a. Obs.*⁻¹ [f. RECOURSE *sb.* + -FUL.] Flowing back; ebbing and flowing.

1612 DRAYTON *Poly-olb.* I. 279 Where Thetis handmaids still in that recoursefull deepe With those rough Gods of Sea, continuall reuells keepe.

re'court, *v.* [RE- 5 a.] To court again.

1675 COCKER *Morals* 45 Philosophy Divine, court and recourt; She can..mount man above a Man.

recover (rɪ'kʌvə(r)), *sb.* Also 4-6 recouer(e, recovere, 5 rekouere. See also RECOUR *sb.* [Orig. (senses 1-3) a. OF. *recovre* (*recouvre*, etc.), f. *recovrer* RECOVER *v.*¹; cf. Sp. *recobro*, It. *ricovero.* In later use directly from the vb.]

†**1.** Recovery, or means of recovery, from misfortune, trouble, illness, error, etc. *Obs.*

1303 R. BRUNNE *Handl. Synne* 7107 What ys loue vnto men pore [*read* povere], Almes to hem ys recouere. *c* **1330** —— *Chron.* (1810) 282 After þat day Scotland may haf gode recouere. **1387-8** T. USK *Test. Love* I. i. (Skeat) I. 45 Without recouer endelesse here to endure. *c* **1450** *Merlin* 332 The grete knowinge and witte of Merlin, in whom was all the recouer. **1555** CARD. POLE *Let. to Cranmer* in Strype *Mem. Cranmer* (1694) App. 212 If I now, that desire your recover, should go about..to bryng yow from your errour to the truth. **1631** CHETTLE *Hoffman* H 3 b, The Princes head being split against a Rocke Past all recouer.

†**2. a.** Recovery (of something lost). *Obs.*

1471 *Arriv. Edw. IV* (Camden) 39 The reentrie and perfect recover of the iuste title and right of owr sayd soueraygne Lord. **1503** HAWES *Examp. Virtue* v. 17 A thynge lost without recouer. **1533** BELLENDEN *Livy* II. xxiii. (S.T.S.) I. 226 þe small pepil rais in grete Ire.., & said thare liberte was endit but recovir.

†**b.** Recovery (of a debt or sum due). *Obs.*

1488 in *Somerset Medieval Wills* (1901) 274 To my lord Dawbeney 10*li.* of the money due unto me..if he help to the rekouere of the same. **1502** in Arnolde *Chron.* (1811) 104 Any other thinge..that may lette..the said aturnais or ani of them of the recouer or recait of the said C. li.

†**3.** *Law.* = RECOVERY 4. *Obs.*

1447 *Rolls of Parlt.* V. 130/2 Atte the tyme of the pursuyt of the Writte, wheruppon the recovere especified in the saide Petition was hadde. **1504-5** in *Plumpton Corr.* (Camden) 195 That all former recovers and other tytles, which your adversaryes hath against you and your heires, may be voyded. **1523** FITZHERB. *Surv.* xviii. 33 The tenant ..cometh nat in by the lorde, but by force of the recouere.

4. The act of bringing or coming back to a former position:

a. *Mil.* (chiefly in phr. ***at, on,*** or ***to the recover***). A position of the fire-arm forming part of the manual exercise: see RECOVER *v.* 12 a.

1799 *Instr. & Reg. Cavalry* (1813) 270 The advanced line of skirmishers are to have their pistols or carbines at the recover. **1809** WELLINGTON in Gurw. *Desp.* (1837) IV. 446 Private O—— J—— having loaded his piece, had it on the recover, when he turned round and saw him. **1847** *Infantry Man.* (1854) 112 Bring the firelock to the recover. **1915** KIPLING *New Army in Training* ii. 10 The squads at bayonet-practice had their balance, drive, and recover already.

b. In general use, in various contexts. Also *fig.*

1818 'T. BROWN' *Brighton* III. ii. 123 'I hold it that a *prime* coachman's a better fellow than a paltry—' peer he was going to say, but he knew how to pull up to a hair; so, making a recover, he added—'man of fortune'. **1819** *Metropolis* II. 45 'Oh! I know their tricks' (making a recover)—'that is to say, I have heard of them'. **1852** THACKERAY *Esmond* III. ii, She..swept a low curtsey, coming up to the recover with the prettiest little foot in the world pointed out. **1888** *Century Mag.* Jan. 449/1 All being done with a quick thrust and recover that does not burn one's finger.

recover (rɪˈkʌvə(r)), *v.*[1] Forms: α. 4–5 **recou-, recoveren,** 4–7 **recouere,** (4 **-coure, -coeure, -covri,** 5 **-couyre),** 4–7 **recouer,** (4 **-cuuer,** 5 **-kouer,** 6 **-couir, -couuer),** 4– **recover.** (See also RECOUR *v.*) β. 4 **rekever, (reck-), -ere,** 4–5 **-keuere,** 5 **-keuer;** 4 **-keouer, -kyuer,** 5 **-kiver.** [ad. AF. *recoverer* (Britton), *rekeverer* (1292–3), OF. *recov(e)rer, -couvrer, -coevrer,* etc. = Sp. *recobrar,* It. *ricoverare*:—L. *recuperāre* to RECUPERATE. Cf. COVER *v.*[2]]

I. *trans.*

1. a. To get (†occasionally, to take) back again into one's hands or possession; to regain possession of (something lost or taken away).

1377 LANGL. *P. Pl.* B. xix. 239 He tauȝte..some to ryde and to recoeure [*v.r.* rekeuere], that vnriȝtfully was wonne. *c* **1400** *Destr. Troy* 10369 The troiens with tene trauailed full sore..The corse to Recouer, & kary to toune. **1484** CAXTON *Fables of Alfonce* ii, I shalle counceylle the how thou shalt recouere thy syluer. **1530** PALSGR. 681/2 This thing is recovred by strength of hande, but it was almost gone. **1560** BIBLE (Genev.) *Hos.* ii. 9, I..wil recouer my woll and my flaxe lent, to couer her shame. **1647** EVELYN *Diary* 22 May, My valet..robb'd me of cloths and plate to the value of threescore pounds, but..I recover'd most of them. **1770** FOOTE *Lame Lover* III. Wks. 1799 II. 93 The recovering my paternal possessions makes me anxious inded. **1857** MAURICE *Ep. St. John* ix. 141 They would stir up endless rebellions, in the hope of recovering what they had lost. **1871** MORLEY *Voltaire* (1886) 5 Humanity had lost its title-deeds, and he had recovered them.

b. To regain (country, territory, etc.) by conquest or main force; to win back (ground lost in fighting).

c **1375** *Sc. Leg. Saints* xxxiii. (*George*) 904 Quhen cristine men tuk on hande to recouer þe haly lande. **1382** WYCLIF *2 Macc.* ii. 23 Thei vengeden al the cuntree..and rekyuerden the most famous temple in al the world. *c* **1450** *Merlin* 654 Than com all the bretouns oute of the wode, and haue recouered the felde. **1513–4** *Act 5 Hen. VIII*, c. 1 *Preamble*, The Kyng..desiring to recover the Royalme of Fraunce his very true patrimonye. **1560** DAUS tr. *Sleidane's Comm.* 34 b, They recovered of the frenchmen Parma and Placence. **1678** WANLEY *Wond. Lit. World* v. ii. §15. 469/2 Justinian, recovered Africk from the Vandals by Belisarius. **1769** ROBERTSON *Chas. V*, VII. III. 8 He..gave the enemy an opportunity of recovering..all the conquests which he had gained. **1841** LANE *Arab. Nts.* I. 117 Having by this means recovered the kingdom. **1861** M. PATTISON *Ess.* (1889) I. 35 To annex to them those districts..which he could recover for the empire.

c. To get back, regain (some non-material thing which may be spoken of as *lost* or *taken away*).

c **1384** CHAUCER *H. Fame* III. 168 For tyme y-lost..Be no way may recoverd be. **1390** GOWER *Conf.* III. 155 He wiste wel his pours was povere, Bot yit he thoght his riht recovere. *c* **1420** LYDG. *Assembly of Gods* 1212 Furst..Baptym go ye to. For by hym sonnest shull ye recouer grace. **1532** SIR J. RUSSEL in Ellis *Orig. Lett.* Ser. II. I. 302 To do your Highnes service, and to helpe you to recouver your right. *a* **1656** BP. HALL *Rem. Wks.* (1660) 106 How unquiet are we..till we have recovered his lost favour. **1769** *Junius Lett.* xxxv. 167 The affections of your subjects may still be recovered. **1791** COWPER *Yardley Oak* 48 Unrecorded facts Recovering, and misstated setting right. **1847** JAMES *Convict* i, I must study hard to recover lost time. **1875** JOWETT *Plato* (ed. 2) III. 694 He recovered the meaning of the several names and re-translated them.

d. To find again, come upon a second time.

1611 COTGR., *Relancer vn lievre,* to recouer her, or put her off the squat. **1856** 'STONEHENGE' *Brit. Sports* 141/1 In that direction [he] will generally succeed in recovering the scent. Most hares..will generally be easily recovered by a cast in the direction of their home. **1888** *Times* 10 Oct. 5/5 When they are at fault,..they will make their own casts and recover the track.

e. To reclaim (land) *from* the sea.

a **1793** ELSTOBB *Bedford Level* (1793) 274 The Romans.. being at the pains of recovering them [marshes] from the sea. **1846** MCCULLOCH *Acc. Brit. Empire* (1854) I. 20 On the south it is low, Sunk Island and some other considerable tracts having been recovered from the sea.

f. To remove (certain substances) from industrial waste in order that they may be reused.

1906 R. W. SINDALL *Paper Technol.* iv. 37 About 75 to 85 per cent. of the soda used in the treatment of esparto can be recovered. **1929** CLAPPERTON & HENDERSON *Mod. Paper-Making* xxii. 315 In almost all mills a large quantity of fibre and clay may be recovered from the back waters of the machines. **1929** *Industr. & Engin. Chem.* May 446 (*caption*) Air filters recover dust from gyratory crushers... This dust is sold as agricultural limestone. **1941** *Coke & Smokeless-Fuel Age* III. 285/1 All coke producers are required to recover benzole from their gas. **1969** D. STEWART *Paper* 33 The caustic soda is recovered in the following way.

2. To regain, acquire again, resume, return to: **a.** a quality, state, or condition.

?*a* **1366** CHAUCER *Rom. Rose* 57 These wodes eek recoveren grene, That drie in wynter ben to sene. **1390** GOWER *Conf.* II. 137 He schal Recovere his ferste astat ayein. **1526** *Pilgr. Perf.* (W. de W. 1531) 10 b, He wolde haue fedde therof: and so a recouered his immortalite that he had lost. **1661** BOYLE *Orig. Formes & Qual.* 172 The Lead ..will not of it self recover its Sphæricity. **1706** LONDON & WISE *Retir'd Gard.* I. xiv. 182 By putting them to the Roots [I] have found that the Leaves have recover'd their Greenness. **1784** COWPER *Task* I. 441 His cheek recovers soon its healthful hue. **1820** SHELLEY *Œd. Tyr.* II. ii. 30 Perhaps I may recover my lost appetite. **1858** FROUDE *Hist. Eng.* xviii. IV. 33 With the assistance of the bishops..they recovered an absolute superiority.

b. *esp.* health or strength.

c **1330** R. BRUNNE *Chron. Wace* (Rolls) 1837 þen was Coryneus aschamed..He recouered his strengþe for tene. **1390** GOWER *Conf.* III. 150 Hou that hir lord of his seknesse ..Recovere myhte his hele ayein. **1477** EARL RIVERS (Caxton) *Dictes* 126 A seke man desireth not to departe from his phisicien till he hath recouerid his helth. **1555** EDEN *Decades* 53 They..sumwhat recouered theyr strengthes muche weakened for lacke of meate. **1594** SHAKS. *Rich. III*, I. iii. 2 Ther's no doubt his Maiesty will soone recouer his accustom'd health. *a* **1691** BOYLE *Hist. Air* (1692) 242 Sick and valetudinary persons used to be sent thither to recover their health. **1841** LANE *Arab. Nts.* I. 112 Had it not been for this, I had recovered my strength. **1849** HELPS *Friends in C.* (1851) II. 3, I had by this time recovered my usual health.

c. a faculty of body or mind, or the use of this; also, ***to recover one's feet*** or ***legs*** (cf. LEG *sb.* 2 f).

14.. in *Tundale's Vis.* (1843) 89 Thys Paynym knyght Only of grace hath recoverd his syght. **1593** SHAKS. *Rich. II*, v. iii. 47 What is the matter..speak, recouer breath. **1596** SPENSER *F.Q.* VI. viii. 17 The Prince to him full nimbly stept And least he should recover foote againe [etc.]. **1617** HIERON *Wks.* (1634) II. 243 It was in his sleepe; but, when he awoke, he recouered his thoughts. **1667** MILTON *P.L.* IV. 357 Satan ..at length fail speech recoverd sad. *Ibid.* x. 966 To whom thus Eve, recovering heart, repli'd. **1725** DE FOE *Voy. round World* (1840) 287 He could hardly speak; but, recovering his breath, said [etc.]. **1749** FIELDING *Tom Jones* XII. xi, Partridge had no sooner recovered his Legs, than [etc.]. **1833** HT. MARTINEAU *Vanderput & S.* i. 19 When he recovered his voice, the pastor turned his attention [etc.]. **1847** MARRYAT *Childr. N. Forest* xiv, They worked another half-hour, when they stopped to recover their wind.

3. a. To get back, or find again (one who has been lost or absent). *rare*[−1].

c **1381** CHAUCER *Parl. Foules* 688 Wele han they cause forto gladen ofte Sethe ech of hem recouerede hathe hys make.

b. To bring, draw, or win back (a person) to friendship or willing obedience; to reconcile.

1576 FLEMING *Panopl. Epist.* 234 Trie not to recouer them, whome you would haue come vnto you in haste, with threatning. **1582** N. LICHEFIELD tr. *Castanheda's Conq. E. Ind.* I. lxiv. 131 Although thou doest loose them, and all the rest of thy subiectes, yet thou doest recouer me. **1604** SHAKS. *Oth.* II. iii. 273 What man, there are more wayes to recouer the Generall againe. *a* **1674** CLARENDON *Hist. Reb.* XVI. §132 They were not willing to despair of recovering their general again to them; and..sent a committee to treat with him. **1797** BURKE *Regic. Peace* iii. Wks. VIII. 293 It was expected, that he would have..endeavoured to recover those whom their fears had led astray. **1869** FREEMAN *Norm. Conq.* (1876) III. xi. 59 Harold's way of recovering rebels differed widely from William's.

c. To recapture, get hold of (an escaped person) again. *rare.*

1585 T. WASHINGTON tr. *Nicholay's Voy.* I. vii, [There] came running diuers other Turkes to recouer him. **1606** G. W[OODCOCKE] *Lives in Hist. Ivstine* Kk iij, The people.. recouering Michaell in his flight, put out his eyes.

†**4.** To get in place of, or in return for, something else. *Obs.*

c **1374** CHAUCER *Troylus* III. 132 (181) For every wo ye shall recover a blisse. *Ibid.* IV. 378 (406) If she be lost, we shul recovere another. **1523** LD. BERNERS *Froiss.* I. 687 If ye do [refuse it], I thynk it wyll be longe or ye recover agayne suche another offre. **1525** *Ibid.* II. 416 If ye have fayled of the duke of Lancasters doughter, ye maye recover another, as great and as good as she is.

5. *Law.* **a.** To get back or gain by judgement in a court of law; to obtain possession of, or a right to, by legal process.

c **1380** WYCLIF *Sel. Wks.* III. 320 ȝif þei kittide þus openly here purses, þei schulden reckevere it bi comyn lawe. **1444** *Rolls of Parlt.* V. 115/2 He that wil sue..shall have the suyte to recovere to hym self the oon half therof, and the Kyng that other half. **1447** *Ibid.* 130/1 Divers Landes and Tenementz, late were recovered, evict and hadde, fro the possession of the Hous of the holy Trinite. **1516** *Test Ebor.* (Surtees) VI. 2 Whereas the Lorde Willuthby [etc.].. recovered all my manors, landes and tenements agaynst me [etc.]. **1542** UDALL *Erasm. Apoph.* 100 He was assured to recouer of Midias so much money for a forfaicte. **1607** COWELL *Interpr.* s.v. *Recovery,* The third man commeth not: whereupon the land is recouered by him that brought the writ. **1710** PRIDEAUX *Orig. Tithes* iv. 167 This Law.. enabled the Clergy to gather and recover Tithes. **1768** BLACKSTONE *Comm.* III. 59 All trivial debts..were to be recovered..in every man's own county. **1817** W. SELWYN *Law Nisi Prius* (ed. 4) II. 737 It was holden, that the plaintiff ..was entitled to recover the value of the goods. **1891** *Law Times Rep.* LXIII. 690/2 This was an action to recover damages for false imprisonment.

b. To have (a judgement or verdict) given in one's favour.

1768 BLACKSTONE *Comm.* III. 404 A defendant, against whom judgment is recovered. **1798** BAY *Amer. Law Rep.* (1809) I. 49 Plaintiff had recovered a verdict for £230.

6. †**a.** To get or obtain; to get hold of. *Obs.*

1398 TREVISA *Barth. De P.R.* XVIII. liii, The amptes gadre grete burthens whych ben more greter than ther owne bodyes: And so they recouer rewarde of lytylnesse of body in yᵉ gretnesse of vertue. *c* **1477** CAXTON *Jason* 70 Considering ..the right hye gladnesse that they hadde recouured. *a* **1533** LD. BERNERS *Gold. Bk. M. Aurel.* (1546) P iij b, The more a man recouereth here renoume among straungers, the more he is persecuted with enuye. **1585** T. WASHINGTON tr. *Nicholay's Voy.* I. xx. 25 b, He found meanes to recouer a barke, intoo the which he and his men got. **1614** RALEIGH *Hist. World* II. (1634) 306 Having beheld the most beautifull and lively among them that he might recover them for his owne use and delights. *a* **1661** FULLER *Worthies* (1840) III. 542 At the ebb thereof you may easily recover a pail or bucket full.

†**b.** To get opportunity for, to give or succeed in giving (another stroke or blow). *Obs. rare.*

c **1450** *Merlin* 342 Arthur hym smote so harde..that he bowed on his horse nekke, and ȝef he myght haue recovered a-nother stroke he hadde fallen of his horse to the erthe. *Ibid.* 391 Whan Pounce wolde have recovered a-nother stroke [etc.]. **1677** MOXON *Mech. Exerc.* No. I. 16 When you draw your file back, to recover an other thrust. **1678** *Ibid.* No. 6. 99 The Saw having run its length, is lifted gently over the Stuff to recover another stroak of the Saw.

†**c.** To reach or attain to (a state). *Obs. rare.*

1575 TURBERV. *Faulconrie* 130 When she is cast off, and beginneth to recouer her gate. **1576** FLEMING *Panopl. Epist.* A ij, All things when they haue recouered perfection.. cannot but then be most acceptable.

d. To get (the wind of one). *Obs.* exc. *arch.*

1602 SHAKS. *Ham.* III. ii. 371 Why do you go about to recouer the winde of mee? *a* **1618** RALEIGH *Inv. Shipping* 30 These hoyes, who will easily recover the wind of any other ships. **1855** KINGSLEY *Westw. Ho!* xx, She is a race ship, and if we can but recover the wind of her [etc.].

7. a. To get to, reach, arrive at, gain (some place or point). Now *rare.* (Common in 16–17th cents.)

c **1350** *Will. Palerne* 2801 Go we on oure gate..to recuuer sum resset þere we vs rest miȝt. **1512** W. KNIGHT in Ellis *Orig. Lett.* Ser. II. I. 195 With..long tribulacion we recovred the saide Porte of Saincte Sebastian. **1585** T. WASHINGTON tr. *Nicholay's Voy.* II. i. 31 b, The sea which so furiously casteth against Malee, is such that without great labour..she is not to be recouered or surmounted. **1603** KNOLLES *Hist. Turks* (1621) 39 At length having recovered the top of an hill,..they there staied, and presently encamped themselves. **1677** W. HUBBARD *Narrative* I. (1865) 121 He kept his Horse till he recovered the next garrison House. **1793** SMEATON *Edystone L.* §226 After labouring at our oars for an hour and an half more, we recovered the buss. **1822** SCOTT *Pirate* xxxi, Without a pocket-compass..I should never have recovered the Fair Isle, for which we run.

transf. **1614** RALEIGH *Hist. World* Pref. 3 Pharaoh slew the Infants of Israel, ere they had recovered their Cradles.

†**b.** To make for, betake oneself to (a place of defence). *Obs.*

c **1500** *Melusine* 252 Philibert was thenne descended from his hors,..and recouered the montayne aboue the pathe. **1600** HOLLAND *Livy* IV. xxxix. 164 Both armies as taking themselves loosers, recovered the mountaines that were next unto them. **1604** E. GRIMSTONE *Hist. Siege Ostend* 14 The Souldiers were forced to recouer the..sande downes.

†**c.** To get back to or into, to return to. *Obs.*

In some cases perh. only a contextual use of 7.

c **1430** *Syr Gener.* (Roxb.) 3824 Abel ashamed began to be, And recouered his sadil hastilie. **1513** DOUGLAS *Æneis* VI. ii. 107 Tharfra to return agane on hycht, And her abufe recovir this airis lycht, That is difficill werk. **1549** in Strype *Eccl. Mem.* (1721) II. App. DD. 104 They turned their backs and recovered the town which they before had fortified for al events. **1618** BOLTON *Florus* IV. x. (1636) 310 That..they should march back, and recover the mountaines. **1675** NEVILE tr. *Machiavelli's Life Castr. Castracani* Wks. 248 The Florentines..recovered the bank, and..searched for a better place.

†**d.** To journey, travel, cover. *Obs.*[−1]

a **1625** FLETCHER *Noble Gent.* I. i, I shall recover twenty miles this night.

†**e.** To remove, transfer. *Obs.*[−1]

1719 LONDON & WISE *Compl. Gard.* 103 We must therefore disburthen its Head, proportionable to the strength and activity we take from it by recovering it to a new place, and retrenching some of its Roots.

8. a. To get back for another; to bring back, restore. Const. *to* (or *unto,* †rarely *into*) a person, country, etc.

1484 CAXTON *Fables of Alfonce* i, [His friend] sente for phisycyens or leches..for to recouere his helthe. **1550** VERON *Godly Sayings* (1846) 16 The body and bloud of our Lorde..have recovered unto mankynde, the love and favour of God. **1647** CLARENDON *Hist. Reb.* VI. §98 This little rest had recovered a strange cheerfulness into all men. **1671** MILTON *Samson* 1098 So had the glory of Prowess been recover'd To Palestine. **1732** LAW *Serious C.* xviii. (ed. 2) 326 Education should be consider'd.. as the art of recovering to man the use of his reason. **1774** CULLEN *Lett. to Ld. Cathcart* (1776) 12 For recovering the heat of the body, it has been proposed, to cover it all over with warm grains. **1851** HUSSEY *Papal Power* iii. 115 The Council thus proposed to restore the Pope to his former condition, by recovering to him all the patrimony [etc.].

b. To bring back, recall (*to* memory). *rare.*

1602 JONSON *Poetaster* III. i. D3, Did you neuer heare any of my verses? *Horace.* No, Sir; but I am in some feare, I must, now. *Crisp.* Ile tell thee some (if I can but recouer 'hem). **1673** MARVELL *Reh. Transp.* II. 320 If he saw what you write, it would recover to his memory his fighting with beasts at Ephesus. **1677** MIÉGE *Fr. Dict.* II. s.v. **1957** L. DURRELL *Justine* IV. 233 It is strange when everything about Alexandria is so vivid that I can recover so little of that lost period.

9. a. To restore or bring back (usu. a person) to life or consciousness.

c **1400** *Cursor M.* 28848 (Cott. Galba) It recouers thurgh grace ogayne al gude werkes þat with syn war slayne. **1600** SHAKS. *A.Y.L.* IV. iii. 151 And now he fainted..Briefe, I recouered him. **1607** *Peele's Jests* (*c* 1620) 14 She fell into a counterfeit swoone, whom the Gentleman soone recouered. **1675** EVELYN *Diary* 22 Mar., Sir William..was grown famous..for his recovering a poor wench that had ben hanged for felony. **1706** E. WARD *Wooden World Diss.* (1708) 101 This effectually recovers him, and makes him as sober as a Bishop. **1798** *Invasion* I. xxiv. 179 Raising her up, he tried by gentler words to recover her. **1841** J. T. HEWLETT *Parish Clerk* I. 153 The squire suddenly recovered her by calling for..a bucket of water.

b. To restore (a person or animal) to health or strength; to cure, heal.

1601 SHAKS. *All's Well* III. ii. 22 Shee hath recouered the King, and vndone me. *a* **1614** DONNE *Βιαθανατος* (1644) 117 He that is as sure that this Medicine will recover him, as that this Poyson will destroy him [etc.]. **1681** tr. *Belon's Myst. Physick* 43 Some Persons..have had occasion to use longer than ordinarily this Remedy before they could be perfectly recovered. **1799** J. ROBERTSON *Agric. Perth* 555 When this happens to be the case, there is little hope of recovering the horse. **1816** JANE AUSTEN *Emma* III. iii. 39 A young lady who faints, must be recovered. **1940** W. FAULKNER *Hamlet* III. i. 179 This legal dollar which would be little enough compensation, not for the time he had spent recovering the cow. **1967** *Listener* 7 Sept. 302/3 Well, I think Mr Wilson would put one well on the way to convalescence, and the Queen would recover one completely.

c. Const. †*of* or *from* (the disease or disorder).

1389 in *Eng. Gilds* (1870) 5 He schal haue, of þe comune box, xiiij*d*, terme of his lyf, but he be recouered of hys mischief. **1606** G. W[OODCOCKE] *Lives Emperors* in *Hist. Ivstine* G g iij, Hee fell madde, of which he was aftirward recoured. **1665** EVELYN *Diary* 5 July, I tooke order for 150 men, who had ben recovered of their wounds [etc.]. **1707** FREIND *Peterborow's Cond. Sp.* 198 A few days rest, good Diet, and Encouragement, soon recover the Souldier of any fatigue. **1808** ELEANOR SLEATH *Bristol Heiress* II. 93 A person..who had already recovered Veney from a similar accident. **1836** MARRYAT *Japhet* lxi, He..recovered her from an imminent and painful disease.

d. Const. *to* or *into* (health, life, etc.).

1594 DRAYTON *Idea* 853 From Death to Life, thou mightst him yet recover. **1654** R. CODRINGTON tr. *Justine* xx. 289 The Crotonians being recovered to their health, were no longer quiet. **1724** SWIFT *Drapier's Lett.* Wks. 1755 V. II. 72 Any more than a dead carcase can be recovered to life by a cordial. **1747** W. HORSLEY *Fool* (1748) II. 271 It is what I always first prescribe to recover great Wits into their right Senses. **1793** *Minstrel* I. 210 She hurried back to the cottage, where she found that Philip had been recovered to sensation.

e. In passive, *to be recovered*: to have got better, to be well again. (Cf. 18.)

13.. *Sir Beues* (MS. A.) 2854 Whan ouer-gon was his smerte And [he] rekeured was of is herte Sir Beues set him vp. **1423** HEN. VI in Ellis *Orig. Lett.* Ser. II. I. 100 And as towardes oure bel Uncle of Excestre, whom oure Lord now late visitid with seknesse,..he is rekiveryd. *a* **1440** *Sir Eglam.* 953 Syr Egyllamowre was hole and sounde, And wele recovryd on hys wounde. **1560** DAUS tr. *Sleidane's Comm.* 280 He commeth there fore to Ulme, whan he was not yet recovered. **1648** *Hamilton Papers* (Camden) 239 Mr. Murray..fell sick; whether he be recovered and gone or not your Lp knowes best. **1733** SWIFT *Let.* 8 Jan., Wks. 1841 II. 694/1 The friend I named, who I was afraid would die, is recovered. **1765** REID *Wks.* I. 43/1, I hope your papa is quite recovered of his cold. **1829** J. JEKYLL *Corr.* (1894) 200 Lady Conyngham has had a bad illness, but is recovered.

†**10.** To restore (a person or thing) to a good or proper estate or condition; to set or make right again. *Obs.*

In quot. *c* 1460 due to a misreading of the Fr. original.

c **1374** CHAUCER *Troylus* I. 327 (383) To hide his desir yn muwe From euery wyght..But he myght ought recouered be þerby. **1388** WYCLIF *Ecclus.* ii. 6 Bileue thou to God and he schal rekeuere thee. *c* **1460** SIR R. ROS *La Belle Dame* 614 There is no Iuge y-sette of suche trespace by which of right one may recouered be. **1523** LD. BERNERS *Froiss.* I. xc. 112 He wolde neuer rest tyll he had so arayed the realme of Scotlande, that it shulde neuer be recouered. **1586** LEICESTER *Corr.* (Camden) 217 God doth knowe what..a ioyfull countreie here was within this month; God send her majestie to recover it soe againe. **1660** BOYLE *New Exp. Phys. Mech.* xiii. 86 The Fire was got out for good and all, and past the possibility of being recover'd by the re-admitted Air. **1706** LONDON & WISE *Retir'd Gard.* I. II. ii. 110 To recover Trees so damnify'd, we perform the following Operation. **1731** P. SHAW *Ess. Artif. Philos.* 126 The Still-Bottoms of Melasses are successfully used to scald and recover musty Casks.

11. †**a.** To rescue or deliver (a person). *Obs.*

c **1430** *Agincourt* 186 in Hazl. *E.P.P.* II. 101 Of truse we wyll beseche the, Vntyll that it be sunday noone, And yf we may not recouered be We will delyuer the towne. **1637** WINTHROP *New Eng.* (1824) I. 244 He fell into the water, near the shore, where it was not six feet deep, and could not be recovered. **1653** H. COGAN tr. *Pinto's Trav.* xxii. 78, I promised..never to part from hence, till by some means or other I have recovered these poor soldiers my companions. **1686** tr. *Chardin's Trav. Persia* 152 Having agreed with my comrade what ways I would take to recover him out of Mingrelia.

b. To bring back, rescue, reclaim *from* or *out of* a state, etc.

1614 CAMDEN *Rem.* (ed. 2) 335, I will onely recouer from obliuion these made vpon the pictures [etc.]. **1635** EARL STRAFFORD *Lett.* (1735) I. 473 To recover them forth of that Superstition and Barbarism which hath hitherto been the reproach almost of the English. **1692** LOCKE *Toleration* III. i. Wks. 1727 II. 311 So men will be well guarded, or recovered from false Religions. **1711** ADDISON *Spect.* No. 10 ¶1 Till I have recovered them out of that desperate State of Vice and Folly, into which the Age is fallen. **1797** *Encycl. Brit.* (ed. 3) XIII. 732/2 The fathers..say that the Indians are but just recovered from a barbarous and dissolute way of life. **1860** WARTER *Sea-board* II. 436, I must recover all from their evil courses by every means in my power.

†**c.** Const. *into* or *to* (a state, etc.). *Obs.*

1647 CLARENDON *Hist. Reb.* VII. §172 They sent a formal commission of both Houses to him..to recover him to his former vigour and zeal in their cause. **1662** H. MORE *Philos. Writ.* Pref. Gen. (1712) 17 That which now deserves to be called Cartesianism for Des-Cartes his so happily recovering it again into view. **1737** WHISTON *Josephus, Hist.* VI. iii. §5 Nor could he expect that such men could be recovered to sobriety.

12. a. To bring back (a weapon) to a certain position. *to recover arms*: (see quot. 1802).

1594 I. G. *Di Grassi's Art Defence* I ij, He must..recouer his owne sworde nimbly, and then deliuer a thrust. **1685** J. S. *Art of War* 27 Recover your Armes. **1796** *Instr. & Reg. Cavalry* (1819) 240 When the rear rank has passed the general ten yards, officers recover their swords with the commanding officer. **1802** JAMES *Milit. Dict.*, *To Recover arms*, a position of the firelock when the piece is held with the lock equal to the left shoulder, and the sling to the front. **1851** MAYHEW *Lond. Labour* III. 167 [Recover arms]. **1859** F. A. GRIFFITHS *Artil. Man.* (1862) 153 The..officers recover and carry their swords.

absol. **1837** DICKENS *Pickw.* iv, The dogs barked, the mob screamed, the troops recovered.

transf. **1711** ADDISON *Spect.* No. 102 ¶2 [The ladies] are exercised by the following Words of Command,..Ground your Fans, Recover your Fans.

b. To pull back (a horse) on its feet again.

1646 EVELYN *Diary* (Milan), Recovering the jade on all foure againe, he desir'd to be taken down. **1857** LAWRENCE *Guy Liv.* xv. 132 [The mare] was down on her head; but Guy recovered her cleverly.

13. a. To get over, get better from (a sickness, misfortune, or affliction).

1340 *Ayenb.* 32 Þanne comþ þe dyeuel and him zayþ 'þou hit sselt wel recouri þou art yong and strang þou sselt libbe long'. **14..** *Isumbras* 336 in Utterson *Sel. Pieces* I. 91 Ye shall be kynge with crowne,..And recover all your wo. **1550** COVERDALE *Spir. Perle* xii. (1560) 130 After the sicke man had recouered his sore, He liued worse then euer he did before. **1597** J. KING *On Jonas* (1618) 73 Hee should recouer his sicknesse. **1615** W. LAWSON *Country Housew. Gard.* (1626) 15 He will safely recouer his wound within seuen yeeres. **1699** R. L'ESTRANGE *Erasm. Colloq.* (1725) 152 One man has a fancy that he shall never recover a fit of sickness. **1764** GOLDSM. *Hist. Eng. in Lett.* (1772) II. 34 This fatal blow the King could never after recover. **1801** JANE AUSTEN *Lett.* (1884) I. 269 The neighbourhood have quite recovered the death of Mrs. Rider. **1875** BRYCE *Holy Rom. Emp.* xix. (ed. 5) 350 The Free Cities had never recovered the famines and sieges of the Thirty Years' War.

b. To annul the effect of (a slip, stumble, etc.). Also in *fig.* context.

1748 RICHARDSON *Corr.* (1804) IV. 227 The accident of a broken thigh, snapped by a sudden jirk, endeavouring to recover a slip. **1768** *Woman of Honor* I. 198 The point with him now was to recover so terrible a stumble. **1886** *Manch. Exam.* 10 Mar. 5/7 Lord C. H. cleverly recovered his *faux pas* by offering a handsome apology.

14. To retrieve, make good, make up for (loss, damage, etc., to oneself).

c **1386** CHAUCER *Man of Law's Prol.* 27 For losse of catel may recouered be, But losse of tyme shendeth vs, quod he. **1481** CAXTON *Myrr.* I. xiv. 43 Yf she lacke on one syde she recouerith it on that other. **1523** LD. BERNERS *Froiss.* I. 506 They determyned to go thyder..to assay if they coude recover any parte of their domage. *Ibid.* 553 To thentent that he shulde recover agayne his losse. **1619** in *Eng. & Germ.* (Camden) 207 Sir Albertus Morton (who hath used more diligence in his journey to recover his detention in England then I feare may be for his health). **1682** G. VERNON *Life Heylin* 34 Many..losses..which he was not able to recover. **1775** C. JOHNSTON *Pilgrim* 210 To try if it was possible to recover the loss which we had been too late to prevent.

15. a. To put right, remedy, make good again (something wrong, a fault, etc.). Now *rare.*

c **1384** CHAUCER *H. Fame* I. 354 Eke though I myght dure ever That I have do rekever I never. **1442** T. BECKINGTON *Corr.* (Rolls) II. 214 This grete hurt, which xx^{m}. li. wol not nowe by many dayes lightly recovere. **1536** *Exhort. to North* in Furniv. *Ballads from MSS.* I. 306 Thes ennormyties to Recoyor [*sic*], now lette vs tayke payne! thynges amysse to Redresse, we oure selff must enforce. **1635** R. JOHNSON *Tom a Lincolne* in Thoms *Prose Rom.* (1828) II. 75 Thou..hast broken thy oath of knighthood, which no excuse can recover. **1721** PERRY *Daggenh. Breach* 106 A Breach..in two Places between Grays and Gravesend, (which, by timely Application, have been recovered). **1811** G. COLMAN *Pref. to J. Palmer's Like Master* I. 21 He had the misfortune to begin wrong in the game of life:—it is difficult to recover blots. **1869** F. W. NEWMAN *Misc.* 286 He was quickly overpowered; yet to recover the mischief he had done..was difficult.

†**b.** To cure, heal (a wound, disease, etc.). *Obs.*

1548 UDALL, etc. *Erasm. Par. Matt.* 11 b, A deadly wounde that can not be recouered. **1576** BAKER *Jewell of Health* 47 b, It doth marvelously recover and helpe..the byte of a mad Dog. **1626** MASSINGER *Rom. Actor* II. i, But grant that I by art could yet recover Your desperate sickness. **1655** MOUFET & BENNET *Health's Improv.* (1746) 199 Many are of opinion, that Caudles..recover the Weakness of Loins. **1748** *Anson's Voy.* II. i. 113 The land, and the refreshments it produces, very soon recover most stages of the sea-scurvy.

II. *refl.* **16. a.** To regain one's natural position or balance. Also *transf.* and *fig.*

1390 GOWER *Conf.* III. 346 Er that thou falle in such a wise That thou ne myht thiself rekevere. **1638** JUNIUS *Paint. Ancients* 41 We daily see..rope-dauncers..handsomly recover themselves after a perillous staggering and reeling. **1706** PHILLIPS (ed. Kersey) s.v. *Cancelier*, When a light-flown Hawk in her Stooping, turns two or three times upon the Wing, to recover her self before she seizes the Prey. *a* **1715** BURNET *Own Time* III. (1724) I. 582 Seeing that he was losing ground at Court, he intended to recover himself a little with the people. **1856** 'STONEHENGE' *Brit. Rural Sports* 533/1 Many careless and low goers are constantly striking their feet against stones, but..easily recover themselves. **1895** *Daily News* 27 Sept. 5/4 There will be ample width for a vessel to 'recover' herself when entering in severe weather.

b. To return to life or consciousness.

1597 GERARDE *Herbal* I. vii. §1. 8 At the approch of winter it dieth, and recouereth it selfe the nexte yeere. **1662** J. DAVIES tr. *Olearius' Voy. Ambass.* 27 Being stunn'd, it was half an hour ere I recover'd my self.

c. To get over a loss or misfortune; to recoup oneself. *rare.*

c **1645** HOWELL *Lett.* I. v. xxvi, I shall pay the wager in the place appointed, and try whether I can recover myself at gioco d'amore. **1797** *Encycl. Brit.* (ed. 3) X. 238/1 From this calamity, great as it was, London soon recovered itself.

d. To get over fatigue or illness. †Also const. *of.*

1745 *Fortunate Orphan* 22 Where we remain'd ten Days..to recover ourselves of the Fatigues of the Journey. **1856** 'STONEHENGE' *Brit. Rural Sports* Introd. 13 The overworked lawyer..has only to bestow an occasional day upon any one of the various sports within his reach, and he speedily recovers himself.

17. †**a.** To retreat, retire *into* a place; to fall back *on* one as an authority. *Obs.*

1606 G. W[OODCOCKE] *Hist. Ivstine* II. 11 Had they not so sodainly recoured themselues againe into their Cittye, he had also bin Lord and conqueror thereof. **1650** HOWELL *Giraffi's Rev. Naples* I. 68 He recover'd himself with four of his confidents..into the next house. **1655** FULLER *Ch. Hist.* VI. i. 268 S. Augustine of Hippo, (on whom these Monks would willingly recover themselves) was S. Benet's Senior by sixty years.

b. To withdraw or escape *from* or *out of*, to return *to*, a position, state, or condition. Now *rare.*

1611 BIBLE *2 Tim.* ii. 26 That they may recouer themselues out of the snare of the deuill. **1613** PURCHAS *Pilgrimage* IV. xii. (1614) 407 The adioyning Princes recouering themselues from Tartarian seruitude. *a* **1660** HAMMOND *Serm.* xxvii. Wks. 1683 IV. 677 He seldom ever recovers himself to a sober countenance. **1720** OZELL *Vertot's Rom. Rep.* II. VIII. 20 Hannibal..was as skilful in recovering himself out of Danger, as in drawing others into it. *a* **1763** SHENSTONE in D'Israeli *Cur. Lit.* (1866) 361/1, I have been at some pains to recover myself from A. Philips' misfortune of mere childishness. **1882** J. H. BLUNT *Ref. Ch. Eng.* II. 297 Ridley's hasty endeavour to recover himself from the pitfall into which he had been precipitated.

III. *intr.* or *absol.*

18. a. To regain health after a wound or sickness; to get well, or become healthy, again. Also *fig.*

c **1350** *Will. Palerne* 3874 No rink þei mi3t of-reche recuuered neuer after. ? *a* **1400** *Morte Arth.* 1572 Thare salle no silver hym save, bot Ewayne recovere. *c* **1470** HENRY *Wallace* x. 785 Byschop Synclar was wesyd with seknas..; and syn throu Goddis grace He recoueryt. *a* **1547** SURREY in *Tottel's Misc.* (Arb.) 3 The winters hurt recouers with the warm. **1596** SHAKS. *2 Hen. IV*, IV. v. 14 If hee be sicke with Ioy, Hee'le recouer without Physicke. **1647** CLARENDON *Hist. Reb.* VI. §97 Whom..he carried..to Oxford, where he wonderfully recovered. **1724** DE FOE *Mem. Cavalier* (1840) 26 My poor captain fell sick..but recovered. **1797** *Encycl. Brit.* (ed. 3) V. 12/2 Most of the young trees that are barked recover and continue healthy. **1845** DARWIN *Voy. Nat.* xii. (1879) 268, I felt very unwell, and from that time till the end of October did not recover. **1891** E. PEACOCK *N. Brendon* I. 254 He recovered slowly, but suffered little pain. **1921** H. CRANE *Let.* 19 Sept. (1965) 64 *The L[ittle] R[eview]*, I was informed..is recovering, will shortly reappear as a quarterly under Pound, Picabia, etc.

b. Const. *of*, *from* (the malady or disease, or that which causes indisposition).

1388 WYCLIF *Isa.* xxxviii. 9 Whanne he hadde be sijk, and hadde rekyuered of his sikenesse. **1535** COVERDALE *2 Kings* viii. 8 Axe councell at yᵉ Lorde by him, and saye: Maye I recouer from this sicknesse. **1597** J. KING *On Jonas* (1618) 73 If it be thy destiny to recouer of such a sicknesse..thou shalt recouer. **1667** MILTON *P.L.* XI. 294 Adam by this from the cold sudden damp Recovering [etc.]. **1766** GOLDSM. *Vic. W.* xvii, The man recovered of the bite, The dog it was that died. **1802** MAR. EDGEWORTH *Moral T.* (1816) I. iv. 18 The dancing-master gradually recovered from his sprain. **1841** BORROW *Zincali* II. iii. 60 Having partially recovered from his malady. **1860** MOTLEY *Netherl.* x. II. 80 Hohenlo recovered of his wound before Zutphen.

transf. **1649** JER. TAYLOR *Gt. Exemp.* I. ad §9 (1667) 144 To recover from a sin is none of the easiest labours that concern the sons of men. **1871** FREEMAN *Norm. Conq.* (1876) IV. xvii. 48 The land had not yet recovered from the mere carnage of the battle.

19. To regain life, consciousness, or composure. Also const. *of*, *from*, *out of.*

13.. *Coer de L.* 425 Tho he recouered of hys swowe, To hys paleys he hym drowe. **1377** LANGL. *P. Pl.* B. XIX. 156 Thus cam it out that Cryst ouer-cam, rekeuered and lyued. **1538** ELYOT *Superuiuo*, to recouer..whan a man semeth to be deade. **1600** SHAKS. *A.Y.L.* IV. iii. 161 Many will swoon when they do look on bloud..Looke, he recouers. **1648** HEYLIN *Relat. & Observ.* I. 47 Before any man that was not privy to the designe, could recover out of his amazement. **1691** tr. *Emilianne's Journ. Naples* 195 We soon recover'd of our Fears, when..we saw them kneel down. **1781** COWPER *Hope* 375, I soon recover from these needless frights. **1810** CRABBE *Borough* xix. 251 He fell, he fainted... As he recover'd, to his mind it came [etc.]. **1877** FROUDE *Short*

Stud. (1883) IV. I. x. 120 The archbishop had seated himself to recover from the agitation of the preceding scene.

†**20. a.** To rally, to return; to make one's way, to succeed in coming or passing (again). Const. *to, unto, over,* etc. Also with *up*. *Obs.*

c **1330** R. BRUNNE *Chron. Wace* (Rolls) 13958 Syn had þey no grace to stande, Ne myghte relye [*Petyt MS.* recouer], but euere fleande. *c* **1330** *Arth. & Merl.* 1650 (Kölbing) þat he fleiȝe in to þe valaye & recouerd [etc.]. *c* **1450** LONELICH *Grail* xiii. 179 ȝif Euere I Mowe rekeuere to sarras, I schal ȝow hyghly qwyten Er that ȝe pas. **1583** GOLDING *Calvin on Deut.* v. 28 Let vs fight against ourselues and daily indeuor to recouer vnto God. **1596** RALEIGH *Discov. Gviana* 97 We found it a wearisome way backe..to recouer vp againe to the head of the riuer. **1639** FULLER *Holy War* IV. vii, With much ado the Christians recovered to Antioch, having scarce a third part of them left. **1668** H. MORE *Div. Dial.* III. xxxiv. I. 535 Lapsed Souls..that recover into Sincerity are saved as we are saved. **1680** —— *Apocal. Apoc.* 184 If..she ever recover unto that plight again.

†**b.** To gain ground again *of* one. *Obs.*$^{-1}$

1654 in *Burton's Diary* (1828) I. 165 A recoiling man may, haply, recover of his enemy; but the courage of an enemy, surely, will be in the keeping of his ground.

21. a. To regain one's footing, position, or balance; †to get *up* again; also, to make a return *from*, †to get the better *of*, a slip, etc.

1494 FABYAN *Chron.* VI. ccxii. 228 It happed one of the Kynges cuppe berers to stumble and to recouer agayne. **1523** LD. BERNERS *Froiss.* I. ccviii. 249 The lorde of Gommegines was ouerthrowen, and coude nat recouer vp agayne. **1745** *Fortunate Orphan* 9 He did not believe it was possible to recover of this Fall. **1796** MORSE *Amer. Geog.* I. 667 A horse's foot having apparently slipped several inches and recovered again. **1856** 'STONEHENGE' *Brit. Rural Sports* 533/1 The ground is not cleared by the toe, and when it is struck there is not power to recover from the mistake.

b. *Fencing.* To return to a position of guard after a thrust.

1705 H. BLACKWELL *Eng. Fencing Master* 22 Advance half a Foot, and make home your Thrust, and as you recover beat on his Foile in Carte. **1809** ROLAND *Fencing* 26 After a thrust is delivered..it is necessary to resume your former position of the guard, which is termed recovering on guard. **1862** *Chambers' Encycl.* s.v. *Fencing*, A thrust can be returned when the adversary thrusts, or when, baffled in his attack, he is recovering to his guard.

c. To rise again after bowing or curtseying.

1711 STEELE *Spect.* No. 240 ¶2 This Person..made a profound Bow and fell back, then recovered with a soft Air, and made a Bow to the next. **1896** A. E. HOUSMAN *Shropshire Lad* xvi, It nods and curtseys and recovers When the wind blows above.

22. a. *Law.* To obtain, by legal process, possession or restoration of the thing claimed; to succeed in a claim or suit of recovery.

1422–61 in *Cal. Proc. Chanc. Q. Eliz.* (1827) I. Introd. 22 Yef that he wolde holde with hym..wherthurgh he myȝt recovere ayenst me, that he sholde have the thridde peny of his recovering. **1515** *Act 7 Hen. VIII*, c. 4 Every Advowaunt ..shall recover their damages and costes..as the playntyf shuld have doo yf they had recoveryd in the said Replevyne. **1607** COWELL *Interpr.* s.v. *Recovery*, A third person afterward by suite of lawe recouereth against me, I have my remedy..to recover in value, that is, to recover so much in mony as the land is worth. *a* **1610** HEALEY *Theophrastus* To Rdr., If the thing bought bee evicted from the buyer..hee may sue the Broker, and recover, as of the owner. **1798** BAY *Amer. Law Rep.* (1809) I. 66 Plaintiff had a right to recover, according to the law and custom of merchants. **1817** W. SELWYN *Law Nisi Prius* (ed. 4) II. 1214 The plaintiff shall recover according to the verdict. **1866** CRUMP *Banking* v. 118 The holder must neither protest nor give notice of dishonour, as he thereby precludes himself from recovering against the acceptor.

b. To make up a loss again.

1870 L. OLIPHANT *Piccadilly* 95 If I can carry on for another fortnight, I have got information which makes it certain I shall recover on them.

recover (riːˈkʌvə(r)), *v.*^{2} Also re-cover. [RE- 5 a.] *trans.* To cover again.

c **1400** *Master of Game* ii. (MS. Digby 182) þen be þei recouerede of her newe here, þat men call polifed, And hir hornes ben keuered with a softe heer. **1579** TOMSON *Calvin's Serm. Tim.* 504/2 It would cost me too much money to set the carpenters a worke to recouer mine house, it would cost me to much in Slate. **1612** *Proc. Virginia* xi. in *Capt. Smith's Wks.* (Arb.) 154 In 3 monthes, we..built some 20 houses; re-couered our Church [etc.]. **1645** FULLER *Good Th. in Bad T.* (1841) 68 Thus in the sight of our soul heaven is covered, discovered, and recovered. **1778** [W. MARSHALL] *Minutes Agric.* 13 May 1775 By plowing in the common way ..the majority of the root-weeds are re-covered in a few minutes. **1896** *Westm. Gaz.* 4 Nov. 8/3 The prisoner brought her the umbrella in question to recover.

recovera'bility. = RECOVERABLENESS.

1855 BAIN *Senses & Int.* II. i. §12 Our sense of their agreement, and their persistence and recoverability in idea. **1964** N. CHOMSKY *Current Issues in Linguistic Theory* ii. 46 But if there are several alternative designated elements, the comments on 'recoverability' must be slightly revised. **1965** G. J. WILLIAMS *Econ. Geol. N.Z.* xviii. 286/1 The recoverability of coal from a thick seam by underground mining is, of course, low. **1968** *Language* XLIV. 234 It will consist of..deletion of the subject of the embedded sentence, subject to the recoverability condition (i.e. only in those cases where it is identical with that of the matrix sentence). **1979** *Sci. Amer.* Jan. 29/3 Estimates of ultimate recoverability vary from one coalfield to another depending on the accessibility of the coal.

recoverable (rɪˈkʌvərəb(ə)l), *a.* [f. RECOVER *v.*^{1} + -ABLE.]

1. a. Capable of being recovered or regained.

c **1470** G. ASHBY *Active Policy* 684, I mene..of wilfulnesse people to supprise, That micht otherwise be recouerable. **1483** *Cath. Angl.* 301/1 Recouerabille, *recuperabilis.* **1591** PERCIVALL *Sp. Dict.*, *Recuperable*, recouerable. **1668** H. MORE *Div. Dial.* IV. xxxvii. (1713) 393 They in a short time may be recoverable to the obedience of the See of Rome. **1685** *Lond. Gaz.* No. 2044/2 The Cannon, some whereof are mounted, and others sunk, though easily recoverable. **1753** RICHARDSON *Grandison* (1781) III. xxi. 195 As giving it up for recoverable, I became for a few moments motionless. **1805** W. SAUNDERS *Min. Waters* 428 When again cooled, the smell is no longer recoverable. **1885** *Manch. Exam.* 26 Aug. 3/2 The publication of every recoverable sentence that fell from his lips or his pen. **1952** F. H. NORRIS *Paper & Paper Making* xiv. 222 Water derived from boiler washings and the rag washers is not recoverable. **1964** N. CHOMSKY *Current Issues in Linguistic Theory* ii. 41 A deleted element is, therefore, always recoverable. **1974** *Canad. Jrnl. Linguistics* XIX. 147 It is clear that not every instance of the operation of vowel deletion in Canadian French results in a recoverable vowel.

b. Capable of being legally recovered or obtained.

1590 SWINBURNE *Treat. Testaments* 15 Legacies..are all at this present recouerable by like actions. *a* **1674** CLARENDON (J.), They promised the good people ease in the matter of protections, by which the debts from parliament men and their followers were not recoverable. **1736** NEAL *Hist. Purit.* III. 494 That there may be a fixed maintenance in every parish recoverable by the incumbent. **1846** MCCULLOCH *Acc. Brit. Empire* (1854) II. 471 A pecuniary penalty, recoverable on summary conviction by a justice of the peace. **1875** JOWETT *Plato* (ed. 2) III. 112 That mere debts should not be recoverable by law.

c. Designating mineral reserves which by reason of their location and purity may be extracted economically.

1950 E. AYRES in L. M. Fanning *Our Oil Resources* vii. 234 The oil-shale regions of Colorado, Utah, and Wyoming.. contain the bulk of recoverable shale oils as well as the bulk of total shale oils. **1959** D. L. KATZ et al. *Handbk. Natural Gas Engin.* xi. 462/2 The initial gas content [of a natural reservoir] minus the content at a selected abandonment pressure gives the recoverable gas. **1973** E. N. TIRATSOO *Oilfields of World* xii. 336 Those volumes of hydrocarbons technically recoverable, to a high degree of certainty, but the exploitation of which is deemed uneconomic. **1976** *Conservation of Resources* (Chem. Soc.) 20 So far we have used up some 16% of total possible recoverable oil reserves, and only about 4% in the case of coal. **1979** *N.Y. Rev. Bks.* 17 May 14/4 The world's recoverable coal reserves are several times those of oil.

2. a. Capable of being restored to a sound, healthy, or normal condition.

1596 SPENSER *State Irel.* Wks. (Globe) 646/2 Having nowe both sowle and bodye greatly diseased, yet both recoverable. **1663** BOYLE *Usef. Exp. Nat. Philos.* II. iii. 70 'Tis one thing to dispute, Whether all Diseases be curable; and another, Whether all Persons be recoverable. **1676** *Phil. Trans.* XI. 652 That it is peculiar to the Thames-water alone, upon Stinking to be recoverable or potable again. **1707–12** MORTIMER *Husb.* (1721) II. 241 The Earth is to be opened to the bottom to find its Distemper; and if the Root be..hard, 'tis recoverable by applying dry Sand and Soot to it. **1774** CULLEN *Lett. to Ld. Cathcart* (1776) 4 Drowned persons are more generally in a recoverable state than has been imagined. **1876** GEO. ELIOT *Dan. Der.* lvi, Her remorse was the precious sign of a recoverable nature.

b. That may be amended; curable.

1616 CHAMPNEY *Voc. Bps.* 1 By how much more the error or deceit in them, is more hurtfull and lesse recouerable. **1652** GAULE *Magastrom.* 240 If you would know..whether the sicknesse or disease be curable and recoverable. **1899** J. HUTCHINSON in *Arch. Surg.* X. 136 It is not more easily recoverable without treatment than is syphilis. **1962** *Times Lit. Suppl.* 28 Sept. 759/1 It was realized that many severe mental disturbances were more recoverable than had previously been supposed.

c. Capable of being retrieved or made good.

1797 MRS. A. M. BENNETT *Beggar Girl* (1813) V. 158 Like vice also, the first lapse was seldom..recoverable. **1833** LANDOR *Imag. Conv., Scipio, Polybius, & Panætius* Wks. 1876 II. 327 Has the name escaped me! no matter,..he would smile at a recoverable lapse. **1848** J. SPEDDING *Even. w. Reviewer* (1881) II. 36 Considering that..a stumble at the threshold [is] scarcely recoverable.

†**3.** Capable of being retraced. *Obs.*$^{-1}$

1607 SHAKS. *Timon* III. iv. 13 A Prodigall course Is like the Sunnes, but not like his recouerable.

Hence **re'coverableness**, the possibility of recovering or of being recovered.

1609 W. SCLATER *Threefold Preserv.* (1610) Bj, Recouerablenesse in the elect, instability of reprobates. **1663** BOYLE *Usef. Exp. Nat. Philos.* II. v. xviii. 275 As may appear by the recoverableness of the metal out of it. **1892** H. DRUMMOND *Programme Chr.* 43 The recoverableness of a man at his worst.

recoverance (rɪˈkʌvərəns). [a. OF. *recoverance, reco(u)vrance*: see RECOVER *v.*^{1} and -ANCE.]

1. Recovery from trouble, misfortune, adversity, etc.; remedy, succour, help. Now only *arch.*

c **1375** *Cursor M.* 25869 (Fairf.) þi saule..sulde drey endeles penaunce & neuer sulde come to recoueraunce. **1423** JAS. I *Kingis Q.* lxxxvii, [They] diuersely happinnit for to deye;..Sum for dispaire, without recouerance. *c* **1440** *York Myst.* xxvi. 101 He coueres all þat comes Recoueraunce to craue. **1525** LD. BERNERS *Froiss.* II. xxxiii. 96 He was a true knyght, by whome in his tyme we had many recoueranses, and good iourneys. *a* **1578** LINDESAY (Pitscottie) *Chron. Scot.* (S.T.S.) I. 121 He persuadit the Earle of Douglas..to interpryse his recoverence in sett battell. **1886** J. PAYNE tr. *Boccaccio's Decameron* II. viii. I. 210 Inasmuch as some means was found for his recoverance.

†**2.** The regaining or recovery *of* some thing or state. *Obs.*

1440 in *Wars Eng. in France* (Rolls) II. 590 The recouerance of the kingis inheritaunce. *c* **1477** CAXTON *Jason* 95 b, For the recouurance of her helth she wolde goo thanke the goddes diane. *a* **1533** LD. BERNERS *Gold. Bk. M. Aurel.* (1546) C vj, The recouerance therof ought to be feared, if a fole haue the guydyng therof.

recovered (rɪˈkʌvəd), *ppl. a.* [f. RECOVER *v.*^{1} + -ED^1.] Restored, regained. †**recovered rubber** = ***reclaimed rubber*** s.v. RECLAIMED *ppl. a.* 2.

1477 EARL RIVERS (Caxton) *Dictes* 1 To dispose my recouerd lyf to his seruyce. **1483** *Cath. Angl.* 301/1 Recouerde, *recuperatus.* **1667** MILTON *P.L.* I. 240 By their own recover'd strength. **1681** FLAVEL *Meth. Grace* XVIII. 331 And shall not the recovered soul..greatly rejoice? **1870** DICKENS *Let. to W. Collins* in *Harper's Mag.* (1891) Nov. 906/2 That it will leave you in a really recovered state of good health. **1892** *Sci. Amer.* 7 May 293/2 Of all the materials used in rubber compounding, none was found to be as effective as recovered rubber, and this for the simple reason that when carefully prepared it *is* rubber. **1897** *India-Rubber & Gutta-Percha & Electr. Trades' Jrnl.* 12 Apr. p. vi (Advt.), G. W. Laughton & Co., manufacturers of recovered rubbers. *Ibid.* p. vii (Advt.), The Recovered Rubber Works, Ltd., Clayton, Manchester. **1902** *Chambers's Jrnl.* Oct. 683/2 This rejuvenated substance is known in New York as 'recovered' rubber. **1906** R. W. SINDALL *Paper Technol.* iv. 37 The organic matter is burnt off, and the mass left behind consists mainly of impure carbonate of soda. This residue is known as 'recovered ash'. **1929** CLAPPERTON & HENDERSON *Mod. Paper-Making* xxii. 317 Most of the recovered stuff will have to be used in a paper of a lower grade. **1952** F. H. NORRIS *Paper & Paper Making* xiv. 225 The most important point is the final recovery cost as compared with the value of the recovered fibre.

recoveree (rɪkʌvəˈriː). [f. as prec. + -EE^1.]

1. *Law.* The person from whom some property is recovered; *spec.* the defendant in an action of common recovery. Now *rare* or *Obs.*

1531–2 *Act 23 Hen. VIII*, c. 10 §3 Euerie persone.. hauinge feoffees recoverees or conisees to his vse. **1594** WEST *2nd Pt. Symbol.* §136 The Tenant is he, against whom the writ is brought, and may be termed the Recoueree. **1607** COWELL *Interpr.* **1766** BLACKSTONE *Comm.* II. 360 If the recoveree should ever obtain a recompense in lands from the common vouchee [etc.]. **1785** *Vermont State Papers* (1823) 501 The recoveree or recoverees in such action..shall..file a declaration..against the recoveror or recoverors, for so much money as the estate is made better.

2. One who is recovering from a disease or an illness.

1957 *Times* 15 Oct. 3/4 There was the Asian influenza casualty..who was replaced gallantly by an influenza recoveree, Mr Robert Harben. **1973** *Washington Post* 5 Jan. B5/2 The survey also showed that employers will hire wheelchair people, ex-convicts, T.B. recoverees, the deaf and the blind ahead of epileptics.

recoveree, obs. form of RECOVERY.

recoverer^1 (rɪˈkʌvərə(r)). Also 4 rekyuerer. [f. as prec. + -ER^1.]

1. One who recovers, regains, restores, etc.

1388 WYCLIF *Ecclus.* xiii. 26 Many rekyuereris [L. *recuperatores*] ben to a riche man disseyued. **1591** PERCIVALL *Sp. Dict.*, *Recobrador*, a recouerer. **1638** MAYNE *Lucian* (1664) 117 Will you permit him..to take Revenge of his Recoverer? **1651** DAVENANT *Gondibert* II. v. ix, Here all Men seem Recov'rers of time past. **1789** J. BROWN *Sel. Rem.* (1807) 244 A regainer of paradise and a recoverer of the tree of life. **1884** TENNYSON *Becket* III. iii. 135 Our recoverer and upholder of customs hath in this crowning of young Henry by York and London..violated the immemorial usage of the Church. **1978** A. PRATT *Directory of Waste Disposal & Recovery* 107 This list does not cover in great depth the more traditional areas of recovery—metals, paper, textiles etc. In these fields there are many recoverers and merchants.

†**2.** *Law.* = RECOVEROR. *Obs.*

1515 *Act 7 Hen. VIII*, c. 4 The recoverers in all suche recoveries..may from hensforth dystreyn for the forseid rentes. **1594** WEST *2nd Pt. Symbol.* §136 The demaundant is he that bringeth the Writ of Entre, and may be termed the Recouerer. *a* **1625** SIR H. FINCH *Law* (1636) 475 The recouerer and the Recognisee shall haue a *Scire facias.* **1766** BLACKSTONE *Comm.* II. 359 Which lands are now absolutely vested in the said recoverer by judgment of law.

†**recoverer**^{2}. *Obs.* Forms: 4–5 recouerer, -co(u)verer(e, -cuuerer(e, -courere; recoverir(e. [a. AF. *recoverer* and *recoverir* (OF. *recovrer, -couvrier*, etc.): see RECOVER *v.*^{1} and -ER^4.]

1. Recovery, remedy, etc. (Cf. RECOVERANCE.)

Common in 14th c.; in Hampole the ending is shown by rimes to be *-ere*, in Gower always *ir(e*.

1340 HAMPOLE *Pr. Consc.* 6095 þai sal þat day for ever be tynt Fra God, with-outen any recoverere. *c* **1380** *Sir Ferumb.* 2471 Ac wan þai seȝe þat of þat þyng recuuerer non þar nas, þay lefte þanne hure mornyng. **1390** GOWER *Conf.* II. 335 Pallas schop recoverir After the will and the desir Of hire. *c* **1450** *Merlin* 185 By that Castell..hadde the saisnes all her recouerer and all her socour of the contrey.

2. *Law.* = RECOVERY 4.

1436 *Rolls of Parlt.* IV. 501/2 Plee personell, wherof ye Jugement of recoverer extendeth to the somme of xl li. **1477** *Ibid.* VI. 181/2 The same Recorde of the same Recoverer.. thenne and their toke..and hadde aweye.

recovering (rɪˈkʌvərɪŋ), *vbl. sb.*^{1} [f. RECOVER *v.*^{1} + -ING^1.] The action of the vb. in various senses.

1375 BARBOUR *Bruce* III. 16 And weill ost, at thar fryst metyng, War layd at erd, but recoveryng. *c* **1400** *Destr. Troy* VIII. *heading*, Of the Counsell of the Grekys for Recoueryng of Elayne. **1483** CAXTON *Gold. Leg.* 339/1, I haue herd of the and of the helthes and recouerynges that thou makyst. **1543–4** *Act 35 Hen. VIII*, c. 9 The recoueringe inclosinge and inninge of..Wappinge marshe. **1593** DALLINGTON *Meth. Trav.* N, So dear was the recouering of Amiens. *a* **1660** HAMMOND *Serm.* xxv. Wks. 1684 IV. 650 The recovering of the Soul to the pure knowledge of God. **1709–10** STEELE *Tatler* No. 145 ¶2 He..made her the most obsequious Bow in the Presence of the whole Theatre..She made him the Recovering or Second Courtesy.

recovering (riːˈkʌvərɪŋ), *vbl. sb.*[2] [f. RECOVER *v.*[2] + -ING[1].] The action of RECOVER *v.*[2].

1904 *Daily Chron.* 28 July 8/5 His umbrella..may want re-covering. **1930** A. D. STUBBS *Pastimes that Pay* 45 When your dining room chairs require re-covering there is no need to send them to the upholsterer. **1967** M. HOLFORD *Photogr. Handbk.* 147 Send them to the local umbrella recovering shop.

recovering (rɪˈkʌvərɪŋ), *ppl. a.* [f. as RECOVERING *vbl. sb.*[1] + -ING[2].] That recovers, in senses of the vb.

1650 BAXTER *Saints' R.* (1836) 56 The Son of God comes with recovering grace. **1693** DRYDEN *Persius* iii. (1697) 446 He..began To mend, and look like a recov'ring Man. **1722** DE FOE *Plague* (1884) 314 These poor recovering Creatures. **1810** LADY GRANVILLE *Lett.* (1894) I. 8 It will be good for him in his recovering state. **1863** I. WILLIAMS *Baptistery* I. i. (1874) 11 The bright recovering year.

Hence **reˈcoveringly** *adv.*

1894 R. BRIDGES *Shorter Poems* 101 From waves of rustling wheat..Recoveringly that pass.

reˈcoverless, *a.* [f. RECOVER *sb.* or *v.*[1] + -LESS.] That cannot be recovered or repaired.

1607 COKE *Charge at Norwich Assizes* 25 This so famous ..monarchie had at one blowe endured a recouerlesse ruine. **1796** *Mod. Gulliver* 159 The Goodwin law his bane, Recoverless he sinks, and joins its ooz-sunk train.

†**reˈcoverment.** *Obs. rare*[−1]. [ad. F. *recouvrement* (11th c.): see RECOVER *v.*[1] and -MENT.] Recovery.

1591 SPARRY tr. *Cattan's Geomancie* III. ii. 159 *Coniunctio* ..signifyeth alwayes a recouerment and restitution of things scattered or lost.

reˈcoveror. *Law.* ? *Obs.* [f. RECOVER *v.*[1] + -OR: cf. RECOVERER[1] 2 and OF. *recovreor.*] The demandant who recovers a judgement, esp. in an action of common recovery.

1628 COKE *On Litt.* 104b, The recoueror should not distreyne, &c. because the conusee against whom the recouerie was had, could not. **1766** BLACKSTONE *Comm.* II. 360 Though the estate-tail is gone from the recoveree, yet it ..will ever continue to subsist (by construction of the law) in the recoveror, his heirs, and assigns. **1818** CRUISE *Digest* (ed. 2) V. 392 In all adversary suits, every recoveror recovered a fee simple. **1841** *Penny Cycl.* XIX. 339/1 On his default the court gave judgment..that the demandant or recoveror should recover the lands against the tenant.

recovery (rɪˈkʌvərɪ). Also 5 recov(e)ree, *Sc.* recouraie. [a. AF. *recoverie*, *-ery* (1302–5) or OF. *recovree*, *-couvree*, f. pa. pple. of *recoverir* or *recov(e)rer*: see RECOVER *v.*[1] and -Y.]

I. † **1.** Possibility or means of recovering, or of being restored to, a normal state; remedy. *Obs.*

1387–8 T. USK *Test. Love* II. xi. (Skeat) l. 127 Now I praie [thee] to enforme me in this, or els I hold me without recouerie. **1523** LD. BERNERS *Froiss.* I. clxx. 208 The frenche kynges thre sonnes..were right yong of age and of counsell; in them was but small recouery. *Ibid.* 743 This domage toucheth us so nyghe that we have no recovery. **1573** TUSSER *Husb.* (1878) 17 To ease thy sicknes speedilie, er helpe be past recouerie. **1686** tr. *Chardin's Trav. Persia* 200 On purpose to ruine past recovery a country that chiefly subsists by making of silk.

2. a. The act of recovering oneself from a mishap, mistake, fall, etc.

1525 LD. BERNERS *Froiss.* II. xlv. 154 What became of the kynge..after this discomfyture, made he ony recouery, or dyd he close hymselfe in ony of his townes? **1662** STILLINGFL. *Orig. Sacræ* II. i. §1 The conditions on which fallen man may expect a recovery. **1734** WATERLAND *Doctr. Holy Trin.* vi. Wks. 1823 V. 233 His mistake had shown some weakness of judgment, but his recovery manifested great strength of mind. **1781** COWPER *Retirem.* 138 To.. search the themes, important above all, Ourselves, and our recovery from our fall. **1860** TYNDALL *Glac.* I. xviii. 133 The effort at recovery is instantaneous.

b. The act of regaining the natural position after curtseying. (Cf. RECOVER *v.* 21 c.)

1712 BUDGELL *Spect.* No. 277 ¶17 The Curtesy and Recovery, the genteel Trip, and the agreeable Jet, as they are now practised in the Court of France. **1867** OUIDA *C. Castlemaine* (1879) 3 And practise their curtsey and recovery before their pier-glass.

c. *Rowing.* The act of returning to the proper position for making a fresh stroke. (Cf. 8.)

1856 'STONEHENGE' *Brit. Rural Sports* 480/1 It is clear.. that swing is not necessarily bad, but that it requires great skill to combine it with the proper recovery. **1884** *Pall Mall G.* 5 Apr. 3/2 They now row much longer than they did, their recovery is better.

d. In general use, the act of regaining an original position, esp. after rhythmic movement.

1876 [see RECURB]. **1949** SHURR & YOCOM *Mod. Dance* 173 Practice slowly at first. Fall: *one, two, three, four*: Recovery. *Ibid.* 190 *Recovery*, a series of movements used in order to return to position after a full sequence.

e. Reversion of a material, object, or property to a former condition following removal of an applied stress or other influence.

1885 P. G. TAIT *Properties of Matter* xi. 218 All elastic recovery in solids is gradual. **1895** *Proc. R. Soc.* LVIII. 132 Recovery of elasticity which the overstrained material undergoes with the mere lapse of time. **1939** WILLIAMS & HOMERBERG *Princ. Metallography* (ed. 4) iii. 73 Complete recovery cannot be attained in polycrystalline metals. **1966** C. R. TOTTLE *Sci. Engin. Materials* vii. 164 Recovery can also take place by annihilation of positive and negative dislocations, with or without the added movements in climb or cross-slip. **1975** E. R. TROTMAN *Dyeing & Chem. Technol. of Textile Fibres* (ed. 5) vi. 129 Recovery from strain [of polynosic fibres] gives good dimensional stability to fabrics which contain them.

3. a. Restoration or return to health from sickness.

1606 SHAKS. *Tr. & Cr.* II. iii. 188 He is so plaguy proud, that the death tokens of it, Cry no recouery. **1647** CLARENDON *Hist. Reb.* I. §60 Grievously Wounded, but not without hope of Recovery. **1713** STEELE *Englishm.* No. 55. 352 The Joy of her Majesty's Recovery very much Contributed to the Diversion. **1781** COWPER *Table-t.* 393 He thought the dying hour already come, And a complete recovery struck him dumb. **1820** SYD. SMITH in Lady Holland *Mem.* (1855) II. 219 Pray tell me how you are, and if you are making a good recovery. **1876** BRISTOWE *Th. & Pract. Med.* (1878) 609 Recovery is generally rapid under suitable treatment.

b. In phr. *in*, *on the*, *upon* (*the*) *recovery*: recovering, convalescent. Cf. *on the mend* s.v. MEND *sb.* 5. ? *Obs.*

1599 H. BUTTES *Dyets drie Dinner* L b, Good in hecticke feuers: restoreth their strength that are in recouery. **1618** *Demeanor of Sir W. Raleigh* 33 When hee was vpon recouerie, he dispatched the Land-forces. **1760–72** H. BROOKE *Fool of Qual.* (1809) I. 83 The strangers..had been treated with great humanity, and were now on the recovery. **1789** COWPER *Let. to Lady Hesketh* 4 Feb., Mrs. Unwin is certainly on the recovery. **1834** H. EVANS *Diary* 27 July in *Chrons. Oklahoma* (1925) III. 206 We found this Camp in a desolate situation... The sick some little on the recovery.

II. 4. *Law.* **a.** The fact or procedure of gaining possession of some property or right by a verdict or judgement of court; *spec.* the process, based on a legal fiction, by which entailed estate was commonly transferred from one party to another (also called ***common recovery***: see b).

For accounts of the nature of (common) recovery, and of the legal process by which it was effected, see West *Symbolæography* (1594) II. §136, Bacon *Max. & Uses of Com. Law* (1596) 62–64, Blackstone *Comm.* (1766) II. II., Cruise *Common Recoveries* (1783) and *Digest* (1818) V. 416. The legal validity of this method of breaking entails rested mainly on the decision of the judges in Taltarum's case in 1472: see *Year-bks. Edw. IV* (1566) an. 12, Mich. pl. 25 fol. 19. Among the enactments regulating its use, the most important are those of 7 *Hen. VIII*, c. 4, 14 *Geo. II*, c. 20, and 3–4 *Will. IV*, c. 74 (see quot. 1833). The party nominally deprived of an estate by such a suit was said ***to suffer a recovery***.

1472–3 *Rolls of Parlt.* VI. 4/2 Londes and Tenementes.. by any manere execution by any Statute or Recovery extended. **1515** *Act 7 Hen. VIII*, c. 4 Where as dyverse as well noble men as other the Kynges Subjectes have sufferid Recoveries ayenst them of dyvers their Maners Lordshippes Landes & Tenementes. **1594** WEST *2nd Pt. Symbol.* §136 The end and effect of such recoueries, is to discontinue and distroy estates tailes, remainders, and reuersions and barre the former owners thereof. **1602** SHAKS. *Ham.* V. i. 114 A great buyer of Land, with his Statutes, his Recognizances, his Fines, his double Vouchers, his Recoueries. **1668** PEPYS *Diary* 7 Feb., Mr. Jackson..hath this day suffered a recovery on his estate, in order to the making her a settlement. **1741** *Act 14 Geo. II*, c. 20 §6 And be it further enacted by the Authority aforesaid, That from and after the Commencement of this Act, every Recovery already suffered, or hereafter to be suffered, shall be deemed good and valid to all Intents and Purposes. **1766** BLACKSTONE *Comm.* II. xxi. 362 In all recoveries it is necessary that the recoveree, or tenant to the *praecipe*, as he is usually called, be actually seised of the freehold, else the recovery is void. **1833** *Act 3 & 4 Will. IV*, c. 74 (*title*) An Act for the Abolition of Fines and Recoveries and for the Substitution of more simple Modes of Assurance. **1861** MAINE *Anc. Law* vii. (1876) 289 Those famous Fines and Recoveries which did so much to undo the harshest trammels of the feudal land-law.

attrib. **1766** BLACKSTONE *Comm.* II. 358 The subsequent proceedings are made up into a record or recovery roll. **1951** KOESTLER *Age of Longing* I. i. 9 Your hand..is on lend-lease to a vicious old man; it is my recovery grant, or whatever you call it.

transf. and *fig.* **1598** SHAKS. *Merry W.* IV. ii. 225 If the diuell haue him not in fee-simple, with fine and recouery [etc.]. **1633** BP. HALL *Hard Texts, O.T.* 30 A pledge..of this covenant of peace, made between us; and an ernest of the recovery, and free grant of this Well. **1635** QUARLES *Embl.* III. xv. 182 My Grief's entayld upon my wastfull breath, Which no Recov'ry can cut off, but death.

b. ***common*** († or ***feigned***) ***recovery*** (see above). ***single recovery***, a suit of recovery in which a single vouchee was called (so ***double***, ***treble recovery***). † ***true recovery*** (see quot. 1607).

1596 BACON *Max. & Uses Com. Law* (1630) 64 If they make a writing, that one of them shall..suffer a common Recouerie to the other [etc.]. **1607** COWELL *Interpr.* s.v., A true Recouerie is an actuall, or reall recouerie of anything, or the value thereof by Judgement. *Ibid.*, A feigned recouerie is (as the Ciuilians call it) *quædam fictio iuris*, a certaine forme, or course, set downe by lawe, to be obserued for the better assuring of lands or tenements vnto us. **1670** BLOUNT *Law Dict.* s.v., This feigned Tenant, if it be a single Recovery, is made to appear and vouch the Bag-bearer of Writs, for the *Custos Brevium*, in the Court of Common Pleas. **1741** *Act 14 Geo. II*, c. 20 (*title*) An Act to amend the Law concerning Common Recoveries. **1818** CRUISE *Digest* (ed. 2) V. 416 A common recovery can in general only be suffered in the Court of Common Pleas at Westminster, because a real action cannot be commenced in any other court.

† **c.** A fine, etc., recovered at law. *Obs. rare*[−1].

1479 in *Eng. Gilds* (1870) 419 [To pay fines, etc.] recovered in the seide Maires Court, vnto the seide Maire and to such personez as the seide recovrees belongeth to of right.

5. The recovering *of* something lost or taken away; the possibility of recovering such a thing.

1538 STARKEY *England* I. i. 24 Suffur not your tyme vaynly to pas, wych, wythout recouery, fleth away. **1555** EDEN *Decades* 168 Th[e]..recouerie of the kyngedome of Granata. **1615** G. SANDYS *Trav.* 26 So farre from endeuouring a recouery..they jested at the losse. **1686** tr. *Chardin's Trav. Persia* 130 The Recovery of Six Thousand Pounds, which I thought I had lost. **1788** GIBBON *Decl. & F.* xlix. V. 120 After the recovery of Italy and Africa by the arms of Justinian. **1863** *Sat. Rev.* 23 May 675 A very interesting recovery of the whole plan of a Norman conventual church.

b. *of* one's health, or other state.

1568 GRAFTON *Chron.* II. 319 That for the better recovery of my health, I should returne into England. **1678** WANLEY *Wond. Lit. World* v. ii. §82. 472/2 He retired for recovery of his health. **1877** WINCHELL *Sci. & Relig.* v. 103 The recovery of that state of equilibrium which had been disturbed.

c. *of* a debt.

1745 *Col. Rec. Pennsylv.* V. 29 An act for the more easy and speedy Recovery of small Debts. **1922** JOYCE *Ulysses* 710 The dun for the recovery of bad and doubtful debts. **1964** W. D. PARK *Collection of Debts* (ed. 2) iii. 37 The court has power, in any action for the recovery of a debt or damages, to order interest at such rate as it thinks fit on the whole or part of the debt for the whole or part of the period it has been due.

d. Something regained or recovered. *rare*[−1].

1771 GOLDSM. *Hist. Eng.* I. Pref. 5 All these minute recoveries could be inserted only to the exclusion of more material facts.

e. The extraction of reusable substances from the waste produced by a process; also, the original extraction of a useful substance from a mixture, raw material, etc.

1885 *Jrnl. Iron & Steel Inst.* I. 216 (*heading*) Recovery of residuals from furnace gases. **1906** R. W. SINDALL *Paper Technol.* iv. 37 (*heading*) Soda recovery. **1923** S. J. TRUSCOTT *Textbk. Ore Dressing* 3 With copper,..though ore containing as little as 2·5 per cent may exceptionally be successfully smelted, a better recovery is obtained when the content is higher. **1923** W. H. WALKER et al. *Princ. Chem. Engin.* vii. 228 (*heading*) Recovery of waste heat from furnaces. **1951** K. K. LANDES *Petroleum Geol.* xi. 621 Modern production methods..result in a much higher percentage of ultimate recovery and, conversely, a lower percentage of residual oil left underground. **1962** F. T. DAY *Introd. Paper* iv. 40 The excess water which falls through the machine wire bed flows away for recovery. **1978** J. UPDIKE *Coup* (1979) vi. 247 Engineer's my title; recovery's my racket... Better recovery in the established fields is the name of the game... It's a miracle, what you can squeeze out of a rock if you know where to pinch it.

f. The return or capture of a ringed or tagged animal after its release; = RETURN *sb.* 15 b.

1909 *Brit. Birds* III. 180 Turning now to..the recovery of marked birds, it is as yet too early perhaps to expect many results of interest. The most interesting recovery that has as yet been reported is ring No. 4308. **1940** H. F. WITHERBY et al. *Handbk. Brit. Birds* III. 23 Twenty-five recoveries of British ringed nestlings indicate movements of comparatively short distances only. **1959** *Listener* 19 Feb. 321/1 We have been marking young seals with identity tags since 1951..and we have had some good recoveries. **1965** P. WAYRE *Wind in Reeds* iii. 36 Of the 284 ducks I ringed at Mileham, forty-five were recovered... Thirteen recoveries were from abroad. **1976** L. BROWN *Brit. Birds of Prey* ix. 114 Most of the recoveries are of birds which died unnatural deaths.

g. An amount recovered, usu. in contrast with that expended or initially available.

1931 *Economist* 17 Jan. 112/2 Total recoveries for December were, for the first time for over three years, slightly (30,000,000 francs) below the expected level. **1958** *N.Z. Timber Jrnl.* May 56/1 *Recovery*, the ratio of final product to log volume in timber conversion. **1973** J. L. GREGOIRE in V. S. White *Mod. Sawmill Techniques* v. 118 Figure 5.2 shows typical recovery on a 9-inch-diameter log 16 feet long with 1/16-inch taper per foot... From this log we are able to obtain a 1 × 4 14 feet long and six pieces of 2 × 4 16 feet long.

h. The retrieval of a satellite or spacecraft after a flight. Freq. *absol.* and *attrib.*

1949 *Jrnl. Brit. Interplanetary Soc.* VIII. 197 Two possibilities for increasing the chances for physical recovery after impact seemed worthy of investigation. **1960** D. E. BAILEY in K. W. Gatland *Spaceflight Technol.* 220 The main problems of satellite recovery are associated with deceleration, heating and tracking. **1961** *Ann. Reg. 1960* 385 Subsequently the U.S. Air Force made two further recoveries of the smaller Discoverer satellites by snatching them in mid-air as they floated down towards the sea by parachute. **1962** D. SLAYTON in *Into Orbit* 22 The recovery techniques which we would put into play to find and rescue the Astronaut and his capsule after they had landed. **1967** *Technol. Week* 20 Feb. 10/3 Orbital telemetry indicated that the capsule battery should have sufficient charge to operate the radio beacon and flashing light that serve as recovery aids.

6. a. The restoration or bringing back *of* a person (or thing) to a healthy or normal condition or to consciousness.

1590 SHAKS. *Com. Err.* V. i. 41 To fetch my poore distracted husband hence,..And beare him home for his recouerie. **1593** —— *3 Hen. VI*, V. v. 45 What? doth shee swowne? vse meanes for her recouerie. **1669** N. MORTON *New Eng. Mem.* 180 This year much of the Wheat is destroyed with Blasting and Mildew,..but the Lord hath sent much Rain for the recovery of the remainder. **1774** CULLEN *Lett. to Ld. Cathcart* (1776) 6 Although the drowned persons have lain for several hours in the water, attempts ought to be made for their recovery.

† **b.** The cure *of* an illness, wound, etc. *Obs.*

1620 E. BLOUNT *Horæ Subs.* 392 In the recovery of some desperate sicknes, wound, or the like. **1761** MRS. F.

SHERIDAN *Sidney Bidulph* I. 14 Ordered by the physicians to Spa for the recovery of a lingering disorder.

7. a. Restoration or return to a higher or better state; reclamation (of persons). Now freq. in economic contexts.

1593 G. HARVEY *New Lett.* Wks (Grosart) I. 289 Were I not content, in some little hope of his finall recouery,.. to do him a meritorious fauour by concealing his vtter discredit [etc.]. **1674** (*title*) Captives bound in Chains,.. the misery of graceless Sinners; and their recovery by Christ. **1736** BUTLER *Anal.* II. Concl. 295 Indeed neither Reason nor Analogy would lead us to think..that the Interposition of Christ.. would be of that Efficacy for Recovery of the World, which Scripture teaches us it was. **1836** J. GILBERT *Chr. Atonem.* i. 24 A modified system, which shall include the provision of means for recovery from a lapsed state. **1853** J. MARTINEAU *Ess.* (1890) II. 310 He is fitted to be among the prophets of recovery, who may prepare for us a more wholesome future. **1932** A. SALTER *Recovery* IV. i. 282 Here what is needed is a moratorium of several years, say four or five, to cover the depression and a period for Germany's recovery after it. **1940** G. CROWTHER *Outl. Money* iii. 115 Prices rose with staggering rapidity, until..they were one million million times the pre-war level. This is 'inflation without recovery'. **1958** *Times* 28 June 11/7 The pound staged a remarkable recovery against the United States dollar. **1974** B. PEARCE tr. *Amin's Accumulation on World Scale* II. iv. 497 In order to explain world recovery, all that remains is to analyze the effects of new techniques.

b. Reclamation (of land). *rare.*

1853 J. H. NEWMAN *Hist. Sk.* (1873) II. I. iii. 121 The special work of his reign was the recovery of the soil.

c. The restoration to working condition of a disused mine.

1932 *Trans. Inst. Mining Engineers* LXXXII. 452 The recovery of two separate underground districts which had been sealed off for several years due to the occurrence of fire.

8. The action of bringing back (an oar) to the original position. (Cf. 2 c.)

1856 'STONEHENGE' *Brit. Rural Sports* 481/1 Keeping Time, is the feathering of the oars, and their recovery.

†**9.** The act or opportunity of reaching. *Obs.*

c **1540** tr. *Pol. Verg. Eng. Hist.* (Camden No. 29) 213 To thintent that his adversaryes showld not have ready recovery of the shore and coome a land. **1653** H. COGAN tr. *Pinto's Trav.* 318 We were already past threescore leagues beyond the Port..; by reason whereof, we were fain to tack about for the recovery of it fifteen days.

III. 10. *attrib.* and *Comb.*, as (sense 3) ***recovery area, room, school, unit, ward***; (sense 5) ***recovery airfield, area, crew, fleet, line, ship, team, vehicle***; (sense 5) ***recovery furnace, plant***; (sense 7) ***recovery area, party***; **recovery time**, (*a*) the time required for an object or material, esp. an item of electronic equipment, to return to some specified condition following an action, e.g. the passage of a current; (*b*) *Railways*, time allowed in a schedule in excess of that which would be required in normal running.

1963 *Dict. U.S. Mil. Terms* 11 It is not expected that combat missions would be conducted from a *recovery airfield. **1965** *Guardian* 23 Aug. 1/2 It was taken for granted that the astronauts would be brought down in the Bermuda '*recovery area' at 12 22 a.m. **1971** *Ibid.* 1 July 1/5 The Soyuz made a..soft landing in the expected recovery area. **1976** *Scotsman* 27 Dec. 2/7 An attempt to have South Ayrshire designated as a recovery area. **1977** *Times* 25 Aug. 2/6 After transfer to the recovery area he [*sc.* a baby] was left in the care of a pupil nurse. **1971** *Guardian* 1 July 1/5 A helicopter-borne *recovery crew..found the cosmonauts.. without any signs of life. **1976** *Daily Times* (Lagos) 26 Aug. 9/3 Landings in darkness are generally avoided by Soviet space controllers as they hamper the work of recovery crews. **1968** *Guardian* 23 Sept. 1/2 The splash-down appears to have been some way from the *recovery fleet. **1942** G. S. WITHAM *Modern Pulp & Paper Making* (ed. 2) viii. 215 The Wagner *Recovery Furnace..embodies an attempt to greatly increase the efficiency of heat utilization in the recovery furnace over what is possible with the traditional rotary furnace. **1963** R. R. A. HIGHAM *Handbk. of Papermaking* v. 107 There are various designs of rotary recovery furnaces although these are generally of the horizontal type. **1976** J. D. LEE *Ninth Man* I. i. 8 One of the deck crewmen started paying out the *recovery line, and the rubber boat bobbed away from the submarine. **1933** *Sun* (Baltimore) 7 Oct. 1/8 McKee named his ticket the '*Recovery Party'. **1929** CLAPPERTON & HENDERSON *Mod. Paper-Making* xxii. 318 The water goes to waste, or back into use, or to a further *recovery plant. **1970** *Adv. in Chem.* XCVII. 223 The performance of butadiene recovery plants improves as solvent selectivity increases. **1916** S. S. GOLDWATER in *Trans. Amer. Hospital Assoc.* XVIII. 476 A large ward designed for an acute surgical service should have *recovery rooms, where postoperative cases may be cared for. **1951** *Anesthesiology* July 476 The use of the recovery room has without question saved lives. **1964** G. L. COHEN *What's Wrong with Hospitals?* iii. 51 She wanted a post-operative recovery room, to avoid crises on a ward ill equipped to deal with them. **1979** *Arizona Daily Star* 1 Apr. K10/1 Hospital auxiliary needs volunteers to make infant sweaters,..blankets and stuffed toys for children coming from the recovery room. **1909** *Westm. Gaz.* 11 Sept. 9/4 The establishment of open-air *recovery schools. **1962** D. SLAYTON in *Into Orbit* 23 The Navy stuck most of its *recovery ships in these big areas. **1976** B. JACKSON *Flameout* (1977) vi. 108 Red Cross volunteers were still carrying coffee and Coke to the *recovery teams. **1944** *Princ. Radar* (Mass. Inst. Technol. Radar School) xi. 18 The time required for elimination of these free ions after disappearance of the main pulse signal is referred to as the *recovery time of the device. **1959** G. R. PARTRIDGE *Princ. Electronic Instruments & Instrumentation* xix. 373 The interval from the end of the dead time to the moment when another full-size pulse can be produced is known as the recovery time. **1961** *Trains Illustrated* Nov. 684/1 Time regaining soon began and by Doncaster, with the joint help of 4 min recovery time and a top speed of 85 m.p.h. on the level at Moss, 6 min had been picked up. **1964** *Proc. IEEE* LII. 1301/1 The time required for full recovery of a gap between silver contacts in vacuum..ranged from about 1 μsec to 30 μ sec... This short recovery time is to be contrasted with the much longer recovery time in gases which is of the order of milliseconds. **1967** R. K. RICHARDS *Electronic Digital Components & Circuits* ii. 31 The time for removal of the minority carriers is called the 'recovery time' of the diode. **1977** *Modern Railways* Dec. 481/3 Nothing more than 81 mile/h was sufficient for even time to Stowmarket and the ensuing sharp 14 min to Diss was just kept from where recovery time should have balanced the arrears. **1965** *Nursing Times* 5 Feb. p. iv/2 (Advt.), *Recovery Unit. *a* **1944** K. DOUGLAS *Alamein to Zem Zem* (1946) 10 Field workshops with huge *recovery vehicles and winches. **1974** A. DOUGLAS *Noah's Ark Murders* i. 6 The recovery vehicle was positioned directly opposite the car. **1965** *Nursing Times* 5 Feb. p. lxii (Advt.), Enrolled Nurses ..For *Recovery Ward to do full-time day duty. **1970** H. MCLEAVE *Question of Negligence* i. 14 Cameron strolled around the recovery ward to inquire, as always, about the patients he had done that day.

recoyle, obs. form of RECOIL.

recraiand, obs. form of RECREANT.

†**recray**, *v. Obs.* Forms: 4 recreye. *Pa. pple.* recreyd, 5 recreiet (see also next). [a. ONF. *recreire, recraire* = OF. *recroire* to yield in a trial by combat = OSp. *recreer*, med.L. *recrēdĕre* to surrender (oneself), f. *re-* RE- + *crēdĕre* to entrust. See Du Cange, s.v. *recredere*, and cf. RECREANT.]

1. *intr.* To yield in a cowardly manner. *rare*$^{-1}$.

c **1330** R. BRUNNE *Chron. Wace* (Rolls) 13873 Loke þat non of ȝow recreye, Ne at þys iourne feynte ne feye!

2. In *pa. pple.* Tired, worn out.

1340 *Ayenb.* 33 Efterward comþ werihede þet makeþ þane man weri and worsi uram daye to daye al-huet he is al recreyd and defayled. **1422** tr. *Secreta Secret., Priv. Priv.* 165 A man a-foote hungry, thursti, and for trauaille recreiet.

†**recrayed**, *ppl. a. Obs.* Also 4 recrei(ȝ)ede, 5 -crayed. [f. prec.]

1. Craven, cowardly; apostate; recreant.

a **1330** *Otuel* 929 Recreiede kniȝtes, whi nele ye fiȝte? **1362** LANGL. *P. Pl.* A. III. 244 Raddest thou neuer *Regum* thou recreiȝede [*v.r.* recrayed] meede. *c* **1440** *York Myst.* xxxviii. 364 Fals recrayed knyght! Combered cowardis I you call. *a* **1529** SKELTON *Replyc.* 45 Ye heretykes recrayed. *a* **1529** —— *Agst. Scottes* 26 He was a recrayed knyght.

2. Slothful, lazy. *rare*$^{-1}$.

1340 *Ayenb.* 195 Ase þe hewe recreyd þet late comþ hom zuo þet þe lhord is oþerhuil euele y-herberȝed.

recrayhande, obs. form of RECREANT.

recreance[1] ('rɛkrɪəns). [ad. L. type **recreantia*, f. *recreāre*: see RECREATE *v.*[1]] Recreation, refreshment.

c **1475** *Lament. Mary Magd.* lxi, I shuld anone deuoid al my greuaunce, For he is the blisse of very recreaunce. **1581** N. WOODES *Confl. Consc.* Prol. iv, Our Author Bethought himselfe, to ease his heart, some recreance to fynde. **1842** TUPPER *Prov. Philos.* Ser. II. 207 Sleep is a recreance to body. **1876** RUSKIN *Fors Clav.* lxiii. 92 Such recreance as that in Mr. Ryman's shop.

'**recreance**[2]. [f. RECREANT *a.*] = next.

1879 HOWELLS *L. Aroostook* xxvi. 314 Grieving at this recreance of her memory to her conscience. **1897** F. THOMPSON *New Poems* 103 To give the pledge, and yet be joined That a pledge should have force to bind, This, O Soul, too often still Is the recreance of thy will!

recreancy ('rɛkrɪənsɪ). [f. RECREANT *a.*: see -ANCY.] The quality of being recreant; mean-spiritedness, apostasy, treachery.

1602 WARNER *Alb. Eng.* Epit. (1612) 377 For his Recreancie in a marriage contracted betwixt him and Williams daughter. **1628** COKE *On Litt.* 391 If a Felon be conuicted by Uerdict, Confession, or Recreancie, he doth forfeit his goods and Chattels. **1851** SIR F. PALGRAVE *Norm. & Eng.* I. 577 Whenever they could, [they] displayed their incorrigible recreancy. **1859** *National Rev.* Apr. 500 France, on pain of recreancy and dishonour, must come to the rescue.

†**recreandise**. *Obs.* [a. OF. *recreandise*, var. *recreantise* (see Godef.), f. *recreant* RECREANT *a.*: see -ISE.] Recreancy, apostasy.

c **1400** *Rom. Rose* 2107, I seye nought for recreaundyse, For I nought doute of your servise. **1480** CAXTON *Ovid's Met.* XIII. viii, Bewaire, that ye doo no such recreandyse.

recreant ('rɛkrɪənt), *a.* and *sb.* Now *poet.* and *rhet.* Forms: 4 recreent, 4–6 -aunt, (4–5 -e), 4– recreant; 4 recrayh-, recreyande, 4, 6 *Sc.* recryand, 5 recraiand. [a. OF. *recreant* adj. and sb., (one) who yields or gives up his cause, pres. pple. of *recroire*: see RECRAY *v.* and cf. OSp. *recreente*. On the northern forms with *-and*, see -ANT[2]. The form CREANT (*a.*[1]) was also current in ME. in the same sense.

The epithet is alluded to by Glanville, and mentioned by Bracton, as a term of the greatest opprobrium. *a* **1190** GLANVILLE II. vii, Perennis infamiæ opprobrium, illius infesti et inverecundi verbi quod in ore victi turpiter sonat consectivum. *a* **1260** BRACTON III. II. xxxiv. §2 Non sufficit ..nisi dicat illud verbum odiosum, quod recreantus sit.]

A. *adj.*

1. Confessing oneself to be overcome or vanquished; surrendering, or giving way, to an opponent; hence, cowardly, faint-hearted, craven, afraid.

a. In predicative use, after *to be* or *become*, *to yield* (oneself), *to make*, etc. †Also const. with *inf.*

13.. *Sir Beues* (MS. A.) 1042 Ich me ȝelde, Recreaunt, to þe, in þis felde. *c* **1330** R. BRUNNE *Chron.* (1810) 9 With dynt of suerde & drede he mad þam recreant. **1375** BARBOUR *Bruce* VI. 258 He..sua stonait the remanand, That thai war weill neir recryand. **1470–85** MALORY *Arthur* I. xxiii, To yelde me vnto the as recreaunt I had leuer dye than to be soo shamed. **1525** LD. BERNERS *Froiss.* II. lxxxi. [lxxvii.] 242 That it sholde not be sayd that the Frensshemen were recreaunt to have made that voyage. **1579** FENTON *Guicciard.* III. (1599) 122 Other peeces of good ability to defend them selues, became recreant, and yeelded. **1634** HEYWOOD *Maidenhead Lost* v. Ij b, Yeeld thy selfe recreant, villaine, or thou dy'st. **1700** DRYDEN *Pal. & Arc.* II. 415 From out the bars to force his opposite, Or kill or make him recreant on the plain. **1781** COWPER *Anti-Thelyphth.* 122 He that does not..Is recreant, and unworthy of his spurs.

b. In attrib. use. (†Occas. placed after the sb.)

c **1386** CHAUCER *Pars. T.* ¶624 Like the Coward Champion recreant þat seith creaunt withouten nede. *c* **1400** *Rowland & O.* 342 Send vnto Rowlande..I calle hym recreyande knyghte. *c* **1477** CAXTON *Jason* 90b, That I be poynted with the finger a reproche and cowardise and as a right recreant knighte. **1513** DOUGLAS *Æneis* XI. Prol. 119 Becum thow cowart, craudoun recryand. **1595** SHAKS. *John* III. i. 129 Hang a Calues-skin on those recreant limbs. **1615** BRATHWAIT *Strappado* (1878) 139 When those that Marshall'd them, Could not with-hold from flight their recreant men. **1725** POPE *Odyss.* VI. 11 Then great Nausithous..retreating from the sound of war The recreant nation to fair Scheria led. **1753** RICHARDSON *Grandison* I. xxvii. 198 What a recreant figure must he make even to himself. **1813** BYRON *Corsair* II. x, The loud recreant wretch who boasts and flies. **1878** BOSW. SMITH *Carthage* 317 It was his resolute bearing which had shamed..the recreant nobles of Rome from deserting the fast sinking ship of the State.

2. Unfaithful to duty; false, apostate.

a. In predicative use. Const. *to*, †*from*.

1643 MILTON *Divorce* II. iii. Wks. 1738 I. 186 If the Law ..shall give out Licence, it foils it self, and turns recreant from its own end. **1671** —— *P.R.* III. 138 Who..Turn'd recreant to God, ingrate and false. **1688** LUTTRELL *Brief Rel.* (1857) I. 453 He writt very severely against the papists and popery, but here of late turn'd recreant, and writt as much for them against the church of England. **1792** BURKE *Let. to Sir H. Langrishe* Wks. 1842 I. 549 Any man, who has not become recreant and apostate from his baptism. **1852** D. G. MITCHELL *Dream Life* 231 You know the careless and the vain purposes which have made me recreant to the better nature.

b. In attributive use. (Also of an action or condition.)

1791–1823 D'ISRAELI *Cur. Lit.* (1866) 286/2 Compelling the unfortunate Bacchanalian to drain the last drop, or expose his recreant sobriety. **1838** LYTTON *Leila* IV. v, That recreant Israelite is he who hath stirred up the Jews of Cordova and Guadix. **1863** W. PHILLIPS *Speeches* i. 3 To rebuke the recreant American.

†**3.** Worn out, exhausted. *Obs. rare*$^{-1}$.

c **1489** CAXTON *Sonnes of Aymon* iii. 109 Now ben the foure sones of Aymon recreaunte & almost wery.

B. *sb.* **1.** One who yields in combat; a cowardly or faint-hearted person.

a **1400** *Sir Perc.* 610 With his craftez ganne he calle, And callede thame recrayhandes alle. **1576** GASCOIGNE *Steele Gl.* Ep. Ded. (Arb.) 44, I should..cast downe mine armoure and hide myselfe like a recreant. **1593** SHAKS. *2 Hen. VI*, IV. viii. 28 You are all Recreants and Dastards, and delight to liue in slauerie to the Nobility. **1799** SHERIDAN *Pizarro* II. iv, Hold! recreants! cowards! What, fear ye death, and fear not shame? **1814** D'ISRAELI *Quarrels Auth.* (1867) 402 The recreant, in silence, was composing the libel, which his cowardice dared not publish. **1894** S. J. WEYMAN *Under the Red Robe* xiv. (1897) 337 Like the recreant..who, lying in the ditch while the battle raged came out afterwards and boasted of his courage.

2. One who breaks allegiance or faith; an apostate, deserter, villain.

1570 LEVINS *Manip.* 25/17 A recreant, *perfidus*. **1589** GREENE *Menaphon* (Arb.) 68, I tell thee, recreant, I scorne thy clownish Arcady with his inferior comparisons. **1607** SHAKS. *Cor.* v. iii. 114 Thou Must as a Forraine Recreant be led With Manacles through our streets. **1688** SHADWELL *Sqr. Alsatia* v, Oh this most wicked Recreant. **1836** J. GILBERT *Chr. Atonem.* ix. 409 Vain will then be the appeals of the recreant. **1869** BROWNING *Ring & Bk.* VIII. 674 We find Saint Paul No recreant to this faith delivered once.

b. *transf.* A runaway (animal).

1856 KANE *Arct. Expl.* I. vi. 65 It cost a pull through ice and water of about eight miles before they found the recreants.

Hence '**recreantly** *adv.*, '**recreantness**.

c **1475** *Partenay* 4436 A gret oth [he] made..That he wold be dede ful recreantly Or discomfite wold this cruell Geant. **1523** LD. BERNERS *Froiss.* I. cccxcix. 693, I trowe there was neuer so vnhappy people, nor more recreantly maynteyned themselfe. **1611** FLORIO, *Recredenza*, a belief changed from that it was, recreantnesse. **1895** *Chicago Advance* 28 Feb. 764/3 Recreantly turning their backs on the sacred doctrine of the rights of man.

†**recrease**, *v. Obs. rare.* [ad. L. *recrēscĕre* (or OF. *recroistre*), after *decrease, increase*.] *intr.* To grow or increase again.

1521 STILE *Let. to Wolsey* in *St. Papers Hen. VIII* (1834) II. 85 Sithe the writeyng of my laste letters sent un to your Grace, here be no newis recresid. **1522** *Ibid.* 97. **1542** *Lam. & Piteous Treat.* in *Harl. Misc.* (Malh.) I. 232 Which [wounds] by the dyffyculte and length of the way recreased and waxed worsse dayly.

recreate ('rɛkrɪeɪt), *v.*[1] [ad. L. *recreāt-*, ppl. stem of *recreāre* to restore, refresh, f. *re-* RE- + *creāre* to CREATE. Cf. F. *récréer* (14th c. in Littré).]

1. a. To restore to a good or normal physical condition from a state of weakness or exhaustion; to invest with fresh vigour or strength; to refresh, reinvigorate (nature, strength, a person or thing). In later use only *refl.* (cf. 4 b).

1535 STEWART *Cron. Scot.* II. 444 Onto the tyme reformit war sic thing.. And recreat agane als war thair strenth. **1555** EDEN *Decades* 106 Sweete sauers greatly recreatynge and comfortynge nature. **1601** HOLLAND *Pliny* II. 152 Wine recreateth and refresheth the stomack. **1624** CAPT. SMITH *Virginia* IV. 112 After hee had recreated and refreshed his Companie, he was sent to the Riuer Patawomeake. **1664** EVELYN *Kal. Hort.* (1729) 199 Stirring the Mould with the Spade, and (as need is) recreating it with Composts.

refl. **1542** ELDER *Let. to K. Hen. VIII* in *Bannatyne Misc.* (1827) I. 11 A certane lady, namede Scota, which.. come out of Egipte.. to recreatt hir self.. in the colde ayre of Scotland. **1555** EDEN *Decades* 279 When Demetrius had.. rested and recreate him selfe. **1797** HOLCROFT *Stolberg's Trav.* (ed. 2) III. lxxxix. 494 We recreated ourselves at two.. springs. **1861** HUGHES *Tom Brown at Oxf.* ii, He stopped at the island, and recreated himself with a glass of beer. **1862** HELPS *Ess., Organ. Daily Life* (1875) 159 That each living being requires a certain portion of air to recreate itself with.

†**b.** To restore to life, revive. *Obs. rare*$^{-1}$.

1631 WEEVER *Anc. Funeral Mon.* 122 They had power to calme stormes and tempests,.. to recreate euen the dead.

†**2. a.** To refresh (a sense or its organ) by means of some agreeable object or impression. *Obs.*

1514 BARCLAY *Cyt. & Uplondyshm.* (Percy Soc.) p. xxxi, What joye haue courtiers in tasting or in smell; For these two wittes in court be recreate. **1578** BANISTER *Hist. Man* VIII. 104 By the which varietie of colours the weryed eyes are recreated. **1621** BURTON *Anat. Mel.* II. iii. I. i, You haue many pleasant obiects, sweet smells, delightsome tasts.. &c. to recreat your senses. **1684** *Contempl. St. Man* II. v. (1699) 172 The eyes shall ever be recreated with the Light of the.. Bodies of the Saints. **1693** EVELYN *De la Quint. Compl. Gard.* I. 144 Speckled with little red spots that recreate the Sight. **1710** STEELE *Tatler* No. 179 ¶ 10 Those Delicacies of Nature recreate two Senses at once.

†**b.** To refresh or enliven (the spirits, mind, a person) by some sensuous or purely physical influence; to affect agreeably in this way. *Obs.*

c **1560** A. SCOTT *Poems* (S.T.S) v. 3 May is the moneth maist amene.. To recreat thair havy hartis. **1578** LYTE *Dodoens* II. lxxi. 241 The later writers say that it [Basill].. recreateth the spirites. **1580** LYLY *Euphues* (Arb.) 395 He that commeth into fine gardens, is as much recreated to smell the flower, as to gather it. **1622** J. HAGTHORPE *Div. Medit.* xix. (1817) 15 Ten thousand flowers to recreate the mind. **1651** tr. *De-las-Coveras' Don Fenise* 1 The various beauties of the Plants and Streames could but very little recreate him. **1712** BLACKMORE *Creation* II. 59 Whose odoriferous exhalations fan The flame of life, and recreate beast and man. **1750** JOHNSON *Rambler* No. 80 ¶ 3 We are very agreeably recreated, when the body, chilled with the weather, is gradually recovering its natural tepidity.

absol. **1778** SIR J. REYNOLDS *Disc.* viii. (1876) 440 Variety.. must be employed to recreate and relieve.

3. To refresh or cheer (a person) by giving comfort, consolation or encouragement. Now *rare*.

c **1470** HENRYSON *Mor. Fab.* ii. (*Town & C. Mouse*) xi, Ane gentill hart is better recreate With blith curage [*Bann. MS.* usage] than seith to him ane kow. **1502** ATKYNSON tr. *De Imitatione* II. xii. 194 Thou shuldest rather chose aduersyte than desyre to be recreate with many consolacions. **1577** tr. *Bullinger's Decades* (1592) 740 Hagar the hand-maid of Sara being in extreme daunger, is recreated by the consolation of an Angell. **1638** *Penit. Conf.* viii. (1657) 235 The holy Spirit recreates and comforts him with the sweet voice. **1749** LAVINGTON *Enthus. Meth. & Papists* (1752) 54 St. Anthony had often familiar Conversations with God, recreating him with extraordinary comforts. **1834** *Oxf. Univ. Mag.* I. 46 The habit.. of being recreated with the cheers of an exhilarated multitude.

4. a. To refresh or enliven (the mind, the spirits, a person) by some pastime, amusement, occupation, agreeable news, etc.

1531 ELYOT *Gov.* I. vii, The mooste noble and valiant princis.., to recreate their spirites,.. enbraced instrumentes musicall. **1584** COGAN *Haven Health* ii. (1636) 19 That learned Lawyer.. was wont to recreat his minde with Tenis-play. **1600** *Hosp. Inc. Fooles* 95 Iesting Fooles, whose intent is no other, but to recreat and make merrie the world. **1629** MAXWELL tr. *Herodian* (1635) 301 Recreating the people (as he thought) with Chariot-races, stage plaies, feasts and night-shewes. **1712** POPE *Let. to Gay* 23 Aug., I am very much recreated and refreshed with the news of the advancement. **1784** SIR J. REYNOLDS *Disc.* xii. (1884) 209 It is.. necessary to intellectual health, that the mind should be recreated and refreshed with a variety in our studies. **1825** LAMB *Elia* Ser. II. *Superann. Man*, No busy faces to recreate the idle man who contemplates them ever passing by. **1838** PRESCOTT *Ferd. & Is.* (1846) I. viii. 361 Some of their sovereigns.. were wont to recreate their spirits with elegant poetry. **1890** *Spectator* 6 Dec., It recreates him to indulge in sayings which leave an impression of rashness and scorn.

absol. **1868** SALA *Lamb's Wks.* I. p. vi, Although he rarely recreated, he never failed to instruct.

b. *refl.* To refresh (oneself) with some agreeable occupation or pastime.

1530 PALSGR. 681/2, I recreate my selfe with some pastyme or sporte. **1600** J. PORY tr. *Leo's Africa* III. 165 Sometimes he recreateth himselfe with hunting, and sometime with playing at chesse. **1669** GALE *Crt. Gentiles* I. III. iii. 45 God contemplating this new framed Image.. rejoiced and recreated himself therein. **1712** STEELE *Spect.* No. 498 ¶ 1 There are many Illustrious Youths.. who frequently recreate themselves by driving of a Hackney-Coach. **1849–50** HT. MARTINEAU *Hist. Peace* IV. xii. III. 158 The Lord Chancellor was recreating himself, after a long stretch of arduous business, with a journey in Scotland.

†**c.** To enliven or gratify (a feeling). *Obs.*

1643 SIR T. BROWNE *Relig. Med.* I. §13 The other Attribute wherewith I recreate my devotion, is His Wisdom. **1681–6** J. SCOTT *Chr. Life* (1747) III. 9 With a Design to mock and ridicule him, and recreate his own inexorable Spleen with the spiteful Pleasure of.. repulsing him.

5. *intr.* To take recreation. Now chiefly *U.S.*

1587 J. RIDER *Bibl. Schol.* s.v., To recreat, neut. or be delighted with, *oblector, acquiesco*. **1606** G. W[OODCOCKE] *Hist. Ivstine* XXXVI. 115 There is in that seate.. a continual shadow to walk and recreat in. **1676** L. ADDISON *State of Jews* 117 They suppose the Souls in Purgatory have liberty to recreate. **1874** HELPS *Soc. Press.* xix. (1875) 282 Let us.. now recreate, lest we should eat and drink too much at dinner. **1978** *Verbatim* Winter 6/1 The President plans to recreate on Labor Day. **1979** *Sunset* Apr. 16/3 (Advt.), Recreate. It's fun in Colorado. For the best in summer fun take yourself and your family away.

transf. **1618** BOLTON *Florus* I. xvi. (1636) 46 Here are the lakes Lucrinus and Avernus, bowers of delight for the sea to recreate in.

†**6.** *trans.* To relieve (an occupation, state, etc.) by means of something of a contrary nature. *Obs.*

1545 ASCHAM *Toxoph.* I. (Arb.) 45 Ernest studie must be recreated with honest pastime. **1597** *1st Pt. Return fr. Parnass.* III. i. 974, I have not onlie recreated thy could state with the warmth of my bountie, but also [etc.]. **1621** G. SANDYS *Ovid's Met.* xv. (1626) 304 Ioues sonne.. entered Heroick Croton's roofe; a welcome Guest: And his long trauell recreates with rest. **1651–3** JER. TAYLOR *Serm. for Year* (1678) 335 A perpetual full table, not recreated with fasting, not made pleasant with intervening scarcity.

Hence '**recreated** *ppl. a.*[1]

1832 HT. MARTINEAU *Each & All* iv. 47 The recreated statesman finds in either case equal pleasure and repose. **1897** *Allbutt's Syst. Med.* III. 484 In order to enable the recreated system to throw off the burden.

recreate (riːkrɪ'eɪt), *v.*[2] Also **re-create.** [f. RE- 5 a + CREATE *v.*] *trans.* To create anew.

1587 GOLDING *De Mornay* Ep. Ded. **ij, Gods wisedome in creating thinges.. nor his goodnesse in recreating or renewing them. **1609** J. DAVIES *Holy Roode* C iv, Nor was't alone for his owne glorie meer That he did man create, or re-create. **1679** PENN *Addr. Prot.* II. v. (1692) 190 They had almost need to be Re-Created in order to be Converted. **1768–74** TUCKER *Lt. Nat.* (1834) I. 300 Could Mr. Locke himself imagine that his person was annihilated every night when he went to sleep, and re-created again when he awoke in the morning? **1813** SHELLEY *Q. Mab* VIII. 107 All things are recreated. **1868** J. H. BLUNT *Ref. Ch. Eng.* I. 63 Four out of the number were recreated, under the name of Regius professorships.

absol. **1860** PUSEY *Min. Proph.* 166 Man.. can destroy; he cannot recreate.

b. To create anew in imagination.

1837 HAWTHORNE *Twice-told T.* (1851) II. xix. 267 While gazing at a figure of melancholy age, to re-create its youth. **1895** W. M. RAMSAY *Paul the Trav.* i. §3. 17 It is always hard to recreate the remote past.

Hence **recre'ated** *ppl. a.*[2], **recre'ating** *vbl. sb.*[2] and *ppl. a.*[2]

1587 GOLDING *De Mornay* xxviii. 524 What counsell wouldest thou giue him for the recreating of thee. **1631** R. BYFIELD *Doctr. Sabb.* 207 Our re-creating or Redemption. **1659** PEARSON *Creed* ii. (1839) 165 Where are the recreated 'principalities and powers'? **1813** SHELLEY *Q. Mab* VI. 56 The blood-stained charter.., Which Nature soon, with re-creating hand Will blot in mercy from the book of earth.

recreate (riːkrɪ'eɪt), *ppl. a.* [Cf. prec. and CREATE *ppl. a.*] Re-created.

1855 BAILEY *Mystic, Spir. Leg.* 134 They.., Through conduct, aspiration and intent Thrice recreate, shall rise. **1877** RUSKIN *Fors Clav.* lxxxiv. 412 The recreate and never to be dissolved order of the perfect earth.

'**recreating,** *vbl. sb.*[1] [f. RECREATE *v.*[1] + -ING[1].] The action of refreshing, reinvigorating, etc.

1580 LYLY *Euphues* (Arb.) 303 After long recreating of hir selfe in the country. **1663** BUTLER *Hud.* I. i. 677 'Twas an old way of recreating, Which learned butchers call Bear-baiting. **1854** FABER *Growth in Holiness* xiv. (1872) 245 Recreating and idling are very different things.

So '**recreating** *ppl. a.*[1], that recreates.

1641 MILTON *Ch. Govt.* II. Introd., Wks. (1851) 147 Some recreating intermission of labour, and serious things. **1695** J. EDWARDS *Perfect. Script.* 223 Other recreating and pleasurable entertainments. **1783** BURKE *Sp. Fox's E. India Bill* Wks. 1842 I. 282 Poverty, sterility, and desolation, are not a recreating prospect. **1849** C. BRONTË *Shirley* xx, Every night yielded her recreating rest.

recreation[1] (rɛkrɪ'eɪʃən). Also 4–6 **-acioun, -acyon,** etc. [a. F. *récréation* (13th c. in Littré), or ad. L. *recreātiōn-em* (Pliny), n. of action f. *recreāre* to RECREATE *v.*[1]]

†**1.** Refreshment by partaking of food; a refection; nourishment. *Obs.*

1390 GOWER *Conf.* III. 100 To sustienen hem and fede In time of recreacion. *c* **1489** CAXTON *Blanchardyn* 145 Blanchardyn, Sadoyne, and his wyff.. were sittyng at the bord takynge their recreacyon. **1538** in Strype *Eccl. Mem.* (1721) I. II. App. xc. 251, I bequest to the Maister, Wardens and Felyshyp of the Drapers, v. pounde, for a recreation or a dyner. **1600** SURFLET *Countrie Farme* III. xlvi. 516 The tree must haue some recreation giuen it in winter, after his great trauell in bringing foorth of his fruite.

†**2. a.** Refreshment or comfort produced by something affecting the senses or body. *Obs.*

1390 GOWER *Conf.* III. 114 [Of the sun] alle erthly creatures.. taken after the natures Here ese and recreacion. *c* **1430** LYDG. *Min. Poems* (Percy Soc.) 14 Wyne is a lycor of grete recreacioun. *c* **1440** *Gesta Rom.* ii. 6 (Harl. MS.) Ofte tyme he vsid to ligge ny the fire, for to haue comfort and recreacion of þe fire.

†**b.** Comfort or consolation of the mind; that which comforts or consoles. *Obs. rare.*

c **1410** HOCCLEVE *Mother of God* 138 The habitacion Of the holy goost our recreacion Be in myn herte. *c* **1440** *York Myst.* xlvi. 20 Vnkyndely þei kidde þem þer kyng for to kenne, With carefull comforth and cold recreacioun. *c* **1475** *Lament. Mary Magd.* cxcvii, My comforte, and al my recreacioun, Fare wel my parpetual saluacioun.

3. a. The action of recreating (oneself or another), or fact of being recreated, by some pleasant occupation, pastime or amusement.

c **1400** MAUNDEV. (Roxb.) xxxiv. 155 New thinges.. to tell off for solace and recreacioun of þaim þat lykez to here þam. **1484** CAXTON *Fables of Alfonce* vi, To take his recreacion he entryd in to his gardyn. **1532** MORE *Confut. Tindale* Wks. 558/1 Tindall is as it semeth.. set vpon readyng of rydles for his recreacion. **1584** COGAN *Haven Health* ii. (1636) 20 Socrates.. for recreation.. blushed not to ride upon a Reed among his little children. **1651** HOBBES *Leviath.* II. xxiv. 129 Forrests, and Chases, either for his recreation, or for preservation of Woods. **1755** YOUNG *Centaur* ii. Wks. 1757 IV. 140 Too much recreation tires as much, as too much business. **1791** COWPER *Iliad* XXI. 56 Eleven days, at his return, he gave To recreation joyous with his friends. **1860** HOOK *Lives Abps.* I. i. 2 He sought his recreation in the study of Ecclesiastical History.

b. An instance of this; a means of recreating oneself; a pleasurable exercise or employment.

c **1430** LYDG. *Min. Poems* (Percy Soc.) 82 Travaile requyrithe a recreacioune. **1477** EARL RIVERS (Caxton) *Dictes* 1 For a recreacion and a passyng of tyme I had delyte and axed to rede somme good historye. **1585** T. WASHINGTON tr. *Nicholay's Voy.* III. x. 86 The Turke hath observed the Palester of the Athletes.. for one of his accustomed recreations. **1631** GOUGE *God's Arrows* III. §11. 206 Such kind of recreations as make men fitter for warre. **1749** LAVINGTON *Enthus. Meth. & Papists* 23 Our love of Recreations and Diversions has indeed confessedly exceeded all bounds. **1849** MACAULAY *Hist. Eng.* vii. II. 169 The chase was his favourite recreation.

c. One who or that which supplies recreation.

1601 SHAKS. *Twel. N.* II. iii. 146 If I do not gull him into an ayword, and make him a common recreation [etc.]. **1863** *Sat. Rev.* 15 Aug. 224 These *Tragedies and other Plays* will live.. not as the recreation of an idle hour [etc.].

†**4.** A place of refreshment or recreation. *Obs.*

c **1440** *Promp. Parv.* 426/1 'Recreacyon', or howse of refreschynge, *recreatorium*. **1618** BOLTON *Florus* (1636) 29 Tiber which is now but a Suburbe, and Præneste but our Summer-recreation.

5. *attrib.* and *Comb.*, as ***recreation area, centre, ground, hall, home, leader, leadership, league, officer, ramble, room, tent, therapy, time, vehicle.***

1961 *Recreation* Dec. 531/1 *Recreation areas are never too large for the future. **1978** *N.Y. Times* 29 Mar. B2/3 Ocean Beach Park, a recreation area on Long Island Sound. **1943** J. S. HUXLEY *TVA* 17 Guntersville, formerly a sleepy market town.. is now becoming.. an important *recreation centre. **1974** M. G. D. DIXEY *Local Recreation Centres* I. 10 Most local authorities recognise the need for indoor recreation centres. **1859** *Act 22 Vict.* c. 27 §8 This Act.. may be cited.. [as] 'The *Recreation Grounds Act, 1859'. **1898** E. HOWARD *Tomorrow* xiv. 147 These wretched slums will be pulled down, and their sites occupied by parks, recreation grounds, and allotment gardens. **1969** I. & P. OPIE *Children's Games* xii. 341 The merry-go-round is a type of swing placed in the recreation ground by the local council. **1981** J. B. HILTON *Playground of Death* iv. 42, I learned on an Essex Recreation Ground. **1943** J. S. HUXLEY *TVA* 75 This method of sectional prefabrication has now been successfully applied to larger buildings, such as.. *recreation halls. **1976** *National Observer* (U.S.) 10 July 6/2 Add to this the boom in *recreation and leisure homes and you have Ozark hills and hollows chock full of people. **1923** *Playground* Apr. 35/2 A *recreation leader should be active in the social work program of his city. **1936** H. R. CLARK *Playground Man.* ii. 32 Discuss the future possibilities for playground and recreation leaders. **1953** H. D. CORBIN *Recreation Leadership* ii. 20 The recreation leader is responsible for the organization, direction, and supervision of recreational activities. **1924** *Playground* Apr. 118 The marked increase in employed *recreation leadership. **1976** *National Observer* (U.S.) 22 May 14/4 (Advt.), Liberal Arts Career Studies... Recreation Leadership. *Ibid.* May 17/2 We were told to scrounge up our own games through local *recreation leagues to get as much experience as possible. **1976** *Evening Times* (Glasgow) 1 Dec. 3/1 The Carstairs patient who died attempting to defend *recreation officer Neil McLellan. **1853** D. F. M'CARTHY *Dramas of Calderon* I. p. viii, *Recreation-rambles into the enchanted regions of foreign song. **1854** *Recreation room [see *coconut matting* s.v. COCO, COCOA 4 e]. **1890** *Harper's New Monthly Mag.* Feb. 342/1 An excellent canteen and a recreation-room are, however, now provided in almost every barrack. **1978** J. WAINWRIGHT *Thief of Time* 99 I'm in the Recreation Room. Playing Ludo. **1930** E. M. BRENT-DYER *Chalet Girls in Camp* v. 75 The two big tents for the commissariat and *recreation tents had ridge-poles. **1977** M. EDELMAN *Polit. Lang.* iv. 60 If they play volleyball, that is *recreation therapy. **1909** 'MARK TWAIN' *Is Shakespeare Dead?* iv. 45 It seriously shortened his.. *recreation-time. **1974** *State* (Columbia, S. Carolina) 15 Feb. 17-B/1 (Advt.), Home sites. Mobile Homes. *Recreation vehicles. **1977** *Globe & Mail* (Toronto) 27 Apr. 35/2 He predicted sales of RVs will continue to rise, 'because the recreation vehicle looks solid when compared with other vacation forms'.

recreation² (riːkrɪˈeɪʃən). Also re-creation. [f. RE- 5 a + CREATION.] The action of creating again; a new creation.

1522 *World & Child* C iij b, Christ,..That craftly made euery creature by good recreacyon. **1584** R. SCOT *Discov. Witchcr.* v. ii. (1886) 74 But to what end should one dispute against these creations and recreations? **1611** BP. HALL *Serm.* v. 52 As in the Creation he could have made all at once, but he would take days for it: so in our recreation by grace. **1664** J. WEBB *Stone-Heng* (1725) 2 Not long after the Re-creation of Mankind we find recorded..the Tower of Babylon. **1850** R. I. WILBERFORCE *Holy Baptism* 42 Regeneration is a re-creation of man's nature. **1873** G. HENSLOW *Evolution* xiii. 204 The cataclysms and recreations of the early geological theorists.

recreational (rɛkrɪˈeɪʃənəl), *a.* [f. RECREATION¹ + -AL¹.] **a.** Of or pertaining to recreation. Also, used for, or as a form of, recreation; concerned with recreation.

1656 E. REYNER *Rules Govt. Tongue* 226 We may use Recreational speeches sometimes, to instruct, reprove or comfort others, in a pleasant way. **1882** JEVONS *Meth. Soc. Ref.* 69 The educational and recreational value of admission to such establishments. **1890** *Century Mag.* June 176 The recreational section has been a most unequivocal Success, and has already proved a boon to East London. **1946** *Q. Jrnl. Forestry* XL. 2 The Americans have a word for it: the 'recreational' use of land. This is primarily what National Parks are for. **1946** *R.A.F. Jrnl.* May 173 There is an extensive technical and recreational library. **1956** A. H. COMPTON *Atomic Quest* 110 The Cook County recreational area. **1973** *Times* 2 Mar. 16/5 Proposals to create the first protected nature reserve..are being discussed by Deal town council with..recreational societies. **1976** *Billings* (Montana) *Gaz.* 20 June 1-F/1 We used to hear about recreational shopping—it was sort of a lark and a lot of fun—but I think now it is a pretty grim, serious business. **1977** *Age* (Melbourne) 18 Jan. 24/1 (Advt.), Caravan Owners!.. Recreational vehicle reports include a 24 ft. Glendale, pronounced ideal for a young couple's first home.

b. ***recreational mathematics***, mathematics studied or indulged in for pleasure or amusement.

1940 KASNER & NEWMAN *Math. & Imagination* 156 Researches in recreational mathematics sprang from the same desire to know, were guided by the same principles, and required the exercise of the same faculties as the researches leading to the most profound discoveries in mathematics and mathematical physics. Accordingly, no branch of intellectual activity is a more appropriate subject for discussion than puzzles and paradoxes. **1973** *Sci. Amer.* Sept. 176/1 It would..be hard to imagine two problems in combinatorial point-set geometry more remote from foreseeable practical applications unless one thinks of recreational mathematics (with its two virtues: amusement and instruction) as a branch of applied mathematics.

Hence **recreˈationalist**, one who advocates or promotes the provision of facilities for recreation; **recreˈationally** *adv.*

1970 *Daily Tel.* 31 Mar. 14 Landowners, farmers, residents, recreationalists, preservationists, conservationists, naturalists, sportsmen and many others have to be considered. **1975** *Nature* 18 Sept. 185/1 Extracts of the poppy plant have been used since the days of the Homeric epics medically and recreationally. **1977** *Jrnl. R. Soc. Arts* CXXV. 257/1 The NCC [*sc.* Nature Conservancy Council] is trying to achieve a revolution in attitudes reconciling the needs of the recreationalists and the conservationists. **1979** *Sci. Amer.* Feb. 52/2 The diver's work is far more demanding than might be supposed by someone who has dived recreationally in clear, warm water.

recreationist (rɛkrɪˈeɪʃənɪst). [f. RECREATION¹ + -IST.] **a.** One who pursues a recreation. **b.** = RECREATIONALIST. (See also quot. 1952.)

1904 *Daily Chron.* 13 Sept. 6/6 The campers had relaxed their vigilance... At a sudden startled shout of 'Police,' the Recreationists discovered helmeted and uniformed stalwarts advancing on them. **1952** D. RIESMAN in *Antioch Rev.* Dec. 420 Students of leisure—'recreationists' perhaps we'd better call them. **1963** *Times* 6 Nov. 13/3 A useful exercise..to bring poachers..round a table with gamekeepers..together with naturalists, architects, town planners, industrialists, and recreationists (if the word will serve). **1977** *Daily Colonist* (Victoria, B.C.) 8 July 13/4 Cougar Air..will be relying heavily on lumber and mining companies for business as well as recreationists.

recreative (ˈrɛkrɪeɪtɪv), *a.*¹ and *sb.* [f. RECREATE *v.*¹ and -IVE, perh. after F. *récréatif* (16th c. in Littré).]

A. *adj.* Tending to recreate or refresh in a pleasureable manner; amusing, diverting.

1549 *Compl. Scot.* Table, The sext cheptor rehersis ane monolog recreatyue of the actor. **1579** E. K. *Spenser's Sheph. Cal.* Gen. Argt. §3 Recreative, such as al those be, which containe matter of love. **1629** *Shertogenbosh* 1 This Boscage was an euen and recreatiue place, fruitfull of wild Deere. **1695** J. EDWARDS *Perfect. Script.* 222 Washing or bathing..was a recreative exercise of the female sex. **1729** SHELVOCKE *Artillery* IV. 207 The form then of the recreative Sort [of crackers] may be much varied. **1814** MME. D'ARBLAY *Wanderer* III. 293 They were only recreative little sylphs amusing themselves with whipping and spurring me on to my own good. **1887** *Spectator* 9 Apr. 492 His contributions to the recreative literature of the day.

†**B.** *absol.* as *sb.* A recreative thing or pursuit.

1615 DANIEL *Hymen's Tri.* Wks. (1717) 90 For these are only Cynthia's Recreatives Made unto Phoebus. **1620** E. BLOUNT *Horæ Subs.* 382, I know few recreatiues that possesse vs more, then the humour of building.

Hence **ˈrecreatively** *adv.*, **ˈrecreativeness**¹.

1611 COTGR., *Recreativement*, recreatiuely, with recreation. **1727** BAILEY vol. II, *Recreativeness*, recreating quality.

recreative (riːkrɪˈeɪtɪv), *a.*² [f. RE- 5 a + CREATIVE *a.*] That creates anew.

1861 J. G. SHEPPARD *Fall Rome* viii. 420 In respect of re-creative energy, there was a boundless difference between Asia and Europe. **1889** *Lux Mundi* xii. (1890) 505 The mysterious facts which lie at the root of the recreative process.

Hence **recreˈativeness**².

1820 L. HUNT *Indicator* No. 42 ¶6 All the living grace.. which the re-creativeness of poetry can give her.

recreator¹ (ˈrɛkrɪeɪtə(r)). [f. RECREATE *v.*¹] One who, or that which, recreates.

1884 H. R. HAWEIS *Musical Mem.* xi. 70 Music's future destiny as a vast civilizer, recreator, health-giver [etc.].

recreator² (riːkrɪˈeɪtə(r)). [RE- 5 a. Cf. RECREATE *v.*²] One who creates again.

1587 GOLDING *De Mornay* Ep. Ded. **ij, We consider not the incomparable worke of our Creator and Recreator, but by piecemeale. **1852** BAILEY *Festus* xv. (ed. 4) 177 Yea even here as everywhere, let man Worship his Recreator.

†**recreatory.** *Obs. rare*⁻¹. [ad. med.L. *recreātōrium*, f. *recreāre*: see RECREATE *v.*¹ and -ORY.] A source of comfort or recreation.

a **1450** *Mankind* (Brandl) 858 O mercy, my..solas and synguler recreatory, My predilecte specyall.

recreaunt(e, obs. forms of RECREANT.

recredence (riːˈkriːdəns). *rare*⁻¹. [Prob. back-formation on RECREDENTIAL *a.* and *sb.*, infl. by CREDENCE *sb.* 4 b.] In phr. ***letters of recredence*** = RECREDENTIALS *sb. pl.*

1855 E. C. GRENVILLE MURRAY *Embassies & Foreign Courts* xxii. 345 In this audience the ambassador presents his letters of recall to the sovereign, and usually makes a farewell speech... He receives at the same time his letters of recredence.

recreˈdential, *a.* and *sb. Obs.* exc. *Hist.* [RE-.]

A. *adj.* Of letters: Serving as credentials to an ambassador returning from a foreign court.

1710 *Lond. Gaz.* No. 4698/1 Count Velo..has insisted upon his having an Audience of Leave, and Recredential Letters from the Emperor. **1725** *Ibid.* No. 6367/1 Prince Galliczin..having been recalled and received his Recredential Letters, is to have..his Audience of Leave of his..Majesty.

B. *sb. pl.* Recredential letters.

1654 WHITELOCKE *Jrnl. Swed. Emb.* (1772) II. 119 To see that..the re-credentialls to Whitelocke, should be perfected and brought to him. **1760** *Francis Lett.* (1901) I. 57, I earnestly hope the next paquet may bring our Recredentials. **1909** *Eng. Hist. Rev.* XXIV. Apr. 256 He obtained his recredentials on 18 October 1666.

recreent, obs. form of RECREANT.

recrei-, recreiȝ-, variants of RECRAY *v. Obs.*

recrement (ˈrɛkrɪmənt). [a. F. *récrément* (1553 in Hatz.-Darm.), or ad. L. *recrēment-um* refuse, dross, etc., f. *re-* RE- 2 + *cernĕre* to separate. Cf. EXCREMENT¹.]

1. The superfluous or useless portion of any substance; refuse, dross, scum, off-scouring.

1599 T. M[OUFET] *Silkwormes* 26 Now what are seedes and egges of wormes or foule But recrements of preexisting things. **1640** BP. HALL *Serm.* Rem. Wks. (1660) 41 Light.. discovers all the foulnesse of the most earthly recrements, it mixeth with none of them. **1707** SLOANE *Jamaica* I. 57 It was thrown up by the waves with other recrements of the sea. **1774** PENNANT *Tour Scotl. in 1772*, 165 [The rocks] did not appear to me a lava, or under any suspicion of having been the recrement of a Vulcano.

fig. **1622** BP. HALL *Serm. 15 Sept.* Wks. (1627) 493 Those other sullen, mopish creatures are the..off-scouring and recrements of the world. **1698** [R. FERGUSON] *View Eccles.* 72 The greatliest offensive Recrements of the Mountebank's Stage. **1819** H. BUSK *Vestriad* I. 748 Some coarse drab, the recrement of earth! **1882** J. B. STALLO *Concepts Mod. Physics* 292 A recrement of ancient tradition.

2. *spec.* **a.** A waste product or excretion of an animal or vegetable body; also *Physiol.*, a fluid which is separated from the blood and again absorbed into it, as the saliva or bile (opp. to *excrement*).

1615 CROOKE *Body of Man* II. ii. (1631) 65 That it [the venter] might better receiue the recrements or excrements of both concoctions. **1660** BOYLE *New Exp. Phys. Mech.* Digress. 351 The superfluous Serosities and other Recrements of the Blood. **1733** TULL *Horse-hoeing Husb.* i. (Dubl.) 7 Plants..have only fine Recrements, which are thrown off by the Leaves. **1802** PALEY *Nat. Theol.* v. §3 (1819) 55 The vestiges of animal or vegetable recrements. **1822–34** *Good's Study Med.* (ed. 4) I. 160 Whatever recrement or other materials are co-acervated in any part of the intestines.

†**b.** The dross or scoria of metallic substances.

1611 COTGR., *Chalcite*, the recrement of brasse, cleauing to the sides of the furnaces wherein tis purified. **1678** *Phil. Trans.* XII. 1051 Slag..is the Recrement of Iron. **1758** J. S. tr. *Le Dran's Observ. Surg.* (1771) Dict., *Lithargyrum*,..a Recrement of Lead thrown off from Silver refined.

recremental (rɛkrɪˈmɛntəl), *a.* ? *Obs.* [f. prec. + -AL¹.] Of or belonging to recrements.

1578 BANISTER *Hist. Man* I. 7 As the brayne had oft occasion, so it should neuer want, the meane of recrementall purging. **1669** W. SIMPSON *Hydrol. Chym.* 121 Carrying away the recremental sordes of those parts. **1744** ARMSTRONG *Preserv. Health* III. 254 'Tis not for those to cultivate a skin Too soft; or teach the recremental fume Too fast to crowd through such precarious ways.

recrementitious (ˌrɛkrɪmənˈtɪʃəs), *a.* [f. as prec. + -ITIOUS.] Of the nature of recrement; drossy, superfluous, separable, unessential.

1650 BULWER *Anthropomet.* ii. 53 That superfluous and recrementitious offspring of haire. **1675–6** BOYLE *Exp. Disc. Quicksilver* Wks. 1772 IV. 226 Common mercury skilfully freed from its recrementitious and heterogeneous parts. **1757** A. COOPER *Distiller* I. xx. (1760) 83 These recrementitious or drossy Parts of the Sugar. **1827** ROBERTS *Voy. Centr. Amer.* 302 The recrementitious earth is thus easily separated. **1857** BRINTON in Todd *Cycl. Anat.* V. 400/2 The importance of these 'recrementitious' secretions.

recreˈmentory, *a. rare.* [-ORY.] = prec.

1822–34 *Good's Study Med.* (ed. 4) I. 141 The recrementory part, which descends on to the large intestines. *Ibid.* 381 A gas recrementory and deleterious to life.

recrescence (rɪˈkrɛsəns). [f. L. *recresc-ĕre* to grow anew: cf. EXCRESCENCE.] The act of growing again; reproduction of a part or member.

1891 *New Rev.* June 533 In lower animals or plants..the fact of recrescence is far more obvious.

†**reˈcrew,** *sb. Obs.* In 7 recrewe, recrue. [a. F. *recrue*, †*recreue*, reinforcement (16th c. in Littré), sb. fem. f. *recrû* pa. pple. of *recroître*: see RECRUIT *sb.* and CREW *sb.*] A body of soldiers intended to reinforce an army. = RECRUIT *sb.* 1.

1619 in *Eng. & Germ.* (Camden) 141 The reinforcing of his broken regiment with newe recrewes. **1641** *Sc. Acts Chas. I* (1814) V. 390 To enact that no leavies,..companies, or recrues of souldiouris, be..sent out of this Kingdome.

†**reˈcrew,** *v. Obs.* In 7 *Sc.* recreu. [f. prec. sb.] *trans.* To reinforce.

1637 MONRO *Expedition* II. 137 Having recreued his Armie againe out of Westfalia, he then marched on Stoade. **1644** *Sc. Acts Chas. I* (1814) VI. 62/1 That þis kingdome may be enabled to..recreu the armie sent forth if neid beis.

recrewte, obs. form of RECRUIT *v.*

recreyande, obs. form of RECREANT.

recreye, variant of RECRAY *v. Obs.*

†**recribrate,** *v. Obs. rare*⁻¹. [RE- 5 a. Cf. med.L. *recrībrāre* (1364 in Du Cange).] *trans.* To sift again.

c **1624** DONNE *Lett.* (1651) 308, I have cribrated, and re-cribrated, and post-cribrated the Sermon.

recriminate (rɪˈkrɪmɪneɪt), *v.* [f. *recrimināt-*, ppl. stem of med.L. *recrimināri*: see RE- 2 and CRIMINATE *v.* Cf. F. *récriminer* (16th c. in Littré).]

1. *intr.* To retort an accusation; to bring a charge or charges in turn against one's accuser.

1611 COTGR., *Recriminer*, to recriminate, retort a crime [etc.]. **1621** ELSING *Debates Ho. Lords* (Camden) 82 Sir H. Y[elverton] came as a delinquent, and dyd recriminate. **1651** TOMBES in Baxter *Inf. Bapt.* 202, I love not to recriminate, for that were to scold. **1777** BURKE *Let. to Sheriffs Bristol* Wks. III. 161 To criminate and recriminate never yet was the road to reconciliation, in any difference amongst men. **1812** D'ISRAELI *Calam. Auth.* (1882) 485 Such are some of the personalities with which Decker recriminated. **1884** CHURCH *Bacon* i. 26 Bacon is able to recriminate with effect, and to show gross credulity and looseness of assertion on the part of the Roman Catholic advocate.

b. Const. *on, upon* (a person, etc.). ? *Obs.*

1693 TATE in *Dryden's Juvenal* i. (1697) 28 How shall such Hypocrites Reform the State, On whom the Brothels can Recriminate? **1752** LADY M. W. MONTAGU *Let. to C'tess. Bute* 20 Oct., I never recriminate on the lives of their Popes and Cardinals, when they urge the character of Henry the Eighth. **1786** *Francis the Philanthropist* II. 72 This circumstance inspired me..to re-criminate on my base accuser.

2. *trans.* **a.** To accuse (a person) in return; to make a counter-charge against (the accuser). Also const. *of.* Now *rare.*

1621 ELSING *Debates Ho. Lords* (Camden) 82 [It] is punishable in the Starr Chamber, yf the defendant dothe recriminate the plaintiff in his aunswere, but to recriminate a third person worse. **1683** *Case of Mixt Communion* 41, I speak not this to excuse our selves, or to recriminate them. **1701** WHITEHEAD *Truth Prevalent* 177 Bitterly Aspersing, and odiously Recriminating us in many things of a publick Nature. **1819** *Metropolis* II. 151 She too recriminated certain characters in turn.

†**b.** To return or retort (a charge or accusation) *against, upon* a person. *Obs.*

1603 FLORIO *Montaigne* III. xii. (1632) 594, I would suspect recriminate, or retorte the fault upon you. **1626** in Ellis *Orig. Lett.* Ser. I. III. 224 While he was in his declaration, the Kings Attorney comes in and recriminates a grievous accusation of High Treason against him. **1653** ASHWELL *Fides Apost.* 266 Athanasius..had the charge of Heresy recriminated also upon him.

recrimination (rɪkrɪmɪˈneɪʃən). [a. F. *récrimination* (1611 Cotgr.), or ad. med.L. *recrīminātiōn-em*: cf. CRIMINATION.]

1. The action of bringing a counter-accusation against a person.

1611 COTGR. s.v., A recrimination, an accusation of an accuser. **1632** *Star Chamb. Cases* (Camden) 147 The

Defendants answere that this Bill is a bill of recrimination. **1662** STILLINGFL. *Orig. Sacræ* I. iv. §10 His Compurgators ..have sought to make good his credit by recrimination. **1771** BURKE *Lett., to Bp. Chester* (1884) I. 295 Avoiding all offensive terms, or any kind of recrimination on their accusers. **1860** MOTLEY *Netherl.* iv. I. 117 When, after so much talking and tampering, there began to be recrimination among the leaguers. **1874** L. STEPHEN *Hours in Library* (1892) I. ix. 313 The dispute lasted for some years, with much mutual recrimination.

2. A counter-accusation; an accusation brought in turn by the accused against the accuser.

1621 ELSING *Debates Ho. Lords* (Camden) 84 Conclusion, denying his recriminacion. **1650** ROW *Hist. Kirk* (1842) 502 It contained many recriminations and fowll aspersions. *a* **1721** SHEFFIELD (Dk. Buckhm.) *Wks.* (1753) II. 101 Neither will I take up your Lordships time with recriminations. **1791–1823** D'ISRAELI *Cur. Lit.* (1859) II. 350 The recriminations of politicians are the confessions of great sinners. **1850** GROTE *Greece* II. lxiv. (1862) V. 535 When they heard the criminations and recriminations between the generals on one side and Theramenês on the other.

recriminative (rɪˈkrɪmɪnətɪv), *a.* [f. as RECRIMINATE *v.* + -IVE.] = RECRIMINATORY.

1828 SOUTHEY in *Q. Rev.* XXXVIII. 234 That [defence] which rests upon recriminative accusation. **1858** CARLYLE *Fredk. Gt.* I. iii. (1872) I. 24 Harsh words, mutually recriminative, rising ever higher.

reˈcriminator. *rare.* [f. as prec. + -OR.] One who recriminates.

1709 MRS. MANLEY *Secret Mem.* (1720) III. 27 Weak, short-sighted Recriminators! **1727** in BAILEY, vol. II.

recriminatory (rɪˈkrɪmɪnətərɪ), *a.* [f. as prec. + -ORY[2]. Cf. mod.F. *récriminatoire.*] Involving, of the nature of, recrimination.

1778 *State Papers* in *Ann. Reg.* 303/2 All recriminatory accusations of subordinate officers against their commanders. **1785** BURKE *Sp. Nabob Arcot* Wks. IV. 195 Returning the prosecution in a recriminatory bill of pains and penalties. **1844** H. H. WILSON *Brit. India* I. I. v. 271 The Government precipitated itself into a career of recriminatory and vindictive acts.

†**reˈcrisple,** *v. Obs. rare*[−1]. In 6 recrispel. [RE- 5 a.] *trans.* To crisp or curl again minutely.

1594 CAREW *Tasso* (1881) 80 The winde new crisples makes in her loose haire, Which nature selfe to waues recrispelled.

recross (riːˈkrɒs, -ɔːs), *v.* [RE- 5 a.]

1. *intr.* and *trans.* To pass over again.

intr. *c* **1470** in *Hors Shepe & G.* (Caxton 1479, Roxb. repr.) 29 A herte..yf he take ouer the ryuer he crossith; Yf he retorne, he recrosseth. **1822** J. FLINT *Lett. Amer.* 11 There is a rudder at each end, so that she can cross and re-cross, without putting about. **1847** LD. LINDSAY *Chr. Art* I. p. cxlvii, Helenus recrossed by himself, many monks looking on.

trans. **1632** LITHGOW *Trav.* I. 41 My purpose reaching for ..Asia, as his was to recrosse the snowy Alpes. **1719** DE FOE *Crusoe* I. vi, By crossing and recrossing the Line. **1795–6** WORDSW. *Borderers* I. 3 Let us..strip the Scottish Foray Of their rich spoil, ere they recross the Border. **1830** J. F. COOPER *Water Witch* xiv, His boat was necessary to enable the party to re-cross the inlet. **1891** T. HARDY *Tess* xlv, Thus absorbed she recrossed the northern part of Long-Ash Lane at right angles.

b. *trans.* To pass by (another).

1862 MERIVALE *Rom. Emp.* xli. (1871) V. 62 The operations of industry, which cross and recross each other in the streets.

2. To hinder or thwart again. *rare.*

1612 J. DAVIES *Muse's Sacr.* (Grosart) 53 For, when we first, to liue well, goe about, w'are crost and recrost by the Reprobate.

3. a. To overlay, mark, etc. (a surface) with repeated crossings.

1598 MARSTON *Pygmal.* III. 148 How his clothes appeare Crost and recrost with lace. **1886** *Pall Mall G.* 18 May 2/1 His back was..crossed and recrossed with bleeding wales.

b. To lay across again.

1893 *Columbus* (Ohio) *Disp.* 24 Aug., With bright ribbons crossed and recrossed about his nimble legs.

Hence **reˈcrossing** *vbl. sb.* and *ppl. a.*

1846 E. FITZGERALD *Lett.* (1894) I. 208 Looking at the sea with its crossing and recrossing ships. **1897** *Daily News* 14 Dec. 8/4 An actor was never allowed to turn his back on the audience. Certain 'crossings' and 're-crossings' had to be rigidly attended to.

reˈcrown, *v.* [RE- 5 a.] To crown again.

1845 LD. CAMPBELL *Chancellors* (1857) I. xxi. 313 Waynflete assisted in re-crowning him. **1884** F. D. HUNTINGTON in J. G. Butler *Bible Work N.T.* (1884) I. 198 To recrown the soul and make it master of the flesh.

reˈcrucify, *v.* [RE- 5 a.] To crucify again.

1618 T. ADAMS *Bad Leaven* Wks. 1862 II. 349 [Our sins were] the hand of Jews recrucifying Christ. **1667** *Decay Chr. Piety* viii. ¶39 The crucified body of our Saviour, which we have..so often recrucified. *a* **1711** KEN *Psyche* Poet. Wks. 1721 IV. 183 My sins, which made incarnate Godhead die, God-man re-crucify.

Hence **reˈcrucifier,** one who recrucifies.

a **1711** KEN *Hymnotheo* Poet. Wks. 1721 III. 69 Whose Love would his Re-crucifyer spare.

reˈcrudency. *rare.* [f. L. *recrūdēscĕre* + -ENCY.] = RECRUDESCENCY.

1603 BACON *Let. to Cecil conc. Irel.* Wks. 1879 II. 22 If the wound be not ripped up again, and come to a recrudency by new foreign succours. **1903** *Jrnl. Hellenic Stud.* XXIV. p. lxii, This success is all the more notable as it synchronises with the recrudency of efforts to circumscribe Greek studies.

recrudesce (riːkruːˈdɛs), *v.* [ad. L. *recrūdēscĕre* to break out again (of wounds, also *fig.*), f. *re-* RE- + *crūdēscĕre* to become raw, f. *crūdus* raw: see CRUDE *a.*] To break out again. *lit.* and *fig.*

1884 E. GURNEY in *Mind* Jan. 118 Particular ideas which have made no part of the waking life, are apt to recrudesce in the sleep-waking state. **1897** *Allbutt's Syst. Med.* III. 12 The acute symptoms..subsiding and recrudescing again and again. *Ibid.* 251 These [boils] slowly develope and frequently recrudesce.

Hence **recruˈdescing** *ppl. a.*

1896 *Allbutt's Syst. Med.* I. 713 Recrudescing attacks of diphtheria.

recrudescence (riːkruːˈdɛsəns). [ad. L. type ***recrūdēscentia*, f. *recrūdēscĕre*: see prec. and -ENCE. Cf. F. *recrudescence* (Littré).] **1.** The state or fact of breaking out afresh. **a.** *fig.* Of a quality or state of things (usually one regarded as bad), a disease, epidemic, etc.

1721 in BAILEY. *a* **1734** NORTH *Exam.* III. viii. §64 (1740) 632 The King required some Regulations should be made for obviating the Recrudescence of those Ignoramus Abuses, for the future. **1863** *Sat. Rev.* 1 Aug. 138/1 The recent victories have occasioned, as might have been expected, a recrudescence of calumny and malignity. **1865** MILL *Comte* 24 The recrudescence..of a metaphysical Paganism in the Alexandrian..schools. **1884** *Standard* 1 Aug., The fears of a recrudescence of the epidemic are now subsiding.

b. Of a wound or sore. Also in fig. context.

1865 *Pall Mall G.* 14 Oct. 7/7 We must not forget what a spirit this has been, or how old and deep was the wound of which this is probably the last recrudescence. **1877** *Daily News* 25 Jan. 6/5 The recrudescence of a varicose ulcer in the leg keeps him in bed most of the day.

2. *transf.* A revival or rediscovery (of something regarded as good or valuable).

1906 H. W. & F. G. FOWLER *King's Eng.* i. 15 A literary tour de force, a *recrudescence*, two or three generations later, of the very respectable William Lamb. **1973** *Times Lit. Suppl.* 3 Aug. 900/2 The first fruit of this act of recrudescence was the catalogue of drawings.

recrudescency (riːkruːˈdɛsənsɪ). Now *rare.* [f. as prec.: see -ENCY.] = prec.

1651 *Life Father Sarpi* (1676) 61 The Disease, which was very long, with divers recrudescencies and prognosticks both of life and death. **1716** M. DAVIES *Athen. Brit.* II. 333 Distempers..heighten'd by a Recrudescency of a Fistula. **1868** BROWNING *Ring & Bk.* I. 578 These I saw, In recrudescency of baffled hate, Prepared to wring the uttermost revenge From body and soul.

recrudescent (riːkruːˈdɛsənt), *a.* [See RECRUDESCE and -ENT.] Breaking out again.

1727 in BAILEY vol. II. **1892** R. WALLACE in *Scott. Leader* 12 July 7 The recrudescent protectionist. **1897** *Allbutt's Syst. Med.* II. 898 These recrudescent pains gradually disappear again.

recrue, variant of RECREW *sb. Obs.*

recruit (rɪˈkruːt), *sb.* Also 7 recrute, -cruite. [a. obs. F. (of Hainault) *recrute* (1592 in Godef. *Compl.*) = F. *recrue* (16th c.) sb., f. *recrû* pa. pple. of *recroître* to increase again: see RECREW *sb.* Hence also Du. *recruut*, G. *rekrut* († *rekrout*, *-krute*), Da. *rekrut* (†*recryt*), Sw. *rekryt*, and Pg. *recruta*, It., Sp. *recluta*. Cf. RECRUIT *v.*]

I. 1. *Mil.* †**a.** A fresh or auxiliary body of troops, added as a reinforcement to an army, regiment, garrison, etc., either to increase or to maintain its strength. *Obs.*

1647 CLARENDON *Hist. Reb.* VI. §87 All the advantage this seasonable Recruit brought them, was to give their old Men so much Courage as to keep the field. **1680** LUTTRELL *Brief Rel.* (1857) I. 46 His majestie hath ordered a recruit of 1200 foot and 300 horse to be sent to reinforce the garrison of Tangier. **1728** MORGAN *Algiers* II. iv. 259 His Deputy returned..with a Recruit of 2000 Janizaries.

transf. **1705** ARBUTHNOT *Coins* (1727) 244 The Rhodians attacked a recruit of vessels, which Antiochus was bringing from Sicily.

b. *pl.* †Fresh or auxiliary troops; reinforcements (*obs.*); the men composing such forces. Hence (in later use) also in *sing.*: One of a newly-raised body of troops; one newly or recently enlisted for service in the army.

1653 URQUHART *Rabelais* I. xlvii, Great supplies and recruits come daily in to your enemies. **1677** G. HICKES in Ellis *Orig. Lett.* Ser. II. IV. 43 My Lord hath taken care to hinder the French officers from levying recruits in this Kingdom. **1707** ADDISON *Pres. St. War* Wks. (Bohn) IV. 351 The grand alliance have innumerable sources of recruits ..in Britain and Ireland. **1722** DE FOE *Col. Jack* (1840) 111 Advanced to the dignity of a footsoldier in a body of recruits raised in the north. **1810** WELLINGTON in Gurw. *Desp.* VI. 22, I sent you a warrant for £150, for bounty, for your recruits. **1844** *Regul. & Ord. Army* 390 No Officer under the degree of Field Officer is competent to approve of a Recruit finally without a special authority. **1876** VOYLE & STEVENSON *Milit. Dict.* 334/1 A recruit remains a recruit from the date of his enlistment until he has passed his drill, which extends generally to 16 weeks.

transf. and *fig.* **1656** HOBBES *Liberty, Necess. & Chance* (1841) 21 Those large recruits of reasons and authorities which offer themselves to serve in this cause. **1791** BURKE *Th. French Affairs* Wks. VII. 53 This supply of recruits to the corps of the highest civil ambition, goes on with a regular progression. **1816** KIRBY & SP. *Entomol.* (1818) II. xvii. 94 The little turf-ants..carry their recruits uncoiled. **1848** DICKENS *Dombey* xxiv, If Sir Barnet had the good fortune to get hold of a raw recruit,..and ensnared him to his hospitable villa [etc.]. **1885** *Daily Tel.* 7 Sept. 3/6 The gap will be filled up by recruits from our schools of art.

†**2.** A fresh supply or number of persons (or animals), either as additional to the previous number, or to make up for a decrease. *Obs.*

c **1645** HOWELL *Lett.* (1650) II. 48 It may be, with this enlargment of dwelling, your Lordship may need a recruit of servants. **1670** R. MONTAGU in *Buccleuch MSS.* (Hist. MSS. Comm.) I. 477 It is believed this business will end with a recruit for the galleys. **1735** SOMERVILLE *Chase* IV. 24 The prudent Huntsman..will supply With annual large Recruits, his broken Pack. **1769** PRICE in *Phil. Trans.* LIX. 106 Supposing the annual recruit from the country to be 7000, the number of inhabitants will be..630,000.

3. A fresh or additional supply of something: **a.** of a material thing or things. Now *rare* or *Obs.*

1650 FULLER *Pisgah* III. xii. §7 Besides the original Utensils of the Temple,..there were severall recruits.. which succeeding Kings made in stead of those instruments, which constant use and age had empaired. **1686** PLOT *Staffordsh.* 67 A constant large flux of water for ten or eleven months together without recruits from rains. **1712** E. COOKE *Voy. S. Sea* 360 Guam, one of the Marian Islands, where we hope to get a Recruit of Provisions. **1801** ELIZ. HELME *St. Marg. Cave* III. 87 Austin carried a lamp with a recruit of oil. **1822–34** *Good's Study Med.* (ed. 4) IV. 174 Till it has lost its own proper supply [of blood] and begins to draw upon the corporeal vessels for a recruit. **1866** *Harper's Mag.* Apr. 677/1, I had gone in for a new recruit of clocks—for you must know I'm a clock peddler.

b. of money. Now *rare* or *Obs.*

1662 GURNALL *Chr. in Arm.* verse 17. II. xxx. §1 (1669) 334/2 Let us endeavour our recruits be suitable to our expence. **1729** GAY *Polly* II. (1772) 171, I was now..forc'd to have recourse to the highway for a recruit to set me up. **1785** G. A. BELLAMY *Apology* II. 77 He was however to return soon, when he was to bring me a recruit of cash. **1818** SCOTT *Rob Roy* xv, This recruit to my finances was not a matter of indifference to me.

†**c.** of health, strength, etc. *Obs.*

1675 TEMPLE *Let. to Ld. Chamberlain* Wks. 1731 II. 339, I hope You find good Recruits of Health in the Country. **1756** H. WALPOLE *Mem. Geo. II*, II. 210 To sacrifice to the moon in order to obtain a recruit of vigour. **1771** MRS. GRIFFITH *Hist. Lady Barton* II. 36 My appearing..seemed to furnish her with such a recruit of strength and spirits.

†**d.** of qualities, etc. *Obs.*

1709 POPE *Ess. Crit.* I. 206 Whatever nature has in worth denied, She gives in large recruits of needful pride.

e. *Ecol.* An animal which has recently reached the size that qualifies it to be counted as a member of the population to which it belongs.

1938 *Jrnl. du Conseil* X. 269 It has been assumed that the same number of recruits would be found. **1948** M. GRAHAM *Rational Fishing of Cod of N. Sea* iii. 86 Codling from the deeper areas of the North Sea grow more slowly and will not enter as recruits until they are..2–3 years old. **1977** J. L. HARPER *Population Biol. of Plants* v. 141 Order and organization appear in populations because of feedback from existing populations to new recruits and because these recruits themselves interact.

II. †**4. a.** *Mil.* Increase or reinforcement (of an army) by the addition or accession of fresh men.

1647 CLARENDON *Hist. Reb.* I. §87 The endeavour to raise new men for the recruit of the Army, by Pressing. **1670** COTTON *Espernon* I. III. 124 The Duke..would now sit no longer idle, but gave immediate order for the recruit of his Troops. **1724** DE FOE *Mem. Cavalier* (1840) 196 Upon this recruit the Earl of Newcastle, being above a thousand strong, made Sir Thomas Fairfax give ground.

b. With reference to population. *Obs. rare.*

1657 HOWELL *Londinop.* 346 By insensible coalition, and recruit of people, they came at last to be united. **1798** MALTHUS *Popul.* (1817) I. 353 The checks to population.. which render a constant recruit of numbers necessary.

5. †**a.** Renewal of stores or supplies. *Obs.*

1650 T. B[AYLEY] *Worcester's Apoph.* 6 To take what Provisions the Countrey would afford, for his present maintenance and recruit. **1673** R. HADDOCK *Jrnl.* 4 June in *Camden Misc.* (1881) 29 Haveing no shot in the fleet for recrute, twas resolved..to saile for the buoy of the Nore.

b. Renewal or repair of something worn out.

1691 T. H[ALE] *Acc. New Invent.* 15 Without..her having any Recruits of her Rudder-Irons in all that time. *Ibid.* 31 [It] appears not to have shifted so much as one Bolt, or received any considerable Recruit of other Iron-work. **1845** *Encycl. Metrop.* (ed. 2) VIII. 749/2 Some hands will wear down a [stocking-] frame in three years; others, however, will work them twelve or even twenty years without serious repairs, or, as it is technically called, a recruit.

6. Renewal of strength or vigour; restoration to a normal state or condition; recovery.

a **1643** W. CARTWRIGHT *On Fletcher's Dram. Poems*, Such pursutes After despair, such amorous recruits. **1650** NEEDHAM *Case Commw.* 85 Though a Nation may have some respit and recruit now and then, by the Vertue and Valour of a Prince, yet this is very rare. **1705** STANHOPE *Paraphr.* I. 16 Necessary indeed this is for the Recruit of these frail and feeble bodies of ours. **1789** MME. D'ARBLAY *Diary* 2 Feb., I was wholly insensible to the effects of a race which, at any other time, would have required an hour's recruit. **1822–34** *Good's Study Med.* (ed. 4) I. 620 The nervous energy..experiences nothing of the decomposition or recruit of every other part of the living frame around it.

7. A means of recruital. Now *rare.*

1655 H. VAUGHAN *Silex Scint.* II. *Resurr. & Immort.* 9 Unbowel'd nature shew'd thee her recruits, And change of suits. **1678** BUTLER *Hud.* III. i. 906 Little quarrels often prove To be but new recruits of love. **1729** BUTLER *Serm. Compassion* Wks. 1874 II. 62 The recruits of food and sleep are the necessary means of our preservation. **1748** HARTLEY *Observ. Man* II. iii. 219 The same active Particles in Foods are probably the Sources and Recruits of that nervous

Power. **1835** LYTTON *Rienzi* x. ii, A treasury which did not require the odious recruit of taxes.

8. *attrib.* and *Comb.*, as ***recruit acquittance, decoy, drill, horse, officer, training.***

1697 LUTTRELL *Brief. Rel.* (1857) IV. 197 A great many recruit horses went on board thereof yesterday for Flanders. **1753** CHAMBERS *Cycl. Supp.* s.v., *Recruit horses* are the horses brought up for compleating the regiments of horse or dragoons every year. **1844** THACKERAY *B. Lyndon* v, He found his calling as a recruit-decoy far more profitable. **1898** *Atlantic Monthly* LXXXII. 481/2 He sent him to the recruiting board and took a recruit acquittance. **1909** A. HUXLEY *Let.* 14 Dec. (1969) 32, I have, in company with Gielgud, accomplished forty recruit drills this half and am now very nearly a full fledge[d] territorial. **1914** (*title*) Recruit training (infantry), 1914: an aid to all instructors. By two Officers of the Dorsetshire Regiment. **1976** *Billings* (Montana) *Gaz.* 30 June 3-B/3 Navy Fireman William G. Jones,.. has completed recruit training at San Diego, Calif.

recruit (rɪ'kruːt), *v.* Also 7 recrute, -crewte, -cruite. [ad. F. *recruter* (17th c.), f. *recrute* RECRUIT *sb.* Hence also Du. *recruteeren*, G. *rekrutieren*, Da. *rekrutere*, Sw. *rekrytera*, and Pg. *recrutar*, Sp. *reclutar*, It. *reclutare*. Cf. RECREW *v.*

The French word first appeared in literary use in gazettes published in Holland, and was disapproved of by French critics in the latter part of the 17th c. (see Littré).

The *l* of the Sp. and It. forms appears in the following early instance: **1652–60** in Gilbert *Contemp. Hist. Irel.* (1879) I. I. 45 Such colonells as had not theire men extant were dismissed to theire severall homes to reclute, himself still in the field.. wheare we leave him recluting his men.]

I. *trans.* **1. a.** *Mil.* To strengthen or reinforce (an army, etc.) with fresh men or troops.

1643 PRYNNE *Sov. Power Parl.* IV. 33 If they might not Levy Moneys, to recrute and maintain their Army. **1655** *Nicholas Papers* (Camden) II. 353 Wee are sending 20 sayle of shippes to recrewte them with 2000 land men. *a* **1727** NEWTON *Chronol. Amended* i. (1728) 181 It was his custom to recruit his army with conquered people. **1788** GIBBON *Decl. & F.* xlii. IV. 214 Public and private distress recruited the armies of the state. **1880** *19th Cent.* Apr. 707 In the Parliamentary papers of 1877, the system of recruiting our native battalions receives considerable attention.

fig. *a* **1735** GRANVILLE *Progr. Beauty*, See in bright array What hosts of heavenly lights recruit the day.

b. To reinforce, to add to or keep up the number of (a class or body of persons or things).

1770 *Junius Lett.* xxxvi. 176 You may find it a very difficult matter to recruit the black catalogue of your friends. **1790** BURKE *Fr. Rev.* 53 You would have had a liberal order of commons, to emulate and to recruit that nobility. **1871** EARLE *Philol. Eng. Tongue* (1880) §266 They drop out of use and are not recruited by fresh members.

†**c.** *transf.* To support, back up, add to. *Obs.*

1648 BOYLE *Seraph. Love* vi. (1700) 42, I could recruit that Question with pretty store of others of the like nature. **1665** —— *Occas. Refl.* IV. x. (1848) 213 Having both applauded and recruited these Commendations.

2. a. To furnish *with* a fresh supply of something; to replenish. Now *rare.*

a **1661** FULLER *Worthies* (1840) III. 208 He used to examine the pockets of such Oxford scholars as repaired unto him, and always recruited them with necessaries. **1697** DRYDEN *Virg. Georg.* IV. 364 With Greens and Flow'rs recruit their empty Hives. **1763** MILLS *System Pract. Husb.* IV. 341 If the neighbouring vines cannot furnish layers, a rooted vine must be brought from the nursery; for it is too late to recruit a vineyard, when we should be gathering it's fruit. **1874** GREEN *Short Hist.* viii. §5. 516 The contributions offered by the English Catholics did little to recruit the Exchequer.

†**b.** To repair (a ship). *Obs. rare.*

1691 T. H[ALE] *Acc. New Invent.* 11 The Plymouth's Rudder-Irons began to be much eaten, doubting his being forced thereby to send her home that Winter, from the incapacity he was in, of getting her recruited abroad.

3. a. To replenish the substance of (a thing) by addition of fresh material.

a **1661** FULLER *Worthies, Essex* I. (1662) 318 Poulterers take them then, and feed them with Gravel and Curds,.. and their flesh thus recruited is most delicious. **1693** J. EDWARDS *Author. O. & N. Test.* 172 They continually.. repaired and recruited it [the vestal fire]. **1733** CHEYNE *Eng. Malady* II. viii. §7 (1734) 202 There remains nothing but to recruit the Solids weakened in the Struggle. **1822–34** *Good's Study Med.* (ed. 4) III. 61 He represents it [the nervous fluid] as never either recruited or exhausted. **1878** STEWART & TAIT *Unseen Univ.* iv. §120. 132 Nature can beget nothing till she is recruited by the death of something else.

b. To increase or maintain (a quality) by fresh influence or operation.

1678 H. VAUGHAN *Thalia Rediv., Daphnis*, Active fires their sluggish heat recruit. **1719** LONDON & WISE *Compl. Gard.* 252 Both to recruit the heat, and to maintain it afterwards. **1788** BURKE *Sp. agst. W. Hastings* Wks. XIII. 320 Fury, rage and malice.. recruiting and reinforcing their avarice, their vices are no longer human. **1870** *Standard* 16 Nov., Since the Crimean war.. Russia has been carefully engaged in recruiting her strength. **1871** B. STEWART *Heat* II. i. §13 If the temperature of the liquid be kept constantly recruited by some natural process.

†**c.** To regain, re-establish (one's credit). *Obs.*

1656 *Artif. Handsom.* 151 If a woman once dash upon this rock of reproach, she hardly ever recrutes her credit.

†**d.** To put right, to make up for. *Obs.*

1673 WOOD *Life* 14 July (O.H.S.) II. 266 What he had uttered to my great disgrace, the vicechancellor in his concluding speech recruited all againe.

e. To become a member of (a natural population). Also *intr.* (const. *to*). Cf. sense 6 d below.

1965 *Oceanogr. & Marine Biol.* III. 357 The stock to which an individual recruits is solely determined by the time at which it attains the critical size. **1967** *Ibid.* V. 415 Before 1950 only a part of each year-class recruited the fishery at three years of age, the remainder recruiting it at age four, but in later years most, if not all, of the members of each year-class recruited at three years of age.

4. a. To increase or restore the vigour or health of (a person or animal); to refresh, re-invigorate (one's spirits, etc.). Also occas. with inanimate object.

1676 WISEMAN *Chirurg. Treat.* 285 He was.. removed.. to Knights-bridge, and there he daily recruited his spirits. **1697** DRYDEN *Virg. Georg.* III. 766 Recruited into Rage, he grinds his Teeth In his own flesh. **1738** WESLEY *Ps.* CIV. iv, Thy Rains from Heav'n parch'd Hills recruit. **1752** HUME *Ess. & Treat.* (1777) I. 287 Indolence.. never is agreeable but when it succeeds to labour, and recruits the spirits. **1842** BARHAM *Ingol. Leg., St. Medard* xiv, When, a little recruited, he rose to go. **1878** BOSW. SMITH *Carthage* 238 When his troops had been sufficiently recruited, and were again eager to advance.

b. *refl.* To refresh or re-invigorate (oneself).

1687 A. LOVELL tr. *Thevenot's Trav.* I. 219 Being asthmatick.. he was forced to go to Acre, there to recruit himself for some days. **1726–31** WALDRON *Descr. Isle Man* (1865) 56 As soon as he had recruited himself with a hearty swill of brandy, he began to relate in this manner. **1856** B. TAYLOR *North. Trav.* xxxv. 374, I sat down.. while our guide recruited himself with a large dish of thick sour milk.

5. a. To fill the place of (a thing). *rare*$^{-1}$.

1707–12 MORTIMER *Husb.* (1721) II. 191 This is the time to carry on your new Poles, to recruit those that are decay'd, and cast out every Year.

b. To renew, or add to, one's supply of (a thing).

1748 *Anson's Voy.* I. vi. 58 As soon as they had there recruited their wood and water, they were to continue cruizing. **1800** *Asiatic Ann. Reg., Misc. Tr.* 244/1 At Anoopsheher I recruited the necessary supplies for the prosecution of my journey.

6. a. *Mil.* (and *Naval*). To raise (men) as recruits; to enlist as soldiers (or sailors); to raise (a regiment, etc.) in this way.

1814 SCOTT *Wav.* xxxi, Such of your troop as were recruited upon Waverley-Honour. **1876** VOYLE & STEVENSON *Milit. Dict.* 334/1 Officers specially appointed.. to recruit men for the several regiments and departments of the army. **1891** PATTERSON *Illust. Naut. Dict.* v. 376 *Receiving Ship*, a man o' war, unfit for sea duty, stationed at a navy yard for recruiting seamen.

transf. **1816** KIRBY & SP. *Entomol.* (1818) II. xvii. 95 The ants that are not yet recruited pursue their ordinary occupations. **1936** [see MONTARÍA]. **1961** NEW ENGLISH BIBLE *Acts* xvii. 5 The Jews.. recruited some low fellows from the dregs of the populace. **1974** *Economist* 11 May 36/2 The neo-fascists among whom many of the stewards at his meetings were recruited.

b. *U.S.* To (attempt to) induce (an athlete) to sign on as a student at a college or university.

1913, etc. [implied in RECRUITED *ppl. a.*]. **1974** *Time* 21 Jan. 62/1 With impressive speed he recruited new talent and turned out a winner his first season. **1979** *Arizona Daily Star* 1 Apr. (Parade Suppl.) 23/1 Like her fellow junior from West Virginia, Earl Jones.., Ostrowski already is being heavily recruited by the country's top college coaches.

c. *Physiol.* To bring (additional muscle fibres or muscular activity) into play by the recruitment of their neurones.

1938 *Amer. Jrnl. Physiol.* CXXII. 49 The manner of recruiting mechanical energy during hyperpnea was extremely variable. **1979** *Sci. Amer.* Sept. 148/3 Slow-twitch units, resistant to fatigue and generating relatively little tension, are the first to be recruited.

d. *Ecol.* Of a natural population: to acquire by recruitment (RECRUITMENT 2 c). Cf. sense 3 e above.

1977 J. L. HARPER *Population Biol. of Plants* v. 116 Even in a controlled, 'homogeneous' environment the numbers of seeds that are recruited into a germinating population are determined by the individual properties of each seed.

II. *intr.* (See also sense 3 e in branch I.)

7. a. *Mil.* To enlist new soldiers; to get or seek for fresh supplies of men for the army.

1655 *Clarke Papers* (Camden) III. 28 Collonel Heane.. hath a commission to raise a regiement of horse in Kent, and every troope in England to recruite up to a 100. **1707** ADDISON *Pres. St. War* Wks. (Bohn) IV. 351 The French have only Switzerland, besides their own country, to recruit in. **1772** *Ann. Reg.* I. 71*/2 That the Company's officers should have liberty to recruit with beat of drum, in the manner practised by the regular forces. **1856** EMERSON *Eng. Traits, Race* Wks. (Bohn) II. 32 If I wanted a good troop of soldiers, I should recruit among the stables.

†**b.** To take fresh stores on board ship. *Obs.*

1725 DE FOE *Voy. round World* (1840) 108 Put in there to recruit and furnish for so long a run. *Ibid.* 109 At the Ladrones, we recruited, and particularly took on board.. near two hundred hogs.

†**8.** To return to a previous number or condition; to recover from diminution. *Obs.*

1646 J. GREGORY *Notes & Obs.* (1650) 125 All the dry Bones shall be reunited.. and the whole Generation of Mankinde recruite againe. **1658** J. JONES *Ovid's Ibis* 194 His heart shall feed the bird and still recruit.

9. To recover vigour or health; to employ means for recovering from exhaustion, etc. Also with *up*.

1635–56 COWLEY *Davideis* IV. 1025 With timely Food his decay'd Spirits recruit. **1697** DRYDEN *Virg. Georg.* I. 404 In Genial Winter, Swains enjoy their Store, Forget their Hardships, and recruit for more. **1800** *Med. Jrnl.* III. 453 Where the powers of the constitution had been previously much exhausted.. and where they appeared to be gradually recruiting. **1814** MME. D'ARBLAY *Wanderer* II. ii, I was so confoundedly numbed.. that I don't think I could have remembered my father.. before I had recruited. **1856** KANE *Arct. Expl.* I. ix. 99 Leaving four of my party to recruit at this station. *Ibid.* xxi. 266 The dogs having now recruited, he started light. **1860** H. J. HAWLEY *Diary* 10 May in *Wisconsin Mag. Hist.* (1936) Mar. 336 We.. stoped [*sic*] giving the teams a fine chance to recruit up a little which they need. **1896** E. DOWSON *Let.* 19 Mar. (1967) 346, I believe I have recruited a little since I came here.

†**10.** To recover what one has expended in trade. *Obs.*

1698 FRYER *Acc. E. India & P.* 121 By the quickness of Merchandise passing thorough this City, they recruit on a suddain. **1727** DE FOE *Eng. Tradesman* vi. (1732) I. 61 They.. may buy sparingly, and recruit again as they sell off.

Hence **re'cruitable** *a.*, capable of being recruited.

1890 *Pall Mall G.* 5 Sept. 3/3 A large highly-trained naval reserve, alone chiefly recruitable from our fisherfolks.

re'cruitage. *rare.* [f. RECRUIT *sb.* + -AGE.] The state of being a recruit.

1890 *19th Cent.* Nov. 843 In the days of his recruitage.

recruital (rɪ'kruːtəl). [f. RECRUIT *v.* + -AL[1].]

†**1.** A new or fresh supply. *Obs.*

1648 in Aikman *Hist. Scot.* (1827) IV. x. 319 *note*, Imploring them for a recruital both of men and money. **1889** W. R. SMITH *Relig. Semites* i. 12 The urban population is maintained only by constant recruital from the country.

2. Restoration to health, etc.

1851 W. HANNA *Life Chalmers* II. 55 Mr. Chalmers sought relief and recruital in an excursion to Fifeshire. **1884** J. PARKER *Apost. Life* III. 107 A time of recruital and renewal.

recruite, obs. form of RECRUIT.

recruited (rɪ'kruːtɪd), *ppl. a.* [f. as prec. + -ED[1].] Strengthened, restored, enlisted, etc. Of an athlete: see sense 6 b of the vb.

1791 COWPER *Iliad* XIX. 278 That we may bear The lengthen'd conflict, with recruited might. **1855** LYNCH *Rivulet* XLVIII. i, That we may ask Recruited vigour for the task Of living as we would. **1913** *Collier's* 1 Mar. 20/2 None of them belongs to the class of 'recruited' athletes, so common in our colleges twenty years ago. **1974** *Anderson* (S. Carolina) *Independent* 19 Apr. 5B/3 One of the most heavily recruited South Dakota schoolboys in history. **1979** *Tucson* (Arizona) *Citizen* 28 Apr. 1B/2 He was one of the state's most highly recruited athletes this season, with every major college swimming power after him.

absol. **1882** *Athenæum* 14 Jan. 56/2 The tricks played by recruiters and recruited are exposed.

recruiter (rɪ'kruːtə(r)). [f. as prec. + -ER[1].]

1. An additional member of Parliament, appointed or elected to bring up the number. *Obs.* exc. *Hist.*

1648 HEYLIN *Relat. & Observ.* I. 166 A List of the Names of the Members of the House of Commons... Note, Reader, that such as have this mark [*].. are Recruiters; illegally elected. *a* **1695** WOOD *Life* (O.H.S.) I. 477 He was chosen a recruiter for that long parliament which began 8 May 1661. **1893** S. R. GARDINER *Hist. Civil War* III. xl. 77 Not far short of 150 new members had been chosen, and these Recruiters, as they were called, counted amongst them men like Ireton and Fleetwood. **1954** BRUNTON & PENNINGTON *Members of Long Parl.* i. 2 The constituency concerned was short of a member until the election of the 'Recruiters'—that is, the members elected from 1645 onwards.

2. One who or that which recruits; *esp.* one who seeks or enlists soldiers, employees, etc., as recruits.

1760 R. ROGERS *Jrnls.* (1883) 153 These three recruiters I do not doubt will bring good men enough to complete us here. **1799** *Ann. Reg.* 118 Tried and punished.. as spies and recruiters for hostile powers. **1816** KIRBY & SP. *Entomol.* (1818) II. xvii. 95 You may stop the emigration.., if you can arrest the first recruiter. **1878** SEELEY *Stein* III. 393 Many innocent lads too are seduced by those recruiters. **1890** *World* 13 Aug. 36/2 Recruiters of flagging energies. **1899** A. CONAN DOYLE *Duet* 301 Frederick William, the half-mad recruiter of the big Potsdam grenadiers. **1944** *Living off Land* viii. 159 The recruiter takes them to District Headquarters. **1970** *Wall St. Jrnl.* 30 Mar. 1/1 One reason for the recent increase in executive recruiters seems to be their value in haggling over perks. **1977** *Graduate* 9 Dec. 15/3 It is also, incidentally, the recruiter's intention to deal with all applicants in an efficient and courteous manner.

re'cruithood. *rare.* [f. RECRUIT *sb.* + -HOOD.] The state of being a recruit.

1884 *Century Mag.* Nov. 108/2 Old soldiers who read this will remember their green recruithood.

recruiting (rɪ'kruːtɪŋ), *vbl. sb.* [f. RECRUIT *v.* + -ING[1].] The action of the vb. RECRUIT.

1646 SIR R. MURRAY in *Hamilton Papers* (Camden) 136 A motion.. concerning the recruiting of the Scots' Regiments in France. **1670** LD. NORTH *Narr. Long Parl.* 60 Before this recruiting of the House of Commons (as it was then called). **1748** *Anson's Voy.* II. vii. 211 A business which.. would occasion some delay.. was the recruiting of our water. **1816** KIRBY & SP. *Entomol.* (1818) II. xvii. 94 When all the neuters are acquainted with the road to the new city, the recruiting ceases. **1840** J. H. NEWMAN *Par. Serm.* (1842) V. xix. 315 Sleep is equally the comfort and recruiting of rich and poor. **1879** J. BURROUGHS *Locusts & W. Honey* (1884) 118 The recruiting of a thunder-storm is often very marked.

b. *attrib.*, as ***recruiting agent, bill, campaign, corps, district, drive, -market, office, officer, party, poster, -schooner, sergeant, sergeantry, service, station.***

In some cases coinciding with the ppl. adj.

1858 FROUDE *Hist. Eng.* III. 423 Confederates who had acted under them as *recruiting agents for Lord Exeter.

1708 ADDISON *Let.* 24 Jan. (1941) 89 The next day,..they cramped the former *Recruiting Bill by a new clause. **1976** *Sunday Mail* (Glasgow) 28 Nov., There have been *recruiting campaigns for both police and teachers since regionalisation. **1802** JAMES *Milit. Dict.* s.v. *Recruits*, The *recruiting corps, professedly so called, and having place in the army list. *Ibid.*, *Recruiting Districts. **1956** *Railway Mag.* May 345/1 A big *recruiting drive for staff..has been launched by British Railways. *a* **1971** R. WHYATT in J. Burnett *Useful Toil* (1974) I. 126 A recruiting drive was on, and her brothers might have to go. **1901** *Macmillan's Mag.* Apr. 476/1 The *recruiting-market is in direct competition with all other avenues of employment. **1848** J. R. LOWELL *Biglow Papers* 1st Ser. viii. 115 He looked through the dirty pane of the *recruiting-office window. **1919** G. B. SHAW *Augustus does his Bit* 244 This is the Town Hall Recruiting Office. Give me Colonel Bogey, sharp. **1706** FARQUHAR (*title*) The *Recruiting Officer; a Comedy. **1710** *Lond. Gaz.* No. 4648/3 This Day arrived the Queen Packet-Boat,..with several Recruiting Officers. **1859** MAX MÜLLER *Chips* (1880) III. iv. 82 A place on the frontier, where he had to act as recruiting officer. **1790** *New Newgate Cal.* V. 149 While he was in the army, and on a *recruiting party in Yorkshire. **1849** MACAULAY *Hist. Eng.* vi. II. 144 The recruiting parties, instead of beating their drums for volunteers at fairs and markets [etc.]. **1909** *Regulations for Recruiting for Regular Army & Special Reserve* (War Office) I. 8 Illustrated *recruiting posters may, with the concurrence of the local postmasters, be exhibited outside post offices. **1940** 'G. ORWELL' *Inside Whale* 184 After the bombs and the food-queues and the recruiting-posters, a human voice! **1971** P. D. JAMES *Shroud for Nightingale* i. 23 She was attractive enough for a recruiting poster. **1923** 'R. DALY' *Enchanted Isl.* i. 16 But you'd have had a more comfortable trip if you'd let him send his *recruiting-schooner for you. **1770** BICKERSTAFF (*title*) The *Recruiting Serjeant; a musical Entertainment. **1814** SCOTT *Wav.* lxi, Introducing Waverley to a recruiting-sergeant of his own regiment. **1849** *Whig Almanac & U.S. Reg. for 1850* 26/2, 23 cents per day, hardships in war, and no hope at all, require the aid of a recruiting sergeant. **1948** *Contact Books* xi. 62/1 When first, as a boy, I got to know boxers, unemployment and hardship were the greatest recruiting sergeants for the ring. **1832** GEN. P. THOMPSON *Exerc.* (1842) II. 50 Let us have no *recruiting-serjeantry. **1772** *Ann. Reg.* I. 71*/2 It would be utterly destructive of the *recruiting service for the army. **1822** *Regul. & Orders Army* 74 Officers on the Recruiting Service. **1845** J. C. FRÉMONT *Rep. Exploring Exped. Rocky Mts.* 160 The bottoms of this river, (the Bear), and of some of the creeks..form a natural resting and *recruiting station for travellers. **1907** G. B. SHAW *John Bull's Other island* p. xxxv, Every school is a recruiting station; every church is a barrack.

So **re'cruiting** *ppl. a.*, that recruits.

1678 BUTLER *Hud.* III. i. 766 Man..had his better half.. T'amend his natural defects And perfect his recruiting sex.

recruitment (rɪ'kruːtmənt). [f. as prec. + -MENT, or ad. F. *recrutement* (Littré).]

1. A reinforcement.

1824 *Blackw. Mag.* XVI. 495 A recruitment to the mob that was inside broke in from the streets. **1864** CARLYLE *Fredk. Gt.* xv. vii. (1872) VI. 30 The sicknesses are ceasing; the recruitments are coming in.

2. The act or process of recruiting: **a.** of a military force or a class of persons.

1843 CARLYLE *Past & Pr.* I. v, Do you expect..that your indispensable Aristocracy of Talent is to be enlisted straightway, by some sort of recruitment aforethought, out of the general population? **1862** MERIVALE *Rom. Emp.* xxii. (1865) III. 44 The rapid decrease of the middle class of citizens..rendered the recruitment of the legions constantly more difficult. **1878** *N. Amer. Rev.* CXXVI. 216 The officer in charge of the recruitment of the army. **1945** in *Amer. Speech* (1946) XXI. 78/2 The material included with this letter describes..the availability of recruitments from this company. **1958** *Times* 26 Mar. (Careers in Industry Suppl.) p. xxiii, One may study the recruitment literature of many employers. **1971** M. E. RAY *Recruitment Advertising* i. 9 Recruitment advertising is but a small part of the wide and varied duties of a Personnel Officer.

b. of the body or health.

1862 *Macm. Mag.* Apr. 518 Sleep..is necessary for the recruitment of the little weary frame. **1896** J. B. THOMSON *Life Jos. Thompson* 116 It required only a week or two..to give him perfect recruitment and re-invigoration.

c. *Ecol.* Increase in a natural population as progeny grow and become recruits (RECRUIT *sb.* 3 e); the extent of such increase.

1938 *Jrnl. du Conseil* X. 266 A stock will be in equilibrium with fishing when..C = A + G − M where C is capture, A is recruitment, G is growth, M is natural mortality. **1938** H. G. CHAMPION in Champion & Trevor *Man. Indian Silviculture* I. v. 146 The extension over the regeneration area as a whole of the light conditions appearing most favourable to regeneration is..the correct first step, always bearing in mind the possibility of different requirements for recruitment, i.e. new seedlings, and establishment, i.e. the further development of seedlings already present. **1954** W. E. HILEY *Woodland Managem.* xx. 357 A number of trees will be included, which have grown..but were omitted from the earlier enumeration because they had not then reached this size. These are called 'recruited trees'... It has been claimed that the volume of these trees—the recruitment—should be omitted from the calculation. **1965** *Oceanogr. & Marine Biol.* III. 357 A problem which has recently received considerable attention is the mechanism underlying recruitment of adolescent fish to the various North Sea Summer—Autumn spawning stocks. **1970** S. H. GARDINER tr. *Assmann's Princ. Forest Yield Study* 459 The lower the threshold of measurable diameter the smaller is the amount of recruitment. **1977** J. L. HARPER *Population Biol. of Plants* v. 144 Changes in the composition of light after it has passed through a leaf canopy may be one of the critical factors hindering the recruitment of seedlings under vegetation.

d. *Anat.* The incorporation into a tissue or region of cells from elsewhere in the body.

1973 *Laboratory Investigation* XXVIII. 56/1 Small bronchioles, bronchi, and tracheas showed cells distributed within all three layers which suggested recruitment by movement of cells from capillaries through the epithelium to airway lumina. **1978** *Nature* 2 Feb. 403/1 These compartments have the property that once the boundary has formed, the cells from the neighbouring compartments can never cross it, so each develops by further subdivision but not by recruitment of cells from outside.

3. *Physiol.* **a.** The involvement of successively more motor neurones in response to an unchanging stimulus.

1923 LIDDELL & SHERRINGTON in *Proc. R. Soc.* B. XCV. 335 The several forms assumed by the course of the ascent indicate the various time relations exhibited by the progressive involvement of additional motoneurones during the development of the reflex. That process may, for convenience of statement, be designated 'recruitment'. **1937** BEST & TAYLOR *Physiol. Basis Med. Pract.* lxv. 1278 Many reflexes gradually increase to a maximum when a stimulus of *unaltered* intensity is merely prolonged. This is due to the activation of a progressively greater number of motoneurons. The phenomenon is called recruitment and is figuratively spoken of as 'inertia' by Sherrington. **1975** A. VANDER el al. *Human Physiol.* (ed. 2) viii. 210 The tension of the muscle can be controlled by the recruitment of additional motor units.

b. The phenomenon shown by an ear which, while having a relatively high threshold for the perception of quiet sounds, perceives louder sounds with undiminished intensity, i.e. increases in objective intensity of sound result in abnormally great increases in perceived loudness.

1937 E. P. FOWLER in *Arch. Otolaryngol.* XXVI. 517 When there is no recruitment of loudness in the poorer ear, i.e., no change in the differences in hearing at the thresholds required to balance the loud sounds binaurally, it means that there is an impedance (conduction) lesion in the poorer ear. **1948** *Proc. R. Soc. Med.* XLI. 517 The deafness of the affected ear present at threshold disappears at higher intensities, and this in its simplest terms constitutes the phenomenon of Loudness Recruitment. **1960** *Jrnl. Speech & Hearing Res.* III. 15/1 The classical technique for the direct measurement of loudness recruitment in subjects with unilateral hearing loss is performed by having the subject equate the loudness of a pure tone on one ear with the loudness of a pure tone of identical frequency on the other ear. **1971** D. E. ROSE *Audiol. Assessment* x. 332 Recruitment came to be viewed..as the distinguishing feature of an ear with a cochlear lesion.

recruity (rɪ'kruːtɪ). [f. RECRUIT *sb.* + -Y.] A humorous diminutive of RECRUIT *sb.* 1 b.

1890 [see ONCE *adv.* A. 8]. **1892** R. KIPLING *Barrack-r. Ballads, Troopin'* iv, Ho, you poor recruities, but you've got to earn your pay.

recrute, obs. form of RECRUIT.

†**recry**, *sb. Sc. Obs. rare*⁻¹. [f. RE- + CRY *sb.*; cf. *recall*.] Recall, revocation.

1535 STEWART *Cron. Scot.* III. 364 The band Betuix thair faderis..maid till stand For euirmoir without ony recry.

recry, *v.* [RE- 5 a.] *trans.* To cry again.

1630 tr. *Camden's Hist. Eliz.* 12 Scarce had he spoken the word, when all from all sides cryed, and recryed, God saue Queene Elizabeth.

recryand, obs. Sc. form of RECREANT.

†**recryat**, *v. Sc. Obs. rare*⁻¹. (Of doubtful origin and meaning, perh. for *recryant*, ad. obs. F. *recreantir*: see RECREANT.)

1508 DUNBAR *Flyting* 88 Suppois thy heid war armit tymis ten, Thow sall recryat, or thy crown sall cleif.

recrystallization (ˌriːkrɪstəlaɪ'zeɪʃən). [RE- 5 a.] **1.** The process of crystallizing again; *spec.* in *Metallurgy*, a rearrangement of the crystalline structure of a metal at high temperatures which tends to reduce distortion of the lattice.

1793 *Trans. Soc. Improv. Med. & Chirurg. Knowledge* 30 (*heading*) A process for preparing pure emetic tartar by recrystallization. **1836-41** BRANDE *Chem.* (ed. 5) 911 The crystals of chromate are..purified by recrystallization. **1881** *Daily News* 7 Dec. 5/1 A breaking up and recrystallisation of ..parties. **1925** *Jrnl. Iron & Steel Inst.* CXII. 474 A formula is derived for establishing the relation between the progress of recrystallisation and the degree of deformation in the hot state. **1937** *Discovery* Feb. 35/2 The firn consists of granular particles of ice..formed by recrystallisation of the snow. **1947** J. C. RICH *Materials & Methods Sculpture* iv. 67 The setting of plaster of Paris after it has been mixed with water is also referred to as a rehydration and occasionally as a recrystallization of the calcined gypsum back to its original hydrated rock form. **1973** B. J. HAZZARD tr. *Becker's Organicum* ii. 38 The most important method for purifying solids is recrystallization. **1976** M. C. NUTT *Metallurgy & Plastics for Engineers* v. 78 Recrystallization occurring at elevated temperatures is a process of the formation and growth of unrestrained grains, supplanting entirely the cold-worked structure.

2. Special Comb.: **recrystallization temperature** *Metallurgy*, the temperature at or above which recrystallization of the crystal lattice of a metal takes place (see quots.).

1927 *Carnegie Scholarship Mem.* XVI. 166 No systematic investigation has been made..into the relation between the degree of cold-work and the recrystallisation temperature. **1948** J. E. GARSIDE in H. W. Baker *Mod. Workshop Technology* I. vi. 135 More precisely, cold working is defined as that process of deformation which is conducted below the recrystallization temperature of the metal or alloy. **1961** G. E. DIETER *Mech. Metallurgy* v. 155 For practical considerations a recrystallization temperature can be defined as the temperature at which a given alloy in a highly cold-worked state completely recrystallizes in 1 hr. *Ibid.*, The recrystallization temperature decreases with increasing purity of the metal. **1976** M. C. NUTT *Metallurgy & Plastics for Engineers* v. 78 When a metal is heated, the internal force changes only slightly, but the movement of the atoms increases sharply. In time a temperature is reached at which movement of the atoms can start, and they can arrange themselves into lattices that are not distorted. This degree of heat is known as the recrystallization temperature.

recrystallize (riː'krɪstəlaɪz), *v.* [RE- 5 a.] *trans.* and *intr.* To crystallize again.

1797 WOLLASTON in *Phil. Trans.* LXXXVII. 397 In marine acid they would re-dissolve, and might be re-crystallized. **1849** D. CAMPBELL *Inorg. Chem.* 118 It may be obtained by dissolving and recrystallizing the impure salt imported. **1935** G. E. DOAN *Princ. Physical Metallurgy* iii. 103 Lead..recrystallizes spontaneously at room temperature, even if only slightly deformed. **1946** *Nature* 5 Oct. 482/2 The hard rolled silver specimens when heated to about 900 °C. recrystallized very rapidly. **1956** *Ibid.* 3 Mar. 429/2 Tyrosine was recrystallized from hot water. **1963** D. W. & E. E. HUMPHRIES tr. *Termier's Erosion & Sedimentation* xvii. 338 Certain rocks are dissolved and recrystallized so readily under the effect of differential pressures, that they can flow as plastic substances toward zones where the pressure is lowest. **1971** I. G. GASS et al. *Understanding Earth* iii. 60/2 The mineral can recrystallize to different and denser crystalline structures.

fig. **1882** FROUDE *Life Carlyle* I. 383 What he took into his mind was dissolved and recrystallised into original combinations of his own.

Hence **re'crystallized, re'crystallizing** *ppl. adjs.* Also **re'crystallizable** *a.*, that may be crystallized again.

1859 *Proc. R. Soc.* IX. 653 The gold-salt is a bright yellow crystalline precipitate, difficultly soluble in boiling water, and not recrystallizable without some alteration. **1878** ABNEY *Photogr.* (1881) 61 Recrystallised silver nitrate. **1908** [see IDIOBLASTIC *a.*]. **1962** SIMPSON & RICHARDS *Junction Transistors* iii. 48 This recrystallized germanium forms a single crystal of the same orientation as the germanium disk and, except for the *p*-type impurity, is indistinguishable from it. **1976** COTTERILL & MOULD *Recrystallization & Grain Growth in Metals* iii. 40 The recrystallized grain size depends chiefly on the degree of deformation and to a lesser extent on the annealing temperature. *Ibid.* 54 'Recovery' will continue until the entire specimen has been consumed by the recrystallizing grains.

†**rect**, *a. Obs. rare.* [ad. L. *rect-us* straight.] **a.** Direct. **b.** Erect, straight. **c.** Right (angle). **d.** *fig.* Upright.

a. 1393 LANGL. *P. Pl.* C. IV. 336 Thus ys mede and mercede as two manere relacions, Rect and indyrect. *Ibid.* 357 Man ys relatif rect yf he be ryht trewe.
b. 1557 *Tottell's Misc.* (Arb.) 156 Running my race as rect vpright: Till teares of truth appease my plight.
c. 1598 SYLVESTER *Du Bartas* II. ii. IV. *Columnes* 200 Th' acute, and the rect Angles too, Stride not so wide as obtuse Angles doe.
d. 1890 E. JOHNSON *Rise Christendom* 102 A rect and good and great soul, what is this but God sojourning in the body of man?

Hence **'rectly** *adv.*, directly. *rare*⁻¹.

1922 JOYCE *Ulysses* 208 Swiftly rectly creaking rectly rectly he was rectly gone.

†**rect**, *v. Obs. rare.* Aphetic f. ERECT *v.*

1432-50 tr. *Higden* (Rolls) V. 153 The sepulcre, whiche was lefte in the see, recte [L. *erexit*] hit selfe with the erthe, and was made an yle. **1638** HEYWOOD *Wise Woman* II. i. Wks. 1874 V. 292 Mistris Mary on the Banke-side, is for recting a Figure.

rectal ('rɛktəl), *a. Anat.* and *Med.* [f. RECT-UM + -AL¹.] Of or belonging to the rectum. **rectal gland**, a gland that excretes into the rectum; *esp.* in cartilaginous fishes, a gland that excretes salt so as to maintain the osmotic balance.

1872 F. G. THOMAS *Dis. Women* (ed. 3) 67 The rectal touch, uterine probe,..and other means, should be resorted to. **1875** H. C. WOOD *Therap.* (1879) 20 The dissolving power of the rectal fluids is very slight. **1887** MARSHALL & HURST *Pract. Zool.* xi. 217 The rectal gland is a thick-walled tube, about three quarters of an inch long, lying in the body-cavity dorsal to the rectum. **1925** R. E. SNODGRASS *Anat. & Physiol. Honeybee* vi. 165 Nothing definite is known of the function of the rectal glands. **1974** D. & M. WEBSTER *Compar. Vertebr. Morphol.* xvii. 442 Excess salt is actively excreted by the rectal, or digitiform gland [of chondrichthyeans].

Hence **'rectally** *adv.*, by way of the rectum.

1906 *Practitioner* Nov. 645 This serum was injected rectally. **1977** *Lancet* 16 Apr. 857/2 We have measured the effect of rectally administered cimetidine on acid secretion in the canine stomach.

rectangle ('rɛktæŋg(ə)l), *sb.* [ad. late L. *rectiangulum* a right-angled triangle (7th c.), neut. of *rectiangulus* adj.: see next. Cf. F. *rectangle* sb.]

1. a. In *Geom.*, a plane rectilinear four-sided figure having all its angles right angles, and therefore its opposite sides equal and parallel; *gen.*, something that has the shape of a rectangle.

Usually limited to figures whose adjacent sides are unequal, and so contrasted with *square*.

1571 DIGGES *Pantom.* I. Elem. Biij b, If one side containing the right Angle, be longer than the other containing side, then is that figure called a Rectangle. **1690** LOCKE *Hum. Und.* IV. iv. §6 The Mathematician considers the Truth and Properties belonging to a Rectangle, or Circle, only as they are in Idea in his own Mind. **1726** tr. *Gregory's Astron.* I. 441 The Rectangle *NQK* is given, since its sides *NQ* and *KQ* are given. **1825** J. NICHOLSON *Operat. Mechanic* 689 To find the area of a rectangle, whose length is 9, and breadth 4 inches, or feet. **1871** TYNDALL *Fragm. Sci.* (1879) I. ii. 43 Its face is a rectangle, which..can be rendered as narrow as desired. **1885** LEUDESDORF *Cremona's Proj. Geom.* 223 Any parallelogram inscribed in a circle must be a rectangle. **1898** G. B. SHAW *Arms & Man* I. 8 For an instant the rectangle of snowy starlight flashes out. **1901** 'LINESMAN' *Words by Eyewitness* iii. 60 The indistinct rectangles of the companies shook themselves out into a single rank. **1925** F. SCOTT FITZGERALD *Great Gatsby* vii. 174 A small rectangle of light which I guessed was the pantry window. **1940** W. FAULKNER *Hamlet* III. i. 168 As if a rectangle of opaque glass had been set into nothing's self. **1965** A. LURIE *Nowhere City* (1977) ix. 103 The shop windows had been painted over in irregular rectangles of red, blue, green and white.

transf. **1671** HOBBES *Three papers* Wks. 1845 VII. 438 A square root (speaking of quantity) is not a line, such as Euclid defines, without latitude, but a rectangle.

†**b.** The product of two quantities. *Obs.*

Used on analogy of *square*: cf. preceding quot.

1674 JEAKE *Arith.* (1696) 616 The Rectangle of the Means is equal to that of the Extreams. **1727–41** CHAMBERS *Cycl.* s.v. *Product*, In lines it is always (and sometimes in numbers) called the rectangle between the two lines, multiplied by one another. **1763** EMERSON *Meth. Increments* 9 The increment of a rectangle or product.

†**2.** A right angle. *Obs.* (Cf. RECT *a.* c.)

1656 in BLOUNT *Glossogr.* **1703** MOXON *Mech. Exerc.* 247 A Large Square, to set their Walls at rectangles, which may also be done..by setting 6 foot from the angle one way, and 8 foot the other way, then if the Diagonal..be exactly 10 feet, the angle is a rectangle. **1795** HERSCHEL in *Phil. Trans.* LXXXV. 388 This machine consists of a bottom frame, and a bar..at rectangles to it.

†**3.** A right-angled triangle. *Obs. rare*$^{-1}$.

1798 CANNING, etc. *Loves Triangles* 76 in *Anti-Jacobin*, The sly Rectangle's too licentious love.

†**rectangle**, *a. Obs.* [ad. late L. *rectiangulus* right-angled (Boethius), f. *rectus* straight + *angulus* ANGLE. Cf. F. *rectangle* adj. (1556).] = next. (Used only with *triangle.*)

1570 BILLINGSLEY *Euclid* I. xlvii. 58 In rectangle triangles, the square whiche is made of the side that subtendeth the right angle [etc.]. **1625** N. CARPENTER *Geog. Del.* I. xii. (1635) 262 The square of the Hypotenuse of a Rectangle Triangle. **1708** *Brit. Apollo* No. 34. *a* **1796** BURNS *Caledonia* in *Works* (1800) IV. 356 Rectangle-triangle, the figure we'll chuse.

rectangled ('rɛktæŋg(ə)ld), *a.* Now *rare.* [f. RECTANGLE *sb.* + -ED^2.] Right-angled.

1570 BILLINGSLEY *Euclid* II. def. i. 60 Euery rectangled parallelogramme, is sayde to be contayned vnder two right lines comprehending a right angle. **1715** A. DE MOIVRE in *Phil. Trans.* XXIX. 339 A rectangled Cone whose Altitude is equal to *AR.* **1798** GREVILLE *Ibid.* LXXXVIII. 416 Gems derived from the rectangled octoedra. **1836–7** SIR W. HAMILTON *Metaph.* xxxvi. (1870) II. 316 The one is a rectangled, and the other an equilateral, triangle.

rectangular (rɛk'tæŋgjʊlə(r)), *a.* [ad. L. type **rectangulār-is*: see RECTANGLE *sb.* and -AR. Cf. F. *rectangulaire* (1571).]

1. a. Shaped like a rectangle; having four sides and four right angles.

1624 WOTTON *Archit.* 19 To resolue vpon Rectangular Squares, as a mean betweene too few, and too many Angles. **1718** QUINCY *Compl. Disp.* 33 In Sugar, the same Pyramids, with oblong and rectangular Bases. **1727–41** CHAMBERS *Cycl.* s.v. *Windmill*, A common windmill, whose sails are rectangular, and their length about five times their breadth. **1831** BREWSTER *Optics* xi. 98 When the termination is rectangular, what are called the crested fringes of Grimaldi are produced. **1861** LEWIN *Jerusalem* 197 The platform..was a rectangular space surrounded by a wall of its own.

Comb. **1898** F. DAVIS *Silchester* 23 Their practice of building city walls rectangularwise. **1960** *Farmer & Stockbreeder* 8 Mar. (Suppl.) 10/3 Rectangular-shaped pods which should be gathered when 1 to 1½ in long. **1976** *Private Eye* 24 Dec. 8/1 They must be true, rectangular-type icebergs, without cracks or crevasses.

b. Of a solid body: Having the sides, base, or section in the form of a rectangle, or with right-angled corners.

1624 WOTTON *Archit.* 47 Bricks moulded in their ordinary Rectangular forme. **1805–17** R. JAMESON *Charac. Min.* (ed. 3) 116 The rectangular hexahedron is named cube. **1812–16** PLAYFAIR *Nat. Phil.* (1819) I. 161 When a rectangular beam is supported at both ends [etc.]. **1871** ROSCOE *Elem. Chem.* 276 Mercuric Chloride..is soluble in water, crystallizing in rectangular octahedra.

c. *fig.* Formal, stiff, rigid.

1842 POE *Marie Roget* Wks. 1864 I. 236 Lawyers, who, for the most part, content themselves with echoing the rectangular precepts of the courts.

†**2.** Of a triangle: Right-angled. *Obs.*

1678 CUDWORTH *Intell. Syst.* I. v. 653 Nor doth every one, who hath an idea of a rectangular triangle, presently understand that the square of the subtense is equal to the squares of both the sides.

3. a. Placed or lying at right angles. (Said also of the relative position of two things.)

1646 SIR T. BROWNE *Pseud. Ep.* 179 The thighes of other animals doe stand at angles with their spine, and have rectangular positions in birds. **1675** OGILBY *Brit.* Introd. I. P ij b, The acute Way on the Left leads to Hogsdon, and the Rectangular Way..over the Fields to Old-Street. **1812–16** PLAYFAIR *Nat. Phil.* (1819) II. 267 The Sun..and..two planets referred to the plane of the ecliptic, each by three rectangular co-ordinates..parallel to the three axes. **1869** TYNDALL *Notes Lect. Light* §465 The elasticity of the ether is different in these two rectangular directions. *Ibid.* §479 The function of the analyzer is to reduce the two rectangular wave-systems to a single plane.

b. *Math.* (See quot.) ? *Obs.*

1727–41 CHAMBERS *Cycl.* s.v., If a cone, cylinder, etc., be perpendicular to the plane of the horizon, it is called a rectangular or right cone, cylinder, etc.

4. a. Having parts, lines, etc. at right angles to each other; characterized or distinguished by some arrangement of this kind.

rectangular hyperbola, a hyperbola having its asymptotes perpendicular to one another. ***rectangular staff***, a lithotomic staff bent at right angles.

1727–41 CHAMBERS *Cycl.* s.v. *Barometer*, Horizontal or rectangular Barometer,..the tube whereof is bent, in form of a square. **1872** T. BRYANT *Pract. Surg.* lii. 558 Buchanan's operation with the rectangular staff, bent three inches from the point. **1882** MINCHIN *Unipl. Kinemat.* 173 The curve denoted by this last equation is a rectangular hyperbola. **1887** W. C. FORD *Amer. Cit. Man.* II. 55 The surveys are conducted on a uniform plan, known as the rectangular system.

†**b.** Of a windmill: Having rectangular sails.

1727–41 CHAMBERS *Cycl.* s.v. *Windmill*, Best form and proportion of rectangular Wind-Mills.

rectangularism (rɛk'tæŋgjʊlərɪz(ə)m). *rare.* [f. RECTANGULAR *a.* + -ISM.] A tendency towards or preference for rectangular forms.

1954 *Archit. Rev.* CXVI. 88/2 But in Holland there was no convulsion change; *de Stijl* won common acceptance by compromise..with existing styles, as in the case of Dudok's romantic rectangularism.

rectangularity (rɛktæŋgjʊ'lærɪtɪ). [f. RECTANGULAR *a.* + -ITY.] The quality or state of being rectangular, or having right angles. Also *fig.* stiffness.

1727 in BAILEY vol. II. **1804** MAR. EDGEWORTH *Ennui* ix, She sketched, in strong caricature, my relaxed elongation of limb, and his rigid rectangularity. **1849** DANA *Geol.* iii. (1850) 281 *note*, The rectangularity in the intersections. **1861** SARAH TYTLER *Papers Thoughtful Girls* (1863) 37 It is almost impossible for a sensitive girl to deviate from the beaten track without a sense of oddity and rectangularity perplexing and harassing her.

rectangularly (rɛk'tæŋgjʊləlɪ), *adv.* [f. as prec. + -LY^2.] In a rectangular manner or direction.

1646 SIR T. BROWNE *Pseud. Ep.* II. ii. 62 At the Æquator thereof the needle will stand rectangularly. **1658** —— *Gard. Cyrus* i, The..Ensigne carried this figure, not..rectangularly entersected, but in a decussation. **1832** G. DOWNES *Lett. Cont. Countries* I. 509 The city is exceedingly handsome, and the streets intersect each other rectangularly. **1880** C. & F. DARWIN *Movem. Pl.* 423 The hypocotyl bends in a few hours rectangularly towards a bright lateral light.

So **rec'tangularness** (Bailey vol. II, 1727).

rec'tangulate, *a.* [f. as RECTANGUL-AR + -ATE.] Rectangular, right-angled. So **rec'tangulate** *v. intr.*, to diverge in a rectangular system.

1852 DANA *Crust.* I. 93 Posterior part of orbital margin salient, not acute, rectangulate. **1893** F. ADAMS *New Egypt* 11 From here radiate, or rather rectangulate, all the new rectilineal thoroughfares.

†**rectanguled**, *a. Obs.*$^{-0}$ = RECTANGLED.

1656 BLOUNT *Glossogr.*, *Rectanguled*, that hath right Corners or Angles; a term of Heraldry.

rectangu'lometer. [f. as RECTANGUL-AR + -(O)METER.] An instrument for testing right angles.

1843 HOLTZAPFFEL *Turning* II. 880 When the work and trial bar, (or rectangulometer), are both laid down, the one side of the bar presents a truly perpendicular face.

†**rec'tangulous**, *a. Obs.*$^{-1}$ [f. as RECTANGUL-AR + -OUS.] = RECTANGULAR.

1680 T. LAWSON *Mite into Treas.* 33 A Natural man through search may apprehend much of the Feats and Terms of this Art, their Points,..Perimeter, Triangle, Rectangulous, Obliquangulous [etc.].

‖**recte** ('rɛkteɪ), *adv.* [L., lit. 'in a straight line, rightly'.] **1.** Correctly: used to indicate that the word or phrase following it within a parenthesis is the correct version of that which immediately precedes the insertion.

1886 *Trans. Philol. Soc.* 621 Leg. *contini* (recte *cointinni*) gen. of *cointinn* s.f. 'strife, controversy'. **1934** *Times Lit. Suppl.* 3 May 325/2 'Tithreks Saga' (*recte* 'Thithriks Saga af Bern'). **1939** JOYCE *Finnegans Wake* (1964) III. 543 The villa of the Ostmanorum to Thorstan's, *recte* Thormars Sraid. **1979** *Trans. Philol. Soc.* 184 Kent translates the portion after my square brackets 'This indeed..(is) my activity (*recte* physical-dexterity).'

2. *Mus.* In phr. ***(per) recte et retro*** [med.L., in the right way and backwards], applied to the movement of a canon cancrizans (see CANCRIZANS *a.*).

[**1801** T. BUSBY *Compl. Dict. Mus.*, *Recte*,..a word signifying forwards and particularly pertaining to the *Canon.*] **1836** *Penny Cycl.* VI. 243/1 The canon *Recte et Retro* has but one peculiarity, and pretends to only one merit, namely, that it may be sung either forwards or backwards. **1876** [see CANCRIZANS *a.*]. **1909** R. DUNSTAN *Composer's Handbk.* x. 155 A Canon 'per Recte et Retro' is one that may be sung *forwards* and *backwards* at the same time, producing two parts in one. **1922** R. O. MORRIS *Contrapuntal Technique* 50 In each pair of voices the part of the lower is that of the upper begun at the end and sung backwards, i.e. a canon *per recte et retro.* **1954** *Grove's Dict. Mus.* (ed. 5) V. 79 Stainer wrote a hymn-tune 'per recte et retro' in 1898.

rectenna (rɛk'tɛnə). [f. *rect(ifying ant)enna.*] A unit combining a receiving aerial and a device for rectifying the current it produces.

1975 *Pop. Sci.* Sept. 66/2 Transmitting electric power from outer space to earth... The rectifying units could be coupled to the receiving antenna or built into it—a combination now called a rectenna. **1977** *Indian Express* 18 Aug. 6 A micro-wave beam is directed to rectenna on the ground. **1978** *Times* 8 Sept. 19/6 The ground antenna which will receive the microwave beam and rectify this energy to direct-current electricity—the name 'rectenna' has been coined—will consist of a grid of wires carried on insulated posts.

rectifiable ('rɛktɪfaɪəb(ə)l), *a.* [f. RECTIFY *v.* + -ABLE.] Capable of being rectified; *spec.* in *Math.* (see RECTIFY 7 b).

1646 SIR T. BROWNE *Pseud. Ep.* 201 The errors of one concoction not [being] rectifiable by another. **1816** tr. *Lacroix's Diff. & Int. Calculus* 120 The curve DF is rectifiable; that is to say we can assign a right line which is equal to it in length. **1887** R. A. ROBERTS *Int. Calculus* I. 307 Charles has given some interesting results connecting circles with arcs whose difference is rectifiable.

rectification (rɛktɪfɪ'keɪʃən). [a. F. *rectification* (14th c. in Littré), or ad. late L. *rectificātiōn-em*, n. of action f. *rectificāre* to RECTIFY.] The action of rectifying.

1. a. The correction of error; a setting straight or right; amendment, improvement, correction. Also *spec.* in Chinese communism, the correction of errors in ideology and practice within the communist party. Also *attrib.*, as ***rectification campaign, drive, movement.***

c **1460** G. ASHBY *Dicta Philos.* 491 The most grettest Rectificacion Ys, from evel thinges to directe a kinge. **1621** BURTON *Anat. Mel.* II. i. IV. i, They haue done more cures in this kind by rectification of Diet, then all other Physick. **1651** C. CARTWRIGHT *Cert. Relig.* I. 119 For though rectification be not error, yet it doth presuppose Errour. **1669** WORLIDGE *Syst. Agric.* 48 *marg.*, Rectification of the Feeder. **1765** WARBURTON *Div. Legat.* v. App., If his Lordship by the present state of things, includes the rectification of them in a future state [etc.]. **1808** SYD. SMITH Wks. (1859) I. 98/1 That they must bear this patiently, and look to another world for its rectification. **1882** LECKY *Eng. in 18th Cent.* (1892) IV. xvi. 355 A few slight rectifications of territory were at the same time made. **1891** *Law Rep.* Weekly Notes 58/2 Such mistake is not capable of rectification as between ordinary adverse litigants. **1956** tr. *Sel. Wks. Mao Tse-Tung* IV. 111 In the rectification campaign of 1943 all bureaux..of the Central Committee of the Party, all regional and district Party Committees should..endeavour to gain experience. **1959** *New Statesman* 17 Jan. 64/3 We make sure that..any professor or student who needs rectification is encouraged to volunteer for three or four weeks of unskilled labour in the steel works. **1962** E. SNOW *Red China Today* (1963) xlvii. 376 It was the opening shot of an official 'rectification' or *cheng-tung tso-feng* movement. **1967** tr. *Quotations from Chairman Mao Tsetung* (ed. 2) 4 As we used to say, the rectification movement is 'a widespread movement of Marxist education'. Rectification means the whole Party studying Marxism through criticism and self-criticism. **1971** J. J. TAYLOR in D. J. Dwyer *China Now* (1974) xxii. 425 The Cultural Revolution is to the international united front what the rectification drives within the CCP in 1941 and 1942 were to the anti-Japanese front in China: an effort to maintain purity and fervour in the revolutionary nucleus. **1977** *Time* 21 Mar. 22/3 Mao's..willingness periodically to shake up the bureaucracy in 'rectification campaigns'.

†**b.** *Astron.* and *Astrol. Obs.*

a **1646** J. GREGORY *Terrestrial Globe* in *Postuma* (1650) 286 This is called Rectification, or right setting of the Globe. **1668** DRYDEN *Even. Love* II. i, What think you..of the best way of rectification for a nativity?

c. *Photogrammetry.* The process of preparing a plan view from an aerial photograph taken at an oblique angle.

1920 M. N. MACLEOD *Mapping from Air Photographs* II. iv. 54 The rectification, or plotting of photos by comparison with fixed points, is at best a roundabout method. **1921** *Geogr. Jrnl.* LVII. 141 The theory of the rectification of photographs that should have been taken vertically, but are really tilted several degrees in an unknown direction, involves propositions in the theory of perspective which are not readily accessible in convenient form. **1928** *Ibid.* LXXI. 589 Whether the tilt is to be eliminated by photographic 'rectification', or by transferring the map grid to the photograph in perspective,..it is first necessary to find the tilt and the height at the moment of exposure. **1944** P. G. MCCURDY et al. *Man. Photogrammetry* ii. 54 Optical rectification is the process of projecting the image of a tilted photograph into a horizontal plane. **1968** *Times* 1 Nov. 6/8 A process known as rectification is already standard practice. This is an automatic method of giving correct positions in plan to elevated features such as hills.

2. *Chem.* The purification or refinement of any substance by renewed distillation or other means.

1605 TIMME *Quersit.* III. 184 Rectification is a reiterated distillation to perfection. **1666** BOYLE *Orig. Formes & Qual.* 339 An indifferent good *Spiritus Nitri*, that even before Rectification would readily enough dissolve Silver. **1712** tr. *Pomet's Hist. Drugs* I. 56 The Oil of Sugar that remains after Rectification. **1787** KEIR in *Phil. Trans.* LXXVII. 267 The acid obtained from vitriol,..deprived by rectification of its smoking quality. **1876** HARLEY *Mat. Med.* (ed. 6) 354 The oily liquid separates, which is purified by rectification.

transf. **1621** BURTON *Anat. Mel.* II. ii. III. 331 To this cure of melancholy..the Rectification of Aire is necessarily required. *a* **1677** HALE *Prim. Orig. Man.* IV. ii. 298 This portion of the lower World seems to be the whole residue of the visible Chaotical Mass, which by the former

Rectification was reduced to a small portion, like the *Caput Mortuum* after Distillation.

3. *Geom.* The finding of a straight line equal in length to a given curve.

1685 WALLIS *Algebra* 293 The Year following (1659), Mr. Heurat, lights on the Rectification of the same Curve, which Mr. Neil had done before. **1727–41** CHAMBERS *Cycl.* s.v., All we need to find the quadrature of the circle is the rectification of its circumference. *Ibid.*, The rectification of curves is a branch of the higher geometry. **1823** J. MITCHELL *Dict. Math. & Phys. Sci.* 413/2 It is..to the doctrine of fluxions that we owe the complete rectification of curve lines, in finite terms. **1892** tr. *H. Schubert's Math. Ess.* 119 The quadrature of the circle stands and falls with the problem of rectification.

4. The process or act of permitting an electric current to flow preferentially in one direction; *esp.* in *Electr.*, the conversion of an alternating current into a direct current; also in *Physiol.*, the action of nerve membranes in allowing electrical impulses to be conducted preferentially in one direction.

anomalous rectification *Physiol.*, the phenomenon of permitting current to flow preferentially from low to high ionic concentrations.

1895 *Electrician* 9 Aug. 488/1 A commutator..to which current is led and from which it is taken, after rectification. **1905** *Proc. R. Soc.* LXXIV. 485 The rectification is less complete in proportion as the temperature of the carbon filament increases. **1922** *Encycl. Brit.* XXXII. 1027/2 The remainder of the plate voltage is created by the rectification by the valve of the speech currents induced in the secondary circuit. **1941** *Jrnl. Gen. Physiol.* XXIV. 562 The most convenient specification of the rectification characteristics of the membrane. **1949** A. L. HODGKIN et al. in *Arch. Sci. Physiol.* III. 139 There is a marked rectification but it evidently takes some time to develop... We therefore propose the use of the term 'delayed rectification' to describe this effect. **1962** *Jrnl. Physiol.* CLXIII. 61 A fall in the membrane conductance when the membrane current flows from the inside to the outside of the fibre, and rise in conductance when the current is in the opposite direction has been called anomalous rectification. **1965** *Math. in Biol. & Med.* (Med. Res. Council) VI. 258 In 1941, Cole and Curtis showed that, in the steady state, the membrane of squid nerve has a much lower resistance to outward (depolarizing) currents than to inward (hyperpolarizing) currents. By analogy with the behaviour of electrical rectifiers this phenomenon was called rectification and the term 'delayed rectification' was introduced—emphasizing the fact that the changes in resistance take an appreciable time (a few milliseconds) to occur. *Ibid.*, Rectification can occur in the absence of [ionic] concentration gradients.., and in skeletal muscle fibres..and in cardiac muscle fibres.. rectification in the opposite direction to that predicted from simple changes in membrane ion concentration occurs. **1966** R. G. KLOEFFLER *Electron Tubes* x. 209 For the purpose of analysis of rectification by diodes, a clear concept may be obtained by assuming that both the device and the load are linear. **1970** J. SHEPHERD et al. *Higher Electr. Engin.* (ed. 2) xxv. 798 The semiconductor diode rectifier is now replacing the mercury-arc rectifier for polyphase rectification in all applications except those involving the highest voltages.

ˈrectificative, *a. rare.* [ad. F. *rectificatif* (Littré): see RECTIFY and -IVE.] That rectifies.

1869 *Daily News* 14 Dec., The total and final amounts of the ordinary, extraordinary, and 'rectificative' Budgets.

† **rectificatory**, *sb. Obs.* [See next and -ORY.] A mathematical instrument used in the construction of dials.

The description given by Sebastian Münster in his *Horologiographia* (1533) 98 is: 'Voco autem rectificatorium, instrumentum triangulare orthogonium, formam habens scaleni, cuius latus breuius basis, medium cathetus, longius vero hypotenusa dicitur'. A figure of the instrument is given on p. 100 of the same work.

1593 FALE *Dialling* A iij, Some teach the making of Dialls by the helpe of the Globe... Munster useth a Rectificatory with a circle, which is unfit for small plats, and faileth in greater, without great heede.

ˈrectificatory, *a.* [ad. L. type **rectificatōrius*: see RECTIFY *v.* and -ORY.] That rectifies; corrective.

1866 *Lond. Rev.* 3 Feb. 133/2 Hypothetical and rectificatory budgets of ordinary and extraordinary expenditure. **1886** *Manch. Exam.* 8 Feb. 5/2 The rectificatory note which Sir H. A. has sent to the papers.

rectified (ˈrɛktɪfaɪd), *ppl. a.* [f. RECTIFY *v.*]

1. a. Made right, corrected. Also (in some cases perh. directly *transf.* from 2), cleared from defects or imperfections, refined.

Common in 17th c., esp. of conscience, reason, will, etc.

1555 PHILPOT in Coverdale *Lett. Mart.* (1564) 221 That wyth a cleane spirite and rectifyed body, we myght serue god iustly. **1612** DONNE *Lett.* (1651) 233 Our..Saviour blesse you with the testimony of a rectified conscience. **1646** J. HALL *Horæ Vac.* 5 Those of more rectified Reasons, can sustaine bright and glistring discoveries to beat in upon them. **1707** NORRIS *Treat. Humility* iv. 176 A juster and more rectifyed sense of things. **1771** FLETCHER *Checks* Wks. 1795 II. 289 A talent of living light and rectified free agency. **1884** H. SPENCER in *Contemp. Rev.* Feb. 158 In the minds of most, a rectified evil is equivalent to an achieved good.

b. *Photogrammetry.* Designating a plan or photograph which has been corrected for errors of perspective (cf. RECTIFY *v.* 1 c).

1920 M. N. MACLEOD *Mapping from Air Photographs* I. iv. 27 A 'rectified' print of the negative is obtained which is true to scale all over and can be traced on to the map. **1969** G. C. DICKINSON *Maps & Air Photographs* xv. 245 All five or nine photographs are printed fused together into one image, the obliques being 'transferred' or rectified into vertical views before printing.

2. *Chem.* Purified or refined by renewed distillation; redistilled. Chiefly used of spirit.

1605 TIMME *Quersit.* I. xv. 74 This humour..doth resemble the rectified animal aquavita. **1667** BOYLE in *Phil. Trans.* II. 608, I made the like Tryal with rectified Oyl of Turpentine. **1747** WESLEY *Prim. Physic* (1762) 90 Three Ounces of rectified Spirits of Wine. **1807** T. THOMSON *Chem.* (ed. 3) II. 376 A fine light transparent liquid, known in commerce by the name of rectified spirits. **1876** HARLEY *Mat. Med.* (ed. 6) 326 Rectified Spirit is alcohol containing 16 per cent. by weight, or 11 per cent. by volume of water, obtained by the distillation of fermented saccharine fluids.

3. †**a.** Straightened, straight. *Obs. rare.*

1597 A. M. tr. *Guillemeau's Fr. Chirurg.* b ij b/1 The rectifyede Lancette, wherewith we open an Apostemation. *Ibid.* 16 b/2 The rectifyede or extendede can or pipe.

b. Of an electric current: (see RECTIFY 7 c).

1892 S. P. THOMPSON *Dynamo-Electric Machinery* (ed. 4) iii. 38 The currents are now 'rectified', or 'redressed', as our continental neighbours say, but are not continuous. *Ibid.* (*caption*) Curve of rectified or commuted alternating current. **1893** SLOANE *Stand. Electr. Dict.* 164. **1910** G. W. PIERCE *Princ. Wireless Telegr.* xviii. 197 The rectified current obtained by applying the alternating voltage *V* could be read on the galvanometer. **1947** R. LEE *Electronic Transformers & Circuits* iii. 48 With large values of capacitance, the rectified voltage..increases to within a few per cent of the peak voltage. **1958** *New Scientist* 10 July 342/2 A wire 'tickled' a crystal of silicon, and when the alternating radio signal was applied to the combination the current would flow only in one direction: this 'rectified' current could then be used to work a Morse receiver. **1965** *Wireless World* July 335/1 The rectified current does not then cause potential changes in the source.

4. Of tulip flowers: having variegated colouring caused by a virus affecting the plant.

1659 T. HANMER *Garden Bk.* (1933) 21 When they [*sc.* the colours of tulips] streame away, as they doe ever wholly in flowers perfected, or rectified (as the tearme is) the leaves retaine not the least blew or yellow in them. **1850** *Beck's Florist* 23 Some say, that as they broke or became rectified, another number was given them. **1881** *Encycl. Brit.* XII. 259/2 The breeder bulbs and their offsets may grow on for years producing only self-coloured flowers, but after a time ..some of the progeny 'break', that is, produce flowers with the variegation which is so much prized. The flower is then said to be 'rectified'. **1911** [see REMBRANDT]. **1929** A. D. HALL *Bk. Tulip* v. 99 This change [in colouring] is called 'breaking', the flower is termed 'broken' or 'rectified', while the original form is known as a 'breeder'. **1948** [see REMBRANDT].

rectifier (ˈrɛktɪfaɪə(r)). [f. as prec. + -ER[1].]

1. *gen.* One who, or that which, rectifies.

1611 COTGR., *Rectificateur*, a Rectifier. **1617** COLLINS *Def. Bp. Ely* I. i. 97 Chrysostome..attributes as much to him, to be rector or rectifyer, as he there speakes, of the whole world. **1663** BUTLER *Hud.* I. ii. 431 He was..Rectifier of Wry Law, And would make three to cure one Flaw. **1741** WARBURTON *Div. Legat.* II. 639, I shall examine this bold Rectifier of prejudices. **1882** SPURGEON *Treas. Dav. Ps.* cxix. 1 They do not consult it now and then as a sort of rectifier of their wanderings, but they use it as a chart for their daily sailing.

b. *Photogrammetry.* A device for preparing, by optical or other means, a plan view from an oblique aerial photograph.

1921 *Geogr. Jrnl.* LVII. 141 The construction of the photographic 'rectifier'..embodies some curious properties of the lens with a flat field. **1932** MCCAW & CAZALET tr. *O. von Gruber's Photogrammetry* xi. 277 If a photograph is projected on a plane (map plane) oriented in a definite manner such that the projection also indicates a definite scale, it is customary to describe the process as rectification and the apparatus therefore as a rectifying camera or simply a Rectifier. **1962** *Photogrammetric Record* IV. 84 The great increase in setting accuracy and definition available in the SEG V (and other modern rectifiers). **1964** *Exhib. Guide 10th Internat. Congr. Photogrammetry* 76 Wild E4 Rectifier-enlarger... Rectification elements: Inclination of table in *x* and *y* directions or across the diagonals.

2. †**a.** An instrument for ascertaining the variation of the compass (see quot. 1704). *Obs.*

1669 STURMY *Mariner's Mag.* II. vi. 68 To know the Variation by the Quadrant.., without the help of the Rectifier before spoken of. **1704** J. HARRIS *Lex. Techn.* I, *Rectifier* (in Navigation,) is an instrument consisting of two Parts, which are two Circles, either laid upon, or let into the other, and so fastned together in their Centres, that they represent two Compasses [etc.].

b. A device or substance which permits an electric current to flow preferentially in one direction; *esp.* in *Electr.*, a device for converting an alternating current into a direct current; in *Physiol.*, a nerve membrane which conducts electrical impulses preferentially in one direction.

1895 *Electrician* 9 Aug. 488/1 An efficiency of 96 per cent. is claimed for the rectifier. **1898** SLOANE *Stand. Elect. Dict.* (ed. 2) App. 616. **1901** *Electrician* 8 Nov. 107/2 The working rectifier is not a mere physical, but also an electro-chemical problem. **1911** *Encycl. Brit.* XXVII. 835/1 A common type of rectifier is another tube containing gas at a low pressure. **1926** R. W. HUTCHINSON *Wireless* 119 Fig. 96 shows a method of using a crystal as a detector or rectifier. **1941** *Proc. Soc. Exper. Biol. & Med.* XLVIII. 293 In a nerve fiber membrane, current may pass more easily in one direction than in the other,..the nerve fiber membrane behaves as a rectifier rather than a simple resistance. **1955** *Amer. Jrnl. Physiol.* CLXXXIII. 671/1 (*heading*) Rectifier properties of Purkinje fibers. **1958** *Times* 11 Feb. 15/2 Thirty years ago we started with the copper oxide rectifier, and 10 years later we introduced the Westalite selenium rectifier. Last year we added the germanium-type rectifier to our range. **1961** [see INVERTER 2 a]. **1970** J. SHEPHERD et al. *Higher Electr. Engin.* (ed. 2) xxv. 795 In its single-phase form the mercury-arc rectifier consists of a graphite or carbon-coated iron anode and a mercury-pool cathode enclosed in an envelope from which all air has been removed.

3. a. One who rectifies spirit.

1727 DE FOE *Eng. Tradesman* vi. (1732) I. 58, I would warn..a distiller or rectifier of spirits to moderate his furnace. **1731** P. SHAW *Ess. Artif. Philos.* 115 When the Rectifier..performs his part masterly, the Spirit receives considerable improvement. **1843** *Penny Cycl.* XXVII. 467/1 In England in 1835 there were 108 rectifiers. **1880** *Act 43 & 44 Vict.* c. 24 §86 Entry must be made by a rectifier before he begins to receive, rectify, or compound any spirit.

b. An apparatus for rectifying spirit.

1854 RONALDS & RICHARDSON *Chem. Technol.* (ed. 2) I. 287 The upper part forming a heater for the wash, while the lower compartment acts as a rectifier.

4. rectifier (photo-)cell, rectifier photo-electric cell, a photovoltaic cell.

1933 *Sci. Proc. R. Dublin Soc.* XX. 538 The selenium rectifier cell of Bergmann. **1935** *Discovery* July 214/2 The so-called rectifier cell has been developed, with its great convenience of being able to dispense with batteries. **1936** [see *light-sensitive* s.v. LIGHT *sb.* 15]. **1952** *Jrnl. Sci. Instrum.* XXIX. 137 Correcting the deviation from the theoretical value of the response of selenium rectifier photo-cells to obliquely incident light.

rectify (ˈrɛktɪfaɪ), *v.* [ad. F. *rectifier* (14th c. in Littré), ad. late L. *rectificāre* (3rd c.), f. *rectus* right + *-ficāre*: see -FY.]

1. a. *trans.* To put or set right, to remedy (a bad or faulty condition or state of things).

c **1400** *Lanfranc's Cirurg.* 51 Wiþ propre eir [*v.r.* cure] to rectifien þe corrupcioun of þilke lyme. **1526** *Pilgr. Perf.* (W. de W. 1531) 136 b, Thus we may se y[t] payne is good, for by it god rectifyeth synne. **1615** BRATHWAIT *Strappado* (1878) 176 For rectifying such abuse as grow, By this foule vice. **1651** HOBBES *Leviath.* II. xxvii. 158 He ought by meditation of the Law, to rectifie the irregularity of his Passions. **1748** HARTLEY *Observ. Man* II. i. 17 It produces Consequences, which in the End rectify the original Disorder. **1829** FARADAY *Exp. Res.* xliii. 255 The bottom gave way..and endeavouring to rectify this..by means of sand [etc.]. **1845** M[c]CULLOCH *Taxation* II. vi. (1852) 285 Though there still remain some anomalies to be rectified, this statute has effected some material improvements.

b. To put right, correct, amend, make good (a mistake, error, omission, etc.).

1659 HEYLIN *Examen Hist.* I. 173, I must make a start to fol. 91 for rectifying a mistake of our Authors. **1699** BENTLEY *Phal.* 250 He discovers his own Omissions, and presently rectifies them. **1718** LADY M. W. MONTAGU *Let. to Abbé Conti* 19 May, An error of his guide, which his short stay hindered him from rectifying. **1837** DICKENS *Pickw.* vii, The slight omission was rectified. **1858** MILL *Liberty* ii. (1865) 12/1 Man..is capable of rectifying his mistakes, by discussion and experience.

c. *Photogrammetry.* To correct errors of perspective in (an oblique aerial photograph, or a position derived from one) in order to obtain a plan view.

1919 *Geogr. Jrnl.* LIII. 390 This method..is..not so satisfactory as our method of rectifying the print in a camera. **1928** *Ibid.* LXXI. 591 The photographed positions of two control points are rectified. **1944** P. G. MCCURDY et al. *Man. Photogrammetry* x. 440 (*heading*) Control and computation to rectify the individual photographs. **1979** *Sci. Amer.* Apr. 28/3 Essentially an orthophoto is an aerial photograph which has been rectified and on which contour lines, spot heights, and other information are superimposed.

2. †**a.** To restore (a diseased or disordered organ) to a sound or healthy condition. *Obs.*

c **1400** *Lanfranc's Cirurg.* 80 If þe lyuere eiþir þe splene ben I-greued,..þou muste rectifien hem. **1620** VENNER *Via Recta* ii. 25 It notably rectifieth the stomacke. **1660** tr. *Amyraldus' Treat. conc. Relig.* III. ix. 498 To reinfuse decayed strength in a moment, and rectifie cripled members after long impotence. **1694** SALMON *Bate's Dispens.* (1713) 580/2 It rectifies a weak and disorderly Stomach.

b. To put or set (a person or thing) right, in various applications of the adj.; to bring or restore to a good or normal condition; †to establish in a proper manner.

a **1529** SKELTON *Col. Cloute* 1265 To rectyfye and amende Thynges that are amys. **1549** LATIMER *1st Serm. bef. Edw. VI* (Arb.) 31 He doth vs rectify in the libertie of the gospel, in that therefore let vs stand. **1599** B. JONSON *Cynthia's Rev.* I, Your trauaile is your only thing that rectifies, or..makes you fit for action. **1640** SIR B. RUDYARD in Rushw. *Hist. Coll.* (1680) II. II. 1358, I have often thought and said, that it must be some great extremity, that would recover and rectifie this State. **1678** *Trans. Crt. Spain* II. 100 The question was only Then of banishing a stranger; but Now the business is to rectify Spain itself. **1796** C. MARSHALL *Garden.* xx. (1798) 376 Espaliers, garden frames, and such things, rectify. **1882** LECKY *Eng. in 18th C.* (1892) IV. xvi. 366 The simplest and most natural way of rectifying his position.

refl. **1809** *Med. Jrnl.* XXI. 294 In this way we may account ..for the manner in which nature tends to rectify herself.

absol. **1830** HOOD *Haunted House* I. xxviii, No hand or foot within the precinct came To rectify or ravage.

†**c.** To restore in right condition *to* something.

1655 FULLER *Ch. Hist.* I. ii. §11 Beholding their Temples ..solemnly continued to a pious end, and rectified to the Service of the true God.

3. *Chem.* To purify or refine (any substance) by a renewed or repeated distillation, or by some chemical process; to raise *to* a required strength in this way; also, to flavour (a liquor) with some substance during rectification. Also *absol.*

c **1450** LYDG. *Secrees* 565 Ffirst departyng of the foure Ellementys, And afftirward..Eurych of hem for to Recteffye. **1460–70** *Bk. Quintessence* 13 Brynge aȝen eurych [element] into 5 beynge [= quintessence]..as tofore, or ellis rectifie. **1594** PLAT *Jewell-ho., Chem. Concl.* 5 When you have divided the oyles from the waters, then you may rectifie or purify them in this manner. **1662** R. Mathew *Unl. Alch.* 155 Its clearness must not come with gentle fire, but with oft rectifying. **1681** tr. *Belon's Myst. Physick* Introd. 35 Pour over it of the best Spirit of Wine, rectified with Pot-ashes. **1731** P. Shaw *Ess. Artif. Philos.* 126 These..refuse parts of Sugar are fermented with Water..; then distill'd into a Spirit, and rectified *per se* to vulgar proof. **1800** tr. *Lagrange's Chem.* II. 248 If you rectify the product found in the receiver, you will obtain prussic acid. **1883** *Hardwich's Photogr. Chem.* (ed. Taylor) 268 To rectify the solution, pour it into the glass bath..and..thoroughly stir up with it four drops of dilute Nitric acid.

transf. **1603** Drayton *Bar. Wars* i. xxii, The temper of that nobler mouing part, With such rare purenesse rectifie'd his blood. **1620** Venner *Via Recta* Introd. 5 The Sunne, which rectifieth the aire. *a* **1677** Hale *Prim. Orig. Man.* i. ii. 45 The assimilation thereof in Animals rectifies this alimental juice into Chyle, and then into Blood. **1727** Pope & Gay *Further Acc. E. Curll*, An Affluence of Animal Spirits rectified and refined to a degree of Purity.

4. a. To correct or reform (a person, one's nature, mind, etc.) from vice or moral defect.

a **1450** *Mankind* (Brandl) 13 O souerence, I be-seche you, yowur condycyons to rectyfye. *c* **1460** G. Ashby *Dicta Philos.* 792 Rectifie a noper if that ye may,..And rectifie youre selfe first euery day. **1548** Udall, etc. *Erasm. Par. John* xx. 113b, Let them therfore put awaye earthly affeccions and rectifie theyr myndes, applying the same to spirituall and heauenly thynges. **1643** Sir T. Browne *Relig. Med.* i. §42 But age doth not rectifie, but incurvate our natures, turning bad dispositions into worse habits. **1667** Flavel *Saint Indeed* Wks. 1716 II. 5/2 Grace hath in great measure rectifyed the Soul, and given it an..heavenly temper. **1714** Addison *Spect.* No. 571 ⁋9 As a Soul within the Soul, to..rectifie its Will, purifie its Passions [etc.]. **1781** Crabbe *Library* 141 Whatever good ye boast, that good impart, Inform the head, and rectify the heart. **1859** Geo. Eliot *A. Bede* ii. xvii, You can neither straighten their noses, nor brighten their wit, nor rectify their dispositions.

†**b.** To correct (one who is mistaken or in error); to set right. *Obs.*

1586 *Exam. Henry Barrowe* A iij b, *Barrowe.* Yow shal not touch one haire of my head, without the wil of my heauenly father. *Arch.* Nay I will doe this to rectifie yow. **1616** B. Jonson *Devil an Ass* ii. i, He do's not know me indeed. I thank you, Ingine, For rectifying him. **1688** Penton *Guard. Instr.* (1897) 1 Pray, Sir, rectifie me if I am mistaken. **1711** Addison *Spect.* No. 93 ⁋4 A Man has frequent Opportunities of..rectifying the Prejudiced.

absol. **1605** Bacon *Adv. Learn.* i. ii. §4 In all these it [learning] doth rectify more effectually than it can pervert.

5. a. To correct by removal of errors or mistakes; to amend or improve in this way.

1494 Fabyan *Chron.* 2, I wyll presume..To ioyne suche a werke or it to rectyfye. **1610** Shaks. *Temp.* v. i. 245 Some Oracle Must rectifie our knowledge. **1674** Marvell *Corr.* Wks. 1872–5 II. 422 In order to the retracting or rectifying ..the reasons formerly given by your House. *a* **1727** Newton *Chronol. Amended* i. (1728) 57 That Chronology is to be rectified, by shortening the times which precede the death of Cyrus. **1777** Watson *Philip II* (1839) 219 He found means, however,..in some measure to rectify their opinion of his conduct. **1830** Seton *Forms Decrees in Equity* 396 It was prayed that the said minutes may be rectified. **1864** Bowen *Logic* i. 12 And of subsequently rectifying and enlarging our Concepts.

b. To correct or emend (a text). *rare.*

1730 *Hist. Litteraria* I. 450 In order therefore to rectify the Text, he collated anew the several Editions. **1778** Bp. Lowth *Transl. Isaiah* Prelim. Diss. (ed. 12) 46 Useful in rectifying as in explaining the Hebrew text.

†**c.** To make (an action) morally right. *Obs.*

1700 S. Sewall *Mem.* in *Diary* (1879) II. 19 *note*, The extraordinary and comprehensive Benefit accruing to the Church of God, and to Joseph personally, did not rectify his brethrens Sale of him.

6. a. To put right by calculation or adjustment.

1559 W. Cunningham *Cosmogr. Glasse* 166 This [figure] semeth to haue a singuler vse in rectifying the longitudes of places. **1669** Sturmy *Mariner's Mag.* i. ii. 6 This is too hard for Practitioners at first to know how to use this Instrument, to rectifie the variation of the Compass. **1679** Moxon *Math. Dict.*, *To Rectify a Nativity*, is to bring the Estimate and supposed time to the true and real time of a persons Birth. **1704** J. Harris *Lex. Techn.* I. s.v., Its Use is to find the Variation of the Compass, to Rectifie the Course at Sea. **1707–12** Mortimer *Husb.* (1721) II. 253 If the Stock be all knotty or crooked..rectifie it with the fittest posture of the Graft you can. **1877** Owen *Mrq. Wellesley's Desp.* Introd. 32 He rectified frontiers, in a military sense, with minute care, so as to make both us and our staunch dependents as defensible as possible.

b. To set right, adjust (an instrument or apparatus). Also in fig. context.

1669 Sturmy *Mariner's Mag.* ii. vi. 67 A most necessary Instrument to rectifie the Compass. **1669** Worlidge *Syst. Agric.* 48 Observe whether it will hold out or super-abound at the end of one or two Furrows, and accordingly proceed and rectifie the Feeder [of the sowing-drill]. *a* **1708** Beveridge *Priv. Th.* i. (1730) 108 Having rectified the Balance of my Judgment according to the Scripture. **1833** Ht. Martineau *Loom & Lugger* i. iv. 45 She..employed herself next in rectifying the time-piece by her own watch.

c. *spec.* To adjust (a globe) for the solution of a problem. Also *absol.*

a **1646** J. Gregory *Terrestrial Globe* in *Postuma* (1650) 286 Lift up the North-Pole aboue the Horizon so manie Degrees as will answer to the Latitude of the Place unto which you mean to rectifie. **1674** Moxon *Tutor Astron.* ii. (ed. 3) 84 Rectifie the Globe, Quadrant, Hour-Index, and Horizon. **1704** J. Harris *Lex. Techn.* I, *To Rectifie the Globe*... Bring the Sun's Place..to the Meridian, and the Hour-Index to 12 at Noon. **1868** Lockyer *Elem. Astron.* 158 When the globe has been rectified, as it is called, in this manner, we have the constellations which are rising on the eastern horizon, just appearing above the eastern part of the wooden horizon.

7. †**a.** To make straight, straighten out (anything crooked, etc.); to bring into line. *Obs.*

1597 A. M. tr. *Guillemeau's Fr. Chirurg.* 39/2 Havinge therfor now rectified this finger by this meanes. **1600** [see rank *v.*[1] 1 b]. **1628** Wither *Brit. Rememb.* Premonit. 2 Rectifying a crooked staffe. *a* **1711** Ken *Christophil* Poet. Wks. 1721 I. 497 O Conscience,..Check me, and rectify my devious Lines. **1793** Smeaton *Edystone L.* §252 The masons proceeded to rectify the face of the work, where it was in any degree wanting thereof.

b. *Geom.* To equate (a curve) with a straight line. (Cf. rectification 3.)

1673 Visc. Brouncker in *Phil. Trans.* VIII. 6150 It was easie..to infer, That, if we can Rectifie the one, we may square the other. **1685** Wallis *Algebra* 293 The same Curve, which Mr. Neil (and so many after him,) had Rectified before. **1721–41** Chambers *Cycl.* s.v. *Rectification*, To rectify the circle, therefore, is to square it. *Ibid.*, To rectify the parabola. **1866** Brande & Cox *Dict. Sci.*, etc. II. 799/1.

c. To permit (an electric current) to flow preferentially in one direction; *esp.* in *Electr.*, to convert (an alternating current) into a direct current.

1892 S. P. Thompson *Dynamo-Electric Machinery* (ed. 4) xxiii. 652 A commutator, which rectified the alternations. **1893** Sloane *Stand. Electr. Dict.* 164. **1895** *Electrician* 9 Aug. 488/1 The town supply of current at a pressure of 3,000 volts is transformed down to 65 volts and rectified. **1901** *Brit. Med. Jrnl.* 9 Mar. 573/2 The current to be 'rectified' is taken direct from alternator to commutator. **1922** *Encycl. Brit.* XXXII. 1024/2 It [*sc.* the valve] can..be used to separate out the two constituents of a high frequency alternating current and 'rectify' them into a direct current. **1962** *Jrnl. Physiol.* CLXIII. 111 The 2–3 membrane was assumed to be permeable only to potassium and to rectify anomalously: the extent of this rectification is illustrated. **1962** A. Lytel *Industr. Electronics* ii. 38 These rectifiers are two-element tubes and are used in power supplies to rectify or convert alternating current to direct current. **1964** B. V. Rollin *Introd. Electronics* v. 65 To rectify a signal by mixing it with a reference voltage of the same frequency and observing the resulting d.c. output.

†**8.** To guide or direct aright. *Obs. rare.*

1603 Daniel *Panegyrike to King* lxiii, Thy iudgement now must only rectifie This frame of pow're thy glory stands vpon. **1618** Bp. Hall *Right. Mammon* Wks. (1625) 693 There is nothing more necessarie..for a Christian heart, then to be rectified in the menaging of a prosperous estate.

†**9.** To declare right, approve of (a thing). *Obs.*

1567 Drant *Horace, De Arte Poet.* A viij, What Tom, and Tib do rectefie What lykes the carter clowne, The wyse men take not in good parte.

†**10.** *intr.* To become straight. *Obs. rare*$^{-1}$.

1597 A. M. tr. *Guillemeau's Fr. Chirurg.* 39/2 If the finger groweth croocked, we must then cause the finger to rectifye and growe straight.

'rectifying, *vbl. sb.* [f. prec. + -ing[1].] The action of the vb. rectify.

1597 A. M. tr. *Guillemeau's Fr. Chirurg.* 39/2 The stretching out or rectifying of the same [finger]. **1634** Sanderson *Serm.* II. 292 There it behoveth the magistrate to set in..for the rectifying and redressing thereof. **1699** Burnet *39 Art.* i. (1700) 21 Matter, after it has pass'd through the highest Refinings and Rectifyings possible. *a* **1708** Beveridge *Priv. Th.* i. (1730) 52 It is not the rectifying of one Faculty, which can make the Whole streight. **1845** G. Dodd *British Manufactures* V. iii. 63 This distillation is the rectifying of the spirit, by which a certain portion of essential oil is removed from it. **1928** *Geogr. Jrnl.* LXXII. 383 When we come to what should be the most interesting chapter on map-plotting, contouring, and rectifying, we find it composed of chunks taken mostly from German propagandist pamphlets. **1960** *Nature* 5 Nov. 495/1 (*heading*) Rectifying properties of heart muscle. **1962** D. F. Shaw *Introd. to Electronics* xi. 246 The rectifying property of a semi-conductor diode is a consequence of the asymmetrical conduction across the contact between a metal and a semi-conductor.

'rectifying, *ppl. a.* [f. as prec. + -ing[2].]

a. That rectifies.

1667 Flavel *Saint Indeed* (1754) 8 Earnest Supplications and instant Prayer for heart purifying and rectifying Grace. **1863** Gladstone *Financ. Statem.* 292 In London a very large rectifying house..sent out in 1861 853,000 gallons. **1892** S. P. Thompson *Dynamo-Electric Machinery* (ed. 4) xxiii. 659 A rectifying commutator. **1901** *Electrician* 8 Nov. 107/2 The patents granted in regard to the application of the rectifying cell. **1906** *Proc. Physical Soc.* XX. 182 Wehnelt.. proposed to employ vacuum-tubes with one electrode covered with..oxides and heated, as rectifying valves for alternating currents. **1932** *Geogr. Jrnl.* LXXX. 463 The Panorama-camera..consists of nine lenses working through prisms, and, in conjunction with a special rectifying printing apparatus, produces the equivalent of a photograph taken with a very wide-angled lens. **1944** P. G. McCurdy et al. *Man. Photogrammetry* ii. 54 Rectifying apparatus is often designed so that a change in scale and tilt removal can be made simultaneously. **1947** R. Lee *Electronic Transformers & Circuits* iv. 86 This circuit requires more rectifying tubes.

b. ***rectifying column***, a distillation column in which the distillate is subjected to successive stages of purification by continually condensing and redistilling the vapour.

1891 S. P. Sadtler *Handbk. Industr. Org. Chem.* vi. 216 An improved Savalle rectifying column as used generally in French and Belgian distilleries. **1923** W. H. Walker et al. *Princ. Chem. Engin.* xvii. 557 An apparatus in which this direct interchange of heat and consequent condensation and evaporation can take place is called a rectifying column. **1946** *Nature* 20 July 105/1 The work..included the design and construction of..a liquid methane rectifying-column. **1955** Coulson & Richardson *Chem. Engin.* II. xviii. 611 A column apparatus may be used for batch or continuous operation. In the former case the column is mounted on a large boiler or still which holds the charge, and the column is said to be a rectifying column.

rectigrade ('rɛktɪgreɪd), *a.* *Zool.* [ad. L. type **rectigrādus*, f. *rectus* rect *a.* + *grādus* grade.] Walking in a straight line; applied to those larvæ which walk with a rectilinear body (Say *Gloss. Entom.* 1825), and to the class of spiders (*Rectigradæ*) which run straight forward (Mayne *Expos. Lex* 1858). Cf. *laterigrade*.

'rectigraph. *Photogr.* [f. as prec. + -graph.] A form of corrected lens.

1890 Woodbury *Encycl. Photogr.* **1891** *Photogr. Ann.* 382 The Combination 'Rectigraph'. *Ibid.* 383 The Narrow-angle 'Rectigraph'.

†**rectiline,** *a.* *Obs.* [ad. late L. *rectilīneus* (Boeth.), f. *rectus* straight + *līnea* line: see rect *a.* and line *sb.*[2] Cf. F. *rectiligne* (14th c. in Littré).] = rectilinear.

1570 Billingsley *Euclid* i. ix. 19 To deuide a rectiline angle geuen, into two equall partes. *Ibid.* vi. def. i. 153 Like rectiline figures are such, whose angles are equall [etc.]. **1660** Stanley *Hist. Philos.* ix. (1701) 382/1 The most simple of all rectiline figures.

rectilineal (rɛktɪ'lɪnɪəl), *a.* [f. as next: see -al[1] and cf. lineal.] = rectilinear.

1646 Sir T. Browne *Pseud. Ep.* 203 Fishes..whose ribs are rectilineall. *a* **1696** Scarburgh *Euclid* (1705) 103 The like transmutation of all Rectilineal spaces into equal Parallelograms. *a* **1774** Goldsm. *Surv. Exp. Philos.* (1776) II. 350 The red ray..is therefore least..bent out of its rectilineal course. **1863** E. V. Neale *Anal. Th. & Nat.* 43 A rectilineal triangle, that is,..the figure produced by three straight lines mutually intercepting each other.

Hence **recti,lineali'zation,** the fact of being arranged in a rectilineal fashion.

1893 F. Adams *New Egypt* 47 The rectilinealisation of the streets is not excessive.

rectilinear (rɛktɪ'lɪnɪə(r)), *a.* and *sb.* [f. as rectiline + -ar. Cf. linear *a.*]

A. *adj.* **1.** Of motion, course, or direction: Taking or having the course of a straight line; tending always to the same point.

1659 H. More *Immort. Soul* iii. xiii. §6 A Bullet..cast up into the Air, would never descend again, but would persist in a rectilinear motion. **1696** Whiston *Th. Earth* i. (1722) 1 All Motion is of it self rectilinear. *a* **1774** Goldsm. *Surv. Exp. Philos.* (1776) II. 350 In proportion as each succeeding ray has less force, it is driven more out of its rectilinear direction. **1830** Kater & Lardner *Mech.* xviii. 247 Continued rectilinear motion is observed in the flowing of a river. **1889** *Nature* 21 Feb. 402/2 The play of forces concerned in rectilinear oscillations.

transf. **1827** Hare *Guesses* Ser. ii. (1866) 340 The course of time is markt, not by the rectilinear flight, but by the oscillations and pulsations of life.

2. Lying in, or forming, a straight line.

1704 Newton *Optics* (1721) 109 When I had caused the rectilinear sides..of the Spectrum of Colours made by the Prism to be distinctly defined. **1811** Pinkerton *Petral.* II. 24 The granite which forms this vein has shrunk..with some rectilinear fissures. **1837** Whewell *Hist. Induct. Sc.* (1857) I. 78 The rays of light are rectilinear. **1875** Blake *Zool.* 252 In the Conidæ the aperture is narrow and rectilinear, or nearly so.

transf. **1858** J. Martineau *Stud. Chr.* 69 It is by no means a rectilinear regiment of incessant priests; but a broken, scattered, yet glorious race of prophets.

3. Of a figure or angle: Bounded or formed by straight lines.

1728 Pemberton *Newton's Philos.* 137 What has here been said upon this rectilinear figure [etc.]. **1840** Lardner *Geom.* 223 If one side of a plane rectilinear angle revolve round its other side as an axis, it will produce the surface of a right circular cone. **1863** E. V. Neale *Anal. Th. & Nat.* 255 A triangle is that plane rectilinear figure which has three sides.

4. Characterized by straight lines.

1727–41 Chambers *Cycl.* s.v. *Map*, Rectilinear Maps are those wherein both the meridians and parallels are represented by right lines. **1827** Steuart *Planter's G.* (1828) 410 The rectilinear Gardens, and elaborate Topiary works handed down from antiquity. **1850** Parker *Gloss. Archit.* (ed. 5) 239 The same rectilinear arrangement also pervaded many of the details. **1861** *Gd. Words* Aug. 433/1 The modern city..has a trim, rectilinear..air about it.

b. *Arch.* Suggested as a substitute for perpendicular.

1826 *Brit. Critic* II. 376 It is not merely the vertical mullions that run in straight lines, but the horizontal transoms also... Hence we would call this the 'Rectilinear style'. **1835** Whewell *Arch. Notes Germ. Churches* Pref. (1842) 21 The term Rectilinear, which has been suggested, would not apparently be an advantageous substitute for Perpendicular; for the mullions, the only members to which the description applies distinctively, are rectilinear only so far as they are perpendicular. **1849** E. Sharpe *Treat. Decor. Wind. Tracery* 8, I propose, then, to name these three styles of window tracery, Geometrical, Curvilinear, and Rectilinear.

c. Of a sawing-machine: Having a straight (in place of a circular) saw.

1843 Holtzapffel *Turning* II. 739 Rectilinear sawing machines are for the most part derived from saws used by hand for similar purposes.

d. Of a spectroscope or lens: (see quots.).

1874 tr. *Lommel's Light* 149 The direct vision or rectilinear spectroscope which instead of a single prism contains a combination of prisms, so that there is no deflection. **1890** Woodbury *Encycl. Photogr.*, *Rectilinear*, a term applied to lenses which have been corrected for aberration as much as possible, so that in photographing architectural subjects the lines appear perfectly straight in the image.

B. *sb.* **1.** A rectilinear figure. *rare*$^{-1}$.

1766 *Complete Farmer* s.v. *Surveying* 7 G 4/2 To return to triangles, the most simple and primitive of all rectilinears.

2. *Photogr.* A rectilinear lens. (Cf. A. 4 d.)

1890 WOODBURY *Encycl. Photogr.* 405 The rapid rectilinear will..be found very useful for copying purposes. **1892** *Photogr. Ann.* II. 39 With rapid rectilinears and the lenses on the same principle distortion is rarely found.

Hence **recti'linearism**, tendency to straight lines.

1854 *Blackw. Mag.* LXXVI. 539 Brooks and rivers leap and run in courses which please all the more because dissimilar from the rectilinearism of utility.

rectiline'arity. [f. prec. + -ITY.] The quality of being rectilinear.

1813–21 BENTHAM *Ontology* Wks. 1843 VIII. 197 Qualities that are qualities of the above-mentioned fictitious entities of the first remove. For example, of motion, rectilinearity, curvilinearity. **1863** LYELL *Antiq. Man* xiii. (ed. 3) 233 The uniformity, parallelism,..and.. rectilinearity of the so-called glacial furrows.

fig. **1840** GEN. P. THOMPSON *Exerc.* (1842) V. 67 The rectilinearity of the law.

recti'linearly, *adv.* [f. as prec. + -LY².] In a straight line, or straight lines.

1801 YOUNG in *Phil. Trans.* XCII. 24 It is easy to show that such a general undulation would in all cases proceed rectilinearly. **1874** W. FROUDE in *Encycl. Brit.* (1886) XXI. 811/2 The particles..are capable of gliding rectilinearly along a perfectly smooth surface.

†rectilined, *a. Obs. rare.* = RECTILINE.

1570 BILLINGSLEY *Euclid* I. 3 *marg.*, Definition of a rectilined angle. *Ibid.* i. 8 A triangle or any other rectilined figure is then said to be set.., when [etc.].

recti'lineous, *a. rare.* = RECTILINEAR.

1691 RAY *Creation* I. (1692) 123 There are only three rectilineous and ordinate figures which can serve to this purpose. **1858** MAYNE *Expos. Lex.*

rectinerved, *a. Bot.* [f. *recti-*, comb. form of L. *rect-us* + NERVED.] (See quot.)

1880 GRAY *Struct. Bot.* iii. §4 (ed. 6) 92 [Leaves] may be Rectinerved, the nerves running straight from origin to apex or margin of the leaf, as the case may be.

rection ('rɛkʃən). *Gram.* [ad. L. *rectiōn-em* government, f. *regĕre* to rule: see RECTOR.] Syntactical government; regimen.

a **1637** B. JONSON *Eng. Gram.* II. vii, Now as before in two articles *a* and *the*, the whole construction of the Latins was contained; so their whole rection is by prepositions near-hand declared. **1673** O. WALKER *Educ.* 131 Which is easily known by the rection of the parts of his Sentence. **1871** EARLE *Philol. Eng. Tongue* xi. 513 Rection, though not necessarily connected with flexion, has ever been found as its close companion and ally. **1953** [see *intraverbal* s.v. INTRA-¹]. **1968** J. LYONS *Introd. Theoret. Linguistics* vi. 241 Concord..is usually distinguished from *government* (or 'rection', in the usage of some authors).

Hence **'rectional** *a.*

1938 *Trans. Philol. Soc.* 115 Where..a given declension implies a given gender, the inflexion may be said to express a rectional category in addition to the categories of case and number. **1949** *Archivum Linguisticum* I. II. 167 Notionally noun compounds are either attributive or rectional (governing).

rectiserial (rɛktɪ'sɪərɪəl), *a. Bot.* [f. L. *recti-*, *rectus* straight + SERIAL.] (See quots.)

1861 BENTLEY *Bot.* 141 All the above varieties of Phyllotaxis in which..the leaves completing the cycles must be necessarily directly over those commencing them, are called rectiserial. **1880** GRAY *Struct. Bot.* iv. §1 (ed. 6) 126 The leaves should be in strict vertical ranks, or, to use the term proposed by Bravais, rectiserial.

rectitude ('rɛktɪtju:d). [a. F. *rectitude* (Oresme, 14th c.), ad. late L. *rectitūdo*, f. *rect-us*: see RECT *a.* and -TUDE.]

1. The quality or fact of being straight; straightness. Now *rare* or *Obs.*

1432–50 tr. *Higden* (Rolls) II. 213 Equalite of complexion was in hit,..rectitude of stature, and pulcritude of figure. **1578** BANISTER *Hist. Man* IV. 47 Perfect sight is had of nothing..but the rectitude of the apple of the eye. **1641** J. JACKSON *True Evang. T.* II. 153 That which is straight shews at once both its owne rectitude, and the crookednesse of the contrary. **1685** BOYLE *Enq. Notion Nat.* vi. 203 If with your Hand you force it a little from its Rectitude, as soon as you remove your Hand, it will endeavour to regain its former straightness. **1729** SHELVOCKE *Artillery* IV. 199 These Slips ..will by their own natural Spring and Energy recover their Rectitude when left at liberty.

fig. *a* **1687** PETTY *Pol. Arith.* v. (1691) 94 And perhaps [these impediments] are but the warpings of time, from the rectitude of the first Institution.

b. Straight line; direction in a straight line.

1578 BANISTER *Hist. Man* I. 36 The first part of the heele ..departyng wholly from the straight lyne, or rectitude of Tibia. **1597** A. M. tr. *Guillemeau's Fr. Chirurg.* 7/2 The Chirurgiane..searchinge for him [the bullet] according to the rectitude of the wounde. **1646** SIR T. BROWNE *Pseud. Ep.* 179 When the spine is in rectitude with the thigh. **1758** J. S. *Le Dran's Observ. Surg.* (1771) 49, I resolved to make another Aperture,..following the Rectitude of the Fibres. **1867** HOWELLS *Ital. Journ.* iii. 23 One may walk long through the longitude and rectitude of many of her streets.

2. Moral straightness or uprightness; goodness, integrity; virtue, righteousness.

a **1533** LD. BERNERS *Gold. Bk. M. Aurel.* (1559) Hhijb, By the rectitude of his iustice. **1633** PRYNNE *1st Pt. Histrio-m.* VII. iii. 593/2 The obscene jests of Stage-players and other vanities, which are wont to soften a Christian soule from the rigour of its rectitude and uprightnesse. **1662** STILLINGFL. *Orig. Sacræ* III. ii. §7 Goodness..imports the necessary rectitude of the Divine Nature. **1711** SHAFTESB. *Charac.* (1737) II. I. III. iii. 55 There is no..Rectitude, Piety or Sanctity in a Creature thus reform'd. **1771** BURKE *Lett., to R. Shackleton* (1844) I. 254 A man of singular piety, rectitude, and virtue. **1856** FROUDE *Hist. Eng.* v. (1858) I. 459 The king was assured of the rectitude of the motives on which he had himself acted. **1879** FARRAR *St. Paul* I. 269 In the decision of momentous questions rectitude of heart is a far surer guarantee of wisdom than power of intellect.

3. Correctness of the (intellectual or artistic) judgement, or of its conclusions.

1651 HOBBES *Leviath.* II. xxvii. 158 Private Iudgement.. according to the rectitude, or errour thereof [etc.] **1756** BURKE *Subl. & B.* Introd., A rectitude of judgment in the arts, which may be called a good taste. **1809** SYD. SMITH *Wks.* (1867) I. 182 There is something extremely contagious in greatness and rectitude of thinking. *a* **1871** GROTE *Eth. Fragm.* i. (1876) 22 Without the possibility of any standard for distinguishing fallacy from rectitude.

4. Correctness of nature, procedure, or application. Also with *pl.*, an instance of this.

1656 STANLEY *Hist. Philos.* v. (1701) 183/1 The rectitude of names is by a certain imposition not temerarious or casual, but seemingly to follow the nature of the things themselves. **1691** HARTCLIFFE *Virtues* 291 That universal Rectitude of all the faculties of the Soul, by which they stand apt and disposed to their receptive Offices and Operations. **1802** PALEY *Nat. Theol.* ix. §6 (1819) 117 They perceive a result, but they think little of the multitude of concurrences and rectitudes which go to form it.

†5. A right. *Obs. rare*$^{-1}$.

1660 R. COKE *Power & Subj.* 190 If any man by force holds the Rectitudes of God [etc.].

Hence **rectitudi'narian**, one who practises rectitude in conduct; **recti'tudinous** *a.*, characterized by rectitude or self-righteousness; also as *sb.*

1671 *True Nonconf.* 308, I heartily pray the Lord, to make all of you, indeed, rectitudinarians. **1897** *Westm. Gaz.* 26 Jan. 2/1 Notoriously and unctuously rectitudinous. **1906** F. S. OLIVER *Alexander Hamilton* v. ii. 381 The rectitudinous inquisition that is enjoyed under the freedom of the press. **1966** 'W. COOPER' *Mem. New Man* I. ii. 27 We were both wearing soberly rectitudinous dark clothes. **1978** *N.Y. Rev. Bks.* 18 May 23/1 It is not so much an appetite for hypocrisy as for the sententious and rectitudinous—for 'expressin' right'—that is a vital impulse in the American folk character.

‖**rectius** ('rɛktɪəs), *adv.* [L., compar. of RECTE *adv.*] More correctly: used similarly to RECTE *adv.* I.

1932 *N. & Q.* 6 Feb. 103/1 'Gallinatia': (*rectius* 'Galimatia(s)')... The more correct spelling is Galimatia(s). **1965** J. S. ROSKELL *Commons & their Speakers* i. 12 A London chronicle says that he was..replaced by William (*rectius* John) Doreward. **1980** *Daily Tel.* 13 Aug. 14, I am by no means sure that Mr Anthony Powell should be allowed to rebuke the editors..for 'oddly' referring to Garter King at Arms (*rectius*, Garter King of Arms).

†rectline, *a. Obs. rare*$^{-1}$. = RECTILINE.

1651 T. RUDD *Euclid* 155 This Book treateth of the Inscription..of rectline Figures, how one right lined Figure may be inscribed within another.

recto ('rɛktəʊ), *sb.* and *adv.* (Abbrev. rº.) [a. L. *recto* (sc. *folio*), abl. of *rectus* right.]

A. *sb.* In *Printing*, the right-hand page of an open book; hence, the front of a leaf, as opposed to the back or VERSO. Also in *Palæography*, the front of a leaf of manuscript.

1824 J. JOHNSON *Typogr.* I. 217 This..volume commences on the recto of the first leaf. **1849** D. ROCK *Ch. of Fathers* I. i. iii. 280 The verses, in a very old hand, at the recto of fol. 258. **1889** H. B. WHEATLEY *How to catalogue* iii. 60 The recto of the additional leaf will range with the verso of the old leaf. **1964** F. BOWERS *Bibliogr. & Textual Crit.* III. vi. 84 A textual critic can find the most desirable combination of recto and verso settings. **1978** *Bodl. Libr. Record* IX. 324 The writing exercises..are confined to the rectos of the pages.

fig. **1873** HENRY *Æneidea* I. Pref. 77 The verso of this agreeable recto of one leaf of my library life.

B. *adv.* On or to the right-hand side.

1888 *Academy* 16 June 405/1 The map is placed..at the end of the volume opening rectò, and not, as too often, made to turn its back upon the reader.

recto-, used as comb. form of RECTUM in various terms of *Anat.* and *Path.*, with the sense 'relating to the rectum in conjunction with some other part of the body', as *recto-coc'cygeal*, *-co'lonic*, *-u'rethral*, *-'uterine*, *-va'ginal*, *-'vesical*, etc. Also more widely in *Surg.* with the sense 'of or pertaining to the rectum', as **'rectopexy** [-PEXY], the fixation of a prolapsed rectum; **'rectoscope** [-SCOPE], an instrument for use in rectoscopy; **rec'toscopy**, visual examination of the rectum.

1836 TODD *Cycl. Anat.* I. 176/1 A tense fibrous..tissue, called the *recto-coccygeal ligament. **1884** KNIGHT *Dict. Mech.* Suppl. 746/2 **Recto-colonic Apparatus*, instruments which reach the rectum and colon. *a* **1898** *Syd. Soc. Lex.*, *Rectopexy. **1902** J. P. TUTTLE *Treat. Dis. Anus* xvii. 691 (*caption*) Rectopexy for procidentia recti—the incision. **1977** *Lancet* 22 Jan. 170/2 On 10 patients a transabdominal rectopexy was performed, using a modified Ripstein procedure. **1890** BILLINGS *Med. Dict.* 442/2 **Rectoscope*, speculum for the rectum. **1906** P. L. MUMMERY *Sigmoidoscope* i. 7 There are several patterns of pneumatic sigmoidoscope or rectoscope now in use. **1977** *Time* 17 Jan. 51/1 The surgeon cuts directly through the urethra with a marvellous combination of scalpel and fibre-optics looking glass called a rectoscope. *a* **1898** *Syd. Soc. Lex.*, *Rectoscopy. **1909** *Index-Catal. Library Surgeon-General's Office, U.S. Army* XIV. 343/1 Rectoscopy. *See* Rectum (Exploration of). **1967** N. S. KAPANY *Fiber Optics* vii. 171 The application of flexible fiberscopes not only to gastroscopy, but also to..rectoscopy. **1879** *St. George's Hosp. Rep.* IX. 273 Two patients were admitted with *recto-urethral fistula. **1857** BULLOCK *Cazeaux' Midwif.* 60 Those formed by it, between the rectum and uterus, are called the posterior, or the *recto-uterine ligaments. **1855** RAMSBOTHAM *Obstetr. Med.* 37 The commissure connecting these two organs is called the *recto-vaginal septum. **1836** TODD *Cycl. Anat.* I. 400/1 The..*recto-vesical operation for stone.

rectocele ('rɛktəsi:l). *Med.* [f. RECTO- + Gr. κήλη a tumour, rupture.] Prolapse of the recto-vaginal wall; vaginal protocele.

1859 TODD *Cycl. Anat.* V. 708/1 Vaginal cystocele and rectocele occur in a similar manner. **1872** T. G. THOMAS *Dis. Women* (ed. 3) 165 Rectocele, or recto-vaginal hernia, occurs in a manner similar to that by which the bladder descends.

rector ('rɛktə(r)). Also 4, 6–8 **rectour.** [a. L. *rector*, agent-n. f. *regĕre* to guide, lead straight, rule, govern.]

†1. a. The ruler or governor of a country, city, state or people. *Obs.*

1387 TREVISA *Higden* (Rolls) III. 55 From Eneas to þis Romulus Italy was vnder fiftene rectoures. **1398** —— *Barth. De P.R.* XV. lv. (Bodl. MS.), Eolas..was rector of þe ylondes þat hatte Eole. **1432–50** tr. *Higden* (Rolls) V. 363 þeke yle was wonte to have a rector..to whom alle the province were subiecte. **1582** STANYHURST *Æneis* III. (Arb.) 72 Priamus, thee Troian rector vnhappye. *c* **1611** CHAPMAN *Iliad* II. 70 The other sceptre-bearing States arose too, and obey'd The people's Rector. **1632** LITHGOW *Trav.* III. 89 It was told me by the Rector of Candy. **1685** H. MORE *Paralip. Proph.* 111 Quirinius made Caius his Rectour till his Recuperation of Armenia. [**1832** tr. *Sismondi's Ital. Repub.* xi. 245 The judicial power was still exercised by two or three *rectors*, aliens to the state.]

†b. *transf.* The queen-bee of a hive. (Cf. KING 8 a.) *Obs. rare.*

1398 TREVISA *Barth. De P.R.* XII. v. (Bodl. MS.), If þe rectoure is on lyue þe males beþ in one partie and þe females in anoþer partye.

†c. Applied to God as the ruler of the world, of mankind, etc. *Obs.* (Common in 17th c.)

1582 STANYHURST *Ps.* iv. in *Æneis*, etc. (Arb.) 132 Our heunlye rectore His sacred darling specialye choosed. **1627** DRAYTON *Agincourt* clv, This Herault from the Rector of the skies In Vision warnes them not to vse delayes. **1676** HALE *Contempl.* I. 229 The great dispenser or permitter and rector of all the events in the world. **1741** WARBURTON *Div. Legat.* IV. vi. §3 The supreme Rector of the Universe.

2. a. One who, or that which, has or exercises supreme or directive control in any sphere. Now *rare*.

1482 *Monk of Evesham* (Arb.) 90 Suche persons kyngys and bysshoppys and other grete men..not beyng rectors and faders, but peruersours and destroyers of her sowlys. **1579–80** NORTH *Plutarch, Flaminius* (1612) 387 Titus was chosen judge and rector of the games that were plaid there [at Argos]. **1601** B. JONSON *Poetaster* v. ii, Reason (which in right should be The special Rector of all harmony). **1632** BROME *Novella* III. i. Wks. 1873 I. 137 We seeke to Art, (Nature's Rector) to restore Us, the strength we had before. **1644** MILTON *Areop.* (Arb.) 51 Who shall be the rectors of our daily rioting? **1835** I. TAYLOR *Spir. Despot.* VI. 264 The imperial regenerator and rector of the Church.

†b. The leader (of a choir). *Obs.*

1546 *Yorks. Chantry Surv.* (Surtees) II. 433 To do suche thinges as they shalbe commaunded to do by the rector of the quere. **1691** WOOD *Ath. Oxon.* (1813) I. 106 He was buried in the choir..under that very place where the rectors of the choir sing the psalm..'Venite exultemus'.

3. a. A parson or incumbent of a parish whose tithes are not impropriate (cf. VICAR). Now also in the Church of England, the leader of a team ministry. In the Roman Catholic Church, a parish priest.

In modern use also sometimes applied to the holders of ancient chapelries and perpetual curacies, and in Scotland and the United States to Episcopal clergymen having charge of a congregation. *lay rector*, a layman receiving the rectorial tithes, or in whom the rectory is vested.

(For continental examples of *rector* in eccl. use see Du Cange. In Brittany the parish priest is styled *recteur* in place of the usual *curé*, the latter term being used in the sense of *vicaire* or curate.)

[**1225** in Wilkins *Concil.* (1737) I. 617/1 Quod rectores ordinentur et serviant ecclesiis. **1237** *Ibid.*, De residentia.. in ecclesiis a rectoribus facienda. **1306** *Rolls of Parlt.* I. 189/2 Henr' de Pynkence, Rectorem Ecclesie de Honyton.] **1393** LANGL. *P. Pl.* C. III. 184 And ich my-self cyuyle and symonye my felawe Wollen ryden vp-on rectours and rich men deuoutours. **1556** [see RECTORAGE]. *a* **1600** HOOKER *Eccl. Pol.* VII. xiii. §2 The bishops..in the time of the primitive Church, all such as parsons or rectors of parishes are with us? **1620** BRENT tr. *Sarpi's Counc. Trent* II. (1676) 234 The superiour did recommend the vacant Church, to some honest and worthy man, to gouern it..until a Rector were provided. **1684** EVELYN *Diary* 11 May, His grandfather and father.., with himselfe, had now ben Rectors of this parish 101 yeares. **1778** [W. MARSHALL] *Minutes Agric., Digest* 6 The Landed Gentlemen, the Clergy, and the Lay Rectors, have industriously propagated this false spirit of farming. **1818** CRUISE *Digest* (ed. 2) III. 58 Payment of tithes to the rector is a sufficient discharge against the vicar, because all tithes of common right belong to the rector. **1866** GEO. ELIOT *F. Holt* (1868) 29 The Rector was helped to this chain of reasoning by Harold's remarks. **1923** S. KAYE-SMITH *End of House of Alard* II. 117 They came to the cottage where the Rector lived, instead of in the twenty-five roomed Rectory. **1927** *Catholic Times* 11 Feb. 21/2 In 1901 he became rector of St. Joseph's, Birkenhead. **1972** *Daily Tel.* 7 Aug. 10/5 Only the leader of the team, usually called 'Rector', is the beneficed freehold incumbent. **1977** MACMORRAN & ELPHINSTONE *Handbk. for Churchwardens* (new ed.) vii. 66 In the context of a team ministry..the incumbent of the benefice or benefices to which a team ministry extends is always styled 'rector'... The other members of the ministry are styled 'vicars'.

†**b.** (See quot.) *Obs. rare*$^{-1}$.

1670 G. H. *Hist. Cardinals* I. III. 90 Amongst these Fathers, there are some that confess people in divers Languages, and one of them in each Church has the Title of Rector.

c. ***missionary-rector***: see MISSIONARY.

4. In scholastic use:

a. The permanent head or master of a university, college, school, or religious institution (esp. a Jesuit college or seminary).

In Eng. use now applied only to the heads of Exeter and Lincoln Colleges, Oxford, and to designate the principal of a higher educational institution, as the Royal College of Art, the Imperial College of Science and Technology, Liverpool Polytechnic, etc. In Scotland common as the designation of the headmasters of secondary schools or academies.

1464 *Rolls of Parlt.* V. 518/1 Provost, Felawes and Scolers, Maister and Felawes, Rector, Felawes and Scolers, President and Felawes of any College, Halle, Hospitall, Hous incorporate, or any other place. **1536** *Act 27 Hen. VIII*, c. 42 §1 That the said acte..be not hurtfull..unto the said Maisters Presidentes Rectours Principalles..within the said Universities. *c* **1570** SIR H. GILBERT in *Q. Eliz. Acad.* (1869) 8 There shalbe one Rector of the said Achademy. **1601** *Imp. Consid. Sec. Priests* (1675) 83 He is Rector of the English Seminary in Rome. **1686** in B. Peirce *Hist. Harvard Univ.* (1833) App. 67 There shall be allowed to the present Rector of the College..the remainder of the income not disposed underneath. **1691** *Case of Exeter Coll.* 5 The Rector and Fellows were convinced in their Consciences of Mr. Colmer's guilt. **1766** T. CLAP *Hist. Yale Coll.* 11 The Trustees chose the Rev. Mr. Abraham Pierson..to take the Care of Instructing and Governing the Collegiate School; under the Title and Character of Rector. **1797** *Encycl. Brit.* (ed. 3) VI. 315/2 (High School, Edinburgh) The rector's place is supposed to be worth not less than 400*l.* per annum. **1837** *Penny Cycl.* IX. 278/1 The Edinburgh Academy..was founded in 1824, and consists of a rector and four other classical masters. **1916** JOYCE *Portrait of Artist* (1969) i. 55 All the fellows would make fun and talk about young Dedalus going up to the rector to tell on the prefect of studies. **1950** *Chambers's Encycl.* XIII. 658/2 [Sir H. T. Tizard] was..rector of the Imperial College of Science and Technology 1929–42. **1973** *Stornoway Gaz.* 3 Mar. 1/4 The Nicolson [School] has had its share of brilliant rectors, teachers and pupils.

transf. **1607** TOPSELL *Four-f. Beasts* Pref., The great Rector and Chancellor of all the Academies in the World Jesus Christ,..the Master of that Colledge wherein he [Moses] was but a Servant or Steward.

b. In the Scottish universities: The holder of one of the higher offices, the precise character and importance of which have undergone considerable changes, esp. in recent times.

At the present time, under the Scottish Universities Acts of 1858 and 1889, the rector (frequently styled *Lord Rector*) is elected by the matriculated students for a period of three years, and is president of the University Court. It is the practice for him to deliver a 'rectorial address' to the students at some time during his tenure of the office. For the older history of the rectorship (which varied considerably in the four universities) see especially the Report of the Universities Commission in *Parl. Papers* (1831) XII.

[**1411–12** *Foundation Charter St. Andrews Univ.*, Quod hujusmodi delinquentes..per rectorem universitatis vestræ intimentur. **1422–3** *Statute St. Andrews Univ.* 24 Mar., Ut dominus Rector antecederet..ita nempe ut..Rector sit episcopo proximus, Rectorem prior sequatur.] **1522** Jas. V in *Rep. St. Andrews Univ. Comm.* (1837) III. 180 The Universitie of Sanctandrois, the rector, doctouris, regentes, maisteris, scolaris,..makand residence therein. **1563–7** BUCHANAN *Ref. St. Andrews* Vernac. Wks. (S.T.S.) 15 The rectour most be..doctor or bachelar in the hyear faculteis, or principal of ane college,..and salbe chosin be the hayl graduattis of the vniuersite... The rectouris tyme to be ane ʒeir. **1640** in *Rep. Comm. Univ. Scot.* (1830) 114 (Edinb.) The Counsall..have resolved and ordaynit.., that yeirlie upon the first Wednesday of December, thair sall be chosen ane Rector. **1666–88** DALLAS *Syst. Stiles* 126 To the Rector and Principal of the University of Glasgow. **1830** *Rep. Comm. Univ. Scot.* App. 317 (Aberdeen) The Rector and his Assessors..constitute a Court, and have frequently exercised control over the University. **1839** J. B. HAY (*title*) Inaugural Addresses by Lord Rectors of the University of Glasgow. **1884** GRANT *Edinb. Univ.* II. 106 Mr. Gladstone thus became [in 1859] the first elected Lord Rector of the University of Edinburgh.

c. The acting head, and president of the administrative body, in most of the continental universities.

In most cases the Rector is one of the professors and is elected annually. In France the title of *Recteur* is now given to the head of an *Académie*.

a **1548** HALL *Chron., Hen. VIII* 199 The Rector of the Vniuersitie called to counsell all the doctors regentes that were that tyme at Tholose. **1611** COTGR., *Recteur de l' Vniversité*, the Rector, the Vicechancelor. **1818** *Autumn near Rhine* 332 The Grand Duke of Baden, in whose territory Heidelberg is comprised, is the nominal head under the title of Rector. **1885** HUTCHISON tr. *Conrad's Germ. Univ.* Transl. Note, An address delivered..by..Dr. Döllinger, Professor of Ecclesiastical History in the University of Munich, in his capacity of rector for the year.

†**d.** = REGENT. *Obs. rare*$^{-1}$.

1535 STEWART *Cron. Scot.* I. 3 Maister in art, rector in theologie, In all science ane profound clerk is he.

†**e.** A proctor or pro-proctor. *Obs.*

1665 J. BUCK in Peacock *Stat. Cambr.* (1841) App. B. p. lxxxiii, The Rector, or Proproctor, who moderates at these two acts hath his cap garnished with Gold Lace. [**1895** RASHDALL *Universities* II. xii. §2. 370 At Oxford the Proctors on one of their earliest appearances in history are styled 'Rectors' instead of Proctors. At Oxford the title Rector is rarely used afterwards. At Cambridge both titles continued in use throughout the medieval period.]

5. *Comb.*, as ***rector-like***: (see RECTORIAL *a.* 1).

†**'rectorage.** *Obs.*$^{-1}$ [f. prec. + -AGE. Cf. obs. F. *rectorage* (Godef.).] = RECTORY 2.

1556 LAUDER *Tractate* 326 Fer les rent, Nor hes sum Vicare for his waige, Or Rector for his Rectoraige.

rectoral ('rɛktərəl), *a.* [f. RECTOR + -AL[1]. Cf. F. *rectoral* (16th c.).] Of or pertaining to a rector or ruler. Cf. RECTORIAL.

1658 R. FRANCK *North. Mem.* (1821) 3 Things thus posited, under such a rectoral governance [etc.]. **1691** W. JANE *Serm. Westminster 26 Nov.* 5 Besides this despotical right of absolute Dominion, there is a Rectoral right in God. **1754** *Session Papers, Petition T. Tullidelph* (Court of Session, Scotland) 5 Mar. 4 The University Meeting requested the Rector to hold a Rectoral Court against the next Day [at St. Andrews]. **1763** WHEELOCK *Serm. 30 June* (1767) 12 His rectoral holiness, and the vindication of the honour of his laws..will require it. **1865** BUSHNELL *Vicar. Sacr.* III. ii. 213 When God forgives sin, without some penal satisfaction, His rectoral honour and character are made equivocal. **1919** A. GORDON *Cheshire Classis* 121 Some of the above provisions cannot fail to remind us of Richard Baxter's 'rectoral' theory of the ministerial office.

rectorate ('rɛktərət). [f. RECTOR + -ATE[1]; cf. med.L. *rectorātus* (1382 in Du Cange), F. *rectorat* (1642).] The office or position of a rector; the period during which the office is held.

1725 tr. *Dupin's Eccl. Hist. 17th C.* I. v. 198 The second was made under his own Rectorate, the last of August, 1652. **1831** E. BALDWIN *Ann. Yale Coll.* 85 He..settled in the ministry, at Windham,..from whence he was removed, fourteen years after, to the Rectorate of the College. **1895** *Westm. Gaz.* 4 Nov. 3/1 The Rectorate of the University [of Berlin] is an annual tenancy.

attrib. **1878** *Pop. Sci. Monthly* XIII. 263 In his very instructive rectorate address..Herr von Littzow deduces [etc.].

rectoress ('rɛktərɪs). [f. RECTOR + -ESS.]

†**1.** A female ruler. = RECTRESS 1. *Obs.*

1599 NASHE *Lenten Stuffe* 13 Our virgin rectoresse most of al, hath shoured downe her bounty vpon them. **1603** DRAYTON *Bar. Wars* I. xxxv, A most perfect Rectoress [**1619** Rect'resse] of her will, Aboue the vsual weakenes of her kind.

2. *colloq.* The wife of the rector of a parish.

1729 W. STUKELEY in *Mem.* (Surtees) I. 225, I think now, my dearest love, I can wish you joy of being rectoress of All Hallows, Stanford. **1844** J. T. HEWLETT *Parsons & W.* xi, Raised by wedlock to the dignity of rectoress. **1880** BLACKMORE *Mary Anerley* III. xii. 181 Those four were.. Robin Cockscroft, and Joan his wife, the rector, and the rectoress.

rectorial (rɛk'toərɪəl), *a.* and *sb.* [f. RECTOR + -IAL.]

A. *adj.* **1.** Of or pertaining to a university rector; connected with the office or election of a rector.

1611 COTGR., *Rectorial*, Rectoriall, Rector-like; belonging to a Rector, or Vicechancelor. **1749** *St. Andrews Univ. Minutes* 8 Apr. (MS.), Principal Munsin caused put the Rectorial robes on Principal Tullideph,..and delivered to him the Rectorial books. **1830** *Rep. Comm. Univ. Scot.* App. 317 A resolution of the Rectorial Court. **1843** *Memorial* in *Rep. St. Andrews Univ. Comm.* (1845) App. XI. 2 At the late Rectorial election. **1884** *Congregationalist* Nov. 951 Many years have passed away since we listened to a rectorial address in the old college hall.

2. Of or belonging to the rector of a parish (esp. ***rectorial tithes***); held by a rector.

1769 BLACKSTONE *Comm.* IV. Index, Rectorial Tithes. **1794** HUTCHINSON *Hist. Cumbld.* I. 79 The church of Bewcastle, dedicated to St. Mary, is rectorial. **1818** BENTHAM *Ch. of Eng.* p. xlvi, In his stall at Canterbury,.. but still more impressively in his Rectorial mansion. **1884** JESSOPP in *19th Cent.* Jan. 119 Every vicarage in England represents a spoliation of the church, whose rectorial tithes had been appropriated by a religious house.

3. Of or pertaining to a ruler or governor. Cf. RECTORAL.

1835 I. TAYLOR *Spir. Despot.* VII. 293 The perpetual rectorial authority [of the popes]. **1853** WHEWELL *Grotius* I. 4 We may call them respectively Equatorial Rights and Rectorial Rights. *Ibid.* II. 425 Justice, also, that is, rectorial justice.

B. *sb.* A rectorial election. *Sc.*

1899 *Student* (Edin. Univ.) 2 Nov. 41 One student writes protesting against the enormities of the Rectorial. **1920** *Glasgow Herald* 27 Nov. 6 The Scottish Universities, to whose noisy 'Rectorials' Viscount Bryce made reference. **1923** *Ibid.* 26 July 6 St David's Day..is March 1, the day of the Rectorial. *Ibid.*, The torchlight procession on the night of the Rectorial. **1968** *Guardian* 30 Oct. 16/4 Edinburgh has never known a rectorial like this.

rec'toriate. [f. RECTOR + -ATE; cf. *vicariate.*] = RECTORATE.

1881 T. S. FRAMPTON *Hund. Wrotham* 64 The long and blighting rectoriate of Peter Alby, the Savoyard.

rectorite ('rɛktəraɪt). *Min.* [See quot. 1891 and -ITE[1].] An aluminosilicate of sodium that is a clay mineral of the montmorillonite group and occurs as large, soft white leaves or plates.

1891 BRACKETT & WILLIAMS in *Amer. Jrnl. Sci.* CXLII. 16 The second hydrous silicate of alumina..is found in the Blue Mountain mining district in Marble Township, Garland county [Arkansas]... We propose the name Rectorite for this,..in honor of Hon. E. W. Rector, of Hot Springs, Ark., who originated and has so unceasingly supported..the bills providing for the Geological Survey of Arkansas. **1950** *Amer. Mineralogist* XXXV. 590 The structural scheme of rectorite consists of contiguous pairs of pyrophyllite-like units separated by pairs of layers of water molecules. An equally apt description would be the alternation of one pyrophyllite unit with one vermiculite unit. **1970** *Clays & Clay Minerals* XVIII. 239 Pyrophyllite is widespread in pelitic rocks of the Manning Canyon Shale in north central Utah, and the association of this mineral with other clay minerals, especially rectorite, is related to the origin. The regular mixed-layer clay mineral rectorite seems to form as a result of the alteration of muscovite—paragonite during late stages of diagenesis... Pyrophyllite subsequently formed from the alteration of rectorite during advancing metamorphism.

rectorship ('rɛktəʃɪp). [f. RECTOR + -SHIP.]

1. The office of ruler or governor; government, rule. Now *rare*.

1607 SHAKS. *Cor.* II. iii. 213 Or had you Tongues, to cry Against the Rectorship of Iudgement? **1695** HUMFREY *Mediocria* 54 Let us take heed..that we set not God aside as Rector or Lord, in it. We must not advance and justifie his Rectorship so as to exclude his Lordship. **1835** I. TAYLOR *Spir. Despot.* VII. 293 Placed under the control of..the church, and under a rectorship—that of its head.

2. The office of rector (of a parish, university, etc.).

1600 W. WATSON *Decacordon* (1602) 109 A good caueat to him to looke to his orders, lest otherwise he lose his Rectorship. **1679** PRANCE *Addit. Narr. Pop. Plot* 43 Dispossessing him of his Rectorship, he appointed his Nephew to be President in his stead. **1753** *Scots Mag.* XV. 64/2 Prebends, rectorships, chapels. **1821–30** LD. COCKBURN *Mem.* 249 His friend and schoolfellow..advised him to stand for the Rectorship [of the High School, Edinburgh]. **1884** GRANT *Edinb. Univ.* I. 211 This terminates the history of the Rectorship of the College of Edinburgh, as distinguished from the Rectorship of the University.

rectory ('rɛktərɪ). [a. obs. F. *rectorie* (1394 in Du Cange), or ad. med.L. *rectoria* (1263 ibid.): see RECTOR and -Y[3].]

1. An educational establishment under the control of a rector. *Obs.* exc. *Hist.*

1536 *Act 27 Hen. VIII*, c. 42 §1 Emolumentes.. apperteynyng..unto the said Houses, Howses Collegiate, Rectories, Halles, Hostelles etc. within the said Universities of Oxford and Cambridge. **1919** J. E. H. THOMSON *Mem. T. Dunlop* ii. 19 All that remained of the Rectory or Pedagogy, that in pre-Reformation days represented the later University.

2. a. A benefice held by a rector.

1594 WEST *2nd Pt. Symbol., Chancerie* §110 One tenement ..within the parish of C...and in the rectorie and personage of C. **1613** SPELMAN *Rights Ch.* Eng. Wks. (1723) I. 1 A Rectory, or Parsonage, is a Spiritual Living, composed of Land, Tythe, and other Oblations of the People [etc.]. **1677** *Act 29 Chas. II*, c. 8 §2 The said Vicars and Curates shall have remedy for the same either by Distress upon the Rectories Impropriate or Portions of Tythes charged therewith. **1765** BLACKSTONE *Comm.* I. xi. 374 When the clerk so presented is distinct from the vicar, the rectory thus vested in him becomes what is called a *sine-cure*. **1818** CRUISE *Digest* (ed. 2) IV. 205 The tenant for life demised the rectory, which consisted of tithes only, reserving a rent. **1886** *Law Times Rep.* LIII. 702/2 The sums payable to Dr. Cox out of the income of the united rectory.

b. The residence appertaining to a rector.

1849 MACAULAY *Hist. Eng.* ii. I. 158 The presentees.. took possession of the rectories, cultivated the glebe lands, collected the tithes [etc.]. **1864** TENNYSON *Aylmer's F.* 38 So that Rectory and Hall, Bound in an immemorial intimacy, Were open to each other.

attrib. **1859** GEO. ELIOT *A. Bede* xvi, Arthur gave his horse to the groom at the Rectory gate.

†**3.** Rectorship; administration. *Obs.*

1640 in *Rep. Comm. Univ. Scot.* (1830) 114 (Edinb.) The ..office of Rectorie sall consist in the free and ample exerceis of the articlis underwriten. **1660** BURNEY *Κέρδ. Δῶρον* (1661) 131 Princes receive a singular Spirit of God for the Rectory of Iustice. **1675** R. BURTHOGGE *Causa Dei* 144 The day of Judgement..: when all Administration, Government, and Rectory shall cease.

rectosigmoid (rɛktəʊ'sɪgmɔɪd), *sb.* and *a. Med.* [f. RECTO- + SIGMOID.] **A.** *sb.* The region of the junction of the rectum and the sigmoid. **B.** *adj.* Of, pertaining to, or designating this region.

1912 *Trans. Amer. Surg. Assoc.* XIII. 159 Carcinoma of the rectum and rectosigmoid remains a local condition until a late stage. **1913** *Jrnl. Amer. Med. Assoc.* 18 Oct. 1489/1 (*heading*) Villous polypus of recto-sigmoid juncture removed by ligation and clamp. **1961** *Lancet* 16 Sept. 624/2 Barium-enema showed a narrow rectosigmoid, with the calibre increasing near the level of the iliac crest. **1962** *Ibid.* 5 May 951/2 Neoplasm of the rectosigmoid region and sigmoid colon. **1977** *Proc. R. Soc. Med.* LXX. 273/1 Anterior resection of the rectum..for..adenocarcinoma of the rectosigmoid.

Also ˌ**recto-sig'moidal** *a.*

1902 J. P. TUTTLE *Treat. Dis. Anus* xvii. 678 Any neoplasm of the sigmoid or upper portion of the rectum may induce a gradual descent until the growth reaches a resting-place in the ampulla of the rectum... Thus, unusual contracture at the recto-sigmoidal juncture..will cause the arrest of the faecal masses. **1914** *Brit. Jrnl. Surg.* I. 683 (*caption*) Small but well-marked recto-sigmoidal anastomosis.

rectress ('rɛktrɪs). Also 7 rect'ress. [See RECTOR, RECTRIX, and -ESS.]

†**1.** A female ruler or governor. *Obs.*

1603 B. JONSON *Sejanus* v. vi, Great mother Fortvne,.. Queene of humane state, Rectresse of Action. **1605** DRAYTON *Man in Moone* 301 The mighty rectres of this globe below. **1656** S. HOLLAND *Zara* (1719) 59 Great Heccat, Rectress of Shades, Plashey Grots, and gloomy Glades.

fig. **1634** T. JOHNSON *Parey's Chirurg.* XXIV. x. (1678) 541 For there [in the head] the soul of life, which is the rectress or governess, is situated.

2. The female head of a school or institution.

a **1843** SOUTHEY *Comm.-pl. Bk.* Ser. II. (1849) 30 Their superior was called the Prepostress, and they had Visitoresses, Rectresses, and other dignitaries, all in the feminine gender. **1893** J. FAHEY *Hist. Kilmacduagh* 419 Rectress of the convent at Clarinbridge.

3. = RECTORESS 2. *rare.*

1906 *Month* July 66 The rector and rectress, and their two delicate-looking, perfectly-dressed daughters.

rectrix ('rɛktrɪks). [a. L. *rectrix* fem. agent-n. f. *regĕre*: cf. DIRECTRIX.]

1. = RECTRESS 1. *rare.* Also ***Queen Rectrix*** (see QUEEN 2 c).

1611 SPEED *Hist. Gt. Brit.* IX. ix. (1623) 629 Lady Blanch, Queene Dowager, and Rectrix of France. **1634** SIR T. HERBERT *Trav.* 195 Which filthy sinne was since corrected by a Queene Rectrix. **1716** *Loyal Mourner* 65 Anna sate A pious Rectrix at the Helm of State. **1823** LINGARD *Hist. Eng.* VI. 22 The king..before his departure appointed 'his most dear consort queen Catharine, rectrix and governor of the realm'.

2. *Ornith.* in *pl.* **rectrices** (rɛk'traɪsiːz). The strong feathers of the tail in birds, by which their flight is directed.

1768 PENNANT *Brit. Zool.* (1776) I. 139 Fig. 14 The tail. Rectrices. **1797** *Encycl. Brit.* (ed. 3) XIII. 506/1 The tail consists of strong feathers (*rectrices*). **1835** KIRBY *Hab. & Inst. Anim.* II. xvii. 163 The tail feathers of birds, called by ornithologists, rectrices or governing feathers. **1893** NEWTON *Dict. Birds* 247 Those papillæ which give rise to the larger feathers, such as the rectrices.

†**rectual** ('rɛktjuːəl). *Obs.*$^{-1}$ [f. RECT-UM + -AL[1], on anal. of *actual*, etc.] = RECTAL.

1727 ARBUTHNOT *Petit. Colliers*, The Sun-beams taken inwardly render the humours too hot, and adust, occasion great sweatings, and dry up the rectual moisture.

rectum ('rɛktəm). *Anat.* and *Med.* [a. L. *rectum* (sc. *intestinum*), neut. of *rectus* straight.] The final section of the large intestine (so called from its form in some animals), extending in man from the sigmoid flexure of the colon to the anus.

1541 R. COPLAND *Guydon's Quest. Chirurg.* H iij b, Fyrste it behoueth to begyn at the ars gut that is called longaum or rectum. **1548–77** VICARY *Anat.* viii. (1888) 66 The syxte and last [gut] is called Rectum or Longaon. **1676** WISEMAN *Chirurg. Treat.* III. v. 238 We found a stop about an inch.. within the *Rectum*. **1727–41** CHAMBERS *Cycl.* s.v., The levatores ani, which serve to raise or pull back the rectum. **1794–6** E. DARWIN *Zoon.* (1801) II. 466 Aloe given internally seems to act chiefly on the rectum. **1873** MIVART *Elem. Anat.* xi. 446 The colon ascends in the abdominal cavity, passes transversely, and then descends to terminate in the rectum.

attrib. and *Comb.* **1863–76** CURLING *Dis. Rectum* (ed. 4) 77 A proper rectum supporter will help to lessen the inconvenience. **1879** *St. George's Hosp. Rep.* IX. 781 If.. there are any remnants of rectum trouble.

rectus ('rɛktəs). Pl. recti ('rɛktaɪ). [L., = straight, right.]

1. *Anat.* **a.** The name of various muscles, esp. of the abdomen, thigh, neck, and eye, so called from the straightness of their fibres.

1704 J. HARRIS *Lex. Techn.* I, *Rectus Femoris* is a Muscel of the Leg, so named from its streight Progress and Situation. **1733** G. DOUGLAS tr. *Winslow's Anat.* (1756) I. 168 The lower extremity of this Muscle..ends in a thin Tendon,..and there it touches the Tendon of the other Rectus. **1831** R. KNOX *Cloquet's Anat.* 274 It arises posteriorly from a tendon common to it with the internal and external recti, and proceeds horizontally towards the ball of the eye. **1840** E. WILSON *Anat. Vade M.* (1851) 258 The rectus must now be divided through its middle, and the two ends turned aside, to bring clearly into view the next muscles.

attrib. **1899** *Allbutt's Syst. Med.* VII. 62 Excessive arm-jerks and knee-jerks,..rectus clonus and ankle-clonus.

b. So ***rectus muscle***.

1801 *Med. Jrnl.* V. 326 Dr. Hosack..maintains, that the *recti* muscles of the eye contribute much in lengthening or shortening the axis of vision. **1840** E. WILSON *Anat. Vade M.* (1851) 218 To dissect the *rectus* muscle, its sheath should be opened by a vertical incision extending..to the front of the os pubis.

2. *Mus.* In a fugal composition, the version of a theme performed in the basic or original, as opposed to the reversed or inverted, order. ***rectus et inversus*** [L., 'and inverted'] = *recte et retro* s.v. RECTE *adv.* 2.

1931 D. F. TOVEY *Compan. to 'Art of Fugue'* 31 The next two fugues are *tours de force*, being compositions that can be inverted note for note from beginning to end. For purposes of comparison Bach writes his *Inversus* under his *Rectus*. **1938** *Oxf. Compan. Mus.* 134/2 The Canon Cancrizans.. other names for it are Canon Recte et Retro or Rectus et Inversus. **1959** *Listener* 30 July 189/3 The English Rite puts the *Gloria* at the end. Rubbra starts it as an elaborate double fugue *rectus et inversus*. **1960** *Times* 30 Nov. 17/3 Fugue, *rectus et inversus*, canon, ostinato..shall these dry bones live? Britten..uses them all. **1962** *Listener* 27 Dec. 1109/2 The rectus versions of the 'mirror' fugues XII and XIII.

3. *Law.* Phr. ***rectus in curia*** [lit. 'right in court'], innocent, acquitted, set right in point of law.

[*a* **1135** in B. Thorpe *Anc. Laws & Inst. Eng.* (1840) I. 240 Omni domino licet submonire hominem suum, ut ei sit ad rectum in curia sua.] *a* **1577** T. SMITH *De Republica Anglorum* (1583) II. iii. 46 Yet with a clause, *modo stet rectus in curia*, that is to say, that no man obiect against the offendor. **1645** J. HOWELL *Lett.* III. vii. 59 He is now come to be again *rectus in curia*, absolutely acquitted and restor'd to all things. *a* **1706** EVELYN *Diary* an. 1680 (1955) IV. 229 Saturday came other Witnesses of the Commons..who tooke off all the former days objections, & set the Kings Witnesses *recti in Curia*. **1816** *Edin. Rev.* XXVII. 122 He must come *rectus in curia*, and swear to the falsehood of the libel. **1866** J. G. MURPHY *Crit. Comm. Exodus* 310 We meet with the propitiation or atoning sacrifice, by which they become *recti in curia*, right in point of law. **1934** E. POUND *Eleven New Cantos* xxxii. 7, I pray you place me rectus in curia in this business with the Emperor.

'**recubate**, *a. rare*$^{-1}$. [ad. L. *recubāt-us*, pa. pple. of *recubāre*: see next.] Laid backwards.

1790 J. WILLIAMS *Shrove Tuesday* (1794) 6 A puzzling archipelago of fat, Where by a recubate and oblique duct They rumbling sunk.

†**recu'bation.** *Obs. rare*$^{-1}$. [f. L. *recubāre* to recline, f. *re-* RE- + *cubāre* to recline, sleep: see -ATION.] The action of reclining, recumbency.

1646 SIR T. BROWNE *Pseud. Ep.* v. v. 244 The French and Italian translations expressing neither position of session or recubation, do onely say that he placed himselfe at the table.

recueil (rəkøj), *sb.* Forms: 5 recuel, recuyle, recuyel(l, 5–6 recule, 6 recueill, -cuoil, -cewle, *Sc.* recoll, 6–7 (9) recueil. [a. F. *recueil* (14th c.), f. *recueillir*: see next.]

1. A literary compilation or collection. (Now only as a Fr. word.)

1474 CAXTON (*title*) Here begynneth the volume intituled ..the recuyell of the historyes of Troye..by..Raoul le ffeure. **1494** FABYAN *Chron.* VII. ccxli. 282 Peter Dysroye, whiche made a recule, or lytle boke of the wynnynge & losynge of Ierusalem. *a* **1529** SKELTON *Sp. Parrot* 232 Thus Parrot dothe pray you..To rekyn with this recule now, And it to remember. **1567** FENTON *Trag. Disc.* 4 In the recewles or commentories of Tuskan. **1656** *Annot. Browne's Relig. Med.* Annotator to Rdr. M 4, I made this recueil meerly for mine own entertainment. **1887** *Athenæum* 1 Jan. 10/3 M. Paul Verlaine has signed his name to one of the most pleasing poetical *recueils* of the day.

†**2.** Reception, welcome; reset. *Obs.*

1490 CAXTON *Eneydos* xviii. 66 The grete recuel that I haue doon to the,..the worshyp that thou hast had of me [etc.]. **1538** *St. Papers Hen. VIII*, I. 583 The high honnour and recueill she had resceyued of the Kinges Majestie, and his subjectes. **1588** A. KING tr. *Canisius' Catech.* 140 Sic as præsume to giwe lodging or recueil to murtherars.

†**recueil**, *v. Obs.* Forms: 5 recuyel, recuylle, 5–6 recule, 6 recuel. [a. F. *recueillir*, *recuillir* (11th c.):—L. *recolligĕre* to collect, gather up, f. *re-* RE- + *colligĕre*: see CUYL, CULL *v.*[1]]

1. *trans.* To gather together.

1474 CAXTON *Chesse* 67 To recuyel and gadre to-gydre the fruyt of his laboure. **1494** FABYAN *Chron.* II. xxix. 21 Brenne had reculid and gaderyd togyder yᵉ more parte of his Nauy. **1566** PAINTER *Pal. Pleas.* I. Ded. 2 All which I haue receleed and bound together in this volume vnder the title of the Palace of Pleasure.

2. To receive hospitably, entertain.

c **1477** CAXTON *Jason* 63 Ye and all your companye had ben dede for honger.. yf I had not recuyellid you in this cyte. **1490** —— *Eneydos* x. 40 In descendynge..in to that countrey [Eneas] was reculed and receyued by dydo.

3. To receive, catch. *rare*$^{-1}$.

1490 CAXTON *Eneydos* x. 39 Alle the nauye descended nyghe to the bottom of the see whiche were anone recuyelled by other wawes & remysed in a momente vp on highe.

Hence †**recueiling** *vbl. sb. Obs.*$^{-0}$

1552 HULOET, Reculynge, *receptio*.

‖**recueillement** (rəkœjmɑ̃). [F., f. *recueillir*: see prec.] = RECOLLECTION[2] 1.

1845 THACKERAY *Picture Gossip* Misc. Ess. (1885) 278 Sabbath repose and *recueillement*. **1886** GURNEY, etc. *Phantasms of Living* II. 224 The majority of hallucinations ..occur to persons who are alone—silence and *recueillement* being apparently favourable conditions. **1897** G. DU MAURIER *Martian* I. 35 The deep stillness and studious *recueillement* that brood over the scene. **1903** E. WHARTON *Sanctuary* II. v. 150 The silence, the *recueillement*, about her. **1931** R. FRY in W. Rose *Outl. Mod. Knowledge* 936 It succeeds in arousing a mood of *recueillement* not unlike that which emanates from some of Giorgione's compositions. **1977** *Times Lit. Suppl.* 20 May 610/4 Every writer required his *recueillement* (a word that appears several times in his letters), his time of in-gathering and collecting.

recuer, -cuire, variants of RECURE *v.*

recuile, -cuilment, obs. ff. RECOIL *v.*, -MENT.

‖**reculade** (rəkylad). [F., f. *reculer* to RECOIL.] Retreat, retirement, going back.

[**1658** PHILLIPS (copying Cotgr.), *Reculade* (French), a recoiling, or going back, also a secret corner.] **1883** *Standard* 14 Sept. 5/6 The French Cabinet..are, perhaps, too sensitive as to what the papers may say about their *reculade*. **1891** *Catholic News* 24 Jan. 3/2 Nothing can show better the 'reculade' of neo-ritualism towards Protestantism.

recule, obs. f. RECOIL *v.*, var. RECUEIL *sb.* and *v. Obs.*

reculement, obs. f. RECOILMENT.

‖**reculer pour mieux sauter** (rəkyle pur mjø sote), *phr.* [Fr., lit. 'to draw back in order to leap better'.] Making use of a withdrawal or setback in such a way as to advance or succeed all the more.

[*c* **1500** J. D'ARRAS *Mesuline* (1895) xx. 113 Alwayes wyse men goo abacke for to lepe the ferther.] **1820** LADY GRANVILLE *Let.* 30 Aug. (1894) I. 170 'Yes,' he said, 'with people in general it is *reculer pour mieux sauter*, with her *sauter pour mieux reculer*.' **1907** G. B. SHAW *Let.* 21 Mar. (1972) II. 675 The sales that are influenced by my name go up steadily from year to year; and all the apparent slumps are cases of 'reculer pour mieux sauter'. **1920** D. H. LAWRENCE *Women in Love* i. 6, I think my coming back home was just *reculer pour mieux sauter*. **1951** R. F. HARROD *Life J. M. Keynes* x. 431 This was, in his mind, a case of *reculer pour mieux sauter*. **1972** *Times* 30 May (Hongkong Suppl.) p. v/4 The hesitation in currency circulation in 1967–1968 following the fall in deposits was a matter of *reculer pour mieux sauter*: growth..took off again.

recull, obs. f. RECOIL *v.*

†**recullisance**, corrupt form of RECOGNIZANCE.

1607 MIDDLETON *Michaelmas Term* III. iv, Come then, and be a witnesse to a Recullisance.

re-'cultivate, *v.* [RE- 5 a. Cf. F. *recultiver* (Cotgr.).] *trans.* To cultivate anew. Also *fig.*

c **1645** HOWELL *Lett.* I. v. ii, A Field that remains fallow for a time..yields a better Crop, being recultivated. **1833** S. AUSTIN *Charact. Goethe* II. 331 Desolate scenes which the liveliest imagination were unable to recultivate and repeople. **1857** TROLLOPE *Barchester T.* III. iv. 61 He had meant, if possible, to recultivate his friendship with Eleanor.

So **re-culti'vation.**

1850 *Proc. Philol. Soc.* IV. 208 It is now just about a hundred years ago that Klopstock paved the way to the recultivation of German. **1857** TROLLOPE *Barchester T.* III. iv. 61 In his present state of mind any such re-cultivation must have ended in a declaration of love. **1887** MOLONEY *Forestry W. Afr.* 237 The balance of time to re-cultivation and fresh harvest.

recumaunde, obs. form of RECOMMAND *v.*[1]

re'cumb, *v. rare.* [ad. L. *recumbĕre*: see RECUMBENT *a.*] *intr.* To lean, recline, rest. Const. *on*, *upon*. Also *fig.*

a **1677** BARROW *Serm.* Wks. 1686 II. 69 The King makes an overture of pardon and favour unto you upon condition, that any one of you will recumbe, rest, lean upon, or roll himself upon the person of his Son. *a* **1711** KEN *Hymnarium* Poet. Wks. 1721 II. 44 Saints, in the most afflictive Hour, Recumb on thy propitious Power. **1761** ALLEN *No Accept. with God by Faith only* 23 What shall we think of the loud and repeated cries..of a faith, which consists in lolling, rolling, and recumbing on Christ? **1906** M. DODS *Later Lett.* (1911) 213 Will you excuse pencil, as I am in a run down condition and my doctor bids me 'recumb' as much as I can. **1925** O. W. HOLMES in *Holmes-Laski Lett.* (1953) I. 693 Now I shall recumb with a hot bottle at my back.

recumbence (rɪ'kʌmbəns). Now *rare.* [f. as next + -ENCE.] = RECUMBENCY.

1676 HALE *Contempl.* I. 378 The next Expedient is Faith and Recumbence upon those Promises of his. **1681** H. MORE *Exp. Dan.* Pref. 100 Breaking off our comfortable recumbence and dependence upon the lovely person of our Lord Jesus. *a* **1711** KEN *Hymnarium* Poet. Wks. 1721 II. 87 The soft, yet firm Recumbence of a Child. —— *Urania* Ibid. IV. 447 Our Dependance on his gracious Care, Should to depending Souls Recumbence teach and Pray'r. **1827** G. S. FABER *Orig. Expiat. Sacr.* 129 The word, which inadequately has been rendered lieth, properly describes the couching or recumbence of an animal.

recumbency (rɪ'kʌmbənsɪ). [ad. L. type **recumbentia*, f. *recumbĕre*: see RECUMBENT *a.*]

1. The state of lying or reclining; a recumbent posture.

1646 SIR T. BROWNE *Pseud. Ep.* III. i. 106 The Tricliniums, or places of festivall Recumbency. **1695** J. EDWARDS *Perfect. Script.* 138 The head or upper end of this bed..was..the chief place of recumbency. **1784** COWPER *Task* I. 82 Relaxation of the languid frame, By soft recumbency of outstretch'd limbs. **1836** E. HOWARD *R. Reefer* lxiv, There was not much room for recumbency. **1866** A. FLINT *Princ. Med.* (1880) 193 If the patient be feeble, constant recumbency on the back is to be avoided.

b. *fig.* Repose.

1653 GAUDEN *Hierasp.* 451 To invite all errours..to a recumbency or rest in their bosome. *a* **1704** LOCKE (J.), When the mind has been once habituated to this lazy recumbency and satisfaction on the obvious surface of things, it is in danger to rest satisfied there.

2. *fig.* Reliance *on* or *upon* a person or thing. Chiefly in religious use. Now *rare.*

1646 FULLER *Wounded Consc.* (1841) 309 The life and formality of faith, which consists only in a recumbency on God in Christ. **1653** GAUDEN *Hierasp.* 178 In some there ought to be an eminency.., upon whom the greatest recumbency of Churches may be laid. **1706** PHILLIPS (ed. Kersey) s.v., He had a great Recumbency upon his Promise. **1738** WESLEY *Serm.* (1838) I. 7 A recumbency upon him as our atonement and our life. **1814** T. BELL *View Cov. Wks. & Grace* 360 He believed this truth not at all as the devils do, but with a recumbency of heart on the Son of God.

b. Without const. Also *pl.*

1642 T. GOODWIN *Christ set forth* v. x. 197 A Faith of Recumbency, or, of Comming unto Christ. **1667** WATERHOUSE *Fire Lond.* 65 His great arrows are..fixed in the very hearts of mens delights and recumbencies. **1675** BAXTER *Cath. Theol.* II. XI. 250 So also all the Affiance or Fiducial Acts are excluded,..even that which they call Recumbency being distinct from Consent. **1826** R. HALL *Wks.* (1832) 394 It produces recumbency, a slothful dependence upon God and neglect of the precautions of religion and the rules of duty.

recumbent (rɪˈkʌmbənt), *a.* (and *sb.*) [ad. L. *recumbent-em*, pres. pple. of *recumbĕre* to lie down, recline, f. *re-* RE- + *-cumbĕre* to lie.]

A. *adj.* **1. a.** Of persons or animals: Lying down, reclining, reposing.

1774 PENNANT *Tour Scotl. in 1772*, 16 He lies in alabaster, recumbent in his gown. **1794** COWPER *Needless Alarm* 47 The sheep recumbent and the sheep that grazed, All huddling into phalanx, stood and gazed. **1856** EMERSON *Eng. Traits, Stonehenge* Wks. (Bohn) II. 129 C. took hold of the recumbent statue's marble hands. **1876** BLACKIE *Songs Relig. & Life* 180 Happy the bard who weaves his rhyme Recumbent on the purple thyme.

b. *transf.* of things. Now chiefly in scientific use; ***recumbent stone circle***, in *Archæol.*, a stone circle characterized by the presence of one large stone lying flat flanked by two tall uprights.

1744 AKENSIDE *Pleas. Imag.* II. 277 Aloft recumbent o'er the hanging ridge, The brown woods wav'd. **1826** KIRBY & SP. *Entomol.* IV. 298. **1867** LAYARD *Birds S. Africa* 223 The nostrils..more or less covered by the recumbent plumes. **1872** NICHOLSON *Palaeont.* 133 In..Pseudocrinus the arms are recumbent and soldered to the calyx. **1933** V. G. CHILDE in *Proc. Soc. Antiquaries Scotland* LXVII. 51 Recumbent Stone Circles may have been erected in late Hallstatt times. **1943** J. & C. HAWKES *Prehist. Britain* iii. 59 Their adaptation of a passage-grave tradition in the remarkable 'Recumbent Stone' circles of north-east Scotland. **1962** GORDON & LAVOIPIERRE *Entomol. for Students of Med.* xx. 134 Like the head and thorax the abdomen is covered with long hairs; on the dorsal aspect of the abdomen the hairs may either lie flat (a condition described as recumbent) or they may be raised. **1963** *Field Archaeol.* (Ordnance Survey) (ed. 4) 40 There is an eccentric type found in North-east Scotland... This is the 'Recumbent' stone circle which has more than seventy examples in this area.

c. *fig.* of qualities personified.

1742 YOUNG *Nt. Th.* IV. 645 What smooth emollients in theology Recumbent Virtue's downy doctors preach. **1842** J. WILSON *Chr. North* (1857) I. 259 The spirit of beauty that lies recumbent there.

2. Of posture: Reclining, leaning or lying.

1705 ARBUTHNOT *Coins* (1727) 134 The Roman recumbent or (more properly) accumbent posture in eating was introduc'd after the first Punic War. **1799** SICKELMORE *Agnes & Leonora* II. 131 A sudden rustling among the trees, against one of which I stood in a recumbent posture. **1848** LYTTON *Harold* VI. iv, Rising proudly from her recumbent position.

3. *Geol.* ***recumbent fold***, a fold whose axial plane is nearly horizontal; so ***recumbent anticline, syncline.***

1909 *Summ. Progr. Geol. Surv. 1908* 52 A discrepancy between the two limbs of the recumbent fold. **1910** *Q. Jrnl. Geol. Soc.* LXVI. 617 The sliding is not confined to the lower limbs of recumbent anticlines. *Ibid.*, The schists of the Highlands of Scotland are disposed in a succession of recumbent folds of enormous amplitude. **1922** [see NAPPE 2]. **1937** [see FAN *sb.*[1] 10 f]. **1962** READ & WATSON *Introd. Geol.* I. viii. 451 A recumbent anticline..faces laterally and a recumbent anticline in which the hinge-region sags or droops faces downwards. **1964** W. C. PUTNAM *Geol.* vi. 131/1 In an extreme case, the whole fold may be forced over on its side so that its axial plane..is horizontal, or very nearly so... Such a structure is called a recumbent fold. **1969** H. ROBINSON *Morphology & Landscape* iii. 34 Sometimes the pressure exerted upon a recumbent fold is sufficiently great to cause it to be torn from its roots and to be thrust forward.

†**B.** *sb.* One who has recumbency or reliance on another. *Obs. rare.*

1642 T. GOODWIN *Christ set forth* v. x. 196 It is more peculiarly fitted into a Recumbents Faith. **1681** FLAVEL *Meth. Grace* ix. 210 'Tis a blessed life to live as a poor recumbent, by acts of trust and affiance.

Hence **reˈcumbently** *adv.*, in a recumbent or reclining posture.

1839 *New Monthly Mag.* LVII. 407 Whom I had passed recumbently sipping his madeira. **1879** SYNGE *Tom Singleton* III. x. 189 Dr. Blandy's sympathetic drops..must be taken recumbently.

†**recumbentibus.** *Obs.* Also 7 -bend-. [A humorous use of L. *recumbentibus*, abl. pl. of *recumbens*: see RECUMBENT. With the later form cf. CIRCUMBENDIBUS.] A knock-down blow.

c **1400** *Laud Troy Bk.* 7490 He ȝaff the kyng Episcropus Suche a recumbentibus, He smot In-two bothe helme & mayle. **1546** J. HEYWOOD *Prov.* (1867) 70 Had you some husbande, and snapt at him thus, I wys he would geue you a recumbentibus. **1593** HARVEY *Pierces Supererog.* Wks. II. 302 Like the dowty fencer of Barnewell, that played his taking-vp with a Recumbentibus. **1675** C. COTTON *Scoffer Scoft* Wks. (1715) 251 A good whirret Bebrix gave him,.. Which Recumbendibus he got By being of an Argonaut.

recuoil, variant of RECUEIL *sb. Obs.*

recuperaˈbility. [f. as next + -ITY.] Ability to recuperate.

1886 C. H. HUGHES in *Alienist & Neurologist* VII. 463 Impairment so slight as to leave the nervous system in a state of almost physiological recuperability. **1899** *Allbutt's Syst. Med.* VI. 864 A lesion..greatly affecting the viability and recuperability of the central mass of the spinal cord.

†**reˈcuperable,** *a. Obs.* [a. OF. *recuperable* (Godef.), or ad. L. type **recuperābilis*: see RECUPERATE and -ABLE.] Recoverable.

14.. *Woman's Chastity* 51 in Chalmers *Eng. Poets* I. 566 And hard it is to rauish a treasour, Which of nature is not recuparable. **1531** ELYOT *Gov.* I. xiii, If thou..by counsaile arte recuperable, Flee thou from idlenesse. **1552** in Strype *Eccl. Mem.* (1721) III. II. xviii. 392 The hoped for and recuperable debts. **1570** LEVINS *Manip.* 4/10 Recuperable, *recuperabilis.*

reˈcuperance. *rare.* [ad. L. type **recuperantia*: see next and -ANCE.] Recuperation.

1887 *Illustr. Lond. News* 22 Oct. 488 To the brain-worker and the hand-worker alike how desirable is this rest and recuperance of mind and body!

recuperate (rɪˈk(j)uːpəreɪt), *v.* [f. L. *recuperāt-*, ppl. stem of *recuperāre*: see RECOVER *v.* Cf. It. *recuperare*, Sp., Pg. *recuperar*, F. *récupérer.*]

1. a. *trans.* To recover (a thing, material or immaterial).

1542 BOORDE *Dyetary* Pref., Your grace recuperatyng your helth. **1603** DEKKER & CHETTLE *Grissil* (Shaks. Soc.) 42 My opinion is, I shall never recuperate the legitimate office of this member, my arm. **1661** BLOUNT *Glossogr.* (ed. 2), *Recuperate*, to recover, rescue or get again. **1896** J. A. H. MURRAY *Let.* 22 Apr. in K. M. E. Murray *Caught in Web of Words* (1977) xiv. 279 We reached the summit however, & recuperated our energies. **1977** *Guardian Weekly* 7 Aug. 11/5 No plant in the world has shown that it can recuperate plutonium on an industrial scale from oxide-bearing fuel.

b. To recover (a loss). *rare.*

1891 M. COLE *Cy Ross* 101 He had recuperated his losses. **1924** *Proc. Classical Assoc.* 13 Both these Associations have fully recuperated any loss which they had made during the war.

2. †**a.** To restore (a thing) to its original condition.

1694 SALMON *Bate's Dispens.* (1713) 309/2 The white Substance of Gold,..which is wont to be called fixed Silver, recovers its pristine Colour, if recuperated with Antimony.

b. To restore (a person) to health or vigour.

1864 T. NICHOLS *40 Yrs. Amer. Life* II. 117 Why..are these sisters not..sent to recuperate themselves in healthier conditions? **1872** M. COLLINS *Two Plunges* III. v. 123 The sparkling wine soon recuperated Ianthe.

3. *refl.* To recoup (oneself). *rare.*

1882 LECKY *Eng. in 18th C.* IV. xvi. 323 More commonly he paid a fixed sum to the clergyman, and recuperated himself by a grinding tyranny of the tenants.

4. *intr.* To recover from exhaustion, ill-health, pecuniary loss, etc.

1864 SALA in *Daily Tel.* 9 Feb., Go into business; smash; recuperate. **1865** —— *Diary Amer.* I. 168 Renowned..for their urbane hospitality to pilgrims. There we recuperated. **1897** *Century Mag.* May 112 In the hope that he might soon recuperate and return to duty.

Hence **reˈcuperating** *vbl. sb.* and *ppl. a.*

1894 'R. ANDOM' *We Three & Troddles* xix. 174 We each mentioned our favoured recuperating localities. **1979** B. PARVIN *Deadly Dyke* xxiv. 128 Recuperating firemen stood watching the thick palls of smoke.

recuperation (rɪk(j)uːpəˈreɪʃən). [ad. L. *recuperātiōn-em*, n. of action f. *recuperāre*: see prec. Cf. F. *récupération* (16th c.).]

1. †**a.** The recovery or regaining *of* a thing. *Obs.*

1481 CAXTON *Godefroy* Prol. 4 For the recuperacion of the holy londe & holy Cyte of Iherusalem. **1620** E. BLOUNT *Horæ Subs.* 250 After them no man euer bore Armes for Recuperation of that gouernment. **1651** BIGGS *New Disp.* ¶270 The conservation or recuperation of health. **1685** H. MORE *Paralip. Proph.* 111 Quirinius made Caius his Rectour till his Recuperation of Armenia.

b. *Rom. Law.* Legal recovery.

1880 MUIRHEAD *Gaius* IV. 105 *note*, Provisions for recuperation in the treaties between Rome and friendly states.

2. Restoration to health, vigour, etc.

1865 *Standard* 4 Feb., The season which has heretofore brought to them rest and recuperation finds them in the trenches. **1889** *Spectator* 19 Oct., That waking rest which is the recuperation of the mind.

3. *Gunnery.* The action of a recuperator (sense 4).

1922 *Encycl. Brit.* XXXI. 1185/2 As the buffer flow-space is greatest at the termination of recuperation, some check is required to prevent a metal-to-metal blow. *Ibid.* 1186/1 Recuperation may be by means of steel springs or compressed air.

recuperative (rɪˈk(j)uːpərətɪv), *a.* (and *sb.*) [ad. late L. *recuperātīvus* recoverable: see RECUPERATE and -IVE.]

A. *adj.* †**1.** Recoverable (Cockeram 1623). *Obs. rare*$^{-0}$.

2. Belonging to, concerned with, the recovery of something lost. ? *Obs.*

1650 R. HOLLINGWORTH *Exerc. Usurped Powers* 14 The known law and practise of all nations..with one vote allow defensive and recuperative arms. *c* **1690** in Lathbury *Non-jurors* (1845) 119 If ever he should recover the throne in a recuperative war. **1858** DE QUINCEY *Wks.* XI. Pref. 10 Lost and hid away in secret chambers of moonshine beyond the 'recuperative' powers (Johnsonically speaking) of Apollonius himself.

3. a. Having the power of restoring (a person or thing) to a proper state.

1861 GLADSTONE *Sp. Ho. Comm.* 2 May, The abolition of these duties is not what is called recuperative. **1872** M. COLLINS *Pr. Clarice* I. vi. 92 Claret-cup, properly administered, is almost as recuperative as salts and senna.

b. Of or belonging to recuperation or recovery of health, vigour, etc.

1860 EMERSON *Cond. Life, Power* Wks. (Bohn) II. 333 We watch in children with pathetic interest the degree in which they possess recuperative force. **1890** G. M. HUMPHRY *Old Age* 154 High breeding in most animals conduces to a marked diminution in the bodily recuperative capacity.

4. Having the power of recuperating.

1862 TROLLOPE *N. Amer.* II. 103 'We are a recuperative people', a west-country gentleman once said to me.

5. Of, pertaining to, or being a recuperator (sense 2), or an air heater using the same principle.

1906 A. L. J. QUENEAU tr. *Damour's Industr. Furnaces* x. 142 The volume..of the recuperative chambers should be calculated to suit the exchange of the calories to be effected, according to the specific heats of the recuperating refractory bricks. **1923** *Iron Age* CXI. 1782 The recuperative installation is adopted where blast furnace or coke oven gas is available. **1930** *Engineering* 31 Jan. 155/2 Two methods of transferring heat from a hot gas to a cold one were in use, and might be distinguished as belonging, respectively, to the recuperative and to the regenerative type. In the recuperative type, the cool and the hot gases were separated by a conducting wall through which the transfer of heat took place. **1938** *Jrnl. Iron & Steel Inst.* CXXXVIII. 327P Of the 848 pit holes surveyed,..6·2% are of the one-way-fired recuperative type, 2·1% are of the bottom-fired recuperative type. **1962** [see RECUPERATOR 2]. **1971** B. SCHARF *Engin. & its Language* xiv. 204 Air heaters are classified as recuperative or regenerative, and the recuperative heaters are further subdivided into tubular or plate-type heaters.

B. *sb.* A substance which restores land to fertility.

1883 J. C. BLOOMFIELD *Fisheries Ireland* 7 (Fish. Exh. Publ.), Such refuse of the cod as its head and backbone turned into a valuable agricultural recuperative.

Hence **reˈcuperativeness.**

a **1901** F. MYERS *Hum. Personality* (1903) I. 194 Can it be some kind of self-suggestion which prevents the mammal from crediting himself with crustacean recuperativeness?

recuperator (rɪˈk(j)uːpəreɪtə(r)). [a. L. *recuperātor*: see RECUPERATE and -OR.]

1. *Rom. Law.* A member of a commission for trying certain cases.

1706 PHILLIPS (ed. Kersey), *Recuperator*, (among the Romans) a Commissioner or Judge appointed by the Prætor to examine private Matters; a Judge Delegate. [**1753** in CHAMBERS *Cycl. Supp.*] **1875** POSTE *Gaius* I. (ed. 2) 53 Recuperators are judges not taken from the panel. **1880** MUIRHEAD *Gaius* I. §20 The council consists in Rome of five senators and five Roman knights of the age of puberty; in the provinces of twenty recuperators, Roman citizens.

2. Formerly, the regenerator of a Ponsard or Siemens furnace. Now restricted to a form of heat exchanger in which hot waste gases, being conducted continuously along a system of flues, impart heat to incoming air or gaseous fuel flowing in the opposite direction in parallel flues by conduction through the dividing walls. Cf. REGENERATOR 2.

1884 W. H. GREENWOOD *Steel & Iron* §638 The Ponsard furnace and recuperator, employed for reheating purposes in the rolling mill, has a gas producer below the floor level. **1884** KNIGHT *Dict. Mech.* Suppl. 746/2. **1906** A. L. J. QUENEAU tr. *Damour's Industr. Furnaces* ii. 47 Two systems are still in practice—the Siemens recuperator with inversion, and recuperation without inversion, by parallel counter currents. **1911** F. W. HARBORD *Metallurgy of Steel* II. xxi. 541 Gorman's furnace..formed a further step in advance, as the waste gases on their way to the chimney passed around horizontal fireclay pipes or 'recuperators'. **1938** H. ETHERINGTON *Mod. Furnace Technol.* vii. 314 In a recuperator, the hot waste gases and the cold air are led through separate channels in close contact..Regenerators operate on a different principle. **1953** D. J. O. BRANDT *Manuf. Iron & Steel* xxviii. 203 Soaking pits are of two kinds, regenerative pits, which are fired in two directions, being reversed at intervals, and recuperative which are fired in one direction only, the heat in the outgoing gases being as far as possible transferred to the incoming air and fuel in a recuperator. **1962** G. R. BASHFORTH *Manuf. Iron & Steel* IV. ii. 39 In the recuperative type of soaking pit, the flow of fuel and air is maintained in one direction... The waste products of combustion pass through a recuperative chamber... These recuperators may either be of the refractory or metallic type.

3. That which restores one's health or spirits.

1905 *Smart Set* 17 Sept. 24 A/2 (Advt.), A day trip on these steamers is calculated to brace the entire system, and the jaded business man will find them a splendid recuperator.

4. *Gunnery.* (See quot. 1922.)

1918 E. S. FARROW *Dict. Mil. Terms* 498 *Recuperator gauge*, in artillery, a gauge for verifying the charge of the recuperator, in liquid and in compressed gas. **1922** *Encycl. Brit.* XXXI. 1184/1 The recuperator returns the gun to the firing position after it has come to rest under the action of the recoil resistance. **1925** *Jrnl. R. Artillery* LII. 38 The recuperator question was taken in hand early on in the war, and by the end of 1918 all springs had been replaced by air recuperators. **1962** *Ordnance Techn. Terminol.* (U.S. Army Ordnance School) (AD 660 112) 86/1 *Counterrecoil mechanism*, a hydraulic, pneumatic, or mechanical system that returns a gun into battery, or firing position, after recoil; a recuperator.

Hence **reˌcuperaˈtorial** *a.*

1976 J. M. KELLY *Stud. in Civil Judicature of Roman Republic* ii. 47 If then we discard the dominant theory, how are we to explain the special recuperatorial jurisdiction otherwise?

re'cuperatory, *a. rare.* [ad. L. *recuperatorius*: see RECUPERATE and -ORY.] Of or belonging to recovery or to recuperators.

1656 BLOUNT *Glossogr.*, *Recuperatory*, belonging to recovering, or to Judges delegate. [Hence in Bailey and later Dicts.] **1875** POSTE *Gaius* IV. (ed. 2) 630 Utrubi was clearly a recuperatory interdict in its original form.

recur (rɪˈkɜː(r)), *v.* Also 7 recurr(e. [ad. L. *recurr-ĕre* to run back, return, have recourse, f. *re-* RE- + *currĕre* to run.]

1. † **a.** *intr.* To run or move back, recede. *Obs. rare.*

1616 BULLOKAR *Eng. Expos.*, *Recurre*, to run backe. **1788** *Trifler* No. 19. 254 There is a point of depression as well as of exaltation, from which human affairs when once arrived, naturally recur in a contrary progress.

b. To return *into* or *to* a place. *rare.*

With first quot. cf. med.L. *recurrĕre* to appeal at law (1369 in Du Cange, s.v. *Recursus* 6).

1468 *Paston Lett.* II. 326 [To remind him] how he promisid bi his feith to my Lord t'obey his rewle and brak it,..and if ye recur in the courte he shal be undo. **1659** WOOD *Life* 24 Oct. (O.H.S.) I. 286 To which lodgings A. W. did recurr dayly, till he had satisfied himself with them [manuscripts]. **1719** WATERLAND *Vind. Christ's Div.* xxvii, Novatian..was intent upon..showing how all recurs to one head and fountain. **1832** [see RECURRING *ppl. a.* 1 b].

† **c.** To resort *to* a place. *Obs. rare.*

1655 STANLEY *Hist. Philos.* I. (1701) 22/1 All the City grew very populous, many recurring thither from all parts of Attica, for liberty and security.

2. To return, go back, in thought, memory, or discourse. Usu. const. *to* (a subject, time, etc.).

1620 T. GRANGER *Div. Logike* 291 But [the mind] recurreth, and discourseth through the axiomes already inuented, and iudged. **1653** H. MORE *Antid. Ath.* II. ii. §7 But first I shall recur and give a touch upon the nature of Gravity. **1780** JEFFERSON *Corr.* Wks. 1859 I. 260, I retain in mind, and recur, almost daily, to your requisitions of August. **1833** HT. MARTINEAU *Berkeley the Banker* I. viii. 163, I know it is painful to her to recur to that terrible time. **1841** CATLIN *N. Amer. Ind.* xxxii. (1844) II. 1 Before I give further account of this downward voyage, however, I must recur back for a few moments, to the Teton River, from whence I started. **1855** MOTLEY *Dutch Rep.* v. iii. (1866) 703 It is necessary to recur for a moment to the Prince of Orange.

3. To go back, resort, have recourse *to* a thing (rarely a person), for assistance or argument.

1529 WOLSEY in Burnet *Hist. Ref.* (1679) I. Rec. II. xxii. 51 For if his Grace were minded,..there were no need to recurr unto the Pope's Holiness for doing thereof. **1646** SIR T. BROWNE *Pseud. Ep.* 195 Scaliger declining this reason hath recurred unto another from the difference of parts in both sexes. **1690** LOCKE *Hum. Und.* II. xvii. §16 If to avoid Succession in eternal Existence, they recur to the *Punctum Stans* of the Schools. **1785** JEFFERSON *Writ.* (1859) I. 485 They have no occasion to recur from his clemency to his justice. **1807** G. CHALMERS *Caledonia* I. I. ii. 99 The sad expedients, to which a rude people were obliged to recur for safety. **1855** MILMAN *Lat. Chr.* VII. iii. (1864) IV. 117 He will recur to the Blessed Virgin to enlighten him.

b. To come back *on* a person.

1838 W. BELL *Dict. Law Scot.* 827 Recourse is the right competent to an assignee or disponee..to recur on the vender or cedent for relief.

4. Of something known, an idea, thought, etc.: To come back or return (†*into*, *in* or) *to* one's thoughts, mind or memory.

a **1704** LOCKE (J.), The idea, I have once had, will be unchangeably the same, as long as it recurs the same in my memory. **1751** JOHNSON *Rambler* No. 175 ⁋3 Sentences, that may be easily impressed on the memory, and taught by frequent recollection to recur habitually to the mind. **1780** BECKFORD *Mem. Painters* 54 The delicacy of her sensations recurred to his memory.

b. Without const.: To return to the mind.

1711 SHAFTESB. *Charac.* III. 197 The Thought it-self will of necessity..the oftner recur. **1719** YOUNG *Revenge* v. ii, Heav'ns! And yet a thousand things recur that swear it. **1784** COWPER *Task* VI. 13 Wherever I have heard A kindred melody, the scene recurs, And with it all its pleasures and its pains. **1806** BYRON *Childish Recoll.* 28 Oft does my heart indulge the rising thought, Which still recurs. **1855** TENNYSON *Will* 14 Acted crime, Or seeming-genial venial fault, Recurring and suggesting still!

c. Of questions, difficulties, etc.: To come up again for consideration; to present themselves, or confront one, again.

1651 W. LYFORD *Serm.* (1654) 4 The question will still recurre, who shall judge of the right? **1732** BERKELEY *Alciphr.* VII. §22 But still, the question recurs, whether man be free? **1828** D'ISRAELI *Chas. I*, I. vi. 202 These critical difficulties were perpetually recurring. **1841** MYERS *Cath. Th.* III. §36. 129 The constant..question will from time to time recur.

d. Of thoughts, statements, etc.: To occur again in the course of a book, etc.

1697 J. SERGEANT *Solid Philos.* 128 Some few Reflexions, which I shall touch on slightly, or omit, because they recurr hereafter. **1863** *Sat. Rev.* 4 July 24/2 In every part of the book two thoughts are continually recurring.

5. Of events, facts, states, etc.: To occur, happen, take place, appear, again. (Common in 19th c.)

The context usually indicates repeated re-occurrence.

1673 O. WALKER *Educ.* 44 When the like occasion recurs. **1692** —— *Grk. & Rom. Hist.* 166 Ordinarily the Solemnity recurred only every 110th year. **1771** T. PERCIVAL *Ess.* (1777) I. 157 The vomiting recurs at short intervals. **1804–6** SYD. SMITH *Mor. Philos.* (1850) 395 One regular set of volitions, constantly recurring at fixt periods. **1851** J. PAGET *Lect. Tumours* ii. 18/1 In some..the disease has appeared to recur. **1878** JEVONS *Prim. Pol. Econ.* 120 Good vintage years on the continent of Europe..recur every ten or eleven years.

† **b.** Of a malady: To return *upon* one. *Obs.*$^{-1}$

1726 *Wodrow Corr.* (1843) III. 248 He was disabled, and for some days since his trouble was recurred upon him.

c. *Math.* Of a figure or figures in a decimal fraction: To return or come again (in the same order), to repeat.

1801 [see RECURRING *ppl. a.* 2 a]. **1823** J. MITCHELL *Dict. Math. & Phys. Sci.* 103/1 A circulating decimal, or..such, that if continued far enough the same figures will again recur. **1875** *Encycl. Brit.* II. 532/1 Subtract the decimal figures that do not recur from the whole decimal.

recurb (rɪˈkɜːb). *rare*$^{-1}$. [f. RE- + -CURB *sb.*: cf. F. *recourber* vb., L. *recurvāre* RECURVE *v.*] The curved shape produced at the repeated climax of systematic oscillation.

1876 G. M. HOPKINS *Wreck of Deutschland* xxxii, in *Poems* (1967) 62 The recurb and the recovery of the gulf's side, The girth of it and the wharf of it and the wall.

† **recure**, *sb. Obs.* Forms: 5 recur, -cuer, -cuire, -keur, 5–7 recure. [f. next, perh. on analogy of RECOVER *sb.*; very common in the 15–16th c.] Recovery; remedy, succour; cure.

1414 BRAMPTON *Penit. Ps.* (Percy Soc.) 28 Whan I do ony forfeture,..Accepte this, Lord, for ry3t rekure. *c* **1480** HENRYSON *Test. Cres.* 335 To thy seiknes sal be na recure. **1545** SURREY *Epit. T. Clere* in Camden *Rem.* (1605) Epit. 50 Hopeles of all recure, Thine Earle halfe dead gaue in thy hand his will. **1591** LYLY *Endym.* III. i, I haue seene him to my griefe, and sought recure with despaire. **1626** T. H. tr. *Caussin's Holy Crt.* 166 It is a lamentable thing, to put purposely the disease into despayre, for feare of recure.

b. In phr. ***but, past,*** or ***without recure***: past or without hope or possibility of recovery.

1423 JAS. I *Kingis Q.* xcv, The thrid [arrow], of stele, is schot without recure. *c* **1470** *Golagros & Gaw.* 1203 It war syn, but recure, The knightis honour suld smure. *a* **1542** WYATT in *Tottel's Misc.* (Arb.) 80 Fierce Tigre, fell, hard rock without recure. **1587** CHURCHYARD *Worth. Wales* (1876) 96 An eating worme, a Cancker past recure. **1603** KNOLLES *Hist. Turks* (1621) 610 Whatsoever fell into the enemies hand, was lost without recure.

† **recure**, *v. Obs.* Also 5 *Sc.* recuir. [ad. L. *recūrāre*, f. *re-* RE- + *cūrāre* to CURE *v.*¹, but also in part repr. RECOVER *v.*¹

The contracted form of *recover* is properly RECOUR *v.*; the use of *recure* for 'recover' in sense 4 is prob. due to the fact that senses 1–3 are common to both verbs.]

1. *trans.* To cure (one) *of* or *from* a disease, wound, trouble, etc.; to restore to health.

1389 in *Eng. Gilds* (1870) 41 He shal han..eueri woke iij pens til þat he be recured. **1430–40** LYDG. *Bochas* VIII. xiii. (1558) 7 Howe Constantine..was recured of his lepre. *c* **1540** HEYWOOD *Four P.P.* 716 Wherefore this woman to recure It was more harde ye may be sure. **1566** DRANT *Horace, Sat.* I. i. A v b, Theyle treate the fyne physition.. thy corps for to recure. **1594** KYD *Cornelia* IV. ii. 143 Nor hath Chyron powre or skill To recure them of their ill. **1621** QUARLES *Argalus & P.* (1678) 32 Drink as thou lov'st me, and it shall secure thee From future dangers, or from past, recure thee. **1628** FELTHAM *Resolves* II. lix. 170 It [opinion] can cast a man into speedy diseases, and can as soon recure him. **1647** H. MORE *Song of Soul* II. i. III. xx, This bow.. Of causeleese grief, I hope, shall thee recure.

absol. **1557** *Tottel's Misc.* (Arb.) 183 As she hath beauty to allure, So hath she a hart that will recure. **1590** GREENE *Never too late* (1600) Q 2 b, Thou hast lent youth..Achilles sword to cut and recure.

refl. **1634** SIR T. HERBERT *Trav.* 193 He has free leaue to recure himselfe.

b. To bring back to a normal state or condition; to restore after loss, damage, exhaustion, etc. Also const. *to* (a better state).

1382 WYCLIF *Ecclus.* ii. 6 3if feith to God and he shal rekure thee; and dresse thi weye and hope in to hym. *c* **1420** *Pallad. on Husb.* I. 313 So that, if mysauenture ffordo thyn hous, a yeer or too [may] recure Hit atte mest. *c* **1430** LYDG. *Reas. & Sens.* 170 Her lignes to sustene, And to Recure.. Ageyn the harmys and gret damage, That wynter wrought. **1590** SPENSER *F.Q.* I. ix. 2 When their powres, empayrd through labor long, With dew repast they had recured well [etc.]. *Ibid.* II. i. 54 Through wise handling and faire governaunce, I him recured to a better will. **1606** J. CARPENTER *Solomon's Solace* viii. 33 They were so ready to inuestigate that, whereof being once certified they did much maruaile at..and could scarsely ease or mitigate, much lesse salue and recure. *a* **1667** COWLEY *Constantia & Philetus* Wks. 1711 III. 11 No Physick can recure my weaken'd State.

2. To cure (a disease, sickness, etc.); to heal, make whole (a wound or sore).

c **1430** LYDG. *Min. Poems* (Percy Soc.) 50 My lord may al my sorowe recure. **1430–40** —— *Bochas* VIII. xxv. (1558) 17 b, To staunche his woundes & hurtes to recure. **1509** HAWES *Conv. Swearers* viii, Grace..recured my sekenes. **1545** RAYNOLD *Byrth Mankynde* 79 The cause knowen, the dysease maye the more readely be recured. **1596** LODGE *Marg. Amer.* 60 Thou hast rubbed the gall, but not recured the wound. **1613** HEYWOOD *Silver Age* III. i, There teares my griefes recure. **1667** MILTON *P.L.* XII. 393 Thy deaths wound Which hee, who comes thy Saviour, shall recure.

b. To remedy, redress, repair, retrieve (a wrong, defect, etc.).

1536 *Exhort. to North* 138 in Furniv. *Ballads fr. MSS.* I. 308 The englysch commontie..your purposse will aide, thes wronges to Rekure. **1579** E. K. *Ded. to Spenser's Sheph. Cal.* ⁋1 Which default when as some endeuoured to salue and recure, they patched vp the holes with peces & rags of other languages. **1590** SPENSER *F.Q.* II. x. 23 Which blott his sonne succeeding in his seat,..Right well recur'd, and did away that blame. **1631** QUARLES *Samson* Medit. viii. 48 Faire language may recure A fault of youth, whilst rougher words obdure.

3. *intr.* Of persons: To become whole; to regain health or a former state.

c **1420–30** *Compl.* 93 in Lydg. *Temple of Glas* (E.E.T.S.) App. i. 60 That I ne schulde..To helthe neuere a-geyn recure, But euere in maledy endure. *c* **1440** *Jacob's Well* 293 Thru3 schryfte he may rekure a3en. *a* **1510** DOUGLAS *K. Hart* I. 254 King Hart sair woundit was, bot..weill he traistit that he suld recure. *a* **1547** SURREY in *Tottel's Misc.* (Arb.) 32 Yet Salomon sayd, the wronged shall recure.

b. Of a wound: To heal.

1616 J. LANE *Cont. Sqr.'s T.* XI. 100 His woundes..closd all vp, and instantlie recurd.

4. *trans.* To recover (something lost).

c **1400** *Rom. Rose* 5124 For tyme lost, as men may see, For no-thyng may recured be. **1432–50** tr. *Higden* (Rolls) II. 263 Artaxerses,..expellenge Nectanabus,..recurede that realme ageyne. *c* **1470** HENRYSON *Mor. Fab.* VI. (*Sheep & Dog*) i, Ane certane breid fra him for to recuir. **1530** PALSGR. 681/2, I recure, I get agayne... I have recured it, but it was with moche a do. **1590** SPENSER *F.Q.* III. v. 34 By this he had sweet life recur'd agayne. **1633** P. FLETCHER *Purple Isl.* I. lvii, So hard was this lost Isle, so hard to be recur'd. [**1746** W. THOMPSON *Hymn to May* xliii, Full suddenly the Seeds of joy recure Elastic spring, and force within empight.]

b. To get, obtain, win.

c **1403** LYDG. *Temple of Glas* 1226 In signe þat 3e haue recured 3oure hole desire. *c* **1430** —— *Min. Poems* (Percy Soc.) 174 With cornerawntys make thy nekke long, In pondys deepe thy prayes to recure. *c* **1450** *Cov. Myst.* x. (Shaks. Soc.) 93 Be prayour grett knowleche men recure. **1509** HAWES *Conv. Swearers* vii, Hope at laste to recure this scyence Exorteth me ryght hardely to wryte.

c. To preserve, save. *rare*$^{-1}$.

c **1430** LYDG. *Hors, Shepe & G.* 248 Thus, bi a Gandre recured was the toun.

Hence † **re'curable** *a.*, that may be cured. *Obs.*

1608 DOD & CLEAVER *Expos. Prov. xi–xii* 15 Neither is it an ordinary euill that is recurable, but a desperate ruine that is remedilesse.

† **re'cureful**, *a. Obs.*$^{-1}$ [Cf. next.] Helpful.

1606 CHAPMAN *Gent. Usher* v. Plays 1873 I. 333 Let me for euer hide this staine of Beauty, With this recureful Maske.

† **re'cureless**, *a. Obs.* [f. RECURE *sb.* + -LESS.] That cannot be cured; incurable. (Freq. *c* 1600.)

1559 FERRARS in *Mirr. Mag.*, *Cobham* xxv, The best salue for my recureles sore Was to despaire of cure for euermore. *a* **1592** GREENE *Jas. IV*, II. ii, 'Tis foolish to bewail recureless things. *c* **1611** CHAPMAN *Iliad* XVI. 302 His speare..on the breast did light..Impressing a recurelesse wound.

Hence † **re'curelessly** *adv.*

1592 GREENE *Groat's W. Wit* (1617) 24 Vntill he perish, recurelessly wounded by his own weapons.

† **re'curement.** *Obs. rare*$^{-1}$. [f. RECURE *v.* + -MENT.] = RECURE *sb.*

1639 G. DANIEL *Ecclus.* xi. 34 And they that Magnifie their follies done Wax Gray in Sin, past all recurement gone.

† **re'curer.** *Obs. rare*$^{-1}$. [f. RECURE *v.* + -ER¹.] One who helps or aids.

1382 WYCLIF *Ecclus.* xiii. 26 To the riche desceyued manye ben rekureres [*v.r.* rekuueers; L. *recuperatores*]; he spac proudli and thei iustefieden hym.

recurrable (rɪˈkɜːrəb(ə)l), *a.* [f. RECUR *v.* + -ABLE.] That can recur.

1935 E. POUND *Let.* 17 Apr. (1971) 273, I don't know that I have been clear enough re *recurrable* epithets—either to be simple and natural so that repeat don't worry one, or else strange and part of definite intended stylization.

recurred (rɪˈkɜːd), *ppl. a.* [f. RECUR *v.* + -ED¹.] *Path.* That has reappeared.

1897 J. HUTCHINSON in *Arch. Surg.* VIII. No. 31. 217 The recurred induration in the site of a primary sore. **1898** *Ibid.* IX. No. 36. 365 The theory of recurred chancres.

recurrence (rɪˈkʌrəns). [See RECURRENT and -ENCE.]

1. a. Return (of a thing, state, event, etc.); renewed, frequent, or periodical occurrence.

1646 SIR T. BROWNE *Pseud. Ep.* III. i. 106 Although the opinion at present be reasonable well suppressed, yet from the..faithfull recurrence of error, it is not improbable, it may revive..againe. **1790** PALEY *Horæ Paul.* i. 12 The perpetual recurrence of names of persons and places. **1861** TRENCH *Ep. 7 Churches Asia* 16 The constant recurrence of this language in all descriptions of our Lord's second advent is very remarkable. **1877** MRS. OLIPHANT *Makers Flor.* vi. 172 So little can the world guard itself as it grows older from the recurrence of the same follies.

b. With *a* and *pl.*, an instance of this.

1759 JOHNSON *Idler* No. 72 ⁋4 Every recurrence [of parts of knowledge] would reinstate them in their former place. **1836** MISS MITFORD in L'Estrange *Life* (1870) III. iv. 62 He brought on a recurrence of an old injury to the tendon under the left knee. **1863** GEO. ELIOT *Romola* lix, An indistinct recurrence of impressions which blended themselves with her agitating fears.

c. Reappearance (of some feature).

1864 H. SPENCER *Princ. Biol.* §83 Atavism, which is the name given to the recurrence of ancestral traits, is proved by many and varied facts.

2. Resort, recourse, reference *to* something. Also without const.

a **1667** JER. TAYLOR (Ogilvie), In the use of this, as of every kind of alleviation, I shall insensibly go on from a rare to a frequent recurrence to the dangerous preparations. **1804** CASTLEREAGH in Owen *Mrq. Wellesley's Desp.* (1877) 262 Such an alliance will occasion frequent recurrence to arms. **1825** JEFFERSON *Autobiog.* Wks. 1859 I. 61 These memoranda were on loose papers, bundled up without order, and difficult of recurrence. **1845** S. AUSTIN *Ranke's Hist. Ref.* I. 153 A permanent imperial council, which might relieve him and the States from incessant recurrence to the diets.

3. The action of going back mentally or in discourse *to* something. Also with *a* and *pl.*, an instance of this.

1751 JOHNSON *Rambler* No. 173 ¶6 By the natural recurrence of the mind to its common employment. **1815** JANE AUSTEN *Emma* xxii, To allow no time for insidious applications or dangerous recurrences to the past. **1834** HT. MARTINEAU *The Farrers* vii. 120 How many recurrences of mind had she to these articles! **1862** C. STRETTON *Chequered Life* I. 115 The announcement of dinner being served, effectually put a stop to any recurrence to the subject.

4. a. Return or reversion *to* a state, occupation, etc.

1812 G. CHALMERS *Dom. Econ. Gt. Brit.* 477 Nothing more is wanting, than recurrence to old habits of diligence. **1855** BROWNING *Ep. Karshish* 197 In sedulous recurrence to his trade Whereby he earneth him the daily bread. **1862** S. LUCAS *Secularia* 68 There is an obvious..difference in the result of a recurrence to this or that particular status.

b. *spec.* in *Biol.* (See quot.)

1862 HUXLEY *Lect. Working Men* 113 A word must be said about what is called Recurrence—the tendency of races which have been developed by selective breeding from varieties to return to their primitive type.

5. *U.S.* Refluence (of sea-water) to a place.

1893 PARKHURST in J. Strong *New Era* 219 The recurrence of the cold polar waters, which return to the Gulf.

6. *attrib.* and *Comb.*, as ***recurrence frequency, interval***; **recurrence formula, relation** *Math.*, an expression which defines the general member of a series in terms of the preceding members; **recurrence surface** [tr. Sw. *rekurrensyta* (E. Granlund 1932, in *Sveriges Geologiska Undersökn.* Ser. C. No. 373. viii. 73)], a horizon in a peat bog between highly decomposed and slightly decomposed peat, indicating the commencement of a period of active peat growth; **recurrence time** *Math.*, the time between two successive occasions when a Markov process enters any given state.

1902 E. T. WHITTAKER *Course Mod. Analysis* x. 210 The *recurrence-formulae. We proceed to establish a group of formulae which connect Legendre functions of different orders. **1925** *Biometrika* XVII. 165 (*heading*) Recurrence formulae for the moments of the point binomial. **1965** *Wireless World* Sept. 431/1 It remains now to provide a suitable pulse generator of variable *recurrence frequency to fire the thyristor. **1965** R. G. KAZMANN *Mod. Hydrol.* iv. 76 Statistical studies made to determine the *recurrence interval of this design-flood resulted in figures ranging from 1000 to 90,000 years. **1933** *Biometrika* XXV. 420 (*heading*) On a *recurrence relation connected with..double Bessel functions. **1961** M. M. NICOLSON *Fund. & Tech. Math. for Scientists* xvi. 369 A set of formulae relating Legendre polynomials of different orders *n*; such relations are called recurrence relations. **1979** PAGE & WILSON *Introd. Computational Combinatorics* ii. 5 If such a recurrence relation can be produced, it can usually be made the basis of an algorithm for computing values of the desired function. [**1934** *Irish Naturalists' Jrnl.* V. 134 To look for Granlund's 'rekurrenz-surfaces'.] **1938** *New Phytologist* XXXVII. 452 Granlund suggests that such layers are due to slowing up of bog growth by unfavourable conditions, and to the level marking the sudden renewal of growth he gives the name 'Rekurrenzflache [*sic*]', which has been translated by Jessen as *Recurrence-surface. **1956** H. GODWIN *Hist. Brit. Flora* iii. 34/2 In his work on the raised bogs of Scania, Nilsson.. has been able to identify no fewer than nine recurrence surfaces between *c.* 3500 B.C. and the present day. **1975** J. G. EVANS *Environment Early Man Brit. Isles* iv. 77 Resumption of peat growth, leading to the formation of 'recurrence surfaces', takes place when conditions of high rainfall return. [**1943** *Rev. Mod. Physics* XV. 54/2 (*heading*) The average time of recurrence of a state of fluctuation in which the molecular concentration in a sphere of air of radius *a* will differ from the average value by 1 percent.] **1949** *Trans. Amer. Math. Soc.* LXVII. 99 A new method of finding the second moment of the *recurrence times of finite or infinite Markov chains. **1971** R. A. HOWARD *Dynamic Probabilistic Syst.* I. v. 287 θ_{ii} is the number of transitions between a departure from state *i* and the first return to *i*; it is called the first passage time from state *i* to state *i*, or the recurrence time of state *i*.

recurrency (rɪˈkʌrənsɪ). [f. as prec. + -ENCY.]

1. †**a.** (See quot.) *Obs. rare*$^{-0}$. **b.** *U.S.* = RECURRENCE 5. *rare.*

1611 FLORIO, *Recorrenza*, a recurrency or running to and fro. **1858** MAURY *Phys. Geog. Sea* vii. §424 A recurrency in the deep water in the middle of the Gut that sets outward to the grand ocean.

2. = RECURRENCE 1. Now *rare.*

a **1661** FULLER *Worthies* (1840) II. 553 The same is reported by Herodotus,..and may be an instance of the recurrency of remarkable accidents. **1749** HARTLEY *Observ. Man* I. I. i. 73 This will be over-ruled by the Recurrency of the Associations. *Ibid.* II. II. iii. 344 The frequent Recurrency of these Fears and Anxieties must embitter all guilty Pleasures. **1928** H. POUTSMA *Gram. Late Mod. Eng.* (ed. 2) I. I. i. 83 The principal verbs used to express recurrency, i.e. the iterative aspect of an action..are *can, to use* and *will.*

re-current (riːˈkʌrənt), *sb.*¹ *rare.* [RE-.] A current flowing in the opposite direction to another.

1873 A. W. WARD tr. *Curtius' Hist. Greece* I. II. iii. 439 They found the same phenomena of currents and re-currents as in their native sound.

recurrent (rɪˈkʌrənt), *a.* and *sb.*² [ad. L. *recurrent-em*, pres. pple. of *recurrĕre* to RECUR. Cf. F. *récurrent* (16th c.).]

A. *adj.* **1.** *Anat.* and *Bot.* Of a nerve, vein, artery, branch, etc.: Turned back so as to run or lie in a direction opposite to its former one. ***recurrent nerves***, the laryngeal and meningeal branches of the pneumogastric nerve.

1611 FLORIO, *Recorrenti vene*, the veines called the recurrant veines. **1664** POWER *Exp. Philos.* I. 68 That pleasant Experiment by tying the recurrent Nerves in a living Dogg. **1712** SLOANE in *Phil. Trans.* XXVII. 499 Two Dogs, which had their Recurrent Nerves cut, lost their Barking and Voice. **1775** J. JENKINSON *Brit. Plants* Gloss., *Recurrent*, running backwards. **1830** LINDLEY *Nat. Syst. Bot.* 190 The corolla, whose tube has five nerves..dividing at top into recurrent branches. **1842** E. WILSON *Anat. Vade M.* (ed. 2) 299 The two recurrent arteries frequently arise by a commmon trunk. **1877** JORDAN *N. Amer. Ichthyog.* II. 71 Its numerous rudimentary rays recurrent above and below the caudal peduncle.

b. *Path.* ***recurrent sensibility*** (see quots.).

1873 A. FLINT *Nerv. Syst.* ii. 82 The sensibility of the anterior root is recurrent, being derived from the posterior root through the periphery. **1877** M. FOSTER *Physiol.* III. i. 343 The phenomena are probably due to the fact, that bundles of sensory fibres of the posterior root after running a short distance down the mixed trunk turn back and run upwards in the anterior root, and by this recurrent course give rise to the recurrent sensibility.

†**2. a.** (See quot.) *Obs. rare*$^{-0}$.

1656 BLOUNT *Glossogr.*, *Recurrent*, returning hastily, running again or back quickly, having recourse to.

†**b.** Of verses: (See quot. and cf. B. 2). *Obs.*$^{-0}$

After L. *recurrentes versus* (Sidonius).

1706 PHILLIPS (ed. Kersey), *Recurrents*, or *Recurrent Verses*, such Verses as are read the same backward and forward.

3. Occurring or coming again (esp. frequently or periodically); reappearing.

1666 HARVEY *Morb. Angl.* xiv. (1672) 33 Short intermittent, or swift recurrent pains do precipitate Patients into Consumptions. **1850** BLACKIE *Æschylus* I. 47 From time to time In children's children recurrent appears The ancestral crime. **1860** TYNDALL *Glac.* II. xxvi. 368 The bands must be due to some regularly recurrent cause. **1893** A. S. ECCLES *Sciatica* 82 Six patients have suffered from recurrent sciatica after periods varying from six months to four years.

†**b.** *Math.* (See RECURRING *ppl. a.* 2 a.) *Obs.*

1763 EMERSON *Meth. Increments* 144 To find the sum of 50 terms of the recurrent series..$1 + 3x + 8x^2 + 21x^3$, etc.

c. Of a crystal: (see quot.).

1816 R. JAMESON *Char. Min.* 203 Recurrent tinstone.. may be described as a rectangular four-sided prism, acuminated on the extremities with four planes, which are set on the lateral edges, and the eight edges formed by the acuminating and lateral planes truncated.

d. Math. ***recurrent relation*** = *recurrence relation.*

1896 *Phil. Trans. R. Soc.* A. CLXXXVII. 522 These recurrent relations between the functions for different values of *n* hold for general complex values of *m* and *n*. **1931** E. W. HOBSON *Theory Spherical & Ellipsoidal Harmonics* ii. 67 Recurrent relations..between the functions $Q_n(\mu)$ for different values of *n*.

B. *sb.* **1.** A recurrent artery or nerve; *esp.* the right or left recurrent laryngeal nerve.

1597 A. M. tr. *Guillemeau's Fr. Chirurg.* 19/2 The muscles which are serviceable to the speach or voyce, as are the recurrentes, or retrogradinge muscles. **1615** CROOKE *Body of Man* 365 When it commeth to the Axillary artery..it transmitteth..three braunches from the inner side..which being reflected toward the head and vnited do make the right Recurrent. **1741** A. MONRO *Anat. Nerves* (ed. 3) 53 The Muscles of the Larynx being in a good measure supplied with Nerves from the Recurrents. **1808** BARCLAY *Muscular Motions* 254 The course of the nervous branches that are called recurrents. **1876** BRISTOWE *Th. & Pract. Med.* (1878) 558 Pressure on the right recurrent, which may be produced by innominate or subclavian aneurysm, will have a corresponding effect on the right vocal cord.

†**2.** A recurrent verse. *Obs. rare.*

1605 CAMDEN *Rem.*, *Rhythmes* 26 Beside these [metres], our Poets hath their knacks as young Schollers call them, as Ecchos.., Serpentine verses, Recurrents, Numeralls, &c. **1656** BLOUNT *Glossogr.* s.v., A kind of verses called Recurrents. **1706** [see A. 2 b]. **1727-41** [see RECIPROCAL *a.* 1 c].

Hence **re'currently** *adv.*

1868 BAIN *Ment. & Mor. Sc.* 720 Only what is instrumental in its production and in most cases customarily or recurrently instrumental. **1877** 'H. A. PAGE' *De Quincey* II. xix. 183 This tendency to real life..declaring itself recurrently and with great strength.

recurrer (rɪˈkʌrə(r)). *rare.* [f. RECUR *v.* + -ER¹.] *Math.* A recurring decimal.

1892 *Black & White* 14 May 623/2 It was a decimal that did me in the Little-Go..a recurrer with complications.

recurring (rɪˈkɜːrɪŋ), *ppl. a.* [-ING².]

1. That recurs, in senses of the vb.

a **1711** KEN *Hymnarium* Poet. Wks. 1721 II. 32 Throughout his annual and re-curring Race, He never stops, but always changes Place. **1804-6** SYD. SMITH *Mor. Philos.* (1850) 168 Every recurring year contributes its remedy to these infringements on justice and good sense. **1851** J. PAGET *Lect. Tumours* v. 55/2 For one group, the name of 'Recurring Fibroid Tumours' may, for the present, suffice. **1875** JOWETT *Plato* (ed. 2) III. 277 The various letters in all their recurring sizes and combinations.

b. With prefixed advbs., as ***ever-, oft-, still-recurring.***

1832 TENNYSON *Sonn., Caress'd or chidden*, Fancy came.. And chased away the still-recurring gnat. **1850** R. G. CUMMING *Hunter's Life S. Africa* (1902) 98/2 The greater part of the forest consisting of the ever-recurring wait-a-bits. **1861** M. PATTISON *Ess.* (1889) I. 45 The Great Hall, serving..as a banqueting-room for the oft-recurring festivities.

2. *spec.* **a.** *Math.* ***recurring curve***, a curve which returns upon itself. ***recurring decimal***: see DECIMAL *sb.* 2. ***recurring series*** (see quot. 1797).

1715 tr. *Gregory's Astron.* v. I. Prop. 2 II. 698 Kepler did not like Circles or other recurring Curves for the Motion of Comets. **1797** *Encycl. Brit.* (ed. 3) XVII. 297/1 Recurring series, a series of which any term is formed by the addition of a certain number of preceding terms, multiplied or divided by any determinate numbers whether positive or negative. **1801** *Ibid.* Suppl. I. 483/2 *Circulating Decimals*, called also recurring or repeating decimals. **1841** *Penny Cycl.* XIX. 342/1 Some use may thus be made of recurring series in various questions of the theory of probabilities. **1886** PENDLEBURY *Arith.* §181 Such a decimal as ·142857, in which all digits recur, is called a pure recurring decimal.

b. *Path.* ***recurring utterances***, a form of aphasia, marked by the repetition of certain words or phrases.

1892 TUKE *Dict. Psych. Med.* II. 1074/1. **1899** *Allbutt's Syst. Med.* VIII. 411 The articulation of such words or 'recurring utterances', as they are now commonly termed.

So **re'curring** *vbl. sb.*, a returning.

1748 RICHARDSON *Clarissa* (1811) VI. 347 Recurrings there will be; hankerings, that will, on every, but remotely-favourable incident..pop up.

recurringly (rɪˈkɜːrɪŋlɪ), *adv.* [f. RECURRING *ppl. a.* + -LY².] In a recurring manner; repeatedly.

1915 'A. HOPE' *Young Man's Year* xxix. 272 It pointedly and recurringly reminded him that there were more women than one in the world. **1923** *Daily Mail* 10 Aug. 4/2 A bogus manager..is 'a manager who engages artists and recurringly fails to pay their salaries'.

recursant (rɪˈkɜːsənt), *a. Her.* [ad. L. *recursant-em*, pres. pple. of *recursāre* to hasten back, return, f. *recurs-*, ppl. stem of *recurrĕre* to RECUR.] Of an eagle: Having the back towards the spectator.

c **1828** BERRY *Encycl. Her.* s.v., *Recursant overture*, or inverted and displayed...is said of an eagle, displayed with the back towards your face. *Recursant volant, in pale*, is said of an eagle as it were flying upwards, showing the back.

†**recurse**, *v. Obs. rare*$^{-1}$. [ad. L. *recurs-āre*: see prec.] *intr.* To recur.

1638 COWLEY *Love's Riddle* II. i, My father, mother, and my brother Recurse unto my thoughts, and straight plucke downe The resolution I had built before.

recursion (rɪˈkɜːʃən). [ad. L. *recursiōn-em*, n. of action f. *recurrĕre* to RECUR.]

1. A backward movement, return. Now *rare* or *Obs.*

1616 BULLOKAR *Eng. Expos.*, *Recursion*, a running backe. **1660** BOYLE *New Exp. Phys. Mech.* xxvi. 203 The Recursions of that Pendulum which was swinging within the Receiver. **1677** GILPIN *Demonol.* (1867) 237 Our passions in their workings do depend upon the fluctuations, excursions, and recursions of the blood and animal spirits. **1720-1** *Lett. fr. Mist's Jrnl.* (1722) II. 33 The present melancholy Prospect of the Recursion of the South-Sea Tide. **1830** T. TAYLOR *Argts. Celsus* 23 The doctrine..that in long periods of time, recursions and concursions of the stars, conflagrations and deluges take place.

2. a. The application or use of a recursive procedure or definition; ***primitive recursion*** [tr. G. *primitive rekursion* (R. Péter 1934, in *Math. Ann.* CX. 613)], definition of a function of natural numbers by induction on a single argument or (equivalently) by simple recursion formulæ; ***recursion formula***, an equation relating the value of a function for a given value of its argument (or arguments) to its values for other values of the argument(s).

[**1871** *Math. Annalen* IV. 113 Man hat also für die Funktion $R^{m,\nu}$ folgende Recursionsformel: $2(\nu - 1)/x \cdot R^{m,\nu} = R^{m+1,\nu-1} + R^{m-1,\nu+1}$.] **1930** *Proc. London Math. Soc.* XXX. 267 For other values of *r* we define $f(r, n, k)$ by recursion formulae. **1933** *Ann. Math.* XXXIV. 863 The recursion formulas, $m + 1 = S(m)$, and $m + (k + 1) = S(m + k)$. **1934, 1974** [see RECURSIVE *a.* 2 a]. **1943** *Trans. Amer. Math. Soc.* LIII. 42 Schema (I) introduces the successor function,..and Schema (V) the schema of primitive recursion. **1961** *Commun. Assoc. Computing Machinery* IV. 65/1 The growing extent and direction of application of recursion in programming research. **1964** E. BACH *Introd. Transformational Gram.* iii. 46 Care must be taken to ensure that unwanted recursion (looping) does not occur. **1967** KLERER & KORN *Digital Computer User's Handbk.* i. 167 Even if recursive procedures are explicitly outlawed,.. recursion can take place unwittingly. **1972** R. A. PALMATIER *Gloss. Eng. Transformational Gram.* 142 Recursion is restricted to the transformational component of the grammar. **1973** C. W. GEAR *Introd. Computer Sci.* v. 232 FORTRAN does not allow recursion. **1975** F. R. PALMER in W. F. Bolton *Eng. Lang.* i. 34 The structure of language involves 'recursion' of the kind illustrated by 'This is the house that Jack built', 'This is the mouse that lived in the house that Jack built' and so on—if necessary *ad infinitum.*

b. A recursive definition.

1936 *Math. Ann.* CXII. 727 There are other definitions of this sort, e.g. certain recursions with respect to two or more variables simultaneously, which cannot be reduced to a succession of substitutions and ordinary recursions. **1963** W. V. QUINE *Set Theory* §11. 79 There are the familiar so-called recursive definitions or recursions. **1966** N. CHOMSKY *Topics Theory Generative Gram.* ii. 33 An utterly fantastic proposal, namely, that a grammar should contain no recursions in its system of rules. **1971** *Computers & Humanities* V. 155 ALGOL is more powerful in that it allows recursions, has block structure, and permits expressions in many places.

recursive (rɪˈkɜːsɪv), *a.* (and *sb.*) [f. L. *recurs-* (see RECURSANT *a.*) + -IVE.]

1. Periodically or continually recurring. Now *rare* or *Obs.*

1790 *Loiterer* 13 Mar. 7 Till your ear be so attuned to one particular measure, that your ideas may be spontaneously absorbed into the same revolving eddy of recursive harmony.

2. a. *Math.* and *Logic.* [after similar uses of G. *rekurrent* (D. Hilbert 1904, in *Verhandl. des dritten Internat. Math. Köngr.*), *rekursiv* (K. Gödel 1931, in *Monatshefte f. Math. u. Physik* XXXVIII. 179).] Involving or being a repeated procedure such that the required result at each step except the last is given in terms of the result(s) of the next step, until after a finite number of steps a terminus is reached with an outright evaluation of the result; ***recursive definition***, a definition (of a function) which is either primitive recursive or (now usu.) general recursive; ***recursive function***, a function which has or which may be given a recursive definition; ***recursive relation***, a property of, or relation between, natural numbers whose truth value for all arguments is a recursive function; ***recursive set***, a set of natural numbers whose defining property is recursive; ***general recursive*** adj. phr., applied to a function or relation which is recursive and is defined for all natural number values of its arguments; ***partial recursive*** adj. phr., applied to a function defined by a recursive process which for some or all values of the arguments does not terminate, leaving the value of the function undefined; ***primitive recursive*** adj. phr., applied to a function or relation which can be generated by primitive recursion and substitution from the zero, successor, and identity functions.

1934 KLEENE & ROSSER *Gödel's Undecidable Propositions Formal Math. Syst.* (typescript) 3 We define the class of recursive functions to be the totality of functions which can be generated by substitution..and recursion..from the successor function $x + 1$, constant functions.., and identity functions. *Ibid.*, A relation R shall be recursive if the representing function is recursive. *Ibid.*, Recursive functions have the important property that, for each given set of values of the arguments, the value of the function can be computed by a finite procedure. Similarly, recursive relations (classes) are decidable in the sense that, for each given set of natural numbers, it can be determined by a finite procedure whether the relation holds or does not hold... The functions $x + y$, xy, x^y and $x!$ are clearly recursive. **1936** *Math. Ann.* CXII. 727 In this paper we offer several observations on general recursive functions, using essentially Gödel's form of the definition. *Ibid.*, Ordinary or 'primitive' recursive functions. *Ibid.* 729 A recursive function (relation) in the sense of Gödel..will now be called a primitive recursive function (relation). **1938** *Jrnl. Symbolic Logic* III. 151 If we omit the requirement that the computation process always terminate, we obtain a more general class of functions, each function of which is defined over a subset (possibly null or total) of the *n*-tuples of natural numbers... These functions we call partial recursive. **1940** *Mind* XLIX. 240 Preliminary considerations, such as..the exact specification of the rules for the use of recursive definitions. **1943** *Mind* LII. 268 Quite elementary theorems, requiring for their proofs recursive arguments to take care of the indefinite number of variables involved. **1943** *Trans. Amer. Math. Soc.* LIII. 44 A system E of equations defines recursively a general recursive function of *n* variables if, for each set $x_1, \ldots, x_n$ of natural numbers, an equation of the form $f(x_1, \ldots, x_n) = x$, where f is the principal function symbol of E, and where $x_1, \ldots, x_n$ are the numerals representing the natural numbers $x_1, \ldots, x_n$, is derivable from E..for *exactly* one numeral *x*. **1944** *Bull. Amer. Math. Soc.* L. 285 In the present paper, 'recursive function' means 'general recursive function'. *Ibid.* 288 Closely related to the technical concept [of a] recursively enumerable set of positive integers is that of a recursive set of positive integers. This is a set for which there is a recursive function $f(x)$ such that $f(x)$ is say 2 when *x* is a positive integer in the set, 1 when *x* is a positive integer not in the set. We may also make this the definition of the set being recursively soluble. For 2 and 1 may be regarded as the two possible truth-values, true, false, of the proposition 'positive integer *x* is in the set'. **1962** R. B. BRAITHWAITE in B. Meltzer tr. *Gödel's Formally Undecidable Propositions* 12 An arithmetical function is recursive if it is the last term in a finite sequence of functions in which each function is recursively defined by a rule involving two functions preceding it in the sequence (or is the successor function or a constant or obtained by substitution from a preceding function). **1964** E. MENDELSON *Introd. Math. Logic* 125 Relations obtained from primitive recursive (or recursive) relations by means of the propositional connectives and the bounded quantifiers are also primitive recursive (or recursive). **1965** HERMAN & PLASSMAN tr. *H. Hermes' Enumerability, Decidability, Computability* i. 29 Today it is generally believed that *every* system of algorithms can be defined by recursive functions. This gives a deeper meaning to Gödel's result. *Ibid.* iii. 82 The essence of Ackermann's proof of the existence of a computable function which is not primitive recursive consists in defining a computable function which increases in a certain sense faster than any primitive recursive function. **1967** *Encycl. Philos.* VII. 92/1 This Herbrand–Gödel–Kleene notion of general recursive function can be put in the context of instructions and computations discussed above. **1970** *Nature* 19 Dec. 1234/1 Turing formulated his concept of an abstract computing machine; the functions computable by these machines are exactly the recursive functions. **1974** A. KENNY tr. *Wittgenstein's Philos. Gram.* 34 Is there a further step from writing the recursive proof to the generalization? Doesn't the recursion schema already say all that is to be said?

b. *Linguistics.* Applied to a grammatical feature or element which may be involved in a procedure whereby that feature or element is repeatedly reintroduced; applied to a grammatical rule in which part of the output serves as input to the same rule.

1955 N. CHOMSKY *Logical Struct. Linguistic Theory* (microfilm, Mass. Inst. Technol.) vi. 248 We will find many other reasons to question the validity of the extension of the notion of *production* to *recursive production*. **1957** —— in *Janua Linguarum* IV. 57 Bar-Hillel has suggested..that Pike's proposals can be formalized without the circularity that many sense in them by the use of recursive definitions. **1968** J. LYONS *Introd. Theoret. Linguistics* vii. 326 The adverb is a recursive category..in the sense that one adverb may modify another. **1970** —— *Chomsky* viii. 90 It will be observed that rules (2), (3) and (4) are recursive, but in different ways. Rule (2) is left recursive; rule (3) is right recursive; and rule (4) is self-embedding. **1972** R. A. PALMATIER *Gloss. Eng. Transformational Gram.* 142 A recursive rule is a rule which reapplies indefinitely to its own output... The recursive power of a grammar, which resides entirely in the syntactic component, is its ability to generate an infinity of sentences... The recursive mechanism is the system of rules which account for the infinite properties of language... A recursive element is one from which strings can be derived that contain the same element... The recursive property of a grammar..is its provision for embedding sentences within other sentences. **1977** *Word 1972* XXVIII. 336 Logicians of the first half of the century had developed and used recursive grammars with such clarity that Chomsky's 'application' can hardly be regarded as a *tour de force*.

c. *Computing.* Applied to a statement, definition, subroutine, or the like, some part of which makes use of the whole of itself, so that its explicit interpretation requires in general many successive executions; applied also to languages, compilers, etc., which allow of such techniques.

Quot. 1958 uses the word in a context where 'iterative' would now be usual.

1958 *Commun. Assoc. Computing Machinery* Aug. 10 The idea of recursive curve fitting has been in use for some time as a graphical technique for fitting curves 'by eye' to observational data. **1959** *Numerische Math.* I. 45 The definition of expressions, and their constituents, is necessarily recursive. **1960** *Ibid.* II. 312 It is then impossible to call in a subroutine while one or more previous activations of the same subroutine have not yet come to an end... We intend to describe..a means of removing the..restriction..; hence the name 'recursive programming'. **1973** C. W. GEAR *Introd. Computer Sci.* v. 233 We can understand recursive procedures by imagining that many different copies of the procedure are available. **1979** PAGE & WILSON *Introd. Computational Combinatorics* vi. 136 Since backtrack programming is closely related to tree searching we can consider using recursive techniques in our implementations.

3. *Phonetics.* A term sometimes used to refer to consonants accompanied by glottal closure or implosion. Also as *sb.*

1924 R. L. TURNER in *Bull. School Oriental Stud.* III. 304 According to one of my informants, an *m* accompanied by glottal closure and distinguished from ordinary *m*, exists in Magarkurā, one of the Mongolian languages of Nepal. Prince Troubetzkoy refers to consonants in the Caucasian languages accompanied by complete closure of the glottis. These he calls 'recoursives', a convenient term I have anglicized as 'recursives'; he indicates them by a dot above or below the letter. **1934** WEBSTER, *Recursive*, adj.,..formed with an inward movement of air caused by lowering the larynx with closed glottis;—said of certain consonants in Sindhi (*g*, *j*, *d*, *b*). **1974** *Encycl. Brit. Macropædia* IX. 448/1 One major feature distinguishing Sindhi from the rest of the northwest group is the development of a series of imploded stops (also called suction stops and recursive stops), for *b*, *d*, *j*, and *g*.

recursively (rɪˈkɜːsɪvlɪ), *adv.* [f. prec. + -LY².] In a recursive manner: esp. ***recursively defined***, having a recursive definition; ***recursively enumerable***, (of a set of natural numbers) generated by a general recursive function having one parameter which ranges through all possible values.

1934 KLEENE & ROSSER *Gödel's Undecidable Propositions Formal Math. Syst.* (typescript) 21 These are arithmetic propositions which involve only recursively defined functions. **1943**, **1944** [see RECURSIVE *a.* 2a]. **1944** *Bull. Amer. Math. Soc.* L. 285 A set of positive integers is said to be recursively enumerable if there is a recursive function $f(x)$ of one positive integral variable whose values for positive integral values of *x*, constitute the given set. **1961** *Commun. Assoc. Computing Machinery* IV. 10/2 Many of the constituents of the ALGOL language are defined recursively. **1962** B. MELTZER tr. *Gödel's Formally Undecidable Propositions* 46 A number-theoretic function $\phi(x_1, x_2, \ldots x_n)$ is said to be recursively defined by the number-theoretic functions $\psi(x_1, x_2, \ldots x_{n-1})$ and $\mu(x_1, x_2, \ldots x_{n-1})$ if for all $x_2, \ldots x_n$, *k* the following hold: $\phi(0, x_2, \ldots x_n) = \psi(x_2, \ldots x_n)$, $\phi(k+1, x_2, \ldots x_n) = \mu(k, \phi(k, x_2, \ldots x_n), x_2, \ldots x_n)$. **1964** *Mem. Amer. Math. Soc.* LI. 8 An index of ϕ_2 is obtainable primitive recursively from an index of ϕ_1, and vice versa. **1968** [see NEST *v.* 4 b]. **1968** *Language* XLIV. 571 The set of all sets of integers is non-denumerable; the set of all Turing machines is denumerable; each recursively enumerable set corresponds to a Turing machine; therefore there are sets of integers which are not recursively enumerable. **1970** *Ibid.* XLVI. 787 Sentence margins are slots where nuclear sentence patterns may recursively be embedded within other sentences. **1970** EILENBERG & ELGOT *Recursiveness* 84 The class of all recursively enumerable sets is countable. **1974** KERNIGHAN & PLAUGER *Elem. Programming Style* iii. 54 Learning to think recursively takes some effort, but that is repaid with smaller and simpler programs... Use recursive procedures for recursively-defined data structures.

recursiveness (rɪˈkɜːsɪvnɪs). [f. as prec. + -NESS.] The property of being recursive.

1936 *Amer. Jrnl. Math.* LVIII. 346 Since the results of the present paper were obtained, it has been shown by Kleene..that analogous results can be obtained entirely in terms of recursiveness, without making use of λ-definability. **1962** R. B. BRAITHWAITE in B. Meltzer tr. *Gödel's Formally Undecidable Propositions* 11 The notion of recursiveness has played a central part in metamathematics since Gödel's work on it. *Ibid.* 12 The importance of recursiveness for metamathematics in general lies in the fact that recursive definition enables every number in a recursively defined infinite sequence to be *constructed* according to a rule, so that a remark about the infinite sequence can be construed as a remark about the rule of construction and not as a remark about a given infinite totality. **1964** E. BACH *Introd. Transformational Gram.* ii. 16 In order to provide for an infinite number of terminal strings, a grammar must have a basic property called recursiveness. **1970** *Nature* 19 Dec. 1234/1 The concept of recursiveness was formulated in Gödel's sensational work in 1931 on the limitations of mechanical languages. **1975** G. SAMPSON *Form of Lang.* v. 89 As soon as we allow 'S' to appear on the right-hand side of one of the rules, the grammar acquires the property of 'recursiveness'.

recurvant (rɪˈkɜːvənt), *a.* *Her.* [ad. L. *recurvant-em*, pres. pple. of *recurvāre* to RECURVE.] Bowed, embowed, recurved. Also of a serpent: Coiled up, with the head raised to strike.

c **1828** BERRY *Encycl. Her.*

recurvate (rɪˈkɜːvət), *a.* [ad. L. *recurvāt-us*, pa. pple. of *recurvāre* to RECURVE.] Recurved.

1776 J. LEE *Introd. Bot.* Explan. Terms 382 *Recurvatum*, recurvate, bent backwards in the Form of an Arch, the convex Side upwards. **1866** *Treas. Bot.* 962/1 *Recurvate*, bent, but not rolled backwards. **1869** GILLMORE tr. *Figuier's Rept. & Birds* Introd. 185 By the anterior series of one barb over-lapping and hooking into the recurvate formation of the barb next to it.

recurvate (rɪˈkɜːveɪt), *v.* Now *rare.* [See prec. and RECURVE *v.*]

1. *trans.* To bend (a thing) back. *rare.*

1597 A. M. tr. *Guillemeau's Fr. Chirurg.* 34 b/2 We must then, with one finger, recurvate the end of the needle. **1656** in BLOUNT *Glossogr.*

b. In *pa. pple.* Bent backwards.

1597 A. M. tr. *Guillemeau's Fr. Chirurg.* lf. xiij b/2 An other bullet-drawer is hookishe and recurvated. **1666** HARVEY *Morb. Angl.* viii. 74 The Nails of those whose Lungs are Ulcerated, are recurvated or turn'd back like the claws of wild beasts. **1683-4** ROBINSON in *Phil. Trans.* XXIX. 482, I had a View of the Ibex..whose large Horns are recurvated almost as far back as the Tail. **1822-34** *Good's Study Med.* (ed. 4) III. 266 The spine is more strongly recurvated than ever, and forms an arch over the bed.

2. *intr.* Of a thing: To bend back; to recurve.

1822-34 [see *ppl. a.* below]. **1860** MAURY *Phys. Geog. Sea* (Low) iii. §174 These gales..march to the N. West until they join it [the Gulf Stream], when they 'recurvate', as the phrase is, and take up their line of march to the N. East.

Hence **re'curvating** *ppl. a.*

1822-34 *Good's Study Med.* (ed. 4) IV. 466 Wherever the skin was scratched, a calcareous fluid oozed from it, that soon hardened and put forth corneous, recurvating excrescences, frequently divaricating.

recurvation (riːkɜːˈveɪʃən). Now *rare.* [ad. L. type **recurvātiōn-em*, n. of action f. *recurvāre* to RECURVE.] The fact of being bent or curved back; a backward bend or curve.

1597 A. M. tr. *Guillemeau's Fr. Chirurg.* 44 b/1 In Fractures, dislocations, recurvatione of Ioynctes. **1599** —— tr. *Gabelhouer's Bk. Physicke* 114/1 Rubbe therwith the recurvatione of the backe. **1646** SIR T. BROWNE *Pseud. Ep.* 172 By a Serpentine and Trumpet recurvation it ascendeth againe into the neck. **1822** GOOD *Study Med.* IV. 326 The term Cyrtosis..among the ancients particularly imported recurvation of the spine, or posterior crookedness.

re'curvature. [See RECURVATE *a.* and -URE.] A backward curvature; recurving.

1729 SHELVOCKE *Artillery* IV. 199 Whalebone..naturally permitting itself to be bent..and inclining to a voluntary Recurvature. **1853** BIRT *Handbk. Storms* (1879) 58 It is very usual to consider that the points of recurvature are, to a certain extent, stable in each hemisphere.

† **recurve**, *a.* *Obs. rare.* [ad. L. *recurv-us*, f. *re-* RE- + *curvus* CURVE *a.*] Recurved.

1702 DRAKE in *Phil. Trans.* XXIII. 1225 In which it very much resembles Water inclos'd in a recurve Tube.

recurve (rɪˈkɜːv), *v.* [ad. L. *recurvāre* to bend (a thing) backwards, f. *re-* RE- + *curvāre* to CURVE.]

1. *trans.* To bend (a thing) back or backwards.

a. In active use. *rare.* Also *refl.*

1623 COCKERAM, *Recurue*, to bow backe againe. **1650** BULWER *Anthropomet.* 118 Unlesse the Larynx at the instant of deglutition should recurve itself upward. **1839-47** TODD *Cycl. Anat.* III. 202/1 Most of the glow-worms..recurve their tails upon their backs. **1890** *Nature* 20 Feb. 367/2 They have muscles by which they may be recurved, so that these points may be directed towards the throat.

b. In *pa. pple.* Bent backwards.
1597 A. M. tr. *Guillemeau's Fr. Chirurg.* 32 b/1 The muscles may lye in ther right places, and not be recurved this way or that waye. **1607** TOPSELL *Four-f. Beasts* (1658) 256 From the bottom to the middle they grow straight, but from thence they are a little recurved. **1748** *Phil. Trans.* XLV. 164 On the Crown of the Head stands a shining black Horn, recurved backward. **1835** KIRBY *Hab. & Inst. Anim.* I. ii. 66 Others, as the Friesland-hen, have the feathers on their body recurved. **1870** HOOKER *Stud. Flora* 241 Stigmas ..persistent, recurved.

2. *intr.* (Chiefly of a wind or current): To turn back in a curve upon its previous direction.
c **1850** *Rudim. Navig.* (Weale) 87 In recurving.., whirlwind storms will have a polar direction. **1853** BIRT *Handbk. Storms* (1879) 80 The direction of the cyclone of April 1847 would lead to the idea of its having recurved. **1875** BEDFORD *Sailor's Pocket-bk.* iv. (ed. 2) 111 A large part recurves to the Eastward, thus flowing into the Indian Ocean.

Hence **re'curving** *vbl. sb.* and *ppl. a.*
1853 BIRT *Handbk. Storms* (1879) 84 The great liability of a commander meeting a recurving cyclone. **1875** BEDFORD *Sailor's Pocket-bk.* iv. (ed. 2) 111 The remarkable recurving of the main body of the current is due to the action of a polar or cold water current flowing from the S.W. **1882** *Garden* 18 Mar. 189/3 A beautiful Orchid..furnished with narrow recurving foliage.

'recurve, *sb. Archery.* [f. the vb.] A backward-curving end of the limb of a bow; a bow designed with this feature. Also *attrib.*
1961 E. BURKE *Archery* i. 10 (*caption*) Named parts of the bow..recurve..upper limb..bowsight..lower limb..nock. **1962** G. H. GILLELAN *Young Sportsman's Guide to Archery* ii. 19 The other important bow design is the recurve, so named because its tips have a reverse curl. **1979** *Country Life* 26 July 287/1 The 'Bowhunter' style involves any type of bow, usually of a recurve construction, that is a combination of glass-fibre and wood..to buy a new bow works out as follows: long bow, £20–£50; recurve, £150–£180. **1980** *Hunting Ann. 1981* 81/3 For targets of opportunity, a recurve or long bow can be handled faster.

recurved (rɪ'kɜːvd), *ppl. a.* [f. RECURVE *v.* + -ED¹.] **a.** Bent back; having a backward curve. (Common esp. in scientific use.)
1597 A. M. tr. *Guillemeau's Fr. Chirurg.* lf. xvj b/2 The recurvede Needle for the sutures of the face. **1607** TOPSELL *Four-f. Beasts* (1658) 127 Having a short recurved body.. and a short tail. **1715** DESAGULIERS *Fires Impr.* 107 A recurv'd Canal with several turnings. **1785** MARTYN *Rousseau's Bot.* xxi. (1794) 297 Aconite has two recurved pedunculate nectaries. **1839** URE *Dict. Arts* 548 The recurved tube must be dipped..under the surface of the tarry liquid. **1870** YEATS *Nat. Hist. Comm.* 265 The common dog is distinguished from the wolf and jackal by its recurved tail. **1925** E. H. WILSON *Lilies E. Asia* 23 Flowers white, fragrant, funnel-shape, dilated, more or less recurved at the apex. **1936** D. WILKIE *Gentians* vi. 33 The calyx is tubular, and the lobes..are ovate and recurved. **1961** J. E. COLLIN *Brit. Flies* VI. I. 71 Proboscis not very stout nor much recurved. **1980** *Plantsman* I. 251 Both [lilies]..have delicate pendant flowers with slightly recurved petals.

b. In plant-names: (see quots.).
1820 T. GREEN *Universal Herbal* II. 860/1 *Ribes recurvatum*, Recurved Black Currant. **1877** S. C. *Ferns Brit. Isles* 27 *Lastrea Fœnisecii* (The Recurved Fern).

†**re'curvity.** *Obs. rare.* [See RECURVE *a.* and -ITY.] The fact of being recurved.
1668–9 SIR T. BROWNE *Let.* Wks. (Bohn) III. 512 Whereby the little incurvitie at the upper end of the upper bill, and small recurvitie of the lower is not discerned.

recurvo-, used in *Bot.* as comb. form of L. *recurvus*, as **re,curvo-'patent**, bent back and spreading; **re,curvo-'ternate**, bend back and divided into three parts.
1829 LOUDON *Encycl. Plants* Gloss. 1104 Recurvo-patent. **1867** J. HOGG *Microsc.* II. ii. 390 Recurvo-ternate defensive and aggressive spicula.

recurvous (rɪ'kɜːvəs), *a. rare.* [f. L. *recurv-us* RECURVE *a.* + -OUS.] Recurved, bent back.
1713 DERHAM *Phys.-Theol.* VIII. 401 *note*, In others I have observed long recurvous tails, longer than their whole bodies. **1832** G. DOWNES *Lett. Cont. Countries* I. 362 These buffaloes were black, with recurvous horns.

recus, obs. Sc. form of RECUSE.

recusal (rɪ'kjuːzəl). [f. RECUSE *v.* + -AL.] An objection to a judge as prejudiced.
1958 *Manch. Guardian* 5 Aug. 5/7 The submission to recusal was based on reports that incorrectly stated the facts. **1980** *Times* 30 Oct. 6/8 They should not feel that by making their applications for his recusal they had prejudiced their case.

recusance ('rɛkjuːzəns, rɪ'kjuːzəns). [f. as next: see -ANCE.] = next.
1597 in *Antiquary* (1881) Oct. 176/1 Being all most willing and ready without any recusance..still to be partakers of the Lorde's Supper at their own Parish Church. **1700** ASTRY tr. *Saavedra-Faxardo* II. 28 By which generous Recusance of that Crown on Earth he merited many more in Heaven. **1863** BARING-GOULD *Iceland* 230 Jon began to show signs of recusance. **1886** 'W. S. GREGG' *Irish Hist. for Eng. Readers* 54 The parliament now passed laws prohibiting Catholic worship, and imposing a fine of one shilling, payable each Sunday for recusance.

recusancy ('rɛkjuːzənsɪ, rɪ'kjuːzənsɪ). [ad. L. type **recūsantia*: see RECUSANT and -ANCY.] The action or practice characteristic of a recusant.
1. *Hist.* Refusal, especially on the part of Roman Catholics, to attend the services of the Church of England; from *c* 1570 to 1791 this was punishable by a fine, and involved many disabilities.
c **1600** NORDEN *Spec. Brit., Cornw.* (1728) 55 It is the howse of one Tregean, who for his and his wives recusancie ..his lande was suspended and himselfe nere 20 yeares imprisoned. **1618** DALTON *Countr. Just.* 82 Any popish Recusant..which is conuicted or indicted for recusancie or which hath not receiued the Communion twice the yeare past. **1679** EVELYN *Diary* 24 Apr., The Duke of York, voted against by the Commons for his recusancy, went over to Flanders. **1732** NEAL *Hist. Purit.* I. 588 He was for extending the Statute of Recusancy to them that went at any time to hear sermons from their own parish church. **1827** HALLAM *Const. Hist.* (1876) I. iii. 145 These grievous penalties on recusancy, as the wilful absence of catholics from church came now to be denominated. **1874** GREEN *Short Hist.* vii. §3. 371 Heavy 'fines for recusancy'..became a constant source of supply to the Royal exchequer.

†**b.** With *a*, an instance of this. *Obs.*
1624 DONNE *Devot.* III. Expost., I cannot say, I will come into thy house... It is not a Recusancy, for I would come, but it is an Excommunication, I must not. **1641** SMECTYMNUUS *Vind. Answ.* ii. 34 The Jesuitish Casuists begun to draw on the Papists to a Recusancie.

2. Refusal to obey some authority or command.
1597 J. KING *On Jonas* (1618) 37 The commission giuen to Ionas, we haue already weighed: it followeth that wee handle his recusancy and disobedience therein committed. **1655** FULLER *Ch. Hist.* VIII. ii. §46 Charging recusancy herein, as a sin on the soul of the refusers. **1816** SCOTT *Old Mort.* xi, There was one of my able-bodied men the other day who plainly refused to attend the wappen-schaw at my bidding. Is there no law for such recusancy, Colonel Grahame? **1868** KINGLAKE *Crimea* (1877) III. iii. 341 This sudden recusancy at the French Headquarters.

†**b.** Const. *of*; also with *inf. Obs. rare.*
1563 FOXE *A. & M.* 1408 He hath..iustly certified Hugh Raulins, person of Tynby, for his wilful recusancy of two other personages. **1655** FULLER *Ch. Hist.* VI. v. *False Miracles* §13 It happened that Abbot Whiting (the last of Glassenbury) was hanged thereon for his Recusancy to Surrender the Abbey.

recusant ('rɛkjuːzənt, rɪ'kjuːzənt), *sb.* and *a.* [ad. L. *recūsant-em*, pres. pple. of *recūsāre* to RECUSE. Cf. F. *récusant* (Littré).]

A. *sb.* **1.** *Hist.* One, especially a Roman Catholic (***Popish recusant***), who refused to attend the services of the Church of England.
1552–3 *Act 7 Edw. VI*, c. 4 §2 The Certificate of Recusauntes made by any of the said Archebyshoppes. **1583** BABINGTON *Commandm.* iv. (1637) 34 In my opinion our recusantes, as wee call them, that is, our refusing papists to come to church, doo greatly offende. **1598** HAKLUYT *Voy.* I. 595 The principall catholique recusants..were sent to remaine at certaine conuenient places. **1630** *R. Johnson's Kingd. & Commw.* 32 Though all our Recusants be the King of Englands subjects, yet too many of them be the King of Spaines servants. **1687** EVELYN *Diary* 10 Mar., They would not promise his Majesty their consent to the repeal of the Test and penal Statutes against Popish Recusants. *a* **1734** NORTH *Exam.* II. v. §78 (1740) 363 To present all Recusants, whereof the legal Definition was the not coming to Church for a Month. **1830** SCOTT *Demonol.* viii. 248 It appears that this remote county was full of Popish recusants. **1881** SHORTHOUSE *J. Inglesant* (1882) I. ii. 46 Many Papists who had conformed to the authority of the English Church..fell away, and became recusants.
transf. *a* **1635** CORBET *Poems* (1807) 73 Imagine now the sceane lyes in the hall; (For at high noone we are recusants all). **1640** SIR J. MENNES & SMITH *Wit's Recreat.* §174 Sith our Church him disciplin'd so sore He (rank Recusant) comes to Church no more.

b. Applied to other religious dissentients.
1777 WATSON *Philip II* (1793) II. XVIII. 370 By which the recusants were banished from the Netherlands. **1861** STANLEY *East. Ch.* iv. (1869) 143 It is impossible at this distance of time..to judge how far the recusants were influenced by an attachment to the positive doctrine of Arius. **1891** S. MOSTYN *Curatica* 121 Five of the recusants took away their hassocks..and worshipped with us no more.

2. One who refuses to submit to some authority, comply with some regulation or request, etc.
1616 BULLOKAR *Eng. Expos.*, *Recusant*, he that refuseth to doe any thing. **1621** FLETCHER *Wild Goose Chase* II. i, Since ye are so angry, And hold your Sister such a strong Recusant [etc.]. **1655** FULLER *Ch. Hist.* II. iv. §14 This Law did not presently find an universall Obedience in all the Land. And the Wonder is not great, if at the first making thereof it met with many Recusants. **1805** WORDSW. *Prelude* III. 67 All studded round... With loyal students faithful to their books, Half and half idlers, hardy recusants, And honest dunces. **1848** W. H. KELLY tr. *L. Blanc's Hist. Ten Y.* I. 521 Some refused compliance with the tariff. The recusants were adjudged to be in the wrong. **1867** FREEMAN *Norm. Conq.* (1876) I. App. 762 Dealing with the dominions of the recusant as being a forfeited fief.

b. Const. *against*, *of*, †*to*.
1599 H. BUTTES *Dyets Drie Dinner* To Country-men Rdrs., They are true Catholiques in matter of Dyet: no Recusants of any thing that is mans meate. **1638** FEATLY *Transubst.* 7 They are no lesse Recusants to your authority, then to our lawes. *a* **1661** HOLYDAY (J.), All that are recusants of holy rites. **1850** GROTE *Greece* II. lv. (1862) V. 23 All being recusants of the recent peace. **1879** *Contemp. Rev.* Oct. 293 All ill-conditioned recusants against the decrees of the local senate should be mulcted in heavy damages.

B. *adj.* **1.** Refusing to attend the parish church; dissenting.
1611 SPEED *Hist. Gt. Brit.* x. i. §54. 892 Catesby like-wise tooke in Ambrose Rookewood and Iohn Grant two Recusant Gentlemen. **1647** CLARENDON *Hist. Reb.* IV. §254 The Major part, albeit the Bishops and all the Recusant Lords were driven from thence, still opposed them. **1852** THACKERAY *Esmond* II. xiii, Do you know that your recusant Bishops wanted to consecrate him Bishop of Southampton? **1870** BURTON *Hist. Scot.* lxvi. (1873) VI. 56 In one instance, where they had failed to bring a recusant clergyman to reason, he rates them in this petulant manner.

2. Refusing to acknowledge authority or to do something commanded or desired.
1659 MILTON *Civ. Power* Wks. 1738 I. 554 The earnest expression of God's Displeasure on those Recusant Jews. **1828** MISS MITFORD *Village* Ser. III. (1863) 47 Master Sims tried his best coaxing and his best double X on the recusant players. **1847** GROTE *Greece* II. xxxiii. (1862) III. 195 The subjugation of the recusant Medes.

b. In predicative use. *rare.*
1820 SCOTT *Abbot* xix, Frieze-jacket wants to dance with stammel-waistcoat, but she is coy and recusant. **1850** GROTE *Greece* II. lv. (1862) V. 2 Though the peace was sworn,.. the most powerful members of the Spartan confederacy remained all recusant.

3. Making a recusation.
1726 AYLIFFE *Parergon* 453 If the Party Recusant has any Cause himself depending with the Judge, in the Judges private Capacity.

recusation (rɛkjuː'zeɪʃən). *Civil* and *Canon Law.* Now *rare.* [a. F. *récusation* (1332 in Godef. *Comp.*), or ad. L. *recūsātiōn-em*, n. of action f. *recūsāre* to RECUSE.] The interposition of an objection or appeal; *esp.* an appeal grounded on the judge's relationship or personal enmity to one of the parties.
c **1529** in Fiddes *Wolsey* II. (1726) 172 Yf this exception shuld be admytted as suffycyent cawse of recusation. *c* **1555** HARPSFIELD *Divorce Hen. VIII* (Camden) 181 The legates declared..that no such recusation..could or might by them be admitted. *a* **1648** LD. HERBERT *Hen. VIII* (1683) 488 After the Protestants had sent him their Recusation of the Council, He made a publick Protestation against it. **1726** AYLIFFE *Parergon* 451 Now this Recusation obtains when a Judge has either before the Suit commenc'd, or on the Cause itself render'd himself suspected to the Parties in Judgment on some Account or other. **1752** CARTE *Hist. Eng.* III. 88 That this might be done without any recusation or appeal, the Pope delegated all his authority to Wolsey. **1853** LADY DUFF GORDON tr. *Ranke's Ferd. & Maxim.* ix. 82 He opposed a formal recusation to the recess of Frankfurt.

†**re'cusative**, *a. Obs. rare*⁻¹. [ad. late L. *recūsātīv-us* prohibitory: see RECUSE and -IVE.] That tends to refuse or prohibit.
1660 JER. TAYLOR *Duct. Dubit.* IV. i. Rule 1 §8 The act of the will..is acquisitive and effective, or recusative and destructive, otherwise than it is in any other faculties.

†**re'cusator**, *a.* and *sb. Sc. Law. Obs. rare.* [f. as next: cf. *declarator*, *interlocutor*, etc.] **a.** *adj.* = next. **b.** *sb.* An exception taken to a judge as incompetent to try a case.
1561 *Reg. Privy Council Scot.* I. 172 Adherand to my recusatouris or declinatouris. **1609** SKENE *Reg. Maj.* 113 He sould not be hard afterward, to propone any exception declinatour, or recusatour against the Judge.

†**re'cusatory**, *a. Obs. rare.* [ad. L. type **recūsātōri-us*: see next and -ORY.] Of or belonging to recusing; containing a recusation.
1529 HEN. VIII in Burnet *Hist. Ref.* I. (1679) Rec. II. xxviii. 78 The Queen..did protest at the said day, putting in Libels Recusatories of the Judges. **1726** AYLIFFE *Parergon* 352 A recusatory Libel or Allegation ought to be offer'd before the Judge recus'd, if he be present in Court.

recuse (rɪ'kjuːz), *v.* Now *rare.* Also 5 *Sc.* recus. [ad. F. *récuser* (13th c. in Littré), ad. L. *recūsāre* to refuse, make an objection, f. *re-* RE- + *causa* CAUSE.]

†**1.** To refuse (a thing offered). *Obs. rare*⁻¹.
1387 TREVISA *Higden* (Rolls) VIII. 165 Wydomarus.. sente a greet deel of the tresour to kyng Richard. And he recused it [*v.r.* refusede; L. *recusavit*], and seide þat he schulde haue al by þe riȝt of his lordschippe.

2. To reject, renounce (a person, his authority, etc.); to object to (a judge) as prejudiced.
1387 TREVISA *Higden* (Rolls) VIII. 189 Kyng Iohn recusede [*v.r.* refused] and wolde in no wise fonge Stevene of Langtoun archebisshop of Caunterbury, þat was confermed by þe pope. *c* **1421** *Lett. Marg. Anjou & Bp. Beckington* (Camden) 28 He therfor hem utterly recuseth, and herto he fully him submitteth. **1563** FOXE *A. & M.* 721/2 And [I] also doo..refuse, recuse, and declyne you my sayde Lorde, and your said Colleages, and your iurisdiction vpon causes aforesayde. **1598** FLORIO, *Ricusare*, to refuse, to renounce, to recuse. **1638** LD. DIGBY, etc. *Lett. conc. Relig.* ii. (1651) 8 Their humility..will not let them be troubled when they are recused as judges. **1726** AYLIFFE *Parergon* 74 Unless he recus'd him as a suspected Judge, he ought to remain under his Jurisdiction. **1812** C. BUTLER in *Alban Butler's Lives Saints* (1836) I. p. xxviii, According to Thomas of Kempis (and what Catholic recuses his authority?). **1897** *Eng. Hist. Rev.* Oct. 634 The defendant would be able to 'recuse' judges against whom a specific charge of presumable partiality could be made.

†**b.** To reject (an appeal). *Obs. rare.*
1529 HEN. VIII in Burnet *Hist. Ref.* I. (1679) Rec. II. xxviii. 78 Yet she..[laid] in her Appeal, which also by the said judges was likewise recused.

†**c.** To refuse to submit to (a decree). *Obs.*
1721 STRYPE *Eccl. Mem.* I. I. xiii. 107 The Queen might at any time recuse and appeal from whatsoever decree or sentence she will.

†**3.** To refuse *to* do something. *Obs.*
1432–50 tr. *Higden* (Rolls) III. 273 The qwene..Vasthi recusenge to comme to hym was despisede. **1438** *Sc. Acts Jas. II* (1814) 32 Geyff þe schirra recus to do his offyce, or

be neclygent. **1521** *St. Papers Hen. VIII* (1830) I. 24 ThEmperours Ambassadors..do nowe recuse to treate junctly wyth the French Ambassadors. **1542** *Ibid.* (1849) IX. 154 The Turke..hath recusid to inprest soche monye as he promissid to the French King.

recussion (rɪˈkʌʃən). *rare.* [ad. L. type **recussiōn-em*, n. of action f. *recutĕre* to strike back.] The action of striking by return or recoil.

1854 *Tait's Mag.* XXI. 674 Wearied by an incessant strain of anxiety and labour for more than a month, and shocked by the recussion of peace.

recut (riːˈkʌt), *v.* [RE- 5 a.] To cut again.

1664 EVELYN *Sylva* (1776) 46 Some repeat the cutting.. the second year, and..recut them at half a foot from the surface. **1862** *Proc. Oxf. Archit. Soc.* 143 The inscription.. not having been altered and recut, as had been suggested. **1897** S. L. HINDE *Congo Arabs* 51 They cut and re-cut the skin from the root of the nose upwards to the hair.

recuyel(le), recuylle, obs. ff. RECOIL *v.*; varr. RECUEIL *sb.* and *v.*

recyclable (riːˈsaɪkləb(ə)l), *a.* [f. RECYCLE *v.* + -ABLE.] Capable of being recycled.

1971 *New Yorker* 4 Dec. 177 Publishers might do well to encase their pages and bindings in some sort of ersatz (but recyclable) horn. **1972** *Guardian* 30 Oct. 12/1 The shape of cars to come—a disposable commuter car which would be 'recycleable' after perhaps two years. **1976** *Nature* 6 May 66/2 Evidence suggests that net water flow from the rectal lumen to haemolymph results from increases in intercellular space osmotic pressure due to the transport across lateral cell membranes of recyclable intracellular solutes. **1979** *Observer* 30 Dec. 3/8 Theoretically they [*sc.* big plastic bottles] are recyclable, but actually they are constructed so as to make reclamation highly improbable.

Hence **reˌcyclaˈbility**.

1973 *Sci. Amer.* July 1 In terms of its attributes, its utility and recyclability, glass is a natural. **1978** *Jrnl. R. Soc. Arts* CXXVI. 609/2 Lifetime and recyclability of the product.

recycle (riːˈsaɪk(ə)l), *v.* Also re-cycle. [RE- 5 a.] **1.** *trans.* **a.** To reuse (a material) in an industrial process; to return to a previous stage of a cyclic process.

1926 [implied in RECYCLING *vbl. sb.*]. **1928** *Jrnl. Inst. Petroleum Technologists* XIV. 766 It is economically more advantageous to stop cracking in the first cycle when coke formation begins and produce more gasoline by re-cycling those fractions which do not form great quantities of coke during cracking. **1929** *Proc. R. Soc.* A. CXXIV. 43 It ought to be possible to obtain nearly the theoretically possible yield by returning to the reaction chamber or 'recycling' all the products formed except the gasoline. **1945** H. D. SMYTH *Gen. Acct. Devel. Atomic Energy Mil. Purposes* ix. 100 Any given sample of material is recycled many times. **1958** *Times* 17 Oct. 5/1 It is envisaged that plutonium produced in the working of the reactor will later be recycled through it. **1964** N. G. CLARK *Mod. Org. Chem.* iv. 62 Using only a small volume of solvent, which is continually re-cycled, it is possible to carry out the equivalent of many hundreds of separate extractions. **1972** *Sci. Amer.* Oct. 69/1 Their new process is the first closed-loop, spray-etching system that electrolytically reverses the chemical reaction of etching. It continuously recycles cupric chloride and has reduced the cost of etching wiring boards by over 90%. **1980** *Times* 7 Mar. 25/3 The uranium is recycled back to an enrichment plant to make new thermal-reactor fuel, and the plutonium is stored.

b. *spec.* To reuse (a waste material), to convert (waste) into or *into* a usable form; also, to reclaim (a material) from waste.

1960 *Aeroplane* XCIX. 521/2 It has systems which reduce all organic waste to a small amount of ash and recycle urine and waste water into drinkable water. **1967** *Technology Week* 23 Jan. 34/3 It would allow us to economically desalt sea and brackish water, recycle water from sewage. **1971** *Sci. Amer.* May 95/1 (Advt.), You bring us the cans and we'll recycle them. **1971** *New Yorker* 16 Oct. 33 What you ecology-minded ladies don't realize is that before a bottle can be recycled it has to be emptied. **1973** *Guardian* 22 Mar. 15/1 The Liberals of Kew..have been recycling paper, and have managed to scrape a regular £25 a month. **1974** *Listener* 28 Feb. 278/1 Such a plant would recycle steel, aluminium, zinc, lead and copper from scrap. **1979** *China Now* Mar./Apr. 31/3 The report covers all methods of recycling organic materials.

c. *transf.* in connection with natural processes. Usu. in *passive*.

1965 G. J. WILLIAMS *Econ. Geol. N.Z.* i. 2/2 These [beds of sediment] are of considerable interest to economic geologists for through them much detrital gold was recycled within and beyond the primary gold-bearing areas. **1970** *Nature* 17 Oct. 273/2 The annual discharge of dissolved sodium in rivers is about 20 × 10⁷ tons, of which 9 × 10⁷ tons have been recycled from the sea through the atmosphere. **1971** I. G. GASS et al. *Understanding Earth* iii. 68/2 Much of the ocean will be recycled in the ocean-floor spreading process. **1973** *Sci. Amer.* Apr. 61/1 Stars continually recycle their material through the interstellar medium.

d. *fig.*

1969 *Guardian* 12 May 1/5 (*heading*) Bankers find way to recycle hot money. **1970** *Nature* 25 July 321/2 It is not possible to recycle the output of the secondary schools without there being some intermediate opportunity for broadening the intellectual experience of the young men and women concerned. **1973** *Ibid.* 2 Mar. 4/2 A further five [cases] may be the result of the virus being recycled in swill. **1973** *Black Panther* 4 Aug. 7/3 Those workers finding themselves without jobs..are re-cycled back to their former jobs at the reduced wages. **1974** *Weekend Mag.* (Montreal) 16 Mar. 2/2 The kids are appropriating the Fifties, proving once more that fads (like garbage) can be recycled. **1974** *Newsweek* 7 Oct. 52/1 A new international banking system to recycle OPEC funds into loans to the poorer nations. **1978** *Washington Post* 8 Aug. C4/5 Many juveniles, he adds, are repeat offenders, 'recycled' through the system.

2. a. *trans.* To repeat (a process) on a computer or counting device; also *absol.* **b.** *intr.* Of a computer: to repeat a procedure.

1962 A. SHEPARD in *Into Orbit* 103 Walt decided to recycle the count—or set it back—to allow for this delay. **1973** *Sci. Amer.* May 110/3 The three input terminals of a NAND gate connected to Q_c, Q_d and Q_e of a series of five flip-flops would cause the apparatus to recycle on the count of 25 (11001). **1970** A. CAMERON et al. *Computer & O.E. Concordances* 47, I made a preliminary run and found a large number of keypunch errors that I had missed originally... I decided therefore to recycle.

3. *intr.* To undergo recycling.

1970 *Nature* 28 Nov. 856/2 The inability of most newly formed lymphocytes to recycle from blood to lymph could explain their truncated life span. **1975** *Ibid.* 24 July 247/1 The PhD degree is a relatively easy target to attack because its recipients do not seem to confer on society the same sort of benefits as, say, medical doctors. More recycle into the educational system than go elsewhere. **1978** *Amat. Photographer* 29 Nov. 128/3, I had noticed the unit appeared to be taking longer than usual to recycle after each shot, but assumed the battery was getting low.

Hence **reˈcycled** *ppl. a.*; **reˈcycling** *vbl. sb.*; ***recycling time*** (*Photogr.*), the time required to recharge the capacitor of a flash unit.

1926 *Petroleum Devel. & Technol. 1925* 338 With the use of higher pressures and temperatures permitting the ultimate cracking of this cut, more recycling of this fraction may be practiced. **1958** *Amat. Photographer* 31 Dec. 2/2 (Advt.), Angle 60°, recycling time 6 sec. **1964** M. GOWING *Britain & Atomic Energy 1939–1945* ix. 258 There were heavy losses of the product and of time in recycling and in washing and cleaning the machines. **1969** *Focal Encycl. Photogr.* (rev. ed.) 636/2 The recycling time and the number of flashes obtainable from a set of batteries..are also the subject of specific measurement methods. **1970** C. S. RUSSELL et al. *Drought & Water Supply* viii. 68 Only 46 percent..indicated a willingness to drink recycled domestic water. **1970** *Daily Tel.* 12 Sept. 5/7 They lived off their recycled body wastes. **1971** *Ibid.* 29 Apr. 14/6 The more than 9·1 million aluminium cans represent about 460,000 lb of litter and solid waste removed for complete recycling. **1972** *Guardian* 6 June 15/4 Recycling enthusiasts are.. collecting..old bottles and tin cans. **1975** *Nature* 17 Jan. 149/2 There is little commercial future for recycled glass in high grade uses at present. **1975** *N.Y. Times* 25 Oct. 27/3 The recycling boom is waning because of unfavorable economic conditions. **1977** *Financial Times* 4 June 5/3 Retreading is a form of recycling, which should be encouraged. **1978** D. BLOODWORTH *Crosstalk* xxiii. 180 He had driven the Deputy Director..half mad with his hesitation, his recycled arguments for accepting and not accepting.

recycle (riːˈsaɪk(ə)l), *sb.* Also re-cycle. [f. the vb.] The operation or process of recycling a material, etc.; also, the material itself. Orig. and freq. *attrib.*, usu. denoting material subjected to or set aside for recycling.

1926 *Petroleum Devel. & Technol. 1925* 339 The gas oil was returned to the cracking system as recycle charging stock. **1936** W. L. NELSON *Petroleum Refinery Engin.* iii. 19 Recycle stock has about the same boiling-range and.. physical characteristics as gas oil. **1939** *World Petroleum* Mar. 104/3 The asphalt bottoms produced are released through exchangers against reduced crude. They are blended with the cracked recycle gas oil and thence through the tar coolers to tankage. **1946** *Nature* 30 Nov. 800/1 The gradual deterioration in the quality of re-cycle benzene is due to the preferential accumulation of paraffins. **1961** *Engineering* 2 June 781/1 Reduce the cost of fuel burned by using plutonium recycle or spikes of fully enriched uranium. **1966** *McGraw-Hill Encycl. Sci. & Technol.* XIII. 185/2 The rich solution from the absorption step must be stripped in order to permit recovery of the absorbed solute and recycle of the solvent. **1975** *Nature* 13 Feb. 496/3 Recycle, or reuse of materials, is an important aspect of the proper management of these resources. *Ibid.* 2 Oct. 369/1 There is a great variety of possible schemes for incorporating a converter, or heat engine, into the heat recycle.

recycler (riːˈsaɪklə(r)). [f. RECYCLE *v.* + -ER[1].] One who or that which recycles (waste products, etc.).

1973 *Nature* 13 Apr. 483/3 Exhaust gas recyclers which cause an increase in the fuel consumption. **1974** *Ibid.* 19 Apr. 641/3 Developing..new manufacturing designs congenial to recyclers. **1976** *National Observer* (U.S.) 13 Mar. 8/2 With the emergence of the week-end home mechanic, the industry has tried to change its image from that of 'junk-yards keepers' to 'recyclers'.

recyclist (riːˈsaɪklɪst). *rare.* [f. as prec. + -IST.] An advocate of the recycling of waste products; a recycler.

1973 *Times* 1 Aug. 12/1 Perhaps pop artists were the first Recyclists.

recydivation, obs. f. RECIDIVATION.

recyt(e, obs. ff. RECEIPT *sb.*, RECITE *v.*

recyve, obs. f. RECEIVE *v.*

red (rɛd), *a.* and *sb.* Forms: 1 réad, 2–6 read(e, 3 ræd(en, 3–6 rede, reed(e, 4–6 redd(e, (*comp.* 4 raddore, 5 -ur), 4–8 *Sc.* reid, (6 rid), 2– red. [Comm. Teut.: OE. *réad* = OFris. *râd*, OS. (M.Du., MLG.) *rôd* (Du., LG. *rood*), OHG., MHG. *rōt* (mod.G. *roth, rot*), ON. *rauðr* (Sw., Da. *röd*), Goth. *rauþs*:—OTeut. **rauðo-z*:—pre-Teut. **roudho-s*, from the *o* grade of the ablaut series **reudh-, roudh-, rudh-*, widely represented in the cognate languages. Of the same grade as the Teut. forms are L. *rūfus*, OIr. *ruad(h)*, Lith. *raũda-s*; the other grades are represented by Gr. ἐρεύθειν to redden, OE. *réod*, ON. *rjóðr* red, ruddy, and L. *ruber*, Gr. ἐρυθρός, OSl. *rŭdrŭ*, Skr. *rudhirá-* red.

The original long vowel is retained in the surname variously written *Read(e, Rede, Reed* and *Reid*. The shortening in the adj. is parallel to the cases of *bread, dead, lead* sb.]

A. *adj.* **I.**

1. a. Having, or characterized by, the colour which appears at the lower or least refracted end of the visible spectrum, and is familiar in nature as that of blood, fire, various flowers (as the poppy and rose) and ripe fruits (whence the frequent similes ***red as blood, fire, a rose, cherry***, etc.).

The precise shades of colour to which the name of *red* is applied vary from bright scarlet or crimson to reddish yellow or brown (the latter esp. of the hair of certain animals). The numerous varieties are distinguished, when necessary, by prefixed nouns or adjectives, as *blood-, brick-, cherry-, fire-, flame-, flesh-, robin-, rose-red; dark, dull, light, lively red; fiery, foxy red; brown-, orange-, yellow-red; brownish, yellowish red*, etc. For examples of these, see the first element.

a **700** *Epinal Gloss.* 404 *Flavum vel fulfum*, read. *c* **725** *Corpus Gloss.* 1758 *Ruber*, read. *c* **888** K. ÆLFRED *Boeth.* xxxii. §3 Æʒðer ʒe hwite ʒimmas ʒe reade. *c* **897** —— *Gregory's Past. C.* xv. 94 On ʒemong ðæm bellum [sceoldon hangian] reade apla. *a* **1000** *Riddles* xxvii. 15 (Gr.) Se reada telg. *c* **1175** *Lamb. Hom.* 83 Alse þe sunne scineð þurh þe glesne ehþurl... ʒif þet gles is red ho schineð red. *c* **1205** LAY. 15940 Þe oder is milcwhit..þe oðer ræd alse blod. **1297** R. GLOUC. (Rolls) 2786 Tueye grete dragons out of þis stones come, þe on was red, þe oþer wyt. **1377** LANGL. *P. Pl.* B. II. 12 Hir fyngres were fretted with golde wyre And thereon red [*v.r.* rede] rubyes as red as any glede. *c* **1400** MAUNDEV. (1839) v. 57 In some place thereof is the Gravelle reede: and therefore Men clepen it the Rede See. **1432–50** tr. *Higden* (Rolls) I. 129 We wryte vn to this tyme the capitalle letters with a redde color. *a* **1500** *Flower & Leaf* 35 Leves new..Some very rede, and some a glad light grene. **1523** FITZHERB. *Husb.* §49 The pockes appere vppon the skyn, and are lyke reed pymples. *a* **1585** MONTGOMERIE *Cherrie & Slae* 229 The starnis..flew sa thick befoir my ein, Sum reid, sum ʒellow, blew, and grein. **1631** CHETTLE *Hoffmann* H ij b, The red lines Mixt with a deadly blacke will tell the world She died by violence. **1683** RAY *Corr.* (1848) 172 A sort of trefoil, with..bright purple or red flowers. **1726–46** THOMSON *Winter* 1060 The red marks Of superstition's scourge. **1794** COWPER *Needless Alarm* 19 Nor yet the hawthorn bore her berries red. **1836–41** BRANDE *Chem.* (ed. 5) 257 The former [sparks] are brilliant,..the latter usually of a paler or redder hue. **1882** G. MACDONALD *Castle Warlock* xxviii, The red wall, mottled and clouded with its lichens.

b. Of fire, flame, lightning, etc. (*lit.* and *fig.*), and of objects lit up by these.

In early use chiefly as a conventional epithet.

a **900** CYNEWULF *Crist* 809 Blac rasetteð recen reada leʒ. *a* **1000** *Cædmon's Gen.* 44 (Gr.) Ðeondfolen fyre & færcyle, rece & reade leʒe. *a* **1225** *Ancr. R.* 356 Fur is hot & read. *c* **1320** *Cast. Love* 719 Þe castel lihteþ al abouten, And is raddore þen euere eny rose schal; þat þuncheþ as hit barnde al. *c* **1374** CHAUCER *Troylus* III. 1633 Also seur as red is euery fir. *a* **1400–50** *Alexander* 4176 Þan fell þar fra þe firmament as it ware fell sparkis Ropand doun o rede fire. *c* **1470** HENRY *Wallace* VII. 428 Quhat euir he be, reskewis off that kyn Fra the rede fyr, him sellf sall pass tharin. **1533** BELLENDEN *Livy* I. xvi. (S.T.S.) I. 88 His hede apperit (as It war blesand) in ane rede low. **1593** SHAKS. *Lucr.* 1353 Two red fires in both their faces blazed. **1667** MILTON *P.L.* I. 175 The Thunder, Wing'd with red Lightning. **1727–46** THOMSON *Summer* 1148 The inconquerable lightning..Ragged and fierce or in red whirling balls. **1819** SHELLEY *Cyclops* 378 He strewed Upon the ground beside the red firelight His couch. **1855** KINGSLEY *Westw. Ho!* xxviii, The hills were red with bonfires in every village.

fig. **1655** tr. *Com. Hist. Francion* IV. 25 My rage doth kindle as red against him as ever. **1795–1804** W. BLAKE *Four Zoas* in *Compl. Writings* (1972) 336 Red rage redounds. **1892** W. B. YEATS *Countess Kathleen* ii. 34 God's red anger seize them. **1938** —— *Herne's Egg* iii. 28 The Great Herne himself And he in a red rage. **1952** DYLAN THOMAS *Coll. Poems* p. x, Of fear, rage red, manalive.

c. Of the sky or sun, esp. at dawn or sunset; hence of dawn, the east, etc.

c **950** *Lindisf. Gosp.* Matt. xvi. 2 Smolt bið; read is.. heofon. *c* **1122** *O.E. Chron.* (Laud MS.) an. 1117 On þære nihte..wæs seo heofon swyðe read ʒesewen. *a* **1400–50** *Alexander* 20 He recouerd..þe regions all clene And all rialme & þe riches into þe rede est. *c* **1440** *York Myst.* xvi. 7 The rakke of the rede sky. **1565** COOPER *Thesaurus* s.v. *Rubesco, Aurora rubescebat*, the morning waxed redde. **1592** SHAKS. *Ven. & Ad.* 453 Like a red morne that euer yet betokend Wracke to the sea man, tempest to the field. **1726–46** THOMSON *Winter* 721 Hence at eve, Steamd eager from the red horison round [etc.]. **1808** SCOTT *Marm.* IV. Introd. 55 When red hath set the beamless sun. **1815** SHELLEY *Alastor* 137 When red morn Made paler the pale moon. **1844** H. STEPHENS *Bk. Farm* I. 292 When the sun rises red, wind and rain may be expected during the day.

d. Of the cheeks (or complexion) and lips (as a natural healthy colour); hence also of persons.

a **1225** *Leg. Kath.* 1432 Mit se swiðe lufsume leores..se rudie & se reade. **13..** *Gaw. & Gr. Knt.* 1205 Wyth chynne & cheke ful swete, Boþe quit & red in-blande. *c* **1386** CHAUCER *Prol.* 153 Hir mouth [was] ful smal and ther to softe and reed. —— *Sir Thopas* 15 Hise lippes rede as rose. *c* **1420** *Anturs of Arth.* 161, I was reddere in rode þan rose in þe rayne. **1530** PALSGR. 322/1 Redde as ones lyppes or their chekes,..*vermeil*. **1601** SHAKS. *Twel. N.* I. v. 266 Two lippes indifferent red. **1687** A. LOVELL tr. *Thevenot's Trav.* I. 39 Women with big black Eyes, and red Cheeks. *a* **1720** SWIFT *Phyllis* 14 She..practised how to place her Head And bit her

Lips to make them red. **1798** COLERIDGE *Anc. Mar.* I. ix, The bride hath paced into the hall, Red as a rose as is she. **1824** BYRON *Juan* XVI. cxxi, A red lip with two rows of pearls beneath. **1894** G. MEREDITH *Lord Ormont* iii, His cheeks are as red as yours now you're blushing.

transf. **1862** BAGEHOT *Lit. Stud.* (1879) I. 246 Pope..had not the large red health that uncivilised women admire.

e. Of the hair (of men and animals) or beard.

1500–20 [implied in RED-HAIRED]. **1538** ELYOT Addit., *Aenobarbus*,..a Roman, so callyd bycause he had a berde as red as brasse. **1593** NASHE *Four Lett. Confut.* Wks. (Grosart) II. 220 [He had] a iolly long red peake,..[which] he cherisht continually without cutting. *a* **1625** FLETCHER *Love's Cure* II. i, Thou art a proper man, if thy beard were redder. **1727** BRADLEY *Fam. Dict.* s.v. *Hart*, The Coats and Colours of this noble Beast..are usually of three several sorts, viz. Brown, Red and Fallow. **1797** PINCKARD *Notes W. Ind.* xxix. (1816) II. 241 The hair,..from being slightly tinged with yellow, assumes..that particular hue, which is, more commonly than correctly, termed red. **1808** SCOTT *Marm.* VI. Introd. 19 While wildly loose their red locks fly. **1819** WARDEN *United States* I. 245 A tail about a foot long, and covered with red hair. **1855** KINGSLEY *Westw. Ho!* ii, A boat rowed by one with a red beard.

f. Of soil, earth, etc. Cf. RED LAND.

1623 CAPT. SMITH *Wks.* (Arb.) 626 The mold is of diuers colours..; the red which resembleth clay is the worst. *Ibid.*, The hardest kinde of it lies vnder the red ground. **1657** W. RAND tr. *Gassendi's Life Peiresc* II. 124 Vapours drawn up out of red earth aloft into the Air. **1706** LONDON & WISE *Retir'd Gard.* I. 371 Above a quarter of Kitchin-Garden Earth well sifted, more than of Red Mould. **1762** MILLS *Pract. Husb.* I. 53 The common opinion, that all hot grounds are red or brown..is..exploded by Columella. **1834** SCHOOLCRAFT *Exped.* 299 Little mounds of red earth frequently appeared above the grass. **1891** Q. *Noughts & Crosses* 217 The thin red soil of the ridge.

g. Combined with other colours in the same object, sometimes forming compound adjectives, as ***red-and-blue, red-and-white***, etc. (Cf. 17 f.) ***red, white, and blue***: the colours of the Union Jack, hence, the flag itself; also *attrib.* or as *adj.*, patriotic, devoted to the service of Britain.

c **1320** *Sir Tristr.* 2404 Þe king a welp he brouȝt..He was rede, grene & blewe. *c* **1330** R. BRUNNE *Chron.* (1810) 174 Þe sailes..som were blak & blo, Som were rede & grene. *c* **1470** HENRY *Wallace* VII. 93 A wand of colour reid and greyne. **1596** SHAKS. *Tam. Shr.* III. ii. 69 A kersey boot-hose..gartred with a red and blew list. **1855** D. T. SHAW *Britannia, Pride of Ocean* 1 May the Service United ne'er sever, And both to their Colours prove true, The Army and Navy for ever! Three cheers for the Red, White and Blue! **1857** LAWRENCE *Guy Liv.* xii. 110 Strong red and white spaniels. **1891** T. HARDY *Tess* xxxix, He observed..a red-and-blue placard. **1912** R. BROOKE *Lett.* (1968) 387 Aren't you, perhaps, going to lecture..about the British Empire, on 'Heart-Cries under the Red White and Blue', or some such title? **1971** *Scope* (S. Afr.) 19 Mar. 30/1 They were all that he was not; British in tradition; red-white-and-blue in sentiment. **1972** P. LOVESEY *Abracadaver* xv. 191 Our careers are *dedicated* to the red, white and blue. There's no need to remind us where our duty lies. **1974** *Times* 24 Aug. 2/2 Anyone joining his organization had his background checked 'to avoid communist infiltration... If the man has a red, white and blue background, then he is okay'. **1977** *Sniffin' Glue* July 21 He just averts his gaze to the red white and blue and exchanges nothings with the silly mayor.

h. ***to paint the town red***: see PAINT *v.*[1] 10.

2. a. As an epithet (chiefly *poet.*) of blood.

c **1205** LAY. 30412 Urnen þa brockes of reden blodes. **1297** R. GLOUC. (Rolls) 1124 Al þe erþe aboute stod as in flode..al of rede blode. *c* **1386** CHAUCER *Sqr.'s T.* 415 The rede blood Ran endelong the tree ther she stood. *c* **1470** *Golagros & Gaw.* 306 Thai brochit blonkis to thair sidis brist of rede blude. **1562** J. HEYWOOD *Prov. & Epigr.* (1867) 135 The red bloud may run downe in thy necke. **1593** SHAKS. *Lucr.* 1437 To Simois reedie bankes the red bloud ran. *a* **1755** *Edom o' Gordon* xix. in Child *Ballads* III. 434/1 Clear, clear was hir yellow hair, Whereon the reid bluid dreips! **1805** SCOTT *Last Minstr.* v. xxi, I have..Seen through red blood the war-horse dashing.

b. In pregnant uses, implying superior quality or value.

1596 SHAKS. *Merch. V.* II. i. 7 Let vs make incision for your loue, To proue whose blood is reddest, his or mine. **1824** SCOTT *Redgauntlet* ch. xi, His blood was too red to be spared when that sort of paint was in request. **1852** DICKENS *Bleak Ho.* xxviii, Inasmuch as very red blood of the superior quality, like inferior blood unlawfully shed, will cry aloud.

3. a. As a conventional (chiefly *poet.*) epithet of gold. Now only *arch.*

This use is also found in other Teut. languages. For *red gold* in mod. technical use see 19 and GOLD *sb.* 5.

a **1000** *Cædmon's Gen.* 2404 (Gr.) Hi..ȝesawon ofer since salo hlifian, reced ofer readum golde. *c* **1000** ÆLFRIC *Hom.* I. 64 He..ða grenan ȝyrda ȝebletsode and hi wurdon to readum golde awende. *c* **1122** *O.E. Chron.* (Laud MS.) an. 1070 Þet fotspure..wæs eall of read golde. *c* **1205** LAY. 23309 He sende..swiðe gode horsses seoluer and red gold. *a* **1300** *Cursor M.* 4763 Þof þai had siluer and gold red þai moght noght find to bi þam bred. *c* **1400** *Destr. Troy* 1742 We haue riches full rife, red golde fyn. **1535** STEWART *Cron. Scot.* II. 98 Sex thousand ȝeirlie..Into tribute of fynest gold so reid. **1818** SCOTT *Br. Lamm.* ii, From the red gold keep thy finger. **1865** SWINBURNE *Chastelard* v. i. 141 The men of Pharaoh's, beautiful with red And with red gold. **1892** W. B. YEATS *Countess Kathleen* i. 18, I am half mindful to go pray to him To cover all this table with red gold. **1931** M. ALLINGHAM *Look to Lady* xiii. 144 The real Chalice..is made of English red gold.

b. Golden, made of gold. Now only *slang.* † ***red ones***, gold coins; also ***red 'un***, a sovereign.

1375 BARBOUR *Bruce* XIII. 463 Sevin hundreth paris of spuris rede War tane of knychtis that war dede. **1377** LANGL. *P. Pl.* B. xv. 501 Now is routhe to rede how þe red noble Is reuerenced or þe Rode. [*a* **1400** *Isumbras* 295, I salle the gyffe tene thowsand pownde of florence that bene rede and rownde.] **1568** T. HOWELL *Poems* (Grosart) I. 91 Besides all this, ich shall not mis of red ones to haue store. *a* **1625** FLETCHER *Mad Lover* v. iv, There's a red rogue to buy thee handkerchiefs. **1816** SCOTT *Antiq.* I. xv. 325 It's a red half-guinea to him every time he mounts his mare. **1879** *Macm. Mag.* Oct. 502/2, I touched for a red toy (gold watch) and red tackle (gold chain). **1890** in Barrère & Leland *Dict. Slang* II. 175/1 The youth, her wish obeying, placed a coin down—gently saying—'There's a red 'un—or in other words "a quid!"' **1896** A. MORRISON *Child of the Jago* 61 Sich a nice watch,—a red 'un an' all. **1899** C. ROOK *Hooligan Nights* ii. 25 Honest work..will bring in but a few shillings a week; and what is that compared to the glorious possibility of nicking a red 'un? **1901** G. B. SHAW *Capt. Brassbound's Conversion* II. 265 E'll give huz fawv unnerd red uns. **1905** *Hackney & Kingsland Gazette* 15 Sept. 3/7 He said 'Here comes a German with a red lot (gold chain, etc.). If you have heart, pull it.' **1981** A. HEWINS *Dillen* iii. 20, I don't think much o' that stone you got. I'll give you a nice red un for it.

c. orig. *U.S.* As an epithet of the cent (formerly made of copper), usually in negative expressions. Also (*U.S.*) in phr. ***nary (a) red (cent)***: see NARY *a.*

c **1839** J. S. JONES *People's Lawyer* (1856) I. i. 8 It would not have cost you a red cent. **1852** BRISTED *Upper Ten Thou.* vi. 144 It was a great catch for Miss Lewison, without a red cent of her own. **1889** *Sir Ch. Danvers* xxix, I don't care a red cent what you say. **1900** W. ARCHER *Let.* 1 Feb. in C. Archer *William Archer* (1931) xii. 263 We have never agreed about plays, and we never will... I have never given a red cent for the ideas in plays. **1904** KIPLING *Traffics & Discoveries* 23 I'd turned in every red cent on the Zigler. **1943** K. TENNANT *Ride on Stranger* xvii. 188 'To think of it,' groaned George Benson. 'We don't get a red cent, not a flaming red cent.' **1958** J. CAREW *Black Midas* ix. 193 He will pay you seven dollar..and not a red cent extra. **1976** T. SHARPE *Wilt* xiii. 135 'I'll alimony you for all the money you've got.' 'Fat chance. You won't get a red cent.' **1979** *Tucson Mag.* Apr. 34/3 In ten years, the city has not spent one red cent from any federal funds for Barrio Historico.

4. Of cloth, clothing, etc.: Dyed with red.

See also RED FLAG, RED SHIRT; *red hat* (of cardinals): see HAT *sb.* 3, and 18 a below.

c **1000** ÆLFRIC *Hom.* II. 252 Hi..hine unscryddon þam readan wæfelse. *c* **1290** *S. Eng. Leg.* I. 302/92 With rede palles huy weren i-heoled þe faireste þat miȝten beo. **13..** *Gaw. & Gr. Knt.* 2036 Vpon þat ryol red cloþe þat riche was to schewe. **1382** WYCLIF *Isa.* lxiii. 2 Why thanne red is thi clothing? **1411** *E.E. Wills* 19 A pallette couerte with reede velwette. *Ibid.*, A reed bedde of worsteyd. **1470–85** MALORY *Arthur* x. lix, Thenne..came a ryche vessel hylled ouer with reed sylke. **1568** GRAFTON *Chron.* II. 633 The Erle of Warwike, whose seruiture were appareiled in red Cotes. **1617** MORYSON *Itin.* II. 177 A valiant Gentleman, marked by a red cap he wore. *a* **1654** SELDEN *Table-t.* (Arb.) 77 All that wear Red Ribbons in their Hats. *a* **1729** SWIFT *Macer* 4 'Twas all th' Ambition his great Soul could feel To wear red Stockings. **1782** COWPER *Gilpin* 75 Then over all..His long red cloak..He manfully did throw. **1895** F. ANSTEY *Lyre & Lancet* I. 7 A..revolutionary poet..in a flannel shirt and no tie—or else a red one.

5. a. Of persons: Having red hair; †of a red or ruddy complexion.

c **1000** ÆLFRIC *Gen.* xxv. 25 Se þe æror com se wæs read and eall ruh and his nama wæs ȝenemned Esau. *c* **1290** *S. Eng. Leg.* I. 76/206 Willam þe rede king þat after willam bastard cam. *Ibid.* 319/686 Ho-so hath of fuyre mest he is smal and red Oþur he is blac with cripse here. **1422** tr. *Secreta Secret., Priv. Priv.* 229 Tho that bene rede men, bene..trechurus, and full of queyntise, i-likenyd to Foxis. **1460** CAPGRAVE *Chron.* (Rolls) 130 William the Rede was crouned in the ȝere of oure Lord m.lxxxvi. **1565** COOPER *Thesaurus*, *Rufus*, somewhat redde; one that hath a redde head. **1598** FLORIO, *Rossa*, red, a red-woman. **1612** DAVIES *Why Ireland*, etc. (1747) 188 Richard Bourk Earl of Ulster (commonly called the Redde-earl). **1774** GOLDSM. *Nat. Hist.* (1776) II. 232 In all regions, the children are born fair or at least red. **1808** SCOTT *Marm.* VI. iv, From Red De Clare, stout Gloster's Earl. **1849** *Fraser's Mag.* XXXIX. 490 Laudations of such persons as Hugh O'Neill and the Red O'Donnell and others. **1922** JOYCE *Ulysses* 23 You know that red Carlisle girl, Lily?

b. Of animals: Having red or reddish hair; tawny, chestnut, or bay.

1382 WYCLIF *Num.* xix. 2 A reede kowe of hool age in the which no spot be. —— *Zech.* i. 8 Loo! a man stynge vp a rede hors;..and after hym horsis dyuerse, rede, and white. *c* **1420** *Pallad. on Husb.* IV. 913 A staloun asse..al blaak Or moushered or reed. **1432–50** tr. *Higden* (Rolls) I. 359 Some of theim causenge redde swyne thro wycchecrafte [etc.]. *c* **1450** *M.E. Med. Bk.* (Heinrich) 203 Tak hony..& grece of a red barow. *Ibid.* 207 Tempre wyþ mylk of a red cow. **1535** COVERDALE *Zech.* vi. 2 In the first charet were reade horse, in the seconde charet were blacke horse. **1651** BARKER *Art of Angling* (1820) 7 The wooll of a red Heyfer makes a good body. **1855** KINGSLEY *Westw. Ho!* vii, The red cattle lowed to each other. **1882** MISS BRADDON *Mt. Royal* III. i. 16 Master had the red setter with him this morning, when he went for his stroll. **1892** R. KIPLING *Barrack-r. Ballads, East & West* 78 The red mare played with the snaffle-bars.

c. Of certain peoples, esp. the North American Indians: Having (or regarded as having) a reddish skin. ***Red Indian***: see INDIAN *sb.* 2 b. See also RED MAN, RED SKIN.

1587 GOLDING *De Mornay* ii. 21 Hee maketh some folkes whyte, some blacke, some read, and some Tawny; and yet is hee but one selfesame Sunne. **1765** in S. P. Hildreth *Pioneer History* (1848) 79 We, red people, are a very jealous people. **1808** PIKE *Sources Mississ.* II. (1810) 122, I was obliged to convince my red brethren that, if I protected them, I would not suffer them to plunder my men with impunity. **1836** W. IRVING *Astoria* II. 8 In the evening the red warriors entertained their white friends with dances and songs. **1889** I. TAYLOR *Orig. Aryans* iv. 198 The half-castes between Europeans and Maoris are unmistakeably red without any tendency to yellow.

6. Wearing red clothing (uniform, livery) or armour. Now *rare.*

a **1400** *Sir Perc.* 50 Wolde he none forsake, The rede knyghte ne the blake. *c* **1470** HENRY *Wallace* IX. 87 The Rede Reffayr thai call him [cf. 106 His cot armour is..ay off reide]. **1470–85** MALORY *Arthur* VII. xvi, The reed knyghte of the reed laundes. **1841** THACKERAY *Chron. Drum* II. xii, He had fought the red English, he said, In many a battle of Spain. **1886** [see *red soldier* in 19].

7. a. Of the face, or of persons in respect of it: Temporarily suffused with blood, esp. as the result of some sudden feeling or emotion; flushed or blushing *with* (anger, shame, etc.); esp. in phr. ***red face***, a sign of embarrassment or shame.

c **1205** LAY. 29597 For þan ilke dede heo habbeð neb rede. *c* **1374** CHAUCER *Troylus* I. 811 (867) He was hit, and wax al red for shame. *c* **1386** —— *Can. Yeom. Prol. & T.* 542 For shame of hym my chekes wexen rede. *c* **1450** HOLLAND *Howlat* 816 The dene rurale worthit reid, Stawe for schame of the steid. **1450–80** tr. *Secreta Secret.* 38 His visage wexith reed.., and the teeres fallen in his eyene whan thou blamyst him. **1592** SHAKS. *Ven. & Ad.* 35 She red, and hot, as coles of glowing fier, He red for shame. **1611** —— *Wint. T.* IV. iv. 54 Addresse your selfe to entertaine them sprightly, And let's be red with mirth. **1653** MILTON *Ps.* vi. 22 Mine enemies shall..then grow red with shame. **1855** KINGSLEY *Westw. Ho!* ii, The churchwardens..bustled themselves hot, and red, and frantic. **1866** G. MACDONALD *Ann. Q. Neighb.* xiv. (1878) 295 Tom's face was as red with delight, as his sister's had been with anger. **1937** PARTRIDGE *Dict. Slang* 692/1 *Red face* (or *neck*), *have a*, to be ashamed. **1973** *Listener* 14 June 786/1 Mediterranean weather caused red faces among long-range weather-men who had to confess they'd got June wrong so far. **1977** *Listener* 30 June 865/1 The celebrated Samuel Palmer fakes..that have left so many red faces in the world of fine art. **1980** B. PARVIN *Death in Past* v. 30 She..grabbed me and said: 'It's true—I'm going to have a baby!' Was my face red! **1981** L. DEIGHTON *XPD* iii. 13 There was secret material..[that] would have caused a few red faces here in Whitehall.

transf. **1820** L. HUNT *Indicator* No. 14 (1822) I. 112 Millions of times did the sense of the impotence of his wish run up in red hurry to his cheeks.

b. Exceptionally high in colour.

1422 tr. *Secreta Secret., Priv. Priv.* 229 Tho that haue the face somewhate ruddy..Tho that have the chekys al reede as thay were dronken. **1483** CAXTON *G. de la Tour* L i j b, He ..was reed as a cok and had a good lyuynge colour. **1577** HARRISON *England* in *Holinshed* I. 85/2 Tyll they be read as cockes. and litle wyser then their combes. **1689** HICKERINGILL *Ceremony-Monger* Concl. iii. Wks. 1716 II. 472 The Lazy Fat Prebend and Ceremony-Monger..is as Red in the Gills as a Turkey-cock, or his Scarlet-hood.

8. a. Stained or covered with blood. Used *absol.*, and const. *with* (†or *of*) blood, gore, etc.

[*a* **1225** *Ancr. R.* 402 Ȝe hit schulen makien of reades monnes blode; þet is Jesu Crist i-readed mid his owune blode oðe rode.] *a* **1300** *Cursor M.* 20075 Mi fete, mi hend, o blod er red. **1375** BARBOUR *Bruce* II. 361 The gres woux off the blud all rede. *c* **1450** *Mirour Saluacioun* 1616 Ye stretes of Jerusalem with thaire blode made he rede. *c* **1500** *Melusine* 352 The grounde was there soone dyed rede with grete effusyon of blood. **1601** SHAKS. *Jul. C.* III. i. 109 Wauing our red Weapons o're our heads, Let's all cry Peace, Freedome, and Liberty. **1738** GRAY *Propertius* III. 46 Sad Philippi, red with Roman Gore. **1796** SCOTT *Will. & Helen* 211 The scourge is red, the spur drops blood. **1808** —— *Marm.* VI. xxxiv, To tell red Flodden's dismal tale. **1855** KINGSLEY *Westw. Ho!* ix, The Fort del Oro was a red shamble. **1893** F. ADAMS *New Egypt* 17 The Ptolemies quenched more than one savage insurrection with red hands.

fig. **1813** COLERIDGE *Sibyl. Leaves, Night Scene* 65, I swore to her that were she red with guilt, I would exchange my unblenched state with hers.

transf. **1816** BYRON *Ch. Har.* III. xxviii, Rider and horse—friend, foe—in one red burial blent. **1894** G. MEREDITH *Lord Ormont* xxv, The dull red facts [of the duel] had to be disengaged from his manner of speech.

b. Shedding blood.

1806 G. GALLOWAY *Poems* 23 Adieu to New Year's din and quarrel, Base chat, red blows. **1882** G. MACDONALD *Castle Warlock* xxix, It cam o' bluid-guiltiness—for 'at he had liftit the reid han' again' his neibour.

c. Of meat: Full of, coloured with, blood. See also *red meat*, sense 19 a.

1837 M. DONOVAN *Dom. Econ.* II. 109 The cow-calf is whiter veal: but the bull-calf, although redder, is better meat.

d. Consisting of blood.

1816 BYRON *Ch. Har.* III. xvii, How that red rain hath made the harvest grow.

9. a. Marked or characterized by blood or fire, or by violence suggestive of these. (In later quots. with implication of b.)

1297 R. GLOUC. (Rolls) 1142 It [the sword] was rede deþ icluped & mid riȝte. *c* **1386** CHAUCER *Knt.'s T.* 889 Ye shal be deed by myghty Mars the rede. **1631** CHETTLE *Hoffman* I. C iv, Till red reuenge in robes of fire, and madding mischiefe runne and raue. *Ibid.* H iij, The heate Of our sad torment, and red sufferings. **1667** MILTON *P.L.* II. 174 What if..from above Should intermitted vengeance Arme again His red right hand to plague us? **1729** SAVAGE *Wanderer* IV, Red Massacres thro' their Republic fly. **1781** COWPER *Truth* 278 Justice..Drops the red vengeance from his willing hand. **1812** BYRON *Ch. Har.* I. xxxviii, Red Battle stamps his foot and nations feel the shock. **1850** TENNYSON *In Mem.* cxxvii, Tho' thrice again The red fool-fury of the Seine Should pile her barricades with dead.

transf. **1851** MAYNE REID *Scalp Hunt.* xvii. 115 You have heard the stories of the mountain men in all their red exaggeration. **1859** JEPHSON *Brittany* xvi. 265 Happy news to the Bretons! and red maledictions to the French!

b. Anarchistic, revolutionary. Also, Bolshevik, communist; freq. *spec.* of or pertaining to the U.S.S.R.; ***red revolution***, a socialist or communist revolution.

Referring originally to the colour of a party badge, but now frequently associated with prec.

1848, etc. [see RED REPUBLIC]. [**1849** *Tait's Mag.* XVI. 402/2 Germany itself is red with Socialism and a desire for Republicanism.] **1864** *Spectator* 16 Apr. 443/2 England is not Red..but she does sympathise heartily with Garibaldi's immediate ends. **1883** *Pall Mall G.* 2 Feb. 1/2 The Dynamitards have not secured the return of a single deputy even for the 'reddest' constituency in France. **1917** [see RED GUARD 1 a]. **1919** *Times* 7 Oct. 4/3 That I was prepared to create a Red Revolution in England..is something which I have never said. **1920** *Blackw. Mag.* Sept. 404/2 The Red Government, still bent upon the destruction of Europe, was ..recognised. **1924** R. MACAULAY *Orphan Island* xix. 252 It is mainly a catalogue of grievances, together with rousing addresses... 'What we call Red journalism.' **1926** *Brit. Gaz.* 12 May 3/6 After an attempt to hold a 'Red' Meeting in Edgware-road, a crowd of about 2,000 people was said to have collected and arrests were made by the police. **1927** W. E. COLLINSON *Contemp. Eng.* 85 The spread of the Bolshevistic propaganda has led to the fear, lest Labour should go red. **1929** J. BUCHAN *Courts of Morning* I. 129 The Scotsman had become their special intimate... Judson, who seemed to have known him before, called him Red Geordie. **1934** *Discovery* Feb. 55/2 All along that frontier, every three hundred yards, there are Red soldiers with rifle and machine-gun. **1940** W. EMPSON *Gathering Storm* 49 Revolt and mercy fired no sparks In the Red argument at all. **1948** E. B. WHITE *Let.* 24 Jan. (1976) 290 My desk got so deep in Red literature that I had to fumigate myself every night before going home. **1951** *Sun* (Baltimore) 19 June 7/1 Count Wolf von Westarp, co-founder of the band of neo-Nazis, .. has indignantly denied any Red ties. **1958** *Spectator* 6 June 723/2 There are still hundreds of writers in gaol all over the Red Empire, not to mention Franco's or Salazar's prisons. **1965** B. PEARCE tr. *Preobrazhensky's New Econ.* 189 The red managers, proletarian engineers, and business executives have no monopoly of the means of production. **1970** M. O'BRINE *Crambo* lii. 193 He is still a Red Navy man. He has the right to be buried at sea. **1972** D. BLOODWORTH *Any Number can Play* ii. 9 He infuriated the communists because he ran too just and egalitarian a kingdom to suit the sacred cause of red revolution. **1976** G. MANSELL *Why External Broadcasting?* 18 Other totalitarianisms, whether of the red or the black variety. **1981** *Times* 3 Mar. 13/2 Anything is better than the horrors of nuclear war..better red than dead. **1981** *Time Out* 24–30 Apr. 7/4 Rosenthal and her fellow-candidates will be..hoping that Sir Horace Cutler's deepest fears of a 'red' London are realized.

10. Heated to redness; red-hot, glowing.

a **1225** *Ancr. R.* 356 Ne kumeð non into Parais bute þuruh þisse leitinde sweorde, þet was hot & read. *c* **1375** *Sc. Leg. Saints* xix. (*Christopher*) 550 þane gert þe kinge ane helme tak & in þe fyre It red al mak. *c* **1385** CHAUCER *L.G.W.* Prol. 235 Twoo firy dartes as the gledes rede. **1430–40** LYDG. *Bochas* IX. xxxii. (1558) 33 b, As I haue tolde, in coles rede His hande he brent for loue of his cite. **1500–20** DUNBAR *Poems* xxvi. 87 They wer full strenge of countenance, Lyk turkass birnand reid. **1605** SHAKS. *Lear* III. vi. 16 To haue a thousand with red burning spits Come hizzing in vpon 'em. **1684** J. PETER *Siege Vienna* 108 Bellows for Red Bullets. **1741** tr. *Cramer's Assaying* 20 Filings of Iron..being presently made red in the Crucible. **1784** COWPER *Task* IV. 289 A waking dream of houses, towers...expressed In the red cinders. **1868** JOYNSON *Metals* 117 Scales that fall from the red iron hammered at the blacksmith's anvil.

11. Of the eyes: (*a*) Naturally of a red colour. (*b*) Bloodshot. (*c*) Inflamed, esp. with weeping.

13.. *Gaw. & Gr. Knt.* 304 Runischly his rede y3en he reled aboute. *c* **1550** LLOYD *Treas. Health* H v b, To haue his mouth open with reed eyes. **1601** SHAKS. *Jul. C.* III. ii. 120 Poore soule, his eyes are red as fire with weeping. **1607** TOPSELL *Four-f. Beasts* (1658) 460 The eies of a Lyon are red, fiery, and hollow. **1676** WISEMAN *Chirurg. Treat.* 313 In the beginning the Eyes look red. **1729** SAVAGE *Wanderer* I I, Death in her Hand, and Frenzy in her Eye! Her Eye all red, and sunk! **1788** COWPER *Death Bullfinch* i, Ye Nymphs if e'er your eyes were red With tears. **1813** SCOTT *Rokeby* III. vi, The snake..Watches with red and glistening eye. **1823** BYRON *Juan* VIII. cxix, Their bloodshot eyes all red with strife. **1855** KINGSLEY *Westw. Ho!* xx, Amyas was pacing the deck, ..his eyes red with rage and weeping.

II. In combinations.

12. a. With substantives, forming attributive compounds as ***red-brick*** (floor), ***red-leather*** (trunk), etc.

1915 J. LONDON *Let.* 5 Nov. (1966) 463, I go ahead content to be admired for my *red-blood brutality. **1925** V. WOOLF *Common Reader* 262 The high-brow public and the red-blood public. **1943** WYNDHAM LEWIS *Let.* 8 Aug. (1963) 360 The vulgarly red-blood American attitude (the lady and gentlemen complex). **1976** A. J. RUSSELL *Pour Hemlock* (1979) ii. 19 I'm not their kind of people... This is a Redblood administration, I'm a Mollycoddle. **1835** WILLIS *Pencillings* I. xi. 83 We obeyed the call of our *red-bonnet guide. **1841** LEVER *C. O'Malley* iii. 19 It's a *red-breeches day, Master Charles. **1918** D. H. LAWRENCE *New Poems* 15 As it guards the wild north cloud-coasts, *red-fire seas runnning through The rocks. **13..** *Gaw. & Gr. Knt.* 1817 Ho ra3t hym a riche rynk of *red golde werkez. **1550** LYNDESAY *Sqr. Meldrum* 8 Hir hair was like the reid gold wyre. **1767** COWPER *Let. to J. Hill* 14 May, I was once the happy owner of a *red-leather trunk. **1913** D. H. LAWRENCE *Love Poems & Others* 33 The subtle, steady rush..of advancing God..Is heard..In the tapping haste of a fallen leaf, In the flapping of *red-roof smoke. **1592** SHAKS. *Ven. & Ad.* 110 Leading him prisoner in a *red-rose chaine. *c* **1610** *Women Saints* 151 Being rinsed in her owne red rose bloud. **1895** W. B. YEATS *Poems* 234 The red-rose-bordered hem. **1942** W. STEVENS *Notes toward Supreme Fiction* 36 The channel slots of rain, the red-rose-red. **1837** THACKERAY *Ravenswing* i, The little *red-silk cottage piano. **1870** MORRIS *Earthly Par.* IV. 52 The *red-throat jay screamed not for nought. **1754** BARTLET *Gentl. Farriery* (ed. 2) 243 Apply..a poultice with *red wine lees. **1877** E. S. DALLAS *Kettner's Bk. of Table* 376 *Matelote Relish*, small onions and mushrooms in a red-wine sauce. *Ibid.* 483 It is difficult to procure the mild red-wine vinegar in London. **1943** E. M. ALMEDINGEN *Frossia* iv. 192 A nice plump partridge, red wine sauce, and cranberry jelly. **1971** *Vogue* 15 Sept. 125/2, I had chicken in red wine sauce with mushrooms and bacon.

b. In specific names or designations, chiefly of animals, birds, and trees, as ***red-bar parrot, red-bead snake***, etc. (see quots.); **red-bead tree**, a leguminous timber-tree, *Ormosia dasycarpa* (also called *bead-tree* and *necklace-tree*), having red bead-like seeds; **red-bead vine**, the coral-bead plant, *Abrus precatorius* (see CORAL *sb.*[1] 9); **red-bean tree**, a species of *Erythrina* (cf. *coral-bean*); **red-ink plant**, the Virginian pokeweed, *Phytolacca decandra*. See also RED-COAT, -HEART, -TOP, -WING.

1811 SHAW *Gen. Zool.* VIII. II. 510 *Red-Bar Parrot. *Psittacus signatus*... It is said to be a native of Brazil. **1802** *Ibid.* III. II. 502 *Red Bead Snake. *Coluber Guttatus*... A native of Carolina. **1756** P. BROWNE *Jamaica* 298 The *Red-Bead Tree. The seeds are pretty large, and well marked with a proportioned black spot. *Ibid.* 297 *Red-Bead Vine. The seeds are of a very beautiful scarlet colour with a black spot on one side. *Ibid.* 288 The Coral or *Red Bean Tree. The seeds of this tree are of a beautiful red colour. **1820** RAFINESQUE in *Smithson. Coll.* XIII. (1877) IX. i. 28 *Red-belly Shiner, *Luxilus Erythrogaster*. **1897** *Westm. Gaz.* 12 May 10/1 Chang is a *red-button mandarin. **1840** HEREMAN *Gardener's Lib.* II. 186 *Graphiphora Festiva*, Primrose Moth... *Red Clay Moth. **1703** DAMPIER *Voy.* (1729) III. 430 *Red-dye Bark. Because it's used in dying that Colour. **1866** *Treas. Bot.* 885/2 Its dark purplish berries..contain a purplish-red juice somewhat resembling red ink, and hence it is sometimes called the *Red-ink Plant. **1880** O. S. WILSON *Larvæ Brit. Lepidopt.* 266 *Orthosia lota*, Linn. The *Red Line Quaker. **1840** HEREMAN *Gardener's Lib.* II. 165 *Orgya Antiqua*, Common Vapourer Moth... *Red Spot Tussock. *c* **1830** *Glouc. Farm Rep.* 11 in *Lib. Usef. Knowl.*, *Husb.* III, The *red-straw-lammas is the kind [of wheat] that is always sown upon this farm. **1802** SHAW *Gen. Zool.* III. I. 242 *Red-Throat Lizard. *Laceria Bullaris*.

13. Prefixed to the names of other colours, forming compound adjs. or sbs., as ***red-black, -brown, -fallow, -gold, -golden, -orange, -pink, -purple, -rose, -white, -yellow***, etc.

1824 SHAW *Gen. Zool.* XII. I. 174 Edged with red..and tipped with a small border of *red-ash. **1910** *Westm. Gaz.* 25 Jan. 5/2 The material employed is the finest *red-black rubber. **1975** R. H. RIMMER *Premar Experiments* II. 174 Even before I touched her, her nipples were engorged, red-black and demanding. **1676** COTTON *Angler* II. vii, The hair ..turns to a *red brown. **1785** BURNS *Ep. Simpson* x, Her moors red-brown wi' heather bells. **1884** *Chamb. Jrnl.* 3 May 273/1 The rich red-brown canvas of a gliding wherry. *c* **1400** *Master of Game* (MS. Digby 182) xiv, þe best hewe is *red falewe with a blacke mosel. **1607** E. TOPSELL *Four-footed Beasts* 661 This beast is of *red-gold-colour. **1871** SWINBURNE *Songs before Sunrise* 237 Till the red-gold harvest-rows, Full-grown, are full of the light. **1896** MARY BEAUMONT *Joan Seton* 112 The diadem of her hair shining red-gold in the light. **1923** D. H. LAWRENCE *Birds, Beasts & Flowers* 98, I have..seen..His red-gold, water-precious, mirror-flat bright eye. **1973** J. CLEARY *Ransom* i. 21 She was ..beautiful, with that red-gold hair that was a sensation on colour television. **1962** I. MURDOCH *Unofficial Rose* 12 Her *red-golden hair. **1879** ROOD *Chromatics* 45 All the *red-orange hues are represented. **1880** E. GLAISTER *Needlework* ix. 101 If the flowers be another colour than yellow, say *red-pink, or blue, the darning may be the same colour. **1951** E. PAUL *Springtime in Paris* xv. 268 The pharmacy had large old-fashioned globes of coloured liquid, red-pink like Corsican wine and transparent blue-green. **1828** DUNLOP in *Mem. R. Astron. Soc.* III. 267 A very singular star..of an uncommon *red purple colour. **1851** *Southern Planter* (Richmond, Va.) July 197/2 Improved Red Purple Straw on corn land. **1929** A. CLARKE *Pilgrimage & Other Poems* 15 Vats of red-purple dye. **1675** *Lond. Gaz.* No. 990/4 One *Red Roan'd Horse, having Pitch-brands on both sides of his Shoulders. *Ibid.* No. 1020/4 A light Red-roan Gelding. **1850** MRS. BROWNING *Swan's Nest* v, The steed shall be red-roan. **1917** G. FRANKAU *Inn of Thousand Dreams* in *City of Fear* 26 Once more I press..Your finger-tips against these lips Your own *red-rose lips knew. **1585** T. WASHINGTON tr. *Nicholay's Voy.* III. xii. 93 b, A high topped cappe, died of *redde scarlet. *c* **1350** *Ipomadon* 2398 Efte come another stede..that was *rede-sore. *a* **1618** SYLVESTER *Wood-Man's Bear* xlv, *Red-white hils, and white-red plaines. **1920** J. MASEFIELD *Enslaved* 9 Little red-white blossoms flecked me. *a* **1578** LINDESAY (Pitscottie) *Hist. Scot.* (S.T.S.) I. 258 He had nothing on his heid bot syde *reid 3allow hair. **1608** SYLVESTER *Du Bartas* II. iv. IV. *Decay* 101 As the fresh red-yellow Apple dangles (In Autumn) on the Tree. **1937** V. WOOLF *Years* 333 There was a red-yellow glow... The sun was sinking through the London dust.

14. Forming parasynthetic adjectives, as ***red-armed, -belted***, etc.

a. In general use. (See also RED-BEARDED, -BLOODED, -CHEEKED, -COATED, -EYED, -HANDED, etc.)

1776 MICKLE tr. *Camoens' Lusiad* 139 The awful blade Of *red-arm'd Justice. **1925** F. SCOTT FITZGERALD *Great Gatsby* iv. 81 A glimpse of *red-belted ocean-going ships. **1852** M. ARNOLD *Lines Kensington Gard.*, Those black-crowned, *red-boled pine-trees. **1922** JOYCE *Ulysses* 657 Dry them..in a long *redbordered holland cloth passed over a wooden revolving roller. **1905** *Westm. Gaz.* 6 Sept. 6/2 There were waiting on the *red-carpeted platform.. officials representing the railway company. **1922** JOYCE *Ulysses* 484 They appear on a redcarpeted staircase. **1948** M. LASKI *Tory Heaven* viii. 106 He climbs the red-carpeted steps under the gay awning. **1976** N. ROBERTS *Face of France* xvi. 165 A red-carpeted dais. **1973** M. AMIS *Rachel Papers* 170 My sister, a swirl of *red-checked nightie, flew through the doorway. **1978** R. LUDLUM *Holcroft Covenant* xxiv. 277 Running across the fronts of the booths were brass rods holding red-checked curtains. **1913** J. MASEFIELD *Daffodil Fields* 2 Some short-grassed fields begin, *red-clayed and pleasant. **1847** EMERSON *Poems* (1857) 12 Little thinks in the field yon *red-cloaked clown Of thee. **1910** W. B. YEATS *Green Helmet* 21 A tall red-headed red-cloaked man stands upon the threshold. **1980** *Jrnl. R. Soc. Arts* Mar. 241/2 Max Ernst's red-cloaked, bird-masked lady in *The Robing of the Bride*. **1763** *Brit. Mag.* IV. 547 The *red-clock'd stocking trims the brawny leg. **1561** HOLLYBUSH *Hom. Apoth.* 6 Then waxeth hys skin *rede colored also. **1719** LONDON & WISE *Compl. Gard'ner* 67 It's pretty red colour'd. **1800** HERSCHEL in *Phil. Trans.* XC. 513 Red-coloured or red-making rays. **1942** S. SPENDER *Life & Poet* 12 Since we believe socialism to be just, novels should preach socialism and see everything through red-coloured spectacles. **1570** J. PHILLIP *Friendly Larum* in Farr *S.P. Eliz.* (Parker Soc.) II. 526 Some wish the *redcombde bird might crow. **1833** TENNYSON *Poems* 104 Lest the redcombed dragon slumber. **1865** DICKENS *Mut. Fr.* I. iii, He turned into a *red-curtained tavern. **1900** W. B. YEATS *Shadowy Waters* 46 A *red-eared hound follows a hornless deer. **1881** O. WILDE *Poems* 80 The dusky *red-eaved sheds. **1918** G. FRANKAU *Judgement of Valhalla* 6 (*title*) The song of the *red-edged steel. **1922** JOYCE *Ulysses* 221 Father Conmee..took his rededged breviary out. **1942** E. SITWELL *Street Songs* 7 Man's threatening shadow Red-edged by the sun like Cain, has a changing shape. **1965** G. MCINNES *Road to Gundagai* xiii. 239 The navy blue red-edged flag. **1892** D. SLADEN *Japs at Home* (ed. 2) xxvi. 283 While in the distance looms the harbour of Yokohama, full of the mighty *red-ensigned steamers of the England he pined for night and day. **1657** W. RAND tr. *Gassendi's Life Peiresc* II. 152 My name I have from my *red-feathered coat. **1870** MORRIS *Earthly Par.* I. I. 313 Seeing..The *red-finned fishes o'er the gravel play. **1697** CONGREVE *Mourn. Bride* IV. vii, What mean those swollen and *red-fleck'd eyes? *a* **1915** JOYCE *Giacomo Joyce* (1968) 16 Poised on its edge a woman's hat, *red-flowered. **1932** BLUNDEN *Face of England* 66 Where the sheep's parsley tops a *red-furred stem. **1838** MARY HOWITT *Birds & Flowers, Ivy-bush* iv, The *red-gemmed holly. **1594** MARLOWE & NASHE *Dido* IV. v, A silver stream, Where thou shalt see the *red-gill'd fishes leap. **1803** SOUTHEY *Eclogues, Alderman's Funeral* 15 One of the *red-gown'd worthies of the city. **1863** GEO. ELIOT *Romola* I. xiii. 222 The boy-cardinal Giovanni de Medici, youngest of the *red-hatted fathers. **1894** FROUDE *Erasmus* 86 A red-hatted lackey of the Holy See. **1918** A. BENNETT *Pretty Lady* x. 52 The young red-hatted officer. **1930** BLUNDEN *Poems* 185 Where the red-hatted cranks Have fixed a portcullis With notice-board—thanks! **1922** JOYCE *Ulysses* 95 The *redlabelled bottle on the table. **1603** HEYWOOD *Wom. killed* II. iii, The *red-leaved table of my heart. **1882** G. MACDONALD *Castle Warlock* xxix, The eye-brows over his *red-lidded blue eyes. **1819** KEATS *Fancy* 13 Autumn's *red-lipped fruitage too. **1881** O. WILDE *Poems* 70 An amorous red-lipped boy. **1611** SHAKS. *Wint. T.* II. ii. 34 Let my tongue..neuer to my *red-look'd Anger bee The Trumpet any more. **1913** KIPLING *Songs from Books* 239 And *red-mouthed shadows racing By, that thrust me from my food. **1934** DYLAN THOMAS *Let.* *c* 26 May (1966) 133 I've wasted some of my tremendous love for you on a lank, redmouthed girl with a reputation like a hell. **1849** ALISON *Hist. Europe* (ed. 2) VIII. xlix. §23. 26 The *red-plumed dragoons of Floyd. **1653** H. MORE *Antid. Ath.* (1662) 73 The *red-puggered attire of the Turkey. **1855** TENNYSON *Maud* I. I. i, The *red-ribbed ledges drip with a silent horror of blood. **1916** JOYCE *Portrait of Artist* (1969) 252, I fear his *redrimmed horny eyes. **1962** I. MURDOCH *Unofficial Rose* xii. 115 The red-rimmed eyes. **1977** P. HILL *Liars* vii. 91 Her eyes were red-rimmed, as if she had been crying. **1857** THORNBURY *Songs Cav. & Roundh.* 184 Through the silent, *red-roofed town. **1790** BURNS *Tam o' Shanter* 135 Five tomahawks wi' blude *red-rusted. **1611** COTGR., *Rason*, a delicate *red-skaled fish. **1647** H. MORE *Song of Soul* III. III. xliii, Red-scaled Dragons with deep burning light In their hollow eye-pits. **1535** in Weaver *Wells Wills* (1890) 208 A *red scoryd cow. **1930** BLUNDEN *Poems* 134 The *red-screened windows of schoolhouse and inn. **1955** E. POUND *Classic Anthol.* II. 94 Fang Shu's black-dappled team of four Drew his red-screen'd car to the war. **1848** THOREAU *Maine W.* (1894) 90 A *red-shirted or green-jacketed mountaineer. **1852** M. ARNOLD *Empedocles* I I, The *red-snooded Phrygian girls. **1880** G. MEREDITH *Tragic Com.* (1881) 299 An immediate death-dealer who stood against *red-streaked heavens. **1865–6** W. WHITMAN *Sequel to Drum-Taps* 19 The *red-striped artilleryman. **1940** BLUNDEN *Poems 1930–40* 209 He ..damned, at each pause, *red-tabbed Brigade, Whose orders for grimness more than the frost-spell made us shiver. **1948** W. FORTESCUE *Beauty for Ashes* xxvii. 207, I accosted a red-tabbed English officer who directed me to it at once. **1977** J. CLEARY *High Road to China* iv. 107 Johnny Silversmith, red-faced and red-tabbed, came to our table. *c* **1612** W. STRACHEY *Hist. Travaile* (1849) 63 A kind of arsenick stone, like..*red tempered oyntments of earth. **1911** G. K. CHESTERTON *Innocence of Father Brown* iv. 105 The *red-tied youth. **1960** D. POTTER *Glittering Coffin* iii. 38 Red-tied adolescent poets. **1844** THACKERAY *Little Trav.* iii, Little old-fashioned, dumpy, whitewashed, *red-tiled houses. **1977** H. OSBORNE *White Poppy* viii. 69 An iron bedstead on a red-tiled floor. **1881** O. WILDE *Poems* 178 The *red-toothed lightning. **1925** BLUNDEN *Eng. Poems* 123 Through red-toothed nettles. **1721** AMHERST *Terræ Fil.* No. 46 (1754) 246 A kick..from a *red-topt shoe. **1859** HAWTHORNE *Marb. Faun* (1878) I. xii. 128 The *red-trousered French soldiers. **1877** C. PATMORE *Unknown Eros* xi. 51 He had put, within his reach, A box of counters and a *red-vein'd stone. **1907** *Daily Chron.* 18 Mar. 6/2 His face is clear, with the red-veined cheeks of a sailor. **1956** R. FINLAYSON in C. K. Stead *N.Z. Short Stories* (1966) 22 He was a thickset florid man with a red-veined nose. **1859** CORNWALLIS *New World* I. 165 The clarion note was sounded from some *red-wattled throat.

b. In the distinctive names of species or varieties of birds, fishes, moths, etc. (See also RED-BACKED, -BELLIED, -BILLED, -BREASTED, etc.)

1781 LATHAM *Gen. Synopsis Birds* I. I. 300 *Red-banded Parrot... On the forehead, from one eye to the other, is a band of red... Inhabits St. Domingo. **1758** G. EDWARDS *Glean. Nat. Hist.* I. 58 The *Red-beaked Toucan. **1857** LIVINGSTONE *Trav.* 613 He put his arm into the hole, and brought out a Tockus or red-beaked hornbill [*Toccus erythrorhyncus*]. **1705** PETIVER in *Phil. Trans.* XXIV. 1953 The *red Beam'd Jamaica Muscle... The dead shells are white and shining, the others have red beams, which shoot from the hinge and are broader at the edges. **1880** O. S. WILSON *Larvæ Brit. Lepidopt.* 39 *Sesia myopiformis*, Bork.

The *Red-belted Clearwing. *Sesia culiciformis*, Linn. The Large Red-belted Clearwing. **1705** Petiver in *Phil. Trans.* XXIV. 1952 The *red-blotted Carolina Crab. **1752** J. Hill *Hist. Anim.* 27 The great *red-bodied Spider, with the white cross. **1840** Hereman *Gardener's Lib.* II. 168 *Megachile Ligniseca*. Carpenter Bee... Red-bodied Bee.—Red Carpenter Bee. **1837** Gould *Birds Europe* IV. Pl. 299 *Red-chested Dotterel... *Charadrius pyrrhothorax*. **1810** Wilson *Amer. Ornith.* II. 103 *Red-Cockaded Woodpecker, *Picus Querulus*. **1837** Gould *Birds Europe* II. Pl. 52 *Red-Collared Goatsucker... *Caprimulgus ruficollis*. **1785** Latham *Gen. Synopsis Birds* III. II. 554 *Red-Crested Duck. **1824** Shaw *Gen. Zool.* XII. II. 188 Red-crested Pochard (*Fuligula rufina*). **1894** Newton *Dict. Birds* 736 The White-eyed or Castaneous Duck,..and the Red-crested Duck, *Nyroca rufina*. **1776** P. Browne *Illustr. Zool.* 30 *Red-Crowned Barbet. **1812** Shaw *Gen. Zool.* VIII. II. 523 Red-crowned Parrot, *Psittacus galeatus*. *Ibid.* IX. II. 446 Red-Crowned Finch (*Fringilla ruticapilla*). **1781** Latham *Gen. Synopsis Birds* I. I. 123 *Red-eared owl, *Strix Asio* (Linn.). **1840** *Cuvier's Anim. Kingd.* 57 Red-eared Monkey (*C. erythrotis*)... From Fernando Po. **1848** Gould *Birds Australia* III. Pl. 79 *Estrelda oculea*..Red-eared Finch. **1937** *Jrnl. Tennessee Acad. Sci.* XII. 45 (*caption*) The Red-Eared Sunfish. Only the males have the red tip on the opercular flap. **1952** A. Carr *Handbk. Turtles U.S. & Canada* II. 251 The red-eared turtle can usually be recognized..by the long, oval expansion of the broad supra temporal stripe, which is usually bright red. **1803** Shaw *Gen. Zool.* IV. II. 413 *Red-Finned Sparus. *Sparus Erythropterus*... Native of Japan. **1882** Day *Fishes Gt. Brit.* II. 210 Red-finned herrings are known as wine-drinkers in Scotland. **1781** Latham *Gen. Synopsis Birds* I. I. 308 *Red-fronted Parrot... Inhabits Brasil. **1815** Shaw *Gen. Zool.* IX. I. 31 Red-fronted Barbet (*Bucco rufifrons*). **1817** *Ibid.* X. I. 91 Red-Fronted Swallow. *Hirundo rufifrons*. **1590** Shaks. *Mids. N.* IV. i. 12 Kill me a *red hipt humble-Bee. **1812** Shaw *Gen. Zool.* VIII. II. 466 *Red-Hooded Parrakeet. *Psittacus capitatus*. **1809** *Ibid.* VII. I. 229 *Red-Horned Owl, *Strix Asio*. **1713** Petiver *Aquat. Anim. Amb.* 3/1 *Red Knobbed Trumpet [shell]. **1910**, etc. *Red-lipped snake [see herald *sb.* 5]. **1729** in *Dampier's Voy.* (ed. 3) III. 415 The *Red-listed Pearch..has large silver Scales with a scarlet Gloss. **1752** J. Hill *Hist. Anim.* 133 The *red-mouthed Buccinum, with the clavicle erect. **1787** Latham *Gen. Synopsis Birds* Suppl. 66 *Red-naped Parrakeet. **1812** Shaw *Gen. Zool.* VIII. II. 543 Red-Naped Parrot, *Psittacus nuchalis*. **1831** Wilson, etc. *Amer. Ornith.* IV. 245 *Red-Shafted Woodpecker. *Colaptes Mexicanus*. **1888** [see flicker *sb.*[4]]. **1812** Shaw *Gen. Zool.* VIII. II. 490 *Red-Sided Parrot. *Psittacus lateralis*. **1860** Gosse *Brit. Sea-Anemones* 198 The *Red-specked Pimplet, *Banodes Ballii*. **1752** J. Hill *Hist. Anim.* 127 The black, *red-streaked, and spotted Nerite. **1898** Morris *Austral Engl.* 385/1 Red streaked Spider, or Black-and-red Spider, an Australasian spider (*Latrodectus scelio*). **1884–5** *Riverside Nat. Hist.* (1888) II. 194 *Caloptenus femur-rubrum*, the *Red-thighed Locust, is found throughout North America. **1880** O. S. Wilson *Larvæ Brit. Lepidopt.* 39 *Sesia formiciformis*, Esp. The *Red-tipped Clearwing. **1812** Shaw *Gen. Zool.* VIII. II. 418 *Red-Topped Parrakeet. *Psittacus Verticalis*. **1776** P. Browne *Illustr. Zool.* 10 *Red-Vented Cockatoo. *Ibid.* 78 Red-vented Warbler. **1812** Shaw *Gen. Zool.* VIII. II. 481 Red-vented Cockatoo, *Psittacus Philippinarum*. **1877** *Nature* XVI. 218/1 Three Red-vented Terrapins (*Clemmys rubriventris*). ?**1711** Petiver *Catal. Gazophyll.* Dec. x. 11/1 *Red-Waved, thread-girdled Heart Cockle.

c. In names of plants.

See also Cooke *Handbk. Fungi* (1871) for *red-cracked*, *-juiced*, etc., in names of fungi.

1634 Johnson *Merc. Botan.* 55 Spurre-flowred Orchis, or *Red-banded Orchis. **1611** Cotgr., *Rosmarin sauvage*, (the *red-branched) wild Rosemarie. **1707** Mortimer *Husb.* (1721) I. 127 They have also a *red-ear'd bearded Wheat. **1762** Mills *Pract. Husb.* I. 362 Their white kind of red ear'd wheat has a white ear and a red grain. **1703** Dampier *Voy.* (1729) III. 446 *Red-edg'd flouring Cane. **1868** Darwin *Anim. & Pl.* I. x. 335 The *red-fleshed orange..fails to reproduce itself. **1777** Lightfoot *Flora Scot.* I. 262 Briar-Rose, *red-flower'd Dogs-Rose, or Hep-Tree. **1832** *Planting* 98 in *Lib. Usef. Knowl., Husb.* III, Red-flowered Bucks-eye-tree, *Pavia rubra*. **1866** *Treas. Bot.* 853/2 *P[avia] rubra*, often called Red-flowered Horse-chestnut. **1846** Mrs. Loudon *Brit. Wild Flowers* 135 The *Red-Fruited Bramble. *Ibid.* 143 The Red-Fruited Dwarf Rose. **1825** J. Neal *Bro. Jonathan* III. 420 The *red-hearted, or upland beech. **1597** Gerarde *Herbal* 84 *Red leafed Cow Wheate. **1819** Warden *United States* II. 522 Andromeda, red leaved. **1911** E. Pound *Canzoni* I Ah! red-leafed time hath driven out the rose. **1923** Blunden *To Nature* 47 There shone the Ancre, red-leafed woods above it. **1763** Mills *Pract. Husb.* III. 183 The *red rooted potatoes have purplish flowers. **1766** *Complete Farmer* s.v. *Turnip*, The red rooted turnip was formerly more cultivated in England than at present. **1753** Chambers *Cycl. Supp.* s.v. *Wall-Moss*, The *red-stalked, transparent, grassy-leaved Bryum. **1764** *Museum Rust.* III. 321 Five coomb of seed red-stalked wheat. **1866** Sowerby *Eng. Bot.* V. 69 *Filago Apiculata*... *Red-tipped Cudweed. **1763** Mills *Pract. Husb.* III. 151 The *red or purple topped, and the large green topped turnips. **1805** R. W. Dickson *Pract. Agric.* II. 640 The red-topped [turnip]..is apt soon to become stringy. **1832** *Planting* 29 in *Lib. Usef. Knowl., Husb.* III, *Red twigged Lime tree, *Tilia Europ. corallina*. *Ibid.* 105 *Red-veined Ash-tree, *Fraxinus rubicunda*. **1878** Hogg & Johnson *Wild Fl. Gt. Brit.* X. Pl. 797 *Rumex Sanguineus*, Red-veined Dock. **1842** Loudon *Encycl. Trees & Shrubs* 174 *Rhamnus Erythoxylon*..The *red-wooded Buckthorn.

15. a. With pa. pples., as ***red-clad***, ***-dabbled***, ***-decked***, ***-dyed***, ***-flushed***, ***-gilded***, ***-lined*** (see also red-line *v.*), ***-lit***, ***-litten***, ***-painted***, ***-plowed***, ***-polished***, ***-struck***, ***-washed***, ***-written***. Also ***red-wet*** (***shod***).

1871 J. Miller *Songs Italy* (1878) 36 The *red-clad fishers row and creep Below the crags. **1857** Thornbury *Songs Cav. & Roundh.* 4 Remember Edge-hill and the *red-dabbled mire. **1923** D. H. Lawrence *Birds, Beasts & Flowers* 66 *Red-decked socialists, Hibiscus-breasted. **1632** Massinger & Field *Fatal Dowry* IV. iv, I, in your case, put on a scarlet robe Of *red-died cruelty. **1871** W. Whitman *Passage to India* 18 The *red-flush'd cheeks, and perfumes. **1943** V. Woolf *Haunted House* 124 The red-flushed clouds. **1949** E. Pound *Pisan Cantos* lxxix. 77 The mountain forest is full of light The tree-comb *red-gilded. **1849** D. J. Browne *Amer. Poultry Yd.* (1855) 242 Opening his *red-lined throat to its utmost extent. **1921** W. de la Mare *Crossings* 31 Unlocks the trunk and pushes back its red-lined lid. **1930** R. Campbell *Gum Trees*, Along the *red-lit rim of space In lofty cadences they rhyme. **1839** Poe *Fall House of Usher* Wks. 1864 I. 301 Travellers..Through the *red-litten windows see Vast forms. **1891** G. F. X. Griffith tr. *Fouard's Christ* I. 259 The red-litten peaks. *a* **1843** Southey *Comm.-pl. Bk.* (1849) II. 566 The *Red-painted Hatchet of War. **1884** Tennyson *Early Spring* 3 The Heavenly Power ..domes the *red-plow'd hills With loving blue. **1934** V. G. Childe *New Light Most Anc. East* iv. 89 Household vessels, always the most sensitive indicator of ethnic change, are radically altered. Though Black-topped and *Red-polished ware continue to be manufactured they are no longer the vehicle for new shapes. **1977** *Jrnl. R. Soc. Arts* CXXV. 476/2 The most important items found in the tombs of *Kotchati* and acquired by the Cyprus Museum are two clay (Red Polished ware) models of sanctuaries. **1923** D. H. Lawrence *Birds, Beasts & Flowers* 82 Since the Lamb bewitched him with that *red-struck flag His fortress is dismantled. **1932** Blunden *Face of England* 50 *Red-washed cottages. **1785** Burns *Ep. Simpson* xi, Still pressing onward *red-wat shod. **1820** *Blackw. Mag.* July 384/2 The hand of her kindred has been red-wat in the heart's blude o' my name. **1871** Browning *Balaustion* 1701 To read *red-written up and down The world [etc.].

b. With pres. pples, in complemental use, as ***red-branching***, ***-burning***, ***-flowering***, ***-gleaming***, ***-glowing***, ***-hissing***, ***-panting***, ***-ripening***, ***-streaming***, ***-swelling***. Also objective, as ***red-making***.

1729 Savage *Wanderer* I, There lies..the ripening Diamond's Ray, And thence *red-branching Coral's rent away. **1625** B. Jonson *Staple of N.* IV. iv, Throw away Her bounties, as they were *red-burning coals. **1816** Warden *Descr. Columbia* 166 Maple (*red flowering). *Acerrubrum*. **1864** Sowerby *Eng. Bot.* II. 129 *Spergularia Rubra*... Red-flowering Field Spurrey. **1889** Maiden *Usef. Native Plants* 471 This rugged-barked variety (Victorian Ironbark) must not be confused with the Red-flowering Ironbark (*E. Sideroxylon*) of New South Wales. **1855** Morris in Mackail *Life* (1899) I. 50 Under the *red-gleaming moonlight. **1936** R. Campbell *Mithraic Emblems* 24 A sombre grape, whose heart, *Red-glowing to the hilted dart, Seems a lit furnace that he fans. **1697** Congreve *Mourn. Bride* II. x, And wrench the Bolt *red-hissing from the Hand Of him that thunders. **1715–20** Pope *Iliad* XIV. 482 The bolt, red-hissing from above. **1704** Newton *Optics* (ed. 3) 168 The homogeneal Light and Rays which appear red, or rather make objects appear so, I call Rubrific or *Red-making. **1797** Brougham in *Phil. Trans.* LXXXVII. 359 If IF *fi* be changed to a red-making beam [etc.]. **1922** Joyce *Ulysses* 47 Unheeded he kept by them.., a rag of wolf's tongue *redpanting from his jaws. **1729** Savage *Wanderer* v, The native Strawberry *red-ripening grows. **1823** Mrs. Hemans *Vespers of Palermo* II. iv, The partial glare Of the *red-streaming lava. **1729** Savage *Wanderer* v, He rolls *red-swelling, tearful Eyes around.

III. In special applications.

16. a. As a distinctive epithet of things in which the colour forms a natural or obvious mark of kind or class.

c **1000** Ælfric *Gloss.* in Wr.-Wülcker 149/8 *Ceraunie*, reade winberiʒe. *a* **1300** *Cursor M.* 4678 Þepe selers..he fild wit wines, quite and red. **1387–8** T. Usk *Test. Love* Prol. (Skeat) l. 15 Some..painten with colours riche..as with red inke. *c* **1450** *M.E. Med. Bk.* (Heinrich) 199 Closed wyþynne þe ere wyþ red wax. *Ibid.* 227 Þen seþ hem wel in red eysel. **1483** *Cath. Angl.* 301/2 Rede grapes, *elbee*. **1523** Fitzherb. *Husb.* §142 Parchmente, reedwax, pommes, bokes. **1617** Moryson *Itin.* I. 143 The white and red Muskedine, one of the most famous Wines in Italy. **1849** Herschel *Outl. Astron.* §851 Many of the red stars are variable. **1851** Carpenter *Man. Physiol.* (ed. 2) 311 The blood of Invertebrated animals, from which the red corpuscles are almost or altogether absent.

b. Applied to various diseases marked by evacuation of blood or cutaneous eruptions.

a **1400–50** *Stockh. Med. MS.* 152 For þe reed flyx. **1417** *Durham Acc. Rolls* (Surtees) 318 De quibus [agnis] in morina lxij, in quodam morbo voc.le redeyll. **1447** [see flux *sb.* 1]. **1493** *Festivall* (W. de W. 1515) 114 b, Cryst..heled Martha her syster of the reed fluxe. **1561** Hollybush *Hom. Apoth.* 6 If yᵉ waking come of yᵉ rede colera, then waxeth hys skin rede colored also. **1563** [see lepry]. **1606** Shaks. *Tr. & Cr.* II. i. 20 A red Murren o' thy Iades tricks. **1610** —— *Temp.* I. ii. 364 The red-plague rid you For learning me your language. **1664** *Meth. Chem. Philos. & Physick* 242 These are the signs of the red Lepry. **1845** Youatt *Dog* (1858) 368 In red mange the whole integument is in a state of acute inflammation. **1878** *Times* 26 Dec., 'Soldier disease or red disease' are names given to any affection in swine accompanied by general or patchy redness of the skin.

c. ***red bogs***, one of the chief classes of bogs in Ireland (see quot. 1846).

1685 W. King in *Phil. Trans.* XV. 955 Every red Bog has about it a deep marshy sloughy ground, which they call the bounds of the Bog. **1737** *Dublin Soc. Weekly Obs.* No. 19 (1739) I. 122 The Crop I mean is Hops; and the Bogs in which I have reared them with most Success, the worst and most useless of all others—the red Bogs. **1846** McCulloch *Acc. Brit. Empire* (1854) I. 347 The colour of the matter of which they are composed is, for the most part, reddish, whence they are usually called red bogs. Exclusive of the red or flat bogs [etc.].

d. ***red squadron***, one of the three squadrons into which the Royal Navy was formerly divided.

1702 *Lond. Gaz.* No. 3835/3 Sir John Munden, Rear-Admiral of the Red-Squadron. **1769** Falconer *Dict. Marine* (1780) s.v. *Fleet*, The ships of the red squadron wear an ensign, whose union is displayed on a red field. **1802** *Naval Chron.* VIII. 223 *note*, The English do not wear the red flag at the main... The distinguishing flag of the red squadron has ever been the Union or flag of the Lord High Admiral. **1891** Hulme *Heraldry* (1897) 262 Until 1864, Great Britain had admirals, and vice and rear-admirals, of the red, white, and blue squadrons.

e. Applied to hearts and diamonds in a pack of cards.

1764 *Suppl. Treat. Quadrille* 27 A Reflection on the Difference in playing the same Hands, in Black and in Red Suits. **1908** R. F. Foster *Auction Bridge* 50 Here is an example of a hand which is not a good red declaration. **1910** W. Dalton '*Saturday*' *Bridge* vii. 100 Doubling an original red-suit declaration cannot be recommended on anything very short of a certainty. **1973** *Times* 29 Sept. 11/7 He needed to find both red aces on the left... His game bid was against the odds.

f. Applied to the representation of British territories on maps: see sense 1 e of the sb.

1916 J. Buchan *Greenmantle* iv. 52 You see that map... South Africa is coloured green. Not red for the English, or yellow for the Germans. **1934** A. Huxley *Beyond Mexique Bay* 36 The non-existent young lady in fancy dress would be mortally offended by the suggestion that the place [*sc.* British Honduras] should be painted anything but red on the map. **1964** *Critical Q.* Winter 320 You shook your finger at the map and said..'Africa, I want it red.' **1975** *Listener* 4 Sept. 297/1 At the beginning of the 20th century, practically every country exporting spices was marked red on the map. **1977** A. Wilson *Strange Ride R. Kipling* iv. 212 Rhodes arranged for Rudyard to make a visit up to the territory of Rhodesia, which he saw as the first step in his dream of an all-red British route from Cape Town to Cairo.

17. Used more or less descriptively and distinctively with the general or generic names of animals, birds, fishes, plants, and minerals.

a. *Animals*, as ***red bot***, ***kangaroo***, ***lemur***, ***mole***, ***slug***, ***snail*** (see quots.); **red adder**, *U.S.*, the copperhead snake; **red ant**, any ant of this colour, esp. (*a*) a common small British ant, *Formica* (or *Myrmica*) *rubra*; (*b*) the hill- or horse-ant, *F. rufa*; (*c*) the American house-ant, *Monomorium pharaonis*; (*d*) (see quot. 1872); †**red antelope**, (*a*) the steen-bok; (*b*) the nagor or Senegal antelope; **red ant-fly** (see ant-fly); **red bat**, *U.S.*, a common American bat; **red bear-cat**, the panda or wah (*Cent. Dict.* 1891); **red buck** = impala, rooibok; **red bug**, *U.S.*, (*a*) the cotton-stainer, *Dysdercus suturellus*; (*b*) = jigger *sb.*[2]; **red cat** *S. Afr.* = rooikat; **red crab**, *U.S.*, an edible crab of the Pacific coast; **red dog**, the dhole, *Cyon* (or *Cuon*) *alpinus*; **red fox**, (*a*) the common European fox, *Vulpes vulgaris*; (*b*) the common North American fox, *V. fulvus*; (*c*) the kit-fox of N. America; **red hare**, (*a*) a variety of the common American hare; (*b*) a southern African hare belonging to the genus *Pronolagus*, distinguished by speckled buff and black fur, with reddish fur beneath the body and a red-brown tail; **red hartebeest**, a variety of hartebeest, *Alcelaphus bucelaphus caama*; **red howler**, a howler monkey, *Alouatta seniculus*, found in forested areas of South America and distinguished by long red-brown fur; **red louse**, the harvest bug, or harvest mite (*Cent. Dict.*); **red lynx**, the bay lynx, *Felis rufa*; **red maggot** (see maggot); **red mite**, (*a*) a blood-sucking mite, *Dermanyssus gallinæ*, which attacks poultry; (*b*) = red spider; **red monkey**, the patas of Western Africa; **red mouse**, the harvest mouse; †**red orang**, the orang-outang; **red panda** = panda 1; **red river hog**, a West African race of the bush pig, *Potamochœrus porcus*; **red setter**, an Irish setter belonging to the breed sometimes so called, distinguished by a long, silky, dark red coat, drooping ears, and a long feathered tail; †**red snake**, a Virginian species of snake (? the red adder); **red squirrel**, (*a*) a small North American squirrel, *Sciurus hudsonicus*, also called the chickaree; (*b*) the common European squirrel, *Sciurus vulgaris*, now relatively rare in Britain; **red tiger**, the cougar (*Cent. Dict.*); **red viper**, (*a*) a species of British viper; (*b*) *U.S.*, the red adder or copperhead; **red wolf**, (*a*) a South American wolf, *Canis jubatus*; (*b*) a North American wolf, *Canis rufus*, native to parts of the south-western states, where it is rare; (*c*) a variety of the common wolf, *Canis lupus*. (For *red admiral*, *arches*, *carpet*, etc., see 19.) Also red deer, red spider, red worm.

1859 Bartlett *Dict. Amer.* s.v. *Copperhead*, It has various other popular names, as Copper-belly, Red Viper, *Red adder. **1667** King in *Phil. Trans.* II. 426 If you put Black Ants into a Bank of the *Red [ants], the Black..will not meddle with the Red, but..run away. **1747** Gould *Acc. Eng. Ants* 11 The Red Ants are to be met with under broad Stones or other Rubbish. **1816** Kirby & Sp. *Entomol.* II. xvii. 97, I found the inhabitants of a nest of the red ant (*Myrmica rubra*) very busily employed. **1872** Wood *Insects at Home* 340 The Red Ant (*Formica sanguinea*) is worthy of some notice, because it is one of the slave-making species. **1781** Pennant *Hist. Quadrup.* I. 76 *Red Antelope. **1790** Bewick *Hist. Quadrup.* 80 The Steen-Bok or Red Antelope of Mr. Pennant. **1797** *Encycl. Brit.* (ed. 3) IV. 146/2 The nagor, or red antelope,..inhabits Senegal and the Cape. **1812** Wilson *Amer. Ornith.* VI. pl. 50 *Red Bat. **1884–5**

Riverside Nat. Hist. (1888) V. 167 The *Atalapha noveboracensis*, or Red Bat, is perhaps the most common of the eastern American bats. **1836** *Penny Cycl.* V. 261/1 A smaller species of bot, called from its colour the *red-bot, is occasionally found in the stomach [of the horse]. **1813** J. CAMPBELL *Jrnl.* 30 Oct. in *Trav. S. Afr.* (1815) xl. 484 The following are the number of creatures killed by our people during the journey..*Redbucks..6..Rhebucks..3. **1883** J. MACKENZIE *Day-dawn in Dark Places* 97, I beheld the gnu and the zebra, the red-buck, the spring buck, and..the lechwe, or water-buck. **1965** Red-buck [see IMPALA]. **1804** D. MCKINNEN *Tour Brit. W. Indies* x. 171 The *red bug.. has stained the cotton so much in some places this year as to render it of little or no value. **1827** J. L. WILLIAMS *View W. Florida* 29 Red bugs are numerous, especially in mossy woods. **1856** *Rep. Comm. Patents 1855: Agric.* (U.S.) 104 The 'red-bugs', or..'cotton-stainers', generally make their appearance about August. **1909** Red bug [see BÊTE ROUGE]. **1939** *Sun* (Baltimore) 18 Aug. 11/2 The chiggers—'red bugs' to some—were terrific. **1955** *Sci. News Let.* 16 July 42/1 Chiggers, called red bugs down South, cause the most exquisite itching. **1731** G. MEDLEY tr. *Kolb's Present State Cape Good-Hope* II. 127 A few that are call'd Wild *Red Cats..have a streak of bright Red running along the ridge of the back. **1781** PENNANT *Hist. Quadrup.* II. 564 Wild Red Cat. **1947** *Cape Times* 3 May 14 Buck which used to be plentiful have been almost exterminated by wild red cats. **1966** E. PALMER *Plains of Camdeboo* x. 180 There could have been lynx or red cats in the mountain behind us... Even in a zoo these animals are wonderful, the size of a small leopard, not spotted but brick red with jet-black pointed ears and emerald eyes. **1825** C. WATERTON *Wanderings S. Amer.* 285 Amongst the bare roots of the trees..a *red crab sometimes makes its appearance. **1887** RATHBUN in Goode *Fisheries U.S.* II. 657 The common crab (*Cancer magister*); the red crab (*Cancer productus*); the rock crab [etc.]. **1862** *Chambers's Encycl.* III. 528/2 The name Dhole is extended to some other very similar species or varieties, natives of Ceylon, Nepaul, and other parts of the East, to which the common name *Red Dogs has been sometimes applied. **1894** KIPLING *Second Jungle Bk.* 178 'What moves?' said Phao... 'The dhole, the dhole of the Dekkan—Red Dog, the Killer!' **1957** P. J. DARLINGTON *Zoogeogr.* vi. 394 *Cuon* (the Dhole or Red Dog), widely distributed in southern and eastern Asia. [**1637** T. MORTON *New Eng. Canaan* II. v. 79 The Foxes are of two colours; the one redd, the other gray.] **1778** in *Essex Inst. Hist. Coll.* (1913) XLIX. 109 Sold..38 *red fox skins. **1816** WARDEN *Descr. Columbia* 159 The grey and the red fox frequent this region. **1875** COPE in *Smithson. Coll.* XIII. I. iii. 62 Our red fox (*Vulpes fulvus*) is nearly related to the European fox (*V. vulgaris*). **1917** H. E. ANTHONY *Mammals Amer.* 72/2 The Red Fox mates in February or early in March. **1974** *Harper's & Queen* Sept. 37/3 *(caption)* Red Fox Jacket £450. **1844** J. BACKHOUSE *Narr. Visit Mauritius & S. Afr.* xxviii. 485 The *Red Hare or Roode Haas..is smaller than the Common Hare. **1879** GOODE *Ibid.* XXIII. iv. 19 *Lepus Americanus*, var. *Washingtonii*.—Red Hare.—West of Rocky Mountains from Columbia River into British Columbia. **1912** J. STEVENSON-HAMILTON *Animal Life Afr.* xvi. 252 The red hare..has only recently acquired the dignity of a separate genus. **1939** [see KLIPBOK]. **1971** C. M. VAN DER WESTHUIZEN in D. J. Potgieter et al. *Animal Life S. Afr.* 396/1 The red hares (*Pronolagus* spp.) are peculiar to Southern Africa, where they inhabit elevated and hilly country. **1947** J. STEVENSON-HAMILTON *Wild Life S. Afr.* xii. 80 The Cape or *red hartebeest..is now found only in the remoter parts of the north-west of the Cape Province and portions of the deserts of Bechuanaland and South-West Africa. **1966** E. PALMER *Plains of Camdeboo* viii. 134 The red hartebeest was almost certainly here for it was once one of the commonest antelope in the Cape. **1979** DELANY & HAPPOLD *Ecol. Afr. Mammals* vii. 152 Blue wildebeest, red hartebeest and eland..are elements of a fauna found further to the south. **1865** *Red howler [see HOWLER 1 b]. **1894** H. O. FORBES *Hand-bk. Primates* I. 194 The Red Howlers always travel in large companies. **1958** J. CAREW *Wild Coast* viii. 109 The forest was full of noises—the roar of red howlers. **1877** *Nature* XV. 419/1 A *Red Kangaroo (*Macropus rufus*), born in the Gardens. **1848** CRAIG s.v. *Red*, *Red lemur, the quadrumanous animal, *Lemur rubra*. **1875** COPE in *Smithson. Coll.* XIII. I. iii. 65 The *red lynx and raccoon are examples.., and several species of wood-warblers. **1894** *Rep. Vermont Board Agric.* XIV. 176 A little kerosene on the roosts will destroy the *red mites that are so troublesome. **1912** J. H. ROBINSON *Princ. & Pract. Poultry Culture* xx. 342 Red mites..secrete themselves about the roosts. **1950** *N.Z. Jrnl. Agric.* Feb. 146/3 Some vegetable crops, including beans, are liable to become severely infested with red mite. *Ibid.* 182/3 Infestations of body lice, red mite, and intestinal worms all weaken the birds' constitution. **1976** WALTERS & PARKER *Keeping Chickens* vi. 61 Red mites. These are in fact greyish in colour, about the size of a pinhead and live in cracks and joints in the woodwork of the house. **1781** PENNANT *Hist. Quadrup.* II. 487 *Red Mole ..*Talpa rubra Americana*. **1840** *Cuvier's Anim. Kingd.* 80 The Red Mole of America..is more likely the *Scalops canadensis*. **1790** BEWICK *Hist. Quadrup.* 403 The Patas, or *Red Monkey. **1848** CRAIG s.v. *Red*, Red or Patas monkey, the *Cercopithecus ruber* of Geoffroy, and *Simia rubra* of Linnæus. *c* **1475** *Pict. Voc.* in Wr.-Wülcker 760/12 *Hic roonideus*, a *redmowse. **1774** G. WHITE *Selborne* lx, As my neighbour was housing a rick he observed that his dogs devoured all the little red mice that they could catch, but rejected the common mice. **1840** *Cuvier's Anim. Kingd.* 55 The Pongo..is known only to occur in Borneo where the *Red Ourang has not been ascertained to exist. **1955** F. BOURLIÈRE *Mammals of World* vi. 184 The *Red Panda is a solitary animal. **1971** L. H. MATTHEWS *Life of Mammals* II. ix. 266 The red or lesser panda..inhabits parts of western China and the slopes of the Himalayas. **1781** PENNANT *Hist. Quadrup.* II. 452 *Red Rat, *Mus Rutilus*... Inhabits Sibiria, from the Oby eastward to Kamtschatka. **1868** *Red river hog [see RIVER *sb.*[1] 6]. **1953** G. M. DURRELL *Overloaded Ark* i. 38 A fully grown pair of Red River Hogs fled... They were the most vivid orange colour with long white tufts on their ears, and a flowing mane of white hair along their backs. [**1872** 'IDSTONE' *Dog* xii. 108 The Irish Setter should be of a pure rich mahogany red.] **1885** *Red setter [see SETTER *sb.*[1] 11 a]. **1893** R. B. LEE *Hist. & Descr. Mod. Dogs (Sporting Div.)* xvii. 343 One cannot say that the Irish red setter, the Irish terrier, and the water spaniel of Ireland, came at any recent date from one stock. **1912** A. HUXLEY *Let.* 23 June (1969) I. 46 For the past week the..beautiful red setter has been ill, refusing nourishment. **1954** M. K. WILSON tr. *Lorenz's Man meets Dog* viii. 78 A Red Setter or a dog of a similar long-haired, long-eared breed. **1977** *Irish Press* 29 Sept. 16/2 (Advt.), Red Setter pups 6 weeks old, male and female, parents F.T.C. **1783** BARBUT *Vermes* 30 *Limax Rufus*... The *Red Slug. **1839** *Penny Cycl.* XIII. 486/2 *Arion rufus*. Red Slug. *Ibid.*, The supposed virtues of a decoction..of Red Slugs in disorders of the chest. **14..** *Stockh. Med. MS.* in *Anglia* XVIII. 297 Late gadre an hep of *red[e] snayl[is] þat crepyn aboute in reyn and haylys. *c* **1450** *M.E. Med. Bk.* (Heinrich) 200 Tak þe water of þe rede sneyl. **1752** J. HILL *Hist. Anim.* 87 *Limax subrufus*... The naked red Snail. **1688** CLAYTON in *Phil. Trans.* XVIII. 134 There is another sort of deadly Snake, called the *Red Snake. [**1637** T. MORTON *New Eng. Canaan* II. v. 81 There are Squirils of three sorts, very different in shape and condition; one..is red, and hee haunts our howses, and will rob us of our Corne.] **1682** T. ASH *Carolina* 22 There are.. the *Red, the Grey, the Fox and Black Squirrels. **1795** *Stat. Acct. Scotland* XV. xxi. 439 The red squirrel..has become extremely common of late years. **1819** WARDEN *United States* I. 230 The Red Squirrel, not so large as the Grey, has its name from a reddish stripe which runs along the back. **1847** AUDUBON & BACHMAN *Vivip. Quad. N.A.* I. 129 Providence has placed much food..within reach of the Red-Squirrel during winter. **1902** W. D. HULBERT *Forest Neighbors* 102 Other sounds there were..the scolding of the red squirrel, disturbed and angry. **1935** [see GREY SQUIRREL]. **1971** *Country Life* 17 June 1538/1 It is not within my memory when red squirrels were about in fair numbers. **1972** *Ecology* LIII. 1142/1 Pasture juniper fruits provide winter food for red squirrels. **1828** *The Crypt* III. 9 A serpent, known to the gamekeepers of Dorsetshire under the name of the *Red Viper,..considered to be more poisonous than the common viper, but is fortunately very rare. **1859** [see *red adder* above]. **1840** *Cuvier's Anim. Kingd.* 91 The *Red Wolf..From the marshes of South America. **1876** GOODE in *Smithson. Coll.* XIII. VI. 69 Red Wolf. **1942** G. M. ALLEN *Extinct & Vanishing Mammals* 229 The typical form of red wolf was slightly the smallest of the three races. **1964** [see *grey wolf* s.v. GREY, GRAY *a.* 8 b]. **1969** J. FISHER et al. *Red Bk.* 75/2 It [*sc.* the giant panda] appears to be without natural enemies, with the possible exception of the leopard and the red wolf. **1978** B. H. LOPEZ *Of Wolves & Men* 279 My wife and I raised two hybrid red wolves.

b. *Birds*, as ***red butcher-bird, creeper, dunlin, heron, humming-bird, oriole, pheasant, sandpiper, sheldrake, shrike, sparrow, wheatear*** (see quots.); **red bishop (bird)**, an African weaver belonging to the genus *Euplectes*, esp. *E. orix*; **red-chatterer**, the Surinam red-bird, *Ampelix carnifex*; **red cock**, the grouse; †**red coot-foot**, = *red phalarope*; **red curassow**, the red Peruvian hen, *Crax rubra*; †**red curlew**, the scarlet ibis; **red duck**, the castaneous or white-eyed duck; **red falcon**, †(*a*) an East Indian falcon, also called *red Indian falcon*; †(*b*) the female peregrine falcon when a year old; (*c*) the merlin; **red fink**, the red grenadier grosbeak, *Ploceus oryx*; **red flammant, flamingo**, the common flamingo, *Phœnicopterus ruber*; **red godwit**, the bar-tailed or black-tailed godwit, *Limosa rufa* or *ægocephala*; **red goose**, *U.S.*, the snow-goose (*Cent. Dict.* 1891); **red grosbeak**, the cardinal grosbeak or Virginia nightingale; **red grouse** (see GROUSE 1 b); **red hawk**, (*a*) a yearling hawk; (*b*) the merlin; **red hoop**, the bullfinch; **red jungle-fowl** (see JUNGLE *sb.* 3 b); **red kite**, the common kite; **red knot**, the sanderling and knot in summer plumage; **red lark**, (*a*) ? the meadow or water pipit; (*b*) the American tit-lark; **red linnet**, (*a*) the common linnet; (*b*) the lesser redpoll; (*c*) the goldfinch; **red lobefoot**, the red phalarope; **red macaw**, the red-and-blue macaw; **red martin**, *U.S.*, the red godwit (*Cent. Dict.*); **red mavis** *U.S.*, the common ground thrush, *Toxostoma rufum*; = *brown-thrasher* s.v. BROWN *a.* 6; **red owl**, *Strix asio*; **red partridge**, the red-legged partridge; **red phalarope**, the grey phalarope in summer plumage; **red ptarmigan**, the grouse; **red rail**, the Virginia rail (*Cent. Dict.*); **red robin**, (*a*) the redbreast; (*b*) = next; **red tanager**, the scarlet tanager; **red thrush**, (*a*) the redwing, *Turdus iliacus*; (*b*) the American red-breasted thrush; **red tiercel**, the male peregrine falcon when a year old. (For *red-back, -bill*, etc., see 18 b, and main words.) Also RED-BIRD, RED-GAME.

1884 E. L. LAYARD *Birds S. Afr.* (ed. 2) 462 *Red Bishop Bird..though not an uncommon bird, is certainly a very local one. **1939** *Nature* 1 Apr. 566/1 The red bishop has never been found to have more than three wives in his large territory. **1955** MACKWORTH-PRAED & GRANT *Birds E. & N.E. Afr.* II. 951 Zanzibar Red Bishop..differs from the South African and Tanganyika Territory races of the Red Bishop. **1966** E. PALMER *Plains of Camdeboo* xii. 197 Here would be red bishop birds in summer plumage, the grenadier of Barrow... Sita saw a bird like a jewel sail past her... It was a red bishop bird, black and glowing scarlet, on its way to the reeds with its drab-coloured harem. **1743** EDWARDS *Nat. Hist. Birds* I. II. 54 The Crested *Red or Russit Butcher-Bird. **1783** LATHAM *Gen. Synopsis Birds* II. I. 97 *Red Ch[atterer]. **1817** SHAW *Gen. Zool.* X. II. 425 Red Chatterer, with a band through the eyes and the tips of the quills and tail-feathers black. **1776** PENNANT *Brit. Zool.* (ed. 4) I. 229 *Red Cock. **1828** FLEMING *Brit. Anim.* 100 *Lobipes hyperboreus*. *Red Coot-foot. **1782** LATHAM *Gen. Synopsis Birds* I. II. 721 *Red Creeper, *Trochilus coccineus*... Supposed to be found in Mexico. **1802** BINGLEY *Anim. Biog.* (1813) II. 142 The Red Creeper. This diminutive inhabitant of New Spain..I mention merely for the purpose of describing its nest. **1819** SHAW *Gen. Zool.* XI. I. 169 The *Red Curassow is the size of a turkey. **1754** CATESBY *Nat. Hist. Carolina* I. 84 The *Red Curlew. **1769** BANCROFT *Guiana* 172 The Curlew of Guiana is the Indian or Red Curlew of Ray. **1785** PENNANT *Arct. Zool.* II. 576 Lapmark, *Red, and Garganey Duck. **1817** T. FORSTER *Nat. Hist. Swallowtribe* (ed. 6) 95 *Anas Nyroca*, Castaneous duck.. Red duck. **1824** SHAW *Gen. Zool.* XII. I. 96 *Red Dunlin (*Pelidna Subarcuata*)..Dunlin with the beak longer than the head. *a* **1672** WILLUGHBY *Ornith.* (1676) Pl. 9 *Falco ruber Indicus*..The *Red Indian Falcon. **1678** RAY *Willughby's Ornith.* 81 The Red Falcon. **1887** SMITH *Birds* 69 (E.D.D.) The female when a yearling was termed a 'Red Falcon'. **1890** WATSON *Nature & Woodcraft* viii, The Keeper's 'red falcon' is the beautiful Merlin. **1867** LAYARD *Birds S. Africa* 185 *Red Fink of Colonists... The 'Red Caffre Fink', though not an uncommon bird, is certainly a very local one. **1785** PENNANT *Arct. Zool.* II. 504 *Red Flammant. **1785** LATHAM *Gen. Synopsis Birds* V. 299 Pl. 93 *Red Flamingo. **1824** SHAW *Gen. Zool.* XII. I. 186 Red Flamingo with the quills black. **1766** PENNANT *Brit. Zool.* (1768) II. 353 The *red godwit is superior in size to the common kind. **1824** SHAW *Gen. Zool.* XII. I. 78 The Red Godwit is found in various parts of Europe, Asia, and North America: in England it is found throughout the year. **1885** SWAINSON *Prov. Names Birds* 199 Black-Tailed Godwit. Also called Red godwit (Ireland). **1731** ALBIN *Nat. Hist. Birds* 55 pl. 57 The *Red Grosbeak, or Virginia Nightingale... Some call it the Virginia Nightingale, and in Virginia, &c. they call it the Red-bird, but more properly the Red Grosbeak. **1776** T. PENNANT *Brit. Zool.* (ed. 4) I. 269 Grous..*Red... The plumage on the head and neck is of a light tawny red. **1794** HUTCHINSON *Hist. Cumbld.* I. 17/2 Moor Game or Red Grous. **1843** YARRELL *Brit. Birds* II. 321 Some authors have called our Red Grouse, the Red Grous Ptarmigan, the Red Ptarmigan, and the Brown Ptarmigan. **1849** M. ARNOLD *Resignation* 70 The red-grouse, springing at our sound. **1910** MALCOLM & MAXWELL *Grouse* i. 1 We shall be almost exclusively concerned with the red grouse. **1927** S. GORDON *Days with Golden Eagle* xiv. 93 The grey or hooded crow is a far more deadly enemy to red grouse than the golden eagle. **1971** *Country Life* 12 Aug. 390/1 It [*sc.* heather] provides the main food of that highly famed bird, the Scottish red grouse. **1500–20** DUNBAR *Poems* xxii. 7, I do lyk ane *reid halk schout. **1828** SIR J. S. SEBRIGHT *Hawking* 32 The young hawks of the year are called red hawks, from the colour of their plumage. **1890** WATSON *Nature & Woodcraft* 13 The great grouse poachers of the Moors are the beautiful little Merlins... The 'red hawk' is plucky beyond its size and strength, and will pull down a partridge. **1678** RAY *Willughby's Ornith.* 283 The greater speckled or *red Heron of Aldrovand. **1802** MONTAGU *Ornith. Dict.* (1831) 59 Bullfinch... *Red-hoop. **1743** EDWARDS *Nat. Hist. Birds* I. I. 32 The Long-tail'd *Red Humming-Bird. **1840** MACGILLIVRAY *Hist. Brit. Birds* III. 265 *Milvus regalis*; The *Red Kite. **1893** NEWTON *Dict. Birds* 491 In some districts this [the black kite] is much commoner than the red kite. **1824** SHAW *Gen. Zool.* XII. I. 90 *Red Knot (*Calidris Islandica*). **1776** PENNANT *Brit. Zool.* (ed. 4) I. 303 *Red Lark. This species is equal in size to the common lark. **1817** T. FORSTER *Nat. Hist. Swallowtribe* (ed. 6) 77 *Alauda Rubra*, Redlark. **1738** ALBIN *Nat. Hist. Birds* III. 68 The *Red Linnet, Cock and Hen. **1831** RENNIE *Montagu's Ornith. Dict.* 298 A male of three years old is distinguished in the spring, by the name of the Red Linnet. **1893** [see LINNET 1]. **1819** CAPT. ROSS *Voy. Discov.* App. II. lix, *Lobipes Hyperboreas* (*Red Lobe-foot), commonly named Red Phalarope. **1703** *Red macaw [see MACAW]. **1831** WILSON, etc. *Amer. Ornith.* IV. 288 Were one to compare..the red macaw with the ground parrot of New Holland. **1854** THOREAU *Walden* 171 Upon the topmost spray of a birch sings the brown-thrasher—or *red mavis, as some love to call him. **1858** *Atlantic Monthly* Dec. 869/2 The Red Mavis ..has many habits similar to those of the Cat-Bird. **1917** T. G. PEARSON *Birds Amer.* III. 179 Brown Thrasher... Other names..Mavis; Red Mavis; Song Thrush. **1781** LATHAM *Gen. Synopsis Birds* I. II. 431 *Red Oriole... Size of our Black bird. **1785** PENNANT *Arct. Zool.* II. 234 *Red Owl. **1812** WILSON *Amer. Ornith.* V. 84 The Red Owl is eight inches and a half long. **1894** NEWTON *Dict. Birds* 678 Now the 'Red Owl' and the 'Mottled Owl' of the older American ornithologists are known to be one species. **1783** LATHAM *Gen. Synopsis Birds* II. II. 767 Greek Partridge or Great *Red Partridge. **1840** *Cuvier's Anim. Kingd.* 229 The Red Partridge (*Tetrao rufus*, Lin.) and five or six others..are peculiar to the eastern hemisphere. **1776** PENNANT *Brit. Zool.* (ed. 4) II. 414 *Red Phalarope. **1831** RENNIE *Montagu's Ornith. Dict.* 366 To these varieties Temminck has added the Red Phalarope. **1894** NEWTON *Dict. Birds* 712 In summer..the whole of the lower parts are bright bay,.. and hence it has in this condition been called the Red Phalarope. **1752** J. HILL *Hist. Anim.* 486 The *red Pheasant. **1819** SHAW *Gen. Zool.* XI. II. 294 The *Red Ptarmigan is in length fifteen inches and a half. **1843** [see *red grouse* above]. **1776** PENNANT *Brit. Zool.* (ed. 4) II. 394 *Red Sandpiper. *Tringa Icelandica*. Birds of this species have appeared in great flocks on the coast of Essex. **1781** LATHAM *Gen. Synopsis Birds* I. I. 192 *Red Shrike..its body is of a bright red colour. Inhabits Surinam. **1783** *Ibid.* III. 271 This [crimson-headed finch] inhabits the thick woods about the Volga and Samara, where it is called the *Red Sparrow. *Ibid.* 217 *Red T[anager]. *Tanagra Rubra*... Inhabits Canada. **1827** AUDUBON in *Journals* (1893) I. 245 The powers of..the *Red Thrush. **1843** *Ibid.* 516 The delightful song of the Red Thrush. **1885** SWAINSON *Prov. Names Birds* 4 Red thrush (Midlands). **1743** EDWARDS *Nat. Hist. Birds* I. I. 31 The *Red or Russit-Colour'd Wheat Ear. **1817** SHAW *Gen. Zool.* X. II. 569 Red Wheatear (*Vitiflora rufa*). ..Taken at Gibraltar and near Bologna.

c. *Fishes*, etc., as ***red dory, lamprey, mackerel, scallop, sea-nettle***; **red bandfish**, the red ribband fish or red snakefish, *Cepola rubescens* (cf. BAND *sb.*[1] III); **red bass**, (*a*) *U.S.* the red drum or red-fish, *Sciæna ocellata*; (*b*) an Australian fish (see quot. 1898); **red bream** (see quot.); **red char**, the case-char before spawning (formerly regarded as a distinct species); **red cod**, (*a*) the rock-cod; (*b*) a New England gadoid fish, *Pseudophycis bacchus*; (*c*) (see quot. 1836); **red crab**, (*a*) the sea cray-fish; (*b*) an American crab (see quot. 1884); **red cusk**, a Californian fish (see quot.); **red dace**, (*a*) the roach; (*b*) *U.S.* the red-fin; **red drum**, = *red bass*; **red garrupa** (see quot.); **red gilthead**, the sea bream; **red groper**, a red-skinned form of the blue groper, *Achœrodus gouldii*, a marine fish found off the coast of southern Australia; **red grouper**, a fish, *Epinephalus morio*, found off the coast of south-eastern North America; **red gurnard** or **gurnet**, (*a*) a species of gurnard, the rocket or rochet, *Trigla cuculus*; (*b*) = next; **red gurnet-perch**, an Australian fish (see quot.); **red lump**, the cock-paddle; **red mullet**, a surmullet; **red paidle**, *Sc.* = *red lump*; **red perch**, (*a*) the rose-fish, *Sebastes marinus*; (*b*) a Tasmanian and Australian fish (see quot. 1898); **red ribband fish** = *red bandfish*; **red rock-cod**, (*a*) one of several Australian fishes (see quot.); (*b*) the orange rock-fish of N. America; **red rock-crab** (see quot.); **red rock-fish**, (*a*) a Bermudan fish (see quot.); (*b*) one of several fishes of the Pacific coast of N. America belonging to the genus *Sebastodes* or *Sebastichthys*; **red sciæna**, = *red bass*; **red snakefish**, = *red bandfish*; **red snapper**, any of several important marine food fishes belonging to the family Lutjanidæ, esp. *Lutjanus campechinus* of eastern North and Central America; **red sole**, the little sole, *Solea lutea*; **red surmullet**, the plain red mullet, *Mullus barbatus*; **red trout**, the lake trout; **red tubs**, the sapphirine gurnard, *Trigla hirundo*; **red wrasse**, the female wrasse, *Labrus mixtus*. (For *red-belly*, *-fin*, *-mouth*, *-sides*; *red-fender*, *-ribbon*, etc., see 18 b and 19.) Also RED-FISH, RED-HORSE.

1828 FLEMING *Brit. Anim.* 204 *Red Band-fish. **1863** COUCH *Brit. Fishes* II. 263 The Red Bandfish is common in the Mediterranean. **1880–84** DAY *Fishes Gt. Brit.* I. 214 Red band-fish or red snake-fish, owing to its colour, appearance, and movements. **1884** GOODE *Nat. Hist. Aquat. Anim.* 372 In the Carolinas, Florida, and the Gulf, we meet with the names 'Bass' and its variations, 'Spotted Bass', '*Red Bass' [etc.]. **1898** MORRIS *Austral Eng.* 383/2 *Red Bass*, a fish of Moreton Bay, *Mesoprion superbus*, family *Percidæ*. **1898** MORRIS *Austral Eng.* 383/2, **Red Bream*, name given to the Schnapper when one year old. **1924** *Truth* (Sydney) 27 Apr. 6 *Red bream*, name given to young schnapper. **1969** *Man* (Austral.) Mar. 87/2 Another prize for the table is the snapper or red bream. **1674** RAY *Fresh-w. Fish* 109 *Red Charre [see CHAR *sb.*[3]]. **1769** PENNANT *Brit. Zool.* III. 258 The two others [specimens] were inscribed, the Red Charr, the Silver or Gilt Charr. **1880–84** DAY *Fishes Gt. Brit.* II. 109 [The case charr] when exhibiting the bright crimson belly which it assumes before spawning,.. is called the red charr. *a* **1705** RAY *Synopsis Pisc.* (1713) 165 A *Red-Cod or Rock-Cod. **1758** BORLASE *Nat. Hist. Cornwall* 268 The Tamlin Cod, Red or Rock-Cod, about two feet long. **1836** YARRELL *Brit. Fishes* II. 148 On the coast of Durham and Northumberland, and at the Isle of Man, the Cod acquire a dark red or reddish brown colour; and are called Red Cod. **1674** RAY *Catal. Fishes* 105 Long Oyster, Sea-gar, *Red Crab. **1884** GOODE *Nat. Hist. Aquat. Anim.* 771 The Red Crab—*Cancer productus*.. is found along the entire Pacific coast of the United States. *Ibid.* 244 A single species is known in California, the so-called *Red-Cusk, *Brosmophycis marginatus*. **1880–84** DAY *Fishes Gt. Brit.* II. 176 [The roach is] sometimes termed *red-dace from the colour of its fins. **1884** [see *red-fin* in 18 b]. **1803** SHAW *Gen. Zool.* IV. II. 292 *Red Dory, *Zeus Aper*. **1709** J. LAWSON *New Voy. Carolina* 156 Black Drums are a thicker-made fish than the *Red Drum. **1884** GOODE *Nat. Hist. Aquat. Anim.* 362 The Red Drum of our coast, *Sciæna ocellata*. **1893** *Outing* (U.S.) XXII. 94/2 About the first of May the large red-drum.. commence to enter the inlets. **1969** *Daily Progress* (Charlottesville, Va.) 25 May 5 B/1 A big Channel Bass, or Red Drum as it is called in some circles, lay on the charmingly beautiful wild-beach. **1884** GOODE *Nat. Hist. Aquat. Anim.* 264 *Red Garrupa (*Sebastichthys caurinus*)... This species is known as 'Garrupa', 'Rock-fish', and 'Rock-cod'. **1776** PENNANT *Brit. Zool.* (ed. 4) III. 212 *Red Gilt-Head. **1880–84** DAY *Fishes Gt. Brit.* I. 37 *Pagellus centrodontus*,.. Common sea bream, sharp-toothed sea bream. Red gilthead. **1893** J. D. OGILBY *Edible Fishes & Crustaceans N.S.W.* 134 (*heading*) *Red Groper. **1962** L. WEDLICK *Fishing in Austral.* IV. 159 The red groper is now considered to be the female of the species. **1829** *Red grouper [see GROUPER 1]. **1884** GOODE *Nat. Hist. Aquat. Anim.* 410 The Red Grouper is extremely abundant in the Gulf of Mexico in company with the red snapper. **1976** *National Observer* (U.S.) 23 Oct. 19/4 This is the place for exotic fish eating, with surprises like.. Florida red grouper. *a* **1672** WILLUGHBY *Icthyogr.*, *Red Gurnard [see GURNARD 1]. **1776** PENNANT *Brit. Zool.* (ed. 4) III. 243 The spines are longer and slenderer in those of the red gurnard. **1884** GOODE *Nat. Hist. Aquat. Anim.* 256 A single specimen of the Red Gurnard of Europe, *Trigla cuculus*, is said to have once been taken at New York. **1883** *Fisheries Exhib. Catal.* 269 The fish that chiefly supply our market are the *red gurnet, ..mullet,..whiting [etc.]. **1882** TENISON-WOOD *Fish N.S.W.* 48 (Morris) *Sebastes percoides*, a fish of a closely allied genus of the same family... In Victoria it is called the *Red Gurnet-perch. **1804** SHAW *Gen. Zool.* V. II. 261 *Red Lamprey, with brownish back. **1873** F. T. BUCKLAND *Fam. Hist. Brit. Fishes* x. 174 Our fishermen consider them to be different species and call them the *Red lump and the Blue lump. **1803** SHAW *Gen. Zool.* IV. 2 *Red Mackrel, silvery beneath, with small scales. **1762** *Ann. Reg.* I. 149 Brills, pipers, dories, and *red mullet. **1809** SHAW *Zool. Lect.* II. 67 One of the principal species is the red Mullet or the Surmullet. **1840** *Cuvier's Anim. Kingd.* 294 There are two species, both of which are European, the Striped Red Mullet, *M. surmuletus*,..and the Plain Red Mullet, *M. barbatus*. **1862** COUCH *Brit. Fishes* I. 217 The Red Mullet appears to be most common in the Mediterranean. **1885** [see *goat-fish* s.v. GOAT 4 b]. **1880–84** DAY *Fishes Gt. Brit.* I. 181 Cock- and hen-paidle or *red- and blue-paidle, according to sex. **1819** WARDEN *United States* I. 431 The following fishes are found in the Lakes Champlain [etc.]..*red-perch, white-perch. **1884** GOODE *Nat. Hist. Aquat. Anim.* 260 The Rose-fish..is also known as 'Red Perch'. **1898** MORRIS *Austral Eng.* 385/1 *Red Perch*, name given in Tasmania to the fish *Anthias rasor*... In Australia, it is *Anthias longimanus*. **1863** COUCH *Brit. Fishes* II. 262 *Red Ribband fish. **1883** RAMSAY *Food Fishes N.S. Wales* 15 The '*Red Rock-Cod'—*Sebastes percoides* and *Scorpæna cardinalis, cruenta*, and *bynoensis*—are rock- and ground-fish, and readily take the hook. **1884** GOODE *Nat. Hist. Aquat. Anim.* 265 Orange Rock-Fish (*Sebastichthys pinniger*)..is usually called simply 'Red Rock-Cod' or 'Red Rock-fish'. *a* **1884** in Goode *ibid.* 778 The *Red Rock Crab—*Echidnocerus setimanus*. **1876** GOODE in *Smithson. Coll.* XIII. v. 57 *Trisotropis guttatus*... With some doubt I refer to this species the *Red Rock-fish of the Bermuda market. **1884** in Goode *Nat. Hist. Aquat. Anim.* 265 Red Rock-fish (*Sebastichthys ruber*)... This species is usually the 'Red Rock-fish' *par excellence*. *Ibid.* 266 Red Rock-fish of Alaska (*Sebastichthys proriger*). **1777** PENNANT *Brit. Zool.* (ed. 4) IV. 86 *Red Scallop. **1803** SHAW *Gen. Zool.* IV. II. 541 *Red Sciæna, with connected dorsal fins, spiny head, and a very long spine on the anterior gill-cover. **1611** COTGR., *Posterol*, the *red sea-Nettle; an ouglie, and imperfect sea-fish. **1822** COUCH in *Trans. Linn. Soc.* (1823) XIV. 76 *Red Snakefish. *Cepola rubescens*. **1840** *Cuvier's Anim. Kingd.* 303 One species..is occasionally found on the south coast of England, where it is known as the..Red Snake-fish. **1775**, etc. *Red snapper [see SNAPPER *sb.*[1] 7 b]. **1879** GOODE in *Smithson. Coll.* XXIII. IV. 47 Red Snapper.—West Indian Fauna and north to Savannah Bank. **1884** —— *Nat. Hist. Aquat. Anim.* 395 In the Gulf of Mexico the Red Snapper is exceedingly abundant. **1973** *Nature* 6 July 49/1 The red snapper, *Etelis marshi* (an Indian Ocean fish). **1978** *Detroit Free Press* 16 Apr. (Detroit Suppl.) 28/2 There is a respectable number of fish dishes, ranging from the irreproachable Florida red snapper to frog legs, scallops and deviled crab. **1978** *Times* 4 Nov. 13/3 Red Snapper baked in a sauce of fresh tomatoes, onions, celery. **1880–84** DAY *Fishes Gt. Brit.* II. 45 *Solea lutea*,..Little sole: *Red sole. **1769** PENNANT *Brit. Zool.* III. 227 *Red Surmullet. **1880–84** DAY *Fishes Gt. Brit.* I. 23 The *M[ullus] barbatus* is known as the red surmullet. **1884** GOODE *Nat. Hist. Aquat. Anim.* 488 The Lake Trout has other appellatives..'Tyrant of the Lake', 'Laker', '*Red Trout'. **1880–84** DAY *Fishes Gt. Brit.* I. 61 *Trigla hirundo*,..tub-fish, or tubbot: sea crows: *red tubs: smooth sides. **1836** YARRELL *Brit. Fishes* I. 286 The *Red Wrasse is a well-marked species, first described by Ascanius. **1880–84** DAY *Fishes Gt. Brit.* I. 258 *Labrus mixtus* ..Female—red wrasse.

d. *Plants*, as ***red asphodel***, ***blite***, ***bramble***, ***briar***, ***cabbage*** (***cole***), ***carrot***, ***catchfly***, ***cinquefoil***, ***colewort***, ***crab-tree***, ***cranesbill***, ***eye-bright***, ***feather-moss***, ***fennel***, ***helleborine***, ***henbane***, ***hickory***, ***oat***, ***onion***, ***passe-flower***, ***potato***, ***sedge***, ***spurry***, ***stonecrop***; **red alder** = *red els*, ROOIELS; **red algæ**, the algæ or seaweeds constituting the class *Florideæ* or *Rhodospermeæ*; rhodosperms; †**red archangel**, = *red dead-nettle*; **red ash**, (*a*) a North American ash, *Fraxinus pennsylvanica*; (*b*) a hard-wooded Australian tree, *Alphitonia excelsa*; (*c*) the silky oak of Australia, *Orites excelsa*; **red bartsia**, the common bartsia, *B. odontites*; **red batata**, a species of Spanish or sweet potato; **red bay**, *U.S.* a lauraceous tree, *Persea borbonia*, of the South-Eastern States; **red bean** (see sense 19 below); **red bear-berry**, the common bear-berry; **red beech**, (*a*) the common North American beech, *Fagus grandifolia*; (*b*) an Australian tree, *Tarrietia trifoliata*; (*c*) a southern beech of New Zealand, *Nothofagus fusca*; **red beefwood**, a Jamaica shrub, *Ardisia coriacea* (*Cent. Dict.* 1891); **red beet**, **behen** (see the sbs.); **red bilberry**, = *red whortleberry*; **red bind**, **-bine** (see BIND *sb.* 2 b); **red birch**, an American species of birch, *Betula nigra*; **red bird's-eye**, (*a*) *Lychnis diurna*; (*b*) Herb Robert (Britten & Holl. 1886); **red box**, a name given to two Australian species of eucalyptus (see quots.), and to the myrtaceous tree *Tristania conferta*; **red broom-rape**, a species of broom-rape, *Orobanche rubra*; **red bryony**, = BRYONY 1; **red buckeye**, the small buckeye, *Æsculus pavia*, of the Southern United States, with red flowers; †**red camomile** (see CAMOMILE 1 b); **red campion** (see CAMPION[2]); **red cherry**, a wild cherry, *Prunus pennsylvanica*, of N. America; **red chickweed**, *U.S.* = *red pimpernel*; **red clover** (see CLOVER *sb.* 1 b); †**red corn-rose**, the red poppy; †**red cow-basil**, = *red valerian*; **red cypress**, a large coniferous timber-tree, *Taxodium distichium*, of the Atlantic States (*Cent. Dict.*); **red darnel**, the common rye-grass; **red dead-nettle**, *Lamium purpureum* (see DEAD-NETTLE); **red dock**, †(*a*) a species of dock, *Rumex sanguineus*; (*b*) the withered stalks of the common dock; **red elder**, the guelder-rose; **red elm**, any of several elms, esp. the American slippery elm, *Ulmus fulva*; **red els**, a South African tree, *Cunonia capensis*; **red fir**, (*a*) (see quot.); (*b*) a fir of western North America belonging to the genus *Abies*, esp. *A. magnifica*; (*c*) the Oregon pine, *Pseudotsuga Douglasii* or *taxifolia*; = *Douglas fir* s.v. DOUGLAS[1]; †**red fitch(ling)**, cock's-head or hen's-bill, *Onobrychis sativa*; **red gooseberry**, †(*a*) (see GOOSEBERRY 2); (*b*) a red variety of the common gooseberry; **red goosefoot**, *Chenopodium rubrum*; **red grass** *S. Afr.*, one of several reddish pasture grasses, esp. *Themeda triandra*; †**red greening**, a kind of apple; **red guayava** (see GUAVA 1); **red haw**, an American species of haw, *Cratægus coccinea*; **red heath**, the common heath or heather, *Calluna vulgaris*; **red hemp-nettle**, *Galeopsis ladanum*; **red horse-chestnut**, (*a*) a variety of horse-chestnut with red flowers; (*b*) the red-flowered buckeye, *Æsculus pavia*; **red iron bark**, a name given to several species of Australian eucalyptus (see quots.); **red jasmine** or **jessamine** (see JASMINE 1 c); **red larch**, a variety of the American larch; **red lily**, †(*a*) ? the red gladiole; (*b*) an American lily, *Lilium philadelphicum*; (*c*) (see quot. 1879); †**red loosestrife** (see LOOSESTRIFE 1 b); †**red lysimachus**, = prec.; **red mahogany**, an Australian species of eucalyptus (see quot.); **red mangrove** (see MANGROVE); **red maple**, a species of maple, *Acer rubrum*, with crimson flowers; †**red mathes** (see MAYTHE); **red mint** (see quots.); **red mulberry**, an American species of mulberry, *Morus rubra*; **red mulga**, an Australian species of Acacia, *A. cyperophylla*; **red myrtle**, an Australian myrtaceous tree, *Eugenia myrtifolia*; **red nightshade**, †(*a*) the winter-cherry, *Physalis Alkekengi*; (*b*) pokeweed (Mayne 1858); **red oak**, a North American oak, *Quercus borealis* (or *Q. rubra*), or a closely related species; **red osier**, (*a*) *N. Amer.* in full, ***red osier dogwood***; one of several species of dogwood, esp. *Cornus stolonifera*; †(*b*) the basket willow, *Salix* × *rubra*; †**red paper-moss**, a red seaweed; **red pepper**, capsicum; **red pimpernel**, the scarlet pimpernel, *Anagallis arvensis*; **red pine**, (*a*) a North American pine, *Pinus resinosa*, also called *Norway pine*; (*b*) a tall evergreen tree of New Zealand, *Dacrydium cupressinum*, also called *rimu* (*Treas. Bot.*); (*c*) an Australian tree, *Frenela Endlicheri*; (*d*) the Japanese pine, *Pinus densiflora*; cf. MATSU; **red plum**, a wild plum of N. America (see quots.); **red poppy** (see POPPY); **red puccoon**, the blood-root of N. America; **red raspberry**, (*a*) the common variety of *Rubus idæus*; (*b*) a wild American species of *Rubus* (*R. strigosus*); †**red ray**, ? rye-grass; **red sallow**, *Salix rubra*; **red sandal tree** or **wood**, (*a*) red sanders wood; (*b*) another East Indian tree, *Adenanthera pavonina*; **red sandwort**, red spurry; †**red satyrion**, some species of orchis; **red sauch**, = *red sallow*; †**red saxifrage**, dropwort, *Spiræa filipendula*; †**red seaweed** or **wrack**, a red alga; **red sorrel**, (*a*) a West Indian name for the tropical plant *Hibiscus sabdariffa*, also called *Indian sorrel*; (*b*) sheep-sorrel; †**red spert**, = *red withy*; **red spruce**, a North American spruce, *Picea rubens*; †**red sumach**, the Sicilian or Venetian sumach; **red valerian**, spur-valerian, *Centranthus ruber*; **red whortleberry** (see COW-BERRY); †**red whorts**, = prec., also ***Spanish red whort***, the strawberry-tree, *Arbutus unedo*; **red willow**, one of several North American willows with reddish bark, esp. *Salix lævigata*; also = *red osier*; †**red willow herb**, the red lysimachia or loosestrife; †**red withy**, = *red sallow*. (For *red berry*, *lac*, *morocco*, *rot*, etc., see 19.)

1907 T. R. SIM *Forests & Forest Flora Cape of Good Hope* xiv. 217 *Red Alder or Red Els. **1852** HARVEY in *Smithson. Coll.* V. II. 1 Rhodospermeæ or *Red Algæ. **1876** GOODE *Ibid.* XIII. v. 60 On the coast of Maine, the bright-red variety of the Cod..is found only on bottoms covered with Red Algæ. **1548** TURNER *Names Herbes* (E.D.S.) 39 Galeopsis after my iudgemente is the herbe, which is called in englishe *red Archaungel. **1634** JOHNSON *Merc. Bot.* 46 *Lamium rubrum*... Red Archangell, small dead Nettle. **1777** LIGHTFOOT *Flora Scot.* I. 309 *Lamium purpureum*. Red Archangel, or Dead-Nettle. **1784** *Mem. Amer. Acad.* I. 492 *Fraxinus*..The White Ash. The *Red Ash. The Black Ash. The Prickley Ash. **1816** WARDEN *Descr. Columbia* 167 Red Ash..*Fraxinus tomentosa*. **1846–50** A. WOOD *Class-bk. Bot.* 464 The red ash is abundant in Penn., and the southern parts of N. England... Leaves of about 7 leaflets, which become reddish underneath. **1889** MAIDEN *Usef. Native Plants* 373 *Alphitonia excelsa*... Variously called 'Mountain Ash', 'Red Ash', 'Leather-jacket', and 'Coopers' Wood'. *Ibid.* 581 *Orites excelsa*... 'Red Ash', 'Silky Oak.' **1965** *Austral. Encycl.* I. 165/2 The red almond (also called red ash, white-leaf, leather-jacket and cooper's wood), is a smooth-barked tree. **1969** T. H. EVERETT *Living Trees of World* 286/2 The red ash forms an irregular head with stout, erect branches. **1597** GERARDE *Herbal* 87 *Red Asphodill. **1846** MRS. LOUDON *Brit. Wild Fl.* 252 The *Red Bartsia.

1857 Miss Pratt *Flower. Pl.* IV. 104 Red Bartsia..is a very common plant in corn-fields, or on dry banks. 1729 in *Dampier's Voy.* (ed. 3) III. 444 *Red Battata's. These are red throughout, and tinge the Hands blue, and a Knife black. 1884 *Health Exhib. Catal.* 159/1 Farinaceous Roots and Fruits.—Red Batata, Fruits of Chayota. 1731 M. Catesby *Nat. Hist. Carolina* I. 63 The *Red Bay... The wood is fine grain'd, and of excellent use for Cabinets. 1734 [see *handboard* s.v. hand *sb.* 65]. 1765 in W. Stork *Acc. E. Florida* (1766) 79 Oak, ash, red bay, spice-tree, papaw-tree, and pine. 1766 J. Bartram *Jrnl.* ibid. 69 That which is called hammocky land is generally full of large evergreen and water-oaks, mixed with red-bay and magnolia. 1838 Loudon *Arboretum* III. xciii. 1299 *Laurus Carolinensis*... The Carolina Laurel, or Red Bay. 1938 M. K. Rawlings *Yearling* iv. 35 The red bay thicket seemed impenetrable. 1846 Mrs. Loudon *Brit. Wild Fl.* 232 The *Red Bear-Berry. [1637 T. Morton *New Eng. Canaan* ii. ii. 63 Beech there is of two sorts, redd and white.] 1810 F. A. Michaux *Hist. Arbres Forestiers de l'Amérique Septentrionale* I. 27 *Red beech..dans les Etats du nord. 1819 Warden *United States* I. 183 Red beech, *Fagus ferruginea.* 1839 Ure *Dict. Arts* 1053 White birch and red beech afford per pound..4 ounces of charcoal. 1846–50 A. Wood *Class-bk. Bot.* 496 The Red Beech is now regarded only as a variety, with the wood softer..and perhaps a slight difference in foliage. 1889 Maiden *Usef. Native Plants* 604 *Tarrietia trifoliata*... 'Red Beech' of Johnstone River (Queensland). It is not unlike common Red Cedar in appearance, but it is harder than that wood. 1894 *Amer. Folk-Lore* VII. 99 *Fagus sylvatica*, white beech, red beech. 1928 Cockayne & Turner *Trees N.Z.* 83 *Nothofagus fusca*..Red-beech. A tall, massive tree. 1970 R. M. Lockley *Man against Nature* x. 204 The native red beech *Nothofagus* takes a hundred.. years to mature. 1578 Lyte *Dodoens* iv. v. 550 The Common *redde Beete is muche lyke vnto the white, in leaues, stalkes, seede, and roote. 1616 [see beet *sb.* 1]. 1882 *Garden* 9 Dec. 510/2 Red Beet is appreciated by most people. 1653 Culpepper *Eng. Phys. Enlarged* (1656) 33 The *Red Bilberry, or Whortle-bush. 1805 R. W. Dickson *Pract. Agric.* II. 744 There is only one species of this plant in cultivation, but which has several varieties, as the *red-bind, the green-bind, the white-bind. 1785 H. Marshall *Arbustrum Americanum* 19 *Red birch..grows to a pretty large size. 1816 Warden *Descr. Columbia* 167 Red Birch... *Betula rubra.* 1846–50 A. Wood *Class-bk. Bot.* 498 Red Birch... Trunk covered with a reddish or chocolate-coloured bark. 1918 N. Duncan *Battles Royal* i. ii. 41 The crew was gathered close about a roaring red birch fire. 1949 Collingwood & Brush *Knowing your Trees* 172 River birch is also called red birch. 1578 Lyte *Dodoens* v. ii. 547 The great *red Bleete is much lyke the other, sauing that his stalkes be very red. *Ibid.*, The small red Blite hath stalkes red as blood. 1653 Culpepper *Eng. Phys. Enlarged* (1656) 38 The Red blite is in all things like the White, but [etc.]. 1889 Maiden *Usef. Native Plants* 273 *Eucalyptus populifolia*... Variously called 'Poplar Box', '*Red Box', 'White Box' [etc.]. *Ibid.* 505 *Eucalyptus polyanthema*... The 'Red Box' of South Eastern Australia. *Ibid.* 608 *Tristania conferta*... In Northern New South Wales it has the following names:—'White Box', 'Red Box', 'Brush Box' [etc.]. c1450 *M.E. Med. Bk.* (Heinrich) 203 Tak hony, may botter.. hemlock & *Red brembel. *Ibid.* 218 Þe croppe of þe Rede bremble. *Ibid.* 177 Croppes of þe rede cool, croppes of þe *rede brere. 1857 Miss Pratt *Flower. Pl.* IV. 78 *Red Broom-rape... This plant..is parasitic upon the common Thyme. 1863 Hogg & Johnson *Wild Fl. Gt. Brit.* II. Pl. 273 *Bryonia dioica*, *Red bryony. Its most common names Red-berried Bryony and Wild Vine scarcely need any explanation. 1860 Darlington *Amer. Weeds*, etc. 88 *Æ. Pavia.* *Red Buckeye. 1881 *Encycl. Brit.* (ed. 9) XII. 206/2 Darwin has observed that *Æ. Pavia* L., the Red Buckeye of North America, exhibits a special tendency..to be double-blossomed. 1611 Cotgr., *Chou cabu rouge*, *Red Cabbage Cole. 1731 Arbuthnot *Aliments* iii. (1735) 63 Red Cabbage is reckon'd a Medicine in Consumptions and Spittings of Blood. 1805 R. W. Dickson *Pract. Agric.* II. 682 This mixed kind..possesses the hardness of the red cabbage. 1611 Cotgr. s.v. *Camomille*, *Red Camomill, red Maithe,.. Adonis red flower. 1710 Salmon *Eng. Herbal* i. 1/1 It is called..in English Adonis flower, Red Camomil, Red Maithes. 1578 Lyte *Dodoens* v. xxxviii. 601 *Staphilinus niger*, *Red Carrot... The red Carrot is lyke to the aforesaid [yellow carrot] in the cuttes of his leaves. 1777 Lightfoot *Flora Scot.* 239 *Lychnis viscaria*,..*Red Catchfly. 1717 *Petiveriana* iii. 12/1 *Red-Cherry. A large Tree in the Woods, not much unlike the Cornel-berry. 1846–50 A. Wood *Class-bk. Bot.* 240 Wild Red Cherry... A small tree, common in woods and thickets in the Northern States. 1845–50 Mrs. Lincoln *Lect. Bot.* App. 73/1 *Anagallis arvensis*, *red chick-weed, scarlet pimpernel. 1578 Lyte *Dodoens* i. lvi. 82 The *redde Cinquefoyle also, is somewhat like to the others, especially like the great yellow kinde. c725 *Erfurt Gloss.* 250 *Calt(h)a*, *reade clabre. [See also clover 1 b.] 1764 *Museum Rust.* I. 110 *note*, A chalky soil, on which the common red clover will not thrive near so well. 1844 H. Stephens *Bk. Farm* II. 556 *Trifolium pratense*, field trefoil or red clover. *Ibid.* 557, I suspect that the true cow-clover.. has been confounded with the perennial variety of red clover. c1450 *M.E. Med. Bk.* (Heinrich) 67 Take a *rede cowle leef, and anoynte hit wyþ þe whit of an eye. [See also *red briar* above.] 1578 Lyte *Dodoens* v. vi. 554 The first kind of the red Cole is called of..Plinie in Latine *Brassica Cumana. Ibid.* 552 The Description of the *redde Colewurtes. The first kinde of red Colewurtes, hath..red greene leaues, with reddish ribbes. 1611 Cotgr., *Chou rouge*, the bitter red Cole; or the garden red Colewort. 1527 *Red corn-rose [see corn-rose]. 1562 Turner *Herbal* ii. 77 Thys kynde [of poppy] is called in English Cornrose or redcornrose. 1597 Gerarde *Herbal* 551 It is also called..in English red Valerian, and *red Cowe Basill. *Ibid.* 1276 *Malus syluestris rubeus.* The great Wilding, or *red Crab tree. 1634 Johnson *Merc. Bot.* 38 *Geranium hæmatodes*, ..*Red or bloody Cranes-bill. 1597 Gerarde *Herbal* 71 *Red Darnell is likewise an unprofitable corne or grasse. 1634 Johnson *Merc. Bot.* 48 *Lolium rubrum*... Red Darnell, great Darnell grasse. 1776 Withering *Botany* I. 66 Red Darnel. The Spike without awns. 1859 Miss Pratt *Brit. Grasses* 127 Common Rye-grass, Red Darnel, or Beardless Darnel. 1846 Mrs. Loudon *Brit. Wild Fl.* 268 The *Red Dead Nettle. 1857 Miss Pratt *Flower. Pl.* IV. 186 Red Dead-nettle... This plant is readily known by the reddish purple tint of its floral leaves. c1000 *Sax. Leechd.* II. 122 Þa fealwan doccan, næs þa *readan. 14.. *Voc.* in Wr.-Wülcker 591/37 *Lapacia* [the rededokke]. *Ibid.* 600/28 *Paradella*, the rede dokke. c1450 *M.E. Med. Bk.* (Heinrich) 87 Take þe rede dokke rootes. 1653 Culpepper *Eng. Phys. Enlarged* (1656) 87 The red Dock which is commonly called Bloodwort. 1880 Jefferies *Gt. Estate* 60 Bird-fowlers..take two large bunches of docks, 'red docks' they call them. 1819 Warden *United States* I. 429 *Red Elder,.. *Vibernum opulus.* 1805 M. Lewis *Jrnl.* 12 Apr. in *Orig. Jrnls. Lewis & Clark Exped.* (1904) I. vii. 299 Some timber..consists of Cotton-wood *red Elm, with a small proportion of small Ash. 1810 [see *moose elm*]. 1819 Warden *United States* I. 190 Red Elm, *Ulmus rubra.* 1878 *Encycl. Brit.* VIII. 152/1 The bark of *Ulmus fulva*,..the Slippery or Red Elm of the United States and Canada. 1956 *Handbk. of Hardwoods* (Forest Prod. Res. Lab.) 88 Elm, English..Other Names. Red elm, nave elm. *Ibid.* 92 Commercial white elm may include some slippery elm (*Ulmus fulva*) also known as red elm. 1880 *S. Africa* (ed. 3) 135 *Red Els..resembles red birch; is used for farm and waggon building purposes. c1710 Petiver *Catal. Ray's Eng. Herb.* §4 Pl. 36 *Red Eye-bright. 1766 *Museum Rust.* VI. 199 Red Eye-bright..has.. purple flowers growing in spikes. 1860 Hogg *Gardener's Year-bk.* 12, July 3... Red Eyebright fl. 1764 G. Edwards *Gleanings* II. iii. Index 346 The *red Feather-moss. c1430 Lydg. *Thebes* Prol., To ward night eate some *Fenell rede. c1450 *M.E. Med. Bk.* (Heinrich) 93 Take of rewe, verueyne, ..red fenel [etc.]. 1844 Lee & Frost *Ten Years in Oregon* 81 The *red fir constitutes the greater part of the timber of the country. 1848 tr. *Hoffmeister's Trav. Ceylon* 498 The red fir or *Picea Morinda.* 1884 [see Douglas[1]]. 1884 [see *mountain hemlock* s.v. mountain 9 d]. 1949 Collingwood & Brush *Knowing your Trees* 106 In close stands the trunks of red fir are clear of branches from sixty to eighty feet. 1957 M. Hadfield *Brit. Trees* 32 Douglas fir,..Oregon pine, red fir. 1974 *Country Life* 12 Dec. 1855/1 A fine Red fir (*Abies amabilis*) a rather rare tree from Washington State and British Columbia. 1671 Salmon *Syn. Med.* iii. xxii. 414 *Ονοβουχίς* *Red-fitch or Cocks-head..rarifies and attenuates. 1653 Culpepper *Eng. Phys. Enlarged* (1656) 71 Cocks-Head, *Red Fitchling, or Medick Fetch. 1857 Miss Pratt *Flower. Pl.* IV. 275 *Red Goosefoot..is quite a frequent plant of salt marshes. 1929 J. W. Bews *World's Grasses* vi. 253 The most important grass in enormous areas of African savanna..is the 'Rooi gras' or '*Red grass' of S. Africa. 1955 J. Cope *Fair House* ii. 37 He [*sc.* a horse] likes the red-grass down here. 1664 Evelyn *Kal. Hort.* (1729) 217 Apples.. Pear-apple, Quince-apple, *Red-greening ribb'd, Bloody Pippin [etc.]. 1716 *Petiveriana* iii. 3/1 *Red Guayava. 1717 *Ibid.* 12/1 *Red Haw. Of an agreeable Taste, and four times as big as ours in Europe. 1851 Schoolcraft *30 Yrs. w. Indian Tribes* 374 We noticed yesterday the red haw. 1863 Wise *New Forest* 285 The three heaths which grow in the New Forest..are respectively known as the bell, black, and *red heaths. 1869 Sowerby *Eng. Bot.* IX. 128 *Cephalanthera rubra*, *Red Helleborine. 1846 Mrs. Loudon *Brit. Wild Fl.* 267 The *Red Hemp Nettle. c1450 *M.E. Med. Bk.* (Heinrich) 231 Leues of mandrake, croppes of þe *rede hennebane. 1717 *Petiveriana* iii. 11/1 *Red Hiccory, the Heart being very red, firm and durable. 1819 Warden *United States* II. 271 *note*, The land is good, and there is abundance of fine tall red hickory trees. 1882 *Garden* 9 Sept. 228/2 The *Red Horse Chesnut..is one of the most handsome flowering trees that enliven our parks and gardens in spring. 1884 A. Nilson *Timber Trees N.S.W.* 65 *E[ucalyptus] leucoxylon.*—Red-flowering Ironbark; Black Ironbark; *Red Ironbark. 1889 Maiden *Usef. Native Plants* 443 *Eucalyptus crebra*... 'White', 'Red', or 'Narrow-leaved Ironbark'. *Ibid.* 471 *Eucalyptus leucoxylon*... Common 'Ironbark'. It is occasionally known as 'Black Ironbark', and from Sydney to the Blue Mountains as 'Red Ironbark', or 'Red-flowering Ironbark'. *Ibid.* 500 *Eucalyptus paniculata*. .. Occasionally called 'Blood wood'. It is the 'Red Ironbark' of the New South Wales coastal districts. 1944 *Living off Land* vii. 137 Slow growers with a dense grain.. include..Snow Gum, Red Ironbark. 1729 in *Dampier's Voy.* (ed. 3) III. 452 *Red Jessamine..At the top grow many red Flowers somewhat cut like the Honeysuckle. 1819 Warden *United States* I. 297 *Red Larch... *Larix Americana.* 1833 *Penny Cycl.* I. 33/1 *Abies microcarpa*, the Red Larch Fir. 1578 Lyte *Dodoens* ii. xliii. 201 There be three kindes of redde or purple Lillies, whereof the first is the small and common *redde Lillie, the second is great. 1847 Audubon, etc. *Quadrup. N. America* I. 343 It..feeds on the meadow-garlic..and red lily (*Lilium Philadelphicum*). 1879 Baron Eggers *Flora St. Croix* 109 *Amaryllis equestris* (Red Lily). 1578 Lyte *Dodoens* i. li. 75 In Englishe, the first [is called] *red Lysimachus, or Wythie herbe, or Louse stryfe. 1884 *Red mahogany [see *forest mahogany* s.v. forest *sb.* 5]. 1889 Maiden *Usef. Native Plants* 508 *Eucalyptus resinifera*... The '*Red' or 'Forest Mahogany' of the neighbourhood of Sydney. 1965 *Austral. Encycl.* III. 404/2 Phillip's 'gum-tree' was the red mahogany, *E[ucalyptus] resinifera.* 1770 J. R. Forster *Trav. N. Amer.* I. 167 The *red Maple, or *Acer rubrum*, is plentiful in these places. 1816 Warden *Descr. Columbia* 193 Scarlet-flowering, red, or swamp-maple. 1846–50 A. Wood *Class-bk. Bot.* 212 The red maple is a common tenant of low woods and swamps throughout the Atlantic States. 1955 [see pace *v.* 2 a]. 1976 *Sci. Amer.* Nov. 111/3 There were other valley species, among them..the sugar maple..and its relatives the silver maple.., the red maple (*A. rubrum*) and the box elder. c1450 *M.E. Med. Bk.* (Heinrich) 70 Tak *rede myntes & rewe. 1548 Turner *Names Herbes* (E.D.S.) 74 Many learned men contayne the red Mynt that groweth by water sydes, and is called of some horse Mynt, vnder sisymbrio. c1710 Petiver *Cat. Ray's Eng. Herb.* §4 Pl. 31 Red Mint. 1846 Mrs. Loudon *Brit. Wild Fl.* 263 The Narrow-Leaved Red Mint. 1717 *Petiveriana* iii. 12/1 Common *red Mulberry. Is very sweet and one of our earliest Fruit, next the Strawberry. 1797 *Encycl. Brit.* (ed. 3) XII. 371/1 The *rubra*, or red Virginia mulberry-tree, grows 30 feet high. 1846–50 A. Wood *Class-bk. Bot.* 509 *Morus rubra.* Red Mulberry. 1896 Baldwin Spencer *Horne Exp. Centr. Austr.* i. 16 We crossed a narrow belt of country characterized by the growth along the creek sides of *red mulga. 1889 Maiden *Usef. Native Plants* 531 *Eugenia myrtifolia*... 'Brush Cherry' or 'Native Myrtle'. Called '*Red Myrtle' in Southern New South Wales. 1597 Gerarde *Herbal* 271 The red winter Cherrie is called..in English *red Nightshade, Winter Cherries and Alkakengie. 1736 Ainsworth *Lat.-Eng. Dict.*, *Halicacabus*,..red nightshade. 1634 W. Wood *New Englands Prospect* 16 Of Oakes there be three kindes, the *red Oake, white, and black. 1663 *Rec. Town of Plymouth* (Mass.) (1889) I. 64 Lott lyeth on the easterly side of the fourth lott and att the south end bounded with a Rid oake stake. 1717 *Petiveriana* iii. 11/1 Red Oak. Is a porous Wood. 1820 T. Green *Univ. Herbal* II. 857/2 *Quercus rubra*, Red Oak-tree. N. Amer. —Varieties, Champion, Scarlet, and Mountain Red Oak. 1846–50 A. Wood *Class-bk. Bot.* 494 The red oak is the most common species in the Northern States and in Canada. 1852 Morfit *Tanning & Currying* (1853) 98 *Quercus Falcata.*—This oak, known..in the Carolinas and Georgia by that of red oak. 1901 H. Robertson *Inlander* 310, I des gwine down to de branch to git me some red-oak bark. 1958 G. A. Petrides *Field Guide Trees & Shrubs* 294 The barks of many red oaks are dark in color. 1976 *Sci. Amer.* Nov. 112/1 The red oak and the white oak, which put down a deep tap root, seldom survive the process of transplantation. 1686 Plot *Staffordsh.* 204 A sort of *Red Oate sowne thereabout. 1762 Mills *Pract. Husb.* I. 409 Red Oats are much cultivated in Derbyshire [etc.]. c1450 *M.E. Med. Bk.* (Heinrich) 97 Take *red oynenons, as many as wolle suffise to make a plasture. c1500 *Bk. Mayd Emlyn* 308 in Hazl. *E.P.P.* IV. 93 A reed onyon wolde she kepe, To make her eyes wepe. 1807 F. Pursh *Jrnl. Bot. Excursion* (1923) 48 Cornus several sorts, among which is the Osier rouge or *Red Osier. 1830 Loudon *Hort. Brit.* 394 *Salix..rubra*, red Osier. 1846–50 A. Wood *Class-bk. Bot.* 296 *Cornus Sericea*, Red Osier. 1857 Thoreau *Maine Woods* (1864) 174 There grew..*Cornus stolonifera*, or red osier. 1864 *Ibid.* 314 *Cornus stolonifera* (red-osier dog-wood), prevailing shrub on shore of West Branch. 1946 T. M. Stanwell-Fletcher *Driftwood Valley* 112 The moose browsed on young twigs of willow and red-osier dogwood. 1971 *Islander* (Victoria, B.C.) 30 May 3/1 A red osier dogwood..shaded our tents. 1972 Fredericksson & East *Silence of North* xx. 182 His [*sc.* a bear's] broad burly rump was vanishing in a thick tangle of red osier halfway down the slope. 1760 G. Edwards *Gleanings* II. iii. Index 346 The *red Paper-Moss. 1597 Gerarde *Herbal* 308 Of bastard Anemones or Pasque flowers..2. *Pulsatilla rubra*, *Red Passe flower. 1591 Percivall *Sp. Dict.*, *Axi*, *red pepper, *Piper rubeum.* 1623 Capt. Smith *Wks.* (Arb.) 629 There is another fruit..of the same or better operation than the red Pepper, and thence borroweth the name. 1792 Mar. Riddell *Voy. Madeira* 87 A variety of the capsicum or red pepper bushes are found here. 1887 Moloney *Forestry W. Afr.* 393 Capsicums, Chillies, Red Pepper, &c. (*Capsicum annuum.* L.). 1611 Cotgr., *Morgeline maste*, *Red Pimpernell. 1809 E. A. Kendall *Trav. U.S.* III. 145, I have referred the sapling of the lumberers to the yellow, *red or Norway pine. 1819 Warden *United States* I. 178 Red or Norway pine, *Pinus rubra.* 1824 Loudon *Encycl. Gard.* (ed. 2) §7046 The pitch or red Canadian pine..is an American tree, introduced in 1756. 1829, etc. [see Norway[1]]. 1839 Ure *Dict. Arts* 1053 Red pine yields per pound..3⅜ ounces of charcoal. 1884, etc. [see matsu]. 1884 A. Nilson *Timber Trees N.S.W.* 81 *F[renela] Endlicheri.*—Red Pine; Black Pine. 1889 Maiden *Usef. Native Plants* 227 *Frenela Endlicheri*... 'Black Pine', 'Murray Pine', 'Red Pine', 'Scrub Pine', 'Cypress Pine'. 1900 A. H. Kent *Veitch's Man. Coniferæ* (new ed.) 145 Two of the species are of great importance in their native countries on account of their valuable timber, viz., the Rimu or Red Pine of New Zealand, *Dacrydium cupressinum*, and the Huon Pine. 1911 [see *Moreton Bay pine* s.v. Moreton Bay a]. 1916 E. Pound *Lustra* 89 The red-pine-tree god looks on him and wonders. 1970 R. M. Lockley *Man against Nature* x. 204 The rimu or red pine *Dacrydium* [takes] two hundred years to mature to the milling stage. 1819 Warden *United States* I. 428 *Red plum, *Prunus sylvestris.* 1846–50 A. Wood *Class-bk. Bot.* 241 *Prunus Americana*, Red Plum, Yellow Plum. 1819 Warden *United States* I. 429 *Red potatoe... *Convolvulus batatas.* 1821 Schoolcraft *Travels* 208 In clambering among the rocks along the river [S. Louis], I found the *red raspberry ripe. 1578 Lyte *Dodoens* iv. xlv. 504 *Phoenix*... This herbe is called..in Englishe Wall Barley or Way Bennet; it may be called *Red-Ray or Darnell. c1000 *Sax. Leechd.* III. 58 genim þu saluian leaf..& *reades seales leaf. 1798 [see *red sauch* below]. 1876 Harley *Mat. Med.* (ed. 6) 646 *Red-Sandal tree is a native of Ceylon and the southern parts of India. 1840 J. Pereira *Elem. Materia Medica* II. 1142 *Red Sandal or red Sander's wood (*lignum santali rubri*; *lignum santalinum rubrum*) is imported in roundish or somewhat angular billets, which are blackish externally, but of blood-red internally. 1889 Maiden *Usef. Native Plants* 369 *Adenanthera pavonina*... The 'Barricarri' (of India). 'Red Sandal-wood'. 1845–50 Mrs. Lincoln *Lect. Bot.* App. 172/2 *Spergula rubra*, *red sandwort. 1578 Lyte *Dodoens* ii. lviii. 225 *Satyrium erythronium*, *Redde Satyrion. 1798 R. Douglas *Agric. Surv. Roxb.* 120 (Jam.) A species of willow, known by the name of *red saugh or sallow, is esteemed next in value to ash, oak, and elm, and brings 1s. 6d. or 1s. 8d. [per foot]. 1578 Lyte *Dodoens* i. xxviii. 41 Som cal this herb in latin *Saxifraga rubea*..in English Filipendula, Dropwurte, and *Redde Saxifrage. 1760 G. Edwards *Gleanings* I. ii. 211 The *Red Sea-wrack or Weed,.. curiously dotted or granulated, and of a beautiful carmine colour. c1000 *Sax. Leechd.* II. 102 Nim niȝontyne snæde eolonan..& endlefan *reades secȝes. 1798 Nemnich *Polygl. Lex.* v. 867 *Red Sorrel. *Hibiscus Sabdariffa.* 1578 *Red spert [see *red-withy* below]. 1777 *Quebec Gaz.* 17 Apr. 2/1 The logs covering the sleepers, shall be of ash or *red spruce. 1797 *Encycl. Brit.* (ed. 3) XIV. 762/1 The *pinus Canadensis* ..includes three varieties, the white.., the red Newfoundland spruce, and the black. 1820 T. Green *Univ. Herbal* II. 858/2 *Pinus nigra*, Black Spruce Fir-tree. N. America.—Red Spruce seems not to be different from this. 1943 R. Peattie *Great Smokies* 157 The red spruce.. crowns only our highest peaks. 1977 J. L. Harper *Population Biol. Plants* xx. 622 At least 50% of the trees in the upper canopy were red spruce. 1634 Johnson *Merc. Bot.* 71 Chick-weede Spurry, *Red Spurry. 1777 Lightfoot *Flora Scot.* I. 235 *Red Stonecrop. 1597 Gerarde *Herbal* 1293 Of *red Sumach..*Cotinus Coriarius* Pliny. *Ibid.* 551 *Red Valerian hath beene so called of the likenesse of the flowres and spoked rundles with Valerian. 1865 Sowerby *Eng. Bot.* IV. 234 Red Valerian. 1777 Lightfoot *Flora Scot.* I. 202 *Vaccinium vitis idæa*,..*Red Whortle-Berries. 1857 Miss Pratt *Flower. Pl.* III. 354 Red Whortleberry, Cowberry... This is a low, somewhat straggling shrub. 1578 Lyte *Dodoens* vi. xi. 670 *Vacinia nigra*, Black Whortes, *Vacinia rubra*, *Red Whortes. 1653 Culpepper *Eng. Phys. Enlarged* (1656) 33 The Red whorts are more binding, and stop..spitting of blood. 1760 J. Lee

Introd. Bot. App. 324 Red whorts, Spanish, *Arbutus.* **1784** *Mem. Amer. Acad.* I. 491 *Salix*... The White Willow. The *Red Willow. The Rose Willow. The Dogwood. **1855** LONGFELLOW *Hiawatha* I. 12 The bark of the red willow. **1895** *Outing* XXVII. 211/1 The lake..was covered with a growth of red willows and rushes. **1969** T. H. EVERETT *Living Trees of World* x. 96/1 Among lower-growing American willows the following are of tree size: the red or polished willow [etc.]. **1578** LYTE *Dodoens* I. li. 72 The second [lysimachion] is the *red willow herbe with Coddes. *Ibid.* VI. lxvii. 744 That whiche hath the reddish barke, is called..in English, *Red Withy, and the better sort therof is called Red sperte. **1611** COTGR., *Osier*, the Ozier, red Withie.

e. *Minerals*, etc., as ***red blende, carnelian, clay, feldspar, jasper, marble, porphyry, sulphur***; **red antimony (ore)**, = KERMESITE; **red arsenic** (see ARSENIC *sb.*[1] 1 b); **red bole** (see BOLE[2]); **red chalk**, (*a*) reddle, ruddle; (*b*) *Geol.* a bed of chalk of a red colour, occurring in Norfolk and elsewhere; **red clay**, (*a*) in general use; (*b*) a fine-grained, red or reddish-brown, abyssal clay of diverse origins, containing windblown particles, meteoric and volcanic dust and debris, and insoluble organic remains; **red cobalt** (†also *red cobalt-ochre* and *ore*), cobalt-bloom, erythrite; **red copper ore**, native red oxide of copper, CUPRITE; **red coral** (see CORAL); **red crag**, *Geol.* a deposit of shelly sand, the upper part of the crag of Suffolk; **red earth**, † (*a*) ruddle; (*b*) a red soil of the tropics and sub-tropics, usu. clayey and highly leached, and coloured by iron; cf. *red loam*; **red hæmatite** (see HÆMATITE); **red iron (ore)**, a variety of specular iron (see quots.); **red iron froth** (see quot.); **red ironstone**, a specular iron ore; **red iron vitriol**, native ferroso-ferric sulphate; **red lead ore**, native chromate of lead, CROCOITE; **red loam**, a red soil of the tropics, usually friable and highly leached; cf. *red earth* (*b*) above; **red manganese (ore)**, native carbonate of manganese, dialogite; **red marl** (see MARL); †**red mercury**, ? cinnabar; **red mud**, (*a*) a marine mud of terrigenous origin, found on continental shelves and in other shallow waters, and coloured by iron oxides; (*b*) a residue from the extraction of alumina from bauxite, coloured red by ferric impurities; †**red mundic**, = next; **red orpiment**, realgar, red sulphuret of arsenic; **red phosphorus**, amorphous phosphorus; **red prussiate**, ferricyanide of potassium; **red rock**, (*a*) *U.S.* (see quot. 1904); (*b*) *Geol.*, a predominantly or wholly granophyric rock of red colour associated with some large gabbroic masses; **red schorl**, titanite, a species of titanium ore; **red silver** (see SILVER ORE); **red soil**, a general name for leached soil of the tropics and sub-tropics, coloured red by ferric compounds; cf. sense A. 1 f; **red tourmaline**, rubellite; **red vitriol**, sulphate of cobalt, also called *bieberite* and *cobalt-vitriol*; **red zinc (ore)**, zincite, manganesian oxide of zinc. See also RED LEAD, OCHRE.

(*Red* is also frequent as the distinctive epithet of those muriates, oxides, precipitates, sublimates, sulphates, etc. of metals, which are of this colour.)

1807 AIKIN *Dict. Chem. & Min.* I. 77/1 *Red antimony has sometimes been confounded with the red silky oxyd of copper. **1816** R. JAMESON *Syst. Min.* (ed. 2) III. 483 Red Antimony-Ore. This species is divided into two subspecies, viz. Common Red Antimony-ore, and Tinder-ore. **1565** COOPER *Thesaurus, Sandaracha*, a bright redde colour vsed of peinters..: some call it *redde Arsenike. **1748** J. HILL *Hist. Fossils* 405 The Authors who have made the distinctions between red Arsenic..and Sandarach. **1839** URE *Dict. Arts* 54 The improper name of yellow and red arsenic, or orpiment and realgar. **1792** *Phil. Trans.* LXXXII. 30 Hoffman discovered that *red blende and feldspat were luminous [etc.]. **1748** J. HILL *Hist. Fossils* 9 The *Red Boles. *Ibid.* 12 Heavy, friable, red Bole, call'd Seal'd Earth of Livonia. *Ibid.* 450* The *red Carnelian. **1875** *Ure's Dict. Arts* I. 732 The colour of red carnelian of Cambray varies from the palest flesh-colour to the deepest blood-red. **1538** ELYOT *Rubrica*, *red chalke, or ruddle wherwith shepe are marked. **1648** HEXHAM, *Roode aerde*, Red earth or Red chaulke. **1748** J. HILL *Hist. Fossils* 62 Indurated Clayey Ochre, called Red Chalk. **1837** DANA *Min.* 382 Under this species [specular iron] must also be included..reddle or red chalk, the common drawing material. **1875** DAWSON *Dawn of Life* viii. 222 The 'red chalk' of Antrim and that of Speeton, contain arenaceous Foraminifera and silicious casts of their shells. **1387** TREVISA *Higden* (Rolls) II. 17 þere is also white cley and *reed [cley]. **1875** DAWSON *Dawn of Life* viii. 222 Red clay ..a sort of ash, composed of silica, alumina and iron oxide. **1827** J. L. WILLIAMS *View of W. Florida* 89 In the gulf [of Mexico], the..red clay lands approach within eighteen or twenty miles of the coast. **1874** *Proc. R. Soc.* XXII. 427 The bottom consists of '*Globigerina*-ooze' or of the red clay produced by the decomposition of the shells of Foraminifera. **1916** H. F. CLELAND *Geol.* vi. 242 Radiolarian ooze and red clay shade into each other in certain places, the deposit being called radiolarian ooze when these organic remains constitute 25 per cent. of the mass. **1926** *Jrnl. Geol.* XXXIV. 140 The *terra rosea* of the Istrian Peninsula, Dalmatia, and Greece consists of red clay, residual from a limestone basement. **1964** W. C. PUTNAM *Geol.* xiv. 371/2 Some workers once thought the red clay consisted mostly of meteoritic dust... Now the evidence appears more convincing that the red clay has a land-derived origin, and that it consists for the most part of the very finest clay and related particles. **1976** *National Observer* (U.S.) 23 Oct. 9/3 But Cooper and his boys are a long way from the red-clay farm he describes so vividly in *Families.* *a* **1977** *Harrison Mayer Ltd. Catal.* 14/2 *Red clay*, a term applied to all the ferruginous bodies, high in iron and manganese. Typified by the clay known as Etruria Marl. **1796** KIRWAN *Elem. Min.* (ed. 2) II. 278 [Cobalt] mineralized by the arsenical acid. *Red Cobalt ore. **1807** AIKIN *Dict. Chem. & Min.* I. 305/2 Red Cobalt. Of this there are two varieties. **1816** R. JAMESON *Syst. Min.* (ed. 2) III. 510 Red Cobalt-Ochre. This species contains three subspecies, viz. Earthy.., Radiated.., and Slaggy Red Cobalt-ochre. **1794** HUTCHINSON *Hist. Cumbld.* I. 51/1 *Red Copper Ore. **1836** T. THOMSON *Mineral., Geol.*, etc. I. 598 This mineral [black oxide of copper] is found in most of the Cornish mines where copper pyrites or red copper ore occurs. *c* **1305** *Land Cokayne* 70 Of grene Iaspe and *red corale. **1752** J. HILL *Hist. Anim.* 97 The large Biota of the red Coral. **1878** HUXLEY *Physiogr.* xv. 249 It is termed a cup coral to distinguish it from other kinds of coral, as red coral. **1851** RICHARDSON *Geol.* (1855) 358 The *red crag is a shelly sand of a deep ferruginous colour. **1879** DANA *Text-bk. Geol.* (ed. 3) 513 Older Pliocene.—Britain.—Coralline Crag and Red Crag of Suffolk. **1601** HOLLAND *Pliny* I. 545 Take ruddle or *red-earth tempered wel with the lees or grounds of oile. **1706** *Lond. Gaz.* No. 4202/3 Red-Earth, lower'd to 4*s.* per C. **1877** C. W. THOMSON *Atlantic* I. iv. 315 Wherever, throughout the islands, a section of the limestone is exposed of any depth, it is intersected by one or two horizontal beds of an ochre-like substance, called locally 'red earth'... This 'red earth', mixed with varying proportions of decayed vegetable matter and coral-sand, forms the surface layer of vegetable soil. **1889** *Bull. U.S. Geol. Survey* No. 52. 25 The red earth of the southern portion of the Great Appalachian Valley is apparently identical, both in composition and in the method of accumulation, with the 'terra rossa' of southern Europe, the 'laterite' of India, and the 'red earth' of Bermuda. **1932** [see *red loam* below]. **1958** C. ACHEBE *Things fall Apart* xxv. 184 There was a small bush behind Okonkwo's compound. The only opening into this bush from the compound was a little round hole in the red-earth wall through which fowls went in and out. **1966** *Official Yearbk. Australia* LII. 878 Red earths associated with old land surfaces are widely distributed throughout the semi-arid areas. **1875** *Ure's Dict. Arts.* II. 739 *Grenada Cocus* or *Grenadillo.* This wood, imported from the West Indies, is called *red ebony by the French cabinet-makers. **1821** SCHOOLCRAFT *Travels* 158 This granite is made up of *red feldspar, quartz, and a little mica. **1796** KIRWAN *Elem. Min.* (ed. 2) II. 169 *Red Hæmatites. **1836** T. THOMSON *Mineral., Geol.*, etc. I. 435 Red hematite (*Rothglaskopf*) is found in masses, stalactites and kidney-form balls. **1868** JOYNSON *Metals* i. 2 'Red hematite', a 'peroxide of iron', a valuable iron, containing as much as 69½ per cent. of ore. **1836** T. THOMSON *Mineral., Geol.*, etc. I. 435 Compact *red iron ore occurs massive or in pseudo-morphous cubic crystals. **1837** DANA *Min.* 382 The varieties of a sub-metallic or non-metallic lustre, were included under the name of red hæmatite, fibrous red iron,..and when [consisting] of slightly coherent scales, scaly red iron, or *red iron froth. **1796** KIRWAN *Elem. Min.* (ed. 2) II. 171 Compact *Red Iron Stone. **1807** AIKIN *Dict. Chem. & Min.* I. 584/2 Red Iron-stone..Of this there are four subspecies. **1837** DANA *Min.* 180 Botryogen..Native *Red Iron Vitriol of Fahlun. **1748** J. HILL *Hist. Fossils* 584 The *Red Jaspers. *Ibid.* 585 Bright, red Jasper, variegated with white. **1843** PORTLOCK *Geol.* 525 The rocks are traversed by strings and nodules of red jasper. **1877** W. JONES *Finger-ring* 268 A bronze ring..set with red jasper. **1816** JAMESON *Min.* (ed. 2) III. 410 *Red Lead-Ore, or Chromate of Lead. **1836** T. THOMSON *Mineral., Geol.*, etc. I. 560 Red lead ore. This mineral was first found in the mines of Beresof in Siberia. **1932** H. GREENE tr. *Vageler's Introd. Tropical Soils* v. 163 The younger the soil, the greater the predominance of unchanged siallitic material, and the soil has then the character of a more or less plastic *red loam. **1932** G. W. ROBINSON *Soils* xiii. 271 P. Vageler draws a distinction between red loams and red earths... In comparatively young soils..the clay is of a siliceous type and the soil is described as a red loam. In the red earths, removal of silicic acid or accession of sesquioxides has proceeded sufficiently to give a weathering complex of a predominantly sesquioxidic character. **1816** JAMESON *Syst. Min.* (ed. 2) III. 334 *Red Manganese-Ore. **1868** WATTS *Dict. Chem.* V. 78 Red Manganese, or Diallogite. **1656** W. D. tr. *Comenius' Gate Lat. Unl.* §87 Alabaster, the whitest marble, and the *red marble (*porphyrites*) are cut out of the quarrie. **1839** URE *Dict. Arts* 801 The red marble of Verona is of a red rather inclining to yellow or hyacinth. **1664** *Method Chem. Phil. & Physick* 245 Sublime the *red Mercury from the Alume. **1885** *Rep. Sci. Results Voy. H.M.S. Challenger: Narrative* I. xxi. 918 *Red muds. **1926** *Jrnl. Geol.* XXXIV. 140 The red muds which Murray found in such quantities in the Atlantic Ocean off the mouth of the Amazon River. **1936** *Metals Handbk.* (Amer. Soc. Metals) 902 The Bayer process is almost universally employed for the purification of bauxite. In this process the bauxite is digested with caustic soda solution under pressure and the alumina dissolved out as a solution of sodium aluminate. The residue, known as red mud, contains the oxides of iron, silicon, and titanium [etc.]. **1972** *Daily Tel.* (Colour Suppl.) 27 Oct. 25/1 There are tentative hopes for a new industry based on 'red mud'. This is the unpleasant-looking residue of the aluminium process... Red mud may yet be pay dirt. **1748** J. HILL *Hist. Fossils* 406, I have lately received a very fine specimen of it [red orpiment] from the tin mines of Cornwall, under the name of *red Mundick, everything that is bright and sparkling being called there by that name. *Ibid.* 405 *Red Orpiment has been a name usually given by the more judicious to Sandarach,..and by the vulgar to red Arsenic. **1837** DANA *Min.* 432 It [light red silver ore] is an important Ore of Silver. Red Orpiment, which it sometimes resembles, differs from it in having a yellow streak. **1865** *Chambers' Encycl.* s.v. *Phosphorus*, *Red phosphorus.. occurs as a deep red amorphous powder, which is perfectly devoid of odour. **1845** DARWIN *Voy. Nat.* xv. (1890) 345, I at first thought it was owing to dust blown from the surrounding mountains of *red porphyry. **1853** W. GREGORY *Inorg. Chem.* (ed. 2) 212 Ferricyanide of potassium (*red prussiate). **1862** MILLER *Elem. Chem.* (ed. 2) III. 685 The red prussiate burns with scintillation when introduced into the flame of a candle. **1880** J. F. CARLL *Geol. Oil Regions* vi. 72 In this record we have two important facts to work upon—the top of the conglomerate and the presence of *red rock beneath it and not far below its base. **1893** *Bull. U.S. Geol. Survey* No. 109. 23 The red rock..is found in three distinct though indefinitely outlined areas... It occupies a position between the gabbro and the fragmental rocks. **1904** *Dialect Notes* II. 387 *Red rock*, the drillers' name for the red shale underlying the Panama Conglomerate. **1908** *Jrnl. Geol.* XVI. 774 The 'red rock dike' of analysis No. 12 is called gabbro-aplite by the author. **1918** *Ibid.* XXVI. 632 The 'red rock' has purposely been left out of the discussion of variations from the gabbro,.. because its geologic relations are very different... The gray gabbro rapidly gives place to a bright red rock... The 'red rock' has become widely known under this name because of its brilliant color and the difficulty of giving it a more accurate classification... The rock here discussed is intrusive and granitoid. **1969** BENNISON & WRIGHT *Geol. Hist. Brit. Isles* xi. 268 Red rocks of Permian and Triassic age outcrop in south-west England. **1800** tr. *Lagrange's Chem.* I. 395 To conclude that the *red schorl is a peculiar metal, united by nature to the state of oxide. **1807** AIKIN *Dict. Chem. & Min.* II. 435/1 Titanite..Red Schorl, of the older mineralogists. *Ibid.* I. 93/2 The substances by which it [realgar] is usually accompanied are native arsenic, *red silver, and galena. **1836** T. THOMSON *Mineral., Geol.*, etc. I. 650 Dark and light red silver were considered by Werner as two subspecies. **1889** *Bull. U.S. Geol. Survey* No. 52. 29 It closely resembles the similar *red soils of Virginia and of many other regions. **1906** E. W. HILGARD *Soils* iii. 34 The 'red' soils formed from the so-called granites and slates of the western slope of the Sierra Nevada of California. **1932** G. W. ROBINSON *Soils* xvi. 323 The red soils which occupy most of southern India outside the black cotton area..are probably similar to the red loams and red earths of East Africa. **1940** G. TAYLOR *Australia* v. 77 All rocks in the west which are not very poor in iron (and not situated in a basin) yield red soils, since the paucity of organic matter allows for a rapid oxidation of the iron in the clay. *Ibid.* viii. 181 The red soils indicate that the material has been peroxidized under a hot sun in an arid climate not subjected to periodic flooding. **1970** *E. Afr. Standard* (Nairobi) 23 Jan. 16/8 (Advt.), Freehold red-soil plot in the most desired residential area. **1748** J. HILL *Hist. Fossils* 402 *Red Sulphur. **1836** T. THOMSON *Mineral., Geol.*, etc. I. 371 The following table exhibits the most recent and exact analyses of the green and *red tourmalins, that have hitherto been made. **1861** C. W. KING *Ant. Gems* (1866) 25 The Red Tourmaline or Rubellite which is as electric as amber itself. **1836** T. THOMSON *Mineral., Geol.*, etc. I. 536 Disulphate of Cobalt. *Red vitriol. This mineral occurs in the rubbish of old mines at Bieber... Colour flesh-red and rose-red. *Ibid.* 541 *Red Zinc. Manganesian oxide of zinc. This mineral has hitherto been found only in Sussex county, New Jersey. .. It was first noticed, described, and analyzed by Dr. Bruce. **1868** WATTS *Dict. Chem.* V. 79 Red Zinc-ore, or Zincite. Oxide of Zinc containing Manganese.

f. Combined with other colours (see quots.); **Red and White Friesian**, a cow or bull belonging to the breed so called, distinguished by its red and white coat from the black and white animals of the older Friesian breed; also *ellipt.*

1678 RAY *Willughby's Ornith.* 114 The red and blue Parrot of Aldrovandus. *Ibid.*, The red and white Parrot of Aldrovandus. **1752** J. HILL *Hist. Anim.* 27 The red and yellow Spider. *Ibid.* 86 The large American red and black Ant. **1760** G. EDWARDS *Gleanings Nat. Hist.* II. 109 The Red and Black Manakin. *Pipra aureola.* **1781** LATHAM *Gen. Synopsis Birds* I. I. 201 Red and yellow Maccaw. **1812** SHAW *Gen. Zool.* VIII. II. 498 Red and green Amazon [parrot]. **1893** NEWTON *Dict. Birds* 528 The Red-and-blue Macaw, *A. macao*, which is even larger and more gorgeously clothed. **1962** *Guardian* 23 Oct. 2/5 A breed of cow making its first appearance at the [Royal Dairy] show this year is the Red and White Friesian. *Ibid.*, One of the Red and Whites has given 8·62 gallons in three milkings at the show. **1975** *N.Z. Jrnl. Agric.* Sept. 65/2 Breeders began experimenting by crossing their purebred cattle with Red and White Friesian and Danish Red bulls.

18. Prefixed to the name of a part (or some distinctive feature) used to denote the whole:

a. of persons, as **red-beard**, one with a red beard, ? a constable or watchman (*obs.*); **red-breeches** (see quot.); **red-clout**, a red-coat (*nonce-wd.*); **red-cowl**, = REDCAP 1 b; **red gown**, a student of St. Andrews University (*nonce-use*); **red-hat**, (*a*) a cardinal; (*b*) a staff officer (*Mil. slang*); **red-jacket**, an attendant wearing a red jacket (cf. RED-COAT 1 b). Cf. also RED SHIRT.

1607 DEKKER & WEBSTER *Northw. Hoe* III. i. D.'s Wks. 1873 III. 39 White haires may fall into the company of drabs as well as *red beardes into the society of knaues. **1868** W. MORRIS *Earthly Paradise* I. 194 Thou laughest—hast thou never heard Of this same valorous Red Beard, And how he died? **1862** in Post *Soldiers' Lett.* II. xxxii. 90 As soon as the rebs saw our *red breeches (the Zouaves) coming through the woods they skedaddled. **1895** CROCKETT *Men of Moss Hags* xxv. 192 His Majesty's *red-clouts. **1816** SCOTT *Antiq.* ix, If you had challenged the existence of *Redcowl in the Castle of Glenstirym. **1828** MOIR *Mansie Wauch* vii, Redcowl, redcowl, come if ye daur. **1773** FERGUSSON *Wks.* (1800) 156 Say, ye *red gowns!.. Gin e'er thir days ha'e had their peer. **1598** BP. HALL *Sat.* v. iii. 74 The *red Hat that tries the lucklesse mayne, For welthy Thames to change his lowly Rhene. **1884** TENNYSON *Becket* II. ii, The King hath bought half the College of Redhats. **1916** W. OWEN *Let.* 3 July (1967) 398 Red-Hats gallup up to us at startling speed .., but they never stay long, or criticise. **1918** A. BENNETT *Pretty Lady* xxii. 146 It was the red hat put me off. **1919** W. DEEPING *Second Youth* xxxiv. 288 When the real job's finished we just throw up our caps and shout. I wish the red-hat element would try to understand that. **1978** A. WAUGH *Best Wine Last* xv. 179 A number of very high-ranking officers were invited... The visiting red hats were not impressed. **1848** THACKERAY *Bk. Snobs* ix, The *red-jackets who hold gentlemen's horses in St. James Street. *Ibid.* x, Slapper's long-tailed..mare in the custody of a red-jacket.

b. *spec.*, forming the names of certain birds, fishes, plants, etc., as **red-beak**, the South African mouse-bird (*Funk's Stand. Dict.*); **red-belly**, (*a*) a species of lake-trout; (*b*) the Welsh char; (*c*) *U.S.* the red-bellied perch or sunfish, the red grouper, the red-fender, etc.; **red-bill**, *Austral.* (*a*) the oyster-catcher; (*b*) the swamp-hen; (*c*) a small bird of the genus *Estrelda*; **red-ear**, (*a*) in full, ***red-ear sunfish***; a North American freshwater fish, *Lepomis microlophus*, which has a red patch on its operculum; (*b*) in full, ***red-ear turtle***; a small North American turtle, *Pseudemys scripta elegans*, distinguished by a reddish stripe behind the eye; also called a slider; **red-face**, a species of love-bird (*Funk's Stand. Dict.*); **red fin**, (*a*) a British fresh-water fish (? *obs.*); (*b*) *U.S.* the shiner and various other American fishes; (*c*) the Australian name for the English perch, *Perca fluviatilis*, which was introduced into Australia in 1868; **red-foot**, an American bird; **red-gullet**, (*a*) the Australian red-throat; (*b*) the red-mouth or grunt (*Cent. Dict.*); **red-knee**, the red-kneed dottrel, *Erythrogonys cinctus*, a species of Australian plovers; **red-knees**, the smartweed, or water pepper; **red-mouth**, a grunt or pig-fish (*Hæmulon*); † **red-neb**, *Sc.* a kind of potato; **red-neck**, a species of brachelytrous beetle (see quot.); **red-root**, *U.S.* (*a*) New Jersey tea, *Ceanothus americanus*; (*b*) the blood-root, *Sanguinaria canadensis* (Webster 1847); (*c*) the stone-weed, *Lithospermum arvense*; (*d*) a plant of the blood-wort family, *Lacnanthes tinctoria*; paint-root; **red-sides**, *U.S.* the red dace or red-fin (*Cent. Dict.*); **red throat**, (*a*) = *redmouth*; (*b*) an Australian singing bird, *Pyrrholæmus brunneus* (Morris); **red-underwing**, a species of moth, *Catocala nupta*; **red-wame**, *Sc.* the char. See also RED-HEART, etc. as main entries.

1792 *Statist. Acc. Scotl., Sutherland* III. 579 Loch-Borley affords, in great abundance, a species of trouts called *Red Bellies. **1836** YARRELL *Brit. Fishes* II. 71 The Welsh Charr is the Torgoch or Red-belly of Wales. **1877** JORDAN in *Smithson. Coll.* XIII. ix. 20 *note*, A fine species called Red-belly, Black-ears, Black-tail Sun-fish [etc.]. **1802** BARRINGTON *Hist. N.S.W.* ix. 345 Taking up his gun to fire at two *red-bills. **1828** P. CUNNINGHAM *N.S. Wales* (ed. 3) II. 18 A long-legged wader, named here a red-bill. **1848** GOULD *Birds Australia* III. Pl. 82 *Estrelda temporalis*, Red-eyebrowed Finch... Red-Bill of the colonists. **1948** *List Common Names Fishes U.S.* (Amer. Fisheries Soc.) 1. 16 *Redear Sunfish *Lepomis microlophus*. **1957** M. B. TRAUTMAN *Fishes of Ohio* IV. 518/1 Three years later the offspring of these 14 Red ears appeared to be..numerous. **1958** R. CONANT *Field Guide Reptiles & Amphibians* 58 Baby Red-ears, commonest of all pet turtles, are sold in enormous numbers. **1977** *N.Z. Herald* 8 Jan. 4-9/5 (Advt.), Miniature red ear turtle, tank, element and thermostat. **1979** *Arizona Daily Star* 1 Apr. C 11/4 A state-record redear sunfish has been reported from Parker Canyon Lake... The big redear was identified by Ft. Huachuca fisheries biologist Bruce Halsted. **1794** HUTCHINSON *Hist. Cumbld.* I. 96 Fishes. Grey trout,..the *redfin, minnow, loach. **1831** WILSON, etc. *Amer. Ornith.* IV. 271, I saw one of them secure a number of red-fins, by wading briskly through the water, and striking at them with his bill. **1884** GOODE *Nat. Hist. Aquat. Anim.* 617 The 'Shiner', 'Red-fin' or 'Red Dace' abounds in all streams from New England to Kansas and Alabama. **1951** T. C. ROUGHLEY *Fish & Fisheries Austral.* 152 English perch (Redfin—*Perca fluviatilis*). **1969** *Southerly* XXIX. 127 Twice, in the dusk, he caught a red-fin. **1819** WARDEN *United States* II. 528 The hatchet-bill, or *red foot. **1848** GOULD *Birds Australia* VI. Pl. 21 Over what extent of country the Banded *Red-knee may range is yet to be determined. **1597** GERARDE *Herbal* Suppl. to Table, *Red-knees is Hydropiper. **1729** in *Dampier's Voy.* (ed. 3) III. 415 The *Red-Mouth. His Back and Gill-fins Scarlet, the rest edged with white. **1884** GOODE *Nat. Hist. Aquat. Anim.* 398 The Grunts or Pig-Fishes..are distinguished by the brilliant red color of the inside of the mouth and throat, from which they have sometimes been called Red Mouths, or Flannel Mouths. **1798** R. DOUGLAS *Agric. Surv. Roxb.* 97 Various other potatoes..of all of which, next to the common white, the one in greatest esteem is the *red-neb. **1872** WOOD *Insects at Home* 81 The present species is one of the few Brachelytra that has a popular name. It is called the *Red-Neck, on account of the bright-red colour of the thorax. **1709** J. LAWSON *New Voy. Carolina* 78 The *Red-Root whose Leaf is like Spear-mint, is good for..sore Mouths. **1788** M. CUTLER in *Life*, etc. (1888) II. 285 Another plant, the characters of which I much wish to know, is called, at Fort Harmar, Red Root. **1838** LOUDON *Arboretum* II. xxxv. 539 The Ceanothus, or Red Root. **1860** EMERSON *Cond. Life, Wealth* Wks. (Bohn) II. 357 He..wakes up from his idiot dream of chickweed and red-root. **1941** R. S. WALKER *Lookout* 59 The commonest shrub..is New Jersey tea or red-root. **1840** *Cuvier's Anim. Kingd.* 296 *Hæmulon* has..the lower jaw compressed, opening very wide and of a bright red. Hence they are called '*Red-throats' in the West Indian Islands. **1720** ALBIN *Nat. Hist. Insects* Descr. facing Pl. 80 It [the moth] is commonly called the *red under Wing. **1832** *Planting* 72 in *Lib. Usef. Knowl., Husb.* III, *Noctua nupta*, red underwing. **1843** WESTWOOD *Brit. Moths* I. 247 *Catocala nupta* (the red underwing). **1793** *Statist. Acc. Scotl.* VIII. 504 This lake abounds with charr commonly called *red wames.

19. a. With miscellaneous sbs., as **red admiral** (see quots. and ADMIRAL 6); **red alert**, a warning of danger; an instruction to be prepared for an emergency, or, in hospitals, to admit only emergency cases; also, a state of readiness for an emergency; also *fig.* and (with hyphen) *attrib.*; **red anchor**, used *attrib.* to designate that period in the history of the Chelsea porcelain factory during which it produced high-quality porcelain with a distinguishing red anchor mark; also applied to porcelain of this period; **red arches**, a British moth (see quots.), also called the *rosy footman*; **Red Arrow**, a familiar name for the nightly express train from Moscow to Leningrad; **red-arse** *Mil. slang*, a recruit; **red ash**, *U.S.* a coal producing a red ash (also *attrib.*); **Red Astrachan**, a red-skinned variety of eating apple; **red atrophy** *Med.*, a later stage of massive necrosis of the liver, in which the organ is red rather than yellow; **red ball** *U.S. slang*, a fast freight train or truck; high priority freight; also *attrib.*; **red-band** *Prison slang* (see quot. 1950); **Red Bank**, the name of an oyster bed in Co. Clare, Ireland, used attrib. in ***Red Bank oyster***; **red banner** = RED FLAG 1, 3 a; also used in the title of various distinctions and orders in the U.S.S.R.; **red bean**, (*a*) the red-skinned seed of one of several legumes; (*b*) an Australian timber tree, *Dysoxylum muelleri*, of the family Meliaceæ; **red beds**, *Geol.*, sedimentary strata deposited in a continental environment, composed largely of sandstone, siltstone, or shale, and coloured red by iron compounds which usu. coat individual grains; *spec.* (with capital initials) a series of W. American strata, of the Jurassic and Triassic; also *attrib.* in *sing.*; **red-berry**, (*a*) any of several North American plants, esp. the red baneberry (*Actæa rubra*); (*b*) (see quot. 1898); **red biddy** *colloq.*, a drink consisting of methylated spirits and cheap red wine; also, inferior red wine; **red blanket** *Austral. slang* (see quot.); **red blood cell** or **corpuscle** = RED CELL; **red board** *U.S. slang*, (*a*) a stop signal on a railway; (*b*) (see quot. 1935); **red body**, in fishes, an aggregation of capillaries on the inside of the swimming-bladder; also, the gland that this aggregation supplies, or both structures together; = *red gland* below; **red bottle-brush**, an Australian myrtaceous plant, *Callistemon lanceolatus*; **red box**, a box (covered with red leather) used by ministers of state for holding official documents; **Red Branch** [tr. Gael. *Craebh Ruaid*], in Irish epic tradition, the name of the most famous of the royal houses of Ulster; **red brass** (see quot.); **Red Brigade(s)**, a left-wing extremist terrorist group operating in Italy from the early 1970s; hence **Red Brigader**, a member of this group; **red card**: in *Assoc. Football*, etc., a card shown by the referee to a player sent off the field; cf. *yellow card* s.v. YELLOW *a.* and *sb.* C. 1 e; **red carpet**, (*a*) a species of moth, *Coremia munitata*; (*b*) the carpet of this colour traditionally laid down on formal occasions to greet important visitors, used *fig.* to indicate a ceremonial welcome or lavish reception; freq. *attrib.*, as ***red carpet treatment***, etc.; **red caviar**, the red roe of fish other than the sturgeon; **Red Centre**, the remote interior of Australia; cf. CENTRE *sb.* 11 h; **Red Chamber**, the Senate chamber of the Canadian Parliament Building, Ottawa; hence, the Senate itself; **red channel**, at a port, airport, etc., the channel through which passengers should pass who have goods to declare; **red charcoal** (see quot.); † **red children**, North American Indians considered as under the guardianship of a white person or agency (*obs.*); **red cock**, a euphemism for fire maliciously raised; **red-cooking** *vbl. sb.*, a form of Chinese cookery in which meat is fried quickly and then stewed in soya sauce; hence (as a back-formation) **red-cook** *v. trans.*; **red core**, a disease of strawberries caused by the fungus *Phytophthora fragariæ*, which attacks the roots, staining the central part of them and making affected plants wilt; **red corpuscle** = RED CELL; **red country**, large tracts of red sand, *spec.* in Australia; **Red Crescent**, the Turkish ambulance society answering to the RED CROSS (sense 2 c); also, the equivalent of the Red Cross in other Muslim countries; **red daddy** (see quot.); **red deal** (see quot. and DEAL *sb.*[3] 2); **red Devon**, a large red-brown bull or cow of the breed so called, usually kept for the production of beef; = DEVON (*a*); **red drops**, = *red lavender*; **red duster** *slang* = *red ensign*; **red dwarf** *Astr.*, an old, relatively cool star lying on the main sequence; also *attrib.*; **red ebony** (see quot.); **red emperor**, an Australian marine fish, *Lutjanus sebæ*, found off parts of the northern coast; **red ensign** (see ENSIGN *sb.* 5); **red eten**, *Sc.* [see ETEN] a monster, a surly person; **red feather**, a species of moth (see quot.); **red fender**, *U.S.* the red-bellied terrapin; **red figure** *Archæol.*, used *attrib.* and *absol.* to designate a technique of vase painting devised in Athens in the late sixth century B.C. in which figures and patterns are outlined and detailed with lines of black paint on a red clay ground and the background filled in with black; so **red-figured** *a.*; **red fire**, a pyrotechnic effect, or the mixture ignited to produce it (see quot. 1869); **red flannel**, flannel dyed red and formerly used esp. for making underwear, nightwear, etc.; also used *colloq.* in *pl.* to designate clothing made from red flannel; also *fig.*; **red flannel hash** *U.S.*, a hash (HASH *sb.* 1) made with beetroot; **red fly**, an artificial fly used in angling (see quot. 1787); **red fog**, (*a*) a sea-haze due to the presence of sand or dust in the air; (*b*) *Photog.* (see FOG *sb.*[2] 4); **red friar**, a Templar; † **red fustian**, *Cant*, red wine; **red giant** *Astr.*, a relatively cool giant star; **red gland** *Zool.*, a gland in the wall of a swim bladder which secretes gas into the bladder so as to increase the buoyancy of the fish; also, esp. formerly, the rete mirabile that supplies the gland, or both structures together; **red gold** (see quot. and GOLD *sb.*[1] 5); **red hackle** (see HACKLE *sb.*[2] 4); **red hardness** *Metallurgy*, the property, exhibited by some steels used for machine tools, of retaining a high degree of hardness up to a low red heat; **red hartshorn**, = *red lavender*; **red hat**, the symbol of a cardinal's office; (see also sense 18 a); **red hay**, *dial.* mow-burnt hay (? *Obs.*); † **red hide** (?); **red Indian**, (*a*) (see INDIAN *sb.* 2 b); (*b*) an Australian marine fish, *Patæcus fronto*, which resembles a blenny; **red judge** (see quot.); *spec.* a high court judge; **Red Kaffir** *S. Afr.* (see quot. 1904); **red lac**, a species of sumach (*Rhus succedanea*, also called ***red lac sumach***), from the fruit of which Japan wax is obtained; **red lamp**, (*a*) a lamp having red glass, used as a doctor's sign; (*b*) = RED LIGHT 2; **Redland** *sb.* and *a.*, the Soviet Union, Russian (*slang*); **red lane**, *colloq.*, the throat; **red lantern** = RED LIGHT 2; **red lavender** (see quot.); † **red leather**, some kind of cosmetic; **red leg** *Zool.*, a bacterial disease of frogs causing hæmolytic septicæmia and a red flush on the ventral surfaces of the hind legs; **red liquor**, a mordant used in calico-printing (see quot. 1839); **red magnetism** (see quot.); † **red mason**, a bricklayer; **red mass** [after F. *messe rouge*], a mass (usually one of the Holy Ghost) at which red vestments are worn by the priest (see also quot. 1896 and cf. Littré s.v. *Messe* 2); **red measures**, *Mining* (see quot.); **red meat**, dark-coloured meat, as beef or lamb (as opposed to chicken, veal, etc.); also *fig.*; **red menace**, the political or military threat regarded as emanating from the Soviet Union; **red metal**, a name given to various alloys of copper having a reddish colour; **redmilk**, a species of mushroom; **red morocco**, the pheasant's eye, *Adonis autumnalis*; **Red Ned** *Austral.* and *N.Z. slang*, inferior red wine or other similar drink; **red noise** (see quots. 1961); **red nucleus** *Anat.*, each of a pair of nuclei in the tegmentum of the midbrain, dorsal to the substantia nigra, which form part of the extra-pyramidal motor system; **red oil**, oleic acid; **Red Paint**, applied to an ancient North American Indian people known from burials in which large quantities of red ochre were used; **red palmer**, an artificial fly (see quot. and PALMER *sb.*[1] 2 b); **red palm oil**, palm oil having a red colour, obtained by boiling the fruit in water instead of by fermentation; **red-pencil** *v. trans.*, to mark (in red) as erroneous or unacceptable; to correct (a piece of written work); **red peril** = *red menace* above; † **red pill** (see quot.); **red planet** (with def. article), the planet Mars; **red poley** = REDPOLL[2]; † **red potter**, a maker of red ware; **red precipitate**, red oxide of mercury, prepared by solution (and repeated distillation) with nitric acid; **Red Prince**, nickname of Prince Frederick Charles of Prussia (1828–85); **red rain**, rain that is red or reddish in colour because of suspended dust or, rarely, red algæ; **red reflex** *Ophthalm.*, a red glow, seen in ophthalmoscopy when the interior of the eye is illuminated, caused by the light reflected from the fundus having passed through the choroid; **red riband, ribbon,** †(*a*) the crimson ribbon worn by Knights of the Order of the Bath, hence, membership of this Order, or the Order itself; (*b*) the band-fish (*Cent. Dict.* 1891); (*c*) *U.S.* as a symbol of temperance; **Red Riding Hood** [f. the fairy tale *Little Red Riding Hood*], used *attrib.* to designate a type of cape with a hood; **red rise,** *U.S.* (see quot.); †**red roan** (see quot. and cf. *red-row*); **red robin,** (*a*) = RUST (in grain); (*b*) the red campion; (*c*) *U.S.*, a perennial herb, *Castilleja coccinea*, which has bright red bracts surrounding small greenish-yellow flowers; **red rock fault** *Geol.*, a fault in Permian red beds, forming part of the boundary of the Cheshire Basin; **red rod,** *U.S.* (see quot.); **red rot,** the sun-dew, *Drosera rotundifolia*; **Red Rover,** a children's chasing game; also, the child who is 'it' in this game; **red row** *dial.* (see quot. and cf. *red-roan*); †**red ruddock** (see RUDDOCK); **red rust,** = RUST (in grain); **red sable,** the fur of the Japanese mink (kolinsky), used esp. for artists' brushes; a brush made from this fur; **red scale,** a scale-insect, *Aonidia aurantii*, infesting orange-trees; †**red scall** (see quot.); **red seed,** a small crustacean on which mackerel feed; **red softening,** a variety of acute softening of the brain, marked by extravasation of blood in the tissue; **red soldier,** (*a*) a pig affected by swine fever or other disease accompanied with redness of the skin; the disease itself; (*b*) a red-coated soldier; **red spinner,** a fly used in angling (see quot. 1858); **red spirit(s** (see quots.); †**red spot,** a pimple or efflorescence of the skin; †**red sprat,** a smoked sprat; **red squill** (see SQUILL); **red star,** a symbol of the Soviet Union; **red steer** *Austral. slang* (see quot. 1941); **red stock,** a kind of red brick (see STOCK); **red-stone,** a stone of a red colour (also *attrib.*); †ruddle; **red stuff,** an iron oxide, as crocus or rouge, used in grinding or polishing; **red tabby,** a cat, esp. a long-haired one, with a reddish-orange coat patterned in a deeper red; **red tag,** name of an artificial fly used in angling; **Red Terror,** the persecution of opponents by the Bolsheviks after the Russian revolution of 1917; also *transf.*; **red tide** = RED-WATER 4; **Red Tory** *Canada*, one of a political group who, while maintaining some conservative principles, yet support many liberal and socialist policies; so **Red Toryism; red twig,** red root (*Ceanothus*); **red varnish** (see quot.); **red vision** *Ophthalm.* = *erythropsia* s.v. ERYTHRO-; **red warning** = *red alert* above; **red wind,** †(*a*) a wind which causes the leaves of trees to shrivel and turn red; (*b*) (see quot. 1857); **red withe,** a tropical American vine, *Combretum Jacquini* (*Treas. Bot.* 1866); †**red wort** (see quot. 1495). See also as main entries: RED ARMY, RED BELT, RED BOOK, etc.

1840 *Cuvier's Anim. Kingd.* 606 This subgenus [*Vanessa*] comprises some of the most beautiful of our British Butterflies, such as..the *Red Admiral. **1872** WOOD *Insects at Home* 399 The splendid, and fortunately common, insect, the Red Admiral (*Vanessa Atalanta*). **1961** WEBSTER, *Red alert. **1962** 'K. ORVIS' *Damned & Destroyed* xxvii. 203 His every move will be under red-alert watch. **1967** *Guardian* 29 Dec. 1/1 The emergency bed service..has put out a 'red alert' to more than 200 hospitals in the London area. **1970** *Daily Tel.* 26 Sept. 1/6 Fearing that the Arabs will attempt to seize another British plane..the Government sent out a 'red alert' to airlines yesterday, warning them to exercise stringent anti-skyjacking precautions. **1972** 'G. BLACK' *Bitter Tea* (1973) xii. 188 It looked as though a phone call to me had resulted in a red alert. **1973** M. AMIS *Rachel Papers* 98 Fortunately, my room was in a state of red alert nowadays and Rachel's telephone call hadn't caught me with my pants down. **1975** *Times* 26 Nov. 1/4 The health authorities at Croydon yesterday put out a 'red' alert of hospital beds... Hospitals in its area will take only emergencies. **1981** W. SAFIRE in *N.Y. Times Mag.* 22 Feb. 9/1 The red alert flashed here a few weeks ago—warning of incoming semantic missiles from the new Secretary of State, Al Haig. **1957** MANKOWITZ & HAGGAR *Conc. Encycl. Eng. Pott. & Porc.* 49/2 Work of the 'raised' (i.e. embossed) and '*red anchor' periods enjoys the highest esteem. *Ibid.*, The resulting quality..was perhaps inferior to 'red anchor' Chelsea. **1966** *Daily Tel.* 26 Oct. 16/4 A Chelsea figure of a Chinaman, Red Anchor period, was sold for £4,200. **1975** *Oxf. Compan. Decorative Arts* 140/2 This factory's [*sc.* Chelsea's] figures of the 'red anchor' period (1748–55 when the factory mark was an anchor painted in red) are among the loveliest in the whole range of European porcelain. **1843** WESTWOOD *Brit. Moths* I. 93 *Miltochrysta miniata* (the *red arches). **1861** MORRIS *Brit. Moths* I. 47 Red-arches (*Calligenia miniata*). **1973** J. SHUB *Moscow by Nightmare* viii. 87 The Krasnaya Strela—the *Red Arrow—leaves Moscow at 11.53 every night. **1974** A. WILLIAMS *Gentleman Traitor* v. 94 You'll be given your ticket on the Red Arrow Express for Leningrad. **1946** R. GRINSTEAD *They dug Hole* I. i. 13 And so it goes on. The everlasting bickering between old sweat and *red-arse! **1947** D. M. DAVIN *Gorse blooms Pale* 193 You were only a bloody redarse in those days. **1874** RAYMOND *Statist. Mines & Mining* 507 To make this..land available for the production of coal, the upper or *red-ash veins having been worked out. **1847** J. M. IVES *New England Bk. Fruit* 36 *Red Astracan.—This beautiful apple is of medium size, of a round and rather flat form. **1860** R. HOGG *Fruit Man.* 21 Red Astrachan... Flesh white, and richly flavoured. **1876** J. BURROUGHS *Winter Sunshine* 128 The red astrachan [is] an August apple. **1948** *Newsweek* 30 Aug. 32/1 The best and most popular American apples are descended from Russian apple trees—Borominka, Titovka, Red Astrakhan, Alma Ata—imported into the United States a hundred years ago. **1977** *N.Z. Herald* 8 Jan. 1-5/5 One store was selling a New Zealand apple, red astrachan, at 33c a pound. **1849** E. SIEVEKING tr. *Rokitansky's Man. Path. Anat.* II. I. ii. 122 Atrophy of the liver, independent of the *marasmus senilis* of the organ, appears in various forms. We first draw attention to two distinct forms which have not been remarked hitherto... Owing to their distinctive colouring, they may be appropriately termed yellow and *red atrophy. **1961** R. D. BAKER *Essent. Path.* xvi. 409 Massive necrosis... If the patient lives several weeks after the onset of jaundice subacute red atrophy is found at autopsy. **1927** *Amer. Speech* II. 388/2 Fast freights are known as **red balls.* **1934** *Sun* (Baltimore) 3 May 12/6 Several who have worked on these 'red ball' runs told me that after a man has been on a truck twenty-four hours he's tired and unstrung. **1944** *N.Y. Times* 8 Oct. IV. 5/4 The famous Red Ball highway—a belt of one-way roads for truck convoys that actually kept pace with General Patton's advance. *Ibid.* 5/5 It was assumed that bullets and butter, and gasoline as important as either, would be delivered. It was—once the Red Ball got rolling. **1968** *T.V. Times* (Austral.) 29 May 18/3 In railway language 'Red Ball' means top priority freight. **1950** P. TEMPEST *Lag's Lexicon* 178 **Redband*, a privileged prisoner. He is allowed to travel freely about the prison in pursuance of his duties. **1952** J. HENRY *Who lie in Gaol* x. 143 That prisoners could walk through the house unaccompanied by a red-band or an officer seemed to her little short of madness. **1976** A. MILLER *Inside Outside* 3, I would then have a cup of coffee brought to me by a 'red band'. **1876** *Encycl. Brit.* V. 803/1 Near Pooldoody is the great Burren oyster bed called the *Red Bank,..from which a constant supply of the excellent Red Bank oysters is furnished to the Dublin and other large markets. **1922** JOYCE *Ulysses* 325 He spat a Red bank oyster out of him. **1935** S. & B. WEBB *Soviet Communism* II. ix. 759 The *Red Banner of Toil is awarded 'by special decision' of the Central Executive Committee (TSIK) of the All-Union Congress of Soviets. **1957** *Encycl. Brit.* XXII. Pl. iv, following p. 704, *Order of the Red Banner*: For conspicuous bravery or self-sacrifice in time of war, special capacity for leadership or some action contributing decisively to the success of soviet arms (military or civil). **1966** tr. Lin Piao in *Quotations from Chairman Mao Tse-tung* (Foreword), The most fundamental task in our Party's political and ideological work is at all times to hold high the great red banner of Mao Tse-tung's thought. **1974** tr. *Sniečkus's Soviet Lithuania* 28 New fighting patriots took the places of those that were killed or jailed, keeping the red banner of revolution flying. **1977** *N.Y. Rev. Bks.* 26 May 24/3 The pilgrims move in ranks, by sections, red banners flying. **1892** T. F. GARRETT *Encycl. Pract. Cookery* 93/2 *Red Haricot Beans à la Bourguignonne... Take 1 qt. of Red Beans, pick out any stones. **1895** [see *black bean* s.v. BLACK *a.* 19]. **1908** J. H. MAIDEN *Forest Flora N.S.W.* III. 115 'Red bean' is, however, the commonest name..because it is supposed to resemble the timber of the Black Bean..except in colour. **1931** E. SHERSON *Bk. Vegetable Cookery* viii. 161 Boil the little red beans in the usual way. **1932** [see *pencil cedar* s.v. PENCIL *sb.*[2] 7b]. **1965** *Austral. Encycl.* I. 468/2 Other trees to which the name [bean] is applied are the red bean.., walnut bean.., and yellow bean. **1977** *Sunday Times* (Colour Suppl.) 4 Dec. 19/1 *Afters*: 'toffee apple', red-bean pancakes. **1980** *Times* 21 June 11/6 Red-bean salad in a sweet, spicy dressing. **1849** *Q. Jrnl. Geol. Soc.* V. 25 The appearance at certain points of the series of stratified deposits of red sandstones and other rocks coloured by the peroxide of iron, in regions where the older formations contain comparatively few *red beds, is a fact observed in many countries. **1888** *Encycl. Brit.* XXIII. 797/2 This group is succeeded by the series of deep-red sandy gypsiferous strata, the 'Red Beds' of the Rocky Mountain geologists. **1922** *Bull. Geol. Soc. Amer.* XXXIII. 107 The thickest beds of such [iron] ore in the Appalachian district are in areas where the underlying red beds of Upper Ordovician age are either very thin or are entirely eroded away. **1946** L. D. STAMP *Britain's Structure & Scenery* xii. 124 In early Permian times conditions repeated those found in early Old Red Sandstone times. The older geologists who used the term New Red Sandstone for the red beds of the Permian and Trias introduced this very useful comparison. **1974** *Encycl. Brit. Macropædia* XVIII. 694/1 Continental sediments, especially of red-bed facies often associated with evaporite deposits, are especially widespread and characteristic of the Triassic. Throughout Eurasia north of Tethys, such rocks are a conspicuous part of the rock record. **1785** G. WASHINGTON *Diary* 28 Jan. (1925) II. 338, I discovered..the *red berry of the Swamp. **1805** M. LEWIS *Jrnl.* 12 Apr. in *Orig. Jrnls. Lewis & Clark Exped.* (1904) I. vii. 299 The under brush is willow, red wood,..the red burry [*sic*], and Choke cherry. **1819** WARDEN *United States* III. 136 The undergrowth consists of hazel, arrow wood, red-berry, crab-apple, wild pea-vine, and rushes. **1898** MORRIS *Austral Eng.* 383/2 *Redberry*, [the] name given to Australian plants of the genus *Rhagodia* bearing spikes or panicles of red berries. **1951** *Dict. Gardening* (R. Hort. Soc.) IV. 1754/1 Rhagodia..Australian Red Berry. **1973** E. GOUDIE *Woman of Labrador* p. xix, Well fortified with her never-ending supply of tea and redberry pie. **1928** *Daily Express* 5 Dec. 13/2 Glasgow has not relaxed its war-time drink restrictions..but nothing is being done to make the sale of this horrible '*Red Biddy' punishable by prison. **1939** JOYCE *Finnegans Wake* (1964) I. 39 Blotto after divers tots of hell fire, red biddy, bull dog, blue ruin and creeping jenny. **1950** E. HYAMS *From Waste Land* 204 Pamphlets issued by the French wine trade..to persuade the customer that the Red Biddy he is drinking is something very special and fine indeed. *a* **1953** DYLAN THOMAS *Adventures Skin Trade* (1955) 85 'I suppose he thinks red biddy's like bread and milk,' Mr. Allingham said. **1961** C. WILLOCK *Death in Covert* iii. 67 Any idea where we could get any of the hard stuff? This flipping red biddy's burning a hole in my stomach. **1977** M. KENYON *Rapist* v. 58 Next time it'd be Majorca..and what if he was not a red biddy man? At five bob a bottle he bloody soon would be. **1926** A. GILES *Exploring in Seventies* 127 Tinned meat in 6 lb tins ('*red blanket' we called it). The tins were painted red without labels or description of contents. **1846** *Phil. Trans. R. Soc.* CXXXVI. 66 Professor Rudolph Wagner was the first to point out the circular form of the *red blood-corpuscle of the Lamprey, but he does not appear to have noticed the existence of a nucleus. **1910** H. W. ARMIT tr. *Ehrlich & Lazarus' Anæmia* i. 3 Tarchanoff proposed that by determining the loss of water during profuse sweating, and by comparative red blood cell counts both before and after the sweating, an estimate of the quantity of blood could be arrived at. **1950** *Sci. News* XV. 87 Thanks to the hæmoglobin in them, the red blood corpuscles of our blood carry oxygen from lungs to muscles and brain, which all the time use it up. **1971** W. M. DOUGHERTY *Introd. Hematol.* v. 135/2 The hematocrit (packed cell volume) is the determination that equates what volume of a given unit of blood is composed of red blood cells (erythrocytes and reticulocytes). **1929** *Bookman* (U.S.) July 527/2 **Red board*, when..a train has to stop for orders. **1935** A. J. POLLOCK *Underworld Speaks* 96/1 *Red board*, board facing the grandstand on which a horse race is declared official by the judges. **1946** *Sun* (Baltimore) 5 Apr. 18/1 After each race there was much 'red board' speculation and betting as to which horse had won. **1968** *Wall St. Jrnl.* 31 Jan., 'One thing about Sam,' he says. 'He never bet the red board.' (In track jargon, to bet the red board is to claim you picked the winner—after the race is over.) **1973** *Amer. Speech 1969* XLIV. 259 *Red board*, stop signal on an overhead signal bridge. **1785** A. MONRO *Struct. & Physiol. Fishes* iii. 28 A red-coloured organ..is found on the inner side of the air-bag of the cod, haddock, etc.: but in those fishes where the air-bag communicates with the alimentary canal, this *red body is either very small and simple..or entirely wanting. **1836** YARRELL *Brit. Fishes* I. 38 The air..found in these bladders..is believed to be secreted by the inner lining membrane, and in some instances by a red body. **1896** KIRKALDY & POLLARD tr. *Boas' Zool.* 375 The vessels..often form close circumscribed retia mirabilia, projecting as 'red bodies' on the inner side of the bladder. **1911** *Proc. Zool. Soc.* I. 184 In the vast majority of cases 'red body' includes both rete mirabile and gas gland. **1963** L. BIRKETT tr. *Nikolsky's Ecol. Fishes* i. 7 In the two red bodies in the swim-bladder of the eel, there are 88,000 venous and 116,000 arterial capillaries. **1889** MAIDEN *Usef. Native Plants* 389 '*Red Bottle-brush'. (The flowers of some species of Callistemon are like bottle-brushes in shape.) *c* **1840** THACKERAY *Misc.* III. 154 Solemn *red-box and tape men. **1865** CARLYLE *Fredk. Gt.* XXI. v. VI. 558 Lee lodges in such and such a Hostelry; bring us his Red-Box for a thirty hours. *a* **1883** E. FITZGERALD *Miscellanies* (1900) 201 It is good for a Counsellor to be attended on his travels with a Red Box. *Ibid.*, A Red Box is as it were a Star Chamber in small. **1723** D. O'CONNOR tr. *Keating's Gen. Hist. Ireland* 91 The Lodge of *Teagh na Craoibhe Ruadhe*, which signifies in English the House of the **Red Branch*, where the most renowned Champions lodged their arms... The Champions..were distinguished by the Title of Champions of the Red Branch. **1772** S. O'HALLORAN *Introd. Study Hist. Ireland* I. v. 40 Long before the birth of Christ we find an *hereditary* order of chivalry in Ulster, called *Curaidhe na Craoibhe ruadh*, or the Knights of the Red Branch, from their chief seat in Emania, adjoining to the palace of the Ulster kings, called Teagh na Craoibhe ruadh, or Academy of the Red Branch. **1879** *Encycl. Brit.* IX. 75/1 Ulster, whose warriors of the *Craebh Ruaid* or Red Branch are the most prominent figures in the Heroic period, had no Fenians. **1889** W. B. YEATS *Wanderings of Oisin* III. 41 Came by me the Kings of the Red Branch with roaring of laughter and songs. **1892** —— *Countess Kathleen* iv. 73 And on tales Of Finian labours and the Red-Branch Kings. **1970** N. CHADWICK *Celts* ix. 268 The ruling king in the [Tain] cycle is Conchobar mac Nessa of the House of the Red Branch at Emain Macha in Ulster. **1839** URE *Dict. Arts* 165 *Red brass, the Tombak of some, ..consists of more copper and less zinc than go to the composition of brass, being from $2\frac{1}{2}$ to 8 or 10 of the former to 1 of the latter. **1973** *Times* 11 Dec. 1/2 Messages found this morning in a telephone booth said that Dr Amerio would be kept in a 'people's jail' as a reprisal against dismissals at Fiat. The messages claimed that the kidnapping was the work of the '*Red Brigades'. **1977** *Time* 18 July 29/1 Some unemployed university graduates..have joined in the terrorism of groups like the 'Red Brigades'. **1978** *Ann. Reg. 1977* 136 Terrorist action with a political flavour was also carried on by other extremist groups, in particular by the left-wing Red Brigade. *Ibid.*, In their efforts to spread terror the Red Brigaders resorted to shooting in the legs or kneecap a number of fairly prominent persons. **1979** *Rolling Stone* 11 Jan. 79 Outside..the Red Brigades are blowing people's knees off. **1976** *Webster's Sports Dict.* 345/1 **Red card*, a red card shown by the referee (as in international soccer) to indicate that a player is being sent off. **1978** S. LOVER *Assoc. Football Match Control* 194 Players who in any way delay the taking of a free kick..will be cautioned (yellow card). On repetition, they will be sent from the field (red card). **1980** D. MORRIS *Tribal Words* (MS) 379 *Early bath*, a slang expression meaning that a player has been given the red card and sent off the field before the end of play. **1984** S. LOVER *Soccer Laws Illustr.* (rev. ed.) 76 In some competitions the Referee is required to display..a red card, indicating a dismissal. **1934** S. LEWIS *Work of Art* 72 He's got to be a certified public accountant, ..or one-night-stand lecturer that blows in and expects to have the *red carpet already hauled out for him. **1938** N. MARSH *Artists in Crime* ii. 28 Be sure to have the red carpet out. **1952** *N.Y. Times* 21 Aug. 21/6 (*heading*) Englewood rolls out red carpet for little baseball league teams. **1960** *Daily Mail* 13 Dec. 7/8 A champagne party was laid on for Mr. Steven Mueller, 2,000,000th passenger to leave London in a TWA jet airliner... There was a hitch when Mr. Mueller arrived. He is just two years and four months old. The red carpet treatment went to his mother. **1966** J. A. MORRIS *Bird Watcher* (1968) ii. 30 We're rolling out the red carpet for him. Nothing will be too good for good old Congressman Herper. **1969** 'G. BLACK' *Cold Jungle* viii. 122 A complete breakdown in red carpet reception arrangements. **1975** *Evening Standard* 23 Sept. 12/1 (Advt.), May we give you the red carpet treatment? Why get footsore and weary comparing notes at all the carpet stores? **1977** *New Yorker* 10 Oct. 67/2 Eaton's interest in the Soviet Union—to which he has made eight red-carpet journeys since 1958—was indirectly whetted by John D. Rockefeller, Sr. **1894** T. F. GARRETT *Encycl. Pract. Cookery* 324/1 **Red Caviare*, this is a very inferior quality, made from the roe of any fish, such as the grey mullet, or carp. **1927** A.

MARTINEAU *Caviare to Candy* iii. 31 *Red Caviare.* This is made from the roe of a hen pike. **1946** G. STIMPSON *Bk. about Thousand Things* 80 Virtually all the red caviar..is displayed as of Russian origin. **1957** V. NABOKOV *Pnin* i. 10 Those stupendous Russian ladies..infuse a magic knowledge of their difficult and beautiful tongue..in an atmosphere of Mother Volga songs, red caviar, and tea. **1964** A. LAUNAY *Caviare & After* i. 21 Red caviare (*Keta*) is made from the salmon roe..bright orange in colour. **1974** M. G. EBERHART *Danger Money* (1975) v. 57 They bought.. some red caviar. 'It would be good with rye bread,' Susan suggested. **1935** H. H. FINLAYSON (*title*) The *red centre: man and beast in the heart of Australia. *Ibid.* ii. 22 The Luritja Country—the south-west portion of Central Australia and contiguous tracts in the adjoining States—.. might well be known as the Red Centre. Sand, soil, and most of the rocks are a fiery cinnabar. **1979** *Jrnl. R. Soc. Arts* Apr. 293/1 Nearly a decade of good rains have turned the famous Red Centre into something approaching a Green Centre. **1905** *Eye Opener* (Calgary, Alberta) 25 Feb. 1/6 The innocent haw-buck who imagines that the *red chamber is full of dignity and high thoughts has never listened to the debates from the galleries. **1948–9** *Parl. Affairs* II. 50 The Senate Chamber at the east end, known from its bright leather upholstery as the 'Red Chamber', is similar in design to the Commons Chamber but is much smaller and has no side galleries. **1955** *Chatelaine* Apr. 13 Canada's first woman senator is Mrs. Norman F. Wilson, who shattered a fifty-year-old tradition that had preserved the Red Chamber as an exclusively men's club when she stepped over the threshold in 1930. **1965** *Globe & Mail* (Toronto) 6 Dec. 6/5 Mr. Pearson..could make no better beginning than to appoint to the Red Chamber 12 such Canadians. **1968** *Red channel [see GREEN *a.* 1 i]. **1979** *Guardian* 2 Aug. 1/8 Customs staff will examine in detail the baggage of all passengers going through the red channel and carry out more spot checks..on those using the nothing-to-declare green channel. **1889** GROVES & THORP *Chem. Technol.* I. 111 Wood imperfectly charred, so as to leave in the product the maximum quantity of combustible matter per volume, is called *red charcoal. **1801** B. HAWKINS *Lett.* (1916) 379 Your father is desirous that his *red children would consent to establish houses of entertainment and ferries on these roads. **1855** J. H. CHAMBERS in *Montana Hist. Soc. Contrib.* (1940) X. 136 Col. Vaughan gave his red children a talk. **1871** *Weekly Manitoban* 5 Aug. 2/4 She wishes her Red children, as well as her White people, to be happy and contented. **1815** SCOTT *Guy M.* iii, We'll see if the *red cock craw not in his bonnie barn yard ae morning before day-dawing. **1972** K. LO *Chinese Food* I. 23 We *red-cook it [*sc.* fish], quick-fry it, clear-simmer it, deep-fry it, steam it, and hot-plunge it. **1956** B. Y. CHAO *How to cook & eat in Chinese* I. vi. 65 *Red-cooking is stewing with soy sauce, some materials needing pre-frying, some not. It is so-called because the soy-sauce juice gives a reddish colour. **1972** K. LO *Chinese Food* I. 12 In red-cooking the meat or poultry is first quick-fried and then simmered in broth or water along with soya sauce and other constituents of the soya herbal sauce. **1936** *Ann. Rep. E. Malling Res. Station 1935* 144 The roots of the affected [strawberry] plants showed the '*red core'. **1952** E. RAMSDEN tr. *Gram & Weber's Plant Dis.* III. 364/1 No method of soil treatment has proved effective against red-core disease. **1970** *Countryman* Spring 111 Red core was first known as a disastrous disease in 1921 in Scotland. **1846** *Phil. Trans. R. Soc.* CXXXVI. 64 The well-known *red corpuscle of the blood of the Frog. **1871** *Q. Jrnl. Microsc. Sci.* XXII. 361 The chemical and formal structure of the red corpuscle. **1911** C. E. W. BEAN *'Dreadnought' of Darling* x. 89 The river came down in flood. People had been forced to clear out of some of the 'frontages' and camp back in the *red country. *Ibid.* xv. 142 The mallee..covers thousands of square miles of red country in Victoria, New South Wales, and South Australia. **1936** A. RUSSELL *Gone Nomad* viii. 60 Picture great wind-scoured plains of red sand ..; a sun glaring wanly day after day from a sky reddened with the dust of incessant sand-storm..—and you will see the great 'Red Country' of the West Darling in the big seven years' drought of 1897–1903. **1877** H. PONSONBY *Let.* 6 Sept. in A. Ponsonby *Henry Ponsonby* (1942) 376 The *Red Cross or Crescent is a valuable association in its attempts to protect the sick and wounded in time of war. **1897** BIGHAM *With Turk. Army Thessaly* iii. 24 Of the two medical services the Red Crescent was excellent. **1959** *Chambers's Encycl.* XI. 552/1 The League of Red Cross Societies (founded 1919) is a federation of national Red Cross and Red Crescent societies. **1970** *Times* 3 Apr. (Arab League Suppl.) p. viii/3 Their own Palestinian Red Crescent facilities. **1971** *Shankar's Weekly* (Delhi) 4 Apr. 10/4, I think it will be a better idea to get some business men and others contribute money, buy medicines and other equipment with that and donate it to the East Pakistan Red Crescent or some other organisation. **1976** G. SEYMOUR *Glory Boys* ii. 23 The big tanks had rumbled into..Nablus. He recalled..the wail of the Red Crescent ambulances. **1869** *Hardwicke's Sci. Gossip* 1 Jan. 23 The insect referred to in your last number under the title of '*Red Daddy', ..is probably *Panorpa communis*, ..commonly called the 'Scorpion-fly'. **1766** *Compl. Farmer* s.v. *Pine*, The Scotch-pine..is the tree that affords the *red or yellow deal. **1843** HOLTZAPFFEL *Turning* I. 101 The roots of some of the red deals..abound in turpentine. **1912** R. LYDEKKER *Ox & its Kindred* v. 101 Attention may be directed to the well-known *red Devons. **1979** V. CANNING *Satan Sampler* ix. 197 A colour gravure of a red Devon heifer. **1925** FRASER & GIBBONS *Soldier & Sailor Words* 237 **Red duster, the*, the Red Ensign of the Mercantile Marine. **1928** *Daily Express* 10 Aug. 15/1 His papers have not yet come through allowing him to fly the White Ensign, so, meanwhile, the Vita sails under the 'red duster'. **1944** *Times* 7 June 6/7 A glance at the ships, with their different flags, the Red Duster of the Merchant Navy, the Stars and Stripes, [etc.]. **1977** *Jrnl. R. Soc. Arts* CXXV. 216/1 Today even the Red Duster is to some extent a flag of convenience. [**1916** *Proc. Nat. Acad. Sci.* II. 17 Differing from the dwarf red stars most conspicuously in density, dimensions, and total brightness.] **1929** J. H. JEANS *Universe around Us* v. 293 The great gulf which lies between the red giants and the *red dwarfs. **1959** *Listener* 26 Feb. 370/1 Instead of cooling steadily down towards the Red Dwarf stage..the Sun is becoming more energetic as it ages. **1978** *Nature* 22 June 645/1 The energies of even the weak radio flares emitted by a red dwarf star are several orders of magnitude greater than those from large and infrequent solar outbursts. **1610** J. MELVILL *Autobiog.* (Wodrow Soc.) 160 The Guisians, and the rest of these monstruus *Read-eattins in France, quha celebrat that bludie drunken feast of Bartholomew in Paris. **1821** *Edinb. Mag. & Lit. Misc.* Apr. 351/2 Sic red-aitens, whase moolie geir is atween them an' their wits. **1951** T. C. ROUGHLEY *Fish Austral.* 68 The *red emperor or king snapper..grows to a weight of at least 40 pounds. **1956** M. WEST *Gallows on Sand* xiii. 145 Fillets of red emperor, caught while we were at the bottom of the sea. **1965** *Austral. Encycl.* IX. 41/1 The juvenile form of the red emperor.. bears a red broad-arrow mark, from which it derives its name of government bream. **1730** *Royal Navy Orders & Instructions* 12 Merchant-Ships are to wear a *Red Ensign; with the Union Jack in a Canton at the upper End next the Staff; and a white Jack, with a red Cross, commonly called *St. George's Cross*, passing quite through the same. **1910** *Encycl. Brit.* X. 459/1 The red ensign is the distinguishing flag of the British merchant service. **1961** B. FERGUSSON *Watery Maze* vi. 123 Red Ensign ships—merchant ships with Merchant Navy crews, requisitioned for Admiralty service—were administered by the Director of Sea Transport. **1976** *Oxf. Compan. Ships & Sea* 695/2 The Red Ensign..is today flown by all British merchant vessels and also by many yachts. **1872** J. G. WOOD *Insects at Home* 522 The *Red Feather (*Tischeria complanella*) so called from its colour and the feathery character of its wings... The name Red Feather is almost a literal translation of Stephen's name *rufipennella*. **1884** in Goode *Nat. Hist. Aquat. Anim.* 154 The 'Red-bellied Terrapin', *Pseudemys rugosa*..is also known under the names 'Potter', '*Red-fender', and 'Slider'. **1893** P. GARDNER *Catal. Greek Vases in Ashmolean Mus.* iv. 22/1 The natural advantages..of the *red-figure method caused it to speedily supersede the older style. **1899** R. GLAZIER *Man. Hist. Ornament* 77 The Transitional period (B.C. 500–470), when the black silhouette figures on a red ground gave way to the red figure period on a black ground. **1918** J. D. BEAZLEY *Attic Red-Figured Vases in Amer. Museums* i. 5 The earliest red-figure vases are mostly amphorae or cups. **1936** *Burlington Mag.* May 253/1 Amongst the fifth-century red-figure vases there are many of high artistic merit. **1960** R. G. HAGGAR *Conc. Encycl. Continental Pott. & Porc.* 211/1 Greek pottery is generally classified by style: Geometric, Oriental influence, Black-figure, Red-figure and mixed styles. **1975** J. BOARDMAN *Athenian Red Figure Vases: Archaic Period* ii. 11 Red figure is the reverse of black figure. *Ibid.* 12 Relief line is so important in early red figure that..a word about it is called for. **1978** K. J. DOVER *Greek Homosexuality* I. 10 An Attic red-figure vase of the early fifth century depicts a man at a dinner party. **1890** HARRISON & VERRALL *Ancient Athens* p. lxxv, The rape..appears on upwards of twenty-five *red-figured vases. **1918** J. D. BEAZLEY *Attic Red-Figured Vases in Amer. Museums* p. v, The Andokides painter, one of the first artists to use the red-figured style. **1919** J. C. HOPPIN (*title*) Handbook of Attic red-figured vases. **1960** E. H. GOMBRICH *Art & Illusion* i. 40 The Greek vase painters made use of this principle of reversal when they switched over from the earlier black-figured technique..to the red-figured style. **1977** *Jrnl. R. Soc. Arts* CXXV. 96/2 It [*sc.* the *anthemion*] was a favourite border design, too, with the painters of Greek pottery of the period, particularly of the red-figured Attic ware. **1820** *Q. Jrnl. Sci., Lit. & Arts* IX. 411 The beautiful *red-fire which is now so frequently used at the theatres, is composed of the following ingredients. **1869** *Pall Mall G.* 13 Oct. 11 This red-fire..is made of nitrate of strontia, calomel, chlorate of potash, and sulphate of copper. **1848** *Santa Fé* (New Mexico) *Republican* 28 June 2/4 A proportionate lot of..Cinto laces, *Red flannel shirts, [etc.]. **1860** *Times* 15 Sept. 10/1 Most of us wear no linen.., the red flannel shirt answering all purposes of outward and inward raiment. **1906** E. NESBIT *Railway Children* vi. 137 'How lucky we *did* put on our red flannel petticoats!' said Phyllis. **1940** L. I. WILDER *Long Winter* (1962) ix. 83 Her red flannel underwear was so hot. *Ibid.* 84 It's too hot for my red flannels, Ma! **1943** *Sun* (Baltimore) 24 Nov. 17/5 It is time for Kent countians to 'get into their red flannels'. **1978** WALKLEY & FOSTER *Crinolines & Crimping Irons* ii. 46 Both natural wool and red flannel became favourite materials for underwear and nightwear. **1907** *Dialect Notes* III. 248 **Red flannel hash*,..beet hash. **1951** E. GRAHAM *My Window looks down East* vii. 59 She had a real hankerin' for red-flannel hash. **1977** J. CHEEVER *Falconer* 60 His mother..served the red flannel hash with poached eggs. **1651** BARKER *Art of Angling* 9 A light Flie for darknesse, the *red Flie *in medio*, and a dark Flie for lightnesse. **1787** BEST *Angling* (ed. 2) 110 The Red-fly comes on about the middle of February..it's wings are made artificially of a dark drake's feather, the body of the red part of squirrel's fur, with the red hackle of a cock. **1860** MAURY *Phys. Geog. Sea* (Low) vi. §322 Seamen tell us of '*red fogs' which they sometimes encounter. **1879** *Encycl. Brit.* X. 266/1 The dust or sand..may descend again..in the form of 'red-fog', 'sea-dust', or 'sirocco-dust'. **1609** SKENE *Reg. Maj., Burrow Lawes* 140 b, Na templair (*Reid Freir..) sall intromet with any merchandise..perteining to the Gilde. **1762** BP. FORBES *Jrnl.* (1886) 178 Dornock of old was a Monastry of Red Friars. *a* **1700** B. E. *Dict. Cant. Crew*, **Red-fustian*, Clarret or red Port-Wine. **1834** H. AINSWORTH *Rookwood* I. viii, Famous wine this..better than all your red fustian. **1916** *Proc. Nat. Acad. Sci.* II. 17 The brightest stars in the cluster are the *red and yellow giants. **1929** J. H. JEANS *Universe around Us* v. 272 The stars of large diameter shewn in the table..are red and have very high luminosities; they are red giants. **1966** *Random House Dict.* 142/3 *Betelgeuse*, a first magnitude red giant star in the constellation Orion. **1977** J. NARLIKAR *Struct. Universe* ii. 39 The red-giant reactions do not take as long to complete as the reactions during the main-sequence stage. **1866** *Jrnl. Anat. & Physiol.* XXX. 550 The *red glands occupy about the anterior half of the internal surface of the ventral wall of the swim-bladder. **1926** H. M. KYLE *Biol. Fishes* xi. 276 The fish is able to exercise some selection of gases, and the 'red glands' or retia mirabilia of the Physoclists are evidently used for this purpose. **1931** J. R. NORMAN *Hist. Fishes* ix. 174 The walls of the bladder are richly supplied with fine blood-vessels, and at certain areas these are accumulated to form the so-called red bodies or red glands, masses of interlacing and tightly packed arteries and veins. **1974** D. & M. WEBSTER *Compar. Vertebr. Morphol.* xv. 368 The rete mirabile here [in teleosts] produces gas, which the red gland secretes into the gas bladder. **1800** tr. *Lagrange's Chem.* II. 141 Jewellers gold, and that used for plate and coins, is allayed with this metal [copper]. When this mixture is made in the arts, the workmen call it *Red Gold. **1651** *Red hackle [see *red palmer*]. **1799** G. SMITH *Laboratory* II. 302 Red-hackle. Body, red silk and gold twist [etc.]. **1910** H. P. TIEMANN *Iron & Steel* 312 *Red hardness is the name they give to the property of a tool when it maintains its cutting edge after its nose is red hot. **1925** *Trans. Amer. Soc. Steel Treating* VIII. 693 Molybdenum when present in sufficient amounts imparts to steel the properties of 'red hardness'. **1937** *Discovery* May 153/1 The forerunner of self-hard steel, ..Musket self-hard steel, employed [carbon and tungsten] ..to confer the then new so-called red hardness... Tungsten contributes to high speed steel the property of red hardness. **1845** *Red hartshorn [see *red lavender*]. **1819** *Orthodox Jrnl.* May 175/2 [He] laboured afterwards most earnestly to counteract its contents, and was honoured with the *red hat by his holiness. **1863** GEO. ELIOT *Romola* I. i. 36 Men who love to see avarice and lechery under the red hat and the mitre. **1969** R. H. BAINTON *Erasmus of Christendom* (1970) i. 44 To receive the red hat he must go to Rome. **1975** R. PLAYER *Let's talk of Graves* vi. 217 Cardinal Cavalle..had got his red hat from Pius the Ninth. **1796** *West Devonsh. Gloss.*, **Red hay*, mow-burnt hay; in distinction to 'green hay', or hay which has taken a moderate heat, and to 'vinny hay', or that which is mouldy. **1710** WHITWORTH *Acc. Russia* (1758) 83 The English export chiefly hemp..*red-hides and caviar; the two last to Leghorne. **1934** *Bulletin* (Sydney) 16 May 20/3 Someone identified the thing as *Patæcus fronto*, better known as the '*Red Indian' in N.S.W., where it is sometimes caught on the reefs. **1965** *Austral. Encycl.* VII. 395/2 Red Indian fish (*Pataecus fronto*), a fish of the southern Australian rocky shore-lines. Its high dorsal fin forms a crest like the feathers of a Red Indian's head dress. **1865** *Pall Mall G.* 8 Aug. 10/1 The '*Red Judges', as the criminal class call her Majesty's judges. **1963** 'J. PRESCOT' *Case for Hearing* viii. 125 There's precious little point in letting him out on bail when a red judge is going to send him back again for at least a couple of years. **1972** *Times* 20 May 3/7, I would very much like to see more work being committed for trial by the red judge. **1977** *Daily Tel.* 19 Oct. 6/5 Since May there have been no visits by 'Red judges' because of a shortage of accommodation. Arrangements have been made for the more important criminal cases—murder and manslaughter—to be tried either at the Old Bailey or Maidstone. **1812** W. J. BURCHELL *Jrnl.* 27 May in *Trav. Interior S. Afr.* (1822) II. viii. 160 They had intended going to the *Roode Kaffers* (*Red Caffres). **1879** R. M. BALLANTYNE *Six Months at Cape* iii. 44 This red-Kafir is in truth a savage. **1904** D. KIDD *Essential Kafir* i. 31 Red ochre and oil are rubbed into the skin, and frequently into the blanket. When this latter is done by a tribe the people are called Red Kafirs. **1829** LOUDON *Encycl. Plants* 226 *Rhus succedanea*, *red Lac. **1838** DICKENS *O. Twist* xiv, I saw her look towards his [a surgeon's] infernal *red lamp. **1846** *Blackw. Mag.* Nov. 595/1 Almost any serial will give hints enough to an acute boy, [and]..guide him to the door with the red lamp. **1894** CONAN DOYLE (*title*) Round the Red Lamp. **1927** W. E. COLLINSON *Contemp. Eng.* 96 The red lamp as the sign of a '*maison tolérée*'. **1929** J. L. HODSON *Grey Dawn* II. ii. 159 You should have seen the queue at the Red Lamp. **1962** H. MYERS tr. *Pingaud's Holland* 51 The dirty little canals near the harbour in the 'red lamp' district. **1942** BERREY & VAN DEN BARK *Amer. Thes. Slang* §491 *Redland, *Russia*. **1966** J. GARDNER *Amber Nine* iii. 44 If Redland have got a finger in the pie then that part of the world could be warmish. **1969** W. GARNER *Us or Them War* i. 15 Morton picked up the camera. .. He said, 'Exacta. Made in Dresden. East Germany. A favourite with Redland agents.' **1977** C. WOOD *James Bond* iv. 40 'You can imagine who the first suspects are?' Bond could. 'Redland.' **1821** M. WILMOT *Let.* 17 Jan. in *More Lett.* (1935) 92 Melodious clang of knives forks and plates to flourish *down the *red Lane* the most magnificent supper that Gourmands ever guttled. **1831** *Lincoln Herald* 15 July, Delicious!—O!—Down the red lane it goes. **1870** *Routledge's Ev. Boy's Ann.* Mar. 165 The tarts e'er this have gone down the red lane! **1958** L. DURRELL *Mountolive* xv. 286 The quarter lying beyond the *red lantern belt. **1973** *Whig-Standard* (Kingston, Ontario) 11 Aug. 7/3 He was on the loose and cutting a swathe in the red lantern district. **1845** COOLEY *Cycl. Pract. Receipts* 752/1 Tincture of Lavender (Compound). *Syn.* Lavender Drops,..*Red Lavender, Red Lavender Drops, Red Hartshorn. **1650** BULWER *Anthropomet.* 156 Now they have too little colour, then Spanish-paper, *Red Leather or other Cosmeticall Rubriques must be had. **1905** EMERSON & NORRIS in *Jrnl. Exper. Med.* VII. 34 The name often given to the disease in these letters is '*red-leg', and this is also the name used by the frog-catchers. **1964** G. DURRELL *Menagerie Manor* iii. 75, I sent them [*sc.* toads] away for post-mortem, and the report came back that they were suffering from an obscure disease called red-leg. **1974** *Amer. Jrnl. Vet. Res.* XXXV. 1243 Since 1890, septicemic frog disease (red-leg) has had a devastating effect on frogs kept under laboratory conditions. **1839** URE *Dict. Arts* 1056 **Red Liquor*, is a crude acetate of alumina..prepared from pyrolignous acid. **1844** E. A. PARNELL *Applied Chem.* I. 280 Red liquor is much more extensively employed as a mordant than any other preparation of alumina. **1893** SLOANE *Electr. Dict.* 345 A two-fluid theory of magnetism has been evolved... It assumes north fluid or '*red magnetism' and a south fluid or 'blue magnetism'. **1703** MOXON *Mech. Exerc.* 237 The *Red Mason, which is the Hewer of Brick. *Ibid.*, The Red Mason (or Bricklayer). **1889** PATER *G. de Latour* (1896) 171 The daily University *red mass,..said to-day according to the proper course of the season. **1896** *Westm. Gaz.* 23 Oct. 1/2 The 'red' mass..by which for some years it has been customary at the ancient Sardinian Chapel in Lincoln's Inn Fields to mark the opening of term at the Law Courts. **1883** GRESLEY *Gloss. Coal-Mining* 200 **Red Measures.* Generally refers to the strata of Permian or Triassic age. **1898** P. MANSON *Trop. Diseases* xxi. 337 Avoid altogether *red meat. **1933** E. O'NEILL *Ah, Wilderness!* I. 24 Poetry's his red meat nowadays, I think—love poetry—and socialism, too, I suspect. **1972** *Times* 3 July 12/2 Colin Carr chose..a lollipop, a Popper Polonaise, rather than good red meat, but it served to show off an enviable fluency on the instrument. **1977** *Jrnl. R. Soc. Arts* CXXV. 369/1 Dairy products, cereal products and red meat account for 60 per cent and 75 per cent respectively of the energy and protein intake of the population. **1925** B. COAN *Red Web* 6 It is time, right now, to get down to cases about this thing we hear called the '*red menace'. **1932** J. F. CARTER *What we are about to Receive* xviii. 204 But once the election is over..we shall quietly lay aside our witch hunting, put the Red Menace in cold storage. **1934** R. V. C. BODLEY *Japanese Omelette* xvii. 174

The substance of his words did not confirm the rather pessimistic views of my soldier friends in Changchun on the subject of the 'Red Menace'. **1977** *Times* 14 Feb. 17/1 Young..was quick to warn Smith that his efforts to gain U.S. support by invoking the 'Red menace' would not succeed. **1882** *Garden* 2 Sept. 207/3 We have the *Redmilk with its flaming juice, as safe as bread. **1777** W. CURTIS *Flora Londin.* I. Pl. 106 The Pheasant's eye..is one of those plants which are annually cried about our streets under the name of *red Morocco. **1819** J. TAYLOR *Naturales Curiosæ* 129 Adonis—Red Morocco... Its flowers are of a bright scarlet, with a black spot or eye at the bottom, and are frequently sold in London under the name of red-morocco. **1931** M. GRIEVE *Mod. Herbal* I. 389/1 'Red Morocco' was a somewhat strange old English name for this plant [*sc.* pheasant's eye]. **1941** BAKER *Dict. Austral. Slang* 59 *Red *Ned*, cheap red wine. **1941** —— *N.Z. Slang* vii. 62 Such terms for strong drink as..*red Ned.* **1972** I. HAMILTON *Thrill Machine* xxvi. 120 Jo clutched the glass of Red Ned that I thrust at him. **1961** WARD & SHAPIRO in *Jrnl. Meteorol.* XVIII. 642/1 The only other characteristic of these spectra is their resemblance to '*red noise', that is, generally higher variance at the lower frequencies (longer periods). [*Note*] The term 'red noise' was suggested by Prof. E. N. Lorenz to describe this phenomenon. *Ibid.* 646/1 The spectrum of a time series of random numbers, which has been modified so that there is a moderate correlation between successive values, exhibits a characteristic damping of the higher frequencies. This type of spectrum, having more power (or variance) at lower frequencies can, by analogy to the spectrum of light, be called a 'red noise'. **1963** *Jrnl. Atmospheric Sci.* XX. 182/1 A general suppression of relative variance at higher frequencies and consequent inflation at lower frequencies, as compared to the even distribution of relative variance across all frequencies shown by the 'white noise' spectrum. Following a suggestion by E. N. Lorenz, Shapiro and Ward have called this phenomenon 'red noise'. **1979** *Nature* 23 Aug. 672/1 The spectra were calculated using a fast Fourier algorithm, the spectral estimates were smoothed, and a white or red noise null continuum was assumed in a significance testing. **1890** W. H. VITTUM tr. *Edinger's Twelve Lect. Struct. Cent. Nerv. Syst.* vi. 93 Below the thalamus is a rounded ganglion,—the nucleus ruber, the *red nucleus of the tegmentum. **1942** F. A. METTLER *Neuroanat.* xiii. 302 The red nuclei are important extrapyramidal relay stations. **1972** M. L. BARR *Human Nerv. Syst.* vii. 110/1 The red nucleus is..involved in pathways through which the cerebellum is able to influence motor function. **1974** D. & M. WEBSTER *Compar. Vertebr. Morphol.* xii. 294 These fibers decussate in the midbrain and then form a large capsule around the red nucleus. **1863** RICHARDSON & WATTS *Chem. Technol.* I. III. 688 *Red Oil or Oleic Soap. Campbell Morfit has patented a process for preparing Soap with red oil and Carbonate of Soda. **1917** W. K. MOOREHEAD *Stone Ornaments used by Indians in U.S. & Canada* 53 Oval forms occasionally found in the *Red Paint People's graves in Maine are much weathered and appear very old. **1947** R. P. T. COFFIN *Yankee Coast* 225 Before the dawn and the Dawn People, there were the Red Paint Men... They had been gone so long now that not even the teeth of them are left, only the red paint, color of life, they smeared their bodies with. **1970** S. TRUEMAN *Intimate Hist. New Brunswick* iii. 43 'Red Paint' Indian burial ground dating back 3,500 to 4,000 years; in the bottom of each grave is a covering of red ochre, bright red oxide. **1651** BARKER *Art of Angling* (1820) 6 A *red Palmer ribbed with gold, and a red hackle mixed with orange cruel. **1884** *St. James's Gaz.* 21 June 6/1 Take, for instance, the 'red palmer'. Originally meant to represent the 'woolly bear' (a caterpillar at least two inches long,) the fly, as now tied, rarely exceeds three quarters of an inch. **1933** *Discovery* May 158/1 *Red palm oil and some samples of maize oil are good sources [of vitamin A]. **1975** *Sci. Amer.* June 126/1 Cereal and vegetable oils are generally poor in carotene—except for red-palm oil, which is very rich. **1959** *Encounter* Dec. 29/1, I have been *red-pencilling student papers for a good many years. **1966** *Eng. Stud.* XLVII. 116 There are many teachers of English who look upon the adjective *corny* as a word to be red-penciled whenever it turns up in a student paper. **1979** *Verbatim* Summer 2/2 To red-pencil is 'to censor or correct'. **1927** *Observer* 4 Dec. 13/1 We have to guard against the *Red Peril on our borders. **1973** *Sat. Rev. Society* (U.S.) Mar. 48/3 At the end of the Fifties the red peril slunk off. **1802** *Med. Jrnl.* VIII. 128 *Red Pills (i.e. any pills rolled in bole armenic, or vermillion). **1873** *Punch* 4 Jan. 1/2 Mars. The *Red Planet salutes you. But you are a slow lot. **1894** J. E. GORE tr. *Flammarion's Pop. Astron.* IV. iv. 374 The red planet varies in brightness according to its position in the sky. **1972** *Nature* 4 Feb. 251/2 They show clearly that the red planet is far from being dead, and that weathering and volcanic activity are taking place on Mars to a significant degree. **1977** *Time* 17 Oct. 45/1 The two Viking landers and their orbiters have spent much of the 15 months since the arrival on Mars snapping pictures of the Red Planet. **1941** *Coast to Coast* 22 The mounted trooper found a couple of *red poley steer skins in Jo Wiggins's slaughter-yard. **1756** *Gentl. Mag.* XXVI. 89 A fire broke out at the kiln-house of Mr. Lemans, *red-potter, at Lambeth. **1754** BARTLET *Gentl. Farriery* (ed. 2) 280 Some make their scalding mixture milder, using *red precipitate instead of the sublimate. **1797** *Encycl. Brit.* (ed. 3) IV. 474/2 These crystals..moderately calcined, assume a sparkling red colour; and are used in medicine as an escharotic, under the name of red precipitate. **1883** *Ibid.* (ed. 9) XVI. 33/1 The oxide is gradually formed as a red powdery solid. This solid has long been known as 'red precipitate'. **1878** DISRAELI *Let.* 13 June in Monypenny & Buckle *Life Disraeli* (1920) VI. ix. 318 Lord B. mistook His Royal Highness for the father of the bride, who soon appeared as 'The *Red Prince'. **1888** *Random Recoll. Courts & Society* vi. 140 The wedding of the Princess of Dessau with Prince Frederick Charles—the Red Prince—in September, 1857, was solemnized in the evening at the Palace with all the customary formalities. **1958** *Everyman's Encycl.* V. 494/1 Frederick Charles of Prussia.., known as the 'Red Prince' because of the uniform he usually wore. **1885** ETHERIDGE & SEELEY *Phillips' Man. Geol.* (ed. 2) I. ii. 18 In the Arctic regions minute spherical particles of iron are sometimes brought down from the air in snow, as though the earth occasionally entered clouds of meteoric dust. A like cause must account for the *red rain which fell at Blankenburg in 1819, and owed its colour to cobalt chloride. **1904** G. S. WEST *Treat. Brit. Freshwater Algæ* 189 *Sph[ærella] lacustris*..is abundant all over the country in ditches, rain-pools, and bog-pools. The cells..frequently become brick-red in colour owing to the presence of hæmatochromin... The curious phenomenon known as 'Red Rain' owes its colour in a few instances to the presence of this Alga. **1933** E. HAWKS *Bk. of Air & Water Wonders* iv. 102 Red rain, accompanied by sand, fell on March 10, 1901, at Vienna and in Italy. **1884** H. E. JULER *Handbk. Ophthalmic Sci. & Pract.* xiv. 364 If the mirror be held at a considerable distance from an emmetropic eye no image of any details of the fundus is seen, but only a *red reflex. **1954** S. DUKE-ELDER *Parsons' Disease of Eye* (ed. 12) vii. 94 If the fundus reflex is seen as a uniform red glow (the red reflex), the eye is emmetropic or approximately so. **1971** *Brit. Med. Bull.* XXVII. 69/1 The 'red reflex' coincides with a very early stage of development of a retinal neoplasm. **1725** J. Wainwright in *Portland MSS.* (Hist. MSS. Comm.) VI. 1 The new institution of Knights of the Bath fills the town with an expectation of *red ribbons. **1732** LORD TYRAWLY in *Buccleuch MSS.* (Hist. MSS. Comm.) I. 382 If any vacancies should happen in the Red Ribbon. **1800** *Asiat. Ann. Reg., Char.* 58/2 The present vacant Red Ribbon has been offered to him. **1853** DISRAELI in *Hansard Commons* 30 June 1045 The very next day his Sovereign elevated him [*sc.* Lord Ellenborough] in the Peerage, and decorated him with the Red Riband. **1879** 'MARK TWAIN' *Lett.* (1917) I. 355 He couched his lance and ran a bold tilt against total abstinence and the Red Ribbon fanatics. **1908** *Costumes Classical & Fashionable* (Liberty & Co.) 16 *Red Riding Hood Cloak in cloth. **1936** N. STREATFEILD *Ballet Shoes* vii. 110 Pauline wore shorts and a shirt, and Petrova an apron and a red-riding-hood cloak over her frock. **1964** M. LASKI in S. Nowell-Smith *Edwardian England* iv. 204 White dresses with sashes..topped, for transit, by a red velvet Red Riding Hood cloak. **1966** M. STEEN *Looking Glass* i. 14, I was taken to parties..in my Red Ridinghood cape. **1888** *Encycl. Brit.* XXIII. 203/1 These freshets, laden with the rich red loam of the plains, usually reach the lower inhabited sections of the State [of Texas] in periods of drought, and are termed '*red rises'. **1762** MILLS *Pract. Husb.* I. 429 Barley is ripe when the *red roan, as farmers call it, meaning a reddish colour, is gone from off the ear. **1826** W. DARLINGTON *Florula Cestrica* 72 *E[uchroma] coccinea*... Painted Cup. *Red Robin. **1851–63** Red robin [see RED RAG 2]. **1882** *Devonsh. Plant Names*, Red Robin, *Lychnis diurna.* **1891** Q. *Noughts & Crosses* 88 My feet trod on bluebells and red-robins. **1855** J. PHILLIPS *Man. Geol.* viii. 190 One [fault] stated to cause a dislocation to the extent of 1,000 yards, is called the '*red rock fault', north of Pendleton near Manchester. **1942** E. M. ANDERSON *Dynamics of Faulting* v. 76 The 'North Staffordshire Boundary Fault'..is not a single fault, as two separate north-north-easterly fractures bound the coalfield... The northern of these is known as the Red Rock Fault. **1969** BENNISON & WRIGHT *Geol. Hist. Brit. Isles* xi. 268 The thickness of the beds in the Cheshire Basin indicates a great amount of downwarping which continued into Triassic times. The basin may have been bounded by faults, such as the Red Rock Fault, which continued to move during Permian times. **1845–50** MRS. LINCOLN *Lect. Bot.* App. 94/1 *Cornus sericea*, red osier, *red rod. **1597** GERARDE *Herbal* III. clv. 1366 [*Ros solis*] is called in English Sunne deaw. In the North parts *Red rot, bicause it rotteth sheepe. **1664** R. TURNER *Brit. Physician* 274 It is called..Sundew, Lustwort, Moor-grass, and of some Red-rot. **1891** *Amer. Folk-Lore* IV. 224 Red Rover. The boy who is 'it' is called the '*Red Rover', and stands in the middle of the street, while the others form a line on the pavement on one side. **1898** A. B. GOMME *Trad. Games* II. 107 The players, except one, take their stand at one side, and one stands at the other side in front of them. When all are ready, the one in front calls out 'Cock', or 'Caron', when all rush across to the other side, and he tries to catch one of them in crossing. This game is called 'Red Rover' in Liverpool... 'Red Rover' is shouted out by the catcher when players are ready to rush across. **1974** J. KEATS *Of Time & Island* v. 82 The little children played Red Rover. **1787** W. MARSHALL *Norfolk* (1795) II. Gloss., When the grains of ripening barley are streaked with red, the crop is said to be in the *red-row. **1879** *Cumbld. Gloss.*, *Reed row.* When barley approaches to ripeness the grains are streaked with red, and are then said to be in the reed row. **1846** J. BAXTER *Libr. Pract. Agric.* (ed. 4) II. 407 In the year 1831, wheat crops were extensively infested with a parasitical fungus, popularly termed the *Red Rust. **1892** A. G. THORNTON *Illustr. Catal. Drawing & Surveying Instruments & Materials* 107 Finest *Red Sable Brushes, Round Black Handles, plated ferrules. **1899** M. MARKS *Cycl. Home Arts* 62/2 The red sables are somewhat too strong for water-colour. **1910** *Encycl. Brit.* XI. 350/2 The fur [of the kolinsky] has often been designated as red or Tatar sable. **1948** F. A. STAPLES *Watercolour Painting* i. 3 The best red sable brushes should be used. **1970** *Oxf. Compan. Art* 169/2 The best soft brush for water-colour is the red 'sable', made from the fur of the Siberian mink. **1893** *Daily News* 23 May 5/2 The '*red scale', so harmful to orange and lemon trees. **1578** LYTE *Dodoens* v. i. 657 Very excellent to annoynt the head against Alopecies, which some calle the *redde scall or falling away of the heare. **1884** GOODE *Nat. Hist. Aquat. Anim.* 291 The various invertebrate animals preyed upon by Mackerel are known to the fishermen by such names as 'shrimp', '*red-seed', and 'Cayenne'. **1884–5** *Riverside Nat. Hist.* (1888) III. 193 The so-called red-seed exercises a deleterious effect on the flesh of the fish. **1854** JONES & SIEV. *Pathol. Anat.* 253 With regard to the locality of *red or inflammatory softening. **1858** AITKEN *Pract. Med.* 499 More partial or local forms of this affection [cerebritis], to which the name of 'red softening', or 'acute ramollissement', has been applied. **1878** *Times* 26 Dec., All pigs not '*red soldiers' will be adjudged innocent of typhoid. **1886** STEVENSON *Kidnapped* xvii, He supposed it was some of the red soldiers coming from Fort William into Appin. **1799** G. SMITH *Laboratory* II. 306 *Red Spinner; begins with July. **1858** KINGSLEY *Misc., Chalk-stream Stud.* (1859) I. 189 [The caperer] may..do duty..for the red spinner or perfect form of the Marchbrown ephemera. **1807** AIKIN *Dict. Chem. & Min.* II. 287/2 It is occasionally used for colouring spirits, as, for example, the *red spirit used for thermometers. **1844** E. A. PARNELL *Applied Chem.* I. 287 Such solutions, which are known among dyers by the name of red spirits or simply spirits, may be obtained by dissolving metallic tin, in a granulated or 'feathered' state, in one of the following liquids. **14..** *Nom.* in Wr.-Wülcker 707/28 *Hec papula*, a *redspott. **1601** HOLLAND *Pliny* II. 125 The root of Onochiles brought into a liniment cureth the lentils or red spots, yea and the infection of the leprosie. *a* **1618** SYLVESTER *Tobacco Battered* 429 Bacon-flitches, *Red-Sprats, red-Herings, and like Chimny-wretches. **1927** M. DEKOBRA tr. *Wainwright's Madonna of Sleeping Cars* xiv. 186 The gorilla with the pallid brow, marked with a *Red star. **1969** G. MACBETH *War Quartet* 73 In his coat He wore the red star. **1979** J. BARNETT *Backfire is Hostile!* xiv. 158 This strange aeroplane..with a red star on its tail. **1941** BAKER *Dict. Austral. Slang* 59 **Red steer, the*, fire, esp. a bush-fire. **1963** J. CANTWELL *No Stranger to Flame* 12 The cane-cutters, made negro by sun and by soot from fires (Red Steers, they called them). **1971** F. HARDY *Outcasts of Foolgarah* 118 Like the bushfires: hadn't he patented the special extinguisher to end the blight of the red steer for all time? **1823** P. NICHOLSON *Pract. Build.* 344 *Red Stocks.. owe their colour to the nature of the clay of which they are made. **1839** URE *Dict. Arts* 184 Place bricks, gray and red stocks,..and cutting bricks. **1598** FLORIO, *Rubrica*, vermillion, red oaker, red-leade, *red stone, or ruddl. **1712** J. MORTON *Nat. Hist. Northampt.* 41 The common Kealy, or Red-stone Land. **1796** KIRWAN *Elem. Min.* (ed. 2) I. 328 Redstone of Rawenstein—Its colour, by reflected light, is rose red. **1848** RICKMAN *Styles Archit. Eng.* (ed. 5) App. p. xvii, The walls being mostly built with rough red-stone rag. **1947** J. C. RICH *Materials & Methods of Sculpture* viii. 222 Many kinds [of sandstones] receive their names from their colors, i.e. bluestone, brownstone, and redstone. **1959** N. SLUMAN *Blackfoot Crossing* 38 On it Sikimi placed a fine revolver, some otter skins, a redstone pipe, and several small sacks of rare pigments. **1976** *Burnham-on-Sea Gaz.* 20 Apr. (Advt.), An attractive redstone detached cottage conveniently close to the town centre. **1876** G. STABLES *Domestic Cat* vi. 51 The first cat of the Tabby kind which claims our attention is the *Red or Sandy Tabby. **1903** F. SIMPSON *Bk. of Cat* xxv. 288/2 Red tabbies..are one of the difficult varieties to obtain. **1948** P. M. SODERBERG *Cat Breeding* 248 Red Tabbies cannot compete with several other breeds for popularity. **1977** D. S. RICHARDS *Handbk. Pedigree Cat Breeding* vii. 107 Ginger cats, or more correctly red tabbies, will invariably be male. **1898** *Red tag [see ZULU *sb.* and *a.* 3]. **1923** *Daily Mail* 11 Aug. 7 Dace..have been caught with fly..and upper parts of the Lea should yield some good specimens of these fish to the black gnat, Zulu, red tag, and coachman. **1918** in J. Degras *Soviet Documents on Foreign Policy* (1951) I. 130, I wish to emphasise that the so-called '*Red Terror'—which is grossly exaggerated and misrepresented abroad—was not the cause but the direct result and outcome of Allied intervention. **1922** 'SAPPER' *Black Gang* xvi. 267 Experts of the Red Terror..butcherers of women and children. **1930** *Morning Post* 13 Aug. 13 Never before, even in 1918–19, when the Red Terror was at its height, have persecutions reached such a terrible level. **1957** *Encycl. Brit.* XIX. 713/1 The beginning of the Red terror coincided with the period of greatest food shortage, before the harvest. **1977** *Socialist Press* 2 Mar. 7/1 His Committee of Public Safety directs accelerating repression (the 'red terror') against 'enemies of the people'. **1947** *Sun* (Baltimore) 3 Sept. 3/4 A tiny sea creature was blamed today for the '*red tides' which destroyed fish. **1970** T. D. BROCK *Biol. Microorganisms* xix. 655 The red tide, an occasional occurrence in inshore areas, results from extensive blooms of red-pigmented dinoflagellate species. Red tides, which probably develop when the seawater becomes unusually enriched with nutrients, are of practical significance because some dinoflagellates produce fish toxins that may cause extensive and unsightly fish kills. **1980** *N.Y. Times* 13 Sept. 8/2 The red tide..usually occurs in much milder form each year in late summer or fall. **1975** *Globe & Mail* (Toronto) 22 Jan. 29/8 But the choice is not merely between the two levels of government; it is between two kinds of conservatism. *Red Tory, blue Tory. **1976** *Weekend Mag.* (Montreal) 10 Jan. 2/1 All good Canadians are on the side of the Red Tories, the Dalton Camp forces who favor family allowances and the welfare state, Canadian nationalism, immigration, bilingualism and multiculturalism, the obviously good and liberal things that keep Canada great. **1974** *Globe & Mail* (Toronto) 29 Oct. 5/3 David Smith could outpace Alderman Anne Johnston in Ward 11, depending on how that ward buys her *Red Toryism as opposed to his knee-deep Liberalism. **1850** HOLTZAPFFEL *Turning* III. 1088 *Red Stuff, a name applied by watch-makers to some kinds of crocus, or the oxide of iron. **1884** F. J. BRITTEN *Watch & Clockm.* 220 Red stuff is prepared of various degrees of fineness. **1816** WARDEN *Descr. Columbia* 196 American *red twig, or Carolina spiræa. **1893** SLOANE *Electr. Dict.* 559 s.v. *Varnish*, *Red Varnish. A solution of sealing wax in 90 per cent. alcohol. [**1879** X. GALEZOWSKI in *Recueil d'Ophtalmologie* I. 534 (*heading*) Sur la vision rouge des opérés de cataracte.] **1883** *Ophthalmic Rev.* II. 281 Purtscher suggests that *red-vision would probably be heard of more frequently..after cataract operations, were it not for the careful protection of the eyes. *Ibid.* 278 He went into the open air and the red vision disappeared. **1959** S. DUKE-ELDER *Parsons' Dis. Eye* (ed. 13) xxiv. 373 Erythropsia (red vision) occurs particularly after cataract extraction if the eyes are exposed to bright light. **1940** *Red warning [see ALERT *sb.* 1 b]. **1963** *Times* 22 Jan. 10/3 Commander J. R. E. Langworthy, secretary of the Emergency Bed Service, said last night that if the cold spell continues a 'red warning' might have to be considered. Under this hospitals are asked to stop admitting any but emergency cases. **1969** *Daily Tel.* 14 Jan. 1/6 The next step, if the position worsened, would be a red warning. This stops all but very urgent admissions, reserves of local nurses are called in, and extra beds are put up in wards. **1575–85** ABP. SANDYS *Serm.* 88 As the goodliest trees in a garden are soonest blasted with *red windes. **1706** LONDON & WISE *Retir'd Gard.* I. 23 The North-East Winds, which are red Winds that blast the Leaves upon your Peach-Trees. **1857** *N. & Q.* Ser. II. IV. 114 There is no sojourner in the Mediterranean.., who has not seen the red wind... It blows from the deserts of Africa, and derives its name from the particles of red sand with which it is charged. *a* **1400** *Stockh. Medical MS.* i. 265 in *Anglia* XVIII. 302 Þe crop of þe *reed worte do þer-to. *c* **1450** *M.E. Med. Bk.* (Heinrich) 232 Tak of redewortes, of fette malwes [etc.]. **1495** *Trevisa's Barth. De P.R.* XVII. lxxiii. (W. de W.) 647 Elutropia highte Solsequium, also the red worte, and many calle it Cicorea.

b. With adjs. (and derived sbs.), as **red-blind**, colour-blind in respect of red (so *red-blindness*); †**red fire-hot**, = RED-HOT;

red-green *a.*, pertaining to or affecting the ability to distinguish between red and green; **red-green-blindness** (cf. *red-blind* and GREEN-BLIND); **red-hearted** (see quot.); **red-mad**, = RED-WOOD *a.*; **red-raw** *a.*, rubbed or irritated until the flesh is exposed and inflamed; also *fig.*; **red-ripe**, fully ripe, as indicated by the red colour (also *fig.* as *sb.*); **red-sensitive** *a.*, sensitive or responding to the colour red; **redward** *a.* and *adv.*, towards the red end of the spectrum; also **redwards**.

1881 LD. RAYLEIGH in *Nature* XXV. 66 That vision would intelligibly be characterized as *red-blind. **1894** ABNEY *Colour Vision* (1895) 63 Taking a red-blind person and examining him with the spectrum, we find that he sees no light at all at the extreme limit of our red. **1876** BERNSTEIN *Five Senses* 115 There are..many degrees of *red-blindness. **1694** SALMON *Bate's Dispens.* (1713) 424/2 Melt the Tin in a Crucible, *red Fire-hot. *Ibid.* 425/1 Put it into a Crucible Red-fire-hot. **1888** *Times* (weekly ed.) 14 Sept. 3/1 Colour-blindness..is either *red-green-blindness or blue-yellow-blindness or total colour-blindness. **1935** *Discovery* Aug. 231/1 According to this theory red-green blindness is due to the red-green nerve being atrophied, leaving the yellow-blue nerve still in action. **1956** C. AUERBACH *Genetics in Atomic Age* 56 A good example for a sex-linked recessive gene in man is red-green colour-blindness. This abnormality is much more frequent in men than in women. **1958** *Listener* 6 Nov. 730/1 He, too, was a red-green colour-defective. **1964** S. DUKE-ELDER *Parsons' Dis. Eye* (ed. 14) xxiv. 364 The red-green cases fall into two main groups, protanopes and deuteranopes. **1971** J. Z. YOUNG *Introd. Study Man* xxxviii. 553 Those who are red-green blind cannot identify ripe or rotten fruit or even see red berries among the leaves! **1832** *Planting* 91 in *Lib. Usef. Knowl., Husb.* III, **Red-hearted*.—A discoloration of the central point or heart-wood of a tree. **1877** *Holderness Gloss.* s.v., He'll be *red-mad ti buy that pony. **1893** STEVENSON *Catriona* 74 She's..red-mad about..proscribed names, and King James. **1924** A. J. SMALL *Frozen Gold* 184 A *red-raw panic. **1957** T. HUGHES *Hawk in Rain* 13 All day he stares at his furnace With eyes red-raw. **1822** GOOD *Study Med.* III. 213 He could perceive cherries on cherry-trees, but only distinguish them even when *red-ripe, from the surrounding leaves by their size and shape. **1868** BROWNING *Ring & Bk.* I. 1396 Human at the red-ripe of the heart. **1936** *Discovery* May 151/2 This..was an advantage in the days of blue-sensitive materials when actinometers were first put forward, but has lost this advantage now green-sensitive and *red-sensitive materials are so universally employed. **1967** KARCH & BUBER *Offset Processes* v. 149 Although it [*sc.* orthochromatic film] is insensitive to red, dyes can be added to make it red-sensitive. **1889** LOCKYER in *Proc. R. Soc.* 10 Jan. 185 Some of the bright lines observed are described as being to the *redward side of dark lines. **1903** AGNES M. CLERKE *Probl. Astrophysics* 224 All showed a much smaller displacement redward than the dark lines. **1927** *Publ. Allegheny Observatory* VI. 136 The redward shifts of the solar lines. **1946** *Nature* 10 Aug. 205/2 The departure from the normal redward shift must be due to changes in the sun, and may readily be attributed to movements of the sodium vapour. **1973** *Sci. Amer.* May 118/1 A scarlet pigment, mercuric sulfide, is in fact a low-frequency reflector, reflecting about equally everything redward of a half-reflecting point in the orange. **1979** *Nature* 19 Apr. 719/1 The IR line moved *redwards by ~150 Å and the red line bluewards by ~70 Å.

B. *sb.* **1. a.** Red colour (dye, stain, etc.); redness.

Also, esp. in modern use, with many defining terms prefixed, as *Adrianople, alizarin, cherry, flesh, indigo, Turkey*, etc. (cf. A. 1).

c **1205** LAY. 24651 Heo wolden of ane heowen heore claðes habben. Sum hafden whit, sum hafden ræd, sum hafden god grene. *c* **1250** *Gen. & Ex.* 640 Ðe rede wid-innen toknet on wreche ðat sal get wurðen sent. *a* **1300** *Cursor M.* 3366 Wit mantel clad o bouen o rede. **13..** *Gaw. & Gr. Knt.* 952 Riche red on þat on [lady] rayled ay quere. *c* **1400** *Destr. Troy* 3988 Hir lippes were louely littid with rede. **1480** CAXTON *Descr. Brit.* 5 Men dyen ther with fyn reed, the redenes ther of is wonder fayr and stable. **1509** HAWES *Past Pleas.* xxxv. (Percy Soc.) 179 In a banner square, All of reade was wrytten Discomfort. **1571** GOLDING *Calvin on Ps.* ii. 9 He consumeth them to nothing with the onely red of his lippes. **1592** SHAKS. *Ven. & Ad.* 901 [The boar's] frothie mouth bepainted all with red. **1629** MILTON *Nativity* 230 The Sun in bed, Curtain'd with cloudy red. *a* **1683** OLDHAM *Wks.* (1685) 15 A deed, for which the day deserves its red Far more than for a paltry Saint, that died. *a* **1711** KEN *Hymnotheo* Poet. Wks. 1721 III. 311 With such rare Mixture of pure Red and White. **1798** COLERIDGE *Anc. Mar.* IV. xi, The charmed water burnt alway A still and awful red. **1808** SCOTT *Marm.* I. Introd. 15 No longer Autumn's glowing red Upon our Forest hills is shed. **1813** —— *Rokeby* v. xxxi, Distinguish'd by the paly red The lamps in dim reflection shed. **1864** BOWEN *Logic* i. 8 Though the red or the white of this object is not the identical red or white of that object.

b. The red colour in roulette or rouge-et-noir.

1849 THACKERAY *Pendennis* xxxvii, A confounded run on the red had finished him. **1866** YATES *Rock Ahead* III. v, I've won a little on the red and black here and there.

c. The red ball in billiards and related games.

1857 J. E. RITCHIE *Night Side of London* 128 'Good stroke'—'Bad flewke'—'On the red'. **1866** in Roberts *Billiards* (1869) 346 Bennett..in the next stroke fluked the red, the 'run' closing for 11. **1895** [see CUSH]. **1928** C. BERGENER *Contrib. Study of Conversion of Adjectives into Nouns* 135 The reds must be potted before you take the colours [in snooker]. **1974** *Rules of Game* 79 Three points if the cue ball hits the red into a pocket. **1977** *Cleethorpes News* 6 May 29/4 Hood potted the last red and this left Barnes in trouble, needing all the colours and a snooker to boot to pull off a win.

d. *to shoot* or *sport the red*: (see quot. 1897).

1849 D. J. BROWNE *Amer. Poultry Yd.* (1855) 163 A safer rule may be fixed at the season called 'shooting the red'. **1897** K. B. B. DE LA BERE *New Poultry Guide* II. 56 Turkeys require considerable attention..until they 'sport the red', as it is termed, i.e., develop the red colouring to the face and wattles.

e. The red colour conventionally used in map-making to represent British territories.

1899 *Manch. Guardian* 2 May 7/1 The destruction of the Transvaal's independence..would blot out from the mass of red on the map of South Africa a spot of brown. **1966** *Observer* (Colour Suppl.) 27 Feb. 5/1 Red on the map tends to be spots, not splashes nowadays—but there are still more than 1,500 British islands. **1975** P. MASON *Kipling* vi. 150 A busy talkative man..preaching war..wanting to paint the map red.

f. *to see red*: to get very angry; to lose self-control.

[**1900** J. K. JEROME *Three Men on Bummel* xiii. 292, I began, as the American expression is, to see things red.] **1901** 'L. MALET' *Hist. Sir R. Calmady* I. v. 39 Happily violence is shortlived, only for a very little while do even the gentlest persons 'see red'. **1923** *Daily Mail* 19 June 15 It maddened me, I think, and I saw red—and before I knew what I was doing I stabbed him. **1937** A. CHRISTIE *Death on Nile* xi. 119 Why—? Because she thinks I'm not her social equal! Pah—doesn't that make you see red? **1953** J. WAIN *Hurry on Down* x. 221 Instead of answering he leaned across and snatched at the packet Charles held in his hand. Charles saw red. His livelihood was in danger. **1974** *Times* 31 Jan. 2/6 'The village was incensed when a woman was left to die in her bath because an ambulance man on a go-slow refused to come out,' he said. 'We saw red and said we would form an action group to drive ambulances and cars.' **1977** *Daily Mirror* 15 Mar. 2 (*heading*) MPs see red over soaring prices.

g. The colour conventionally (now less commonly) used to indicate debit items and balances in accounts, used esp. in phrases ***in the red***: in debt, overdrawn, losing money (also *fig.*); ***out of the red***: in credit, making a profit. Hence, debt, an overdraft. Cf. BLACK *sb.* 2 d.

1926 MAINES & GRANT *Wise-Crack Dict.* 10/1 *In the red*, losing money in show parlance. **1927** *Scribner's Mag.* Apr. 380/2 'We've got to put forth our best efforts from now till the end of the month, or we'll be in red on the books,' he announced. **1928** *Publisher's Weekly* 10 Nov. 1957/2 About 966 copies more and the title will be out of the red. **1931** F. L. ALLEN *Only Yesterday* viii. 212 The Philadelphia Sesquicentennial was sinking deeper and deeper into the red. **1949** *Harper's Mag.* Mar. 62/2 The corporation was nearly a million dollars in the red. **1955** *Times* 28 June 3/3 With Tordoff and Saeed opening Somerset's second innings with commendable vigour, Leicestershire went further into the red. **1960** *Times* 15 Feb. 11/6 The British Transport Commission is already in the red to the tune of at least £30m. **1966** O. NORTON *School of Liars* i. 5, I don't think the manager at Barclays has ever heard of the Married Women's Property Act,..my red is Andrew's red. **1977** D. WILLIAMS *Treasure by Degrees* xviii. 169 A quarter of a million pounds ..would be more than sufficient to keep the College out of the red for the foreseeable future. **1978** S. BRILL *Teamsters* vii. 268 CCC has never run in the red.

h. A red light, lamp, etc., meant as a signal to stop. Also *fig.*

1970 'W. HAGGARD' *Hardliners* xiv. 155 At the top of Whitehall he jumped his first red, slipping left to the Mall against the signal. **1972** D. BLOODWORTH *Any Number can Play* xvi. 153 'We go by the position of the lights, not the colours,' soothed Ivansong, as they roared through a red. **1976** 'P. B. YUILL' *Hazell & Menacing Jester* vi. 67, I was doing over fifty and jumping reds.

2. a. Stuff, cloth, or the like, of a red colour (usually as the material of a dress).

c **1380** WYCLIF *Wks.* (1880) 475 He..made hym & his cardenals ride in reed on hye ors. *c* **1386** CHAUCER *Prol.* 294 Twenty bookes clad in blak or reed. **1523** in Turner *Sel. Rec. Oxf.* (1880) 44 For ij yards of Red for Crosses, price the yarde xij^{d}. **1590** SPENSER *F.Q.* II. ix. 27 There sate, y-clad in red Downe to the ground, a comely personage.

b. Ruddle (now *dial.*); †rouge.

1398 TREVISA tr. *Barth. De P.R.* XVI. lxxx, Off it gendreth seemliche colour and faire, as rewli, reed [*Caxton* redy], and stibium. **1538** ELYOT, *Rubricatus*, coloured with redde or ruddelyd, as shepe are. **1558** WARDE tr. *Alexis' Secr.* IV. 75 Another kinde of redde verye good for the face. **1700** CONGREVE *Way of World* III. i, *Lady.* Fetch me the Red—The Red, do you hear, Sweet-Heart?.. *Peg.* The red Ratifia does your Ladyship mean..? *Lady*... Paint, dost thou understand that? *c* **1720** DUCHESS OF MONTAGU in *Buccleuch MSS.* (Hist. MSS. Comm.) I. 367, I made myself as French as I could.., but they wear such loads of red, and powder, that it is impossible for me to come up to that. **1727-41** CHAMBERS *Cycl.*, *Red* in cosmetics, a fucus or paint wherewith the ladies enliven their cheeks and lips. **1869** *Lonsdale Gloss.*, *Red*, ruddle for marking sheep.

3. †**a.** Gold. *Obs. rare.*

c **1374** CHAUCER *Troylus* III. 1335 (1384) They shul for-go þe white and eke þe rede. **1390** GOWER *Conf.* II. 88 To the rede and to the whyte This Ston hath pouer to profite. **1677** W. HUGHES *Man of Sin* II. x. 187 The most Gracious See (saith he) rejecteth none where White or Red (Silver or Gold) makes Intercession.

b. Red wine.

c **1386** CHAUCER *Pard. T.* 198 Whan man so drynketh of the whyte and rede. **1709** *Rambling Fuddle-Cups* 11 Came in with a Friend for a whet of good Red. **1721** RAMSAY *To R. H. B.* iii, If ram'd wi' red, they rant and rair, Like mirthfu' men. **1842** TENNYSON *Will Waterproof* 82 No pint of white or red Had ever half the power. **1927** E. HEMINGWAY *Men without Women* 207 You tried the red?..we'll have a round of the red. **1961** J. B. PRIESTLEY *Saturn over Water* viii. 113 We drank a bottle of Chilean red, and she made coffee. **1969** *Listener* 27 Mar. 417/3 A bottle of red with this, which lasted right through the half-pound of Brie cheese that followed. **1974** K. MILLETT *Flying* (1975) III. 286 Nell goes off to seek another bottle of red.

4. = *red squadron* (cf. A. 16 d).

1690 *Lond. Gaz.* No. 2541/3 A second Rate, and Rear-Admiral of the Red. **1707** CHAMBERLAYNE *State Gt. Brit.* III. 600 Rear-Admiral of the Red. **1805** *Admiralty Notice* in *Naval Chron.* XIV. 439 His Majesty having been pleased to order the rank of Admirals of the Red to be restored to His Majesty's Navy. **1833** *Penny Cycl.* I. 126/2 Admirals of the Red bear their flag at the main-top-gallant-mast-head.

5. *pl.* (rarely *sing.* with *a.*)

a. Shades or tints of red.

1633 BP. HALL *Occas. Medit.* (1851) 59, I do not like these reds, and blues, and yellows, amongst these plain stalks and ears. **1635-56** COWLEY *Davideis* I. 87 No dawning Morn does her kind Reds display. **1812** SIR H. DAVY *Chem. Philos.* 243 It does not destroy even reds and yellows when fixed by mordants. **1884** *Times* (weekly ed.) 19 Sept. 5/2 The bodies and bars of the carts were..painted in blues and reds.

b. Red kinds or varieties of cloth, wine, wheat, etc.; red cattle, ants, herrings, etc. Also, potatoes of variety bearing red-skinned tubers or the tubers themselves.

1566 A. EDWARDS in Hakluyt *Voy.* (1599) I. 357 Your London reds are not to be sent hither. **1641** FRENCH *Distill.* Pref. (1651) *iiij b, They..have brought a great Odium upon it by..vending their whites, and reds. **1829** G. GRIFFIN *Collegians* II. xxx. 333 The English reds are a nate pratie. **1868** *Chambers' Encycl.* s.v. *Wine*, The Italian wines are very numerous. The best reds are Lambrusco, Barbera, etc. **1881** *Daily News* 23 Aug. 3/6 There were a few parcels of new wheat shown... Reds realized 55s. to 58s., and fine whites up to 60s. per quarter. **1890** 'R. BOLDREWOOD' *Col. Reformer* (1891) 121 He's got a real turn for the roans and reds. **1902** A. BENNETT *Grand Babylon Hotel* xxii. 251 The 'Spanish reds' from Catalonia, including the dark 'Tent' so often used sacramentally. **1926** R. N. SALAMAN *Potato Varieties* v. 28 A red,..when selfed, gives rise to three plants bearing red tubers to one bearing white. **1929** W. FAULKNER *Sartoris* II. v. 125 Got an old red we been saving for you... John would have enjoyed that fox. **1961** *Guardian* 24 Oct. 8/6 Some Russian dry whites and reds, selling at as little as 7s. 6d. a bottle. **1968** *Ibid.* 23 Feb. 9/6 No Swiss reds are of real distinction. **1968** K. WEATHERLY *Roo Shooter* 8 A number of roos were resting. The big buck was typical of the reds, standing on his tips about seven feet. **1972** E. HARGREAVES *Fair Green Weed* vii. 93 I'm to buy in more cattle, good reds, in the herd book. **1976** *Southern Evening Echo* (Southampton) 18 Nov. 16/6 Least wastage was 1½oz. from a pound of 'Reds'. **1977** *Age* (Melbourne) 18 Jan. 13/2 Let me forecast in no uncertain terms that this policy can lead only to a severe shortage of high quality reds in five years' time. **1977** *Grimsby Even. Tel.* 24 May 12/4 Principal sorts were: Cod.., coley.., rockfish.., reds.

†**c.** The menses. *Obs.*

1563 HYLL *Art Garden.* (1593) 69 Cummine seeds..doth stay the much bleeding at the nose, and womens excesse of the Reddes. **1601** HOLLAND *Pliny* II. 268 Herb Robert.. and Hyocisthis..do stay the flux of reds or whites. **1664** R. TURNER *Brit. Physician* 189 [copying Gerarde].

†**d.** Red cheeks. *nonce-use.*

1616 J. LANE *Contn. Sqr.'s T.* x. 212 Canace, whose bothe reddes paeld deadlie teene.

6. a. *pl.* Red men; North American Indians.

1804 C. B. BROWN tr. *Volney's View Soil U.S.* 351 A body ..capable of defending itself both against whites and reds, the savage on the one hand, and the land jobber on the other. **1889** *Boston* (Mass.) *Jrnl.* 11 May 1/7 A fight occurred between Indians and cowboys near that post, and..three of the reds were killed.

b. A radical, republican, or anarchist. Also, a Russian Bolshevik; a communist, or extreme socialist. Phr. ***reds under the bed***, used to denote an exaggerated or obsessive fear of the presence and harmful influence of communist sympathizers in a particular society, institution, etc.

1851 *Punch* XX. 245/2, I dreamt that I stood in the Crystal Halls, With Chartists and Reds at my side. **1864** TENNYSON *Aylmer's F.* 251 The next day came a neighbour. Blues and reds They talk'd of. **1882** *Spectator* 2 Dec. 1535 They fret as if they were Reds under a Cæsar. **1892** MRS. H. WARD *David Grieve* II. 349 My father was a Red—an Anarchist. **1922** S. LEWIS *Babbitt* v. 56 Say, juh notice in the paper the way the New York Assembly stood up to the Reds? **1928** D. L. SAYERS *Lord Peter views Body* iii. 44 I'm a Tory, if anything. I'm certainly not a Red. Why should I help to snatch the good gold from the Primrose Leaguers and hand it over to the Third International? **1931** P. HODGES *Britmis* i. 20 The Orenburg Army,..had been operating against the Reds south of the Trans-Siberian Railway. **1940** [see LIBERAL *sb.* 1 c]. **1947** *Partisan Rev.* XIV. 354 'All those guys,' he said, 'are just sore because they are not rich. Give any one of them a million dollars and they would forget all about being reds.' **1957** *Economist* 7 Dec. 882/2 Dr Villeda..has been at pains to show the Americans that he is no red. **1972** *Times* 24 May 16/3 This sort of 'reds under the bed' scare..could only be counter-productive. **1974** *Socialist Worker* 23 Nov. 16/1 The question now is whether the Broad Left leadership has the guts to campaign openly against the Social Contract and for a £30 a week claim in the face of mounting hostility from the government and an increasingly bitter Reds under the Bed campaign from the forces of reaction inside and outside the NUM leadership. **1976** C. BERMANT *Coming Home* I. i. 16 There came the depredations of the Russian civil war, first from the Reds then the Whites. **1976** *West Lancs. Evening Gaz.* 15 Dec., Apparently it is usual practice for Tory writers, if they think an election is imminent, to re-hash previous pre-election writings, same methods, reds under the bed, Communists, or other disguises becoming members of the Labour Party. **1977** 'J. LE CARRÉ' *Hon. Schoolboy* xiii. 303 There's a story that you people had some local Russian embassy link... Any Reds under your bed.. if I may ask?

7. Chiefly *U.S.* A red cent (see sense 3 c of the adj.).

1849 *Alta California* (San Francisco) 12 July 1/5 Silver is not Plenty on the Pharaoh and his host's Tables, and any body can sea it, and bet a red on any card he chuses. **1856** 'OCKSIDE' & 'DOESTICKS' *Hist. & Rec. Elephant Club* 244 Judge—'Have you got ten dollars?' Mr. W.—''Tis true, I hain't a red.' **1865** 'MARK TWAIN' in Harte & 'Twain' *Sk. Sixties* (1926) 199 Greely would ante up money on him as long as he had a red. **1905** J. LONDON *Let.* 1 June (1966) 173, I don't care a red how much the Lazar-sheets roast me. **1922** JOYCE *Ulysses* 151 Didn't cost him a red. **1936** J. A. MCKENNA *Black Range Tales* 267 Many who came into Frisco had not a dad-blasted red left to their name.

8. *ellipt.* for *red alert* (sense 19a of the adj.).

1943 B. NIXON *Raiders Overhead* iii. 28 Every night, and all night, there were raids. On the evening of the 16th the 'red' came up at 8.5 p.m. **1943** G. GREENE *Ministry of Fear* IV. i. 223 Yellow's up... About time for the Red I should think.

9. *Naut.* The port side of a ship. Also quasi-*advb.*

1948 PARTRIDGE *Dict. Forces' Slang* 153 *Red, the*, the port side of a ship. It shows a red light. **1956** 'TAFFRAIL' *Arctic Convoy* xi. 103 Someone shouted: 'There they are, sir! Bearing red nine-oh!'—otherwise ninety degrees on the port beam. **1958** W. KING *Stick & Stars* 66 Object bearing red five oh.

10. = RED-BIRD 2, RED DEVIL 3. *slang.*

1967 W. MURRAY *Sweet Ride* vii. 107 It's pills, mostly. Reds, goofballs, all kinds. And grass, of course. **1969** *Oz* May 21/1 Mixing 'reds' & alcohol can lead to a one way trip because the two drugs potentiate each other, i.e. 1 + 1 = more than 2. **1972** J. WAMBAUGH *Blue Knight* (1973) xvi. 293 What've you got, boy? Bennies or reds? Or maybe you're an acid freak?

11. *Comb.*, as (sense 6b) ***red-hunting*** *vbl. sb.* and *ppl. a.* See also RED-BAITING *vbl. sb.*

1927 U. SINCLAIR *Oil!* 313 Sure thing! He's nuts on this red-hunting business, and the pinks are worse than the reds, he says. **1935** H. L. ICKES *Secret Diary* (1953) I. 402 He feels about Red hunting just as I do and thinks it is absurd to deny communists an opportunity to express themselves or to have a ticket on the ballot. **1962** M. MCCARTHY *On Contrary* 37 Such Red-hunting publications as *Counter-attack*.

†**red**, *v. Obs.* [OE. *réadian*, f. *réad* RED *a.* Cf. OHG. *rôtên* (MHG. *rôten*), f. *rôt* red.]

1. *intr.* **a.** To be red. **b.** To become or grow red; to blush; = REDDEN *v.* 2 and 2b.

*c*975 *Rushw. Gosp.* Matt. xvi. 3 To-dæge biþ hreanis, readaþ forþon unrotlice þe heofun. *c*1000 *Sax. Leechd.* I. 330 Nim.. hwitne æppel þe þonne ȝyt ne readiȝe. *a*1310 in Wright *Lyric P.* ix. 34 Eyther cheke [is] Whit y-noh ant rode on eke ase rosen when hit redes. **1390** GOWER *Conf.* II. 7 For oght that is befalle Mai noman do my chekes rede. **1422** tr. *Secreta Secret., Priv. Priv.* 168 Muche sholde oure crystyn Prynces reede and be ashamyd.

2. *trans.* To make red; = REDDEN *v.* 1.

*a*1225 *Ancr. R.* 356 And nes Godes rode þuruh his deorewurðe blode iruded & ireaded. *Ibid.* 402 Jesu Crist ireaded mid his owune blode oðe rode. **1570** FOXE *A. & M.* (ed. 2) 695/1 He did redde and dyed them with their own bloud. **1611** COTGR., *Aynets*, little rods, or twigs, wherin herrings are threaded, and layed on hurdles to be redded. **1676** MOXON *Print Lett.* 12 By Redding or Blacking the Backside of your Paper. *a*1703 BURKITT *On N.T., 1 John* iii. 13 The prosecutor goes about with Cain's club in his hand, redded with blood. **1736** AINSWORTH *Lat. Dict.* s.v. *Rubidus*, Bread redded in the oven, and scorched.

red, var. RAD *a.*[2]; obs. f. (pa. t., etc.) of READ *v.*, var. REDD, obs. f. REDE *sb.* and *v.*, REED *sb.*

red, variant of READ *sb.*[1]

-red, *suffix*, representing OE. *rǽden* condition, which was freely used as a second element in combs. In ME. the full form *-rǽden, -rēden, -rāden* was by the general dropping of final *-n* reduced to *-rēde*, and this was subsequently shortened to *-red*. (In some cases the *-ēde* was confused with the synonymous *-hēde*.) In Sc., by an early metathesis of *n*, the suffix assumed the form *-rend* (*-rand*), later *-rent* (*-rant*).

Of the numerous words thus formed in OE. (see Bosw.-Toller, s.v.) only a few were retained in ME., as *brother-, fer-, folk-, frend-, love-, man-, sibrede(n, -red)*, repr. OE. *bróðor-, ȝefér-, folc-, fréond-, luf-, man(n)-, sibrǽden*. In addition to these, ME. had a few forms not recorded in OE., as *felawrede, neȝeburrede*, and the surviving representatives of the class, GOSSIPRED, HATRED and KINDRED. (*Cousinred*, used by Scott, is a hybrid and app. an individual formation.)

†**redabsolve**, *v. Obs. rare*[−0]. [ad. L. type **redabsolvĕre*: see RE- and ABSOLVE.] 'To discharge or dispatch' (Cockeram 1623).

†**re'dact**, *pa. pple. Obs.* [ad. L. *redact-us*, pa. pple. of *redigĕre*: see next.]

1. Brought together in a written form.

1432-50 tr. *Higden* (Rolls) III. 255 The grete Pompeius was the firste whiche willede to haue redacte the lawes in to bokes. *Ibid.* VII. 309 Whiche descripcion [of England] was redacte into oon volume.

2. Brought or reduced *into* (*in*), *to* a state, condition, etc., or *under* one's power.

1432-50 tr. *Higden* (Rolls) VII. 51 Ynglonde was redacte iiij. tymes into servitute. **1502** in Arnolde *Chron.* (1811) 163 So the[y] be redacte vnder the pour of the Soudane. **1513** *Ballad* in *Bradshaw's St. Werburge* 202 Thy bretherne were .. With diuers of thy kynne.. Redact in the catholique papall. **1539** in Froude *Hist. Eng.* (1858) III. 419 Wales is redact to that state that one thief taketh another, and one cow keepeth another. **1560** ROLLAND *Crt. Venus* IV. 528 Sa at all time I bruik my priuilage, That it be not redact vnto thirlage.

b. Of material things: Reduced *to* or *into* ashes, dust, etc.

1432-50 tr. *Higden* (Rolls) I. 119 Whiche apples y-taken be redacte vn to esches. **1545** JOYE *Exp. Dan.* iv. D. iij, Then was ye test or potsherd, the brasse, gold & sylver redacte into duste. **1558** WARDE tr. *Alexis' Secr.* I. (1568) 29b, Take drie Camomill redact into powder.

redact (rɪ'dækt), *v.* Also *pa. t.* 5 **redact**. [f. L. *redact-*, ppl. stem of *redigĕre* to bring back, collect, reduce, etc., f. *re(d)-* RE- + *agĕre* to drive, etc.: see ACT *v.* The form *redact* for the pa. t. (cf. prec.) is frequent in the later version of Higden. In its mod. use, the verb has been reintroduced in the 19th c. (after REDACTION); Ash (1775) and Todd (1818) mark it as 'not used'.]

†**1.** *trans.* To bring (matter of reasoning or discourse) *into* or *to* a certain form; to put *together* in writing. *Obs.*

1432-50 tr. *Higden* (Rolls) III. 251 Aristotille redacte hit [logic] in an arte. *Ibid.* 253 The Romanes didde redresse and redacte these lawes of Salon [*sic*] in to x. tables. *c*1550 LLOYD *Treas. Health* Y vj b, The aphorismes of Hippocrates redacted vnto a certayne order. **1597** A. M. tr. *Guillemeau's Fr. Chirurg.* *iiij b, They have redacted them together, because they might the easyer be vnderstoode. **1639** DRUMMOND *Conv. w. B. Jonson* Wks. (1711) 225 Ben Johnson.. cursed Petrarch for redacting verses into sonnets.

†**b.** To bring or insert (a thing) *into* a scheme or body. *Obs. rare.*

1570 FOXE *A. & M.* (ed. 2) 451/1 Although this law is not redacted into y[e] body of the law, yet.. it is not abrogated.

†**c.** To reduce (a subject) *to* a person's understanding. *Obs. rare.*

1657 TOMLINSON *Renou's Disp.* To Rdr. 1b, Here the whole Pharmaceutical Art is denuded, and redacted to the clear intelligence of the meanest capacity.

†**2.** To bring together *into* one body. *Obs.*

1432-50 tr. *Higden* (Rolls) I. 209 After that Romulus redacte alle the cites in to oon. *Ibid.* II. 273 Augustus.. redacte in to oon monarchy the realmes of alle the worlde. **1550** VERON *Godly Sayings* (1846) 50 Those things whiche can be redacted into some one thynge of manye.

†**3.** To reduce (a person or thing) *to, into* a certain state, condition, or action. Also rarely with *inf. Obs.* (Common in 17th c., esp. *Sc.*)

1542 BECON *News out of Heaven* Wks. 1564 I. 13 Ye see into how miserable a case ye are redacted and fallen by the sin of Adam. **1582-8** *Hist. Jas. VI* (1804) 90 In respect of the greatt desolatioun that the commonweill was redactit into. **1637** MONRO *Exped.* I. 3 The Baron of Fowles, being .. a little prodigall in his spending, redacted his estate to a weeke point. **1678** *Trans. Crt. Spain* II. 121 They will be ever redacted to shift for that where of they shall stand in need. **1731** *Plain Reas. Presbyt. Dissent.* 115 Poor people are squeezed and redacted to most pinching straits, thro' gentlemen's racking their rents.

†**b.** To reduce (a material thing) *to* a certain form. *Obs. rare.*

1634 BP. HALL *Character of Man* (1635) 26 Metalls whereby they might make use of those plants, and redact them to any forme or instruments of work, were yet.. to seek.

4. In modern use: **a.** To draw up, frame (a statement, decree, etc.).

1837 CARLYLE *Fr. Rev.* I. v. ii, The oath is redacted; pronounced aloud by President Bailly. **1845** —— *Cromwell* (1871) I. 101 The House of Commons.. was busy redacting a 'Protestation'. **1860** W. G. CLARK in *Vac. Tour.* 46 A council of ministers was held in the palace..: they were engaged in redacting the two proclamations.

b. To put (matter) into proper literary form; to work up, arrange, or edit.

1851 CARLYLE *Sterling* III. v, Sterling.. redacts it in a *Times* leader. **1884** *Times* 1 Nov. 9 Their observations are recorded, tabulated, digested, and redacted in every possible way.

Hence **re'dacted** *ppl. a.*

1676 COLES, *Redacted*, forced back. **1898** G. B. GRAY in *Expositor* May 347 The present redacted text of Genesis.

redacter, var. REDACTOR.

‖**rédacteur** (redaktœr). [F.] = REDACTOR.

1804 *Edin. Rev.* IV. 2 These materials.. left nothing to the *redacteur*, but the occasional labour of selection, arrangement, and compression. **1844** J. W. CROKER *Ess. Fr. Rev.* vii. (1857) 478 The careful *rédacteur*.. exercised some degree of judgment in correcting these unseemly blunders. **1848** J. G. LOCKHART *Let.* 4 Jan. in *N. & Q.* (1946) 9 Mar. 90, I wrote only yesterday to thank him for the Life of the Chancellor.. tho' not to congratulate him on his redacteur. The book is awfully ill done. **1883** *Daily News* 2 Oct. 5/6 Other *rédacteurs* of the once famous *Journal des Débats*. **1962** *Economist* 27 Jan. 334/3 In the French tradition, the *Dépêche* .. hands the big news of the day to a star rédacteur who comments on the story as he tells it.

Hence **re'dacteurship**.

1820 *Blackw. Mag.* VI. 619 In your two or three busy days of redacteurship.

redaction (rɪ'dækʃən). [In sense 1, ad. late L. *redactiōn-em* (Boeth.), n. of action f. *redigĕre* (see REDACT *v.*), or f. *redact-*, ppl. stem of *redigĕre*; in sense 2, a. F. *rédaction* (1690).]

†**1.** The action of driving back, resistance, reaction. *Obs. rare.*

1621 S. WARD *Life of Faith* 71 [Faith] takes away all reluctation and redaction, infuseth a plyable willingnesse. *a*1659 BP. BROWNRIG *Serm.* (1674) I. xxx. 385 There is a redaction and repercussion in resistance.

2. a. The action or process of preparing for publication; reduction to literary form; revision, rearrangement.

1785 T. JEFFERSON *Writings* (1894) IV. 68 The English of which is, that the redaction of the paper had been taken from the imprisoned culprit, and given to another. **1803** W. TAYLOR in *Ann. Rev.* I. 448 His redaction is neater, his range of study more comprehensive [etc.]. **1835** ARNOLD in Stanley *Life* (1858) I. vii. 357 Patches put together from various quarters without any redaction. **1883** A. ROBERTS *O.T. Revis.* ii. 43 The Pentateuch must have been subjected to many redactions before receiving its final shape.

b. The result of such a process; a new edition; an adaptation; a shortened form, an abridged version.

1810 *Edin. Rev.* XVI. 480 A sort of redaction, or new edition, of the subsisting statutes. **1860** ADLER *Fauriel's Prov. Poetry* xi. 221 The great poem of the Nibelungen is a redaction of several detached songs and poems.. more ancient than itself. **1948** *Observer* 30 May 3/3 Finally, we have.. what is described as a 'redaction' or compression—this dangerous device grows in popularity—of Lytton's *The Last Days of Pompeii*, by S. Fowler Wright. **1977** *New Yorker* 8 Aug. 2/3 Vinnette Carroll's singing-and-dancing redaction of the Book of Matthew. **1978** *Amer. N. & Q.* Mar. 103/2 In 1661 Samuel Smithson produced a prose redaction of the old metrical romance of Guy of Warwick.

3. The action of bringing or putting *into* a definite form.

1867 *Q. Rev.* Oct. 441 About 200 A.D. the redaction of the whole unwritten law into a code.. was completed.

4. *attrib.* and *Comb.*, as **redaction criticism** (see quot. 1976); hence ***redaction critic***, ***redaction-critical*** adj.

1970 N. PERRIN *What is Redaction Criticism?* i. 22 Although he does not use the term, Lightfoot was actually the first redaction critic. **1976** *Christian Believing* 47 The redaction critic returns by way of the work of form criticism to the Synoptic Gospels as wholes. **1976** *Times Lit. Suppl.* 8 Oct. 1285/3 As far as I know, all redaction critics begin by considering how Luke or 'Matthew' has altered the Marcan narrative. **1968** D. M. BARTON tr. *Rohde's Rediscovering Teaching of Evangelists* i. 15 Various basic theological ideas in the individual gospels were presented through redaction-critical work on the synoptic gospels. **1970** N. PERRIN *What is Redaction Criticism?* ii. 27 Bornkamm's article.. is the first thoroughgoing redaction- critical investigation of the theological peculiarities and theme of Matthew's Gospel. **1966** KECK & MARTYN *Stud. in Luke-Acts* (1968) I. 65 At the present time the method called redaction-criticism is luring us into a one-sided concentration on the work of editors. **1968** D. M. BARTON tr. *Rohde's Rediscovering Teaching of Evangelists* ii. 37 Redaction criticism.. endeavours to understand the gospels in their entirety against the background of a definite theological situation in the church. **1970** N. PERRIN *What is Redaction Criticism?* i. 1 Redaction criticism is an attempt to represent in English the German word *Redaktionsgeschichte*, which Willi Marxsen proposed as the designation for a discipline within the field of New Testament studies. **1976** *Times Lit. Suppl.* 8 Oct. 1285/3 What is called redaction criticism, the attempt to discover the theological and cultural presuppositions of the gospel writers by examining how they have edited ('redacted') their material.

Hence **re'dactional** *a.*, of or belonging to redaction; of the nature of redaction; also, of or belonging to a particular redaction.

1891 DRIVER *Introd. Lit. O.T.* 19 Making such slight redactional adjustments as the unity of his work required. **1968** *Language* XLIV. 15 In this theory also, RV [*sc.* Rigvedic] *deyām* would probably be redactional for original **dayām*. **1971** *Ibid.* XLVII. 65 Emeneau's hunch was that some forms beginning with *dy-* which occur in environments interdicted by the Sievers-Edgerton theory might actually be puristic redactional substitutions for Middle Indicisms in *j-*. **1971** *New Testament Abstracts* XV. 285 A minute analysis of vocabulary in this parable shows that before redactional activity it dealt with a king (God) who acted like a shepherd who separated the sheep from the goats with sure judgment.

redactor (rɪ'dæktə(r)). Also **redacter**. [a. L. type **redactor*, agent-n. f. *redigĕre* to REDACT. Cf. RÉDACTEUR.] One who redacts; an editor.

1816 SCOTT *Tales of my Landlord* 1st Ser. I. 8, I am not the writer, redacter, or compiler, of the Tales of my Landlord. **1831** CARLYLE *Misc.* (1857) II. 299 The first German redactor of this Fable. **1877** DAVIDSON *Canon Bible* 19 The idea naturally arises that he was the final redactor of the Pentateuch.

Hence **redac'torial** *a.*, of or belonging to a redactor; editorial.

1865 *Even. Standard* 6 June, To assume the redactorial charge of a new Republican daily paper. **1897** *Expositor* Sept. 167 The redactorial insertions of the later Judaism.

redactoral (rɪ'dæktərəl), *a.* [f. REDACTOR + -AL.] = REDACTORIAL *a.*

1970 R. S. FOSTER *Restoration of Israel* v. 110 The first redactoral addition in [*2 Kings* xvii.] v. 24-28 explains that the Samaritans were a mixed race.

red alert: see RED *a.* 19a.

†**redamancy**. *Obs. rare*[−1]. [f. L. *redamāre* to love in return, f. *re(d)-* RE- + *amāre* to love: see -ANCY.] The action of loving in return.

1656 BLOUNT *Glossogr.* (citing Montague *Missive Consol.*).

†**reda'mation**. *Obs. rare*[−1]. [See prec. and -ATION.] = prec.

1658 in PHILLIPS. **1678** J. J[ONES] *Brit. Church* 571 Where Christ is not exemplified, in three conformities: in his death, in his life, in his redamation.

†**re'dambulate**, *v. Obs. rare*$^{-0}$. [f. ppl. stem of L. *redambulāre*: see RE- and AMBULATE.] *intr.* 'To walk back' (Cockeram 1623).

redam'nation. *rare*$^{-1}$. [RE- 5 a.] Renewed damnation.
a **1652** BROME *Queen & Conc.* II. viii, Until the world be vindicated from The redamnation such an error threatens.

redan (rɪ'dæn). Also 8 reden(t, **redant** (and *erron.* **redans, -ens**). [a. F. *redan* (1677) for *redent* 'a double notching or iagging, as in the teeth of a saw' (Cotgr.), f. *re-* RE- + *dent* tooth.]

1. *Fortif.* A simple form of field-work, having two faces which form a salient angle.
1689 [see b]. **1704** J. HARRIS *Lex. Techn.* I, *Redent*, in Fortification [etc.]. **1706** PHILLIPS (ed. Kersey), *Redan* or *Redent.* **1727–41** CHAMBERS *Cycl.* s.v., Redens are frequently used in the fortifying of walls, where it is not necessary to be at the expense of building bastions. **1762** STERNE *Tr. Shandy* VI. xxi, A number of small piquets driven into the ground at the several angles and redans. **1776** in Sparks *Corr. Amer. Rev.* (1853) I. 159 It was..my intention to throw up a great number of large flèches or redans at certain distances, one behind another. **1828** J. M. SPEARMAN *Brit. Gunner* (ed. 2) 213 The distances of the redans from each other should not exceed 120 yards, in order that the fire from the faces of one redan may defend the saliants of the next. **1864** BURTON *Scot Abr.* I. v. 294 The long ranges of bastions and redans which covered miles of land under..Vauban.
transf. **1878** T. HARDY *Ret. Native* I. vi, Not on the level ground, but on a salient corner or redan of earth, at the junction of two converging bank fences.

b. *attrib.*
1689 *Lond. Gaz.* No. 2478/2 Having view'd the Ground, [he] staked out a Redent Work with Redoubts. **1834–47** J. S. MACAULAY *Field Fortif.* (1851) 31 To reduce the number of points of attack in a continued redan line, the salient of the large redan may be placed more in advance.

2. (See quot.)
1848 CRAIG, *Redan*, a projection in a wall on uneven ground to render it level. [Hence in Ogilvie (1850), and later Dicts., but it is doubtful whether this sense of the Fr. word has ever been adopted in Eng.]

redar(e, obs. forms of READER.

†**redarguate**, *v. Obs. rare*$^{-0}$. [irreg. f. L. *redarguĕre*: see next.] 'To reprove' (Cockeram 1623). So †**redarguation**, = REDARGUTION.
c **1485** *Digby Myst.* II. 47 To persue all tho that do reprobacion A-gayns owur lawes by ony redarguacion. **1721** BAILEY, *Redarguation*, a disproving or confuting.

redargue (rɛ'dɑːgjuː), *v.* Now *Sc.* [ad. F. *rédarguer* (14th c. in Littré), or L. *redarguĕre* to disprove, etc., f. *re(d)-* RE- + *arguĕre* to ARGUE.]

†**1.** *trans.* To blame, reprove (a person or persons, an action, etc.). Also const. *of, for. Obs.*
c **1400** *Apol. Loll.* 6 Poule aȝenstod him in þe face, & redarguid him, for he was reprouable. **1547** BOORDE *Brev. Health* lxviii. 19 b, A power of the soule the whiche doth reluct agaynst vyces and synne, and redargueth or reprehendeth synne. *a* **1578** LINDESAY (Pitscottie) *Chron. Scot.* (S.T.S.) I. 33 Quhen he had pansit in this maner wp and doun and ressonit [*MS. I*, redarguit] himself for his slouthfulness. **1648** LIGHTFOOT *Horæ Hebr.* (1684) II. 604 The Holy Spirit..could not but reprove and redargue the world of Sin. **1677** GALE *Crt. Gentiles* II. III. 136 Basil.. severely redargues Origen's allegoric mode of Theologising.

2. To confute (a person) by argument. (In later use only Sc.; cf. next sense.)
c **1380** WYCLIF *Sel. Wks.* I. 79 Rekke we not of argumentis þat sophistis maken, þat we ben redargued grantynge þat we denyen. **1632** B. JONSON *Magn. Lady* III. iv, Sir, I'll redargue you By disputation. **1671** [R. MACWARD] *True Nonconf.* 3 It is your part, by this your conference more solidly to redargue him. **1704** EARL OF CROMARTY in *Lond. Gaz.* No. 4037/5 That we may redargue one another with Kindness and Civility. **1877** BLACKIE *Wise Men* 327 All these Love's vouchers stand, beyond the craft Of sophist to redargue.

3. To refute or disprove (an argument, statement, etc.). (Since *c* 1700 only *Sc.*, chiefly *Law.*)
1627 HAKEWILL *Apol.* III. §4 (1635) 310 Nathaniel Carpenter thus fully redargues that forgerie. **1641** J. JACKSON *True Evang. T.* I. 68 The error which this point is profitable to confute and redargue is twofold. **1679** *Prot. Conformist* 3 It has been so fully and clearly redargued, that I need not meddle with it. **1751** MCDOUALL *Inst. Laws Scot.* I. 359 The presumption lies..that he has the drawer's effects, which he must redargue by the letter of advice. **1771** SMOLLETT *Humph. Cl.* Introd. p. vi, The objections you mention, I humbly conceive are such as may be redargued, if not entirely removed. **1847** HAMILTON *Let. to De Morgan* 4, I may..redargue your claim and statements, as the result of a mistake. **1885** *Law Rep. 10 App. Cases* 383 *note*, This fact afforded a degree of real evidence which no parole testimony could redargue.

†**b.** To argue (a case) in opposition to another person. *Obs. rare.*
a **1633** W. AMES *Saint's Secur.* (1652) 8 When Job's three Friends had spent much time in arguing and redarguing the case with Job, Elihu..speaketh after this manner.

4. *absol.* or *intr.* To reprove or refute; to employ argument for the purpose of refuting.
1641 J. JACKSON *True Evang. T.* I. 55 Men love truth when it shines, but not when it redargues. **1644** BULWER *Chirol.* 170 The bowing downe of the Fore-Finger for a checke of silence, and to redargue, is an action often found in the Hands of men.

Hence **re'darguing** *vbl. sb.*
1627–77 FELTHAM *Resolves* II. xii. 184 It was the redarguing of his misguided friends..that moved him. **1656** STANLEY *Hist. Philos.* IV. (1701) 147/1 A great lover of Contention, and therefore called *Ἐλέγξινος* from redarguing.

redargution (rɛdɑː'gjuːʃən). Now *rare.* [a. OF. *redargucion, -tion* (12th c. in Godef.), ad. L. *redargūtiōn-em*, f. *redarguĕre*: see prec.]

†**1.** Reproof, reprehension (of a person, an action, etc.). *Obs.* (Common in 17th c.)
1483 CAXTON *Gold. Leg.* 435/2 He sheweth hymself worthy of redargucion or rebuke. **1533** MORE *Apol.* 160 b, The open reprofe and redargucyon therof may not..well bycome those that are no more spyrytuall than I. **1593** BELL *Motives conc. Rom. Faith* (1605) 129 The whole scripture.. is profitable to doctrin, to redargution, to correction. *a* **1690** BP. HOPKINS *Serm. Lev.* xix. 17 Wks. 1809 IV. 489 To expose the vice that we reprove..keeping still within the bounds of a sober and friendly redargution.

†**b.** An instance of this. *Obs. rare.*
1610 WILLET *Hexapla Dan.* 157 There is first a redargution and reprehension of the king. **1620** BRENT tr. *Sarpi's Counc. Trent* VIII. (1676) 675 To make an excuse to Lorain, saying that his redargutions were not meant of his Excellency..but of the Divines of the Sorbone.

2. Confutation (of a person); refutation, disproof (of a statement, etc.). Now *rare.*
1529 MORE *Dyaloge* I. Wks. 149/2 Thei coulde not endure yᵗ redargucion that should sometime fall to their part in dispysicions. **1597** J. KING *On Jonas* (1618) 544 Therefore they must be vanquished..both by written demonstrations, and by vnwritten redargutions. **1640** *Consid. Ch. Eng.* 9 It is a matter Volumes have beene compiled of, and therefore cannot receive a briefe redargution. **1697** C. LESLIE *Snake in Grass* (ed. 2) 46 Which Plea leads us Naturally and Necessarily into this sort of Redargution. **1882** GOUGH & COWELL *Sarva-darshana-samgraha* 66 As if then we had thrown their best wrestler, the redargution of the rest of their categories may be anticipated.

†**re'dargutive**, *a. Obs. rare.* [ad. L. type **redargūtīvus*: see REDARGUE and -IVE.] = next.
1609 R. BARNERD *Faithf. Sheph.* 60 The first [use] is Redargutiue, when the doctrine is vsed to confute and ouerthrow an error or heresie. **1623** in COCKERAM.

†**re'dargutory**, *a. Obs. rare.* [ad. L. type **redargūtōrius*: see REDARGUE and -ORY.] Pertaining to refutation or reproof.
1634 T. CAREW *Cœlum Brit.* Wks. (1824) 154 My privileges are an ubiquitary,..interrogatory, redargutory immunity over all the privy lodgings. **1650** *Let. Cens. & Redargution Lieut.-Col. Lilburne* 1 This censorious, redargutory address of mine.

Red Army. [see RED *a.* 9 b.] **a.** The name given to the Russian Bolshevik army and later to that of the Soviet Union.
1918 *Manch. Guardian* 13 Dec. 7/4 The Bolshevik Government..is engaged in creating a Red Army of over a million men. **1935** N. MITCHISON *We have been Warned* II. 172 In Moscow..on May Day there are great processions.. and marching by the Red Army. **1943** J. B. PRIESTLEY *Daylight on Saturday* viii. 51 The Red Army is still showing what a workers' republic can do. **1976** 'M. BARAK' *Secret List H. Roehm* viii. 81 After the Revolution he remained an officer in the Red Army. **1978** *Detroit Free Press* 16 Apr. (Record) 15/3 At last, in January 1944 the Red Army advance made it safe for the Kranzbergs and little Miriam to leave their hiding place. **1980** M. BAR-ZOHAR *Deadly Document* x. 164 The band chimed in with..the Red Army song.

b. Adopted as the name of the army in other, esp. communist, countries.
1926 *Encycl. Brit.* II. 393/1 The [Hungarian] Red Army was organised, primarily to ensure the maintenance of the dictatorship. **1934** tr. *Mao Tse-Tung's Red China* 21 The Chinese Soviets and their Red Army have grown out of the development of the agrarian revolution, which liberates the masses of the peasants from oppression and exploitation. **1965** M. MICHAEL tr. *J. Myrdal's Report from Chinese Village* i. 4 The peasants of northern Shensi..set up their own soviet republic and formed their own Red Army. **1974** tr. *Sniečkus's Soviet Lithuania* 20 Many joined the ranks of the Lithuanian Red Army. **1975** *Times Lit. Suppl.* 14 Feb. 163/2 Horthy came to power in the winter of 1919–20..after Romania's military victory over the Hungarian Red Army. **1977** *Time* 21 Mar. 26/3 The Communists' Red Army had just completed its epic Long March from the Southeast to its new headquarters at Yenan in remote northern Shensi province.

c. The name of a left-wing extremist terrorist organization in Japan.
1972 *Sat. Rev.* (U.S.) 24 June 30/1 The Red Army, an extremist terrorist group in Japan, sponsored and trained by the radical Popular Front for the Liberation of Palestine. **1974** *Times* 7 Feb. 5/1 The Popular Front for the Liberation of Palestine and the Red Army of Japan in a statement issued yesterday sought to justify the attack on the Singapore oil storage tanks—where it is claimed 15 tanks were blown up. **1976** K. BENTON *Single Monstrous Act* ii. 19 The Libyans.. seem to have dished out money to every revolutionary group there is, from the Japanese Red Army to the Provos.

d. Red Army Faction, the name of a terrorist organization of West Germany.
1977 *Time* 19 Sept. 8/3 The initials represent the now familiar Red Army Faction, which had murdered both Buback and Ponto. **1979** R. PERRY *Bishop's Pawn* ix. 174 The terrorists..were definitely operating under the Red Army Faction umbrella.

re'dart, *v.* [RE-.] *trans.* To dart (a thing) back in return. Hence **re'darted** *ppl. a.*
1613 PURCHAS *Pilgrimage* IX. iv. (1614) 842 They sometimes are said to catch an arrow with the hand, and redart it at the shooter. **1640** [R. BRATHWAIT] *Two Lancashire Lovers* 63 Let but one line redart one small beameling of love. *a* **1711** KEN *Anodynes* Poet. Wks. 1721 III. 449 Soon as a bearded Dart I feel, Redarted Pray'r the Wound shall heal.

re'date, *v.* [RE- 5 a.] *trans.* To change the date of; to assign a new date to. Hence **re'dating** *vbl. sb.*
1611 COTGRAVE *Dict.*, *Redater*, to redate, or adde a new date vnto. **1864** *Spectator* 31 Dec. 1498 Instead of rewriting or redating the previous part of my letter I prefer to send it as it was written. **1935** HUXLEY & HADDON *We Europeans* ii. 54 A recently propounded re-dating of a fragment of a skull. **1980** *Early Music* Jan. 103/2 The new madrigal was not really published in appreciable quantity until the late 1530s, and the re-dating of a central group of manuscript sources shows that dissemination in manuscript was the main way in which the repertory circulated during the years 1520–40.

re'dawn, *v.* [RE- 5 a.] *intr.* To dawn again. Hence **re'dawning** *ppl. a.*
1837 DE QUINCEY *Revolt Tartars* Wks. 1854 IV. 175 Peace and prosperity..re-dawned upon the tribes. **1896** *Q. Rev.* Oct. 334 This faint gleam of redawning freedom died away.

red-back.
1. *U.S.* The American dunlin or red-backed sandpiper, *Tringa americana*; also, the wax-bill (? error for *red beak*).
1813 WILSON *Amer. Ornith.* VII. 25 This bird..[is] known in England by the name of the Dunlin; and in the United States, along the shores of New Jersey, by that of the Red-back. [Cf. Newton *Dict. Birds* (1894) 770.] **1851** MAYHEW *Lond. Labour* II. 72 In St. Helena birds, known also as wax-bills and red-backs, there is a trade to the same extent.

2. *Austral.* In full, ***red-back spider***; = *jockey spider* s.v. JOCKEY *sb.* 9.
1933, etc. [see *jockey spider* s.v. JOCKEY *sb.* 9]. **1936** K. C. MCKEOWN *Spider Wonders Austral.* xi. 152 The Red-back Spider..has adapted itself to a life in close association with man. **1953** A. UPFIELD *Murder must Wait* xiv. 130 Five red-back spiders..lying in wait to inject their poison. **1956** *Coast to Coast 1955* 59 Look, there's a red-back in it. **1978** *Telegraph* (Brisbane) 11 Aug. 4/4 The six were victims of a wolf spider—of a type previously unknown and potentially as dangerous as a redback. **1979** *Ibid.* 22 Feb. 3/1 It's a battle to the death. Redback spider versus poisonous dugite snake.

red-backed, *a.* **a.** Having a red back; chiefly of birds, *esp.* the red-backed butcher-bird or shrike (*Lanius collurio*), and the red-backed sandpiper (*Erolia alpina*); also, the red-backed mouse or vole (*Clethrionomys gapperi*), and the Australian red-backed spider (= RED-BACK 2).
1709 J. LAWSON *New Voy. Carolina* 126 The Red-back'd Snake [is found in Carolina]. **1768** PENNANT *Brit. Zool.* I. 163 The Red backt Butcher Bird [1776 Shrike]..The upper part of the back and coverts of the wings are a bright ferruginous color. **1802** BINGLEY *Anim. Biog.* (1813) The mode in which a Red-backed Pelecan..stowed its food into its pouch. **1813** WILSON *Amer. Ornith.* VII. 25 Red-backed Sandpiper, *Tringa Alpina.* **1819** WARDEN *United States* II. 411 The rattle-snake,..red-backed snake. **1822** LATHAM *Gen. Hist. Birds* VI. 286 The Red-backed Lark. **1839** AUDUBON *Ornith. Biog.* V. 335 Red-Backed Woodpecker. **1840** *Penny Cycl.* XVIII. 263/2 One species..is known by the names Variegated Sole, Red-backed Flounder, etc. (*Monochirus linguatulus*). **1894** NEWTON *Dict. Birds* 845 Much smaller than this is the Red-backed Shrike,..the best-known species in Great Britain, where it is a summer visitor. **1897** *Proc. Biol. Soc. Washington* XI. 113 The following brief synopsis of the Red-backed Voles is based on a study of specimens in the collection of the U.S. Biological Survey. **1934** *Bulletin* (Sydney) 6 June 20/3 In the Chillagoe..district the red-backed spider is known as 'the jumping red-back'. **1936** D. MCCOWAN *Anim. Canad. Rockies* viii. 71 The Red-backed mouse is a forest dweller.. of medium size and has a coat that is marked by a fairly broad belt of chestnut brown hair over the spine. **1940** GABRIELSON & JEWITT *Birds Oregon* 263 The handsome Red-backed Sandpiper is a common migrant on the coast. **1942** Red-backed spider [see KATIPO]. **1962** M. E. MURIE *Two in Far North* II. iii. 117 Olaus was interested in learning all he could about the distribution of..the red-backed mouse. **1963** *Times* 5 June 14/4 There was still to come the red-backed shrike. **1966** 'J. HACKSTON' *Father clears Out* 134 Safe from..red-backed spiders, and spiders without red backs. **1977** J. L. HARPER *Population Biol. Plants* xv. 465 The seed was collected and buried mainly by..redbacked voles.

b. Of books: Backed with, bound in, red.
1866 HOWELLS *Venet. Life* xvi. 246 We *forestieri* of the red-backed books.

red-bait ('rɛdbeɪt). *S. Afr.* [tr. Afrikaans *rooiaas.*] A large sea-squirt, *Pyura stolonifera*, an ascidian which is used as bait by anglers.
1895 *Agricultural Jrnl.* (Dept. of Agric., Cape Colony) 912 The bait most in use is crayfish, and 'rooiaas' (red bait) a species of Zoophyte. **1905** J. GILCHRIST in Flint & Gilchrist *Science in S. Afr.* III. iv. 192 One of the features of the rocky parts of the coast line from Cape Point eastwards is the clusters of 'rooias' or 'red-bait'. **1930** C. L. BIDEN *Sea-Angling Fishes of Cape* xii. 217 The name 'red-bait' is the English interpretation of the Dutch 'rooi aas'. **1945** *Cape Times* 20 Oct. 7 Red bait could be cut by the sackful. **1957** S. SCHOEMAN *Strike!* iii. 29 Not a single fish would take redbait or mussel. **1971** *Stand. Encycl. S. Afr.* III. 205/2 'Sea-squirts', including the common 'red-bait' (*Pyura*) and the transparent *Ciona*, live permanently attached to rock surfaces.

'Red-baiting, *vbl. sb.* orig. *U.S.* Also with small initial. [RED *sb.*[1] 6 b.] Harassment of those of known or suspected communist sympathies; also *attrib.* So (as a back-formation) **'red-bait** *v.*

trans. and *intr.*, to oppose, thwart, or persecute because of communist associations; **'Red-baiter, red-baiter**, one who seeks out and harasses supposed communists.

1929 *Nation* 2 Oct. 343/1 Red-Baiters... Mr. Woll and his underlings have become..obsessed with an anti-Communist spirit. **1934** M. H. Weseen *Dict. Amer. Slang* 386 *Red-baiting*, looking for communists. **1937** *Nation* 14 Aug. 167/2 A new red-baiting campaign. **1939** *Sun* (Baltimore) 22 Mar. 12/1 It was well-nigh impossible to say a word for capitalism and against the vagaries of Communism without being accused of Red-baiting. **1940** G. Seldes *Witch Hunt* p. xi, Nevertheless, that program was redbaited into compromise and failure. **1943** F. Scully *Rogue's Gallery Hollywood* 83 Fugitives from red-baiting America..they all rallied 'round leaders like Pirandello. **1946** *Sun* (Baltimore) 19 July 20/1 The War Department hasn't gone off half-cocked to 'witch hunt, red bait or to bust' unions. **1950** *Manch. Guardian Weekly* 15 June 15 The 'Amerasia' case is something that the Red-baiters have wanted to open up again ever since the conviction of Alger Hiss. *Ibid.* 16 Nov. 9 The defeat of the Liberals..suggests that vociferous 'Red-baiting' is, however silly, good politics. **1962** D. Lessing *Golden Notebk.* iv. 483 The fanciest bit of red-baiting I've heard in a long time. **1969** *Listener* 13 Feb. 214/2 One might sneer away the Red-baiting of the Hearst press and shrug off the ceaseless cries of 'Fascists!' from the Left, and yet be uneasy about the future. **1974** *Socialist Worker* 2 Nov. 12/5 The information could be used to red-bait or victimise workers involved in the present disputes. **1976** *Times Lit. Suppl.* 23 Jan. 89/1 Professor Nove may be in danger of incurring from some of our red-baiters the ludicrously unjustifiable charge of being an apologist for Stalin. **1977** *Time* 7 Feb. 46/3 Boyle, 40, stars as the Red-baiting chairman of the Senate Permanent Subcommittee on Investigations.

red-banded: see red *a.* 14 b, 14 c.

red bark. A variety of Cinchona-bark.

1782 W. Saunders *Superior Efficacy of Red Peruvian Bark* (ed. 2) 7 The diversity both in size and colour of the Red Bark from the common Peruvian Bark. **1837** *Penny Cycl.* VII. 173/2 Red bark has been known for 130 years, but was not much used in Europe till 1779. **1880** C. R. Markham *Peruv. Bark* 41 The species yielding 'red bark', the richest and most important of all the Chinchonæ.

attrib. **1861** R. Spruce (*title*) Report on the Expedition to procure Seeds and Plants of the Cinchona Succirubra, or Red Bark Tree. **1880** C. R. Markham *Peruv. Bark* 218 Now the 'red bark' grounds are confined to the ravine of the river Chasuan, and its tributaries. *Ibid.* 305 The dry season in the 'red bark' region.

red-bead snake, tree, vine: see red *a.* 12 b.

red-bearded, *a.* Having a red beard.

1576 Newton *Lemnie's Complex.* (1633) 207 That red-bearded men are seldome of any good disposition. **1611** L. Barry *Ram Alley* E ij b, Fetch me a red-bearded sargeant. **1751** H. Walpole *Lett.* (1846) II. 403 He is..red-bearded, and not comely. **1843** Carlyle *Past & Pr.* iv. iv, Thor red-bearded, with his blue sun-eyes.

red-bellied, *a.* Having a red belly.

Frequent in the names of American birds and fishes.

1709 J. Lawson *New Voy. Carolina* 126 Red-bellied Land-Snakes. **1731** M. Catesby *Nat. Hist. Carolina* I. 19 The Red-bellied Wood-pecker... The belly near the vent..is stained with red. **1743** G. Edwards *Nat. Hist. Birds* I. 22 The Red-belly'd Blue-Bird. **1782** Latham *Gen. Synopsis Birds* I. ii. 485 Red-bellied Curucui, *Trogon Curucui*. **1808** Wilson *Amer. Ornith.* I. 43 Red-bellied black-capt nuthatch, *Sitta varia*. *Ibid.* 114 Red-bellied woodpecker, *Picus Carolinus*. **1819** Warden *United States* II. 411 The..red-bellied land snake. **1847** Audubon & Bachman *Vivip. Quadrup. N. Amer.* I. 292 Red-bellied Squirrel. **1876** Goode in *Smithson. Coll.* XIII. vi. 60 Red-bellied terrapin (*Pseudemys rugosa*). **1917** T. G. Pearson *Birds Amer.* II. 161/2 The Red-bellied Woodpecker..evinces a decided taste for fruit. **1934** Dylan Thomas *Let.* 15 Apr. (1966) 108 If there must be a worm in our letters let it be the jolly, red-bellied one you told me about. **1965** Mrs. L. B. Johnson *White House Diary* 3 June (1970) 281 Most startling of all was a fish whose every scale stood out..the red-bellied angelfish. **1973** M. Crowell *Greener Pastures* 109 It is the red-bellied woodpecker that visited the feeder last week. **1977** C. McCullough *Thorn Birds* iv. 75 Of snakes the variety was almost endless..red-bellied black snakes.

red-belly: see red *a.* 18 b.

red belt. 1. [red *a.* 9 b.] **a.** Territory under the political control or influence of the U.S.S.R. **b.** Elsewhere, an area of communist strength or influence.

1947 *Sun* (Baltimore) 22 Dec. 2/1 The 'Red Belt' states of Europe are moving into a fairly solid bloc. **1966** M. R. D. Foot *SOE in France* ix. 257 The French communist organizations in the 'red belt' round Paris. **1969** P. Allum in Henig & Pinder *European Political Parties* 233 The dc is strongest in the 'white provinces' where it regularly polls half the vote and it is weakest in the 'red belt' where its vote is only around 30 per cent. **1977** *Time* 4 Apr. 22/3 But much as Moscow might like a Red belt across Africa, even Angola and Mozambique are not anxious to be totally under Soviet control. **1978** *Sunday Star* (Toronto) 26 Feb. A4/3 When voters of the Paris red-belt suburb of Kremlin-Bicetre attend election meetings, the gloves are off.

2. [red *a.* 16.] A belt worn by one who has attained a certain degree of proficiency in judo or karate; also, a person qualified to wear such a belt.

1952 E. J. Harrison *Judo* i. 14 A black belt is worn in the first five Dan grades..and a red belt in the tenth and higher Dan grades. **1958** *Radio Times* 7 Feb. 9/4, I am only a Red Belt. **1967** P. Urban *Karate Dojo* 44 A solid red belt is worn by the highest grand masters. **1971** *Rand Daily Mail* 27 Mar. 6/8 Executive members of the South African division of the Japanese Karate Association put their heads together and came up with a new belt—a red one symbolising a junior brown belt. **1976** B. Jacks *Judo* 8 The adult beginner wears a white or red belt and the grades then progress.

red-belted: see red *a.* 14 a, b.

red-berried, *a.*

1. Bearing red berries.

1731 P. Miller *Gardeners Dict.* s.v. *Sambucus*, The Mountain red-berry'd Elder. **1739** *Ibid.* II. s.v. *Casia*, Red-berried Shrubcasia. **1819** Warden *United States* II. 242 *note*, Mountain maple, red-berried elder, and witch hazle. **1865** Sowerby *Eng. Bot.* IV. 36 Red-berried Bryony. **1891** T. Hardy *Tess* (1900) 32/2 The tall red-berried hedges. **1930** J. Masefield *Wanderer of Liverpool* 19 Red-berried blackthorn. **1972** *Hilliers' Man. Trees & Shrubs* 360 *Sambucus..racemosa* L. 'Red-berried Elder'. A medium-sized to large shrub.

2. Resembling red berries.

1881 *Macm. Mag.* XLIV. 345 The child with ripe red-berried lips.

red-bill: see red *a.* 18 b.

red-billed, *a. Ornith.* Having a red bill.

1729 in *Dampier's Voy.* (ed. 3) III. 408 The Red-bill'd Starling. **1781** Latham *Gen. Synopsis Birds* I. i. 355 Red billed Hornbill. *Ibid.* 390 Red-billed Jay. **1814** Wilson *Amer. Ornith.* Index, Red-billed Rail. **1864–5** J. G. Wood *Homes without H.* xi. (1868) 200 Our first example of the African Weavers is the Red-billed Weaver Bird. **1884–5** *Riverside Nat. Hist.* (1888) IV. 106 Of this very remarkable form only one species, the red-billed curlew..is known.

'red-bird. 1. A name given to various small American birds with red plumage, esp. the summer tanager (*Piranga rubra*), scarlet tanager (*P. olivacea*), Baltimore oriole (*Icterus galbula*), and cardinal grosbeak (*Richmondena cardinalis*).

1669 [see Baltimore]. **1670** D. Denton *Descr. New York* (1845) 5 There is also the red Bird, with divers sorts of singing birds. **1723** Blackmore *Alfred* vii. 224 When on Indian Plains a Rattle-Snake Perches a Red-Bird in a shady Brake. **1783** Latham *Gen. Synopsis Birds* II. i. 27 At Hudson's Bay it [the red-breasted thrush] is known by the name of Red bird. **1856** Bryant *Murdered Trav.* ii, The red-bird warbled, as he wrought His hanging nest o'erhead. **1885** Lady Brassey *The Trades* 423 The red-birds, or 'Cardinal gros-beaks'..are a kind of Virginian nightingale. **1929** W. Faulkner *Sartoris* iv. iv. 337 They saw redbirds darting like arrows of scarlet flames. **1938** M. K. Rawlings *Yearling* ix. 81 A red-bird swung in an arc across the sink-hole. **1959** E. B. White *Let.* Feb. (1976) 459 It's a nice place to be, what with the..red-bird saying 'Portugee, Portugee'.

2. The drug secobarbital (Seconal); also, a tablet of this drug (coloured red). *slang.*

1969 R. R. Lingeman *Drugs from A to Z* 219 *Seconal*... Slang names: red birds, red devils, reds. **1976** *Billings* (Montana) *Gaz.* 11 July 9-A/1 In order on DAWN's list of drugs most frequently recorded in crisis situations—in which a drug user sought help or died—were heroin, marijuana, aspirin, LSD, secobarbital (marketed as Seconal and known as 'red devils, Mexican reds and red birds'), [etc.].

red-blind(ness): see red *a.* 19 b.

'red-blooded, *a.* [red *a.* 14 a.] **1.** Having red blood.

1802 *Med. Jrnl.* VIII. 370 These organs are the same in the white as in the red-blooded animals. **1840** *Cuvier's Anim. Kingd.* 388 The Annelides,..or Red-blooded Worms, constitute the first [class].

2. Restored to health and strength after weakness or exhaustion.

1877 Tennyson *Harold* iv. iii. 131 Sit down, sit down, and eat, And, when again red-blooded, speak again.

3. *transf.* Virile, vigorous, full of life, spirited.

1881 A. A. Hayes *New Colorado* xi. 155 [Nothing] can be conceived more exasperating to a strong red-blooded man than to..have a villain take his watch and money. **1888** W. Whitman in *Cent. Mag.* (1911) Dec. 254/2 John's letter appeals to me..because of its uncompromising red-blooded espousal of the book. **1914** E. R. Burroughs *Tarzan of Apes* xix. 257 Tarzan..did what no red-blooded man needs lessons in doing. **1923** *Daily Mail* 28 Feb. 10 (Advt.), It's a rip-roaring, red-blooded yarn that no man or woman will be able to read unmoved. **1941** B. Schulberg *What makes Sammy Run?* vii. 159 The play was..about two red-blooded guys who are always scrapping. **1966** Wodehouse *Plum Pie* i. 11 A redblooded loony doctor under the influence of the divine passion ought surely to have put the thing through months ago. **1978** M. Puzo *Fools Die* xxxiii. 387 To me he sounded like any red-blooded American businessman.

'redbone. *U.S.* A hound belonging to a variety distinguished by a red or red and tan coat, which was once used to hunt racoons. Also *attrib.*

1916 W. H. Miller in *Field & Stream* XXI. 177/1 Good Redbone, Pennsylvania or Portsmouth hound stock is what we want up North. **1919** —— *Amer. Hunting Dog* iii. 57 Two strains are well known, the Redbone, an ancient breed of Southern coon-hound, and the J. E. Williams dogs. **1948** W. Faulkner *Intruder in Dust* i. 5 A true rabbit dog, some hound, a good deal of hound, maybe mostly hound, redbone and black-and-tan. **1975** E. Wigginton *Foxfire 3* 38, I had a *good* stock a' dogs—blue tick and redbone mix.

red book, red-book. A book bound in red.

1. a. As the name of individual books of an official character, or otherwise important.

Red Book of the Exchequer, a miscellaneous volume, containing copies of charters, statutes, surveys, etc., originally compiled in the 13th century, and printed in 1896 (Rolls Series); see also quot. 1820. ***Red Book of Hergest***, a Welsh manuscript of the 14–15th c. (now the property of Jesus College, Oxford), containing the tales known as the Mabinogion and other pieces in prose and verse.

1479 *Bristol Rec.* in *Eng. Gilds* (1870) 419 All the chauntry preestis whos composicions are enrolled in the rede boke. **1574** in W. H. Turner *Select. Rec. Oxford* (1880) 352 A certifycatt sent downe from London to this cytye as the same appearith in the redd booke. **1699** Bp. W. Nicolson *Eng. Hist. Library* iii. iii. (1714) 213 There is also, in the keeping of the King's Remembrancer, an antient Miscellany of several notable Treatises; which Volume is commonly cited, and call'd by the Name of *Liber ruber Scaccarii*, or Red-Book of the Exchequer. **1700** Tyrrell *Hist. Eng.* II. 828 The Copy of this Charter..is entred in the Red Book of the Exchequer at Dublin. **1715–6** in *Catal. MSS. Wales in B.M.* (1903) 408 Since I perceived Jesus College had an undoubted right to the Red Book of Hergest. **1800** in *Rep. on Ossian* (1805) App. 278 He remembers that his father had a book which was called the Red Book,..which..contained a good deal of the history of the Highland Clans. **1820** *Trans. Royal Irish Acad.* XIII. iii. 181 An antient book of record, called the Red Book of the Exchequer, which is preserved in the office of the chief remembrancer of that court in Ireland. **1896** H. Hall *Red Bk. Exchequer* (Rolls) I. Pref. i The Red Book of the Exchequer belongs to the class of Entry Books usually termed Precedent Books, but more correctly Registers, or Books of Remembrance.

†**b.** A book containing the names of all persons holding office under the State or receiving pensions from it. *Obs.*

1800 *Asiatic Ann. Reg., Proc. E. Ind. Ho.* 93/1 The proprietors of India Stock would soon have a Red-book of their own, which would rise with the Red-book of England. **1820** (*title*) The Extraordinary Red Book: An Account of all Places, Pensions, Sinecures, Grants, &c. The Expenditure of the Civil List, the Finances and Debt of Great Britain.

†**2.** (See quot.) *Obs. rare*$^{-0}$.

1688 Miége *Gt. Fr. Dict.* ii. s.v. *Red*, A Witche's red Book, a Catalogue of such as have sealed to the Devil with their own bloud, *la rouge liste*.

3. A popular name for the 'Royal Kalendar, or Complete..Annual Register' (published from 1767 to 1893); also, the title of a similar work of later date (see quot. 1847).

1788 *Observer* No. 98 ¶6 He measures his devoirs with an exactitude that bespeaks him a correct interpreter of The Red Book. **1814** Moore *Poems, Epigram*, We've lost the Court-Guide, Ma'am, but here's the Red Book. **1823** Hazlitt *Liber Amoris* 55 Is the name on the frank: see if you can decypher it by a Red-book. **1830** Gen. P. Thompson *Exerc.* (1842) I. 278 Dukes, earls, viscounts, and so on to any extent down the ladder of honour in the Red Book. **1847** (*title*) Webster's Royal Red Book; or Court and Fashionable Register: comprising..an alphabetical list of the nobility and gentry, with their town and country residences, etc. etc. **1888** Rider Haggard *Mr. Meeson's Will* xiv, He..seized a Red Book, in which he discovered that Lord Holmhurst's..London house was in Hanover Square.

4. ***Little Red Book***: a popular name used in Western countries for 'Quotations from Chairman Mao Tse-tung' (published in English in 1966). Also in extended and allusive use.

1967 [see Maoism]. **1970** G. Jackson *Let.* 17 Apr. in *Soledad Brother* (1971) 225 Burn it; all the fascist literature, burn that too. Then equip yourself with the Little Red Book. **1971** D. Bagley *Freedom Trap* viii. 193 Communist Albania has ceased to hew to the Moscow line. Enver Hoxha, the Albanian party boss, has read the Little Red Book and thinks the thoughts of Mao. **1974** *Times* 21 Oct. 12/8 A hotelier in..Lübeck has arranged to provide in all bedrooms..a German translation of Chairman Mao's little red book. **1976** J. Crosby *Nightfall* x. 47 If I write my own little Red Book, that will be in it. Hit the pricks—or they get ideas. **1977** *N.Y. Rev. Bks.* 12 May 22/3 Photos showed rampaging teenagers waving their little red books of Mao quotations.

'redbreast.

1. a. The robin (see also *Robin redbreast*).

c **1401** Lydg. *Flower Courtesy* 58 The sely wrenne, the titmose also, The litel redbrest. *c* **1440** *Promp. Parv.* 426/2 Redbreste, byrde, *rubellus*. **1530** Palsgr. 261/2 Reed breest a byrde, *rovgegorge*. **1604** Drayton *Owle* 87 Covering with Mosse the deads unclosed eye, The little Red-brest teacheth Charitie. **1647** Ward *Simp. Cobler* 74 Should I heare..a Horse whistle like a Red-breast, it would scare me. **1708** Prior *Turtle & Sparrow* 18 Ye pious Redbreasts, deck his Hearse. **1750** Gray *Elegy* 119 The Redbreast loves to build and warble there. **1847** Lytton *Lucretia* (1853) 300 The spray of the willow trembles with the wing of the redbreast. **1894** Newton *Dict. Birds* 771 Even those Redbreasts which stay in Britain during the winter are subject to a migratory movement.

attrib. and *Comb.* **1576** Gascoigne *Philomene* (Arb.) 110 As the red breast byrds, Whome prettie Merlynes hold. **1596** Shaks. *1 Hen. IV*, iii. i. 265 'Tis the next way to turne Taylor, or be Redbreast teacher. **1783** Wolcott (P. Pindar) *Odes to R. A.'s* i. 29 May some good Christian Bard..Turn Redbreast kind, and with the sweetest song Bewail our hapless fate with watry eye! **1876** T. Hardy *Ethelberta* (1890) 115 Bright auburn, several shades nearer to redbreast-red than was Ethelberta's hair.

b. Applied to other red-breasted birds, esp. *U.S.* to the migratory thrush (also called *robin*).

1775 Clayton in *Phil. Trans.* LXVI. 105 Of small birds there are several sorts; the red breast, speckled on the back like a partridge [etc.]. **1828–32** in Webster.

2. *transf.* (See quots.)

1862 Dickens *Lett.* 18 Apr. (1880) II. 178 The Bow Street runners..had no other uniform than a blue dress-coat, brass buttons..and a bright red cloth waistcoat. The waistcoat was indispensible, and the slang name for them was 'red-breasts' in consequence. **1899** *London Letter* 10 Nov. 701/2 The 'Redbreasts', or New South Wales Lancers, who have been at Aldershot for a year.

3. *U.S.* The long-eared sunfish, *Lepomis megalotis*.

1888 G. B. GOODE *Amer. Fishes* 66 In Pennsylvania it [*sc.* the long-eared sun-fish] is called 'Sun Perch' and 'Red Headed Bream', elsewhere it is the 'Red Breast'. 1948 *New Hanover Fishing Club Prize List* 30 Annual prizes for freshwater fish..Red Breast.

red-breasted, *a.* Having a red breast. Chiefly *Ornith.* In quot. 1609 *fig.*

red-breasted duck, the white-eyed duck. **r. finch**, = *r. grosbeak.* **r. godwit**, the bar-tailed godwit, *Limosa rufa.* **r. goosander**, = *r. merganser.* **r. goose**, *Anser* or *Bernicla ruficollis.* **r. grosbeak**, the rose-breasted grosbeak. **r. merganser**, *Mergus serrator.* **r. rail**, (*a*) the king-rail, *Rallus elegans*; (*b*) the Virginia rail. **r. sandpiper**, the knot in summer plumage. **r. snipe**, the dowitcher, *Macrorhamphus griseus.* **r. thrush**, the American robin or red-breast.

1609 B. JONSON *Case is Altered* v. i, O [my] fair-feather'd, my red-breasted birds, Come fly with me. 1678 RAY *Willughby's Ornith.* 194 The red-breasted Indian Blackbird, perchance the Jacapu of Marggrave. 1729 in *Dampier's Voy.* (ed. 3) III. 406 The Red-breasted Parrot. *Ibid.* 409 The Red-breasted Woodpecker. 1750 G. EDWARDS *Nat. Hist. Birds* III. 138 Red-breasted Godwit. 1776 PENNANT *Brit. Zool.* (ed. 4) II. Pl. 93 Red breasted Goosander. Red breasted Merganser. *Ibid.* 467 Red-breasted Shoveler. 1785 —— *Arct. Zool.* II. 335 Red-breasted Thrush. *Ibid.* 350 Red-breasted Grosbeak. *Ibid.* 372 Red-breasted Finch. *Ibid.* 571 Red breasted Goose. 1802 MONTAGU *Ornith. Dict.* (1831) 580 The red-breasted snipe is a variety of this species [yarwhip]. 1813 WILSON *Amer. Ornith.* VII. 43 Red-breasted Sandpiper, *Tringa rufa.* 1817 T. FORSTER *Nat. Hist. Swallowtribe* (ed. 6) 95 *Anas Nyroca*,..Red-breasted duck. 1835 AUDUBON *Ornith. Biog.* III. 27 The Great Red-Breasted Rail, or Fresh-Water Marsh-Hen. 1886 C. TAYLOR in *Ibis* No. 15. 380 The Red-breasted Goose, *Bernicla ruficollis*, is not now found in Upper Egypt.

red-brick. Also red brick, redbrick. **1.** A red building-brick. Freq. *attrib.*

1712 J. MORTIMER *Whole Art Husbandry* II. 150 The black Mould..will in time degenerate into a red-brick Earth. 1835 J. ROMILLY *Diary* 11 Mar. (1967) 70 They are nasty red-brick churches, in the worst stile of 1760. 1839 URE *Dict. Arts* 184 The finest kind of marl and red bricks, called cutting bricks. *a* 1847 ELIZA COOK *Rhymes by Roadside* iv, The child upon the red-brick floor. 1888 *Lockwood's Dict. Terms* 280 Red Brick Dust, used for parting Sand. 1916 E. F. BENSON *David Blaize* v. 101 His horizon and aspirations stretched no farther than this red-brick arena. 1943 'B. TRUSCOT' *Redbrick University* 17 The material used in them [*sc.* universities] was..a hideously cheerful red brick suggestive of something between a super council-school and a holiday home for children. 1960 J. BETJEMAN *Summoned by Bells* v. 46 But for me, Less academic, red-brick Chalfont Road Meant great-aunt Wilkins, tea and buttered toast. 1977 *Western Mail* (Cardiff) 5 Mar. 7/3 For the Opposition leader, it was a nostalgic return to the red brick establishment of Kesteven and Grantham girls' school which she left 34 years ago.

2. (Also with capital initial.) Used *attrib.* or quasi-*adj.* to denote a British university founded in the late nineteenth or early twentieth century in a large industrial city, with buildings of red-brick, as distinct from the older universities (esp. Oxford, Cambridge, the ancient universities of Scotland, and some of the London colleges) built predominantly in stone, and also as distinct from the new universities founded after the 1939–45 war; of or pertaining to such a university; also *ellipt.*, a red-brick university; *collect.*, such universities in general. Also *transf.*

1943 'B. TRUSCOT' *Redbrick University* 18 The range of interests represented in a Redbrick staff common-room. *Ibid.* 19 It may be natural enough for him to go on to Red-brick, but to..enter Oxbridge is something infinitely more exciting. 1944 'H. ASHTON' *Yeoman's Hospital* ix. 197 Marriner took his professorship at that frightful red-brick university. 1950 *Times Educ. Suppl.* 10 Mar. 183 (*heading*) Redbrick criticized. 1958 *Times Lit. Suppl.* 17 Jan. 30/4 Talk of..'the red-brick intellectuals', though no Movement founder-member had done more than *teach* at one of the provincial universities. 1958 *Observer* 16 Feb. 12/3 One of the new 'redbrick actors', neither actorish in aspect nor conventionally po-voiced. 1958 *New Statesman* 22 Feb. 233/1 Under education, the correct entry is: 'Educated Thomas Cooks, American Express, Wayfarers, etc., etc.' Europe has been my Redbrick. 1960, etc. [see OXBRIDGE]. 1966 G. SINSTADT *Whisper in Lonely Place* iii. 33 He's a research engineer, degree from one of the red-bricks, middle twenties. 1975 D. LODGE *Changing Places* i. 9 Rummidge.. had lately suffered the mortifying fate of most English universities of its type (civic redbrick). 1976 M. HINXMAN *End of Good Woman* i. 13 They kept introducing her to eligible mates. Revolutionaries at the London School of Economics, posh chums from Oxford..budding scientists and engineers at the 'red-brick' universities. 1977 *Jrnl. R. Soc. Arts* CXXV. 670/1 Some of the best safety managers I know left school at 14 or 15 years of age. Conversely, we have seen people who come from red bricks and grey stones but are quite unable to do the job at all.

'red-bud. **a.** A tree belonging to one or other of the American species of *Cercis*, esp. *Cercis canadensis*; the Judas tree. Also *attrib.* †**b.** (See quot. 1798.) *Obs.*

1705 R. BEVERLEY *Hist. & Present State Virginia* IV. 56 They dish up [roots, herbs, etc.] various ways, and find them very delicious Sauce to their Meats;..such are the Red-buds, Sassafras-Flowers, Cymnels, Melons, and Potatoes. 1709 J. LAWSON *New Voy. Carolina* 100 The Red-Bud-Tree bears a purple Lark-Heel. 1717 *Petiveriana* III. 11/2 Red-bud. Bears a purple Blossom. 1732 *Gentl. Mag.* II. 670 No verdant leaves the lovely Red-Bud grace. 1798 NEMNICH *Lex. Polygl.* v. 867/1 Redbud, *Andromeda racemosa.* Caroline Red bud, *Andromeda nitida.* 1816 BRACKENRIDGE in *Views Louisiana* (ed. 2) 202 The red-bud, the tree which blooms earliest in our woods,..appears in a few places. 1868 *Rep. U.S. Commissioners* (1869) 201 European red-bud (*Cercis siliquastrum*). 1883 *Century Mag.* July 379/1 The pink tassels of the redbud lit up the dark mass of foliage. 1931 W. FAULKNER *Sanctuary* xviii. 164 Lilac and wistaria and redbud..had never been finer. 1946 D. C. PEATTIE *Road of Naturalist* v. 58 The red-bud trees begin to bloom. 1977 *New Yorker* 2 May 51/2 The dogwoods and redbuds blossomed.

'redcap, red-cap, red cap.

1. a. Applied to one who wears a red cap.

1550 *Acts Privy Council* (1891) III. 6 Captaine Redde Cappe, one of the rebelles of the last yere. 1602 DEKKER *Satiromastix* L iv, Runne Red-cap, ware hornes there. *a* 1687 COTTON *Poet. Wks.* (1765) 99 Her Grace Finds me among a Crew of mad-caps, Æneas, at one Mother Red-Cap's. 1795 WOLCOTT (P. Pindar) *Wks.* (1812) III. 118 Since Impudence, assuming Freedom's form Near Mother Redcap brews the dangerous storm. 1841 LEVER *C. O'Malley* xxxvii. 205 Now push along old red-cap. 1883 STEVENSON *Treas. Isl.* xxv, There were the two watchmen, sure enough: red-cap on his back, as stiff as a handspike.

b. *spec.* as the name of a sprite or goblin.

a 1802 LEYDEN *Lord Soulis* lxi. in *Minstr. Bord.* II. 348 But Redcap sly unseen was by, And the ropes would neither twist nor twine. 1802 SCOTT *ibid.* 335 Redcap is a popular appellation of that class of spirits which haunt old castles. 1886 *Rochdale Gloss.*, *Redcap*, that which induces a person to run away from his work. The people say such a one 'has seen Redcap'.

†**2.** A red-hat, a cardinal. *Obs. rare.*

1539 *St. Papers, For. & Domestic Hen. VIII*, XIV. I. 68 That divorce should lead to the utter fall of the said Red Cap ..and after much misery the land should by another Red Cap be reconciled. 1609 [BP. W. BARLOW] *Answ. Nameless Cath.* 236 A silly frumpe of a White-liverd Red-cap.

3. †**a.** Some kind of shell. *Obs. rare*$^{-1}$.

? 1711 PETIVER *Catal. Gazophyll.* Dec. 11/2 Red-Cap, [or] Spoon-egg... Each of these Valves resembles a Tea-Spoon; and both shut, a small Egg.

b. The goldfinch.

1785 *Gentl. Mag.* LV. II. 534/2 Many birds..seem to have particular names in these parts [Yorkshire]. Woodpeckers ..[are called] pickatrees, [and] gold-finches, red-caps. [1795 COWPER *Pairing Time* 37 My dear Dick Redcap, what say you?] 1827 CLARE *Sheph. Cal.* 6 The red-cap, hanging over head, In cage of wire. 1842 TENNYSON *Gardener's D.* 94 The redcap whistled; and the nightingale Sang loud. 1864–89 in dial. glossaries (Yks., Linc., Shropsh., etc.).

c. The red field-poppy.

1846 MRS. LOUDON *Brit. Wild Fl.* 25 The farmers call it Red-weed, Red Cap, Corn Rose.

4. *Mil. slang.* A military policeman.

1919 *Athenæum* 1 Aug. 695/1 In your July 18 issue a correspondent mentions 'red-hat' as an army policeman. I have always found 'red-cap' to be the more familiar term. 1949 G. COTTERELL *Randle in Springtime* 7 'Mind yourself, there are some redcaps in that jeep.' 'I seen 'em,' the driver grinned, slowing down to below forty miles an hour, as another jeep, containing three Military Policemen, approached and passed them. 1964 J. HALE *Grudge Fight* viii. 127 The redcaps and the R.A.F. police. 1976 J. O'CONNOR *Eleventh Commandment* iv. 53 She used to take me to night-clubs tucked away which no officers or redcaps knew about.

5. Chiefly *U.S.* A porter at a railway station.

1919 S. LEWIS *Free Air* xxiv. 245 A factory illuminated by arc-lamps,—the baggage—the porter.. red caps. 1929 M. DE LA ROCHE *Whiteoaks* x. 145 A 'redcap' darting into the throng, the bag clutched in his hand. 1931 W. FAULKNER *Sanctuary* xxi. 227 A man shouted 'taxi' at them; a redcap tried to take Fonzo's bag. 1942 *Sun* (Baltimore) 10 Oct. 10/2 There are only thirty-five red caps to help the anxious passengers with their luggage. 1960 B. KEATON *Wonderful World of Slapstick* iii. 59 Kelly didn't explain that there were no redcaps at Victoria Station. 1969 J. A. MCPHERSON in A. Chapman *New Black Voices* (1972) 156 He had redcaps in the Chicago stations telling the soldiers who to ask for on the train. 1977 *Times* 19 Apr. 15/7 In France and Switzerland the larger stations have 'red cap' porters who shift baggage on a prescribed tariff.

red-capped, *a.* Wearing a red cap; capped with red. Chiefly *Ornith.*

1848 GOULD *Birds Australia* VI. Pl. 17 The Red-capped Dottrel is universally dispersed over every part of the sea-shores of Australia that I have visited. 1865 —— *Handbk. Birds Austr.* I. 280 Red-capped Robin of the Colonists. 1877 *Nature* XV. 461/2 A Red-capped Parrot (*Pionopsitta pileata*) from Brazil. 1880 OUIDA *Moths* I. 64 Sailors in dark blue jerseys, and red capped.

red carpet: see RED *a.* 19 a.

red cedar. **a.** A North American species of juniper, esp. *Juniperus virginiana*, or the western conifer, *Thuja plicata*. Also *attrib.* **b.** The toon-tree or Moulmein cedar, *Cedrela toona.* **c.** An Australian timber-tree, *Flindersia australis.*

1682 S. WILSON *Acct. Province Carolina in Amer.* 12 This Country hath..divers sorts of lasting Timber that England hath not, as Cedar white and red, Cypress, Locust, Bay and Laurel Trees. 1717 *Petiveriana* III. 11/2 Red Cedar. An Evergreen, its Wood sweet, very durable. 1832 *Planting* 122 in *Lib. Usef. Knowl., Husb.* III, The red cedar..attains to the size of a timber tree in deep sandy loam soils. 1843 HOLTZAPFFEL *Turning* I. 80 The wood of *Juniperus virginiana* is called Red or Pencil Cedar. In New South Wales the term..red cedar [is applied] to that of *Flindersia australis*, as well as to the wood of the Toon-tree, or *Cedrela Toona.* 1884 C. S. SARGENT *Rep. Forests N. Amer.* 7 The hemlock, and the red cedar (*Thuya*) are still important elements of the forests. 1889 MAIDEN *Usef. Native Plants* 400 *Cedrela Toona*... The 'Cedar', or 'Red Cedar' (a universal appellation in Australia). 1904 E. STEP *Wayside & Woodland Trees* 81 The Virginian Juniper..or 'Red Cedar', as it is called on the American continent, is..frequently planted in our parks and gardens. 1958 G. A. PETRIDES *Field Guide Trees & Shrubs* 22 The junipers (including the Red Cedar) may bear either scaly or hollowed 3-sided needles. 1969 T. H. EVERETT *Living Trees of World* iv. 63/1 Western red-cedar..is native along the Pacific Coast of North America. 1972 *Ecology* LIII. 1141/2 'Fruits' of pasture juniper and red cedar are important foods for red squirrels.

attrib. 1797 *Deb. Congress U.S.* 10 Feb. (1849) 2113 It would be expedient..to secure some of the lands in South Carolina and Georgia, well clothed with live oak and red cedar timber, for the purpose of building ships of war. 1825 *Field's Geog. N. S. Wales* App. 502 Red cedar tree. *Cedrela toona.* 1851 *Knickerbocker* XXXVII. 377 The country-bred traveller..inhales the odor of the red-cedar buckets.

red cell. A blood cell containing hæmoglobin; an erythrocyte; = *red blood cell, red corpuscle*, both s.v. RED *a.* 19 a.

1885 DELAFIELD & PRUDDEN *Handbk. Path. Anat. & Histol.* (ed. 2) II. 50 In the extravasation of blood by diapedesis, the white blood-cells may pass through the walls of the vessels..; the red cells, on the other hand,..are.. carried passively through the walls by minute amounts of fluid. 1896 *Boston Med. & Surg. Jrnl.* CXXXV. 131/2 Nucleated red cells have usually been classified as microblasts, normoblasts, megoblasts..and those with dividing nuclei. 1936 *Lancet* 11 July 88/2 A..study of the permeability of red cells. 1968 PASSMORE & ROBSON *Compan. Med. Stud.* I. xxvi. 2/1 The red cells are by far the most numerous of the blood cells; for every white cell there are about 500 red cells and about 30 platelets.

b. *attrib.*

1917 C. PRICE-JONES *Blood Pictures* i. 11 Assuming the average red-cell count of a woman to be 4,450,000 per c.mm. 1941 *Science* 24 Jan. 87/1 (*heading*) Red cell volume circulating and total as determined by radio iron. 1947 *Radiology* XLIX. 303/2 After acutely toxic doses of such agents as Sr^{89} and Pu^{239}, the minimum red cell count occurs in survivors at a period later than the time of death of non-survivors. 1968 PASSMORE & ROBSON *Compan. Med. Stud.* I. xxvi. 5/1 Red cell precursors normally account for one third to one tenth of the bone marrow cells. 1976 *Med. Clin. N. Amer.* LX. 945 Pure red cell aplasia is a disorder in which patients cease making new red cells. 1976 I. CHANARIN et al. *Blood & its Dis.* ii. 11 The normal..red cell count at sea level is..$10^6/\mu l$ 5·0 ± 0·6 [for men].

red cent: see RED *a.* 3 c.

red-cheeked, *a.* Having red cheeks. Also *transf.*, esp. of apples.

1602 MARSTON *Antonio's Revenge* v. iv. sig. K1 Red cheekt Bacchus. 1606 *Sir G. Goosecappe* I. i. in Bullen *O. Pl.* III. 5 Here's a red cheeckt apple to take him up with. 1611 BARKSTED *Hiren* (1876) 100 The red-cheek't morning opens now her gate. 1664 EVELYN *Pomona* 26 Red-cheek'd and Red-strak'd Musts of several kinds. 1725 RAMSAY *Gentle Sheph.* II. iv. Song xi, Red-cheek'd ye compleatly ripe appear. 1764 G. EDWARDS *Glean. Nat. Hist.* III. 258 The Red-cheeked Wood-pecker. 1786 BURNS *Halloween* xxi, She gies the Herd a pickle nits An' twa red cheeket apples. 1872 GEO. ELIOT *Middlemarch* II. xxxvii. 254 Pratt, a red-cheeked man. 1923 E. O'NEILL *Anna Christie* I. 7 He is a boyish, red-cheeked, rather good-looking young fellow of twenty or so. 1960 *Farmer & Stockbreeder* 16 Feb. (Suppl.) 3/1 From the car he waved goodbye to her. Red-cheeked, in her felt shoes, one hand clutching her dress at the neck, she waved back.

Red China. [RED *a.* 9 b.] Communist China; the People's Republic of China. Hence **Red Chinese** *sb.* and *adj. phr.* Cf. *mainland China* s.v. MAINLAND 2 b.

1934 tr. Mao Tse-Tung (*title*) Red China. 1937 E. SNOW *Red Star over China* i. 17 There has been perhaps no greater mystery among nations, no more confused an epic, than the story of Red China. 1966 'G. BLACK' *You want to die, Johnny?* viii. 151 You couldn't stop junks landing... I'm thinking of Red Chinese. 1967 R. J. SERLING *President's Plane is Missing* (1968) vii. 138 Is there any reason to suspect the Red Chinese or Russians? *Ibid.* 139 Suppose, sir, Red Chinese agents had somehow kidnaped Mr. Haines. 1971 J. HENDERSON *Copperhead* (1972) xv. 195 Targets inside Russia and Red China. 1972 J. BALL *Five Pieces of Jade* ii. 27 A systematic new campaign by the red Chinese to pump narcotics..into the United States. 1972 'G. BLACK' *Bitter Tea* (1973) iii. 44 Plenty of people in Malaysia still hate Red China. 1978 *Listener* 8 June 721/1 The entry permit into what we used to call 'Red China' is stamped on your passport.

red-circle, *v.* To separate out by circling in red ink; usu. *fig.*; *spec.* (see quots. 1974 and 1977). Hence **red-circling** *vbl. sb.*

1965 E. BROWN *Big Man* xxiii. 202 The night had been red-circled for pleasure and for entertainment. 1973 *Maclean's Mag.* July 63/1 This was not a problem peculiar to the Trudeau regime, but it grew worse when the Treasury Board approved a plan to 'red circle' my 28 senior officers, the heart of my department. *Ibid.*, He suggested that if a committee were set up, the impending red circling might be avoided. 1974 *Globe & Mail* (Toronto) 14 Feb. 1/2 [The secretaries] fear their position will be further downgraded by a reclassification scheme undertaken by the Treasury Board, whereby secretaries could be red-circled—held in their current pay bracket until the new secretarial classifications catch up to them. The possibility of red-circling has stalled salary negotiations between the Treasury Board and the Public Service Alliance of Canada. 1976 *Ibid.* 15 Sept. 1/2 The alliance said red-circling is not permitted and that an employee can only be demoted if he is proved to be incompetent or incapable of performing the duties of his position. 1977 *Spare Rib* May 22/1 Certain men at Vauxhall's were 'red circled', placed in a special category to preserve their higher rate of pay. (It is called 'red circling' when workers moved on to a job with a lower rate of pay take their previous higher rate with them.)

redco, variant of REDCOLL *Obs.*

'redcoat, red-coat, red coat.

1. One who wears a red coat; *spec.* **a.** A soldier of the British army. Now *Hist.*

In the Civil War commonly applied to the Parliamentary troops or some regiments of them, though each side had red-coated soldiers.

1520 *Song Lady Bessy* (Percy Soc.) 74 Sir William Standley.. Ten thowsand read coates that had hee. **1644** VICAR *God in Mount* 200 Colonell Hollis his regiment of Red-coats.. did most gallant service. **1660** *Trial Regic.* 192, I do not charge you that you commanded those Halbertiers, but those Red-coats; you were all in Red. **1725** B. HIGGONS *Rem. Burnet* II. Hist. Wks. 1736 II. 114 They.. violently drove the Orthodox Ministers from their Livings, by the Help of their ruffianly Red-coats. **1775** SHERIDAN *St. Patr. Day* I. ii, Egad, he'll make the redcoats keep their distance. **1810** WELLINGTON in Gurw. *Desp.* VII. 69 It would be still necessary to keep your picquets, etc. upon the river, and some red coats in Chamusca. **1862** *Sat. Rev.* 8 Feb. 141/2 The police constable would immediately make his appearance on the scene; and if his efforts were fruitless, the red-coats would come too.

b. An attendant wearing a red coat.

1848 THACKERAY *Bk. Snobs* xxxiv, The red-coats wish to be Briareian, so as to hold all the gentlemen's horses.

c. A steward at a Butlin's holiday camp.

1950 L. BLAIR *Butlin Holiday Bk. 1949–50* 66 The snow eventually disappeared and the 'Redcoats' prepared to return to the Holiday Villages. **1962** R. NORTH *Butlin Story* v. 61 Charlie was a Redcoat at Filey for four seasons. **1966** P. J. KAVANAGH *Perfect Stranger* iii. 23 To counteract my snobbism, he sent me to Butlin's Holiday Camp to do a month as a Holiday Uncle, or Redcoat. **1979** *Daily Tel.* 2 Aug. 3/3 A holiday camp 'redcoat'.. claimed a world record at Brighton yesterday, by eating 100 peanuts in 46 seconds.

d. The title of a particular attendant at the door of the House of Lords.

1972 *Times* 22 July 12/5 Redcoat is the only attendant dressed in red in the House, a reminder that his was a royal appointment of Charles II's originally. The King, visiting the Lords and finding no one to greet him, made his own appointment on the spot. **1974** *Daily Tel.* (Colour Suppl.) 6 Dec. 29/2 C. D. Maxted, known as Red Coat, is a familiar figure to all peers as they arrive at the Lords.

2. *Bot.* A small Brazilian tree (*Erythrochiton*).

1866 *Treas. Bot.* 962/1.

3. *attrib.* in sense 'red-coated', as ***redcoat bully, guard, type***; also **red-coat mite** (see quot. 1867).

1773 *Gentl. Mag.* XLIII. 572 The field with red-coat bullies glow'd, Who cut each other's throats. **1843** CARLYLE *Past & Pr.* IV. iii, One sees.. 'United Services' quite other than the redcoat one. **1867** *Nat. Encycl.* I. 100 *Trombidiidæ*, or garden mites, as *T. holosericeum*, or 'red-coat' mite. **1895** *Daily News* 25 June 3/3 His Highness.. inspected the Redcoat guard of honour. **1906** *Westm. Gaz.* 6 Sept. 2/1 The British markets want large, bright apples, preferably of the red-coat type.

red-coated, *a.* **a.** Wearing a red coat or red coats. **b.** Coated with red.

1662 *Rump* I. 298 Now we must desert thee,.. And the Red-coated Saints domineer. **1719** D'URFEY *Pills* V. 86 A Red-coated Face Frights a Searjeant at Mace. **1823** MOORE *Fables* 49 Woe to the Monarch, who depends Too much on his red-coated friends. **1844** THACKERAY *Little Trav.* III, A man of peace has no right to be dazzled by that red-coated glory.

†redcoll. *Obs.* Forms: 5 radcolle, 6 redco, -cole, 7 -col. [Of obscure formation, perh. based on *radik*, obs. var. of RADISH.] Horse-radish.

1483 *Cath. Angl.* 298/1 Radcolle, *raphanus.* **1548** TURNER *Names Herbes* (E.D.S.) 78 Thys kynde [of thlaspi] groweth in Morpeth in Northumberland and there it is called Redco. **1562** —— *Herbal* II. (1568) 35 In Freseland, some make a sauce of redco for sodden meat. **1597** GERARDE *Herbal* II. vii. §2. 187 Horse Radish.. is called in the north part of England red-cole. **1673** *Wedderburn's Voc.* 18 (Jam.) *Raphanus rusticanus*, red-col.

red-collared, -coloured, -combed, -crested: see RED *a.* 14 a, 14 b.

red cross, red-cross.

1. A cross of a red colour; *esp.* **a.** as the national emblem of England; St. George's Cross.

c **1430** *Agincourt* 89 in Hazl. *E.P.P.* II. 96 On euery panes a crosse rede,.. Saynt Georges stremers sprede ouer hede. *a* **1578** LINDESAY (Pitscottie) *Chron. Scot.* (S.T.S.) II. 29 The Scottis.. war all faine.. to tak on the reid crose and to be sworne as natiue subiectis of the king of Ingland. **1601** J. WHEELER *Treat. Comm.* 30 Wearing the red Crosse or Cognizance of England. **1652** EVELYN *Diary* 6 Mar., Heraulds carrying the armes of the State (as they cal'd it), namely, the red crosse and Ireland. **1805** SCOTT *Last Minstr.* I. vi, To see St. George's red cross streaming. **1838** HALIBURTON *Clockm.* Ser. II. i, On fresh or on salt water,.. down comes the red cross and up go the stars.

b. as the mark made on the doors of infected houses during the London plagues of the 17th century.

1636 *Direct. Cure Plague* H 2 b, That euery house visited be marked with a Red Crosse of a foot long, in the middle of the doore. **1654** WHITLOCK *Zootomia* 529 A Door,.. and a red Crosse on it would.. effectually bring a licentious Gallant out of conceit with a Brothell-house. **1664** KILLIGREW *Parson's Wedding* IV. iii, Let us not forget ourselves in our grief; I am not ambitious of a Red Cross upon the door. **1665** *Orders Ld. Mayor & Alderman City Lond.* B. 2 [as in quot. 1636 above].

c. as the badge of an ambulance service (see 2 c); the Geneva cross (see GENEVA²).

1863 *Resolutions*, etc. *Conf. Geneva* §8 They shall wear round the arm.. a white band with a red cross upon it. **1891** HULME *Heraldry* (1897) 269 The doctors, nurses, and assistants have a white armlet with the red cross, the sacred badge that proclaims their errand of mercy.

2. *transf.* †**a.** An English ship. *Obs.*⁻¹

1622 CAPT. SMITH *New-Eng. Trials* Wks. (Arb.) 262 More afraid.. then the smallest red crosse [that] crosses the seas would be.. of any French Piccaroun [etc.].

b. The Christian side in the Crusades.

1801 SCOTT *Fire-King* xxvi, The Red-cross wax'd faint, and the Crescent came on. *Ibid.* xxxvii, How the Red-cross it conquer'd, the Crescent it fell.

c. With capital initial. An ambulance or hospital service organized in accordance with the Geneva convention of 1864, and distinguished by a cross (see 1 c); a person attached to an ambulance or hospital of this kind.

1877 W. E. FORSTER in Reid *Life* (1888) II. iv. 169, I went down with Russian Red Crosses in the Austrian steamer. **1897** C. BIGHAM *With Turkish Army in Thessaly* xiv. 121 Detachments of the Red Cross, who worked efficiently and generously throughout.

3. *attrib.* **a.** (sense 1) as ***red cross ensign, flag, knight, power, rank, shield.***

1889 DOYLE *Micah Clarke* 23 He.. had fought under the *red cross ensign against Frenchman, Don, Dutchman, and Moor. **1820** SOUTHEY *Portr. Bp. Heber*, All seas have seen thy *red-cross flag In war triumphantly display'd. *a* **1850** WORDSWORTH *Prelude* (1959) x. 385 The proud fleet that bears the red-cross flag. **1590** SPENSER *F.Q.* I. vi. 38 The *Redcrosse knight was slain with Paynim knife. **1833** TENNYSON *Lady of Shalott* III. i, A red-cross knight for ever kneel'd To a lady in his shield. **1811** SCOTT *Don Roderick* III. ii, Till.. their own sea hath whelm'd yon *red-cross powers. **1777** T. WARTON *Poems* 64 When Arthur rang'd his *red-cross ranks On conscious Camlan's crimson'd banks. **1811** SCOTT *Don Roderick* II. lvi, Fast as they land the red-cross ranks unite. **1814** —— *Ld. of Isles* VI. xxix, Alone, De Argentine Yet bears on high his *red-cross shield.

b. (sense 1 c or 2 c) as ***Red Cross Association, hospital, man, Society, work.***

1873 C. A. GORDON *Lessons Hygiene* Introd., Societies and individuals connected with the Red Cross Associations. **1876** W. E. FORSTER in Reid *Life* (1888) II. iii. 124 The steamer was crowded with Russians, but many of them really Red Cross men, an ambulance from Kazan. **1878** *Temple Bar Mag.* LIV. 525 Women.. who left their.. homes to work almost day and night in the rough barracks of the Red Cross hospitals. **1914** W. OWEN *Let.* 23 Sept. (1967) 284 There are already *too many* ladies offering to help with red cross work.

So **red-crossed** *a.*

1643 QUARLES *Emblems* v. xiii, Tell me, my wishing soul, didst ever trie How fast the wings of red-crost faith can flie? **1900** W. S. CHURCHILL in *Morning Post* 17 Feb. 8/1 White-hooded, red-crossed ambulance waggons. **1916** 'BOYD CABLE' *Action Front* 165 Another [ambulance wagon] was overturned,.. and in the Red-Crossed canvas tilts of others gaped huge tears and rents. **1935** C. S. FORESTER *Afr. Queen* ii. 30 The Mediterranean squadron.. with the red-crossed Admiral's flag in the van. **1962** J. B. PRIESTLEY *Margin Released* II. iv. 113 The starched and red-crossed debs.

'red-cross, *v. rare.* [f. the sb.] *trans.* To mark with a red cross.

1869 BROWNING *Ring & Bk.* IV. xi. 128 You would have .. forced me.. find my way submissive to the fold. Be red-crossed on the fleece, one sheep the more.

red-crowned: see RED *a.* 14 b.

red currant. **a.** The fruit of the *Ribes rubrum* (see CURRANT, sense 2) or the shrub itself. **b.** (See quot. 1898.)

1629 [see CURRANT 2]. **1661** RABISHA *Cookery* 37 To make a Made-dish of Apples and Red Currans. **1753** CHAMBERS *Cycl. Supp.* s.v. *Grossularia*, The common red currant,.. the great fruited red currant. **1797** *Encycl. Brit.* (ed. 3) XVI. 231/1 All these sorts are varieties of one species, *ribes rubrum*, or common red currant. **1865** SOWERBY *Eng. Bot.* IV. 42 In France the Red Currant seems to have been known long before the Gooseberry. **1898** MORRIS *Austral Eng.* 384/1 *Red Currant*, another name for the Native Currant of Tasmania, *Coprosma nitida*.

c. *attrib.*, as ***red currant cream, jam, jelly, tart, tree, water, wine.***

1661 RABISHA *Cookery* 30 To make Red Currans Cream. **1769** MRS. RAFFALD *Eng. House-kpr.* (1778) 211 To make Red Currant Jelly. *Ibid.* 323 To make Red Currant Wine. **1788** J. WOODFORDE *Diary* 8 July (1927) III. 36 We had for Dinner to Day some Peas and Beans, a Piggs Face.. and black and red currant Tarts. **1797** *Encycl. Brit.* (ed. 3) XVI. 231/1 Rubrum, common red-currant tree, &c., hath a shrubby stem. **1861** MRS. BEETON *Bk. Househ. Managem.* 771 Red-currant jam. **1866** J. BLACKWOOD *Let.* 10 Sept. in *Geo. Eliot Lett.* (1956) IV. 307 My little boy.. declined red currant tart. **1898** *Allbutt's Syst. Med.* V. 122 Tamarind or red-currant water may be given. **1899** *Ibid.* VI. 148 Frequent hæmoptysis with red-currant jelly expectoration. **1958** R. PAGE *Let.* 11 Oct. in R. McDouall *Clubland Cooking* (1974) 166 Another member had a weakness for Red Currant and Raspberry Tart.

redd (rɛd), *sb.*¹ *Sc.* and *north. dial.* 5–6, 9 red, 9 redd (*north.* rid). [f. REDD *v.*²]

1. The act of clearing away, removing, setting in order, etc.; also the result of this, a clearance, riddance, arrangement. Also with *up.* (See also quot. 1893–4.)

For other dialect uses, see the *Eng. Dial. Dict.*

c **1470** HENRY *Wallace* VIII. 1076 Befor the ȝett, quhar it was brynt on breid, A red thai maid. **1496** *Sc. Treas. Acc.* 15 Oct., Giffin to Rolland Robysone, for the red of the Inglismen to the see. *c* **1557** SIR R. MAITLAND in Pinkerton *Anc. Sc. Poems* (1786) I. 282, I trow that sic sall mak ane red Of all thair paks this yeir. **1846** JAS. WILSON *Let.* in *Life* vii. (1859) 236 They seem to be giving every thing a thorough redd. **1893–4** R. O. HESLOP *Northumb. Words* II. 569 By inversion, 'A fine *red* up' is sometimes used to indicate a scene of disorder. **1917** 'H. H. RICHARDSON' *Fortunes R. Mahony* II. ii. 105 She herself, in proper wifely fashion, proposed to give her little house a good red-up, in its master's absence.

2. That which is, or is to be, cleared away; rubbish, refuse.

1527–8 *Burgh Rec. Edinb.* (1869) 233 Till caus the waist land of the townis.. to be fillit vp with red. **1560** *St. Giles Charters* (1859) p. xlv, For bering of the red and staines thairof away, £11 15*s.* **1867** in Ramsay *Remin.* iii. (ed. 18) 68, I just fan' a doo in the redd o' my plate. *a* **1894** in *Northumbld. Gloss.* s.v., Some quarrymen were clearing the redd from the bank top of a quarry.

attrib. **1883** GRESLEY *Gloss. Coal-mining* 200 *Redd Bing*, a spoil heap on the surface. **1887** P. M'NEILL *Blawearie* 104 Downhill.. swept the redd-box, full of unwieldy blocks for the building.

redd, *sb.*² orig. *Sc.* and *north. dial.* Also 7 *Sc.* raid, 9 read(d, red, rid(d. [Of obscure origin: separately or in combs. (see PADDOCK *sb.*¹ 3), the word also appears as *reed, ride, rod, roud, rudd* and *rude*, the mutual relationship of which is far from clear.]

1. The spawn of fish and frogs; also *attrib.* in **redd-time**, spawning-time.

1648 *Aberd. Reg.* (Jam.), For keiping of the fischings in raid tyme fra all maner of nettis,.. and all uthir instrumentis. **1805** ANDREW SCOTT *Twa Frogs* Poems (1808) 48 Wow, friend, to meet you here I'm glad, Wham I've ne'er seen sin' time o' redd. **1894** *Northumbld. Gloss.* s.v., The fish were lying on their red in the stream.

2. The nest made by a fish, esp. a salmon, in which to spawn.

1808 JAMIESON s.v. Red, Redd. With their snouts they form a hollow in the bed of the river, generally so deep, that, when lying in it, their backs are rather below the level of the bed. This is called the redd. **1838** HOLLOWAY *Prov. Dict.*, *Rid* or *Red*, a hollow place in the gravel, where salmon deposit their roe. **1844** *Zoologist* II. 505 Shedding its spawn on the 'redds' or spawning-ground. **1864** WALSH in Buckland *Salmon & Trout Hatching* 18 The female works away at the ridd, and after she has made a kind of trough she lies in it. **1875** *Rep. Maine Fisheries Comm.* 12 (Cent. Dict.), Favourite grounds where the trout make their rids. **1880** *Times* 21 Dec. 6/4 During the winter months, when the fish are.. engaged in preparing the beds or 'redds' for the reception of the ova. **1913** F. M. HALFORD *Dry-Fly Man's Handbk.* III. i. 307 An observant man will detect the heaps of clean gravel or redds where the ova have been deposited by the trout... If there are salmon in the river, their redds too will be visible. **1916** *Trans. Inverness Sci. Soc.* VIII. 324 Salmon and all kinds of trout are very much alike in their spawning habits. The spawning bed, often called a 'redd', is composed of gravel or rough sand. **1960** *New Scientist* 2 June 1392/1 A study of the nature of redds—the gravel banks chosen by the female trout to receive her eggs—has shown that an essential feature is the presence of water currents. **1971** W. HILLEN *Blackwater River* xi. 105 The alevins emerge from the spawning nest, or redd, in late winter. **1977** *New Yorker* 2 May 47/2 Everywhere, in fleets, are the oval shapes of salmon. They have moved the gravel and made redds.

redd (rɛd), *ppl. a. Sc.* and *north. dial.* Also red. [f. REDD *v.*²]

1. *Sc.* In predicative use, in the legal phr. ***void and redd*** (common in 16th c.): Cleared; left clear for a new occupant.

1545 *Reg. Privy Council Scot.* I. 4 The Sheriff.. sall remoiff furth of the said abbay.., and leiff the samyn void and red. **1581** N. BURNE *Disput.* in *Cath. Tract.* (S.T.S.) 170[They compel them] to deluge and leue the grounde voyd and red to thame selfis. **1817** SCOTT *Let. to W. Laidlaw* 5 Apr. in *Lockhart*, Of free will he leaves my premises void and redd at Whitsunday.

2. In attributive use: Put in order; clean; cleaned or tidied *up.* Also *ill-* or *well-redd* (*up*).

For other dialect uses, see the *Eng. Dial. Dict.*

1765 A. DICKSON *Treat. Agric.* (ed. 2) 124 A strong-made Scots plough, with a well redd beam. *Ibid.* 240 The plough that.. makes the best work, is the one that makes a redd fur below. **1838** A. RODGER *Poems* 293 A weel redd-up housie, a snug elbow chair. **1854** MRS. GASKELL *North & S.* xxxvi, Mrs. Boucher was sitting in a rocking-chair on the other side of the ill-redd up fireplace.

redd (rɛd), *v.*¹ *Obs.* exc. *Sc.* Forms: 1 hreddan, 2–3 redden(n), 5–6 redde; *Sc.* 5–7, 9 red, redd. *Pa. t.* 3 readde, 4, 7 *Sc.* redde, 9 *Sc.* red. *Pa. pple.* 4, 6 red, 6–7 redde. [OE. *hreddan* (also *áhreddan* AREDDE) = OFris. *hredda*, MDu. (and Du.) *redden* (hence Da. *redde*, Sw. *rädda*), OHG. (and G.) *retten* to save, deliver, etc.:—OTeut. **hradjan* of doubtful relationship. In later use, and esp. in sense 2, the word can hardly be distinguished from REDD *v.*²]

†**1.** *trans.* To save, deliver, rescue, free (a person). Const. *from, out of. Obs.*

a **900** CYNEWULF *Crist* 274 We.. sculon ermþu dreoȝan, butan þu usic.. hreddan wille. *c* **1200** *Trin. Coll. Hom.* 19 Ure louerd ihesu crist.. redde hem ut of eche sicnesse. *c* **1275** LAY. 20155 His hors.. readde hine fram deaþe. *c* **1330** *Florice & Bl.* 785 The children ther with fram dethe he redde. **1584** J. MELVILL *Autobiog.*, etc. (1842) 180 Your tender King, and sweit native countrey, to be redde from the abbusars and misrewlares of the sam. *c* **1635** SIR W. MURE *Ps.* cxliv. 11 O, red and save me from their hand, Whose mouths doe lyes relate.

b. To save from burning; to put out (fire).

So mod. G. *den brand* or *das feuer retten.*

1375 BARBOUR *Bruce* IV. 132 The fyre our all the castell spred, Thar mycht no fors of men it red. *Ibid.* XIX. 677

Quhen the man Saw his mantill ly byrnand than, Till red it ran he hastely. **1871** W. ALEXANDER *Johnny Gibb* xvii. 124 He comes..like a man gyaun to redd fire.

2. To make (one) free or clear *of* something; to rid (oneself or another) *of*. Also in phr. ***to be*** or ***get redd of***.

14.. in *Pol. Rel. & L. Poems* (1866) 100 For to redde me of this payne They haue no power for to helpe me. **1450** *Burgh Rec. Edinb.* (1869) 12 It sall be lefull to thame to red their handis of it..betwix this and Candilmes. **1570** *Satir. Poems Reform.* x. 50 We haif him taine out of that wickit lyfe, And red him of all miserie and stryfe. *a* **1578** LINDESAY (Pitscottie) *Chron. Scot.* (S.T.S.) I. 108 Be quhat moyane sall I red me of this mischeif. **1768** ROSS *Helenore* 45 (Jam.), But to get red, the lad contrives a sham, To send her back for something. **1879** G. MACDONALD *Sir Gibbie* vi, Gien he red himsel' o' a' 'at was left, it was sma' won'er.

†**3. a.** *refl.* To clear (oneself) in money-matters. **b.** To take away, remove (cf. REDD *v.*[2] 4). *Obs.*

1509 BARCLAY *Shyp of Folys* (1570) 49 He that still borowes shall scant him quite or redde. *Ibid.* (1874) II. 117 Bytter Pryson doth deth clene quyte and red. By it all fetters and Chaynes lowsyd be.

redd (rɛd), *v.*[2] *Sc.* and *north. dial.* (exc. in sense 6 a). Forms: 5- red, 6- redd, (7, 9 redde), 8 rade. *Pa. t.* and *pa. pple.* 7- redd, 9 red; also 5 reddyt, 6 reddit. [= MLG. and Du. *redden*, in the same senses, but the origin and relationship of the forms is not clear. It is possible that they are independent developments from ME. *rēden* and the equivalent LG. *rêden, reiden* (see REDE *v.*[2]), in Eng. by assimilation of the vowel of the pres. and inf. to that of the pa. t. and pa. pple. (cf. KEP *v.*). Most of the senses of the word are also represented under RID *v.*]

1. a. *trans.* To clear (a space, the way, etc.).

c **1425** WYNTOUN *Cron.* v. xii. 1180 Thare he begowth to red a grownd Quhare that he thowcht a kyrk to fownd. *c* **1470** HENRY *Wallace* x. 404 All hym about was reddyt a gret rowm. **1513** DOUGLAS *Æneis* x. vii. 30 With swerdis dynt behuffis ws,..Throw amyddis our ennemys red our way. *a* **1578** LINDESAY (Pitscottie) *Chron. Scot.* (S.T.S.) I. 314, I sall pase and put ȝone theiffis of the ground, and red the gaitt into ȝour grace. **1822** SCOTT *Nigel* iv, It wad have red the gate for my ain little bill. **1880** *Antrim & Down Gloss., Red the road!* clear the way!

b. To clear or clean out (something that is stopped up).

1497 *Sc. Treas. Acc.* 14 May, Item, for ane cabil tow to stede the well of Dunbar quhen it was red. **1541** *Records of Elgin* (New Spald. Club) I. 66 That all channellis and wennellis be red be the ownaris. *a* **1795** *Robin Hood & Beggar* lxxx. in Child *Ballads* III. 163/2 Or any one of them could red their eyne, Or yet a glimmering could see. **1813** W. BEATTIE *Poems* 21 (Jam.), Now and then, to red her head, She takes a pickle snuff. **1881** GREGOR *Folk-lore* ix. 51 A bunch of stars..to redd the tobacco pipes.

2. a. To disentangle. Also in fig. context.

1513 DOUGLAS *Æneis* v. i. 28 Commandis he every feir, Do red thair takillis, and stand hard by thair geir. **1725** RAMSAY *Gentle Sheph.* I. i, Ye..have sae kind Redd up my ravel'd doubts, and clear'd my mind. **1782** [D. GRAHAM] *Hist. Buckhaven* 5 They can neither bait a hook nor redde a line. **1876** *Mid-Yorksh. Gloss., Red*, to unloose, or unravel; to unriddle. **1895** P. H. HUNTER *J. Inwick* iii. 32 It was a raivelled hasp he had to redd.

absol. **1737** RAMSAY *Sc. Prov.* (1750) 26 Fools revle, and wise men redd. **1768** ROSS *Helenore* II. 86 Among us a' a ravell'd hesp ye've made, Sae now, put too your hand, an help to red.

b. To arrange, put right (business of any kind); to clear up (one's affairs).

1500–20 DUNBAR *Poems* lx. 44 His erandis for to ryne and red. **1824** SCOTT *Redgauntlet* let. ix, Nor do I know if his affairs are yet well redd.

c. ***to redd the marches***: to fix the boundaries exactly. Also *fig.*

1596 [see REDDING *vbl. sb.*[2] 1]. **1683** in Shields *Faithful Contendings* (1780) 70 Mr. Gillespie, and many others, have redd marches so well, that they have left nothing for us to do. **1835** T. ROSE *Rambles* 163 (Northumbld. Gloss.), In this neighbourhood—between Keilder and Larriston—the precise boundaries of each kingdom are 'ill to red'.

3. a. To put in order, make tidy, by clearing away whatever is in disorder or is unnecessary.

a **1568** *Sym & his Bruder* (Bann. MS.) 31 Thus quhen thai had reddit thair ragis, To Rome thay war inspyrit. **1582–8** *Hist. Jas. VI* (1804) 236 The Regent..causit masonis to begin to redd the bruisit wallis, and to repaire the foirwork. **1637** RUTHERFORD *Lett.* (1862) I. 323 Waiting on till..the great hall be redd for the meeting of that joyful couple. **1786** *Har'st Rig* cxxxix, The stalwart Chelsea man (Whase now ta'en in to redd the barn). **1829** BROCKETT *N.C. Words, Red*, to put in order, to clear. **1847** H. S. RIDDELL *Poems* 16 To redd the house and sweep the floor.

b. To comb, arrange (the hair).

1715 RAMSAY *Christ's Kirk Gr.* II. v, Some redd their hair, some set their bands. **1879** MISS JACKSON *Shropsh. Word-bk., Red*,..to comb out the hair.

4. To remove (persons or things) from a place; to clear *away*.

1546 *Reg. Privy Council Scot.* I. 50 Apoun xv dayis warnyng that scho may red hir geir furth of the samin. **1569** *Ibid.* 675 To remove, devoid, and red thame selffis, thair servandis and propir gudis..furth of the said College. **1826** J. WILSON *Noct. Ambr.* (1856) III. 349 The shielings that we used to come upon..have 'been a' red awa!'

5. a. To part or separate (combatants).

15.. *Pebbles to Play* xv, For dust that day Mycht na man se ane styme To red thame. **1593** *Sc. Acts Jas. VI*, c. 35 Hurt slayne or mutilat in redding and putting sindre parties meitand in armes. **1725** RAMSAY *Gentle Sheph.* IV. i, A stout battle. Mause endeavours to redd them. **1814** SCOTT *Wav.* lxvi, To fetch the Chevalier to redd Mr. Wauverley and Vich Ian Vohr. **1830–3** CARLETON *Traits Irish Peas.* (1843) I. 68 We endeavoured all in our power to red them.

absol. **1535** STEWART *Cron. Scot.* II. 667 Cum on! God schaw the richt! Now is moir tyme quhen no man is to red. **1573** *Satir. Poems Reform.* xli. 75 Allace! what sall cum of the rest Except repentance rin and red?

b. To settle, decide (a plea), put an end to (a quarrel, fray, etc.).

c **1575** *Raid of Reidswire* xi, Up rose the laird to red the cumber, Which would not be for all his boast. **1629** SIR W. MURE *True Crucifix* 140 God..Sent in the flesh his Christ the plea to redde. **1681** COLVIL *Whigs Supplic.* (1751) 55 When they the fray intend to redd. **1768** ROSS *Helenore* II. 78 Come here, and red this threap, for ye can tell The very truth. **1814** SCOTT *Wav.* liv, To stick him under the other gentleman's arm while he was redding the fray.

6. a. With *up*. To put in order; to make neat or trim. (Also in *U.S.* and general use.)

Also, to clear up by discussion or explanation, to criticize sharply, assail with invective, etc. (see *Eng. Dial. Dict.*).

1718 RAMSAY *Christ's Kirk Gr.* III. vii, Right well red up and jimp she was. **1768** ROSS *Helenore* III. 121 Anither forward unto Bony-Ha', To tell that there things be red up an' bra'. **1820** SCOTT *Abbot* xxvi, Doctor Lundin failed not to be a confused sloven, and his..housekeeper, whose life, as she said, was spent in 'redding him up' [etc.]. **1842** *Spirit of Times* (Philad.) 12 Aug. (Th.), I never used to red up their chamber without thinking of it. **1854** MRS. GASKELL *North & S.* xxxvii, To do something that she suggested towards redding up the slatternly room. **1864** ELIZ. A. MURRAY *E. Norman* I. 160, I left her and Kristy redding up their hair, and making themselves grand. **1887** P. M'NEILL *Blawearie* 99 The other pair on having the wall-face redd up fell to 'holing' once more. **1896** E. HIGGINSON *Flower that grew in Sand* 120 'You got your front room red up, Emarine?' 'No; I ain't had time to red up anything.' **1909** A. QUILLER-COUCH *True Tilda* xix. 258 They tumbled out and redded up the place in a hurry. **1912** MULFORD & CLAY *Buck Peters* I. 19, I guess you two men can take care of each other while I red up. **1951** L. CRAIG *Singing Hills* xix. 181 You take this baby while I redd up the room. **1977** J. AIKEN *Five-Minute Marriage* ix. 141 The rooms..are all clean and redd up, sir.

b. With *out*: To bring out from disorder, to comb out, etc.

1818 SCOTT *Rob Roy* xxii, I canna see how you..can redd out the business ye're come down about. **1881** *Leicestersh. Gloss.* s.v., As I was reddin' out my hair. **1893** STEVENSON *Catriona* 193 If his story was properly redd out [etc.].

redd(e, varr. RAD *a.*[2] *Obs.*, obs. pa. t. and pa. pple. READ *v.*, obs. ff. RED *a.*, REDE *sb.*[1], Sc. varr. REDE *v.*[1]

reddar, obs. Sc. f. REDDER *sb.*[1]

†**redde**, *v. Obs. rare*$^{-1}$. [Of obscure origin.] *trans.* To strike.

a **1330** *Otuel* 535 Roulond..vp wiþ þe brond,..& in þe heued he þoute to redde Otuwel, bote nouȝt he ne spedde.

red deer. a. A species of deer, *Cervus elaphus*, so named from its reddish-brown colour, widely distributed in Europe, Western Asia, and Northern Africa, and still existing in a wild state in the Highlands of Scotland and some other parts of Great Britain. **b.** The Virginia deer, *Cariacus virginianus*, the common deer of N. America. **c.** The Caspian or Persian deer, *Cervus maral*.

1470–85 MALORY *Arthur* x. lxi, He chaced at the reed deer. **1485** *Rolls of Parlt.* VI. 373/1 A Reed Dere called an Hert. **1546** *Plumpton Corr.* (Camden) 251 Or any red deare be fatt, it will be July, as far as my experience serves. **1620** VENNER *Via Recta* iii. 55 Some doe suppose Venison of Fallow-Deere to be of a middle nature betweene the flesh of Red-Deere and of Weathers. **1655** MOUFET & BENNET *Health's Improv.* (1746) 156 They are good roasted, sodden, or baked as Red Deer. **1710** CHAMBERLAYNE *St. Gt. Brit.* 335 Woods which were once well stock'd with Red and Fallow Deer. **1789** G. WHITE *Selborne* vi, The red-deer, which toward the beginning of this century amounted to about five hundred head. **1819** WARDEN *United States* III. 172 Of deer there are three kinds—1. The common red deer [etc.]. **1837** HOWITT *Rur. Life* I. iii. (1862) 27 The herds of red-deer trooping away from the sounds of wheels in the silent park. **1884–5** *Riverside Nat. Hist.* (1888) V. 292 The Stag, or Red deer, attains a length of seven feet. *Ibid.* 293 For fleetness and agility the red deer is unexcelled.

attrib. **1625** B. JONSON *Staple of N.* v. ii, Where is your venison now? Your red-deer pies? **1693** *Lond. Gaz.* No. 2903/4 A Red-Deer-Horn-Hafted Knife. **1815** SCOTT *Guy M.* xxxix, A bit of red-deer venison. **1895** CORNISH *Wild England* 120 Every year the largest red-deer stags are caught and removed to Windsor Park.

reddely, variant of REDLY *adv. Obs.*

redden (ˈrɛd(ə)n), *v.* [f. RED *a.* + -EN[5].]

1. *trans.* To make red, to impart a red colour to (a substance or thing).

1611 COTGR., *Saurir les harencs*, to redden Herrings. **1697** DRYDEN *Virg. Georg.* III. 741 Scarcely the Knife was redden'd with his Gore. —— *Æneid* VII. 703 Refulgent Arms appear, Red'ning the Skies. **1725** POPE *Odyss.* XIII. 219 The blazing altars redden all the shore. **1800** tr. *Lagrange's Chem.* I. 132 This gas..reddens blue vegetable colours. **1837** M. DONOVAN *Dom. Econ.* II. 235 It may be mixed with..salt-petre to redden the meat. **1855** TENNYSON *Maud* I. XIX. vi, This was what had redden'd her cheek When I bow'd to her on the moor. **1871** B. TAYLOR *Faust* (1875) II. II. iii. 129 All have fallen.., Reddening with their blood the water.

2. a. *intr.* To grow or become red, to assume a red appearance.

1700 CONGREVE *Way of World* II. iii, I have seen the warm confession reddening on your cheeks. **1710** POPE *Windsor For.* 394 For me the balm shall bleed,..The coral redden. **1791** COWPER *Iliad* XXI. 27 The waters as they ran, redden'd with blood. **1827** KEBLE *Chr. Y., Burial Dead* ii, Bright leaves, reddening ere they fall. **1847** TENNYSON *Princ.* IV. 367 This anger reddens in the heavens.

b. To become red (in the face) *with* shame, rage, etc.; to flush, blush.

a **1648** LD. HERBERT *Autobiog.* (1886) 38 When occasion of offence was given him, I have seen him redden in the face. **1701** W. WOTTON *Hist. Rome* 450 He would redden with Rage. **1781** COWPER *Anti-Thelyphth.* 204 Reddening with a just and generous pride. **1834** HT. MARTINEAU *Farrers* ii. 32 There was no more to be said; but Jane reddened all over. **1866** GEO. ELIOT *F. Holt* (1868) 62 She reddened..and said, ..'I have a great admiration for Byron'.

c. To grow ruddy with health.

1807 CRABBE *Par. Reg.* III. 554 Here cloth'd and fed, no sooner he began To round and redden, than away he ran.

d. Of a pullet: to acquire a deeper shade of red in the comb and wattles as the bird approaches maturity and prepares to begin laying.

1909 T. W. STURGES *Poultry Man.* vii. 106 When a pullet is about to redden up and develop her comb previous to laying, the change from one pen to another will check this development. **1950** *N.Z. Jrnl. Agric.* Oct. 332/3 If any [pullets] appear unlikely to start 'reddening up' for a month or more, they should..be sold immediately. **1967** T. R. MORRIS in T. C. Carter *Environmental Control in Poultry Production* ii. 27 Once the flock has begun to 'redden up' it is usually too late to alter sexual maturity.

‖**reddendo** (rəˈdɛndəʊ). *Sc. Law.* [L., (abl. of REDDENDUM), the first word of the clause *reddendo inde annuatim*, etc.]

1. The clause in a charter which specifies the duty to be paid to the superior.

1693 STAIR *Instit.* II. iii. §29 Infeftments upon Apprysing or Adjudication..do require Charters to be granted by the Superiors of the Appryzed Lands..their *Reddendo* is ordinarly general [etc.]. *a* **1768** ERSKINE *Instit. Law Scot.* II. iii. §24 The next clause in a charter is the *Reddendo*. **1788** RUSSELL *Theory Conveyancing* 131 It is therefore necessary to mention it in the reddendo in a proper manner. **1838** W. BELL *Dict. Law Scot.* 145 The original charter contains the following clauses..4. The *reddendo*, which expresses the duty in money or services to be paid by the vassal to the superior [etc.].

attrib. **1830** G. J. BELL *Princ. Law Scot.* (ed. 2) §762 The *Reddendo* clause expresses the regular return to be made by the vassal of services [etc.].

2. The service rendered, the sum of money, etc. paid by a vassal to his superior.

1674 SIR G. MACKENZIE *Instit. Law Scot.* 96 The fourth Clause is that which expresses what the vassal is to pay to the Superiour, and this duty is called the Reddendo. **1693** STAIR *Instit.* II. iii. §15 If it be a Charter *à se*, bearing, to be holden from the Disponer of the King, and expressing the *Tenendas* and *Reddendo*. **1774** in A. McKay *Hist. Kilmarnock* (1864) App. iii. 305 The reddendo of this feu-right is £7 Scots yearly. **1860** COSMO INNES *Scot. in Mid. Ages* v. 167 The reddendo for the toft and six acres, twelve pence.

‖**reddendum** (rəˈdɛndəm). *Law.* [L., neut. sing. of *reddendus*, gerundive of *reddĕre* to give in return, RENDER.] A reserving clause in a deed (see quots. 1607 and 1766).

1607 COWELL *Interpr., Reddendum* is vsed many times substantiuely for the clause in a lease, &c. Whereby the rent is reserued to the leasour. **1744** JACOB *Law Dict.* s.v., Where special Days are limited in the *Reddendum*, the Rent must be computed from those Days, and not according to the *habendum*. **1766** BLACKSTONE *Comm.* II. xx. 299 Next follow the terms or stipulations, if any, upon which the grant is made: the first of which is the reddendum or reservation, whereby the grantor doth create or reserve some new thing to himself out of what he had before granted. **1862** E. WASHBURN *Amer. Law Real Prop.* II. III. v. 645 If any thing is to be reserved out of the property granted, it is usually done by the clause of *reddendum*.

reddened (ˈrɛd(ə)nd), *ppl. a.* [f. REDDEN *v.* + -ED[1].] Made red, heated to redness, inflamed, etc.

1611 COTGR., *Rubesié*, redned, made red. **1765** *Universal Mag.* XXXVII. 84/1 It separates the..ingredients from the reddened steel. **1799–1805** S. TURNER *Hist. Anglo-Sax.* (1836) I. III. iii. 167 Biers with the dead and reddened men. **1863** *Sat. Rev.* 4 July 22 Reasons for discontent in the shape of fifty years and a reddened nose. **1899** *Allbutt's Syst. Med.* VIII. 461 Extensive areas of reddened skin.

reddening (ˈrɛd(ə)nɪŋ), *ppl. a.* [f. as prec. + -ING[2].] Becoming, growing, or turning red.

1701 ADDISON *To Ld. Halifax* 114 The poor inhabitant beholds in vain The red'ning Orange and the swelling grain. **1726** POPE *Odyss.* XVII. 517 The redning dawn reveals the hostile fields Horrid with bristly spears. **1801** SOUTHEY *Thalaba* II. xiii, Anon a deeper rage Inflamed her reddening eye. **1894** S. J. WEYMAN *Under Red Robe* ii. (1897) 49 The trees stood up black against the reddening sky.

reddening, *vbl. sb.* [f. REDDEN *v.* + -ING[1].] The action of making or becoming red. Also *attrib.*

1847 T. T. STODDART *Angler's Compan. Scotl.* 116 Worms on their transference to the moss-jar still undergo the process of scouring..that of toughening, and..the further one of reddening. *Ibid.*, The reddening matter..is a species of high-coloured earth, reduced to a powder. **1927** HALDANE & HUXLEY *Animal Biol.* vii. 150 Impulses..run directly to the local vessels, which open up, causing reddening of the skin. **1978** PASACHOFF & KUTNER *University Astron.* xxiii. 579 Traditionally, studies of reddening and extinction have been used to find the distances to stars.

redder (ˈrɛdə(r)), *sb.*[1] *Sc.* and *north.* Also 6 *Sc.* reddar. [f. REDD *v.*[2] + -ER[1].]

1. One who tries to separate combatants or to make peace in a quarrel. ***redder's lick*** = ***redding-stroke*** (see quot. 1802 and REDDING *vbl. sb.*[2] 2).

1453 in *14th Rep. Hist. MSS. Comm.* App. III. 9 That nouther of thaim sal tak part with thaire awyn men bot be euynly reddaris and stanchearis of euill and debatis. **1579–80** *Reg. Privy Council Scot.* Ser. I. III. 268 The said provest..interponit himself as reddar betuix the saidis partiis. **1637** MONRO *Exped.* II. 70 The maker of a quarrell ..drawing a sworde, when he knowes of twentie Parters, or Redders. *a* **1676** GUTHRY *Mem.* (1748) 261 They..were in an hour upon the place before any redders came; so that they had leisure enough to have fought, if they had been willing. **1774** MACLAURIN *Crim. Cases* 54 The defunct, interposed as a redder between them, did casually receive the wound libelled. **1802** SIBBALD *Chron. S.P.* Gloss. s.v. *Red*, Hence *Redding blow* or *Redder's part*, viz., a blow or hatred from both parties. **1820** SCOTT *Abbot* vii, He may come by the redder's lick, and that is ever the worst of the battle. **1848** in EVANS *Leicestersh. Gloss.*

2. One who clears up, puts in order, etc. Also ***redder-up***.

1890 *Daily News* 7 Nov. 5/1 The agreeable objects which salute the eye of the 'redder up'. **1894** *Northumbld. Gloss.*, *Redder*, a shiftman at a colliery employed in reddin.

†**ˈredder**, *sb.*[2] *Obs. rare*$^{-0}$. [f. RED *v.* + -ER[1].] One who reddens or makes red.

1611 COTGR., *Saurisseur*, a redder of Herrings.

†**ˈredder**, *v. Obs. rare.* [Of obscure origin.] Of cattle: To be in heat. Hence ***reddring-time***.

1577 B. GOOGE *Heresbach's Husb.* III. 128b, Aristotle woulde haue him all the reddring time to goe in pasture with the Kine. *Ibid.* 127* The Cowe should when she is reddring, haue but short pasture.

reddere, variant of REDDOUR *Obs.*

red devil. 1. A type of Italian hand grenade. Also *attrib.*

a **1944** K. DOUGLAS *Alamein to Zem Zem* (1946) vi. 44 The little tin 'red devil' grenades, bombastic little crackers that will blow a man's hand off and make a noise like the crack of doom. **1967** *Sunday Times* (Colour Suppl.) 10 Sept. 45/4 *Red devils*, Italian hand grenades painted red. They made a lot of noise but caused little damage.

2. ***the Red Devils***: popular name for the Parachute Regiment of the British Army.

1943 in G. G. Norton *Red Devils* (1971) ii. 24 General Alexander directs that I Para Brigade be info[rmed] that [they] have been given name by Germans of 'Red Devils'. **1948** M. PACKE *First Airborne* vii. 78 They..inspired the German paratroops..to christen them the Red Devils. **1974** *Times* 19 Apr. 15/4 The Red Devils free-fall team is giving another display. **1977** *Times* 8 June 4/1 The Red Devils, the Army's daring freefall parachute team.

3. = RED-BIRD 2.

1967 *Boston Sunday Herald* 26 Mar. I. 12/2 Friday's 'goof ball' raid in a South End apartment (where 3,600 so-called 'red-devils' were confiscated) was the result of three months investigatory work. **1971** 'D. SHANNON' *Murder with Love* (1972) iv. 67 Quite a collection of the pills..the Blue Angels and Red Devils and Yellow Submarines. **1974** M. C. GERALD *Pharmacol.* xi. 205 Short-acting barbiturates such as..secobarbital ('red devils').

†**ˈreddiness.** *Obs. rare*$^{-0}$. [f. REDDY *a.* + -NESS.] Redness, ruddiness.

1611 FLORIO, *Robicondita*, rednesse, reddinesse, rubicondity.

ˈredding, *sb.*[1] Also 3, 5 redyng(e, 6 redinge. [f. RED *a.* + -ING[3].]

1. Red ochre, ruddle. Now only *dial.*

[**1292–3** in T. Bond *Corfe Castle* (1883) 108 Colours called 'redyng' and 'rugeplum' were brought from Salisbury for ornamenting the walls of the chamber.] *c* **1440** *Promp. Parv.* 427/1 Redynge, colowre, *rubiculum, rubratura.* **1598** FLORIO, *Sinópio*..red leade, ruddle, red okre, or redding. **1729** *Seasonable Remarks Trade* 98 The Goods which they take from these Dominions are Coals,..Clay, Redding [etc.]. **1778** *Eng. Gazetteer* (ed. 2) s.v. *Chew Magna*, That red bolus, called Redding, which is used for the marking of sheep. **1878** T. HARDY *Ret. Native* I. ii, A reddleman—a person whose vocation it was to supply farmers with redding for their sheep.

b. *U.S.* A compound used to redden the hearth and sides of a fireplace.

1867 MRS. WHITNEY *L. Goldthwaite* vii. 149 The brick hearth and jambs aglow with fresh 'redding'.

2. A kind of apple; the ruddock. *rare.*

1611 COTGR., *Rouveau, Pomme de rou*, the Ruddocke, Redding, Summer Goulding. **1898** SLOSSON *Dumb Foxglove* 55 The little Denison reddings, all crimson and shining outside.

†**ˈredding**, *sb.*[2], var. READING *sb. Obs.*

(The source of Cotgrave's F. *redins* is obscure.)

1611 COTGR., *Redins*, redding clothes.

ˈredding, *vbl. sb.*[1] [f. RED *v.* + -ING[1].] **1.** The action of making red.

1572 *Ludlow Churchw. Acc.* (Camden) 149 Payd for xvj *li.* of rede lede for the redinge of the churche. **1632** SHERWOOD, A redding, growing or making red, *rubrication.*

2. [See RED-OUT.] ***redding-out***: the process of undergoing or experiencing a red-out.

1933 *Jrnl. R. Aeronaut. Soc.* XXXVII. 407 The phenomenon of 'redding out' is essentially and solely ocular in origin due to postural congestion of the vascular retina. **1951** NAYLER & OWER *Flight To-day* (ed. 3) i. 24 Accelerations..in the other direction, i.e., upwards towards the pilot's head, of more than 2g [are common] in bunts, which lead to risks of 'redding out' in contrast to 'blacking out'. **1961** R. L. CHRISTY in H. G. Armstrong *Aerospace Med.* xvi. 250/2 Occasionally there may be a temporary loss of vision and there have been a few scattered reports that objects appear red and produce the phenomenon commonly referred to as 'redding out'.

redding (ˈrɛdɪŋ), *vbl. sb.*[2] [f. REDD *v.*[2]]

1. The action of separating combatants, or of arranging, tidying, clearing up, etc. Also ***redding up***.

1496 *Sc. Treas. Acc.* 15 Oct., Item, for redding of the werkhous in the Castel to hous the artailȝery, xij*d.* **1529** LYNDESAY *Compl.* 353 Euerilk lord did stryue for stait, That all the realme mycht mak no reddyng. **1596** in J. Melvill *Autobiog.*, etc. (1842) 381 With whome the King enterit in actioun for redding of merches. **1812** CHALMERS *Let.* in *Life* (1851) I. 293 My aunt..has been..exercising her peculiar talent for redding-up. **1899** F. T. BULLEN *Log of Sea-waif* 212 In order that the bulk of the 'redding-up' may be done before crossing the line.

2. *Comb.* **a. redding-blow** or **-stroke**, a blow received by a person trying to separate combatants.

a **1649** in *Wodrow Soc. Sel. Biog.* (1845) I. 384, I hope Jesus Christ shall give death the redding stroke. **1737** RAMSAY *Sc. Prov.* (1750) 45 He that meddles with toolies comes in for the redding streak. **1802** [see REDDER *sb.*[1] 1]. **1815** SCOTT *Guy M.* xxvii. *note*, The redding straik..is proverbially said to be the most dangerous blow a man can receive.

b. redding-comb, an ordinary hair-comb.

1821 SCOTT *Pirate* xv, Ye might as weel give it a ritt with the teeth of a redding kame. **1829** BROCKETT *N.C. Words*, *Redding-comb*, a comb for the hair. **1876–** in dial. glossaries (Yks., Lancs., Chesh., Shropsh., Antrim).

reddingite (ˈrɛdɪŋaɪt). *Min.* [f. the name of *Redding* township, Fairfield County, Connecticut, where the mineral was first found: see -ITE[1].] A hydrated phosphate of ferrous iron and bivalent manganese (the latter predominating), $(Mn,Fe)_3(PO_4)_2.3H_2O$, which forms an isomorphous series with phosphoferrite and occurs as pinkish, yellowish, or colourless, translucent or transparent, orthorhombic crystals.

1878 BRUSH & DANA in *Amer. Jrnl. Sci.* CXVI. 35 In addition to the above minerals, as original constituents of the same deposit, are amblygonite (hebronite), and a phosphate of manganese isomorphous with scorodite which we shall describe under the name reddingite. **1955** [see *phosphoferrite* s.v. PHOSPHO-]. **1964** *Amer. Mineralogist* XLIX. 1122 Landesite, a rare hydrated manganous-ferric phosphate, is an alteration product of reddingite which, in turn, is derived from the hydration and alkali-leaching of lithiophilite-triphylite at the Berry Quarry, Poland, Maine. **1971** *Mineral. Abstr.* XXII. 18/1 Iron-manganese phosphate minerals, new to the Congo are..reddingite-phosphoferrite, bermanite, phosphosiderite, [etc.].

reddish (ˈrɛdɪʃ), *a.* Also 4 redische. [f. RED *a.* + -ISH[1].]

1. a. Somewhat red, red-tinted.

1398 TREVISA *Barth. De P.R.* VI. xxii. (Tollem. MS.), Some [wine] is reed or redische, and is more hote þan oþer. *Ibid.* XVII. vi, The Aloe þat is calde Epaticum..is broune redische as þe lyuoure. **1545** RAYNOLD *Byrth Mankynde* 18 The lytel small vaynes which ye se reddisshe in a mans eye. **1597** A. M. tr. *Guillemeau's Fr. Chirurg.* 21 b/1 Then is the swellinge reddishe of colour, or purple-coloured. **1660** F. BROOKE tr. *Le Blanc's Trav.* 192 They delight much to parget their bodies with a reddish earth. **1712** ADDISON *Spect.* No. 281 ⁋5 This Pericardium..contains in it a thin reddish Liquor. **1774** GOLDSM. *Nat. Hist.* (1776) IV. 339 The two former are of a brown dusky colour, but this of a beautiful reddish. **1836** MACGILLIVRAY tr. *Humboldt's Trav.* x. 122 A reddish vapour rose in the evening. **1886** RUSKIN *Præterita* I. 407 A reddish and rather vacant face.

b. In names of animals and plants.

1777 LIGHTFOOT *Flora Scot.* II. 846 *Lichen rubescens*, Reddish Ground Liverwort. **1785** PENNANT *Arct. Zool.* II. 447 Reddish Egret. **1809** SHAW *Zool. Lect.* I. ii. 37 The species which makes the nearest approach to the human figure, is the chesnut-coloured or reddish Oran Otan. **1835** AUDUBON *Ornith. Biog.* III. 411 The Reddish Egret is a constant resident on the Florida Keys. **1869** SOWERBY *Eng. Bot.* IX. 31 *Polygonum Rufescens*,..Reddish Pondweed. **1889** *Cent. Dict.* 5018/3 *Reddish light-arches*, a British noctuid moth. **1907** R. SOUTH *Moths Brit. Isles* 1st Ser. 279 The Reddish Light Arches..occurs in beech woods. *Ibid.* 321 The Reddish Buff... The female is much smaller than the male. **1968** *Oxf. Bk. Insects* 82/1 It is easy to confuse this moth with the less common Reddish Light Arches.

2. *Comb.* **a.** Qualifying adjs. and sbs. of colour; esp. ***reddish-blue***, ***-brown***, ***-purple***, ***-violet***, ***-yellow***.

reddish-grey bat, Natterer's bat (see quot. 1837).

1629 J. PARKINSON *Paradisi in Sole* I. 518 The scales..are eyther of a reddish browne, whitish, or greenish colour. *Ibid.* viii. 55/2 A white [flowring Tulipa], speckled with reddish purple, more or lesse, of diuers sorts, with white, yellow, or blew bottomes. **1659** HOWELL *Vocab.* II, A reddish bay [horse], *Rabicano.* **1685** W. KING in *Phil. Trans.* XV. 953 The reddish black colour of the turf. *a* **1728** WOODWARD *Hist. Fossils* I. 226 Internally the Colour is a reddish brown. **1739** C. LABELYE *Short Acc. Piers Westm. Bridge* 53 A dirty reddish yellow. **1831** BREWSTER *Optics* xiv. 115 Of a dull reddish-white colour. **1837** T. BELL *Brit. Quadrup.* 42 *Vespertilio Nattereri.* This species, to which I have applied the English name of Reddish-grey Bat from its prevailing colour, was first described by Kuhl, and named by him after..Dr. Natterer. **1849** D. CAMPBELL *Inorg. Chem.* 76 Its vapour is reddish-green. **1855** J. PHILLIPS *Man. Geol.* 411 Over all is a continuous widely spread reddish-brown clay. **1856** *Rep. Comm. Patents 1855: Agric.* 273 The *Red-striped* [sugar] cane,..and the *Violet* or *Reddish-violet*, which is only a variation from the former,.. will generally prosper..[in] the Southern States. **1879** ROOD *Chromatics* xi. 168 The resultant tint would always have been a reddish-grey. **1934** *Webster*, Reddish-blue. **1962** I. MURDOCH *Unofficial Rose* xviii. 179 A dark reddish-blue sky. **1963** A. LUBBOCK *Austral. Roundabout* 108 The granite ridges round Cloncurry, reddish-purple and bare. **1964** S. DUKE-ELDER *Parsons' Dis. Eye* (ed. 14) x. 102 The ciliary form for the most part a diffuse reddish-violet blush. *Ibid.* xxi. 296 The anterior ciliary veins are dilated, and a reddish-blue zone surrounds the cornea. **1971** L. A. BOGER *Dict. World Pott. & Porc.* 278/2 Inscriptions were often painted on the black background in red (or reddish purple). **1980** *Catal. Fine Chinese Ceramics* (Sotheby, Hong Kong) 16 The unglazed stoneware burnt reddish-brown in the firing. *Ibid.* 92 Covered with a bright reddish-purple glaze attractively streaked and mottled in milky blue.

b. Parasynthetic, as ***reddish-bellied***, ***-coloured***, ***-haired***, ***headed***, and similative, as ***reddish-looking***.

1597 A. M. tr. *Guillemeau's Fr. Chirurg.* 34/1 The matter whyte, or reddishe coloured, and without stincke. **1653** R. SANDERS *Physiogn.* 157 The persons are white-breasted, reddish-hair'd. **1678** RAY *Willughby's Ornith.* 369 Our smaller reddish-headed Duck. **1752** J. HILL *Hist. Anim.* 480 The gray-breasted and reddish-bellied Charadrius. **1807** T. THOMSON *Chem.* (ed. 3) II. 394 A reddish-coloured acrid solution. **1876** *Clin. Soc. Trans.* IX. 76 Discharging about 8 ozs. of offensive reddish-looking fluid.

Hence **ˈreddishly** *adv.*; **ˈreddishness**.

1663 BOYLE *Exp. Hist. Colours* II. Exp. xiii, Whether or no this White mixture..would not let go its Arsenick,..and return to the Reddishness of Copper. **1881** C. A. YOUNG *Sun* 306 We should doubtless believe this reddishness the natural color of the glowing, naked carbons. **1946** R. CAPELL *Simiomata* II. 47 He is donnish, tall and reddishly fair.

reddish, obs. form of RADISH.

reˈddition. Now *rare.* [a. F. *reddition* or ad. L. *redditiōn-em*, n. of action f. *reddĕre* to give back, to RENDER. See also RENDITION.]

1. †**a.** Restoration of something taken or received; also, surrender of a thing, a town, army, etc. *Obs.*

1449 *Rolls of Parlt.* V. 167/1 As sone as that office [comes] to your hand..by deth, cession,..reddicion or surrendre. **1593** BELL *Motives conc. Romish Faith* (1605) 31 So as the reddition be of that, which is equivalent and not otherwise due. **1641** PRYNNE *Antip.* 310 The Bishops [were] apprehended and compelled to a reddition of their possessions. **1643** —— *Sov. Power Parlt.* IV. 167 [To be taken] if warlike necessitie require it, yet with a pact of reddition. **1679** EVERARD *Prot. Princes Europe* 26 In examining what hath befallen it.., since that fatal Reddition [of Rochelle]. **1755** CARTE *Hist. Eng.* IV. 39 They had frequently for some years past solicited.. the reddition of those towns which were held as a pledge. **1774** PENNANT *Tour Scotl.* 67 The shameful reddition of the Scotch army. **1794** *Hist.* in *Ann. Reg.* 39 The same motives that operated the reddition of the one effected the surrender of the other.

†**b.** *Law* (see quot. 1607). *Obs.*

1535 tr. *Littleton's Nat. Brev.* (1544) 128 A man that hath recouered by assise of mort dauncestour..or by reddycyon or by any maner enquest. **1607** COWELL *Interpr.*, *Reddicion* ..is a iudiciall confession, and acknowledgement, that the land or thing in demaund belongeth to the demaundant, or at the least, not to himselfe. **1642** tr. *Perkins' Prof. Bk.* v. 164 Against whom the heire of the disseisor doth recover by reddition, or by default in a writ of entry.

†**c.** Retaliation, retort. *Obs. rare.*

1656 HOBBES *Six Lessons* 55 Whatsoever is added of contumely, either directly, or scommatically, is want of Charity, and uncivil; unless it be done by way of Reddition from him that is first provoked to it.

d. Recompense or restitution. *poet.*

1929 R. BRIDGES *Testament of Beauty* IV. 143 And for her soilure make Reddition to Nature.

†**2.** The application of a comparison, or the clause containing the application. (Common in 17th c.) *Obs.*

1579 FULKE *Confut. Sanders* 615 This reddition is false, for ye image of the Trinitie..hath no essentiall trueth. *a* **1603** T. CARTWRIGHT *Confut. Rhem. N.T.* (1618) 350 The similitude that the Apostle useth in the verse next before, whereof this is the reddition or part that answereth unto it. **1678** GALE *Crt. Gentiles* III. 80 We know that al Parables consiste of two parts, the proposition and Reddition or moral. *a* **1714** M. HENRY *Wks.* (1835) II. 356 He does not come to the reddition of the comparison till ver. 27. **1786** A. GIB *Sacr. Contempl.* II. ii. 87 It is evidently but..one half of a sentence in one side of a comparison. And the other side of it, or what is called the reddition, is not to be found in the verse next following.

3. Rendering, translation. *rare.*

1609 [BP. W. BARLOW] *Answ. Nameless Cath.* 317 Which is the naturall Interpretation in the sense, though not the grammatical reddition of the words. *a* **1685** KNATCHBULL *Annot. N. Test.* (1693) 159 In most Interpreters you have in this place..a deficiency in the reddition of the sense. **1950** J. N. D. KELLY *Early Christian Creeds* ii. 36 This solemn rehearsal, or reddition, of the creed before baptism was universally observed in the West.

†**ˈredditive** *a.* and *sb. Obs.* [ad. L. *redditīvus*: see prec. and -IVE.]

A. *adj.* That answers to something already said; corresponding, correlative.

1614 T. ADAMS *Fatal Banquet* IV. Wks. 1861 I. 216 This sad sequel is, if not a relative, yet a redditive demonstration of their misery. **1657** J. SERGEANT *Schism Dispatch't* 296 The redditive part of the testimony. **1659** O. WALKER *Oratory* 20 Conjunctions, Discretive, Redditive, Conditional. [**1721** in BAILEY, and hence in later Dicts.]

B. *sb. Gram.* A word which answers to one already used; a correlative.

1590 STOCKWOOD *Rules Constr.* 2 The word that asketh a question, and the word that answereth vnto the same question, the which they call the interrogatiue and his redditiue. *a* **1638** MEDE *Wks.* (1672) 767 The causal *Quoniam*, and the redditive thereto *Ideo.* **1668** WILKINS *Real Char.* III. iv. 312 The former being Comparative General, the other the Redditive of it.

reddle (ˈrɛd(ə)l), *sb.* [var. RUDDLE: cf. also RADDLE.] Red ochre, ruddle.

1727–41 CHAMBERS *Cycl.*, Reddle, Ruddle, or Red oker. **1748** J. HILL *Hist. Fossils* 47 This is the substance commonly called in English Reddle, and is the *Rubrica fabrilis.* **1805** R. W. DICKSON *Pract. Agric.* II. 1147 Smearing the fore-bows of the rams with reddle, ochre, or some similar substance that has the property of marking. **1879** RUTLEY *Stud. Rocks* x. 155 Hematite also occurs in a granular state, sometimes earthy as reddle.

Hence **ˈreddle** *v. trans.*, to paint or wash over with reddle.

1796 G. M. WOODWARD *Eccentric Excursions* vii. (1796) 81 The floor is reddled, the walls white-washed. **1854** MISS BAKER *Northampt. Gloss.* s.v. *Plough Monday*, A number of boys with their faces blacked and reddled.

ˈreddleman. [f. prec.] = RADDLEMAN.

[*a* **1661** (see RADDLEMAN).] **1878** T. HARDY *Ret. Native* I. ii, The traveller with the cart was a reddleman—a person whose vocation it was to supply farmers with redding for their sheep.

red dog.

1. *U.S.* A banknote formerly in circulation (also *red dog money*).

1848 BARTLETT *Dict. Amer.* 357 *Red Dog Money*, a term applied, in the State of New York, to certain bank-notes which have on their back a large red stamp. **1859** *Ibid.* 357 The community stigmatized them..as red dogs.

2. A low grade of flour.

1889 in *Cent. Dict.* **1931** *Hearings U.S. Congress House Comm. Ways & Means* 131 That would probably include 'red dog' flour, which is a very low grade flour which is considered feed. **1946** *Sun* (Baltimore) 14 Feb. 14/1 'Red dog' is fine bran particles and small quantities of wheat flour.

3. Either of two card games (see quot. 1934).

1930 *Sun* (Baltimore) 18 Aug. 6/1 Playing red dog for money. **1934** *Webster*, *Red dog*... 3. a. A game in which players hold each five cards and bet, for a pool, that they hold a higher card in the same suit than the top card of the stock. b. A variety of stud poker played with seven cards, the first two and the last one being dealt face down, in which all buried red cards are wild. **1935** *Encycl. Sports* 400/1 *Red dog.* This is a card game for any number of players from three to eight. **1938** J. D. CARR *Crooked Hinge* xxi. 290 It was, in the terms of an American pastime called Red Dog, 'high, low, jack, and the goddam game'. **1945** A. A. OSTROW *Compl. Card Player* 47 (*heading*) Red Dog (Also known as high-card pool). *Ibid.* 48 Six-Spot Red Dog... In this variant of red dog each player receives 3 cards. **1974** *Hoyle's Mod. Encycl. Card Games* 289 Despite its simplicity, red dog can build up to high stakes.

4. A manœuvre in American football, in which an opponent rushes the player who is passing the ball. Also as *v. trans.*, to rush (a player) in this way.

1959 *Washington Post* 17 Nov. C1/3 A variety of defenses which stress red-dogging the passer. **1959** *Time* 30 Nov. 56/2 Huff is at his rugged best when he knifes through the line and 'red-dogs' a quarterback as he fades to pass. The crash of Huff's tackle can stir the Giant bench to bellowing glee. **1966** ROTE & WINTER *Lang. Pro Football* iii. 132 *Red dog*,..surprise defensive maneuver where one or more linebackers..charge across line of scrimmage after ball carrier.

reddon, obs. pl. pa. t. READ *v.*

†**reddour.** *Obs.* Forms: 4–5 reddure, -our, (4 -owr, 5 -ur, *Sc.* -oure), 4 redd(e)re; 5 redur, (-yur), *Sc.* -oure; 5 riddour. See also RADDOUR². [a. ONF. *reddur*, *redor*, *reidur*, etc. (mod.F. *raideur*, *roideur*), f. *redde*, *rede*, etc. (mod.F. *raide*, *roide*):—L. *rigida* RIGID.] Severity, strictness, rigour; also, harshness, harsh treatment.

1340 HAMPOLE *Pr. Consc.* 5357 Þat day..Sal noght be shewed but ryghtwysnes, Wyth gret reddour til synful. **1387** TREVISA *Higden* (Rolls) III. 313 He bated nevere contenaunce, noþer reddere of his þouȝt [L. *de animi rigore*]. *c* **1430** LYDG. *Min. Poems* (Percy Soc.) 57 To do reddour alwey without grace or mercy. *c* **1470** HARDING *Chron.* XCVII. ix, That they put nought reddour ne punissyon..On trespassours that dyd violence.

reddour, variant of RADDOUR¹. *Sc. Obs.*

reddring: see REDDER *v.*

reddsman (ˈrɛdzmən). *Sc.* [f. REDD *sb.*¹ + -S- + MAN.] *Mining.* A man employed in clearing away rubbish from the workings of a mine.

1808 in JAMIESON. **1883** GRESLEY *Gloss. Coal-mining* 200. **1887** P. M'NEILL *Blawearie* 59 Down came another cage, out of which stepped the manager accompanied by the chief oncost or reddsman.

reddur(e, variants of REDDOUR *Obs.*

reddure, variant of RADDOUR¹. *Sc. Obs.*

reddy (ˈrɛdɪ), *a.* Also 4–6 redy. [f. *rede* RED *a.* + -Y.] †**a.** Red, ruddy. *Obs.* **b.** (With names of colours.) Reddish.

a. *c* **1374** CHAUCER *Boeth.* II. met. iii. 39 (Addit. MS.) Whan þe wode wexeþ redy [*v.r.* rody] of rosene floures. *a* **1400–50** *Alexander* 3369 Þe ferd was a granate, goules althire fynest, Is nane so redy, as I rede, of all þe riche stanes. **1483** *Cath. Angl.* 103/1 A redi dok, *lappacium acutum.* **1557** ?HEYWOOD in *Tottell's Misc.* (Arb.) 163 Her rosiall colour comes and goes..More redier to then doth the rose. **1579** *Poore Knights Palace* G, My reddy blood this terror did expell,..which in my cheekes was plaste. **1605** TIMME *Quersit.* II. v. 130 The saphiric and reddy colour of those that are ripe. *a* **1661** FULLER in Spurgeon *Treas. Dav. Ps.* xxv. 7, I will not conclude that David was of a wanton constitution because of a reddy complexion.

b. **1888** *Pall Mall G.* 17 May 2/2 Thin sheet iron, painted a reddy brown. *Ibid.* 4 Aug. 5/1 A powder which imparts to the hair a 'bronze reddy gold'. **1946** G. MILLAR *Horned Pigeon* i. 1 A bedside light shone into her reddy-brown curls. **1968** D. IRELAND *Chantic Bird* i. 5 Ma's photos..were in a flat, wooden box, covered with flowered paper. Reddy brown. **1970** A. DRAPER *Swansong for Rare Bird* vi. 45 My best shirt was reddy mauve. **1977** 'M. UNDERWOOD' *Murder with Malice* ii. 24 The reddy-brown stain on the mushroom-pink carpet showed where her head had lain.

reddy, var. READY *sb.* 1.

reddyly, obs. form of READILY.

reddynn, obs. pa. pple. of READ *v.*

rede (riːd), *sb.*¹ Now *arch.* or *poet.* and *dial.* Forms: 1–3 ræd, 3 reæd, ræid, (reað), 3–6, 9 read, 3–7 (9 *Sc.*) reade, 3 (4–6 *Sc.*) reid, (5 *Sc.* -e), 3–7 reed, (5–7 -e), 2–7 (8 *Sc.*), 9 rede; 1–5 (6 *Sc.*) red, 5 redde, 7 *Sc.* redd, 2–3 (7 *Sc.*) rad, 3–4 rade. [Common Teut.: OE. *rǽd* masc. = OFris. *rêd*, OS. *râd* (MDu. *rāt*, *rād-*, Du. *raad*), OHG. *rât* (G. *rath*, *rat*), ON. *ráð* neut. (Sw. *råd*, Da. *raad*):—OTeut. **rǽđo-z* (? and **rǽđom*), f. the stem of the vb. **rǽdan* to READ or REDE.

The word is very frequent in OE. and early ME., and remained in literary use till the beginning of the 17th c. After that date it is rarely found until revived in archaic and poetic diction in the 19th c.]

1. a. Counsel or advice given by one person to another.

Beowulf 3080 (Z.) Ne meahton we ȝelæran..rices hyrde ræd ænigne þæt he ne grette gold weard þone. *c* **1000** ÆLFRIC *Exod.* xviii. 19 Ac ȝehyr mine word and minne ræd. *c* **1175** *Lamb. Hom.* 63 Þe luste nulleð þesne red wisliche he scal wurðen ded. *c* **1205** LAY. 5293 Þeos eorles comen to Rome..axeden heom ræddes. *a* **1300** *Cursor M.* 15139 A rede i sal yow giue, And herkens all to me. **13..** *K. Alis.* 6165 He..so longe criede and bade, That him com from heven, rade, How he scholde heom distroye. **1375** BARBOUR *Bruce* II. 122 Tak him as off thine awyne heid, As I had gevyn thar-to na reid. *c* **1412** HOCCLEVE *De Reg. Princ.* 411 My rede in happe yit the profite may. **1509** BARCLAY *Shyp of Folys* (1570) 17 The reade and aduisement, Of wise men,..Helpeth thine owne, be thou neuer so prudent. **1550** CROWLEY *Last Trump.* 942 If thou be calde a counseller, And many men do seke thy read. **1607** J. CARPENTER *Plaine Mans Plough* 84 Refusing all vaine babling and unprofitable reeds of fools. **1632** HOLLAND *Cyrupædia* 185 If according to your rede, I had bin a hoarder of gold. **1786** BURNS *Ep. Young Friend* xi, May you better reck the rede, Than ever did th' Adviser! **1814** SCOTT *Ld. of Isles* III. iii, Is this thy rede? **1876** MORRIS *Sigurd* IV. 371 That he hearken the council of night and the rede that to-morrow saith.

Prov. *a* **1235** ROGER OF WENDOVER *Chron.* (E.H.S.) II. 18 [Unus ex illis cujus arbitrium omnes exspectabant, præcipitanter patria lingua dixit,] Schort red, god red; slea ye the bischop. *a* **1250** *Prov. Ælfred* 336 in *O.E. Misc.* 122 Hit is ifurn iseyd þat cold red is quene red. **1599** PORTER *Angry Wom. Abingd.* (Percy Soc.) 82, I could haue said to you, syr, Take heede is a good reede.

†**b.** In phr. ***by*** (***after***, ***through***, ***with***) ***one's rede***; also ***to do by one's rede***, to accept one's advice. *Obs.*

c **1122** *O.E. Chron.* (Laud MS.) an. 1043 Be þæs cynges læfe & ræda. *Ibid.* an. 1100 Be þære ræde þe him abutan wæran. *a* **1225** *Leg. Kath.* 6 Constentin ferde þurh þe burhmenne reað into Fronclonde. *a* **1300** *Cursor M.* 2290 Lik til his fader þat was ded A wygur was mad wit his red. **13..** *Guy Warw.* (A.) 1238 Leue sone,..Þou do bi þi faders rede. *c* **1412** HOCCLEVE *De Reg. Princ.* 1119 Sone, by my rede thow shalt do so. *c* **1420** *Chron. Vilod.* st. 562 So þey dedon trewelyche after his redde. **1554** *Interl. Youth* A ij b, And yet syr do by my rede. **1587** M. GROVE *Pelops & Hipp.* (1878) 73 Leaue of I pray you by my reade.

†**c.** ***to give to rede***: to give by way of counsel or advice. *Obs.*

13.. *Cursor M.* 10791 (Gött.) Ne had he neuer gyuen to rede, þat iesu crist war don to dede. *c* **1400** *Destr. Troy* 12002 The grekys..gyffon to red, Ilion to ouerturne. *c* **1430** *Syr Tryam.* 634 Moche warre began to sprede Yn hur lande..Therfore sche ys gevyn to rede, To take a lorde.

2. a. Counsel, decision, or resolve taken by one or more persons; a plan, design, or scheme devised or adopted.

c **1000** ÆLFRIC *Vet. Test.* 2 (Gr.) Se ræd wæs æfre on his rædfæstum ȝeþance, þæt he wircan wolde þa wundorlican ȝesceafta. *c* **1050** in Thorpe *Dipl. Angl. Sax.* (1865) 322 Ic þa feng on minne aȝenne red. **1297** R. GLOUC. (Rolls) 11198 An vewe wilde hinen a liȝt red þer of nome. *c* **1330** *Arth. & Merl.* 2048 (Kölbing) Bi comoun dome, bi comoun rade, Vterpendragon coroun nam & king of Inglond bicam. *c* **1386** CHAUCER *Doctor's T.* 146 Whan þat assented was this cursed reed, Glad was this Iuge. *c* **1425** *Seven Sag.* (P.) 226 Sone aftir that scho was dede, Hys fadir hadde anothir rede. *c* **1440** *York Myst.* iv. 44 Lovyng be ay to suche a lord, ..[who] mayd vs after his owen read. **1870** MORRIS *Earthly Par.* III. IV. 316 Therefore swift rede I take with all things here.

†**b.** ***to take to rede***: to adopt as one's decision or plan; to decide, resolve. Also with dative (refl.) pronoun. *Obs.*

c **893** K. ÆLFRED *Oros.* IV. v. §2 Hanno..him to ræde ȝenom þæt he hie ealle to ȝereordum to him ȝehete. *c* **1205** LAY. 440 Seoþen he nom to rede..þat he an wriht makede. *Ibid.* 20210 Heo nomen heom to ræden þat aȝæin heo wolden riden. *a* **1300** *Cursor M.* 4032 Þir breþer tuam þam tok to red To dele þair landes þam bi-tuixs. *c* **1330** R. BRUNNE *Chron.* (1810) 52 Þo childre tok to rede, to com vnto þis lond. **1390** GOWER *Conf.* III. 214 Gedeon..tok him to rede, And sende in al the lond aboute.

†**c.** ***to take rede***: to take counsel, resolve, decide. *Obs.*

c **1330** *Arth. & Merl.* 286 (Kölbing) [Þai] tok rede bi tvixen hem to, Þe to childer ouer þe se bring. *c* **1375** *Sc. Leg. Saints* xxi. (*Clement*) 636 Clement wysly tuk rede, þat he wald nocht next petir be. *c* **1400** *Destr. Troy* 8996 Palamydon..All his Renkes had arayet, as he rede toke.

†**3. a.** A scheme, plan, or method for attaining some end; a principle or course of action, mode of procedure. *Obs.*

For the obs. Sc. phr. ***will of rede***, see WILL *a.*

Beowulf 1376 (Z.) Nu is se ræd ȝelang eft æt þe anum. *c* **893** K. ÆLFRED *Oros.* IV. x. §8 Scipia..Romanum to ræde ȝelærde, þæt hie foren mid scipum on Hannibales land. *c* **1205** LAY. 30576 Ofte he hine biðohte what he don mahte and biþohten him enne ræd. *a* **1250** *Gen. & Ex.* 309 Ic wene I can a red, ðat hem sal bringen iwel sped. *a* **1300** *Cursor M.* 14254 Leif lauerd, sco said, quat rede? Mi broþer nu es fra me ded. **1382** *Pol. Poems* (Rolls) I. 252, I leeve this beo ur best red, To thenke on this warnyng and be ware. *c* **1420** *Sir Amadace* (Camden) xxii, Take the tille a bettur rede. *c* **1470** HENRYSON *Mor. Fab.* II. *Town & C. Mouse* xx, So desolate and will of ane gude reid. **1549–62** STERNHOLD & H. *Ps.* cxix. 100 To keepe thy lawes, I held it aye best reede.

†**b.** ***to be to rede***: to be an advisable or possible course of action (for one). *Obs.*

971 *Blickl. Hom.* 205 Hie befrinon & beahsodan hwæt him þæs to ræde þuhte. *a* **1200** *Moral Ode* 90 Hwat scal us to rede. *c* **1205** LAY. 13527 Whæt maȝe we nu to rade [*c* **1275** Wat his vs nou to reade], whæ scal us nu ræden. *c* **1330** R. BRUNNE *Chron. Wace* (Rolls) 864 Brutus..nyste what was best to red. *c* **1350** *Will. Palerne* 903, I not in þe world what is me to rede. *Ibid.* 3885 He..seide after anon 'Alas! what to rede!'

†**c.** With *no* or *no other*: no (or no other) plan, device, or way to act, *esp.* in order to help or save oneself. *Obs.*

1297 R. GLOUC. (Rolls) 9121 Alas alas of engelond ne can ich nanne red. **1375** BARBOUR *Bruce* I. 568 Quharfor syne he tholyt ded; Than he couth set tharfor na rede. *c* **1400** *Rom. Rose* 3859, I was astoned, and knew no rede, But fledde awey for verrey drede. *c* **1470** HENRY *Wallace* v. 588 The madyn than wyst off no othyr rede, Bot..purchest had king Eduardis protectioune. *a* **1542** WYATT *Poet. Wks.* (1861) 69 For in despair there is no rede.

†**d.** Occurrence, event, hap, lot. *Obs.*

c **1205** LAY. 3910 Seoððen her com a strong ræd þat Riwald kinge iwerð deað. *Ibid.* 8164 þe oðer wolde him habben dæd; hit þuhte him swiðe hærd ræd. *c* **1420** *Sir Amadace* (Camden) xvi, Thus carefulle is my rede. *a* **1425** *Cursor M.* 14295 (Trin.) My broþer lazer þi frend is deed And þat is to me a colde reed. *c* **1440** *Sir Gowther* 661 [He] halp holy chirche with his myght, Thus cawght he better rede.

†**4. a.** What is advisable, advantageous or profitable for one; aid, help, succour; remedy. *Obs.*

805–31 *Charter* in *O.E. Texts* 444 He brytnie swæ hiȝum maest red sie. *a* **1000** *Boeth. Metr.* ii. 12 [Hi] me þa berypton rædes & frofre. *c* **1000** ÆLFRIC *Saints' Lives* xii. 122 Bið nu micel ræd þam þe his sylfes recð. *c* **1175** *Lamb. Hom.* 63 Gif us to dei ure deies bred Lauerd god al ure red. *c* **1315** SHOREHAM (E.E.T.S.) ii. 32 And ȝyf þe lyues [= living] mylse and grace þe dede red and reste. *c* **1375** *Cursor M.* 8376 (Fairf.) Peraunter þer wil rise strife bot ȝe do rede in ȝoure life. *c* **1420** *Sir Amadace* (Camden) xxxv, Lord, I aske the rede, Hastely that I were dede. *c* **1485** *Digby Myst.* (1882) III. 1793 Blyssyd mavdleyn, be hyr rede!

†**b.** ***to take rede to***: to seek help for. *Obs.*⁻¹

a **1225** *Leg. Kath.* 1379 Þe deore Drihtin areaw us, & toc read to ure alde dusichipes.

5. The faculty of deliberation, or the exercise of this; judgement, prudence, reason. ***rede-craft*** (see quot. 1880). *Obs.* exc. *arch.*

a **900** CYNEWULF *Elene* 553 (Gr.) Is eow rædes þearf on meðelstede, modes snyttro. *a* **1200** *Moral Ode* 4 (Trin. Coll. MS.) Þeih i bie a winter eald, to ȝung ich am on rade. *a* **1250** *Owl & Night.* 682 Never nis wit so kene, So wane red him is ayene. **1399** LANGL. *Rich. Redeles* III. 125 Ho is riall of his ray..light reede him ffolwith. *a* **1650** *Merline* in Furniv. *Percy Folio* I. 424 A doughtye man he was of deed, & right wise he was of reede.

Comb. *a* **1250** *Owl & Night.* 694 Ȝif þat he forleost his wit, þonne is his redpurs al toslit. **1880** W. BARNES (*title*) An outline of rede-craft (logic) with English wording.

†**6.** The act of taking counsel together, or of assembling for this purpose; a council. *Obs.*

Beowulf 172 (Z.) Moniȝ oft ȝesæt rice to rune, ræd eahtedon. *c* **1000** ÆLFRIC *Saints' Lives* xix. 201 Þa wæs se acitofel mid absalone on ræde, and rædde him [etc.]. *c* **1000** —— *Hom.* II. 242 He sona eode to ðæra Iudeiscra ræde [etc.]. *c* **1205** LAY. 374 Alle þe weren at þisse reade biluuede þeos runen. *a* **1300** *Cursor M.* 4550 Þe barunnage mikel ferli thoght þat suilk to king red was broght. *c* **1330** R. BRUNNE *Chron.* (1810) 48 Þe clergie & þe baronage samned at a reade. *c* **1375** *Cursor M.* 7901 (Fairf.) Shortly wiþ-out mare rede þai sulde [him take] and bringe to dede.

7. a. Tale, narrative, story; †a saying, proverb. (Cf. READ *v.* 14.)

c **1375** *Sc. Leg. Saints* xxiii. (*Seven Sleepers*) 362 Wes nane þat euire hard tel of ony of þame in red na spel. **1579**

SPENSER *Sheph. Cal.* July 11 This reede is ryfe, that oftentime, great clymbers fall vnsoft. 1665 BRATHWAIT *Comment Two Tales* 82 Read your Rede to me then boldly, you shall find me an honest old woman. 1808 SCOTT *Marm.* VI. L'Envoy, A final note..to bid the gentles speed Who long have listened to my rede. 1868 BROWNING *Ring & Bk.* x. 227 All's a clear rede, and no more riddle now.

†**b.** Speech. *Obs. rare*⁻¹.

1596 SPENSER *F.Q.* IV. x. 34 Concord she cleeped was in common reed, Mother of blessed Peace.

c. Interpretation.

1871 BROWNING *Pr. Hohenst.* 11 Sphynx in wise old age, Grown..jealous for her riddle's proper rede.

†**rede**, *sb.*[2] *Obs. rare.* Also 5 reede. [Of obscure origin.] A small trench or furrow.

c1420 *Pallad. on Husb.* IV. 219 Sperage is sowe..In redes [L. *fossulis*] smale, ymaad by lyne, in wete And fat lond. *Ibid.* XII. 73 Maak redes [L. *sulcos*] in the bord, and ther bistowe Hem in the coppe.

†**rede**, *sb.*[3] *Sc. Obs. rare*⁻¹. Sound.

c1470 HENRY *Wallace* VIII. 1191 The cler rede amang the rochis rang, Throuch greyn branchis quhar byrdis..sang.

rede (riːd), *v.*[1] Now *arch.* or *poet.* and *dial.* Forms: *Infin.* 1 rǽdan, -en, 2 readan, 3 reden, 4 redyn; (and *Pres.*) 3–6 (9 *Sc.*) read, (3, 6–7 -e), 4–6 reed, (5, 7 -e), 4, 5–6 *Sc.* reid, 5 reyd, 3–7 (8 *Sc.*) 9 rede; 4–6, 8–9 *Sc.* red, 4, 8–9 *Sc.* redd, (9 *Sc.* -e), 5 *Sc.*, 6 rid; *Subj.* 2–3 rade; 3 *sing. Pres. Indic.* 1 ræt, 4 ret. *Pa. t.* 1 reord, 1, 3 rædde, 3–4 radde, 3–5 redde, 4–5 redd, 4–6 red, 6 reade. *Pa. pple.* 1 ȝeræd, 4 rad, 5 rade, 8 *Sc.* red, 9 *Sc.* rede. [The same word as READ *v.*, the common ME. spelling being usually retained to distinguish the archaic from the current senses of the word. In dial. the vowel of the infin. and pres. is sometimes shortened (*red, redd*) on analogy of the pa. t. and pa. pple.: cf. REDD *v.*[2]]

I. †**1.** *trans.* To have or exercise control over; to rule, govern, guide. *Obs.*

Beowulf 2056 (Z.) Þone maðþum..þe ðu mid rihte rædan sceoldest. c888 K. ÆLFRED *Boeth.* xxxv. §3 He riht & ræt eallum gesceaftum, swa swa good stiora anum scipe. a1000 *Daniel* 8 (Gr.) Þat wæs modiȝ cyn, þenden hie þy rice ræden moston. c1205 LAY. 16956 He makede per hueþ þan uolke to reden. c1290 *S. Eng. Leg.* I. 179/26 To þe al mi truste was mi lond to wissi and rede. c1325 *Chron. Eng.* 499 in Ritson *Metr. Rom.* II. 291 Hou he myhte him wise and rede, Ant ys lond ariht lede. c1375 *Cursor M.* 5292 (Fairf.) Þe lorde-hede of al þis lande, to wisse and rede I haue in hande.

†**b.** To bring, deliver; *refl.* to direct (oneself) *to* a place. Also *absol.* to arrive. *Obs. rare.*

a1000 *Rect. Sing. Pers.* c. 4 §1 He sceal ælcre wucan erian .i. æcer and rædan sylf ðæt sæd on hlafordes berne. c1330 R. BRUNNE *Chron. Wace* (Rolls) 14088 Arthur dide his flete eft dight, To Romeneye þey redde þem right. *Ibid.* 15892 His wey he tok..ful faste he spedde, Þat til Oxenforde algate he redde.

†**2.** Of God, Christ, etc.: To take care or charge of (one); to guide, guard, or protect. *Obs.*

a1200 *Moral Ode* 158 (Trin. Coll. MS.) On þe daie and on þe dome us helpe crist and rade. c1250 *Orison Our Lady* 39 in *O.E. Misc.* 160 Ich bidde hire to me bi-seo, And helpe me and rede. a1300 *Cursor M.* 8397, I sai noght yon, sa godd me rede, For nan vpbraid ne for na nede. c1384 CHAUCER *H. Fame* II. 559 Also wis god rede me But o thinge y wil warne the. c1450 HOLLAND *Howlat* 463 The gud king gaif the gaist to God for to reid. c1470 *Golagros & Gaw.* 809 Gif I de doughtely, the les is my dere, Thoght he war Sampsone himself, sa me Criste reid!

†**b.** To save, deliver. *Obs. rare.*

a1300 *Cursor M.* 906 Þou sal be slan wit duble dedd, Herd it es þe for to redd [*other MSS.* dede: rede]. c1374 CHAUCER *Anel. & Arc.* 340 But me to rede out of this drede or guye Ne may my wit, so weyke is hit, not streche.

†**3.** To decree, appoint. *Obs.*

c1205 LAY. 18100 Swa þe is nu iræd, þer on þu ært ded. a1225 *Juliana* 62 Þu..reddest him [David] to rixlen in sawmueles riche. c1330 R. BRUNNE *Chron.* (1810) 17 Right in þe mornyng in aldermost nede Com þe kynges sonnes tuo, als Crist wild it rede. 1362 LANGL. *P. Pl.* A. v. 180 Þei couþe not..acorde to-gedere, Til Robyn þe Ropere weore Rad forte a-ryse, And nempned for a noumpere.

II. †**4.** *intr.* To take counsel together or *with* another, to deliberate. Also of one person: To take counsel *for* others. *Obs.*

c893 K. ÆLFRED *Oros.* I. xiv. §1 Þa redon hi him betweonum, cwædon þæt hie to raðe wolde fultumlease beon [etc.]. a900 tr. *Bæda's Hist.* I. xi. [xiv.] (1890) 50 Þa ȝesomnedon hi ȝemot & þeahtedon & ræddon, hwæt him to donne wære. c1000 ÆLFRIC *Saints' Lives* v. 323 Wið þone rædde chromatius, and be his ræde [etc.]. c1122 *O.E. Chron.* (Laud. MS.) an. 1010 Man þonne ræden scolde hu man þisne eard werian sceolde. c1131 *Ibid.* 1131 Crist ræde for þa wrecce munecas of Burch. c1205 LAY. 32128 Þær heo gunnen ræde, þer heo gunnen rune. 1494 FABYAN *Chron.* VI. cxcix. 206 The kynge..called his counsayl to rede what were best to be done.

†**5.** *trans.* To agree upon, resolve, decide, after consultation or deliberation. *Obs.*

c1000 ÆLFRIC *Hom.* I. 162 Ðæt folc rædde be him, þæt hi woldon hine..ahebban to cyninge. c1205 LAY. 25002 Nu ȝe habbeoð iherd..what Romanisce men redeð heom bitwenen. *Ibid.* 26221 [They] radden heom bitwenen enne castel to areren. c1250 *Gen. & Ex.* 2861 He redden samen he sulden gon wid wise men to pharaon. 1297 R. GLOUC. (Rolls) 4060Þei ech of vs sete al day þe best red to rede [etc.]. 1559 *Mirr. Mag., Mowbray's Banishment* xxi, The king through counsayle of the Lordes thought good To banysh bothe, whiche iudgement strayt was rad.

III. 6. *trans.* To advise or counsel (a person). With various constructions: †**a.** Simple (dative or) accusative. Also const. *of. Obs.*

a900 CYNEWULF *Elene* 1023 (Gr.) On þam stedewange ȝirwan Godes tempel, swa hire gasta weard reord of roderum. c1175 *Lamb. Hom.* 115 Wise men him scule readan. c1205 LAY. 7427 He wes cniht swiðe ræh to ræden ane kinge. 1297 R. GLOUC. (Rolls) 7422 An stounde he gan abide & is kniȝtes rede. c1350 *Will. Palerne* 1301 Riȝt as william wold þat wisly him radde. a1400–50 *Alexander* 5194 Latt se þi witt in þis werke & wysely me rede. a1450 MYRC 7 Whenne þey scholde þe pepul rede In to synne þey do hem lede. a1586 SIDNEY *Arcadia* (1622) 224 Thou heardst euen now a young man sneb me sore, Because I red him, as I would my sonne. 1615 BRATHWAIT *Strappado* (1878) 133 Be stately Billy (and I doe thee rede).

refl. c1385 CHAUCER *L.G.W.* 2217 *Ariadne*, I can mine selue In this case nat rede.

†**b.** Double accusative (or acc. and dat.); sometimes with cognate object. *Obs.*

c1205 LAY. 11403 Þe king heom hauede [it] isæid, & bæd heom ræden him ræd. *Ibid.* 24783 Wha hit þe durre ræden þat þu swa reh ært iwurðen. a1330 *Otuel* 326 Cristers cors vppon his heued, þat me radde such a red. c1330 R. BRUNNE *Chron.* (1810) 283 To wite what ȝe me rede, I set þis parlement. a1400–50 *Alexander* 244 A riall roune þou me redis, a reson of blis. c1450 *Merlin* 80 He shall not rede yow no-thynge but for youre profite.

†**c.** Accusative (or dative) with objective clause, introduced by *that, what, where,* etc. *Obs.*

c1200 ORMIN 18336 Forrþi ræde icc ȝuu..þatt ȝure nan ne dwelle nohht. c1205 LAY. 6681 Heo him redden wher his lich mihte bezst leggen. a1330 *Cursor M.* 3450 At pray to godd ai was sco prest To rede hir quat þat hir was best. 1340 HAMPOLE *Pr. Consc.* 3502 Þarfor I rede ilk man,..þat he use þa ten thinges sere. a1400–50 *Alexander* 2464, I anely ȝow rede, þat þe end of ȝoure eldirs enterely ȝe be-hald.

d. Accusative and infinitive with *to.*

a1225 *Juliana* 40 Ich redde nerrun..to bihefden pawel ant don peter on rode. c1290 *Beket* 916 in *S. Eng. Leg.* I. 132 To queme þe kinge we redez þe, hov-so it euere gon. 1362 LANGL. *P. Pl.* A. IV. 97 Þenne summe Radde Reson to haue reuþe of þat schrewe. c1450 *Merlin* 25, I rede you to fle out of the londe for drede of the kynges peple. 1530 TINDALE *Pract. Prelates* Wks. (1573) 376/1, I reede them to break their bondes, and to follow right by the playne and open way. a1592 GREENE *Jas. IV*, I. iii, I rid thee to view the picture still. 1786 *Har'st Rig* xxiii, The next rig redds them to take care To cut their fur. 1876 FARRAR *Marlb. Serm.* iv. 36 If any one of you is in the habit of using oaths, I rede his sleeping conscience to beware of their guilt and folly.

e. Acc. and inf. without *to*, in later use (with *thee* or *you* as object) passing into next.

c1290 *S. Eng. Leg.* I. 386/338 Þe Quiene..radde hire to hire louerd go. c1300 *Harrow. Hell* 64 Ich him rede speke na more. c1386 CHAUCER *Doctor's T.* 285 Ther-fore I rede yow this conseil take. a1450 *Knt. de la Tour* (1868) 14 Y rede you be curteys and humble to gret and smale. 1500–20 DUNBAR *Poems* li. 22 Madame, I red ȝou get a less ane. 1598 R. BERNARD tr. *Terence, Eunuch* II. ii, In troth I read you stay. 1786 *Har'st Rig* ci, The master..redds them mind their wark indeed. 1818 SCOTT *Hrt. Midl.* xxxii, I redd thee keep hand off her. 1870 MORRIS *Earthly Par.* I. I. 248 Therefore, my son, I rede thee stay at home.

f. Accusative, with imperative clause (following or preceding).

a1300 *Cursor M.* 783 Of it ȝee ette, sua red i ȝow. 1377 LANGL. *P. Pl.* B. I. 173 For-þi I rede ȝow riche, haueth reuthe of þe pouere. c1425 *Seven Sag.* (P.) 1163 Let hym lyve, I wylle the rede. 1470–85 MALORY *Arthur* x. xxii, Beware, I rede the, of treason. a1601 NORTH *Plutarch* (N.), Dispatch, I read you, for your enterprize is betrayed. 1785 BURNS *Death & Dr. Hornbook* ix, I red ye weel, tak care o' skaith. 1853 READE *Chr. Johnstone* 210 Put them off your hands, I rede ye.

†**g.** With acc. and *to* prep. *Obs. rare.*

1297 R. GLOUC. (Rolls) 2758 Min enchantors quaþ þe king me abbeþ þer to yrad. 1362 LANGL. *P. Pl.* A. v. 103 'Ȝus, rediliche', quod Repentaunce and Radde him to goode. c1400 *Destr. Troy* 5129 And rede hym to redurs, þat rixles to shame!

†**7.** To advise (a thing); to give as advice or counsel. *Obs.*

c1205 LAY. 875 Ȝif ȝe hit rædeð ȝe beod mine riche men. c1230 *Hali Meid.* 26 Oþer is þet godd hat, & oþer is þet he ret [*v.r.* reades]. c1300 *Cursor M.* 8352 O mi kingrike quat redes þou? 13.. *E.E. Allit. P.* C. 406 [They] parformed alle þe penaunce þat þe prynce radde. 1390 GOWER *Conf.* I. 44 This wolde I rede, That every man ensample take [etc.]. c1450 *Merlin* 81 The kynge..toke Vlfin in counseile and asked hym what he redde in this mater. c1560 A. SCOTT *Poems* (S.T.S.) xxxiv. 5 Thairfoir I reid remeid, To leife and lat it be. a1650 *Robin Hood's Death* 5 in Furniv. *Percy Folio* I. 52 'That I reade not' said will Scarllett.

†**b.** With clause as object. *Obs.*

c1205 LAY. 414 Assaracus hit redde..þat þat Troynisce folc..makeden hine to duke. a1300 *Cursor M.* 13467 Hu redes þou we wit þam dele? c1320 *Sir Tristr.* 984 Tristrem seyd:—'y rede þat he þe barnes mis'. 1375 BARBOUR *Bruce* VII. 534 Tharfor I rede, all preualy We send a voman hym to spy. c1450 *Merlin* 115, I rede that thou go and serue hym. 1526 SKELTON *Magnyf.* 1011 Pease, man, pease! I rede, we sease. 1591 SPENSER *M. Hubberd* 114 Now read..What course ye weene is best for us to take.

†**c.** With infinitive as object. *Obs.*

a1300 *Cursor M.* 19358 Þai..badd þam fle als þai wald ded, To neuen iesus namar þai red. c1330 R. BRUNNE *Chron. Wace* (Rolls) 1199 Wheþer þey redden hym for to slo, Oþer quytly let hym go. a1400–50 *Alexander* 2601 'Þare I rede', quod þe kyng, 'our bakis neuir to turne'. c1450 *Merlin* 91 [The king] asked theire counseile. And the barons redden to be avenged vpon hem.

†**8.** *intr.* To give advice. *Obs.*

a1000 *Byrhtnoth* 18 (Gr.) Byrhtnoð..rad and rædde, rincum tæhte, hu hi sceoldon standan. c1290 *Beket* 865 in *S. Eng. Leg.* I. 131 Þe bischop Robert of lincolne radde wel þare-to. 1340 HAMPOLE *Pr. Consc.* 1677 Bodily ded, Ogayns þe whilk no man may help ne red. c1425 *Seven Sag.* (P.) 1253 Forsoth I can no rede nowe: Leve fadir, how reddyst thow? c1450 *Merlin* 80 Than seide the kynge to Merlyn, 'And how rede ye of this thinge?' 1591 GREENE *Maiden's Dreame* xvi, For wars or peace right wisely could he rede.

†**b.** Used at the end of a sentence, or parenthetically. *Obs.*

c1230 *Hali Meid.* 26 Hwa se hit mei underneomen, underneome, ich reade. c1320 R. BRUNNE *Medit.* 177 By þese vertues folue hym, y rede. 1377 LANGL. *P. Pl.* B. XI. 378 'For-þi I rede', quod reson, 'rewle þi tonge bettere'. c1460 *Towneley Myst.* xiii. 467 Go we theder, I rede, and ryn on oure feete. 1513 DOUGLAS *Æneis* XI. vi. 167 Be war with thame for till debait, I reid. c1530 H. RHODES *Bk. Nurture* in *Babees Bk.* (1868) 81 Or thou be olde, beware, I rid, least thou doe get a fall. 1603 HOLLAND *Plutarch's Mor.* 38 His counsell take, I reede, and then [etc.].

†**c.** In clauses introduced by *as* or *so. Obs.*

c1290 *S. Eng. Leg.* I. 44/335 Þov ne miȝht me neuere paye wel bote þov do ase ich rede. 1387 TREVISA *Higden* (Rolls) VI. 339 Þe Norþhombres hadde i-doo awey here kyng Osbrucus, as þe devel hem radde. 1393 LANGL. *P. Pl.* C. xx. 106 'He seide soth', quaþ þe samaritan, 'and so ich rede þe also'. 1412–20 LYDG. *Chron. Troy* IV. xxxiv, It shall not be As Anthenor hath rade in no degree.

†**9.** *trans.* To teach or give (one) a knowledge *of* (something). *Obs. rare*⁻¹.

13.. *Guy Warw.* (A.) 170 Gii a forster fader hadde þat him lerd & him radde Of wodes & riuer & oþer game.

10. *Sc.* To think, imagine, guess. = READ *v.* 1.

1768 [see READ *v.* 1 a]. 1790 SHIRREFS *Poems* 86 He's ane, I red, that ye can eithly spare. 1806 JAMIESON *Pop. Ballads* I. 237 And this black hour be past, I rede ye'll rue it sair.

11. To interpret, explain. = READ *v.* 2.

1725 RAMSAY *Gentle Sheph.* III. ii, Nor come I to redd fortunes for reward. 1728 —— *Robt., Richy & Sandy* 34 Ah! now my dream its red. a1810 TANNAHILL *Poems* (1846) 19 O, dool and wae, my dream's been rede right soon! 1831 CARLYLE *Sart. Res.* I. viii, The secret of Man's being is still ..a riddle that he cannot rede. 1837 —— *Fr. Rev.* v. iii. (1872) III. 185 Rede us this riddle, O Collot!

12. To relate, tell. = READ *v.* 14.

1840 BARHAM *Ingol. Leg.* Ser. I. *Witches' Frolic* i, I'll rede ye a lay of Grammerye. *Ibid.*, *Lay St. Nicholas* xli, Now rede me aright the most wonderful sight, Thou Palmer gray, that thine eyes have seen.

rede (riːd), *v.*[2] *Obs.* exc. *dial.* Forms: 1 (ȝe)-rǽdan, redan, 4, 6, 9 rede, 6 *Sc.* reyd, 8–9 reed, 9 read. [OE. *rǽdan* (rare) = MDu. and MLG. *rêden, reiden* (Du. *reeden*) to make ready, set in order, etc. (hence Da. *rede*, Sw. *reda*). OE. had also *ȝerǽdan* (rare) = MDu. *gherêden*, ON. *greiða* to GRAITH. The base is that of the adj. READY.]

1. *trans.* To put in order; to comb (the hair); to clear (a way); to clean up or out; etc. (see REDD *v.*[2]).

[a900 tr. *Bæda's Hist.* III. vii. [ix.] (1890) 180 Heo þwoh & hyre feax ȝerædde.] 944 in Earle *Land Charters*, etc. 179 On fealuwes lea þær ælfric biscep redan het to þære ealdan dic. c1330 *Arth. & Merl.* 7896 (Kölbing) Þai..large roume about hem redde. c1440 *York Myst.* xii. 124 He saide, 'sonne I sall sende by-fore Myne Aungell to rede þe thy way'. 1470 *Extr. Aberdeen Reg.* (1844) I. 30 To devoyde and rede a certaine lande and Tenement..to oure louyt Agnes Lilburne. 1507 *Ibid.* 76 Evere fyrhouse..sale furnis and sende ane sufficient work seruand..to help to rede the common loche. 1513 DOUGLAS *Æneis* VII. xii. 86 Buskis wythdrawis..To reyd thair renk, and rovmis thaim the way. 1791 *Cottingham Incl. Act* 28 Ditches to be well and effectually reeded, scoured and cleansed. 1822 AINSLIE *Land of Burns* 271 I'll rede room for thee, Jock. 1876 *Whitby Gloss.* s.v., Rede thy hair menseful.

†**b.** *absol.* (also with *dat.*) To clear a way (for oneself). *Obs. rare.*

c1330 *Arth. & Merl.* 3334 (Kölbing) Þo he was opon his stede, Wiþ swerd he gan about rede. *Ibid.* 8277 Ich [= each] dede his launce go..& redden hem wiþ miȝt fin.

2. *spec.* (See quots.)

1825 JENNINGS *Obs. Dial. W. Eng.*, *Read*, to strip the fat from the intestines. 1878 *Cumbld. Gloss.* s.v. *Reed*, Butchers reed the entrails of slaughtered animals to obtain the fat.

Hence **'reding** *vbl. sb.* in ***reding-comb.***

1894 HALL CAINE *Manxman* III. xii. 170 Take the redyng comb and lash your hair out, it's all through-others.

rede, var. obs. Sc. REID.

rede, var. RAD *a.*[2] *Obs.*, obs. f. READ *sb.*[1] and *v.*, RED *a.*, REED *sb.*

redeal, *v.* [RE- 5 a.] To deal again. Also as *sb.*, a fresh deal.

1935 *Sun* (Baltimore) 11 Jan. 1/2 The New Deal is to be 'redealt'. 1959 T. REESE *Bridge Player's Dict.* 182 If the pack is deficient in any respect there must always be a redeal. 1964 *Official Encycl. Bridge* 287/2 When there is a redeal, the current deal is canceled; the same dealer deals again, unless he was dealing out of turn. *Ibid.* 450/1 Hands are never redealt at duplicate except in special cases.

redeamer, obs. form of REDEEMER.

red-eared: see RED *a.* 14 a, b, c.

rede'bate, *v.* [RE- 5 a. Cf. F. *redébattre* (Cotgr.).] *trans.* To debate (a subject) again. Hence **rede'bating** *vbl. sb.*

1611 COTGR., *Redebatre*, to redebate the matter; to cauill, or brabble about it againe. 1880 BURTON *Reign Q. Anne* II. xii. 261 To have that point settled by redebating and revoting the settlement of the throne. 1896 *Daily News* 7 Oct. 5/1 The re-debating of Parliamentary questions.

rede'cide, *v.* [RE- 5 a.] To decide again. So **rede'cision**.

1850 CARLYLE *Latter-d. Pamph.* i. (1872) 13 The rigorous fact..which will one day..demand practical decision or redecision of it from us. 1885 *Law Times* LXXVIII. 168/1 Cases which if not obsolete have been in principle re-decided in more modern decisions.

re'deck, *v.* [RE- 5 a.] *trans.* **a.** To array again. **b.** To furnish with a new deck.

1771 MRS. GRIFFITH *Hist. Lady Barton* I. 125 Think what it will be, when summer shall redeck it in its leafy pride. 1897 *Westm. Gaz.* 20 July 4/1 The Temple landing-stage..has cost about £1,000 to be re-decked.

rede'clare, *v.* [RE- 5 a. Cf. F. *redéclarer* (Cotgr.).] To declare again.

1611 COTGR., *Redeclarer*, to redeclare, to reexpresse. 1876 S. MILLER in T. Smith *Mem.* (1883) 130 He came to redeclare this truth. 1883 *Daily News* 11 Oct. 2/7 All mine hot-blast pigs were redeclared, at 65s. to 62s. 6d.

re'decorate, *v.* [RE- 5 a. Cf. F. *redécorer* (Cotgr.).] *trans.* To decorate again. Hence **re'decorated** *ppl. a.*

1611 COTGR., *Redecorer*, to redecorate, or bedecke againe. 1835 LYTTON *Rienzi* IV. i, The redecorated, refurnished, and smiling shops. 1861 *Times* 29 Aug., All the..wide and lofty rooms had been redecorated.

So **redeco'ration**.

1857 W. COLLINS *Dead Secret* (1861) 48 To survey the neglected north rooms, with a view to their redecoration. 1881 *Athenæum* 30 Apr. 599/3 The projects for the re-decoration of the dome of St. Paul's.

re'dedicate, *v.* (Also as *pa. pple.*) [RE- 5 a.] *trans.* To dedicate anew.

1611 COTGR., *Rededier*, to rededicate, to consecrate or hallow anew. 1703 HEARNE in Plummer *Elizab. Oxford* (O.H.S.) 108 After 'twas quite finished, 'twas rededicated to the same Saint as before. 1839–48 BAILEY *Festus* x. 105 All being shall be rebegotten, all Worship rededicate. 1839–52 *Ibid.* xxvii. 457 Canst thou..reconsecrate the heart, Re-dedicate the temple? 1872 SPURGEON *Treas. Dav.* Ps. lvi. 12 Those who..have re-dedicated themselves unto the Lord.

So **rededi'cation**; **re'dedicatory** *a.*

1883 *Harper's Mag.* May 895/2 A rededication of the Egyptian obelisk to its ancient deity. 1896 *Daily News* 11 July 3/6 There was a re-dedication service at the church. 1896 *Chicago Advance* 24 Sept. 418 The re-dedicatory services will be held Oct. 4.

†**re'deem**, *sb. Sc. Obs. rare*$^{-1}$. In 5 radem. [f. the vb.] The act of redeeming; redemption.

*c*1470 HENRY *Wallace* x. 1005 The Roman buikis at than was in Scotland, He gart be brocht..And, but radem, thai brynt thaim thar ilkan.

redeem (rɪ'diːm), *v.* Forms: 5 *Sc.* rademe, radeym, 5–6 redeme, (5 redem), 6 *Sc.* redeime, 6–7 redeeme, 7– redeem. [ad. F. *rédimer* (15th c. in Godef.), or L. *redimĕre* to buy back, etc., f. *re(d)-* RE- + *emĕre* to buy. The popular OF. form *raembre* is represented in ME. by RAIM *v.*

The vowel of the second syllable in *redeem* and *exeme* (in place of **redime* and **exime*) may have originated in the pa. t., after L. *redēmit, exēmit*, and its retention would be favoured by the existence of *redemption* and *exempt*.]

1. *trans.* To buy back (a thing formerly possessed); to make payment for (a thing held or claimed by another).

*c*1425 WYNTOUN *Cron.* II. v. 365 Off Egipte al þe tenendreis He redemyt þaim agayn, And maid þaim to the kynge demayn. 1535 COVERDALE *Lev.* xxv. 25 Then shall he redeme that his brother solde. 1596 DALRYMPLE tr. *Leslie's Hist. Scot.* VI. 339 Thair was the peace maid, and with a smal soume redeimet the hail Iles. 1665 BOYLE *Occas. Refl.* IV. xvii. (1848) 268 That precious Time, which no sum..can either purchase or redeem. 1710 PRIDEAUX *Orig. Tithes* ii. 80 The Firstling of the Ass which was to be redeemed with a Lamb. 1838 W. BELL *Dict. Law Scot.* 828 A clause, whereby the granter..may, on payment of a certain sum, redeem the lands or subjects conveyed.

absol. 1651 HOBBES *Leviath.* III. xli. 262 He that redeemeth, hath no title to the thing redeemed, before the Redemption. 1838 W. BELL *Dict. Law Scot.* 828 Rights of reversion..must be exercised within forty years from the time at which the proprietor is allowed to redeem.

b. To regain, recover (an immaterial thing).

1526 *Pilgr. Perf.* (W. de W. 1531) 11 b, Who may redeme grace or recouer it whan he hath lost it? 1596 SHAKS. *1 Hen. IV*, v. iv. 48 Thou hast redeem'd thy lost opinion. 1646 J. HALL *Horæ Vac.* 82 He would redeeme (if possible) his health with the losse of halfe his Learning. 1697 DRYDEN *Virg. Georg.* III. 365 Then, to redeem his Honour at a Blow, He moves his Camp. 1865 TROLLOPE *Belton Est.* xviii. 206 If this friend..had since redeemed, or in part redeemed, her position by a second marriage.

c. To regain or recover by force. (Cf. 4.)

1666 DRYDEN *Ann. Mirab.* clxvii, The toils of war we must endure And from the injurious Dutch redeem the seas. 1742 GRAY *Propertius* ii. 54 Redeem what Crassus lost, and vindicate his name. 1810 SCOTT *Lady of L.* v. vii, The Gael, of plain and river heir, Shall with strong hand redeem his share.

2. a. To free (mortgaged property), to recover (a person or thing put in pledge), by payment of the amount due, or by fulfilling some obligation.

*c*1470 HENRY *Wallace* VI. 86 Thow sall loss a gage Quhilk neuir in erd sall be redemyt agayne. 1538 ELYOT, *Repignero*, to quite or redeme a pledge or gage. 1568 GRAFTON *Chron.* II. 856 He redemed the Marques Dorcet, and Sir John Bourchier whome he hadde left as pledges at Paris for money there before borowed. 1600 J. PORY tr. *Leo's Africa* VI. 266 They are constrained to lay their sonnes to gage, and then goe rob and rifle trauellers to redeeme them againe. 1766 BLACKSTONE *Comm.* II. 159 They will allow the mortgagor at any reasonable time to re-call or redeem his estate. 1791 J. NICHOLS in *Boswell's Johnson* an. 1784, Dr. Johnson collected a sum of money to redeem his friend's clothes, which in two days after were pawned again. 1810 SCOTT *Lady of L.* VI. xxvii, To him thy woes, thy wishes, bring. He will redeem his signet ring. 1861 M. PATTISON *Ess.* (1889) I. 42 The Crown jewels had been pledged... Edward was not in a condition to redeem them.

absol. 1818 CRUISE *Digest* (ed. 2) IV. 387 On a bill by a mortgagee, to redeem or foreclose.

fig. 1597 SHAKS. *2 Hen. IV*, II. iii. 8 My Honor is at pawne, And but my going, nothing can redeeme it.

b. To buy off, compound for (a charge or obligation) by payment or some other way.

1494 FABYAN *Chron.* v. lxxvi. 55 It was answered that they hadde redemed the sayde Trybute with the Pryce of theyr bloode. 1600 E. BLOUNT tr. *Conestaggio* 298 To the ende they should redeeme this voyage with money. 1606 G. W[OODCOCKE] *Hist. Ivstine* XXXVIII. 119 Now that there was no remedy to redeem their slauery but by resistance. 1818 CRUISE *Digest* (ed. 2) II. 59 A judgement against a purchaser of an equity of redemption, or to redeem incumbrances, &c. 1844 H. H. WILSON *Brit. India* III. 504 A guarantee fund, which..should be sufficient at the end of that term to redeem the annuity at the rate proposed.

transf. 1633 FORD *'Tis Pity* III. vi, Is there no way left to redeem my miseries?

c. To fulfil, perform (a pledge, promise, etc.).

1840 MACAULAY *Ess., Clive* (1887) 559 Clive redeemed his pledge. He..effected one of the most..difficult and salutary reforms. 1847 JAMES *Convict* viii, I call upon you to redeem that promise. 1861 M. PATTISON *Ess.* (1889) I. 38 Some consciousness of not having redeemed their engagements.

3. To ransom, liberate, free (a person) from bondage, captivity, or punishment; to save (one's life) by paying a ransom.

1432–50 tr. *Higden* (Rolls) IV. 61 Hanibal offrede to the Romanes that thei scholde redeme the Romanes in captiuite. 1500–20 DUNBAR *Poems* xxxviii. 37 The weir is gon,..The ransoun maid, the presoneris redemit. 1590 SHAKS. *Com. Err.* I. i. 8 Wanting gilders to redeeme their liues. *Ibid.* IV. iv. 86, I sent you Monie to redeeme you, By Dromio heere. 1639 MASSINGER *Unnat. Combat* v. ii, The Turkish empire offer'd for his ransom Should not redeem his life. *a*1711 KEN *Preparatives* Poet. Wks. 1721 IV. 101 The Christians, Slaves to Pagans sold, Whom he redeem'd with Gold. 1785 JEFFERSON *Writ.* (1859) I. 477 In order to justify ourselves for undertaking to redeem you, without orders. 1852 MRS. STOWE *Uncle Tom's C.* xix. 201 His mistress is going to send down money to redeem him.

refl. 1641 BAKER *Chron.* (1653) 120 One Abraham, found a Delinquent, redeems himself for seven hundred Marks. 1660 F. BROOKE tr. *Le Blanc's Trav.* 301 He had been a slave 9 years, then redeemed himself. 1849 MACAULAY *Hist. Eng.* V. I. 657 He was therefore suffered to redeem himself by giving a bond for forty thousand pounds.

b. Const. *from, out of, to.* Also with adverbs of place, as *hence, thence, home.*

1508 FISHER *Wks.* (E.E.T.S.) 228 In his tresour hous is ryches innumerable, wherwith..he may redeme all the worlde from thy pryson and captyuyte of the deuyll. 1596 SHAKS. *1 Hen. IV*, I. iii. 86 Shall our Coffers then, Be emptied, to redeeme a Traitor home? 1611 BIBLE *Deut.* vii. 8 The Lord..redeemed you out of the house of bondmen, from the hand of Pharaoh. 1686 HORNECK *Crucif. Jesus* xvii. 471 He that redeems a slave out of Turkish captivity [etc.]. 1856 OLMSTED *Slave States* 282 It was, for a long time, generally expected..that the State would thus be redeemed to freedom.

4. To rescue, save, deliver. †Also with *out.*

*c*1470 HENRY *Wallace* IX. 231 Wallace, that has rademyt Scotland. 1590 SPENSER *F.Q.* I. viii. *heading*, Faire virgin, to redeeme her deare, Brings Arthure to the fight. 1591 JAS. VI *Lepanto* Chorus Venetis, Their netts were sett about, But yet our dearest Father in Heauen, He hath redeemed vs out. 1683 WOOD *Life* 11 Apr. (O.H.S.) III. 42 The rout..laid wait for Charlet's comming out of the Castle. He therefore sends a letter to the vice-chancellor to redeem him. 1700 DRYDEN *Ovid's Met.* XII. 325 He thrusts aside The crowd of centaurs and redeems the bride. 1871 BROWNING *Balaust.* 903 The man was like some merchant who, in storm, Throws the freight over to redeem the ship.

refl. 1607 SHAKS. *Timon* IV. iii. 507 How faine would I haue hated all mankinde, And thou redeem'st thy selfe.

absol. *c*1470 HENRY *Wallace* II. 183 Bot thow redeme, na liff thai ordand me. 1591 SHAKS. *1 Hen. VI*, II. v. 88 Leuied an Army, weening to redeeme, And haue install'd me in the Diademe. 1611 BIBLE *Isa.* l. 2 Is my hande shortened at all, that it cannot redeeme?

b. Const. *from, out of, to.*

1588 SHAKS. *Tit. A.* III. i. 181 Let me redeeme my brothers both from death. 1591 SPENSER *M. Hubberd* 1331 Arise, and doo thy selfe redeeme from shame. 1611 BIBLE *Ps.* xxv. 22 Redeeme Israel, O God, out of all his Troubles. 1665 MANLEY *Grotius' Low C. Warres* 156 When nothing now could be looked for by Antwerp but extremity, behold it redeemed from that, by the Conquerours Clemency. 1697 DRYDEN *Æneid* VI. 493 Redeem from this Reproach my wand'ring Ghost. 1788 GIBBON *Decl. & F.* l. V. 225 They redeemed themselves with prayers and promises from their hands. 1819 SHELLEY *Julian* 332 My creed should have redeemed me from repenting. 1843 E. MIALL in *Nonconf.* III. 209 We trust we have said enough to redeem the voluntary principle from contempt.

c. To reclaim (land). Also const. *from.*

1721 PERRY *Daggenh. Breach* 11 Those Levels which are of large extent, and not easy to be redeemed when a Breach is made. 1820 BYRON *Mar. Fal.* II. ii. 112 Where palaces have sprung On banks redeem'd from the rude ocean's ooze. 1830 LYELL *Princ. Geol.* I. 138 We find evidence that considerable spaces were redeemed from the original ocean and converted into dry land after the chalk was formed.

5. To free from a charge or claim.

1494 FABYAN *Chron.* VI. ccvi. 217 He..redeemed the scole of Saxons, fre of all former trybute. 1790 BURKE *Fr. Rev.* 178 The clergy in the old provinces did not pay the capitation; but they had redeemed themselves at the expence of about 24 millions. 1871 FREEMAN *Norm. Conq.* (1876) IV. xviii. 210 It would almost seem as if a yearly tribute of thirty pounds..redeemed the borough from all claims.

6. Of God or Christ: To deliver from sin and its consequences.

1500–20 DUNBAR *Poems* lxx. 25 Thow, that on rude ws ransomit and redemit. 1558 GOODMAN *How to Obey* 233 Subiecte your selues whollye to God: for he hath redemed you. 1651 HOBBES *Leviath.* III. xli. 262 Our Saviour..was not King of those that he Redeemed, before hee suffered death. 1715 DE FOE *Fam. Instruct.* I. i. (1841) I. 20 God manifested in the flesh, sent from heaven to redeem a lost world. 1781 COWPER *Truth* 279 A soul redeemed demands a life of praise. 1827 POLLOK *Course T.* x, The others, who refused to be redeemed,—They stand unsanctified.

b. Const. *from, to, unto.*

*c*1460 *Hymn Virgin* 6 in *Pol. Rel. & L. Poems* (1866) 81 The hevynly kyng enteryd thy close virgynall, Man to redeme from dedely synne. 1530 PALSGR. 682/1 Christ redemed us by his passyon from our gostly enemy. 1557 N. T. (Genev.) *Rev.* v. 9 Thou wast killed, and hast redemed vs to God by thy bloude. 1567 *Gude & Godlie B.* (S.T.S.) 78 Christ als discendit to the hell, And vs redemit from that paine. 1732 LAW *Serious C.* x. (ed. 2) 141 To redeem Souls unto God, to fill Heaven with Saints. 1754 C. WESLEY *Hymns* (ed. 3) xxxii, A slave redeem'd from death, and sin.

†**7.** To obtain by purchase, to buy. *Obs.*

*c*1520 BARCLAY *Jugurth* xvii. 25 b, This Jugurth redemed of Calphurnius but onely delayng and deferinge of the warre. 1560 DAUS tr. *Sleidane's Comm.* 125 The tyme woulde come, wherin they would wyshe to have redemed his frendshyp derely. 1603 KNOLLES *Hist. Turks* (1621) 693 The Emperour must in many things yeeld to the requests of the French king, and redeme his good will. 1645 FULLER *Good Th. in Bad T.* (1841) 38 But aged folk will find it harder and dearer to redeem this the last volume than if they had been chapmen for all three at the first.

†**b.** To go in exchange for. *Obs.*

1591 SHAKS. *1 Hen. VI*, II. v. 108 Would some part of my young yeeres Might but redeeme the passage of your Age. 1602 MARSTON *Ant. & Mel.* v. Wks. 1856 I. 66 Oh! that my life..Would but redeeme one minute of his breath!

8. To save (time) from being lost.

After the N.T. passages *Eph.* v. 16 and *Col.* iv. 5, in which the Vulgate has *tempus redimentes*, rendering ἐξαγοραζόμενοι τὸν καιρόν.

1526 TINDALE *Col.* iv. 5 Walke wysely to them that are with out, and redeme the tyme. 1596 SHAKS. *1 Hen. IV*, I. ii. 241 Redeeming time, when men thinke least I will. 1742 YOUNG *Nt. Th.* II. 75 Redeem we time?—Its loss we dearly buy. 1781 COWPER *Retirement* 561 Not to redeem his time, but his estate. 1880 J. F. CLARKE *Self-Culture* iii. (1889) 78 He worked, not by faith, but by sight,..with indefatigable energy, redeeming the time.

9. Of persons: To make amends or atonement for, to compensate (an error, fault, etc.).

1526 *Pilgr. Perf.* (W. de W. 1531) 14 b, Syth man may by almesdede redeme all his synnes. 1553 EDEN *Treat. Newe Ind.* (Arb.) 18 Yf any man wound another..he redemeth thoffence. 1630 LORD *Banians* Introd., The President, was urgent with me, to redeeme their omissions. 1667 MILTON *P.L.* III. 214 Which of ye will be mortal to redeem Mans mortal crime..? *a*1715 BURNET *Own Time* II. (1724) I. 257 They will labour to redeem all that is pass'd by turning..violently against them. 1790 GIBBON *Misc. Wks.* (1814) III. 414 The naked heir might often complain, that his father's sins had been redeemed at too high a price. 1867 FREEMAN *Norm. Conq.* (1876) I. App. 765 Snorro makes him redeem former misdeeds by saving Cnut when in great danger.

†**b.** To make up to oneself for (some wrong sustained); to repay. *Obs. rare*$^{-1}$.

1596 SHAKS. *1 Hen. IV*, III. ii. 132, I will redeeme all this on Percies head.

c. To make good (a loss). *rare.*

1629 MILTON *Nativity* 153 The Babe..That on the bitter cross Must redeem our loss. 1818 JAS. MILL *Brit. India* II. V. v. 528 The English were eager to redeem by a victory the loss of Trincomalee.

10. Of qualities, actions, etc.: To make up for, compensate for, counterbalance (some defect or fault).

*a*1586 SIDNEY (J.), Extremely faulty; and yet having no good thing to redeem these. 1592 *Nobody & Someb.* in Simpson *Sch. Shaks.* (1878) 314 The wrongs that you haue seene In me, my future vertues shall redeeme. *a*1628 SIR J. BEAUMONT *Bosworth F.* 178 Then doubled haste redeems his former pause. 1788 GIBBON *Decl. & F.* xlviii. V. 27 His want of virtue was not redeemed by any superior talents. *a*1826 GIFFORD *Ford's Plays* (1827) I. Introd. 15 There is nothing to redeem the absurdity of the plot. 1874 GREEN *Short Hist.* ii. §6. 87 His bravery had redeemed much of his earlier ill-fame.

b. To save (a person or thing) *from* some defect or blot. Also without const.

1601 SHAKS. *All's Well* IV. iii. 306 He hath out-villain'd villanie so farre, that the raritie redeemes him. 1781 COWPER *Table Talk* 664 A spark, Sufficient to redeem the modern race From total night and absolute disgrace. 1833 LYTTON *Godolphin* xxxviii, His ambition made Augustus odious; his occasional forgetfulness of ambition alone redeems him. 1842 TENNYSON *Morte d'Arth.* 279 Perhaps some modern touches here and there Redeem'd it from the charge of nothingness. 1849 RUSKIN *Stones Ven.* (1874) I. xxix. 334 A blank ceiling is not to be redeemed by a decorated ventilator.

11. †**a.** To restore or bring *into* a condition or state. Also *intr.* To turn *to* a state. *Obs.*

*c*1470 HENRY *Wallace* x. 1054 For Goddis saik radeym anys to grace, And tak the croun. 1613 MIDDLETON (*title*) The Triumphs of Truth... Directed, Written, and redeem'd into Forme, from the ignorance of some former times. 1688 NORRIS *Theory Love* 203 As to the redeeming us into the ability of closing with what is discern'd best.

b. To restore, set right again. *rare.*

1575 GASCOIGNE *Flowers* Wks. 28 Hee wyll redeeme our deadly drowping state. 1814 SCOTT *Rokeby* I. xix, With his barb'd horse..Stout Cromwell has redeem'd the day.

†**12.** To gain, reach (a place). *Obs. rare*$^{-1}$.

1648 HERRICK *Hesper.*, *Oberon's Palace*, By many a crosse-Track they redeem a bank of mosse Spungie and swelling.

redeema'bility. *rare.* [f. next + -ITY.] Capability of being redeemed.

1882 in OGILVIE. **1888** GÖSCHEN *Sp. Ho. Comm.* 5 July, The Act regulating the redeemability, if he might use the word, of these stocks.

redeemable (rɪˈdiːməb(ə)l), *a.* and *sb.* [f. REDEEM *v.* + -ABLE.] **A.** *adj.* Capable of being redeemed, in various senses of the vb.

1611 COTGR., *Rachetable*, redeemable; ransomable; recouerable for money. *c* **1642** *Contra-Replicant's Compl.* 16 Nations..are not congregable, nor consultable, nor redeemable from confusion (pardon the hardnesse of words). **1768–74** TUCKER *Lt. Nat.* (1834) II. 216 To say, that we are not yet actually redeemed, but only made redeemable. **1850** HAWTHORNE *Scarlet L.* Introd. (1852) 36 His forfeited powers may be redeemable. **1892** *Sat. Rev.* 26 Mar. 349/2 Its defeat will be honourable and redeemable.

b. *spec.* Of property sold or mortgaged, bonds, stock, annuities, etc.: Capable or admitting of being repurchased or bought in again.

1646 Z. BOYD in *Zion's Flowers* (1855) App. 31/1 The said Laird wodset sold and disponed to us..the lands of the barronie..under reversion alwayes redeemable from us. **1681** STAIR *Inst. Law Scot.* II. iii. §22 (ed. 2) 205 Redeemable Rights are not so secure, because they may be evacuat by order of Redemption. **1723** *Lond. Gaz.* No. 6199/1 The Royal Demesnes which have been alienated shall be redeemable by the Crown. **1825** HONE *Every-day Bk.* I. 165 The debt which the nation had incurred.., whether redeemable or irredeemable. **1868–9** BROWNING *Ring & Bk.* VIII. 1805 The very pearls that..Pietro pawned..Redeemable by somebody. **1882** *Globe* 24 July 8/3 The same is hereby created to the amount of £600,000 as a redeemable stock.

fig. **1868** M. PATTISON *Academ. Org.* App. 341 A brilliant lecture-list is a paper issue which may, or may not, be redeemable at par.

B. *sb. pl.* Redeemable property, stocks, annuities, etc. Now *rare.*

1720 STRYPE *Stow's Surv.* (1754) II. v. xvii. 367/2 Directors..applied themselves to take in the remainder of the Annuities and Redeemables. **1727–41** CHAMBERS *Cycl.*, *Redeemables*, are lands, funds, &c. sold with a reservation of the equity of redemption. **1882** *Standard* 3 Nov. 6/3 For Perpetual Threes they ranged from 20 c. to 23 c.; for Redeemables, from 22 c. to 24 c.

Hence **re'deemableness**, capability of being redeemed; **re'deemably** *adv.*, so as to be redeemable.

1727 BAILEY vol. II, *Redeemableness.* [Hence in JOHNSON and later Dicts.] **1827** in *Law Times Rep.* (N.S.) L. 708/2 Real security for payment..heritably, but redeemably always in terms of the said bond. **1892** BRUCE *Apologetics* I. i. 6 Christianity has faith in the redeemableness of human beings.

redeemed (rɪˈdiːmd), *ppl. a.* [f. REDEEM *v.* + -ED¹.] **a.** Delivered, atoned for, etc. Also *absol.*

1535 COVERDALE *Isa.* xxxv. 9 The redemed of the Lorde shal conuerte, and come to Sion with thankesgeuinge. **1604** SHAKS. *Oth.* II. iii. 350 All Seales, and Simbols of redeemed sins. **1667** MILTON *P.L.* XI. 43 Where with mee All my redeemed may dwell in joy and bliss. **1753** C. WESLEY *Hymns for Watch-Night* ix, We..singing remove, With all the redeem'd to the Sion above. **1816** J. SCOTT *Vis. Paris* (ed. 5) p. lxiv, The shout of a redeemed and rejoicing people. **1832** LYTTON *Eugene A.* v. viii, The greater villain had escaped, the more generous and redeemed one fallen.

b. Of land: reclaimed. *rare.*

1838 H. COLMAN *1st Rep. Agric. Mass.* (Mass. Agric. Survey) 37 From one acre of redeemed meadow 4½ tons of English Hay were weighed and sold in 1836–7.

redeemer (rɪˈdiːmə(r)). Also 6 redeamer, redemer, -ar, *Sc.* redemour, redimar. [f. REDEEM *v.* + -ER¹.]

1. One who redeems, in religious sense; God or Christ regarded as saving man from sin or its effects. (Cf. REDEMPTOR.)

1432–50 tr. *Higden* (Rolls) VIII. 201 A man.. havynge woundes in his body lyke to the woundes of Criste, seyenge that he was redemer of man. **1500–20** DUNBAR *Poems* ix. 2 My King, my Lord, and my Redeemer sweit. **1540** CROMWELL in Merriman *Life & Lett.* (1902) II. 278, I pray the eternall Redemer to preserue you all in long lyffe. **1594** SHAKS. *Rich. III*, II. i. 123 The precious Image of our deere Redeemer. **1667** MILTON *P.L.* x. 61 Mans Friend, his Mediator, his design'd Both Ransom and Redeemer voluntarie. **1712** ADDISON *Spect.* No. 273 ¶9 The whole God-head..under the Three-fold Distinction of a Creator, a Redeemer and a Comforter! **1794** PALEY *Evid.* III. iv. (1817) 309 The Redeemer and the destined Judge of the human race. **1897** *Catholic Dict.* (ed. 5) 776/1 The older heresies directly impugned the Person of the Redeemer.

2. One who redeems, in other senses of the vb.

1552 HULOET, Borower or redeamer of his gage, *repignerator.* **1590** SPENSER *F.Q.* II. v. 20 He would algates with Pyrochles fight, And his redeemer chaleng'd for his foe. **1605** VERSTEGAN *Dec. Intell.* iv. 91 The redeemer of the remainder of the captiue Troyans that were in Greece. **1672** *Life & Death J. Alleine* vi. 60 He was a careful redeemer of his time. *a* **1720** SHEFFIELD (Dk. Buckhm.) *Wks.* (ed. 2) I. 340 Rome..riots in the Blood of her Redeemers.

†**3.** [tr. L. *redemptor.*] A contractor. *Obs.*

a **1610** HEALEY *Theophrastus* To Rdr., These Redeemers (so tearmed) were such as did hire scaffolds or stages, instantly to be made. *Ibid.* (1636) 47 He sendeth them..for the redeemers of the Theaters.

Hence **re'deemeress**, a female redeemer; **re'deemership**, the office of a redeemer.

1612 R. SHELDON *Serm. St. Martin's* 42 A Sauiour of their Sauiours and Sauiouresses: a Redeemer of their Redeemeresses. **1880** L. WALLACE *Ben-Hur* 501 Could any one then deny the Redeemership of the Christ?

redeeming (rɪˈdiːmɪŋ), *vbl. sb.* [-ING¹.] The action of the vb. REDEEM, in various senses.

c **1470** HENRY *Wallace* VI. 195 Quhar gret dulle is, bot redemyng agayne, Newyn off it is bot ekyng off payne. **1535** COVERDALE *Ruth* iv. 7 This was an olde custome in Israel concernynge the redemynge & chaunginge. **1575** *Galway Arch.* in *10th Rep. Hist. MSS. Comm.* App. V. 425 For redeming and ramsoning of the Illes of Aren which..[are] in mortgadge and other wyse in pledge. **1604** E. GRIMSTONE *Hist. Siege Ostend* 187 They parled about the redeeming of prisoners. **1643** MILTON *Divorce* Pref., That tends to the redeeming and restoring of none but such as are the object of compassion.

re'deeming, *ppl. a.* [f. as prec. + -ING².] That redeems, in various senses of the vb. Commonly used with *feature*, *quality*, etc.

1754 WESLEY *Hymns* (ed. 3) xlv, I shall live to prove..The length and breadth..Of thy redeeming love. **1827** POLLOK *Course T.* v. 738 Redeeming features in the face of Time. **1836** MARRYAT *Japhet* xxxi, The major, with all his faults, had redeeming qualities. **1862** STANLEY *Jewish Ch.* (1877) I. xiii. 261 The disorder of their times sets forth the more clearly the one redeeming element of trust.

redeemless (rɪˈdiːmlɪs), *a. rare.* [f. as prec. + -LESS.] Incapable of being redeemed, irrecoverable; admitting of no redemption.

1631 CHETTLE *Hoffman* v. K, [We] will change his pleasures into wretched And redeemelesse misery. **1632** QUARLES *Div. Fancies* III. No. 52 Dragd to the redeemlesse Iayle. **1812** H. & J. SMITH *Rej. Addr.*, *Archit. Atoms* 48 He is doom'd to toss In legal shipwreck and redeemless loss.

rede'fection. [RE- 5 a + DEFECTION.] Return to a country from which one has previously defected. Hence (as a back-formation) **rede'fect** *v. intr.*; **rede'fector.**

1957 *Britannica Bk. of Year* 814/1 *Redefection, n*, the returning of exiles to their native country. **1959** *Washington Post* 7 Apr. A 16/2 Many months before the Hungarian Revolution, the Communist propaganda mills began an elaborate campaign to encourage the 'redefection' of home-sick or otherwise dissatisfied or disillusioned refugees from satellite countries. *Ibid.*, The destiny that awaited these 'redefectors' was of course easily predictable. **1963** *Punch* 13 Feb. 249/3 Defected Western scientist who wishes to redefect. **1963** *Daily Progress* (Charlottesville, Va.) 7 Aug. 36/2 West German social workers concede the justice of complaints by many of the re-defectors that they are treated as 'outcasts' in West Germany. **1974** 'J. LE CARRÉ' *Tinker, Tailor* xxi. 179 What's Tarr supposed to be doing now: redefecting to us?

rede'fine, *v.* [RE- 5 a.] To define again.

1872 MINTO *Eng. Prose Lit.* Introd. 14 One of the ancient terms it might be well to revive and redefine. **1881** RUSSELL *Haigs* v. 97 A jury..to re-define the marches. **1946** *Nature* 14 Dec. 885/1 Since inequality in the number of filaments in *Spirographis* was the only positive character distinguishing it from *Sabella*, that distinction is no longer valid, and both should be united under *Sabella*, as re-defined. **1951** R. FIRTH *Elem. Social Organiz.* v. 163 Let us..re-define the notion of primitive. **1964** *Ann. Reg. 1963* 231 A Trades Union Council re-defined the duties of unions on 3 July. **1979** *Listener* 16 Aug. 212/3 The many attempts..to get round the decline of religion and worship by re-defining them in various Pickwickian senses.

So **redefi'nition**; hence **redefi'nitional** *a.*

1865 MASSON *Rec. Brit. Philos.* 106 The whole tenor of his labours was towards an assertion, purification, and redefinition of Transcendentalism. **1944** J. S. HUXLEY *On Living in Revolution* 13 A re-definition of the status of colonies. **1949** *Mind* LVIII. 146 It will be convenient to call a statement in which a word is used in a high or in a low sense a *redefinitional statement.* **1956** *Nature* 25 Feb. 370/2 Many, and perhaps all, scientific advances involve the re-definition of terms. **1970** S. L. BARRACLOUGH in I. L. Horowitz *Masses in Lat. Amer.* iv. 125 Another effect of changing technology is to force a redefinition of the traditional relations between peasants and management. **1977** *New Society* 5 May 225/1 There is a very close concern with the meanings of words and their definition or re-definition.

†**'redeful,** *a. Obs.* Forms: see REDE *sb.*¹; also 3 redesful, rætful. [f. REDE *sb.*¹ + -FUL.] Wise, prudent, full of counsel.

c **1205** LAY. 129 Hey [he] wes riche; & he wes redesful. *Ibid.* 3008 þa answærde [she] mid rætfulle worden. *Ibid.* 6537 He wes..radful and rihtwis. *c* **1320** *Cast. Love* 612 Wonderful God, and of miht, And redeful, and Fader ariht Of al þe world.

redefy, obs. form of RE-EDIFY *v.*

†**rede-ȝive.** *Obs. rare.* [OE. *rǽdȝifa, -ȝyfa* = OFris. *redgeva, -ieva*, OS. *râdgebo*, OHG. *râtgebo, -kepo* (MHG. *-gebe*), ON. *ráðgjafi*; f. *rǽd* REDE *sb.*¹ + *-ȝifa* f. *ȝifan* to GIVE.] One who gives rede or counsel; a counsellor, adviser.

1006 *Laws of Ethelred* VI. *heading*, Ðis sindon þa ȝerædnessa þe Engla rædȝifan ȝecuran and ȝecwædan. *c* **1100** *O.E. Chron.* (MS. F.) an. 1051 Stigand, þe was þes cinges ræd ȝifa & his hand prest. *c* **1205** LAY. 11615 Cleope nu to ræde þine ræd-ȝiuen wise. *Ibid.* 24888 þer men gunnen rune, his redȝeuen wise.

re'deify, *v.* [RE- 5 a.] To deify again.

1839–48 BAILEY *Festus* iv. 31 Till the soul shall be By grace redeified.

redeime, obs. Sc. form of REDEEM *v.*

redel(e, obs. forms of RIDDLE, varr. RIDEL.

redeless (ˈriːdlɛs), *a. Obs.* exc. *arch.* Forms: 1 rǽd-, 3 redleas; 3 redliese; 3–6 red-, 4–5 redeles, (4 redelees, -lis, rydelles); 5 reed-, 6 red-, rydlesse; 5 red-, 9 redeless. [OE. *rǽdléas* = OFris. *rêdlâs*, MDu. *raedloos* (Du. *radeloos*), OHG. *ratelôs* (G. *ratlos*), ON. *ráðlauss* (Sw. *rådlös*, Da. *raadløs*): see REDE *sb.*¹ and -LESS.] Devoid or destitute of counsel; *esp.* of persons, having no resource in a difficulty or emergency, not knowing what to do.

a **1000** *Daniel* 177 (Gr.) Gleaw ne wæs gumrices weard, reðe & rædleas. *c* **1122** *O.E. Chron.* (Laud MS.) an. 1009 Wæs þa swilc hit eall rædleas wære. *c* **1250** *Gen. & Ex.* 3754 'Nai, for gode', quad moyses, 'It is a song wikke and redles'. *a* **1300** *Cursor M.* 15695 O þam redles him reud sare. **13..** *E.E. Allit. P.* B. 1197 Þenne wern þo rowtes redeles in þo ryche wones. **1399** LANGL. *Rich. Redeles* I. 1 Now, Richard the redeles, reweth on ȝou-self. *c* **1450** HOLLAND *Howlat* 968 Fra rule, ressoun and richt redless I ran. **1494** FABYAN *Chron.* v. cxxviii. 110 This woman, beynge reedlesse,..went vnto hym. **1536** in Ellis *Orig. Lett.* Ser. II. II. 79, I am sokerles and as a redles createwr bot only fro the gret tr[ust I] have in the Kyngs grace. [**1883** GREEN *Conq. Eng.* vii. 339 The opponents of Eadward..dreaded that..he would be..what they afterwards called Æthelred,—a king 'redeless' or unconselled.]

absol. **12..** *Prayer to Our Lady* 27 in *O.E. Misc.* 193 Rede þe redliese þat is wið-ute rede. **13..** *E.E. Allit. P.* C. 502 Rwe on þo redles þat remen for synne.

redeli(che, varr. REDELY *adv. Obs.*

redeliver (riːdɪˈlɪvə(r)), *v.* [RE-.]

1. *trans.* To give back, return, restore:

a. a thing.

1494 FABYAN *Chron.* VII. 341 All rollys..were delyueryd vnto the sayde Iohn Mansell, the whiche he there sealyd and redelyuered them vnto the chamberleyne. **1539** TAVERNER *Gard. Wysed.* I. 31 The money shulde nat be redelyuered to the one without the other. **1592** *Nobody & Someb.* in Simpson *Sch. Shaks.* (1878) I. 311 Will you be King againe? If they agree, Ile redeliver all my royaltie. **1634** SIR T. HERBERT *Trav.* 125 The Gentleman when the storme was past, re-deliuered her her Jewels. **1693** CONGREVE *Old Bach.* III. vii, Go, and force him to redeliver you the note. **1788** JEFFERSON *Writ.* (1859) II. 438 They will re-deliver it and disavow their officer who accepted it. **1868** *Act 31 & 32 Vict.* c. 101 §142 Deeds..shall be registered..and thereafter re-delivered to the parties with certificates of due registration.

b. a person kept in custody as a hostage, etc.

1494 FABYAN *Chron.* VII. 408 He..redelyuered vnto hym all suche hostages & pledges as his brother Alphons had before tyme of hym receyued. **1580** *Reg. Privy Council Scot.* Ser. I. III. 318 Quhilk Robert, being deliverit..to him, wes alsua immediatlie redeliuerit agane be him to Elizabeth Hay. **1620–6** QUARLES *Feast for Wormes* VII, God..bespoke the whale, To redeliuer Ionah to his hand. *a* **1648** LD. HERBERT *Hen. VIII* (1683) 416 He..should desist from Hostility..and redeliver their Children.

2. To make or set free again.

1601 CHESTER *Love's Mart.* cxxiv, Iudith..that redeliuered the strong besieged Citie of Bethulia. **1623** BP. HALL *Contempl.*, *O.T.* XIX. i, His mercy..both in fore-warning, and redelivering Ahab.

3. To deliver (a message, etc.) again.

1856 FROUDE *Hist. Eng.* I. 301 The ready damsel redelivered his instructions to the world in her moments of possession. **1865** SEELEY *Ecce Homo* iii. 21 The Jewish statesman was the prophet, and his business was to redeliver to each successive generation, a proclamation [etc.].

†**4.** To repeat, report. *Obs. rare*⁻¹.

1602 SHAKS. *Ham.* v. ii. 186 *Osr.* Shall I redeliuer you e'en so? *Ham.* To this effect Sir.

Hence **rede'livering** *vbl. sb.*

1633 T. STAFFORD *Pac. Hib.* I. xii. (1810) 139 About the redelivering thereof to Her Majesties use.

So †**rede'liverage**, discharge; **rede'liverance**, †(*a*) redelivery; (*b*) a fresh deliverance; **rede'liverer**, one who delivers again.

1612 COTTA *Disc. Dang. Pract. Phys.* I. iii. 12 Neuer eating nor hauing..redeliuerage at the posternes, but ensensiblie. **1535** *Act 27 Hen. VIII*, c. 7 §5 If any of the said fosters..do deny the redeliueraunce of all such cattel. **1847** MRS. A. KERR tr. *Ranke's Hist. Servia* 340 He had effected the re-deliverance of the nation. **1816** HAZLITT *Pol. Ess.* (1819) 91 No weathercock deliverers and redeliverers of mankind.

redelivery (riːdɪˈlɪvərɪ). [RE-.] The action of giving back again, restitution; restoration; also, the action of setting free again, liberation.

1494 FABYAN *Chron.* III. 501 To ayde and assyst, euery man after his power, for yᵉ redelyuerey of their prynce agayne. **1530** RASTELL *Bk. Purgat.* III. xiii, Payment or redelyvere of the goodes is a satisfaccyon. **1577** FENTON *Gold. Epist.* 72 Iacob prayed for the redeliuerie of Beniamin. **1628** COKE *On Litt.* 161 A Repleuin which is a redeliuery of the distresse by the Sherife. **1668** CLARENDON *Vindic.* Tracts (1727) 80 They answer'd, that they had..sent Orders for the Re-delivery of it. **1768** BLACKSTONE *Comm.* III. ix. 147 A re-delivery of the pledge, or thing taken in distress, to the owner. **1831** *Act 3 & 4 Will. IV*, c. 120 §14 The expiration of such notice and the re-delivery of such licence. **1875** POSTE *Gaius* III. Comm. (ed. 2) 423 There is usually a delivery and a redelivery.

redell, variant of RIDEL *Obs.*

redels, obs. form of RIDDLE *sb.*¹

†**redely,** *adv. Obs.* Forms: 3 reade-, 4 redeliche, -lyche, redeli, 4–6 redely. *Comp.* 5 redelyer. [App. a var. of REDLY *adv.*², but metrical examples freq. indicate that the connecting *e* was pronounced. The various senses are not

easily distinguished, and in some cases (see sense 4) the form is perh. written for *redily* READILY (cf. also REDILY).]

1. Clearly, plainly, distinctly.

a **1225** *Ancr. R.* 344 Al he wule a domesdai reden ful readeliche [*v.r.* witterliche] uorte bicleopien þe mide. *a* **1300** *Cursor M.* 25852 Qua þat dees in dedli sin sal duell in bale, ..And sua we find ful redeli. **1390** GOWER *Conf.* II. 139, I schal thee redely Devise hou men therinne stonde. *c* **1400** *Beryn* 3116, I am wiser then yee ween, For there nys noon of ȝewe woot redely what I mean. **1470–85** MALORY *Arthur* VII. xxxiv, Whan she sawe syr Gareth redely in the vysage she..fell doun in a swoune.

2. Certainly, assuredly.

c **1350** *Will. Palerne* 461 Redeli bi resoun þerfore hem rette i mai mi sorwe. *c* **1384** CHAUCER *H. Fame* I. 130 Wel wyste I Hyt was of Venus redely The temple. *c* **1394** *P. Pl. Crede* 811 On his fader riȝt hand redeliche he sitteþ. *c* **1440** *Gesta Rom.* lxx. 324 (Harl. MS.) 'We ben redy', quoþ thei, 'to do this deede redely'.

3. Carefully, attentively.

1390 GOWER *Conf.* I. 93 This knyht behield hir redely. *c* **1400** *Master of Game* (MS. Digby 182) xxv, þei do drawe hem nere hym as redely and warely as þei may.

4. ? Readily, quickly.

c **1380** *Sir Ferumb.* 270 Euere suþþe y haue me raid redely to þy seruyse. *c* **1400** *Song Roland* 102 Redely the right ere he pullid from the hed. **1443** *Paston Lett.* I. 48, I sopose that I xal redelyer have tydyngys from yow herr dan I xulde have ther. *c* **1489** CAXTON *Sonnes of Aymon* ii. 64 She felle doun all in a swoune, and Reynawde toke her vppe redely. **1550** MARBECK (*title*) A Concordance, that is to saie a Worke wherein..ye maie redely finde any worde conteigned in the Whole Bible.

† **redelyng**, app. a var. of *radelyng* RATLIN.

1466 *Mann. & Househ. Exp.* (Roxb.) 347 Paid to Thomas Fuller, for xvij. li. of redelynge yerne, xij.*d*... Paid for the lynenge of the toppe armynge and for the toppe maste xx*d*.

redem, obs. form of REDEEM *v.*

rede'mand, *sb. rare*⁻⁰. [RE-.] The act of redemanding, 'a demanding back again'.

1828–32 in WEBSTER.

redemand (riːdɪ'mɑːnd, -æ-), *v.* [RE-. Cf. F. *redemander* (12th c.).]

1. *trans.* **a.** To demand the return of (a thing).

1576 FLEMING *Panopl. Epist.* 18 That the expences are.. also redemaunded and taken away. **1603** KNOLLES *Hist. Turks* (1621) 1223 Which places hee had oftentimes by as just right redemanded, as they were by unjust forces usurped. **1656** EARL MONM. tr. *Boccalini's Advts. fr. Parnass.* I. li. (1674) 66 [He] re-demanded the moneys which he had given him. **1711** W. KING tr. *Naude's Ref. Politics* iv. 140 He is always wavering,..relinquishes what he sought, then redemands what he relinquished. **1818** COLEBROOKE *Obligations* 98 If payment be made before-hand,..it cannot be redemanded and recovered. **1861** THORNBURY *Turner* (1862) I. 399 He declares that Turner after-wards re-demanded it, and charged two guineas for the loan.

b. To demand again.

1849 LYTTON *K. Arthur* II. cxxi, Once more forsake the throng Call childhood back, and redemand the song. **1883** J. PARKER *Apost. Life* II. 332 All the wondrous works of Jesus Christ were redemanded by Nature.

2. To ask or inquire again.

a **1572** KNOX *Hist. Ref.* Wks. 1846 I. 176 The Cardinall askyne, 'Who calles?' he answeris, 'My name is Leslye'. He re-demandis, 'Is that Normond?' **1613** SIR E. SACKVILLE in *Guard.* No. 133 ¶3, I redemanded if he would request his life.

Hence **rede'manded** *ppl. a.*, **rede'manding** *vbl. sb.*

1611 COTGR., *Repetition*,..a redemanding. **1859** LOWELL *Biglow P.* Ser. I. Introd. (1866) 21 Rewards..More solid than the redemanded praise With which the world be-ribbons later days.

So **rede'mandable** *a.*, that may be redemanded (Webster 1828–32).

redeme, obs. form of REDEEM *v.*

redemer, obs. form of REDEEMER.

rede'mise, *sb.* [RE-.] *Law.* The retransfer of land to one who has demised it.

1797 *Encycl. Brit.* (ed. 3) V. 748/2 *Demise* and *Redemise*, denote a conveyance where there are mutual leases made from one to another of the same land, or something out of it. **1828–32** in WEBSTER.

So **rede'mise** *v.*, to demise (land) back again.

1828–32 in WEBSTER (citing *Encyc.*).

rede'molish, *v.* [RE- 5 a. Cf. F. *redémolir* (Cotgr.).] *trans.* To demolish again.

1611 COTGR., *Redemolir*, to redemolish, resubuert, ouer-throw againe. **1736** LD. HERVEY *Mem.* I. 140 Bragging that their industry had re-demolished Dunkirk.

† **re'demp**, *v. Obs.*⁻¹ [f. next.] To redeem.

1527 W. KNIGHT in Ellis *Orig. Lett.* Ser. I. I. 281 The kyng hath sayde that in case Philip be taken by ennymyse his Highnesse will redempe hym and pay his rawnesome.

† **re'dempt**, *pa. pple.* and *ppl. a. Obs. rare.* [ad. L. *redempt-us*, pa. pple. of *redimĕre* to REDEEM.] Redeemed.

a **1450** *Mankind* 798 (Brandl) Aryse, my precyose redempt sone; ȝe be to me full dere. *c* **1500** *Everyman* 548, I cum with Knowlege for my redemcyon Redempt with herte and full of contrycyon.

So † **re'dempt** *v. Obs. rare*⁻⁰.

1623 COCKERAM, *Redempted*, redeemed.

redempteur, obs. variant of REDEMPTOR.

re'demptible, *a.* [ad. L. type **redemptibilis*: see REDEMPT and -IBLE.] Redeemable.

1882 in OGILVIE.

re'demptine. [f. REDEMPT-OR + -INE.] Redemptoristine.

1889 *Cath. Household* 29 June 7/2 Miss D...was received into the Order of the Redemptines.

redemption (rɪ'dɛm(p)ʃən). Also 4–6 -cio(u)n, -cyo(u)n, etc., 5–6 redemcion, 6–7 redemtion. [a. F. *rédemption* (12th c. in Littré), or ad. L. *redemptiōn-em*, n. of action f. *redimĕre* to REDEEM.]

1. a. Deliverance from sin and its consequences by the atonement of Jesus Christ.

a **1340** HAMPOLE *Psalter* xx. 1 Swa þat we be parcenel in his redempcioun. **1340** —— *Pr. Consc.* 7251 'Ffor in hell', he says, 'es na redempcyoune'. *c* **1380** WYCLIF *Sel. Wks.* II. 161 God ȝaf his sone to make it free, for noon oþer redempcioun was ynowȝ for mannis synne. **1426** AUDELAY *Poems* 55 In tyme of his passcion, Here fore our redemcion, His blesful blod he bled. **1509** FISHER *Funeral Serm. C'tess Richmond* Wks. (1876) 307 Byleuynge that he..came in to this worlde for the redempcyon of synners. **1593** SHAKS. *Rich. II*, III. ii. 129 Oh Villains, Vipers, damn'd without redemption. **1603** —— *Meas. for M.* V. i. 29 You bid me seeke redemption of the diuell. **1667** MILTON *P.L.* XII. 408 Proclaming Life to all who shall believe In his redemption. **1777** BLAIR *Serm.* (1810) I. v. 83 This was the hour in which Christ.. accomplished our eternal redemption. **1845** S. AUSTIN *Ranke's Hist. Ref.* III. 191 The doctrine of original sin, on which the whole scheme of redemption rests. **1884** J. TAIT *Mind in Matter* (1892) 228 Miracles and prophecy..bore directly or indirectly on one point,—redemption.

b. *Year of Redemption* = ANNO DOMINI.

1513 MORE in Grafton *Chron.* (1568) II. 756 The .ix. day of Aprill, the year of our redemption .1463. **1599** SHAKS. *Hen. V*, I. ii. 60 Who died within the yeere of our Redemption, Foure hundred twentie six. **1835** W. IRVING *Conq. Spain* i, Such was the state of Spain when, in the year of Redemption 701, Witiza was elected to the Gothic throne.

2. a. The action of freeing a prisoner, captive, or slave by payment; ransom.

c **1374** CHAUCER *Troylus* IV. 80 (108) Ye haue now kaught & fetered in preson Troians y-nowe, and yf youre wille be, My chyld with on may haue redempcion. **1432–50** tr. *Higden* (Rolls) IV. 21 Pirrus..sende to Rome his prisoners withowte eny redempcion. **1460** CAPGRAVE *Chron.* (Rolls) 269 That thei schuld gader a certeyn summe for her lordis redempcion. **1560** DAUS tr. *Sleidane's Comm.* 219 b, They shoulde bee slayne withoute redemption, whersoever they were found. **1604** SHAKS. *Oth.* I. iii. 138 Of being taken by the Insolent Foe, And sold to slauery. Of my redemption thence. **1671** MILTON *Samson* 1482 For his redemption all my Patrimony, If need be, I am ready to forgo. **1709** STEELE *Tatler* No. 105 ¶2 Which purchased his Redemption out of the Hands of the Bailiffs. **1785** JEFFERSON *Corr.* Wks. 1859 I. 477 Mr. Adams..and myself have agreed to authorize the bearer hereof..to treat for your redemption. **1855** MILMAN *Lat. Chr.* III. v. (1864) II. 47 The redemption of captives —that is the repurchase of slaves in order to restore them to freedom—is esteemed an act of piety.

b. *Jewish Law.* The ceremony of redeeming the eldest son by an offering (Numb. xviii. 15).

14.. in *Tundale's Vis.* (1843) 132 Lyke as the custom of the law was Sche mekely made hys redempcion. **1892** ZANGWILL *Childr. Ghetto* I. 83 The ceremony of the Redemption of her grandson.

3. a. The action of freeing, delivering, or restoring in some way. *without* or *past redemption*: without or beyond the possibility of deliverance, recovery, or restoration.

c **1470** HENRY *Wallace* VIII. 1261 The flour of France, withoutyn redempcioun, Throuch that foull deid, was brocht to confusioun. **1650** H. BROOKE *Conserv. Health* 175, I shall for the redemption of such as are deceived by it [etc.]. **1769** BURKE *Late State Nation* Wks. II. 95 The great ground-work of his plan for the national redemption. **1818** BYRON *Ch. Har.* IV. cxlv, Rome and her Ruin [are] past Redemption's skill. **1840** DICKENS *Barn. Rudge* xxxii, Though our contract is at an end, and broken past all redemption. **1851** GALLENGA *Italy* 441 The battle of Custoza..might have marked the day of redemption for Italy.

b. Improving (of time); reclaiming (of land).

1755 YOUNG *Centaur* ii. Wks. 1757 IV. 147 Have you never heard, my good Ladies, of the redemption of time? **1862** D. WILSON *Preh. Man* ii. 37 Spots mapped off for redemption from river or lake.

c. That which redeems; a redeeming feature.

1860 FORSTER *Gr. Remonstr.* 72 The improvement in literary studies and pursuits which was one of the redemptions of his reign. **1863** COWDEN CLARKE *Shaks. Char.* v. 128 Roderigo has so much of redemption in him, that we commiserate his weakness.

4. a. The action of redeeming oneself from punishment; way or means of doing this; atonement made for a crime or offence.

1553 DK. NORTHUMBLD. in *Four C. Eng. Lett.* (1880) 22 Alas, my lord is my cryme so heynous as noe redemcion but my blood can washe awaye the spottes thereof? **1603** SHAKS. *Meas. for M.* II. iv. 113 Lawfull mercie Is nothing kin to fowle redemption. **1647** N. BACON *Disc. Govt. Eng.* I. xxxix. (1739) 59 If the circumstances favoured the Delinquent, he was admitted to redemption of Life or Member, by Fine. **1800** *Asiatic Ann. Reg., Misc. Tr.* 335/1 If he be able to purchase the redemption of his crime, that redemption shall be facilitated. **1873** BROWNING *Red Cott. Nt.-cap* III. 301 Vanity Was ended: its redemption must begin—And, certain, would continue.

† **b.** A recompense. *Obs. rare*⁻¹.

1625 BACON *Ess., Envy* (Arb.) 512 They..thinke other Mens Harmes a Redemption of their owne Sufferings.

5. The fact of obtaining a privileged status, or admission to a society, by means of purchase.

c **1500** in Arnolde *Chron.* (1811) 89 That noo man com in to bee made free of this Citee by redempcion wythout he bee borne under the dominacion of our Soueraigne Lorde the Kyng. **1606** in *Vicary's Anat.* (1888) App. iii. 162 It is ordered that [he].. shalbe made free of this Cittye by Redempcion in the Companie of barborsurgeons. **1884** *Times* 28 June 6 It is only possible to become a member of a Livery Company by patrimony, by apprenticeship, or by redemption, which last means by purchase or gift.

6. The action of clearing off a recurring liability or charge by payment of a single sum.

1494 FABYAN *Chron.* VI. ccvi. 218 Canutus..redemed the scole of Saxons, fre of all former trybute graunted..; which redempcyon of trybute..was called Rome Scot. **1523** *Churchw. Acc. St. Giles', Reading* 19 Paid to Thomas Burard for redemption of the new rents vij[li]. **1844** H. H. WILSON *Brit. India* III. 500 Whatever the amount might be, at the period fixed by Parliament for the redemption of the annuity, it should be applied in or towards that redemption. **1867** FREEMAN *Norm. Conq.* (1876) I. App. 751 Florence describes his alms and his redemption of the tolls by which pilgrims were troubled.

7. The action of redeeming or buying back from another, in various applications. *equity of redemption*: see EQUITY 5 b.

a **1548** HALL *Chron., Hen. VIII* 109 b, The tributes and other paimentes, whiche he should paie to the kyng of Englande, for redempcion of Tornay. **1563–4** *Reg. Privy Council Scot.* I. 262 [He] grantis the saidis landis..to be lauchfullie redemit..and oblissis him to warrand the said redemptioun. **1611** BIBLE *Lev.* xxv. 24 In all the land of your possession, ye shall grant a redemption for the land. **1697** POTTER *Antiq. Greece* III. xi. (1715) 100 Whence it appears, that Redemption of the Dead was practis'd in those Days. **1734** *Act 7 Geo. II*, c. 20 (*title*) An Act for the more easy Redemption and Foreclosure of Mortgages. **1752** FIELDING *Amelia* Wks. 1775 X. 20 The first thing, after redemption of the coat..was to supply himself with snuff. **1838** W. BELL *Dict. Law Scot.* 829 The order of redemption is prescribed by the clause of redemption in the redeemable right. **1876** GEO. ELIOT *Dan. Der.* xxxiv, This crude young gentleman, who apparently supposed that redemption was a satisfaction to pawnbrokers.

8. *attrib.*, as *redemption fee*, *money*, *work*; **redemption yield**, the yield of a stock calculated as a percentage of the redemption price and allowing for any capital gain or loss which that price represents relative to the current price.

1535 COVERDALE *Num.* iii. 49 Then toke Moses yᵉ redempcion money. **1828–40** TYTLER *Hist. Scot.* (1864) I. 145 Levying from the towns and monasteries..large sums of redemption money. **1859** G. BUSH *On Swedenborg's Doctr.* (1875) 42 The sum total of these conquests constituted his redemption-work. **1897** MARY KINGSLEY *W. Africa* 498 Without claiming the redemption fees as they become due. **1948** G. CROWTHER *Outl. Money* (ed. 2) ii. 74 If the price of this bond in the market is 101, that means that for every £101 invested now, the purchaser will get £6 in interest, but he will also lose £1 in capital value—that is to say, the 'redemption yield' is 2½ per cent per annum. **1972** *Daily Tel.* 2 Dec. 24 The redemption yield is defined as that rate of interest at which the present price is made to equal the present discounted value of the future stream of interest payments plus the present discounted value of the eventual capital repayment. The rate of interest used for the purpose of discounting these future interest and capital values is the redemption yield rate of interest itself. **1973** *Ibid.* 7 Mar. 21 At the issue price of £99¾ the 1980 stock will give a running yield of 9·05 p.c. and a gross redemption yield of 9·10 p.c. to 1980.

Hence **re'demptional** *a.*, of or belonging to redemption.

1840 DE QUINCEY *Essenes* Wks. 1859 X. 261 There might still have remained the great redemptional and mediatorial functions for Christ. **1854** *Tait's Mag.* XXI. 174 Not only is all religion redemptional in its principal interests.., but it is the only redemptional attribute.

† **re'demptionary.** *Obs. rare*⁻¹. [f. prec. + -ARY.] One who enters a society by purchase (cf. REDEMPTION 5).

1589 PECKHAM in Hakluyt *Voy.* III. 176 None..are to be admitted in the seid society, but as Redemptionaries, which will be very chargeable.

redemptioner (rɪ'dɛm(p)ʃənə(r)). [-ER¹.]

1. *U.S.* An emigrant who received his passage to America on the condition that his services there should be disposed of by the master or owners of the vessel, until the passage-money and other expenses were repaid out of his earnings.

1775 *Rivington's New York Gazett.* 30 Mar. 4/2 To be disposed of, for a term of years, a number of Servants and Redemptioners, just arrived from England. **1796** W. PRIEST *Trav.* (1802) 145 The law respecting the redemptioners are very severe: they were formed for the English convicts before the revolution. **1805** JEFFERSON *Writ.* (1830) IV. 38 With respect to the German redemptioners, you know I can do nothing. **1864** SALA in *Daily Tel.* 29 Sept., Passengers to the States may be brought out, not as free emigrants, but as 'redemptioners', owing their passage-money to the company, who are to have a lien on their earnings until this debt is discharged.

2. One who clears off a charge by redemption.

1897 *Board Agric. Leaflet* No. 39 No fee is payable by a redemptioner for such information.

re'demptionist. [f. as prec. + -IST.] † **a.** A redeemer. *Obs.* **b.** = RANSOMER 2 a.

1647 SALTMARSH *Spark. Glory* 162 The generall Redemptionist. **1866** *Chambers' Encycl.*, *Redemptionist*, one of the names of an order of monks devoted to the redemption of Christian captives from slavery.

re'demptionless, *a.* [f. as prec. + -LESS.] Incapable of redemption.

1846 J. BROWN *Let.* 12 Aug. (1912) 93 By the bye, is not he a redemptionless devil that Sir Robert? **1866** *Daily News* 12 Feb. 6/3 The persons who have been foremost in proclaiming the redemptionless character of the Jamaica labourers are principally those who have had little intercourse or practical acquaintance with them.

redemptive (rɪ'dɛm(p)tɪv), *a.* [ad. L. type **redemptīv-us*: see REDEMPT and -IVE.] Tending to redeem, redeeming.

1647 M. HUDSON *Div. Right Govt.* Introd. 7 Redemptive Divine Right is that which is grounded upon the will of God concerning the manifestation of his mercy in the preservation of Man-kind. **1825** COLERIDGE *Aids Refl.* (1848) I. 250 The Redemptive Act, as the transcendant cause of salvation. **1883** H. DRUMMOND *Nat. Law in Spir. W.* xii. (1884) 414 These silent and patient processes..are the early stages in the redemptive work.

redemptivism (rɪ'dɛm(p)tɪvɪz(ə)m). *rare.* [f. prec. + -ISM.] The desire to redeem. So **re'demptivist** *a.*

1924 C. MACKENZIE *Heavenly Ladder* xxiii. 289 You are obsessed by redemptivist phantoms... I perceive you the victim of an absurd idea that you have to save other people. Even your own God Jesus Christ made no attempt to do that. *Ibid.* 290 You misunderstand what you call my redemptivism... I regard myself as an automatic purveyor of Almighty God's bounteous Grace by administrating His Sacraments.

redemptor (rɪ'dɛm(p)tə(r)). Now *rare.* Also 5 -ure, 5-6 -our, 6 *Sc.* -eur. [a. or ad. F. *rédempteur* (OF. *redemptor*, Godef.), or L. *redemptor*, agent-n. f. *redimĕre* to REDEEM.]

†**1.** = REDEEMER 1. *Obs.*

[**1377** LANGL. *P. Pl.* B. xi. 201 And after his resurreccioun *Redemptor* was his name.] *c* **1400** *26 Pol. Poems* (E.E.T.S.) 140/589, I wote ryght well that myn redemptour Lyueth yet. **1483** CAXTON *Cato* D iij, Hit was a moche precious yefte whyche our redemptour gaue to us. *c* **1510** BARCLAY *Mirr. Gd. Manners* (1570) D v, That is a speciall grace of our dere redemptour. **1512** *Helyas* in Thoms *Prose Rom.* (1828) III. 38 The savyour and redemptor Jesu Chryst. **1600** J. HAMILTON *Facile Tract.* in *Cath. Tract.* (S.T.S.) 223 For the loue ye aucht to the honor of your redempteur. **1634** *T. Norton's tr. Calvin's Inst.* Table Script. Quot., The Redemptor shall come to Sion.

2. A redeemer, in other senses of the word. *rare.*

1880 L. WALLACE *Ben-Hur* v. xi. 347 And..now, O redemptor of the flesh of swine, let us on. **1896** *Speaker* 18 July 53/2 Its redeemability converts the redemptors into rent-chargers.

3. = TRINITARIAN *sb.* 1.

1880 MRS. OLIPHANT *Cervantes* ii. 25 The friar, Jorge Olivar, one of the Brothers of Mercy, and official Redemptor for the province of Aragon.

redemptorial (rɪdəm(p)'tɔərɪəl), *a. rare.* [f. as REDEMPTORY *a.* + -AL^1.] = REDEMPTORY *a.*

1900 R. W. BARBOUR *Thoughts* 6 He pleads His own crucified person. His very redemptorial existence is His plea.

Redemptorist (rɪ'dɛm(p)tərɪst). [ad. F. *rédemptoriste*: see REDEMPTOR and -IST.]

1. A member of the Roman Catholic Congregation of the Most Holy Redeemer, founded at Naples in 1732 by St. Alphonsus Liguori, and devoted chiefly to work among the poor.

1835 J. B. ROBERTSON in *Schlegel's Philos. Hist.* I. p. xlii, In conjunction with..some of the Redemptorists—a most able, amiable, and exemplary body of ecclesiastics at Vienna—he established in 1820, a religious and political journal. **1840** J. R. HOPE-SCOTT *Diary* in R. Ornsby *Mem. J. R. Hope-Scott* (1884) I. xii. 227 Viewed as instruments of the Church, he thinks that most of the orders are now of little use. Those of the Jesuits and Redemptorists, with one or two more of the same kind as the latter, he conceives to be the only effectual orders. **1863** SALA *Capt. Dangerous* III. ix. 287, I did as the good Redemptorist bade me. **1897** *Catholic Dict.* (ed. 5) 654/2 In his third edition Ballerini replies to the charges of laxity which the Redemptorists made against him. **1915** *Encycl. Relig. & Ethics* VIII. 68/1 The Redemptorists have remained sturdily faithful to their primary work of giving missions and retreats. **1975** *Church Times* 27 June 14/5 It [*sc.* the Roman clerical collar] is still worn by Redemptorists, Passionists and Oratorians.

2. *attrib.* or as *adj.* Belonging to the Order of the Redeemer.

1863 SALA *Capt. Dangerous* III. ix. 283 The Blessed Old Man that was a Redemptorist Father appeared. **1876** TREVELYAN *Macaulay* (1880) I. 73 A religious house of the Redemptorist Order.

Hence **Redempto'ristine**, a member of a recluse and contemplative order of nuns, associated with the Redemptorists (see quot. 1884); also *attrib.* or as *adj.*

1884 *Catholic Dict.* 711/1 The nuns.., commonly called Redemptoristines, form the Order of the Most Holy Redeemer, as distinguished from the Congregation of missionaries. **1886** T. LIVIUS tr. *Saintrain's Our Lady of Perpetual Succour* (ed. 3) I. xxiv. 211 In the public chapel attached to the convent of the Redemptoristine Nuns, St. Alphonsus, Dublin, the Holy Picture has a beautiful shrine. **1931** *Tablet* 8 Aug. 183/2 The Redemptoristine nuns from Clapham went into their new home at Chudleigh in 1925. *Ibid.*, The Redemptoristines are established also in a number of convents in Canada, Italy, Austria, France, Belgium, Spain, Holland and Brazil. **1969** *Observer* (Colour Suppl.) 13 Apr. 54/1 *Redemptoristines.* Founded by St Alphonsus Liguori at Amalfi, Italy, in 1731.

redemptory (rɪ'dɛm(p)tərɪ), *a.* Now *rare.* [ad. L. type **redemptōrius*: see REDEMPT and -ORY.] Of or pertaining to redemption; redemptive.

1598 CHAPMAN *Iliad* I. 94 Till to her loved sire The black-ey'd damsell be resign'd; no redemtorie hire Tooke for her freedome. **1602** T. FITZHERBERT *Apol.* 61 That redemptory & absolut sacrifice, which was to be offred but once. **1675** BROOKS *Golden Key* Wks. 1867 V. 255 Λύτρον signifies a redemptory price, a valuable rate. **1886** H. JAMES *Bostonians* III. III. xxxvii. 126 A woman could live on persistently, clinging to a great, vivifying, redemptory idea.

redemptour, obs. form of REDEMPTOR.

redemptress (rɪ'dɛm(p)trɪs). [After REDEMPTOR.] A female redeemer; = next.

1865 [see RESTORESS].

re'demptrice. *rare.* [ad. L. *redemptrīcem*, *-trix*, fem. of *redemptor*.] A female redeemer.

1755 T. H. CROKER *Orl. Fur.* IV. xlii, Well he knows, She had been solely his redemptrice [It. *redentrice*] kind.

redempture, obs. f. REDEMPTOR.

redemtion, obs. f. REDEMPTION.

redemyte, var. REDIMITE *a.* and *v. Obs.*

reden, obs. f. READ *v.*, REDAN, REDE *v.*^{1}, obs. pa. pple. RIDE *v.*

re-'denigrate, *v.* [RE- 5 a.] To blacken or darken again.

1664 POWER *Exp. Philos.* I. 74 If you super-add a few drops of oyl of Tartar..it re-denigrates it again. **1721** BAILEY, *Redenigrate*, to recover in Blackness.

redens, redent, obs. forms of REDAN.

†**re'dented**, *ppl. a. Obs. rare*$^{-1}$. [f. *redent* (see REDAN) + -ED^2.] Formed like the teeth of a saw; dented, indented.

1753 CHAMBERS *Cycl. Supp.* s.v. *Redens*, The parapet of the corridor also is frequently redented, or carried on in the way of redens.

rede'ploy, *v.* [RE- 5 a.] **a.** *intr.* To carry out redeployment; to change employment to increase overall efficiency. **b.** *trans.* To move (troops, labour, materials, etc.) from one area of activity to another.

1945 *Sunday Times* 27 May 7 Re-deploying to crush Japan. **1945** *Sat. Rev. Lit.* (U.S.) 16 June 12/1 Others stated that the plan to redeploy troops from Europe was a great mistake. **1948** *Picture Post* 3 Apr. 11/2 Labour forces had to be redeployed. **1949** *Manch. Guardian Weekly* 28 Apr. 3/3 A very extensive proportion of this industry could be redeployed within six months. **1958** *Times Lit. Suppl.* 22 Aug. 473/2 Organized labour cannot be induced to redeploy over the day-shift, thus releasing labour for a second day (and sometimes a third night) shift. **1966** *Hansard Commons* 20 June 628 Action is needed equally to deal with the problem of internal demand, public and private, and to redeploy resources, both manpower and capacity, according to national priorities, and check inflation. **1970** *New Society* 5 Mar. 389/1 The unification of hitherto separate services.. should make it easier to recruit and redeploy social service staff. **1971** *Brit. Jrnl. Industrial Relations* July 160 Some believed that there was a vast pool of under-used labour and that a short sharp burst of deflation would force companies to release surplus manpower which could then be redeployed into the essential export industries. **1980** *Times* 29 Feb. 19 Hawker's philosophy since aerospace nationalization has been to redeploy its resources into the electrical and mechanical engineering business it knows well.

Hence **rede'ployable** *a.*, available for redeployment, able to be redeployed.

1946 I. SHAW in *New Yorker* 2 Feb. 24/2 'I'm redeployable,' Olson sang.

rede'ployment. [RE- 5 a.] Movement or reallocation (of troops, labour, resources, etc.); reorganization for greater efficiency; transfer to alternative employment.

1945 *Time* 12 Feb. 17/2 The new blueprint for U.S. redeployment calls for an army of 6,500,000 men to defeat Japan. **1945** *Newsweek* 28 May 28/3 The redeployment of three and four star generals from the European theater. **1949** *Manch. Guardian Weekly* 28 Apr. 3/3 Only by redeployment of labour can higher wages, greater productivity, and lower costs be achieved. **1955** *Times* 7 July 13/1 The growth of deposits had been checked (partly, as with Martins, by the redeployment of funds by large customers). **1959** *Economist* 3 July 42/1 Redeployment of liquid resources in this way, incidentally, can also keep directors and managers in the powerful style to which they are accustomed. **1966** *Daily Tel.* 2 Nov. 1/2 Temporary bridging finance for house purchase also has a special importance at a time when the redeployment of labour needs to be encouraged. **1970** *New Scientist* 24 Sept. 613/2 If they all have similar reserves of manpower, there should soon be no shortage for the Soviet Union's developing economy. The question may then be one of retraining and redeployment. **1974** *Financial Times* 20 Mar. 18/8 If they cancel the entire venture now, some 21,000 workers on the programme in Britain and a similar number in France will face either redundancy or redeployment.

rede'posit, *sb.* [RE- 5 a.] A new depositing.

1875 *7th Rep. Dep. Kpr. Irel.* 6 This duty, involving much detail of arrangement, separation, and redeposit.

rede'posit, *v.* [RE- 5 a.] To deposit again. Also *absol.*

1856 MRS. GORE *Life's Lessons* I. vii. 112 After..he had re-deposited the poor cripple on her couch. **1862** ANSTED *Channel Isl.* II. xi. (ed. 2) 292 The water..had slowly re-deposited lime. **1889** G. FINDLAY *Eng. Railway* 8 The Bill was re-deposited in the ensuing session of Parliament. **1905** *Westm. Gaz.* 8 Feb. 9/3 The Bill which the Board proposes to redeposit in Parliament. **1963** A. J. HALL *Textile Sci.* vi. 282 At the same time that soil is passing out of the fabric into the main bulk of detergent liquor some of this soil is passing from this liquor into the fabric and there being re-deposited on the fibres. **1975** *New Yorker* 17 Nov. 37/2 'I never heard of a bank saying "Do not redeposit",' she said.

Hence **rede'posited** *ppl. a.*; **rede'positing** *vbl. sb.*; **redepo'sition.**

1863 LYALL *Antiq. Man* 49 Changes..brought about by the deposition, removal, and redeposition of gravel, sand, and fine sediment. **1905** *Westm. Gaz.* 8 Feb. 9/3 The Board had decided to take an early opportunity of redepositing their bill. **1946** F. E. ZEUNER *Dating Past* vi. 169 Re-deposited Younger Loess (probably result of ploughing), with Neolithic. **1965** G. V. WILLIAMS *Econ. Geol. N.Z.* xix. 334/2 These rocks consist of conglomerates, black shales, re-deposited sandstones, mudstones and pseudo-tillites. **1977** *Antiquaries Jrnl.* LVII. 235 There are tips of redeposited sands and loams..associated with features in the timber building sequence.

†**'reder.** *Obs. rare.* [f. REDE *v.*^{1} + -ER^1; cf. OFris. *redir*, OHG. *râtiri* (MHG. *râtære*, G. *rater*).] An adviser, counsellor.

1340 *Ayenb.* 184 Ac loke..uram kueade rederes, and ne akse no red at foles. **1534** WHITINTON *Tullyes Offices* I. (1540) 1 Thou..must needs habounde in preceptes and rules of phylosophye..for the synguler authoritie of thy reder.

reder(e, obs. forms of READER.

rederi'vation. *rare*$^{-1}$. [RE- 5 a.] A second derivation, †drawing or leading off.

a **1631** DONNE *Serm.* cxxi. V. 138 In each of these three there is a Rederivation into three Branches.

rede'rive, *v.* [RE- 5 a.] To derive again.

1968 P. A. P. MORAN *Introd. Probability Theory* vii. 293 It has probably been independently rederived by more writers than almost any other result. **1968** C. G. KUPER *Introd. Theory Superconductivity* xiv. 237 Thus all the results of Chapter 12 may be rederived.

redescend (riːdɪ'sɛnd), *v.* [RE- 5 a. Cf. F. *redescendre* (13th c.).] To descend again:

a. *intr.* (Cf. DESCEND 1-9.)

1597 MIDDLETON *Wisd. Solomon* vi. 1 Forthwith the voice of God did redescend. **1650** HOWELL *Lett.* II. liii. 67 O let them redescend, and still My soul with holy raptures fill. **1766** *Compl. Farmer* s.v. *Sap*, Through these it re-descends to the root, and thence to the earth again. **1821** SHELLEY *Prometh. Unb.* III. i. 24 That fatal child..Who waits..To redescend and trample out the spark. **1868** LOCKYER *Guillemin's Heavens* (ed. 3) 459 The sea..by degrees re-descends to its point of departure.

b. *trans.* (Cf. DESCEND 11.)

1819 W. TAYLOR in *Monthly Mag.* XLVII. 398 He was obliged to re-descend the pulpit. **1836-7** SIR W. HAMILTON *Metaph.* xxxv. (1859) II. 295 Having reached the pinnacle of generalisation, we may redescend the ladder.

Hence **rede'scending** *ppl. a.*

1883 STEVENSON *Treas. Isl.* III. xiv, Only the rustle of the redescending birds..disturbed the langour of the afternoon.

So **rede'scent**, a fresh descent.

1836-9 TODD *Cycl. Anat.* II. 755/1 Such pressure will be sufficient to prevent a re-descent.

rede'scribe, *v.* [RE- 5 a.] To describe again.

1871 BROWNING *Pr. Hohenst.* 302, I can redescribe..where some segment silver-true Stays clear. **1897** *Allbutt's Syst. Med.* IV. 28 Urochrome first described by Dr. Thudichum in 1864 and recently..redescribed by Dr. A. E. Garrod.

So **rede'scription.**

1884 GOODE *Nat. Hist. Aquat. Anim.* 337 The numerous redescriptions to which almost all widely distributed forms have been subjected.

redesful, variant of REDEFUL *a. Obs.*

rede'sign, *v.* [RE- 5 a.] To design again.

1891 MORRIS in Mackail *Life* (1899) II. 262 The t does not look well: I shall have to re-design it. **1895** *Westm. Gaz.* 18 Feb. 2/3 We want our stamps re-designed. **1914** *Jrnl. Inst. Electr. Engineers* LIII. 94/2 It would be safe to re-design on a scientific basis all the cables mentioned in the British Standard Specification. **1930** G. B. SHAW *Apple Cart* p. xxix, Wren was not content to redesign and rebuild St Paul's: he wanted to redesign London as well. **1969** *Jane's Freight Containers 1968-69* 185/1 This berth was re-designed and re-constructed to handle the London-Gothenburg passenger, car and cargo service of the England Sweden Line. **1973** *Sci. Amer.* Apr. 17/1 A further need is to redesign medical education so that physicians and other health personnel are trained and challenged to provide primary care and to deal with the chronic diseases.

Hence **rede'signed** *ppl. a.*, **rede'signing** *vbl. sb.*

1943 *Mind* LII. 63 Though minor improvements and modifications of traditional language and its categories are permissible, any radical 'redesigning' of them must necessarily distort reality and be ultimately unintelligible. **1946** *Nature* 21 Dec. 897/2 Many of the re-designed features were not amenable to accepted strength computation methods. **1978** *Dumfries Courier* 20 Oct. 10/3 (*caption*) The 900 series has a 5 cm. longer wheelbase and a completely redesigned chassis.

rede'sign, *sb.* [f. the vb.] A fresh design; designing again.

1930 *Daily Express* 6 Oct. 1/4 The re-design of the air-ship's hull. **1946** *Nature* 28 Sept. 439/1 Redesign of existing roads and the planning of new roads must serve two purposes, circulation and safety. **1963** *Guardian* 15 May 6/8 This is a redesign..of the regular Tuscan pattern. **1973** *Sci. Amer.* Sept. 69/1 Most of the work being done on the problem of air pollution resulting from the internal-combustion engine is focused on redesign of the engine or on adding emission-control devices to it. **1977** *Time* 15 Aug. 5/2 Our last redesign came in 1971.

rede'sire, *v.* [RE-.] To desire or request again; to desire the return of (a thing).

1599 B. JONSON *Ev. Man out of Hum.* III. ii, Therefore, good father, these are..to re-desire you, that [etc.]. **1614** LODGE *Seneca, Epist.* 167 There is nothing the losse whereof is more easie to be supported then of that which, being lost, cannot be redesired.

redesman ('riːdzmən). *Obs.* exc. *arch.* Forms: 1–3 rædes-, 3 reades-, reaðes-, 4 (9) redes-. [OE. *rædesmann*, f. *ræd* REDE *sb.*[1] + MAN; cf. Du. *raadsman*, G. *ratsmann*, ON. *ráðsmaðr*.] Counsellor, adviser, †steward.

1039 in Earle *Land Charters*, etc. (1888) 298 Æt steorran þe þa wæs þæs kinges rædesmann. *c* **1122** *O.E. Chron.* (Laud MS.) an. 1039 His rædes menn hit syððon strange forguldon. *a* **1225** *Leg. Kath.* 573 Ʒe schulen beon mine readesmen [*v.r.* reaðesmen] in all mine dearne runes. **1258** *Procl. Hen. III* (1868) 21 This wes idon ætforen vre isworene redesmen. *c* **1320** *Cast. Love* 1225 Nas þis a good redes-mon þat vs so deore for-buggen con? **1892** BROOKE *Early Eng. Lit.* II. 68 Bishop Daniel..was his most trusted redesman.

redespatch: see REDISPATCH.

rede'termine, *v.* [RE- 5 a.] To determine again.

1611 COTGR., *Rappoincter*,..to redetermine, redecree. *Ibid.*, *Redeliberer*, to rédeliberate, redetermine of. **1828** HERSCHELL in *Mem. R. Astron. Soc.* III. 197 [A star] as since observed, and the place &c. redetermined. **1862** DRAPER *Intell. Devel. Europe* iv. (1864) I. 91 To redetermine their boundaries after the subsidence of the flood.

So **redetermi'nation**, a fresh determination.

1867 G. F. CHAMBERS *Astron.* I. i. 3 The importance of a re-determination was thus rendered more and more obvious. **1881** *Athenæum* 21 May 691/3 He proposes to undertake a redetermination of the constant of aberration.

†**redevable**, *a.* (and *sb.*) *Obs.* Forms: 6 redueable, 7 reduable, redewable; 7 redivable, 6–8 redevable. [ad. F. *redevable* (15th c. in Littré), f. *redevoir* (see RE- and DEVOIR) + -ABLE. Some of the forms are influenced by DUE *a.*] Beholden, indebted. Also as *sb.*, a debtor.

1502 *Ord. Crysten Men* (W. de W. 1506) IV. xiii. R vij b, Whan..the dettour hath not of Justyce excusacyon that he sholde not..paye, than such redeuable is contynually in the state of dedely synne. **1627** W. D. tr. *Audiguier's Lisander* 13, I thanke God and your good helpe, unto whom I am redueable for my life. **1647** BOYLE *Let. to Hartlib* 8 May, Wks. 1772 I. p. xl, To the former..I am also redevable for a very handsome complimental letter. **1711** *Fingall MSS.* in *10th Rep. Hist. MSS. Comm.* App. V. 152 The King would have been redevable unto their prowess.

rede'velop, *v.* [RE- 5 a.] **a.** *trans.* and *intr.* To develop again.

1882 H. SPENCER *Princ. Sociol., Pol. Inst.* 553 There survived in them, or were re-developed in them, the family-organization, rights, and obligations. **1889** *Anthony's Photogr. Bull.* II. 82 Bleach it with mercury,..wash and redevelope with hydroquinone. **1967** *Oceanogr. & Marine Biol.* xiv. 363 After a short time polarity in growth redevelops. **1978** *SLR Camera* Nov. 9/2 The image will then re-develop to a warm brown tone.

b. *spec.* in *Town Planning.*

1936 E. E. FINCH & C. G. EVE *Rep. Town Planning Scheme* (Corporation of London Publ. Health Dept.) 3 It therefore appears that nearly a quarter of the building site area has been redeveloped in the last 30 years. **1947** *Act 10 & 11 Geo. VI* c. 51 §5(3) For the purposes of this section, a development plan may define as an area of comprehensive development any area which in the opinion of the local planning authority should be developed or re-developed as a whole. **1956** N. LICHFIELD *Econ. Planned Devel.* x. 129 Where an area is to be re-developed, demolition and clearance may be required. **1971** P. GRESSWELL *Environment* 91 *Comprehensive* development covers a large area, usually in towns—perhaps including a number of streets which are to be redeveloped to one comprehensive plan.

Hence **rede'veloped** *ppl. a.*, **rede'veloper**, **rede'velopment** (esp. in *Town Planning*).

1873 SPON *Workshop Rec.* Ser. I. 265/1 Removing the bromine..by means of redevelopment. **1879** *Cassell's Techn. Educ.* III. 143 In ordinary cases one application of the re-developer will be sufficient. **1882** H. SPENCER *Princ. Sociol., Pol. Inst.* 576 The re-development of military organization in modern times. **1890** *Anthony's Photogr. Bull.* III. 341 The redeveloped bromide print. **1935** *Act 25 & 26 Geo. V* c. 40 §13 It shall be the duty of the local authority to cause the area to be defined on a map, and to pass a resolution declaring the area so defined to be a proposed re-development area. **1938** *New Statesman* 25 June 1060/1 As to the great city itself, no satisfactory redevelopment of it is possible so long as population and business pour into it and its overall density is increasing. **1940** *Economist* 28 Dec. 794/2 The committee recommends that in cases where private ownership presents an obstacle to planned development, redevelopment or conservation on an economical basis, the areas should be bought outright by planning authorities. **1941** H. J. MANZONI in F. E. Towndrow *Replanning Britain* iv. 99 (*heading*) Relating the redeveloped units. **1944** in D. Tyerman *Ways & Means of Rebuilding* iii. 59 Mr Cadbury had been considering plans of redevelopment schemes at thirty to the acre. **1952** L. KEEBLE *Princ. & Pract. Town & Country Planning* xvi. 345 In towns where a great deal of redevelopment overspill will have to be accommodated..it will often be possible to plan some completely new neighbourhoods for development at later stages. **1964** J. B. CULLINGWORTH *Town & Country Planning* xii. 241 Housing, comprehensive redevelopment and traffic. **1966** N. LICHFIELD *Cost Benefit Anal. Town Planning Cambridge* iv. 26 The projects comprise a group of interrelated redevelopment areas, roads and car parks. **1972** R. QUILTY *Tenth Session* 136, 61 Sainsbury Road is bang in the middle of a redevelopment area. One of those decaying streets back of Kentish Town. **1976** *Star* (Sheffield) 29 Oct. 10/2 Our re-developed city has been advertised as a tourist and conference centre,..and yet the horrible menace of litter continues. **1977** *Grimsby Even. Tel.* 13 May 1/3 The 'shocking conditions' they have to live in while their area goes through a redevelopment phase.

rede'vote, *v.* [RE- 5 a.] To devote anew.

a **1711** KEN *Hymnarium* Poet. Wks. 1721 II. 68 To thee I re-devote my Heart.

redewable, variant of REDEVABLE *a. Obs.*

†**'redewise**, *a. Obs. rare*⁻¹. [f. REDE *sb.*[1] + WISE *a.*] Wise in counsel.

a **1225** *St. Marher.* 13 Ruffines of helle, the rehest ant the redewisest of alle theo in helle.

'red-eye.

1. A European fish, the rudd, *Leuciscus erythrophthalmus.*

a **1672** WILLUGHBY *Icthyogr.* (1686) Tab. v. 10 Red eye, *Belgis*, i.e. *oculus Coccineus.* *a* **1704** RAY *Synopsis Pisc.* (1713) 116 *Rootaug*..The Red-Eye. **1740** R. BROOKES *Art of Angling* 55 The Red-Eye..is very much like a Bream, but thicker. **1836** YARRELL *Brit. Fishes* I. 412 To this second division [Cyprinidæ] belong four British species, the largest of which, the Rudd or Red-eye, is a very common fish in Europe. **1884** *Chamb. Jrnl.* 3 May 273/2 The rudd, or red-eye, a beautiful active fish, is very abundant.

2. a. The name of several American fishes, as (*a*) the rock-bass, (*b*) the red-fish, (*c*) the green or blue-spotted sunfish.

1820 RAFINESQUE in *Smithson. Coll.* (1877) XIII. IX. i. 22 Red-Eye, *Aplocentrus.* **1877** JORDAN *Ibid.*, The name 'Red-Eye' in the region which this fish is supposed to inhabit is chiefly applied to the Rock-Bass (*Ambloplites rupestris*). **1884–5** *Riverside Nat. Hist.* (1888) III. 131 More closely allied to American Cyprinidæ are the roach,..the red-eye (*Scardinius*).

b. Used attributively.

1820 RAFINESQUE in *Smithson. Coll.* (1877) XIII. IX. i. 20 Red-Eye Sunfish, *Icthelis Erythrops.*

3. *U.S.* The red-eyed vireo (*Cent. Dict.* 1891).

1857 THOREAU *Maine Woods* (1864) 172 The birds sang quite as in our woods,—the red-eye, red-start, veery, wood-pewee, etc. **1917** T. G. PEARSON *Birds Amer.* III. 103/2 Mr. Job..photographed several times a female Red-eye solicitously feeding two voracious young Cowbirds. **1953** D. A. BANNERMAN *Birds Brit. Isles* II. 252 The red-eye has been called 'preacher-bird' because of its unceasing vocal efforts.

4. *U.S. slang.* Coarse fiery whisky.

1819 J. A. QUITMAN *Diary* in J. F. H. Claiborne *Life & Corr. J. A. Quitman* (1860) I. 42 Whiting and I had to treat to 'red-eye' or 'rot-gut', as whiskey is here called. **1838** *Yale Lit. Mag.* III. 12 An Indian tribe that..seldom ever passed the prairie except to sell their skins, and purchase 'red-eye'. *a* **1859** in Bartlett *Dict. Amer.* 358, I promised the overseer ..a demijohn of red-eye if all went straight. **1903** *Sun* (N.Y.) 15 Nov., Ben made for the nearest red-eye plant, and inside an hour he was riotous and shooting up the town. **1910** in J. Lomax *Cowboy Songs* 305 Drink that rot gut, drink that rot gut, Drink that red eye, boys. **1911** C. E. MULFORD *Bar-20 Days* viii. 95 Anybody'd think you was full of red-eye, th'way you act. **1949** A. HYND *We are Public Enemies* ii. 44 Barrow put down a slug of red eye and walked up to her. **1957** J. STEINBECK *Short Reign of Pippin IV* 69 Serving red-eye in shot-glasses. **1976** *Observer* 5 Dec. (Colour Suppl.) 18 (Advt.), Most of the liquor to be had [in New Orleans] at that time [*sc.* 1865] was known as 'redeye'. Because that's what it did.

5. *U.S. slang.* Tomato ketchup.

1923 G. H. MCKNIGHT *Eng. Words* 56 *Red eye* for 'catsup'. **1947** *Sun* (Baltimore) 7 Aug. 10/3 Red-Eye..that great disguise, ketchup. **1960** WENTWORTH & FLEXNER *Dict. Amer. Slang* 423/2 *Redeye*.., ketchup. *W.W.I and W.W.II Armed Forces use.*

6. *Austral.* A cicada, *Psaltoda mœrens.* Also *attrib.*

1925 [see FLOURY *a.* d]. **1945** BAKER *Austral. Lang.* xii. 214 Most noted among our appellations for cicadas are: baker, floury baker,..red eye and double drummer. **1965** *Austral. Encycl.* II. 379/2 (*caption*) Red-eye cicadas. *Ibid.* 380/1 Other well-known cicadas are the red-eye..and the aptly named cherry-nose.

7. ***red-eye gravy***: gravy made by adding liquid to the grease from cooked ham or other lean meat. *U.S.*

1947 *Reader's Digest* Apr. 130/1 Pinky brown slices of cured ham that almost floated in red-eye gravy. **1949** *Newsweek* 11 July 6/2 Truman had..'good Missouri hams, red-eye gravy, and hominy grits'. **1959** *Washington Post* 29 Oct. D5/1 To the folks in the hominy grits and red-eye gravy belt there is only one game this week—Louisiana State vs. Mississippi. **1977** *Time* 24 Oct. 27/2 Dennis serves up his baked ham and red-eye gravy, grits, green beans, carrots, buttermilk biscuits and coffee.

8. *U.S. colloq.* Used *attrib.* to designate an aeroplane flight on which the traveller is unable to get adequate sleep because of the hour of arrival or because of differences in time zones.

1968 MRS. L. B. JOHNSON *White House Diary* 31 Mar. (1970) 642 Lynda was coming in on 'the red-eye special' from California, about 7 A.M., having kissed Chuck good-by at Camp Pendleton last night as he departed for Vietnam. **1972** 'J. LANGE' *Binary* 19 They all looked tired... Phelps had brought them out to California on a red-eye flight, let them sleep a few hours, then dragged them up for a meeting. **1973** *Time* 25 June 8/3 He took two 'red-eye' flights from Seattle to the capital. **1976** *National Observer* (U.S.) 4 Sept. 5/1 Schweiker..and Newhall took the red-eye special back to Washington that same night. Newhall just wanted to sleep, but Schweiker was, in Newhall's words, 'euphoric'.

9. *Canada.* A drink made from beer and tomato juice.

1973 *Daily Colonist* (Victoria, B.C.) 29 Aug. 2/2, I did manage to acquire a fair liking for 'red-eye'..a mixture of beer and tomato juice. **1975** 'S. MARLOWE' *Cawthorn Jrnls.* (1976) xiii. 107 'I'll have a redeye,' Lester told the barman, who mixed tomato juice and beer for him, half and half. **1976** *Maclean's Mag.* 22 Mar. 51/2 The red-eye, a murky combination of beer and tomato juice.

red-eyed, *a.*

1. Having the iris of a red colour. Also *transf.*

1646 CRASHAW *Steps to Temple* 80 Bid the golden god, the sun,..Put all his red-eyed rubies on. **1653** R. SANDERS *Physiogn.* 158 They are reddish- or red-eyd, which signifies their malice. **1752** J. HILL *Hist. Anim.* 525 The red-eyed Lepus, with a very short tail. **1838** DICKENS *O. Twist* xv, At his feet sat a white-coated, red-eyed dog. **1911** J. MASEFIELD *Everlasting Mercy* 47 Old parson, red-eyed as a ferret. **1934** C. CARMER in B. A. Botkin *Treas. S. Folklore* (1949) III. ii. 490 Two-Toe is a red-eyed 'gator and about fourteen feet long.

2. a. In the specific names of certain birds: Having red eyes, or eyes surrounded by a red ring.

1752 J. HILL *Hist. Anim.* 370 The red-eyed Parrot. **1754** CATESBY *Carolina* I. 54 The red ey'd Fly-catcher. *Muscicapa olivacea.* The iris of the eyes are red. **1783** LATHAM *Gen. Synopsis Birds* II. I. 211 Red-eyed Bunting. Round the eyes naked, and of a rose-colour. **1831** SWAINSON *Fauna Bor. Amer.* II. 233 *Vireo olivaceus*.., Red-eyed Greenlet. **1831** WILSON, etc. *Amer. Ornith.* II. 270 Their manners very much resemble those of the red-eyed, or towhe bunting. **1834** AUDUBON *Ornith. Biog.* II. 287 The Red-eyed Fly-catcher is an inhabitant of the whole of our forests. **1883** *Century Mag.* Sept. 683/1 The nest of the red-eyed vireo is one of the most artfully placed in the wood.

b. In the names of certain insects.

1934 *Nat. Geogr. Mag.* May 612/2 Spiders and red-eyed flies are numerous. **1937** C. LONGFIELD *Dragonflies Brit. Isles* 170 The Red-eyed Damsel-fly should be easy enough to tell by its eyes alone.

3. Having the eyelids reddened by tears, want of sleep, or the like. Also *transf.*

1865 DICKENS *Mut. Fr.* IV. xv, It was as heavy on him in his scanty sleep, as in his red-eyed waking hours. **1894** FENN *Real Gold* 227 No sleep came to the restless lads; and the next morning found them red-eyed and feverish.

red-faced, *a.* Having a red face. Also *transf.*

1579–80 NORTH *Plutarch* (1595) 369 He was somewhat giuen to be redfaced. **1599** SHAKS. *Hen. V*, III. ii. 34 For Bardolph, hee is white-liuer'd, and red-fac'd. **1712–13** J. TILLARD in Hearne *Collect.* (O.H.S.) IV. 81 Yᵉ most red-faced Topers in either university. **1727** BOYER *Dict. Royal* I, *Rougeaud*,..a red-faced or ruddy complexion'd Man or Woman. **1829** B. HALL *Travels* I. 349 A village of birch-bark wigwams, thinly inhabited by a dirty set of red-faced inhabitants. **1847** TENNYSON *Princ.* v. 114 But red-faced war has rods of steel and fire. **1880** C. R. MARKHAM *Peruv. Bark* 197 The red-faced man whom I had met on the road to Sandia.

b. In names of birds, etc.

1784 PENNANT *Arct. Zool.* II. 584 Red-faced Corvorant. **1816** SHAW *Gen. Zool.* IX. II. 448 Red-faced Finch (*Fringilla afra*). **1817** *Ibid.* X. II. 340 The Red-faced Flycatcher is found in Siberia. **1882** *Proc. Zool. Soc.* App. 798 Red-faced Saki (*Brachyurus rubicundus*).

Red Fed ('rɛd fɛd). *N.Z. colloq.* Also redfed. [f. RED *a.* 9 b + FED(ERATION.] A member of the Federation of Labour (founded 1909); now *gen.*, one who rebels against the established order, a left-winger. Hence **'Red-Fed-ism.**

1914 *Evening Post* (Wellington, N.Z.) 14 Jan. 10/5 The charge you prefer against the 'Red Feds'. **1916** *Chrons. N.Z. Expeditionary Force* 15 Nov. 134/1 I'll poke the fellow in the jaw that calls me a 'Red Fed'. **1931** N. E. COAD *Such is Life* 24 They are on the look-out for Bolshevists, Red-Feds and I.W.W.s. **1948** D. W. BALLANTYNE *Cunninghams* I. xxxi. 152 That crazy young redfed..who landed himself in trouble over at the works with his gabbing. **1959** K. SINCLAIR *Hist. N.Z.* iii. 199 In contrast to the United Labour Party, the 'Red Feds' eschewed political action. *Ibid.*, The 'Red Fed's' rejection of the principle of industrial arbitration. **1959** *N.Z. Listener* 26 June 4/1 Those dark days when many a university lecturer and many a student were being hauled across the coals for radicalism, Communism, red-Fed-ism, and all sorts of other nonsense. **1969** F. SARGESON *Joy of Worm* iv. 134 And when besides he's Red Fed, Maoriland worker, not to mention *Das Kapital* all rolled into one—well, it's a toss-up whether he can continue to survive. **1970** D. M. DAVIN *Not Here, not Now* VI. i. 280 He sounded a bit of a red-fed, though. No time for Baldwin or any of that lot over in England.

Redfern ('rɛdfɜːn). [f. the name *Redfern*, Maddox.] (See quot. 1909.) Also *attrib.*

1909 J. R. WARE *Passing Eng.* 207/2 *Redfern* (*Soc.*, 1879), perfectly-fitting lady's coat or jacket. From the vogue obtained, 1879 on, by Redfern, Maddox, W. Regent Street, whose lady's tailoring became celebrated over the whole world. **1932** N. COWARD *Cavalcade* I. iii. 24, I am now going home to have a bath and put on my new Redfern model.

Red Fife (rɛd faɪf). Also **Red Fyfe.** [f. RED *a.* + the name of David *Fife* (1804?–77), Canadian botanist.] A rust-resistant variety of spring wheat, developed in Canada during the 1870s by David Fife.

[1851 *Watchman* (St. Thomas, Ontario) 1 Feb. 2/4 In another column will be found an article on the 'Fife Wheat' which is held in such high estimation..by all who have tried it.] **1883** *Prince Albert* (Saskatchewan) *Times* 3 Oct. 6/2 Try it and be convinced, and by all means give the 'red fyfe' the preference. **1889** *Experimental Farms: Rep. 1888* (Canada Dept. Agric.) 29 One sample of the Red Fyfe was grown in Ontario. **1900** *Westm. Gaz.* 28 Dec. 2/1 The quantity and quality of Red Fife..is as fine as ever. **1932** *Discovery* Mar. 73/2 The suitable wheat [for prairie farming], Red Fife, was discovered by accident. **1936, 1965** [see MARQUIS 4]. **1973** H. ROBERTSON *Grass Roots* iii. 56 Home-steaders were able to purchase high-quality Red Fife wheat.

red-fin, -finned: see RED *a.* 14a, 14b, 18b.

red fish, 'red-fish.

1. A male salmon in the spawning season, when it assumes a red colour. Also *Comb.*

14.. *Ordo Justiciarie* in *Sc. Acts Parl.* (1814) App. iv. 343 All reid fische slaeris in forbodin tyme. **1457** *Sc. Acts Jas. II*, c. 33 (1814) 51 Anentis rede fische it is ordanyt [etc.]. **1585** *Reg. Privy Council Scot.* Ser. I. III. 739 [They] sall desist and ceis..fra slaying of ony reid and blak fische. **1836** YARRELL *Brit. Fishes* II. 10 The body partakes of the golden orange tinge, and the Salmon in this state is called a red-fish. The females are dark in colour, and are as commonly called black-fish. **1870** PENNELL *Mod. Pract. Angler* 146 'Foul fish' before spawning are, if males, termed 'red fish'.

b. The salmon, in contrast to 'white' fish.

1851 MAYHEW *Lond. Labour* I. 62/2 The fish sent to London is known to Billingsgate salesmen as 'red' and 'white' fish. The red fish is confined to salmon.

2. a. The red gurnard, *Trigla cuculus.*

1611 COTGR., *Rougette*, the Red-fish; verie like a Gurnard, and by some held to be the same. **1611** FLORIO, *Grincio*,.. a Gournet, a Rochet or red fish. **1743** *Phil. Trans.* XLII. 612 There are..Sharks, Holly-butts, Red-fish, Trout. **1862** COUCH *Brit. Fishes* II. 19 Red-Fish. Soldier. Red Gurnard.

b. The name of various American or North Atlantic fishes, *esp.* the blue-backed salmon (*Oncorhyncus nerka*), the red perch or rose-fish, and the red-drum.

1763 tr. *Le Page du Pratz's Hist. Louisiana* II. 26 This Gulf abounds with delicious fish; as..red fish, cod, sturgeon,..and many other sorts. **1843** *Southern Lit. Messenger* I. 121/2 The waters too, furnished their finny.. treasures,—the red fish, buffalo [etc.]. **1876** GOODE in *Smithson. Coll.* XIII. VI. 14 *Teleocephali acanthopteri*..red-fish, rock cod [etc.]. *Ibid.* 62 Red fish or spotted bass (*Sciænops ocellatus*). **1877** JORDAN *Ibid.* IX. 32 *note*, Anomal Fallfish, *Rutilus Anomalus*..Vulgar names: Chub, Redfish, Fallfish. **1882** —— in Goode *Nat. Hist. Aquat. Anim.* 477 This species [*Oncorhynchus nerka*] is known as the 'Red-fish' to the English speaking inhabitants of Alaska and Kamtchatka. **1884-5** *Riverside Nat. Hist.* (1888) III. 249 The *S[ebastes] marinus* is variously known as the rose-fish, red-fish, red-perch, Norway haddock [etc.]. **1897** [see *channel bass*]. **1955** S. A. GRAU *Black Prince* 190 He had not lifted his head from the redfish he was cleaning. **1962** K. F. LAGLER et al. *Ichthyol.* viii. 247 The giant redfish (*Arapaima gigas*) of the Amazon is one of the largest freshwater bony fishes. **1969** A. WHEELER *Fishes Brit. Isles & N.-W. Europe* 480/1 The red-fish is widely distributed in the North Atlantic.

3. †**a.** Fish cured in a certain way (see quot.). *Obs.*

1727-41 CHAMBERS *Cycl.* s.v. *Fish*, Red Fish is some fresh fish broiled on the gridiron, then fried in oil of olives, and barrelled up with a proper liquor, as new olive-oil, vinegar, salt, pepper, cloves, and laurel leaves, or other herbs.

b. (See quot. 1883.)

1865 DAY *Fishes Malabar* 237 A delicious condiment known under the name of 'Red-fish'. **1883** SIMMONDS *Usef. Anim., Red Fish*,..a delicious condiment prepared in the Straits Settlements with *Engraulis commersonianus*, salted, with vinegar, spices and powdered red rice.

4. *Austral.* = NANNYGAI.

1951 T. C. ROUGHLEY *Fish & Fisheries Austral.* 26 The nannygai, or redfish..occurs round the southern half of Australia. **1966** [see NANNYGAI]. **1979** *Verbatim* Summer 7/2 Australian fishermen found that redfish sold better than nannygai though the difference is entirely linguistic.

red flag.

1. A red flag as a sign of battle, etc.

1602 DEKKER *Satirom.* Wks. 1873 I. 233 What, dost summon a parlie, my little Drumsticke? tis too late: thou seest my red flag is hung out. **1666** *Lond. Gaz.* No. 91/4 That the Red Flag was out, both Fleets in sight of each other, expecting every hour fit weather to Engage. **1727-41** CHAMBERS *Cycl.* s.v. *Flag*, The red flag is a signal of defiance and battle. **1891** HULME *Heraldry* (1897) 271 Others were decking their houses with red flags, the symbols of revolution and bloodshed. *a* **1895** LD. C. E. PAGET *Autobiog.* (1896) iv. 98 [He came] to tell me that the [Russian] forts were in sight, and a red flag flying. 'Odds bones!' said I, 'don't they mean to give any quarter, then?'

2. As a sign of danger, a warning, or a signal to stop. Also *attrib.* and *fig.*

1777 P. THICKNESSE *Year's Journey* I. iii. 23 There is a red flag hoisted gradually higher and higher, as the water flows into the harbour [at Calais]. **1856** *N.Y. Herald* 12 Jan. 1/4 James Flood is road master of his section; any obstruction being on the track it is the duty of the flagman to exhibit his red flag. **1885** C. M. YONGE *Nuttie's Father* I. xiii. 153 They went into a hole and stuck fast, while the red-flag traction engineman prodded her with an umbrella. **1908** KIPLING in *Flag* (Union Jack Club) 8 Thou didst flee up Cheepe, calling ..for a red flag. **1968** J. UPDIKE *Couples* ii. 146 You're sore as hell about some silly thing, maybe Harold's snubbing you, maybe you have the red flag out, but you're right there. **1973** 'C. AIRD' *His Burial Too* iii. 32 The roadmen went and got into a muddle with their flags... One of them.. apparently gets a power complex every time anyone puts a red flag into his hand. **1976** *Billings* (Montana) *Gaz.* 17 June 2-A/4 Time and time again, Eizenstat addressed the members and urged them to avoid 'red flag' words or issues —such as homosexual rights, amnesty, opposition to capital punishment, full federalization of welfare costs. **1977** *Time* 17 Oct. 39/3 He..warned present and future White House aides to be on the alert for 'red flags' of moral dilemmas that may arise while serving a President.

3. a. As a symbol of revolution, socialism, or communism, freq. *spec.* of Soviet Russian communism. Also *attrib.* and *fig.*

1848 A. H. CLOUGH *Let.* 26 Feb. in T. Arnold *N.Z. Lett.* (1966) 78 The Red Flag flying at Paris. **1857** C. M. YONGE *Dynevor Terrace* I. xx. 322 Muskets and pikes were here and there seen, and once he recognized the sinister red flag. **1878** *Indianapolis Sentinel* 23 May 4/6 We denounce the red flag communism imported from Europe. **1888** E. BELLAMY *Looking Backward* xxiv. 353 They were paid by the great monopolies to wave the red flag and talk about..blowing people up. **1889** J. CONNELL in *Justice* 21 Dec. 3/2 Then raise the scarlet standard high! Within its shade we'll live and die! Though cowards flinch, and traitors jeer, We'll keep the Red Flag flying here! **1891** [see RED *a.* 4b]. **1909** *Westm. Gaz.* 19 Oct. 2/1 The Socialists who in such circumstances would be returned in many constituencies.. would be the real thing, of the red-flag order. **1914** CHESTERTON *Flying Inn* xxiii. 274 A very coarse strip of red rag..had been tied round the wooden sign-post by way of a red flag of revolution. **1922** W. J. LOCKE *Tale of Triona* xvii. 199 The only positive ideal in England at the present moment is Bolshevism. The only flag waved..is the red flag. **1957** *Encycl. Brit.* XIX. 711/1 In the urban centres the victory was won under the red flag of class warfare. **1967** *Guardian* 4 Dec. 1/4 The purpose of the visit is political—to show the Red Flag over Cairo. **1973** *Times* 21 Nov. 6/8 Red flag on Cunarder. The former Cunard liner Franconia..left Southampton yesterday flying the hammer and sickle. She was bought..by..the Far Eastern Steamship Company, of Vladivostock. **1974** P. GORE-BOOTH *With Great Truth & Respect* 210 The country was infested with various hostiles, Red Flag Communists, White Flag Communists, Karens or simply dacoits. **1977** *Time* 4 Apr. 24/3 There was little of the tedious Red-flag waving 'revolutionary culture' with which visitors to Peking are entertained.

b. ***the Red Flag***: a socialist song by James Connell (see quot. 1889 above).

1909 R. BROOKE *Let.* 2 Jan. (1968) 154 Yes! yes! Herbert Samuel..is a Socialist... He used to sing *The Red Flag* after dinner every night instead of grace. **1935** H. NICOLSON *Let.* 1 Nov. (1966) 222 He..left the hall while they sang the *Red Flag*. **1968** A. DIMENT *Bang Bang Birds* ix. 160 A covey of West German millionaires who were singing the Red Flag in a hypnotised dirge. *a* **1974** R. CROSSMAN *Diaries* (1976) II. 507 As an outgoing member I went down to the last debate and took part in singing the 'Red Flag' and 'Auld Lang Syne'. **1976** *Whitaker's Almanack 1977* 361/1 Labour M.P.s in their jubilation sang 'The Red Flag', shouted, and waved order papers in the air.

4. = *red ensign* s.v. RED *a.* 19a. See ENSIGN 5.

1901 W. C. RUSSELL *Ship's Adventure* v. 78 He..had begun the sea life in the Royal Navy as midshipman, but.. had quitted the white for the red flag.

Hence **red 'flagger**, one who carries a red flag, a communist; **red 'flaggery**, communist doctrines.

1920 R. MACAULAY *Potterism* II. i. 54, I hate red-flaggery, and all other flaggery. **1921** *Times* 4 Feb. 11/6 The common enemy..what Belfast of today calls the 'red-flaggers'. **1923** *Glasgow Herald* 23 June 8/3 That modest pattern which.. Mr. Kirkwood is finding it so difficult to assimilate with Red Flaggery. **1934** G. B. SHAW *On Rocks* II. 231 That's the way to dish these Labor chaps and Red flaggers.

red-flowered, -flowering: see RED *a.* 14a, c, 15b.

redfol, -ful, varr. REDEFUL *a. Obs.*

red-footed, *a.* Having red feet. Chiefly *Ornith.*, esp. in ***red-footed falcon***, the orange-legged hobby (*Falco rufipes* or *vespertinus*).

1785 LATHAM *Gen. Synopsis Birds* III. II. 572 Red-Footed P[enguin]. **1831** WILSON, etc. *Amer. Ornith.* IV. 358 Red-footed tern. *Sterna hirundo.* **1837** GOULD *Birds Europe* I. Pl. 23 Red-footed Falcon..*Falco rufipes*... Our bird is the Orange-legged Hobby and Ingrian Falcon of Dr. Latham. **1843** YARRELL *Brit. Birds* I. 44 The Red-footed Falcon is a species of small size. **1872** WOOD *Insects at Home* 162 We.. take for our first example of these Beetles the Red-footed Weevil (*Bruchus rufimanus*).

red-fronted: see RED *a.* 14b.

Red Fyfe, var. RED FIFE.

red game. The red grouse, *Lagopus scoticus* (see GROUSE). ? *Obs.*

1674 RAY *Coll. Words, Eng. Birds* 85 The Redgame: *Grygallus minor.* **1676** —— *Willughby's Ornith.* II. 128 The Gor-cock or Moor-cock, or Red-game. **1761** *Act 2 Geo. III*, c. 19 §1 No Person..shall..take, kill..buy [etc.],..any grouse, commonly called Red Game, between the first Day of December and the twenty-fifth Day of July, in any Year. **1797** *Encycl. Brit.* (ed. 3) XVIII. 398/2 The *scoticus*, red game, or moor-fowl is peculiar to the British islands. **1819** SHAW *Gen. Zool.* XI. II. 294.

redgeling, variant of RIDGELING *Obs.*

†**red-gown(d, -gowm.** *Obs.* Forms: 5 **red gownd**, 6 **reed gounde**, 7 **red gowm**, 9 **gown.** [App. f. RED *a.* + GOUND *sb.*, but perh. an alteration, by popular etym., of RADEGOUND.] = RED GUM, RED-GUM[1].

c **1440** *Promp. Parv.* 426/2 Red-gownd, sekenesse of yonge chyldryne, *scrophulus*. **1530** PALSGR. 261/2 Reed gounde sicknesse of chyldren. **1657** C. BECK *Univ. Char.* K iij b, Red gum or red gowm a sickness in Children. **1678** LITTLETON *Lat. Dict.*, *Strophulus*, Red-gowm, a sickness of young children. **1812-20** THOMPSON *Cullen's Nosol. Meth.* (ed. 3) 321 *Strophulus intertinctus*, the red gum or gown, occurs chiefly within..the two first months after birth.

Red Guard. [RED *a.* 9b.]

1. a. A member of an organized detachment of workers during the Russian Bolshevik revolution of 1917; also, such units collectively.

1917 *Times* 12 Nov. 8/5 In Moscow, the 'Red Guard' was defeated. *Ibid.* 13 Dec. 8/5 The fighting at Tamarovka seems to have been between detachments of shock battalions ..and local troops, with sailors, 'Red Guards', infantry, and armoured cars. **1943** E. M. ALMEDINGEN *Frossia* x. 407 At the corner of Sredny a red guard picket awaited them. **1957** *Encycl. Brit.* XIX. 710/2 Definitely expecting a crushing defeat of Trotsky's Red guards, the committee of public defense gave orders to the cadets of the military schools to arrest the military revolutionary committee. **1961** *Everyman's Conc. Encycl. Russia* 388 Kerensky's Provisional Government..was overthrown..with the aid of the Red Guards. **1977** *N.Y. Rev. Bks.* 9 June 46/3 The role of the Petrograd Red Guard in the October seizure of power has been greatly exaggerated.

b. A member of a paramilitary group of Russian soldiers and Finnish communist sympathizers who seized power in Finland in 1918; the group itself.

1922 *Encycl. Brit.* XXXI. 74/1 Whole trainloads of revolutionary *soldateska* arrived from Petrograd... They entered the so-called Finnish 'Red Guards', and ransacked the country. The reactionaries..organized the 'White Guards'. **1956** A. G. MAZOUR *Finland between East & West* iii. 43 In this manner there came into being the so-called Red Guard.

2. A name given to (*a*) the armed units of village people in the Second Revolutionary Civil War in China, 1927-37, (*b*) a youth movement during the Cultural Revolution in the People's Republic of China, 1966-76; also, a member of one of these movements.

1966 *Guardian* 24 Aug. 9/7 The teenage demonstrators, who are known as the 'Red Guard'..appeared to have taken over permanently the churches serving Peking's Christians. **1966** *Economist* 27 Aug. 813/1 The rioters were clearly identified as a new youth group of secondary school and university student activists called the Red Guard. The Red Guard made its first appearance at the monster rally on August 18th, when the students were publicly congratulated for their revolutionary zeal by Mao Tse-tung. **1967** *Listener* 19 Jan. 80 The Red Guards damaged a number of temples and old buildings, destroyed old books. **1971** T. W. ROBINSON *Cultural Revolution in China* p. vii, The Red Guard phase of the Great Proletarian Cultural Revolution began in the late summer of 1966. **1973** M. LINDSAY in Yuan-li Wu *China* vi. 142 Mao insisted that the Red Guards (local village militia) had an important function in harassing small enemy forces and assisting the Red Army. **1977** *N.Y. Rev. Bks.* 12 May 22/3 To purge the party bureaucrats Mao mobilized these adolescents as Red Guards, but millions of them later had to be dispersed to the countryside. **1978** *China Now* July/Aug. 25/1 During the Cultural Revolution in the late 1960's, the influx of Red Guards from all over the country swelled the numbers to nine million.

3. *transf.* Applied to various other radical groups and their members.

1966 *Observer* 25 Sept. 1 In his winding-up speech to the Liberal Assembly..Mr Grimond yesterday hit back at the party's youthful 'Red Guard'. **1966** *Time* 4 Nov. 35 Japan's Red Guards are members of the Socialist opposition—aided by Communists and the *Komeito* (Clean Government Party). **1967** *Guardian* 17 July 14/3 The growing anger of the Liberal Party's leadership at the outspoken criticism by the party's young 'Red Guards'. **1968** *N.Y. Times* 10 Feb. 2 As in all such movements there is an extremist group, called 'Red Guards' in Turin, that seeks to eliminate virtually all traditional authority, to elect professors and to confer marks based on the findings of student committees. **1968** *Listener* 10 Oct. 482/2 A young Red Guard of British music recently expressed to me his concern about form in pop music. **1969** *Guardian* 20 Nov. 3/5 West Bengal's Red Guards, as the Marxist volunteers have been nicknamed. **1970** *Ibid.* 8 Apr. 12/3 India's most turbulent politician, Jyoti Basu, was addressing maybe 100,000 Marxists on the Maidan in Calcutta. He was surrounded by his own Red Guards; tough, supple, and enormously well-disciplined young men.

Hence **Red Guardism**, the Chinese Red Guard movement.

1967 *N.Y. Times* 5 Mar. 2 By November last year Red Guardism was in full cry, and zealous youths were swarming across China..holding aloft little red books containing quotations from Mr. Mao.

red gum, red-gum[1]. [Alteration of RED-GOWN(D, -GOWM, after GUM *sb.*[2] 4.]

1. A papular eruption or rash (*Strophulus intertinctus*) incident to young children, esp. during dentition, consisting of red pimples and patches irregularly disposed on the skin. ***rank red gum***, a virulent form of this (*Strophulus confertus*).

1597 GERARDE *Herbal* 218 The leaues stamped and strained into milke..helpeth the red gumme and frets in children. **1598** SYLVESTER *Du Bartas* II. i. III. *Furies* 531 Their heads are hid wth skalls; Their Limbs with Red-gums and with bloudy bals Of Menstruall humour. **1601** HOLLAND *Pliny* II. 127 A proper liniment..to annoint young children that haue the red gum and be all broken out. **1698** FRYER *Acc. E. India & P.* 378 Red Gum, which besets our Children in Europe, is pernicious to Old Age here. **1749** *Phil. Trans.* XLVI. 234 There appeared an Eruption all over his Skin, which was at first taken by the Nurse for the Red-Gum. **1796** JANE AUSTEN *Sense & Sens.* xxxvii, The child.. was all over pimples... 'Lord! my dear', says I, 'it is nothing in the world but the red-gum'. **1822-34** *Good's Study Med.* (ed. 4) I. 36 A rash appears on the skin, usually the red-gum.

1899 *Allbutt's Syst. Med.* VIII. 586 *Lichen strophulosus* or *strophulus*, 'red gum', 'teething rash', usually regarded as a sweat rash.

2. A form of rust in grain. Also *attrib.*

1807 VANCOUVER *Agric. Devon* (1813) 147 The burnt, red-gum, or cockle-eared, are diseases little, indeed almost wholly unknown. **1851** J. M. WILSON *Rural Cycl.* s.v. *Rust*, The red-gum variety occurs only on the ear, and appears like gummy exudations.

red gum, red-gum[2].

1. A reddish resinous substance exuded from the bark of various tropical or semi-tropical trees and shrubs, esp. that obtained from various Australian species of Eucalyptus.

1738 STIBBS *Voy. Gambia* 267, I shall now describe the Pau de Sangue, or Blood-wood, so called from a red gum which issues from it. **1788** J. WHITE *Voy. N.S. Wales* (1790) 178 At the heart they are full of veins, through which an amazing quantity of an astringent red gum issues. **1865** TENISON-WOODS *Discov. & Expl. Australia* I. 42 The usual red gum was observed oozing out from the bark... This gum is a species of Kino.

2. A tree of one or other of the Australian species of Eucalyptus yielding a red gum, esp. *E. camaldulensis* or one of a group of closely related species; also, the wood of these trees.

1821 MART in Field *Geog. Mem. N.S. Wales* 316, I found also the red.. and blue gum. **1846** HAYDON 5 *Yrs. Australia Felix* 33 Red gum, a wood which has of late years been exported to England in great quantities; it has all the properties of mahogany. **1870** TUCKER *The Mute*, etc. 85 Then the dark savage 'neath the red gum's shade Told o'er his deeds. **1889** MAIDEN *Useful Native Plants* 429 *Eucalyptus amygdalina*... This Eucalypt has even more vernacular names than botanical synonyms... In Victoria it is one of the 'Red Gums'. **1911** E. M. CLOWES *On Wallaby* ix. 249 Farther eastward iron bark and stringy bark prevail, and red gum follows the course of the Murray and its tributaries. **1920**, etc. [see MARRI]. **1955** M. R. JACOBS *Growth Habits of Eucalypts* vi. 219 The red gums form one of the most widespread and stable groups of the eucalypts.

3. *U.S.* The sweet gum, *Liquidambar styraciflua*, an important timber tree.

1839 *Southern Lit. Messenger* V. 113/2 Dislodge the rackoon from its lofty hole in the red-gum tree. **1916** E. T. SETON *Woodcraft Man.* 288 Sweet Gum, Star-Leaved, or Red Gum, Bilsted, Alligator Tree, or Liquidambar. **1942** W. M. HARLOW *Trees Eastern U.S.* 193 Now that veneered furniture has so largely replaced solid pieces, redgum wood has come into prominence.

4. *attrib.*, as ***red-gum pitcher, tree, wood.***

1790 J. WHITE *Voy. N.S. Wales* App. 231 The Red Gum Tree, *Eucalyptus Resinifera.* **1843** HOLTZAPFFEL *Turning* I. 86 There is.. a variety of a redder tint called red Gum-wood. **1868** CARLETON *Austr. Nights* 14 While she, the younger, went to fill Her red-gum pitcher at the rill.

red-haired, *a.* [See RED *a.* 1 e.] Having red or reddish hair. (Chiefly of persons.)

1500–20 DUNBAR *Poems* xxxii. 16 He wes ane lusty reid haird [*v.r.* rid-harit] lowry. **1530** PALSGR. 322/1 Reed heared, *roux, rouse.* **1607** CHAPMAN *Bussy d'Ambois* III. i, Worse than the poison of a red-hair'd man. **1715** HEARNE *Collect.* (O.H.S.) V. 129 The famous D[r] Hammond was a red-hair'd Man. **1777** LIGHTFOOT *Flora Scot.* II. 1002 Red-haired Byssus. **1815** SCOTT *Guy M.* xviii, Is my future friend red-haired? **1889** I. TAYLOR *Orig. Aryans* ii. 110 The tall, red-haired brachycephalic Irishman and Scot.

absol. **1726** SWIFT *Gulliver* IV. viii, It is observed, that the Red-haired of both Sexes are more libidinous and mischievous than the rest.

transf. *a* **1704** T. BROWN *Wks.* (1720) III. 187 The red-hair'd Charioteer of the Day, meaning the Sun. **1813** W. S. WALKER *Gustavus Vasa* III. 101 But see! the red-haired sun to ocean bends.

red hand, red-hand, *a.* and *sb.*

A. *adj.* **1.** *Sc.* (orig. *Law*). = REDHANDED 1. (Common in 16th c.)

1432 *Sc. Acts Jas. I*, c. 2 Gif he may be ouretakyn he salbe put in sikkir festines quhil þe law be done on hym.. Ande be it red hand it salbe done w[t]in þat sonne. **1535** STEWART *Cron. Scot.* III. 274 That samin carle.. Come the thrid nycht,.. To steill the irnes, and wes tane reid hand. **1580–81** *Reg. Privy Council Scot.* Ser. I. III. 346 The said justice and warden sall tak na mannis tennent or servand for executing of justice upoun him, except he be tane reid-hand. **1678** SIR G. MACKENZIE *Crim. Law* 136 If he be not taken red-hand the sheriff cannot proceed against him. **1700** in Hector *Judic. Recs. Renfrewsh.* (1876) 188 Taken red hand with soume small goods a little from the house. **1768** ERSKINE *Inst. Law Scot.* II. iv. §4 The case where the murderer is seized red-hand or in the act. **1881** MRS. WALFORD *Dick Netherby* vii, We'll tak' the hoos i' the flank, an' catch the twa o' them reid-hand.

2. = RED-HANDED 1 c.

1894 CROCKETT *Raiders* (ed. 3) 381, I was known for a gypsy and a red-hand follower of the chief persecutor.

B. *sb.* **1.** In phr. ***with (the) red hand*** = A. 1. (Orig. *Sc.* only, and now *rare.*) Also †***without red hand***, without clear evidence of guilt.

1577–8 *Reg. Privy Council Scot.* Ser. I. II. 666 The said Alexander Winsister wes not takin with reidhand. **1597** SKENE *De Verb. Sign.* s.v. *Schireff*, Gif he beis apprehended with reid hand Justice sall be done within that Sunne. And gif he be taken and apprehended without read hand, Hee salbe put in prison. **1609** —— *Reg. Maj., Quoniam Attach.* c. 39 §2 Gif he is takin with reid or hait hand of slauchter. **1878** LEA *Superst. & Force* (ed. 3) 23 *note*, A murderer was allowed to rebut with his single oath all testimony as to his guilt, unless he chanced to be caught with the red hand.

2. *Her.* (See quot. 1863, and cf. BLOODY *a.* 2 b.)

1856 *N. & Q.* 2nd Ser. I. 226/2 The Red Hand of Ulster. **1863** CHAMBERS *Bk. of Days* 22 May, I. 670/2 From the connexion of the first baronets with Ulster, they were allowed to place in their armorial coat the open red hand heretofore borne by the forfeited O'Neils, the noted *Lamh derg Eirin*, or red hand of Ulster.

red-handed, *a.*

1. In the very act of crime, having the evidences of guilt still upon the person, esp. in phr. ***to take,*** or ***be taken, redhanded.***

App. first in Scott: the older Sc. phrase was REDHAND.

1819 SCOTT *Ivanhoe* xxv, I did but tie one fellow, who was taken redhanded and in the fact, to the horns of a wild stag. **1857** G. LAWRENCE *Guy Liv.* iv, The fact of the property being found in our possession constituted a *flagrans delictum* —we were caught 'red-handed'. **1893** EARL DUNMORE *Pamirs* I. 306 A notorious thief was caught red-handed in the act of breaking open a lock.

b. Fresh from the commission of murder or homicide; having the hands red with blood.

1861 *Reynolds' Newsp.* 24 Nov., Call a drum-head court-martial, and hang the murderer red-handed! **1885** MABEL PEACOCK in *Academy* 10 Oct. 239/3 When Abel in thine arms lay dead, And Cain red-handed turned and fled.

fig. **1878** BOSW. SMITH *Carthage* 175 While Hamilcar was returning redhanded from his desperate victory.

c. That sheds or has shed blood; bloody, sanguinary, violent.

1879 TOURGEE *Fool's Err.* (1883) 16 He had hitherto been .. a red-handed slayer of men! **1894** CROCKETT *Raiders* (ed. 3) 38 The evil gypsies of the hill—red-handed men.

2. Having red hands. **a.** As the distinctive epithet of certain monkeys.

1828 STARK *Elem. Nat. Hist.* I. 53 *M. rufimanus*,.. The Red-handed Howler. Fur black; hands red. **1882** *Proc. Zool. Soc.* App. 789 Red-handed Tamarin.

b. Applied to a species of orchis.

1805 DUNCUMB *Agric. Hereford* 172 The northern parts of the county produce the following:.. *Orchis conopsia*, Red-handed Orchis.

'red-head, 'redhead.

1. *attrib.* Having a red head or hair.

1664 WOOD *Life* 26 Jan. (O.H.S.) II. 4 Read the red-hed boy. **1738** ALBIN *Nat. Hist. Birds* III. 61 The Red Head Sparrow. **1892** in Cozens-Hardy *Broad Nrf.* (1893) 46 Pochard, male sometimes called Redhead Drake.

2. One who has a red head.

a **1843** SOUTHEY *Comm.-pl. Bk.* (1849) II. 444 There is the sect of Nakhoodi.. who surpass seventy times all the impiety of the Redheads (the Persians). **1893** KOHLER in Barrows *Parlt. Relig.* I. 366 You see man divided into groups of blackheads (the race of Ham) and redheads (Adam).

b. A name given to various birds, *esp.* the American pochard and red-headed woodpecker.

1814 WILSON *Amer. Ornith.* VIII. 110 The Red-head is twenty inches in length. **1831** AUDUBON *Ornith. Biog.* I. 145 As soon as the Red-heads have begun to visit a Cherry or Apple tree, a pole is placed along the trunk of the tree. **1858** LEWIS in Youatt *Dog* (N.Y.) iii. 89 The Chesapeake bay and its tributaries, where the canvass-back and red-heads resort in such numerous quantities every fall. **1863** WISE *New Forest* 312 Pochard.. known along the coast as the 'redhead' and 'ker'. **1898** MORRIS *Austral Eng.* 146/1 In New South Wales *Æ[gintha] temporalis* is known as the Red-head.

3. *Bot.* Bastard ipecacuanha. ? *Obs.*

1798 NEMNICH *Polygl. Lex.* v. 867 Redhead, *Asclepias currasavica.*

red-headed, *a.*

1. = RED-HAIRED. Also *fig.*

1565 COOPER *Thesaurus, Ruber crine*, a redde headed felowe. **1580** HARVEY *Wks.* (Grosart) I. 69 No such Orators againe, as red-headed Angelles. **1632** MASSINGER & FIELD *Fatal Dowry* IV. i, He has made me smell for all the world like a flax, or a red-headed woman's chamber. **1736** AINSWORTH *Lat. Dict.* s.v. *Red*, Red haired, or red headed, *rufus, rufis capillis.* **1865** KINGSLEY *Herew.* iii, Here is a pretty coil about a red-headed brute of a Pict! **1894** *Outing* (U.S.) XXIV. 123/2 His motto is: 'A red-headed man never squeals'.

2. Having a red head. **a.** In names of birds, as ***red-headed macao, parrot, starling,*** etc.

red-headed duck, the red-crested duck, *Nyroca* or *Fuligula rufina*; also = *r. widgeon.* **r. lark**, a South African bird of the family *Alaudidæ* (see quot.); †**r. linnet**, the common linnet, and lesser redpoll. **r. pochard** = *r. widgeon.* **r. smew**, the female of the smew, *Mergus albellus.* **r. widgeon**, the pochard, *Fuligula ferina.* **r. woodpecker**, an American woodpecker, *Melanerpes erythrocephalus.*

1678 RAY *Willughby's Ornith.* 364 The great *red-headed Duck. **1814** WILSON *Amer. Ornith.* VIII. 110 Red-headed duck. *Anas ferina.* **1838** AUDUBON *Ornith. Biog.* IV. 198 The Red-headed Duck reaches the Middle and Southern States by passing overland or following our great streams. **1867** LAYARD *Birds S. Afr.* 212 *Megalophonus cinereus*... The *red-headed lark is common throughout the colony. **1674** RAY *Catal. Eng. Birds* 88 The greater *red-headed Linnet... The lesser red-headed Linnet. **1752** J. HILL *Hist. Anim.* 360 The *red-headed Macao. *Ibid.* 370 The *red-headed Parrot. **1802** BINGLEY *Anim. Biog.* (1813) II. 77 The Guinea or little Red-headed Parrot. **1824** SHAW *Gen. Zool.* XII. II. 193 *Red-headed Pochard. (*Fuligula ferina.*) **1768** PENNANT *Brit. Zool.* II. 439 *Redheaded smew. The head is slightly crested, and of a rust color. **1729** in *Dampier's Voy.* (ed. 3) III. 408 The *Red-headed Starling. **1678** RAY *Willughby's Ornith.* 367 The Poker, or Pochard, or great *red-headed Wigeon. **1828** STARK *Elem. Nat. Hist.* I. 321 Red-Headed Widgeon. Head and neck bright red. **1754** CATESBY *Carolina*, etc. I. 20 The *Red-headed Woodpecker. The whole head and neck are of a deep red. **1831** AUDUBON *Ornith. Biog.* I. 144 The Red-headed Woodpecker is found in all parts of the United States. **1850** LYELL *2nd Visit U.S.* II. 269 The loud tapping of the large red-headed woodpecker, so common a sound in the American forests.

b. In names of animals and plants.

1744 W. ELLIS *Let.* 11 Aug. in *Mod. Husbandman* (1750) VI. xxi. 161 The red-headed Thistle is growing on the Hills. **1774** GOLDSM. *Nat. Hist.* (1776) VIII. 172 The small red-headed earth worm. **1777** LIGHTFOOT *Flora Scot.* II. 717 Red-headed Bryum. **1802** SHAW *Gen. Zool.* III. I. 236 Red-headed Lizard. **1845** WESTWOOD *Moths* 207 *Microsetia ruficapitella* (the red-headed pigmy). **1901** E. MOUNTS *Islands in Ocean of Memory* 58 You may throw the bait out within three feet of the boat and a red-headed hag or gony will make a dive at it. **1947** J. STEVENSON-HAMILTON *Wildlife S. Afr.* xxx. 249 The red-headed squirrel (*Paraxerus palliatus*), is distinguished by the rufous colour of the head and underparts.

'red-heart. 1. A cherry belonging to a variety bearing heart-shaped fruit with red flesh; also, the fruit of a tree of this kind. Also *attrib.*

[**1664** J. EVELYN *Kalendarium Hortense* 68 June.. Cherries,.. Heart, Black, Red, White.] **1707** [see *black heart* s.v. BLACK *a.* 19]. **1764** EDWARDS *Gleanings* II. III. 346 Index, The Red-heart Cherry. **1833** H. BARNARD *Let.* 25 May in *Maryland Hist. Mag.* (1918) XIII. 377 Here were.. numerous trees of ripe cherries, black hearts and red hearts. **1887** *Harper's Mag.* Dec. 31/1 Under the largest of two red-heart cherry-trees sat a girl shelling pease. **1904** E. A. G. GLASGOW *Deliverance* 238, I used to cut round old Fletcher's pasture.. to keep from passin' by his red-heart cherry-tree.

2. One of several trees with reddish bark or wood, esp. the western North American *Ceanothus spinosus*, an evergreen shrub or small tree belonging to the family Rhamnaceæ and bearing clusters of blue or white flowers.

1926 J. MASEFIELD *Odtaa* xiv. 231 He saw a footmark in some soft earth close to a red-heart. **1937** *Range Plant Handbk.* (Forest Service, U.S. Dept. Agric.) B39 The branches of a number of species [of *Ceanothus*], such as.. redheart, or spiny myrtle (*C. spinosus*), end in spines. **1951** W. L. JEPSON *Flowering Plants Calif.* 620 Red-heart. Straggling shrub 5 to 10 ft. high, or forming a small tree up to 24 ft. **1965** *Austral. Encycl.* V. 225/2 *Dissiliaria baloghioides* (hauer or redheart). **1973** G. M. CHIPPENDALE *Eucalypts W. Austral. Goldfields* 93/1 Redheart [sc. *Eucalyptus decipiens*] is a spreading, twisted, gnarled tree. **1973** *Stand. Encycl. S. Afr.* IX. 266/1 Red-heart.. (*Acacia nilotica* = *A. benthami*) Thorn-tree with a spreading rounded canopy.

red heat, red-heat. The state or condition of being red-hot; the degree of heat present when a substance is red-hot.

1686 PLOT *Staffordsh.* 161 It is so brittle it would crack in the red-heat. **1807** T. THOMSON *Chem.* (ed. 3) II. 209 He dried a quantity of crystallized carbonate of soda in a red heat. **1831** BREWSTER *Nat. Magic* xiii. (1883) 319 This vapour, being consumed without flame, keeps the wick at its red-heat. **1886** A. WINCHELL *Walks Geol. Field* 134 They could only be separated by bringing the residue to a red-heat.

fig. **1898** WATTS-DUNTON *Aylwin* (1900) 45/2, I awoke in about an hour with red-heat at my brain.

red-heeled, *a.*

1. Of shoes, etc.: Having red heels.

1709 STEELE *Tatler* No. 67 ¶1, I gave Mr. Didapper a private Reprimand for wearing red-heel'd Shoes. **1725** RAMSAY *Gentle Sheph.* IV. ii, I come hame strutting in my red-heel'd shoon. **1801** MRS. ROBINSON *Sylphid* III. 66 (Jod.), His redheeled pumps for a pair of squaretoed boots. [**1899** H. G. GRAHAM *Soc. Life Scot.* (ed. 2) 19 Young men .. displaying their new fashions, their red stockings and red-heeled shoes.]

2. Wearing shoes with red heels. Also *transf.*

1840 THACKERAY *Paris Sk.-bk.* (1867) 395 Ancient French Tragedy, red-heeled, patched, and beperiwigged, lies in the grave. **1894** DU MAURIER *Trilby* II. 206 Lords and ladies gay —red-heeled, patched, powdered.

So **red'heelery.** *nonce-wd.*

1818 *Blackw. Mag.* III. 532 Whence, like a rascal's visage in the pillory, Stares, fringed and flounced with flannel, the redheelery.

red herring. [Cf. HERRING 1 b.]

1. a. *collect.* Herring to which a red colour is imparted in the process of curing them by smoke.

c **1420** *Liber Cocorum* (1862) 54 Cover þy white heryng ..þen cover red heryng and set abufe. **1466** *Mann. & Househ. Exp.* (Roxb.) 207 Paid.. for j. cade of rede heryngе vs. **1577** B. GOOGE *Heresbach's Husb.* I. (1586) 12 Here is a good handsome rooffe.. well stored with redde Hearing, Bacon, and Martilmas beefe. **1633** HART *Diet of Diseased* I. xxi. 91 Some are salted, and afterwards hung up and dried: and then we call them Red-hering.

b. A single herring cured in this way.

1495 *Naval Acc. Hen. VII* (1896) 162, ccc Redde Heryngs —iij[s]. **1561** in *Child-Marriages* (1897) 70 Stockfishe, red heringes and such marchaundrie wares. **1620** VENNER *Via Recta* iv. 77 Red Herrings and Sprats giue a very bad and adusted nourishment. **1686** N. COX *Gentl. Recreat.* v. (ed. 3) 65 The trailing or dragging of a dead Cat, or Fox, (and in case of necessity a Red-Herring) three or four miles.. and then laying the Dogs on the scent. **1714** MANDEVILLE *Fab. Bees* (1725) I. 263 Red-herrings, pickled-sturgeon,.. and every thing that was proper to make their liquor go down with pleasure. *a* **1818** M. G. LEWIS *Jrnl. W. Ind.* (1834) 106 The slaves also receive.. a regular weekly allowance of red herrings and salt meat, which serves to relish their vegetable diet. **1885** ANSTEY *Tinted Venus* 87 A display of joints, cauliflowers, and red herrings.

c. *slang.* A soldier.

1853 in *Househ. Words* (1854) 75/2 A soldier [is called] a swaddy, a lobster, a red herring.

2. In phrases, or allusively: **a.** ***neither fish, (nor) flesh, nor good red herring,*** etc.: (see FISH *sb.*[1] 4 c).

1542 [see FISH *sb.*[1] 4 c]. **1605** BRETON *I pray you be not Angrie* To Rdr., They that are neither of both, but betwixt both, neither Fish nor Flesh, but plaine Red-Hearing. **1698** FRYER *Acc. E. India & P.* 123 To me it seems.. neither Fish nor Flesh, nor good Red Herring. **1711** ADDISON *Spect.* No. 165 ¶6 A Letter that was neither Fish, Flesh, nor good Red-Herring. **1850** SMEDLEY *F. Fairleigh* liii, A brat that's neither fish, flesh, nor fowl, nor good red herring.

b. ***to draw a red herring across the track*** (cf. quot. 1686 in 1 b): to attempt to divert attention from the real question; hence ***red herring***, a subject intended to have this effect.

1884 *Liverpool Daily Post* 11 July 5/4 The talk of revolutionary dangers is a mere red-herring. **1892** *Spectator* 12 Mar. 360/2 These red-herrings drawn across the path. **1900** *Westm. Gaz.* 2 Feb. 2/1 Not to be put off the main line of attack by the red-herrings of an unreformed War Office. **1928** *Manch. Guardian Weekly* 10 Aug. 105/1 Both the Opposition parties are trying to drag in the Protectionist red herring in the vain hope of causing dissension. **1956** [see CHIVVY *v.*[1]]. **1967** G. F. FIENNES *I tried to run Railway* iv. 48 The Coroner's opinion that the detonators were 'something of a red herring'. **1975** M. RUSSELL *Murder by Mile* xi. 116 This could be a side-issue or red herring designed to.. turn me from the genuine scent. **1976** *Southern Even. Echo* (Southampton) 13 Nov. 9/3 He accused Mr. Deacon of introducing a red herring into the issue.

3. *attrib.*, as ***red-herring cob, house, sort.***

1594 [see COB *sb.*[1] 8]. **1598** HAUGHTON *Englishmen for my Money* (1616) B 2 b, [I] looke like nothing but Red-Herring Cobbes, and Stock-Fish. **1727–41** CHAMBERS *Cycl.* s.v. *Herring*, Such as are kept to make red herrings.. are hanged up in the herring-hangs, or red-herring houses. **1833** MARRYAT *P. Simple* xxvii, He has his wife on board, who is a red-herring sort of a lady, and very troublesome to boot.

redhibition (rɛdhɪˈbɪʃən). *Civil Law.* [a. F. *rédhibition* (16th c.), or ad. L. *redhibitiōn-em*, n. of action f. *redhibēre* to take back or give back, f. *red-* RE- + *habēre* to have.] (See quot. 1727–41.)

The nature of the evidence leaves it doubtful whether the word has ever been actually in English use; the entry in Chambers is translated from the *Dict. de Trévoux* (1721).

1656 BLOUNT *Glossogr.* (copying Cotgr.), *Redhibition*, restitution of a thing to him that sold it; the causing of one by Law to take that again, which he sold. **1727–41** CHAMBERS *Cycl.*, *Redhibition*, in the civil law, an action allowed a buyer, whereby to annul the sale of some moveable,.. upon the buyer's finding it damaged, or that there was some personal cheat, etc. **1852–6** in BOUVIER *Law Dict. U.S.* [Hence in Worcester and later Dicts.]

redhibitory (rɛdˈhɪbɪtərɪ), *a. Civil Law.* [ad. F. *rédhibitoire* (14th c. in Hatz.-Darm.), or late L. *redhibitōri-us*: see prec. and -ORY.] Of or pertaining to redhibition.

Chambers copies the *Dict. de Trévoux*: see prec.

1727–41 CHAMBERS *Cycl.* s.v. *Redhibition*, If a horse was sold that had the glanders, were broken-winded, or foundered, it was a redhibitory case. **1851** BURRILL *Law Dict.*, Redhibitory action. *Ibid.*, Redhibitory defect. [Hence in Worcester and later Dicts.]

red horse, red-horse. *U.S.*

1. a. An American fish of the genus *Moxostoma* (esp. *M. macrolepidota*). **b.** The red-fish, *Sciæna ocellata.*

1796 MORSE *Amer. Geog.* I. 663 Catfish, buffaloe-fish, red horse, eels [etc.]. **1818** RAFINESQUE in *Smithson. Coll.* (1877) XIII. IX. i. 13 *Catostomus Erythrurus*.. Red Horse. **1877** JORDAN *Ibid.* 32 The coloration [of the black-tail fallfish] is that of a young 'Red-Horse'. **1884** GOODE *Nat. Hist. Aquat. Anim.* 372 The 'Red Fish' and 'Red Horse' of Florida and the Gulf States. *Ibid.* 614 The common 'Red Horse' or 'Mullet' abounds in most streams westward and southward of New York.

2. A nickname given to natives of Kentucky.

1835 HOFFMAN *Winter in West* I. 210 The spokesman was evidently a 'red-horse' from Kentucky. **1835–40** HALIBURTON *Clockm.* (1862) 318 These last have all nicknames. There's the hoosiers of Indiana,.. the red horses of Kentucky.

3. *slang* (orig. *Mil.*). Corned beef.

1864 I. JACKSON *Let.* 28 June in *Some of Boys* (1960) 184 Supper.. is coffee & Red Hoss. **1905** J. BOWE *With 13th Minnesota in Philippines* 24 Of bean-soup, hard-tack, and red horse.. we have had our fill. **1920** W. B. ELLINGTON *Company 'A', 23rd Engineers* 27 We have red horse and rice pudding for dinner. **1941** J. SMILEY *Hash House Lingo* 46 *Red horse*, corned beef.

red-hot, *a.* (and *sb.*). (Now usually written with hyphen, rarely **redhot**: in predicative use still occas. **red hot.**)

1. a. Heated to redness.

c **1375** *Sc. Leg. Saints* xlv. (*Christina*) 242 He ane oyne gert be mad red het. *c* **1460** *Play Sacram.* 682 To make an ovyn as redd hott as euer yt can be made wt fere. **1595** SHAKS. *John* IV. i. 61 The Iron of it selfe, though heate red hot [etc.]. **1665** MANLEY *Grotius, Low C. Warres* 707 To prevent fire, which they greatly fear'd from the Red hot Bullets shot into it. **1756–7** tr. *Keysler's Trav.* (1760) III. 25 Stones.. glowing hot, and when broken exactly resembling red-hot iron. **1819** SHELLEY *Cyclops* 384 He.. placed upon the fire A brazen pot to boil, and made red hot The points of spits. **1878** HUXLEY *Physiogr.* 189 This crack then serves for the passage of steam and other vapours, with showers of red-hot ashes.

b. *absol.* as *sb.* Red-hot metal. Also *fig.*

1832 BABBAGE *Econ. Manuf.* ii. (ed. 3) 21 It is usual to set the engine at work a short time before the red-hot is ready to be removed from the furnace to the rollers. **1865** CARLYLE *Fredk. Gt.* XXI. v. VI. 545 A stratum of red-hot kindling in Ziethen too.

2. *fig.* **a.** Of persons: Highly inflamed or excited; fiery; violently enthusiastic, extreme (in some view or principle). Also, outstanding, uninhibited, lively, sexy, passionate; esp. in phr. ***red-hot momma***, (*a*) a woman who sings in a particular earthy style; (*b*) a girlfriend, lover. Hence *transf.* in jazz; cf. HOT *a.* 8 g. Occas. as *sb.* (quot. 1835).

1608 MIDDLETON *Fam. Love* III. iii, I shall expect my wife anon, red-hot with zeal. **1610** SHAKS. *Temp.* IV. i. 171, I told you Sir, they were red-hot with drinking. **1758** WESLEY *Wks.* (1872) II. 464 A red-hot Predestinarian, talking of God's 'blowing whole worlds to hell'. **1835** C. BRONTE in Mrs. Gaskell *Life* viii. (1858) 107 The opposition is divided, Red-hots, and Luke-warms. **1845** COL. HAWKER *Diary* (1893) II. 255 It has.. ridded Keyhaven of a redhot young gunner. **1870** DICKENS *E. Drood* viii, Edwin's coolness, so far from being infectious, makes him red-hot. **1888** J. RUNCIMAN *Chequers* 116 You take the fellows in town that make their living after dark... There's some red-hot ones up—you know where—in Piccadilly. **1926** WHITEMAN & MCBRIDE *Jazz* viii. 169 A red hot mama song. **1934** S. R. NELSON *All about Jazz* ii. 58 Dorsey is a red-hot stylist and technician [on the saxophone]. **1934** C. LAMBERT *Music Ho!* III. 210 The negro associations of jazz, the weary traveller, the comforting old mammy, the red-hot baby, have become a formula of expression only, as empty and convenient as the harlequin and columbine of the nineteenth century. **1935** *Time* 21 Jan. 58 Sophie Tucker, famed as 'the last of the red hot mamas'. **1936** WODEHOUSE *Laughing Gas* ii. 24 The bride-to-be is probably some frightful red-hot mamma. **1940** O. NASH *Face is Familiar* 87 Affection.. leads to breach of promise If you go round lavishing it on red-hot momise. **1942** Z. N. HURSTON in A. Dundes *Mother Wit* (1973) 223/2 A red hot pimp like you *say* you is, ain't got no business in the barrel. **1950** A. LOMAX *Mister Jelly Roll* 69 A red-hot bass player, seventy-nine years old, a proud Creole. **1957** R. HOGGART *Uses of Literacy* v. 132, I first heard 'Paper Doll' sung in the 'red-hot' fashion by an American star crooner. **1976** in D. Villiers *Next Year in Jerusalem* 204 (*caption*) 'The Last of the Red Hot Mommas', Sophie Tucker. **1977** J. WAINWRIGHT *Do Nothin'* xi. 183 It was jive and blues; either red-hot or smoochy.

b. Of things, actions, etc.: Burning, scorching, urgent, violent, furious, etc. Also, sensational, lively, exciting, intense.

1647 WARD *Simp. Cobler* (1843) 38, I will.. leave the red-hot question to them that dare handle it. *c* **1790** WOLCOTT (P. Pindar) *Lousiad* v. Wks. 1812 I. 236 Then quick he aim'd, of red-hot anger full, His nails of vengeance. **1852** MOTLEY *Corr.* (1889) I. v. 142 Some singeing, scorching, red-hot review. **1865** CARLYLE *Fredk. Gt.* XVIII. xiii. (1872) VIII. 37 Of Fermor's redhot savagery on Cüstrin, it is lamentably necessary we should say something. **1879** MISS E. K. BATES *Egypt. Bonds* II. viii. 207 Oscar strikes up a red-hot flirtation with some.. country beauty. **1887** *Lantern* 19 Feb. 6/1 A red-hot newsy journal. **1891** 'MARK TWAIN' in *Harper's Mag.* Dec. 97 Suddenly a red-hot new idea came whistling down into my camp. **1904** J. C. LINCOLN *Cap'n Eri* xi. 205 '"Fightin' Fred Starlight, the Boy Rover of the Pacific",' he read aloud. 'Humph! Is it good?' 'Bet your life! It's a red-hot story.' **1915** WODEHOUSE *Psmith Journalist* v. 33 My idea is that *Cosy Moments* should become red-hot stuff. I could wish its tone to be such that the public will wonder why we do not print it on asbestos. **1955** *Times* 16 May 3/3 Local propaganda on the virtues of nationalization has resembled rather the cooing of lethargic doves than the strident militancy of red hot Socialism. **1969** *John Edwards Mem. Foundation Q.* V. ii. 60 An urban audience more accustomed to 'red hot' fox trots than to barn dances. **1977** *Belfast Tel.* 24 Jan. 18/6 The clinching of these red-hot finals must be hailed as another major breakthrough for the sport.

c. Very warm (as the favourite for a race).

1882 *Daily Tel.* 30 Jan., The first-named won three races.. and was each time a 'red hot' favourite.

d. *Austral. slang.* Unfair, unreasonable.

1896 H. LAWSON *While Billy Boils* 281 When.. she paused for breath, he drew a long one, gave a short whistle, and, said: 'Well, it's red-hot!' **1907** A. WRIGHT *Keane of Kalgoorlie* 107 'It's red 'ot,' put in Dave, 'th'way these 'ere owners makes er pore man give 'em a lump in th' sweep.' **1941** BAKER *Dict. Austral. Slang* 59 A red hot price.

3. ***red-hot poker,*** a tall perennial herb of the genus *Kniphofia* (formerly *Tritoma*), esp. *K. uvaria*, belonging to the family Liliaceæ, native to southern or tropical Africa, and bearing spikes of red, yellow, or white flowers.

1887 'F. ANSTEY' *Talking Horse* (1892) 216 The dahlias and 'red-hot pokers' and gladioli.. burnt with a sinister glow. **1897** *Westm. Gaz.* 22 Nov. 2/1 Red Hot Poker. **1916** M. HAMPDEN *Flower Culture* xvii. 206 Red-hot pokers are not over [in November]. **1934** G. A. R. PHILLIPS *Aristocrats of Flower Border* xiii. 191 Far more descriptive of its vivid beauty are the common names of torch lily and red hot poker. **1971** H. EVANS *How to cheat at Gardening* xi. 168 The Red Hot Poker.. looks marvellous mixed with Sea Holly.

4. as *sb.* A frankfurter; a hot dog. *U.S. slang.*

1892 *Chicago Figaro* VI. 157/2 The appetizing savors of 'red hots'. **1934** J. T. FARRELL *Calico Shoes* 46 Don leaned against the thrown-together red hot stand, munching at a hot-dog sandwich. **1971** B. MALAMUD *Tenants* 143, I got this redhot with mustard on it I'm gonna eat my meat.

redi, obs. form of READY *a.*

‖**redia** (ˈriːdɪə). Pl. **rediæ** (ˈriːdɪiː). [mod.L., f. *Redi*, the name of an Italian naturalist.] *Zool.* An asexual stage in some trematodes, as the liver-fluke (*Distomum hepaticum*), hatched from eggs formed within the sporocyst, and in turn developing into a cercaria.

1877 HUXLEY *Anat. Inv. Anim.* iv. 203 The Redia, as this form is called, has a mouth and a simple caecal intestine, but no other organs. **1882** A. P. THOMAS in *Proc. R. Med. Soc.* 14 Nov. 15 These assume the forms of rediae, or nurse forms more highly organised than the simple sporocysts.

re'dial, *v.* [f. RE- 5 a + DIAL *v.* 4.] *intr.* and *trans.* To dial again.

1961 'E. LATHEN' *Banking on Death* (1962) viii. 70 His daughter broke the connection. He started to redial then put the phone down. **1966** 'A. HALL' *9th Directive* xiv. 132 All three lines were busy and I began redialling the numbers. **1973** 'E. MCBAIN' *Let's hear It* xiii. 193 In as long as it took for the caller to re-dial, the phone began to ring again. **1976** 'D. CRAIG' *Faith Hope & Death* xvi. 111, I re-dialled and still engaged, so it was not a wrong number.

redich, obs. form of RADISH.

redic'tate, *v.* [RE- 5 a.] *trans.* To dictate again. Also *absol.* So **redic'tation.**

a **1631** DONNE *Serm.* lxxxix. IV. 142 Whether.. the books of the Law.. were re-inspired and redictated again by the Holy Ghost to Esdras. **1890** *Pall Mall G.* 2 July 2/2 The typesetter setting up his 'copy' direct from the phonograph's redictation. **1964** T. L. KINSEY *Audio-Typing & Electric Typewriters* iii. 12 After a recording has been transcribed the dictator need only re-dictate over the existing work and it is automatically erased, the new dictation being recorded in its place. **1974** R. CROSSMAN *Diaries* (1975) I. 15, I decided therefore to re-dictate this whole first transcript in plain intelligible English.

redicule, obs. form of RIDICULE.

'redient, *a. rare*$^{-0}$. [f. L. *redīre* to return, after *ambient, transient.*] Returning.

1656 BLOUNT *Glossogr.*, *Redient*, returning, coming or going back; the Redient moon.. the new moon. **1828–32** WEBSTER cites E. H. SMITH. Hence in later Dicts.

‖**redif** (rɛˈdɪf). [Turkish, a. Arab. *redif* one who follows, a second.] The reserve of the Turkish military force; a soldier belonging to the reserve.

1879 FIFE-COOKSON *Armies of Balkans* i. 16 About twelve battalions.. inferior in quality, owing to being principally composed of redifs. **1889** *Daily News* 12 Nov. 5/4 The Turkish Government is also perplexed by the recent mutiny of four battalions of redifs (reserves) who have already been sent home.

redi'ffuse, *v. Broadcasting.* [RE- 5 a.] *trans.* To disseminate, broadcast, or rebroadcast by rediffusion. So **redi'ffused** *ppl. a.* Also **redi'ffuser,** a person who or company which rediffuses a programme.

1931 *Times Educ. Suppl.* 1 Aug. p. iv/1 In order to receive such rediffused signals the listener requires an ultra-short wave adapter. **1932** *B.B.C. Year-bk. 1933* 70 Apart from the purely copyright aspect.. the BBC.. may very reasonably question the equity of the public rediffuser being able to use its programmes for the same.. fee as is paid by the private listener. **1948** *Architect Rev.* CIV. 131/2 A public address system enables broadcast programmes to be received and rediffused throughout the school. **1950** *Sport* 7–11 Apr. 22/4 It may not be long before television programmes are rediffused through cinemas.

rediffusion (riːdɪˈfjuːʒən). *Broadcasting.* [RE- 5 a.] **a.** The dissemination, broadcasting, or rebroadcasting of a programme by (*a*) reproduction on loudspeakers and screens in public places, (*b*) transmission by a broadcasting company which was not responsible for making it, or (*c*) publication by other media of items from a radio or television programme.

1927 *Observer* 13 Nov. 19/5 The best programmes of the British service will be available for re-diffusion throughout the Continent as well as throughout the Empire and the rest of the world. **1933** *B.B.C. Year-bk. 1934* 28 It was found possible to apply the [Copyright] Act.. to public loud-speaker 'rediffusion'. **1948** *Daily Tel.* 9 June 6/5 The Association for the Protection of Copyright in Sport set out to secure certain safeguards, particularly against general 'rediffusion' of television on big cinema screens. **1950** *Sport* 7–11 Apr. 22/4 Sporting events will, I think, be among the most popular types of rediffusion. **1967** W. SOYINKA *Kongi's Harvest* 2 Who but a lunatic Will bandy words with boxes With government rediffusion sets Which talk and talk and never Take a lone word in reply.

b. *spec.* The distribution of radio or television transmissions within a community by cable from a single receiver.

1935 *Nature* 2 Feb. 196/1 'Rediffusion' is a method of distributing a broadcast programme over an independent line network to a number of subscribers. **1968** BETHELL & BURG tr. *Solzhenitsyn's Cancer Ward* I. xix. 295 Vadim.. was happily surprised to discover there was no radio... (The reason for this omission was that for years they had been planning to move the clinic into better-equipped quarters, and the new place.. was going to be wired with rediffusion points throughout.) **1975** C. STUART in J. Reith *Diaries* ii. 179 Wireless or relay exchange (also called rediffusion) was the practice of wiring broadcast programmes to individual subscribers by commercial companies operating under licence from the Post Office.

redify(e, obs. forms of RE-EDIFY *v.*

re'dig, *v.* [RE- 5 a.] *trans.* To dig again. So **re'digging** *vbl. sb.*

1907 *Church Q. Rev.* July 470 This division seems to entail some redigging of ground already trenched. **1922** G. BELL *Let.* 16 Feb. (1927) II. xxii. 633, I must tell you the Yusufiyah is one of the oldest canals in the world... Julian sailed down it to Ctesiphon and the Abbasids re-dug it. **1963** *Times* 4 June 12/5 A year later the tree can be lifted out after the trench is redug. **1965** J. A. MICHENER *Source* 892 Couldn't they have redug the tunnel?

† **redige**, *v. Obs. rare*⁻¹. [ad. F. *rédiger* (1455 in Godef.), or L. *redigĕre*: see REDACT *v.*] *trans.* To reduce, translate.

1550 *Kalender of Sheph.* N v, Of ye which I wil declare as I haue found written in ye latin tong, I will redige it to our English maternal.

redi'gest, *v.* [RE- 5 a. Cf. obs. F. *redigérer* (Cotgr.).] *trans.* To digest again. Chiefly *fig.*

1611 COTGR., *Redigerer*, to redisgest, redigest. **1836** F. MAHONEY *Rel. Father Prout, Songs Hor.* I. (1859) 374 To redigest..whatever might have been crude and unmatured in his juvenile lucubrations. **1865** MASSON *Rec. Brit. Philos.* 281 Kant ate up all Hume and redigested him.

So **redi'gestion**.

1817 KEATS *Let.* 22 Nov., The redigestion of our most ethereal musings upon earth.

redilis, obs. form of RIDDLE *sb.*[1]

† **'redily**, *adv. Obs.* Forms: 4 redilie, -lyche, 4–5 redyly, redili(che, 5 -lich, (? rydilich), 4–6 redily. *Comp.* 4 redilokar, redylyer. [f. REDY *a.* + -LY[2]; but in many cases app. written for REDELY.]

a. Wisely, discreetly, prudently. **b.** Precisely, certainly, assuredly.

a **1300** *Cursor M.* 6297 Als i sal tel yow redili For-þer mar in þis stori. *c* **1330** R. BRUNNE *Chron.* (1810) 105 If any man wille witen, & se of hir storie, At Westmynster written er þei redilie. **1362** LANGL. *P. Pl.* A. IV. 153 Bote Rediliche [*v.r.* redelyche] Reson þou Rydest not heonnes. **1387** TREVISA *Higden* (Rolls) VI. 47 Ȝe helde forþ ȝoure purpose rediliche [*v.r.* redyly, L. *caute*] inow. **1413** *Pilgr. Sowle* (Caxton) I. xxvii. (1859) 31 Ther nys no pylgrym that goth so redyly but that oftymes he mote foruoyen. *c* **1449** PECOCK *Repr.* I. xx. 129 The first premisse is redili trewe.

redily, obs. form of READILY *adv.*

redimar, obs. Sc. form of REDEEMER.

redi'minish, *v.* [RE- 5 a.] *trans.* To diminish anew.

1611 COTGR., *Rededuire*, to rededuct, rediminish. *a* **1743** SAVAGE *Animalcule* ix, In Britain, Halifax it rose; (By Halifax, bloom'd Congreve's strains); And now it rediminish'd glows, To glide through godlike Rutland's veins.

† **redimite**, *a. Sc. Obs.* In 6 redomyt, redem-, redymyte. [ad. L. *redimīt-us*, pa. pple. of *redimīre*: see next.] Wreathed or crowned; adorned, ornate, beautiful.

1500–20 DUNBAR *Poems* xlvi. 77 Hir goldin tressit hairis redomyt. **1513** DOUGLAS *Æneis* VI. xi. 60 The blomyt lillyis quhyte, And vthir fragrant blosumys redemyte. *Ibid.* XII. Prol. 128 Hevinly lylleis..schew thar creistis redymyte.

† **redimite**, *v. Obs. rare.* In 6 redymite, redemyte. [f. L. *redimīt-*, ppl. stem of *redimīre* to bind, crown, wreathe.] *trans.* To bind, crown.

1592 R. D. *Hypnerotomachia* 53 The head of which image was redymited with an azure Diademe. **1599** LINCHE *Fount. Anc. Fict.* F ij, Wreaths and garlands, with which his temples were girt and redemyted.

Red Indian: see INDIAN *sb.* 2 b.

redines, obs. form of READINESS.

† **'rediness.** *Obs.* Also 4 redy-, reedy-. [f. REDY *a.* + -NESS.] **a.** Wisdom, discretion, prudence. **b.** Certainty, certain knowledge.

1382 WYCLIF *Judith* xi. 6 Forsothe the redynesse [L. *industria*] of thin inwit is told to alle folkis. **1387** TREVISA *Higden* (Rolls) V. 245 Hit byfalleþ to ȝoure redynesse and wisdom [L. *prudentiæ*] to conspire aȝenst þe tyraunt. *c* **1400** *Master of Game* (MS. Digby 182) xxv, It were good redinesse to loke if þei myght se ony deere. *c* **1400** *Beryn* 3291 Met I nevir creature that me coude wissh or say Reedynes of my ffadir, dede othir a lyue.

reding, *vbl. sb.*: see REDE *v.*[2]

† **reding-king.** *Obs. rare.*

Of obscure origin and meaning. The suggestion that it stands for *riding-king* (though favoured by the reading of one MS.), and that this had the same sense as RADKNIGHT, involves obvious difficulties.

1362 LANGL. *P. Pl.* A. v. 166 A ribibor, a ratoner, a rakere of chepe, A ropere, a redyng-kyng. **1393** *Ibid.* C. III. 112 Bette þe budele of banneburies sokne, Reynauld the reue and redyngkynges menye.

redingote ('rɛdɪŋgəʊt). [a. F. *redingote* (1725), corruption of Eng. *riding-coat.*]

a. (In France.) A double-breasted outer coat for men, with long plain skirts not cut away in the front. **b.** A similar garment worn by women, sometimes cut away in front.

1793 F. BURNEY *Let.* *c* 9 Feb. (1972) II. 13 He was quite wet through his *redingotte.* **1802** C. WILMOT *Let.* 3 Jan. in *Irish Peer* (1920) 22 Benches..where servants are generally stretch'd in 'Redingotes' (Great coats) and cock'd hats. **1835** *Court Mag.* VI. p. xviii/2 Silks are the only materials for promenade robes and *redingotes.* **1880** *Cassell's Mag.* June 441 The Directoire redingote is not as yet common in England. **1883** *Ibid.* Oct. 698/1 One of the useful redingotes which..will be found suitable as an additional wrap. **1890** *Athenæum* 28 June 838/2 The Emperor [Napoleon], buttoned up in his legendary grey *redingote* and seated on a white horse stands motionless on a small rise of ground. **1930** *Times* 17 Mar. 9/4 Some of the new redingotes are made to give the effect of a coat and skirt with pleated lingerie vest. **1939** *Country Life* 11 Feb. p. xxxviii/2 This Matita two-piece redingote and dress is in a tone-on-tone effect in light and dark grey. **1965** [see CLOQUÉ]. **1973** *Times* 14 Nov. 16/8 The Queen will wear a classic redingote of blue silk.

attrib. **1888** *Daily News* 14 June 5/8 Redingote gowns are also in great favour.

redingtonite ('rɛdɪŋtənaɪt). *Min.* [f. the name of the *Redington* mine, Knoxville, Napa Co., Calif. + -ITE[1].] A hydrous sulphate of iron, magnesium, chromium, and aluminium occurring as fibrous masses of a white, yellowish, or purple colour.

1888 G. F. BECKER in *Monogr. U.S. Geol. Survey* No. 13. 279 A hydrous chromium sulphate occurs in fissures in silicified serpentine... It seems appropriate to give the name redingtonite to this hitherto unknown mineral. **1965** G. J. WILLIAMS *Econ. Geol. N.Z.* x. 149/1 He found deep lilac or purple earthy redingtonite associated with the folia of the fuchsite.

red ink. 1. *slang.* Cheap red wine; also applied to some other inferior alcoholic drinks. Chiefly *U.S.*

1919 *Red Cross Mag.* Nov. 22/3 He at once took ten of his fellow students to a sixty-cent 'red-ink' and spaghetti dinner down on Tenth Street. **1926** J. BLACK *You can't Win* xii. 153 Barrels of the deadly 'foot juice' or 'red ink', as the winos called it. **1930** *N.Y. Times Mag.* 16 Feb. 19 Today's word 'rum' used in a broad sense to designate all kinds of forbidden liquors, may refer to..the 'red ink' of Greenwich Village. **1942** H. W. VAN LOON *Lives* 631 The wine problem was easily settled. Any kind of 'red ink'—any kind of that cheap Chianti..would be satisfactory. **1952** E. O'NEILL *Moon for Misbegotten* III. 140 You'd lie awake..with..the wine of passion poets blab about, a sour aftertaste in your mouth of Dago red ink! **1976** W. H. CANAWAY *Willow-Pattern War* iii. 28 Lunch..was a real workaday snack this time: *raclettes* and *rösti* with a half-bottle of red ink.

2. *U.S. colloq.* The debit side of an account: cf. RED sb.[1] 1 g. Also in extended use.

1929 *Century* Mar. 605/2 Red ink returns were as prolific as asparagus, which meant you..dug deep for the freight money. **1939** S. BENT *Newspaper Crusaders* ii. 35 The long-drawn crusade whereby St. Louis was taken out of political red ink and put on the credit side of the electoral ledger merits examination. **1948** *Sun* (Baltimore) 31 Jan. 1/3 We cannot play with red ink when we're financing a great government. **1967** *Boston Sunday Herald* 7 May IV. 9/2 Give us enough red ink and make money plentiful enough and the economic skies will soon clear. **1977** *Time* 28 Feb. 26/1 Carter's projected $57·4 billion deficit is an improvement over the $68 billion in red ink anticipated for fiscal 1977, which ends on Sept. 30. **1979** *Financial Rev.* 19 Oct. 27/1 The company would report a loss of more than $US 3 million for the third quarter, bringing the red-ink figure for nine months close to $US 6 million.

† **re'dintegral**, *a. Obs. rare*⁻¹. [f. as next: see INTEGRAL.] Tending to redintegration.

1651 BIGGS *New Disp.* ¶288 The ferment [of the stomach] is redintegral and redivivous.

redintegrate (rɛ'dɪntɪgreɪt), *pa. pple.* ? *Obs.* [ad. L. *redintegrātus*, pa. pple. of *redintegrāre*: see next.] Restored to a perfect state, renewed.

1501 in *Lett. Rich. III & Hen. VII* (Rolls) I. 154 The said amitie and confederacion [shall] be redintegrate aftre the maner and fourme..in tyme passed. **1564** in Froude *Hist. Eng.* (1863) VIII. 460 [He recommended her to allow] the trafic with the low countries to be redintegrate. **1622** BACON *Hen. VII*, 40 The Kingdome of France..being redintegrate in those principall members, which anciently had beene portions of the Crowne of France. **1655** JER. TAYLOR *Unum Necess.* v. iv. ¶35 That every wound may have its balsam, and every broken bone be bound up and redintegrate. **1819** H. BUSK *Vestriad* v. 653 With strength redintegrate the stage he cross'd.

redintegrate (rɛ'dɪntɪgreɪt), *v.* [f. ppl. stem of L. *redintegrāre* to make whole again, restore, renew, f. *red-* RE- + *integrāre* to INTEGRATE.]

1. *trans.* To restore to a state of wholeness, completeness or unity; to renew, re-establish, in a united or perfect state.

1432–50 tr. *Higden* (Rolls) III. 255 Sone after that Iustinianus redintegrate [L. *redintegravit*] the lawes of the digeste. **1632** B. JONSON *Magn. Lady* IV. iii, Redintegrate the fame first of your house, Restore your ladyship's quiet. **1678** CUDWORTH *Intell. Syst.* 814 The dæmoniack body, being divided, is quickly redintegrated by coalescence, as air or water. *a* **1734** NORTH *Exam.* I. i. §4 (1740) 16 To redintegrate the Honour and Credit of that exploded Faction. **1811** *Chron.* in *Ann. Reg.* 578 To restore or redintegrate the ancient representation of the commons. **1862** F. HALL *Hindu Philos. Syst.* 64 Often as the universe has been redintegrated, the Veda has as often been produced.

absol. **1647** WARD *Simp. Cobler* 66 In Breaches integrant, 'tween Principalls of States, Due Justice may suppresse, but Love redintegrates.

b. Const. *to* (a person), *into* (a state). *rare.*

1680 J. AUBREY in *Lett. Eminent Persons* (1813) III. 611 Here his Majesty's favours were redintegrated to him. **1724** R. WELTON *Chr. Faith & Pract.* 12 The grave shall surrender our crumbled ashes, redintegrated into a more perfect vivacity.

† **2.** To re-establish (a person) *in* a place. Also *refl. Obs. rare.*

1630 WOTTON in *Reliq.* (1685) 452 The King of Sweden hath landed..with intention..to redintegrate his near Kinsman in Mecklebúrge. **1649** CROMWELL *Let.* 14 Nov. in *Carlyle*, Inchiquin..did strongly endeavour to redintegrate himself there, but without success.

b. To re-establish (a person) *in* (†*into*) a position, condition, etc. Chiefly *pass.* Now *rare.*

1622 E. MISSELDEN *Free Trade* (ed. 2) 115 They and We ..may be redintegrated, renewed, and revnited, in vnfaigned Amitie. **1643** *Answ. Ld. Digby's Apol.* 5 That you may be firmly redintegrated in that esteem with your Countrey. **1698** *Christ Exalted* 59 And so the Rebuker here ..would redintegrate the said Mr. Williams into the good esteem of those [etc.]. **1860** THACKERAY *Lovel* ii, I..had to pay the..taxes..before I could be redintegrated in my own property.

† **c.** With other than personal obj. *Obs. rare*⁻¹.

1670 G. H. *Hist. Cardinals* II. III. 194 That he should as much as possible redintegrate into the favour of his Majesty ..the opinion the Chigi had lost in France.

† **d.** Without const.: To restore to the previous state or position. *Obs.*

1645 WITHER *Vox Pacif.* 108 Such an one, if we redintegrate, When of his penitence good proofes appeare. **1679** J. GOODMAN *Penit. Pardoned* I. iv. (1713) 111 It was too late to think of redintegrating himself by taking up and changing his course. *a* **1734** NORTH *Lives* (1826) I. 14 He was in the same advanced post at the bar, fully redintegrated as before.

3. *intr.* † **a.** To regain favour or friendship *with* one. *Obs.* **b.** To become united again.

1670 G. H. *Hist. Cardinals* II. III. 182 The Knight had intelligence of all, and made all imaginable submission to redintigrate with Cardinal Flavio. **1788** SIR W. JONES in Ld. Teignmouth *Life* (1807) 400, I lament the sad effects of party, or rather faction, in your Maidstone Society, but hope (to use a word of Dr. Johnson) that it will redintegrate.

Hence **re'dintegrated** *ppl. a.*

1666 BOYLE *New Frigor. Exp.* Wks. 1772 III. 148 The redintegrated sal armoniac. **1715** CHEYNE *Philos. Princ. Relig.* II. 114 His regenerated, redintegrated and established Estate. **1727–41** CHAMBERS *Cycl.* s.v. *Medal*, Redintegrated Medals are those wherein we find the letters *Rest.* which shew that they have been restored by the emperors. **1870** HUXLEY *Lay Serm.* xii. (1874) 261 The redintegrated limb.

redintegration (rɛdɪntɪ'greɪʃən). [ad. L. *redintegrātiōn-em*, n. of action f. *redintegrāre* to REDINTEGRATE. Cf. AF. *redintegration* (1397, mod.F. *réintégration*).]

1. The action of redintegrating; restoration, re-establishment, reconstruction, renewal.

a. of conditions, qualities, results of action, etc.

1501 in *Lett. Rich. III & Hen. VII* (Rolls) I. 155 The redintegracion of the said peax. **1583** STUBBES *Anat. Abus.* I. (1877) 90 They conclude that whordome is a badge of loue,..a redintegration of loue, and an ensigne of vertue, rather meritorious than damnable. **1617** BP. ANDREWES 96 *Serm., Holy Ghost* x. (1629) 709 The redintegration of the favour of God. **1666** J. SMITH *Old Age* (1676) 239 It cannot return to the Fountain, for a redintegration of its life and spirit. **1757** MRS. GRIFFITH *Lett. Henry & Frances* (1767) I. 175 The redintegration of our affections..is to be considered more as an alliance than as a conquest. **1855** THACKERAY *Newcomes* xxiv, A redintegration of love began to take place between the Colonel and his relatives in Park Lane.

b. of material things. Now *rare* or *Obs.*

1666 J. SMITH *Old Age* (1752) 46 That wonderful redintegration of the sight and teeth of the old minister. *a* **1677** HALE *Prim. Orig. Man.* II. ix. 217 In the Redintegration of the World after these Destructions there is also a Re-production of Mankind.

2. *spec.* **a.** *Chem.* The restoration of any body or matter to its former state. ? *Obs.*

1471 RIPLEY *Comp. Alch.* IX. xi. in Ashm. (1652) 176 By naturall conspysacyon Of thyngs dysseveryd, a dew redyntegracyon. **1666** BOYLE *Orig. Formes & Qual.* 252 It were not impossible to make an adæquate Redintegration of a Chymically Analiz'd Body. **1669** W. SIMPSON *Hydrol. Chym.* 55 A redintegration of the glyssent ferments of the blood. **1758** REID tr. *Macquer's Chym.* I. 102 Such redintegrations are the only means we have of satisfying ourselves that we know all the principles which constitute a body. **1802** JAMES *Milit. Dict.* s.v., The redintegration of nitre from damaged gunpowder.

b. *Math.* (See quot.)

1801 *Encycl. Brit.* (ed. 3) Supp. II. 395/2 *Redintegration*, is the taking or finding the integral or fluent again from the fluxion.

c. *Psychol.* (See quots.)

1836–7 SIR W. HAMILTON *Metaph.* xxxi. (1870) II. 238 The law of Redintegration or Totality... This law may be thus enounced,—Those thoughts suggest each other which had previously constituted parts of the same entire or total act of cognition. **1912** B. DUMVILLE *Fund. Psychol.* x. 208 All suggestion of things not present is due to a process of redintegration; things found or put together in past experience tend to call one another up. **1920** H. L. HOLLINGWORTH *Psychol. Functional Neuroses* ii. 19 Redintegration is to be conceived as that type of process in which a part of a complex stimulus provokes the complete reaction that was previously made to the complex stimulus as a whole. This is not precisely Hamilton's use of the term 'redintegration', but the process is so similar that the term may be used here without injustice. **1938** G. W. ALLPORT *Personality* xix. 525 One variation of the associational theory is the doctrine of redintegration. **1947** G. MURPHY *Personality* viii. 172 If the term canalization marked off no specific kind of event but were purely an alternative for such terms as conditioning, positive adaptation, or redintegration, there would be no justification in using it.

† **3.** The restoration of a person to a previous condition. *Obs.*

1604 BACON *Apol.* Wks. 1879 I. 439, I made it my task and scope to take and give occasions for my lord's redintegration in his fortunes. *c* **1645** HOWELL *Lett.* (1892) II. 657 My Lord Bishop of Lincoln's Pardon is ready to pass the great seal with a perfect Redintegration into the King's Favour. **1652** SPARKE *Prim. Devot.* (1663) 278 Shall I (at length) redintegration have? **1727–41** CHAMBERS *Cycl.*, *Redintegration*, in the civil law, the act of restoring a person to the enjoyment of a thing whereof he had been illegally dispossessed.

†4. Reconciliation. *Obs. rare.*

1663 Cowley *Cutter Colman St.* II. v, We'll drink up a whole Vessel there to Redintegration. **1667** J. Corbet *Disc. Relig. Eng.* 41 A looking back to former discords marrs the most hopeful Redintegration.

re'dintegrative, *a.* [f. as prec. + -IVE.] Tending to redintegrate. Hence **re'dinte,gratively** *adv.*

1839–52 Bailey *Festus* xx. 358 Next comes the truth divine, Redintegrative. **1870** S. H. Hodgson *Theory of Practice* I. 370 States of consciousness which the redintegrative activity has the tendency to produce. **1890** W. James *Princ. Psychol.* I. xiv. 581 The forms of its transitions, whether redintegrative, associative, or similar, are due to unknown regulative or determinative conditions. **1920** H. L. Hollingworth *Psychol. Functional Neuroses* ii. 18 The redintegrative mechanism, whereby a part reinstates a previous whole, is one of the most enlightening concepts ever offered to psychology. **1933** G. Murphy *Gen. Psychol.* xviii. 352 All about us are objects to which we do not respond redintegratively because this would involve dozens of *conflicting* action patterns. **1941** *Brit. Jrnl. Psychol.* Oct. 167 Three of the six CO stimuli aroused reactions of a redintegrative character. Some of them went back to situations of childhood and early life. **1946** C. Morris *Signs, Lang. & Behavior* 292 The requirement for redintegrative (or 'part-whole') efficacy. **1960** *Encounter* Jan. 81/1 This book has been for me..a remarkable redintegrative experience.

re'dintegrator. *rare*[−1]. [f. as prec. + -OR.] That which redintegrates.

1858 Lowell *Wks.* (1890) V. 9 The last trial of the virtues of the Patent Redintegrator [*sc.* compromise]..has ended like all the rest.

†**redintegre,** *v. Obs. rare*[−1]. [ad. L. *redintegrāre* to REDINTEGRATE.] To redintegrate.

1501 in *Lett. Rich. III & Hen. VII* (Rolls) I. 156 They in noo wise redintegre nor renewe..the treatie.

re'dip, *v.* [RE- 5 a.] *trans.* (also *absol.*) To dip again; *spec.* to rebaptize. Hence **re'dipping** *vbl. sb.*

1660 Fuller *Mixt Contempl.* (1841) 234, I am utterly against the rebaptizing of Christians, but I am for the redipping of ships. **1712** *Act 10 Anne* in *Lond. Gaz.* No. 5031/6 In Case any Chandler..shall..encrease the Weight of such Candles..by re-dipping the same. **1736** Chandler *Hist. Persec.* 329 One Felix was drowned at Zurich, upon the sentence pronounced by Zuinglius,..'He that re-dips, let him be drowned'.

redi'rect, *a.* [RE- 5 a.] *U.S. Law.* The term applied to the further examination of a witness by the party calling him, after cross-examination by the opposing party.

1891 in *Cent. Dict.*

redi'rect, *v.* [RE- 5 a.] *trans.* To direct anew; to send in a new direction.

1873 W. M. Williams *Sci. in Short Chapt.* (1882) 225 It is the industry and skill of our workmen..that has..redirected for human advantage the buried energies of ancient sun-beams. **1884** *Law Times* LXXVII. 339/2, I must content myself by simply redirecting attention to the second query.

b. *esp.* To direct (a letter) to a fresh address.

1844 *Regul. & Ord. Army* 221 Their Letters are not liable to Postage if re-directed. **1874** Trollope *Lady Anna* xli. 318 The note was delivered..at his old abode, and was re-directed from Wyndham Street late on Monday evening.

So **redi'rection.** Also *attrib.*

1865 Trollope *Belton Est.* xvii. 202 He would give special orders as to the re-direction of his own letters from the post-office. **1892** Sir J. Fergusson *Sp. Ho. Comm.* 25 Feb., It is ..in contemplation to abolish the redirection charges on letters generally.

redis'burse, *v. rare.* [RE- 5 a.] *trans.* To pay back again. So **redis'bursement.**

1596 Spenser *F.Q.* IV. iii. 27 Then backe againe His borrowed waters forst to redisbourse, He sends the sea his owne with double gaine. **1655** tr. *Com. Hist. Francion* x. 19 He demanded of him Letters of Change,..and gave him others..for the re-disbursement of the money which he was to borrow.

redis'charge, *v.* [RE- 5 a.] *trans.* To discharge or disburden again.

1603 Daniel *Philotas* 1319 Poor Ceballinus not a moment stayes To redischarge himselfe of such a weight.

rediscount, *v.* [RE- 5 a.] *trans.* To discount again. So **re'discount** *sb.*; also *attrib.*, as ***rediscount rate.***

1866 Crump *Banking* ix. 193 Giving great facilities by credit and discounts; which latter were immediately re-discounted. **1892** *Pall Mall G.* 2 Feb. 7/2 A liability on re-discounts and foreign bills negotiated. **1896** *N. Amer. Rev.* CLXIII. 750 A central bank of issue and re-discount. **1927** *New Republic* 21 Sept. 108/2 The action of the Reserve Board in ordering the Chicago bank to reduce its rediscount rate from 4 to 3½ percent has resulted in a direct challenge of the Board's authority to compel such a change. **1929** *Times Lit. Suppl.* 21 Mar. 218/3 This..should be corrected by the raising of the Reichsbank rediscount rate and the forcing down of German prices. **1951** *N.Y. Herald Tribune* 15 Nov. 20/2 The rise in the Bank of England rediscount rate from 2 to 2½ per cent. **1970** G. Jackson *Let.* 17 Apr. in *Soledad Brother* (1971) 223 The missionaries, with the benefits of christendom, school us on the value of symbolism, dead presidents, and the rediscount rate.

redis'countable, *a.* [RE- 5 a.] That may be discounted again.

1964 *Economist* 8 Aug. 573/1 Restrictions on the eligibility of rediscountable paper.

re'discounting, *vbl. sb.* [f. REDISCOUNT *v.* + -ING[1].] The action of discounting again. Also *attrib.*

1931 *Economist* 2 May 946/2 This, in its turn, has occasioned a very decided increase in rediscounting. **1961** *Ann. Reg. 1960* 491 Gerrard and Reid, discount brokers, were granted borrowing and rediscounting facilities at the Bank of England. **1974** B. Pearce tr. *Amin's Accumulation on World Scale* II. iii. 429 The commercial banks in the under-developed countries do without rediscounting by the bank of issue.

redis'cover, *v.* [RE- 5 a.] *trans.* To discover again.

1752 T. Salmon *Univ. Trav.* I. Introd. 4 The Continent of America was rediscovered about 250 Years ago. **1837** Whewell *Hist. Induct. Sc.* I. 229 Tycho Brache rediscovered the same lunar inequality. **1858** Kingsley *Misc.* (1859) I. 153 Excellencies the world will in some saner mood rediscover. **1883** *Century Mag.* July 417/1 He has been re-discovered and eulogized afresh.

Hence **redis'coverer.**

1895 *Proc. 14th Conv. Amer. Instruct. Deaf* 103 The re-discoverer and popularizer of the intuitive method.

redis'covery. [RE- 5 a; cf. prec.] The act of discovering again; a renewed discovery.

1862 M. Hopkins *Hawaii* 82 The..re-discovery of the islands thirty years afterwards. **1878** Newcomb *Pop. Astron.* III. iii. 324 Its rediscovery became a difficult problem.

redi'scuss, *v.* [RE- 5 a.] To discuss again.

1804–6 Syd. Smith *Mor. Philos.* (1850) 165 This is the question that has been discussed and re-discussed from time immemorial. **1874** Sully *Sensat. & Intuit.* 2 Spencer has recently rediscussed the phenomena of consciousness.

So **redi'scussion.**

1805 W. Taylor in *Ann. Rev.* III. 202 A right of sending back to the commons for rediscussion any unwelcome law. **1878** Newcomb *Pop. Astron.* 539 Rediscussion of the observations of the transit of Venus.

redish, obs. form of RADISH.

†**redishing knife.** *Obs. rare*[−1]. A knife (see quot.) used by comb- and card-makers.

1688 R. Holme *Armoury* III. 383/1 The second [tool] is termed a Redishing Knife; it is a Knife with a long Blade, and sharp pointed like a Scotch Bibby, with a little bending in the back towards the point.

redi'spatch, *v.* [RE- 5 a.] *trans.* To dispatch again.

1620 Brent tr. *Sarpi's Council Trent* VII. (1629) 660 Ventimiglia, redispatched by the Pope; returned to Trent the nine and twentieth of January. **1780** Earl Malmesbury *Diaries & Corr.* I. 300, I..certainly shall redespatch my messenger before the Empress's departure.

redi'sperse, *v.* [RE- 5 a.] To disperse again.

1621 Brathwait *Nat. Embassie*, etc. 232 Thy darknesse is displayd, Which can by no meanes re-disperse her shade. **1946** *Nature* 28 Dec. 946/2 Elutriation methods of size separation redisperse coagulæ into their ultimate particles, thereby producing erroneous results. **1956** *Ibid.* 17 Mar. 521/2 The precipitates were then..redispersed by high-speed stirring.

redi'spone, *v.* [RE- 5 a.] To dispone again.

1734 [see RECONVEY *v.* 2].

redi'spose. [RE- 5 a.] *trans.* To dispose again. Also with *of.*

1733 A. Baxter *Enq. Nat. Soul* I. 339 Spirit hath no parts; and therefore it stands in need of no reparation, or redisposing its parts. **1859** Cornwallis *New World* I. 62 The very land that had only just been sold, was being re-disposed of at a considerable advance.

So **redispo'sition.**

1866 Lowe *Sp. Reform Bill* 31 May, I deny that a case is made out for this redisposition. **1867** Ld. Houghton in *Ess. Reform* III. 63 Under any redisposition of the constituent body.

redi'spute, *v.* [RE- 5 a.] To dispute again.

1641 Sir E. Dering in Rushw. *Hist. Coll.* III. (1692) I. 392 Your late Order and Declaration..are much debated and disputed abroad; perhaps it may be a good occasion for us to Re-dispute them here. **1650** B. *Discolliminium* 25 Nor must I..re-dispute what our Supreme Power doth.

redis'seise, *v. Law.* [RE- 5 a, prob. after an AF. **redisseisir*: cf. next.] *trans.* To disseise (a person) a second time.

1628 Coke *On Litt.* 154 b, If the recouery in the Assise were against two Disseisors, and one of them redisseise him againe, he shall haue a Redisseisin against him. **1700** Tyrrell *Hist. Eng.* II. 1106 Disseisors that have redisseis'd those who have recovered Seisin..from them.

redisseisin (riːdɪs'siːzɪn). *Law.* [a. AF. *redisseisine* (Britton): see RE- and DISSEISIN.] Repeated disseisin (see quot. 1607).

1535 tr. *Littleton's Nat. Brev.* (1544) 127 b, Where a man is disseised,..and after y[t] is disseysed by the same disseysour, he shall have this wryt of Redysseyson agaynste him. **1607** Cowell *Interpr.*, *Redisseisin* is a disseisin made by him, that once before was found, and adiudged to haue disseised the same man of his lands, or tenements. For the which there lyeth a speciall writ, called a writ of redisseisin. **1670** in *Phoenix* (1721) I. 428 The Judgment in the Re-disseisin is also Revers'd. **1768** Blackstone *Comm.* III. x. 188. **1865** Nichols *Britton* II. 233 Where the plaintiff is tenant of the tenement which he lost..by his own intrusion, or by redisseisin.

redis'seisor. *Law.* [a. AF. *redisseisour* (Britton): see RE- and DISSEISOR.] One who disseises another a second time.

1647 N. Bacon *Disc. Govt. Eng.* I. lxix. (1739) 183 Redisseisors and Postdisseisors found upon verdict before the Sheriff, Coroners, and Knights, shall be imprisoned. **1768** Blackstone *Comm.* III. x. 188 If he recover therein, the re-disseisor shall be imprisoned. **1865** Nichols *Britton* II. 354 Neither does it [essoin] lie..in the persons of disseisors or redisseisors.

re'dissoluble, *a.* [RE- 5 a.] That may be redissolved.

1796 Kirwan *Elem. Min.* (ed. 2) II. 285 The solutions are precipitable by and re-dissoluble by Blue Volalkali, mild or caustic. **1835–6** Todd *Cycl. Anat.* I. 90/1 These precipitates are..redissoluble in excess of liquid albumen.

redisso'lution. [RE- 5 a.] A second or renewed dissolution.

1790 Keir in *Phil. Trans.* LXXX. 379, I observed..a solution of part of the iron, a redissolution of the precipitated silver. **1875** Darwin *Insect. Plants* x. 243 After the protoplasm in a tentacle has been aggregated, its redissolution always begins in the lower part.

redi'ssolvable, *a.* [RE- 5 a.] Redissoluble.

1790 Crawford in *Phil. Trans.* LXXX. 413 A slight white precipitate not re-dissolvable in a large quantity of water. **1801** Chenevix *ibid.* XCI. 197 *note*, If all is re-dissolvable, [he] concludes there is no silica or alumina.

redi'ssolve, *v.* [RE- 5 a.] *trans.* and *intr.* To dissolve again.

a. *trans.* **1605** Sylvester *Quadrains* xvii, Hee..re-dissolves them with that breath of His. **1666** Boyle *Orig. Formes & Qual.* II. vii. 357 By reduction of it into a Body, re-dissolving it again [etc.]. **1771** T. Percival *Ess.* I. 163 Acids, he says, destroy its blackness by redissolving the ferrugineous particles. **1815** W. Phillips *Outl. Min. & Geol.* 64 These two earths were re-dissolved by a final analysis into silex. **1845** Darwin *Voy. Nat.* ii. (1879) 29 As the light wreaths of cloud passed over the ridge,..they were immediately redissolved. **1941** J. S. Huxley *Uniqueness of Man* 98 The mineral framework of the bones is redissolved to be used up by the living cells. **1946** *Nature* 7 Sept. 350/2 The precipitates are..redissolved in a 3 per cent solution of sodium dihydrogen phosphate. **1965** Phillips & Williams *Inorg. Chem.* I. xv. 567 It dissolves in an excess of the base, and can then be reprecipitated by addition of thionyl chloride, but excess of this acid does not, however, redissolve the aluminium sulphite.

b. *intr.* **1790** Wedgwood in *Phil. Trans.* LXXX. 312 The precipitate..re-dissolves in marine acid as easily as that made by water. **1854** J. Scoffern in *Orr's Circ. Sc.*, *Chem.* 86 The oxide of silver re-dissolves. **1897** *Allbutt's Syst. Med.* IV. 299 The deposit will redissolve on cooling.

Hence **redi'ssolving** *vbl. sb.*

1888 H. W. Parker *Spir. Beauty* (1891) 156 Re-dissolvings..just sufficient to liquefy the smaller crystals.

redi'stend, *v.* [RE- 5 a.] To distend again.

1684 R. Waller *Nat. Exper.* 65 The Lungs..were so shrunk up together for want of the air: but by blowing with a Straw..they were redistended.

redi'stil, *v.* [RE- 5 a.] To distil again. Hence **redi'stilled** *ppl. a.*

1666 Boyle *Orig. Formes & Qual.* 392 To redistill the same portion of Water. **1758** Reid tr. *Macquer's Chym.* I. 108 If they be redistilled, they recover their former tenuity. **1800** tr. *Lagrange's Chem.* II. 397 Crell recommends re-distilling it from off more of the sebate. **1877** Huxley & Martin *Elem. Biol.* 10 Redistil this after saturation with potassic carbonate. **1930** *Engineering* 21 Mar. 394/1 A parcel of redistilled magnesium of exceptional purity. **1956** *Nature* 21 Jan. 130/2 Using the normal procedure of shaking infective fluid with 20 per cent of freshly redistilled ether and leaving overnight.

redisti'llation. [RE- 5 a.] The action of redistilling; renewed distillation.

1666 Boyle *Orig. Formes & Qual.* 281 Neither do liquors, that have already been distill'd, obtain that colour upon redistillation. **1823** J. Badcock *Dom. Amusem.* 21 By more care and re-distillation [it] may be increased to six times. **1873** Ralfe *Phys. Chem.* 49 The different beakers are in turn submitted to redistillation.

redi'stribute, *v.* [RE- 5 a. Cf. F. *redistribuer* (Cotgr.).] *trans.* To distribute anew.

1611 Cotgr., *Redistribuer*, to redistribute, or deale backe againe. **1836** T. Hook *G. Gurney* (L.), This was settled by redistributing the tickets. **1846** Grote *Greece* II. vi. II. 503 He redistributed the whole territory belonging to Sparta. **1863** Fawcett *Pol. Econ.* III. viii. 406 The precious metals which are thus poured into England she again redistributes.

redistri'bution. [RE- 5 a.] A fresh distribution, esp. of Parliamentary seats.

1837 Syd. Smith *Let. to Archd. Singleton* Wks. 1859 II. 281/1 The Commissioners had already carried the principle of re-distribution as far as they thought that it could..be carried. **1866** *Ch. Times* 6 Jan. 1/1 He does not ask for the ballot, nor for a redistribution of seats. **1882** H. Spencer *Princ. Sociol.*, *Pol. Inst.* 576 A redistribution of military obligations.

redi'stributive, *a.* [RE- 5 a.] Of or belonging to redistribution (of wealth, seats, etc.).

1883 in *Pall Mall G.* 8 Sept. 12/1 The Government may try and compromise matters by promising a Redistributive Bill immediately. **1931** G. B. Shaw *Fabian Ess.* p. viii, Redistributive taxation within Capitalist limits means dole for idleness. **1971** *Morning Star* 2 Sept. 3 Taxation structure should be much more progressive and redistributive and should include effective taxation of wealth, capital gains and gifts and a heavier tax on unearned income. **1974** *Guardian* 27 Mar. 15/4 The Budget is redistributive in favour of the working man.

So **redi'stributory** *a.*

1884 *St. James's Gaz.* 20 Oct. 4/2 The..meetings..were allowed to pass without any redistributory interruptions.

re'district, *v. U.S.* [RE- 5 a.] *trans.* To divide or apportion anew into districts. Hence **re'districting** *vbl. sb.*; also *attrib.*

1850 in *Hist. Pelham, Mass.* (1898) 198 Voted..a committee to redistrict the town. **1870** *Trans. Illinois Agric. Soc.* VII. 510 Mr. Flag moved that the subject of redistricting the State be referred to a special committee of nine. **1888** BRYCE *Amer. Commw.* I. I. xiii. 165 *note*, When Massachusetts was being re-districted. **1890** *N.Y. Weekly Tribune* 22 Oct. 12/3 Democratic rascalities in redistricting and in voting and counting will not prevent but will hasten and insure the passage of a bill to secure fair Congressional elections in future. **1949** *Illinois State Register* (Springfield) 1 Feb. 6/4 States throughout the nation are eyeing the Illinois plan for redistricting schools which has proved to be a tax saver as well as a more efficient means of educating youths. **1973** *Time* 25 June 18/3 He supports busing and the redistricting of the Richmond school system to achieve racial balance. **1977** *Time* 21 Mar. 57/2 The mock rebellion is a protest against a redistricting plan under which Martha's Vineyard will lose the seat that it has had in the Massachusetts legislature for 285 years. **1980** *Christian Sci. Monitor* (Midwestern ed.) 4 Dec. 5/1 The shift will be reflected in a gain of congressional seats by the region, when the US House of Representatives is redistricted on the basis of the 1980 census.

†**re'dition.** *Obs. rare.* [ad. L. *reditiōn-em*, n. of action f. *redīre* to go or come back, f. *re(d)-* RE- + *īre* to go.] The action of going or coming back; return.

1595 CHAPMAN *Ovid's Banquet Sence* E 2, Because shee [echo] weaker is In that redition, then when first shee fled. **1615** —— *Odyss.* VI. 486 Address suit to my mother, that her mean May make the day of your redition seen. **1656** in BLOUNT *Glossogr.*

redition, obs. form of REDDITION.

†**Redituary.** *Obs. rare.* [ad. med.L. *redituārius* (Du Cange), f. *reditus* revenue, vbl. sb. f. *redīre*: see prec. Cf. obs. F. *redituaire* (1565 in Godef.).] (See quot. 1656.)

1607 R. C[AREW] tr. *Estienne's World of Wonders* I. xx. 168 Both blacke and white Friers, both Mendicants and Redituaries (if I may vsurpe this goodly Latin word *Redituarij*). **1656** BLOUNT *Glossogr.* (copying Cotgr.), *Redituaries*, an order of Franciscan Friers, which have Lands and Revenues; therein differing from the Mendicants or begging Friers, who are to possess nothing.

redivable, variant of REDEVABLE *a. Obs.*

re'dive, *v.* [RE- 5 a.] *intr.* To dive again.

1864 DASENT *Jest & Earnest* (1873) I. 22 Strange sea-birds flock about us, and dive and redive in the waves. **1879** JEFFERIES *Wild Life in S. Co.* 382 At other times this bird will dive and redive, and double about in the water.

redi'vide, *v.* [RE- 5 a. Cf. F. *rediviser.*] To divide again. Hence **redi'viding** *vbl. sb.*

1603 HOLLAND *Plutarch's Mor.* 1360 By the meanes whereof, that which is composed and mixed is redivided, and separate againe. **1611** FLORIO, *Ridiuisione*, a re-deuiding. **1647** N. BACON *Disc. Govt. Eng.* I. lxi. (1739) 120 The King re-divided the Land into four Circuits. **1846** GROTE *Greece* II. vi. II. 522 Aristotle clearly did not believe that Lycurgus had redivided the soil. **1866** FELTON *Anc. & Mod. Gr.* II. II. v. 349 The Empire was redivided, and territorially reorganized.

redi'vision. [RE- 5 a.] Renewed division.

1597 A. M. tr. *Guillemeau's Fr. Chirurg.* 57/1 Re-divisione of the first kinde of Ligament. *a* **1631** DONNE in *Select.* (1840) 45 The schools have made so many divisions, and sub-divisions, and re-divisions, and post-divisions of ignorance. **1846** GROTE *Greece* II. vi. II. 522 Plato..never hints..that an entire subsequent redivision had been resorted to by Lycurgus. **1862** S. LUCAS *Secularia* 400 A series of divisions and re-divisions and exchanges.

†**redivival,** *a. Obs.*⁻¹ [f. L. *rediviv-us* (see next) + -AL¹.] Of renewed vitality.

a **1734** NORTH *Lives* (1826) III. 274 In this manner some lives have become redivival.

redivive ('rɛdɪvaɪv), *a. rare.* [ad. L. *redivīvus* that lives again, f. *re(d)-* RE- + *vīvus* living, alive.] Revived, come to life again.

1685 H. MORE *Paralip. Prophet.* xliii. 371 This Beast redivive was not the eighth King and seventh Head. **1829** *Examiner* 371/1 The part..of the 'black priest' is the staple mystery... It is Radcliffe redivive.

†**'redivive,** *v. Obs.*⁻¹ [f. prec.] *trans.* To restore to life. So **'redivived** *ppl. a.*

1634 G. CRYMES in *Ford's Wks.* (Rtldg.) p. vi, Perkin is rediviv'd by thy strong hand, And crown'd a king of new. *a* **1656** BP. HALL *Revelation Unrevealed* §11 Beware of all either new divised or redivived errors of opinion. **1809** A. KNOX in *Jebb's Corr.* (1834) I. 527 Hannah More's new book, Coelebs, an odd sort of redivived religious courtship.

†**redivivous,** *a. Obs.* [f. L. *rediviv-us* + -OUS.] Liable to revive; reappearing.

1651 BIGGS *New Disp.* ¶288 The ferment is redintegral and redivivous. **1654** GAYTON *Pleas. Notes* III. vii. 114 A sort of these Theeves are now redivivous.

‖**redivivus** (rɛdɪ'viːvəs), *a.* Also fem. **rediviva**, fem. pl. **-æ**. [L., see REDIVIVE *a.*] Come back to life; = REDIVIVE *a.*

Always placed after the sb.

1675 R. HEAD (*title*) Proteus redivivus: or the art of wheedling. **1681** H. NEVILE (*title*) Plato redivivus. **1843** H. JAMES *Let.* 11 May in R. B. Perry *Tht. & Char. W. James* (1935) I. 47, I believe Jonathan Edwards *redivivus* in true blue would, after an honest study of the philosophy that has grown up since his day, make the best possible reconciler and critic of philosophy—far better than Schelling *redivivus.* **1856** C. M. YONGE *Daisy Chain* II. xxii. 589 He walked round and round his friend, called him Nicholas Randall *redivivus*, quoted Dogberry. **1937** *Mind* XLV. 492 Paton.. has written the sort of defence of Kant against his critics which a Kant *redivivus* might have written in self-defence. **1939** JOYCE *Finnegans Wake* (1964) III. 490 She's write to him she's levt by me, Jenny Rediviva! **1974** *Listener* 28 Feb. 284/3 The belligerent women of all parties, tricoteuses *redivivae.* **1975** *Times* 5 May 15/2 Some still believe in Stormont Redivivus. **1979** *Amer. N. & Q.* June 167 There isn't much more to say about this first volume of GW [sc. *Gesamtkatalog der Wiegendrucke*] *redivivus.*

Redjang, var. REJANG.

red-knee(s): see RED *a.* 18 b.

red land. [RED *a.* 1 f.]

1. *Sc.* Ploughed land; fallow; arable land.

a **1578** LINDESAY (Pitscottie) *Chron. Scot.* (1814) 499 It was ane fauch eard and Rid land quhair they moved for the tyme. *a* **1800** *Elfin Knight* xi. in Child *Ballads* I. 16/2 Ye'll get an acre o gude red-land..And ye maun aer it wi your horn. **1805** FORSYTH *Beauties Scotl.* II. 67 Lands under summer fallow in this county [Roxburgh] correspond correctly..with the common Scottish appellation of red land. *a* **1848** KERR *Maggie o' the Moss* (1891) 84 We will never try to slim Red-land or lea.

2. Sandy or clayey soil of a reddish colour.

1712 J. MORTON *Nat. Hist. Northampt.* 40 Red-Land is a Term much us'd by the Husbandmen here, and in Neighbour Counties... They always apply it to a Sandy Soil of a Reddish Hue, interspersed..with Pieces of Sand-Stone of the same Colour. **1813** YOUNG *Agric. Oxfordsh.* 3 This county contains three distinctions of soil..1. The red-land of the northern district; which, in fertility, much exceeds that of any other portion of equal extent. **1856** [see LAND *sb.*¹ 2]. **1857** OLMSTED *Journ. Texas* 67 This tract is known as the Red Lands of Eastern Texas.

attrib. **1712** J. MORTON *Nat. Hist. Northampt.* 41 In most of the Red-land Soil..there is more Sand than Earth. *Ibid.* 48 In all Red-land Fields..we may see..many Iron-colour'd Stones. **1813** YOUNG *Agric. Oxfordsh.* 4 The Red-land District.

red lattice. *Obs.* exc. *arch.* A lattice painted red as the mark of an alehouse or inn; hence *transf.* an alehouse, tavern, inn.

1575–97 [see LATTICE 1 b]. **1612** BRETON *Wits Private Wealth* (1879) 11/2 The world goes hard with pride, when a Lady lyes at a red Lattice. **163.**, **1689** [see LATTICE 1 b]. *a* **1704** T. BROWN *Wks.* (1708) III. II. 107 Drinking burnt Brandy..at the next Red Lattice.

attrib. **1598** SHAKS. *Merry W.* II. ii. 28 Your Cat-a-Mountaine-lookes, your red-lattice phrases. **1827** HOR. SMITH *Tor Hill* (1838) II. 191, I will not be letted by any such red-lattice swaggerer.

red lead, red-lead. [See LEAD *sb.*¹ 2.]

1. A red oxide of lead, largely used as a pigment.

c **1450** *M.E. Med. Bk.* (Heinrich) 202 Tak ceruse..Redled ..litarge [etc.]. **1466** *Mann. & Househ. Exp.* (Roxb.) 349, ij. li. of rede lede..viijd. **1507** *Acc. Ld. High Treas. Scot.* (1902) IV. 90 Item, payit to Pieris, the payntour, for.. caddes, verneis, Rede lede,..gold fulze [etc.] xxxijs. viij. **1578** LYTE *Dodoens* II. viii. 157 Of the colour of Red-lead, or lyke to the colour of the Orenge pill. **1612** PEACHAM *Gentl. Exerc.* 17 To draw with drie colours, you may make long pastils, which you shall doe by grinding red lead, or any other colour with strong wort. **1675** A. BROWNE *App. Ars Pict.* 7 A Temperature of White Carmine and a little Red Lead. **1744** BERKELEY *Siris* §196 Mr. Hales attributes this effect to air enclosed in the red lead. **1800** tr. *Lagrange's Chem.* I. 388 The nitric acid produces no change in the nature of the red lead. **1868** JOYNSON *Metals* 122 Paint containing red-lead must be carefully eschewed.

b. *attrib.* and *Comb.*, as ***red-lead cask, colour, maker*** (1885), ***mill***, †***pen*** (= pencil), ***pencil, putty***.

1670 PETTUS *Fodinæ Regales* xxv. 37 At the Red Lead Mill. *Ibid.*, Several sets of Coopers Tools..necessary for making Red Lead Cask. **1678** RAY *Willughby's Ornith.* 364 The Eyes are red like the Bill, or rather of a red-lead colour. **1684** T. GODDARD *Plato's Demon* 12, I perceive indeed that your red Lead Pen hath examin'd it very strictly. **1766** *Compl. Farmer* s.v. *Surveying* 7 I 2/1 We would commend for expedition a red-lead pen, whereby you may mark out every angle neatly. **1807** AIKIN *Dict. Chem. & Min.* I. 587/2 What are vulgarly called Red-lead pencils are composed of thin slips of the finer kinds of reddle inclosed in a wooden case. **1891** PATTERSON *Illust. Naut. Dict.* I. 146 *Red Lead Putty*, a mixture of white lead and red lead used for various purposes.

†**2.** ***red lead of Siberia***, red lead-ore (see RED 17 e). *Obs.*

1816 J. SMITH *Panorama Sc. & Art* II. 411 Chromium was discovered by Vauquelin, in analyzing a beautiful mineral called red lead of Siberia.

3. *Naval slang.* **a.** Tomato ketchup. **b.** Tinned tomatoes.

1918 R. W. KAUFFMAN *Our Navy at Work* 6 'Red lead' is catsup, which it hugely resembles. **1919** G. M. BATTEY *70,000 Miles in Submarine Destroyer* 261 Beans and 'red lead' for breakfast. **1945** 'TACKLINE' *Holiday Sailor* v. 55 Everything went into a pot-mess—meat, spuds, peas, beans, rice, oxo, 'red-lead' (tinned tomatoes)—and the result was invariably good. **1959** W. L. CORZINE *Sailors in Nightgowns* vii. 100 We were having those delicious beans for breakfast, which we always camouflaged with red lead (catsup).

Hence **red-lead** *v. trans.*, to paint with red lead; **red-leader**, a workman in the shipbuilding industry who scrapes iron plates and paints them with red lead.

1882 *Standard* 13 Oct. 2/3 A non-union man was employed as red leader. **1890** *Daily News* 30 Sept. 3/2 The work of chipping, scraping, and red-leading her iron work is being proceeded with.

redleas, variant of REDELESS *a. Obs.*

red-leaved: see RED *a.* 14 a, 14 c.

red-legged, *a.* Having red legs.

a. In the specific names of birds (and animals), as ***red-legged crane, duck, heron, parakeet, thrush, turtle, wallaby***, etc.

red-legged chough or **crow**, the Cornish chough. **r. falcon**, the red-footed falcon (*Falco rufipes*). **r. gull**, the black-headed gull (*Larus ridibundus*). **r. horseman**, the redshank (*Totanus calidris*). **r. kittiwake**, *Rissa brevirostris*. **r. mew** = *r. gull*. **r. partridge**, the French partridge (*Caccabis rufa*); also *fig.* a cardinal (quot. 1813). **r. plover**, *U.S.* the turnstone (Cent. Dict. 1891). **r. sandpiper**, (*a*) the redshank; (*b*) the purple sandpiper.

1840 *Cuvier's Anim. Kingd.* 208 European or *Red-legged Chough. *a* **1705** RAY *Synopsis Avium* (1713) 193 The *red-legged Crane. **1776** PENNANT *Brit. Zool.* (ed. 4) I. 196 *Red legged Crow. The legs and bill are of a bright orange, inclining to red. **1875** MCILWRAITH *Guide Wigtownshire* 139 These precipices are frequented by the red-legged crow. **1729** in *Dampier's Voy.* (ed. 3) III. 403 The *red-legg'd Duck. The feet of these when roasted dye both Hands and Linnen red. **1836** EYTON *Rare Brit. Birds* 5 *Red-legged Falcon. **1785** LATHAM *Gen. Synopsis Birds* III. II. 381 *Red-legged Gull, *Larus cinerarius*. **1802** MONTAGU *Ornith. Dict.* (1831) 291 The Red-legged Gull of authors is only this bird before it is arrived at maturity. **1753** CHAMBERS *Cycl. Supp.*, *Ibis*..by some confounded very erroneously with the hæmatopus, or *red-legged heron. **1678** RAY *Willughby's Ornith.* 299 We take this to be the bird the French call *Chevalier aux pieds rouges*, the *red-leg'd Horseman. **1734** ALBIN *Nat. Hist. Birds* II. 63 The *Totanus* or Red-leg'd Horseman. **1892** *Within an hour of London* xiii. 256 The redshank, pool-snipe,..red-leg, red-legged horseman. **1752** J. HILL *Hist. Anim.* 372 The *red-legged Parroquet... This species is a native of many places both in the East and West Indies. **1611** COTGR., *Perdrix gaille*,..the great browne-bodied, and *red-legd Partridge, the French Partridge. **1678** RAY *Willughby's Ornith.* 167 The Red-leg'd Partridge, *Perdrix ruffa* Aldrov. **1756–7** tr. *Keysler's Trav.* (1760) III. 20 Red-legged partridges are natives of Numidia. **1813** *Examiner* 31 May 344/2 Did you ever see one of us red-legged partridges before? **1840** *Penny Cycl.* XVII. 437/1 They are most determined runners, and few birds are more calculated to injure the behaviour of a well-bred pointer or setter than the Red-legged Partridge. **1824** SHAW *Zool.* XII. I. 135 *Red-legged Sandpiper (*Totanus calidris*). **1831** RENNIE *Montagu's Ornith. Dict.* 412 Little difference seems to exist between this [the redshank] and the red-legged sandpiper (*T. Bewickii*, Montagu) which is doubtless a variety of this species. **1754** CATESBY *Nat. Hist. Carolina* (ed. 2) I. 30 The *red-leg'd Thrush, *Turdus viscivorus plumbeus*. **1729** in *Dampier's Voy.* (ed. 3) III. 409 The *Red-legg'd Turtle. **1898** MORRIS *Austral Eng.* 494/2 *Red-legged W[allaby], *M[acropus] wilcoxi.*

b. Of persons: Wearing red stockings.

1835 WILLIS *Pencillings* I. xv. 111 The motley troop of cardinals and red-legged servitors passed out.

'red-legs, red-leg.

1. *Ornith.* A name given to various birds with red legs; *esp.* the redshank (*Totanus calidris*), the purple sandpiper (*Tringa maritima*), the red-legged partridge (*Caccabis rufa*), and (*U.S.*) the turnstone (*Strepsilas interpres*).

1802 MONTAGU *Ornith. Dict.* (1831) 392 Two [purple sandpipers] were shot there.., and were called by the fishermen red-legs. *Ibid.* 407 Red-legs. A name for the Red-shank. **1831** RENNIE *Montagu's Ornith. Dict.* 291 Laughing gull (*Larus ridibundus*)..Red Legs. **1878** *Daily News* 12 Sept. 3/1 The red-legged partridge is not a native of this country... In 1826 the red-legs were reported 'now plentiful in Suffolk'. **1892** [see *red-legged horseman* in prec.].

2. (See quot. and cf. REDSHANK 1 a.)

1887 N. D. DAVIS *Cavaliers & Roundheads of Barbados* 83 *note*, The descendants of the old clansmen form a peculiar people at the present time, in Barbados, where they are known as Red Legs.

3. The plant bistort (*Polygonum bistorta*). Also = RED-SHANKS 3 a.

1820 *Q. Jrnl. Sci. Lit. & Arts* IX. 422 The juices of some plants contain nitrate of potash; among others, I have detected it in the *polygonum bistorta*, called in English 'red-legs'. **1866** *Treas. Bot.* 962/2. **1886** BRITTEN & HOLLAND *Dict. Eng. Plant-Names* 399 Red Legs. From the general redness of the stems. (1) *Polygonum bistorta*... (2) *Polygonum Persicaria*. **1960** *Oxf. Bk. Wild Flowers* 126/1 Spotted Persicaria or Red-legs..can usually be easily recognized by the red stems and the dark blotch in the middle of the leaves. **1971** *Countryman* Winter 126 The redleg..was flowering in late summer.

4. *U.S. Mil. slang.* An artilleryman.

1900 P. REVERE *Cleveland in War with Spain* 164 The battery marched down the street... Cleveland's 'red-legs' were off. *Ibid.*, For once the 'dough boys' were envied by the 'red legs'. **1927** *Amer. Legion Monthly* July 16 Reilly's redlegs..admired the advance guard of Bengal lancers. **1969** S. N. SPETZ *Rat Pack Six* 71 Anyway, you'll get a chance to cool it down there, just guarding a bunch of Red Legs.

redles(e, obs. variants of REDELESS *a. Obs.*

red letter.

1. a. (Chiefly *pl.*) A letter made with red ink, or with some red pigment, esp. as used in ecclesiastical calendars to indicate saints' days and church festivals. Also in *fig.* context.

14.. *A.B.C. Poem* 13 in *Pol. Rel. & L. Poems* (1866) 244 Red letter in parchemyn Makyth a chyld.. Lettrys to loke & se. **1490** CAXTON *Eneydos* xxii. 83 We wryte yet in oure kalenders the hyghe festes wyth rede lettres of coloure of purpre. **1570** FOXE *A. & M.* (ed. 2) 695/1, I did but onely colour them with red letters. And thus for matter of my Calendare enough. **1593** SHAKS. *2 Hen. VI*, IV. ii. 97 He's a Booke in his pocket with red Letters in't. *Cade.* Nay then he is a coniurer. **1658** H. PLUMPTRE in *12th Rep. Hist. MSS. Comm.* App. V. 6 Enter it into your Calendar with red letters, that when it comes, it may be celebrated. **1679** V. ALSOP *Melius Inquirendum* 17 If this were the Character of Primitive Saintship, the Apostle Paul must not have worn a Red Letter in our Enquirer's Calendar. **1879** SPURGEON *Serm.* XXV. 411 The hour which sovereign grace has marked with a red letter in the calendar of love!

†**b.** *transf.* The Roman Catholic Church, as being prominently given to the observation of saints' days and festivals. *Obs.*

1679 OATES *Narr. Popish Plot* Ded. a ij, He that was caught and executed.. was of the same Red-Letter, and had Masses sung for him after his death. *c* **1688** in Hardwick *Trad. Lanc.* (1872) 269 The fountain is called Saint Ellen's Well, to which place the vulgar neighbouring people of the Red letter do much resort.

c. As the name of a moth.

1845 WESTWOOD *Moths* II. 180 *Depressaria ocellana* (the red letter).

2. a. *attrib.*, as ***red-letter almanac, mark, name***; †**red-letter man**, a Roman Catholic (cf. 1 b).

1677 MARVELL *Season. Argum.* Wks. 1776 II. 570 A red letter man, if of any religion. *a* **1700** B. E. *Dict. Cant. Crew*, *Red-letter-man*, a Roman-catholic. **1816** COLERIDGE *Lay Serm.* (Bohn) 315 These are red-letter names even in the almanacs of worldly wisdom. **1843** (*title*) The Red Letter Almanack. **1878** *N. Amer. Rev.* CXXVI. 81 My desire.. gained me some red-letter marks at the war-office.

b. red-letter day, a saint's day or church festival indicated in the calendar by red letters; hence, any memorable, fortunate, or specially happy day. (So ***red-letter night.***)

1704 S. KNIGHT *Diary* in *Amer. Speech* (1940) XV. 231/2 Red letter day. **1740** *Mock Campaign* 18 Their empty Eccho only now displays Great —'s Power on Red Letter Days. **1776** BRAND *Pop. Antiq.* (1777) Pref. 8 The Calendar was crowded with Red-Letter Days, nominally.. consecrated to Saints. **1782** MISS BURNEY *Cecilia* x. vi, 'To-day is a red-letter day, so that's the reason of it'. 'A red-letter day?' **1811** COLERIDGE *Lett.* II. 566 To sit at the same table with Grattan, who would not think it a memorable honour, a red letter day in the almanac of his life? **1887** T. A. TROLLOPE *What I remember* I. xvii. 354, I used to dine and pass the evening with Dr. Jeune; and these were my red-letter days. **1894** D. C. MURRAY *Making of Novelist* 6 My red-letter nights were when he came over to my native town. **1905** PROCTOR & FRERE *New Hist. Bk. Common Prayer* (ed. 3) ix. 338 It is difficult to see clearly the motive which determined the selection of the black letter Saints' Days. In the case of the red letter days it was clearly the desire to bring the festivals to the test of the Bible. **1919** *Granta* 1 May 4/1 January 18th, 1889 should be a red-letter day in the history of Cambridge University, for it was on that date that *The Granta*, like a new planet, swam into our ken. **1965** C. E. POCKNEE *Parson's Handbk.* (ed. 13) xvi. 145 The 1928 Book classifies days as holy, special, and ordinary. To *Holy* (or *Red-letter*) *Days* 1928 has added St. Mary Magdalene, 22 July, and the Transfiguration of our Lord, 6 August.

Hence **red-lettered** *a.* (and *pa. pple.*), distinguished by, marked with, red letters; **red-letter** *v.* to mark in this way (*rare*).

1707 J. STEVENS *Quevedo's Com. Wks.* (1709) 327 Why should we make red letter'd Saints? **1784** COWPER *Let.* 21 June, It is reasonable to suppose, that in the next year's almanack we shall find the name of Handel among the red-lettered worthies. **1832** SOUTHEY in *Q. Rev.* XLVIII. 281 The bonfires of persecution and St. Bartholomew's red-lettered day. **1868** BROWNING *Ring & Bk.* III. 640 Assuredly it shall be salve to mine [ear] When this great news red-letters him, the rogue! **1898** *Daily News* 11 Oct. 8/1 The efficiency of the action being evidenced by a red-lettered shutter. **1940** A. UPFIELD *Bushranger of Skies* xiv. 160 The history of his life was red-lettered with luck.

redliche, variant of READLICHE *Obs.*

red light. 1. A warning light, esp. one instructing traffic to stop. Hence *fig.*, a sign of danger; a warning; a signal to pause or desist in some course of action or thought; esp. in phr. ***to see the*** (or *a*) ***red light.***

1849 C. BRONTË *Shirley* III. iii. 44 He is one of Mrs. Yorke's warning-examples—one of the blood-red lights she hangs out to scare young ladies from matrimony. **1862** ANON. *Railway Traveller's Handy Bk.* 99 *Danger, to stop*, is shown by a red light fixed upon a pole being turned full upon the line... *Caution, to go slowly*, is shown.. by a green light. *All right, to go on*,.. by a white light. *c* **1864** BROUGH & HALLIDAY in M. R. Booth *Eng. Plays of 19th Cent.* (1973) IV. 239 There, that's our signal—that's the red light on our railway, and means 'danger'. **1907** A. QUILLER-COUCH *Major Vigoureux* xxiii. 234, I fancy the man has begun to see the red light. **1927** *Daily Tel.* 15 Nov. 9/3 Men see a red light when they find that things they have called their own—like intelligence—may be given to women too. **1931** E. WALLACE *On Spot* x. 120 If Con had been better acquainted with Tony he would have seen the red light. **1938** *Mag. Digest* Jan. 66 (*heading*) A red light for the pugnacious. **1946** *Sun* (Baltimore) 29 Jan. 11/1 What in fact the Associated Press has done is to put up the red light. **1948** G. V. GALWEY *Lift & Drop* vii. 190 Roberts' carelessness in getting pinched showed them the red light and they ceased operations. **1958** *Spectator* 28 Feb. 251/1 The French Government may see the red light. **1974** E. AMBLER *Dr. Frigo* II. 97 He's hit by a drunk driver running a red light and killed. **1977** *New Yorker* 24 Oct. 52/3 He drove through a red light in Pennsylvania and.. was picked up by police.

2. The sign of a brothel. Freq. *attrib.*, as ***red light district***, etc.

1900 *N.Y. Jrnl.* Nov. 19 (*caption*) Children of the 'red light district'. **1900** *Boston Transcript* 4 Dec. 14/3 The disorderly houses in the 'red-light' district were all closed last night. **1925** H. L. FOSTER *Trop. Tramp with Tourists* 276, I was amazed to find that about two thirds of every city consisted of red-light district. **1928** *Daily Express* 26 Sept. 11/1 It is further asserted that he has elevated the 'red light' houses to the level of a business in New York. **1947** [see GEISHA]. **1951** E. PAUL *Springtime in Paris* xi. 205 Strangers in cities of Spain or Italy, who want to locate the red-light district, are advised to seek a point equidistant between the principal seminary and the main barracks of the Guardia Civil. **1962** *Coast to Coast 1961–62* 131 Harry was rough, tough and hairy, and he knew where to find a swy game, a sly-grog joint or a red light in every capital city. **1967** O. WYND *Walk Softly* vi. 91 He is reported to have sizeable interests in the Naboshima Red Light district, and many bars. **1973** *Islander* (Victoria, B.C.) 17 June 16/3 At one time there were about 2,000 men in the camp, and except for the red-light girls at the other end of town, only two women. **1978** *Detroit Free Press* 16 Apr. 11A/2 Besides, she said, a legal red-light district would probably be bad for business. **1981** *Observer* 2 May 3/4 The trial will seem far removed from the red-light districts and suburbs where Sutcliffe struck.

3. A children's game in which one participant turns his back on the others, who try to sneak up on him without being seen moving.

1953 P. G. BREWSTER *Amer. Nonsinging Games* 35 Red Light (Mississippi). The player who is 'It' counts rapidly to ten and then cries, 'Red Light!'.. At the cry of 'Red Light!' each must stop and hold the position in which he was when he heard it. **1969** I. & P. OPIE *Children's Games* vi. 195 Other names [for 'Peep behind the Curtain'] include.. 'Red Light' (Liverpool, Blackburn, Spennymoor, Peterborough, Helensburgh, and Edmonton, Alberta), [etc.]. **1975** *New Yorker* 10 Mar. 38/1 Evenings, screen doors bang behind children rushing out to meet each other for hide-and-seek, giant steps, dead dog, red light.

Hence **red-'lighter**, a prostitute.

1913 A. STRINGER *Shadow* 37 He could hobnob with bartenders and red-lighters.

red line, *sb. phr.* Used to describe the British army, esp. in phr. ***thin red line***; also *transf.*

1855 F. DUBERLY *Let.* 8 June in E. E. P. Tisdall *Mrs. Duberly's Campaigns* (1963) v. 147 They advance, supported by the impenetrable red line, our infantry. **1877** W. H. RUSSELL *Brit. Exped. Crimea* III. ii. 156 The Russians.. dashed on towards that *thin red line tipped with steel*. **1890** KIPLING *Departmental Ditties* (U.S. ed.) 61 It's 'Thin red line of 'eroes' when the drums begin to roll. **1935** 'G. ORWELL' *Clergyman's Daughter* iv. 226 Napoleon Buonaparte.. soon found that in the 'thin red line' he had more than met his match. **1971** *Guardian* 24 Feb. 10/1 Trade unionists.. are beginning to give physical support to the Union of Post Office Workers as their 'thin red line'. **1974** *Times* 19 Apr. 14 Home of the thin red (or khaki) lines. .. 'Home of the British Army', say the road signs leading into Aldershot.

'red-line, *v.* Also redline, red line. To circle or mark in red ink; freq. *fig.* (see quots.). Hence **'red-lining** *vbl. sb.*; **'red-lined** *ppl. a.*

1820 KEATS *Lamia & Other Poems* 57 Why were they proud? Because red-lin'd accounts Were richer than the songs of Grecian years? **1942** *Yank* 23 Sept. 14/1 Who is it the yardbird sees when he gets red-lined on the payroll for signing his name wrong? **1945** *Amer. Speech* XX. 261 To *redline* a soldier is to cross off his name on the payroll for a particular month because of an improper signature or some other irregularity on anyone's part. **1961** *Richmond* (Va.) *Times-Dispatch* 18 Jan. 4/1 The American Automobile Association may 'red-line' Prince George county because of its policy toward traffic violaters. 'Red-lining' is a method used by the AAA to warn motorists of possible speed traps. **1966** *Sunday Times* (Colour Suppl.) 4 Dec. 73/3 [GI Jargon] *Red-lined*, cancelled or classified unserviceable. **1973** *Times* 7 Feb. 20/4 They found that Laurelton had been 'red-lined' by the bank, which meant that it was not possible to get a normal mortgage. **1973** *Black Panther* X. XXVIII. 4/4 'Red-lining' is a corrupt scheme whereby real estate developers.. arrange unofficial agreements with banks to have them refuse to grant improvement loans for particular buildings. Eventually the homes fall into a state of such disrepair that the owner is willing to sell it. **1976** *In Common* VI. II. 4/1 Common Cause Governing Board.. voted CC support of legislation aimed at discouraging 'redlining'—the practice by lending institutions of discriminating arbitrarily against certain city neighborhoods in making home mortgage loans. **1977** *Listener* 9 June 763/1 The policy of so-called 'red-lining', that is, drawing a line round certain undesirable areas and refusing to lend money on property within the red line. **1979** *N.Y. Times* 24 Jan. B18/1 Redlining has an undeniable racial component whereby redlined neighborhoods often coincide with nonwhite neighborhoods. **1979** *Verbatim* Summer 2/2 To redline an aircraft, thus, is 'to ground' it.

†**'redling.** *Obs. rare*[−1]. [f. RED *a.* + -LING[1].] = REDSHANK 2.

1655 MOUFET & BENNET *Health's Impr.* 109 Redlings or Water Redschancks feed as Water-railes do and be of the like nourishment.

†**'redly**, *a. Obs. rare*[−1]. [app. f. RED *a.* + -LY[1], but perh. a misprint for *redy*.] Red, reddish.

1482 *Bk. St. Albans, Her.* A iij b, The .vi. stone is calde a Rudy a [1486 ruby or] redly stone, gowlys it is calde in armys.

'redly, *adv.*[1] [f. RED *a.* + -LY[2].] **a.** In a red manner, with a red appearance or colour.

1611 COTGR., *Rougement*, redly. **1814** BYRON *Lara* II. xiv, Blood is mingled with the dashing stream, Which runs all redly till the morning beam. **1843** BORROW *Bible in Spain* (ed. 2) III. xvii. 333 The blaze was redly reflected in the waters of the strait. **1883** STEVENSON *Treas. Isl.* I. iv, A full moon peered redly through the upper edges of the fog.

b. *Comb.*, as ***redly-lipped, -squirting*** adjs.

1910 J. MASEFIELD *Ballads & Poems* 91 Maids that were redly-lipped and comely-skinned. **1930** R. CAMPBELL *Adamastor* 90 Its steel-shot bulk with redly-squirting Nose and lolling tongue.

†**'redly**, *adv.*[2] *Obs.* Forms: 1 **rædlíce**, 3 **readliche**, 4 **redlych**, *comp.* **reedloker**; 4 **redli**, 4–5 **reddely**, 4–6 **redly**, (6 **readly**). [OE. *rædlíce*, f. *rædlic* adj.: see REDE *sb.*[1] and -LY[2], and cf. ON. *ráðliga*. See also REDELY and REDILY.] Prudently, carefully, distinctly, clearly, correctly, certainly.

c **897** K. ÆLFRED *Gregory's Past. C.* xviii. 131 Ðæt he meahte ðæt folc ðy wislicor & ðy rædlicor læran. *c* **1000** in Assmann *Homilies* etc. (1889) xviii. 195 Deofol.. hine oft rædlice mid mænig-fealdum costningum costnode. *a* **1250** *Owl & Night.* 1279 Nu thu miȝt wite readliche, That eavere thu spekest gideliche. *c* **1350** *Will. Palerne* 2143 þe real emperour of rome þanne redli him thonked. **1387** TREVISA *Higden* (Rolls) I. 145 þe men of þat lond beeþ rediloker [*v.r.* reedloker] i-cleped Gothy þan Gogi. *c* **1425** WYNTOUN *Cron.* II. vi. 499 For redly wilys in women Sonnar apperis þan in men. **1448** *Paston Lett.* I. 74 As he stombled, on of Harcourts men smot hym in the bak with a knyfe; men wotte not ho hyt was reddely. **1513** DOUGLAS *Æneis* VI. iii. 79 He prentit baith his futsteppis in the erd, Behaldand redly quhat singnis thai schaw.

redly, -lyd, varr. of RADLY, RIDLED *Obs.*

†**redlys.** *Obs. rare.* [Repr. OE. *réadlęsc*: see LASCH.] Some kind of red leather.

1408 *Mem. Ripon* (Surtees) III. 139 In iiij correis quæ vocantur redlys,.. pro prædictis cathedris cooperiendis.

red-making: see RED *a.* 15 b.

red man. Also **red-man.**

†**1.** *Alchemy.* ? Red sulphide of mercury. *Obs.*

1610 B. JONSON *Alch.* II. iii, Your red man, and your white woman, with all your broths, your menstrues [etc.].

2. a. [See RED *a.* 5 c.] A (*or* the) North American Indian.

1744 VAUDREUIL in *Pres. State Louisiana* 37 The English .. aimed at nothing so much as the Destruction of the red Men. **1794** S. WILLIAMS *Vermont* 187 The Indian or the Red Man seems to have been the most ancient, or the original man of America. **1804** C. B. BROWN tr. *Volney's View Soil U.S.* 187 The fancied superiority of the red men has been exploded ever since the settlement of emigrants from Europe along the frontiers. **1858** LONGF. *M. Standish* VII. 42 Ready to be let loose, and destroy his brother the red man. **1878** *N. Amer. Rev.* CXXVII. 477 A few scattered tribes of red-men.

b. One of the extinct Beothuk people of Newfoundland.

1955 L. E. F. ENGLISH *Historic Newfoundland* 9/2 They [*sc.* Beothuks] were described as of ordinary height—yet there are recorded instances of giant Red Men of seven feet in stature. **1969** H. HORWOOD *Newfoundland* xi. 78 The original Red Men, who, because of their attachment to red ochre, gave their nickname to all the other native tribes of North America.

3. *U.S.* The squirrel-fish, *Holocentrus ascensionis.*

1891 in *Cent. Dict.*

4. = ROMAN *sb.*[3] 2.

1966 E. PALMER *Plains of Camdeboo* xiv. 235 The Red Men come into the house at night... Of medium size—perhaps three inches with the legs fully spread.. orange-red, hairy, fast, with great snapping beak-like jaws which, most horrifyingly, they can move at the same time up and down and from side to side.

†**redmod**, *a. Obs. rare*[−1]. [f. *red* RAD *a.*[1] + *mod* MOOD.] Hasty, rash.

c **1175** *Lamb. Hom.* 105 Wreððe hafð wununge on þes dusian bosme, þet is þenne þe mon bið to redmod.

Redmondite ('rɛdməndaɪt), *a.* and *sb.* [f. the name *Redmond* (see below) + -ITE[1].] **A.** *adj.* Of or pertaining to the Irish politician John Edward Redmond (1856–1918) or his nationalist ideas. **B.** *sb.* A supporter of Redmond or his policies.

1895 *Notes from Ireland* 2 Feb. 47 The Redmondite manifesto. *Ibid.*, The past week has seen the issue of two familiar appeals.. one from the McCarthyites, and one from the Redmondites. **1905** T. D. SULLIVAN *Recoll. Troubled Times in Irish Politics* xxxvii. 339 At the first blush one might suppose that the Tory party would scoff at the Redmondite motion. **1910** *Westm. Gaz.* 9 Feb. 2/2 He cannot even pretend he is entitled to a Redmondite summons. **1913** *Times* 30 Dec. 3/2 Mr John MacNeill denies that his friends are actuated by hostility towards the Redmondites. **1928** T. M. HEALY *Lett. & Leaders of my Day* II. xxxi. 391 In the middle of the negotiations with the Liberal Cabinet as to the Home Rule Bill—which the Redmondites were certain to denounce as inadequate—Dillon tried to get control of the *Freeman*. **1962** GREENE & LAURENCE in G. B. Shaw *Matter* *with Ireland* 142 *Sinn Féin*, which..had already won two by-elections against Redmondite candidates. **1973** S. LEVENSON *James Connolly* xvii. 208 He accused the Redmondites of accepting partition without a struggle. **1978** D. MURPHY *Place Apart* ii. 17 My mother, whose ancestry was Redmondite at best.

Hence '**Redmondism**, the ideas or policies associated with Redmond.

1914 R. CASEMENT *Let.* 29 July in R. MacColl *Roger Casement* (1956) vii. 133 Redmondism has no real support here at all.

red-mouth: see RED *a.* 18 b.

red-mouthed: see RED *a.* 14 a and b.

rednase, -nes, Sc. varr. RADNESS *Obs.*

'**redneck.** Also red-neck, red neck.

1. *U.S.* **a.** A member of the white rural labouring class of the southern States; one whose attitudes are considered characteristic of this class; freq., a reactionary.

Originally, and still often, derogatory, but now also used with more sympathy for the aspirations of the rural American.

1830 A. ROYALL *Southern Tour* I. 148 This may be ascribed to the *Red Necks*, a name bestowed upon the Presbyterians in Fayetteville. **1893** H. A. SHANDS *Some Peculiarities of Speech in Mississippi* 53 *Red-neck*,..a name applied by the better class of people to the poorer inhabitants of the rural districts. **1904** *Dialect Notes* II. 420 *Redneck, n.*, An uncouth countryman. 'The hill-billies came from the hills, and the *rednecks* from the swamps.' **1913** J. DAVIS *Life & Speeches* iii. 42 If you red-necks or hill billies ever come to Little Rock be sure and come to see me—come to my house. **1936** W. FAULKNER *Absalom, Absalom!* 122 Rich and poor, aristocrat and redneck. **1959** *Times Lit. Suppl.* 28 Aug. 491/4 The ugly faces and, under prompting or provocation, the uglier actions of a handful of red-necks, crackers, tar-heels and other poor white trash here and there in the South. **1960** *Spectator* 15 Jan. 83/2 The old patrician families who are opposed to the graft, blackmail and demagogy by which the Boss, the tribune of the rednecks, keeps himself in power. **1969** *Observer* 7 Dec. 25/3 They [*sc.* communes] all shared two experiences: the search for new values, and attention from local rednecks and the police. **1971** J. BISHOP *Days of Martin Luther King, Jr.* IV. 329 The fearful Southern red-neck, committed to the credo that the black man is a bridge between the animal kingdom and the human, derided the speech as typical 'coon shouting'. **1973** *Black World* Mar. 56 Carload of rednecks came with the darkness to Slim's house. Blew the horn until Slim's daddy opened the door. **1975** *Daily Tel.* 15 Oct. 17/7 Was it because they might think his [*sc.* Govenor George Wallace's] reputation as a Right-wing 'red neck' a political embarrassment? **1976** *Time* 27 Sept. 47/1 That was the point Carter was attempting to make when he said in 1970 that Maddox 'has compassion for the little man', and when he said that a Humphrey-Wallace ticket in 1972 'would do well in the South', and when he called himself 'basically a redneck'. **1977** D. JAMES *Spy at Evening* x. 71 Middle-class rednecks like you..get all worked up about it. **1978** J. UPDIKE *Coup* v. 192 Her momma's a washrag and her daddy's a redneck.

b. *attrib.* or as *adj.*

1961 D. ALEXANDER *Bloodstain* xi. 134 You should never have come out here alone. This is redneck country. Every man in every one of these houses is a Night Rider. **1965** *Listener* 20 May 730/2 His general manner and accent suggest a person who might hold the racist views of a red-neck Southern bigot. **1971** B. MALAMUD *Tenants* 60 'I' grows up in redneck Mississippi in pure black poverty. **1972** R. BLOCH *Night-World* (1974) vii. 43 See how far you can march through Georgia today before some redneck sheriff busts you for vagrancy. **1973** *Freedomways* XIII. 52 Even Faulkner's ability was distorted by the pervasive racism of his redneck traditionalism. **1974** *New Yorker* 25 Feb. 102/3 He seems Southern redneck—a common man who works outdoors in the sun—to the soul. **1976** *National Observer* (U.S.) 17 July 4/1 Quite possibly Mississippi's only self-avowed redneck Republican. **1979** *Arizona Daily Star* 22 July 1. 5/4 Carter..ran on a virtually redneck platform for the 1970 nomination... After running a redneck campaign, [he] pledged an end to discrimination in his inaugural address.

2. (See quot.)

1900 *Westm. Gaz.* 25 Apr. 2/3 'Red-neck' used to be applied to Roman Catholics in Lancashire as a term of opprobrium.

3. *S. Afr.* = ROOINEK.

1900 A. H. KEANE *Boer States* p. xviii, *Rooinek*, 'Red-neck', in reference originally to some merinos introduced by an English farmer into the Free State, and marked with a red brand on the neck. These were spoken of as *red-necks*—an expression afterwards extended to the English themselves, and then as a term of contempt to the British troops in red uniform. **1921**, etc. [see ROOINEK]. **1936** R. CAMPBELL *Mithraic Emblems* 111 To find a red-neck cheap upon this day You do not need to wander far away. **1972** J. MCCLURE *Caterpillar Cop* ii. 18 What's with this Red-neck?.. Another bloody English immigrant?

red-necked, *a.* **a.** Having a red neck; used *spec.* in names of birds (and animals).

red-necked avocet, the Australian avocet, *Recurvirostra rubricollis*. **r. bernacle**, the red-breasted goose, *Bernicla ruficollis*. **r. coot-foot** = *r. phalarope*. **r. dabchick** = *r. grebe*. **r. footman**, a British moth. **r. francolin**, a South African francolin, *F. rubricollis*. **r. goatsucker** = *r. night-jar*. **r. grebe**, *Podiceps rubricollis* or *griseigena*. **r. kangaroo** = *r. wallaby*. **r. lobe-foot** = *r. phalarope*. **r. night-jar**, *Caprimulgus ruficollis*. **r. partridge** = *r. francolin*. **r. phalarope**, *Phalaropus* or *Lobipes hyperboreus*. **r. pheasant** = *r. francolin*. **r. (purre) sandpiper** (see quot. 1802). **r. wallaby**, *Macropus ruficollis*.

1874 J. E. HARTING in *Ibis* July 259 The *Red-necked Avocet, which is perhaps the most beautiful of the four known species, chiefly inhabits Australia. **1831** WILSON, etc. *Amer. Ornith.* IV. 348 *Red-necked Bernacles. **1896** MORRIS & TEGETMEIER *Nests Brit. Birds* III. 65 *Red-Necked Coot-Foot. **1817** T. FORSTER *Nat. Hist. Swallowtribe* (ed. 2) 89 *Rednecked dobchick. **1845** WESTWOOD *Moths* I. 99 *Gnophria rubricollis* (the *red-necked Footman). **1819** SHAW *Zool.* XI. II. 35 *Red-necked Francolin. **1847** P. H. GOSSE *Birds of Jamaica* 334 The *red-necked gaulin—*Egretta ruficollis*. **1862** HANCOCK in *Ibis* 39 Notice on the occurrence of the *Red-necked Goat sucker (*Caprimulgus ruficollis*) in England. **1785** PENNANT *Arct. Zool.* (1792) II. 499 *Red-necked Grebe, *Colymbus Parotis*. **1889** APLIN *Birds Oxfordsh.* 180 The Red-necked Grebe is an occasional winter visitor. **1893** NEWTON *Dict. Birds* 382 The larger Red-necked Grebe, *P. griseigena*,..a native of the sub-arctic parts of both Europe and America. **1841** WATERHOUSE *Nat. Hist. Mamm.* I. 125 The *Red-necked Kangaroo was discovered by MM. Peron and Lesueur. **1840** *Cuvier's Anim. Kingd.* 246 The *Red-necked Lobefoot. **1896** MORRIS & TEGETMEIER *Nests Brit. Birds* I. 128 The *Red-necked Night-jar has only once been recorded as occurring in Great Britain; it breeds in the South of Europe. **1783** LATHAM *Gen. Synopsis Birds* II. II. 771 *Red-necked Partridge. **1817** T. FORSTER *Nat. Hist. Swallowtribe* (ed. 6) 88 *Red-necked phalarope. **1882** NEWTON *Yarrell's Birds* III. 315 The Red-necked Phalarope is at once distinguished from the Grey Phalarope ..by its smaller size, with a longer and more slender beak [etc.]. **1971** *Country Life* 27 May 1292/3 The red-necked phalarope..though still Ireland's rarest breeding bird, has shown an increase. **1867** LAYARD *Birds S. Afr.* 268 The '*red-necked pheasant' is only found in wooded districts. **1785** LATHAM *Gen. Synopsis Birds* III. I. 183 *Red-necked Purre Sandpiper. **1802** MONTAGU *Ornith. Dict.* (1831) 408 Red-necked sandpiper. The young of the Dunlin. **1894-5** LYDEKKER *Royal Nat. Hist.* III. 241 One of the largest species is the *red-necked wallaby. **1926** Red-necked wallaby [see *brush wallaby* s.v. BRUSH *sb.*[1] 4]. **1782** J. LATHAM *Gen. Synopsis Birds* I. II. 558 (*heading*) *Red-necked W[oodpecker].

b. Holding redneck views; characteristic of a redneck (sense 1); conservative. orig. *U.S.*

1960 *Washington Post* 30 Apr. A6 'Uncle Earl' cavorted in typically 'red-necked' style at a fashionable luncheon. **1973** *Publishers' Weekly* 2 Apr. 58/2 A villain (red-necked political appointee with shady family connections to an equally red-necked but powerful Senator). **1977** *Arab Times* 13 Dec. 6/4 The white, red necked, blue collared worker is more interested in better wages, lower taxes, improved Social Security than justice in the Middle East.

redness ('rɛdnɪs). [f. RED *a.* + -NESS.] **a.** The state or quality of being red; red colour.

c **900** tr. *Bæda's Hist.* IV. xxi. [xix.] (1890) 322 Mid þy me nu..of swiran forðhlifað seo readnis [L. *rubor*] & bryne þæs swiles & wærces. **971** *Blickl. Hom.* 7 Seo readnes þære rosan lixeþ on þe. *c* **1374** CHAUCER *Boeth.* I. pr. i. 3 (Camb. MS.), Shewynge by rednesse [L. *rubore*] hyr shame they passeden sorwfully the thresshfold. *c* **1430** *Pilgr. Lyf Manhode* IV. lix. (1869) 204 Whyt milk it bicometh whan it is soden, and þe rednesse goth al awey. **1485** CAXTON *St. Wenefr.* 4 A lytil redenes in maner of a threde wente aboute the neck. **1544** PHAER *Regim. Lyfe* (1553) Biv, A desease called Gutta rosacea, or copper face, in Englishe,..is an excessiue rednesse aboute the nose. **1615** CROOKE *Body of Man* 72 Where blood aboundeth..a rosie rednesse mingleth it selfe with the white. **1661** LOVELL *Hist. Anim. & Min.* 220 Towards winter they wax kipper,..and loose both their rednesse and taste. *a* **1756** MRS. HEYWOOD *New Present* (1771) 25 Fresh fish in general may be judged by the redness of their gills. *a* **1822** SHELLEY *Chas. I*, I. 118 We see the redness of the torches Inflame the night. **1855** LONGF. *Hiaw.* xxii. 212 The evening sun descending Set the clouds on fire with redness. **1976** *Lancs. Evening Post* 7 Dec. 3/9 He grabbed witness by the collar, causing scratches to the neck and redness. **1981** G. HAMMOND *Revenge Game* xii. 137 In Keith's mind, a set of vague ideas solidified into a herring of most extraordinary redness.

b. The state or quality of being politically 'red'.

Under Chairman Mao the concept of 'redness' as opposed to 'expertness' was of great significance in the People's Republic of China.

1940 R. S. LAMBERT *Ariel & all his Quality* iii. 84 Press campaigns against alleged BBC 'redness'. **1973** R. TAYLOR *Educ. & Univ. Enrolment Policies in China, 1949–1971* 39 The subordination of expertise to ideology (or 'redness'). **1973** T. R. TREGEAR *Chinese* iii. 57 In the industrial field 'expertness' assumed greater importance than 'redness'. **1975** I. C. Y. HSÜ *Rise of Mod. China* (ed. 2) xxvi. 796 The government in 1957 initiated a 'socialist education movement' among the industrial and agrarian population, followed by the dispatch of military and civil leaders to physical labor as an example to the people. The importance of 'redness', i.e., ideology over expertise, was very much emphasized.

red nettle.

1. † **a.** A variety of the stinging nettle. *Obs.* **b.** The red dead-nettle.

c **1000** *Sax. Leechd.* III. 52 Seo reade netele ðe þurh ærn inwyxð. *a* **1400** *MS. Sloane* 282 in *Alphita* (Anec. Oxon.) 193 *Urtica greca*, rouge urteie, reed netel. **14..** *Stockh. Med. MS.* in *Anglia* XVIII. 302 þe crop of þe reed nettyle forȝet þou noȝt. *c* **1450** *M.E. Med. Bk.* (Heinrich) 75 Take gromylle,..þe rede netelle, violet [etc.]. **1530** PALSGR. 261/2 Reed nettyll, *ortiegriache*. **1561** HOLLYBUSH *Hom. Apoth.* 3 Take sedes of red nettels, and braye them to pouder in a morter. **1611** COTGR., *Ortie griesche*, the small stinging red Nettle. *Ortie rouge*, the red Nettle. **1877** HULME *Fam. Wild Flowers* I. 63 The upper leaves of the red nettle are sometimes densely clothed with silky hairs.

†**2.** (See quot.) *Obs. rare*[−1].

1611 COTGR., *Cul de cheval*, a small and ouglie fish,.. called, the red Nettle.

‖**redningskoite** ('rɛdnɪŋz,kɔɪtə, 'rɛdnɪŋz,ʃɔɪtə). Also **redningschoite, redningsshöite,** and with capital initial. [Norw., f. *redning* rescue + *skøyte* a type of fishing vessel.] A kind of Norwegian lifeboat. Also *attrib.*

1906 H. W. SMYTH *Mast & Sail* 434 *Redningskoite*, a Norwegian sea-keeping lifeboat for assisting the Northland fishing fleets in bad weather. **1925** *Yachting Monthly* XXXVIII. 135/1 The original Redningschoites were designed, by the late Colin Archer, to be the best heavy weather boats in the world. **1935** C. E. T. LEWIS *Lifeboats & their Conversion* ii. 39 The cruising lifeboats of Scandinavia and Russia as typified by the Norwegian ketch-rigged redningsshöites. The main duty of these craft is to keep in touch with the herring fleets throughout the winter, and render any help required. **1937** *Yachting Monthly* LXII. 508/1, I wanted to try out the conventional *redningskoite* sail plan. **1962** D. PHILLIPS-BIRT *Fore & Aft Sailing Craft* vii. 177 The redningskoite is illustrated in Figs 89, 90, and 91. The Norwegian term is rendered literally as 'rescue sailing ship'.

red-nose.

1. a. *attrib.* Red-nosed. **b.** One who has a red nose, a toper.

1589 NASHE *Anat. Absurd.* Wks. (Grosart) I. 34 Our new found songs.., which euery rednose Fidler hath at his Fingers end. [**1591** —— *Prognost.* ibid. II. 162 The ancient order of the redde noses.] **1636** W. DURHAM in *Ann. Dubrensia* (1877) 10 Their red-nose pimple-faced deitie. **1638** BRATHWAIT *Barnabees Jrnl.* III. (1818) 137 Down the staires..To a knot of brave boyes fell I, All red-noses, no dye deeper. **1798** NEMNICH *Polyg. Lex., Nat. Hist.* v. 867 Red nose kidneys; a sort of potatoes.

2. A name locally given to various species of molluscs.

1864 GOSSE in *Gd. Words* 191 The fishermen..use them for bait, applying to them the..expressive soubriquet of Red-noses [Note. *Saxicava rugosa*]. *Ibid.* 353 The cottagers about Paignton well know the 'red-noses', as they call the great cockles [Note. *Cardium rusticum*].

red-nosed, *a.* Having a red nose. Also *transf.* in names of birds, etc.

1607 SHARPHAM *The Fleire* II. D, Shall we haue red-nos'd Corporals here? **1666** PEPYS *Diary* (1879) III. 467 A long red-nosed silly jade. **1782** WOLCOTT (P. Pindar) *Odes to R.A.'s* vi. 16 Old red-nos'd Wilson's art. **1805** R. W. DICKSON *Pract. Agric.* II. 602 Red-nosed kidney [potato]. **1821** LATHAM *Gen. Hist. Birds* I. 201 Red-Nosed Falcon... Inhabits Senegal. **1840** DICKENS *Old C. Shop* xlvi, The doctor was a red-nosed gentleman. **1861** H. KINGSLEY *Ravenshoe* xlviii, Here's the rid-nosed oysther of Carlingford.

re'do, *v.* Also re-do. [RE- 5 a.]

1. *trans.* To do over again or afresh.

1597 A. M. tr. *Guillemeau's Fr. Chirurg.* 15/2 Redoinge the same soe often as the greatnes of the wounde shall require. **1615** G. SANDYS *Trav.* 262 Prodigality and luxurie are no new crimes, and..we do but re-do old vices. **1680** J. AUBREY in *Lett. Eminent Persons* (1813) III. 555 'Tis pitty it is not re-donne. **1837** C. LOFFT *Self-formation* I. 131 This we must do, and redo, and as nearly as we can overdo. **1892** *Daily News* 2 Aug. 6/1 The boots must either be redone, or he would not pay.

b. To redecorate (a room).

1864 TROLLOPE *Can you forgive her?* ii, I'll go halves with you in the expense of redoing it. **1895** *Blackw. Mag.* Feb. 36/2 My father redid the interior of the East room.

c. To do *up* again.

1845 *Economy* 48 It is to be patched..and re-done up.

†**2.** To do back or in return. *Obs.*[−1]

1650 LOCKYER *Olive-Leafe* 73 What evil men doe to good shall be re-done to them, done back again upon them.

'**redo**, *sb.* Also re-do. [f. the vb.] A doing over again (in various senses); a repetition.

a **1953** DYLAN THOMAS *Quite Early One Morning* (1954) 79 The decorators were in at the mortuary, giving the old home a bit of re-do like. **1961** D. B. SHIELDS in *Webster* s.v., No pleasanter prospect than a redo of our South American trek. **1977** *Surgery* LXXXI. 41 (*heading*) 'Redo' surgery after operations for aneurysm and occlusion of the abdominal aorta.

red ochre. A variety of OCHRE, commonly used for colouring with; reddle or ruddle.

1572 *Churchw. Acc. St. Dunstan's, Canterb.* (M.S.), Payed for red oker iijd. **1601** HOLLAND *Pliny* II. 417 This floure of salt is..commonly coloured with red ocre. **1681** CHETHAM *Angler's Vade-m.* IV. §7 (1700) 35 Some ingenious Anglers.. use to shave Riddle or red Oker into the Moss they keep their Worms in. **1725** *Phil. Trans.* XXXIII. 395 About Winford..it turns to Ruddle, or Red-Okre, used chiefly for marking of Sheep. **1774** GOLDSM. *Nat. Hist.* (1776) II. 240 They use many methods to darken their skins by art, painting them with red ochre [etc.]. **1836-7** DICKENS *Sk. Boz* (1850) 69/2 The company are now promenading outside in all the dignity of wigs, spangles, red-ochre, and whitening. **1884** W. H. GREENWOOD *Steel & Iron* iii. 34 The soft and more earthy varieties [of red hæmatite] constitute red ochre.

attrib. **1609** DEKKER *Lanth. & Candle-lt.* viii, No Red-oaker man caries a face of a more filthy complexion. **1623-4** MIDDLETON & ROWLEY *Span. Gipsy* II. i, No red-ochre rascals umbered with soot and bacon as the English gipsies are.

Hence **red-ochre** *v.* Also **red-ochreing** *vbl. sb.*

1884 BARING-GOULD *Mehalah* x, The roof was tiled and looked very red, as though red ochred every morning. **1899** *Strand Mag.* Mar. 278/1 A little staining and red-ochreing.

redolence ('rɛdələns). [a. OF. *redolence* (Godef.), f. *redolent*: see -ENCE.]

1. Sweet smell, fragrance, perfume. Also *fig.*

c **1420** LYDG. *Assembly of Gods* 1611 The wordys of Doctryne yaue gret redolence, In swetness of sauour, to her dysciples all. *c* **1530** *Remedy Love* 213 Breathyng an Aromatike redolence Surmountyng Olibane. *c* **1570** *Pride*

& Lowl. (1841) 8 So paynted and so coloured.. Nas Floras land.. Ne with such verdure, and such redolence. *a* **1691** BOYLE (J.), We have all the redolence of the perfumes we burn upon his altars. **1791** HUDDESFORD *Salmag., Illus. Fancy* 15 Whose undulating folds dispense Cassia's ambrosial redolence. **1845** *Blackw. Mag.* LVIII. 750 Was not this feeling an echo, a redolence, of the happy, lively sensations [etc.]. **1897** *Chr. Herald* (N.Y.) 13 Oct. 764/2 Migrating into groves of redolence and perpetual fruitage.

†**2.** Smell, stench. *Obs. rare*$^{-1}$.

1599 NASHE *Lenten Stuffe* 58 Al these hee graunted, to bee ridde of his filthy redolence.

So †'**redolency**. *Obs.* [See -ENCY.]

1610 GUILLIM *Heraldry* III. vii. (1611) 116 Flowers for beauty, varietie of colour, and pleasant redolencie. **1658** EVELYN *Fr. Gard.* (1675) 89 The flies so much frequent their flowers and leaves, which attract them with their redolency and juyce. [Copied by Mortimer *Husb.* (1721) II. 268, whence in Johnson and later Dicts.]

redolent ('rɛdələnt), *a.* [a. OF. *redolent* or L. *redolent-em*, pr. pple. of *redolēre*, f. *re(d)-* RE- + *olēre* to emit a smell. Cf. OLENT *a.*]

1. Having or diffusing a pleasant odour; sweet-smelling, fragrant, odorous. Now *rare*.

c **1400** *Beryn* 2765 This gardeyn is evir green, & ful of maye flowers.. the wich been so redolent, & sentyn so aboute. **1432–50** tr. *Higden* (Rolls) VII. 485 The body.. was founde redolente and incorrupte by ij. yere after his dethe. **1528** PAYNEL *Salerne's Regim.* H b, Fragrant and redolent wyne conforteth moste. **1600** FAIRFAX *Tasso* x. lxi, A lothsome lake of brimstone, pitch and lime, Oregoes that land, earst sweet and redolent. **1634** H. R. *Salerne's Regim.* 66 A toast wet in redolent Wine is good to eate. **1828–30** TENNYSON in *Life* (1897) I. 64 Every flower and every fruit the redolent breath Of the warm seawind ripeneth.

transf. **1509** HAWES *Past. Pleas.* XXXVIII. (Percy Soc.) 198 Her redolente wordes of swete influence Degouted vapoure moost aromatyke.

†**b.** In fig. context. *Obs.*

14.. LYDG. *Commend. Our Lady* 39 Fructif olyve, of foyles faire and thikke, And redolent cedre.. Remembre on sinners. **1513** BRADSHAW *St. Werburge* I. 1815 A redolent floure all vertue to augment. **1542** BECON *Christmas Banquet* I. Wks. 1564 I. 18 b, The most odiferous, redolent, and swete smellyng floures of the holy Scriptures. **1629** R. BRUCE *Let.* in Wodrow *Life* (1843) 138 To pour in after this his redolent balm on the bleeding wounds of a festered conscience. **1643** UDALL *Serm.* in *Shute's Sermons* (1645) 8 The substance of this Text, and.. the pretious fragrant redolent oyntment in it.

2. Of smell, odour, etc.: Pleasant, sweet, fragrant.

c **1450** LYDG. & BURGH *Secrees* 2371 Lyk a gardeyn of Redolent savour. **1568** T. HOWELL *Arb. Amitie* (1879) 19 The Violets trim.. Doe not alwayes.. florishe gay, with smell most redolent. **1629** MAXWELL tr. *Herodian* (1635) 297 All manner of redolent Odors. **1652** C. B. STAPYLTON *Herodian* 6 Leaving behind a redolent perfume.

3. Odorous or smelling *of* or *with* something; full of the scent or smell *of*. Also *fig.*

1700 DRYDEN *Ovid's Met.* xv. 109 While Kine to Pails distended Udders bring, And Bees their Hony redolent of Spring. **1742** GRAY *Eton* ii, The gales.. seem.., redolent of joy and youth, To breathe a second spring. **1821** LAMB *Elia* Ser. I. *My Relations*, The odour of those tender vegetables comes back upon my sense, redolent of soothing recollections. **1871** ALABASTER *Wheel of Law* 125 The Grand Being entered his magnificent palace, redolent with fragrant perfumes.

b. *fig.* Strongly suggestive or reminiscent *of*, or impregnated *with*, some quality, feeling, etc.

1828 E. IRVING *Last Days* 369 Their craft.. all redolent with Popish superstition. **1837–9** HALLAM *Hist. Lit.* II. II. v. 226 It is a strain redolent of a bridegroom's joy. **1856** EMERSON *Eng. Traits, Universities* Wks. (Bohn) II. 90 On every side Oxford is redolent of age and authority. **1876** HOLLAND *Sev. Oaks* xxiii. 328 The lawyer's hands were as pale,.. and his lips as redolent of scorn.

†**redoling**, *ppl. a. Obs. rare*$^{-1}$. [f. L. *redol-ēre* (see prec.) + -ING^2.] Redolent.

c **1450** *Mirour Saluacioun* 556 Above both rose and lyllye candent redoling.

redomyt, variant of REDIMITE *a. Sc. Obs.*

†**redonable**, *a. Obs. rare.* [f. RE- + DONABLE *a.*] That may be given back.

1641 EARL MONM. tr. *Biondi's Civil Warres* II. 69 Artillery, munition, or victualls, prisoners of quality, or other-wise redonable, doe properly belong to them.

†**redonate**, *v. Obs. rare*$^{-0}$. [f. L. *redōnāt-*, *redōnāre*: see RE- and DONATE *v.*] (See quot.)

1656 BLOUNT *Glossogr.*, *Redonate*, to give again a thing that is taken.

†**redo'nation**. *Obs. rare*$^{-1}$. [See prec. and -ATION.] The action of giving back.

1623 COCKERAM, *Redonation*, a giuing backe of a thing. **1648** LIGHTFOOT *Horæ Hebraicæ* (1684) II. 561 We have.. heard of the Holy Ghost's departure,.. but of his return and redonation of him, we have not yet heard.

redond(e, obs. form of REDOUND.

‖**redondilla** (redon'diʎa). [Sp., dim. f. *redonda* fem. of *redondo* round.] In Spanish poetry, a stanza of riming verse; *spec.* a stanza of four trochaic lines consisting of six or eight syllables, in which the first line rimes with the fourth, and the second with the third.

1837 HALLAM *Hist. Lit.* I. ii. §41. 163 The favourite metre in lyric songs and romances was the redondilla. **1868** GEO. ELIOT *Sp. Gipsy* III. 257, I am a thing of rhythm and redondillas.

redondite (rə'dɒndaɪt). *Min.* [f. the name of *Redonda* Island, W. Indies + -ITE^1.] A hydrated phosphate of aluminium and iron, (Al,Fe)$PO_4.2H_2O$, occurring as whitish amorphous masses.

1870 C. U. SHEPARD in *Amer. Jrnl. Sci.* C. 96 Barrandite has gr. = 2·576. Redondite gives gr. = 2·019. **1964** *Amer. Mineralogist* XLIX. 445 X-ray powder data are given on redondite from Ponikla and Listenec, Czechoslovakia, from Redonda Island, and for tangaite from Tanganyika... Redondite (and tangaite) give patterns that are identical and distinct from those of variscite and clinovariscite... The authors feel that the name redondite should be used for all material of this type with Al > Fe and the name tangaite is superfluous. **1975** *Mineral Abstr.* XXVI. 225/2 Variscite, crandallite, and redondite, relatively rare phosphate minerals, are found in phosphatic rocks associated with carbonatites and syenites in the Grande islet (Brava island) Cape Verde.

re-'doom, *v.* [RE- 5 a.] To doom again.

1738 A. HILL *Wks.* (1753) I. 286 If preferring the peace of poor England to your Lordship's, I should even wish you redoom'd to her helm.. the wish would deserve pardon.

redor, variant of REDVORE *Obs.*

redorse, redos, obs. variants of REREDOS.

redoub(e, redoubbe, varr. REDUB *v. Obs.*

†**re'double**, *sb.*^{1} *Obs.*$^{-1}$ [Cf. REDOUBLE *v.*^{1} and obs. F. *redouble* (Godef.).] Repetition, anadiplosis.

1589 PUTTENHAM *Eng. Poesie* III. xix. (Arb.) 210 Ye haue another sort of repetition when with the worde by which you finish your verse, ye beginne the next verse... The Greeks call this figure Anadiplosis, I call him the Redouble as the originall beares.

redouble, *sb.*^{2} *Bridge.* [f. REDOUBLE *v.*^{2}] A call that redoubles a bid.

1906 'CUT-CAVENDISH' *Compl. Bridge Player* 98 The redouble is the *rara avis* of the Bridge world. **1910** J. B. ELWELL *Auction Bridge* 103 The laws of Auction, as embodied for club play, limit the doubling feature to one double and one re-double. **1925** [see BUSINESS 21 d]. **1964** *Official Encycl. Bridge* 450/1 Ill-judged doubles of game or slam contracts may lead to redoubles. **1975** *Times* 20 Dec. 10/7 The Double of a No trump is primarily for a penalty: what does the opener mean to convey by a Redouble?

redouble (rɪ'dʌb(ə)l), *v.*^{1} Also 6–7 redub(b)le. [a. F. *redoubler* (f. *re-* RE- + *doubler* to DOUBLE) = Sp. *redoblar*, Pg. *redobrar*, It. *raddoppiare.*]

1. *trans.* To double (a thing); to make twice as great or as much.

c **1477** CAXTON *Jason* 18 b, I haue yet good wil that to-morne I shal redouble that. *c* **1489** —— *Blanchardyn* xlii. 159 These tydynges dyde redouble her ioye ouer mesure. **1555** EDEN *Decades* 249 By this meanes are the customes redoubeled. **1594** SOUTHWELL *M. Magd. Fun. Tears* (1823) 73 Thy losse hath redoubled the torment of my owne [grief]. **1603** HOLLAND *Plutarch's Mor.* 219 The feare which she hath lest her little one should take harme redoubleth her courage. **1698** S. CLARKE *Script. Just.* iv. 18 When God justified Job,.. he return'd and redoubled all his Temporal Blessings to him again. **1748** *Anson's Voy.* II. vi. 192 This made our people redouble their efforts. **1797–1809** COLERIDGE *Three Graves* 345 There was a hurry in her looks, Her struggles she redoubled. **1868** FREEMAN *Norm. Conq.* (1876) II. x. 520 The King's alms and prayers and fastings are redoubled.

b. *intr.* To be doubled; to become twice as great or as much. Also, to become doubly strong *in* some respect.

1490 CAXTON *Eneydos* xxiv. 90 Redoublen her sorowes and her trystesses enforce more vpon her. **1530** PALSGR. 682/1 Whan I thynke upon his dethe my sorowes redouble. *a* **1627** HAYWARD *Four Y. Eliz.* (Camden) 62 The Englishe.. redublinge in courage upon the importance of their danger,.. drave the French againe home to the towne. **1666** HARVEY *Morb. Angl.* xxxi. (1672) 94 The heat of the body reflecting at the fingers ends, redoubles, and is more intense than in any other part. **1715** POPE *Iliad* I. 296 Nor yet the rage his boiling breast forsook, Which thus redoubling on Atrides broke. **1831** JEKYLL *Corr.* (1894) 281 The morning papers redouble in fury. **1855** MACAULAY *Hist. Eng.* xvii. IV. 46 The clamour redoubled when it was known that the convert.. had accepted the Deanery of Saint Paul's.

†**c.** To be (so many times) greater than. *Obs.*

1611 SPEED *Hist. Gt. Brit.* VII. xxii. §5. 338 The Armie of this enemie is reported to redouble thirty times his.

†**2.** *trans.* **a.** To repay doubly. **b.** To cause to be repeated. *Obs. rare.*

1531 ELYOT *Gov.* II. xii, Thus my kyndenesse hathe he well acquyted, or (as I mought saye) redoubled, delyvering me from the death. *Ibid.* III. xxi, Often tymes the omittynge of correction redoubleth a trespace.

3. To repeat; to do, say, etc., a second time.

1581 J. BELL *Haddon's Answ. Osor.* 344 b, Of the greatnesse of Sinne.. hath bene spoken so much already that it is needelesse now to redouble the same agayne. **1626** T. H. tr. *Caussin's Holy Crt.* 71 There is not a visitant.. that will not roame from house to house.. and redouble iourney after iourney heerevpon. **1645** MILTON *Tetrach.* Wks. (1847) 180/1 (Gen. i. 27) He.. said also in the same verse, 'in the image of God created he him', and redoubled it. **1845** STODDART *Gram.* in *Encycl. Metrop.* I. 91/1 It is sufficient.. that the negative conception should be once expressed in a simple sentence; but we generally find it redoubled in old English.

b. *esp.* To repeat (a blow, etc.).

1593 SHAKS. *Rich. II*, I. iii. 90 Let thy blowes doubly redoubled, Fall like amazing thunder. **1598** GRENEWEY *Tacitus, Ann.* VI. viii. (1622) 134 He.. being carried away with his horse, was not able to redouble his stroke. **1646** EARL MONM. tr. *Biondi's Civil Warres* VI. 40 *e*, He was.. wounded in the side by one who was come thither to kill him, and who did not redouble his thrust.

†**c.** *absol.* To repeat a thrust or stroke in fencing.

1640 tr. *Verdere's Romant of Rom.* III. 220 He ran him with his sword into the thigh, and instantly redoubling on his helmet, he overturned him. **1692** SIR W. HOPE *Fencing-Master* 98 When you Redouble or give in another Thrust.

†**4.** *trans.* To repeat (a sound); to return, reproduce, re-echo. *Obs.*

a **1542** WYATT in *Tottel's Misc.* (Arb.) 75 To me they do redubble still of stormy sighes the voyce. **1596** SPENSER *Prothalamion* 111 So ended she; and all the rest around To her redoubled that her undersong. **1655** MILTON *Sonn. Mass. Piedmont*, Their moans The Vales redoubl'd to the Hills, and they To Heav'n. **1679** DRYDEN *Limberham* III. i, Hollow mountains my groans redouble.

b. *intr.* To re-echo, resound.

1725 POPE *Odyss.* VI. 136 Loud shrieks the virgin train, And the loud shriek redoubles from the main. **1781** COWPER *Truth* 240 Peal upon peal redoubling all around. **1817** SHELLEY *Rev. Islam* VII. xi, A stunning clang of massive bolts redoubling Beneath the deep.

5. *trans.* To duplicate by reflection.

1827 MONTGOMERY *Pelican Isl.* I. 11 The sun Sole in the firmament, but in the deep Redoubled. **1869** RUSKIN *Q. of Air* §18 As you may trace new forms and softer colours in a hillside, redoubled by a lake.

†**6.** To pass or sail round, to double. *Obs.*$^{-1}$

1611 SPEED *Hist. Gt. Brit.* v. i. §4. 155 The huge enorme tract of ground beyond Caledonia.. was first redoubled with the Romane fleet by Iulius Agricola.

redouble (riː'dʌb(ə)l), *v.*^{2} [RE- 5 a.] **a.** *trans.* and *intr.* To double again.

1530 PALSGR. 682/1 It is a sporte to se an hare doubyll and redoubyll. **1589** PUTTENHAM *Eng. Poesie* II. x[i]. (Arb.) 100 The maker will double or redouble his rime or concords, and set his distances farre or nigh. **1603** KNOLLES *Hist. Turks* (1638) 283 Doubling and redoubling the praises of the king. **1771** LUCKOMBE *Hist. Print.* 403 As the volume that is doubled or re-doubled is imposed in the whole Chase.

b. *spec.* in *Bridge*, to double again (a bid which an opponent has already doubled). Also *absol.* or *intr.*

1894 'BOAZ' *Pocket Guide to Bridge* 6 The leader has then to ask the adversaries whether either of them wishes to redouble. **1898** [see DOUBLE *v.* 1 g]. **1910** J. B. ELWELL *Auction Bridge* 102 The partner.. may be well satisfied with the double, and, perhaps, in a position to redouble... The general Auction laws do not limit the number of times that a declaration may be doubled and re-doubled. **1921** *Sat. Westm. Gaz.* 1 Oct. 17/1 The player who doubles would not lose much if the rule was that *his* double could not be re-doubled. **1980** *Times* 12 Jan. 10/6 South doubles for a take-out and West redoubles.

†**re'double**, *v.*^{3} *Obs.* Also 6 -dub(b)le, -doble. [a. obs. F. *redoubler*, *-dobler* (15th c.), app. an erroneous form of *redouber* to REDUB.] *trans.* To put right, amend, redress.

c **1555** HARPSFIELD *Divorce Hen. VIII* (Camden) 55 They would fain reduble and redress this error. **1571** DK. NORFOLK in *14th Rep. Hist. MSS. Comm.* App. IV. 574 Manye men have runne astraie who.. have afterwardes, with good service, redobled ther former follies. **1596** *Foxe's A. & M.* 1001/2 No man shall by colour of dutie omitted by their curates, deteine their tithes, and so redouble [1570 redubbe] one wrong with another.

redoubled (rɪ'dʌb(ə)ld, riː-), *ppl. a.* [f. REDOUBLE *v.*^{1} (and *v.*^{2}) + -ED^2.]

1. a. Increased to double; repeated.

a **1542** WYATT in *Tottel's Misc.* (Arb.) 59 Who geueth willingly, Redoubled thankes aye doth deserue. **1590** SPENSER *F.Q.* II. ii. 23 He.. with redoubled buffes them backe did put. **1591** —— *Tears Muses* 22 Th' hollow hills from which their silver voyces Were wont redoubled Echoes to rebound. **1631** QUARLES *Div. Poems, Samson* sec. viii, His quicke redoubled paces make His stay amends. **1671** MILTON *Samson* 923 Where my redoubl'd love and care.. May ever tend about thee. **1711** W. KING tr. *Naude's Ref. Politics* iii. 105 The king persisted in his resolution.. which was followed by the redoubled complaints of his people. **1776** GIBBON *Decl. & F.* xi. I. 330 The angry and selfish passions of the soldiers.. soon broke out with redoubled violence. **1869** J. MARTINEAU *Ess.* II. 228 The memory will.. require redoubled precautions against mistake.

b. *Music.* Increased by an octave.

1811 BUSBY *Dict. Mus.* (ed. 3) s.v., The thirteenth composed of a sixth and octave is a redoubled sixth; and the fifteenth containing two octaves is a redoubled octave.

c. *spec.* in *Bridge*.

1964 *Official Encycl. Bridge* 450/1 When the standard of play is high, redoubled contracts are rare.

2. Doubled, or folded, back or again.

1601 DENT *Pathw. Heaven* (1831) 37 These doubled and redoubled ruffs which are now in common use. *c* **1825** BEDDOES *Poems, Kisses* 115 Soft as a snow-tuft in the dewless cup Of a redoubled rose. **1827–8** STEUART *Planter's G.* (ed. 2) 248 Taking care, by redoubled folds of mat, to secure the bark against.. damage.

re'doublement. [a. F. *redoublement* (16th c.), or f. REDOUBLE *v.*^{1} + -MENT.]

1. = REDOUBLING *vbl. sb.* 1.

1611 COTGR., *Redouble*, a redoublement;.. a redoubling. **1768** *Woman of Honor* III. 256 To that circumstance it was so plain, my owing her redoublement of attention to me, that I never [etc.]. **1867** MILL in *Even. Star* 10 May, This bill..

will have the unrivalled feat of making a redoublement of agitation both inevitable and indispensable.

†**2.** *Med.* An increase in severity; a paroxysm. *Obs.* (Cf. REDOUBLING *vbl. sb.* 2.)

1740 tr. *De Mouhy's Fort. Country-Maid* (1741) II. 304 A frightful Crisis, which at first was thought to be a Redoublement of the Fever. **1753** N. TORRIANO *Gangr. Sore Throat* 93 Any Diminution in the Redoublements of the Fever.

transf. **1878** FR. A. KEMBLE *Rec. Girlhood* I. viii. 215, I fell into a redoublement of weeping.

re'doubler. [f. REDOUBLE *v.*[1] or [2] + -ER[1].]

1. One who redoubles. *rare.*

1611 COTGR., *Redoubleur*, a redoubler. **1959** T. REESE *Bridge Player's Dict.* 182 At the slam level the odds in favor of the redoubler are better yet.

2. A machine for redoubling yarn.

1884 M^c^LAREN *Spinning* 241 It is only necessary to put from six to twelve turns per yard into the yarn. The best frame for doing this is Messrs. Boyd's redoubler.

redoubling (rɪˈdʌb(ə)lɪŋ, riːˈdʌblɪŋ), *vbl. sb.* [f. REDOUBLE *v.*[1] (and *v.*[2]) + -ING[1].]

1. a. The action of REDOUBLE *v.* in various senses.

1580 HOLLYBAND *Treas. Fr. Tong*, *Redoublement*, a redoubling. **1610** J. MORE in *Buccleuch MSS.* (Hist. MSS. Comm.) I. 87 By the redoubling of her griefs on all hands. *a* **1665** J. GOODWIN *Filled w. the Spirit* (1867) 111 The redoubling of the negative particle..fortifying the negation. **1681** [see ANADIPLOSIS]. **1748** HARTLEY *Observ. Man* I. iv. 458 The Progress, Windings, and endless Redoublings of Self-love. **1893** *Daily News* 3 Feb. 5/4 The next re-doubling of the present number of his co-religionists.

b. *techn.* in spinning (see quot.).

1884 M^c^LAREN *Spinning* 239 There is a second form of twisting called re-doubling, which is chiefly used for carpet yarn. It is for twisting two or more threads together that have already been each made into two-fold.

c. *spec.* in *Bridge.*

1899 A. DUNN *Bridge* 63 Doubling and Redoubling... After the trump suit is announced, the adversaries may 'double' the value of the suit selected... The dealer and his partner may redouble. **1908** *Laws of Auction Bridge* §55 Doubling and redoubling affect the score only, and not the value in declaring. **1963** G. F. HERVEY *Handbk. Card Games* 134 Doubling and redoubling do not..increase the size of a contract.

†**2.** A paroxysm. *Obs.* (Cf. REDOUBLEMENT 2.)

1747 tr. *Astruc's Fevers* 265 A pestilential fever, particularly of the malignant and continued kind with redoublings.

fig. **1756** NUGENT *Montesquieu's Spir. Laws* XIII. xvii, A new distemper has spread itself over Europe, infecting our princes... It has its redoublings, and of necessity becomes contagious.

re'doubling, *ppl. a.* [f. as prec. + -ING[2].] Doubling, increasing; re-echoing, resounding.

1632 LITHGOW *Trav.* VIII. 349 Wars..the issue whereof, but retorted to the Duke a redoubling disaduantage. **1717** POPE *Iliad* XII. 298 Redoubling clamours thunder in the skies. **1762–9** FALCONER *Shipwr.* I. 799 Redoubling cords the lofty canvas guide. *Ibid.* II. 73 One in redoubling mazes wheels along. **1817** SCOTT *Harold* v. xii, Redoubling echoes roll'd about. **1822** GOOD *Study Med.* II. 26 The dicrotic, coturnising, and inciduous [pulses], proposed..as mere subvarieties of the rebounding, or redoubling.

redoubt (rɪˈdaʊt), *sb.* Also 7, 9 **redout(e.** [ad. F. *redoute*, †*redote*, *ridotte* (first recorded in 1616), ad. It. *ridotto* (= Sp. *reducto*, Pg. *reducto*, *reduto*, F. *réduit*: see REDUIT):—med.L. *reductus* a secret place, a refuge, f. L. *reductus* retired, pa. pple. of *redūcĕre* to REDUCE.

The *b* in Eng. is intrusive, an analogy of *redoubt v.*]

1. *Fortif.* †**a.** A small work made in a bastion or ravelin of a permanent fortification, or (***detached redoubt***) at some distance beyond the glacis, but within musket-shot from the covert-way. *Obs.* **b.** A species of out-work or field-work, usually of a square or polygonal shape, and with little or no means of flanking defence.

a **1608** SIR F. VERE *Comm.* (1657) 4 Because there were upon it certain small redoubts held by the enemie, we took along with us two small field-pieces. **1625** B. JONSON *Staple of N.* IV, When my muster-master..tells you of redoubts, of cats, and cortines. **1673** SIR J. MOORE *Mod. Fortif.* 95 Plain Redoubts, are either small or great; the small are fit for Court of Guards in the Trenches. **1704** J. HARRIS *Lex. Techn.* I. s.v., In Marshy Grounds, these Redoubts are often made of Mason's Work for the Security of the Neighbourhood. **1794** MRS. RADCLIFFE *Myst. Udolpho* xxxiii, They were fired from that redoubt yonder, and rare execution they did. **1834–47** J. S. MACAULAY *Field Fortif.* (1851) 13 The defects of a circular redoubt are, that it is difficult to apply to irregular sites, and that it distributes its fire equally on every part whether required or not.

c. *fig.* and in fig. context.

1629 B. JONSON in Sir J. Beaumont *Bosworth F.*, etc. a j b, Yet, who dares offer a redoubt to reare? To cut a Dike? or sticke a Stake vp, here, Before this worke? **1663** BUTLER *Hud.* I. i. 326 [The rats] till th' were stormed and beaten out Ne'er left the fortified Redoubt. **1712** SWIFT *Sid Hamet* 51 A magical Redoubt To keep mischievous Spirits out. **1781** COWPER *Conversat.* 689 They..Enlarge and fortify the dread redoubt, Deeply resolved to shut a Saviour out. **1841** EMERSON *Lect. on Times* Wks. (Bohn) II. 249 This great fact of Conservatism, entrenched in its immense redoubts. **1955** *Times* 16 May 3/4 Labour's most south-westerly redoubt is in acute danger. **1963** *Times* 30 May 13/2 It would be too embarrassing for all concerned if Ebbw Vale and the other Labour redoubts were to be presented on nomination day with official Labour candidates on top of the sitting 'independents'. **1970** R. LOWELL *Notebk.* 72 Let's face it, English is a racist redoubt. **1977** *Time* 21 Mar. 10/3 Like his predecessors, he has tried—and failed—to overcome the age-old linguistic dispute that makes Belgium the staunchest redoubt of tribalism in Western Europe.

2. *Fortif.* = REDUIT.

1802 JAMES *Milit. Dict.*, *Redoubt*,..a place more particularly intrenched and separated from the rest by a ditch. **1841** *Penny Cycl.* XIX. 348/2 Any works constructed within others, in order to prolong their defence, or to afford a retreat for the troops who occupy them, are also called redoubts.

3. A public assembly-hall in Germany used for gambling and entertainments; also *transf.* an assembly held there, esp. a masked ball.

1787 [see ASSEMBLÉE]. **1818** *Autumn near Rhine* 509 The Redoubt is a large handsome building, the ground-floor open with a colonnade in front. **1858** CARLYLE *Fredk. Gt.* VI. iii. (1872) II. 150 The two Kings, after dinner, went in domino to the redoubt (*ridotto*, what we now call *rout* or evening party).

†**redoubt,** *ppl. a. Obs.* [f. next.] Redoubted.

1417 in Ellis *Orig. Lett.* Ser. II. I. 54 Our righte redoubt and righte soveraiyne liege Lord. **1502** *Ord. Crysten Men* (W. de W. 1506) v. iii. M M ij b, How moche is this horryble thynge cruell and redoubte as to offende god and his commaundementes to trespasse.

redoubt (rɪˈdaʊt), *v.* Now *rhet.* Also 4–7 **redoute**, 5–6 **redowt**, (4 **-e**). [ad. F. *redouter*, †*redoubter* (11th c.), f. *re-* RE- + *douter* to DOUBT. Cf. obs. It. *ridottare*.] *trans.* To dread, fear, stand in awe or apprehension of: **a.** a person, nation, etc. (Chiefly in *pa. pple.*)

c **1374** CHAUCER *Boeth.* II. pr. vii. 45 (Camb. MS.), Yit was ..Roome wel waxen and gretly redowted of the parthes [L. *Parthis..formidolosa*]. **1456** SIR G. HAYE *Law Arms* (S.T.S.) 2 Charles the Sext..the quhilk is lufit and redoubtit our all the warld. *c* **1500** *Melusine* 200 Regnald.. made so grete appertyse of armes that alle his enemyes redoubted hym. **1590** C'TESS PEMBROKE *Antonie* 947, I conquer'd Rome, that Nations so redoubt. *a* **1648** LD. HERBERT *Hen. VIII* (1683) 2 He seem'd to hold that strong temper of Authority, which made him esteem'd and redoubted both at home and abroad. **1728** MORGAN *Algiers* II. i. 212 Algiers formidable and redoubted as it renders itself to many of the Coasts of Europe measures barely one League about. **1866** *Edin. Rev.* Oct. 363 The Sawflies are those most to be redoubted by the English farmer.

b. a thing or event.

c **1374** CHAUCER *Boeth.* I. pr. iii. 5 (Camb. MS.) Sholde I thanne redowte my blame. **1491** CAXTON *Vitas Patr.* (W. de W. 1495) I. xlviii. 92/2 They had seen his Iugements, whyche ben moche to be fered and redoubted. **1523** LD. BERNERS *Froiss.* I. cclxxv. 412 Whiche thynges they sayd ought greatly to be redoubted and consydered. *c* **1586** C'TESS PEMBROKE *Ps.* CXXI. ii, March lustily on, redoubt no falling. **1653** H. COGAN tr. *Pinto's Trav.* ix. 27 Here is the cause that makes me so much redoubt the coming of mine enemies. **1782** ELPHINSTON *Martial* I. lxx. 61 Yet, bold approach; thou canst redoubt no pride. **1889** J. J. THOMAS *Froudacity* 198 Whiteness of skin was both redoubted and tremblingly crouched to by negroes.

redoubtable (rɪˈdaʊtəb(ə)l), *a.* (and *sb.*) Now *rhet.* Also 4 **redowt-**, 4–6 **redout-**. [a. F. *redoutable*, †*redoubt-* (12–13th c.): see prec.]

1. To be feared or dreaded; formidable. †Also, of persons: To be reverenced or revered, commanding respect. **a.** In predicative use.

c **1374** CHAUCER *Boeth.* IV. pr. v. 102 (Camb. MS.) No wyse man hath leuere ben exiled, poore and nedy, and nameles, than for to..flowren of Rychesses, and be redowtable by honour [L. *honore reverendus*]. **1481** CAXTON *Myrr.* I. viii, For the evyll was helle maad..whiche is horryble stynking and redoubtable. **1530** PALSGR. 383 He was wont to be so redoubtable to them. **1638** R. BAKER tr. *Balzac's Lett.* (vol. III.) 108 In such equipage hee would be more ridiculous than redoubtable. **1685** *Gracian's Courtier's Orac.* 53 By one word he rendred himself more redoubtable, than by all his power. **1787** BURNS *Death Sir J. H. Blair* vi, Revers'd [is] that spear, redoubtable in war. **1816** KIRBY & SP. *Entomol.* xxiii. (1818) II. 358 A spider-wasp..whose sting is redoubtable. **1889** *Spectator* 14 Sept., As a fighting race, they will always be redoubtable.

b. In attributive use. (Chiefly of persons, and now freq. in humorous or ironical application.)

1421 SIR H. LUTTRELL in Ellis *Orig. Lett.* Ser. II. I. 84 Redoutabel and souveraine Lord. **1484** CAXTON *Chivalry* 4 He thought of the ryght redoubtable sentence of our lord. **1550** BALE *Eng. Votaries* (title-p.), Dedicated to our most redoubtable soveraigne kynge Edward the syxte. **1621** MOLLE *Camerar. Liv. Libr.* v. xiv. 377 Ridiculous redoubtable rellicks which the ancient Pagans were wont to carrie. **1657** CROMWELL *Sp.* 23 Jan. in *Carlyle*, That you marry this redoubtable couple together—Righteousness and Peace. **1716** POPE *Let. to Earl of Burlington* Wks. 1886 X. 205 The enterprising Mr. Lintot, the redoubtable rival of Mr. Tonson. **1825** J. NEAL *Bro. Jonathan* II. 163 A little to their left was a female.., a redoubtable speaker of the society. **1877** MRS. OLIPHANT *Makers Flor.* xi. 270 They fell on the redoubtable Swiss, then 'the finest infantry in the world'.

2. *sb.* A formidable person.

1844 BROWNING *Colombe's Birthday* III, Had you sought the lady's court..Faced the redoubtables composing it [etc.].

Hence **re'doubtableness.**

1672 PENN *Spir. Truth Vind.* 67 Behold then the redoubtableness of this Adversary.

redoubted (rɪˈdaʊtɪd), *ppl. a.* [f. REDOUBT *v.* + -ED[1].] Feared or dreaded; reverenced, respected; noted, distinguished.

Very common in 15–17th c. in addressing sovereigns.

1417 in Ellis *Orig. Lett.* Ser. II. I. 55 Unto there soveraigne and redoubted liege Lord. **1464** *Rolls of Parlt.* V. 527/2 Oure right redoubted Fader of noble memorie. **1509** HAWES *Past. Pleas.* XI. (Percy Soc.) 42 How redoubted Hercules by puyssaunce Fought with an ydre. **1547** in *Vicary's Anat.* (1888) App. iii. 131 Our late most redowtyd souereygn lorde, Kinge Henrye the viij^th^. **1600** HOLLAND *Livy* XXI. xli. 416 Can it be thought then, that..I fell by chance and at unwares upon this drad and redoubted enemie? **1774** WARTON *Hist. Eng. Poetry* Diss. i. 14 Arthur having killed this redoubted knight. **1815** SCOTT *Ld. of Isles* v. xxix, Nor better their lot who fled, And met..The Douglas's redoubted spear! **1861** THACKERAY *Four Georges* iv. (1862) 204 The prime minister himself, the redoubted William Pitt.

re'doubting, *vbl. sb. rare.* [f. as prec. + -ING[1].] Respect, reverence; apprehension.

c **1386** CHAUCER *Knt.'s T.* 1192 With soutil pencel was depeynted this storie In redoutynge of Mars and of his glorie. **1611** FLORIO, *Ridottanza*, a redoubting or fearing.

redound (rɪˈdaʊnd), *sb. rare.* [f. the vb.]

1. Reverberation, echo; a resounding cry.

a **1665** CODRINGTON *Q. Curtius* III. (1670) 55 The redound of the Hills and the Rocks, which doubled every voice of theirs. **1825** G. M^c^CANN *Right Private Judgem.* 239 Against whomsoever we direct our clamours, our last redound is against heaven.

2. The fact of redounding or resulting.

1847 TENNYSON *Princ.* II. 28 We give you welcome: not without redound Of use and glory to yourselves ye come.

redound (rɪˈdaʊnd), *v.* Forms: α. 4–6 **redund(e**, 5–6 *Sc.* **redond(e**; 4–6 **redounde**, 6 **redownd**, 6– **redound.** β. 5 *Sc.* **radoun**, 6 **redoun**, 6, 7 **redown(e.** [ad. F. *rédonder* (12th c.) = Sp., Pg. *redundar*, It. *ridondare*:—L. *redundāre*, f. *re(d)-* RE- + *undāre* to surge, f. *unda* a wave.

In the obsolete uses the precise sense is not always clear; in 4 and 5 there is probably some confusion with REBOUND *v.*]

I. *intr.* †**1.** Of water, waves, etc.: To swell or surge up, to overflow. *Obs.*

1382 WYCLIF *Esther* xi. 10 A litle welle wex in to the moste flod, and in to manye watris redundede. **1382** —— *Eccl.* i. 7 Alle flodis entren in to the se, and the se redoundith not. **1596** SPENSER *Hymn Heav. Love* 165 Their streames yet never staunch, But stil do flow, and freshly stil redound. **1684** T. BURNET *Th. Earth* I. 121 These must have subterraneous out-lets..: otherwise they would redound and over-flow the brims of their vessel. **1725** POPE *Odyss.* IV. 578 Round the descending nymph the waves redounding roar.

†**b.** Of other liquids, esp. of moisture in the body: To overflow, superabound. *Obs.*

1568 SKEYNE *The Pest* (1860) 37 Purge al superflew flewme as may redunde in all naturall partis. **1596** SPENSER *F.Q.* IV. x. 1 For every dram of hony therein found A pound of gall doth over it redound. **1596** BARROUGH *Meth. Physick* III. liv. (1639) 187 We say, that menstruis do redound and overflow in women, when [etc.]. **1684** tr. *Bonet's Merc. Compit.* x. 362 The Mercury..may more easily mix it self with the Phlegm redounding in the Body.

†**c.** *transf.* To be in excess or superfluous. *Obs.*

1599 B. JONSON *Cynthia's Rev.* v. ii, It is a strange outrecuidance: your humour too much redoundeth. **1631** JORDEN *Nat. Bathes* ii. (1669) 9 If any of these properties be wanting, or any redound, it is mixed [etc.]. **1653** ASHWELL *Fides Apost.* 17 Some old Latine Copies of the Creed.. wherein (In) redounds by the like Hebrew Pleonasme. **1667** MILTON *P.L.* v. 438 What redounds, transpires Through Spirits with ease.

†**2.** To be plentiful, abound. *Obs.*

1382 WYCLIF *Ecclus.* xlvii. 30 Ful manye redoundeden the synnes of hem gretli. **1413** *Pilgr. Sowle* (Caxton) I. xv. (1859) 15 But this were soth grete peryl most redounde, Al mortal folk with meschyef to confounde. **1528** LYNDESAY *Dreme* 840, I maruell gretlie..That Ryches suld nocht in this realme redound. **1581** T. HOWELL *Deuises* (1879) 223 Who are brought downe, by thy most forwarde frownes, Still subiect liue, and trouble them redownes.

†**3.** To abound *in* (a thing); to overflow or be filled *with* (a thing or quality). *Obs.*

1483 CAXTON *Gold. Leg.* 373/2 Thenne hyr body was put in a monumente whyche after was founden to redounde in oyle. **1582** STANYHURST *Æneis* I. (Arb.) 37 Theare stud vp Æneas, with glittring beautye redowning. **1591** SPENSER *Virgil's Gnat* 189 A pleasant bowre..To rest their limbs with wearines redounding. **1656** [? J. SERGEANT] tr. *T. White's Peripat. Inst.* 421 When the Earth redounded with well-digested moisture. *a* **1661** FULLER *Worthies* (1841) III. 241 Ramus himself doth not so much redound in dichotomies as they do.

†**b.** To be redundant in some respect. *Obs.*

1612 BRINSLEY *Pos. Parts* (ed. 2) 53 Those words which redound, or which haue more in declining than Nounes haue commonly. **1650** BULWER *Anthropomet.* viii. (1653) 162 They which onely fall short or redound in number [of parts of the body]..live many years.

†**4.** To flow, come, or go back; to return (*to* a place or person); to come again. *Obs.*

1382 WYCLIF *2 Chron.* xix. 6 What euer ȝe shul demyn, in to ȝou it schal redoundyn. **1456** SIR G. HAYE *Law Arms* (S.T.S.) 12 As to the see agayne passis all wateris, sa..all sciencis in this warld redoundis agayne to haly scripture. *c* **1470** HENRY *Wallace* x. 413 Sum wytt agayn to Wallace can radoun; In hys awn mynd so rewllyt him resoun. **1526** *Pilgr. Perf.* (W. de W. 1531) 181 b, Lyke as all flodes commeth out of ye see, and in to ye see they redounde agayne. **1596**

SPENSER *Hymn Heav. Beauty* 75 So those likewise doe by degrees redound And rise more faire.

†**b.** To rebound after impact, to recoil, spring back. *Obs.*

c **1500** *Melusine* 175 Hys swerd redounded vpon hys hors nek by suche myght that nygh he cutte his throtte of. **1545** ASCHAM *Toxoph.* II. (Arb.) 159 For the wynd whych commeth in dede against you, redoundeth bake agayne at the wal. *a* **1625** FLETCHER *Nice Valour* IV. i, I never yet took box o' th' eare, But it redounded.

†**c.** To pass, make way, penetrate. *Obs. rare.*

1500–20 DUNBAR *Poems* lxxxi. 17 Thair pleasant sang,.. Nor ȝett thair joy did to my heart redoun. *c* **1560** A. SCOTT *Poems* (S.T.S.) xiv. 7 Þe bewty of my lady stoundis Outthroucht my breist, vnto my hairt redoundis.

†**5.** To resound, reverberate, re-echo. **a.** Of sounds. *Obs.*

1470–85 MALORY *Arthur* I. xvi, He cam in so fiersly that the strokes redounded ageyne fro the woode and the water. **1526** *Pilgr. Perf.* (W. de W. 1531) 159 Whan ye swete songes and hymnes of ye chirche redounded to his eares. **1550** LYNDESAY *Sqr. Meldrum* 740 Quhilk on the Sey maid sic ane sound, That in the Air it did redound. **1632** LITHGOW *Trav.* VIII. 343 What else redounds But sighes and sobs?

†**b.** Of places. *Obs.*

c **1400** *Destr. Troy* 10183 The skrew, for þe skrykyng & skremyng of folke, Redoundet with dyn drede for to here. **1491** CAXTON *Vitas Patr.* (W. de W. 1495) 116 The devyll apperyd to hym.. makynge a crye soo merveylous, that alle the place redounded. **1509** HAWES *Past. Pleas.* XXXVI. vi, My ryght lusty and stormy blast, That made the walles therof to redounde. **1573** TWYNE *Æneid* XI. H h iij, All the bankes about with cracklinge noyse agayn redound.

6. To result in, have the effect of, contributing or turning *to* some advantage or disadvantage for a person or thing. †Also const. *into.*

1432–50 tr. *Higden* (Rolls) II. 215 The passiones of the body redunde in to the perturbacion of the sawle. **1481** CAXTON *Myrr.* III. xiii. L 6, They retche not for to lerne, sauf that whiche they knowe shal redounde to their singular prouffyt. **1547** J. HARRISON *Exhort. Scottes* F viij, It hath redounded to no lesse discomfiture of our nacion, then of the Frenchemen. **1587** FLEMING *Contn. Holinshed* III. 1346/2 Falling to an other matter, for that this redounded to his owne confusion. **1644** MILTON *Educ.* Wks. 1738 I. 140 Which could not but mightily redound to the good of the Nation. **1718** *Free-thinker* No. 89 ⁋3 This Objection.. redounds only to the Damage of the Student. **1813** H. & J. SMITH *Horace in Lond.* 1 If the granting it redound to my advantage. **1860** LD. BROUGHAM *Brit. Const.* Ded., Redounding to the security of the Crown.

b. To turn *to* one's honour, disgrace, etc.

1474 *Rolls of Parlt.* VI. 103/2 For als moche as the seid rescuse redondez.. to the reproche of his seid Chaunceller. **1502** ATKYNSON tr. *De Imitatione* I. xix. 167 Those thynges that shulde redounde to the honour of god. **1560** DAUS tr. *Sleidane's Comm.* 30 b, Affyrming that it would redounde to the perpetuall shame of Germany. **1635** BARRIFFE *Mil. Discipl.* lxx. (1643) 188 The benefit redounds to the Reputation and Honour of our Countrey. **1711** BUDGELL *Spect.* No. 161 ⁋3 Something redounding more to their Honour than a Coat of Arms. *a* **1845** BARHAM *Ingol. Leg.* Ser. III. *Blasph. Warning*, I think it redounds to their praise. **1879** SEGUIN *Black For.* v. 77 A tale.. remarkable among German legends for redounding to the credit of the clergy.

†**c.** To bring credit or honour *to* something.

1681 LUTTRELL *Brief Rel.* (1857) I. 104 An action highly redounding to the English valour.

7. a. Of advantage, damage, praise, etc.: To result, attach, accrue *to*, *unto* (a person).

1500–20 DUNBAR *Poems* xlvi. 63 The thank redoundis to him in every place. **1542** UDALL *Erasm. Apoph.* 212 He enterpreted.., that to hym thereby had redounded more good then eiuill. **1608** WILLET *Hexapla Exod.* 334 The sinnes of the wicked fathers doe not redound to the children. **1704** SWIFT *T. Tub* ix, The clear gain redounding to the Common-wealth. **1794** GODWIN *Cal. Williams* 99 The mischief that redounded to an unfortunate patron from the transactions of that day. **1861** TRENCH *Ep. 7 Ch. Asia* 13 Benefits which redound to us through the sacrifice of the death of Christ.

†**b.** Of revenue, wealth, etc.: To come or fall *to* a person, etc. *Obs.*

1587 HARRISON *England* II. v. (1877) I. 114 They are of custome punished by a fine, that redoundeth vnto his cofers. **1600** J. PORY tr. *Leo's Africa* III. 162 A new gouernour ouer euery citie, vnto whom all the tributes and reuenues of the same place redound. **1655** FULLER *Hist. Cambr.* 144 At this day much emolument redowneth to the antient Colledges in each University.. by the passing of this Act.

8. Of honour or disgrace, advantage, etc.: To recoil or come back, to fall, *upon* a person.

1589 NASHE *Anat. Absurd.* B iv, The infamie of their ignorance did redound onelie upon themselves. **1606** G. W[OODCOCKE] *Hist. Ivstine* I. 2 Wisely casting the inconuenience that might redound hereby vpon himselfe. **1692** BEVERLEY *Disc. Dr. Crisp* 9 Christ taking us as his Members, whatever unworthiness we have, must redound upon him. **1818** JAS. MILL *Brit. India* I. II. x. 430 The portion of that flattering sentiment, which would redound upon themselves. **1852** J. H. NEWMAN *Scope Univ. Educ.* 254 The blessings.. are so great, while they are close to it and redound back upon it and encircle it.

†**b.** To cast opprobrium, to reflect unfavourably, *upon* one. *Obs. rare*$^{-1}$.

1581 SAVILE *Tacitus, Hist.* IV. xlv. (1591) 203 Many skornefull and reprochfull speeches redounding [L. *jacerentur*] vpon the whole Senate.

9. To proceed, issue, arise *from* or *out of* something. ? *Obs.*

1590 SPENSER *F.Q.* I. vi. 30 Trew sacred lore, which from her sweet lips did redound. **1596** —— *State Irel.* Wks. (Globe) 617/2 The pleasure which would redounde out of theyr history. **1605** BACON *Adv. Learn.* I. i. §3 The anxietie of spirit which redoundeth from knowledge. **1700** ASTRY tr. *Saavedra-Faxardo* I. 233 The Prince's Reputation redounds from that of the State. **1796** MORSE *Amer. Geog.* I. 70 The benefits which might redound from its success.

†**10.** To result, turn out. *Obs. rare.*

1586 A. DAY *Eng. Secretary* I. (1625) 89 The ill conceit of your L. should redound to be of all others most grieuous. **1589** PUTTENHAM *Eng. Poesie* II. xi[i]. (Arb.) 123 Vpon the transposition I found this to redound.

II. *trans.* †**11.** To reflect (honour, blame, etc.) *in, to, upon* a person. *Obs.*

c **1477** CAXTON *Jason* 88, I may not requyre Jason of loue, for that sholde redounde in me grete blame. **1485** —— *Chas. Gt.* 34 Whyche moche redounded to hym grete honour & vyctorye. **1595** T. EDWARDS *Cephalus & Procris* (1878) 43 Iems valued past their worth, Redoune small honor to their bringer forth. **1712** STEELE *Spect.* No. 486 ⁋1 For fear they should redound Dishonour upon the Innocent.

†**b.** To reckon *to* one's dishonour. *Obs.*$^{-1}$

1494 FABYAN *Chron.* VII. 568 All men shall redounde this dede to my dyshonour and shame.

†**12.** *Sc.* To return, refund (money); to make good (expenses). *Obs.*

1574 *Sc. Acts Jas. VI* (1814) III. 90 The takaris to redound all proffeittis that thay haue takin vp of thay landis agane to the king. *a* **1578** LINDESAY (Pitscottie) *Chron. Scot.* (S.T.S.) I. 155 Promissand to them to cause the King of France his master to redound to them the costis.

†**b.** To give or render in return. *Obs. rare.*

1597 BEARD *Theatre God's Judgem.* (1612) 323 The love that parents beare their children is greater than that which children redound to their parents. **1632** LITHGOW *Trav.* V. 182, I redounded thankes for my imbraced courtesies.

†**13.** To add, yield, cause to accrue. Also *refl.*

1612 R. SHELDON *Serm. St. Martin's* 11 He.. vouchsafed by a great miracle to stop, and conteine the glory of his soule, from communicating, or redounding it selfe, to his body. **1690** CHILD *Disc. Trade* (1694) 88 It would redound some hundreds of thousands of pounds per annum to the publick advantage.

Hence **re'dounded** *ppl. a.*; **re'dounding** *vbl. sb.* and *ppl. a.*

1523 LD. BERNERS *Froiss.* I. cxcv. 232 Y^e watchmen.. herde clerely the redoundyng of the nauerryse. **1541** R. COPLAND *Galyen's Terap.* G gj, It is nat the redoundyng of blode y^t indicateth the phlebotomye. **1590** SPENSER *F.Q.* I. iii. 8 Redounding teares did choke th' end of her plaint. **1632** LITHGOW *Trav.* II. 75 After my redounded thankes, they.. returned. *a* **1679** HOBBES *Rhet.* (1840) 532 Bragging of no proof, is when that which is brought is too much, called redounding. **1667** MILTON *P.L.* II. 889 So wide they stood, and like a Furnace mouth Cast forth redounding smoak.

†**re'doundance.** *Obs.*$^{-1}$ [f. prec. + -ANCE: cf. *redundance.*] A redounding influence.

1638 FEATLY *Strict. Lyndom.* II. 81 How can a Prayer whereof never a syllable is understood.. cause.. a better redoundance from the soule to the body, by a vehement affection.

So †**re'doundancy**, redundance. *rare*$^{-0}$.

1623 COCKERAM, *Redoundancie*, superfluitie.

redoure, Sc. var. RADDOUR[1], REDDOUR. *Obs.*

re'dout, *a. Her. rare.* (See quot.)

c **1828** BERRY *Encycl. Her.* II. s.v. *Redout*, The cross potent, rebated, is, by some writers, called a Cross Redout, from its resemblance to a bulwark, or fortification.

red-out ('rɛdaʊt). [f. RED *a.* and *sb.*; cf. BLACK-OUT.] A reddening of the vision resulting from an accumulation of blood in the head when the body is accelerated downwards.

1942 *Richmond* (Va.) *Times-Dispatch* 21 Dec. 13/1 The doctors learn airplane ambulance work... They learn about grayouts, blackouts and redouts. **1943** *Effects of Flight* (U.S. Navy Training Div., Bur. Aeronaut.) iv. 70 High numbers of *g*'s acting upward through the vertical axis of the body can be produced.. and when these are excessive there may be the sensation of everything turning red, followed by unconsciousness. This has been called 'red-out'. **1946** R. A. MCFARLAND *Human Factors in Air Transport Design* ix. 363 Values of − 2 or − 3*g* produce fullness and a throbbing pain in the head. The vessels of the eyes become congested, and reddening of vision, or 'red-out', may occasionally occur. **1962** F. I. ORDWAY et al. *Basic Astronautics* xii. 463 If the acceleration is applied in the opposite direction, then a condition known as red-out occurs... The blood.. increases in weight to the point where the heart can no longer pump it. **1970** *Daily Tel.* (Colour Suppl.) 10 July 25/2 With a severe bout of negative G you get a red-out, when so many vessels burst that your vision becomes crimson and you see through a haze of blood. **1980** *Verbatim* Winter 19/1 Too many positive G's may cause loss of consciousness—a *red-out.*

Hence **red 'out** *v. intr.*, to undergo or experience a red-out. See also REDDING *vbl. sb.*[1] 2.

1955 M. RELFER *Dict. New Words* 175 *Red out*, to experience a red field of vision, congestion of the face and, in particular, the eyes, pressure in the head, etc., as a result of blood rushing to the head in certain aerial maneuvers, such as a rapid climb, inverted spins, outside loops, etc. **1980** *Verbatim* Winter 19/1 A pilot is in danger of redding out when an aerial maneuver puts a strong positive-G stress on his body.

redout(e, obs. forms of REDOUBT *sb.* and *v.*

‖**redowa** ('rɛdəvə). Also **redowak.** [a. F. or Ger. *redowa*, ad. Czech *rejdovák*, f. *rejdovati* to steer, manipulate (as with a carriage pole), to wheel about.] A Bohemian folk dance, in Western Europe developed into a dance in relatively quick triple time; the music for such a dance.

1845 J. R. PLANCHÉ *Graciosa & Percinet* II. 9 Charming Polka—Redowa Polka! Pink of Polkas thou'rt to me! **1855** E. R. SMITH *Araucanians* vi. 65 The schottisches and redowas of the modern ball-room. **1862** E. PAUER *Programme* 8 Mar., *Redowak*, Bohemian dance in 3/4 or 3/8 time. **1881** GROVE *Dict. Mus.* s.v., The ordinary Redowa is written in 3–4 time. The dance is something like a Mazurka with the rhythm less strongly marked. **1885** A. DODWORTH *Dancing* viii. 62 *Redowa.* When first introduced this dance had the time of a polka mazourka... Our beautiful waltz of to-day is a subdued redowa. **1903** W. LAMB *How & what to Dance* vii. 70 The Redowa, when first introduced, began with a promenade movement, but it is now generally commenced with the circular figure. **1960** P. J. S. RICHARDSON *Social Dances of 19th Cent. Eng.* ix. 99 As late as 1894 or 1895 I can clearly remember being present at a popular assembly in London when the Redowa was announced, but only about three veteran couples.. were able to perform it.

redown(d, -downe, obs. ff. REDOUND *v.*

redowt, obs. form of REDOUBT *v.*

redox ('ri:dɒks, 'rɛdɒks). *Chem.* [f. RED(UCTION + OX(IDATION.] A reversible reaction in which one species is oxidized and another reduced; usu. *attrib.*, indicating (some connection with) such a reaction, or a simultaneous oxidation and reduction, as ***redox couple, electrode, indicator, potential, reaction***, etc.

1928 MICHAELIS & FLEXNER in *Jrnl. Biol. Chem.* LXXIX. 689 The success met on application of the theoretical fundamentals of oxidation-reduction potentials (hereinafter to be referred to by us as 'redox' potentials).. to organic redox systems.. has given great impetus to more elaborate study of physiological materials. **1938** *Nature* 15 Oct. 723/1 Increasing use of redox indicators is being made with marked success in analytical chemistry. **1940** GLASTONE *Text-bk. Physical Chem.* xii. 932 A reversible oxidation-reduction electrode.. sometimes abbreviated to.. 'redox' electrode. **1959** *Engineering* 2 Jan. 25/2 A mercaptan modifier and redox catalyst are employed to obtain the desired molecular structure in the shortest possible reaction time. **1965** PHILLIPS & WILLIAMS *Inorg. Chem.* ix. 312 Since galvanic cells consist essentially of two redox couples opposed one against the other, it is convenient to choose one couple arbitrarily and regard it as having zero potential. **1970** AMBROSE & EASTY *Cell Biol.* ii. 66 Note.. that a favourable redox potential does not necessarily mean that a particular reaction will take place, but simply that it is thermodynamically feasible. **1971** *Nature* 4 June 311/2 An internal redox apparently occurs, and the electron moves from cation to anion. *Ibid.* 12 Nov. 89/1 The red colour of Mars suggests the presence of ferric iron which is not readily explained by the redox state implied by the second hypothesis. **1978** P. W. ATKINS *Physical Chem.* xii. 362 In a redox titration a reduced form of an ion (e.g., Fe^{2+}) is oxidized by the addition of some oxidizer (e.g., Ce^{4+}).

'redpoll[1], **-pole.** [f. RED *a.* + *pole* POLL.]

1. A name given to several species of the family *Fringillidæ* characterized by bright red feathers on the crest. **a.** The greater redpoll, the male of the common LINNET in summer plumage. **b.** The lesser or common redpoll, formerly often kept as a cage-bird, *Linota rufescens* or *Ægiothus linaria.* **c.** The mealy or stone redpoll, *Ægiothus canescens*, a somewhat rare winter visitant to the British Islands. Also, the allied American species (*Æ. exilipes*).

1738 ALBIN *Nat. Hist. Birds* III. 70 The Red Pole is a very small, but an exceeding pretty feathered Bird. **1772** BARRINGTON in *Phil. Trans.* LXII. 312 There is another bird,.. called a redpoll, which is taken in numbers during the Michaelmas and March flights by the London bird-catchers. **1811** WILSON *Amer. Ornith.* IV. 42 Lesser Red-Poll. **1831** RENNIE *Montagu's Ornith. Dict.* 298, I [Bechstein] hope to shew.. that our common Linnet, the greater Redpole, and.. the Mountain Linnet, are one and the same species. **1839** AUDUBON *Ornith. Biog.* V. 88 On two occasions I have seen the Mealy Redpoll associated with the American Siskin. **1882** H. LANSDELL *Through Siberia* I. 202 Flocks of redpoles and shore-larks, bramblings and wagtails. **1894** NEWTON *Dict. Birds* 773 The geographical range of the Lesser Redpoll is apparently limited to Western Europe... On the other hand, the Mealy Redpoll.. is much more widely distributed.

attrib. **1831** WILSON, etc. *Amer. Ornith.* IV. 112 We.. can perceive scarcely any resemblance.. to a similar state of the red-poll finch. **1882** J. HARDY in *Proc. Berw. Nat. Club* IX. No. 3. 561 The Redpole Linnet arrives with them.

2. ***yellow red-poll***, an American warbler, *Dendræca palmarum*; the palm-warbler. Also *attrib.*

1764 G. EDWARDS *Glean. Nat. Hist.* II. III. 295 The Yellow Red-pole. **1811** WILSON *Amer. Ornith.* IV. 19 Yellow Red-Poll Warbler, *Sylvia Petechea. Ibid.*, Length of the Yellow Red-poll five inches, extent eight.

So **red-polled** *a.*, red-headed.

1787 WOLCOTT (P. Pindar) *Instr. Celebr. Laureat* 42 Large red-poll'd, blowzy, hard, two-handed jades.

'redpoll[2], **-polled.** *pl.* Red-haired polled cattle. Also *attrib.*

1891 J. MACDONALD *Stephens's Bk. Farm* (ed. 4) III. VI. 416/1 The Norfolk and Suffolk Red Polled breed stands highest for dairying purposes. The Red Polls are handsome symmetrical animals of medium size. **1895** *Westm. Gaz.* 29 Mar. 7/2 [The celebrated.. herd of Red-Polled cattle.] The Duke of York is getting together a large and choice herd of Red-Polls. **1896** *Daily News* 8 Dec. 5/1 The breed cup for red-polleds. **1898** RIDER HAGGARD in *Longm. Mag.* Oct. 508 Red-polls have many advantages. *Ibid.*, Pedigree animals of the Norfolk red-poll breed. **1949** *Caribbean Q.* I. II. 36 A small herd of grade red poll cattle was maintained. **1970** G. E. EVANS *Where Beards wag All* viii. 95, I have kept Red Polls, because they are harmless, and the Suffolk breed for a Suffolk man.

redpurs: see REDE *sb.*[1] 5.

redraft (riːˈdrɑːft, -æ-), *sb.* Also 7 **-draught.** [RE- 5 a. Cf. next.]

1. A bill of re-exchange. (Cf. REDRAW *v.*[2] 1.)

1682 SCARLETT *Exchanges* 144 The Payment of the Redraught from the place where the Bill was to be paid. **1826** G. J. BELL *Comm. Law Scot.* III. I. ii. (1870) I. 430 This redraft is to be made directly on the place of the original draft.

2. A second or new draft.

1847 in WEBSTER. **1890** *Times* 28 Nov. 7/1 The part of the Bill which dealt with the congested districts was very little more than a redraft of the original measure.

redraft (riːˈdrɑːft, -æ-), *v.* [RE- 5 a.] *trans.* To draft again (a writing or document).

1798 I. ALLEN *Hist. Vermont* 183 Colonel Allen..gave it to the late Roger Sherman,..praying him to redraft it, and propose it as his own. **1847** WEBSTER, *Redraft*, to draw or draft anew. **1884** *Manch. Exam.* 29 Mar. 5/2 The bill..is likely to be entirely redrafted.

red rag, red-rag.

1. *slang.* The tongue.

a **1700** B. E. *Dict. Cant. Crew*, *Red-rag*, a Tongue. **1785** GROSE *Dict. Vulgar T.* s.v., Shut your potatoe trap, and give your redrag a holiday. **1820** COMBE *Syntax, Consol.* IV, If your red rag did not show it, By your queer fancies I should know it. **1876** W. S. GILBERT *Dan'l Druce* i, Stop that cursed red rag of yours, will you.

2. A variety of rust in grain.

1851 J. M. WILSON *Rural Cycl.* s.v. *Rust*, The rust, the red-rag, and the red-robin varieties [of mildew] make the plants look as if they were dusted with a rustiness of some colour from yellow to brown. **1863** *N. Brit. Rev.* May 375 The leaf and chaff of the cereals are subject to a disease called rust, red-rag or red-robin (*Uredo Rubigo*).

3. (From the phr. *like a red rag to a bull.*) A source of extreme provocation or annoyance; something which excites violent indignation.

1873 C. M. YONGE *Pillars of House* II. xviii. 151 Jack will do for himself if he tells Wilmet her eyes are violet; it is like a red rag to a bull. **1875** 'MARK TWAIN' in *Atlantic Monthly* Feb. 219 'What do you suppose I told you the names of those points for?' 'Well, to—to be entertaining, I thought.' This was a red rag to a bull. **1885** C. MARVIN *Russians at Gates of Herat* 98 These opinions cannot but be so many red rags to English Russo-phobists. **1887** SAINTSBURY *Hist. Elizab. Lit.* v. (1890) 167 Shakesperian clowns are believed to be red rags to some experienced playwrights. **1965** *Listener* 25 Nov. 874/3 Professor Allen has adopted more an 'inquiry programme' style to examine some of the sacred cows and red rags of American life.

4. *Naut. slang.* = *red ensign, red duster.*

1910 D. W. BONE *Brassbounder* 129 Pluggin' a Dutchman's naethin'; it's th' 'Rid Rag' that Kelly's doon oan. **1929** D. J. MUNRO *Roaring Forties* 23 Up went Old Glory... We followed suit with the 'Red Rag' waving in defiance.

Hence **red-ˈraggish** *a.*, of the nature of a red rag.

1887 in *Chicago Advance* 30 June, Prohibition sounds a little harsh, and is red-raggish to many.

red rattle, red-rattle. [See RATTLE *sb.*[1] 3.] Louse-wort, *Pedicularis sylvatica* or *palustris.* †Also called ***red rattle-grass.***

1578 LYTE *Dodoens* IV. lvi. 517 Redde Rattel is taken of the Physitions in these dayes. **1597** GERARDE *Herbal* II. ccccxxi. 913 Red Rattle..hath very small, rent, or iagged leaues, of a browne redde colour. It is called..in English Rattle Grass, red Rattle grasse, and Lousewoort. **1653** CULPEPPER *Eng. Physic. Enlarged* (1656) 312 The common Red Rattle, hath sundry reddish hollow stalks..rising from the Root. *c* **1710** PETIVER *Catal. Ray's Eng. Herb.* §4 Pl. 36 Tall Red Rattle. **1756** C. LUCAS *Ess. Waters* II. 131 All over it [grow] rushes, red rattle, marsh-marygold, &c. **1846** MRS. LOUDON *Brit. Wild Fl.* 251 The Pasture Louse-Wort, or Dwarf Red Rattle. *Ibid.* 252 The Marsh Louse-wort, or Tall Red-Rattle. **1883** *Gd. Words* XXIV. 574/1 The golden bog-asphodel,..the rosy red-rattle.

†**redraw**, *v.*[1] *Obs. rare*$^{-1}$. [f. RE- + DRAW *v.*, after F. *retraire.*] *trans.* To draw back, reclaim (a person) *to* (something).

1480 CAXTON *Ovid's Met.* XIII. xvi, I..and hys parents dide what we myghte to redrawe hym to hys fyrst nature.

redraw (riːˈdrɔː), *v.*[2] [RE- 5 a.]

1. *intr.* To draw a fresh bill of exchange to cover a former one.

a **1692** POLLEXFEN *Disc. Trade* (1697) 13 Their correspondents to reimburse themselves, Redraw on them, or on their Agents in other places. **1776** ADAM SMITH *W.N.* II. ii. (1869) I. 309 The well-known shift of drawing and redrawing. **1847-** in WEBSTER and later Dicts.

2. *trans.* To draw or take out again.

1805 [see *redrawn* below]. **1825** *Act 6 Geo. IV*, c. 50 §26 To try any issue with the same jury..without their names being returned to the box and redrawn. **1898** *Westm. Gaz.* 22 Oct. 3/1 Four torpedo-boat destroyers..have been instructed to redraw their returned stores.

3. To draw (a picture, etc.) again. Also *fig.*

1830 H. COLERIDGE *Grk. Poets* (1834) 291 That remorseless iteration, with which the battles..of the Iliad have..been redrawn and recoloured. **1894** BARING-GOULD *Deserts S. France* I. 171 The sketcher was dissatisfied with the position in which he had drawn the legs, and he re-drew them.

4. To draw up again, to compose again.

1815 A. CONSTABLE *Let.* 26 Apr. in J. Constable *Corr.* (1962) I. 126 My father has had his *will redrawn*, leaving *out* the objectionable clause.

Hence **reˈdrawer**; **reˈdrawing** *vbl. sb.*; **reˈdrawn** *ppl. a.*

1682 SCARLETT *Exchanges* 55 In the Redrawing of a Bill, the Redrawer is looked upon, as the absolute and first Drawer. **1790** BURKE *Fr. Rev.* Wks. V. 428 It is as little worth remarking any farther upon all their drawing and re-drawing. **1805** SOUTHEY *Madoc* II. xvi, Breath and blood Followed the re-drawn shaft. **1858** HOMANS *Cycl. Commerce* 176/2 The law does not require an actual re-drawing. **1889** *Pall Mall G.* 19 Jan. 3/3 Each redrawing [of a portrait] takes us a step..further from the probable fact.

Red Republic. Also with small initials. [RED *a.* 9 b.] A republic based on socialist principles, *spec.* the French Second Republic, proclaimed in 1848. So **Red Republican**, one who holds radically republican views and advocates the use of force to realize them, esp. a supporter of the European revolutions of 1848; **Red Republicanism**, the principles and views of Red Republicans.

1848 *Illustr. London News* 1 July 415/1 The 'Red Republicans' have justified their name. They have filled the streets of Paris with blood... The working classes, or 'Red Republicans', were imbued with the doctrines of Communism. **1848** *Tablet* 2 Sept. 566/4 The red republic is now in a situation somewhat analogous to that of the Jacobins under Bonaparte. **1850** (*title of newspaper*) The Red Republican. **1850** E. P. WHIPPLE *Washington & Principles of Revolution* 29 We are proposing all those intricate problems which red republicanism so swiftly solves. **1857** C. M. YONGE *Dynevor Terrace* I. xx. 327 Raise our barricade for the rights of the Red Republic, and cry *La liberté, l'égalité, et la fraternité. Ibid.* II. ii. 23 All I am clear about is, that even a Red Republican is less red than he is painted. **1858** *N.Y. Tribune* 11 Jan. 2/5 When Mr. Bigler was in Kansas last summer, he was the known, open and enthusiastic advocate of what some hereabout call Red Republicanism. **1874** TROLLOPE *Phineas Redux* I. xxxiii. 276 One..advocates the personal government of an individual ruler, and the other that form of State which has come to be called a Red Republic. **1875** P. K. O'CLERY *Hist. Ital. Revolution* v. 185 The other [was] a soldier and nothing more, knowing nothing of politics beyond a rabid red-republicanism. **1960** R. K. WEBB *Harriet Martineau* xi. 322 Only Cavour was capable..of steering his way between the reactionary agents and the red republicans. **1972** T. COLEMAN *Passage to Amer.* xiv. 221 Kossuth came to America in 1851... He came to be seen as a continental red republican.

redress (rɪˈdrɛs), *sb.* Also 4-7 **redresse**, 5-6 *Sc.* **redres.** [a. AF. *redresse, -dresce* (14th c.), f. *redresser* to REDRESS.]

1. Reparation of, satisfaction or compensation for, a wrong sustained or the loss resulting from this.

1375 BARBOUR *Bruce* XIX. 198 The King send oft till ask redress, Bot nocht thar-of redress ther wes. *c* **1400** *Destr. Troy* 2051 Redresse for þe dethe of his dere fader. **1456** SIR G. HAYE *Law Arms* (S.T.S.) 190 He salbe for hir part herd in jugement, and have redress and reformacioun of lawe for hir. **1567** *Reg. Privy Council Scot.* I. 578 To seik redres be the ordinar magistrattis. **1597** SHAKS. *2 Hen. IV*, II. i. 118 But for these foolish Officers, I beseech you, I may haue redresse against them. **1654** BRAMHALL *Just Vind.* iv. (1661) 75 If the Archbishop failed to do justice, the last complaint must be to the King to give order for redress. **1741** BUTLER *Serm. Ho. Lords* Wks. 1874 II. 266 Whilst redress is delayed,..wrong subsists. **1784** COWPER *Task* VI. 822 God..would else..endure Dishonour, and be wronged without redress. **1819** SHELLEY *Cenci* III. i. 194 Think not But that there is redress where there is wrong, So we be bold enough to seize it. **1875** JOWETT *Plato* (ed. 2) V. 119 He who gives credit, and is cheated, will have no redress.

†**b.** Possibility or means of redress; appeal against a decision. *Obs. rare.*

1467 in *Eng. Gilds* (1870) 408 Thereof notice to be made to the Bailies,..[and] they to reforme wᵗ out accion or redresse suche maters. **1771** GOLDSM. *Hist. Eng.* II. 406 The king was empowered to issue a proclamation to destroy the lives, or take away the properties, of any of his subjects; and the only redress was to himself in council.

†**2.** Remedy for, or relief from, some trouble; assistance, aid, help. *Obs.*

c **1374** CHAUCER *Compl. Mars* 162 The grounde and cause of al my peyn..I wol reherse; not for to haue redresse, But to declare my grounde of heuynesse. **1523** LD. BERNERS *Froiss.* I. xviii. 21 They trusted than to fynde some redresse for themselfe and for their horses. *c* **1586** C'TESS PEMBROKE *Ps.* LXXVII. i, To nightly anguish thrall, From thee I sought redresse. **1596** SPENSER *F.Q.* v. iv. 41 He..ranne to his redresse. *a* **1619** FOTHERBY *Atheom.* II. vi. §4 (1622) 255 There is no sicknesse, but it hath his redresse. **1671** MILTON *Samson* 619 My griefs..finding no redress, ferment and rage. **1759** GOLDSM. *Bee* No. 3 ¶2 He who best knows how to conceal his necessity and desires is the most likely person to find redress.

†**b.** Correction, amendment, or reformation of something wrong. *Obs.*

1526 SKELTON *Magnyf.* 2443 Full many thynges there be that lacketh redresse. **1595** DANIEL *Civ. Wars* II. xliii, So that there were some orderly redresse In those disorders. *a* **1656** BP. HALL *Rem. Wks.* (1660) 121 Too long have we driven off the applying of our redress. **1764** *Museum Rust.* III. 286 The pernicious effects, to farmers, of this abominable practice, are notorious, and cry aloud for redress.

†**c.** In phr. ***beyond, past, without redress***: beyond the possibility of remedy, aid, or amendment. *Obs.*

1593 SHAKS. *Rich. II*, II. iii. 171 Things past redresse, are now with me past care. **1697** DRYDEN *Æneid* v. 771 As the Cretan Labyrinth of old,..Involv'd the weary feet, without redress. **1700** J. JACKSON in *Pepys' Diary* (1879) VI. 232 And were immediately smothered without redress. **1764** GOLDSM. *Hist. Eng. in Lett.* (1772) II. 189 Damaged their transports beyond redress.

†**3. a.** With *a* and *pl.* A means or way of redress; an act or arrangement whereby a person or thing is redressed; an amendment, improvement. *Obs.*

1472-5 *Rolls of Parlt.* VI. 163/1 That the Lordes..have full auctorite, to discusse and set theryn a redresse after their discretions. **1544** *Supplic. to Hen. VIII* (E.E.T.S.) 57 Grant ..that he wyll ernestly go a boute to se a redresse a monge them. **1547** *Reg. Privy Council Scot.* I. 77 Redressis suld be maid of all dampnaiges. **1579** LYLY *Euphues* (Arb.) 150 So the father..causeth a redresse and amendement in his childe. **1645** MILTON *Tetrach.* Wks. (1851) 194 (Deut. xxiv. 1, 2), The guiltles therfore wert not depriv'd thir needful redresses. **1728** R. MORRIS *Ess. Anc. Archit.* 33 The sick Man just expiring for want of a speedy Redress by..proper Remedies.

†**b.** One who, or that which, affords redress.

c **1530** *Crt. of Love* 591 They seid: Venus, redresse of all division, Goddes eterne [etc.]. **1596** SPENSER *State Irel.* Wks. (Globe) 650/1 Is not the swoord the most violent redress that may be used for any evill? **1697** DRYDEN *Æneid* I. 838 Fair majesty, the refuge and redress Of those whom fate pursues and wants oppress.

4. Const. *of.* The act of redressing; correction or amendment of a thing, state, etc.

1538 STARKEY *England* II. i. 156 To theyr cure schal be commyttyd the redresse of many grete dyseasys in thys polytyke body. **1598** BARRET *Theor. Warres* II. i. 30 For the redresse of many casualties chancing in the night. **1643** *Ord. Parlt. regul. Print.* in *Milton's Areop.* (Arb.) 26 The bill in preparation, for redresse of the said disorders. **1709** STEELE *Tatler* No. 12 ¶6 There might be some Hopes of Redress of these Grievances. **1819** SHELLEY *Cenci* IV. iv. 121 Arming familiar things To the redress of an unwonted crime. **1874** GREEN *Short Hist.* iii. §5. 138 The great principle that redress of wrongs precedes a grant to the Crown.

redress (rɪˈdrɛs), *v.*[1] Also 4 **redresce**, 4-7 **redresse**, 5-6 *Sc.* **redres**, (5 **ra-**). [ad. F. *redresser*, OF. *redrecier, -drechier*, etc. = Sp. *redereçar*, It. *ridirizzare*: see RE- and DRESS *v.*]

†**1.** *trans.* To set (a person or thing) upright again; to raise again to an erect position. Also *fig.* to set up again, restore, re-establish. *Obs.*

c **1374** CHAUCER *Boeth.* IV. pr. ii. 89 (Camb. MS.), As thise leches ben wont to hopyn of sike folk, whan they aperceyuen þat nature is redressed [L. *erectæ*] and withstondith to the maledie. **1481** CAXTON *Godfrey* cxcviii. 289 Incontinent he redressyd and reysed on heygthe his baner alle blody. *c* **1500** *Melusine* 290 [They] supposed wel to haue redressed thadmyrall vpon his hors but it was for nought, For he was deed. **1583** STOCKER *Civ. Warres Lowe C.* IV. 34 The Catholique Romishe Religion shall bee redressed..in the Cities and places..where it is banished. **1643** PRYNNE *Popish R. Favourite* 46 He caused the Image of the Crosse to be redressed, and that men should not foule it under their feete. **1669** WORLIDGE *Syst. Agric.* (1681) 107 Cut through all the Collateral Roots, till..you can inforce him upon one side, so as to come..at the Tap-Root; cut that off, redress your Tree, and so let it stand. [Copied in Mortimer's *Husb.* (1721) II. 69, and other works.] **1711** SHAFTESB. *Charac.* (1737) III. 133 Some ambitious Architect..being call'd perhaps to prop a Roof, redress a leaning Wall [etc.].

†**b.** *refl.* To raise (oneself) again; to reassume an upright posture. *Obs.*

c **1374** CHAUCER *Troylus* II. 920 (969) Right as floures.. stoupen in hire stalk lowe, Redressen hem a-yen þe sonne bryght. *c* **1450** *Merlin* 328 As soone as the spere was spente the kynge Boors redressed hym in his sadell. **1727-41** CHAMBERS *Cycl.* s.v. *Redressing*, Trees and other plants have a natural faculty of redressing themselves, when, by any external cause, they are forced out of the perpendicular.

†**c.** *intr.* To rise, become erect. *Obs.*

1480 CAXTON *Ovid's Met.* XIII. xv, Thou oughtest not to despyse me, Galathee, thoughe my heere redresse a lytyl & brustle. **1584** HUDSON *Du Bartas' Judith* II. in *Sylvester's Du Bartas* (1621) 700 Yet like the valiant Palme they did sustaine Their peisant weight, redressing vp againe.

†**2.** To set up, erect, build. *Obs. rare*$^{-1}$.

1481 CAXTON *Godfrey* clxxix. 264 The other that were nyghe the corner..redressyd a castel of tree moche hye.

†**b.** ? To spread out. *Obs. rare*$^{-1}$.

c **1450** LONELICH *Grail* xli. 276 Thanne Josephes bothe Schirte and water gan blesse, And Anon God gan it for to Redresse, and wax moche largere hem vntylle.

†**3.** To put right again, repair, mend (a house or wall). *Obs.*

1480 CAXTON *Chron. Eng.* lxv, How the kyng Aurilambros let amend and redresse the hous of Amlesbury. *c* **1540** tr. *Pol. Verg. Eng. Hist.* (Camden) I. 47 Disposinge himselfe to the beutifienge of the cittee of London, [he] redressed the walles,..beinge ruinus throughe yeares, strengtheninge the same with divers turrets.

†**4.** *fig.* To bring back (a person) to the right course; to correct or direct aright. *Obs.*

c **1366** CHAUCER *A.B.C.* 129 Redresse me mooder and me chastise. *c* **1400** *Rom. Rose* 3423, I wole swere for evermo To be redressid at youre likyng, If I trespasse in ony thyng. *c* **1430** *Syr Gener.* (Roxb.) 358 An Emperoure..Whom no mannes counsel might redres. **1573** L. LLOYD *Marrow of Hist.* (1653) 263 Anger out not to be in any Prince..toward his equal, for he might be redressed with power. **1615** BRATHWAIT *Strappado* (1878) 174 You..Would see your Towne..By selfe-same censures to be soone redrest. **1689** POPPLE tr. *Locke's 1st Let. Toleration* L.'s Wks. 1727 II. 235 In teaching, instructing, and redressing the Erroneous by Reason.

†**b.** *Hunting.* To bring back (the hounds or deer) to the proper course. *Obs.*

c **1400** *Master of Game* Prol. (MS. Digby 182), He hath ynogh at done..to loke wherafter he hunteth..and redresse and bryng his houndes into right whann thei haue envoised or fallen in to rascall. **1659** HOWELL *Vocab.* III, To redresse the deer, or putt her off her changes;..*redresser le cerf*. 1706 PHILLIPS (ed. Kersey), *To redress a Stag*, (a Term in Hunting) to put him off his changes.

†**c.** To direct or amend (one's acts or ways). *Obs.*

1422 tr. *Secreta Secret., Priv. Priv.* 158 To the Offyce of Prudencia appendyth the dedis of all othyr vertues redresse. 1560 BIBLE (Genev.) *Ps.* cxix. 9 Wherewith shal a yong man redresse his waie? —— *Jer.* vii. 7 If you amend and redresse your waies and your workes. [Hence in 16–17th c. writers, down to *c* 1635.]

†**5.** To direct or address (a thing) *to* a destination or in a specified course. *Obs.* Also *refl.*

c 1386 CHAUCER *Pars. T.* ¶965 Preyeres is for to seyn a pitous wyl of herte that redresseth it in god. 1390 GOWER *Conf.* III. 177 So were it good to taken hiede That ferst a king his oghne dede Betwen the vertu and the vice Redresce. *c* 1440 *Gesta Rom.* lii. 230 (Harl. MS.), This hope owithe to be Redressid vnto god. 1461 *Rolls of Parlt.* V. 484/1 That the same Duches have..such Writtes and Warantes.., directed or redressed to the seid Custumers.

†**b.** *intr.* and *refl.* To address oneself *to* a person or place. *Obs. rare.*

c 1460 *Play Sacram.* 607 All manar off men yt haue any syknes To master brentberecly loke yt yow redresse. *c* 1598 ROLLOCK *Passion* vi. (1616) 58 A man that redresses himselfe to a kingdome, would euer take delite to speake of it.

†**c.** To guide or lead (a person) *to* oneself. *Obs.*

c 1477 CAXTON *Jason* 113 b, She dide do make fires and a light..for to redresse Iason and Argos to herward.

†**6.** To put (things) in order; to arrange. *Obs.*

1413 *Pilgr. Sowle* (Caxton 1483) IV. v. 60 Lete the Iugement be yeuen as ryght wylle rewarden and soo may fynal pees be redressyd bitwene bothe partes. 1432–50 tr. *Higden* (Rolls) III. 253 The Romanes didde redresse and redacte these lawes of Salon in to x tables. *c* 1500 *For to serve a Lord* in *Babees Bk.* 371 Thenne the kerver shall goo unto the cuppebord, and redresse and ordeyn wafers in to towayles. *c* 1500 *Doctr. Gd. Servaunts* (Percy Soc.) 6 Erly in the mornynge se ye ryse, Your werke and laboure to redresse. *c* 1585 R. BROWNE *Answ. Cartwright* 15 They redresse and order matters by money, Brybes, Fees, Ciuill penaltyes.

†**b.** To bring back *to* the proper order; to shift *to* the proper place. *Obs. rare.*

c 1500 *Melusine* 193 The two bretheren..went fro bataill to batayll and there as fawte was of ordynaunce, they redressed theire peple to it. 1588 J. MELLIS *Briefe Instr.* G j, If any parcell were put by error in any other parcell there as it should not bee, and that you would redresse it vnto the proper place there it ought to be set.

†**c.** To make conformable *to* something. *Obs.*

1538 STARKEY *England* II. ii. 182 Thys conseyl schold euer be occasyon to redresse the affectys of the prynce to the ordur of the law.

7. †**a.** To restore or bring back (a thing or person) to a proper state; to put right, or in good order, again; to mend, repair. *Obs.*

c 1386 CHAUCER *Frankl. T.* 709 Another Theban mayden ..ffor oon of Macidonye hadde hire oppressed She with hire deeth hir maydenhede redressed. 1422 tr. *Secreta Secret., Priv. Priv.* 241 Goynge afor mette dryuth away the ventositeis, redressith the body. 1483 CAXTON *Gold. Leg.* 206/2 In lystris was a contracte which he losed and redressid. 1590 SPENSER *F.Q.* I. v. 36 Sad Aesculapius far apart Emprisond was..For that Hyppolytus rent corse he did redresse. 1630 WADSWORTH *Pilgr.* ii. 7 The ship redrest as well as time and place could afford, we still made forward.

†**b.** To put (a matter, or state of things) right again; to reform, amend, improve. *Obs.*

c 1386 CHAUCER *Clerk's T.* 375 Whan that the cas required it, The commune profit koude she redresse. 1477 EARL RIVERS (Caxton) *Dictes* 20 Alle thynges may be redresshed and reformed, saue euil dedis. *c* 1540 tr. *Pol. Verg. Eng. Hist.* (Camden) I. 135 The estate of relligion and orders of priesthoode were newlie sifted and redressed. 1560 DAUS tr. *Sleidane's Comm.* 182 b, That they redresse and pourge their churches. 1648 MILTON *Ps.* lxxxii. 26 Rise God, judge thou the earth in might, This wicked earth redress. 1716 POPE *Iliad* VI. 91 Now had..frighted Troy within her Walls retir'd; Had not sage Helenus her State redrest. 1764 GOLDSM. *Trav.* 176 E'en here content can spread a charm, Redress the clime, and all its rage disarm.

c. To correct, emend. *rare.*

1710 SHAFTESB. *Charac.* (1737) I. III. ii. 325 Nor am I out of my own Possession, whilst there is a Person left within; who has Power to dispute the Appearances, and redress the Imagination. 1796 HAMILTON in *Washington's Writ.* (1892) XIII. 190 *note*, You mentioned to me your wish, that I should redress a certain paper, which you had prepared. 1868 M. PATTISON *Academ. Org.* iv. 73 The material estimate of worth should be redressed by a moral standard.

d. To adjust again. (Chiefly with *balance*.)

1847 EMERSON *Poems* (1857) 213 [He] sees aloft the red right arm Redress the eternal scales. 1849 MACAULAY *Hist. Eng.* i. I. 44 Unless the balance had been redressed by a great transfer of power from the crown to the parliament. 1874 GREEN *Short Hist.* iv. §5. 197 At an earlier time the personal greatness of Edward might have redressed the balance.

†**8.** To restore (a person) to happiness or prosperity; to save, deliver *from* misery, death, etc. *Obs.*

a 1425 *Cursor M.* 22737 (Trin.) Whenne he coom furst vs to redresse He coom al wiþ mekenesse. 14.. *Hymn Virg.* 25 in *Pol. Rel. & L. Poems* (1866) 82 Redres mans sowle from alle mysery. 1483 CAXTON *G. de la Tour* G vj, Saint Eustace ..lost goodes and children for the space of xiii yere and then god redressed hym ageyne. 1535 *Goodly Prymer* (1834) 132 Wash me O Lord, in his blood,..redress me in his resurrection. *a* 1550 in *Dunbar's Wks.* (S.T.S.) 324 The hevynnis King is cled in our nature, Ws fro the deth with ransoun for to redress. 1583 GOLDING *Calvin on Deut.* cxc. 1183 So as hee may..not onely forgiue vs all our sinnes,.. but also rid vs cleane of them, and redresse vs.

9. To set (a person) right, by obtaining, or (more rarely) giving, satisfaction or compensation for the wrong or loss sustained.

c 1430 *Chev. Assigne* 204 Go brynge hym to his fader courte... Ryȝte by þe mydday to redresse his moder. 1574 *Reg. Privy Council Scot.* II. 368 That thai suld redres all Scottismen offendit be thame. 1650 HOWELL *Giraffi's Rev. Naples* I. 109 They came..to be redressed by him for divers grievances. 1700 DRYDEN *Pal. & Arc.* I. 59 'Tis thine, O King, the afflicted to redress. 1753 FOOTE *Englishm. in Paris* II. Wks. 1799 I. 55, I indeed have wrong'd, but will redress you. 1797 *Monthly Mag.* III. 491 If our gracious sovereign does not order us to be redressed in fifty-four hours, such steps will be taken, as will astonish our dear countrymen. 1820 BYRON *Mar. Fal.* I. ii. 339 You..will redress Him, whom the laws of discipline and Venice Permit not to protect himself. 1863 S. L. J. *Life in South* I. xix. 375 How am I to be redressed for the loss of my property?

refl. 1860 L. HARCOURT *Diaries G. Rose* I. 168 The time had..arrived for the people to redress themselves.

10. To remedy or remove (trouble or distress of any kind).

c 1374 CHAUCER *Compl. Mars* 192 Who may me helpe, who may my harm redresse. *c* 1375 *Canticum de Creatione* 953 in Horstm. *Altengl. Leg.* (1878) 136 God shel come.. And shel redressen mannes nede In riȝt and in leute. *c* 1410 HOCCLEVE *Mother of God* 41 Swich an advocatrice who can dyvyne..our grieves to redresse. *c* 1500 *Lancelot* 1359 For thyne estat is gewyne to Redress Thar ned. 1579 LYLY *Euphues* (Arb.) 106, I can neither remember our miseries without griefe, nor redresse our mishaps without grones. 1617 FLETCHER *Valent.* II. iii, Their duty And ready service shall redress their needs. 1714 *Spect.* No. 611 ¶2, I flatter my self, you will..if possible, redress a Misfortune my self and several others of my Sex lie under. 1764 GOLDSM. *Trav.* 214 Every want that stimulates the breast Becomes a source of pleasure when redrest. 1870 EMERSON *Soc. & Solit.*, *Eloquence* Wks. (Bohn) III. 25 There is no calamity which right words will not begin to redress.

b. To cure, heal, relieve (a disease, wound, etc.). Also in fig. context.

1470–85 MALORY *Arthur* XII. xii, Syr Tristram now be we mette for or we departe we wille redresse our old sores. *a* 1529 SKELTON *Knowl., acquaint.*, etc. 8 Allectuary arrectyd to redres These feuerous axys, the dedely wo and payne [etc.]. *a* 1542 WYATT in *Tottel's Misc.* (Arb.) 45 The frosty snowes may not redresse my heat. 1601 DANIEL *Civ. Wars* VII. lxxii, Or, whether 'tis not time we should have rest And this confusion, and our wounds redrest. 1633 BP. HALL *Hard Texts, N.T.* 383 Which may be to thee instead of.. eyesalve to redresse thy blindnesse. *a* 1687 VILLIERS (Dk. Buckhm.) *Poems* (1775) 143 Such carbuncles..As no Hungarian water can redress. 1784 COWPER *Task* VI. 521 The frenzy of the brain may be redress'd By medicine well applied. 1835–6 TODD *Cycl. Anat.* I. 160/2 This is a species of fracture..which can..be readily redressed.

†**c.** To remove, take away (a disability). *Obs.*

1560 DAUS *Sleidane's Comm.* 290 To pardon his fault, to redresse the outlawery dew for his offence.

†**d.** To put away, get over (sorrow). *Obs.*

1583 GREEN *Mamillia* Wks. (Grosart) II. 240 Mamilia had by the space of a weeke..something redressed her sorrow.

11. To set right, repair, rectify (something suffered or complained of): **a.** a wrong.

c 1374 CHAUCER *Troylus* III. 959 (1008) Þer-with mene I fynally the peyne,..Fully to slen and euery wrong redresse. 1422 tr. *Secreta Secret., Priv. Priv.* 158 To hym longyth nedes to Esplete,..wronges to redresse. *c* 1470 HENRY *Wallace* VI. 224 It slakis ire off wrang thai suld radres. 1551 CROWLEY *Pleas. & Pain* 308, I woulde se all theyr wrongis redreste. 1660 WALLER *To the King on his return* 62 Armies and fleets..Owned their great Sovereign, and redressed his wrong. 1749 SMOLLETT *Regicide* III. viii, The sword of Athol Was never drawn but to redress the wrongs His country suffer'd. 1784 COWPER *Task* IV. 795 A heart To feel, and courage to redress her wrongs. 1862 SHIRLEY (J. Skelton) *Nugæ Crit.* x. 444 The wrong indeed was redressed, as far as redress was possible.

absol. 1601 SHAKS. *Jul. C.* II. i. 47 Speake, strike, redresse. Brutus, thou sleep'st: awake.

b. damage, injury, etc.

c 1400 *Destr. Troy* 4917 [To] redresse vs the domage, þat he don has. 1591 SHAKS. *1 Hen. VI*, II. v. 126 Those bitter Iniuries..I doubt not, but with Honor to redresse. 1628 DIGBY *Voy. Medit.* (1868) 16 He hoped the King of England would redresse some iniuries done to subiectes of this state by some of his. 1863 KINGLAKE *Crimea* (1876) I. xiii. 209 It rested with Austria to prevent or redress the threatened outrage. 1878 P'CESS ALICE *Mem.* (1884) 367 The Opposition seems to me..to have done her a greater harm than can ever be redressed.

c. a grievance or complaint.

1597 SHAKS. *2 Hen. IV*, IV. i. 170 This containes our generall Grieuances: Each several Article herein redress'd [etc.]. 1713 STEELE *Englishm.* No. 8. 52, [I] bring a Complaint before you, which it is your Province to redress. 1761 HUME *Hist. Eng.* II. xxxvi. 293 Some persons.. believed that it would be safer to prevent than to redress grievances. 1863 GEO. ELIOT *Romola* xxi, At present it was not understood that he had redressed any grievances.

12. To correct, amend, reform or do away with (a bad or faulty state of things, now *esp.* an abuse).

c 1386 CHAUCER *Wife's Prol.* 696 They wolde han writen of men more wikkednesse Than all the mark of Adam may redresse. 1390 GOWER *Conf.* III. 268 To redresce At hom the grete unrihtwisnesse. 1449 *Rolls of Parlt.* V. 149/2 To redresse the defaultes of the said maire and constables. 1538 STARKEY *England* I. iii. 71 The general fautys and mysordurys.., wych by commyn counsely and gud pollycy may be redressyd. 1577 tr. *Bullinger's Decades* (1592) 130 Our detestable cursings..which very few magistrates..go about to redresse. 1634 H. R. *Salerne's Regim.* 33 For such Wines redresse and amend the coldnesse of Complexion. 1675 MARVELL *Let. to Mayor of Hull* Wks. 1872–5 I. 258 The Atheism, Profanenesse, and Impiety among the people were one point to be redressed. 1712 ADDISON *Spect.* No. 446 ¶4 That the Lewdness of our Theatre should be..so well exposed, and so little redressed. 1781 COWPER *Table T.* 632 Ever anxious to redress The abuses of her sacred charge. 1835 I. TAYLOR *Spir. Despot.* II. 77 Spiritual despotism is necessarily redressed or excluded when theology is reformed. 1874 GREEN *Short Hist.* v. §5. 254 In a vigorous campaign he pacified Ireland while redressing the abuses of its government.

†**b.** To settle (discord or debate). *Obs.*

1387 TREVISA *Higden* (Rolls) IV. 191 ȝif þere fil ony discord bytwene the tweyn, þe þridde schulde redresse it. 1389 in *Eng. Gilds* (1870) 4 [If] eny debat chaunselich falle .., þe same maistres and breþeren shul do her diligence trewly to redresse it.

†**c.** To repair the want of. *Obs. rare*$^{-1}$.

1765 BLACKSTONE *Comm.* I. 437 The consent of the mother or guardians, if unreasonably withheld, might be redressed and supplied by the judge.

†**13.** To repair (an action); to atone for (a misdeed or offence). *Obs.*

c 1325 *Know Thyself* 56 in *E.E.P.* (1862) 131 Who-so greueþ hym is worþi to go To helle fuyr but he hit redres. 1390 GOWER *Conf.* I. 241, I am al redy to redresce The gilt of which I me confesse. *c* 1400 *Rom. Rose* 3302 And eke thee caste, If that thou maist, to gete thee defence For to redresse thi first offence. 1597 HOOKER *Eccl. Pol.* v. lxii. §18 Vnlawful vsurpation a penitent affection must redresse.

†**14.** *Sc.* **a.** To restore, give back. *Obs. rare.*

1533 BELLENDEN *Livy* II. ii. (S.T.S.) I. 134 Gif þe gudis of tarquinis war nocht redressit [L. *reddita*]. 1536 —— *Cron. Scot.* (1821) II. 328 The nobillis of Ingland..causit all the saidis guddis to be redressit.

†**b.** To make good (a bill). *Obs.*

1565 [see REDRESSING *vbl. sb.*1]. 1573 *Reg. Privy Council Scot.* II. 307 He wilbe compellit to answer and redresse the said bill.

†**15.** ? To win or take by force. *Obs. rare*$^{-1}$.

1592 WARNER *Alb. Eng.* VII. xxxvi. 153 The Cleonæan Lyons spoyles for her I would redresse. I would the Lernan Hydras heads with sword and fire suppress.

Hence **re'dressed** *ppl. a.*1, **re'dressing** *ppl. a.*

1845–6 DE QUINCEY *Shelley* Wks. 1857 VI. 3 *note*, The boyish period in which these redressing corrections occurred to me. 1893 SLOANE *Stand. Electr. Dict.* 164 Current, Rectified... Synonym—Redressed Current.

redress (riː'drɛs), *v.*2 Also **re-dress**. [RE- 5 a.] To dress again, in senses of the vb.

1739 G. OGLE *Gualtherus & Griselda* 88 Griselda may redress her, or retire. 1834 *Fraser's Mag.* IX. 609 Yet was Chaucer to him a poet whom he might re-dress with advantage. 1847 SINGER *Wayland Smith* p. xxxix, The maidens, not being able to re-dress themselves, utter loud cries of terror. 1859 *Six Yrs. Trav. Russia* II. v. 67 It appears that the Russians re-dress all furs that they import. 1897 MARY KINGSLEY *W. Africa* 560 But I..shut up the doors and windows..while I am dressing, or rather redressing.

Hence **re'dressed** *ppl. a.*2

1872 *City Press* 6 Apr., The Engineers had reported that this street could be repaved with re-dressed stone.

redressable (rɪ'drɛsəb(ə)l), *a.* [f. REDRESS *v.*1] That may be redressed; admitting of redress.

1688 *Pr. of Orange's Declar., with Animadv.* 14 Are they not Redressable by a Parliament? 1803 W. TAYLOR in *Ann. Rev.* I. 398 It would be well..if these societies occupied themselves more with specific and redressable grievances.

redressal (rɪ'drɛsəl). [f. as prec. + -AL1.] = REDRESS *sb.*

1867 *Pall Mall G.* 24 June 1 The redressal of the balance of representation. 1884 *Contemp. Rev.* May 689 All hope of the redressal of her grievances had become extinct.

redresser (rɪ'drɛsə(r)). [f. as prec. + -ER1. Cf. F. *redresseur* (16th c.).] One who redresses or rectifies (esp. a wrong). Also = REDRESSOR (*Syd. Soc. Lex.* 1897).

c 1430 *Pilgr. Lyf Manhode* III. xxxiv. (1869) 154 Of redressere ne of vndertakere thei taken no keepe. 1540 PALSGRAVE tr. *Fullonius' Acolastus* III. iii, That same moste beste redresser or reformer is God, whose hande gouerneth ..all thynges. 1565 JEWEL *Def. Apol.* VI. 742 For feare lest they feele him once a redresser, and reuenger of his owne cause. 1612 SHELTON *Quix.* I. IV. xxv, The famous Don Quixote of the Mancha, the righter of wrongs, the redresser of injuries. 1799 HAN. MORE *Fem. Educ.* (ed. 4) I. 27 The fighter of the duel no longer pretends to be a glorious redresser of the wrongs of strangers. 1851 ROBERTSON *Serm.* Ser. I. xvii. (1866) 298 The redressers of the poor man's wrongs. 1871 B. TAYLOR *Faust* (1875) II. IV. iii. 266, I also in my time must meet the sure Redresser.

redressing (rɪ'drɛsɪŋ), *vbl. sb.*1 [f. REDRESS *v.*1] The action of REDRESS *v.*1 in various senses.

c 1449 PECOCK *Repr.* I. xvi. 86 It nedith forto haue a redressing of it into accordaunce with lawe of kinde. 1526 *Pilgr. Perf.* (W. de W. 1531) 169 b, For redressynge and releuynge of mannes necessytees. 1565 *Reg. Privy Council Scot.* I. 404 For redressing of the saidis billis and expenssis. 1634 SANDERSON *Serm.* II. 292 It behoveth the magistrate to set in..for the rectifying and redressing thereof. 1693 *Lond. Gaz.* No. 2843/2 To take care about Redressing of the Mint. 1711–12 SWIFT *Let. on Eng. Tongue* Wks. 1755 II. I. 183 A grievance, the redressing of which is to be your own work. 1774 GOLDSM. *Nat. Hist.* (1862) I. 183 Every want thus becomes a means of pleasure, in the redressing. 1884 *Manch. Exam.* 10 Dec. 5/2 A straight way to the redressing of grievances.

redressing (riː'drɛsɪŋ), *vbl. sb.*2 [f. REDRESS *v.*2] The action or result of dressing again.

1889 JACOBS *Aesop* I. 156 The majority are a redressing of the ordinary Æsop.

re'dressive, *a. rare.* [f. REDRESS *v.*[1] + -IVE.] Seeking to redress, bringing redress.

1726–46 THOMSON *Winter* 360 The generous band, Who, touch'd with human woe, redressive search'd Into the horrors of the gloomy jail. **1965** H. KAHN *On Escalation* ii. 45 The first use of nuclear weapons..is likely to be less for the purpose of destroying the other side's military forces.. than for redressive, warning,..or deterrence purposes.

re'dressless, *a. rare*[−0]. [f. REDRESS *sb.* + -LESS.] Without redress, or the possibility of this.

1611 COTGR., *Irremediable*, remedilesse, redreslesse.

re'dressment. [f. REDRESS *v.*[1] + -MENT, perh. after F. *redressement* (12th c.).] The act of redressing; redress.

1643 HUNTON *Treat. Monarchy* I. ii. 11 It must be yeelded to..without repeale or redressement by any created power. **1644** —— *Vind. Treat. Monarchy* ii. 8 If they come with pretence of Authority, there may be seeking redressement above from Authority. **1822** JEFFERSON *Writ.* (1830) IV. 353 The redressment of mental vagaries would be an enterprise more than Quixotic. **1897** *Syd. Soc. Lex., Redressment*, reduction of a dislocation, or correction of a deformity.

re'dressor. [f. REDRESS *v.*[1] + -OR[1].] One who, or that which, redresses; *spec.* in *Surg.* (see quot. 1884).

1884 KNIGHT *Dict. Mech.* Suppl. 746/2 *Redressor* (Surgical), a replacing instrument, e.g. the uterine redressor. **1894** *Daily News* 11 Dec. 4/7 The Power which has long been the redressor of Christian grievances against the Turk.

re-'drill, *v.*[1] [RE- 5 a + DRILL *v.*[3]] *trans.* To drill again.

1802 JAMES *Milit. Dict.* s.v., It is observed, page 2, of General Rules and Regulations, that every soldier, on his return from long absence, must be re-drilled before he is permitted to act in the ranks of his company. **1822** *Regul. & Ord. Army* (1844) 90 Soldiers, on returning from Furlough, are to be re-drilled until reported fit to rejoin their Troops or Companies.

re'drill, *v.*[2] [f. RE- 5 a + DRILL *v.*[4]] *trans.* To drill (crops or ground) again in the same season. So **re'drilling** *vbl. sb.*

1959 *Times* 5 Aug. 4/1 (Advt.), Aldrin wettable powder, used as a seed dressing, has proved outstandingly successful against the Black Cutworm.., eliminating time and money-wasting re-drilling and reducing handling and application costs. **1961** *Times* 24 July 6/6 Wheat bulb fly is in some years a very serious pest. In 1953 the estimated total loss in this country, taking into account crops which had to be redrilled or patched, was estimated at £1,250,000.

re'drive, *v.* [RE-.] To drive back (again).

1594 WILLOBY *La Avisa* xl. 8 Penelope With all her wordes could not redryue Her sutors. *a* **1700** DRYDEN, etc. *Ovid's Amours* II. x. (1724) 285 As to and fro the doubtful Galliot rides, Here driven by Winds, and there redriven by Tydes. **1847** WEBSTER cites SOUTHEY.

Red River. *Canad.* The name of a river flowing from North Dakota, U.S.A., to Lake Winnipeg, Manitoba, Canada, used *attrib.* in **Red River cart** *Hist.* (see quot. 1875); **Red River fever,** typhoid fever; **Red River frame** *Hist.*, used in a particular style of architecture (see quot. 1921); **Red River jig,** a fast, intricate jig.

1857 J. PALLISER *Jrnl.* 14 July (1863), The Red River cart is one admirably suited to the exigencies of the country. **1875** J. CARNEGIE *Saskatchewan & Rocky Mts.* ii. 13 Red River cart, a stout two-wheeled vehicle of the toughest quality though entirely made of wood, wheels, body, shafts, and all, being fitted together without a single particle of iron. **1968** [see *ox-train* s.v. OX 5]. **1975** *Whig-Standard* (Kingston, Ontario) 21 Nov. 25/1 I've been here [*sc.* at Calgary] for three days and I haven't seen one buffalo, or a Red River cart or a redcoated Mountie or a saloon shoot-out. **1880** D. CURRIE *Lett. of Rusticus* 62/1 Red River fever was very prevalent at the Portage. **1889** J. G. DONKIN *Trooper & Redskin in Far North-West* iii. 41 In fact it is the typho-malarial scourge known as Red River fever in Manitoba, jungle fever in India,..and Rocky Mountain fever in British Columbia. **1945** K. M. HAIG *Brave Harvest* 40 Aunt Alice's heart sank. The Red River fever! **1966** M. KAVANAUGH *Assiniboine Basin* xxxv. 223 Fisher spent six weeks in the hospital suffering from typhoid—sometimes called Red River fever. **1882** *Edmonton Bull.* 29 July 4/1 They are of the style known as Red River frame and are for use as storehouses. **1921** *Beaver* Feb. 15/2 The 'big house' was a two-and-a-half storey building, with a large kitchen behind, built from the same plan as the officers' dwellings in Fort Garry, and known as a Red River frame building. **1963** MACLEOD & MORTON *Cuthbert Grant of Grantown* 93 There on the western limit of his seigniory, Cuthbert Grant built the great log house, in the Red River frame style. **1872** *Canad. Monthly* Oct. 305/1 The principal dance, in fact the only one, is called a Red River jig, which somewhat resembles a horn-pipe, male and female participating in it. **1930** L. MUNDAY *Mounty's Wife* iii. 44 The jigging by the men, known as the Red River jig, is really done very cleverly and is so swift. **1965** G. SHEPHERD *West of Yesterday* x. 74 Two compatriots came out on the floor and danced a Red River jig.

redross, obs. variant of REREDOS.

red rot. [f. RED *a.* + ROT *sb.*[1]] **a.** Fungal decay of standing trees or of timber characterized by red-brown rotted tissue; *esp.* that caused by *Trametes pini* in conifers.

1894 W. SOMERVILLE tr. *Hartig's Text-bk. Dis. Trees* 1 The damping-off of seedling beeches,..the red-rot of the spruce, &c., were known to foresters more than a hundred years ago. **1925** HAWLEY & HAWES *Man. Forestry* (ed. 2) vii. 127 The practice..of leaving for seed purposes trees diseased with red rot is unsafe because it tends to perpetuate the disease, not through the seed of the old trees, but by the fungus upon them. **1934** [see CONK *sb.*[2]]. **1950** R. MOORE *Candlemas Bay* 119 The house was starting in to go right now, the way all the fine old houses went, as surely as if red rot had got into its solid beams and were eating it hourly down.

b. A fungal disease of sugar cane characterized by red patches within the canes.

1907 *Bull. Hawaiian Sugar Planters' Assoc. Exper. Station* VII. 25 The fungus is *Colletotrichum falcatum*, and the disease it causes is called the 'red rot' of the cane. **1928** F. S. EARLE *Sugar Cane* v. 154 The red rot fungus gains entrance to the stalks through borer holes and other injuries. **1944** *Phytopathology* XXXIV. 210 The lesions produced on the inoculated leaves were in all ways similar to lesions produced by virulent red-rot cultures. **1975** *Mycologia* LXVII. 56 Perithecia produced by *C*[*olletotrichum*] *graminicola* most closely resemble those of *Glomerella tucumanensis*, the causal agent of the red rot of sugarcane... Carvajal and Edgerton..connected the conidial state, *C. falcatum*, with *P*[*hysalospora*] *tucumanensis*. The perfect state of this fungus was transferred by von Arx and Müller ..to the genus *Glomerella*, and the name generally accepted today is *G. tucumanensis*.

red rot (the plant): see RED *a.* 19.

red-rumped, *a. Ornith.* Having a red rump.

1752 J. HILL *Hist. Anim.* 367 The red-rumped Parrot..is one of the largest of the Parrot-kind. **1776** P. BROWN *Illustr. Zool.* 70 The Red-rumped wax-billed Finch. **1782** LATHAM *Gen. Synopsis Birds* I. II. 420 Red-rumped Oriole. *Oriolus hæmorrheus.* **1815** SHAW *Gen. Zool.* IX. I. 194 Red-Rumped Woodpecker (*Picus capensis*). *Ibid.* 405 Red-Rumped Bunting (*Emberiza quadricolor*). **1817** T. FORSTER *Nat. Hist. Swallowtribe* (ed. 6) 75 *Fringilla Montium*, twite, or Redrumped linnet. **1894** *Northumbld. Gloss., Red-rumped thrush*, the missel thrush.

redruthite ('rɛdru:θaɪt). [f. *Redruth*, the name of a town in Cornwall + -ITE[1].] A native sulphide of copper; copper glance, chalcocite.

1849 J. NICOL *Manual Mineral.* 473. **1873** FOWNES *Chem.* 399 Cuprous Sulphide occurs native as copper-glance or redruthite.

red sanders. Also 7 saunder, 8–9 **saunders.** [See SANDERS.] Red sandalwood or rubywood; the wood of an East Indian tree, *Pterocarpus santalinus*, used in dyeing, and formerly employed in medicine as an astringent and tonic.

1553 EDEN *Treat. Newe Ind.* (Arb.) 23 There are also in this Iland many woddes that bringe foorth redde sanders. **1568** TURNER *Herbal* III. 67 Rede sanders hinder the flowinge of humores to the partes of the bodye, and strengthen the gummes and stomach. **1647** LILLY *Chr. Astrol.* x. 68 The Hearbs..are such as come neare to a rednesse..Horehound, Hemlock, red Sanders. **1698** SLOANE in *Phil. Trans.* XX. 73 Of Red Saunder, of *Lignum Aloes*, each half an Ounce. **1736** BAILEY *Househ. Dict.* 206 If you would have the comfits red infuse some red Saunders in the water. **1838** T. THOMSON *Chem. Org. Bodies* 410 Red sanders is the name given in this country to the wood of the *pterocarpus santalinus*, a large tree which grows upon the Coromandel coast and other parts of India, especially Ceylon. **1868** W. RITCHIE *Script. Test. agst. Intox. Wine* viii. 196 Tincture of red Sanders or cudbear were extensively used.

attrib. **1807** AIKIN *Dict. Chem. & Min.* II. 287/1 Red Saunders Wood..is also brought from the East Indies. **1872** OLIVER *Elem. Bot.* II. 165 Red Sanders-wood,..a reddish-brown dye, used for woollen cloths.

†red-sear, *v. Obs.* Also 8 -seer. [app. f. *red-share* RED-SHIRE *a.*, with assimilation of the second element to SEAR *v.*] (See quots.)

1677 MOXON *Mech. Exerc.* i. 8 If it be too hot it will Red-sear, that is break or crack under the Hammer while it is working between Hot and Cold. *Ibid.* 13 Spanish Iron would be as good as Swedish Iron were it not subject to Red-sear (as Work-men phrase it) that is to crack betwixt hot and cold. [Hence in Holme *Armoury* (1688), Harris *Lex. Techn.* II. (1710), Chambers *Cycl.* (1727–41), etc.]

So **red-sear** *a. rare.* = RED-SHORT *a.*

1798 NEMNICH *Polygl. Lex.* v. 867 Red-short or Red-sear iron. Malleable when cold, but brittle when red-hot. **1876** VOYLE *Milit. Dict.* 334/2 *Red-sear Iron*, a defect in iron which causes it to become brittle when heated, and to break when forged.

'red-shank(s, 'redshank.

1. One who has red legs; *spec.* **a.** (chiefly in *pl.*) One of the Celtic inhabitants of the Scottish Highlands and of Ireland. Now only *Hist.*

The name was app. given in allusion to the colour of the bare legs reddened by exposure, and not for the reason assigned in quot. 1818.

1542 ELDER *Let. to Hen. VIII* in *Bannatyne Misc.* (1827) I. 10 The Yrische lordes of Scotland, commonly callit the Reddshanckes, and by historiographouris, Pictis. *Ibid.* 13 Wherfore they call ws in Scotland Reddshankes,..goynge alwaies bair leggide and bair footide [etc.]. **1547** BOORDE *Introd. Knowl.* iii. (1870) 132 The other parte of Irland is called the wilde Irysh; and the Redshankes be among them. **1596** SPENSER *State Irel.* Wks. (Globe) 658/2 The O-Neales are neerelye allyed..to the Earle of Argile, from whom they use to have all theyr succours of those Scotts and Redd-shankes. **1611** L. BARRY *Ram Alley* D ij b, I will rather wed a most perfidious Redshanke. **1648** MILTON *Observ. Art. Peace* Wks. (1851) 580 By thir actions we might rather judg them to be a generation of High-land Theevs and Red-shanks. **1681** COLVIL *Whigs' Supplic.* II. (1741) 137 That Red-shank sullen, Once challenged for stealing Beef. **1771** SMOLLETT *Humph. Cl.* 18 July, Let. i, The mountaineers of Wales, and the redshanks of Ireland. **1818** JAMIESON in *Burt's Lett. N. Scotl.* I. 74 *note*, In the Lowlands of Scotland, the rough-footed Highlanders were called red-shanks, from the colour of the red-deer hair. **1893** STEVENSON *Catriona* 182 There might be knives again; these red-shanks are unco grudgeful.

b. (See quot.)

1846 *New Monthly Mag.* Feb. 181 'Yer dinner's ready, sir', screamed a red-shank from the house. [*Ibid.* 180 *note*, A term applied in Connaught to ladies, who consider stockings a superfluity.]

c. A red-stockinged person; a cardinal.

1824 BYRON *Def. Transf.* II. ii. 6 What have we here? A cardinal or two..How the old red-shanks scamper!

2. *Ornith.* **a.** A wading bird (*Totanus calidris*) of the snipe family (*Scolopacidæ*), so called from the colour of its legs. See also RED-LEGS 1.

to run (quot. 1804) *like a redshank* is a common dialect phrase (and is also recorded in N.Z.).

1525 *L'Estrange Househ.-bk.* in *Archæologia* XXV. 487 Item vj plovers..iiij redshancks. **1549** *Compl. Scot.* vi. 39 The rede schank cryit my fut my fut. **1570** LEVINS *Manip.* 24/36 Readshanke, *hæmocopedus.* **1620** VENNER *Via Recta* iii. 64 The Puet, the Red-shanke,..are..to be reiected, as vnwholsome. **1623** CAPT. SMITH *Wks.* (Arb.) II. 629 The gray and greene Plouer, some wilde Ducks and Malards, Coots and Red-Shankes. *a* **1682** SIR T. BROWNE *Tracts* 108 [The description] seems more agreeable unto some kind of Red-shank. **1768** PENNANT *Brit. Zool.* II. 368 Redshank; this species is found on most of our shores; in the winter time it conceals itself in the gutters; and is generally found single, or at most in pairs. **1804** MAR. EDGEWORTH *Ennui* vi, He'll run like a red-shank with the news to the castle. **1843** YARRELL *Brit. Birds* II. 525 Redshanks are not uncommon in Cornwall, Devonshire, and Dorsetshire. **1873** E. WAUGH *Snowed-Up* v. 88 They're off like red-shanks! An' they'n come noan back to-neet, noather. **1891** G. CHAMIER *Philosopher Dick* 466 Without another thought or look behind us we were off like red shanks. **1894** NEWTON *Dict. Birds* 774 The body of the Redshank is almost as big as a Snipe's, but its longer neck, wings and legs make it appear a much larger bird. **1901** W. F. BARRY *Wizard's Knot* vi. 53 Don't be running from us that way like a redshank. **1903** *N.Z. Illustr. Mag.* VIII. 93 They would be off into the bush like redshanks.

b. (See quot. 1894.)

1776 PENNANT *Brit. Zool.* (ed. 4) II. 377 Spotted Redshank... In size it is equal to the greenshank. **1843** YARRELL *Brit. Birds* II. 523 As the white spots on the wings ..are permanent in this bird at all ages and seasons, I have preferred calling it the Spotted Redshank. **1863** *Spring & Summer in Lapland* 349 The dusky redshank..seems a stranger here, but breeds further up in the valley of the Munio. **1894** NEWTON *Dict. Birds* 775 The name Red-shank, prefixed by some epithet as Black, Dusky, or Spotted has also been applied to a larger but allied species—the *Totanus fuscus* of ornithologists.

†c. *Cant.* A duck or drake. *Obs.*

1567 HARMAN *Caveat* 83 A quakinge chete or a red shanke, a drake or ducke. **1725** *New Cant. Dict.* Song 18 On Red-shanks, and Tibs thou shalt ev'ry Day dine.

3. a. A name given to various species of *Polygonum*, esp. *P. persicaria*, the spotted persicaria.

1674–91 RAY *N.C. Words* 57 Redshanks; Arsmart. **1798** NEMNICH *Polygl. Lex.* v. 867 Red Shanks, *Polygonum persicaria.* **1869–** in northern dial. glossaries.

b. Herb Robert, *Geranium Robertianum.*

1757 LISLE *Obs. Husb.* 345 (E.D.S.). **1828** CARR *Craven Gloss.* II. 78.

c. *Sc.* (See quot.)

1810 J. ROBERTSON *Agric. Surv. Kincard.* 376 (Jam.) Should dock-weeds be allowed to remain till they begin to ripen (then called red-shanks) they are not so easily pulled.

4. (See quots.)

1805 YOUNG *Annals Agric.* XLIII. 628 (E.D.D.) The wheat began to change colour, or get into what is called the red shank preparative to ripening. **1891** *Sheffield Gloss.* Suppl. s.v., When the straw is in the red-shank wheat is said to be nearly ripe.

5. *attrib.*, as (sense 1) *red-shank rebel*; **red-shank gambet** = sense 2; **red-shank gull,** the black-headed gull, *Larus ridibundus*; **†red-shank pea,** a variety of field-pea.

c **1650** SIR H. SPOTTISWOODE in Maidment *Spottiswoode Misc.* (1844–5) I. 179 In bloud he made The red-shank rebells wade. **1707** MORTIMER *Husb.* (1721) I. 138 They reckon the Henley grey and the red-shank Pease are the best for never broke-up Ground. **1840** *Cuvier's Anim. Kingd.* 246 A fourth [species].., the Redshank Gambet, is very abundant in Britain. **1885** SWAINSON *Prov. Names Brit. Birds* 209 From the bright vermilion of its feet and legs it is called Red-shank gull (Ireland).

red shift, *sb.* Chiefly *Astr.* Also **red-shift, redshift.** [f. RED *a.* and *sb.* + SHIFT *sb.*] Displacement of spectral lines towards the red end of the spectrum; increase in the wavelength of electromagnetic radiation. Also *fig.*

1923 A. S. EDDINGTON *Math. Theory Relativity* v. 164 The red shift in the spiral nebulae. **1936** *Five Halley Lectures* 17 This telescope should penetrate to distances where the effects of red-shifts are so great that the requisite data will lie well above the threshold. **1958** *Listener* 11 Dec. 971/2 When we look at these distant regions we find that the light is reddened, indicating that the galaxies are receding from us. As far as we can see, the red shift of the most distant nebulae is still increasing linearly with distance. **1967** *Daily Tel.* 30 Jan. 10/4 The gigantic red-shift of quasars is therefore considered proof by some astronomers that they may be as much as six to eight thousand million light years away from our earth. **1971** *Sci. Amer.* May 56/3 Red shifts are commonly expressed as a fraction or percentage obtained by dividing the measured displacement of a line by the wavelength of the undisplaced line. **1973** A. GARNER *Red Shift* 155 Next time it'll be all right, every time, and it isn't. Next time will make up for him—and me. Never...

Galactic. Red shift. The further they go, the faster they leave. The sky's emptying. God, this wind's cold. **1976** *Pract. Electronics* Oct. 793/3 During 1975 two teams of astronomers in the United States recorded a red-shift of z = 0·5240 in the optical spectrum of a quasar. **1979** *Nature* 11 Oct. 498/1 Hyperpolarisation of the membrane causes a blueshift of the spectrum when probe is applied to the inside and a redshift for probe bound to the outer surface.

Hence **red-shifted** *a.*, exhibiting a red shift; also *transf.*; (as a back-formation) **red-shift** *v. trans.*

1963 *Nature* 16 Mar. 1041/1 Some broad lines..may be red-shifted hydrogen lines. **1964** *Listener* 20 Aug. 266/2 Matthews and Greenstein were able to identify the lines of 3C 48, which they found to be red shifted by 37 per cent. **1973** *Nature* 3 Aug. 264/1 As the 3 cm radiation propagates through an expanding Universe it will be redshifted. *Ibid.* 21/28 Dec. 517/1 The report..seems to provide a rare parallel to the visual pigments of the freshwater Osteichthyes, and to raise the question whether its pigment is a porphyropsin or a redshifted rhodopsin. **1976** *Pract. Electronics* Oct. 793/3 They set up their apparatus to scan for the 21 cm line at what could be its redshifted wavelength. **1979** *Nature* 5 July 20/1 The apparent colours of the faint galaxy identifications (presumably at redshifts of about 0·5) are considerably bluer than expected from redshifting the spectrum of nearby giant ellipticals such as M87.

†'**redship.** *Sc. Obs.* [ad. obs. Du. *reedschap* (Kilian), f. *reeden* to set in order, fit out: see REDE *v.*²] Equipment, tackle. Also *attrib.*

1565 *Aberdeen Burgh Reg.* (Jam.), Ane Norroway yaucht, callit the James, with her haill redschip graicht. **1593** *Compt Bk. D. Wedderburne* (S.H.S.) 93 A crear callit the Lamb and hir redschip.

'**redshire, -share,** *a. Metall.* ? *Obs.* [ad. Sw. *rödskör*: see RED-SHORT *a.*, and cf. RED-SEAR; also the forms *cold-share, -shire* under COLD-SHORT. In first quot. associated with SHARE *sb.*] Red-short.

1665 D. DUDLEY *Mettalum Martis* (1854) 30 The Iron thereof made is very Redshare, which is that if a workman should Draw or Forge out a Share mould fit for a Plough in that red heat, it would crack and not be fit for the use of the Husbandsmans Plough or Share. **1674** J. STURDIE in *Phil. Trans.* XVII. 696 Some makes Coldshire-Iron, that is, such as is brittle, when it is Cold; another sort makes Redshire, that is, such as is apt to break if it be hammered, when it is of a dark red Heat. **1794** S. WILLIAMS *Vermont* (1809) II. 361 It does not answer so good a purpose; though it is neither coldshire, nor redshire.

red shirt, redshirt. 1. a. A supporter of Garibaldi, esp. one of the thousand who sailed with him in 1860 to conquer Sicily.

1864 YOUNG & STEVENS *Garibaldi: Life & Times* lxxv. 200 Naples had gone mad with joy: men, women, ragamuffins, priests, Redshirts, ex-Bourbon *sbirri*, *lazzaroni*,..—all lent their voices to..the general cry of '*Viva Garibaldi!*' *Ibid.* lxxvi. 202 Some of them mended their lives when Garibaldi came, and fought well in the ranks of the Redshirts before Capua. [**1868** MARRIOTT *Vest. Chr.* p. xviii, The red shirt of Garibaldi's troops.] **1948** F. FRENAYE tr. *Levi's Christ stopped at Eboli* xvii. 168 When King Franceschiello had to leave Naples.., Garibaldi and his Red Shirts set out to attack him. **1979** *Guardian* 12 June 9/4 It took a march on Rome..—echoes of Garibaldi's thousand Red Shirts—to get water and elementary sewerage installed.

b. In more general use, a revolutionary, an anarchist, a communist.

1889 GUNTER *That Frenchman!* xi, The red-shirts of Messieurs Rochefort and Fleurens are uttering their cries of rage at law and order. **1905** *Daily Chron.* 12 Sept. 3/2 Because I made a stand in my native town for municipal ownership of public utilities, I was branded a 'red-shirt', a 'dynamiter', and an 'Anarchist'. **1911** H. S. HARRISON *Queed* xviii. 234 Queed wrote a stinging little article.. holding up to public scorn journalistic red-shirts who curry-combed the masses. **1934** T. S. ELIOT *Rock* i. 42 Enter *redshirts* in military formation. **1940** G. GREENE *Power & Glory* I. i. 13 You remember this place—before the Red Shirts came?

c. *spec.* A member of a Pathan nationalist organization formed in North-West Province in 1921 and lasting until the creation of Pakistan in 1947; also *attrib.* or as *adj.*

1930 *Civil & Milit. Gaz.* (Lahore) 1 June 1/5 In Mardan and Charsadda..the activities of the 'Red Shirts' have again increased. **1932** *Ann. Reg. 1931* 156 An organisation closely allied with Congress, the 'Red Shirt' Army under Abdul Ghaffar Khan, was a source of much anxiety in the North-west Frontier Province. **1948** G. CUNNINGHAM *Diary* in N. Mitchell *Sir George Cunningham* (1968) vii. 152, I could tell he felt he was on rather weak ground in talking about the Red Shirt activities by the twiddling of his bare toes. **1968** N. MITCHELL *Sir George Cunningham* v. 87 He records a recruiting meeting at Swabi..on 11th February, and the fact that four notorious ex-Red Shirts had publicly given him purses towards any war fund purpose.

2. *U.S.* A college athlete whose course is extended by a year during which he does not take part in university events, in order to develop his skills and extend his period of eligibility at this level of competition. Also *attrib.*, as ***redshirt year***.

1955 *Life* 5 Dec. 144/2 Although he is what the pros call 'redshirt', a player with one more year of college eligibility, five pro clubs are eyeing him. **1970** *Time* 7 Dec. 78 He worked even harder in his sophomore year as a 'redshirt', practicing with the varsity but not playing in any games—so that he would have an additional year of eligibility. **1976** *Honolulu Star-Bull.* 21 Dec. H-2/1 Crowe was coming off a redshirt year last season while Bonup was going through one.

So as *v. trans.*, to keep out of university competition for a year for the above reasons; so '**red-shirting** *vbl. sb.*

1950 *Birmingham* (Ala.) *News* 27 Sept. 35/1 He coached all the juniors and senior linemen and the boys red shirted. *Ibid.* 19 Nov. C1/2 There are not enough players to have a 'B' squad or red shirt promising sophomores. **1958** *Tuscaloosa* (Ala.) *News* 8 Jan. 6/8 An anticipated argument over 'red shirting'—the practice of holding athletes out of competition to prolong their eligibility—failed to develop. **1963** *San Francisco Chron.* 3 Dec. 44 He could have been red-shirted but he was an uncertain commodity last year. **1966** *Time* 14 Oct. 49 They [*sc.* the Big Ten] also are forbidden to 'red-shirt' prospects—putting them on a five-year program, keeping them out of action as sophomores in order to beef them up. **1968** *Daily Progress* (Charlottesville, Va.) 10 Apr. A10 Edwards supported continuation of red-shirting, a common practice that permits an athlete to use four years to complete three years of varsity eligibility.

'**red-short,** *a. Metall.* [ad. Sw. *rödskört* (sc. *jern* iron) neut. of *rödskör*, f. *röd* red + *skör* brittle: cf. COLD-SHORT and see REDSHIRE, -SHARE *a.*] Of iron: Brittle while in a red-hot condition, owing to excess of sulphur in the metal. Cf. HOT-SHORT.

1730, 1773 [see COLD-SHORT]. **1795** PEARSON in *Phil. Trans.* LXXXV. 342 There is another variety called red short, which is malleable when cold, but brittle when ignited. **1824** *Mechanic's Mag.* No. 52. 383 Notwithstanding the superior quality of this iron, the bars made from it were ..so completely red-short, as to drop asunder. **1868** JOYNSON *Metals* 13 The ore also being free from phosphoric acid, the iron was generally red-short. **1884** W. H. GREENWOOD *Steel & Iron* x. 208 Antimony..produces when present in small quantities in malleable iron, a metal which is both cold-short and red-short.

Hence **red-shortness**, the quality or state of being red-short.

1868 JOYNSON *Metals* 14 Where much sulphur is present in the ore, it produces in the iron the quality known as 'red-shortness'. **1874** J. A. PHILLIPS *Elem. Metallurgy* (1887) 323 The exact cause of red-shortness in welded iron is not always very clear.

red-shouldered, *a. Ornith.* Having the shoulder or bend of the wing red, esp. the ***red-shouldered buzzard, falcon,*** or ***hawk*** of N. America (*Buteo lineatus*).

1785 PENNANT *Arctic Zool.* II. 206 Red Shouldered F[alcon]. **1790** WHITE *Voy. N.S. Wales* App. 263 The Red Shouldered Paroquet..*Psittacus Discolor.* **1792** PENNANT *Arctic Zool.* (ed. 2) II. 143 Red-Shouldered Heron. **1809** SHAW *Gen. Zool.* VII. II. 421 Red-Shouldered Oriole. *Oriolus phœniceus.* **1812** WILSON *Amer. Ornith.* VI. 86 Red-Shouldered Hawk. *Falco Lineatus*... The Red-Shouldered Hawk is nineteen inches in length. **1884** *Harper's Mag.* Mar. 622/1 The red-shouldered hawk is a handsome bird.

'**redskin.** Also red-skin. [See RED *a.* 5 c.] **1.** A North American Indian. (Not the preferred term.)

1699 S. SMITH in H. E. Smith *Colonial Days* (1900) 49 Ye firste Meetinge House was solid mayde to withstande ye wicked onsaults of ye Red Skins. **1823** E. JAMES *Long's Exped.* I. 160 The whites will not harm the red-skins when they have them thus in their power. **1851** DIXON *W. Penn* xxiii. (1872) 205 A strong believer in the native virtues of the Redskins, when these savages were treated well. **1890** *Times* 27 Dec. 3/2 After dark the whole band..renewed the attack, Kicking Bear himself leading the redskins.

attrib. **1699** S. SMITH in H. E. Smith *Colonial Days* (1900) 49 My Honoured Father was as Active as ye Red-skin Men and sinewy. **1871** LUBBOCK in *Jrnl. Anthrop. Inst.* (1872) I. 3 Though the Redskin family is constituted in a manner very unlike ours [etc.]. **1883** *Athenæum* 20 Jan. 81/1 A picture of redskin life.

2. A variety of potato.

1908 *Chambers's Jrnl.* Oct. 702/1 The chief products grown are..potatoes... Tasmanian 'redskins' are.. exported. **1973** *Courier & Advertiser* (Dundee) 21 Feb. 2/8 Scandinavia demands Redskin..and Maris Piper.

red snow. 1. Snow reddened by a kind of alga (*Protococcus nivalis*) common in Arctic and Alpine regions.

1678 *Phil. Trans.* XIII. 976 On St. Josephs day, upon the Mountains call'd Le Langhe, there fell..a great quantity of red, or if you please of bloody Snow. **1820** BAUER in *Ibid.* CX. 165 The fungi, which constitute the colouring matter of the red snow, discovered in Baffin's Bay..1818. **1820** *Edin. Phil. Jrnl.* III. 307 (*heading*) Observations on the red snow of Mount St. Bernard. *Ibid.*, Some imperfect observations on the red snow of the Alps were made by M. Saussure in 1778, and the result of them appeared in the 3d volume of his Travels. **1866** *Chambers' Encycl.* s.v., It is not impossible that animal as well as vegetable life may exist in red snow, and that real animalcules may have been observed. **1894** J. W. MOORE *Meteorol.* xx. 236 Red snow and green snow have been observed in the Arctic Regions and elsewhere. **1912** *Q. Jrnl. R. Meteorol. Soc.* XXXVIII. 220 The red snow first attracted attention because the hoof-prints of the pack animals..were observed to be 'splotched with red as if the snow-crust had cut the mules feet and dyed the snow with drops of blood'. **1933** E. HAWKS *Bk. of Air & Water Wonders* vii. 145 Red snow was known to Pliny, and was attributed by him to a dust with which the snow became covered after it had lain for some time on the ground... The phenomenon of red snow is due to the presence of some genus of algæ, scientifically known as *Protococcus nivalis.* **1973** *Islander* (Victoria, B.C.) 17 June 5/2 The three explorers saw white ptarmigan, and the unique 'red snow' of the area.

2. *transf.* The alga which gives a red colouring to snow.

1825 CARMICHAEL in *App. Parry's Jrnl. 2nd Voy.* 429 On the whole, I should think..that you may safely arrange the Red Snow among the *Palmellæ.* **1845** DARWIN *Voy. Nat.* xv. (1890) 345 On several patches of the snow I found the *Protococcus nivalis*, or red snow. **1861** H. MACMILLAN *Footn. fr. Page Nature* 145 Red snow..has been discovered spreading over decayed leaves and mosses on the borders of small lakes.

3. *attrib.*, as ***red-snow shower***; **red-snow alga** or **plant** = sense 2.

1826 in Loudon *Encycl. Plants* 928 The most remarkable red-snow shower was that which fell..[in] March 1823,..in Tuscany. *Ibid.*, The Lepraria Kermesina, which..is considered only a particular state of the red-snow plant itself. **1866** *Chambers' Encycl.* s.v., The red snow plant consists, in its mature state, of brilliant globules like fine garnets, seated on, but not immersed in, a gelatinous mass. **1869** SPENCER *Princ. Psychol.* (1872) I. III. ii. 295 Of those classed with the vegetal kingdom, may be instanced the.. red snow alga.

red spider. A small red spider-like mite (*Tetranychus* or *Acarus telarius*) infesting plants, especially in hothouses. (See also quot. 1824.)

1646 SIR T. BROWNE *Pseud. Ep.* III. xxv. Table, Of the Tainct or small red Spider. **1793** *Trans. Soc. Arts* (ed. 2) V. 58 Destroying the Red Spider and other noxious insects. **1816** KIRBY & SP. *Entomol.* (1843) I. 161 The red-spider (*Erythræus telarius*) spinning its web over the under surface of the leaves draws out their juices with its rostrum. **1824** LOUDON *Encycl. Gardening* (ed. 2) §2271 The red spider is the *Acarus telarius*, and the same name is also applied by gardeners to the scarlet acarus (*A. holosericeus*), the only two British species of the genus which infest plants. **1871** H. MACMILLAN *True Vine* v. 232 In this country, the greatest pest of the vinery is the little red spider, whose movements over the leaves and fruit are exceedingly nimble.

red spot. 1. *Astr.* = *great red spot* s.v. GREAT *a.* 20.

1879 *Monthly Notices R. Astron. Soc.* XL. 86 The very remarkable red spot which has attracted the attention of every observer during the present opposition. **1962** *Listener* 26 July 136/1 After 1882 the Red Spot began to fade, and since then it has undergone various changes. **1977** *Times Educ. Suppl.* 21 Oct. 21/2 Neither is it true to say that with regard to the Red Spot on Jupiter, 'scientists do not know what causes it'.

2. A defect of cheese in which there are fine red spots throughout.

[**1900** *Bull. N.Y. Agric. Exper. Station* No. 183. 189 The evidence seems to be conclusive that the red spots are produced by the growth of a minute plant which finds its way into the curd before it is put to press.] **1932** *Discovery* Feb. 59/2 The trouble in cheese known as 'open-ness' is being investigated and red spot in cheese and oiliness in butter have been studied with some success. **1955** J. G. DAVIS *Dict. Dairying* (ed. 2) 662 The peculiar fault known as 'red spot' in Cheddar cheese is due to an organism biochemically resembling the mastitis streptococcus which apparently lives a saprophytic existence in the udders of certain cows.

red-spotted, *a.* Marked with red spots.

1713 PETIVER *Aquat. Anim. Amb.* 1/1 *Cancer ruber*..Red spotted Crab. **1782** LATHAM *Gen. Synopsis Birds* I. II. 736 Red spotted Creeper, *Certhia cruentata* (Linn.).. Its native place is Bengal. **1802** SHAW *Gen. Zool.* III. II. 496 Red-Spotted snake. *Coluber Coccineus*... Black snake, with yellow back spotted with red. **1883** *Century Mag.* Dec. 163/2 That beautiful inhabitant of fresh water, the red-spotted trout.

redstart ('rɛdstɑːt). *Ornith.* [f. RED *a.* + START (ME. *stert*, OE. *steort*) tail: cf. RED-TAIL 1. Parallel forms are Du. *roodstaartje*, Flem. *-steertje* (†*-steertken*), Da. and Sw. *rödstjert*, G. *rotsterz*.]

1. a. A small European and North African bird belonging to the genus *Phœnicurus* of the family Turdidæ, esp. *P. phœnicurus*, so named from its red tail, which it has a habit of moving quickly from side to side.

1570 LEVINS *Manip.* 33/41 Redstarte, *ruticilla.* **1632** SHERWOOD, The Redstert, or Redtaile, *rossignol de muraille, rubienne.* **1657** TOMLINSON *Renou's Disp.* To Rdr. c 2 Who can determine what becomes of Cranes, Cuckoes,..Red-starts, that some are seen onely in Summer, some in Winter? **1678** PHILLIPS (ed. 4), *Redstert* (Rubicilla), a certain Bird so called from its red tail. **1774** G. WHITE *Selborne* lx, The song of the redstart is superior, though somewhat like that of the whitethroat. **1829** E. JESSE *Jrnl. Naturalist* 204 We have no bird more assiduous in attentions to their young than the red-start. **1840** *Cuvier's Anim. Kingd.* 190 The White-fronted Redstart..is a common summer visitant in many parts of Britain. **1884** JEFFERIES in *Chamb. Jrnl.* 1 Mar. 131/1 A brightly coloured bird, the redstart, appears suddenly in spring. **1925** C. E. RAVEN *In Praise of Birds* vi. 76 Not far off was a Redstart's nest in a piece of old iron piping. **1950** J. BUXTON *Redstart* xi. 132 Am I to describe as redstarts only those species which are placed in the genus *Phoenicurus*? **1973** T. SOPER *New Bird Table Bk.* iii. 31 Redstarts and woodpeckers are hole-nesters.

b. ***black redstart***, a related species, *Ruticilla titys*, occurring in southern England and common on the European continent.

1836 EYTON *Rarer Brit. Birds* 7 Black Redstart. *Ficedula Tithys.* This Redstart inhabits chiefly the warmer parts of Europe. **1894** NEWTON *Dict. Birds* 776 The males of the Black Redstart seem to be more than one year in acquiring their full plumage.

c. *attrib.* with *warbler* (= prec. senses).

1817 SHAW *Gen. Zool.* X. II. 670 Redstart Warbler. (*Sylvia Phœnicurus.*) *Ibid.* 673 Grey Redstart Warbler. (*Sylvia Gibraltariensis.*)

2. An American fly-catching warbler, *Setophaga ruticilla*, outwardly resembling the common European redstart but generically distinct from it.

1731 M. CATESBY *Nat. Hist. Carolina* I. 67 The Red-Start... These Birds frequent the shady Woods of Virginia. **1796** MORSE *Amer. Geog.* I. 211 Red Start, *Ruticilla Americana*. **1808** WILSON *Amer. Ornith.* I. 105 The American Redstart builds frequently in low bushes. **1812** *Ibid.* V. 119 The Redstart extends very generally over the United States. **1831** AUDUBON *Ornith. Biog.* I. 202 The insect secured, the lovely Redstart reascends, perches, and sings a different note. **1894** NEWTON *Dict. Birds* 777 The American Redstart.., belonging to the purely New-World Family *Mniotiltidæ*, and to a genus which contains about a dozen species. **1947** R. T. PETERSON *Field Guide to Birds* (ed. 2) 208 The Redstart is one of the most butterfly-like of birds.

†**3.** (See quot.) *Obs.*

1738 ALBIN *Nat. Hist. Birds* III. 52 This Bird was brought from Bengall in the year 1734, without any Name being affixt to it;.. I shall beg leave to call it by the Name of the Bengall Redstart.

'red-streak. Also 7 -strake.

1. A red-streaked apple formerly highly esteemed for making cider.

1664 EVELYN *Pomona* i. 6 Thus the famous Red-strake of Hereford-shire is a pure Wilding, and within the memory of some now living surnamed the Scudamores Crab. **1676** WORLIDGE *Cyder* (1691) 209 Above all Cider-fruit, the Redstreak hath obtain'd the preference. **1708** J. PHILIPS *Cyder* I. 32 Let every Tree in every Garden own The Red-Streak as supream. **1750** SHENSTONE *Rural Elegance* 31 Is not the red-streak's future juice The source of your delight? **1807** VANCOUVER *Agric. Devon* (1813) 238 The species called the red-streak, is mostly preferred; but of late years, these orchards have been much subject to a blight. **1875** F. J. SCUDAMORE *Day Dreams* 16 We began to pass through apple-orchards, in which the 'redstreak' flourished in its native soil.

b. The cider made from this. (Cf. 3.)

1671 *Phil. Trans.* VI. 2129, I have had as good Red-strake as ever I drank in any place. **1709** E. SMITH *Poem J. Philips* 64 Redstreak he quaffs beneath the Chianti Vine, Gives Tuscan yearly for thy Scud'more's Wine. **1778** *Eng. Gazetteer* (ed. 2) s.v. *South-Hams*, That noble rough cyder which is generally preferred to the soft sickly Hereford redstreak.

2. *transf.* A girl with red cheeks.

1771 SMOLLETT *Humph. Cl.* 26 June, Then turning to Liddy, he added—'What say you, my pretty Redstreak?' **1776** R. GRAVES *Euphrosyne* (1776) VI. 219 The rural lass with ruddy cheeks, The Redstreak we may name.

3. *attrib.*, as ***red-streak apple, cider, face***.

1664 EVELYN *Pomona* 25 So does the Red-strake-Cider of the Vale excell any other Cider of the forcible soil. *Ibid.* 27 M. Philips.. shewed me a very fair large Red-strake apple. **1712** W. ROGERS *Voy.* (1718) 12, I gave him a dozen bottles of Red-Streak Cyder. **1712** ARBUTHNOT *John Bull* I. xii, That redstreak country face. **1797** *Encycl. Brit.* (ed. 3) XVI. 721/1 Those most esteemed for cyder are.. the redstreak apple, the whitsour [etc.].

Hence †**red-streaked** *a.*, made from red-streaks.

For other uses of the comb., see RED *a.* 14 a, 14 b.

1664 EVELYN *Pomona* 26 Red-cheek'd and Red-strak'd Musts of several kinds. *Ibid.*, A richer Red-strak'd-cider of a.. fulvous or ruddy colour.

red-tail ('rɛdteɪl).

1. = REDSTART 1 (and 1 b).

1552 ELYOT, *Ruticilla*, a little birde called a red tayle. **1611** COTGR., *Rubienne*, the Red-taile, or Starke; a small bird. **1661** LOVELL *Hist. Anim. & Min.* Introd., Bunting, redtaile. **1736** AINSWORTH *Lat. Dict.* s.v. *Red*, A red tail, *Phoenicurus*. **1783** LATHAM *Gen. Synopsis Birds* II. II. 425 Red Tail. *Motacilla erithacus*. A Trifle bigger than the Redstart. **1802** MONTAGU *Ornith. Dict.* (1831) 412 *Redstart*... Provincial. —Redtail. Brantail. Firetail. **1869–** in dial. glossaries (Northumbld., Lonsd., E. Anglia, Som.). **1896** MORRIS & TEGETMEIER *Nests Brit. Birds* II. 66 Black Redstart.—Black Red-Tail.

b. *U.S.* The red-tailed buzzard (*Buteo borealis*).

1812 WILSON *Amer. Ornith.* VI. 75 Early next morning the unfortunate Red-tail was found a prisoner.

2. †**a.** The rudd. *Obs.* **b.** A name of several American fishes (see quots.).

1740 R. BROOKES *Art of Angling* Index, The Rud or Red-tail. **1876** GOODE in *Smithson. Coll.* (1877) XIII. v. 15 *Carassius auratus*.. Red-tail. **1877** JORDAN *Ibid.* IX. 29 *note*, Vulgar names [of Kentuckian Shiner]: Indian Chub, Red-tail, Shiner. *Ibid.* 37 *note*, Vulgar names [of Red-tail Sucker]: Red-horse, Red-tail, Horse-fish [etc.].

3. *attrib.*, as ***red-tail hawk, lizard, parrot, sucker, warbler***.

1802 SHAW *Gen. Zool.* III. I. 244 Red-tail Lizard. *Lacerta Cruenta*. **1817** *Ibid.* X. II. 674 Red-Tail Warbler (*Sylvia Erithracus*). **1820** RAFINESQUE in *Smithson. Coll.* (1877) XIII. IX. 37 Red-tail Sucker, *Catostomus Erythrurus*. **1894** *Outing* (U.S.) XXIII. 406/1 The red-tail hawk has his story of a cold wintry day. **1897** MARY KINGSLEY *W. Africa* 58 The wearer's hair aglow with red-tail parrots' feathers.

red-tailed, *a.* Having a red tail.

red-tailed buzzard or ***hawk***, a common North American hawk; the upper side of the tail is red in the adult bird.

1601 SHAKS. *All's Well* IV. v. 7 That red-tail'd humble Bee I speake of. **1611** COTGR., *Rosse*,.. a small red-tayld lake-fish. **1771** PENNANT *Synopsis Quadrup.* 133 Red-tailed Monkey:.. rump and half the tail deep orange-colored, almost red. **1785** LATHAM *Gen. Synopsis Birds* III. II. 259 Red-Tailed Gallinule... This species inhabits Ceylon. **1807–8** W. IRVING *Salmag.* (1824) 335 The chattering of the red-tailed parrot. **1812** WILSON *Amer. Ornith.* VI. 75 The Red-tailed Hawk is most frequently seen in the lower parts of Pennsylvania during the severity of winter. **1824** SHAW *Gen. Zool.* XII. I. 222 Red-tailed Crake (*Ortygometra phœnicura*). **1839** AUDUBON *Synopsis Birds N. Amer.* 6 *Buteo borealis*. Red-tailed Buzzard. Red-tailed Hawk. **1857** DUFFERIN *Lett. High Lat.* 199 Pirouetting on the deck below with a red-tailed demon.

red-tape, red tape.

a. Tape of a red colour such as is commonly used in securing legal and official documents. Hence **b.** Excessive formality or attention to routine; rigid or mechanical adherence to rules and regulations.

1696–1715 *Maryland Laws* IV. (1723) 11 The Map.. upon the Backside thereof sealed with his Excellency's Seal at Arms on a Red Cross with Red Tape. **1736** LD. HERVEY *Poet. Epistle to Queen* in *Mem.* (1848) II. 156 Let Wilmington, with grave, contracted brow, Red tape and wisdom at the Council show. **1814** SCOTT *Wav.* lxxi, Drawing from his pocket a budget of papers, and untying the red tape. **1837** C. G. F. GORE *Stokeshill Place* I. vii. 142 My dear, you mistake John Barnsley... Dearly as he loves a bit of red tape, you never saw him try to inspire any other man with the love of business. **1839–40** W. IRVING *Wolfert's R.* (1855) 274 His brain was little better than red tape and parchment. **1869** LONGF. in *Life* (1891) III. 141 All the morning at the custom-house, plagued with red tape. **1873** SPENCER *Stud. Sociol.* vii. 170 After ceaseless ridicule of red-tape, the petition is for more red-tape. **1938** *Daily Progress* (Charlottesville, Va.) 18 Aug. 4/1 The trial time has been about cut in half by the preliminary clearing away of red tape. **1956** A. WILSON *Anglo-Saxon Attitudes* I. i. 4 He resigned from the Labour Party and the House of Commons to fight your battle without the restraints of red tape. **1977** *Time* 14 Feb. 24/3 Straw-bossing the operation was Energy Chief James Schlesinger, who helped draft the natural gas bill and cut red tape to get gas supplies moving.

attrib. and *Comb.* **1838** LYTTON *Alice* III. i, The men of more dazzling genius began to sneer at the red-tape minister as a mere official manager of details. **1840** CARLYLE *Heroes* (1858) 353 Keep your red-tape clerks, your influentialities, your important businesses. **1863** P. BARRY *Dockyard Econ.* 144 Those who framed the red-tape code were not men of business. **1897** *Dublin Rev.* Oct. 304 The regions of red-tape-tied officialism.

Hence **red-taped** *a.*, tied with red tape; affected with the spirit of red-tape; also, restricted by red-tape. **red-'tapedom**, the sphere or spirit of red-tape. **red-'taper** = RED-TAPIST. **red-'tapery** = RED-TAPISM. **red-'tap(e)y** *a.* [-Y¹] = RED-TAPISH *a.* **red-'tapified** *a.*, characterized by red-tape.

1835 MARRYAT *Olla Podr.* vii, Documents, numbered, scheduled, and *red-taped. **1890** *Nature* 29 May 106/2 The unimpressionable mind of the red-taped official. **1928** E. E. CUMMINGS *Enormous Room* iv. 61 The whole rotten red-taped Croix Rouge. **1954** *Sun* (Baltimore) 19 July 26/6 Red-taped—Jimmy Kennedy.. wants to work but can't. **1850** *Times* 31 Aug. 4/4 Mr. Carlyle has, we know, denounced *red-tapedom in all its forms. **1845** DISRAELI *Sybil* (1863) 33 Calling at clubs, closeted with *red-tapers. **1893** *Ch. Times* 20 Oct. 1065/1 The clergyman who refuses .. is a miserable red-taper. **1831** *Fraser's Mag.* III. 654 These were the great heroes of the *red-tapery. **1884** *Nonconf. & Indep.* 14 Feb. 153/1 [To] lessen the rates and provide an antidote to red-tapery in education. **1889** *Columbus* (Ohio) *Dispatch* 21 Jan., Whether the newspaper reports are extravagant, or the official reports are too *red-tapy or timid,.. it is hard to say. **1905** D. SLADEN *Playing the Game* iv. 37 He'll be more red-tapey than ever, so as not to let the Japanese suspect anything. **1975** *Daily Tel.* 21 July 5/8 There is.. 'a strictly Christian name approach' so that they are as different as possible to the 'red-tapey concept' of the social services. **1895** *Longm. Mag.* Aug. 386, I had not.. exaggerated the.. *redtapefied way in which things were done.

red tapeworm. *joc.* [Blend of RED-TAPE and TAPEWORM.] Red-tapism or a red-tapist regarded as parasitic or as a disease of society.

1917 *Times* 26 Oct. 8/3 Send the papers to the Christchurch Museum in New Zealand as an example of the Red Tape-worm of England. **1918** *Studies* Dec. 664 The State ought to provide it; but the mechanism is clogged by the red-tapeworm. **1939** *Amer. Speech* XIV. 6 Others refer disparagingly to 'poluticians',.. and 'red tapeworms'.

red-'tapish, *a.* [f. RED-TAPE, RED TAPE + -ISH.] Characterized or infected by red-tapism.

1850 CARLYLE *Latter-d. Pamph.* iii. (1872) 94 One Intellect still really human, and not redtapish. **1855** *Fraser's Mag.* LI. 635 Close bodies tend to become narrow and red-tapish.

red-'tapism. Also -tapeism. [f. as prec. + -ISM.] The spirit or system of red-tape.

1855 (*title*) Red-tapeism; its cause, by one behind the scenes. **1858** J. B. NORTON *Topics* 79 There appears to have prevailed the usual red-tapeism and circumlocution. **1882** M. WILLIAMS *Leaves Life* (1890) II. 296 Was there ever a greater piece of red-tapism than the letter which has been read from the Home Office?

red-'tapist. Also -tapeist. [f. as prec. + -IST.] One who adheres strictly or mechanically to official routine.

1842 R. FORD in Knapp *Life Borrow* (1899) II. App. i. 315 Red-tapists hatched in the hotbeds of jobbery. **1856** DORAN *Knights & Days* xxii. 374 There is a good deal of the red-tapist in our moralist after all. **1884** *Fortn. Rev.* June 817 The official red-tapeists who seek to carry minutes, memoranda, and returns into every department of life.

red-throated, *a. Ornith.* Having a red throat.

1743 G. EDWARDS *Nat. Hist. Birds* I. I. 38 Red-throated Huming Bird. **1752** J. HILL *Hist. Anim.* 365 The red-throated Parrot; this is an extreamely beautiful species; it is of the size of a large pigeon. **1781** LATHAM *Gen. Synopsis Birds* I. I. 97 Red-throated Falcon... Inhabits Cayenne, and other parts of South America. **1809** SHAW *Zool. Lect.* I. v. 187 One of the most common, as well as one of the most beautiful of all the Humming-birds is the *Trochilus Colubris* or red-throated Humming-bird. **1896** MORRIS & TEGETMEIER *Nests Brit. Birds* I. 152 The only claim of the Red-throated Pipit to be considered as a British bird [etc.].

b. *esp.* **red-throated diver,** †**ducker,** or **loon** (see quots. and DIVER 2 a).

1747 G. EDWARDS *Nat. Hist. Birds* I. II. 97 Red-throated Ducker or Loon. **1768** PENNANT *Brit. Zool.* II. 415 The Red throated Diver. **1840** *Cuvier's Anim. Kingd.* 253 The Red-throated Loon.. [is] still smaller and much commoner. **1843** YARRELL *Brit. Birds* III. 337 The Red-throated Diver is the smallest species of the genus, as well as the most common. **1893** NEWTON *Dict. Birds* 152 The common species of *Colymbus* is *C. septentrionalis*, known as the Red-throated Diver from an elongated patch of dark bay colour which distinguishes the throat of the adult in summer-dress.

'red-top.

1. *attrib.* Having a red top; red-topped.

c **1800** T. GIBBS *Catal. Seeds*, Red-top Turnip. **1840** J. BUEL *Farmer's Companion* 331/1 Red-top grass. **1884** E. P. ROE in *Harper's Mag.* July 247/1 They began with red-top clover.

2. *N. Amer.* One of several pasture grasses, esp. *Agrostis stolonifera* or one of its varieties. Also *attrib.* ***false red-top*** (see quots.). ***tall red-top***, a tall reddish grass, *Triodia cuprea*.

1790 S. DEANE *New-England Farmer* 115/1 The red top grass is so natural to every soil in this country, that all our old fields.. are full of it. **1819** WARDEN *United States* II. 8 The grasses are: White clover, white top and red top. **1829** LOUDON *Encycl. Plants* 65 *Tricuspis*... This grass is called Red-top in the Southern States of N. America. **1840** J. BUEL *Farmer's Companion* 228 Red-top, the herds-grass of the middle and southern States.. is indigenous, perennial, and valuable for hay and pasture. **1846–50** A. WOOD *Class-bk. Bot.* 613 *Tricuspis seslerioides*. False Red-top. *Ibid.* 614 *Poa serotina*. Meadow Red-top. **1856, 1889** [see FINETOP]. **1860** DARLINGTON *Amer. Weeds*, etc. 382 *Poa serotina*, Late Poa. Fowl Meadow Grass. False Red-top. **1891** M. E. WILKINS *Humble Romance* 92 The whole yard.. [was] covered with a tall waving crop of red-top. **1937** *Range Plant Handbk.* (Forest Service, U.S. Dept. Agric.) G8 It seems preferable to use redtop, as a generic name for most of the native range species of *Agrostis*. **1958** J. G. MACGREGOR *North-West of 16* v. 65 In bays, mostly on the west side and shaded from the afternoon sun, grew Red Top, the glory of the wild hay meadows. In places it was six feet high. **1972** *Daily Colonist* (Victoria, B.C.) 9 Mar. 5/3 The birds [*sc.* prairie chickens] would survive when redtop grass was raised, since it was combined in midsummer.

3. A variety of turnip.

c **1830** *Glouc. Farm Rep.* 6 in *Lib. Usef. Kn., Husb.* III, About one-third of the whole crop consists of Swedish turnips,.. the remainder of the white Norfolk and the red-tops.

red-topped: see RED *a.* 14 a, b, c.

reduable, variant of REDEVABLE *a. Obs.*

†**re'dub,** *sb. Obs. rare*⁻¹. In 6 redoube. [f. the vb., or ad. F. *radoub* (16th c. in Godef. *Compl.*).] Remedy, improvement.

1549 EDW. VI in Strype *Eccl. Mem.* (1721) II. I. xxv. 211 [The King] thought good.. straightly to charge and command him that.. he should have an earnest and special regard to the redoube of these things.

†**re'dub,** *v. Obs.* Also 6 redubb(e, -doub(e, -do(u)bbe. [ad. AF. *redubber* (13th c., hence also AL. *redubbare*), f. *re-* RE- + *dubber* DUB *v.*¹ Cf. F. *radouber* (15th c.). See also REDOUBLE *v.*³

The word is very frequent in 16th c. English, esp. in state papers and other official documents.]

1. *trans.* To repair or restore (a damaged thing).

1522 *St. Papers Hen. VIII* (1830) I. 113 Many of your shippes were disgarnysshed of their mastes, cables, ankers, and other takelyng, in such wise that fewe or none of theym can be sufficiently redubbed or furnisshed to do any service on the see for this yere. **1536** *Ibid.* 470 That our honour, touched by this your assemblee and insurrection, may.. again be redubbed, to the knowleage of the world.

2. To put right, remedy, improve (a bad state of things).

1528 GARDINER in Pocock *Rec. Ref.* I. 109 If every one of their college had with such good heart regarded that calamity.. it had been much less and sooner redubbed. *a* **1547** SURREY *Æneid* IV. 444 If desteny.. would have permitted me After my wil my sorrow to redoub. **1562** CHALONER in Froude *Hist. Eng.* (1863) VII. v. 440 *note*, I told him that the state of things was easely so redubbed, as he should haue cause.. to be of another opinion.

3. To make up for, amend, correct (a mistake, fault, etc.).

1537 CROMWELL in Merriman *Life & Lett.* (1902) II. 110 Redubbe yt my lord in the Just punyshment of his Traytours Carkas. **1542** in *Lett. & Pap. Hen. VIII*, XVII. 592 A wise grave man, to redubbe the lightness of your late Governour. **1548** UDALL *Erasm. Par. Luke* Pref. 5 b, This imperfeccion I haue to my litle power so laboured to redoub.

4. To remedy, redress (something suffered).

1547 EDW. VI *Injunct.* §18 No man shall.. redubbe and requite one wronge with another, or be his awne judge. **1553** *Act 1 Mary* Sess. 2 c. 1 §2 Unlesse so great an iniustice .. be redubbed,.. plagues and strokes are like to increase. **1568** GRAFTON *Chron.* II. 1353 A dishonor where-with this realm shall be blotted, vntyll God shall giue power to redubbe it with some like requitall to the French.

b. To requite (a person) *with* something. Also with double obj. *rare.*

1557–8 PHAER *Æneid* VI. Rj, O gods redubbe them vengeance iust. **1565** JEWEL *Def. Apol.* (1611) 459 Yet hitherto we haue not redubbed you with any one Lie.

5. To make up, restore (money expended).

1536 Cromwell in Merriman *Life & Lett.* (1902) II. 48 Suche a revenue..as maye..in time of peax bothe redubbe that which shalbe in warre expended [etc.].

Hence †**re'dubbing** *vbl. sb. Obs.*

1527 Wolsey in *St. Papers Hen. VIII* (1830) I. 228 Praying God that I may have grace..for the redubbing of the premisses. 1547 *Privy Council Acts* (1890) II. 537 It may partely tende to a redobbinge of that they have done. 1555 J. Proctor *Hist. Wyat's Rebell.* 41 What was to be done for the redubbing of that vnhappie chaunce?

re'dubber. *Obs.* exc. *Hist.* Also -our, -or. [ad. AF. *redubbour, redobeour* (Britton), agent-n. f. *redubber* to redub. App. never actually current as an Eng. word.] (See quots.)

[1284 *Act 12 Edw. I* (*Stat. Wallie*) c. 4 De Redobatoribus [*v.r.* Redubatoribus] pannorum furatorum, eos in novam formam redigentibus et veterem mutantibus. 1292 Britton I. xxx. §3 De redubbours achatauntz a escient dras emblez, et les attirent en autre fourme.]

1616 Bullokar *Eng. Expos.*, *Redobbour*, he that wittengly buieth stollen cloth, and turneth it into some other fashion. 1656 Blount *Glossogr.*, *Redubbours*, are those that buy cloth, which they know to be stoln, and turn it into some other form or fashion. 1704 J. Harris *Lex. Techn.* I, *Redubbor*. 1823 Crabb *Technol. Dict.*, *Redubber*. 1865 Nichols *Britton* I. 83 *note*, It is forbidden that any redubber of clothes..shall dwell elsewhere than in cities or boroughs.

redubble, obs. form of redouble *v.*

†**re'duce,** *sb. Obs.*⁻¹ [f. next.] Reduction.

1549 Edw. VI in Foxe *A. & M.* (1563) 692/1 That from hencefourth ye haue an earnest & special regard to the reduce of these things.

reduce (rɪ'dju:s), *v.* Also 5 reduyse, 5–7 reduse. [ad. L. *redūcĕre* to bring back, restore, replace, f. *re-* re- + *dūcĕre* to lead, bring. Cf. F. *reduire* (14th c., Oresme) and †*reducer* (15th c.), Sp. *reducir*, It. *ridurre*.]

The original sense of the word, 'to bring back', has now almost entirely disappeared, the prominent modern sense being 'to bring down' or 'to diminish'. A clear arrangement of the various uses (many of them found only in the language of the 15–17th centuries) is rendered difficult by the extent to which the different shades of meaning tend to pass into or include each other.

I. *trans.* †**1. a.** To bring back, recall (a thing or person) *to* one's memory, mind, etc. *Obs.* (Common in 16th c.)

c 1375 *Sc. Troy-bk.* (Horstmann) II. 2973 Redusand to his fresche memore His deidly dreme, he saw before. 1432–50 tr. *Higden* (Rolls) IV. 383 Leste that he scholde reduce to his mynde the dethe of his sonne by the siȝhte of theyme. 1513 Douglas *Æneis* VII. Prol. 45 Ane similitude of hell, Reducyng to our mynd..Goustly schaddois of eild and grisly deid. 1559 in Knox *Hist. Ref.* Wks. 1846 I. 437 It will pleise your Grace reduce to your remembrance, how..we required [etc.]. 1594 Peele *Battle of Alcazar* III. iv, So freshly to my mind Hath this young prince reduced his father's wrong. 1624 Wotton *Archit.* II. in *Reliq.* (1672) 66 Reducing often to my memory that conceit of the Roman Stoick.

†**b.** To bring back, recall (the mind, thoughts, etc.) *from* or *to* a subject. Also without const. *Obs.*

1432–50 tr. *Higden* (Rolls) III. 205 His disciples cowthe reduce theire myndes from wickede thouȝhtes thro musike and songe. 1563 Foxe *A. & M.* 403/1 Luther diligently reduced the mindes of men to the Sonne of God. *a* 1633 Austin *Medit.* (1635) 292 Then cease,..And with these words reduce thy Thoughts that Roame. 1655 Stanley *Hist. Philos.* II. (1701) 65/2 Pericles..could easily reduce the exercise of his mind from secret abstrusive things to publick popular causes. 1700 Prior *Carmen Sec.* 317 To Janus' Altars, and the numerous Throng,..Ambitious Muse reduce the roving Song. 1706 *Reflex. upon Ridic.* 58 Whatever digressions I made, he still reduc'd the discourse to the same subject.

†**c.** To bring (one) back *to* a recollection of something. *Obs. rare*⁻¹.

1541 R. Copland *Galyen's Terap.* 2 F iij, He reduceth vs to mynde of that he hath sayde before.

†**2.** To lead or bring back (a person) *to, into, from*, etc. a place or way, or *to* a person. *Obs.*

a. In figurative context. (Common in 16–17th c.)

c 1400 *Apol. Loll.* 1 Preying also ilke man to reduce me in to þe riȝt wey,..if I haue gon beside þe wey. *a* 1535 Fisher *Wks.* (E.E.T.S.) 439 So must yᵉ heretickes be reduced vnto yᵉ wayes of yᵉ churche. 1563 Grindal *Rem.* (Parker Soc.) 263 Excommunication..is the ordinary mean..to reduce men to God. 1641 Milton *Prel. Episc.* Wks. (1851) 74 Doing my utmost endeavour..to reduce them to their firme stations under the standard of the Gospell. 1678 R. Barclay *Apol. Quakers* i. 15 He that Errs in the Entrance is not so easily reduced again into the Right Way. 1726–31 Tindal tr. *Rapin's Hist. Eng.* XVII. (1743) II. 52 Their attempt to reduce the Protestants within the Pale of the Romish Church.

absol. 1650 W. Brough *Sacr. Princ.* (1659) 473 This..Reduces to a Paradise both of Joy and Innocence.

b. In literal sense.

1483 Caxton *Gold. Leg.* 54/1 God..shal reduce and brynge you agayn unto the londe of your faders. 1513 Douglas *Æneis* VI. ii. 84 Gif Orpheus mycht reduce agane ..From hell his spousis gost. 1563 Golding *Cæsar* VI. (1565) 174 Wyth the losse of two cohorts he reduced the rest to Duracort. *a* 1636 Fitz-Geffray *Compass. Captives* i. (1637) 19 Extend your charity..towards the redeeming and reducing them home. *a* 1677 Barrow *Wks.* (1830) I. 276 Blessed be God, who..did reduce him to his country. *a* 1727 Newton *Chronol. Amended* ii. (1728) 223 Bacchus appeased him with wine, and reduced him back into heaven.

c. (Without const.) To bring back again.

1579 Lyly *Euphues* (Arb.) 91 For all his trauayle he reduced (I cannot say reclaymed) but a straggeler. 1609 Bible (Douay) *2 Kings* xix. 10 How long are you stil, and reduce not the king? 1642 Sir E. Dering *Sp. on Relig.* xvi. 83 Reduce, replant our Bishop President. 1684 tr. *Bonet's Merc. Compit.* Pref. 1 Mercury's Statue was placed in the Cross-ways, to guide Men in the right way, and to reduce them that were out.

†**3.** To bring (a thing) back *to* or *into* a place; also *Sc.*, to bring (coin) in again to the mint. *Obs.*

1432–50 tr. *Higden* (Rolls) VIII. 488 Newe statutes were ordeynede..of the staple to be reducede from Mirbonrach to Caleys. 1581 *Reg. Privy Council Scot.* Ser. I. III. 463 The late silver cunyie..sould be reducit and brocht in agane, to be cunyeit of new. 1588 D. Rogers in Ellis *Orig. Lett.* Ser. II. III. 152 He causeth manie superstitious and popish ceremonies to be reduced into the Church. 1627 Sybthorpe *Apostol. Obed.* 20 So the papists lye at waite..to reduce superstition into England.

†**4. a.** To take back, refer (a thing) *to* its origin, author, etc. *Obs.*

c 1450 tr. *De Imitatione* III. lix. 139 Grace reduciþ all þinges to god, of whom þei welliþ oute groundely & originaly. 1607–12 Bacon *Ess.*, *Great Place* (Arb.) 284 Reduce thinges to the first Institucion, and observe wherein and how they have degenerate. 1660 R. Coke *Power & Subj.* 47 All regular motions and actions may be reduced to one certain beginning.

†**b.** To carry back in time. *Obs. rare*⁻¹.

a 1619 Fotherby *Atheom.* II. xii. §4 (1622) 342 But Plutarch himselfe reduceth it higher; not allowing of any mortall man to bee the first inuentor.

5. To bring back, restore (a condition, state of things, time, etc.). Now *rare.*

c 1477 Caxton *Jason* 120 b, To reduce his yongth in suche wise as he shall seme..in the aage of xxxij yere. 1549 *Compl. Scot.* xi. 90 Ȝour foir fathers..reducit there liberte, quhilk vas ane lang tyme in captiuite. 1580 Lyly *Euphues* (Arb.) 232 Rage can neither reduce thy fathers life, nor recouer his treasure. 1594 Shaks. *Rich. III*, v. v. 36 Abate the edge of Traitors..That would reduce these bloudy dayes againe. 1630 *R. Johnson's Kingd. & Commw.* 207 The States..cannot on the sudden reduce perfection in the profession of Religion. *c* 1665 Mrs. Hutchinson *Mem. Col. Hutchinson* (1846) 98 The endeavours to reduce popery and subvert the true protestant religion. 1821 Lamb *Elia* Ser. I. *Old Benchers Inner T.*, While childhood, and while dreams, reducing childhood, shall be left.

6. *Surg.* To restore (a dislocated, fractured, or ruptured part) to the proper position.

1541 R. Copland *Guydon's Quest. Chirurg.* N iv b. The .vj. place is vpon the matryce, and vpon the bowelles for to reduce and withdrawe them to theyr places. 1643 J. Steer tr. *Exp. Chyrurg.* xvi. 66 If any bones be broken, they are to be reduced. 1658 Rowland *Moufet's Theat. Ins.* 912 Salt with meal and honey, takes away the pain of a joynt that is dislocated,..and makes it more apt to be reduced. 1720 De Foe *Capt. Singleton* xi. (1840) 197 He reduced the splinters of the bone, and calling for help, set it. 1803 *Med. Jrnl.* IX. 202 A man who had dislocated his shoulder, and had had it reduced by a celebrated bone-setter.

b. To adjust, set (a dislocation or fracture).

1836 Marryat *Japhet* vii, We reduced the dislocation. *a* 1859 Macaulay *Hist. Eng.* xxv. V. 306 The jolting of the rough roads..made it necessary to reduce the fracture again.

†**7. a.** To draw or pull back again. *Obs. rare.*

1611 L. Barry *Ram Alley* I. i, By her actiuity she got it [her leg]..Crosse her shoulder: but not with all her power Could she reduce it. 1621 G. Sandys *Ovid's Met.* XI. (1632) 379 The Seamen..Reduce their oares, vp-rising from their Banks With equall strokes.

†**b.** To take *back* (a reckoning). *Obs. rare*⁻¹.

c 1595 Capt. Wyatt *R. Dudley's Voy. W. Ind.* (Hakl. Soc.) 57 The master himselfe was deceaved in the swifte gate of our shipp, and caused our Generall to reduce his reckninge back some 50 leagues.

II. †**8. a.** To lead or bring back from error in action, conduct, or belief, *esp.* in matters of morality or religion; to restore to the truth or the right faith. *Obs.* (Very common *c* 1600 to 1700.)

1412–20 Lydg. *Chron. Troy* II. 183 (Digby MS. 232 lf. 29) Of that arte I hadde as tho no gyde Me to reducen whan I went awrong. *c* 1485 *Digby Myst.* v. 313 Whan I erryd, thu reducyd me, Iesus. 1556 in W. H. Turner *Select. Rec. Oxford* 245 One Friar John..travelled with him to reduce him. But it would not be. 1590 A. Hutchinson in Greenwood *Collect. Sclaund. Art.* C, To confer with him about his seperating of himself from the Church of England, if I might reduce him. 1643 Milton *Soveraigne Salve* 1 If any of these erring men may be reduced, I have my end. 1674 Allen *Danger of Enthusiasm* 20 This very thing.. would in great part reduce you, and set you to rights. 1710 R. Ward *Life More* 62 Philotheus presently reduceth him with this sober and edifying Discourse. 1788 V. Knox *Winter Even.* II. IV. xi. 69 So is the knowledge of the passions..necessary to him whose office it is to reduce those who have erred.

†**b.** Const. *from* (an error, etc.). *Obs.*

1560 Daus tr. *Sleidane's Comm.* 19 b, Howe they of Boheme should be reduced from their errours. *a* 1614 Donne *Βιαθανατος* (1644) 91 It is not a better understanding of nature, which hath reduced us from it. 1686 Parr *Life Usher* 93 This Holy Primate..laboured instantly to reduce Popish Recusants and Sectaries from their Errors. 1713 Berkeley *Hylas & Phil.* Pref., If these principles..are admitted for true..men [will be] reduced from Paradoxes to common Sense.

†**9. a.** To bring back or restore (a person, etc.) *from* or *to* a state or condition. *Obs.*

1502 *Ord. Crysten Men* (W. de W. 1506) IV. i. 166 To reduce a synner from the estate of mortall synne, unto the estate of grace. 1598 Barckley *Felic. Man* II. (1603) 94 To reduce him againe to his former gravitie and course of life. 1646 Sir T. Browne *Pseud. Ep.* VII. xix. 384 For the satisfaction of their revenge they..would have reduced them unto life again. 1660 Boyle *New Exp. Phys. Mech.* xli. 334 By letting in the Air again, we soon reduc'd him to his former liveliness. 1695 Woodward *Nat. Hist. Earth* II. (1723) 106 Reducing him from the most abject and stupid Ferity, to his Senses, and to sober Reason.

†**b.** To bring (a thing, institution, etc.) back *to* a former state. Also without const. *Obs.*

1599 Shaks. *Hen. V*, v. ii. 63 Which to reduce into our former fauour You are assembled. 1639 Fuller *Holy War* IV. viii. (1840) 192 Matters for the main [were] reduced to the same estate they were at the first peace. 1666 Evelyn *Diary* 17 Aug., I entreated [him] to visit the Hospital of the Savoy and reduce it..to its original institution. 1709 Strype *Ann. Ref.* I. xxii. 225 So that the Church of England was reduced to the same good state wherein it was in the latter years of K. Edward. 1726 Swift *Gulliver* IV. ii, As if he would signify that I should reduce them to their former Shape. 1765 *Museum Rust.* IV. 21 If once a fruit is become deformed, no art will then reduce it.

†**c.** To redress, repair (a wrong). *Obs. rare*⁻¹.

c 1592 Marlowe *Jew of Malta* I. ii, Till they reduce the wrongs done to my father.

†**10. a.** To bring (a person or thing) *to* or *into* a certain state or condition. *Obs.*

a 1450 *Fysshynge w. Angle* (1883) 1, I aske þis questyon wyche bynne þe menys & cause to reduse a man to a mery spryte. 1485 Caxton *Chas. Gt.* 12 Fraunce was enhaunced & reduced to mageste ryal. 1538 Starkey *England* I. iv. 103 The prynce ys no thyng in boundage therby, but rather reducyd to true lyberty. 1581 Lambarde *Eiren.* IV. xvi. (1588) 582 This Fine (that is reduced to certaintie by the discretion of the Iustices). 1611 Bible *Transl. Pref.* ¶2 Seeking to reduce their Countrey-men to good order and discipline. 1649 Blithe *Eng. Improv.* (title-p.), By reducing Boggy or Drowned Land to sound Pasture. 1664 J. Webb *Stone-Heng* (1725) 76 The Romans..reduced the natural Inhabitants from their Barbarism to the Society of civil Life. 1713 Swift *Cadenus & Vanessa* Wks. 1751 VII. 17 With pleasing Arts she could reduce Men's Talents to their proper Use. 1719 De Foe *Crusoe* II. i, She was..the engine that by her prudence reduced me to that happy compass I was in.

refl. 1633 Bp. Hall *Occas. Medit.* (1851) 103 All things, the more perfect they are, the more do they reduce themselves towards that unity, which is the centre of all perfection. 1677 Gale *Crt. Gentiles* III. 56 These proud Philosophers aspired..to reduce themselves to a friendship with the great though unknown God.

†**b.** To bring (a person) *to* some belief or opinion. Also *absol. Obs.*

1563 Foxe *A. & M.* 1008/1 Whom I besech the Lorde to reduce to a better truth. 1570 *Ibid.* (ed. 2) 67/1 At what time, the wholsome doctrine of the Gospell allured and reduced the hearts of all sorts of people vnto the true religion of God. 1586 A. Day *Eng. Secretary* I. (1625) 21 The natures..of the other [being] to withdraw, disswade or reduce to another meaning. 1712 [see reduction 4 c].

†**c.** With *inf.* To lead or induce *to* do something. *Obs.*

1568 Grafton *Chron.* II. 672 The lorde Marques could by no meanes be reduced to take any part against king Edwarde. 1571 Digges *Pantom.* Pref. A iv, Suche two footed Moules and Todes..maye not possibly..be reduced or moued to taste or sauour any whitte of vertue. 1628 Ford *Lover's Mel.* I. ii, He knows no reason but he may reduce The courtiers to have women wait on them. 1656 Stanley *Hist. Philos.* VI. (1701) 257/1 That which moveth the Taste, and reduceth it to act.

d. To bring (a theory, etc.) *to* (or *into*) practice, action, etc.

1625 C. Brooke *On Sir A. Chichester* Poems (1872) 209 Of armes and arts, he had the theorie, which he reduc't to practise. 1668 Howe *Bless. Righteous* 116 Heretofore some gracious dispositions have been to seek..when there was most need and occasion for their being reduced into act. 1709 Pope *Let. to Cromwell* 7 May, I thought your observation..not a rule without exceptions, nor that ever it had been reduc'd to practise. 1781 Cowper *Conversat.* 139 Reduced to practice, his beloved rule Would only prove him a consummate fool. *a* 1871 Grote *Eth. Fragm.* iv. (1876) 81 Dispositions..reduced into action.

†**e.** To bring to a determination, to settle. *Obs.*⁻¹

1616 Sir C. Mountagu in *Buccleuch MSS.* (Hist. MSS. Comm.) I. 250 They say they have now reduced it to have the money brought in, in eight years.

†**11. a.** To adapt (a thing) *to* a purpose. Also without const., to apply, expound, explain. *Obs. rare.*

c 1440 *Gesta Rom.* xxix. 216 (Add. MS.), This Emperour may be saide herode, the kyng..Or els it [the story] may be reduced on a nother maner. 1523 Fitzherb. *Husb.* §7 To reduce and brynge the same text to my purpose, I take it thus. 1530 Palsgr. 682/1 All the artycles whiche he hath layde agaynst me I truste to reduce them to my purpose. 1609 Sir T. Bodley *Let.* in *Pietas Oxon.* (1903) 8, I could not busie myselfe to better purpose, then by redusing that place..to the publique vse of Students.

†**b.** To make conformable or agreeable *to* a standard. *Obs.*

1647 Clarendon *Hist. Reb.* VI. §116 It admitted an interpretation of reducing the government of the Church in Scotland to this of England. 1662 Gerbier *Princ.* 38 By the not reducing whatsoever is represented to the true Lines of Perspective.

c. *Astron.* To adapt (an observation) *to* a particular place or point; to correct by making the necessary allowances for position and other modifying circumstances. (Cf. reduction 6 c.)

1633 Gellibrand in T. James *Voy.* R 3, The [moon's] true place at midnight reduced to the Ecliptique. 1812 Woodhouse *Astron.* x. 73 Observations, therefore, seen at the surface, must be reduced to the center. 1866 Herschel *Fam. Lect. Sc.*, *Comets* (1871) 101 From these observations so far as they have as yet been communicated and reduced [etc.]. 1881 Donnelly in *Nature* No. 625. 594 To collect..

all information on this subject, and finally to reduce the Indian observations.

†**12. a.** To bring *into* another language; to render, translate. *Obs.*

1484 CAXTON *Curiall* 1 At whos instance and requeste I have reduced it in to Englysshe. **1513** DOUGLAS *Æneis* I. Prol. 410 Lo he repreifis..Ay word by word to reduce ony thing. *a***1533** LD. BERNERS *Gold. Bk. M. Aurel.* (1546) O o vij, The translatours, that haue laboryously reduced this treatyce out of Greke into Latin. **1581** LAMBARDE *Eiren.* I. i. (1588) 5 Bracton (who reduced the body of our law into Latine).

†**b.** To set down or record in writing; to put down or draw in a map. *Obs.*

1485 CAXTON *Chas. Gt.* 1 Al thynges that ben reduced by wrytyng ben wryton to our doctryne. *c***1532** DU WES *Introd. Fr.* in Palsgr. 897 To reduce and to put by writtynge the maner how I have proceded. **1576** FLEMING *Panopl. Epist.* 46 He..being nowe inflamed with the admiration of your martiall exploites,..is very desireous, to reduce them in a Chronicle. **1603** OWEN *Pembrokeshire* i. (1891) 5 Amonge diuerse other thinges of the xiii Sheres of Wales reduced according to arte.

†**13.** To bring *to* one by way of acquisition. *Obs.*

1491 *Act 7 Hen. VII*, c. 1 The King..hath determyned hym self to passe..in to his Realme of Fraunce and to reduce the possession thereof..to hym and his heires Kinges of Englond. **1596** BACON *Max. & Uses Com. Law* i. (1636) 2 The admission of my Clerke, whereby the inheritance is reduced to mee, is the act of the Ordinary.

14. a. To bring (†*into* or) *to* a certain order or arrangement.

1570 FOXE *A. & M.* (ed. 2) 8/1 The said Ezechias also reduced the Priests and Leuits into their orders. **1612** BRINSLEY *Lud. Lit.* xxi. 248 *marg.*, The way might be more compendious by the rootes reduced to Classes. **1666** PEPYS *Diary* 25 Dec., Reducing the names of all my books to an alphabet. **1729** BUTLER *Serm. Self-deceit* Wks. 1874 II. 125 A great part..of the intercourse amongst mankind, cannot be reduced to fixed determinate rules. **1756** C. LUCAS *Ess. Waters* I. Ded., The rules..were..reduced to the just order in which they now stand. **1837** WHEWELL *Hist. Induct. Sc.* (1857) I. 167 When one set of anomalies had been discovered, and reduced to rule. **1875** JOWETT *Plato* (ed. 2) IV. 21 The infinite would be no longer infinite, if limited or reduced to measure.

b. To bring *to* (†*into* or *under*) a specified number of classes or heads; also, to assign or refer *to* a certain class.

In some cases passing into sense 26.

1526 *Pilgr. Perf.* (W. de W. 1531) 146 b, All the counseyles of our lorde Jesu Chryst may be reduced to these nyne. *c***1560** *(title)* Summe of Christianitie, reduced unto eight propositions. **1647** MAY *Hist. Parl.* Pref., I will only professe to follow that one Rule, Truth, to which all the rest ..may be reduced. **1676** H. PHILLIPS *Purch. Patt.* 1 Many things..may all be reduced to these three general heads. **1697** POTTER *Antiq. Greece* II. xii. (1715) 302 Hither may also be reduc'd another sort of Divination. **1713** STEELE *Englishm.* No. 7. 43 Those who set up for Criticks in Poetry ..may be reduced to two Classes. **1718** *Free-thinker* No. 62 ¶5 These Presages..may be reduced under Seven Principal Denominations.

†**c.** (Without const.) To bring into proper order; to assign to the proper class or classes. *Obs.*

1668 WILKINS *Real Char.* Ded. a j b, The species of Natural bodies,..if they were (so far as they are yet known and discovered) distinctly reduced and described. **1692** RAY in *Lett. Lit. Men* (Camden) 198 The..reducing and settling the severall histories and relations of species, will be a thing of eminent use. *Ibid.* 203 He hath abundance of Jamaica plants, which if in your Catalogue it is very difficult to reduce them, especially his Felices.

15. a. To bring (†*into* or) *to* a certain form or character. (Cf. 12 a.)

*c***1592** MARLOWE *Massacre Paris* I. viii, I knew the Organon to be confus'd, And I reduc'd it into better form. **1612** WOODALL *Surg. Mate* (1639) Pref. 3 Galen..reduced the Science [medicine] into a more perfect Art. **1662** J. DAVIES tr. *Olearius' Voy. Ambass.* 216 The Ambassador ordered me to reduce Persia and Turkie into one Map. *a***1693** WOOD *Antiq. Oxf.* (1786) 56 They began..to pull down their buildings, which stood without any method, and to reduce them..into a quadrangular pile. **1726** SWIFT *Gulliver* IV. i, A second Word, much harder to be pronounced; but reducing it to the English Orthography may be spelt thus, Houyhnhnm. **1836** H. ROGERS *J. Howe* ii. 26 Nevertheless, it may be very useful..to attempt to reduce it to such a form.

refl. **1590** SIR J. SMYTH *Disc. Weapons* 12 Whilest the Piquers and other weapons doo reduce themselues into forme vnder their Ensignes.

b. To put *into*, commit *to*, writing. (Cf. 12 b.)

1659 HEYLIN *Examen Hist.* I. 230 Why was not the Protestation reduced into writing? **1711–12** SWIFT *Let. Eng. Tongue* Wks. 1751 IV. 243 All which reduced to writing would entirely confound Orthography. **1747** *Col. Rec. Pennsylv.* V. 78 Having reduc'd into writing the Transaction ..touching the Delivery of the three Negroes. **1875** MAINE *Hist. Inst.* i. 10 A small body of Aryan customs reduced to writing in the fifth century B.C.

16. a. *Arith.* To change (a number or quantity) from one denomination *into* or *to* another.

Commonly conveying some suggestion of sense 26, as resulting either in a smaller number or in one composed of smaller units.

1579 DIGGES *Stratiot.* 23 The Numerator of the last Fragment to be reduced. **1594** BLUNDEVIL *Exerc.* I. xxvii. (1636) 75 Then in like order reduce your Divisor into the smallest Fraction, and you shall find the totall summe [etc.]. **1674** JEAKE *Arith.* (1696) 156 To reduce the Denominations of Measure, Weight,..&c. of one Kind or Countrey to another. **1766** *Compl. Farmer* s.v. *Surveying* 7 G 2/2 If the content to be reduced, be cast up into acres, roods, and perches, reduce all into perches, and then in other respects work as before. **1823** MITCHELL *Dict. Math. & Phys. Sci.* 419/2 Reduce the compound quantity to its lowest denomination, and the whole integer to the same denomination.

absol. **1766** *Compl. Farmer* s.v. *Surveying* 7 G 1/2 Multiply the number of half feet contained in a pole of that measure you would reduce into.

b. To change (a quantity, figure, etc.) *into* or *to* a different form. Also *absol.*

1579 DIGGES *Stratiot.* I. xii. 21 To reduce, is to bring Integers into Fractions or contrarie. **1669** STURMY *Mariner's Mag.* I. ii. 43 To reduce a Trapezia into a Triangle. **1676** H. PHILLIPS *Purch. Patt.* A v, There will be 18 rod of Brick-work in the Wall, which may all be reduced to a brick and an half thick. **1706** W. JONES *Syn. Palmar. Matheseos* 89 To Reduce an Integer into an Improper Fraction. **1743** EMERSON *Fluxions* 82 The given Fluxion may be reduced to another Expression. **1797** *Encycl. Brit.* (ed. 3) I. 405/1 To reduce an Integer to the Form of a Fraction. **1833** LOUDON *Encycl. Archit.* §88 In estimating the price of brick-work in Britain, the quantity, of whatever nature and thickness it may be, is always reduced to walls of one and a half brick in thickness.

c. To resolve by analysis. Const. *to.*

1860 TYNDALL *Glac.* II. xxix. 399, I shall now endeavour to reduce the ripples to their mechanical elements.

17. a. To turn *to*, convert *into*, a different physical state or form; esp. to break down, grind, or crush *to* powder, etc.

1605 TIMME *Quersit.* I. xiii. 56 The black feces..being reduced..into a calxe. **1662** J. DAVIES tr. *Mandelslo's Trav.* 15 They reduce dates into a paste, and it serves them instead of bread. **1687** A. LOVELL tr. *Thevenot's Trav.* I. 39 Their Bodies being reduced into Ashes,..God shall create them a-new. **1753** CHAMBERS *Cycl. Supp.* s.v. *Urine*, The first step is to reduce that liquor to the consistence of a rob or thick extract. **1816** J. SMITH *Panorama Sc. & Art* II. 825 Reduce the tartrate and sugar to powder. **1839** *Penny Cycl.* XIII. 33/1 The first process is that of reducing the iron-stone or ore..into a metallic state by means of fusion. **1884** W. H. GREENWOOD *Steel & Iron* vi. 92 Since ferrous carbonates are reduced to the state of ferric oxide [etc.].

b. *Metall.* To convert into metal; to smelt.

1758 REID tr. *Macquer's Chym.* I. 361 When the ore of an Iron mine is found difficult to reduce, it is usually neglected even though it be rich. **1839** URE *Dict. Arts* 687 By the year 1788, several attempts had been made to reduce iron ore with coaked coal. **1866** ROGERS *Agric. & Prices* I. xxiii. 599 In the infancy of the metallurgic arts lead was much more easily reduced than iron.

c. *Chem.* To decompose (a compound); to resolve into a simpler compound or into the constituent elements. Hence in mod. use, the opposite of OXIDIZE *v.*; to cause to undergo reduction.

1741 tr. *Cramer's Assaying* 51 When refractory Calx of Iron is to be reduced by a great and long lasting Fire. **1800** HENRY *Epit. Chem.* (1808) 213 To reduce the oxide of iron, charcoal must be added. **1872** *Mining Mag. & Rev.* I. 250 When oxides are heated with carbon, the oxygen they contain combines with the carbon to form two invisible gases..which pass away into the air, the ore being thus 'reduced'. **1873** RALFE *Phys. Chem.* 202 Since uric acid also has the power of reducing cupric sulphate [etc.]. **1890** W. JAGO *Inorg. Chem.* iii. 48 There are other examples of reduction in which the bodies are simply reduced to a lower stage of oxidation. **1935** J. W. MELLOR *Comprehensive Treat. Inorg. & Theoret. Chem.* XIV. lxvii. 608 Cobaltic fluoride in hydrogen at 200°..is reduced to cobaltous fluoride. **1955** *Sci. News Let.* 7 May 297/2 Using heats as high as 3,100 degrees Fahrenheit, quartzite rock is reduced with coke and charcoal. **1971** *Nature* 1 Jan. 13/1 The resulting electrons are used to reduce carbon dioxide to carbohydrate. **1974** *Sci. Amer.* Dec. 68/3 The molecule that has lost electrons is said to have been oxidized; the one that has received them is said to have been reduced. Thus in photosynthesis water is oxidized and carbon dioxide is reduced.

d. To break up (soil) into fine particles.

1763 *Museum Rust.* I. 144 The land cannot be stirred too deep:..the more the earth is reduced the more nourishment will it afford. **1805** R. W. DICKSON *Pract. Agric.* II. 604 It is the custom..to reduce the cloddy surface well by means of harrowing.

18. *Logic.* To bring a syllogism (†or proposition) into a different but equivalent form, *spec.* to one of the moods of the first figure.

1727–41 CHAMBERS *Cycl.* s.v. *Reduction of propositions*, The proposition preceding the particle is reduced. **1845** WHATELY *Logic* II. iii. §4 All arguments may be in one way or other brought into some one of the four Moods in the First Figure: and a Syllogism is, in that case, said to be reduced. **1864** BOWEN *Logic* vii. 195 The motives for reducing the three lower Figures to the First.

III. 19. a. To bring *to* (or *into*) order, obedience, reason, etc., by constraint or compulsion.

1490 CAXTON *Eneydos* xxii. 78 The resolucion..of his courage is euer reduced to thobeyssaunce of yᵉ goddes. **1541** *Act 33 Hen. VIII*, c. 9 §2 The subiectes therof..subdued and redused diuers and many regions and countreis to their due obeisance. **1560** DAUS tr. *Sleidane's Comm.* 198 They requested them to reduce and frame [L. *adducerent*] him to his dewtie. **1654** BRAMHALL *Just Vind.* i. (1661) 5 Whensoever they have occasion to reduce the Pope to reason. **1687** A. LOVELL tr. *Thevenot's Trav.* I. 241 The King of Æthiopia..marched out against them [Jews], reduced them to duty. **1751** EARL ORRERY *Remarks Swift* (1752) 32 His first step, was to reduce to reason and obedience his reverend brethren the chapter of St. Patrick's. **1841** MYERS *Cath. Th.* IV. §46. 412 Nor can any one [church] ..reduce all the others to subjection. **1877** FROUDE *Short Stud.* (1883) IV. I. x. 108 The clergy could not be allowed to reduce Crown and barons into entire submission to their own pleasure.

†**b.** To make subject *to* one; to cause to give obedience or adherence *to*; to bring *under* one, *into* or *under* one's power, *within* bounds, etc. *Obs.*

1569 STOCKER tr. *Diod. Sic.* II. xxii. 73/2 He reduced likewise..all the townes and cities of the Messenians to him. **1590** SPENSER *F.Q.* III. iii. 32 He the six Islands comprovinciall In auncient times unto great Britainee, Shall to the same reduce. **1628** ABP. WILLIAMS *Serm.* 34 When shall I see the day, when all my Affections reduc't vnder reason, I may pronounce this happy word, *Vici*, I haue ouercome them. **1655** STANLEY *Hist. Philos.* I. (1701) 17/2 Solon perswaded also the Athenians to reduce into their power the Thracian Chersonesus. **1697** DAMPIER *Voy.* (1729) I. 544 The Shot tumbled out..; neither was it an easie matter to reduce them again within Bounds. **1737** WHISTON *Josephus, Antiq.* VI. ix. §3 God..will yet reduce him under my power.

†**c.** To place *under*, to bring or unite *to*, one. *Obs.*

1588 *Copy of Letter to Mendoza* in *Harl. Misc.* (Malh.) II. 65 Governed by the principal noblemen..and reduced under captains of knowledge. **1604** E. G[RIMSTONE] *D'Acosta's Hist. Indies* VII. xxvii. 584 The greate difficultie they haue founde to reduce those Indians to Christ. **1630** CAPT. SMITH *Trav. & Adv.* 49 Some English and Irish..he reduced to his company and to leave the Dutch.

d. *Law.* To bring (a thing or right) *into* (†*to*) possession.

1766 BLACKSTONE *Comm.* II. 433 Unless he reduces them to possession, by exercising some act of ownership upon them, no property vests in him. **1845** STEPHEN *Comm. Laws Eng.* (1874) II. 45 Rights not yet reduced into possession. **1884** *Law Times Rep.* L. 199/2 All that the husband has a right to do is to reduce such property into possession if he can.

20. a. To bring (a place) into subjection, to subdue, conquer; *spec.* to capture (a town, fortress, etc.); to compel to submit or surrender.

1612 DAVIES *Why Ireland*, etc. (1787) 8 The late king of Spain could sooner win the kingdom of Portugal, than reduce the states of the Low Countries. **1665** MANLEY *Grotius' Low C. Warres* 253 To leave the French..untill the Netherlands were wholly reduced or quieted. **1724** DE FOE *Mem. Cavalier* (1840) 295 Chester was reduced by famine. **1780** COXE *Russ. Disc.* 187 A body of troops whom he sent before him to reduce the fortress found it quite deserted. **1815** ELPHINSTONE *Acc. Caubul* (1842) I. 405 The whole of Persia and the Uzbek country were invaded and reduced by the Arabs. **1867** SMILES *Huguenots Eng.* viii. (1880) 132 The young King set out with his army to reduce the revolted towns.

b. To bring (a person) under control or authority, to subdue, conquer. †Also, to reclaim or domesticate (animals).

1598 SYLVESTER *Du Bartas* II. ii. I. *Ark* 518 Reducing, with industrious care, The Flocks and Droves cover'd with wool and hair. **1666** EVELYN *Diary* 7 Sept., The clamor and peril..made the whole Court amaz'd, and they did with.. greate difficulty reduce and appease the people. **1700** PRIOR *Carmen Sec.* 32 The Son of Mars reduc'd the trembling Swains. **1719** DE FOE *Crusoe* I. xvii, If they were reduced, they should be brought to the gallows. **1777** JOHNSON *Let. to Mrs. Thrale* 5 Aug., Do you think..you shall be able to manage me again? I suppose..that you are thinking how to reduce me. *a***1842** ARNOLD *Hist. Rome* (1846) II. xxxv. 403 Ptolemy reduced the several petty kings of the island, and made himself master of it. **1865** TYLOR *Early Hist. Man.* iii. 35 Those of the natives who have but lately been reduced.

c. With *inf.* To constrain, compel, force (a person) *to* do something.

1622 BACON *Hen. VII* (1876) 17 To reduce aliens being made denizens, to pay strangers customs. **1710** PRIDEAUX *Orig. Tithes* iii. 156 Having reduced them to receive Christianity, he imposed the same Law upon them. **1727–41** CHAMBERS *Cycl.* s.v. *Reduction*, The other [method].. whereby the person..is reduced to assert or grant something absurd and impossible. **1749** FIELDING *Tom Jones* V. xi, A blow..reduced him to measure his length on the ground. **1894** MEREDITH *Ld. Ormont* ii, Poor gentlemen reduced to submit to any but a young woman's hug.

†**d.** To overcome, subdue, repress, moderate (a desire, temper, etc.). *Obs.*

1643 MILTON *Divorce* 10 Mariage cannot be honourable for the meer reducing and terminating lust between two. **1704** HEARNE *Duct. Hist.* (1714) I. 417 Not being able to reduce the Temper of the Tyrant or procure Justice. **1706** STANHOPE *Paraphr.* III. 13 We reduce and restrain our Desires of things agreeable here. **1725** DE FOE *Voy. round World* (1840) 45 It was necessary..their tempers be reduced by my kindness to them.

†**e.** To crush (a rebellion). *Obs. rare*$^{-1}$.

*a***1687** PETTY *Pol. Anat.* (1691) 6 The Army who reduced the Rebellion, did..consist of near 35000 Men.

f. To make (land) fit for cultivation. ? *Obs.*

1762 J. MILLS *Syst. Pract. Husb.* I. 151 Another method of reducing barren boggy land, in Ireland, is by laying upon it a little dung or straw, and covering this with shells.

21. a. To bring down *to* a bad or disagreeable condition.

1572 in *Buccleuch MSS.* (Hist. MSS. Comm.) I. 23 Scotland wes reducet to gret extremeties. **1662** J. DAVIES tr. *Mandelslo's Trav.* 22 The continual rains reduced it [a province] to..a deplorable condition. **1671** MILTON *Samson* 1468 Having reduc't Thir foe to misery. **1713** STEELE *Englishm.* No. 8. 54 Thousands of their Fellow-Subjects may be reduced to Want. **1748** *Anson's Voy.* III. ii. 219 Thus were we all..reduced to the utmost despair. **1777** WATSON *Philip II*, II. I. 27 His children..had reduced him to the painful necessity of taking arms against them. **1820** W. IRVING *Sketch Bk.* I. 41 He found himself reduced almost to penury. **1868** GLADSTONE *Juv. Mundi* i. (1870) 4 The Dorian conquest had the immediate effect of reducing Mycenae to obscurity. **1875** JOWETT *Plato* (ed. 2) V. 216 Are not those who train in gymnasia, at first beginning reduced to a state of weakness?

b. In *pass.*, with *inf.* To be compelled by want *to* do something; also, to be hard put to it.

1693 DRYDEN *Juvenal* i. 163 The poor Patrician is reduc'd to keep, In Melancholly Walks, a Grazier's Sheep. **1709** STEELE *Tatler* No. 59 ¶6 The Garrison is brought to the utmost Necessity;..they were reduced to eat Horse-Flesh. **1743** H. WALPOLE *Let.* 4 May, Poor creature! he was reduced..to borrow five guineas of Sir Francis Dashwood. **1768** —— *Hist. Doubts* 100 Henry was so reduced to make out any title to the crown that he catched even at a quibble. **1807** *Trans. Highl. Soc.* III. 472, I rather think they are poisoned by being reduced to eat such unwholesome food. **1834** MRS. CARLYLE *Lett.* I. 6 She is every other day reduced to borrow my tumblers, my teacups.

c. To bring down *to* a smaller allowance.

1819 SHELLEY *Cenci* II. ii. 13 If you..were reduced at once From thrice-driven beds of down, and delicate food,..To that which nature doth indeed require.

d. To weaken physically.

1767 GOOCH *Treat. Wounds* I. 80 An ulcer..which had reduced the patient exceedingly, and brought her life into imminent danger. **1838** DICKENS *O. Twist* xxxii, Fever and ague..hung about him for many weeks, and reduced him sadly. **1856** KANE *Arct. Expl.* II. xxix. 288 The men seemed half crazy: I had not realized how much we were reduced by absolute famine.

e. To diminish the strength of (spirit).

1880 *Act 43 & 44 Vict.* c. 24 §67 A distiller may..reduce with water any plain spirits.

f. *Photogr.* To decrease the density of (a negative or print).

1889 E. J. WALL *Dict. Photogr.* 158 Bromide prints may be reduced in exactly the same way as negatives. **1903** A. WATKINS *Photogr.* 118 Do not throw away paper prints which are too dark from over printing. They can be reduced. **1956** *Focal Encycl. Photogr.* 950/1 Before starting to reduce a negative or print it should be well soaked in water. **1963** P. MOYES *Murder à la Mode* iv. 65 'What does "reducing" mean, exactly?' 'Makin' the print lighter... If the neg's too contrasty, like you can't get the light part to print without the dark's too dark. So you reduce it. By nibbin' the dark part with cyanide.'

22. a. To bring down *to* a lower rank or position, dignity, etc. Also without const. and with *inf.*

1641 MILTON *Ch. Govt.* II. Concl., Wks. (1851) 177 The protestant religion..must undresse them of all their guilded vanities, and reduce them as they were at first to the lowly and equall order of Presbyters. **1667** —— *P.L.* v. 843 More illustrious made, since he the Head One of our number thus reduc't becomes. **1727** POPE, etc. *Art of Sinking* ix, The book of Job is acknowledged to be infinitely sublime, and yet has not the father of the Bathos reduced it in every page? **1751** HARRIS *Hermes* Wks. (1841) 180 The articles *a* and *the*..circumscribe the latitude of genera and species by reducing them for the most part to denote individuals. **1788** GIBBON *Decl. & F.* xlix. V. 146 The ambition of the popes was reduced to the empty honour of crowning and anointing these hereditary princes. **1811** JEFFERSON *Writ.* (1830) IV. 164 The moment they usurp their direction and that of their government, they will be reduced to their true places. **1864** BRYCE *Holy Rom. Emp.* vii. (1875) 111 By setting the Emperor at the head of the Church to reduce the Pope to the place of chief bishop of his realm. **1941** *Sun* (Baltimore) 17 Feb. 18/4 He was a top sergeant there. His cooking career began in France in July, 1918, when he was 'reduced' and made a mess sergeant. **1948** PARTRIDGE *Dict. Forces' Slang* 154 *Reduced*, reduced in rank. (Services' colloquialism verging on jargon.) **1953** K. TENNANT *Joyful Condemned* xxiii. 220 The deputy-governor..had been reduced..because of some trouble in a gaol of which he had been governor.

b. *Mil.* in phr. ***to reduce to the ranks***, to degrade (a non-commissioned officer) to the rank of private.

1802 JAMES *Milit. Dict.* s.v., If a serjeant be reduced to the ranks, his clothing is to be given in for the use of his successor. **1844** *Regul. & Ord. Army* 149 Non-commissioned Officers may be reduced to the Ranks by the Sentence of a Regimental or other Court-Martial.

†**c.** To assign (a person) to a more recent date.

1704 HEARNE *Duct. Hist.* (1714) I. 398 The Chaldæan Traditions carried the Age of the first Zoroaster very high, ..but the Examinations made by learned Men reduc'd him almost to the Age of Nimrod.

23. *Sc. Law.* To rescind, revoke, annul.

1553 KENNEDY *Compend. Tractive* in *Wodrow Soc. Misc.* (1844) 139 The subjectis mon evir stand at quhilk is done be the hiear poweris,..aye and quhill the samyn be reducit be sufficient ordour. **1574** *Reg. Privy Council Scot.* Ser. I. II. 392 Their infeftment salbe reducit and decernit null. **1609** SKENE *Reg. Maj.* 127 (*Form of Proces* xxxvi. §2) Na Iudge may reduce his awne decreit, except the Lords of session. **1646** BP. MAXWELL *Burd. Issach.* in *Phenix* (1708) II. 303 No Judgment pass'd there can be rectify'd or reduc'd by any Judicatory..but by themselves. **1742** *Acts of Sederunt* (1790) 372 [The] arbitrers, who pronounced the decreet now reduced. **1838** W. BELL *Dict. Law Scot.* 829 The object of this class of actions..is to reduce and set aside deeds, services, decrees, and rights. **1865** *Glasgow Herald* 25 Mar., His first thought was to have the marriage settlement reduced.

absol. **1838** W. BELL *Dict. Law Scot.* 831 The creditors of an apparent heir may also pursue a reduction..without previously adjudging the right to reduce.

24. *Mil.* **a.** To break up, disband (an army or regiment). ? *Obs.*

1706 PHILLIPS (ed. Kersey) s.v. *Reform*, In Military Affairs, to Reform is to reduce a Body of Men, either disbanding the Whole,..or only breaking a Part. **1746** H. FOX in *Buccleuch MSS.* (Hist. MSS. Comm.) I. 409 The Regiments..should be marched into their own counties before reduced,..the other three Regiments not immediately to be disbanded. **1802** JAMES *Milit. Dict.* s.v., When a regiment is reduced, the officers are generally put upon half-pay.

b. To break up (a square, etc.) and restore the component parts to line or column.

1802 JAMES *Milit. Dict.*

IV. 25. To bring or draw together. Also *refl.*

In later use only as implying diminution of bulk.

c **1374** CHAUCER *Boeth.* III. pr. viii. 63 (Camb. MS.), Of alle whyche forseyde thinges I may reducen [L. *redigere*] this shortly in somme. **1481** CAXTON *Myrr.* II. xv. 100 Yf he mete ony beste that wold doo hym harme he reduyseth hym self as rounde as a bowle. *c* **1532** DU WES *Introd. Fr.* in Palsgr. 940 To reduce narowly, *coarter*. **1600** E. BLOUNT tr. *Conestaggio* 4 Portugall was then obscure, vntilled, poore, and reduced into streight limits. **1655** STANLEY *Hist. Philos.* III. (1701) 74/2 This was one of those small Villages scattered through Attica, before Theseus Reduc'd the People within the Walls of a City. **1777** WATSON *Philip II*, II. I. 48 He..reduced the water into a canal large enough to receive some small boats. **1788** GIBBON *Decl. & F.* xlviii. V. 2 The Roman name..is reduced to a narrow corner of Europe. **1807** SYD. SMITH *Plymley's Lett.* ii, Reduce this declamation to a point, and let us know what you mean. **1834** DICKENS *Sk. Boz, Horatio Sparkins*, The unfortunate Tom reduced himself into the least possible space.

26. a. To bring down, diminish *to* a smaller number, amount, extent, etc., or *to* a single thing.

1560 DAUS tr. *Sleidane's Comm.* 341 b, When thys..semed over long, Clement the sixt reduced [L. *redegit*] the same unto fifty yeres. **1627** MAY *Lucan* VII. M viij b, To what small number is mankind reduc'd. **1662** STILLINGFL. *Orig. Sacræ* II. vi. §4 But Aquinas doth better reduce the two former to one. **1667** MILTON *P.L.* I. 790 Thus incorporeal Spirits to smallest forms Reduc'd thir shapes immense. **1678** BUTLER *Hud.* III. iii. 330 All dangers are reduc'd to Famine. **1762** *Ann. Reg.* I. 147/1 What remained..were further reduced to half-price. **1781** COWPER *Conversat.* 403 Recovering..The faculties that seemed reduced to nought. **1827** SCOTT *Napoleon* Introd., Wks. 1870 IX. 218 Danton and Robespierre, reduced to a Duumvirate might have divided the power betwixt them. **1853** SOYER *Pantroph.* 271 Wine, reduced to two-thirds by boiling, was added. **1871** DAVIES *Metric System* III. 187 He finds by experience that these [two] may with increased convenience be reduced to one. **1903** E. A. ROSS in *Amer. Jrnl. Sociol.* IX. 197 There never has been a good reason for supposing we shall be able to reduce everything social to a single element. *Ibid.* 198 It is certain, nevertheless, we cannot reduce the whole man to a 'cell' in a 'social organism'. **1920** *Psychol. Rev.* XXVII. 71 The psychological simplification of human behaviour, which reduces instinctive conduct to the functioning of psychical dispositions or impulses.

b. To lower, diminish, lessen.

1787 BENTHAM *Def. Usury* vii. 69 No law can reduce the rate of interest below the lowest ordinary market rate, at the time when the law was made. **1833** I. TAYLOR *Fanat.* vi. 169 Every attempt to reduce the plain import of certain passages in the Gospels. **1856** KANE *Arct. Expl.* I. x. 114 Step by step ..we went on reducing our sledging outfit. **1878** HUXLEY *Physiogr.* 42 If a current of warm and moist air meet a colder current its temperature is reduced.

c. *intr.* To become lessened or limited. Also, to condense, come down *to*.

1811 L. M. HAWKINS *C'tess & Gertr.* II. 368 Miss Mendax has now lived, for a long time, on a biscuit *per diem*. .. She certainly does not reduce on it. **1885** *Pall Mall G.* 25 June 4/2 Diseased he was, and of a harsh Northern strain, but all the carping reduces at last to this. **1895** J. R. HARRIS in *Expositor* Nov. 352 They reduce to two classes. **1924** *Times Lit. Suppl.* 6 Nov. 704/2 His success or failure hangs ..on the degree of intensity with which he fuses his material —and perhaps the old distinction between fancy and imagination reduces in the end to that. **1953** J. B. CARROLL *Study of Lang.* iii. 78 The problem of describing verbal behaviour..reduces to the problem of describing the strengths..of verbal responses under various stimulus conditions. **1956** E. H. HUTTEN *Lang. Mod. Physics* iii. 109 The equations of motion for a material particle as given by the general theory reduce to the equations of motion of Newton, when we consider the simplest case of a Euclidean, limited, region of space. **1971** *Ideal Home* Apr. 69/1 The size of houses in sq. ft. has tended to reduce quite rapidly over the last few years. **1973** *Daily Tel.* 15 May 19 (Advt.), After only 8 years the amount you need to pay in cash will reduce and if present conditions continue you pay nothing after 10 years. **1978** *Amer. Polit. Sci. Rev.* Sept. 964/1 Over time those claims reduce to nothing more than rationalizations to maintain power. **1979** *Daily Tel.* 1 Dec. 27 (Advt.), The Company invests 98% to 113% of each payment (depending on your starting age), except in the first two years when these figures reduce to 73% to 89%.

d. *trans.* To articulate (a speech sound) in a way requiring less muscular effort; to form (a vowel) in a more neutral, centralized articulatory position; to weaken, obscure.

1874 A. J. ELLIS *Early Eng. Pronunc.* IV. 1099/1 Reducing (r_0) from a consonant to a pure glide. *Ibid.* 1315 So that (oo') often falls into the juncture (AA), or else (ee', oo') are reduced to two syllables. **1892** W. W. SKEAT *Primer Eng. Etymol.* ii. 25 The *day* in *Monday* has been reduced to *-dy* (di) in familiar speech. **1909** D. JONES *Pronunc. Eng.* I. 46 Cases occur in which almost all other vowels may be reduced to ə when unstressed. **1934** C. DAVIES *Eng. Pronunc.* 12 Back-rounded vowels were unrounded and reduced to an indistinct sound similar to [ʌ] or [ə]. **1957** E. J. DOBSON *Eng. Pronunc. 1500–1700* II. x. 871 The unstressed back vowels seem not to have been reduced to [ə] as early as ME *ĕ*. **1962** A. C. GIMSON *Introd. Pronunc. Eng.* vii. 143 In present RP the secondary accent has been lost and the former [e] or [ɛː] reduced to [ə] or elided.

e. *intr.* To lessen one's weight, to slim.

1926 MAINES & GRANT *Wise-Crack Dict.* 12/2 *Perpendicular your outline*, reduce a little. **1929** E. LINKLATER *Poet's Pub* xii. 145 'And how did they reduce?' asked Jean... 'They perspired without shame,' said the professor. **1958** *Times Lit. Suppl.* 13 June 334/5 A commendably simple and, at the same time, reliable guide for those who wish to 'reduce' without too much trouble. **1963** R. WOLFF *I, Keturah* (1964) II. xvii. 230 Miss Hawthorne said abruptly 'I think you ought to reduce, Keturah.' So she bought a book on dieting. **1971** *Homes & Gardens* Sept. 65/3, I try continually to reduce, but you cannot take a couple out for a gay evening and be on a diet.

†**re'duceable**, *a. Obs.* [f. prec. + -ABLE. Cf. OF. *reduisable* (Godef.).] = REDUCIBLE.

1570 LEVINS *Manip.* 4/7 Reduceable, *reducibilis*. **1638** R. BAKER tr. *Balzac's Lett.* (vol. II.) 160 Those..which serve for use, and are reduceable to action. *a* **1661** FULLER *Worthies, Carnarvonsh.* IV. (1662) 31 There is an Island called Berdsey justly reduceable to this County. **1736** BUTLER *Anal.* II. iv. 188 A great Part of the natural Behaviour of living Agents, is reduceable to general Laws. **1778** SIR J. REYNOLDS *Disc.* viii. Wks. 1797 I. 178 To consider every excellence as reduceable to principles.

Hence †**re'duceableness**. *Obs.*

1680 *Disc. Tangier* in *Harl. Misc.* (1745) V. 527 The Reduceableness and Extirpation..of the Piracy of Sallee.

reduced (rɪ'djuːst), *ppl. a.* [f. as prec. + -ED[1].]

†**1. a.** Brought back. *lit.* and *fig. Obs.*

1699 HOWE *Redeemer's Domin. Invis. World* Wks. 1724 II. 70 That he might have these Keys to open the Heavenly Hades to reduc'd Apostates [etc.]. **1721** STRYPE *Eccl. Mem.* III. II. xvi. 376 Providing for the public credit of this your reduced daughter.

†**b.** Of a leaf: Indented at the outer end. *Obs.*

1676 GREW *Anat. Flowers* App. §11 The Top is..either Produced, that is, Poynted, or at least, Roundish,..or else Reduced, as in Woodsorrel.

2. a. *Mil.* Of officers: Discharged from active service and put on half-pay. ? *Obs.*

a **1631** DONNE *Elegies* xvii. 4 To..brave Reformed or reduced captaine. **1716** *Lond. Gaz.* No. 5488/5 Who..enjoy the Benefit of half Pay..as reduced Officers. **1792** BURKE *Pres. St. Aff.* Wks. VII. 105 A theatrical, vapouring, reduced captain of cavalry. **1817** *Parl. Deb.* 1073 Reduced officers of his Majesty's land forces. *Ibid.* 1074 The reduced adjutants of the Local Militia.

b. Of persons, their circumstances, etc.: Impoverished.

1629 FORD *Lover's Mel.* Dram. Pers., Rhetias, (a reduced Courtier) Servant to Eroclea. **1807** tr. *Goede's Trav.* II. 73 Reduced clergymen, schoolmasters and mechanics. **1851** MAYHEW *Lond. Labour* (1864) I. 331/2, I dare say he was some poor musicianer, or singer, or a reduced gentleman. **1886** RUSKIN *Præterita* I. 408 Retired to the rural districts in reduced circumstances.

c. Weakened, impaired.

1689 BOYLE *Let.* 22 Aug., Wks. 1772 I. p. cxxviii, You will not find me more backward than formerly to serve you faithfully in my reduced capacity. **1797** BURKE *Affairs Irel.* Wks. IX. 453 In the reduced state of body, and in the dejected state of mind, in which I find myself. **1818** JAS. MILL *Brit. India* II. IV. iv. 152 *note*, The English leaders appear to have had no conception of the extremely reduced state of the French.

d. Subdued, subjugated.

1732 BERKELEY *Alciphr.* VI. §22 The Phœnicians, Assyrians, and Chaldeans were each a conquered and reduced people.

†**3.** Brought to a state of gravity and composure. *Obs.* (In Fuller only.)

1642 FULLER *Holy & Prof. St.* IV. iv. 257 The heat of his youth was tamed in his reduced age. *Ibid.* xiii. 304 Yet in her reduced thoughts she makes all the sport she hath seen earnest to her self. *a* **1661** —— *Worthies* (1840) I. 119 The grave, sage, and reduced Scottish-men in this age.

4. Brought into another form. **a.** *Logic.* Of a proposition: (see REDUCE *v.* 18). †**b.** Of charts: (see first quot.). *Obs.* **c.** Of brick- or stone-work: (see REDUCE *v.* 16 b). **d.** ***reduced eye***, a diagrammatic eye employed to simplify the treatment of various optical problems (*Cent. Dict.* 1891; *Syd. Soc. Lex.* 1897).

1727–41 CHAMBERS *Cycl.* s.v. *Chart*, Reduced Chart..is that wherein the meridians are represented by right lines converging towards the poles; and the parallels by right lines parallel to one another, but unequal... Another kind of reduced charts has been invented, wherein the meridians are parallel, but the degrees thereof unequal; these are called Mercator's Charts. *Ibid.* s.v. *Reduction of propositions*, To a reduction, therefore, there are two propositions required, the reduced, and the reducing. **1825** J. NICHOLSON *Operat. Mechanic* 558 What is the quantity of reduced brick-work in a wall containing 4540 superficial feet, 2 bricks thick? **1833** LOUDON *Encycl. Archit.* §88 One rod, eighty-two feet of reduced stone-work (the stone walls are reduced to one and a half brick in thickness).

e. Mathematically modified to a more convenient form.

1862 E. ATKINSON tr. *Ganot's Elem. Treat. Physics* X. ix. 724 The resistance offered by the element and galvanometer is equal to the resistance of 4·08 yards of such copper wire, and this is said to be the reduced length of the element and galvanometer in terms of the copper wire. **1916** W. C. McC. LEWIS *Syst. Physical Chem.* II. iii. 90 It is more convenient to make use of the reduced form [of van der Waals' equation], i.e. pressures, volumes, and temperatures will be expressed as fractions..of their critical values. **1930** L. BRAND *Vectorial Mech.* xiv. 445 This is the same as the equation..for a simple pendulum of length $l = k^2/b$. For this reason l is called the reduced length of the pendulum. **1934** H. E. WHITE *Introd. Atomic Spectra* ii. 34 The preceding equations will apply to two masses m and M rotating about their center of mass, if m be replaced by $mM/(m + M) = m/(1 + m/M) = \mu$. μ is called the reduced mass and approaches m as $M \to \infty$. **1950** CORBEN & STEHLE *Classical Mech.* iv. 54, μ is called the reduced mass of the system and is given by $\mu = m_1 m_2/(m_1 + m_2)$. **1973** *Sci. Amer.* July 25/2 The 'reduced', or simplified, form of the horn equation shows similarly that at any point in the horn the acoustic wavelength depends on the square root of the difference between the squared frequency and a 'horn function' U that depends in a rather simple way on the nature of the horn flare.

5. a. Of metals and chemical substances: (see REDUCE *v.* 17 b, c).

1797 *Encycl. Brit.* (ed. 3) XI. 474/1 To prevent this calcination of the reduced metal a larger quantity of charcoal is used. **1839** URE *Dict. Arts* 685 The reduced iron would be apt to remain scattered in little globules. **1849** NOAD *Electricity* (ed. 3) 60 A zig-zag black line of reduced mercury. **1900** *Allbutt's Syst. Med.* V. 630 It is changed into reduced hæmoglobin.

b. ***reduced indigo*** (see quot. 1862). ***reduced iron***, a fine iron powder, obtained by treating ferric oxide with hydrogen.

1862 MILLER *Elem. Chem.* III. (ed. 2) 617 When blue indigo is treated with deoxidising agents,.. a yellow solution is formed, containing reduced indigo, a compound in which one equivalent more of hydrogen is present than in blue indigo. **1863** W. AITKEN *Pract. Med.* (1866) II. 62 The reduced iron—the *ferrum reductum* of the British Pharmacopœia—is also a remedy which does not possess the astringent properties of the other preparations.

c. Broken into fine particles.

1805 R. W. DICKSON *Pract. Agric.* II. 622 In this way the crop is rendered clean, and the fine reduced mold well laid up to the stems of the plants.

6. a. Diminished in number, quantity, amount, or size.

1762 *Ann. Reg.* I. 147/2 To direct that no fish be sold at reduced price on the day of their arrival. **1809** R. LANGFORD *Introd. Trade* 57 At the reduced rate of 3 per Cent. per annum. **1820** W. JAY *Prayers* 294 Yet are they all diminished by another irreparable loss; and the reduced remainder [etc.]. *c* **1860** H. STUART *Seaman's Catech.* 14 Load the gun with a reduced charge. **1880** C. R. MARKHAM *Peruv. Bark* 48 I.. reproduced some of his plates on a reduced scale.

b. *Phonetics.* Of a vowel sound: articulated less distinctly than a stressed vowel; weakened and centralized; become more obscure than the vowel of which it is a reflex.

Much used in descriptions of the reduced grade of ablaut theory in Indo-European philology.

1894 V. HENRY *Short Compar. Gram. Eng. & German* I. iii. 76 To a normal grade *ĕy*, *ĕw*, there corresponds a reduced grade *ĭ*, *ŭ*. **1909** O. JESPERSEN *Mod. Eng. Gram.* I. xv. 423 Besides this 'full' [ə] we have a reduced [ə]. **1938** *Language* XIV. 41 Statements that the reduced grade preceded the accent and the zero grade followed it conflict with some of the best established and most pervading ablaut schemes. **1957** E. J. DOBSON *Eng. Pronunc. 1500–1700* II. x. 868 Gil uses *ē* as the symbol for the reduced vowel from ME *ŭ* in *oner* 'honour'. **1962** A. C. GIMSON *Introd. Pronunc. Eng.* vii. 120 As the great variety of spellings indicates, /ə/ may represent the reduced (obscured, 'schwa') form of any vowel or diphthong in an unaccented position. **1964** *Language* XL. 156 Indo-European reconstructions would require a consideration of laryngeals or reduced-grade vowels or both. **1968** CHOMSKY & HALLE *Sound Pattern Eng.* 28 The segment represented as ə will be referred to as the 'reduced vowel'. **1972** A. A. PRINS *Hist. Eng. Phonemes* I. 38 Indo-European had the following vowel system:.. Reduced Vowels: $ə_1$, $ə_2$.

c. *spec.* Lowered in price.

1939 JOYCE *Finnegans Wake* (1964) I. 166 A real fur, reduced to 3/9. **1941** E. BOWEN *Look at all these Roses* 8 She came up to London.. and bought reduced coats and shoes for the little girls. **1975** M. KENYON *Mr Big* xviii. 174 It's *reduced*. And it really fits.

reduceless (rɪˈdjuːslɪs), *a.* [f. REDUCE *v.* + -LESS.] Incapable of reduction, that cannot be lessened.

c **1864** E. DICKINSON *Poems* (1955) II. 641 As an Estate perpetual Or a reduceless Mine. **1954** W. FAULKNER *Fable* 16 They wore.. the same regimental numerals, to the rest of the regiment which had not only preceded them by that reduceless gap but which had even seemed to be fleeing from them.

†reˈducement. *Obs.* [f. as REDUCED *ppl. a.* + -MENT. Cf. It. *riducimento*, Sp. *reducimiento*.]

1. The act of bringing back to a previous state (or position), *esp.* to right belief or conduct.

1592 WARNER *Alb. Eng.* VII. iii. 156 Erickmon.. of her loue and witts did wish reducement all in vayne. **1604** N. D. [PARSONS] *3rd Pt. Three Convers. Eng.* 471 What labour and charity was vsed towards them, for their instruction and reducement. **1635** BARRIFFE *Mil. Discip.* ix. (1643) 34 Face to your Leader, a word of Reducement. **1668** HOWE *Bless. Righteous* (1825) 26 He manages in order to the reducement of lost Sinners.

b. Const. *to* a specified state.

1649 BLITHE *Eng. Improv.* (*running title*) Englands Improvement: or, a Reducement of Land to pristine Fertility. **1691** WOOD *Ath. Oxon.* (1813) I. 618 That he.. plotted the reducement of the R. religion to its ancient vigour.

2. Reduction *to* (*unto*) or *into* a specified quality, state, form, etc.

1609 SIR R. BOYLE in *Lismore Papers* Ser. II. (1887) I. 142 They maie.. become instruments in reducement of that part of the kingdome to civillety and obedience. **1649** MILTON *Eikon.* ix. Wks. (1851) 401 A universal distemper, and reducement of law to arbitrary power. *a* **1670** RUST *Disc. Truth* (1682) 192 The reducement of a general principle into a particular action.

b. The act of bringing one thing *into* another.

1641 MILTON *Ch. Govt.* I. vi. Wks. (1851) 130 That ancient Prelaty which you say was first constituted for the reducement of quiet and unanimity into the Church.

3. Assignment to a particular kind or class; deduction, inference.

1624 R. B. in F. White *Repl. Fisher* App. 71 The Errors were Fundamentall, *reductiue*, by a Reducement, if they which embraced them, did pertinaciously adhere to them, hauing sufficient meanes to be better enformed. *a* **1750** A. HILL *Wks.* (1753) II. 228 You are a species in a single pen, and are not to be judg'd by any of the bold reducements of a criticism, drawn from other writers' practice.

4. Conquest, subjugation, reduction (of a town or country).

1617 MORYSON *Itin.* II. 270 For a future absolute reducement of this Countrey. **1650** CROMWELL *Let.* 20 June in *Carlyle*, When we lay before Bristol.. we considered.. of what importance the reducement thereof would be to the good of the commonwealth. **1692** WAGSTAFFE *Vind. Carol.* i. 22 They had no sooner gotten an Army and Money together .. for the reducement of Ireland [etc.].

5. Reduction, diminution; abatement.

1619 *Hist. Patient Grisel* (Percy Soc.) 40 After a little reducement of his passion. **1646** SIR T. FAIRFAX in H. Cary *Mem. Gt. Civ. War* (1842) I. 77 The committee of Northampton have applied to me for the reducement of the forces of that garrison. **1661** SIR T. CULPEPPER *Abat. Usury* (1670) 22 Usury had its first reducement from ten to eight per Cent. **1736** CARTE *Ormonde* II. 367 The King had deferred the reducement of the establishment of that kingdom.

6. Decline, decay. *rare*$^{-1}$.

1667 WATERHOUSE *Fire Lond.* 35 The Translations of Empires, the advance and reducement of families,.. all these are circumacted by God.

reducend. *Arith. rare.* [ad. L. *redūcend-um*, neut. gerundive of *redūcĕre* to REDUCE.] A number which is given to be reduced.

1674 JEAKE *Arith.* (1696) 152 The Number given to be reduced is called the Reducend. **1847** G. BOOLE *Math. Anal. of Logic* 45 Reducend Mood, *Baroko*. **1880** W. H. S. MONCK *Introd. Logic* xvi. 181 Both extremes of the Reducend Syllogism occur in its conclusion.

reducent (rɪˈdjuːsənt), *a.* (and *sb.*) [ad. L. *redūcent-em*, pr. pple. of *redūcĕre* to REDUCE.]

A. *adj.* **1.** *Bot.* and *Zool.* Of a vein, channel, etc.: That carries something back from a certain part. (Opp. to *adducent*; cf. *abducent*.)

1805 tr. *Willdenow's Botany* v. 236 The reducent vessels only appear, when the plant is cut at the top, and put inverted in the liquid. **1848** LINDLEY *Introd. Bot.* (ed. 4) II. II. iv. 173 Both the adducent and reducent channels of the sap.

2. *Med.* Lowering.

1822–34 *Good's Study Med.* (ed. 4) III. 444 A reducent treatment.. cannot be laid down as the proper plan to be pursued in general. *Ibid.* IV. 92 Copious venesections, purgatives and a reducent diet.. will often indeed be found highly beneficial.

B. *sb.* That which reduces.

1847 in WEBSTER.

reducer (rɪˈdjuːsə(r)). [f. REDUCE *v.* + -ER[1].]

1. One who reduces, in various senses.

c **1530** WYER *C. Hyst. of Troye* A b, Excuse thy reducer [= translator] blamyng his ygnoraunce. **1533** BELLENDEN *Livy* II. xv. (S.T.S.) I. 187 Þocht he was.. reducear [*v.r.* redussar] of þame to þe ciete. *a* **1586** SIDNEY *Arcadia* (1622) 120 The reducer of them into order. **1611** SPEED *Hist. Gt. Brit.* IX. xxi. (1623) 1046 The first reducer of the University of Cambridge from rudenesse and barbarity, vnto good literature and learning. **1868** G. MACDONALD *R. Falconer* I. 243 We shall have more compilers and reducers,.. and fewer inventors. **1877** RAYMOND *Statist. Mines & Mining* 286 Reducers cannot now buy directly of the miner. **1923** W. S. MAUGHAM *Our Betters* I. 23 He's the great reducer... What does he reduce?.. The Duchess of Arlington told me he'd taken nine pounds off her.

2. That which reduces. *spec.* **†a.** *Arith.* A multiplier used to reduce an amount to another denomination. *Obs.* **b.** A reducing coupling (Knight *Dict. Mech.* Suppl. 1884). **c.** *Chem.* A reducing agent (cf. also sense 2 e.) **d.** A reducing valve.

1674 JEAKE *Arith.* (1696) 152 The several Denominations are Reducers. **1894** *St. James's Gaz.* 17 Feb. 6/2 It was a great reducer of crime. **1899** *Westm. Gaz.* 29 June 2/1 The reducers for regulating the air-pressure in the cylinders. **1935** J. N. FRIEND *Text-bk. Physical Chem.* II. vii. 302 When E_0 is negative the ion in the lower state of oxidation.. functions as a reducer or reductant. **1973** *Sci. Amer.* Oct. 128/2 The oxidant, hydrogen peroxide, is stored in a plastic bag within the pressure vessel and mixed in the exit opening with reducer in the soap.

attrib. **1884** McLAREN *Spinning* 128 It is necessary to have a great many reducer and roving spindles.

e. *Photogr.* A chemical used to reduce the density of a print or negative.

1878 ABNEY *Photogr.* (1881) 298 Plain pyrogallic acid is a much less energetic reducer than alkaline pyrogallate. **1897** E. J. WALL *Dict. Photogr.* (ed. 7) 500 Belitski's Reducer. This is the most convenient as it is one solution. *Ibid.* 501 If the negative has been dried, soak in water till wet, then cover with the reducer. **1905** *Westm. Gaz.* 25 Feb. 14/2 This [*sc.* Farmer's] reducer is compounded of potassium ferricyanide solution, and a solution of hypo. **1911** [see BLEACHER 4]. **1960** G. A. GLAISTER *Gloss. Bk.* 342/2 Proportional reducers exert a uniform action on the negative, thus preserving the tone. **1977** J. HEDGECOE *Photographer's Handbk.* 242 Persulfate reducer.. makes a better reducer for negatives which are over-developed and therefore need less density and contrast.

f. A means of reducing one's weight.

1903 E. SANDYS in *Athletics for Women* 99 For those able to dispense with a few pounds of surplus adipose tissue, it [*sc.* swimming] is one of the best of reducers.

g. *Printing.* (See quot. 1968).

1963 KENNEISON & SPILMAN *Dict. Printing* 161 *Reducers*, the addition of varnish, boiled oils, etc., to printing inks to enable them to work more easily. **1968** *Gloss. Terms Offset Lithogr. Printing* (*B.S.I.*) 26 *Reducer*. 1. A liquid, miscible with ink, used to reduce its consistency. 2. A substance for addition to a printing ink to reduce its colour strength without necessarily affecting its consistency.

reduciˈbility. [f. next + -ITY.] **a.** The fact or quality of being reducible.

1676 COLLINS in Rigaud *Corr. Sci. Men* (1841) II. 10 The reducibility of Davenant's problem to infinite series. **1842** PARNELL *Chem. Anal.* (1845) 89 The easy reducibility of its compounds to the metallic state. **1889** *Lancet* 18 May 1002/1 The complete reducibility of the tumour.

b. *spec.* in *Logic*, as ***axiom of reducibility*** (see quot. 1952).

1910 WHITEHEAD & RUSSELL *Principia Math.* I. 168 (*heading*) The hierarchy of types and the axiom of reducibility. *Ibid.* 174 We assume, then, that every function of one variable is equivalent, for all its values, to some predicative function of the same argument. This assumption seems to be the essence of the usual assumption of classes; at any rate, it retains as much of classes as we have any use for... We will call this assumption the *axiom of classes*, or the *axiom of reducibility*. **1930** L. S. STEBBING *Mod. Introd. Logic* xxiii. 463 Ramsey has suggested a reconstruction of the system of *Principia Mathematica* in which the axiom of reducibility is no longer needed. **1942** D. D. RUNES *Dict. Philos.* 266/2 As an indication or rough description of the axiom of reducibility, it may be said that it cancels a large part of the restrictive consequences of the prohibition against impredicative definition.. and, in approximate effect, reduces the ramified theory of types to the simple theory of types. **1952** S. C. KLEENE *Introd. Metamath.* iii. 44 To escape this outcome, Russell postulated his *axiom of reducibility*, which asserts that to any property belonging to an order above the lowest, there is a coextensive property (i.e. one possessed by exactly the same objects) of order 0. **1963** W. V. O. QUINE *Set Theory & its Logic* xi. 251 The axiom of reducibility regales us after all with attributes unspecifiable except by quantifying over attributes whose order is as high as their own.

reducible (rɪˈdjuːsɪb(ə)l), *a.* [ad. L. type **redūcibilis*: see REDUCE *v.* and -IBLE.] That may be reduced; capable or admitting of reduction.

†1. a. Of persons: That may be brought back to right conduct; reclaimable. *Obs. rare.*

a **1450** *Mankind* 821 (Brandl), '*Nolo mortem peccatoris*', *inquis*, yff he wyll [be] reducyble.

b. Of things: That may be restored to a former (†state or) position. *rare.* (Now only *Surg.*)

1646 SIR T. BROWNE *Pseud. Ep.* III. vi. 117 Once omitted or perverted.. it is not reducible by any other whatsoever. **1655** MRQ. WORCESTER *Cent. Inv.* §13 Without blowing the Decks up, or destroying them from being reducible. **1878** T. BRYANT *Pract. Surg.* I. 646 When a hernia comes down into a sac and goes up again, it is called reducible.

2. a. That may be referred or assigned *to* some other thing, *to* some class or specified number of classes.

1529 MORE *Dyaloge* I. Wks. 170/1 Some.. rule of oure liuing, whiche is also depending vppon faith & reducible therto. **1577** HARRISON *England* III. xiv. (1878) II. 97 Our yeare is counted after the course of the sunne, and although the church hath some vse of that of the moone.. yet it is reducible to that of the sunne. **1639** FULLER *Holy War* v. x. 246 These millions of miracles are reducible to one of these foure ranks. **1698** W. CHILCOT *Evil Thoughts* v. (1851) 57 Every thought.. unsuitable.. to his glorious attributes, is reducible to this first kind of evil thoughts. **1791** HAMILTON *Berthollet's Dyeing* I. I. I. i. 25 Facts which are not reducible to any theory. **1806–7** J. BERESFORD *Miseries Hum. Life* (1826) I. Introd., Such items of anguish only as may be reducible to that specific class of 'miseries'.

†b. That may be referred *to* a place or person.

1655 FULLER *Hist. Camb.* (1840) 45 Brought up in Cambridge, but not reducible, with probability, to any College now in being. **1661** BOYLE *Style of Script.* (1675) 169 Wise men.. will not easily lose good thoughts or good expressions, because they are not reducible to them.

3. That may be brought *to* (†or *into*) some more definite state, arrangement, or principle.

1651 G. W. tr. *Cowel's Inst.* 184 It is necessary that the thing sold be certain or reducible to certainty. **1668** HALE *Pref. Rolle's Abridgm.* b ij, The Common-Law is reducible into a competent method, as to the general Heads thereof. **1710** STEELE *Tatler* No. 234 ¶9 Our English Tongue.. is the most determinate in its construction, and reducible to the fewest Rules. **1756** C. LUCAS *Ess. Waters* I. 4 Into some or all of these principles, all bodies are reducible by art, as well as nature. **1818** CRUISE *Digest* (ed. 2) III. 377 There is no title in the English law reducible to a more technical system than the title of descent in fee simple.

4. a. That may be brought, altered or converted *to* or *into* another (*esp.* a simpler) form.

c **1645** HOWELL *Lett.* (1655) II. 69 In the new World.. there is no root, flower, fruit or pulse but is reducible to a potable liquor. **1666** BOYLE *Orig. Formes & Qual.* 33 A salt easily reducible.. into Chrystalline Grains. **1699** BENTLEY *Phal.* 465 Thus reducible to Trochaics. **1754** LEWIS in *Phil. Trans.* XLVIII. 640 All are reducible.. into powder. **1777** PRIESTLEY *Philos. Necess.* 182 Complex reasoning is all reducible to acts of simple judgment. **1838–9** HALLAM *Hist. Lit.* (1847) I. 23 The words.. seem reducible, with a little emendation, to short verses. **1881** MIVART *Cat* 253 Nervous tissue is reducible into water. **1932** LEWIS & LANGFORD *Symbolic Logic* ix. 282 Functions like this one, which can be expressed in equivalent form by means of functions of a lower degree of generality, will be said to be *reducible*. **1967** R. A. GEORGE tr. *Carnap's Logical Struct. of World* I. 6 An object (or concept) is said to be reducible to one or more other objects if all statements about it can be transformed into statements about these other objects.

b. Without const. (see REDUCE *v.* 16, 17).

1674 JEAKE *Arith.* (1696) 299 Square Surdes.. not thus reducible.. are to be joyned together with the sign.. +. **1842** PARNELL *Chem. Anal.* (1845) 263 Metals whose compounds are reducible with soda on charcoal in the reducing flame. **1884** W. H. GREENWOOD *Steel & Iron* vi. 93 These silicates (which are only reducible with difficulty). **1957** G. E. HUTCHINSON *Treat. Limnol.* I. xi. 707 Some of both oxidizable and reducible iron was no doubt in organic combination. **1976** *Nature* 15 Jan. 147/1 These bulk membranes, being less dense than water, separated aqueous reducing agents and potentially reducible substrates.

†**5.** That may be brought *to* a belief, *under* a standard. *Obs. rare.*

1639 Fuller *Holy War* iv. ii. 170 Now it seemeth the Tartars are reducible with most facility to our religion. **1760–72** H. Brooke *Fool of Qual.* (1809) IV. 78 There is no ..virtue, that is not reducible under the standard of..Love.

6. *Sc. Law.* Of a deed, contract, decree, etc.: That may be annulled by a court.

1754 Erskine *Princ. Sc. Law* (1809) 108 No deed, granted with consent of the interdicters, is reducible. **1838** W. Bell *Dict. Law Scot.* 832 All deeds executed by a minor..are reducible on the head of minority and lesion. **1888** Ld. Watson in *Law Times Rep.* LIX. 4/2 To determine whether the marriage contract is reducible.

7. That may be lessened in number or amount.

1742 Richardson *Pamela* IV. 370 The number of the old ones will be always reducible..in a greater Proportion, than the new ones will increase. **1852** Mill *Pol. Econ.* iii. xviii. (ed. 3) §8. 365 These two influencing circumstances are in reality reducible to one.

Hence **re'ducibleness; re'ducibly** *adv.*

1666 Boyle *Orig. Formes & Qual.* 201 The thing itself is made plausible by the reducibleness of ice back again into Water. **1680** —— *Scept. Chem.* iii. Wks. 1772 I. 538 Its reducibleness, according to Helmont, into alcali and water. **1854** C. Forster *Monum. Assyria* (1859) 1 The consequent reducibleness of all the postdiluvian dialects to the one primeval language. **1882** Ogilvie, Reducibly.

reducine (rɪ'djuːsaɪn). *Chem.* Also **-in.** [f. reduce *v.* + -ine⁵.] An alkaloid found in small quantities in urine.

1878 Kingzett *Anim. Chem.* 229 The filtrate..was then found to contain kreatinine and the new body reducine. **1899** Cagney tr. *Jaksch's Clin. Diagn.* vii. (ed. 4) 370 Certain basic substances have recently been isolated from urine by precipitation with phosphoric acid.., such as urochrome, urotheobromin, omichol and reducin.

reducing (rɪ'djuːsɪŋ), *vbl. sb.* [-ing¹.]

1. a. The action of the vb. reduce in various senses; reduction.

?**1488** Caxton *Ryall Bk.* (Colophon), Whyche translacon or reducyng..was achyeved fynysshed and accomplysshed the xiii day of Septembre. **1591** Percivall *Sp. Dict.*, *Reduzimiento*, bringing backe, reducing. **1646** Massey in H. Cary *Mem. Gt. Civ. War* (1842) I. 90, I made an humble request..on behalf of..my brigade, upon a report made unto me of some command for the reducing of them. **1683** Cave *Ecclesiastici, Athanasius* 53 They had done it in order to the reducing and reclaiming of him. **1720** *Lond. Gaz.* No. 5813/1 To facilitate the reducing of Palermo. **1790** Beatson *Nav. & Mil. Mem.* I. 106 Although the reducing of the Havannah was strongly recommended by his Majesty's instructions, yet..success could not now be looked for. **1863** Dana *Man. Geol.* 558 The reducing of the level of the rivers.

b. Const. *to, into.*

1489 *Rolls of Parlt.* VI. 434/2 For the reducyng of the said monastery into the old auncyen order. **1532** Cromwell in Merriman *Life & Lett.* (1902) I. 349 For the reducing of the same his vntrew purpose to effecte. **1596** Spenser *State Irel.* Wks. (Globe) 646/1 The reducing of such a greate people to Christianitye. **1607** T. Rogers *39 Art.* Ded. ¶2 *marg.*, Praiers..for the reducing of true religion into the realme. **1645** Milton *Colast.* Wks. (1851) 358 The reducing of a minde to this or that fitnes. **1711** *Fingall MSS.* in *10th Rep. Hist. MSS. Comm.* App. V. 197 The reduceing of them to mendicancy and hard shifts of liveing.

2. *attrib.* and *Comb.*, as ***reducing action, enterprise***; (in sense 26 e of the vb.) ***reducing belt, pill, treatment***; **reducing box** (see quot.); **reducing compasses**, compasses adapted for copying figures on a smaller scale; **reducing coupling** or **piece**, a pipe-coupling with ends of different diameters, used in joining pipes of different sizes; **reducing gear** = *reduction gear* s.v. reduction 13; **reducing machine**, an apparatus for producing scale models; **reducing scale** (see quot.); **reducing valve**, a valve serving to reduce the pressure in a steam-engine; **reducing works**, a place at which metallic ore is reduced.

Also *reducing furnace, press, square, tee* (see Knight *Dict. Mech.*). In *reducing action, effect, power*, etc., the vbl. sb. can hardly be distinguished from the ppl. adj.

1889 *Anthony's Photogr. Bull.* II. 151 This *reducing action may produce a sub-oxide, sub-chloride, etc. **1928** A. Huxley *Point Counter Point* v. 69 No idea how comfortable those rubber *reducing belts are till you've tried them. **1894** *Labour Commission Gloss.*, **Reducing boxes*, the machines in which the operation before roving is performed by female labour. **1823–5** Fosbroke *Encycl. Antiq.* ix. (1843) 294/1 A pair of *reducing compasses, which have, like ours, four points, forming two angles,..one large, the other small. **1877** Raymond *Statist. Mines & Mining* 185 The final results of several mining and *reducing enterprises..are very discouraging. **1917** E. Butler *Transmission Gears* iii. 66 The first use of a planetary *reducing gear as a transmission between a petrol motor and the driving wheel of an automobile, was made in 1888–9 by Edward Butler on his petrol cycle. **1947** J. C. Rich *Materials & Methods of Sculpture* vi. 191 In using platinum or palladium for medals, the original model is first cast in a hard bronze, and by means of a *reducing machine a small steel die is cut of the precise size of the medal. With this die the copies are struck. **1968** *Canad. Antiques Collector* July 10/1 Benjamin Cheverton's 'reducing machine' had been employed for the scale model. This ingenious machine kept proportions exact, so that a six-inch statuette would lose nothing of the artistry of the original. **1901** *Feilden's Mag.* IV. 432/1 There would be a good many special pieces used, such as..12-in. to 9-in. *reducing pieces, besides many bends. **1955** W. Gaddis *Recognitions* ii. vii. 608 I'm taking *scads* of these marvelous *reducing pills that simply take your appetite away. **1701** Moxon *Math. Instr.* 17 **Reducing Scale*,..a thin broad piece of Box with several different Scales of equal Parts, and Lines to turn Chains and Links into Acres and Roods, by Inspection. **1907** F. H. Burnett *Shuttle* xix. 195 Mina is growing fat, and spends her days in taking *reducing treatments. **1884** Knight *Dict. Mech.* Suppl. 746/2 *Reducing Valve. **1889** *Nature* 24 Oct. 631 The pressure..is controlled by means of a reducing-valve. **1859** *Jrnl. Geog. Soc.* XXX. 48 Several owners of smelting and *reducing works. **1877** Raymond *Statist. Mines & Mining* 281 As yet there are no reducing-works on the spot.

re'ducing, *ppl. a.* [f. as prec. + -ing².] That reduces, in senses of the vb.

1741 tr. *Cramer's Assaying* 42 Borax..is classed, though improperly, among reducing Bodies, that is, among those which restore Metals, howsoever destroyed, to their metallick Form. *Ibid.* 185 Melting Metals and Ores together with saline and reducing Fluxes. **1805–17** R. Jameson *Char. Min.* (ed. 3) 299 Reducing Agents..either abstract oxygen from the mineral, or protect it from the action of that gas. **1836** T. Thomson *Mineral., Geol.*, etc. I. 599 In the reducing flame it [disulphuret of copper] becomes covered with a coat and does not melt. **1897** *Allbutt's Syst. Med.* II. 77 The reducing remedies..have been strongly recommended.

†**re'duct**, *sb. Obs.* Also 7 **-duck.** [f. as next, or ad. med.L. *reductus* a retired place, retreat.]

a. *Arith.* A number or quantity which has been reduced. **b.** (See quot.) **c.** = reduit. **d.** (See quot.)

a. 1579 Digges *Stratiot.* 23 Yee shal multiply..the Denominator of the Reduct into the Numerator of the last Fragment to be reduced.

b. 1678–96 Phillips, *Reduck*, a Chymical term, signifying a Powder by which calcined Metals and Minerals are dissolved, and return again to their Metalline Regulus. **1706** —— (ed. Kersey), *Reduct.* **1727–41** Chambers *Cycl.*, *Reduct*, or *Redux*, among chemists, is a powder [etc.].

c. 1704 J. Harris *Lex. Techn.* I, *Reduct*, a Military term, signifying an advantageous piece of Ground, entrenched and separated from the rest of the Place, to retire to in case of surprize. [Hence in Chambers (1727–41) and later Dicts.]

d. 1727–41 Chambers *Cycl.*, *Reduct*, in building, a quirk, or little place, taken out of a larger, to make it more uniform and regular; or for some other convenience, as for a little cabinet aside of a chimney, for alcoves, etc. [Hence in Crabb, Gwilt, Craig, and later Dicts.]; but in Chambers merely translated from the article *réduit* in the *Dict. de Trévoux* (1721).]

†**re'duct**, *pa. pple. Obs.* [ad. L. *reduct-us*, pa. pple. of *redūcĕre* to reduce: cf. next.]

1. Brought *into* or *to* a certain form, state, etc.; reduced to order.

1398 Trevisa *Barth. De P.R.* xix. cxvi. (1495) 920 Al pertyculer thynges the whyche eche is perfite in himself ben perfighte whan they be reducte in to one. *c* **1535** in Ellis *Orig. Lett.* Ser. iii. III. 14 Nowe ye may boldely affirme that Wales is reduct to that state that oone thief taketh an other. *a* **1548** Hall *Chron., Edw. IV* 220 All the kynges host there beyng assembled and reduct into one company. **1640–1** Ld. J. Digby *Sp. in Ho. Com.* 9 Feb. 17, I meane Episcopacy so ordered, reduct and limitted as..it may be by..sollid boundaryes.

2. Brought back (*into* a place).

1545 Joye *Exp. Dan.* ix. T viij b, He prayed for the remission of their sinnes and to be reducte into theyr land. **1635** Heywood *Hierarch.* vi. Dial. 348 Menippus..Dy'de from amongst us, without taking leave And is again reduct.

†**re'duct**, *v. Obs.* [f. ppl. stem of L. *redūcĕre*: cf. prec. and reduce *v.*]

1. *trans.* To bring *into, to* or *from* a state or form.

1558 Warde tr. *Alexis' Secr.* i. (1562) 6 b, To resolue and reducte gold into a potable licoure. **1624** T. Scott *Belg. Souldier* 24 Their resolutions to reduct the gouernment to electiue Suffrages. **1639** G. Daniel *Ecclus.* xxiii. 59 The Man of Scorne and of a bitter Tongue Will never..Be from his Sin reducted. **1816** Lamb in *Final Mem.* vi. 247, I fear lest it should be discovered by..clear reducting to letters no better than nonsense.

2. To lead back, lead *to* a place.

c **1580** Munday *View Sundry Examples* (Shaks. Soc. 1851) 86 Hee..was led to the place where he committed this murderous offence,..was reducted back, and..was executed. **1632** Lithgow *Trav.* x. 428, I was neuer before reducted to such a floting Laborinth.

3. To deduct (a sum).

1599 B. Jonson *Ev. Man out of Hum.* iv. v, Master Snip, pray let me reduct some two or three shillings for points and ribands. **1615** Jackson *Creed* iv. vii. §15 If we compare the several growth of steadfast faith and hypocrisy, they much resemble the order..of laying or reducting sums in accounts. **1738** [G. Smith] *Curious Rel.* II. 213 But this Capital was paid again,..it being reducted out of the three millions of Crowns.

reductant (rɪ'dʌktənt). *Chem.* [f. reduct(ion + -ant¹, after oxidant.] A reducing agent.

1925 *Chem. Rev.* II. 128 The heroic efforts to measure the potential of a pure solution of a reductant are evidence of the tenacity of a preconception. **1935** [see reducer 2 c]. **1968** J. March *Adv. Org. Chem.* xix. 853 In some cases both the oxidant and reductant are organic. **1976** *Sci. Amer.* July 71/2 The process is termed gaseous direct reduction or solid direct reduction depending on the state of the reductant.

reductase (rɪ'dʌkteɪz). *Biochem.* [ad. F. *réductase* (M.-E. Pozzi-Escot 1902, in *Bull. de la Soc. Chim. de Paris* XXVII. 559), f. *réduct-ion* reduction: see -ase.] **a.** Any enzyme which promotes chemical reduction.

1902 *Jrnl. Chem. Soc.* LXXXII. i. 655 The author [*sc.* Pozzi-Escot] has discovered a new class of diastases which he calls 'reductases'. **1914** [see dehydrase a]. **1938** *Ann. Rev. Biochem.* VII. 112 The protein of acetaldehyde reductase has been obtained in a crystalline condition. **1974** *Nature* 13 Dec. 579/1 The enzymes responsible for the first step in nitrate assimilation and for nitrate respiration are the nitrate reductases, both these processes involving the conversion of nitrate to nitrite. **1977** *Proc. R. Soc. Med.* LXX. 617/1 Thurnham..measured the erythrocyte glutathione reductase activity.

b. reductase test, a method of estimating the bacterial content of a sample of fluid, usu. milk, by measuring its reducing power.

1910 *Analyst* XXXV. 207 (*heading*) Reductase test for milk. **1932** *Discovery* Feb. 59/2 In the north of Europe..general use is made of the 'reductase' test, which takes the time required to decolourize a definite solution of methylene blue as a measure of the purity of milk. **1964** *Biol. Abstr.* XLV. 3876/1 Application of the reductase test to 261 randomly selected staphylococcus strains showing a positive plasma coagulase test yielded reductase times of 15 minutes or less in 96·6% of the cases.

reducti'bility. [ad. F. *réductibilité*, or f. as reduct *v.* + -ible, -ity.] Reducibility (Ogilvie 1882).

‖**reductio** (rɪ'dʌktɪəʊ). Pl. **reductiones** (rɪdʌktɪ'əʊniːz). [L., = reduction.] Used in various Latin phrases: **1. reductio ad impossibile**, reduction to the impossible: a method of proving a proposition by drawing an absurd or impossible conclusion from its contradictory.

1552 T. Wilson *Rule of Reason* (ed. 2) f. 56 The other croked waye (called of the Logicians, *Reductio ad impossibile*) is a reduccion to that, whiche is impossible. **1843** J. S. Mill *Logic* I. iii. iii. 265 We shall thus discover the error in our generalisation, by what the schoolmen termed a *reductio ad impossibile*. **1869** W. S. Jevons *Substitution of Similars* 44 This indirect or negative method is closely analogous to the *indirect proof*, or *reductio ad absurdum*, so frequently used by Euclid and other mathematicians, and a similar method is employed by the old logicians in the treatment of the syllogisms called *Baroko* and *Bokardo*, by the *reductio ad impossibile*. **1884** J. N. Keynes *Formal Logic* iii. iv. 181 This method of reduction is called *Reductio ad impossibile*, or *Reductio per impossibile*, or *Deductio ad impossibile*, or *Deductio ad absurdum*. **1962** W. & M. Kneale *Devel. Logic* i. 8 What Aristotle attributed to Zeno was presumably the discovery of the use of the *reductio ad impossibile* in metaphysics.

2. reductio ad absurdum: reduction to the absurd (see reduction 9 b). Also with superl. **reductio ad absurdissimum** (the most absurd, the greatest absurdity).

1741 I. Watts *Improvement of Mind* i. xiii. 181 *The Respondent* may be attack'd either upon a Point of his own Concession, which is call'd *Argumentum ex concessis*, or by reducing him to an Absurdity, which is call'd *Reductio ad absurdum*. **1824** J. S. Mill in *Westm. Rev.* II. 34 This we admit: and we regard it as a decisive *reductio ad absurdum* of his own argument. **1865** —— *Exam. Hamilton's Philos.* iv. 44 Hegel..has fairly earned the honour..of having logically extinguished transcendental metaphysics by a series of *reductiones ad absurdissimum*. **1896** G. B. Shaw *Our Theatres in Nineties* (1932) II. 170 Madame Sarah Grand's position is a *reductio ad absurdum* of our whole moral system. **1931** *Times Educ. Suppl.* 10 Jan. 9/4 A *reductio ad absurdissimum* is seen in the fact that an aspirant for employment in a business house, who has actually qualified for exemption from matriculation by virtue of the subjects endorsed on his school certificate, is not infrequently informed that his application cannot be entertained unless he produces the actual matriculation certificate. **1939** *Canadian Forum* July 126/2 It..may prove to be no more than the *reductio ad absurdum* of his own introspectiveness. **1955** *Times* 23 June 11/3 When the House of Commons regards even nationalized boards as little more than civil servants, and piles a committee on top of their committee we approach the *reductio ad absurdum*. **1963** [see *Christocentricity* s.v. Christo-]. **1969** L. Ruby *Art of Making Sense* (rev. ed.) viii. 84 Here is a more complex sample of the reductio ad absurdum. **1976** *Times Lit. Suppl.* 3 Dec. 1522/4 Whether the result represents anything more than a reductio ad absurdum of the traditional musicological pastime of theme-spotting. **1977** *Time* 7 Feb. 51/1 *Reductio* is always *ad absurdum*.

reduction (rɪ'dʌkʃən). Also 5–6 **reduccion, -cyon.** [a. F. *réduction* (13–14th c.), or ad. L. *reductiōn-em*, n. of action f. *redūcĕre* to reduce.]

I. †**1. a.** The action of bringing (back) *to* or *from* a state, condition, belief, etc. *Obs.*

1483 *Rolls of Parlt.* VI. 241/2 Desyryng..the peas..of this Lande, and the reduccion of the same to the auncien honourable estate and prosperite. **1557** in Burnet *Hist. Ref.* (1681) II. Records ii. ii. No. 34 For reduction of your Majesty's Realm of Ireland to the Unity of the Church. **1609** Bible (Douay) *Haggai* i. *comm.*, Reduction of soules from sinne, and amending of il maners. **1651** Hobbes *Leviath.* iii. xli. 263 God having determined his sacrifice, for the reduction of his elect to their former covenanted obedience. **1677** Gale *Crt. Gentiles* iii. 98 The reduction of the soul from its night-day to the true Light of Being.

†**b.** Without const.: Reclamation. *Obs.*

1620 tr. *Augustine's Confess.* Ep. Ded. *4 Whose ioy was no lesse in the reduction of sinners, then it would haue been, in their preseruation.

†**c.** *Metall.* (See quot.) *Obs. rare.*

1741 tr. *Cramer's Assaying* 186 Metals destroyed, and changed into Scoria or Ashes, are, by their Union with the same matter, again restored to their metallick Form. This Operation is called Reduction.

†**2. a.** The action of bringing back (a person, thing, institution, etc.) to a place previously occupied; restoration. Also const. *to*, *from*, *out of*. *Obs.*

a **1548** HALL *Chron., Hen. VIII* 144 b, To..entreate with the nobles of the Countrey for the reduccion of kyng Cristierne, to his realme, Croune, and dignitie. **1557** KNOX *Sel. Writ.* (1845) 184 After their reduction, their lives did nothing amend. **1655** FULLER *Ch. Hist.* VIII. i. §22 In the Convocation..there were found but six which opposed the Reduction of Popery. **1668–84** OWEN *Exp. Hebr.* (1790) IV. 430 The reduction of Christ from the dead by 'the God of peace'. **1741** WARBURTON *Div. Legat.* II. 322 The whole History of their Reduction out of Egypt.

†**b.** *Sc.* The action of bringing back (money) to the mint again. (Cf. REDUCE *v.* 3.) *Obs. rare.*

1581–2 *Reg. Privy Council Scot.* III. 463 For inbringing and reductioun of quhilk money thair wes nominat and appointit William Napier and Thomas Aitchesoun..to ressave all the said cunyie.

3. *Surg.* The restoration of a dislocated part to its normal position; the action of reducing a displacement, etc.

[**1612** WOODALL *Surg. Mate* Wks. (1653) 87 The reduction of parts disjoynted and dislocated to union.] **1656** RIDGLEY *Pract. Physick* 161 That which is longwaies is soonest cured, for there needs no reduction. **1727–41** CHAMBERS *Cycl.*, *Reduction*, in surgery, denotes an operation whereby a dislocated, luxated, or fractured bone, is restored to its former place. **1879** *St. George's Hosp. Rep.* IX. 288 Reduction of displacement could not be effected till 1 inch of lower fragment was cut off.

II. 4. a. Conquest or subjugation *of* a place, esp. a town or fortress.

c **1500** *Melusine* 369 After the reducyon of the Fortres. **1665** SIR T. HERBERT *Trav.* (1677) 276 Babylon thus taken, it gave the Turk the easier reduction of Diarbec. **1756–7** tr. *Keysler's Trav.* (1760) I. 204 The famous reduction, as it was called, was carried so far, that all the fundamental laws ..were entirely subverted and destroyed. **1776** GIBBON *Decl. & F.* xiii. (1782) I. 442 The reduction of Egypt was immediately followed by the Persian war. **1838** THIRLWALL *Greece* III. 407 Thus the reduction of Syracuse would lead ..to the subjugation of Greece. **1877** BROCKETT *Cross & Cr.* 49 The first exploit which Basil's successor..attempted, was the reduction of Kazan.

b. The action of reducing *into* possession (see REDUCE *v.* 19 d). Also without const.

1647 TRAPP *Comm. 1 Cor.* iii. 22 (*All are yours*) Though not in possession, yet in use, or by way of reduction, as we say. **1840** *Penny Cycl.* XVIII. 453/2 It is still doubtful whether the assignment by a husband of his wife's immediate choses in action is a reduction into possession.

c. *Hist.* [ad. Sp. *reduccion.*] A settlement or colony of South American Indians converted and governed by the Jesuits.

1712 W. ROGERS *Voy.* (1718) 89 This is the way of living in those cantons, which the missionaries call Reductions; because, if you'll believe them, they have reduced them to Christianity by their preaching. **1822** SOUTHEY in *Q. Rev.* XXVI. 286 The number of converted Indians..amounted to about 120,000 in thirty Reductions. **1881** *Encycl. Brit.* XIII. 649/1 Governing and civilizing the natives of Brazil and Paraguay in the missions and 'reductions'.

5. *Sc. Law.* The action of reducing a deed, decree, etc. (See REDUCE *v.* 23.)

reduction reductive: see REDUCTIVE *a.* 2 (quot. 1838). ***reduction-improbation***: see 13 below.

1546 *Reg. Privy Council Scot.* I. 37 Tuiching the reductioun of the infeftmentis, chartour or chartouris of talye. **1578–9** *Ibid.* III. 91 The mater dependand under reductioun befoir his Hienes and the saidis Lordis of Secreit Counsale. **1630** *Acts of Sederunt* (1790) 43 The forming and directing of Summonds of reductioune of Retours. **1706** *Act 6 Anne*, c. 11 Art. 19 All reviews reductions or suspensions of the sentences in maritime cases. *a* **1768** ERSKINE *Inst. Law Scot.* IV. 1 §24 (1773) 647 Simple reductions, where improbation is not also libelled, are now seldom made use of. **1838** W. BELL *Dict. Law Scot.* 833 The effect of a decree of reduction is, that the deed thereby reduced ceases to be of any effect against the party who has obtained it.

6. a. *Arith.* (*a*) The process of changing an amount from one denomination to another. ***ascending r.***, from a lower to a higher denomination; ***descending r.***, from a higher to a lower (Phillips 1706). (*b*) The process of bringing down a fraction to its lowest terms.

1542 RECORDE *Gr. Artes* (1575) 192 Reduction is, by whiche all summes of grosse denomination may bee turned into summes of more subtile denomination: And contrary wayes. **1594** BLUNDEVIL *Exerc.* I. xxvii. (1636) 75 The Division is to be done either by Reduction into the smallest Fractions, or without Reduction. **1674** JEAKE *Arith.* (1696) 152 Reduction of Fractions declareth the proportion of one number to another, or of broken parts to broken parts. **1682** SCARLETT *Exchanges* 17 Of the Reduction of Exchanges. **1727–41** CHAMBERS *Cycl.* s.v., To expedite the practice, several compendious ways of reduction have been invented. **1798** HUTTON *Course Math.* (1806) I. 74 This operation is the same as Reduction Descending in whole numbers. **1823** J. MITCHELL *Dict. Math. & Phys. Sci.* 420/1 Reduction of algebraic fractions is performed in exactly the same manner as the reduction of common fractions. **1859** BARN. SMITH *Arith. & Algebra* (ed. 6) 96 Reduction is the method of expressing numbers of a superior denomination in units of a lower denomination, and conversely.

b. *Alg.* (See quots. 1702–4.)

1702 RALPHSON *Math. Dict.*, *Reduction of Equations* (in Algebra) is the reducing them into a fit and proper Order or Disposition for a Solution. **1704** J. HARRIS *Lex. Techn.* I, *Reduction of Equations*, in Algebra, is the clearing of them from all superfluous Quantities, and the separating of the known Quantities from the unknown [etc.]. **1743** EMERSON *Fluxions* 36.

c. *Astron.* (*a*) (See quot. 1704.) ? *Obs.* (*b*) The correction of observations by allowance for modifying circumstances, as parallax, refraction, etc.

1704 J. HARRIS *Lex. Techn.* I, *Reduction*, in Astronomy, is the difference between the Argument of Inclination and the Eccentrical Longitude. **1812** WOODHOUSE *Astron.* x. 73 The reduction of a star's place seen from the surface, to the center. **1833** HERSCHEL *Astron.* v. (1858) 215 The complete reduction..of an astronomical observation, consists in applying..five distinct and independent corrections.

d. *Geom.* The process of reducing (a curve, etc.) to a straight line.

1798 HUTTON *Course Math.* (1807) II. 63 The high roads ..hardly ever lie in a right line between the stations; which must cause endless reductions, and require great trouble to make it a right line.

e. *transf.* The process of explaining behaviour, social or mental activity, etc., by reducing it to its component factors or to a simpler form; also by ascribing a complex result to the operation of a few or one of its factors.

1916 A. A. BRILL tr. *Freud's Wit & its Relation to Unconsc.* ii. 28 The briefest reduction of the meaning by which one could replace this joke would be..[etc.]. **1927** W. M. WHEELER in *Proc. 6th Internat. Congr. Philos., 1926* 34 The reduction of these new properties to those of the parts in the sense of identification, and the finding of a causal determination also in this sense is impossible. **1928** H. G. & C. F. BAYNES tr. *Jung's Contrib. to Analytical Psychol.* 56 When the unsuitable structures have been reduced, and the natural course of things restored, the possibility of a normal life being thus attained, reduction is not to be pushed further. **1950** H. HARTMANN *Ess. Ego Psychol.* (1964) vi. 112 We may refer to such simplifications as 'theories by reduction'. They see one specific phase..as the sole causative factor for a character type. **1960** J. STRACHEY in *Freud's Compl. Wks.* VIII. 23 Here and elsewhere in this work Freud uses the word 'reduction' in the sense of taking something back to its original form. **1960** R. F. C. HULL tr. *Jung's Gen. Aspects of Dream Psychol.* in *Coll. Wks.* VIII. 240 Obviously this reduction is quite unsatisfying from the scientific point of view... The discovery of a single antecedent is by no means sufficient.

f. *Computers.* The transformation of data into a simpler or more amenable form.

1958 *Jrnl. Assoc. Computing Machinery* V. 89 (*heading*) Special purpose analog machine for data reduction. **1969** P. B. JORDAIN *Condensed Computer Encycl.* 423 Reduction can take several forms: changing the encoding to eliminate redundancy, or extracting significant details from the data and eliminating the rest or choosing every second or third out of the totality of available points.

7. *Logic.* The process of reducing a syllogism (†or proposition) to another, esp. to a simpler or clearer, form; *spec.* by expressing it in one of the moods of the first figure (***direct*** or ***ostensive reduction***). Also, the process of establishing the validity of a syllogism by showing that the contradictory of its conclusion is inconsistent with its premisses (***indirect*** or ***apagogical reduction***).

1551 T. WILSON *Logike* (1567) 27 b, To make a thing otherwise then it was before, to reduce it, or to bring it to more plaine understanding, in the shape and forme of the first figure, is called reduction. **1697** [see OSTENSIVE *a.* 1]. **1727–41** CHAMBERS *Cycl.*, *Reduction of propositions* is used in a more general sense, for any expression of one proposition, by another proposition equivalent thereto. *Ibid.*, *Reduction of syllogisms* is a regular changing or transforming of an imperfect syllogism into a perfect one. **1827** WHATELY *Elem. Logic* II. iii. §6 in *Encycl. Metrop.* (1845) I. 211 In these ways (which are called Ostensive Reduction..) all the imperfect Moods may be reduced to the four perfect ones. **1891** [see DIRECT *a.* 4 c]. **1896** [see INDIRECT *a.* 2 b].

b. ***reduction sentence***: a sentence giving conditions for the use of a concept less strict than a definition.

1936 R. CARNAP in *Philos. of Sci.* III. 441 We shall call R_1 and R_2 reduction sentences for 'Q_3' and '$\sim Q_3$' respectively. **1949** [see *non-dispositional* s.v. NON- 3]. **1963** A. PAP *Introd. Philos. of Sci.* ii. 32 The virtue of the reduction sentence, then, is that it permits us to ascribe a disposition *D* to an object only if the relevant experiment has been performed and found to have a positive outcome. **1965** P. CAWS *Philos. of Sci.* viii. 54 Carnap..closes the loophole in the definition by rewriting it as a *reduction sentence*.

†**8.** The action of reducing *to* a standard or class.

1597 BROUGHTON (*title*) Daniel his Chaldie Visions.. expounded..by reduction of heathen most famous stories vnto the exact proprietie of his wordes.

9. a. Conversion *into* or *to* a certain state, form, etc.

1605 BACON *Adv. Learn.* I. v. §4 Another Errour..is the over-early and peremptorie reduction of knowledge into Arts and Methodes. **1626** JACKSON *Creed* VIII. xviii. §1 God ..did prevent the reduction of that possibility..into act. **1656** BRAMHALL *Replic.* vi. 263 If it had been only the reduction of these new mysteries into the form of a Creed, that did offend us. **1850** ROBERTSON *Serm.* Ser. III. vii. (1853) 95 The reduction of society to that state in which the monster injustice has been perpetrated.

b. ***reduction to the absurd*** or ***to absurdity***, a method of proving the falsity of a premiss, principle, etc., by showing that the conclusion or consequence is absurd; also loosely, the pushing of anything to an absurd extreme. (More freq. used in the Latin form *reductio ad absurdum.*)

1856 MISS YONGE *Daisy Chain* II. xv. 506 [The Doctor] had a courteous clever process of the reduction to the absurd, which seldom failed to tell. **1865** MILL *Exam. Hamilton* 369 There is no such thing as a reduction to absurdity if this is not one. **1892** *Pall Mall G.* 26 May 1/2 Such reductions to absurdity of the universal eight hours day are..less necessary now.

10. a. The action or process of reducing (a substance) to another (usually a simpler) form, *esp.* by some chemical process; *spec.* in *Chem.*, the opposite of OXIDATION (senses 1 a and b): the removal of oxygen from, or addition of hydrogen to, a compound; partial or complete donation of an electron to an atom or molecule; a decrease in the proportion of electronegative constituents in a molecule or compound.

1666 J. SMITH *Old Age* 186 Glandules in the body of man ..that serve either to Excretion, to Reduction, or to Nutrition. **1727–41** CHAMBERS *Cycl.* s.v., The reduction of metals into their first matter, or principles. **1796** KIRWAN *Elem. Min.* (ed. 2) II. 504 As appears both by precipitation and reduction. **1851** CARPENTER *Man. Phys.* (ed. 2) 266 The action of the Stomach is restricted, in the higher animals, to the reduction of the food by the solvent powers of the gastric juice. **1862** MILLER *Elem. Chem.* III. (ed. 2) 61 Processes of reduction are less completely under the control of the chemist than those of oxidation. **1884** W. H. GREENWOOD *Steel & Iron* vi. 92 The chemical reactions..are very simple, involving only the reduction of ferric oxide. **1900** W. A. SHENSTONE *Inorg. Chem.* 177 The terms oxidation and reduction are no longer confined to changes in which oxygen plays a part... The term reduction may be applied to any change which involves a decrease in the relative amount of the negative radicle present in a compound. **1913** J. B. COHEN *Org. Chem. Adv. Students* II. ii. 100 The difference between the two catalysts is also brought out in the case of heptine C_7H_{12}, copper giving heptene C_7H_{14} and polymerisation products.., and nickel effecting complete reduction to heptane. **1930** L. B. FLEXNER tr. *L. Michaelis's Oxidation- Reduction Potentials* 10 We shall simply collect together as equivalent processes (1) the addition of oxygen, (2) the loss of hydrogen, and (3) the loss of electrons and call them all oxidations, and their converses, reductions. **1950** N. V. SIDGWICK *Chem. Elements* II. 1327 Ferrous compounds are formed either from the metal or by the reduction of the ferric. **1964** N. G. CLARK *Mod. Org. Chem.* x. 177 Aldehydes readily undergo reduction to alcohols. **1970** AMBROSE & EASTY *Cell Biol.* ii. 62 Reduction is regarded conversely as involving a gain of electrons, and substances which have the characteristic of giving up electrons to other substances are called reducing agents. **1979** *Archaeology* July–Aug. 21/2 When there is a lack of oxygen in the 'reduction' the iron oxide constituent of the earthenware clay remains in its ferrous or black state.

b. The conversion of ore into metal; smelting.

1797 *Encycl. Brit.* (ed. 3) XI. 453/2 The reduction of iron-ore..requires a violent and long-continued heat. **1839** URE *Dict. Arts* 710 The reduction of a portion of the roasted ore is begun at the same time. **1890** W. J. GORDON *Foundry* 98 Just below the top, where reduction takes place by the contact with the carbonic oxide, the fire is a dull red.

c. *Philos.* In phenomenology, the process of reducing an object of consciousness or an idea to its pure essence through elimination of all reference to extraneous things, in particular by eliminating (or 'bracketing') all reference to the real world of material objects; esp. as ***eidetic***, ***phenomenological***, ***transcendental reduction***. (See quot. 1943.)

1914 *Mind* XXIII. 590 He [*sc.* Husserl] deals in a most valuable section with the relation of consciousness to natural reality, with the province of pure consciousness, and with the phenomenological reductions. **1924** *Monist* XXXIV. 520 To carry out the 'phenomenological reduction', i.e., to isolate an object from its existential or systematic connections, is equivalent to considering it as it is originally given, without the distorting influences of 'theory'. **1931** W. R. B. GIBSON tr. *Husserl's Ideas* 44 The corresponding Reduction which leads from the psychological phenomenon to the pure 'essence', or,..from factual ('empirical') to 'essential' universality, is the eidetic Reduction. *Ibid.* 114 We propose to speak..of phenomenological reductions... From the epistemological viewpoint we would also speak of transcendental reductions. **1943** M. FARBER *Found. Phenomenol.* i. 20 The 'reduction' opens up a universal field for philosophical investigation which is free from all pre-judgements and assumptions, hence its crucial methodological importance. Husserl is careful to distinguish eidetic reduction (proceeding from fact to essence) from transcendental reduction, according to which the phenomena are characterized as 'irreal'... The method of phenomenological reduction is applied in order to achieve the presuppositionless field of philosophy. **1966** A. GURWITSCH *Stud. Phenomenol. & Psychol.* v. 111 Performance of the transcendental without the eidetic reduction discloses the flow of 'my' transcendentally purified mental states in phenomenal time. **1970** A. GIORGI *Psychol. as Human Sci.* iii. 148 By means of the phenomenological reduction, i.e., by a change in attitude, the world can be considered as phenomenon. **1972** H. SPIEGELBERG *Phenomenol. in Psychol. & Psychiatry* ii. 76 He did not believe in a strict separation between the world of essences and the world of facts, thus rejecting Husserl's 'eidetic reduction'.

11. a. Diminution, lessening, cutting down.

a **1676** HALE (J.), Some will have these years to be but months;..yet that reduction will not serve. **1730–4** WATERLAND *Script. Vind.* Postscr., Wks. 1823 VI. 186 Let him therefore first make the proper reduction in the account, and then see what it amounts to. **1769** BURKE *Late St. Nat.* Wks. II. 46 Not one shilling towards the reduction of our debt. **1796** C. MARSHALL *Garden.* xii. (1813) 178 If they [lilacs] need much reduction let them be cut down as soon..as they have got off flower. **1874** GREEN *Short Hist.* viii. §6. 526 The general opinion was in favour of a reduction of the power and wealth of the Church.

b. The action or process of making a copy on a smaller scale; also, a copy of this kind. *spec.* of the size of a copy or photographic image in photography, microphotography, etc.

1727–41 Chambers *Cycl.* s.v., The great use of the proportional compasses is in the reduction of figures, &c., whence they are also called compasses of reduction. **1786** Jefferson *Writ.* (1859) I. 536 It is as particular as the four-sheet maps from which it is taken, and I answer for the exactness of the reduction. **1876** Geo. Eliot *Dan. Der.* xxx, The little faces beside her, almost exact reductions of her own. **1889** E. J. Wall *Dict. Photogr.* 158 Whereas in enlargements the greater distance is between lens and sensitive surface, in the case of reduction the greater distance must be between the lens and negative. **1959** F. Luther *Microfilm* 1 Reductions greater than those now in common use were employed to produce microfilms that could meet the rule-of-thumb test of quality, that is, be enlarged back to original size without substantial loss of definition or legibility. **1962** A. Günther *Microphotogr. in Libr.* 5 The advantages of the use of photographic reduction in recording documents are so obvious that it is not surprising that the first microphotograph was made shortly after the invention of photography. **1965** *Focal Encycl. Photogr.* II. 1255/1 Reduction in printing, in copying and graphic arts work applies to reproduction at a scale of less than 1:1 or same size. **1973** D. A. Spencer *Focal Dict. Photogr. Technol.* 518, A 1:3 reduction is a copy that is one-third of the linear size of the original.

c. *Photogr.* Diminution of the density of a print or negative.

1889 E. J. Wall *Dict. Photogr.* 158 Reduction will proceed in proportion to the amount of ferridcyanide [*sic*] present. **1902** A. Watkins *Photogr.* 93 Where a rapid plate (of poor quality) does not seem to give sufficient contrast before it fogs over, a knowledge of reduction and intensifying will often give a good negative. **1956** *Focal Encycl. Photogr.* 951/2 The object of reduction is to make a very dense negative easier to print, or to lighten undesirably black areas of a print. **1977** J. Hedgecoe *Photographer's Handbk.* 242 Assess the progress of reduction by removing the negative at frequent intervals.

d. *Mus.* Transcription of a full orchestral score for a smaller number of instruments, esp. for piano; the reduced score thus produced.

1884 F. Niecks *Dict. Mus. Terms* 273 *Riduzione*, reduction. **1966** [see *piano reduction* s.v. piano *sb.*[2] 2 d]. **1973** L. Lockwood in A. Tyson *Beethoven Stud.* 118 (*caption*) Reduction of *Sehnsucht*, bars 3–6. **1979** [see *open score* s.v. open *a.* (*adv.*) 22 c]. **1980** *Times* 28 June 9/7 Mahler songs, not in their familiar orchestral settings but in piano versions. Some are originals, some reductions, and some fall in between.

e. *Cytology.* The halving of the number of chromosomes per cell that occurs at one of the two anaphases of meiosis (cf. postreduction, prereduction); chiefly *attrib.* in **reduction division**, the meiotic cell division during which reduction occurs. [The senses are due to A. Weismann, who used G. *reduktion*, *reduktionstheilung* (*Über die Zahl der Richtungskörper und über ihre Bedeutung für die Vererbung* (1887) i. 14, ii. 35).]

1891 *Jrnl. R. Microsc. Soc.* 461 There is a 'reduction-division', for twelve chromosomes are found in each new cell. **1896** E. B. Wilson *Cell* v. 182 The process of reduction is very obviously a provision to hold constant the number of chromosomes characteristic of a species. **1906** *Rep. Brit. Assoc. Adv. Sci. 1905* 570 Weissman predicted that a transverse division of the chromosomes would be found to take place by which the reduction would be brought about. *Ibid.*, A true reduction division is found to occur in the heterotype stage. **1927** Haldane & Huxley *Animal Biol.* ii. 59 Instead of the chromosomes dividing, the members of a pair come to lie side by side; and at division one whole chromosome of a pair is separated from the other. This process is called the reduction of the chromosomes, for owing to it, each of the two cells produced at this division possess only half of the ordinary number of chromosomes for the species. **1931** E. B. Ford *Mendelism & Evolution* i. 12 Each chromosome must contain many factors. These will be inherited together for, at the reduction division, they will pass into the same germ cell without the opportunity of random assortment. **1948** H. P. Riley *Genetics & Cytogenetics* iv. 65 The reduction division reduces the *number* of chromosomes and centromeres. **1971** D. J. Cove *Genetics* i. 7 This type of cell division whereby a diploid cell can give rise to haploid cells is called reduction division. **1979** *Sci. Amer.* Feb. 104/1 Meiosis, the 'reduction division' whereby one male germ cell divides to form four sperm cells, each of which has half the normal complement of chromosomes.

f. *Phonetics.* Weakening; obscuring (of a vowel); substitution of a sound which requires less muscular effort to articulate.

1909 O. Jespersen *Mod. Eng. Gram.* I. ix. 260 Weak /iu/ has in some words kept both sounds, though with an early reduction of /i/ to /j/. **1953** K. Jackson *Lang. & Hist. Early Brit.* 293 The reduction of pretonic ǭ to ǭ in Welsh. **1959** C. L. Wrenn *Word & Symbol* (1967) 39 *Gerrans*.. shows the regular Cornish reduction of the final *t* to *s*. **1962** A. C. Gimson *Introd. Pronunc. Eng.* vii. 120 This reduction of unaccented vowels, typical of a stress-accent language such as English, has been a feature of the English sound system for over a thousand years. **1970** B. M. H. Strang *Hist. Eng.* vi. 342 The reduction of vowels is a sign that these formal distinctions were no longer functionally important.

g. Reducing or limiting the use of addictive drugs. Usu. *attrib.*

1914 Jackson & Hellyer *Vocab. Criminal Slang* 69 *Reduction*.., the reduction cure for a 'habit'. Example: 'The only sensible way of getting off is on the reduction'. **1953** W. Burroughs *Junkie* iii. 39 The 'thirty-day cure'. This is not a reduction cure. They don't give any junk... All they offer the addict is thirty days' detention. *Ibid.* viii. 73, I have never known one of these self-administered reduction cures to work. **1962** 'K. Orvis' *Damned & Destroyed* ii. 18 You've tried everything with your daughter, haven't you?.. Forced her to take cold-shock and reduction treatments.

12. *Mil.* Degradation to a lower rank.

1806 Pike *Sources Mississ.* (1810) 78, I examined into the conduct of my sergeant, and found that he was guilty and punished him by reduction, &c.

13. *attrib.* and *Comb.*, as *reduction product*, etc.; **reduction compasses**, reducing compasses; **reduction division**: see sense 11 e above; **reduction gear** *Engin.*, a system of gear wheels in which the driven shaft rotates more slowly than the driving shaft; so **reduction gearing**; **reduction-improbation** *Sc. Law*, a form of rescissory action, in which it is suggested that the deed, or other document in question, is not genuine; **reduction negative, print** *Photogr.*, a negative or print made from a larger original; so **reduction printing**; **reduction-works**, (*a*) works for the reduction of metallic ore; (*b*) (see quot. 1894).

1875 Knight *Dict. Mech.* 1903/1 **Reduction-compasses*, proportional dividers or whole-and-half dividers. **1896** E. T. Carter *Motive Power & Gearing* xxviii. 532 The double *reduction gear used on the Frankfort-Offenbach tramcars. **1942** *R.A.F. Jrnl.* 3 Oct. 18 The port propeller and reduction gear casing were wrenched off. **1971** B. Scharf *Engin. & its Lang.* xii. 161 Any system of gears in which the speed of the driven shaft is lower than the speed of the driving shaft may be described as a reduction gear. **1896** E. T. Carter *Motive Power & Gearing* 617/1 (Index), *Reduction gearing. **1934** *Jane's Fighting Ships* 94 Turbines with single reduction gearing. **1942** J. Liston *Aircraft Engine Design* viii. 146 The inherent tendency for the propeller efficiency to drop at high speeds can be offset by suitable reduction gearing. *a* **1768** Erskine *Inst. Law Scot.* iv. i. §19 (1773) 644 The most effectual method of setting aside deeds granted to one's prejudice, is by the action of *reduction-improbation. **1838** W. Bell *Dict. Law Scot.* 485 Under the certification of an action of reduction-improbation, the deed, if not produced, will be held as false and forged. **1868** *Act 31 & 32 Vict.* c. 100 §17 It shall not be necessary to obtain the concurrence of Her Majesty's Advocate to any summons of reduction-improbation. **1945** *Jrnl. Soc. Motion Picture Engineers* Apr. 290 This process [*sc.* reduction printing] is commonly used in making 16-mm negatives or prints from 35-mm originals. Film thus made is referred to as a *reduction negative or reduction print, as the case may be. **1943** *Ibid.* Dec. 507 An effort was made to learn if the wows introduced into the *reduction prints by the printer itself could be reduced by an increase in the speed of the printer. **1973** D. A. Spencer *Focal Dict. Photogr. Technol.* 420 The assembly is also used to make reduction prints—e.g. by projecting 35 mm film on to 16 mm raw stock in the camera. **1945** *Jrnl. Soc. Motion Picture Engineers* Apr. 290 *Reduction printing is the process of producing and recording photographically a smaller image, usually on a smaller film, from a larger image. **1891** *Anthony's Photogr. Bull.* IV. 159 A silver chloride *reduction product. **1872** Raymond *Statist. Mines & Mining* 26 During one month when all the *reduction works were producing. **1894** Gould *Dict. Med.* etc., *Reduction works*, a cremating establishment for disposing of the filth and refuse matter of a city.

re'ductional, *a.* [f. reduction + -al[1].] Characterized by reduction. (*spec.* in *Cytology*: cf. reduction sense 11 e above). Hence **re'ductionally** *adv.*

1674 Jeake *Arith.* (1696) 49 Reductional Operation ended, Probation follows. **1816–30** Bentham *Offic. Apt. Maximized, Extract Const. Code* (1830) 45 Each bidding will be either reductional, or emptional, or compound. **1903** *Biol. Bull.* IV. 266 Van Winiwarter.. considers it probable that one of these divisions is reductional. **1905** *Proc. Acad. Nat. Sci. Philadelphia* LVII. 195 There is no evidence that chromosomes divide in different ways in the first maturation mitosis, some equationally and some reductionally. **1914** *Jrnl. Morphol.* XXV. 622 The univalent chromosomes.. conjugate first in the equator of the first maturation spindle and there separate reductionally. **1920** etc. [see equational *a.* 3]. **1939** Sansome & Philp *Rec. Adv. Plant Genetics* (ed. 2) vi. 183 Muller's Theory implies that the whole chromosome divides reductionally at the first division of meiosis. **1975** *Nature* 8 May 111/1 Normally fertilisation stimulates both the completion of the reductional first meiotic division and the subsequent equational second division.

reductionism (rɪˈdʌkʃənɪz(ə)m). [f. reduction + -ism.] In philosophy, the practice of trying to show that certain entities may be eliminated by reducing all reference to them to reference to some other entities. In more general use, the practice of describing a phenomenon (particularly one involving human thought and action) in terms of an apparently more 'basic' or 'primitive' phenomenon, to which the first is then said to be equivalent; for example, the practices of describing mental states in terms of the behaviour that expresses them, of describing organic processes in terms of the physico-chemical reactions which underly them, of describing social and political transformations in terms of the economic changes which engender them. In each case it is supposed that 'reduction' both explains, and also simplifies; 'reductionism' is therefore often used as a term of abuse for those theories which simplify too much, by reducing one phenomenon to another that is too basic to explain it.

1948 A. L. Kroeber *Anthropol.* (rev. ed.) xv. 576 The whole problem of the double aspect of our phenomena can also be seen as hingeing on how far we wish.. to carry or not to carry what might be called intellectual reductionism. **1952** R. M. Hare *Lang. Morals* 180 Nor am I committing the sin of 'reductionism' which, because of its excessive prevalence, has become a fashionable target for philosophical heresy-hunters. **1953** W. V. O. Quine *From Logical Point of View* 20 The other dogma is *reductionism*: the belief that each meaningful statement is equivalent to some logical construct upon terms which refer to immediate experience. **1960** B. G. Andreas *Exper. Psychol.* viii. 212 In theory construction reductionism refers to the use of constants and laws from one scientific discipline to explain the relationship found in another realm of investigation. **1965** *Jrnl. Politics* XXVII. 783 Reductionism. In its belief that every major irritation in society has a simple cause, a simple explanation and a simple solution, the radical right reduces such irritations to Communism. **1969** *Daily Tel.* 1 Nov. 7/7 It [*sc.* the minute dissection of music's anatomical structure] can easily succumb to the kind of 'reductionism' which.. claims that any organism can be fully explained by a careful analysis of its smallest components. **1969** *Times Lit. Suppl.* 20 Nov. 1341/1 Reductionism.. assumes that all properties of organisms.. are ultimately reducible to physics and chemistry. **1971** R. F. Murphy *Dialectics of Social Life* (1972) ii. 68 Durkheim.. directed his critique against theories that sought to reduce social explanation to areas of psychology and biology that were not known at the time... Such 'reductionism' to the unknown is indeed a shallow gambit. **1976** *Nature* 3 June 439/1 Reductionism rests on the belief that the whole can be fully explained in terms of the parts. **1979** *Bull. Amer. Acad. Arts & Sci.* Apr. 20 What would be needed instead is what I once heard Etienne Gilson describe as a dogmatic basis for dogmatic tolerance. For that we must go beyond the reductionism that has shaped all of us to a historical awareness of the deepest issues that have divided the two communities. **1981** *Times Lit. Suppl.* 6 Feb. 137/4 Structuralism.. has offered certain threats to reductionism.

re'ductionist, *sb.* and *a.* [f. reduction + -ist.]

a. One who favours reduction (in the number of licensed houses).

1895 *N.B. Daily Mail* 5 Oct. 2/1 Neither progressive prohibitionists nor moderate reductionists could afford to fight without each other's help.

b. An advocate of reductionism; one who attempts to analyse or account for a complex theory or phenomenon by reduction. Also *attrib.* or as *adj.*

1934 in Webster. **1943** *Mind* LII. 129 The behaviour field which, as a whole, is molar from the reductionist's point of view. **1953** K. Britton *John Stuart Mill* iii. 86 Here it was Comte who maintained a reductionist view, holding that all the laws of psychology must find their ultimate explanation in terms of bodily changes. **1956** A. J. Ayer in H. D. Lewis *Contemp. Brit. Philos.* 60 The reductionist's hero is the average man who is patently a logical construction. **1960** J. Cohen *Chance, Skill & Luck* i. 13 It does not follow that psychology lacks the status of an independent science and must be 'reduced' to neurophysiology, though this is what latter-day reductionists in effect demand. **1964** I. L. Horowitz *New Sociol.* 9 It succeeds in re-tooling the 'culture-lag' doctrine by making it conform to its own reductionist image of society. **1974** M. Wiles *Remaking of Christian Doctrine* i. 5 Reductionists who in the face of the evolution of the human species want to say that man is really nothing but his animal ancestry in another form. **1977** *Times Lit. Suppl.* 1 Apr. 409/2 While the interpretation may be reductionist, it is a plausible one.

reductio'nistic, *a.* [f. reduction + -istic.] = reductionist *a.* Hence **reductio'nistically** *adv.*

1960 B. G. Andreas *Exper. Psychol.* viii. 213 In psychology a theory may be considered reductionistic if, in addition to describing behavioral events, it employs constructs from physiology. **1965** *Jrnl. Politics* XXVII. 783 The list of problems and events treated reductionistically is enormous. **1971** *Jrnl. Gen. Psychol.* LXXXIV. 152 It is quite easy to see how each generation of reductionistically oriented theorizers was so easily seduced into using the most current, exciting, interesting, and potentially useful technology as the basis for its ideas. **1974** B. F. Skinner *About Behaviourism* xiv. 240 A science of behaviour has been said to dehumanize man because it is reductionistic. **1976** Smythies & Corbett *Psychiatry* i. 7 Current sociological theory is just as fragmented, disorganized and reductionistic as Freudian psychology.

reductive (rɪˈdʌktɪv), *a.* and *sb.* [f. as reduct *v.* + -ive. Cf. F. *réductif* (14th c.).]

A. *adj.* **1. a.** That leads or brings back. Also with *of*.

1655 Stanley *Hist. Philos.* I. (1701) 11/2 The Zoroastrian Oracles mention reductive Angels, which reduce Souls to them, drawing them from several things. **1677** Gale *Crt. Gentiles* iv. 389 God is.. of those things that ascend up to him the way and reductive manuduction. **1821** Lamb *Elia* Ser. i. *Old Benchers Inner T.*, Her prettiest blushing curtsy .. reductive of juvenescent emotion!

b. *Psychol.* That leads back to an earlier state.

1928 H. G. & C. F. Baynes tr. *Jung's Contrib. to Analytical Psychol.* 58 If now, by means of a reductive procedure, we uncover the infantile pre-stages of an adult psyche, we find as the ultimate foundation the infantile seeds. **1950** J. A. Hadfield *Psychol. & Mental Health* xvi. 410 We style our method direct reductive analysis: it is reductive in that we analyse back to the deep-seated and predisposing causes as well as the more recent and precipitating causes. **1962** *Listener* 29 Mar. 568/2 Psychoanalysis is primarily historical and reductive, deducing the analysand's present situation from his past history. **1967** J. A. Hadfield *Introd. Psychotherapy* xxii. 182 By reductive analysis I mean all those systems of psychotherapy whose methods are to go into the past to discover the causes of the neurosis in childhood experiences.

2. a. That reduces, or serves to reduce, in various senses of the vb.; connected with, of the nature of, reduction. Also with *of*.

1633 H. GELLIBRAND in T. James *Voy.* R 2 b, [The moon's] Reductive Scruples. **1651** JER. TAYLOR *Holy Dying* iv. §6 Repentance..productive of fixed Resolutions of holy Living, and reductive of these to act. **1674** JEAKE *Arith.* (1696) 156 So such kind of Reductive Questions become transient. **1694** SALMON *Bate's Dispens.* (1715) 326/2 They can never be separated without some reductive Salt. **1741** tr. *Cramer's Assaying* 51 Artificers compose a great many Fluxes with the above-mentioned Salts and with the reductive ones. **1822–34** *Good's Study Med.* (ed. 4) II. 295 The important question before us, under what circumstances it may be expedient to employ a palliative plan, and under what a cooling and reductive? **1838** W. BELL *Dict. Law Scot.* 834 An action of reduction reductive is an action in which a decree of reduction, which has been erroneously or improperly obtained, is sought to be reduced. **1898** *Westm. Gaz.* 29 Nov. 6/3 The Imperial Government do not expect to be recouped one penny on the reductive move. **1924** C. E. MONTAGUE *Right Place* iii. 29 Calvin cast his reductive shadow over the naturally high spirits of Scotland. **1957** G. E. HUTCHINSON *Treat. Limnol.* I. ix. 626 Reductive organic sediments. **1969** *Listener* 14 Aug. 203/3 A British cinema..need not be one that seeks to indoctrinate foreigners in some reductive British image. **1974** *Times* 19 Nov. 9/4 Mr. Wilson..is not a reductive writer: he wants to recreate Crowley, not to explain him away. **1979** *Quarto* Oct. 3/4 There may be something reductive in Wolfe's constant harping on the rivalry and the petty resentments of the astronauts and their wives.

b. That tends to reduce, or is connected with reduction, esp. REDUCTION 6 e and 7 b. (See also REDUCTIONISM.)

1937 T. PARSONS *Struct. Social Action* v. 181 He [*sc.* Pareto] is thus free at the outset at least from the 'reductive' tendencies so prominent in the older positivism. **1957** P. LAFITTE *Person in Psychol.* v. 62 Reductive tendencies in social psychology can now be considered. The first of these is the tendency to see the person as an object which is pushed around in a field of force. **1966** O. WOJTASIEWICZ tr. *Kotarbinski's Gnosiology* IV. i. 221 All reasonings are usually divided into deductive and reductive, the former being from reason to consequence, and the latter, from consequence to reason. **1977** R. WILLIAMS *Marxism & Lit.* I. iv. 62 What is in fact idealized, in the ordinary reductive view, is 'thinking' or 'imagining'. **1979** *Dædalus* Summer 96 The search for a common denominator can prove fruitful—if it does not degenerate into a reductive maneuver.

c. *Art.* = MINIMAL *a.* c.

1967 *New Yorker* 25 Feb. 99 To judge by art magazines and museum programs, nothing new has been done in the past few years but Happenings, optical displays, and so-called primary structures and reductive paintings. **1970** *Britannica Bk. of Year 1969* 798/3 *Rejective art*, a simplified and often depersonalized art (as painting or sculpture) based on the principle of the artist rejecting the various options open to him; called also *reductive art, reductivism, rejectivism*.

†**3.** That may be referred to or derived from something else; reducible. *Obs.*

1660 JER. TAYLOR *Duct. Dubit.* III. iii. rule 6 §32 The church makes laws either by her declarative and direct power, or by a reductive and indirect power. **1662** GURNALL *Chr. in Arm.* verse 19. viii. (1679) 502/1 His Commission is to make known the Gospel; to deliver that..which is not reductive to this, is besides his instruction. **1691** W. NICHOLLS *Answ. Naked Gospel* 59 There is a guilt contracted from this reductive Heresy as well as from the other.

B. *absol.* as *sb.* That which tends to reduce. *rare.*

a **1676** HALE *Prim. Orig. Man.* II. ix. 215 There needed no other Reductive of the Numbers of Men to an Equability, than the Wars that have happened in the World. **1681** CHETHAM *Angler's Vade-m.* xxxviii. §14 (1689) 249 All sorts of Creatures whatever have their Reductives and Corrections, else would the World be over-stocked. **1871** T. D. HAYE tr. *Taine's On Intelligence* I. II. i. 53 It is the *special reductive*, that is to say, the contradictory sensation, which fails in the conflict, and, instead of depriving the image of its externality, becomes itself effaced. **1890** W. JAMES *Princ. Psychol.* II. 125 The usual explanation of hypnagogic hallucinations is that they are ideas deprived of their ordinary reductives.

re'ductively, *adv.* Now *rare.* [f. prec. + -LY[2].] By reduction; by consequence or inference, indirectly. (Common in 17th c.)

1631 J. BURGES *Answ. Rejoined* Pref. 37 Ceremonies called Sacred are of two sorts, Properly so called, or Reductively. **1661** BOYLE *Style of Script.* (1675) 129 Insinuating, that all the laws that regulate man's duty are virtually or reductively comprised there. **1702** *Eng. Theophrastus* 298 Tho' they are not matter of conscience, simply and apart, they are so reductively, with a regard to other considerations. **1817** J. BROWN *Gospel Truth Stated* (1831) 141 There is not a conditional promise in the Bible but what is reductively absolute. **1853** WHEWELL *Grotius* I. 11 Some things are said to be according to Natural Law, which are not so properly, but, as the schools love to speak, reductively.

reductivism (rɪ'dʌktɪvɪz(ə)m). [f. REDUCTIVE *a.* and *sb.* + -ISM.] **1.** *Art.* = MINIMALISM.

1967 *Listener* 17 Aug. 220 Bernard Cohen's *White Plant* dates from the period when his earlier 'linguistic' style had degenerated into a hothouse aestheticism; the rather self-conscious reductivism of his recent exhibition was far less cloying. **1970** [see REDUCTIVE *a.* 2 c].

2. = REDUCTIONISM.

1972 *Village Voice* (N.Y.) 1 June 74/3 Dylan had been moving toward Duchamp's brand of Cartesian reductivism and public withdrawal. **1975** *Times Lit. Suppl.* 23 May 566/1 The reductivism implied in this enterprise—the reducing of ideas to another level of meaning or set of causes.

So **re'ductivist** *a.* and *sb.* = MINIMALIST B. 2 and A. 2.

1967 *Listener* 13 July 45/3 Harold and Bernard Cohen were the two foremost British painters during the early 'sixties who were trying to evolve a visual language to correspond to what 'the artist thinks'. Now both seem to have given this up as a bad job and fallen in line with current reductivist tendencies. **1967** *Sat. Rev.* (U.S.) 23 Sept. 23 New York..is dominated by large numbers of artists who swim in one or two schools producing closely related works—lately, the reductivists and the remainders of the Pop people.

reduc'torial, *a. rare.* [f. as REDUCT *v.* + -ORIAL.] = REDUCTIVE *a.*

1788 T. TAYLOR *Proclus* (1792) II. 409 Every reductorial cause..in the gods differs both from a cathartic or purifying cause, and from convertive genera. **1816** —— in *Pamphleteer* VIII. 478 Intellect is of a reductorial or convertive nature.

redueable, variant of REDEVABLE *a. Obs.*

‖**reduit** (redɥi). *Fortif.* Also 7 reduite. [F. *réduit*:—L. *reductus*: see REDUCT *sb.* c, and cf. REDOUBT *sb.*] A keep or stronghold into which a garrison may retire when the outworks are taken, and so prolong the defence of the place.

1604 E. GRIMSTONE *Hist. Siege Ostend* 215 A Blockehouse or reduite inuironed with the Sea. [**1619** GILL *Logon. Angl.* (1621) 29 *Redvite*, nupera vox est à reduco, munimentum pro tempore aut occasione factum.] **1706** PHILLIPS (ed. Kersey) s.v., In Fortification, *Reduit* or *Reduct* [etc.]. **1802** JAMES *Milit. Dict.* s.v., Reduits are sometimes used for the purpose of securing different posts in a town independent of its citadel. **1841** *Penny Cycl.* XIX. 346/1 Thus were formed good defensive posts, to each of which the mill served as a reduit or keep. **1876** VOYLE & STEVENSON *Milit. Dict.* (ed. 3) 334/2 Blockhouses form the most suitable reduits for fieldworks.

†**re'dulcerate,** *v. Obs.*[−0] [f. ppl. stem of L. *redulcerāre*: see RE- and ULCERATE.] (See quot.)

1656 BLOUNT *Glossogr.*, *Redulcerate*, to begin to make sore again, to renew a wound.

red 'un: see RED *a.* 3 b.

†**re'duncate,** *a. Obs. rare*[−1]. [f. L. *reduncus*, after ADUNCATE (q.v.).] Of horns: Bent or curved backwards.

1661 LOVELL *Hist. Anim. & Min.* Introd., Some have robust [horns] for butting,..some aduncate, others reduncate.

redund (riː'dʌnd), *v. rare.* [Shortened f. REDUND(ANT *a.* and *sb.*] **a.** *intr.* To be redundant; to contain a redundancy. **b.** *trans.* To make redundant.

1905 *Daily Chron.* 16 Jan. 4/7 The phrase 'inadvertently forgotten' does not redund so much as appears. **1959** *Guardian* 23 Dec. 4/1 'I've worked here before,' said another, 'but I was redunded in May.'

redundance (rɪ'dʌndəns). [ad. L. *redundantia*: see REDUNDANT and -ANCE, and cf. F. *rédondance* (14th c.).] = REDUNDANCY.

1620 T. GRANGER *Div. Logike* 227* Redundance, or amplification, is, when either the same argument is repeated, or else some others are added to the principall parts. **1621** BURTON *Anat. Mel.* I. ii. II. iv, When there is a manifest redundance of bad humors and melancholy blood. **1681** FLAVEL *Meth. Grace* ii. 42 If he gives even to redundance unto his enemies. *a* **1763** SHENSTONE *Elegies* xvi. 27 Loose flow'd the soft redundance of her hair. **1788** REID *Aristotle's Log.* vi. §2. 144 A redundance rather than a defect of first principles. **1876** J. PARKER *Paracl.* I. v. 47 Such redundance of power as will carry him through all his engagements with the most perfect ease.

redundancy (rɪ'dʌndənsɪ). [See prec. and -ANCY.] **1. a.** The state or quality of being redundant; superabundance, superfluity. Also with *a* and *pl.*, an instance or case of this.

1601–2 FULBECKE *1st Pt. Parall.* 74 There is in them me thinketh great redundancie of wordes, which might wel be spared. **1678** CUDWORTH *Intell. Syst.* I. iv. §20. 375 A Love of Redundancy and Overflowing Fulness, delighting to communicate it self. **1706** WALSH *Let. to Pope* 20 July, The redundancy of Wit..is not what ever pleases the best judges. **1765** *Museum Rust.* IV. 14 Such trees as run into wood, whose redundancy must be moderated before they will throw out any bearing branches. **1821** BYRON *Juan* IV. cxvii, I'm sensible redundancy is wrong, But could not for the muse of me put less in't. **1875** HELPS *Soc. Press.* xiv. 207, I can perceive defects and redundancies in his way of treating them.

b. A redundant thing or part.

1631 GOUGE *God's Arrows* III. §9. 201 This particle (*us*) is an usuall redundancy in the Hebrew tongue. **1651** N. BACON *Disc. Govt. Eng.* II. xxvi. (1739) 114 As touching the Pontifical Benediction, himself took that but as a redundancy. **1770** FOOTE *Lame Lover* I. Wks. 1799 II. 61 A leg! a redundancy! a mere nothing at all. **1816** T. L. PEACOCK *Headlong Hall* vii, The remaining one wallows in all the redundancies of luxury. **1875** GLADSTONE *Glean.* VI. xxxii. 160 There is no redundancy that can be safely parted with.

c. That which is redundant; the surplus.

1733 CHEYNE *Eng. Malady* II. vii. §2 (1734) 186 That Function..throwing off the Redundancy and Feculence. **1795** J. SULLIVAN *Hist. Maine* 35 Here a fall of water.. empties the redundancy of Damariscota Ponds into the channel. **1832** HT. MARTINEAU *Homes Abroad* ii. 25 It is not the whole of the people... It is only the redundancy that we have to take care of.

2. *spec.* **a.** *Engin.* The presence in a framework of more members than are needed to confer rigidity.

1904 J. B. JOHNSON et al. *Theory & Pract. Mod. Framed Structures* (ed. 8) I. xxv. 260 Another common example of redundancy is where two diagonals are used in the same quadrilateral. **1923** W. L. MARSH *Internat. Air Congr., London, 1923* 828 Owing to the extreme redundancy of the structure [of the airship] the calculations cannot be tackled by the graphical methods employed on most types of girder work construction. **1950** J. C. GRASSIE *Elem. Theory Structures* ix. 129 (*heading*) Conditions for internal and external redundancy in structures. **1966** J. L. MERIAM *Statics* iii. 81 For a truss that is statically determinate externally, there is a definite relation between the number of its members and the number of its joints necessary for internal stability without redundancy.

b. The condition of having more staff in an organization than is necessary. Hence, the state or fact of losing a job because there is no further work to be done; a case of unemployment due to reorganization, mechanization, loss of orders, etc.

1931 *Economist* 11 Apr. 780/1 Such economics create redundancy of staff and unemployment rather than increased employment. **1934** *Planning* II. xxvi. 3 The shipbuilding and wool textiles industries have succeeded in establishing common instruments with which to combat redundancy. **1952** *Economist* 12 July 77 The strike against redundancy is a comparatively new phenomenon in industrial relations. **1955** *Times* 31 Aug. 4/6 The men stopped work after a dispute..over the way to handle redundancy at the works because of a reorganization scheme. **1956** *Economist* 7 July 12/2 The unions now appear ready to lay rather more emphasis on bargaining for higher severance pay, and rather less on demonstrations against the fact of redundancies. **1957** *Observer* 8 Sept. 9/4 This [*sc.* Gloucester] is a rather troubled city, with 15,000 people—nearly a third of the insured population—in the aircraft industry, and the prospect of substantial redundancy as defence contracts run out. **1972** *Accountant* 5 Oct. 420/1 Should a staff surveyor become redundant, redundancy pay would be considered, the maximum benefit being limited to one month's pay (based on salary at the date of redundancy) for every completed year's service. **1976** J. R. L. ANDERSON *Redundancy Pay* i. 11 The terms of the final merger called for heavy redundancies. **1977** M. DRABBLE *Ice Age* II. 240 There isn't any work. There's large-scale unemployment. Redundancies everywhere. **1977** I. SHAW *Beggarman, Thief* III. vi. 267 We live in the age of what the British call redundancy.

c. *Linguistics.* The element or degree of predictability in a language arising from knowledge of its structure; the fact of superfluity of information in a piece of language.

1948 *Bell Syst. Techn. Jrnl.* XXVII. 398 The redundancy of ordinary English, not considering statistical structure over greater distances than about eight letters, is roughly 50%. **1954** G. A. MILLER et al. in J. S. Bruner *Beyond Information Given* (1974) iii. 59 When missing or ambiguous portions of a stimulus pattern can be supplied correctly..on the basis of the context alone, the missing portions carry little or no information. This fact is referred to as the redundancy of the language. **1972** J. L. DILLARD *Black English* vii. 283 What the linguist calls redundancy—a technical term..which explains how we are able to understand sentences which we have not heard plainly or to read paragraphs in which a great deal of the print has been scrambled. **1977** A. SHERIDAN tr. *J. Lacan's Écrits* iii. 86 This notion of redundancy in language originated in research that was all the more precise because a vested interest was involved. **1979** E. H. GOMBRICH *Sense of Order* iv. 104 It is easy to understand how our grasp of ordinary language profits from high redundancies. We can afford to miss or mishear individual sounds or even words without losing the meaning.

d. *Engin.* The incorporation of extra parts in the design of a mechanical or electronic system in such a way that its function is not impaired in the event of a failure.

1962 J. GLENN in *Into Orbit* 38 The engineers had a word for this insistence on inserting backups into the system. They called it the principle of 'redundancy'. **1972** L. M. HARRIS *Introd. Deepwater Floating Drilling Operations* viii. 84 Redundancy implies that alternate methods of well control and operating subsea equipment will be available in the event of failure of any one component or group of components. **1972** *Sci. Amer.* Jan. 46/2 Perhaps the most unusual feature of the grand-tour spacecraft will be a computer called STAR ('self-test and repair'), provided with enough redundancy to operate for at least 10 years.

3. *attrib.* and *Comb.*, as (sense 2 b) ***redundancy agreement, pay, payment, scheme***; (sense 2 c) ***redundancy rule***; **redundancy check** *Computers*, a check on the correctness of processed data that involves a comparison with accompanying data derived from them prior to processing.

1951 *Public Administration* XXIX. 374/1 Examples, in the years between the two wars, of competitive industries being turned into monopolies, sometimes with the help of the State—the agricultural schemes, or the redundancy agreements, as in tinplate and shipbuilding. **1969** *Guardian* 3 July 12/1 The dockers and the port employers should start thinking about the sort of redundancy agreement that would meet their needs. **1962** *Gloss. Terms Automatic Data Processing (B.S.I.)* 33 *Redundancy check, redundant check*, a check that uses extra digits, which do not themselves fully represent the data concerned. **1970** O. DOPPING *Computers & Data Processing* ii. 49 The most common form of redundancy check is the parity check. **1969** *Times* 7 Nov. 21/7 (*heading*) Redundancy pay. **1976** J. R. L. ANDERSON *Redundancy Pay* i. 11 The terms of the final merger called for heavy redundancies... There would be a bit of redundancy pay. **1980** *Times Lit. Suppl.* 31 Oct. 1240/4 Gus Baedecker, the London adman of *Events Beyond the Heartlands*, who uses his redundancy pay to take Kate and the children away from it all to a cottage on the Welsh coast. **1965** *Act 13 & 14 Eliz. II* c. 62 §1 Where on or after the appointed day an employee who has been continuously employed for the requisite period—..is dismissed by his employer by reason of redundancy,..then,..the employer shall be liable to pay to him a sum (in this Act referred to as a 'redundancy payment'). **1966** *Listener* 17 Mar. 391/2 We carried out too, our pledge to introduce redundancy payments for those who were temporarily out of a job through the speeding of the process of industrial change. **1972** M. Jones *Life on Dole* II. i. 98 The Redundancy Payments Act of 1965..compels the employer to pay out a lump sum..to each employee who is dismissed. **1965** N. Chomsky *Aspects of Theory of Syntax* 214 More generally the *phonological redundancy rules*, which determine such features as voicing of vowels.., can be supplemented by analogous syntactic and semantic redundancy rules. **1972** *Archivum Linguisticum* III. 14 A morphological feature.. must be recognized as being syntactically relevant, by means of a lexical redundancy rule. **1976** *Language* LII. 296 Lexical redundancy rules define the set of possible underlying morphemes in a language, in addition to minimizing the feature specifications required in the lexicon. **1969** *Guardian* 3 July 12/2 A generous redundancy scheme for dockers could save money.

redundant (rɪˈdʌndənt), *a.* and *sb.* [ad. L. *redundant-em*, pple. of *redundāre* to REDOUND.]

A. *adj.* **1. a.** Superabundant, superfluous, excessive.

1604 R. Cawdrey *Table Alph.*, *Redundant*, ouerflowing, or abounding too much. **1642** Fuller *Holy & Prof. St.* III. xv. 190 An Heteroclite in Nature, with some member defective or redundant. **1697** Dryden *Virg. Georg.* I. 129 When the latent Vice is cur'd by Fire, Redundant Humours thro' the pores expire. **1763** Emerson *Meth. Increm.* 23 To expunge any redundant factor, put in its stead any other factor which is equivalent to it. **1794** S. Williams *Hist. Vermont* 97 The beavers always leave sluices or passages near the middle for the redundant waters to pass off. **1855** Macaulay *Hist. Eng.* xix. IV. 320 Devising new schemes for the employment of redundant capital. **1869** E. A. Abbott *Shaks. Gram.* 96 A somewhat different case of the redundant object. **1879** T. Bryant *Pract. Surg.* II. 5 The redundant mass is to be dissected off.

b. Characterized by superfluity or excess in some respect; having some additional or superfluous part, element, or feature. Also const. *in.*

1645 Fuller *Good Th. in Bad T.* (1841) 25 It grieved me at the first to see our translation defective; but it offended me afterwards, to see the other redundant. **1655** —— *Ch. Hist.* II. i. §5 This..will make our Belief to demurre to the Truth of his so frequent Miracles, being so Redundant in working them on Triviall Occasions. **1674** Jeake *Arith.* (1696) 169 Improper Fractions are redundant. **1725** Watts *Logic* III. ii. §6 All these four kinds of syllogisms..may be called redundant, because they have more than three propositions. **1751** Johnson *Rambler* No. 88 ¶15 Milton frequently uses ..the hypermetrical or redundant line of eleven syllables. **1830** Mackintosh *Progr. Eth. Philos.* Wks. 1846 I. 148 The naturally copious and flowing style of the author is generally redundant. **1856** Macready in *Four C. Eng. Lett.* (1880) 513 You make inquiry of me whether it is true that, in my youth, my action was redundant, and that I took extraordinary pains to chasten it?

c. *spec.* in ***redundant chord, hyperbola, interval, noun***: (see quots.).

1706 Phillips (ed. Kersey), *Redundant Nouns*, (in Grammar) are those that have a Number or particular Case more than is usual. **1710** J. Harris *Lex. Techn.* II, *Redundant Hyperbola* is one so called, because it exceeds the Conical Sections, in the Number of its Hyperbolical Legs; being a Triple Hyperbola with six Hyperbolical Legs. **1753** Chambers *Cycl. Supp.*, *Redundant interval*, in music, is used for an interval exceeding the truth by a comma. Some apply redundant to an interval exceeding a diatonic interval by a semitone minor; but this is more usually called a superfluous interval. **1797** *Encycl. Brit.* (ed. 3) XVI. 36/1 What the French call *une accord superflue*, which we have translated *a redundant chord*. **1866** Cayley *Math. Papers* (1892) V. 360 In the former case, the asymptotes are all real, and we have the redundant hyperbola.

d. *Engin.* Of a component of a framework, or a force or moment on it: capable of being removed without causing loss of rigidity. Hence of a framework: containing more than the minimum number of components necessary for rigidity.

1890 *Jrnl. Assoc. Engin. Societies* IX. 242 (*heading*) Deflection of framed structures and the distribution of stresses over redundant members. **1908** E. S. Andrews *Theory & Design of Structures* xi. 290 Redundant frames have the following disadvantages:—(1) Any stress in one member caused by bad fitting or change of temperature causes stress in all the other members. **1929** Niles & Newell *Airplane Structures* xiv. 316 In any redundant structure, the distribution of stresses will be such that not only are the conditions of equilibrium satisfied, but also that the deformations of all parts of the structure will be consistent with respect to each other. **1953** C.-K. Wang *Statically Indeterminate Structures* i. 4 In analyzing indeterminate structures it is necessary to have as many extra conditions, in addition to those of statics, as there are redundant reactions. **1976** A. C. Palmer *Structural Mech.* vii. 147 Determine the number of redundant forces (or moments) for each of the plane frames in Figure 7.22.

e. Of a person: no longer needed at work; unemployed because of reorganization, mechanization, change in demand, etc.

1928 *Britain's Industr. Future* (Liberal Industr. Inquiry) xxv. 358 We reach, finally, the pressing, but difficult, problem of the redundant workers. When everything possible has been done..there is little doubt that we shall still have to deal with a large surplus of labour in the coal-mining industry. **1934** J. B. Priestley *Eng. Journey* x. 346 You may do a good stroke of work by declaring the Stockton shipyards 'redundant', but you cannot pretend that all the men who used to work in those yards are merely 'redundant' too. **1956** *Times* 21 July 7/5 Redundant workers.. workers dismissed on the score of redundancy. **1958** *Spectator* 30 May 713/3 Over five thousand other men were rendered redundant. **1969** H. E. Bates *Vanished World* xii. 156 Nowadays,..it would no doubt be said that I became redundant. I prefer the old way: I was unexpectedly sacked. **1974** C. Hill *Scorpion* 49, I rang his office... He doesn't work there any more. He was made redundant about two months ago. **1976** *Milton Keynes Express* 30 July 9/3 He had been made redundant and needed money.

f. Of a language: containing material which is predictable from context or a knowledge of its structure; also of a language feature, predictable in this way.

1954 G. A. Miller et al. in J. S. Bruner *Beyond Information Given* (1974) iii. 59 If a language is highly redundant, the relative information per symbol is much lower than it would be if successive symbols in a message could be chosen independently. **1965** W. S. Allen *Vox Latina* 78 Towards the end of a word sounds tend to become more 'redundant', i.e. predictable in terms of what has already been uttered. **1979** E. H. Gombrich *Sense of Order* iv. 104 If the message reads that the meeting was suspended for lack of a q.u.o.r.u.m. every successive letter can be said to be increasingly redundant.

2. Abounding to excess or fullness; plentiful, copious, exuberant: **a.** of material things.

In mod. examples only after Milton's use.

1671 Milton *Samson* 568 These redundant locks Robustious to no purpose clustring down. **1730** Arbuthnot *Aliments* iv. 83 Notwithstanding the redundant Oil in Fishes, they do not increase Fat so much as Flesh. **1755** Doddridge in Palmer *Bk. of Praise* (1862) 286 Thy hand in autumn richly pours Through all our coasts redundant stores. **1789** E. Darwin *Bot. Gard.* II. i. 201 Redundant folds of glossy silk surround Her slender waist, and trail upon the ground. **1814** Wordsw. *Laodameia* 59 Redundant are thy locks. **1848** Mrs. Jameson *Sacr. & Leg. Art* (1850) 49 Rubens gives us strong well-built youths with redundant yellow hair.

b. of immaterial things, qualities, etc.

1695 J. Edwards *Perfect. Script.* 3 Where words are few, but the sense is full and redundant. **1784** Cowper *Task* I. 226 With foliage of such dark redundant growth. **1853** Kane *Grinnell Exp.* viii. (1856) 57 The materials thus afforded in redundant profusion are rapidly converted into icebergs. **1893** Liddon, etc. *Life Pusey* I. xvii. 397 This petition, marked by the redundant earnestness and sustained intensity, which were his characteristics.

c. Characterized by copiousness, fullness, or abundance. Also const. *of*, *with.*

a **1653** G. Daniel *Vpon Reading*, etc. 24 Yᵉ Copious East Ransack'd, & ioyn'd to yᵉ Redundant West. **1755** Young *Centaur* iv. Wks. 1757 IV. 203 Thou Father of all mercies! of mercy redundant, inexhaustible, source! **1814** Southey *Ode during War w. Amer.* xii, Queen of the Seas! enlarge thyself; Redundant as thou art of life and power. **1853** Marsden *Early Purit.* 243 Henry Smith had preached at St. Clement Danes in rich redundant periods. **1876** Blackie *Songs Relig. & Life* 233 Growth the fairest and the sweetest In the green redundant bower.

†**3. a.** ? In swelling waves, wave-like. *Obs.*

1667 Milton *P.L.* IX. 503 His circling Spires, that on the grass Floted redundant. **1726** Pope *Odyss.* XVIII. 342 Down from the swelling loins, the vest unbound Floats in bright waves redundant o'er the ground.

†**b.** Swelling up; overflowing. *Obs.*

1719 Young *Busiris* IV. i, Redundant Nile, Broke from its channel, overswells the pass. **1768–74** Tucker *Lt. Nat.* (1834) II. 30 Nor will it be incongruous to represent Him.. riding in whirlwinds, upheaving redundant seas.

†**4.** Redounding, resulting. *Obs. rare*⁻¹.

1654 tr. *Scudery's Curia Pol.* 154 With glory or dishonour redundant to my self in those mighty undertakings.

B. *sb.* **1.** †**a.** Something redundant; *spec.* a redundant noun or chord (see 1 c). Also *fig. Obs.*

1612 Brinsley *Pos. Parts* (1669) 106 Heteroclits called Redundants. **1640** Fuller *Joseph's Coat* 174 Let us not willingly bee Heteroclites from his will; either Defectiues, to doe too little, or Redundants, to doe too much. **1650** —— *Pisgah* II. x. 217 The Giants bred in Philistia..being Heteroclites, redundants from the rules of nature. **1797** *Encycl. Brit.* (ed. 3) XVI. 36/2 The third redundant consists of two tones and a semi-tone.

b. *Engin.* A redundant component of a framework (see sense A. 1 d above).

1953 C.-K. Wang *Statically Indeterminate Structures* i. 5 When the equations are solved and the redundants found, they can be put back on the given indeterminate structure and the remaining reactions solved by the equations of statics. **1976** A. C. Palmer *Structural Mech.* vii. 138 Although the frame was three times redundant, this extra piece of information enabled us to reduce the number of unknown redundants to two.

2. A person who leaves his job because of redundancy (sense 2 b); = REDUNDANTEE.

1975 *Times* 4 Aug. 12/1 A call for volunteer redundants has not fallen on deaf ears.

Hence **reˈdundantize** *v. trans.*, to make (a person) redundant (fortunately *rare.*—R.W.B.); **reˈdundantly** *adv.*

1680 Dalgarno *Deaf & Dumb Man's Tutor* 17 The one is still running the same round,..hearing the same words redundantly. **1717** Berkeley *Jrnl. Tour in Italy* 27 Jan., Façade of the Jesuits' church ornamented but not redundantly. **1755** Redundantly, in Johnson and later Dicts. **1783** Mason tr. *Du Fresnoy's Art Paint.* 768 Yet more than these to meditation's eyes, Great Nature's self redundantly supplies. **1949** *Picture Post* 19 Nov. 22/1 The blameless little men, so many of whom have been and will be 'redundantised'.

redundantee (rɪˌdʌndənˈtiː). *rare.* [f. REDUNDANT *a.* + -EE¹.] A person who has been made redundant.

1963 *Times* 8 May 13/7 Could not redundancies due to the Beeching plan be handled in a similar way? I am sure that industrialists would cooperate to try to find work for these men, possibly on the basis of one redundantee (?) to so many regular employees. **1971** *Selling Today* Sept. 8/2 Much is offered by way of genius. Like the recent 'redundantee' who offered a world of experience, expertise, exuberance and enthusiasm.

†**redunˈdation.** *Obs.*⁻¹ [ad. L. *redundātio*, n. of action f. *redundāre* to REDOUND.] Overflow.

a **1659** Bp. Brownrig *Serm.* (1674) II. x. 122 Repentance ..rises in the heart, then by a natural flux, and redundation, shews it self in the body.

redunde, obs. form of REDOUND.

reduplicate (rɪˈdjuːplɪkeɪt), *a.* and *sb.* [ad. late L. *reduplicāt-us*: see RE- and DUPLICATE *a.*, and cf. next.]

A. *adj.* **1.** Doubled, repeated.

1647 H. More *Song of Soul* II. ii. II. xxxvi, Lesse active, lesse reduplicate, lesse free. **1822–34** *Good's Study Med.* (ed. 4) IV. 48 It exhibits the two following varieties:.. Reduplicate menstruation. **1827** Hood *Mids. Fairies* lxii, By silver trouts upspringing from green sheen, And winking stars reduplicate at night, Spare us. **1879** Khory *Princ. Med.* 57 Very often the sounds are more or less doubled or repeated and are called reduplicate sounds.

b. *Gram.* Reduplicated; connected with or involving reduplication.

1841 Latham *Eng. Lang.* xvi. 276 In the present English there is no Perfect or Reduplicate form. **1844** *Proc. Philol. Soc.* I. 265 Buttmann conjectures it to be nothing more than a mutilation of the reduplicate prefix of the perfect. **1880** Earle *Philol. Eng. Tongue* (ed. 3) §285 The German *ging*.. indicates a reduplicate form which was lost in English.

2. *Bot.* Valvate, with the edges reflexed.

1856 Henslow *Dict. Bot. Terms.* **1870** Bentley *Man. Bot.* (ed. 2) 211 When the margins are turned outwards under the same circumstances, the æstivation is reduplicate.

B. *sb.* A double (one), a duplicate.

1657 Gaule *Sapientia Justificata* 73 Therefore then (the illative is a reduplicate, and concludes so much the stronger) etc. **1803** G. S. Faber *Cabiri* II. 275 *note*, It is manifest, that both these stories are in substance the same, for the second is merely the reduplicate of the first. **1816** —— *Orig. Pagan Idol.* II. 238 Which number [14] is the mere reduplicate of seven.

reduplicate (rɪˈdjuːplɪkeɪt), *v.* [f. ppl. stem of med.L. *reduplicāre*, f. *re-* RE- + *duplicāre* to DUPLICATE: cf. prec.]

1. a. *trans.* To make double; to repeat, redouble.

1570 Levins *Manip.* 42/13 To Reduplicate, *reduplicare.* *a* **1657** R. Loveday *Lett.* (1663) 256, I think it will prove no unwelcom Office to you, to reduplicate the old token. **1660** Jer. Taylor *Duct. Dubit.* III. i. rule 1 §20 When the preceptive or prohibitive clauses are reduplicated. **1717** L. Howel *Desiderius* (ed. 3) 79 He reduplicates his consolatory Grace. **1812** G. Chalmers *Dom. Econ. Gt. Brit.* 428 The Irish people..augmented their gains, and reduplicated their capital. **1850** B. Taylor *Eldorado* I. iv. 23 The firmament.. reduplicating its hues on the glassy sea. **1878** H. C. Lea *Superst. & Force, Wager of Law* (ed. 3) 27 The plan of reduplicating oaths on different altars was an established practice among the Anglo-Saxons.

b. *Gram.* To repeat (a letter or syllable); to form (a tense) by reduplication.

1832 Lee *Hebr. Gram.* (ed. 2) vii. 105 Those [nouns] which are augmented,..reduplicating, or not, at the same time, any of their letters or syllables. **1869** Farrar *Fam. Speech* iii. (1873) 88 In the perfect the second letter is often reduplicated, as in Rabab. **1894** Henry *Comp. Gram. Eng. & Germ.* 307 Hence the perfects of type G were clearly reduplicated in Pregermanic.

2. *intr.* To become double or doubled. *rare.*

1866 *London Rev.* 6 Jan. 6/2 The people..went on reduplicating with a fecundity which [etc.]. **1973** *Sci. Amer.* Feb. 59/1 The manner in which two-syllable adjectives reduplicate is different... A verb reduplicates by the entire word, but the adjective reduplicates in terms of its constituent syllables.

reˈduplicated, *ppl. a.* [f. prec. + -ED¹.]

1. Doubled, repeated.

1597 A. M. tr. *Guillemeau's Fr. Chirurg.* 2 b/1 The reduplicated semicircle. **1658** Earl Monm. tr. *Paruta's Wars Cyprus* 166 The Pope..sent reduplicated Briefs to Don John, to make him speedily depart. **1860** O. W. Holmes *Prof. Breakf.-t.* iv. (Paterson) 84 Like the reduplicated echo of a cry among the ..hills!

b. *Gram.* (See REDUPLICATE *v.* 1 b.)

1832 Lee *Hebr. Gram.* (ed. 2) vii. 107 Of reduplicated words. *Ibid.* viii. 139 The second class of reduplicated nouns. **1874** Sayce *Compar. Philol.* iv. 149 Other forms, such as the reduplicated perfect or the optative. **1882** Monro *Gram. Homeric Dial.* 42 These forms may be either connected with the Perfect..or with the Reduplicated Aorist. **1888** King & Cookson *Sound & Inflection*, etc. 417 The vowel of the reduplicated syllable.

†**2.** Folded double. *Obs. rare*⁻¹.

1599 A. M. tr. *Gabelhouer's Bk. Physicke* 36/2 Applye this water with reduplicatede clothes, or with a Sponge.

reˈduplicating, *ppl. a.* [f. as prec. + -ING².] That reduplicates; causing, or connected with, reduplication.

1727–41 Chambers *Cycl.* s.v. *Reduplication*, The usual reduplicating words are *quatenus*, as, so far as [etc.]. **1814** Southey *Roderick* XVIII, The thundering shout, Rolling among reduplicating rocks. **1883** A. S. Hardy *But yet a*

Woman 254 Windows whose reduplicating mirrors were arranged to catch the eye of the loiterer.

reduplication (rɪdjuːplɪˈkeɪʃən). [ad. late L. *reduplicātiōn-em*: see REDUPLICATE *v.* and -ATION, and cf. F. *réduplication* (1520).]

†**1.** The action of doubling or folding. *Obs.*$^{-1}$

1589 PUTTENHAM *Eng. Poesie* III. xix. (Arb.) 210 The Greekes name this figure *Symploche*, the Latins *Complexio*, perchaunce for that he seemes to hold in and to wrap vp the verses by reduplication, so as nothing can fall out.

b. A double or fold. *rare.* Cf. REDUPLICATURE.

1698 TYSON in *Phil. Trans.* XX. 115 A Reduplication of the Skin inwards, which forms a Bag. **1881** MIVART *Cat* 296 The cartilage of the pinna is large and complexly-shaped, with a reduplication in front.

2. The action of making or becoming double or two-fold; repetition; also, an instance of this, a double or counterpart.

1649 JER. TAYLOR *Gt. Exemp.* Ad Sect. IX. §2 When Jesus by reduplication of his desire, fortifying it with a Command [etc.]. **1659** H. MORE *Immort. Soul* I. ii. Ax. 9 To both these may be apply'd the termes of Reduplication and Saturation: The former, when Essence or Substance is but once redoubled into it self, or into another. **1812** G. CHALMERS *Dom. Econ. Gt. Brit.* 475 We have seen the reduplications of populousness, in both our Isles. **1841** L. HUNT *Seer* (1864) 86 A crowd is but the reduplication of ourselves. **1876** BRISTOWE *Th. & Pract. Med.* (1878) 509 There is frequently a tendency,..either to disregard the true second sound, or to look upon it as a mere reduplication.

b. Repetition of a word (or phrase). †Also *spec.* (see quot. 1656).

a **1619** FOTHERBY *Atheom.* Pref. (1622) A viij b, Marke heere againe, how the Prophet resumeth his first admiration, by a Poeticall Epanalepsis or reduplication. **1656** BLOUNT *Glossogr.*, *Reduplication*..is a figure in Rhetoric, when the same word that ends one part of a verse or sentence, is repeated in that which follows. *a* **1680** CHARNOCK *Attrib. God* (1834) II. 685 Intimating the greatness of their sins by the reduplication of the word. **1729** POPE *Dunc.* III. 266 *note*, Which reduplication of the word gives a much stronger emphasis to Violante's concern. **1860** PUSEY *Min. Proph.* 537/2 What meaneth that reduplication, 'and He shall rule on His Throne', but that [etc.].

c. *Path.* (See quot. and cf. REDOUBLEMENT 2.)

1858 MAYNE *Expos. Lex.*, *Reduplication*,..applied to the paroxysms of ague of a double type.

†**3.** The repetition of a term with a limiting or defining force; hence, the addition of some limiting term to one already used, or the sense of a term as thus limited. *Obs.*

1620 T. GRANGER *Div. Logike* 279 Euery good thing is to be desired, ªas it is good. *marg.*, ªThis is called reduplication, or the redoubling of a terme. **1656** JEANES *Fuln. Christ* 149 Yet the word considered, as Christ, as incarnate, as subsisting in two natures, may under this reduplication be said to be after the manhood, and to depend upon it. **1678** GALE *Crt. Gentiles* III. 101 God doth not deliver up men to judicial hardnesse simply as hardnesse, under that reduplication. **1727–41** CHAMBERS *Cycl.* s.v., Reduplication, in logic, is a kind of condition expressed in a proposition, indicating or assigning the manner wherein the predicate is attributed to the subject.

4. *Gram.* Repetition of a syllable or letter, *esp.* in the case of verbal forms (chiefly the perfect tense) in Greek and other Indo-European languages.

Attic reduplication, the form exemplified in Gr. ἀκήκοα from ἀκουω, ἤγαγον from ἄγω.

1774 J. BRYANT *Mythol.* I. 36 They seem to have sometimes used this term with a reduplication: for we read of a city in Canaan called Sansanah. **1832** LEE *Hebr. Gram.* (ed. 2) vii. 112 These are nouns which are thought to have an intensive signification, without presenting any reduplication either in the vowels or consonants. **1839** *Penny Cycl.* XIII. 314/1 The third conjugation..is characterized by the reduplication of the first letter of the verb with a short vowel. **1869** FARRAR *Fam. Speech* ii. (1873) 74 It also retained the reduplication of the perfect.

attrib. **1894** LINDSAY *Latin Lang.* viii. §39. 494, ĕ being the usual Reduplication-vowel. *Ibid.* §43. 503 The older writers used ĕ in the Reduplication-syllable.

b. A word-form produced by repetition of a syllable.

1862 D. WILSON *Preh. Man* iv. (1865) 65 They are traceable in many reduplications, and influence the choice of vowel-sounds in a large class of words. **1868** GLADSTONE *Juv. Mundi* xiii. (1869) 489 Tartaros is taken to be the reduplication of the 'tar' in 'tarik'.

†**5.** Exact reproduction. *Obs. rare*$^{-1}$.

1794 MATHIAS *Purs. Lit.* (1798) 137 The uniform and constant reduplication of the old spelling of every word in Mr. Ireland's new Volume by Shakspeare.

†**6.** The action of doubling a second time.

1674 JEAKE *Arith.* (1696) 24 Reduplication..or Multiplication by 4 is to double the Duplication.

reduplicative (rɪˈdjuːplɪkətɪv), *a.* and *sb.* [f. L. *reduplicāt-*, ppl. stem of *reduplicāre* + -IVE.]

A. *adj.* **1.** Of the nature of, pertaining or relating to, expressing or implying, reduplication of terms. (See prec. 3.) Now *rare.*

1605 *Answ. Supposed Discov. Rom. Doctr.* 48 Our Priests, neither vnder that reduplicatiue formalitie (as Priests) nor otherwise maintaine by our religion any position or practise seditious. **1657** J. SERGEANT *Schism Dispach't* 260 That 'as such' depends upon Dr. H's invention; no such reduplicative expression being found in the testimony. **1674** HICKMAN *Hist. Quinquart.* Ep. (ed. 2) a ij b, Not knowing.. that, in such kind of Syllogisms, the Reduplicative particle ought alway to be put to the major term of the Syllogism. **1710** tr. *Werenfels's Disc. Logom.* 25 Whether the word *As* be reduplicative or specificative. **1864** BOWEN *Logic* v. 147 The second sort of Restriction is called Reduplicative, as it consists in a repetition of the restricted Term.

b. Of propositions: Having a limiting repetition of the subject expressed.

1704 J. HARRIS *Lex. Techn.* I, *Reduplicative Propositions*, are such wherein the Subject is repeated: Thus, Men, as Men, are Rational; Kings, as Kings, are subject to none but God. **1725** WATTS *Logic* II. ii. §6 Some logicians refer reduplicative propositions to this place. **1788** REID *Aristotle's Logic* iv. §7. 100 The first class comprehends the syllogism into which any reduplicative proposition enters.

†**2.** Capable of repetition. *Obs.* (In H. More only.)

1647 H. MORE *Philos. Poems* 231 Like quantity it self out stretched right Devoid of all reduplicative might. *Ibid.* Interpr. Gen. 433 That is reduplicative, which is not onely in this point, but also in another. **1668** —— *Div. Dial.* I. xxv. 100 Whence again it is a sign that it has an Extension of its own, reduplicative into it self.

†**3.** Of pronouns: (see quot.). *Obs. rare*$^{-1}$.

1668 WILKINS *Real Char.* III. ii. 305 The Modifications of Pronouns..are of two kinds. 1 Possessive... 2 Reduplicative, denoting a particular Emphasis, whereby a word is raised and intended in its signification; as I my self.

4. Formed by reduplication.

1833 *Cambr. Philol. Museum* II. 378 Of these [conjugations] the first six or reduplicative, exist as such only in Gothic. **1873** EARLE *Philol. Eng. Tongue* (ed. 2) §286 The earliest extant forms are not reduplicative.

5. *Bot.* = REDUPLICATE *a.* 2.

1866 *Treas. Bot.* **1876** *Encycl. Brit.* IV. 130/2 Diagram to illustrate reduplicative or reduplicate æstivation, in which the parts of the whorl are slightly turned outwards.

B. *sb.* †**1.** A reduplicative particle (see A. 1).

1569 J. SANFORD tr. *Agrippa's Van. Artes* viii. 22 b, Of Reduplicatiues, of Exclusiues,..and other intollerable and vaine wordes which are writen in the little Logicals.

2. A reduplicating verb.

1833 *Cambr. Philol. Museum* II. 378 Comparing with the Gothic reduplicatives above given, the following Anglo-Saxon verbs.

Hence **reˈduplicatively** *adv.* (Cf. A. 1 above.)

1652 URQUHART *Jewel* Wks. (1834) 293 As they suppone for things reduplicatively as things in the first apprehension of the minde by them signified. **1678** GALE *Crt. Gentiles* III. 31 'As' here must not..be taken reduplicatively but only specificatively. **1840** G. S. FABER *Prim. Doctr. Regen.* 26 Throughout his Treatise, identifying Conversion with Regeneration, he reduplicatively expresses himself.

reˈduplicatory, *a. rare*$^{-1}$. [f. as REDUPLICATE *v.* + -ORY.] Repetitional.

1780 M. MADAN *Thelyphthora* II. 242 Another instance of the reduplicatory emphasis in the Hebrew language.

reduplicature (rɪˈdjuːplɪkeɪtjʊə(r)). [f. as prec. + -URE. Cf. DUPLICATURE.] = REDUPLICATION 1 b.

1836–9 TODD *Cycl. Anat.* II. 587/2 The reduplicature of the lining membrane. **1884** SEDGWICK & HEATHCOTE tr. *Claus' Zool.* I. 416 A..laterally compressed bivalve shell, formed by a reduplicature of the skin.

redur(e, varr. RADDOUR, REDDOUR *Obs.*

reduviid (rɛˈdjuːvɪɪd), *a.* and *sb.* Also **reduvid.** [f. mod.L. *Reduvi-us* (J. C. Fabricius *Systema Entomologiæ* (1775) 729) + -ID.] **A.** *adj.* Belonging to the *Reduviidæ*, a family of predaceous bugs, of which *Reduvius* is the typical genus. **B.** *sb.* An insect of this family. So **reˈduvioid,** *a.* and *sb.*

1888 J. S. KINGSLEY *Riverside Nat. Hist.* II. 267 These are strongly suggestive of certain tropical forms of Reduviids. **1891** in *Cent. Dict.* **1900** *Ibis* April 245 The stomachs contain diptera, reduviid bugs, and occasionally cheniform spiders and wasps. **1909** *Lancet* 20 Nov. 1495/2, I have recently suspected a reduviid bug..as having some relationship with the causation of kala-azar in Madras. **1962** GORDON & LAVOIPIERRE *Entomol.* xxxix. 237 Triatomines may be distinguished from other reduviid bugs. **1965** B. E. FREEMAN tr. *Vandel's Biospeleol.* xii. 182 Certain reduviid bugs are frequently found in the entrances of tropical caves.

‖**redux** (ˈriːdʌks), *a.* [L., f. *redūcĕre* to bring back, REDUCE.] **1.** *Path.* Of crepitation or other physical signs: indicating the return of an organ to a healthy state.

1898 *Allbutt's Syst. Med.* V. 99 The 'redux' crepitation is sometimes indistinguishable from that of pulmonary hæmorrhage. *Ibid.* 360 Friction sound, indicative of restored contact between the pleural surfaces, redux friction as it is usually called.

2. Brought back, restored.

[**1662** DRYDEN (*title*) Astraea Redux. A poem on the happy restoration and return of His Sacred Majesty.] **1873** TROLLOPE (*title*) Phineas redux. **1971** J. UPDIKE (*title*) Rabbit redux.

red-veined: see RED *a.* 14 a, 14 c.

red-vented: see RED *a.* 14 b.

†**redvore,** app. a variant of RADEVORE *Obs.*

The precise sense is not clear; but the general import of the passage seems to make the current explanation of *radevore* doubtful.

c **1425** WYNTOUN *Cron.* I. v. 256 (Royal MS.) Scho begowth on hand to ta Wewyng that nevyr than before Wes oysyd be cavale na reduore [*v.rr.* reduoir, redor, rhetour].

redward, *a.* and *adv.*: see RED *a.* 19 b.

red ware[1]. *Sc.* [See WARE *sb.*] A kind of seaweed, *Laminaria digitata*; common tangle.

1806 P. NEILL *Tour Orkney & Shet.* 29 On deep shores.. great quantities of red-ware or sea-girdles (*F. digitatus*) are collected with long hooks at low water. **1808** FORSYTH *Beauties Scotl.* V. 155 In Loch Erriboll..red-ware, or sea-weed is produced in such quantity as to afford yearly ten or twelve tons of Kelp.

b. *attrib.*, as **red-ware cod** or **codling,** a small brownish cod found among seaweed; **red-ware fishick,** the rockling or whistle-fish.

1707 SIBBALD *Fife* 52 *Osellus varius vel striatus Shonfeldii*, the Redware Codling. **1805** G. BARRY *Orkney Isl.* 289 The Wrasse..is very often found in company with what we call the red-ware cod. *Ibid.* 292 The Whistle Fish (*gadus mustela* ..) or, as it is here named, the red-ware fishick, is a species very often found under the stones among the sea-weed.

red ware[2]. A coarse kind of unglazed pottery. Also, a type of fine, glazed pottery. Also *attrib.* as ***red-ware potter, pottery.***

1699 M. LISTER *Journey to Paris* 139 As for the Red Ware of China, that has been and is done in England, to a far greater perfection than in China, we having as good Materials. [**1797** *Encycl. Brit.* (ed. 3) XVII. 810/1 The coarse yellow, red, black, and mottled wares.] **1832** G. R. PORTER *Porcelain & Gl.* 41 The oxide of iron, when present in any sensible degree, renders the clay unfit for all purposes, except that of forming the common red ware. **1852** *Hist. Co. Oxford* 856 Leafield has been noted for some time for its red-ware pottery. **1885** *Census Instruct.* 88 Red Ware Potter. **1934** *Discovery* June 166/2 Plain burnished red ware. **1959** *Chambers's Encycl.* XI. 137/2 Unglazed red-ware was made till about 1770... Thomas Astbury (1688–1743) is supposed to have been the first to glaze this finely potted red ware and to decorate it with pads of white clay stamped in patterns. **1965** E. TUNIS *Colonial Craftsmen* v. 121 Redware as it came from firing was no harder than a modern flowerpot and it was just as porous. To make it useful, the potters glazed it. **1975** *Country Life* 26 June (Suppl.) 56/2 Christie's... Fine English Porcelain and Pottery..Astbury glazed redware..bell-shaped mug. **1977** *New Hampshire Times* 27 July 17/2 The potter had only one type of clay available, the local glacial clay underlying most of the coastal area. This clay fires in a kiln to a red color and therefore is called redware. Redware collapses past a certain firing temperature.

red-water. Also red water, redwater.

1. a. A disease in cattle and sheep, now recognized as of malarial affinities, and characterized by the presence of free hæmoglobin in the urine.

1594 O. B. *Quest. Profit. Concern.* 12 b, Their cattell should rot and die of the murrion or read-water. **1644** QUARLES *Sheph. Orac.* i, In those past daies our Shepheards knew not what Red-water meant. **1707** MORTIMER *Husb.* (1721) I. 245 The Rot, Red-water, and most of the Distempers that Sheep are subject to. **1778** [W. MARSHALL] *Minutes Agric.* 29 Aug. an. 1774, Yesterday one of the Lancashire cows died of the red-water. **1834** YOUATT *Cattle* 161 It is said that the young Galloway cattle are more exposed than others to Redwater. **1879** ATCHERLEY *Boërland* 257 Some of the oxen showed symptoms of red water.

b. (See quot.)

1807 *Trans. Highl. Soc.* III. 428 Redwater..consists in an inflammation of the skin, that raises it into blisters, which contain a thin, reddish, and watery fluid.

†**2.** (See quot.) *Obs. rare*$^{-1}$.

1712 J. MORTON *Nat. Hist. Northampt.* 273, I now proceed to the Acidulæ, or the Medicinal Springs... A Spring of this Kind is here commonly known by the Name of the Red-Well, or the Red-Water, the Iron Water.

3. The poisonous red juice of the sassy-tree of West Africa (*Erythrophlæum guineense*), hence called ***red-water tree.***

a **1759** N. OWEN *Jrnl. Slave-Dealer* (1930) 30 If they are found out they are obliged to drink a large quantity of poyson, comonly caled red watter, which soon puts an end to thier days. **1830** LOUDON *Hortus Brit.* 168 *Erythrophleum* ..Red Water Tree. **1878** H. C. LEA *Superst. & Force* (ed. 3) 222 Throughout a wide region of Western Africa, one of the most popular forms of ordeal is that of the red water, or 'sassy-bark'. **1887** MOLONEY *Forestry W. Afr.* 338 Mancone of the Portuguese, Bourane, Red-water Tree, Ordeal Bark, &c.

4. A mass of water made red by pigmented plankton, esp. dinoflagellates.

1856 *Edin. New Philos. Jrnl.* IV. 264 Alphonse Albuquerque..saw, from the stern of his vessel, issuing from the strait, and expanding outside, a stream of red water, which flowed towards Aden. **1902** *Amer. Naturalist* XXXVI. 189 The 'red water' occurred for two hundred miles..along the coast, from the region of Santa Barbara to San Diego. **1933** *Science* 7 July 13/1 *Provocentrum* is more frequently prominent in production of 'red water' than reports have indicated. **1948** *Jrnl. Marine Res.* VII. 57 The presence of this [human respiratory] irritation was reported as associated with 'red water', dying fish and onshore winds. *Ibid.* 60 'Red water' containing 56 × 10⁶ dinoflagellates per liter.

red weed, red-weed.

1. An American plant or plants. Now applied to a species of *Phytolacca* (Treas. Bot. 1866).

1624 CAPT. SMITH *Virginia* 170 Here is also frequently growing a certaine tall Plant, whose stalke being all ouer couered with a red rinde, is thereupon termed the red weed. **1667** *Phil. Trans.* II. 796 There grows a Berry (by report) both in the Bermudas and New England, call'd the Summer-Island-Redweed, which Berry is as red as the Prickle-Peare.

2. The corn poppy (*Papaver rhœas*).

1641 BEST *Farm. Bks.* (Surtees) 35 The most usuall and best way for tythinge of hey is..to make use of reade-weedes for wikes. *a* **1722** LISLE *Husb.* (1757) II. 285 Poppy or redweed seldom grows in the deep and wet lands of Hants. **1788** *Trans. Soc. Arts* VI. 113 A county like this, overrun with red weeds. **1846** MRS. LOUDON *Brit. Wild Fl.* 25 The farmers call it Red-weed, Red-cap, and Corn Rose. **1881-** in dial. glossaries (E. Anglia, Berks, Hants, Wilts, Devon, etc.). **1899** RIDER HAGGARD *Farmer's Year* 13 Jan., That part of the field produced more poppies than anything else—red weed we call it.

3. a. Herb Robert. **b.** Knot-grass.

1877 *Hardwicke's Sci. Gossip* Jan. 39 *Geranium Robertianum*.—The cottagers on Delamere Forest call this 'Rubwort' and 'Red weed'. **1882** *Devon Plant Names*, Redweed, *Polygonum aviculare*. 'Redweed and Assmart usually occur together', said a farmer.

red wheat. A variety of the common wheat, of a reddish colour.

1523 FITZHERB. *Husb.* §34 Red wheate hath a flat eare,.. and is the greatteste corne. **1578** LYTE *Dodoens* IV. i. 453 The first kinde, whiche of Columella is iudged the best,.. is called *Robus*, and of Plinie *Triticum*: in English Red Wheat. **1597** SHAKS. *2 Hen. IV*, v. i. 17 Shall we sowe the head-land with Wheate? *Shal.* With red Wheate Dauy. **1611** COTGR., *Rousset*,.. also, red wheat, Duck-bill wheat, Normandie wheat. **1712** J. MORTON *Nat. Hist. Northampt.* 476 *Triticum spica* and *granis rubentibus*,.. red Wheat, [called] in some places Kentish Wheat; here red Lammas. Its Stalk, Ear, and Grain are all of them red. **1762** MILLS *Syst. Pract. Husb.* I. 361 The red-wheat, and the Poland bearded wheat. **1844** H. STEPHENS *Bk. Farm* II. 349 Most of the red wheats belong to this class of grain. **1868** *Chambers' Encycl.* s.v. *Wheat*, Red wheats are therefore preferred for comparatively poor soils.

red, white, and blue: see RED *a.* 1 g.

'redwing, red-wing.

1. *Ornith.* **a.** A European thrush belonging to one of the subspecies of *Turdus musicus* (or *T. iliacus*), distinguished by red patches on the flanks and under sides of the wings.

1657 W. RAND tr. *Gassendi's Life Peiresc* III. 157 He undertook among other things to send.. a pair of *Phœnicopteri*, or Red-wings, birds so-called. **1674** RAY *Catal. Eng. Birds* 86 The Thrush-kind... The Redwing or Swine-pipe: *Turdus Iliacus*. **1752** J. HILL *Hist. Anim.* 494 The orange-grey Turdus, with a white breast, the Redwing; this is smaller than the common thrush. **1771** G. WHITE *Selborne* xlv, Redwings are some of the first birds that suffer with us in severe weather. **1802** MONTAGU *Ornith. Dict.* (1831) 414 The Redwing is a migrative species, coming to us in great flocks about the latter end of September. **1863** BARING-GOULD *Iceland* 332 A coppice of birch, among which darted the redwing and white wagtail. **1894** A. NEWTON *Dict. Birds* 778 The notes of the Redwing are indeed pleasing in places where no better songster exists. **1954** D. A. BANNERMAN *Birds Brit. Isles* III. 192 To these islands the Continental redwing is a winter visitor. **1977** J. L. HARPER *Population Biol. Plants* ii. 47 Redwings.. eat the fleshy receptacles [of rose hips].

b. The red-winged blackbird (*Agelaius phœniceus*) of North America.

1778 J. CARVER *Trav. N. Amer.* 474 The second sort [of blackbird] is the red wing, which is rather smaller than the first species. **1831** AUDUBON *Ornith. Biog.* I. 348 As soon as spring makes its appearance, almost all the Redwings leave the Southern States. **1859** THOREAU *Autumn* (1894) 68, I see .. no red-wings for a long time. **1947** *Chicago Tribune* 2 Sept. 7/3 The grackles and redwings also are having a high old time these days roaming around the country. **1974** A. DILLARD *Pilgrim at Tinker Creek* xi. 201 By the creek, where .. redwings scatter.

c. The red-winged francolin of South Africa.

1878 T. J. LUCAS *Camp Life & Sport S. Afr.* vi. 85 We had a sprinkling of 'red wing', but the game grey partridge was more predominant. **1893** NEWTON *Dict. Birds* 292 No fewer than ten [species are].. found within the limits of the Cape Colony, *Francolinus levaillanti*, the 'Redwing' of English settlers, being especially numerous. **1962** MACKWORTH-PRAED & GRANT *Birds Southern Third Afr.* 208 Red-wing... Top of head brown with darker centres to feathers. [Cf. quot. 1867 in 3.]

2. *transf.* A small sailing-boat with red sails.

1897 *Westm. Gaz.* 19 Aug. 7/1 Every kind of craft is likely to find representation, from the big racers to the little red-wings with their rosy sails.

3. *attrib.*, as ***red-wing blackbird, fieldfare, partridge, thrush.***

1767 G. WHITE *Selborne* x, The martins and red-wing fieldfares were flying in sight together. **1828** FLEMING *Brit. Anim.* 65 *Turdus iliacus.* Redwing Thrush. **1840** *Cuvier's Anim. Kingd.* 185 The Redwing Thrush.. is a common winter visitant in Britain. **1867** LAYARD *Birds S. Afr.* 270 *Francolinus Levaillantii*... Red-wing-Partridge of Colonists. **1883** *Century Mag.* Sept. 653/1 Among the most common birds are the meadow-lark.., the red-wing blackbird [etc.].

red-winged, *a.* Having red wings. Also *fig.*

1712 BLACKMORE *Creation* v. 247 The red-wing'd Fire must to the Moon arise. **1752** J. HILL *Hist. Anim.* 54 The red-winged Cantharus, with a red thorax. **1781** LATHAM *Gen. Synopsis Birds* I. I. 246 Little Red-winged Parakeet. **1831** WILSON, etc. *Amer. Ornith.* I. Contents p. vii, Red-winged Waxwing. **1898** *Westm. Gaz.* 6 Sept. 8/2 Millions of red-winged ants.

b. ***red-winged blackbird, icterus, oriole, starling,*** or ***troopial***: The American marsh blackbird, *Agelaius phœniceus* (formerly called *Icterus phœniceus*).

1754 CATESBY *Nat. Hist. Carol.* (ed. 2) I. 13 The red wing'd Starling. **1768** PENNANT *Arct. Zool.* I. 300 The Red-winged Orioles build their nests in bushes. **1803** MITCHILL in *Med. Repository* (1805) 122 Redwing'd blackbird. **1831** WILSON, etc. *Amer. Ornith.* IV. 49 The bill is.. formed exactly like that of the red-winged troopial. **1839** AUDUBON *Ornith. Biog.* V. 3 Their habits are similar to those of the Red-winged Icterus. **1864-5** WOOD *Homes without H.* 537 One of the most variable of birds in its nesting is the well known Red-winged Starling of North America. **1893** NEWTON *Dict. Birds* 530 *Maize-bird*, a local name for *Agelæus phœniceus*, often called the Red-winged Blackbird.

'redwood, *sb.*[1] Also **red wood, red-wood.**

1. a. Wood of a red colour, obtained from many different trees, chiefly of tropical regions; formerly applied esp. to such as were used for dyeing.

1619 W. PHILLIP tr. *Schouten's Relation Wonderfull Voiage* 37 In each Canoe.. there lay two whole broad planckes of fayre redde wood. **1634** *Copy Court Roll (Wakefield)*, One milne.. used for the grinding of red wood. **1640** *Jrnl. Ho. Comm.* II. 33 The sole importing of the Red-wood. **1686** *Lond. Gaz.* No. 2186/1, 150 thousand pounds of Red Wood. **1722** *Ibid.* No. 6040/7 Red Wood or Guinea Wood the Hundred Weight,.. one Pound ten Shillings. **1725** SLOANE *Jamaica* II. 185 Red-wood. This is very red, more porous, lax, and lighter than any of the foregoing woods. **1812** J. SMYTH *Pract. of Customs* (1821) 285 *Cam Wood*, a fine red wood of Africa and of the Brazils, principally used in turnery... Cam Wood and Red Wood are considered in London as one and the same article. **1857** R. TOMES *Amer. in Japan* vi. 135 The jamana.. is very like the red-wood of Brazil and Mexico. **1887** MOLONEY *Forestry W. Afr.* 139 Redwood comes chiefly from Old Calabar, gives a stronger colour than barwood, and is worth a little more. **1957** *Handbk. Softwoods* (Forest Prod. Res. Lab.) 42 Timber of this species [sc. *Pinus sylvestris*] imported from the Continent is commonly called redwood, red deal, or simply 'red'. **1963** [see KAPUR].

b. = ***compression wood*** s.v. COMPRESSION 6.

1825 JAMIESON, *Red-Wood*, the name given to the reddish, or dark-coloured, and more incorruptible, wood found in the heart of trees. **1925** [see *compression wood*].

2. A name given to various trees having a red wood, *esp.* a tall Californian timber-tree, *Sequoia sempervirens*.

1716 *Petiveriana* III. 4/1 Red Wood [of Barbadoes]. **1756** P. BROWNE *Jamaica* 278 Red-wood or Iron-wood. This is a small but beautiful tree. **1819** WARDEN *United States* III. 97 In the lower parts are found oak, elm,.. red-wood, sumach. **1850** B. TAYLOR *Eldorado* I. vii. 47 A few miles west of the Pueblo there is a large forest of redwood, or Californian cypress. **1883** *Harper's Mag.* Jan. 210/2 When the glade began to narrow into a cañon the redwoods appeared—magnificent specimens.. rising straight two hundred feet.

3. *attrib.*, as ***redwood bark, fir, lumber, tree,*** etc.

1745 P. THOMAS *Jrnl. Anson's Voy.* 168 There are several others [trees] among which is one we call'd the Red-Wood-Tree, or Iron-Wood, from its great solidity. **1825** J. NICHOLSON *Operat. Mechanic* 84 The arms are of redwood fir, 6 inches square. **1883** *Harper's Mag.* July 815/2 Extensive yards of the attractive redwood lumber. **1885** B. HARTE *Maruja* ii, A quaint stockade.. thatched with redwood bark.

Redwood ('rɛdwʊd), *sb.*[2] [The name of Sir Boverton *Redwood* (1846–1919), British chemist.] **a.** ***Redwood viscometer***: either of two types of viscometer (differing in the ranges of viscosity for which they are suitable), which were designed by Redwood and are used esp. to measure the viscosity of petroleum and its products.

[**1886** *Jrnl. Soc. Chem. Industry* 29 Mar. 131/1 He had been in the habit of using one of Mr. Redwood's instruments for determining viscosities.] **1896** B. REDWOOD *Petroleum* II. ix. 605 The Redwood viscometer.. is a modification, designed by the author in 1885, of the instrument formerly used at the Battersea Works of Price's Patent Candle Company. **1931** G. BARR *Monogr. Viscometry* iv. 96 Liquids for which the Redwood No. II viscometer is specified.. are difficult to free from suspended impurities. **1949** A. C. MERRINGTON *Viscometry* v. 58 The calibration of a Redwood viscometer with a number of oils using an apparatus of the Thorpe and Rodger type. **1972** HARKER & ALLEN *Fuel Sci.* vii. 98 The instrument most commonly used in the United Kingdom to measure viscosity is the Redwood Viscometer... The two standard instruments are the No. 1 and the No. 2 Redwood viscometers. The former is used for thin oils having viscosities of less than 2,000 Redwood seconds, and the latter for more viscous oils. **1973** A. L. MILLS in Hobson & Pohl *Mod. Petroleum Technol.* (ed. 4) xx. 730 These instruments are now rarely used except perhaps for black oils... In fact, the method of viscosity determination using the Redwood viscometer has been deleted from the Institute of Petroleum 'Standard Tests'.

b. ***Redwood second*** (also ***second Redwood***): a unit of viscosity used in conjunction with Redwood viscometers and equal to one second of the time required for a given quantity of fluid to pass through a capillary in the instrument. So ***Redwood time, unit, viscosity,*** etc., and with ellipsis of second word.

1913 *Petroleum World* June 272/1 The remaining three columns respectively give their colour, density at 20° C. and viscosity at 20° in Redwood units. **1930** *Engineering* 5 Sept. 308/1 The fuel used throughout this test was Mexican boiler oil with.. a viscosity of 200 secs. Redwood. **1949** A. C. MERRINGTON *Viscometry* v. 57 The results are normally expressed as 'Redwood seconds' at the temperature of the test. *Ibid.* A Redwood time of T_R seconds. **1967** A. S. BRUNJES in Bland & Davidson *Petroleum Processing Handbk.* xii. 32 The Kinematic, Saybolt, Universal, redwood [*sic*] No. 1, and Engler scales. **1973** P. J. KING et al. in Hobson & Pohl *Mod. Petroleum Technol.* (ed. 4) vi. 215 Reference to .. viscosities expressed in terms of Redwood seconds.. is still found in the literature. **1973** J. G. C. POPE in *Ibid.* xviii. 654 The viscosity of relatively mobile oils is recorded as so many seconds Redwood I @ 100° F. **1973** W. H. THOMAS in *Ibid.* xxv. 860 When the Redwood viscosity requirements are quoted in specifications the usual procedure is to determine viscosity in kinematic or dynamic units and to convert these into Redwood by means of a conversion chart.

red-wood, -wud, *a. Sc.* [See WOOD *a.*] Stark mad, completely mad; furious, distracted.

c **1560** A. SCOTT *Poems* (S.T.S.) ii. 102 Than to Dalkeith thai maid thame boun, Reidwod of this reproche. *a* **1585** MONTGOMERIE *Cherrie & Slae* 934 Will ran reid-wood almaist. **1719** RAMSAY *2nd Answ. Hamilton* i, Gin ony higher up ye drive her, She'll rin red-wood. **1786** BURNS *Cry & Prayer* xvi, Now she's like to rin red-wud About her whisky. **1882** J. WALKER *Jaunt to Auld Reekie*, etc. 46 The Carle.. Rowtes and roars like ane redwud.

red worm, red-worm.

1. A variety of earth-worm much used as bait in rod-fishing.

a **1450** *Fysshynge w. Angle* (1883) 30 He hath but one manere of bayte & that is a red worme, which is moost cheyf for all manere of fysshe. **1613** DENNYS *Secrets Angling* II. D ib, The Pearch, the Tench, and Eele, doe rather bite At great red wormes, in Field or Garden bred. **1740** R. BROOKES *Art of Angling* 12 The Brandling, Gilt-Tail and Red-Worm, are all to be found in old Dunghills. **1856** STONEHENGE *Brit. Sports* 236/2 The Red-Worm is about the same size as the brandling.

2. A worm or grub attacking grain.

1764 *Museum Rust.* III. 171 My wheat.. was cut off, last May, by a little insect called the red-worm. **1780** YOUNG *Tour in Irel.* I. 6 Soot he buys at Dublin for sowing over the wheat in April to kill the red worm. **1792** *Trans. Soc. Arts* X. 59 Materially injured by the wire or red worm.

3. A parasitic nematode worm belonging to the family Strongylidæ, esp. to the genus *Strongylus*, which infests the intestine and other organs of many vertebrate animals, causing severe anæmia and general debility.

1891 R. WALLACE *Rural Econ. Austral. & N.Z.* xxviii. 374 Sheep also suffer from the red worm.. in their fourth stomach. **1951** *Chambers's Jrnl.* Oct. 587/1 Red-worms belong to the Strongyle family. **1970** MILLER & WEST *Black's Vet. Dict.* (ed. 9) 768/1 Thiabendazole is a useful drug for the removal of red worms in horses.

† **'redy,** *a. Obs.* [f. REDE *sb.*[1] + -Y: cf. G. *rätig*, Da. and Sw. *rådig*, ON. *ráðugr*.] Wise, prudent.

1297 R. GLOUC. (Rolls) 11699 Ouȝ, he sede, redi folk & wel iwar is þis, & more conne of bataile þan hii coupe biuore. **1387** TREVISA *Higden* (Rolls) I. 205 Here moder Gambara, þat was ful redy and wise [L. *prudentissima*]. *Ibid.* III. 181 þe kyng.. byhiȝte hem ȝiftes þat ȝaf þe redieste answere [L. *prudentius respondenti*]. **1422** tr. *Secreta Secret., Priv. Priv.* 234 Who-so hath the face straght.. he is wyse and redy in his dedys. *c* **1450** LONELICH *Merlin* 1560 (Kölbing), He was so wis, so redy and so bold.

redy, obs. form of READY, REDDY, REEDY.

re-dye (riːˈdaɪ), *v.* [RE- 5 a.] *trans.* To dye again. Hence **re-'dyeing** *vbl. sb.*

1611 COTGR., *Retaindre*, to put into a new colour, to re-die, or die againe. *Ibid.*, *Reteinture*, a re-dying, a second or new dying. **1851** MAYHEW *Lond. Labour* II. 70 When canaries are 'a bad colour' or have grown a paler yellow from age, they are re-dyed.

redyfy, obs. f. RE-EDIFY *v.*

redyl-, obs. f. RIDDLE *v.*

redyli, -ly, obs. ff. READILY; varr. REDILY *Obs.*

redymite, -yte, varr. REDIMITE *v. Obs.*

redyn, obs. inf. REDE *v.*[1], obs. pa. pple. RIDE *v.*

redyness, variant of REDINESS *Obs.*

† **ree,** *sb.*[1] *Obs.* Also 6 **rhe.** [Of obscure origin.] A stream, channel, river.

Perh. repr. OE. *éa* with the *r* of the fem. article in such phrases as *on* or *ofer þǽre éa*: see Hempl in *An Engl. Miscellany* (1901) 155 and Skeat *Student's Pastime* 400. But connexion with Flem. *reie* and *rui* (in Kilian *reye, ruye*) in the same sense seems possible.

1422 *Will of Kyt* (Somerset Ho.), Quodquid tenementum .. abuttet erga le Hye Ree. **1455** in Willis & Clark *Cambr.* (1886) I. 212 [From Mylnstrete to the water called] 'le Ree'. **1502** ARNOLDE *Chron.* (1811) 252 Mary ouer the ree in Southwerke, a priorye of Chanons. **1587** HARRISON *England* in *Holinshed* I. 46/1 Euen to this daie in Essex I haue oft obserued, that when the lower grounds by rage of water haue beene ouerflowen, the people beholding the same, haue said; All is on a Rhe, as if they should haue said; All is now a riuer. *a* **1669** SOMNER *Rom. Ports Kent* (1693) 69 By Gilford to (what in all likelyhood ows it's name to that Ree or channel) Rye. [**1724** BAILEY (ed. 2), *Ree*, as *all is on a Ree* .. all is on a River, or overflowed with Water. *Essex*.]

ree (riː), *sb.*[2] [Variant of REEVE *sb.*[2] It is not clear which is the more original form.] The female of the ruff.

15.. *Inthron. Abp. Nevill* in *MS. Bodl. Rolls* 8 Of the foules called Rees cc dosen. **1750** POCOCKE *Trav. through Eng.* (Camden) I. 67 Among the game they have the ruffs and rees, the former cocks, the latter hens. **1768** *Ann. Reg.* I. 171 The bill of fare at the king of Denmark's table was as follows:.. Leveret, Ruffs and Rees, Wheat ears [etc.]. **1801** H. SKRINE *Rivers Gt. Brit.* 28 Those rare and delicate birds, the Ruff and Ree are found here. **1819** H. BUSK *Banquet* III. 316 Point out the speckled pairs of ruffs and rees.

ree (riː), *sb.*[3] *Sc.* [Of obscure origin: the form *reeve* also occurs locally.]

1. A walled enclosure for sheep, cattle, or swine. (See also *sheep-ree*.)

1824 MACTAGGART *Gallovid. Encycl.* 406 Ree is often confounded with bught, but a sheep-ree and a sheep-bught are different. **1875** W. McIlwraith *Guide Wigtownshire* 62 It seems as if the stones of this old castle had been gathered together to form rees for sheep. **1894** Crockett *Raiders* (ed. 3) 238 A great swine that lies..in the filth of the ree.

2. A yard where coal is stored for sale.

1880 in Jamieson. **1902** *Scotsman* 2 Oct., The person in charge of the ree admitted using the weight.

ree (riː), *a. Sc.* [Of unknown origin.] Excited, esp. with drink; elevated; crazy, delirious.

1788 R. Galloway *Poems* 23 (Jam.) Until their noddle twin them ree And kiss the causey. **1790** A. Wilson *2nd Ep. Clark* Poet. Wks. (1846) 99, I..Read and leugh,..Till my pow grew haflins ree. **1828** Moir *Mansie Wauch* xv, Tammie..was a whit ree with the good cheer. **1886** 'H. Haliburton' *Horace in Homespun* (1900) 144 Here's Willie wi' a warlike ee,..Dave amorous daft, an' Roger ree.

ree (riː), **rye** (raɪ), *v. dial.* Also 7, 9 **ray**. [Of obscure origin: the various forms indicate a ME. *rēȝe(n)*, but their relationship to the synonymous reeve *v.*[2] and *rew* or *rue* (Devonshire) is not clear.] *trans.* To clean or sift (winnowed grain, peas, etc.), *spec.* by giving a circular motion to the contents of the sieve, so that the chaff, etc. collects in the centre.

α. **1400–1** [see reeing *vbl. sb.* 1]. **1523** Fitzherb. *Husb.* §36 Whan thou haste thresshed thy pees, and beanes, after they be wynowed,..let theym be well reed with syues. **1615** Markham *Eng. Housew.* ii. vii. (1668) 171 After it is well rubbed, and winnowed, you shall ree it over in a fine sieve. *Ibid.*, After the malt is ree'd, you shall sack it up. **1669** Worlidge *Syst. Agric.* (1681) 330 To *Ree*, or *Ray*; to handle Corn in a Sieve, so as the chaffy or lighter part gather to one place. **1824** Mactaggart *Gallovid. Encycl.* 406 To ree grain is to whirl it through a riddle, so that the tares in it may be seen. **1828–** in northern dial. glossaries (Northumbld., Cumbld., Lonsd., Yks., Sheff., Leic.). **1875** W. Dickinson *Cumbriana* 231 Fwok ree's a lock wheat in a seive, if they hev't, And that was their deetin' machine.

β. **1641** Best *Farm. Bks.* (Surtees) 103 A sieve to rye the corne with; we make the miller sitte on his knees and rye it. **1744–50** W. Ellis *Mod. Husb.* VI. iii. 64 (E.D.S.) This practice of rying, or cleaning better than ordinary. **1788** W. Marshall *Yorksh.* II. Gloss., *To Rie*; to turn corn in a sieve; bringing the 'capes' into an eddy. **1854** Anne E. Baker *Northampt. Gloss.* s.v. *Ree*, A labourer who works it expertly is said to 'rye it up well'.

γ. **1669** [see α above]. **1813** T. Davis *Agric. Wilts.* 266 Corn well arrayed, or rayed. Corn well dressed and cleaned. **1893** *Wilts. Gloss.*, *Ray*, or *Array*, to dress and clean corn.

ree (riː), *int.* Now *rare*. A call to horses, usually a command to turn to the right.

Hence the dial. phrase *neither heck nor ree*, (to go) neither to the left nor right; (to be) intractable or obstinate.

1548 *J. Bow & Mast Parson* 164 in Hazl. *E.P.P.* IV. 16 Have a gayne, bald before, hayght, ree, who! **1599** Middleton *Micro-cyn.* Wks. (Bullen) VIII. 121 Whipstaff in his hand, Who with a hey and ree the beasts command. *c* **1603** Heywood & Rowley *Fortune by Land* ii. i. H.'s Wks. 1874 VI. 384 Come Ile go teach ye hayte and ree, gee and whoe, and which is to which hand. **1832** Mrs. Bray *Descr. Tamar & Tavy* (1836) I. ii. 24 He soon found that some or other of the crook horses invariably crossed him on the road ..owing to two words of the driver, namely *gee* and *ree*.

ree, sing. of *rees* = reis (Pg. money).

ree, reean, reeaum, obs. forms of rye[2], reean, realm.

‖**reebok** ('rɪəbɒk, 'riː-). Also 8 **-bock**, 9– **rhe(e)boc, -bok, -buck**, 20 **ribbok**. [Du. *reebok* roebuck.] A small South African antelope, *Pelea capreola*, with sharp horns.

1775 Masson in *Phil. Trans.* LXVI. 270, I spent a whole day in search of plants, and hunting a sort of antelope called Ree Bock. **1790** Bewick *Hist. Quadrup.* 77 The Ree-Bok is a gregarious animal. **1834** *Penny Cycl.* II. 80/1 The Rheebok (*Antilope capreolus*). *Ibid.* II. 80/2 The rheeboks live in small families of five or six individuals. **1834** Pringle *Afr. Sk.* 22 Along the grassy meads Where the skipping reebok feeds. **1834** A. Smith *Jrnl.* 14 Nov. (1939) I. 137 Saw the common rheebok. **1839** W. C. Harris *Wild Sports S. Afr.* 384 *Redunca Capreolus.* The Rhee Buck. Rhee-bok of the Cape Colonists. **1850** R. G. Cumming *Hunter's Life S. Afr.* I. i. 18 The rhooye-rheebok, or red rheebuck. **1862** J. S. Dobie *Jrnl.* 10 Sept. in *S. Afr. Jrnl.* (1945) 23 Saw both oribi and rhebuck, the former very pretty animals. **1881** Selous *Wanderings S. Afr.* 2, I..had managed to bag one bushbuck ram..and eight gray and red rhebucks. **1889** H. A. Bryden *Kloof & Kerroo* xvi. 297 The Voal or Grey Rhebock..is..plentiful on most of the mountain ranges. **1910** J. Buchan *Prester John* xiv. 230 There were droves of smaller game—rhebok and springbok and duikers. **1947** H. C. Bosman *Mafeking Road* xii. 67 He remembered having had that same feeling once before when he had shot a ribbok. **1950** *Cape Argus* 17 July 4/4 Two dainty rhebuck stood and gazed at us. **1953** *Cape Argus* 25 Apr. 8/4 The animals include ribbok, grysbok,..and one blue wildebeest. **1958** L. van der Post *Lost World of Kalahari* v. 91 Barely fifty feet from me five rhee-buck got up from their warm beds behind a ledge of rock. **1959** *Encounter* Sept. 53 These mountains of up-pointed spears Hold eland, oribi and rhebok. **1966** E. Palmer *Plains of Camdeboo* vii. 124 'The skull is ribbok,' he said, 'and that's the tibia of a buffalo.'

re-e'bullient, *a.* [re- 5 a.] Boiling up again.

1817 Coleridge *Biog. Lit.* xiii. (1882) 141 The power which acts in them is indestructible; it is therefore inexhaustibly re-ebullient.

reech, smoke: see reek *sb.*[1] and *v.*[1]

reechily: see reechy.

re-'echo, *sb.* [f. next, or f. re- + echo *sb.*] An echo; also, a second or repeated echo.

1613–16 W. Browne *Brit. Past.* i. iv. 75 The hills and vallies here and there resound With re-ecchoes of the deepe-mouth'd hound. **1828–32** Webster, *Re-echo*, the echo of an echo. **1862** *Rep. Ecclesiol. Soc.* 20 He was glad to hear Mr. Digby Wyatt's re-echo of the President's aspirations. **1895** J. A. Beet *New Life in Christ* ii. x. 79 The re-echo of this voice in our own spirit.

re-'echo, *v.* [f. re- + echo *v.*]

1. *intr.* To echo (again), resound:

a. of a sound, noise, or cry.

1590 Spenser *F.Q.* ii. i. 38 A deadly shrieke..That through the wood re-echoed againe. **1725** Pope *Odyss.* x. 472 Sobs of joy re-echoed through the bower. **1740** Pitt *Æneid* xi. 641 A thousand notes re-echoing thro' the wood. **1801** Southey *Thalaba* xi. xix, The thunder of the avalanche Re-echoes far behind. **1865** F. Boyle *Dyaks of Borneo* 51 The crash of some giant branch..re-echoes widely for the moment.

b. of places. Const. *to*, *with*.

a **1599** Spenser *F.Q.* vii. vi. 52 All the woods and dales.. Did ring againe, and loud re-echo to the skie. **1712–14** Pope *Rape Lock* v. 86 With starting tears each eye o'erflows, And the high dome re-echoes to his nose. **1786** tr. *Beckford's Vathek* (1883) 64 The city re-echoed with shouts of joy, and flourishing of trumpets. **1851** Longf. *Gold. Leg.* v. *Devil's Bridge*, The rocks re-echoed with peals of laughter.

2. *trans.* **a.** To echo back; to return (a sound), reverberate, multiply by repetition.

1595 Chapman *Ovid's Banq. Sence* E 2 [Echo] the selfe same way shee came doth make retreate, And so effects the sounde reecchoed. **1656** H. More *Enthus. Tri.* (1712) 32 Thunder, whose sound is so great and terrible, because it is re-ecchoed from the arched roof of Heaven. **1757** Gray *Bard* 54 Severn shall reecho with affright The shrieks of death. **1784** Cowper *Task* i. 343 The consecrated roof Re-echoing pious anthems! **1814** Scott *Wav.* xlvi, The Highlanders set up a tremendous yell, which was re-echoed by the heights behind them.

fig. **1847** Longf. *Ev.* ii. v. 5 The streets still re-echo the names of the trees of the forest. **1863** Hawthorne *Our Old Home* I. 247 The many peaks in which the structure ascends, and..the pinnacles which, as it were, repeat and re-echo them into the sky.

b. To repeat like an echo.

1636 Massinger *Bashf. Lover* iv. iii, The princess' name, Matilda, oft re-echoed! **1797** Mrs. Radcliffe *Italian* xii, 'In this chamber', re-echoed Vivaldi, in a voice of desperation. **1849** Macaulay *Hist. Eng.* i. I. 85 Those acclamations were reechoed by the voice of the capital and of the nation. **1875** T. Hill *True Ord. Stud.* 130 Those who still re-echo Ricardo and Malthus.

Hence **re-'echoed** *ppl. a.*; **re-'echoing** *vbl. sb.* and *ppl. a.*

1611 Florio, *Ribombo*, a hollow re-ecchoyng. **1668** H. More *Div. Dial.* v. xxxviii. (1713) 516 There was a re-echoing noise round about the Heavens. **1678** Cudworth *Intell. Syst.* i. iii. §37. 160 Ravished with the Re-ecchoing of its own Harmony. **1801** Southey *Thalaba* v. xxvi, When the long re-echoing ceased. **1810** —— *Kehama* i. iii, Rising over all..Is heard the echoed and re-echoed name.

reechy ('riːtʃɪ), *a. Obs.* exc. *dial.* Also 5 **rechy**, 6 **rechie**. [f. *reech* reek *sb.*[1] + -y[1].] Smoky; squalid, dirty; rancid.

c **1460** J. Russell *Bk. Nurture* 359 Raw, resty, and rechy [meats], ar comberous vndefied. **1599** Shaks. *Much Ado* iii. iii. 143 Like Pharaoes souldiours in the rechie painting. **1607** —— *Cor.* ii. i. 225 The Kitchin Malkin pinnes Her richest Lockram 'bout her reechie necke. **1660** Blount *Boscobel* 41 His face and hands made of a reechy complexion by the help of the Walnut-tree leaves. **1879** Miss Jackson *Shropsh. Word-bk.* s.v., A grimy, reechy lookin' thing. *Ibid.*, That butter's nasty reechy stuff.

Hence **'reechily** *adv. rare*[−1].

1618 D. Belchier *Hans Beer-pot* D j b, Bad him goe And wash his face, he lookt so reechilie, Like Bacon hanging on the Chimnies roofe.

reed (riːd), *sb.*[1] Forms: 1 **hréod**, **(h)réad**, 2–5 **reod**, (3 **rode**, **ræode**), 3–6 **rede**, (4 **riede**, 6 **ride**), 4–5 **red**, (4 **rued**, **rehed**, 5–6 **reid**), 4–7 **reede**, 6– **reed**. [Common W. Germ.: OE. *hréod* = OFris. *(h)reid*, OS. *hriad-*, OLG. *ried* (MLG. *riet*, mod.LG. *rêd*, *rêt*; MDu. *ried-*, *riet*, Du. *riet*), OHG. *(h)riot* (MHG., mod.G. *riet*):—OTeut. **hreudo*[m], not traceable in the cognate languages.

An early form of the word is preserved in the place-name *Hreutford* or *Hreudford* 'id est vadum harundinis' in Bæda's *Eccl. Hist.* iv. xvi.]

I. 1. a. One of the tall straight stalks or stems formed by plants of the genera *Phragmites* and *Arundo* (see 4 and 5); †also, a cane.

c **725** *Corpus Gloss.* 1007 *Harundo*, canna, hreod. *c* **950** *Lindisf. Gosp.* Luke vii. 24 Forhuon foerdon ȝie on woestern, ȝesea hread..from wind ȝecerred? *c* **1000** Ælfric *Hom.* II. 252 [Hi] for cyne-ȝyrde him hreod forȝeafon. *c* **1160** *Hatton Gosp.* Matt. xxvii. 30 [Hi] namen reod ænd beoton hys heafod. *c* **1265** *Voc. Names Pl.* in Wr.-Wülcker 556/42 *Arundo*, rosel, reod. **13..** *K. Alis.* 6433 A reod they putteth in heore mouth And they sowketh by the reod. *c* **1400** Maundev. (Roxb.) xxi. 95 Beside þat logh growez redez of a wonderfull lenth... Of þir redez þai make þare houses. **1484** Caxton *Fables of Æsop* iv. xx, A reed whiche was at his foote bowed hym self as moche as the wynd wold. **1590** Spenser *F.Q.* iii. vi. 6 A little cottage, built of stickes and reeds In homely wize. **1617** Moryson *Itin.* i. 213 This Iland yeeldeth Canes or Reedes of sugar. **1671** Milton *P.R.* ii. 26 By a Creek: Where winds with Reeds, and Osiers whisp'ring play. **1756** Nugent *Gr. Tour, Italy* III. 304 The common habitations..are mostly huts made of reeds. **1797** *Encycl. Brit.* (ed. 3) VII. 255 The reeds [for a fire-ship] are made up in small bundles of about a foot in circumference. **1815** J. Smith *Panorama Sc. & Art* I. 215 Reeds are used instead of laths in some parts of the country. **1877** Bryant *Odyss.* v. 557 He, meanwhile, Withdrawing from the brink, lay down among The reeds.

b. *fig.* and in fig. context.

c **1450** tr. *De Imitatione* ii. vii. 47 Truste not ner leene not upon a windy rede. **1562** A. Bernher *Ep. Ded. Latimer's Serm.* A iv b, He was contented rather to be cast into the Tower..then to be found a wauering reede. *c* **1593** T. Deloney *Garland of Goodwill* (1631) iii. sig. B1, But senselesse man, what de I meane, Upon a broken reede to leane. **1611** Bible *Isa.* xxxvi. 6 Loe, thou trustest in the staffe of this broken reede, on Egypt. **1617** J. Chamberlain *Let.* 20 Dec. (1939) II. 123 Yf you trusted to him you trusted to a rotten reede who wold have failed you in the end. **1621** *House of Lords Jrnls.* 30 Apr. 101/1 Their lordships.. reported, That they..demanded of his lordship [*sc.* F. Bacon] whether it were his Hand..who answered 'My lords, it is my Act, my Hand.. I beseech your Lordships, be merciful unto a broken Reed.' **1657** *Penit. Conf.* vii. 152 Penitents are taught more to rely upon that reed and arm of flesh. **1757** Smollett *Reprisal* i. i. 7 You lean upon a broken reed if you trust to their compassion. **1810** Scott *Lady of L.* v. xi, I only meant To show the reed on which you leant. **1821** Byron *Sardanap.* v. i. 135 The last frail reed of our beleaguer'd hopes. **1893** *Baily's Mag.* Oct. 271/1 The reeds on which they depended were Ravensbury and Self Sacrifice. **1926** R. H. Tawney *Relig. & Rise of Capitalism* ii. 108 Human efforts, social institutions, the world of culture, are at best irrelevant to salvation, and at worst mischievous. They distract man from the true aim of his existence and encourage reliance upon broken reeds. **1961** I. Murdoch *Severed Head* xiii. 118 A nervous shrinking which was not exactly dislike made me hesitate to probe the motives of such a being. Therewith some vague yet powerful train of thought led me to say, 'I'm a broken reed after all.' **1973** *Times Lit. Suppl.* 23 Mar. 311/3 The history of the opposition shows what bruised reeds the generals were.

2. *collect.* Reeds (as plants); a growth or bed of reeds.

a **800** *Erfurt Gloss.* 290 *Carectum*, hreod. *a* **900** tr. *Bæda's Hist.* iii. xvii. [xxiii.] (1890) 230 In þæm cleofun..wære upyrnende grownes hreodes & rixa. *c* **1205** Lay. 20170 Hundes in þan reode mid reouðe hine imeteð. *Ibid.* 21741 þat is a seolcuð mere..mid fenne & mid ræode. **13..** *K. Alis.* 5064 The water was ful of longe reede. **1481** Caxton *Godfrey* xxix. 63 A fewe of them that withdrewe them in to the mareys and hydde them in the reed. **1560** Bible (Genev.) *Job* xl. 21 [16] Lyeth he vnder the shady trees in the couert of the rede and fennes? **1579–80** North *Plutarch* (1595) 469 He..couered him with a great deale of reede and bent. **1865** Kingsley *Herew.* xxxi, The morass to right and left, which had been a minute before deep reed.

b. Reeds employed for firing or thatching, or used as lath for plastering upon.

1494 Fabyan *Chron.* vii. 368 They fyryd the gates, and after forced the fyre with rede and drye wood. **1556–7** in Willis & Clark *Cambridge* (1886) II. 455 Y[e] reede over the cloyster and y[e] gystes of the same. **1568** Grafton *Chron.* II. 277 He..set the houses like streetes, and couered them with Reede and Broome. **1596** Dalrymple tr. *Leslie's Hist. Scot.* I. 10 Thay Reid for wod use..to thair fyre. **1669** E. Byland in *St. Papers, Dom.* 151, I have fetched a boat-load of reed from Ham Creek. **1703** T. N. *City & C. Purchaser* 260 They Thatch with Reed instead of Straw... Reed is sold by the Thousand, *viz.* A Thousand handfuls.

c. *transf.* Wheat-straw prepared for thatching.

1415–16 *Durham Acc. Rolls* (Surtees) 612 Item in tectura straminea vocat. rede empt. **1523** Fitzherb. *Husb.* §27 All the wheate-strawe that they pourpose to make thacke of, they..cutte of the eares, and bynde it in sheues, and call it rede. **1669** Worlidge *Syst. Agric.* (1681) 329 *Reed*, is.. Straw bound up for thatching, by some called Helm. **1797** *Encycl. Brit.* (ed. 3) XVI. 36/2 *Reed*, a term used in the west of England for the straw used by thatchers, which is wheat straw finely combed. **1805** R. W. Dickson *Pract. Agric.* I. 74 The Somersetshire-reed; which is nothing more than the strongest wheat-straw which can be met with [etc.]. **1848** *Jrnl. R. Agric. Soc.* IX. ii. 465 A large proportion of the wheat-straw is made into reed for thatching.

3. Without article, as a material. †Also *in reed*, as or like a reed.

a **1240** *Lofsong* in *Cott. Hom.* 207 Ich bide þe..bi þe þornene crununge, bi ðe kineȝerde of rode. **1388** Wyclif *2 Kings* xviii. 21 Whether thou hopist in a staf of rehed and broken Egipt. **1535** Coverdale *2 Kings* xviii. 21 Beholde puttest thou thy trust in this broken staffe of reed, in Egipte? **1604** E. G[rimstone] *D'Acosta's Hist. Indies* iv. xvi. 257 It is a graine, as he saies, that growes in reede, and covers it selfe with a leafe. **1667** Milton *P.L.* vi. 519 Part incentive reed Provide, pernicious with one touch to fire. **1866** Livingstone *Last Jrnls.* (1873) I. vi. 158 A flake of reed is often used in surgical operations by the natives.

4. With *the*, as the distinctive name of the class of plants forming the genera *Phragmites* and *Arundo*, having a firm stem and growing in water or marshy ground; *esp.* the common species *Phragmites communis*, abundant in Britain and on the Continent; †also, the sugar-cane.

1382 Wyclif *Isa.* xix. 6 The reed and the ressche shal welewen. **1667** Milton *P.L.* vii. 321 Up stood the cornie Reed Embattell'd in her field. **1672** W. Hughes *Amer. Phys.* 29 Of the Juyce of this Reed or Cane is made Sugar. **1688** R. Holme *Armoury* ii. 57/2 The Reed is between an Herb and a Tree. **1785** Martyn *Rousseau's Bot.* xiii. (1794) 142 The woollyness of the flowers in the Reed will shew you this genus as soon as it unfolds its panicle. **1850** Tennyson *In Mem.* ciii, We glided winding under ranks Of iris, and the golden reed.

5. With distinctive epithets, denoting various species of reeds, or plants resembling these.

aromatic reed (see calamus 2). **Dutch reed** = Dutch rush (see Dutch A. 3 c). **great reed**, a reed of the genus *Arundo*, esp. *A. donax*. **Indian reed**, canna. **small reed**, a grass of the genus *Calamagrostis* (or *Deyeuxia*). Also *bur*, *canary*, *paper*, *sea*, *trumpet*, *water*, *wood reed*: see these sbs.

1597 Gerarde *Herbal* i. v. 6 Wilde Reede.., called also *Calamogrostis*, is far lesser [1633 bigger] than Couch grasse, or Dogs grasse. *Ibid.* xxvi. 36 *Harundo florida*: in English the Flowring Reede. **1611** COTGR. s.v. *Calame, Calame aromat*, the sweet Arabian reed, or cane, tearmed *Calamus odoratus*, or the Aromaticall reed. **1613** DENNIS *Secrets Angling* I. B 2, Shutes as are.. In shape and beautie like the Belgicke Reed. **1640** PARKINSON *Herbal* 1629 *Cannæ Indicæ*.. Indian Reede staves. **1733** MILLER *Gard. Dict.* (ed. 2) s.v. *Cannacorus*, The Indian Reed. **1739** *Ibid.* II. s.v. *Arundo*, The species.. are the common Reed, the large manured Reed,.. the variegated Reed, the Bambu Cane,.. and Dark red reed. **1743** JAMES *Med. Dict.*, *Arundo Donax*,.. the Great Reed. *Ibid.*, *Calamus odoratus*, Aromatic Reed. **1797** *Encycl. Brit.* (ed. 3) II. 384/1 The debax, or manured reed, is a native of warm countries. **1842** R. PARNELL *Grasses Scot.* 37 *Calamagrostis stricta*. Small Close Reed. **1859** MISS PRATT *Brit. Grasses & Sedges* 67–8 *Calamagrostis lanceolata*. Purple-Flowered Small-reed. *Calamagrostis stricta*. Narrow Small-reed.

II. 6. a. A reed used as a dart or arrow; hence *poet.* an arrow.

1377 LANGL. *P. Pl.* B. XVIII. 30 Aue, *rabby!* quod that ribaud, and threw redes [*v.r.* reodes] at hym. **1387** TREVISA *Higden* (Rolls) VII. 77 þe childe losed and schette, and hitte þe charbuncle stoon wiþ a reed. *a* **1709** PRIOR *To a Lady* 31 With cruel Skill the backward Reed He sent, and, as he fled, he slew. **1791** COWPER *Iliad* IV. 146 Whizz'd the bowstring, and the reed Leap'd off. **1813** SCOTT *Trierm.* II. x, The frantic steed rush'd up the dell, As whistles from the bow the reed. **1830** TENNYSON *Poet* 13 The viewless arrows of his thoughts.. Like Indian reeds blown from his silver tongue.

b. In Biblical use (rendering L. *calamus* and *arundo*, Gr. κάλαμος, Heb. *qāneh*): A reed employed as a measuring-rod; hence, a Jewish measure of length (also called ***Ezekiel's reed***), equal to six cubits.

c **1375** *Sc. Leg. Saints* vi. (*Thomas*) 201 Thomas.. tuk a lange red in his hand as man of craft þat vare cunnand. **1388** WYCLIF *Ezek.* xlii. 16 He mat.. with the rehed of mesure bi cumpas fyue hundrid rehedis. —— *Rev.* xxi. 15 And he.. hadde a golden mesure of a reed. [Also in Tyndale, Coverdale, etc.] **1611** BIBLE *Ezek.* xlii. 16 He measured the East side with the measuring reede, fiue hundreth reedes. **1858** LONGF. *M. Standish* IV. 9 Over its turrets uplifted Glimmered the golden reed of the angel who measured the city. **1863** W. L. BEVAN in W. Smith *Dict. Bible* III. 1736/2 With the exception of the notice that the reed equals six cubits (Ezek. xl. 5), we have no intimation that the measures were combined in anything like a scale.

†**c.** *pl.* Papyrus. *Obs. rare*$^{-1}$.

1551 ROBINSON tr. *More's Utop.* II. vi. (1895) 219 Where as before they wrote onelye in skynnes, in barkes of tryes, and in rides, now they haue attempted to make paper and to imprint letters.

7. a. A reed made into a rustic musical pipe. Also applied to the hollow stems of other plants used for the same purpose, esp. ***oaten reed***.

c **1384** CHAUCER *H. Fame* III. 131 That craftely begunne to pipe Bothe in doucet and in riede. **1390** GOWER *Conf.* II. 162 He the ferste.. Was which the melodie fond Of Riedes,.. With double pipes forto pipe. **1530** PALSGR. 261/1 Rede to playe or pype with, *anche*. **1634** MILTON *Comus* 345 Might we but hear The.. sound of pastoral reed with oaten stops. **1697** DRYDEN *Virg. Past.* v. 2 Since my Voice can match your tuneful Reed. **1805** SCOTT *Last Minstr.* IV. i, As if thy waves.. Had only heard the shepherd's reed, Nor started at the bugle-horn. **1878** B. TAYLOR *Deukalion* I. i. 18 To the musical reeds and the glasses.., farewell.

b. *fig.* as the symbol of rustic or pastoral poetry.

1582 STANYHURST *Æneis* I. (Arb.) 1, I that in old season wyth reeds oten harmonye whistled My rural sonnet. **1721** RAMSAY *Petit. Whin-bush Club* ii, Etling wi' spite to rive my reed, And give my muse a fa'. **1783** BURNS *Poor Mailie* viii, Come, join the melancholious croon O' Robin's reed! **1821** CLARE *Vill. Minstr.* I. 105 Sweetest of subjects are ye for my reed. **1867** WHITTIER *Tent on Beach* 86 Making his rustic reed of song A weapon in the war with wrong.

8. A part of various musical instruments.

a. In the oboe and bassoon: A part of the mouth-piece, consisting of two slightly concave wedge-shaped pieces of reed or cane fixed face to face on the end of a metal tube, and producing a musical sound by vibration when the instrument is blown into. Also, a similar device fixed in the chanter of a bagpipe. (Now freq. called a ***double reed*** in distinction to c: also, with hyphen, *attrib.*)

1530 PALSGR. 261/2 Rede of a weyght the instrument, *anche*. **1727** BOYER *Dict. Royal* I, *Anche*,.. the Reed of a Hoboy, or some other Wind-Instrument of Musick. **1727–41** CHAMBERS *Cycl.* s.v. *Bagpipe*, The third [pipe] has a reed, and is played on by compressing the bag under the arm. *Ibid.*, *Hautboy or Hoboy*, a sort of musical instrument of the wind kind, with a reed to blow or play it withal. **1797** *Encycl. Brit.* (ed. 3) VIII. 342/1 It [the oboe] spreads and widens towards the bottom, and is sounded through a reed. **1835** *Penny Cycl.* IV. 10/1 It [the bassoon] consists of.. a brass craned neck in which the reed is inserted. **1876** STAINER & BARRETT *Dict. Mus. Terms* 137/2 *Double reed*,.. the vibrating reed of instruments of the oboe class. **1879** W. H. STONE in Grove *Dict. Mus.* I. 123/2 The chaunter reed is .. made of two approximated edges of cane tied together, and is thus essentially a double reed, like that of the oboe or bassoon. **1879** GROVE *Dict. Mus.* I. 151/2 *Bassoon*.., a wooden double-reed instrument of eight-foot tone. **1931** G. JACOB *Orchestral Technique* iii. 26 The bassoon also agrees well with its double-reed cousin the oboe. **1961** A. BAINES *Musical Instruments* ix. 233 The European shawm reed is of harder material prepared like all Western double reeds by folding over a strip of seasoned cane, shaping and binding the ends together, and paring down and finally separating the tip. **1974** *Encycl. Brit. Macropædia* XIX. 848/1 The human voice.. may be classified as a double-reed aerophone in which the vocal chords act as a double reed.

b. (*a*) In the organ: A small metal tube fixed at the lower end of a pipe, having a longitudinal opening covered or closed by a metal tongue, which is made to vibrate by the air entering the tube. ***free reed*** (see quot. 1855 and cf. note to c). (*b*) In a bagpipe drone: A piece of hollow reed, closed at one end by a joint, and having a tongue made on one side by splitting from a cross-cut near the joint backwards in the direction of the open end.

1727–41 CHAMBERS *Cycl.* s.v. *Organ*, A reed-pipe consists of a foot.., which carries the wind into the shallot, or reed .., which is a hollow demi-cylinder [etc.]. **1855** HOPKINS *Organ* xviii. 93 The reed is a small cylindrical tube of brass. .. In the front of the reed, an opening is left, running lengthways, presenting an appearance as though a portion of the reed had been cut away, at which the wind enters. *Ibid.* 95 A third kind of reed is used on the continent, called the free-reed. In this variety.. the tongue,.. instead of striking on the edges of the reed, is impelled into the opening by the wind. **1879** W. H. STONE in Grove *Dict. Mus.* I. 123/2 The drone reeds.. somewhat resemble the reed in organ pipes, the loose flap of cane replacing the tongue, the uncut part the tube or reed proper.

c. (*a*) A metal tongue used to produce sound by vibration, *esp.* that used in an organ-pipe; (*b*) a slip of cane used for the same purpose, as in the clarinet. (Sometimes called ***single reed***, in distinction to a.)

beating or ***striking reed***, one which strikes against its seat; in the organ, against the edges of the opening in the tube. ***free reed***, one which produces sound by vibration only, esp. one which vibrates in the opening of a tube without touching the edges, as in instruments of the reed-organ type.

1811 BUSBY *Dict. Mus.* (ed. 3), *Reed*,.. the name given by organ-builders to a kind of tongue, consisting of a thin narrow plate of brass [etc.]. **1837** *Penny Cycl.* VII. 234/2 Clarinet, a musical instrument made of wood,.. having a fixed mouth-piece containing a reed. **1867** TYNDALL *Sound* v. 193 The metal reed commonly employed in organ-pipes. **1879** W. H. STONE in Grove *Dict. Mus.* I. 361/1 The clarinet consists essentially of a mouth-piece furnished with a single beating reed [etc.]. **1889** D. J. BLAIKLEY in *Proc. Mus. Assoc.* 152 The reed of a Dobell's fog-horn.. is as truly a reed in its action as the most delicate reed of the clarinet.

d. A reed-instrument. ***double reed***: see sense 8 a.

1838 C. FOX *Jrnl.* 5 June (1972) 50 Professor Wheatstone .. then played the Chinese reed, one of the earliest instruments constructed. **1871** H. CALDERWOOD *Let.* 23 June in Calderwood & Woodside *Life H. Calderwood* (1900) 216 The orchestra mostly reeds and strings. **1877** G. B. SHAW *How to become Musical Critic* (1960) 26 The strings and reeds were a little better than usual. **1879** W. H. STONE in Grove *Dict. Mus.* I. 151/2 Some of the older forms.. possess a contrivance which does not exist at the present day on any reed. *Ibid.* 153/2 The curious dialogue.. between strings and reeds. **1926** WHITEMAN & MCBRIDE *Jazz* ix. 199 In the double reeds, I am planning to add a bassoon. **1939** JOYCE *Finnegans Wake* (1964) 408 Brass and reeds, brace and ready! **1959** 'F. NEWTON' *Jazz Scene* vi. 107 Three trumpets, three trombones, four reeds, piano. **1961** J. A. MACGILLIVRAY in A. Baines *Musical Instruments* x. 244 The clarinet.. marked (like the oboe among the double reeds) the arrival of the fully lip-controlled instrument. **1974** *Encycl. Brit. Macropædia* XIX. 855/1 Shawms were a particularly important family of loud double reeds. **1975** *New Yorker* 19 May 6/3 Joe Muranyi on reeds, and Bobby Pratt on trombone.

9. †**a.** A piece of reed on which yarn is wound; a bobbin, spool. *Obs. rare.*

1530 PALSGR. 261/2 Rede to wynde yarne on or suche lyke, *tuyau*. **1721** RAMSAY *Elegy Patie Birnie* Prol. *note*, The pirn, or little hollow reed which holds the yarn in the shuttle.

b. *Mining.* A tube containing the powder-train for igniting the charge in blasting.

1875 KNIGHT *Dict. Mech.* 1903/2.

10. a. A weaver's instrument for separating the threads of the warp and beating up the weft, formerly made of thin strips of reed or cane, but now of metal wires, fastened by the ends into two parallel bars of wood. ***fly reed***: see FLY *sb.*[2] 8.

1611 COTGR., *Lame*,.. the reed, or slay of a weuers loome. **1688** R. HOLME *Armoury* III. 107/2 *Reed*,.. like the Barrs of a Grate through which the Warp or Yarn runs. **1714** *Fr. Bk. of Rates* 188 The Combs, Reeds, and other Parts of the Loom. **1789** E. DARWIN *Bot. Gard.* II. (1791) 56 Quick beat the reeds, the pedals fall and rise. **1825** NICHOLSON *Operat. Mech.* 412 The reed.. has one or two threads of the warp passed between each of its wires, which wires are termed dents. **1894** *Labour Commission Gloss.* s.v., *Reeds* are reckoned by the number of interstices per inch, thus, a 64 reed has 64 interstices to the inch.

b. A make of cloth, as distinguished by the number of threads which go to an inch of the reed.

1881 *Manch. Guard.* 18 Jan., Printing cloth of all kinds is also very steady, especially 72 reeds. **1888** *Daily News* 27 Aug. 7/2 Printers of medium reeds have been in better request.

11. A comb used in the making of tapestry for pressing down the threads of the weft, so as to produce a close surface.

1727–41 CHAMBERS *Cycl.* s.v. *Tapestry*, The reed or comb is.. of wood, eight or nine inches long, and an inch thick at the back. *Ibid.*, The silk or wool being placed, he beats it with his reed or comb. **1842** *Penny Cycl.* XXIV. 46/1 The thread of woof or shoot thus inserted is finally driven close up.. by means of a reed or comb formed of box-wood or ivory.

12. One of a set of small semicylindrical mouldings, resembling a number of reeds laid beside each other. ***reed-and-tie***, used of a style resembling reeds bound together. (Cf. REEDING *vbl. sb.* 2.)

1745 POCOCKE *Descr. East* II. II. III. x. 169 The lower part filled with cablins of reeds, is of one stone, and the upper part of another. **1823** P. NICHOLSON *Pract. Build.* 161 When a piece of wood is formed into two or more semi-cylinders, touching each other, the semi-cylinders are called Reeds. **1842** GWILT *Archit.* §2129 A repetition of equal semicylindrical mouldings, springing from a plane or cylindrical surface, is called reeds. **1875** T. SEATON *Man. Fret Cutting & Wood Carving* vi. 68 Make a little reed round the uncarved or T part of the bracket and the support... This will form a neat reed, and give a pretty finish to your work. **1960** H. HAYWARD *Antique Coll.* 235/1 *Reed-and-tie moulding*, an ornament composed of contiguous parallel convex mouldings bound together by straps simulating ribbons. **1971** *Country Life* 1 Apr. 766/1 The grandiloquence of Louis XVI's France, with heavy reed-and-tie borders.. also had a place at fashionable West-End silversmiths.

13. *attrib.* and *Comb.* **a.** Simple attrib., as ***reed-bank, blade, boat, bush, case, fence, ground, land, marsh, pen, pit, plot, seed, sheaf, spire, stem, -swamp, top, whisper, -whistle***, etc.; (sense 8) ***reed action, cap, instrument, register, section***; (sense 10) as ***reed hook, -motion, space, -split***. Also similative, as ***reed-green***; ***reed-like*** adj.

1889 D. J. BLAIKLEY in *Proc. Mus. Assoc.* 152 The manner of *reed action has been the subject of much mathematical investigation. **1589** RIDER *Bibl. Scholast.*, A *reede banke, or place where reeds growe, *arundinetum, cannetum*. **1827** CLARE *Sheph. Cal.* 147 Lapping up love-knot plaits.. With broad green *reed-blades. **1894** MEREDITH *Ld. Ormont* xxv, The bordering flags amid the reed-blades dipped and streamed. **1902** *Encycl. Brit.* XXV. 377/1 The catamaran and the *reed boat were known to the Peruvians. **1977** *Time* 28 Nov. 60/1 Now Heyerdahl is about to take a reed boat down the Tigris River. **1535** COVERDALE *Isa.* ix. 18 As it were out of a fyere in a wod or a *redebush. **1964** S. MARCUSE *Musical Instruments* 441/1 **Reed cap*, a small wooden cap with a blowhole on top; it enclosed the reed of some 16th-c. double-reed instrs. **1976** Reed-cap [see RAUSCHPFEIFE]. **1886** R. F. BURTON *Arab. Nts.* (abr. ed.) I. 115, I.. took the *reed-case and reed; and wrote. **1807** CRABBE *Par. Reg.* I. 148 The *reed-fence rises round some fav'rite spot. **1894** *Daily News* 28 Apr. 6/4 There is a considerable demand for a soft tint of *reed-green. **1629** *Drayner Conf.* (1647) Bj, If the water be drayned, and the cold moisture removed from the root of *Reed-ground. **1910** L. HOOPER *Hand-Loom Weaving* (1920) 328 **Reed hook*, hook for entering reed. **1914** H. NISBET *Preliminary Operations of Weaving* I. ix. 359 The reacher, with the right hand, then proceeds to select the warp threads from a bunch held in the left hand, and delivers them in consecutive rotation to a reed-hook which is inserted through successive eyes of the harness by the drawer-in. **1957** SIMPSON & WEIR *Weaver's Craft* (ed. 8) viii. 97 (*caption*) Reed hooks. **1867** TYNDALL *Sound* v. 195 The most perfect of *reed instruments is the organ of voice. **1876** tr. *Blaserna's Sound* i. 20 The clarinet, the oböe and all the trumpet class, are reed instruments. **1769** *St. James's Chron.* 10–11 Aug. 2/2 Several Parcels of *Reed-land, lying before.. the March Walls. **1605** SYLVESTER *Du Bartas* II. iii. I. *Vocation* 358 With *Reed-like Lance, and with a Blunted blade. **1829** LOUDON *Encycl. Plants* 58 Reed-like Canary-grass. **1766** J. BARTRAM *Jrnl.* 7 Jan. in W. Stork *Acc. E. Florida* 26 Being generally good *reed-marsh and some cypress-swamps. **1877** A. B. EDWARDS *Up Nile* iii. 63 Scrawling upon it in rude Arabic characters with a *reed-pen of his own making. *c* **1440** *Promp. Parv.* 426/1 *Reed pytte, or fenne, *cannetum, arundinetum*. **1611** COTGR., *Caneliere*, a *Reed-plot; a ground thats full, or set full, of reeds. **1852** SEIDEL *Organ* 20 Even in the course of the sixteenth century some of the *reed-registers were invented. **1939** D. BAKER *Young Man with Horn* III. i. 117 Rick.. started setting chairs together the way they should go, in threes: *reed section, brass section, rhythm section, and the extras one on top of another. **1975** *New Yorker* 21 Apr. 8/3 Billy Harper, a young and very exciting tenor saxophonist.. steams up the reed section of the Thad Jones-Mel Lewis band. **1830** J. D. HOY in Loudon *Mag. Nat. Hist.* III. 329 Their food is not entirely the *reed seed. **1810** in W. Marshall *Rev. Rep. Agric., N. Som.* II. 515 *note*, The sheaves thus prepared are called *reed-sheaves. **1874** T. HARDY *Far fr. Mad. Crowd* xxxvii, You can bring up some reed-sheaves to me, one by one. **1919** *Brit. Manufacturer* Nov. 35/2 Wide hand looms of high *reedspace scarcely require more effort than those for narrower weaving. **1585** HIGINS tr. *Junius' Nomencl.* 117 *Arundinum oculi, vel bulbi*,.. *Reede spier. **1875** KNIGHT *Dict. Mech.* 1903/1 Two threads of yarn pass between each of the *reed-splits or dents. **1843** *Zoologist* I. 97 Shell-snails .. covering the lower part of the *reed-stems. **1971** *Nature* 11 June 364/2 Here the invasion of *reedswamp from the north and west was incomplete. **1975** J. G. EVANS *Environment Early Man Brit. Isles* iii. 58 The vegetation.. passes through a variety of stages—reed swamp, carr.. and raised bog. **1830** TENNYSON *Dying Swan* 10 Ever the weary wind went on, And took the *reed-tops as it went. *a* **1835** MRS. HEMANS *Elysium*, Low *reed-whispers, making sweet reply. **1864** J. A. GRANT *Walk across Afr.* xi. 245 On his arm he carried a *reed-whistle three inches long, but it seemed to be more for ornament than use. **1962** R. P. JHABVALA *Get Ready for Battle* ii. 101 A toyman with toys stuck on the end of a long pole.., blowing on a reed-whistle.

b. Objective or objective genitive, as ***reed-cutter, -drawer, -maker; reed-burning, -cutting, -drawing, -making, -rustling***.

1591 PERCIVALL *Sp. Dict.*, *Bruscar*, to heate a ships side with *reede burning. **1829** in Loudon *Mag. Nat. Hist.* II. 222 The *reed-cutters having even then commenced their operations. **1974** *Country Life* 3 Oct. 922/1 In winter.. the reed cutters took the harvest that served for thatch all over Britain. **1973** R. ADAMS *Watership Down* xxxiii. 260 The 'boat' was a miniature punt, used for *reed-cutting. **1891** T. HARDY *Tess* xliii, Noted *reed-drawers were they too. **1874** HARDY *Far from Madding Crowd* I. vi. 74 Oak seized the cut ends of the sheaves, as if he were going to engage in the operation of '*reed-drawing'. **1891** T. HARDY *Tess* xliii, Reed-drawing is fearful hard work. **1946** N. WYMER *Eng. Country Crafts* v. 50 The preparation of the straw—variously known as yelming, reed-drawing, or gabbling—consists of removing all unsuitable pieces and arranging the strands level. **1639** *Canterb. Marriage Licences* (MS.), Peter Beiseu of All Saints', Canterbury, *reedmaker. **1885** *Census Instruct.* 43 Reed Maker. **1854** MRS. GASKELL *North & S.* xii, I shall be glad to procure her admission to print-works, or *reed-making. **1884** BLAKELEE *Industr. Cycl.* 342/1 *marg.*, Reed-making Machine. **1797** SOUTHEY *Comm.-pl. Bk.* (1851) IV. 45 The *reed-rustling breeze.

c. Instrumental and parasynthetic, as ***reed-bordered, -bottomed, -capped, -choked, -clad, -compacted, -crowned, -encumbered, -fringed, -grown, -roofed, -stemmed, -throated.***

1890 'R. BOLDREWOOD' *Col. Reformer* (1891) 192 A *reed-bordered lagoon. **1835** C. MATHEWS *Let.* 7 Feb. in A. Mathews *Mem. Charles Mathews* (1839) IV. 343 Then behold six *reed-bottomed, ragged, ricketty chairs. **1977** *Early Music* July 342/2 A rauschpfeife, a relatively easy (i.e. non-embouchure) instrument, presumably derived from a *reed-capped bagpipe chanter. **1952** V. CANNING *House of Seven Flies* viii. 125 The narrow, *reed-choked mouth of an old cut. **1850** R. G. CUMMING *Hunter's Life S. Afr.* (1902) 63/2 The *reed-clad margin of the western branch of the stream. **1777** POTTER *Æschylus, Prom. Bd.* 36 Hoarse sounds the *reed-compacted pipe. *a* **1608** SYLVESTER *Hymn to St. Lewis* 181 This River makes the *Reed crown'd banks to kiss, By th' arched favour of a Bridge. **1744** MASON *Musæus* 32 His reed-crown'd locks shall shake. *a* **1835** MRS. HEMANS *Last Constantine* iv, The shore Of the reed-crown'd Eurotas. **1892** W. B. YEATS *Countess Kathleen* iii. 55 Leave marshes and the *reed-encumbered pools. **1906** A. B. COOPER *Flood-Tides* 4 By wold and wilderness, by *reed-fring'd lake. **1952** V. CANNING *House of Seven Flies* viii. 124 Flat, reed-fringed islands. **1887** *Westm. Rev.* June 338 These semi-stagnant, *reed-grown meres. *c* **1820** S. ROGERS *Italy* (1839) 167 A *reed-roofed cabin by a river-side. **1942** W. FAULKNER *Go down, Moses* 266 She held a *reed-stemmed clay pipe but she was not smoking it. **1914** W. B. YEATS *Responsibilities* 76 From that *reed-throated whisperer Who comes at need.

14. Special combs., as **reed-babbler**, the reed-warbler; **reed back**, the wooden bars of a weaving-reed; **reed bat** = *reed legget* below; †**reed-beere**, a reed-bed; **reed bent-grass**, small reed, *Calamagrostis*; **reed-buck**, the rietbok, or other antelope frequenting reeds; **reed canary-grass**, canary-reed, *Phalaris arundinacea*; **reed fescue**, slender wheat-grass, *Festuca sylvatica*; **reed-flush** (see quot.); **reed-horn**, (*a*) a fog-horn in which the sound is produced by a current of air blowing on a reed (sense 8 c); (*b*) *slang*, a saxophone; **reed-knife**, a knife-like instrument used in tuning a reed-organ; **reed legget** = LEGGET; **reed-machine**, a machine for making weaving-reeds; **reed-man**, (*a*) a player of a reed instrument; (*b*) one who works with reeds; **reed-mark** (see quots.); **reed-marked** *a.*, of cloth, having the warp threads lying unevenly; **reed meadow-grass**, a tall coarse grass, *Poa* or *Glyceria aquatica*; **reed moth**, a European moth, *Macrogaster arundinis*; **reed-organ**, a musical instrument of the organ type in which the sounds are produced by means of reeds; **reed-pheasant**, the bearded titmouse; **reed-plane**, a reeding-plane (Knight 1875); **reed-press**, a press for straw which is to be made into reed; **reed-rand** (or **-rond**) (see quots.); **reed relay** *Electr.*, a small, high-speed, switching device consisting of a pair of contacts, enclosed in a glass tube, which can be brought together by an external magnetic field; **reed-roll** (see quot.); †**reed sedge**, ? reeds; **reed-stop**, an organ-stop composed of reed-pipes; **reed-thrush** = REED-WARBLER b; **reed-tree** (see CALAMODENDRON); **reed voice**, a reedy or squeaking voice; †**reed-yard**, a sceptre of reed. Also REED-BED, -BIRD, etc.

1840 *Cuvier's Anim. Kingd.* 191 The Sedge Babbler.. is also a common summer visitant in Britain, more generally distributed than the *Reed Babbler (*Sylvia arundinacea*). **1895** *Reed back [see *reed-machine* below]. **1969** *Reed bat [see LEGGET]. **1585** HIGINS *Junius' Nomencl.* 388/1 *Arundinetum*,.. a place where reedes grow: a *reedebeere. **1822–34** *Good's Study Med.* (ed. 4) I. 179 Horses feed with avidity and thrive to fatness on the *agrostis arundinacea*, or *reed bent-grass. **1860** DARLINGTON *Amer. Weeds*, etc. 376 *Calamagrostis.* Reed Bent-Grass. **1834** *Penny Cycl.* II. 79/2 The reitbok.. or *reedbuck, so called from its habit of frequenting the reedy banks and beds of dry water-courses. **1893** SELOUS *Trav. S.E. Africa* 160 A reed-buck, with a fine head, jumped out of the long grass. **1759** B. STILLINGFL. *Misc. Tracts* (1791) 182 The *reed canary grass serves for thatching houses. **1860** DARLINGTON *Amer. Weeds*, etc. 400 *P. arundinacea*.. Reed-like Phalaris. Reed Canary Grass. **1859** MISS PRATT *Brit. Grasses & Sedges* 103 *Reed Fescue, .. its stem is from 2–4 feet high.. the leaves are long, and of somewhat yellowish green. **1876** *Encycl. Brit.* IV. 490/2 Reeds are generally struck on the panel in the direction of the grain, and laid in on the panel across it, or along the ends; this is termed *reed-flush. **1902** *Encycl. Brit.* XXX. 266/2 At the Trinity House experiments with fog signals at St. Catherine's (1901) several types of *reed-horn were experimented with. **1936** *Metronome* Feb. 61/2 *Reed horn*, sax. **1876** STAINER & BARRETT *Dict. Mus. Terms* 339/2 An organ is tuned by means of hollow cones and *reed-knives. **1961** *Thatcher's Craft* (Rural Industries Bureau) vii. 205/1 (*caption*) Norfolk *reed leggett used for dressing reed into position. **1895** R. MARSDEN *Cotton Weaving* iv. 106 The *reed machine is furnished with the parts of the machine termed the reed back, composed of two strips of wood each for the top and bottom. **1872** *Reed-man [see *brass-man* s.v. BRASS *sb.* 6]. **1938** D. BAKER *Young Man with Horn* I. v. 47 There was the band playing 'Home, Sweet Home' as a one-step with the reed man getting into clear and going absolutely wild on a clarinet. **1951** WALLACE & BAGNALL-OAKLEY *Norfolk* vii. 84 The old villages.. began as trading places for the eel-fishers, the reed-men and the smugglers from the sea. **1977** *New Yorker* 6 June 128/2 It consists of eleven Laurence studio performances (about forty minutes in all), backed by two reedmen (Paul Quinichette or the late Bobby Jaspar) and two rhythm sections. **1931** E. MIDGLEY *Techn. Terms Textile Trade* I. 261 **Reed marks*, a type of defect in woven fabrics due to the warp threads running in 'twos' or 'threes'. **1961** BLACKSHAW & BRIGHTMAN *Dict. Dyeing* 145 *Reed marks*, marks or streaks running the warp of a cloth and caused by defects in the functioning of the reed during weaving. **1894** T. W. FOX *Mechanism of Weaving* iii. 37 Sometimes warp threads are allowed to run in pairs throughout the piece without being looked upon as a serious defect; such material is said to be *reed-marked, or without cover. **1842** R. PARNELL *Grasses Scot.* 101 *Poa aquatica.* *Reed Meadow-Grass. **1858** SIMMONDS *Dict. Trade* s.v. *Melodeon*, Seraphine, harmoneon, *reed-organ, &c. are names for essentially the same instrument. **1879** A. J. HIPKINS in Grove *Dict. Mus.* I. 667 Of late the name Reed-Organ has been used to express both the harmonium and the American organ. **1831** RENNIE *Montagu's Ornith. Dict.* 26 Bearded Tit.—*Reed Pheasant. **1848** *Zoologist* VI. 2186 The bearded titmouse is the 'reed pheasant', and indeed with its long graduated tail it is not unlike a miniature pheasant. **1891** T. HARDY *Tess* xliii, There had already been placed in the *reed-press.. as many sheaves of wheat as would be sufficient for the women to draw from during the day. **1840** SPURDENS *Suppl. Forby* s.v. *Rand*, A *reed-rand, on our rivers and broads is a margin overgrown with reeds. **1865** KINGSLEY *Herew.* Prel., Long lines of reed-rond, emerald in spring. **1947** *Electr. Engin.* LXVI. 1104 (*heading*) Glass enclosed *reed relay. **1966** *Times* 16 Dec. 11/6 The key component in the Ambergate exchange is a miniature reed relay. **1975** FINK & MCKENZIE *Electronics Engineers' Handbk.* xxiii. 41 Figure 23-46 shows the reed relay, combining small size and high reliability. A magnetic field induced by an external coil follows the path of the encapsulated contact arm, causing a force to pull the two arms together. *a* **1825** FORBY *Voc. E. Anglia*, *Reed-roll, a thicket of reeds on the borders or shallow parts of a river. *a* **1490** BOTONER *Itin.* (Nasmith, 1778) 288 Shevys de *reede segge. **1727** BOYER *Dict. Royal* II, *Reed-stop of an Organ, *anche d'orgue.* **1811** BUSBY *Dict. Mus.* (ed. 3) s.v. *Reed*, Those stops of an organ which consist of pipes so furnished are called Reed Stops. **1871** HILES *Dict. Mus. T.*, *Hautboy-clarion*, a 2 ft. reed stop in an organ. **1871–4** NEWTON *Yarrell's Brit. Birds* I. 365 There seems no reason to doubt their having been specimens of the Great Reed-Warbler or *Reed-Thrush, to use its oldest English name. **1596** SHAKS. *Merch. V.* III. iv. 67 Ile.. speake betweene the change of man and boy, With a *reede voyce. *a* **1240** *Wohunge* in *Cott. Hom.* 281 Siðen ȝette buffetet and to dunet i þe heaued wið þe *red ȝerde.

reed (riːd), *sb.*[2] *Mining.* [Of obscure origin.] **a.** The split or fracture in a coal seam at right angles to the bedding; the cleat. **b.** The parting between strata.

1839 URE *Dict. Arts* 962 The lamellæ (reed of the coal) are always parallel to the bed or plane on which the coal rests. *Ibid.* 974 It is often divided and intersected, with its concomitant strata, by what are named partings, backs, cutters, reeds, or ends. **1883** GRESLEY *Gloss. Coal-mining.*

reed (riːd), *v.* [f. REED *sb.*[1]]

1. *trans.* To thatch with reed. Chiefly *pass.* (cf. REEDED *ppl. a.* 2.)

c **1440** *Promp. Parv.* 426/2 Redyn' howsys, *arundino, calamo.* **1538** LELAND *Itin.* (1768) III. 125 The Abbay Chirch and Paroch Chirch [being] then be chaunce readid or thatchid. **1573** TUSSER *Husb.* (1878) 111 Where houses be reeded.. now pare off the mosse.

2. To make (straw) into reed. (See REED *sb.*[1] 2 c.)

1817–18 COBBETT *Resid. U.S.* (1822) 339 If this straw be reeded, as they do it in the counties of Dorset and Devon, it will last thirty years. *Ibid.* 341 Only think of the expense of drawing or of reeding straw in England!

3. To fashion into, or decorate with, reeds; to furnish with a reed-moulding. (See REED *sb.*[1] 12.)

1823 P. NICHOLSON *Pract. Build.* 161 When a piece of wood is formed into two or more semi-cylinders, touching each other.. the piece of wood is said to be reeded. **1848** B. WEBB *Cont. Ecclesiol.* 42 Two of the pillars are reeded.. in opposite directions. **1890** *Athenæum* 9 Aug. 199/1 The chalice.. has a mullet-shaped base, reeded vertically.

4. *Weaving.* To pass (warp threads) through the splits of a reed.

1894 T. W. FOX *Mechanism of Weaving* ii. 17 It will be noticed that the threads from shaft 4 are reeded two in a dent, and those from the remaining shafts three in a dent. **1957** *Textile Terms & Definitions* (Textile Inst.) (ed. 3) 79 *Reed, v.*, to draw ends through a reed (local, to sley, to bob the reed or to enter the reed).

reed, var. READ *sb.*[1]; obs. f. READ *v.*, RED *a.*, REDE *sb.*[1] and *v.*; obs. var. ROOD.

†**'reedal**, *a.* and *sb. Obs. rare.* [f. REED *sb.*[1] + -AL[1].] **a.** *adj.* Of the nature of a reed. **b.** *sb.* A device of this kind.

1728 NORTH *Mem. Music* (1846) 26, I guess it was voiced either by the lipps, as a cornett, or else by some reedall. *Ibid.* 37 The tibia were pipes that sounded by a reedall device like those affixed to bagpipes.

reed-bed. [REED *sb.*[1]] A bed or growth of reeds. (Common in recent use.)

c **1000** ÆLFRIC *Exod.* ii. 3 Heo.. asette hyne on anum hreodbedde be þæs flodes ofre. **1483** *Cath. Angl.* 302/1 Rede bede, *arundinetum, cannetum.* **1732** AINSWORTH *Lat. Dict.* I. s.v. *Reed*, A reed bed, bank, or plot, *arundinetum.* **1843** *Zoologist* I. 97 The reed-beds on the banks of the Thames. **1897** E. CONYBEARE *Hist. Cambridgesh.* 5 The Great Copper butterfly.. no longer brightens the reed-beds.

reed-bird. [REED *sb.*[1]]

1. A bird which frequents reeds. *rare*$^{-1}$.

1648 HEXHAM, *Een riet-meese*, a Reede-bird like a Tit-mouse.

2. *spec.* **a.** A North American singing-bird, *Dolichonyx oryzivorus*; the bobolink or rice-bunting. Also *attrib.*

1795 W. PRIEST *Trav. U.S.* (1802) 90 A wonderful variety of small birds, among which, the reed bird, or American ortolan, justly holds the first place. **1810** WILSON *Amer. Ornith.* II. 48 Rice Bunting, *Emberiza oryzivora*... This is the Boblink of the eastern and northern states, and the Rice and Reed-bird of Pennsylvania and the southern states. **1893** LELAND *Mem.* I. 55 The reed-bird, which is quite as good as the ortolan of Italy. *Ibid.* 57 Then we all had reed-bird suppers or lunches.

b. (*a*) The reed-warbler; (*b*) the sedge-warbler.

1848 *Zoologist* VI. 2186 The sedge warbler is the 'reed-bird'. **1871–4** NEWTON *Yarrell's Brit. Birds* I. 370 Its partiality for reeds.. make[s] the names of Reed-bird or Reed-Wren, by which it is commonly known, sufficiently applicable.

reed-bunting. [REED *sb.*[1]] The reed-sparrow (*Emberiza schœniclus*).

1785 PENNANT *Arct. Zool.* II. 368 Reed B[unting]. **1840** *Cuvier's Anim. Kingd.* 198 The Reed Bunting.. has a black head and gorget, and white ring round the neck. **1871** DARWIN *Desc. Man* II. xiii. II. 95 In the spring the feathers on the head of the male reed-bunting.. acquire a fine black colour.

reede, obs. f. READ *v.*, RED *a.*, REDE *sb.*[1] and *v.*

reeded ('riːdɪd), *ppl. a.* [f. REED *v.* and *sb.*[1]]

1. Overgrown with reeds.

1876 GROSART *Introd. A. Wilson's Poems* I. p. xli, He journeyed—gun in hand—in forest, brushwood, reeded swamp. **1891** E. R. PENNELL *Stream Pleas.* 65 The campers pitch their tents on the reeded islands.

2. Thatched with reed.

1778 J. BAMPFYLDE *Sixteen Sonnets* 16 Counting the frequent drop from reeded eaves. **1819** H. BUSK *Vestriad* v. 263 Grassy fences.. That glittering hang the reeded eaves beneath. **1848** LYTTON *Harold* I. iv, Blunt, cone-headed turrets.. rose often from the low, thatched and reeded roofs.

3. Ornamented with reed-moulding.

1829 H. FOOTE *Compan. to Theatre* 36 The upper circle and tiers, including both the slips and lower gallery, are each supported in part by 14 slender shafts, reeded, of iron. **1833** J. HOLLAND *Manuf. Metal* II. 80 When the [sword] blade.. is required to have a reeded back or some similar sort of ornament. **1858** *Ecclesiologist* XIX. 165 Circular shafts, with reeded caps. **1889** PATER *G. de Latour* (1896) 79 Frames of reeded ebony or jewelled filigree. **1935** *Archit. Rev.* LXXVIII. 33 The window is glazed with reeded glass. **1952** [see AGBA]. **1978** R. RENDELL *Sleeping Life* ii. 14 No one came when they rang the bell on the neighbouring front door, a far more trendy and ambitious affair of wrought iron and reeded glass.

4. Furnished with musical reeds.

c **1865** *Wylde's Circ. Sc.* I. 284/1 The usual mode of forming reeded and tongued instruments.

5. Of wood: having a specified kind of reed.

1839 URE *Dict. Arts* 972 A quantity of well-seasoned and clean reeded deal is required for forming the joints.

6. *fig.*

1926 T. E. LAWRENCE *Seven Pillars* (1935) lxxxix. 495, I knew that Sherif Abd el Main should be still at Shobek, so rode boldly up the silent street in the reeded starlight, which played with the white icicles.

reedel, obs. form of RIDDLE *sb.*[1]

reeden ('riːd(ə)n), *a.* Now *rare.* Also 6–7 readen. [f. REED *sb.*[1] + -EN[4].]

1. Made or consisting of reed; reed-like.

1382 WYCLIF *2 Kings* xviii. 21 Whether hopist thou in the reeden [L. *arundineo*] staf and broken. **1586** BRIGHT *Melanch.* Pref., Philosophie.. is but a readen staffe to beare up so heauy a burthen. **1597** GERARDE *Herbal* I. iii. 4 A long slender reeden stalke. **1611** CORYAT *Crudities* 262 The women of Venice.. put on a readen hat, without any crowne at all. **1697** DRYDEN *Virg. Georg.* IV. 385 Thro' reeden Pipes convey the Golden Flood. **1817** *Sporting Mag.* L. 25 The thresher in his shirt and reeden fillet.

†**2.** = REEDY 1. *Obs. rare*$^{-1}$.

1387 TREVISA *Higden* (Rolls) VII. 487 Whanne þey were unneþes i-passed a reden marys.

reeder ('riːdə(r)). Also 5 redare, 6 reider. [f. REED *v.* and *sb.*[1] + -ER[1].]

1. One who thatches with reeds, a thatcher. ? *Obs.*

c **1440** *Promp. Parv.* 426/2 Redare, of howsys, *calamator, arundinarius, cannarius.* **1552** HULOET, Reider of houses or thacker, *arundinarius.* **1610** in *Eng. Hist. Rev.* (1898) XIII. 524 Thatcher, Reeder, or Fleeker vii *d.*

2. A thatched frame used to protect blocks or tiles of china-clay from rain.

1880 *Spons' Encycl. Manuf.* I. 637 The blocks [of china-clay] are then collected, and piled away in sheds, under a number of thatched gates or 'reeders'.

reed-grass. [REED *sb.*[1]]
1. A name given to various reed-like grasses, as the bur-reed, bent, reed bent-grass, etc.
1578 LYTE *Dodoens* IV. lv. 515 Rede grasse hath long narrow leaues..with a sharpe crest or backe, raysed vp. **1585** HIGINS tr. *Junius' Nomencl.* 120 *Butomum*,.. reedgrasse, or oxbane. **1611** COTGR., *Roseau des estangs*, reed-grasse, the Burre Reed. **1743** JAMES *Med. Dict.* s.v. *Arundo*, The *Gramen Arundinaceum*, Reed Grass, enumerated amongst the Reeds by Dale, agrees in Virtues with the common Reed. **1777** LIGHTFOOT *Fl. Scot.* I. 107 *Arundo arenaria*, Sea Reed Grass. **1813** H. DAVIES *Welsh Botanol.* I. 12 *Arundo colorata*, Canary Reed-grass.
2. The name of various American grasses.
salt reed-grass, a tall stout grass (*Spartina polystachya*) of the Atlantic coast. *small reed-grass*, a species of *Calamagrostis*. *sweet* or *wood reed-grass*, the tall sweet-scented grasses *Cinna arundinacea* or *C. pendula*.
1756 P. BROWNE *Jamaica* 341 The Mountain Reed-Grass. I found this curious little plant at Cold Spring. **1846-50** A. WOOD *Class-bk. Bot.* 601 *Calamagrostis canadensis*, Reed Grass, Blue-joint.

†**re-edificate,** *pa. pple. Obs. rare*[−1]. [See RE-EDIFY and EDIFICATE.] Rebuilt.
1432-50 tr. *Higden* (Rolls) II. 79 That cite [Chester], somme tyme destroyede by men of Northumbrelonde, but reedificate by Elfleda, lady of the marches.

re-edifi'cation. [a. OF. *reedification* (14th c.) or med.L. *reædificātiōn-em*, n. of action f. *reædificāre* to RE-EDIFY.] The action of rebuilding or the state of being rebuilt. Now *rare* or *Obs.*
1473 *Rolls of Parlt.* VI. 94/2 The reparations and reedifications of the houses..within the Toune. **1538** LELAND *Itin.* (1768) III. 125 The Toun was compellid to help to the Reedification of it. **1597** BEARD *Theatre God's Judgem.* (1612) 534 That rich and renowned Citie..after her reedification to be debased into so low.. an estate. **1651** HOBBES *Leviath.* III. xxxiii. 202 The re-edification of the walls and houses of Jerusalem. **1726** DART (*title-p.*) The History..of the Cathedral Church of Canterbury,.. Containing, An Account of its First Establishment, Building, Re-edifications [etc.]. **1796** JEFFERSON *Writ.* (1859) IV. 134, I have begun the demolition of my house, and hope to get through its re-edification in the course of the summer. **1815** WRAXALL *Hist. Mem.* I. 68 Its re-edification ..and improvement in every sense, occupied his capacious mind.

re-'edifier. [RE- 5 a; or f. next + -ER[1].] One who rebuilds, a rebuilder. Now *rare*.
1538 LELAND *Itin.* (1769) IV. 8 He thinketh that the Vaulx were Reedifiers of it. **1579** FENTON *Guicciard.* (1618) 24 An old opinion..that Charlemaine was the reedifier of their citie. **1675** SHERBURNE *Sphere Manilius* 66 [Philippi] afterwards renamed from Philip..its Reedifier. **1767** S. PATERSON *Another Trav.* I. 425 Re-edifiers of fallen temples! and quickeners of dead laurels! **1832-4** DE QUINCEY *Cæsars* Wks. 1862 IX. 35 She looked up to him..as the re-edifier of her husband's honours.

re-edify (riː'ɛdɪfaɪ), *v.* Forms: see EDIFY. Also β. 5-6 **redifye,** 6 **redyfy,** 6-7 **redefy.** [ad. OF. *reedifier* (and *redifier*) = Sp., Pg. *reedificar*, It. *riedificare*:—late L. *reædificāre* to rebuild, f. *re*-RE- + *ædificāre* to EDIFY.]
1. *trans.* To rebuild (a house, or other building, a wall, city, street, etc.).
1420-22 LYDG. *Thebes* II. (Laud MS.) lf. 26 Þis olde Neemie Gat hym licence to reedifie The walles newe of Ierusalem. **1485** *Rolls of Parlt.* VI. 313/2 Your Besecher.. myght not be suffred to reedifie and make ageyn the said two Forges. **1513** BRADSHAW *St. Werburge* II. 641 This noble duchesse..Reedified Chestre and fortified it full ryght. **1594** WEST *2nd Pt. Symbol., Chancerie* §85 They yet doe deny and refuse..to repaire and reedify the said tenements and premisses. **1631** WEEVER *Anc. Funeral Mon.* 267 The Langleys..did either found or reedifie this Church. **1688** EVELYN *Diary* 23 Aug., Northampton, having ben lately burnt and re-edified. **1722** DE FOE *Plague* (1756) 109 To beautify the City, and re-edify the Buildings. **1775** CHANDLER *Trav. Asia M.* (1825) I. 241 Hadrian is said to have reedified and named it Hadrianopolis. **1818** MILLS *Hist. Crusades* (1822) I. i. 4 The impious and vain attempt of the Emperor Julian to re-edify the walls of the holy city. **1894** BARING-GOULD *Deserts S. France* II. 103 Men began everywhere to erect churches, and re-edify those that were ruinous.
absol. **1608** TOPSELL *Serpents* (1658) 706 If it happen at any time that a house be burned,..when the people come to re-edifie, they can very hardly displant their number.
β. **1432-50** tr. *Higden* (Rolls) III. 173 This Cambises wolde not suffre the temple to be redifiede in his tyme. *c* **1475** *Partenay* 3700 Which church he shall weile redyfy. **1545** JOYE *Exp. Dan.* vi. Lv, For yᵉ walls of Jerusalem & temple to be redefied. **1568** GRAFTON *Chron.* II. 755 Edmond Shaw..of his awne costs redefied Cripplegate.
†**b.** To rebuild (a ship). *Obs. rare*[−1].
1570-6 LAMBARDE *Peramb. Kent* (1826) 315 All these ships Queen Elizabeth hath either wholy built upon the stockes, or newly reedified upon the olde moaldes.
2. *fig.* To rebuild, restore, re-establish.
1540-1 ELYOT *Image Gov.* 43 This publike weale, which beyng subuerted,..I haue reedified. **1592** DANIEL *Compl. Rosamond* Wks. (1717) 62 Thy favourable Lines Re-edified the Wreck of my Decays. **1603** DRAYTON *Bar. Wars* I. xxiii, Re-edify'd king Arthur's ancient Boord. *a* **1652** BROME *New Acad.* IV. ii. Wks. 1873 II. 79 The least syllable of your fair testimony, is able to re-edifie the ruines of a decayed commendation. **1822** HAZLITT *Table-t.* Ser. II. xiv. (1869) 289 My public and private hopes have been left a ruin,..I would wish them to be re-edified.
3. *transf.* To build up again physically.
1897 *Allbutt's Syst. Med.* III. 479 As the gastralgia subsides the patient must be re-edified in the usual way.

Hence **re-'edified,** *ppl. a.*
1600 J. PORY tr. *Leo's Africa* III. 197 The inhabitants of this reedified towne are Moores. **1633** BP. HALL *Hard Texts, O.T.* 562 There shall be holy service performed to my name, in the re-edified Temple.

re-edifying (riː'ɛdɪfaɪɪŋ), *vbl. sb.* [f. prec. + -ING[1].] The action of the vb. RE-EDIFY in various senses.
1481 CAXTON *Godfrey* vii. 27 For the reedefyeng of this holy werke. **1534** *Act 26 Hen. VIII*, c. 8 (*title*) An act for reedifiying of voide groundes in the citie of Norwich. **1579** W. WILKINSON *Confut. Fam. Love* 26 The redyfiyng of the Church by Christ is prophecied. **1615** G. SANDYS *Trav.* 11 Vpon the reedifying of Corinth it [Delos] was held by the Athenians. **1668** *Lond. Gaz.* No. 245/1 Great care is taken for the speedy re-edifying of the late ruined Palace here. **1747** CARTE *Hist. Eng.* I. 329 He readily swallowed all pretences of dreams for the re-edifying of monasteries. **1851** D. WILSON *Preh. Ann.* (1863) II. IV. i. 194 The re-edifying of churches and monasteries on a larger..scale.

reediness ('riːdɪnɪs). [f. REEDY *a.* + -NESS.] The state or quality of being reedy, in various senses of the adj.
1844 H. STEPHENS *Bk. Farm* II. 365 The straw of the former kind is strong and inclined to reediness. **1869** SIR E. REED *Shipbuild.* xviii. 397 To try..the quality of the iron and to develope indications of any reediness, or looseness of structure it may possess. **1888** *Sci. Amer.* 30 June 402/3 The Liszt organ..possesses great freedom from reediness in sound. **1899** *Westm. Gaz.* 16 May 2/1 There is a harshness, a reediness about it, and sometimes an absence of modulation. **1931** E. MIDGLEY *Techn. Terms Textile Trade* I. 20 The warp threads..must lie in the cloth an equal distance apart, or a defect known as 'reediness' is created.

†**reeding,** *sb. Obs.* (See quot. and READING *sb.*[1])
1688 R. HOLME *Armoury* III. 348/2 Reedings..[is] House-wives Cloth made of Hemp or Flax.

reeding ('riːdɪŋ), *vbl. sb.* [f. REED *v.* + -ING[1].]
1. The action of the verb in various senses.
c **1440** *Promp. Parv.* 427/1 Redynge, of howsys. *Arundinacio.* **1710** HILMAN *Tusser Rediv.* No. 5. 5 Reeding is no where so well done as in Norfolk and Suffolk... [It] will bear a better Slope than any other Thatch. **1885** *Harper's Mag.* July 256/1 Reeding and harnessing are subsidiary processes in putting the warp in proper shape on the loom.
2. a. A small semicylindrical moulding (cf. REED *sb.*[1] 12); ornamentation of this form.
1815 J. SMITH *Panorama Sc. & Art* I. 173 Several beads placed together, or sunk in a flat face, are called reedings. **1854** F. REINNEL *Carpenters' Compan.* 50 When reeding is introduced on flat surfaces, there should always be an odd number. **1862** RAWLINSON *Anc. Mon.* I. II. vi. 362 The plaster of which they are composed is formed into sets of half pillars or reedings.
b. The milling on the edge of coins. (Knight *Dict. Mech.* 1875.)
3. *Comb.* **reeding-plane,** a plane used for making reeds in wood.
1825 JAMIESON *Suppl.* **1829** ELMES *Metrop. Improv.* 22 Wood scored by a carpenter's reeding plane.

†**'reedish,** *a. Obs. rare.* [f. REED *sb.*[1] + -ISH[1].] Of the nature of a reed.
1628 GAULE *Pract. The.* (1629) 233 His Hand mildly swayes the Reedish Scepter. **1652** —— *Magastrom.* 108 What reedish, nay strawy, suppositors doe they stand upon?

re-'edit, *v.* Also 9 **-edite.** [RE- 5 a.] *trans.* To edit again. Hence **re-'editing** *vbl. sb.*
1797 *Monthly Mag.* III. 91 Some progress will be made in re-editing a German edition of a forgotten classic. **1807** SOUTHEY *Spec. Eng. Poets* I. p. vii, When Dr. Aikin began to re-edite Johnson's collection [of the poets]. **1865** M. ARNOLD *Ess. Crit.* ii. 42 A book like the history of the French Academy..which M. Charles Livet has lately re-edited. **1898** *Daily News* 23 Sept. 4/6 The re-editing of liturgical forms upon simpler and more Scriptural lines. **1953** K. REISZ *Technique Film Editing* ii. 168 The picture and words were slightly re-edited to fit in with the music. **1975** *Listener* 21 Aug. 242/2 Not as severely compromised by studio re-editing and reshooting as some of his earlier films had been.

re-e'dition, *sb.* [RE- 5 a.] A second edition; a re-editing.
1655 FULLER *Wounded Consc.*, etc. (1867) 278 Gerard himself..must have been forced to a re-edition of his Herbal. **1716** M. DAVIES *Athen. Brit.* III. I. 30 Before this re-edition of Quintilian appear'd. **1876** FURNIVALL in *Thynne's Emblems* (E.E.T.S.) p. v. *note*, This re-edition is more than four times the size of our 1st edition. **1881** E. FITZGERALD *Lett.* (1889) I. 464 To re-edit his Works, which did not want any such re-edition.

†**re-e'dition,** *v. Obs. rare.* [RE- 5 a.] *trans.* To issue again. Hence †**re-e'ditioning** *vbl. sb.*
1716 M. DAVIES *Athen. Brit.* II. To Rdr. 44 Mr. Beomet's History of the Primitive usage of Forms of Prayers, re-edition'd at Cambridge, 1707. *Ibid.* III. I. 30 'Tis impossible to imagine any necessity there was of re-editioning of it.

reedle, obs. form of RIDDLE *sb.*[1]

'reedless, *a. rare*[−1]. [f. REED *sb.*[1] + -LESS.] Destitute of reeds.
1628 MAY *Virg. Georg.* IV. 134 Youths, that tomb'd before their parents were; Whom foule Cocytus' reedlesse bankes enclose.

reedles(se, varr. REDELESS *a. Obs.*

reedling ('riːdlɪŋ). [f. REED *sb.*[1] + -LING.]
1. The bearded titmouse, *Panurus biarmicus*. Also called ***bearded reedling***.
1840 *Cuvier's Anim. Kingd.* 198 There is only one known species, the Bearded Reedling.., extensively diffused over Europe and Asia, and not rare in some parts of Britain. **1871-4** NEWTON *Yarrell's Brit. Birds* I. 522 Reedling, used for it by several authors, would certainly be preferable to Titmouse, had not some of the aquatic warblers been also so called. **1896** *Daily News* 28 Nov. 3/6 Bearded tit, reedling or reed pheasant.
2. A reed-bed.
1830 J. D. HOY in Loudon *Mag. Nat. Hist.* III. 329 The very young shell-snails of different kinds which are numerous in the bottom of the reedlings.

reedloker, compar. REDLY *adv.*[2] *Obs.*

reed-mace. [REED *sb.*[1]] **a.** An aquatic plant, *Typha latifolia*, common on the margins of ponds and lakes, having long ensiform leaves and tall stems, the latter terminated by dense cylindrical spikes of small brownish flowers. (Also called *cat's-tail* or *cat-tail*, and *bulrush*.) **b.** The smaller species, *Typha angustifolia*.
The two species are sometimes distinguished as *greater* (or *broad-leaved*) and *lesser reed-mace*.
1548 TURNER *Names Herbes* (E.D.S.) 79 Typha groweth in fennes and water sydes among the reedes... It is called in englishe cattes tayle, or a Reedmace. **1562** —— *Herbal* II. 159 b, It maye be..called rede mace, because boyes vse it in theyr handes in the stede of a mace. **1578** LYTE *Dodoens* IV. liii. 513 Turner calleth it in Englishe, Reede Mace, and Cattes tayle. **1668** WILKINS *Real Char.* II. iv. §3. 73. **1691** RAY *Creation* I. (1692) 100 The number of seeds produced at once in some one Plant, as for example Reed-mace..may amount to a Million. **1777** FORSTER *Voy. round World* I. 217 The seams between them are caulked with the downy or woolly substance of the reed-mace. **1785** MARTYN *Rousseau's Bot.* xxviii. 431 The greater, or broad-leaved Cat's-tail, otherwise called Reed-mace. **1817** J. BRADBURY *Trav. Amer.* 116 There was a considerable quantity of the down of reedmace, (*Typha palustris*). **1842** W. R. WADE *Journey N. Zealand* (Morris), The raupo, the reed-mace of New Zealand, always grows in swampy ground. **1884** JEFFERIES *Red Deer* ix. 176 By the shore flourishes the tall reed-mace (so rarely distinguished from the lesser bulrush).

reedmergnerite (riːd'mɜːgnəraɪt). *Min.* [See quot. 1954 and -ITE[1].] A colourless triclinic silicate of sodium and boron, $NaBSi_3O_8$.
1954 C. MILTON et al. in *Bull. Geol. Soc. Amer.* LXV. 1286 Cores and cuttings from the Green River formation in Utah contain two new minerals, reedmergnerite and eitelite, ..in dolomitic shale. Reedmergnerite..occurs in many wells in Duchesne and Uintah counties as crystals rarely more than 1 mm long, colorless, triclinic..; habit stubby prismatic... The name honors Frank S. Reed and John L. Mergner, technicians of the Geological Survey. **1974** *Amer. Mineralogist* LIX. 79/1 This study was undertaken to determine more precisely the bond lengths and angles of danburite..for comparison with topologically similar paracelsian ($BaAl_2Si_2O_8$) and hurlbutite ($CaBe_2P_2O_8$) and with structurally similar feldspars: anorthite ($CaAl_2Si_2O_8$) ..; albite ($NaAlSi_3O_8$); and reedmergnerite ($NaBSi_3O_8$).

reed-pipe. [REED *sb.*[1]]
†**1.** A reed-pen. *Obs. rare*[−1].
a **1300** *E.E. Psalter* xliv. 2 Mi tunge rede-pipe [L. *calamus*] mot..be Writer of swiftli writande.
2. A musical pipe made of reed.
1648 HEXHAM, *Een riet-pijpe*, a Reede-pipe. **1801** STRUTT *Sports & Past.* III. v. 177, I saw three itinerant musicians.. One of them turned the winch of an organ.., another blew a reed-pipe. **1885** tr. *Schurer's Hist. Jew. People* I. 272 Reed-pipes were introduced into the choir on the high festivals.
3. An organ-pipe fitted with a reed.
1727-41 CHAMBERS *Cycl.* s.v. *Organ*, The degree of acuteness and gravity in the sound of a reed-pipe, depends on the length of the tongue. **1840** *Penny Cycl.* XVI. 493/1 The bells of all reed-pipes should be as large as their places in the organ will admit of. **1881** BROADHOUSE *Mus. Acoustics* 172 The reed pipes of organs and the vibrators of harmoniums produce their tones in the same way.

reed-sparrow. [REED *sb.*[1]]
a. A common British bird, *Emberiza schœniclus*, frequenting reedy places. Also called REED-BUNTING. **b.** The sedge-warbler.
The two were formerly sometimes distinguished as (*a*) *greater* and (*b*) *lesser reed-sparrow*. The former is not a song-bird (cf. quot. 1802).
14.. *Nom.* in Wr.-Wülcker 702 *Hic palustris*, a rede-sparowe. **1658** ROWLAND tr. *Moufet's Theat. Ins.* 1088 Larks, Gnat-snappers, Reed-sparrows, and many other birds,..do feed on the Worms of trees and herbs. **1676** WILLUGHBY *Ornith.* II. 99 The lesser Reed-sparrow. *Ibid.*, The greater Reed-sparrow. **1752** J. HILL *Hist. Anim.* 501 The Reed-sparrow. The Fringilla, with a black head, brown at the sides and with a white ring. **1769** G. WHITE *Selborne* xxiv, The person that shot it says that it sung so like a reed-sparrow that he took it for one. **1802** MONTAGU *Ornith. Dict.* (1831) 416 There can be no doubt..that the nest, as well as the song of the sedge bird, have been taken..for those of the Reed Sparrow. **1884** *Public Opin.* 5 Sept. 299/1 Here a reed-sparrow, deep-nested and brown, and there a snipe darting away.

Reed-Sternberg (riːd 'stɜːnbɜːg). *Path.* [The names of Dorothy M. *Reed* (1874-1964), U.S. pathologist, and C. *Sternberg* (1872-1934), Austrian pathologist, who described the cell in 1902 and 1898 respectively.] *Reed-Sternberg* *cell*: a binucleate or multinucleate giant cell characteristic of Hodgkin's disease.

[**1937** *Surg., Gynecol. & Obstetr.* LXIV. 466/1 Hodgkin's disease,..with its Sternberg Reed cells, fibrosis, necrosis, and eosinophilic infiltration, needs no introduction.] **1947** JACKSON & PARKER *Hodgkin's Dis. & Allied Disorders* i. 7 The fact that the Reed-Sternberg cells are frequently scattered, isolated, and often separated widely by cells of other cell types favors an inflammatory process rather than a neoplasm. **1980** *Brit. Med. Jrnl.* 29 Mar. 903/1 The dermis was infiltrated by lymphocytes,..mononuclear Hodgkin's cells, and classical binucleate Reed-Sternberg cells.

re-'educate, *v.* [RE- 5 a.] *trans.* To educate again. Now often *spec.* with the object of changing political beliefs or social behaviour.

1808 MRS. C. KEMBLE *Day after Wedding* 7 Then you must re-educate her. **1836** SIR W. HAMILTON *Discuss.* (1852) 322 These tutors, educated in the older system, were unable or unwilling to re-educate themselves for teachers of the new. **1899** *Allbutt's Syst. Med.* VI. 899 Gymnastics are also of advantage in re-educating the nerve centres. **1947** *Hansard Commons* 15 Dec. 1434 The work of the *Kulturbund zur demokratischen Erneuerung Deutschlands* in re-educating the German people in the spirit of democracy and international understanding. **1955** *Treatment of Brit. P.O.W.'s in Korea* (H.M.S.O.) 4 'Re-educating' the prisoners. The Chinese technique of 're-education' embraced every phase of daily life in the prison camps. **1967** *Listener* 18 May 653/1 The aim..is to re-educate the prisoner rather than to punish him. **1975** *Chinese Econ. Stud.* VIII. IV. 3 Chairman Mao teaches us that 'it is necessary for educated youths to go to the countryside to be reeducated by the poor and lower-middle peasants'. **1976** *New Yorker* 26 Jan. 110/2 The Chinese considered him sufficiently important to be spared and 'reëducated', or brainwashed. **1976** W. H. CANAWAY *Willow-Pattern War* vi. 64 Agricultural communes which specialized in re-educating professors and other intellectuals as labourers.

So **re-edu'cation** (also *attrib.*).

1888 *Voice* (N.Y.) 2 Feb., A..Theological Seminary for their re-education. **1899** *Allbutt's Syst. Med.* VII. 578 The re-education of the sense of hearing. **1906** *Trans. Assoc. Amer. Physicians* XXI. 724 Re-education is undoubtedly one of the most important factors in producing lasting cures. **1944** J. S. HUXLEY *On Living in Revolution* 151 This gang has succeeded in imposing its ideas on a considerable minority of the German people, and..this constitutes a grave problem of re-education. **1945** 'G. ORWELL' *Animal Farm* iii. 26 He formed..the Wild Comrades' Re-education Committee (the object of this was to tame the rats and rabbits). **1945** *Times* 8 May 7/5 It is becoming clear that the 're-education' of Germany by the allies will not be a pious aspiration, but an unavoidable duty. **1951** KOESTLER *Age of Longing* ix. 337 You don't like revolutionary vigilance,..and discipline, and re-education camps. **1974** N. FREELING *Dressing of Diamond* 133 A year of physiotherapy..in a re-education centre. **1976** SCOTT & KOSKI *Walk-In* (1977) xiii. 79, I am once again politically unreliable. I once again face re-education. **1977** *Time* 9 May 22/1 Also targetted for resettlement are most of the 30,000 political prisoners the regime admits are still interned in 're-education' camps.

reed-warbler. [REED *sb.*^{1}] **a.** A common British sylvioid bird, *Acrocephalus streperus*, frequenting reed-beds. **b.** A related species, *A. arundinaceus* (also called *reed-thrush* and ***great reed-warbler***), occasionally seen in Britain.

1802 MONTAGU *Ornith. Dict.* (1831) 418 In Wiltshire and Somersetshire, where the sedge warbler is found in abundance.., not a single Reed Warbler is to be found. **1843** H. DOUBLEDAY in *Zoologist* I. 13 A single reed-warbler was shot at a pond close by the town [Epping] in 1835. **1884** *Public Opin.* 5 Sept. 299/1 The birds essentially of the mere are the sedge warbler, the reed warbler [etc.].

reed-wren. [REED *sb.*^{1}] The reed-warbler; also a name of various allied North American birds.

1783 LIGHTFOOT in *Phil. Trans.* LXXV. 12 As we have already a bird, called in English the Willow-wren; ours, being nearly of the same size and shape, as well as the same genus, may, from its haunts, not improperly be denominated the Reed-wren. **1787** LATHAM *Gen. Synopsis Birds* Suppl. 184 Reed Wren. Size of the Willow Wren. **1802** MONTAGU *Ornith. Dict.* (1831) 27 Others have undoubtedly taken the nest of the reed wren for it. **1862** ANSTED *Channel Isl.* II. ix. (ed. 2) 207, I have put the reed wren as doubtful for Guernsey.

reedy ('ri:dɪ), *a.* Also 4 **reeddy**, 6 **redy**. [f. REED *sb.*^{1} + -Y^1.]

1. Abounding with, full of, reeds; characterized by the presence of reeds.

1382 WYCLIF *Wisd.* iii. 7 As sparcles in reeddy places [L. *in arundineto*] thei shuln renne hider and thider. **1398** TREVISA *Barth. De P.R.* XVIII. xc. (Bodl. MS.), Some [frogs] beþ icleped calamite for þei wone among reede..& in reedy places. **1538** LELAND *Itin.* (1769) V. 91 Lesse then a Quarter of a Mile from that Place is a greate redy Poole. **1593** SHAKS. *Lucr.* 1437 To Simois reedie bankes the red bloud ran. **1658** T. WALL *Charact. Enemies Ch.* 30 Some perillous beast, which out of the cover of their reedy thickets, attends the opportunity of their desired prey. **1727-46** THOMSON *Summer* 482 The adjoining brook..Now scarcely moving through a reedy pool. **1840** THIRLWALL *Greece* lv. VII. 103 On the reedy margin of the lake stood here and there some monuments. **1869** FREEMAN *Norm. Conq.* (1876) III. xiv. 357 The Derwent itself, a reedy and somewhat sluggish stream.

2. Made or consisting of reed or reeds; reeden.

a **1763** SHENSTONE *Elegies* x. 31 How must Velino shake his reedy crest! **1794** SOUTHEY *Poems Slave Trade* iv, The o'erwearied slave..Rests on his reedy couch. **1853** FELTON *Fam. Lett.* xxvii. (1865) 247 A shepherd, who charmed his weary hours..by playing rustic airs upon his reedy pipe.

3. Resembling a reed or reeds in some respect: **a.** Weak like a reed.

1628 FELTHAM *Resolves* II. xix. 61 She rests full, in her owne approuement, without the weak Worlds reedy under-propping. **1832** *Examiner* 721/2 He is reedy—he wants strength of character. **1890** G. MEREDITH *Let.* 26 Mar. (1970) II. 993 A reedy state of health forbids my going to Dinners.

b. Of straw or grass: Stiff or coarse like reeds.

1743 W. ELLIS *Mod. Husbandman* Dec. viii. 419 As..they make good Part of their Rent by the Sale of their Wheat Straw, they are very careful to preserve it as reedy or long as they can. **1778** [W. MARSHALL] *Minutes Agric.* 5 Apr. an. 1777 Nothwithstanding it was weedy, and the barley-straw reedy, they have eaten it up very clean. **1863** FR. A. KEMBLE *Resid. Georgia* 50 A small bank of mud and sand, covered with reedy coarse grass. **1883** F. M. PEARD *Contrad.* viii, She had pulled a root of reedy grass from the sand.

c. Having the form or texture of a reed.

1807 CRABBE *Par. Reg.* I. 140 The leek with crown globose and reedy stem. **1830** LYTTON *P. Clifford* xxxi, A horse..of the lengthy, reedy, lank, yet muscular race. **1834** DE QUINCEY in *Tait's Mag.* I. 797 Carriages of our present light and reedy (almost, one might say, corky) construction. **1842** LOUISA S. COSTELLO *Pilgr. Auvergne* I. 29 The groups of reedy pillars which support the body of the church.

d. Of iron bars or plates: Having the character of being formed of small rods imperfectly united.

1869 [implied in REEDINESS].

e. Of cloth: having the warp threads unevenly distributed.

1931 E. MIDGLEY *Techn. Terms Textile Trade* I. 261 *Reedy*, a term applied to a cloth which shows reed marks.

†**4.** Partaking of the nature of reed (as being derived from the sugar-cane). *Obs.*$^{-1}$

1658 ROWLAND tr. *Moufet's Theat. Ins.* 912 Do not use sugar that is earthly, reedy, and so full of dregs.

5. a. Having a tone resembling that produced by a musical reed.

1811 BUSBY *Dict. Mus.* (ed. 3) s.v. *Reed*, A kind of tongue ..which..produces a reedy thickness of tone. **1823** MOORE *Mem.* (1853) IV. 79 Ronzi, notwithstanding her thin reedy voice, [is] very charming. **1866** A. MACDONALD *Ann. Q. Neighb.* ii, A good many tones were rough..and reedy.

Comb. **1823** CRABB *Technol. Dict.*, *Reedy-toned*, an epithet for any voice which..partakes of the tone of the reed. **1905** *Westm. Gaz.* 1 Nov. 1/3 The valley of the reedy-voiced little Ervola.

b. Having a reedy voice.

1855 DICKENS *Dorrit* I. xxxi, A poor little reedy piping old gentleman, like a worn-out bird.

reedyness, variant of REDINESS *Obs.*

reef (ri:f), *sb.*^{1} Forms: 4, 8 **riff**, 6 **ryft**, **refe**, 7- **reef.** *Pl.* 8 **reeves**, 8- **reefs**. [ME. *riff*, *refe* = Du. *reef*, *rif*, LG. *reef*, *reff*, G. *reff* (*riff*, *reef*), Sw. *ref*, Norw. *riv*, Da. *rev*, *reb*: the ultimate source is ON. *rif* in the same sense (formally identical with *rif* rib, and perh. only a transferred use of that word: cf. next), but the precise manner in which the word passed into the other tongues is obscure. F. *ris* (12th c., Wace) is app. a pl. form, for **rifs*.]

1. *Naut.* One of the horizontal portions of a sail which may be successively rolled or folded up in order to diminish the extent of canvas exposed to the wind; they are usually three or four in number, and situated at the top of square sails and at the bottom of fore-and-aft sails. Freq. in phr. ***to take in a reef*** (also in fig. context).

1390 GOWER *Conf.* III. 341 The wynd was good, the See was plein, Hem nedeth noght a Riff to slake. *c* **1515** *Cocke Lorell's B.* 12 Some yᵉ longe bote dyde launce..Mayne corse toke in a refe byforce. *a* **1547** SURREY in *Tottell's Misc.* (Arb.) 28 And so wisely, when lucky gale of winde All thy puft sailes shall fil, loke well about: Take in a ryft. **1684** *Lond. Gaz.* No. 1933/4 Her Main-Sail a Lug Sail with four Reefs at the bottom, and her Fore-Sail three aloft. **1711** W. SUTHERLAND *Shipbuild. Assist.* 115 Reeves to take up part of the Sail as the Wind rises. **1762** FALCONER *Shipwr.* II. 158 The folding reefs, in plaits inroll'd, they lay. **1807** CRABBE *Par. Reg.* I. 328 When tempests plough the deep We take a reef, and to the rocking sleep. **1862** *Lond. Rev.* 16 Aug. 139 When the morning breaks we [yachtsmen] are beating into Weymouth with two reefs down.

transf. **1846** *Swell's Night Guide* 48 Ruttum turned out a quid as big as a moke's egg, took a reef in his patter trap. **1884** 'MARK TWAIN' *Huck. Finn* xxxi. 316, I lit out, and shook the reefs out of my hind legs. **1885** *Spectator* 30 May 715/1 He is wasting away, and is obliged to take in reefs in his waistcoat. **1903** SOMERVILLE & 'ROSS' *All on Irish Shore* i. 2 'I dunno, Master Freddy; it might be 'twas a hare,' returned Patsey, taking in a hurried reef in the strap that was responsible for the support of his trousers. **1924** E. POUND *Let.* 3 Dec. (1971) 190 Am also letting out another reef in my long job. Installment of which should soon be inspectable.

2. †**a.** The act of reefing. *Obs. rare*$^{-0}$.

1704 J. HARRIS *Lex. Techn.* I. s.v., This contracting or taking up the Sail, they call a Reef or Reefing the Sail.

b. A mode of reefing.

1829 MARRYAT *F. Mildmay* v, We tried a Spanish reef, that is, let the yards come down on the cap.

3. *attrib.* and *Comb.*, as ***reef-cringle***, ***-earing***; **reef-band** (see quot. 1762); **reef-hank** = *reef-point*; **reef-jig**, **-jigger**, a tackle sometimes used to pull the reef-band taut before tying the points (*Cent. Dict.* 1891); **reef-knot**, (*a*) a knot made in tying the reef-points; (*b*) a certain form of knot used for this and other purposes; hence **reef-knot** *v. trans.*, to tie with a reef-knot; **reef-line** (see quot. 1769); **reef net** *N. Amer.*, a type of net used for catching salmon; also *attrib.*; hence **reef netter**, a fisherman who uses a reef net; **reef-pendant** (see quot.); **reef-point**, one of a set of short ropes fixed in a line along a reef-band to secure the sail when reefed; **reef-tackle** (see quot. 1769); also *attrib.*

1762 FALCONER *Shipwr.* II. 153 *note*, The *reef-band is a long piece of canvas sewed across the sail, for strengthening it in the place where the reef-holes are made. *c* **1860** H. STUART *Seaman's Catech.* 45 The reef bands and bellybands stretch from leech to leech, for strengthening the sail. **1841** R. H. DANA *Seaman's Man.* 29 Having the head and first *reef cringles..out. *Ibid.*, Fasten the head and *reef earings to their cringles. **1883** *Man. Seamanship for Boys' Training Ships R. Navy* (Admiralty) (1886) 51 Reef-earrings are pieces of rope, in size according to the size of the leech-rope, as when a topsail is reefed the reef-earring, when passed is supposed to bear the same amount of strain as the leech-rope. **1888** E. J. MATHER *Nor'ard of Dogger* 162 The fourth hand and myself were getting the reef-earings adrift. **1974** P. WRIGHT *Lang. Brit. Industry* xv. 148 Over the mainsail came, broke all the reef-ear-rings, an' then we'd full sail on. **1823** CRABB *Technol. Dict.*, **Reef-hanks*, short pieces of small line sewed at certain distances on the reefs of boom-sails. **1841** R. H. DANA *Seaman's Man.* 40 This is sometimes called a *Reef-knot. **1859** *All Year Round* No. 17. 400 The faces of the men, as they lay along the yard, tying the reef knots. **1974** *Maclean's Mag.* Nov. 10/1 Show the other lads the difference between a reef knot and a granny. **1883** *Man. Seamanship for Boys' Training Ships R. Navy* (Admiralty) (1886) 87 For a topgallant sail or royal,..[a roband-hitch] is ..not clove-hitched, the two nearest robands being *reef-knotted together. **1886** J. M. CAULFEILD *Seamanship Notes* 2 Take your boat's grapnel, and reef-knot it round boat. **1762** FALCONER *Shipwr.* II. 156 The *reef-lines next..Thro' eye-lid-holes and roband-legs are reev'd. **1769** —— *Dict. Marine* (1789) Hh iv, The courses of large ships are either reefed with points or small cords, which are thence called reef-lines... The line is passed spirally through the eyelet-holes of the reef, and over the head of the sail alternately, and ..strained..tight. **1882** NARES *Seamanship* (ed. 6) 124 In reefing, the end of the becket is passed under the reef line. **1917** *Pacific Fisherman Yearbk.* 60 (*heading*) The Siwash *reef net. *Ibid.*, Reef net fishing was confined to the flood tide. **1970** *National Fisherman* Feb. 21-B/1 In 1969 there were 63 pairs of reefnet vessels registered in Puget Sound. **1974** B. & R. HILL *Spirit in Stone* iii. 35 A man whom we will call the ritualist and several assistants are fishing for salmon with a reef net. **1939** *Pacific Fisherman* June 45/2 With the increase in gear, considerable friction arose between purse seiners and *reef netters. **1867** SMYTH *Sailor's Word-bk.*, **Reef pendant*, a rope..with a tackle attached to its end to bowse the after-leech down to the boom. **1805** SOUTHEY *Madoc in W.* iv, The *reef-points rattled on the shivering sail. **1840** R. H. DANA *Bef. Mast* iv. 8, I was of some service on a yard, and could knot my reef-point as well as anybody. **1750** BLANCKLEY *Nav. Expos.* 129 Reefing..is done with the *Reef Tackle Pendants, Tyes, and Falls. **1769** FALCONER *Shipwr.* II. 150 *note*, Reef-tackles are ropes employed to facilitate the operation of reefing, by confining the extremities of the reef close up to the yard. **1840** R. H. DANA *Bef. Mast* v. 10 We had got..the topsail reef-tackles hauled out. *c* **1860** H. STUART *Seaman's Catech.* 23 Reeve it through the reeftackle block.

reef (ri:f), *sb.*^{2} Forms: 6 **riffe**, 6–8 **riff**, 8- **reef.** [= Du. *rif* (in Kilian also *riffe*), MLG. *rif*, *ref*, G. *riff*, Sw. *ref*, Norw. *riv*, Da. *rev* (*rif*), ultimately from ON. *rif* in the same sense (prob. a transferred use of *rif* rib: cf. prec.). The immediate source of the Eng. word is prob. Du. or LG.]

1. A narrow ridge or chain of rocks, shingle, or sand, lying at or near the surface of the water. †Formerly also ***reef of rocks***.

See also CORAL REEF, *barrier-reef* s.v. BARRIER *sb.* 5, *fringing-reef* s.v. FRINGING *ppl. a.*

1584 NORMAN *Safegard of Saylers* 11 The riffe lyes alongst betweene Bombergen and the holmes west. *Ibid.* 15 From the northwest corner of Burckum, doth lie a riff of sand. **1695** *Phil. Trans.* XIX. 35 The Riff or Ridge..descending a little towards the Eastward. **1742** [RICHARDSON] *Tour Gt. Brit.* (ed. 3) I. 297 Though Portland stands a League from the main Land of Britain, yet it is almost join'd by a prodigious Riff of Beach, that is to say, of small Stones cast up by the Sea. **1748** *Anson's Voy.* II. iv. 157 There is also a reef of rocks running off the eastern point of the Island. **1813** BAKEWELL *Introd. Geol.* (1815) 88 Islands and reefs of coral rocks are raised from vast depths in the course of a few years. **1864** TENNYSON *En. Ard.* 585 The league-long roller thundering on the reef. **1868** MISS BRADDON *Dead Sea Fr.* I. i. 2 Leaving it far away across a level waste of reef and sand. **1883** SIR A. HOBHOUSE in *Law Rep.* 9 *App. Cases* 177 A reef of shingle which extends to the right bank of the river.

fig. **1875** LONGF. *Masque Pandora* iv, To the reefs of doom he drifts! **1896** *Daily News* 4 Nov. 7/1 On this reef the hypothesis..is shattered.

transf. **1877** BARING-GOULD *Myst. Suffering* 93 The blackness which was falling reef on reef, over mind and soul.

2. *Gold-mining* (orig. *Austral.*). **a.** A lode or vein of auriferous quartz.

1857 in *Occasional Papers Univ. Sydney Austral. Lang. Res. Centre* (1966) No. 9. 21 On this gold-field the word reef shall be taken to mean any seam of quartz, the average thickness of which..shall exceed three (3) feet. **1858** MCCOMBIE *Hist. Victoria* xiv. 213 A party..discovered gold in the quartz reefs of the Pyrenees. **1873** C. ROBINSON *N.S. Wales* 38 Mining and engineering skill, and..powerful machinery are brought to bear on such reefs. **1939** C. W. TOWNE *Her Majesty Montana* 114 Even before the end of placer mining, Butte prospectors had located quartz on a black-stained reef. **1955** *Times* 9 May 18/3 The total development footage driven was 48,295 ft., and of the 21,085 ft. on basal reef and sampled 12,990 ft., or 62 per cent., proved payable. **1966** 'J. HACKSTON' *Father clears Out* 16 An offshoot from our old reef provided the quartz.

b. The bed-rock.

1869 R. B. Smyth *Gold Fields Victoria* Gloss. s.v., The term is applied to the up-turned edges of the palæozoic rocks. The reef is composed of slate, sandstone, or mudstone. The bed-rock anywhere is usually called the reef.

c. *S. Afr.* (With capital initial.) = RAND *sb.*[2] 1 b. Also (usu. with small initial), rock in a mine which is not gold- or diamond-bearing.

1893 T. Reunert *Diamonds & Gold S. Afr.* I. 21 The surface shales and basalt surrounding the pipes are called 'Reef'. *Ibid.* 22 In the upper levels of the mines intrusive masses of shale and igneous rock are met with, called 'Floating Reef'. They are destitute of diamonds. *Ibid.* 28 The encasing rock of the mine (or the 'Reef', as the diggers called it) being exposed by the removal of the diamondiferous ground, began to disintegrate, and fall into the mine... The reef troubles..more than once threatened to involve the whole mine in ruin. **1905** L. Phillips *Transvaal Probl.* ii. 49 Meetings took place along the Reef from Boksburg to Krugersdorp. **1926** S. G. Millin *S. Africans* 77 The richest road in the world, whose sixty miles run over the gold-mines of the Reef. **1970** W. Smith *Gold Mine* xvi. 44 Free gold..rapidly worked its way down..its journey accelerated by the vibration of the conveyor and bin as mine reef was dropped. **1975** 'D. Jordan' *Black Account* xvii. 89 One of the houses with the Reef's pre-war style of flat roofs and enormous bay windows.

3. Short for *reef-sponge* (see 4).

1883 *Fisheries Exhib. Catal.* (ed. 4) 160 The principal varieties [of sponges], in the order of their value, are known as sheep-wool, white reef,..dark reef.

4. *attrib.* and *Comb.*, as (sense 1) ***reef-channel***, ***-ground***, ***-mass***, ***-region***, ***-rock***, etc.; ***reef-building***, ***-forming***, ***-making***, ***-strewn*** adjs.; (senses 2 a, 2 c) ***reef development***, ***-matter***, ***share***, ***town***, ***value***; **reef-bass**, an American fish; **reef-break** *Surfing* (see quot. 1970); **reef-builder**, a cœlenterate or other marine organism which builds reefs; **reef-drive** (see quot.); **reef-eel**, an Australian murænoid eel, as *Muræna tessellata* (*Funk's Stand. Dict.* 1895); **reef flat**, the horizontal upper surface of a reef; **reef-goose**, the common N. American wild goose, *Bernicla canadensis* (*Cent. Dict.* 1891); **reef-heron**, an Australian heron of the genus *Demiegretta*, as *D. jugularis* or *D. sacra* (Funk); **reef-knoll**, a hillock, usu. of limestone, formed from ancient coral; **reef-limestone**, limestone which was formed in reefs; **reef-oyster**, an oyster growing on, or forming, reefs; a coarse oyster (*Cent. Dict.*); **reef-sponge**, a kind of sponge obtained in the West Indies; **reef-trout**, an American species of lake-trout; **reef-wash** (see quot.).

1884 Goode *Nat. Hist. Aquat. Anim.* 372 In the Carolinas, Florida, and the Gulf, we meet with the names 'Bass', and its variations, 'Spotted Bass', 'Red Bass', 'Sea Bass', '*Reef Bass', and 'Channel Bass'. **1966**, **1968** *Reef break [see *point break* s.v. POINT *sb.*[1] B. 14]. **1970** *Studies in English* (Univ. of Cape Town) I. 26 A reef break, surf breaking over a reef, will provide a good, fast ride. **1869** *Amer. Naturalist* III. 352 We could find no evidence that the *reef-builders at the present time..are working upon so high a northern line. **1877** Huxley *Anat. Inv. Anim.* 167 Even within the coral-zone, the distribution of the reef-builders appears to be singularly capricious. **1972** *Sci. Amer.* June 54/1 The chief animal reef-builders today are the corals, but many other marine invertebrates are important members of the reef community. **1861** J. R. Greene *Man. Anim. Kingd., Cœlent.* 193 External conditions which seem favourable..to the growth of *reef-building Corals. **1850** Dana *Geol.* ii. 40 The reef of New Holland has been instanced as affording an example of one of the larger *reef-channels. **1971** *Daily Tel.* 11 Oct. 17 A limited amount of *reef development in the lower western portion of the mine yielded reasonable values. **1869** R. B. Smyth *Gold Fields Victoria* Gloss. 619 *Reef-drive—A drive cut or constructed entirely through the bed rock,..or along the face of the reef, or partly in the reef. **1886** *Trans. R. Soc. Edin.* XXXII. 557, I..came upon the coral rock exposed in flat surfaces resembling those of the ordinary *reef-flat. **1931** J. S. Gardiner *Coral Reefs & Atolls* ii. 35 Such rock masses as are visible on the reef flat do not stand up above the high tide level. **1976** R. C. Selley *Introd. Sedimentol.* viii. 297 There are three main morphological elements to a reef: the fore-reef, the reef flat and the back-reef. *Ibid.* 299 Tidal channels..traverse the reef-flat. **1967** *Oceanogr. & Marine Biol.* V. 330 Tethyan corals include such *reef-forming genera as *Stylina*, *Isastraea*, and *Thamnastrea*. **1850** Dana *Geol.* ii. 40 The *reef-grounds being in some parts twenty-five miles wide. **1890** R. H. Tiddeman in *Rep. Brit. Assoc. Adv. Sci. 1889* 602 At the foot of these mounds, or *reef-knolls as I would call them, we have in many places a breccia formed of fragments of the limestone. **1969** Bennison & Wright *Geol. Hist. Brit. Isles* ix. 211 Extensive sheet reefs, not necessarily primarily organic in origin, as well as reef-knolls are widespread, the reef-knolls occurring on the flanks of massifs. **1893** P. Lake tr. *E. Kayser's Textbk. Compar. Geol.* iii. 225 In these *reef limestones..the greater part of the rock is formed not by corals, but by the rock-building algae..*Gyroporella* and *Diplopora*. **1938** M. Black *Hatch & Rastall's Petrol. Sedimentary Rocks* (ed. 3) viii. 163 The term 'reef limestone' has been used in geological literature with varying significance. In this discussion, shelly or structureless, unbedded limestones which show no clear connection with sessile benthonic organisms will be left out of consideration. **1956** W. Edwards in D. L. Linton *Sheffield* 6 Shirley and Horsfield..have described the reef-limestones of the northern fringe of the main outcrop near Castleton. **1855** J. Phillips *Man. Geol.* xvi. 491 The *reef-making madrepores are seldom found below 100 feet. **1876** Page *Adv. Text-bk. Geol.* iii. 68 The *reef-mass formed by their aggregate labours. **1896** *African Critic* 24 Oct. 546/2 The mine shows over two and a-half feet of *reef matter. **1872** Dana *Corals* ii. 129 The cruiser in untried *reef-regions. **1820** Keats *Hyperion* II. 306 Sullen waves In the half-glutted hollows of *reef-rocks. **1890** 'R. Boldrewood' *Miner's Right* (1899) 52/1 An agency for the purchase of *reef shares. **1883** W. S. Kent *Fisheries Bahamas* 45 (Fish. Exh. Publ.) The *reef or glove sponge,..technically known as *Spongia officinalis*, var. *tubulifera*. **1885** Lady Brassey *The Trades* 311 There were little black balls of reef-sponges. **1961** *Times* 14 Dec. 17/5 Ice and *reef-strewn channel. **1938** N. Devitt *Spell of S. Afr.* 185 At a military court held in a certain *Reef town, a civilian was charged with murder. **1884** Goode *Nat. Hist. Aquat. Anim.* 488 About Grand Traverse Bay, Lake Michigan, two varieties [of lake trout] are also recognised, one being..known as '*Reef Trout'. **1955** *Times* 3 May 17/2 *Reef values to the south-west of the fault are expected to be similar to those encountered in the President Brand and Western Holdings mines. **1869** R. B. Smyth *Gold Fields Victoria* Gloss. 620 *Reef-wash—A deposit of washdirt spread over an expanse of flat or undulating reef (i.e., bed-rock), or lodged in a hollow in the reef.

reef, *sb.*[3], modernized form of REAF, mantle.

1842 Sir H. Taylor *Edwin* I. viii, This shaveling's meagre face, With his mass-hackle and his reef and stole.

reef, northern Sc. form of ROOF.

reef (riːf), *v.*[1] [f. REEF *sb.*[1]; cf. Du. *reven*, Da. *reve*, *rebe*, Sw. *refva*, Icel. *rifa*.]

I. 1. a. *trans.* To reduce the extent of (a sail) by taking in or rolling up a part and securing it.

1667 Davenant & Dryden *Tempest* I. i, Up aloft Lads. Come, reef both Top-sails. **1687** B. Randolph *Archipelago* 103 We hoised our main-saile, with which and our fore-saile (both reeft) we stood in. **1726** Swift *Gulliver* II. i, We reeft the Fore-sail and set him. **1762** Falconer *Shipwr.* II. 141 Again to reef the main-sail they repair. **1862** *Catal. Internat. Exhib.* II. xii. 6/1 By this invention, the topsails can be reefed and unreefed from the deck, without sending any one aloft. **1888** *Encycl. Brit.* XXIV. 599/2 Mills are exposed to great danger if the sails are not reefed or furled in high winds.

absol. **1762** Falconer *Shipwr.* II. 12 At ev'ry hatchway, 'Reef!' they call again. **1816** 'Quiz' *Grand Master* Pref. 3 He might have call'd them out to reef. **1862** *Catal. Internat. Exhib.* II. xii. 6/2 Fitted..with reef lines, &c., in the topsail, to reef in the old plan if required for purposes of exercise.

b. *transf.* To draw up or gather in, after the manner of reefing. Hence in *Criminals' slang*, to pull up (the lining of a pocket) so as to steal the contents; to pick (a pocket); hence, to steal or obtain dishonestly in any fashion; also more *gen.* to remove, to take or strip *off*, to pull *down*.

1836 E. Howard *R. Reefer* xxx, The clues of my hammock were not reefed. **1887** J. Ashby Sterry *Lazy Minstrel* (1892) 68 Dear little damsels..Face the salt spray, reef their petticoats pluckily. **1899** [see LEATHER *sb.* 2 e (*a*)]. **1901** M. Franklin *My Brilliant Career* xvii. 142 She was the only one who bothered with a bathing-dress. The rest of us reefed off our clothing. **1903** Farmer & Henley *Slang* VI. 10/1 *Reef*..(thieves'), to draw up a dress-pocket until the purse is within reach of the fingers. **1926** *Variety* 29 Dec. 7/4 The cleverest wire who ever reefed an insider would be astonished to hear that a 'milk man' was a hambo, who stole more bows than the applause warranted at the finish of his act. **1938** *Surg., Gynecol. & Obstetr.* LXVI. 200/2 An attempt was made to shorten the quadriceps by reefing the tendon and fastening the aponeurosis of the internal vastus to the patella under tension. **1944** L. Glassop *We were Rats* xviii. 102 'Where'd you get all the smash?' asked Pat. 'The Harday organization,' said Gordon, 'works fast. I reefed it off a few Parsees like steam.' **1949** —— *Lucky Palmer* xiv. 124 Mugs deserve to have their dough reefed off them. **1953** K. Tennant *Joyful Condemned* xxiii. 223 They vowed it [*sc.* a magpie] ran squawking to inform on anyone who was reefing down a bit of lightning conductor to make an aerial. **1955** *Publ. Amer. Dial. Soc.* xxiv. 95 Some careful tools reef every score. **1959** *Economist* 7 Feb. 505/1 Where public servants..feather their nests when they are not reefing money off honest citizens. **1967** K. Giles *Death in Diamonds* vi. 104 If I go near the car pool they'll reef it off me. **1976** *Courier-Mail* (Brisbane) 17 July 24/9 Collins 'reefed' his $140 watch from his left hand. **1977** *Times* 13 July 5/4 As the talent suckers chummy, the wire reefs his leather... A slick pickpocket team has a private language for its dirty work.

c. To feel the genitals of (a person). *coarse slang.*

1962 Parker & Allerton *Courage of his Convictions* i. 33, I enjoyed reefing girls much more than lessons. The girls enjoyed it too. **1972** B. Rodgers *Queens' Vernacular* 101 Cop a feel..reef (Brit gay sl); take somebody's pulse.

2. a. To shorten (a topmast) by lowering, or (a bowsprit) by sliding inboard. Also *intr.* (see quot. 1875).

1704 [see REEFED *ppl. a.* 1]. **1745** P. Thomas *Jrnl. Anson's Voy.* 138 We found our own Main-top-mast sprung,..whereupon we reef'd it twenty Inches, that is we lower'd it so much and secured it there. **1867** Smyth *Sailor's Word-bk.* 565 The lower piece is cut off, and a new fid-hole cut, by which the mast is reefed or shortened. **1875** Knight *Dict. Mech.* 1904/1 The bowsprit of a cutter or that of a ship-of-war..is said to reef when it is run-in or shortened by sliding in-board. **1883** *Harper's Mag.* Aug. 449/2 The bowsprit and topmast can be reefed or housed.

b. To alter (a paddle) by moving the float-boards nearer to the centre of the wheel, in order to diminish the dip when the vessel is deep.

1838 Barlow in Tredgold *Steam Eng.* (ed. Woolhouse) App. 61 This serious loss of speed in a laden vessel..would be more effectually saved by reefing the paddles. **1858** Murray *Marine Eng.* xii. 143 When the wheels are too deeply immersed, they may sometimes be 'reefed' by disconnecting the boards, and securing them near the centre.

3. *intr.* (See quot.)

1889 *Atlantic Monthly* July 115/1 When the driver moves the bit to and fro in his mouth, the effect is to enliven and stimulate the horse... If this motion be performed with an exaggerated movement of the arm, it is called reefing.

II. *Comb.* **reef-topsail**, used *attrib.* to designate a breeze of a strength in which topsails are reefed; also *fig.* ? *Obs.*

1840 R. H. Dana *Two Yrs. before Mast* xxxi. 235 We had a steady 'reef-topsail breeze' from the westward. **1849** H. Melville *Redburn* 1648 By night it was a reef-topsail-breeze. **1909** B. Lubbock *Deep Sea Warriors* 16 The sail-maker's reef-topsail voice drowned my question.

reef, *v.*[2] [f. REEF *sb.*[2]] *intr.* To work at a (mining) reef. So **'reefing** *vbl. sb.*[2]; also *attrib.*

1861 [see QUARTZ *sb.* 2 b]. **1865** *Mining Surveyors' & Registrars' Rep.* (Dept. Mines, Victoria) Sept. 46 The southern or Gipps Land slope of the Great Dividing Range ..will become one vast reefing district. **1874** A. Bathgate *Colonial Experiences* viii. 95 Quartz crushing for gold..gives abundant promise for the future, notwithstanding that the interest of the speculating public has been somewhat shaken in 'reefing'. **1874** C. Holloway *Jrnl. Visit N.Z. 1873–75* I. 121 (typescript), These Block's [*sic*] are distant about 20 miles from the rising reefing district of Lyell. **1890** 'R. Boldrewood' *Miner's Right* (1899) 21/2 Patiently sinking, driving, sluicing, or reefing as the case might be. **1906** J. M. Bell in P. Galvin *N.Z. Mining Handbk.* 5 Reefing is being carried out at a number of places.

reefable ('riːfəb(ə)l), *a.* [f. REEF *v.*[1] + -ABLE.] Capable of being reefed.

1909 *Westm. Gaz.* 26 Oct. 5/1 Instead of having two rigid planes or wings, set one on either side of the body, it has a single transversal span of canvas which is reefable, like that of the sail of a ship.

reefe, obs. form of RIFF, midriff.

reefed (riːft), *ppl. a.* [f. REEF *v.*[1] + -ED[1].]

1. Of masts: Shortened.

1704 J. Harris *Lex. Techn.* I. s.v. *Reef*, When a Top-Mast is Sprung,..they cut off the lower piece that was near broken off, and setting the other part, now much shorter, in the Step again, they call it a Reeft Top-Mast.

2. a. Of sails: Having a reef or reefs taken in. Also with *up*, and *transf.*

1748 *Anson's Voy.* I. vii. 73 We were obliged..to continue under a reefed mizen till eleven at night. **1814** Scott *Ld. of Isles* I. xxi, The helm..Gave the reef'd sail to meet the wind. **1863** S. R. Graves *Yachting Cruise* 84 We took in the trysail, and ran under reefed square sail and foresail. **1874** K. H. Digby *Temple of Memory* iv. 78 The windmills with the reef'd-up sails. **1962** *Into Orbit* 245 *Reefed*, the condition of a parachute which is not fully deployed, in order to reduce the initial stress.

b. With *single-*, *double-*, etc.

1803 *Naval Chron.* XXIII. 398 Treble-reefed main-top-sail. **1836** Marryat *Midsh. Easy* xxvi, Another ten minutes, and then they were under double-reefed topsails. **1857** in *Merc. Marine Mag.* (1858) V. 1 Under double-reefed top-sails, courses, jib, and single-reefed main-try-sail.

reefer[1] ('riːfə(r)). [f. as prec. + -ER[1].]

1. One who reefs; *spec.* a slang name given to midshipmen 'because they have to attend in the tops during the operation of taking in reefs' (Smyth).

1818 'A. Burton' *Adventures J. Newcome* I. 40 'Hoy! Reefers! Reefers!—with your sport you seem to make a *Dover Court*.' **1829** Marryat *F. Mildmay* ii, I..was saluted by the females with the appellation of 'royal reefer' (midshipman). **1840** R. H. Dana *Bef. Mast* xxix. 104 A lad ..who went by the name of the 'reefer', having been a midshipman in an East India Company's ship. **1888** *Harper's Mag.* July 166 The steerage or gun-room was..the home of darling reefers. **1939** Joyce *Finnegans Wake* (1964) 323 Reefer was a wenchman.

2. A reefing jacket. Also (*N. Amer.*), an overcoat.

1878 C. Hallock *Amer. Club List & Sportsman's Gloss.* p. ix/2 *Reefer*, a short jacket worn by sailors. **1883** *Tailoring World* 20 Oct. 1/2 The forms of garments known as Reefers and Lounges. **1894** R. H. Davis in *Harper's Mag.* May 891/1 A tall, handsome woman..with her hands in the pockets of her reefer. **1921** [see *covert cloth*]. **1935** A. J. Pollock *Underworld Speaks* 96/1 *Reefer*, an overcoat. **1947** *Words: New Dict.* 480/1 *Reefer*, *n. Slang.* 2. A short, double-breasted overcoat. **1968** [see LOUNGE *sb.* 2 c]. **1970** J. H. Gray *Boy from Winnipeg* 47 Our winter overcoats—'reefers' we called them—lasted so well that one might serve as many as three boys before being discarded.

attrib. **1885** *Pall Mall G.* 13 Mar. 10/2 The man..was dressed in a reefer jacket and light-coloured trousers. **1901** G. B. Shaw *Capt. Brassbound's Conversion* II. 241 Sprawl supine on the floor, with their reefer coats under their heads. **1928** R. Macaulay *Keeping up Appearances* xv. 170 Cary spoke with a hint of nervous defiance, thrusting her hands into the pockets of her reefer coat. **1936** N. Streatfeild *Ballet Shoes* x. 161 On the day of the interview, Nana cleaned Pauline's reefer coat, and blue beret. **1955** *Times* 20 Aug. 3/3 He was wearing a reefer jacket and uniform trousers under a blue naval raincoat. **1969** N. W. Parsons *Upon Sagebrush Harp* i. 4 Rena and I shivered in our white serge reefer coats. **1978** *Jrnl. R. Soc. Arts* CXXVI. 702/2 Pugin shocked his contemporaries by attending important meetings with aristocratic clients dressed in a seaman's jersey and reefer jacket.

3. [Or perh. ad. Mexican Sp. *grifo* marijuana, one who smokes marijuana.] A cigarette containing marijuana; marijuana; one who smokes marijuana. Also *attrib.* *slang* (orig. *U.S.*).

1931 [see CAMP *a.* (and *sb.*[5])]. **1932** *Melody Maker* Sept. 749/2 'Song of the Weed', 'Got the South in my Soul', 'I

Heard', and 'Reefer Man' are all worth your half-crowns. **1933** *Chicago Defender* 2 Dec. 5 The humble 'reefer', 'the weed', the marijuana, or what have you by way of a name for a doped cigarette has moved to Park Ave. from Harlem. **1940** R. CHANDLER *Farewell, My Lovely* xxxiii. 256 He sold reefers... With the right protection behind him. **1946** S. JACKSON *Indiscreet Guide to Soho* 120 'Reefers' (cigarettes made from marihuana) used to sell in thousands in the West End before the war. **1952** *Amer. Speech* XV. 335/2 One who smokes is a nicotine-hound or a reefer (especially a smoker of marihuana). **1952** M. TRIPP *Faith is Windsock* ix. 137 Got any reefers?.. Gimme some skin man. **1956** 'N. SHUTE' *Beyond Black Stump* 279 And then we got to smoking those reefers... Those cigarettes! **1959** *News Chron.* 26 Aug. 1/2 'Reefer' cigarettes, made up from hashish, are sold in the West End and in Notting Hill at 5s. apiece. **1967** M. M. GLATT et al. *Drug Scene* iv. 49 Quite a few were on heroin and cocaine, most smoked reefers, but not too many were on Purple Hearts. **1972** W. LABOV *Lang. in Inner City* p. xxii, Reginald then makes another disruptive move, suggesting that they get a bag of reefer (marijuana). **1976** *Milton Keynes Express* 2 July 9/6 [He].. was fined £100 after three ounces of cannabis, enough to make 240 'reefers', was found at his home. **1979** *High Times* Mar. 25 Louisiana state cop displays a pot of pot discovered among 30 tons of Columbian reefer.

4. *Criminals' slang.* (See quots.)

1935 N. ERSINE *Underworld & Prison Slang* 62 *Reefer*,.. a pickpocket. **1941** BAKER *Dict. Austral. Slang* 59 *Reefer*... (2) A pickpocket's accomplice.

'reefer². [f. REEF *sb.*² or *v.*² + -ER¹.]

1. *Austral.* and *N.Z.* One who works on a gold-reef.

1859 *Adelong Mining Jrnl.* 15 Apr. 4/2 On Monday last he made known to a few of our old reefers his discovery. **1890** 'R. BOLDREWOOD' *Col. Reformer* (1891) 285 He was not a miner, a speculator, a reefer, nor an engine-driver. **1940** BAKER *N.Z. Slang* iv. 28 Gold-fields brought [to N.Z.] the reefer, the deep lead, the gutter, the monkey shaft.

2. *U.S.* A reef-oyster (*Cent. Dict.* 1891).

3. *Austral.* One associated with the Great Barrier Reef.

1951 J. DEVANNY *Travels N. Queensland* xv. 78 We plunged into the water up to our knees.. holding the sticks which experienced 'reefers' invariably carry.

'reefer³. Alteration of REFRIGERATOR. Usu. = *refrigerator car* or *ship*. Also *attrib.*, and as *adj.* = REFRIGERATED *ppl. a.*

1914 *Wells Fargo Messenger* III. 39 Ten thousand halibut must be packed in Wells Fargo 'reefers' between sun-up and sunset. **1924** 'DIGIT' *Confessions 20th Cent. Hobo* 12 *Reefer*, a refrigerator box car for perishable goods with an ice-box at each end. **1926** *Amer. Speech* I. 652/2 *Reefer*, refrigerator. **1951** *Manch. Guardian* 27 Sept. 14/2 Denmark also provides examples of English, or rather American naming, in the African Reefer and the Indian Reefer—'Reefer' being an Americanism for a vessel carrying refrigerated cargo. **1953** *Sun* (Baltimore) 7 Nov. (B ed.) 6/3 Then.. to San Francisco for 'reefer' cargo—refrigerated fruit. **1958** J. KEROUAC *On Road* I. 19 We didn't know.. what boxcars and flats and de-iced reefers to pick. **1961** *Amer. Speech* XXXVI. 273 *Reefer box*, a refrigerated trailer. **1963** *North* (Ottawa) May-June 14/1 Price had been showing them how to can the local fruit and prepare it for freezing in the Indian Affairs reefer. **1963** T. PYNCHON *V.* i. 22 To the mezuzah nailed up over the vegetable reefer and the Zionist banner hanging in back of the salad table Da Conho added this prize. **1965** R. B. ORAM *Cargo Handling* (1969) vi. 99 Refrigerated space is now commonly referred to as 'reefer' space. **1968** P. DURST *Badge of Infamy* iv. 32 Steaks are in the reefer, the french fries are all out and in the wire basket. **1971** *Maclean's Mag.* Sept. 34/1 Reefers are insulated vans with Thermo King refrigerated units on them. They can carry anything from ice cream to corpses. **1976** *Times* 6 Oct. 21 The underlying strength of the refrigerated ship (reefer) business. **1978** *Jrnl. R. Soc. Arts* CXXVI. 186/1 At present in the Dry Cargo Fleets of the World the United Kingdom is first in Reefers, second in Containers and, it would seem, is leaving Bulkers and General Cargo to others. Reefer and Container ships certainly need high grade officers who are good navigators and capable ship handlers in traffic.

reeffe, obs. form of REEVE *sb.*¹

†re-efformation. *Obs. rare*⁻¹. [RE- 5 a.] Renewal of form, re-formation.

1626 DONNE *Serm.* xxi. 206 The resurrection from this fall is by Re-efformation.

reefing ('ri:fɪŋ), *vbl. sb.*¹ *Naut.* [f. REEF *v.*¹ + -ING¹.] **a.** The action of REEF *v.*¹

1750 BLANCKLEY *Nav. Expos.* 129 This contracting or taking up the Sail they call Reefing. **1758** J. BLAKE *Plan Mar. Syst.* 7 Exercising those who are received into the service.. in handing and reefing of sails. **1829** MARRYAT *F. Mildmay* viii, Many a sail is split by bad reefing. **1862** *Catal. Internat. Exhib.* II. XII. 6/1 The old defective and dangerous method of reefing by the men going aloft and out on the yards.

b. *attrib.*, as ***reefing breeze, gear, hook, point, spindle, topsail, wheel***; **reefing-jacket**, a particular form of close-fitting jacket made of stout heavy cloth.

1897 *Outing* (U.S.) XXX. 362/2 The race was sailed with a *reefing breeze. **1956** A. F. LOOMIS *'Hotspur' Story* 118, I was sailing in a reefing breeze. **1911** J. BARTEN *Compl. Naut. Pocket Dict.* 156/2 **Reefing gear*, Mechanismus zum Segelreffen. **1961** F. H. BURGESS *Dict. Sailing* 169 *Reefing gear*, patent roller fittings used in some small sailing boats, to dispense with the use of reef points. **1860** 'VANDERDECKEN' *Yarns* 36 The topmast shrouds.. should have.. *reefing hooks and thimbles. **1882** OGILVIE, *Reefing-jacket. **1894** *Idler* Sept. 220 A reformed world, in which every man should.. sit down in a reefing jacket to a dinner of pork and beans. **1856** 'STONEHENGE' *Brit. Rural Sports* 461/1 Tying round the boom a corresponding line of the '*reefing points',.. hanging on the lower part of the mainsail. **1962** *Roving Commissions 1961* 43 Mr 'Christie' Mahoney arranged for our *reefing spindle to be mended. **1878** A. H. MARKHAM *Gt. Frozen Sea* i. 3 Both ships were fitted with.. patent *reefing and furling topsails. **1840** *Civil Engin. & Archit. Jrnl.* III. 104/1 This vessel.. has the *reefing wheels after Mr. Hall's patent.

reefort, Sc. variant of RAIFORT. *Obs.*

'reefous, *a. rare*⁻¹. [f. REEF *sb.*²] Reefy.

1859 R. F. BURTON in Lady Burton *Life* (1893) I. 272 An occasional glimpse through its green veil showed a reefous surface, flecked with white froth.

reeft, obs. f. RIFT *sb.*; obs. pa. pple. of REAVE *v.*

reefy ('ri:fɪ), *a.* [f. REEF *sb.*²] Full of reefs.

1847 in WEBSTER. **1893** SIR H. HOWORTH *Glacial Nightmare* II. 625 It has brought down a lot of loose material to a reefy coast.

'reeing, 'rying, *vbl. sb.* Also 5 rey(i)ng, 9 reean, rieing, rayen. [f. REE *v.* + -ING¹.]

1. The action of reeing corn; hence ***reeing-sieve, -machine***.

α. **1400–1** *Durham Acc. Rolls* (Surtees) 603 In j ridella et j reyingsife empt. ijs. vjd. **1485–6** *Ibid.* 649, 1 Reyng syff, iijd. **1620** MARKHAM *Farew. Husb.* (1625) 115 With small reeing siues to dresse it from the Corne, and so preserue the dust. **1844** H. STEPHENS *Bk. Farm* II. 283 Reeing-machines have been invented for cleansing corn. **1878** *Cumbld. Gloss.*, *Ree*, to riddle corn in a 'ree-an sieve'.

β. **1744–50** W. ELLIS *Mod. Husbandm.* VI. III. 64 (E.D.S.) A brass or iron wire round hand-sieve, which we call a rying-sieve. **1879** MISS JACKSON *Shropsh. Word-bk.*, *Rieing-sieve*, same as Blind-sieve.

γ. **1863** W. BARNES *Dorset Gloss.*, *Rayen-zieve*.., a sieve, used chiefly in cleansing clover.

†2. Such a quantity as can be reed at once. *Obs.*

1641 BEST *Farm. Bks.* (Surtees) 104 A bushell of pease, and a bushell of rye, into which we putte a ryinge, or two, or three, of barley.

re-e'jaculate, *v.* [RE- 5 a.] *trans.* To ejaculate or emit again.

a **1711** KEN *Hymnarium* Poet. Wks. 1721 II. 113 A Love which Love celestial may With re-ejaculated Love repay.

re-e'jection. [RE- 5 a.] Ejection again or a second time.

1831 T. HOPE *Ess. Origin Man* II. 185 The separation of those substances fit for absorption and nutrition, from those only fit for re-ejection. **1881** JUDD *Volcanoes* iv. 69 By constant re-ejection these [fragments] were gradually reduced in size.

reek (ri:k), *sb.*¹ Forms: α. 1 réc, 3–7 reke, 4 rek, rike, 4 *Sc.*, 5 reyk, 4–6 *Sc.* reik, 6–7 reeke, 7 reake, 7, 9 *Sc.* reak, (8 wreak), 9 *north. dial.* rik, rick, 5– reek. β. 4–5 (9 *dial.*) reech, 4–5 reche, 5 rich. [Comm. Teut.: OE. *réc* = OFris. *rek, reek*, OS. *rôk* (MDu. *rooc*, Du. *rook*), OHG. *rouh* (MHG. *rouch*, G. *rauch*), ON. *reykr* (Sw. *rök*, Da. *rög*):—OTeut. **rauki-z*, from a stem *reuk-, rouk-* (cf. REEK *v.*¹), app. not found outside of Teutonic. As the word has chiefly survived in northern use the palatalized form *reech* is comparatively rare.]

1. Smoke from burning matter. (Still the general word in *Sc.* and *north. dial.*; in standard Eng. only in literary use, and chiefly applied to dense or unctuous smoke.)

α. *c* **825** *Vesp. Psalter* xvii[i]. 9 Astaȝ rec in eorre his. *a* **1000** *Cædmon's Gen.* 325 (Gr.) [Hi] þoliað.. brand & brade liȝas, swilce eac þa biteran recas. *a* **1300** *Cursor M.* 3105 It brend, þe reke raght vp euen. **1340** HAMPOLE *Pr. Consc.* 9431 Þair throtes sal ay be filled.. Of lowe and reke. **1375** BARBOUR *Bruce* IV. 130 The fyre out syne in blasis brast, And the reik rais richt vounder fast. *c* **1400** tr. *Secreta Secret., Gov. Lordsh.* 81 With sandell confyt ennoynt his body, reekyd with reek of ensens. **1466** *Paston Lett.* II. 268 To the glaser for takyn owte of ii. panys of the wyndows.. for to late owte the reke of the torches. ? **1531** FRITH *Answ. Rochester* Wks. 56/2, I shall offer vnto thee fat sacrifices with the reke of wethers. *a* **1572** KNOX *Hist. Ref.* Wks. 1846 I. 42 For the reik of Maister Patrik Hammyltoun hes infected as many as it blew upoun. **1598** SHAKS. *Merry W.* III. iii. 86 As hatefull to me as the reeke of a Lime-kill. **1630** J. TAYLOR (Water P.) *Praise Clean Linen* Wks. II. 169/1 The suddes vnto the Sea I may compare, The Reake or smocke, the wind. **1664** H. MORE *Myst. Iniq.* vii. 21 The diffused reek of the things sacrificed. **1703** T. N. *City & C. Purchaser* 47 The Reek which ascends out on the top of the Kiln. **1725** RAMSAY *Gentle Sheph.* v. ii. Prol., The rising sun shines motty throw the reek. **1821** SCOTT *Pirate* xi, The reek that's rising out of yon lums. **1864** DASENT *Jest & Earnest* (1873) I. 43 The miner makes a little explosion.., which fills the air.. with a sulphurous reek. **1895** CROCKETT *Men of Moss-Hags* xli. 292 The whole interior was full of the smoor of reek.

β. **13..** *E.E. Allit. P.* B. 1009 Suche a roþun of a reche ros fro þe blake, Askez vpe in þe ayre & vsellez þer flowen. *a* **1425** *Cursor M.* 3105 (Trin.), Hit brent; reche roos vp ful euen. **1879** WAUGH *Chimney Corner* 251 There's bin nought nobbut reech (smoke) an' rain sin I coom.

b. In comparisons, with reference to the lightness or other qualities of smoke.

c **825** *Vesp. Psalter* xxxvi[i]. 20 Aspringende swe swe rec. *c* **1000** *Ags. Ps.* (Th.) lxvii. 2 Rece hi ȝelicast ricene geteoriað. *a* **1300** *Cursor M.* 26994 Quat es mans lijf bot fam, And a rek þat mai noght last. *c* **1375** *Sc. Leg. Saints* xxxii. (Justin) 442 He had na langare mycht to byde bot fled as reke & can hym hyde. **1513** DOUGLAS *Æneis* v. xii. 138 Thus has he said; and.. Vanist away, as the reik in the air. **1858** M. PORTEOUS *'Souter Johnny'* 8 But sic pretension I, like reek will puff aside.

c. *fig.* in various applications.

a **1300** *Cursor M.* 2744 Þe word es wers þan man mai neuen; þe reke [*Trin. MS.* reech] es raght vn-to þe heuen. *c* **1440** *York Myst.* xxvi. 34 Thurgh his romour in þis reme Hath raysede mekill reke. **1529** LYNDESAY *Compl.* 367 Than rais ane reik, or euer I wyste, The quhilk gart all thare bandis bryste.

d. *transf.* A house, as having a fire burning in it (cf. 5 and HEARTH¹ 2).

1626 *Act. 31* in Barry *Orkney* App. ix. (1805) 469 Whatever persone shall slay the earn or eagle shall have.. 8d. from every reik within the parochine. **1822** HIBBERT *Descr. Shetl. Isl.* 321 To feed these birds a hen was demanded from every house; or (as it is called) from every reek.

2. Vapour or steam arising from, or given off by, something in a moist or heated state, as wet or marshy ground (hence also *Sc.*, fog or mist), wet clothes, boiling water, etc.

c **1400** tr. *Secreta Secret., Gov. Lordsh.* 79 Whenn þe erthe ys clene with-oute roche, and with-oute reke, þe water of þat stede ys light. *c* **1400** *Sege Jerus.* 790 Þe wedes dropeden doun, d[r]yed ȝerne, Rich rises hem fro. **1607** SHAKS. *Cor.* III. iii. 121 Curs, whose breath I hate, As reeke a'th rotten Fennes. **1685** BOYLE *Salubr. Air* 22 He found the Reeks ascending from them into the Air.. make him as it were Asthmatical. **1696** BP. PATRICK *Comm. Exod.* iv. (1697) 63 He added these words.. I am a reek from a pot. **1843** BORROW *Bible in Spain* II. viii. 149 They lay immersed in the tepid waters.. overhung with steam and reek. **1879** BROWNING *Ned Bratts* 17 Like threshers, one and all, Of a reek with laying down the law in a furnace.

fig. **1681** J. SCOTT *Chr. Life* iv. (1684) 287 Melancholy.. overwhelms the Fancy with black Reeks and Vapours. **1819** SHELLEY *Cenci* v. iii, That eternal honour which should live Sun-like, above the reek of mortal fame. **1856** BOKER *Poems* (1857) II. 96 My heart boils sometimes, and the reek is death To such as stir it.

b. *spec.* The vapour given off by hops in drying.

1846 J. BAXTER *Libr. Pract. Agric.* (ed. 4) I. 401 The instantaneous abstraction of the 'reek', which maintains the best colour [in the hops]. **1881** WHITEHEAD *Hops* 64 A current of air, heated by the fire below, is passed perpetually thro' the green hops in the upper floor, and their 'reek' is carried quickly off.

c. Haziness, indistinctness. *rare.*

1876 R. F. BURTON *Gorilla L.* II. 201 The most delicate sharpness and purity of outline took the place of meridian reek and blur.

3. An exhalation; a fume emanating from some body or substance; in mod. use, a strong and disagreeable fume or smell.

1659 H. MORE *Immort. Soul* III. ii. §7 That our Substance is in a manner lost, and nothing but a tenuious reek remains. **1674** N. FAIRFAX *Bulk & Selv.* 182 It shall be or may be alwayes body,.. sending forth and taking in of steams and reeks, even all along. **1685** BOYLE *Enq. Notion Nat.* 320 The closeness of the Place, or the over charging of the Air with the fuliginous Reeks of Mens Bodies. **1871** DIXON *Tower* IV. xxxi. 330 A reek of gin and powder filled the chamber. **1886** *All Year Round* 4 Sept. 103 From the engine-room hatch there came up a reek of oil.

fig. **1870** LOWELL *Among my Bks.* Ser. I. (1873) 49 Nor does Dryden's lewdness leave such a reek in the mind as the filthy cynicism of Swift.

b. Impure, fetid atmosphere.

1873 DIXON *Two Queens* II. XI. vii. 260 Amid the reek and squalor of a Spanish hamlet. **1891** E. GOSSE *Gossip in Library* iv. 52 The sweet, pure meadows lie just outside the reek of Southwark.

4. Applied to fine dust or snow in motion, having the appearance of smoke or steam.

1854 DICKENS *Hard T.* II. xi, The reek of her own tread in the thick dust that felt like velvet. **1894** BLACKMORE *Perlycross* 270 The shattered roof yawning to the reek of the snow-slides.

5. *attrib.* and *Comb.*, as **†reek-fowl** or **-hen**, an ancient Scottish tax of a hen paid annually by each householder on an estate; **reek penny**, *north.* a tax paid to the clergy by each house in the parish; **†reek-poultry**, = *reek-fowl*.

1592 *Sc. Acts Jas. VI* (1814) III. 607 Togidder wᵗ the haill teynd wictuall.. *reikfowlis custumes and vtheris dewties quhatsumeuir. **1567** *Sc. Acts Mary* (1814) II. 556 Duodecem lie *reik hennis. **1795** *Statist. Acc. Scotl.* XV. 451 The cotters and sub-tenants pay.. a reek hen, and one day's shearing in harvest. **1871** W. ALEXANDER *Johnny Gibb* xix. (1873) 114 It had been the practice.. to bind every tenant to pay yearly to the laird a 'reek hen'. **1255** *Memorandum Sherburn Hospital, Bishopton* No. 4 (MS.), De *Rekepeni v sol. **1351–2** *Durham Acc. Rolls* (Surtees) 552, xiijs. iiijd. de Rekepenys parochiarum de Jarowe et Wermouthe. **1735** *Visitation of Chollerton* in Hodgson *Northumbld. County Hist.* (1897) IV. 270 All tithes and Easter offerings (except reek penny and communicants). **1832** HODGSON *Northumbld.* II. II. 356 *note*, The [Christmas] offering here [Bedlington] for communicants.. is three-halfpence each; each family also pays one penny, under the name of smoke or reek penny. **1585** *Charter* (Jam.), Decem capones.. cum lie *reik pultreis solitis. *c* **1592** *Registr. Arbroath* (Bann. Club) II. App. p. xxxvii, With the reik pultreis vseit and wount.

†reek, *sb.*² *Obs.* Forms: 6 reke, reek(e, reake, 7 reike, riek. [Of obscure origin: perh. an alteration of REIT.]

1. *collect.* Water-plants, seaweed.

1555 EDEN *Decades* 55 Amonge the reke or weedes of the maryshes, they espyed a multitude of wylde bores. **1567** GOLDING *Ovid's Met.* XIV. (1593) 324 First trees shall grow.. in the sea, and reeke shall thrive On tops of hilles. **1601** HOLLAND *Pliny* I. 445 Sea-weeds or Reike, rushes and reeds growing vpon the washes and meers.

2. With *pl.* A water-plant, a seaweed.

1566 DRANT *Horace, Sat.* II. iv. G viij b, The bore is yll in Laurente soyle, that feedes on reakes and reeds. **1591** PERCIVALL *Sp. Dict., Alga marina*, reeks or sea weede.

Reek (riːk), *sb.*³ *Ireland.* [Var. of RICK *sb.*¹: cf. REEK *v.*³] A mountain, used *spec.* in *pl.* in ***Macgillicuddy's Reeks*** (also, ***the Reeks***), county Kerry. Also in *sing.*, as pop. name for Croaghpatrick, county Mayo. ***Reek Sunday***, the last Sunday in July, on which pilgrimages are made to Croaghpatrick.

1780 A. YOUNG *Tour in Ireland* I. 381 Nothing stops the eye till Mangerton and Macgilly Cuddy's Reeks point out the spot where Killarney's lake calls for a farther excursion. *Ibid.* II. 3 Mangerton, and the Reeks, in Kerry; the Galbies in Corke..these are the principal in Ireland. **1808** J. MILNER *Let.* 22 Sept. in *Inquiry concerning Ireland* (ed. 2, *c* 1810) 326 The forked, cloud-capped Reeks, overlooking the Atlantic Ocean. **1870** P. W. JOYCE *Irish Local Names* 36 Croagh; *Cruach*, a rick or stacked up hill... Croaghpatrick; St. Patrick's rick or hill. **1871** T. C. POPE *Council of Vatican* 236 He required a period of nearly six weeks to complete the remaining portion of the journey to Rome. He commenced the ascent of the Alpine reeks on a Friday. **1922** JOYCE *Ulysses* 290 From the streamy vales of Thomond, from M'Gillicuddy's reeks the inaccessible and lordly Shannon the unfathomable. **1930** *Irish Rosary* May 321 From our drawing-room windows one had a perfect view of the Reek. **1959** D. D. C. P. MOULD *Peter's Boat* iii. 31 Carrauntual, the 3414 foot height at the western end of the great ridgeway of the MacGillycuddy's Reeks. *Ibid.* 32 The ridge of the Reeks springs up suddenly, a wall of rock, from the plains of Kerry. **1960** [see GARLAND *sb.* 9]. **1964** B. WHELPTON *Unknown Ireland* vii. 98 The Gap of Dunloe between the Reeks and the Purple Mountains.

reek, obs. form of RICK *sb.*

reek (riːk), *v.*¹ Forms: 3–6 reke, 5–7 *Sc.* reik, 6 rik-, 6–7 reake, reeke, 6–8 reak, (8 wreak), 7, 9 *dial.* reech, 6– reek. [Comm. Teut.: OE. *réocan* (north. *réca*: see also sense 5) = OFris. *riaka*, *reka*, OLG. *riecan* (MDu. and Du. *rieken*; also MDu. *rûken*, Du. *ruiken*), OHG. *riohhan* (G. *riechen*), ON. *rjúka* (Sw. *röka*, Da. *ryge*):—OTeut. **riukan* (see REEK *sb.*¹). G. *riechen* and Du. *rieken*, *ruiken* now mean only 'to smell', the orig. sense being expressed by the new formations *rauchen* and *rooken*.]

1. *intr.* To emit smoke: **a.** of something burning.

c **1000** *Ags. Ps.* (Th.) ciii. [civ.] 30 ʒif he mid his mihte muntas hrineð, hi ful ricene reocað sona. **1300** *E.E. Psalter* cxliii[i]. 5 Laverd..Negh hilles, and reke þai salle. **1483** *Cath. Angl.* 302/2 To Reke, *fumare*. **1513** DOUGLAS *Æneis* II. xi. 34 Thair followis a streme of fire,..Quhill all enveron rekit like brintstane. **1585** JAS. I *Ess. Poesie* (Arb.) 72 Earth dois tremble, mountains reikis, afraid. **1617** SIR W. MURE *Misc. Poems* xxi. 78 With Iberian fyres the Alpes doe reik. **1698** FRYER *Acc. E. India & P.* 124 The only Structure standing in the Town, it..was then reaking in its Ashes. **1830** SCOTT *Demonol.* x. 368 Not long after the civil war, the embers of which were still reeking. **1846** KEBLE *Lyra Innoc.* (1873) 149 While temples crash, and towers in ashes reek.

b. of a building, chimney, etc. Also *transf.*

Also common in dial. use of a chimney which 'smokes', i.e. sends out smoke into the room or house.

c **1420** *Avow. Arth.* xv, Alle wroth wex that sqwyne,..As kylne other kechine, Thus rudely he rekes. *c* **1500** *Felon Sewe of Rokeby* ix, The kilne began to reeke. **1572** *Satir. Poems Reform.* xxxvi. 115 In the craft expert, And þerby garis ȝour kitchingis daylie reik. **1579** SPENSER *Sheph. Cal.* Sept. 117 Fewe chymneis reeking you shall espye. **1625** LISLE *Du Bartas, Noe* 132 And shall I never see my country chimnies reake? **1795** MACNEILL *Will & Jean* xxi, White the wa's, wi' roof new theeckit,..Lown 'mang trees and braes it reekit. **1820** SCOTT *Abbot* xxxiv, Observing that the chimney of the kitchen had reeked that whole day in a manner which contradicted the supposition [of famine].

2. To emit hot vapour or steam; to smoke with heat; to exhale vapour (or fog). Now chiefly *dial.*

a. of hot liquids, food, etc., and of moist things under the influence of heat, or when warmer than the atmosphere.

c **1000** *Sax. Leechd.* II. 18 Wel on wætere; læt reocan on þa eaȝan þonne hit hat sie. **1538** LELAND *Itin.* (1768) II. 66 The Water of the Baynes..rikith like a sething Potte continually. **1573** TUSSER *Husb.* (1878) 21 With some vpon Sundaies, their tables doe reeke. *a* **1635** CORBET *Poems* (1807) 138 Your cold meate comes in reaking, and your wine Is all burnt sack. **1658** tr. *Porta's Nat. Magic* v. iii. 168 When the fume..is exhaled from them, that they have left reaking, make a powder of them. **1724** RAMSAY *Tea-t. Misc.* Ded. vi, The tea's fill'd reeking round. **1742** *Lond. & Country Brew.* I. (ed. 4) 3 In the Warmth of Well Waters, that are often seen to wreak in the cold Seasons. **1796** MORSE *Amer. Geog.* I. 133 The most severe cold..is so piercing in February and March, that..the sea reeks like an oven. **1889** *N.-W. Linc. Gloss.* (ed. 2) s.v., When fog arises the land is said to reek.

b. of persons and animals in a heated and perspiring state.

c **1430** LYDG. *Min. Poems* (Percy Soc.) 114 He ran in a fyrryd gowen, he cast of alle hys clothys, alle his body gan reke. **1530** PALSGR. 684/1 I reke, as a horse dothe that is laboured. *Je fume.* *a* **1599** SPENSER *F.Q.* VII. vii. 40 His browes with sweat did reek and steem. **1611** SHAKS. *Cymb.* I. ii. 2 The Violence of Action hath made you reek as a Sacrifice. **1706** E. WARD *Wooden World Diss.* (1708) 84 His Phiz is everlastingly reaking with Sweat and Grease. **1790** BURNS *Tam o' Shanter* 148 They reel'd, they set, they cross'd, they cleekit, Till ilka carlin swat and reekit. **1852** MRS. STOWE *Uncle Tom's C.* vi. 39 Sam appeared..with Haley's horse by his side, reeking with sweat.

transf. **1616** R. C. *Times Whistle* I. 433 Six dayes in the weeke Are not sufficient, but the seventh must reeke With sweat of their vngodly labour. *a* **1661** FULLER *Worthies* (1840) III. 319 It is ill for a soul to go reeking with anger out of this world.

c. of blood freshly shed, or of things smeared with this. (Also of the air, etc.) Const. *with*, †*in*.

1593 SHAKS. *Lucr.* 1377 The red bloud reek'd to shew the Painter's strife. **1601** —— *Jul. C.* III. i. 158 Now, whil'st your purpled hands do reeke and smoake, Fulfill your pleasure. *a* **1674** CLARENDON *Hist. Reb.* XI. §252 Whilst these perfidious wretches had their hands still reeking in the precious blood of their sovereign. **1733** POPE *Ess. Man* III. 265 Altars grew marble then, and reek'd with gore. **1785** G. A. BELLAMY *Apology* (ed. 3) II. 74 Plunging the same weapon, which was reeking with the blood of her favourite boy, into her own bosom. **1805** SCOTT *Last Minstr.* I. xxx, Till gallant Cessford's heart-blood dear Reek'd on dark Elliot's Border spear. *a* **1892** TENNYSON *Bandit's Death* v, For he reek'd with the blood of Piero.

3. To emit an unwholesome or disagreeable vapour or fume; hence, to smell strongly and unpleasantly; to stink. Chiefly const. *of*, *with*.

1710 SWIFT *Jrnl. to Stella* v, I was forced to go to a blind chop-house,..and then go reeking from thence to the First Minister of State. **1752** FOOTE *Taste* I. i, Two Domitians reaking from the Dunghill. **1798** COLERIDGE *Anc. Mar.* IV. viii, The cold sweat melted from their limbs, Nor rot nor reek did they. **1838** DICKENS *Nich. Nick.* xvi, The small apartments reek with the breath of deputations and delegates. **1881** W. H. MALLOCK *Rom. 19th Cent.* I. 140 She literally reeked of garlic. **1888** A. K. GREEN *Behind Closed Doors* vii, I found a broken phial reeking with the smell of bitter almonds.

b. *transf.* or *fig.*

1679 OWEN *Christol.* xvii. (1851) I. 223 God will not take us into heaven..with our heads and hearts reeking with the thoughts and affections of earthly things. **1772** FLETCHER *Logica Genev.* 92 Do you not plunge it in muddy stygian waters till it..reeks with poisonous error? **1846** J. BAXTER *Libr. Pract. Agric.* (ed. 4) I. p. xxx, Reeking from the filthy communion of crime. **1879** FARRAR *St. Paul* (1883) 455 The vicinity of the great Temple at Ephesus reeked with the congregated pollutions of Asia. **1961** *Newark Evening News* 21 Nov. 12 The day before Election Day, to which we are entitled as a legal holiday, we were informed to report to our respective polls to work as 'workers of the party'... Such tactics reek of totalitarianism! **1969** *Listener* 3 Apr. 467/3 The plot fairly reeks of the confessional.

†**4.** Of smoke, vapour, perfume, etc.: To be emitted or exhaled; to rise, emanate. *Obs.*

c **1325** *Metr. Hom.* 97 For rekeles rekes upward evin, And menskis him that wonis in hevin. *c* **1385** CHAUCER *L.G.W.* 2612 *Hypermnestra*, Thencence out of the fire reketh sote. **1513** DOUGLAS *Æneis* III. viii. 131 The blak laithly smuke that oft did rise..rekand as the pyk. **1542** UDALL *Erasm. Apoph.* 96 Perfume beeyng poured vpon the hedde, reketh out into the aier. **1563** WINȜET tr. *Vincent. Lirin.* Wks. (S.T.S.) II. 64 Thai knaw thair stink to na man almaist..to be plesand, gif it stewit and reikit out naikit and plane. *c* **1600** SHAKS. *Sonn.* cxxx, In some perfumes is there more delight Then in the breath that from my Mistres reekes. *fig.* **1553** T. WILSON *Rhet.* 79 If you come to him in a hotte sommers day, you shal se his honestye in such sort to reeke [etc.]. **1588** SHAKS. *L.L.L.* IV. iii. 140, I heard your guilty Rimes,..Saw sighes reeke from you. **1599** —— *Hen. V*, IV. iii. 101 The Sun shall greet them, And draw their honors reeking vp to Heauen.

b. Of snow: To whirl in fine particles like smoke or vapour.

1828 CARR *Craven Gloss.* s.v., 'It reeks and blaws', that is, the snow is driven with such violence as to resemble smoke. **1837** R. MUDIE *Spring* 266 The snow still darkens the air, and reeks along the curling wreaths, as if each were a furnace.

5. *trans.* To expose to smoke; to dry or taint with smoke; to fumigate. Also *techn.*, to coat (moulds for steel) with soot.

The OE. trans. *récan* is distinct from the intr. *réocan*.

a **1000** *Gloss.* in Wr.-Wülcker 244/36 *Fumarat*, reohte. *c* **1000** *Sax. Leechd.* I. 346 Þæs ylcan drinces smyc heora eaȝan onfon & mid þam broþe recen. *c* **1430** *Two Cookery-bks.* 29 Þen reke hem on þe colys tyl þey ben tendyr. **1500–20** DUNBAR *Poems* xxxiv. 57 Ane browstar swoir the malt wes ill, Bath reid and reikit on the kill. **1611** COTGR., *Soré*, reeked, made red or sorrell, as a Herring by the smoake. **1661** LOVELL *Hist. Anim. & Min.* 220 The sides may be pickled, and the chine broiled or fried. Some reech them. [**1864** COCKAYNE *Sax. Leechd.* I. 347 Let them receive with their eyes the smoke..and reek them with the broth.] **1884** W. H. GREENWOOD *Steel & Iron* xviii. 423 Emitting large quantities of unconsumed carbon, which is deposited upon the surface of the moulds. After the halves are so coated or reeked, they are fitted together.

fig. **1868** BUSHNELL *Serm. Living Subj.* 188 They are reeking themselves in all kinds of disorder bodily and mental.

6. To emit (smoke, steam, etc.). Chiefly *fig.*

1598 R. HAYDOCKE tr. *Lomazzo* II. 11 Alexander the Great ..was seene to reake forth from his bodie fier and light. **1602** MARSTON *Antonio's Rev.* V. ii, Swart Pieros lips reake steame of wine. **1641** MILTON *Reform.* I. Wks. 1851 III. 10 Our Ministers,..like a seething pot set to coole, sensibly exhale and reake out the greatest part of that zeale. **1867** MACGREGOR *Voy. Alone* (1868) 68 A great human sink reeking out crime, disease, and disloyalty on the whole nation.

7. To cause (a place) to smell of blood.

1880 L. WALLACE *Ben-Hur* VIII. v. 503 The slaughter of lambs in offering reeked the fore-courts of the Temple.

Hence **reeked** (riːkt, *Sc.* 'rikɪt), *ppl. a.*, smoked.

1785–6 BURNS *Address to Deil* xvii, Wi' reekit duds, an' reestit gizz. **1792** —— *Kellyburn Braes* x, A reekit wee deevil looks over the wa'. **1832** J. COLE *Scarborough Guide* 109 A delicious relish for the breakfast table,..called Reek'd Haddocks.

reek, *v.*² *Sc.* Also 8 reick. [Of obscure origin: connexion with *reek* REACH *v.* or REKE *v.* is not clear.] *trans.* (and *intr.*) To fit or rig *out* (†also with *forth*). Hence '**reeking** *vbl. sb.*²

Sometimes used without the adv.: see the *Eng. Dial. Dict.*

1590 JAS. VI in *R. Bruce's Life* (1843) 20 The reeking out of three or four ships to meet me here and convey me home. **1591** R. BRUCE *Serm.* (1843) 296 His great army quhilk was so long in reeking forth. **1676** Row *Contn. Blair's Autobiog.* (1848) 509 The King could not get his navy so soon reeked out. **1715** *Wodrow Corr.* (1843) II. 113 Some were taken by some passage-boats that were reicked out [equipped] by way of privateers from Leith harbour. **1798** D. CRAWFORD *Poems* 20 Had I but siller I cou'd spare, To reek me out and pay my lare. *a* **1800** in Maidment's *N. Cy. Garland* (1824) 50 Dinna ye mind..How we a' reek'd out, an' a' to Shirramuir?

reek, *v.*³ Now *dial.* Also 7 reeke. [app. f. *reek*, var. RICK *sb.*] *trans.* To pile up.

1693 BROWNLOW *Entries* 145 Ad fodiendum scindendum (*Anglice* hew)..cumulandum (*Anglice* reeke). **1780** YOUNG *Tour Irel.* I. 262 Women 3ᵈ. and 4ᵈ. a day in reeking corn. **1886** *S.-W. Linc. Gloss.* s.v., The snow was that reek'd up.

†**reek**, *v.*⁴ *Obs. rare*⁻⁰. (See quot.)

1674–91 RAY *N.C. Words* s.v., His sickness will reek him, that is so wast him as to kill him.

reek, Sc. variant of REACH *v.*¹

reekes, variant of REAKS *Obs.*

reekes-doller, obs. form of RIX-DOLLAR.

reeking ('riːkɪŋ), *vbl. sb.*¹ [f. REEK *v.*¹ + -ING¹.] The action of REEK *v.*¹ Also *concr.*, smoke, vapour.

1483 *Cath. Angl.* 302/2 A Rekynge, *fumositas*. **1558** PHAER *Æneid* II. E iij, Mixt with dust & smoke thick streames of reekings rise. **1604** R. CAWDREY *Table Alph.*, *Vapor*, moisture, ayre, hote breath, or reaking. **1674** N. FAIRFAX *Bulk & Selv.* 90 The least steams or reekings of bodies. **1705** A. VAN LEUWENHOEK in *Phil. Trans.* XXV. 1856 A great Hay-rick.., after some Reaking and Fermentation took fire. **1884** W. H. GREENWOOD *Steel & Iron* Index 531/1 Reeking of ingot-moulds.

reeking, *vbl. sb.*²: see REEK *v.*²

reeking ('riːkɪŋ), *ppl. a.* [f. REEK *v.*¹ + -ING².]

1. That emits smoke. ***a reeking house***, an inhabited house. *Sc.*

c **950** *Lindisf. Gosp.* Matt. xii. 20 Recende *vel* smecende [flax]. **1483** *Cath. Angl.* 302/2 Rekynge, *fumalis*. **1779** DOUGAL GRAHAM *Writ.* (1883) II. 228 A reeking house and a rocking cradle. **1837** R. NICOLL *Poems* (1842) 77 Where the shepherd's reeking cot Peeps from the broomy glen. **1894** CROCKETT *Raiders* (ed. 3) 170 Not one reeking house or any place where kindly folk dwelt.

2. That emits vapour or steam.

c **1000** ÆLFRIC *Saints' Lives* vii. 20 Agnes..þæra maðma ne rohte þe ma þe reocendes meoxes. *c* **1400** tr. *Secreta Secret., Gov. Lordsh.* 79 Salt water, and bitter, and rekand, ar euyl. **1601** HOLLAND *Pliny* I. 97 Breathing forth vapors out of reeking rockes. **1781** COWPER *Anti-Thelyphth.* 93 From many a steaming lake and reeking bog. **1822** LAMB *Elia* Ser. I. *Praise Chimney-Sweepers*, Indiscriminate pieces of those reeking sausages. **1888** MISS BRADDON *Fatal Three* I. v, A reeking heap of stable manure.

fig. **1784** COWPER *Task* III. 503 The impatient fervour which it first conceives Within its reeking bosom.

b. of dead or mangled bodies or their parts while still warm.

a **1000** *Judith* 314 (Gr.), Cirdon cynerofe,..wælscel oninnan, reocende hræw. **1700** DRYDEN *Ovid's Met.* XII. 211 The reeking Entrails on the Fire they threw. **1735** SOMERVILLE *Chase* III. 214 The Jest of Clowns, his reeking Carcase hangs. **1821** SHELLEY *Hellas* 434 Where'er..The obscene birds the reeking remnants cast Of these dead limbs. **1864** BURTON *Scot Abr.* I. i. 30 A feudal lord..would ..warm his feet in their reeking vitals.

c. of blood and wounds freshly shed or made, or of things smeared with warm blood.

1573 TWYNE *Æneid* XII. (1584) T vj, Their foule black reaking blood, with channel large doth fall to ground. **1605** SHAKS. *Macb.* I. ii. 39 Except they meant to bathe in reeking Wounds. **1695** LD. PRESTON *Boeth.* IV. 186 They..stain their Swords in their own reeking Gore. **1720** POPE *Iliad* XVII. 415 A sanguine torrent steeps the reeking ground. *a* **1839** PRAED *Poems* (1864) II. 352 From out the reeking wound. **1877** L. MORRIS *Epic of Hades* I. 19 With the reeking blade Wet with the heart's blood of my child I smote.

d. of persons or animals in a heated state.

1605 SHAKS. *Lear* II. iv. 30 Came there a reeking Poste, Stew'd in his haste. **1735** SOMERVILLE *Chase* I. 181 Tumultuous soon they plunge into the Stream, There lave their reeking Sides. **1782** COWPER *Gilpin* 122 Bowing down His reeking head full low. **1840** DICKENS *Barn. Rudge* ii, Holding the light to his panting and reeking beast.

3. That rises as vapour or steam.

c **1000** ÆLFRIC *Saints' Lives* xviii. 57 Butan ren-scurum & reocendum deawe. *c* **1586** C'TESS PEMBROKE *Ps.* CXXXV. iii, In flaky mists, the reeking vapors rise. **1650** W. D. tr. *Comenius' Gate Lat. Unl.* §48 Reaking steam drawn out of moist places. **1667** MILTON *P.L.* VIII. 256 In Balmie Sweat, which with his Beames the Sun Soon dri'd, and on the reaking moisture fed. **1899** RODWAY *Guiana Wilds* 33 The great drawback was the reeking moisture.

fig. **1607** SHAKS. *Timon* III. vi. 103 [Timon] washes it off and sprinkles in your faces Your reeking villany.

4. Sending out, full of, unwholesome or unpleasant fumes or smells.

1832 LYTTON *Eugene A.* I. x, Washing the walls of the reeking town. **1850** KINGSLEY *Alt. Locke* i, Poor wretches who sit stifled in reeking garrets and workrooms. **1871** FARRAR *Witn. Hist.* iii. 122 God..purged the pestilence from the reeking atmosphere with fire and storm.

5. *Comb.*, as ***reeking hot, red.***
1615 G. SANDYS *Trav.* 103 Whom reeking hote, with heart yet panting, they greedily devoured. **1668** CULPEPPER & COLE *Barthol. Anat.* 359 It comes reaking hot as it were from the fire. **1810** SCOTT *Lady of L.* II. xiv, But can I clasp it reeking red?

Hence **'reekingly** *adv.*
1611 COTGR., *Fumeusement*, smoakily, fumingly, reekingly.

reeks, variant of REAKS *Obs.*

reek-staffold, -staval: see RICK *sb.*

reeky ('ri:kɪ), *a.* Forms: 5, 6 *Sc.* **reky**, 6 *Sc.* **reikie**, 6–9 *Sc.* **reekie**, 7 **reaky**, 7– **reeky**. [f. REEK *sb.*[1] + -Y[1]. See also REECHY.]

1. a. That emits vapour; steamy; full of rank moisture.
c **1400** tr. *Secreta Secret., Gov. Lordsh.* 79 Waters þat spryngyn yn stony lond and ys reky Abundandly, er heuy & noyant. **1641** BEST *Farm. Bks.* (Surtees) 15 A meanes..to keepe them reeky and moyst till such time as they can bee gotten peel'd. **1808** SCOTT *Marm.* v. Introd. 131 Her wavering lamp I'd rather trim.. Than gaze abroad on reeky fen, And make of mists invading men. **1861** LYTTON & FANE *Tannhäuser* 11 Their lips, Spurning the reeky pasture, yearn for draughts Of rock-rebounding rills.

b. Emitting smoke, smoky.
1604 JAS. I *Counterbl. to Tobacco* (Arb.) 110 You must haue a reekie cole brought you..to kindle your Tobacco with. *a* **1849** H. COLERIDGE *Ess.* (1851) I. 276 The dens and caverns..where daylight never entered, and the reeky tapers are never extinguished.

2. Consisting of or resembling smoke.
1513 DOUGLAS *Æneis* XI. v. 14 The hevynnis hye dyd walxin dyrk, Involuyt with the reky stewis myrk. *a* **1578** LINDESAY (Pitscottie) *Chron. Scot.* (1814) 479 He saw ane gritt mistie and reikie cloud ryse and move fordwardis till it cam aboue Dunpenderlaw. **1892** LD. LYTTON *King Poppy* Prol. 614 Above his sallow couch a reeky cloud Its poison-dropping canopy suspends.
fig. **1629** Z. BOYD *Last Battell* 511 All the joys which are heere, are but reekie pleasures, purchased with teares, wher with the eyes of men are made bleared.

3. Full of smoke.
1576 NEWTON *Lemnie's Complex.* (1633) 226 As bright and handsome things in a reaky house that are besmeared, dusked and smoaked. **1718** BP. NICOLSON in Ellis *Orig. Lett.* Ser. II. IV. 318 The wretches lie in reeky sod-hovels. **1827** CARLYLE in Froude *Life* I. 380 Thus we pass our days..far from all the uproars..of the reeky town. **1859** JEPHSON *Brittany* vi. 69 As my eyes became accustomed to the reeky atmosphere.

b. Blackened with smoke; †black as with smoke.
a **1585** POLWART *Flyting w. Montgomerie* 539 Bot, reikie rooks and ravens, or ȝee ryue him, Desist, delay his death, whill I descriue him. **1859** R. F. BURTON in *Jrnl. Geog. Soc.* XXIX. 46 A long upper room, with reeky rafters.

reel (ri:l), *sb.*[1] Forms: 1 **hréol, réol**, 5–6 **rele**, (5 **real, re(y)lle**, 6 **reill**, 8 **reil**), 5–7 **reele**, 7– **reel**. [OE. *hréol*, not represented in the cognate languages: cf. REEL *v.*[1]
Both sense and form are against connexion with ON. *hræll*, weaver's slay, which has been suggested. Gaelic *ruidhil* is from Eng.]

1. a. A rotatory instrument on which thread is wound after it is spun, or silk as it is drawn from the cocoons, and from which it may again be easily wound off upon bobbins or spools.
The reel now commonly used is an open framework, consisting of a horizontal axis with radiating arms at each end, which carry bars extending parallel to the axis, so that the whole has a cylindrical form. The circumference of the reel is in some cases made of such dimensions that in a given number of revolutions it takes up a certain length of thread, forming a skein or hank. The older reels used in connexion with the spindle or spinning-wheel were of simpler forms (cf. quot. 1727–41).
c **1050** *Suppl. Ælfric's Gloss.* in Wr.-Wülcker 187/19 *Alibrum*, hreol. *a* **1100** *Gerefa* in *Anglia* IX. 263 Spinle, reol, gearnwindan. *c* **1400** *Laud Troy Bk.* 5939 Sche halpe him wel with Real & Rok. **14..** *Voc.* in Wr.-Wülcker 564/32 *Appendium*, a yernwynder, or a reel. *c* **1440** *Promp. Parv.* 428/2 Reel, womannys ynstrument, *alabrum*. **1530** PALSGR. 261/2 Rele for yarne, *deuidover*. **1560** ROLLAND *Crt. Venus* II. 693 Ilk ane [had] in hand ane Reill..To reill thair hankis so small of reid gold wyir. **1611** COTGR., *Guindre*, a reele, or wheele to wind silke on. **1697** DRYDEN *Virg. Georg.* IV. 493 The Sisters turn the Wheel, Empty the woolly Rack, and fill the Reel. **1727–41** CHAMBERS *Cycl.* s.v., Those most in use are, 1°, A little reel, held in the hand, consisting of three pieces of wood;..2°, The common reel, or windlace, which turns upon a pivot..whereon the skain to be reeled is put. **1766** FRANKLIN *Lett.* Wks. 1887 III. 458 The reels are to screw on the edge of the table, when you would wind silk or thread. **1825** J. NICHOLSON *Operat. Mechanic* 387 These reels are of a sufficient breadth to wind off about 50 cops.. at the same time. **1839** URE *Dict. Arts* 1114 The arm..is capable of being bent inwards,..so as to permit the hanks, when finished, to be taken off, as in every common reel. **1894** *Cassell's New Techn. Educ.* IV. 369 The reel is now almost always driven by power, the driving gear being a friction pulley on a cross shaft.
Phr. c **1460** *Towneley Myst.* iii. 298 Ther is garn on the reyll other, my dame.

b. A similar framework on which other materials are wound at some stage in the process of manufacture, as the separate spun-yarns in rope-making, paper as it comes from the machine (hence also, the continuous roll of paper thus produced, as used in web-printing), etc.
1797 *Encycl. Brit.* (ed. 3) XVI. 483/2 The first spinner takes it off the whirl hook, joins it to his own, that it may follow it on the reel, and begins a new yarn. **1825** J. NICHOLSON *Operat. Mechanic* 369 The paper..is passed between a series of similar cylinders, and finally delivered to a reel, and wound off in a coil. *Ibid.* 370 The frame in being forced towards the reel of paper presses the arms down. **1890** W. J. GORDON *Foundry* 198 Forty-three years ago Applegath proposed to print from the reel.

c. An upright revolving frame used in wire-drawing.
1825 J. NICHOLSON *Operat. Mechanic* 347 The wire to be drawn is placed upon a reel..which turns upon a vertical pin. **1833** J. HOLLAND *Manuf. Metal* II. 338 As soon as the wire is entirely drawn off the reel..and has passed through the plate [etc.].

2. a. An apparatus (of varying form and dimensions) capable of easy revolution, by which a cord, line, etc., may be wound up and unwound as required.
1727–41 CHAMBERS *Cycl.* s.v. *Log-line*, a little cord.. wound round a reel, fixed for that purpose in the gallery of the ship. **1765** *Museum Rust.* IV. 310 That mine might stand with all possible exactness, each man had a garden-line and reel. **1769** FALCONER *Dict. Marine* s.v. *Log*, The reel,..about which the log-line is wound. **1867** SMYTH *Sailor's Word-bk.* 566 The log-reel for the log-line, deep-sea reel (which contains the deep-sea line),..&c. 'She went 10 knots off the reel'—i.e. by the log-line. **1884** BLAKELEE *Industr. Cycl.* 123 Cheap Garden Reel.

b. A device of this kind attached to the butt of a fishing-rod, on which the line is wound up.
The usual type consists of two circular metal plates, so joined by a few small rods as to form a cylindrical case with open sides, and having a central barrel on which the line is wound.
1726 *Gentleman Angler* 3 He must have a Landing-Hook, Reels for his Silk Lines [etc.]. **1740** R. BROOKES *Art of Angling* 9 Your Line must be of Silk..; there must likewise be a Reel to wind it upon. **1833** J. RENNIE *Alph. Angling* 55 The..angler is provided with a long line wound on a reel. **1861** H. KINGSLEY *Ravenshoe* III. 201 The old gentleman began to wind up his reel, and then the lad..lifted the fish. **1892** NIVEN *Brit. Angler's Lex.* 190 Reels are made in several designs, such as plain, check, revolving plate, multipliers [etc.].

c. ***off the reel***, without stopping, in an uninterrupted course or succession; also, immediately, quickly; so ***right*** (or †***sharp***) ***off the reel***.
1825 J. NEAL *Bro. Jonathan* I. vi. 156 So then, says he to me, says he; sharp off the reel;—as 'cute a feller, that, as ever you seed. **1833** J. K. PAULING *Banks of Ohio* II. v. 78 I'd as good a mind as I ever had to shoot a wild deer, to have a fight with him off the reel, and settle the right of soil at once. **1835** *Gentleman's Vade-Mecum* (Philadelphia) 14 Feb. 3/1 Where's my old man—tell me that..where's Tom Bloomberg—tell us right off the reel. **1866** DICKENS *Let.* 20 Feb., [The story] seems to me to be so constituted as to require to be read 'off the reel'. **1880** SALA in *Illustr. Lond. News* 25 Dec. 619 Can you always say pusillanimity right off the reel? **1884** *St. James's Gaz.* 13 June 4/1 He won five races off the reel. **1900** ADE *Fables in Slang* 27 He could tell you quick—right off the reel. **1927** *Daily Tel.* 3 May 17/2 The Eton XI..were undefeated, having scored four victories off the reel. **1941** J. SMILEY *Hash House Lingo* 40 *Off the reel*, added to an order to signify a 'rush order'. **1946** *Sunday Dispatch* 8 Sept. 6/5 Won six races off the reel for Wembley Cubs. **1951** F. YERBY *Woman called Fancy* ii. 44 'You want to bring me back?' Court said. 'Why, little Fancy?' 'Can't answer that—not right off the reel. Don't rightly know myself.'

3. a. A small cylinder, usually of wood, with a rim or wider part at each end, on which thread is commonly wound to be convenient for ordinary use; a quantity of thread made up in this way.
1784 COWPER *Task* IV. 264 Weaving nets..Or twining silken threads round ivory reels. **1814** SCOTT *Wav.* lxv, He looked not unlike that ingenious puzzle called a reel in a bottle. **1840** HOOD *Kilmansegg, Death* xi, Her golden scissors, and thread and reels. **1866** GEO. ELIOT *F. Holt* v, Dispersing on the floor reels, thimble, muslin-work [etc.].

b. A small cylinder on which any flexible substance is wound, as the coil of wire in a magneto-electric machine, the strip of paper in a recording telegraph, etc. *spec.* the flanged cylinder or core on which magnetic tape or punched paper tape is wound; also *transf.*, a length of tape wound on such a cylinder.
1839 G. BIRD *Nat. Philos.* 270 Winding on a wooden reel, about three inches in length, with a hollow axis, about sixty feet of insulated copper wire. **1939** *Wireless World* 19 June 611/2 (*caption*) The necessary controls, together with the reels of steel tape, are mounted on top of the [recording] cabinet. **1953** E. T. CANBY *Home Music Syst.* xiii. 227 The reel size is seven inches. **1956** *RCA Rev.* XVII. 366 The tape is unwound from a reel..and after passing over the video heads, is pulled by the capstan. **1958** H. G. M. SPRATT *Magnetic Tape Recording* iii. 55 The tape..when wound on the normal type of spool employed, will result in a reel ranging from 5–12 in. in diameter. **1964** *Communications Assoc. Computing Machinery* VII. 630/1 This standard covers the physical dimensions of take-up (or storage) reels, with either fixed or separable flanges, so that reels of perforated tape may be interchanged among machines of various manufacturers. **1977** T. ALLBEURY *Man with President's Mind* ix. 101 The video tapes..were..sent in a special top priority diplomatic bag to Moscow. The priority was so high that the reels were not even rewound before despatch.

c. *Cinemat.* and *Photogr.* A flanged cylinder on which film is wound; usu. *transf.*, a length of film wound on such a cylinder; *loosely*, a (long) portion of a motion picture; also, †the spool on which photographs were mounted in a mutoscope (see quot. 1901).
In early usage in Cinemat., *reel* was restricted in signification to a fixed length of film, normally one thousand feet at 35 mm. gauge, complete films being called *two-reelers*, etc. (see REELER[1] 3). The word is now used of other fixed lengths, of standard lengths of film at other gauges, and also without regard to length.
1896 QUEEN VICTORIA *Jrnl.* 3 Oct. (1980) 222 The new cinematograph process,—which makes moving pictures by winding off a reel of film. **1901** *Everybody's Mag.* Aug. 230/2 Ordinary photographs are printed from the negative film and mounted on a central spool, from nine hundred to twenty-seven hundred pictures to a 'reel', as it is called. **1912** *Maclean's Mag.* Apr. 634/1 It is comprised in three 'reels', which means that there are 3,000 feet of film, requiring a full hour to run. **1915** *Chicago Herald* 1 Nov. 8/5 'The Sentimental Lady' is five reels of whipped cream lightness and frothy texture. **1916** F. H. RICHARDSON *Motion Picture Handbk.* (ed. 3) 198 There has been some inclination to increase the size of reels to two and even three thousand feet... One thousand feet of film has been and should continue to be the standard reel of film. **1921** B. SCHULBERG *What makes Sammy Run?* iv. 51 People.. become characters in Hollywood movies... In the last reel the good brother has to be killed off so that the bad brother can be regenerated. *Ibid.* xi. 193 Two-reel horse-operas. **1968** *Tamarack Rev.* Spring 9 He was waiting for the others to arrive so they could run through the second reel together. **1972** *Daily Tel.* 19 June 24/4, I don't know what I took. I know I shot three reels—36 pictures on each—but don't ask me what is on them.

d. ***reel-to-reel*** attrib. phr.: applied to a form of tape-recorder in which tape passes between two reels which are mounted separately on the recorder (cf. *open-reel* s.v. OPEN *a.* 22 c; contrast CASSETTE d and CARTRIDGE 1 d (iii)); also to the tape used in such a machine; also *absol.*
1961 *N.Y. Times* 10 Sept. II. 15/3 'Reel-to-reel' machines move the tape..from an open supply reel to a take-up reel. **1967** *Tape Recording Mag.* Jan. 12/2 Transferring recording material on to an orthodox quarter-inch tape reel-to-reel model. **1975** *Gramophone* Jan. 1389 (Advt.), It will make going in for tape much more worthwhile—cassette or reel-to-reel or both. **1976** *Broadcast* 29 Nov. 15/1 Capitol Records..wants..listeners..to send cassettes or reel-to reel tapes of their vocal efforts. **1977** *Design Engin.* July 97/2 A range of two and four channel cassette tape recorders offers recording facilities usually associated with reel-to-reel instruments.

4. a. A rotatory apparatus facilitating or causing motion of the material in the processes of dyeing cloth or tarring yarn.
1839 URE *Dict. Arts* 421 [The 'long reel' is described.] The continuous motion of the series of pieces of goods.. which are made to travel by the incessant rotations of the reel. *Ibid.* 1072 In tarring the yarn, it is found favourable.. to allow it to pass around or under a reel or roller in the bottom of the kettle. **1894** *Cassell's New Techn. Educ.* IV. 24 This [band] is supported and drawn continuously through the liquor by means of a reel or winch placed above, and driven by power.

b. In milling, the drum on which the bolting-cloth is fastened.
1845 *Encycl. Metrop.* (ed. 2) VIII. 366/2 The bolting-mill consists of a reel fitted to an axle which revolves with great rapidity; the reel is covered with cloth..in the inside of which the flour is to be prepared is placed.

c. A revolving frame, having radiating arms with pans attached, in which bread is placed for baking.
1875 KNIGHT *Dict. Mech.* 1905/2 The reel has a horizontal axis, which is rotated by gearing on the outside. To each arm of the reel..is a pendulous shelf or bread-pan.

d. In a reaping-machine, an arrangement of radial arms with horizontal bars at their extremities, which by its rotation presses the grain towards the knives.
1875 KNIGHT *Dict. Mech.* 1890/2 The machine..had a reel with twelve vanes to press the grain toward the cutters.

†**5.** A humming or buzzing noise, like that of a reel in motion. *Obs. rare*[−1]. (Possibly connected with REEL *sb.*[2] 3; but cf. REEL *v.*[2] 4.)
1747 R. MAXWELL *Bee Master* (1750) 35 By this time also, the Drones will begin to make their Appearance, and your Hive will be making a Reel, as we call it, once every Day.

6. *attrib.* and *Comb.*, as ***reel-arm, -clutch, line, -maker, measure, -plate, protector, -seat, -shaft, stand, swift; reel-winding*** adj.; **reel-backing** *U.S. local* (see quot. 1976); **reel barge**, a barge, carrying extended lengths of pipe coiled on a reel, which is used to lay submarine pipelines; also *attrib.*; **reel boy**, a boy attending to the reeling of yarn, etc.; **reel-fed** *a. Printing*, using reeled paper; **reel-land** *nonce-wd.*, the world of the cinematograph; **reel man**, a sailor who holds the reel from which a log-line depends; **reel oven** (see quot. and 4 c above); **reel-printing** (see quot. and 1 b); **reel-room**, the room in a cinema where reels of cinematographic films are kept; **reel ship**, a self-powered ship performing the function of a reel barge; †**reel-staff**, ? a hank or skein; **reel-tenter**, one who attends upon a silk-reel; **reel timing**, a method of playing certain kinds of slot machine (see quot.).

Also in many other combs. relating to fishing-reels, as *reel-band, -bed, -brake, -check, -click, -keeper*, etc.

1875 KNIGHT *Dict. Mech.* 1905/2 The pans, instead of being pendulous, are placed above the *reel-arms. **1959** W. FAULKNER *Mansion* xii. 346 His uncle had the gun..a black strong small-gauge length of *reel-backing running from the trigger through a series of screw eyes to the sash of the window screen. **1976** C. S. BROWN *Gloss. Faulkner's South* 161 *Reel-backing*.., a heavy (often old) length of fishing-line wound as the first layer on a fishing reel, and hence the last piece if the entire line is reeled out. **1972** *Study of Potential Benefits Offshore Oil & Gas Devel.* (Internat. Managem. & Engin. Group of Brit. Ltd.) x. 80 There is also the highly promising *reel-barge technique, which, however, has so far been limited to comparatively small diameter pipe. **1975** *Offshore* Aug. 121/1 Santa Fe International Corp's reel barge Chickasaw has successfully laid a 10-in pipeline in more than 1,000 feet of water. **1975** [see PIPE-LAY *sb.*]. **1975** *Offshore Progress* (Shell Internat. Petroleum Co.) 17 Another technique which has been used for some time in the Gulf of Mexico for small-diameter pipelines is the reel barge: the pipe is welded together on-shore (thereby minimizing expensive offshore time) and coiled on a reel. The barge is then pulled along the right of way, unreeling pipe behind it. **1918** *Nation* (N.Y.) 7 Feb. 130/1 Defeating the man in whose flax mill he had worked as a *reel boy. **1877** RAYMOND *Statist. Mines & Mining* 224 For throwing the *reel-clutches in and out of gear. **1946** V. S. GANDERTON in H. Whetton *Pract. Printing & Binding* xii. 153/1 Multi-colour rotaries and methods have been brought to a high degree of perfection... They are either sheet- or *reel-fed, but the delivery is flat. **1971** D. POTTER *Brit. Eliz. Stamps* xiv. 150 Reel-fed printing takes the paper into the press on a continuous reel, and the printed sheets are later divided. **1926** *Chambers's Jrnl.* Aug. 605/1 Some..would fain have treated her much in the style of those who at the present day mob the stars of *reel-land. **1837** J. KIRKBRIDE *Northern Angler* 3 With regard to the reel and *reel-line I need say nothing. **1867** *Routledge's Handbk. Fishing* 12 Reel Lines are mostly made of silk and horse-hair. **1885** CUMMINS *Fishing Tackle Catal.* 50 The best reel lines will soon rot if wound wet on the reel and left in that condition. **14..** *Nominale* in Wr.-Wülcker 686/37 *Hic citaciarius*, a *relmaker. **1776** ADAM SMITH *W. N.* I. x. II. I. 150 Artificers subservient to them, wheel-makers, reel-makers, &c. **1884** BLAKELEE *Industr. Cycl.* 451 The *Reel Measure. A reel for measuring land is made as follows. **1875** KNIGHT *Dict. Mech.* 1905/2 **Reel oven*, a baker's oven in which the bread-pans are swung on the horizontal arms of a rotating reel. **1893** *Outing* (U.S.) XXII. 122/2 Let the *reel-plate..be on the extreme end of the butt. **1890** W. J. GORDON *Foundry* 198 Printing from continuous paper is known as 'web-printing', 'roll-printing', or '*reel-printing'. **1876** PREECE & SIVEWRIGHT *Telegraphy* 260 This '*reel' protector..was adopted for a considerable time in both the needle and Morse instruments. **1851** H. MELVILLE *Moby Dick* III. xxxix. 226 The towering resistance of the log caused the old *reelman to stagger strangely. **1928** *Daily Express* 8 Oct. 2/1 Hundreds of children..filed from the..Cinema..while the staff tackled a fire in the reel-room behind the gallery. **1883** *Century Mag.* July 378/1 Adjusting a light, German-silver click reel..to the *reel-seat at the extreme butt of the rod. **1877** RAYMOND *Statist. Mines & Mining* 224 The crank-shaft is 8 inches in diameter, the *reel-shaft 10 inches. **1976** *Offshore Platforms & Pipelining* 143/2 Santa Fe expects to launch its new *reel ship in 1977. **1653** *Public Gen. Acts* 183 All yarns called Worstead-yarns shall be..reeled on a Reel of a full yard about, every *Reel-staff containing Forty thrids. **1889** *Cent. Dict.*, *Reel-stand. **1961** *World's Press News* 6 Jan. 7 (Advt.), A..Rotary Newspaper Press. The machine will be arranged with..six 3-arm magazine reelstands. **1969** E. H. PINTO *Treen* 320 The silk on the spool of the cocoon winder was then transferred to the lead-weighted reel stand. **1891** *Textile Industries* 12 Dec. 61/2 The end of the frame..carries two standards—the back one supporting the *reel swift. **1839** URE *Dict. Arts* 1114 Announcing to the *reel-tenter that a measured length of silk has been wound upon her reel. **1964** A. WYKES *Gambling* iii. 71 But another method, called '*reel timing', was not easy to track down... First, the player had to determine the exact number of seconds that each reel spun before coming to rest after the handle was pulled. Secondly, he had to memorize the sequence of all 60 symbols on the three reels... He had to be able to count..a certain number of seconds between the insertion of the coin and the pulling of the lever. **1866** *Chambers' Encycl.*, *Reel-winding machine, a beautiful contrivance, now used by the manufacturers of sewing-thread.

reel (riːl), *sb.*[2] Also 6 *Sc.* reill. [f. REEL *v.*[1]; but sense 3 may have some other origin.]

1. A whirl or whirling movement; an act of reeling; a roll or stagger. Also *fig.*

1572 *Satir. Poems Reform.* xxxi. 93 Fortoun, with a Reill, Hes wrocht thame ane vnabill charr,..With turnin of hir Quheill. *c* **1585** MONTGOMERIE *Misc. Poems* iii. 29 Quhen with a quhisk sho quhirlis about hir quheill, Rude is that rattill running with a reill. **1642** SIR T. BROWNE *Relig. Med.* I. §3 Those unstable judgements..cannot consist in the narrow point or centre of justice without a reele or stagger to the circumference. **1679** ALSOP *Melius Inq.* II. v. 295 They ran from Superstition to Prophaneness; the common reel of those who, to avoid one extreme, run into the opposite. **1851** HAWTHORNE *Ho. Sev. Gables* xvi, To steady herself from the reel and vibration which affected her more immediate sphere. **1878** BROWNING *Poets Croisic* clvii, The drunken reel Of vice and folly round him.

†**b.** *pl.* Revels, revelry. *Obs. rare.*

1602 SHAKS. *Ham.* I. iv. 9 The king doth wake to night and takes his rouse, Keeps wassels and the swaggering vpspring reeles. **1606** —— *Ant. & Cl.* II. vii. 100 Drinke thou: encrease the Reeles.

†**2.** *Sc.* A rapid careless delivery. *Obs. rare*$^{-1}$.

1573 *Satir. Poems Reform.* xlii. 536 Sic Preichouris..That thinkis thame selfis dischargit weill, Quhen they haue run ouir with ane reill Thair sairles Sermone.

3. *Sc.* A noise, tumult, disturbance; a crash, peal.

The vb. *reel* to rattle, etc., is also found in mod. Sc.

1573 *Satir. Poems Reform.* xli. 101 He said thair suld not mis ane reill That suld the cheifest walkin vp. **1724** RAMSAY *Vision* iii, To rare with rackless reil. **1813** PICKEN *Poems* II. 135 He pou'd at the bell, an it gae sic a reel. **1871** WADDELL *Ps.* xxix. 7 *marg.*, Atween bleezes o' light comes a reel o' thunner.

reel (riːl), *sb.*[3] Also 6 reill. [Perh. the same word as prec. Gaelic *righil, ruithil*, etc., commonly given as the source, is prob. from Lowland Sc.]

1. a. A lively dance, chiefly associated with Scotland, usually danced by two couples facing each other, and describing a series of figures of eight. †Also *reel-dance* (in quot. *fig.*).

Virginia reel, an American country-dance supposed to be derived from the English *Sir Roger de Coverley*: see VIRGINIA 1 d.

a **1585** MONTGOMERIE *Flyting w. Polwart* 511 Litill tent to their time the toone leit them take, Bot ay rammeist red-wood, and raveld in their reeles. **1591** *Newes fr. Scot.* (Roxb.) B j b, They..tooke handes..and daunced this reill or short daunce. **1702** R. CURRIE in *Coll. Dying Testim.* (1806) 61 Though He seem to linger, yet He is upon His journey coming, and there will be a reel-dance ere long. **1745** in R. Forbes *Lyon in Mourning* (Scott. Hist. Soc. Ser.) (1895) I. 208 He..took his share in several dances, such as minuets, Highland reels (the first reel the Prince called for was, 'This is not mine ain house'). **1788** J. O'KEEFE (*title*) The Highland reel. **1790** BURNS *Tam o' Shanter* 117 Hornpipes, jigs, strathspeys, and reels, Put life and mettle in their heels. **1806** SURR *Winter in Lond.* (ed. 3) II. 207 The jolly duchess..became the patroness of reels, a lively species of dancing. **1814** [see FOURSOME *a.* 2]. **1818** B. DUN *Nine Quadrilles* Pref., There are two kinds of music to which the Scotch reel is danced, viz. the reel properly so called, and the strathspey. **1827** PRAED *Poems* (1865) II. 214, I danced one day an Irish reel. **1840** LYTTON *Money* III. v. 85 Do you remember her dancing the Scotch reel with Captain Macnaughten? **1843** [see EIGHTSOME *a.* or *adv.*]. **1864** LOWELL *Lincoln* Pr. Wks. 1890 V. 198 There were..persons who seemed to think this as simple a thing to do as to lead off a Virginia reel. **1913** *Times* 3 June 11/3 The old Scotch reel is rarely danced today, as the young folk prefer eight-somes as more 'romping'. **1950** *Oxf. Jun. Encycl.* IX. 278/2 The chief dances performed at the [Highland] Games are the Sword Dance, the Foursome Reel, the Reel of Tulloch, the Highland Fling, and the Seann Triubhas. **1955** *Highland Dancing* ii. 61 During the Highland Reel the distance between the points may be reduced. **1964** W. G. RAFFE *Dict. Dance* 414/2 *Reel o' Tulloch*... This and other Scottish Reels in 4/4 time, come from ancient periods. *Ibid.*, This Reel is a variant of the Foursome Reel. **1971** *Country Life* 23 Dec. 1790/1 Get up and take a whirl in an eightsome reel. **1974** *Encycl. Brit. Micropædia* VIII. 468/3 Popular reels include the Irish Sixteenhand Reel and the Scottish reels Maury's Wedding and the Duke of Perth.

b. *transf.* (perh. sometimes associated with *sb.*[2]).

1768 ROSS *Helenore* 69 (Jam.) In mony a reel they scamper'd here and there, Whiles on the yerd, and whiles up in the air. **1798** COLERIDGE *Anc. Mar.* II. xi, About, about, in reel and rout The death-fires danced at night. **1850** KINGSLEY *Alt. Locke* xi, I used to lie..and watch the flies dancing reels between me and the ceiling.

2. The music or (*U.S. dial.*) a song for such a dance (see quot. 1811).

1591 *Newes fr. Scot.* (Roxb.) B j b, Geilles Duncane did goe before them, playing this reill or daunce vpon a small Trumpe. **1811** BUSBY *Dict. Mus.* (ed. 3), *Reel*, a lively Scotch dance, generally written in common-time of four crotchets in a bar, but sometimes in jig time of six quavers. **1818** [see sense 1 above]. **1883** GROVE *Dict. Mus.* III. 92/1 The Irish reel is played much faster than the Scotch. **1964** *Amer. Folk Music Occasional* I. 61 From such a man you will hear ballads, breakdowns, reels. **1968** J. ARNOLD *Shell Bk. Country Crafts* 320 In the form of the reel, strathspey, or pibroch it has a primitive echo which is evocative for all its convention and sophistication.

reel (riːl), *v.*[1] Forms: 5 relyn, 5–6 rele, reyll, 6 reyle, *Sc.* reill, 6–7 reele, 7– reel. [Of uncertain origin: possibly related to REEL *sb.*[1] Early examples are chiefly northern or Sc.]

1. *intr.* To whirl round or about; to go with a whirling motion; †to wheel suddenly.

13.. *E.E. Allit. P.* C. 147 [The ship] reled on round vpon þe roȝe ypes. *Ibid.* 270 He glydes in by þe giles..Relande in by a rop, a rode þat hym þoȝt. *c* **1400** *Laud Troy Bk.* 12761 Hedes reled aboute ouer-al, As men playe at the fote-bal. **1500–20** DUNBAR *Poems* xxvii. 75 The sowtaris horss scart with the rattill, And round about cowd reill. **1594** DRAYTON *Idea* 710 Thus the World doth, and evermore shall Reele. **1813** SCOTT *Trierm.* III. xxi, Zarah's sands in pillars reeling Join the measure that we tread. **1820** SHELLEY *Witch Atl.* xxviii, She saw the constellations reel and dance Like fireflies.

†**b.** Of a drinking cup: To go round, circulate. *Obs.*$^{-1}$ (Cf. REEL-POT.)

c **1460** *Towneley Myst.* xii. 270, *1 pastor.* I drynk for my parte. *2 pastor.* Abyde, lett [the] cop reyll.

2. Of the eyes: To whirl, with dizziness or excitement.

1513 DOUGLAS *Æneis* III. Prol. 35 Few knawis all thir coistis sa fer hence; To pike them wp perchance ȝour eene suld reill. **1737** RAMSAY *Sc. Prov.* (1750) 121 Ye never saw green cheese but your e'en reel'd. **1768** [see REELING *ppl. a.* 1]. **1835** LYTTON *Rienzi* I. iv, His eyes began to wink and reel beneath the glare of the tossing torches.

b. Of the mind, head, etc.: To be in a whirl, to be or become giddy or confused.

a **1796** BURNS *O leave novels* 6 Your fine Tom Jones and Grandisons, They make your youthful fancies reel. **1810** SCOTT *Lady of L.* v. xvi, For, while the dagger gleam'd on high, Reel'd soul and sense, reel'd brain and eye. **1855** TENNYSON *Maud* II. IV. iv, When all my spirit reels At the shouts. **1881** BESANT & RICE *Chapl. of Fleet* I. 261 My head reels, doctor.

c. To have, or seem to have, a rapid quivering motion.

1847 TENNYSON *Princ.* VII. 336 All the rich to-come Reels, as the golden Autumn woodland reels Athwart the smoke of burning weeds. **1856** BRYANT *Damsel of Peru* iv, The silent hills and forest-tops seem reeling in the heat.

†**3.** To rush, dash, or prance about in a rude or violent manner; to run riot, behave in a reckless or riotous fashion. *Obs.*

13.. *Gaw. & Gr. Knt.* 2246 Here ar no renkes vs to rydde, rele as vus likez. **1375** BARBOUR *Bruce* XII. 513 Sum of the horss, that stekit wer, Ruschit and relit richt [roydly]. **14..** *Sir Beues* (MS. M.) 510 There myght men se mekyll on-hele Whan that Beues be-gan to rele. *c* **1460** *Towneley Myst.* xiii. 274 Now were tyme for to reyll. *a* **1510** DOUGLAS *K. Hart* I. 227 So Bewte with hir wangarde gane to reill, The greitest of thair ost scho can ourryd. **1513** —— *Æneis* IV. vi. 42 Sic vise as quhen thir nunis of Bacchus Ruschis and relis our bankis, brayis, and bus. **1570** *Satir. Poems Reform.* xviii. 39 Lat neuer þai Ruffians within ȝour rowmis reill. **1715** RAMSAY *Christ's Kirk Gr.* II. xvii, His wife did reel, And rampage in her choler. **1791** LEARMONT *Poems* 23 Wi' rude Mars To reel, and get themselves made lame.

transf. **1570** *Satir. Poems Reform.* xvii. 34 Quhat vice rais vp, reuolue into ȝour minds; Quhat sin, quhat shame in hir last dayis did reil.

4. Of an army, rank, line of battle, etc.: To waver, become unsteady, give way.

1375 BARBOUR *Bruce* VIII. 328 The king..saw thame reland to and fra. *a* **1572** KNOX *Hist. Ref.* Wks. 1846 I. 212 Whill that everie man laubouris to draw from the north, whense the danger appeired, thei begyne to reyll. **1613** SHAKS. *Hen. VIII*, IV. i. 79 Great belly'd women..would shake the prease, And make 'em reele before 'em. **1648** MILTON *Ps.* lxxxiii. 51 Giddy and restless let them reel Like stubble from the wind. **1814** SCOTT *Ld. of Isles* VI. xxix, De Argentine..Renews the ranks where they have reel'd, And still makes good the line.

b. Of persons (or animals): To sway or stagger as the result of a blow or encounter. Often with *back, backward*.

?*a* **1400** *Morte Arth.* 2795 The renke relys abowte and rusches to þe erthe. *c* **1460** *Towneley Myst.* xii. 122, I shall the hytt on thi pate, lo, shall thou reyll. **1470–85** MALORY *Arthur* VII. xvii, Eyther gafe other suche buffets..that they relyd bacward. *c* **1489** CAXTON *Sonnes of Aymon* viii. 196 He made bothe the man and the horse to rele sore. *a* **1548** HALL *Chron., Hen. VIII* 49 When they saw the Almayne rele and staggar, then they fall the rayle betwene them. **1590** SPENSER *F.Q.* II. v. 6 So sore a buff to him it lent, That made him reele. **16..** *Robin Hood & Tinker* xxxi. in Child *Ballads* III. 142/2 The Tinker laid him on so fast That he made Robin reel. **1809** MALKIN *Gil Blas* VI. i. ¶ 15 [He] reeled two steps backward, just as if some one had given him a blow in the bread-basket. **1855** TENNYSON *Lt. Brigade* 35 Cossack and Russian Reel'd from the sabre-stroke Shatter'd and sunder'd.

fig. *a* **1862** BUCKLE *Civiliz.* (1873) III. ii. 69 He reeled under the double shock; a slow fever wasted his strength. **1887** BOWEN *Virg. Æneid* VI. 857 When Rome reels with the shock of the wild invaders alarm.

†**c.** To waver (in an argument). *Obs.*$^{-1}$

1529 MORE *Suppl. Soulys* Wks. 331/2 Yet said he therwith one thyng or twayn, that could not stand therwith: and therby may ye see that he began to reele.

5. Of persons (or animals): To sway unsteadily from side to side, as if about to fall; to swing about with the whole body in trying to walk or stand, as the result of intoxication, faintness, etc.

c **1477** CAXTON *Jason* 8 The dronkardes that went relyng on all sydes in the feldes. **1530** PALSGR. 684/1 It is a goodly syght to se you rele on this facyon lyke a dronken man. **1582** BATMAN *Trevisa's Barth. De P.R.* VII. lxix. 115 b, It maketh the hound to reyle and stagger, as hee were dronken. **1596** DRAYTON *Legends* iv. 276 With faintness she began to reele. **1615** G. SANDYS *Trav.* 75 A common souldier..rising from among the dead bodies, and reeling with his wounds. **1687** T. BROWN *Saints in Uproar* Wks. 1730 I. 80 How many gallons have you guzzled for your morning's draught, that you reel and stagger so? **1728** POPE *Dunc.* III. 337 Till Isis' Elders reel, their pupils' sport. **1813** SCOTT *Trierm.* II. x, Reeling from the desperate race, He stood, exhausted, still. **1843** LYTTON *Last Bar.* I. iv, Now reeling,—now falling, he still dragged on his limbs. **1865** KINGSLEY *Herew.* ii, He saw the huge carcass bend, reel, roll over slowly to one side, dead.

b. *transf.* of parts of the body, etc.

1590 SPENSER *F.Q.* I. viii. 20 Whiles yet his feeble feet for faintnesse reeld. **1818** SHELLEY *Rev. Islam* x. viii, His footsteps reel On the fresh blood. **1858** KINGSLEY *Poems* 62 Knees which reel as marches quicken.

c. *fig.* in various applications.

1654 WHITLOCK *Zootomia* 162 They are..swelled with pride,..and even reeling with Sedition. **1726** BOLINGBROKE *Study Hist.* viii. Wks. 1754 II. 448 [France] went on indeed, but she staggered and reeled under the burden of the war. **1858** O. W. HOLMES *Aut. Breakf.-t.* vii. 61 We are hustled into maturity reeling with our passions and imaginations.

6. Of things: To shake, rock, or swing violently; to totter, tremble; †to become unsteady.

1495 [see REELING *vbl. sb.*[1]]. *a* **1591** H. SMITH *Six Serm.* (1594) 89 The water vnder him tossing, the ship about him reeling. **1607** SHAKS. *Cor.* II. i. 121, I will make my very house reele to night. **1648** MARKHAM *Housew. Gard.* III. x, Stakes rot and reel, Rain and Weather eat your hives and covers. **1660** F. BROOKE tr. *Le Blanc's Trav.* 335 The vessel reeling quite down on one side..was immediately filled with water. *c* **1720** *Ship in a Storm* x, The faithless Flood forsook her Keel,..Stun'd she forgot awhile to reel. **1791** COWPER *Iliad* I. 651 All around The Sov'reign's..head his curls Ambrosial shook, and the huge mountain reeled. **1814** CARY *Dante, Inf.* XXXI. 97 By violent earth-quake rock'd Ne'er shook a tower, so reeling to its base, As Ephialtes. **1864** TENNYSON *Voyage* 15 So quick the run, We felt the good ship shake and reel. **1869** PHILLIPS *Vesuv.* ii. 12 Making the whole country reel and totter.

transf. **1818** BYRON *Ch. Har.* IV. lxiii, An earthquake reel'd unheededly away! None felt stern Nature rocking at his feet.

b. *fig.* of kingdoms or institutions. †Also const. *from* (a state or condition).

fig. **1577–87** HOLINSHED *Chron.* I. 140/1 The kingdome of Britaine began now to reele from their owne estate, and leane to an alteration. **1628** FORD *Lover's Mel.* I. ii, When commonwealths totter and reel from that nobility and ancient virtue which renowns the great. **1663** BUTLER *Hud.* I. i. 271 To stand fast As long as Monarchy should last; But when the state should hap to reel [etc.]. **1868** STANLEY *Westm. Abb.* iv. 341 When Church and State were reeling to their foundations.

c. To fall or roll hurriedly. *rare.*

1593 DRAYTON *Eclog.* viii. 36 From whose high top the high soon'st downward reele. **1818** BYRON *Juan* I. cxxiv, The showering grapes In Bacchanal profusion reel to earth, Purple and gushing.

7. To walk with the body swinging violently from side to side; to make one's way in a swaying or staggering manner, esp. under the effects of intoxication. Also in fig. context.

1607 MIDDLETON *Five Gallants* III. iii, Take him when he reels from a tavern late. **1615** G. SANDYS *Trav.* 291 Drunkards reeling along the shore. **1726–31** WALDRON *Descr. Isle of Man* (1865) 22 Being unable to reel any further, he lay down at the door. **1761** CHURCHILL *Night* Poems 1767 I. 74 Reel in a drunkard, and reel out a saint. **1819** SHELLEY *Peter Bell 3rd* III. vii, Those patriots..Who gorge, before they reel to bed. **1821** —— *Prometh. Unb.* II. iv. 22 Each one reels Under the load towards the pit of death. **1849** MACAULAY *Hist. Eng.* v. I. 633 Permitting them to sleep on watch, to reel drunk about the streets.

transf. **1592** SHAKS. *Rom. & Jul.* II. iii. 3 Darknesse like a drunkard reeles From forth daies path. *c* **1600** —— *Sonn.* vii, When from high-most pich..Like feeble age he reeleth from the day. *a* **1704** T. BROWN *Praise Drunkenness* Wks. 1730 I. 32 Epicurus whose drunken atoms reel'd into order.

fig. **1650** FULLER *Pisgah* IV. vii. 138 Shunning open profaneness, they reeled into spirituall pride. *a* **1661** —— *Worthies* (1840) III. 432 This age, wherein so many have reeled into damnable errors. *a* **1679** W. OUTRAM *Serm.* (1682) 53 Christianity..now is reel'd to the other extreme.

b. To move, fly, or dash, rapidly and unsteadily.

1727–46 THOMSON *Summer* 183 All th' extinguish'd stars, would loosening reel Wide from their spheres. **1860** HOLLAND *Miss Gilbert* iv. 73 He..watched the little gig as it reeled off toward the mill at the highest speed. **1878** BROWNING *Poets Croisic* ii, Redly up and out and off they reeled Like disconcerted imps, those thousand sparks.

8. *trans.* To cause to roll, whirl, or stagger; to impel violently. Now *rare.*

13.. *Gaw. & Gr. Knt.* 304 Runischly his rede ȝȝen he reled aboute. **1513** DOUGLAS *Æneis* II. vii. 130 With the preis we war relet of that steid. **1590** SPENSER *F.Q.* I. v. 35 Sisyphus an huge round stone did reele Against an hill. **1595** BARNFIELD *Cynthia* v, In his hand was placed Fortunes wheele: The which he often turn'd, and oft did reele. **1613** J. DAVIES *Muse's Teares* B 2 b, Our Hopes, Which now this Blast doth reele, and backward beare! **1800** MOORE *Anacreon* ii. 12 Our feet shall catch the elastic bound, And reel us through the dance's round.

b. *refl.* To throw (oneself) with a stagger.

1890 CLARK RUSSELL *Ocean Trag.* I. ix. 191 He..swung, or rather reeled, himself into [a chair].

9. To reel through or along (a street). *rare*$^{-1}$.

1606 SHAKS. *Ant. & Cl.* I. iv. 20 To sit And keepe the turne of Tipling with a Slaue, To reele the streets at noone.

reel (riːl), *v.*[2] Forms: 4 rely, reole, 4–5 rele, (5 relyn), 6 reele, *Sc.* reill, 7– reel. [f. REEL *sb.*[1]]

1. a. *trans.* To wind (thread, silk, etc.) on a reel. Also *absol.*, to perform, or be engaged in, this kind of work.

1393 LANGL. *P. Pl.* C. x. 81 Boþe to karde and to kembe ..To rube and to rely [*v.rr.* rele, reole]. **14..** *Voc.* in Wr.-Wülcker 586/31 *Girgillo* [to rele]. *c* **1440** *Promp. Parv.* 429/1 Relyn, wythe a reele, *alabriso.* *c* **1462** *Wright's Chaste Wife* 349 Thowe schalt rubbe, rele, and spynne, And þou wolt eny mete wynne. **1548** THOMAS *Ital. Dict.* (1567), *Innaspare*, to reele, as they reele silke or thread. **1560** ROLLAND *Crt. Venus* II. 694 Ilk ane in hand ane Reill..To reill thair hankis so small of reid gold wyir. **1629** MASSINGER *Picture* IV. ii, You should reel well What he spins, if you give your mind to it. *Ibid.* v. i, The other too reels well For his time. **1641** R. BAILLIE *Lett. & Jrnls.* (1841) I. 334 Proclamations were read dischargeing to sell any yarne but reeled in such a fashion. **1732** *Acc. Workhouses* 138 That fit persons be appointed to reel the work. **1789** *Gentl. Mag.* Suppl. 1200/2 He invented a machine to spin and reel Cotton at one operation. **1825** J. NICHOLSON *Operat. Mechanic* 387 If the yarn has to be packed for the market, it is reeled upon a frame. **1886** *Mag. of Art* Dec. 46/1 The silk used was..the same as that reeled at the present time by the Indians, Chinese, and Japanese.

b. *Angling.* To wind (the line) on the reel. Also with *up*, and *absol.*

1854 L. LLOYD *Scandin. Adv.* I. 194 The line..is reeled around the two pins in the handle. **1873** G. C. DAVIES *Mount. & Mere* ii. 10 We reel up and seek the shelter of the wood. **1883** *Century Mag.* July 381/2 Then he reeled slowly, keeping the minnow near the surface. **1884** BRAITHWAITE *Salmonidæ Westmld.* v. 21 The angler reels up his line as quickly as possible.

c. To fill (a spool) with thread.

1774 KEITH *Farmer's Ha'* vii, The auld gudewife the pirney reels Wi' tenty hand.

2. to reel off. a. To take *off* by reeling.

1530 PALSGR. 684/1 Rele this skayne of the blades and than come dyne. **1756** *Gentl. Mag.* XXVI. 138 The sixth book describes the manner of reeling off the silk from the pod. **1789** *Trans. Soc. Arts* (ed. 2) II. 164, I reeled off every single thread. **1880** C. M. MASON *Forty Shires* 94 The silk is called raw after it has been reeled off the cocoons. **1884** BLAKELEE *Industr. Cycl.* 123 Twine wound upon this may be reeled off at pleasure.

b. *transf.* To rattle *off* (a story, song, etc.) without pause or effort. Also, to cover (a distance, etc.) rapidly; to accomplish or perform without pause or effort. Also const. *out* (*rare*).

1837 MARRYAT *Dog-fiend* ix, Well reeled off, Billy. **1870** 'MARK TWAIN' in *Galaxy* Dec. 883/2 The hands [of my watch] would straightway begin to spin round and round... She would reel off the next twenty-four hours in six or seven minutes. **1872** —— *Roughing It* iv. 46 We reeled off ten or twelve miles. **1885** *Pall Mall Budget* 19 June 31/1 General Butler..can reel off nautical stories by the yard. **1890** MCCARTHY *French Revol.* I. 118 He reeled off a world of insipid verses. **1928** *Granta* 30 Nov. 172/2 Milton just reeled out bits about Christmas when he was up here. **1961** *Trains Illustr.* Nov. 685/2 The 11 miles between posts 137 and 148 were reeled off at an average of 93.8 m.p.h. **1972** J. MOSEDALE *Football* iv. 50 The Rams became the most exciting team in football, reeling off six straight victories. **1976** *0–10 Cricket Scene* (Austral.) 33/2 In a fine performance in which he reeled off 35.5 overs, he captured 5–148 in the Third Test in Australia at Adelaide in 1974.

3. a. To draw *out*, as with a reel; to draw *through* (something), or cause to move, by means of a reel. Also, to draw *in*, as with a reel.

1855 BROWNING *Childe Roland* xxiv, That harrow fit to reel Men's bodies out like silk. **1868** JOYNSON *Metals* 105 Wire is reeled through the zinc, into which it is forced to dip by a fork or other contrivance. **1891** *Textile Industries* 12 Dec. 69 Reel the stuff well in the solution. **1942** *Tee Emm* (Air Ministry) II. 57 A large passenger aircraft was struck while its trailing aerial was still reeled out. **1975** *Offshore* Aug. 121/1 The test pipeline was reeled from the Chickasaw into water depths of approximately 1,000 to 1,040 feet. **1978** *Sci. Amer.* Feb. 158/1 To launch a kite hold it about 20 degrees forward of the vertical and in approximately the correct flying attitude, release it as a gust of wind passes and slowly reel out line. *Ibid.* 158/2 To bring the kite down you probably will reel in the kite line. **1979** *Amat. Photographer* 10 Jan. 73/2 It's also dangerous, and illegal, to have permanent power points in a bathroom, so you must reel in an extension cable each time so you can use your enlarger, safelights, etc.

b. *Angling.* To draw in (a fish, etc.) by reeling up the line. Also in fig. context, and *intr.* (const. *out*) to become uncoiled from a reel. So **'reel-out** *sb.*

1881 *Confess. Frivolous Girl* 181 Once hook him and you are all right... You can reel him in then at your pleasure. **1883** *Century Mag.* July 379/2 The Professor..soon reeled the bass within a few feet. **1894** *Outing* (U.S.) XXIV. 228/2 The minnow is reeled nearly to the tip of the rod. **1975** *Daily Tel.* 11 Sept. 3/7 Three cases of seat belts reeling out with no load being taken by the belt until all the webbing was off the reel, and four cases of excessive reel-out.

4. *intr.* To make a noise like that of a reel when in motion.

1747 [see REELING *vbl. sb.*[2] 2]. **1899** *Longm. Mag.* Dec. 154 The grasshopper warblers which were reeling from many a 'tangled watercourse' a fortnight ago are now silent.

reel (riːl), *v.*[3] [f. REEL *sb.*[3]] *intr.* and *trans.* To dance a reel.

1768 ROSS *Helenore* I. 21 The summer cauls were dancing here an' there, An' clouds of midges reeling in the air. **1790** BURNS *Tam o' Shanter* 147 The dancers quick and quicker flew; They reel'd, they set, they cross'd, they cleekit. **1833** MARRYAT *P. Simple* xxxv, Troubridge opened the ball.., making them reel 'Tom Collins', whether or no. **1843** NICHOLSON *Hist. & Tradit. Tales* 241 Loud laughed Old Nick and danced and reeled.

reelable ('riːləb(ə)l), *a.* [f. REEL *v.*[2] + -ABLE.] That can be reeled or wound on a reel.

1887 *Encycl. Brit.* XXII. 60/1 At least six species of Bombyx..form reelable cocoons. *Ibid.* 60/2 The reelable fibre is as a rule thickest..at the middle portion.

'reel-bird. [f. REEL *sb.*[1]] (See quot.)

1888 NEWTON in *Encycl. Brit.* XXIV. 367/1 In those parts of England where it [the grasshopper lark or warbler] was formerly most abundant it was known as the Reeler or Reel-bird.

re-e'lect, *v.* [RE- 5 a.] *trans.* To elect again.

1601 HOLLAND *Pliny* I. 181 Those Senators..whom he had either chosen or re-elected in his Censorship. **1681** LUTTRELL *Brief Rel.* (1857) I. 127 One Mr. Broom being some time since chosen, but not qualified,..he was this day ..reelected. **1769** *Junius Lett.* xix. (1771) 103 [He] was expelled, re-elected, and admitted to take his seat in the same parliament. **1844** THIRLWALL *Greece* lxv. VIII. 361 Philopœmen was re-elected for the following year. **1863** H. COX *Instit.* I. viii. 128 A member expelled may, upon the issue of a new writ, be re-elected by his former constituents.

Hence **re-e'lected** *ppl. a.*; **re-electa'bility**.

1838 J. L. ADOLPHUS in J. G. Lockhart *Life Scott* VII. vi 221 He spoke very beautifully and warmly of the re-elected candidate who sat by him. **1898** B. GREGORY *Side Lights* 421 The re-electability of the best known Wesleyan Methodist minister. **1974** *Times* 4 Mar. 2/7 Re-elected Conservatives are anxious to make their views known.

re-e'lection. [RE- 5 a; cf. RE-ELECT *v.*] The action of re-electing; a fresh election; the fact of being re-elected.

a **1745** SWIFT (J.), Several acts have been made and rendered ineffectual by leaving the power of re-election open. **1756** H. WALPOLE *Lett. to Mann* 29 Nov., The Parliament meets on Thursday, but will adjourn for about ten days for the re-elections. **1824** BYRON *Juan* XVI. xcv, Safe conduct through the rocks of re-elections. **1884** *Law Times* 8 Mar. 3 The Examiners above named are re-eligible, and intend to offer themselves for re-election.

reeled (riːld), *ppl. a.* [f. REEL *v.*[2]] Wound on a reel.

1776–7 *Act 17 Geo. III*, c. 11 § 14 The reeler..of such false or short reeled yarn. **1831** G. R. PORTER *Silk Manuf.* 152 To obtain one pound of reeled silk, requires 12 pounds of cocoons. **1851** L. D. B. GORDON in *Art Jrnl. Illustr. Catal.* p. ii **/1 Samples of the cocoons, and of the reeled or raw silk of these countries.

reeler[1] ('riːlə(r)). [f. REEL *v.*[2] + -ER[1].]

1. a. One who reels or winds yarn, cord, etc., upon a reel; also, one who employs such workers.

1598 FLORIO, *Innaspatore*, a reeler or winder of yarne. **1611** COTGR. s.v. *Garde, Faire la garde*, to make fast; (a phrase vsed by reelers, or winders of yarne). **1776–7** [see REELED *ppl. a.*]. **1825** J. NICHOLSON *Operat. Mechanic* 395 The slubs which may have been left in the silk by the negligence of the foreign reeler. **1844** G. DODD *Textile Manuf.* vi. 175 When the winder or reeler has purchased the cocoons [etc.]. **1891** *Textile Industries* 12 Dec. 61/1 However careless the reeler may be, the reel is stopped instantly.

b. (See quot.)

1893 L. KELLERN *Soldiers at Sea* 50 Told off as Reelers, to haul in the reel, which tests the ship's rate of progress.

c. The grasshopper-warbler, *Locustella nævia.*

1871–4 NEWTON *Yarrell's Brit. Birds* I. 385 In the more marshy parts of England..this bird has long been known as the 'Reeler'—from the resemblance of its song to the noise of the reel used..by the hand-spinners of wool.

d. *Cant* (after *peeler*). A policeman.

1879 *Macm. Mag.* Oct. 502/1 A reeler came to the cell and cross-kiddled (questioned) me.

2. An instrument for reeling. In mod. use, a machine which winds paper, yarn, etc., on to reels.

1598 FLORIO, *Indeuenatoio*, a reeler or reeling sticke. **1629** MASSINGER *Picture* v. i, *Ubaldo.* I have not spittle enough to wet my fingers When I draw my flax from my distaff. *Ricardo.* Nor I, strength To raise my hand to the top of my reeler. **1906** [see RE-REEL *v.*]. **1907** [see *cop-winder* s.v. COP *sb.*[2] 8]. **1929** CLAPPERTON & HENDERSON *Mod. Paper-Making* xvi. 246 Many defects in the paper..will..cause a break at the reeler, owing to the high tension of the paper as it passes from the roll to the reeler bar. **1952** F. H. NORRIS *Paper & Paper Making* xvii. 246 The reeler is equipped with a yardage counter and may have four winding drums. **1955** S. C. GILMOUR *Paper* vi. 59 On most modern machines..a drum reeler is more common.

3. *Cinemat.* Used with a qualifying number, as *two-reeler* or *two reeler*, to designate a film consisting of the given number of reels. orig. *U.S.* Cf. REEL *sb.*[1] 3 c.

1916 *Chicago Herald* 17 Feb. 3/4 Essanay will make an international release of the eight-reeler. **1922** H. L. WILSON *Merton of Movies* v. 90, I got another two reeler to pull off after this one. **1938** F. H. RICKETSON *Managem. Motion Picture Theatres* 121 Coming-attraction trailers can be spotted after the newsreel. A two-reeler, if the length of the feature permits, or a one-reel comedy can follow. **1976** L. KENNEDY *Presumption of Innocence* ii. 88 A kind of mad, surrealistic quality, like an early Chaplin two-reeler.

Hence **'reelerman**, one who operates a reeler (sense 2).

1929 CLAPPERTON & HENDERSON *Mod. Paper-Making* xvi. 247 The yardage is kept on two different tickets by the reelerman.

reeler[2] ('riːlə(r)). [f. REEL *v.*[1] + -ER[1].] **a.** A stagger; esp. in slang phr. *to cop a reeler*, to get drunk. **b.** One who sways or staggers; a drunken person.

1937 J. CURTIS *You're in Racket, Too* v. 60 Make him swear blind he'll be quiet as he comes up the stairs, see? Of course, if he's copped a reeler you'll have to skip it. **1960** A. CLARKE *Later Poems* (1961) 76 Though every firework has been banned, Student or reeler from a band Flung it.

re-'elevate, *v.* [RE- 5 a.] To elevate again.

a **1834** COLERIDGE cited by WORCESTER (1846). **1873** J. GEIKIE *Gt. Ice Age* xxii. 290 Then, finally, the land was re-elevated to its present level. **1895** *Minutes 9th Nat. Counc. Congreg. Ch.* (U.S.) 242 To re-elevate the standard of scholarship which has been so unfortunately..lowered.

So **re-ele'vation.** (Chiefly *Geol.*)

1817 J. SCOTT *Paris Revis.* (ed. 4) 395 Resting its re-elevation on the foundation of popular choice. **1868** LYELL *Princ. Geol.* II. xxxi. (ed. 10) II. 187 It seems impossible to explain the position of this buried hut, without imagining, first a subsidence..then a re-elevation. **1876** PAGE *Adv. Text-bk. Geol.* xiv. 258 The frequent subsidences and re-elevations.

reel foot. *Sc.* [? f. REEL *sb.*[1]] A club-foot. So **reel-footed** *a.*

1867 H. SCOTT *Fasti Eccl. Scotic.* II. 586 A reel foot marred his personal appearance. **1887** SERVICE *Dr. Duguid* I. xxiii. 155 James being reel-fitted. **1902** *Brit. Med. Jrnl.* 19 July 209 A child..is 'reel-footed' if there is a club-foot.

re-eligi'bility. [f. next + -ITY.] Eligibility for re-election to the same office.

1787 HAMILTON *Federalist* No. 72 With a positive duration [of the presidency]..I connect the circumstance of re-eligibility. **1788** JEFFERSON *Let.* 7 Feb., There is another strong feature in the new constitution, which I..strongly dislike. That is, the perpetual re-eligibility of the President. **1888** BRYCE *Amer. Commw.* II. xli. II. 103 The governor.. is elected directly, not..by a college of electors... Some States limit his re-eligibility.

re-'eligible, *a.* [RE- 5 a.] Capable of being re-elected to the same office.

1802 *Ann. Reg.* 644 The president is to exercise his functions for ten years, and to be indefinitely reeligible.

1843 *Penny Cycl.* XXVI. 26/2 The person so appointed to vacate is not re-eligible for the ensuing year. **1884** *Law Times* 8 Mar. 3 The Examiners above-named are re-eligible.

reeling ('riːlɪŋ), *vbl. sb.*[1] [f. REEL *v.*[1] + -ING[1].] The action of staggering, etc.

1375 BARBOUR *Bruce* XIII. 265 The king Robert be thair relyng Saw thai war neir discomfyting. **1495** *Trevisa's Barth. De P.R.* (W. de W.) v. xx. 126 The passyons of the teeth ben dyuers..brekynge, and brusynge.., relynge and wag[ging] and fallynge. *a* **1500** *Peebles to Play* ii, For reiling thair micht na man rest, For garray and for glew. *a* **1591** H. SMITH *Six Serm.* (1594) 89 As if he should say, neither the winds blowing..nor the ships reeling..should..waken him from his sleepe. **1607–12** BACON *Ess., Counsel* (Arb.) 312 They will..be full of inconstancye,..like the reeling of a drunken Man. **1664** H. MORE *Myst. Iniq.* 329 Singing and dancing and drinking and reeling were usual concomitants of all the Pagan Holy-days. **1736** E. ERSKINE *Serm.* Wks. 1871 II. 406 The Avenger of thy blood will take care of thee in public reelings. **1781** COWPER *Conversat.* 862 Though such continual zigzags in a book, Such drunken reelings, have an awkward look. **1899** *Allbutt's Syst. Med.* VII. 69 [A gait] in which there is unsteadiness, titubation, and reeling like a drunken man.

Comb. **1610** SHAKS. *Temp.* v. i. 279 Trinculo is reeling ripe: where should they Finde this grand Liquor that hath gilded 'em? **1706** E. WARD *Wooden World Diss.* (1708) 100 When he's reeling drunk ashore, he takes it for granted to be a Storm abroad.

reeling ('riːlɪŋ), *vbl. sb.*[2] [f. REEL *v.*[2] + -ING[1].]

1. a. The action of winding on a reel. Also *concr.*, reeled yarn or the like.

1589 RIDER *Bibl. Schol.*, A Reeling, *alabratio.* **1603** DEKKER *Grissil* v. i, Janiculo, leave your fish-catching, and you your reeling. **1653** *Public Gen. Acts* 179 Abuses..in the Reeling of the Yarns. **1727–41** CHAMBERS *Cycl.* s.v. *Reel*, The reel used..in the reeling or winding of silks. **1789** *Trans. Soc. Arts* VII. 143 It was..afterwards reeled off from those bobbins, and in the reeling passed through warm water. **1803** W. TAYLOR in *Ann. Rev.* I. 432 The purchases [of silk] are made about the end of August when the reelings terminate. **1884** MCLAREN *Spinning* (ed. 2) 235 The processes of twisting, reeling, and scouring. **1894** *Cassell's New Technical Educator* IV. 369/1 The reelings are then weighed and made up into bundles. **1906** W. MACFARLANE *Princ. & Pract. Iron & Steel Manuf.* iv. 47 Bars for certain purposes are straightened by reeling. **1952** F. H. NORRIS *Paper & Paper Making* xvii. 246 There are also the faults.. which in turn will add their quota of troubles in supercalendering and reeling. **1973** J. G. TWEEDDALE *Materials Technol.* II. iv. 95 A simplified form of a two-high mill of this kind can be used for straightening rolls and tubes by causing spiral flexture [*sic*] in the cold condition, a process called reeling. **1974** *Encycl. Brit. Macropædia* XVIII. 173/2 Reeling is the process of unwinding raw silk filament from the cocoon directly onto a holder.

b. *attrib.* and *Comb.*, as ***reeling apparatus, arrangement, drive, establishment, machine, stick.***

1598 FLORIO, *Indeuenatoio*, a reeler or reeling sticke. **1835** URE *Philos. Manuf.* 265 The reeling apparatus used in France. **1853** —— *Dict. Arts* (ed. 4) II. 616 The cocoons are prepared at the reeling establishment into raw silk. *Ibid.*, The reeling machines in the Tyrol. **1887** *Encycl. Brit.* XXII. 61/2 A sectional view of the reeling apparatus and arrangements..is shown in fig. 12. **1904** HARBORD & HALL *Metallurgy of Steel* xxxii. 506 Both are passed through the reeling machine. This consists of a pair of conical rolls, revolving both in the same direction, and lying side by side, their axes being placed, not horizontally, but inclined to the horizon a few degrees in opposite directions, so as to cross each other at a slight angle in the middle of their length. **1926** J. B. WALKER *Story of Steel* xii. 117 The next step is to pass the tube..through what is known as the reeling machine... In this operation any mill-scale is removed; the tubes are given a smooth, burnished surface. **1962** G. A. T. BURDETT *Automatic Control Handbk.* vii. 9 This is the basis of a large number of electronic control schemes embracing ..coiling and reeling drives [etc.]. **1971** W. K. V. GALE *Iron & Steel Industry: Dict. Terms* 168 *Reeling machine*, a machine which straightens round steel bars by passing them between specially shaped rollers which induce reverse bending.

2. The production of a humming sound.

1747 R. MAXWELL *Bee-Master* (1750) 35 This reeling is occasioned, by a great many of the Bees flying, and making a confused Motion and Noise in the..Hive. **1899** *Longm. Mag.* Dec. 152 It was more sustained than the longest reeling of the grasshopper warbler that I have heard.

reeling ('riːlɪŋ), *ppl. a.* [f. REEL *v.*[1] + -ING[2].]

1. That reels, in senses of the vb.

1577 HOLINSHED *Chron.* I. 69/1 Honorius, perceiuing the reeling state of the empire, determined foorthwith to recouer it. **1602** MARSTON *Ant. & Mel.* I. Wks. 1856 I. 17 With that he totterd from the reeling decke, And downe he sunke. **1649** JER. TAYLOR *Gt. Exemp.* III. Ad §16. 177 With troubled spirits and a reeling faith. **1697** DRYDEN *Virg. Past.* v. 46 Daphnis did Rites to Bacchus first ordain; And holy Revels for his reeling Train. **1768** ROSS *Helenore* I. 55 The man..in his fury, an' in his reeling eyn, Thinks that the ane he wanted she had been. **1781** COWPER *Expost.* 306 War lays a burden on the reeling state. **1849** LONGF. *Building the Ship* 242 The stress and the strain Of the wind and the reeling main.

2. Characterized by reeling; causing to reel.

1614 MARKHAM *Cheap Husb.* IV. x. (1668) 99 If your Goats be troubled with the Staggers or Reeling Evil. **1875** MANNING *Mission H. Ghost* ii. 54 That sort of gross reeling intoxication by which men..shame themselves in the streets. **1896** *Westm. Gaz.* 27 Feb. 1/1 The Liberal Party suffered a reeling blow yesterday.

Hence **'reelingly** *adv.*

1621 LADY M. WROTH *Urania* 481 Suddenly, and reelingly he ran with his last fury vpon him. **1657** J. SERGEANT *Schism Dispach't* 62 Is this a sober discourse, which falls reelingly to the ground of it self, when none pushes it?

†**reel-pot.** *Obs. rare*[−1]. [f. REEL *v.*[1]] One who makes the (drinking) pot go round.

1604 T. M. *Black Bk.* in *Middleton's Wks.* (Bullen) VIII. 28 There I heard..how many perjurds [were] in France, and how many reel-pots in Germany.

reely, reelly ('riːlɪ). Representing a vulgar pronunciation of REALLY *adv.*[2]

In quot. 1792 representing the pronunciation of a German speaker.

1792 F. BURNEY *Jrnl.* May (1972) I. 152 Mrs. Schwellenberg exclaimed 'But, Miss Berner, I hear it bin reelly true you will Marry!' **1910** H. G. WELLS *Hist. Mr. Polly* vi. 158 Thought my bicycle was on fire... All right reely. **1933** E. A. ROBERTSON *Ordinary Families* x. 222 'E's a good boy to us, reelly, Ted is. **1939** JOYCE *Finnegans Wake* (1964) II. 527 Of course it was downright verry wickred of him, reely meeting me disguised. **1967** N. MARSH *Death at Dolphin* i. 9 'Well—I don't know, reely, if we've anybody free at the moment,' said the clerk.

‖**reem** (riːm). [a. Heb. *rᵉʾēm* (also *rēym* in Job xxxix. 9–10), rendered in the Vulgate by *rhinoceros* and *unicornis*, and by Wyclif and later Eng. versions, *unicorn*.] The Hebrew name of an animal mentioned in the Old Testament, now identified with the wild ox.

1719 YOUNG *Par. Job* Wks. 1757 I. 215 Will the tall Reem, which knows no Lord but Me, Low at the crib, and ask an alms of thee? [**1845** KITTO *Cycl. Bibl. Lit.* s.v., From the fact that the reëm is classed in scripture with bulls or bullocks.. it has been concluded that he was of the bovine species, and probably the buffalo or wild ox. **1886** W. HOUGHTON in *Academy* 24 Apr. 292 The identification of the Hebrew *reêm* with the wild ox (*Bos primigenius*) is one of the most certain of all Bible animal names.]

reem, obs. f. REALM, REAM; var. REME *v.*, to cry, shout; obs. f. RIME, hoarfrost.

re-embark (riːɛm'bɑːk), *v.* Also 7–8 reim-. [RE- 5 a. Cf. F. *rembarquer* (1549), It. *rimbarcare* (Florio), Sp. *reembarcar.*]

1. *trans.* To put (a person or thing) on board ship again. Also †const. *into.*

1611 COTGR., *Rembarquer*, to reimbarke, to put into a ship againe. **1654** H. L'ESTRANGE *Chas. I* (1655) 18 The Admirall re-imbarques all and..plies for the Southward Cape. **1687** LOVELL tr. *Thevenot's Trav.* II. 171 Goods.. which..he was necessitated to reimbark. **1702** *Lond. Gaz.* No. 3850/3 They were reimbarking the Troops on board the Ships. **1758** *Ann. Reg.* I. 101/1 They were..hoisted into the ship, and ..re-imbarked into the boats. **1836** MACGILLIVRAY tr. *Humboldt's Trav.* xviii. 250 The boat having been got up, they re-embarked their instruments and provisions.

refl. **1622** CAPT. SMITH *Wks.* I. 257 Reimbarking myselfe in a Bark of 60 Tuns.

fig. **1647** WARD *Simp. Cobler* (1843) 80 It may re-imbarque themselves and you all into a deadly relapse of scorne and calamity.

2. *intr.* To go on board ship again. Also const. *in.*

1585 T. WASHINGTON tr. *Nicholay's Voy.* II. v. 35 We had made our accompt to reembarke and depart. **1747** CARTE *Hist. Eng.* I. 288 The Danes still re-imbarking when they found opposition in any place, and landing in some other. **1777** ROBERTSON *Hist. Amer.* II. v. 23 He..issued orders that the army should be in readiness next day to reimbark for Cuba. **1856** KANE *Arct. Expl.* II. xxviii. 279, I called my officers together..and prepared to re-embark. **1878** GLADSTONE *Prim. Homer* xi. 131 After re-embarking, he exasperates the monster with his pungent addresses.

fig. *a* **1711** KEN *Edmund* Poet. Wks. 1721 II. 159 His Soul, which while he slept at Anchor lay, Began to reimbark. **1812** *Examiner* 24 Aug. 542/2 In such a cause his very selfishness is a security for his not re-embarking.

transf. **1751** SMOLLETT *Per. Pic.* ci, He re-embarked in his hackney-coach.

Hence **re-em'barking** *vbl. sb.*

1611 FLORIO, *Rimbarcamento*, a re-imbarking. **1790** BEATSON *Nav. & Mil. Mem.* I. 321 Brigadiers Graham and O'Farrel..agreed to the reimbarking of the troops.

re-embar'kation. Also 8 re(-)im-. [RE- 5 a.] The action of re-embarking.

1716 *Lond. Gaz.* No. 5470/2 They knew nothing of the Re-imbarkation. **1757** SMOLLETT *Hist. Eng.* xviii. §5 After the re-embarkation of the troops. **1790** BEATSON *Nav. & Mil. Mem.* I. 323 They unanimously declared themselves for the reimbarkation. **1847** GROTE *Greece* II. xxxvi. IV. 471 They repulsed the Athenians from the sea-shore and secured a safe re-embarkation.

So **re-em'barkment.** [Cf. F. *rembarquement.*]

1728 G. CARLETON *Mem. Eng. Officer* 95 The heavy artillery landed for the siege was return'd aboard the ships, and everything in appearance prepar'd for a re-imbarkment. **1758** *Ann. Reg.* I. 66/1 The smaller [squadron]..was designed..to favour the landing and reimbarkment. **1915** J. CHURCHILL *Jrnl.* 21 Mar. in M. Gilbert *Winston S. Churchill* (1972) III. Compan. I. 722 The re-embarkment would take longer.

re-em'battle, *v.* In 7 reim-. [RE- 5 a.] *trans.* To draw up again in battle array.

1667 MILTON *P.L.* VI. 794 They..at the sight Took envie, and aspiring to his highth, Stood reimbattell'd fierce.

re-em'bellish, *v.* Also 7 re-im-. [RE- 5 a.] *trans.* To embellish anew. Hence **re-em'bellishing** *vbl. sb.*

1611 FLORIO, *Rimbellire*, to re-imbellish. *Ibid.*, *Rabbellimento*, a rebeautifying, a re-embellishing. **1655** tr. *Com. Hist. Francion* II. 43 Ceruse and Vermillion were not capable to re-imbellish my face.

re-em'bodied, *ppl. a.* [f. RE-EMBODY *v.* + -ED[1].] Reincarnated. So **re-em'bodiment.**

1901 'A. HOPE' *Tristram of Blent* xiii. 175 That re-embodiment or resurrection of her in the girl who moved and talked and sat like her, who had her ways though not her face. **1924** W. B. SELBIE *Psychol. Relig.* 271 In Indo-European folk-lore, dogs, wolves, and hares represent such re-embodied spirits.

re-em'body, *v.* Also 7, 9 reim-. [RE- 5 a.] To embody again. **a.** *trans.*

1802 JAMES *Milit. Dict.* s.v., The militia is disbanded, and partially reimbodied for 28 days in every year during peace. **1862** MERIVALE *Rom. Emp.* lvii. (1865) VII. 121 It became necessary to re-embody the praetorian and the urban guards. **1873** in B. Stewart *Conserv. Force* vii. 173, I propose ..now to reëmbody my views in a more popular form.

†**b.** *intr.* for *refl.* (See EMBODY 5 b.) *Obs.*

a **1691** BOYLE (J.), Quicksilver broken into little globes, the parts brought to touch immediately reimbody.

re-em'bosom, *v.* Also 7 reim-. [RE- 5 a.] *trans.* To embosom again.

1641 HEYLIN *Hist. Episc.* II. (1657) 369 Some..had been Reconciled and reimbosomed with the Church. **1656** —— *Surv. France* 56 [Henry IV. of France] once more re-embosom'd himself into the Roman Synagogue. **1878** BROWNING *La Saisiaz* 129 Treasure oft was disembosomed. .. Disembosomed, re-embosomed.

re-em'brace, *v.* Also 7 re-im-, reim-. [RE- 5 a. Cf. F. *rembrasser*, †*rembracier.*] *trans.* and *intr.* To embrace again, in *lit.* and *fig.* senses.

1611 FLORIO, *Rimbracciare*, to imbrace againe, to re-imbrace. **1633** PRYNNE *1st Pt. Histrio-m.* 57 Why should you re-embrace..the things, which you haue thus abiured? **1655** tr. *Com. Hist. Francion* IX. 4 His Daughter and her Sweet-heart coming to re-imbrace each other. *a* **1711** KEN *Preparatives* Poet. Wks. 1721 IV. 48 When their Souls they re-embrace. **1742** YOUNG *Nt. Th.* v. 1044 He takes his Leave, To re-embrace in Extasies, at Eve. **1855** BROWNING *In a Year* i, Bitterly we re-embrace, Single still. **1858** CARLYLE *Fredk. Gt.* VIII. iii. (1872) III. 13 His Majesty, who wept like a paternal bear, on reëmbracing Wilhelmina.

So **re-em'brace** *sb.*, a renewed embrace; **re-em'bracement.**

1611 FLORIO, *Rabbracciamenti*, re-imbracements. **1868** BROWNING *Ring & Bk.* XI. 2316 If, fighting quietly, the jaws enjoy One re-embrace in mid back-bone.

re-em'broider, *v.* [RE- 5 a.] *trans.* To ornament with additional embroidery. So **re-em'broidered** *ppl. a.*; **re-em'broidering** *vbl. sb.* (also *attrib.*).

1927 *Daily Express* 8 Apr. 5 The gown is of ivory silk lace, re-embroidered with small china beads. *Ibid.*, Interesting example of the re-embroidering vogue. In this case an embroidery of coloured taffeta and bugle beads was applied to black Spanish lace. **1963** *Times* 24 Jan. 12/4 Re-embroidered white lace is used. **1968** J. IRONSIDE *Fashion Alphabet* 235 *Re-embroidered*: This is a lace with an all-over motif outlined and emphasised by re-embroidering either with silk thread, ribbon, braid or metallic yarns. **1974** *Times-Picayune* (New Orleans) 15 Aug. v. 6/1 The bride.. wore a peau de soie gown styled with a sculptured yoke of re-embroidered lace and a cameo neckline.

re-em'broil, *v.* [RE- 5 a.] To embroil again.

1718 BLACKMORE *Alfred* x. (1723) 363 Lest this audacious Tribe..Disturb the Throne and re-embroil the State.

re-emburse, -ment, obs. ff. REIMBURSE, -MENT.

reeme, obs. f. REALM, REAM *sb.*[3], RIME.

re-e'merge, *v.* [RE- 5 a.] To emerge again.

1775 CHANDLER *Trav. Asia M.* (1825) I. 94 It will gradually re-emerge, and become dry and green as before. **1837** CARLYLE *Fr. Rev.* III. II. iii, A question emerges,..is put off, submerged; but always reemerges bigger than before. **1879** M. ARNOLD *Mixed Ess., Falkland* 227 But is it meant,..that after all, political liberty re-emerged in England..?

So **re-e'mergence**; **re-e'mergent** *a.*; **re-e'mersion.**

1801 COLERIDGE *Lett.* (1895) 365 Flashes of lightning, that seemed almost to alternate with the flash-like re-emersions of the waning moon. **1837** CARLYLE *Fr. Rev.* III. II. iii, By its frequent reemergence and by its rapid enlargement of bulk,.. this question [etc.]. **1865** GEIKIE *Scen. & Geol. Scot.* ix. 248 Since its first re-emergence it has doubtless been often sunk and raised anew. **1895** *Forum* (N.Y.) Apr. 254 Cases of fallen and still fitfully re-emergent nobility.

reeming ('riːmɪŋ), *vbl. sb.* Also **reaming.** [See REAM *v.*[3]] (See quot. 1846.) Also *Comb.*, as ***reeming-beetle, -iron.***

1750 BLANCKLEY *Nav. Expos.* 130 *Reeming Irons*, are used by the Caulkers for opening the Seams of the Planks of Ships on the Stocks before caulked. **1846** A. YOUNG *Naut. Dict.*, *Reeming*, in shipbuilding, opening the seams of the planks with iron wedges, called reeming-irons, in order that the oakum used in caulking may be more readily admitted. **1867** SMYTH *Sailor's Word-bk.* 566 *Reeming-Beetle*, a caulker's largest mallet. **1875** KNIGHT *Dict. Mech.* 1905/2 The tool is a reeming-iron struck by a reeming-beetle.

re-e'mission. [RE- 5 a.: cf. next.] A second or subsequent emission; a re-issue.

1740 W. DOUGLASS *Disc. Curr. Brit. Plant. Amer.* 10 In the following Years no more new Emissions, but some Re-emissions of the remainder. **1801** YOUNG in *Phil. Trans.* XCII. 46 Its remaining many months as if in a latent state, and its subsequent re-emission by the action of heat. **1955** FRIEDMAN & WEISSKOPF in W. Pauli *Niels Bohr* 136 These states..have a finite lifetime, since they can decay by the re-emission of the incident particle. **1968** G. M. B. Dobson *Exploring Atmosphere* (ed. 2) iii. 62 As a result of this complicated process of constant absorption and re-emission of radiation,..the ground..absorbs about half of the incoming solar radiation.

re-ˈemit, *v.* [re- 5 a.] *trans.* To emit again; esp. *U.S.*, to reissue (bills, bank-notes, etc.). Hence **re-ˈmitting** *vbl. sb.* (in quot. *attrib.*).

1740 W. Douglass *Disc. Curr. Brit. Plant. Amer.* 10 The Province..have since a. 1702 emitted and re-emitted Bills of public Credit. *Ibid.* 17 The three Upper Counties.. emitted 30,000 *l.* which have generally been continued out by re-emitting Acts from Time to Time. **1759** Franklin *Ess.* Wks. 1840 III. 203 The trustees of the loan office might reëmit the same sums. **1884** *American* VIII. 311 The notes are not held, when redeemed, but re-emitted. **1924** *Proc. Physical Soc.* XXXVI. 422 It is possible that the α-particle is in some way attached to the residual nucleus. Certainly it cannot be re-emitted with any considerable energy, or we should be able to observe it. **1955** *Bull. Atomic Sci.* Mar. 92/1 Several neutrons are re-emitted when a uranium atom is exploded by one neutron. **1969** *Times* 19 Feb. 13/6 Atoms and molecules of the atmosphere absorb sunlight and then reemit the energy at wavelengths which are characteristic of the particular type of atom or molecule.

re-ˈemphasize, *v.* [re- 5 a.] *trans.* To emphasize again, to place renewed emphasis on. So **re-ˈemphasis**.

1857 E. B. Browning *Aurora Leigh* i. 26 From many a volume, Love re-emphasised. **1894** J. R. Illingworth *Personality, Human & Divine* i. 18 This intimacy and immediacy of possible union between the soul and God.. had long vanished from the popular religion. Luther re-emphasized it. **1934** Webster, Re-emphasis. **1948** J. Towster *Polit. Power in U.S.S.R.* viii. 174 The changes or re-emphases that took place. **1971** *Nature* 23 Apr. 490/3 He also reemphasizes his original contention that an anomalous situation does exist.

re-emˈploy, *v.* [re- 5 a.] *trans.* To employ again; to take back into employment. So **re-emˈployment**.

1611 Cotgr., *Remployer*, to reimploy. **1883** Stevenson *Silverado Sq.* 147 Begging me to re-employ him again. **1893** *Columbus* (Ohio) *Disp.* 7 Aug., It is to be hoped that relief will come, in the way of re-employment, before cold weather sets in.

Reemy, var. R.E.M.E., REME.

reen (riːn). Also **reene, rheen.** A variant (and more phonetic) spelling of the south-western rhine, a ditch.

1829 J. L. Knapp *Jrnl. Nat.* 142 A pale blue shrew..has been seen about the margin of our reenes, and the deep marsh ditches. **1864** G. F. Berkeley *Life & Recoll.* I. 241 The wide deep reens or ditches that intersect these marshy meadows. **1867** *Macm. Mag.* June 164 It is intersected..by several large dykes, called in the language of the country 'rhines' or 'rheens'.

reen, var. rean; obs. f. rein(deer).

re-eˈnable, *v.* Also 6–7 re-in-. [re- 5 a.]

†**1.** *trans.* To rehabilitate, restore. *Obs.*

1586 T. B. *La Primaud. Fr. Acad.* i. (1594) 600 The re-inabling of such as before were not capable of offices or dignities. **1611** Speed *Hist. Gt. Brit.* ix. xiv. §7. 612 They were also forbidden..to reenable the late King against the authoritie of this Parliament. **1629** Donne *Serm.* V. 440 When God hath thus created a new heart, that is, Re-enabled me by his Ordinance.

2. To make able again.

1633 T. Adams *Exp. 2 Peter* iii. 18 Thus are we re-enabled to pay him the debt of glory. **1834** *Good's Study Med.* (ed. 4) II. 616 To require..many months before the patient was re-enabled to take his station in society.

So †**re-eˈnablement.** *Obs.*

1648 W. Mountague *Devout Ess.* i. Ep. Ded. A 4 b, The propitiating of Almighty God, towards Your reinablement to afford them all..succors.

re-eˈnact, *v.* [re- 5 a.]

1. *trans.* To enact (a law, etc.) again. Hence **re-eˈnacting** *vbl. sb.*

a **1676** Hale *Prim. Orig. Man.* iv. viii. (1677) 369 That Precept..was no other than the re-enacting of that old Commandment. **1705** Arbuthnot *Coins*, etc. (1727) 259 The Construction of Ships was forbidden to Senators, by a law made by Claudius, Tribune of the people,..and re-enacted by the Julian Law of Concussions. **1832** Babbage *Econ. Manuf.* xxxiii. (1835) 363 *note*, In 1825 an attempt to re-enact some of the most objectionable was made. **1865** H. Phillips *Amer. Paper Curr.* II. 38 All the regulations of the prior resolution..were herein re-enacted.

2. To act or perform again; to reproduce.

1854 J. S. C. Abbott *Napoleon* (1855) I. v. 89 Napoleon had no desire to see the Reign of Terror re-enacted in the cities of Italy. **1856** 'Stonehenge' *Brit. Rural Sports* 464/1 My yachting friends need never expect to see her with her present rig re-enacting the America.

So **re-eˈnaction, re-eˈnactment.**

1803 *Hist. Europe* in *Ann. Reg.* (1804) 14/2 Lord Limerick positively asserted that the re-enactment of those bills was absolutely necessary for the tranquility of the country. **1855** H. Clarke *Dict.*, Reenaction. **1860** Forster *Gr. Remonstr.* 2 The Petition..was but the affirmation and re-enactment of the precedents of the three foregoing centuries.

re-eˈnamour, *v.* [re- 5 a.] *trans.* To inflame again with love. In *pass.*

a **1711** Ken *Anodynes* Poet. Wks. 1721 III. 417 Love saw me cool, I by his Rod Shall re-enamour'd be of God.

re-enˈchain, *v.* Also 7–8 re-in-. [re- 5 a.] *trans.* To enchain again.

1611 Cotgr., *Renchainer*, to reinchaine, to chain, or bind in chaines, againe. **1718** *Free-thinker* No. 90 ¶7 He becomes an easy Captive to the first Person, who shall endeavour to re-inchain him. **1837** R. Wilson *Pleas. Piety* iv. 93 Ham's haughty King collects his armed hosts To re-enchain the ransomed of the Lord.

†**re-enˈcharge,** *v. Obs. rare*$^{-1}$. [re- 5 a.] ? To charge again.

1600 Holland *Livy* viii. xxxix. 310 The Dictator..cried unto the Colonels..to reencharge and renew the medley againe with him.

†**re-enˈcloister,** *v. Obs.* In 7 re-in-. [re- 5 a.] *trans.* To shut up again in a cloister.

1632 Lithgow *Trav.* vi. 286 Bidding farewell to the Church of St. Saluatore, and being re-incloystred againe.

re-enˈclose, *v.* [re- 5 a.] To enclose again.

1598 Florio *Worlde of Wordes* 307/2 *Racchiúdere*,..to re-enclose or shut vp againe. *Racchiuso*, re-enclosed or shut vp againe. **1849** E. A. Poe *Let.* 13 Jan. (1948) II. 416 Please re-enclose me the printed papers. **1870** 'Mark Twain' *Lett. to Publishers* (1967) 31, I re-enclose the Express letter, as you desire. **1907** R. Brooke *Let.* 29 Oct. (1968) 114 You probably know all this already from Mrs Leon. I re-enclose her letter.

re-enˈcounter, *sb.* Also 6–7 rein-, re-in-. [f. re- + encounter *sb.*; cf. rencontre *sb.*, rencounter *sb.*] †**a.** A meeting, encounter, *esp.* a hostile one. *Obs.* **b.** A renewed meeting.

1525 Ld. Berners *Froiss.* II. xxix. 34/1 Without any busynesse or reencounter we came to the captall. **1577–87** Holinshed *Chron.* I. 85/2 The Saxons had the victorie in that reincounter. **1603** Holland *Plutarch's Mor.* 443 So many pleasant speeches and lively reencounters. **1611** Florio, *Rancontro*, a reincounter, a meeting againe. **1666** S. Parker *Free & Impart. Censure* (1667) 32 After many reiterated controversial Re-incounters with Aurelius. **1737** L. Clarke *Hist. Bible* (1740) I. i. 68 This Re-encounter had not a little ruffled Jacob's mild disposition. **1794** Godwin *Cal. Williams* 77 Mr. Falkland's servants, hearing the bustle of the re-encounter [etc.]. **1904** *Daily Chron.* 28 July 8/5 If she is wise she will..avoid disenchanting re-encounters in the flesh. **1948** *Times Lit. Suppl.* 18 Sept. 526/3 Mr. Sassoon ..sets down his personal experience of the re-encounter. **1974** Frith & McLauchlan in R. K. Harris *Nuclear Magnetic Resonance* (Chem. Soc. Specialist Periodical Rep.) III. xii. 387 This..broadens our definition of cage recombination to include reaction of the original partners in the radical pair on re-encounter after their initial diffusive separation.

re-enˈcounter, *v.* Also 6–7 re-in-. [f. re- + encounter *v.*; cf. rencontre *v.*, rencounter *v.*] †**a.** To encounter, *esp.* in a hostile manner. *Obs.* **b.** To encounter or meet again.

1523 Ld. Berners *Froiss.* I. ccxiv. 267 They..robbed all that countrey, for there was none that reencountred them. **1577–87** Holinshed *Chron.* I. 164/2 Bicause the Danes.. were reencountred..so often as they did encounter [etc.]. **1600** *Gowrie Conspir.* C 2, His owne seruants..hauing put his maiestie in safetie, re-encountred the sayd Earle and his seruantes. **1611** Florio, *Rancontrare*, to reincounter or meete againe. *c* **1630** Risdon *Surv. Devon* §65 (1810) 63 Both armies met again, and re-encountered. **1639** Fuller *Holy War* ii. x. (1840) 63 The Pagans, little suspecting to be reencountered, gave themselves over to mirth and jollity.

†**re-enˈcountry.** *Obs.*$^{-1}$ = re-encounter *sb.*

1568 Grafton *Chron.* II. 266 For I thinke verely that your aduersarie king Phillip will meete with you to fight, and ye shall find many streight passages and reencountries.

re-enˈcourage, *v.* In 6–7 rein-. [re- 5 a.] *trans.* To encourage again.

1598 Florio, *Rinfrancare*, to reincourage. **1670** Milton *Hist. Eng.* iv. 138 The Abbot Austin.., reincourag'd by the exhortations of Gregory.., came safe to the Ile of Tanet.

So **re-enˈcouragement.**

a **1766** J. Browne *Willie & Old Wernock* 329 But O, (my Wernock) how am I to thee Obligen, for thy keene re-encouragements.

re-endear, *v.* In 6–7 re-in-. [re- 5 a.] *trans.* To endear again. So **re-enˈdearment.**

1626 Bp. Hall *Contempl.*, *O.T.* xx. xii, As a man..puts himself into some deserving action, whereby he may hope to re-indeare him selfe. **1654** H. L'Estrange *Chas. I* (1655) 212 Resolued he was no opportunity should escape him which might promove his re-endeerment with them.

re-enˈdow, *v.* Also 8 re-in-. [re- 5 a.] *trans.* To endow again.

1607 Hieron *Wks.* I. 390 How much is vented away by such meanes, by which..many an impouerished and spoiled church [might be] re-endowed. **1761** *London & Environs* IV. 102 The hospitals..being built, and re-indowed at the public expence. **1869** *Spectator* 24 July 861/1 Concessions which re-endow the Free Church with an extra half-million.

So **re-enˈdowment.** Also *attrib.*

1869 *Spectator* 24 July 861/1 Re-endowment even with half a million is re-endowment. **1884** *Manch. Weekly Times* 11 Oct. 4/6 A re-endowment of the Protestant denomination. **1897** *Daily News* 10 Mar. 9/4 In aid of the Re-endowment Fund of Guy's Hospital.

reene, var. rean, reen; obs. f. rein.

re-ˈenergize, *v.* [re- 5 a.] *trans.* To energize anew, impart fresh energy to.

1803 Anna Seward *Lett.* (1811) VI. 108 You, my friend, have..affectionate interests, which combine to reenergize your mind. **1887** *Chicago Advance* 5 May 274 The true way to re-energize the languishing institution.

re-enˈfeoff, *v.* Also 7 rein-, re-in-. [re- 5 a; cf. refeoff *v.*] *trans.* To enfeoff anew; to enfeoff in return (the original feoffor).

1540 in *Eng. Gilds* (1870) 256 Who, soe being seised, shall re-enfeoffe the said seaven who shall survive. **1628** Coke *On Litt.* 208 b, If the Condition be, That the Feoffee shall re-infeoffe the Feoffor [etc.]. **1642** tr. *Perkins' Prof. Bk.* iii. §241. 107 If my Feoffee in Fee of one Acre of Land, doe reinfeoff mee of the same acre [etc.]. **1765** *Act 5 Geo. III*, c. 26 *Preamble*, With power also to the surviving trustees..to re-enfeoff other trustees to the same uses. **1865** Nichols *Britton* II. 209 *note*, It was not uncommon for a layman to enfeoff a church on condition of being reenfeoffed to hold of the church.

So **re-enˈfeoffment.**

1661 J. Stephens *Procurations* 55 So warranty is extinguished by Re-infeoffment or Descent of Land to the same person that had the Warranty. **1870** *Eng. Gilds* 256 *marg.*, When only seven feoffees remain living, a re-enfeoffment, to fourteen, shall be made.

re-enflame, variant of reinflame.

re-enˈforce, *sb.* = reinforce *sb.*

1886 *American* XII. 141 The gun is a small one,.. composed of two concentric cylinders, the inside one being of steel, the outside or reënforce of cast iron.

re-enˈforce, *v.* [f. re- + enforce *v.*; cf. reinforce and renforce. Now rare in English, but common in American use.]

1. *trans.* To strengthen, give fresh or additional strength to.

c **1586** C'tess Pembroke *Ps.* lxxxvi. v, Thou, Jehova,.. With strength my weaknesse re-enforce. **1625** K. Long tr. *Barclay's Argenis* v. x. 364 He was with these and the like speeches re-enforcing his anger. *a* **1630** S. Page *Broken Heart* (1637) 177 To magnifie him, and to reenforce his Petition, he calleth him *Deum salutis*. *a* **1711** Ken *Hymnarium* Poet. Wks. 1721 II. 49 Thou to thyself dost Glory raise, By re-enforcing our Decays. **1883** *Harper's Mag.* Nov. 886/2 The sonority of this reservoir is expected materially to re-enforce the volume of tone. **1888** Stevenson *Gentlemen in Fiction*, The opinions.., though.. re-enforced with excellent images, are not peculiar..to Hamlet.

b. *refl.* To strengthen or encourage (oneself) afresh. *rare.*

1589 in Hakluyt *Voy.* (1812) V. 588 Who after one battle were never able to reenforce themselves against him. **1599** B. Jonson *Cynthia's Rev.* iii. iii, And then, if she shall coily recoil, and signify your repulse, you are to reenforce yourself with [etc.].

2. *Mil.* To strengthen with additional forces (†or supplies); to support by fresh numbers.

1596 Danett tr. *Comines* (1614) 24 Then vsed we to re-enforce them with new supplies. **1613** Purchas *Pilgrimage* iv. ii. 295 The Magi..himselfe re-enforcing his power, and bidding battell..was taken aliue. **1693** *Mem. Cnt. Teckely* iv. 62 They thought only upon reposing themselves, and re-enforcing their Army by detachments out of the neighbouring Garrisons.

transf. **1885** J. L. Allen in *Harper's Mag.* Apr. 709/2 With my house re-enforced by a housekeeper,..there would be nothing more to desire. **1896** *Paterson Mag.* VI. 305/1 The pioneers have been re-enforced.

†**b.** To collect again; to reassemble. *Obs.*

1594 Kyd *Cornelia* Argt., His purpose was to have re-enforc'd a newe Armie. **1599** Shaks. *Hen. V*, iv. vi. 36 The French haue re-enforc'd their scatter'd men.

3. To strengthen (any part of an object) by additional support.

1883 *Harper's Mag.* Nov. 887/1 The re-entrant angles.. are re-enforced..with..pilasters. **1897** *Outing* (U.S.) XXX. 278/2 It goes to the brazing furnace, where the joints are re-enforced and solidified.

†**4.** *intr.* To renew one's efforts; to insist. *Obs.*

1624 Bp. Mountagu *Gagg* 3 Though he fall off to-day, hee will re-enforce to-morrow, though he faile to-day, he will assay to-morrow. **1642** Jer. Taylor *Episc.* (1647) 325 This account we have from S. Cyprian, and he reenforces againe upon the same charge in his Epistle.

Hence **re-enˈforceable** *a.*, capable of being re-enforced (*Funk's Stand. Dict.* 1895); **re-enˈforcer**, one who re-enforces; also, something which re-enforces; **re-enˈforcing** *vbl. sb.*

1611 Florio, *Rafforzamento*, a re-enforcing. **1884** *Century Mag.* Mar. 929/1 Writers who are more properly feeders and reënforcers of life itself. **1914** W. McDougall *Social Psychol.* 404 The energy of the sex impulse..may function as a re-enforcer of purely intellectual activities.

re-enˈforcement. [f. as prec. + -ment: cf. reinforcement and renforcement.] The act of re-enforcing, or the state of being re-enforced; that which re-enforces; a fresh supply.

1601 R. Johnson *Kingd. & Commw.* (1603) 139 Populous, because of reenforcements after checks or ouerthrows. **1621** Bp. Mountagu *Diatribæ* 41 Without a generall re-enforcement from authority. **1681** Glanvill *Sadducismus* ii. 126 Having resolved upon this Reenforcement, I writ again to my Honoured Friend. **1775** P. Schuyler in Sparks *Corr. Amer. Rev.* (1853) I. 78 That a reënforcement may be speedily sent into Canada. **1853** Kane *Grinnell Exp.* xlv. (1856) 411 We devoured eagerly the seal, of which, by good fortune, we had several re-enforcements. **1882** *Rep. to Ho. Repr. Prec. Met. U.S.* 472 The natural head of water needs the re-enforcement of pumping apparatus to enable it to reach the highest point of the mine.

re-enˈfranchise, *v.* Also 7 re-in-. [re- 5 a.] *trans.* To enfranchise (†set free) again. So **re-enˈfranchisement.**

1611 Florio, *Raffrancare*, to re-enfranchise or set at libertie. **1660** Ingelo *Bentiv. & Ur.* ii. (1682) 147 A price paid down for the re-infranchising of inslav'd Men. **1888** G. W. CABLE in *Libr. Mag.* (U.S.) May 16 The slow doling out of re-enfranchisement to the best intelligence of Southern white society.

re-en'gage, *v.* Also 7 rein-, re-in-. [RE- 5 a. Cf. F. *rengager* (16th c.).] To engage again. Hence **re-en'gaging** *vbl. sb.* **a.** *trans.*

1611 COTGR., *Rengager*, to reingage. **1825** J. NICHOLSON *Operat. Mechanic* 20 The disengaging and reengaging of the moving parts. **1828** SOUTHEY *On a Picture*, etc. xiv, If then the power to thee were given In that cold form its life to re-engage. **1870** *Act 33 & 34 Vict.* c. 67 §8 Any soldier who being in army service has commenced the twelfth year from his first enlistment.. may.. be reengaged.

b. *intr.*

1678 BUTLER *Hud.* III. iii. 182 It put him in so fierce a Rage He once resolv'd to re-ingage. **1864** CARLYLE *Fredk. Gt.* XVII. i. (1872) VII. 3 Brühl has ever since rather held back; would not reëngage at all. **1876** VOYLE & STEVENSON *Milit. Dict.* 335/1 Soldiers who have declined to re-engage abroad, and have been sent home at the public expense, will not be permitted to re-engage in this country.

So **re-en'gagement**.

1731 BAILEY Vol. II. (ed. 2), *Re-ingagement*, an engaging again. **1828** *Lights & Shades* II. 286 He stayed to see Madame Vestris commence her re-engagement. **1870** *Act 33 & 34 Vict.* c. 67 §8 Re-engagement of soldiers.

re-en'gender, *v.* In 6-8 rein-, re-in-. [RE- 5 a. Cf. F. *rengendrer* (13th c.).] To engender again. Hence **re-en'gendering** *ppl. a.*

1545 RAYNOLD *Byrth Mankynde* 3 Y^e thynne or superficial skyn, skale it, or fall it of, neuer so often, yet in the place of it is reingendryd nue. **1611** COTGR., *Rengendrer*, to reingender. **1641** MILTON *Animadv.* iv. Wks. 1851 III. 219 As if a man should taxe the renovating and re-ingendring Spirit of God with innovation. **1751** tr. *Rousseau's Discourse* 35 What star may be inhabited, what insects reingender themselves in an extraordinary manner..?

So **re-en'genderer**.

1611 COTGR., *Rengendreur*, a reingendrer.

re-'engine, *v.* [f. RE- 5 a + ENGINE *v.* 4.] *trans.* To furnish (a ship, or aeroplane) with new engines. Hence **re-'engined** *ppl. a.*; **re-'engining** *vbl. sb.*

1888 *Daily News* 9 Nov. 3/7 The Admiralty have decided to re-engine those ships [etc.]. **1889** *Standard* 9 Mar., Certain ships required to be re-engined. **1941** *Sun* (Baltimore) 20 Jan. 2/7 Reengined and rearmed Hurricanes, new Tornadoes.. and improved Defiants. **1955** *Times* 23 Aug. 5/1 The Grants Scheme should be extended to include the re-engining and re-conditioning of suitable trawlers. **1967** *Jane's Surface Skimmer Syst. 1967–68* 36 (*caption*) A re-engined version of the BHC SR.N5. **1973** *Stornoway Gaz.* 2 June 2/5 The cruising speed will be 14½ knots—she has not been re-engined.

,re-engi'neer, *v.* [RE- 5 a.] *trans.* To design and construct anew; also *transf.* and *fig.*, to arrange or contrive anew.

1944 *Sun* (Baltimore) 14 Dec. 4-0/3 Management and labor should decide now.. whether jobs re-engineered for women will be restored to provide work for servicemen. **1946** *Jrnl. Inst. Electr. Engineers* XCIII. IIIA. 59/2 It was decided therefore to re-engineer the system using aerial arrays. **1958** J. K. GALBRAITH *Affluent Society* xiii. 194 The first task of the public relations man is to 're-engineer' his image to include something besides the production of goods. **1974** W. REES-MOGG *Reigning Error* v. 104 The most fundamental relationships of human life have been re-engineered in order to prevent sufferings which turned out to represent the unavoidable limitations of human existence. **1977** *Gramophone* Feb. 1346/2 The new GT55P arm has been completely re-engineered.

So **re-engi'neered** *ppl. a.*, **re-engi'neering** *vbl. sb.*

1962 *Rep. Comm. Broadcasting 1960* 337 in *Parl. Papers 1961–2* (Cmnd. 1753) IX. 259 The importance.. of planning the use of Bands IV and V (and when the time comes the re-engineered Bands I and III).. as an integrated whole. **1973** C. SAGAN *Cosmic Connection* (1974) xxii. 150 Our motivations for planetary re-engineering must be clear. **1977** *Time* 18 Apr. 46/2 What would happen, they ask, if by accident or design, one variety of re-engineered *E. coli* proved dangerous?

†**re-en'gorge**, *v. Obs.* Also 7 rein-. [RE-.] *refl.* Of water: To pour back *into*, *in* a place.

1610 HOLLAND *Camden's Brit.* I. 208 When the sea re-engorgeth it selfe backe againe into the sea. **1632** LITHGOW *Trav.* x. 466 My head hanging downeward, and the water reingorging it selfe in my throat with a strugling force.

re-engraft: see REINGRAFT.

re-en'grave, *v.* [RE- 5 a.] *trans.* To engrave again. Hence **re-en'graved** *ppl. a.*

a **1711** KEN *Hymnarium* Poet. Wks. 1721 II. 99 They joy to see God's Image re-engrav'd. **1776** DA COSTA *Elem. Conchol.* ii. 35 He had them re-engraved; and therefore many shells appear twice in his work. **1806** W. TAYLOR in *Monthly Mag.* XXII. 133 Doppelmayer had a fac-simile of this chart re-engraved. **1889** *Pall Mall G.* 1 Feb. 2/1 The re-engraved plates are nine in number.

re-en'join, *v.* Also 7 rein-. [RE- 5 a.] *trans.* To enjoin again.

1611 COTGR., *Rejoindre*, to reinioyne, reordaine vnto, reimpose vpon. **1748** RICHARDSON *Clarissa* (1811) V. 36, I besought Miss Lloyd to re-enjoin secrecy to every one. **1892** *Current Hist.* (U.S.) Aug. 134 Re-enjoining the duty of loyalty to the Republican Government in France.

re-en'joy, *v.* Also 7 rein-. [RE- 5 a.] *trans.* To enjoy again.

1605 EARL STIRLING *Alexandr. Trag.* I. Chor., Those that th'earth chargde.. Theyr ashie lodgings leaue, To re-enioy the light. *a* **1648** LD. HERBERT *Hen. VIII* (1683) 159 That Charles, Duke of Bourbon should re-injoy his former estate. **1670** COTTON *Espernon* II. v. 241 To the end they might re-enjoy the licence of War. *a* **1711** KEN *Hymns Evang.* Poet. Wks. 1721 I. 53 'Tis Heav'n to me to re-enjoy my Dear. **1751** ELIZA HEYWOOD *Betsy Thoughtless* II. 221, I am preparing to return to my country-seat, where I hope to re-enjoy.. tranquility.

So **re-en'joyment**.

1611 COTGR., *Rejouïssance*, a reinioyment, repossession, reinioying. **1631** QUARLES *Div. Poems, Samson* Medit. xx, Whose sweet enjoyment.. leaves a thirst Of reenjoyment, greater than the first. **1668** FRANCO *Truth Springing* 46 The re-injoyment of those infinite Delights the Soul lost. **1815** MRS. PILKINGTON *Celebrity* III. 148 The result was, a re-enjoyment of illicit pleasures.

re-en'kindle, *v.* Also 7 re-in-. [RE- 5 a.] *trans.* and *intr.* To kindle again, *lit.* and *fig.*

1650 JER. TAYLOR *Holy Living* i. §2 ¶4. 20 Renew and re-inkindle your purpose by short ejaculations. **1651** —— *Serm. for Year* I. xii. 156 They went out, never to be re-enkindled. *a* **1711** KEN *Anodynes* Poet. Wks. 1721 III. 394 Love re-enkindled in my frozen Soul. **1713** [see RADIAL *a.* 1]. **1879** L. SHEPHERD tr. *Guéranger's Liturg. Year* I. 195 The piety of her children was re-enkindled.

re-en'large, *v.* Also 7 rein-. [RE- 5 a.] *trans.* To enlarge, set at large, again.

1611 FLORIO, *Ringrandire*,.. to re-enlarge. **1631** QUARLES *Div. Poems, Samson* VI, When time,.. By his benignant power, had reinlarg'd Their captive senses. **1823** BENTHAM *Not Paul* 376 Peter imprisoned, enlarged, recommitted, examined, and reenlarged.

re-en'lighten, *v.* [RE- 5 a.] *trans.* To enlighten again.

1691 E. TAYLOR tr. *Behmen's Divine Essence* xviii. 275 Re-enlightening the Soul.

re-en'list, *v.* Also rein-. [RE- 5 a.] *intr.* and *trans.* To enlist again.

1828–32 in WEBSTER. **1837** *Penny Cycl.* IX. 443/1 At the end of his time of service a seaman may re-enlist for a like period. **1850** R. G. CUMMING *Hunter's Life S. Afr.* (1902) 109/1 He declared himself.. penitent,.. and, expressing a wish again to join the service, I re-enlisted him. **1869** *Pall Mall G.* 7 Jan. 1/2 Many men.. take the bounty with no other intention than that of deserting in order to re-enlist.

So **re-en'listment** (also *attrib.*); **re-en'lister**, a person who enlists again.

1847 in WEBSTER. **1866** *Pall Mall G.* 3 Jan., This draw-back would be greatly lessened if we could secure re-enlistments in greater numbers. **1908** *Daily Chron.* 8 May 8/2 The majority of the re-enlisters 'are the discontented, the thriftless, the criminal class'. **1953** R. WELLS (*song-title*) Re-enlistment blues. **1970** *Times* 28 May 7/7 A source of much resentment is the iniquitous system whereby the Army maintains a high re-enlistment rate.

re-en'liven, *v.* [RE- 5 a.] *trans.* To inspire with new life or vigour.

a **1660** HAMMOND *Wks.* (1684) IV. 660 To clear up as much as we can, and re-inliven this light within us. **1681** *Whole Duty Nations* 31 When the times.. of Re-enlivening all things shall come. *a* **1711** KEN *Psyche* Poet. Wks. 1721 IV. 293 May Love, they cry'd, Lord, re-enliven'd be. **1809–10** COLERIDGE *Friend* (1865) 145 Does not war create or re-enliven numerous branches of industry as well as peace?

re-en'rol(l, *v.* [RE- 5 a.] *trans.* To enrol again. So **re-en'rolment**.

1889 *Voice* (N.Y.) 8 Aug., The third and final day of the Republican re-enrollment. **1893** *Daily News* 27 Dec. 5/5 Dr. Jameson.. is re-enrolling many of the men to form a permanent police force.

re-en'shrine, *v.* [RE- 5 a.] *trans.* To enshrine again.

a **1711** KEN *Preparatives* Poet. Wks. 1721 IV. 48 God-man his Angels will enjoyn, Saints hallow'd Dust to re-enshrine. **1815** J. C. HOBHOUSE *Substance Lett.* (1816) I. 104 Relics.. to be re-adjusted and re-enshrined by a second St. Louis.

re-en'slave, *v.* Also 7 rein-, re-in-. [RE- 5 a.] *trans.* To enslave again. Hence **re-en'slaving** *vbl. sb.*

1657 HAWKE *Killing is M.* 12 The Army presaging what dangerous.. consequences might ensue to the reinslaving of the people. **1691** BEVERLEY *Mem. Kingd. Christ* 3 It would be wholly impossible to Re-inslave these Nations. **1807** HAZLITT *Pol. Ess.* (1819) 406 If this increase would be an evil.. the re-enslaving the country would be a good. **1856** OLMSTED *Slave States* 95 A man who had been free, but.. was reënslaved.

So **re-en'slavement**.

1859 LD. LYONS *Let.* 6 Dec. in Ld. Newton *Lord Lyons* (1913) I. ii. 19 The reenslavement of all the emancipated negroes. **1883** *Contemp. Rev.* Nov. 686 The whites would undoubtedly disfranchise the blacks if they could.. but none assuredly would ever again consent to their re-enslavement.

re-en'sphere, *v.* Also 7 re-insphear. [RE- 5 a.] *trans.* To ensphere again.

1684 T. HOCKIN *God's Decrees* 152 He could not re-ensphere himself into the same happy condition he did lose. *Ibid.* 277 The faln angels could not be re-inspheard'd into their primitive blessed condition.

re-en'stamp, *v.* Also 8 rein-. [RE- 5 a.] *trans.* To enstamp or imprint again.

a **1703** BURKITT *On N.T.*, *Romans* viii. 39 Will he leave them after his image is engraven, and reinstamped upon them? *c* **1750** J. NELSON *Jrnl.* (1836) 191 He doth actually destroy the works of the devil, and re-enstamp the image of God in their souls. **1776** JOS. NEILL *23 Serm.* 257.

†**re-'enter**, *sb. Obs.* [RE- 5 a.] = RE-ENTRY.

1574 tr. *Littleton's Tenures* 74 Yelding to the lessoure.. a certeine rent, and for defaut of paiment a reenter. **1639** *Records of Dedham* (Mass.) (1892) III. 58 In case y^t payment be not yearly made.. it shall be lawfull for ye said Town to make a Reenter vpon ye premises.

re-enter (riːˈɛntə(r)), *v.* [RE- 5 a + ENTER *v.* Cf. F. *rentrer* (12th c.).]

1. a. *intr.* To enter again. Const. †*in*, *into*, *upon*.

1483 CAXTON *Gold. Leg.* 129/1, I shal reentre nakyd agayn in to therthe. **1494** FABYAN *Chron.* VI. clxxxix. 191 He warred vpon the Danys that then were reentrede into Northumberlande. **1515** BARCLAY *Egloges* i. (1570) Aiij 2 When the good is gone.. Seldome the better re-entreth in the place. **1551** ROBINSON tr. *More's Utop.* II. (1895) 283 The other, at theyre retourne home, agayn reentre euery one into his own place. **1618** ROWLANDS *Sacred Mem.* 35, I doe commaund and charge that forth thou come, And neuer to reenter any more. **1651** HOBBES *Leviath.* II. xxix. 174 There is no possibility for the Soveraignty to re-enter. **1726** POPE *Odyss.* XXI. 246 Re-enter then, not all at once. **1825** J. NICHOLSON *Operat. Mechanic* 499 An air was then performed by bells; after which the two figures reentered. **1861** tr. *Montalembert's Monks of West* I. 354 He descended.. to re-enter into a rustic solitude. **1870** *Act 33 & 34 Vict.* c. 67 §5 When any such soldier is directed to re-enter upon army service.

b. *Law.* To enter again upon possession of lands or tenements.

1461 *Rolls of Parlt.* V. 485/1 In the same halfendele to reentre, and it in their first state to hold. **1485** *Ibid.* VI. 321/2 The forsaid Blaunch and her said Feoffes to reenter into the said Ten[emen]ts. **1503–4** *Act 19 Hen. VII*, c. 29 *Schedule*, It shalbe lefull to the seid Abbas.. to reentre into the seid grounde. **1607** COWELL *Interpr.* s.v. *Reentry*, If I doe condition with the Leasee, that for nonpayment of the rent at the day it shalbe lawful for me to reenter. **1622** CALLIS *Stat. Sewers* (1647) 45 If A. or his heirs pay to B. Ten pounds within a certain day, that they might re-enter. **1818** CRUISE *Digest* (ed. 2) I. 396 The feoffee will re-enter, or bring an action to recontinue the possession. **1849** MACAULAY *Hist. Eng.* ii. I. 179 The royalist nobility and gentry reentered on their confiscated estates.

c. In stage-directions; hence, also in wider contexts. (Cf. ENTER *v.* 1 b.)

1693 CONGREVE *Old Batchelour* v. i, Enter Sharper... Re-enter Sharper. **1803** G. COLMAN *John Bull* IV. i. 56 Re-enter Dan booted. **1937** 'M. INNES' *Hamlet, Revenge!* II. iii. 137 And so—just conceivably—re-enter the spies.

2. a. *trans.* To enter (a place, etc.) again.

1442 T. BECKINGTON *Corr.* (Rolls) II. 246 The Lord Usak.. re-entred the said cite by the same ladder. **1494** FABYAN *Chron.* VI. cxcviii. 205 In whiche season he made great prouysion to reenter the lande of Englande. **1570** FOXE *A. & M.* (ed. 2) 255/2 He was content that Thurstinus should reenter hys realme. **1667** MILTON *P.L.* II. 397 Those bright confines, whence.. we may chance Re-enter Heav'n. *a* **1711** KEN *Hymnotheo* Poet. Wks. 1721 III. 220 Once more we to re-enter Bliss will try. **1778** MISS BURNEY *Evelina* (1791) II. xxxi. 195, I re-entered the drawing-room. **1830** LYTTON *P. Clifford* xxv, Mauleverer slowly re-entered his carriage. **1898** *Allbutt's Syst. Med.* V. 111 The air re-enters the minute bronchi and air-vesicles.

†**b.** To enter again into possession of (a thing); to regain (possession). *Obs. rare.*

1590 SOUTHWELL *M. Magd. Funeral Teares* (1823) 115 Hee should after death re-enter possession of that inheritance which Adam lost. **1706** PHILLIPS (ed. Kersey), *To Re-enter*, to enter upon, or take Possession of again.

c. *spec.* of spacecraft. Also *absol.*

1961 *Times* 6 May 8/2 Seven minutes after take-off the report came through that the capsule was beginning to reenter the earth's atmosphere. **1962** S. CARPENTER in *Into Orbit* 56 The capsule should not re-enter too quickly or the deceleration will be too great. **1968** *Times* 16 Dec. 7/3 A second crucial phase begins when Apollo 8 reenters the earth's atmosphere. **1977** G. SCOTT *Hot Pursuit* x. 90 The Americans.. spotted it... It looked as though it was about to reenter.

d. In the drilling of offshore oil wells and similar holes: to enter (a borehole) again with a drilling bit.

1961 W. BASCOM *Hole in Bottom of Sea* xii. 244 Two parallel guide lines, stretched between the ship and fittings on the bottom, had a sliding crossbar to guide the bit so that the hole could be re-entered at will. **1967** *Ocean Industry* June 15/1 Sonar system for hole re-entry which makes it possible to re-enter a small diameter borehole in three-mile-deep water. **1968** *Proc. Offshore Exploration Conf.* 241 The drilling personnel have found it necessary to remove the drill string and desire to reenter it at a later time. **1975** *Proc. Offshore Technol. Conf.* I. 27/1 One beacon.. is attached to the object being re-entered (well head) and the other beacon.. is attached to the re-entry tool.

†**3.** *Sc.* To lodge (a person) again *in* a place.

1566 *Reg. Privy Council Scot.* I. 454, I am content.. that my saidis freindis tak and reentir and put me within the castellis. **1574** *Ibid.* II. 379, I sall re-enter agane the said Roger in presoun quhen I sall be requirit.

4. To enter again in a book or register.

1838 W. HOWITT *Rural Life Eng.* I. i. v. 81 On applying to the steward he found that he was actually re-entered as tenant to the farm. **1839** *Act 2 & 3 Vict.* c. 11 §4 The Senior Master shall forthwith re-enter the same [judgment] in like Manner as the same was originally entered. **1885** *Law Times* LXXIX. 25/1 Another [notice] must be given before the plaintiff can re-enter the cause for trial.

5. *techn.* **a.** In hand calico-printing: To apply (the secondary colours), to ground in.

1839 [see the *vbl. sb.* below].

b. In engraving: To cut (imperfect or worn lines) deeper in the plate.

1854 FAIRHOLT *Dict. Terms Art* s.v., [The] line is re-entred with a sharp graver, and cut to the proper depth.

Hence **re-'enterable** *a.*, capable of being re-entered; **re-'entering** *vbl. sb.*

1638 JUNIUS *Paint. Ancients* 309 The very.. reentring into the presence of things will instantly suggest unto us.. how to order and place every figure. 1839 URE *Dict. Arts* 216 The grounding in or re-entering (*rentrage*) of the other colours is the next process. 1969 P. B. JORDAIN *Condensed Computer Encycl.* 423 A reenterable program can service several tasks concurrently by switching from one task to another task at high speed.

re-'entering, *ppl. a.* [f. prec. + -ING[2].]

1. a. ***re-entering angle***, an angle pointing inward.

1696 PHILLIPS (ed. 5) s.v. *Angle*, Re-entring Angle, is that which re-enters into the body of the place. 1723 CHAMBERS tr. *Le Clerc's Treat. Archit.* I. 95 The Inner or Re-entering Angles. 1805–17 R. JAMESON *Char. Min.* (ed. 3) 175 Salient, and never re-entering angles. 1877 HUXLEY & MARTIN *Elem. Biol.* 43 The branches spring from the re-entering angle between the stem and the leaf.

b. So ***re-entering bend, line, order, place, wall.***

1830 E. S. N. CAMPBELL *Mil. Dict.* 182 The object of the Re-entering Places of Arms is to flank the branches of the covered way. 1841 *Penny Cycl.* XIX. 346/1 To break the lines of parapet near the gorges, so as to form re-entering bends. 1873 TRISTRAM *Moab* v. 74 Each of the flanking or re-entering walls extending in an obtuse angle from it. 1876 VOYLE & STEVENSON *Milit. Dict.* 335/1 Re-entering order of battle. 1885 W. C. COUPLAND *Spir. Goethe's Faust* vi. 208 The industrialism of the present is only a point in a re-entering historic line.

2. Returning into a place.

1850 GROTE *Greece* II. lxvi. (1862) VI. 9 The re-entering exiles from Peiræus, and the Horsemen.. blended again together into one harmonious.. democracy. 1958 *Punch* 17 Sept. 361/1 Re-entering nose-cones. 1959 *Daily Tel.* 14 Apr. 1/7 The proposed American attempt to catch a re-entering satellite is a very long shot indeed. 1974 *Encycl. Brit. Macropædia* XV. 938/2 In the early 1960s a new technique.. was developed, using materials similar to those employed as heat shields for re-entering space vehicles.

re-enter'tain, *v.* [RE- 5 a.] To entertain again; to readmit. So **re-enter'tainment.**

1611 SPEED *Hist. Gt. Brit.* IX. xi. §4. 555 Peirs of Gaueston.. whose reentertainement the dying King had so seriously forbidden. *a*1680 CHARNOCK *Attrib. God* (1834) I. 191 Till the true sense of God be reentertained in the soil where it ought to grow.

re-en'thrall, *v.* Also 7 rein-. [RE- 5 a.] *trans.* To enthrall again.

1622 DONNE *Serm.* cxix. V. 107 Neither is this.. to re-enthrall you to a necessity of communicating all your sins. 1632 LITHGOW *Trav.* VI. 241 Ierusalem was reinthralled and seazed vpon by Saladine. 1644 HEYLIN *Stumbling-block* Tracts (1681) 651 That.. we should not re-inthral our selves to the lusts of men.

re-en'throne, *v.* [RE- 5 a; cf. REINTHRONE.] *trans.* To enthrone again.

1654 tr. *Scudery's Curia Pol.* 117, I am at last.. ready to invest and re-enthrone John King of Hungary. *a*1711 KEN *Hymns Festiv.* Poet. Wks. 1721 I. 368 When Jesus re-enthron'd on high, His Spirit sent. —— *Preparatives* ibid. IV. 72 My Mind, which now I re-enthrone.

So **re-en'thronement** (Webster 1847); †**re-en'thronize** *v.* = REINTHRONIZE.

1620–55 I. JONES *Stone-Heng* 43 Vortigern was re-enthronis'd.

re-en'tice, *v.* In 6 rein-. [RE- 5 a.] *trans.* To entice again.

1589 WARNER *Alb. Eng.* v. xxvi, And reintise the Club-God Dys, And all his diuells to daunt.

re-en'toil, *v.* [RE- 5 a.] To entoil again.

1606 SYLVESTER *Du Bartas* II. iv. II. *Trophies* 777 What frantick fury art thou mov'd with-all..(By powr-full Charms) to re-entoyl my Cares?

re-'entrance. [RE- 5 a.] A renewed or repeated entrance.

1594 HOOKER *Eccl. Pol.* IV. ix. §2 Their whole religion in time will have reentrance. 1597 *Ibid.* V. xxii. §4 The first step of their re-entrance into Life. 1661 GLANVILL *Van. Dogm.* 32 That the pores of the brain.. are more easily opened to the spirits which demand re-entrance. 1775 ROMANS *Florida* App. 62 It being too dark to attempt a re-entrance of the reef, I was forced to heave the vessel too. 1883 H. DRUMMOND *Nat. Law in Spir. W.* (ed. 2) 168 The successful re-entrance of importunate desires.

re-'entrancy. [f. RE-ENTRANCE + -Y[3].]

a. *Electr.* The state of being re-entrant; also, a measure of the number of complete turns required to trace out an armature winding (see RE-ENTRANT *a.* 2 a).

1901 SHELDON & MASON *Dynamo Electr. Machinery* iii. 47 Any closed-coil winding, single or multiple, may be singly or multiply re-entrant, the re-entrancy being reckoned as great as that of any single winding on the armature. 1902 *Jrnl. Inst. Electr. Engineers* XXXI. IV. 933 A few writers.. take the re-entrancy as being the number of times we must go around the armature in tracing out the whole winding. *Ibid.* 935 Condition of Re-entrancy.—The first condition to be fulfilled by a proposed winding is that it should re-enter upon itself. 1907 HOBART & ELLIS *Armature Construction* viii. 157 Multiplicity and re-entrancy of multiplex windings.

b. The capability of being entered again.

1976 P. C. SANDERSON *Minicomputers* iv. 72 For some applications, hardware should allow re-entrancy. This allows the same procedures to be performed on different blocks of data. 1976 *Nature* 11 Mar. 176/2 There is an absence of detailed comment on.. modern programming techniques which are important for memory-starved mini-computers, such as subroutine re-entrancy.

re-'entrant, *a.* (and *sb.*). [f. RE- + ENTRANT. Cf. F. *rentrant.*] **A.** *adj.* **1. a.** = RE-ENTERING *ppl. a.* 1 and 1 b.

1781 J. T. DILLON *Trav. Spain* 462 He could find nothing which seemed to confirm the opinion relating to the salient and reentrant angles. 1825 J. NICHOLSON *Operat. Mechanic* 588 When the faces form a re-entrant angle, common dove-tailing is preferable. 1876 TAIT *Rec. Adv. Phys. Sc.* v. (ed. 2) 108 Any re-entrant line whatever may be supposed to be traced. 1883 *Harper's Mag.* Nov. 887/1 The re-entrant angles of the splay. 1967 M. CHANDLER *Ceramics in Mod. World* iv. 122 It is difficult to form reentrant shapes between two dies. 1973 J. G. TWEEDDALE *Materials Technol.* II. iv. 94 There are limits on the shapes of the grooves in grooved rolls, re-entrant angles are completely unusable. 1975 D. G. FINK *Electronics Engineers' Handbk.* IX. 49 Magnetron oscillators are single-port devices. Both the slow-wave circuit and the electron stream are reentrant; i.e., the circular geometry is always used.

b. *Mus.* Designating a form of tuning of the open strings of the citole, cittern, and ukulele, in which the fourth course is tuned to a higher pitch than the third, as e′, d′, g, b or e′, d′, g, a for the cittern.

1948 *Galpin Soc. Jrnl.* I. 48 The cittern's curious re-entrant tuning gives simply-fingered versions of all the chords commonly used in contemporary music. 1961 A. BAINES *Mus. Instruments* vii. 166 Its [*sc.* the cittern's] tunings.. were re-entrant, with the fourth course higher in pitch than the third, as on the modern ukelele. 1976 D. MUNROW *Instruments Middle Ages & Renaissance* iv. 27/1 The instrument which Tinctoris describes [*c.* 1487] is unquestionably the ancestor of the renaissance cittern, with .. a re-entrant tuning for its four metal strings. *Ibid.*, The earliest account of the tuning of any stringed instrument, that of Jerome of Moravia (*c.* 1250), described three fiddle tunings, one of which is re-entrant.

2. a. Of or pertaining to something which returns upon itself, as in *Electr.*, applied to a form of armature winding (see quot. 1901); in *Acoustics*, applied to a form of horn loudspeaker in which the bore is divided and folded upon itself before expanding to the flare, in order to reduce space.

1901 SHELDON & MASON *Dynamo Electr. Machinery* iii. 46 A singly-re-entrant winding is one in which, by successive angular advances, all the coils have been laid when an advance of 360° has been made. To be doubly-re-entrant wound the angular advance between successive coils, in the order of their winding, is doubled; and the whole winding is not complete until the armature has been gone around, angularly, twice, i.e., through an advance of 720°. 1902 *Jrnl. Inst. Electr. Engineers* XXXI. IV. 933 A winding is re-entrant if it comes back to the starting point and is then complete. 1928 *Gramophone* Jan. 345/1 There are now listed three models (called 're-entrant') in which a relatively broad acoustic system is, by means of embodying a double reflexion of tone, enabled correctly to expand to quite a wide-mouthed horn in no greater depth from front to back than is allowable in the relatively shallow American pattern cabinet. 1940 *Chambers's Techn. Dict.* 710/1 The majority of windings are singly re-entrant. 1960 *Practical Wireless* XXXVI. 395/2 Speakers of the re-entrant type will be found most suitable. 1961 BRIGGS & COOKE *A to Z in Audio* 79 One of the earliest applications of this principle [*sc.* that of the exponential horn] to sound reproduction was probably the re-entrant gramophone produced by HMV in 1927.

b. *Computers.* Of, pertaining to, or designating a program or subprogram which may be called or entered many times concurrently from one or several programs without alteration of the results obtained from any one execution.

1964 *Proc. Fall Joint Computer Conf.* I. 45 (*heading*) Method of control for re-entrant programs. *Ibid.* 45/1 A routine which permits unlimited multiple entrances and executions before prior executions are complete is called a re-entrant routine. 1970 O. DOPPING *Computers & Data Processing* xiv. 221 A form of programming which allows re-entry into a partially used subroutine is called re-entrant programming. 1976 H. D. BAECKER in *Virtual Storage* (Infotech International Ltd.) 195 Allocation of and access to local variables in recursive or re-entrant environments. *Ibid.*, Re-entrant programs are not only a good thing because of their alleged economy of space.

B. *sb.* **a.** *Geogr.* A prominent, angular indentation into a landform, such as an inlet between two coastal promontories or a valley extending into a hill or mountain side.

1893 [see *pocket-beach* s.v. POCKET *sb.* 13]. 1899 R. T. HILL *Geol. Jamaica* i. 18 The interior mountains are marked by deeply etched knife-edged salients.. and angular re-entrants. 1936 *Bull. Amer. Assoc. Petroleum Geologists* XX. 1224 The profound reëntrant between the escarpment of the Serra das Furnas and that of the Serra de São Joaquim. 1962 J. ONSLOW *Bowler-Hatted Cowboy* v. 53 Dense spruce spread from the valley upwards, following the big re-entrants. 1973 C. BONINGTON *Next Horizon* xviii. 248 The road was like a switchback gone mad, as it bucked from valley floor, over spurs, round re-entrants and down again.

b. A re-entrant angle in a fortification.

1900 'LINESMAN' *Words by Eyewitness* iii. (1902) 41 A.. crackle of musketry from the occupants of the re-entrant.

re-entry (riːˈɛntrɪ). [RE- 5 a. Cf. F. *rentrée.*]

1. a. *Law.* The act of re-entering upon possession of lands, tenements, etc., previously granted or let to another.

1461 *Rolls of Parlt.* V. 485/1 With lyke clause of reentre reserved. 1473 *Ibid.* VI. 70/1 Though he wold entre into the seid maneres,.. yet anon theruppon reentre is made ayen uppon hym. 1540 *Act 32 Hen. VIII*, c. 17 The leassor.. to haue no action reentre or other remedy for nonpayment of the same. 1581 in W. H. Turner *Select. Rec. Oxford* (1880) 414 Wth a clause of re-entre for none payment of the rente .., and also a re-entrye for not doinge reparacions. 1611 BARRY *Ram Alley* H, Although thou boughtst the heyre, Yet hath the slaue made a re-entry. 1644 QUARLES *Sheph. Orac.* xi, They plead for want of dressing Our Garden's forfeited, and they are pressing Hard for reentry. 1766 in Burrow *Rep.* (1776) IV. 1936 No Re-entry shall in such Case be given, unless the Demand be precisely and strictly followed. 1818 CRUISE *Digest* (ed. 2) IV. 113 No right of entry or re-entry can be assigned. 1876 DIGBY *Real Prop.* x. §1. 381 A lease usually contains a proviso for re-entry by the lessor in the event of the breach of any of the covenants entered into by the lessee.

†**b.** Resumption *of*, return *to*, a right or station.

1471 *Arriv. Edw. IV* (Camden) 39 The reentrie and perfecte recover of the iuste title and right of owr sayd soveraygne Lord Kynge Edward the Fowrthe, to his realme and crowne of England. 1586 T. B. *La Primaud. Fr. Acad.* I. (1589) 374 Convicted for conspiring the reentrie of Tarquinius race unto the Kingdome of Rome.

2. a. The act of re-entering or coming back into a place, etc.; a second or new entry.

1494 FABYAN *Chron.* VII. 636 To haue his counceyll for maters concernyng theyr charge as reentre into this lande & other. 1601 DANIEL *Civ. Wars* VII. xxxi, Every Port And Shore close-shut debarres their reentry. 1603 HOLLAND *Plutarch's Mor.* 922 Those of Phila had made a reentrie into the citie, and chased out the tyrants. *a*1653 GOUGE *Comm. Hebr.* iii. (1655) 8 To return to sinne.. is to make way for the Devils re-entry. *a*1680 CHARNOCK *Attrib. God* (1834) II. 127 Will [he] lose the glory.. by suffering his foiled adversary to make a re-entry? 1821 SCHOOLCRAFT *Trav.* 98 We.. effected the crossing and re-entry of the lake. 1884 'CAVENDISH' *Whist* (ed. 14) 5 A player cutting into one table, whilst belonging to another, loses his right of re-entry into that latter.

b. ***card of re-entry***, in Whist, a card which by winning a trick gives the lead to a player at an advanced stage of the hand; also, in Bridge, a card which by winning a trick gives the lead (in his own hand or in dummy) to a player who has previously had it. So ***re-entry card*** and *ellipt.* as ***re-entry.***

1884 'CAVENDISH' *Whist* (ed. 14) 127 Plain suits should be led like trumps.. if all the trumps are out, and the leader or his partner has certain cards of re-entry in other suits. 1899 A. DUNN *Bridge* 22 If the long suit hand has no card of re-entry, he will be prevented from bringing in his suit. 1905 [see DUCK *v.* 6]. 1908 R. F. FOSTER *Auction Bridge* 84 In planning the play of a no-trumper, the declarer must be careful to provide for re-entry cards. 1958 *Listener* 9 Oct. 572/1 If he had a suit headed by KQJ and a re-entry he would pass, not overcall. 1967 COHEN & BARROW *Bridge Players' Encycl.* 405/1 *Re-entry*, a card by which a player who had the lead (including the opening lead) can regain it.

c. *Astronautics.* The return of a spacecraft into the earth's atmosphere.

1948 *Jrnl. Brit. Interplanetary Soc.* VII. 34 The technique of atmospheric re-entry will be developed from progressively daring excursions into space. 1961 *Guardian* 6 May 1/3 The vapour trail caused by the re-entry of the capsule. 1968 *Times* 16 Dec. 7/2 The reentry of the first rocket stage into the atmosphere. 1970 *Guardian* 18 Apr. 1/1 The spacecraft.. appeared to be badly scarred by the heat of re-entry. 1977 G. SCOTT *Hot Pursuit* x. 89 Clearly it had not been programmed to come down where it did; you've seen how it was damaged in re-entry and landing.

d. The act of re-inserting a drilling bit into a borehole during the drilling of an offshore oil well or similar hole.

1961 W. BASCOM *Hole in Bottom of Sea* xiii. 271 There would be no riser pipe or other means of hole re-entry. If the bit were once withdrawn, the hole would be lost. 1962 *Design of Deep Ocean Drilling Ship* (U.S. Nat. Research Council) 64 A riser pipe may be the best means of hole re-entry... When re-entry is attempted—after a bit change, for example—as the pipe tip approaches bottom a sensing sonde will be lowered into position at the bit which will be able to sense the tip of the projecting casing. 1968 *Proc. Offshore Exploration Conf.* 242 Reentry was attempted by two engineers with only one reentry for a number of attempts. 1974 *Geotimes* Dec. 16/2 The casing broke just below the reëntry core, and was displaced downward.. after 4 successful reëntries, eventually preventing further reëntry.

e. *Surfing.* (See quot. 1968.)

1968 W. WARWICK *Surfriding in N.Z.* 14/1 A re-entry is a roller coaster, taken a stage further. To perform this tactic, your board must be moving roughly parallel to the top of the wave and as the wave begins to break, kick your board to the top so that it is sitting on top of the curl with virtually no water covering its deck. Your board will appear to have stalled at the top of the wave for a second then it will be sucked back down with the curl. 1970 *Surf* I. x. 11/2 Finishes it off with a re-entry.

f. Return to one's usual place or mode of living.

1972 *Listener* 31 Aug. 270/1 The standard pattern of war veterans.. a difficulty in what is called 're-entry', in getting back into the civilian society. 1974 *N.Y. Times* 8 July 1/3 'Country' is where you go.. to escape from your city responsibilities, and when country-time ends, re-entry can be traumatic.

†**3.** *Sc.* The act of putting (a person) back *in* a place. *Obs. rare*$^{-1}$.

1566 *Reg. Privy Council Scot.* I. 454 For re-entre of the said Erle..in ward.

4. a. The act of setting down or recording again; the fact of being so set down; the entry thus made.

1839 *Act 2 & 3 Vict.* c. 11 §4 Such officer shall be entitled for any such Re-entry to the Sum of One Shilling. **1885** *Law Times Rep. LII.* 574/2 The re-entry was erroneous, and ought to be struck out. **1887** *48th Rep. Dep. Kpr. Records* 628 A memorandum..of the judgment, &c., was to be left for the purpose of re-entry in the book.

b. *Philately.* (See quots.)

1916 F. J. MELVILLE *Postage Stamps in Making* I. ix. 96 The varieties of the first British stamps which are best described as having had the roller applied twice, or 're-entries' known to have existed on Plate 145 of the 1d., Small Crown, imperforate, and other plates of Great Britain. **1951** R. J. SUTTON *Stamp Collector's Encycl.* 191 *Re-entry*, duplication of part of a stamp design due to a first impression having been inadequately erased, and thus enabling traces of its 'entry' to appear in conjunction with the new impression, causing a doubling of a part of the image... Known in the U.S.A. as 'shift'. **1971** D. POTTER *Brit. Eliz. Stamps* xiv. 159 On recess-printed stamps the entry die may momentarily make contact in part, twice, and slight doubling of the design results. This is known as a re-entry. **1972** D. & M. PATRICK *Hodder Stamp Dict.* (1973) 204/1 *Re-entry*, a second attempt to rock in the stamp design on a steel plate for engraving postage stamps... A perfect re-entry leaves no second line on the stamps. **1975** B. GUNSTON *Philatelist's Compan.* 247 *Re-entry*, characteristic doubling or thinning of portions of the design of a line-engraved stamp caused by the impression having been entered more than once on the plate.

5. *attrib.* (*a*) in sense 2 c, as ***re-entry angle, black-out, capsule, heating, parachute, problem, vehicle***; (*b*) in sense 'giving permission for re-entry into a country', as ***re-entry permit, visa***; **re-entry card**: see sense 2 b above; **re-entry point** *Computers* (see quots.).

1970 *Daily Tel.* 17 Apr. 6/1 Without this burn, the spacecraft would miss by 100 miles the critical re-entry angle, between 5·6 and 7·2 degrees. **1966** *Electronics* 14 Nov. 54 Reentry blackout has plagued every flight in the Mercury and Gemini series. **1967** *Technology Week* 20 Feb. 10/2 *Biosatellite I's* re-entry capsule containing biological specimens and data on magnetic tape..is believed to have re-entered in or near Australia. **1962** F. I. ORDWAY et al. *Basic Astronautics* i. 5 A review of the problems of reentry heating. **1976** P. CAVE *High Flying Birds* i. 11 Originally designed as a possible re-entry parachute device for space capsules, the flying sail designed by Francis M. Rogallo in the early sixties has come a long way. **1948** F. FRENAYE tr. *Levi's Christ stopped at Eboli* xiii. 123 Before they are aware of it..their re-entry permit [to the US] has expired, and they have to stay at home. **1972** R. PERRY *Fall Guy* iv. 73 Wondering whether I'd be granted a re-entry permit. **1922** *Gloss. Terms Automatic Data Processing* (*B.S.I.*) II. 39 The point at which a routine is re-entered from a subroutine is a re-entry point. **1977** *Gloss. Terms Data Processing* (*B.S.I.*) VII. 8/1 *Reentry point*, the address or the label of the instruction at which the computer program that called a subroutine is reentered from the subroutine. **1957** *Times* 9 Nov. 6/5 The President's positive claim that the United States has solved the so-called re-entry problem of bringing space missiles back to earth. **1965** *New Scientist* 2 Dec. 638/1 Further improvement is being made with re-entry vehicles which embody penetration aids against anti-missile defence. **1973** *Times* 26 Feb. (Arms for Peace Suppl.) p. ii/4 The United States, by possessing the ability to put multiple independently targeted reentry vehicles on her launchers, has many more nuclear warheads than the Soviet Union. **1973** J. SHUB *Moscow by Nightmare* xi. 125 I'm not coming back... The Soviet Embassy called me yesterday. They've cancelled my re-entry visa. **1977** *Times* 11 May 7/8 The Soviet authorities had given him a permanent reentry visa so that he can return to Moscow.

re-e'nunciate, *v.* [RE- 5 a.] *trans.* To enunciate again. So **re-enunci'ation**.

1881 LE CONTE *Sight* 97 After this explanation we reenunciate the law of corresponding points. **1888** *Chicago Advance* 20 Dec. 832 The New Testament does not re-enunciate and re-enact the old law. **1895** A. J. BALFOUR in *Daily News* 9 Sept. 5/1 A mere re-enunciation of my belief.

†**re-en'verse**, *v.* *Obs.* [ad. F. *renverser* to RENVERSE.] *trans.* To reverse.

1603 FLORIO *Montaigne* II. xii. (1632) 322 Plato saith, that ..the Starres, and the Sunne do some times re-enverse the motion we perceive in them. **1610** DONNE *Pseudo-martyr* x. 274 Bridgewater, which cals himselfe Aquipontanus, ouerturning and re-enuersing his name with his conscience.

reepe, obs. form of REAP.

reeper, reaper ('ri:pə(r)). *Anglo-Indian.* [ad. Mahratti *rīp* (Yule).] (See quots.)

1734 in J. H. Wheeler *Madras in Olden Time* (1862) III. 148 Paid the Banksall Merchants for the house poles, country reapers, &c. necessary for house building. **1858** SIMMONDS *Dict. Trade, Reepers*, laths, or longitudinal sections of the palmyra palm, used for building purposes in the East; the trunk of the tree is split into 8 for reepers, and these are dressed with an adze. **1886** YULE & BURNELL *Anglo-Ind. Gloss., Reaper.* The small laths, laid across the rafters of a sloping roof to bear the tiles, are so called in Anglo-Indian house-building.

re-e'pitomize, *v.* [RE- 5 a.] *trans.* To present again in smaller compass.

1655 FULLER *Wounded Consc., Antheologia* (1867) 277 A small scantling of some three acres, which..re-epitomized the delicacies of all the rest.

re-e'quip, *v.* [RE- 5 a.] *trans.* To equip again. So **re-e'quipment**.

1804 LARWOOD *No Gun Boats* 12 Re-equipping Line-of-Battle Ships. *Ibid.* 17 The process of re-equipment being thus obvious. **1823** SOUTHEY *Penins. War* I. 743 The government had already begun to take measures for re-equipping them. **1889** *Voice* (N.Y.) 24 Oct., To get education and re-equipment for Christian Work. **1919** J. L. GARVIN *Econ. Foundations Peace* viii. 158 Their industrial centres, wherever existing, have to be re-equipped. **1944** J. S. HUXLEY *On Living in Revolution* 148 Neither the profit motive nor political considerations should be allowed to interfere with the job of re-equipping Europe. **1960** *Farmer & Stockbreeder* 19 Jan. (Suppl.) 6/1 Currently engaged in re-equipping many leading breeding and research farms.

ree-raw ('ri:'rɔ:), *a.* (and *sb.*). [Anglo-Irish, prob. of echoic origin.] Rough, riotous, noisy.

1842 S. LOVER *Handy Andy* xxxvii, The joining of many voices in a 'ree-raw' chorus indicated that a carouse was going forward within. **1863** LE FANU *House by Churchyard* (ed. 2) II. 44 There was something cynical in his ree-raw independence. **1864** ANSTER tr. *Faustus* pt. II. I. (1887) 48 A wild, ree-raw, self-willed tumultuous throng.

b. *sb.* A drinking-bout; a noisy romp.

1854 DICKENS in *Househ. Wds.* VIII. 75/2 For the one word drunk,..I find..on the ran-tan, on the re-raw, groggy. **1867** KENNEDY *Banks Boro* xxxi, Wouldn't the little boys..have a fine ree-raw at prison bars at play time!

†**reere.** *Obs. rare.* Also 4 rere. [Of obscure origin, perh. related to ROAR *v.*, but cf. also REAR *sb.*[1]] Noise, shouting; a shout.

c **1330** R. BRUNNE *Chron. Wace* (Rolls) 10207 Alle þe ernes ..Schul crie & ȝelle, & make rere. **1567** GOLDING *Ovid's Met.* XIII. (1593) 320 These words were spoke with such a reere as verie well became An angrie Giant. **1571** —— *Calvin on Ps.* xvii. 1 Hypocrites make stout bragges, and lift up their voyce with lowd reere, in token of affiance.

re-e'rect, *v.* [RE- 5 a.] *trans.* To erect again, *lit.* and *fig.* Hence **re-e'recting** *vbl. sb.*

1598 DRAYTON *Heroic. Ep.* (1605) 89 Bring marble mines to re-erect those walls. **1631** HEYLIN *St. George* 220 Temples demolished..in the time of Diocletian: and reerected by..Maximinianus. **1679** PRANCE *Addit. Narr. Pop. Plot* 30 This re-erecting of Abbies by Q. Mary. *a* **1711** KEN *Preparatives* Poet. Wks. 1721 IV. 14 Conscience, thy Throne I'll re-erect. **1835** in Willis & Clark *Cambridge* (1886) I. 333 To re-erect or restore on some other site, the Old Gateway. **1882–3** SCHAFF *Encycl. Relig. Knowl.* III. 2172 He re-erected the Court of High Commission in 1664.

So **re-e'rection.**

1655 FULLER *Ch. Hist.* VI. vi. 359 She was legally empowred for the re-erection of these Convents. **1861** SMILES *Engineers* II. 28 He also had regard to durability as an important point in its re-erection.

reermouse, variant of REARMOUSE.

reer-supper, variant of RERE-SUPPER. *Obs.*

rees, variant of REIS (Pg. money), RESE.

re-'escalate, *v.* [f. RE- 5 a + ESCALATE *v.* 2.] *trans.* To escalate (a war or conflict) again. Also *absol.*

1965 H. KAHN *On Escalation* xii. 237 Further bargaining is rarely successful unless the conflict is re-escalated. **1965** *Punch* 4 Aug. 165/1 Up and down this ladder nations may escalate, de-escalate and re-escalate. **1972** *Sat. Rev.* (U.S.) 6 May 34/1 President Nixon has always kept for himself the option of re-escalating the war.

So **re-esca'lation**, the act or process of re-escalating. Also *attrib.*

1965 H. KAHN *On Escalation* xii. 231 De-escalation dominance might also involve being in a good position to resume fighting if the other side forced further action. The latter property could also be called 're-escalation dominance'. *Ibid.* 234 Of course, de-escalation cannot guarantee that re-escalation will not occur.

re-e'scape, *v.* [RE- 5 a.] To escape again.

1727 BROOME *Poems* 120 Lest hid in Shades, Thro' the dusk Air he re-escape to Troy. **1902** *Daily Chron.* 15 Aug. 3/6 After sundry depredations he was recaptured, only to re-escape.

†**reescate**, *v.* *Obs. rare*[−1]. [ad. It. *riscattare*, Sp. *rescatar*:—pop.L. **re-ex-captāre*.] *trans.* To redeem, ransom.

c **1645** HOWELL *Lett.* v. xxxii. (1650) I. 168 The great honour you have acquir'd by your gallant comportment in Algier in reescating so many English slaves.

reese, reeze (ri:z), *v.*[1] *Obs.* exc. *dial.* [? Back-formation from REESED.] *intr.* To become rancid.

1784 TWAMLEY *Dairying* 712 Butter..will reeze or get of a tallowy nature; fat Bacon will reeze so far as the fat melts. **1886** *Rochd. Gloss., Reese*, to grow rancid, as bacon.

†**reese, reeze**, *v.*[2] *Obs.* [Of obscure origin: cf. REEST *v.*[2]] *trans.* To burn, scorch, smoke.

1618 T. ADAMS *Heaven made sure* Wks. (1629) 902 For a while they bee reezed in Purgatory. **1633** —— *Exp. 2 Peter* ii. 4 His priests..were reesed or smoked with the incense offered to the idol. **1698** M. LISTER *Journ. Paris* (1699) 147 It is little less than Quicklime, and burns and reeses all it touches.

reese, var. RESE *sb.* and *v.*; dial. var. ROOSE *v.*

reesed, reezed (ri:zd), *ppl. a.* Also 5 resside, 6 re(e)z'd, 7 reised; 8 reased, 9 reazed. [Later form of REST *a.*; cf. REASTY.] Rancid.

1486 *Bk. St. Albans* C vij, Upon that powdre do a litill larde that is resside. **1598** BP. HALL *Sat.* IV. ii. 36 Once a weeke, perhaps, for nouelty, Reez'd bacon soords shall feast his familie. **1598** MARSTON *Sco. Villanie* I. iii. 183 What Academick starued Satyrist Would gnaw rez'd Bacon? **1607** MARKHAM *Caval.* VII. (1617) 56 Their insides are..in colour yellow like reesed bacon. **1641** *Curates Conference* in *Harl. Misc.* (Malh.) IV. 376 He..looks like a piece of reesed bacon, ever since the plot failed. **1727** BRADLEY *Fam. Dict.* s.v. *Garget*, Put in a little reased bacon and boil them altogether. **1883** *Almondbury Gloss., Reezed* or *Reazed*, a term applied to rancid bacon.

reeshle: see REESLE.

reesk (ri:sk). *Sc.* Forms: 5 reysk, 6 resk, 9 reisk, reisque, reesk. [a. Gael. *riasg* 'a moor, fen, or marsh; coarse mountain-grass'.]

1. A piece of moorish or mossy ground producing coarse worthless grass or rushes; unproductive soil or land of this description.

1466 *Reg. Arbroath* (Bann. Club) II. 152 The marchis of Gwtheryn..passand eist the Greyn Reysk to Laithan Den. **1540** in *5th Rep. Hist. MSS. Comm.* 609/1 The..merchis.. begynnand at the west in the myddis of the resk betuix the ..landis. **1804** TARRAS *Poems* Gloss. 156 *Reesk*, ground full of rough-rooted weeds, something like rushes. **1813** G. ROBERTSON *Agric. Kincardinesh.* 317 The greater part of the original soil..is either a moss..or it is, what in this and in the adjacent county of Aberdeen, is provincially called Reisque, or Reisk.

2. Coarse grass growing on moorish ground.

1794 *Statist. Acc. Scotl.* XII. 576 Large tracks of ground producing a coarse kind of grass, called by the country people reesk. **1812** D. SOUTER *Agric. Banffsh.* App. 59 If a field be cold and canker'd, or overgrown with reesk, year old fauch will agree best.

Hence **'reesky** *a.*, producing reesk.

1804 TARRAS *Poems* 7 Aft we've seen them fain, Dink owre the bent to the reiskie den.

reesle ('ri:s(ə)l), **reeshle** ('ri:ʃ(ə)l), *sb.* *Sc.* Also reestle. [Of onomatopœic origin.] A loud clatter; a rattling blow.

a **1774** FERGUSSON *Tron Kirk Bell* Poems (1845) 44 I'd bring ye wi' a reesle down. *a* **1810** TANNAHILL *Come hame* Poems (1846) 145 I'll lend you a reestle wi' this, owre your back. **1880** JAS. E. WATT *Poet. Sketches* 52 A reeshle like thunder was heard at the door.

'reesle, 'reeshle, *v.* *Sc.* Also reessil, reishle, etc. [Cf. prec.]

1. *intr.* To make a loud clattering noise.

1819 TENNANT *Papistry Storm'd* (1827) 44 Doors reessil'd up, and made a blatter. **1826** D. ANDERSON *Poems* 92 Gar'd ..their shin-banes reeshle i' their hose. **1895** CROCKETT *Men of Moss-hags* 31 That blind and unkindly wind reestling and soughing about the house.

2. *trans.* To beat with rattling blows.

1853 WATSON *Poems* 91 (E.D.D.), Whan Scotlan' had reissl't the rascals [etc.]. **1887** SERVICE *Life Dr. Duguid* v. 31 He reishled the main author o' thae tricks weel.

reeso(u)n, obs. forms of REASON *sb.*[1]

re-e'spouse, *v.* [RE- 5 a.] To espouse again.

a **1618** SYLVESTER *Elegie to Marg. Wyts* 80 Metkerk had her Mother re-espous'd. **1652** BENLOWES *Theoph.* XIII. lxxvi, The Corps but falls to be refin'd And re-espous'd unto the Glorifi'd high Minde.

Hence **re-e'spousal**.

1817 G. S. FABER *Eight Dissert.* (1845) I. 357 *note*, The repudiation, long desolation, and ultimate reëspousal, of the Levitical Church, are described at large in Isaiah liv. 1–14. **1827** —— *Sacr. Cal. Prophecy* (1844) III. 299 The set time of the Reëspousal of Judah.

reest (ri:st), *sb.* *Obs.* exc. *dial.* Forms: 1 réost, 7, 9 reest, 9 reist, riest, reost, reece; 6–7 (9) rest. Also *wreest* WREST. [OE. *réost*, of obscure origin: cf. G. *rist* ploughshare (Grimm), Sw. *rist* (MSw. *rist-iern*) coulter.

G. *rist* may be for *riest*, repr. an OHG. **rîost*: cf. OHG. *riostra, riostar, riester, rister*, etc. (mod.G. dial. *riester, rister*) ploughshare, plough-handle, the stem of which agrees with the OE. form. It is doubtful, however, whether Sw. *rist* can be separated from ON. *ristill* ploughshare (mod.Norw. *ristel* coulter, also Gael. *risteal* a kind of plough used in the Hebrides), which may rather be a derivative of *rista*, to cut, than an adaptation of the OHG. word. The Du. or Flem. equivalent of the latter is given by Kilian as *ryster, reyster*, with the meaning 'plough-staff'.]

†**a.** The share-beam of a plough. *Obs.* **b.** A mould-board. **c.** A piece of wood or iron fixed beneath the mould-board.

c **725** *Corpus Gloss.* 656 *Dentalia*, sules reost. *a* **1000** *Gloss.* in Wr.-Wülcker 219/2 *Dentale, s. est aratri pars prima in qua uomer inducitur quasi dens*, sule-reost, *uel proc.* ? **14..** *MS. Lansdowne* 560 fol. 47 b, *Restis*, a rest of a plow. **1523** FITZHERB. *Husb.* §3 The rest is a lyttell pece of woode, pynned fast vpon the nether ende of the stylt, and to the sharebeame in the ferther ende. **1616** SURFL. & MARKH. *Country Farme* v. vi. 532 The spindles, the rest,..the plowfoot, the culture, and the share. **1688** R. HOLME *Armoury* III. 333/2 The Reest, is the Boards on the side of the Plow that turns over the Furrow. **1886** *Chesh. Gloss., Reest*, the mould-board of a plough. **1887** *Kentish Gloss., Chef*, the part of a plough on which the share is placed, and to which the *reece* is fixed.

attrib. **1894** *Northumbld. Gloss., Reest-, reost-cloot*,..a thin piece of iron fastened under the lower edge of the mowdy-boord (mould-board) of a plough.

reest (riːst), *v.*[1] *Obs.* exc. *dial.* Also 7 **reast**, 7, 9 **reist**. [Of obscure origin: cf. REST *a.* and REESED.] *intr.* Of bacon, etc.: To become rancid. Hence **'reested** *a.*, rancid.

c**1440** *Promp. Parv.* 431/1 Reestyn', as flesche, *ranceo.* **1530** PALSGR. 688/2, I reest, I waxe of yll taste, as bacon dothe. **1616** SURFL. & MARKH. *Country Farme* I. xxiv. 107 The scalding of Hogges keepeth the flesh whitest,..neither is the Bacon so apt to reast as the other. **1634** W. WOOD *New Eng. Prosp.* (1865) 39 This kind of fish..is so fat, that it can scarce be saved against winter without reisting. **1869** *Lonsdale Gloss.*, *Reested*, rancid, spoiled, as bacon from being badly kept. **1894** *Northumbld. Gloss.*, *Reest*, to become rancid. Reested or reesty bacon—rancid bacon.

reest (riːst), *v.*[2] *Sc.* and *north. dial.* Also 6, 9 **reist**. [Of obscure origin: cf. REESE *v.*[2] and Da. *riste* to grill or broil, f. ON. *rist* gridiron.]

1. *trans.* To dry or cure (herring, bacon, etc.) by means of heat or smoke.

1508 DUNBAR *Flyting* 187 Thow purehippit, vgly averill, ..Reistit and crynit as hangit man on hill. a**1590** MONTGOMERIE *Sonn.* xxv, Rau rid herring reistit in the reik. **1692** *Sc. Presbyt. Eloq.* (1738) 138 Take them up by the Heels, reest them in the Chimney of Hell, and dry them like Bervy Haddocks. **1816** SCOTT *Bl. Dwarf* ix, Let us cut up bushes and briers,..set fire to them, and smoke that auld devil's dam as if she were to be reested for bacon. **1832-53** W. CROSS in *Whistle-Binkie* Ser. III. 16 But ne'er say a herring is dry until it be reestit and reekit.

2. *intr.* To become smoke-dried.

1725 RAMSAY *Gentle Sheph.* II. i, A large ham hangs reesting in the neuk. **1829** SCOTT *Guy M.* xxvi. *note*, The salmon is usually dried by hanging it up, after being split and rubbed with salt, in the smoke of the turf fire.., where it is said to reist, that preparation being so termed.

reest (riːst), *v.*[3] *Sc.* and *north. dial.* Also **reist**. [Prob. a var. of REST *v.*, or identical with *reest*, aphetic form of Sc. *arreest*, to ARREST. The precise relationship to RESTIVE *a.* is not clear.] *intr.* Of horses: To stop suddenly and refuse to proceed. Hence **'reesting** *vbl. sb.* and *ppl. a.*

1786 BURNS *To Auld Mare* xiv, In cart or car thou never reestet. **1816** SCOTT *Antiq.* xv, Our powny reists a bit, and it's dooms sweer to the road. *Ibid.* xxiv, The butcher's reisting powny. **1826** J. WILSON *Noct. Ambr.* Wks. 1855 I. 250 Like horses that never reest. **1895** CROCKETT *Men of Moss-hags* xxvi. 197 Reesting and terror among horses are mostly but over-sharpness in hearing.

fig. **1890** SERVICE *Notandums* xix. 124, I was like to reist and to sten at the doctor's orders.

reest, obs. form of REST.

re-establish (riːɪ'stæblɪʃ), *v.* [RE- 5 a. See also RESTABLISH.] *trans.* To establish again.

1. To establish (a person or thing) again *in* a former place, position, or state; to restore to a previous place or position. Also const. *among*.

1483 CAXTON *Gold. Leg.* (1493) 268 b/1 Thus was the precious tree of the crosse reestablyshid in his place. **1586** WILKES in Motley *Netherl.* x. (1860) II. 99, I had not much to do..to re-establish in her Majesty..a singular good opinion of you. **1606** G. W[ODCOCKE] *Hist. Ivstine* XVI. 67 He could now deliuer them..and re-establish them in their former peace. a**1648** LD. HERBERT *Hen. VIII* (1683) 87 He purpos'd to re-establish Henry d'Albret in the Kingdom of Navarre. **1728** ELIZA HEYWOOD tr. *Mme. de Gomez's Belle A.* (1732) II. 215 A Nation on whose Throne his Ancestors had sat for a long Series of Ages, would not fail to protect and re-establish him. **1838** LYTTON *Alice* I. ix, He has been kind to me, and re-established me among my flock. **1858** FROUDE *Hist. Eng.* IV. 311 He expected that..he could re-establish the English party in a decisive superiority.

b. To fix or set up again. *rare.*

1669 J. ROSE *Eng. Vineyard* (1675) 35 Re-establish your props, and with your foot tread the earth close to the roots. **1827** STEUART *Planter's G.* (1828) 24 The same writer.. mentions, that it was a common practice to reestablish large Trees..that had been blown down. **1847** GROTE *Greece* II. xxxiv. (1862) III. 233 The bridge was re-established.

2. To set up again in a status or condition similar to the former one; to restore.

1559 *Fabyan's Chron.* II. 571 In the foresaied parliament also was the booke of seruice..reestablished. **1579** FENTON *Guicciard.* II. 77 The better to reestablish their gouernment, they had in their parliament..instituted a kind of pollicie. **1631** WEEVER *Anc. Funeral Mon.* 137 One hundred and sixe Abbeyes of this Order were built and reestablished. **1676** TOWERSON *Decalogue* 161 The great design of the gospel was to re-establish natural worship. **1705** ARBUTHNOT *Coins*, etc. (1727) 257 Theodosia..was..afterward re-established and possessed by the Genoese, under the name of Cafa. **1769** GOLDSM. *Hist. Rome* (1786) I. 62 Some young men.. undertook to re-establish monarchy. **1863** BRIGHT *Sp., Amer.* 26 Mar. (1876) 127 He had a fair chance of re-establishing his business. **1866** CRUMP *Banking* ix. 193 America was..re-establishing a metallic currency.

3. To restore (one's health or strength) to the usual state; to set (ill-health) right again. Usually in *pass.* (†also with person as subj.).

1697 [see the *vbl. sb.* below]. **1709** STEELE *Tatler* No. 7 ¶ 18 His Health being so well re-established by the Baths. **1735-6** BERKELEY *Let. to Johnson* 12 Mar. in Fraser *Life* vii. 245 My ill-health, which is now pretty well re-established. **1766** J. WILKES *Let.* 3 May, I thank my dearest daughter for her obliging solicitude about my health. I am now quite re-established. c**1850** *Arab. Nts.* (Rtldg.) 268 The jeweller.. felt his strength re-established. a**1859** MACAULAY *Hist. Eng.* xxv. V. 288 With health so far re-established that he was able to take exercise on horseback.

b. To restore to a proper condition.

1812 G. CHALMERS *Dom. Econ. Gt. Brit.* 144 To see her.. reestablish her financial affairs, in so short a period, after the conclusion of war. **1822** DE QUINCEY *Confess.* 61 About fifteen shillings I had employed in re-establishing..my dress.

4. To reassure. *rare*[−1].

1722 DE FOE *Plague* (1754) 212 These things re-establish'd the Minds of the People very much.

Hence **re-e'stablishable** *a.*; **re-e'stablisher**; **re-e'stablishing** *vbl. sb.*

1599 SANDYS *Europæ Spec.* (1632) 162 The soveraigne restorers of vertue, and re-establishers of an happy world. **1611** COTGR., *Restablissable*, reestablishable. **1611** SPEED *Hist. Gt. Brit.* VI. xlvi. §9. 260/2 He addressed himselfe with his Armie to the reestablishing of the Ilands subiection. **1697** DRYDEN *Virgil, Life* *2 b, The wholesomness of the Air ..contributed..to the re-establishing of his Health.

re-e'stablishment. [f. as prec. + -MENT.] The act of re-establishing; the fact or condition of being re-established; restoration to a previous position or state.

1586 T. B. *La Primaud. Fr. Acad.* I. (1594) 302 Their creation after the image of God,..and..their reestablishment into the same image. **1651** HOBBES *Leviath.* III. xliii. 331 The re-establishment of the Kingdome of God in Christ. a**1679** W. OWTRAM *Serm.* (1682) 43 The reestablishment of the nation upon its antient laws. **1751** SMOLLETT *Per. Pic.* lxxxi, I repaired to Bath for the re-establishment of my health. **1788** GIBBON *Decl. & F.* lxx. VI. 575 All persons should assemble..to provide for the re-establishment of the good estate. **1817** SHELLEY *Rev. Islam* Pref., The re-establishment of successive tyrannies in France. **1884** BLACK *Jud. Shaks.* v, The re-establishment of the Catholic faith.

†**b.** Restoration to health. *Obs.*

1753 N. TORRIANO *Gangr. Sore Throat* 101 His Recovery must be slower, and..it must take up more Time for his entire Re-establishment. **1783** JOHNSON *Let. to Mrs. Thrale* 8 July, I am..willing..to persuade myself that a short succession of trifles may contribute to my re-establishment.

re-e'state, *v.* Now *rare.* [RE- 5 a.] *trans.* To reinstate, re-establish. (Very common in 17th c.)

1611 SPEED *Hist. Gt. Brit.* VII. xxxi. §3. 348 They againe sought to reestate themselues in so glorious a possession. **1630** *R. Johnson's Kingd. & Commw.* 362 The old Duke was re-estated with both their consents. a**1662** HEYLIN *Laud* (1668) 468 A day..on which the Bishop of Lincoln was re-estated with such Triumph. **1681** WALLIS *Two Serm.* i. (1682) 26 Had there not been a Degeneration..there had been no need of a Regeneration, to reestate us in it. a**1945** E. R. EDDISON *Mezentian Gate* (1972) ix. 82 Kallias's meaning was by this alliance to re-estate his power in the Meszrian Marches.

'reested, *ppl. a. Sc.* and *north. dial.* [f. REEST *v.*[2] + -ED[1].] Dried by heat or smoke.

1549 D. MUNRO in Hume Brown *Scot. bef. 1700* (1893) 263 The said stewart receives thir dewties in meill and reistit mutton, wyld foullis reistit and selchis. **1681** COLVIL *Whigs Supplic.* (1751) 19 His hands were hued like reisted hams. **1785** BURNS *Addr. to Deil* xvii, Wi' reekit duds, an' reestit gizz. **1818** SCOTT *Br. Lamm.* xxvi, Such boiling of reested hams. **1894** *Northumbld. Gloss.*, *Reested*, salted, dried, and roasted; applied to fish, particularly to herrings.

reested, rancid: see REEST *v.*[1]

'reesty, *a. Sc.* [f. REEST *v.*[3] + -Y.] Inclined to reest or stop; given to reesting.

1739 A. NICOL *Nature without Art* 8 If e'er my grov'ling reesty Rills of Sense Shall fail to glide in easy Eloquence. **1824** MACTAGGART *Gallovid. Encycl.* s.v., A horse is reestie when it stands fast, and will not move for the whip. **1895** CROCKETT *Men of Moss-hags* iv, Gay Garland was aye a reesty beast.

reesty, reesy, varr. REASTY, REASY, rancid.

reet (riːt), *a.* U.S. dial. var. RIGHT *a.* (usu. in sense 8).

Also a common dial. var. in the U.K.: see *Eng. Dial. Dict.* **1934** in WEBSTER. **1942** *Amer. Mercury* July 85 Jelly got into his zoot suit with the reet pleats. **1943** *Crisis* July 201/2 Negro youths will crack at anyone of any race who is nice looking. They will say, 'A fine queen..a reet cheet'. **1946** B. TREADWELL *Big Bk. Swing* 125/1 *Reet*, fine, O.K. **1977** *Hot Car* Oct. 42/3 People I've spoken to who went last year said it was reet good and very alcoholic.

reet, dial. variant of RIGHT, ROOT.

reeuel, obs. form of REVEL *sb.*

re-e'valuate, *v.* [RE- 5 a.] *trans.* To evaluate again.

1945 *Physiol. Rev.* XXV. 126 Those same changes which were originally considered slight and of no consequence have more recently been re-evaluated in the light of new experiments and are now spoken of as 'worthy of emphasis'. **1964** M. A. K. HALLIDAY et al. *Linguistic Sci.* p. xiii, As theories develop so must applications thereof be re-expounded, and books continually re-evaluated. **1972** *Jrnl. Social Psychol.* LXXXVII. 145 The modified semantic differential was translated into Afghan colloquial speech and reevaluated according to the criteria of excellence. **1976** *Nature* 29 Apr. 740/2 It asked the Secretary of the Department of Health, Education and Welfare (of which NIDA is a part) to reevaluate the project and determine whether Rubin is suitably qualified to conduct the research. **1979** *Time* 2 Apr. 2/3 Their music has the power to force people to reevaluate their ideas and institutions.

Hence **re-evalu'ation**, a second or further evaluation.

1946 *Nature* 16 Nov. 689/2 In view of the great progress made in recent years on the pancreatic enzymes, there is no doubt that much of the older work on the peptidases, etc., of the intestinal canal will need re-evaluation. **1959** *Encounter* Sept. 58/1 These re-evaluations called into question the accepted idea of the populist basis of American radicalism. **1970** *Publishers' Weekly* 8 June 152/1 This capability is worth noting; it may cause a reevaluation of short-run publishing. **1972** *Maclean's Mag.* Sept. 12/2 It is too much to hope that it will cause a re-evaluation in the selection of officers from the top down. **1976** *Nature* 29 Apr. 740/2 The reevaluation was carried out on March 11 at a closed meeting.

re-e'vaporate, *v.* [RE- 5 a.] To evaporate again. So **re-evapo'ration**.

1839 URE *Dict. Arts* 297 The solution..[must be] re-evaporated and re-crystallized. **1862** ANSTED *Channel Isl.* IV. xx. (ed. 2) 470 The rain-fall, part of which is immediately re-evaporated. *Ibid.*, When the necessary deductions are made for re-evaporation. **1878** THURSTON *Growth Steam-Eng.* 107 The condensation and reëvaporation of steam.

reeve (riːv), *sb.*[1] Now chiefly *Hist.* Forms: 1 **ᵹi-, ᵹeroefa, ᵹeréfa, réfa**, 2 **irefe**, 3 **ref-**, 5, 7 **refe**, 6 **reeffe**, *Sc.* **reif**; 2–8 (9) **reve**, 4 **reyve**, 5 **rive**, 6–7 **reave**, 4, 6– **reeve**. [OE. *ᵹeréfa*, earlier *ᵹirǽfa*, of uncertain etym.; app. not in any way related to the continental forms cited under GRAF, GRAVE *sb.*[3] and *sb.*[4] Old Northumbrian had also the form *grǽfa* whence GRIEVE *sb.*]

1. *Hist.* **a.** An Old English official of high rank having a local jurisdiction under the king; the chief magistrate of a town or district. †Also, in OE., applied to prefects, governors, etc., of Roman and Jewish times.

On the position of the *ᵹeréfa* in OE. times see Kemble *Saxons in England* (1876) II. v. 151-181; and cf. the articles on BOROUGH-REEVE, PORTREEVE, and SHERIFF. Modern writers have sometimes used the OE. form of the word.

a**700** *Epinal Gloss.* 197 *Censores*, ᵹiroefan. *Ibid.* 223 *Commentariensis*, ᵹiroefa. **805** *Charter* in *O.E. Texts* 442 Æðelnoð se ᵹerefa to eastoreᵹe. c**850** *O.E. Martyrol.* 25 Dec. 4 þa het se ᵹerefa hie belucan in carcerne. a**900** tr. *Bæda's Hist.* II. xiii. [xvi.] (1890) 144 þa ærest to Drihtnes ᵹeleafan [he] ᵹecerde Lindcylene ceastre ᵹerefan [L. *præfectum*].. mid his heorode. c**1000** *Ags. Gosp.* Mark xv. 43 þa com iosep se æðela ᵹerefa of abarimathia. c**1175** *Lamb. Hom.* 115 [The king] scal soðfeste men setten him to irefen. c**1205** LAY. 15597 þa wes inne Kair-Merðin a reue þe hehte Eli. a**1225** *Juliana* 8 He bi-ȝet et te keiser, þat he ȝettede him reue to beonne. c**1300** *Havelok* 1627 Wile ich speke with non oþer reue, But with þe, þat iustise are. a**1577** SIR T. SMITH *Commw. Eng.* (1609) 69 The sherife (which is asmuch to say as the Reeue or Baily of the shire). **1593** NORDEN *Spec. Brit.*, *M'sex* I. 7 The Saxons called him *Scyreᵹerefa*, the Reeve of the Shire. **1710** PRIDEAUX *Orig. Tithes* iv. 199, I Athelstan..do command all my Reves in my Kingdom [etc.]. **1839** KEIGHTLEY *Hist. Eng.* I. 24 When the reeve of the next town attempted to make them prisoners, they slew him, and escaped to their vessels. **1867** FREEMAN *Norm. Conq.* (1876) I. v. 318 Hugh, a Frenchman, was now the royal reeve in Exeter. **1874** GREEN *Short Hist.* i. §6. 55 The royal reeves, officers despatched to levy the royal revenues and administer the royal justice.

b. *high reeve* (OE. *heahᵹeréfa*).

The precise nature of the rank or office denoted by this title is uncertain: see Kemble (as above) 156-7.

?c**900** *Wergilds* c. 2 §4 in Thorpe *Laws* I. 186 Holdes & cyninges heah-ᵹerefan [ᵹild] .iiii. þusend þrymsa. c**950** *Lindisf. Gosp.* Mark xiii. 9 Befora undercyningum *vel* hehᵹeroefum [L. *præsides*] & cyningum ᵹie biðon stondende. c**1002** *O.E. Chron.* (Parker MS.) an. 1001 Ðær wearð Æþelweard cinges heahȝerefa ofsleᵹen..and Leofwine cinges heahᵹerefa. a**1225** *Juliana* 8 Maximian hehest in rome, þat is heh reue. **1848** KEMBLE *Saxons in Eng.* II. v. (1876) II. 157 These high-reeves were therefore probably military officers of Æðelred. **1872** E. W. ROBERTSON *Hist. Ess.* 177 Amongst the Northumbrians, the place of the Ealderman seems to have been filled by the High-Reeve.

2. †**a.** A bailiff, steward, or overseer; a minor officer appointed by a landowner to superintend his estates, tenants, or workmen. *Obs.* (Cf. GRIEVE.) **b.** A local official of minor rank; an overseer of a parish, a churchwarden, or the like. (See also *church-*, *fen-*, *field-reeve*.)

a**1300** *Beket* 49 Gilbert and his felawes..Prisoun breke. ..The reve amorwe that hem scholde to here labour lede, Nuste he tho he miste hem what him was to rede. a**1300** *Vox & Wolf* 26 in Hazl. *E.P.P.* I. 58 For he com in withouten leue Bothen of haiward and of reue. **1340** *Ayenb.* 37 þe ontrewe reuen, prouos, and bedeles and seruons þat steleþ þe amendes and wyþdraȝeþ þe rentes of hire lhordes. **1362** LANGL. *P. Pl.* A. II. 78 Rondulf þe Reue of Rotelondes sokene. **1377** *Ibid.* B. v. 427, I can holde louedayes, and here a reues rekenynge. c**1380** WYCLIF *Wks.* (1880) 195 Oure prestis ben so bysye aboute worldly occupacioun þat þei semen bettere bailyues or reues þan gostly prestis of ihesu crist. **1419** *Liber Albus* (Rolls) I. 14 Hoc nomen 'reve' Saxonice sonat 'villicum' vel 'ballivum', qui sæpius in ore populi nominatur. c**1440** *Promp. Parv.* 431/2 Reve, lordys serwawnte, *prepositus.* **1511-12** *Act 3 Hen. VIII*, c. 23 §9 The said accomptauntes..that is to saye, Feodaries Bailliffes Reves Heywardes and Bedelles. **1574** tr. *Littleton's Tenures* 17 b, Hee may surrender hys landes unto the Bayliffe or to the Reeve. **1603** OWEN *Pembrokeshire* (1892) 191 The Landlord by his bailiffe or reave vseth to arrest so much of the tenantes goods vpon the land as ys found of decaye. **1686** PLOT *Staffordsh.* 434 To this Hobby-horse dance there also belong'd a pot, which was kept by turns, by 4 or 5 of the cheif of the Town, whom they call'd Reeves. **1710** J. HARRIS *Lex. Techn.* II, *Reeve* of a Church is the Guardian of it; or the Church-Warden. **1765** BLACKSTONE *Comm.* I. xi. 377 Neither can he be chosen to any temporal office; as bailiff, reeve, constable, or the like. **1791** in *15th Rep. Commissioners Woods, Forests*, etc. (1793) 40 The Cattle of the Commoners are marked by the Reeves of the respective Parishes. **1871** *Daily News* 21 Sept., The reeve of Leyton..reported encroachments in Wanstead Flats.

c. A foreman or overseer in a coal-mine.
1863 *Edin. Rev.* Apr. 417 The Reeve went on a few yards in advance of the party—his unlighted Davy-lamp in one hand. **1879** Miss Jackson *Shropsh. Word-bk.*, *Reeve*, the underground overlooker of the pits.
d. In Canada, the president of a village- or town-council.
1853 S. Strickland *27 Yrs. Canada West* II. 271 Counties.. choose their reeves, and deputy reeves where the population admits of it, and these form the county council. **1884** *Brandon* (Manitoba) *Blade* 17 Jan. 8/3 The Reeve, in a few well chosen remarks, dwelt on the duties and responsibilities devolving on them as servants of the people. **1890** Dilke *Probl. Greater Brit.* I. i. ii. 112 The council of every village or township [in Canada] consists of one reeve and four councillors, and the county council consists of the reeves and deputy-reeves of the townships and villages within the county. **1945** G. W. Brown *Canad. Democracy in Action* vii. 89 The town council consists of a mayor, a reeve, and two or three councillors elected for each of the wards. **1965** *Victoria* (B.C.) *Daily Times* 20 July 11/8 The reeve said the general principle of regional planning is good but the mechanics need improving. **1968** *Globe & Mail* (Toronto) 5 Feb. 1/3 Dresden Reeve Wilfred Shaw said 61 families had been removed from their houses by firemen and other town employees.
3. *attrib.* (in *obs.* or *arch.* terms), as ***reeve-ham***, ***-land***, ***-mead***, ***-pole*** (see quot. 1813), ***-roll***, ***-sheaf***.
969 *Charter* in Birch *Cartul. Saxon.* (1893) III. 532 We writað him... vi. æcras mæde on þa gerefmæde. *c* **1000** *Gloss.* in Wright *Vocab.* (1873) II. 45 *In tribulano territorio*, on þæm sundor ʒereflande. **1235–52** *Rentalia Glaston.* (Som. Rec. Soc.) 34 Pro iiij^or acris que vocantur Reflond iij *sol.* *Ibid.* 93 Et debet qualibet die in autumpno.. unum revesef. *Ibid.* 118 Et [prepositus] habebit j pratum quod appellatur Refmede. *Ibid.* 140 [Prepositus] debet habere ij hammes prati.. que vocantur Refhammes. **1393** Langl. *P. Pl.* C. xxii. 465 With *spiritus intellectus* thei toke þe reeue-rolles. **1778** *Eng. Gazetteer* (ed. 2) s.v. *Taunton*, The tenures here are copyhold-lands, over-lands, and reve-lands. **1813** *Guide to Watering Places* 459 The landlord of the Portland Arms usually has it in his power to shew the Reevepole, or Saxon mode of keeping accounts. **1897** Maitland *Domesday & Beyond* 169 Besides this he seems to have 'reveland' which belongs to him as sheriff.

reeve (riːv), *sb.*² [Of obscure origin: the form REE *sb.*² is found earlier, but is less frequent.] The female of the RUFF (*Tringa pugnax*).
1634 *Althorp MS.* in Simpkinson *Washingtons* (1860) App. 12 Ruff and reeve 3 dozen. *Ibid.* 15 For 20 dozen and 5 ruffs and reeves. **1648** Herrick *Hesper., Panegyr. Sir L. Pemberton*, The phesant,.. reeve, ruffe, raile. **1678** Ray *Willughby's Ornith.* 302 The Ruff, whose Female is called a Reeve. **1768** Pennant *Brit. Zool.* II. 364 The Reeves, or females are said never to change their colors. **1831** Rennie *Montagu's Ornith. Dict.* 445 When the Reeves begin to lay, both those and the Ruffs are least shy, and.. easily caught. **1871** *Athenæum* 3 June 689/2 The ruff and the reeve, now reduced to only a few pairs in a single locality, must also soon be lost if not protected by the law.

reeve (riːv), *sb.*³ [Of obscure origin: the two senses may represent different words.]
1. A string or rope (of onions). Now only *dial.*
1678 Sampson in *Phil. Trans.* XII. 1001 All distended with Liquor, and ty'd, like a Reeve of Onions altogether. **1854–96** in dial. glossaries (Northampt., Leic., Warw.).
2. A long narrow strip. ? *Obs.*
1725 Dudley in *Phil. Trans.* XXXIII. 258 Both the Finbacks and Humpbacks are shaped in Reeves longitudinal from Head to Tail on their Bellies and their Sides, so far as their Fins. **1770** Franklin *Lett.* Wks. 1840 VI. 335 The edges of two sheets are laid down so as to lap or cover each other an inch, and a slip of the same copper, about three inches and a half broad, called the reeve, is introduced between them.

reeve (riːv), *v.*¹ Chiefly *Naut.* Also 7 rieve, 8 reif. *Pa. t.* and *pa. pple.* rove and reeved; also 9 *pa. pple.* roven. [Of obscure origin; usually referred to Du. *reven*, but this means 'to reef'. The earlier form of the pa. t. and pa. pple. is *reeved*.]
1. a. *trans.* To pass (a rope) through a hole, ring, or block. Also const. *through*.
1627 [see REEVING *vbl. sb.*]. **1658** Phillips, *To Reeve*, a Term in Navigation, and spoken of ropes, signifieth as much as to put in or to put through. **1667** Sir H. Mainwayring *Sea-Man's Dict.* 81 When we would expresse that the Tack is put through the Ches-trees, we say it is reeved through. **1743** Bulkeley & Cummins *Voy. S. Seas* 14 Reev'd the Top Ropes, and lower'd the Yard. **1748** *Anson's Voy.* I. x. 104 We exerted ourselves.. to reeve new lanyards, and to mend our sails. **1794** Nelson Mar. in Nicolas *Disp.* (1845) I. 379 Purchases will be rove to drag the guns. **1803** *Phil. Trans.* XCIII. 322 With great difficulty.. I got small lines rove through four of the ports on the starboard side. **1825** Waterton *Wand. S. Amer.* III. iv. 264 One end of the new rope.. was reeved through the chain of the shark-hook. **1898** F. T. Bullen *Cruise Cachalot* 321 All hands were kept busily employed preparing for stormy weather—reeving new running-gear.
b. *transf.* To thrust or pass (a rod, etc.) *through* any aperture or opening.
1681 R. Knox *Hist. Ceylon* I. vii. 28 Then they.. take them [fish] out. And rieve a Rattan thro their gills. **1706** E. Ward *Wooden World Diss.* (1708) 54 With the Reigns reif'd through both Hands, he streight hawls them aft like Main-Sheets. **1867** F. Francis *Angling* viii. (1880) 259 The tackle is not reeved through the gill. **1869** Sir E. Reed *Shipbuild.* v. 80 One of the angle-irons at each transverse frame is reeved through a score just above the upper edge of the side bar.
c. *intr.* Of a rope: To pass *through* a block, etc.
1860 *Merc. Marine Mag.* VII. 113 The.. lines are to reeve through a.. block. **1882** Nares *Seamanship* (ed. 6) 9 Chocks of wood.. for the fore-topmast stays to reeve through.
2. *trans.* To place *in*, *on*, or *round*, to fix *to*, something by reeving.
1667 Sir H. Mainwayring *Sea-Man's Dict.* 81 Instead of putting a rope through a block, we say, Reeve it in that block (as the Halliards are reeved in the Knights and Ram-heads). **1752** Smeaton in *Phil. Trans.* XLVII. 496 From this construction arises a new method of reeving the line upon the shieves. *Ibid.*, The last line.. being reeved round those till it comes at the opposite side. **1821** Scott *Pirate* xxii, He would willingly reeve a rope to the yard-arm for the benefit of an unfortunate buccanier. **1833** Marryat *P. Simple* (1863) 100 Double breechings were rove on the guns.
3. a. To fit (a block) with a rope by reeving; to attach in this way; to tie.
1639 R. Gibson in *Harper's Mag.* (1883) Mar. 597/2 The block was reeved at the mainyard to have ducked her. **1793** Smeaton *Edystone L.* §143 Those blocks being reeved and brought together. *Ibid.* Expl. Pl. 18 The greater sheaves are reeved as far as can be on them. **1807** Vancouver *Agric. Devon* 130 A hook, reeved at one end of the tackle-rope, takes the middle band. **1850** Scoresby *Cheever's Whalem. Adv.* iii. 37 They proceeded to reeve the huge blocks that are always made fast.. to the fore and main mast head. **1895** Crockett *Men of Moss-hags* li. 365 Nigh halfway up the steep bank stood our little Margaret, loosely reeved to a sunken stob.
b. Of a rope: To pass through (a block).
1775 Falck *Day's Diving Vessel* 27 Above and below were eyes on each side, through which went the rope that reeved the block.
c. *transf.* Of a ship: To thread (shoals or ice-pack).
1860 *Merc. Marine Mag.* VII. 122 After a day of hair-breadth escapes, literally reeving the shoals, by conning from the mast-head and jib-boom, the fair channel was reached. **1867** Smyth *Sailor's Word-bk.* 566 *Reeving*, in polar voyaging, following up serpentine channels in the ice, till the vessel reaches open water, or reeves the pack.
d. *fig.* To gather together.
1876 G. M. Hopkins *Wreck of Deutschland* xii, in *Poems* (1967) 55 Yet did the dark side of the bay of thy blessing Not vault them, the millions of rounds of thy mercy not reeve even them in?
Hence **reeved** (riːvd), *ppl. a.*
1775 Falck *Day's Diving Vessel* 51 Reeve them at an equal distance,.. tie the reeved parts together with a rope-yarn.

reeve (riːv), *v.*² Now only *dial.* [Of obscure origin.] = REE *v.* Hence **'reeving** *vbl. sb.*² (also in comb. ***reeving-sieve***).
1688 R. Holme *Armoury* III. 74/1 Reeving, is to sift the Corn, to cleanse it from small seeds. *Ibid.* 331/1 The Reeving Sieve is to cleanse Corn at the time of Winnowing from the dreggs of Chaff. **1820** Wilbraham *Chesh. Gloss.* (ed. 2), *Reeve*, to separate corn that has been winnowed from the small seeds which are among it; this is done with what they call the reeving sieve. **1880** *W. Cornw. Gloss.*, *Reeve*, to separate by means of a sieve [etc.]. **1886** Elworthy *W. Som. Word-bk.*, Reive. *Ibid.*, Reiving-zieve.

reeve (riːv), *v.*³ *dial.* [Of obscure origin.] *intr.* To twine, twist, wind or unwind.
1821 Clare *Vill. Minstr.* I. 114 Medicinal betony, By thy wood-side railings, reeves With antique mullein's flannel-leaves. **1876** S. C. J. Ingham *White Cross & Dove of Pearls* xliii. 281 How difficult it was.. to keep the threads from twitching and the silk from reeving. **1890** *Gloucestersh. Gloss.*, *Reeve*,.. to twist round, unwind.

'reever. *rare*—¹. [Of obscure origin.] A wooden instrument for collecting the crushed apples from the cider-mill.
1833 Loudon *Encycl. Archit.* §1314 The Reever.. to push it [apple-pulp] up together for removal when ground.

Reeves (riːvz). The name of John Reeves (1774–1856), English naturalist, used *absol.*, *attrib.*, or in the possessive in **Reeves('s) pheasant** to designate a long-tailed Chinese pheasant, *Syrmaticus reevesii*, introduced to Europe by him and named in his honour by J. E. Gray in 1829.
1829 J. E. Gray in E. Griffith et al. tr. *Cuvier's Anim. Kingdom* VIII. 25 (*heading*) Reeves' Pheasant, *Phasianus Reevesii*. **1834** G. Bennett *Wanderings in N.S.W.* II. iv. 55 In the aviary [at Macao], the beautiful.. Reeves's Pheasant, was seen. **1922** W. Beebe *Monogr. Pheasants* III. 146 Then came my first view of a live Reeves in its wild home. **1926** J. S. Huxley *Ess. Pop. Sci.* 47 If a female Reeves pheasant is crossed with a male of another race, the males among the hybrid offspring show many characters of the male Reeves pheasant. **1951** J. Delacour *Pheasants of World* ix. 227 Reeves's Pheasants are found on all the higher wooded hills of Central China north of the Yangtze River. **1975** *Islander* (Victoria, B.C.) 19 Oct. 4/3 We now have.. the rare Reeves pheasant. **1976** *Shooting Times & Country Mag.* 18–24 Nov. 28/2 He is, however, incorrect in his remarks about the Reeves pheasant.

'reeveship. Forms: 1 ʒerefscipe, 3 refschipe, 7 reeveship. [f. *ʒeréfa* REEVE *sb.*¹ + -SHIP.] The office of a reeve.
c **1000** ÆLFRIC *Hom.* II. 94 Ne heora nan ʒerefscipe oððe mangunge ne drife, forðan ðe hi sind ʒecorene of woruld-mannum to Godes teolungum. *a* **1225** *Leg. Kath.* 11 Maxence steorede þe refschipe in Rome. *a* **1225** *Juliana* 9 Se riche refschipe to rihten and to readen. **1631** *Charter* in Bingham *Rep.* V. 340 A grant by Charles I.. of.. the reeveship of Greetham and the bailiwick of Greetham.

reevesite ('riːvzaɪt). *Min.* [f. the name of Frank *Reeves*, Australian geologist + -ITE¹.] A hydrated basic carbonate of nickel and iron, $Ni_6Fe_2CO_3(OH)_{16}.4H_2O$, occurring as yellowish plates.
1967 J. S. White et al. in *Amer. Mineralogist* LII. 1182 Reevesite: This mineral occurs as bright yellow fine-grained aggregates lining cavities and cracks in the weathered meteorites. *Ibid.* 1193 The mineral is named reevesite in honor of Dr. Frank Reeves, who was responsible for the discovery of the Wolf Creek meteorite crater in 1947. **1971** *Ibid.* LVI. 1077 Reevesite.. has been found in the nickel ore from the Bon Accord area in the Barberton Mountain Land, South Africa.

reeving ('riːvɪŋ), *vbl. sb.*¹ [f. REEVE *v.*¹ + -ING¹.] The action of passing a rope through a block, etc.; the manner in which this is done.
1627 Capt. Smith *Seaman's Gram.* v. 23 Reeuing is.. drawing a rope thorow a blocke or oylet to runne vp and down. **1793** Smeaton *Edystone L.* Expl. Pl. 18 The principle whereon the reeving is performed. **1844** H. Stephens *Bk. of Farm* II. 321 The reeving of the pulleys and chains will be more clearly seen in the perspective views. **1892** Kipling *Life's Handicap* 182 The reeving and unreeving of the bed-tapes.
attrib. *c* **1860** H. Stuart *Seaman's Catech.* 24 They are usually rove with a reeving line. **1969** E. H. Pinto *Treen* 266 The pear-shaped, elm object is a reeving block. **1971** *Gloss. Terms Materials Handling* (*B.S.I.*) v. 18 *Reeving thimble*, a thimble.. of sufficient internal length and breadth for one thimble to pass through another. **1975** *Offshore* Sept. (Dutch Suppl.) 49–12/3 The actual pulling wires, also 57-mm diameter, ran from the Pontra Maris to a sheave pontoon anchored 2 km away by eight 7·2-ton capacity delta anchors. The reeving system allowed a total pulling force of 600 tons.

reeving, *vbl. sb.*²: see REEVE *v.*²

reewe, obs. form of RUE *v.*

re-e'xalt, *v.* [RE- 5 a.] *trans.* To exalt again.
1670 Milton *Hist. Eng.* v. Wks. 1851 V. 192 Ethelred like in fortune to the former Ethelred, was re-exalted to his Seat.

re-e'xaminable, *a.* [RE- 5 a.] Capable of being re-examined.
1847 Webster cites Story. **1893** *Voice* (N.Y.) 20 Apr., That conclusion is not re-examinable here.

† **re-examinate**, *pa. pple. Sc. Obs.* [RE- 5 a: cf. next.] Re-examined.
1573 *Reg. Privy Council Scot.* II. 213 My Lord Regentis Grace.. ordanit David Nicholl and Johnne Barclay witnessis, sworne and examinat of befoir.. to be re-examinat.

re-exami'nation. [RE- 5 a.] A second or further examination.
1604 Bacon *Apol.* Wks. 1879 I. 440 Afterwards upon a re-examination of some that charged him,.. I went instantly to the queen. **1611** Cotgr., *Revision*, a reuision, reuise, reuiew, reexamination. **1642** in Clarendon *Hist. Reb.* IV. §290 Or if, upon their re-examination, they did not find particular evidence [etc.]. **1713** Derham *Phys.-Theol.* To Rdr., By a critical Re-examination, I find.. they are not so true as mine. **1748** Richardson *Clarissa* (1768) IV. xxxv. 215 And if, upon a re-examination of my own heart, I find [etc.]. **1814** Scott *Wav.* xlix, I found that.. from a re-examination of the persons engaged in the mutiny.. he was much softened towards you. **1869** M. Pattison *Serm.* (1885) 181 A re-examination of the received principles of natural religion.

re-e'xamine, *v.* [RE- 5 a.] *trans.* To examine again; *spec.* in legal use, of a counsel, to examine (a witness) again, after cross-examination by the opposing counsel.
1594 Hooker *Eccl. Pol.* Pref. vi. §5 Spend the time in re-examining more duly your cause. **1605** Bacon *Adv. Learn.* II. To King §12 As most of the usages.. were derived from more obscure times, it is the more requisite they be re-examined. *a* **1639** Wotton in *Reliq.* (1651) 463 The false Accusers.. might be re-examined likewise about their Uncle. **1737** Waterland *Eucharist* i. Wks. 1843 IV. 477 A learned and considerate writer, who very lately has re-examined the chronology of that Epistle. **1776** G. Semple *Building in Water* 66 If you turn back and re-examine the Borings. **1827** Lytton *Falkland* I. 6, I am not unwilling to re-examine the past. **1898** *Allbutt's Syst. Med.* V. 513 For a year thereafter she must be re-examined.

re-'excavate, *v.* [RE- 5 a.] *trans.* To excavate again. So **re-exca'vation**.
1851 Lyell *Elem. Geol.* x. 119 Thus the original valleys might have been re-excavated. *Ibid.* 120 The filling up and re-excavation of the valleys. **1873** J. Geikie *Gt. Ice Age* xxiv. 317 Rivers.. re-excavated the gravels that were laid down during the previous period.

re-ex'change, *sb.* [RE- 5 a.]
1. *Comm.* (See quots. and cf. RECHANGE *sb.* 1.)
1707 Justice *Treat. Monies* 3 The Re-Exchange is the like Sum of Money, payable by the Drawer of a Bill which is return'd protested; for the Exchange of the Sum, contain'd in the Bill, back again to the place whence it was drawn. **1727–41** Chambers *Cycl.* s.v., The occasion of re-exchange is, when the bearer of a bill of exchange, after protesting it.. draws a bill of exchange in the place where the payment was to be made, on the person who furnished the first. **1809** R. Langford *Introd. Trade* 22 Re-exchange means the damages incurred by non-acceptance and non-payment, and they consist of protest charges on the amount of the bill, commission, bill brokerage, interest, stamps, and postages. **1877** *Law Rep.* 7 *Chanc. Div.* 641 Re-exchange is defined.. to be the difference in the value of a bill occasioned by its being dishonoured in a foreign country in which it was payable.
2. A second or fresh exchange.
1856 Olmsted *Slave States* 566, I asked the landlord what I should do to effect a reëxchange.

So **re-ex'change** *v. trans.*, to exchange again. **1873** *Routledge's Young Gentlm. Mag.* Dec. 117/2 Opportunity to re-exchange the cards.

re-ex'cite, *v.* [RE- 5 a.] *trans.* To excite again. Hence **re-ex'cited** *ppl. a.*; **re-ex'citing** *vbl. sb.* and *ppl. a.*

1697 J. SERGEANT *Solid Philos.* 195 Some short time must be allow'd for the coming of Impressions from without.. and the Re-exciting them in the Fancy. *Ibid.* 438 Such Sounds, thro' the *use* of the Words are apt to re-excite the Memory. **1804-6** SYD. SMITH *Mor. Philos.* (1850) 269 New ..fields of knowledge, which have re-excited those faculties ..and improved them by exercise. **1816** KIRBY & SP. *Entomol.* xxvii. (1818) II. 507 The instinct..lies dormant: but transfer the bees to a new hive..and it is instantly re-excited. **1822-34** *Good's Study Med.* (ed. 4) I. 567 The increased action and re-excited energy that restore the system to a balance of health. **1868** *Chambers's Encycl.* X. 221/1 (*Wine*) Before it [fermentation] is quite finished, the whole liquid mass is stirred up so as to re-excite the process. **1899** *Allbutt's Syst. Med.* VIII. 483 In this way eruptions are repeatedly re-excited. **1964** J. Z. YOUNG *Model of Brain* xiii. 211 Here we may notice that because it contains re-exciting circuits it could provide an increase in the 'command to attack' by what amounts to a positive feed-back.

So **re-exci'tation.**

1880 *Fraser's Mag.* May 664 The partial re-excitation of some faded current of parental instinct.

re-'execute, *v.* [RE- 5 a.] *trans.* To execute again. So **re-exe'cution.**

1858 LD. ST. LEONARDS *Handy-Bk. Prop. Law* xvii. 128 Generally speaking, it will not now be necessary to re-execute your will. *Ibid.* xviii. 139, I will presently explain to you the object of a re-execution of your will. **1884** *Law Times Rep.* L. 630/1 The work..was not executed..in a workmanlike manner, and..he had been compelled to take it out and re-execute it.

re-'exercise, *v.* [RE- 5 a.] *trans.* To exercise again.

1657 HAWKE *Killing is Murder* 12 To make way for the readmitting of the then King, to the reexercising that power which had produced such bloody and fatal effects.

re-e'xert, *v.* [RE- 5 a.] To exert again.

1782 SMEATON in *Phil. Trans.* LXXII. 346 The operation of half the mechanic power is..only locked up and suspended, and capable of being re-exerted.

re-ex'hale, *v.* [RE- 5 a.] To exhale again.

a **1676** HALE *Prim. Orig. Man.* III. iv. (1677) 267 Grass, which is..most visited with the Dew of Heaven, and re-exhaled again. **1733** TULL *Horse-hoeing Husb.* xi. 138 Most of the Dew that falls on it is re-exhal'd from untill'd Land.

re-e'xhaust, *v.* [RE- 5 a.] To exhaust again.

a **1711** KEN *Hymnarium* Poet. Wks. 1721 II. 113 Give me a Love which thou wilt re-exhaust.

re-e'xhibit, *v.* [RE- 5 a.] To exhibit again.

a **1648** LD. HERBERT *Hen. VIII* (1683) 528 So the Book was re-exhibited to the Emperor. **1654** H. L'ESTRANGE *Chas. I* (1655) 129 At Guildhall, where the resplendent shew was iterated and re-exhibited. **1836** LYTTON *Athens* (1837) II. 518 That a chorus should be granted to any poet who chose to re-exhibit his dramas. **1857** DUFFERIN *Lett. High Lat.* (ed. 3) 25 After a few minutes, each in turn re-exhibited itself with monotonous punctuality.

So **re-exhi'bition.**

1816 BENTHAM *Chrestom.* Wks. 1843 VIII. 15 Supplying the deficiency by repetitions and re-exhibitions made for this express purpose.

re-e'xist, *v.* [RE- 5 a.] *intr.* To exist again.

1841 EMERSON *Misc.* (1855) 173 That they may re-exist and reappear in the finer world of rational souls. **1853** G. S. FABER *Revival* 40 It plainly will reëxist, should that last Head be restored to political power.

So **re-e'xistence; re-e'xistent** *a.*

1664 H. MORE *Myst. Iniq.* 291 Understanding the revived or re-existent Beast of the persecuting Empire under Julian the Apostate. **1806** G. S. FABER *Diss. Prophecies* (1814) II. 207 The existence, the non-existence, and the re-existence, of the Roman beast. **1847** F. W. NEWMAN *Hist. Hebrew Monarchy* 305 A doctrine of future personal re-existence. **1973** *Times Lit. Suppl.* 14 Dec. 1536/2 He builds up imaginary examples of transmigration, re-existence, etc.

re-ex'pand, *v.* [RE- 5 a.] *trans.* and *intr.* To expand again. Hence **re-ex'panding** *vbl. sb.*

1660 BOYLE *New Exp. Phys. Mech.* ii. 40 The Box they are inclos'd in would as much resist their re-expanding of themselves. **1873** DARWIN in *Life & Lett.* (1887) III. 323 One was taken out and placed in cold water, and it re-expanded. **1884** *Athenæum* 16 Aug. 215/2 Nitrogen compressed,..refrigerated,..and then re-expanded, falls down in snow-like flakes.

So **re-ex'pansion.**

1873 DARWIN in *Life & Lett.* (1887) III. 323 Not the least power of re-expansion. **1898** *Allbutt's Syst. Med.* V. 386 Followed by slight re-expansion of lung.

†**re-ex'pect,** *v. Obs.* [RE- 5 a. Cf. late L. *re-expectāre* (Vulg.).] *trans.* To expect again.

1620 BRENT tr. *Sarpi's Counc. Trent* VI. 577 Hee sendeth, and countermandeth, expecteth, and reexpecteth.

re-ex'pel, *v.* [RE- 5 a.] To expel again.

1864 in WEBSTER. **1899** *Daily News* 14 Jan. 5/4 On the expiration of the sentence he will be re-expelled.

re-ex'perience, *v.* [RE- 5 a.] *trans.* To experience again.

1789 MRS. PIOZZI *Journ. France* I. 12, I was pleased to.. re-experience that particular sensation. **1831** T. HOPE *Ess. Origin Man* I. 90 No portion of time appears..again able to be recallable, so as to be re-experienced.

So **re-ex'perience** *sb.*, a renewed experience.

1848 G. J. MACKENZIE *Year's Ministry* 95 We wish the re-experience of his favour.

re-'export, *sb. Comm.* [RE- 5 a.]

1. A commodity re-exported. Also (chiefly in *pl.*), the amount (*of* something) re-exported.

1761 *Descr. S. Carolina* 48 The Re-exports of imported Commodities and Manufactures. **1828-32** WEBSTER, *Re-export*, any commodity re-exported. **1874** RAYMOND *Statist. Mines & Mining* 524 Tabular statement of imports, exports, and re-exports of gold and silver coin and bullion.

2. = RE-EXPORTATION.

1761 J. GLEN *Descr. S. Carolina* 48 The Exports of South Carolina Produce are inserted in one Account, and the Re-exports of imported Commodities and Manufactures in another. **1775** *Jrnls. Continental Congress U.S.* (1905) III. 502 The reëxport employs ships, sailors [etc.]. **1792** A. YOUNG *Trav. France* 494 Where they see navigation, re-export, commercial profit, and a great circulation. **1841** W. SPALDING *Italy & It. Isl.* III. 389 For re-export to other parts of the Mediterranean. **1885** *Manch. Exam.* 8 Apr. 5/5 The statistics of the re-export of raw cotton for the three years show a steady increase.

re-ex'port, *v. Comm.* [RE- 5 a.] *trans.* To export (imported goods) again.

1690 CHILD *Disc. Trade* ix. 162 Commodities to be further Manufactured here, or re-Exported. **1719** W. WOOD *Surv. Trade* 276 Whereof a very small value is Re-exported to Foreign Countries. **1769** BURKE *Late St. Nation* Wks. II. 71 Such an immense quantity of goods exported and re-exported. **1861** GOSCHEN *For. Exch.* 16 If they are re-exported to America..they would again affect the exchanges in the contrary direction.

re-expor'tation. [RE- 5 a.] The exportation of imported goods.

1729 *Seasonable Remarks Trade* 98 Their great Wealth arises from the Re-exportation of the Growth of other Countries. **1761** *Descr. S. Carolina* 49 The Re-exportation of British Commodities and Manufactures from our Northern Colonies. **1804** *Edin. Rev.* IX. 114 The reexportation of this superfluous specie. **1876** BANCROFT *Hist. U.S.* III. xi. 452 Rice might be warehoused in England for re-exportation.

re-ex'pound, *v.* [RE- 5 a.] *trans.* To expound again.

1867 BUSHNELL *Mor. Uses Dark Th.* 249 The topic is in the hospitals and the courts expounded and re-expounded. **1888** *Centen. Confer. Missions* (U.S.) II. 61 The principle [of marriage] was re-expounded by the Lord Jesus Christ.

re-ex'press, *v.* [RE- 5 a.] *trans.* To express again. Hence **re-ex'pressing** *ppl. a.*

1649 J. ECLISTON tr. *Behmen's Epistles* vi. (1886) 66 A former of the re-expressing or re-spirating will. **1858** A. LINCOLN in *Voice* (N.Y.) (1890) 20 Nov., I was glad to express my gratitude at Quincy, and I re-express it here. **1889** *Spectator* 13 Apr., [A] desire to see the Ornaments Rubric re-expressed in a more comprehensive spirit.

So **re-ex'pression.**

1832 AUSTIN *Jurispr.* (1879) II. 1057 A re-expression and arrangement of statute law.

re-ex'pulsion. [RE- 5 a.] A second expulsion.

1655 FULLER *Ch. Hist.* II. v. §47 The next Archbishop of Canterbury, endeavoured the re-expulsion of the Priests.

†**re-ex'struct,** *pa. pple. Obs.*$^{-1}$ [RE- 5 a.] Rebuilt.

1594 CHAPMAN *Shadow of Night* E, Thy glorious temple ..shall now againe, Be reexstruct, and this Ephesia be Thy countries happie name.

re-ex'tend, *v.* [RE- 5 a.] To extend again.

1611 COTGR., *Restendre*, to reextend, or to reinlarge. **1882** SPENCER *Princ. Sociol.*, *Pol. Instit.* 750 When, as at home, an extended franchise, very soon re-extended, vastly augments the mass of those who [etc.].

†**re-ex'tent.** *Law. Obs.* [f. RE- 5 a + EXTENT *sb.* 2.] (See quot.)

1607 COWELL *Interpr.*, *Reextent*, is a second extent made vpon lands, or tenements, vpon complaint made, that the former extent was partially performed. [Hence in Phillips (ed. Kersey 1706) and in later Dicts.]

reeze, variant of REESE, ROOSE *v.*

reezed, rancid: see REESED.

reezy, variant of REASY, rancid.

ref (rɛf), *sb.*^{1} Colloq. abbrev. of REFEREE *sb.* 3 b.

1899 R. H. BARBOUR *Halfback* xxii. 233 De Farge (the referee) is awfully down on holding and off-side plays. Last year he penalized us eight times during the game. But he's all right... He's the finest little ref that ever tossed a coin. **1939** *War Illustr.* 9 Dec. 394/3 Prisoners taken from U-boats and merchant ships are spending a happy hour kicking the ball about... An armed guard stands by, but not to protect the 'ref'. **1941** *London Opinion* Sept. 45/2 The referee goes to examine the eye while the crowd roars. Can he go in? The ref. moves away. He can. He does. **1957** I. CROSS *God Boy* (1958) 108 You're a pretty good ref, Sister. **1962** *Observer* 9 Sept. 16/2 A mob stormed outside the club offices shouting: 'We want the ref.' **1966** F. SHAW et al. *Lern Yerself Scouse* 51 *Buy a bewk, ref!* The referee appears to have forgotten the rules of the game. **1972** A. DRAPER *Death Penalty* iii. 18 He detested referees who were continually blowing their whistles... A ref could make or mar a game. **1976** *Listener* 29 Jan. 117/1 Adam is able to make good jokes about Cambridge..and there is no ref to blow the whistle on him.

ref (rɛf), *sb.*^{2} Colloq. abbrev. of REFERENCE *sb.*

a. In sense 3.

1926 F. M. FORD *Let.* 9 Mar. (1965) 168 Yours of the 23d ult. Ref German Translation of *No More Parades.* **1967** WODEHOUSE *Company for Henry* ix. 149 'I want his advice.' 'With ref. to what?' 'Oh, something that's coming up'. **1971** —— *Much Obliged, Jeeves* xi. 108 It's with ref to that book you pinched from the Junior Ganymede.

b. In sense 6 b.

1901 [see BOVRILIZE *v.*]. **1907** WESTBROOK & WODEHOUSE *Not George Washington* xvii. 183 Your refs. must be A1, or you don't stand an earthly. **1934** H. G. WELLS *Exper. Autobiogr.* I. iv. 161 Such questions seemed to me already of far more importance than satisfying J.K. or securing a satisfactory 'ref.' when my apprenticeship was up. **1974** P. WRIGHT *Lang. Brit. Industry* xii. 102 *Refs* (references).

ref (rɛf), *v. trans.* and *intr.* Colloq. abbrev. of REFEREE *v.*

1929 R. C. SHERRIFF *Journey's End* II. i. 50 *Raleigh.* Did you play Rugger? *Osborne.* Yes. But mostly reffing at school in the last few years. **1964** J. HALE *Grudge Fight* viii. 125 A scrum developed while Windy who was supposed to be reffing blew his whistle and went red in the face and didn't dare come too close. **1968** *Punch* 2 Oct. 457/3 Who says the game was badly reffed? The sending-off of Nobby Stiles, For nothing, was supremely deft. **1975** *Times* 4 Jan. 12/3 Muhammad Ali..was fighting Mildenberger and Teddy Waltham was reffing. **1977** *Gay News* 24 Mar. 2/2 Norman has recently been booked to ref games in California.

ref, obs. Sc. variant of REIF, plunder(ing).

†**re'fabric,** *v. Obs.*$^{-1}$ [RE- 5 a.] *trans.* To reconstruct. In **re'fabricking** *vbl. sb.*

1632 J. HAYWARD tr. *Biondi's Eromena* 158 Their departure was deferred for no other cause, than for the refabricking [It. *rifabricare*] of its ruines.

refaccimento, variant of RIFACIMENTO.

re'face, *v.* [RE- 5 a.]

1. *trans.* To put a new face or surface on (a building, stone, etc.).

1852 C. BRONTE in Mrs. Gaskell *Life* (1857) II. xi. 225 On Friday I..visited the churchyard and stone. It must be re-faced and relettered. **1886** WILLIS & CLARK *Cambridge* II. 155 The tower had been repaired, refaced, and strengthened.

2. (See FACE *v.* 15.)

1887 *Pall Mall G.* 5 Oct. 5/1 Of late years there has been a tremendous deterioration in Chinese tea... No doubt spent leaves have been refaced in quantities.

3. To face (a person, a concept) again.

1906 *Daily Chron.* 18 Apr. 3/4 Rather than re-face Mag McGhie..David prefers to 'face an angry Maker'. **1979** R. RENDELL *Make Death love Me* xii. 106 It would teach her to assume responsibility and re-face reality.

Hence **re'facing** *vbl. sb.*

1883 *Pall Mall G.* 29 Sept. 3/1 The great refacing of the Schools quad. **1898** J. T. FOWLER *Durh. Cath.* 26 Modern 'restorations' and refacings.

refacimento, variant of RIFACIMENTO.

†**re'faction.** *Obs.* [a. F. *réfaction* (17th c.): see RE- and FACTION.] Recompense, satisfaction.

1640 HOWELL *Dodona's Gr.* 174 The Soveraign Minister ..was commanded to require refaction and satisfaction against the Informers. **1656** FINETT *For. Ambass.* 248 That the King..hath commanded him to demand refaction and satisfaction of your Majesty against the said Marquis. **1755** MAGENS *Insurances* I. 297 For Refaction and to make good the loss and damage suffered..in the said Cargo of Wheat.

refained (rɪ'feɪnd), *a.* Also **refaned, refayned, refeened** (-'fiːnd). Repr. an affected pronunc. of REFINED *ppl. a.* (with reference to sense 2). Freq. joc. or derogatory.

1930 A. HUXLEY *Brief Candles* 25 Altogether too much the lady—refained; you know the type. A Governess;..the genteel, Jane Eyre, daughter-of-clergyman kind. **1932** *New Statesman* 9 Jan. 36/2 Few audiences could take seriously a performance of *Hamlet* in which..Horatio [spoke] in what is known as the 'refaned' accent. **1939** R. CAMPBELL *Flowering Rifle* II. 46 The most 'refayned' of all that breed. **1940** W. DE LA MARE *Pleasures & Speculations* 137 His [*sc.* the advertiser's] tone is usually genteel and refaned. **1940** H. G. WELLS *New World Order* 53 A friendly adviser..protests against 'the wombs of associated labour'... My adviser produces..'the lap of social labour', which is more refained but pure nonsense. **1940** *John o' London's* 3 May 149/3 Edinburgh being very 'refained', the word [*sc.* keelie] is seldom used in the more polite society. **1941** V. WOOLF *Between Acts* 122 The old lady..looked too refined. 'Refeened'—Mrs. Manresa qualified the word to her own advantage... She could span the old lady's 'refeenment'. **1961** *Radio Times* 27 Apr. 63/4 *The Kilt Is My Delight* is indeed a delightful programme, but..may I suggest that it sometimes takes on a less 'refaned' air? Always these immaculately dressed ladies and gentlemen prance around in some 'stately home'. **1962** N. MARSH *Hand in Glove* i. 28 Nicola..wondered if Mr. Period would find the phrase 'refeened,' a word he often used with humorous intent. **1962** *Punch* 14 Feb. 297/3 An appalling gold-digger with a refained accent. **1969** M. O'BRINE *Mills* xi. 43 The Sangsters were much too 'refained' to argue with someone they were meeting for the first time. **1972** A. MACVICAR *Golden Venus Affair* v. 53 Her accent was 'refained', but it betrayed a Glasgow East End origin. **1976** *Listener* 25 Mar. 386/4 The blowzy, mini-skirted divorcee with a loutish son and an impossibly 'refeened' mother.

Hence **re'fainment, re'feenment** (with reference to REFINEMENT 2).

1933 H. MATHESON *Broadcasting* iii. 63 Universal education may mean a universal hybrid speech..often overlaid with a veneer of what can only be called 'refainment'. **1941** [see above]. **1960** J. MITFORD *Hons &*

Rebels i. 17 Nancy [Mitford], even in those early days preoccupied with U and Non-U usage, made up a poem illustrative of the main 'refainments' of Miss Broadmoor's speech.

re'fall, *v.* [RE- 5 a.]
1. *intr.* To fall a second time.
1620 SHELTON *Don Quix.* IV. x. II. 137 Stumbling here, falling there, getting up again on the other side, and re-falling on this. **1632** J. HAYWARD tr. *Biondi's Eromena* 173 For one of a perfect sight to fall and refall so fouley..is a thing altogether prodigious.
2. To fall back or again *into* a state.
1570 FOXE *A. & M.* (ed. 2) 617/1 He had decreed to procede to the degradation..of the sayd William Sautrie, as refallen into heresie. **1647** FULLER *Wounded Consc.* viii. 53, I..have often re-fallen into the same offence. **1658** J. WEBB *Cleopatra* VIII. I. 4 She was againe re-fallen into that captivity from whence they thought her entirely delivered.
So **re'fall** *sb.*, a repeated fall.
1727 BRADLEY *Fam. Dict.* s.v. *Distillation of Oil*, Falling back into the Vessel, they are dissolved again, and at last, by continual Thickening and Refalls, are wasted and come to nothing.

re-'fallow, *v.* [RE- 5 a.] *trans.* To fallow (land) again.
1812 SINCLAIR *Syst. Husb. Scot.* I. 174 He laid on, (when the land came to be re-fallowed), 20 or 25 bolls more.

re-'fan, *v.* [RE- 5 a.] *trans.* To fan again.
a **1618** SYLVESTER *Maiden's Blush* 308 They..almost staid withall His Brethren's rage; till Ruth-lesse Issachar Re-fand the fire. *c* **1620** Z. BOYD *Zion's Flowers* (1855) 98 His dev'lish thoughts did still refanne the fire.
2. (Chiefly unhyphened.) [RE- 5 c.] *Aeronaut.* To fit (a turbo-fan) with a new fan. So **re'fanned** *ppl. a.*, **re'fanning** *vbl. sb.*
1973 *Internat. Aerospace Abstr.* XIII. 2222/1 (*heading*) Refanned commercial gas turbine engines. **1974** *Ibid.* XIV. 2236/1 (*heading*) Reduction of JT8D powered aircraft noise by engine refanning. **1975** *Times Lit. Suppl.* 21 Mar. 318/3 Improved engine design has produced a new generation of quieter aircraft, earlier and noisier types can be refanned and further progress in the direction of peace and quiet may be expected. **1978** *Flight Internat.* 18 Feb. 429/1 United Airlines' flirtation with the refanned 727-300B in 1975 marked the end of this transport's major development.

refan ('riːfæn), *a.* and *sb. Aeronaut.* [f. prec. vb.] **A.** *adj.* **a.** = REFANNED *ppl. a.* **b.** = REFANNING *vbl. sb.* (used *attrib.*). **B.** *sb.* A refanned engine.
1974 *Internat. Aerospace Abstr.* XIV. 2236/1 This would be accomplished by retrofitting the existing fleet with quieter refan engines and new acoustically treated nacelles. **1975** *Ibid.* XV. 2764/2 The objective of the refan program is to demonstrate the technical feasibility of substantially reducing the noise levels of existing JT8D powered aircraft. **1978** *Flight Internat.* 18 Feb. 428/2 The principal advantage of refans (whether cropped or sized up) over new engines can be summarized as lower development, acquisition and ownership costs; [etc.].

refar, obs. Sc. form of REAVER.

refar(re, obs. forms of REFER.

re'fashion, *v.* [RE- 5 a. Cf. F. *refaçonner* (16th c.).] *trans.* To fashion anew.
1803 W. TAYLOR in Robberds *Mem.* (1843) I. 459, I have begun to modernize—no, to refashion—Drayton's battle of Azincour. **1816** —— in *Monthly Rev.* LXXXI. 471 They..have been much nationalized and refashioned in the transplantation. *a* **1880** GEO. ELIOT *A. Bede* xvii, I might re-fashion life and character entirely after my own liking.
Hence **re'fashioning** *vbl. sb.*
1799 W. TAYLOR in Robberds *Mem.* (1843) I. 277 Milton and Klopstock, poets too good to undergo a refashioning. **1890** *Athenæum* 1 Nov. 583/2 The genuine Chaucer poems in the same MS. have not been subjected to any such wholesale refashioning.
So **re'fashioner**.
1800 W. TAYLOR in *Monthly Mag.* VIII. 597 From that period the balance of erudition and talents began to incline toward the side of the reformers or refashioners. *a* **1861** MRS. BROWNING *Lett. R. H. Horne* (1877) I. xxi. 108 The refashioners stand..too far from Chaucer's side.

re'fashionment. [f. as prec. + -MENT, after It. RIFACIMENTO.] The action of refashioning; also *concr.*, something refashioned.
1830 W. TAYLOR *Hist. Surv. Germ. Poetry* II. 3 These epic poems are mere Swabian refashionments (*rifacimento* is the Italian word which I attempt to recoin..) of pre-existing Lombard story-books. **1831** *Fraser's Mag.* IV. 542 Danish and Icelandic versions and refashionments..exist. **1862** BORROW *Wales* II. 305 A re-fashionment of the work of Richard Parry.

re'fasten, *v.* [RE- 5 a.] *trans.* To fasten again. Hence **re'fastening** *vbl. sb.*
1598 FLORIO, *Risaldatura*, a resoldring, a refastning. *a* **1832** SCOTT (Webster 1864), It was so negligently re-fastened. **1897** BARING-GOULD *Bladys of the Stewponey* xviii, Bladys hastily re-fastened the case.

re-'father, *v. nonce-wd.* [RE- 5 a.] *trans.* To make (one) again a father.
1847 TENNYSON *Princ.* VI. 113 At the happy word 'he lives' My father stoop'd, re-father'd o'er my wounds.

re'favour, *v.* [RE- 5 a.] To favour again.
1632 LITHGOW *Trav.* IX. 423 Vpon the seauenth day the winds refauouring vs, were safely arriued at London.

refe, obs. f. REAVE *v.*, REEF *sb.*[1], REEVE *sb.*[1]; Sc. var. REIF, plunder(ing); obs. pa. t. RIVE *v.*

†**re'fect**, *pa. ppl. Obs.* [ad. L. *refectus*, pa. pple. of *reficĕre*: see next.] Refreshed, restored.
c **1374** CHAUCER *Boeth.* IV. pr. vi. 111 (Camb. MS.), Tak thanne this drawht; and whan þow art wel refresshed and refect [L. *refectus*], thow shal be moore stydefast to stye in to heyere questyouns. **1456** SIR G. HAYE *Law Arms* (S.T.S.) 53 Quhen he was wele refect, he passit in Affrik, to mak were on Hanyball.

refect (rɪ'fɛkt), *v.* Also 5 *Sc.* refeck. [Orig. f. L. *refect-*, ppl. stem of *reficĕre* to remake, restore, renew, etc., f. *re-* RE- + *facĕre* to make: in later use a back-formation from REFECTION.
The word app. fell out of use before 1700 and was revived in the 19th c., but has always been rare and is now somewhat rhetorical in sense 1.]
1. a. *trans.* To refresh, esp. with food or drink; to restore after fatigue. Now usually *refl.*
c **1470** HENRY *Wallace* III. 9 Fyscheis in flude refeckit rialye Till mannys fude. **1570** LEVINS *Manip.* 47/47 To Refect, *reficere.* **1614** LODGE *Seneca, Epist.* 259 So like-wise ought we sometimes to recreate our spirit, and refect the same with some delights. **1646** SIR T. BROWNE *Pseud. Ep.* IV. vii. 196 A man in the morning is lighter in the scale,..and is also lighter unto himselfe, because he is refected. *Ibid.* V. vi. 241 After which they commonly retired to bed, and refected themselves with repast. **1813** T. BUSBY *Lucretius* I. Diss. p. iii, The world itself is refected and nourished by a perpetual accession of these corpuscles. **1822** T. L. PEACOCK *Maid Marian* iii, The knight and the friar..proceeded to refect themselves after their ride. **1859** SALA *Tw. round Clock* (1861) 195, I remember once refecting myself at a public dinner.
b. *intr.* (for *refl.*) To take a refection.
1886 SALA in *Illustr. Lond. News* 27 Mar. 312/1 While you are refecting in the saloon.
2. *trans.* To eat (fæcal pellets).
1960 M. BURTON *Wild Animals Brit. Isles* 60 The droppings refected are different from those discarded. **1964** R. M. LOCKLEY *Private Life of Rabbit* x. 102 Termites may refect food as much as six times.

refection (rɪ'fɛkʃən), *sb.* Forms: 5 refeccioun(e, reffecio(u)n, refectioun (-tyon), 5–6 refeccion (-cyon), 4– refection, (6 -e). [a. F. *réfection* (12th c. in Littré), ad. L. *refectiōn-em*, n. of action f. *reficĕre*: see prec.]
1. a. Recreation or refreshment received through some spiritual or intellectual influence. (Freq. *transf.* from 2 or 3.)
a **1340** HAMPOLE *Psalter* lix. 8 Moab, þat is, ill men, that tourments me, are potte, þat is refection of my hope. **1413** *Pilgr. Sowle* (Caxton 1483) V. iii. 94 The vision of the good lord, that is al their ioye, theyr reste, and their refection. **1450–1530** *Myrr. our Ladye* 87 He..hathe ordeyned vs to haue hymselfe to our endeles refeccyon in blysse. **1509** HAWES *Past. Pleas.* XI. (Percy Soc.) 37 To the artyke eres swete and dylycious The golden rethoryke is good refeccion. **1581** MARBECK *Bk. of Notes* 109 The comfort of Gods spirite shoulde coole it to his euerlasting refection. **1630** BRATHWAIT *Eng. Gentlem.* (1641) 4 The only sight of God is the true food and refection of our minds. **1717** L. HOWEL *Desiderius* (ed. 3) 170 It is the true and solid Refection of the holy Mind. **1858** NEALE *Bernard de M.* (1864) 30 O sacred, sweet refection.
b. Refreshment or relief due to some sensuous or physical cause. Now *rare* or *Obs.*
1450–80 tr. *Secreta Secret.* 24 When the spirit hath take refeccioun in good odoures. **1567** MAPLET *Gr. Forest* 20 There is no greater refection to the eies than the sight of this. **1576** FLEMING *Panopl. Epist.* 40 At night I cast vp much choler, after the eiection whereof, I felt such a refection [etc.]. **1725** POPE *Odyss.* VI. 261 Since this worn frame refection knew, What scenes have I survey'd of dreadful view?
2. a. The action of refreshing or partaking of refreshment: the fact of being refreshed, or of refreshing oneself, with food or drink after hunger or fatigue. Also, an instance or case of this.
1398 TREVISA *Barth. De P. R.* IX. xxxi. (Bodl. MS.), Ester daie is a tyme..of ioiful refeccion and fedinge. *c* **1450** tr. *De Imitatione* I. xviii. 20 For gret swetnes of contemplacion som tyme was foryeten þe necessite of bodely refeccion. **1483** CAXTON *G. de la Tour* M iv, She..toke only for her refection brede and water. **1579** FULKE *Heskins' Parl.* 109 Melchizedech..for refection as well of him, as of his warriours, brought forth breade and wine. **1615** CROOKE *Body of Man* 121 From these veines come those sodaine refections of the spirits by sweete and strong Wine, Broths, and Cordials. **1646** SIR T. BROWNE *Pseud. Ep.* 196 After a draught of wine a man may seeme lighter in himselfe from sudden refection, although he be heavier in the balance. **1720** POPE *Iliad* XXIV. 754 Now the peaceful hours of sacred night Demand refection, and to rest invite. **1820** SCOTT *Monast.* xvi, Sorrow it were..if we were now either to advance or retard the hour of refection. **1872** R. F. BURTON *Zanzibar* I. 150 The cocoa-nut, manioc, and broiled fish, offered by squatting negresses for their refection.
†**b.** In phr. *to take* (*one's*) *refection. Obs.*
c **1440** *Cast. Persev.* (E.E.T.S.) 1828 In abstinens lede þi lyfl take but skylful refeccyon. **1483** CAXTON *G. de la Tour* D viij b, After they had taken their refection and wel dronken. **1568** GRAFTON *Chron.* II. 823 He was so diseased in his stomacke that he could take eyther refection or rest. **1600** HAKLUYT *Voy.* (1810) III. 375 They would rather haue perished with hunger and thirst, then haue taken their refection at any mans hand but mine. **1634** *Malory's Arthur* (1816) II. 276 When he was armed, she prayed him for to take his refection.

Comb. **1489** CAXTON *Faytes of A.* II. xxxvii. 158 Yf they may knowe that theyre aduersaryes be not upon theyre warde or that they be at theyre refeccyon taking.
c. Entertainment with food and drink; the right of demanding, or duty of supplying, such entertainment. Now only *Hist.*
1601 HOLLAND *Pliny* I. 240 They deserued a better reward than one daies refection and victuals. **1635** QUARLES *Embl.* V. vi. 5 Without thy presence Earth gives no refection, Without thy presence Sea affords no treasure. **1689** R. COX *Hist. Irel.* I. Expl. Index, Refection, is a priviledge the Lord has of claiming Entertainment for one Meal, and no more. **1727–41** CHAMBERS *Cycl.* s.v., Refection is also used, in antient authors, for a duty or service incumbent on any person to provide meals, for ecclesiastics, or even for princes. **1875** MAINE *Hist. Inst.* vi. 161 This 'right of refection' and liability to it are among the most distinctive features of ancient Irish custom.
d. The eating of fæcal pellets, practised by rabbits and some other animals.
1939 *Nature* 10 June 982/1 The pellets frequently constitute more than one third of the stomach contents [of the rabbit] and refection to such a degree seemed too improbable. **1952** L. H. MATTHEWS *Brit. Mammals* vi. 136 In 1939 the habit of 'refection' was rediscovered in the rabbit. **1964** R. M. LOCKLEY *Private life of Rabbit* x. 102 Many animals, including insects as well as hares and rabbits, have this habit of refection. **1973** *Bk. Brit. Countryside* (Automobile Assoc.) 367/2 Feeding is by refection, a similar method to chewing the cud. Food is eaten then excreted in semi-digested form as soft moist pellets. These are eaten again and passed through the intestines to be fully digested.
3. a. An occasion of partaking of food; a meal.
1432–50 tr. *Higden* (Rolls) VI. 43 Herynge that Cristen men usede diversites of meytes at oon refeccion. **1542** BOORDE *Dyetary* xii. (1870) 265 Eatynge of moche butter at one refection is not commendable. **1617** MORYSON *Itin.* I. 94 After this refection we went the rest of our iourney through pleasant fields. **1655** FULLER *Ch. Hist.* IX. iv. §2 At a publick refection of those Ministers together..the next time of their meeting was appointed. **1856** FROUDE *Hist. Eng.* X. (1858) II. 435 One of the brethren, at every refection, was to read aloud a chapter of the Old or New Testament.
b. A portion of food or drink; a meal or repast, esp. a slight one.
1482 *Monk of Evesham* (Arb.) 27 With a ful litil refeccion ther of he brake his faste. **1531** ELYOT *Gov.* III. xxi, A man ..shall in the mornyng..with a litle refection,..haue his inuencion quicker, his iugement perfecter, his tonge rediar. **1542** BOORDE *Dyetary* ix. (1870) 252 The last refeccyon or meale wyll let the dygestyon of the fyrste. **1625** K. LONG tr. *Barclay's Argenis* II. xx. 130 With these words, the Herald was led aside to take a short refection. **1664** H. MORE *Myst. Iniq.* xviii. 69 Birds..that ever smel out a comfortable refection from the fall of every such Carcass. **1727–41** CHAMBERS *Cycl.*, *Refection*, among monks and ecclesiastics, a spare meal or repast, just sufficing for the support of life. **1748** RICHARDSON *Clarissa* (1811) VIII. xvi. 88 Though our little refection was just brought in. **1856** MRS. CARLYLE *Lett.* II. 295 A miserable refection of weak tea and tough toast. **1870** DISRAELI *Lothair* l, The cheerful fire, the judicious refection on a side table.
†**c.** A particular form of food or refreshment.
1502 *Ord. Crysten Men* I. iii. (W. de W. 1506) C iij b, In tastynge this fyrst refeccion of salte. **1625** USSHER *Answ. Jesuit* 54 The sonnes which he begat..he nourisheth with a peculiar refection and food, and meat and drink.
4. †**a.** Resetting of a dislocation. *Obs. rare.*
1646 T. WHITAKER *Uzziah* 40 Till..it..gangrene, and then after far greater pain, no hope of cure but by refection.
b. Repair, restoration. *rare.*
1656 BLOUNT *Glossogr.*, *Refection*,..a repairing or mending a thing that is worn and decayed. **1684** tr. *Bonet's Merc. Compit.* XVIII. 659 When Patients stand in need of refection of their strength. **1845–56** BOUVIER *Law Dict.*, *Refection*, reparation, reëstablishment of a building.
5. *attrib.*, as *Refection Sunday*, the fourth Sunday in Lent, Refreshment Sunday.
1872 SHIPLEY *Gloss. Eccl. Terms.*

†**re'fection**, *v. Obs.* Also refeccion, etc. [ad. F. *réfectionner* (15th c. in Godef.), f. *réfection*: see prec.] *trans.* To refresh, furnish with a refection.
a **1450** *Knt. de la Tour* (1868) 97 In the whiche arke was manna where with the children of israel were refeccioned. **1502** *Ord. Crysten Men* I. iv. (W. de W. 1506) D ij b, The baptem refeccyoneth the soule and kepeth it..from deth. **1550** VERON *Godly Sayings* (1846) 62 Thou art so refectyoned, that thou canste not lacke, whereof to be refectioned. **1629** WADSWORTH *Pilgr.* iii. 11 After they had been well refectioned by the Rector, thay tooke their leaue.

re'fectionary, *a. rare*⁻¹. [f. REFECTION *sb.* + -ARY[1].] Of or belonging to refection.
1823 GALT *Entail* vii, As the critics hold it indelicate to describe the details of any refectionary supply, however elegant, we must not presume to enumerate the series and succession of Scottish fare.

re'fectioner. [f. REFECTION *sb.* + -ER[1].] In a monastery or convent, the person having charge of the refectory and supplies of food.
1820 SCOTT *Monast.* xv, Two most important officers of the Convent, the Kitchener and Refectioner. **1886** *Athenæum* 13 Mar. 361/3 The documents..include..two accounts of the infirmarer and one of the refectioner.

refective (rɪ'fɛktɪv), *a.* and *sb.* ? *Obs.* [f. as REFECT *v.* + -IVE. Cf. obs. F. *refectif*, *-ive* (15th c. in Godef.).] **a.** *adj.* Refreshing, restoring, nourishing. **b.** *sb.* A medicine that restores the strength.
a. 1611 FLORIO, *Refettiuo*, refectiue, refreshing. **1657** W. MORICE *Coena quasi Κοινὴ* Def. xv. 229, I may [then].. beleeve the Supper of the Lords may be alimental and

refective to the soul, by seeing, as well as by partaking. **1665** HARVEY *Advice agst. Plague* 25 Repeat the said sudorifick, and thereupon the Refective Cordial.

b. **1667** L. STUCLEY *Gospel Glass* xxxii. (1670) 334 Cordials, and sweet refectives, after all our wearisome labours. **1706** PHILLIPS (ed. Kersey), *Refectives*, medicines that refresh and renew strength. [Hence in BAILEY and later Dicts.]

‖**refectoire.** *Obs. rare*$^{-1}$. [F., ad. L. *refectōrium*: see REFECTORY *sb.*] Refectory.

1667 PEPYS *Diary* 23 Jan., I was in the refectoire, where every man his napkin, knife [etc.].

refecto'rarian. *rare.* [See next and -AN.] = REFECTIONER.

1886 *Athenæum* 3 July 14/1 The refectorarian by virtue of his office held certain estates in Winchester. **1892** KITCHIN *Compotus Rolls St. Swithun's Priory* Introd. 32 The Refectorarian.. received all the eatables, etc.

re'fectorary. *rare*$^{-1}$. [ad. med.L. *refectorari-us* (Du Cange): see REFECTORY *sb.* and -ARY[1].] = REFECTIONER.

1844 S. R. MAITLAND *Dark Ages* 409 While he was refectorary.. he made himself as annoying as he dared.

re'fectorer. *rare.* [See prec. and -ER[1].] = REFECTIONER.

1794 W. TINDAL *Hist. Evesham* 109 As often as our potation shall be made after noon.. the refectorer shall be allowed two measures of ale from the cellar. **1892** KIRK *Abingdon Acc.* p. xli, There is only one account of the Refectorer, and that is very brief.

refectorial (rɪfɛkˈtɔərɪəl), *a.* [f. as next + -AL[1].] Of or belonging to refection.

1843 *Blackw. Mag.* LIV. 255 Merrily the beards wagg'd round the refectorial board. **1872** *Daily News* 3 Aug., The Abbots' lodging-house was for the day devoted.. to refectorial purposes.

refec'torian. [f. med.L. *refectōri-um* (see next) + -AN.] = REFECTIONER.

1660 F. BROOKE tr. *Le Blanc's Trav.* 376 At St. Croix, the Refectorian of the Dominicans was beaten dead. **1679** *Trials of White & Other Jesuits* 57, I was a servant there... A Refectorian, a Butler. **1869** *Echo* 16 Feb., I had given directions to the refectorian.. because she was so difficult to please in her food.

refectory (rɪˈfɛktərɪ), *sb.* Also 6–7 -orie. [ad. med.L. *refectōrium* (Du Cange), f. *reficĕre*: see REFECT *v.* and -ORY[1]. Cf. F. *réfectoire* and REFRECTORE.] **a.** A room for refreshment; *esp.* in religious houses and colleges, the hall or chamber in which the meals take place.

The stressing *'refectory* was at one time somewhat prevalent (see Walker's note, and is still used by some Roman Catholics.)

1483 CAXTON *Gold. Leg.* 241/2 There cam two yong men of yͤ same habite & forme whiche entrid in to yͤ refectory or fraitour. **1526** *Pilgr. Perf.* (W. de W. 1531) 65 Seruynge at meet & in other places, redynge in yͤ refectory, or in the chapyter hous at collation. **1582** N. T. (Rhem.) *Mark* xiv. 14 The Maister saith Where is my refectorie, where I may eate the Pasche..? **1617** MORYSON *Itin.* I. 95 Their refectory or place where the Monkes eat, is faire and large. **1687** DRYDEN *Hind & P.* III. 530 He.. cells, and refectories did prepare, And large provisions laid of winter fare. **1756** NUGENT *Gr. Tour, France* IV. 71 In the refectories where the soldiers eat, most of the famous battles and sieges.. are painted on the walls. **1797** MRS. RADCLIFFE *Italian* vi, She passed through the refectory where the nuns had just returned from vespers. **1820** SCOTT *Abbot* xii, A spacious chamber, which had once been the refectory of the convent. **1879** SIR G. SCOTT *Lect. Archit.* I. 296 Round this cloister you still trace the plan of the refectory.

b. *ellipt.* for *refectory table.*

1913 L. V. LOCKWOOD *Furniture Collector's Gloss.* 51/2 *Refectory*, an early long, narrow table upon which was served a meal.

transf. **1876** GEO. ELIOT *Dan. Der.* xiv, To tell of the food that was eaten in that green refectory.

c. *attrib.*, as ***refectory-bell, man***; **refectory table**: see quots. 1948, 1960.

1772 NUGENT tr. *Hist. Friar Gerund* I. 544 An old lay brother.. who had been refectory man above forty years. **1850** S. DOBELL *Roman* v. Poet. Wks. (1875) 72 Soft excitements of refectory-bell. **1923** H. STANLEY-BARRETT *Old World Galleries A.B.C. Hist. Eng. Antique Furnit.* (ed. 2) 118 The Elizabethan trestle refectory table usually had heavily carved bulbous legs. **1928** *Daily Express* 18 Apr. 4, Refectory tables.. were the principal pieces of furniture in medieval and Tudor times. **1948** *Antique Collector* Aug. 127/1 In the late 16th and 17th centuries the common dining-table was an oblong one with either four or six turned legs connected by square sectioned stretchers. In contemporary inventories it was usually called a 'long table', but in order to conjure up a picture of jovial monks dining, the long table has been renamed a 'refectory table', which inaccurate term is often used today. **1960** H. HAYWARD *Antique Coll.* 235/1 *Refectory table*, popular modern term for a long table of the type in use in the second half of the 16th cent. until the Restoration. **1971** D. FRANCIS *Bonecrack* iv. 51 We sat.. with our feet up on a sixteenth century Spanish walnut refectory table. **1976** *Cumberland News* 3 Dec. 29/5 (Advt.), We are most interested in old oak furniture—dressers, court cupboards—kitchen presses, bedding chests, kitchen and refectory tables as well.

†**re'fectory,** *a. Obs.*$^{-1}$ [ad. L. *refectōrius* (4th c.): see REFECT *v.* and -ORY[2].] Refreshing.

1691–8 NORRIS *Pract. Disc.* (1711) III. 123 This is that Divine Consolation.., that Refectory Grace.

†**re'fectuary.** *Obs.* [Cf. med.L. *refectuāri-us* refectioner.] = REFECTORY.

1611 COTGR., *Refectouër*, a Refectuarie, or Fratrie; the roome wherein Friers eat together. **1658** PHILLIPS, Refectory or Refectuary. **1694** MOTTEUX *Rabelais* v. v. (1737) 18 He led us into a.. Refectuary, or Fratrie-room.

refeed (riːˈfiːd), *v.* Also re-feed. [RE- 5 a.] *trans.* To feed again, esp. after a period of starvation.

1884 *Manch. Exam.* 19 Dec. 5/3 In refeeding a fire in a large grate. **1943** *Nutrition Abstr. & Rev.* XII. 637/2 [The birds] were then refed on maize until the original weight was regained. **1971** *Jrnl. Nutrition* CI. 1564/2 Rats were starved 48 hours and were refed the high carbohydrate diet for 0, 1, 2, 3, 4, and 7 days.

So **re'fed** *ppl. a.*, **re'feeding** *vbl. sb.*

1932 *Biol. Abstr.* VI. 410/2 (*heading*) Re-feeding after starvation. **1950** *Arch. Biochem.* XXVII. 177 The percentage of nitrogen in the extracts obtained from the livers of the rats refed with a high-carbohydrate diet was significantly lower than the percentage of nitrogen in the extracts obtained from the pellet-refed and the fat-refed rats. **1964** *Proc. Soc. Exper. Biol. & Med.* CXV. 441/1 The data for refed rats reflect a marked increase in liver lipid upon refeeding. **1967** M. KENYON *Whole Hog* viii. 94, I put them [*sc.* laboratory animals] on controlled feeding after a period of starvation and their reactions to the re-feeding.. would be similar to human reactions.

re'feel, *v.* [RE- 5 a.] *trans.* To feel again.

1757 MRS. GRIFFITH *Lett. Henry & Frances* (1767) II. 102 The heart-rending fears, which Providence.. decreed should never be re-felt. **1847** *Simmonds' Colonial Mag.* July 360 The effect she then produced upon his senses was refelt in pristine force.

refeet, variant of REFETE *Obs.*

refeff, obs. form of REFEOFF *v.*

re'feign, *v.* [RE- 5 a.] *trans.* To feign again.

1652 GAULE *Magastrom.* xxvi, A certain playing upon allegories, which idle men.. do feign and refeigne, &c.

†**re'fel,** *v. Obs.* Also 6 refelle, 6–7 refell. [ad. L. *refellĕre* to disprove, refute, f. *re-* RE- + *fallĕre* to deceive, etc.: the sense of the compound is unusual. Senses 2 and 3 are purely English applications of the word.]

1. *trans.* To refute, confute, disprove (an argument, opinion, error, etc.); to prove to be false or untenable. (Very common in the 16–17th c.)

1530 PALSGR. 682/1, I can nat refell your argument, it is so evydent. *a* **1540** BARNES *Wks.* (1573) 207/2 Was not this a charitable argument to refell myne aunswere with? **1578** BANISTER *Hist. Man* VIII. 98 It is most certainly otherwise, and his opinion therein easely refelled. **1630** PRYNNE *Anti-Armin.* 77 Such of those Tenets which haue beene constantly oppugned, refelled, disclaimed. **1655** FULLER *Ch. Hist.* XI. viii. §60 He took occasion to refell that slander, which some cast on Lecture-Preachers. **1686** GOAD *Celest. Bodies* I. ix. 33 Who can refell this with any better Argument than a Smile? **1713** BENTLEY *Rem. Disc. Freethink.* II. §47. 259 Not to coin Articles, but to explain them, and refell the adversaries objections. *a* **1734** NORTH *Exam.* I. ii. §80 (1740) 72 It was the Case of a Peer,.. else the Pretence had been refelled upon the Opening.

b. To refute or confute (a person).

1553 BALE *Gardiner's De Vera Obed.* F viij b, To refelle him yͭ calleth him selfe chief untruly. **1583** STUBBES *Anat. Abus.* II. (1882) 72 Neither.. able to.. explane the scriptures, nor yet to refell and conuince the aduersarie. **1610** WILLET *Hexapla Daniel* 268 Junius may be refelled by his own chronicle. **1657** REEVE *God's Plea* 21 He is refelled, and he hath instantly done with anger and argument. **1692** SOUTH *12 Serm.* (1717) V. 480 Why then did not those profound Rabbies.. baffle and refel these Babblers..?

c. *absol.*

1598 GRENEWEY *Tacitus, Ann.* III. xiv. (1622) 85 Tiberius himselfe.. asked him many questions; not giuing liberty to refell or replie. **1654** GATAKER *Disc. Apol.* 83 The manner of them both is rather to rail and revile, then by arguing and reasoning to refel and refute. **1697** tr. *Burgersdicius' Logic* II. xviii. 85 Places from like and unlike are of no great Use to prove or refel.

d. To cast doubt upon, deny. *rare*$^{-1}$.

c **1611** CHAPMAN *Iliad* IX. 36 As thou then didst refell My valour first of all the hoast.

2. To reject; to refuse to accept, admit, or give heed to (a request, a thing offered, etc.).

a **1548** HALL *Chron., Hen. IV* 28 This my lowly requeste.. (whiche I thynke your clemencie will not reiect nor refell). **1583** FULKE *Defence* xv. 398 The other signification of imposing handes is gone, which Mayster Whitgift defendeth, and the popular election is brought in, which he refelleth. **1598** DRAYTON *Heroic. Ep.* iv. 21, I once determin'd, still to haue been mute, Onely by Silence to refell thy Sute. **1603** KNOLLES *Hist. Turks* (1621) 599 Your offered favours.. I deserve not; neither is my present estate and desert towards you such, as that I dare or ought to refell the same.

3. To repel, repulse, force or drive back, repress: **a.** a person.

a **1548** HALL *Chron., Hen. V* 56 b, He determined as he might to refell and withstande the comen enemies of the realme. **1556** J. HEYWOOD *Spider & F.* lx. 95 They either had miserable ouer throw In rebelling, or streight after refelled. **1621** B. JONSON *Gipsies Metam.* Wks. (Rtldg.) 626/1 Friends, not to refel ye, Or any way quell ye [etc.]. *c* **1650** *Robin Hood & Tanner's Dau.* xxii. in Child *Ballads* I. 110/2 The tanners bold they fought right well,.. But Robin did them both refell.

b. an attempt, undertaking, danger, etc.

a **1548** HALL *Chron., Hen. V* 22 b, Not one of them would take hede how to resist and refell the present ieopardye which was commyng out of England. *Ibid., Edw. IV* 192 All enterprises afterward against hym attempted had either evill successe, or were sone refelled. **1573** *Satir. Poems Reform.* xli. 51 Sic foly faill not to refell. **1584** HUDSON *Du Bartas' Judith* vi. 102 One while her feare refeld her first entent. **1652** BENLOWES *Theoph.* IX. xlii, Binde up what's loose, what's rash new-mould, refell what's ill.

c. To clear (the mind) *of* something. *rare*$^{-1}$.

1575 *Appius & Virginia* A j b, Refel your minde of mourning plaints, deare mother rest your minde.

Hence †**re'feller,** one who refels or refutes.

1652 GAULE *Magastrom.* Ep. Ded., A teacher of truth,.. a refeller of falshood.

†**re'felling,** *vbl. sb. Obs.* [f. prec. + -ING[1].] The action of the vb. REFEL.

c **1530** L. COX *Rhet.* (1899) 71 The confutacyon is the soylynge and refellynge of other mennes sayenges agaynste our purpose. **1581** N. BURNE *Disput.* in *Cath. Tract.* (S.T.S.) 154 Nocht villing to spend tyme in farder refelling of your vanitie. **1649** ROBERTS *Clavis Bibl.* 344 His refelling of Zophar's Thesis. **1697** tr. *Burgersdicius' Logic* II. xvi. 66 The Confirming and Refelling of Notional Problemes.

†**re'feoff,** *v. Obs.* In 5 refeff(e, 5–6 refeoffe. [ad. AF. *refeffer* (1304 in Godef.): see RE- and FEOFF *v.*] *trans.* To feoff (one) again, to re-enfeoff.

c **1420** *Anturs of Arth.* 685, I shall refeff him in felde, in forestes so faire. *c* **1450** *Merlin* 479 The kynge Arthur refeffed hym a-gein in his londe that he hadde be-fore. **1461** *Rolls of Parlt.* V. 492/2 To refeffe the seid persone. **1532** *Dial. on Laws Eng.* II. vii. (1638) 71 The feoffour.. is driven to cause him to refeoffe him againe.

So †**re'feoffment.** *Obs.*

1441 in W. P. Baildon *Sel. Pl. Chanc.* (1896) 132 To refeoffe hem accordyng to thentent of the first feoffement. **1580** EGERTON in Ld. Campbell *Chancellors* (1857) II. xlvii. 312 You have all but the dede of refeffment layed together.

†**re'fer,** *sb. Sc. Obs.* [f. next.]

1. A matter referred for consideration.

1637–50 ROW *Hist. Kirk* (Wodrow Soc.) 59 [The] Moderator.. haveing been absent fra the last Assemblie, and so not acquaint with the referres, did choose assessors to assist him. **1671** *Rec. Presbyt. Inverness* (S.H.S.) 14 Ye minister.. being inquired of the refer of John McIntosh [etc.].

2. A reference in a book. *rare*$^{-1}$.

1697 DALLAS *Stiles* I. Ded., Your Lordship will find, that by Referrs from one place to another, it is of Large Extent.

refer (rɪˈfɜː(r)), *v.* Also 4–6 **refere**, 4, 6–7 **referre**, 7–8 **referr**, 5 **reffer**, 6 **refar-**. [ad. OF. *referer* (14th c., Oresme; mod.F. *référer*), or L. *referre*, f. *re-* RE- + *ferre* to bear, carry, etc. Cf. Sp. and Pg. *referir*, It. *referire*.]

I. Transitive senses.

†**1. a.** To bring back, reduce again. *Obs. rare*$^{-1}$.

c **1374** CHAUCER *Boeth.* III. pr. xi. 78 (Camb. MS.), Either alle thinges ben referred and browht to nowht [L. *ad nihilum referuntur*], and floteryn with owte gouernour,.. or elles [etc.].

†**b.** To convey or give back, to restore. *Obs.*

c **1547** SURREY in *Tottel's Misc.* (Arb.) 222 And when thys carcas here to earth shalbe refarde, I do bequeth my weried ghost to serue her afterwarde. **1629** QUARLES *Argalus & Parth.* II. (1677) 83 One while his tired fancy does refer His thoughts to silence.

†**c.** To reproduce, represent, refigure. *Obs. rare.*

1700 DRYDEN *Ovid's Met.* xv. 550 His tail in circles toss'd Refers the limbs his backward father lost. **1727** POPE, etc. *Art of Sinking* x. 93 The figures must be so turned, as.. to refer exactly the mold, in which they were formed, in all its inequalities,.. and distortions.

2. To trace (back), assign, attribute, impute (something) *to* a person or thing as the ultimate cause, origin, (author,) or source.

c **1374** CHAUCER *Boeth.* v. pr. iii. 123 (Camb. MS.), Thanne folweth it that owre vices ben referred to the makere of alle good. *c* **1450** tr. *De Imitatione* I. xv. 17 He ascriueþ to no man eny good þinge, but holy referriþ all þynges to god, of whom þei proceden originaly. **1494** FABYAN *Chron.* VI. clxxvi. 173 They.. hadde nat therfore gyuen due thanke vnto God, but referred it to theyr owne strengthes and vertue. **1526** *Pilgr. Perf.* (W. de W. 1531) 40 Rest not to moche therto, but referre all to the gyuer. **1596** DALRYMPLE tr. *Leslie's Hist. Scot.* I. 70 To.. Gathel thay refer our hail stock, and him to be author of our hail natione. **1611** BIBLE *Ecclus.* Prol. *marg.*, Some referre this Prologue to Athanasius, because it is found in his Synopsis. **1646** SIR T. BROWNE *Pseud. Ep.* 366 While we referre it unto the Moon, we give some satisfaction for the Ocean, but no generall salve for Creeks, and Seas which know no floud. **1841** MISS MITFORD in L'Estrange *Life* (1870) III. viii. 129 It seems impossible to refer all these well-attested stories to imposition. **1871** BLACKIE *Four Phases* i. 9 The God to whom he habitually referred his highest inspirations.

3. a. To assign *to* a thing, or class of things, as being properly included or comprehended in this; to regard as naturally belonging, pertaining, or having relation *to*; to attach or attribute *to*.

c **1374** CHAUCER *Boeth.* III. pr. ii. 52 (Camb. MS.), Certes, now am I redy to referren the goodes of the body to thise forseyde thinges abouen. *c* **1450** tr. *De Imitatione* III. xxxix. 109 What eurere of gode þinge þei fynde in creatures, all þat þey referre to þe preising [L. *ad laudem referunt*] of her maker. **1538** STARKEY *England* I. i. 16 Thys law [of nature] ys the ground and end of the other, to the wych hyt must euer be referryd. **1597** GERARDE *Herbal* I. xviii. 24 Their nature and vertues are to be referred vnto Dogs grasse. **1641** WILKINS *Math. Magic* I. i. (1648) 2 To the second [study] may be referred all that Knowledge which concerns the Frame of this great Universe. **1697** tr. *Burgersdicius' Logic* I.

xxii. 91 Those which .. are said to be of the Opposites, or in any other manner are referred to them. **1812–16** PLAYFAIR *Nat. Phil.* (1819) II. 267 Let S be the Sun and P and P′ two planets referred to the plane of the ecliptic. **1875** JOWETT *Plato* (ed. 2) V. 32 You went wrong when you referred all legislation to a part of virtue, and to an inferior part.

†**b.** To put *into*, place *among*, a certain class.

1577 HANMER *Anc. Eccl. Hist.* VIII. xiv. (1619) 152 Constantius .. was first referred of them into the number of the gods. **1633** P. FLETCHER *Elisa* xliii, He lives in heaven, among the saints referred.

c. To assign *to* a particular place or date.

a **1604** HANMER *Chron. Irel.* (1633) 85 Stanihurst in his description of Ireland, referreth it to the yeere 155. **1788** PRIESTLEY *Lect. Hist.* IV. xvii. 148 A person thus prepared will be able to refer any particular history he takes up to its proper place in universal history. **1828** ABERCROMBIE *Dis. Brain* 311 An obscure affection, referred chiefly to the stomach. **1863** LYELL *Antiq. Man* 26 In a few of the most modern lake-dwellings .. (which the antiquaries refer to the sixth century).

d. Used with advbs., as *here* (†*hither*), *there*.

1605 CAMDEN *Rem.* 34 Hither also may be referred that [name] of Claudius Rutilus. **1655** STANLEY *Hist. Philos.* I. I. 12 Hither we must likewise referre what is cited under his name by the same Stobæus. **1715** tr. *Gregory's Astron.* (1726) I. 66 And the Place of the Sun .. will be there, .. for there the Eye plac'd in the Centre of the Earth refers it. **1830** LINDLEY *Nat. Syst. Bot.* 49 Adoxa, .. which is always referred here, appears to me far more anomalous than Parnassia.

†**e.** To give or bear (trust) *to* one. *Obs.*$^{-1}$

1594 WEST *2nd Pt. Symbol., Chancerie* §85 Your said orator then referring especiall trust and confidence to the said J. T. and A. L.

†**4. a.** To bring into relation *to* a thing or person; to order with reference *to*. *Obs. rare.*

c **1460** FORTESCUE *Abs. & Lim. Mon.* viii. (1885) 127 Wherfore all that he dothe owith to be referred to his kyngdome. **1538** STARKEY *England* I. i. 21 To thys euery man ought to referre al hys actys, thoughtys and dedys.

†**b.** To apply (a word) *to* a thing. *Obs.*

1509 HAWES *Past. Pleas.* v. (Percy Soc.) 24 The Latyn worde whyche that is referred Unto a thynge whych is substancyall, For a nowne substantyve is wel averred. **1553** T. WILSON *Rhet.* 93 When a woorde hath a proper signification of the owne, & beyng referred to an other thyng, hath an other meanyng, the Grecians call it Metonymia. **1664** H. MORE *Myst. Iniq.* v. 13 Εἴδωλον is to be referred also to those things that are not carved Images.

5. *refl.* To betake, commit, commend, entrust (oneself) *to* some person or thing for assistance, advice, etc., or in a spirit of submission, acquiescence, or confidence. Now *rare* or *Obs.*

c **1450** HOLLAND *Howlat* 581 Tharfor I end heir, Refferis me to harraldis, to tell ȝow the hale. **1500–20** DUNBAR *Poems* lvii. 24, [I] with ane humill cheir and face, Referris me to the Kyngis grace. **1555** CRANMER *Let. to Queen Mary* in *Misc. Writ.* (Parker Soc.) II. 453, I refer me to the judgment of all indifferent hearers. **1585** T. WASHINGTON tr. *Nicholay's Voy.* III. viii. 82 b, As for my part I referre me too that which it may be, and will not otherwise assure it to bee true. **1611** SHAKS. *Wint. T.* III. ii. 116, I doe referre me to the Oracle: Apollo be my Iudge. **1642** FULLER *Holy & Prof. St.* II. xvii. 115 He makes not advantage of his chapmans ignorance, chiefly if referring himself to his honesty. **1729** BUTLER *Serm. Love God* i. Wks. 1874 II. 179 The conclusion of the whole would be, that we should refer ourselves implicitly to him. **1748** RICHARDSON *Clarissa* (1811) VI. 48, I refer myself to your generosity. **1824** SCOTT *Redgauntlet* let. xi, I refer myself to God's pleasure, and not to yours.

6. a. To commit, submit, hand over (a question, cause, or matter) *to* some special or ultimate authority for consideration, decision, execution, etc. Also rarely without const.

1456 SIR G. HAYE *Law Arms* (S.T.S.) 19 Thare he referrit the fontayne of humanitee to the will of the fader, as him lykit best for mannis hele. **1535** COVERDALE *2 Macc.* xi. 36 As concernynge the thinges which he referred vnto the kynge, sende hither some with spede. **1560** DAUS tr. *Sleidane's Comm.* 6 Referryng the whole matter to the judgement of the same. **1590** NASHE *Pref. Greene's Menaphon* (Arb.) 14, I had rather referre it as a disputatiue plea by diuines, than set it downe as a determinate position. **1614** SIR R. DUDLEY in *Fortescue Papers* (Camden) 8 Referring the recompence to his gratiousnes. **1687** A. LOVELL tr. *Thevenot's Trav.* I. 248 When they fall out .., they refer their controversie to the next man they meet, who makes them good friends again. **1725** POPE *Odyss.* I. 510 To heav'n alone Refer the Choice to fill the vacant Throne. **1769** ROBERTSON *Chas. V*, VII. III. 30 The King referred the matter to the council. **1822** SHELLEY tr. *Calderon* I. 255 And thus to me .. You may refer the merits of the case. **1875** JOWETT *Plato* (ed. 2) I. 44 Socrates proposes at last to refer the question to some older person.

absol. **1853** WHARTON *Pennsylv. Digest* 113 An attorney's agreement to refer binds his client.

b. *Sc. Law.* To submit the fact at issue in a legal action (as the existence of a debt) *to* the oath of the defendant. Also *absol.* (quot. 1681).

1579–81 *Reg. Privy Council Scot.* II. 254 [The amount owing] wes referrit .. to the said Petiris aith. **1681** STAIR *Instit.* IV. xliv. §14 Where in any Affair, a Party who Referrs to Oath, pitches upon Particulars sufficient to Infer the Conclusion. **1752** MCDOUALL *Inst. Laws Scot.* II. IV. xxxii. 655 In an action where .. the pursuer refers his libel or declaration to the defender's oath. **1797** *Encycl. Brit.* (ed. 3) IX. 724/1 Crimes cannot, like debts, be referred to the defender's oath. **1853** *Act 16 Vict.* c. 20 §5 It shall not be competent .. to refer the cause or any part of it to his oath.

†**c.** To commit (a person) *to* trial or prison. *Obs.*

1645 WHITELOCKE *Memorials* 26 Aug., Lieutenant-colonel Lilburne was committed by order of the house, and referred to a legal trial. **1723** *Acct. Tryal Pyrates* 34 The Prisoner pleaded Force, and an affidavit made by his Captain appearing to the same purpose, he was referred to Marshalsea.

†**7. a.** To defer, postpone, put off (something) *to, unto, till, until* another time or season. *Obs.*

1573 PHILIP MORE *Almanack & Prognost.* B j, Hillarie Tearme, beginneth the xxiij of Januarie, if it be not Sundaye, which then is referred untill the next day after. **1586** T. B. *La Primaud. Fr. Acad.* I. (1594) 6 They had not the patience to refer the rest of that matter unto the afternoone. **1642** FULLER *Holy & Prof. St.* v. xvi. 422 Some advised to referre it to another time. **1670** COTTON *Espernon* III. XII. 645 The Duke .. referr'd it till the next morning. **1751** ELIZA HEYWOOD *Betsy Thoughtless* IV. 38 She would refer what she had farther to say on these subjects, 'till another opportunity.

†**b.** Without const. = DEFER *v.*^{1} 2. Also, to vote for postponement. *Obs.*

1611 BEAUM. & FL. *King & no K.* III. ii, The first is no madder of fighting than I; so that that's referred: the place where it must be ended is four days' journey off. **1640** LAUD *Wks.* (1853) III. 290 It came to voting in that House, the first article was denied by eighteen, and referred by eight. **1734** tr. *Rollin's Anc. Hist.* XIX. ii. (1827) VIII. 100 One of the five magistrates who refused to refer the debate.

c. To reserve (a subject, etc.) for later treatment. Also const. *to* and with *inf.* Now *rare.*

1559 W. CUNNINGHAM *Cosmogr. Glasse* 43, I will speake nothing of the Water (but referre it until we intreat of Navigation). **1585** T. WASHINGTON tr. *Nicholay's Voy.* II. vii. 37 b, I doe referre the description of the sayde Ile .., for that it appertayneth vntoo the seconde tome. **1617** MORYSON *Itin.* I. 287, I will referre the change of the value of Coynes in the Low-Countries, to the proper place. **1660** BARROW *Euclid* Explic. Signs, Other Abbreviations .. the Reader will without trouble understand of himself; saving some few, which, being of less general use, we refer to be explained in their places. **1726** SWIFT *Gulliver* I. viii, My Account of this Voyage must be referred to the Second Part of my Travels. **1815** KIRBY & SP. *Entomol.* xii. (1818) I. 404 A description of these, however, which will require a detailed survey, I must refer to another letter.

†**d.** To remit the treatment of (a word, subject, etc.) *to* another word or section of a work. *Obs.*

1611 COTGR. Errata, *Ceincture de dueil* (vnder Ceincture) referred vnto Dueil, where it was forgotten. *a* **1661** FULLER *Worthies* (1840) II. 265 What remaineth concerning mastiffs is referred to the same topic in Somersetshire.

†**e.** To carry or bring forward (a sum). *Obs.*$^{-1}$

1588 J. MELLIS *Briefe Instr.* F j, The rest [= balance] you shall referre and rescribe it in another leafe of the Leager.

f. To postpone the passing of (a candidate) in an examination or the acceptance of (an application for a degree), provision being made for re-examination at a later date.

1907 *Practitioner* June 795 A student, who should venture to put upon an examination paper what is the only logical outcome of the teaching of text-books, ought, without hesitation, to be referred. **1908** A. S. M. HUTCHINSON *Once Aboard Lugger* I. i. 32 'I had forgotten. Your examination?' .. 'I failed. I was referred for three months.' **1927** *Univ. Oxford Examination Statutes* vi. 227 The examiners shall have power .. to recommend the Board to refer the Student's application for leave to supplicate back to him in order that he may present himself for re-examination. **1976** *Daily Times* (Lagos) 3 Nov. 31/2 Twenty-four students drawn from the states and the Armed Forces passed the prescribed test while four students were referred. **1979** *Jrnl. R. Soc. Arts* Dec. 9/1 The candidates for this session's examination were exclusively restricted to those who had been referred in a previous examination or who were resitting in order to obtain higher grades.

8. a. To send or direct (one) *to* a person, a book or its author for information. Also const. *back to.*

1601 in Moryson *Itin.* II. (1617) 152 Wee beseech your Lordships giue vs leaue to referre you for your information in that point to the Iournall which herewithall we send. **1696** WHISTON *Th. Earth* II. (1722) 143, I must refer my Reader to my Short View of the Chronology. **1712** HEARNE *Collect.* (O.H.S.) III. 381, I refer'd him to the Decem Scriptores. **1766** GOLDSM. *Vic. W.* xi, My wife .. referred her to all the neighbours for a character. **1838** DICKENS *O. Twist* xxxiii, The ostler .. after hearing all he had to say again, referred him to the landlord. **1875** JOWETT *Plato* (ed. 2) I. 352, I will refer you to a witness who is worthy of credit. **1927** W. E. COLLINSON *Contemp. Eng.* 123 The elements of committee English which I had picked up in the Debating Society were soon reinforced by the constantly heard expressions: standing orders, terms of reference (defining the scope of a committee's labours), to refer back (to a committee for further consideration). **1934** G. B. SHAW *On Rocks* II. 267, I must really refer you back to him for further consideration and report. **1961** NEW ENG. BIBLE *Luke* xxiii. 15, I have myself examined him in your presence and found nothing in him to support your charges. No more did Herod, for he has referred him back to us. **1976** [see sense 8 d below].

absol. **1737** WATERLAND *Eucharist* 413 For the avoiding of prolixity, I choose rather to refer, than to repeat.

b. To direct (one) *to* a fact, event, or thing, by drawing attention to it or pointing it out.

1605 SHAKS. *Macb.* I. v. 9 These weyward Sisters saluted me, and referr'd me to the comming on of time. *a* **1715** BURNET (J.), Those causes the divine historian refers us to, and not to any productions out of nothing. **1864** D. G. MITCHELL *Sev. Stor.* 271, I wrote De Courcy that very day, referring him to the paragraph I had read.

†**c.** To refer any one (for an account) *to* some book. *Obs. rare*$^{-1}$.

1634 SIR T. HERBERT *Trav.* 36, I referre the description of their [the Banians'] Religion to a Booke late written by Master Lord a Preacher to the Merchants in Surat.

d. To send or direct (a person) to a medical consultant or institution for specialist treatment.

1961 *Lancet* 2 Sept. 517/2 We are indebted to Dr. J. F. O'Connell for referring this patient. **1970** H. MCLEAVE *Question of Negligence* xxii. 186 She did consult me, but she was referred by someone else. **1973** *Guardian* 9 Mar. 13/2 The slum Doctor round the corner who never examines his patients before referring them. **1973** *Listener* 19 Apr. 507/1 They're all referred by the GP... They're all psychogeriatrics. **1976** *Women's Report* Sept./Oct. 2/1 Yet the clinic makes use of the NHS because all clients needing surgery or expensive treatment have to be referred back to NHS hospitals or clinics.

9. To relate, recount, report, record. Now *rare.*

1568 GRAFTON *Chron.* II. 733 King Edward aunswered that .. he woulde referre and report the truth to him. **1577–87** HOLINSHED *Chron.* I. 81/2 In that meane time he builded a strong castle, .. which some referre to be builded in his second returne into Wales. **1649** JER. TAYLOR *Gt. Exemp.* I. Ad Sect. ii. §8 So it happened .. as she related to her Cousin Elizabeth, and so it happened not to be as she referred to her husband Joseph. *a* **1825** *Prince Robert* x. in Child *Ballads* II. 286/2 With sichin and sabbin and wringing his hands, No message he could refer. **1851** MRS. BROWNING *Casa Guidi Wind.* I. 136 So keep your stone .. To cover up your grave-place and refer The proper titles!

†**10.** To hand over, give, transfer. Also *refl.* *Obs.*

c **1611** CHAPMAN *Iliad* XXIV. 111 Juno did receive Her entry with a cup of gold, in which she drank to her, .. and the cup did to her hand refer. **1611** SHAKS. *Cymb.* I. i. 6 His daughter, and the heire of's kingdome .. hath referr'd her selfe Vnto a poore but worthy Gentleman. **1705** in Picton *L'pool Munic. Rec.* (1886) II. 83 It is order'd in Councell that to encourage a horse race to be run at ye Waterside, tenne guineas be referr'd to Mr. Mayr for one year.

II. Intransitive senses.

†**11.** To return, recur *to* some person or thing.

c **1374** CHAUCER *Troylus* I. 210 (266) As touchyng þis matere, For I it gan, I wil þer-to referre. *c* **1430** LYDG. *Min. Poems* (Percy Soc.) 78 To Phebus my wittes gan refere, And on this wise he sayde to me [etc.].

12. a. To have reference or relation *to* a thing; *esp.* to have allusion, to apply, *to.*

c **1386** CHAUCER *Can. Yeom. Prol. & T.* 530 To go to the conclusioun That refereth to thy confusioun. **1530** PALSGR. 322/1 Refarryng one to another, *relatif.* **1647** CRASHAW *Poems* 149 Awake, my glory, soul, if such thou be, And that fair word at all refer to thee. **1678** MOXON *Mech. Exerc.* No. 6. 107, I marked some Terms in Joynery with superiour Letters .. intending at the latter end of these Exercises to have explained the Terms those Letters referr'd to. **1718** ATTERBURY *Serm.* (1734) I. vii. 196 Breaking of Bread: A Phrase, which in the Acts manifestly referrs to the Eucharist. **1791** BURKE *App. Whigs* Wks. VI. 134 All such institutions .. must originate from their Crown, and in all their proceedings must refer to it. **1860** TYNDALL *Glac.* II. xxi. 345 My measurements refer to the ice at and near the surface. **1891** E. PEACOCK *N. Brendon* I. 314 His words referred to Mildred only.

†**b.** To have relationship *to* one. *Obs.*$^{-1}$

1640 BP. REYNOLDS *Passions* xxxi, [This is] the reason why this difference between men nearly referring each to other should work a greater anger between them.

†**c.** To matter, be of consequence *to* a thing.

1677 GALE *Crt. Gentiles* IV. 437 Either because he conceives it no way refers to the whole, if small things are neglected: or, if he thinks it doth refer, yet .. he neglectes it.

d. To make reference or allusion, to give a reference, direct the attention, *to* something.

1691 T. H[ALE] *Acc. New Invent.* p. lx, Any other Engine .. than this I have referred to. **1725** POPE *Wks. Shaks.* I. Pref. p. xxii, Some suspected passages .. are degraded to the bottom of the page; with an Asterisk referring to the places of their insertion. **1828** MACAULAY *Hallam's Const. Hist.* Wks. 1898 VII. 317 With all deference to the eminent writers to whom we have referred, we may venture to say [etc.]. **1860** TYNDALL *Glac.* I. ix. 61, I at length found myself on the peak referred to. **1875** JOWETT *Plato* (ed. 2) I. 422 He refers to passages of his personal history.

†**13.** To suggest, or leave, *to* a person to do something. *Obs. rare.*

1585 T. WASHINGTON tr. *Nicholay's Voy.* IV. xxxiii. 156 Ordinances, which I passe with silence, referring vnto the reader, to see that which Plutarch hath written. **1586** J. HOOKER *Hist. Irel.* in *Holinshed* II. 162/2 The lord iustice sent his letters .. to the earle of Desmond, for his repaire vnto him, .. referring vnto him to come either to Cashell or to Limerike. **1645** WHITELOCKE *Memorials* 1 Aug., The house referred to the committee of the army to audit their arrears.

14. To have recourse, make application, *to* a thing; to turn or appeal *to* for some purpose.

1595 DANIEL *Civ. Wars* II. xxxiii, Doe but referre to time, and to small time; And infinite occasions you shall finde. **1813** WELLINGTON in Gurw. *Desp.* (1838) XI. 51 He is to refer to and obey all orders of the army referrible to the mode of treating the Spanish Colonel. **1849** DICKENS *Dav. Copp.* xvi, 'Mother will be expecting me,' he said, referring to a .. watch in his pocket.

Hence **re'ferring** *vbl. sb.* and *ppl. a.*

1572 *Reg. Privy Council Scot.* II. 165 Notwithstanding the referring interpretatioun and declaratioun foirsaid. **1611** COTGR., *Renvoy*, .. a referring from one vnto another. **1628** T. SPENCER *Logick* 168 The predication it selfe is no more, but an absolute referring of a thing signified, vnto the subiect. **1771** LUCKOMBE *Hist. Print.* 392 The Contents .. are generally set in Italic ..; with the referring figures justified to the ends of the respective lines. **1950** P. F. STRAWSON in *Mind* LIX. 320 We very commonly use expressions of certain kinds to mention or refer to some individual person or single object or particular event or place or process... I shall call this way of using expressions the 'uniquely referring use'. *Ibid.* 326 'Mentioning', or 'referring', is not something an expression does; it is something that some one can use an expression to do.

referability (ˌrɛfərə'bɪlɪtɪ). *rare*. [f. REFERABLE *a*. + -ILITY.] The fact or quality of being referable.

1964 R. H. ROBINS *Gen. Linguistics* vi. 233 Non-favourite sentences of class I have no such referability to a longer sentence in which they may be incorporated.

referable ('rɛfərəb(ə)l, rɪ'fɜːr-), *a*. [f. REFER *v*. + -ABLE: cf. *inferable*, *preferable*, and see also REFERRABLE and REFERRIBLE.] Capable of being referred or assigned *to*, †*unto* (some person or thing); assignable, ascribable.

1646 SIR T. BROWNE *Pseud. Ep.* 345 All parts of time are alike unto him, unto whom none are referable. **1720** WELTON *Suffer. Son of God* I. vii. 137 The Names..are not possibly Referable to those they are generally given to. **1823** H. J. BROOKE *Introd. Crystallogr.* 147 It is probable..that there is not any mineral whose crystals are strictly referable to this class of octahedrons. **1879** PROCTOR *Pleas. Ways Sc.* ii. 28 All the phenomena of weather are directly referable to the sun as their governing cause.

referee (rɛfə'riː), *sb*. Also 7 referree. [f. REFER *v*. + -EE[1].]

†**1. a.** One appointed by Parliament to examine and report on applications for monopolies or letters patent. *Obs*.

1621 in *Crt. & Times Jas. I* (1848) II. 235 The Lords and Commons met in the afternoon, to consult what punishment to inflict upon monopolists, and the referees, who are in chiefest fault. **1640** *Resol. Ho. Comm.* in Rushw. *Hist. Coll.* III. (1692) I. 53 That the Patent for the Monopoly of Tobacco be forthwith brought into this House; And that the Referrees, to whom the Legality of this Patent was referred, attend the said Committee at the same time. **1663** in *Milton's Wks.* (1738) I. p. lxxxv, We have received your Letter..together with several Petitions,..all which we likewise transmitted to the Lords Referees.

b. One to whom the management or superintendence of something is entrusted.

1705 in Brewster *Life Newton* (1854) II. App. xv, To refer the care and management of the said impression to the said ..S[r]. Is. Newton [etc.];..the said referees..have treated with the said Mr. Aunsham Churchill for printing the same. **1845** *Act 7 & 8 Vict.* c. 84 §2 The Term 'Official Referees' to mean the Persons appointed in pursuance of this Act to be Official Referees of Metropolitan Buildings.

c. A member of certain committees and courts appointed by the House of Commons to deal with private bills.

For details see Bonham-Carter's edition of *May's Parl. Practice* (1893) III. 726–8. Since 1868 the only *Court of Referees* has been one for deciding questions as to the *locus standi* of petitioners; the office of ***Referee on Private Bills*** ceased in 1902.

1865 *Private Bills* April 54 Referees on Private Bills. **1867** *Ibid.* April 35 Bills Referred to the Court of Referees. **1876** in Bonham-Carter *May's Parl. Practice* (1893) III. 728 That it be an instruction to committees on private bills that referees appointed to such committees may take part in all the proceedings thereof, but without the power of voting.

2. *Law*. **a.** A person to whom (either alone or with others) a dispute between parties is referred by mutual consent; an arbitrator.

1690 CHILD *Disc. Trade* vi. 121 While we choose our Judges our selves..they can be no more too arbitrary than too much can be given to Referees, when both parties desire an end of their Differences. **1712** ADDISON *Spect.* No. 481 ¶7 As the case now stands, if you will have my Opinion, I think they ought to bring it to Referees. **1781** H. WALPOLE *Lett.* (1902) 60 He offers to compromise, and has desired me to be a Referee [to a will], and Mozzi has named Mr. Morrice for the other. **1841** W. SPALDING *Italy & It. Isl.* III. 375 A Conciliatore, who is a sort of judicial arbiter or referee, chosen from among the resident landholders.

b. *spec*. (See quots.)

1733 [? WORSLEY] *Observ. Const. Middle Temple* (1896) 184 The Referees are not properly officers of the Society but are two Barristers appointed by Cha: Cox Esq[r]. by deed bearing date 30 Septr. 1637 [etc.]. **1828–32** WEBSTER s.v., In New England, a referee differs from an arbitrator in being appointed by the court to decide in a cause which is depending before that court. An arbitrator is chosen by parties to decide a cause between them.

3. a. One to whom any matter or question in dispute is referred for decision; an umpire.

1670 COTTON *Espernon* I. IV. 162 Neither did his Majesty altogether..trust to the Referree he had in publick honoured with that Office. **1710** STEELE *Tatler* No. 169 ¶3 The good Offices of an Advocate, a Referee, a Companion, a Mediator, and a Friend. **1798** W. HUTTON *Autobiog.* 37, I considered myself overcharged. We agreed to leave it to reference. The referees appeared warm in his favour. **1844** DISRAELI *Coningsby* I. v, Clear-sighted, unprejudiced, sagacious;..he was the universal referee. **1878** BROWNING *La Saisiaz* 277 Were we two the earth's sole tenants, with no third for referee, How should I distinguish?

transf. **1853** LYNCH in *Lett. to Scattered* (1872) 349 They sought to the Referee; they searched the Old Scriptures. **1868** M. PATTISON *Academ. Org.* v. 162 These institutions have become the referees to whose verdict every product of mind must be unconditionally submitted.

b. In games or sports.

1840 *Spirit of Times* 25 Jan. 559/3 He was a general referee and umpire, whether it was a horse swap, a race, a rifle match, or a cock fight. **1856** *Porter's Spirit of Times* 6 Dec. 229/1 In [baseball] matches, an umpire is chosen on each side, and a referee to decide, when the umpires cannot agree. *c* **1860** *Rules of the Ring* in *Boxiana* 76 That a referee shall be chosen by the umpires..to whom all disputes shall be referred. **1880** *Henning's Bk. Rules Billiards*, etc. 2 In all games for stakes an umpire or referee should be appointed. **1887** G. A. HUTCHISON *Football* ii. 11 In case of infringement, the referee shall..order a scrummage to be formed. **1889** *Sportsman* 10 Apr. 7/1 Britton claimed the fight on a foul, but the referee disallowed the claim. **1906** *Daily Chron.* 7 Sept. 9/4 No great blame attaches to the referee, who probably did not notice the forward till he was apparently off-side. **1936** H. B. T. WAKELAM *Game goes On* 17 Other innovations during the Daring 'Eighties were the appointment of neutral referees and the provision of whistles for those functionaries. **1951** F. N. S. CREEK *Soccer for Boys* iii. 18 The duration of the game is mainly the responsibility of the referee. **1977** *Times* 16 Mar. 12/1 The main topic of conversation..was the alleged attempt to bribe the Danish referee before the first leg.

Comb. **1895** *Daily News* 7 Feb. 5/4 An abolition of the brutal practice of referee-baiting.

c. A person appointed to examine a scientific or other learned work and comment on its suitability for publication.

1884 *Proc. London Math. Soc.* XV. 160 The original paper has been divided into two..at the suggestion of the referee. **1926** A. E. HOUSMAN *Let.* 14 Oct. (1971) 242 A report of mine..decided the Syndics not to accept a treatise of Richmond's... A. W. Ward..told him that I was the referee. **1970** *Physics Bull.* Jan. 2/2 The majority of authors expressed their appreciation of the value of the constructive criticism of the referees in improving the quality of their papers. **1971** *Nature* 22 Oct. 571/3 Each paper was carefully scrutinized by one senior referee and by one of the two distinguished editors-in-chief.

4. A person who may be referred to for information or guidance on the character or other qualities of someone, *spec*. of an applicant for employment, for an academic or other award, or the like.

1862 H. MAYHEW *London Labour* IV. 12 Classification of the workers and non-workers of Great Britain... Referees, or those who give characters to professional beggars when a reference is required. **1882** *Sydney Slang Dict.* 7/2 *Referees*, those who give characters to enable dishonest persons and thieves' accomplices to obtain situations. **1944** *Oxf. Univ. Gaz.* LXXIV. 316/1 Candidates are requested to send in their names with eight copies of any statement that they may wish to make..giving the names of not more than three referees. **1971** *Reader's Digest Family Guide to Law* 689/2 One way an employer can assess the abilities of an applicant is to ask for references from former employers. It may also be useful to telephone the referee, who may be prepared to give more information informally than he can provide in writing. **1972** *Library Assoc. Record* Nov. 224/1 On three occasions lately I have sent for an application form and job description only to find that these did not arrive until two or three days before the closing date, this making it very difficult..to arrange referees, etc. **1976** *Oxf. Univ. Gaz.* CVII. 209/1 Applications, including a *curriculum vitae*,.. and the names of two academic referees, should be sent to the Secretary of the Marjory Wardrop Fund.

referee (rɛfə'riː), *v*. [f. prec.]

1. *trans*. To preside over (a match) as umpire. Also *intr*.

1889 *Sportsman* 10 Apr. 7/1 Those fights that I want to referee, I will referee. **1895** *Westm. Gaz.* 22 Mar. 6/3 When next he referees at Sunderland an organised attack will be made upon him.

2. *trans*. and *intr*. To examine and evaluate (a scientific paper, thesis, or book); to act as referee (in sense 3 c of the sb.).

1966 *Rep. Comm. Inquiry Univ. Oxf.* II. 452 Editing or refereeing for journals. **1970** *Physics Bull.* 3/1 If a referee is unable to referee a paper himself, he is invited to pass it to an appropriate colleague. **1970** *Computers & Humanities* IV. 312 All submitted papers will be refereed. **1971** *Nature* 24 Sept. p. xvi/2 (Advt.), All papers are scrupulously refereed and the journal is guided by an editorial board of distinguished scientists whose activities cover all aspects of polymer research.

Hence **refe'reed** *ppl. a.*; **refe'reeing** *vbl. sb.*

1894 *Westm. Gaz.* 29 Sept. 7/1 Regret was expressed that more players of renown did not lend their aid in refereeing. **1966** [see sense 2 of the vb.] **1970** *Physics Bull.* Jan. 2/2 (*heading*) Refereeing of research papers. **1975** *Nature* 6 Nov. 1/1 The Scientific Information Committee of the Royal Society has recently put forward a set of guidelines for the refereeing of papers for publication. **1978** *Maledicta* II. 10 Unfortunately for them, our journal is not a 'refereed' academic publication.

reference ('rɛfərəns), *sb*. [f. REFER *v*. + -ENCE; cf. *conference*, *deference*, *inference*, etc. and mod.F. *référence*.]

1. a. The act or expedient of referring or submitting a matter, esp. a dispute or controversy, to some person or authority for consideration, decision, or settlement (in legal use *spec*. to the Masters in Ordinary of the Court of Chancery).

1589 PUTTENHAM *Eng. Poesie* III. xix. (Arb.) 234 *Epitropis*, or the Figure of Reference. This manner of speech is vsed when..hauing said inough already, we referre the rest to their consideration. **1609** DANIEL *Civ. Wars* VIII. lv, We will our selfe take time to heare Your Cause at large: wherein we wil you haue No other reference, but repaire to vs. **1642** FULLER *Holy & Prof. St.* v. xiii. 408 References and compositions he hates as bad as an hangman hates a pardon. **1678** WYCHERLEY *Plain Dealer* III. i, Art thou a solicitor in chancery, and offer a reference? **1745** *De Foe's Eng. Tradesman* xxxix. (1841) II. 119 When two tradesmen of this pacific temper meet, a reference never fails to put an end to all disputes between them. **1834** *Penny Cycl.* II. 251/1 If the arbitrator refuses or ceases to act, the reference is at an end. **1836** *Ibid.* VI. 484/1 It would be impossible to specify every head of reference to the Masters. **1863** H. COX *Instit.* I. vii. 71 In some instances the peerage has been allowed without reference to the House of Lords.

b. *spec*. in *Sc. Law*. (See REFER *v*. 6 b.)

1752 M[c]DOUALL *Inst. Laws Scot.* IV. xxxii. II. 655 This reference to the deferrors oath will not be allowed if it is done invidiously or fraudulently. **1797** *Encycl. Brit.* (ed. 3) IX. 714/1 The reference is a virtual contract between the litigants. **1853** *Act 16 Vict.* c. 20 §5 The adducing of any party as a witness..shall not have the effect of a reference to the oath of the party so adduced.

c. The authority or standard referred to. *rare*.

1599 MASSINGER, etc. *Old Law* v. i, Whom, for his manifest virtues, we make such judge and censor of youth, and the absolute reference of life and manners. **1861** GOLDW. SMITH *Lect. Mod. Hist.* ii. 69 Universal expediency and the fitness of things are ultimate and distant references, if they are not altogether beyond the range of our vision.

†**2.** Assignment. *Obs*.[−1]

1604 SHAKS. *Oth.* I. iii. 238, I craue fit disposition for my Wife, Due reference of Place, and Exhibition.

3. a. Relation, relationship, respect, regard *to* some thing or person.

1593 G. HARVEY *Pierce's Super.* Wks. (Grosart) II. 108 In every enterprise..[Resolution] hath..a regard to worth, a respect to assurance, and a reference to the end. **1600** SHAKS. *A.Y.L.* I. iii. 129 What will you be call'd? *Cel.* Something that hath a reference to my state. *a* **1641** BP. MOUNTAGU *Acts & Mon.* (1642) 456 Man in this consideration stands in a two-fold respect and reference to God, publick and private. *a* **1704** T. BROWN *Sat. Antients* Wks. 1730 I. 14 *Satura* is an Adjective, which has Reference to a Substantive understood. **1736** BUTLER *Anal.* II. v. Wks. 1874 I. 223 The world is a..system, whose parts have a mutual reference to each other. **1821** SCOTT *Kenilw.* xviii, A strange smile, which yet bore a greater reference to the human character. **1850** M[c]COSH *Div. Govt.* I. ii. (1874) 39 All things sublunary have a reference more or less direct to man.

b. ***in*** or ***with reference to***, with respect or regard to; †with a view to, according to.

1594 HOOKER *Eccl. Pol.* I. viii. §6 The knowledge of that which man is in reference unto himself, and other things in relation unto man. **1662** GERBIER *Princ.* 35 Neither are the Vessels of Silver but in reference to the Neatness which ought to be observed in all Cookery. **1662** STILLINGFL. *Orig. Sacræ* I. vi. §9 The contradictions in reference to the Ægyptian History between Manetho, Herodotus [etc.]. **1700** MAIDWELL in *Collect.* (O.H.S.) I. 311 The scholars, in reference to his thoughts, are not to exceed the number of 60. **1704** SWIFT *T. Tub* ix, If we take this Definition of Happiness, and examine it with Reference to the Senses, it will be acknowledged wonderfully adapt. **1840** LARDNER *Geom.* 289 The same notation as was used to express the properties of the ellipse in reference to its axes. **1894** H. DRUMMOND *Ascent Man* 266 All existing lives must, with reference to their environment, be the best possible lives.

c. ***without reference to***, without regard to, without consideration of or for.

1846 LANDOR *Imag. Conversat., Southey & Porson* II. Wks. I. 74/2, I will tell you what is applicable on all occasions..without reference to weak or common minds. **1877** *Cassell's Techn. Educ.* III. 373/1 By these means the whole of the area treated as a plane surface—that is, without reference to its differences of level—will be mapped.

d. *Logic* and *Linguistics*. The act or state of referring through which one term or concept is related or connected to another or to objects in the world; also as ***objective reference***, and *attrib*. as ***reference class***, ***property***.

1883 F. H. BRADLEY *Princ. Logic* I. i. ii. 55 Judgment is not the synthesis of ideas, but the reference of ideal content to reality. *a* **1914** C. S. PEIRCE *Coll. Papers* (1933) III. xix. 366 Dyadic relations..which can only subsist between two subjects of different categories of being..may advantageously be termed a reference. **1927** OGDEN & RICHARDS *Meaning of Meaning* (ed. 2) i. 9 It is Thought (or, as we shall usually say, *reference*) which is directed and organized, and it is also Thought which is recorded and communicated. **1946** C. I. LEWIS *Knowledge & Valuation* x. 270 This property ψ may be called the *reference property*. *Ibid.* 271 The class of things having it [*sc*. a property] may be called the *reference class*. **1951** G. HUMPHREY *Thinking* viii. 228 In its original form as the 'problem of meaning' the question has to be obscured by the invention of new descriptive terms such as *transcendent reference*, *objective reference* or *context* in order to satisfy the scientific conscience. **1956** G. RYLE in A. J. Ayer *Revol. in Philos.* 7 Both [Frege and Bradley] saw that it is..intrinsic to a thought to be true or false, or to have 'objective reference'. **1959** K. R. POPPER *Logic Sci. Discovery* viii. 155 This class α, which is assumed to be *non-empty*, serves, as it were, as a frame of reference, and will be called a (finite) *reference-class*. **1972** *Language* XLVIII. 446 In order to understand problems of semantic theory, it is crucial to understand why most philosophers think of the notion of reference as the key element in such theories. Reference is the relation between singular term and bearer, as well as between general predicate and the entities of which the predicate is true. With the notion of reference go the notions of naming, describing, and—therefore—truth. **1974** P. F. STRAWSON *Subject & Predicate* ii. 47 Hearer and speaker should each understand the name..as having a certain unique reference; and..the reference should be the same for each of them.

e. *Sociol*. and *Psychol*. The process by which or the extent to which an individual establishes a relation with elements in society as a standard for comparing status and values (see also ***frame of reference*** s.v. FRAME *sb*. 4 d (ii)). Freq. *attrib*. (see also ***reference group*** in sense 8 a below).

1937 G. MURPHY et al. *Exper. Social Psychol.* (rev. ed.) iv. 220 A laboratory situation is set in which social factors determine a reference frame which must be used by the subject in perceiving. **1947** SHERIF & CANTRIL *Psychol. of Ego-Involvements* vi. 137 Judgments of the physical characteristics of others..become..ego-involving judgments in which an individual uses himself..as a central point of reference. **1948** M. & C. SHERIF *Outl. Social Psychol.* xviii. 621 This ordering of responses held whether a respondent made as many as nineteen consensual references or as few as one. **1956** GARDNER & THOMPSON

Social Relations & Morale v. 23 Displacements of the distributions of scores along the reference continuum. *Ibid.* vii. 43 The most general reference population.. would be: 'All the persons (living or dead) you have.. known in any way'.

4. a. An allusion or directing of attention *to* some thing or person.

1613 CAWDREY *Table Alph.*, *Reference*, a pointing at, or alluding to. **1754** RICHARDSON *Grandison* VI. xxxi. 203 By his eye (taking the reference, as I may call it, of hers) turned as often towards me. **1784** COWPER *Ep. J. Hill* 13 Were I called to prove the assertion true, One proof should serve —a reference to you. **1818** CRUISE *Digest* (ed. 2) III. 171 Without a reference to any word in the writ which connected the person with the tenure. **1865** TROLLOPE *Belton Est.* xxiii. 271 No reference had been made to the former conversation. **1875** JOWETT *Plato* (ed. 2) IV. 387 The later dialogues of Plato contain many references to contemporary philosophy.

b. Without article.

1825 SCOTT *Talism.* xxviii, The shield of the Marquis bore, in reference to his title, a serrated and rocky mountain. **1858** HAWTHORNE *Fr. & It. Note-bks.* II. 21 Demonstrating it.. by reference to the points which he criticised. **1891** H. MATTHEWS in *Law Times* XCII. 96/1, I briefly summarise them, so that reference to previous circulars on the subject may not be necessary.

5. a. A direction to a book, passage, etc., where certain information may be found; an indication of the author, work, page, etc., to be looked at or consulted. Also without article.

1612 BRINSLEY *Lud. Lit.* xiii. (1627) 188 If they had but only bookes of References, it would be exceeding profitable. **1716** M. DAVIES *Athen. Brit.* III. 192 Not one Reader in a hundred takes the pains to turn backwards and forwards, as such appendicular References require. **1727–41** CHAMBERS *Cycl.* s.v., References are also used in books, where things being but imperfectly handled, the reader is directed to some other part or place where they are more amply explained. **1779–81** JOHNSON *L.P.*, *Fenton*, Illustrations drawn from a book so easily consulted, should be made by reference rather than transcription. **1864** MAX MÜLLER *Chips* (1880) III. vi. 137 He does not load his pages with references and learned notes. **1875** JOWETT *Plato* (ed. 2) III. 4 By numerous references from one part of the work to another.

b. A mark or sign referring the reader to another part of a page or book (*esp.* from the text to a note), or serving to indicate the part of a figure or diagram referred to.

1678 MOXON *Mech. Exerc.* No. 6. 107, I have.. left out the Superiour Letters.. and instead of those References give you this Alphabetical Table of Terms. **1706** PHILLIPS (ed. Kersey). **1771** LUCKOMBE *Hist. Print.* 257 References are all such Marks and Signs as are used in matter which has either side or bottom Notes. [**1806** O. GREGORY *Treat. Mech.* II. 163 The same letters of reference being put to the corresponding parts in these figures.] **1862** *Catal. Internat. Exhib.* II. xiii. 18/2 References—A. Cylinder. B. Stern [etc.].

6. a. The act of referring one person to another for information or an explanation; hence, a person to whom one is (or may be) referred for this purpose. *spec.* = REFEREE *sb.* 4.

1815 SCOTT *Guy M.* li, I request.. that you will refer Mr. Bertram to me for the reason. You will naturally wish to know what is to be the issue of such a reference. **1837** DICKENS *Let.* 24 Feb. (1965) I. 238, I have.. taken the liberty of mentioning your name, among those of other references, to testify to my being 'sober and honest'. **1865** DICKENS *Mut. Fr.* I. ii., Like the advertising people, I don't ask you to trust me, without offering a respectable reference. Mortimer there is my reference, and knows all about it. **1884** *Law Times Rep.* L. 121/1 P. was not called upon by the auctioneer for any references as to his alleged agency. **1934** D. L. SAYERS *Nine Tailors* II. ii. 95 'Did he give you any references?'.. 'Yes.. he did. He give me the name of a garridge in London.. and.. said if I was to write to the boss, he'd put in a word for him.'

b. A (usu. written) report produced by a referee (REFEREE *sb.* 4); a testimonial.

1895 in *Funk's Stand. Dict.* **1924** GALSWORTHY *White Monkey* II. ix. 197 That was my first job since the war, so I can whistle for a reference. **1936** *Punch* 21 Oct. 467/1 'I have references, excellent references... Here is one from a lady in Eaton Square.' (Hands it to the employer.) **1940** G. D. H. & M. COLE *Counter-Point Murder* viii. 85 Corcoran said he wrote to us taking up the reference, and got back a letter speaking very highly of the firm. **1976** 'P. B. YUILL' *Hazell & Menacing Jester* ii. 27 'Did Thornton get another job?' 'Nobody's asked me for a reference.'

7. ***book***, etc. ***of reference***, one intended to be, or suitable for being, referred to or consulted. ***for reference***, for the purpose of consulting or being consulted.

1836 *Penny Cycl.* V. 455/1 Dictionaries and lexicons in all languages, with more than 8000 books of reference. **1845** STOCQUELER *Handbk. Brit. India* (1854) 172 The advantages of a library of reference and a circulating library. **1859** E. EDWARDS *Mem. Libraries* II. 634 What are in a special sense termed books of reference such as Collections, Encyclopædias, Lexicons, Dictionaries, etc. **1890** 'R. BOLDREWOOD' *Col. Reformer* (1891) 137 [They have] got an album, for reference, at all the chief police stations.

8. *attrib.* **a.** *gen.*, as ***reference bible***, ***book***, ***catalogue***, ***librarian***, ***library***, ***mark***, ***point***, ***room***; **reference book**, (*a*) a book used for reference purposes; cf. *book of reference* in sense 7; (*b*) *S. Afr.*, an identity document or group of documents officially introduced in 1952 or the name for a pass (see PASS *sb.*^{2} 8 f), regulating movement in particular areas, which all non-white residents must carry (replaced in 1977 by 'travel documents': see quot. 1977 s.v. PASS *sb.*^{2} 8 f); **reference electrode** *Electr.*, an electrode the potential of which can be accurately maintained and reproduced, and in relation to which other potentials can be measured; **reference frame** = *frame of reference* s.v. FRAME *sb.* 4 d; occas. *transf.*; **reference group** *Sociol.* and *Psychol.*, a group to which a person may or may not belong but which he, perhaps subconsciously, refers to as a standard in forming his attitudes and behaviour; **reference tube** *Electr.*, a cold-cathode gas-filled tube which can maintain an accurately fixed voltage across itself for long periods.

1860 G. M. [F. W. Robinson] *Grandmother's Money* VI. vi, A little reference-bible on the dressing-table. **1889** *Cent. Dict.*, Reference book. **1952** [see PASS *sb.*^{2} 8 f]. **1954** L. G. GREEN *Under Sky like Flame* xii. 174 On the Gold Coast cooks carry a reference book. **1960** *Observer* 27 Mar. 16/4 Failure to produce a reference book on demand is a criminal offence. **1967** [see AUTHOR *v.*]. **1969** *Golden City Post* July 3 The thugs.. robbed him of his money, reference book and personal documents. **1970** C. L. CLINE *Lett. George Meredith* I. p. xxxii, The inaccessibility of reference books in provincial towns may also have contributed to the slothfulness of the editing. **1971** *Drum* Mar. 4 They walked purposefully towards the women who searched themselves for their reference books. But it was not the reference books the policemen wanted. **1971** *Rand Daily Mail* 27 Mar. 2/2 The vast majority of short-term prison sentences are for minor statutory offences connected with Bantu influx control, taxation and reference book regulations. **1972** *Physics Bull.* Apr. 225/2 For a reference book the index is inadequate. **1885** *Athenæum* 14 Mar. 346/2 The new volume of Mr. Whitaker's 'Reference Catalogue'. **1926** *Jrnl. Amer. Chem. Soc.* XLVIII. 34 The effect of temperature upon the potential of reference electrodes. **1948** GLASSTONE *Textbk. Physical Chem.* (ed. 2) xii. 940 There is no reliable method known for determining the absolute potential of a single electrode. The only sound procedure is to combine the electrode with a reference electrode of known potential difference and to measure the E.M.F. of the resulting cell. **1975** M. R. JENKINS in Williams & Wilson *Biologist's Guide to Princ. & Techniques Pract. Biochem.* vii. 202 Calomel electrodes.. are the most common reference electrodes and they consist of a solution of mercurous chloride (calomel) and potassium chloride in contact with solid mercurous chloride and mercury. **1921** J. M. BIRD *Relativity & Gravitation* ii. 36 (*heading*) The reference frame for space. **1940** C. S. SHERRINGTON *Man on his Nature* ii. 62 There was as yet no reference-frame of natural law, of chemistry or physics, by help of which to orientate the natural fact. **1967** [see FRAME *sb.* 4 d (i)]. **1970** *Nature* 17 Oct. 272/2 In deriving the equations of the electromagnetic field in a rotating reference frame, Schiff used the explicit transformation to rotating co-ordinates. **1942** H. H. HYMAN *Psychol. of Status* ii. 37 Satisfaction with status is consequently also a function of the reference group, since the reference group is a variable of the judgment. **1957** *Jrnl. Abnormal & Social Psychol.* LV. 360/1 Attention has also been given to the influence of his reference groups: the groups in which he aspires to attain or maintain membership. **1969** *Times* 14 Apr. 7/3 The two groups of farmers have different reference groups, a different set of individuals with which they will compete for status and recognition. **1970** C. T. RESTREPO in I. L. Horowitz *Masses in Lat. Amer.* xiv. 542 The absence of contacts—and hence the lack of visibility of reference groups —has kept the peasants unaware even of their own needs. **1973** 'J. PATRICK' *Glasgow Gang Observed* xiii. 115 Tim's reference group for clothes was the teenage record scene. **1977** R. HOLLAND *Self & Social Context* v. 119 The area of social theory most closely related to that of role, namely 'reference group' research. **1951** L. I. EDWARDS in J. D. Stewart *Reference Librarian* iii. 61 Theoretically the reference librarian should know something about everything because of the varied nature of the queries received. **1978** W. WHITE in *W. Whitman's Daybks. & Notebks.* I. 87 For this information and other help I am grateful to George A. Masterton, reference librarian at Wayne State University. **1858** in E. Edwards *Mem. Libraries* (1859) II. 707 The large hall for the reference Library. **1860** [see *art gallery* s.v. ART *sb.* 18]. **1976** *Nature* 1 Apr. 466/3 This book is a 'must' and it certainly deserves space on a shelf of every reference library. **1977** *Evening Post* (Nottingham) 24 Jan. 3/2 Now there is a reference library, a craft work base, and two other areas into which children can move for private reading and study. **1856** *N. & Q.* 1st Ser. Index, Reference marks. **1884** Reference-point [see BENCH-MARK b]. **1936** M. SHERIF *Psychol. of Social Norms* vi. 96 This subjectively established standard or norm serves as a reference point with which each successive experienced movement is compared and judged to be short. **1977** *Rolling Stone* 5 May 33/1, I really do think Rod Stewart, Bruce Springsteen and the Who are the most appropriate reference points for rock and roll. **1960** *Electronic Engin.* XXXII. 218 Studies were confined to neon-filled tubes.. having molybdenum anodes and cathodes and employing high-stability reference-tube manufacturing techniques. **1962** G. A. T. BURDETT *Automatic Control Handbk.* vii. 23 The primary duty of the reference tube.. is to provide voltage which can be accurately maintained within close limits for long periods.

b. In extended scientific and technical use denoting an object, property, value, or the like, used as a basis for comparative measurement or standardization. Also *absol.*

1878 J. W. DRAPER *Sci. Mem.* ii. 57, I had previously passed through the slit a beam of sunlight reflected from a mirror, so as to have a reference spectrum with fixed lines. **1901** *Shop & Foundry Pract.* III. XXVII. 23 Reference gauges are gauges that represent either an accurate subdivision of the imperial yard, or some arbitrary size or shape adopted for some purpose and required to be preserved. **1941** C. O. FAIRCHILD et al. *Temperature* 305 It is not always possible to maintain the reference junctions.. at a desired temperature during the calibration of a thermocouple. **1941** K. HENNEY *Radio Engin. Handbk.* (ed. 3) xxi. 775 A convenient and consistently accurate method of measuring the amplitude of the signals is required, as well as a reference level common to the entire system. **1952** MARKUS & ZELUFF *Electronics for Communication Engin.* ix. 342/1 This cavity has a high Q and is used as the frequency reference. **1953** AMOS & BIRKINSHAW *Television Engin.* I. i. 20 D.c. restoration is only possible provided the picture signal contains a reference signal related to black level and the television waveform therefore includes such a signal. **1966** WILLIAMS & FLEMING *Spectrosc. Methods Org. Chem.* iv. 81 The positions of proton resonances in an NMR spectrum are measured relative to the resonance position of the twelve equivalent protons of an arbitrary reference substance, tetramethylsilane. **1975** D. G. FINK *Electronics Engineers' Handbk.* xix. 3 The reference pressure for sounds in air, corresponding to 0 dB, has been defined as a sound pressure of 0·0002 microbar. **1978** P. W. ATKINS *Physical Chem.* xxix. 968 The potentiometer reading is used in the normal way to find its new potential relative to the reference.

reference ('rɛfərəns), *v.* [f. prec.]

1. †**a.** *trans.* To refer, assign *to* a thing. *Obs. rare.*

1621 W. SCLATER *Tythes* (1623) 93 Where the dutie is Religious, and the injunction meerely referenced to pietie. **1627** —— *Exp. 2 Thess.* (1629) 20 Particular proceedings, referenced as well to good as bad.

b. To relate (a measurement) *to* a defined base or zero level.

1971 *Nature* 3 Sept. 51/2 A complete separation of the explosion population from the earthquake population is obtained when referenced to the arbitrary decision line. **1972** *Science* 23 June 1349/3 The intensity of the sound was as high as 80 db (referenced to 0·0002 dyne/cm^2).

2. To provide with references; to give a reference to (a passage); to find by reference.

1891 *N. & Q.* 7th Ser. XII. 303/2 This loose method of indexing adds greatly to the labour of referencing a passage. **1894** *Daily News* 28 Feb. 6/2 The passages illustrating the use of words.. have.. been duly referenced. **1971** *Nature* 3 Sept. 71/3 Each chapter is very fully referenced. **1972** *Physics Bull.* May 295/3 The book is well produced and well referenced. **1975** *Nature* 3 Apr. p. iv (Advt.), Published as a two-book set for easier handling, each part is fully referenced and illustrated. **1977** *Jrnl. R. Soc. Arts* CXXV. 451/2 One BCS paper is referenced on page 35 of the White Paper Cmd. 6354. **1978** *Sci. Amer.* Jan. 28/3 The version we see (not explicitly referenced) is probably from an edition of about 100 years ago or from a 20th-century reprint. **1980** *Encounter* May 16/2 It is enough to remember that Ferrar and Debenham's formulation of the sequence of Beacon rocks is still referenced today.

3. *intr.* To make out a return of the number of people to be displaced by proposed railway extension. Also *trans.* to schedule (property) for this purpose.

1884 [implied at REFERENCING *vbl. sb.* below]. **1891** *Daily News* 31 Oct. 3/8 To acquire certain important properties, which are now being referenced, for the purpose of greatly enlarging.. Victoria Station.

Hence **'referenced** *ppl. a.*, **'referencing** *vbl. sb.*; also **'referencer**.

1884 *Cassell's Mag.* Apr. 287/1 The solicitors.. send out men called 'referencers' to ascertain the names of all the owners, lessees, and occupiers of the property within the limits of deviation. **1884** *Cassell's Mag.* Apr. 288/2 The united cost for.. surveys, referencing, printing, fees, parliamentary agents, and so on. **1971** *Nature* 30 Apr. 602/1 It is a very good book indeed—but it could have been excellent if just a little extra thought had gone into the original plan and an extra month into the final editing and referencing. **1972** *Science* 5 May 503/3 The authors.. give an additional line of the frequently quoted but never referenced turbulence poem by Richardson (1922) beginning 'Big whorls have little whorls'. **1978** *Nature* 14 Dec. 739/2 The referencing, which includes entries up to the first half of 1976, is impressive.

referend ('rɛfərɛnd, rɛfə'rɛnd). [ad. L. *referendum*, gerund or neut. gerundive of *referre* to REFER.] That by which or, more commonly, to which reference is made, *spec.* that which is signified by a particular sense of a word.

1925 *Monist* XXXV. 427 By the content of a judgment is meant the referend plus that which is predicated of the referend, and by the referend is meant that to which the judgment refers. **1930** L. S. STEBBING *Mod. Introd. Logic* ii. 13 We shall find it convenient to use the word 'referend' to stand for that which is signified. *Ibid.*, It is perhaps unfortunate to have to introduce new terminology, but the word 'object' is not suitable for the purpose for which I use the technical term 'referend'. The referend is that which is being referred to. **1939** *Trans. Philol. Soc.* 74 How can we disentangle ourselves from the close meshwork of our native language and find a *tertium quid* or set of neutral referends to serve as a measure for both languages compared? **1940** *Kenyon Rev.* 269 The monosign is referential in the sense that what it means.., its referend, is something distinct from itself. **1941** *Mind* L. 151 He thinks he is holding fast to some identical referend throughout, whereas in truth he has only an identical symbol which is changing its referend. **1956** J. WHATMOUGH *Language* 262 Referend. That which is symbolized or referred to by a verbal symbol, e.g. the referend of *rain* is 'the moisture of the atmosphere condensed and falling in visible drops'. **1957** S. POTTER *Mod. Linguistics* vii. 141 The bird, the living creature that we see with our eyes, we may call the *referend*, and the picture of it that we have in our minds as we speak.. may be called the *image*. **1977** *Word 1972* XXVIII. 162 The auxiliary is invariably present when the referend is not the subject of the clause.

referen'darial, *a.* *rare*$^{-1}$. [Cf. next and -AL^1.] To which matters are referred for decision.

1840 *Penny Cycl.* XVIII. 325/2 The referendarial tribunals, which had jurisdiction without appeal.

referendary (rɛfə'rɛndərɪ), *sb.* [ad. med.L. *referendārius*: see REFERENDUM and -ARY[1]. Cf. F. *référendaire* (14–15th c.).]

1. One to whom a matter in dispute is referred for decision; a referee. Now *rare.*

1546 *St. Papers Hen. VIII*, XI. 23 In this matier Monsr. Skepperus was referendary between us and them, and wery of us both. **1625** BACON *Ess., Suitors* (Arb.) 45 Let him chuse well his Referendaries, for else he may be led by the Nose. **1865** *Fortn. Rev.* 15 May 123 Just at the moment when a great referendary and umpire in many European questions is likely to be needed.

b. An adviser or assessor to a commission.

1876 *Times* 17 May, We find the native section of the Supreme Council charged with the audit of the accounts of Egypt. It is true that the members of this section are to be assisted by six referendaries.

2. *spec.* **a.** A title given at various times to certain officials in the papal, imperial, and some royal courts, charged with the duty of examining and reporting on petitions, requests, use of the seal, and similar matters.

On the older uses of the title, see Du Cange s.v. *Referendarii*, and cf. Littré s.v. *Référendaire*.

1528 in Strype *Eccl. Mem.* (1721) I. App. xxiii. 58 Which words being spoken..in the presence of Simonetta, oon of the referendaries [etc.]. **1587** HARMAR tr. *Beza* 426 The princes of this world, who haue their Referendaries, or masters of Request. **1656** BLOUNT *Glossogr., Referendaries*, Officers..who made relation of Petitions or Requests, exhibited to the Emperors... The like Officers are under the Pope, as also under the Masters of Requests in France. **1670** G. H. *Hist. Cardinals* I. III. 85 These thirteen Prelates are called Referendaries, or Remembrancers of the one and the other Court. **1699** LUTTRELL *Brief Rel.* (1857) IV. 535 On the 1st instant the crown referendary of Great Poland was elected speaker of the diet. **1704** *Collect. Voy.* (Churchill) III. 123/1 Then are the [Spanish] Officers call'd the Chancellor, Secretaries, Referendaries. **1801** A. RANKEN *Hist. France* I. I. iii. 261 The referendary was the keeper of the king's seal. **1848** W. H. KELLY tr. *L. Blanc's Hist. Ten Y.* I. 45 The grand referendary accompanied the marshal to the coach. **1866** *Chambers' Encycl.* VIII. s.v., The office of Great Referendary to the monarchy of France merged eventually in that of Chancellor.

†**b.** Applied to the prolocutor in the Lower House of Convocation. *Obs.*

1553 in Strype *Eccl. Mem.* (1721) III. I. iv. 43 The Reverend Fathers..had..enjoined them to meet together and..conclude upon the Choice of a Referendary, which they commonly called a Prolocutor. **1709** STRYPE *Ann. Ref.* I. xxvii. 281 The Bishop of London..bad the Inferior Clergy depart and chuse them a Prolocutor or Referendary.

c. An official attached to the Patriarch of Constantinople. (See Du Cange, s.v. *Chartophylax*.)

1716 M. DAVIES *Athen. Brit.* II. 278 Another Orthodox Greek Poet, Chartophylax or Referendary of the great Church of Constantinople.

†**3.** One who, or that which, furnishes news or information; a reporter. *Obs.*

1581 MULCASTER *Positions* Ep. Ded. (1887) 5 Other mens report..will proue a referendarie, and certifie your highnesse how they finde me appointed. **1614** DONNE *Let.* in Gosse *Life* (1899) II. 48 Sir, when these places afford anything worth your knowledge, I shall be your referendary. *a* **1636** FITZ-GEFFRAY *Holy Transp.* (1881) 178 A Glorious Angel is the Referendarie Who first these things unto men doth carry.

†**4.** An appendix or epilogue referring to what has gone before. *Obs. rare*$^{-1}$.

1581 FLEMING *Sch. of Skill* 208 A Referendarie to the Premisses.

Hence **refe'rendaryship**. *rare*$^{-1}$.

1620 BRENT tr. *Sarpi's Counc. Trent* (1676) 617 He spake of..Benefices conferred upon some of the kinsmen of some Prelates, and a Referendarieship to the Secretary of the Portugal Ambassador.

refe'rendary, *a.* [ad. L. type **referendāri-us*: see prec. and -ARY[1].]

†**1.** Containing references or documents referred to. *Obs. rare*$^{-1}$.

1716 M. DAVIES *Athen. Brit.* II. 191 Baronius's Referendary Appendixes to most of his tedious Annals.

2. Pertaining to, of the nature of, a referendum.

1894 *Westm. Gaz.* 2 Sept. 2/1 In the period 1469–1524 the city of Berne took no fewer than sixty Referendary votes.

referendum (rɛfə'rɛndəm). Pl. **referendums, -enda.** [L., gerund or neut. gerundive of *referre* to REFER.]

1. The practice or principle (in early use chiefly associated with the Swiss constitution) of submitting a question at issue to the whole body of voters.

In terms of its Latin origin, *referendums* is logically preferable as a modern plural form meaning ballots on one issue (as a Latin gerund *referendum* has no plural); the Latin plural gerundive *referenda*, meaning 'things to be referred', necessarily connotes a plurality of issues. Those who prefer the form *referenda* are presumably using words like *agenda* and *memoranda* as models. Usage varies at the present time (1981), but *The Oxford Dictionary for Writers and Editors* (1981) recommends *referendums*, and this form seems likely to prevail.

1847 G. GROTE *Let.* 25 Sept. in *Seven Lett. concerning Politics Switzerland* (1847) iv. 81 The clergy made efficient use of their influence over the popular *referendum*. **1870** *Sat. Rev.* 7 May 602/1 The *veto* or *referendum* has this much in common with the Bonapartist *plebiscitum*, that it is submitted to a body which is not an assembly and which cannot discuss. **1870** *Rep. Mass. Bureau of Statistics of Labor* I. 358 We want the referendum. **1882** *Daily News* 30 May 7/2 An immense number of signatures..has been obtained to the requisition for a referendum, or appeal to the people against the..vaccination law passed by the Federal Council or Chamber. **1885** *Manch. Exam.* 2 Mar. 5/4 It is quite open to discussion whether the *referendum* is really an advantage to the Swiss. **1889** F. O. ADAMS *Swiss Confederation* vi. 77 In Federal matters there are now two Referendums. **1895** *Edin. Rev.* July 265 When would Catholic emancipation have become law had the Referendum been part of the British Constitution? **1911** W. S. CHURCHILL *Let.* 29 Mar. in R. S. Churchill *Winston S. Churchill* (1969) II. *Companion* II. xiv. 1061 The collapse of the Referendum policy in the House of Lords was the subject of comment in the Lobbies yesterday. **1945** —— in *Times* 22 May 4/1 If you should decide to stand on with us, all united together until the Japanese surrender is compelled, let us discuss means of taking the nation's opinion, for example, a referendum, on the issue whether in these conditions the life of this Parliament should be further prolonged. **1945** C. ATTLEE in *Ibid.* 4/2, I could not consent to the introduction into our national life of a device so alien to all our traditions as the referendum, which has only too often been the instrument of Nazism and Fascism. Hitler's practices in the field of referenda and plebiscites can hardly have endeared these expedients to the British heart. **1965** H. V. WISEMAN *Britain & Commonwealth* II. iii. 86 Referenda have been held in New Zealand on the question of prohibiting the sale of intoxicating liquors. **1975** *Referendum on U.K. Membership of European Community* (Cmnd. 5925) i. 3 The present White Paper is concerned only with the organisation of the referendum. *Ibid.* iii. 5 The Government propose to ensure that the postal and proxy voting facilities which are available for general elections are also available for the referendum poll. **1975** *Times* 10 Apr. 5/1 The Liberals think that Referendum Day should be a public holiday. **1975** *Act Eliz. II* c. 33 §1 A referendum shall be held on the question whether the United Kingdom is to remain a member of the European Economic Community. **1976** H. WILSON *Governance of Brit.* iii. 75 There was great interest in constitutional circles in my announcement on 23 January 1975 that collective responsibility would be relaxed for the period of the referendum campaign on membership of EEC —the famous 'agreement to differ'. **1976** *Ann. Reg. 1975* 53 Two referenda had already been held in Wales in 1975. **1976** *Times* 22 Dec. 11/7 Since we are now likely to hear much about referendums, could we ask the BBC not to continue calling them referenda? **1977** *Daily Tel.* 16 Feb. 1/3 Proposed referenda on the plan for Scottish and Welsh Assemblies should be consultative only and not binding on Parliament. **1977** *Times* 17 Mar. 19/3 They did not tell us at the time of the referendum that Brussels was to reform the English language. **1977** *Time* 21 Nov. 28/2 The many referendums on the ballots reflected a growing public demand for more efficient and less meddlesome government.

2. A note from a diplomatic agent to his government, requesting instructions on a particular matter (*Cent. Dict.* 1891).

referent ('rɛfərənt), *sb.* (and *a.*) [ad. L. *referent-em*, pres. pple. of *referre* to REFER.]

1. One who is referred to or consulted.

1844 J. CAIRNS *Let.* in *Life* ix. (1895) 205, I have indeed lost a friend and theological referent of the highest order. **1921** *Contemp. Rev.* Mar. 315 The whole administration is conducted by the provincial government in Bratislava (Pressburg), under the Minister for Slovakia and his thirteen 'Referents' or State Secretaries.

2. *Gram.* **a.** A word referring to another. Also as *adj.* referring, containing a reference.

1899 R. C. TEMPLE *Univ. Gram.* 35 This relation may be expressed..by the addition of referent words expressing it, or referents. A referent word may express the inter-relation of connected sentences by conjoining them [etc.]... Referents are therefore conjunctors or substitutes.

b. That to which something has reference; *spec.* that which is referred to by a word or expression. Also in *Comb.* (*appositively*), as ***referent-object***.

1923 OGDEN & RICHARDS *Meaning of Meaning* i. 13 The word 'thing' is unsuitable for the analysis here undertaken, because in popular usage it is restricted to material substances—a fact which has led philosophers to favour the terms 'entity', 'ens' or 'object' as the general name for whatever is. It has seemed desirable, therefore, to introduce a technical term to stand for whatever we may be thinking of or referring to. 'Object', though this is its original use, has had an unfortunate history. The word 'referent', therefore, has been adopted. **1931** F. C. S. NORTHROP *Sci. & First Principles* ii. 49 This theory [*sc.* the physical theory of nature] is untenable unless there is a referent for atomicity and motion in something other than the microscopic particles. **1937** *Harper's Monthly Mag.* Dec. 49/2 Knowledge about technological unemployment..is not advanced by the syllogisms of classical economists. The classicists treat the term as a thing-in-itself without finding the referents which give it meaning. **1938** *Mod. Lang. Rev.* Oct. 547 The reinterpretation of the term [*baroque*] has sprung, not..from the feeling that it could be better applied to some other type of art, but from the revaluation of its original referent. **1950** *Papers Mich. Acad. Sci., Arts & Lett.* XXXVI. 323 The same question may..be phrased by asking how to bridge the gap between..sign and referent. **1958** S. STUBELIUS *Airship, Aeroplane, Aircraft* 7 As a rule, there has been no difficulty in ascertaining the referents in my linguistic material, with the aid of context. **1964** *Eng. Stud.* XLV. 385 Gender distinctions had always been functional in English as indicating either the sex of the referent or the non-significance of sex-distinction of the referent. **1964** *Language* XL. 229 The much-studied relations of words to their referent-objects. **1968** [see DENOTATUM]. **1970** *New Society* 5 Mar. 394/2 Clearly, if the ongon is to have any meaning at all, there must be some way of knowing at what level the symbols are to be interpreted, bearing in mind that each drawing or material object will have several referents. **1973** *Times Lit. Suppl.* 26 Oct. 1306/3 Canada often provides the landscape for his fable or the referents of his argument. **1976** *Archivum Linguisticum* VII. 17 Most Castilian loanwords from other languages have been borrowed to refer to referents, or fulfil functions, when Latin had originally an apparently good word for the same purpose. **1979** *Dædalus* Summer 97 'Official' discourse is reproached for being without a referent in psychic or social reality.

3. *Logic.* Any member of the class of all terms bearing a given relation to any term. (The correlative of *relatum*.)

1903 [see DOMAIN *sb.* 4 f]. **1933** L. S. STEBBING *Mod. Introd. Logic* (ed. 2) vii. 111 Every relational proposition has a converse, which consists in interchanging the terms with, or without, a change in the relation asserted to hold between them. The term *from* which the relation proceeds is called the referent; the term *to* which it proceeds is called the relatum. **1947** H. REICHENBACH *Elem. Symbolic Logic* iii. 115 There will be more than one relatum with respect to Peter if Peter has other children... The class of referents is also called the domain of function, and the class of relata is called the converse domain. **1967** R. A. GEORGE tr. *Carnap's Logical Struct. of World* III. 60 A relation extension is called one-many if, for each relatum, there exists only one referent.

referential (rɛfə'rɛnʃəl), *a.* [f. REFERENCE, on anal. of *inferential*, etc.] **a.** Having reference (*to* something); belonging to, or of the nature of, (a) reference; containing a reference or references, etc.

1660 WATERHOUSE *Arms & Arm.* 21 There are also Families whose bearings are referential to their names, and have a kind of consanguinity with them. *a* **1750** A. HILL *Wks.* II. 157 To compleat your picture..by strong referential proofs of a superiority [etc.]. **1775** SHERIDAN *Rivals* II. i, This we call the oath referential, or sentimental swearing. **1806** *Monthly Mag.* XXI. 133 The referential mark..referring to the note annexed.

b. Of or pertaining to a referent (sense 2 b); *spec.* of language or symbolism: that indicates a referent or has a referent as object.

1884 SIR E. E. KAY in *Law Times Rep.* LII. 88/2 These are referential words, and referential words always receive a liberal construction. **1922** T. C. POLLACK *Nature of Lit.* IX. 195 In *phatic communion*, one person uses words to come into relation with another. In *referential symbolism*, one person uses words to direct the attention of another to certain referents... In *evocative symbolism*, one person uses words to evoke a controlled experience in another. **1923** OGDEN & RICHARDS *Meaning of Meaning* i. 13 Besides this referential use which for all reflective, intellectual use of language should be paramount, words have other functions which may be grouped together as emotive. *Ibid.* ix. 318 Unless the referential and the affective-volitional aspects of mental process are clearly distinguished, no discussion of their relation is possible. **1946** C. MORRIS *Signs, Lang. & Behavior* 60 The current distinction between 'referential' and 'emotive' terms, a basic distinction in the work of C. K. Ogden and I. A. Richards. **1946** H. JACOB *On Choice of Common Lang.* 116 The never entirely separable functions of language roughly classified as 'emotive' and 'referential'. **1964** [see EXTRASOMATIC *a.*]. **1964** S. JACOBSON *Adverbial Positions in Eng.* i. 38 Several adverbs and adverbial phrases, especially such as express restriction or particularization, refer to, i.e. direct attention to, some particular constituent within the sentence. They may be called referential adverbials, and together with the constituent referred to, which may be a word, phrase, or clause, they form a structure of reference... Thus..'Only a Person can forgive' .., where *only* refers to *a Person*. **1964** R. H. ROBINS *Gen. Linguistics* 29 Word translation, or the finding of lexical equivalents, is easiest..with words in other languages which are such as to have a referential meaning more or less uniform in all cultures. **1971** *Archivum Linguisticum* II. 40 Nor is there any compulsion to believe in the primacy of any subdivision of meaning, for instance in the referential 'table'-ness of 'table'. **1980** *Mind* LXXXIX. 601 The truth of the speaker's belief q is neither necessary nor sufficient for the referential use of his definite description.

Hence **refe'rentially** *adv.*

1855 OGILVIE *Suppl.* **1922** W. E. JOHNSON *Logic* II. 120 Those so-called constants which are dependent upon context are only referentially constant. **1963** J. LYONS *Structural Semantics* iii. 39 Each of the [colour-] terms is referentially, or denotationally, vague in the sense that it denotes an area of the spectrum whose boundaries are not fixed precisely. **1966** *Philos. Rev.* LXXV. 11 Some of Socrates' substitutions are within intensional or referentially opaque contexts. **1975** *Nature* 10 Apr. 510/1 [He] is not bound by referentially constrained situations in his use of VIC [*sc.* Visual Communication, a therapeutic programme]. **1980** *Mind* LXXXIX. 599 Has the definite description been used referentially? No doubt the students took it in the attributive way... They do not even realize that the teacher intends his description referentially.

'referently, *adv. rare.* [f. as REFERENT + -LY[2].] In reference or relation *to* something.

1650 B. *Discolliminium* 39 All other things..were so subservient to that, that they stand and fall referently to that great worke. **1799** COLERIDGE *Lett.* (1895) I. 285 Consider it referently to non-existence, and what a manifold and majestic Thing does it not become?

†**'referism.** *Obs. rare*$^{-1}$. [f. REFER *v.* + -ISM.] A report made by a referee (sense 1).

1621 in *Crt. & Times Jas. I* (1848) II. 241 This day Sir Henry Yelverton is to be heard in parliament about some of his referisms.

†**re'ferment.** *Obs.* [f. REFER *v.* + -MENT.]

1. The act of referring, a reference, to a place or passage in a book.

a **1558** SIR R. BROOKE *La Graunde Abridgm.* (1586) Tab. Titles 2nd pt., Where in these Tables after the titles is a referrement by *Vide* unto other titles, there the matters..are under the Title whereunto that referrement is made. **1620–55** I. JONES *Stone-Heng* (1725) 53 The same

Referment in like Manner he makes for the Ornaments of the Peripteros.

2. Reference to something else, to the care or decision of another, etc.

1603 OWEN *Pembrokeshire* I. (1892) 154 By the saied referrement to the Customes of Northwales. **1617** HIERON *Wks.* II. 391 This referment of our selues in our prayers to the Lord,..our Saviour taught two wayes. **1636** STRAFFORD *Lett.* (1739) II. 14, I..approve of your Referment of Causes to be ended by Consent.

re-fer'ment, *v.* [RE- 5 a.] To ferment again.

1712 BLACKMORE *Creation* VI. (1786) 194 Th' admitted nitre agitates the flood, Revives its fire, and referments the blood.

†**re'ferrable,** *a. Obs. rare.* [f. REFER *v.* + -ABLE.] Referable, referrible.

a **1661** FULLER *Worthies, Westmld.* III. (1662) 140 Anne Clyfford..because having her greatest Residence and Estate in the North, is properly referrable to this County. **1676** TOWERSON *Decalogue* 532 Those motions..are aptly enough referrable..to those several commandments.

referral (rɪ'fɜːrəl). [f. REFER *v.*: see -AL II. 5.] **a.** The act of referring; *spec.* the referring to a third party of personal information concerning another.

1934 in WEBSTER. **1943** *Sun* (Baltimore) 27 Nov. 6/3 The publication by Senator Butler of his report and his referral of it to the Truman Committee. **1968** *Globe & Mail* (Toronto) 15 Jan. 24/7 (Advt.), Television and newspaper advertising will supply starting work followed by constant referral jobs. **1969** *Ithaca* (N.Y.) *Jrnl.* 27 Nov. 32/2 The name of the woman who was two months pregnant was apparently given secretly to the..company by one of her friends, who was paid for the 'referral' with a vaporizer or other small appliance. **1971** *Nature* 30 Apr. 545/1 The Unisist committee asks that associated countries should survey information services of national, regional or international scope and make plans to integrate these into a 'world referral network'. **1971** *N.Y. Law Jrnl.* 23 Nov. 20/4 After referral to me by order of Mr. Justice McInerney, this motion for a withdrawal order is granted. **1981** *Times* 10 Mar. 18/6 The senior management of these businesses comes out well from these referrals.

b. The referring of an individual to an expert or specialist for advice; *spec.* the directing (usu. by a general practitioner) of a patient to a medical consultant for specialist treatment (see REFER *v.* 8 d). Also *attrib.*

1955 D. M. DEED in C. Morris *Social Case-Work in Gt. Brit.* (ed. 2) iii. 70 At the time of referral [to a family caseworker] the child was in a temporary hostel. **1958** *Times* 8 Nov. 7/5 The public..is in turn increasingly unwilling to trust themselves to the care of their N.H.S. practitioner, thus reinforcing the habit of unnecessary referral to hospitals. **1960** in L. Pincus *Marriage* II. 58 At the time of their referral to the Bureau, they had been married for nine and a half years. **1966** *Lancet* 24 Dec. 1403/1 The referral system, whereby consultants see patients only at the request of the family doctor, came into being at the end of the 19th century. **1968** *World Medicine* 26 Nov. 35/1 The referral diagnosis was Addison's disease. **1972** *Where* May/June 136/3 He can go to his family doctor who will either examine him and take the necessary tests to establish the diagnosis before giving treatment, or will send him to the nearest hospital clinic with a letter of referral. **1976** *Proc. R. Soc. Med.* LXIX. 949/1 Our surgical unit is no less busy than most in the country: it has its share of medical ward referrals, urgent admissions and emergencies. **1978** *Times* 2 Nov. 14/2 They [*sc.* the Samaritans] can, and do, act as a medical or psychiatric referral agency.

†**re'ferrance.** *Sc. Obs. rare*$^{-1}$. [f. REFER *v.* + -ANCE.] Reference.

1583 *Reg. Privy Council Scot.* III. 581 Quhilk submissioun and referrance..being acceptit be his majestie [etc.].

referred (rɪ'fɜːd), *ppl. a. Path.* [f. REFER *v.* + -ED[1].] Proceeding from some other part or organ.

1899 *Allbutt's Syst. Med.* VI. 746 Marked superficial tenderness of the referred visceral type. *Ibid.* VIII. 84 The pain in the head differs..from the referred pain set up in different parts of the body by disorders of the viscera.

referree, obs. form of REFEREE *sb.*

†**re'ferrent.** *Obs. rare*$^{-1}$. [f. REFER *v.* + -ENT.] A relative, or word indicating a relation.

1635 *Gram. Warre* D 6 b, In what manner the referred, and the referrent, agreed with the Antecedent.

referrer[1] (rɪ'fɜːrə(r)). [f. REFER *v.* + -ER[1].] One who refers; *esp.* in *Sc. Law* (see REFER *v.* 6 b).

1683 STAIR *Instit.* IV. xliv. §13 Oaths of verity referred to parties are sometimes by them deferred back to the referrer. **1838** W. BELL *Dict. Law Scot.* 371 It appears even to be doubtful whether the deposition of the bankrupt on reference to his oath..will be admitted as good evidence in favour of the referrer.

†**re'ferrer**[2]. *Obs. rare*$^{-1}$. [f. REFER *v.* + -ER[4].] Reference.

1650 ELDERFIELD *Tythes* xxv. 198 The latter [law] mentions the remanding or dismissing suits of Dismes back from the secular Judge..; And for the two former which might be answered to create that referrer [etc.].

referrible (rɪ'fɜːrɪb(ə)l), *a.* [f. REFER *v.* + -IBLE: cf. REFERRABLE.] = REFERABLE.

1596 BELL *Surv. Popery* III. ix. 381 No sin, no, not the least of al is referrible to God. **1659** H. MORE *Immort. Soul* I. vi. Ax. 19 Acknowledging..the Secondary to be referrible also to the Primary or Centrall Substance by way of causal relation. **1795** BURKE *Let. to W. Smith* Wks. IX. 404 To this the merit or demerit of every measure (with me) is referrible. **1846** J. BAXTER *Libr. Pract. Agric.* (ed. 4) II. 139 The staggering is principally referrible to the hindquarters. **1891** M. DODS *Gosp. John* XV. (1892) I. 234 A stainless life is..referrible to no freak of nature.

Hence **re'ferribleness.**

1865 MOZLEY *Mirac.* vi. 114 The question..of the referribleness of miracles to an unknown law.

referring, *vbl. sb.* and *ppl. a.*: see REFER *v.*

†**referse,** *v. Obs.*$^{-1}$ [ad. L. *refercīre*, f. *re-* RE- + *farcīre* to FARCE.] *trans.* To stuff, cram.

1580 T. M. *To Rdr.* xiv. in *Baret's Alv.* A vj/2 So Barret ..Hath left behind..This Hiue of his, referst with honie meates.

†**refert,** *pa. pple. Obs. rare*$^{-1}$. [ad. L. *refertus*, pa. pple. of *refercīre*: see prec.] Stuffed, crammed, filled. So also †**re'ferted.**

1642 H. MORE *Song of Soul* II. iii. II. xxiv, But tell me then how is their quantity If every part with each part is refert? **1657** *Physical Dict., Referted,* replenished, well furnished.

†**re'fet(e,** *v. Obs.* Also 6 **reuet.** [f. as REFETE, REFET *pa. pple.*]

1. *trans.* To refect, refresh.

13.. *E.E. Allit. P.* A. 88 As fode hit con me fayre refete. *c* **1375** *Sc. Leg. Saints* xlvi. (*Anastas*) 294 þat scho suld duel but drink or mete, or ellis ocht mycht hir refete. **1382** WYCLIF *Acts* xxviii. 2 Forsoth a fyer kyndlid, thei refetiden, or refreischiden, vs alle. *c* **1400** *Sc. Trojan War* (Horstm.) II. 1766 Quhene þat þai ware þaire Sumquhat refettyd, þai gane faire To seike þare lord. *c* **1440** [see prec. 1].

2. To nourish, feed, fatten. *rare*$^{-1}$.

1422 tr. *Secreta Secret., Priv. Priv.* 245 Vse in this tymes hote mettys..as chykenys well refeted.

3. *intr.* To recover, recuperate. *rare*$^{-1}$.

c **1480** HENRYSON *Orph. & Eur.* 365 Were scho at hame in hir contree of Trace, Scho wald refete [*Bann. MS.* rewert] full sone in fax and face.

Hence †**re'feting** *vbl. sb.*

c **1400** *Sc. Trojan War* (Horstm.) II. 1445 And syne þat refectiouns seire Thame prayed he for his refetyne.

re'fetch, *v.* [RE-.] *trans.* To bring back; †to bring to life again. Hence **re'fetching** *vbl. sb.*

1623 J. REYNOLDS *God's Revenge* III. xii. 96 The Prouidence and Iustice of God, doth now againe refetch bloudy Petro to act another part upon the Stage and Theatre of this History. *Ibid.* Hist. xiii. 134 Shee faints twice in a chayce betwixt their armes, and all the cold water they threw in her face, could very hardly refetch her. **1624** T. SCOTT *Votivæ Angliæ* A j, Incite and stirre vp your Royall resolutions, for the refetching and reconquering therof.

†**re'fete, re'fet,** *sb. Obs. rare.* Also 5 **refett,** 6 **reuet.** [a. OF. **refet*, var. *refait* sb. (cf. next), which however is app. not recorded in this sense.] Nourishment, food, *spec.* that of fishes; the contents of a fish's stomach.

c **1460** J. RUSSELL *Bk. Nurture* 577 Codde, haddok, by þe bak splat þem in þe dische liynge, pike owt þe boonus, clense þe refett in þe bely bydynge. *Ibid.* 839 Playce with wyne, & pike withe his reffett. *c* **1490** *Promp. Parv.* 427/1 (MS. K), Refet of fisshe [*Pynson* reuet], *refectio, refectura.* *a* **1500** *Piers of Fullham* 82 in Hazl. *E.P.P.* II. 5 Eteth of the fysche and be not so lykerows,..ffor thogh the bottomles belyes be not ffyllyd with such refete, Yet the saver of sauze may make yt good mete.

†**re'fete, re'fet,** *pa. pple. Obs.* Also 5 **refeet.** [a. OF. *refet* (= L. *refectus*), var. *refait*, pa. pple. of *refaire*, f. *re-* RE- + *faire* to make.]

1. Refreshed with food. Also *fig.*

13.. *E.E. Allit. P.* C. 20 þay ar happen also þat hungeres after ry3 t, For þay schal frely be refete ful of alle gode. *c* **1374** CHAUCER *Boeth.* IV. pr. vi. 143 (Addit. MS.), Whan þou art wel refresshed and refet [*L. refectus*] þou shalt ben more stedfast to stye in to heyere questiouns. *c* **1440** *Promp. Parv.* 427/1 Refetyd [*Pynson* reueted], or refeet, *refectus.*

2. Nourished, fed, fattened.

c **1380** *Sir Ferumb.* 1736 Of grete hertes refet at al y asky of 3ow an hundred. **1496** *Bk. St. Albans, Fishing* l ij, The dace is a gentyll fysshe to take & yf it be well refet then is it good meete. **1602** CAREW *Cornwall* 28 They are refettest (that is fattest) at their first comming from the Sea.

reff(e, obs. form of REIF, plunder(ing).

reffayr, obs. Sc. form of REAVER.

reffo ('rɛfəʊ). *Austral. slang.* [Abbrev. REFUGEE *sb.*] A European refugee; *spec.* a refugee who left Germany or German-occupied Europe before the war of 1939–45. Now *Obs.* exc. *Hist.*

1941 BAKER *Dict. Austral. Slang* 59 *Reffo*, a refugee from Europe. **1951** CUSACK & JAMES *Come in Spinner* 278 'The woman's a Viennese.' 'Oh, a reffo?' **1955** J. CLEARY *Justin Bayard* x. 137 She talked even now in her letters of the Dagoes and Balts and reffos, the New Australians, who were taking over the country. **1960** *Times Lit. Suppl.* 3 June 349/3 Stefan is the refugee—from Bulgaria... Lionel.. considers Stefan 'a bloody reffo' and a nuisance. **1961** P. WHITE *Riders in Chariot* 221 He was..a blasted foreigner, and bloody reffo, and should have been glad he was allowed to exist at all. **1965** *Listener* 2 Sept. 339/2 Australians..had their full quota of terms such as wogs, dagos, and so on, and refugees were commonly referred to as 'bloody reffos'. **1976** *Australasian Post* 8 Apr. 54/2 Several decades ago, the normal expression for migrants was 'reffo', which was then officially changed to 'migrant'.

reffrein, reffreshe, reffus, obs. ff. REFRAIN, REFRESH, REFUSE.

†**re'fibulate,** *v. Obs.*$^{-0}$ [f. L. *refibulāre*: see FIBULA.] 'To unbuckle' (Cockeram 1623).

†**reficiate,** *v. Obs.*$^{-0}$ [Irreg. f. L. *refic-ĕre* + -ATE.] *trans.* To restore, refresh.

1657 *Physical Dict., Reficiates,* amends, comforts.

re'fight, *v.* [RE- 5 a.] *trans.* To fight again.

1827 *Gentl. Mag.* XCVII. II. 42/1 Every battle is refought by the historian with minute exactness. **1862** MARG. GOODMAN *Exper. Eng. Sist. Mercy* 86 If we could each of us refight our battles, doubtless our tactics would be different.

†**refigu'ration.** *Obs. rare*$^{-1}$. [RE- 5 a: cf. next.] Reproduction, representation.

c **1470** HARDING *Chron.* LXXVIII. xii, In token of the table refyguracion, Of the brotherhede of Christes supper & maundie Afore his death.

refigure (riː'fɪg(jʊ)ə(r)), *v.* [ad. obs. F. *refigurer* or late L. *refigurāre* (Vulgate).]

1. *trans.* To figure again; to represent anew.

c **1374** CHAUCER *Troylus* v. 473 Refigurynge here shape, here womanhede, Wiþ-inne his herte. *c* **1470** HARDING *Chron.* XXXIII. iv, His triumphes all..Well wrought about, in ymagerie and scripture, Full royally wrought for to refigure. *c* **1600** SHAKS. *Sonn.* vi, Ten times thy selfe were happier then thou art, If ten of thine ten times refigur'd thee. **1642** MILTON *Apol. Smect.* ii. Wks. 1851 III. 285 The child doth not more expresly refigure the visage of his Father, then that book resembles the stile of the Remonstrant. **1776** DA COSTA *Elem. Conchol.* viii. 171 Plancus describes and figures some very minute Nautili... Gualtieri refigures three species of them. **1867** LONGF. tr. *Dante, Inferno* XXXI. 35 When the fog is vanishing away, Little by little doth the sight refigure Whate'er the mist..conceals.

2. *spec.* To restore (a metallic speculum) to the original parabolic figure.

1888 *Encycl. Brit.* XXIII. 146/1 If such a mirror is much exposed,..frequent repolishing will be necessary. This involves refiguring, which is the most delicate and costly process of all.

refill ('riːfɪl, riː'fɪl), *sb.* (and *a.*) [RE- 5 a: cf. next.]

a. That which serves to refill anything; a fresh fill for a memorandum or pencil case, etc.

1886 *Athenæum* 25 Dec. 847/1 (*Advt.*) The Student's Writing Tablets..Refills for size No. 1. **1888** *Advt.*, Pencil ..with Box of Eight Patent Black Copying Ink Refills.

b. The renewed contents of a glass; a second or further drink.

1929 'E. QUEEN' *Roman Hat Mystery* iii. 53, I asked her if it was time to go in for my orangeade refills. **1960** C. MACINNES *Mr Love & Justice* 79 The star ponce beckoned for refills... The girl..brought the glasses. **1966** M. SHARMAN *Seeds of Violence* ii. 11 'I think we'd better have refills.' He busied himself with the drinks. **1968** 'R. RAINE' *Night of Hawk* xxxiii. 156 Drink up and I'll give you a refill. **1977** *Rolling Stone* 30 June 25/1 She lets go with a loud, decidedly unsentimental laugh that startles a room-service waiter trying to set down refills on a coffee table hopelessly cluttered with empty glasses and Heineken bottles.

c. *adj.* That requires or serves as a refill.

1907 *Yesterday's Shopping* (1969) 345/1 Nickel Pencil..4 in. long, with refill leads. **1918** W. OWEN *Let.* 9 Sept. (1967) 574 I'd like a parcel with re-fill battery, cigarettes, & chocolate. **1921** *Edin. Rev.* Jan. 158 Perhaps in time each party will provide not only its own refill ministers and kitchenmaids but even its own king. **1961** *Lebende Sprachen* VI. 103/2 *Refill cartridge*, die Nachfüllmine..für Kugelschreiber.

re'fill, *v.* Also 8–9 **refil.** [RE- 5 a.] *trans.* and *intr.* To fill again.

a. *trans.* **1687** in *Magd. Coll. & Jas. II* (O.H.S.) 96 To have all the places of the College refilled..with..Priests. *a* **1745** BROOME *Anacreon, Ode* I, See! how the mimic clusters roll, As ready to refil the bowl. **1816** BYRON *Ch. Har.* III. lxxxii, Dungeons and thrones, which the same hour refill'd. **1830** LYTTON *P. Clifford* ix, The watchman was good-natured enough to assist him in re-filling the barrow. **1863** *Sat. Rev.* 22 Aug. 245 To re-fill the places where the foremost assailants of the breach had been struck down.

b. *intr.* **1744** WARRICK in *Phil. Trans.* XLIII. 15 Hence, to the latter End of October, she [a dropsical patient] re-filled incredibly. **1897** *Allbutt's Syst. Med.* IV. 451 If they [the cysts] refill, they should be laid open.

refillable (riː'fɪləb(ə)l), *a.* [f. REFILL *v.* + -ABLE.] Capable of being refilled.

1920 in WEBSTER. **1961** R. A. FORESMAN in H. R. Shepherd *Aerosols* iii. 48 Although disposable aerosols are the only real market factor at this writing, the refillable units were of some consumer importance as late as 1958. **1962** *Harper's Bazaar* Aug. 65 An elegant new black and gold refillable atomiser. **1971** *Nature* 23 July 274/1 For electrophoresis, refillable glass cannulae containing 25% KCl and a coiled silver wire were implanted chronically. **1977** *Private Eye* 13 May 23/3 (Advt.), Refillable ballpens and cartridge pens that look good and feel good.

re'finage. *rare*$^{-1}$. [f. REFINE *v.* + -AGE. Cf. F. *raffinage.*] The right of refining (metals).

1842 *Blackw. Mag.* LI. 56/2 The regent gave his bank the monopoly of tobacco, and the sole refinage of the gold and silver.

re'finance (also -fɪ'næns), *v.* [RE- 5 a.] *trans.* To finance again; to provide with further capital. So **refinanced** *ppl. a.*; **refinancing** *vbl. sb.* and *ppl. a.*

1908 *Standard* 6 Apr. 6/4 Plans have been drafted for the refinancing of the Erie Railway Company. **1921** *Glasgow Herald* 6 July 8/2 The first important refinancing operation, since the Funding and Victory issues, was the Conversion Loan announced with the Budget statement. **1922** *Daily Mail* 26 Oct. 3 The conditions of the Government guarantee and the details of the scheme for re-financing the company were first officially announced. 1930 *Times Lit. Suppl.* 30 Oct. 893/1 Oscar, generously refinanced through 'Gamy', is sailing..safely into harbour. 1934 *Planning* I. xix. 3 Refinancing in the post-war boom had left an evil legacy: the practices of local finance, of the issue of part-paid shares and of calling up unpaid capital had intensified the problem and to a large extent control had passed into the hands of the banks. 1971 *Flying* Apr. 25/2 The R. J. Enstrom Helicopter Company..is being reactivated and refinanced as a wholly owned subsidiary of Franklin Capital Corp. of Michigan. 1976 *Economist* 16 Oct. 102/2 Instead of forcing foreigners to convert their sterling holdings into other reserve assets once and for all, such a scheme would allow Britain to refinance any rundown in its sterling balances, both private and official, as and when it occurred. 1979 *Jrnl. R. Soc. Arts* CXXVII. 428/1 There would be danger, if interest rates fell substantially, that mortgages would be redeemed and refinanced.

Hence **re'finance** *sb.*, renewed or additional finance; chiefly *attrib.* in ***refinance credit*** (see quot. 1970); **refi'nanceable** *a.*, capable of being refinanced.

1959 *Economist* 28 Feb. 817/1 The authorities have not lifted the ban on 'refinance' credits... These are usance credits, usually of three months' duration, opened in order to meet sight drafts payable in London. 1965 *Ibid.* 19 June p. ix/1 What of 'refinanceable credits'— the portions of medium-term advances for export credits which now allow the banks to grant such advances with no impact on their liquidity ratio? 1970 *Penguin Dict. Commerce* 276 *Refinance credits*, credits obtainable by an overseas buyer, where the exporter cannot provide credit and the buyer does not wish to pay cash. 1976 *Bank of England Q. Bull.* XVI. 194 Cash flow may well be negative in the earlier years, thus requiring refinance at uncertain interest rates.

re'find, *v.* [RE- 5 a.] *trans.* To find again.

1621 G. SANDYS *Ovid's Met.* III. (1632) 88 Seuen Autumns past, he, in the eighth the same Refinding, said [etc.]. 1624 QUARLES *Sion's Elegies* iv. 17 Ægypt, that once did feel heauen's scourge,..would now refinde it. 1830 LYTTON *P. Clifford* viii, Tomlinson..was glad to re-find a person who had known him in his *beaux jours*. 1878 HOOKER & BALL *Marocco* 42 Maw refound the plant in 1869.

†**re'fine**, *a.* (and *sb.*) *Obs.* [Related to next. Cf. Sp. *refino* refined, and obs. F. *refin* fine wool or cloth.] Refined. Also *absol.* as *sb.*, fine metal.

a 1635 CORBET *Poems* (1807) 92 Thine own rich studies, and deep Harriots mine, In which there is no dross, but all refine. 1646 S. BOLTON *Arraignm. Err.* 47 The understanding it is the purest, spirituallest and refinest part. *a* 1656 HALES *Gold. Rem.* (1688) 50 The thing which in an especial refine dialect of the new Christian language, signifies nothing but morality and civility. 1704 *Lond. Gaz.* No. 3986/4, 5 Yards and a half of superfine Woman's Black, 12 Yards and a half of refine Black, both Spanish.

refine (rɪ'faɪn), *v.* [f. RE- + FINE *v.*³; cf. Sp. *refinar*, and F. *raffiner*, It. *raffinare* (see AFFINE *v.*).]

1. *trans.* To purify or separate (metals) from dross, alloy, or other extraneous matter; in iron-working, to convert grey pig-iron into white or plate metal by partial decarburization.

1582 STANYHURST *Æneis* I. (Arb.) 37 Touch stoane brazed with deepe gould purelye refined. 1592 DAVIES *Immort. Soul* Introd. xl, So doth the Fire the drossy Gold refine. 1604 E. G[RIMSTONE] *D'Acosta's Hist. Indies* IV. iii. 209 As much quicke-silver as is necessarie to refine their gold and silver. 1674 RAY *Coll. Words* 117 All lead oar dig'd in England hath a proportion of silver mixt with it, but some so little, that it will not quit cost to refine it. 1727–41 CHAMBERS *Cycl.* s.v. *Refining*, There are two ways of refining silver; the one with lead, the other with saltpetre. 1796 MORSE *Amer. Geog.* I. 591 Furnaces for running this ore into pigs..and forges to refine pig-iron into bars. 1839 URE *Dict. Arts* 324 The operation of refining copper is delicate. *Ibid.* 1124 The *teller* silver is refined in quantities of 160 or 170 marcs. 1884 W. H. GREENWOOD *Steel & Iron* xiii. 246 The loss is greater in refining hot-blast than it is with cold-blast pig-iron.

b. *fig.* and in fig. context.

1596 SPENSER *Hymn Beauty* 47 It more faire..it makes, And the grosse matter of this earthly myne Which clotheth it thereafter doth refyne. 1720 WELTON *Suffer. Son of God* I. xi. 294 When Thou refinest all the Dross, all that is base and Earthly in me by the Fire of Thy Love. 1754 COWPER *Ep. Lloyd* 89 Nor needs [he] his genuine ore refine; 'Tis ready polished from the mine. 1827 KEBLE *Chr. Y.* 23 Sund. Trin., The world's rude furnace must thy blood refine. 1871 BROWNING *Pr. Hohenst.* 1321 The special gold, whate'er the form it take, Head-work or heart-work, fined and thrice-refined I' the crucible of life.

2. To free from impurities; to purify or cleanse (in general sense).

1601 CHESTER *Love's Mart., K. Arthur* (1878) 61 Our vnpure Sinne by him being full refind. 1628 DIGBY *Voy. Medit.* (1868) 40 Because the windes can not refine the aire. 1667 MILTON *P.L.* XII. 548 To..raise From the conflagrant mass, purg'd and refin'd, New Heav'ns, new Earth. 1709 WATTS *Hymn*, '*And must this Body die*' ii, Corruption, Earth and Worms Shall but refine this Flesh. 1781 COWPER *Progr. Err.* 344 To purge and skim away the filth of vice, That so refined it might the more entice.

b. *spec.* To purify or clarify (a substance or product) by means of some special process; to make purer or of a finer quality; *esp.* to subject (raw sugar) to the processes of clarifying, condensing, and crystallizing.

1613 PURCHAS *Pilgrimage* V. xii. (1614) 507 The raw Lac is of a darke red colour, but being refined, they make it of all colours. 1630 *R. Johnson's Kingd. & Commw.* 371 Selling their Sugars unextracted from the Cane to the Venetians, and buying it againe from them after it is refined. 1678 BUNYAN *Pilgr.* I. 59 Now the Table was furnished with fat things, and with Wine that was well refined. 1706 E. WARD *Wooden World Diss.* (1708) 83 Tho' the Extraction be very gross, it's so well refin'd, that it does not, in the least, smell of the Kettle. 1799 G. SMITH *Laboratory* I. 8 The nitre is thoroughly refined. 1836–41 BRANDE *Chem.* (ed. 5) 1076 It cannot be doubted that much improvement may be made in refining sugar, by the aid of chemistry, so as to produce a larger quantity of refined from raw sugar.

absol. 1883 *Century Mag.* July 332/2 The United [Company] stores and transports [oil]; the Standard buys, refines, sells, and exports.

†**3. a.** To clear (the spirits, mind, etc.) from dullness; to make clearer or more subtle. *Obs.*

1589 PUTTENHAM *Eng. Poesie* I. iii. (Arb.) 23 They came by instinct diuine, and by deepe meditation, and much abstinence (the same assubtiling and refining their spirits) to be made apt to receaue visions. 1591 SYLVESTER *Du Bartas* I. i. 5 Thou glorious Guide..Lift up my Soule, my drowsie Spirits refine. 1690 *School of Politicks* I With sober Liquour to refine my Head. *a* 1704 T. BROWN *Praise Drunkenness* Wks. 1730 I. 35 Wine..refines the judgment of the doctors, and makes their opinions most canonical. 1728 ELIZA HEYWOOD tr. *Mme. de Gomez's Belle A.* (1732) II. 107 A Relaxation of Thought is certainly a help to the refining it.

†**b.** To free or cleanse from moral imperfection; to raise to a higher spiritual state. *Obs.*

1667 MILTON *P.L.* XI. 63 Tri'd in sharp tribulation, and refin'd By Faith and faithful works. 1672 DRYDEN *2nd Pt. Conq. Granada* IV. iii, Blessed souls are there refined, and.. prepared for light. 1711 ADDISON *Spect.* No. 257 ¶8 What Actions can express the entire Purity of Thought which refines and sanctifies a virtuous Man?

4. To free from imperfections or defects; to bring to a more perfect or purer state.

c 1670 HOBBES *Dial. Com. Laws* (1840) 5 The law of England..hath been fined and refined by an infinite number of grave and learned men. *a* 1703 E. CHAMBERLAYNE *Pres. St. Eng.* III. iv. (1707) 287 King James the Fifth refined the Order of St. Andrew in Scotland. 1717 J. KEILL *Anim. Oecon.* Pref. 19 The whole Practice of Physick by the Invention of many useful Remedies..is so much refined that [etc.]. 1813 SHELLEY *Q. Mab* VIII. 139 Lending their power to pleasure and to pain, Yet raising, sharpening, and refining each. 1889 PAGER *G. de Latour* (1896) 7 Cheerful daylight, refined, but hardly dimmed at all, by painted glass.

b. To polish or improve (a language, composition, etc.); to make more elegant or cultured.

1617 MORYSON *Itin.* IV. v. i. (1903) 438 The English tounge..hath beene in late ages excellently refyned and made perfitt for ready and breefe deliuery both in prose and verse. 1634 *Malory's Arthur* title-p., The Most Ancient and Valiant History of the Renowned Prince Arthur..newly refined. 1674 PLAYFORD *Skill Mus.* I. xi. 56 Of late our Language is much refined, and so is our Musick. 1750 JOHNSON *Rambler* No. 37 ¶8 They may as well refine the speech as the sentiments of their personages. 1841 LANE *Arab. Nts.* I. 75 He took the trouble of refining the language of a copy of them which he possessed.

5. To free from rudeness, coarseness, or vulgarity; to imbue with culture or polish, delicate feelings or instincts, etc.

1667 MILTON *P.L.* VIII. 589 Love refines The thoughts, and heart enlarges. *a* 1703 E. CHAMBERLAYNE *Pres. St. Eng.* III. iii. (1707) 272 The Britains or Welch, more lately refin'd, did not take Surnames till of late Years. 1781 COWPER *Charity* 98 Ingenious Art..Steps forth to fashion and refine the race. 1781 —— *Retirem.* 240 Love..Refines his speech, and fashions his address. 1838 LYTTON *Alice* I. iii, He had sought less to curb, than to refine and elevate her imagination. 1848 L. HUNT *Jar Honey* iii. 32 When reproached for carrying off paintings..from Sicily, he said he did it to refine the minds of his countrymen.

absol. 1781 COWPER *Charity* 332 All truth is precious,.. And what dilates the powers must needs refine.

6. With const. **a.** To bring *into*, raise *to*, a certain state by purifying or subtilizing.

1647 N. BACON *Disc. Govt. Eng.* I. xxxviii. (1739) 57 Time and experience refined this way of trial into a more excellent condition. 1864 SKEAT *Uhland's Poems* 270 Dante, who could earthly passion To celestial love refine. 1877 E. R. CONDER *Bas. Faith* ii. 68 To refine this discussion into the wire-drawing of verbal controversy.

b. To purify or cleanse *from* something.

1633 FORD *Broken Heart* II. iii, What heaven Refines mortality from dross of earth [etc.]. 1712 BLACKMORE *Creation* III. (ed. 2) 135 By the driving Wind The Air from noxious Vapours is refin'd. 1754 SHERLOCK *Disc.* (1759) I. i. 30 Its Worship is refined from the Errors and Idolatries of Superstition. 1810 SCOTT *Lady of L.* II. xxii, A human tear From passion's dross refined and clear.

c. To clear *away*, or *out of*, by refining.

1857 BUCKLE *Civiliz.* I. ix. 588 This was a simple alternative; which might indeed be kept out of sight, but could not be refined away. 1893 FORBES-MITCHELL *Remin. Gt. Mutiny* 3 A class of writers..who would if it were possible, refine even God Himself out of creation.

7. *intr.* To become pure; to grow clear or free from impurities.

1604 E. G[RIMSTONE] *D'Acosta's Hist. Indies* IV. xiv. 250 The Emeralds grow in stones..and they seeme by little and little to thicken and refine. 1690 NORRIS *Beatitudes* (1694) I. 54 They presently began to behave themselves more orderly; and seemed, like Gold, to refine upon the Trial of the Furnace. 1713 ADDISON *Cato* I. vi, The pure stream.. Works it self clear, and as it runs, refines. 1734 WATTS *Reliq. Juv.* xxviii. (1789) 86 Let it lie and refine from all the dregs of sin and sensual impurities. 1809 BYRON *Bards & Rev.* 496 That head,..though the thickening dross will scarce refine, Augments its ore, and is itself a mine.

8. To improve in polish, elegance, or delicacy.

c 1620 FLETCHER & MASSINGER *False One* III. ii, Did you live at court, as I do, gallants, You would refine, and learn an apter language. 1709 POPE *Ess. Crit.* 421 Let a Lord once own the happy lines, How the wit brightens! how the style refines! 1762 GOLDSM. *Cit. W.* lxxv, In proportion as society refines, new books must ever become more necessary. 1821 CLARE *Vill. Minstr.* I. 31 As his years increas'd his taste refin'd.

9. To employ or affect a subtlety of thought or language.

1713 SWIFT *Cadenus & Vanessa*, This tempts Free-thinkers to refine, And bring in doubt their pow'rs divine. 1774 GOLDSM. *Retal.* 35 Who, too deep for his hearers, still went on refining, And thought of convincing, while they thought of dining. 1875 JOWETT *Plato* (ed. 2) III. 316 Suppose the objector to refine still further, and to draw the nice distinction [etc.].

b. Const. *on* or *upon* a subject, etc.

1669 R. MONTAGU in *Buccleuch MSS.* (Hist. MSS. Comm.) I. 449 The politicians here, that refine upon everything. 1837 HT. MARTINEAU *Soc. Amer.* III. 291 The company who sit at the feet of the pastor while he refines upon abstractions. 1883 *Contemp. Rev.* Aug. 163 To creep out of a difficulty..by refining upon words in defiance of the intention.

10. To improve *on* or *upon* something, by introducing refinements.

1662 EVELYN *Chalcogr.* 50 Canferri, and..Barlacchi graved divers things:..which afterwards Sebastian Serli refining upon composed the better part of that excellent book of his. 1719 YOUNG *Revenge* I. i, Not only die, But plunge the dagger in my heart myself? This is refining on calamity. 1765 BLACKSTONE *Comm.* I. xviii. 590 Our laws have considerably refined and improved upon the invention. 1815 JANE AUSTEN *Emma* ix, You must not refine too much upon this charade.

Hence **re'finable** *a.*, that may be refined.

1607 HIERON *Wks.* I. 238 To purifie that which is refineable as gold and siluer.

refined (rɪ'faɪnd), *ppl. a.* [f. prec. + -ED¹.]

1. Purified; freed from impurities or extraneous matter. **a.** In general use. *rare.*

1596 SPENSER *Hymn Love* 193 It all sordid basenesse doth expell, And the refyned mynd doth newly fashion [etc.].

b. Of metals. Now *spec.* with *iron* (or *metal*) and *tin*.

1595 SHAKS. *John* IV. ii. 11 To gilde refined Gold, to paint the Lilly..Is wastefull, and ridiculous excesse. 1611 BIBLE *1 Chron.* xxix. 4 Seuen thousand talents of refined siluer. 1843 HOLTZAPFFEL *Turning* I. 186 [The iron] is..cast into a plate about four inches thick, which is purer, finer in the grain than pig-metal, and also much harder and whiter; it is then called refined metal. 1855 J. R. L[EIFCHILD] *Cornwall Mines* 209 Refined tin, though not equal in quality to grain tin, is made from selected ores... It is used by most of the tin-plate manufacturers. 1884 W. H. GREENWOOD *Steel & Iron* xiii. 245 The plate of fine metal, refined iron, plate metal, or simply metal, as the product of the refinery is variously called.

c. Of sugar, salt, etc. Also *ellipt.*

1727–41 CHAMBERS *Cycl.* s.v. *Sugar*, Sugar-candy..is better made of earthed sugar, than refined sugar. 1791 NEWTE *Tour Eng. & Scot.* 108 By an Act passed in 1786, refined English Rock-salt is allowed to be imported into Scotland. 1839 URE *Dict. Arts* 1207 Six tons of refined sugar can be turned out daily in a three-pan house. 1895 *Daily News* 8 Apr. 3/7 Sugar.—..Foreign refined market remains steady.

2. Characterized or distinguished by the possession of refinement in manners, action, or feeling.

1588 SHAKS. *L.L.L.* I. i. 164 A refined trauailer of Spaine, A man with all the worlds new fashion planted. 1638 R. BAKER tr. *Balzac's Lett.* (vol. III.) 101 The most refined Frenchman that ever ranne afoote. 1663 GERBIER *Counsel* 7 In this refined Age, which abounds in Books. 1713 STEELE *Englishm.* No. 21. 135 It repeats only such things as are proper for a refined Ear. 1781 COWPER *Table T.* 511 Modern taste Is so refined and delicate and chaste. 1835 MARRYAT *Jac. Faithf.* xlii, The more refined the society may be—the more civilized its parts—the greater is the mutual dependence. 1878 BOSW. SMITH *Carthage* 404 The refined soul and Hellenic sympathies of the general.

Comb. 1835 WILLIS *Pencillings* I. iv. 31 There is a delicate, refined-looking little marchiones here.

b. Free from, or devoid of, rude, gross, or vulgar elements.

1650 FULLER *Pisgah* IV. ii. 21 [Dromedaries are] of as much more refined service above Camells, as Hackneis are above Packhorses. 1659 *Gentl. Calling* (1696) 12 That Advantage..of an ingenuous and refined Education. 1781 COWPER *Hope* 500 The gross idolatry blind heathens teach Was too refined for them, beyond their reach. 1804–6 SYD. SMITH *Mor. Philos.* (1850) 313, I am not speaking of the highest-refined London grief,—the grief of civilisation and softness; but the grief of a savage and a child. 1856 EMERSON *Eng. Traits, Wealth*, The proudest result of this creation [wealth] has been the great and refined forces it has put at the disposal of the private citizen.

c. Of language, speech, etc.: Cultivated, polished, elegant.

1611 BIBLE *Transl. Pref.* ¶2 Certaine [men]..could not be brought for a long time to giue way to good Letters and refined speech. 1673 *Remarques Humours Town* 6 The fountain of the refinedst conversation. 1708 SWIFT *Wks.* (1841) II. 185 It is to be understood that this refined way of speaking was introduced by Mr. Locke. 1763 J. BROWN *Poetry & Mus.* xii. 209 Certain Greeks..brought a refined and enervate Species of Music to Rome. 1866 GEO. ELIOT *F. Holt* (1868) 23 She spoke with a refined accent.

3. † **a.** Having or affecting a subtlety of mind or judgement. *Obs.*

1574 HELLOWES *Gueuara's Fam. Ep.* (1577) 133 There be men..so ouer sharpe or refined, that..they holde it for an office to diuine thoughts. 1594 NASHE *Terrors of Night* Wks. (Grosart) III. 243 Complement-mungers they are, who would faine be counted the Court's Gloriosos, and the refined judges of wit. 1681 TEMPLE *Mem.* III. Wks. 1731 I. 345 The refined Courtiers, who observe Countenances and Motions, had no Opinion of it. 1714 SWIFT *Pres. St. Aff.* Wks. 1751 IV. 266 Others were yet more refined; and thought it neither wise nor safe wholly to extinguish all Opposition from the other side.

b. Raised to a high degree of subtlety, nicety, or precision.

1668 DAVENANT *Man's the Master* III. i, This reasoning does appear too much refin'd. **1726** LEONI tr. *Alberti's Archit.* III. 1 The Mathematician considers the nature and forms of things..absolutely distinct from all kind of matter: whereas..it will be necessary for me to consider them in a way less refined. **1769** ROBERTSON *Chas. V*, x. III. 232 Maurice employed artifices still more refined to conceal his machinations. **1812** R. HALL *Wks.* (1833) I. 292 Nothing subtle or refined should enter into the views of a Christian missionary. **1878** HUXLEY *Physiogr.* 53 Both instruments are but refined modifications of our familiar experiment.

refinedly (rɪˈfaɪnɪdlɪ), *adv.* [f. prec. + -LY[2].] In a refined manner; with refinement, nicety, precision, etc.

c **1679** MULGRAVE *Ess. Sat.* 135 Will any dog Refinedly leave his bitches and his bones To turn a wheel? **1740** tr. *De Mouhy's Fort. Country-Maid* (1741) II. 134 Always complaisant, always refinedly polite. **1819** MOORE *Mem.* (1853) II. 276 Too vulgar a subject..for the refined readers, and too refinedly executed for the vulgar ones. **1866** CARLYLE *Remin.* (1881) II. 290, I noticed only how refinedly beautiful she was.

re'finedness. [f. as prec. + -NESS.] Refinement.

1612 HEYWOOD *Apol. Actors* I. 27 The sages..of Grecia—who, for the refinednesse of their language, were in such reputation through the world. **1687** BURNET *Six Papers* 23 Our Flattery has come short of the Refinedness of the Romans. **1711** SHAFTESB. *Charac.* (1737) III. Misc. v. ii. 291 To laugh as agreeably, and with as much Refinedness. **1717** *Censor* II. sig. A4[v], The sensible Part of the World in their Pleasures, as well as graver Conduct, are proud of being influenc'd by Examples that give them the Credit of Discernment, and a Refinedness of Taste. *a* **1945** E. R. EDDISON *Mezentian Gate* (1972) xxxviii. 227 'Your son, I said. There are other names for bastards.' 'I have always admired the refinedness of your language.'

refinement (rɪˈfaɪnmənt). [f. REFINE *v.* Cf. F. *raffinement* (Cotgr.), It. *raffinamento.*]

1. The act or process of refining; the result of refining, or the state of being refined.

1611 COTGR., *Raffinage*, the refinement, or quintescence of. **1659** H. MORE *Immort. Soul* III. i, The Soul of Man is capable of very high refinements, even to a condition purely Angelical. **1688** BOYLE *Final Causes Nat. Things* ii. 85 The renovation and refinement of the present world by the last fire. **1709** STEELE *Tatler* No. 108 ¶7 Religion which does not only promise the entire Refinement of the Mind, but the glorifying of the Body. **1764** GOLDSM. *Trav.* 229 For, as refinement stops, from sire to son Unalter'd, unimprov'd the manners run. **1816** J. SCOTT *Vis. Paris* (ed. 5) 309 The refinement of nitre, from its rough state in the nitre bed, to the packing of the pure salt in casks. **1861** W. FAIRBAIRN *Iron* 99 The surface of iron thus exposed undergoes refinement.

†**b.** A refining influence. *Obs. rare*[−1].

1712 HUGHES *Spect.* No. 525 ¶6 If Love be any Refinement, Conjugal Love must be certainly so in a much higher Degree.

2. Fineness of feeling, taste, or thought; elegance of manners; culture, polish.

1710 SWIFT *Jrnl. to Stella* v, I must tell you a great piece of refinement of Harley. **1784** COWPER *Task* IV. 359 That sensibility of pain with which Refinement is endued. **1816** J. SCOTT *Vis. Paris* (ed. 5) 170 Louis le Grand encouraged every thing that shed refinement over the world. **1843** PRESCOTT *Mexico* (1850) I. 393 It is too much to ask of any man..to be in advance of the refinement of his age. **1874** GREEN *Short Hist.* iii. §5. 139 There was a certain refinement in Henry's temper which won him affection.

b. An instance of this; a particular feature, custom, or thing indicating refined manners, feelings, or taste.

1708 SWIFT *Sacram. Test* Wks. 1751 IV. 166 We of Ireland are not yet come up to other Folks Refinements, for we generally love and esteem our clergy. **1714** —— *Pres. St. Aff.* ibid. 282 Affecting German Modes and Refinements in Dress or Behaviour. **1794** S. WILLIAMS *Hist. Vermont* 151 Not until the refinements of society have taken place. **1820** W. IRVING *Sketch Bk.* I. 6 The refinements of highly cultivated society. **1833–6** J. H. NEWMAN *Hist. Sk.* (1873) II. I. i. 39 Timour..had the command of every refinement not only of luxury, but of gluttony.

3. The act or practice of refining in thought, reasoning, or discourse; an instance of this.

1712 ADDISON *Spect.* No. 303 ¶13 It is the Poet's Refinement upon this Thought which I most admire. **1714** SWIFT *Pres. St. Aff.* Wks. 1751 VI. 259 Opportunities of shewing their skill in Mystery and Refinement. **1754** EDWARDS *Freed. Will* IV. xiii. (1762) 279 There is no high Degree of Refinement and abstruse speculation, in determining, that a Thing is not before it is. **1823** ROSCOE tr. *Sismondi's Lit. Eur.* (1846) II. 184 He abandoned himself to that refinement and false wit, which the Spaniards mistook for the language of passion.

b. A piece of subtle reasoning; a subtlety.

1708 SWIFT *Ch. Eng. Man* Wks. 1751 IV. 71 [To] draw in fresh Proselytes by some further Innovations or Refinements. **1769** *Junius Lett.* xv. (1788) 92 The people of this country are neither to be intimidated by violent measures, nor deceived by refinements. **1822** HAZLITT *Table-t.* Ser. II. xvi. (1869) 327 Sound conclusions come with practical knowledge, rather than with speculative refinements. **1875** E. WHITE *Life in Christ* III. xxi. (1878) 302 No even colourable escape from this criticism seems possible except by refinements unintelligible to the common people.

4. An instance of improvement or advance towards something more refined or perfect; the state or thing thus arrived at or obtained.

1710 SWIFT *Tatler* No. 230 ¶6 The Breaks at the End of almost every Sentence; of which I know not the Use, only that it is a Refinement. **1732** LAW *Serious C.* xviii. (ed. 2) 333 For Emulation..is nothing else but a refinement upon envy. **1841** ELPHINSTONE *Hist. Ind.* II. 595 All the refinements of his artful policy. **1851** PENROSE *Princ. Athenian Arch.* (title-p.), The optical refinements exhibited in the construction of the ancient buildings. **1871** FREEMAN *Norm. Conq.* (1876) IV. xviii. 156 A countermine was a refinement beyond their skill.

b. The most refined form *of* something.

1880 *Chr. World* No. 1195. 138 It would be the refinement of exquisite cruelty.

refiner (rɪˈfaɪnə(r)). [f. REFINE *v.* + -ER[1].]

1. a. One who or that which refines or purifies substances; *spec.* one who makes a business of refining (metal, sugar, etc.).

1598 BARRET *Theor. Warres* V. iii. 133 Two or three Refiners of powder. **1611** BIBLE *Mal.* iii. 2 He is like a refiners fire, and like fullers sope. **1648** BOYLE *Seraph. Love* v. (1700) 38 'Tis not the custom of Refiners to snatch the belov'd Metal out of the Fire..till it have stood its due time. **1720** STRYPE *Stow's Surv.* V. xv. II. 244 The former Refiners of Sugar added thereunto corrupt Mixtures to their own private Gain. **1832** HT. MARTINEAU *Hill & Valley* iv. 61 They saw the refiners take it by turns to run out their moulds of metal. **1858** SIMMONDS *Dict. Trade, Refiner's-sweeps*, the refuse filings or dust collected from the workshops of silver-smiths and jewellers to be re-smelted. **1865** DICKENS *Mut. Fr.* I. vii, The enriched water in which they wash them is bought for the refiners.

fig. **1629** W. SIMONS *Proc. Virginia* III. in *Capt. Smith's Wks.* (1819) I. 169 The worst was our guilded refiners with their golden promises made all men their slaues in hope of recompences.

b. An apparatus for refining. *spec.* a machine used in paper-making in which knots and lumps in the pulp are broken down by scissoring between blades or discharged by centrifugal action.

1624 CAPT. SMITH *Virginia* III. vii. 68 We spent some time in refyning, having..a refyner fitted for that purpose. **1902** *Encycl. Brit.* XXXI. 458/2 One form of beater [for paper making] has already been referred to..but engines of quite a different construction are now used largely in American mills, and also to some extent in Great Britain. These are known as 'refiners'. *Ibid.* 459/1 By the use of the refiner the time occupied in the beater can be reduced by nearly one half. **1929** CLAPPERTON & HENDERSON *Mod. Paper Making* vi. 68 The final clearing of knots, and the reduction of the longer fibres to a uniform length, are often performed by a refiner or perfecting engine. **1963** R. R. A. HIGHAM *Handbk. Papermaking* ii. 55 The Bauer refiner consists of two discs which rotate in opposite directions, the bars of which form a variety of cutting surfaces according to the character of the stock and the grade of paper to be manufactured.

2. One who, or that which, imparts elegance, polish, or culture; a remover of rudeness, grossness, or vulgarity.

1605 CAMDEN *Rem.* 28, I may be charged by the minion refiners of English [etc.]. **1625** tr. *Decameron* title, The Modell of Wit,..by the Renowned John Boccacio, the first Refiner of Italian prose. **1633** WOTTON *Let.* in *Reliq.* (1685) 463 War it self is a greater refiner of spirits in little time. **1715** M. DAVIES *Athen. Brit.* I. 30 The two first Refiners of the English Tongue. **1794** G. ADAMS *Nat. & Exp. Philos.* II. xxi. 421 A destroyer, a consumer, and refiner of grossness. **1801** HAN. MORE *Wks.* I. 26 Hail, Conversation ..Refiner of the social plan! **1855** LEWES *Goethe* I. 229 There can be no sweeter, tenderer refiners in the world than German ladies. **1873** SYMONDS *Grk. Poets* v. 145 The three refiners of language.

3. One who refines in speculation or reasoning.

1586 PUCKERING in *Plea Sacram. Test* 82 The Writings of godly and learned Men, neither answered nor answerable by these new-fangled Refiners. **1654** JER. TAYLOR *Real Pres.* A 4 The zeal of prevailing in it hath so blinded the refiners of it in this age, that they still urge these miracles for proof. *c* **1685** TEMPLE *Ess., Poetry* Wks. 1731 I. 248 There are no where..so many Reasoners upon Government, so many Refiners in Politicks. **1754** EDWARDS *Freed. Will* II. vii. (1762) 64, I wish such Refiners would thoroughly consider whether they distinctly know their own Meaning.

refinery (rɪˈfaɪnərɪ). [f. REFINE *v.* + -ERY.]

1. a. A place, building, or establishment, where refining (of sugar, oil, metal, etc.) is carried on. Also *attrib.*

1727–41 CHAMBERS *Cycl.* s.v. *Sugar*, In a refinery there are usually two coppers, the one serving to clarify, the other to boil the clarified liquor. **1758** REID tr. *Macquer's Chym.* I. 389 The large refineries of Gold and Silver by the means of Lead furnish a great quantity of this material. **1804** W. TAYLOR in *Ann. Rev.* II. 327 American and other settlers would have had..their refineries in every island. **1841** W. SPALDING *Italy & It. Isl.* II. 165 The capital had silk-works of all kinds,..to these it added soap-works, refineries, chemical-works, lace-works. **1939** *Thorpe's Dict. Appl. Chem.* (ed. 4) III. 348/2 The largest refinery plant in this country is at Prescot, where copper is refined..from blister copper. **1951** DYLAN THOMAS *Let.* Jan. (1966) 351 Today I was taken to see a great new black-towered hissing and coiling monster, just erected in the middle of the refinery. **1954** *Thorpe's Dict. Appl. Chem.* (ed. 4) XI. 187/1 Refined sugar presupposes treatment with bone charcoal in refineries as distinct from factories dealing with sugar beet or sugar cane. **1959** *Listener* 2 Apr. 582/1 Refinery gases, oil, and now refrigerated methane. **1970** W. G. ROBERTS *Quest for Oil* ix. 93 The newest refineries use desulphurisation processes of this kind to treat a wide cut from the light end of the crude oil right up to kerosine or gas oil. **1981** J. SIMPSON *Moscow Requiem* II. v. 159 The coast of Saudi Arabia and the peninsula where stood the second largest oil refinery in the world.

b. A furnace for the conversion of cast into malleable iron.

1825 J. NICHOLSON *Operat. Mechanic* 334 The method of releasing the pig-iron of its carbon, or of converting it into what is called wrought or malleable iron is, by placing it in an open furnace, termed a refinery. **1884** C. G. W. LOCK *Workshop Receipts* Ser. III. 250/2 When grey pig-iron is used for making malleable iron, it must first be converted into white iron by the 'whitening' process in a 'refinery'.

attrib. **1839** URE *Dict. Arts* 712 One of the numerous refinery furnaces. *Ibid.*, D is the refinery hearth.

†**2.** Refinements; a refinement. *Obs. rare.*

1746 W. HORSLEY *Fool* (1748) I. 272 Painted it over with silly Glosses and Refinery. *Ibid.* 291 That play in Circumlocutions and Refineries.

re'finger, *v.* [RE- 5 a.] To finger again.

1873 BROWNING *Red Cott. Nt.-cap* II. 748 Lucie, much solaced, I re-finger you, The medium article.

refining (rɪˈfaɪnɪŋ), *vbl. sb.* [-ING[1].]

1. The action of the vb. REFINE in various senses.

1604 E. G[RIMSTONE] *D'Acosta's Hist. Indies* IV. iii. 210 That [metal] which remaines of the refining of gold and silver. **1672** DRYDEN *Def. Epil. Conq. Granada* Ess. (Ker) I. 170 A turning English into French, rather than a refining of English by French. **1712** tr. *Pomet's Hist. Drugs* I. 57 The next thing to be consider'd is the Refining of Sugar. **1797** *Encycl. Brit.* (ed. 3) XVI. 37/2 The vessel in which the refining is performed is flat and shallow. **1863** TREVELYAN *Compet. Wallah* (1866) 56 The opium goes through a series of processes which may generally be described by the epithet 'refining'. **1881** RAYMOND *Mining Gloss.* s.v., The refining of 'base bullion' (silver-lead) produces nearly pure lead and silver.

b. With *a* and *pl.* An instance of this.

a **1652** J. SMITH *Sel. Disc.* iv. 75 After many refinings, macerations, and maturations. **1686** HORNECK *Crucif. Jesus* v. 75 Men..are strangely tickled with new things, which are often called refinings, or improvements of old truths. *a* **1715** BURNET *Own Time* III. (1724) I. 407 This was such a refining in a point of honour. **1754** EDWARDS *Freed. Will* II. vii. (1762) 64 This seems to be a Refining only of some particular Writers, and newly invented.

2. *attrib.*, as ***refining basin, forge, furnace, hearth, house, mould, process, room***, etc.

In many cases hardly distinct from the *ppl. a.*

a **1658** CLEVELAND *Poems* (1687) 1 The Still of his refining Mold Minting the Garden into Gold. **1674** RAY *Coll. Words* 114 These bars they bring to the refining Furnace. **1727–41** CHAMBERS *Cycl.* s.v. *Sugar*, As soon as the earth is on the sugar, all the windows of the refining-room are shut. **1731** P. SHAW *Ess. Artif. Philos.* 126 The Washings..and Waste of a Sugar-Baker's Refining House. **1839** URE *Dict. Arts* 608 The gold produced by the refining process with lead, is free from copper and lead. *Ibid.* 712 The German refining forge. **1855** J. R. L[EIFCHILD] *Cornwall Mines* 211 Plunging billets of green wood into the melted tin in the refining basin.

re'fining, *ppl. a.* [f. REFINE *v.* + -ING[2].] That refines. (See also prec. 2.)

1676 MARVELL *Mr. Smirke* I, Some of the Bishops were so ignorant and gross, but others so speculative, acute and refining in their conceptions. **1736** HERVEY *Mem.* (1848) I. 40 Like many other refining historians, I attribute that to prudence which was only owing to accident. **1774** BURKE *Sp. Amer. Tax.* Wks. 1842 I. 175/1 Whether [sufficiently] to serve a refining speculatist,..I know not. **1875** *Ure's Dict. Arts* I. 943 In washing, the metal and refining fluxes are projected together into the crucible. **1885** *Athenæum* 27 June 828/2 Where the refining power of a genuine master would begin to display itself.

Hence **re'finingly** *adv.*

1822 *Examiner* 10/2 The general eye would be refiningly familiarised to the relish and knowledge of Art.

refit (ˈriːfɪt, riːˈfɪt), *sb.* [RE- 5 a.] An act or instance of refitting (*esp.* of a ship); a fresh fitting-out.

1799 NELSON 12 Sept. in Nicolas *Disp.* (1845) IV. 11 The Seahorse, whose state requires docking and a thorough refit. **1833** MARRYAT *P. Simple* (1863) 387 Your vessel is strained to pieces,..no orders for a refit. **1870** ANDERSON *Missions Amer. Bd.* II. xvi. 123 A large number of whaling vessels resorted to Lahaine for their annual refit. **1945** *Jane's Fighting Ships 1944–45* 432 A contract was signed..for the repair and refit of this battle-cruiser. **1955** *Times* 7 May 8/1 An explosion occurred last night in the diesel room of H.M.S. Daring under refit in Devonport dockyard. **1975** *Drive* New Year 28/2 Is it more economical to write off a damaged car and pay the client out or make him wait for a re-fit? **1976** *Gramophone* Sept. 453/3 The Canterbury instrument is now in need of a refit.

refit (riːˈfɪt), *v.* [RE- 5 a.]

1. *Naut.* **a.** *trans.* To fit out (a ship, fleet, etc.) again; to restore to a serviceable condition by renewals and repairs. Also *refl.*, and const. *with.*

1666 PEPYS *Diary* 4 July, Ships, when they are a little shattered, must..refit themselves the best they can. **1697** DRYDEN *Æneid* I. 777 Permit our Ships a Shelter on your Shoars, Refitted from your Woods with Planks and Oars. **1725** POPE *Odyss.* XIV. 422 Ulysses on the coast of Crete Staid but a season to refit his fleet. **1790** BEATSON *Nav. & Mil. Mem.* I. 64 They met with a violent storm, and put into Port Louis to refit their ships. **1853** KANE *Grinnell Exp.* xxxvi. (1856) 324 To prepare for our closing struggle with the ice-fields..it was determined to refit the Rescue.

b. *intr.* To get refitted; to have renewals or repairs executed.

1669 H. SALESBURY in *St. Papers, Dom.* 175 The Portland has come in to refit, having lost her masts. **1703–4** *Lond. Gaz.* No. 3880/1 The Captains of Our Ships of War, which are come into Port to Clean and Refit. **1833** MARRYAT *P. Simple* (1863) 110 We anchored in Gibraltar Bay, and the ship was stripped to refit. **1854** H. MILLER *Sch. & Schm.* (1858) 5 The enemy drifted to leeward to refit.

2. a. *trans.* To fit, arrange, or set in order, again; to fit out afresh in some respect. Also with *up*.
1676 MARVELL *Mr. Smirke* Wks. 1875 III. 62 When it shall come out new vamped and refitted, it will be a question .., whether it be the same sermon. **1716** M. DAVIES *Athen. Brit.* II. 223 Those harmless Doctrines have been .. refitted up again by a still later set of Modern Montanists. **1782** MISS BURNEY *Cecilia* VII. ix, That all expedition might be used in refitting the other chaise for their reception. **1812** BYRON *Ch. Har.* II. vi, Can all sage, saint, or sophist ever writ People this lonely tower, this tenement refit?
b. *intr.* To renew supplies or equipment.
1802 H. MARTIN *Helen of Glenross* III. 261, I want to go and refit at Cheltenham; and thence I shall vagabondize somewhere or other. **1841** ELPHINSTONE *Hist. Ind.* II. 405 The exhausted condition of the army .. compelled Aurangzib .. to halt and refit at Cabul.
3. *trans.* To fit (a person) again *for* something.
1792 MME. D'ARBLAY *Diary* Jan. (1842) V. VII. 278 An old attendance I was so little refitted for renewing.

re'fitment. [f. prec. + -MENT.] The act of refitting; a refit.
1706 E. WARD *Wooden World Diss.* (1708) 62 Sometimes his Captain .. repairs to him for a refitment. **1748** *Anson's Voy.* III. vii. 366 The Viceroy of Canton's warrant for the refitment of the Centurion. **1799** MOORE *Mem.* (1853) I. 90 Indeed, I want a total refitment; my best black coat .. is quite shabby. **1832** SOUTHEY *Penins. War* III. 199 His troops .. were equally in need of rest and of refitment. **1863** *Morn. Star* 28 Aug., She will immediately commence her refitments to enable her to take in a new cable.

re'fitting, *vbl. sb.* [f. REFIT *v.* + -ING[1].] The action of the vb. in various senses.
1695 WOODWARD *Nat. Hist. Earth* III. i. (1723) 163 He will not allow .. that there was so great care taken in the re-fitting of it up again at the Deluge. **1748** *Anson's Voy.* II. iv. 159 The thorough refitting of the Anna Pink .. was .. impossible. **1838** THIRLWALL *Greece* III. xx. 153 These commissioners .. applied themselves to the refitting of the ships engaged in the last action. **1886** WILLIS & CLARK *Cambridge* I. 59 The Church was also undergoing repairs and refittings.
attrib. **1894** *Times* 24 Aug. 9/4 The port now boasts of a large refitting basin.

re'fix, *v.*[1] [RE- 5 a.] *trans.* To fix again; to establish anew.
1611 FLORIO, *Riffiggere*, to refix, to fix againe. *a* **1711** KEN *Hymns Evang.* Poet. Wks. 1721 I. 174 They both believe, yet Doubts were intermix'd, Till fresh Illuminations Faith refix'd. **1769** FALCONER *Marine Dict.* (1780) s.v. *Jigger*, To jam the latter to the windlass, and prevent it from running out till the jigger is refixed. **1816** BYRON *Siege Cor.* v, A hundred years have roll'd away Since he refix'd the Moslem's sway. **1837** CARLYLE *Fr. Rev.* I. VII. iii, One individual picks his [cockade] up again; .. attempts to refix it. **1870** E. PEACOCK *Ralph Skirl.* I. 7 It had not refixed life on its old basis.

†**re'fix,** *v.*[2] *Obs. rare*$^{-1}$. [ad. L. *refix-*, ppl. stem of *refigere*: see RE- 2 d and FIX *v.*] *trans.* To abrogate, annul (a law).
1621 BP. MOUNTAGU *Diatribæ* 50 This is enough to proue in the iudgement of those that made the Law, it was held a thing of common right, and ought to be receiued as Law, vntill as good authoritie did refixe it.

refi'xation. [RE- 5 a: cf. REFIX *v.*[1]] A renewed fixing.
1899 *Allbutt's Syst. Med.* VII. 572 The daily passive movements which will be necessary to prevent refixation.

refize, obs. form of REFUSE *sb.*

†**reflac, revelaik.** *Obs.* Forms: 1–2 **réaflác,** 2 refloc, 3 ræflac, raflak, reflac, 4 reuelaic(k, -laike, 5 *Sc.* reyflake, revelayk. [OE. *réaflác*, f. *réaf* REIF + *-lác* -LOCK (cf. *wedlock*).] Rapine, robbery, reavery.
c **888** K. ÆLFRED *Boeth.* xxvi. §2 Ælc bit þæs reaflaces þe him on ʒenumen bið. *c* **1000** ÆLFRIC *Hom.* II. 102 Þa ælmessan þe of reaflace beoð ʒesealde. *c* **1154** *O.E. Chron.* (Laud MS.) an. 1135, On þis kinges time wes al unfrið & yfel & ræflac. *c* **1200** *Trin. Coll. Hom.* 79 ȝif þe unfele man .. teð him to unwrenches to stele oðer refloc oðer swikedom. *a* **1225** *Ancr. R.* 208 Etholden oðres hure, ouer his rihte terme, nis hit strong reflac? *c* **1250** *Gen. & Ex.* 436 Ðeft and reflac ðhugte him no same. *a* **1300** *Cursor M.* 27825 Þe first sin es o couaitise .. O þis cums blindnes and tresun, Reuelaic, theft, extorsiun. **14..** in *Sc. Acts Parl.* (1844) I. 381 Of soyt to be mayd of reyflake and uþir crymis. Alsua na man aw to be herd of revelayk na of haymesokyn.

†**re'flair,** *sb. Obs.* Also 4, 6 -flayr. [prob. a. OF. or AF. **reflair*, f. *re-* RE- + *flair* FLAIR *sb.*[1]] Odour, scent, redolence.
13.. *E.E. Allit. P.* A. 46 ȝif hit was semly on to sene, A fayr reflayr ȝet fro hit flot. *c* **1400** MAUNDEV. (Roxb.) xviii. 84 Þe water þeroff has a swete sauour and reflaire. *a* **1529** SKELTON *P. Sparowe* 524 To make a fumigation, Swete of reflayr And redolent of ayre.

†**re'flair,** *v. Obs.* Forms: 5–6 reflar-, 6 -flayre, -fleyre, -flere. [Cf. prec. and F. *flairer* to smell.]
1. *intr.* To arise or issue; to distil.
c **1440** *York Myst.* xli. 367 The odour of thy goodnes reflars to vs all. **1509** HAWES *Past. Pleas.* XIV. (Percy Soc.) 53 Morall Gower, whose sentencious dewe Adowne reflayreth with fayre golden bemes.
2. *trans.* To emit, send forth, give out, shed.
1509 HAWES *Past. Pleas.* XI. (Percy Soc.) 42 O clere fountayne replete wyth swetenes, Refleryng out the dulcet delicacy Of iiii. ryvers. *Ibid.* xx. 96 Habundant teres theyr hertes do refleyre.

Hence †**re'flairing** *ppl. a.*, redolent. *Obs.*
1523 SKELTON *Garl. Laurel* 977 My mayden Isabell, Reflaring rosabell, The flagrant camamell.

re'flame, *v.* [RE-.]
†**a.** To reflect light. *Obs.* **b.** To burst into flame again; to rekindle.
1481 CAXTON *Myrr.* II. xxxi. 125 In the mone is a body polysshyd .. whiche reflaumbeth and rendrith lyght and clerenes whan the rayes of the sonne smyteth therin. **1875** TENNYSON *Q. Mary* I. v, Stamp out the fire, or this Will smoulder and re-flame.

reflate (riː'fleɪt), *v.* [f. RE- 5 a after DEFLATE *v.* 3, INFLATE *v.* 4.] **a.** *absol.* To raise the pressure of demand (in an economy) after a period of falling pressure. Also *trans.*, to expand (the money supply or the flow of expenditure) or raise (prices) after a period of contraction or reduction. **b.** *intr.* for *pass.* Of an economy: to be affected by or subject to reflation. Hence **re'flating** *vbl. sb.*
1932 *Sun* (Baltimore) 12 Apr. 10/2 There are plenty of ways to inflate or 'reflate' without putting the Federal Government $2,000,000,000 more into debt to accomplish the purpose. **1939** *Ibid.* 18 Dec. 13/6 The Administration was pleased to see farm prices on the rise for the New Deal dedicated a large part of its recovery promotion energies to schemes for 'reflating' commodity quotations. **1958** *Engineering* 21 Mar. 354/2 The rest of the world is afraid that the American determination not to reflate is going to start a deflation abroad. **1960** *Economist* 15 Oct. 220/2 Britain's present poor export performance makes it imperative that we should not reflate too early. **1966** *Daily Tel.* 2 Nov. 1/1 It is not a sign that the Government has begun to reflate the economy to halt unemployment and start industrial production moving forward. **1971** *Ibid.* 10 Sept. 19 The banks have 'saved' £600 million and .. the authorities will probably want a substantial slice of it locked up again in case the economy reflates too fast again. *a* **1974** R. CROSSMAN *Diaries* (1976) II. 134 If we wait until the officials tell us it's wise to reflate, the results won't show for years ahead and we'd have no prospect of winning the election. **1975** *Washington Post* 31 Aug. C7/4 The French and Germans are now having to reflate their economies by massive government expenditures. **1979** *Dædalus* Spring 43 Governments are .. taking pains not to reflate the economy enough to wipe out unemployment for fear of rekindling inflation and a balance of payments crisis.

reflation (riː'fleɪʃən). [f. RE- 5 a after DEFLATION 3, INFLATION 6.] The process of reflating or taking measures designed to allow an expansion in economic activity to be resumed.
1932 *Economist* 20 Feb. 394/2 Its purpose has been aptly described as 'reflation', to prevent further deflation .. and to undo some of the present extreme deflation. **1932** *Sun* (Baltimore) 12 Apr. 10/2 It does seem in order to ask why, if inflation or 'reflation' or whatever they may choose to call it is really the principal concern, they do not .. come forward with a straight inflation or 'reflation' project. **1932** *Hansard Commons* 20 Apr. 1582, I propose a different thing altogether [from inflation]. I would describe it as reflation, which I would define as controlled expansion of the note issue to keep pace with increased production. **1933** *Daily Tel.* 24 Apr. 11/3 The fight in Congress to beat depression by inflation—reflation, as some call it—grows more heated. **1940** G. CROWTHER *Outl. Money* iii. 116 The custom has grown up of referring to what happens during the upward phase of the normal trade cycle not as 'inflation' but as 'reflation'. For the present, we can think of 'reflation' as being restricted to a rise of prices that merely restores the *status quo ante*—the position before the start of the preceding deflation—and inflation to any further rise in prices after this point. **1959** *Economist* 17 Jan. 194/2 Every pound's worth of income tax relief this year would bring less risk to sterling than every ten shillings' worth of reflation made in any other way. **1971** *New Scientist* 10 June 606/1 A reflation stimulus is urgently needed now to fill the yawning gap in consumer demand. **1975** *Evening Standard* 24 July 36/2 (*heading*) It's reflation time says EEC. **1977** *Times* 29 Aug. 9/3 An electorally opportunistic government .. might be strongly tempted to chance some reflation in the run up to a general election next year.

reflationary (riː'fleɪʃənərɪ), *a.* [f. REFLATION + -ARY[1].] Characterized by, suggestive of, or tending to reflation.
1932 *Times Lit. Suppl.* 8 Dec. 931/3 The 'reflationary' policy of the American Government will in the end, he thinks, set prices rising again. **1940** *Economist* 7 Dec. 704/2 As long as the bulk of the gold inflow in the United States was the counterpart of a movement of capital there was no inherent reflationary or inflationary virtue to be found in it. **1957** *Ibid.* 26 Oct. 286/1 No small reflationary measures taken by Britain now, however, would make the situation then any better. **1963** *Indian Econ. Rev.* Feb. 32 As it proved, what expansion of the money supply there was in the 1930s was not inflationary but .. reflationary—that is, it served to increase national income without inducing a significant rise in prices. **1969** *Daily Tel.* 28 Oct. 16 An election just after a reflationary Budget would be cynically received. **1974** *Guardian* 27 Mar. 15/3 The TUC wanted a mildly reflationary Budget and Mr Healey has given them .. a mildly deflationary one. **1976** LD. SELWYN-LLOYD *Mr. Speaker, Sir* vii. 150 Many heads had already been shaken at the reflationary measures of the first two years or so of the Parliament and the idea of bursting through to growth and success.

reflationist (riː'fleɪʃənɪst). [f. REFLATION + -IST.] One who supports or advocates a policy of reflation.
1959 *Economist* 31 Jan. 393/1 The next questions that eager reflationists put to him should presumably be about the date of that budget and about investment allowances. **1972** *Guardian* 24 Jan. 6/8 Mr Macleod was a natural reflationist. **1980** *Spectator* 1 Nov. 4/2 What *is* unique to Britain is the great strength of the reflationists in the party of the Right.

reflect (rɪ'flɛkt), *sb.* Now *rare.* [f. the vb.] = REFLECTION, in various senses, *lit.* and *fig.* (Chiefly in 17th c. use.)
1596 LODGE *Marg. Amer.* 15 As the rainbow which .. Lives by the sunnes reflect and opposition. **1615** MARKHAM *Pleas. Princes* ii. (1635) 4 Their colour will be so darke that they will give no reflect into the water. *a* **1653** G. DANIEL *Idyll* i. 58 Perhaps I have To my owne Private, had reflects as grave On my Condition. **1687** WINSTANLEY *Lives Eng. Poets* 91 This tart reflect so wrought upon the Queen, that she gave strict order .. for the present payment of the hundred pounds. **1727–41** [see REFLEX *sb.* 1 b]. **1829** CARLYLE *German Playwr.* Misc. (1840) II. 63 Aiming apparently at some Classic model, or at least at some French reflect of such a model.

†**reflect,** *a. Obs.* [f. the vb., on analogy of ppl. forms in *-ct*.] Reflex, reflected.
1645 USSHER *Body Div.* (1647) 200 It is the reflect act of faith that justifieth. *a* **1660** HAMMOND *Serm.* xx. Wks. 1684 IV. 610 When looking in the glass, he sees all far more glorious in that reflect beam, than it is in the direct. **1662** SIR A. MERVYN *Sp. Irish Aff.* 12 Our spirits on both sides exercised not so much the reflect Act .. as the direct Act.

reflect (rɪ'flɛkt), *v.* [a. OF. *reflecter* (14th c., Oresme) or L. *reflectĕre*, f. *re-* RE- + *flectĕre* to bend (cf. *deflect, inflect*), whence also It. *riflettere*, Sp. *reflectir*, F. *réfléchir*.]
I. Transitive senses.
1. To turn or direct in a certain course, to divert; to turn away or aside, to deflect.
1412–20 LYDG. *Chron. Troy* II. xi. (1555), By arches stronge his course for to reflecte Through condite pipes .. By certayne meanes artifyciall. *c* **1450** tr. *De Imitatione* III. lix. 139 Nature reflectiþ [L. *reflectit*] all þynge to himself, & for himself he striueþ & arguiþ. **1540** ELYOT *Image Gov.* (1556) 34 b, No kynde of affection .. moughte reflect hym from the sharpe execution of his lawes. **1613** PURCHAS *Pilgrimage* (1614) 13 Dazled with this greater light [the sun] I would reflect mine eyes to that reflexion of this light in the sober, siluer countenance of the .. Moone. **1796** MORSE *Amer. Geog.* I. 61, I conceive that, when easterly and westerly winds meet with unequal force, one of them may be reflected northward. **1827** HOOD *Mids. Fairies* liv, It raised my bile To see him so reflect their grief aside.
2. a. To bend, turn, or fold back; to give a backward bend or curve to (a thing); to recurve; †to bend (the legs). (Chiefly in *pa. pple.*, denoting the position of parts.)
1578 BANISTER *Hist. Man* I. 13 The neither iawe is Orbicular .. the vtmost endes wherof are ascendently reflected. **1609** W. M. *Man in Moone, Parasite* E iij b, He fleareth not in your face for nothing, nor reflects his legges without some surmised reason. **1646** SIR T. BROWNE *Pseud. Ep.* 342 The coccyx sometime more reflected to give the easier delivery. **1693** *Phil. Trans.* XVII. 762 The Flowers come out in Clusters, are monopetalose, with five *Laciniæ* or Incisures, all reflected. **1768** PENNANT *Brit. Zool.* II. 353 The bill is .. not quite strait, but a little reflected upwards. **1776–96** WITHERING *Brit. Plants* (ed. 3) I. 297 Anthers strap-shaped, upright, reflected at the top. **1846** BRITTAN tr. *Malgaigne's Man. Oper. Surg.* 195 The horizontal incision being made, convert it into a T by a vertical incision .. and reflect the two flaps. **1869** H. USSHER in *Eng. Mech.* 3 Dec. 271/2 From the under surface of the eyelid a thin membrane is reflected on the ball.
fig. **1608** TOPSELL *Serpents* (1658) 691 A deadly antipathy reflecting themselves upon themselves. **1650** BULWER *Anthropomet.* 60 Whence the spirits streined and reflected, rise again.
†**b.** *fig.* To bring back from anger or estrangement; to appease. *Obs. rare.*
c **1611** CHAPMAN *Iliad* IX. 180 Such rites beseeme Ambassadors: and Nestor vrged these, That their most honours might reflect enrag'd Æacides. *Ibid.* XXI. 353 And prayd her, that her sonne Might be reflected.
†**3.** To turn (back), cast (the eye or thought) *on* or *upon* something. *Obs.*
1607 in Harington *Nugæ Ant.* (ed. Park 1804) II. 166 When I reflect my thought and eye upon that I have formerly written. **1655** FULLER *Ch. Hist.* IX. vii. §22 Let me minde the Reader to reflect his eye on our Quotations. *a* **1677** BARROW *Serm.* Wks. 1716 I. 127 If we reflect our thoughts on the first ages of Christianity.
4. a. To throw or cast back again; to cause to return or rebound.
1611 SHAKS. *Wint. T.* IV. iv. 758 Reflect I not on thy Basenesse Court-Contempt? **1613** WITHER *Abuses Stript, Envy* Juvenilia (1633) 25 The shafts are aim'd at me, but I reject them, And on the shooters may perhaps reflect them. **1656** tr. *Hobbes' Elem. Philos.* III. (1839) 274 A body falling upon the superficies of another body and being reflected from it. **1722** WOLLASTON *Relig. Nat.* vi. 132 It is that violence, of which he is the author, reflected back upon himself. **1799** J. WOOD *Princ. Mech.* VI. §206. 121 Each body will therefore be reflected with a velocity equal to that which it had before impact.
transf. **1656** tr. *Hobbes' Elem. Philos.* (1839) 274 If two strait lines drawn from the same point fall upon another strait line, the lines reflected from them, if they be drawn out the other way, will meet in an angle equal to the angle of the incident lines.
b. *spec.* Of bodies or surfaces (cf. REFLECTED *ppl. a.*): to cast or send back (heat, cold, or sound) after impact. Also used with reference to other forms of wave or radiation.
1718 PRIOR *Solomon* II. 636 The vocal triumphs bound Against the hills: the hills reflect the sound. **1774** GOLDSM. *Nat. Hist.* (1776) I. 351 The land .. receives a greater quantity of heat, and reflects it more strongly. **1794** J. HUTTON *Philos. Light*, etc. 138 To suppose that cold may be

irradiated like light, and be reflected and concentrated as well as heat. **1822** IMISON *Sc. & Art* I. 230 Buildings constructed of certain shapes..have this property of reflecting sounds in a remarkable manner. **1878** HUXLEY *Physiogr.* 53 A cloud..reflects or throws back upon the earth the heat. **1902** *Chem. News* 24 Jan. 47/2 (*heading*) Rays capable of being reflected in radiation emitted by a mixture of chlorides of radium and barium. **1909** *Proc. R. Soc.* A. LXXXII. 495 The fraction of the incident α-particles which are reflected. **1937** *Discovery* Jan. 3/2 The ionosphere—that region in the upper atmosphere where free electrons reflect wireless waves. *Ibid.* 4/1 Pulses are radiated in all directions: some reach the receiver by travelling direct along the ground, others by travelling high up into the atmosphere, where they are reflected downwards by one or more of the conducting layers. **1950** D. HALLIDAY *Introd. Nuclear Physics* vi. 247 A substance with a positve scattering length should..reflect neutrons totally at small external glancing angles. **1960** K. N. TONG *Theory Mech. Vibration* iv. 308 If the bar has an end, the disturbance wave will be reflected as it reaches that end. In a certain subsequent time period the reflected wave and the incident wave co-exist in the bar. Afterward, only the reflected wave remains. The manner in which the reflection takes place depends on the end condition. **1974** S. W. FLAX et al. in R. S. Reneman *Cardiovascular Applications Ultrasound* ii. 19 Another factor is how blood cells reflect ultrasound.

c. *Physiol.* To give out (an impulse) along a motor nerve, in response to one received along a sensory nerve. Usu. *pass.*

1833 *Proc. Royal Soc.* III. 210 [A function] by which an impression made upon the extremities of certain nerves is conveyed to those two portions of the nervous system, and reflected along other nerves to parts different from those which received the impression. **1855** BAIN *Senses & Int.* I. ii. §18 When an action takes place on this inner surface,.. there is reflected a stimulus to the muscle that closes the [eye] lids. **1859** J. C. DALTON *Treat. Human Physiol.* II. i. 314 The function of the gray matter is..to receive the impulse conveyed to it, and to reflect or send back another. **1906** H. W. SYERS tr. *J. P. Morat's Physiol. of Nerv. Syst.* ii. 218 The impulse is reflected from the posterior roots to the tracts of the spinal cord, in conscious impressions. **1931** H. G. WELLS et al. *Sci. of Life* I. iii. 86/1 The impulse may be wholly reflected in a reflex or pass on in part and more or less modified to the hemispheres. **1950** P. D. F. MURRAY *Biol.* vii. 68 The term 'reflex'..refers to the manner in which the impulse, having passed in to the central nervous system, is 'reflected' outwards from it.

5. a. Of bodies or surfaces, esp. such as are smooth or polished: To turn, throw, or cast back (beams, rays, or light). Also in fig. context.

1573 P. MORE *Alman. & Prognost.* D vj b, Whether the sayd beames [the sun's] be extended unto the Earth, or reflected backwardes again, do forshew tempest of windes comming. *c***1586** C'TESS PEMBROKE *Ps.* CXXI. iv, No sunne shall hurt thee With beames too violently right reflected. **1602** MARSTON *Ant. & Mel.* I. Wks. 1856 I. 61 Marry but shine, and ile reflect your beames. **1622** DRAYTON *Poly-olb.* xxii. 134 As when you see the sunbeams in a glass, That.. on the earth reflects the very same. **1664** POWER *Exp. Philos.* I. 43 The Crystal Sands..refracting and reflecting the Suns rays, seem here and there of Rainbow-colours. **1692** BENTLEY *Boyle Lect.* viii. 259 The Light of the Moon reflected from frozen Snow. **1781** COWPER *Charity* 398 As diamonds, stripp'd of their opaque disguise, Reflect the noonday glory of the skies. **1831** BREWSTER *Optics* Introd. 2 When light falls upon any body whatever, part of it is reflected or driven back. **1875** BRYCE *Holy Rom. Emp.* (ed. 5) Pref., The great events of 1866 and 1870 reflect back so much light upon the previous history of Germany.

absol. **1730** A. GORDON *Maffei's Amphith.* 351 The red.. and yellow Coverings of the Theatre reflected back on the Assembly of Spectators,..undulating the whole with their Colours. **1869** TYNDALL in *Fortn. Rev.* 1 Feb. 244 It [a cloud] is absolutely incompetent to reflect upwards or downwards.

b. To emit, give out (a light), as the result of reflection.

1719 DE FOE *Crusoe* I. xii, The Walls reflected a hundred thousand Lights to me from my two Candles. **1727-46** THOMSON *Summer* 170 The briny deep,..Restless, reflects a floating gleam.

6. a. Of mirrors or other polished surfaces: To give back or exhibit an image of (a person or thing); to mirror. Also *absol.*

1592 SHAKS. *Ven. & Ad.* 1130 Two glasses where herself herself beheld A thousand times, and now no more reflect. **1713** ADDISON *Cato* I. vi, The floating mirrour shines, Reflects each flow'r that on the border grows. **1765** GOLDSM. *Double Transf.* 82 The glass..Reflected now a perfect fright. **1790** COWPER *Mother's Pict.* 93 The floods that show Her beauteous form reflected clear below. **1816** SHELLEY *Alastor* 501 The rivulet..Reflecting every herb and drooping bud That overhung its quietness. **1836** LANDOR *Peric. & Asp.* Wks. 1846 II. 386 A shallow water may reflect the sun as perfectly as a deeper. **1864** BOWEN *Logic* I It is like a mirror reflecting the objects that are held up before it.

b. *fig.* and in fig. context. To reproduce or exhibit after the fashion of a mirror.

*a***1771** GRAY *Dante* 63 When I beheld My Sons, and in four Faces saw my own Despair reflected. **1784** COWPER *Tiroc.* 92 If all we find possessing earth, sea, air, Reflect his attributes who placed them there. **1821** SHELLEY *Prometh. Unb.* II. iv. 84 And mothers, gazing, drank the love men see Reflected in their race. **1858** FROUDE *Hist. Eng.* III. xvii. 498 The law..reflects the plain sentiments of the better order of average men. **1874** GREEN *Short Hist.* viii. §1. 455 This balanced attitude of the Crown reflected faithfully enough the balanced attitude of the nation.

7. a. Of persons: To throw or cast (blame, dishonour, etc.) *on* or *upon* a person or thing. *rare.*

1670 BAXTER *Cure Ch. Div.* Addit. Direct. Pastors §14 When you reprove those weak Christians..reflect not any disgrace upon piety itself. **1700** CONGREVE *Way of World* II. iii, Do you reflect that guilt upon me, which should lie buried in your bosom? **1809** E. CHRISTIAN in *Blackstone's Comm.* II. 160 If it were not presumptuous to reflect a censure upon a doctrine..sanctioned by illustrious names.

b. Of actions, circumstances, etc.: To cast or bring (dishonour, credit, etc.) *on* or *upon* a person or thing.

1675 R. BURTHOGGE *Causa Dei* 45 All the Aggravations Reflected on the faulty Action by this Transcendent Object. **1769** ROBERTSON *Chas. V*, VI. Wks. 1813 VI. 103 Of all the transactions in the emperor's life, this..reflects the greatest dishonour on his reputation. **1834** PRINGLE *Afr. Sk.* xi. 351 The attention given to education in this district..reflects the highest credit on the inhabitants. **1884** *Manch. Exam.* 7 May 5/4 The contest..reflects more credit upon the intrepidity than upon the wisdom of the belligerents.

8. With direct statement, question, or exclamation as obj. (For indirect uses, see sense 13 b.)

1862 MRS. H. WOOD *Channings* II. vii. 102 'No, no; it would not be right of him to make me his wife now,' she reflected. **1881** MRS. J. H. RIDDELL *Senior Partner* II. xi. 223 'She has the Pousnett kind of talk,' he reflected, 'and the same uppish way with her.' **1906** E. PHILLPOTTS *Portreeve* I. vi. 50 'Let what will come, there's amusement in it,' she reflected. ''Tis hunting of a sort. Fox-hunting—man-hunting—what more has life for me?' **1919** V. WOOLF *Night & Day* xxxiii. 506 Even if she started the very moment that she got it [*sc.* a letter], he reflected, she would not be home till Tuesday night.

II. Intransitive senses.

†**9. a.** Of beams or rays of light: To return, turn back, after striking or falling upon a surface. *Obs.*

1530 PALSGR. 682/2, I reflecte, as the sonne beames do that strike upwards from the grounde agayne. *Je reflecte. Je reuerbere.* I can nat abyde here, the sonne beames reflecte so sore. **1624** QUARLES *Sion's Sonn.* v. 1 From Thee Reflect those rayes, that haue enlightned mee. **1625** N. CARPENTER *Geog. Del.* I. ix. (1635) 205 The Sunne darts forth his Rayes at right Angles, which reflect backe vpon themselues. **1687** A. LOVELL tr. *Thevenot's Trav.* I. 260 Sore Eyes are..caused by the burning heat of the Sun, which reflects from the Ground upon the Eyes. **1703** MOXON *Mech. Exerc.* 346 When the Sun Shines upon the Glass at Nodus, its Beames shall reflect upon the Hour of the Day.

†**b.** To shine, cast a light. *Obs.*

1588 SHAKS. *Tit. A.* I. ii. 226 Lord Saturnine, whose Vertues will I hope, Reflect on Rome as Tytans Rayes on earth. **1590** GREENE *Never too late* (1600) G, When the glister of your beauty surpassing them both [Venus and Diana], reflected like the pride of Phœbus on my face, I perceiued it was my good Mistresse. **1653** BINNING *Serm.* Wks. (1735) 11 It is that Love of God, reflecting upon our Souls, that carries the Soul upward to him.

c. To appear imaged or mirrored.

1819 KEATS *Lamia* I. 380 A silver lamp whose phosphor glow Reflected in the slabbed steps below. **1821** CLARE *Vill. Minstr.* I. 208 Brooks curl o'er their sandy bed; On whose tide the clouds reflect.

†**10.** To deviate, to go *to* or come away *from* a place. *Obs. rare.*

1547 BOORDE *Brev. Health* §236 This impediment doth come of the corruption of humours reflectynge more to a pertyculer place then to vnyversall places. **1593** R. BARNES *Parthenophil*, Madr. xxiv. in Arb. *Garner* V. 405 Then from her sphere did Venus down reflect, Lest Mars by chance her beauty should affect.

†**11. a.** To return; to turn, come, or go back. *Obs.*

1608 T. MORTON *Preamb. Encounter* 1 To throw dust against the wind, which will reflect and returne with greater violence upon his own face. **1614** RALEIGH *Hist. World* I. (1634) 41 Where the River of Euphrates reflecteth from the Desart of Palmirena. *Ibid.* II. 217 At Etham he rested but one night, and then he reflected back from the entrance thereof and marched away directly to the South. **1654** tr. *Scudery's Curia Pol.* 127 These Cogitations reflected on me with shame to my selfe. **1692** BENTLEY *Boyle Lect.* vii. 25 Inanimate unactive Matter moves always in a streight Line, and never reflects in an Angle, nor bends in a Circle.., unless [etc.]. **1717** J. KEILL *Anim. Oecon.* (1738) 118 They must necessarily hit one against another, and being elastic, reflect from one another.

†**b.** To bend or be bent back. *Obs.*

1756 P. BROWNE *Jamaica* 352 The leaves stand in the same manner, reflecting a little backwards from the direction of the foot-stalks. **1797** *Encycl. Brit.* (ed. 3) VIII. 465/2 A Chain affixed thereto, reflecting over the back.

†**12. a.** To cast a look or glance *upon* a thing; to have a bearing *upon*, etc. *Obs.*

1613 FLETCHER, etc. *Captain* IV. v, Let thine eyes Reflect upon thy soul, and there behold How loathed black it is. **1653** R. SANDERS *Physiogn.* 36 The hands are big, and of a pale colour, reflecting somewhat on the Æthiopian. **1657** HAWKE *Killing is M.* 46 That it reflected not so much upon his own good, as the welfare of the Commonwealth, that he should be safe. **1662** H. MORE *Philos. Writ.* Pref. Gen. (1712) 17 Which latter in all likelihood was a glance at the third day's work. But the former part, that affirms the ground eternal, reflects upon the first.

†**b.** To bestow attention or regard *upon* a person or thing; to set a value *on*. *Obs. rare.*

1611 SHAKS. *Cymb.* I. vi. 24 He is one of the Noblest note. .. Reflect vpon him accordingly, as you value your trust. *a***1661** FULLER *Worthies* (1840) III. 213 He became a favorite to the duke of Florence, who highly reflected on his abilities.

13. a. To turn one's thoughts (back) *on*, to fix the mind or attention *on* or *upon* a subject; to ponder, meditate *on*; †think *of* (quot. 1751). Also occas. with *over*.

1605 B. JONSON *Volpone* II. i, Would I reflect on the price? Why, the whole world is but..as a private purse to the purchase of it. **1652** NEEDHAM tr. *Selden's Mare C.* 500 That I may reflect a little upon the point of sea Dominion. **1687** A. LOVELL tr. *Thevenot's Trav.* I. 134 Having reflected a little on the Danger which we had escaped, we viewed the second Pyramide. **1726** BUTLER *Serm. Hum. Nat.* i. Wks. 1874 II. 9 We are plainly constituted such sort of creatures as to reflect upon our own nature. **1751** *Female Foundling* II. 10, I would for ever blot out of my Memory, and reflect of nothing for the future but my Obligations to you. **1860** TYNDALL *Glac.* I. xxii. 155, I paused here for a moment, and reflected on the work before me. **1879** LUBBOCK *Addr. Pol. & Educ.* viii. 147 It is a melancholy subject to reflect on. **1906** W. S. MAUGHAM *Bishop's Apron* ix. 137 Winnie reflected over this for a moment.

b. With objective clause introduced by *that*, *what*, *how*, etc.

1703 MAUNDRELL *Journ. Jerus.* (1732) 14, I have sometimes reflected for what reason the Turks should [etc.]. **1709** MRS. MANLEY *Secr. Mem.* (1736) 2, I sat down in an Easy Chair to reflect what I had best to do. **1777** SIR W. JONES *Ess. Poetry E. Nat.* in *Poems*, etc. 178 They do not reflect that every nation has a set of images, and expressions, peculiar to itself. *a***1854** H. REED *Lect. Eng. Hist.* i. (1856) 11 Reflect how often our sense of truth is impaired or impeded. **1894** HALL CAINE *Manxman* v. xxi, He reflected that he had no right to do this.

c. Without const.: To employ reflection.

1704 NORRIS *Ideal World* II. iii. 121 There is but here and there a man that reflects..and carefully observes what's doing in his own mind. **1715** DE FOE *Fam. Instruct.* I. i. (1841) I. 7 Reflect, argue, and know both yourself, and Him that made you. **1772** PRIESTLEY *Inst. Relig.* (1782) I. 124 It is necessary..that we think and reflect before we act. **1825** COLERIDGE *Aids Refl.* (1831) 3 The noblest object of reflection is the mind itself, by which we reflect. **1841** JAMES *Brigand* xxv, I wish you to pause, reflect, and judge before you decide.

14. To cast a slight or imputation, reproach or blame, *on* or *upon* a person or thing; to pass a censure *on*. Also without const. (quot. *a* 1718).

1631 MASSINGER *Emperor East* IV. v, In this you reflect Upon my empress? **1644** CROMWELL *Sp.* 9 Dec. in *Carlyle*, I am far from reflecting on any. I know the worth of those commanders. **1676** DRYDEN *Aurengz.* III. i, But since my Honour you so far suspect, 'Tis just I should on your Designs reflect. *a***1718** PENN *Maxims* Wks. 1726 I. 833 Reflect without Malice but never without Need. **1756** C. LUCAS *Ess. Waters* II. 61, I would not be thought to reflect upon this very eminent physician's practice. **1794** in Bloomfield *Amer. Law Rep.* 21 Divers Expressions reflecting on the Authority of the Court. **1849** MACAULAY *Hist. Eng.* vi. II. 115 The clergy were strictly charged not to reflect on the Roman Catholic religion in their discourses.

15. a. Of actions, circumstances, etc.: To cast or bring reproach or discredit *on* a person or thing.

1647 CLARENDON *Hist. Reb.* I. §200 Not the less pleased to find, that the Prejudice of that whole Transaction reflected solely upon the Arch Bishop. **1654** BRAMHALL *Just Vind.* ii. (1661) 7 These were but personal heats, which reflected not upon the publick body of the Church. **1691** NORRIS *Pract. Disc.* 167 We are generally more impatient of what reflects upon our Intellectuals, than of what reflects upon our Morals. **1709** STEELE *Tatler* No. 39 ¶13 Ill Language, and brutal Manners, reflected only on those who were guilty of 'em. **1749** FIELDING *Tom Jones* XVII. vi, Mrs. Miller.. related everything concerning that fact, suppressing only those circumstances which would have most reflected on her daughter. **1828** SCOTT *F.M. Perth* viii, I cannot endure to see our townsman beaten and rifled... It reflects upon the Fair Town. **1878** BOSW. SMITH *Carthage* 329 A series of terrible atrocities..which reflects seriously on the state in whose service the worst offenders were.

b. To cast a certain light or character *on*.

1856 FROUDE *Hist. Eng.* (1858) I. v. 399 His conduct, though creditable to his ingenuity, reflects less pleasantly on his character. **1979** *Nature* 11 Jan. 84/1 If the flight control centre was indeed 'astounded', this surely reflects on the rate at which the Soviet team get access to the data from US missions.

Hence †**re'flectant**, a reflecting substance. *Obs.*—[1]

1706 FRAZER *Disc. Second Sight, Ess. Witchcr.* (1820) 171 Any lucid, smooth and solid reflectant.

reflectance (rɪˈflɛktəns). *Physics.* [f. REFLECT *v.* + -ANCE.] The proportion of the light incident upon a surface, which is reflected or scattered by it; *spec.* a complex number whose modulus is the proportion of the radiant flux (at some specified wavelength or range of wavelengths) which is reflected, and whose argument indicates the change of phase undergone by the reflected light. Cf. *reflection coefficient, factor.* Also *attrib.*

1926 *Jrnl. Optical Soc. Amer.* X. 178 Reflectance..is the ratio of reflected to incident radiant energy. **1932** [see INFRA-RED *a.* and *sb.* A. 1]. **1956** *Nature* 14 Jan. 74/2 The assessment of particular reflectance characteristics of cotton may be made on the automatic Nickerson-Hunter cotton colorimeter. **1957** V. J.-R. KEHOE *Technique Film & Television Make-Up* viii. 96 Black velvet has approximately 2 per cent reflectance, while some white paper is as high as 90 per cent. **1960** *Illuminating Engin.* LV. 228/1 The concepts of transmittance and reflectance can be extended to cover the separation of specular and diffuse components which are functions of angles. **1975** D. H. BURRIN in Williams & Wilson *Biologist's Guide to Princ. & Techniques Pract. Biochem.* v. 138 Reflectance spectrophotometers, which measure the radiation absorbed when a light beam is reflected by the sample, allow the determination of absorption spectra of pastes and suspensions of micro-organisms which are too opaque to transmit radiation. **1977** J. HEDGECOE *Photographer's Handbk.* 132 (*caption*) Meter reads direct off mid-gray (ideally 16 percent reflectance) card which simulates subject mid-tone.

reflected (rɪˈflɛktɪd), *ppl. a.* [f. REFLECT *v.*]

1. Bent, folded, or turned back; recurved.

1611 SPEED *Hist. Gt. Brit.* VI. xxiii. 227 His haire for more ornament long hee wore in reflected curles vpon his shoulders. **1861** HULME tr. *Moquin-Tandon* II. III. ii. 84 A thick peristome, terminating in an abrupt or reflected margin.

2. a. Turned, cast, or thrown back; sent in a reverse direction; coming indirectly. In later use chiefly *transf.* from b.

c **1380** WYCLIF *Sel. Wks.* II. 299 þe first siȝt is even siȝt, as man seeþ þing þat is bifore him; þe secounde siȝt is reflectid whan it is turned aȝen bi myrour. **1656** tr. *Hobbes' Elem. Philos.* III. (1839) 275 If two strait lines, which fall upon another strait line, be parallel, their reflected lines shall be also parallel. **1773** *Life N. Frowde* 116 You can feel no Anxiety..but what must assail my Bosom, with reflected Force. **1826** LAMB *Elia* Ser. II. *Wedding*, On these occasions I am sure to be in good-humour for a week or two after, and enjoy a reflected honey-moon. **1840** *Penny Cycl.* XVI. 153/1 The motions that result from the reflected influence evince design. **1875** MCLAREN *Serm.* Ser. II. ii. 30 The prayer that prevails is a reflected promise.

b. *esp.* of light, colour, or heat. Also used of other waves and radiations Cf. REFLECT *v.* 4 b.

1667 MILTON *P.L.* III. 723 That Globe whose hither side With light from hence, though but reflected, shines. **1704** J. HARRIS *Lex. Techn.* I, *Reflected Ray*, or *Ray of Reflection*, is that whereby the Reflection is made upon the Surface of a reflecting Body. **1746–7** HERVEY *Medit.* (1818) 142 Beautified..with colourings of reflected crimson. **1794** J. HUTTON *Philos. Light*, etc. 109 Another term for that which has been called obscure or reflected heat. **1827** POLLOK *Course T.* x, In native and reflected blaze of bright Celestial equipage. **1830** *Encycl. Metrop.* II. 753 A tendency in the reflected Sound to confine itself to the direction which a ray of Light regularly reflected at the echoing surface would follow. **1862** R. MALLET *First Princ. Observational Seismol.* II. III. xvi. 356 Ottajano and Somma..sustained the subordinate shock, of reflected waves from the N.E. flank of Vesuvius. **1869** TYNDALL in *Fortn. Rev.* 1 Feb. 237 The blue light of the sky is all reflected light. **1909** *Proc. R. Soc.* A. LXXXII. 497 For β-particles the number of reflected particles..decreases with the atomic weight of the reflector. **1925** *Year-bk. Wireless Telegr. & Telephony* 13 A system of telegraphy employing reflected beams was not only possible, but possessed very many advantages. **1960** [see REFLECT *v.* 4 b]. **1975** LEOPOLD & ASHER *Fund. Abdominal & Pelvic Ultrasonography* p. vii, One can obtain information from all areas of the body by suitably observing the reflected ultrasound pulses.

†**c.** Of dialling: (see quot.). *Obs. rare*$^{-0}$.

1710 J. HARRIS *Lex. Techn.* II, *Reflected Dialling* is the Art of describing..all the Furniture of Dials on such Places as the Suns direct Rays can never come to directly, but only by the help of some reflecting Surface.

†**d.** *Gram.* = REFLEXIVE 5.

1727–41 CHAMBERS *Cycl.* s.v. *Verb*, [A verb is called] reflected, where the action returns upon the agent.

3. Mirrored, imaged on some surface.

1784 COWPER *Task* I. 702 A lucid mirror, in which Nature sees All her reflected features. **1818** SHELLEY *Rev. Islam* I. xxii, That strange boat..did sway Amid reflected stars that in the waters lay. **1886** SHELDON tr. *Flaubert's Salammbô* 12 The reflected torch flames quivered to the very bottom.

Hence **re'flectedly** *adv.*, **re'flectedness.**

1727–41 CHAMBERS *Cycl.* s.v. *Mirror*, The object A radiates reflectedly, in the same manner as it would do directly. **1863** S. WILBERFORCE *Ess.* (1874) I. 323 He had neither the theological learning nor the calm sagacious reflectedness necessary for working out..such tangled threads.

†**re'flectent**, *a. Obs. rare*$^{-1}$. [ad. L. *reflectent-em*, pres. pple. of *reflectĕre* to REFLECT.] That reflects, reflecting.

1644 DIGBY *Nat. Bodies* xiii. (1658) 134 Refraction at the entrance into the reflectent body is towards the perpendicular.

reflecter (rɪˈflɛktə(r)). [f. REFLECT *v.* + -ER[1]. Cf. REFLECTOR.]

1. One who makes or casts reflections on another.

1686 SHERLOCK *Papist not Misrep.* 2 The Reflecter craftily insinuates that we grant all his Misrepresentations..to be ignorant, childish, or wilful Mistakes. **1704** SWIFT *Tale T.* Apol., For the greater part, the Reflecter is entirely mistaken. **1726** —— *Gulliver* IV. xii, The Tribes of Answerers, Considerers.., Observers, Reflecters. **1748** RICHARDSON *Clarissa* I. xlii, I was a reflecter again..Such venom in words!

2. A lamp provided with a reflector. *rare*$^{-1}$.

1782 *Gentl. Mag.* LII. 588 The miserable lanthorns and candles..have given place..to 1200 *reverberes* (or reflecters) made of polished tin.

reflecti'bility. *rare*$^{-1}$. [See next + -ITY.] Capacity for being reflected.

1705 C. PURSHALL *Mech. Macrocosm* 256 And therefore they have all the same Degree of Reflectibility.

re'flectible, *a.* [f. REFLECT *v.* + -IBLE.] That may be reflected.

1828–32 WEBSTER cites GREGORY.

reflecting (rɪˈflɛktɪŋ), *vbl. sb.* [f. as prec. + -ING[1].] The action of the vb. in various senses.

1530 PALSGR. 261/2 Reflectyng, *reflection, reuerberation.* **1578** BANISTER *Hist. Man* I. 35 This maner of the ioynt serueth to the bowyng, and reflectyng of the foote. **1594** CHAPMAN *Shadow Night* D iv, As when the sunnebeams..dance vpon a wall, that is the subiect of his [the sun's] faire reflectings. **1666–7** PEPYS *Diary* 14 Feb., My Lord Bellassis would not take notice of their reflecting on him. **1711** *Brit. Apollo* III. No. 156. 2/1 The Earth's reflecting of the Sun's Light. **1712** ADDISON *Spect.* No. 418 ¶5 We are delighted with the reflecting upon Dangers that are past.

attrib. **1826** HENRY *Elem. Chem.* I. 477 In general the reflecting power was found..to be proportionate to the degree of polish.

reflecting (rɪˈflɛktɪŋ), *ppl. a.* [-ING[2].]

1. a. That reflects, or casts back, light or images of things; †*reflecting glass*, a mirror. Also, that reflects waves or radiation of other kinds (cf. REFLECT *v.* 4 b).

1591 *Troub. Raigne K. John* (1611) 59 The murtherers That rob me of your faire reflecting view. **1592** KYD *Sol. & Pers.* I. iii. 130, I am now captiuated with the reflecting eye Of that admirable comet Perseda. **1601** SIR W. CORNWALLIS *Ess.* II. xlv. (1631) 258 The truest reflecting glasses, are those that present particular mens lives. **1734** WATTS *Reliq. Juv.* Pref. (1789) 8 When a reflecting glass shews the deformities of a face so plain as to point to the person [etc.]. **1823** J. BADCOCK *Dom. Amusem.* 51 The two reflectors..or as we term them—'reflecting surfaces'. **1841–4** EMERSON *Ess.*, *Friendship* Wks. (Bohn) I. 92 It never troubles the sun that some of his rays fall wide..and only a small part on the reflecting planet. **1850** W. & R. CHAMBERS *Nat. Philos. Acoustics* 26 The reflected [sound] waves have the same form as if they diverged from a point on the other side of the reflecting surface, directly opposite to the origin of the waves and equally distant from the surface. **1869** J. TYNDALL *Sound* (ed. 2) i. 13 Like sound also, light and radiant heat, when sent through a tube with a reflecting interior surface, may be conveyed to great distances with comparatively little loss. **1937** *Discovery* Jan. 3 The reflecting ionosphere layer. **1953** REED & RUSSELL *Ultra High Frequency Propagation* 513 The amplitude of the reflected energy is dependent..upon the dynamic mechanics of the reflecting media.

b. Provided or fitted with some arrangement or apparatus serving to reflect light or images; esp. *reflecting telescope.*

1704 J. HARRIS *Lex. Techn.* I, *Reflecting*, or *Reflexive Dyals*, are made by a little piece of Looking-Glass-Plate, duly placed, which reflects the Sun's Rays to the top of a Ceiling, &c. where the Dyal is drawn. *Ibid.*, *Reflecting Telescope.* **1722** POPE *Let. to R. Digby* 10 Oct., Have ye not Reflecting Telescopes whereby ye may innocently magnify her Spots and Blemishes? **1772** in Picton *L'pool Munic. Rec.* (1886) II. 242 The reflecting lights fixed up at the Light-houses for this Port. **1802** *Brookes' Gazetteer* (ed. 12) s.v. *Port Patrick*, The..quays..with a reflecting light-house. **1831** BREWSTER *Optics* v. 51 The two constitute a reflecting microscope. **1842** BRANDE *Dict. Sci.*, etc. s.v. *Telescope*, In reflecting telescopes the speculum or mirror performs the office of the object glass in those of the refracting kind. **1849** SIR F. B. HEAD *Stokers & Pokers* x. (1851) 96 Lighted by four large reflecting lamps.

2. Casting reflections on a person or thing. (In common use from *c* 1690 to 1715.)

1687 A. FARMER in *Magd. Coll. & Jas. II* (O.H.S.) 74 Certificates, the most reflecting contents of which they disown. *a* **1715** BURNET *Own Time* VII. (1734) II. 412 The Lower House..brought up injurious and reflecting Addresses to the Upper House. **1768** BLACKSTONE *Comm.* III. 125 Neither..are any reflecting words made use of in legal proceedings, and pertinent to the cause in hand, a sufficient cause of action for slander.

3. Having or exercising reflection or thought; characterized by reflection.

1711 SHAFTESB. *Charac.* (1737) II. II. II. i. 119 Every reasoning or reflecting Creature. **1712** BLACKMORE *Creation* I. (ed. 2) 6 To pursue That End..Demands a Conscious, Wise, Reflecting Cause. **1823** LAMB *Elia* Ser. II. *Poor Relations*, With a reflecting sort of congratulation, he will inquire the price of your furniture. **1849** MACAULAY *Hist. Eng.* iv. I. 478 Grave and reflecting men..augured from such beginnings the approach of evil times.

Hence **re'flectingly** *adv.*

1688 BOYLE in *Wks.* (1772) I. Life, p. cxxvi, Sometimes naming him [the true author] as it were incidentally, and peradventure reflectingly. **1701** NORRIS *Ideal World* I. i. 21 He may not indeed think of it reflectingly and distinctly. **1838** *New Monthly Mag.* LIII. 541 Well and reflectingly hath Wordsworth told us that the simplest flower [etc.].

reflection, reflexion (rɪˈflɛkʃən). Also 5–6 **refleccio(u)n**, 6 **reflyxyon, reflextion.** [a. F. *réflexion* (14th c.), or ad. late L. *reflexiōn-em* (med.L. also *reflectiōn-em*): see REFLECT *v.* and FLEXION.

The etymological spelling with *x* is the earliest, and is still common in scientific use, perh. through its connexion with *reflex*; in the general senses the influence of the verb has made the form with *ct* the prevailing one.]

†**1.** ? A reflexive influence on the mind. *Obs.*$^{-1}$

c **1384** CHAUCER *H. Fame* I. 22 As yf folkys complexions Make hem dreme of reflexions.

2. a. The action, on the part of surfaces, of throwing back light or heat (rays, beams, etc.) falling upon them; the fact or phenomenon of light and heat being thrown back in this way. Also, the similar action of surfaces on other waves and radiations. Cf. REFLECT *v.* 4 b.

angle of reflection, the angle which the reflected ray makes with a perpendicular to the surface (†or with the surface itself).

c **1386** CHAUCER *Sqr.'s T.* 222 It myghte wel be Naturelly by composicions Of Anglis and of slye reflexions. **1412–20** LYDG. *Chron. Troy* I. iii. (1555) B vi/2 Whan Phebus beames ..cause the eyer by reflection To be full hoote. **1481** CAXTON *Myrr.* II. xxxi. 125 Of the reflexion yᵉ myrrour smyteth on the walle and shyneth theron as longe as the rayes of the sonne endure in the glasse. **1559** W. CUNNINGHAM *Cosmogr. Glasse* 42 The lower region..is thorowe the reflextion of the Sonne beames rebounding from th' earth also made hoote. **1613** PURCHAS *Pilgrimage* I. viii. (1614) 43 The reflection or refraction of the Sunne-beames in a waterie cloud. **1660** R. COKE *Justice Vind.* 10, I therefore probably conclude, that the heat in summer is caused from the reflexion of the sun. **1726** SWIFT *Gulliver* III. iii, Twenty Lamps..which, from the Reflection of the Adamant, cast a strong Light into every Part. **1753** CHAMBERS *Cycl. Supp.* s.v., Rays of light being supposed.. to be reflected by a given curve, so as to make the angle of reflexion equal to the angle of incidence. **1841** *Penny Cycl.* XIX. 349/2 Heat being capable of reflection, like light, the rays of the sun may be collected by a concave speculum in its principal focus. **1869** TYNDALL in *Fortn. Rev.* 1 Feb. 240 When a luminous beam impinges at the proper angle on a plane glass surface it is polarized by reflexion. **1902** *Chem. News* 24 Jan. 47/2 Certain rays existed in the radiation emitted by certain radio-active bodies which were capable of reflection. **1909** *Proc. R. Soc.* A. LXXXII. 497 The diffuse reflection of the α-particles is a consequence of their scattering. **1929** *Jrnl. Sci. Instruments* VI. 34 Sound has all the properties of a wave motion..and exhibits the phenomena of reflection, interference, diffraction and resonance. **1941** A. B. WOOD *Textbk. Sound* (ed. 2) iii. 311 The direct reflection of a sound of short duration from a surface of large area such as the wall of a building or a cliff is generally discribed as an echo. **1960** [see REFLECT *v.* 4 b]. **1969** *Times* 28 Aug. 3/3 Seismic reflections indicate the thickness of the rocks.

fig. **1606** SHAKS. *Tr. & Cr.* III. iii. 99 Man..Cannot make boast to haue that which he hath; Nor feeles not what he owes, but by reflection. **1651** N. BACON *Disc. Govt. Eng.* II. xv. (1739) 79 They are like the Sun gone down, and must rule by reflection, as the Moon in the night.

b. The result of such reflecting of light; reflected light or heat.

1555 EDEN *Decades* 246 The raynebowe is a reflection of the beames of the soonne in the vapoure of a clowde. **1601** SIR W. CORNWALLIS *Ess.* II. xxix. (1631) 33 Rather choosing to be a glimmering reflexion, then a true and reall light. **1667** MILTON *P.L.* III. 428 That side which from the wall of Heav'n..som small reflection gaines Of glimmering air. **1727–46** THOMSON *Summer* 439 In vain the sight, dejected to the ground, Stoops for relief; thence hot-ascending steams And keen reflection pain. **1796** MORSE *Amer. Geog.* II. 312 Almost blind and with their skin terribly burnt by the reflection of the snow.

fig. **1598** BARCKLEY *Felic. Man* (1631) 686 If we examine our coldness in our love to God; wee shall perceive the reflexion of it to our neighbour to bee frozen. **1611** SHAKS. *Cymb.* I. ii. 33 Shee's a good signe, but I haue seene small reflection of her wit. **1686** tr. *Chardin's Coronat. Solyman* 64 The Lustre of Gold cast such a powerful reflection upon his Lordly senses.

3. a. The action of a mirror or other polished surface in exhibiting or reproducing the image of an object; the fact or phenomenon of an image being produced in this way.

c **1430** LYDG. *Reas. & Sens.* 5757 This welle most royall Was y-pavyd with cristall, Shewyng by refleccioun Al the estris enviroun. **1601** SHAKS. *Jul. C.* I. ii. 53 The eye sees not it selfe but by reflection, By some other things. **1653** H. MORE *Antid. Ath.* III. xvi, Reflexion makes the images more dim then direct sight. **1777** SIR W. JONES *Ess. Poetry E. Nat.* in *Poems*, etc. 186 Both drew their images from nature herself, without catching them only by reflection. **1809–10** COLERIDGE *Friend* (1865) 26 Occasioning us at first to mistake images of reflection for substances. **1831** BREWSTER *Nat. Magic* ii. (1833) 34 The image was as distinct and perfect as if it had been formed by reflexion from a piece of mirror glass. **1860** TYNDALL *Glac.* I. xv. 101 In its blue depths each ice mass doubled itself by reflection.

b. An image or counterpart thus produced.

1587 GOLDING *De Mornay* v. 57 It was of necessitie, that this vnderstanding of God should yeeld a reflexion backe againe to it self, as a face doth in a Lookingglasse. **1692** DRYDEN *Eleonora* 137 As the sun in water we can bear, Yet not the sun, but his reflection there. **1839** *Athenæum* 26 Jan., An apparatus..to receive a reflection of the scene without. **1870** J. H. NEWMAN *Gram. Assent* II. vi. 188 The mind is like a double mirror, in which reflexions of self within self multiply themselves till they are undistinguishable. **1877** BLACK *Green Past.* ii. (1878) 11 There was not a breath of wind to break the reflections of the trees on the glassy surface.

fig. **1821** SHELLEY *Epipsych.* 118 A tender Reflection of the eternal Moon of Love. *a* **1854** H. REED *Lect. Eng. Hist.* (1855) 346 Poetry is a glorified reflection of life and nature. **1882** FARRAR *Early Chr.* II. 29 We might perhaps see in this fact a reflexion of the unbending character of the writer.

c. The fact of colour being thrown by one thing upon another; a colour, hue, or tint received in this way; also *Zool.* a colour varying in different lights, an iridescence.

1614 RALEIGH *Hist. World* II. (1634) 219 This Sea was so called from a reflection of rednesse..from the banks, clifts and sands of many Ilands. **1638** JUNIUS *Paint. Ancients* 285 Goe to then, Painter, confound red roses with good store of lillies, and what reflexion the aire taketh of them, let that be the colour of her face. **1805** A. KNOX *Rem.* (1844) I. 16 The purple and gold..seems clearly an unconscious reflection of that yet unrisen sun. **1840** *Penny Cycl.* XVIII. 64/1 Feathers..golden-green, with grey edges, and all are glossed with brilliant metallic reflections. **1874** *Ibis* July (1886) 258 The greater wing-coverts..with greenish black reflections, but without any white.

4. a. The action of bending, turning, or folding back; recurvation. Also *fig.*

1553 BRENDE *Q. Curtius* 167 Croked Erymanthus with hys many turnynges and reflexions is consumed by the inhabitours with wateryng their grounde. **1587** GOLDING *De Mornay* v. 62 This Vnderstanding, by a certeine Reflexion of it selfe vpon it selfe, hath begotten vs a second person. **1610** GUILLIM *Heraldry* II. iv. 44 A Bunched Line is that which is carried with round reflections or bowings vp and downe, making diuers hollow Crookes or Furrowes. *a* **1667** JER. TAYLOR *Apol. Liturgy* Pref. §8 The first reflexions of a crooked tree are not to straightness, but to a contrary incurvation. **1692** BENTLEY *Boyle Lect.* vii. 25 Inanimate unactive Matter moves always in a streight Line, nor ever reflects in an Angle, nor bends in a Circle (which is a continual Reflexion), unless [etc.]. **1758** I. LYONS *Fluxions*

vii. §191. 142 If a curve instead of being continued beyond the ordinate is reflected from it,..that ordinate is said to pass through a point of Reflection or Cusp. **1870** ROLLESTON *Anim. Life* 47 [The] umbilicus is partly concealed by the reflection over it of the peristome.

†b. The action of bringing back from a state of anger or estrangement. *Obs. rare*$^{-1}$.

1598 CHAPMAN *Iliad* XVIII. 404 Mightie suppliance, By all their graue men hath bene made, gifts, honors, all proposde For his reflection.

†c. The action of turning back from some point; return, retrogression. *Obs. rare.*

1605 SHAKS. *Macb.* I. ii. 25 As whence the Sunne gins his reflection, Shipwracking Stormes, and direfull Thunders [break]. **1662** J. BARGRAVE *Pope Alex. VII* (1867) 123 Ashes of the Mount Vesuvius, near Naples, which was 4 times the poynt of my reflection,—I facing about for England from the topp, or crater,..of that mountain.

†d. *Astron.* (See quots.) *Obs. rare*$^{-0}$.

1704 J. HARRIS *Lex. Techn.* I, *Reflexion* of the Moon, is (according to Bullialdus) her 3d inequality of Motion: this Tycho calls by the Name of her Variation. **1710** *Ibid.* II, *Reflection* in the..Copernican System is the Distance of the Pole from the Horizon of the Disk; which is the same thing as the Sun's Declination in the Ptolemaick Hypothesis.

5. a. The action of throwing back, or fact of being thrown or driven back, after impact. (Said of material objects, sound, etc., and *fig.*)

1642 FULLER *Holy & Prof. St.* III. iii. 157 It sheweth more wit but no lesse vanity to commend ones self not in a strait line but by reflection. **1656** tr. *Hobbes' Elem. Philos.* III. (1839) 274 In this place..let it be supposed that the angle of incidence is equal to the angle of reflection. **1662** HOBBES *Seven Prob.* Wks. 1845 VII. 21 The air comes out again with the same violence by reflection. **1703** KELSEY *Serm.* 149 It is but like the rebounding of a Ball betwixt the Hardness of two Walls, where the Reflection is continued till the Force be spent. **1799** J. WOOD *Princ. Mech.* VI. 130 The velocity of the body after reflection is equal to it's velocity before incidence. **1831** BREWSTER *Nat. Magic* ix. (1833) 221 Many remarkable phenomena in the natural world are produced by the reflexion and concentration of sound. **1884** A. DANIELL *Princ. Physics* xiv. 413 Reflexion of sound is familiarly illustrated by the Echo.

b. *Phys.* The action, on the part of a nerve-centre, of returning an impression received; reflex action.

1836 SIR J. PAGET in *Mem.* v. (1901) 93 He is certainly a sharp fellow, but I should think rather monomaniac on the reflections. **1840** *Penny Cycl.* XVI. 153/1 In all these cases sensation coexists with the reflection of the impression through the motor nerves.

6. a. Animadversion, blame, censure, reproof.

1651 N. BACON *Disc. Govt. Eng.* II. xiv. (1739) 78 As their work is full of reflection, so formerly they had met with many sad influences for their labour. **1693** DRYDEN *Juvenal* Ded. (1697) 47 For in English, to say Satire, is to mean Reflection, as we use that Word in the worst sence. **1707** HEARNE *Collect.* 23 Dec. (O.H.S.) II. 82 The Duke was oppos'd by yᵉ Dr...not without some sharpness and Reflection. **1748** RICHARDSON *Clarissa* I. vi, If I have deserved reflection, let me not be spared. **1818** SCOTT *Hrt. Midl.* ii, Robertson uttered not a word of reflection on his companion for the consequences of his obstinacy.

b. A remark or statement reflecting, or casting some imputation, on a person.

1647 CLARENDON *Hist. Reb.* IV. §49 All those sharp Reflexions which could be made upon the King himself. **1658–9** in *Burton's Diary* (1828) III. 238 It is a reflexion upon the whole House. I am sorry to hear that said. **1675** R. BURTHOGGE *Causa Dei* 11, I abhor Reflections and Hard Words, as neither Philosophical, nor Civil, nor Christian. **1718** PRIOR *Solomon* III. 459 May no reflection shed Its poisonous venom on the royal dead. **1788** PRIESTLEY *Lect. Hist.* IV. xx. 161 The Baeotians were Plutarch's countrymen and he could not bear that any reflection, though ever so just, should be cast upon them. **1839** HALLAM *Hist. Lit.* III. v. §43 He cannot restrain himself from reflections on kings and priests when he is most contending for them. **1870** MAX MÜLLER *Sc. Relig.* (1873) 395 Had his personal reflections concerned myself alone.

c. An imputation; a fact or procedure casting an imputation or discredit *on* one.

1663 GERBIER *Counsel* 5 An ill built Palace leaves a perpetual reflection of Ignorance on the Builder. **1673** GREW *Anat. Roots* Ep. Ded., To insist hereon too much, might be a reflection upon Your Judgments. **1711** ADDISON *Spect.* No. 189 ¶7 It is one of the greatest Reflections upon Human Nature that Paternal Instinct should be a stronger Motive to Love than Filial Gratitude.

†7. Reference, relation, connexion. *Obs.*

1628 T. SPENCER *Logick* 20 Those 10. things, are propounded, not as meere and simple beings: but, in respect of that reflection, or relation which ariseth out of them, vnto our vnderstanding. *Ibid.* 191 They haue no reflexion, or relation to any thing before man. **1664** MARVELL *Corr.* Wks. 1875 II. 177 That His and Your present prosperity may have as strong a sympathy and reflexion.

8. a. The action of turning (back) or fixing the thoughts on some subject; meditation, deep or serious consideration.

a **1674** CLARENDON *Surv. Leviath.* (1676) 20 We shall with less reflexion pass over his fourth Chapter. **1704** NORRIS *Ideal World* II. iii. 122 By reflection we come to know the true state of human nature. **1726** BUTLER *Serm. Hum. Nat.* ii. Wks. 1874 II. 28 Our real nature leads us to be influenced in some degree by reflection and conscience. **1771** *Junius Lett.* lix. (1788) 319 Upon reflection, his conduct accounts naturally for itself. **1785** PALEY *Mor. Philos.* I. vii. 37 Mankind act more from habit than reflection. **1837** LANDOR *Pentam.* Wks. 1846 II. 309 It is only the hour of reflection that is at last the hour of sedateness and improvement. **1869** TYNDALL *Notes Lect. Light* §373 A moment's reflection will make it plain [etc.]. **1873** M. ARNOLD *Lit. & Dogma* (1876) 43 *note*, Surely it must on reflexion appear that this is by no means so.

†b. Recollection or remembrance *of* a thing. Also without const. *Obs.*

1655–87 H. MORE *App. Antid.* (1712) 193 This torture arising..out of reflexion of what it has suffered. **1694** CONGREVE *Double Dealer* II. vii, Though it made you a little uneasy for the present, yet the reflection of it must needs be entertaining. *a* **1704** T. BROWN *Eng. Satire* Wks. 1730 I. 25 Making them [vices] as bitter in the Reflection as..they might be suppos'd pleasant in the Enjoyment.

c. *Philos.* The mode, operation, or faculty by which the mind has knowledge of itself and its operations, or by which it deals with the ideas received from sensation and perception.

1690 LOCKE *Hum. Und.* II. i. §4 By Reflection then,..I would be understood to mean, that notice which the Mind takes of its own Operations, and the manner of them. **1692** NORRIS *Refl. Locke's Ess. Hum. Und.* 61 Ideas of Reflection are but a Secondary sort of Ideas [etc.]. **1797–1803** FOSTER in *Life & Corr.* (1846) I. 177 A knowledge of sensation more than of reflexion. **1847** LEWES *Hist. Philos.* (1867) I. 98 Was there nothing to guide man but the reports of his senses? Democritus said there was Reflection. **1853** ABP. THOMSON *Laws Th.* §48 Reflection is ascertainment of points of resemblance and points of difference.

9. a. A thought or idea occurring to, or occupying, the mind.

1647 CLARENDON *Hist. Reb.* I. §25 These reflections were so terrible to him that they robbed him of all peace and quiet of mind. **1671** R. MONTAGU in *Buccleuch MSS.* (Hist. MSS. Comm.) I. 510 See whether upon second reflections the King will say anything to me. **1716** LADY M. W. MONTAGU *Let. to C'tess Bristol* 22 Aug., These reflections draw after them others that are too melancholy. **1791** COWPER *Retired Cat* 108 Then stepped the poet into bed, With this reflection in his head. **1833** N. ARNOTT *Physics* (ed. 5) II. 84 The reflection will naturally occur here [etc.]. **1866** CRUMP *Banking* ix. 207 A fact suggesting rather a singular reflection.

b. A thought expressed in words; a remark made after reflection on a subject.

1659 HAMMOND *On Ps.* Pref. 3 Beside his many incidental reflexions on this Book of Psalms. *a* **1704** T. BROWN *Eng. Satire* Wks. 1730 I. 25 The reflections are beautiful, founded upon true learning and give a just reputation to their author. **1750** JOHNSON *Rambler* No. 31 ¶3 When an account was brought him of his son's death, he received it only with this reflection, 'I knew that my son was mortal'. **1819** SHELLEY *Peter Bell 3rd* v. xii, Odd collections Of saws and proverbs, and reflections Old parsons make in burying-grounds. **1839** HALLAM *Hist. Lit.* II. vii. §36 The reflections are usually of a moral cast.

10. *Cryst., Math., Physics.* The conceptual operation of inverting a system or event with respect to a plane, each element being transferred perpendicularly through the plane to a point the same distance the other side of it. Freq. *attrib.*

1899 W. J. LEWIS *Treat. Crystallogr.* iii. 18 We shall often express the relation of two planes, or two lines, to a plane of symmetry bisecting the angle between them by the statement that they are reciprocal reflexions in the plane. **1910** *Nature* 26 May 368/1 Its 880 known solutions (8 × 880, if we admit reversals and reflections of the same square to be 'different'). **1955** W. PAULI *Niels Bohr* 30 The mathematical group was further amplified by including the reflections of space and time. *Ibid.* 33, I am restricting myself..to the discussion of the reflection of all coordinates simultaneously while I do not consider the reflection of space or time separately. **1965** A. F. BROWN tr. *Zhdanov's Crystal Physics* v. 144 Symmetry groups containing only the operations of reflection, rotation and inversion, and not containing any translations, are called point groups. **1965** *Sci. Amer.* Dec. 28/1 Until December, 1956, they [*sc.* physicists] had assumed that if an event is possible, its mirror image is also possible, and that if one looks at some real event in a mirror, what one sees could also actually happen. This was known as reflection symmetry. **1971** I. G. GASS et al. *Understanding Earth* i. 19/1 The stereogram of zircon..shows a four-fold rotation axis in the centre and also shows a number of reflection planes. **1972** F. J. BUDDEN *Fascination of Groups* xxvi. 507 The two-dimensional pattern of fig. 26·051 contains translations and glide reflections, but no rotations.

11. *attrib.* and *Comb.*, as ***reflection-coiner***, ***oscillator***, ***time***; ***reflection-reducing*** adj.; **reflection coefficient, factor** *Physics* = REFLECTANCE; **reflection nebula** *Astr.*, a nebula which is visible only by virtue of the light which it reflects; **reflection profiling** *Geol.*, profiling (sense 3) by means of reflection shooting; **reflection shooting** *Geol.*, seismic prospecting in which shock waves generated at the earth's surface are detected up to a mile away after having been reflected at the interface between strata, the depth of which is deduced from their time of arrival.

1942 A. HUND *Frequency Modulation* i. 139 The reflection coefficient for horizontal polarization. **1959** BORN & WOLF *Princ. Optics* xiii. 627 The complex reflection and transmission coefficients of the film may immediately be evaluated. **1975** E. HEIGHT *Optics* iii. 43 Determine the values of the amplitude reflection coefficients for light incident at 30° on an air-glass interface. **1711** SHAFTESB. *Charac.* (1737) III. 95 The celebrated wits.., casual discoursers, reflection-coiners, meditation-founders [etc.]. **1920** Reflection factor [see REFLECTOMETER]. **1971** E. SKUDRZYK *Acoustics* xv. 302 The amplitude reflection factor represents the ratio of the reflected to the incident pressure wave with respect to magnitude and phase. **1936** *Astrophysical Jrnl.* LXXXIV. 219 (*heading*) Reflection nebulae. **1974** *Sci. Amer.* Oct. 34/3 These reflection nebulas are useful for studying the properties of the interstellar dust grains, but they are distinguished from the true emission nebulas, which shine as a result of the atomic processes going on within them. **1938** B. MCCOLLUM in A. E. Dunstan et al. *Sci. of Petroleum* I. VIII. 396/2 (*heading*) Accuracy of reflection profiling. **1964** CURRAY & MOORE in van Andel & Shor *Marine Geol. Gulf of Calif.* 193 The sedimentary structure of the continental terrace of the Costa de Nayarit ..has been investigated geophysically by means of continuous acoustic reflection profiling. **1971** I. G. GASS et al. *Understanding Earth* xvi. 243/2 Reflecting horizons..can be mapped over vast areas by continuous reflection profiling. **1962** CORSON & LORRAIN *Introd. Electromagn. Fields* xi. 406 Do reflection-reducing coatings on lenses improve the transmission significantly? **1929** *Trans. Amer. Inst. Mining & Metall. Engineers* LXXXI. 606 The distances are short in reflection shooting compared with those in refraction shooting. **1951** K. K. LANDES *Petroleum Geol.* ii. 48 Refraction shooting has recently become important again as a method of detailing rock structure where reflection shooting is not practicable. **1973** R. E. CHAPMAN *Petroleum Geol.* ii. 45 More detailed structural information is obtained from reflection shooting, in which the elastic waves are partly reflected by surfaces of contrasting density. **1971** *Physics Bull.* June 333/1 Reflection spectroscopy concerns the measurement of the frequency dependence of the specular reflectivity of the material to determine either the positions and strengths of features in its absorption spectrum or its optical constants. **1889** *Anthony's Photogr. Bull.* II. 285 In my case the reflection time is over.

Hence **re'flectional** *a.*, due to reflection; **re'flectioning**, the action of reflecting; **re'flectionist**, one who theorizes on the subject of reflection; **re'flectionless** *adv.*, without a reflection; also as *adj.*, not giving rise to any reflection.

1748 RICHARDSON *Clarissa* (1811) VI. 3 But reflectioning apart, thou seest, Jack, that her plot is beginning to work. **1861** RUSKIN *Arrows of Chace* (1880) I. 300 Whenever I have seen a rainbow over water..it has stood on it reflectionless. **1862** F. HALL *Refut. Hindu Philos. Syst.* 63 The bondage of the soul, consisting in its connexion with misery, which is reflexional, is unreal. *Ibid.* 243 Such as say thus, the reflexionists [etc.]. **1878** S. H. HODGSON *Philos. Reflection* II. v. I. 226 Idealist (or rather Reflectionist) in philosophy. **1951** *Rev. Sci. Instruments* XXII. 828/1 A reflectionless wave-guide termination. **1956** *Nature* 25 Feb. 392/1 A thin transverse film having a surface resistivity equal to the wave impedance of the waveguide forms a reflexion-less termination when [etc.].

reflectious (rɪˈflɛkʃəs), *a. nonce-wd.* [f. REFLECT *v.* + -IOUS. Cf. REFLEXIOUS *a.*] = REFLECTIVE *a.*

1874 HARDY *Far from Madding Crowd* II. xxv. 311 'Justice is come to weigh him in the balance,' I said in my reflectious way.

reflective (rɪˈflɛktɪv), *a.* and *sb.* [f. REFLECT *v.* + -IVE. Cf. REFLEXIVE, and mod.F. *réflectif*.]

A. *adj.* That reflects, in various senses.

1. a. That gives back an image or reflection of an object; that mirrors or reproduces.

1627 FELTHAM *Resolves* II. lxxix. 226 Domitian's reflectiue Galleries, could not guard him from the skarfed arme. **1718** PRIOR *Solomon* III. 795 In the reflective stream the sighing bride, Viewing her charms impair'd, abash'd shall hide Her pensive head. **1791** E. DARWIN *Bot. Gard.* I. 156 Each bright stream.., Reflective fountain, and tumultuous tide. **1867** ELLACOMBE in *Trans. Exeter Dioc. Archit. Soc.* Ser. II. I. 105 All the panels are filled with plate glass, the reflective power of which is greatly admired. **1886** RUSKIN *Præterita* I. vi. 175 The polished floor..as reflective as a mahogany table.

fig. **1848** GILFILLAN in *Tait's Mag.* XV. 511 A man's times are reflective of the man, as well as a man of the times.

b. That throws back something striking or falling upon the surface; *esp.* that reflects light.

1742 tr. *Algarotti on 'Newton's Theory'* II. 205 Where the attractive Force is greatest, the reflective and repulsive is greatest also. **1867** G. F. CHAMBERS *Astron.* 81 When viewed by the naked eye the Moon presents a mottled appearance; this arises from our satellite being unequally reflective. **1871** tr. *Schellen's Spectr. Anal.* xviii. 64 The reflective substance of a prism.

c. *Gram.* = REFLEXIVE 5.

1843 *Penny Cycl.* XXVI. 253/1 The so-called Reflective verb is in form either a transitive verb..or a passive verb.

2. a. Of light: Produced by reflection, reflected, borrowed.

1666 DRYDEN *Ann. Mirab.* ccliii, His beams he to his royal brother lent, And so shone still in his reflective light. **1773** J. ROSS *Fratricide* IV. 357 (MS.), Now their broad blades encount'ring in mid air Shot through the darkness a reflective light. **1867** BAILEY *Univ. Hymn* 6 Moon, whose gleam Reflective, types the God-light, wherewith shines Man's soul.

b. Reflex, reciprocal.

1839 I. TAYLOR *Anc. Chr.* I. 386 Could such things happen without producing a reflective effect on the religious sentiments and manners of the men most nearly concerned?

†3. That makes or contains reflections or censures *on* or *upon* a person. *Obs.*

1668 PEPYS *Diary* 13 Sept., Little [is] said reflective on me, though W. Pen and J. Minnes do mean me in one or two places. **1677** GILPIN *Demonol.* (1867) 334 At such times men are too apt to entertain cruel thoughts of God, and sadly reflective upon His mercy or justice.

4. a. Of mental faculties: Of or pertaining to reflection (on what is presented to the mind).

1678 NORRIS *Misc.* (1699) 276 The Soul, whose reflective Faculty will not fail to give her information. **1718** PRIOR *Solomon* I. 739 Forc'd by reflective reason, I confess, That human science is uncertain guess. **1858** O. W. HOLMES *Aut. Breakf.-t.* vi. 50 The Poet says, that rapidly growing towns are most unfavourable to the imaginative and reflective faculties.

b. Given to, commonly exercising, thought or reflection; meditative, thoughtful.

1820 *Blackw. Mag.* VI. 688 The very model of an accomplished, reflective, and affectionate English matron. **1833** COLERIDGE *Table-t.* 23 Oct., Elegy is the form of poetry natural to the reflective mind. **1870** DICKENS *E. Drood* iii, Until her face, which has been comically reflective, brightens.

c. Proceeding from, due to, reflection.

1863 E. V. NEALE *Anal. Th. & Nat.* vi. 71 The first half of such a judgment as 'the bridge is of iron, therefore it is strong', is only reflective. **1934** M. BODKIN *Archetypal Patterns in Poetry* 314 An hypothesis..that archetypal patterns, or images, are present within the experience communicated through poetry, and may be discovered there by reflective analysis. **1961** *Manas* 5 Apr. 1/2 Mr. Lyford gives voice to a temper that represents..an achieved plateau of reflective thinking.

B. *sb.* †**1.** A mirror. *Obs. rare*$^{-1}$.

1720 MRS. MANLEY *Secret Mem.* II. 251 If any one were but for ten Years forbid that View, and then to have the Reflective brought,..they would be..at a loss to know their own outward Form.

2. *pl.* The organs or faculties of reflection.

1895 *Funk's Stand. Dict.*

re'flectively, *adv.* [f. prec. + -LY^{2}.]

1. After reflection or consideration; deliberately.

1774 WRAXALL *Tour North. Europe* (1776) 260 Our English papers, which are reflectively and on principle the avowed vehicles of falshood over all Europe. **1875** WHITNEY *Life Lang.* ii. 16 A peculiar red..was, reflectively and artificially, called by its inventor magenta.

2. In a reflective or thoughtful manner; thoughtfully, meditatively.

1825 HONE *Every-day Bk.* I. 810 They..go homewards, reflectively. **1865** E. C. CLAYTON (Mrs. Needham) *Cruel Fortune* I. 244 'It does seem like it, to be sure, when one comes to think it over', observed Jessop, reflectively. **1887** *Spectator* 2 Apr. 458/2 Any one who looks back on it reflectively, and remembers rather than reads.

3. By way of reflection (from one thing to another); indirectly, in consequence.

1855 MISS COBBE *Intuit. Mor.* 70 It cannot be because the happiness of our brethren will reflectively produce our own. *a* **1876** HT. MARTINEAU *Autobiogr.* (1877) I. II. 101 We had ..a great reverence for Mrs. Barbauld and, reflectively, for Dr. Aikin, her brother.

re'flectiveness. [f. as prec. + -NESS.] The state or quality of being reflective.

1857 LEVER *Fortunes of Glencore* viii. (1873) 52 A charming union of reflectiveness with repartee. **1873** SYMONDS *Grk. Poets* i. 31 Music attains independence.. only in an age of intellectual reflectiveness.

reflec'tivity. [f. REFLECTIVE *a.* + -ITY.] = REFLECTIVENESS; *spec.* (*a*) the degree to which anything incident on a surface is reflected; (*b*) the degree to which a surface reflects what is incident upon it.

1881 MRS. LYNN LINTON *My Love* II. iii. 55 The value of the image is its comprehensiveness,..the facetted quality of its reflectivity. **1916** *Physical Rev.* VIII. 152 The reflectivity of metal atoms striking surfaces of the same metals at room temperature (or lower) is zero. **1936** *Discovery* Aug. 237/1 Steel mirrors of high reflectivity. **1946** [see ALUMINIZE *v.* 2]. **1966** *McGraw-Hill Encycl. Sci. & Technol.* XI. 395/1 Typical curves of the reflectivity of the polarized components versus angle of incidence are given in Fig. 7. **1974** *Mineral. Abstr.* XXV. 267/1 Reflectivities of pyrite.. and sphalerite were measured with POH microscope and SPS-1 microscope photometer.

†**re'flectly,** *adv. Obs.*$^{-1}$ [f. REFLECT *a.* + -LY^{2}.] In a reflected manner; by reflection.

1635 SWAN *Spec. M.* (1670) 293 The Optick Masters confess and prove, that the forms of the Stars are comprehended of the sight reflectly, and not rightly.

reflec'tometer. [See -OMETER.] Any of various instruments for measuring quantities associated with reflection; *spec.* (*a*) one for measuring the critical angle of a transparent solid so that its refractive index may be calculated; (*b*) one for measuring the intensity of light reflected or scattered by a surface so that its reflectance may be calculated.

1891 *Jrnl. Chem. Soc.* LX. 513 (*heading*) Measurement of refractive indices at high temperatures by means of the total reflectometer. **1895** *Times* 14 Jan. 4/6 Among new.. methods introduced by recent discoveries were the use of the reflectometer. **1920** *Sci. Papers U.S. Bureau of Standards* XVI. 435 The use of an incomplete sphere as a reflectometer furnishes two new absolute methods for the determination of diffuse reflection factors. **1935** *Sci. Abstr.* A. XXXVIII. 1223 (*heading*) Ultrasonic total reflectometer to measure speed of sound and elastic constants of solids. **1962** R. H. KAY in J. Thewlis *Encycl. Dict. Physics* VI. 240/1 Instruments primarily designed to measure reflecting power of materials are known as reflectometers and usually compare the test specimen against such a standard as magnesium oxide or aluminium. **1977** *Sci. Amer.* Feb. 88/3 (Advt.), A time domain reflectometer (TDR) works in a manner similar to radar. It generates repetitive pulses of energy that are sent down a cable and displayed on a cathode-ray tube screen. Any cable faults (impedance changes) cause pulse reflections. **1977** BOXALL & VON FRAUNHOFFER *Conc. Paint Technol.* ix. 193 The contrast ratio is the reflectometer reading obtained over the black tile after the reflectometer has been set to 100% over the white tile.

Hence **reflec'tometry.**

1967 *Jrnl. Optical Soc. Amer.* LVII. 445 (*heading*) Terms, definitions, and symbols in reflectometry. **1977** *Sci. Amer.* Feb. 88/2 (Advt.), I knew that the TV industry used time domain reflectometry a lot.

reflector (rɪˈflɛktə(r)). [f. REFLECT *v.* + -OR^{2}. Cf. REFLECTER and mod.F. *réflecteur*.]

1. One who reflects or meditates. *rare.*

1665 BOYLE *Occas. Refl.* Disc. Occ. Medit. (1848) 53 In that which we suppose our Reflector now considering. **1790** T. WILKINSON *Mem.* IV. 132 By which means [*sc.* comparing cast lists of 1747 and 1789] the unprejudiced reflector may draw a fair conclusion. **1921** W. C. BOOTH *Rhetoric of Fiction* I. vi. 157 It was not until authors had discovered the full uses of the third-person reflector that they could effectively show a narrator changing *as he narrates.*

†**2.** One who casts reflections; a censor, critic.

1688 in Somers *Tracts* (1748) I. 304 Had he been a Foreigner, as our Reflector terms him, it might have looked like an intended Conquest. **1748** RICHARDSON *Clarissa* lxxxvii. (1768) VII. 327 Mighty generous, I said,..in such insolent reflectors.

3. A reflecting telescope, microscope, etc.

1767 MICHELL in *Phil. Trans.* LVII. 261 To obtain such a pencil, we must not make use of a refracting telescope..of less than 15 inches, nor a reflector of less than nearly two feet aperture. **1794** G. ADAMS *Nat. & Exp. Philos.* I. xxii. 471 No reflector was heard of for near half a century after [Newton's]. **1837** GORING & PRITCHARD *Microgr.* 15 [Reflecting Engiscope.] A clasp of diaphragms to be applied to the tube of reflectors itself. **1868** LOCKYER *Guillemin's Heavens* (ed. 3) 485 Telescopes, both refractors and reflectors, are eagerly sought after.

4. a. A body or surface which reflects (rays of) light, heat, sound, etc. *spec.* in *Geol.*, a stratum or interface that reflects seismic waves.

1800 HENRY *Epit. Chem.* (1808) 30 Metals, therefore, are much better reflectors [of heat] than glass. **1863** J. G. MURPHY *Comm., Gen.* i. 16–19 The full-orbed reflector of the solar beams, as she is during the night. **1879** ROOD *Chromatics* 12 As a general thing polished metallic surfaces are the best reflectors of light. **1933** *Bull. Amer. Assoc. Petroleum Geologists* XVII. 258 The geologic section contains many strata which act as good reflectors of wave energy. **1952** C. H. DIX *Seismic Prospecting for Oil* xi. 217 In areas where the reflectors are almost planes with small dip and small variations of dip, the reflections carry across the records with little change in character or amplitude. **1965** *Bull. Amer. Assoc. Petroleum Geologists* XLIX. 352/1 Lateral continuity of these reflectors appears to be large compared to those within the..aprons and sea fans of the basins. **1978** *Nature* 29 June 744/1 The tilt of the terraces parallels a northwards dip of subsurface reflectors toward a sedimentary basin off Hudson Strait.

b. *spec.* A specially prepared surface of metal or glass (usually of a curved or concave form), for the purpose of reflecting rays of light or heat in a required direction. Also, something designed to reflect other forms of radiation (as radio waves or neutrons); e.g. part of a nuclear reactor designed to reflect escaping neutrons back into the core.

1797 *Encycl. Brit.* (ed. 3) X. 54/2 The effect of these [lamp-lights] may be increased by placing them.. before properly disposed glass or metal reflectors. **1801** *Ibid.* Suppl. II. 395/2 Reflector for a lighthouse is composed of a number of square plane glass mirrors. **1826** KIRBY & SP. *Entomol.* I. IV. 519 Cause a lanthorn to be made with a concave back, and furnished with a reflector. *c* **1860** FARADAY *Forces Nat., Electric Light* 153 At Teignmouth, some of the revolving lights have ten lamps and reflectors. **1897** *Strand Mag.* Mar. 277/1 How far have you sent a telegraphic despatch on the air?.. Did you use a reflector? **1909** *Proc. R. Soc.* A. LXXXII. 496 The zinc sulphide screen S..was fixed behind the lead plate P, in such a position that no α-particles could strike it directly. When a reflector was placed in the position RR at about 1 cm. from the end of the tube, scintillations were at once observed. **1923** E. W. MARCHANT *Radio Telegr. & Telephony* i. 11 The strength of the signal received, when reflectors were used, was estimated to be about 200 times as great as when there were no reflectors. **1943** *Gloss. Terms Telecomm.* (*B.S.I.*) 66 A passive aerial placed behind an active aerial is usually called a reflector. **1945** *Chemical Age* 27 Oct. 390/1 And the escape of neutrons from the system can be reduced (relatively) by increasing the size of the system, and by a reflector (*e.g.*, a layer of graphite). **1958** *Times* 1 July 7/3 It consists of an arrangement of enriched reactor fuel in ordinary water and will be used to investigate..the use of different materials as 'reflectors' (to reflect neutrons, which might otherwise escape, back into the core). **1977** N. FREELING *Gadget* I. 21 Cast a near-crit mass... Put a high-class reflector round it. **1978** *Nature* 9 Feb. 497/3 Chain reaction is unlikely, since the mass of uranium used in such satellites is normally subcritical, and special methods, e.g. a reflector, must be used to keep sufficient neutrons within it to maintain a chain reaction.

c. A piece of reflective material, now commonly a red disc, mounted at the rear of a vehicle or by the roadside so as to show its presence by reflecting the light from headlights.

1909 *Cyclist Touring Club Gaz.* Dec. 544/1 If a rearward indication is considered desirable, the Lea Reflex reflector and lens does everything needful... It throws back the light of the overtaking vehicle in a red glow through a wide angle. **1931** *Highway Code* 13 If you do not use a red rear lamp remember to keep your red reflector clean and properly fixed. **1962** *Which? Car Suppl.* Oct. 133/1 We checked the position of all lamps and reflectors. **1972** A. PRICE *Colonel Butler's Wolf* vii. 68 'He came directly down the road... His headlight 'ud pick up the first of the reflectors. Even my bicycle light picks 'em up.'.. 'Then supposing a car came round the corner as he was approaching it—could it have cut off the reflectors and then blinded him?' 'Mmmm—it could have, I suppose—but it would have lit 'em all up first and warned him there was a corner here.' **1978** *Highway Code* 35 Make sure your cycle is safe to ride. At night you must have front and rear lamps and a rear reflector.

5. a. A polished surface exhibiting images of objects; also *spec.* (see quot. 1894).

1831 BREWSTER *Nat. Magic* vi. (1833) 147 Where or what the reflector could be which exhibited this image, I cannot conceive. **1839** G. BIRD *Nat. Philos.* 300 The images of the objects placed between the reflectors are seen most beautifully arranged when the latter form an angle, which is an even aliquot part of a circle. **1894** *Westm. Gaz.* 23 Apr. 3/1 Sometimes..the sharper..has recourse to..'reflectors'. These are exceedingly well-made little instruments..used to 'reflect'..the cards held by the players.

fig. **1837** HT. MARTINEAU *Soc. Amer.* III. 32 The children are such faithful reflectors of this spirit as to leave no doubt of its existence, even amidst the nicest operations of cant.

b. *spec.* The speculum of a reflecting telescope.

1815 J. SMITH *Panorama Sc. & Art* I. 492 [Gregorian Telescope.] At the bottom of the tube..is placed the large concave reflector. **1871** ROSCOE *Elem. Chem.* 185 An alloy of 33 parts of tin to 67 of copper..is known as speculum-metal and employed for the reflectors of telescopes.

6. That which reflects, in other senses.

1840 *Penny Cycl.* XVI. 153/1 They..lose themselves in its central grey matter—the recipient and reflector of the impressions which they convey.

Hence **re'flectored** *a.*, of a lamp: fitted with a reflecting surface or surfaces.

1916 A. BENNETT *These Twain* xix. 429 The glittering light of the latest triple-jetted and reflectored gas-lamps which the corporation..had placed in Crown Square. **1978** *Amer. N. & Q.* Dec. 65/2 Pierre Patte's early advocacy of reflectored lights in the auditorium.

reflec'torially, *adv. rare.* [f. as REFLECTORY *a.* + -AL^{1} + -LY^{2}.] Reflexly, by reflex action.

1876 BRISTOWE *Th. & Pract. Med.* (1878) 759 Peristaltic movements, for the most part reflectorially excited from the mucous surface.

reflectorize (rɪˈflɛktəraɪz), *v.* orig. *U.S.* [f. REFLECTOR + -IZE.] *trans.* To treat or coat with a substance that reflects light. Chiefly as **re'flectorized** *ppl. a.*

1942 *New Hampshire Highway Signs & Road Marking* 56 Route markers 24" × 24" white or black. Plain or reflectorized. **1947** *Sun* (Baltimore) 22 May 2/5 A bus accident in Texas has resulted in one of several attempts by that state to reflectorize curb surfaces to enhance driving safety. *Ibid.*, A traffic circle where the reflectorized surface now warns fast drivers that the road does not go straight on. **1951** *Richmond* (Va.) *Times-Dispatch* 15 Feb. 7/6 More and more 'reflectorized' paint—the kind that gleams brilliantly under automobile lights at night—is being used to mark traffic lanes on Virginia highways. **1959** *B.S.I. News* Mar. 4/2 (*caption*) Left to right: sign with button reflectors, sign reflectorized all-over, painted sign. **1961** *Evening Star* (Dunedin, N.Z.) 28 Mar. 1/7 They signalled with torches and skipped out of the path of the oncoming traffic which even knocked down large reflectorised stop signs. **1967** *New Scientist* 26 Jan. 225/2 A great improvement on the type of number plate now in use in Britain would be one with black letters on a white, 'reflectorized' background. **1973** *Houston Chron.* 21 Oct. 9 (Advt.), Bicycle has black saddle and grips. 20" × 1·75" tires. Fully reflectorized for safety. **1978** *Highway Code* 15 Watch out for blind people who may be carrying white sticks (white with two red reflectorised bands for deaf/blind people).

re'flectory, *a. rare*$^{-0}$. [f. REFLECT *v.* + -ORY.] Capable of being reflected (*Cent. Dict.*).

reflectoscope (rɪˈflɛktəskəʊp). [f. REFLECT *v.* + -O + -SCOPE.] An instrument for investigating opaque bodies by transmitting ultrasound into them and measuring its reflection.

1944 *Sun* (Baltimore) 26 May 9/1 The invention, credited to Dr. Floyd A. Firestone, physicist and acoustics expert, is known as the 'supersonic reflectoscope'... The machine can gauge thickness of metal when one side is inaccessible. **1964** I. EDLER in D. Gordon *Ultrasound as Diagnostic & Surg. Tool* xiv. 124 The apparatus used for ultrasound-cardiography is an ultrasound reflectoscope.

re'fledge, *v.* [RE- 5 a.] *trans.* To fledge again. Hence **re'fledging** *vbl. sb.*

1829 SOUTHEY *Pilgr. Compostella* II. xxi, In flew the feathers,..And the Cock and the Hen in a trice were refledged. **1850** BROWNING *Easter Day* xxiv, Scared if the South firmament With North-fire did its wings refledge! **1889** PATER *G. de Latour* (1896) 63 The flush and re-fledging of the black earth itself in that fervent springtide.

reflee, *v.* [RE- 5 a.] *intr.* To flee again.

1598 SYLVESTER *Du Bartas* II. ii. IV. *Columnes* 672 Yet thence, re-fled, it [astronomy] doth th' Arabians try.

‖**reflet** (rəflɛ). [F., earlier *reflés*, ad. It. *riflesso* reflection, REFLEX *sb.*: the modern spelling has app. been influenced by L. *reflectere*.] Colour due to reflection, lustre, iridescence; *spec.* a metallic lustre on pottery.

1862 H. MARRYAT *Year in Sweden* II. 258 Black wool, with a silvery 'reflet', or iron gray. **1888** *Athenæum* 6 Oct. 454/1 The pottery..errs in the extreme of coppery tints and too emphatic *reflets* of the metallic sort.

attrib. **1886** S. G. W. BENJAMIN *Persia & the Persians* 287 The reflêt tiles in which a copper tint is prominent may be considered as generally coming from Nathenz.

reflex (ˈriːflɛks, rɪˈflɛks), *sb.* [ad. late L. *reflex-us*, a bending back, recess, return, f. ppl. stem of *reflectĕre* to REFLECT. Cf. Sp. *reflejo* (*-flexo*), It. *riflesso*.]

1. a. Reflection of light (or heat); reflected light; light or colour resulting from reflection.

App. not in common use from *c* 1660 to 1840.

1508 DUNBAR *Gold. Targe* 33 Bewis bathit war in secund bemys Throu the reflex of Phebus visage brycht. **1594**

BLUNDEVIL *Exerc.* III. II. iii. (1636) 377 The lowest Region is hot by the reflexe of the Sunne, whose beames first striking the earth, do rebound back againe to that Region. **1615** W. LAWSON *Country Housew. Gard.* (1626) 3 Quinches..will not like in our cold parts, vnlesse they be helped with some reflex of Sunne. **1621** QUARLES *Argalus & P.* Wks. (Grosart) III. 261 Shall every day, wherein the earth does lack The Sun's reflex, b' expell'd the Almanack? *a* **1711** KEN *Hymns Festiv.* Poet. Wks. 1721 I. 222 Who taught her Love to Heav'n the readiest way On his Reflex of Fontal Godhead's Ray. **1843** CARLYLE *Past & Pr.* II. ii, The illimitable Ocean, tinting all things with its eternal hues and reflexes. **1853** C. BRONTE *Villette* xiv, The reflex from the window..lit his face. **1874** LAWSON *Dis. Eye* 159 The margin of the lens exhibiting a brilliant yellow reflex.

trans. and *fig.* **1602** FULBECKE *2nd Pt. Parall.* 74 If God doe still vouchsafe the Moone-diall of this darksome life, with the reflexe of his intellectuall illumined influence. **1647** CLARENDON *Contempl. Ps.* Tracts (1727) 437 We shall have always some such rays of comfort from the reflex of that beautiful prospect. **1862** MERIVALE *Rom. Emp.* (1865) V. xl. 8 The fame of ancient Hellas was mainly a reflex from the preeminent glory of Athens. **1866** FENTON *Anc. & Mod. Gr.* II. v. 358 The transient reflex of ancient prosperity..sank in the long night of slavery.

b. *spec.* in *Art* and *Arch.* The light reflected, or supposed to be reflected, from a surface in light to one in shade.

1695 in Dryden tr. *Dufresnoy Obs.* ¶200 The fineness of stuffs or garments which is not to be discern'd but by the Colours, the Reflexes, and more especially by the Lights and Shadows. **1727–41** CHAMBERS *Cycl., Reflex, Reflect*, in painting, is understood of those places in a picture which are supposed to be illuminated by a light reflected from some other body represented in the same piece. **1784** J. BARRY in *Lect. Paint.* v. (1848) 182 Masses of light, half-lights, darks and half-darks, and reflexes. **1807** OPIE *ibid.* iii. 296 Gradations of middle tint, local colour, and reflexes. **1842** GWILT *Archit.* §2484 The varieties of reflexes are almost infinite.

2. a. The reflection or image of an object, as seen in a mirror or surface acting as such.

1638 SIR T. HERBERT *Trav.* (ed. 2) 146 Black shining Marble..so bright and jetty, as we could easily view our reflex, no steel mirror comparing with it. **1663** *Aron-bimn.* 12 Spots in the Sun and Moon are better discovered by observing them in their Reflexes and Images in the Water. **1805** WORDSW. *Prelude* I. 450 To cut across the reflex of a star That..gleamed Upon the glassy plain. **1830** TENNYSON *Poems* 124 So their wan limbs no more might come between The moon and the moon's reflex in the night.

fig. **1643** SIR T. BROWNE *Relig. Med.* I. §13 We behold Him but asquint, upon reflex or shadow.

b. *fig.* An image, reproduction; something which reproduces certain essential features or qualities of another thing. (The usual sense in current use.)

1683 KENNETT tr. *Erasm. on Folly* 5 My Visage, the exact reflex of my Soul. **1816–17** COLERIDGE *Lay Serm.* (Bohn) 416 As the motley reflexes of my experience move in long procession..before me. **1847** DISRAELI *Tancred* VI. viii, It was the race that produced these inimitable forms, the idealised reflex of their own peculiar organisation. **1878** LECKY *Eng. in 18th C.* I. ii. 180 It may even very materially contribute to make legislation a reflex of the popular will.

c. *Linguistics.* A form (word, sound unit, etc.) corresponding to, or derived from, another comparable form.

1890 S. PRIMER in *PMLA* V. II. 196 It is doubtful whether it [*sc.* the *a*-sound] is a reflex of the older pronunciation. **1945** Y. MALKIEL in *Univ. Calif. Publ. Linguistics* I. IV. iii. 51, -entia seems to have taken root in Italy more than anywhere else, as follows from the..reflexes of *absentia, haerentia, licentia, negligentia, scientia*. **1965** A. ZETTERSTEN *Stud. Dial. & Vocab. Ancrene Riwle* 67 It is necessary to emphasize that this Mercian sound coalesced with the reflexes of /æ/ and /a/ in ME. **1970** *Publ. Amer. Dial. Soc.* LIV. 4 This chapter presents the regionally divergent reflexes of Middle English parent phonemes. **1971** J. ANDERSON in A. J. Aitken et al. *Edin. Stud. Eng. & Scots* 110 The permutation of *may* and the subject [in *May your cabbages wither away*] is the superficial reflex of this underlying structure [*I wish that your cabbages may wither away*]. **1975** *Language* LI. 983 The assumption is..that the different reflexes of the same unit are due to phonetic change, either in the lending or the borrowing language, and that therefore the borrowings took place at different times.

†**3. a.** The act of bending or turning the mind (back) *upon* a subject; reflection. *Obs.*

1594 HOOKER *Eccl. Pol.* I. iv. §3 It seemeth therefore that there was no other way for angels to sin, but by reflex of their understanding upon themselves. **1643** SIR T. BROWNE *Relig. Med.* I. §7 A serious reflex upon my own unworthiness did make me backward from challenging this prerogative of my Soul. **1658** T. WALL *Charact. Enemies Ch.* 46 Pride was first begot in Heaven by the reflex of an Angels understanding upon his own excellency.

b. A reflection; a remark made after consideration. *Obs.*

a **1641** BP. MOUNTAGU *Acts & Mon.* (1642) 377 Saint Jerom's Reflexe upon a passage of Tertullian's examined. **1660** HOWELL (*title*) The Parly of Beasts,..with Reflexes upon the present State of most Countries in Christendome.

†**4.** A glance or side look (*lit.* and *fig.*); indirect reference or allusion. *Obs.*

1630 BRATHWAIT *Eng. Gentlem.* (1641) 15, I have not a little wondered..how any man, having reflex, by the eye of his Soule, to his first fall, should glory in these..rags of shame. **1646** J. GREGORY *Notes & Obs.* (1650) 96 The præcepts in the Law..are still set downe with a reflex upon the Heathen Rites. **1650** ELDERFIELD *Tythes* 148 Sometimes in direct assertion, oftner by glance and occasionall reflexe, but by supposition constantly ever.

†**5.** Return, rebound; indirect action or operation. *Obs.*

a **1613** OVERBURY *A Wife*, etc. (1638) 45 Whence in their face, the Faire no pleasure have, But by reflex of what thence other take. **1626** LAUD *Serm.* v. Wks. 1847 I. 131 Some directly concern God, and some only by reflex. **1683** D. A. *Art Converse* 44 Let us abstain from railery least it return by reflex upon our selves.

6. *Phys.* **a.** A reflex action. Also in literary use.

1877 LEWES *Phys. Basis Mind* 461 The sensations of contact and temperature will excite reflexes. **1899** *Allbutt's Syst. Med.* VI. 905 In the early stages of the disease the reflexes are increased. **1921** G. B. SHAW *Back to Methuselah* v. 238 Martellus: Control your reflexes, child. The Newly Born: My what! Martellus: Your reflexes. The things you do without thinking.

b. *attrib.*, as ***reflex apparatus, mechanism, movement, stimulus, therapy, time***; **reflex arc**, the connected set of nerves concerned in the production of a reflex action. Cf. REFLEX *a.* 5.

1924 R. M. OGDEN tr. *Koffka's Growth of Mind* iii. 77 This statement..agrees..with what we have already learned about the reflex-apparatus. **1882** B. BRAMWELL *Dis. Spinal Cord* i. 24 Every half segment of the spinal cord with its sensory and motor nerve roots is, in theory and probably also in fact, a perfect reflex arc. *Ibid.* 25 The multipolar nerve cells of the anterior cornua probably constitute the centre of this reflex arc. **1924** R. M. OGDEN tr. *Koffka's Growth of Mind* iii. 69 Always beginning with a sensory neurone and ending with a motor neurone, this apparatus is called a reflex-arc. **1976** *Radiol. Clin. N. Amer.* XIV. 432/2 The reflex arcs controlling normal esophogeal motility are interrupted by disease of the medullary nuclei. **1885** *Encycl. Brit.* XIX. 29/1 Stimulation of a sensory surface may simultaneously produce, by a reflex mechanism, movement, secretion and consciousness. **1924** R. M. OGDEN tr. *Koffka's Growth of Mind* iii. 69 A reflex-mechanism is..conceived as a pre-determined, inherited connection between afferent (receptor) and efferent (effector) pathways. *Ibid.* 91 A stimulus excites a reflex-movement. **1937** *Discovery* Nov. 341/1 When the reasoning powers are great, as in man, the mind is less responsive to outside influences or reflex stimuli. **1956** A. HUXLEY *Adonis & Alphabet* 31 Unorthodox medicine tries to influence the autonomic system by direct mechanical action in the form of osteopathy, chiropractic, reflex therapy and acupuncture. **1913** *Amer. Jrnl. Physiol.* XXXI. 309 How soon, after administering a minimal and also stronger dose of alcohol, does a change in reflex time appear? **1964** L. MARTIN *Clin. Endocrinol.* (ed. 4) iii. 135 Delayed tendon reflexes are characteristic, and particularly the ankle jerks. Sherman *et al.* (1963) measured the reflex-time in 50 hypothyroid cases and considered that the increase had a diagnostic significance.

7. *Photogr.* A reflex camera. Cf. REFLEX *a.* 7.

1926–7 *Army & Navy Stores Catal.* 969/2 Reflex cameras. The 'Mentor' Folding Reflex is constructed..of the finest materials. **1940** *Wall's Dict. Photogr.* (ed. 15) 548 A twin-lens reflex consists of a rigid box which forms the camera, on top of which is mounted a structure such as that shown in the sketch, but with the mirror fixed in position. **1948** H. S. NEWCOMBE *Twin-Lens Camera Compan.* 15 Other people also find it difficult to hold a normal reflex steady. **1958** *Oxford Mail* 19 May 7/3 In the single-lens reflex you actually focus by looking through the camera lens with a mirror. **1977** J. HEDGECOE *Photographer's Handbk.* 14/1 The single lens reflex is the most highly developed and deservedly popular camera for advanced work.

reflex ('riːflɛks, rɪ'flɛks), *a.* [ad. L. *reflex-us*, pa. pple. of *reflectĕre* to REFLECT. Cf. F. *réflexe* (16th c.), Sp. *reflejo* (*-flexo*), It. *riflesso*.]

1. a. Bent or turned back; recurved.

1658 ROWLAND *Moufet's Theat. Ins.* 957 They couple sometime with their tails averse, sometimes reflex. **1752** J. HILL *Hist. Anim.* 64 A number of white, reflex hairs. **1753** CHAMBERS *Cycl. Supp.* s.v. *Leaf, Reclinate* or *reflex Leaf*, one which has its summit lower than its base. **1791** COWPER *Iliad* III. 418 At the disk, with blunted point Reflex, his ineffectual weapon stay'd. **1869** DUNKIN *Midn. Sky* 15 The reflex zenith-tube.

Comb. **1825** *Greenhouse Comp.* II. 25 *M*[*alva*] *tridactyloides*, reflex-flowered Mallow,..a shrub introduced from the Cape of Good Hope in 1791.

†**b.** Of motion: Reversed or changed after impact.

1704 NORRIS *Ideal World* II. iii, We say a motion is..reflex when there is a change of its determination upon the rencontre of another body which it cannot move or displace.

2. a. Of light, rays, etc.: Reflected.

1681 FLAVEL *Right. Man's Ref.* 256 Our love to God is but the reflex beam of his love to us. *c* **1705** BERKELEY *Commonpl. Bk.* Wks. 1871 IV. 465 No more than a deformed person ought to cavil to behold himself by the reflex light of a mirror. **1772** MASON *Eng. Garden* I. 23 Whose mighty mind,..mirror like, Receiv'd, and to mankind with ray reflex The sov'reign Planter's primal work display'd. **1881** SHORTHOUSE *J. Inglesant* (1882) II. 152 A reflex light, ethereal and wonderful, coming from the sky behind him.

fig. **1847** EMERSON *Repr. Men, Montaigne* Wks. (Bohn) I. 349 The last class must needs have a reflex or parasite faith.

b. Reflected, as in a mirror. *rare*$^{-1}$.

1678 CUDWORTH *Intell. Syst.* I. v. 638 A kind of Notional World, which hath some Reflex Image, and correspondent Ray,..to whatsoever is in the true and real world of being.

3. a. Of acts of thought: Directed or turned back upon the mind itself or its operations. Chiefly in ***reflex act***.

1649 JER. TAYLOR *Gt. Exemp.* I. III. §9 The Soul..can produce the same effects by reflex acts of the understanding. *a* **1676** HALE *Prim. Orig. Man.* I. i. (1677) 24 Which I call the reflex act of the Soul, or the turning of the intellectual eye inward upon its own actions. **1704** NORRIS *Ideal World* II. iii. 120, I conceive that then thought is said to be..reflex, when the same act of thought terminates upon itself, or is its own object. **1768–74** TUCKER *Lt. Nat.* (1834) I. 129 There is a reflex act, whereby the mind turns inward upon herself to observe what ideas arise in her view. **1850** MCCOSH *Div. Govt.* (1852) 312 The delightful sensations of moral approbation which rise up on the reflex contemplation of such affection. **1870** J. H. NEWMAN *Gram. Assent* II. vi. 158 An act of consciousness..is a reflex act with its own object, viz. the act of knowledge itself.

b. Derived from, consisting in, the conversion of the mind or thought upon itself.

a **1652** J. SMITH *Sel. Disc.* iv. 82 This reflex knowledge whereby we know what it is to know. **1665** GLANVILL *Scepsis Sci.* i. 14 A pure intellectual eye may have a sight of it in reflex discoveries. **1736** BUTLER *Anal.* Diss. ii. 311 It does not appear, that Brutes have the least reflex Sense of Actions as distinguished from Events. **1850** MCCOSH *Div. Govt.* III. i. (1874) 331 When the reflex moral faculty, or the conscience, surveys virtuous action, it proclaims it good.

4. Coming by way of return or reflection.

1822 HAZLITT *Table-t.* Ser. II. xviii. (1869) 376 It is the immediate pursuit, not the remote or reflex consequence that gives wings to the passion. **1833** CHALMERS *Const. Man* (1834) I. ii. 100 The secondary or reflex gratification which there is in the consciousness of benevolence. **1866** DK. ARGYLL *Reign Law* i. (ed. 4) 12 That knowledge has a reflex influence on our knowledge of ourselves.

5. *Phys.* **a.** ***reflex action***, involuntary action of a muscle, gland, or other organ, caused by the excitation of a sensory nerve being transmitted to a nerve-centre, and thence 'reflected' along an efferent nerve to the organ in question; also in extended or *fig.* use.

1833 *Proc. Royal Soc.* III. 210 He [Dr. M. Hall] distinguishes muscular actions into three kinds:..thirdly, those resulting from the reflex action above described [see REFLECT *v.* 4]. **1840** *Penny Cycl.* XVI. 153/1 In decapitated animals (in which the reflex actions are more remarkable than under any other circumstances). *a* **1846** B. R. HAYDON *Autobiogr.* (1927) III. xv. 278 He [*sc.* Wordsworth]..had a portion of the spirit of the mighty ones..but..did not possess the power of using that spirit otherwise than with reference to himself and so as to excite a reflex action only. **1851** CARPENTER *Man. Phys.* (ed. 2) 518 From the best judgment we can form of the actions of the Star-fish,..we may fairly regard the greater number of them as simply reflex. **1872** DARWIN *Emotions* i. 35 Coughing and sneezing are familiar instances of reflex actions. **1917** KIPLING *Diversity of Creatures* 159 Only the Lord can understand.. How much is reflex action and How much is really sin.

b. Of the nature of, characterized by, or connected with, such action.

1833 M. HALL in *Proc. Royal Soc.* III. 210 On the Reflex Function of the Medulla Oblongata and Spinalis. **1840** *Penny Cycl.* XVI. 151/2 When the spinal chord remains, its passage may be indicated by the phenomena of reflex motion. **1878** FOSTER *Phys.* II. i. §2. 208 The ganglion in fact acted as a reflex centre. **1899** *Allbutt's Syst. Med.* VII. 618 The natural and imperious reflex cough being diminished.. by the depth of coma.

6. *Gram.* Reflexive.

1873 EARLE *Philol. Eng. Tongue* (ed. 2) §469 The accusative pronoun of all the persons performed for a long period the double office of a direct and a reflex pronoun.

7. *Photogr.* Applied to a camera in which the image from the main lens (or from a duplicate of it) is reflected by means of a mirror on to a glass screen and can be seen and adjusted up to the moment of exposure.

1895 W. DE W. ABNEY *Instantaneous Photogr.* p. v (Advt.), The 'Reflex' Manufacturing Company..Patentees and Sole Manufacturers of the 'Reflex' Camera... The actual working lens also serves for the finder. **1911** *Encycl. Brit.* XXI. 505/2 Although reflex cameras are rather heavy and bulky as hand cameras, they have many advantages over the ordinary hand camera. **1946** R. J. C. ATKINSON *Field Archaeol.* v. 157 The chief advantage of the reflex type of camera is the full-sized focusing-screen, which is a valuable aid to composing the photograph and to exact focusing. **1976** *Daily Mail* (Hull) 30 Sept. 2/6 (Advt.), Edixa SL, 35 mm. Reflex Camera, flash gun, quartz, cine camera, lenses, etc; £32. **1976** J. TATE tr. *A. Bodelsen's Operation Cobra* v. 27 As neither his mother nor his father earned so much money now, he knew he could not reckon on getting a reflex camera.

8. *Electronics.* **a.** Applied to a circuit, amplifier, etc., in which the same valves or transistors are used for amplification of both high- and low-frequency signals (usu. the radio and audio frequencies respectively); also applied to the action of such a device.

1923 *Radio News* Feb. 1455/1 Very much discussion has been carried on as to the practicability of the so-called reflex circuit—a circuit designed, developed and patented in April and November of 1917 by Mr. Marius Latour, a French radio engineer. **1924** W. JAMES *Construction Two-Valve & Crystal Reflex Receiver* 3 The first valve is connected to operate as a dual or reflex amplifier; that is, it gives high-frequency and low-frequency-amplification. **1928** LAUER & BROWN *Radio Engin. Princ.* (ed. 2) vii. 163 (*heading*) Reflex amplification. **1934** *Pract. Wireless* 1 Sept. 723/1 Reflex circuits are rarely used at the present time, although they were extremely popular between 1922 and 1924. *Ibid.*, It is possible to obtain the same output from two valves wired in a reflex arrangement as from three valves connected in a more conventional circuit. **1957** R. F. SHEA *Transistor Circuit Engin.* xi. 375 When size and cost are of extreme importance, reflex circuits may be used. **1961** J. M. CARROLL *Design Man. for Transistor Circuits* viii. 154 Reflex circuits in which i-f and a-f gain are achieved in the same transistor stage have recently been incorporated into economy broadcast receivers.

b. Applied to an oscillator, esp. a klystron, in which the same resonant cavity serves to modulate the electron beam and to produce an amplified microwave signal.

1942 J. G. BRAINERD et al. *Ultra-High-Frequency Techniques* x. 339 A reflex klystron oscillator, in which a single resonator acts both as the buncher and the catcher. **1945** *Proc. IRE* XXXIII. 112/2 Reflex oscillators can be considered as oscillators in which an electron stream passes through a longitudinal radio-frequency field across a 'gap' between two electrodes, then into a drift space in which there is a retarding electric field produced by a negative repeller electrode, and finally returns through the radio-frequency field across the gap. 1969 *IEEE Trans. Industr. Electronics* XVI. 103/1 The oscillation frequency of a reflex klystron is determined by..the size of the cavity resonator. 1975 D. G. FINK *Electronics Engineers' Handbk.* IX. 31 Reflex Klystrons are used as test signal sources, receiver local oscillators, pump sources for parametric amplifiers, and low-power transmitters for FM line-of-sight relays.

9. Applied to a photocopying process in which the original document is illuminated by light passing through a piece of sensitized paper placed in contact with it, a negative image being formed on the paper according to the amount of light reflected by the original; also applied to equipment or materials connected with such a process.

1943 *Jrnl. Sci. Instruments* XX. 18/1 The Kodak Reflex plate has been introduced to solve the problem of the exact preservation of scale in copying maps, machine drawings and other line diagrams. *Ibid.*, The latter [distortion] is eliminated by the nature of reflex copying. *Ibid.*, Reflex printing has been carried out with photographic paper for a number of years. 1947 *Jrnl. R. Aeronaut. Soc.* LI. 318/1 The exposure is made through the paper with a yellow reflex screen. *Ibid.*, A plasticising solution is applied to the cellulose film and the exposed reflex paper is then laminated on to the material. 1956 'C. BLACKSTOCK' *Dewey Death* vii. 149 We then take a piece of..reflex contact document paper—the shiny side is the business end. 1958 T. LANDAU *Encycl. Librarianship* 267/2 The principle of reflex copying was established by Albrecht Breyer of Berlin,..who in 1839 produced reflex prints by placing silver chloride papers in contact with printed pages. 1972 A. TYRRELL *Basics of Reprography* xiii. 210 Reflex printing by the diffusion-transfer technique has been very popular... Attempts have been made to use diazo-sensitizers in reflex copying.

reflex (rɪˈflɛks), *v.* [f. L. *reflex-*, ppl. stem of *reflectĕre* to REFLECT.]

1. *trans.* To bend, fold back, recurve; = REFLECT *v.* 2. Chiefly *Her.* and *Bot.*, and only in pa. pple. (cf. REFLEXED *ppl. a.* 4).

1572 BOSSEWELL *Armorie* II. 48 The fielde is verte, twoo Apes..combattante, with tayles reflexed. 1610 GUILLIM *Heraldry* VI. vii. (1611) 280 A chaine..passing betweene his fore legs and reflexed ouer his backe. 1655 FULLER *Wounded Consc., Ornithologie* (1867) 244 This Eagle had its bill..reflexed back again into his mouth. 1760 J. LEE *Introd. Bot.* II. xvii. (1765) 107 The Stigma bipartite and acute, with the lower Lacinia reflexed. 1771 *Antiq. Sarisb.* 182 A monster lying at his feet, with his head reflext on his tail. 1861 MRS. LANKESTER *Wild Fl.* 125 The petals are reflexed, and turn over. 1868 CUSSANS *Her.* 209 *note*, Their tails passing between their legs, and reflexed over their backs. 1875 DARWIN *Insectiv. Pl.* iv. 71 With the outer tentacles slightly reflexed.

†**2.** To reflect (light, vision, etc.). *Obs.*

c1380 [see REFLEXED *ppl. a.* 1]. a1586 *Satir. Poems Reform.* xxxvii. 22 Ay moir brycht and burning is þe beymis Off Phebus face, þat fastast ar reflexit. 1594 R. ASHLEY tr. *Loys le Roy* 4 The Sun beames reflexed doe heate. 1658 tr. *Porta's Nat. Magic* VIII. 230 The Cockatrice..giveth venimous wounds with the beams of his eyes: which being reflexed upon himself,..kill the Author of them.

†**b.** To throw, cast (beams) *on* a place. *Obs.*

1586 MARLOWE *1st Pt. Tamburl.* III. i, For neither rain can fall upon the earth, Nor sun reflex his virtuous beams thereon. 1591 SHAKS. *1 Hen. VI*, v. iv. 87 May neuer glorious Sunne reflex his beames Vpon the Countrey where you make abode.

†**3.** To reflect, mirror, image (an object). *Obs.*

1633 DRUMM. OF HAWTH. *Entertainm. Charles* Wks. (1856) 228 When Iber's streams reflex'd thy glorious face! 1657 W. RAND tr. *Gassendi's Life Peiresc* II. 96 Contemplate the Image being reflexed by the Retina and restored.

†**4.** *intr.* Of heat: To strike *upon* a thing, and be reflected. *Obs.*⁻¹

1632 LITHGOW *Trav.* VI. 292 What with..the great heate reflexing vpon the sand, and from the sand to our faces, we were miserably turmoiled.

†**5.** To reflect, meditate, etc., *on* a subject. *Obs.*

1631 R. H. *Arraignm. Whole Creature* iv. 22 To drive this naile further to the very head: reflexing more fully on the Prodigals huskes.

†**reflexcye.** *Obs. rare*⁻¹. [app. f. REFLEX *sb.* or *a.* + -CY, but perhaps a misprint.] Reflection.

1589 *Almond for Parrat* 16 The very reflexcye of my fury, shall make thee driue thy father to the gallows, for begetting thee.

reflexed (rɪˈflɛkst), *ppl. a.* [f. REFLEX *v.*]

1. Of light, etc.: Reflected, thrown back; due to, or caused by, reflection.

c1380 WYCLIF *Sel. Wks.* II. 299 Þe þridde siȝt is reflexid whan it comeþ bi dyvers meenes, and þei ben on divers kyndis, as þe moone is seen aȝens niȝt. 1595 J. KING *Queens Day Serm.* in *Jonas* (1618) 690 Our loue to other..comming as broken and reflexed beames from our loue to God. 1615 JACKSON *Creed* IV. III. viii. §5 Any reflexed splendour from the favourable aspect of earthly majesty. 1662 BARGRAVE *Pope Alex. VII* (1867) 134 This glass..will render the reflexed species of the outward object full and large.

†**2.** Directed backwards. Cf. REFLEX *a.* 3. *Obs.*

1656 in Clarendon *Hist. Reb.* xv. §113 When we take a reflexed [1704 reflex] view of our past actions. 1659 *Gentl. Calling* (1696) 102 Cheating has usually a reflexed efficacy, and deceives none more than those that use it. a1676 HALE *Prim. Orig. Man.* I. i. (1677) 20 By considering the reflexed acts of our Understanding, whereby we know many acts of our own minds and Soul.

†**3.** = REFLEX *a.* 4. *Obs. rare*⁻¹.

1667 *Decay Chr. Piety* v. ¶11 This secondary and reflext apologie for Christs law.

4. Turned, bent, or folded back. Cf. REFLEX *v.* 1.

1733 MILLER *Gard. Dict.* (ed. 2) s.v. *Cassia*, Barbadoes Cassia, with a reflex'd Cup, and pointed leaves. 1818 KIRBY & SP. *Entomol.* xxi. (ed. 2) II. 238 The reflexed head simulating a tail curled over its back. 1854 HOOKER *Himal. Jrnls.* II. xx. 77 Inflated reflexed bracts, that conceal the flowers. 1882 *Garden* 7 Oct. 312/2 A very handsome and full reflexed flower.

Comb. 1777 LIGHTFOOT *Flora Scot.* II. 755 Reflex'd-leav'd Hypnum.

b. (See quot.)

1836 RAFINESQUE *Amer. Nations* I. ii. 66 The Resupinate or Reflexed Group [of American languages]: where the roots or nouns substantive are reversed, following the adjectives or epithetes, which are prefixed.

reflexiˈbility. [f. next + -ITY. Cf. F. *réflexibilité* (14th c., Oresme; but in mod. use adopted from English).] Capability of being reflected.

1673 NEWTON in Rigaud *Corr. Sci. Men* (1841) II. 351 Whence it is that the same rays exhibit the same colours, when separated by any other means; as by their different reflexibility. 1728 PEMBERTON *Newton's Philos.* 370 The sun's light differs in reflexibility, those rays being most reflexible, which are most refrangible. 1797 BROUGHAM in *Phil. Trans.* LXXXVII. 375 It is evident, that neither reflexibility nor refrangibility will account for either sort of rings. 1808 HERSCHEL *ibid.* XCIX. 267 In consequence of the different reflexibility of the differently coloured rays.

reflexible (rɪˈflɛksɪb(ə)l), *a.* [f. REFLEX *v.* Hence F. *réflexible.*] Capable of being reflected.

1706 W. JONES *Syn. Palmar. Matheseos* 301 The Light of the Sun consists of Rays that are differently Reflexible and Refrangible. 1794 J. HUTTON *Philos. Light*, etc. 29 Such an opinion, as that heat is a thing eradiated and reflexible. 1822 IMISON *Sc. & Art* I. 229 The waves of sound being thus reflexible, nearly in the same manner as the rays of light.

So **reˈflexile** *a. nonce-wd.*

1797 BROUGHAM in *Phil. Trans.* LXXXVII. 384 The rays which are most flexible..are most refrangile, reflexile, and flexile.

†**reˈflexing,** *ppl. a. Obs. rare.* [f. REFLEX *v.* + -ING².] That reflects, in senses of the vb.

1606 J. RAYNOLDS *Dolarney's Prim.* (1880) 62 The hot reflexing rayes Of bright Apollo. 1632 LITHGOW *Trav.* x. 488 This reflexing heart..Can by experience conster well, your Churches Sire and Dame.

ˈreflexing, *vbl. sb. Electronics.* [f. REFLEX *a.* + -ING¹.] The use or action of a reflex circuit.

1925 A. H. MORSE *Radio* ii. 60 The modern practice of 'reflexing', or amplifying both audio and radio-frequency in a single triode. 1939 *A. W. A. Techn. Rev.* IV. 37 Reflexing does not appreciably reduce the higher audio note response. 1961 J. M. CARROLL *Design Man. for Transistor Circuits* viii. 154/1 The reflexing circuit, normally used as a second i-f amplifier and first audio amplifier, can provide gain from a single transistor only a few db less than the gain obtained from two transistors in conventional circuits.

reflexion, -al, -ist: see REFLECTION.

†**reˈflexious,** *a. Obs. rare*⁻¹. [f. REFLEX *sb.* + -IOUS.] Of the nature of a reflection.

1680 J. AUBREY in *Lett. Eminent Persons* (1813) II. 255 But shee needed neither borrowed shades, nor reflexious lights, to set her off.

†**reˈflexity.** *Obs.* [f. as REFLEX *a.* + -ITY.]

1. Shining, reflection. *rare*⁻¹.

c1485 *Digby Myst.* (1882) III. 441 Heyl, oryent, as þe sonne In his reflexite!

2. Reflexibility. *nonce-use.*

1797 BROUGHAM in *Phil. Trans.* LXXXVII. 361, I now tried to measure the different degrees of reflexity, &c. of the different rays.

reflexive (rɪˈflɛksɪv), *a.* and *sb.* [ad. L. type **reflexivus*: see REFLEX *v.* and -IVE. Cf. F. *réflexif, -ive* (Cotgr. 1611), Sp. *reflexivo*, It. *riflessivo*, and see also REFLECTIVE.] **A.** *adj.*

1. a. Capable of turning or bending back. *rare.*

1588 J. READ tr. *Arcæus' Compend. Meth.* 60b, Who would not feare the force, the pearcing and power reflexiue of Quicksiluer. 1884 A. DANIELL *Princ. Physics* xiv. 413 The reflexive power of flame is nearly the same as that of tracing-paper.

†**b.** Capable of reflecting light. *Obs. rare.*

1676 BOYLE in *Phil. Trans.* XI. 787, I found the Confining surface very strongly reflexive.

†**c.** Reflected (as light). *Obs. rare*⁻¹.

1676 HALE *Contempl.* II. 201 Though the Glory of thy Essence, cannot receive any increase by this reflection, yet thou art pleased everlastingly to perpetuate this thy reflexive Glory.

2. †**a.** Of mental operations: Turned or directed back upon the mind itself. *Obs.*

1640 BP. REYNOLDS *Passions* xxviii. 295 In those two Offices of Reason, the Transient and Reflexive act, that whereby we looke Outward on others; or Inward on our selves. 1656 JEANES *Mixt. Schol. Div.* 42 Then the mind in it's reflexive workings can proceed *in infinitum.* a1708 BEVERIDGE *Priv. Th.* I. (1730) 1 Being not capable of a reflexive act, they know it not.

†**b.** †Capable of, inclined to, or characterized by, reflection or serious thought; reflective. *Obs.*

1653 H. MORE *Antid. Ath.* II. v. (1712) 53 Man, in whom there is a principle of more fine and reflexive Reason. 1655–87 —— *App. Antid.* (1712) 193 This must be in a knowing, passive, and reflexive Subject. 1684 T. BURNET *Th. Earth* I. 287 To the attentive and reflexive, to those that are unprejudic'd. 1752 *School of Man* (1753) 37 Their sensitive soul bears such marks of a reflexive intelligence.

c. *Social Sciences.* Applied to that which turns back upon, or takes account of, itself or a person's self, esp. methods that take into consideration the effect of the personality or presence of the researcher on the investigation.

1934 G. H. MEAD *Mind, Self & Society* xxi. 173 Cooley and James..endeavor to find the basis of the self in reflexive affective experiences, i.e., experiences involving 'self-feeling'. 1957 P. LAFITTE *Person in Psychol.* 17 All learning depends on the reflexive interpretation of one's experience together with the experience of others. *Ibid.* 21 The psychologist's reflexive judgements will be limited by his knowledge of himself in some of the ways that his subjects' reports are limited. 1970 A. GOULDNER *Coming Crisis of Western Sociol.* xiii. 489 The historical mission of a Reflexive Sociology is to transcend sociology as it now exists. *Ibid.* 490 A Reflexive Sociology means that we sociologists must..acquire the ingrained *habit* of viewing our own beliefs as we now view those held by others. 1972 M. LANDAU *Polit. Theory & Polit. Sci.* i. 32 A reflexive prediction is one in which the prediction is itself a factor which may materially alter the projected or anticipated outcome. 1977 DOUGLAS & JOHNSON *Existential Sociol.* p. xiii, Our emphasis on the problematic and situated nature of meaningful experience contrasts..with the structuralism of Alvin Gouldner's 'reflexive sociology'. 1977 R. HOLLAND *Self & Social Context* v. 82 In both cases the person producing the theory is included within the subject matter he attempts to understand. The usual term for this kind of approach is 'reflexive', a word which has begun to appear in the human sciences..but which has long been implicit in social theory.

†**3.** Reciprocal, correspondent. *Obs.*

c1642 *Contra-Replicant's Complaint* 18 There is likewise a neare consanguinity, and reflexive benevolence of aspects between Lawes and Princes. 1681 FLAVEL *Right. Man's Ref.* 178 Nor..are our thoughts as Gods in respect of reflexive comprehension.

†**4.** Reflecting on a person. *Obs. rare*⁻¹.

a1716 SOUTH *Serm.* (1744) X. 174, I would fain know what man..there is that does not resent an ugly reflexive word.

5. *Gram.* and *Linguistics.* Of pronouns, verbs, phrases, and their signification: Characterized by, or denoting, a reflex action on the subject of the clause or sentence.

1837 G. PHILLIPS *Syriac Gram.* 114 The ordinary method of expressing a reciprocal or reflexive sense. 1861 MAX MÜLLER *Sc. Lang.* viii. 299 The mere addition of certain letters, which give to every verb a negative, or causative, or reflexive, or reciprocal meaning. 1867 J. HADLEY *Ess.* xi. 205 A shortened form of the reflexive pronoun. 1933 L. BLOOMFIELD *Language* xii. 193 In English we say ***he washed him*** when actor and goal are not identical, but ***he washed himself*** (a *reflexive* form) when they are the same person. 1979 *Trans. Philol. Soc.* 11 We might of course propose to handle such facts by a purely local reflexive deletion rule.

6. Of a reflex character.

1871 FARRAR *Witn. Hist.* iv. 138 He reduced religion to a reflexive ceremony of empty proprieties. 1888 J. T. GULICK in *Linn. Soc. Jrnl.* XX. 200/2 Reflexive Selection is the exclusive generation of those better fitted to the relations in which the members of the same species stand to each other. 1927 *Jrnl. Nerv. & Mental Dis.* LXV. 463 We..succeeded in producing in apes..a reflexive contraction of the adductor muscles of the thigh. 1971 L. KOPPETT *N.Y. Times Guide Spectator Sports* i. 13 To have any chance at all, the batter, whose action must be entirely reflexive, needs protection from additional trickery. 1971 *Sci. Amer.* Aug. 74/1 A number of biologists..adopted the radical hypothesis that animal behavior was almost wholly reflexive. On this view the continually changing array of stimuli that an animal encounters as it moves through its environment was thought to produce a large part of the animal's repertory of behavior by reflexes and their mutual interactions. 1975 *New Yorker* 13 Jan. 30/2 At the end, the audience rose in an ovation—but at concerts like this one standing ovations have become reflexive. 1976 *Nature* 1 Apr. 392/1 To suggest..that the evolutionary considerations which determine the mating systems of mammals and birds have any light..to shed on the tensions and asymmetries commonly observed in human sexual relationships is to invite reflexive dismissal as a 'sexist'.

7. *Math.* and *Logic.* Applied to any relation which always holds between a term and itself. [The sense is due to G. Vailati, who used It. *riflessività* reflexivity (*Rivista di Matematica* (1891) I. 134).]

1903 B. RUSSELL *Princ. Math.* xix. 159 All kinds of equality have in common the three properties of being reflexive, symmetrical, and transitive. 1937 R. CARNAP *Logical Syntax of Lang.* iv. 261 Conditions which require for symmetrical, reflexive, and transitive relations the property of non-emptiness. 1953 A. A. FRAENKEL *Abstract Set Theory* i. 34 Any set is equivalent to itself... Equivalence is a reflexive relation. 1972 F. J. BUDDEN *Fascination of Groups* xx. 374 Conjugacy is a relation between the elements of a group. It is evidently reflexive (since $y = 1y1^{-1}$).

B. *sb.* †**1.** An object reflecting light. *Obs.*⁻¹

1686 GOAD *Celest. Bodies* I. ix. 27 That there may be found as much variety in them as in other Reflexives, i.e. Plain, Convex or Concave Glasses.

2. A reflexive verb or pronoun.

1866 *Trans. Phil. Soc.* 88 We are still capable of forming a double set of reflexives. 1867 J. HADLEY *Ess.* xi. 209 The reflexive which serves to express the passive is a causal reflexive.

reˈflexively, *adv.* [f. prec. + -LY².] **a.** In a reflexive or reflecting manner, by way of reflection (in various senses).

1674 *Govt. Tongue* 223 Not only directly..but reflexively also, in respect of what may rebound to our selves. 1678 CUDWORTH *Intell. Syst.* I. v. 636 Reflexively examining himself whether he have a phantasm, or sensible idea, belonging to every word, or no. *a* **1716** South *Twelve Serm.* (1717) VI. 105 Ay, but he spoke slightly and reflexively of such a Lady. **1858** Caswall *Poems* 192 Thyself by nurture, meditation, grace, Reflexively reveal'd. **1867** C. J. Smith *Syn. & Antonyms, Abeyance*, The term has been transferred reflexively from the person waiting to the thing waited for.

b. = reflexly *adv.*; in the manner of a reflex action, automatically. *rare.*

1952 *Mind* LXI. 252 As is usual with such reflexively repeated dicta, this one is true but never practical to follow. **1966** D. F. Galouye *Lost Perception* xvi. 172 Instantly the three men twisted round. The closest was Wellford. Reflexively, he loosed a laser discharge.

re'flexiveness. [f. as prec. + -ness.] The state or quality of being reflexive.

1667 H. More *Div. Dial.* I. ii. 234 There not being that Reflexiveness..in Brutes in their suffering as in rational Creatures. **1881** Westcott & Hort *Grk. N.T.* II. App. 144 The reflexiveness is so direct that a refusal to admit the rough breathing introduces language completely at variance with all Greek usage. **1903** B. Russell *Princ. Math.* xxvi. 219 The property of a relation which insures that it holds between a term and itself is called by Peano *reflexiveness.* **1933** *Mind* XLII. 36 In the *Principia Mathematica* $p \supset p$ assigns to the relation $\supset$ the property of reflexiveness. **1968** *New Scientist* 16 May 339/1 Three properties of conditions are frequently mentioned: reflexiveness, symmetry and transitivity... A reflexive condition is a relation between an idea and itself... An example is equality.

So **refle'xivity.**

1653 H. More *Antid. Ath.* iii. xvi. 137 Ready from every part to be reflected if the clouds had any such reflexivity in them. **1891** Mrs. H. Ward tr. *Amiel's Jrnl.* 32 Less reflexivity and more plasticity..would raise the style of Vinet. **1940** W. V. Quine *Math. Logic* iii. 138 A natural extension of the notions of reflexivity and commutativity which were applied to a statement composition. **1950** L. M. Hammond et al. tr. *Hilbert & Ackermann's Princ. Math. Logic* iv. 135 The properties of reflexivity, symmetry, and transitivity of dyadic predicates. **1965** *Canad. Jrnl. Linguistics* X. 175 They [*sc.* classifiers] refer most clearly to the voice of the verb:..passivity, reflexivity. **1977** Douglas & Johnson *Existential Sociol.* v. 172 Reflexivity refers to the mutual interdependence of observer or knower to what is seen or known.

reflexivization (rɪˌflɛksɪvaɪ'zeɪʃən). *Linguistics.* [f. next + -ation.] The action of making (a verb, noun phrase, etc.) reflexive; the process or fact of being made reflexive. Cf. reflexive *a.* 5.

1965 N. Chomsky *Aspects of Theory of Syntax* iii. 145 In a sentence such as..'the boy hurt the boy', the two phonetically identical Noun Phrases are necessarily interpreted as differing in reference; sameness of reference requires reflexivization of the second Noun Phrase. *Ibid.*, The reflexivization rule can be formulated as an erasure operation that uses the Noun Phrase to delete another. *Ibid.* 146 The reflexivization rule..will apply only when the integers assigned to the two items are the same. **1966** P. M. Postal in F. P. Dinneen *Rep. 17th Round Table Meeting Linguistics & Lang. Stud.* 182, I view the process of reflexivization as a complex of a number of partially independent operations. **1972** *Language* XLVIII. 390 The interactions of other pro-nominals with indirect object, shown in reflexivization properties for example, suggest that postpositions are two-place predicates rather than one-place (intransitive) predicates. **1978** *Studies in Eng. Lit.: Eng. Number* (Tokyo) 65 Reflexivization, which converts the simple personal pronoun into the compound refl. pronoun in *-self*, is apparently optional in ME.

reflexivize (rɪ'flɛksɪvaɪz), *v. Linguistics.* [f. reflexive *a.* + -ize.] **a.** *trans.* To make (a verb, noun phrase, etc.) reflexive. **b.** *intr.* To become reflexive. Hence **re'flexivizing** *ppl. a.*

1965 S.-Y. Kuroda *Generative Gram. Stud. in Japanese Lang.* (Mass. Inst. Technol. thesis) v. 144 The object of a subordinate clause which is coreferential with the matrix subject will be Provincialized rather than Reflexivized. **1967** J. R. Ross *Constraints on Variables in Syntax* (Mass. Inst. Technol. thesis) vi. 254 It would be expected that the leftmost occurrence of *Bill* would be able to reflexivize the rightmost. **1971** *Language* XLVII. 160 It appears that in Japanese the subject can optionally reflexivize (with *zibun*) an identical NP [= noun phrase] in an embedded sentence, if that embedded sentence is a part of the VP. **1976** J. S. Gruber *Lexical Struct. Syntax & Semantics* i. iii. 73 The expression of Accompaniment must, like the expression of Location, not be generated in construction with the verb. This follows from phrase order and also the fact that they do not reflexivize. **1978** *Language* LIV. 142 Level III DA usages in our data always include *on-* along with the reflexivizing apparatus and reverential elements.

reflexly ('riːflɛkslɪ, rɪ'flɛkslɪ), *adv.* [f. reflex *a.* + -ly².] In a reflex manner.

1839 Hallam *Hist. Lit.* iv. iii. §20 No body can act reflexly on itself. **1875** H. C. Wood *Therap.* (1879) 255 Contraction of the pupil before dilatation..is probably caused reflexly by irritant action of the atropia. **1932** S. Zuckerman *Social Life Monkeys & Apes* ix. 146 It seems reasonable to surmise that when the sexual skin is swollen with oedema, its sensory nerve endings are stimulated by pressure and that this reflexly rouses the animal to sexual behaviour. **1961** *Lancet* 12 Aug. 367/2, I thought of..Superdiagnostex, lying in the cupboard where I hurled it reflexly when a salesman left it on trial last month. **1974** *Sci. Amer.* Oct. 100/1 A coordinated motor performance could be described as being differentiated into many parts along the time dimension, so that each part is reflexly triggered by the sensory components of its predecessor.

refle'xogenous, *a. Path.* [f. reflex *a.*: see -o¹.] Producing reflex action. So **reflexo'genic** *a.*

1891 *Cent. Dict.*, Reflexogenic **1899** *Allbutt's Syst. Med.* VI. 521 Certain bone surfaces are similarly very dependably 'reflexogenous'. **1933** *Ann. Rep. London Co. Council* IV. iii. 133 Sometimes the epileptic fit is intimately bound up with the appropriate stimulus... Much depends on the nature of the reflexogenous stimulus. **1969** *Jrnl. Compar. Neurol.* CXXI. 124/2 Stimulation of the skin of the head and of the rostral half of the belly elicited reflex movements of the ipsilateral forelimb, and this area is referred to as the forelimb reflexogenous zones. **1973** *Nature* 3 Aug. 310/1 These calculations..predict very high pressures in the aorta, and imply reflexogenic control over cerebral perfusion pressures.

reflexology (ˌriːflɛk'sɒlədʒɪ). *Psychol.* [f. reflex *sb.* + -ology; cf. G. *reflexologie.*] **a.** The theory that the behaviour of organisms is made up of established patterns of simple or complex reflex responses; the scientific study of reflex action as it affects behaviour.

[**1912** W. von Bechterew in *Deutsche Med. Wochenschr.* 8 Aug. 1481 (*heading*) Was ist Psychoreflexologie?] **1927** *Psychol. Abstr.* I. 590 Thanks to its objective method, reflexology has rendered service to applied sciences, psychiatry and pedagogy. **1933** E. & W. Murphy tr. A. Gerver in *Bechterev's Princ. Human Reflexology* 8 Bechterev ..founded this Institute in 1918, and its chief aim was the study of the anatomy and physiology of the central nervous system and also the study of the principles of reflexology, a new branch of science created by him... The Institute is now called the Reflexological Institute for the Study of Brain. **1957** T. Kilmartin tr. *Aron's Opium of Intellectuals* vi. 198 'Reflexology' does not solve the riddle of existence any more than materialistic sociology. **1973** C. D. Kernig *Marxism, Communism & Western Society* VII. 144/1 (*heading*) Results of recent research in reflexology. **1975** C. Burt *ESP & Psychol.* iv. 54 The physiological psychologists (materialistic monists) who adopted Huxley's reflexology.

b. A technique for relaxing nervous tension through a method of foot massage.

1976 M. Segal *Reflexology* i Known also as compression foot massage, reflexology is a natural art of healing. *Ibid.*, Like acupuncture, reflexology has been used by the Chinese for 5,000 years. **1976** *Seed* V. v. 31 (Advt.), Reflexology (compression massage of the feet). **1977** D. Berkson *Foot Bk.* ii. 13 Various kinds of pressure-point therapy and reflexology as well as shiatsu.

Hence **ˌreflexo'logical** *a.*; **ˌrefle'xologist.**

1927 *Psychol. Abstr.* I. 650 Therapeutics ought to investigate..the methods of reflexological orthopedics applicable to the cure of mental diseases. **1933** Reflexological [see sense a above]. **1933** E. & W. Murphy tr. A. Gerver in *Bechterev's Gen. Princ. Human Reflexology* 13 Not only have psychiatrists, reflexologists, and neuropathologists been in close touch with him [*sc.* Bechterev], but also teachers, both rural and urban, have always given him a ready ear. **1938** *Brit. Jrnl. Psychol.* Jan. 337 Behaviourists and reflexologists who do not believe that a rat has any mental life involving anticipations or foresights which govern his behaviour. **1957** *Listener* 31 Oct. 689/1 Another analogy was suggested by the experiments of the Russian reflexologists, Bechterev and Pavlov. **1976** M. Segal *Reflexology* i. 3 We, as reflexologists, do the same by trying to relax the patient and relieve nerve tension.

†**re'flexure.** *Obs. rare*⁻¹. [See reflex *v.* and flexure.] A bend or fold.

1578 Banister *Hist. Man* viii. 100 The thinne Membran ..made in reflexures, should nourish the substaunce of the brayne.

†**re'flirt,** *v. Obs. rare*⁻¹. In 7 reflurt. [re-.] *trans.* To toss back again.

1652 *News fr. Low-Countr.* 11 If carping Momes shall flurt in Podex's face A Flout,..Podex, with a full Breath, reflurts it back.

†**re'float,** *sb. Obs. rare.* [ad. obs. F. *reflot*: see re- 2 a and float *sb.* 2.] A flowing back; reflux, ebb (of the tide).

1594 [see float *sb.* 2]. **1626** Bacon *Sylva* §907 The Maine Float and Refloat of the Sea..which is..Part of the Diurnal Motion.

So †**re'float** *v.*¹ *intr.*, to flow back, ebb. *Obs.*⁻⁰

1632 Sherwood, To reflote, *refloter.*

refloat (riː'fləʊt), *v.*² [re- 5 a.] **a.** *trans.* To float, set afloat, again. Also *transf.* in *Econ.*

1871 *Daily News* 14 Jan., The necessary operations for the refloating of the French war vessel. **1883** *Manch. Exam.* 24 Oct. 7/1 The company undertook to refloat, at their own expense, any vessel that went ashore in the canal. **1973** *Oxf. Mag.* 1 June 1/2 He gallantly accepted the responsibility of re-floating it [*sc.* the *Magazine*]. **1974** B. Pearce tr. *Amin's Accumulation on World Scale* II. iii. 434 If a slump in cotton sales should occur, the central bank would refloat the producers through an additional issue. **1977** *Economist* 3 Sept. 67/1 Portugal refloats the escudo downwards.

b. *intr.* To float again.

1906 *Daily Chron.* 23 June 6/3 On the rising tide the Talisman refloated.

Hence **re'floating** *vbl. sb.*; also **refloa'tation.**

1892 *Pall Mall G.* 22 Nov. 2/1 The refloating of all the colonial loans... By such a refloatation there would be a saving of about one per cent.

refloenge, obs. form of reflowing *vbl. sb.*

refloo, obs. form of reflow *v.*

†**re'flore,** *v. Sc. Obs. rare*⁻¹. In 6 refloir. [f. re- 5 a + *-flore*, as in *deflore* deflower.] *trans.* To cause to flourish again; = reflower *v.* 1.

1560 Rolland *Crt. Venus* i. 295 With superabundant Mirth, melodie, thow dois my hart refloir.

reflo'rescence. [re- 5 a; or f. L. *reflōrēscĕre* to flower again + -ence.] A blossoming again, a second florescence.

1721 in Bailey. *a* **1792** Horne *Disc.* xvi. Wks. 1809 IV. 302 By the reflorescence of that mortal part which he drew from the stem of Jesse. **1880** Swinburne *Stud. Shaks.* 17 A famous..example of this reflorescence.

So **reflo'rescent** *a.*

1897 *Dublin Rev.* Oct. 398 The classic forms so exuberantly reflorescent in the sixteenth century.

reflourish (riː'flʌrɪʃ), *v.* [f. re- 5 a + flourish *v.*, orig. after L. *reflōrēscĕre.*] *intr.* To flourish anew. Chiefly *fig.* (Common in 17th c.)

a **1340** Hampole *Psalter* xxvii. 10 And my fleysse reflorist [L. *refloruit*]. **1544** Leland *N.Y. Gift* in *Itin.* (1768) I. p. xxiii, The old Glory of your renowmid Britaine [shall be seen] to reflorisch thorough the Worlde. **1558** Phaer *Æneid* Gen. Sum. aij b, A land where their Kyngdome should reflorishe. **1615** G. Sandys *Trav.* 83 Cypresse: a tree destinated to the dead; in that once being cut it neuer reflourisheth. **1675** Plume *Life Hacket* in *Cent. Serm.* p. i, Afterwards, when Christian religion reflourished, the Christian Church resumed these studies again. **1776** R. Chandler *Trav. Greece* (1825) II. 135 He saw the city reflourishing under the auspices of the emperor Hadrian. **1853** G. Johnston *Nat. Hist. E. Bord.* I. 229 The love of flowers..reflourishes..in the autumn of our age.

†**b.** Const. with *inf.* (after the Vulgate). *Obs.*

1582 N. T. (Rhem.) *Phil.* iv. 10, I rejoyced in our Lord excedingly, that once at the length you have reflorished to care for me [L. *refloruistis pro me sentire*]. **1613** Day *Dyall* x. (1614) 266 Little haue they Reflourished to care for them, to use a phrase of theirs.

Hence **re'flourishing** *vbl. sb.* and *ppl. a.*

1621 H. Farley *St. Paul's* title-p., All such as beare good will to the reflourishing estate of the said Chvrch. **1627** Hakewill *Apol.* (1630) 230 Their resurrection, and reflouresshing agaıne. **1657** W. Rand tr. *Gassendi's Life Peiresc* ii. 238 The reflourishing Glory of that most excellent and Beneficent King Renatus. **1728** Earbery tr. *Burnet's St. Dead* II. 108 The Wicked are no Objects of Hope nor of Reflourishing. **1775** S. J. Pratt *Liberal Opin.* xciv. (1783) III. 191 The reflourishing fortunes of the benevolent Blewitt.

So **re'flourishment.** *rare*⁻¹.

1611 Speed *Hist. Gt. Brit.* ix. ix. §95. 535/2 The Welsh seeing these round proceedings in England, the peace and reflorishment whereof they feared, labored for reconciliation.

reflow, *sb.* [re- 2 a.] **a.** A reflux, refluence, ebb of the tide.

1610 Holland *Camden's Brit.* i. 37 By the reflow or ebbe of the Ocean. **1793** Smeaton *Edystone L.* §197 This matter ..would in time block up the Humber, was it not for the powerful re-flow of that river's tide. **1832** De la Beche *Geol. Man.* (ed. 2) 131 A quick flow or reflow of the water. **1860** Maury *Phys. Geog. Sea* §136 (Low) 47 The grand equatorial flow and reflow which is performed by the waters of all the great oceans.

b. *fig.*

1969 *Daily Tel.* 4 Sept. 1/4 The re-flow of funds into London after the wave of speculation which followed devaluation was not as large as the initial outflow. **1975** *Washington Post* 19 Feb. A15/2 May I ask at that point if you have had an opportunity to examine the reflow in the purchase of goods and services.

re'flow, *v.*¹ Now *rare.* [re- 2 a, orig. after L. *refluĕre.*] *intr.* To flow back; *esp.* of the tide, to ebb. Freq. in phr. ***flow and reflow.***

1387 [see reflowing *vbl. sb.*]. **1432-50** tr. *Higden* (Rolls) I. 57 The see Pontike reflowethe not as other sees. *Ibid.* 425 A lytelle welle in the costes of Ruthlande,..whiche dothe not floo and refloo in the maner of a see. **1535** Stewart *Cron. Scot.* I. 373 Syne as the flude begouth for till reflow [etc.]. **1555** Eden *Decades* 119 They see the seas by increase and decrease to flowe and reflowe. **1589** Fleming *Virg. Georg.* iv. 71 At creekes reflowing past the which the water cannot go. **1776** Burrow *Rep.* IV. 2163 It is said that the king has a right, as high as the sea flows and reflows. **1810** Crabbe *Borough* i. 216 The billows..strike with furious force, And then re-flowing, take their grating course. **1852** *Humber Conserv. Act* 2038 So far as the tide flows or reflows.

b. *fig.* and in fig. context.

1609 J. Davies *Holy Roode* Ded., Those [pleasures] will runne to Helles impure, While these to Eden faire reflow againe. **1677** Gale *Crt. Gentiles* iv. 15 As al Creatures flow and reflow to God, as the Ocean or plenitude of al Being. **1721** R. Keith tr. *T. à Kempis, Solil. Soul* xii. 197 My Affection floweth and refloweth here and there and every where. **1818** Byron *Ch. Har.* iv. xcii, An universal deluge, which..ebbs but to reflow!

re'flow, *v.*² *rare.* [re- 5 a.] To flow again.

1817 Byron *Mazeppa* xiv, Life reassumed its lingering hold.., My blood reflow'd, though thick and chill. *a* **1823** Crabbe *Woman* i, She..bids the spring of hope re-flow That languish'd in the fainting heart.

re'flower, *v.* [re- 5 a.]

†**1.** *trans.* To cause to flower or flourish again.

1598 Sylvester *Du Bartas* ii. ii. i. *Ark* 66 As the Sommer sweet-distilling drops..Re-greens the Greens, and doth the Flowrs re-flowr [F. *refleurir*]. **1606** *Ibid.* iv. ii. *Magnificence* 805 Her sight re-flowres th' Arabian Wilderness. *a* **1649** Drumm. of Hawth. *Poems* Wks. (1711) 39 To make peace prosper, justice to reflow'r.

2. *intr.* To flower again (Ogilvie *Suppl.* 1855). Also *fig.*

1878 Swinburne *Poems & Ballads* 2nd Ser. 178 Out of the herbs on the walls reflowering. **1977** *Arab Times* 13 Dec. 7/3 This technology has reflowered in the sports hall, where highly specialised surfaces are needed.

Hence **re'flowered** *ppl. a.*, covered with flowers again.

1907 E. NESBIT in *Daily Chron.* 19 Feb. 6/7 Hark to the sigh of the reflowered tomb: 'Ah, live, live, live, for Spring goes by, goes by!'

re'flowing, *vbl. sb.* [f. REFLOW *v.*[1] + -ING[1].] The action of the vb.; refluence.

1387 TREVISA *Higden* (Rolls) III. 369 The floenge..of the see þer as at oon tyme and refloenge to gedre. **1555** EDEN *Decades* 58 Whiche rowghnes or reflowinge, the Spanyardes caule Resacca. **1613–16** W. BROWNE *Brit. Past.* I. v, Our teares should make the flood, not her reflowing. **1654** EARL MONM. tr. *Bentivoglio's Warrs Flanders* 224 The flowing and reflowing of the Tide will oppose them. **1813** J. C. HOBHOUSE *Journey* (ed. 2) 454 The change which..took place in the flowing and reflowing of the stream.

So **re'flowing** *ppl. a.*

1609 HOLLAND *Amm. Marcell.* 196 With a returne of the current and reflowing waves it dasheth upon the temple of Apollo Sminthius. **1896** *Daily News* 29 Feb. 5/5 Coming up ..on the crest of the re-flowing tide.

refluction, variant of REFLUXION *Obs.*

refluctu'ation. *rare*$^{-0}$. [RE- 2a.] A flowing back (Webster 1828–32).

†**reflue**, *v. Obs. rare.* [ad. L. *refluĕre*: see REFLUENT and REFLOW *v.*[1]] *intr.* To flow back.

1545 RAYNOLD *Byrth Mankynde* 30 This skynny flappes close the passage and defende, that nothynge canne rebound, ne reflue backe agayne. *Ibid.* 44 Sum part therof refluеth, and is reuerted to the womans brestes, ther to becum mylke.

refluence ('rɛfluːəns). [See REFLUENT and -ENCE.] A flowing back; a reflux.

c **1592** MARLOWE *Jew of Malta* III. iv, The wastfull sea, Whose billowes..Shall ouerflow it with their refluence. **1615** CROOKE *Body of Man* 167 To hinder the refluence or returne of the..vnprofitable humors. **1621** LODGE *Summary of Du Bartas* 106 In the sea, betwixt Norway, and Scotland, there is clerely obserued a flow and refluence. **1817** SHELLEY *Rev. Islam* XII. ix, Like the refluence of a mighty wave Sucked into the loud sea. **1861** MRS. BROWNING *Psyche & Pan* 4 The gentle river..cast up Psyche, with a refluence brave, Upon the flowery bank.

transf. and *fig.* *a* **1592** GREENE *Jas. IV*, IV. iii, One hornpipe further, a refluence back, and two doubles forward. **1842** ALISON *Hist. Europe* lxxiv. §78 The refluence of its legions over the Rhine and the Pyrenees..prostrated the financial affairs of the Empire.

So †**'refluency**. *Obs. rare.*

1615 CROOKE *Body of Man* 400 By..what affluencies and refluencies this perpetuity is accomplished. **1648** W. MOUNTAGUE *Devout Ess.* I. vi. §2. 58 How all things sublunary move..in an interchangeable flowing and refluencie.

refluent ('rɛfluːənt), *a.* [ad. L. *refluent-em*, pres. pple. of *refluĕre* to flow back, f. *re-* RE- 2a + *fluĕre* to flow.]

1. Flowing back, reflowing:

a. of the sea, waves, rivers, etc.

1712 BLACKMORE *Creation* III. 139 Do not the Rivers..to the Hills convey the Refluent Wave..? **1725** POPE *Odyss.* v. 549 Then backward sweep The refluent tides, and plunge him in the deep. **1791** COWPER *Iliad* XII. 30 All those [rivers] with refluent course Apollo drove Nine days against the rampart. **1812** BRACKENRIDGE *Views Louisiana* (1814) 37 In lower Louisiana, there are a great number of lakes from the refluent waters of the Mississippi. **1873** T. W. HIGGINSON *Oldport Days* ii. 36 All night the phosphorescent water.. washes with long, refluent waves along their sides.

transf. **1842** ALISON *Hist. Europe* lxxxiv. §1 The once triumphant Peninsular hosts, refluent through the passes of the Pyrenees. **1856** R. A. VAUGHAN *Mystics* (1860) II. 78 To give him a hold against any refluent doubt that might threaten to sweep him back.

b. of blood, the spirits, life, etc.

1699 GARTH *Dispens.* 91, I show'd of old, how vital Currents glide, And the Meanders of their refluent Tide. **1714** *Spring* in Steele *Poet. Misc.* 109 When to his Heart the refluent Spirits came. **1789** E. DARWIN *Bot. Gard.* II. (1791) 77 Slow-ebbing life with refluent crimson breaks O'er their wan lips. **1816** SOUTHEY *Lay of Laureate* lxix, I felt the refluent blood forsake my face. **1872** GEO. ELIOT *Middlem.* xxxii, Too languid to sting, he had the more venom refluent in his blood.

c. *Phys.* of blood or other fluids.

1704 RAY *Creation* II. (ed. 4) 319 To discharge the refluent Blood into the next adjacent Trunk. **1822–34** *Good's Study Med.* (ed. 4) IV. 347 The ammoniacal salt of the refluent urine. **1898** *Allbutt's Syst. Med.* V. 924 The heading back will..fill the ventricle still more with refluent aortic blood.

2. Characterized by refluence, *esp.* tidal.

1741 MONRO *Anat. Nerves* (ed. 3) 21 This..Reflux it was .., which gave Rise to another Division of the Nerves into arterious or effluent, and venous or refluent. **1798** *Anti-Jacobin* No. 28 Wherever man is found, or refluent oceans roll. **1864** TENNYSON *Boädicea* 28 A phantom colony smoulder'd on the refluent estuary.

†**3.** Directed backwards. *Obs. rare*$^{-1}$.

1741 SHENSTONE *Judgm. Hercules* 424 If o'er their lives a refluent glance they cast, Their's is the present who can praise the past.

†**'refluous**, *a. Obs. rare.* [f. L. *reflu-us* refluent + -OUS.] Refluent; recurring.

1628 SIR W. MURE *Spirit. Hymn* 274 That Day shall rest Heauen's rolling spheares, Earth's refluous tumults. **1650** FULLER *Pisgah* II. 62 Seeing the stream of Jordan..was not supplied with any reciprocall or refluous tide out of the Dead Sea.

reflurt: see REFLIRT *v. Obs.*

reflux ('riːflʌks), *sb.* [f. RE- 2a + FLUX: cf. F. *reflux* (16th c.), Sp. *reflujo* (*-fluxo*), It. *riflusso*.]

1. A flowing back, return, refluence: **a.** of the sea (esp. in phr. ***flux and reflux***), rivers, water, air, etc.

c **1430** LYDG. *Min. Poems* (Percy Soc.) 194 Man hath of erthe the slowthe and hevynesse, Flux and reflux by watir made unstable. **1601** HOLLAND *Pliny* I. 43 Hereunto addeth Aristotle..that no liuing creature dieth but in the reflux and ebbe of the sea. **1686** PLOT *Staffordsh.* 56 Which in some measure may cause the flux and reflux of the green Sea. **1719** DE FOE *Crusoe* I. xv, The great draught and reflux of the..river. **1761** *Ann. Reg.* I. 95 Fluxes and refluxes of the sea..continued till six o'clock next morning. **1804** C. B. BROWN tr. *Volney's View Soil U.S.* 67, I cannot determine how far eastward the Delaware then extended the reflux of its waters. **1830** LYELL *Princ. Geol.* I. 117 The heat and cold which surround the globe are in a state of constant and universal flux and reflux. **1869** E. A. PARKES *Pract. Hygiene* (ed. 3) 110 Ill-contrived sewers permitting a large reflux of air into the houses.

b. in *transf.* and *fig.* uses.

1632 J. HAYWARD tr. *Biondi's Eromena* 129 The refluxes of so unjust a fortune in a Princesse of so great merit. **1670** R. COKE *Disc. Trade* 69 After all this flux and re-flux of vexation and charge to the certain undoing of one or both parties. **1711** SHAFTESB. *Charac.* (1737) I. 271 The alterations which happen in manners, and the flux and reflux of politeness, wit, and art. **1800** COLQUHOUN *Comm. Thames* Introd. 25 The flux and reflux of Commercial Property..on the Thames. **1849** MACAULAY *Hist. Eng.* vii. II. 189 A violent and rapid reflux of public feeling.

c. *Phys.* of the blood and the contents of the stomach or intestine.

1653 HARVEY *Anat. Exerc.* I. xiii. (1673) 81 [The blood] comes..into the ear of the heart in so great abundance, with so great flux, and reflux [etc.]. **1707** FLOYER *Physic. Pulse-watch* 15 The Circulation of our Blood, whose reflux to the Heart is promoted by..Respiration. **1834** J. FORBES *Laennec's Dis. Chest* (ed. 4) 511 The reflux of blood into the jugular veins from coughing or a prolonged expiration. **1899** *Allbutt's Syst. Med.* VI. 40 The intra-ventricular pressure becomes lowered from reflux through the valve. **1937** R. SCHINDLER *Gastroscopy* xiv. 275 The continuous unregulated reflux of intestinal juice containing bile and pancreatic juice may play the greatest role. **1978** T. C. JEWETT in E. Lebenthal *Digestive Dis. Children* 414 The redundant mucosa which forms a rosette at the cardio-esophageal area may also act as a barrier to reflux of gastric contents up the esophagus.

d. *Chem.* The condition, process, or action of refluxing; also *concr.*, the condensed vapour involved in this. Freq. in adverbial phr., as ***at*** or ***under reflux***, in a vessel fitted with a reflux condenser.

1897 *Jrnl. Chem. Soc.* LXXI. 1036 The operation is carried out under reflux. **1923** H. M. BUNBURY *Destructive Distillation of Wood* xii. 213 It is sometimes necessary to make a total reflux, i.e. to return all the condensed vapours to the column. **1936** W. L. NELSON *Petroleum Refinery Engin.* xv. 278 The reflux flows down the column but it changes composition from plate to plate so that all of the material that is originally put into the top of the column as reflux is vaporized and returns to the product storage tank. **1958** F. H. GARNER et al. in H. W. Cremer *Chem. Engin. Pract.* V. vii. 422 Liquid-liquid extraction with reflux is usually applied to the separation of homologous substances where both the separation factor and distribution coefficient are low. **1959** *Petroleum Handbk.* (Shell Internat. Petroleum Co.) (ed. 4) 172 The light product returned in this manner to the top of the column is called the reflux. **1962** J. T. MARSH *Self-Smoothing Fabrics* xxii. 372 Melamine..may be determined gravimetrically after hydrolysing a known weight of the treated fabric in 0·2N HCl for 30 min. under reflux. **1968** *Inorg. Syntheses* XI. 20 The mixture is stirred at reflux for 6 hours. *Ibid.* 38 The reflux and stirring are continued for an additional 5–6 hours. **1975** *Jrnl. Chem. Soc.: Perkin Trans.* I. 297/1 The mixture..was heated at reflux under nitrogen. *Ibid.* 344/2 Ethyl cyclo-oct-4-enylideneacetate (1·0 g) was added to sodium hydroxide solution (20 ml; 2N) and brought to reflux.

2. *attrib.* and *Comb.*, as ***reflux current, theory, tide***; **reflux catheter**, a double-channel catheter, in which the liquid passes by one duct and returns by the other (Knight *Dict. Mech.* Suppl. 1884); **reflux condenser** *Chem.*, a condenser so mounted or designed that condensed vapour runs back into the stock of boiling liquid; **reflux œsophagitis** *Med.*, œsophagitis caused by the flow of fluid into the œsophagus from the stomach or intestine; **reflux trap**, a trap in a drain or sewer to prevent a back current of foul air; **reflux valve** = *check-valve* s.v. CHECK-.

1891 F. W. STREATFIELD *Pract. Work in Org. Chem.* 64 The operation is most conveniently conducted in a tubulated retort to the neck of which is attached a reflux condenser. **1939** *Inorg. Syntheses* I. 82 The mixture is placed in a small flask fitted with a reflux condenser and kept at a temperature of about 40 °C. for approximately 48 hours. **1962** J. T. MARSH *Self-Smoothing Fabrics* xxii. 368 The flask is then cooled and the reflux condenser washed down with about 50 cc of distilled water. **1898** *Allbutt's Syst. Med.* V. 975 The current impelled by the right ventricle..is met by the reflux current from the left ventricle. **1952** R. BELSEY in F. A. Jones *Mod. Trends Gastro-Enterol.* I. vii. 144 Reflux oesophagitis leads to thickening of the oesophageal wall, not penetration or perforation. **1980** *Brit. Med. Jrnl.* 29 Mar. (Advt. facing p. 946) 'Tagamet' represents a mark of reliability in reducing gastric acid, and has revolutionised the treatment of disorders such as peptic ulcer and reflux oesophagitis, where acid plays a part. **1899** *Allbutt's Syst. Med.* VI. 234 The reflux theory seems at present the more probable for most cases. **1852** WIGGINS *Embanking* 51 This is to sustain any current that may take place at the reflux tide. **1892** *Daily News* 30 Dec. 3/4 As far as practical, the up current of air (when existing) is prevented by reflux traps. **1888** *Lockwood's Dict. Mech. Engin.* 282 *Reflux valve*,..a flap valve used for the purpose of taking off the pressure of a head of water acting in a backward direction against a set of pumps. **1893** TURNER & BRIGHTMORE *Princ. Waterworks Engin.* vi. 375 'Re-flux' valves are introduced at such points as the inlets to reservoirs or towards the 'delivery' sides of deep depressions in the pipe-line. **1962** L. B. ESCRITT *Pumping Station Equipment & Design* vii. 72 If a reflux valve sticks open..water will rush backwards from the rising main.

reflux ('riːflʌks), *v. Chem.* [f. the sb.] **a.** *intr.* Of a liquid: to boil in circumstances such that the vapour returns to the stock of liquid after condensing. **b.** *trans.* To boil (a liquid) in this way, esp. in a flask fitted with a reflux condenser; also *absol.*

1923 H. M. BUNBURY *Destructive Distillation of Wood* xii. 229 The steam is then almost completely shut off and the contents allowed to reflux gently for about two hours. **1926** LOWY & BALDWIN *Lab. Bk. Elem. Org. Chem.* 45 After all the alcohol or acetone has been added, reflux the mixture on a water bath for half an hour. **1938** A. A. MORTON *Lab. Technique in Org. Chem.* iv. 83 The stopcock is closed, and the liquid allowed to reflux until the thermometer records the lowest temperature possible. **1958** A. I. VOGEL *Elem. Pract. Org. Chem.* xvii. 420 Place 0·5 g. of the dry acid..into the flask, add 2·0–2·5 ml. of redistilled thionyl chloride and reflux gently for 30 minutes. **1965** ADAMS & RAYNOR *Adv. Pract. Inorg. Chem.* v. 49 Reflux equimolar quantities of vanadyl acetylacetonate and pyridine in ether. **1973** *Nature* 9 Mar. 113/2 The reincorporation of 1 molecule of H_2O into the partially dehydrated talc was achieved by refluxing the material with 50 volumes of benzene/water azeotropic mixture.

Hence **'refluxing** *vbl. sb.* and *ppl. a.*

1923 H. M. BUNBURY *Destructive Distillation of Wood* xii. 213 The bulk or the whole of the condensate from the rectifier, which contains most of the less volatile constituent, is returned to the column; this operation is termed 'refluxing'. **1959** R. J. HENGSTEBECK *Petroleum Processing* iii. 49 If bubble-cap trays are used, actual tray requirements are usually estimated by means of empirical correlations of 'tray efficiency' against the properties of the refluxing liquid. **1962** J. T. MARSH *Self-Smoothing Fabrics* xxii. 368 Refluxing for 30 min. is generally enough to hydrolyse the amino-aldehyde. **1975** L. F. & M. FIESER *Reagents for Org. Synthesis* V. 381 Raney nickel which had been deactivated by treatment with refluxing ethanol.

†**re'fluxion**. *Obs.* Also **refluction**. [ad. med.L. *refluxiōn-em*, n. of action f. *refluĕre*: see REFLUENT.] = REFLUX *sb.*

1597 A. M. tr. *Guillemeau's Fr. Chirurg.* 4b/1 The refluxione of badd humors vnto the wounded parte. **1635** SWAN *Spec. M.* vi. §2 (1643) 202 The next..question propounded, was concerning the fluxion and refluxion of the sea. **1654** GAYTON *Pleas. Notes* IV. xvii. 259 Are they more daring at the ebullition of the blood, or at the circular refluxion?

re'fly, *v.* [RE-.] *intr.* To fly back or again.

1611 FLORIO, *Riuolare*, to flie againe, to refly. *a* **1711** KEN *Hymns Evang.* Poet. Wks. 1721 I. 142 Thus spake the Seraph, and to Bliss reflew. —— *Hymns Festiv.* ibid. 351 Gabriel..to Heav'n reflown, Attended at the Throne. **1866** CRICHTON *Nat. Ramble Orcades* 63 Many individuals were flying and reflying from and to the spot.

re'focillate, *v.* Now *rare.* [ad. late L. *refocillāre* to warm into life again, revive: see RE- 5a and FOCILLATE.] *trans.* To revive, refresh, reanimate, comfort (a person, the spirits, senses, etc.).

1611 CORYAT *Crudities* 93 The first view thereof did euen refocillate my spirits and tickle my senses with inward joy. **1680** AUBREY *Lives* (1898) II. *Prynne* 174 About every 3 houres his man was to bring him a roll and a pott of ale to refocillate his wasted Spirits. **1694** MOTTEUX *Rabelais* v. (1737) 230 In Arbors, some themselves refocillate. **1760** STERNE *Tr. Shandy* III. xxxviii, The nose was comforted, nourish'd, plump'd up, refresh'd, refocillated, and set a growing for ever.

Hence †**re'focillating** *ppl. a. Obs.*

1697 R. PEIRCE *Bath Mem.* II. ii. 279 These Disorders.. were greatly increased..so that she was not fit for any, but refocillating Means (to palliate the most urging Symptomes).

refoci'llation. Now *rare.* [ad. med. or mod. L. *refocillātiōn-em*, n. of action f. *refocillāre*: see prec. + -ATION.] The action of the verb; refreshment, reanimation, reinvigoration.

1576 FOXE *A. & M.* (ed. 3) 1615/1 What paynes..would not hee willyngly haue suffered, to haue had some refocillation and tyme of refreshyng? **1620** DONNE *Serm.* xlii. 414 He..kindly performed all offices of ease and refocillation to these way-faring strangers. **1656** E. REYNER *Rules Govt. Tongue* 225 For recreation of the minde, and refocillation of the spirits. **1814** COLERIDGE *Lett.* (1895) II. 621, I need for myself solace and refocillation of animal spirits. **1872** JACOX *Asp. Authorsh.* 3 Refocillation is a favourite resource—whatever the word may be—with authors not a few.

†**b.** A means of refreshment. *Obs. rare*$^{-1}$.

1608 MIDDLETON *Mad World* III. ii, Some precious cordial, some costly refocillation.

re'focus, *v.* [RE- 5a.] *trans.* and *intr.* To focus again.

c **1865** J. WYLDE in *Circ. Sc.* I. 149/2 Having..refocussed the lenses, the brass cap..should be put on. **1895** *N. Amer. Rev.* Feb. 173 A pulpit..capable of re-focusing religion. **1943** A. W. JUDGE *Automobile Electr. Maintenance* (ed. 2) viii. 222 Provided the correct bulb is used as a replacement it should be unnecessary to re-focus after bulb renewal.

1971 S. HILL *Strange Meeting* i. 55 Then, he seemed to come to abruptly, and his eyes re-focused. **1981** J. GARDNER *Licence Renewed* vi. 70 Bond just had time to refocus his glasses. The horses were off.

re'fold, *v.* [RE- 5 a.] *trans.* To fold again. Hence **re'folding** *vbl. sb.*

1594 DANIEL *Cleopatra* Wks. (1717) 293 And having ended, with a Sigh refolds Thy Letter up. **1611** FLORIO, *Riduplicare*, to redouble or refold. *Ibid.*, *Ripiego*, a refolding vp againe. **1852** SURTEES *Sponge's Sp. Tour* (1893) 327 Having mastered its contents, the captain refolded and replaced it where he found it. **1892** ZAEHNSDORF *Bind. Books* (1892) 7 Refolding would in such a case be most detrimental. **1899** *Allbutt's Syst. Med.* VIII. 344 She will refold and rearrange all clothing and bedding in the store-room.

re'font. *rare.* [ad. F. *refonte*: see FONT *sb.*[2] and cf. REFOUNT.] A recast, recasting.

1833 *New Monthly Mag.* XXXVII. 47 The impending refont of the political structure of Germany. **1833** S. AUSTIN *Charact. Goethe* iii. 220 The fragment of the *Achilleis*, or his refont of *Reinecke Fuchs*.

refoorme, obs. form of REFORM *v.*

re'foot, *v.* [RE- 5 a.] *trans.* To put a new foot in (a boot or stocking).

1851 MAYHEW *Lond. Labour* II. 6/2 Stocking-legs for the supply of 'jobbing worsted', and for re-footing. *Ibid.* 34/1 The back and the remainder of the front having been used for refooting boots. **1880** *Plain Hints Needlework* 116 It is in this last meaning probably that this word [*sc.* stilt] is used in Lincolnshire to describe the re-footing a stocking.

†**reforce,** *v. Obs.* [ad. OF. *reforcier*, *reforcer*, f. *re-* RE- + *forcer*: see FORCE *v.*]

1. *trans.* To reinforce, strengthen, make stronger.

c **1489** CAXTON *Blanchardyn* 113 He byganne to reforce his callynge, cryinge wyth a hyghe voyce. *c* **1500** *Melusine* 175 Thus bygan ayen the batayll to be reforced. **1546** *Reg. Privy Council Scot.* I. 54 He sall send men of experience for reforsing of strenthis and biggein of the samyn.

2. *intr.* To become stronger, be reinforced.

c **1489** CAXTON *Blanchardyn* 110 Nothyng coude playse nor brynge hym tyll his hertys ease, But euer more reforced and redoubled his sorowe. *c* **1500** *Melusine* 290 There reforced the batayll.

re'forest, *v.* Chiefly *N. Amer.* [RE- 5 a.] *trans.* To cover again with forest; = REAFFOREST *v.* 2. Also *absol.*

1881 *Q. Rev.* July 56 Large tracts of land are being re-forested. **1882** *Nature* XXV. 527 Attention is called to the necessity of re-foresting. **1918** *Jrnl. Forestry* XVI. 335 It has been assumed that 75 per cent of the State-owned land must be reforested artificially. **1939** *Geogr. Jrnl.* XCIV. 178 The French have spent 317 million francs on reforesting over a million acres. **1969** S. M. JEPSEN *Trees & Forests* i. 27 During 1965, more acres..of national forest land were reforested by planting and seeding than in any previous year.

So **refore'station; reforesti'zation** (Ogilvie 1882); **re'forestize** *v.* (Webster 1897).

1887 MOLONY *Forestry W. Afr.* 90 How different would it have been had there been some system of conservancy or re-forestation. **1918** *Jrnl. Forestry* XVI. 889 It is absolutely essential to ameliorate the rivers, especially the Hun Ho, in the mountainous collecting basin, by reforestation. **1976** T. WALKER *Spatsizi* xi. 121 Natural re-forestation was well advanced in the burn with pines ten feet high.

re'forfeit, *v.* [RE- 5 a.] To forfeit again.

1667 *Decay Chr. Piety* v. ¶ 12 Those who by a new set of impossible commands should..reforfeit themselves again.

re'forge, *v.* [RE- 5 a. In early use prob. ad. OF. *reforgier* (15th c.; mod.F. *reforger*).]

1. *trans.* To forge (metal or articles of metal) over again.

1426 LYDG. *De Guil. Pilgr.* 16048 Take ageyn ther olde Armure..Wych they ha broke, and lost in veyn; Lat hem reforge hem newe ageyn. **1813** *Metrical Remarks* 42 To reforge the fetters they had broke. **1846** HOLTZAPFFEL *Turning* II. 536 Continually re-forging the blade, to the manifest deterioration of the steel.

2. To refabricate, fashion afresh.

1542 UDALL *Erasm. Apoph.* 144 b, Thou dooest disguyse and reforge thyn ownself into a woman. **1614** SYLVESTER *Bethulia's Rescue* IV. 242 There, did no drunken Groom.. against Heav'n blasphemous Oathes re-forge. **1899** *Daily News* 20 Apr. 3/2 Whether they should retain this Act..or whether they should throw it aside and leave the necessity of re-forging it at some future time.

Hence **re'forger,** one who forges anew. *rare.*

1548 UDALL *Erasm. Par. Luke* xxiv. 187 Christe beeyng a newe reforger of the olde lawe.

reform (rɪ'fɔːm), *sb.* [f. next, or ad. F. *réforme* (1640) = Sp. *reforma*, It. *riforma*.]

1. a. The amendment, or altering for the better, of some faulty state of things, *esp.* of a corrupt or oppressive political institution or practice; the removal of some abuse or wrong.

1663 BUTLER *Hud.* I. ii. 538 No Sow-gelder..but cry'd Reform! **1706** PHILLIPS (ed. Kersey), *Reform*, Reforming, Reformation. **1730–6** BAILEY (folio), *Reform*,..a reestablishment or revival of a former neglected discipline; also a correction of reigning abuses. **1786** HAN. MORE *Florio* Dramas, etc. (1827) 181 He said when any change was brewing, Reform was a fine name for ruin. **1820** SHELLEY *Œd. Tyr.* I. 113 Bœotia, choose reform or civil war! **1844** H. H. WILSON *Brit. India* II. 118 His unwilling consent.. rendered him still more than ever hostile to all projects of reform. **1874** MICKLETHWAITE *Mod. Par. Churches* 80 Reform was needed, and not total abolition.

b. A particular instance of such amendment; a change for the better.

1781 COWPER *Conversat.* 804 Great changes..have occurred, And blest reforms, that I have never heard. **1795** BURKE *Regic. Peace* iv. Wks. IX. 58 This new constitution of theirs, which had been announced as a great reform. **1855** MACAULAY *Hist. Eng.* xii. III. 209 To reduce those endowments..would have been a reform worthy of a good prince and of a good parliament. **1883** *Law Times* 20 Oct. 408/1 The public and the Profession were alike urgent in calling for sweeping reforms.

c. *ellipt.* (with capital initial), the Reform Club (see 6 a below).

1853 *London Clubs* 51 *The Reform Club.* Next [to Boodle's] in order amongst political clubs stands the *Reform*, although we are not sure that it is not surpassed in seniority by its great rival..the *Carlton*. Both had their origin in the exciting era of 1830, and the Reform Bill. **1860** A. J. MUNBY *Diary* 18 Mar. in D. Hudson *Munby* (1972) 56, I feel no interest in..Reform and Carlton conflicts. **1886** B. POTTER *Jrnl.* 14 Jan. (1966) 163 It was rumoured yesterday, 13th, that Morley was going to leave the Reform. Harrison has left the Athenaeum. **1940** H. NICOLSON *Let.* 14 July (1967) 102, I dined..at the Reform and we listened afterwards to Winston. **1978** G. GREENE *Human Factor* III. i. 97 They made a habit of lunching alternately at the Reform and the Travellers once a month on a Saturday.

2. a. Amendment of conduct; reformation of persons or character.

1784 COWPER *Task* II. 321 What vice has it subdued? whose heart reclaimed By rigour, or whom laughed into reform? *Ibid.* v. 618 Remorse begets reform. **1843** *Penny Cycl.* XXV. 155/2 Institutions auxiliary to those for Punishment (Houses of Reform).

b. ***reform through labour*** [tr. Chinese *láodòng gǎizào*], in China, an element of ideological reformation whereby criminals and dissidents are made to work as a part of their political re-education.

1957 P. S. H. TANG *Communist China Today* v. 247 The theoretical basis for the policy of 'reform through labor' was stated by Mao Tse-tung in his 1949 report *On People's Democratic Dictatorship*..promising that 'reactionaries' who desisted from counter-revolutionary activities would not be put to death but would be given work in order to 'reform themselves through labour so as to become new men'. **1962** E. SNOW *Red China Today* (1963) xxi. 156 He inspects reform-through-labour farms. *Ibid.* xlvii. 361 No one is entitled to assume that 'reform through labor' in China is administered by humanitarians. **1977** *China Now* July/Aug. 13/3 Bao spent seven years undergoing Reform Through Labour (Lao Dong Gai Zao) having been arrested in 1957.

3. Improvement or rectifying of something faulty or inexact.

1856 EMERSON *Eng. Traits, Wealth,* Roger Bacon explained precession of the equinoxes, [and] the consequent necessity of the reform of the calendar.

4. a. A religious order created by the reduction of another to stricter observances. Also (with capital initial) preceded by designating adj. *rare.*

Copied by Chambers from the *Dict. de Trévoux* (1721).

1727–41 CHAMBERS *Cycl.* s.v., In this sense the order of St. Bernard is said to be only a reform of that of St. Benedict. **1869** *Chambers' Encycl.* s.v. *Recollet*, A reform of the Cistercian order of nuns in Spain was called by the same name. **1873** LADY G. FULLERTON *Life L. de Carvajal* II. viii. 243 Her beloved friends..were both nuns of the Augustinian Reform. **1893** *Mod. Lang. Notes* VIII. 344 (*heading*) History and texts of the Benedictine reform of the tenth century. **1911** A. BRENNAN *St. Lawrence of Brindisi* xvi. 147 The Fathers of St. Giles, who belonged to the Alcantarine Reform, were delighted to receive him [*sc.* Father Lawrence] as their guest. **1953** K. SISAM *Stud. Hist. Old Eng. Lit.* VI. ii. 106 The second half of the tenth century was the period of the Benedictine Reform.

†**b.** A reformed person. *Obs. rare.*

1756 AMORY *Buncle* (1770) I. 118, I became a thorough reform from that hour.

†**5.** *Mil.* A discharge or dismissal. *Obs. rare*[−1].

1698 LUTTRELL *Brief Rel.* (1857) IV. 416 Another reform of 25 men more will be made out of each troop of guards, which will reduce them to 150 each troop.

6. a. *attrib.*, as ***reform*** or ***Reform Convention, Democrat, League, mayor, movement, Parliament, party, politician, school***; **Reform Act** or **Bill,** an act or bill to amend the system of parliamentary representation, especially those brought in and passed in 1831–2; **Reform Club,** a club instituted to promote (usu. political) reform; *spec.* the name of a London club in Pall Mall founded in 1836; **Reform(ed) Neutral** *Philol.*, an international language developed by Rosenberger and de Wahl from *Idiom Neutral* (see IDIOM 5); **reform school** orig. *U.S.*, a reformatory for young persons.

1832 F. N. ROGERS (*title*) Parliamentary Reform Act, 2 Will. 4. c. 45. With notes. **1831** (*title*) A Chart exhibiting a list of the Names of the Majority and Minority, on the Second Reading of the English Reform Bill. **1835** *Times* 16 June 5/6 People have heard of the Middlesex Reform Club. It seems that this formidable 'corporation' is on the eve of dissolution. **1837** *Times* 27 Nov. 5/1 A numerous meeting of Whig-Radical members of the House of Commons was held to-day (Saturday), at 12 o'clock, at the Reform Club-house, Pall-mall. **1877** *Public Acts Michigan* 42 Reform club temperance societies may be incorporated in pursuance of the provisions of this act. **1884** B. POTTER *Jrnl.* 22 Feb. (1966) 68 Lord Rollo..is a member of the Reform Club, but seldom goes. *a* **1974** R. CROSSMAN *Diaries* (1975) I. 42 One of the Reform Club dinners at which Charles Snow took the chair and captivated Harold Wilson. **1851** *Documentary Hist. Amer. Industr. Society* (1910) VIII. 317 A National Reform Convention is however to be held. **1887** *Courier-Jrnl.* (Louisville, Kentucky) 8 Feb. 1/2 (*heading*) The Reform Democrats manage to get Mr. Randall into very deep water. **1866** BRIGHT *Sp., Reform* 27 Aug. (1876) 377, I am not afraid of the principles of the Reform League. **1968** *Listener* 5 Sept. 290/1 His machine had just taken a terrible beating at the hands of a reform mayor. **1839** J. S. MILL in *Westm. Rev.* XXXII. 476 The question is not now about particular reforms, but how to carry on the Reform movement. **1922** A. L. GUÉRARD *Short. Hist. Internat. Lang. Movement* II. vi. 139 Reformed-Neutral of 1907 looked more natural than the primitive form. The restitution of international *c* wherever it had been replaced by *s* or *k* greatly improved the appearance of the language. But one of the most obvious blemishes of the Idiom was not corrected: the accumulation of final consonants as in *nostr. Ibid.* viii. 172 He [*sc.* Prof. Peano] is, like Dr. Molenaar, and like Messrs. Rosenberger and de Wahl in their Reform-Neutral, a radical, a posteriorist. **1946** H. JACOB *On Choice Common Lang.* iii. 27 Idiom Neutral, the early product of the Akademi, under the influence of Rosenberger and de Wahl, soon became Reform-Neutral, and when Rosenberger died de Wahl carried on his studies until, in 1922, he published his own system, Occidental. **1862** C. KNIGHT *Pop. Hist. Eng.* VIII. xvii. 310 The dreaded Reform Parliament was to assemble at the end of January, 1833. **1839** J. S. MILL in *Westm. Rev.* XXXII. 477 No reformer can hope to realize any reforms of importance, but by means of a strong and united Reform party. **1851** BORROW *Lavengro* c, I think of the two, the liberal or reform party were the most inveterate. **1970** D. GOLDRICH et al. in I. L. Horowitz *Masses in Lat. Amer.* v. 189 It is much more common for 'reform' parties to symbolize the *peasant* as the forgotten. **1904** A. FRENCH *Barrier* iii. 22 The reform politicians, those bees who buzzed continually and occasionally stung, had been after the young man. **1859** BARTLETT *Dict. Amer.* 359 *Reform School.* **1860** C. E. DELONG *Jrnl.* 7 Dec. in *Calif. Hist. Soc. Q.* (1931) X. 258 In the afternoon a crowd of us went out to view the site of the [state] Reform School [for boys]. **1913** J. LONDON *Valley of Moon* i. 3 An' her with seven, an' two of 'em in reform school. **1958** *New Statesman* 6 Sept. 294/3 A reform-school boy whose criminal side has been straightened up by the analysts. **1973** J. CLEARY *Ransom* i. 12 Even the Police Commissioner's wife didn't go to finishing school—some of us reckon he found her in a reform school.

b. Reform Judaism, a liberalizing movement initiated in Germany by the philosopher Moses Mendelssohn (1729–86), to accommodate the Jewish faith to the European intellectual enlightenment. Also in various related *attrib.* collocations, as ***Reform Jew, party, Synagogue,*** etc. Occas. *ellipt.* as predic. adj.

In Britain, Reform Judaism occupies a middle position between Orthodox and Liberal Judaism.

1843 *Voice of Jacob* 27 Oct. 21/2 The Frankfort Reform Association..meets with great sympathy among a large portion of the Jews here... The Anti-reform party.. seriously proposes to counteract the..'reformers' in an honourable manner. **1844** *Southern Q. Rev.* Apr. 325 The Reform party maintain that the old written law,—the law of Moses and the Prophets, is the only divine..law, but that the Talmud and the decisions of the Rabbins..are not divine. *Ibid.* 333 An important effort was made in London ..establishing a Reform Synagogue. **1845** *Voice of David* 15 Aug. 219/1 The 'Berlin Reform Association'..is said to have declared..that should the Synod not agree with its (the Reform Association's) views, the latter would independently pursue its own course. **1860** *N.Y. Times* 6 Aug. 8/3 The innovations of the 'reform party'..which he [*sc.* Rabbi Isaacs] attributed to religious pride... The congregation..remained uncontaminated by these pretended reforms. **1870** R. D-C. LEWIN *What is Judaism?* 8 The signal triumphs which have attended the efforts of the Reform School of Judaism. *Ibid.*, Charitable institutions which are so largely supported by Reform Jews. **1892** I. ZANGWILL *Childr. Ghetto* III. 36 The paper was founded to inculcate..the principles of true Judaism... But this is rank Reform; it's worse than the papers we came to supersede. *Ibid.* 143 The Reform Synagogue, though a centre of culture and prosperity, was cold, crude, and devoid of magnetism. **1916** H. SACHER *Zionism & Jewish Future* 48 Why should not all Jews recover their spiritual unity through Reform Judaism? **1959** *Tamarack Rev.* Summer 12 Try to convince Gershon that she'd joined the Orthodoxes in protest against her sons' becoming Anglican-like Reform Jews. **1966** 'A. BLAISDELL' *Date with Death* xvi. 208, I never was very religious, we were Reform but not much given to..keeping up with temple. **1977** H. FAST *Immigrants* IV. 238 What about the Reform Jews? The capacity of the rich is always larger than the capacity of the poor. **1980** *Times* 18 July 4/3 It is intended to broadcast a service from a Reform synagogue in London..the first occasion that an established non-Christian religious service has been included in the regular output.

reform (rɪ'fɔːm), *v.*[1] Also 4 refoorme, reffourme, 4–7 refourme. [ad. OF. *reformer* (12th c.; mod.F. *réformer*), or L. *reformāre*, f. *re-* RE- + *formāre* to form; hence also Sp. *reformar*, It. *riformare*.

For early examples of the purely literal sense 'to form again', see *v.*[2]]

†**1.** *trans.* To renew, restore, re-establish (peace).

c **1340** HAMPOLE *Prose Tr.* 3 This name Ihesu..wastys discorde, reformes pese. **1387** TREVISA *Higden* (Rolls) VII. 103 Pees was reformed in þis manere [L. *pax reformata est*]. **1483** CAXTON *Gold. Leg.* 182/1 In theyr solempnytees pees was reformed bytwene the lombardes and the emperour of Rome. **1556** *Chron. Gr. Friars* (Camden) 16 That pesse shulde be reformyd be-twene Yngland and France.

†**2. a.** To convert, bring back, or restore (a thing or person) *to* the original form or state, or to a previous condition. *Obs.*

c 1340 Hampole *Prose Tr.* 14 Whene þe myghtes of þe saule er refourmede by grace to þe dignyte and þe state of þe firste condicione. c 1375 *Sc. Leg. Saints* v. (*John*) 136 Sancte Iohne..tuk vpe þe pecis small, and..be his prayere þar futhate reformyt þam to þe fyrste state. 1390 Gower *Conf.* I. 144 His mannes forme aȝein he tok, And was reformed to the regne In which that he was wont to regne. c 1430 Lydg. *Min. Poems* (Percy Soc.) 206 Suche as be pensyff make hem glad and murye, Distrauhte in thouhte refourme hem to resoun. c 1485 *Digby Myst.* (1882) v. 120 What reformyth the sovle to his first light? *Ibid.* 127 Baptem..reformyth the soule..to the glorious lykenesse of god eternall. 1579 Tomson *Calvin's Serm. Tim.* 815/2 It is true nowe that God is reuealed to vs when he reformeth vs to his image.

b. Without const. To restore (a person) to a normal state of mind, or to consciousness. *Obs.*

1382 Wyclif *1 Sam.* xvi. 23 Dauid took an harp, and smoot with hys hoond, and Saul was refourmyd [L. *refocillabatur*], and liȝter he hadde. —— *Judith* xiii. 30 [xiv. 7] After forsothe that, the spirit taken aȝeen, he is reformed [L. *recreatus*], he fel doun to hir feet, and honourede hir.

†3. To restore (a building) after destruction, decay, or damage; to rebuild, repair. *Obs.*

c 1375 *Sc. Leg. Saints* xxii. (Laurence) 582 Lumbardis had brynt it in were... þane gat he men of craft to wyrk & to reforme þis haly kyrk. 1480 Caxton *Chron. Eng.* III. (1520) 23 b/2 He refourmed the temple of God better and encreased the cytee of Jherusalem. a 1578 Lindesay (Pitscottie) *Chron. Scot.* (S.T.S.) I. 57 The castell..was reformit againe new better nor it was befoir. 1606 Warner *Alb. Eng.* xiv. lxxxvii, Reforming first their thrise-reard wall. 1667 Milton *P.L.* ix. 101 Seat worthier of Gods, as built With second thoughts, reforming what was old!

4. a. To convert into another and better form; to amend or improve by some change of form, arrangement, or composition; to free from previous faults or imperfections. †Also const. *unto, into.* Now *rare.*

13.. *Gaw. & Gr. Knt.* 378 Þen carppez to syr Gawan þe knyȝt in þe grene, 'Refourme we oure for-wardes, er we fyrre passe'. 1382 Wyclif *Phil.* iii. 21 Oure Lord Jhesu Crist, the which schal refoorme the body of oure mekenesse. c 1450 Holland *Howlat* 77 His halynace Throw prayer may purchace To reforme my foule face. 1495 *Act 11 Hen. VII*, c. 24 §1 Panells..shall herafter be refourmed by addicions and taking oute of names of persones by discrecion of the same Justices. 1565 Jewel *Repl. Harding* (1611) 315 The Water of Baptisme by the working of the holy Ghost, is reformed vnto a Diuine power. 1589 Greene *Menaphon* (Arb.) 79 Those eyes, faire eyes, too faire to be describde, Were those that earst the Chaos did reforme. 1615 W. Lawson *Orch. & Gard.* xi. (1623) 34 Neither let any man euer so much as thinke,..it is vnprobable..to reforme any tree. 1634 W. Tirwhyt tr. *Balzac's Lett.* (vol. I) 208 He would neede reforme all the fortifications of those strong places we passed by; he trode on no earth at which he carped not. 1687 Dryden *Hind & P.* III. 1030 'Tis prudence to reform her into ease. 1727–41 Chambers *Cycl.* s.v. *Calendar*, Romulus's calendar was reformed by Numa, who added two more months. 1769 Sir W. Jones *Palace Fortune* Poems (1777) 23 Describ'd the seasons, and reform'd the year. 1796 H. Hunter tr. *St.-Pierre's Stud. Nat.* (1799) II. 26 Persons who have been disfigured..have it in their power to reform their looks. 1853 J. H. Newman *Hist. Sk.* (1873) II. I. ii. 95 He patronised learning and poetry, and he reformed the calendar.

absol. 1340 *Ayenb.* 81 Þis uayrhede..reformeþ and agrayþeþ and him yelt his ryȝte pryente.

†b. To correct, emend (a book, writing, chart, etc.); to recast, improve by revision and alteration. *Obs.*

1498 in *Archæol. Jrnl.* XLIII. 169 Pd..for mendyng and reformyng an Article of our ordinances viijd. 1528 in *Vicary's Anat.* (1888) App. xiv. 249 To peruse, oversee, examyne, Refourme, & correcte suche Bookes and ordynaunces. 1568 North *Gueuara's Dial. Pr.* (ed. 2) title-p., Now newly revised and corrected.., refourmed of faultes escaped in the first edition. 1621 Burton *Anat. Mel.* II. ii. III. 320, I would..Correct those errors in Navigation, reforme Cosmo-graphicall Chartes, and rectifie longitudes. 1631 Weever *Anc. Funeral Mon.* 489 Geffery Chaucer, whose life is written at large, by Thomas Speght, (who by old copies, reformed his workes). 1705 Hearne *Collect.* 8 Sept. (O.H.S.) I. 42 The original Author of the *Private Devotions*, wch Dr. Hicks..reform'd. c 1779 R. Cumberland in *Lett. Lit. Men* (Camden) 412, I have reformed the passages you pointed out and..written a Prologue.

c. *Law.* To revise and amend a judgement (*obs.*); to allow an instrument to be corrected or construed according to the original intention, when an error has been committed in it.

c 1670 Hobbes *Dial. Com. Laws* (1681) 63 Erroneous Judgments are only to be reform'd by the High Court of Parliament. 1755 Magens *Insurances* I. 440 His Majesty is disposed..to have the Judgement reformed, in case the Pleas of the adverse Party, so suing, should be found valid. 1824 Simons & Stuart *Rep. Cases Chanc.* I. 210 *marg.*, A Court of Equity will reform an Instrument which, by the mistake of the Drawer, admits of a construction inconsistent with the true Agreement of the Parties, although the Party seeking to reform it himself drew the Instrument.

5. a. To make a change for the better in (an arrangement, state of things, practice or proceeding, institution, etc.); to amend or improve by removal of faults or abuses.

1432 *Rolls of Parlt.* IV. 405/1 To have ye saide first Statute of newe reformed. 1494 Fabyan *Chron.* II. l, Callynge a counsayl he refourmed many thynges for the weale of hys realme. 1560 Daus tr. *Sleidane's Comm.* 180 b, Howe the state of the weale publike, as well ciuile, as ecclesiasticall maye or ought to be reformed [L. *emendari*]. 1594 Hooker *Eccl. Pol.* IV. viii. §4 There hath arisen a sect in England, which..seeketh to reform even the French reformation. 1651 Hobbes *Leviath.* II. xxx. 177 To doe no more than reforme the Common-wealth. 1727 Gay *Fables* I. xiv, A Monkey to reform the times, Resolv'd to visit foreign climes. 1788 Gibbon *Decl. & F.* xlix. V. 155 After a long series of scandal, the apostolic see was reformed and exalted by the austerity and zeal of Gregory VII. 1845 S. Austin *Ranke's Hist. Ref.* I. 121 He was bound by the concessions he made in 1489 to reform the administration of justice. 1867 Smiles *Huguenots Eng.* i. (1880) 2 There were many eminent churchmen who sought to reform it [the Church] from within.

absol. 1480 *Bury Wills* (Camden) 63 And the seid priour of the same monasterie to refourme and to make a direccion therof. 1643 Denham *Cooper's H.* 116 May no such storm Fall on our Times, where ruine must reform. 1849 Macaulay *Hist. Eng.* i. (1890) I. 49 A body of members anxious to preserve, and a body eager to reform.

†b. *ironically.* To alter *to* a worse state. *Obs.*

1649 C. Walker *Relat. & Observ.* II. 35 For, in the interim, they garrisoned Black Fryars and S. Pauls, reforming it, from the Church of God, to a den of thieves, &c.

c. To take away, remove entirely, by (or by way of) reformation.

1660 South *Serm. Matt.* xiii. 52 In those Days, when the Revenues of the Church were not wholly reformed from it. 1694 Atterbury *Serm. 1 Peter* iv. 8 (1726) I. 78 Our Adversaries..who cry'd us down, as Men that were Reforming away Good Works. 1897 Labouchere in *Daily News* 17 Mar. 3/7 His idea of reform was to reform the Armenians off the face of the globe.

6. a. To put a stop or end to (an abuse, disorder, malpractice, etc.) by enforcing or introducing a better procedure or conduct; †to amend (a fault committed).

1390 Gower *Conf.* III. 136 Wherof full many a gret debat Reformed is to good astat. 1399 Langl. *Rich. Redeles* Prol. 21 If reson ne had reffourmed the myssecheff and the mysserule. c 1430 *Stans Puer ad Mensam* 89 (Lamb. MS.), A rodde reformeþ al her neclígence. 1530 Palsgr. 682/2 If I have done any thynge amysse, I wyll reforme it. 1545 Brinklow *Compl.* 6 Such abuses as are to be reformed in the realme. 1596 Spenser *F.Q.* v. ii. 28 Sir Artegall undid the evill fashion, And wicked customes of that Bridge refourmed. 1619 Sir R. Naunton in *Fortescue Papers* (Camden) 96 The best remedies they can for reforming what they find faultie. 1687 T. Brown *Saints in Uproar* Wks. 1730 I. 83, I am resolved..to reform these disorders. 1715 De Foe *Fam. Instruct.* I. iii. (1841) I. 63 We are resolved to reform several practices..in their behaviour. 1802 Mar. Edgeworth *Moral T.* i, He could reform every abuse.

†b. (Chiefly *Sc.*) To repair, redress (a wrong, loss, damage, etc.), to make up, make good. *Obs.*

1456 Sir G. Haye *Law Arms* (S.T.S.) 185 To reforme all harmes and scathis that suld be done throu his men. 1461 *Paston Lett.* II. 15 Seyng they have had gret wrong, besechyng my Lorde that it myght be reformed. 1535 Stewart *Cron. Scot.* I. 459 Beseikand him..to reforme the greit dampnage and cryme Tha had sustenit. 1549 *Compl. Scot.* ix. 77 Ther eftir thai reformit the distructione of the tempil. 1609 Skene *Reg. Maj.*, *Forme of Proces* 126 b, Vntill ..he be summoned,..and his expenses payed and reformed to him.

c. To correct, put right (an error or mistake).

1542–3 *Act 34 & 35 Hen. VIII*, c. 27 §113 Al errours in plees personall shalbe reformed by billes, to be sued before the saied presidente. 1571 Digges *Pantom.* III. xi. R iv b, But if ye finde any discrepance or variaunce betweene them, ye shall by the ayde of some skilfull Artificer refourme it in the lesser. 1784 Cowper *Tiroc.* 445 Young heads are giddy,.. And make mistakes for manhood to reform.

†d. To remove (a fault or blemish) by some treatment. *Obs. rare.*

1589 Puttenham *Eng. Poesie* III. xxiv. (Arb.) 293 Euery man may..reforme by arte, the faultes and imperfections that nature hath wrought in them. 1675 Hobbes *Odyssey* (1677) 290 Then we bare your body to the fleet, And there the blemishes thereof reform With water fair and warm.

7. a. To bring, lead, or force (a person) to abandon a wrong or evil course of life, conduct, etc., and adopt a right one; to bring about a thorough amendment in (a person, his conduct, etc.).

1413 *Pilgr. Sowle* (Caxton) II. lii. (1859) 54 Sathan.. myght not be refourmyd by cause of his vnchangeablylyte. 1494 Fabyan *Chron.* v. lxxxiii. 61, ii. holy Byshoppes.. came into Brytaygne to refourme the Kynge, and al other that erryd from the waye of trouth. 1535 Coverdale *Prov.* v. 23 Because he wolde not be refourmed, he shal dye. 1575–85 Abp. Sandys *Serm.* 60 Those wilful cubbes, which neither by teaching nor by example will be reformed must feele the smart of the rod. 1631 Gouge *God's Arrows* I. §46. 81 What usurer, what deceiver is reformed by this Plague? 1680 Burnet *Rochester* (1692) 61 A man is never thoroughly reformed till a new principle governs his thoughts. 1715 De Foe *Fam. Instruct.* I. iv. (1841) I. 84 Will you call my father's desire to reform your life, a putting hard upon you? 1796 H. Hunter tr. *St.-Pierre's Stud. Nat.* (1799) III. 540 As we must not go to ruin the men whom we wish to reform. 1819 Shelley *Cenci* I. i. 74 You give out that you have half reformed me. 1846 J. Baxter *Libr. Pract. Agric.* (ed. 4) I. p. xxxi, Far be it from us to discourage any effort made to reform juvenile offenders. 1871 Ruskin *Fors Clav.* ix. 6, I have not the slightest intention..of setting myself to mend or reform people.

b. Const. *from*, †*of*, †*to*, †*unto.*

1422 tr. *Secreta Secret., Priv. Priv.* 204 He rebukid the forsayden breenys and bourkeyns..and ham to Pees reformed. c 1450 Holland *Howlat* 875 To reforme the Howlat, of faltis full fell. 1477 Earl Rivers (Caxton) *Dictes* 16 To reforme the euyl disposed vnto goodnesse. 1697 Potter *Antiq. Greece* III. xi. (1715) 99 The Grecians were much reform'd from the Inhumanity..of their own Ancestors. 1714 Swift *Pres. St. Aff.* Wks. 1755 II. I. 214 The house of Hanover..is the nearest branch of our regal line reformed from popery. 1858 Carlyle *Fredk. Gt.* x. i. (1872) III. 204 Lieutenant Buddenbrock..is now reformed from those practices.

†c. To reprove, punish, chastise (a person) for some fault. *Obs.*

1484 Caxton *Fables of Æsop* II. Pref., By cause they were not customed to be refourmed ne chastysed, whan ony of them was corrected and punysshed, they were gretely troubled. 1535 Coverdale *Jonah* (heading), Ionas is angrie, and complayneth of God which refourmeth him. 1577 Harrison *England* II. iv. (1877) I. 103 At these meetings also ..roges, and runnagates, are often reformed for their excesses. 1596 Spenser *F.Q.* v. i. 21 He..The lady to alight did eft require, Whilest he reformed that uncivill fo.

d. *refl.* (also with *heart, life,* etc. as obj.) To improve one's own conduct, character, etc.

1512 *Act 4 Hen. VIII*, c. 19 *Preamble*, The seid Frensche Kyng..the Decree of the enterdiccion dispysyng will not therby reforme himselfe. 1535 Coverdale *2 Esdras* xiv. 34 Yf so be that ye wil subdue youre owne vnderstandinge, and refourme youre hert [etc.]. 1597 Shaks. *2 Hen. IV*, v. v. 72 And as we heare you do reforme your selues, We will according to your strength, and qualities, Giue you aduancement. 1727 De Foe *Syst. Magic* I. i. (1840) 14 How justly might they bid him hold his tongue, and go and reform his life, before he pretended to instruct them.

transf. 1552 Latimer *Serm. & Rem.* (Parker Soc.) 182 The wind and waters obeyed him, and reformed themselves according to his word.

†8. To instruct, inform (a person). *Obs. rare.*

1535 Coverdale *Isa.* xl. 12 Who hath refourmed [1611 directed] the mynde of the Lorde? Or who is of his councel to teach him? 1560 Becon *New Catech.* II. Wks. 1564 I. 312 The Prophete Esaye also sayeth, who hath refourmed the Spiryte of the Lorde?

†9. a. *Hawking.* (See quot.) *Obs. rare*$^{-1}$.

1486 *Bk. St. Albans* A vj b, Sum tyme yowre hawke countenansis as she piked hir, and yet she proynith not, and then ye most say she Reformith hir federis and not piketh hir federis.

b. To cut down or back to a desired length; to trim, prune. *Obs.*

1574 R. Scot *Hop Gard.* (1578) 17 You must pyle them vp immediately after they are cut, sharped, reformed in length and smoothed. 1615 W. Lawson *Country Housew. Gard.* (1626) 35 Snub his top..with a sharpe knife, and take him cleane away, and so you may vse any Cyon you would reforme. 1667 Milton *P.L.* IV. 625 We must be ris'n And at our pleasant labour, to reform Yon flourie Arbors. 1697 Dryden *Virg. Georg.* II. 605 Shall we doubt..To sow, to set, and to reform their growth?

c. To bring into a better state, to improve.

1607 Norden *Surv. Dial.* v. 237 This peece of ground.. hath had much labour and great cost bestowed on it, and the ground little or nothing the more reformed.

†10. *Mil.* [After F. *réformer.*] To form into a new regiment or company; to break up, partially or completely, for this purpose; hence also, to disband, dismiss from the service. *Obs.*

1604 E. Grimstone *Hist. Siege Ostend* 188 He hath casziered and dismissed aboue 600 men, as well Commanders and Sargeants, as commissaries and Treasurers,..hee hath also reformed the common soldiers. 1629 Wadsworth *Pilgr.* vii. 71 His regiment being reformed into one company, was giuen to Captaine Rhisby. 1664 Pepys *Diary* 31 Oct., If you must reform two of them, be sure let him command the troop that is left. 1706 Phillips (ed. Kersey) s.v., In Military Affairs, to Reform, is to reduce a Body of Men, either disbanding the Whole, and putting the Officers and Soldiers into other Bodies, or only breaking a Part, and retaining the rest. 1768 Sterne *Sent. Journ.* II. 51 (*Le Patissier*) At the conclusion of the last peace, his regiment being reformed,..he found himself.. without a livre.

11. *intr.* (for *refl.*) To abandon wrong-doing or error; to free oneself from misconduct or fault.

1582 N. Lichefield tr. *Castanheda's Conq. E. Ind.* I. xxi. 54 The Catuall did reforme, and make himselfe friendes with him. 1643 Sir T. Browne *Relig. Med.* I. §3 We have reformed from them, not against them. 1680 H. More *Apocal. Apoc.* 356 How necessary it is to reform from the Roman impurities. 1736 Butler *Anal.* I. iii. 47 Those who have gone on for some time in the ways of Vice, and have afterwards reformed. 1769 *Junius Lett.* xiv. 61 It is possible the young man may, in time, grow wiser and reform. 1865 Pusey *Truth Eng. Ch.* 80 If..the Church of England reformed by herself [etc.]. 1867 Freeman *Norm. Conq.* (1876) I. App. 637 He reformed and rose to the rank of Ealdorman.

12. Also **re-form.** To subject (petrol, hydrocarbons, etc.) to reforming *vbl. sb.* 2.

1924 *Proc. 31st Ann. Convention Pacific Coast Gas Assoc.* 724 The artificial gas portion of the commercial mixture may be manufactured by 'reforming' natural gas rather than by producing this gas from oil. 1931 *U.S. Bureau of Mines Techn. Paper* No. 483. 1 There is a definite demand for a means and process for re-forming hydrocarbon gases, including refinery gas. 1941 W. L. Nelson *Petroleum Refinery Engin.* (ed. 2) xxiv. 527 These authors conclude that it is not economical to top the light gasoline and reform the naphtha separately. 1966 *McGraw-Hill Encycl. Sci. & Technol.* XI. 403/2 In a typical operation, a Pennsylvania straight-run gasoline of 44 octane number may be reformed to give a product with an octane number of 80..with a yield of 66%. 1974 *Sci. Amer.* Oct. 67/2 The carbohydrates decay exoergically to form fossil fuels such as methane..which can then be re-formed endoergically to yield hydrogen gas.

re-form, reform (riːˈfɔːm), *v.*² Also 4 refourme, 5 *Sc.* refurm. [Orig. identical with prec., but in later use a new formation from re- 5 a and form *v.* Cf. F. *reformer.*] *trans.* and *intr.* To form a second time, form over again.

trans. a 1340 Hampole *Psalter* iv. 7 Þe light of his grace þat refourmes in vs his ymage. 1390 Gower *Conf.* I. 273 And riht so in the same forme In fleissh and blod he schal reforme the qwike and dede. c 1425 Wyntoun *Cron.* II. vi. 484 Til wyttyr þaim for hir pete How mankynde mycht refurmyt be. 1594 Kyd *Cornelia* II. 360 The formes of things doe neuer die, Because the matter that remaines Reformes another thing thereby. 1656 Stanley *Hist. Philos.* v. (1701) 181/1 When the Soul by cogitation reforming these things, which are conceived in Opinion by Memory and Sense [etc.]. **1695** WOODWARD *Nat. Hist. Earth* II. (1723) 105 Its prime Errand was to Re-form and New-mold the Earth. **1798** LANDOR *Gebir* IV. 128 She had words to speak, She form'd them and reform'd them. **1821** BYRON *Juan* III. lix, Our little selves re-form'd in finer clay. **1875** *Ure's Dict. Arts* (ed. 7) II. 924 The formation goes on continuously, so that..a fresh deposit..is re-formed in about twenty years.

intr. **1899** CAGNEY tr. *Jaksch's Clin. Diagn.* v. (ed. 4) 158 This precipitate re-formed on the further addition of the dye.

b. *Mil.* (See FORM *v.* 8.)

trans. **1802** JAMES *Milit. Dict.* s.v., When a line of several battalions hath passed another..it may be reformed in the following manner. **1835** LYTTON *Rienzi* II. iii, Order was again restored, and the line reformed. **1859** F. A. GRIFFITHS *Artil. Man.* (1862) 13 Unfix Swords. Re-form Company.

intr. **1847** *Infantry Man.* (1854) 97 No advanced guard.., after carrying a post, should..be permitted to advance without reforming. **1854** J. S. C. ABBOTT *Napoleon* (1855) II. xx. 311 At that well known..voice, the flying troops immediately re-formed.

reforma'bility. *rare.* [f. REFORMABLE *a.*: see -ITY.] Capacity for being reformed.

1904 *Daily Chron.* 29 Nov. 6/1 The Council has made provision for all women sent from London courts, regardless of the question of reformability.

reformable (rɪ'fɔːməb(ə)l), *a.* [f. REFORM *v.*[1] + -ABLE: cf. F. *réformable* (16th c. in Godef. *Compl.*).] Capable of being reformed; admitting or susceptible of reformation.

1483 in *Eng. Gilds* (1870) 337 Provided allway..that hit be reformabyll and corrigabill by the Mayre. **1533** CRANMER *Let. to Hen. VIII* in *Misc. Writ.* (Parker Soc.) II. 271, I find them as conformable and reformable as any number with whom I have communed. **1563** ABP. PARKER in Ellis *Orig. Lett.* Ser. II. II. 271 Other disorders reformable by ecclesiasticall lawes. **1647** HAMMOND *Power of Keys* iv. 76 To make the Christian offender by that meanes ashamed and reformable. **1711** G. HICKES *Two Treat. Chr. Priesth.* (1847) I. 163 The reformable mal-administration of church censures. **1832** *Fraser's Mag.* VI. 486 The boy was criminal, but in my judgment reformable.

Hence † **re'formableness.** *rare*[−1].

a **1591** R. GREENHAM *Wks.* (1599) 32 Little children, whether in teachablenes to good, or reformablenes from sinne.

† **reformade.** *Obs.* [ad. next: see -ADE 3.] = REFORMADO I.

c **1645** T. TULLY *Siege of Carlisle* (1840) 8 With him came some white coats, and about 200 of reformades. **1661** *Sir A. Haslerig's Last Will & Test.* 3 Our baffled Reformades, and desperate Decoys of our late disbanded Army. **1696** tr. *Du Mont's Voy. Levant* xiv. 176 A sort of Officers that never go to War, almost like our Reformades. **1733** NEAL *Hist. Purit.* II. 525 David Hyde, one of the Reformades, first drew his sword in Palace yard.

attrib. *c* **1645** T. TULLY *Siege of Carlisle* (1840) 26 The partye, consisting of 42, all reformade officers. **1685** CROWNE *Sir C. Nice* I. 8 They..march in Publick with their Baggage,..and a whole train of Reformade sinners.

b. *to ride reformades*, to serve as volunteers.

1682 BUNYAN *Holy War* 104 There were also some from the Court that rode Reformades, for the love that they had to the King Shaddai.

So † **reformader.** *Obs.* (In quot. *attrib.*)

c **1642** in *Glover's Hist. Derby* (1829) I. App. 71 Two hundred and forty of the Lord Brooke's reformader troupe, which behaved themselves all very gallantly.

reformado (rɛfɔː'meɪdəʊ). [a. Sp. *reformado* (= Pg. *reformado*, It. *riformato*, F. *réformé*): ad. L. *reformātus*, pa. pple. of *reformāre* to REFORM.]

1. *Mil.* **a.** An officer left without a command (owing to the 'reforming' or disbanding of his company) but retaining his rank and seniority, and receiving full or half pay; a 'reformed' officer. **b.** A volunteer serving in the army (or navy) without a commission, but with the rank of an officer. Now only *Hist.*

1598 B. JONSON *Ev. Man in Hum.* III. v, Into the likenesse of some of these Reformado's had he moulded himselfe so perfectly. **1640** in Rushw. *Hist. Coll.* III. (1692) I. 68 That the Earl of Crauford's Troop, and those other Officers in the Army that go under the name of Reformadoes, are an unnecessary Charge. **1647** SPRIGGE *Anglia Rediv.* III. ii. (1854) 143 The castle was manned with 700 men, divers of them reformadoes. **1660** PEPYS *Diary* 1 Oct., Mr. Mansell, a poor Reformado of the Charleses, came to see me. **1724** DE FOE *Mem. Cavalier* (1840) 85 There was about thirty officers, who, having no soldiers,..served as reformadoes with the regiment. **1755** CARTE *Hist. Eng.* IV. 311 Moving his majesty that the loyal Scotch officers, formed into a company of reformadoes.., might be cashiered. **1814** SCOTT *Wav.* xliv, Jinker..had been reduced, with several others, by the advice of the Baron of Bradwardine, to the situation of what he called reformed officers, or reformadoes. **1891** GARDINER *Hist. Civil War* III. liii. 177 The Reformadoes were at last to be actually ejected from London.

transf. **1643** TRAPP *Comm. Gen.* xiv. 16 Kings cared not for souldiers (no more did the King of Sodome for Abraham, and his Reformadoes). *a* **1679** T. GOODWIN *Christ the Mediator* v. xviii. Wks. 1863 V. 331 The devil again put out of trade, and made a reformado.

2. One who is (or has) reformed in some respect; also, one who favours reform; a reformer.

a **1632** WEEVER (T.), This was one of Celestin the pope's caveats for his new reformadoes. **1642** *View Print. Book int. Observat.* 22, I promise him upon that to turn Reformado. **1654** WHITLOCK *Zootomia* 502 Now see the Rocks our false Reformado splits on. *a* **1734** NORTH *Exam.* II. iv. §146 (1740) 310, I promise hereafter to be a Reformado, or no Writer at all. **1787** *Gentl. Mag.* LVII. II. 1053/1 Never surely did any Turkish or Algerine reformado slash his subject of conversion with a spirit so zealous. **1823** BYRON *Juan* x. xiii, Even shuffling Southey..Would scarcely join again the 'reformadoes', Whom he forsook to fill the laureate's sty. **1857** *Blackw. Mag.* LXXXI. 394 Have I not set fast brothers by the ears..And sometimes roused the reformado's zeal?

3. a. *attrib.*, as ***reformado officer, saint, Scot, sect, soldier***, etc.

1644 *Ordinance* 26 Mar. in Husband *Coll. Pub. Ord. Ho. Parlt.* (1646) 446 The condition of Reformadoe Officers. **1664** BUTLER *Hud.* II. ii. 116, I grant You are a Reformado Saint. *Ibid.* 648 She..o'er her shoulder Chastiz'd the Reformado Soldier. *a* **1680** —— *Rem.* (1759) II. 128 Three Reformado Sects joined in one..will not serve to maintain one Pedant. **1724** DE FOE *Mem. Cavalier* (1840) 85 My reformado Scots having observed that the town port [etc.].

b. Used after a sb., as ***captain, gentleman, knight reformado***.

1609 B. JONSON *Sil. Wom.* v. ii, His Knights reformados are wound vp as high, and insolent, as euer they were. **1617** MORYSON *Itin.* II. 166 Wee tooke thirteene prisoners, among whom was a Captaine Reformado (as they terme them, for honour of antiquitie). **1691** *Proc. agst. French* in *Select. fr. Harl. Misc.* (1793) 475 Himself leading his own guard of gentlemen reformadoes.

† **re'formalist.** *Obs. rare*[−1]. [irreg. f. REFORM *sb.*, perh. an error for REFORMATIST: cf. next.] A reformer.

1611 SPEED *Hist. Gt. Brit.* IX. xv. §44. 636/2 By instigation of the discontented reformalists.

† **re'formalizing,** *ppl. a. Obs. rare*[−1]. [Perh. an error for *reformatizing*: cf. prec.] Seeking or pretending to reform.

1614 W. LOE *Serm. Bliss of Br. Beauty* 25 (T.), Christ's doctrine [is] pure, correcting all the impure glosses of the reformalizing Pharisees.

reformate (rɪ'fɔːmeɪt). [f. REFORM(ING *vbl. sb.* + *-ate*, after *distillate*, *filtrate*, etc.] The end-product of the process of reforming petroleum products.

1949 *Industr. & Engin. Chem.* Oct. 2185/1 The crude reformate was condensed at 32°F. **1951** *World Petroleum* Nov. 73/2 In recent weeks two new processes have been announced for separating and purifying the aromatics from reformate. **1958** W. L. NELSON *Petroleum Refinery Engin.* (ed. 4) xxi. 813 Reformate normally has an end point 15 to 30°F higher than that of the feedstock. **1973** HADLEY & TURNER in Hobson & Pohl *Mod. Petroleum Technol.* (ed. 4) xii. 442 Catalytic reforming of straight-run material yields a C_6–C_8 reformate rich in the aromatic hydrocarbons, benzene, toluene, ethylbenzene, and the xylenes.

reformation (rɛfə'meɪʃən). Also 6 refourmation. [ad. L. *reformātiōn-em*, n. of action f. *reformāre* to REFORM: cf. F. *réformation* (13th c. in Godef. *Compl.*).]

† **1.** Restoration (of peace). Cf. REFORM *v.*[1] I.

c **1440** *Gesta Rom.* I. xlvii. 196 (Harl. MS.), Wher so euer he knewe þat eny discorde or vnrest was Regnynge, he labovrid to make Reformacion of pes. **1568** GRAFTON *Chron.* II. 156 The Legate..laboured so to the king, that a reformation of peace was spoken of.

2. Improvement in form or quality; alteration to a better form; correction or removal of defects or errors; †reparation, rebuilding.

c **1425** WYNTOUN *Cron.* II. i. 108 Off Babilon bathe towire and town Scho made gude reformacion. **1468** *Paston Lett.* II. 314 Maister John Smyth, that..was none holsom counceller yn the reformacion of the last testament. **1528** in *Vicary's Anat.* (1888) App. xiv. 249 [To] examine, Refourme, & correcte..alle suche of the saide Actes and Ordynaunce As vppon the examinacion and Reformacion of theym they shalle thynke to be good and Resonable. *c* **1543** in Parke *Dom. Archit.* (1859) III. 79 To make..a new halle ..and reformacon honourable for the quenes loggyng. *Ibid.*, With reformation of your conduyts there. **1594** BLUNDEVIL *Exerc.* III. I. xvi. (1636) 311 Unlesse the Kalenders be reformed..(for the Roman reformation is not so exactly true as it might be). **1600** ROWLANDS *Lett. Humours Blood* xii. 18 Fine Phillip comes vnto the Barbers shopp, Wheer's nittie lockes must suffer reformation. **1663** GERBIER *Counsel* d 3, All such as the very aspects of number of Brick-buildings, since the reformation of a Gotis relick building, hath manifested to have been the main cause **1776** ADAM SMITH *W.N.* I. v. I. 49 Even before the late reformation of the gold coin of Great Britain. **1829** SIMONS & STUART *Rep. Cases Chanc.* I. 218 Whether a Court of Equity will refuse to reform an Instrument..because it happened to be drawn by the Party seeking that reformation. **1855** BREWSTER *Newton* II. xxiii. 311 When the public attention was called to the reformation of the Kalendar.

† **b.** Improvement in health. *Obs. rare*[−1].

1772 JOHNSON *Let. to Mrs. Thrale* 19 Oct., This is to be my home long enough to receive a letter, which will, I hope, tell me that you are busy in reformation.

3. Improvement of (or in) an existing state of things, institution, practice, etc.; a radical change for the better effected in political, religious, or social affairs.

c **1460** FORTESCUE *Abs. & Lim. Mon.* xv. (1885) 148 How also þe lawes mey be amendet in suche thynges as thay neden reformacion in. *a* **1548** HALL *Chron., Hen. VIII* 60, I will do for a reformacion of this matter as muche as a priest may do. **1588** BURGHLEY in Ellis *Orig. Lett.* Ser. I. III. 28 Yf I fynde not a due and spedye reformation of all disorders among you. **1662** J. DAVIES tr. *Olearius' Voy. Ambass.* 3 In consequence of the Reformation of Religion, both lost the Authority they had in this City. **1713** BERKELEY *Guardian* No. 62 ¶10 The reformation of the church and that of learning began together. **1782** COWPER *Flatting Mill* 14 Alas for the poet! who dares undertake To urge reformation of national ill. **1833** ALISON *Hist. Europe* ii. II. 65 If they [bands] are slowly and cautiously unbent, it is Reformation; if suddenly removed,..it is Revolution. **1856** FROUDE *Hist. Eng.* (1858) I. ii. 99 Wolsey talked of reformation, but delayed its coming.

b. *spec.* (with capital). The great religious movement of the 16th century, having for its object the reform of the doctrines and practices of the Church of Rome, and ending in the establishment of the various Reformed or Protestant Churches of central and north-western Europe.

1563 WINȜET *Wks.* (S.T.S.) I. 67 We ar sa tribulit be ȝow ..for nocht assenting generalie to ȝour prætendit reformatioun. **1588** FREGEVILLE *Reformed Politicke* 44 To the end to ship the Clergy in the League, they wer perswaded, that within six moneths the Reformation should be vtterly extinguished. **1657** TRAPP *Comm. Ps.* cl. 4 That grave and simple Psalmodie..(so much used of old, and by this blessed Reformation restored to the Church). **1685** EVELYN *Diary* 22 Dec., The first Popish Nuncio that had ben in England since the Reformation. *a* **1715** BURNET *Own Time* I. 10 Some few..did lean so grosly to Popery, that the heat and violence of the Reformation became the main subject of their sermons. **1772** T. WARTON *Sir T. Pope* 133 The liberal Pontiff did not consider.., that he was undermining the papal interest, and bringing on the Reformation. *a* **1862** BUCKLE *Misc. Wks.* (1872) I. 85 The English Reformation..during the early period of its progress,..did not produce a single man of genius.

† **c.** A reformed order (of friars). *Obs. rare*[−1].

1706 tr. *Dupin's Eccl. Hist. 16th C.* II. IV. xi. 449 These [friars] also being divided yet farther into different Reformations, Leo X. commanded them all to be reduced under the single Title of Reformed.

† **4.** Reparation, redress. *Obs.* Cf. REFORM *v.*[1] 6 b.

1442 *Rolls of Parlt.* V. 65/2 To have reformation made to the Kynges poeple, of certein Injuries and Wronges done to hem. **1583** *Wills & Inv. Durh.* (Surtees) 82, I do humble craue theme, that they will se my said wiffe and children maynteaned in lawe, for reformation of this crewell murder, committed vpon me.

5. The action of reforming (one's own or another's) conduct or morals; improvement or amendment in this respect; correction. ***house of reformation***, a reformatory.

1509 HAWES *Past. Pleas.* XI. xxxi. (Percy Soc.) 45 Their fruitfull problemes for reformacion, To make us lerne to lyve directly. **1542** BOORDE *Dyetary* xxxvii. (1870) 299 Excepte it be for reprehensyon or gentyll reformacyon. **1588** SHAKS. *L.L.L.* v. ii. 879, I shal finde you emptie of that fault, Right ioyfull of your reformation. *a* **1628** PRESTON *Breastpl. Love* (1631) 192 If there be no reformation in their lives, if a man deny not himselfe in his beloved sinne [etc.]. **1678** BUNYAN *Pilgr. Prog.* (1900) 127 My trouble came tumbling upon me again, and that over the neck of all my Reformations. **1715** DE FOE *Fam. Instruct.* I. i. (1841) I. 23 Earnest endeavours after reformation and amendment. **1780** BENTHAM *Princ. Legisl.* xvii. §15 The punishment most subservient to reformation. **1843** *Penny Cycl.* XXV. 137/2 Institutions in England auxiliary to those for punishment, or Houses of Reformation. **1885** H. CONWAY *Family Affair* ix, The work of reformation is child's play to that of making your friends believe you have reformed.

† **6.** Control, direction, authority. *Obs. rare*[−1].

1523 *Act 14 & 15 Hen. VIII*, c. 2 All maner of personnes beyng Alyens..occupieng any mistery or handy craft.. shalbe under the Serche and Reformacion of the Wardens and the Felowshyppes of handy craftes.

† **b.** In phr. ***under*** (or ***saving***) ***your reformation***: subject to your amendment or correction. *Obs.*

1558 LD. WENTWORTH in Arb. *Garner* IV. 194 Under your Majesty's Reformation..I am of opinion there would be enow. **1616** COKE in *Buccleuch MSS.* (Hist. MSS. Comm.) I. 173, I shall be able..to make the case (saving your Majesty's reformation) without all question. **1617** MORYSON *Itin.* II. 189 Wee thinke it (vnder your Lordships reformation) very expedient, that in euery of them, Cittadels were raised.

† **7.** A disbanding, dismissal (of troops); the removal of an officer from the active list. *Obs.*

1668 *Lond. Gaz.* No. 282/2 His Most Christian Majesty having resolved upon the discharge and reformation of the greatest part of his forces. **1670** [see REFORMED *ppl. a.* 4].

8. *attrib.* and *Comb.*, as ***reformation act, -cut, -monger, principles, statute***; ***reformation-bitten***, adj.

1661 J. GUTHRIE (*title*) The great Danger of backsliding and defection from Covenanted Reformation-principles. **1681** OTWAY *Soldier's Fort.* IV. i, That grave hypocritical Beard, of the Reformation-cut. **1723** DK. WHARTON in *True Briton* No. 45. II. 396 That many of these pretended Reformation-mongers, have proved themselves as bad Christians, as their Ancestors were Subjects. **1848** KINGSLEY *Saint's Trag.* v. i, A kindly youth and a godly, but reformation-bitten, like the rest. **1898** SIR W. HARCOURT in *Westm. Gaz.* 4 July 2/3 The great Reformation Act of Elizabeth. *Ibid.*, The Reformation statutes by which the doctrines and practice of the Church of England were established by law.

re-formation (riːfɔː'meɪʃən). [Orig. the same word as prec.; in later use f. RE- 5a + FORMATION (cf. RE-FORM *v.*).] The action of forming again; a second or new formation.

c **1425** WYNTOUN *Cron.* II. vi. 520 (MS. Cott.), Til conclusion Off þis reformacion [of mankind] þis Owide maid þis ilka wersse. **1541** R. COPLAND *Guydon's Quest. Chirurg.* B iv b, One is very regeneracion, whiche is very reformacion of the membre in the same selfe substaunce, forme [etc.]. **1695** WOODWARD *Nat. Hist. Earth* VI. 265 There were the same Measures taken..in this Re-Formation of it, that were when 'twas first built. **1761** *Ann. Reg.* II. 38/1 The first formation of the earth at the creation, the reformation after the deluge. **1831** BREWSTER *Nat. Magic* iv. (1833) 93 The re-formation of distorted pictures by reflection from cylindrical and conical mirrors. **1875** CROLL *Climate & T.* xxii. 361 The materials composing our stratified beds may have passed through many cycles of destruction and re-formation.

reformational (rɛfəˈmeɪʃənəl), *a.* [f. REFORMATION + -AL^1.] Belonging to, concerned with, the Reformation or with reform.

1861 BP. EWING in Ross *Mem.* xxi. (1877) 329 Theologies, Reformational and Roman, have heretofore obscured the light. **1884** *Manch. Exam.* 20 Oct. 3/6 The black gown..is reformational, and it stands in the way of making an 'altar' the great centre of worship.

So **reforˈmationary** *a.*

1827 CARLYLE *Germ. Rom.* III. 219 My feeble attempt, in regard to this Reformationary advocate [etc.].

reforˈmationist. [f. REFORMATION + -IST.] One who supports or advocates reformation.

1906 *Macmillan's Mag.* June 589 One who is proved incorrigible..may indeed be secluded, but..if the reformationists are right, his seclusion should have no penal character. **1928** *Sunday Express* 17 June 12/5 The chaos in the Church may harden into bitter anarchy and disintegrating conflict between Reformationists, Adorationists, and Modernists. **1969** *Listener* 17 July 87/3 'To make them better citizens,' says the Reformationist.

†**reˈformatist.** *Obs.* [f. L. *reformāt-*, ppl. stem of *reformāre* to REFORM, + -IST.] A reformer.

1620 BRENT tr. *Sarpi's Counc. Trent* v. (1676) 395 The king [Francis II], by his Edict, pardoned all the reformatists, until they returned to the Church. **1653** ASHWELL *Fides Apost.* 216 The Power and cleerenesse of this Truth..may serve to stop the violence of some zealous Reformatists.

reformative (rɪˈfɔːmətɪv), *a.* [f. as prec. + -IVE.] Inclined to reform; that tends to, or makes for, reform; reformatory.

1593 *Tell-Troth's N.Y. Gift* (1876) 37 Fy, fy, sweet hart, ..Will strike so deepely into a reformative conscience, as there shall not neede out vpon thee. **1641** *Short View Prel. Ch. Eng.* 10 Whither their Courts bee reformative or deformative. **1883** M. DAVITT in *Contemp. Rev.* Aug. 173 Under conditions that would lessen the evils just referred to, separate confinement might become a reformative kind of punishment.

Hence **reˈformatively** *adv.*, **reˈformativeness.**

1824 MᶜCULLOCH *Highlands Scot.* IV. 161 There is an Organ of Reformativeness. **1874** BUSHNELL *Forgiven. & Law* ii. 124 A law that undertakes the training of men..reformatively out of ways of self-indulgence.

re-ˈformative (riː-), *a.* [RE- 5 a.] Having the power of forming again.

1847 WEBSTER cites GOOD. **1900** *Q. Rev.* July 49 Earth is the most potent disinfectant known:..it is resolvent and reformative as well.

†**reformator.** *Obs.* [a. L. *reformātor*, agent-n. f. *reformāre* to REFORM: cf. F. *réformateur* (14th c.).] A reformer.

1538 ELYOT *Dict.*, *Reformator*, a reformatour. **1632** *Contin. Forraine Avisoes* No. 18. 14 Apr. 13 (Stf.), The Reformators came to Schoole, and caused the Swedes..to bee whipt in their presence. **1657** HEYLIN *Ecclesia Vind.* 24 Such points of Controversie, as were in difference betwen the Reformators of the Church of England, and the Church of Rome.

reformatory (rɪˈfɔːmətərɪ), *a.* and *sb.* [f. L. ppl. stem *reformāt-* + -ORY.]

A. *adj.* Having a desire or tendency to reform (a person or thing); designed for reforming.

1589 NASHE *Pref. Greene's Menaphon* (Arb.) 14 The vpstart discipline of our reformatorie Churchmen. **1709** STRYPE *Ann. Ref.* I. xvii. 209 Much was done not long after according to this Reformatory Platform. **1791** BENTHAM *Panopt.* II. Postscr. 189 The business of reformatory instruction may be transferred to the Chapel. **1831** MACKINTOSH *Sp. Ho. Comm.* 4 July, Wks. 1846 III. 535 Such objections..would exclude most important questions, and, certainly, all reformatory measures. **1851** MARY CARPENTER (*title*) Reformatory Schools for the Children of the Perishing and Dangerous Classes, and for Juvenile Offenders. **1884** *Manch. Exam.* 21 Aug. 4/7 The object of the discipline..is not so much retributive as reformatory. **1932**, etc. [see APPROVED *ppl. a.* 5]. **1933** J. MASEFIELD *Conway* II. 61 H.M.S. reformatory-ship *Clarence* was fired and burned by the boys on board her.

B. *sb.* An institution to which juvenile incorrigibles or offenders against the law are sent with a view to their reformation. Also *N. Amer.*, a reforming institution for women or for first offenders. Also *attrib.*

1834 J. S. MILL in *Monthly Repos.* VIII. 735 He proposes that those who are convicted of offences..should be no otherwise ill-treated than by being compelled to live as a community apart... If all who, in any manner violated the laws, were removed into such a place of reformation, the inhabitants of the reformatory would speedily outnumber the remainder of the community. **1837** *Edin. Rev.* LXIV. 353 They recommend a general Reformatory for England and Wales. **1843** *Penny Cycl.* XXV. 154/2 With the establishment of the Parkhurst Reformatory, in the Isle of Wight, the commencement of a systematic improvement.. has been made. **1870** *N.Y.* (State) *Laws* I. 320 The action of the commissioners..in locating said prison or industrial reformatory..at Elmira..is hereby approved. **1878** *Harper's Mag.* Dec. 109/1 Our reformatories..do not check the first steps in wrong-doing. **1885** *Encycl. Brit.* XIX. 764/1 The average reformatory population [in the United States] is about 15,000. **1912** M. NICHOLSON *Hoosier Chron.* iii. 53 They were going to cut down the Reformatory's appropriation last winter. **1950** *Times* 20 Mar. 5/3 As the result of the laudable impulse for reformatory treatment, the expectation may have been fostered among criminals that they will find that the salutary discomforts of prison have been reformed away. **1970** *Globe & Mail* (Toronto) 26 Sept. 2/2 [He] was sentenced to two years less a day definite and 18 months indeterminate in reformatory after admitting that he stole about \$50,000 from Sunnybrook Hospital. **1975** *Washington Post* 27 Feb. B1/7 Michael Craddock.. thinks the reformatory is a danger, a 'public nuisance'. **1977** *Ibid.* 25 Feb. A2/1 About 200 inmates at the Ohio State Reformatory hurled trays and food and fought guards during a disturbance today in the institution dining room.

reformed (rɪˈfɔːmd), *ppl. a.* and *sb.* [f. REFORM *v.*^{1} + -ED^1.] **A.** *ppl. a.*

1. a. Of religion, churches, etc.: Brought to a better or purer state by the removal of errors or abuses, esp. those imputed to the Church of Rome. Also *transf.* of persons, times, etc.

The name of ***Reformed Church(es)*** sometimes includes all the Protestant churches, and sometimes is specifically restricted to the Calvinistic bodies as contrasted with the Lutheran. The adj. also forms part of the specific names of various churches and religious bodies in different countries.

1563 FOXE *A. & M.* To Persecutors, In Countries..and Churches reformed, your errours and superstitious vanities bee so blotted out [etc.]. *Ibid.* 1 In these reformed dayes. **1588** FREGEVILLE *Reformed Politicke* Ded. A ij, So it is that the Reformed Princes haue bene sclandered by the Pope. *Ibid.* 73 The Reformed Church began by poore men. **1646** EVELYN *Diary* (Geneva), The French Protestants would make no scruple to submitt to it.., had they a King of the Reform'd Religion. **1727–41** CHAMBERS *Cycl.* s.v. *Church*, The Reformed Church is again divided into the Lutheran Church, the Calvinist Church, the Church of England, &c. **1772** T. WARTON *Sir T. Pope* 150 The English reformed clergy, who..had fled into Germany, now returned in great numbers. **1794** T. COXE *View U.S.* ix. 373 There are and have been in the legislative, executive and judicial branches of the general government, persons of the following denominations—Episcopalian,..Reformed, Roman, and probably others. **1837** J. M. PECK *Gazetteer Illinois* (ed. 2) 73 A Seminary is about being established in a settlement of Reformed Presbyterians. **1841** *Penny Cycl.* XIX. 355/1 Many of the followers of the Reformed doctrines suffered death. **1844** I. D. RUPP *He Pasa Ekklesia* 466 The Reformed Methodists took their origin from a feeble secession from the Methodist Episcopal Church, in..1814. **1847** R. DAVIDSON *Hist. Presbyterian Church Kentucky* viii. 216 Campbellites..affected the title of Reformers, or Reformed Baptists, and spoke of 'The Reformation' as if there had never been any Reformation before. **1894** EARLE *Psalter Gt. Bible* Introd. 63 The original hymns of the Lutheran worship constituted a feature which distinguished it from that of the Calvinistic or 'Reformed' branch of the continental Protestants. **1928** W. D. BROWN *Hist. Reformed Church in Amer.* i. 7 The Reformed Church in America is the direct outgrowth of the emigration from the Netherlands. **1954** *Collier's* 20 Aug. 21/3 Three allocations were decided upon—..the third to an Evangelical Reformed Church. **1967** R. MCA. BROWN *Ecumenical Revolution* viii. 142 In 1934 the Evangelical Synod of North America merged with the Reformed Church in the United States to form the Evangelical and Reformed Church, while a few years later both of these new groups merged to form what is now the United Church of Christ. **1969** T. F. TORRANCE *Theol. Sci.* ii. 87 So far we have been thinking of this mainly in terms of strictly Reformed theology but in some respects it had an even greater development in Lutheran theology. **1977** *Washington Post* 18 Mar. D18/3 The signers included Billy Graham and leaders of the.. Reformed Church in America. **1978** *Church Times* 29 Dec. 1/3 The consultation is proposing to the sponsoring bodies that a dialogue programme at world level be implemented between the Anglican and Reformed traditions.

b. In general use.

1605 BACON *Adv. Learn.* II. xx. §9 The reformed school of the Epicureans.

c. Of parliament, *spec.* of that which met after the Reform Act of 1832.

1822 COBBETT *Weekly Reg.* 2 Feb. 290 We forbear to speculate on the manner in which a Reformed Parliament would be engaged at a crisis like this. **1862** C. KNIGHT *Pop. Hist. Eng.* VIII. xviii. 324 The first session of the Reformed Parliament. **1873** EDITH THOMPSON *Hist. Eng.* xliii. 234 The Reformed Parliament, the object of great hopes and greater fears, met January 29, 1833.

d. *Judaism.* (With capital initial.) Subscribing to, or characteristic of, Reform Judaism (see REFORM *sb.* 6 b).

1844 *Voice of Jacob* 19 July 188/2 There is a 'reformed Synagogue at Liverpool'..that..is to take no part in the election of a Chief Rabbi. **1859** *N.Y. Times* 30 Sept. 1/5 At the tabernacle of the Reformed Society..Dr. Adler preached in German. **1876** GEO. ELIOT *Dan. Der.* II. IV. xxxii. 298 He was affectionately directed by a precocious Jewish youth, who entered cordially into his wanting not the fine new building of the Reformed but the old Rabbinical school of the orthodox. **1898** W. J. LOCKE *Idols* vi. 70 Think of Simeon Goldberg, a good friend, a man..of the Reformed faith. **1918** H. BARNETT *Canon Barnett* II. xxxiv. 65 Minister of Reformed Synagogue in New York. **1971** *Guardian* 16 Nov. 8/6 Grandfather had been a warden of a reformed synagogue. **1977** *Church Times* 12 Aug. 5/5 On our last day we went with a party to a service in the Reformed synagogue in Haifa.

2. †**a.** Improved in manners; cultivated. *Obs.*$^{-1}$

1574 HELLOWES *Gueuara's Fam. Ep.* (1577) 181 Very noble and refourmed [Sp. *enmendado*] knight, by the words of your letter, I understood [etc.].

b. Improved in character, conduct or morals.

1579 LYLY *Euphues* (Arb.) 53 Then doubtlesse women either do or should loue those best whose vertue is best, not measuring the deformed man, with the reformed minde. **1592** GREENE *Disput.* 11 Iacke Rhoades is now a reformed man,..he is growne a correcter of vice. **1715** DE FOE *Fam. Instruct.* I. iv. (1841) I. 85 So at last we may be a sober family, a reformed family. **1837** HT. MARTINEAU *Soc. Amer.* III. 199 When I asked how reformed offenders were to put their reformation in practice.

c. Reduced to stricter observance.

1706 [see REFORMATION 3 c]. **1863** GEO. ELIOT *Romola* xliii, First came a white stream of reformed Benedictines.

3. a. Altered in form or content; *esp.* put into a better form, corrected, amended.

1584 PARSONS *Leycester's Commw.* (1641) 148 He cousened most notably her Majesty, by shewing her a reformed Copie of the said letter, for the letter it selfe. **1727–41** CHAMBERS *Cycl.* s.v. *Calendar*, *Reformed*, or *Corrected Calendar*, that which..determines the equinox.. by astronomical computation, according to the Rudolphine tables.

b. Also **re-formed.** Of petroleum products: subjected to or obtained by REFORMING *vbl. sb.* 2.

1924 *Proc. 31st Ann. Convention Pacific Coast Gas Assoc.* 725 Reformed natural gas. **1931** *U.S. Bureau of Mines Techn. Paper* No. 483. 2 The natural gas employed was composed almost entirely of methane (CH_4) and ethane (C_2H_6), but the re-formed product comprised methane.. and hydrogen..as the chief combustible constituents. **1952** KIRK & OTHMER *Encycl. Chem. Technol.* VIII. 793 Generally a greater part of the natural gas is re-formed, and a smaller amount is mixed with air and added to the reformed gas in order to control the specific gravity and burning characteristics of the mixture. **1966** *Petroleum Handbk.* (Shell Internat. Petroleum Co.) (ed. 5) 73/2 Reformed natural gas..can usually be blended to give a gas interchangeable with manufactured gas.

†**4.** *Mil.* Of officers: Left without a command (see REFORM *v.*^{1} 10 and REFORMADO 1 a). *Obs.*

1629 WADSWORTH *Pilgr.* vii. 71 Those that continued tooke their pay of reformed Captaines. **1670** R. MONTAGU in *Buccleuch MSS.* (Hist. MSS. Comm.) I. 468 The late reformation amongst all the reformed officers. **1715** *Lond. Gaz.* No. 5323/3 Robert Rich, a Reformed Lieutenant in.. Major General Rook's late Regiment of Foot. **1758** SMOLLETT *Hist. Eng.* (1800) II. 281 With respect to the reformed officers he declared he had given orders for their being immediately paid. **1814** [see REFORMADO 1].

†**B.** *sb.* **a.** as *pl.* Adherents of the Reformed religion; Protestants. **b.** *sing.* A Protestant. *rare.*

1588 FREGEVILLE *Reformed Politicke* Ded. A ij b, The fidelitie of the Reformed, and the conspiracies of the League. **1620** BRENT tr. *Sarpi's Counc. Trent* v. (1676) 391 The Kings death in France, which the reformed did ascribe to miracle, increased their courage. **1655** (*title*) A Collection or Narrative..Concerning the..Massacres, Murthers, and other Cruelties, committed on many thousands of Reformed, or Protestants dwelling in the Vallies of Piedmont. **1741** S. A. LAVAL *Hist. Reform.* IV. VIII. 1122 That Child was born a Reformed, and had been educated in that Religion. **1772** T. WARTON *Sir T. Pope* 50 Mary.. persecuted the reformed with the most barbarous severities.

Hence **reˈformedly**, *adv. rare*$^{-1}$.

1653 MILTON *Hirelings* (1659) 57 Yet a late hot Quærist for tithes..would send us back, very reformedly indeed, to learn reformation of Tyndarus and Rebuffus.

reformer^1 (rɪˈfɔːmə(r)). [f. as prec. + -ER^1.]

1. One who reforms another. *rare.*

1526 *Pilgr. Perf.* (W. de W. 1531) 88, I sholde accompte it amonge my great lukers and vauntages..to be reproued or correcte of my reformer or mender. **1570** DEE *Math. Pref.* b ij, That any..Sober Student..will..become a Reasonable Reformer of three Sortes of people, about these Influentiall operations, greatly erring from the truth.

transf. **1869** LOWELL *Under the Willows* 348 God's passionless reformers, influences, That purify and heal and are not seen.

2. One who reforms, or effects a reform in, a state of things, practice, etc.

1548 ELYOT *Dict.*, *Reformator*, a reformer, he that bryngeth to a new or better facion. **1553** M. WOOD (Bale) tr. *Gardner's True Obed.* To Rdr. B ij, God hath appointed them..to be priuate persons, and not reformers of common causes. **1585** T. WASHINGTON tr. *Nicholay's Voy.* IV. xxxiii. 155 Solon beyng..chosen for the generall reformer of their lawes. **1660** R. COKE *Justice Vind.* 16 These are the glorious Reformers of our Church and State. **1767** GOOCH *Treat. Wounds* I. 447 *note* Ambroise Paré was a great Reformer of Surgery. **1788** GIBBON *Decl. & F.* l. V. 222 The elders of the city..affected to despise the presumption of.. the reformer of his country. **1846** MᶜCULLOCH *Acc. Brit. Empire* (1854) II. 499 The plan..advocated by the early reformers of prison discipline. **1853** MAURICE *Proph. & Kings* xxii. 381 Have we yet to learn that a great teacher or reformer..does that which swords cannot do..?

3. *spec.* **a.** One of the leaders in the reformation of religion in the 16th century.

1561 WINȜET *Cert. Tract.* i. Wks. (S.T.S.) I. 12 Sum for saying only to our ruid reformearis..hes libertie to bruke the kirk rentis. **1563** *Ibid.* I. 83 Of the ceremonies among the new reformaris. **1616** CHAMPNEY *Voc. Bps.* 29 The question between the Catholike Roman Church, and the pretended Reformers. **1714** SWIFT *Pres. St. Aff.* Wks. 1751 IV. 284, I think Luther and Calvin seem to have differed as much as any two among the Reformers. **1796** T. GREEN *Diary Lover of Lit.* (1810) 14, I should have conducted myself just as he did, towards the pope and the reformers. **1839** KEIGHTLEY *Hist. Eng.* II. 28 Fourteen Dutch reformers, who had taken refuge in England. **1880** SWINBURNE *Stud. Shaks.* 304 The struggle of episcopalian with Calvinistic reformers.

b. An advocate or supporter of political or parliamentary reform; *esp.* one who took part in the reform movement of 1831–2.

radical reformer: see RADICAL *a.* 3 c.

1780 G. SELWYN in *15th Rep. R. Comm. Hist. Manuscripts* App. VI. 443 in *Parl. Papers 1897* (C. 8551) LI. 1 My best and ablest friends here are dead; their survivors supine and superannuated; their connections new Whiggs and Reformers, and Associators. **1785** PITT *Sp.* 18 Apr. in Hansard *Parl. Hist.* (1815) XXV. 435/1 Such a House of Commons it was the wish of every reformer now to establish. **1817** COBBETT *Weekly Reg.* 8 Feb. 169/1 How do you trace that riot to the Reformers? **1832** DISRAELI *Let.* 22 Feb., I am still a Reformer, but shall destroy the foreign policy of the Grey faction. **1868** *Daily News* 8 Nov., In Birmingham, of all places, he cannot be required to stand on his defence as a Reformer.

c. *U.S.* A member of one of the reformed sects of various Protestant denominations in the 19th century, *esp.* the Campbellite Baptists. *Obs.* exc. *Hist.*

1831 J. M. PECK *Guide for Emigrants* 258 The Reformers, or Methodist Protestant church, have several societies and preachers in the State [of Illinois]. **1834** [see CAMPBELLITE 1]. **1871** E. EGGLESTON *Hoosier Schoolmaster* xii. 101 Squire Hawkins..had become a member of the 'Reformers'..who now call themselves 'Disciples', but whom the profane will persist in calling 'Campbellites'. **1931** W. W. SWEET *Relig. on Amer. Front* I. ii. 26 Between 1829 and 1832, something like 10,000 Kentucky Baptists withdrew to form the Disciples Church. Besides the Campbell followers, who were known as *Reformers*, there were several thousand anti-mission Baptists in Kentucky.

d. An advocate or adherent of Reform Judaism (cf. REFORM *sb.* 6 b).

1855 *Jewish Chron.* 20 July 245/3 The two parties, orthodox and reformers. **1870** *N.Y. Times* 3 Apr. 3/3 The tenets of Mr. Lewin represent the most advanced opinions of the Reform School, and are therefore shared in full by a minority only of the Reformers themselves. **1892** I. ZANGWILL *Childr. Ghetto* III. II. iv. 39 'By worshipping bare-headed, and by seating the sexes together, they have defiled Judaism.' 'Stop..who told you the Reformers do this?' **1934** *Times Lit. Suppl.* 10 May 334/3 The 'Reformers', too, are unlikely to have much material earlier than their foundation, though, no doubt, their papers throw light on the schism and their *ritualia* are of great beauty. **1976** B. WILLIAMS *Making of Manchester Jewry* iv. 105 To Reformers the future of Judaism..appeared to depend upon..a degree of accommodation to the values of the surrounding milieu.

4. A reviser, corrector, improver. *rare.*

1656 EARL MONM. tr. *Boccalini's Advts. fr. Parnass.* I. xxviii. (1674) 30 Apollo..received the Poem, and..gave it to the Reformer [It. *censore*] of the Library..that it might be revewed. **1837** HALLAM *Hist. Lit.* I. viii. §7 *note*, This reformer of Boiardo [Domenichi] did not alter the text nearly so much as Berni.

5. An installation or apparatus for the reforming of petroleum products (REFORMING *vbl. sb.* 2).

1934 *Jrnl. Inst. Petroleum Technologists* XX. 347 One of the new refineries in France..includes a cracking still, a viscosity breaker and a naphtha reformer. **1958** *Times Rev. Industry* May 24/3 The pilot scale installation incorporates ..a catalytic reformer in which gaseous hydrocarbons interact with steam to produce the hydrogen. **1971** *Daily Tel.* 6 Dec. 6/7 The board found it necessary to retain specialist workers employed on a hydro-carbon reformer plant. **1974** *Times* 22 Mar. 21/4 A 'reformer' unit which processes the fuel (natural gas or propane) to produce a hydrogen-rich feed for the fuel cell. **1978** *Trends in Oil & Gas Refining* (Shell Internat. Petroleum Co.) 3 In a simple refinery there are few secondary units—perhaps..a catalytic reformer (for the improvement of octane quality of motor gasoline).

Hence **re'formeress**, a female reformer.

1611 COTGR., *Emendatrice*, she that correcteth..[or] reformeth..; a correctresse, reformeresse. *a* **1843** SOUTHEY *Doctor* ccxiii. (1848) 575 Holy Colette of portentous sanctity, the Reformeress of the Poor Clares. **1849** SARA COLERIDGE *Mem. & Lett.* II. 234 Substantially the reformeresses must be in the right.

†reformer^2, **-ier.** *Obs. rare.* [irreg. f. REFORM *v.*^{1} 10 + -ER, -IER.] = REFORMADO^1.

1644 SIR W. MURE *Let.* in *Wks.* (S.T.S.) Introd. p. xvi, For the most part they are reformer officers under the commandment of the Earle of Craufurd and Mackay. **1645** LITHGOW *Siege Newcastle* (1820) 25 Lieutenant Colonell Henderson, a Reformier.

re-'former^3. [RE- 5 a: cf. RE-FORM *v.*] One who forms again.

1839–52 BAILEY *Festus* xxviii. 475 The Former and Re-Former of the world.

reforming (rɪˈfɔːmɪŋ), *vbl. sb.* [f. REFORM *v.*^{1}]

1. The action of the vb. in various senses.

a **1400** HYLTON *Scala Perf.* II. iv, He delaiede þe ful reformynge of mannys soule vnto þe laste ende. **1560** DAUS tr. *Sleidane's Comm.* 81 b, For the debating of controversies, and refourming of vices. **1598** STOW *Surv.* 134 He gaue towardes the reforming of that church fiue hundred markes. *a* **1660** HAMMOND *Serm.* (1851) II. 540 A reforming of every thing which was either formally or indirectly contained in their ignorance. **1743–4** MRS. DELANY *Autobiog. & Corr.* (1861) II. 283, I wish you had the reforming of the family you are in. **1752** J. LOUTHIAN *Form of Process* (ed. 2) p. iii, I have been prevailed upon..to undertake the reforming of the former Edition.

2. Also **re-forming.** The treatment of hydrocarbons so as to produce changes in composition; *spec.* (i) increasing the octane number of petrol by heating it under pressure over a catalyst (the major effects being an increase in the proportions of aromatic and other unsaturated cyclic compounds, and loss of hydrogen); (ii) partially or completely converting gaseous hydrocarbons to carbon monoxide and hydrogen by heating with steam over a catalyst.

Not all the early reforming processes used a catalyst.

1924 *Proc. 31st Ann. Convention Pacific Coast Gas Assoc.* 724 The 'reforming' or 'cracking' of natural gas is a process of much interest to several of the Southern California gas utilities. **1932** *Jrnl. Inst. Petroleum Technologists* XVIII. 262 In the cracking or 're-forming' of gasoline, one company uses a De Florez furnace, heating the gasoline to 925° F. at about 1000 lb. pressure, obtaining a recovery of 86 to 88 per cent. of gasoline of high octane number from a straight-run paraffin type gasoline. **1941** *Oil & Gas Jrnl.* 27 Mar. 87/1 A catalytic process for the 'reforming' or converting of low-octane to high-octane gasolines at high temperatures in the presence of hydrogen gas. **1966** *Kirk-Othmer Encycl. Chem. Technol.* (ed. 2) X. 417 A basic problem in catalytic steam reforming and cracking is that the pyrolysis reactions.. compete with the steam-hydrocarbon reactions. **1971** *Sci. Amer.* Dec. 57/2 During the 1950's new platinum-alumina-halogen catalysts were introduced to carry out the catalytic reforming of low-octane oil fractions. **1974** *Ibid.* Oct. 68/2 In the U.S. methane is the customary commercial source of hydrogen. In the process called re-forming it is treated with high-temperature steam, producing carbon monoxide (CO) and molecular hydrogen.

reforming (rɪˈfɔːmɪŋ), *ppl. a.* [f. as prec. + -ING^2.] That reforms.

1641 MILTON *Ch. Govt.* I. vi. Wks. 1851 III. 124 The expected reforming grace that God hath bid us hope for. **1692** E. WALKER tr. *Epictetus' Mor.* xvi, 'Tis better he were hanged, than thou should'st share A moment's Grief by thy reforming Care. **1849** MACAULAY *Hist. Eng.* i. I. 64 Elizabeth..put herself at the head of the reforming party. **1878** SEELEY *Stein* II. 166 We must retrace our steps, and examine his reforming legislation.

Hence **re'formingly** *adv. rare*$^{-1}$.

1649 ROBERTS *Clavis Bibl.* 346 It would better have become Iob to have submitted himselfe reformingly and humbly to his hand.

reformism (rɪˈfɔːmɪz(ə)m). [f. REFORM *sb.* + -ISM.] A policy of social, political, or religious reform, *spec.* in *Politics*, the theory that socialism can be established in an evolutionary way by reforms within a country's existing legislative system rather than by revolution. Cf. REVISIONISM.

1904 R. C. K. ENSOR *Mod. Socialism* p. xxvi, The germs of all Von Vollmar's reformism may be found in his own speeches before Bernsteinism appeared. *Ibid.* p. xxvii, The concrete spirit of reformism, which is careful of national peculiarities in its domestic politics, cannot overlook them wholly in foreign affairs. **1920** *Contemp. Rev.* Dec. 872 Your Right leaders are favouring reformism on those questions which I have called fundamental and decisive. **1926** *Socialist Rev.* Jan. 317 Industrial Conferences where working men..are learnedly lectured by middle-class apostles of reformism. **1937** 'C. CAUDWELL' *Illusion & Reality* xii. 309 Since this Kingdom of Heaven was to be achieved by non-resistance, by heavenly forces and a general change of heart, it was bound to become mere reformism and end as a machine for tying the oppressed of the Empire to the throne of Constantine. **1957** R. N. C. HUNT *Guide to Communist Jargon* xli. 139 Reformism was the view..that the evils of the capitalist system could be exorcised by reforms. **1964** P. G. CASANOVA in I. L. Horowitz *New Sociol.* 72 The transformation of social structures in the twentieth century has brought both sides to make partial concessions to reformism. **1970** F. C. WEFFORT in I. L. Horowitz *Masses in Lat. Amer.* xi. 403 Reformism was conceived within an ideological framework of consecration of the State as the only solution to social and economic problems. **1973** C. D. KERNIG *Marxism, Communism & Western Society* VII. 154/2 On the international level contemporary reformism is represented by the Socialist International founded in 1951. **1976** *Times* 9 Aug. 11/3 Their convictions, constancy and devotional practices form in fact a needed counterweight within the church to the prevalence of reformism.

reformist (rɪˈfɔːmɪst). [f. REFORM *v.*^{1} + -IST.]

1. a. One who advocates reform in the Church; a Reformer. (Common in 17th c.)

1589 G. HARVEY *Pierce's Super.* II. Addit. Ff, The forward Zeale of dowtie Martin Seniour,..and some other bragge Reformistes. **1608** H. CLAPHAM *Errour Left Hand* 36 He differs much from the most of our Reformistes heere at home. **1693** J. EDWARDS *Author. O. & N. Test.* 310 Among the reformists you will see this more plainly attested. **1791** MME. D'ARBLAY *Diary* 3 Aug., The Winton inhabitants.. ran up a slight wall before it [the altar], and deceived the Reformists. **1826** W. E. ANDREWS *Crit. Rev. Fox's Bk. Mart.* II. 312 Their judges were cold and calculating reformists. **1850** *Elder's House* 97 So you see that all the Reformists have not given up the doctrine of confession.

attrib. **1590** GREENWOOD *Confer.* Pref. A ij, Considering the reformist Preachers are now become the BB's trustie actors. **1882** *Macm. Mag.* XLV. 449 Mrs. Ashley..was put into the Tower, apparently on suspicion of Reformist sympathies.

b. An advocate or supporter of political reform; (common *c* 1792 to 1830). Later *spec.* an advocate or supporter of REFORMISM. Also as *adj.*

1641 *News from Hell*, etc. in *Harl. Misc.* (Malh.) IV. 393 The subtle practices of some parliamentary reformists. **1792** WINDHAM *Speeches Parl.* (1812) I. App. C. 155 Yet these [the Jacobins] are the men whom our Reformists are known to correspond with. **1817** BENTHAM *Parl. Reform Catech.* (1818) 104 By a radical reformist, the Householder plan could not be refused to any Electoral District. **1830** LADY GRANVILLE *Lett.* (1894) II. 62, I have been to see the Staffords, violent reformists. **1893** *Columbus* (Ohio) *Disp.* 10 July, The general policy of the party has been enough to break the strength of the so-called Reformists. **1906** M. MINTURN tr. *Jaurès's Stud. in Socialism* p. vi, The situation reached its climax in 1899 with the entrance of the Reformist Millerand into the Waldeck-Rousseau coalition cabinet. **1913** V. G. SIMKHOVITCH *Marxism versus Socialism* 292 Whether they call themselves revisionists, reformists, laborites or plain socialists..the overwhelming majority of the socialists of today are tending to be reformers. **1941** KOESTLER *Scum of Earth* xi. 113 The sectarian hatred between Stalinists, Trotskyists, and Reformists still existed.

attrib. *a* **1849** POE *Marginalia* Wks. 1864 III. 523 The modern reformist Philosophy..and the late reformist Legislation. **1904** R. C. K. ENSOR *Mod. Socialism* 164 We are revolutionaries, because..we are not at all sure, Citizen Millerand, of attaining our desired solution by the reformist method. **1920** *19th Cent.* Aug. 206 England..allowed the right of private judgment to her middle classes in the seventeenth century and allowed every kind of Reformist literature to enter the country. **1927** H. J. LASKI *Communism* i. 39 The growth of capitalism..seemed to suggest that the day of its end was far distant. Everywhere there grew up reformist socialism. **1950** E. H. CARR *Bolshevik Revolution* I. i. 12 The 'Economists'..reached the same practical conclusion as the legal Marxists that it was necessary to postpone to an indefinite future the revolutionary socialist struggle of the proletariat and to concentrate meanwhile on a reformist democratic programme in alliance with the bourgeoisie. **1969** *Daily Tel.* 1 Feb. 19/3 An article published in Soviet newspapers yesterday blamed 'reformist' journalists for the 'moral tenor' in Czechoslovak life. **1974** tr. *Sniečkus's Soviet Lithuania* 12 A reformist opportunist trend..had developed on the basis of the petty-bourgeois nationalistic ideology. **1977** *Time* 14 Nov. 16/3 The situation in Italy is too critical for a reformist policy like the one the Communists propose.

†2. A member of a reformed religious order.

1611 COTGR., *Reformez*, reformists, an Order of Franciscan Fryers. **1706** PHILLIPS (ed. Kersey), *Reformists*, Monks, whose Discipline, or Rules have been reformed.

†re'formitor. *Obs. rare*$^{-1}$. [irreg. f. REFORM *v.*^{1}, perh. for REFORMATOR.] A reformer.

1537 in *Lett. Suppress. Monast.* (Camden) 157 Abusys.. clokyde and coloryde by the reformitors (so namede) of evere religion.

So **†Re'formity**, Protestantism. *Obs. rare*$^{-1}$.

1606 WARNER *Alb. Eng.* xv. xcviii, Yet whatsoeuer Papistrie exacted, payed yet, His scrupulous Reformitie, will nought therof remit.

†re'formling. *nonce-wd.* [irreg. f. REFORM *v.*^{1} + -LING.] An amended pamphlet.

1662–3 J. B[IRKENHEAD] *Assembly-Man* To Rdr., A copy of that Reformling had crept to the Press.

re'formulate, *v.* [RE- 5 a.] *trans.* To formulate anew.

1882 *Academy* 14 Jan. 29/1 As Luther's doctrine of justification by faith reformulated Gospel truth for the Reformation era. **1896** *Westm. Gaz.* 17 June 4/1 A reformulation of the indictments against society. **1962** E. E. EVANS-PRITCHARD *Ess. Social Anthropol.* 9 Our knowledge has increased and some of our theoretical propositions have had to be reformulated accordingly. **1968** C. G. KUPER *Introd. Theory Superconductivity* iv. 55 These questions must be carefully reformulated before they can be answered. **1970** *Times* 20 Apr. 4/4 It might be necessary to reformulate existing trace mineral mixtures where this material was used. **1970** G. GERMANI in I. L. Horowitz *Masses in Lat. Amer.* xvi. 586 Class and mass theories must be reformulated within a more general framework.

Hence **re'formulated** *ppl. a.*; **reformu'lation.**

1922 A. G. HOGG *Redemption from this World* iv. 135 We are keeping well within the limits of legitimate reformulation when we say [etc.]. **1951** E. E. EVANS-PRITCHARD *Social Anthropol.* v. 86 The theories have been shaped and reshaped by this steady growth in knowledge and they have.., in each reformulation, directed observation into deeper layers. **1957** J. S. HUXLEY *Relig. without Revelation* (rev. ed.) ix. 220 The crude distinction in terms of ethical absolutes like 'good' and 'evil' requires reformulation in the light of psychology and history. **1965** *Mod. Law Rev.* XXVIII. 536 Alternative policies.. embodied in a reformulated principle. **1968** FOX & MAYERS *Computing Methods for Scientists & Engineers* x. 195 For this purpose we would prefer a reformulation of the problem. **1970** G. GERMANI in I. L. Horowitz *Masses in Lat. Amer.* xvi. 586 Such reformulation has been suggested by the mass and 'national-popular' movements in Latin America. **1979** *Dædalus* Winter 38 The deeper cause of this popular success surely lies in the new philosophy's reformulation of the antipolitics of May.

refortifi'cation. [Cf. next.] The action of fortifying again; a new fortification.

1598 BARRET *Theor. Warres* v. ii. 128 What order is there to be taken in such refortifications? **1878** A. FORBES in *Daily News* 15 Aug. 5/7 The reduction of the size of the city by the Venetians, and its refortification on a more contracted circumference.

re'fortify, *v.* [RE- 5 a; cf. F. *refortifier* (15th c. Godef.).] *trans.* To fortify again. Hence **re'fortifying** *vbl. sb.*

1598 BARRET *Theor. Warres* v. ii. 128 More commonly old Castels..be repaired and refortified. **1611** FLORIO, *Rinforzamento*,..a refortifying. **1641** EVELYN *Diary* 6 Aug., This was our continual duty till the Castle was re-fortified. **1692** *Lond. Gaz.* No. 2801/2 Above 6000 are summoned in with Shovels and Pickaxes..to re-fortifie the Town of Old-Manheim. **1778** *Eng. Gazetteer* (ed. 2) s.v. *Harwich*, This town..has since been ordered to be refortified. **1807** G. CHALMERS *Caledonia* I. I. iv. 182 He reoccupied and refortified such of those posts as promoted his vengeful designs. **1896** W. H. HUTTON *Philip Augustus* iii. 76 The island taken, Philip refortified it and rebuilt..the bridge.

fig. **1889** SKRINE *Mem. Thring* 140, I am repeating a judgment formed long ago, and often refortified.

†re'fossion. *Obs. rare*$^{-1}$. [f. RE- + FOSSION, after L. *refodĕre.*] A digging up again.

c **1625** BP. HALL *St. Paul's Combat* I. Wks. 1808 V. 372 Hence are..refossion of graves, torturing of the surviving, worse than many deaths.

refound (ri:ˈfaʊnd), *v.*[1] [f. RE- 5 a + FOUND *v.*[2]; cf. OF. *refonder* (12th c.).] *trans.* To found (a town, etc.) again; to re-establish. Also *fig.*

1500–20 DUNBAR *Poems* xxxviii. 28 The grit victour agane is rissin on hicht..; our fayth is now refoundit. **1641** W. CARTWRIGHT *Lady-Errant* v. ii, Her service hath Preserv'd the Kingdom, and refounded Cyprus. **1702–3** ATTERBURY *Let.* Misc. Wks. 1739 I. 159 The other bill is to enable the Queen to re-found the Savoy. **1761** *London & Environs* IV. 296 This hospital was..suppressed by Henry V and re-founded by Edward IV. **1869** GOLDW. SMITH *Lect. Mod. Hist.* iv. 16 This Colony did not..require to be refounded. **1879** FARRAR *St. Paul* I. 505 Cassander had re-founded it, and changed its name from Therma to Thessalonica.

Hence **reˈfounding** *vbl. sb.*

1754 POCOCKE *Trav.* (Camden) II. 112 The first foundation of the church by Wilfrid, and the refounding by K. H. 8th. **1893** MALLESON (*title*) The Refounding of the German Empire.

refound (ri:ˈfaʊnd), *v.*[2] [f. RE- 5 a + FOUND *v.*[3]; cf. F. *refondre* (12th c.).] *trans.* To cast (objects of metal) again; to recast.

a **1649** DRUMM. OF HAWTH. *Jas. III*, Wks. (1711) 60 Why ..when these old medalls were defaced..he might not refound them,..he thought no sufficient reason could be given. **1781** WARTON *Hist. Kiddington* 8 Perhaps they are all antient bells refounded. **1865** CARLYLE *Fredk. Gt.* XXI. ii. (1872) IX. 265 All our Cannon..needed to be refounded.

†**reˈfound**, *v.*[3] *Sc. Obs.* [var. of REFUND *v.*[1]; cf. *confound*, *infound*.]

1. *trans.* To refund, restore.

1546 *Reg. Privy Council Scot.* I. 41 The saidis Eirle and Lord..oblissis thame..to refound and deliver the samin agane to the persone fra quhame the samin hapins to be taikin. **1572–3** *Ibid.* II. 186 For warrandice to the said Archibald..and refounding to him of the pryces thairof acclamit be him. **1632** LITHGOW *Trav.* x. 476 Thy money and Patents shall be refounded.

b. To make good, repair, redress.

a **1578** LINDESAY (Pitscottie) *Chron. Scot.* (S.T.S.) I. 42 Cause all enormities and crymes committet..to be refoundit and randerit witht in ȝour boundis. *Ibid.* 82 To refound the skaythtis and iniurieis done be thame of befoir.

2. To cast the blame of (something) *on* or *upon* a person or thing.

a **1653** BINNING *Serm.* (1845) 438 They do not refound it upon God, Who is righteous in all His ways, but retort it upon themselves. *c* **1680** MACWARD *Contend.* (1723) 144 The want whereof is to be refounded on this court stratagem. *Ibid.* 147 The marring of that unity..is to be refounded upon that intimacy.

refounˈdation. [RE- 5 a; cf. REFOUND *v.*[1]] The action of founding again; a new foundation.

a **1661** FULLER *Worthies, Lancs.* II. (1662) 120 This Colledge hath passed many Dissolutions and refoundations. **1864** J. RAINE *Hexham* (Surtees) I. Pref. 148 There is some valuable information..about the refoundation of their house. **1890** GASQUET & BISHOP *Edw. VI & Bk. Com. Prayer* (1891) 5 On the refoundation of the monastic cathedrals.

refounder (ri:ˈfaʊndə(r)). [f. REFOUND *v.*[1] + -ER[1].] One who refounds.

1528 in *Lett. Suppress. Monast.* (Camden) 2 Alen Niger, summe tyme erele of Richemound, and our secounde re-founder. **1782** PENNANT *Journ. Chest. to Lond.* 57 This Enysan..was the true re-founder [of Stone Priory]. **1824** SOUTHEY *Bk. of Ch.* (1841) 408 That Church, and the Queen, its refounder, are clear of persecution, as regards the Romanists. **1865** MASSON *Rec. Brit. Philos.* 95 He was..the refounder of Transcendentalism in modern Europe.

†**reˈfoundiment.** *Sc. Obs. rare*$^{-1}$. [Cf. REFOUND *v.*[3]] The act of refunding; reparation.

1555 *Sc. Acts Mary* (1814) 497/2 Vnder the pane of refoundiment of the dampnage and skaith to the parteis.

reˈfoundress. *rare*$^{-1}$. [f. REFOUND *v.*[1]; see -ESS.] A female refounder.

1655 FULLER *Ch. Hist.* III. ix. §23 Nor let not our Virgin Queen be forgotten, as in effect Refoundresse of this from the third year of her reign.

refount (ri:ˈfaʊnt). [ad. F. *refonte* REFONT.] A recasting.

1832 AUSTIN *Jurispr.* (1879) II. 1081 Though the refount of form, now recommended, would not touch necessarily the substance or effect.

refourme, obs. form of REFORM *v.*

refows, -foys, obs. forms of REFUSE *a.*

refract (rɪˈfrækt), *pa. pple. rare.* [ad. L. *refractus*, f. *refringĕre*: see next.] Refracted.

1625 GILL *Sacr. Philos.* Pref., If the eye bee not able to behold the beames of the Sunne,..yet it joyes to see that shining lampe when his beames are refract, or as it were broken off. **1880** SWINBURNE *Songs of Spring-t., Birthday Ode* 38 With moonlight-coloured gold And rays refract from the oldworld heaven of time.

refract (rɪˈfrækt), *v.* [f. L. *refract-*, ppl. stem of *refringĕre*, f. *re-* RE- + *frangĕre* to break. Cf. F. *réfracter* (1752).]

1. a. *Physics.* Of substances: To break the course of (light or other waves) and turn (it or them) out of the direct line; *esp.* to deflect at a certain angle at the point of passage from one medium into another of different density.

1612 SELDEN *Pref. Drayton's Poly-olb.* (1876) I. p. xliv, By ..rash collecting (as it were,) from visual beams refracted through another's eye. **1646** SIR T. BROWNE *Pseud. Ep.* 345 Some reflected, others refracted beget that semicircular variety we generally call the Rainebow. **1668** CULPEPPER & COLE *Barthol. Anat.* III. viii. 148 The glassie Humor may give a passage to the Species to the Retina, and may refract them from Perpendiculars. **1728** PEMBERTON *Newton's Philos.* 375 All transparent bodies refract part of the light incident upon them, and reflect another part. **1794** J. HUTTON *Philos. Light*, etc. 218 The powers in bodies for variously reflecting, absorbing, transmitting, and refracting light. **1800** HENRY *Epit. Chem.* (1808) 31 Caloric is refracted, also, according to the same law that regulates the refraction of light. **1872** HUXLEY *Physiol.* ix. 225 Glass refracts light more strongly than water does. **1874** *Proc. R. Soc.* XXII. 532, I have dealt with the effect of the atmosphere to refract sound upwards. **1944** A. HOLMES *Princ. Physical Geol.* xiv. 284 The waves advance more rapidly through the deeper water opposite a bay than through the shallower water opposite a headland... The waves thus become curved or refracted..towards parallelism with the shore line. **1966** *McGraw-Hill Encycl. Sci. & Technol.* XI. 408/1 Waves propagated through the solid earth are refracted by changes of material or changes of density. **1974** HARVEY & BOHLMAN *Stereo F.M. Radio Handbk.* vii. 144 The sky-wave..may be refracted back towards the earth by the layers of ionized gas.

absol. **1678** HOBBES *Decam.* x. Wks. 1845 VII. 172 It will follow that all transparent bodies that equally refract are equally hard; which I think is not true.

transf. and *fig.* **1656** tr. *Hobbes' Elem. Philos.* (1839) 381 The sine of the angle refracted in one inclination is to the sine of the angle refracted in another inclination [etc.]. **1790** BURKE *Fr. Rev.* Wks. V. 125 These metaphysick rights.., like rays of light,..are, by the laws of nature, refracted from their straight line. **1869** LECKY *Europ. Mor.* v. II. 355 No other body of men have ever exhibited a more single-minded and unworldly zeal, refracted by no personal interests.

b. To produce by refraction. *rare.*

1728–46 THOMSON *Spring* 202 Meantime, refracted from yon eastern cloud..the grand ethereal bow Shoots up immense. **1762–9** FALCONER *Shipwr.* II. 277 His languid fires..Refract along the dusk a crimson blaze.

c. *intr.* To undergo refraction.

1964 *Oceanogr. & Marine Biol.* II. 84 If waves reach the beach unaffected by offshore underwater topography one has an easier task than if waves are breaking and refracting around an offshore bar.

†**2.** *trans.* To throw back; to reflect, return. *Obs.*

1621 BURTON *Anat. Mel.* I. ii. II. v. 109 The Turkes weare great Tulipantes..to refract the Sun beams. **1658** ROWLAND tr. *Moufet's Theat. Ins.* Ep. Ded., The air..beating against the rough-cast walls of the hollow place, and refracted, makes a sound. **1694** WESTMACOTT *Script. Herb.* 1 [Algum wood] was most precious,..fit to refract sounds.

†**3. a.** To break up; to impair. *Obs. rare.*

1647 HAMMOND *Power of Keys* Pref. A 4 The several excellencies of the other three..may..be found at least, as in mixture, refracted and compounded in this fourth. *a* **1676** HALE *Prim. Orig. Man.* IV. iii. (1677) 318 Those common Notions which yet remain in the Humane Nature, though refracted and abated by the Fall of Man.

b. *Chem.* To analyse (nitre) in order to discover the percentage of impurities (cf. REFRACTION 6).

1842 PARNELL *Chem. Anal.* (1845) 478 The most usual method of refracting nitre consists in determining, 1°, the amount of water lost by exposure to a moderate heat; 2°, the amount of insoluble matter [etc.].

4. *Ophthalm.* To measure the focusing characteristics of (an eye) or of the eyes of (a person). Also *absol.*

1897 J. THORINGTON *Retinoscopy* v. 45 To give a patient thus refracted with the retinoscope his emmetropic correction..an allowance must always be made, in all meridians, of one diopter. **1904** —— *Refraction & how to Refract* (ed. 3) ix. 235 If a young subject must be refracted without drops, then the fogging method must be followed. *Ibid.*, The [manifest] method by which the eyes of patients past forty-five years of age are refracted. **1953** N. BIER *Contact Lens Routine & Pract.* iv. 56 If the measurements.. in the corneal fit were 8·75/13, do not refract with a trial lens of 8 mm radius and 13 mm diameter. **1968** *Sci. Jrnl.* Dec. 21/1 Normally when 'refracting' human patients an ophthalmologist relies on verbal reports and applies corrective lenses until the subject says that he sees most clearly.

Hence **reˈfractable** *a.*, refrangible. *rare*$^{-1}$.

1676 H. MORE *Remarks* 100 For as bodies are only tangible, so they are only reflexible and refractable.

†**reˈfractarily**, *adv. Obs. rare.* [f. as next + -LY[2].] = REFRACTORILY.

1623 COCKERAM II, Obstinately, *Refractarily*. **1654** H. L'ESTRANGE *Chas. I* (1655) 62, I cannot but totally acquit King Charles of blame in proscribing such as refractarily offended.

†**reˈfractariness.** *Obs.* [f. REFRACTARY *a.* + -NESS.] = REFRACTORINESS.

1624 DONNE *Devot.* (ed. 2) 80 Take from me, O Lord, her peruersenese, her wilfulnesse, her refractarinesse. **1636** CHAS. I in Rushw. *Hist. Coll.* III. (1692) I. 320 May not the Kings..by Law compel the doing thereof in case of Refusal or Refractariness? **1693** LOCKE *Educ.* 85 She had..by her unprevailing Blows only confirmed her refractariness.

†**refracˈtarious**, *a. Obs. rare*$^{-1}$. = next.

1614 JACKSON *Creed* III. xiii. §10 The life of the world censured to death for an hereticke, or refractarious Scismatique.

†**reˈfractary**, *a.* and *sb. Obs.* [ad. L. *refractārius* (Seneca) obstinate, stubborn: see REFRACT *v.* and -ARY[1], and cf. F. *réfractaire* (16th c.).

In the Earl of Stirling's *Domesday* (1614) x. xlii. the stressing is '*refractary*: cf. the note to REFRACTORY.]

A. *adj.* = REFRACTORY. (Common in 17th c.)

1604 R. CAWDREY *Table Alph.*, *Refractarie*, wilfull in opinion, obstinate. **1613** PURCHAS *Pilgrimage* II. xix. (1614) 215 The woman which rendereth not her husband his due, is rebellious and refractarie. **1660** MARVELL *Corr.* Wks. 1875 II. 41, I am sorry to heare that Mr. Wilson has been so refractary. **1694** FALLE *Jersey* v. 171 And in case the said Minister continues refractary, the Dean..shall proceed even to Deprivation.

B. *sb.* A refractory person.

1599 B. JONSON *Cynthia's Rev.* v. ii, Render not your selfe a refractarie, on the sudden. **1657** TRAPP *Comm. Job* vii. 12 God looked not upon him as he doth upon these refractaries, who to their impatience adde impenitence.

refracted (rɪˈfræktɪd), *ppl. a.* [f. REFRACT *v.* + -ED[1].]

1. Of light, etc.: Bent aside, deflected. Also *transf.* of things connected with, or produced by, refraction.

1638–48 G. DANIEL *Eclog* iii. 352 Homeward wend, Whilst the refracted West some Lights yet lend. **1678** VAUGHAN *Thalia Rediv.*, *Pious Th.* 212 Whose fires by refracted chance Burnish some neighbour rock. **1691** NORRIS *Pract. Disc.* 244 We look upon Truth..by a refracted Ray, which makes it to appear where it is not. **1740** SOMERVILLE *Hobbinol* III. 292 She darts along, and with refracted Rays Paints the gay Clouds. **1789** E. DARWIN *Bot. Gard.* II. (1791) 133 O'er heavens wide arch refracted lustres flow. **1831** BREWSTER *Optics* iii. 22 The ray HR is called the incident ray, and R b the refracted ray. **1871** B. TAYLOR *Faust* (1875) II. I. i. 7 Life is not light but the refracted color.

fig. **1654** H. L'ESTRANGE *Chas. I* (1655) 146 The information being somewhat lame, as being taken upon refracted and second hand report. **1856** R. A. VAUGHAN *Mystics* (1860) II. 230 According to Swedenborg, all the mythology and the symbolisms of ancient times were so many refracted or fragmentary correspondences.

†**b.** *refracted angle*, angle of refraction. *Obs.*

1704 J. HARRIS *Lex. Techn.* I, *Refracted Angle*, in Opticks, is the Angle contained between the refracted Ray and the Perpendicular. **1797** *Encycl. Brit.* (ed. 3) XIII. 234/1 Before this time Kepler had published a New Table of refracted Angles.

†**2.** Driven back, repelled. *Obs. rare*$^{-1}$.

1635 SWAN *Spec. M.* v. §2 (1643) 169 [The wind] with a refracted and disjoynted force..is driven hither and thither.

†**3.** Broken down, diminished. *Obs. rare*$^{-1}$.

1639 FULLER *Holy War* II. xxxv. (1840) 96 If they [mercenary soldiers] be not entertained in too great numbers, but in such refracted degrees, that the natives may still have the predominancy.

Hence **reˈfractedly** *adv.*, **reˈfractedness**.

1667 SPRAT *Hist. R. Soc.* 216 Experiments of the Transparency, and Refractedness of Flames. **1854** KINGSLEY *Alexandria* 67 Even if he sees a truth, he can only see it refractedly.

†**reˈfracter.** *Obs.* [f. REFRACT *v.* + -ER[1].] = REFRACTOR 3 b.

1761 HIRST in *Phil. Trans.* LII. 397 A 4 feet refracter, of Mr. Dollond's new construction. **1763** SHORT *ibid.* LIII. 341 He used an 18 foot refracter.

refractile (rɪˈfræktɪl, -taɪl), *a.* [f. as prec. + -ILE.] Capable of producing refraction. Hence **refracˈtility**.

1847–9 TODD *Cycl. Anat.* IV. 514/1 The bands appear.. to..become more refractile. *Ibid.* 517/1 These cells, in respect of their..refractility..resemble those seen in articular cartilage. **1880** *Nature* XXI. 411 A well-defined highly refractile fibrous network.

refracting (rɪˈfræktɪŋ), *ppl. a.* [-ING[2].]

1. Causing refraction; refractive.

1704 NEWTON *Optics* (1721) 4 Def. iv, The Perpendicular to the reflecting or refracting Surface at the Point of Incidence. **1743** EMERSON *Fluxions* 282 To find the Motion of a Ray of Light passing into a refracting Medium. **1837** GORING & PRITCHARD *Microgr.* 182 The rays..should traverse both the refracting surfaces without any obliquity. **1851** NICHOL *Archit. Heav.* (ed. 9) 115 The magnitude of its reflecting disc, or refracting lens. **1898** *Allbutt's Syst. Med.* V. 886 The fibres..present a few refracting granules.

b. Provided with some apparatus or arrangement for refracting light; esp. ***refracting telescope***, a telescope in which the rays of light are converged to a focus by an object glass.

1764 HORNSBY in *Phil. Trans.* LIV. 145 An excellent refracting telescope of 12 feet focus. **1823** J. BADCOCK *Dom. Amusem.* 119 Expose it..to the light of a refracting lamp. **1870** *Daily News* 8 Oct., A magnificent refracting telescope, with an object-glass of 25 inches diameter. **1896** ORFORD *Mod. Optical Instr.* 95 In the refracting stereoscope the rays of light..are always bent towards the thicker part of the lens.

c. ***refracting angle***, the angle between two faces of a prism or lens.

1796 H. BROUGHAM in *Phil. Trans.* LXXXVI. 262 An hollow prism made of fine plate-glass,..its refracting angle being 55°. **1890** WOODBURY *Encycl. Photogr.* 394 A divergence from the axis will take place, becoming more and more marked as the refracting angles become greater towards the edge of the lens.

2. Undergoing refraction. *rare*$^{-1}$.

1718 ROWE tr. *Lucan* IV. 119 Unvary'd by the Light's refracting Beam She stoop'd to drink from Ocean's briny Stream.

3. That resists fire; = REFRACTORY A. 4.

1894 *R. S. Burn's Steam Engine User* 145 The interior, especially of the furnace proper,..and the combustion chamber being lined with 'refracting' bricks, generally termed fire-bricks.

refraction (rɪˈfrækʃən). [ad. late L. *refractiōn-em* (Boethius), n. of action f. *refringĕre*: see REFRACT *v.* and cf. F. *réfraction* (16th c.).]

† **1. a.** The action of breaking open or breaking up. *Obs. rare.*

1578 BANISTER *Hist. Man* VII. 91 This bloud by styrring.. is made thinne, and together with the ayre mixed, which thus, by the same refraction, and beatyng together, is prepared. **1611** FLORIO, *Refrattione*, a bursting or refraction. **1661** BLOUNT *Glossogr.* (ed. 2), *Refraction*, a breaking open.

b. Rebound, recoil. *Obs. rare.*

1653 HARVEY *Anat. Exerc.* II. (1673) 135 The blood being forc'd against the hand, did by its reverberation and refraction, fly back four or five foot. **1661** BLOUNT *Glossogr.* (ed. 2), *Refraction*,.. a rebound.

2. a. The fact or phenomenon of a ray of light, heat, (†the sight), etc., being diverted or deflected from its previous course in passing obliquely out of one medium into another of different density, or in traversing a medium not of uniform density. More widely, change in direction of propagation of any wave as a result of its travelling at different speeds at different points along the wave front.

angle of refraction, the angle between the refracted ray and the perpendicular to the surface of the refracting medium at the point of incidence (†or that between the refracted ray and a continuation of the incident ray). †***axis of refraction***, the perpendicular to the surface of the refracting medium at the point of incidence. ***double refraction***, the fact of a ray of light being split up by certain minerals into two divergent, unequally refracted rays. ***index of refraction***: (see INDEX *sb.* 9 a).

1603 HOLLAND *Plutarch's Mor.* 1295 The rainbow is.. distinguished by sundry colours, by the refraction of our eie-sight against a cloud. **1646** SIR T. BROWNE *Pseud. Ep.* 347 The colours are made by refraction of light, and the shadows that limit that light. **1677** GREW *Anat. Fruits* iv. §6 By Refraction, Objects of all Sizes are represented on the Walls of the Eye. **1706** W. JONES *Syn. Palmar. Matheseos* 301 The Refraction out of a Rarer Medium into a Denser is made towards the Perpendicular. **1797** *Encycl. Brit.* (ed. 3) XIII. 279/2 The phenomena of refraction are explained by an attractive power in the medium through which light passes. **1831** BREWSTER *Optics* xvii. 144 The refraction of the two pencils is called double refraction and the bodies which produce it are called doubly refractive bodies. *c* **1860** FARADAY *Forces Nat., Electric Light* 177, I can employ the principle of refraction to bend and direct the rays of light. **1874** *Proc. R. Soc.* XXII. 532 This refraction explains the well-known difference which exists in the distinctness of sounds by day and by night. **1880** LE CONTE *Sight* 32 All refraction is accompanied by dispersion. **1914** [see ABSORPTION 4 (*d*)]. **1944** A. HOLMES *Princ. Physical Geol.* xiv. 297 (*caption*) Diagram to illustrate the development of a hooked spit by the refraction of oblique waves. **1971** *Nature* 12 Feb. 452/2 T. D. Krishna Kartha describes his work on the variation of velocity (refraction) of microseisms approaching Cochin in southern India. **1974** HARVEY & BOHLMAN *Stereo F.M. Radio Handbk.* vii. 144 Refraction of the radio wave occurs due to the effects of the varying density of the gas layers in which the wave is travelling.

fig. **1614** SELDEN *Titles Hon.* Pref. C 4, I.. euer.. vsd that Medium only, which would not at all, or least, deceiue by Refraction. **1873** SPENCER *Stud. Sociol.* i. 12 To make allowance for the refraction due to the historic medium.

b. With *a* and *pl.* An instance of this.

1619 J. BAINBRIDGE *Descr. Late Comet* 10 A second refraction of the Sunne beames. **1660** BOYLE *New Exp. Phys. Mech.* xviii. 136 The various refractions that may happen in the Air. **1743** EMERSON *Fluxions* 284 The Sum of all the Refractions will be equal to the single Refraction [etc.]. **1796** KIRWAN *Elem. Min.* (ed. 2) I. 241 It causes a double refraction. **1867** J. HOGG *Microsc.* I. i. 2 A table of the refractions which light experiences under different angles of incidence in passing from air into glass.

fig. **1827** HARE *Guesses* Ser. I. (1873) 2 When among the manifold refractions of Knowledge, Wisdom is almost lost sight of. **1860** EMERSON *Cond. Life, Illusions*, Even the prose of the streets is full of refractions.

†**c.** *pl.* Refracted beams. Also *fig. Obs. rare.*

1648 BOYLE *Seraph. Love* xxv. (1700) 152 Variety.. such as we may see in the diversify'd refractions of the same sparkling Diamond. **1649** G. DANIEL *Trinarch., Hen. IV*, ccclxxxvii, Now.. the Refractions of his Spirit Gild Only the Hemme of Life.

3. a. *Astron.* The deflection of the beams or light from heavenly bodies when not in the zenith, due to the refracting power of the atmosphere, which increases their apparent elevation.

Spec. called ***atmospheric*** and ***astronomical refraction***.

1603 HEYDON *Jud. Astrol.* 137 There lieth a deceipt or fallacie in the refraction of beams, which cheifly happeneth about the Horizon, where the aire is alwaies thickest. **1669** STURMY *Mariner's Mag.* II. 118 The Refraction of the Sun, Moon and Stars, causeth them to appear higher above the Horizon than they are. **1715** tr. *Gregory's Astron.* (1726) I. 279 The uncertain Refractions will render the Operation doubtful; and besides, then the Sun ascends and descends too obliquely [etc.]. **1812** WOODHOUSE *Astron.* x. 74 Refraction, by which a star, to appearance, is elevated above its true place. **1868** LOCKYER *Guillemin's Heavens* (ed. 3) 186 The Sun, actually already below the horizon, is raised up by refraction, and remains visible to us.

fig. **1850** TENNYSON *In Mem.* xcii, Such refraction of events As often rises ere they rise.

b. The effect of the atmosphere in making terrestrial objects appear higher than they are.

Spec. called ***terrestrial refraction***; see also quot. 1831.

1698 KEILL *Exam. Th. Earth* (1734) 173 He seems to allow too much, both for refraction and errors in the Observations. **1831** BREWSTER *Optics* III. xxxi. 255 Great local heats or local colds will produce great changes of refractive power, and give rise to optical phenomena of a very interesting kind. Such phenomena have received the name of unusual refraction. **1853** KANE *Grinnell Exp.* x. (1856) 69 My sketches of the coast.. show what strange diversities of outline may be induced by refraction.

4. The action *of* a medium in refracting light; refractive power or effect. Also *fig.*

1664 POWER *Exp. Philos.* I. 34 Which is helped and advantaged also by the refraction of the water wherein they swim. **1796** H. HUNTER tr. *St.-Pierre's Stud. Nat.* (1799) III. 27 Allowing one degree for the refraction of the Atmosphere in winter. **1849** KINGSLEY *Misc.* (1860) II. 246 A deep pool.. paved with sandstone slabs and boulders, distorted by the changing refractions of the eddies. **1870** LOWELL *Among my Bks.* Ser. I. (1873) 279 The willful refraction of a clear mind, twisting awry whatever enters it.

†**5.** A reduction on a charge or bill. *Obs.*

1727–41 CHAMBERS *Cycl.* s.v., I will deduct or make you a refraction of 30s. charged inadvertently in my bill. **1782** *Gentl. Mag.* LII. 364 Mr. K. mentioned the refraction which the Company had on their side of their bargains with Government, as very advantageous.

6. The process of ascertaining the percentage of impurities contained in a sample of nitre; the sum of the impurities as thus ascertained.

1842 PARNELL *Chem. Anal.* (1845) 478 The total amount of these impurities in 100 parts of a sample of nitre is technically termed the 'refraction' of that sample. **1876** VOYLE & STEVENSON *Milit. Dict.* 335/1 Government.. generally purchases saltpetre at 5 per cent. refraction.

7. *Ophthalm.* Measurement of the focusing characteristics of eyes. Also *attrib.* Cf. REFRACT *v.* 4.

1900 J. THORINGTON *Refraction & how to Refract* ix. 229 The great danger in any refraction.. is an overcorrection. **1928** W. S. DUKE-ELDER *Pract. Refraction* xxi. 302 Test.. the depth of cycloplegia by testing the accommodation before the refraction is done. **1953** N. BIER *Contact Lens Routine & Pract.* iv. 56 The practitioner's contact lens refraction set. *Ibid.*, An alteration of 0·5 mm in the corneal radius is approximately equivalent to 3·00 D.S. in refraction. **1961** *Lancet* 30 Sept. 760/2 An ophthalmologist holds refraction clinics weekly in the surgery. **1975** M. RUBEN *Contact Lens Pract.* iv. 67/2 The cylinder found by refraction is −3·00 D.

8. *attrib.*, as ***refraction error***, ***-index***; also **refraction-circle**, one of two or more graduated circles attached to a refracting telescope in order to adjust its direction; **refraction profiling** *Geol.*, profiling (sense 3) by means of refraction shooting; **refraction shooting** *Geol.*, seismic prospecting in which shock waves generated at the earth's surface are detected at several points along a line some miles long, the relation between the time of arrival at each point and its distance giving information about the nature and depth of the underlying strata.

1875 KNIGHT *Dict. Mech.* 1909/2 The refraction-circle of the Washington Observatory. **1879** *St. George's Hosp. Rep.* IX. 489 The pulsation was more marked in the eye with inferior sight. There was absolutely no refraction error. **1889** *Anthony's Photogr. Bull.* II. 167 The relation between the refraction-index and the dispersion. **1929**, **1963** Refraction profiling [see PROFILING *vbl. sb.* 3]. **1929**, **1951** Refraction shooting [see *reflection shooting* s.v. REFLECTION 11]. **1960** C. GATLIN *Petroleum Engin.* iii. 37/1 Refraction shooting is used primarily as a reconnaissance tool to select areas and obtain interpretative data for the more detailed reflection method. **1978** *Nature* 27 Apr. 789/1 Seismic refraction shooting near the Isle of Lewis in the Outer Hebrides has shown the presence of major sedimentary units.

Hence **reˈfractional** *a.*; **reˈfractionist**, one skilled in the application of the laws of refraction, esp. for the correction of visual defects.

1871 HUTTON *Ess.* II. 84 He rejected 'refractional' theories of light with scorn. **1899** *Daily News* 23 Feb. 5/1 An exhibition organized.. in the interest of the refractionist.

†**reˈfractious**, *a. Obs. rare.* [f. REFRACT *v.* + -IOUS: cf. FRACTIOUS.] = REFRACTIVE I.

a **1691** BOYLE *Hist. Air* xx. (1692) 192 The Difference betwixt clear Weather and misty refractious Weather... I have seen the Land elevated by reason of the refractious Air.

refractive (rɪˈfræktɪv), *a.* [ad. late L. *refractīv-us* (Priscian), or f. REFRACT *v.* + -IVE. Cf. F. *réfractif, -ive* (1752).]

1. a. That refracts light, etc.; possessed of, characterized by, the power of refracting.

1673 FLAMSTEED in Rigaud *Corr. Sci. Men* (1841) II. 168 The refractive air reaches some height above our heads. *a* **1691** BOYLE *Hist. Air* (1692) 190 The air.. was filled with vapours and exhalations, that made it much more refractive than formerly. **1754** DOLLOND in *Phil. Trans.* XLVIII. 552 Rays, which, by the refractive quality of the glass, are made to converge. **1854** J. SCOFFERN in *Orr's Circ. Sc., Chem.* 75 Tourmaline is a doubly refractive substance. **1872** PROCTOR *Ess. Astron.* vi. 84 Its outline should be distorted if the planet has a refractive atmosphere.

b. ***refractive power***, the power which a transparent body has of refracting the light passing through it.

1709 BERKELEY *Th. Vision* §34 By the refractive power of the crystalline. **1769** WALES in *Phil. Trans.* LX. 131 The very great refractive power of the air in these parts. **1831** BREWSTER *Optics* I. iii. 22 The power by which bodies produce this effect is called their refractive power, and bodies that produce it in different degrees are said to have different refractive powers. **1874** tr. *Lommel's Light* 60 In this way every transparent substance has its own refractive power.

c. ***refractive index***, index of refraction. (See INDEX *sb.* 9 a.)

1839 G. BIRD *Nat. Philos.* 394 The refractive indices of the different refracting structures of the eye. **1873** W. LEES *Acoustics* II. iii. 52 In the passage [of light] from one medium to another of a different refractive index.

2. a. Due to, caused by, refraction.

1717 BERKELEY *Jrnl. Tour Italy* 19 Sept., Wks. 1871 IV. 589 The refractive curve in an atmosphere of different density. **1879** *Cassell's Techn. Educ.* IV. 313/1 Three defects —spherical aberration, chromatic aberration, and refractive aberration. **1881** CLARK RUSSELL *Ocean Free-Lance* I. v. 234 Little blobs of hazy film trembled upon the white refractive line about the dark waters of the horizon.

b. Refrangible.

1890 *Anthony's Photogr. Bull.* III. 417 Thereby it has been shown that the gelatine absorbs the most refractive rays most energetically.

3. Relating to refraction.

1727 THOMSON *To Mem. Newton* 124 Ev'n now the setting sun and shifting clouds,.. declare How just, how beauteous, the refractive law. **1953** N. BIER *Contact Lens Routine & Pract.* iv. 58 [Temporary spasm of accommodation] may persist throughout the refractive examination. **1969** J. R. GREGG *How to communicate in Optometric Pract.* iii. 31 At key spots along the refractive procedure, build in ways of showing confidence and understanding.

4. Refractory. *rare.*

1709 J. NIMMO *Narr.* (S.H.S.) 19 Kinstirie seemd not verie refractive if Park desired him to take the burthin of all thes off my hand. **1845** [implied in REFRACTIVENESS].

Hence **reˈfractiveness**, **refracˈtivity**.

1843 J. CAIRNS *Let.* in *Life* vii. (1895) 140 Is there not too much refractiveness in his exegetical atmosphere..? **1845** JANE ROBINSON *Whitehall* xlv, He was detained.. apparently with the intention of subduing the refractiveness of his nature. **1889** *Philos. Mag.* Ser. v. XXVIII. 400 The refractivity of a substance is the difference between the index of refraction of the substance and unity.

refracˈtometer. [f. as REFRACT *v.* + -OMETER.] An instrument for measuring the indices of refraction of various substances.

1876 *Catal. Sci. App. S. Kens.* 133. **1883** *Nature* 15 Mar. 473/1 On a refractometer for measuring the indices of refraction and the dispersion of solid bodies.

refractometry (rɪfrækˈtɒmɪtrɪ). [f. REFRACT *v.* + -O + -METRY.] The measurement of refractive indices of media.

1902 *Encycl. Brit.* XXX. 239/2 Refractometry by total reflection. **1950** *Engineering* 10 Feb. 143/2 Increased attention has been devoted to methods of high-precision refractometry. **1958** *Oxf. Univ. Gaz.* 23 Apr. 892 Studies in refractometry of living cells with particular reference to the investigation of osmoregulatory function. **1974** *Encycl. Brit. Macropædia* IX. 633/2 Of the many laboratory principles employed in the process analytical instruments, the three in widest use today are refractometry, absorption spectroscopy, and gas chromatography.

Hence **refractoˈmetric** *a.*, of or pertaining to a refractometer; made by means of refractometry; **refractoˈmetrically** *adv.*

1904 *Nature* 4 Feb. 334/2 A simple thermostat for use in connection with the refractometric examination of oils and fats. **1920** *Amer. Jrnl. Physiol.* LI. 278 Reading refractometrically the serum non-protein increase after the intra-venous injection of a known amount of acacia or gelatin solution. **1929** *Canad. Jrnl. Res.* I. 13 The total solid content was determined refractometrically. **1937** *Discovery* June 180/2 The application of refractometric work to observe the progress of essential processes in the production of plastics may not be so commonly known. **1970** *Nature* 26 Dec. 1269/1 The relative values [of purity] given by the four methods were: Lowry, 1·0; gravimetric, 0·93; refractometric, 0·87; ultraviolet absorption, 0·32. *Ibid.*, The protein concentration.. was also determined refractometrically and gravimetrically.

refractor (rɪˈfræktə(r)). [f. REFRACT *v.* + -OR.]

†**1.** A refractory person. *Obs. rare*$^{-1}$.

1638 LAUD *Wks.* (1853) V. 206, I have received an answer not much in effect differing from this petition, from two or three refractors in different parts.

†**2.** That which breaks or repels. *Obs. rare*$^{-1}$.

1682 GREW *Exp. Luctat. Menstruums fr. Bodies* i. §13 For which reason.. the best Correctors, or Refractors of the force of Colocynthis, are some kinds of Alkalies.

3. a. A medium which refracts light; a refracting lens.

1836–41 BRANDE *Chem.* (ed. 5) 191 The ultimate direction of a refracted ray of light is influenced by the relative position of the surface of the refractor. *c* **1860** FARADAY *Forces Nat., Electric Light* 190 As yet no attempt has been made to construct special.. refractors for it.

b. A refracting telescope. Cf. REFRACTER.

1769 *Phil. Trans.* LIX. 308 The situation of the telescopes, the reflector being within the observatory, and the two refractors.. without it, favoured this purpose. **1794** G. ADAMS *Nat. & Exp. Philos.* II. xxii. 471 [Newton's telescopes] in power were compared to a six feet refractor. **1891** *Anthony's Photogr. Bull.* IV. 369 A reflector can always be mounted at far less cost than a refractor of equal aperture.

4. *Geol.* A stratum, or an interface between strata, detected in refraction shooting.

1946 *Geophysics* XI. 40 The production in refraction shooting varies widely, depending on the surface conditions and also on the depth of the refractors. **1976** W. M. TELFORD et al. *Appl. Geophysics* iv. 365 Where a single refractor is being followed, a series of short refraction profiles are often shot rather than a long profile.

refractorily (rɪˈfræktərɪlɪ), *adv.* [f. REFRACTORY *a.* + -LY^{2}.] In a refractory manner.

c **1646** *True Relat.* in *Glover's Hist. Derby* (1829) I. App. 62 She still refractorily and willfully said, that shee would not give them one penny. **1657** *Penit. Conf.* viii. 273 If any person..behaved himself refractorily to the decrees of the Council. **1736** NEAL *Hist. Purit.* III. 464 He behaved very refractorily towards the Visitors. **1825** HONE *Every-day Bk.* I. 1168 One keeper of a..stall..refractorily persisted.

refractoriness (rɪˈfræktərɪnɪs). [f. REFRACTORY *a.* + -NESS.] The quality or state of being refractory.

1. a. Of persons: Obstinacy, perversity; stubborn disobedience or resistance *to* some authority or control. (Common in 17th and 18th c.)

a **1642** SIR W. MONSON *Naval Tracts* II. (1704) 295/1 Those that repine at Princes Actions out of Stubbornness, or Refractoriness. **1686** HORNECK *Crucif. Jesus* xvii. 497 Your refractoriness to reformation and amendment makes you unworthy. **1752** CARTE *Hist. Eng.* III. 677 They now showed their disaffection as well as refractoriness in refusing to give thanks. **1807** *Edin. Rev.* X. 96 He was..abused for his refractoriness in this particular. **1859** HAWTHORNE *Marb. Faun* ii. (1878) 25 Donatello's refractoriness..had evidently cost him something.

fig. **1658** A. FOX *Wurtz' Surg.* I. viii. 33 If Wounds in the dressing be abused..what can be expected, but Natures unwillingness and refractoriness..?

b. Power of resistance *to* some influence.

1805 FOSTER *Ess.* I. iv. (1806) I. 62 Unless you had brought into the world some extraordinary refractoriness to the influence of evil. **1886** E. R. LANKESTER *Advancem. Sc.* (1890) 148 A state of refractoriness to the poison of rabies.

c. *Physiol.* Temporary inability to respond fully to nervous or sexual stimuli.

1932 W. BURRIDGE *Excitability* xxi. 172 Refractoriness is here defined as a condition of inexcitability of an excitable tissue which follows the receipt of an adequate stimulus. **1937** *Wilson Bull.* XLIX. 251 Birds invariably passed the climax of activity after a time and underwent regression. This was due to 'throwing out of gear' or development of refractoriness at some part of the sexual mechanism. **1949** *Ibid.* LXI. 221 This refractoriness must 'wear off' before external stimuli can induce a new gonadal activation. **1963** S. OCHS in E. E. Selkurt *Physiol.* ii. 28 In the alpha group of A fibers of the frog sciatic nerve, this period of absolute refractoriness lasts only a little longer than 1 msec.

2. Of things: Resistance to treatment or manipulation, *esp.* to the action of heat.

1839 URE *Dict. Arts* 299 Its refractoriness allows of a harder glaze being applied to the ware formed from it. **1870** *Academy* 12 Feb. 122 The vigour and skill with which they coped with its [granite's] refractoriness. **1893** SIR R. BALL *Story of Sun* 289 The two conditions of refractoriness and low atomic weight.

†**refracˈtorious**, *a. Obs.* [f. next + -OUS.] = REFRACTORY.

1555 RIDLEY in Foxe *A. & M.* (1563) 1360/2 Because he was verye refractorious, I said to him [etc.]. **1608** TOPSELL *Serpents* (1658) 639 Rebellious persons, refractorious, obstinate, and such as will not be ruled. **1613** T. GODWIN *Rom. Antiq.* (1658) 252 Punishments used..towards refractorious and disobedient soldiers.

refractory (rɪˈfræktərɪ), *a.* and *sb.* Also 7 -urie. [var. REFRACTARY, on anal. of adjs. in -ORY[2].

'It is now accented on the first syllable, but by Shakespeare on the second' Johnson (1755): cf. mod. dial. ˈ*refertory*, ˈ*refatory*, and see the note to REFRACTARY.]

A. *adj.* **1.** Stubborn, obstinate, perverse; unmanageable, rebellious. **a.** of persons.

1613 R. CAWDREY *Table Alph.* (ed. 3), *Refractorie*, Stubborne, which will not bend. **1646** BP. MAXWELL *Burd. Issach.* 19 If He be obstinately refractorie, He is not worthy to hold His Crowne. **1699** BURNET *39 Art.* xxxiii. (1700) 368 There is no other way of proceeding but by cutting off those who are so refractory. **1719** DE FOE *Crusoe* II. ii, They were a parcel of refractory, ungovernable villains. **1769** *Junius Lett.* i. (1788) 34 The most refractory of the colonies were still disposed to proceed by..constitutional methods. **1818** JAS. MILL *Brit. India* II. v. iv. 436 The honour of his government was concerned in chastising a refractory dependant. **1859** J. H. NEWMAN *Hist. Sk.* (1873) III. v. iii. 455 The old Roman law..gave to the father the power even of life and death over his refractory offspring.

absol. **1685** BAXTER *Paraphr. N.T.*, Matt. x. 11 More worthy, (or less unworthy) than the refractory. **1772** JOHNSON in *Boswell* (Argt. for Hastie), The refractory must be subdued by harsher methods. **1847** PRESCOTT *Peru* (1850) II. 343 The refractory were ejected..from their offices.

b. of character, disposition, actions, etc.

1606 SHAKS. *Tr. & Cr.* II. ii. 182 To curbe those raging appetites that are Most disobedient and refracturie. *a* **1653** BINNING *Serm.* (1845) 558 There are different tempers of mind among men, some more smooth and pliable, others more refractory and froward. **1720** WELTON *Suffer. Son of God* I. vii. 130 All those Refractory Dispositions that were Opposites to the Love, and to the Law of God. **1748** *Anson's Voy.* II. iii. 148 A Midshipman..had appeared the foremost in all the refractory proceedings of the crew. **1777** WATSON *Philip II*, XIV. (1839) 313 The factious and refractory spirit of the Walloons and Flemings. **1836** J. GILBERT *Chr. Atonem.* ix. (1852) 278 The thoughts and feelings may have still their refractory range.

†**2. a.** Strongly opposed, not amenable, refusing compliance, *to* something. *Obs.* (freq. in 17th c.)

1617 MORYSON *Itin.* II. 299 The Citizens of Mounster.. were now growne most refractory to all due obedience. **1671** SHADWELL *Humourists* III, I can no longer be refractory to your honourable Desires. **1723** *Pres. St. Russia* I. Pref. 2 A People formerly..so refractory to all Culture.

b. Undesirous *of* something. *Obs. rare*$^{-1}$.

c **1610** SIR J. MELVIL *Mem.* (1735) 174 He seemed somewhat refractory of accepting the Government.

3. *Med.* **a.** Of wounds, diseases, and the like: Obstinate, not yielding *to* treatment.

1663 BOYLE *Usef. Exp. Nat. Philos.* II. v. xix. 290 Stubborn Diseases that had been found refractory to all ordinary Remedies. **1836–9** TODD *Cycl. Anat.* II. 515/2 The wound was at first refractory.

b. Able to offer resistance *to* a disease; not susceptible to morbid agencies.

1884 *Science* III. 744/1 A dog..being rendered refractory to rabies by hypodermic inoculation. **1897** *Allbutt's Syst. Med.* II. 591 It is conceivable that with a weak virus in a strongly 'refractory' individual, the appearance of erysipelas might be delayed.

4. Resisting the action of heat; difficult to fuse (or work in any way).

1758 REID tr. *Macquer's Chym.* I. 359 All Iron ores in general are refractory, and less fusible than any other. **1777** PRIESTLEY *On Air* III. 21 The earth of tin is the most refractory, little differing..from flint, the most refractory of all the earths. **1833** N. ARNOTT *Physics* (ed. 5) II. 151 His blow-pipe fed with mixed oxygen and hydrogen, whose flame is capable of melting the most refractory substances. **1871** B. STEWART *Heat* (ed. 2) §109 The most refractory substances, such as carbon, can be made to appear as gases.

fig. **1836** EMERSON *Nature, Idealism* Wks. (Bohn) II. 161 To him [the poet] the refractory world is ductile and flexible. **1857** BUCKLE *Civiliz.* I. iii. 140 Where the products of the external world have been refractory [etc.].

5. *Physiol.* Temporarily unresponsive or not fully responsive to nervous or sexual stimuli; *esp.* in ***refractory period***, a period of reduced responsiveness following a response to such a stimulus.

1879–80 *Jrnl. Physiol.* II. 400 The same absence of response was observed whenever the second excitation occurred 'during the commencement of the systole of the ventricle' (termed by Marey the 'refractory period'). **1900** J. BURDON-SANDERSON in E. A. Schäfer *Text-bk. Physiol.* II. 449 This rhythmicality is attributed to the liability of the heart to be 'refractory' for a certain period after each excitation. **1937** L. V. HEILBRUNN *Outl. Gen. Physiol.* xxxvi. 415 In skeletal muscle, the refractory period is much shorter than in cardiac muscle. **1950** *Nature* 16 Dec. 1034/2 During this time, experimental birds are 'refractory'—they cannot be forced into spermatogenesis by means of photostimulation. **1952** *Jrnl. Physiol.* CXVII. 534 After the earliest stimulus the membrane potential falls again with hardly a sign of activity, and the membrane can be said to be in the 'absolute refractory period'. The later stimuli produce action potentials of increasing amplitude, but still smaller than the control; these are in the 'relative refractory period'. **1967** J. L. MCCARY *Human Sexuality* xi. 176 After orgasm, the man enters the refractory period..; the sexual stimulation that was previously effective and pleasurable now becomes unavailing and distasteful. Women, on the other hand, usually do not go into a refractory period. **1971** M. B. V. ROBERTS *Biol.* xviii. 268 The importance of the refractory period is that, together with transmission speed, it determines the frequency at which an axon can transmit impulses. **1972** *Nature* 18 Feb. 366/1 A substance from the male accessory glands..rendered the female permanently refractory to further insemination. **1974** P. SVENDSEN *Introd. Animal Physiol.* xi. 119 The very long action potential and refractory period in cardiac muscle are of great importance. They ensure that..two successive contractions cannot add together without a period of relaxation between them.

B. *sb.* †**1.** A refractory person. *Obs.*

1627 ABP. ABBOT in Rushw. *Hist. Coll.* (1659) I. 442 My Reply was, By what then doth he coerce those Refractories? **1633** T. ADAMS *Exp. 2 Peter* ii. 5 Like a bladder, which the peevish refractory puts under his arm. **1860** DICKENS *Uncomm. Trav.* in *All Year Round* II. 394/1 The Refractories were picking oakum... The oldest Refractory was, say twenty; youngest Refractory, say sixteen.

2. A piece of refractory ware employed in the process of glazing pottery. More widely, any refractory material.

1839 URE *Dict. Arts* 1019 Occasionally also a very fusible composition is thrown upon the inner surface of the muffle, and 5 or 6 pieces called refractories are set in the middle of it. **1875** KNIGHT *Dict. Mech.* 1910/1. **1907** *Jrnl. Iron & Steel Inst.* LXXIII. 384 The plant, which has only recently been laid down by the American Refractories Company at Joliet, represents the first successful attempt at manufacturing refractory materials in the west of America. **1931** *Daily Express* 15 Oct. 14/1 For many months manufacturers of refractories have had to struggle against the dumping of large quantities of Belgian sand. **1957** *New Scientist* 9 May 44/1 It was inevitable that factories making fire-bricks—the original refractory—should spring up alongside iron- and steel-works. **1962** *Science Survey* III. 344 The tundish that evens out the flow between the ladle and mould is usually a simple refractory-lined box. **1967** M. CHANDLER *Ceramics in Mod. World* v. 140 A high proportion of refractories must serve also as structural materials.

†**reˈfracture**, *sb.*[1] *Obs. rare*$^{-1}$. [f. REFRACT *v.* + -URE.] Refractory opposition or action.

1659 GAUDEN *Tears Ch.* IV. xx. 562 More veniall and excusable may those verball reluctancies, reserves, and refractures..seem.

reˈfracture, *sb.*[2] [RE- 5 a.] Renewed fracture (of a bone).

1908 *Practitioner* Oct. 535 Instances of refracture in long bones, at an old site of previous similar injury.

re-ˈfracture, *v.* [RE- 5 a.] *trans.* To fracture (a bone) again.

1876 *Clin. Soc. Trans.* IX. 161 Mr. Maunder proposed to try and re-fracture the thigh. **1898** *Daily News* 22 July 5/7 He unfortunately re-fractured the left bone.

refræne, obs. form of REFRAIN *v.*

†**refragable**, *a. Obs.*$^{-0}$ [= obs. F. *refragable*, It. *refragabile*, med.L. *refragābilis*: see IRREFRAGABLE *a.*] That may be refuted or gainsaid.

1611 FLORIO, *Refragabile*, refragable, that may be repugned or gaine-stood. **1721**– in BAILEY and later Dicts.

Hence †**refragaˈbility**, †**refragableness**.

1721–31 in BAILEY. [Hence in some mod. Dicts.]

†**refragate**, *v. Obs.* [f. L. *refragāt-*, ppl. stem of *refragārī* to resist, withstand.] *intr.* To oppose, controvert, gainsay.

1593 NASHE *Christ's T.* (1613) 119 Stoutly they refragate and withstand, that the Firmament is not his handy-worke. **1623** COCKERAM, *Refragate*, to gainesay. **1661** GLANVILL *Van. Dogm.* 179 If upon further enquiry, any were found to refragate, they were to be discharg'd by a distinction.

†**refragatory**, *a. Obs. rare*$^{-1}$. [f. as prec. + -ORY[2].] Disposed to controvert or refute.

1716 M. DAVIES *Athen. Brit.* II. To Rdr. 45 As to the severer sort of the High-Church Aristarchi, I shall not be very Refragatory.

refraiche, obs. form of REFRESH *v.*

†**refraidour**. *Obs. rare.* Also 5 refraydeur. [a. ONF. **refreidure*, var. OF. *refroidure*: see REFROIDOUR and REFREID *v.*] Cooling, coolness.

1483 CAXTON *Gold. Leg.* 250 b/1 He was cold of the fyrst refraydeur whiche is desyre of heuenly glorye..which within hym posseded the refraidour of paradis.

refrain (rɪˈfreɪn), *sb.*[1] Forms: 4 **refreyne**, 5 **refreyn**, 6 **refreine**, (7 **reffrein**); 6 **refraynt**, 7– **refrain**, (8 **-e**). [a. OF. *refrein*, *refrain* = Prov. *refranh*, Cat. *refrá*, Sp. *refran*, Pg. *refrão*, in the same sense, ultimately f. pop. L. **refrangĕre* (OF. *refraindre*) to break back, break again. See also REFREIT.] A phrase or verse recurring at intervals, esp. at the end of each stanza of a poem or song; a burden, chorus. Also *transf.*

App. not in very common use before the 19th century.

c **1374** CHAUCER *Troylus* II. 1522 (1571) But euere more allas was his refreyn. *c* **1430** LYDG. *Min. Poems* (Percy Soc.) 128 Remembre sothely that I the refreyn tooke, Of..my maister Chaucier, chief poete of Bretayne. **1530** PALSGR. 261/2 Refraynt of a balade, *refraynt.* **1580** HOLLYBAND *Treas. Fr. Tong*, *Envoy*, the refreine of a Ballade, that is, the foot of a song. **1603** HOLLAND *Plutarch's Mor.* 1271 In all the actions of Alexander, a man may use this for a reffrein or faburden, All Philosophically. **1778** BP. LOWTH *Transl. Isaiah* Notes xl. 191 Dancing and throwing in alternately the refrain or burthen of the song. **1795** MASON *Ch. Mus.* 213 To confine the Organist to a slightly ornamented Refraine, or Ritornello at the end of each Stave or Stanza. **1835** WILLIS *Melanie* 36 When another sang the strain, I mingled in the old refrain. **1860** ADLER *Prov. Poet.* xviii. 408 The song was divided into several stanzas, each of which terminated in a refrain. **1877** BLACK *Green Past.* xiv. (1878) 114 These old phrases and chance refrains seemed to suggest themselves quite naturally.

†**reˈfrain**, *sb.*[2] *Obs. rare*$^{-1}$. In 6 refrane. [f. REFRAIN *v.*] Restraint.

c **1560** A. SCOTT *Poems* (S.T.S.) iv. 86 The denkest sounest doun, The farest but refrane, The gayest grittest loun.

refrain (rɪˈfreɪn), *v.* Forms: 4–5 **refreyne(n**, 5 **-nyn)**, 5–6 **refreyn**, (5 *Sc.* **ra-**), 6–7 **refrein(e**; 4, 6 **refreigne**, (4 *Sc.* **refrenȝe**), 4–6 **refrene**, (7 **refræne**); 4–6 **refrayn(e**, 5–6 **refrane**, 5–7 **refraine**, 6– **refrain**. [ad. OF. *refrener* (12th c.); mod.F. *refréner*): ad. L. *refrēnāre* to bridle, f. *re-* RE- + *frēnum*, *frænum* bridle.]

I. *trans.* †**1.** To restrain, hold back, check (a person or thing). *Obs.*

c **1380** WYCLIF *Wks.* (1880) 278 þat meyntenours of false causes..be wisly refreyned & scharply ponyschid. **1388** —— *Bible, Ezek.* xxxi. 15, I forbede his flodis, and Y refreynede [*L. coercui*] many watris. **1483** CAXTON *Gold. Leg.* 292 b/2, I shalle soo refrayne hym that he shalle no more dare demaunde suche thyng. **1533** BELLENDEN *Livy* II. xxv. (S.T.S.) I. 232 Nowthir schame nor fere of þare Inemyis mycht refrene þame. **1548** UDALL, etc. *Erasm. Par. Matt.* xxvi. 99 b, Jesus refrayned them saying: Why be ye greued with this woman? **1633** G. HERBERT *Temple* Ded. 6 Turn their eyes hither, who shall make a gain: Theirs, who shall hurt themselves or me, refrain. **1645** M. CASAUBON *Orig. Temp. Evils* 42 What then..would they do, if God did use no such means, no such examples to refrain them?

b. *refl.* To restrain, put restraint upon (oneself); to repress any manifestation of emotion, impatience, etc. Now *arch.*

1387 TREVISA *Higden* (Rolls) III. 317, I am suche oon by kynde, but I refreyne [*v.r.* refreigne] me by vertue. *c* **1400** *Beryn* 2745 Wherfor refreyne the, And blowe but fair & sofft. **1535** COVERDALE *Gen.* xlv. 1 Then coude not Ioseph refrayne him self before all them that stode aboute him. *a* **1861** CLOUGH *Poems on Life & Duty, In a London Square* ii, And thou, O human heart of mine, Be still, refrain thyself, and wait. **1895** *Westm. Gaz.* 4 Oct. 1/2 For the first six months..the Party..refrained themselves and kept low.

†**c.** (In lit. sense.) To rein back, rein in (a horse).

c **1430** *Syr Gener.* (Roxb.) 6387 He..Refreyned his hors, and come hem too. *Ibid.* 6431 Gentil knight, refreyn youre stede. **1515** BARCLAY *Egloges* iv. (1570) C iij b/1 But if this same colte be broken at the last, His sitter ruleth and him refrayneth fast.

†**d.** *Astrol.* in *pass.* Of a planet: To receive a check and become retrograde before attaining conjunction with another. *Obs.*

1598 G. C. *Math. Phisicke* E iv b, Venus seeking the conjunction of Saturn by retr[ogradation] is refrayned. [1606 Fage *Spec. Ægrot.* E iv, Sometimes by accidents.. their friendship and familiaritie is refrained.]

†**e.** *Sc.* To hold, contain. *Obs. rare*$^{-1}$.

1542 *Inv. R. Wardr.* (1815) 72 Item twa doubill planttis [? *read* plattis] to refrane heit watter in maner of schoufer.

2. To hold back, restrain (a person or thing) *from* something, esp. some act or course of action. †Also const. *of*. Now *rare*.

c 1375 *Sc. Leg. Saints* xvi. (*Magd.*) 230 Scho.. presyt hyre in mony wyse þame to refrenȝe fra sik seruice of ydolis. *c* 1400 *Destr. Troy* 11305 Eneas.. Refraynit Amphimacus of his frike wille. 1450–80 tr. *Secreta Secret.* 5 God comfort the .. and refrayne the from flesshely and bestly desires. 1494 Fabyan *Chron.* vii. ccxxiii. 249 In auoydynge wherof.. he lytell & lytell refrayned theym of theyr outrage. 1535 Coverdale *Ps.* cxviii. [cxix.] 101, I refrayne my fete from euery euell waye. 1551 Robinson tr. *More's Utop.* ii. (1895) 222 They.. cowlde not for all that be refreyned from mysdoynge. 1602 Nixon *Eliza's Mem.* cxxxi. in Farr *S.P. Eliz.* (1845) II. 556 To make us of true light participate, Whereby our steps from darknes are refrain'd. 1667 Milton *P.L.* vi. 360 Nor from the Holie One of Heav'n Refrein'd [he] his tongue blasphemous. 1883 Tennyson *Charge Heavy Brig.* Epil. 14 Trade [might] refrain the Powers From war.

absol. *c* 1400 *Rom. Rose* 4956 But Eelde gan ageyn restreyne From sich foly, and refreyne.

†**b.** *refl.* To restrain (oneself) *from* some action, etc. *Obs.* (cf. 9).

a 1400–50 *Alexander* 4638 If ȝe refreyne ȝow þar-fra.. ȝow writhis with ȝour wele. 1450–80 tr. *Secreta Secret.* 22 He that wille.. refrayne him from ouirmoche etyng and drynkyng. 1535 Coverdale *Acts* v. 38 And now I saye vnto you: refrayne youre selues from these men, and let them go. 1561 T. Norton *Calvin's Inst.* i. 3 She doth not for onely feare of punishment refraine her self from sinning. 1581 Rich *Farew.* viii. A a iij, Thei haue not bin able to refraine themselues, from prosecuting their follie to the ende.

†**c.** Const. with *inf.* or *that*. *Obs.*

c 1450 *St. Cuthbert* (Surtees) 7782 þe enmys to wende him refreynd. *c* 1500 *Three Kings' Sons* 192 Assone as.. he knewe it was Le Surnome, he coude not refrayne him to kisse him. 1535 Coverdale *Acts* xiv. 50 They scarse refrayned the people, that they dyd not sacrifice vnto them. *c* 1570 *Pride & Lowl.* (1841) 12 Ill can I take at thy hand such despit, And that to dooe thee force I mee refrayn.

†**3.** To restrain, curb, check, stay (an action, proceeding, feeling, quality, etc.). *Obs.*

c 1375 *Sc. Leg. Saints* xxviii. (*Margaret*) 8 Vertu It is blud to restrenȝe, & flux of wame refrenȝe. *c* 1380 Wyclif *Wks.* (1880) 278 þat þe grete blasphemye of goddis name.. be refreyned bi drede of peynes. *c* 1450 *St. Cuthbert* (Surtees) 1592 He was euer mare in his office Bysy to refreyn vice. 1483 Caxton *G. de la Tour* F iv, By curtosye and by swete langage ought the good wymmen to refreyne the yre and wrathe of their lord. 1538 Starkey *England* i. iv. 120 Yf we coude fynd a way to tempur and refrayne thayr malyce. 1561 Hollybush *Hom. Apoth.* 15 b, The same refrayneth the breaking up of the stomake. 1585 T. Washington tr. *Nicholay's Voy.* iv. xxxi. 153 b, To the intent to refraine superfluity and dayntinesse. 1637 R. Ashley tr. *Malvezzi's David Persecuted* 227 It is not altogether impossible to refraine nature a long time. 1683 Tryon *Way to Health* 107 [When] the continual use hath made this weak Quality strong, then it oft-times proves.. a difficulty to Refrain it.

†**b.** To withhold or keep back *from* another.

1503 Hawes *Examp. Virt.* vii. l, And I dyd my power from hym refrayne All his labour were lost in vayne. *a* 1586 Sidney *Arcadia* (1622) 37 A strange nicenesse were it in mee to refraine that from the eares of a person representing so much worthines.

4. To put a restraint or check upon (one's own desires, feelings, actions, etc.).

13.. *E.E. Allit. P.* B. 756, I schal.. my rankor refrayne for þy reken wordez. 1382 Wyclif *Jas.* i. 26 If ony man gessith him silf for to be religious, not refreynynge his tunge,.. the religioun of him is veyn. 1413 *Pilgr. Sowle* (Caxton 1483) iv. xx. 67 We haue no myght oure sorowe to refreyne. 1483 Caxton *Cato* B v b, Thou oughtest to refrayne thyn yre. 1560 Daus tr. *Sleidane's Comm.* 64 Certainly ye ought to.. refraine your prodigalitie and riot. 1584 Cogan *Haven Health* Ep. Ded. ¶3 A great punishment it is for a man to refraine his appetite. 1647 Lilly *Chr. Astrol.* ii. 312 She refraines and restraines her Concupiscence very much, and casts off her Suitors. 1672 Marvell *Reh. Transp.* i. 85 That even then Mr. Bayes alone should not be able to refrain his Malignity. 1725 Pope *Odyss.* i. 100 Neptune aton'd, his wrath shall now refrain. 1773–83 Hoole *Orl. Fur.* xii. 258 Say—whither would ye go?—your course refrain. 1846 Kingsley *Misc.* (1859) II. 348, I.. meddled in matters too high for me, instead of refraining my soul, and keeping it low. 1875 Jowett *Plato* (ed. 2) I. 498 When we heard that, we were ashamed, and refrained our tears.

b. To confine, keep *within* bounds. *rare*$^{-1}$.

1814 Cary *Dante, Paradise* xxii. 49 My brethren, who their steps refrain'd Within the cloisters.

†**5.** To keep from (an action), desist from, give up.

1593 Shaks. *3 Hen. VI*, ii. ii. 110 Scarse I can refraine The execution of my big-swolne heart Vpon that Clifford. 1606 G. W[oodcocke] *Hist. Ivstine* xii. 55 One of the wise men gaue him aduice to refrain his cumming there, for it was the fatal place of his death. 1676 Marvell *Gen. Councils* Wks. 1875 IV. 154 Whereas if men could have refrain'd this cunning.. governing of Christianity [etc.]. 1725 Pope *Odyss.* iv. 907 Must my servant train Th' allotted labours of the day refrain..?

†**b.** Const. with gerund or vbl. sb. *Obs.* (cf. 9 b).

1561 T. Hoby tr. *Castiglione's Courtyer* i. (1577) D iv, They come so to purpose, that hee can not refraine telling them. 1611 Bible *Job* xxix. 9 The princes refrained talking, and laid their hand on their mouth. 1620 Venner *Via Recta* (1650) 5 Those that have tender bodies shall do well to refraine travelling abroad in such a disordered change of the aire. 1678 Otway *Friendship in F.* ii. 13 A spark can no more refrain running into love after a Bottle [etc.]. 1725 De Foe *Voy. round World* (1840) 276 We could not refrain smiling at one another. 1745 Eliza Heywood *Female Spect.* No. 14 (1748) III. 104 Impossible was it for her to refrain being merry at the first part of this intelligence. 1791 Mrs. Radcliffe *Rom. Forest* v, She resolved, however, to refrain for some time walking in the forest.

†**c.** To keep back (laughter or tears). *Obs. rare.*

1638 Mayne *Lucian* (1664) 16, I could not refraine laughter, when he proceeded, and said [etc.]. 1719 De Foe *Crusoe* ii. vi, This.. man could not refrain tears.

†**6.** To abstain from (a habit or practice); to give up, avoid, eschew. *Obs.*

1560 Daus tr. *Sleidane's Comm.* 28 That his adversaries may refraine theyr wonted rayling. 1567 *Gude & Godlie B.* (S.T.S.) 16 Als oft as we repent, and sin refraine. 1606 G. W[oodcocke] *Hist. Ivstine* xii. 55 He began anew his feastings and ryot, which of some long time he had refrayned. 1658 *Whole Duty Man* viii. §15 Which would certainly kill thee if thou didst not for some little time refrain immoderate drinking. 1738 tr. *Guazzo's Art Conversation* 42 We ought to refrain Conversation with such sort of Persons. 1751 Eliza Heywood *Betsy Thoughtless* II. 267 Having been advised.. to refrain the use of any of these liquors, on account of some disorder.

†**b.** To abstain from using or partaking of (some article of food or drink). *Obs.*

1568 Hyll *Gard.*, *Yearly Conject.* v, Sharpe meates refraine in this moneth. 1580 Lyly *Euphues* (Arb.) 447 They refraine wine, bicause they fear to take too much. 1641 Baker *Chron.* (1679) 401/1 She would sit silently, refrain her meat, and not admit of any conference. 1691 Tryon *Wisd. Dictates* 21 Refrain all salt sharp Foods, as Cheese, Flesh.

†**c.** To keep the hands off (something). *Obs.*$^{-1}$

1600 Tourneur *Transf. Metam.* liv, Thou monstrous fiend (quoth he) thy pray refrain.

†**7.** To avoid, shun, eschew (one's company). *Obs.*

1547–64 Bauldwin *Mor. Philos.* i. (Palfr.) 54 A king ought to refraine the company of vicious persons. 1579 Lyly *Euphues* (Arb.) 145 Not disdayning their cockemates or refraining their company. 1629 Wadsworth *Pilgr.* vi. 53 Father Boniface.. gaue order to his tutor to refraine my company. 1697 Sir T. P. Blount *Ess.* 148, I refrain no man's company because his opinion comes not up to mine. 1716 Bp. Wilson in Keble *Life* (1863) I. xi. 371 [He at once excommunicates the offender] that the Society of Christians may utterly refrain his company.

†**b.** To avoid, keep or stay away from (a place); also, to go away from, to leave. *Obs.*

1577 Hanmer *Anc. Eccles. Hist.* (1619) 290 Such as refrained the Churches and publike assembly. 1605 *Play of Stucley* in Simpson *Sch. Shaks.* (1878) I. 229 It is most certain there are many sick And therefore good my Lord refrain the place. 1621 Lady M. Wroth *Urania* 8, I must my Lord (said she) intreate you to refraine this place. *a* 1723 *Robin Hood & Little John* xxxviii. in Child *Ballads* III. 136/2 Then all the whole train the grove did refrain, And unto their caves they did go. 1748 Johnson *Van. Hum. Wishes* 149 Should tempting Novelty thy cell refrain.

†**c.** To avoid or shun (danger). *Obs. rare*$^{-1}$.

c 1560 A. Scott *Poems* (S.T.S.) xxxii. 23 To refrane that denger plane, Fle alwayis frome þe snair.

II. *intr.* **8.** To abstain, forbear.

c 1400 *Destr. Troy* 2957 [þou] might faire haue refraynit with þi fre wille. *c* 1430 Lydg. *Min. Poems* (Percy Soc.) 69 Over salt mete doth grete oppressioun To fieble stomakes, whan they can nat refreyne. 1549 Coverdale, etc. *Erasm. Par. Rom.* Prol. 24, I may of myne owne strength refraine that I do mine enemy no hurte. 1560 Daus tr. *Sleidane's Comm.* 306, I wyll refrayne and wil aske him but this question only. 1605 Shaks. *Macb.* ii. iii. 122 Who could refraine, That had a heart to loue..? 1648 Milton *Sonn. to C. Skinner*, Heav'n.. disapproves that care, though wise in show, That.. when God sends a cheerful hour, refrains. 1715 De Foe *Fam. Instruct.* i. viii. (1841) I. 148, I am persuaded had you been there, you could not have refrained. 1780 Cowper *Progr. Err.* 456 Let the wretch refrain, Nor touch the page he cannot but profane. 1807 Crabbe *Par. Reg.* ii. 18 Till age, refrain not—but if old, refrain. 1875 Gladstone *Glean.* VI. xx. 154, I might, I believe, add other instances.. but it is needless and I gladly refrain.

transf. 1522 Skelton *Why not to Court* 36 But whan age seeth that rage Dothe aswage and refrayne. 1886 Winter *Shaks. Eng.* ii. (1893) 21 Fog has refrained, though it is understood to be lurking in the Irish Sea.

†**b.** Const. with *to* and *inf.* *Obs.*

1554–9 *Songs & Ball. Philip & Mary* (1860) 9 To synge the truthe, why shulde I refrayne? 1561 Daus tr. *Bullinger on Apoc.* Pref. (1573) 5 Lawrence Ualla.. could not refrayne to enveygh against the Popish clergie. 1633 G. Herbert *Temple, Providence* v, He that to praise and laud thee doth refrain. 1671 Milton *Samson* 1565, I refrain, too suddenly To utter what will come at last too soon. 1718 Rowe tr. *Lucan* v. 284 Why did your wary Oracles refrain To tell what Kings, what Heroes must be slain?

9. To abstain, keep oneself, *from* some act or feeling, †using or partaking of something, interference with a person, etc.

1538 Starkey *England* ii. ii. 191 Thys schold cause the attorneys and prokturys to refrayne from theyr crafty inuentyonys. 1579 Lyly *Euphues* (Arb.) 110 Learne of Romulus to refraine [1581 abstaine] from wine. 1604 Shaks. *Oth.* iv. i. 99 (Qq.) He, when he heares of her, can not refraine From the excesse of Laughter. 1611 Bible *Acts* v. 38 And now I say vnto you, refraine from these men, and let them alone. 1679 Dryden *Troil. & Cress.* Pref., Consider the wretchedness of his Condition.. and refrain from pitty if you can. 1711 Addison *Spect.* No. 106 ¶3 Some of them could not refrain from Tears at the Sight of their old Master. 1777 Watson *Philip II*, vii. (1839) 123 That their preachers should refrain from all invectives against the established church. 1819 Shelley *Julian* 498, I refrain From that sweet sleep which medicines all pain. 1875 Jowett *Plato* (ed. 2) V. 304 A man should refrain from excess either of laughter or tears.

b. Const. *from* with gerund or vbl. sb. (cf. 5 b).

1528 Roy *Rede me* (Arb.) 30 Howe shall we from hevy wepynge refrayne? 1579 Lyly *Euphues* (Arb.) 152 Refraine from dicing. 1620 tr. *Boccaccio's Decam.* 98 Refraine from weeping and observe attentively what I shall say. 1816 J. Wilson *City of Plague* ii. ii. 275 For one single day I must refrain From visiting the sick. 1867 Smiles *Huguenots Eng.* viii. (1880) 134 Richelieu refrained from pushing his advantage to an extremity.

†**refrai·nation.** *Astrol. Obs.* [var. of refrenation, after prec.] = refrenation 2.

1598 F. Wither tr. *Dariot's Judgem. Starres* H b, Prohibition or let is done by retrogradation or going backward..: and this let is properly called a Refreynation, or houlding backe. 1679 Moxon *Math. Dict.*, *Refraination*, 'Tis a kind of weakning to a Planet which is called so by Astrologers when a Planet going to an Aspect with another, before they come up to it becomes Retrograde, and thereby is as it were pluckt back. 1704 Eland *Tutor to Astrol.* 58 Refraination is, when a Planet is applying to another, either by Conjunction or Aspect, and before he comes to Conjunction he becomes retrograde.

†**refrained,** *ppl. a. Obs. rare.* [app. from refrain *v.* + -ed[1], but perh. an error for *refrayed* refreid.] Of a hawk: ? Affected with a cold.

1486 *Bk. St. Albans* C vij, Whan ye se your hawke nesynge & casting water thorugh her noesthrilles on her nares: then dowteles she is Refraned. *Ibid.*, A medecyne for hawkis that bene Refreyned. [Hence in later works.]

re'frainer. *rare*$^{-1}$. [f. refrain *v.* + -er[1].] One who restrains.

a 1548 Hall *Chron.*, *Hen. VII* 56 These .ii. persons were euer cohibetors and refreiners of the kinges wilfull skope.

†**re'fraining,** *vbl. sb.*[1] *Obs. rare*$^{-1}$. [f. refrain *sb.*[1]] Singing of a refrain; caroling.

? *a* 1366 Chaucer *Rom. Rose* 749 Noon.. couthe make in song sich refreynynge, It sat hir wondir wel to synge.

refraining (rɪ'freɪnɪŋ), *vbl. sb.*[2] [f. refrain *v.* + -ing[1].] The action or fact of restraining, abstaining, etc.

c 1340 Hampole *Prose Tr.* 20 In fastynge, wakeynge, and in refreynynge of thi fleshly lustis. 1398 Trevisa *Barth. De P.R.* xviii. viii. (Bodl. MS.), þe asse.. is [led] heder and þedre.. bi refreynynge of þe bernacle. 1526 *Pilgr. Perf.* (W. de W. 1531) 45 They profyte moche in ye refreynynge or leuynge of vnlawfull pleasures. 1611 Cotgr., *Refrenation*, a refraining. 1857 Susanna Winkworth tr. *Life Tauler* 56 All her works and refrainings will give her no content. 1875 Whitney *Life Lang.* xv. 312 The refraining from pushing conclusions beyond what the evidences warrant.

refrainment (rɪ'freɪnmənt). *rare.* [f. as prec. + -ment.] Refraining, abstinence.

1711 Shaftesb. *Charac.* (1737) III. vi. vi. 386 Forbearance and Indurance, or what we may otherwise call Refrainment and Support. 1884 Mrs. F. E. Pirkis *J. Wynne* II. vii. 91 Her night's rest and refrainment having evidently sharpened the edge of her appetite for pretty things.

refraite, variant of refreit *Obs.*

reframe (riː'freɪm), *v.* [re- 5 a.] *trans.* To frame, fashion anew. Hence **re'framing** *vbl. sb.*

1590 C'tess Pembroke *Antonie* i. 99 So long thy loue with such things nourished Reframes, reformes it selfe. 1598 Barret *Theor. Warres* vi. i. 183 The ready reframing of them [maniples] againe into their grand square. 1627 Hakewill *Apol.* (1630) 274 It was.. unframed and reframed in the Grand Signiours presence by the maker. *a* 1711 Ken *Christophil* Poet. Wks. 1721 I. 498 My Jesus, who dost Souls reframe, To a true God-like Height. 1768–74 Tucker *Lt. Nat.* (1834) I. 285, I shall be content with it,.. without regarding whether he had made it up of the same materials as the former, reframed, or of fresh stuff. 1839–52 Bailey *Festus* xx. 354 All things reframed themselves before mine eyes. 1884 *Law Times* LXXVI. 294/1 The promoters.. would be more likely to meet with general support.. if they would reframe their Bills.

†**refra·nation,** irreg. var. of refraination or refrenation. *Obs.* Chiefly *Astrol.*

1583 T. Heth *Confut. Astrol. Disc.* B vij b, Although they bee in application, yet is the same.. preuented by refranation, afore they come to the full conjunction. 1597 A. M. tr. *Guillemeau's Fr. Chirurg.* 49/1 The refranatione or bridlinge of this furiouse humoure. 1658 Phillips, *Refranation*, is, when a Planet is Applying to another,.. and before he comes joyned, he becomes retrograde. 1819 J. Wilson *Dict. Astrol.* 220 Refranation is the most certain symptom of a breach between the parties.

refrane, obs. form of refrain *v.* (and *sb.*[2]).

refrangent (rɪ'frændʒənt), *a. rare.* [f. pres. pple. of L. **refrangĕre* (for *refringĕre*): see refract *v.*] Refracting; breaking up again.

1880 Swinburne *Songs of Spring-t.*, *Gard. Cymodoce* 304 The beam.. refrangent again from the wave. 1883 Sternberg *Bacteria* 269 The anthrax bacillus.. develops refrangent, endogenous spores.

refrangi'bility. [f. next + -ity.]

1. The property of being refrangible; the degree to which this property is present.

1673 Newton in *Phil. Trans.* VIII. 6090 The Sun's light consists of rays differing by indefinite degrees of Refrangibility. 1706 W. Jones *Syn. Palmar. Matheseos* 302 Homogeneal Rays (or those of like Refrangibility). 1717 J. Keill *Anim. Oecon.* (1738) 147 Rays of Light, of different Refrangibilities. 1808 *Phil. Trans.* XCIX. 268 This.. is only the consequence of the different refrangibility of light. 1879

Proctor *Pleas. Ways Sc.* i. 24 A gas when glowing absorbs rays of the same refrangibility as it emits.

2. Refracting power. *rare*⁻¹.

1774 Goldsm. *Nat. Hist.* (1860) I. xxi. 140 Glasses of different refrangibilities.

refrangible (rɪˈfrændʒɪb(ə)l), *a.* [ad. L. type **refrangibilis* f. **refrangĕre* (for *refringĕre*): see refract *v.*] Capable of being refracted; admitting of, susceptible to, refraction.

1673 Newton in *Phil. Trans.* VIII. 6090, I call that Light homogeneal, similar, or uniform, whose rays are equally refrangible. **1706** W. Jones *Syn. Palmar. Matheseos* 301 The Light of the Sun consists of Rays that are differently.. Refrangible. **1770** *Monthly Rev.* XLII. 507 All the different images of the object produced by the differently refrangible rays. **1822** Imison *Sc. & Art* II. 33 The invisible rays of heat being more refrangible than those of light. **1851** Nichol *Archit. Heav.* (ed. 9) 218 The red or least refrangible end of the spectrum.

Hence **reˈfrangibleness**.

1731 in Bailey vol. II, and hence in some mod. Dicts.

†**reˈfrangile**, *a. Obs.* [f. the vbl. stem **refrang-* (see prec.) + -ile.] Liable to be refracted at a certain point or distance. So †**reˈfrangity**.

1797 Brougham in *Phil. Trans.* LXXXVII. 384 The rays which are most flexible have also the greatest refrangity, reflexity, and flexity; or are most refrangile, reflexile, and flexile. [Cf. *ibid.* 360.]

†**reˈfraught**, *v. Obs. rare*⁻¹. [f. re- 5 a + fraught *v.*] *trans.* To freight again. So †**reˈfraught** *pa. pple.*, reladen.

1612 *Proc. Virginia* in *Capt. Smith's Wks.* (Arb.) 122 Captaine Newport vndertook to fraught the Pinnace with corne, in going and returning in his discoverie, and to refraught her again from Werawocomoco. **1765** E. Thompson *Meretriciad* 26 Entomb'd sev'n years, and lo! she rose again! Refraught with goods.

refrayed: see refreid *pa. pple.*

refrayn(e, -fraynt, obs. forms of refrain *v.*

†**reˈfrayne**, *v. Obs.* [f. re- + frayne *v.*, perh. after *require*.] *trans.* To question or examine.

c **1425** *Seven Sag.* (P.) 22 He toke thaym, and refreynde alle, Whilk of thaym he myght take. *c* **1450** Lonelich *Merlin* 1188 (Kölbing), The jugge gan hire refreyne And axede hire [etc.]. **1526** Skelton *Magnyf.* 2503, But frendly I wyll refrayne you ferther or we flyt, Whereto were most metely my corage to knyt.

refrech, obs. form of refresh *v.*

†**reˈfrectore**. *Obs. rare*⁻¹. [ad. med.L. *refrectōrium* for *refectōrium*: cf. OF. *refreitur*, *refretor*, etc. and see frater *sb.*¹] = refectory.

1432–50 tr. *Higden* (Rolls) VI. 183 Also he did write in the belle in the ffrater or refrectore [etc.].

refreeze (riːˈfriːz), *v.* [re- 5 a.] *trans.* and *intr.* To freeze again.

a. *trans.* **1794** J. Williams in *A Cabinet*, etc. p. vii, He can ..thaw coagulation, and refreeze the billows. **1860** Tyndall *Glac.* i. xi. 77 The surface of the snow had been partially melted by the sun and then refrozen.

b. *intr.* **1853** Kane *Grinnell Exp.* xli. (1856) 377 The surface thaw..is protected from re-freezing by the very snow through which it has descended. **1875** Croll *Climate & T.* App. vi. 554 The water..refreezes the moment it is relieved from pressure.

†**refreid**, *v.* (and *pa. pple.*) *Obs. rare.* In 4–5 **refreyd(e, refrayed; refre(i)t, refreyt.** [a. ONF. *refreider* (*-ier, -ir*) to cool, to make or become cold; see also refroid *v.* and refraidour.]

1. *trans.* To cool, make cold, chill. Also in *pa. pple.*, affected with a cold.

With the second quot. *c* 1410 cf. OF. 'cheval qui estoit refroidié' (1456–7 in Godef. VI. 727/3).

c **1374** Chaucer *Rosemounde* 21 My love may not refreyd be nor afounde; I brenne ay in an amorous plesaunce. *c* **1386** —— *Pars. T.* ¶ 267 If he were al refreyded by siknesse or by malefice of sorcerie or colde drynkes. *c* **1410** *Master of Game* v. (MS. Digby 182), And for cause þat þe sowe shall be refreted [*v.r.* refreited; F. *refroidees*], þe boore goth not frome hir. *Ibid.* xii, Houndes somtyme beth refrayed, as horse, when þai haue renne to longe and commeth hoote in some water.

2. *intr.* To become or grow cold.

c **1374** Chaucer *Troylus* ii. 1294 (1343) Troylus..[did] writen to hire of his sorwes sore. Fro day to day he leet it not refreyde. *Ibid.* v. 507 God wot refreyden may þis hote fare, Er Calkas sende Troylus Cryseyde.

Hence †**reˈfreiding** *vbl. sb.*, cooling. *Obs.*

1382 Wyclif *2 Macc.* iv. 46 So Tholome wente to the kyng, sett in sum porche, as for grace of refreytyng [L. *refrigerandi*], or colyng.

refreigne, -frein(e, obs. ff. refrain *v.* (and *sb.*).

refreische, -ss(c)h, obs. ff. refresh *v.*

†**refreit, refret.** *Obs.* Forms: 5 refreit(e, refreyt, (reffreyt, refreyd), 5–6 refraite, 6 refrayte; 5–7 refret, (5 refrect, 6 refrete). [a. OF. *refrait*, *refret*, etc.:—L. *refract-um*, pa. pple. of *refringĕre* (or **refrangĕre*, OF. *refraindre*) to refract. Cf. refrain *sb.*¹] A refrain or burden.

1387–8 T. Usk *Test. Love* iii. i. (Skeat) l. 156 For euer sobbynges and complaintes be redy refrete in his meditacions. *c* **1420** *Chron. Vilod.* 4103 Þis was þe refret of þat caroulle, y wene. **1443** Lydg. in *Pol. Poems* (Rolls) II. 211 Of ther song the refreit was of pees. *c* **1500** Medwall *Nature* 516 (Brandl), These .ii. folk harp both on refrayte. **1532** More *Confut. Tindale* Wks. 686/2, I shal yet ones agayn..fal to my rude refraite, & sing him mine olde song. **1585** Higins tr. *Junius' Nomencl.* 11 *Versus intercalaris..*, *Refrein de ballade*, a verse often interlaced: the foote, refret, or burden of the dittie. **1623** tr. *Favine's Theat. Hon.* ii. xiii. 222 Taking the Refret or burthen of the Song. **1727–41** Chambers *Cycl.*, *Ritornello* or *Refret*, in music, the burden of a song.

refreit, variant of refreid *v.*

†**refrenate**, *v. Obs. rare*⁻¹. [ad. L. *refrēnāt-*, ppl. stem of *refrēnāre* to refrain.] *trans.* To check, restrain.

1599 A. M. tr. *Gabelhouer's Bk. Physicke* 130/1 It [a drug] violently refrenateth the laske, although it hath bin of a longe continuance.

†**refrenation.** *Obs.* [ad. L. *refrēnātiōn-em*, n. of action f. *refrēnāre*; see refrain *v.* and -ation.]

1. The action of refraining or restraining.

c **1450** tr. *De Imitatione* iii. xii. 80 It is expedient amonge to use refrenacion, yea, in gode studies & desires, lest by importunyte þou falle into distraccion of mynde. **1560** Rolland *Crt. Venus* Prol. 229 Oftimes be dantit refrenatioun, A man may weill alter his Inclinatioun. **1652** Sparke *Prim. Devot.* (1663) 187 The fast of refrenation, we all much stand in need of.

2. *Astrol.* The prevention of a conjunction by the retrogression of one of the planets. See also refraination and refranation.

1598 G. C. *Math. Phisicke* E ij b, Also in aspects these things ought to be considered; that is to say. 1. Reception. 2. Collection... Refrenation. *Ibid.* E iv b, Refrenation [is] when an Inferiour planet seeketh the ☌ [conjunction] or aspect of another [and] before he bee joyned becometh Retrograde. **1647** Lilly *Chr. Astrol.* xix. 111 There's another manner of Prohibition; by some more properly called Refrenation. **1706** Phillips (ed. Kersey), *Refrenation*... The Word [is] us'd among Astrologers, when a Planet applying to another, by Conjunction, or Aspect, before it draws near becomes retrograde. [Hence in Bailey (1721) and later Dicts.]

refrene, -frenȝe, obs. forms of refrain *v.*

re-ˈfrenzy, *v.* [re- 5 a.] *trans.* To throw again into a frenzy.

1796 Anna Seward *Lett.* (1811) IV. 275 What a wonderful performance is Mr. Burke's late attempt to re-frenzy the nation!

refresh (rɪˈfrɛʃ), *sb.* [f. next: cf. Sp. *refresco*, It. *rinfresco*.]

†1. The act of refreshing; refreshment; renewal of supplies. *Obs.*

1592 Daniel *Delia* Poems (1717) 414 Like the Morning Dew, Whose short Refresh upon the tender Green, Chears for a Time. **1615** —— *Hymen's Tri.* ibid. 133 Render sweet Refresh Unto his weary Senses, whilst he rests. **1648** Gage *West Ind.* xvii. 114 The Indians helped one another to unload and load the mule that came of refresh.

2. *colloq.* A refreshment (esp. of liquor) taken by a person; a refresher.

1884 *Telegraphist* Jan. 27/2 A man may be compared to a battery when he gets a 'refresh'.

3. The process of renewing the data stored in a memory device or displayed on a cathode-ray tube. Usu. *attrib.*

1967 *Technology Week* 20 Feb. 22/3 The complete refresh memory is made up of 16 parallel magnetostrictive delay-line loops that store all of the picture elements for one frame. **1972** D. Lewin *Theory & Design of Digital Computers* vii. 264 To produce a steady picture on the CRT the contents of the display file must be periodically cycled through (a word at a time) and passed to the display unit; this procedure is known as the refresh cycle. **1977** J. C. Boyce *Digital Computer Fundamentals* viii. 211 Typically the refresh operation must be performed about every 2 milliseconds. **1977** *Sci. Amer.* June 57/2 (Advt.), Every [memory] board is fast. With 'hidden refresh' and *no* 'wait state'.

refresh (rɪˈfrɛʃ), *v.* Forms: α. 4 **refressch, -frech, -fres**, 4–6 **refresch(e, refressh(e**, 5 **reffreshe**, 6 **refreshe**, 4– **refresh**. β. 4 **refreische, -freissh**, 6 **refraiche**. [a. OF. *refrescher*, *-ier*, *refraischer* (12th c.; cf. Sp. *refrescar*, med.L. *refrescāre*, It. *rinfrescare*) or *refreschir*, f. *re-* re- + *fresche* fresh *a.*, *adv.* and *sb.*¹ Cf. also OF. *rafreschir*, *rafraischir* (12th c.; mod.F. *rafraîchir*).]

1. a. *trans.* Of physical agents (esp. water): To impart freshness to (a place or thing, the air, etc.) by means of cooling or wetting. (Sometimes with suggestion of next.) Also, to plunge (cooked vegetables, etc.) into cold water as part of the cooking process.

14.. *Circumcision* in *Tundale's Vis.* (1843) 92 Hit is the well with iiij stremes..That thorow the world refrescheth all reemis. **1535** Coverdale *Ecclus.* xliii. 22 Whan a dew commeth vpon the heate, it shalbe refreszshed agayne. **1585** T. Washington tr. *Nicholay's Voy.* iii. i. 69 b, The snow.. serueth in whotte weather to refreshe..his drinke. **1660** F. Brooke tr. *Le Blanc's Trav.* 373 In this Countrey it never rains, snows, or thunders, nor anything that may refresh it. **1697** Dryden *Virg. Georg.* i. 388 Moisture then abounds, and Pearly Rains Descend in silence to refresh the Plains. **1756–7** tr. *Keysler's Trav.* (1760) III. 368 The neighbourhood of the mountains constantly refreshes this city in the heats of summer with a cool evening breeze. **1824** B'ness Bunsen in Hare *Life* (1879) I. vii. 239 In the evening the atmosphere is never sufficiently refreshed to be enjoyable till about a quarter after dark. **1861** Mrs. Beeton *Bk. Househ. Managem.* xxv. 591 Let the herbs be as fresh as possible for a salad, and, if at all stale or dead-looking, let them lie in water for an hour or two, which will very much refresh them. **1877** E. S. Dallas *Kettner's Bk. of Table* 45 Some..prefer to eat them [*sc.* asparagus] with oil and vinegar. In this case they are, as the French say, to be *refreshed* with cold water. **1972** *Guardian* 18 Aug. 11/3 Lasagne... Boil the pasta for ten minutes then drain and run under the cold tap, and drain again... Cannelloni: these are boiled like lasagne, and refreshed in the same way.

absol. **1604** E. G[rimstone] tr. *D'Acosta's Hist. Indies* ii. xi. 107 In some ports and havens, the salt water doth refresh. **1611** Bible *Ecclus.* xliii. 22 A dew comming after heate, refresheth.

†b. *fig.* To cool (desire). *Obs. rare.*

1588 A. King tr. *Canisius' Catech.* Deuot Prayers 17 b, Refraiche thairfor, o lord, my concupiscence with the vatter of thy grace.

2. a. To make (one) feel fresher than before; to impart fresh vigour to (a person, the spirits or mind, the eyes, etc.) when fatigued or exhausted; to reanimate, reinvigorate physically, mentally, or spiritually; to provide with refreshment.

Said of food, drink, rest, sleep, etc., or of persons providing or bestowing these; also freq. in passive without specified agent.

c **1374** Chaucer *Boeth.* iv. pr. vi. 111 (Camb. MS.), Tak thanne this drawht, and whan þou art wel refresshed and refect [etc.]. **1375** Barbour *Bruce* xiii. 614 The erll Patrik.. gert with met and drink alsua Refresche thame weill. **1398** Trevisa *Barth. De P.R.* xv. lvii. (Bodl. MS.), þere beþ fayre feeldes..to refressche and comfort yȝen þat beþ wery in studye. *c* **1440** *Partonope* 6061 Her beaute shall so me refresch. **1508** Fisher *7 Penit. Ps.* cxlii. Wks. (1876) 239 Beddes to refresshe theyr wery lymmes. **1560** Daus tr. *Sleidane's Comm.* 148 Whiche thinge refresheth their spirites to thinke vpon. *c* **1595** Capt. Wyatt *R. Dudley's Voy. W. Ind.* (Hakl. Soc.) 5 Our Generall..refreshed his men, and withall renued his store of victuall. **1634** Massinger *Very Woman* iii. v, This air will much refresh you. **1671** Milton *P.R.* iv. 591 Ambrosial drink, That soon refresh'd him wearied. **1717** S. Sewall *Diary* 23 Sept., I was greatly refreshed by reading..Psal. 66. **1747** Chesterf. *Lett.* 27 Mar., The mixed companies of men and women of fashion..unbend and refresh the mind. **1784** Cowper *Task* iii. 19, I feel myself at large, Courageous, and refreshed for future toil. **1835** Lytton *Rienzi* i. i, The rest will refresh you. **1860** Tyndall *Glac.* i. ii. 20 We rose with the sun, refreshed and strong. **1875** J. P. Hopps *Princ. Relig.* i. (1878) 7 A beautiful picture which thrills the heart and refreshes the eye.

absol. **1585** T. Washington tr. *Nicholay's Voy.* i. viii. 8 b, Another frute..giuing a water as it were sugred and serue greatly to refresh and digest. **1849** Thackeray *Pendennis* xli, Those [writings] that..are pleasant at the first draught, when they refresh and sparkle.

b. *refl.* (of persons): To make (oneself) fresher, by partaking of food or drink, by resting, †or by taking the air.

c **1375** *Sc. Leg. Saints* xxv. (*Julian*) 292 Þat mornyng Iulyane was gane to þe feld hym to refres. *c* **1400** Maundev. (Roxb.) xiv. 62 Þare he refreschez him and puruays him of vitailes. **1494** Fabyan *Chron.* vi. cxcviii. 205 Wherfore yͤ Danys..spoyled both those townes, and there refresshed theym. **1555** Eden *Decades* 53 With the vytayles..they refresshed theym selues. **1590** Spenser *F.Q.* ii. i. 24 There sate a knight..Himselfe refreshing with the liquid cold, After his travell long. **1655** *Clarke Papers* (Camden) III. 20 The next day..his Highnesse refresht himselfe with the aire in Hyde Parke. **1754** Fielding *Voy. Lisbon* Wks. 1882 VII. 66 That my wife and her company might refresh themselves with the flowers and fruits with which her garden abounded. **1828** Scott *F. M. Perth* xxxiii, That they might have the interval of Saturday to rest, refresh them-selves, and prepare for the combat. **1876** J. Saunders *Lion in Path* x, Is there any quiet inn near, where one might rest and refresh oneself?

transf. **1599** Shaks. *Hen. V*, ii. ii. 37 Labour shall refresh it selfe with hope To do your Grace incessant seruices.

†c. To relieve *of*, to set free or clear *of*. *Obs.*

c **1385** Chaucer *L.G.W.* 1081 *Dido*, Refreschede muste he been of his distresse. **1399** Langl. *Rich. Redeles* Prol. 32 This made me..to meuve him of mysserewle his mynde to reffresshe. **1546** Langley tr. *Pol. Verg. De Invent.* iii. vi. 71 By reason pͭ thei wer refreshed of their extreme colde by fyre & such houses as they had deuised. **1760** *Impostors Detected* iii. viii. II. 80 A sound sleep..perfectly refreshed me of the fatigues of the foregoing night.

3. a. To freshen up (the memory), to make clear or distinct again. Also with personal obj. (cf. refresher 2 and 3).

1542 Boorde *Dyetary* viii. (1870) 244 Moderate slepe.. doth acuate, quycken, & refressheth the memory. **1665** Dryden *Ind. Emp.* i. ii, But you, I see, Take care still to refresh your memory. **1705** Addison *Italy* Pref., For before I enter'd on my Voyage I took care to refresh my Memory among the Classic Authors. **1789** Mme. D'Arblay *Diary* 26 Aug., I did not refresh his memory with the severities he practised in that marine education. **1825** Lamb *Elia* Ser. ii. *The Convalescent*, He was to be seen trudging about upon this man's errand.., jogging this witness, refreshing that solicitor. **1867** Trollope *Chron. Barset* lxx. III. 270, I have had some trouble to refresh my memory as to all the particulars.

†b. To renew, revive. *Obs. rare.*

1628 Donne *Serm. John xiv.* 26, Wks. 1839 I. 545 When he refreshed many errors formerly condemned, concerning the Holy Ghost. **1692** Dryden *St. Euremont's Ess.* 3 They have refreshed their Alliance with the Gods by the Fabulous Nativity of Romulus.

†4. To restore, renovate (a building). *Obs. rare.*

c **1375** *Sc. Leg. Saints* xxii. (*Laurence*) 531 A prest..thocht he wald a kyrk refresch,..þe quhilk sic ned had of mending, þat it was nere þe done-cummyng. **1538** Leland *Itin.* (1768) I. 7 There be very fair Lodgyns in the Castel. And as I hard

Catarine of Spaine did great Costs in late tyme of refresching of it. *a* **1548** HALL *Chron., Hen. V* 45 b, The Kyng..repaired the walles, fortefied the bulwarkes, refresshed the rampiers.

5. a. To restore to, or keep at, a certain level or condition by furnishing (†or procuring) a fresh supply of something.

c **1450** *M.E. Med. Bk.* (Heinrich) 78 Let hit lye þreo dayes ..& on þe þridde day, ȝef hit be nede, refresshe hit wyþ newe. **1495** *Trevisa's Barth. De P.R.* XIII. xiv. (W. de W.) 448 To renewe and refresshe pondes fresshe water is ladde and brought by gutters, conduytes and pipes. **1569** SIR J. HAWKINS *Voy.* (Hakl. Soc.) 80 We determined there to refresh our water, and so..to take the Sea. **1604** E. G[RIMSTONE] tr. *D'Acosta's Hist. Indies* II. x. 105 A small fire continued, heats more, then a greater that lastes but little, especially if there be any thing to refresh it. **1876** PREECE & SIVEWRIGHT *Telegraphy* 19 Batteries such as those described ..will remain in constant action for a month... At the expiration of a month it becomes necessary to refresh them. **1895** SCULLY *Kafir Stories* 26 They went into the hut, and they refreshed the fire. **1977** A. P. MALVINO *Digital Computer Electronics* vii. 180 Because capacitor charge leaks off, the stored data must be refreshed every few milliseconds. **1977** *Sci. Amer.* Sept. 139/3 A memory used to refresh the information presented in a conventional video display, which is scanned point by point in a repeating linear pattern, does not require a memory with random access.

†**b.** To furnish *with* fresh supplies. Also without const. *Obs.*

1458 *Paston Lett.* I. 427, I have desirid hym to move the Counsell for refresshing of the toun of Yermowth with stuff of ordnance and gonnes and gonne powdre. **1555** EDEN *Decades* 1 To the intente there to refreshe his shyppes with freshe water and fuell. **1598** BARRET *Theor. Warres* II. i. 16 Let him prouide to be first refreshed with victuals. **1634** SIR T. HERBERT *Trav.* 6 Sierra Leoon, a place in Afrique,.. famous for refreshing that aduenturous Captaine Sir Francis Drake. **1756** COLLINS *Peerage* (ed. 3) II. II. 625 They..refreshed the garrison..with victuals and money.

†**c.** To furnish *with* reinforcements. Also const. *of*. *Obs.*

c **1470** *Golagros & Gaw.* 196, I may refresch yow with folk, to feght gif you nedis, With thretty thousand tald. *c* **1500** *Melusine* 121 Syn the paynemyes have refresshed themself twyes of new folke. **1557** in Burnet *Hist. Ref.* (1681) II. Records II. 320 They return again to fetch more, always to refresh their camp with fresh souldiers, in the lieu of such as be perished.

6. a. To restore (a thing) to a fresh or bright condition; to brighten or clean up; to give a fresh or new appearance to. ? *Obs.*

c **1400** *Destr. Troy* 9215 He..Asket water at his weghes, wesshed hym anone, Refresshing his face for facyng of teres. *c* **1402** LYDG. *Compl. Bl. Knt.* 103 This welle..wolde.. evermore refresshe the visage Of hem that were in any werinesse. **1587** HOLINSHED *Chron.* III. 932/2 The conduit was newlie painted, and all the armes and angels refreshed. **1599** BARNFIELD in *Pass. Pilgr.* 176 As vaded gloss no rubbing will refresh,..So beauty blemish'd once's for ever lost. **1647** N. BACON *Disc. Govt. Eng.* I. xliii. (1739) 69, I have endeavoured to refresh the Image of the Saxon Commonwealth, the more curious lineaments being now disfigured by time. **1697** DRYDEN *Æneid* VIII. 580 The rest refresh the scaly Snakes, that fold The Shield of Pallas, and renew their Gold. **1739** CIBBER *Apol.* xiv. 361 He would order two or three Suits to be made, or refresh'd, for Actors of moderate Consequence. **1818** SCOTT *Hrt. Midl.* xliii, The old hat looked smarter;..the lace had been refreshed.

b. To make (a surface) fresh, esp. by cutting.

1658 EVELYN *Fr. Gard.* (1675) 66 Nor can the graffe joyn to its trunk, unless the rind be refreshed, and cut to the quick with the knife. **1846** BRITTAN tr. *Malgaigne's Oper. Surg.* 336 We shall say nothing of refreshing the edges by means of a blister. **1880** MACCORMAC *Antisept. Surg.* 208 The distal and proximate ends of the gut were now 'refreshed', and the margins accurately united with sutures.

7. a. *intr.* (for *refl.*) To refresh oneself (cf. 2 b); to take refreshment in some way; now *spec.* to partake of some refreshing liquor.

1650 CROMWELL *Let.* 30 July in *Carlyle*, In the morning.. we resolved to draw back to our quarters at Musselburgh, there to refresh and revictual. **1706** FARQUHAR *Recruiting Officer* I. i, Tell her I shall only refresh a little, and wait upon her. **1777** EARL OF CHATHAM *Sp.* 2 Dec. in *Hansard's Parl. Hist.* (1814) XIX. 476 Not men sufficient to man the works, while those fatigued with service and watching go to refresh, eat, or sleep. **1856** OLMSTED *Slave States* 612 Working this way for three weeks, and then refreshing for about one. **1895** *Cornh. Mag.* Oct. 396 Young men..danced and perspired and refreshed.

b. To lay in fresh supplies.

1685 R. BURTON *Eng. Emp. Amer.* i. 5 One of the Canary Islands, where having refresht, after many days, they encountered the Sea. **1748** *Anson's Voy.* II. iv. 157 It was not the most eligible place for a ship to refresh at. **1853** KANE *Grinnell Exp.* xli. (1856) 411 It had been determined..that we should refresh at Whale Fish Islands.

Hence **re'freshed** *ppl. a.*

1646 *Mem. Occurrences* D ij, His daily refreshed memory. **1701** NORRIS *Ideal World* I. iii. 175 After this little devotional interlude my refreshed reader may accompany me with new vigour. **1812** L. HUNT in *Examiner* 14 Sept. 587/2 The numbers and the refreshed vigour which Bonaparte will be able to pour into Spain. **1871** RUSKIN *Fors Clav.* xi, They came out in a highly refreshed state.

refreshen (riː-, rɪ'frɛʃ(ə)n), *v.* [RE- 5 a.] *trans.* To make fresh again; to restore to freshness.

1782 SIR J. REYNOLDS *Notes Mason's tr. Dufresnoy* xxviii, In order to keep the mind in repair, it is necessary to replace and refreshen those impressions of nature which are continually wearing away. **1801** *Lusignan* III. 52 He..felt the breath of Heaven descend to refreshen his feverish brain. **1882** *Fraser's Mag.* XXVI. 203 You may refreshen your eyes and quicken your thoughts.

Hence **re'freshened, re'freshening** *ppl. adjs.*

1790 A. WILSON *Poems & Lit. Prose* (1876) II. 204 Exulting with refreshened glee. **1829** LANDOR *Imag. Conv., Penn & Ld. Peterborough*, The refreshening sweetness of well-ripened society. **1865** *Pall Mall G.* 13 July 11/2 The list of refreshened pictures is given in the appendix.

re'freshener. [f. prec.] That which refreshens; an article of refreshment.

1833 T. HOOK *Parson's Dau.* II. viii, Miss Jarman.. turned her head..towards Miss Budd, whenever she wanted a refreshener [of the memory]. **1888** 'L. SCOTT' *Tuscan Stud.* II. vii. 264 [Medlars] are the favourite refresheners until the water melon takes their place.

refresher (rɪ'frɛʃə(r)). [f. REFRESH *v.* + -ER[1].]

1. a. One who or that which refreshes.

c **1420** LYDG. *Commend. Our Lady* 45 Paradyse of plesaunce,..refressher of our food. **1581** T. ROGERS *St. Aug. Praiers* ix. (1597) 45 Come thou hope of the poore, and refresher of them which be ready to faint. **1678** OTWAY *Friendship in F.* II. 16 Tho' Love like Wine be a good refresher, yet 'tis much more dangerous to be too busie withall. **1727–46** THOMSON *Summer* 1257 The kind refresher of the summer-heats. **1845** W. SEWELL *Hawkstone* (1846) II. 281 Miss Mabel Brook, who had been permitted to come in as a refresher in the evening.

b. A refreshment; *colloq.* a drink.

1822 COBBETT *Weekly Reg.* 30 Mar. 795/1 When the press has taken a refresher, let it burst forth again in new peals of praise. *a* **1841** T. HOOK in *Casquet of Lit.* (1896) I. 313/2 A few friends at dinner and some refreshers in the evening had prevented Harding from saying a word. **1861** FLOR. NIGHTINGALE *Nursing* (ed. 2) 53 Taking a piece of bread instead of a cup of tea or coffee as a refresher.

2. A reminder.

1837 DICKENS *Pickw.* xxxi, His memory had received a very disagreeable refresher on the subject of Mrs. Bardell's action. **1856** J. W. CROKER in *C. Papers* 4 Dec. (1884) I. 5, I don't think that this noble ambition had recurred to my memory..up to the receipt of your refresher of yesterday.

3. In legal use: **a.** An extra fee paid to counsel in prolonged or frequently adjourned cases. Also *attrib.* **b.** (See quot.)

a. **1826** F. REYNOLDS *Life & Times* I. iv. 148 For the cause, after refresher on refresher, came on within the space of a few months. **1831** —— *Playwright's Adventures* vi. 108 He also knew that barristers..can only be kept alive by refreshers. **1881** *Times* 19 Feb. 10/3 It is therefore recommended that daily refreshers should be abolished, as being one of the principal causes of the undue lengthening of trials. **1892** *Pall Mall G.* 28 Oct. 7/1 A master in chambers, who had disallowed the 'refresher' fees of his learned leader.

b. **1853** DE QUINCEY *Autobiog. Sk.* ii. Wks. I. 72 Every fortnight or so I took care that he should receive a 'refresher', as lawyers call it,—a new and revised brief memorialising my pretensions.

4. *attrib.*, applied to training or instruction provided as a review of material previously studied or to instruct a person in new developments, techniques, etc., esp. in ***refresher course***; ***refresher leave***, leave granted for the purpose of attending a refresher course.

1907 *Interim Rep. War Office Comm. Provision of Officers* 10 Given a short term of liability, and short periods of recall to the Colours for 'refresher' training, many officers..would remain therein. **1914** HAMEL & TURNER *Flying* x. 209 Others ..go direct into the Royal Flying Corps Reserve..where they are available for periodical 'refresher' courses and for employment in the event of war. **1930** *Times Educ. Suppl.* 20 Sept. 403/4 Refresher courses for teachers. **1945** *Jrnl. Amer. Med. Assoc.* 12 May 141/1 A clinical refresher training program for..medical officers. **1959** *Listener* 17 Dec. 1085/1 This is not an introduction to Kipling, but a splendid refresher course. **1972** *Accountant* 17 Aug. (Suppl.) 14/3 (Advt.), Terms of appointment include generous refresher leave periods. **1976** H. WILSON *Governance of Britain* vi. 121 A major conference would involve one or two, or more, full briefing meetings at No. 10..with refresher briefings to review the progress of the conference and decide tactics to meet a changing situation. **1977** *New Yorker* 12 Sept. 103/1 A refresher training course in the basic sciences that I was teaching at the Armed Forces Institute of Pathology in the fall of 1969. **1980** R. PERRY *Grand Slam* v. 42 [He] was making a complete pig's ear of shadowing me... He was in dire need of a refresher course.

refreshful (rɪ'frɛʃfʊl), *a.* [f. REFRESH *v.* + -FUL.] Full of refreshment, refreshing.

a **1676** BP. GUTHRIE *Mem.* (1702) 73 These Emergents were very refreshful to the Covenanters. **1727–46** THOMSON *Summer* 364 They spread their breathing harvest to the Sun, That throws refreshful round a rural smell. *a* **1790** WARTON *Ode to Evening* v, Pleas'd with the cool, the calm, refreshful hour. **1885** MEREDITH *Diana* xxii, It was refreshful to look abroad after his desperate impulse.

Hence **re'freshfully** *adv.*

1818 KEATS *Endym.* I. 898 Refreshfully There came upon my face, in plenteous shower, Dewdrops. **1885** MEREDITH *Diana* xxxv, We are brought refreshfully to acknowledge that the world is right.

refreshing (rɪ'frɛʃɪŋ), *vbl. sb.* [f. REFRESH *v.* + -ING[1].]

1. The action of the vb. in various senses; also, an instance of this; refreshment given or received; the plunging of cooked vegetables, etc., into cold water.

1382 WYCLIF *Acts* iii. 19 Whanne the tymes of kelynge, or refreischinge [L. *refrigerium*]..schulen come. *c* **1400** *Melayne* 1207 Othere refreschynge noghte many hade Bot blody water of a slade. *c* **1430** LYDG. *Min. Poems* (Percy Soc.) 217 Quyk lusty sprynges..Do gret refresshyng and coumfort to the sihte. **1482** *Monk of Evesham* (Arb.) 93 Y haue euermore had yn al my peynys a swyfte refreschyng and releuyng of helpe. **1523** LD. BERNERS *Froiss.* I. ccxxv. 297 Than euery man drewe to his logynge and toke their ease, and refresshing of suche as they had. **1561** T. HOBY tr. *Castiglione's Courtyer* I. I iij, The tunablenes of musicke is a very great refreshing of..griefs. **1604** E. G[RIMSTONE] tr. *D'Acosta's Hist. Indies* II. x. 104 The nights being cold and moist, give a refreshing. *a* **1656** BP. HALL *Rem. Wks.* (1660) 35, I [had] a comfortable refreshing of sufficient sleep. **1671** MILTON *Samson* 665 Some sourse of consolation from above; Secret refreshings, that repair his strength, And fainting spirits uphold. **1719** LONDON & WISE *Compl. Gard.* 27 The refreshings and helps they are to receive by Rain, or Dew. **1845** MRS. S. C. HALL *Whiteboy* v, Such improvements need perpetual refreshing, and, above all, Patience. **1897** *Westm. Gaz.* 15 Apr. 2/3 At what point.. could it be said that the refreshing leaves off and the poisoning begins? **1961** S. BECK et al. *Mastering Art of French Cooking* viii. 422 A second important French technique is that of refreshing. As soon as green vegetables have been blanched..they are plunged for several minutes into a large quantity of cold water.

†**2.** Fresh supplies of food. Also *pl.*, and const. *of* (meat, etc.). *Obs.*

1480 CAXTON *Chron. Eng.* ccxxviii. 236 For defaute of vytaylles and of refresshynge they eten hors, houndes, cattes and myse. **1585** T. WASHINGTON tr. *Nicholay's Voy.* I. xi. 13 b, The refreshings of flesh, bread and fruites which he gaue vs. **1586** T. B. *La Primaud. Fr. Acad.* (1589) 194 As he passed with his armie by the countrey of the Thasians, they sent him certaine refreshing of floure, and of daintie cates. **1634** SIR T. HERBERT *Trav.* 13 The good water and refreshing here obtained. **1650** S. CLARKE *Eccl. Hist.* I. (1654) 182 Giving them corn, wine, flesh, fish, cheese, and many other refreshings. **1725** DE FOE *Voy. round World* (1840) 185 The English at St. Helena are enriched by the refreshing which the East India ships find that meet there.

re'freshing, *ppl. a.* [f. as prec. + -ING[2].]

1. That refreshes: **a.** physically.

c **1580** SIDNEY *Ps.* XLII. i, As the chafed hart which braieth Seeking some refreshing brooke. **1610** SHAKS. *Temp.* IV. i. 79 Upon my flowres [thou] Diffusest hony drops, refreshing showres. **1693** CONGREVE in *Dryden's Juvenal* xi. (1697) 297 Let us repose, While round our Heads refreshing Ointment flows. **1730** FIELDING *Rape upon Rape* I. vii, I'll take but one refreshing turn, and come back to the tavern to thee. **1797** MRS. RADCLIFFE *Italian* i, The air rose from the bay with most balmy and refreshing coolness. **1871** L. STEPHEN *Playgr. Eur.* (1894) v. 132 My thoughts turned to a refreshing cup of tea and a bed.

b. mentally or spiritually. Freq. in 19th c. in phr. ***it is (quite, etc.) refreshing.***

1697 S. SEWALL *Diary* 28 Jan., These thoughts were very refreshing to me. **1723** in *Sewall's Lett.-Bk.* (1886) I. 14 It was exceedingly refreshing to me to hear from an ancient Acquaintance and so worthy a Friend as your Self. **1774** J. ADAMS in *Fam. Lett.* (1876) 10 This is very refreshing news. **1823** BYRON *Juan* VIII. xc, One good action in the midst of crimes Is 'quite refreshing', in the affected phrase Of these ambrosial, Pharisaic times. **1867** LOWELL *Rousseau* Pr. Wks. 1890 II. 235 There is always a refreshing heartiness in his growl.

2. Used for freshening a thing.

1856 KANE *Arct. Expl.* I. xv. 169 The decks are cleaned, ..the refreshing beef-nets examined.

3. Of a fee: (see REFRESHER 3 a).

1716 *Parish Rec. Kenilworth* in *Mod. Lang. Rev.* (1951) XLVI. 327 Paid to Mr. Palmer a Refreshing fee at Christmas Sessions. **1775** SHERIDAN *Rivals* Prol., We did amend our plea, Hence your new brief, and this refreshing fee.

Hence **re'freshingly** *adv.*

1817 KEATS *Calidore* 16 To see it..Dip so refreshingly its wings and breast 'Gainst the smooth surface. **1886** F. M. CRAWFORD *Tale Lonely Parish* vi, She had made the acquaintance of a refreshingly young scholar.

re'freshingness. [f. prec. + -NESS.] The quality of being refreshing.

1658 DURHAM *Exp. Revelation* vii. 34 His countenance is as the Sun shining in his strength for the refreshingnesse of it. **1683** PORDAGE *Mystic Div.* 120 Coldness, Refreshingness [of water]. **1825** *Blackw. Mag.* XVII. 224 The most engaging elegance and sparkling refreshingness of style.

refreshment (rɪ'frɛʃmənt). [a. OF. *refreschement* (*-fresshe-*, *-fraische-*, etc.), f. *refrescher* to REFRESH + -MENT. Cf. mod.F. *rafraîchissement*.]

1. The act of refreshing, or fact of being refreshed, in a mental or spiritual respect.

1387–8 T. USK *Test. Love* II. xiii. (Skeat) l. 122 Sithen mercie and pite..might neuer been shewed [unto] refreshement of helpe, and of comforte. **1549** COVERDALE, etc. *Erasm. Par. Rev.* xxi. 35 The eternal springynge floode of refreshment vnto saluacion. **1651** CROMWELL *Let.* 24 Mar. in *Carlyle*, With singleness of heart to His glory, and the refreshment of His people. **1675** TRAHERNE *Chr. Ethics* 248 All the misery that is lodged in infinite despair has comfort and refreshment answerable to it in infinite hope. **1717** S. SEWALL *Diary* 18 Nov., Mr. Baxter came in and Pray'd with us to my great Refreshment. **1796** JANE AUSTEN *Pride & Prej.* xviii, She danced next with an officer, and had the refreshment of talking of Wickham. **1873** HOLLAND *A. Bonnic.* viii, I most devoutly trust we are going to have a season of refreshment.

2. a. The act of refreshing, or fact of being refreshed, physically, by means of food, drink, rest, coolness, etc.; †recreation. Also, that which refreshes in this way; the means of restoring strength or vigour, mental or physical. Freq. in phr. ***to take refreshment.***

1481 CAXTON *Godfrey* cxl. 209 This refresshement was not only in the men, but alle theyr horses were anon so stronge, so fresshe [etc.]. **1624** CAPT. SMITH *Virginia* v. 182 Hee recouered about foure spoonefuls of raine water to his vnspeakeable refreshment. **1667** MILTON *P.L.* IX. 237 When we need Refreshment, whether food, or talk between, Food of the mind. **1703** MAUNDRELL *Journ. Jerus.* (1707) 67

Having taken a little refreshment, we went to the Latin Convent. **1784** COWPER *Task* I. 390 The sedentary stretch their lazy length When custom bids, but no refreshment find. **1849** THACKERAY *Pendennis* xv, May I offer you any refreshment..? **1856** SIR B. BRODIE *Psychol. Inq.* I. iv. 142 The absence of its natural refreshment would powerfully affect the nervous system. **1872** YEATS *Techn. Hist. Comm.* 125 All these establishments for shelter and refreshment early attracted the attention of governments.

†**b.** ***quarters of refreshment***: (see QUARTER *sb.* 15). *Obs.*

1678 *Lond. Gaz.* No. 1318/4 On the side of Catalonia the Kings Troops are all in quarters of refreshment. **1702** *Ibid.* No. 3810/7 His Forces were in Quarters of Refreshment in some Towns. **1812** *Examiner* 31 Aug. 549/2 His Majesty has sent the army into quarters of refreshment.

†**c.** ***Sunday of Refreshment***: (see quot. and 7).

So called because the Gospel for the day is from John vi.

1710 WHEATLY *Bk. Com. Prayer* v. §12 (1720) 225 The fourth [Sunday in Lent] is with us generally called Midlent Sunday; tho' Bishop Sparrow, and some others, term it, *Dominica Refectionis*, the Sunday of Refreshment.

3. With *a* and *pl.* **a.** In general sense.

1387-8 T. USK *Test. Love* III. vii. (Skeat) l. 31 The grete bounties & worthy refreshements that she..ofte hath me rekened. **1611** COTGR., *Frescades*, refreshments, or things refreshing. **1651** HOBBES *Leviath.* II. xxix. 173 The small refreshments of such things as coole for a time. **1696** STANHOPE *Chr. Pattern* (1711) 38 The inward refreshements and unspeakable consolations of the Blessed Spirit. **1747** WESLEY *Charac. Methodist* 10 His Business and Refreshments, as well as his Prayers, all serve to this great End. **1829** *Good's Study Med.* (ed. 3) IV. 473 The kneading-friction, or shampooing..which has of late become a fashionable refreshment in the watering-places of our own country. **1888** BURGON *Lives 12 Gd. Men* II. v. 68 Such matters were evidently a favourite refreshment of his spirit.

b. Applied to food and drink. Now only *pl.* of a light repast, and often *spec.* of drink.

1665 G. HAVERS *P. della Valle's Trav. E. India* 109 A Present of Sugar Canes and other refreshments to eat. **1729** LAW *Serious C.* ix. 125 To make their use of liquors a matter of conscience, and allow of no refreshments but such as are consistent with the strictest rules of Christian Sobriety. **1780** *Act 21 Geo. III*, c. 49 §2 The common and usual Prices at which the like Refreshments are commonly sold. **1829** LYTTON *Disowned* II. 5 Have you had any refreshments, Mamma..? **1829** LANDOR *Imag. Conv.*, *Odysseus*, etc., While the goats are being milked, and such other refreshments are preparing for us as the place affords.

†**4.** *pl.* Fresh supplies of men or provisions. *Obs.*

1481 CAXTON *Godfrey* clxxiv. 258 To them cam newe ayde & grete refresshementes of men and vytaylle. **1585** T. WASHINGTON tr. *Nicholay's Voy.* I. xvii. 19 Fiue and twentie Muttons, and certain other refreshments. **1706** *Lond. Gaz.* No. 4197/3 They had [taken] one within the Streights, laden with Refreshments. **1772-84** *Cook's Voy.* (1799) 31 Several of the chiefs came on board bringing with them hogs, and other refreshments. **1803** NELSON 6 Oct. in Nicolas *Disp.* (1845) V. 225 The Boats employed in bringing the necessary refreshments to the Garrison.

†**5.** ***place of refreshment***, a place for vessels to renew supplies at. *Obs.*

1772 *Ann. Reg.* I. 5/1 It was supposed that it would have been an useful station and place of refreshment..for the French East India ships. **1800** *Asiatic Ann. Reg., Hist. Ind.* 20/1 A place of refreshment for the fleets on their passage from India to Europe.

6. The action of refreshing the memory.

1873 FORSTER *Life Dickens* II. 320 Notwithstanding the refreshment of his memory by this letter.

7. *attrib.*, as ***refreshment bar, car, counter, house, room, saloon, stall, stand, station, stop, table, tent***, etc.; **Refreshment Sunday**, the fourth Sunday in Lent, refection Sunday (cf. 2 c).

1860 DICKENS *Uncomm. Trav.* in *All Year Round* II. 418/2 Crowds of us had sandwiches and ginger-beer at the refreshment-bars..in the Theatre. **1889** E. DOWSON *Let.* 17 Mar. (1967) 50, I..searched through the Law Court refreshment bars. **1973** 'B. MATHER' *Snowline* vi. 68 The first class refreshment bar at Sealdah Station. **1886** *Encycl. Brit.* XX. 247/1 Refreshment cars are also attached to trains. **1908** *Busy Man's Mag.* Jan. 89/2 The dance over, he took them to the refreshment counter for a cup of coffee and a sandwich. **1979** *National Trust* Spring 14/3 Nowhere perhaps is the transformation more apparent than in the Tea Room, now freed from the unsightly refreshment counter. **1860** *Act 23 Vict.* c. 27 (*title*), An Act..for regulating the licensing of Refreshment Houses. **1835** DICKENS in *Evening Chron.* 7 Mar. 3/4 The Militia-man..repaired to Bellamy's kitchen—a refreshment room where persons who are not members [of the House of Commons] are admitted on sufferance, as it were. **1849** THACKERAY *Pendennis* xxvi, The refreshment-room..was a room set apart for the purposes of supper. **1966** G. W. TURNER *Eng. Lang. in Austral. & N.Z.* vii. 157 Because the narrow-gauge lines necessary for a mountainous country preclude corridors, and therefore dining cars, in our trains, the New Zealand *refreshment rooms* on railway stations are notable. **1976** *Flintshire Leader* 10 Dec. 3/5 Mrs Parry worked in the refreshment room at Chester railway station. *a* **1828** J. BERNARD *Retrospections of Stage* (1830) II. x. 318, I..purchased a cottage..surrounded by..meadowland; the former being small enough for a refreshment saloon. **1936** A. RUSSELL *Gone Nomad* ii. 8, I..sauntered down the corridors to the refreshment saloon at the first suggestion of thirst. **1855** HAWTHORNE *Eng. Note-bks.* (1870) I. 357, I bought a bun of a little hunchbacked man, who kept a refreshment-stall. **1976** *Honolulu Star-Bull.* 21 Dec. A-3/1, I have two gripes about the refreshment stand operation at Blaisdell Center Arena. **1860** DICKENS *Uncomm. Trav.* in *All Year Round* II. 513/2, I travel by rail-road... I am hungry when I arrive at the 'Refreshment' station where I am expected. **1977** C. MCCULLOUGH *Thorn Birds* iii. 67 Our next refreshment stop is a place called Blayney. **1841** HAMPSON *Medii Aevi Cal.* II. 94 *Dominica Refectionis*, Refreshment Sunday, the fourth in Lent. **1912** *Encycl. Relig. & Ethics* V. 770/2 The fourth Sunday in Lent, when the Gospel for the day narrates the Feeding of the Five Thousand, has long been called *Dominica Refectionis*, or 'Refreshment Sunday'. **1974** [see LÆTARE]. **1977** *Church Times* 1 Apr. 5/4 'The God of love my Shepherd is' set in *The English Hymnal* for Refreshment Sunday. **1860** DICKENS *Uncomm. Trav.* in *All Year Round* II. 514/2 You are going off by railway, from any Terminus. .. You present to your mind, a picture of the refreshment-table at that terminus. **1885** A. EDWARDES *Girton Girl* I. xiv. 276 Let us bend our steps to the refreshment tent. **1928** E. WAUGH *Decline & Fall* I. ix. 94 The refreshment tent looked very nice.

refret, refrain: see REFREIT.

refrete, refreyd, -t, varr. REFREID *v. Obs.*

refreyn(e, obs. ff. REFRAIN *sb.*[1] and *v.*

refreynation, var. REFRAINATION *Obs.*

†**'refricate**, *v. Obs. rare.* [f. ppl. stem of L. *refricāre* to rub open again, f. *re-* RE- + *fricāre* to rub.] *trans.* To open up again, renew (a wound or grief); to stimulate (the memory) afresh.

1570 FOXE *A. & M.* (ed. 2) 2121/1 They..began to refricate and rippe vp the old sore. **1600** HOLLAND *Livy* XXVI. xviii. 597 Euery man began afresh to refricate and renue the former greefe. **1657** HAWKE *Killing is M.* 29 To refricate your memories, The first Question was whether his Highness was a Tyrant or no?

†**refri'cation.** *Obs. rare.* [f. prec. on L. types: cf. FRICATION.] The action of rubbing open or rubbing up again. Also *fig.*

1590 BARROUGH *Meth. Physick* III. xiv. (1639) 123 The eating of sharp things..causeth a certaine refrication and rubbing open again of the scarre. **1633** BP. HALL *Hard Texts, N.T.* 337 In these legall sacrifices there is a continuall refrication of the memory of those sinnes.

†**re'friction.** *Obs.* [RE- 5 a.] Renewed friction.

1615 CROOKE *Body of Man* 216 By friction and refriction the seede is called out of the like parts.

refrigerant (rɪˈfrɪdʒərənt), *a.* and *sb.* [a. F. *réfrigérant* (16th c.), or ad. L. *refrīgerant-em*, pr. pple. of *refrīgerāre*: see REFRIGERATE *v.*]

A. *adj.* **1. a.** Of medicinal agents or appliances: Cooling the body or part; allaying heat or fever. Also with *property*, etc.

1599 A. M. tr. *Gabelhouer's Bk. Physicke* 324/2 And if you applye theron a refrigerante Playster cut then therin a hole. **1626** BACON *Sylva* §961 There be divers Sorts of Bracelets fit to Comfort the Spirits: And they be of three Intentions: Refrigerant, Corroborant, and Aperient. **1686** GOAD *Celest. Bodies* III. i. 392 'Tis known to have a greater Virtue, as the Endive and Succory, to be refrigerant. **1765** GALE in *Phil. Trans.* LV. 203 Every morning,..a portion of the refrigerant powder is given. **1804** *Med. Jrnl.* XII. 406, I..sent a cathartic with a refrigerant lotion. **1861** BENTLEY *Man. Bot.* 510 They generally possess refrigerant properties. **1875** H. C. WOOD *Therap.* (1879) 193 In fevers, lemonade often affords a very refreshing and useful refrigerant drink.

†**b.** Refreshing, otherwise than by cooling. *Obs.*

1626 BACON *Sylva* §788 Wherein you must beware of Dry Heat, and resort to Things that are Refrigerant with an inward Warmth and Vertue of Cherishing.

2. In general use: Cooling, producing coolness.

1766 G. CANNING *Anti-Lucretius* v. 339 In the recess of some refrigerant cave. **1830** W. PHILLIPS *Mt. Sinai* I. 383 The rays Fall mild, refrigerant.

B. *sb.* **1. a.** A medicinal agent or appliance employed to reduce abnormal heat, as in inflammation or fever; a cooling medicine.

1676 WISEMAN *Surg. Treat.* v. ix. 277 If the tumour be large, feel pappy and increase, notwithstanding your application of refrigerants, you may suspect [etc.]. *a* **1763** SHENSTONE *Economy* I. 168 In what lonely vale Of balmy med'cine's various field aspires The blest refrigerant? **1822** GOOD *Study Med.* II. 519 The injury produced..by an injudicious use of evacuants and refrigerants. **1880** GARROD & BAXTER *Mat. Med.* 38 In a dilute form, [it is] a refrigerant, tonic, and astringent.

b. *transf.* or in general use: A means of cooling; *esp.* a cooling or refreshing drink.

1826 SOUTHEY *Vind. Eccl. Angl.* 323 We read of Saints who resorted to such refrigerants as the ice bath and the bed of snow. **1841** LEVER *C. O'Malley* xxx, Discussing by way of refrigerant our eighth tumbler of whisky-punch. **1869** O. W. HOLMES *Cinders fr. Ashes* in *Old Vol. of Life* (1891) 245 The saline refrigerant struck a colder chill to my despondent heart.

c. *fig.* of immaterial things.

1783 BLAIR *Lect.* xxxii. II. 191 This almost never fails to prove a refrigerant to passion. **1829** SOUTHEY *Sir T. More* II. 397 It is a consideration, Sir Poet, which may serve as a refrigerant for their ardour.

†**2.** In distillation, a cooling vessel or apparatus at the head of a still; a refrigerator, refrigeratory.

1696 in PHILLIPS (ed. 5). **1727** BRADLEY *Fam. Dict.* s.v. *Distilling*, The Parts of the Matters distill'd are raised up in the Form of Vapours,..and being sometimes help'd by a Refrigerant or Cooler, fall Drop by Drop into the Recipient.

3. A freezing agent; anything which reduces the temperature below freezing point. Also, a substance used as the working fluid in a refrigerator.

1885 *Sci. American* 9 May 291/3 Some experiments recently made..appear to show that liquid oxygen is one of the best of refrigerants. **1901** [see *champagne gas*]. **1926** *Encycl. Brit.* III. 319/1 In the refrigerating cycle, the refrigerant is made to pass into the evaporating coils so as to enable heat to be absorbed from the commodity to be cooled. **1964** *Listener* 7 May 776 (Advt.), ICI salesmen are today successfully selling..refrigerants to Icelanders (where you'd think it would be cold enough already). **1970** *Times* 16 June 2/7 The water is mixed with a liquid hydrocarbon freezing agent such as butane. The refrigerant takes heat from the water which in turn produces ice crystals and concentrates unwanted solids and salts into a brine slurry.

re'frigerate, *ppl. a.* Now *rare.* [ad. L. *refrīgerātus*, pa. pple. of *refrīgerāre*: see next.] Made or kept cold, cooled. †Also const. *from.*

c **1420** *Pallad. on Husb.* VII. 62 Nowe benes..Made clene, and sette up wel refrigerate, From grobbes save wol kepe up thaire estate. **1483** CAXTON *Gold. Leg.* 108 b/1 He was colde and refrigerat fro all concupyscence of the flesshe. *a* **1548** HALL *Chron., Hen. VII* 16 b, Their fury was asswaged and refrigerate. **1647** A. ROSS *Mystag. Poet.* iii. (1675) 62 When the stomachical nerves are too much refrigerate. **1896** *Westm. Gaz.* 15 Dec. 3/1 Antiquity has become doubly refrigerate.

refrigerate (rɪˈfrɪdʒəreɪt), *v.* [ad. L. *refrīgerāt-*, ppl. stem of *refrīgerāre*, f. *re-* RE- + *frīgerāre*: see FRIGERATE *v.* Cf. F. *réfrigérer* (16th c.).]

1. *trans.* To cause to become cold, to cool: **a.** the body or its parts, or heat in these.

1534 MORE *Comf. agst. Trib.* II. Wks. 1179/1 Ye shadow of hys holy shoulders, which are brode & large, sufficient to refrigerate & refreshe the man in that heate. **1545** RAYNOLD *Byrth Mankynde* 82 These medycynes do refrigerate and coole the vehement heate wont to be in apostumes. **1615** CROOKE *Body of Man* 24 Where he saith..that the Braine was made onely to refrigerate or coole the heart. **1668** H. MORE *Div. Dial.* I. 481 The gentle fresh morning Air..refrigerating my bloud and spirits. **1797** J. DOWNING *Disord. Horned Cattle* 69 This medicine..refrigerates the heat of the blood. **1833** *Cycl. Pract. Med.* I. 247 Not..with the view of refrigerating the surface, but of suddenly cutting short the disease.

absol. **1612** WOODALL *Surg. Mate* Wks. (1653) 75 Camphora..refrigerateth and calefieth. **1658** ROWLAND tr. *Moufet's Theat. Ins.* 1000 They do refrigerate and bind,..and help the weakness of the stomach.

b. the air, earth, or other things.

1637 SALTONSTALL *Eusebius' Constantine* 139 The ayre, which from on high descends downe to refrigerate and coole the world. *a* **1691** BOYLE *Hist. Air* (1692) 164 He was able to find..that part of the beer or the wine that was next to the sides of the bottle to be refrigerated. **1777** G. FORSTER *Voy. round World* II. 493 The air was refrigerated by the abundance of snow on the mountains. **1854** TYNDALL *Fragm. Sci.* (1879) I. xi. 342 Hence [the blade of grass] becomes more and more refrigerated.

absol. **1626** BACON *Sylva* §398 The great Brizes which the motion of the Air in great Circles..produceth, which do refrigerate. **1671** R. BOHUN *Wind* 177 All Winds..doe actually refrigerate, and oftentimes so intensly, that they prove the fittest instruments for the Congelation of Liquids.

c. To expose to extreme cold for the purpose of freezing or preserving.

1875 KNIGHT *Dict. Mech.* 1165/2 The vessels to be refrigerated are sustained on a carriage. **1957** *Times* 1 Nov. 11/7 Operations which cannot be undertaken at normal temperature may be performed if the body is refrigerated. **1979** *Arizona Daily Star* 5 Aug. J 5/2 Refrigerate overnight before using.

2. *intr.* To grow cold.

1559 P. MORWYNG tr. *Gesner's Treasure of Evonymus* 151 A man must put les wyne to new routes then to dry: and perauentur, les also to them whiche ought to refrigerat and coule. **1563** T. GALE *Antidot.* II. 17 Takynge it from the fyre when as it begynne to refrigerate and waxe colde. **1603** SIR C. HEYDON *Jud. Astrol.* xii. 314 He receiveth the Sunnes beames but weakely, and therefore can not heat by them, but rather refrigerate. **1794** SULLIVAN *View Nat.* II. 142 The lavas..either overflow the land above the sea, and refrigerate there, or..they refrigerate again within the volcanos. **1864** LOWELL *Fireside Trav.* 149, I will make a fire, and leave them to refrigerate as much longer as they please.

Hence **re'frigerated** *ppl. a.*, cooled, frozen; also applied, by extension, to the container in which food is kept, displayed, transported, etc., in a refrigerated condition.

1666 BOYLE *Orig. Formes & Qual.* 173 We lately discours'd touching heated and refrigerated water. **1836** MACGILLIVRAY tr. *Humboldt's Trav.* xxiv. 347 The great heats are occasionally tempered by strata of refrigerated air. **1884** *Pall Mall G.* 26 July 5/2 The trade in refrigerated meat. **1943** J. S. HUXLEY *TVA* xv. 128 TVA, in collaboration with the University of Tennessee, designed and built refrigerated barges..to encourage the fruit and vegetable freezing industry in the Valley. **1958** *Brit. Standard Specification* No. 3053 (*title*) Open and closed refrigerated display cabinets (for the retail sale of frozen packaged foods in temperate climates). **1962** [see GONDOLA 4 d]. **1967** *Economist* 7 Jan. 29/2 Bulgaria has bought a fleet of..long-distance refrigerated trucks (built on the standard American pattern)... There has been heavy investment in refrigerated rail cars bought from Hungary and Poland. **1967** *Commercial Fisheries Rev.* Dec. 53/1 The catch of the refrigerated tuna boats was 7,985 tons in 1966. **1976** *Southern Even. Echo* (Southampton) 3 Nov. (Advt.), Cunard have bought 10 fast refrigerated ships.

refrigerating (rɪˈfrɪdʒəreɪtɪŋ), *vbl. sb.* [f. REFRIGERATE *v.* + -ING[1].] The action of the vb. REFRIGERATE. Also *attrib.*

1684 R. WALLER *Nat. Exper.* 72 It was cooled first, lest..upon the first Refrigerating it should Contract. **1877** *Patents Abridgm.* 1819-66, 15 The first part of this invention relates to the refrigerating of beverages. **1898** *Westm. Gaz.* 30 Mar. 10/3 An illustrated monthly dealing with ice, ice-making, refrigerating, cold storage, and all the allied industries that employ forced cold. **1909** *Chambers's Jrnl.* Jan. 23/1 The refrigerating-engineer..claims to play the chief part in the successful maintenance of the overseas trade in chilled meat.

re'frigerating, *ppl. a.* [f. as prec. + -ING².] That refrigerates; producing, pertaining to, connected with, natural or artificial refrigeration.

1634 SIR T. HERBERT *Trav.* 47 A coole and refrigerating sleeping-place. **1650** BULWER *Anthropomet.* (1653) 316 Refrigerating repercussive medicaments, which driue backward the matter to the profundity. **1676** WORLIDGE *Cyder* (1691) 143 A cool refrigerating spring-water. **1799** *Med. Jrnl.* II. 149 The situation..suggested to me an idea that refrigerating, and also sedative remedies, might be used externally with advantage. **1833** N. ARNOTT *Physics* (ed. 5) II. 108 The brine is at first a refrigerating mixture, which cools still more the pavement and the neighbouring ice. **1881** *Nature* 18 Aug. 364 These differences being due..to the refrigerating power of snow.

refrigeration (rɪfrɪdʒə'reɪʃən). Also 5 refrygeracion, 6 -cyon. [ad. L. *refrīgerātiōn-em*, n. of action f. *refrīgerāre* to REFRIGERATE. Cf. F. *réfrigération* (16th c. in Littré).]

1. a. The action of refrigerating, cooling, or freezing; the process of becoming cold.

1471 RIPLEY *Comp. Alch.* VIII. iii. in Ashm. (1652) 171 So hyt rejoysyth wyth refrygeracion I the tell. **1555** EDEN *Decades* 263 Suche thynges..are hyndered by refrigeration or coulde. **1646** SIR T. BROWNE *Pseud. Ep.* 59 Irons heated in the fire..contract a verticity in their refrigeration. **1684** BOYLE *Porousn. Anim. & Solid Bod.* vi. 104 These thin flaws, which upon the slow refrigeration of the Stones.. might lock up the tinging Particles. **1748** *Anson's Voy.* II. v. 185 That refreshment and pleasing refrigeration of the air, which is sometimes produced in other climates by rains. **1847** T. MILNER *Gallery Nature* (1855) 296 The vapours cannot become visible by refrigeration. **1871** TYNDALL *Fragm. Sci.* (1879) I. ii. 60 By nocturnal refrigeration, the aqueous vapour of the air is condensed.

b. *Geol.* The gradual cooling of the earth from natural causes.

1794 SULLIVAN *View Nat.* I. 71 That the successive cooling or refrigeration of the earth is a groundless notion. **1841** TRIMMER *Pract. Geol.* 469 The secular refrigeration of the heated interior of our planet. **1873** tr. *Schmidt's Desc. & Darwinism* 11 We may..infer that, at a definite epoch of refrigeration, life appeared in a natural manner.

c. The freezing of provisions for the purpose of preserving them.

1881 *Marine Engineer* 1 Jan. 225 The refrigeration of provisions for transhipment either as a cargo for sale in England, or simply as provisions in our large passenger liners, becomes daily of more importance.

2. Reduction of heat in the body (now only *Med.*); †cooling and refreshing of the blood or spirits.

1502 *Ord. Crysten Men* (W. de W. 1506) I. iv. D ij, The water gyueth refrygeracyon, The baptym taketh & coleth the inclynacyon. **1607** TOPSELL *Four-f. Beasts* (1658) 100 By smelling, they prevent the air that should come unto them for refrigeration. **1635** PERSON *Varieties* I. 35, I could allow for fishes a kind of respiration called refrigeration. **1681** CHETHAM *Angler's Vade-m.* xxxviii. §11 (1689) 247 Though they receive some refrigeration by their Guills, yet that refrigeration is not so continual, as when it is by breathing. **1833** *Cycl. Pract. Med.* I. 246/1 Refrigeration, to a certain extent, must of necessity result immediately from immersion in the cold bath. **1876** BRISTOWE *Th. & Pract. Med.* (1878) 229 Actual refrigeration, and bleeding.

transf. **1606** J. CARPENTER *Solomon's Solace* ii. 8 We hoped for some consolatory refrigeration and ease.

3. *attrib.* and *Comb.*, as ***refrigeration company, machinery, unit.***

1976 *National Observer* (U.S.) 28 Aug. 7/2 Les Whitely, who owns a refrigeration company in the San Francisco Bay area. **1943** J. S. HUXLEY *TVA* 30 The production of new refrigeration machinery. **1969** *Coast to Coast 1967–68* 103 The Natwicks sat on the front veranda to watch the traffic.. the semi-trailers and refrigeration units, the decent old-style sedans, [etc.]. **1979** *Tucson* (Arizona) *Citizen* 20 Sept. 1B/4 We have two refrigeration units in our house.

refrigerative (rɪ'frɪdʒərətɪv), *a.* and *sb.* [prob. ad. med.L. **refrīgerātīvus*: see REFRIGERATE *v.* and -IVE, and cf. F. *réfrigératif* (14th c., Oresme).]

A. *adj.* Tending to cool, refrigerant.

1558–66 WARDE tr. *Alexis' Secr.* III. I. 49 It [a plaster] is repercussiue, refrigeratiue and desiccatiue. **1601** HOLLAND *Pliny* II. 24 All Lectuces are by nature refrigeratiue, and do coole the body. **1665** J. WEBB *Stone-Heng* (1725) 82 Lead hath naturally commixt with it a certain Mineral..of such a refrigerative Quality, as in a very short Time it will consume even the Metal it self. **1727** BRADLEY *Fam. Dict.* s.v. *Cookoo bread*, This Plant is refrigerative like Sorrel. **1852** *Patents Abridgm.* 1819–66 (1877) 16 Improvements in machinery applicable to the manufacture of ice and to refrigerative purposes generally.

B. *sb.* A cooling medicine. *rare*⁻⁰.

1706 in PHILLIPS (ed. Kersey). **1727–41** in CHAMBERS *Cycl.* and in later Dicts.

Hence **re'frigerativeness.**

1731 in BAILEY vol. II. (ed. 2).

refrigerator (rɪ'frɪdʒəreɪtə(r)). [f. REFRIGERATE *v.* + -OR. Cf. obs. F. *refrigerateur* (Cotgr.).]

1. That which refrigerates or cools. In later use *transf.* from 2.

1611 COTGR., *Refrigerateur*, a refrigerator, refresher, cooler. **1862** RAWLINSON *Anc. Mon., Assyria* ii. I. 267 Trees, those great refrigerators. **1876** *Fortn. Rev.* Mar. 347 An enormous natural refrigerator in the shape of the Rosegg glacier.

transf. and *fig.* **1809** MALKIN *Gil Blas* VII. x. ¶4 A reflection..so virtuous acted as a refrigerator on my spirits. **1852** DICKENS *Bleak Ho.* xl, He moves among the company, a magnificent refrigerator.

2. An apparatus, vessel, or chamber for producing or maintaining a low degree of temperature.

The following are some of the commoner specific applications of the term: **a.** A chamber or vat for cooling worts in a brewery. **b.** Any vessel, chamber, or apparatus in which the contents are preserved by maintaining a temperature near, at, or below freezing point, esp. in the cold storage of food. **c.** An ice-making machine. **d.** = REFRIGERATORY *sb.* 1. **e.** That part of a surface-condenser in which the steam evaporated from salt-water is condensed into fresh water to supply the boilers of marine engines. **f.** (Incorrectly applied to) an arrangement whereby the feed-water is warmed on its way to the boiler of a marine engine by a current of hot waste brine pumped from the boiler.

1824 *Specif. Maudslay & Field's Patent* No. 5021. 3 Passing the hot brine and the supply water for the boiler through a system of tubes or vessels of extended surface called a refrigerator. **1839** URE *Dict. Arts* 1183 [The vapour] may be conducted to a worm or refrigerator, to be cooled in the ordinary way. **1841** C. CIST *Cincinnati in 1841* (Advt.), Refrigerators or Ice Chests. **1861** WYNTER *Soc. Bees* 192 Every man who possesses a refrigerator has the power of arresting for a time the natural decay of animal and vegetable substances. **1881** *Marine Engineer* 1 Jan. 226 We think the time is not far distant when all Australian and Eastern liners will be fitted throughout with refrigerators. **1958** *Times* 13 Jan. 11/2 Only 10 per cent. of the population of this island have refrigerators, against 90 per cent. in the United States. **1975** *N.Z. Jrnl. Agric.* Sept. 39/1 My first impression was that the New Zealand farm equipment manufacturers were attempting to 'sell refrigerators to the Eskimos', because, among the massive displays by the British manufacturers, a comparative handful of New Zealand firms were trying to enter an overcrowded market.

3. *attrib.* and *Comb.*, as ***refrigerator beef, car, engineer, -freezer, -maker, ship, truck.***

1881 *Chicago Times* 4 June, American refrigerator beef sold at London and Liverpool to-day at 5½d. **1875** KNIGHT *Dict. Mech.* 1911/1 *Refrigerator-car.* (Railway.) **1883** GOODE *Fish. Indust. U.S.A.* 9 (Fish. Exh. Publ.), Refrigerator cars carry unfrozen fish from sea and lake inland. **1909** *Westm. Gaz.* 6 Sept. 5/3 The second refrigerator-engineer..informed us that the boats had put off. **1960** M. SPARK *Ballad of Peckham Rye* ii. 27 Humphrey Place, refrigerator engineer of Freeze-eezy's. **1963** *Which?* 6 Feb. 42/1 The combined refrigerator-freezer..will hold more frozen food than a refrigerator's freezing compartment. **1976** *Woman's Day* (U.S.) Nov. 125 Self-defrosting refrigerator-freezer has built-in energy-saving condenser. **1950** *Manch. Guardian Weekly* 7 Dec. 15/3 The Sullivan tunes in the interest of the butcher and baker and refrigerator-maker. **1877** in *Sci. Amer.* (1977) Jan. 14/3 A despatch from M. Tellier to the French Academy of Sciences announces the arrival of the refrigerator ship *Frigorific* at Pernambuco, Brazil. **1921** *Daily Colonist* (Victoria, B.C.) 21 Oct. 12/5 The Moliere, another refrigerator ship..is at Seattle loading. **1976** *Islander* (Victoria, B.C.) 12 Sept. 10/1 A refrigerator ship carrying, eggs, bacon and steel to England. **1971** P. O'DONNELL *Impossible Virgin* x. 211 Get Brunel boxed up and put in the refrigerator truck. **1974** R. B. PARKER *God save Child* vi. 48 A big refrigerator truck lumbered by on the highway.

refrigeratory (rɪ'frɪdʒərətərɪ), *sb.* [See next and -ORY¹. Cf. obs. F. *refrigeratoire* (Cotgr.).]

1. A vessel at the head of a still filled with cold water through which the worm passes, for condensing alcoholic and other vapours; any vessel or apparatus employed for a similar purpose.

1605 TIMME *Quersit.* III. 186 Thy vessell..must be such as the chymicall distillars do use;..furnished with their refrigeratories (as they terme them). **1641** FRENCH *Distill.* i. (1651) 34 The liquor..must be distilled in an Alembick with a refrigeratory or Copper Stil with a worm. **1727** BRADLEY *Fam. Dict.* s.v. *Distillation of oil*, When the cold Water in the Tub grows hot, you must let it out thro' the Canal of the Refrigeratory, and put fresh in the room of it. **1782** WITHERING in *Phil. Trans.* LXXII. 328, 1st, By water, is always meant water distilled in glass vessels, or by means of a large tin refrigeratory. **1821** URE *Dict. Chem.* s.v. *Laboratory*, Instead of using a refrigeratory or receiver, the spirit is made to pass through a spiral pipe called a worm. **1875** KNIGHT *Dict. Mech.* 2456/1 The refrigeratory consists of three compartments.

attrib. **1839** URE *Dict. Arts* 1179 The alcohol..will proceed onwards into the refrigeratory tube.

2. Any medium, appliance, vessel or chamber by or in which the process of cooling or freezing is effected.

1653 R. G. tr. *Bacon's Hist. Winds* 17 Enquire concerning ..Artificiall windes, as Bellowes, Refrigeratories, or Coolers in Parlours. **1664** EVELYN *Sylva* (1679) 28 The leaves of Oaks abundantly congested on Snow, preserves it as well for wine, as a deep pit, or the most artificial Refrigeratory. **1707** MORTIMER *Husb.* (1721) II. 352 It will be a delicate, palatable, rich Wine,..and in a Refrigeratory very durable. **1849** *Blackw. Mag.* LXV. 411 Vast refrigeratories are provided at both the poles. **1875** KNIGHT *Dict. Mech.* 1165/1 If now the end containing the compound be plunged in a refrigeratory and the other in water [etc.].

refrigeratory (rɪ'frɪdʒərətərɪ), *a.* [ad. L. *refrīgerātōri-us*: see REFRIGERATE *v.* and -ORY².] Tending to cool or make cold; cooling.

1721 in BAILEY. **1744** BERKELEY *Siris* §120 This grateful acid spirit..is..highly refrigeratory, diuretic, sudorific. **1798** in *Spirit Pub. Jrnls.* (1799) II. 150 Close to the stream I was showed this lady's bower; it is umbrageous and refrigeratory. **1839** *Blackw. Mag.* XLVI. 42 Trinity term.. replaces these delicacies with the more refrigeratory victual of cold boiled lamb and salad. **1889** *Pall Mall G.* 23 May 4/3 The pumping of cold air for refrigeratory purposes.

†refri'gerium. *Obs.* [a. late L. *refrīgerium* a cooling, mitigation. Cf. next.]

1. A respite granted to the souls of the damned; also *transf.* hymns or prayers for such a respite.

c **1645** HOWELL *Lett.* III. xxxvi. (1650) I. 164 To sing Dirges and Refrigeriums for the soul of the deceased Duke. **1652** —— tr. *Giraffi's Rev. Naples* II. 26 Raising up their beads and voices..with requiems and refrigeriums to his soul. **1667** SOUTH *Serm. Prov.* x. 9 (1697) II. 12 Some of the Ancients..have talked much of Annual Refrigeriums, Respites, or Intervals of Punishment to the Damned.

2. A place of cooling. *rare*⁻¹.

a **1670** HACKET in Plume *Life* (1865) 182 Heaven is so large, and spacious, that it is fit to admit divers quarterings and mansions in it, the archangel's throne..[and] the refrigerium of the faithful before His Ascension.

†re'frigery. *Obs.* [ad. late L. *refrīgeri-um* (see prec.), or a. OF. *refrigerie* (Godef.).] Cooling, refreshing, comfort, consolation.

c **1450** *Mirour Saluacioun* 3053 If the aungels presence to the childre in the fire refrigery made. **1483** CAXTON *Gold. Leg.* 263/2 To this deserte place gyue the refrygery and comfort of thy grace. **1535** JOYE *Apol. Tindale* (Arb.) 41 Luke remembreth thys perfeccion..callyng yt the tyme of refrigery and confort. **1565** JEWEL *Def. Apol.* (1611) 512 Yee haue stepped from the place of Spiritual refrigery, into the frying pan of Schismes & Heresies.

refrined, erron. form of REFRAINED *Obs.*

†re'fringe, *v. Obs.* [ad. L. *refringĕre*: see REFRACT *v.*]

1. *trans.* To infringe (one's liberties). *rare*⁻¹.

1530 PALSGR. 683/1, I am nat aboute nor never was to refrynge your lybertyes.

2. To refract (light). Also *fig.*

c **1610** SIR C. HEYDON *Astrol. Disc.* (1650) 11 We are first to agree how deep or thick this cloudy Region of the air that refringeth the Sunbeams may be. **1675** BAXTER *Cath. Theol.* I. II. 95 Vapors..by which the light of divine immutable verity, seemeth to us to be refringed, and to waver.

b. To knock or drive back. *rare*⁻¹.

1692 NORRIS *Curs. Refl.* 24 How can they do it in such troops and numbers without justling, refringing, and inverting one another?

refringency (rɪ'frɪndʒənsɪ). [f. as prec. + -ENCY.] = REFRACTIVITY.

1882 in OGILVIE. **1885** GOODALE *Physiol. Bot.* (1892) 211 Minute granules which have a high degree of refringency.

refringent (rɪ'frɪndʒənt), *a.* [ad. pres. pple. of L. *refringĕre* to REFRACT.] = REFRACTIVE.

1778 *Phil. Trans.* LXVIII. 541 Considering.., that the changes of refringent power and of density are two co-effects of very different nature. **1863** ATKINSON tr. *Ganot's Physics* VII. iii. §432 According as the refracted ray approaches, or deviates from the normal, the second medium is said to be more or less refringent or refracting than the first. **1898** P. MANSON *Trop. Diseases* xxxvii. 587 The spores..are twice the size of tricophyton spores, and remarkably refringent.

†refriscative, *a. Obs. rare*⁻¹. [f. med.L. *refriscāt-*, ppl. stem of *refriscāre* to REFRESH + -IVE.] That refreshes, refreshing.

1582 HESTER *Secr. Phiorav.* II. xi. 91 You shall purge hym with apperatiue thynges, and refriscatiue that purge the bloud.

†re'froid, *v. Obs. rare.* [a. OF. *refroider, -ier, -ir*, f. *re-* RE- + *froid* cold. Cf. REFREID *v.*] *trans.* To cool.

c **1450** *Merlin* 500 Nevew, be not so wroth, refroide youre maltalente. *c* **1477** CAXTON *Jason* 18 b, For to hyde her wil and to refroide and cole her a litil..she left him.

So **†re'froidour** [OF. *refroidure*], coolness.

1483 CAXTON *Gold. Leg.* 250 b/1 He had within forth thre refroydours or coldes..by whiche he assuaged by coldenes all the fyre withoute forth.

re'front, *v.* [RE- 5 a.] *trans.* To supply with a new front; to renew the front of.

1855 HAWTHORNE *Eng. Note-bks.* (1879) I. 326, I should take it to have been at least refronted since Johnson's time. **1895** DOYLE *Stark Munro Lett.* iv. 68 My linen had gone to Belfast to be refronted and recuffed.

re'frustrate, *v.* [RE- 5 a.] *trans.* To frustrate again.

1662 HICKERINGILL *Jamaica* 56 Being so often refrustrated in their reattempts.

refry (riː'fraɪ), *v.* [RE- 5 a.] *trans.* To fry again. So **re'fried** *ppl. a.*, esp. in ***refried beans*** (U.S.) [Sp. *frijoles refritos*], a dish consisting of pinto beans boiled and fried in advance and refried when required; also *fig.*

1957 *House Beautiful* Sept. 126/2 Main course is a barbecue, Yucatan fashion, accompanied by refried beans. **1960** *N.Y. Times Mag.* 1 May 72/1 The sales of such canned items as tortillas, refried beans and green chilies..have shown marked increases in recent months. **1967** V. BENNETT *Compl. Bean Cookbk.* iv. 117 To refry the beans: heat them in the balance of the bacon drippings. **1976** *Sat. Even. Post All-Amer. Cookbk.* 130/2 California refried beans with cheese. This is one of the best and heartiest dishes for which we have to thank the Spanish and the Mexicans. *Ibid.*, The beans are ready to refry at your convenience. **1977** MCKNIGHT & TOBLER *Bob Marley* ix. 113 Of the ten songs, three are re-fried oldies.

refrygeracion, -cyon, obs. ff. REFRIGERATION.

†**reft**, *sb.*[1] *Sc. Obs. rare.* [Alteration of REIF, after the pa. pple. of REAVE *v.*[1], or on analogy of *theft.*] Robbery.

1456 SIR G. HAYE *Law Arms* (S.T.S.) 132 Suppos that gude war nouthir tane be violence, fors, na reft. **1552** ABP. HAMILTON *Catech.* (1884) 10 Resettaris of theft and reft.

reft, *sb.*[2] *rare.* [Alteration of RIFT, after the pa. pple. of REAVE *v.*[2], or on analogy of *cleft.*] A rift, fissure.

1811 PINKERTON *Petral.* I. 495 It..had most probably dropped into a reft, afterwards filled by stalactitic matter. **1851** ANGUS *Serm.* viii. (1862) 156 The mountain has been shivered..; and spiritual churches..have come out of the enormous reft.

reft, *ppl. a.*[1] [See REAVE *v.*[1]] Robbed, bereft of something.

1847 LYTTON *Lucretia* (1853) 257 Through all this the reft tigress mourned her stolen whelp.

reft, *ppl. a.*[2] [See REAVE *v.*[2]] Split, cleft.

1763 *Museum Rust.* I. lxxx. 336 If..it should not be convenient to the farmer to get these wicker hurdles, but he should be obliged to take up with those made of reft stuff in form of a gate [etc.].

refter, obs. form of RAFTER *sb.*[1]

†**refu.** *Obs. rare*$^{-1}$. [ad. OF. *refu, refui*:—L. *refugium* REFUGE *sb.*] Refuge.

1340 *Ayenb.* 138 He is hire refu and ham ssel souy.

refuce, obs. form of REFUSE *sb.* and *v.*

re'fuel (riː-), *v.* [RE- 5 a.] **1.** *trans.* To supply again with fuel; to fill up the fuel-tank of (a car, an aircraft, etc.).

1811 COLERIDGE *Lett.* (1895) II. 567 The necessity of ever re-fuelling the moral feelings of the people. **1973** D. ROBINSON *Rotten with Honour* 186 He refuelled the middle-aged Saab. **1974** *Guardian* 25 Jan. 13/1 The Italian attitude has been one of reciprocity: you refuel our aircraft and we'll refuel yours. **1976** C. EGLETON *State Visit* iii. 31 A tanker would roll out of the BP hangar to refuel a Trident which was on turn round for Amsterdam.

2. *absol.* or *intr.* To take on more fuel.

1940 N. MONKS *Squadrons Up!* i. 18 They [*sc.* the pilots] dropped down to reload, refuel, and grab a sandwich. **1958** *Sat. Even. Post* 20 Sept. 129/1 The first waves of F-100 and F-101 fighters have already passed through.., the second waves are air-refueling. **1973** D. KYLE *Suvarov Affair* xiv. 173 He..decided to drop down to the seaplane station at Port Hardy, refuel and report. **1977** *R.A.F. News* 11–24 May 4/5 Flt Lt Hermer then flew to the Olna to refuel... He was unable to shut down his aircraft while refuelling.

re'fuelling, *vbl. sb.* [f. prec. + -ING[1].] The action of the verb. Freq. *attrib.*

1917 W. S. CHURCHILL in M. Gilbert *Winston S. Churchill* (1977) IV. Compan. I. 93 A sheltered anchorage with refuelling facilities, the whole properly netted and surrounded by an extensive system of mines, will have been created. **1930** *Engineering* 9 May 612/1 If we permit refuelling in flight. **1935** *Jrnl. R. Aeronaut. Soc.* XXXIX. 267 The refuelling system in the centre portion of the wing is an interesting time saving device. **1954** W. TUCKER *Wild Talent* (1955) xv. 203 They're setting up refuelling bases and they hope to send that ship completely around the world. **1955** *Times* 12 July 7/5 An R.A.A.F. Canberra jet bomber will make a round-Australia flight to-morrow, making only two refuelling stops. **1968** J. SANGSTER *Touchfeather* xviii. 205 The other crewman was standing with the refuelling mechanic. **1978** R. LUDLUM *Holcroft Covenant* 9 It was a refueling station never detected by Allied Intelligence.

refuge ('rɛfjuːdʒ), *sb.* Also 5 reffuge. [a. F. *refuge* (12th c.), ad. L. *refugium*, f. *re-* RE- back + *fugĕre* to flee. See also REFU and REFUTE *sb.*[1]]

1. a. Shelter or protection from danger or trouble; succour sought by, or rendered to, a person. †*to do refuge*, to give refuge or aid *to* one.

c **1386** CHAUCER *Knt.'s T.* 862 Yeue vs neither mercy ne refuge But sle me first. **1426** LYDG. *De Guil. Pilgr.* 448 The grete Reffuyt and Reffuge that thow dost to alle synful men. **1494** FABYAN *Chron.* v. cvii. 81 The .ii. sones of Mordred were constrayned of pure force to seche stronge holdes for theyr refuge. **1513** BRADSHAW *St. Werburge* I. 1095 To the prophet Hely a rauen dyd refuge, Brought hym his sustenaunce and saued his lyue. **1582** STANYHURST *Æneis* I. (Arb.) 39 Of the[e] request I refuge, with meeke submission humbled. **1667** MILTON *P.L.* XI. 673 So violence Proceeded ..Through all the Plain, and refuge none was found. **1755** WARBURTON *Serm. Luke xiii.* 1–2 Wks. 1788 V. 297 The hapless Unbeliever..hath no where to fly for refuge from his terrors. **1784** COWPER *Task* I. 238 The dweller in that still retreat Dearly obtains the refuge it affords. **1807** SIR R. WILSON *Jrnl.* 28 June in *Life* (1862) II. viii. 286 All patriotism and honour has in Prussia sought refuge among the women. **1878** BROWNING *La Saisiaz* 429 Is he sad? there's ready refuge.

b. *of refuge*, adapted or intended for shelter or protection, as in *city* (see CITY 1 f), *country, harbour, place, port*, (†*weapon*,) *of refuge*; also *house of refuge*, an institution for sheltering the homeless or destitute.

c **1430** LYDG. *Bochas* II. xxviii. 61/1 This Asylum..Was a place of refuge and socours. **1482** CAXTON *Trevisa's Higden* I. xv. 29 Sychem..was a Cyte of refuge and of socoure. **1540** BIBLE (Cranmer) *Josh.* xx. 2 Appoynte out from among you cyties of refuge. **1560** DAUS tr. *Sleidane's Comm.* 49 b, The rest..shall be banisshed to have no place of refuge. **1590** SIR J. SMYTH *Disc. Weapons* 3 b, Swords..have been in all ages ..the last weapon of refuge both for horsemen, and footmen. **1797** *Encycl. Brit.* (ed. 3) XVI. 50/2 The cities of refuge were required to be well supplied with water and necessary provisions. **1838** ARNOLD *Hist. Rome* I. 7 He [Romulus] set apart a place of refuge, to which any man might flee, and be safe from his pursuers. **1866** *Act 29 & 30 Vict.* c. 117 §31 Provided that such House of Refuge, School, or Institution is certified as a Reformatory School under this Act. **1867** SMILES *Huguenots Eng.* Pref. (1880) 5 The geographical position of Britain has, from the earliest times, rendered it a country of refuge.

c. *to take refuge*, to seek safety or shelter *in* (or *at*) a place; also *transf.* (const. *in*), to betake oneself, have recourse, to (something) as a means of escape, consolation, etc.

1764 BURN *Poor Laws* 228 The Portuguese have a notion of honour, that if a murderer takes refuge in their house, they are bound to protect him. **1791** MRS. RADCLIFFE *Rom. Forest* iv, We must take refuge in Switzerland, I think. **1841** ELPHINSTONE *Hist. Ind.* II. 397 The king..was borne down by the superior force of his enemies, and was constrained to take refuge in his capital. **1874** GREEN *Short Hist.* iii. §7. 147 A thunderstorm once forced the King..to take refuge at the palace of the Bishop of Durham.

transf. **1708** ATTERBURY *Serm.* vi. (1726) II. 202 These Persons..take Refuge in Reflections on the..Goodness of God. **1788** MME. D'ARBLAY *Diary* 18 Feb., I..would have taken refuge in some other topic: but he seemed bent upon pursuing his own. **1852** MRS. STOWE *Uncle Tom's C.* xviii. 175 Dinah perfectly scorned logic and reason in every shape, and always took refuge in intuitive certainty. **1877** MRS. FORRESTER *Mignon* I. 113 Capt. Carlyle goes to his own room,..and takes refuge in a cigar.

2. One who, or that which, serves to give shelter, protection, aid, comfort, etc.

c **1430** LYDG. *Min. Poems* (Percy Soc.) 205 Reste and refuge to folk disconsolat, Fadir of pite and consolacioun, Blissid Leonard! **1481** CAXTON *Myrr.* I. xiii. 39 He that is the very reffuge of alle creatures. **1555** EDEN *Decades* 85 The byshoppe of Burges beinge the chiefe refuge of this nauigation. **1607** SHAKS. *Timon* III. iii. 11 Must I be his last Refuge? *a* **1660** HAMMOND *Serm.* xxiii. Wks. 1684 IV. 635 In the midst of his Ship wrack, when there be planks and refuges enough about him. **1784** COWPER *Task* IV. 396 Sleep seems their only refuge: for, alas! Where penury is felt the thought is chained. **1821** SHELLEY *Prometh. Unb.* I. 311 Howl, Spirits of the living and the dead, Your refuge, your defence lies fallen and vanquished. *c* **1886** KIPLING *Departm. Ditties*, etc. (1899) 101, I go back To Rome and leisure... Or books—the refuge of the destitute.

3. a. A place of safety or security; a shelter, asylum, stronghold; *spec.*, an establishment that offers shelter to a woman who has been physically ill-treated by her husband (or another man with whom she has cohabited). Also in *fig.* context.

14.. in *Tundale's Vis.* (1843) 136 And lyke a dowve fle to his refuge. **1535** COVERDALE *1 Macc.* x. 14 Onely at Bethsura remayned certayne of the Iewes.., for Bethsura was their refuge. *a* **1548** HALL *Chron., Hen. VI* 131 Thei had no certain refuge nor place to resorte to. **1598** GRENEWEY *Tacitus, Ann.* IV. xi. (1622) 106 With small bloudshed of the barbarians, by reason of their refuges at hand. **1667** MILTON *P.L.* II. 168 This Hell then seem'd A refuge from those wounds. **1784** COWPER *Task* VI. 310 Drawn from his refuge in some lonely elm..ventures forth..The squirrel. **1814–15** SHELLEY *Wordsworth* 9 Thou hast like to a rock-built refuge stood Above the blind and battling multitude. **1860** TYNDALL *Glac.* I. xv. 103 [The chamois] flew with the speed of the wind to its refuge in the mountains. **1976** *Lancaster & Morecambe Guardian* 7 Dec. 27/3 (Advt.), Battered Women's Refuge—Women's Information Centre. **1977** *New Society* 25 Aug. 389/1 The Hastings Refuge Group began campaigning in January 1976 in the hope of getting a house from the council to use as a refuge. Meanwhile they set up an emergency service for battered wives.

b. (See quot.)

1891 H. MATTHEWS in *Law Times* XCII. 96/2 Female convicts..are in certain cases released to refuges nine months before the ordinary time for release on licence.

c. A portion of the roadway marked off at busy crossings, for securing the safety of foot passengers.

1869 [see ISLAND *sb.* 2 c]. **1881** GRANT WHITE *England* xiv. 320 The contrivance called a 'refuge' which is placed at intervals more or less convenient in the roadway of the street. **1896** *Daily News* 11 Sept. 4 The erection of a large refuge, which would separate the two lines of traffic. **1930** V. SACKVILLE-WEST *Edwardians* iii. 122 Standing upon the refuge waiting to cross Park Lane, he had seen her drive out of Stanhope Gate. **1976** *Cumberland & Westmorland Herald* 4 Dec. 1/1 It was ludicrous that Belisha beacons could not be erected. People would be running the gauntlet from the pavement to the central refuge.

d. A mountain hut in which climbers and walkers can shelter.

1817 H. C. B. CAMPBELL *Jrnl.* 4 Sept. in G. de Beer *Journey to Florence* (1951) 62 We were eight hours in reaching the top of this wondrous mountain... We stopped at the Refuge No 2. **1873** *Young Englishwoman* Nov. 524/2 Napoleon appointed that ten or twelve 'refuges' should be built for storm-harassed travellers here. **1899** G. BELL *Let.* 28 Aug. (1927) I. 51 We..walked up to the Refuge de l'Alpe in two hours. Two German men turned up at the Refuge. **1933** G. D. ABRAHAM *Mod. Mountaineering* i. 8 The hut is situated less than an hour below the Shoulder... To use this refuge for ordinary mountaineering is an abuse; it is only intended and equipped for special parties *in extremis*. **1956** G. RÉBUFFAT *Mont Blanc to Everest* 42 'There's the refuge. Look, they're signalling to us with lanterns!' How I wished they were. But I knew that the Solvay hut was at least 600 feet lower. **1967** 'G. CARR' *Lewker in Tirol* vi. 84 He had not been inside an Alpine hut for years, but this one was very different from the penitential refuges he remembered in Haute Savoie. **1973** *Guardian* 25 Apr. 1/8 The boys had only to be a short distance off route to walk right past their assessors, who were waiting in the safety of the mountain refuge on Foel Grach's summit.

e. *Biol.* A region in which a natural population can survive through a generally unfavourable period.

1929 *Bull. Geol. Soc. Amer.* XL. 663 On the west coast of Norway the ice seems to have reached out into the sea, but it was probably so thin that many islands and high peninsulas rose above it and formed places of refuge for arctic plants and animals. **1946** *New Phytol.* XLV. 235 The tundra refugees could survive only in the tundra refuges but not in those offered by the coastal mountains. **1954** A. J. CAIN *Animal Species* v. 60 Its [*sc.* the arid period's] effect was to confine forest-living animals of all sorts to several refuges where rainfall was sufficient to maintain the sort of habitat necessary for them. **1979** *Guardian* 28 Aug. 3/2 The Dartford warbler..suffered population crashes seven times between 1860 and 1945, but recovered each time because a breeding population of several dozen pairs remained in a habitat refuge.

f. *U.S.* A bird sanctuary.

1933 *Sun* (Baltimore) 9 May 14/5 The refuge..is under the supervision of Mrs. R. L. Duke, who since 1931 has played host to the waterfowl which make it a winter 'resort'. **1956** PETERSON & FISHER *Wild Amer.* xxix. 320 At the Refuge headquarters they told us that their census of nesting grebes on Tule Lake..showed 3500 pied-bills. **1976** *National Observer* (U.S.) 24 Jan. 9/4 The conservation group..succeeded in setting up a 150-acre refuge in central Wisconsin... It is a roosting site where eagles have been stopping..as they migrate southward.

4. †**a.** A way or means of obtaining shelter or safety; a resource; recourse *to* a practice. *Obs.*

1529 MORE *Dyaloge* I. Wks. 163/1 He..hath a sure and vndoubtable refuge..to brynge him out of all perplexite, in that God hath commaunded him in all such doutes to byleue his churche. **1541** R. COPLAND *Galyen's Terap.* Gj, We must somtyme come and haue refuge to the sendyng of blode. **1607** SHAKS. *Cor.* V. iii. 11 Their latest refuge Was to send him. **1638** JUNIUS *Paint. Ancients* 313 These shifts and by-ways..are meer refuges to shelter our infirmitie. **1670** CLARENDON *Life* (1760) I. v. 177 The king then, as the last Refuge, calls for the English Mastiffs. **1734** tr. *Rollin's Anc. Hist.* (1827) II. II. ii. 12 A general..has no other refuge left, than continually to raise the expectation of his allies by some fresh exploits.

†**b.** *to have* or *make one's refuge*: to betake oneself for refuge *to* a person or place. *Obs.*

1579 TOMSON *Calvin's Serm. Tim.* 248/1 To the end we may haue our refuge to his mercie. *a* **1648** LD. HERBERT *Hen. VIII* (1683) 439 The offenders making their refuge from one lordship marcher to another, were continued without punishment and correction.

c. A plea, pretext, excuse, or answer, in which one takes refuge.

1549 in Burnet *Hist. Ref.* (1681) II. Records I. 177 His refuge was only, That they would fain learn how they might honestly answer the French. **1591** SHAKS. *1 Hen. VI*, V. iv. 69 She and the Dolphin haue bin iugling, I did imagine what would be her refuge. **1699** BENTLEY *Phal.* Pref. 19 The Starters of this Calumny..betook themselves to this Refuge, That [etc.]. **1724** WATERLAND *Farther Vind. Christ's Div.* ii. §15 The boasted pretence.., the last refuge both of Socinians and Arians, is entirely routed and baffled. **1775** JOHNSON in *Boswell* 7 Apr., Patriotism is the last refuge of a scoundrel. **1891** *Daily News* 24 Nov. 4/7 As patriotism is sometimes the last refuge of a scoundrel, so economy..is the last refuge of a Reactionary.

5. *attrib.*, as *refuge house, hut, place, tower*; **refuge hole** (see quot. 1883); **refuge room**, a gas-proof room.

c **1586** C'TESS PEMBROKE *Ps.* LXXI. iii, Lord,..Be my rock, my refuge tower. **1813** SCOTT *Rokeby* VI. vi, I've sought for refuge-place in vain. **1856** KANE *Arct. Expl.* II. xviii. 187 This little refuge-hut..was the means of saving the lives of these four men. **1869** J. KER *Serm.* (1874) 339 To make the death of Christ a mere refuge-house for pardons. **1883** GRESLEY *Gloss. Coal-mining*, *Refuge Hole*, a place formed in the side of an underground plane or horse road..in which men can take refuge during the passing of a train, or when firing shots. **1938** *Times* 10 Mar. 11/1 An internal passage will form a very good refuge-room if it can be closed at both ends. **1940** [see GOOF *v.* 1 a].

refuge ('rɛfjuːdʒ), *v.* Now *rare.* [f. the sb., or ad. F. *réfugier*, †*refuger* (15th c.), usually refl. *se réfugier*, to take refuge.]

1. a. *trans.* To afford a refuge, asylum, or retreat to (a person); to shelter, protect. Also occas. in pass., *to be refuged*, to have taken refuge.

1594 O. B. *Quest. Profit. Concern.* 13 b, A strong couert and sanctuarie..to refuge the wronged. **1613** SHERLEY *Trav. Persia* 34 Hauing promise of the Turke that he should be detained in Corassan where he was refuged. **1681** TEMPLE *Mem.* III. Wks. 1731 I. 358 Prince William..[has] been refuged and supported by that Crown against..the Emperor. **1720** MRS. MANLEY *Power of Love* VII. (1741) 359 Castruchio..promised to receive and refuge her at a fair House he had at Tivoli. **1779** G. KEATE *Sketches fr. Nat.* II. 145 They found all the people on board, refuged [1790 retired] in different places beneath the deck. **1818** SHELLEY *Eugan. Hills* 205 So shall be The city that did refuge thee. **1867** J. B. ROSE tr. *Virgil's Aeneid* 22 Thou who alone hast refuged our distress.

transf. **1593** SHAKS. *Rich. II*, V. v. 26 Like silly Beggars, Who sitting in the Stockes, refuge their shame That many haue, and others must sit there.

†**b.** *refl.* To take refuge; to flee for refuge *to* a place. *Obs.*

1618 T. ADAMS *Serm.* 9 Sensualitie is the voluptuous man's mountaine, there he refugeth himselfe against all reproofes. **1643** T. COLEMAN *Serm.* in Kerr *Covenants* (1895) 173 The ministers of the Lord that have refuged themselves to this little Sanctuary. **1709** MRS. MANLEY *Secret Mem.* (1720) III. 240 He was expell'd the Empire, and refuged himself in the Persian Court. **1748** RICHARDSON *Clarissa* (1811) II. 304, I have refuged myself in his family.

2. a. *intr.* To take refuge; to seek shelter or protection. Also *fig.*

1638–48 G. DANIEL *Eclog.* v. 302 And now, the King Is pleas'd to refuge there. **1709** MRS. MANLEY *Secret Mem.* I. 4, I was reported to have refug'd among the Villagers. **1720** —— *Power of Love* I. (1741) 116 He..refuged in the Greatness of his Courage. **1790** MRS. A. M. JOHNSON *Monmouth* I. 47 She had heard that pirates refuged formerly in the Hebrides. **1805** SOUTHEY *Madoc in Azt.* xxvii, Upon the heights Eastward, how few have refuged! **1899** RIDER HAGGARD in *Longm. Mag.* Oct. 535 They move in short dipping flights, refuging in every convenient tree. **1929** R. BRIDGES *Testament of Beauty* III. 85 What grave lore had refuged with the Ishmaelite was stealing back from exile to its western home.

†**b.** To flee for refuge. *Obs. rare.*

1656 FINETT *For. Ambass.* 111 The Duke de Soubise refuged hether from France upon miscarriage of some undertakings of his there.

Hence **'refuged** *ppl. a. rare.*

1725 tr. *Dupin's Eccl. Hist. 17th C.* I. II. iii. 39 If the refug'd Person is guilty, he shall agree to make proper Satisfaction for him.

refuge, obs. (or dial.) var. of REFUSE *sb.* and *v.*

refugee (rɛfjuːˈdʒiː), *sb.* Also 7–8 refugie. [ad. F. *refugié*, pa. pple. of *refugier*: see REFUGE *v.* The Anglicized form in *-ee* appears almost as early as that in *-ie*, and soon became the standard one.]

1. a. One who, owing to religious persecution or political troubles, seeks refuge in a foreign country; orig. applied to the French Huguenots who came to England after the revocation of the Edict of Nantes in 1685.

α. **1685** BURNET *Tracts* (1689) I. 27 Zurich demanded the Estates of the refugies. **1691** *Lond. Gaz.* No. 2679/1 The Troops in the Town behaved themselves very well, and particularly the French Refugies. **1709** STEELE *Tatler* No. 13 ¶2 That all the French Refugies in those Dominions are to be naturalized.

β. **1687** EVELYN *Diary* 12 June, The poore and religious refugees who escaped out of France in the cruel persecution. **1696** PRIOR *Secretary* 8 The long-winded cant of a dull refugee. **1707** *Lond. Gaz.* No. 4334/4 There was also an humble Address from the French Refugees in the Kingdom of Ireland. **1783** *New York during Amer. Rev.* (1861) 141 A very considerable embarkation of Refugees took place last week bound for Nova Scotia and Canada. **1797** *Encycl. Brit.* (ed. 3) XVI. 51/1 Since the revolt of the British colonies in America, we have frequently heard of American refugees. **1814** MACKINTOSH *Rev. Lives Milton's Nephews* Wks. 1846 II. 503 Some of those ingenious and excellent Protestant refugees, whose writings contributed to excite all Europe against Louis XIV. *a* **1842** ARNOLD *Later Hist. Rome* (1846) I. v. 203 Attending the lectures of Philo, then a refugee from Athens. **1879** FIFE-COOKSON *Armies of Balkans* i. 5 A large number of refugees from the Tunja Valley had already arrived.

b. A runaway; a fugitive from justice, etc. *rare.*

1760–72 H. BROOKE *Fool of Qual.* (1809) III. 108, I held myself as the refugee Jonas, whose crimes brought perdition on all in the vessel. **1816** SCOTT *Old Mort.* vi, With a promise on Morton's part that he would call the refugee when it was time for him to pursue his journey.

†**c.** *transf.* of migratory birds. *Obs. rare*$^{-1}$.

1764 HARMER *Observ.* x. xiv. 413 Among other refugees of that time Maillet elsewhere expressly mentions quails.

d. Someone driven from his home by war or the fear of attack or persecution; a displaced person. Also *fig.*

1914 E. A. POWELL *Fighting in Flanders* vii. 190 The road from Antwerp to Ghent..was a solid mass of refugees. **1926** T. E. LAWRENCE *Seven Pillars* (1935) VI. lxxix. 436 Then there were the guests and refugees whom we might expect so soon as the news of our establishment was rumoured in Damascus. **1944**, etc. [see DISPLACED *ppl. a.* b]. **1957** L. DURRELL *Justine* I. 39 You are a mental refugee of course, being Irish. **1976** *National Observer* (U.S.) 6 Mar. 18/4 Robert MacNeil, a 44-year-old refugee from NBC and the British Broadcasting Corp., opens with a succinct summary of the program's topic.

2. *U.S.* A name given, esp. in New York State, to parties of marauders in the American revolutionary war who claimed British protection; = COWBOY 2. *Obs.* exc. *Hist.*

1780 ANDRÉ (*title*) Cow-Chace, in Three Cantos published on Occasion of the Rebel General Wayne's attack of the Refugees Block-House on Hudson's River. **1781** J. ADAMS in *Fam. Lett.* (1876) 403, I expect all the rancor of the refugees will be poured out upon Cornwallis for it. **1821** F. COOPER *Spy* vii, The more cunning refugees dispersed in small bands;..the dispersion of a troop of Cow-boys was only the extension of an evil.

3. a. Used appositively, as ***refugee family***, ***scholar***, ***tutor***, etc.; **refugee capital** = *hot money* s.v. HOT *a.* 12.

1721 R. NEWTON *Univ. Educ.* 181 Grooms, and footmen, and nurses, and refugee tutors. **1791** GOUV. MORRIS in Sparks *Life & Writ.* (1832) II. 143 The aristocrats are gone and going in great numbers to join the refugee princes. **1833** HT. MARTINEAU *Vanderput & S.* iv. 63 Our refugee divines preach to more purpose. **1858** CARLYLE *Fredk. Gt.* IX. xi. (1872) III. 188 Stanislaus has abundance of useless refugee Polish Magnates about him. **1936** *Discovery* Apr. 98/1 The most distinguished of the refugee scholars. **1936** Refugee capital [see *hot money* s.v. HOT *a.* 12]. **1940** *Manch. Guardian Weekly* 23 Feb. 147 Contracts have just been signed admitting 500 refugee families from Germany and Poland to San Domingo. **1950** *N.Y. Times* 12 Sept. 11/2 Since the Korean invasion began, as much as $300,000,000 to $400,000,000 in 'refugee capital' has flowed here from Europe. **1978** P. SUTCLIFFE *Oxf. Univ. Press* VII. iv. 260 Some of the refugee scholars eventually made their way to America.

b. *attrib.* Characteristic of a refugee. Also, of or pertaining to a refugee or refugees, as ***refugee camp***, ***centre***, ***colony***, ***project***, ***style***, ***train***.

1855 MACAULAY *Hist. Eng.* xx. IV. 407 Animated by the true refugee hatred of the country which had cast him out. **1864** K. CUMMING *Jrnl. Hospital Life* (1866) ix. 146/2 His two daughters were with him, and were keeping house in *two* rooms, refugee style. **1888** M. GRIGSBY *Smoked Yank* xxvi. 224 General Hazen asked me to take charge of the refugee train that was assigned to his division. **1902** J. BUCHAN in J. Adam Smith *J. Buchan & his World* (1979) 38/2 [Milner] has turned over to me..the Boer refugee camps. **1906** *Westm. Gaz.* 23 Apr. 7/1 In the refugee camps yesterday rude altars were erected. **1940** *Manch. Guardian Weekly* 23 Feb. 147 This is the first step in an ambitious plan for a large refugee colony..that will be one of the most important refugee projects in the New World. **1941** KOESTLER *Scum of Earth* 177 Refugee-centre besieged by crowd but said there is some British ambulance in Périgueux. **1953** *News Chron.* 2 June 1/4 The Mall looked like a gigantic refugee camp. Over 30,000 people were bedding down along the pavements. **1975** O. SELA *Bengali Inheritance* ii. 18 Kids, spawned in refugee camps, brought up in squalor.

Hence **refu'geeism**, the condition of a refugee; **refu'geeship**, the personality of a refugee. (*nonce-wds.*)

1784 in Southey *Life Andrew Bell* (1844) I. 293 All will go on admirably with your refugeeship. **1876** GEO. ELIOT *Dan. Der.* III. xxii, A Pole, or a Czech, or something of that fermenting sort, in a state of political refugeeism.

refugee (rɛfjuˈdʒiː), *v.* [f. the sb.] **a.** *trans.* To cause (someone) to become a refugee. **b.** *intr.* To be or become a refugee; to depart or live as a refugee. Chiefly *U.S.* Hence **refu'geeing** *vbl. sb.*

1750 CARTE *Hist. Eng.* II. 373 Whether the report was raised by the English rebels refugee'd at Paris [etc.]. **1806** in B. Hawkins *Lett.* (1916) 429 It will be some time before the Greek young will get rid of the remains of that alloy which debased the agents and refugeed their associates. **1862** K. STONE *Jrnl.* 25 Aug. in *Brokenburn* (1955) 139 The planters generally are moving back to the hills as fast as possible. There are two families refugeeing in our neighbourhood. **1864** K. CUMMING *Jrnl. Hospital Life* (1866) x. 157/2 Many of the citizens of Mobile..had *refugeed* from fear of an attack. **1866** W. REID *After War* 250 Many of his pupils were..negroes that had been 'refugeed' from the Red River country. **1874** L. COLLINS *Hist. Sk. Kentucky* I. 162/1 [There have been] about 1,200 deaths..among the negroes refugeed at Camp Nelson. **1904** R. E. LEE *Recoll. & Lett. Gen. R. E. Lee* xv. 270 In the early years of the struggle, my mother and sisters, when 'refugeeing' had boarded..at his home. **1936** M. MITCHELL *Gone with Wind* xviii. 324 The exodus of women, children and old people from the city began... Many..who took the train that night had already refugeed five and six times before. **1942** J. LEES-MILNE *Ancestral Voices* (1975) 43 The two were very entertaining about their refugeeing with the niece of an old friend near Chedworth. **1965** 'HAN SUYIN' *Crippled Tree* xxix. 412 The house in which Aunt Number One refugeed herself when her husband, Uncle Liu, wanted to give her baby number twelve.

refu'geedom. [f. REFUGEE *sb.* + -DOM.] The condition of (being) a refugee.

1967 P. E. H. DURSTON *Mortissimo* xv. 120 He had come to dislike the paraphernalia of refugeedom—votive masses for the unlikely deliverance of the homeland. **1968** *Guardian* 20 Sept. 9/3 Today, the possibilities of social refugeedom are just as great..but few if any parents are worth running away from.

refugium (rɪˈfjuːdʒɪəm). *Biol.* Pl. -ia. [a. L. *refugium* place of refuge (see REFUGE *sb.*).] A refuge (sense 3 e), *spec.* one in which a species survived a period of glaciation.

1955 *Canad. Jrnl. Bot.* XXXIII. 442 (*heading*) Nature of the evidence in support of glacial refugia. **1967** M. E. HALE *Biol. Lichens* ix. 142 It occurs as a disjunct in the celebrated unglaciated refugium of south-western Wisconsin. **1976** *Islander* (Victoria, B.C.) 16 May 7/1 The presence of endemic mammals on the Island suggests that suitable survival areas (refugia) existed there during the peaks of the last two glaciations.

†**refugy.** *Obs. rare*$^{-1}$. [ad. L. *refugium*: see REFUGE *sb.*] A place of refuge.

1535 COVERDALE *1 Macc.* xi. 41 To dryue them out which were in the castell at Ierusalem and in the other refugies.

refuis(s, obs. Sc. forms of REFUSE *v.*

refuissall, obs. Sc. form of REFUSAL.

refulgence (rɪˈfʌldʒəns). [ad. L. *refulgentia*: see REFULGENT and -ENCE.] The quality of being refulgent; splendour, brightness, radiance.

1634 SIR T. HERBERT *Trav.* 194 The refulgences of those Carbuncles. **1692** KNATCHBULL tr. *Annot. N. Test.* 259 The refulgence of the eternal light. **1774** WRAXALL *Tour North. Europe* (1776) 169 A bar of ore, the heat and refulgence of which were almost insupportable to me at ten feet distance. **1825** SCOTT *Talism.* ii, The calm, clear, blue refulgence of a winter's lake. **1847** L. HUNT *Men, Women & B.* I. xiv. 269 All this bloom and rosy refulgence, which are phrases of the poets.

refulgency (rɪˈfʌldʒənsɪ). ? *Obs.* [See prec. and -ENCY.] = REFULGENCE.

1616 CHAPMAN *Homer's Hymn Venus* 95 Giue me the refulgencie Of most renown'd and rich posteritie. *c* **1645** HOWELL *Lett.* (1650) II. li. 60 Her sight is presently dazled and disgregated with the refulgency and coruscations thereof. **1741–2** STACKHOUSE *Hist. Bible* IV. ii. (1752) I. 461/1 [Moses] was oblig'd then to keep at a more awful Distance from the tremendous Throne of God, and not come within the Circle of its refulgency. **1796** T. SCOTT *Comm. Daniel* x, To behold, with our bodily eyes, the refulgency of his personal and mediatorial excellences.

refulgent (rɪˈfʌldʒənt), *a.* [ad. L. *refulgent-em*, pres. pple. of *refulgēre*, f. *re-* RE- + *fulgēre* to shine.] Shining with, or reflecting, a brilliant light; radiant, resplendent, gleaming.

1509 [see b]. **1598** J. DICKENSON *Greene in Conc.* (1878) 127 Haires of a goldlike hewe; (not purest gould so refulgent). **1635** QUARLES *Embl.* IV. ii. 194 Enrich mine eyes with thy refulgent ray. **1661** GLANVILL *Van. Dogm.* 238 The most refulgent colours are the result of light and shadows. **1717** POPE *Iliad* XI. 204 In blazing heaps, the grove's old honours fall, And one refulgent ruin levels all. **1788** WESLEY *Wks.* (1872) VI. 292 There will be no clouds or fogs; but one bright, refulgent day. **1807** J. BARLOW *Columb.* IV. 474 Freedom..here shall rise, Light her new torch in my refulgent skies. **1864** TENNYSON *Experiments, Milton* 13 Some refulgent sunset of India.

b. *transf.* or *fig.*

1509 HAWES *Past. Pleas.* XI. (Percy Soc.) 45 These poetes ..Devoyde our rudenes wyth grete fyry lemes; Theyr centencious verses are refulgent. **1624** QUARLES *Div. Poems, Sion's Elegies* (1717) 385 Sion, the glory of whose refulgent Fame Gave earnest of an everlasting name. **1821** SHELLEY *Adonais* v, Others more sublime..Have sunk, extinct in their refulgent prime. **1840** DICKENS *Barn. Rudge* xxvii, Bestowing upon the locksmith a most refulgent smile, he left them.

†**c.** As a term of compliment applied to a lady.

1602 MARSTON *Ant. & Mel.* II. Wks. 1856 I. 25 Bright and refulgent ladie, daine your eare. **1656** S. HOLLAND *Zara* (1719) 83 Who wait upon the high-born, illustrious, and refulgent Maulkina.

Hence **re'fulgently** *adv.*; **re'fulgentness**.

1626 T. H. tr. *Caussin's Holy Crt.* 204 This Iewell.. refulgently shining with the rayes of a constant equality of spirit. **1664** H. MORE *Myst. Iniq., Apol.* 501 How refulgently bright and glorious the bodies of the blessed are at the Resurrection. **1730–6** BAILEY (folio), *Refulgentness*, brightness, splendor.

refund (rɪˈfʌnd, ˈriːfʌnd), *sb.* [f. next.] Repayment.

1866 *Morn. Star* 6 Mar. 6/3 He instituted this suit to obtain a refund of the sum. **1884** *Harper's Mag.* June 42/1 That claims for drawback or refund be paid upon due proof only.

refund (rɪˈfʌnd), *v.*[1] [ad. OF. *refunder* (*refonder*) or L. *refundĕre*, f. *re-* RE- + *fundĕre* to pour: see FOUND *v.*[3]]

1. a. *trans.* To pour back, pour in or out again (*lit.* and *fig.*). Now *rare* or *Obs.*

1386 *Almanak for Year* 8 þe vertu or þe influens þat it hace or receyves of þe hyer planetys..it refundes and puttys til þe erthe by his bemys. *c* **1450** tr. *De Imitatione* II. x. 53 þe giftes of god mowe not flowe in us, for..we refunde not ayen all to þe originall welle. **1653** H. MORE *Antid. Ath.* II. xii. Schol. §1 (1712) 160 It is at last refunded into the Body by the left Ventricle of the Heart. **1674** *Govt. Tongue* v. 56 One may as easily perswade the thirsty earth to refund the water she has suckt into her veins. **1725** POPE *Odyssey* XII. 132 Thrice in dire thunders she refunds the tide. **1765** *Antiq.* in *Ann. Reg.* 181/1 The waves play, absorbed in each other and again refunded. [**1818** SCOTT *Hrt. Midl.* i, Two lawyers, whose wetted garments..would refund a considerable part of the water they had collected.]

b. To give back, restore. Also *absol.*

1432–50 tr. *Higden* (Rolls) II. 179 The membres inferialle supporte and do seruyce, the..membres mediate receyve, and refunde. **1694** CROWNE *Regulus* IV. 43 This body..Asks the refunding all our victories. **1699** WOODWARD in *Phil. Trans.* XXI. 217 These..being Vegetable Substances, when refunded back again into the Earth, serve for the formation of other like Bodies. **1856** DOVE *Logic Chr. Faith* v. i. §2. 215 An animal nature which..is compelled to refund its constituent matter to the planet..on which it grew.

c. *Philos.* To put back *into* something antecedent. *rare.*

1696 J. SERJEANT *Meth. Science* 222 They cannot.. without making use of Principles, refund Effects into their Proper Causes. **1697** —— *Solid Philos.* 452 So that all the Certainty of Authority is to be refunded into Intrinsecal Arguments. [**1836–7** SIR W. HAMILTON *Metaph.* iv. (1877) I. 77 The intellectual necessity of refunding effects into their causes.] **1920** A. S. PRINGLE-PATTISON *Idea of God* i. 9 If any one prefers to use the term universe for the sum of created or dependent beings, he may, of course, refund the universe into God as its creative source.

2. To make return or restitution of (a sum received or taken); to hand back, repay, restore.

1553 *Reg. Privy Council Scot.* I. 146 To refund, content, and pay to ane honorable man..the sowme of ye lib. **1661** PEPYS *Diary* 20 Oct., I am to refund to..Lord Peterborough what he had given us six months ago. **1674** tr. *Scheffer's Lapland* xxv. 116 The maid's Father is sentenced to refund either the entire sum, or half of it, as the case stands. **1723** WODROW *Corr.* (1843) III. 10 Whatever charges you are at in copying I shall willingly refund. **1727** POPE, etc. *Art of Sinking* 95 If you would describe a rich man refunding his treasures, express it thus. **1784** COWPER *Task* III. 799 Some private purse Supplies his need with a usurious loan, To be refunded duly. **1844** H. H. WILSON *Brit. India* I. 441 They ..refunded to the peasantry of the country the money which had been extorted from them. **1875** JOWETT *Plato* (ed. 2) V. 134 A thief, whether he steals much or little, must refund twice the amount.

3. To reimburse, repay (a person).

1736 SWIFT *Let. to Bp. Hort* 12 May, The printer has a demand..to be fully refunded, both for his disgraces, his losses, and the apparent danger of his life. **1862** J. M. LUDLOW *Hist. U.S.* 204 A proposal to refund him out of the Treasury was now made in Congress. **1895** *Daily News* 30

Oct. 6/7 If you are out of pocket by this business, [I] shall be glad to contribute towards refunding you.

4. *absol.* To make repayment.

1655 FULLER *Ch. Hist.* VIII. iii. §43 As none were Losers employed in that service,.. so we finde few refunding back to charitable uses. **1706** MRS. CENTLIVRE *Basset-Table* v, I believe you are the first Gamester that ever refunded. **1755** SMOLLETT *Quix.* (1803) IV. 60 He not only refuses to refund, but also denies that I ever lent him the ten crowns. **1841** MACAULAY *Ess., Hastings* (1850) 606 The majority.. voted.. that Hastings had corruptly received between thirty and forty thousand pounds; and that he ought to be compelled to refund.

Hence **re'funded** *ppl. a.*; **re'funding** *vbl. sb.*[1] Also **re'funder**[1], one who refunds.

1691 T. BROWN *Reas. New Converts taking Oaths* 3 A City Usurer turn'd into a Refunder of his ill-gotten Estate. **1825** LAMB *Elia* Ser. II. *Barbara S——*, Ravenscroft.. in silence took back the refunded treasure. **1843–56** BOUVIER *Law Dict.* (ed. 6) s.v. *Refund*, On a deficiency of assets, executors .. are entitled to have refunded to them legacies which they may have paid..; they are generally authorized to require a refunding bond.

re'fund (riː-), *v.*[2] [RE- 5 a.] *trans.* To fund again or anew. Hence **re'funding** *vbl. sb.*[2]; also **re'funder**[2].

1860 in WORCESTER. **1896** *Columbus* (Ohio) *Disp.* 22 Apr. 4/2 When the bonds are sold and the floating indebtedness is refunded.. let us join in well-wishing to the refunders. **1900** *Westm. Gaz.* 23 Apr. 8/1 The disbursements of the Treasury in connexion with the re-funding of bonds.

refundment (rɪ'fʌndmənt). [f. REFUND *v.*[1] + -MENT.] The act of refunding.

1826 LAMB *Elia* Ser. II. *Pop. Fallacies* ii, The denunciators have been fain to postpone the prophecy of refundment to a late posterity. **1896** *Westm. Gaz.* 18 Feb. 5/1 The guarantees .. for the refundment of such a loan.

refurbish (riː'fɜːbɪʃ), *v.* [RE- 5 a.] *trans.* To furbish anew; to repolish, do up again.

1611 COTGR., *Refourbir*, to refurbish, repolish. **1824** LANDOR *Imag. Conv., Abbé Delille & Landor* Wks. 1853 I. 100/1 It requires a better poet to refurbish a trite thought than to exhibit an original. **1874** GLADSTONE *Ritualism* in *Contemp. Rev.* Oct. 674 She has refurbished and paraded anew every rusty tool.

Hence **re'furbished** *ppl. a.*; **re'furbishing** *vbl. sb.*; also **re'furbishment**.

1866 GEO. ELIOT *F. Holt* xlii, It was a charming little room in its refurbished condition. **1879** *Daily News* 31 Dec. 5/2 The refurbishing of an old and faded political celebrity. **1885** *Sat. Rev.* 5 Dec. 732 The figures which are in process of refurbishment at Madame Tussaud's.

refurnish (riː'fɜːnɪʃ), *v.* [RE- 5 a.] *trans.* To furnish anew, in various senses.

1531 ELYOT *Gov.* I. xxiv, [Henry VII] refurnisshed his dominions, and repayred his manours. **1598** BARRET *Theor. Warres* IV. iii. 109 If any men.. be hurt or slaine,.. how are these rankes to be refurnished. *a* **1676** HALE *Prim. Orig. Man.* II. vii. (1677) 187 The Brutes and Birds.. might easily refurnish the same Continent after the subsiding of the Flood. **1829** LYTTON *Disowned* xxv, You will refurnish the house, I suppose? **1849** STOVEL *Canne's Necess.* Introd. 48 The Reformed church of England was never adapted to overthrow, however it might modify and refurnish, the fabric of superstition.

Hence **re'furnished** *ppl. a.*; **re'furnishment**.

1835 LYTTON *Rienzi* IV. i, The redecorated, refurnished, and smiling shops. **1880** L. WALLACE *Ben-Hur* VIII. i, The refurnishment was in a style richer than before.

refus, obs. form of REFUSE *sb.* and *v.*

refusable (rɪ'fjuːzəb(ə)l), *a.* Now *rare.* [f. REFUSE *v.*[1] + -ABLE, or ad. obs. F. *refusable.*]

1. That may be rejected or refused (when offered).

1570 LEVINS *Manip.* 4/8 Refusable, *recusabilis.* **1611** COTGR., *Rejectable*, reiectable, refusable. **1659** H. THORNDIKE *Wks.* (1846) II. 512 No act of theirs.. is refusable by the Church. **1698** NORRIS *Pract. Disc.* IV. 138 Since those Sufferings were absolutely refusable as not being the very same which the Law demanded.

†**b.** Deserving of rejection. *Obs.*

1658 A. FOX tr. *Würtz' Surg.* III. xvii. 271 If a patient hath bled nere so much, they will phlebotomize him further, which is an ill and refusable way. **1666** BP. S. PARKER *Free Censure* (1667) 143 The Sensation of.. displeasing Objects, which makes their Existence full of nothing but Sadness and Misery, and utterly refusable.

2. That may be refused (when asked for).

1652 WARREN *Unbelievers* (1654) 17 Payment was refusable. **1668** MARVELL *Corr.* Wks. 1875 II. 258 My Lord .. did wish [etc.]... Which, all circumstances considered, seeming not refusable, my Lord Bellasis writ this letter. **1818** BENTHAM *Ch. Eng., Catech. Exam.* 404 An indulgence refusable, and not to be granted but upon conditions.

†**refusado.** *Obs. rare*⁻⁰. [app. a. Pg. *refusado*, pa. pple. of *refusar* to REFUSE.] (See quots.)

1598 FLORIO, *Refusati*, the coursest veluets that be, called refusados. *Ibid.*, *Setanino*, a kind of thin veluet called refusados. *Ibid.*, *Velutino*, fine, slender, course, refusado veluet.

refusal (rɪ'fjuːzəl). Also 5 **refusaile**, 5–7 **refusall**, **-fusel(l**, 7 *Sc.* **refuissall.** [f. REFUSE *v.*[1] + -AL[1] 4.]

1. The act of refusing; a denial or rejection of something demanded or offered.

1474 *Rolls of Parlt.* VI. 118/2 Any of the said Commyssioners or Collectours provyng the same refusell. **1523** *Act 14 & 15 Hen. VIII*, c. 2 The same estranger.. to whom such refusel shalbe made. **1560** DAUS tr. *Sleidane's Comm.* 107 b, Where the reasons of theyr refusall may be heard. **1607** NORDEN *Surv. Dial.* I. 35 It were very foolishness in a Tennant, for wilfull refusall thereof, to indanger the same. **1671** MILTON *Samson* 1330 Do they not seek occasion of new quarrels, On my refusal, to distress me more..? **1776** GIBBON *Decl. & F.* xiv. I. 404 It was impossible long to refuse so natural a request.. without maintaining his refusal by arms. **1847–9** HELPS *Friends in C.* (1851) I. 15 Accepting only for the fear of giving offence by refusal. **1875** JOWETT *Plato* (ed. 2) V. 448 If he refuse, he shall be liable to be convicted by law of refusal to serve.

b. *spec.* in the game of écarté, the action of the dealer in refusing to allow a discard. Hence ***refusal hand***, a hand on which the dealer should refuse to allow a discard.

1877 *Encycl. Brit.* VII. 621/1 Proposal, acceptance, or refusal made cannot be retracted. **1878** 'CAVENDISH' *Ecarté* 53 The cases are few in which, with a refusal, he will only make three or four tricks. *Ibid.* 58 His hand should be stronger than those given in the refusal hands.

c. Of a horse: (see REFUSE *v.* 3 c).

1856 'STONEHENGE' *Brit. Rural Sports* 383 A refusal is never desirable, as the horse.. is apt to repeat it. **1857** LAWRENCE *Guy Liv.* xiv. 131 The mare was so savage and sulky still that a refusal seemed a certainty.

d. Absolute resistance of a pile to further driving; the point at which this takes place.

1847 CRESY *Encycl. Civ. Engin.* (1856) 1070 The refusal of a pile to advance does not always insure it having arrived at a proper bed. **1875** KNIGHT *Dict. Mech.* 1911/2 The refusal of a pile intended to support 13½ tons may be taken at 10 blows of a ram of 1,350 pounds [etc.].

†**2. a.** Repudiation (of a wife), divorce. **b.** Abandonment (of a party). *Obs. rare.*

1531 *Dial. Laws Eng.* I. xxvi. F vij, Mosyes suffred a byll of refusell to the Iues. **1568** GRAFTON *Chron.* II. 845 Many others, leuyng king Richarde, turned and came to the part of the Erle of Richmonde... Which refusall of king Richardes parte [etc.].

3. The chance of refusing some thing, office, or the like before it is offered to others; the privilege or right of having it placed at one's disposal for acceptance; *esp.* in phr. ***to have the refusal of.***

1571 *Reg. Privy Council Scot.* II. 80 His Presentatioun —togidder with the refuissall of the kirk abone-writtin. **1613** PURCHAS *Pilgrimage* v. xvii. (1614) 546 If any of his subiects hath any precious stone of value, and make not him the offer of it, it is death to him; he must haue the refusall of all. **1640** *Boston* (U.S.) *Rec.* (1877) II. 54 Chrystopher Stanley is promised the refusall of six acres of upland.. yf it be there to be sould. **1708** SWIFT *Sacram. Test* Wks. 1755 II. I. 126 When employments go a begging for want of hands, they shall be sure to have the refusal. **1812** SINCLAIR *Syst. Husb. Scot.* I. Add. 17 The stock kept upon turnips or clover, have the refusal of water at all times when soiling. **1887** *Times* (weekly ed.) 14 Oct. 15/1 They had the first refusal of any concessions he might obtain.

4. That which has been refused or rejected.

1746 H. WALPOLE *Lett.* (1846) II. 166 Ireland is to be offered to Lord Harrington, or the Presidentship; and the Duke of Dorset, now president, is to have the other's refusal. **1748** RICHARDSON *Clarissa* (1811) II. 102 And next, with her pride, to take her sister's refusals, as she once phrased it.

†**refusant**, *a. Obs. rare*⁻¹. [a. F. *refusant*, pres. pple. of *refuser*, or f. REFUSE *v.*[1] + -ANT[1].] Refusing to take an oath, recusant.

1577 in W. H. Turner *Select. Rec. Oxford* (1880) 389 Some of the Aldermen and Burgesses refusants [are required] to make their repaier hither to declare what lawfull causes they may have to the contraryе.

†**re'fuse**, *sb.*[1] *Obs.* Also 4 **refous**, 4–5 (7) **refus**, 5 **reffus(e**, 6 **refuce**, *Sc.* **refuis(e.** [a. OF. *refus*, f. *refuser* to REFUSE.]

1. = REFUSAL 1. (Common in 15–16th c.)

1390 GOWER *Conf.* III. 298 Thei made hem naked as thei scholde,.. Amonges hem was no refus. *c* **1420** LYDG. *Assembly of Gods* 848 Refuse of Rychesse & Worldly Veynglory. **1477** EARL RIVERS (Caxton) *Dictes* (1877) 53 The reffuses of a nygard ben bettir than the largesces of a prodygall waster. **1525** LD. BERNERS *Froiss.* II. cci. [cxcvii.] *heading*, Of the refuce of them of Acquytayne made to the Duke of Lancastre. **1568** GRAFTON *Chron.* II. 513 As of the refuse made vnto my Lorde of Gloucester, of openyng the tower to him,.. he aunswereth [etc.]. **1600** FAIRFAX *Tasso* XII. xiii, Readie with a proud refuse Argantes was his proffred aid to scorne. *a* **1639** SPOTTISWOOD *Hist. Ch. Scot.* v. (1677) 280 His refuse would have made a great Commotion.

b. *of refuse* (OF. *de refus*), not worth hunting. So ***without refuse*** (OF. *sans refus*), that ought to be hunted.

c **1330** R. BRUNNE *Chron.* (1810) 115 Siþen wan þei Inglond.. & now er þise bot mansbond, rascaile of refous. *c* **1410** *Master of Game* (MS. Digby 182) xxiv, If a man se a wylde boore þe whiche seme hym gret ynogh, as men seye of þe herte chaseable of x., he shall saye a wylde boore of þe thred yere, þat is withoute refuse.

2. = REFUSAL 3.

1753 SMOLLETT *Cnt. Fathom* (1784) 92/2 A certain lady of quality bespoke the refuse of the jewel.

refuse ('rɛfjʊs), *a.* and *sb.*[2] Forms: 4 **refus**, **reffuys**, 5, 7 **refuce**, 6 **refuze**, **refows**, 6–7 **reffuse**, (6 **reffize**), 6–7 (9) **refuge**, 4– **refuse**. [app. an irregular adoption of OF. *refuse* (= mod.F. *refusé*), pa. pple. of *refuser* to REFUSE.]

A. *adj.* †**1.** Refused or rejected. Const. *of* (= by). *Obs. rare.*

c **1374** CHAUCER *Troylus* I. 514 (570) My langwysshynge, That am refus of euery creature. **1508** DUNBAR *Flyting* 105 Forworthin fule, of all the warld reffuse.

2. a. Rejected or thrown aside as worthless or of little value; discarded, useless: †odd (money).

[**1425** in Kennett *Par. Ant.* (1818) II. 250 De lana refuse vendita.. hoc anno.] **1464** *Rolls of Parlt.* V. 567/2 All the refuse Hornes.. to sell. **1503–4** *Churchw. Acc., Croscombe* (Som. Rec. Soc.) 26 More over in the box of refows money resteth.. xis. iiijd. **1530** PALSGR. 261/2 Refuse woll, *layne refusee.* **1611** BIBLE *1 Sam.* xv. 9 Euery thing that was vile, and refuse, that they destroyed vtterly. **1638** EARL OF CORK *Diary* in *Lismore Papers* Ser. I. (1886) V. 52, I sould 7 tonnes of refuge steele. **1659** HAMMOND *On Ps.* xxxi. 12 As that refuse potsheard, cast out as good for nothing. **1754** HAWKINS *Refl. Card-playing* 19 Seizing on a Heap of Refuse Cards that lay by him, began playing them away. **1827–35** WILLIS *Parrhasius* 6 A dog Crunching beneath the stall a refuse bone. **1869** E. A. PARKES *Pract. Hygiene* (ed. 3) 25 Certain trades pour their refuse water into rivers.

transf. **1770** LANGHORNE *Plutarch* (1879) I. 98/1 He ordered the Milesians to bury him in a certain refuse and neglected place. **1879** CHR. ROSSETTI *Seek & F.* 59 A refuse burial in heat and frost and without lamentation.

b. of persons. *rare.*

1579–80 NORTH *Plutarch* (1656) 207 The refuse and scattered People of the overthrowne Army his Father had lost before. **1660** J. PORY tr. *Leo's Africa* III. 156 Another kinde of reffuse people of one family and disposition with the former. **1820** LAMB *Elia* Ser. I. *Two Races Men*, As distasteful as Priam's refuse sons.

B. *sb.* **1. a.** That which is cast aside as worthless; rubbish or worthless matter of any kind; the rejected or rubbishy part of anything.

c **1440** *Promp. Parv.* 375/1 Owte caste, or refuse, or coralyce of corne. *Ibid.* 427/2 Refuce, or owt caste, what so euer hyt be, *caducum, purgamentum.* **1455** *Rolls of Parlt.* V. 325/1 No Silke.. but of ye wurst refuse that they mowe have. **1547** *Act 1 Edw. VI*, c. 3. §2 Giving the same slaue.. such reffuse of meate as he shall thinke meete. **1597** BACON *Coulers Good & Evill* Ess. (Arb.) 141 Many kindes [of things] haue much refuse which counterualе that which they haue excellent. **1662** J. DAVIES tr. *Olearius' Voy. Ambass.* 223 The best Wollen Tapistry in the whole Countrey, whereof there is brought into Europe but the refuse. **1709** STANHOPE *Paraphr.* IV. 513 In themselves they are no better than Chaff and Refuse. **1755** MAGENS *Insurances* I. 257 The Company alledged.. that there generally was some Refuse among a whole Cargo of Hemp. **1832** BABBAGE *Econ. Manuf.* xxxii. 319 Light almost solar has been extracted from the refuse of fish. **1865** DICKENS *Mut. Friend* I. iii, Slipping over the stones and refuse on the shore.

transf. **1569** E. HAKE *Newes out of Powles Churchyarde* (1579) F ij, Was euer seene.. such monstrous kinde of men, Such vomite, reffize, Dunghill drosse? **1599** PORTER *Angry Wom. Abingdon* (Percy Soc.) 80 Why, thou whorson refuge of a tayler [etc.]. **1709** STEELE *Tatler* No. 109 ¶5 The Refuse of a Heart long before given away to a Coxcomb. **1749** SMOLLETT *Gil Blas* (1797) III. 87 Miserable authors whose works are the refuse of libraries and players.

b. The worthless or outcast portion *of* some class of persons; the scum, offscourings, dregs, etc.

1603 KNOLLES *Hist. Turks* (1621) 145 But the greater part void of judgement, and the refuce of the people in simple attire, ran roguing abroad. **1687** A. LOVELL tr. *Thevenot's Trav.* I. 23 These.. are the refuse of the tribute Children. **1711** ADDISON *Spect.* No. 99 ¶8 [This] has given Occasion to the very Refuse of Mankind.. to set up for Men of Honour. **1813** SHELLEY *Q. Mab* IV. 181 The refuse of society, the dregs Of all that is most vile. **1858** NORTON *Topics* 118 Jones, Brown, and Robinson, the 'refuse', remain with the regiment to be slaughtered by their sepoys.

c. The leavings *of* (= what is left by) something.

1665 MANLEY *Grotius' Low C. Warres* 101 He had with him, something more than Eight Hundred Horse, and Six Thousand Foot, the Refuse and Remains of the French Troubles and Tumults. **1704** SWIFT *Batt. Bks.* Misc. (1711) 260 Some Carcass half devour'd, the Refuse of gorg'd Wolves or ominous Ravens. *a* **1800** COWPER *Heroism* 70 Yet man.. Gleans up the refuse of the general spoil.

2. *attrib.* and *Comb.*, as ***refuse bin, can, cart, collection, collector, disposal, eater, heap, matter, sack, tip, tipping***; **refuse consumer** or **destructor**, a furnace in which refuse of various kinds is burned; **refuse sifter**, one who is employed in separating the more useful parts of refuse from the utterly worthless.

1959 J. KIRKUP tr. *de Beauvoir's Mem. Dutiful Daughter* III. 212 In the evenings, there would be the refuse bin to empty. **1976** 'W. TREVOR' *Children of Dynmouth* i. 14 The wind.. rattled the refuse-bins on the ornamental lamp-posts. **1955** W. GADDIS *Recognitions* II. v. 539, I knew it, said Mr. Sinisterra, standing behind a refuse can. **1974** J. WAINWRIGHT *Hard Hit* 33 Along the street, the refuse cart is collecting the empties. **1945** *Listener* 12 July 35/1 For three months now there has been no refuse collection of any kind [in Berlin]. **1974** *Listener* 19 Sept. 368/3 There's a restaurant in Kensington Park Road. It needs six refuse collections a week. **1958** *Daily Mail* 25 Oct. 5/2 It happened to the rat-catcher (*he's now a rodent operator*), the dustman (*refuse collector*), and the sweeper (*street orderly*). **1976** BOTHAM & DONNELLY *Valentino* iii. 24 A string of unskilled jobs. Messenger, refuse collector, dishwasher and laundry assistant. **1906** *Westm. Gaz.* 10 Jan. 2/3 Owing to the narrow limits of Manhattan Island the problem of refuse-disposal is far more difficult in New York than in any other great city in the world. **1972** *Country Life* 28 Dec. 1790/2 Whereas refuse disposal will be a county function, refuse collection will be that of the district. **1895** *Daily News* 3 Aug. 3/3 The burning, fiery furnace.. was simply a refuse consumer. **1895** *Pall Mall G.* 26 Jan. 8/1 That most essential sanitary apparatus, a refuse destructor. **1889** J. JACOBS *Fables of Æsop* I. 66 The refuse-eater and the offal-eater Belauding each other. **1816** W. PHILLIPS in *Trans. Geol. Soc.* III. 112 In 1805, I noticed some crystals of the oxyd of uranium on the refuse heaps of Tin Croft mine. **1863** LYELL *Antiq. Man* 22 The contents of the Danish refuse-heaps. **1921** R. A. S. MACALISTER *Text-bk. European Archaeol.* I. x. 556 Most

Danish archaeologists . . call these remains *affaldsdynger* (refuse-heaps) or *skaldynger* (shell-heaps). **1848** DICKENS *Dombey* xv, The miserable waste ground, where the refuse-matter had been heaped of yore. **1972** *Police Rev.* 1 Dec. 1557/2 Does he, at the moment of picking up your dustbin or refuse-sack, become the owner . . of its contents? **1977** *Cornish Times* 19 Aug. 7/2 (Publ. Notice) Refuse sacks will be provided for premises which would normally receive a collection on these days. **1884** J. SHARMAN *Hist. Swearing* i. 1 The bone-sellers and refuse-sifters of . . Clare Market. **1969** M. PUGH *Last Place Left* xviii. 132 We reached a quarry where we buried Nell's craft lightly in the refuse tip. **1981** *Observer* 17 May 3/3 Refuse tips are probably the richest wildlife refuges in cities. **1974** *Country Life* 3 Oct. 940/3 This valley . . one of the loveliest in the south west . . is threatened by refuse tipping.

refuse (rɪ'fju:z), *v.*¹ Forms: 4 (5–6 *Sc.*) **refus**, (4 **refusy**, 5 **refusen, -yn**), 4–6 **reffus(s)-**, 5–6 **refuce**, *Sc.* **refoys-**, (6 **refuge**), 6–7 *Sc.* **refuis(s)-**, 4– **refuse**. [ad. F. *refuser* (12th c. = Pg. *refusar*, Sp. *rehusar*, obs. It. *rifusare*):—pop.L. **refūsāre*, f. *refūsum*, pa. pple. of *refundĕre*: see REFUND *v.*¹]

I. †1. a. To disclaim, disown, decline to countenance (an act). *Obs.*⁻¹

13.. *Coer de L.* 4669 Cursyd be he that thy werk alowe! . . Thou hast done us gret schame: Thou wer wurthy to have blame; Al swylke werkes I refuse.

†b. To avoid, keep clear of or free from (sin, vice, etc.). *Obs.*

1357 *Lay Folks Catech.* 58 The seuen vertues that ilk man sal use, And . . the seuen dedely sinnes that man sal refuse. **1390** GOWER *Conf.* III. 164 If a Prince wolde him reule . . This vice sholde be refused, Wherof the Princes ben assoted. **1526** *Pilgr. Perf.* (W. de W. 1531) 3 What we shold ensewe & folowe, and what we sholde refuse & forsake. **1534** MORE *Comf. agst. Trib.* II. Wks. 1207/2 Geue the Emperor those thinges that are his, refusing al extorsion and bribery beside. **1587** *Induct. Mirr. Mag.* viii, Examples there, for all estates you find, . . the gentleman vngentlenes refuse. **1691** HARTCLIFFE *Virtues* 399 By his being well directed in his Morals, to refuse evil and to do good.

2. To decline to take or accept (something offered or presented); to reject the offer of (a thing).

13.. *K. Alis.* 396 Theo falce god dude al his wille . . ; Theo game refuse scheo n'olde. *c* **1330** R. BRUNNE *Chron.* (1810) 103 Þorgh conseile of som of hise, refused [F. *refusa*] he þat present. **1393** LANGL. *P. Pl.* C. XIV. 142 Ich seih . . how þat men mede token, and mercy refuseden. *c* **1425** WYNTOUN *Cron.* II. v. 338 Bot he refoysitt þat curtassy, For þe worschep of his larde. **1513** DOUGLAS *Æneis* IV. iii. 34 Quhat wickit wycht wald ever Refuse sic proffer . . ? **1596** SHAKS. *Merch. V.* v. i. 211 No Woman had it, but a ciuill Doctor, Which did refuse three thousand Ducates of me. **1671** MILTON *P.R.* II. 329 Meats by the Law unclean . . young Daniel could refuse. **1710** *Swift Jrnl. to Stella* let. v, Lord Halifax began a health to me to-day; . . which I refused. **1755** COLMAN & THORNTON *Connoisseur* No. 60 ¶4 A leads a strong Club, which B refuses. **1774** GOLDSM. *Nat. Hist.* (1776) VII. 82 Four days after they refuse all vegetable food. **1820** SHELLEY in Lady Shelley *Memorials* (1859) 138 It was refused at Drury Lane . . on a plea of the story being too horrible. **1847** MRS. A. KERR tr. *Ranke's Hist. Servia* 242 Rather let the duty be undertaken by those who refuse foreign assistance.

b. To reject (a thing or person) in making a choice or selection. †Also const. *from*. Somewhat *rare*.

1526 TINDALE *Matt.* xxi. 42 The same stone which the bylders refused, is set in the princypall parte of the corner. **1556** LAUDER *Tractate* 508, I haue maid knawin . . How that ȝe suld Elect . . Ȝour Iugis . . And quhome ȝe aucht for to refuse Frome that gret office. **1611** BIBLE *Isa.* vii. 15 That hee may know to refuse the euill, and choose the good. **1633** HERBERT *Priest to Temple* iv, They say it is an ill Mason that refuseth any stone. **1725** WATTS *Logic* IV. i, By this means they [poets and orators] will better judge what to chuse and what to refuse.

3. To decline to accept or submit to (a command, rule, instruction, etc.) or to undergo (pain or penalty).

1375 BARBOUR *Bruce* XII. 205 Nane payn sall refusit be Till we haue maid our cuntre fre. *c* **1386** CHAUCER *Clerk's T.* 72 Accepteth thanne of vs the trewe entente That neuere yet refuseden thyn heeste. *c* **1440** *Cursor M.* 28678 (Cott. Galba), Þis man . . es in will to sin nomare, And refuses penance neuer þe lese. **1484** CAXTON *Fables of Æsop* v. xvi, He that reffuseth the good doctryne of his fader, yf euyl happe cometh to hym it is but ryght. **1560** DAUS tr. *Sleidane's Comm.* 112 [They] graunted out proces against certen, . . whose judgement, unles they surceased they would refuse. *a* **1618** RALEIGH *Sceptick* in *Rem.* (1651) 15 This creature chuseth his food, refuseth the whip, fawneth on his Master. **1667** MILTON *P.L.* VI. 41 To subdue By force, who reason for thir Law refuse. **1784** COWPER *Task* v. 874 Yet thus we dote, refusing while we can Instruction. **1856** 'STONEHENGE' *Brit. Rural Sports* 363/1 The orders to ride behind . . could scarcely be refused by the jockey.

b. *transf.* of things, in various contextual senses.

1490 CAXTON *Eneydos* x. 40 Her membres refuseden the swete reste of slepe. **1684** tr. *Bonet's Merc. Compit.* XVIII. 643 A young Man had been ill of an Ulcer in his Chin for 3 years, which refused all Medicines. **1726** LEONI tr. *Alberti's Archit.* I. 75/2 We must . . have such a depth, in . . the Haven, as will not refuse Ships of burthen, though ever so deep laden. **1794** *Rigging & Seamanship* II. 325 Clubhauling is practised when it is expected that a ship will refuse stays upon a lee shore. **1873** SPON *Workshop Rec.* Ser. I. 152/1 The acid . . causes the stone to refuse the printing ink except where touched by the chalk.

c. Of a horse: To stop short at (a hedge, water, etc.) instead of leaping. (Cf. 13 b.). Also *transf.*

1840 DE QUINCEY *Style* iii. Wks. 1862 X. 227 We shall endeavour to bring up our reader to the fence . . But as we have reason to fear that he will 'refuse' it [etc.]. **1881** *Encycl. Brit.* XII. 197/2 However bold the horse may be, he will soon refuse water if his rider be perpetually in two minds when approaching a brook.

4. †a. To reject (a person); to decline to admit to a certain position, or to some relationship with oneself. *Obs.*

1390 GOWER *Conf.* III. 180 Every jugge was refused Which was noght frend to comun riht. *c* **1400** *Destr. Troy* 12978 Þai meuit vnto messan with þere men hole; All refusit hom the folke of þe fyne plase. *a* **1548** HALL *Chron., Hen. VIII.* 219 b, She them utterly refused for her servauntes. **1611** BIBLE *Acts* vii. 35 This Moses whom they refused, saying, who made thee a ruler and a Iudge? **1671** MILTON *P.R.* IV. 496 [Thou] wouldst be thought my God, And storm'st refus'd. **1683** *Songs Lond. Prentices* (Percy Soc.) 79, I for my part will utterly refuse thee.

b. To reject, decline to have, as a (†lover, paramour) wife or (now usually) husband.

c **1375** *Sc. Leg. Saints* xxxi. (*Eugenia*) 358 Quhen scho schaw [= saw] scho wes sa refusit, scho can sorou ma. *c* **1400** MAUNDEV. (1839) xvii. 179 Alle the Wommen there . . forsake no man. And thei seyn, thei synnen, ȝif thei refusen ony man. **1484** CAXTON *Fables of Alfonce* xi, A yonge man . . was so moche esprysed of her loue that by cause she reffused hym he deyde for her loue. **1600** E. BLOUNT tr. *Conestaggio* 266 Bicause she had refused so many great Kings and Princes in former times. **1722** DE FOE *Relig. Courtsh.* I. i. (1840) 10, I dare say she won't refuse him. **1773** GOLDSM. *Stoops to Conq.* v, You know I can't refuse her till I'm of age, father. **1866** G. MACDONALD *Ann. Q. Neighb.* i. (1878) 5, I had been refused a few months before.

†c. To decline to meet (an opponent). *Obs. rare.*

a **1513** FABYAN *Chron.* (1811) II. 538 Syr Wyllyam Darell refusyd his appellant, or they had ronne theyr full coursys. **1606** SHAKS. *Ant. & Cl.* III. vii. 40 No disgrace Shall fall you for refusing him at Sea, Being prepared for Land.

†d. *Venery.* To reject (a stag) as not proper for the chase. *Obs. rare*⁻¹.

The Fr. text has *il n'a point de refuz* (cf. REFUSE *sb.*¹ 1 b).

c **1410** *Master of Game* (MS. Digby 182) xxiv, He shall saye þat it is an hert þat farne yer was of x.; þat shuld not be refused.

II. †5. To renounce: **a.** To resign, give up (something valued or attractive). *Obs.*

c **1375** *Sc. Leg. Saints* iii. (*Andrew*) 920 Manis falowschipe haf I refoysit euir-mare halely. *c* **1430** LYDG. *Min. Poems* (Percy Soc.) 120 Ther was a kyng . . Refused his corowne and gan to advertise [etc.]. **1472–3** *Rolls of Parlt.* VI. 54/1 The Tenauntes of your said Suppliauntes have refused their tenures, and the said maner lefte waste. **1500–20** DUNBAR *Poems* xxx. 5 Reffus the warld, for thow mon be a freir. **1568** GRAFTON *Chron.* II. 308 *marg.*, The king here agreeth to refuse the name of the French king, and no more to call himselfe by that name. **1684** BUNYAN *Pilgr.* II. Introd. A 2 b, Yea tell them . . how they still Refuse this World, to do their Father's will.

†b. To decline to bear (a name). *Obs.*

1393 LANGLAND *P. Pl.* C. IV. 369 Þat is noȝt reisonable ne rect to refusy my syres sorname. **1592** SHAKS. *Rom. & Jul.* II. ii. 34 Denie thy Father and refuse thy name. **1652** C. B. STAPYLTON *Herodian* 36 Yea to such drunken dotage he was growne, He now refused flat his Fathers Name.

†c. To abandon, forsake, give over (a practice, way of life, action, etc.). *Obs.*

1377 LANGL. *P. Pl.* B. XIX. 365 Thanne alkyn crystene saue comune wommen, Repenteden & refused synne. **1432–50** tr. *Higden* (Rolls) II. 339 Iosue . . renewede circumcision, refusede [L. *intermissam*] by xl^{ti} yere. *Ibid.* V. 407 They myȝhte not refuse [L. *renunciare*] theire olde rites. **1509** BARCLAY *Shyp of Folys* (1874) I. 165 This day begyn thy lewde lyfe to refuse. **1589** R. ROBINSON *Gold. Mirr.* (1851) 10 The traueller, his jorney doth refuse.

†d. To abandon, leave, depart from (a place).

c **1350** *Leg. Holy Rood* iv. 125 Þan cristen men þat place refused, None of þam efter þeder vsed. **1568** GRAFTON *Chron.* II. 15 In the ende King William was faine to refuse the fielde, and gat at that tyme none aduauntage of his . . sonne. *a* **1600** *Flodden F.* iii. (1664) 23 First of all refuse this place And down to yonder Valleys draw The walls.

†6. To renounce (God or Christ); to cast off (a person); to divorce (a wife). *Obs.*

1390 GOWER *Conf.* III. 80 Whan he for lust his god refuseth, And tok him to the dieules craft. **1432–50** tr. *Higden* (Rolls) III. 389 He hade refusede [L. *repudiata*] Olimpias the moder off kynge Alexander, for cause of adowtery. **1531** *Dial. Laws Eng.* I. xxvi. F vij, Thoughe suche a byll of refusell was lawfull, so that they that refused theyr wyves therby shulde be without payne in the lawe. **1562** *Child Marriages* 191 Now in her old age she wold not hurt her soule, and refuge Christ . . in speakinge any thinge apon her othe but the truthe. **1566** STERNHOLD & H. *Ps.* 389 Refuse me not that am vniust. **1599** SHAKS. *Much Ado* IV. i. 186 Refuse me, hate me, torture me to death.

†b. In (*God*) *refuse me*, as an oath. *Obs.*

1612 WEBSTER *White Devil* I. i, God refuse me. *c* **1626** *Dick of Devon* II. i. in Bullen *O. Pl.* II. 27 They should have found . . another manner of noise than *dam me and refuse me*. **1640** tr. *Verdere's Romant of Rom.* II. 84 God refuse me, said Arnides, if ever I come neer it.

†c. *transf.* Of things: To decline, or cease, to remain with (a person); to abandon, desert. *Obs.*

14.. *Prov. Gd. Counsel* 12 in *Q. Eliz. Acad.* 68 He þat yn yowþe no vertue wyll vse, In Age all honour wyll hym Refuse. **1500–20** DUNBAR *Poems* xxxvi. 6 Gif it be thyne thy self it vsis, Gif it be nocht the it refusis. **1582** STANYHURST *Æneis* III. (Arb.) 88 Thee winds and soonbeams vs, poore souls weerye, refused. *a* **1590** MONTGOMERIE *Misc. Poems* x. 36 Vhat better ar they nor a beist, Fra tym that reson thame refuisis?

†d. To let go, dismiss. *Obs. rare*⁻¹.

c **1440** *York Myst.* xxxiii. 315 Now I recorde wele þe right, ȝe will no raþere refuse hym, To he be dreuen to his dede and demed to dye.

†7. To put or drive away, get rid of. *Obs. rare.*

1387 TREVISA *Higden* (Rolls) V. 53 So þat ȝif he knewe eny þat kepte of here owne catel for to lyve by, he refused hem þat [*read* and] wolde nouȝt have hem in his loore. **1426** LYDG. *De Guil. Pilgr.* 4534 Thus my smerte yerde I vse, Alle synnes to refuse, And do with-al correccioun. *c* **1450** *St. Cuthbert* (Surtees) 7586 Walchere began forto moyse how he þat menȝe moght refoyse, And forto bryng in monkys agayne. **1483** CAXTON *G. de la Tour* K v b, They whiche were worthy to be blamed were refused and separed oute of the felaushipe of the other.

†8. To deny (a charge or allegation). *Obs. rare.*

1390 GOWER *Conf.* I. 76 Thei of the suggestioun Ne couthen noght a word refuse. ? *c* **1475** *Sqr. lowe Degre* 400 Thou may not thyselfe excuse; This dede thou shalt no wise refuse. **1752** MACCOLL in *Scots Mag.* (1753) Sept. 449/2 The deponent refusing his having seen him. **1753** in *Stewart's Trial* App. 139 This letter was . . shown this day to Allan Stewart his son, who refuses it to be his hand-writing.

III. 9. With *inf.* To decline positively, to express or show a determination not *to* do something. Also *transf.* of things.

1390 GOWER *Conf.* II. 43 Bot otherwise, if thou refuse To love, thou miht so per cas Ben ydel. *c* **1450** LONELICH *Grail* lii. 791 Thanne myht he Refusen . . with ȝow to fyhten In bataylle. **1477** *Rolls of Parlt.* VI. 187/2 If . . the Pleyntif or Pleyntifs, or their attourney, refusen to be sworn in fourme aforeseid. **1560** DAUS tr. *Sleidane's Comm.* 6 He . . will not refuse to stande in judgement herein of the universities of Germany and Paris. **1591** SPENSER *M. Hubberd* 21 Seeing kindly sleep refuse to doe His office. **1667** MILTON *P.L.* II. 451 Wherefore do I assume These Royalties, and not refuse to Reign . . ? **1719** YOUNG *Busiris* III. i, My trembling limbs Refuse to bear their weight. **1780** COWPER *Progr. Err.* 498 If stubborn Greek refuse to be his friend, Hebrew or Syriac shall be forced to bend. **1874** GREEN *Short Hist.* viii. §3. 483 Eliot refused to move from his constitutional ground.

b. Const. with gerund. *rare.*

1753 L. M. *Accomplished Woman* II. 252 One of the principal actors . . refused going upon the stage. **1766** *Burrows' Reports* II. 1152 The Officer of the inferior Court can not refuse paying obedience to the Writ.

10. To decline to give or grant; to deny (something asked) *to* a person (or thing).

1585 T. WASHINGTON tr. *Nicholay's Voy.* I. xvii. 19 b, [To] obtaine of the great Lord that which by his lieuetenaunt was refused. **1607** SHAKS. *Cor.* v. i. 33 If you refuse your ayde . . yet do not Vpbraid's with our distresse. **1734** tr. *Rollin's Anc. Hist.* (1827) II. II. 186 He could not refuse his tears to the unhappy fate of Carthage. **1821** SHELLEY *Hellas* 587 The Georgians Refuse their living tribute. **1859** TENNYSON *Enid* 448 When I . . Refused her to him, then his pride awoke.

†b. *refl.* To abstain from giving (oneself) over, to refrain from yielding, *to* (something). *Obs.*

1753 CHESTERF. *Lett.* (1792) IV. ccxcviii. 12, I have refused myself to every thing that my own experience did not justify and confirm. **1788** GIBBON *Decl. & F.* lxiv. VI. 288 Nor can I refuse myself to those events which . . will interest a philosophic mind. **1809** MALKIN *Gil Blas* VII. i. ¶11 She would fancy she had her death to answer for, had she refused herself to any of her whims.

c. *Mil.* To decline to oppose (troops) to the enemy; to withdraw or move back from the regular alignment.

1796 *Instr. & Reg. Cavalry* (1813) 176 The echellons on one flank will be refused, and on the other they will advance . . to envelope the enemy. **1802** JAMES *Milit. Dict.* s.v., The French during the whole of the action . . refused their right wing. **1875** KINGLAKE *Crimea* V. vi. 92 If the disposers of ordnance . . should desire . . to refuse their right, they might bend off that part of their artillery line along the crest.

11. With double acc.: To decline to give, deny (something) to (a person, or thing).

1621 ELSING *Debates Ho. Lords* (Camden) 53 That John Birde . . [was arrested] by John Gillett . . and refused baylle. **1746** H. WALPOLE *Let.* 17 Jan., On their refusing him entrance, he burst open the door with his foot. **1782** MISS BURNEY *Cecilia* VI. x, I feel already that I can refuse you nothing. **1817** SHELLEY *Otho* 16 Such pride as from impetuous love may spring, That will not be refused its offering. **1891** *Law Times* XC. 462/1 Where the court refuses a parent the custody of his child.

b. With personal object (or subject) only.

1784 COWPER *Task* IV. 418 These ask with painful shyness, and refused Because deserving, silently retire. **1818** SHELLEY *Rev. Islam* II. xxvii, Soon I could not have refused her. **1865** TROLLOPE *Belton Est.* x. 110 If refused once, he might probably ask again.

†12. To refuse (one) leave *to* do something; to prohibit or keep back *from* something. *Obs.*

1617 MORYSON *Itin.* I. 171 The Guard refused me as a foot-man to passe into the Citie. **1657** in *Burton's Diary* (1828) II. 308 They refused the magistrates of Edinburgh from the sacrament, for three years. **1688** *Exped. Pr. Orange* in *Select. Harl. Misc.* (1793) 471 Sir William W—— who had been at Ford with the prince, to see Sir William C——, were both refused to be seen of him.

IV. 13. *intr.* To make refusal; to decline acceptance or compliance; to withhold permission; *spec.* in écarté (see REFUSAL 1 b).

13.. *Gaw. & Gr. Knt.* 1772 Nede hym bi-houed, Oþer lach þer hir luf, oþer lodly re-fuse. **1535** COVERDALE *1 Sam.* xxviii. 23 But he refused, and sayde, I wil not eate. **1560** DAUS tr. *Sleidane's Comm.* 130 b, He not refusyng, toke his offer in very good part also. **1611** SHAKS. *Wint. T.* II. iii. 137 If thou refuse, And wilt encounter with my Wrath, say so. **1668** SEDLEY *Mulb. Gard.* I. iv, Sister, tho' Laws of Decency refuse, We shining Swords, and glitt'ring Armour use. **1717** PRIOR *Alma* I. 160 Before they're ask'd, can maids refuse? **1780** COWPER *Progr. Err.* 25 Free in his will to choose or to refuse, Man may improve the crisis, or abuse. **1877** *Encycl. Brit.* VII. 620/1 (*Ecarté*), The dealer may either accept or refuse. . . If the dealer refuses the hand is played without discarding.

b. Of a horse: (see 3 c above).

1525 Ld. Berners *Froiss.* II. clxviii. 190/2 The first course they fayled for their horses refused at yͤ cope. **1857** G. Lawrence *Guy Liv.* ix, The Axeine swerves, and refuses at rather an easy fence.

c. Of a pile: To resist further driving.

1879 Sir R. Ball in *Cassell's Techn. Educ.* V. 276 When the pile 'refuses', as it is technically termed..it..is capable of supporting the buildings.

re-fuse, *v.*[2] [RE- 5 a.] To fuse or melt again.

1875 *Ure's Dict. Arts* (ed. 7) I. 943 If the fusion has been properly made, the slag will not require..to be re-fused.

re'fused, *ppl. a.* [f. REFUSE *v.*[1] + -ED[1].] Rejected, cast off; declined; denied.

1560 A. L. tr. *Calvine's Foure Serm. Songe Ezech.* (1574) i, He was a wicked and refused man. **1606** *Wily Beguiled* H iij b, My father got me of a refus'd Hagge. **1790** *Acts Sederunt* Index 91 The Ordinary, shall write on the back of a refused bill of suspension, his special reasons for so doing. **1883** L. Z. Joncas *Fisheries Canada* 19 (Fish, Exh. Publ.) The merchantable, the inferior, and the 'refused', that is, the heavy salted and broken fish.

b. *Mil.* (See REFUSE *v.*[1] 10 c.)

1796 *Instr. & Reg. Cavalry* (1813) 156 The rear of the column which was destined to become the refused flank of the new line. **1888** *Times* 8 Oct. 7/2 They opened fire on the enemy's two guns on his right, and a refused flank on his left.

refusel(l, obs. forms of REFUSAL.

refusenik (rɪˈfjuːznɪk). Also **refusnik.** [Partial tr. Russ. *otkáznik*, f. stem of *otkazát'* to refuse: see -NIK.] A Jew in the Soviet Union who has been refused permission to emigrate to Israel.

1975 *Nature* 31 Jan. 297/2 If, as is often the case with scientists, the initial application is rejected, one may spend months or years as a 'refusnik', with neither the opportunity nor the necessary time to keep up one's reading or think about one's own research. **1976** *Listener* 26 Aug. 237/1 Hundreds of people all over Britain make regular telephone calls to refuseniks every week. **1978** *Daily Tel.* 19 Dec. 11/4 The couple..have recently been putting on a satirical show ..mainly to keep up the morale of their 'refusenik' friends. **1980** *Jewish Chron.* 18 July 18/1 The dissidents languishing in exile, in prison camps and insane asylums, and the refuseniks cut off from family and friends and..from their sources of livelihood. **1980** *Radio Times* 29 Oct. 63/4 Tonight Avital talks about her life since she left Russia, a life of waiting and campaigning to free her husband and other Jewish refusniks from jail in the USSR.

refuser (rɪˈfjuːzə(r)). [f. as REFUSE *v.*[1] + -ER[1].] One who refuses; *esp.* a recusant (common in 17th c.).

1474 *Rolls of Parlt.* VI. 118/2 And over that the same refuser [is] to make fyne and raunson to your Highnes. **1550** *Reg. Privy Council Scot.* I. 106 The disobearis and refusaris of the said mony. **1567** *Ibid.* 535 The refusaris and contravenaris to be secludit fra the bosum of the Kirk. **1610** Donne *Pseudo-martyr* 246 Drawing scandall vpon the whole cause, and afflictions vpon euery particular Refuser. **1687** Jas. II in *Magd. Coll. & Jas. II* (O.H.S.) 211 All the Bishops in England should not excuse a refuser. **1754** Richardson *Grandison* (1766) V. 18 The requester of a favour..perhaps shews as much self in the application as the refuser does in the denial. **1864** Raine *Priory Hexham* (Surtees) I. Pref. I. p. xxiii, The modesty of the refuser only whetted the eagerness of the offerers.

b. Of a horse: (see REFUSE *v.*[1] 3 c).

1886 *Sat. Rev.* 6 Mar. 327/1 That he [a horse] should become a confirmed refuser at water.

refusing (rɪˈfjuːzɪŋ), *vbl. sb.* [f. REFUSE *v.*[1] + -ING[1].] The action of the vb. in various senses.

c **1330** R. Brunne *Chron.* (1810) 216 At his dome suld it be, withoute refusyng. *c* **1440** *Promp. Parv.* 427/2 Refusynge, *refutacio, recusacio. a* **1533** Ld. Berners *Huon* xxiv. 70 They shal derely by the refusynge of theyr answere. **1611** Cotgr., *Repudiement*, a refusing. **1660** Jer. Taylor *Duct. Dubit.* II. ii. rule 2 §4 Single life, and abstinence from certain meats, and refusing of blood. **1705** Stanhope *Paraphr.* II. 348 What forced Constructions do we put upon every Indignity, that it may not pass for a final Refusing? **1901** *Chambers's Jrnl.* Sept. 663/2 He will, if not instantly checked, learn a lot of bad tricks, such as..slipping his head-collar at night, and 'refusing' in the hunting-field.

re'fusing, *ppl. a.* [-ING[2].] That refuses.

1583 Babington *Commandm.* iv. (1637) 34 Our recusantes, as wee call them, that is, our refusing papists to come to church. **1627** in Rushw. *Hist. Coll.* (1659) I. 445 After his going,..the refusing Londoners were pursued more fervently then before. **1723** *Pres. State Russia* II. 264 The King of Sweden..returned a refusing Answer.

Hence **re'fusingly** *adv.*

c **1477** Caxton *Jason* 35 Why haue ye than answerd him so coldly and refusingly? **1659** Torriano *A-rifúso*, refusingly.

†**re'fusion**[1]. *Obs. rare.* [a. F. *réfusion* (16th c. in Littré), ad. late L. *refūsiōn-em*, n. of action f. *refundĕre* to REFUND *v.*[1]]

1. The action of pouring back; re-infusion (of the soul).

1656 Blount *Glossogr.*, *Refusion*, a pouring back again. **1741** Warburton *Div. Legat.* II. II. App. 46 He owns..that neither Gataker in his notes, or Casaubon, had any Notion that the Doctrine of Refusion was here alluded to.

2. The action of refunding (money).

1726 Ayliffe *Parergon* 351 A Person thus amending his Libel..is oblig'd to a Refusion of such Expences.

re-fusion[2] (riːˈfjuːʒən). Also **refusion.** [f. RE- 5 a + FUSION.] A renewed or repeated fusion; the result of this, a recast. Also *fig.*

1811 Pinkerton *Petral.* II. 460 This tumefaction usually accompanies a refusion, in our fires, of solid glasses and volcanic enamels. **1863** Cowden Clarke *Shaks. Char.* xii. 308 Leonato is a re-fusion of old Capulet, but without his fussiness and dollying.

refuta'bility. *rare.* [f. next + -ITY.] Capability of being refuted.

1654 Whitlock *Zootomia* 141 The Heretick (guilty and consciencious to himselfe of Refutability) taketh place first. **1957** C. A. Mace *Brit. Philos. in Mid-Century* 160 One can sum up all this by saying that falsifiability, or refutability, is a criterion of the scientific status of a theory.

refutable (rɪˈfjuːtəb(ə)l, ˈrɛfjuːtəb(ə)l), *a.* [ad. late L. *refūtābilis*, f. *refūtāre* to REFUTE. Cf. F. *réfutable.*] That may be (†rejected,) refuted, or disproved.

1560 Rolland *Crt. Venus* III. 175, I think part of thame refutabill Of the assyis, and vtheris acceptabill Into thair steid. **1600** F. Walker *Sp. Mandeville* 26 b, Your proofe and information is not refutable. **1646** Sir T. Browne *Pseud. Ep.* 181 That the heart of man is seated in the left side, is an asseveration which strictly taken, is refutable by inspection. **1771** *Junius Lett.* liv. (1788) 301 He alters the text, and creates a refutable doctrine of his own. **1802** *Edin. Rev.* I. 22 It refutes the very refutable positions of Mr. Godwin. **1871** *Echo* 13 Apr. 2 It is not in the abstract; but only in the concrete that it is refutable.

Hence **re'futably** *adv.*

1806 W. Taylor in *Ann. Rev.* IV. 724 Speaking intelligibly, and therefore refutably, concerning the phænomena of animal life.

refutal (rɪˈfjuːtəl). [f. REFUTE *v.* + -AL[1].] Refutation.

1605 Verstegan *Dec. Intell.* iv. (1628) 102 What refutall is this, when it can bee prooued that they so were. **1736** in Bailey. **1816** O'Meara in *Century Mag.* (1900) Feb. 626/2 Such a work carries with it its own refutal. **1885** *National Baptist* XXI. No. 13. 1 A living refutal of the lie that a good soldier must needs be depraved.

refutation (rɛfjuːˈteɪʃən). [ad. L. *refūtātiōn-em*, n. of action f. *refūtāre* to REFUTE. Cf. F. *réfutation.*]

1. The action of refuting or disproving a statement, charge, etc.; confutation.

a **1548** Hall *Chron., Hen. VIII* 149[2] It was answered by another boke called the Refutacion or Ouercommyng of the apollogie of the conuencion of Madrill. **1628** T. Spencer *Logick* 233 Thereby we know how to apply an Answer for the refutation, and disproofe of such a proposition. **1692** Bentley *Boyle Lect.* iv. 119 An effectual refutation of his own Principles. **1769** *Junius Lett.* xxxiv. (1788) 168 A charge which called immediately for the clearest refutation. **1792** *Anecd. W. Pitt* II. xxix. 129 The idea..does not deserve a serious refutation. **1865** Tylor *Early Hist. Man.* ii. 14 The deaf and dumb man is the living refutation of the proposition. **1877** Northcote *Rom. Catacombs* I. i. 8 This might be allowed to stand as a peremptory refutation of the theory in question.

Comb. **1819** Shelley *Julian* 194 You might Make such a system refutation-tight, As far as words go.

†**2.** Military repulse *of* a person. *Obs. rare*[−1].

1596 Dalrymple tr. *Leslie's Hist. Scot.* v. 267 Achai..is present with speid, with ane armie of ten thousand Scotis.. to the supplie of Hung, and refutatioune of Athelstane.

refutative, *a. rare.* [f. ppl. stem of L. *refūtāre* to REFUTE + -IVE.] That tends to refute; belonging to refutation.

1652 Urquhart *Jewel* Wks. (1834) 292 Proleptically with the refutative schemes of anticipation and subjection. **1837** *Fraser's Mag.* XV. 303 Strepsiades is delighted with his complexion, which is both 'negative and refutative', with the true Attic stamp.

So **refutatory** *a.* [cf. med.L. *refūtātōri-us*, F. *réfutatoire*]. (Webster 1847.)

†**refute,** *sb.*[1] *Obs.* Forms: 4 refuit, 4–6 refuyt(e, (5 reffuyt), 4–6 refut(e. [a. OF. *refuite*, f. *refuir*, f. *re-* RE- + *fuir* to flee: cf. REFUGE *sb.*]

1. = REFUGE *sb.* 1.

a **1325** *Prose Psalter* xxx[i]. 3 Be to me in-to God defendour, & in-to þe hous of refut, þat þou mak me sauf. *c* **1400** *Rom. Rose* 3840 Thou shalt be bounde, And fast loken in a tour, Withoute refuyt or socour. *c* **1420** in Lydg. *De Guil. Pilgr.* 16696 The grete Reffuyt and Reffuge that thow dost to alle synful men. **1494** Fabyan *Chron.* Prol. 3, I nyll presume wythout other refute, To ioyne suche a worke. **1535** Stewart *Cron. Scot.* II. 275 Justice and law..to execute To puir and riche, without ony refute.

2. = REFUGE *sb.* 2.

a **1325** *Prose Psalter* xxx[i]. 4 For þou art my strengþe and my refut. **1382** Wyclif *Ps.* lxxxix. [xc.] 1 Lord, refut thou art maad to vs. *c* **1450** *Merlin* 622 A kynge that ought to be refute and counfort to alle the hoste. **1509** Hawes *Conv. Swearers* 13 Yet I to you am chefe refuyte and boote.

3. = REFUGE *sb.* 3.

c **1374** Chaucer *Troylus* III. 965 (1014) Allas þat he.. Shuld haue his refuyt in so digne a place. **1432–50** tr. *Higden* (Rolls) II. 279 To be a refute of gilty men fleenge to hit. *c* **1450** *St. Cuthbert* (Surtees) 5541 At tynemouth' his refuyt he make, To kepe him fra skathe.

†**refute,** *sb.*[2] *Obs.* [f. the vb.] Refutation.

1646 Sir T. Browne *Pseud. Ep.* 312 We finde no concurrent determination of ages past, and a positive and undeniable refute of these present. **1657** J. Sergeant *Schism Dispach't* 1 Schism Dispatcht,..containing..a refute of Dʳ. Hammonds Defence of his first three Chapters.

refute (rɪˈfjuːt), *v.* [ad. L. *refūtāre* to repel, repress, rebut: see RE- and CONFUTE *v.* Cf. F. *réfu-er* (*c* 1549 in Godef.).]

†**1.** *trans.* To refuse, reject (a thing or person). *Obs. rare.*

1513 Bradshaw *St. Werburge* I. 1535 Her royall dyademe and shynynge coronall Was fyrst refuted for loue of our sauyoure.

2. To prove (a person) to be in error, to confute.

1545 Joye *Exp. Dan.* Argt. 5 b, Which reiecteth and refuteth the iewes and vs castinge away god and his gospel as thei did. **1579** Fenton *Guicciard.* III. (1599) 116 He refuted the Admirall, who..assayed to qualifie indirectly the wills of the councell. **1641** Hinde *J. Bruen* xxii. 68 Who might also have received their answer and beene evidently refuted to their faces, if they had but observed his ordinary practices. **1692** Washington tr. *Milton's Def. Pop.* M.'s Wks. 1738 I. 544 That you, my Countrymen, refute this adversary of yours yourselves. **1768** tr. *Rollin's Anc. Hist.* (ed. 5) I. p. xlix, In his second [book], wherein he refutes his brother Quintus.

refl. **1869** *Daily News* 14 Dec., But Mr. M. is good enough, for all practical purposes, to refute himself.

3. To disprove, overthrow by argument, prove to be false: **a.** a statement, opinion, etc.

1597 Hooker *Eccl. Pol.* v. lxxx. §7 It is some greife to spende thus much labour in refuting a thing that hath so little grounde to vphold it. **1664** Power *Exp. Philos.* I. 39 An errour so gross and palpable, that it needs not the Microscope to refute it. **1710** Lady M. W. Montagu *Let. to Bp. Burnet* 20 July, They bring them a thousand fallacious arguments, which their excessive ignorance hinders them from refuting. **1780** Cowper *Table-t.* 104, I grant the sarcasm is too severe, And we can readily refute it here. **1838** Lytton *Alice* II. vii, Unconsciously his whole practice began to refute his theories. **1875** Jowett *Plato* (ed. 2) I. 194 They can refute any propostion whether true or false.

b. an imputation, accusation, etc.

1611 Speed *Hist. Gt. Brit.* IX. xxiv. §231 Which imputation in sundry languages he refuted in Print. **1725** Pope *Odyss.* VIII. 270 Well thy gen'rous tongue With decent pride refutes a public wrong. **1784** Cowper *Task* II. 824 Let the arraigned Stand up unconscious, and refute the charge. **1838** Thirlwall *Hist. Greece* V. 375 The plan which he has suggested..is the surest way to refute such calumnies. **1875** Manning *Mission H. Ghost* x. 277 Would you not seek everywhere for proofs to refute the accusation?

4. *absol.* To demonstrate error.

1742 Young *Nt. Th.* VII. 1343 Instead of racking fancy, to refute, Reform thy manners, and the truth enjoy. **1805** *Med. Jrnl.* XIV. 174 Those, whose only object is to cavil where they cannot refute.

¶**5.** *trans.* Sometimes used erroneously to mean 'deny, repudiate'.

1964 C. Barber *Ling. Change Present-Day Eng.* v. 118 For people who still use the word in its older sense it is rather shocking to hear on the B.B.C., which has a reputation for political impartiality, a news-report that Politician A has *refuted* the arguments of Politician B. **1978** *Observer* 7 May 4/9 Mr O'Brien, who was first elected general secretary three years ago, refutes the allegations. **1979** *Daily Mail* 17 Feb. 15/3 He refuted allegations that she took her own life because of police harassment. **1980** *Bookseller* 19 July 257/1, I refute Mr Bodey's allegation that it is our policy not to observe publication dates, and to display new titles in newsagents immediately on receipt from the publisher.

Hence **re'futed** *ppl. a.*, **re'futing** *vbl. sb.*

c **1555** Harpsfield *Divorce Hen. VIII* (Camden) 239 In the refuting of which impure and unchaste proviso..I trust the reader will bear with me. **1638** R. Baker tr. *Balzac's Lett.* (vol. II.) 33 Such of their objections, that seeme worth the refuting. **1646** Sir T. Browne *Pseud. Ep.* I. viii. 30 He often..seems to confirme the refuted accounts of Antiquity. **1780** Cowper *Progr. Err.* 550 His still refuted quirks he still repeats. **1818** in Lady Morgan *Autobiog.* 241 Commonplaces, repeated a hundred times over with a refuted tone.

refuter (rɪˈfjuːtə(r)). [f. prec. + -ER[1].] One who refutes.

1620 Bp. Hall *Hon. Mar. Clergy* III. ii, No lesse vaine is my refuter, that spends many waste words [etc.]. **1645** Milton *Colast.* Wks. 1851 IV. 345, I was still waiting, when these light arm'd refuters would have don pelting at their three lines. **1710** Shaftesb. *Charac.* (1737) III. I. ii. 11 Some living Antagonist, who..pretends to..refute the Refuter upon every Article he has advanc'd. **1890** C. U. R. Cooke *4 Yrs. in Parlt.* 60 An easy and effective exposure of them brings to the refuter some momentary credit.

refyn(e, obs. Sc. pa. pple. of RIVE.

Reg.[1], abbrev. of REGINA.

1792 W. Boscawen *Treatise on Convictions on Penal Statutes* 48 *Reg.* v. *Matthews.* **1848** E. W. Cox *Reports Cases in Criminal Law* II. 422 *Reg.* v. *Hawkes*..settles that question, about which some doubt had been previously entertained. **1976** *Law Rep. Queen's Bench Div.* 417 (*heading*) Reg. v. Michael (Crown Ct.).

reg[2] (rɛg). *Physical Geogr.* [N. African Arab.] A flat area of desert covered with gravel or boulders; stony desert.

1904 A. Knox *Gloss. Geogr. & Topogr. Terms* 324 *Reg*, firm level ground, generally without vegetation, a barren, naked plain. **1926** *Chambers's Jrnl.* June 341/1 Beyond the harbour,..away to the east, lies open stony 'Reg', and thence the vast, empty desert. **1963** D. W. & E. E. Humphries tr. *Termier's Erosion & Sedimentation* ii. 38 *Regs* and *serirs* are planed areas with a covering of boulders, which tumble from the surface of the hamadas or from the plains below them. The term reg is generally reserved for the low plains used by caravans. Moreover, this term is applied commonly to all bouldery ground which has been subjected to deflation. **1966** M. Woodhouse *Tree Frog* xxvi. 196, I was somewhere near the edge of a *reg*, one of those huge flat plains of gravel which are, more than anything, the true desert. **1976** L. Deighton *Twinkle, twinkle, Little Spy* xxiii. 226 The going changed to the gravelly surface of the 'reg' and then to rough 'washboard'.

reg^3 (rɛg), colloq. abbrev. of REGULATION.

1952 M. SHAARA in *Mag. of Fantasy & Sci. Fiction* Oct. 4 Wisher had decided..to follow the regs without question. For without the regs, the Mapping Command was a death trap. **1971** J. SANGSTER *Your Friendly Neighbourhood Death Pedlar* iv. 86 I'm sorry I can't do what you ask. Company regs. **1977** *Hot Car* Oct. 53/2 In Germany it will possibly do well because of their strict regs about modding a car.

reg, obs. form of *rig* RIDGE *sb.*, RIG *v.*

regain (rɪˈgeɪn, riː-), *v.* [ad. F. *regagner* (earlier spelling *regaigner*): see RE- and GAIN *v.*]

1. *trans.* To gain or get anew; to recover possession of (something). Also *absol.*

a **1548** HALL *Chron., Hen. VIII* 260 b, One daie thone parte lost, and the other gained, and likewise the losers regained. **1568** GRAFTON *Chron.* II. 645 Is not Normandy, which is father gat, regayned and conquered agayne, by the insolencie of him? **1631** GOUGE *God's Arrows* III. §43. 260 Obtaining or re-gaining any publique, or private blessings. **1667** MILTON *P.L.* IV. 665 Least total darkness should by Night regaine Her old possession. **1710** LADY M. W. MONTAGU *Let. to W. Montagu* 25 Apr., Could I deceive one minute, I should never regain my own good opinion. **1838** LYTTON *Leila* IV. iv, Regaining thee once more, a new and a soft existence opens upon my eyes. **1875** JOWETT *Plato* (ed. 2) I. 13, I began by degrees to regain confidence.

†**b.** To reclaim (land). *Obs. rare*$^{-1}$.

1652 BLITHE *Eng. Improv. Impr.* (ed. 3) title-p., The Drainage of Fen Lands, Regaining Sea Lands, &c.

†**2.** To win back, recover, for another. *Obs. rare.*

1590 C'TESS PEMBROKE *Antonie* 1077 When I regainde him his rebellious Realme. **1599** H. BUTTES *Dyets Drie Dinner* B vj, Constrained to implore the ayde of Mithridate..in regaining to them the Castle of health.

†**b.** To win or bring back *to* a state or condition.

1639 FULLER *Holy War* IV. ix. (1840) 194 Thus this city..was won by this barbarous people, never since regained to our religion. **1679** *Establ. Test* 6 Little hope of help was to be expected.., to regain England to Obedience.

†**3.** With *inf.* To succeed in coming again. *Obs.*

1644 MILTON *Educ.* Wks. 1851 IV. 381 By regaining to know God aright, and out of that knowledge to love him.

4. To get back to, succeed in reaching (a place) again; to rejoin (a person).

1634 MILTON *Comus* 274 Extreme shift How to regain my sever'd company Compell'd me to awake the courteous Echo. **1725** POPE *Odyss.* I. 409 Let me now regain the Reithrian port. **1775** R. CHANDLER *Trav. Greece* (1825) II. 209, I made my egress.., glad to revisit day and regain a purer atmosphere. *a* **1859** L. HUNT *Glove & Lions* iv, The leap was quick, return was quick, he has regain'd his place. **1878** HUXLEY *Physiogr.* 41 The cloud descends, and regaining the lower and warmer regions, returns to its original state.

b. To recover (one's feet).

1814 SIR R. WILSON *Autobiog.* in *Life* (1862) I. ii. 90, I was up and down several times; but my dear little mare..always regained her feet.

Hence **reˈgained** *ppl. a.*, **reˈgaining** *vbl. sb.* and *ppl. a.* Also **reˈgainable** *a.*, **reˈgainer**.

a **1548** HALL *Chron., Hen. VI* 134, I thought here, to omit and ouerpasse the regainyng and conquest of the strong toune of Harflew. **1621** BURTON *Anat. Mel.* III. ii. III. iv, With a regaining retrait, a gentle reluctancy. **1666** BOYLE *Orig. Formes & Qual.* 203 The Form..was reproduc'd by God, upon the regain'd Disposition of the Matter to receive it. **1682** BUNYAN (*title*) The Holy War..for the Regaining of the Metropolis of the World. *a* **1787** J. BROWN *Sel. Rem.* (1807) 244 To behold him a regainer of paradise. **1869** RUSKIN *Q. of Air* §153 Your liberty of choice has simply destroyed..so much life and strength, never regainable.

reˈgain, *sb.* [f. the vb.] **1.** An act of regaining; recovery. Also, an amount regained or recovered.

1927 *Observer* 2 Oct. 19/5 Take into consideration..wages cost, depreciation and interest on working capital, general expenses, discount, regain, and waste. **1927** *Morning Post* 4 Oct. 4/4 Progress of time will see..a regain of position of the horse in the ranks of industry.

2. The weight of moisture in a textile fibre or fabric expressed as a proportion of the weight of the material when thoroughly dry.

1904 J. M. MATTHEWS *Textile Fibres* iii. 46 The amount of normal wool is obtained by adding to the dry weight of the wool the amount of moisture supposed to be present in the air-dried material under normal conditions of humidity and temperature. The added amount is termed 'regain', and is officially fixed by the conditioning house. The permissible percentage of regain varies with the form of the manufactured wool. **1941** *Nature* 4 Oct. 408/2 Dry wool shows strong polarization under an applied potential, but as its regain is increased its conductivity increases exponentially. **1961** A. F. W. COULSON *Man. Cotton Spinning* II. I. ii. 285 The changes in moisture regain depend on temperature.

reˈgainment. [f. REGAIN *v.* + -MENT.] The action of regaining.

1642 *Declar. Lords & Comm.* 4 July 3 The regainment of the ancient..Rights. **1646** EARL MONM. tr. *Biondi's Civil Warres* VI. 30 Being advertised..of the regainment of the Kingdome. **1871** *Daily News* 22 Sept., Our actual occasional rallies and temporary regainment of ground.

regal (ˈriːgəl), *a.* and *sb.*^{1} Also 4–5 **regalle**, (5 **-ale**), 5–7 **regall**. [a. OF. *regal, -ale*, or L. *rēgālis*, f. *rēg-, rex* king: see -AL^1.]

A. *adj.* **1. a.** Of or belonging to a king; royal.

c **1374** CHAUCER *Boeth.* I. pr. iv. 9 (Camb. MS.), The iustice Regal [L. *regia*] hadde whilom demed hem bothe to gon in to exil. **1432–50** tr. *Higden* (Rolls) II. 323 In the regalle cite of Saba. **1503** HAWES *Examp. Virt.* VII. xlii, That sheweth his dygnyte to be regall. *c* **1510** *Gesta Rom.* Add. Stor. v. (1879) 438 [They] brought hym with grete reuerence and worshyp vnto his regal sete. **1591** SPENSER *M. Hubberd* 1111 The Ape thus seized of the Regall throne [etc.]. **1667** MILTON *P.L.* v. 739 When they see all Regal Power Giv'n me to quell thir pride. **1735** BOLINGBROKE *On Parties* 8 They, who could never brook a Regal, will have the Merit of saving their Country from the Danger of a Ministerial Tyranny. **1788** GIBBON *Decl. & F.* liii. V. 505 The regal title was assumed by the most ambitious chiefs. **1825** JEFFERSON *Autobiog.* Wks. 1859 I. 36 Our legislation, under the regal government, had many very vicious points. **1876** HUMPHREYS *Coin-coll. Man.* xxvi. 403 The Macedonian series includes the earliest regal coin known.

†**b.** ***regal fishes***: (see quots.). *Obs. rare.*

1562–3 *Act 5 Eliz.* c. 5 §5 Such fyshes as be knowen and vsed to be called Regal fyshes, whereunto her maiestie..shal haue right. **1670** BLOUNT *Law Dict.* (1691) *Regal Fishes*..Are Whales, and Sturgeons; some add Porpusses.

†**2. a.** ***regal water***: (see quot.). *Obs. rare*$^{-1}$.

Cf. F. *eau régale*, a mixture of hydrochloric and azotic acid, used for dissolving gold and platinum (Littré).

1576 BAKER *Jewell of Health* 102 This then is named the regall water, or water of a kyng, which separateth Golde.

b. Ruling, governing. *Obs. rare.*

1653 R. SANDERS *Physiogn.* 240 The brain and heart are the two regal and principal parts of man. **1656** STANLEY *Hist. Philos.* v. (1701) 198/1 Thus Plato in Philebo avers by Jove is understood a Regal Soul, meaning the principal part of the World which Governs the other.

3. Befitting, or resembling, a king; kingly; hence, splendid, magnificent, stately, etc.

1799 WORDSW. *Danish Boy* iii, A regal vest of fur he wears, In colour like a raven's wing. **1816** SHELLEY *Alastor* 619 A rare and regal prey He hath prepared, prowling around the world. **1858** LYTTON *What will He do* I. xiv, Then they emerged into the noble garden, with its regal trees. **1862** STANLEY *Jew. Ch.* (1877) I. xv. 290 Every one of them was like a prince; and not the least regal was the sole survivor Gideon.

transf. **1825** LAMB *Elia* Ser. II. *Convalescent*, If there be a regal solitude, it is a sick bed. **1859** SMILES *Self-Help* xii. 319 Beethoven's admiration for Cherubini was regal.

4. ***regal lily*** = REGALE *sb.*^{1} 4; ***regal pelargonium***, a house plant belonging to a group of varieties of *Pelargonium × domesticum*, flowering in spring and early summer.

1925 E. H. WILSON *Lilies E. Asia* 38 The bulbs of the Regal Lily are often part yellow-brown or orange-coloured. **1939** D. T. MACFIE *Lilies* vii. 102 It is difficult to be moderate in the choice of words when talking of the regal lily. **1980** *Observer* 4 May 44/7 Charles Lyte..discovered in his research the extraordinary exploits of the men who introduced delights like the..Regal Lily into Britain. **1903** T. W. SANDERS *Amateur's Greenhouse* 311 Pelargonium..Decorative and Regal Kinds. These are grown in great quantities for Covent Garden Market. **1951** J. E. CROSS *Bk. Geranium* xii. 104 The plant which still bears the name Pelargonium in commerce is *Pelargonium domesticum*, known in England generally as Show or Regal Pelargonium. **1955** *Times* 26 May 12/3 At Chelsea this year are several large groups of pelargoniums, both the zonal forms for outdoor bedding and the regal types for the greenhouse. **1962** R. PAGE *Educ. Gardener* ix. 260 Pots of palest pink regal pelargoniums..line the steps. **1966** ROCHFORD & GORER *Rochford Bk. Flowering Pot Plants* viii. 116 The Regal Pelargoniums..are generally known simply as Pelargoniums.

5. ***regal (walnut) moth***, a large brown and yellow moth, *Citheronia regalis*, found in the eastern United States.

1854 E. EMMONS *Agric. N.Y.* V. 238 Regal Walnut-moth..feeds on the walnut. **1887** S. W. DENTON *Pages from Naturalist's Diary* (1949) 121, I have..caught eight sphinx moths, and many others, one like the regal walnut moth. **1912** *Country Life in Amer.* 1 Aug. 38 The blue horned hickory devil..turns into the Regal moth. **1972** SWAN & PAPP *Common Insects N. Amer.* xix. 270 Regal moth..Also known as hickory horned moth and royal walnut moth.

B. *sb.* †**1. a.** Royalty, sovereignty, royal authority.

c **1330** R. BRUNNE *Chron.* (1810) 71 Nien monethes beforn kept Harald þe regalle. *c* **1350** *Will. Palerne* 282 Al þe regal of rome to riȝtleche y weld. **1455** *Rolls of Parlt.* V. 300/2 The drede wheryn here tofore they have been..of youre myghty regalle and of your said lond. **1460** *Pol. Poems* in *Archaeologia* (1842) XXIX. 338 To remeve his heuynesse Whiche to his regalle is no þyng conservyng.

†**b.** *Sc.* A regality. *Obs. rare.*

1440 *Sc. Acts Jas. II* (1814) II. 33/1 Lordis of Regaliteis within thare Regalis. Ande alsua the kingis balȝeis of his Regalis. [Hence in Skene *Reg. Maj.* (1609) 163.]

c. A royal right or privilege. Cf. REGALE *sb.*^{1} 2. *Obs.*

a **1540** BARNES *Wks.* (1573) 201/2 But how commeth S. Peter by these regalles..? All the worlde knoweth, that regalia belongeth to kinges. **1641** PRYNNE *Antip.* 116 *marg.*, Peter was acquainted with his nets but not with Regals. **1797** W. JOHNSTON *Beckmann's Invent.* II. 324 When and where originated the term *jus grutiæ*, under which this regal is known by jurists?

†**2.** A prince, ruler. *Obs. rare.*

c **1385** CHAUCER *L.G.W.* 2128 *Ariadne*, We be duchessis bothe I & ȝe And sekerede to the regalys of Athenys And bothe hereafter likly to ben quenys. *c* **1395** *Plowman's Tale* I. 202 'All-holyest' they clepen hir heed, That of hir rule is regall.

3. a. ***the regal of France***: (see quots.). *Obs.* exc. *Hist.*

? *a* **1400** *Morte Arth.* 4208 With rynges and relikkes, and þe regale of ffraunce, That was ffowndene one syr ffrolle, whene he was feye levyde. **1560** DAUS tr. *Sleidane's Comm.* 160 Thomas of Canturbury..was shryned in siluer, and hanged rounde about with costly Jewelles of Gold and precious stones... And amonges others, there was one riche Jewell, called the Regal of Fraunce. **1656** BLOUNT *Glossogr.* s.v., A Jewel or Ring of great value, which a King of France offered at St. Thomas shrine at Canterbury, called the Regal of France, which Henry the Eighth, upon the dissolution, took thence, and wore on his own finger. **1905** R. H. BENSON *King's Achievement* III. xi. 482 He noticed for a moment a wonderful red stone on the thumb, and recognized it. It was the Regal of France that he had seen years before at his visit to St. Thomas's shrine at Canterbury.

transf. **1631** BRATHWAIT *Whimzies, Traveller* 92 Styling..Paris the regall of France; Venice the eye of Italy.

†**b.** ***the regal of Scotland***, the Coronation Chair.

c **1470** HARDING *Chron.* CLXII. vi, The regall there of Scotlande then he brought, And sent it forth to Westmynster for ay.

†**c.** (See quot.; perh. = 3 a.) *Obs.*

1485 *Rutland Papers* (Camden) 18 [Coronation of Henry VII.] The said Cardinall shall blesse the ring with a ruby, called the regall, for the King, to be sett on the iiijth fynger of the right hand.

†**d.** The chalice used for the communion at the coronation of British sovereigns. *Obs.*

1603 *Cerem. Coron. Jas. I* (1685) 3, 1. The Regal. 2. The Paten. **1626** in Chr. Wordsw. *Coron. Chas. I*, Introd. (1892) p. lii, Regale, the chalice of Saphire and gold carried by the Bishop of London. **1662** SIR E. WALKER *Acc. Coron. Chas. II* (1820) 92 The Bishop of London (haueing in the interim placed the Regall vpon the Altar).

†**4.** Some kind of precious stone. *Obs.*$^{-1}$

c **1430** LYDG. *Min. Poems* (Percy Soc.) 223 Wythe stones and perles ryally pyghte, Regalles, rubies, saffyres blewe.

†**5.** *pl.* = REGALIA^1 2. *Obs.*

c **1485** in Wickham Legg *Coron. Rec.* (1901) 237 The said chamberlayn shall take for the king all the Regalls aforesaid, and peace by peace deliuer them to the Abbot of westminster. **1533** *Coron. Q. Anne* in Arb. *Garner* II. 50 The Abbot of Westminster with his rygals came into the Hall *in pontificalibus*. **1556** *Chron. Gr. Friars* (Camden) 4 Thys yere kynge Edward toke..the cheffe regalles in Scotland, his crowne and hys cepter, and browte it to Westmyster. **1603–4** in A. Taylor *Glory of Regality* (1820) 311 The orbe, the scepter, the armill, And suche other regalls as hee hath in his custodye.

regal (ˈriːgəl), *sb.*^{2} Also 6 **reygalle, reyggal, regol**, 6–7 **rigoll, -ole**, 7 **rigalle**, 6–9 **regall**, (6 **-alle**). [a. F. *régale* (16th c., in Rabelais *regualle*), of obscure origin, perh. f. *régal* REGAL *a.*: cf. It. *regale* (Florio).]

1. Chiefly *pl.* A small portable organ formerly in use, having one, or sometimes two, sets of reed-pipes played with keys by the right hand, while a small bellows was worked by the left hand. Now chiefly *Hist.* (common *c* 1550–1625).

c **1550** L. WAGER *Life Marie Magd.* 735 *Infid.* Can ye not play on the virginals? *Mary.* Yes..that I can, and also on the regals. **1556** in Rimbault *Hist. Organ* (1855) 39 Payd to James Hewet for playing of his regols in the payggeant, viij d. **1589** PUTTENHAM *Eng. Poesie* II. i. (Arb.) 79 Vocall Musike, or that of melodious instruments, as Lutes, Harpes, Regals, Records and such like. **1598** FLORIO, *Regali*, a musicall instrument called rigoles. **1626** BACON *Sylva* §172 In Regals (where they have a pipe they call the Nightingale pipe which containeth water). **1767** in Rimbault *Hist. Organ* (1855) 39 *note*, [Bernard Gates received a salary of £56, as] tuner of the regalls [in the Royal Chapel. The same gentleman, in 1770, is styled 'tuner of the organs']. **1776** HAWKINS *Hist. Music* IV. IV. viii. 503 *note*, Raphael has painted her singing, with a regal in her hands. **1801** STRUTT *Sports & Past.* III. v. 201 Assisted by the music of the regals and the bagpipes. **1899** DE MORGAN in Mackail *W. Morris* I. 223, I recollect his playing on a regal.

Comb. **1770** in *Archaeologia* (1775) III. 32 Our kings had a regall-maker amongst their musical establishment.

2. One of certain reed-stops (*esp.* the *vox humana*) in organs.

1799 YOUNG in *Phil. Trans.* XC. 141 His reasoning has fully shown the analogy between the voice and the *voix humaine* and regal organ-pipes. **1944** W. APEL *Harvard Dict. Mus.* 633/2 The reed stops of the later organs are frequently called 'regal'. **1976** *Gramophone* Nov. 837/2 This is instanced by his almost spooky use of the 16-foot regal from the top manual coupled to the pedals.

ˈregal, *sb.*^{3} *Obs.* exc. *dial.* Forms: 5 **regyll**, 6–7 **regal(l**, 7 **reigle**, 9 *dial.* **riggle**. [ad. F. *rigole*: cf. RAGGLE *sb.*] A groove, a slot.

1458 *Church-w. Acc., Yatton* (Som. Rec. Soc.) 101 It. to make a regyll abowte the batylmente xv^d. **1577** HARRISON *England* II. xi. (1877) I. 227 The engine..dooth ride vp and downe in a slot, rabet, or regall. **1602** CAREW *Cornwall* 104 b, In one of the corners next the sea standeth a flood-gate to bee drawne vp and let downe through reigles in the side postes. **1608** WILLET *Hexapla Exod.* 605 In the sides of the boord shal be two regals or incisians wherby they shal one be ioyned to another. **1886** ELWORTHY *W. Som. Word-bk.*, *Riggle*, a groove cut round some article... The groove on a pulley is a riggle.

regald, obs. form of RIGGALD.

‖**regale** (rɪˈgeɪlɪ, F. regal), *sb.*^{1} [a. F. *régale* (ad. L. *rēgālia*), or L. *rēgāle*, neut. sing. of *rēgālis* REGAL *a.* See also REGALIA^1.]

1. *Eccl. Hist.* The right, on the part of the kings of France, of enjoying the revenues of vacant bishoprics and abbacies, and of presenting to benefices dependent on these.

'The enjoyment of the fruits of the see is called the *temporal regale*; that of presenting the benefices, the *spiritual regale*'. Chambers *Cycl.* (1727–38), copying the *Dict. de Trévoux*.

1611 COTGR. s.v. *Regale*, In Normandie when diuers Lords are at suit for the Patronage of a vacant Benefice, the King, by this right of Regale, enioyes the profits of it vntill the suit be ended, or they agreed. **1682** *News fr. France* 16, I know your Curiosity in this affair of the Regale makes you more than ordinary concerned to know the true State of it. *a***1715** BURNET *Own Time* III. (1724) I. 595 The Pope.. found also fault with many of the proceedings in France, with relation to the Regale. **1839** HALLAM *Hist. Lit.* IV. ii. §2 Louis XIV.. extended in 1673 the ancient prerogative, called the regale, by which the king enjoyed the revenues of vacant bishoprics, to all the kingdom.

†**2.** A privilege or prerogative of royalty. *Obs.* More frequently used in *pl.*; see REGALIA¹ 1.

1714 NICOLSON *Eng. Hist. Libr.* II. iv. (ed. 2) 117 We must (in this place) so understand the Author, as if he had not any Design to state the extent of the Regale. **1797** W. JOHNSTON tr. *Beckmann's Invent.* III. 20 The State.. availed itself of that regale called by Leyser *regale falsae monetae*, and returned the capital in money of an inferior value.

†**3.** *Chem.* (See quot.) *Obs.*$^{-0}$

1650 J. F[RENCH] *Chym. Dict.*, *Regale* is a Ciment whereby Gold is purged. [Hence in Phillips (1678) and Bailey.]

4. The specific epithet of *Lilium regale*, used to designate a fragrant, white-flowered lily of the species so called, which was discovered in China by E. H. Wilson in 1903 and named by him in 1912 (*Horticulture* XVI. 110). Also *attrib.*

1935 WOODCOCK & COUTTS *Lilies* i. 3 Then came the epoch-making introduction of that choice representative of the genus, justly called *regale*. **1949** H. NICOLSON *Let.* 15 June (1968) 171 Out of this jungle growth I wish regale to rise. I know it means keeping regale seeds each year. **1962** R. PAGE *Educ. Gardener* viii. 236 The regale lilies open their cream-pink trumpets. **1963** W. BLUNT *Of Flowers & Village* 174 The Madonna lily is to the Regale lily as is the Parthenon to the Mansion House. *Ibid.*, Regale smells like a Bond Street hairdresser's.

regale (rɪˈgeɪl), *sb.*² [a. obs. F. *régale* fem. (now *régal* masc.), ad. It. *regalo* REGALO.]

1. a. A choice repast, feast, or banquet; †an entertainment or fête.

1670 R. MONTAGU in *Buccleuch MSS.* (Hist. MSS. Comm.) I. 483 My Lord Duke will not be able to get away yet.., all the regales that are intended for him not being yet at an end. **1691** J. WILSON *Belphegor* III. i, I beseech ye Gentlemen,.. I hope you'll take share of a short Regale. **1726-31** WALDRON *Descr. Isle of Man* (1865) 70 A little valley.. was the place they made choice on for their rendezvous and regale. **1784** COWPER *Tiroc.* 834 Their breath a sample of last night's regale. **1849** C. BRONTE *Shirley* xv, This sort of impromptu regale, it was Shirley's delight to offer any chance guests. **1897** E. COUES *New Light Early Hist. Greater Northwest* I. 8 All were merry over their favorite regale, which is always given on their departure, and generally enjoyed at this spot, where we have a delightful meadow to pitch our tents, and plenty of elbow-room for the men's antics. **1922** E. R. EDDISON *Worm Ouroboros* xxxiii. 429 That night was supper set in Lord Juss's private chamber: a light regale, yet most sumptuous.

b. Const. *of* (the dainties provided).

1791 F. BURNEY *Jrnl.* Aug. (1972) I. 46 There was a grand regale of sweetmeats, fruits, & cakes. **1796** STEDMAN *Surinam* (1813) II. xvi. 22 Another negro also brought me a regale of groe-groe or cabbage tree worms. **1835** W. IRVING *Tour Prairies* xxii, Tonish served up to us his promised regale of buffalo soup and buffalo beef.

c. *transf.* or *fig.*

1684 *Contempl. St. Man* II. vi. (1699) 188 The Damned.. would take it for a great Regale, to have a Dunghil for their Bed, instead of the burning Coals of that Eternal Fire. **1728** MORGAN *Algiers* I. iv. 98 The Camels are to them the very Nerves of War and the Regales of Peace. **1773** MME. D'ARBLAY *Early Diary* (1889) I. 192, I venture at no further opinion than that to me the sight was a great regale. **1842** W. IRVING in *Life* (1866) III. 225 This pageant.. is a regale of which we never get tired.

2. A choice article of food or form of refreshment; a dainty.

1673 RAY *Journ. Low C.* 37 The Indian Betle which is very stomachical and a great Regale at visits. **1725** *Portland MSS.* (Hist. MSS. Comm.) VI. 140 This regale is composed of an ordinary broth well stuffed with bread. **1791** *Gentl. Mag.* LXI. II. 720, I may therefore hope.. to see the tables adorned with the regale of Devonshire cream. **1845** BROWNING *Englishman in Italy* 92 The snails Tempted out by this first rainy weather,—Your best of regales.

3. Regalement, refreshment.

1753 *School of Man* 101 The whole skill of Cookery is employed in food the most delicate for its regale. **1820** LAMB *Elia* Ser. I. *Christ's Hosp.*, Viands of higher regale than those cates which the ravens ministered to the Tishbite. **1841** D'ISRAELI *Amen. Lit.* (1867) 262 That volume probably reposes for the regale of the next century.

†**4.** A complimentary present. *Obs. rare.*

1728 MORGAN *Algiers* II. iv. 275 Don Juan wrote to the Spanish Governor of Bujeya, that among the Presents and Regales he was to send him and his Companions, against Christmas, he should not forget a But filled with Swords. **1744** H. WALPOLE *Lett.* (1846) II. 2, I had been threatened with a regale of hams and Florence wine.

re-gale, *sb.*³ [f. RE- 5a + GALE *v.*³] A new arrangement or division of a mining gale.

1884 *Law Times Rep.* LI. 76/2 They made a similar application for a re-gale of the Union Gale.

regale (rɪˈgeɪl), *v.* [ad. F. *régaler* (Cotgr.), It. *regalare*, Sp. and Pg. *regalar*: see REGALO.
Mabbe (1622) in his translation of Aleman's *Guzman d'Alfarache* I. 230 and 242, uses the Sp. infinitive *regalar*.]

1. *trans.* To entertain or feast (a person, etc.) in a choice manner. Also *ironical* (quot. 1822).

1656 BLOUNT *Glossogr.*, *To Regale*,.. to Feast or entertain with rarities. **1687** A. LOVELL tr. *Thevenot's Trav.* I. 34 When they would regale any Friend that comes to see them, they cause a Dish of Coffee to be brought to him. **1713** STEELE *Guard.* No. 6 ¶3 Sir Harry has for ever a year's income, to extend his charity, serve his pleasures, or regale his friends. **1774** GOLDSM. *Nat. Hist.* (1776) VIII. 102 It will.. plunder them of their honey-bag, with which it flies triumphantly loaded to its nest to regale its young. **1822** COBBETT *Weekly Reg.* 29 June 795/1 Those beans and other .. wholesome materials with which the honest contractors used to regale us. **1837** W. IRVING *Capt. Bonneville* II. 42 Regaling each other in the best style their respective camps afforded. **1848** DICKENS *Dombey* viii, She was regaled with rice.

b. Of things: To furnish (one) with a choice feast or refreshment.

*a***1721** PRIOR *Wand. Pilgr.* 12 Adam's Ale, Pure Element no Life can give, Or mortal Soul regale. **1727** GAY *Fables* I. xvii, The thefts of night regal'd the day. **1853** J. H. NEWMAN *Hist. Sk.* (1873) II. I. i. 39 The food which regaled the old Scythians in the heroic age of Greece.

2. To gratify or delight (the mind) by some pleasing influence or occupation; to entertain (a person) in a highly agreeable manner. Also *ironical* (quot. 1856).

1671 WOODHEAD *St. Teresa* I. x. 56 If in these reflections, the party be possessed and seized with any love of God, the Soul is all regaled. **1751** JOHNSON *Rambler* No. 89 ¶4 The art of regaling his mind with those airy gratifications [of fancy]. **1785** MME. D'ARBLAY *Diary* 16 Dec., These fancies, however, only regaled me while I continued a quiet spectator. **1856** KANE *Arct. Expl.* II. ix. 95 Then the few tired out-workers are regaled by the groans and tossing of the sick. **1875** JOWETT *Plato* (ed. 2) II. 77 Until he has delivered up the speech with which Lysias has regaled him.

b. To affect with a pleasurable sensation.

1703 J. PHILLIPS *Splendid Shilling* 19, I.. with a warming Puff Regale chill'd Fingers. *a***1763** SHENSTONE *Elegies* x. 23 The peach's vernal bud regal'd his eye. **1784** COWPER *Task* III. 621 The sight is pleased, The scent regaled. **1850** H. ROGERS *Ess.* (1874) II. ii. 119 The eye and the ear, and all the senses, are regaled amidst woodland scenery on a fine spring day.

3. To gratify, please, delight, by a gift, deference, etc. *rare.*

1671 tr. *Frejus' Voy. Mauritania* 17 Whom I regaled with some small present,.. and afterwards caused them to be rowed to land. **1751** JOHNSON *Rambler* No. 172 ¶13 The sycophant.. regales his [a patron's] reigning vanity.

4. *refl.* To entertain or recreate (oneself) with food, drink, or amusement.

[**1656** BLOUNT *Glossogr.*, *To Regale*, to make as much account, and take as great a care of ones self, as if one were a King.] **1719** DE FOE *Crusoe* I. viii, I repos'd my self here a Week, to rest and regale my self after my long Journey. **1771** J. ADAMS *Diary* 8 June, I must make a pool.. for the cool spring water.. that the cattle and hogs and ducks may regale themselves here. **1827** *Perils & Captivity* (Constable's Misc.) 219 Our masters regaled themselves with the raw fat of the goat. **1869** LECKY *Europ. Mor.* I. 298 Heliogabalus and Galerius are reported.. to have regaled them-selves with the sight of criminals torn by wild beasts.

5. *intr.* To feast; const. *on*, *upon*, *with*.

1678 in A. Duncan *Mariner's Chron.* (1810) III. 150, I killed a peacock... We regaled upon it, and ate it as if it had been the most delicious morsel we had yet met with. **1749** FIELDING *Tom Jones* VIII. viii, While Tom Jones.. was regaling in the parlour. *Ibid.* x. iv, To regale with.. dainties. **1783** COWPER *Epit. on a Hare* 17 On twigs of hawthorn he regaled. **1849** C. BRONTE *Shirley* i, Mr. Donne had kindly invited his brethren to regale with him. **1860** GOSSE *Rom. Nat. Hist.* 57 Some browsing on the juicy trees,.. and others regaling on the fresh roots of high mimosas.

transf. **1814** JANE AUSTEN *Mansfield Park* ii, Mrs. Norris .. thus regaled in the credit of being foremost to welcome her.

regalement (rɪˈgeɪlmənt). [f. prec. + -MENT; cf. It. *regalamento*, Sp. *-miento*.]

1. The act of regaling, refreshment, entertainment.

1708 J. PHILIPS *Cyder* II. 73 The Muses still require Humid regalement. **1799** MRS. J. WEST *Tale of Times* I. 68 The long oaken tables.. which used to administer to the regalement of his tenants at Christmas. **1852** *Blackw. Mag.* LXXII. 231 With no other regalement for the ear than the hoarse braying of the beaters.

2. A means of regaling; a dainty.

1818 SOUTHEY *Lett.* (1856) III. 89 Sweet butter, caudle, and other such regalements.

re'galer. [f. REGALE *v.* + -ER¹.] One who or that which regales (Ogilvie, 1882).

‖**regalia**¹ (rɪˈgeɪlɪə). Also 7-8 **regalia's**. [L., pl. of *rēgāle* REGALE *sb.*¹]

1. a. Rights appertaining to a king; royal powers or privileges.

α. *a***1540** BARNES *Wks.* (1573) 201 All the worlde knoweth, that *regalia* belongeth to kinges, and to like power of kynges. **1656** BLOUNT *Glossogr.*, *Regalia*, the Rights of a King, which the Civilians say are six, *viz.* 1. Power of Judicature [etc.]. **1691** T. H[ALE] *Acc. New Invent.* 65 The administration of the Banks of Rivers is a part of the *Regalia*. **1754** ERSKINE *Princ. Sc. Law* (1809) 180 There are certain rights naturally consequent on property, which are deemed to be reserved by the crown, as *regalia*, unless they be specially conveyed. **1797** W. JOHNSTON tr. *Beckmann's Invent.* II. 323 [The floating of wood seems] to have been considered among regalia. **1838** W. BELL *Dict. Law Scot.* 840 There are also certain *regalia* connected with the right of land. **1885** *Encycl. Brit.* XIX. 672/1.

β. **1644** HOWELL *Twelve Treat.* (1661) 253 There are six *Jura Regalia*, six Regal Rights... Among these Regalia's, we find that Arming.. is among the chiefest. **1702** *Reflect. Case W. Penn* 6 Levying Men and Money, Calling Assemblies,.. and all the other Regalia's of Government.

†**b.** *Eccl. Hist.* (See REGALE *sb.*¹ 1.) *Obs. rare*$^{-1}$.

1688 *Answ. Talon's Plea* 4 With what Charity did this great Pope represent to his Christian Majesty the Injustice Committed.. by extending the Regalia upon four Provinces that had ever been free?

†**c.** (See quot. and cf. REGALITY¹ 5 b.) *Obs.*$^{-0}$

1727-38 CHAMBERS *Cycl.*, *Regalia*, of the church, are those rights and priviledges which cathedrals, etc. enjoy by grants, and other concessions of kings.

2. The emblems or insignia of royalty; the crown, sceptre, and other distinctive ornaments of a king or queen which are used at coronations. Also erron. as sing.

1626 D'EWES in Ellis *Orig. Lett.* Ser. I. III. 216 Upon a table placed on the left hand of the Estate, were the regalia laied. **1661** EVELYN *Diary* 23 Apr., The Deane and Prebendaries brought all the regalia, and deliver'd them to severall Noblemen to beare before the King. **1700** ASTRY tr. *Saavedra-Faxardo* I. 173 Ezekiel commanded King Zedekiah to lay down his Crown and other Regalia. **1756** NUGENT *Gr. Tour, Germany* II. 31 As soon as the day and place of the coronation is settled, the magistrates.. send their deputies with the regalia or coronation ornaments committed to their care. **1818** J. W. CROKER in *C. Papers* 9 Jan. (1884), I have gotten the warrant for searching for the old regalia of the Scottish Crown. **1855** MILMAN *Lat. Chr.* IX. ii. (1864) V. 215 If he had the majority of voices and the possession of the regalia, on the other hand must be taken into account the illegality of his coronation. **1953** *Times* 29 May 15/4 The regalia which will be used at the Coronation .. is that which is normally used at the Coronations of our kings.

transf. **1742** YOUNG *Nt. Th.* IX. 1686 The Mighty Potentate, to whom belong These rich Regalia pompously display'd. **1811** *Ora & Juliet* II. 110 A coach and six, a regalia of jewels,.. sideboards of plate. *a***1861** MRS. BROWNING *De Profundis* xx, The sharp regalia are for Thee.

3. The decorations or insignia of an order.

Noted as an improper use in Edmondson's *Compl. Body of Heraldry* (1780) II. Gloss.

1676 *Lond. Gaz.* No. 1143/1 The Regalia of the Mayoralty were delivered into the hands of the new Lord Mayor. **1788** *Gentl. Mag.* LVIII. I. 83/1 [He] was escorted to the grave by upwards of 200 Free-masons, dressed in all their regalia. **1880** *Daily Tel.* 27 Sept., A large number of Orangemen, dressed in regalia,.. were present.

regalia² (rɪˈgeɪlɪə). [a. Sp. *regalía* royal privilege (see REGALY).] A Cuban or other large cigar of superior quality.

1819 H. BUSK *Dessert* 379 Amber ginseng, and purified eringoes, Regalia's, and imperial's, and *maringoe's*. **1841** S. WARD in *Life Longfellow* (1891) I. 386, I rejoice that Allston should have enjoyed the 'regalias'. **1851** MAYNE REID *Scalp-Hunt.* ii. 19 We commenced smoking regalias and drinking madeira. **1874** M. COLLINS *Transmigr.* III. vii. 117 My chief conversation that evening had been puff after puff of the regalia.

regalia, obs. variant of *regalio* REGALO.

regalian (rɪˈgeɪlɪən), *a.* [ad. F. *régalien* (1690): see REGAL *a.* and -IAN.] Pertaining to a sovereign, regal.

1818 HALLAM *Mid. Ages* iii. I. (1841) I. 235 He defined the regalian rights, as they were called, in such a manner as to exclude the cities and private proprietors from coining money. **1882** ROGERS *Agric. & Prices* IV. 31 All those regalian rights which belonged to the county Palatine.

regalio, obs. variant of REGALO.

regalism (ˈriːgəlɪz(ə)m). [f. REGAL *a.* + -ISM.] The doctrine or practice of the supremacy of the sovereign in ecclesiastical matters.

1869 MANNING *Petri Privileg.* (1871) II. 53 Gallicanism is also the last form of Regalism yet lingering in the Church. **1890** *Dublin Rev.* Apr. 245 The clergy who had submitted to the regalism of Henry and the Protestantism of Edward.

regalist (ˈriːgəlɪst). [a. F. *régaliste* (16th c.): see prec. and -IST.] †**a.** A royal partisan. *Obs.*

1591 CONINGSBY *Jrnl. Siege Rouen* in *Camden Misc.* I. 44 The greate severitie used by Villiers unto those suspected to be regalists. **1617** MORYSON *Itin.* I. 193 The bell of that Church was sounded.. to giue a signe to the Regalists and Guisians, that they should kill those of the reformed Religion.

b. A supporter of regalism.

1894 *Tablet* 7 July 35 The principles and practice of the Regalists have been revived with increased virulence.

regality¹ (rɪˈgælɪtɪ). Also 5-6 **-ite, -yte**, 6 **-itye, -itee**, 6-7 **-itie**; 5, 6 *Sc.* **rigalitie**. [a. AF. (and OF.) *regalité* (Langtoft, etc.), or ad. med.L. *rēgālitāt-em*: see REGAL *a.* and -ITY.]

1. a. Royalty, sovereignty, kingship, sovereign rule or jurisdiction.

1422 tr. *Secreta Secret., Priv. Priv.* 199 He foryaue manasses his orribill Synnes, and hym agayn broȝt into Ierusalem, and the regalite hym yaue. *c***1485** *Digby Myst.* (1882) IV. 36 Nobyll prelates and princes of Regalyte. *c***1540** tr. *Pol. Verg. Eng. Hist.* (Camden No. 36) 177 Adelredus.. was bolde to take on him the charge of regalitie. **1590** SPENSER *F.Q.* II. i. 57 When raging Passion with fierce tyranny Robs Reason of her dew regalitie. **1631** WEEVER *Anc. Funeral Mon.* 217 Stephen died, and Henry.. succeeded him in the Regalitie. **1678** MARVELL *Growth Popery* Wks. (Grosart) IV. 249 We have the same right.. in our propriety that the prince hath in his regality. *a***1734** NORTH *Exam.* III. vi. §15 (1740) 434 He never.. differed with his parliament, but.. complied so far, as, consistent with his entire Regality, he might do. **1814** SOUTHEY *Roderick* III. 170 Now from its state Of proud regality debased and fallen. **1878** STUBBS *Const. Hist.* xix. III. 331 Things which touch the king, his crown, regality, or realm. *fig.* *a* **1861** G. MASSEY *Wedded Love* Wks. (1861) 219 Thou hast put a queenlier presence on With thy regality of Womanhood!

b. Royal dignity or demeanour. *rare.*

1582 STANYHURST *Æneis* I. (Arb.) 34 Such was Dido ioying, so she with regalitye passed With Princely presence the wurcking coompanye cheering. **1966** *New Statesman* 22 July 140/2 Her firmness is deeply satisfying and, in the final act, that excessive regality was lost in the gentle girlhood.. which she can present when she chooses. **1979** *Daily Tel.* 4 Dec. 15/1 She is a narrator whose regality, though it is all natural style and never affectation, proves oddly inhibiting to those she interviews.

†**c.** Rule or sovereignty *of* a place. *Obs. rare*$^{-1}$.

1626 in Rushw. *Hist. Coll.* (1659) I. 353 There needs no Argument.. but one, The Regality of our narrow seas, the Antient Inheritance of our Princes lost or impeached.

2. †**a.** Local rights or jurisdiction properly appertaining to the king. *Obs. rare*$^{-1}$.

1414 *Rolls of Parlt.* IV. 58/1 The Priour and Chanons of Barnewell.. hav cleymed, and ȝit cleymen, the regalite and the frehold of the Kynges Lordshippe and Towneshipe of Chestreton.

b. *Sc.* Territorial jurisdiction of a royal nature granted by the king. Now only *Hist.* (abolished by Act 20 Geo. II, c. 43).

lord of regality, the person to whom such jurisdiction was granted. ***burgh of regality***, one having a lord of regality for its superior. ***court of regality***, the court held by a lord of regality. Also ***bailie, clerk***, etc., ***of regality***.

1436 *Sc. Acts Jas. I* (1814) II. 23/2 Vndir þe payn to þe lordis of Regalite doing in þe contrary of tynsall of Regaliteis. **1535** STEWART *Cron. Scot.* I. 127 This nobill King hes gevin till him than.. tha landis frie, Euir till be haldin in regalitie. **1569** *Reg. Privy Council Scot.* II. 33 The said Abbay of Halieruidhous hes had, thir mony and diverse yeris bipast, fre Regalitie within all the townis. *c* **1680** DALLAS *Stiles* (1697) 579 To hold and affix Courts of Regality within the said Burgh. *Ibid.* 581 The said Burgh of Regality, and Heretable Offices of Regality, Bailliary and Justiciary. **1746–7** *Act 20 Geo. II*, c. 43 §1 All Heretable Jurisdictions of Justiciary, and all Regalities and Heretable Baillieries.. within.. Scotland, belonging unto.. any Subject or Subjects,.. shall be.. abrogated, taken away, and totally dissolved and extinguished. **1799** J. ROBERTSON *Agric. Perth* 2 Methven had the regality of its own estate. **1838** W. BELL *Dict. Law Scot.* 840 The civil jurisdiction of a lord of regality was equal to that of the sheriff; but his criminal jurisdiction was much more extensive.

†**c.** Land or territory subject to such jurisdiction. *Obs.*

1545 *Reg. Privy Council Scot.* I. 6 All Sheriffis Stewartis Ballies alswele Regalitie as Ryalte. *Ibid.* 371 Fensabill personis alsweill dwelland to burgh as to land, within Regalitie as Rialtie. **1681** *Act Secur. Prot. Rel.* (Scotl.) in *Lond. Gaz.* No. 1649/3 All Magistrates, Deans of Gild, Counsellors and Clerks of Burroughs Royal and Regality.

3. a. *Sc.* A particular territory or area subject to a lord of regality.

1438 *Sc. Acts Jas. II* (1814) II. 32/1 Geyff the offisaris of þe regalyteys fulfillis noȝt þis act It sall be leyfful to the kyngis schirraye to fulfill it. **1540** *Charters Edinb.* (1871) 212 Inhabitaris of the north syde of the brig of Leith whilkis duellis in the regalite of Halyrudehous. **1565** *Reg. Privy Council Scot.* I. 368 Baillie of the regalitie of Pettinweme. *c* **1680** DALLAS *Stiles* (1697) 580 The Tennants and Inhabitants of the said Barony and Regality. **1708** *Royal Proclam.* 6 Mar. in *Lond. Gaz.* No. 4416/2 We do.. hereby Charge.. all our Lord-Lieutenants,.. Sheriffs, Bailiffs of Regalities,.. to put in Execution all Laws.. now in Force.., against such Persons. **1799** J. ROBERTSON *Agric. Perth* 2 The duke of Athol had the same authority in Athol as a separate regality. **1820** SCOTT *Monast.* xiii, The cultivators of each barony or regality, temporal or spiritual, in Scotland, are obliged to bring their corn [etc.].

b. ***regality of Hexham***, a district in Northumberland over which the Bishops of Hexham, Lindisfarne, and Durham, and the Archbishop of York, successively for centuries exercised a quasi-royal jurisdiction.

For historical details see Hinds *Hist. Northumberland* (1896) III. 20 ff. Cf. also REGALY 1 b.

1515 in Hinds *Hist. Northumb.* (1896) III. 46 As touching all your causes withynne your regallity of Hexham, there hath bene of late some business. **1608** *Ibid.* 104 Ther are noe parkes or game within the regalitie of Hexham. **1703** in Wright *Hist. Hexham* (1823) I. ii. 28 *note*, Within the said regality and manor of Hexham aforesaid there is a custom [etc.]. **1823** WRIGHT *Ibid.* I. v. 54 The Fenwicks.. afterwards purchased the regality or manor of Hexham from the crown. **1865** RAINE *Priory of Hexham* (Surtees) II. Pref. I. xxv, The registers at York contain many documents relating to the Archbishop's regality of Hexham and his officers.

†**c.** *pl.* The bounds or limits of a royalty.

1666 *Ormonde MSS.* in *10th Rep. Hist. MSS. Comm.* App. V. 7 Persons.. within the Regalities and liberties of Tipperary. *Ibid.*, The Seneschall and Chancellor of the said Regalityes and Libertyes.

4. A country or district subject to royal authority, a kingdom; a monarchical state.

1486 in *Surtees Misc.* (1888) 54 Most reverend, rightwose regent of this rigalitie. **1600** W. WATSON *Decacordon* (1602) 316 Territories, seigniories, regalities and dominions. **1827** G. S. FABER *Sacr. Cal. Prophecy* (1844) III. 106 They are seven regalities or seven forms of supreme government. **1864** BURTON *Scot Abr.* I. v. 260 Over Europe there were inexhaustible varieties of palatinates, margravates, regalities, and the like, enjoying their own separate privileges.

5. a. A right or privilege pertaining or appropriate to a king. Chiefly *pl.*

1523 LD. BERNERS *Froiss.* I. ccxii. 258 The honours, regalities, obeisaunce, homages.. and souerainties, that apperteyneth.. to the crowne of Fraunce. **1592** *Nobody & Someb.* in Simpson *Sch. Shaks.* (1878) I. 335 Before Ile be halfe a king, and contrould In any regality, ile hazard all. **1640** *Prerog. Parlt. Eng.* in *Select. fr. Harl. Misc.* (1793) 241 A prince that suffereth himself to be besieged, forsaketh one of the greatest regalities belonging to a monarchy. **1671** F. PHILLIPS *Reg. Necess.* 273 If a restless Spirit of opposition to the Kings Rights or Regalities shall not permit an acquiescence. **1765** BLACKSTONE *Comm.* I. (ed. 2) 108 Proprietary governments, granted out by the crown to individuals,.. with all the inferior regalities. **1862** S. LUCAS *Secularia* 261 The Crown abdicated its regalities in favour of a Proprietary, yet claimed to bind him by its fiscal regulations.

†**b.** *pl.* = REGALIA[1] 1 c. *Obs. rare.*

a **1641** BP. MOUNTAGU *Acts & Mon.* (1642) 73 Coming short of the enlarged Regalities of the Church. **1761** HUME *Hist. Eng.* II. xxxv. 281 The regalities of the see, which included the jurisdiction of a court palatine, were given by the king to Northumberland.

†**6.** *pl.* = REGALIA[1] 2. *Obs. rare*$^{-1}$.

1531 ELYOT *Gov.* II. ii. (R.), For what purpose was it ordeyned, that Christen kynges.. shulde in an open and stately place, before al theyr subiectes, receiue their crowne and other regalities.

7. *attrib.* (sense 2 or 3), as ***regality books, court, land***, etc.

1752 in J. Louthian *Form of Process* (ed. 2) 278 At the Time, when the Suits were carried on against them, before the Regality-court. **1797** *Encycl. Brit.* (ed. 3) IX. 650/1 Such regality lands as happened to fall to the crown by forfeiture. *Ibid.* 650/2 A regality-jurisdiction, called the Principality. **1876** GRANT *Burgh Sch. Scot.* II. ii. 112 An obligation.. registered in the regality books of Dunfermline.

†**re'gality**[2]. *Obs. rare*$^{-1}$. [irreg. f. REGALE *v.* + -ITY.] Regalement, entertainment.

1672 *Lond. Gaz.* No. 695/3 The King closed all with a regality of the season, and an exercise of his own Regiment.

'regalize, *v. rare.* [f. REGAL *a.* + -IZE.]

†**1.** *Chem.* To convert into 'regal water'. *Obs.*

1694 SALMON *Bate's Dispens.* (1713) 498/1 Its Mechanical use is for Refiners, who Regalize their Aqua fortis therewith, to make it able to dissolve Gold.

2. To make regal or royal.

1873 BROWNING *Red Cott. Nt.-cap* I. 745, I trust Clairvaux thus renovated, regalized.. Answers that question.

regally ('ri:gəlɪ), *adv.* [f. REGAL *a.* + -LY[2].] In a regal manner.

1436 *Libel Eng. Policy* in *Pol. Poems* (Rolls) II. 196 To saile and rowe.. So regaliche aboute the Englisshe yle. **1611** COTGR., *Regalement*, regally, kingly, royally. **1670** MILTON *Hist. Eng.* v. 212 Alfred.. was buried regally at Winchester. **1852** MRS. JAMESON *Leg. Madonna* (1857) 28 Both figures are regally attired. **1890** H. G. DAKYNS *Xenophon's Wks.* I. p. lxxxvii, Regally the sun-god smiled upon his going.

‖**regalo** (re'galo). Now *rare.* Also 7–8 **regalio, regalia.** [ad. It. (also Sp. and Pg.) *regalo* a present, gift, etc., the sb. related to *regalare* to REGALE; the etym. of the stem is obscure (see Diez and Körting). The erroneous form *regalio* is common in the second half of the 17th century: *regalia* is less usual.] A present, esp. of choice food or drink; a choice or elegant repast or entertainment, etc. (see REGALE *sb.*[2]).

α. **1622** MABBE tr. *Aleman's Guzman d'Alf.* I. 24 Sending their servants laden with baskets of regalo's, and delicate choice Dainties. **1654** JER. TAYLOR *Real Pres.* 159 It was a present for a Prince,.. a Regalo fit for so great a person. **1668** *Lond. Gaz.* No. 324/1 She was.. presented from the Pope with a Regalo of all sorts of Fowl, Fruits, Wines, and other Delicacies. **1758** H. WALPOLE *Let. to Mann* 8 July, I congratulate you on your regalo from the Northumberlands. **1847** DISRAELI *Tancred* IV. xi, I will not demand more than a third of the profits, leaving it to your own liberality to make me any regalo in addition.

fig. **1671** WOODHEAD *St. Teresa* I. xi. 54, I.. durst never advisedly desire any regalos, or spiritual delights at his hands. **1749** LAVINGTON *Enthus. Meth. & Papists* II. (1754) 57 God for many Years did hide himself from her, withdrawing the Regalo's and Joys of his Presence.

β. **1652** BENLOWES *Theoph.* IV. xciv, How mid'st regalios of Loves Banquet I Dissolve in sweets Extremitie. **1697** *Phil. Trans.* XIX. 143 A small round nut,.. some eat them, and account them as great a Regalio as Pistaches. **1727** A. HAMILTON *New Acc. E. Ind.* I. xxi. 249 Candied and preserved Fruits are their Regalio in all Seasons. *a* **1734** NORTH *Lives* (1826) II. 473 A jewel of fifteen purses was to be the vizier's *regalio.*

fig. **1667** DRYDEN *Sir Martin Mar-all* Prol. 2 Fools.. Are yet the great regalios of a play. **1686** W. DE BRITAINE *Hum. Prud.* xi. 53, I am not much delighted with the Regalio's or Gaiety of the World.

γ. *c* **1640** [SHIRLEY] *Capt. Underwit* I. in Bullen *O. Pl.* (1883) II. 330 There's a Ball to night in the Strand... I ha' bespoke regalias there, too. **1685** COTTON tr. *Montaigne* xxx. (1869) 172 After having a long time treated their prisoners very well, and given them all the regalia's they can think of. **1721** D'URFEY *Two Queens Brentford* I. (D.), The Town shall have its regalia: the Coffee-house gapers, I'm resolv'd, shan't want their Diversion.

†**'regalty.** *Obs.* Forms: 4 **regaute**, 4–5 **regalte**, (4 -tee), 6–7 **regaltie**, (7 -tye), 7–8 **regalty.** [Prob. a. AF. **regalté, regauté*: see REGAL *a.* and -TY and cf. ROYALTY.] = REGALITY[1].

c **1330** R. BRUNNE *Chron.* (1810) 15 Egbriht of alle þe lond had þe regaute. *Ibid.* 57 To coroune Kyng Edward, Als he þat had gode right vnto þe regalte. **1388** WYCLIF *Wisd.* vi. 22 If ȝe kyngis of the puple, deliten in seetis, and kyngis ȝerdis, ether regaltees. *c* **1440** CAPGRAVE *Life St. Kath.* II. 726 Þat hye degre, Grettest of all, I mene þe regalte. **1588** ALLEN *Admonit.* 34 Queene Maacha.. was deposed from her regaltie by her owne sonne. **1601** R. JOHNSON *Kingd. & Commw.* (1603) 20 The kingdome is deuided into many Regalties and principalities, as Burgundie, Britaine, Aniou and Normandie. **1614** SELDEN *Titles Hon.* 206 To speake here of particular Dukedomes their rights, Regalties and such like were from our purpose. **1703** *Lond. Gaz.* No. 3950/4 With all the several Regalties, Free-Fisheries, &c.

†**'regaly.** *Obs.* Forms: 4–5 **regalye**, 4–6 **-ly, -lie**; 5 **regall(i)e**, 5–6 **regally**, (5 **-ye**, 6 **-ey**), 6 **rigalie.** [a. AF. *regaly, regalie* = It. and Sp. *regalía*: see REGAL *a.* and -Y[1].]

1. Royalty, royal prerogative, kingship; kingdom. (Very common *c* 1380–1500.)

c **1368** CHAUCER *Compl. Pite* 65 Your contraire, Crueltee, Allyed is ageynst your regalye. *c* **1380** WYCLIF *Sel. Wks.* II. 88 Here Crist shewide his regaly, and tauȝte how lordis shulde chastise symonye. **1432–50** tr. *Higden* (Rolls) III. 399 Too egles.. that signifiede ij. regalies, of Asia and of Europe. **1494** FABYAN *Chron.* VI. cli. 138 After he had.. depryuyd Sygebert, theyr Kynge, from his auctorite, & regally. **1513** BRADSHAW *St. Werburge* I. 407 Ercombert .xxx. yere reynynge in his regaly Had a noble progeny. **1558** G. CAVENDISH *Poems* (1825) II. 46 Farewell the pieussant prynce, flower of all regally.

b. = REGALITY[1] 3 b.

1467–8 *Rolls Parlt.* V. 633 In Regalie, and Court of the Archbishop of York in Hexhamshire. **1515** in Hinds *Hist. Northumb.* (1896) III. 47 Th' enhabitauntes of yo[r] regalie of Hexam. *c* **1530** in Raine *Priory Hexham* (Surtees) I. p. cviii, The rigalie of Hexham, belonging my lord archebusshop his grace of York.

2. *pl.* = REGALIA[1] 2.

c **1430** LYDG. *Min. Poems* (Percy Soc.) 128 Erthely princes, reigneng in theyr glorye, Withe theyre sceptres and theyr regalyes. **1494** FABYAN *Chron.* VII. 399 The castell, in the whiche were founde y[e] regalies of Scotlande; that is to meane y[e] crowne w[t] the sceptre & cloth of astate.

regante, error for *regaute* REGALTY.

regard (rɪ'gɑ:d), *sb.* Also 4, 7–8 **reguard**, 5–7 **regarde**, 7 **regaurd**, 5–6 *Sc.* **regaird.** [a. F. *regard* (OF. also *regart, regars*, and *reguart, reguard*: cf. REWARD *sb.*), vbl. sb. to *regarder* REGARD *v.* Hence also med.L. *regardum* (see Du Cange).]

I. 1. Aspect, appearance (*obs.*); look (of persons); habit or manner of looking; air.

c **1380** *Sir Ferumb.* 1297 Þe erld of montdisdier, þat was þe fairest kniȝt of regard of alle þe doþþeper. **1483** CAXTON *Gold. Leg.* 416 b/2 He was gracious and curtoys in maners and playsant in regarde. **1484** —— *Chivalry* 6 He hadde a regard or countenaunce of moche hooly lyf. **1576** GASCOIGNE *Steele Gl.* (Arb.) 56 Wherein I see a Sampsons grim regarde Disgraced yet with Alexanders bearde. **1604** E. G[RIMSTONE] *D'Acosta's Hist. Indies* IV. xxxvii. 309 They .. have so lively and pleasing a regard, as the Painter cannot exceede it with his pencill and colours. **1667** MILTON *P.L.* IV. 877 To whom with stern regard thus Gabriel spake. **1858** M. ARNOLD *Merope* 740 The prince at start seem'd sad, but his regard Clear'd with blithe travel and the morning air.

2. a. A look, glance, or gaze.

c **1477** CAXTON *Jason* 19 Yn these regardes and in these semblances they passid the soupper. **1483** —— *Gold. Leg.* 201/2 Deuyls and wicked spirites went out of the bodyes of creatures by his symple regarde and syghte. **1592** R. D. *Hypnerotomachia* 75 b, Her regards were wanton, lascivious, and unconstant. **1606** SHAKS. *Tr. & Cr.* III. iii. 255 He.. bites his lip with a politique regard. **1725** POPE *Odyss.* IV. 201 Such quick regards his sparkling eyes bestow. **1791** MRS. RADCLIFFE *Rom. Forest* i, From these objects she turned her regard upon Monsieur and Madame La Motte. **1815** SHELLEY *Alastor* 488 When his regard Was raised by intense pensiveness. **1859** HAWTHORNE *Marb. Faun* xxiii, Miriam, with a long regard from the threshold, bade farewell to this doves' nest.

†**b.** Prospect, view. *Obs. rare.*

c **1500** *Melusine* 313 The which chambre had regarde toward the gardyns. **1599** B. JONSON *Cynthia's Rev.* II. i, You are now within regard of the presence.

†**c.** An object of sight. *Obs. rare.*

1586 WHETSTONE (*title*) The English Myrror, a Regard wherein al Estates may behold the Conquests of Envy. **1604** SHAKS. *Oth.* II. i. 40 To throw-out our eyes for braue Othello, Euen till we make the Maine, and th' Eriall blew, An indistinct regard.

†**d.** The position of two geomantic figures in relation to each other. (Cf. ASPECT *sb.* 4.) *Obs.*

1591 SPARRY tr. *Cattan's Geomancie* III. xvii. 187 The regard of opposition in the fygure formed, is, when the fyrst doth beholde the 7th.

3. a. The official inspection of a forest in order to discover whether any trespasses have been committed in it; the right of such inspection, or the office of one appointed to make it. *Obs.* exc. *Hist.*

[? *a* **1184** in Hoveden *Chron.* (Rolls) II. 243 Hæc sunt videnda in regardis Forestæ. *Ibid.*, Essarta post ultimum regardum facta. **1217** *Carta de Foresta* in *Stat. Realm* (1810) I. 20 Reguardores nostri eant per Forestas ad faciendum Reguardum sicut fieri consuevit. **1278** *Rolls of Parlt.* I. 9/2 E si unt la chartre meyme le Roi Henry.. ke les acquite de Reguard de Foresters e de Verders.]

1502 ARNOLDE *Chron.* 79 b/2 For Inquisicion and Regarde... Our raungers shall goo by our forest too make regarde as they were wont to doo the tyme of the furst coronacion of the forsaid kyng herry our graundsir. **1598** MANWOOD *Lawes Forest* xvi. §9. 96 b, Mastives are not to be Expeditated, but onely where the Regard is to be made, and that is in Forrestes and not in Chases. **1615** *Ibid.* (ed. 2) xxi. §3. 194 The King hath the regard of all the woods and wast grounds and other lands which are afforested. **1670** BLOUNT *Law Dict.* (1691) s.v. [and in various later Dicts.]. **1768** BLACKSTONE *Comm.* III. 72 The court of regard, or survey of dogs, is to be holden every third year for the lawing or expeditation of mastiffs. **1868** STUBBS *Hoveden* (Rolls) I. Pref. 76 As a sort of Appendix to this work are given.. the Articles of Regard and Assize of the Forest.

b. The district within the jurisdiction of the official regarders.

1594 CROMPTON *Jurisd.* 193 It appeareth.. that within the regard of any Forest, no man may buyld either houses or barcaryes. **1598** MANWOOD *Lawes Forest* vii. §4. 40b, All such woods and landes, as are parcell of the Forrest, the same is within the regard. **1667–8** *Act 19 & 20 Chas. II*, c. 8 §11 All Lands and Grounds lying within the Perambulation and Reguard of the said Forrest [of Dean]. **1837** HOWITT *Rur. Life* v. i. (1862) 356 The forests were.. systematically divided into walks, or keepings, wards or regards, over which was a properly subordinate succession of officers. **1873** *Q. Rev.* CXXXV. 153 The 'regards' or limits of the 'foresta regis' are indicated by a circle running from point to point.

4. †**a.** Reference *to* a person or thing. Chiefly in phr. ***to have (a) regard to***. *Obs.*

1559 BP. SCOT in Strype *Ann. Ref.* (1709) I. II. App. x. 446 Neyther dothe the preste take the bread in his handes, neyther yet hathe any regard or respect to the bread. **1561** T. NORTON *Calvin's Inst.* III. 262 We see howe this accepting hath not regarde to the righteousnesse of man. **1649** EARL MONM. tr. *Senault's Use Passions* (1671) 23 The passions of the concupiscible appetite have a regard to good and to evil, as absent, or as present. *a* **1677** BARROW *Serm.* Wks. 1716 III. 1 We may be said to do that in another person's name, which we do with any kind of reference or regard to him.

b. Respect, point, particular.

1602 FULBECKE *1st Pt. Parall.* 57, I must therefore request you to stretch your sinewes in this regarde. *a* **1617** BAYNE *On Eph.* (1658) 87 The Gospel of salvation may bee called a Mystery in three regards. **1726** LEONI tr. *Alberti's Archit.* I. 4/2 If it is of Service in a publick Regard, I cannot find Fault with it. **1821** SHELLEY *Ess. & Lett.* (1852) II. 265, I will pay every possible attention to your instructions in this regard. **1875** WHITNEY *Life Lang.* vii. 132 Each tongue has its own way in this regard.

†**c.** ? Intention, design, purpose. *Obs. rare.*

1599 SHAKS. *Hen. V*, I. i. 22 The King is full of grace, and faire regard. **1601** —— *Jul. C.* III. i. 224 Our Reasons are so full of good regard, That were you, Antony, the sonne of Cæsar, You should be satisfied.

II. †**5. a.** Repute, account, or estimation, in which anything is held. *Obs.*

c **1400** in *Hampole's Wks.* (Horstm.) I. 182 Þat he be meke in his awen felynge, and halde þis mynde in regarde nouȝt til he may.. fele þe fyre of lufe. **1553** GRIMALDE *Cicero's Offices* III. (1556) 154b, So greatly was an othe had in regard, at those dayes. **1591** SPENSER *M. Hubberd* 60 Thus manie yeares I now have spent.. In meane regard. **1606** SHAKS. *Tr. & Cr.* III. iii. 128 What things there are Most abiect in regard, and deare in vse. What things againe most deere in the esteeme, And poore in worth. **1632** LITHGOW *Trav.* v. 180 These commanders haue euer best prospered, which haue.. had in singular regard, Military Arts and Souldiers.

†**b.** ***of.. regard***, of (small, great, etc.) account, estimation, importance, or value. (Also *Sc.* without *of.*) *Obs.*

1556 LAUDER *Tractate* 216 Thocht thay ryde on mulis or hors, Itt is bot small regarde or fors. **1591** SPENSER *M. Hubberd* 685 A noble Gentleman of high regard. **1597** BEARD *Theatre God's Judgem.* (1612) 465 A thousand men of base regard. **1622** SIR R. HAWKINS *Voy. S. Sea* (1847) 215 In fights, all receipts which add courage and spirit, are of great regard, to be allowed and used. **1670** WALTON *Lives* III. 252 [This] is a Point in my Opinion of great regard. **1742** SHENSTONE *Schoolmistress* 21 Whilome a twig of small regard to see. **1785** BURNS *Jolly Beggars* 7th Air, I am a bard of no regard Wi' gentlefolks, an' a' that.

†**c.** ***in*** (one's) ***regard***, in one's opinion, estimation, or judgement. *Obs. rare.*

1596 SHAKS. *1 Hen. IV*, IV. iii. 57 Sicke in the Worlds regard, wretched, and low. **1604** —— *Ham.* IV. vii. 76 (Q. 2) That one,.. in my regard, Of the vnworthiest siedge.

6. a. Observant attention or heed bestowed upon or given *to* a matter; †consideration of a question or problem, doubt. Also *pl.* (cf. sense 2).

1456 SIR G. HAYE *Law Arms* (S.T.S.) 192 Touchand the quhilk debate thare is grete regarde and avis. **1469** *Paston Lett.* II. 369, I cannot understand what regard my Lords concell takyth to my Lords letter. **1523** LD. BERNERS *Froiss.* I. ccxii. 261 By the aduise and regarde of the frenche kyng, and of his Counsaile. **1589** NASHE *Martins Months minde* To Rdr., This man, like a madde dogge runneth at euerie man without regarde. **1601** DOLMAN *La Primaud. Fr. Acad.* (1618) III. 833 If he see.. an Horse come neere vnto him, he neuer taketh regard who rides him. **1625–8** tr. *Camden's Hist. Eliz.* III. (1688) 280 Beseeching him that these my.. Lamentations may now at length find Regard with you. **1764** REID *Inquiry* vi. §3 They no sooner appear, than quick as lightening the thing signified succeeds, and engrosses all our regard. **1818** JAS. MILL *Brit. India* II. v. viii. 661 The conduct pursued by the Governor-General is the next object of regard. **1881** WESTCOTT & HORT *Grk. N.T.* Introd. §10 There is no special concentration of regard upon the language.

Comb. **1632** J. HAYWARD tr. *Biondi's Eromena* 13 Finding in her at first sight regard-worthy objects, hee thought well of her.

pl. **1586** WHETSTONE *Eng. Myrror* Ded., The reach of my duetie.. simply laboreth to publish these regards, that common faults may be amended. **1665** J. SPENCER *Prodigies* ii. §3 (ed. 2) 75 We shall accordingly observe Omens.. to command the most solemn regards of Persons, whose Imagination is more busie and active then their Reason. **1758** S. HAYWARD *Serm.* xvii. 536 Creatures.. so much beneath his regards. **1770** LANGHORNE *Plutarch* (1879) I. 220/2 Socrates was the only one whose regards were fixed upon the mind. **1820** W. JAY *Prayers* 322 We.. implore thy favorable regards to the privileged country in which we live.

†**b.** Attention, care, or interest directed *to* some end. Chiefly in phr. ***to have*** or ***take regard to*** (a thing); also const. *that*. *Obs.*

1542–3 *Act 34 & 35 Hen. VIII*, c. 27 §70 Which two constables.. shall haue especial regarde to the conseruacion of the kinges peace. **1585** T. WASHINGTON tr. *Nicholay's Voy.* II. viii. 41 They haue a regarde that in the plague time no shippe.. do enter into their port. **1631** WEEVER *Anc. Funeral Mon.* To Rdr., Out of the respect I bore to venerable Antiquity, and the due regard to continue the remembrance of the defunct to future posteritie. **1699** BENTLEY *Phalaris* 407 It were no difficult contrivance, if the Publick had any regard to it, to make the English Tongue immutable.

c. Care in doing something; close attention *to* some principle or method.

1575 F. WITHER tr. *Indaquie's Chirom.* III. N vij b, They shall receive hurt by them, without great regarde be had. **1576** GASCOIGNE *Steele Gl.* (Arb.) 65 A souldiour cannot haue Too great regarde, whereon his knife should cut. **1727** BOYER *Dict. Royal* II. s.v., So great Regard [F. *circonspection*] there was amongst the Ancients in making of War. **1748** J. MASON *Elocution* 31 So much for Pauses, Emphasis, and Cadence: A careful Regard to all which is the first Rule for attaining a right Pronunciation.

7. †**a.** ***to take*** or ***have regard to*** or ***of***, to give protective attention or heed *to*, to take care *of* (a person, one's life, etc.). *Obs.*

1523 LD. BERNERS *Froiss.* I. ccvi. 99 b/2 They desyred his noblenes to take some regarde to them. **1535** COVERDALE *Ezek.* xxxiv. 8 Seynge that my shepherdes take no regarde off my shepe. **1553** GRIMALDE *Cicero's Offices* III. (1556) 145b, The man must haue regarde to his owne life, and helth. **1573** L. LLOYD *Marrow of Hist.* (1653) 185 Was not .. Alexander warned by a vision to take more regard to his life then he did? **1611** BIBLE *Tobit* iii. 15 Command some regard to be had of me, and pitie taken of me. **1671** MILTON *P.R.* II. 315 Of thee these forty days none hath regard, Forty and more deserted here indeed. **1747** WESLEY *Prim. Physic* (1762) 51, I earnestly advise every one who has any regard to his health to try this.

†**b.** The task of taking care *of*; (in) the care or charge *of* a person. *Obs. rare.*

1596 DALRYMPLE tr. *Leslie's Hist. Scot.* I. 106 *marg.*, Preistes haueng the regarde of the saules. **1611** TOURNEUR *Ath. Trag.* II. vi, Left I not My worthy Father i' the kind regard Of a most louing Uncle?

c. Care or concern *for* something.

1836 J. GILBERT *Chr. Atonem.* ix. (1852) 285 It was a free regard for our happiness which we are called to contemplate. **1871** FREEMAN *Norm. Conq.* (1876) IV. xviii. 152 Even regard for the safety of the hostages did not move men who had made up their minds not to yield.

8. a. Attention, heed, or consideration, given to a thing or person, as having an effect or influence on one's actions or conduct; respect or deference paid *to*, or entertained *for*, some authority, principle, etc. Orig. in phr. ***to have*** (†***make*** or ***take***) ***regard to***; in later use also const. *of*, *for*. †Formerly sometimes in *pl.*

c **1477** CAXTON *Jason* 20 My herte jugeth that ye shall haue grete regard unto my good wil. **1512** in Ellis *Orig. Lett.* Ser. II. I. 195 When I remembre the small regarde that dyvers made unto the saide lettyr. **1542** UDALL *Erasm. Apoph.* 231 Thei tooke no regarde vnto his woordes, but persisted in their querele & noyse makyng. **1560** DAUS tr. *Sleidane's Comm.* 6b, [He] had to little regarde to the Byshop of Rome his authoritie. **1603** KNOLLES *Hist. Turks* (1638) 53 Without regard that he had but the other day worne vpon his head the imperiall crowne. **1667** MILTON *P.L.* XII. 16 Fearing the Deitie, With some regard to what is just and right. **1744** BERKELEY *Siris* §182 A religious regard was paid to fire. **1784** COWPER *Task* IV. 679 Disclaiming all regard For mercy and the common rights of man. —— *Tiroc.* 242 Where no regard of ord'nances is shown. **1827** SOUTHEY *Penins. War* II. 288 Due regard was paid to the feelings.. of the people. **1875** JOWETT *Plato* (ed. 2) V. 31 A divine lawgiver must surely have had regard to all the different kinds of virtue.

pl. **1695** J. EDWARDS *Perfect. Script.* Ded., I now attempt to express my infinite regards and veneration of Your Grace's transcendent undertakings. **1738** WESLEY *Ps.* CIII. iv, So much his boundless Love transcends The small Regards that we can pay.

b. ***without regard*** (†***of*** or) ***to***, without (†taking heed or thought, *of* or) giving consideration or weight *to* a thing; without reference *to*.

1564 *Reg. Privy Council Scot.* I. 298 Without regaird of the propinctie of bluid. **1632** LITHGOW *Trav.* II. 68 He extorted the most part of my money.. without any regard of conscience. **1727** SWIFT *Circumcis. E. Curll* Wks. 1755 III. I. 163 The heaping together a superfluity of wealth without the least regard of applying it to its proper uses. **1736** BUTLER *Anal.* I. iii. Wks. 1874 I. 48 A disposition to produce the greatest.. happiness, without regard to persons behaviour. **1857** BUCKLE *Civiliz.* I. vii. 348 Those political writers who judge events without regard to that intellectual development of which they are but a part.

9. a. A thing or circumstance looked to, or taken into account, in determining action; a consideration, a motive.

1579 TOMSON *Calvin's Serm. Tim.* 188/2 Therfore must we haue an other regard to cause vs to come nigh to God, to wit, our Lord Iesus Christ. **1601** HOLLAND *Pliny* I. 130 Their king was alwaies chosen by the voices of the people: wherein they had these regards; that hee were aged, milde, and childlesse. **1633** BP. HALL *Hard Texts, N.T.* 24 This conjunction of Grace in the Soule doth more indeare my Mother and Kinsmen unto me than all earthly and bodily regards whatsoever. **1708** SWIFT *Predict.* 1708 Wks. 1755 II. I. 155 My fortune hath placed me above the little regard of writing for a few pence. **1790** BURKE *Fr. Rev.* Wks. V. 350 Those higher and more large regards by which alone men come to be affected. **1844–7** EMERSON *Ess., Love* Wks. (Bohn) I. 71 A benevolence which shall lose all particular regards in its general light.

†**b.** A looking *to* another in order to direct one's actions or conduct. *Obs. rare.*

1726 BUTLER *Serm. Hum. Nat.* ii. Wks. 1874 II. 34 Throw off all regards to others, and we should be quite indifferent to infamy and to honour. **1732** LAW *Serious C.* xi. (ed. 2) 163 That it will be made too anxious a state, by thus introducing a regard to God in all our actions.

10. a. Esteem, affection, kindly feeling.

1591 SHAKS. *Two Gent.* II. iv. 60 A Son, that well deserues The honor, and regard of such a father. **1667** MILTON *P.L.* I. 653 A generation, whom his choice regard Should favour equal to the Sons of Heaven. **1712** STEELE *Spect.* No. 304 ¶2, I have no Reason to fancy my Mistress has any Regard for me. **1777** SHERIDAN *Sch. Scand.* III. i, I have heard enough to convince me that he is unworthy my regard. **1828** SCOTT *F.M. Perth* xxxiii, He resolved to trust in the warm regard of Simon.. and the friendship of the Provost. **1860** TYNDALL *Glac.* I. xxvii. 219 There is no guide of my acquaintance for whom I have a stronger regard.

†**b.** A token or evidence of esteem or affection.

1747 *Col. Rec. Pennsylv.* V. 151 They were pleased with the Regards shown to them. **1829** LANDOR *Imag. Conv.*, *Barrow & Newton*, Think how gratifying.. are the regards and attentions of such wise and worthy men as you.

c. *pl.* in epistolary expressions of good-will.

1775 J. ADAMS in *Fam. Lett.* (1876) 103 My regards.. to my relations and yours. **1796** in Carus *Life Simeon* (1847) vi. 133 We all join in most affectionate and respectful regards to you. **1835** MRS. CARLYLE *Lett.* I. 29 With kindest regards to every one of you. **1847** DICKENS *Dombey* (1848) xxvi. 265 'Your regards, Edith, my dear?' said Mrs. Skewton, pausing, pen in hand, at the postscript. **1978** W. J. BURLEY *Wycliffe & Scapegoat* ix. 160 Give my regards to your father and tell him not to worry.

†**11.** A payment by way of acknowledgement. *Obs. rare.* (So med.L. *regardum*, F. *regard.*)

c **1581–90** in Willis & Clark *Cambridge* (1886) II. 411 The Towne doth receaue.. an anuall regard for the same.

III. In prepositional phrases.

12. a. ***in regard of***, in comparison with. Now *arch.* †So also ***in regard to***, ***at regard of***, (***as***) ***to*** or ***unto*** (***the***) ***regard of*** or ***to***. *Obs.*

1340 HAMPOLE *Pr. Consc.* 8114 Bot se we noght how schort a day es here To regard of a hundreth yhere? *Ibid.* 8998 Alle þir blysses.. War als noght, als to regard to þe blys of heven. *c* **1381** CHAUCER *Parl. Foules* 58 Thanne shewede he hym the litel erthe that here is At regard of the heuenys quantite. **1413** *Pilgr. Sowle* (Caxton) II. xlvi. (1859) 53 Al this erdely fyre is but thyng depeynted in regard of that other. **1481** CAXTON *Myrr.* II. i. 61 Syth that the erthe is so lytil,.. lytil may we preyse the goodes therof vnto the regard of heuen. **1523** LD. BERNERS *Froiss.* (1812) I. 322 The companyons were but a fewe in regarde to the Frenchmen. *c* **1530** —— *Arth. Lyt. Bryt.* 92 The valure of al other knyghtes wer as nothing to the regard of his noblesse. **1596** SPENSER *F.Q.* VI. xi. 14 At last when all the rest them offred were,.. They all refused in regard of her. **1630** *R. Johnson's Kingd. & Commw.* 247 He spendeth but little in the warres, in regard of that, that.. the King of Spaine disburseth. **1755** WASHINGTON *Lett.* Writ. 1889 I. 195 Sensible how confined their punishments are, in regard to what they ought to be. **1868** MORRIS *Earthly Par.* (1870) I. I. 311 In regard of mine, a little thing His kingdom was.

†**b.** ***at*** or ***in regard***, in comparison, comparatively. *Obs.*

c **1475** *Rauf Coilȝear* 652 Thay countit not the Coilȝear almaist at regaird. **1511–2** *Act 3 Hen. VIII*, c. 3 *Preamble*, Archers.. with litell nombre and puyssaunce in regarde have done many notable actes. **1540–1** ELYOT *Image Gov.* 104 Howe meruailousely did a few Romaines in regarde.. defende this little territory.

†**c.** ***as to regard of***, after the fashion of. *Obs.*

c **1500** *Doctr. Gd. Servaunts* 9 As to regarde of the fete of an harte, They sholde ever theyr mayster socoure.

13. a. ***in regard of*** or ***to***, ***with regard to***, †***as to the regard of***, in respect of, with respect or reference to.

c **1477** CAXTON *Jason* 35 The more parte of men haue no verite ne loyaulte as to the regard of loue. **1512** *Helyas* in Thoms *Prose Rom.* (1827) III. 101 As to the regarde of my londe and duchi of Boulion, I give it freely to this valiaunt knight. **1599** SHAKS. *Hen. V*, I. i. 77 In regard of Causes now in hand. **1680** BOYLE *Scept. Chem.* IV. 219 There are divers sorts of compound Bodies, even in regard of all or some of their Ingredients. **1713** BERKELEY *Hylas & Phil.* I. Wks. 1871 I. 266, I speak with regard to sensible things only. **1747** GOULD *Eng. Ants* 37 There does not seem to be any considerable Variation in regard of the Eggs. **1792** *Monthly Rev.* May VIII. 77 In regard to the matter,.. he had, no doubt, been misled. **1842** GROVE *Corr. Phys. Forces* 94 The world was believed fixed until.. it was found to change its place with regard to them. **1869** GOULBURN *Purs. Holiness* viii. 66 Of the affinity between God and Man, in regard of man's wants and God's fulness.

b. ***in one's regard***, with regard, respect, or reference to one.

1634 W. TIRWHYT tr. *Balzac's Lett.* (vol. I.) 340, I shall in mine own regard bee very glad. **1686** F. SPENCE tr. *Varillas' Ho. Medicis* 174 Nothing more was there to do than two things in his regard. **1740** tr. *De Mouhy's Fort. Country-Maid* (1741) I. 37, I was very sensible of her Coldness, or rather her Envy, in my Regard. **1821** BYRON *Let. to Murray* 24 Sept., My feelings are like the dead, who.. feel nothing.. that is said or done in their regard. **1865** F. OAKELEY *Hist. Notes* 94 If God have any other will in our regard.

†**14. a.** ***in regard of***, ***for the regard of***, for the sake of; on account of, by reason of. *Obs.*

1576 FLEMING *Panopl. Epist.* 147 A great multitude, who for the regard of their health,.. have recourse to these quarters. *a* **1604** HANMER *Chron. Irel.* (1633) 127 It would please them (some in regard of neighbourhood, othersome in regard of naturall affection unto their natiue soile). **1662** STILLINGFL. *Orig. Sacræ* II. vi. §1 A matter of very difficult tryall, in regard of the goodness.. of God so frequently interposing between the prediction and the event.

b. ***in regard of*** or ***to***, out of consideration for.

1593 SHAKS. *Rich. II*, I. iii. 216, I thanke my Liege, that in regard of me He shortens foure yeares of my sonnes exile. *a* **1677** BARROW *Serm.* Wks. 1716 III. 152 What hath occurred..to my meditation, I must at present, in regard to your patience, omit. *a* **1713** ELLWOOD *Autobiog.* (1765) 39 Although they were somewhat unwilling to yield to it, in regard of me, yet my Importunity prevailed. **1724** SWIFT *Reas. agst. Exam. Drugs*, In regard of our common Interest ..we presume to lay the following Reasons before the Publick, against the said Bill.

†**15. a.** ***in regard***, since, because, inasmuch as, considering that. *Obs.*

1591 SHAKS. *1 Hen. VI*, v. iv. 124 In regard King Henry giues consent,..To ease your Countrie of distressefull Warre. **1664** J. WEBB *Stone-Heng* (1725) 16 They could not belong to any of the circular Courses; in regard they are raised so clearly without the..Circle. **1723** CHAMBERS tr. *Le Clerc's Archit.* I. 8 The Roman Order is usually call'd the Composite, in regard its Capital is composed of the..other Orders. **1821** SCOTT *Pirate* xxviii, I cannot say that I ever saw an adder, in regard there are none in these parts.

†**b.** With *that*. *Obs.*

1615 G. SANDYS *Trav.* 83 On Saturdayes they feast, in regard that it was the old Sabboth. **1695** WOODWARD *Nat. Hist. Earth* IV. (1723) 204 In regard that..the mineral and metallick Matter..was different in different Parts of it. **1719–20** J. HUGHES in J. Duncombe *Lett.* (1773) I. 271 This is the more generous..in regard that I have given up this play to the importunity of my friends.

IV. 16. ***attrib.***, as **regard ring** (see quots.).

1889 in *Cent. Dict.* **1890** W. JONES *Finger-Ring Lore* viii. 414 'Regard rings', of French origin, were common even to a late period, and were thus named from the initials with which they were set forming the acrostic of these words: Ruby Emerald Garnet Amethyst Ruby Diamond Lapis lazuli Opal Verd antique Emerald. **1912** O. M. DALTON *Franks Bequest Catal. Finger Rings* 302 A 'regard ring', so called from the fact that the initial letters of the gems composing the bezel form that word. **1951** M. FLOWER *Victorian Jewellery* 253 *Regard ring*, a ring set with a row of small stones of different kinds, the initial letters of which spell a word. **1973** *Country Life* 29 Nov. (Suppl.) 56/1 A tiny antique 'Regard' ring, the word spelt by the first letters of the stones: ruby, emerald, garnet, amethyst, ruby and diamond. **1978** *Illustr. London News* Nov. 129/2 (*caption*) Early Victorian 'regard' ring, £140.

regard (rɪˈgɑːd), *v.* Also 6 **reguard, regarde,** 6–7 *Sc.* **regaird.** [ad. F. *regarder*, †*reguarder* (OF. also *rewarder*: see REWARD *v.*), f. *re-* RE- + *garder* to GUARD *v.*]

I. *trans.* **1. a.** To look at, gaze upon, observe.

1523 LD. BERNERS *Froiss.* I. cxci. 227 Howbeit to regarde hit the fortresse was impregnable, yet he wanne hit by scalynge. **1539** TONSTALL *Serm. Palm Sund.* (1823) 91 We that haue vsed our eyes all the yere in regardyng worldly pleasures. **1599** SHAKS. *Much Ado* v. iv. 22 Your neece regards me with an eye of fauour. *a* **1677** BARROW *Serm.* (1683) II. vi. 91 Who doth attently regard a locust or a caterpillar? **1713** YOUNG *Last Day* III. 106 Th' almighty judge bends foreward from his throne, These scars to mark, and then regards his own. **1813** SHELLEY *Q. Mab* VI. 216 Thou Regard'st them all with an impartial eye. **1878** H. M. STANLEY *Dark Cont.* II. xiii. 367 He..drove his axe into the tree with a vigour which was delightful to regard.

†**b.** Of places, etc.: To look or face toward.

1585 T. WASHINGTON tr. *Nicholay's Voy.* II. ii. 32 b, This Ile..regardeth towards yᵉ west yᵉ cape Malee. **1645** EVELYN *Diary* June (Venice), One of the sides is yet much more Roman-like than the other which reguards the Sea. **1693** *Mem. Cnt. Teckely* IV. 61 The Right Wing attacked those, who regarded the Camp of the Imperialists. **1750** *Phil. Trans.* XLVI. 346, I hastened to the other Front [of the house], which regards the NE.

2. To take notice of, bestow attention or notice upon; to take or show an interest in; to give heed to; †to look after, take care of.

c **1430** LYDG. *Min. Poems* (Percy Soc.) 104 Many I found earnyng of pence, But none at all once regarded mee. ?*a* **1500** *Chester Pl.* xiii. 27 Other sheep I haue,..they be not of this flocke, yet will I them regarde. **1526** TINDALE *Heb.* viii. 9 They continued nott in my testament, and I regarded them not sayth the lorde. **1592** SHAKS. *Ven. & Ad.* 377 Then loue's deep groans, I neuer shall regard, Because Adonis heart hath made mine hard. **1548–9** (Mar.) *Bk. Com. Prayer, Publ. Baptism*, Regarde we beseche thee, the supplicacions of thy congregacion. **1648** MILTON *Ps.* lxxxii. 9 Regard the weak and fatherless. **1671** —— *Samson* 1157 Presume not on thy God, what e're he be, Thee he regards not. **1738** WESLEY *Ps.* v. i, 'Till thou regard my ceaseless Cries. **1834** DISRAELI *Revol. Epick* II. xxiv, As the shells upon the silent shore, That none regardeth.

†**3. a.** To look to, have a care of or for (oneself, one's own interest, health, etc.). *Obs.*

1494 FABYAN *Chron.* v. cxvii. 92 Thou well knowest our owne [part] is moost to be regardyd. **1509** HAWES *Past. Pleas.* XLV. (Percy Soc.) 219 Set not your mynde upon worldly wealth, But evermore regarde your soules health. **1560** DAUS tr. *Sleidane's Comm.* 27 Admonisheth al men that regarde theyr salvation, to beware of that Bishoppes kyndom. **1576** FLEMING *Panopl. Epist.* 40 It is my..desire, that you regard your owne health. **1671** MILTON *Samson* 1333 Regard thyself, this will offend them highly.

b. To look to, consider, take into account.

1591 SHAKS. *Two Gent.* III. i. 256 As thou lou'st Siluia.. Regard thy danger, and along with me. **1615** W. LAWSON *Country Housew. Gard.* (1626) 50 It is good for some purposes to regard the age of your fruit trees. **1628–9** DIGBY *Voy. Medit.* (Camden) 91 For the soundinges..the depths and the substance of the ground that you bring vp are to be regarded. **1642** FULLER *Holy & Prof. St.* III. vii. 168 Beauty remains behind as the last to be regarded.

4. †**a.** To take notice of (a thing), as being of special value, excellence, or merit; to value or set store by. *Obs.*

1509 FISHER *Funeral Serm. C'tess Richmond* Wks. (1876) 291 Tryfelous thynges that were lytell to be regarded she wolde let passe by. **1535** COVERDALE *1 Kings* x. 21 All kynge Salomons drynkynge vessels were of golde,..for syluer was not regarded in Salomons tyme. **1582** STANYHURST *Æneis* II. (Arb.) 46 Then we were of reckning; our feats weare duelye regarded. **1604** E. G[RIMSTONE] *D'Acosta's Hist. Indies* I. xxii. 72 Origene, who so much regardes the writings of Plato. **1638** JUNIUS *Paint. Ancients* 80 It did grieve him to see how little the rare workes of Protogenes were regarded. *a* **1656** HALES *Gold. Rem.* I. (1673) 241 But, for that superfluous stuff of the world, he wills us not to regard that.

b. To hold (a person) in great (†respect or) esteem; to have a regard for (one).

1513 MORE in Grafton *Chron.* (1568) II. 785 They were before greatly esteemed among the people, but after that, neuer none of these two were regarded. *a* **1548** HALL *Chron., Hen. VIII* 105 b, For refusyng of this office therle of Northumberland was not regarded of his owne tenauntes. **1647** N. BACON *Disc. Govt. Eng.* I. lix. (1739) 115 Thus the English Bishops that formerly did but regard Rome, now give their Estates, Bodies and Souls unto her service. **1675** BAXTER *Cath. Theol.* II. XI. ii. 226 Why do you and all men regard or reward a loving thankful obedient child..? **1702** STEELE *Funeral* I. (1724) 25, I have in vain done all I can to make her regard me. **1775** SHERIDAN *Duenna* I. i, She does not regard you enough. **1848** THACKERAY *Van. Fair* xxiii, I regard him so much—for you know we have been like brothers—that I hope..the quarrel may be settled.

5. a. To heed, or take into account, in regulating one's actions or conduct.

1512 *Act 4 Hen. VIII*, c. 2 *Preamble*, The persons so offendyng litell regarde the punysshment therof by..the Comen lawe. **1560** DAUS tr. *Sleidane's Comm.* 4 b, Regarding the authoritie of no man. *Ibid.* 34 We ought not to regard such inconveniences. **1611** BIBLE *Ecclus.* x. 19 They that regard not the Law are a dishonourable seed. **1667** MILTON *P.L.* IX. 787 Eve Intent now wholly on her taste, naught else Regarded. **1713** STEELE *Englishm.* No. 55. 356 They regard not speaking Truth, but making their Fortunes. **1875** JOWETT *Plato* (ed. 2) V. 109 The perfect citizen is he who regards not only the laws but the precepts of the legislator.

b. To have respect for or dread of (a person).

1526 TINDALE *Luke* xviii. 2 There was a Iudge in a certaine cite, which feared not god nether regarded man. **1549** LATIMER *2nd Serm. bef. Edw. VI* (Arb.) 73 Regarde no person, feare no man. **1591** SHAKS. *1 Hen. VI*, I. iii. 60 Here's Beauford, that regards not God nor King. **1868** FREEMAN *Norm. Conq.* (1876) II. viii. 210 Tyrants who neither fear God nor regard man.

c. To pay heed or attention to (one speaking or something said).

1535 COVERDALE *Zech.* i. 4 They wolde not heare, ner regarde me, saieth the Lorde. **1596** SHAKS. *1 Hen. IV*, I. ii. 97 Hee talk'd very wisely, but I regarded him not. **1667** MILTON *P.L.* XII. 174 The lawless Tyrant, who denies To know thir God, or message to regard. *a* **1715** BURNET *Own Time* II. (1724) I. 213 The Earl..said, he knew Sharp too well to regard any thing that came from him. **1728** T. SHERIDAN tr. *Persius* Ded., Having so faithfully regarded the last Advice, which I gave you.

d. To show consideration for (a thing or person).

1513 MORE in Grafton *Chron.* (1568) II. 769 Which Sanctuary good men as me thinketh might without sinne, somwhat lesse regard then they do. **1671** MILTON *P.R.* III. 427 Should I of these the liberty regard..? **1788** GIBBON *Decl. & F.* l. V. 229 Without regarding the sanctity of days or months, to pursue the unbelieving nations of the earth. **1865** TENNYSON *Love thou thy land* 24 Gentle words are always gain; Regard the weakness of thy peers. **1871** FREEMAN *Norm. Conq.* (1876) IV. xvii. 13 We may be led to think that the rights of England were..strictly regarded.

6. a. To consider, look on, *as* being something. Also occas. with other constructions. (Now the most usual sense.)

1607 SHAKS. *Cor.* v. vi. 144 Let him be regarded As the most Noble Coarse, that euer Herald Did follow to his Vrne. *a* **1719** ADDISON (Ogilvie), They are not only regarded as authors, but as partisans. **1781** COWPER *Prog. Err.* 148 If he the tinkling harpsichord regards As inoffensive, what offence in cards? **1836** J. GILBERT *Chr. Atonem.* vii. (1852) 194 Whatever constitutes atonement, therefore, must..be regarded a safe..remedy. **1853** F. W. NEWMAN *Odes of Horace* 7 Dr. Leonard Schmitz regards it to indicate the looseness of popular opinion. **1856** FROUDE *Hist. Eng.* (1858) I. ii. 120 The interests of the nation..entitled him to regard his position under another aspect. **1877** —— *Short Stud.* (1883) IV. I. iii. 39 He regarded his submission as the end of the dispute.

b. To look upon *with* some feeling.

1615 SIR W. MURE *Misc. Poems* xiv. 17 That hyer Powares be wᵗ feir regairdit. **1784** COWPER *Tiroc.* 156 The stamp of artless piety..The youth..Regards with scorn. **1833** HT. MARTINEAU *Manch. Strike* v. 62 The shortest way to a good issue was to regard the claims of the people with respect. **1884** *Manch. Exam.* 22 May 5/2 A war which the great majority of the nation regarded with unaffected dislike.

7. a. To concern, have relation or respect to.

1603 B. JONSON *Sejanus* v. v, Business of high nature with your lordship,..and which regards you much. **1709** STEELE *Tatler* No. 72 ¶1, I have few Notices but such as regard Follies and Vices. **1739** HUME *Hum. Nat.* (1874) I. Introd. 307 Morals and criticism regard our tastes and sentiments. **1819** SHELLEY *Cenci* IV. iv. 47 The deed is done, And what may follow now regards not me. **1865** CARLYLE *Fredk. Gt.* XVIII. v. (1872) VII. 176 If these things regarded only myself, I could stand it with composure.

b. In *pres. pple.* Concerning, relating to.

1793 SMEATON *Edystone L.* §307 Every thing, regarding the light, operated in a proper manner. **1897** W. J. TUCKER *E. Europe* 194, I have an advantageous offer to make him regarding the cattle.

c. ***as regards, as regarding***, so far as relates to.

1824 SOUTHEY *Bk. of Ch.* (1841) 408 That Church, and the Queen, its refounder, are clear of persecution, as regards the Romanists. **1884** BROWNING *Ferishtah's Fancies* 111, I am in motion, and all things beside That circle round my passage through their midst,—Motionless, these are, as regarding me. **1885** *Law Times Rep.* LII. 651/1 He was in a thoroughly sound condition as regards intellect.

II. 8. *absol.* or *intr.* **a.** To look, gaze. *rare.*

1523 LD. BERNERS *Froiss.* I. ccxxxvii. 338 Then the prince of Wales opened his Eyen and regarded towarde heuen. **1847** TENNYSON *Princ.* IV. 363 We with blind surmise Regarding, while she read.

b. To pay attention, give heed; to bestow attention *on* a thing.

1611 BIBLE *Prov.* i. 24, I haue stretched out my hand, and no man regarded. **1667** MILTON *P.L.* v. 44 Now reignes Full Orb'd the Moon..; in vain, If none regard. **1747** WESLEY *Prim. Physic* (1762) 118 Regard not tho' it prick or shoot for a time. **1784** COWPER *Task* VI. 1019 In vain the poet sings, and the world hears, If He regard not. **1855** DE MORGAN in Graves *Life Hamilton* (1889) III. 502 Airy, regarding thereon, found out a more simple mode.

†**9. a.** To consider. Also with dep. clause. *Obs.*

1523 LD. BERNERS *Froiss.* (1812) I. 716 It behoveth us to regarde wisely, and to take counsayle in this mater. *a* **1533** —— *Huon* lxxxii. 255 Therfore, sir, regarde well in what place ye wyll haue one of your peeres iugyd.

b. To look *to*; to refer *to*. *Obs.*

1525 LD. BERNERS *Froiss.* II. lxxxiv. 96/2 Refrayne your euyll wyll and moderate your courage and regarde to reason. *a* **1586** SIDNEY *Arcadia* (1613) 269 The under ones..cannot, by nature, regard to any preservation but of themselves. **1659** H. L'ESTRANGE *Alliance Div. Off.* 249 To this custome the Angel in the Revelation is thought to regard.

†**10.** Const. with *inf.* **a.** To endeavour, seek, or plan. *Obs. rare*⁻¹.

a **1533** LD. BERNERS *Gold. Bk. M. Aurel.* (1536–7) H j b, They that be yll, regarde to distroy the good.

b. To take heed or care. *Obs.*

1542 UDALL *Erasm. Apoph.* 333 Thei neither regarded to sette hym to schoole, nor..to paie his schoolemaisters duetie. **1577** B. GOOGE *Heresbach's Husb.* I. (1586) 41 b, In reapyng, you must regarde to goe with the wynde. **1642** J. EATON *Honey-c. Free Justif.* 202 Little remembering and lesse regarding to lay the blame where it is. **1673** S. C. *Art of Complaisance* 17 They who play at Tennis..regard not onely to toss back the ball dextrously, but also [etc.].

c. To be inclined or desirous. *Obs. rare*⁻¹.

1550 BALE *Image Both Ch.* III. xviii. B b b iij b, Neyther regarde they to kneele anye more downe and to kisse their pontificall rings.

d. To be concerned, to reck. *Obs. rare.*

1557 NORTH *Gueuara's Diall Pr.* 23 For covetous parsons lytle regard to shorten their life, so that they may augment their ryches. *c* **1600** *Constance of Cleveland* in Child *Ballads* (1857) IV. 229 The Knight nothing regarded To see the Lady scoffed.

†**11.** Const. with *that*. **a.** To see to it; to take care. *Obs. rare*⁻¹.

c **1550** R. BIESTON *Bayte Fortune* B iv, But yet he must regarde,..That all his goodes be got by way of rightousnes.

b. To consider, take into account. *Obs.*

1586 A. DAY *Eng. Secretary* I. (1625) A 2 b, Regarding that by a reuiew of the same, it hath now receiued some shape, and proportion. **1591** SHAKS. *Two Gent.* III. i. 70 Neither regarding that she is my childe, Nor fearing me.

c. To appreciate, to think it well. *Obs.*⁻¹

1621 BP. MOUNTAGU *Diatribæ* 385 Those..will not much admire, nor yet greatly regard, that a Patron of Sacriledge for Lay-Vsurpers, should become a Practiser for Lay-elders.

12. To look, appear. *rare*⁻¹.

1819 SHELLEY *Prometh. Unb.* IV. 213 The hills and woods ..Regard like shapes in an enchanter's glass.

Hence **reˈgarded** *ppl. a.*

1586 WHETSTONE *Eng. Myrror* Ded., It then followeth, most regarded Queene, that the reach of my duetie [etc.]. **1596** SHAKS. *Merch. V.* II. i. 10 The best regarded Virgins of our Clime Haue lou'd it to.

re-gard: see REGUARD *v.*

reˈgardable, *a.* ? *Obs.* [f. REGARD *v.* + -ABLE, or a. F. *regardable* (14th c.).] Worthy of being regarded, noticeable. (Common in 17th c.)

1591 SPENSER *Muiopot.* Ded., Nor for name or kindreds sake by you vouchsafed, being also regardable. **1602** CAREW *Cornwall* 144 Generally, it is more regardable for profit, then commendable for pleasure. **1656** [? J. SERGEANT] tr. *T. White's Peripat. Inst.* 261 Seeing these objects to be unworthy and not regardable. **1704** NORRIS *Ideal World* II. vi. 321 These mean and ignoble essences,..the less regardable pieces of his workmanship. **1785** *Hist. York* II. 293 A circumstance not regardable by any but a true antiquary.

†**reˈgardage.** *Obs. rare*⁻¹. [? f. REGUARD *v.* + -AGE.] ? An allowance for providing fresh guards for robes.

1684 E. CHAMBERLAYNE *Pres. St. Eng.* II. (ed. 15) 272 Note that out of the Sergeants afore-mentioned, the King by Writ usually calls some to be of his Council at Law, allowing each one wadage, feodage, vesturage and regardage.

regardance: see NON-REGARDANCE.

†**reˈgardancy.** *Obs. rare.* [See next and -ANCY.] The fact of being regardant.

1628 COKE *On Litt.* 124 b, The law doth favor the villein in this issue..for otherwise he ought to answer to the speciall matter, viz. to the regardancy. **1771** in Howell *State Trials* (1814) XX. 42 Regardancy necessarily implies prescription.

regardant (rɪˈgɑːdənt), *a.* and *sb.* Also 6 (9) **-aunt, -and.** [a. F. *regardant*, pres. pple. of *regarder* to REGARD.]

A. *adj.* **1.** *Law* (now only *Hist.*) Attached to a manor; only in ***villein regardant*** (†also const. *to*).

[**1316** *Year Bk. 9 Edw. II, Trin.* 294 Le manoir de H... a quel manoir cest vileyn est regardant. **1356** *Ibid. 29 Edw. III, Trin.* (1561) 41 b, Villeyns regardants al maneres sont de droyt al seignour de prendre lez a sa volunte.]

1443–50 in Baildon *Sel. Cas. Chanc.* (1896) 135 He and his auncestres.. haue been seised of the said John Bysship and of his auncestres as villeyns regardantz to the said Maner fro the tyme that no mynde is. **1531** *Dial. on Laws Eng.* I. xx. 33 b, But he hathe nother ryghte to the aduowsons appendaunt if any be, nor to the vylleyns regardant. *a* **1577** SIR T. SMITH *Commw. Eng.* II. viii. (1584) 108 These were not bond to the person but to the mannor or place,.. and in our lawe are called villaines regardantes. **1628** COKE *On Litt.* II. ii. §189. 123 b, And there is no diuersitie herein whether he be a villeine regardant, or in grosse although some haue said the contrarie. **1766** BLACKSTONE *Comm.* II. vi. 93 These villeins, belonging principally to lords of manors, were either villeins regardant, that is, annexed to the manor or land; or else they were in gross. **1818** HALLAM *Mid. Ages* viii. (1868) 569 The statute de donis must have operated very injuriously to prevent the enfranchisement of villeins regardant. **1892** VINOGRADOFF *Villainage in Eng.* I. i. 48 Most modern writers on the subject have laid stress upon a difference between *villains regardant* and *villains in gross*, said to be found in law books.

†**b.** *transf.* Bound or subject *to* something. *Obs.*

1651 N. BACON *Disc. Govt. Eng.* II. xxxvii. 167 Whereas formerly Bishops were regardant both to the Crown and Presbytery,.. now they are made the birth of the King's own breath.

2. *Her.* Looking backward.

c **1500** *Sc. Poem Heraldry* 130 in *Q. Eliz. Acad.*, etc. 98 First, a lionne [statant]; on-vthir, lyone rampand;.. the viij dormand; the ix regardand is. **1562** LEIGH *Armorie* 83 He beareth Azure .ij. Lyons passaunt regardant, Or. *Ibid.* 83 b, Some haue thought, that these Lyons be regardaunt, whereof by proofe, you see the contrarye. **1594** KYD *Cornelia* v. 207 Passant regardant softly they [two lions] retyre. **1610** GUILLIM *Heraldry* III. xxvi. 184 Hee beareth or, a Lion Rampand, Regardant Sable,.. This action doth manifest an inward and degenerate perturbation of the mind. **1864** BOUTELL *Her. Hist. & Pop.* x. (ed. 3) 58 The Lion Passant Reguardant.. looks back to the Sinister. *Ibid.* xxxii. 474 Two griffins reguardant sa., crowned or.

transf. *a* **1502** in Arnolde *Chron.* (1811) 239 Frumenty and venyson, syngnet rosted, graunt luce in sarris, roo roested regardaunt, feusaunt roosted [etc.].

3. Observant, watchful, contemplative.

1588 KYD *Househ. Phil.* Wks. (1901) 242, I might shew myselfe mindful and regardant. **1630** B. JONSON *New Inn* IV. iv, You might haue known that by my looks, and language, Had you been or regardant, or observant. **1814** SOUTHEY *Roderick* XI, The heroic Prince (who passing now.. the dangerous track, Turns thither his regardant eye). **1834** —— *Doctor* (1848) 1/1 The look which accompanied the words was rather cogitative than regardant.

†**b.** Full of regard or consideration. *Obs.*

1647 N. BACON *Disc. Govt. Eng.* I. lvii. (1739) 105 Towards his Lay-Subjects he was more regardant for the settling of Laws, and executing of Justice.

4. ? Looking towards each other. *rare*$^{-1}$.

1856 J. C. ROBINSON *Catal. Soulages Collection* 133 An unfinished relievo of two regardant portraits of a lady and gentleman exists at the back of the slab.

B. *sb.* † **1.** A beholder, spectator. *Obs.* (So also F. *regardant.*)

1596 Z. J. tr. *Lavardin's Hist. Scanderbeg* 8 An incredible kind of care intermingled with griefe did assaile the hearts of the regardants. **1602** MUNDAY *Palmerin of Eng.* xii, To the no small pleasure of the Emperor and his nobility as also the regardants.

2. A villein regardant, a serf. ? *Obs.*

1795 BURKE *Regic. Peace* iv. Wks. IX. 72 The Helots of Laconia, the Regardants to the Manor in Russia and in Poland, even the Negroes in the West Indies, know nothing of.. so penetrating, so heart-breaking a slavery.

regarder (rɪˈgɑːdə(r)). Also 6 -or. [f. REGARD *v.* + -ER[1], in early use after AF. *regardour*, med.L. *reg(u)ardor* and *regardator*.]

1. An officer charged with the supervision of a forest. Now only *local* and *Hist.*

[**1217** (see REGARD *sb.* 3). ? **1278** in *Stat. Realm* (1810) I. 244/2 Licitum est ei.. habere.. tot porcos quot boscus per visum forestariorum & viridariorum Regardatorum agistatorum & aliorum proborum hominum possit pati [etc.]. **1312** *Rolls of Parlt.* I. 283/1 Que les Forestiers.. presentent meismes les trespas as precheins Swanimotz devaunt Forestiers, Verdiers, Regardours, Agistours, & autres Ministres de meismes les Forestes.]

1502 ARNOLDE *Chron.* (1811) 210 Noo forestir.. make any gaderyng, but be the sight and othe of xij. regarders when they make regard. **1523** FITZHERB. *Surv.* 28 b, The kepars, regarders, goysters, and other offycers of suche forest and chases. **1594** CROMPTON *Jurisd.* 169 If a man be indited of Trespasse done in the forrest before verdors, regardors, agistors, and other Ministers of the Forrest [etc.]. **1615** MANWOOD *Lawes Forest* (ed. 2) xxi. §3. 193 b, It seemeth that at that time [Hen. II] no man was called to the place of a Regarder but he that was a Knight. **1667–8** *Act 19 & 20 Chas. II*, c. 8 §5 New Elections shall be made.. of all Verderors, Reguarders and other Officers of and for the Governing of the said Forrest [of Dean]. **1796** *Sporting Mag.* VIII. 164 Mr. Renshaw, one of the regarders of the New Forest. **1840** *Penny Cycl.* XVI. 175/1 The verderers and regarders are chosen by the freeholders of Hampshire. *Ibid.* The regarders.. attend the marking of all trees to be felled, value the timber for sale [etc.]. **1865** *Morn. Star* 13 Apr., The Crown has neglected to appoint a warden, forester, regarder, and verderer of the said [Epping] forest. **1882** *Spectator* 18 Feb. 227/1 If you extinguish the regarder, you extinguish with it the regard.

2. One who or that which regards; †a spectator.

1525 LD. BERNERS *Froiss.* II. lxii. [lxv.] 209 Al theyr feats were nobly accomplysshed, to the grete pleasure of all the lordes and ladyes and other regarders. **1542** RECORDE *Gr. Artes* Pref. a ij b, Where so fewe regarders of learnynge are, howe greately they are to bee estemed that doeth fauour and further it. **1598** FLORIO, *Riguardatore*,.. a regarder. **1630** LENNARD tr. *Charron's Wisd.* I. liii. (1670) 190 Where there is neither Judge nor Controller, nor regarder. **1682** SOUTHERNE *Loyal Brother* I. i, Thou kind regarder of my Fame. **1804** COLLINS *Scripscrap* 97 Old Reynard kept a Larder, Of neighbours' wants a kind regarder.

regardful (rɪˈgɑːdfʊl), *a.* [f. REGARD *sb.*]

1. Heedful, attentive, observant.

a **1586** SIDNEY *Arcadia* II. (1622) 103 The sexe of woman-kinde.. is most bound to haue regardfull eyes to mens iudgements. **1610** GUILLIM *Heraldry* VI. i. (1611) 251 For the better instruction of the regardfull reader. **1657** BAXTER *Call to Unconverted* Wks. (1846) 168 You will hear such a message with more awakened regardful hearts. **1715** POPE *Iliad* I. 287 With regardful ear 'Tis just, O goddess! I thy dictates hear. **1827** HOOD *Mids. Fairies* xlii, The dear curl on a regardful brow. **1849** RUSKIN *Sev. Lamps.* v. §22. 158 The difference, when the touches are rude and few, between those of a careless and those of a regardful mind.

b. Const. *of*, †*to.*

1611 SPEED *Hist. Gt. Brit.* VII. xxviii. (1623) 369 A great number.. who were more intentiue and regardfull to the Feast, than to any defence. **1653** GATAKER *Vind. Annot. Jer.* 14 They ar more regardful of their worldly gain.. then they ar of a good conscience. **1748** RICHARDSON *Clarissa* (1811) III. xlvi. 267 A libertine in his riper years, hardly regardful of appearances. *c* **1850** NEALE *Hymns East. Ch.* (1866) 109 Regardful of that day. **1876** FARRAR *Marlb. Serm.* i. 7 A life regardful of duty is crowned with an object, directed by a purpose.

2. Respectful; indicative of regard or esteem.

1607 *Schol. Disc. agst. Antichr.* I. i. 27 The very name it selfe of an Idoll ought to be left, and euery regardfull remembrance of him. **1651** JER. TAYLOR *Holy Dying* iv. §8 To use all.. persons upon whom his name is called.. with a regardful and separate manner of usage. **1707** NORRIS *Treat. Humility* vi. 228 Much more should we his poor petitioners on earth, put up our humble supplications to him with the most regardful concern. **1821** SCOTT *Kenilw.* iii, The drawer says—'Coming, friend', without any more reverence or regardful addition. **1872** BLACKIE *Lays Highl.* 69 Was it a lady fair.. to whom Her lord, with proud, regardful grief, Upreared this stately tomb?

†**3.** Worthy of regard or attention. *Obs.*

1621 BP. MOUNTAGU *Diatribæ* 219 Their authority in the Church is so awfull, and so regardfull, that it will much preiudice your Negatiue against their Affirmatiue. **1650** GENTILIS *Considerations* 89 Taking away honorable and regardfull subjects, whose valour and worth are the Sanctuary to which wronged subjects flye.

reˈgardfully, *adv.* [f. prec. + -LY[2].] Attentively, respectfully.

1607 SHAKS. *Timon* IV. iii. 81 Is this th' Athenian Minion, whom the world Voic'd so regardfully? **1647** CLARENDON *Hist. Reb.* VII. §144 He thought himself not regardfully enough used. **1685** BAXTER *Paraphr. N.T.* Mark iv. 23 Let him.. see that he hear God's word regardfully. **1821** *Examiner* 12/2 Fixing public attention most regardfully upon the loftiest of its objects.

So **reˈgardfulness**.

1571 GOLDING *Calvin on Ps.* x. 4 The beginning of weldooing in all a man's whole lyfe is regardfulnesse. **1611** W. SCLATER *Key* (1629) 112 That reuerent esteeme, and regardfulnesse in vsing, as is due to such ordinances. *a* **1864** J. D. BURNS *Memoir & Remains* (1869) 290 With strong and unwearied regardfulness for me.

reˈgarding, *vbl. sb.* [f. REGARD *v.* + -ING[1].] The action of the vb.; †distinction.

1526 *Pilgr. Perf.* (W. de W. 1531) 157 b, With lytell regardyng of our duty. **1611** COTGR., *Regardement*, a.. regarding. *c* **1680** *Roxb. Ball.* (1891) VII. 468 He told her that he would marry with she, for he was a Man of regarding. **1885** *Athenæum* 19 Sept. 368/2 The contemplative regarding of modern life.

†**reˈgardively**, *adv.* *Obs.* *rare*$^{-1}$. [irreg. f. REGARD *v.*] Attentively.

1602 WARNER *Alb. Eng.* XIII. lxxviii. 324 Thy vnderstanding Minde.. casts and conceiues the Sum: And all th' aforesaid Vnities, regardiuely, obserues.

regardless (rɪˈgɑːdlɪs), *a.* [f. REGARD *sb.*]

1. a. Heedless, indifferent, careless, without regard *of*. †Also const. *at*, *for*, *to*.

1591 SPENSER *Muiopot.* 384 He likest is to fall into mischaunce, That is regardles of his governaunce. **1667** MILTON *P.L.* III. 408 Regardless of the Bliss wherein hee sat. **1725** MANDEVILLE *Ess. Charity* in *Fab. Bees*, etc. I. 305 Reprobate parents that take ill courses and are regardless to [1723 of] their children. **1743** BULKELEY & CUMMINS *Voy. S. Seas* Pref. 16 Indolent and regardless for the Preservation of the People. **1756** TOLDERVY *Hist. 2 Orphans* IV. 153 Would.. the soldier be regardless at the thundering of cannon? **1784** COWPER *Task* II. 775 Regardless of her charge, She needs herself correction. **1863** GEO. ELIOT *Romola* xix, A man who had been openly regardless of religious rites.

b. Without const. (Chiefly in attrib. use.)

1601 YARINGTON *Two Lament. Trag.* F ij b, Grim imperious death, Reguardlesse instrument of cruell fate. *c* **1695** J. MILLER *Descr. New York* (1843) 7 The most part ignorant and conceited, fickle and regardless. **1718** POPE *Iliad* XVI. 659 What thoughts, regardless chief! thy breast employ? **1784** COWPER *Task* V. 350 You the regardless author of its woes. **1868** WHITTIER *Among the Hills* Prel. 78 Treading the May-flowers with regardless feet.

c. *ellipt.* (passing into *adv.*) for 'regardless of expense' or 'regardless of consequences', used postpositively. orig. *U.S.* Phr. ***to press on regardless***: see PRESS *v.*[1] 14 a.

1872 'MARK TWAIN' *Roughing It* xlvii. 334 We are going to get the thing [*sc.* a funeral] up regardless, you know. **1896** *Advance* (Chicago) 30 July 150 Miss Bond got herself up regardless, and came in resplendent in ruby velvet and white swansdown. **1898** J. D. BRAYSHAW *Slum Silhouettes* 40 Who do yer think is down 'ere, got up regardless? D'Arcy's mash, Daisy Chapman. **1911** H. QUICK *Yellowstone Nights* xi. 289 We got a bulletin from his doctors and messages from him to rush S.F. 41144 to its passage, regardless, or he'd accept a bid he'd got for the Bottle Imp. **1920** W. J. LOCKE *House of Baltazar* xvii. 205 I've a jolly good mind to set him up regardless, like a pre-war nut. **1928** T. E. LAWRENCE *Let.* 16 Apr. (1938) 587, I thought some plutocrat publisher was backing you, regardless: the price he offered was so fantastic. **1928** E. O'NEILL *Strange Interlude* II. 58 *Evans.* (*Blundering on regardless now.*) I know it's hardly the proper time—. **1940** M. DICKENS *Mariana* iii. 63 'It's a shilling. Is that too much?' He laughed at her. 'I told you—we're dining out regardless to-night.' **1960** *Observer* 24 July 17/6 What a marvellous feeling when you find the boat is sailing on regardless. **1962** *Listener* 19 Apr. 687/2 The microphone picks everything up, and transmits it regardless. **1980** J. SCOTT *Gospel Lamb* vii. 103 San fairy anne, as the Frogs used to say. He was clobbered, regardless.

2. Unregarded, slighted; unworthy of regard.

a **1591** H. SMITH *Wks.* (1867) I. 153 A precious head-tire, which all day is worn,.. but at night that riches is laid aside, and the head muffled with some regardless tire. **1611** SPEED *Theat. Gt. Brit.* (1614) 107/2 From a princely castle [it] is become no better then a regardlesse cottage. **1697** CONGREVE *Mourn. Bride* II. ix, Zara.. Is a regardless suppliant, now, to Osmyn. **1714** H. GROVE *Spect.* No. 626 ¶7 They dazzle every one but the Possessor: To him that is accustomed to them they are cheap and regardless Things. **1853** G. JOHNSTON *Nat. Hist. E. Bord.* I. 154 Producing a very pleasing and picturesque effect with materials, which, separately viewed, are of a mean and regardless character.

reˈgardlessly, *adv.* [f. prec. + -LY[2].] In a regardless manner.

1601 WEEVER *Mirr. Mart.* E iij, With watrie lockes about her shoulders spred Regardlessely. **1676** TOWERSON *Decalogue* 143 His Name [is].. not either slightly or regardlesly to be mentioned. **1814** SOUTHEY *Roderick* XXI, Time was when in our fathers' ways we walk'd Regardlessly alike.

reˈgardlessness. [f. as prec. + -NESS.] Heedlessness, carelessness.

1611 W. SCLATER *Key* (1629) 280 Regardlesnesse of choyse in marriage. **1681** FLAVEL *Meth. Grace* Ep. Ded. 14 Such is the supineness and inexcusable regardlessness of most men. *a* **1732** T. BOSTON *Crook in Lot* (1805) 61 With a holy contempt and regardlessness of the hardships. **1823** SOUTHEY *Penins. War* I. 422 It was.. shocking to humanity to behold their sufferings, and the cruel regardlessness of their comrades. **1875** JOWETT *Plato* (ed. 2) III. 105 This exclusive love of freedom and regardlessness of everything else.

†**reˈgardship.** *Obs.* *rare*$^{-1}$. [f. REGARD *sb.*] Consideration, carefulness.

1494 FABYAN *Chron.* VII. 644 This Lewis.. wolde goo more lyker a yoman.. than lyke a prynce: yᵉ which was for no regardshyp nor sparynge of good.

reˈgarment, *v.* [RE- 5 a.] To clothe anew.

1814 CARY *Dante, Par.* XIV. 39 Our shape, regarmented with glorious weeds, Of saintly flesh.

reˈgarnish (riː-), *v.* [In early use ad. F. *regarniss-*, *regarnir*; later f. RE- 5 a + GARNISH *v.*] *trans.* To garnish afresh.

1480 CAXTON *Ovid's Met.* XIV. viii, Ulixes dyde do repayre & regarnysshe hys shyppes. **1611** COTGR., *Regarnir*, to regarnish, to new furnish. *a* **1680** CHARNOCK *Attrib. God* (1834) II. 382 Not regarnishing an earthly, but providing a richer palace. **1901** CLIVE HOLLAND *Mousmé* 67 The surface of the earth regarnished with jewels of flowers.

regasify (riːˈgæsɪfaɪ), *v.* Also **re-gasify**. [RE- 5 b.] *trans.* To convert back into gas.

1926 [implied in REGASIFIED *ppl. a.* below]. **1940** *Gas Age* 24 Oct. 47/1 The liquefied natural gas would be stored in special insulated tanks, to be withdrawn.. and regasified when need arose. **1946** *Nature* 20 July 105/2 The methane would be extracted and stored as liquid at periods of low demand, and re-gasified to enrich water gas at periods of high demand. **1967** *Sci. Amer.* Oct. 32/1 Natural gas is liquefied, stored and regasified for use in a city on days of peak demand.

So **reˈgasified** *ppl. a.*; also **regasifiˈcation**, the action or process of regasifying.

1926 R. W. LAWSON tr. *Hevesy & Paneth's Man. Radioactivity* xxiii. 167 The uncondensed impurities (nitrogen, hydrogen, rare gases) are then pumped off, and after removal of the liquid air, the regasified emanation is allowed to stream into the vessel in which it is to be used. **1940** *Oil & Gas Jrnl.* Oct. 51/1 We began an intensive study of natural-gas liquefaction, its storage and subsequent regasification. **1967** *Sci. Amer.* Oct. 32/1 Regasification involves heating liquid natural gas (*LNG*), which is at a temperature of −259 degrees Fahrenheit, so that it vaporizes and is raised to a safe temperature of 40 degrees F. **1978** *Liquefied Natural Gas* (Shell Internat. Petroleum Co.) 8 The heat required for re-gasification can be taken from a variety of sources—sea water, power station effluent or gas-fired heaters.

reˈgather, *v.* [RE- 5 a; cf. RECOLLECT *v.*[1] 2.]

1. a. *trans.* To collect or bring together again.

1589 GREENE *Menaphon* (Arb.) 66 At length regathering his spirits.. he strained foorth this dittie. **1598** BARRET *Theor. Warres* V. i. 140 Having regathered his disordered troupes. **1676** OTWAY *Don Carlos* III. i, I'll regather yet my strength. **1838–40** [see the *vbl. sb.* below]. **1868** SILL *Poems, Hermitage* xv, As the image of God Is broken and re-gathered in the soul.

refl. **1598** BARRET *Theor. Warres* V. ii. 144 Time to regather themselues into order againe.

b. *intr.* To meet or come together again.

1855 [see the *ppl. a.* below]. **1890** *Pall Mall G.* 16 Aug. 7/1 When the House of Commons..regathered yesterday afternoon.

2. *trans.* To gather (a garment) again.

1856 Miss Yonge *Daisy Chain* xviii, Margaret..was..regathering a poor child's frock. **1875** *Plain Needlework* 20 The child can probably sew the gathers in..instead of having to regather the whole.

Hence **re'gathering** *vbl. sb.* and *ppl. a.*

1838 De Quincey *Lamb* Wks. 1858 IX. 112 The regathering and restoration of the total word from its scattered parts. **1840** Poe *William Wilson* Wks. 1864 I. 421 An indistinct regathering of feeble pleasures and phantasmagoric pain. **1855** Lynch *Rivulet* xxxii. i, 'Twas hard the unbroken dark to bear, But harder still re-gathering night. **1955** *Times* 9 Aug. 10/2 They are kept together by a rule of life, by monthly meetings on the mainland, and a 10-day regathering on the island each June.

regatta (rɪ'gætə). Also 7 regatto, 7–8 regate, 8 regata. [It. (Venetian) *regatta* (and *regata*) 'a strife or contention or struggling for the maistrie' (Florio): hence also F. *régate*.]

1. The name given at Venice to certain boat-races held on the Grand Canal.

1652 S. S. *Secretaries Studie* 265 The rarest [show] that ever I saw, was a costly and ostentatious triumph, called a *Regatto*, presented on the Grand-Canal. **1677** *Govt. Venice* 315 Regates, are the Courses or Combats of their Boats upon the Grand Canal for a Prize, not unlike the Carrousels. **1754** Drummond *Trav.* 84 Though I stayed in this city [Venice] longer than I could have wished, I was extremely well entertained with the sight of a regatta. **1866** Howells *Venet. Life* (1883) II. xvii. 65 The picturesque and exciting pastime of the regatta.

2. A boat- or yacht-race, or (usually) an organized series of such races, forming a more or less prominent sporting and social event.

The first English regatta was held on the Thames on the 23rd of June 1775: see the *Annual Register* for that year, pp. 133 and 216.

1775 *Public Advertiser* 24 May 2/2 The Regatta will keep at home many of our Nobility and wealthy Commoners. **1775** Johnson *Let. to Mrs. Thrale* 21 June, I am glad that you are to be at the regatta. **1775** *Newcastle Courant* 16 Sept., Monday, the keelmen, the great watermen on this river, were much engaged in a Regatta. **1843** E. FitzGerald *Lett.* (1889) I. 117 Regattas at Lowestoft, and at Woodbridge. **1856** 'Stonehenge' *Brit. Rural Sports* 469/2 Sailing regattas are held in many of our rivers and lakes, but chiefly at Cowes, Kingstown, and other seaport towns. **1887** Miss Braddon *Like & Unlike* xix, He took her to race-meetings, and cricket grounds, and regattas.

attrib. **1848** Thackeray *Van. Fair* xxxix, They penetrated to Cowes for the race-balls and regatta-gaieties there. **1887** J. Ashby-Sterry *Lazy Minstrel* (1892) 204 Regatta-time's pleasant, Thrice pleasant is Henley in laughing July!

3. A cotton fabric, usu. made in twill; a striped garment made in this fabric. Also *attrib.*, esp. as ***regatta shirt***, an informal light-weight striped shirt.

1861 T. Baines *Jrnl.* 21 July in *Explorations S.-W. Afr.* (1864) 59, I gave Hendrick a couple of regatta shirts and elastic braces. **1910** *Westm. Gaz.* 7 Feb. 5/5 (Advt.), Woven Ginghams, Zephyrs, Regattas, and heavier grades, good for tub frocks. **1910** *Encycl. Brit.* VII. 278/1 *Regatta* is a stout, coloured shirt cloth similar in make to a jeanette. It was originally made in blue and white stripes and was used largely and is still used for men's shirts. **1962** *B.S.I. News* Jan. 8/2 The cloths are coloured-woven regatta fabrics, one of which is all cotton and the other a blend of cotton with one-third rayon staple. *Ibid.* 9/1 The blend has been evolved more recently; requirements for it have been based on regattas submitted to comprehensive trials by hospitals and local authorities. **1963** *New Yorker* 1 June 115 *These* shirts ..in regatta, sky blue..navy or red. **1972** *Canad. Antiques Collector* Nov.–Dec. 10/1 The Langley records list substantial quantities of Chesterfields, frock coats, Scotch tweeds,..regatta shirts.

Hence **re'gatting** *vbl. sb.* (*nonce-wd.*)

1843 Thackeray *Irish Sk.-bk.* x, We had talked of hunting, racing, regatting, and all other sports.

re'gauge, *v.* [re- 5 a.] *trans.* To gauge anew. Also **re-'gauge** *sb.*

1812 J. Smyth *Pract. Customs* (1821) 413 Re-gauged Ullage Contents. [See also Re- 5 a.] **1891** *Imperial Tariff* 269 On a warrant for the re-gauge or re-test of Wine.., the officer is to allow the regauge or re-test thereof.

regaute, variant of regalty *Obs.*

rege, obs. Sc. form of rage *sb.* and *v.*

†**re'geal,** *v. Obs.*$^{-1}$ [ad. L. *regelāre*: see re- 2 d and geal *v.*] *intr.* To thaw, melt.

a **1658** Cleveland *Gen. Poems* (1677) 10, I feel thou art consenting ripe By that soft gripe, And those regealing Crystal Spheres.

regelate (riːdʒɪ'leɪt), *v.* [f. re- 5 a + ppl. stem of L. *gelāre* to freeze: perh. after F. *regeler* (1461).] *intr.* (and *refl.*) To freeze together again.

1860 Tyndall *Glac.* ii. xxiv. 358 The confused fragments regelated to a compact continuous mass. **1863** *Sat. Rev.* 1 Aug. 148 The ice fragments round him had regelated so as to form a solid case.

fig. **1874** Ruskin *Fors Clav.* xliii. 158 It..regelated itself into a somewhat compact essay on glaciers.

regelation (riːdʒɪ'leɪʃən). [See prec. and gelation[1].] The action of freezing together again; *spec.* the fusion of two pieces of ice, having moist surfaces, at a temperature above freezing-point.

1857 Tyndall & Huxley in *Phil. Trans.* CXLVII. 329 On the Regelation of Ice, and its application to Glacial Phenomena. **1871** B. Stewart *Heat* §100 Provided the surfaces be smooth, when they are brought into the slightest contact regelation ensues.

attrib. **1897** *Edin. Rev.* July 45 The viscous and regelation theories only account for the moulding of the glacier to its trough.

regement, obs. form of regiment.

†'**regence**[1]. *Obs. rare.* [a. F. *régence*: see regency and -ence.] = regency.

c **1470** Harding *Chron.* lix. ii, She was able, by wytte and sapience, The realme to rule, and haue therof regence. *Ibid.* lxii. ii, He had..A lyons chere in felde, with good regence. **1669** Gale *Crt. Gentiles* i. ii. ii. 2 The regence or presidence of the Moon..over the Air. **1678** Butler *Hud.* iii. ii. 275 Some..That swore to any human regence Oaths of supremacy and allegiance.

Régence[2] (reʒɑ̃s). [Fr.: see regence[1].] Used, chiefly *attrib.*, to designate the style of costume, furniture, and interior decoration, characteristic of the first third of the eighteenth century in France, during which occurred the French Regency (see regency 5).

1919 H. Nicolson *Let.* 1 Feb. in J. Lees-Milne *H. Nicolson* (1980) vii. 114 A huge Régence writing table. **1930** R. Cuthill tr. *J. Schober's Silk & Silk Industry* iv. 272 *Regeance* [sic], a Jacquard fabric with small designs and also stripes in the warp direction; usually in striking colours. **1930** *Morning Post* 18 July 14/5 A Regence settee and four fauteuils. **1963** *House & Garden* Mar. 79/2 The term Régence..is used for the period 1710 to 1730. **1968** *Ibid.* May 47 (*caption*) The sitting-room, showing one of the bergères, Régence overmantel and Austrian clock. **1973** *Country Life* 10 May 1307/1 Slender *Régence* ribbonwork displaced the more plastic forms of the Baroque. **1977** *Times* 16 June 18/6 An ormolu-mounted Régence commode at 53,000 francs..or £6,235.

regency ('riːdʒənsɪ). [ad. med.L. *regentia* (1418 in Du Cange), or f. regent: see -ency. Cf. F. *régence*.]

1. The position or office of ruler; exercise of rule or authority; government, dominion, control.

a. on the part of persons. Now *rare* or *Obs.*

c **1485** *Digby Myst.* (1882) iii. 212 Heyll, reytyus rewlar in þi regensy! **1597** Hooker *Eccl. Pol.* v. li. §3 The scepter of Christs regencie euen in the kingdom of heauen. **1601** Holland *Pliny* I. 128 She..had the prerogatiue of the regencie ouer the greatest kingdome. **1651** N. Bacon *Disc. Govt. Eng.* ii. xxxiv. (1739) 157 Custom in Government.. made her Regency at last taste somewhat stale and spiritless. **1711** *Fingall MSS.* in *10th Rep. Hist. MSS. Comm.* App. V. 114 Mankind might wish to be under the regency of such a monarch. **1760–72** H. Brooke *Fool of Qual.* (1809) III. 116, I had made a vow..to forsake her and the country the very day after her regency [as Queen of the May].

b. *transf.* or *fig.* of things.

1635 Valentine *Foure Sea-Serm.* 24 This Planet hath a regencie, and dominion ouer moist bodies. **1681** Flavel *Meth. Grace* xxvii. 457 The deposing of corruption from its regency and dominion in the soul. **1840** *Fraser's Mag.* XXII. 457 His passions,..spurning the regency of judgment, exercised..undivided sway. *a* **1890** Austin Phelps *My Note-Book* (1891) vii. 169 Conscience claims regency in everything that a man should aim to do or to be.

2. a. The office and jurisdiction of a regent or vicegerent; government by a regent or by a body exercising similar authority.

1429–30 *Rolls of Parlt.* V. 416/1 It was advised and thoght, that as toward the Regencie of France occupied theire by my Lorde of Bedford, that anoon..that name and Office shuld cesse. *c* **1470** Harding *Chron.* cxxxvii. iii, For constable then was he Of Englande hole to haue the regency. *c* **1600** Drayton *Miseries Q. Margaret* xxvi, York then, which had the regency in France, They force the King ignobly to displace. **1660** R. Coke *Power & Subj.* 101 How came.. Mary de Midici wife of Henry the Fourth..to manage the Regencie of France..? **1727–38** Chambers *Cycl.* s.v. *Regent*, Some have urged that women being incapable of succeeding to that crown, were incapable of the regency; but custom has declared in their favour. **1791** Burke *Corr.* (1844) III. 255 The rebels say they will declare a regency if the king refuses to accept. **1828** Scott *F.M. Perth* xxxv, He transferred the regency which he had so foully acquired, to his son Murdoch. **1878** Stubbs *Const. Hist.* (1896) III. xviii. 169 The king's illness placed the queen and the duke of York in direct rivalry for the regency.

b. *personified.* = regent *sb.* 2.

1814 Byron *Diary* 18 Feb., The avowal and republication of two stanzas on Princess Charlotte's weeping at Regency's speech to Lauderdale in 1812.

3. †**a.** The governing body of certain (chiefly European) towns and Muslim states. *Obs.*

1706 *Lond. Gaz.* No. 4239/1 Deputies from the neighbouring Regencies [in Germany]. **1748** *Anson's Voy.* iii. ix. 389 When these prisoners got to Canton, the Regency sent for them. **1769** *Lloyd's Even. Post* 22–5 Sept. 295/1 The Regency of Venice have sent orders that no more bodies shall be dug out of the ground. **1796** Washington *Lett.* Writ. 1892 XIII. 240 The purport of your private letter ..(that part of it I mean which relates to the Frigate for the Regency of Algiers) has surprised me exceedingly.

b. A body of men appointed to carry on the government during the absence, minority, or incapacity of the sovereign or hereditary ruler; a Government so constituted. Also in *transf.* or extended senses: a group that manages or administers in the absence of a manager or political leader; an inside group or clique controlling affairs.

1721 Bailey, *Regency*, the Government or Governours of a Kingdom during the Minority or absence of a Prince. **1750** H. Walpole *Lett. to Mann* (1834) II. 321 We expect some chagrin on the new Regency at the head of which is to be the Duke. **1788** in Dk. Buckingham *Court & Cabinets Geo. III* (1859) II. 18 The Opposition..are exceedingly embarrassed, even supposing the Regent, or Regency, to venture on the change of Ministry. **1845** S. Austin *Ranke's Hist. Ref.* II. 45 It made no difference whether the States supported the Regency or not. **1852** Hawthorne *Stories fr. Hist. & Biog.* ix. 72 A number of..statesmen, who were called a regency. **1940** *Sun* (Baltimore) 13 Aug. 15/5 Secretary Knox named a three-man 'regency' to publish and edit the *News* while he holds his Cabinet post. **1956** *New Republic* 9 Jan. 2/3 There's some evidence the Administration 'Regency' is using Ike's absence to even old scores. **1963** *Daily Tel.* 12 Jan. 15/3 Leading members of the Parliamentary Labour party have been angered by a suggestion..that a 'Regency' has been set up to rule in the absence of Mr. Gaitskell.

†**c.** A council or meeting of the members of a regency. *Obs.*$^{-1}$

1748 H. Walpole *Lett.* (1846) II. 242 There was a great Regency kept in town.

d. ***Albany regency***, a group of politicians who controlled the Democratic party in the state of New York from *c* 1820 to 1850.

1888 A. Johnston in Winsor *Hist. Amer.* VII. v. 283 The methods of the 'Albany Regency', whose members..made it their rule never to desert a party friend or forgive disobedience or breach of party discipline.

4. A district under the control of a regent or regency (3 a).

1667 Milton *P.L.* v. 748 Regions they pass'd, the mightie Regencies of Seraphim and Potentates and Thrones. **1780** *Ann. Reg.* 5 The territory appertaining to the regency of Burghausen. **1817** Raffles *Hist. Java* iii. I. 142 The rice fields of a regency are divided among the whole of the population. **1838** *Sparks' Biogr.* IX. *Eaton* vii. 245 The Bashaw gave permission to the American agent to leave the Regency.

5. The period during which a regent governs; *spec.* the periods in French and English history during which Philip, Duke of Orleans (1715–23), and George, Prince of Wales (the Prince Regent, 1810–20), acted as regents.

1727 Boyer *Dict. Royal* I. s.v. *Reistre*, The German Horse that came into France during the Regency of Queen Catherine of Medicis. **1841** *Penny Cycl.* XIX. 358/2 It was during the English regency that the power of Napoleon was broken, and peace was restored to Europe. **1869** Lecky *Europ. Mor.* II. v. 326 The moral tone..was..lower, probably, than in France under the Regency, or in England under the Restoration.

6. a. The office or function of a university regent.

1639 in Spalding *Troub. Chas. I* (1850) I. 233 *note*, In regaird of the vacancie of the place of regencie of the thrid classe. *a* **1670** Spalding *Ibid.* (1851) II. 74 Mr. Alex[r] Scrogie..deposit fra his regency..had gottin sum pensioun fra the King. **1691** Wood *Ath. Oxon.* I. 548 In 1446, he being then in his Regency, he became one of the Commissaries of the University. **1771** *Gentl. Mag.* XLI. 19 Every fellow is obliged to leave that College after he has completed eighteen years from his Regency in Arts. **1841** Peacock *Stat. Cambr.* 11 Every master of arts..was sworn to continue his regency for five years. **1895** Rashdall *Univ. Mid. Ages* xii. II. 475 The privilege of studying Theology after Regency in Arts.

b. (See quot.) *rare*$^{-1}$. [After F. *regence*.]

1839 Hallam *Hist. Lit.* iv. i. §5 The Jesuits write and speak Latin well..owing to their keeping regencies (an usual phrase for academical exercises) from their early youth.

7. *attrib.* and *Comb.*, as ***regency act, bill, cap, post***; **regency point**, a kind of lace (see quots.); also *attrib.*

1705–6 Luttrell *Brief Rel.* (1875) VI. 5 The committee, to whom the regency bill is committed. **1743** H. Walpole *Let.* 14 Apr., The Earl of Bath and Mr. Pelham, neither of them in regency-posts, are to be of the number. **1865** F. B. Palliser *Hist. Lace* xxx. 364 A 'point' lace, with the 'cloth' or 'toilé' on the edge, for many years was in fashion, and in compliment to the Prince, was named..'Regency Point'. It was a durable and handsome lace. **1867** C. Grey *Early Years Prince Consort* 351 The Regency Bill..will to-day be read for a third time in the House of Lords. **1900** E. Jackson *Hist. Hand-Made Lace* 193 Regency Point Lace. This lace, made in Bedfordshire, was in great demand during the Regency early in the nineteenth century. The edge is thick, the ground, a complicated réseau, or hand-made mesh. **1930** T. Wright *Romance of Lace Pillow* xv. 219 During the Regency (1810–1820) there was made in Northamptonshire a striking lace, with fillings of a bold character, which was called Regency Point.

b. Passing into *adj.* Applied to styles of architecture, clothing, furniture, etc., characteristic of the English Regency (sense 5), and, more generally, the late eighteenth and early nineteenth century.

The isolated early use in quot. *c* 1793 may possibly reflect the public controversy surrounding the Regency Bill of 1788.

c **1793** Jane Austen *Volume Third* in *Minor Works* (1954) 211 'She sends me a long account of the new Regency walking dress Lady Susan has given her... She says nothing indeed except about the Regency.' 'She *must* write well thought Kitty, to make a long letter upon a Bonnet & Pelisse.' **1880** E. Glaisher *Needlework* viii. 86 Shield-backed chairs of the Regency fashion. **1887** Lecky *Eng. in 18th C.* V. 145 Whig ladies appeared in society with caps that were known as 'regency caps' and with ribands indicating their politics. **1909** *Cent. Dict.* Suppl., Regency style. **1918** A. Bennett *Pretty Lady* vi. 25 He had furnished his flat in the Regency style of the first decade of the nineteenth century. *Ibid.* vii. 33 Regency furniture and china. **1936** *Discovery* Oct. 321/2 The short 'Brutus' curls of regency mock-classical beauties. **1938** C. Day Lewis *Overtures to Death* 18 We gaze At a Regency terrace, curved Like the ritual smile. **1954** J. Betjeman *Few Late Chrysanthemums* 43, I pulled aside the thick magenta curtains—So Regency, so Regency, my dear—. **1958** —— *Coll. Poems* 250 It's for Regency now I'm enthusing So we've Regency stripes on the wall. **1963** N. Freeling *Because of Cats* iii. 47 There were Regency-striped silk cushions. **1973** P. Moyes *Curious Affair of Third Dog* v. 57 The Regency-stripe wall-paper. **1976** *Denbighshire Free Press* 8 Dec. 16/7 (Advt.), Curtains... Regency stripe/gold, 2 width each side, length 53 in. £20. **1977** C. McCullough *Thorn Birds* iii. 64 The Louis Quinze sofa and chairs, the Regency escritoire. **1977** *S. Wales Echo* 18 Jan. (Advt.), Only four remaining on a small development of just 10 Regency style Detached Houses.

regend, obs. variant of regent.

†**re'gender**, *v. Obs.* [f. re- 5 a + gender *v.*, after L. *regenerāre*: see next.] *trans.* To beget again; to make or create afresh; to form anew. (Cf. re-engender.) Hence **re'gendered** *ppl. a.*, **re'gendering** *vbl. sb.* and *ppl. a.*

c **1400** *Lanfranc's Cirurg.* 38 If þat a leche wolde bisie him ..to regendre fleisch in a wounde. *Ibid.* 211 Mundificatiuis ..wiþ regendring þingis & drijng þingis. **1532** More *Confut. Tindale* Wks. 431/1 Enabling the new regendred creature to inheritaunce of heauen. **1533** —— *Apol.* 54 The regendrynge of the soule by fayth. **1582** Stanyhurst *Æneis* II. (Arb.) 59 With toonge three forcked furth spirts fyre freshlye regendred. **1597** Lowe *Chirurg.* II. i. (1634) 39 The continuall inspiration..for their refreshing, as also for the regendring of the spirit Animall.

†**re'gener**, *v. Obs.* [ad. OF. *regenerer* (11th c.; mod.F. *régénérer*) or L. *regenerāre*: see re- and gener *v.*] = prec.

c **1400** *Lanfranc's Cirurg.* 38 Aftirward we schulen clense þe quytture, & aftir þat regenere fleisch. **1456** Sir G. Haye *Law Arms* (S.T.S.) 295 With haly unctioune annoyntit, and regenerit be new generacioune. *c* **1500** *Melusine* 140 The feyth of Jeshu Cryste, of the whiche he vs alle hath regenered and saued.

regenerable (rɪˈdʒɛnərəb(ə)l), *a.* [f. regener(ate *v.* + -able.] Capable of being regenerated.

1920 in Webster. **1927** A. Kocourek *Jural Relations* x. 140 Regenerable relations..are mesonomic relations which are convertible into zygnomic relations by means of a jural act or event. **1976** *Nature* 24 June 660/1 Microparticles were needed in the thermally regenerable ion-exchange process to ensure rapid rates of ion-exchange.

regeneracy (rɪˈdʒɛnərəsɪ). [f. regener-ate *ppl. a.* + -acy.] The state of being regenerate.

1626 Huit (*title*) Anatomy of Conscience; or, the Sum of Paul's Regeneracy. *a* **1660** Hammond *Serm.* Wks. 1683 IV. 686 Though Saul were..called from the depth of sin to regeneracy and salvation. **1755** Amory *Mem.* (1769) I. 105 A religion of regeneracy and holy spiritual life. **1853** Lynch *Onward* in *Lett. to Scattered* 340 The things they have just left behind, which in their first regeneracy are like those 'fleshpots of Egypt'.

re'generant, *a.* and *sb.* [See next and -ant.]

A. *adj.* Regenerating. *rare*⁻¹.

1855 Bailey *Spir. Leg.* in *Mystic*, etc. (ed. 2) 66 Of talismanic and regenerant force.

B. *sb.* A regenerating agent.

1961 in Webster. **1963** *Engineering* 13 Sept. 338/3 The regenerant for the anion column can be either sodium carbonate or sodium hydroxide.

regenerate (rɪˈdʒɛnərət), *ppl. a.* and *sb.* [ad. L. *regenerāt-us*, pa. pple. of *regenerāre*: see next.]

A. *ppl. a.* †1. Re-born; brought again into existence; formed anew. *Obs.*

1471 Ripley *Comp. Alch.* v. viii. in Ashm. (1652) 150 Guydo..seyth by rottyng dyeth the compound corporall, And then..Uprysyth agayne Regenerat, Sympill, and Spyrytuall. **1593** Shaks. *Rich. II*, I. iii. 70 The earthy author of my blood, Whose youthfull spirit in me regenerate, Doth with a two-fold rigor lift mee vp. **1593** G. Harvey *Pierce's Super.* 58 A canker..neuer perfectly healeth, vnlesse the rootes and all be vtterly extirped; and the fleshe regenerate. **1610** Healey *St. Aug. Citie of God* 794 For our flesh shalbe regenerate by incorruption, as our soule is by faith.

2. In religious use: Spiritually re-born.

1526 *Pilgr. Perf.* (W. de W. 1531) 221 b, Excepte a man be regenerate & borne agayne of water & the holy goost. **1561** T. Norton *Calvin's Inst.* II. 84 Which excuse belongeth only to the regenerate, which do with the chief part of their soule tend vnto good. **1605** Bacon *Adv. Learn.* II. xxv. §20 By the Holy Ghost are the elect regenerate in spirit. **1667** Milton *P.L.* XI. 5 Grace..had remov'd The stonie from thir hearts, and made new flesh Regenerate grow instead. **1746** Hervey *Medit.* (1818) 93 An innumerable race of regenerate children. **1875** Manning *Mission H. Ghost* ii. 35 We are born again, we are regenerate, we are sons of God. **1883** J. W. Reynolds *Supernat. in Nature* 24 The remarkable betterment which is wrought in those who are called 'regenerate'.

b. Restored to a better state, reformed.

1647 N. Bacon *Disc. Govt. Eng.* I. viii. (1739) 16 It had been a wonder if Episcopacy..should by transplanting become regenerate into their original condition of meekness and humility. **1860** Froude *Hist. Eng.* V. 459 Organs still pealed through the aisles in notes unsuited to a regenerate worship.

c. Of nations: Restored or raised again from a sunk or base condition.

1811 Scott *Don Roderick* III. xiv, O who shall grudge him Albuera's bays, Who brought a race regenerate to the field. **1865** Freeman *Hist. Ess.* Ser. I. (1871) vi. 130 The righteous and generous sympathy which we all feel towards regenerate Italy.

†3. Degenerate, renegade. *Obs. rare.*

1596 *Edward III*, I. i, Regenerate traitor, viper to the place Where thou wast foster'd. **1607** Topsell *Four-f. Beasts* (1658) 360 So forth went this regenerate English Moor, more like a mad man then an advised champion, to kill this lion.

4. *Biol.* Formed or modified by regeneration.

1952 *Q. Rev. Biol.* XXVII. 169/2 Intimacy of morphological relation between the regenerate and the adult tissue has demanded that study of the process of regeneration be made against the background of the anatomy and physiology of adult tissues.

B. *sb.* †1. A regenerate person. *Obs.*

a **1569** Kingesmyll *Comf. Afflict.* (1585) C vij, The blessed posteritie of the blessed Abraham, and true regenerates of God by our Saviour Christ. **1652** Bp. Hall *Invis. World* III. §5 Casting undue fears into the tender hearts of weak regenerates.

2. *Biol.* A limb or other part formed by regeneration.

1952 *Q. Rev. Biol.* XXVII. 169/2 The histology of the regenerate emphasizes the continuity and interrelation between adult and regenerating tissue. *Ibid.*, The regenerate ..is nourished by the adult blood stream. **1960** [see dedifferentiation]. **1964** [see *melanogenesis* s.v. melano-]. **1977** *Sci. Amer.* July 69/3 A graft between a proximal level of a host cockroach leg and a distal level of a donor leg gives rise to a normally oriented intercalary regenerate and forms a normal leg segment.

regenerate (rɪˈdʒɛnəreɪt), *v.* [ad. ppl. stem of L. *regenerāre*: see re- and generate *v.*, and cf. F. *régénérer* (11th c.).]

1. a. *trans.* In religious use: To cause to be born again in a spiritual sense; to invest with a new and higher spiritual nature. Also *refl.*

a **1557** Mrs. M. Basset tr. *More's Treat. Passion* M.'s Wks. 1378/2 These I meane whom he hath by his wholesome sacramentes & faith regenerated & renewed. **1587** Golding *De Mornay* xxxi. (1617) 503 But yet hath he circumcised our hearts by regenerating vs. **1679** Penn *Addr. Prot.* II. 112 The Family of the Faithful, regenerated and redeemed from the Earth. **1740** Waterland *Regeneration* Wks. 1823 VI. 352 No man regenerates himself at all. **1788** Gibbon *Decl. & F.* lviii. VI. 267 She was regenerated and crowned in St. Sophia, under the more orthodox appellation of Anne. **1850** Robertson *Serm.* Ser. III. iv. (1872) 48 Man need not be regenerated in order to possess the power of reasoning. **1885** Finlayson *Biol. Relig.* 86 Perhaps he thinks that infants dying in infancy are regenerated in the article of death.

b. To reform completely; to effect a thorough moral change in (a person or state of things, etc.).

1849 Alison *Hist. Europe* III. xiv. §45. 179 Your brothers ..desire to be regenerated, and to become men. **1863** W. Phillips *Speeches* iii. 54 The church has to be regenerated. **1891** *Spectator* 23 May, Where the West rules Mussulmans, it 'regenerates' their social system.

c. To convert *into* something better. *rare.*

1850 W. Collins *Antonina* iv, Pagan images regenerated into portraits of saints.

2. *Path.* and *Biol.* To reproduce, form afresh (some part of the body). Chiefly in *pass.*

1597 A. M. tr. *Guillemeau's Fr. Chirurg.* 33/2 Round aboute the vlceration is regenerated a tender and viscouse flesh. **1646** Sir T. Browne *Pseud. Ep.* 127 That the limbs of Hyppolitus were set together, not regenerated by Æsculapius, is the utmost assertion of Poetry. **1678** Cudworth *Intell. Syst.* I. iii. 167 Which regenerates and repairs Veins consumed or cut off. **1784** M. Baillie *Wks.* (1825) I. 193, I found many old scars where the Rete Mucosum was regenerated. **1813** J. Thomson *Lect. Inflam.* 471 The dark-coloured fungous mass..on being removed is quickly regenerated. **1895** *Arch. für Entwicklungsmech. der Organismen* II. 122 The power of an adult animal to regenerate lost parts. **1897** *Trans. Amer. Pediatric Soc.* IX. 89 The exsected rib had been regenerated. **1909** R. H. Lock *Rec. Progress Study of Variation* iii. 61 The power of regenerating a lost part must clearly often be of service to the creatures which possess it. **1959** [see regeneration 3]. **1961** Lenhoff & Loomis *Biol. Hydra* 409 Hydra treated with $10^{-5}M$ lipoic acid for short periods immediately after removal of their hypostomes and tentacles completely lose the capacity to regenerate those structures. **1970** Ambrose & Easty *Cell Biol.* i. 21 The capacity to regenerate certain tissues, possessed by most embryonic animals, is still present in some mature animals and plants.

3. a. To reproduce, re-create; to form or bring into existence again.

1608 Topsell *Serpents* (1658) 728 Out of the ashes of a Toad burnt, not only one, but many Toads have been regenerated the year following. **1712** Blackmore *Creation* II. (ed. 2) 65 [The sun] Through all the Soil a genial Ferment spreads, Regenerates the Plants. **1731** Arbuthnot *Aliments* IV. ii. §39 (1735) 109 The Salts, of which the Acid was compos'd, will be regenerated. **1816** J. Scott *Vis. Paris* (ed. 5) 284 The soil in which nitre is produced or regenerated. **1962** *Which?* Oct. 294/1 After a time, the resin [in a water softener] has no sodium left, and has to be 'regenerated' by adding sodium chloride.

b. With immaterial object.

1612 Davies *Why Ireland*, etc. (1787) 156 Yet could not the King's grace regenerate obedience in that degenerate house. **1790** Burke *Fr. Rev.* 29 In both cases they regenerated the deficient part of the old constitution through the parts which were not impaired. **1837** Ht. Martineau *Soc. Amer.* III. 185 The great point to be gained with the criminal is to regenerate self-respect. **1869** Claridge *Cold Water-cure* 77 Mankind may still turn back, and regenerate health.

c. *Chem.* and *Textiles.* To re-precipitate (a natural polymeric substance, as cellulose, proteins) following chemical processing, esp. in the form of fibres; to make (fibres) in this way. Cf. regenerated *ppl. a.* 2.

1925 *U.S. Patent 1,528,219*, I..have invented certain new and useful Improvements in a Process of Regenerating Cellulose from Viscose. **1948** J. T. Marsh *Textile Sci.* i. 8 It has not been possible to regenerate fibres from wool, but successful attempts have been made with silk. **1950** R. W. Moncrieff *Artificial Fibres* 90 Some of the sodium cellulose xanthate decomposes, regenerating cellulose which is maintained in emulsion form by that part of the sodium cellulose xanthate which is still undecomposed. **1955** Cockett & Hilton *Basic Chem. of Textile Preparation* iv. 82 Attempts have been made to regenerate both silk and wool in which the protein raw material is in a linear or near linear form. **1972** M. A. Taylor *Technol. of Textile Properties* 30 Azlon is the generic term given..to fibres regenerated from natural protein, such as casein from milk. **1973** *Materials & Technol.* VI. iv. 277 The extruded filaments were injected into a bath of dilute sulphuric acid to re-precipitate, or 'regenerate', the original cellulose and form textile threads.

4. To reconstitute on a higher plane; to place on a new basis. Also *refl.*

1789 Coxe *Trav. Switz.* (1801) I. Introd. 39 To regenerate Switzerland is not to disturb it. **1791** Paine *Rights of Man* (ed. 4) 58 The country has never yet regenerated itself and is therefore without a constitution. **1864** Raine *Priory of Hexham* (Surtees) I. Pref. I. 63 When his nephew Thomas II wished to regenerate Hexham. **1891** *Pall Mall G.* 5 May 2/1 Is capital required to 'regenerate', as you term it, the non-paying mines?

5. *intr.* a. To form again. Chiefly *Path.* and *Biol.*

1541 R. Copland *Guydon's Quest. Chirurg.* C j, I saye fyrste that all sanguyne membres may regenerate and knyt by very regeneracion and consolidacion. **1691** Ray *Creation* I. (1692) 89 Metals and Minerals..shoot, ferment, and as it were vegetate and regenerate. **1755** Brady in *Phil. Trans.* XLIX. 249 We have not tried, if it does not regenerate, when cut, like polypes. **1822** Good *Study Med.* I. 464 When extracted imperfectly it [a polypus] is very apt to regenerate. **1899** *Allbutt's Syst. Med.* VII. 79 Before regenerating they must be destroyed. **1901** T. H. Morgan *Regeneration* i. 20 A piece of hydra regenerates without the formation of new material. **1928** J. S. Huxley *Ess. Pop. Sci.* 251 When small pieces of a planarian regenerate, they exhibit what we may call polarity. **1971** [see regulate *v.* 5].

b. To reform, become regenerate.

1786 tr. *Swedenborg's Chr. Relig.* 510 The fellowship or communion called the church..gains admission into every one when he is regenerating. **1835** I. Taylor *Spir. Despot.* III. 105 No corporation regenerates by spontaneous energy: it must be brought back to duty..by a hand from without.

regenerated (rɪˈdʒɛnəreɪtɪd), *ppl. a.* [f. regenerate *v.* + -ed[1].] 1. Re-born, re-formed, etc.

1594 T. B. *La Primaud. Fr. Acad.* II. 203 Hee..loueth them also as regenerated and newe creatures in Iesus Christ his Sonne. **1758** Reid tr. *Macquer's Chym.* I. 125 The other name, Regenerated Tartar, which is also given it. **1776** Cruikshank in *Phil. Trans.* LXXXV. 182, I supposed the regenerated nerves might now be performing their offices. **1806** R. Fellowes tr. *Milton's 2nd Defence* 228 At present he makes his appearance as a regenerated book-seller at the Hague. **1839** Murchison *Silur. Syst.* I. xxxviii. 526 Moulds of regenerated red Sandstone. **1877** Froude *Short Stud.* (1883) IV. I. x. 109 His personal religion was not the religion of a regenerated heart.

2. *Chem.* and *Textiles.* Of natural polymeric materials (as cellulose, proteins): re-precipitated (esp. in the form of fibres) following chemical treatment. Of fibres: prepared from a substance in this way.

1904 *Jrnl. Soc. Chem. Industry* 29 Feb. 177/1 The next operation..is one for the purpose of denitrating the cellulose, in order that the fibre may ultimately consist of what might be termed 'regenerated' cellulose. **1933** *Trans. Faraday Soc.* XXIX. 230 Regenerated celluloses are more highly activated than cotton which has merely been swollen. **1941** *Thorpe's Dict. Appl. Chem.* (ed. 4) V. 121/2 Viscose and regenerated cellulose rayons in general show a much higher moisture adsorption at all relative humidities than do native cellulose fibres. **1948** J. T. Marsh *Textile Sci.* i. 8 Regenerated fibres may be classified according to the nature of the parent material, cellulose or protein. **1963** A. J. Hall *Textile Sci.* ii. 66 Several types of protein are satisfactory for the production of regenerated protein fibres and among those most used are casein..and the natural proteins.. extracted from groundnuts and soya beans. **1964** N. G. Clark *Mod. Org. Chem.* xvii. 363 Regenerated fibres are derived from naturally occurring fibrous material by first converting it into a soluble derivative, forcing a solution of this through a minute jet to give a 'thread' of solution, and finally recovering the original or its derivative from solution as a solid thread or fibre. **1973** *Materials & Technol.* VI. iv. 277 Wool and silk are both protein fibres, and it is not surprising that attempts have been made to produce regenerated protein fibres.

re'generateness. *rare*⁻⁰. [-ness.] Regeneration.

1731 in Bailey vol. II.

regenerating (rɪˈdʒɛnəreɪtɪŋ), *ppl. a.* [-ing[2].] That regenerates.

1681 Flavel *Meth. Grace* xxxi. 532 The principal internal cause of spiritual life is the regenerating spirit of Christ. **1707** *Curios. in Husb. & Gard.* 339 We may conclude them to be the first Principles of the regenerating Plant. **1776** *Phil. Trans.* LXXXV. 183 The regenerating nerve..converting the whole of the surrounding extravasated blood into its own substance. **1836–9** Todd *Cycl. Anat.* II. 45/2 The star-fish affords an example of great regenerating power. **1861**

GOLDW. SMITH *Lect. Mod. Hist.* i. 22 Men, who..have left a great and regenerating example to mankind.

b. *techn.* = REGENERATIVE 2.

1842 GROVE *Corr. Phys. Forces* (1874) 65 Under the term 'regenerating-engine' various ingenious combinations have lately been suggested. **1875** KNIGHT *Dict. Mech.* 1911/2 Regenerating furnace.

regeneration (rɪdʒɛnəˈreɪʃən). Also 4–6 -acion, etc. [ad. L. *regenerātiōn-em*, n. of action f. *regenerāre* to REGENERATE: see -ATION. Cf. F. *régénération* (12th c.).]

1. a. The action of regenerating; the process or fact of being regenerated; re-creation, re-formation, etc.

13.. *Propr. Sanct.* (Vernon MS.) in *Archiv neu. Spr.* LXXXI. 103/49 In þe Regeneracion good Of alle men to flesch and blood. **1382** WYCLIF *Matt.* xix. 28 In regeneracioun, or gendrynge aȝein, whenne mannes sone shall sitte in the sete of his mageste. **1561** T. NORTON *Calvin's Inst.* I. 24 After the generall flood, there was as it were a new regeneration of the world. **1694** SALMON *Bate's Dispens.* (1713) 317/1 This is made a Regeneration of Nitre. **1707** *Curios. in Husb. & Gard.* 324 The Miracle of the Regeneration, or even of the Resurrection of Plants from their Ashes. **1785** WILKINS tr. *Bhagvat* vi. 50 But such a regeneration into this life is the most difficult to attain. **1860** WARTER *Sea-board* II. 206 The throes the grave has to undergo before the regeneration in the resurrection. **1882–3** SCHAFF *Encycl. Relig. Knowl.* II. 1690/2 [The olive-tree has] almost inexhaustible power of regeneration.

b. *fig.* Revival; renascence, re-constitution on a higher level.

1627 HAKEWILL *Apol.* (1630) 255 Together with the regeneration of other kindes of learning Poetrie likewise grew in request. **1792** A. YOUNG *Trav. France* 119 What they call the regeneration of the kingdom, a favourite term, to which they affix no precise idea. **1835** LYTTON *Rienzi* I. viii, All great regenerations are the universal movement of the mass. **1847** MRS. A. KERR tr. *Ranke's Hist. Servia* 217 The military regeneration of the Turkish Empire.

c. *Forestry.* The natural regrowth of a forest which has been felled or thinned. Freq. *attrib.*

1888 E. E. FERNANDEZ *Man. Indian Sylviculture* i. 6 The name regrowth will be specially given to the new crop obtained by coppice regeneration. **1909** P. T. MAW *Pract. Forestry* ix. 183 A Seed Felling or Regeneration Felling is made when a good seed year has come. As its name implies, it is the felling made for the actual regeneration of the area. It consists in the removal of all the trees except a few, which are left as mother trees, to seed the whole area; and also, to form a light canopy or shelter wood for the young crop. **1928** R. S. TROUP *Silvicultural Syst.* iv. 38 Where regeneration is sufficiently well advanced it should be freed from overhead cover. *Ibid.* 45 The latter will be retained as regeneration areas under the revised working plan. **1979** *Biol. Abstr.* LXVII. 2139/2 The conditions of regeneration and growth of seedlings varied with stands and plots.

2. a. In religious use: The process or fact of being born again in a spiritual sense; the state resulting from this.

c **1420** LYDG. *Assembly of Gods* 2101 That we may haue a place, Accordyng to oure regeneracion, With heuynly spyrytes. **1513** BRADSHAW *St. Werburge* I. 2936 By the seconde byrthe..At fonte of baptym we haue regeneracyon. **1597** HOOKER *Eccl. Pol.* v. l. §1 They haue the seede of their regeneration by the ministerie of the Church. **1607** ROWLANDS *Guy Warw.* 72 Nature's corruption I do strive to leave, A new regeneration to receive. **1701** NORRIS *Ideal World* I. v. 284 Considering that our Regeneration implies only the restoration of our nature. *a* **1805** PALEY *Serm.* vii. (1810) 116, I am not unwilling to admit..that, when this Spirit is given, there is a new birth, a regeneration. **1883** FROUDE *Short Stud.* IV. III. 263 Spiritual regeneration begins naturally among the poor and the humble.

b. (See quot.)

App. based on a wrong punctuation of Matt. xix. 28.

1651 HOBBES *Leviath.* III. xlii. 263 And therefore it is, that the time of his preaching is often by himself called the Regeneration.

3. *Path.* and *Biol.* The formation of new animal tissue; the reproduction of lost parts or organs.

1541 R. COPLAND *Guydon's Quest. Chirurg.* Biv b, In asmoche as they haue..regeneracyon as the membres, they be called membres. **1612** WOODALL *Surg. Mate* Wks. (1653) 89 The medicaments incarnative, or for regeneration of the flesh. **1646** SIR T. BROWNE *Pseud. Ep.* 127 Spermaticall parts..will not admit a Regeneration. **1776** CRUIKSHANK in *Phil. Trans.* LXXXV. 183 The regeneration of the nerves which took place in the first dog. **1836–9** TODD *Cycl. Anat.* II. 45/2 We are not aware that the process of regeneration in these animals has been carefully traced. **1872** HUXLEY *Physiol.* i. 18 The local death of some tissues is followed by their regeneration. **1901** T. H. MORGAN *Regeneration* i. 23 The word 'regeneration' has come to mean, in general usage, not only the replacement of a lost part, but also the development of a new, whole organism, or even a part of an organism, from a piece of an adult, or of an embryo, or of an egg. **1959** W. ANDREW *Textbk. Compar. Histol.* xii. 478 While asexual reproduction is not common among the echinoderms, a high power of regeneration is present and a single arm can regenerate a whole starfish. **1978** *Nature* 27 July 374/1 Can re-innervation take place not only by regeneration of the original axons but also by collateral sprouting of..undamaged fibres?

4. *Electronics.* Positive feedback (see FEEDBACK, FEED-BACK *sb.* a).

1922 *Proc. IRE* X. 244 The effect of regeneration (that is, the supplying of energy to a circuit to reinforce the oscillations existing therein) is equivalent to introducing a negative resistance reaction in the circuit. **1943** [see REACTION 3 e]. **1957** *Practical Wireless* XXXIII. 694/1 The hole is used..in the next stage for a regeneration control. **1969** J. J. SPARKES *Transistor Switching* iii. 74 Regeneration will only commence provided the loop gain A_v..is greater than 1.

5. *Chem.* and *Textiles.* The action or process of regenerating fibres, etc. Cf. REGENERATE *v.* 3 c.

1925 *U.S. Patent 1,528,219* The regeneration of cellulose from viscose solutions. **1950** R. W. MONCRIEFF *Artificial Fibres* ii. 20 The original cotton had consisted of short, hairy, nearly opaque fibres, and after regeneration it consisted of very long, smooth, transparent filaments, but it was still the same essential material. **1953** *Chem. Abstr.* XLVII. 643 (*heading*) Regeneration of egg albumins under pressure. **1972** M. A. TAYLOR *Technol. Textile Properties* 28 The regeneration and polymerisation of the cellulose occurs after the filament has been coagulated and stretched.

regenerative (rɪˈdʒɛnərətɪv), *a.* (and *sb.*). [ad. F. *régénératif, -ive* (14th c.), or med.L. *regenerātīv-us*: see REGENERATE *v.* and -IVE.]

1. a. Tending to or characterized by regeneration. (Common in recent use in fig. senses.)

c **1400** *Lanfranc's Cirurg.* 38 If þat a leche wolde besie him wiþ a medicyn regeneratijf to regendre fleisch in a wounde. **1432–50** tr. *Higden* (Rolls) IV. 257 The strenȝhte regeneratiue ȝiffen to waters. **1624** F. WHITE *Repl. Fisher* 428 To alter the property of naturall water, and to giue regeneratiue force and vertue to it. *a* **1652** BROME *City Wit* v. i, I pray you what is Lady Luxury? a woman regenerative? **1839–52** BAILEY *Festus* 545 Idolatry Worshipped God meanly,..Not as man's great Regenerative Lord. **1871** BLACKIE *Four Phases* i. 26 The great regenerative work which he undertook.

†**b.** *sb.* An application to regenerate flesh. *Obs.*$^{-1}$

c **1400** *Lanfranc's Cirurg.* 38 þe quytture schal be clensid or þou leie ony regeneratijf to holowȝ woundis.

2. *Mech.* **a.** Constructed on, or employing the principle of the REGENERATOR (sense 2).

1861 FAIRBAIRN *Iron* 66 The prospective advantages of these regenerative stoves are greater economy..and the higher temperature attainable by the blast. **1864** PERCY *Metallurgy, Iron & Steel* 428 Mr. Siemens, the inventor of the so-called regenerative furnaces. **1890** *Athenæum* 19 July 101/1 The application of the regenerative system to the firing of gas retorts.

b. Applied to a principle or technique of refrigeration by which the uncooled portion of the working fluid loses some heat prior to the major cooling step by exchange with the cooled portion.

1896 *Proc. Chem. Soc.* XI. 222 In all continuously working circuits of liquid gases used in refrigerating apparatus the regenerative principle applied to cold first introduced by Siemens in 1857..has been adopted. *Ibid.* 231 If..hydrogen, previously cooled by a bath of boiling air, is allowed to expand at 200 atmos. over a regenerative coil..a liquid jet can be seen. **1922** GLAZEBROOK *Dict. Appl. Physics* I. 565/1 The usual process [for the commercial liquefaction of gases] is a regenerative one, first successfully developed by Linde, in which the Joule-Thomson effect of irreversible expansion in passing a constrictive orifice..serves as the step-down in temperature, and a cumulative cooling is produced by causing the gas which has suffered this step-down to take up heat in a thermal interchanger from another portion of gas that is on its way to the orifice. **1961** F. E. HOARE et al. *Exper. Cryophysics* i. 4 Dewar was employing regenerative cooling to produce a jet of cold hydrogen gas which could be used for cooling other systems.

c. *Astronautics.* Applied to a method of cooling the walls of a rocket engine by circulating the fuel through them.

1947 *Amer. Jrnl. Physics* XV. 131/2 In the motor, between 2 and 3 percent of the heat due to combustion passes through the chamber and nozzle walls into the coolant, which returns again to the combustion chamber when regenerative cooling is utilized. **1949** G. P. SUTTON *Rocket Propulsion Elements* vi. 142 In regenerative cooling the motor parts are cooled by means of a built-in jacket or cooling coil in which the oxidizer or the fuel are used as the coolant fluid. **1962** F. I. ORDWAY et al. *Basic Astronautics* x. 413 This regenerative cooling method serves two purposes. It cools the walls of the thrust chamber and adds thermal energy to the propellant. **1974** *Encycl. Brit. Macropædia* XV. 938/2 The conventional method of cooling [in rocket engines] is known as regenerative cooling.

3. Applied to any method of braking in which energy is extracted from the parts braked, to be stored and re-used.

1904 *Electrical Mag.* I. 600/1 The regenerative braking action comes into play automatically. **1930** *Engineering* 6 June 722/2 Regenerative braking had been adopted on the majority of the electric locomotives recently placed in service. **1958** *Ibid.* 14 Mar. 340/1 A bus using the regenerative transmission... In this system, when the vehicle is braked..energy is absorbed in accelerating a..flywheel... Then when the vehicle is restarted the energy of the flywheel is used to accelerate it, resulting in a saving of fuel. **1973** *Sci. Amer.* Dec. 23/2 A regenerative braking system would employ the vehicle's electric motors as generators during braking or downhill driving, thus putting the kinetic energy of the vehicle back into the storage system.

4. *Electronics.* Pertaining to or employing positive feedback (see FEEDBACK, FEED-BACK *sb.* a); ***regenerative feedback***, positive feedback.

1915 *Proc. IRE* III. 231 It is always better practice to use the cascade circuits for the radio frequencies, even if the regenerative circuits are not employed with each individual audion system. **1919** *Wireless World* Aug. 250/2 By using regenerative feed back much higher amplification can be realized, but the operation becomes less stable. **1922** *Sci. Amer.* Sept. 160/1 Armstrong's regenerative receiver, now so widely employed, is ever so much more sensitive than the ordinary vacuum tube receiver. **1947** R. LEE *Electronic Transformers & Circuits* ix. 254 The next pulse occurs when the negative grid voltage decreases sufficiently so that regenerative action starts again. **1969** J. J. SPARKES *Transistor Switching* iii. 59 The cross-coupling resistor..can be shunted by a capacitor..to speed up the regenerative switching of the circuit. **1971** *Physics Bull.* July 385/2 The high spectral intensity results from the fact that, since the laser is a regenerative oscillator, the oscillation linewidth decreases with increasing laser power—in contrast to the behaviour of any thermal source. **1975** G. J. KING *Audio Handbk.* ii. 35 Positive feedback means that the phase of the signal fed back is coincident with the phase of the source or input signal. This is regenerative feedback which results in sustained oscillation.

Hence **reˈgeneratively** *adv.*

1882 in OGILVIE. **1892** WHITNEY *Max Müller* 64 Some changes result more regeneratively than others. **1947** *Amer. Jrnl. Physics* XV. 131/1 The coolant liquid absorbs heat as it circulates in ducts around the motor and is then injected into the combustion chamber (regeneratively cooled type). **1949** G. P. SUTTON *Rocket Propulsion Elements* vi. 142 The German Me 163 motor has a steel cooling jacket in which fuel cools the motor regeneratively. **1969** J. J. SPARKES *Transistor Switching* iii. 74 When T_2 is conducting, raising V_1 until it is about equal to V_{B2} turns T_1 on so that T_2 is switched off regeneratively.

regenerator (rɪˈdʒɛnəreɪtə(r)). [f. REGENERATE *v.* + -OR. Cf. F. *régénérateur* (14th c.).]

1. One who or that which regenerates.

1740 WATERLAND *Regeneration* Wks. 1823 VI. 352 He is not his own regenerator, or parent, at all, in his new birth. **1844** *Mem. Babylonian P'cess* II. 205 She expected a regenerator of the world, or second Messias. **1861** MAY *Const. Hist.* viii. (1863) II. 10 He at once became the regenerator and leader of the Tory party.

2. *Mech.* A fuel-saving device attached to a furnace, consisting of layers of fire-brick which, becoming heated by the hot air and gases from the furnace, impart the heat to an incoming current of cold air or combustible gas acting alternately with the outgoing current. Also *attrib.*

1835 J. MALAM in *Lond. Jrnl. Arts & Sc.* (1836) VIII. 144 A front elevation of three retorts, with their 'regenerators' and conducting pipes. **1877** RAYMOND *Statist. Mines & Mining* 335 Using the Siemens producer and regenerators if necessary. **1884** KNIGHT *Dict. Mech.* Suppl. 748/2 Regenerator Furnace. **1897** *Daily News* 22 Sept. 6/7 The Regenerator system of gas burning.

b. *transf.* in *Electr.* (See quot.)

1873 MAXWELL *Electr. & Magn.* (1881) I. 299 This conductor, by which the carrier is enabled to be connected to earth without a spark, answers to the contrivance called a Regenerator in heat-engines. We shall therefore call it a Regenerator.

regeneratory (rɪˈdʒɛnərətərɪ), *a.* [f. as REGENERATE *v.* + -ORY^{2}.] Of the nature of regeneration; regenerative.

1803 G. S. FABER *Cabiri* II. 351 Mr. Maurice imagines, that these regeneratory sacrifices shewed the deep and unanimous conviction of the pagan world, that man had fallen. **1831** W. H. MILL *Christa Sangitá* Pref. 17 Those proselytes who by a regeneratory initiation were introduced to all the privileges of Abraham's children.

reˈgeneratress. *rare*$^{-1}$. [-ESS: cf. next.] A female regenerator.

1894 *Dublin Rev.* Oct. 307 The regeneratress of France.

reˈgeneratrix. [See REGENERATOR and GENERATRIX.] A female regenerator.

1871 M. COLLINS *Mrq. & Merch.* II. v. 125 Miss Pinnock regarded herself as fit to be the regeneratrix of the world. **1890** *Pall Mall G.* 8 Nov. 2/1 Ireland..should..aim at becoming a great spiritual force, and the regeneratrix, in the religious sense, of the British Empire.

re-ˈgenesis. [RE- 5 a.] The state, fact, or process, of reproducing or being reproduced.

1831 CARLYLE *Sart. Res.* I. v, Not Mankind only, but all that Mankind does or beholds, is in continual growth, re-genesis and self-perfecting vitality. **1858** SPENCER *Ess.* I. 19 In Christian art we may trace a parallel re-genesis. **1973** *Black World* June 90/2 Sister [Sherley Anne] Williams breaks her book [sc. *Give Birth to Brightness*] down into three major parts. Part 1 is called 'Regenesis'.

regent (ˈriːdʒənt), *sb.* [Subst. use of next.]

1. a. That which rules, governs, or has supremacy; a ruling power or principle. Now *rare.*

c **1412** HOCCLEVE *De Reg. Princ.* 3827 Whan resoun is regent Of man, þan regneþ no delicacie. **1526** SKELTON *Magnyf.* 38 Lyberte may somtyme be to large, But yf reason be regent and ruler of your barge. **1601** DOLMAN *La Primaud. Fr. Acad.* (1618) III. 771 The moone..beeing as the regient of the seas and waters. **1667** MILTON *P.L.* VII. 371 First in his East the glorious Lamp was seen, Regent of Day. **1762–9** FALCONER *Shipwr.* I. 554 Thou moon, fair regent of the night! **1781** COWPER *Retirement* 724 Flowers by that name promiscuously we call, But one, the rose, the regent of them all. **1805** FOSTER *Ess.* IV. v. II. 197 If Christianity ought really..to be the supreme regent of all moral feelings.

b. One who rules or governs; a ruler, governor, director. Now *rare* or *Obs.*

1480 CAXTON *Chron. Eng.* ccl. 169 The duchesse hauyng full power of hir lord as Regent and lady of his londes. **1533** BELLENDEN *Livy* III. iii. (S.T.S.) I. 252 Valerius publicola on þe thrid day eftir þat he was made regent, was chosin consul. **1589** PUTTENHAM *Eng. Poesie* III. xvi. (Arb.) 188 Elizabeth regent of the great Brittaine Ile, Honour of all regents and of Queenes. **1649** MILTON *Eikon.* xviii. Wks. 1851 III. 471 As farr as Reason, Honour, Conscience, and the Queen who was his Regent in all these, would give him leave. **1670** G. H. *Hist. Cardinals* I. III. 84 This Penetentiary has a Prelat under him, that is call'd the Regent of the Penitentiary office. **1725** Pope *Odyss.* II. 42 Assist him, Jove! thou regent of the skies! **1847** Longf. *Ev.* I. ii. 37 Regent of flocks was he when the shepherd slept.

2. a. One who is invested with royal authority by, or on behalf of, another; *esp.* one appointed to administer a kingdom during the minority, absence, or incapacity of the sovereign.

1425 *Rolls of Parlt.* IV. 277/1 [That power be given to] my Lord ye Regent of France..to receyve and take ye said debate into ye Kyngs hand. *c* **1477** Caxton *Jason* 5 b, I.. constytute the[e] Regent and gouernour of my royaume. **1560** Daus tr. *Sleidane's Comm.* 101 The Lady Mary..came into Flaunders, whom the Emperour made Regent of all the base countreis. **1593** Shaks. *2 Hen. VI*, I. i. 66 Cosin of Yorke, We heere discharge your Grace from being Regent I'th parts of France. **1610** Willet *Daniel* 211 Alexanders 4. captaines were at the first regents under Alexander. *a* **1648** Ld. Herbert *Hen. VIII* (1649) 193 When Madame Louise the Regent had declared [etc.]. **1759** Robertson *Hist. Scot.* VI. Wks. 1813 I. 440 A king, they told him, had often reason to fear, seldom to love, a regent. **1811** *Edin. Rev.* XVIII. 76 It has been said, that the name and office of Regent are unknown to our Law and Constitution. **1878** Stubbs *Const. Hist.* xviii. III. 89 He accepted Henry as his son-in-law, regent and heir of France.

†**b.** The name formerly given to the municipal authorities of some continental cities, and to the native chiefs in Java. *Obs.*

1724 *Lond. Gaz.* No. 6291/1 A Vessel which the Regents of Berne have caused to be built. **1795** Thunberg *Travels* (ed. 2) II. 309 The Regent in the island of Madura is stiled ..a free prince or regent. **1817** Raffles *Hist. Java* ii. I. 79 Governors of provinces, called by the Dutch *Regents*,..are ranked among the chief nobility of the country.

3. In the Universities:

a. At Oxford and Cambridge, a Master of Arts ruling or presiding over disputations in the Schools, a duty originally discharged for one, and afterwards for five, years after graduation; hence, in later use, a Master of not more than five years standing. Now only *Hist.*

1432–50 tr. *Higden* (Rolls) VIII. 213 Thabbot and chanons of Oseney with regentes of the universite. **1494** Fabyan *Chron.* VII. 330 The regentis and masters of that vnyuersytie, were lastly compellyd..to aske of hym forgyuenes. **1504** *Will of Archer* (Somerset Ho.), To euery Regente et non Regente being at my burying vj^d & j^d. **1574** M. Stokys in Peacock *Stat. Cambr.* (1841) App. A. p. xi, The Father..shall dispute with the old Bachilour, and after hym two Regents. **1604** Tooker *Fabrique of Church* 120 Congregations of the Masters or convocation of Regents, and not Regents, is a needlesse thing. **1681** *Lond. Gaz.* No. 1656/2 When their Majesties were come into the Schools, they found the Regent-walk crouded on both sides with Regents, non-Regents, and Batchelors of Divinity. **1797** *Cambr. Univ. Calendar* 147 The Senate is divided into two bodies or houses, 1st. Those who have not been A.M. five years, and are called Regents. **1841** Peacock *Stat. Cambr.* 15 *note*, The house of regents was composed of those masters or doctors who were actually regent, or engaged in teaching or reading lectures in the university, without reference to standing. **1895** Rashdall *Univ. Mid. Ages* App. xxxiii. II. 791 Probably by an oversight on the part of the framers of the Act of 1854, the ancient Congregation of Regents [at Oxford] was left in existence for certain purposes.

b. In the Scottish universities, one of several instructors forming part of the teaching staff of a college, who undertook the tuition of a certain number of students from the time of their entrance to the end of the course. Now only *Hist.*

[**1414** *Acta Facult. Artium* (St. Andrews) 25 Mar., Quod determinantes admitterentur per decanum Facultatis et regentes qui habeant considerare eorum sufficientiam.] **1522** Jas. V *Let.* in *Rep. Univ. Comm., St. Andrews* (1837) 180 The Universite of Sanctandrois, the rector, doctouris, regentes,..makand residence therin. **1563–7** Buchanan *Reform. St. Andros* Wks. (S.T.S.) 8 The regent sal writ thayme in hys rol, and assigne thayme place in hys classe diuidit in decuriis. **1641** *Sc. Acts Chas. I* (1870) V. 581/2 þe principall professoures regentes and remanent maisteres and members of the samen colledge. **1708** J. Chamberlayne *St. Gt. Brit.* II. III. x. (1710) 469 In Philosophy there are Four Regents or Professors; they teach Philosophy and Greek. Every Regent has his Class, which Classes are divided according to the Years that the Students have been entred in the University. **1771** Smollett *Humph. Cl.* 3 Sept., The students are..taught in public schools or classes, each science by its particular professor or regent. **1867** Masson *Edinb. Sk.* 40 The four general or circulating professors were the essential complement of the Arts Faculty. They were called 'regents', by way of distinction.

c. In France, the title usually given to those who taught the more elementary classes; an instructor in arts or science. (See quot. 1727–38.)

1611 Cotgr., *Regent*,..a Regent, Reader, Teacher, Moderator of a forme in a Colledge. **1653** Urquhart *Rabelais* II. v. 29 It was told him by one of his Teachers (there called Regents,) that the paine of the eyes was the most hurtful thing of any to the sight. **1727–38** Chambers *Cycl.* s.v., Regent is generally restrained to the lower classes, as regent of rhetoric, regent of logic, &c., those of philosophy are rather called professors. **1863** Draper *Intell. Devel. Europe* xviii. (1864) II. 126 In Montpellier, he was for long one of the regents of the faculty of medicine. **1875** M. Pattison *Casaubon* 89 The regents in medicine and law had a salary secured by patent.

d. *U.S.* (*a*) A member of the governing board of a State University (and of the Smithsonian Institute, Washington). (*b*) At Harvard, an officer having supervision of the students' conduct.

(*a*) **1813** *Niles' Reg.* V. 79/2 The regents of the university, expressly endeavored to effect this important object. *a* **1817** T. Dwight *Trav. New Eng.*, etc. (1821) II. 485 This seminary..is under the superintendence of a Board, styled the Regents of the University of Columbia. **1843–56** Bouvier *Law Dict.* (ed. 6) s.v., In New York..the board who have the superintendence of all the colleges, academies and schools, are called the regents of the University of the state of New York. **1877** (*title*) A Memorial to the Regents of the University of the State of Iowa. **1969** *Morning Star* 13 Oct. 5/3 The Director of Afro-American Studies declares her sacking raises grave doubts about the Regents' desire to encourage black participation. **1976** *New Yorker* 26 Apr. 32/2 One of the Smithsonian's regents..is chairman of the House Appropriations Committee. **1977** *Detroit Free Press* 11 Dec. 11-D/1 Regents for Oklahoma State University Friday honoured Terry Miller by retiring his No. 43 football jersey and approving a commendation to be awarded at the next regents meeting.

(*b*) **1888** A. P. Peabody *Harvard Reminisc.* 199 The students who were not present at evening prayers were obliged..to register their names with the regent.

†**4.** The head master of a school. *Obs.*

1583 Stubbes *Anat. Abus.* II. (1882) 20 Except one be able to giue the regent or prouost of the house a peece of mony.. he comes not there, I warrant him. *a* **1652** Brome *New Acad.* IV. ii, By your leave, Sir, Are you the Regent of this Academy? **1718** Addison *Chr. Relig.* v. viii, Origen was appointed Regent of the Catachetic school in Alexandria. **1796** H. Hunter tr. *St.-Pierre's Stud. Nat.* (1799) I. 391 Those infamous punishments, which produce a disgraceful effect, at once, on the morals of both scholars and regents.

5. A variety of potato.

1846 [see early *sb.* a]. **1868** M. Jewry *Warne's Model Cookery & Housekeeping Bk.* 14 Potatoes.—*We* think the best are..the regents for winter use. **1892** I. Zangwill *Childr. Ghetto* II. 6 'Kidneys or regents, my child?'..said Guedalyah the greengrocer. **1927** T. P. McIntosh *Potato* ii. 20 Not much appears to be known about Regent, which was a later introduction [*sc.* after 1836].

6. A chairman of a branch of the Daughters of the American Revolution.

1890 *Constitution & Bye-Laws, Daughters Amer. Revolution* 4 When twelve or more members of the Society shall be living in one locality they may organize a Chapter. They may elect a presiding officer whose title will be Regent. **1928** *Harper's Mag.* Oct. 529/2 The Daughters upheld Mrs Brousseau and the contention of the Massachusetts State Regent. **1946** *Nat. Historical Mag.* Mar. 144/2 Please read over the foregoing statement again, Madam Regent. **1974** *Marlboro Herald-Advocate* (Bennettsville, S. Carolina) 18 Apr. 4/2 Mrs. Walter Hughes, local regent, also attended the Congress.

7. *attrib.* **a. regent bird** or **oriole**, an Australian bird, *Sericulus melinus*, named in compliment to the Prince Regent, afterwards George IV; **regent honeyeater**, a bird, *Zanthomiza phrygia*, of the family Meliphagidæ, having black plumage with yellow bars and spots and found in the eucalyptus forests of south-east Australia.

1825 Field *Geog. N.S. Wales* App. 503 Regent bird or Kinghoney-sucker, *Sericulus chrysocephalus.* **1847** Leichhardt *Jrnl.* v. 161 Mr. Gilbert observed the female of the Regent-bird. **1913** G. M. Mathews *List Birds Austral.* 270 *Zanthomiza phrygia phrygia.* Regent Honey-eater. **1967** A. Rutgers *Birds Austral.* 262 Regent Honey-eaters make a lot of noise and have a loud laughing call. **1840** *Cuvier's Anim. Kingd.* 189 The Regent Oriole of authors (*Sericulus regens*, Lesson), the plumage of which is fine silky black.

b. Regent (congregation or) **house**, the upper of the two houses into which the Senate of Cambridge University was formerly divided; **Regent walk**, the former name of certain walks or alleys in Christ's and Queens' Colleges and at the Schools, Cambridge.

1895 Rashdall *Univ. Mid. Ages* xii. II. 365 *note*, Even in the Fifteenth Century Register..we find that in a *Regent Congregation the graces are 'pronounced'..by a Proctor. **1573** G. Harvey *Letter-bk.* (Camden) 18, I have not yit bene so courst and galled in our own House as I am like hereafter to be pincht and nipt in the *Regent Hous. **1641** Milton *Reform.* II. Wks. 1851 III. 67 They come furnish't with no more experience then they learnt..at the Colledge audit, or the regent house. **1681** *Lond. Gaz.* No. 1656/3 Then their Majesties went up to the Regent-House, and by their particular Command, Mr. Montague..was Admitted, and Created Doctor of Divinity. **1635** Quarles *Embl.* II. iv. 77 To follow Natures too affected Fashion, Or travell in the *Regent walk of Passion. **1681** [see 3 a above]. **1719** in Willis & Clark *Cambridge* (1886) II. 213 At dinner and supper in Summer they met upon ye Regent Walk, and there waited till they knew what Seniors would come down. **1886** *Ibid.* II. 54 The gate-house and the central alley [at Queens' College], called 'Regent-walk', were flagged. *Ibid.* 215 This doorway was exactly opposite to the Great Gate, and the walk leading to it from the gate is 'the Regent Walk'.

regent ('riːdʒənt), *a.* [a. F. *regent* (14th c.) or L. *regent-em*, pres. pple. of *regĕre* to rule.]

1. In special senses (usu. placed after the sb.).

a. Holding the position of a University regent. Now only *Hist.*

1387 Trevisa *Higden* (Rolls) VIII. 213 þe abbot and þe chanouns of Osenay and maisters regentes [L. *magistri regentes*] of Oxenforde. *a* **1548** Hall *Chron., Hen. VIII* 199 The Rector of the Uniuersitie called to counsell all the Doctors regentes..to shew their myndes on this question. **1570** Foxe *A. & M.* (ed. 2) 1384/1 Angry with the vnmanerly multitude that would giue no rowme vnto the Doctours, Bachelers, Maisters, & other graduates and regent masters. **1682** *Lond. Gaz.* No. 1720/8 First, One of the Esquire Beadles, then the Regent-Masters, afterwards the Non-Regents, and Officers. **1895** Rashdall *Univ. Mid. Ages* xii. II. 364 The 'Decree and Statute' is issued 'by the authority of the Chancellor and Masters Regent.'

b. Acting as, having the position of, regent of a country, esp. ***Queen regent***; †ruling as sovereign.

1555 Eden *Decades* 215 The lady Regente moother vnto the frenche kynge. *a* **1578** Lindesay (Pitscottie) *Chron. Scot.* (S.T.S.) I. 10 Than schaw ȝow him how queine regent Reft frome the Duik the authoritie. *c* **1645** Howell *Lett.* I. xviii. (1650) 30 She was made Queen Regent of France during the Kings Minority. **1690** *Lond. Gaz.* No. 2533/1 Next the Princes who are not Regents or Soveraigns, the Princes Regents, the Heralds. **1705** *Lond. Gaz.* No. 4161/2 His Imperial Majesty..intends..to receive the Homage of the States of Austria, as being the Regent Arch-Duke. **1727–38** Chambers *Cycl.* s.v., In France, the queen mother has the regency of the kingdom, under the title of queen regent, while the king is a minor. **1765** Blackstone *Comm.* I. iv. 212 The queen regent, regnant, or sovereign, is she who holds the crown in her own right. **1841** *Q. Rev.* LXVII. 316 Though himself a Protestant, he had in early life warmly defended Mary of Guise, the Queen Regent.

2. Ruling, governing, controlling. Now *rare.*

1613 M. Ridley *Magn. Bodies* 1 The great regent Globes of Saturne, Mars, Jupiter, the Sunne and the Earth. **1680** Baxter *Answ. Stillingfl.* 8, I entreat you to tell me more plainly, which is the constitutive Regent part of a National Church? **1762–9** Falconer *Shipwr.* II. 184 The regent helm her motion still commands. **1844** Mrs. Browning *Drama of Exile* Poems 1850 I. 71 This regent and sublime Humanity, Though fallen, exceeds you.

regent ('riːdʒənt), *v.* Now *rare.* [f. regent *sb.*]

1. a. *trans.* To superintend or teach (a college, class, etc.), as a regent.

1623 tr. *Favine's Theat. Hon.* II. xiii. 248 All these Vniuersities are Regented by Professors of singular Pietie, and exquisite Learning. **1715** M. Davies *Athen. Brit.* I. Pref. 36 The Colleges..are regented by the Secular Clergy. **1882** M. Pattison in *Jrnl. Educ.* 1 Mar. 70 Graduates engaged in instructing or regenting the boys.

b. *intr.* To act as a University regent.

1631 in Craufurd *Hist. Univ. Edin.* (1808) 119 Mr. William King, (after he had regented in the colledge 23 years), was called to the ministry at Crammond. **1846** *Life J. Guthrie* 142 He regented in the University of St. Andrews and there taught as Professor of Philosophy.

2. To control (a person) as a regent.

a **1797** H. Walpole *Mem. Geo. II* (1847) I. 99 Even the black Princes widow..was passed over and her son regented by his Uncles.

Hence **'regenting** *vbl. sb.* and *ppl. a.*

a **1693** *Urquhart's Rabelais* III. xviii. 147 The well-payed Incomes of Regenting Doctors. **1884** *Edin. Rev.* Apr. 427 The comparative economy of the plan of regenting.

'regental, *a. rare*$^{-1}$. [f. regent *sb.* + -al[1].] Of or pertaining to a regent.

1883 Besant *All in Garden Fair* I. xiv, If the supper had been of royal or regental character, he could not have assumed a more courtly air.

'regentess. [-ess.] A female regent.

1611 Cotgr., *Regente*, the Regentesse, or Protectresse of a Kingdome. **1830** W. Taylor *Hist. Surv. Germ. Poetry* III. 318 A characteristic scene is that..between the Regentess and Macchiavel. **1877** *Tinsley's Mag.* XX. 147 Penetrating to the cabinet of the regentess.

†**'regentry.** *Sc. Obs.* [f. regent *sb.* + -ry.] The office or function of a regent, regency.

1558 *Sc. Acts Mary* (1814) II. 504/2 To desyre our souerane ladie..To mak ane commissioun of regentrie.. vnto hir derrest moder. **1579** *Reg. Privy Council Scot.* III. 244 The saidis place and charge of regentrie within the said college.

'regentship. [f. regent *sb.* + -ship.] The office or position of a regent.

1579 Fenton *Guicciard.* II. (1599) 93 The gouernement of a little sonne whom she had left, to which Regentship aspired..the Marquise of Saluce. **1593** Shaks. *2 Hen. VI*, I. iii. 107 If Yorke haue ill demean'd himselfe in France, Then let him be denay'd the Regent-ship. **1848** *Fraser's Mag.* XXXVIII. 338/1 The Liberal ladies of Germany..seem to consider this act as his chief recommendation to the regentship.

re'germinate (riː-), *v.* [re- 5 a.] To germinate again. Hence **re'germinating** *ppl. a.*

1623 Cockeram, *Regerminate*, to spring againe. **1656** Blount *Glossogr.*, *Regerminate*, to burgen again, to spring anew, to grow a fresh. **1753** Smollett *Cnt. Fathom* (1784) 100/1 Even amidst the rank productions of vice, they regerminate to a sort of imperfect vegetation. **1794** T. Taylor *Pausanias* III. 54 This tree regerminates perpetually. **1826** Good *Bk. Nature* I. 187 This organ will regerminate and the whole plant be renewed. **1881** W. Siemens in *Nature* No. 624. 568 The resulting seeds are not at any rate devoid of regerminating power.

So **regermi'nation**.

1646 J. Gregory *Notes & Obs.* xxvi. 124 The Jewes commonly expresse Resurrection by Regermination, or growing up againe like a Plant. **1658** in Phillips. **1731** in Bailey vol. II. **1819** G. S. Faber *Dispensations* (1823) II. 104 He expresses an assured hope, that the time of his renovation or regermination would come. **1849** *Fraser's Mag.* XL. 188 The paschal eggs, symbol of vital essence and regermination, are rolled upon the turf.

†**re'gest,** *sb.*[1] *Obs. rare*$^{-1}$. [f. regest *v.* 2.] The act of casting back, retort.

1609 T. Morton *Answ. Higgons* 24 Being twise conuicted in himselfe, both by the friuolousnesse of his reasons, and also by the regest of their owne like contradictions.

† **re'gest**, *sb.*[2] *Obs. rare.* [ad. late L. *regesta* (pl.) a list, register, f. *regerĕre*: see next, and cf. F. *regeste*.] A register.

1670 MILTON *Hist. Eng.* III. 123 Others of later time have sought to assert him by old legends and Cathedrall regests. *Ibid.* 134 Teudric King of Glamorgan, whom the regest of Landaff recounts to have bin alwaies victorious in fight.

† **re'gest**, *v. Obs.* [f. L. *regest-*, ppl. stem of *regerĕre*, f. *re-* RE- + *gerĕre* to bear, carry, etc.] **1.** *trans.* To register.

1520 *Churchw. Acc. St. Giles, Reading* (ed. Nash) 9 Paidd to Willm Edmunds for makyng and regestyng of the last accompte iij[s] iiij[d]. **1555** W. WATREMAN *Fardle Facions* I. v. 62 Thei also declare vnto them, the stories of men of olde tyme, regested in their holy Scripture.

2. To cast back, return, retort.

1614 JACKSON *Creed* III. v. §2 Vnto the obiected dreadfull consequences of their decrees,..they would regest disobedience to the Church. **1641** *Answ. Vind. Smectymnuus* 102, I have..indeed anticipated all those thred-bare objections which are here againe regested to the weary Reader. **1657** W. MORICE *Coena quasi Κοινὴ* xv. 228, I shall regest, that to what end shall they look on, if they can look for no fruit or good effect thereby?

† **regestary**. *Obs. rare*[−1]. [f. as prec. + -ARY: cf. REGISTRARY.] = next.

1523 SKELTON *Garl. Laurel* 522 Lo, hither commyth a goodly maystres, Occupacyon, Famys regestary.

† **regester**. *Obs.* Also 6 -our. [f. as prec. + -ER[1], or var. of REGISTER *sb.*[2]] One who registers; a registrar.

1555 W. WATREMAN *Fardle Facions* II. xi. 248 When the batteile is done, all the armie is presented to the Regestour, ..that it maye bee knowen who is slain. **1597** *Child-Marriages* 161 The Serchers, sealers & Regesters of all Tanned lether..in the county of the citie of chester.

regestery, obs. variant of REGISTRY.

† **re'gestion**. *Obs. rare.* [See REGEST *v.* and -ION[1].] Retort, reply.

1565 CALFHILL *Answ. Treat. Crosse* (1846) 60 But because ..we are only burdened with the name of Fathers give us leave sometime to use a Regestion. **1620** T. GRANGER *Div. Logike* 125 Our Sauiour Christ answereth to the Pharisees question by regestion. *a* **1640** JACKSON *Creed* x. xxiii. §5 The manner of the regestion seems to imply, that they had now begun to be sorry that they had so far believed on him.

† **regesture**. *Obs. rare*[−1]. [Alteration of REGISTER *sb.*, as if f. REGEST *v.* + -URE.] Register.

1598 T. BASTARD *Chrestoleros* (1880) 61 After the brauer sorte haue cast them off, Like fashions counting booke, or regesture.

regestyr, obs. form of REGISTER.

reget (riː'gɛt), *v. rare.* [RE- 5 a] *trans.* To obtain again, get back.

1604 DANIEL *Civ. Wars* VI. lxxi, And then desire in Gascoign to re-get The glory lost..Advantaged the Duke. **1611** J. DAVIES *To Worthy Persons* Wks. (Grosart) II. 52/2 Tovy, although the mother of vs all Regetts thee in her womb [etc.]. **1654** EARL MONM. tr. *Bentivoglio's Warrs Flanders* 161 All the Provinces would revolt; which when they should once be lost, they would not be so easily regotten.

† **re'get**. *Obs.* (Of obscure origin and meaning.)

13.. *E.E. Allit. P.* A. 1064 Þe almyȝty was her mynyster mete, Þe lombe Þe saker-fyse Þer to reget.

reggae ('rɛgeɪ). Also **Reggae**, **Reggay**. [Origin unknown; perh. connected with Jamaican English *rege-rege* quarrel, row (in Cassidy and Le Page, *Dict. Jamaican Eng.* (1967) 380/1).] A kind of popular music, of Jamaican origin, characterized by a strongly accentuated off-beat and often a prominent bass; a dance or song set to this music. Also *attrib.*

1968 (*song-title*) Do the Reggay. **1969** *Daily Mirror* 10 Oct. 19/1 *Reggae*, West Indian music. **1969** *Observer* 23 Nov. 25/8 The visiting American executives..dancing the Reggae, Jamaica's successor to the Ska. **1969** *Listener* 25 Dec. 905/2 A very dapper and jaunty Reggae group called the Pioneers. **1970** *Melody Maker* 3 Oct. 25/6 If I ever did reggae again, it would have to be darned good reggae, and there's not much of that around. It's such a blank type of music. **1971** *Advocate-News* (Barbados) 17 Sept. (Guyana Suppl.) p. vi (Advt.), A rum punch..served to an atmosphere of reggae, calypso and steelband music. **1973** G. SIMS *Hunters Point* xiii. 120 I'm a reggae fan. West Indian music. And early Beatles like 'From Me to You'. **1973** *Black World* Jan. 77/2, I heard the Rastas credited with starting everything from the island's most popular dance, 'Reggae', to the embryonic Black Consciousness movement. **1975** *Globe & Mail* (Toronto) 16 July 7/3 The reggaes..should be viewed as songs of social protest in which the dispossessed describe their personal experience and comment upon the social injustice of the system. **1976** *Telegraph* (Brisbane) 28 Apr. 58/4 As reggae grows in popularity, ever more artists are performing material with a reggae flavour. **1977** MCKNIGHT & TOBLER *Bob Marley* iii. 42 So we come to reggae, which the British initially found difficulty in pronouncing, let alone understanding. **1978** *Sunday Times* 29 Jan. 43/2 Althea and Donna met at a reggae festival in Ochos Rios. **1979** *Spectator* 1 Dec. 13/3 The bulk of the reggae-blacks were born here and yet feel themselves to be foreigners.

Regge ('reɪdʒeɪ). *Nuclear Physics.* The name of T. E. *Regge* (b. 1931), Italian physicist, used *attrib.* to designate certain concepts in the theory of the scattering of sub-atomic particles, as **Regge pole**, a pole of a complex function relating the scattered amplitude of partial waves to angular momentum; **Regge trajectory**, a path traced in the complex angular momentum plane by a Regge pole as the energy varies; esp. a plot of spin against the square of the rest mass for a group of particles.

1961 *Physical Rev. Lett.* VII. 394/2 We may satisfy Feynman's principle therefore by postulating that all poles of the *S* matrix are of this type (Regge poles). **1962** *Ibid.* VIII. 41/2 Each point is supposed to lie on a Regge trajectory. **1962** *Physical Rev.* CXXVI. 2204/2 This perturbation theory behavior is very different from that of the Regge case. *Ibid.*, Strongly interacting particles may exhibit the Regge behavior. **1973** [see POLE *sb.*[2] 10]. **1973** B. H. BRANSDEN et al. *Fundamental Particles* viii. 163 (*caption*) The Regge trajectories of some meson states. Mesons differing in spin by one unit appear to lie on the same Regge trajectory. **1973** L. J. TASSIE *Physics Elem. Particles* xii. 170 Most work on Regge theory is concerned with describing collision processes, and in this respect the Regge pole model is not a theory with a high predictive power. **1975** *Sci. Amer.* Feb. 62/3 The Regge trajectories turn out on observation to be nearly linear, meaning that the angular momentum of the particles on a particular trajectory is given to a good approximation by a linear function of the mass of the particle squared. **1977** P. D. B. COLLINS *Introd. Regge Theory* ii. 69 When such a Regge pole occurs for a physical integer value of l it will correspond to a physical particle or resonance. **1977** *Nature* 21 July 207/2 Hadrons on the same Regge trajectory have a remarkably simple relation between mass and angular momentum: $J = a'M^2 + a_0$, where J is the total angular momentum of the hadron, M is its mass and a' and a_0 are called the Regge 'slope' and 'intercept' respectively.

regge, obs. form of *rig*, RIDGE *sb.*

Reggeization (ˌrɛdʒeɪaɪ'zeɪʃən). *Nuclear Physics.* [f. REGGE: see -IZATION.] Treatment or modification in accordance with Regge theory.

1964 *Rev. Mod. Physics* XXXVI. 641/1 We have throughout considered the theory of spin ½ fermions, which as stated above shows the factoring property which is necessary for the success of the Reggeization procedure. **1975** *Physics Bull.* Jan. 25/2 Schnitzer's study of the Reggeization of non-abelian gauge theories is now seen to have been prophetic.

So **'Reggeized** (also r-) *a.*

1971 N. DOMBEY in Cumming & Osborn *Hadronic Interactions of Electrons & Photons* ii. 37 Now assume instead that the pion is Reggeized; i.e. S_7 has a moving pole at $J = a_\pi(t)$. **1973** *Physics Bull.* Feb. 99/1 Reggeized baryon exchange models give poor quantitative agreement with the results. **1973** *Jrnl. Physics* A. VI. 506 A reggeized absorption model with no free parameters..is applied to spin-2$^+$ production reactions.

Reggeon ('rɛdʒeɪɒn). *Nuclear Physics.* [f. as prec. + -ON[1].] (A particle represented by a) Regge pole or trajectory, or a virtual particle regarded as exchanged in the type of scattering they represent. Hence **regge'onic** *a.*

1964 *Physics Lett.* IX. 269/1 Mandelstam has given some arguments that moving branching points may appear in a relativistic theory as a result of singularities to the right in the *j*-plane for particles with spin. These new singularities correspond to the production threshold of resonance states (reggeons) with negative orbital momenta. *Ibid.* XII. 153/2 If this fact is correct it would modify the reggeonic branch points and the elastic scattering asymptotic amplitude. **1974** *Physics Bull.* May 206/4 High energy backward scattering is studied by (i) covariant reggeization techniques, (ii) the use of a super multiplet reggeon propagator model to generate polynomial residues. **1977** P. D. B. COLLINS *Introd. Regge Theory* ii. 71 The power behaviour expected from the exchange of a Regge trajectory (sometimes called 'Reggeon') ..may be contrasted with that from a fixed-spin (elementary) particle. **1978** *Nature* 19 Jan. 214/2 Reggeons with arbitrarily high spin can be exchanged with equanimity.

reȝȝn, obs. f. RAIN *sb.*[1]

reȝȝsenn, obs. f. RAISE *v.*

† **reȝhel-boc**. *Obs. rare*[−1]. [f. OE. *reȝol* rule + *bóc* BOOK.] A book of monastic rules.

c **1200** ORMIN Ded. 8 Þurrh Þatt witt hafenn takenn ba An reȝhellboc to follȝhenn.

† **'regian**. *Obs.* [f. L. *rēgi-us* royal + -AN.] An upholder of regal authority; a royalist.

1653 A. WILSON *Jas. I* 202 Then they strive to make a Division of Regians and Republicans. **1655** FULLER *Ch. Hist.* II. iii. §38 This is alleadged and urged by our Regians, to prove the Kings Paramount Power *in Ecclesiasticis*. *a* **1670** HACKET *Abp. Williams* I. (1692) 39 Art. Wils[on]..favours all Republicans, and never speaks well of Regians, (it is his own distinctions) if he can possibly avoid it.

† **regibbe**, *v. Obs.*[−1] [ad. OF. *regiber* (mod. F. *regimber*); see note to JIB *v.*[2]] *intr.* To kick.

a **1225** *Ancr. R.* 138 Al so sone so Þet flesh haueÞ al his wil, hit regibbeð anon, ase uet kelf & idel.

† **'regible**, *a. Obs. rare*[−1]. [ad. L. *regibilis*, f. *regĕre* to rule: see -IBLE.] Governable.

1609 HOLLAND *Amm. Marcell.* XVI. xii. 69 (If occasion require) the same [boldness] ought to be regible, advised, and considerate. **1656** in BLOUNT *Glossogr.* **1721** in BAILEY.

Hence † **'regibleness**.

1731 BAILEY vol. II.

regicidal (ˌrɛdʒɪ'saɪdəl), *a.* [f. REGICIDE + -AL[1].] Pertaining to, characterized by, inclined to, regicide.

a **1779** WARBURTON *Wks.* X. 136 (R.), One might suspect this regicidal collection to be the spiritual breathings of an enlightened Methodist. **1813** GRATTAN *Parl. Deb.* 11 May, This oath abjured the regicidal power attributed to the Pope. **1834** DISRAELI *Rev. Epick* II. xxiv. 127 The regicidal steel that shall redeem A nation's sorrow with a tyrant's blood. **1883** GOLDW. SMITH in Ward *Eng. Poets* II. 381 Marvell, far less compromised and by no means regicidal, remained in public life.

† **regicidation**. *nonce-wd.* = REGICIDE[2].

1661 K. W. *Conf. Charac.*, To Rdr. (1860) 11 Tyrannicall usurpation and murderous regicidation spoiled the markets of their swelling honour.

regicide[1] ('rɛdʒɪsaɪd). [f. L. *rēgi-*, stem of *rex* king + -CIDE 1: cf. F. *regicide* (16th c.).]

1. One who kills a king, esp. his own king; one who commits the crime of regicide.

a **1548** HALL *Chron., Hen. IV* 14 b, Our posterite shal be reproved as children of Homecides, ye of Regicides & prince quellers. **1607–15** [see REGNICIDE]. **1651** HOBBES *Govt. & Soc.* xiv. §20. 229 Of which sort are Traytors, Regicides, and such as take up armes against the City. **1690** DRYDEN *Don Sebastian* IV. iii, That I miss'd [your life] Was the propitious errour of my fate, Not of my Soul, my Soul's a Regicide.

2. *spec.* **a.** *Eng. Hist.* One of those who took part in the trial and execution of Charles I.

1654 EVELYN *Diary* 27 Aug., He who publish'd those bold sermons of..the Jewes crucifying Christ, applied to the wicked regicides. **1660** *Ibid.* 11 Oct., The Regicides who sat on the life of our late King, were brought to tryal in the Old Bailey. **1679** in Somers *Tracts* I. 51 When there are still so many of the old Regicides not only alive, but in Vogue and Authority. *a* **1715** BURNET *Own Time* II. (1724) I. 162 The Regicides were at that time odious beyond all expression. **1818** CRUISE *Digest* (ed. 2) I. 374 Where by the statute 12 Cha. II. all the lands, tenements, and hereditaments of the regicides were forfeited to the Crown. **1874** GREEN *Short Hist.* ix. §2. 605 In the punishment of the Regicides indeed, a Presbyterian might well be as zealous as a cavalier.

b. *Fr. Hist.* One of those Revolutionists concerned in the execution of Louis XVI.

1796 BURKE *Regic. Peace* i. (1892) 21 The Regicides were the first to declare war. We are the first to sue for peace. **1809** SYD. SMITH *Wks.* (1859) I. 161/1 The regicides of France were poor theatrical imitators. **1848** W. H. KELLY tr. *Le Blanc's Hist. Ten Y.* II. 508 The king had granted a pardon to Meunier who had been condemned by the Court of Peers as a regicide.

3. *attrib.* passing into *adj.*

c **1645** HOWELL *Lett.* I. xviii. (1650) 30 The Regicide villain was apprehended. **1790** BURKE *Fr. Rev.* 108 A groupe of regicide and sacrilegious slaughter. **1796** —— *Regic. Peace* i. (1892) 25 The Regicide Directory..charge us with eluding our declarations. **1804** W. TAYLOR in *Ann. Rev.* II. 244 The Cordeliers were the regicide portion of the Jacobins. **1839** MARRYAT *Phant. Ship* viii, The murder of his regicide ambassador.

regicide[2] ('rɛdʒɪsaɪd). [f. as prec. + -CIDE 2.] The killing or murder of a king.

1602 WARNER *Alb. Eng.* IX. li. 232 That doth Rebellion, Regecide, and breach of Othes allow. **1644** SIR E. DERING *Prop. Sacr.* b iv, The first Regicide..was that of the Emperour Mauritius. **1683** EVELYN *Diary* 12 Feb., The late Rebells usurpation and regicide. **1725** POPE *Odyss.* I. 48 Did fate, or we, when great Atrides died, Urge the bold traitor to the regicide? **1796** BURKE *Regic. Peace* i. (1892) 8 The Republick of Regicide..has actually conquered the finest parts of Europe. **1816** SCOTT *Antiq.* xviii, A crime only inferior to sacrilege, or regicide. **1884** SYMONDS *Shaks. Predec.* xv. 662 Marlowe..shows Edward smothered, sparing only one incident of that unnatural regicide.

'regicidism. [f. prec. + -ISM.] The practice or principle of regicide.

1660 R. COKE *Justice Vind.* Ep. Ded. 10 Sacriledge, Regicidism and Murder. **1676** *Doctrine of Devils* 77 Any Crime, Villany, or Piacle whatever, Murther,..Regicidism [etc.]. **1795** W. TAYLOR in *Monthly Rev.* XVI. 522 The stimulus required is—Regicidism. **1800** ANNA SEWARD *Lett.* (1811) V. 370 Our great and truly religious poet, Milton, published in defence of regicidism.

regiculture ('rɛdʒɪˌkʌltjʊə(r)). *rare.* [f. L. *rēgi-*, *rex* king + CULTURE *sb.*] Honour or homage to kings.

1880 SWINBURNE in T. H. Ward *Eng. Poets* III. 281 For all her evil report among men on the score of passive obedience and regiculture.

‖ **regidor** (rexi'dor). Pl. **regidores**, **regidors**. [Sp. *regidor* alderman, f. *regir* to rule.] In Spain and the former Spanish dominions in America, a member of a cabildo or municipal council; a councillor; a village official.

1622 J. MABBE tr. *Aleman's Rogue* I. I. iii. 33 Thus it fared with a Regidor, who being espied by an old man,..call'd him unto him. **1755** SMOLLETT *Cervantes' Don Quixote* I. p. xiv, Dedicated to the alcaides, regidors, and gentlemen of the noble town of Argamasilla. **1834** A. PIKE *Prose Sketches & Poems* 170 The Regidor, or Assistant Alcalde, Miguel Sena, has only perjured himself three times. **1848** E. BRYANT *What I saw in California* xxii. 283 The first of these pueblos is governed by its corresponding body of magistrates, composed of an alcalde or judge, four regidores or municipal officers, a syndic and a secretary. **1895** G. E. KING *New Orleans* vii. 115 Instead of a superior council, there was a cabildo, with regidores, alcaldes, [etc.]. **1934** *Hist. Soc. Southern California Publ.* XVI. 142 He was *regidor* of Los Angeles in 1838–39. **1950** G. BRENAN *Face of Spain* vi. 143 He introduced himself as the *regidor* of the village municipality. **1969** *Femina* (Bombay) 26 Dec. 41/1 One of the labourers summoned the *regidor*, a village official, to the scene. **1974** *Encycl. Brit. Micropædia* II. 422/1 In local affairs, each municipality in Hispanic America was governed by its *cabildo*, or city council... Its members, *regidores* (councillors) and *alcaldes ordinarios* (magistrates), along with the local *corregidor* (royally appointed judge), enjoyed considerable prestige and power.

‖**régie** (reʒi). Also with capital initial. [Fr., f. *régir* to rule.] In France and certain other countries: a government department that administers a state-controlled industry or service; formerly *esp.*, one responsible for taxation, customs and excise, etc.; a government monopoly used as a means of taxation, *esp.* the tobacco monopoly in the former Turkish Empire. Also *attrib.*

1791 LD. GOWER in *Despatches Earl Gower* (1885) 61 The 4th [article of a decree] allows tobacco in leaves to be stored, for a year, in the ware-houses of the *Régie*. **1879** *Encycl. Brit.* IX. 738/1 Unfortunately, he [*sc.* Frederick the Great] adopted the French ideas of excise, and the French methods of imposing and collecting taxes,—a system known as the Regie. **1883** *Pall Mall Gaz.* 9 May 5/1 The Turkish tobacco régie..is designed to include a company having the exclusive right of preparing tobacco for home consumption and of selling it to the public. **1884** *Ibid.* 5 Sept. 6/2 Ladies ..smoke the strong régie cigar with evident enjoyment. **1890** *Athenæum* 11 Oct. 474/3 All the frequenters of a country inn [in France]..consume the tobacco of the *régie*. **1923** *Glasgow Herald* 26 Feb. 10 The exploitation of the railways of the Ruhr and the Rhineland by a Franco-Belgian 'regie' is believed to have been decided. **1929** W. RAY tr. *Hegemann's Frederick the Great* 122 The King indeed was thoroughly well satisfied with his Régie escapades... The patient Prussians had barely two more years to wait before death came to rid them of their great king, the extortions of the French *Régie*, [etc.]. **1958** G. T. MATTHEWS *Royal Gen. Farms 18th Cent. France* I. ii. 43 Prior to 1548 the various salt taxes and commercial concessions constituting the *grandes gabelles* were partly farmed to individual tax-farmers and partly managed by government *régies*. **1964** RIDLEY & BLONDEL *Public Administration in France* II. vii. 181 Finally we come to the revenue or, as the French call them, fiscal divisions. Until recently there were four more or less autonomous services (or *régies*). These had remained virtually unchanged since the Revolution and corresponded roughly to the main sources of state revenue: direct taxes, indirect taxes, customs duties, and registration fees, stamp duties and the national domain... After the war it was decided that the four *régies* should be transformed into two divisions of the ministry. *Ibid.* x. 239 Traditionally there were two ways of organizing a public service, the *régie* and the concession; the former operated by a government department or a local authority, the latter on contractual terms by private enterprise. **1977** S. J. & E. K. SHAW *Hist. Ottoman Empire & Mod. Turkey* II. iii. 233 In 1883 the Public Debt Commission turned the tobacco monopoly over to a private German-French company called the *Régie cointéressée de tabacs de l'Empire Ottoman*, which paid a fixed annual fee..in return and then divided the profits with the Ottoman treasury. The Régie had the sole right to buy and process all tobacco sold in the empire and regulate its cultivation... The tobacco..was stored in the Régie warehouses.

regient, obs. form of REGENT *sb.*

†**re'gifical**, *a.* *Obs. rare*⁻⁰. [f. L. *rēgific-us* + -AL¹.] 'Royal, princely, pompous, sumptuous' (Blount *Glossogr.* 1656).

regifuge ('rɛdʒɪfju:dʒ). *Rom. Hist.* [ad. L. *rēgifugium*, f. *rēgi-*, *rex* king + *fuga* flight.] The flight or expulsion of the kings from Rome.

L. *rēgifugium* occurs only as the name of the festival (on 24 Feb.) commemorative of the expulsion.

1654 VILVAIN *Epit. Ess.* II. xxviii, Tarquins expulsion or Regi-fuge. *a* **1727** NEWTON *Chronol. Amended* i. (1728) 49 The old Records of the Latines were burnt by the Gauls, an hundred and twenty years after the Regifuge. **1770** SWINTON in *Phil. Trans.* LXI. 88 They prevailed at Rome.. till after the regifuge. **1847** GROTE *Greece* II. xxxi. IV. 206 At the epoch of Kleisthenês, which by a remarkable coincidence is the same as that of the regifuge at Rome.

regild (ri:'gɪld), *v.* [RE- 5 a.] *trans.* To gild again. Also *fig.*

1583 STUBBES *Anat. Abus.* I. To Rdr. (1879) p. xii, With their swoords, daggers, and rapiers guilte and reguilte. **1841** F. E. PAGET *S. Antholin's* 3 He neither regilt the weathercock, nor raised the height of his own pew. **1857** DUFFERIN *Lett. High Lat.* (ed. 3) 10 Destined to regild his spurs in future years on the soil of Spain.

‖**régime, regime** (reɪ'ʒi:m). [F., ad. L. *regimen* REGIMEN.]

1. = REGIMEN 2.

1776 EARL CARLISLE *Let.* 13 Sept. in Jesse *Selwyn & Contemp.* (1844) III. 157 Regime is better than physic. **1908** A. BENNETT *Old Wives' Tale* I. iii. 45 She was a shrivelled little woman, capable of sitting twelve hours a day in a bedroom and thriving on the *régime*. **1943** *Ann. Allergy* I. 33 Others in whom the psychic element is important are nevertheless improved by a hygienic régime or by symptomatic medication. **1973** *Daily Tel.* 13 Feb. 16 This is not a diet to enter upon without medical prescription... To embark on this régime without due regard to the consequences may delay diagnosis of other disorders.

2. a. A manner, method, or system of rule or government; a system or institution having widespread influence or prevalence. Now freq. applied disparagingly to a particular government or administration.

1792 [see b]. **1805** *Edin. Rev.* VI. 471 The short sentence about the *regime* of the Roman provinces affords two instances of inadvertence. **1833** CHALMERS *Const. Man* I. vi. (1834) I. 250 These first and second principles of natural justice, whatever violence may have been done to them at the overthrow of a former regime [etc.]. **1848** MILL *Pol. Econ.* III. xvi. §1 Under the regime of competition, things are ..exchanged for each other at such values [etc.]. **1898** BODLEY *France* I. Introd. 32 Under previous parliamentary regimes this evil was not patent. **1955** *Times* 2 May 8/3 But none of us is prepared, either, to bolster up the aging régime of Chiang Kai-shek. *Ibid.* 11/5 Only King Saud and the régime in the Yemen (which recently survived in undiminished medieval splendour an abortive *coup d'État*) remain patently faithful to Egypt. **1973** *Guardian* 16 Apr. 1/6 The Smith regime in Rhodesia.

b. *spec.* in phr. ***the ancient***, or ***old, regime*** (tr. F. *l'ancien régime*), the system of government in France before the Revolution of 1789. Also *transf.*, the old system or style of things.

1792 GOUV. MORRIS in Sparks *Life & Writ.* (1832) II. 195 Some are for absolute monarchy, some for the ancient regime. **1808** SIR J. MOORE in Jas. Moore *Narr. Campaign* (1809) 76 They have acted with all the imbecility of an old established weak government of the old regime. **1816** W. SCOTT in *Q. Rev.* XIV. 192 A crime against sentiment which no author, of moderate prudence, would have hazarded under the old *régime*. **1825** JEFFERSON *Autobiog.* Wks. 1859 I. 104 The Aristocracy was cemented by a common principle, of preserving the ancient regime, or whatever should be nearest to it. **1842** GEO. ELIOT *Let.* 30 Aug. (1954) I. 144 There ought to be..a few spectral clingers to the memory of the old régime in the era of political regeneration. **1884** *Harper's Mag.* Mar. 554/2 The habits of the last century in respect to decorum were just receding... The old *régime* was dying. **1912** F. A. TALBOT *Moving Pictures* xii. 136 Under the old *régime* darkness prevailed from one end of the programme to the other, save, perhaps, during a short interval. **1971** R. BENDIX in A. Bullock *20th Cent.* xv. 352/2 Their overthrow of an 'old regime' fulfils the first task of their [*sc.* revolutionary movements'] ideological mission. **1976** J. B. HILTON *Gamekeeper's Gallows* xv. 159 'Take her back home again tomorrow.'.. The old regime was over.

3. *Physical Geogr.* **a.** The condition of a watercourse with regard to changes that may be occurring in its form or bed and the possibility of an equilibrium in which there is neither erosion nor deposition; = REGIMEN 5.

[**1779** P. L. G. DU BUAT *Principes d'Hydraulique* I. iv. 73 Ainsi, par le terme régime, nous entendons proprement la vitesse du courant, comparée à la résistance du terrain qui forme le lit.] **1856** *Min. Proc. Inst. Civil Engineers* XV. 241 The case of the River Clyde, at Glasgow, should be carefully examined, when considering any measure for the *régime* of the Thames. *Ibid.* 242 To regulate the low-water *régime*, by removing the shoals below London Bridge. **1895** *Ibid.* CXIX. 282 Observations were made at thirty sites... Each was known by long local experience to have been in a state of permanent regime, the canal having been flowing for years on its self-silted bed. **1925** F. REEVES *Notes & Data Rly. Engin.* 30 One frequently sees the results of this absence of accurate knowledge of the *régime* of the stream in washaways, bridges of unnecessary size, etc. **1927** *Min. Proc. Inst. Civil Engin.* CCXXIII. 268 The conditions of great rivers in unstable regime, presenting every kind of irregularity of flow. **1957** *New Scientist* 26 Dec. 30/3 The regime theory of canals was originally developed in India.. and stemmed from field observations of the self-adjusting character of these artificial alluvial canals. *Ibid.*, From the regime viewpoint the behaviour of a river is visualised as fluctuation about equilibrium or 'regime' dimensions. **1965** A. HOLMES *Princ. Physical Geol.* (ed. 2) xviii. 543 The whole régime of sandbanks and inner channels eventually reaches an all-over width that meets the requirements of all but the very greatest floods.

b. The condition of a body of water with regard to the rates at which water enters and leaves it.

1874 *Chem. News* 27 Feb. 101/2 (*heading*) Pluvial régime of the torrid zone in the basin of the Atlantic Ocean. **1933** *Geogr. Jrnl.* LXXXII. 174 While some writers have thought the régime of the lake (the balance between gains and losses) to depend almost entirely on the precipitation on and evaporation from the lake-surface, Mr. Gillman finds that the mean inflow from tributary basins is by no means negligible. *Ibid.*, Theeuws held that the old régime of the lake was changed once and for all by the *débâcle* of about 1875.

4. The set of conditions under which a system occurs or is maintained.

1890 *Rep. Brit. Assoc. Adv. Sci. 1889* 502 We should expect that, after the change of loads has been frequently repeated so that a cyclic *régime* is established, the wire will, for any value of load between the two extremes, be longer during unloading than during loading. **1920** A. FAGE *Airscrews in Theory & Exper.* xii. 176 The study of the working régime of a helicopter. **1942** *Electronic Engin.* XIV. 665/3 It has been found that the duration of this low voltage régime may be increased to..20–30 microseconds by connecting an additional condenser directly between anode and cathode. **1957** J. K. CHARLESWORTH *Quaternary Era* II. xlviii. 1410 Pluvial conditions over vast areas of the world.. were replaced by a régime of desiccation. **1971** *Sci. Amer.* Sept. 118/1 Without altering the horticultural regime of keeping 90 percent of the land fallow the Tsembaga's 1,000 best acres might have supported a population of 200 or more per square mile. **1978** *Nature* 29 June 752/1 Anemones were ..maintained in circulating seawater at 10°C for 6 months before experimentation in a 12-h light and 12-h darkness regime.

regimen ('rɛdʒɪmən). Also 5 *Sc.* regemen. [a. L. *regimen*, f. *regĕre* to rule, direct, etc. Cf. OF. *regimen* (14th c.).]

1. a. The act of governing; government, rule.

1456 SIR G. HAYE *Law Arms* (S.T.S.) 66 Quhare thare is na hede, regemen na ordinaunce, thare resoun naturale failis. **1535** STEWART *Cron. Scot.* I. 52 Baith sword and sceptour, regimen and croun. **1647** CLARENDON *Hist. Reb.* II. §128 The General himself, and the Martial affairs, were subject to this Regimen and Discipline as well as the Civil. **1678** CUDWORTH *Intell. Syst.* I. iv. 491 Others commonly assign him the Regimen of Separate Souls after Death. **1765** BLACKSTONE *Comm.* I. 25 In the inns of court all sorts of regimen and academical superintendance..are found impracticable. **1827** HALLAM *Const. Hist.* I. i. 2 The forms and principles of political regimen in these different nations became more divergent from each other. **1875** TENNYSON *Q. Mary* III. i, Sir, no woman's regimen Can save us.

b. A particular form or kind of government; a regime; a prevailing system.

a **1734** NORTH *Lives* (1826) III. 362 Gentlemen's sons in the college, under the influence of such a regimen, will be exposed to the mischiefs of idleness, expense, and debauchery. **1792** A. YOUNG *Trav. France* 529 Under the regimen of land-taxes, all foreigners residing in a kingdom absolutely escape taxation. **1837** HALLAM *Hist. Lit.* I. vii. §45 Nothing is so apt to follow as sedition from a popular regimen. **1860** MILL *Repr. Govt.* (1865) 19/1 What sort of human beings can be formed under such a regimen?

†**c.** The aggregate of those under some government; a class or kind. *Obs. rare.*

[**1660** STANLEY *Hist. Philos.* IX. (1701) 347/2 The Soul of Pythagoras, being of the Regimine of Apollo, (whether as a Follower, or some other way more near to him).] **1709** STEELE *Tatler* No. 68 ¶2, I have also a long List of Persons of Condition, who are certainly of the same Regimen with these Banditti.

2. *Med.* **a.** The regulation of such matters as have an influence on the preservation or restoration of health; a particular course of diet, exercise, or mode of living, prescribed or adopted for this end; †a course of treatment employed for the cure of a wound. Cf. REGIMENT 5.

c **1400** *Lanfranc's Cirurg.* 60 In anoþer maner regimen Vndirstonde þat þe man.. schal not be lete blood in þe bigynnynge [etc.]. *Ibid.* 289 Þou schalt kepe him wiþ good regimen, & he schal vse no metis ne drinkis þat engendrith scharp blood & greet. **1646** G. DANIEL *Wks.* (Grosart) I. 41 Things.. Very behoofull to the Regimen Of health. **1693** tr. *Blancard's Phys. Dict.* (ed. 2), *Regimen*, a Word us'd in Physick, about ordering Diet, and the like. **1707** FLOYER *Physic. Pulse-Watch* 197 If thereby the Pulse be alter'd to more frequency, we use a cool Regimen. **1764** REID *Inquiry* i. §3 Would he not hope for his cure from physic and good regimen? **1830** SCOTT *Demonol.* i. 19 His physician received a grateful letter from him acknowledging the success of his regimen. **1899** *Allbutt's Syst. Med.* VI. 425 A strict regimen ..being at the same time observed.

b. *transf.* and *fig.*

1751 JOHNSON *Rambler* No. 89 ¶7 Active employment.. is generally a necessary part of this intellectual regimen. **1777** SHERIDAN *Sch. Scand.* III. iii, There's Sir Harry diets himself for gaming, and is now under a hazard regimen. **1862** BURTON *Bk. Hunter* 97 'A course of reading' as it is sometimes called, is a course of regimen for dwarfing the mind.

3. *Gram.* The government of one word by another; the relation which one word in a sentence has to another depending on it.

1600 HOLLAND *Livy* 2nd Index s.v. *H–S*, You must in this manner of speech understand *millia* for the regimen of the Genitive case. **1668** WILKINS *Real Char.* IV. 448 The Regimen of words doth concern their government of others. **1751** HARRIS *Hermes* Wks. (1841) 193 Hence..arises the grammatical regimen of the verb by its nominative, and of the accusative by its verb. **1824** L. MURRAY *Eng. Gram.* (ed. 5) I. 328 The following sentences, which give the passive voice the regimen of an active verb, are very irregular. **1872** F. HALL *False Philol.* 84 The grammarians posit the absence of regimen as one of the differential features of a conjunction.

†**4.** *Alch.* (See quot.) *Obs. rare*⁻⁰.

1727–38 CHAMBERS *Cycl.*, *Regimen*, in chymistry and alchymy, is the method of ordering and conducting any thing, that it may answer it's intention. Thus, regimen of fire, is the manner of making and ordering fire, and the degrees thereof. [From *Dict. de Trévoux* s.v. *Régime*.]

5. *Physical Geogr.* = RÉGIME, REGIME 3 a.

1810 *Encycl. Brit.* XVIII. 65/1 We shall..learn the mutual action of the current and its bed, and the circumstances which ensure the stability of both. These we may call the regimen or the conservation of the stream, and may say that it is in regimen or in conservation. **1851** *Min. Proc. Inst. Civil Engineers* X. 231 Experiments and observations were made on the velocity and regimen of the stream. **1966** *McGraw-Hill Encycl. Sci. & Technol.* XI. 584/2 Most natural streams are in regimen. **1971** R. F. FLINT *Glacial & Quaternary Geol.* iii. 47 It will be useful to follow the practice of engineers in reference to streams of water, and refer to the system or activity of the glacier as a whole, based on its meteorology, economy, rate and possible type of flow, and fluctuation, as the regimen of the glacier. The term, applied to glaciers as well as streams, is not quantitatively precise; it is broadly descriptive.

Hence **re'gimenal** *a.* = REGIMINAL.

1866 FLINT *Princ. Med.* (1880) 215 The correctness of this view of the regimenal management of the disease. **1874** BUCKNILL & TUKE *Man. Psych. Med.* (ed. 3) 687 The treatment is medicinal and regimenal.

†**regimence.** *Obs. rare.* [Alteration of next, after sbs. in -ENCE.] = REGIMENT 1.

c **1470** HARDING *Chron.* Proem v, Vnto your sapience I wyll remember a notabilytee Of your elders rule and regymence. *Ibid.* XCVIII. xiii, Full greate intelligence Of all good rule and noble regimence.

regiment ('rɛdʒɪmənt), *sb.* Also 5–6 **regement.** [ad. late L. *regimentum*, f. L. *regĕre* to rule: see -MENT, and cf. F. *régiment* (1314).]

1. Rule or government over a person, people, or country; *esp.* royal or magisterial authority. Now *rare* (very common *c* 1550–1680).

1390 GOWER *Conf.* III. 233 Pite is the foundement Of every kinges regiment, If it be medled with justice. *a* **1502**

Charter London cxi. in Arnolde *Chron.* (1811) 43 Hens forth yͭ he be vnder the regement and gouernaunce of the Mayr and Aldirmen. *c* **1557** ABP. PARKER *Ps.* xcii, But thou.. as Lord and president For ever standst unmoveable and wyse in regiment. **1576** FLEMING *Panopl. Epist.* 33 What place is there in all the world, not subiect to the regiment and power of this citie? *a* **1617** BAYNE *On Eph.* (1658) 153 The King hath a more intimate.. regiment over his Queen than over any other subject. **1698** [R. FERGUSON] *View Eccles.* 100 Without which there could be no Superiority, nor Subordination and consequently no Regiment in the World. **1826** E. IRVING *Babylon* II. VII. 177 He tried, by all human wisdom, to gain security and steadfastness to his regiment. **1832** AUSTIN *Jurispr.* vi. (1879) I. 261 The powers of ecclesiastical regiment which none but the church should wield.

†**b.** Manner, method, or system of ruling or governing; a form of polity, a regime. *Obs.*

1474 in Tighe & Davies *Windsor* (1858) I. 400 The Statutes for the Order and Regiment to be hadde, used, and contynued in the Corporacion. **1535** COVERDALE *Bible* Ded. ¶6 In all godly regimentes of olde tyme the kynge and temporall iudge was obeyed of euery man. **1576** FLEMING *Panopl. Epist.* 197 You account tyrannicall regiment, an execrable regiment. **1605** BACON *Adv. Learn.* II. ii. §13 History Civill, in respect of the Habitations, Regiments, and Manners of the people. *a* **1676** HALE *Prim. Orig. Man.* (1677) 6 The knowledge of History, of Humane Laws,.. of Political and Oeconomical regiments.

2. †**a.** The office or function of a ruler. *Obs.* (Common *c* 1550–1610, chiefly with verbs of receiving, accepting, etc., and their opposites.)

1390 GOWER *Conf.* I. 218 Whan this king was passed thus, This false tunged Perseus The regiment hath underfonge. **1494** FABYAN *Chron.* VI. clviii. 147 He obteynyd the regyment and gouernaunce of the abouesayde Kynge. *a* **1572** KNOX *Hist. Ref.* Wks. 1846 I. 431 Ane man.. maist unworthy of ony regiment in ane weill rewlit commun-wealth. **1591** *Troub. Raigne K. John* II. (1611) 86 To seeke a meane To dispossesse Iohn of his regiment. **1596** SPENSER *F.Q.* II. x. 30 When he had resigned his regiment. **1630** B. JONSON *New Inn* II. ii, A rare stateswoman! I admire her bearing In her new regiment.

†**b.** The time or period during which one rules; a reign. *Obs.*

1566 CECIL in Strype *Ann. Ref.* (1709) I. xlvii. 481 Otherwise her Regiment will prove very troublesome and unquiet. **1582** *Reg. Privy Council Scot.* III. 473 Laitlie, in the regiment of umquhile James, sumtyme Erll of Mortoun. **1609** HOLLAND *Amm. Marcell.* 203 During his regiment there was hardly any man.. could have remedie were it never so just and reasonable. **1630** PRYNNE *Anti-Armin.* 85 During all the time of his exile for Religion in Queene Maries bloody Regiment.

†**3.** Government or control over oneself, one's feelings or actions. *Obs.*

c **1412** HOCCLEVE *De Reg. Princ.* 2052 Of Gyles of regyment Of princes, plotmel thynke I to translate. **1483** CAXTON *Cato* 2 b, This is a singuler book and may well be callyd the regyment or gouernaunce of the body and sowle. **1605** BACON *Adv. Learn.* II. xxi. §6 For it concerneth the Regiment & gouernment of euery man, over himself, & not ouer others. **1679** PENN *Addr. Prot.* II. 219 Speculations that have no influence upon holy Living, or tendency to the Regiment of our Passions.

†**b.** Control or influence exercised by one thing over another, or over a person. *Obs.*

1390 GOWER *Conf.* III. 115 Whom this planete under-fongeth To stonde upon his regiment, He schal be meke and pacient. **1528** PAYNELL *Salerne's Regim.* C iij, The membres or places of mans body, in whiche is the regiment, that is, the digestion of meates and humours. **1591** SYLVESTER *Du Bartas* I. ii. 95 Not, that at all times, one same Element In one same Body hath the Regiment. **1635** SWAN *Spec. M.* (1670) 179 Sith this lunar regiment is pertinent to most seas. **1674** GREW *Nat. Mixture* II. §6 Yet doth not this vast Diversity take away the Regiment and Subordination of Principles.

†**c.** *Gram.* = REGIMEN 3. *Obs. rare*$^{-1}$.

1591 PERCIVALL *Sp. Dict.* E iv, Regiment is, when any part of speech requireth or gouerneth in construction, any case or moode to be set before him or after him.

†**4.** The ruling or governing *of* a person, people or place. *Obs.*

a **1529** SKELTON *Sp. Parrot* 431 For o ower regente the regimente he hathe. **1555** EDEN *Decades* 22 Leauinge the hole regiment of the Iland with his brother the Lieuetenaunte. **1610** J. DOVE *Advt. Seminaries* 49 Saints departed have the regiment of whole Provinces. **1652** NEEDHAM tr. *Selden's Mare Cl.* Auth. Pref., The consent of men and gods.. would have the regiment of Sea and Land bee in thy power. **1702** C. MATHER *Magn. Chr.* IV. vii. (1852) 136 Could we see the unseen regiment of the world.. what an awe would it strike us with!

†**b.** The management, guidance, or control *of* a thing or affair. *Obs. rare.* Cf. REGIMEN 4.

1477 NORTON *Ord. Alch.* vi. in Ashm. (1652) 101 Now lerne the Regiment of your Fiers. **1651** N. BACON *Disc. Govt. Eng.* II. v. (1739) 26 The greatest Lords thought the Regiment of Sea-affairs worthy of the best of their Rank. **1741** BETTERTON *Eng. Stage* vi. 82 We shall proceed to the Regiment and proper Motions of the Head.

†**5.** *Med.* Rule of diet or mode of living. = REGIMEN 2. *Obs.* (Common in phr. *regiment of health.*)

1525 LD. BERNERS tr. *Froiss.* II. clxxxix. [clxxxv.] 577 If they had ordred hym in his youthe, and so contynued by a reasonable regement,.. this syckenesse had nat fallen to hym nowe. **1582** HESTER *Secr. Phiorav.* I. xxiii. 26 Let them keepe a good regemente of life. **1612** WOODALL *Surg. Mate* Wks. (1653) 87 The particular Regiment is in remedies which conserve and strengthen [etc.]. **1669** *Pref. Digby's Closet Opened*, According to that old Saw in the Regiment of Health, *Incipe cum Liquido*, etc. **1768** FOOTE *Devil on 2 Sticks* III. (1778) 46 What signifies a palliative regiment, with such a rotten constitution.

†**6.** A rule, regulation, ordinance. *Obs.*

1546 BALE *Eng. Votaries* I. (1560) 13 b, After he had furnished it with new regiments and lawes. *a* **1548** HALL *Chron., Rich. III* 42 The metrician coulde not obseruynge the regimentes of metre ende the seconde verse in Bore. *a* **1617** BAYNE *On Coloss.* (1634) 349 The worke is double, internall or externall: regiments, or direction.

†**b.** *Naut.* (See quots.) *Obs.*

1574 BOURNE *Regiment for Sea* Pref. (1577) A iij b, A Table of Declination calculated for fowre yeres,.. which the See-men doo call a Regiment. **1594** J. DAVIS *Seaman's Secr.* (1607) 18 You must also by your Regiment or other tables, search to know the declination of that body which you obserue.

†**7.** A place or country under a particular rule; a kingdom, province, domain, district. *Obs.*

1390 GOWER *Conf.* III. 127 The ferste regiment Toward the part of Orient.. Governed is of Signes thre. **1590** SPENSER *F.Q.* II. ix. 59 An auncient booke.. That of this lands first conquest did devize, And old division into Regiments. **1601** HOLLAND *Pliny* I. 113 So much for the principall nations of this countrey. As for the States, Tetrarchies, and regiments, there be in all 195. **1635** PAGITT *Christianogr.* II. vi. (1636) 39 That Councell divided the Regiment of the Church into foure Patriarchall Sees. **1662** in *Buccleuch MSS.* (Hist. MSS. Comm.) I. 540 A company of foot raised or to be raised in Long-acre or thereabouts in the Regiment of Westminster and the Liberty thereof.

transf. **1602** L. LLOYD *Confer. Lawes* 1 The elements are commaunded to staie within their owne regiments, without trespassing one of another. **1623** WEBSTER *Duchess Malfi* Ded., Men who never saw the sea, yet desire to behold that regiment of waters. **1625** JACKSON *Creed* V. iii. 14 Speculatiue notions are seated in the head or vtmost confines of the soules regiment.

8. *Mil.* A considerable body of troops, more or less permanently organized under the command of a superior officer, and forming a definite unit of an army or military force; since the 17th c. the specific name of the largest permanent unit of the cavalry, infantry, and foot-guards of the British Army. ***regiment of the line***: see LINE *sb.*[2] 21 b.

The precise application of the term in the British Army was considerably altered by the changes made in 1881, when the old numbered infantry regiments (see quot. 1876) were converted into battalions of the new Territorial Regiments finally formed in that year.

1579 DIGGES *Stratioticos* III. vii. 96 If his Regiment amount to the number of a fiue or sixe thousande [etc.]. **1590** SIR J. SMYTH *Disc. Weapons* 6 It was verie meete and conuenient that all that whole regiment should bee reduced into bands of 150. soldiers to an Ensigne. **1598** BARRET *Theor. Warres* Gloss. 252 *Regiment*, a Dutch word, is a number of sundry companies vnder the charge of a Colonell. **1603** KNOLLES *Hist. Turks* (1621) 67 To that purpose was every mans regiment appointed what place to assaile. **1630** *R. Johnson's Kingd. & Commw.* 147 These companies.. are now againe of late yeares dissolved, and in their place the Regiments now entertained, are five in number. **1665** MANLEY *Grotius' Low C. Warres* 834 The hope of the Venetian Warr being deferred,.. the Spanish Regiments came thence into the Netherlands. **1710** STEELE *Tatler* No. 100 ¶4 As idle People use to gather about a Regiment, that are exercising their Arms. **1775** SHERIDAN *Rivals* I. ii, He is at present with his regiment. **1853** STOCQUELER *Milit. Encycl.* 230/1 The ordinary strength of a regiment of infantry of a single battalion is 750. **1876** VOYLE & STEVENSON *Milit. Dict.* 51/1 The 109 regiments of the line include 12 Highland regiments, and the first twenty-five have 2 battalions each. **1881** (*title*) Report of Committee on the Formation of Territorial Regiments as proposed by Colonel Stanley's Committee.

b. *transf.* and *fig.* in various contexts; *esp.* a large array or number (of anything).

1605 SYLVESTER *Du Bartas* II. i. III. *Furies* 484 The fell fourth Regiment, is outward Tumours. *c* **1645** HOWELL *Lett.* (1650) II. 37, I find as high examples of vertue in women as in men: I could produce heer a whole regiment of them. **1722** DE FOE *Col. Jack* (1840) 27 You look as if you belonged to the ragged regiment. **1768–74** TUCKER *Lt. Nat.* (1834) I. 236 If they find you invulnerable in front, they will detach a regiment of secret motives to take you in rear. **1849** MRS. CARLYLE *Lett.* II. 84 A cat.. to eat the regiments of mice. **1860** *All Year Round* No. 70. 475 Regiments of old vellum-bound books.

†**c.** A number of individuals formed into a body or group; a class or kind. *Obs.*

1610 HEALEY *St. Aug. Citie of God* X. ix. Comm. 354 Proclus diuides the diuels into fiue regiments rather then fiue kinds, distinguishing them by their functions. **1634** W. WOOD *New Eng. Prosp.* (1865) 30 Although an Eagle be counted King of that feathered regiment, yet is there a certaine blacke Hawke that beats him. **1656** EARL MONM. tr. *Boccalini's Advts. fr. Parnass.* I. xlvii. (1674) 63 [He] was forced to send.. for a new Regiment of Dogs, to bring his Sheep to better obedience.

†**9.** *pl.* Regimentals. *Obs. rare*$^{-1}$.

1759 H. WALPOLE *Lett., to G. Montagu* 19 July (1846) III. 464 The regiments, too, are very becoming, scarlet faced with black, buff waistcoats, and gold buttons.

10. *attrib.* and *Comb.*, as (sense 8) ***regiment commander, piece, sword.***

1684 J. PETER *Siege Vienna* 109 Regiment Pieces of Prince Rupert's Invention. **1722** DE FOE *Col. Jack* (1840) 115 They stood upon their defence having the regiment swords on. **1886** *Pall Mall G.* 8 Oct. 2/1 An appeal to Russia to send us.. brigade and regiment commanders.

regiment (ˈrɛdʒɪmənt), *v.* [f. prec.]

1. *trans. Mil.* To form into a regiment or regiments. (Chiefly in *passive.*) Also *transf.*

1617 COLLINS *Def. Bp. Ely* 546 Diuers kinds of fishes are ranked and regimented vnder the conduct of some one fish. **1689** G. WALKER *Siege Derry* 41 Of 7500 Men Regimented we had now alive but about 4300. **1748** *Anson's Voy.* II. vi. 196 There were two hundred horse.., properly trained and regimented. *a* **1797** H. WALPOLE *Mem. Geo. III* (1845) I. x. 144 A plan for regimenting twenty-five thousand papists in Ireland for the same service. **1827** SCOTT *Napoleon* lxxiv. Wks. 1870 XV. 79 A great part of the inhabitants were regimented and embodied. **1898** *19th Cent.* Feb. 223 The rebel force, regimented and armed throughout the country, was estimated at close upon three hundred thousand men.

refl. **1788** *Hist.* in *Ann. Reg.* 200* The peasants arming and regimenting themselves in considerable numbers.

absol. **1845** CARLYLE *Cromwell* (1871) I. 177 The new General is full of business, regimenting, discharging, enlisting.

b. To form (persons, now esp. workers) into a definitely organized body or group.

1718 *Free-thinker* No. 50 (1733) 239 He lives in a degenerate Age, and in a Nation regimented into Factions. **1731** FIELDING *Letter-writers* III. vii, Why, the rogues are incorporated, they are regimented. **1847** GROTE *Greece* II. xxxi. IV. 175 They continued to be a separate fraternity, and would not submit to be regimented anew under an altered category and denomination. **1878** *Fraser's Mag.* XVIII. 194 They must be 'regimented' under captains of industry who will compel them to their task.

c. To bring or put (things) *into* some definite order or system; to organize, systematize.

1698 [R. FERGUSON] *View Eccles.* Pref., Yet being otherwise Regimented and Marshal'd into sentences. **1866** CARLYLE in *Morning Star* 4 Apr. 5/5 Very many things could be regimented and organised into the mute system of education that Goethe evidently adumbrates there. **1873** A. L. PERRY *Elem. Pol. Econ.* (ed. 8) 535 The.. folly of law-makers, who.. have struggled to regiment all industry.

2. To assign to a regiment or group.

1774 KAMES *Sketches* II. ix. (1807) II. 261 In Switzerland ..every male who can bear arms is regimented, and subjected to military discipline. **1856** FROUDE *Hist. Eng.* I. i. 13 Every man was regimented somewhere;.. the restrictions both on masters and servants were.. severe.

regimental (rɛdʒɪˈmɛntəl), *a.* and *sb.* [f. REGIMENT *sb.* + -AL[1].]

A. *adj.* **1.** Of or belonging to, associated with, a regiment, or with some particular regiment.

1659 J. JONES *Let.* 1 Dec. in J. Mayer *Inedited Lett. Cromwell & Other Regicides* (1861) 112 But crosse windes stayed the messenger at the water side till saturday last, soe that the tyme of meeteing at whitehall is come upon us before wee canne have any regimental meetings of o[u]r offic[e]rs. **1702** *Lond. Gaz.* No. 3843/4 He is 5 foot 9 inches, in his Regimental Clothes. **1753** CHAMBERS *Cycl. Supp.*, *App.* s.v. *Hospital*, Regimental hospitals are of the greatest importance. **1776** J. ADAMS *Wks.* (1854) IX. 406 It is right, I believe, to make the rule of promotion among captains and subalterns regimental only. **1829** *Regul. & Ord. Army* (1844) 10 The Regimental, or Second, Standard, or Guidon, is to be of the Colour of the Facing of the Regiment. **1880** GEN. ADYE in *19th Cent.* April 703 With only seven officers in a regiment, a system of pure regimental rise by single battalions cannot well be applied.

fig. **1845** J. SAUNDERS *Pict. Eng. Life* 8 Chaucer had not much relish for the regimental school of rhythm. **1848** CLOUGH *Amours de Voy.* I. 110 With metallic beliefs and regimental devotions.

2. *Mil. slang.* Maintaining or observing strict discipline.

1919 *Athenæum* 1 Aug. 695/1 *Regimental*, an Old Army adjective for a strict disciplinarian. **1948** PARTRIDGE *Dict. Forces' Slang* 154 *Regimental*... As an adjective, applied to an officer or N.C.O. who was a stickler for details. 'So-and-so's too regimental for words.'

B. *sb.* **1. a.** *pl.* The dress proper to or characteristic of any particular regiment; military uniform.

1742 *Lond. Mag.* 610 The Gold Lace on their Regimentals. **1766** GOLDSM. *Vic. W.* xxxi, He.. entered, handsomely dressed in his regimentals. **1812** BYRON *Ch. Har.* II. Notes 159 Regimentals are the best travelling dress. **1863** *Sat. Rev.* 19 Sept. 375 When he.. was no nearer Empire than a tame eagle and some sham regimentals could carry him.

fig. **1749** FIELDING *Tom Jones* VI. ix, The pale livery of death succeeds the red regimentals in which love had before drest her cheeks. **1832** LYTTON *Eugene A.* ix, Miss Nelly blushes when he speaks, scarlet is love's regimentals.

b. *transf.* Prison clothes.

1838 DICKENS *O. Twist* xviii, Stating that his 'time' was only out an hour before; and that.. having worn the regimentals for six weeks past [etc.].

†**2.** A military or regimental uniform. *Obs. rare.*

a **1794** COLMAN *Man of Business* II. (D.), If they had been ruled by me, they would have put you into the guards. You would have made a sweet figure in a regimental. **1795** ANDERSON *Brit. Emb. China* 7 The regimental consisting of a very coarse blue jacket, with a vest and breeches of the same colour.

Hence **regiˈmentalism**; ˌ**regimenˈtality**; **regiˈmentalled** *ppl. a.*

1768–74 TUCKER *Lt. Nat.* (1834) II. 190 Gypsiety and regimentality can never be turned into one another. **1789** *Poetry* in *Ann. Reg.* 156 The regimental'd and the trowser'd trains. *a* **1896** LADY BURTON in Wilkins *Rom. Lady Burton* (1897) I. x. 364 Peppering their conversation with an occasional Hindustani word,.. and plentiful regimentalisms.

regimentally (rɛdʒɪˈmɛntəlɪ), *adv.* [-LY[2].]

1. According to regiment; by regiments.

1713 *Lond. Gaz.* No. 5086/3 The rest of the Out-Pensioners are to appear at the said Hospital Regimentally on such Days as will be advertised. **1799** *Instr. & Reg. Cavalry* (1813) 278 The trumpet flourish, in drawing swords, is used regimentally on their own ground. **1834** NAPIER *Penins. War* XV. ii. (Rtldg.) II. 300 All things requisite for the subsistence.. of troops should be organised regimentally. **1885** *Manch. Exam.* 14 Apr. 4/7 The Government intended to call out the reserves regimentally.

2. In point of regimental rank.

1864 *Realm* 18 May 6 The close of the occupation of France found him still only, regimentally, a major in the 43rd.

regimentary (rɛdʒɪˈmɛntərɪ), *sb.* and *a.* [f. REGIMENT *sb.* + -ARY¹: cf. mod.F. *régimentaire.*]

†**A.** *sb.* The title of a Polish military officer. *Obs.*

1733 BUDGELL *Bee* IV. 295 The Regimentary of the Crown will enter into Saxony with an Army of 60,000 Men. **1774** *Ann. Reg.* 18 The regimentary Krazewski, who commanded in Great Poland, opposed these encroachments.

B. *adj.* Regimental.

1869 *Daily News* 30 Mar., I followed in the wake of a regimentary fragment through the streets to the Priory station. **1901** *N. Amer. Rev.* Feb. 216 With an implacable regularity, with a regimentary rigidity.

,regimenˈtation. [f. REGIMENT *v.* + -ATION.] The action or process of regimenting or organizing. (Common in recent use, esp. with ref. to workers, industries, and societies.) Also with ref. to a whole society.

1882 SPENCER *Princ. Sociol.* v. xviii. §553 The process of militant organization is a process of regimentation, which.. affects the whole community. **1890** BOOTH *Darkest Eng.* 35 The regimentation of industrial workers who have not got regular work is not so very difficult. **1936** *Sun* (Baltimore) 6 July 8/4 Let us..take the word 'regimentation'.. One dictionary has its meaning as 'enforced socialism'. **1937** *Liberty* 10 July 4/2 The same sort of regimentation that we find in Russia. **1943** J. S. HUXLEY *TVA* i. 7 The possibility of obtaining the efficiency of a coordinated plan without totalitarian regimentation. **1958** A. HUXLEY *Let.* 15 Feb. (1969) 845 Uniformity and tidiness..are so admirable in a work of art or a scientific theory but..in human life spell regimentation.

regimented (ˈrɛdʒɪməntɪd), *ppl. a.* [f. REGIMENT *v.* + -ED¹.] Formed into regiments or organized groups.

1702 DE FOE *Mock Mourners* 14 A Regimented Few we had indeed, Who serv'd for neither Pride nor Fame, but Bread. **1781** COWPER *Truth* 422 His books well trimmed.. Like regimented coxcombs rank and file. **1829** SOUTHEY *Sir T. More* II. 327 They became objects of jealousy to the whole regimented forces of the Romish Church. **1849** GROTE *Greece* II. liv. (1862) IV. 529 The superiority of disciplined and regimented force over disorderly numbers.

regiminal (rɪˈdʒɪmɪnəl), *a. Med.* [f. REGIMEN, on L. types, as *criminal*: cf. REGIMENAL.] Of or pertaining to, of the nature of, regimen.

1832 J. THOMSON *Life Cullen* I. 179 To employ..all the means, medicinal, dietetic, and regiminal, which may assist in restoring the diseased economy. **1867** W. FOX *Dyspepsia* iv. 101 Treatment..may be conveniently divided into regiminal and dietetic, and medicinal.

Regina (rɪˈdʒaɪnə). [L. *rēgīna.*] A queen; used to designate the prosecution in criminal proceedings during the reign of a queen, as in law reports.

1717 W. SALKELD *Rep. Cases adjudg'd in Court of King's Bench* I. 460 Domina Regina *versus* Wigg. **1792** W. BOSCAWEN *Treat. on Convictions on Penal Statutes* 36 In the earliest case, indeed, upon the statute of 5 An. viz. *Regina* v. *Matthews*, the Court seem to have thought otherwise. **1976** *Law Rep. Queen's Bench Division* 372 Regina v. Kellett.

reginal (rɪˈdʒaɪnəl), *a.* [ad. med.L. *rēgīnāl-is*, f. *rēgīna* queen + -AL¹; cf. obs. F. *reginal* (Godef.).] **a.** Of or pertaining to a queen; queenly, queenlike. **b.** Taking the side of the queen.

1568 in Hay Fleming *Mary Q. of Scots* (1897) 512 To gif over our authoritie and powar reginall. **1824** MOORE *Mem.* (1853) IV. 261 Dined at Denman's, the party a most Reginal one;..Talked of the Regency Question. **1845** CAMPBELL *Chancellors* (1857) II. xxxviii. 150 It raised the question whether, by a disparaging alliance, the reginal precedence was not lost. **1898** BESANT *Changeling* xvii, With reginal gesture, tall and commanding.

†**reˈgine.** *Obs.*⁻¹ [ad. L. *rēgīna.*] Queen.

Evidently used only for the sake of rhyme.

1500–20 DUNBAR *Poems* lxxxv. 6 Haile, sterne superne! Haile, in eterne,..Angelicall regyne!

†**reˈginist.** *Obs.*⁻¹ [f. L. *rēgīna* + -IST; cf. QUEENIST.] A partisan of a queen.

1646 BUCK *Rich. III*, I. 12 Those of the blood Royall (with whom the ancient Barons sided) and the Reginists.

region (ˈriːdʒən). Also 4–5 -youn(e, 5 -yowne, 4–6 -ioun(e, -yon, etc. [a. AF. *regiun* (mod.F. *région*), ad. L. *regiōn-em* direction, line, boundary, quarter, district, etc., f. *regĕre* to direct. The earliest English uses show association with *regĕre* in the sense of 'to rule'.]

1. †**a.** A realm or kingdom. *Obs.* **b.** A large tract of land; a country; a more or less defined portion of the earth's surface, now esp. as distinguished by certain natural features, climatic conditions, a special fauna or flora, or the like.

Wyclif, Tindale, and the Genevan version (1557) have *regions* in place of *fields* in John iv. 35, after *regiones* of the Vulgate. Similarly *tree of the region* in Wyclif, Jer. xii. 20.

c **1330** R. BRUNNE *Chron.* (1810) 282 Merlyn..of him has said, þat þre regions, in his bandons, salle be laid. *c* **1385** CHAUCER *L.G.W.* 1445 *Hypsipyle*, If..That thou this famous tresor mightest winne, And bryngyn it myn regioun with-inne. **1432–50** tr. *Higden* (Rolls) I. 59 The grete see is namede in diuerse maners for diuerse regiones, yles, cites, and peple that hit compassethe. **1485** CAXTON *Chas. Gt.* i. 12 There was a kyng..which, whan he departed fro Troye came in to the regyon of fraunce. *a* **1533** LD. BERNERS *Huon* lxxxii. 255 In what place of your regyon thynke you that ye ought too iuge of the peeres of Fraunce? **1542** UDALL *Erasm. Apoph.* II. 188 Whiche Lybia is a region or coste of the countree of Afrike, boundyng vpon Aegypte. **1607** SHAKS. *Cor.* IV. vi. 101 All the Regions Do smilingly Reuolt, and who resists Are mock'd for valiant Ignorance. **1625** N. CARPENTER *Geog. Del.* II. i. (1635) 5 Nauigatours haue discouered few or no Regions wanting inhabitants. **1671** MILTON *P.R.* IV. 67 Embassies from Regions far remote In various habits on the Appian road. **1726–46** THOMSON *Winter* 414 Amongst those hilly regions, where embrac'd In peaceful vales the happy Grisons dwell! **1814** SCOTT *Ld. of Isles* III. xvii, But late you said No steps these desert regions tread! **1857** SCLATER in *Jrnl. Proc. Linn. Soc., Zool.* (1858) II. 143 South America is the most peculiar of all the primary regions in the globe as to its ornithology. **1870** YEATS *Nat. Hist. Comm.* 1 The inhabitants of any one region may, by exchange, become possessed of the abundance and variety of all other regions.

c. Without article: Land, territory. *rare*⁻¹.

1697 DRYDEN *Virg. Georg.* IV. 415 That length of Region, and large Tract of Ground.

d. An area, space, or place, of more or less definite extent or character.

1726 LEONI *Alberti's Archit.* I. 2/1 The Region..shall be the whole large open Place in which we are to build, and of which the Seat or Platform shall be only a Part. **1838** DICKENS *Nich. Nick.* xvi, Within the precincts of the ancient city of Westminster, is a narrow and dirty region. **1871** MRS. EDWARDS *Ought we to visit her?* III. viii. 131 The ginger-beer stalls and Aunt Sallies of the back regions.

†**2.** The rule or government of a kingdom. *Obs.*

c **1400** *Apol. Loll.* 86 þey reyse not a king to regioun, þey schal not ȝeue reyn to men. *c* **1470** HARDING *Chron.* CLXXVI. ix, He prayed the lordes at parlyement His sonne to admytte into the regyon, Syth he vnable was to the regyment.

3. a. A separate part or division of the world or universe, as the air, heaven, etc.

1340 *Ayenb.* 268 þe zuete smel ine hare regyon [*sc.* heaven] zuo zuete ys þet alle manyre zuete smelles ouercomþ. *c* **1384** CHAUCER *H. Fame* II. 421 For in this Region [the air] certeyn Duelleth many a Citezeyn. *c* **1477** CAXTON *Jason* 73 Bulles of fyre so grete that they enflamed alle the regyon of the ayer. **1591** SHAKS. *1 Hen. VI*, V. iii. 11 Ye Familiar Spirits, that are cull'd Out of the powerfull Regions vnder earth. **1602** —— *Ham.* II. ii. 509 Anon the dreadfull Thunder Doth rend the Region. **1667** MILTON *P.L.* III. 349 Heav'n rung With Jubilee, and loud Hosannas fill'd Th' eternal Regions. **1726–46** THOMSON *Winter* 116 In what far-distant region of the sky, Hush'd in deep silence, sleep ye when 'tis calm? **1820** SHELLEY *Liberty* x, As light may pierce the clouds when they dissever In the calm regions of the orient day! **1866** G. MACDONALD *Ann. Q. Neighb.* xxix. (1878) 497 We know nothing of the region beyond the grave!

b. *fig.* A place, state or condition, having a certain character or subject to certain influences; the sphere or realm *of* something.

1526 TINDALE *Matt.* iv. 16 To them which sate in the region and shadowe of deeth. **1548–9** (Mar.) *Bk. Com. Prayer, Burial of Dead*, That he escaping the..paynes of eternall derkenes May euer dwel in the region of lighte. **1601** DANIEL *To C'tess Cumbld.* ii, With how free an eye doth he looke downe Vpon these lower regions of turmoyle. **1667** MILTON *P.L.* I. 65 Darkness visible Serv'd only to discover sights of woe, Regions of sorrow. **1751** JOHNSON *Rambler* No. 83 ⁋2 Barbarians, by whom every region of science is equally laid waste. **1843** MIALL *Nonconf.* III. 1 We have passed beyond the region of early perils. **1875** JOWETT *Plato* (ed. 2) IV. 234 He has followed philosophy into the region of mythology.

4. a. One of the successive portions into which the air or atmosphere is theoretically divided according to height (see quot. 1704). Also similarly of the sea according to depth.

1563 W. FULKE *Meteors* (1640) 7 Some part of it being caryed up into the highest Region, by the fiery heat is set on fire. *Ibid.* 11 Generated in the highest region of the ayre. **1626** BACON *Sylva* §81 Raines [are condensed] by the Cold of that, which they call the Middle Region of the Aire. **1671** BOYLE *Temp. Submarine Regions* iii. 8 To justifie my ascribing of this Coldnesse to the second, or lower Region of the Sea, I shall now subjoin some Relations. **1704** J. HARRIS *Lex. Techn.* I. s.v., Regions of the Air, are distinguished into Upper, Middle, and Lower. **1843** RUSKIN *Mod. Paint.* I. ii. III. ii. §2. 196, I shall therefore consider the sky as divided into three regions: the upper region, or region of the cirrus [etc.]. **1860** TYNDALL *Glac.* I. xxvii. 203 The wind was high in the upper regions.

fig. **1598** SHAKS. *Merry W.* III. ii. 74 He is of too high a Region, he knows too much.

†**b.** = CLIMATE 1. *Obs. rare.*

1551 RECORDE *Cast. Knowl.* (1556) 91, I meane by a Region that whiche the Grekes do call a Climate;..the climates may well be accompted 48 betwene the two polare circles.

5. a. An administrative division of a city or district.

1593 BILSON *Govt. Christ's Ch.* 282 Every Bishop had his region or Diocese besides his Citie. *a* **1600** HOOKER *Eccl. Pol.* VII. viii. §7 The Roman governor..gave charge that Macedonia should be divided into four regions or diocesses. **1781** GIBBON *Decl. & F.* xvii. II. 21 He divided Constantinople into fourteen regions or quarters. **1841** W. SPALDING *Italy & It. Isl.* I. 319 No new nomenclature seems to have been introduced, each province being merely called a Region... The following were the Augustan Regions. **1854** CDL. WISEMAN *Fabiola* (1855) 80 One of the seven regions into which Pope Cajus..had divided the city.

b. A relatively large subdivision of a country for economic, administrative, or cultural purposes that freq. implies an alternative system to centralized organization; *spec.* one of the nine local government areas into which the mainland of Scotland has been divided since 1975, when the former system of counties was abolished. ***standard (administrative) region***: one of the eight (formerly nine) areas into which England is divided for industrial planning, demographic surveying, etc.

1921 G. D. H. COLE *Future of Local Govt.* ii. 15 What is really needed is..a systematic scheme of development including both towns and rural areas over the whole of a wide Region. **1933** H. FINER *Eng. Local Govt.* vii. 160 The largest area of government..which would comprehend the main large-scale services, to be managed or regulated by a Council popularly elected for the whole of the Region. **1950** ORMROD & WALKER *Butterworth's Annotated Legislation Service: Statutes Suppl. No. 63* I. 10 England and Wales are divided into fourteen hospital regions, each administered by a Regional Hospital Board. Each region is based on a town in which there is a University Medical School. **1958** *Britain: Official Handbk. 1959* (H.M.S.O.) i. 14 Table 2 shows the distribution of the population by urban and rural districts and the populations of the standard administrative regions, of the seven major conurbations and of 16 large cities. **1959** W. ISARD et al. *Industrial Complex Anal.* i. 6 Until the 'ultimate' is achieved in social science theory, analysts must be content with sets of regions—or hierarchies of sets of regions—which tend to differ from problem to problem. **1966** *Census 1961: Occupation Tables* p. xix, (*heading*) Areas for which statistics are given. Standard Regions. The constitution of the Standard Regions of England and Wales used in this volume is as follows. **1973** *Times* 23 May 16/6 The Government were confident of their ability to continue giving the regions the assistance they needed. **1973** *Act 21 & 22 Eliz. II.* c. 65 §1 Scotland (other than Orkney, Shetland and the Western Isles) shall be divided into local government areas to be known as regions. **1976** *Scottish Daily Express* 23 Dec. 6/6 Even in booming Aberdeen and the thriving Grampian Region there are troubles between the two councils.

c. An area of the world made up of neighbouring countries that, from an international point of view, are considered socially, economically, or politically interdependent.

1925 W. S. CULBERTSON *Internat. Econ. Policies* App. ix. 549 Regional or world conferences..to establish in regions, or with respect to subjects in the agenda, 'a workable basis of coöperation among the nations of the earth'. **1948** G. A. JOHNSON in K. M. Panikkar et al. *Regionalism & Security* 45 There are..yet few who would..divide the world into regions, each a federation. **1959** W. ISARD et al. *Industrial Complex Anal.* i. 5 For a long time economists, geographers, sociologists, political scientists, city and regional planners, and other social scientists have been concerned with the concept of 'region'. **1970** CANTORI & SPIEGEL *Internat. Politics of Regions* i. 1 We will consider regions to be areas of the world which contain geographically proximate states forming, in foreign affairs, mutually interrelated units. **1977** M. HUDSON *Global Fracture* xiii. 167 Regional consolidation is occurring within five broad geopolitical blocs... Each of these regions is characterized by a broad range of complementary products.

d. *Broadcasting.* A part of the country covered by a particular programme service or broadcasting company; *transf.*, the company itself.

1929 *Radio Times* 8 Nov. 442/1 The Northern Region—Manchester 2ZY 797 kc/s. (376·4 m.) **1949** *Ibid.* 15 July 12/4 In Other Regions—Midland (296·2 m)..North (449·1 m), [etc.]. **1956** *B.B.C. Handbk. 1957* 124 The expansion of television resources in the Regions. **1968** *Listener* 25 July 123/2 This was a good effort by a small ITV region—Anglia—and the old companies of ITV have been putting on quite a brave show. **1974** *B.B.C. Handbk. 1975* 56/2 The Manchester site will eventually accommodate network production centre, television region and local radio station.

6. A part or division of the body or its parts:

a. *spec.* in *Anat.* and *Med.*

1398 TREVISA *Barth. De P.R.* VII. liii. (Bodl. MS.), Ofte such a passion and yuel is ycured by bloode letting and by medicyns..and namelich vppon þe regioun of þe lyuoure. **1579** LANGHAM *Gard. Health* (1633) 133 Applyed to the region of the milt, it doth soften it. **1626** BACON *Sylva* §65 To draw away the Reliques of the Humours, that may haue descended to the Lower Regions of the Body. **1707** FLOYER *Physic. Pulse-Watch* 350 The celiac Branches of the Artery ..send Branches to all the Viscera in the middle Region. **1835–6** TODD *Cycl. Anat.* I. 2/2 The outline of the anterior wall or proper abdominal region constitutes an oval. **1881** MIVART *Cat* 60 The skull is said to be divided into certain regions.

b. in general use.

1604 SHAKS. *Oth.* IV. i. 84 The Gybes, and notable Scornes That dwell in euery Region of his face. **1605** —— *Lear* I. i. 147 Let it fall rather, though the fork invade The region of my heart. **1839** DE QUINCEY in *Tait's Mag.* Jan. 9/1 The mouth, and the region of the mouth..were about the strongest feature in Wordsworth's face. **1892** HARDY *Tess* li. (ed. 5), A sudden rebellious sense of injustice caused the region of her eyes to swell with the rush of hot tears.

c. Phr. ***in the region of***: round about, approximately.

1966 'A. HALL' *9th Directive* x. 97 The breech-pressure is in the region of 20 tons p.s.i. **1972** *Country Life* 5 Oct. (Suppl.) 7/2 Delightful house... Offers in the region of £40,000. **1979** *Solihull News* 26 May (Classified Section) 24/1 (Advt.), A superb and spacious centrally heated residence... Price: offers in the region of: £29,500.

7. A space occupied by a thing.

1664 POWER *Exp. Philos.* I. 35 Oyle (which floated on the Vineger in a distinct Region by it self). **1876** TAIT *Rec. Adv. Phys. Sc.* xiii. (ed. 2) 334 We indicate on the diagram the region within which our given quantity of water can exist partly as vapour and partly as liquid. **1882** MINCHIN *Unipl. Kinemat.* 194 Let *DEF*..be a contour enclosing any portion of a moving fluid. We may speak of the whole of this space as a region.

8. *attrib.*, as ***region cloud, kite, planting, whisper***; (in sense 5 b) ***region-planning***.

c **1600** SHAKS. *Sonn.* xxxiii, The region cloude hath mask'd him from me now. **1602** —— *Ham.* II. ii. 607, I should haue fatted all the Region Kites With this Slaues Offal. *a* **1821** KEATS *Hyperion* I. 349 Ere half this region-whisper had come down, Hyperion arose. **1832** *Planting* 44 in *Lib. Usef. Kn., Husb.* III, The forest trees to be planted should be selected according to the above principles. In practice this may be termed region planting. **1921** G. D. H. COLE *Future of Local Govt.* ii. 14 What is really needed is plainly not mere town-planning, but region-planning. **1931** W. A. ROBSON *Devel. of Local Govt.* I. ii. 143 Similar problems are presented in connection with other fundamental region-planning requirements.

regional ('riːdʒənəl), *a.* and *sb.* [ad. late L. *regiōnāl-is*: see prec. and -AL[1], and cf. mod.F. *régional*.]

A. *adj.* **1. a.** Of or pertaining to, connected with, a particular region or district.

1654 HAMMOND *Answ. Animadv. Ignat.* vi. 159 The Apostles.. planting a Church in a chief Citie, and extending the Faith to the Region about it,.. annext the Regional-Church to the City-Church. **1675** EVELYN *Terra* (1729) 11 Especially if.. we could skill to modify also the Air, about them, and make the Remedy as well regional as topical. **1861** *Times* 10 July, He asked how he meant to deal with Tuscany, .. where the regional system was still kept up in all its integrity. **1882** GEIKIE in *Nature* 7 Dec. 122 It is evident that an enormous area of regional metamorphism extends across Scandinavia. **1888** *Times* 23 June 5/5 The regional shows held in the different departments of France.

b. *Geol.* ***regional metamorphism*** [tr. F. *métamorphisme régional* (G. A. Daubrée *Études et Expériences Synthetiques sur le Métamorphisme* (1860) II. ii. 59)]: metamorphism affecting rocks over an extensive area as a result of the large-scale action of heat and pressure.

[**1859** T. S. HUNT in *Q. Jrnl. Geol. Soc.* XV. 489 We must commence by distinguishing between the local metamorphism which sometimes appears in the vicinity of traps and granites and that normal metamorphism which extends over wide areas and is apparently unconnected with the presence of intrusive rocks.] **1871** —— in *Amer. Naturalist* V. 494 The problem to be solved in regional metamorphism is the conversion of sedimentary strata.. into aggregations of crystalline silicates. **1937** WOOLDRIDGE & MORGAN *Physical Basis Geogr.* x. 133 Much more important are the great masses of metamorphic rock which have resulted from what is often called regional metamorphism, *i.e.* deep burial of rock masses.. due to earth-movement. **1971** I. G. GASS et al. *Understanding Earth* i. 35/1 Regional metamorphism is accompanied by more or less intense deformation.

c. Of, pertaining to, or connected with a region (esp. in senses 5 b and c). So ***regional board, planning***, etc.

1921 G. D. H. COLE *Future of Local Govt.* ii. 15 There is an overwhelming case, from the standpoint of public convenience and efficiency of service, for the regional planning of publicly owned road transport services. **1927** *Rep. Comm. Publ. Libraries Eng. & Wales* 151 in *Parl. Papers (Cmd. 2868)* XII. 231 Our conclusion is that a national system should be built up on.. the grouping of public libraries round regional centres, which will generally be the great urban libraries. **1933** H. FINER *Eng. Local Govt.* vii. 164 If the regional solution were adopted it would.. furnish an area large enough to include most of those services for which a large area has been found necessary. **1941** *Economist* 18 Jan. 68/2 Lord Nuffield.. envisaged regional boards throughout the country which would co-ordinate hospital finance and policy. **1943** in J. S. Huxley *TVA* 5 The Tennessee Valley Authority initiated regional planning on a scale never before attempted in history. **1956** G. N. FLEMMING *Organisation of Technical Coll.* 1 There are at present three main types of technical college,.. described in this circular as local, area and regional colleges. **1957** G. L. GOODWIN *Brit. & United Nations* 459 The prospects of world peace will turn not on the United Nations but on the effectiveness of global and regional balances of power. **1959** W. ISARD et al. *Industrial Complex Anal.* i. 6 The concept of regional structure has come to be relativistic. **1962** *Lancet* 27 Jan. 219/2 The unit would be organised on regional-board level. **1965** HAAS & SCHMITTER *Polit. of Econ. in Lat. Amer. Regionalism* i. 1 One of the first prolonged attempts at regional economic integration between independent developing countries. **1969** *Times* 3 Feb. 10/8 Farming is not a subject which often enters the realm of regional planning. **1972** W. ISARD et al. *Ecologic-Economic Anal. for Regional Development* p. xv, We constantly assert that no longer can regional development and regional planning be treated in their traditionally narrow contexts. **1976** C. A. SMITH *Regional Anal.* I. p. xi, Careful field studies of markets and regional economics.. would have identified regional patterns not predicted by central-place theory.. thereby stimulating the development of new regional system theories. **1977** M. HUDSON *Global Fracture* xiv. 178 The currency-debt of a nation or regional grouping of nations not politically associated with the creditor central bank. **1978** *Dumfries Courier* 13 Oct. 2/6 The modernisation project at Templand had been praised by the Regional Planning Committee.

d. Of or pertaining to a broadcasting region (sense 5 d). Also, designating a B.B.C. radio service which operated during the 1930s.

1929 *Radio Times* 8 Nov. 403/3, 2BE *Belfast*.. 9.0 Regional News. **1930** *B.B.C. Year-bk.* 30 The Regional Stations of Daventry, London, and Manchester will cover about 75 per cent. of the population. **1962** *Rep. Comm. Broadc. 1960* 157 The four major companies having been appointed [by the ITA], this consideration prompted the appointment of the relatively large number of relatively small 'regional' companies. *Ibid.* 221 The present sound programmes of the BBC are.. basically national programmes. Within them, regional programmes are accommodated. **1965** [see NATIONAL *a.* 1 d]. **1968** *Writing for BBC* (ed. 2) 12 A particularly worth-while opportunity for would-be contributors exists in the Regional editions of programmes.

2. Pertaining to a special part of the body.

1861 O. W. HOLMES *Med. Ess.* Wks. 1891 IX. 224 It is curious that the Japanese should have anticipated Europe in a kind of rude regional anatomy. **1899** *Allbutt's Syst. Med.* VII. 271 The regional diagnosis of cerebral disease is, in some instances, comparatively easy.

B. *sb.* **1.** A B.B.C. radio service which operated during the 1930s.

1936 J. REITH *Diary* 20 Jan. (1975) iii. 185 We got it [*sc.* a statement] out at 9.38 as we had to collect all the Regionals and Empire. **1938**, **1971** [see NATIONAL *a.* 1 d]. **1978** *Broadcast* 27 Feb. 4/2 A balance between the majors and regionals has emerged.

2. The part of a gravity anomaly or magnetic anomaly that is due to deep features and varies only gradually from place to place.

1940 L. L. NETTLETON *Geophys. Prospecting for Oil* xii. 222 If this regional is properly estimated and removed,.. the local features will show up in their proper form and relief. **1954** *Geophysics* XIX. 1 The problem of regionals and residuals arises in all geophysical methods which are based on measurement of a 'potential' field. **1967** *Bull. Amer. Assoc. Petroleum Geologists* LI. 2388/1 The 13th-order regional fits closely the observed data.

3. In general use, *ellipt.* for *regional (stock) exchange, newspaper, stamp*, etc.

1958 *Gibbons Stamp Monthly* 1 Sept. 2/3 Pictorials can be captioned—to most people these Regionals will be confusingly anonymous. **1965** *Time* 3 Sept. 58 Because of this growth.. the cost of seats on the regionals has been rising steadily. **1969** *Times* 5 May (Wall Street Suppl.) p. v/7 Many of the regionals even encouraged institutional, or mutual fund, business... The major brokerage houses handling institutional transactions could thus buy a relatively inexpensive seat on a regional exchange. **1971** D. POTTER *Brit. Eliz. Stamps* iv. 59 Jersey and Guernsey stamps were withdrawn on 1 October 1969, and the two islands issued their own stamps. But the regionals remained valid for postage elsewhere in the United Kingdom. **1974** *State* (Columbia, S. Carolina) 27 Feb. 3-B/4 The South Atlantic regional at Norfolk, Va. **1975** B. GUNSTON *Philatelist's Companion* 247 *Regional*, a stamp issued for use in only part of the territory under the authority of a postal administration (eg Scotland, in the case of the UK). **1975** *Times* 13 Aug. 12/1 While national newspaper managements were still thinking in the fifties of hot metal.. modernization ran across Britain and the regionals profited.

Hence '**regionally** *adv.*

1879 PARKER in *Trans. Linn. Soc.* (1882) II. 166 Regionally, these walls answer to the orbitosphenoids and alisphenoids of the higher Vertebrata. **1886** *Science* 10 Sept. 233/2 The preservation of rock-oils in every formation, of every geological age, all over the world; subject, however, locally or regionally, to subsequent change or destruction. **1962** *Rep. Comm. Broadc. 1960* 151 We have examined the BBC on its allocation of money between its sound and television services, both nationally and regionally. **1974** *Nature* 1 Nov. 28/1 Viewed regionally, the area of greatest regressive tendency within the depositional regime can be identified as the central and northern North Sea.

regionalism ('riːdʒənəlɪz(ə)m). [f. prec. + -ISM.] **1.** Tendency to, or practice of, regional systems or methods; localism on a regional basis. Also, on a national or international scale: the theory or practice of regional rather than central systems of administration, or of economic, cultural, or political affiliation; the study of such phenomena as they relate to geographic factors.

1881 *Manch. Guard.* 4 Feb., That unfortunate 'regionalism' of Italy which has been described by.. recent writers in the country. **1887** *Edin. Rev.* Jan. 107 The spirit of local individualism,—in politics somewhat inharmoniously dubbed 'regionalism'. **1919** GEDDES & BRANDFORD in C. B. Fawcett *Provinces of England* p. ii, 'Regionalism' was, indeed, first a French word: and this not merely in geography, but also in politics, and long before the war. From Brittany to Provence its studies have been long preparing. **1923** G. M. TREVELYAN *Manin & Venetian Revolution* xiv. 244 He abandoned his Republican faith and his Venetian 'regionalism' in view of the new circumstances of Italy. **1931** E. C. MOWER *Internat. Govt.* v. 89 Regionalism, it is claimed, is justified both from the defensive value of natural frontiers and on sound economic principles, having regard to the needs of modern industrial life. **1934** *Encycl. Soc. Sci.* XIII. 208/2 Regionalism has been called a manifestation of 'world federalism' and an intermediate stage between administrative decentralization and federalism. **1936** *Columbia Univ. Quart.* Mar. 268 Regionalism can.. be defined as the study of the relation of man to geographic areas, and the potentialities which this relation presents in terms of human welfare and progress. **1948** G. A. JOHNSON in K. M. Panikkar *Regionalism & Security* 45 Of these claims on behalf of regionalism the United Nations Charter is concerned directly with only one. **1959** A. H. ROBERTSON *Europ. Institutions* i. 4 As the idea of universalism waned,.. that of regionalism developed. **1962** L. GOLDING *Dict. Local Govt.* 332 When War broke out in 1939 regionalism was applied in practice by dividing the country for purposes of civil defence and the administration of other emergency services into twelve large areas, each of which was placed in the charge of a Commissioner. **1965** HAAS & SCHMITTER (*title*) The politics of economics in Latin American regionalism. **1970** CANTORI & SPIEGEL *Internat. Polit. of Regions* i. 1 Sometimes 'regionalism' has been studied exclusively in terms of regional organization. **1977** M. HUDSON *Global Frontiers* xv. 195 (*heading*) The new regionalism.

2. A regional word, phrase, or peculiarity of pronunciation which is not part of the standard language of a country; regional distinctiveness in literature.

1953 S. A. BROWN in A. Dundes *Mother Wit* (1973) 40/1 We go then to what is called the New Negro Movement, then to Regionalism. **1954** F. G. CASSIDY *S. Robertson's Development Mod. English* v. 126 The third [sc. *you-all*] is a regionalism. **1955** *Times* 7 May 9/4 The regionalism of American writing falls into place beside that of Scotland or Ireland. **1964** *Language* XL. 93 Intellectual leaders of the Seicento.. did not hesitate to use, as nonce-forms, regionalisms like *parapaglia* 'butterfly' (based on Bolognese *parpaja*..) and *sfragaro* 'wastrel' (Calabrese-Sicilian). **1974** R. A. HALL *External Hist. Romance Lang.* 216 Some lexical regionalisms have been inevitable in films made in, say, Mexico or Argentina. **1978** *Amer. Speech* LIII. 13 The layman applies the term imprecisely to a large body of lexemes including true slang, jargon, regionalisms, and colloquialisms, which are vaguely perceived as slang by such groups as college students.

So '**regionalist**, one inclined to regionalism (also *attrib.* and as *adj.*); **regiona'listic** *a.*

1898 *Contemp. Rev.* Sept. 325 As Catalonian Leagues, Regionalistic propagandas.., and Press protests testify. **1900** *Daily Express* 10 July 1/7 The regionalists of Catalonia are preparing a violent campaign against bull-fights. **1919** GEDDES & BRANFORD in C. B. Fawcett *Provinces of Eng.* p. iii, The most discerning.. regionalists of to-day are also among the most appreciative of truly comprehensive politics. **1925** L. MUMFORD in *Survey* 15 Apr. 151/1 The regionalist attempts to plan such an area so that all its sights and resources.. may be soundly developed. **1934** *Encycl. Soc. Sci.* XIII. 216/1 There was a revival of regionalist feeling in Italy after the World War. **1937** F. BORKENAU *Spanish Cockpit* i. 59 The Basque provinces, naturally, voted for the Basque regionalists. **1941** J. MASEFIELD *In Mill* 112 The Regionalist novel-writers. **1944** A. BRECHT in *Regionalism & World Organization* 11 The universalists want a world-wide organization; the major-regionalists recommend federations of continental scope; the minor-regionalists propose federal groupings of smaller countries; and the ideological unionists advocate a confederation of democracies or a league of the United Nations. **1977** *Economist* 23 Apr. 56/1 The three major regionalist parties [in Belgium]—the Walloon Rally, the Volksunie and the Francophone Front. **1977** G. P. ATKINS *Lat. Amer. in Internat. Polit. System* i. 9 Regionalists were primarily concerned with security arrangements for and keeping the peace in delineated geographical areas.

regionality (riːdʒə'nælɪtɪ). [f. REGIONAL *a.* + -ITY.] Nature or character connected with or pertaining to a region.

1961 in WEBSTER. **1966** *New Statesman* 8 Apr. 510/1 The zone of time-space that middle-class western man mostly inhabits is the continuous present of the Western World: the particularities of the particular place he happens to live in are often little more than a backdrop to home and work and leisure—unless he's feeling jolly, when he is sometimes prepared to wear his regionality as a mask or humour. **1976** *Amer. Speech 1973* XLVIII. 282 For obvious reasons, the concept of 'regionality' in regard to language is a pre-occupation of the editors of the *Dictionary of American Regional English*. **1979** *Dictionaries* I. 27 Many of the statements about regionality are qualified in some way.

regionali'zation. [f. REGIONAL *a.* + -IZATION.] The action of adapting economic, political, social, or cultural organization to a geographical or administrative region.

1920 A. R. ORAGE in C. H. Douglas *Credit Power & Democracy* 152 The suggested regionalisation of the administration of the industry may be regarded as acceptable to the Miners' Federation. **1930** *Aberdeen Press & Jrnl.* 3 Nov. 5/6 We have just completed.. what might be called the first try-out of programme regionalisation. **1938** ODUM & MOORE *Amer. Regionalism* I. ix. 216 The present regionalization of the country. **1952** *Property Owners' Jrnl.* Jan. 10/2 The other major factor is.. regionalisation. Bricks are expensive things to carry... Consequently, brick houses must be built as near the brick-fields as possible. **1963** *Times* 23 Apr. 13/3 The fashion for regionalization is strengthening in Britain today. **1970** *Nature* 26 Dec. 1250/2 In regions.. which have urban populations large enough for regionalization of intake to be a real possibility, less than half the students accepted in 1969 came from the region in which the universities are situated. **1975** *Church Times* 18 July 12/3 It may be believed that SCM is committing itself to increased regionalisation and student work from within. **1978** *Nature* 2 Feb. 403/2 The development of the adult fly involves first the regionalisation of the embryo into a number of territories.

regionalize ('riːdʒənəlaɪz), *v.* [f. REGIONAL *a.* + -IZE.] *trans.* To bring under the control of a region for administrative purposes; to divide into regions; to organize on a regional basis. So '**regionalized** *ppl. a.*, '**regionalizing** *vbl. sb.*

1921 G. D. H. COLE *Future of Local Govt.* xii. 112 May it not be possible to escape the disadvantages of central ownership and control by regionalizing instead of nationalizing many industries and services. **1938** ODUM & MOORE *Amer. Regionalism* I. viii. 188 We have 'regionalized' our nation and subregionalized and districted our states. **1962** *Times* 23 Jan. 4/2 The draw for the second round of the F.A. Amateur Cup—to be played on February 3 and no longer regionalized. **1962** *Daily Tel.* 8 May 1/7 Miners' M.P.s repeatedly voiced suspicion that Lord Robens's real intention.. is to 'regionalise' the coal industry by creating autonomous boards in Scotland, Lancashire and elsewhere. **1972** *Times of India* 28 Nov. 1/2 Various service cadres will be regionalised. **1978** *Jrnl. R. Soc. Arts* CXXVI. 218/1 It costs just as much to broadcast to half a million people as to broadcast to fifty million, so that the more you regionalize your output the more expensive it becomes. **1978** *Radio Times* 11–17 Mar. 15/4 In future years Ceefax will offer regionalized news.

regionary ('riːdʒənərı), *a.* and *sb.* [ad. late L. *regiōnāri-us* (Quicherat and Du Cange): see REGION and -ARY[1].]

A. *adj.* Of or pertaining to a region. ***regionary bishop*** (see quots. 1727–38 and 1869).

1657–83 EVELYN *Hist. Relig.* (1850) I. 104 They attributed their successes..to the topical and regionary deities. **1727–38** CHAMBERS *Cycl.* s.v., A regionary bishop was properly a missionary invested with an episcopal character, but without being attached to any particular see. **1833** WATERWORTH *Rule Cath. Faith* 16 Decisions passed, in what are called by St. Austin the regionary councils. **1869** MACLEAR *Apost. Med. Europe* viii. 113 He was consecrated regionary bishop, without any particular diocese, but with a general jurisdiction over all whom he might win over.

b. ***regionary deacon***, etc. (see quots.).

1727–38 CHAMBERS *Cycl.* s.v., At Rome there were antiently seven regionary deacons, who presided over a kind of hospitals, and looked to the distribution of alms. There were also regionary subdeacons, and regionary notaries. **1854** CDL. WISEMAN *Fabiola* II. i. 138 Our holy Pope will be there, with the priests of the titles, the regionary deacons, the notaries [etc.].

B. *sb.* An account or description of the regions of Rome.

1818 J. C. HOBHOUSE *Hist. Illustr.* (ed. 2) 54 Panvinius dedicated his description of Rome, which he added to the old regionaries, to the Emperor Ferdinand, in 1558.

'regioned, *ppl. a.* [f. REGION + -ED[2].] Divided into regions; placed in a region.

a **1821** KEATS *Hyperion* I. 119 Space region'd with life-air, and barren void. **1872** A. DE VERE *Legends St. Patrick, Mount Cruachan* 160 His prayer Rose and far spread; nor roused alone those Powers Regioned with God.

regi'onic, *a. rare.* [-IC.] Regional.

1891 *Cent. Dict.* (citing *Buck's Handbk. Med. Sci.*).

† **'regious,** *a. Obs. rare*[−1]. [f. L. *rēg-*, *rex* king + -IOUS.] Taking the side of a king.

a **1677** J. HARRINGTON *Grounds Monarchy* Wks. (1700) 11, I would fain ask the Regious Defenders, by what Law they can maintain Governments to be inherent in one?

‖ **regisseur** (reʒisœr). *Theatr.* and *Ballet.* [Fr.] A stage manager or artistic director. Also *transf.* in *Cinemat.*

1828 J. EBERS *Seven Yrs. of King's Theatre* ii. 58 He had been a kind of manager of the Opera at Bologna, and subsequently Regisseur of the Théâtre Italien at Paris. **1925** *Daily Herald* 20 May 9/3 The three main streams of the revolutionary theatre..derive from the three *regisseurs.* **1935** A. REVUSKY *Jews in Palestine* x. 173 Piscator, the leading theatrical regisseur of Germany. **1949** *Ballet Ann.* III. 27 *Prince Igor*, revised by that experienced and excellent *régisseur*, Nicolas Beriosoff. **1954** 'E. Box' *Death in Fifth Position* i. 10, I was introduced to..the *regisseur* or director of the [ballet] company. **1965** *New Statesman* 16 Apr. 621/2 Shaw, Chekhov and Brecht wrote for a producers' theatre, intervening when necessary as their own *régisseurs* to bully their actors into subordination to their texts. **1968** *Listener* 14 Mar. 357/1 Zeffirelli is a *régisseur* in the grand 19th-century naturalistic manner. **1977** *New Yorker* 16 May 79/3 Serge Grigoriev, who was Diaghilev's regisseur, restaged it for the Royal Ballet.

register ('rɛdʒɪstə(r)), *sb.*[1] Forms: 4–6 **regestre, -gistre,** 5–6 **regester,** (5 **-tyr**), **regyster,** (5 **-tre**), 6 **regesto(u)r,** 5– **register.** [a. F. *registre*, †*regestre* (12th c.), or med.L. *registrum*, *regestrum*, for *regestum*, from the late L. pl. *regesta* matters recorded, a record, list, f. *regerĕre* to record, set down, f. *re-* RE- + *gerĕre* to carry (see *congest*, *digest*, etc.).

The intrusive *r* of the F. and med.L. forms is due to the analogy of other sbs. in F. *-istre* (for *-iste*), L. *-istrum*. Some of the senses placed under II have app. arisen by false association with F. *regir*, L. *regĕre*, to rule, regulate.]

I. 1. a. A book or volume in which regular entry is made of particulars or details of any kind which are considered of sufficient importance to be exactly and formally recorded; a written record or collection of entries thus formed; †a list, catalogue; a record of attendance at a school.

1377 LANGL. *P. Pl.* B. xx. 269, I wolde witterly þat ȝe were in þe registre, And ȝowre noumbre vnder notaries sygne. ? *a* **1400** *Morte Arth.* 113 Thy fadyr mad fewtee, we fynde in oure rollez, In the regestre of Rome. *c* **1460** FORTESCUE *Abs. & Lim. Mon.* xv. (1885) 149 Oper artycles..mowe be..putt in a boke, and that boke kept in this counseill as a registir or a ordinarye. **1479** in *Eng. Gilds* (1870) 421 A Registre of the same to remayn with the Maire. **1560** DAUS tr. *Sleidane's Comm.* 347 There is a register of bokes, which thuniversity of Louain hath rejected. **1581** J. BELL *Haddon's Answ. Osor.* 129b, It is not needefull to make a Register of all yᵉ testimonies of writers. **1641** J. JACKSON *True Evang. T.* I. 28 Seven Scribes..who had.. enough to doe to..keep Registers of the Martyrs that were put to death. *a* **1715** BURNET *Own Time* I. (1724) I. 88 He kept a register of all the King's promises. **1778** [W. MARSHALL] *Observ. Agric.* 151, I began, on Tuesday the 19th of August, an Experimental Register of the State of the Atmosphere. **1805** *Med. Jrnl.* XIV. 195 He was so good as to visit his patient, and examine his register. **1844** H. H. WILSON *Brit. India* III. 294 The results of the general survey were embodied in a map; those of the field survey were preserved in village registers. **1865** DICKENS *Mut. Fr.* I. x, With a number of leathery old registers on shelves. **1887** C. D. WARNER *Their Pilgrimage* (1888) vi. 165 Mr. King discovered by the register that the Bensons had been there. **1888** C. M. YONGE *Our New Mistress* ii. 14 She called over the names... The registers had got into a muddle, and there was no knowing who had left school and who was only absent. *a* **1930** D. H. LAWRENCE *Phoenix II* (1968) 22 One day my bread-stealer arrived at half past two, when the register was closed. **1955** E. BLISHEN *Roaring Boys* IV. 183, I called the register... The ginger-haired boy answered to the name of Grange. **1961** M. SPARK *Prime of Miss Jean Brodie* iii. 59, I must mark the register for today before we forget. There are two new girls. **1978** R. MILLS *Comprehensive Educ.* 44 His lessons..began with the calling of the register.

transf. and *fig.* **1555** W. WATREMAN *Fardle Facions* II. viii. 182 Thei entre into the regestre of their stories. **1598** SHAKS. *Merry W.* II. ii. 195 As you haue one eye vpon my follies, as you heare them vnfolded, turne another into the Register of your owne. **1642** FULLER *Holy & Prof. St.* III. x. 176 Abuse not thy Memory to be Sinnes Register. **1726** POPE *Odyss.* xx. 91 The God supreme, to whose eternal eye The registers of fate expanded lie. **1817** CHALMERS *Astron. Disc.* ii. (1852) 65, I may put into the registers of my belief, all that comes home to me through the senses of the outer man. **1863** DANA *Man. Geol.* 734 The Pacific Ocean..has registers of subsidence all over it, in its coral islands.

b. A note or mark serving as a record.

1883 *Hardwich's Photogr. Chem.* (ed. Taylor) 343 On a corner of the glass is scratched with a diamond 1, 2, &c., as the case might be. The register will serve for future printings from the same Negative.

c. A person's face, regarded as an indication of feeling or emotion. *slang.*

1899 'J. FLYNT' *Tramping with Tramps* II. iv. 271, I hain't seen your register for many a day.

†**2.** As a title: **a.** of the Epistles of Gregory the Great. *Obs.*

After the L. title *Registrum* or *Regestum* (*epistolarum*).

c **1380** *Antecrist* in Todd *Three Treat. Wyclif* (1851) 118 As seynte Gregore seiþ in þe fyveþe boke of his regestre. **1494** FABYAN *Chron.* v. cxix. 95 Which answers are wrytten with other questions in the regestre of Gregory.

b. of a compilation containing the forms of writs of the Common Law, cited by English lawyers of the 16–17th c. *Obs.*

The full title was 'the Register of Writs', or 'of the Chancery'; see Cowell *Interpr.* and Blount *Law Dict.* s.v.

1544 tr. *Littleton's Tenures* 3 b, So it shalbe sayd in dyuers other wryttes..as it appereth by the register. **1598** MANWOOD *Lawes Forest* ix. §5. 53 In the Register in the writ of *Ad quod dampnum*, there the woord is *Assertare*. **1628** COKE *On Litt.* 73 b, It appeareth by the Register that the king shal haue escuage of his tenants which hold of him.

3. a. In *Sc.* use, the general term (current from the 15th c.) for records of a legal, parliamentary, or public character; in later use *spec.* those instituted by the Act of 1617, in which all documents affecting landed property are recorded.

1425 *Sc. Acts Jas. I* (1814) II. 9/1 Þat all & sindry.. present þar lettres..at þai may be putt in þe kingis Register til perpetuale memore. **1566** (*title*) The Actis and Constitutiounis of the Realme of Scotland..viseit, correctit, and extractit furth of the Registers. **1577** in *Acts Parl. Scot.* (1844) I. Pref. 25 *note*, The Registeris of the decreittis gevin be the Lordis of Counsale. **1617** *Sc. Acts Jas. VI* (1816) IV. 546/1 Thair salbe ane publick Register In the whiche all Reuersiones,..grantis off redemptioun and siclyik all enstrumentis of seasing salbe registrat within thriescore dayes efter þe date of the same. **1708** J. CHAMBERLAYNE *St. Gt. Brit.* II. III. v. (1710) 443 The Law of Scotland is easy and regular, by reason of Public Registers,..for recording Conveyances of the Lands and Possessions of private Subjects. **1837** *Penny Cycl.* IX. 274/2 What is almost peculiar to this part of the empire, the register of all deeds conveying or changing territorial property. **1877** *Act 40 & 41 Vict.* c. 40 §5 The keeper..of the register of deeds and probative writs. *Ibid.* §6 Where any writ..shall have been registered in the General Register of Sasines.

b. ***Clerk of* (*the*) *Register***, now ***Lord Clerk Register***: originally the clerk who kept the King's register, in later times a Scottish officer of state, who formerly had custody of the national records or registers, but is now represented in that capacity by the Deputy Clerk Register.

In early use the Latin genitive *registri* sometimes appears: in the modern form there is perh. confusion with *sb.*[2]

1457 *Sc. Acts Jas. II* (1814) II. 52/2 Þe lordis thinkis speidfull þat oure souerane lorde commande all his schirrefis and commissaris of burowis to cum to þe clerk of his Regestre [etc.]. **1542** *Sc. Acts Mary* (1814) II. 414/1 Hir hienes..ordanis þe clerk of registri and Justice clerk [etc.]. *Ibid.* 415/2 Maister James foulis of colintoun Clerk of registeris askit Instrumentis. **1607** in *Acts Parl. Scot.* (1844) I. Pref. 13 Proclamation is made throughout the Kingdome, to deliver in to the King's Clearke of Register (whom you heere [at Whitehall] call the Master of the Rolles) all Bills to be exhibited that Session. **1644** D. HUME *Hist. Ho. Douglas* 358 Master John Skeene, Clerk-Register, and Master of the Rols. **1705** *Lond. Gaz.* No. 4139/1 A Commission to Sir James Murray to be Clerk-Register. **1794** *Inv. R. Wardrobes* (1815) App. ii. 358 And there was produced to the Commissioners, by the Lord Clerk Register's Deputies for keeping the records, a public and solemn instrument. **1844** C. INNES *Pref. Acts Parl. Scot.* I. 13 *note*, The Fourth Annual Report of the Deputy Clerk Register of Scotland. **1879** *Act 42 & 43 Vict.* c. 44 §2 The Lord Clerk Register shall continue to be one of the officers of state of Scotland. *Ibid.* §4 In his absence..the Deputy Clerk Register shall have and may exercise the said rights.

4. As the name of certain official or authoritative records or books of record having some public or commercial importance: e.g.

a. of the baptisms, marriages, and burials in a parish, kept by the clergyman; or (in later use) of births, marriages, and deaths, kept by an official (a REGISTRAR) appointed for the purpose.

1538 CROMWELL in Merriman *Life & Lett.* (1902) II. 154 That yow and euery parson vicare or curate within this diocese shall for euery churche kepe one boke or registre wherein ye shall write the day and yere of every weddyng christenyng and buryeng. **1603** *Constit. & Canons Eccl.* lxx, Ministers to Keepe a Register of Christenings, Weddings, and Burials. *a* **1676** HALE *Prim. Orig. Man.* II. viii. (1677) 205 The strict and vigilant Observance of the..Registers of the Bills of Births and Deaths. **1753** *Act 26 Geo. II*, c. 33 §14 Immediately after the Celebration of every Marriage, an entry thereof shall be made in such Register. **1791** BOSWELL *Johnson* (1831) I. 1 His baptism is recorded, in the register of St. Mary's parish. **1836** *Act 6 & 7 Will. IV*, c. 86 §49 *marg.*, Registers of Baptisms and Burials may be kept as heretofore. **1848** DICKENS *Dombey* v, The register signed, and the fees paid [etc.]. **1874** *Act 37 & 38 Vict.* c. 88 §49 The registrar..who keeps the register in which the birth or death ..is..registered.

b. of seamen in the British mercantile marine.

1695–6 *Act 7 & 8 Will. III*, c. 21 §1 In the said Register or Registers, there shall be truly and faithfully Entred..the Names, Sirnames [etc.]. **1754** *Ess. Manning Fleet* 9 In, or about the Year 1696, a Register for Seamen was opened..by what Accidents it fail'd, I cannot say. **1835** *Act 5 & 6 Will. IV*, c. 19 §19 And whereas it is expedient that a Register should be formed and maintained of all the 'Mariners and Seafaring Men of the United Kingdom'. **1863** A. YOUNG *Naut. Dict.* (ed. 2) 306 The register being compiled from the agreements with seamen &c.

c. of shipping, containing particulars of construction, materials, size, ownership, etc.; also, a cetificate issued by the registering official, esp. as evidence of the nationality of the vessel.

1825 *Act 6 Geo. IV*, c. 110 §48 The Force and Effect of any Register granted to any Ship or Vessel. **1836** MARRYAT *Midsh. Easy* xxxviii, The brigantine, which had taken out her British register and licence under the name of the Rebiera, went out of harbour. **1842** DICKENS *Amer. Notes* (1850) 1/1 The Britannia steam-packet, twelve hundred tons burthen per register. **1846** A. YOUNG *Naut. Dict.* 195 Lloyd's Register of British and Foreign Shipping, which is published yearly, is an alphabetical list of vessels ranked in different classes according to their qualifications.

d. of those entitled to vote in Parliamentary or municipal elections.

1832 *Act 2 Will. IV*, c. 45 §37 Whereas it is expedient to form a Register of all Persons entitled to vote [etc.]. **1843** LD. BROUGHAM *Pol. Phil.* III. ix. 69 The necessity for a register, assumes that the franchise is confined to particular classes. **1870** *Act 33 & 34 Vict.* c. 92 *marg.*, Preparation of municipal registers in burghs which do not return members to Parliament.

5. a. An entry in a register (esp. in sense 4 a).

1535 COVERDALE *Ezra* ii. 62 These soughte the register of their byrth, and founde none. **1726** ARBUTHNOT *It cannot rain but it pours*, There being no Register of his Christening, his Age is only to be guessed at by his Stature and Countenance. **1769** *Junius Lett.* xii. (1788) 76 You have better proofs of your descent..than the register of a marriage. **1825** *Act 6 Geo. IV*, c. 110 §11 *marg.*, Book of Registers to be kept. *a* **1832** MACKINTOSH *Revolution of 1685*, Wks. 1846 II. 20 Three persons were executed illegally at Taunton for rebellion, the nature and reason of their death being openly avowed in the register of their interment.

b. A quantity recorded or registered.

1904 T. HOLDICH *India* xii. 351 At this point the rainfall is extraordinary, 50 or 60 feet being a not unusual register at Cherra Punji on the edge of the plateau.

6. Registration, registry.

1653 *Acts & Ordin. Parl.* c. 6 (Scobell) 227 And the person so elected..shall continue three years in the said place of Register. **1677** YARRANTON *Eng. Improv.* Ep. Rdr., The Free Lands of England being put under a Voluntary Register by Act of Parliament. **1860** *Merc. Marine Mag.* VII. 245 Her port of register is Liverpool. **1886** RUSKIN *Præterita* I. iv. 129 Elaborate pencil and pen outlines, of which perhaps half-a-dozen are worth register and preservation.

II. 7. †**a.** A bookmark. [So med.L. *registrum.*]

1530 PALSGR. 261/2 Regyster of a boke, *signet.*

b. An index; a table of contents. *rare.*

1585 HIGINS tr. *Junius' Nomencl.* 8 *Syllabus, index libri*,.. the index, table, or register of a booke. **1890** *Durham Diocesan Gaz.* IV. 59 Register. 1. Letter from the Bishop.. page 33 [etc.].

c. The series of signatures in a printed book; the list of these at the end of early printed books.

1885 *Brit. Mus. Catal.*, *Caxton* Game and Playe of the chesse..(2nd ed.) Without titlepage or pagination; the register commences on the eighth leaf bj, and extends to I vi.

8. a. A slider in an organ; hence, a set of pipes controlled by a slider, a stop; also, a stop-knob.

1585 HIGINS tr. *Junius' Nomencl.* 354/2 *Pleuritides regulæ*, ..the side rules which are put in and pulled out, either to stop or to open the holes: the registers. **1659** LEAK *Waterwks.* 30 The three Registers marked GHI, are different the one from the other. And..it is good that there be a Wall of a foot thick between the Registers and the said motion. **1766** HAWKINS *Hist. Mus.* IV. I. x. 148 By means of the Registers that command the several orders of pipes, the wind is either admitted into or excluded from them severally. **1797** *Encycl. Brit.* (ed. 3) XIII. 487/2 To fit these channels, there are the same number of wooden sliders or registers running the whole length. **1862** *Catal. Internat. Exhib.* II. xvi. 104/2 The whole of the accessory movements are labelled similar to the registers. *Ibid.*, The total number of pipes is 2475, and of registers 45.

transf. **1727** POPE, etc. *Art of Sinking* xiii, Every Composer will soon be taught the use of this Cabinet, and how to manage all the Registers of it, which will be drawn out much in the manner of those in an Organ.

b. The compass of a voice or instrument; the particular range of tones which can be produced by certain voices.

Freq. used with distinguishing terms as *upper*, *middle*, and *lower register*; *head*, *chest*, and *throat register*, etc.

1811 BUSBY *Dict. Mus.* (ed. 3), *Register*, a term applied to the compass, or graduated notes, of a voice. **1843** *Penny*

Cycl. XXVI. 418/2 The compass of soprano and some other voices are divided into registers, of which there are two, viz. the natural and the falsetto. **1876** GEO. ELIOT *Dan. Der.* x, The sounds too were very pleasant to hear.., musical laughs in all the registers.

c. *Art.* One of a number of bands or sections into which a design is divided.

1937 *Discovery* Sept. 287/1 As a rule these plant designs [on Jhukar pottery] were painted in black, or a deep purple, the red being used for the broad bands separating the registers. **1966** RONIGER & DUNN tr. *Lazarev's Old Russ. Murals & Mosaics* i. 39 In the middle register of the apse is the great monumental composition of the *Eucharist*. **1977** *Times Lit. Suppl.* 4 Feb. 137/3 The outside [of a conical drinking-horn] is decorated in paint or in enamel. There are two upper registers with scenes of animals and hunters. **1980** *Catal. Fine Chinese Ceramics* (Sotheby, Hong Kong) 222 Two groups of nine bosses arranged in three registers within rectangular enclosures, the registers alternating with bands of repeated curlicues.

d. *Linguistics.* A variety of a language or a level of usage, *spec.* one regarded in terms of degree of formality and choice of vocabulary, pronunciation, and (when written) punctuation, and related to or determined by the social role of the user and appropriate to a particular need or context.

1956 T. B. W. REID in *Archivum Linguisticum* VIII. 32 He will on different occasions speak (or write) differently according to what may roughly be described as different social situations: he will use a number of distinct 'registers'. **1962** *Canadian Jrnl. Linguistics* VII. 69 Interference may also vary according to the social role of the speaker in any given case. This is what the Edinburgh School has called *register.* **1966** G. N. LEECH *Eng. in Advertising* vii. 68 Varieties of English distinguished by use in relation to social context are called *registers.* **1971** P. YOUNG in J. Spencer *Eng. Lang. W. Afr.* 173 A novel, then, can be seen as an amalgam of registers within a wider register of literary endeavour. **1972** *N. & Q.* Dec. 446/2 Chaucer must therefore have used what was, for the London of his time, a more formal, possibly more archaic, register. **1977** P. STREVENS *New Orientations Teaching of Eng.* x. 119 They are aware..of the idea of 'varieties' of English, and they probably know the term 'register'—a variety related to a particular use of the language, a particular subject or occupation.

e. *Phonetics.* A type of phonation, essentially controlled by the larynx, but distinct from tone, employed contrastively in some languages (e.g. Cambodian).

1964 J. C. CATFORD in D. Abercrombie et al. *Daniel Jones* 34 'Register' differences..are associated with tone-differences in several S.E. Asian languages. **1967** D. ABERCROMBIE *Elem. Gen. Phonetics* 101 In Cambodian, for example, every syllable is spoken with one of two registers, which are mainly distinguished from each other by the position of the larynx in the throat. The same is true of Gujerati spoken in Surat, the difference here being between 'tight' and 'breathy' phonation.

9. a. A contrivance, usually consisting of a metal plate or plates by which an opening may be wholly or partially closed, used for regulating the passage of air, heat, or smoke.

In ordinary use now chiefly applied to the adjustable plate which regulates the draught of a common fire-grate, or (*orig. U.S.*) to the perforated or open-work plate by which warm air is admitted to an apartment.

1610 B. JONSON *Alch.* II. iii, Looke well to the register, And let your heat, still, lessen by degrees. **1664** EVELYN *Kal. Hort.* (1729) 231 Which Hole is to be left open, or govern'd with its Register, to attemper the Air..entering by the Furnace-pipes. **1758** REID tr. *Macquer's Chym.* I. 264 Make a small passage through the dome, by opening some of its registers, that the flame may just begin to draw. **1801** *Trans. Soc. Arts* XIX. 326 A double register;—first to close the back flue. **1860** EMERSON *Cond. Life, Culture* Wks. (Bohn) II. 373 People..who coddle themselves, who toast their feet on the register. **1920** E. FROST *Let.* Mar. in *Lett. R. & E. Frost* (1972) 86, I am writing to you with a pencil generally these days, because I can sit and warm my feet over the register at the same time if I use a pencil. **1950** R. MOORE *Candlemas Bay* II. 86 Two rooms were warmed by hot-air registers through the kitchen ceiling. **1957** V. NABOKOV *Pnin* vi. 145 A cranky-looking oil furnace in the basement did its best to send up its weak warm breath through registers in the floors. **1967** *Gloss. Terms Gas Industry* (*B.S.I.*) 91 *Register*, a fitment equipped with a damper or movable louvres which permit adjustment or closure. **1970** *Daily Tel.* (Colour Suppl.) 25 Sept. 14 (Advt.), Built-in ducts waft warm air to each room through small, skirting-level registers.

†**b.** A regulator in a steam engine. *Obs.*$^{-0}$

1797 *Encycl. Brit.* (ed. 3) XVI. 54/2 There are also registers in the steam engine.

c. *Rope-making.* A disc containing concentric circles of holes through which the component yarns of a strand pass, the rotation of the disc serving to twist them together. Also ***register plate.***

1793 J. HUDDART *Brit. Patent 1952* 5 The register is calculated to form the strand into shells of yarns, and therefore they must be made of different sizes. **1846** G. DODD *Brit. Manuf.* VI. 199 The system for attaining any required intensity of twist is called the 'register'. **1855** W. COTTON *Brief Memoir Capt. Joseph Huddart* 20 His great principle (concentric circles) was accomplished by what he called a register plate. **1950** A. E. HAARER *Ropes & Rope-Making* vii. 43 This..is what we call a register plate. Behind it you can see the yarns passing together into a short tube. **1957** D. HIMMELFARB *Technol. of Cordage Fibres & Rope* v. 127 Register plates are generally heavy castings of curved cross section, with holes approximately ½-inch to 1-inch in diameter.

10. a. A registering device; a mechanical contrivance or apparatus by which data of some kind are automatically recorded; an indicator.

[**1677** PLOT *Oxfordsh.* 228 He contrived a Thermometer to be its own Register.] **1830** DANIELL in *Phil. Trans.* CXX. 262 The pyrometer..consists of two distinct parts, which I shall designate as the Register and the Scale. **1862** *Catal. Internat. Exhib.* II. xv. 80 Clock with perpetual register of day, week, and month. **1875** KNIGHT *Dict. Mech.* 1912/1 Among the applications of gearing..applicable to registers, may be cited epicyclic and differential gears.

b. = *cash register* s.v. CASH *sb.*[1] 3 a. Chiefly *U.S.*

1895 in *Funk's Stand. Dict.* **1911** *Daily Colonist* (Victoria, B.C.) 29 Apr. 13/4 Two robbers..took $160, all the money in the register, and made good their escape. **1976** 'E. MCBAIN' *Guns* vii. 148 Colley wishes he could see into the open drawer of the register. **1977** *Transatlantic Rev.* LX. 40 He..then counted the cash in the register.

c. In mechanical calculators, a device in which numbers representing data or the results of arithmetical operations are stored or displayed; in an electronic computer or calculator, a location in store having a small capacity but negligible access time and used for a specific purpose (hence with qualifying sbs., as ***address, control, storage register***).

1928 *Monthly Not. R. Astron. Soc.* LXXXVIII. 451 Their principal deficiencies were the absence of tens transmission in the multiplier register,..and the excessive labour of zeroising or clearing the registers. **1946** *Math. Tables & Other Aids to Computation* II. 151 The Brunsviga Dupla..had two product registers..and had red and white figures as in the multiplier register. **1947** *Proc. I.R.E.* Aug. 759/1 The counter advances one stage on receiving a pulse, and hence is an adder as well as a register. **1956** [see ADDRESS *sb.* 7 c]. **1959** *Commun. Assoc. Computing Machinery* Oct. 3/2 Besides the internal memory, the arithmetic unit has four fast access cells. In these cells, the words are stored in dynamic form, in registers. **1964** F. L. WESTWATER *Electronic Computers* i. 13 This number, when placed in a special register called the control register, will cause the machine to obey the instruction. **1973** *Sci. Amer.* Aug. 102/2 (Advt.), In addition to its computer-like operational stack, the HP-35 has a constant storage register which lets you store any number and recall it as often as you want for repeat operations, with-out ever having to re-enter it. **1977** *Ibid.* Sept. 86/3 In microprocessors registers are employed for the temporary storage of data, of partial results, of instructions and of the addresses where other data or instructions are to be found.

11. †**a.** A part of a type-mould (see quot. 1727–38).

1683 MOXON *Mech. Exerc., Printing* xv. ¶7 The Register ..is made of an Iron Plate about a Brevier thick. **1727–38** CHAMBERS *Cycl.*, *Register*, among letter-founders, is one of the inner parts of the mould wherein the printing types are cast... It's use is to direct the joining of them justly together.

b. *Printing.* Precise adjustment of the type or printing; *esp.* exact correspondence of the printed matter on the two sides of a leaf. More widely, exact coincidence of position of superimposed images, esp. in colour printing; so ***in, out of register.*** Also *transf.*

1683 MOXON *Mech. Exerc. Printing* xxiv. ¶7 *Making Register* is to Quoin up a Form [etc.]. *Ibid.*, Then he observes how the Register of the Head and Foot agrees. **1683–4** *Ibid.* (1962) 348 Out of register, bad register. **1706** PHILLIPS (ed. Kersey) s.v., In the Art of Printing, Register is a Rule for the equal Distribution of the Lines and Pages. **1771** P. LUCKOMBE *Hist. & Art of Printing* 500 *Out of register*, when pages are not worked even on each other. **1816** SINGER *Hist. Cards* 159 The right hand margin is not in register, the lines being of unequal length. **1825** J. NICHOLSON *Operat. Mechanic* 305 In order to..be printed on both sides, without destroying the register (or coincidence of the pages on the opposite sides of the sheet). **1890** ZAEHNSDORF *Bookbinding* I. i. 3 The binder is perfectly justified in rejecting any sheets..not in register. **1907** [see DUOTONE]. **1915** [see PRINT *v.* 15 a]. **1947** *Electronics* Jan. 75/2 Color fringing..is also not present in the simultaneous system [of colour television], but a similar effect due to lack of register among the three simultaneous images may be present. **1950** *Proc. R. Soc.* A. CCI. 189 It [*sc.* a diffraction grating] is then cut in half, perpendicular to the rulings, and the two halves are put together face to face in register. **1966** H. WILLIAMSON *Methods Bk. Design* (ed. 2) xxii. 366 Colour printing usually costs more per colour than does black printing because of the laborious work of getting and maintaining register. **1967** V. STRAUSS *Printing Industry* xi. 735/2 Printers distinguish several kinds of register, depending on the intricacy of a job. No-register means that the several color areas are completely independent of each other, loose register that minor variations in their relations are inconsequential; tight, close, or hairline register indicates that these relations must be quite exact. **1975** J. B. HARLEY *O.S. Maps* ix. 138 Road casings were omitted..to assist with colour register when printing. **1975** *Nature* 25 Sept. 331/2 It is a rod-shaped, coiled-coil molecule, about 410 Å long, composed of two parallel α-helical chains which are in register. **1978** *Amat. Photogr.* 11 Jan. 69/2 A bas relief is made by printing through a negative and a positive, sandwiched together slightly out of register.

c. *Photogr.* In a camera, proper correspondence between the focussing screen and the sensitive plate or film.

1890–1 WOODBURY *Encycl. Photogr.* 607.

12. *attrib.* and *Comb.*, as (sense 1) ***register clerk***; (sense 4) ***register act, box, certificate, keeper, ticket, vessel***; (sense 8) ***register valve***; (sense 9) ***register furnace, grate, plate, stove***; (sense 10) ***register frame, head, pyrometer, thermometer***; (sense 11 b) ***register point, sheet***; **register board**, a flat surface with pegs or guides such that sheets of paper or film placed on it may be brought into the same relative position; **register mark** *Printing* (see quots.). See also REGISTER BOOK, HOUSE, OFFICE, SHIP.

1818 CRUISE *Digest* (ed. 2) IV. 538 To remedy this inconvenience..several acts of parliament have been made, called the *Register Acts. **1840** SHEE *Abbott's Merchant Ships* (ed. 6) 58 The old Register Acts contained no provision for registering ships in the territories under the government of the East India Company. **1967** KARCH & BUBER *Offset Processes* viii. 331 The *register board.. performs a very important part in obtaining accurate registration by providing a mechanism to jog each sheet into exactly the same position for entry into the head of the press. **1977** J. HEDGECOE *Photographer's Handbk.* 245 (*caption*) Take a negative 2¼ ins sq..and attach it to a strip of film which has been punched to fit the register board. **1836** *Act 6 & 7 Will. IV*, c. 86 §14 The Register Books..shall be always kept in the *Register Box, and the Register Box shall always be left locked. **1696** *Pub. Gen. Acts* (1697) 489 Divers evil disposed Persons so Registred..have fraudulently lent their *Register Certificates to divers Mariners..who were not Registred. **1887** C. D. WARNER *Their Pilgrimage* (1888) iii. 63 The *register clerk stood fingering the leaves of the register with a gracious air. **1885** C. G. W. LOCK *Workshop Receipts* Ser. IV. 213/1 The *register-frame is placed on the bed, and black-leaded, the forme is placed inside. **1641** FRENCH *Distill.* i. (1651) 3 Some Furnaces have three partitions, as the Furnace for Reverberation, and the *Register Furnace. **1833** LOUDON *Encycl. Archit.* §1458 Among the fixtures of the bar may be included a folding *register grate. **1800** MUDGE in *Phil. Trans.* XC. 558 The disturbances to which the *register-heads were liable, did not discover themselves till a mile of the base had been measured. **1687** in Dallas *Stiles* (1697) 109 Compter, and *Register-keeper of all Wares and Merchandice imported in to the said Kingdom. **1727** DE FOE *Syst. Magic* I. ii. (1840) 52 We must have been deluded..by all the writers and register-keepers that ever have been, are, or are in being. **1927** H. HUBBARD *Colour Block Print Making* 208 **Register marks*, in colour printing, marks for controlling the position of the paper in printing to ensure register. **1937** *Discovery* Oct. 300/2 Register marks are drawn on the stones just off the edge of the design. These the printer uses for placing the paper in exactly the right place on the stones used in subsequent printings. **1971** D. POTTER *Brit. Eliz. Stamps* xv. 174 Autotron marks, long bars, provide the electronic check for colour registration. Register marks..serve a similar purpose. **1715** DESAGULIERS *Fires Impr.* 52 A *Register Plate of Iron towards the top of the Funnel. *Ibid.* 53 These Register Plates will serve to keep in the warm Air. **1839** URE *Dict. Arts* 280 In building chimneys..we can readily reduce it to any desired size, by means of a sliding register plate near its bottom. **1875** KNIGHT *Dict. Mech.* 1905/2 These are the equivalents of the *register-points of the chromo-lithographic process or the typographic printing in colors. **1830** DANIELL in *Phil. Trans.* CXX. 257 A new *Register-Pyrometer, for measuring the Expansion of Solids. **1683** MOXON *Mech. Exerc., Printing* xxiv. ¶7 He lays another Sheet even upon the Tympan-sheet, for a *Register Sheet. **1795** *Specif. Crook & German's Patent* No. 2032. 8 *Register stoves and every other project commonly supposed to be useful by those who profess to cure smoking chimnies. **1838** DICKENS *O. Twist* iii, A nice small pattern, just the thing for register stoves. **1820** *Q. Jrnl. Sci.* XIV. 316 The maximum and minimum of temperature in the course of the twenty-four hours, as marked by a *register thermometer. **1844** *Act 7 & 8 Vict.* c. 112 §20 Every Person ..intending to serve on board any Ship..is hereby required to provide himself with a *Register Ticket. **1880** E. J. HOPKINS in Grove *Dict. Music* II. 583/2 A metal pin.. rested on the front end of the '*register-valve' as it was called. **1727–38** CHAMBERS *Cycl.* s.v. *Register ships*, In the years 1702, 1703, &c. these *register vessels..sold their commodities for above three hundred per cent. profit.

register ('rɛdʒɪstə(r)), *sb.*[2] Now *rare.* [Prob. for REGISTRER, q.v.] **a.** The keeper of a register; a REGISTRAR. (In common use *c* 1580–1800.)

1531–2 *Act 23 Hen. VIII*, c. 19 All judges, aduocates, registers and scribes, proctours.. and apparitours and all other. **1570–6** LAMBARDE *Peramb. Kent* (1826) 175 Thomas Laurence the Register of Canterbury was attainted of misprision of the same treason. **1651** N. BACON *Disc. Govt. Eng.* II. iv. (1739) 23 At the first, he was no better than a Register, or the King's Remembrancer, or Secretary. *a* **1704** T. BROWN *Two Oxford Scholars* Wks. 1730 I. 4 The Bishops Secretary or Register will present me with some Parchments and wax. **1788** JEFFERSON *Writ.* (1859) II. 500 To discharge the functions of notaries and registers of the consulate. **1816** SCOTT in Raine *Mem. Surtees* (1852) 166 My friend Thomas Thomson, the Deputy Register of Scotland. **1837** *Lett. fr. Madras* (1843) 93 There will also be in time a Registrar, or, as they spell it here, 'Register', but none is appointed yet. [**1873** SIR R. PHILLIMORE *Eccles. Law* II. IV. v. 1330 Schoolmasters are within the canons of 1603 as well as registers.] **1948** *Daily Progress* (Charlottesville, Va.) 7 Apr. 13/7 He is the Register of Wills. That's what the state constitution calls him. **1972** *Publishers' Weekly* 21 Aug. 58/1 Now Acting Register of Copyrights on leave to UNESCO, Miss Ringer has been opposing appointment of George D. Cary as Register.

attrib. and *Comb.* **1603** *Humble Petit. Ministers Ch. Eng.* §4 That none having jurisdiction or Register places, put out the same to farme. **1650** *Pub. Gen. Acts* 1681 Trustees, Treasurers, Register, Register-Accomptant [etc.].

†**b.** *Sc.* ***Lord Register*** = Lord Clerk Register (see *sb.*[1] 3 b). *Obs.*

1686 DALLAS *Stiles* (1697) 111 His Majesties right trusty and well beloved Cousin and Counsellor G. V. of T. Lord Register. **1708** J. CHAMBERLAYNE *St. Gt. Brit.* II. (1710) 407 The Four Lesser Officers of State [before the Union] were The Lord Register, The Lord Advocate [etc.]. **1794** *Inv. R. Wardrobes* (1815) App. ii. 355 One of the Lord Register's Deputies for Keeping the Records.

register ('rɛdʒɪstə(r)), *v.* Also 5–6 **regystre**, 5–7 **-gestre**, (6 **-gester**). [ad. F. *registrer* (13th c.), or med.L. *registrāre*, f. *registrum* REGISTER *sb.*[1]]

1. a. *trans.* To set down (facts, names, etc.) formally in writing; to enter or record in a precise manner.

1390 GOWER *Conf.* I. 261 Of whom the wrytinge is yit now Registered, as a man mai hiere. **1433** LYDG. *S. Edmund* III. 604 As it is remembryd in historie And registred be old antiquyte. **1494** FABYAN *Chron.* 5 Of bothe landes the Cronycles entyere, With other matyers whiche Regystred be. **1568** GRAFTON *Chron.* II. 433 Rychard Whittyngton.. hath right well deserued to be regestred in the boke of fame. **1615** G. SANDYS *Trav.* 90 Those that had bin sicke, vpon recouery there registered their cures, and the experiments wherby they were effected. **1667** MILTON *P.L.* XII. 335 Such follow him, as shall be registerd Part good, part bad, of bad the longer scrowle. **1758** JOHNSON *Idler* No. 17 ¶3 Some register the changes of the wind. **1784** COWPER *Task* v. 530 The fatal hour Was registered in heaven ere time began. **1815** J. SMITH *Panorama Sc. & Art* II. 36 Observations on the hygrometer have not been.. so diligently registered.. as appears desirable. **1872** LIDDON *Elem. Relig.* i. 21 To know all that can be known about his wishes and character, and to register this knowledge in exact terms.

transf. or *fig.* c **1530** *Crt. of Love* lxvii, Register this in thine remembraunce. **1590** GREENE *Orl. Fur.* Wks. (Rtldg.) 91/1 With my trusty sword.. I'll register upon his helm what I dare do. *a* **1806** H. K. WHITE *Lett.* Poet. Wks. (1837) 281 Many a flower, which in the passing time My heart hath register'd. **1878** HUXLEY *Physiogr.* 211 Such appears to have been the succession of events registered by these ruins. **1891** 'L. MALET' *Wages of Sin* I. iii. 53 He was always thinking, doing, feeling, experiencing something... Always registering impressions, making observations. **1946** D. C. PEATTIE *Road of Naturalist* iv. 49 All I could do was.. register on the one hand my sympathy with Abie and, on the other, the isolation of my own interests. **1955** W. HEISENBERG in W. Pauli *Niels Bohr* 22 The observer has.. only the function of registering decisions. **1972** *Daily Tel.* 31 Jan. 7 Those responsible for the television serialisation of Heinrich Mann's *Man of Straw*.. worked hard to register the idea that the novel.. prophesied the rise of the Nazis.

†**b.** To set (one) down *for*, or as, something.

1597 HOOKER *Eccl. Pol.* v. lxxvi. §5 Him we may register for a man fortunate. **1604** T. WRIGHT *Passions* III. i. 81 He deserueth to be registred for a foole. **1611** BIBLE *1 Macc.* viii. 20 That we might be registred, your confederats and friends.

†**c.** Const. with *inf.* To record. *Obs. rare.*

1614 RALEIGH *Hist. World* II. (1634) 444 He.. was the first that is registred to haue set up Irreligion by force. **1631** WEEVER *Anc. Funeral Mon.* 806 In the Manuscript.. these Carmelites following are registered to haue beene buried in this Monastery.

†**d.** To set *down* in a record or register. *Obs.*[−1]

1683 WOOD *Life* 26 Oct. (O.H.S.) III. 76 They framed themselves into a solemn meeting, had discourses, and the discourses were registered down by Dr. Plot.

2. *spec.* **a.** To make formal entry of (a document, fact, name, etc.) in a particular register; also, to get (a document, etc.) entered in the register by the person entitled to do so.

1463 *Bury Wills* (Camden) 43 He that registerith it to haue a competent reward for his labor, and that this forseyd wryting be registerid also. **1530** PALSGR. 683/1 My fathers wyll is regystred in the bysshops courte. **1547** *Reg. Privy Council Scot.* I. 79 Ordanis the Clerk of Register to extend the samyn act.. and to register the samin in the bukis of Counsale. **1617** *Sc. Acts Jas. VI* (1816) IV. 546/2 So proportionallie for everie page.. for registring of everie ane of þe saidis evidentis. **1677** YARRANTON *Eng. Improv.* 12, I can both in England and Wales Register my Wedding, my Burial, and my Christening,.. and that which is Register'd there, is good by our Law. **1794** in Bloomfield *Amer. Law Rep.* 9 The Term.. fixed in the said Act for registering Slaves. **1825** *Act 6 Geo. IV*, c. 110 §2 The said Ship or Vessel .. has been duly registered at the Port. **1858** HAWTHORNE *Fr. & It. Note-bks.* (1872) I. 3 The great bulk of our luggage had been registered through to Paris. **1864** BLACKMORE *Clara Vaughan* (1872) 119 My last letter.. was registered for security.

absol. **1787** JEFFERSON *Writ.* (1859) II. 231 The edict for the stamp tax has been the subject of reiterated orders and refusals to register. **1930** N. R. STEPHENSON *Nelson W. Aldrich* iii. 48 The Senate passed the bill, Aldrich and Platt registering against it.

b. *refl.* (also with *as.*)

1529 RASTELL *Pastyme* (1811) 282 [She] there regystarde herselfe as a sentwary woman. **1568** GRAFTON *Chron.* II. 706 [She] departed to a Seminarie there by called Beaulieus.. and registred her selfe and hers, as persons there priuileged. **1695** *Act 7 & 8 Will. III* (1696) 478 A Natural born Subject of this Realm.. Who shall be willing to Enter and Register himself for the Service of His Majesty. **1866** GEO. ELIOT *F. Holt* Introd., They.. could have registered themselves in the census.. as members of the Church of England.

c. *trans.* and (now chiefly) *intr.* (for *refl.*) To enter the name of (a guest or visitor) in the register of a hotel or guest-house; to enter one's name in such a register. orig. *U.S.*

1848 *Lit. Amer.* 14 Oct. 237/1 Sixty miles down the Monongahela brought us to Pittsburgh, and about half past 7 P.M., I was registered at the 'Monongahela House'. **1850** M. REID *Rifle Rangers* I. v. 52 Take your supper, engage a snug room, and wait for me. Don't register till I come—I'll attend to that. **1891** 'MARK TWAIN' in *Harper's New Monthly Mag.* Dec. 96/2, I arrived in Washington, registered at the Arlington Hotel, and went to my room. **1905** A. BENNETT *Tales of Five Towns* II. 264 'You haven't registered,' Nina called to him... He advanced to sign. **1922** H. TITUS *Timber* xv. 136 She.. stopped her car at the Commercial Hotel where she registered and was given a room. **1936** G. B. SHAW *Millionairess* IV. 187 You have allowed my husband to bring a woman to my hotel and register her in my name. **1967** BEAVIS & MEDLIK *Man. Hotel Reception* ii. 12 The receptionist should hand the pen to the guest when asking him to register. **1977** *Rolling Stone* 30 June 81/1 We then registered at the Airport Inn.

d. *intr.* (for *refl.*) To enter oneself or have one's name recorded in a list of people (freq. as a legal requirement), as being of a specified category or having a particular eligibility or entitlement.

1940 *Economist* 26 Oct. 521/2 Special delivery certificates have been issued for householders who must register with a single coal merchant. **1941** M. B. LOWNDES *Diary* 7 Nov. (1971) 225, I registered for my rations, sugar, bacon, butter, etc. at Fortnum's, where quality is *excellent*. **1952** B. PYM *Excellent Women* xxvi. 243, I told them of a laundry, a grocer and a butcher where they might register. **1965** *Listener* 10 June 875/3 To intimidate Negroes who might be tempted to register as voters. **1973** 'B. MATHER' *Snowline* vii. 85, I tried to get him to register.. as an addict. You get a scrip to buy the damned stuff on prescription. **1975** S. BRIGGS *Keep smiling Through* 149/2 You could even.. choose where to shop without being tied to the grocer where you were registered for basic rations. **1976** *Southern Even. Echo* (Southampton) 13 Nov. 8/4 The next day he registered as unemployed. **1977** *Time* 17 Jan. 24/2 This presumably would include all those civilians who fled the country to avoid the draft, simply failed to register or refused to submit to induction.

3. a. Of instruments: to record by some automatic device; to indicate. (Cf. REGISTER *sb.*[1] 10.)

1797 *Encycl. Brit.* (ed. 3) XVIII. 498/2 He proposes to adapt clock-work to this thermometer, in such a way as to register.. the degrees of heat and cold. **1862** *Catal. Internat. Exhib.* II. xv. 65 Improved Watchman's Clock.. for indicating punctuality and registering the neglect of it. **1877** *Nature* 24 May 59/1 In the hottest province.. the thermometer never registered above 74° before sunrise.

absol. **1875** KNIGHT *Dict. Mech.* 1838/2 Many of these instruments register up to 1000° Centigrade.

b. Of a person: to indicate or express (a particular feeling or emotion), esp. by facial expression.

1901 'L. MALET' *Hist. Sir R. Calmady* VI. viii. 568 The brightness died out of Honoria's face. She registered sharp annoyance against herself. **1915** WODEHOUSE *Something Fresh* iii. 56 A stage-director of a moving-picture firm would have recognized the look; Lord Emsworth was 'registering' interest. **1925** A. P. HERBERT *Laughing Ann* 32 For I don't have no adventure in the street, Men don't register emotion when we meet. **1977** *Private Eye* 29 Apr. 3/3 On being told, her face registered shock and horror.

c. *intr.* Of a person (orig. and esp. a film actor): to portray a particular role with conviction. Also of the ideas or feelings concerned: to communicate themselves successfully, to be convincing. Hence *gen.* of feelings, thoughts, utterances, etc.: to produce the desired effect, to make an appropriate impression on the person intended. Freq. const. (*up*)*on*, *with*.

1913 ESENWEIN & LEEDS *Writing Photoplay* 24 It is sometimes said that an effect, a bit of business, or an emotion which an actor is endeavoring to portray, 'will not register', meaning that it will not 'get across' or be understood by the audience in the way intended by the producer. **1915** *N.Y. Times* 1 Nov. 11 This new movie star 'registers', as the film folk have it. **1928** *Sunday Dispatch* 16 Dec. 14/4 It looks.. as though the producers had not been willing to risk spending money on it in case Miss Eagels did not register well. **1934** H. G. WELLS *Exper. Autobiogr.* II. ix. 704 He never did as he intended or the hint was too feeble to register upon our minds. **1939** *Punch* 6 Sept. 255/1, I give a cough. A significant cough... The cough registers. Deep silence ensues. **1951** N. BALCHIN *Way through Wood* iv. 60 Even that didn't register. You see I didn't know *where* Joe had been knocked down. **1951** M. MCLUHAN *Mech. Bride* (1967) 141/2 The slick-chick and the corporation executive, as they now register on the popular imagination, are already inside the totem machine. **1964** 'A. GILBERT' *Knock, knock, who's There?* i. 14, I couldn't help seeing the name... I looked sharply at Ted, wondering if it was going to register with him. **1966** *Listener* 17 Feb. 253/1 Sixteen-year-old Alexandra can only hope to register with her mother, so she finds out sadly. **1977** *Daily Mirror* 16 Mar. 5/3 With the five-year-old it did not register.

d. *intr.* To appear or produce a response on a recording or measuring instrument.

1947 *Math. Tables & Other Aids to Computation* II. 356 When two pure imaginaries are multiplied together a minus sign will register. **1974** *Nature* 6 Sept. 19/1 The ion energies were too small to register.

4. a. *intr.* To coincide or correspond exactly.

1839 *Penny Cycl.* XIV. 45/2 The printer superadds the impressions.. taking great care that the two fit well, or 'register', as it is technically called. **1890** W. J. GORDON *Foundry* 175 They are.. adjusted until the impressions fit —'register', as it is called—as intended by the engraver.

b. *trans.* To adjust with precision, so as to secure the exact correspondence of parts.

1839 [see REGISTERING *vbl. sb.* b]. **1891** *Anthony's Photogr. Bull.* IV. 92 The cardboard form is first placed in the printing frame, then the negative,.. then the sensitive paper, care being taken.. to register every part as perfectly as possible. **1976** *Physics Bull.* May 200/1 The images of the projected mask and the structure on the silicon wafer are superimposed and alignment is accomplished by registering the two images.

c. *Mil.* To adjust a gun in relation to (its target); to align (artillery) with its target.

1958 *Observer* 9 Feb. 11/4 The American Polaris.. will free still further the Western nuclear deterrent from dependence on large static bases.. which can be registered in advance. **1958** *Listener* 11 Sept. 386/3 The position had been liberally registered by Russian gunners from the city; hence the cannon balls. **1959** H. MACLENNAN *Watch that ends Night* IV. vii. 166, I had to spend ten hours in that hole with the body, for the machine guns were registered so close to the ground a rat couldn't have escaped.

5. *intr.* To manipulate the registers of an organ.

1891 *Times* 22 Oct. 14/2 Admirably calculated to exhibit the player's skill in 'registering'.

6. *trans. Rope-making.* To form (a strand) by the use of a register. Cf. REGISTER *sb.*[1] 9 c. Also *absol.*

1793 J. HUDDART *Brit. Patent 1952* 3 The spindle is turning in, registering the strand. **1800** *Remarks on Patent Registered Cordage* (Huddart & Co.) 3 He has invented a method of manufacturing cordage, whereby every yarn holds a situation in the strand, in which it bears its proportion of the strain of the rope. This is termed registering the strands. **1855** W. COTTON *Brief Memoir Capt. Joseph Huddart* 26 In order to render them impervious to water, it was necessary to register them at a higher angle. **1968** W. TYSON *Rope* I. iii. 10 In 1799 Huddart patented.. a means of registering the strands at a short length from the tube and winding up the rope as made, thus preserving a uniformity of twist.

registerable: see REGISTRABLE *a.*

registerary, obs. form of REGISTRARY.

'register book. = REGISTER *sb.*[1] 1 or 4.

1515 *Galway Arch.* in *10th Rep. Hist. MSS. Comm.* App. V. 396 He to fynd suficient surties to be recordid in the Regester-Booke. **1622** B. JONSON *Masque Augurs* Wks. (Rtldg.) 630/2 This, the register-book of my function, shews me no less than a clerk at all points. **1677–8** in J. T. Wheeler *Madras* (1862) III. 434 The.. Customer.. is alsoe to keepe the Register bookes for all private trade. **1771** LUCKOMBE *Hist. Printing* 31 A register book of wills.. wherein registrations were made. **1846** A. YOUNG *Naut. Dict.* 195 Their [ships] title to be on any class is determined by certain rules laid down in the register-book. **1869** in *Phillimore's Eccles. Law* (1873) II. VI. i. 1772 The registering of the deeds and the act in the register book of the diocese.

registered ('rɛdʒɪstəd), *ppl. a.* [f. the vb. + -ED[1].] **1.** Recorded or entered in some book or list; *spec.* of postal items recorded at the point of dispatch and indemnified against loss or damage. Also *ellipt.* as *sb.*

1674 BREVINT *Saul at Endor* 298 But the Registred Brethren or Sisters should not care much for Conversion. **1716** *Lond. Gaz.* No. 5467/1 The Value of the registred Effects brought by this Flota, is computed at 12 Millions of Pieces of Eight. **1782** WEDGWOOD in *Phil. Trans.* LXXII. 307 By these have I made my registered experiments. **1837** *Act 1 Vict.* c. 34 §25 All registered Letters shall be delivered to the Post Office, and also be delivered by the Post Office, under all such Regulations in every respect as the Postmaster General shall from Time to Time appoint. **1846** MCCULLOCH *Acc. Brit. Empire* (1854) I. 407 The proportion of registered baptisms to the population. **1855** MRS. GASKELL *Let.* 21 July (1966) 359, I am going to send it by registered parcel post. **1860** *Merc. Marine Mag.* VII. 214 Her registered tonnage was 686 tons. **1864** D. G. ROSSETTI *Let.* 5 Feb. (1965) II. 498 It shall.. fly in a registered letter to you as soon as may be. **1874** in Phillimore *Suppl. Eccles. Law* (1876) 52 The representation.. shall be.. sent by post in a registered packet. **1921** *Daily Colonist* (Victoria, B.C.) 9 Apr. 17/7 Three bandits.. last night held up a United States mail truck here and robbed it of three pouches of registered mail. **1930** J. B. PRIESTLEY *Angel Pavement* xi. 553 Don't forget you've got three registereds there; bring me the receipts in the morning. **1946** W. STEVENS *Let.* 12 Nov. (1967) 537 The proofs.. are being returned by registered mail today. **1962** *John o' London's* 11 Jan. 27/3 *Postman* ..'Ere, I got a registered for yer. **1967** E. RUDINGER *Wills & Probate* ii. 85 He enclosed a short covering letter listing the enclosures, and sent it by registered post. **1976** *New Yorker* 8 Mar. 90/3 She found waiting for her on the kitchen table the mail in response to the registered letters she had sent to the United States senators. **1981** *Guardian* 15 May 4/3 The registered envelopes, posted in Dublin and Waterford, have been handed to police but most people have held on to the money.

2. *Rope-making.* Formed by means of a register. Cf. REGISTER *sb.*[1] 9 c.

1800 *Remarks on Patent Registered Cordage* (Huddart & Co.) 5 But this loss of proportional strength, increases with the number of internal yarns contained in the first strands, while the registered strands bear a proportional strength to their number of yarns. **1846** G. DODD *Brit. Manuf.* VI. 199 A registered strand, or the strand produced by twisting the yarns together by this machine, is a smooth, uniform piece of cordage, all the yarns twisting round in one direction.

3. ***registered nurse***, a nurse who has been entered on an official register. See also *state-registered nurse* s.v. STATE *sb.* 41 a.

1896 *Brit. Med. Jrnl.* 18 Jan. 158/1 The precedent of the General Medical Council should be followed, and an analogous body created, composed of representatives of the nursing interests, the medical profession, the Privy Council, and the registered nurses. **1903** *Outlook* 14 Mar. 604/1 Such a person shall be given a Regents' certificate of proficiency and be privileged to bear the title of 'Registered Nurse' (R.N.). **1905** *Rep. Sel. Comm. Registration of Nurses* p. iv in *Parl. Papers* VII. 733 No person should be entitled to assume the designation of 'Registered Nurse' whose name is not upon the Register. **1949** *Reader's Digest* June 91/1 They passed with flying colors the examinations for registered nurse. **1976** L. HOCKEY *Women in Nursing* v. 50 After the age of twenty-five years, registered nurses are likely to move into a variety of other designations, mostly probably becoming ward sisters.

'registerer. *rare*[−1]. [f. as prec. + -ER[1].] One who registers.

1565 GOLDING *Cæsar* Pref., The Grekes the chiefe Registerers of worthy actes, called all thinhabiters from the river of Danow northward by the name of Celtes or Galles.

ˈ**Register House.** *Sc.* The house appointed for the keeping of the registers, now a special bulding, called the ***General Register House*** (erected at various dates from 1774 onwards), at the east end of Princes Street, Edinburgh.

1542 *Inv. R. Wardrobes* (1815) 71 The silver wark quhilk is in the register hous within the castell of Edinburgh. **1581** *Reg. Privy Council Scot.* III. 373 In his majesties Register Hous in the Castell of Edinburgh. **1740** *Acts Sederunt* (1790) 348 Ten hogsheads more of the records..ly still unopened in the general register-house. **1794** *Inv. R. Wardrobes* (1815) App. ii. 354 Within the Lord Clerk Register's Office in the General Register House at Edinburgh. **1844** C. INNES *Pref. Acts Parl. Scot.* I. 18 *note*, These three rolls were brought to the General Register House by a person who could give no information where he had got them. **1877** *Encycl. Brit.* VII. 663/2 The General Register House for Scotland..is an important adjunct to the Supreme Courts.

registering (ˈrɛdʒɪstərɪŋ), *vbl. sb.* [f. REGISTER *v.* + -ING[1].] The action of recording, or entering in a book, etc.

1576 FLEMING *Panopl. Epist.* 59 Yᵉ registring of our tumultuous times & daungerous chaunces. **1605** BACON *Adv. Learn.* II. viii. §5 The registering of doubts hath two excellent uses. **1653** *Acts & Ordin. Parl.* c. 6 (Scobell) 227 A Book of good Vellum or Parchment for the Registring of all such Marriages. **1712** PRIDEAUX *Direct. Ch.-wardens* (ed. 4) 99 For the Registring of such Baptisms. **1825** *Act 6 Geo. IV*, c. 110 (*title*), An Act for the registering of British Vessels.

b. *techn.* (See quots.)

1839 URE *Dict. Arts* 258 The means by which the successive impressions..are to be brought exactly to join each other..; this is by printers called registering. **1852** SEIDEL *Organ* 111 By registering, we here understand, the mode in which the various registers of an organ are combined.

ˈ**registering,** *ppl. a.* [-ING[2].] That registers.

1836 *Act 6 & 7 Will. IV*, c. 86 §31 Every such Registering Officer of the Quakers [etc.]. **1863** GEO. ELIOT *Romola* lxiii, A temporary post as an extra *cancelliere* or registering secretary under the Ten. **1877** *Nature* 13 Sept. 421/2 The metallic spiral must be placed very close to the registering apparatus.

ˈ**register** ˈ**office. a.** An office at which a register of any kind of kept, or where registration is made. **b.** *spec.* the office of a registrar of births, marriages, and deaths.

The officially correct form in the U.K. at the present time (1981). Cf. REGISTRY OFFICE 2.

1760 FOOTE *Minor* I. Wks. 1799 I. 247, I have advertis'd this morning, in the register-office, for servants under seventeen. **1779** SHERIDAN *Critic* I. i, My drawing-room is an absolute register-office for candidate actors, and poets without character. **1810** WALSH *Genius & Dispos. Fr. Gov.* (ed. 5) 108 Register offices abound in every part of the empire. **1835** *Act 5 & 6 Will. IV*, c. 19 §19 There shall be established in the Port of London an office to be called 'The General Register Office of Merchant Seamen'. **1893** MARY CHOLMONDELEY *Diana Tempest* i, The marriage at the local register office. **1954** T. S. ELIOT *Confidential Clerk* III. 121 We'd meant to be married very quietly In a register office. **1976** *Southern Even. Echo* (Southampton) 2 Nov. 6/5 Colours are gradually creeping into the dresses in shades of palest pinks and blue satin ribbon edging, and cream is a favourite for register office weddings. **1980** *Times* 13 Aug. 1/8 Couples [in Russia] intending to get married apply to the local register office.

Comb. **1782** MISS BURNEY *Cecilia* VII. ix, No register-office keeper has been pestered with more claimants.

†ˈ**registership**[1]. *Obs.* [f. REGISTER *sb.*[2] + -SHIP.] The office of registrar.

1574 ABP. PARKER *Corr.* (Parker Soc.) 460 Extend still your good will, if in case he be your officer for the registership. **1625** USSHER *Lett.* (1686) 335 For the former of these, which doth concern the Registership; I signified unto him..that I had made promise of it already. *a* **1645** LAUD *Rem.* (1700) II. 183 The Registership..of the Vice Chancellor's Court. **1726** AYLIFFE *Parergon* 163 See the case of Vaughan and Compton 14 Jac. at the Assizes for the Office of the Registership of Suffolk.

ˈ**register-ship**[2]. *Obs.* exc. *Hist.* A Spanish ship having a registered licence authorizing it to trade with the Spanish possessions in America.

1727–38 CHAMBERS *Cycl.* s.v. *Register ships*, or *ships of register*. **1739** in *Descr. Windw. Passage* (ed. 2) 3 There are another Sort of Vessels imploy'd in the Trade to the Indies, which are called Register-Ships. **1742** H. WALPOLE *Corr.* (1837) I. xxvii. 118 One of our men of war..has taken another register-ship of immense value. **1777** ROBERTSON *Hist. Amer.* VIII. Wks. 1851 VI. 139 All the register-ships destined for the South seas must still take their departure from Cadiz, and are obliged to return thither.

†**registery.** *Obs. rare.* [ad. med.L. *registeri-um*, or f. REGIST(ER *v.* + -ERY.] = REGISTRY.

1483 *Cath. Angl.* 302/1 A Regestery, *registerium*. **1686** PLOT *Staffordsh.* 445 A Copy of King Johns Charter taken out of the black book of the said Arch-Bishops Registery at Dublin. **1693** J. EDWARDS *Author. O. & N. Test.* 65 The Canon of Scripture is taken out of authentick registeries.

registrable (ˈrɛdʒɪstrəb(ə)l), *a.* Also **registerable.** [f. REGISTER *v.*] That may be registered.

1765 *Act 5 Geo. III*, c. 49 §4 A protest..shall be registerable in the Courts of Session or other competent judicatories. **1802–12** BENTHAM *Ration. Judic. Evid.* (1827) II. 667 Contracts registrable, contracts fit to be included in the system of registration. **1883** *Law Times* LXXV. 180/1 An office copy of a will..under such a seal, is to be registrable in the same way as a will. **1886** *Fortn. Rev.* Jan. 26 Suppose she is content with the cheapest registerable diploma obtainable. **1918** *Brit. Med. Jrnl.* 31 Aug. 212/2 In speaking of the minimum period, it is to be remembered that that time is only sufficient to gain a registrable qualification. **1960** *Times* 28 Apr. 3/3 (Advt.), Qualifications: Medical qualification registerable in New South Wales. **1962** *Economist* 20 Jan. 246/1 These agreements, which may become registrable. **1971** *Daily Tel.* 1 July 2/6 Places where Jews and Quakers celebrated marriage should become registerable in the interests of inter-religious harmony. **1976** *Sunday Times* (Lagos) 26 Sept. 11/1 At least, in some alert official's estimation, 4,000 registrable voters might just call at the centre. **1977** *Nature* 6 Jan. p. xiv/3 (Advt.), Applicants must have a veterinary qualification which is registerable in the United Kingdom.

Hence ˌ**registraˈbility.**

1885 *Law Times* LXXIX. 172/1 To make the registrability of words depend..upon the novelty of the mode of application.

ˈ**registral,** *a.* [f. REGISTER *sb.*[1] + -AL[1].] Pertaining to, derived from, authenticated by, a register.

1632 *Bishops Transcripts, Bilsington* (MS.), A coppy-registral of all such Xᵗnings Marriages and Burials as have been in..Bilsington. **1885** *Athenæum* 26 Dec. 843/1 It will contain copies of the registral acts of birth and death of all the Foscolos. **1967** E. SALZMAN *20th-Cent. Music* xiv. 173 Tiny, cell-like structures which retain their..identity through every kind of registral, rhythmic, dynamic, and color shift. **1970** *Language Sciences* Oct. 11/1 Rules that change this basic competence into dialect forms, into registral forms. **1980** *Dædalus* Spring 189 The expansion of registral sonority..and the appoggiatura, G-sharp, strongly stress the arrival of the A.

registrant (ˈrɛdʒɪstrənt). orig. *U.S.* [f. REGISTER *sb.*[1] or *v.* + -ANT[1].] One who registers (in various senses), esp. one who thereby gains a particular entitlement.

1890 in WEBSTER. **1928** *Index Trade-Marks U.S. Patent Office 1927* 5 (*heading*) Alphabetical list of registrants of trade-marks for the year 1927. **1942** *Nation* (N.Y.) 27 Apr. 41 Up to Jan. 1, 1942, the Army rejected 8 per cent of the registrants passed as physically fit by Selective Service. **1955** W. W. DENLINGER *Compl. Boston* 65 The many registrants carrying this name in the studbooks since 1934. **1964** *Economist* 24 Oct. 360/2 The registrants are more likely to be Democrats. **1976** *Century of Trade Marks* (Patent Office) 8/2 The definition specifically includes marks 'proposed to be used'; though the Courts have held that this means that the registrant must have a 'present intention' to use the mark. **1977** E. AMBLER *Send no more Roses* ii. 18 The subject of that particular seminar was of fairly general interest..and the number of registrants was high. **1979** *Rescue News* Mar. 2/6 The registration fee for the symposium is £4... Registrants will receive the definitive Symposium programme.

registrar (ˈrɛdʒɪstrɑː(r), rɛdʒɪˈstrɑː(r)). [f. REGISTER *v.* + -AR[2]: cf. the earlier REGISTRER and REGISTRARY.

The form is noted by Vesey, *Decline of the Eng. Lang.* (1841) 82, as a 'novelty..recently, within the memory of persons now living, introduced'.]

1. a. One whose business it is to keep a register; an official recorder. *spec.* the title of (*a*) a senior officer with administrative responsibility in certain universities; (*b*) a local official responsible for maintaining an index of births, marriages, and deaths in the area under his authority.

1675 BATHURST in Warton *Life* (1761) 136 The patent was sealed and delivered, and the person admitted, sworne before the public registrar. **1768** BLACKSTONE *Comm.* III. xxvii. 451 The minutes of it are taken down, and read openly in court by the registrar. **1812** *Act 52 Geo. III*, c. 146 §7 The Registrar of every Diocese in England. **1835** *Act 5 & 6 Will. IV*, c. 19 §21 A due Return should be made to the said Registrar of Merchant Seamen. **1868** FARRAR *Silence & V.* iii. (1875) 57 Every great historian should be no dull registrar of events.

(*a*) **1756** *Reply to Dr. Huddesford's Observations relating to Delegates of Press* 4 A Convocation being appointed to be held in the Theater on the second of July, the Vice-Chancellor gave directions to the Registrar to prepare the forms of nomination. **1797** *Encycl. Brit.* (ed. 3) XVI. 54/2 *Registrar*, an officer in the English universities, who has the keeping of all the public records. **1870** D. P. CHASE *Registrarship of University* 5 The Registrar has been relieved of a great amount of labour connected with the University accounts. **1900** *Statuta et Decreta Univ. Oxon.* 283 The Registrar of the University shall be elected in Convocation. He..is required to attend..all meetings of the Houses of Congregation and Convocation and of the Congregation of the University,..and generally to perform all duties necessary for carrying on the business of the Houses. **1943** 'B. TRUSCOT' *Redbrick Univ.* iii. 59 After a pause for breath we come to the whole of the University [of Bristol] Council, the Deans of Faculties, the Professors and Professores Emeriti, the Librarian, the Registrar, twenty-nine representatives of Convocation, [etc.]. **1953** K. AMIS *Lucky Jim* i. 16 He'd been passing behind the Registrar's chair.., had stumbled and had knocked the chair aside just as the other man was sitting down. **1975** J. MANN *Captive Audience* i. 10 The crowd of students..far from being calmed by the duplicated communication which the registrar had delivered had become wild and agitated. **1980** *Times* 1 Aug. 15/7 (Advt.), In view of the forthcoming retirement of the present Registrar, applications are invited for the post of Registrar of the University of Wales.

(*b*) **1864** DICKENS *Mut. Fr.* I. xi. 106 There were the Inquests and the Registrar's returns. **1876** C. M. YONGE *Three Brides* II. xiii. 242 They put up their banns at the Union at Brighton, and were married by the Registrar. **1880** A. TROLLOPE *Duke's Children* II. xxvii. 325 None of your private chaplains... Just the registrar, if there is nothing better. **1892** I. ZANGWILL *Childr. Ghetto* II. I. xxv. 218 Let us be married honestly by a registrar. **1967** *Guardian* 1 Aug. 4/3 The shot-gun marriages tend to take place in the registrar's office under the mistaken impression that the church does not marry pregnant brides.

b. ***registrar general.*** (See GENERAL *a.* 10.)

1836 *Act 6 & 7 Will. IV*, c. 86 §6 The Registrar General shall send..a General Abstract of the Numbers of Births, Deaths, and Marriages. **1863** A. YOUNG *Naut. Dict.* (ed. 2) 306 A general register and record office of seamen in the mercantile marine, under the direction of a registrar-general.

2. = REGISTER *sb.*[1] 8 and 10.

1840 *Penny Cycl.* XVI. 492/2 (*Organ*), A shows the reservoir;..DD, the registrars, by which the equal rising of the reservoir is ensured. **1879** in Sladen *Gunnery* App. ii, The electro-magnet, B, sustains a shorter rod, F.., named the 'registrar'.

3. A doctor of a certain grade in a hospital: orig. a junior doctor whose duties included the maintenance of a register of patients; now usu. a senior officer undergoing training as a specialist or consultant. Cf. RESIDENT *sb.* 3.

1862 *Med. Times & Gaz.* 18 Oct. 411/2 Besides these there are a Resident Medical Officer, or Physician's Assistant..; a Medical and Surgical Registrar at a salary of £25 a year; two House Surgeons. **1894** *Brit. Med. Jrnl.* 10 Nov. 1089/1 Rayner, Herbert E., F.R.C.S.Eng., appointed Surgical Registrar and Anæsthetist to the Hospital for Sick Children, Great Ormond Street. **1937** *Ibid.* 4 Sept. 470/2 Qualified students of the school can obtain appointments as house-physicians and house-surgeons, obstetric assistants, surgical, gynaecological, and medical registrars. **1961** *Lancet* 29 July 264/2 There would seem to be intra-professional divisions in which interests do not quite coincide—e.g., the unplaced registrars and the established consultants. **1965** P. FERRIS *Doctors* iii. 59 What senior registrars want is to be appointed consultants. **1977** *Western Morning News* 30 Aug. 3/3 Some new patients have to wait as long as two to three years before they are seen, because the consultant surgeons spend so much of their time with follow-up cases; these could be handled easily and effectively by registrars. **1980** *Times Lit. Suppl.* 1 Aug. 879/2 In interviews with residents (in Britain, registrars) she found that they expressed strong preference for the middle-class patient.

Hence ˈ**registrarship** (also stressed *regiˈstrarship*), the office of registrar.

1847 in WEBSTER. **1852** *Tait's Mag.* XIX. 622 His registrarship of £10,000 a-year. **1889** *Brit. Med. Jrnl.* 9 Nov. 1077/1 London Hospital,..—Surgical Registrarship. Salary £100 per annum. **1891** *Law Times* XC. 419/2 A mastership in lunacy, and a registrarship in bankruptcy. **1937** *Brit. Med. Jrnl.* 4 Sept. 467/2 In addition, the following appointments are open to all qualified students of the hospital:..two medical registrarships at £100 per annum. **1963** *Lancet* 12 Jan. 117/2 After he was demobilised in 1946 he held registrarships in Bristol at Southmead Hospital and the Children's Hospital.

registrary[1] (ˈrɛdʒɪstrərɪ). [ad. med.L. *registrāri-us* (Du Cange): see REGISTER *sb.*[1] and -ARY[1].] A registrar. Chiefly in University use, and now retained only at Cambridge.

c **1541** in Hearne *Collect.* 11 Dec. an. 1705 (O.H.S.) I. 124 Tho. Key Registrarie of the University. **1625** LAUD *Diary* 10 Oct. in *Hist.* (1695) 24, I and my Company dined in the open Air, in a place called Pente-Cragg, where my Registrary had his Country-House. **1691** WOOD *Ath. Oxon.* I. 1 The publick Scribe or Registrary of the University of Oxon. **1707** *Lond. Gaz.* No. 4294/3 The several Lists of Incumbents..are reduced to An. 1700. by the present Registrary. **1829** in Willis & Clark *Cambridge* (1886) III. 103 The Registrary's Office and Record Room. **1894** *Circular*, Fellow of Trinity College, and Registrary of the University from 1862 to 1891.

transf. **1853** MERIVALE *Rom. Rep.* vi. (1867) 166 The senate, reduced to the mere registrary of its haughty champion's decrees.

†ˈ**registrary**[2]. *Obs. rare*[−1]. [Cf. prec. and -ARY[1] B. 2.] A register or registry.

1716 M. DAVIES *Athen. Brit.* II. 173 For, say they, Godwin 'transcribes out of Josseline and Mason, as if he had them immediately from the Archives and Registraries'.

†ˈ**registrate,** *pa. pple.* (and *a.*). *Sc. Obs.* Also 5–6 **registrat(t,** 6–7 **regestrat.** [ad. med.L. *registrāt-us*, pa. pple. of *registrāre*, f. *registrum* REGISTER *sb.*[1]] Registered, recorded.

1425 *Sc. Acts Jas. I* (1814) II. 11/2 Þe King..has ordanit þat all statutis & ordinance of þis parliament..be registrat in the kingis Registir. **1543** *Sc. Acts Mary* (1814) II. 440/1 Þat þis present contract be actit and registrat in þe buikis of parliament sessioun. **1588** A. KING tr. *Canisius' Catech.* 118 b, Ye determination of Jouinian..registrat in the buuk callit the Code. **1639** *Procl. Chas. I to Scot.* 9 It is his Majesties will, that this be insert and registrate in the books of assembly. *c* **1680** DALLAS *Stiles* (1697) 472 By Vertue of Arrestments founded upon Registrat Bonds, Decreets, or the like. **1752** J. LOUTHIAN *Form of Process* (ed. 2) 135 Persons charged upon Criminal Letters..are..denounced, and registrate to the Horn.

fig. **1616** SIR W. ALEXANDER *Alexis to Damar* in *Drummond's Wks.* (1894) I. 183 Those madrigals we sung.. Are registrate by echoes in the rocks.

†ˈ**registrate,** *v. Obs.* Chiefly *Sc.* [f. ppl. stem of med.L. *registrāre*: see prec.] *trans.* To register (in *lit.* and *fig.* uses).

1570 in *Westm. Gaz.* (1897) 16 June 10/2 Fame shall registrate her princelie deeds. **1574** *Reg. Privy Council Scot.* II. 359 Commanding our clerkis..to registrate the samyn. **1617** *Sc. Acts Jas. VI* (1816) IV. 546/2 To receave fra the pairties thair euidentis and to registrat þe same. **1676** W. ROW *Contn. Blair's Autobiog.* xii. (1848) 372 They would registrate that sense of it in the books of Parliament. **1776** J.

NEILL 23 *Serm.* 60 These and other Young Saints God hath registrated in his book.

Hence †**'registrated** *ppl. a.*, **-ating** *vbl. sb.*

a **1598** ROLLOCK *Serm.* Wks. 1849 I. 406 The registrating of thair speiches is na thing to his schame. **1687** A. HAIG in J. Russell *Haigs* xi. (1881) 331 Item, For registrating of the signetor. **1732** E. ERSKINE *Serm.* Wks. 1871 II. 146 It is his registrated word: his sealed word.

registration (rɛdʒɪ'streɪʃən). [ad. med.L. *registrātiōn-em*, n. of action f. *registrāre* to REGISTER. Cf. obs. F. *registration* (16th c.).]

1. a. The act of registering or recording.

clause of registration, in Sc. Law, a clause in deeds providing for their being properly registered.

? **1566** *Acts Parl. Scot.* (1814) II. Chron. Table 4/1 Anent the registracione of letteris of newe infeftment confirmacion &c. *Ibid.* 33/2 Registratioun of ane appunctuament betuix my lord Governour and James Hammiltoun. *c* **1680** DALLAS *Stiles* (1697) 705 Remember, that immediately before the Clause of Registration, ye insert the Faculty reserved by the Father to himself. **1776** ADAM SMITH *W.N.* v. ii. II. 471 Duties upon registration [have become] extremely common. **1836** *Act 6 & 7 Will. IV*, c. 86 §1 So much of the said Acts as relates to the Registration of Marriages. **1877** *Nature* 23 Sept. 421 The registration of temperature is one of the most difficult of meteorological problems.

b. With *a* and *pl.* An instance of this; an entry made in a register. Also (occas. without article) *ellipt.*, = *registration number* below.

1611 FLORIO, *Registratione*, a registration, an enroulement, a recording. **1617** *Sc. Acts Jas. VI* (1816) IV. 546/1 Oure said souerane Lord..ordanis the same registeris and registratiounes foirsaidis to be insert thairin. **1712** PRIDEAUX *Direct. Ch.-wardens* (ed. 4) 97 A Page is filled with such Registrations. **1741–2** STACKHOUSE *Hist. Bible* VIII. i. Objection (1752) II. 1260/1 Their [censors] Business was to make a Registration of all the Roman Citizens. **1771** LUCKOMBE *Hist. Printing* 31 A register book of wills.. wherein registrations are made. **1973** J. PATTINSON *Search Warrant* vii. 111 A blue Chrysler... It had a New York registration. **1973** 'I. DRUMMOND' *Jaws of Watchdog* xii. 152 His car..was a Ferrari but with British registration. **1976** L. DEIGHTON *Twinkle, twinkle, Little Spy* x. 111 'The same registration!' said Mann excitedly. 'That makes four times the same number.'

c. *attrib.*, as ***registration act, court, fee, law***, etc.; (with reference to the registration of motor vehicles) ***registration book, number, plate***.

1885 WILKINSON *Cox & Grady's Law of Registration* 3 Persons acting as town clerks under the Parliamentary Registration Acts. **1922** *Michelin Guide Gt. Brit.* III. 711 When disposing of his car the motorist must fill in the name and address of the new owner in the registration book. **1968** 'D. RUTHERFORD' *Skin for Skin* ii. 17 The Morris 1000 was parked at the kerbside... I had the registration book and the cover note ready. **1843** COX *Registration of Voters* Pref. 1 Practical experience in the registration courts. **1869** *Bradshaw's Railway Man.* XXI. 14 Certificates are required for transfers. Registration fee 2*s.* 6*d.* each deed and seller. **1967** *Post Office Guide* 85 The registration fee must be paid by postage stamps affixed to the cover. **1977** J. BINGHAM *Marriage Bureau Murders* ii. 24 There would be a down payment, a registration fee..and further annual payments. **1868** G. DUFF *Pol. Surv.* 24 The Danish Government.. passed two new measurement and registration laws. **1903** *Act 3 Edw. VII* c. 36 §6 A person driving a motor car shall, ..if an accident occur to any person,..or to any horse or vehicle..owing to the presence of the motor car on the road, stop and, if required, give his name and address, and also.. the registration mark or number of the car. **1911** *Motor Man.* (ed. 13) viii. 260 A registration number once issued cannot be transferred to another car. **1959** M. GILBERT *Blood & Judgement* xii. 128 Are you the owner of a blue Riley saloon car, registration number GKR 692? **1977** B. PYM *Quartet in Autumn* v. 39 The car was an important status symbol and large sums of money could be paid for particularly desirable registration numbers. **1956** Registration plate [see ALL OVER *advb. phr.* 1 b]. **1974** F. NOLAN *Oshawa Project* xviii. 170 A black Volkswagen with a Darmstadt registration plate. **1977** 'D. CORY' *Bennett* v. 133 Relatively few cars, and fewer still with foreign registration plates.

2. In organ-playing: (see quot.). Also used with reference to other keyboard instruments, esp. the harpsichord.

1881 *Edin. Rev.* Jan. 238 The awkward..word 'registration', which is the only expression we have for the study of effect and combination of tone on the organ, and means the same in regard to it that 'orchestration' means in regard to the orchestra. **1921** G. A. AUDSLEY *Organ-Stops* 1 Haphazard methods of registration must be shunned. **1961** R. RUSSELL in A. Baines *Mus. Instr. through Ages* iv. 80 Undue preoccupation with such things as registration.. tends to obscure the fundamental musical requirements of the instrument [*sc.* the harpsichord]. **1966** *Listener* 19 May 737/3 He is the most characterful harpsichord player since Landowska. Purists may question his frequent changes of registration. **1974** *Daily Tel.* 18 Feb. 11/1 The excesses to which Bach's 'Goldberg' Variations can easily lend themselves were strictly avoided by George Malcolm..on the harpsichord... Registration was also kept within reasonable limits. **1976** *Gramophone* May 1761/2 Chorzempa's [organ] registration balances happily with the orchestra.

3. The state of being in register (REGISTER *sb.*[1] 11 b), or the action of obtaining this.

1890 JACOBI *Printing* 178 The sole object of points is to obtain perfect registration in backing. **1901** *Chambers's Jrnl.* June 364/1 The skilled attendant replaces them in the clip, one upon another, taking a little care to ensure perfect 'registration'..and, lo! there is a finely painted lantern slide! **1949** *Electronics* Dec. 69/2 The three color images in camera and picture tube must be very precisely aligned, both electrically and optically, to secure accurate registration. **1959** HALAS & MANVELL *Technique Film Animation* III. xix. 218 Background artists should know what registration manipulation is possible under the camera. **1962** W. H. STEVENS in G. A. T. Burdett *Automatic Control Handbk.* viii. 61 Separate panels are now cut from the multiple boards, and the fixing and component holes are drilled or punched... Registration of the holes with the circuit is achieved by means of the pilot holes. **1967** *Listener* 30 Mar. 424/2 The three pictures are equally focused and accurately in registration one with the other. **1971** D. POTTER *Brit. Eliz. Stamps* iii. 37 The line was printed in two operations as part of the tricolour production, and the very accurate registration required was not forthcoming. **1975** J. B. HARLEY *O.S. Maps* i. 11 A second sheet of plastic material carrying an opaque coating is placed in exact registration with the first.

Hence **regi'strational** *a.*

1889 *Lancet* 30 Nov. 1135 The above-named exceptional effort to obtain registrational accuracy.

'registrative, *a. rare* [f. as REGISTRATE *v.* + -IVE.] Of the nature of registration.

1862 J. BROWN *Horæ Subs.* (ed. 2) 410 Looking is a voluntary act,..seeing is a state,—passive and receptive, and at the best, little more than registrative. **1878** W. JAMES in *Jrnl. Specul. Philos.* XII. 11 At one time, 'scientific' thought, mere passive mirroring of outward nature, purely registrative cognition..would seem to be his [*sc.* Spencer's] ideal.

'registrator. *rare.* [a. med.L. *registrātor*, agent-n. f. *registrāre* to REGISTER. Cf. G. *registrator*, F. *régistrateur*.] One who registers, a registrar.

1802–12 BENTHAM *Ration. Judic. Evid.* (1827) I. 523 In case of registration..publicity serves as a security for the correctness..of the work of the registrator.

†**registrature.** *Obs. rare*⁻¹. [ad. G. *registratur* = It. *registratura*: see REGISTRATE *v.* and -URE.] A registry.

1762 tr. *Busching's Syst. Geog.* V. 432 The princely, spiritual and temporal colleges, together with their chanceries and registratures.

registree (rɛdʒɪ'striː). [f. REGISTER *v.* + -EE[1].] One who is registered (in various senses).

1923 G. B. SHAW in *Daily News* 18 Dec. 6/1 My refusal to credit the trade union known as the General Medical Council with the power to confer Omniscience and Infallibility on its registrees. **1966** *Punch* 28 Dec. 945/3 Miss Shuter at the desk had hysterics when an irate would-be registree broke into her glassy sanctuary and shook her by the shoulders.

'registrer. Now *rare.* Also 4 **regystrere**. [Orig. a. AF. **registrere* = OF. *registreur*: in later use f. REGISTER *v.* + -ER[1].] †**a.** One who registers; a registrar. *Obs.* **b.** = REGISTER *sb.*[1] 10.

1377 LANGL. *P. Pl.* B. II. 173 Erchdekenes and officiales and alle ȝowre regystreres. **1433** LYDG. *S. Edmund* III. 165 Burchardus..Was his Registrer and also his notarye. *c* **1450** —— *Secrees* 436 Callyd Registrer of ther tresoury. **1576** FLEMING *Panopl. Epist.* 59 Such as be the registrers & writers of their owne actes. **1598** FLORIO, *Registratore*, a registrer.., a remembrancer, a keeper of records. **1831** PALMER in *Phil. Trans.* CXXI. 209 Description of a Graphical Registrer of Tides and Winds.

So †**registrour**. *Obs. rare*⁻¹.

1556 OLDE *Antichrist* 88 b, Platina (the most registrour of the popes names).

registry ('rɛdʒɪstrɪ). [f. REGIST(ER *v.* + -RY: cf. REGISTERY.]

1. The act of registering, registration.

1589 PUTTENHAM *Eng. Poesie* I. x. (Arb.) 39 The memoriall and registry of all great fortunes, the praise of vertue [etc.]. **1653** in Somers *Tracts* (1748) I. 514 The whole City of Bristol (as to the Place of Registry, and Matters to be Registered) is to be accounted Part of the County of Somerset. **1694** *Act 6 & 7 Will. III*, c. 6 And if any undue preference..shall be made, either in point of Registry or Payment [etc.]. **1789** *Hist.* in *Ann. Reg.* 15 They had presumed to assert that no edict could be valid without their registry. **1817** W. SELWYN *Law Nisi Prius* (ed. 4) II. 1282 *note*, An action of trover for the certificate of registry itself. **1825** *Act 6 Geo. IV*, c. 110 §11 At every Port where Registry shall be made. *Ibid.* §21 If..the Master..cannot attend at the Port of Registry [etc.]. **1869** MOZLEY *Univ. Serm.* i. (1876) 27 A great volume of time is now shutting, the roll is folded up for the registry, and we must open another.

2. A place where registers are kept.

1603 *Constit. & Canons Eccles.* cxxvi, Bishop's Registrie. ..All such Possessours..shall once in euery yere exhibite into the publike Registrie of the Bishop of the Diocesse.. euery originall Testament. **1712** PRIDEAUX *Direct. Ch.-wardens* (ed. 4) 64 Many Instruments of such Consolidations may be seen in the Episcopal Registries of this Realm. **1803** S. PEGGE *Anecd. Eng. Lang.* 284 The place where such documents are deposited..is the Registry. **1874** *Act 37 & 38 Vict.* c. 85 §2 All documents..shall be.. sent to the registry of the Arches Court of Canterbury..or the registry of the Chancery Court of York.

3. A register, a book of record; also, an entry in a register.

1622 J. HUGHES *St. Pauls Exerc.* 7 A Chronicle, or a Registrie, wherein all our workes are written. *a* **1687** PETTY *Pol. Arith.* i. (1690) 28 There hath been much discourse, about introducing of Registries into England. **1770** *Monthly Rev.* 349 All registries agree in this, that the S.E. and N.W. winds are nearly equal. **1817** W. SELWYN *Law Nisi Prius* (ed. 4) II. 1282 The certificate may be proved to have been granted to the plaintiff by the production of the registry, from which it was copied. **1825** *Act 6 Geo. IV*, c. 110 §11 A Book shall be kept by the Collector..and every Registry shall be numbered in Progession. **1884** BROWNING *Ferishtah, Shah Abbas* 45 A useful registry,—Which therefore we—'believe'? **1891** MAYSTON *Index Customs Gen. Ord.* 194 Every entry in registry is to be signed.

†**4.** Registership. *Obs. rare*⁻¹.

1727–38 CHAMBERS *Cycl.* s.v. *Register*, The lord register, ..before the union, was the fifth officer of state, and besides the registry, was clerk of the parliament, treasury, exchequer, and session.

5. *attrib.*, as ***registry act, ticket***.

1838 W. BELL *Dict. Law Scot.* 841 *Registry Acts*, that body of enactments..as to the enregistering of all ships which are to have the privileges of British vessels. **1863** A. YOUNG *Naut. Dict.* (ed. 2) 306 The registry tickets which for some time were given to seamen are now abolished.

So †**registy**. *Obs. rare*⁻¹. In quot. *attrib.*

1562 *Child-Marriages* 50 As..doth more plainelie appere recorded in the registie boke within the parishe of Bunburye.

'registry ,office. 1. = REGISTER OFFICE a., *spec.* †a place where a register of positions in domestic employment is kept (*obs.* exc. *hist.*).

1728 SWIFT *Let.* c 10 May in *Works* (1766) XVII. 169, I will take up the bones, and make of it a skeleton, and put it in my registry office. **1834** J. S. MILL in *Monthly Repos.* VIII. 439 Prying into the records of the..registry office. **1836** *Act 6 & 7 Will. IV*, c. 86 §4 All Expences of carrying on the Business of the General Registry Office. **1839** J. ROMILLY *Cambr. Diary* 16 Sept. (1967) 178 Lucy went..to the Registry Office..to get a place for Frances Wilderspin. **1892** C. M. YONGE *Cross Roads* xv. 157 She was in communication with the registry office there; but she would not take what the matron of the lodge called 'rackety situations'. **1910** E. M. FORSTER *Howards End* vii. 59 Would you come round with me to the registry office? There's a housemaid who won't say yes but doesn't say no. **1964** M. LASKI in S. Nowell-Smith *Edwardian England* iv. 144 Registry offices abounded, but for really high-class servants the best method was..use of the advertisement columns of the *Morning Post*.

2. = REGISTER OFFICE b.

1911 G. B. SHAW *Getting Married* 236 Marriages gave place to contracts at a registry office. **1931** J. S. HUXLEY *What dare I Think?* vi. 205 The marriage ceremonial among most primitive peoples..contains a religious motive, just as much as does a Christian wedding ceremony (and just as little as does a wedding in a registry office). **1974** 'R. TATE' *Birds of Bloodied Feather* iii. 67 Can't we just make a date? It only means slipping into a registry office. **1976** *Daily Times* (Lagos) 27 Aug. 16/4 Workers at the registry office explained to Ajar that according to the law his wife could retain her maiden name. **1980** J. CARTWRIGHT *Horse of Darius* ii. 27 They..were married in the registry office.

†**'regitive**, *a. Obs. rare.* [a. OF. *regitif*, *-ive*, prob. ad. med.L. **regitīvus*, irreg. f. *regĕre* to rule: see -IVE.] Ruling, governing.

Godef. explains OF. *regitif* as 'qui rejette, qui expulse', app. in error.

a **1412** LYDG. *Two Merchants* 330 Whan nature of vertu regitiff Thoruh malencolye is pressyd and bor doun. **1574** NEWTON *Health Mag.* 4 Nothynge is more hurtful to the vertue regitive then cold. **1603** LODGE *Treat. Plague* iii, Feeblenes and weaknes of the regitiue vertue of the body. **1659** *Gentl. Calling* i. §5 Their regitive Power over the world, saith Gerson, is not so suitable an ingredient for a Magnificat of their composing.

Regius professor: see PROFESSOR *sb.*

regive (riː'gɪv), *v.* [f. RE- + GIVE *v.*, perh. after L. *reddĕre* or F. *redonner*.] *trans.* To give again, give back, restore, give in return.

1575 G. HARVEY *Letter-bk.* (Camden) 90, I regive you a pottle of howedyes. **1621** J. REYNOLDS *God's Revenge* I. Hist. i. 24 Remembring the former courtesie he had receiued of Grand-Pre, in regiuing him his sword, hee..vowes now to requite it. **1658** J. WEBB *Cleopatra* VIII. i. 25 Coriolanus, to whom the Africans had re-given the name of Juba his father. **1742** YOUNG *Nt. Th.* II. 309 Bid Day stand still,..and reimport The period past, regive the given hour. **1815** WORDSW. *Let. to Mrs. Clarkson*, The Soul..may be re-given when it has been taken away. *a* **1863** FABER *Hymns* (1875) 180 Not for worlds would I have him regiven.

reg'lar ('rɛglə(r)), *a.* and *adv.* Repr. a colloq. pronunc. of REGULAR *a.* and *adv.*

1842 DICKENS *Let.* 17 Feb. (1974) III. 69 The Newhaven serenade was not so good; though there were a great many voices, and a 'reg'lar' band. **1843** —— *Martin Chuzzlewit* (1844) xxv. 306, I says 'my half a pint of porter fully satisfies; perwisin', Mrs. Harris, that it is brought reg'lar, and draw'd mild.' **1899** F. W. MAITLAND *Let.* 10 Oct. (1965) 201 Wherever I go I shall expect my E.H.R. 'reglar'. **1950** *Collier's* 6 May 56/2 (*caption*) I'm a 'real pal'—a 'reg'lar fellow'—a 'good scout'!

re'glaze (riː-), *v.* [RE- 5 a.] *trans.* To glaze again. Hence **re'glazing** *vbl. sb.*

a **1618** SYLVESTER *Job Triumphant* II. 63 He dwels in Houses..By him, re-built, re-gilt, re-glost, re-glas'd. **1874** *Contemp. Rev.* Oct. 769 The windows require reglazing.

†**regle**, *sb. Obs. rare.* [a. OF. *regle* (13th c.; mod.F. *règle*), ad. L. *rēgula* rule: see REGULAR, etc.] A rule, regulation.

1483 CAXTON *G. de la Tour* K v b, Worship is not kepte in her ryght regle ne in her ryght estate. **1548** HOOPER *Commandm.* i. Wks. (Parker Soc.) 275 From this right line and true regle of God's word man erreth divers ways.

†**regle, reigle**, *v. Obs.* [ad. F. *régler*, †*reigler*, ad. L. *rēgulāre* to REGULATE.] *trans.* To rule, regulate. Hence †**'regling** *vbl. sb.*

1591 J. ELIOT *Disc. Warre* 57 He is farre deceived, who, to reigle himselfe well, regardeth what is..wont to be done. **1637** J. WILLIAMS *Holy Table* 57 To reigle and direct the English Churches. *a* **1661** FULLER *Worthies, Wales* IV. (1662) 9 All ought to regle their lives, not by the Popes Decrees, but Word of God. *a* **1670** HACKET *Abp. Williams* I. (1692) 92 My letter written to the Justices for the regling of the same.

regle, obs. form of *riggel* RIGGALD.

‖**'reglement**, †**reiglement**. [a. F. *règlement*, †*reiglement*, f. *régler*: see REGLE *v.*]

†**1.** The act of regulating or controlling. *Obs.* (Common in 17th c.)

1598 DALLINGTON *Meth. Trav.* Q iv, This *Conseil d'Estat* was wont only to determine publike affaires, as..the Reglement of Finances. **1625** BACON *Ess., Usury* (Arb.) 544 The Reformation and Reiglement of Vsury. **1683** TEMPLE *Mem.* Wks. 1731 I. 428 Offering privately..such a Reglement of Commerce as they could desire. *a* **1734** NORTH *Lives* (1826) III. 367 They used all means..to reduce this master under the like reglement as the former.

2. A regulation. (Now only as French.)

1668 *England's Wants* 24 In the Orders and Reglements set forth by his Grand Mareschals. **1673** SIR L. JENKINS *Let.* in Wynne *Life* (1724) I. 88 The other two reglements of trade in Indies they likewise passed over without making any exceptions to them. **1797** *Encycl. Brit.* (ed. 3) XVI. 575/1 By that reglement she divided the whole empire into 43 governments. **1898** *Schedule Articles Grk. Loan* art. i, The conditions of this Loan..will form the subject of a Règlement which will be sanctioned by a Royal Decree.

regle'mentary, *a. rare.* [ad. F. *règlementaire*: see prec. and -ARY.] Regular, according to regulations.

1870 *Daily News* 20 Sept., Grumbling as the Parisians did at the reglementary four hours daily drill. **1882** *Mech. World* 4 Mar. 139 The reglementary alloy now adopted. **1937** M. COVARRUBIAS *Island of Bali* iii. 58 The independent village is called a *desa*, a term we shall employ to designate the legal, 'complete' village that has the three reglementary temples.

reglet ('rɛglɪt), † **riglet**. [a. F. *réglet* (14th c.): see REGLE *sb.* and -ET[1], and cf. It. *regoletto*.]

†**1.** A narrow division of a page of a book; a column. *Obs. rare*$^{-1}$.

1576 HANMER *Chronogr.* in *Anc. Eccl. Hist.* 1 The fourth riglet contineweth the raigne of the Kings of Judæa.

2. *Arch.* A narrow flat band used to separate mouldings or other parts from each other.

The definition in Chambers *Cycl.* (1727–38), copied by Bailey, Nicholson, Gwilt, etc., is translated from the *Dict. de Trévoux*.

1664 EVELYN tr. *Freart's Archit.* xvii. 44 He has..made it [the height of the cornice] less, and cut off three or four small Reglets which renders it very dry and trifling. **1726** LEONI tr. *Alberti's Archit.* II. 34/2 The length of these reglets [It. *regoletti*] was twelve minutes, and the spaces from one reglet [It. *regolo*] to the other were eighteen. **1789** P. SMYTH tr. *Aldrich's Archit.* 12 The fillet, or plat band.., is a kind of plinth of a more oblong shape. From this the reglet..and the listel..differ only by their being smaller.

†**3.** A thin, flat piece or strip of wood used in carpentry or frame-making. *Obs. rare.*

1678 MOXON *Mech. Exerc., Joinery* I. vi. 112 *Riglet* is a thin square peece of Wood: Thus the peeces that are intended to make the Frames for small Pictures, &c. before they are Molded are called Riglets. [Hence in Holme *Armoury* (1688), and Bailey (1731), vol. II.] **1683** *Ibid., Printing* iv, On the..Fore-Rail..is nailed a small Riglet about half an Inch high, and a quarter and half quarter of an Inch thick.

b. *Printing.* A thin, narrow strip of wood, used (†as a head- or side-stick, etc., or) to make wide blanks between the lines in a page (see quots.).

More rarely applied to pieces of metal of similar form and use.

1683 MOXON *Mech. Exerc., Printing* II. 28 And Note, that the Head and Side-sticks are called Riglets, if they are not an English thick. *Ibid.* 207 The Compositer seeks among the Furniture for a Riglet,..or else he cuts a Riglet to that length (this Riglet is called a Destributing-stick). **1727–38** CHAMBERS *Cycl.* s.v., The reglets make the chief part of what they call the furniture of the chase. **1771** LUCKOMBE *Hist. Printing* 278 Reglets..are more proper for Whites than Quadrats, because Reglets are capable to interrupt the hanging and crookedness of Matter. **1898** SOUTHWARD *Mod. Printing* I. 82 Reglets, generally made of oak or beech,..vary in thickness from diamond up to 2-line great primer.

c. Collectively, or as a material. Also *attrib.*, as *reglet plane*.

1846 HOLTZAPFFEL *Turning* II. 487 The reglet plane.. derives its name from being employed in making the parallel slips of wood, or reglet, used by the printer for the wide separation of the lines of metal type. *a* **1885** CASLON *Catal. Printing Material*, Metal Reglet of the most beautiful finish and accuracy, in yard lengths.

reglorship: see RAGLER.

re'gloss, *v. rare.* [RE- 5 a.] *trans.* To put a fresh gloss upon.

1609 J. DAVIES *Humours Heauen on Earth* Wks. (Grosart) I. 6 Grease.., which so re-glosst the Sattens glosse that it Was varnisht like their vailes that turn the Spit. *a* **1618** SYLVESTER *Job Triumphant* II. 63 He dwels in Houses..By him, re-built, re-gilt, re-glast, re-glos'd.

re'glow, *sb.* [RE- 5 a.] The act of glowing again. So **re'glowing** *vbl. sb.*

1887 *Proc. Physic. Soc.* Apr. (1888) 116 There should be at least two points at which a sudden reheating takes place; but not necessarily two sensible reglows. *Ibid.* 117 The alternate darkening and reglowing. **1890** *Nature* 4 Sept., The phenomenon of recalescence or the re-glowing of..iron and steel at certain stages during the cooling process.

†**re'glutinate**, *v. Obs. rare*$^{-0}$. [f. L. *reglūtināre*: see RE- 2 a, 2 d and GLUTINATE.] *trans.* To unglue (Cockeram 1623), or glue again (Blount 1656). So †**re'glutination**, an ungluing (Cockeram); a gluing again (Phillips 1658).

regm(e, obs. forms of REALM.

‖**regma** ('rɛgmə). *Bot.* Pl. '**regmata**. [a. Gr. ῥῆγμα a break or fracture.] In Mirbel's classification, a dry fruit formed of three or more cells which break open when ripe.

1839 LINDLEY *Introd. Bot.* (ed. 3) I. ii. 237 *Regma.* Three or more celled, few-seeded,..dry, the cells bursting from the axis with elasticity into two valves. *Ibid.*, Such regmata are drupaceous. **1861** BENTLEY *Man. Bot.* 319 When a capsule consists of three or more cells, which separate from the axis, and burst with elasticity,..it has been termed a *Regma.*

regn, obs. form of REIGN.

regnacioune, -acyon, varr. REGNATION *Obs.*

regnal ('rɛgnəl), *a.* [ad. med.L. *regnālis*, f. *regn-um* kingdom, REIGN *sb.*]

1. a. ***regnal year***, the year of a sovereign's reign, dated from the moment of his accession.

1612 HOPTON *Concord. Years* Ded. A iij, I obserued the inconueniences..occasioned..by the participation of euery one Regnall yeare with two Ecclesian yeares. **1685** *Chron. Jurid.* Pref. in Nicolas *Chronol. Hist.* (1833) 272 Thirdly, there is what we call the year regnal; and that beginneth on the day, and at the immediate moment, of the decease of each last preceding king. **1833** NICOLAS *Ibid.* 272 The exact day from which the regnal year is calculated. **1876** FREEMAN *Norm. Conq.* (ed. 2) I. vi. 457 He dated his public acts by the regnal years of the King.

b. ***regnal day***, the anniversary of a sovereign's accession.

1877 C. GEIKIE *Christ* (1879) 55 On the regnal day of Herod, in the year B.C. 14 the..structure was consecrated.

2. Of or pertaining to a reign, kingdom, or king, in various applications.

1643 PRYNNE *Sov. Power Parlt.* Ded. A iij b, The true originall grounds of Regall, Regnall, Popular, or Parliamentary Jurisdictions. **1846** MCCULLOCH *Acc. Brit. Empire* (1854) II. Index 769/1 Regnal Table; from the Conquest. **1869** RAWLINSON *Anc. Hist.* 32 An intentional duplication of the regnal and other periods mentioned by Herodotus.

'**regnancy**. [f. L. *regn-āre* to REIGN: see -ANCY.]

1. The fact of reigning, predominance. *rare*$^{-1}$.

a **1834** COLERIDGE in *Lit. Rem.* (1838) III. 159 The third and last cause..is the presence and regnancy of a false and fantastic philosophy.

2. *Psychol.* In the sense of REGNANT *ppl. a.* 2 c.

1938 [see REGNANT *ppl. a.* 2 c]. **1963** S. R. MADDI in Wepman & Heine *Concepts of Personality* vii. 185 Murray.. with his concept of regnancy, has gone a bit further than Allport in attempting to conceptualize relevant brain processes. **1964** GOULD & KOLB *Dict. Soc. Sci.* 352/2 The authors point to Allport's biophysical traits and Murray's regnancies as illustrations of hypothetical constructs.

regnant ('rɛgnənt), *ppl. a.* [ad. L. *regnant-*, pres. pple. of *regnāre* to REIGN. Cf. F. *régnant*.]

1. a. Of sovereigns or other persons: Reigning, ruling.

1600 W. WATSON *Decacordon* Pref. (1602) A iv b, Queene Elizabeth our Soueraigne now regnant. **1670** G. H. *Hist. Cardinals* II. III. 205 Giving Orders that he should be treated like a Nephew of the regnant Pope. **1718** D'URFEY *Grecian Heroine* II. Operas, etc. (1721) 112 A marbled Cæsar pinnion'd to a Throne, The People regnant, and the Monarch Stone. **1856** C. R. KENNEDY tr. *Demosthenes' Leptines* App. iv, Some time afterwards the power of government passed from the regnant house into the hands of the Eupatridæ. **1884** BROWNING *Ferishtah, Shah Abbas* 49 Our liege, the Shah Happily regnant, hath become assured [etc.].

transf. or *fig.* **1600** J. HAMILTON in *Cath. Tract.* (S.T.S.) 222 Thair saules regnant now in gloire with..Christ Iesus. **1642** JER. TAYLOR *Episc.* 253 The Church of Martyrs,..now regnant in heaven. **1862** B. TAYLOR *Poet's Jrnl.* ii, Serfs of the regnant moon. **1875** M. COLLINS *Sweet & Twenty* I. iv, A full moon was regnant over breadths of lawn.

b. Placed after the sb., esp. ***queen regnant***.

1632 H. SEILE *Augustus* 212 With th' one [face] looking on the King Regnant; with th' other, on the Prince successive. *a* **1639** WOTTON in *Reliq.* (1685) 168 There may be reasonably supposed in Queens Regnant, a little proportion of tenderness that way, more than in Kings. **1765** BLACKSTONE *Comm.* I. iv. 212 The queen regent, regnant, or sovereign, is she who holds the crown in her own right. **1818** CRUISE *Digest* (ed. 2) IV. 144 Neither the king, nor a queen regnant, can convey in this manner, nor can a corporation. **1859** WRAXALL tr. *R. Houdin* xix. 284 Each of my performances was honoured by the presence of one or more of the princes regnant of the Germanic Confederation.

2. a. Of things, qualities, etc.: Ruling, exercising sway or influence, predominant, dominating.

1621 BP. MOUNTAGU *Diatribæ* 32 This humour being Regnant in you, bred those Inuectiues of lazie Ignorance. **1687** WALLER *Divine Love* 65 The Law was regnant, and confined his thought. **1799** SICKELMORE *Agnes & Leonora* II. 30 Her passion for controversy and reproach was so regnant, that the most poignant misery would hardly subdue it. **1847** EMERSON *Poems, Musketaquid*, And by the order in the field disclose The order regnant in the yeoman's brain. **1885–94** R. BRIDGES *Eros & Psyche* Apr. vii, Their fames..Do battle with the regnant names of eld, To win their seats.

b. Prevalent, wide-spread.

1625 CHAS. I *Sp.* Wks. 1662 I. 360, I must mind you of the Mortality now regnant in this City. **1676** WORLIDGE *Cyder* Pref., Drunkenness..is not now so regnant in this isle. ? **1757** H. I. (*title*) The Players Scourge, or a Detection of the ranting prophanity and regnant impiety of stage plays. **1877** M. ARNOLD *Last Ess.* 25 The belief in witchcraft and diabolical contracts which was regnant in his day.

c. ***regnant process*** (Psychol.): in the theory of personality, a hypothesis that dominant brain processes exist which determine behaviour (see quot. 1938).

1938 H. A. MURRAY *Explor. Personality* ii. 45 It may prove convenient to refer to the mutually dependent processes that constitute dominant configurations in the brain as *regnant* processes; and, further, to designate the totality of such processes occurring during a single moment..as a *regnancy*. **1974** W. B. ARNDT *Theories of Personality* xii. 237 We must infer the characteristics of regnant processes from the behavior of organisms.

†**Regnard**, obs. f. REYNARD. Hence †**regnardism**; †**regnardize** *v.*

1602 CAREW *Cornwall* (1769) 22 Then Master Regnard ransacketh every corner of his wily skonce. **1656** BLOUNT *Glossogr.* [after Cotgr.], *Regnardism*, Fox-like subtilty, sliness, craftiness,..; and to *Regnardise*, to play the Fox.

†**reg'nation**. *Obs. rare.* Also 5 **-acioune, -acyon**. [a. OF. *regnacion, -ation*, or ad. med.L. *regnātiōn-em*, n. of action f. *regnāre* to REIGN.] Reign; the act of ruling.

1418–20 J. PAGE *Siege of Rouen* in *Hist. Coll. Citizen Lond.* (Camden) 27 Cryste for Hys Passyon Kepe hym in Hys regnacyon! **1422** tr. *Secreta Secret., Priv. Priv.* 182 In the begynnynge of his regnacioune, he was an oppressoure. **1668** WILKINS *Real Char.* 397 The proper notion expressed by this Character is Regnation,..which is the Substantive of Action, as King is of Person.

regne, obs. form of REIGN.

†**regnee**. *Obs. rare*$^{-1}$. [a. OF. *regné* (see Godef.), f. *regner* to REIGN.] A kingdom.

c **1380** *Sir Ferumb.* 2386 þe Amyral clypede to him þan Maubyn of egremolee; A such þef as he was an was non in his regnee.

†'**regnicide**. *Obs. rare.* [f. L. *regni-, regnum* kingdom + -CIDE I.] One who destroys a kingdom.

1607 BP. J. KING *Serm.* 5 *Nov.* 28 They..become paricides, Regicides, Regnicides at once. **1615** T. ADAMS *England's Sickness* Wks. 1861 I. 418 Regicides are no less than regnicides,..for the life of a king contains a thousand thousand lives.

†**re-go**, *v. Obs.*$^{-1}$ [RE-.] To return, go back.

c **1640** J. SMYTH *Lives Berkeleys* (1883) I. 369 Hee shall regoe to his prison at the said time.

†**regolate**, *v. Obs. rare*$^{-1}$. [ad. It. *regolare*:—L. *rēgulāre*.] *trans.* To regulate.

1585 DYER *Praise of Nothing* Poems (Grosart) 78 We were (as having our minds regolated by the good order of nature) the lovers of virtue.

regolith ('rɛgɒlɪθ). *Geol.* [erron. f. Gr. ῥῆγο-ς rug, blanket + -LITH.] The unconsolidated solid material covering the bedrock of a planet.

1897 G. P. MERRILL *Treat. Rocks* v. 299 This entire mantle of unconsolidated material, whatever its nature or origin, it is proposed to call the regolith, from the Greek words ῥῆγος, meaning *a blanket*, and λίθος, *a stone*. **1935** *Jrnl. Geol.* XLIII. 745 'Regolith' was introduced by Merrill to include all unconsolidated surficial material and therefore embraces far more than residual weathered rock. **1949** F. J. PETTIJOHN *Sedimentary Rocks* ix. 282 Residual soils (regolith of Merrill, saprolith of Becker, and sathrolith of Sederholm) are the products of weathering formed *in situ*. **1970** *Nature* 24 Jan. 321/2 The solid rocks at Tranquillity Base are covered by a 4–6 m thick regolith or dust layer composed of local rock fragments..and spheres or fragments of glass. **1976** J. KLECZEK *Universe* iv. 155 The solid lunar globe is covered by a layer of loose broken rock material called regolith. **1977** A. HALLAM *Planet Earth* 16/1 Meteorite debris [on the moon] amounts to only about 2% of the sampled regolith.

Hence **rego'lithic** *a.*

1955 *Trans. R. Soc. N.Z.* LXXXII. 1015 Under the soil of the upland surface of the Belmont plateau there are arrested streams or sheets..of formerly regolithic debris now forming deposits of head on slopes. **1977** *Nature* 6 Jan. 38/2 Since the returned sample is of regolithic materials it could also contain basalt fragments.

regorge (riː'gɔːdʒ), *v.* [ad. F. *regorger* (14th c.), or f. RE- + GORGE *v.*, perh. after L. *regurgitāre* to REGURGITATE.]

1. *trans.* To disgorge or cast up again; to throw or cast back. *lit.* and *fig.* †Also with *of*.

1605 M. SUTCLIFFE *Brief Exam.* 84 It is not much materiall, what is regorged out of such a gulfe of impieties. **1673** DRYDEN *Marr. à la Mode* I. i, When you have regorged what you have taken in, you are the leanest things in nature. **1727** *Philip Quarll* 27 Those Curses your populous and celebrated Cities regorge of. **1804** R. W. DICKSON *Pract. Agric.* I. 386 That water..must soon have reached the bottom, and there have been regorged back upon the soil. **1844** DISRAELI *Coningsby* II. i, Ever fearful that they might be called upon to regorge their..spoil.

absol. **1850** BROWNING *Easter-Day* xv, Then, each cleft The fire had been sucked back into, Regorged.

b. *intr.* To gush or flow back again.

1654 EARL MONM. tr. *Bentivoglio's Warrs Flanders* 359 He therefore resolved to block up the Arches of the Bridg..so as the water might regorge back again into the fields. **1733** CHEYNE *Eng. Malady* II. viii. §2 (1734) 193 The regorging Fluids..struggling and labouring under the Animal Functions. **1850** ALISON *Hist. Europe* (ed. 2) X. lxvii. §15. 217 The least east wind..makes their waters regorge and overspread a vast extent of level ground.

† **c.** *intr.* Of a place: To be flooded. *Obs.*⁻¹
1621 MOLLE *Camerar. Liv. Libr.* v. iii. 329 The Narses ouerthrew..so many of the Franci in a set battell, that the territories about Capua regorged with humane blood.

2. *trans.* To engorge or swallow again. *rare.*
1700 DRYDEN *Sigism. & Guisc.* 186 But as extremes are short, of ill and good, And tides at highest mark regorge the flood. **1894** WHISTLER in *Speaker* 10 Nov. 516, I question if it be not without precedent that a writer ever before so abjectly regorged his spleen.

Hence †**re'gorgement**, what has been regorged.
1641 R. BROOKE *Eng. Episc.* I. x. 58 But what he hath done in that kind, he hath done many times by gathering up the regorgements of others.

regorgitate, obs. variant of REGURGITATE.

†**re'gort.** *Obs. rare*⁻¹. [a. OF. *regort* (Godef.).] A deep place in the sea; a gulf.
c **1477** CAXTON *Jason* 69 b, The noble arke was caste in a meruayllous regorte of the see.

regosol ('rɛgəʊsɒl). *Soil Sci.* [erron. f. as REGOLITH + -SOL.] A poorly developed soil without definite horizons, overlying and formed from deep, unconsolidated deposits such as sand or loess.
1949 THORP & SMITH in *Soil Sci.* LXVII. 120 Soon after the definition of Lithosols was published in the 1938 Yearbook, it was realized that many weakly developed soils occur in deep soft-rock deposits, like loess and sand, that are not *stony* in the ordinary sense of the word. These nonstony soils were called lithosols for a time, but a practical need was felt for distinguishing deep soft soil materials from very stony ones. Hence the proposal of the name *Regosol*. This new term is not yet fully established in the literature, and it may prove desirable eventually to give the concept some other status than that of a great soil group. **1968** R. W. FAIRBRIDGE *Encycl. Geomorphol.* 523/1 Soil scientists sometimes use 'regosol' for soils developed without distinct horizons over deep unconsolidated 'rock', e.g., a mature alluvial formation. **1976** *Sci. Amer.* Sept. 174/3, ·7 billion hectares of sandy, undifferentiated soils called regosols are nonarable.

Hence **rego'solic** *a.*
1956 *Proc. Soil Sci. Soc. Amer.* XX. 268/2 The Iowan loess is separated from the Farmdale loess by a regosolic buried soil.

†**re'grace.** *Obs. rare*⁻¹. [See next and GRACE *sb.* 19, and cf. obs. F. *regraciation*, med.L. *regrātiātio*.] *pl.* Thanks.
1463 *Plumpton Corr.* (Camden) 7 Right worshippfull my singuler good mastre, as my dewtie is, with intier regraces I recomend me unto you.

†**re'gracy,** *v. Obs. rare.* [ad. OF. *regracier*, med.L. *regrātiāre*: see RE- and GRACE *v.*] *trans.* To thank, give thanks to (one).
1483 CAXTON *Gold. Leg.* 438/2 Thus the creature shal mowe thanke and regracye god by deuoute contemplacion. *c* **1500** *Melusine* 23, I oughte to preyse to thanke and to regracy the hertily in thy highe mageste.

†**regra'dation.** *Obs. rare*⁻¹. [See REGRADE *v.*² and GRADATION.] Regression, retrogradation.
1607 *Lingua* III. vi, Starres, Orbes, and Plannets, with their motions, The Orientall Regradations [etc.].

†**re'grade,** *v.*¹ *Obs.*⁻¹ [ad. L. *regradāre*, f. *re-* RE- + *gradus* GRADE.] *trans.* To degrade.
1605 SALTERN *Anc. Laws* I j b, Elutherius..ordained that none should be regraded before he were condemned.

regrade (rɪ'greɪd), *v.*² *rare.* [f. L. *re-* RE- + *gradī* to go. The correct L. comb. is *regredī*: see REGREDE *v.*] *intr.* To retire, recede, fall back.
1811 HALES *New Anal. Chronol.* II. 897 They saw the darkness commence at the eastern limb of the sun, and proceed to the western, till the whole was eclipsed; and then regrade backwards from the western to the eastern, till his light was fully restored.

re'grade (riː-), *v.*³ [RE- 5 a.] *trans.* To grade again, in senses of the vb. Also *absol.*
1826 A. MACOMB Letr. 18 Nov. in *Reg. Deb. Congr. U.S.* (1829) III. 1572 The road..is to be regraded. **1869** *Rep. Comm. Agric. 1868* (U.S. Dept. Agric.) 362 They may be readily and rapidly leveled in the construction of a new road, or regraded when displaced by wear. **1884** *Century Mag.* Mar. 649/2 The city was torn up from one end to the other, and regraded. **1886–7** *Proc. Amer. Instruct. Deaf* 141 You may start out..with a class well graded, and before you have been at work three months you will find that you ought to regrade. **1960** *Farmer & Stockbreeder* 26 Jan. 70/2 The pigs are..regraded by the Association's own system of selective grading. **1977** *Times* 18 Mar. 4/5 Unless the corporation offers to regrade the cameramen there is little chance that their union..will allow the programme to go ahead.

Hence **re'graded** *ppl. a.*, **re'grading** *vbl. sb.*
1920 *Glasgow Herald* 1 Sept. 6 They have agreed to a conference to consider regrading. **1923** *Ibid.* 28 Mar. 10 Heavy extraordinary expenditure has to be budgeted for, including three-quarters of a million for arrears of regraded salaries. **1956** D. L. LINTON *Sheffield* 41 The regrading consequent on these changes would favour the Froggart stream. **1962** A. BATTERSBY *Guide to Stock Control* 105 Transferring from one stock to another, e.g. re-grading.

regraft (riː-), *v.* [RE- 5 a.] *trans.* To graft again. Hence **re'grafting** *vbl. sb.*
1626 BACON *Sylva* §454 It may bee, that oft Regrafting of the same Cions, may likewise make Fruit greater. **1803** KNIGHT in *Phil. Trans.* XCIII. 282 When a large tree has been deprived of its branches, to be regrafted, it often becomes unhealthy. **1861** J. A. ALEXANDER *Gospel of Jesus Christ* xiii. 177 There is no regrafting of exscinded boughs into the heavenly olive-tree.

regrait, var. of REGRATE *sb.*¹ and *v.*¹ *Obs.*

regrant (riː'grɑːnt, -æ-), *sb.* [RE- 5 a: cf. next.] The act of granting again; the renewal of a grant.
1617 MORYSON *Itin.* II. 10 MacMahown..had surrendered this his Countrey..into her Maiesties hands, and receiued a regrant thereof. *a* **1734** NORTH *Exam.* III. viii. §64 (1740) 632 This was for Caution, lest some Customs or Duties..might fall and not revive upon a Regrant. **1855** MACAULAY *Hist. Eng.* xx. IV. 427 As soon as it appeared that the Old Company was likely to obtain a regrant of the monopoly. **1876** FREEMAN *Norm. Conq.* V. xxii. 16 As there had been no forfeiture, no regrant was needed.

regrant (riː'grɑːnt, -æ-), *v.* [RE- 5 a.] *trans.* To grant (a privilege, estate, etc.) again.
1591 HORSEY *Trav.* (Hakl. Soc.) 169 [He] regrants a privaleges..to towns..and merchants, upon new composicion. **1617** MORYSON *Itin.* II. 6 He..surrendring his Inheritance..had his land regraunted to him from the King. **1682** *Lond. Gaz.* No. 1739/3 To the intent that Your Majesty will be graciously pleased to regrant to the said Burrough their said Messuages. **1750** CARTE *Hist. Eng.* II. 274 The King had indeed regranted several privileges to the citizens. **1818** CRUISE *Digest* (ed. 2) V. 559 A surrender is a yielding up of the estate by the tenant to the lord, for the purpose of being regranted to some other person. **1876** DIGBY *Real Prop.* i. 35 A vast quantity of the land of the kingdom was deemed to have been forfeited or surrendered to the king, and regranted by him.

re'grass (riː-), *v.* [RE- 5 c.] To put (land) under grass again. So **re'grassing** *vbl. sb.*
1901 *Yearbk. U.S. Dept. Agric.* 30 Experiments in regrassing were undertaken at Tucson, Ariz., in cooperation with the agricultural experiment station. **1940** *Advisory Bull. War Food Production* No. 1. 1 Ploughable grassland too poor to be initially cereal-worthy should..be ploughed and immediately re-grassed. *Ibid.* 28 Re-grassing properly and methodically undertaken enormously extends the effective grazing season.

regratar(y, varr. of REGRATER(Y *Obs.*

†**re'grate,** *sb.*¹ *Sc. Obs.* Also 5–6 **regrait.** [f. REGRATE *v.*¹, or a. OF. **regrat*, var. of *regret* REGRET *sb.*]

1. Lamentation, complaint; expression of grief, distress, or sorrow. Also with *a* and *pl.*
c **1375** *Sc. Leg. Saints* xvi. (*Magdalene*) 468 Þat gret pitte wes to here his regrat & sorowful chere. **1456** SIR G. HAYE *Law Arms* (S.T.S.) 64 Thai maid grete regrate and lamentacioun for the noble prince. *c* **1480** HENRYSON *Test. Cres.* 397 Yit thay presumit, for hir hy regrait And still murning, sho was of nobill kin. **1513** DOUGLAS *Æneis* v. xiii. 35 In the meyn sesoun Venus..Spak to Neptune with sic peteous regrait. *c* **1614** SIR W. MURE *Dido & Æneas* I. 445 Such regrates vnable more to hear: 'Brave Trojane be encourag'd' Venus sayes. *a* **1653** BINNING *Serm.* (1845) 399 The first word is, to the Heavens and to the earth: a weighty and horrible regrate of this people. **1671** MACWARD *True Nonconf.* 23 You still your..regrate, for the neglect and ruine of the work of God; by the Consideration of Gods Power and Providence.

2. Sorrow, regret.
1456 SIR G. HAYE *Law Arms* (S.T.S.) 55 Thai had sa grete regrate to leve it, that all maid sik sorow..that pitee was to se. **1581** J. HAMILTON in *Cath. Tract.* (S.T.S.) 95 They brocht hir hienes in contempt of certane rebellious subiectis to hir vnnaturall banishment, and gret regrait of all treu Scottis-men. *a* **1639** SPOTTISWOOD *Hist. Ch. Scot.* VI. (1677) 373 They had expressed their great regrate for the disappointment of his Preparations. **1704** *Let. to Sc. Parlt.* in *Lond. Gaz.* No. 4037/1 Animosities, that to Our great Regrate we discovered among you.

†**re'grate,** *sb.*² *Obs. rare*⁻¹. [? f. RE- + GRATE *v.*; cf. REGRATE *v.*⁴] Oppression.
1621 QUARLES *Esther* Introd. 116 Degenerate Cambyses.. Sits crowned King, to vexe the Persian state With heauy burthens, and with sore regrate.

†**regrate,** *sb.*³ [Of obscure origin.] Request.
c **1450** *Craft of Lovers* xii. in Stow *Chaucer* (1561) 341/2 Me semeth by langage ye be some potestate..What is your name mekely I make regrate.

†**regrate,** *v.*¹ *Sc. Obs.* Also 7 **regrait.** [ad. OF. *regrater*, var. of *regreter*, *regretter* to REGRET.]

1. *trans.* To lament, to feel or express grief or sorrow at (some injury, loss, or event).
c **1375** *Sc. Leg. Saints* xvii. (*Martha*) 24 Of þat [town] come þane bath ȝung & ald, þare skath regratand. **1513** DOUGLAS *Æneis* I. iv. 106 The petefull Eneas Regratis oft the hard fortune and cais Of sterne Orontes new drownit in the se. **1581** J. HAMILTON in *Cath. Tract.* (S.T.S.) 74 Albeit this is to be hauelie regraitit..yit all youre graces faythfull subiectis hes confort. **1632** LITHGOW *Trav.* IV. 140, I cannot but regrate, the great losse Sir Thomas Glouer receiued. **1671** W. RAIT *Vind. Reformed Relig.* 252 You would father a contradiction on me, because I regrate our rents [= divisions]. *a* **1712** T. HALYBURTON *Five Serm.* (1721) 14 You have many onlookers, sin Satan and the world who regrate your prosperity.

b. With obj. clause introduced by *that.*
c **1375** *Sc. Leg. Saints* xvi. (*Magdalene*) 455 [He] regratit ofte be-twene, þat euir he had þe magdelan sene. **1653** R. BAILLIE *Dissuas. Vind.* (1655) 77 You regrate that such men as your self and other Anabaptists..were misregarded. **1704** EARL SEAFIELD in *Lond. Gaz.* No. 4037/4 It is to be Regrated, that the Nation is in so low a Condition.

2. To lament or mourn for the loss or death of (a person or thing).
1375 BARBOUR *Bruce* xv. 233 Schir Eduuard..regratit his gret manhede, And his worschip with douchty dede. *c* **1375** *Sc. Leg. Saints* xii. (*Mathias*) 207 Regratand alswa hyr husband þat ded. *a* **1649** DRUMM. OF HAWTH. *Hist. Jas. IV* Wks. (1711) 78 He had..a natural son, arch-bishop of St. Andrew's, so much admired and regrated by Erasmus. **1685** *Gracian's Courtiers Orac.* 258 The Phœnix it self makes use of retirement and desire, to make it self to be the more esteemed and regrated.

3. *intr.* To lament, mourn.
1616 SIR W. MURE *Misc. Poems* xi. 18 Eyes, by 30ʳ streames of silwer trickling teares, Regrait, since sche is butt [= without] remorce!

regrate (rɪ'greɪt), *v.*² *Obs.* exc. *Hist.* [a. OF. *regrater*, mod.F. *regratter*, usually regarded as f. *gratter* to scrape, GRATE *v.*, but the form of the synonymous It. *rigattare* (Florio), Sp. *regatear*, makes this doubtful.]

1. *trans.* To buy up (market commodities, esp. victuals) in order to sell again at a profit in the same or a neighbouring market.

The practice was formerly regarded as hurtful to the community, and was forbidden by various enactments: see the quots. here and under REGRATER, REGRATING, REGRATOR.

1467 in *Eng. Gilds* (1870) 381 That Bakers..regrate no corne commynge to the market, in peyne of lesynge xx.*s.* **1551–2** *Act 5 & 6 Edw. VI*, c. 14 §2 Whatsoever person.. shall by any meanes regrate obteyne or gett into his.. possession in any fair or market, anye corne wyne fishe [etc.],..and doe sell the same agayne in anye fayre or markett holden or kepte in the same place, or..within fower myles thereof, shalbe..taken for a Regrator. **1612** T. TAYLOR *Comm. Titus* i. 7 As by monopolies, enhansing, ingrossing, and regrating corne or other commodities. **1697** in Strype *Stow's Surv.* (1754) II. v. xxi. 413/1 No man shall regrate any victuals in the Markets..under pain of forfeiture of the victuals so regrated. **1707** *Ibid.* (1720) I. *Billingsgate* 166/2 Without fail, they cause all Persons that..shall Regrate Fish (that is to say Buy Fish and Sell the same again in the said Market) to be apprehended.

2. To sell again (articles so bought), to retail.
1582 N. LICHEFIELD tr. *Castanheda's Conq. E. Ind.* I. xliii. 99 His going thether was..also for to regrate their gold, and this was done in xxv. dayes. **1623** COCKERAM, *Forestall*, to buy any Merchandize by the highway, ere it come into the marquet for to regrate it againe. **1859** RILEY *Liber Albus* Pref. (Rolls) I. p. lxii, The keepers of ale-taverns or ale-houses, who regrated the ale which they had purchased from the brewery.

†**regrate,** *v.*³ *Obs. rare.* [ad. med.L. *regratiāre*: see REGRATIATE *v.*] *trans.* To reward, repay, requite (a person).
c **1540** tr. *Pol. Verg. Eng. Hist.* (Camden No. 36) 146 That cruell tyrants showlde bee regrated with juste penaltie for there great impietie. *Ibid.* 166 To the ende he might seeme to regrate Allmightie Godd for his victorie.

†**re'grate,** *v.*⁴ *Obs. rare.* [app. f. RE- + GRATE *v.*¹: cf. next.] **a.** *intr.* To grate *on* something. **b.** *trans.* To grate upon, offend (the eye).
1652 FELTHAM *Low-Countries* (1661) 62 Too much to regrate on the patience of but fickle Subjects, is to press a Thorn till it prick your finger. **1713** DERHAM *Phys.-Theol.* IV. xii. 224 Those that are the least beautified with Colours, or rather whose Clothing may regrate the Eye. *Ibid.*, By an incurious view it rather regrateth than pleaseth the Eye.

re'grate, *v.*⁵ *rare*⁻⁰. [ad. F. *regratter*, f. *gratter* to GRATE *v.*¹] (See quot.)
1727–38 CHAMBERS *Cycl.* s.v. *Regrater*, Among masons, etc. to Regrate, is to take off the outer surface of an old hewn stone, with the hammer and ripe, in order to whiten, and make it look fresh again. [Taken from the *Dict. de Trévoux*: hence in Crabb, Parker, Gwilt, and recent Dicts.]

regrater (rɪ'greɪtə(r)). Also 5 *Sc.* **-tar.** [a. AF. *regrater* m., *regratere* f., = OF. *regratier* (1180; mod.F. *regrattier*), f. *regrater* to REGRATE *v.*²: cf. It. *regattiere*, Sp. *regatero* in the same sense. See also REGRATOR.]

1. One who regrates victuals or other commodities; a buyer-up for sale; a retailer. Now chiefly *Hist.* or with reference to France.
[**1301** *Rolls of Parlt.* I. 254/1 Agnes la Regratere..in pane venal. xvd. **1353** *Act 27 Edw. III*, c. 3 Les hostelers des herbergeries & autres Regraters de vitailles.] **1377** LANGL. *P. Pl.* B. III. 90 Of alle suche sellers syluer to take,..Ringes or other ricchesse þe regrateres to maynetene. *Ibid.* v. 226 Rose the regratere was hir riȝte name. *c* **1450** *Merlin* 168, I ne knowe nought of the kynge that loueth tresoure, and is regrater and a wysshar. *a* **1500** *Iter Camer.* c. 19 in *Acts Parl. Scot.* (1844) I. 699 Of Regrataris..þai by gudis befor þe lauchfull hour. **1537** CROMWELL in Merriman *Life & Lett.* (1902) II. 75 The oversight..of forstalers and regraters..within the town of Cambridge. **1592** *Sc. Acts Parl.* (1597) c. 148 Forasmeikle as sindry acts of Parliament hes bene maid for punishment of fore-stallers and regraters [etc.]. **1613** WELWOD *Abridgem. Sea-Lawes* 12 Against the forestallers, regraters, and dearthers of corne, fish, drinke, fire-wood, victuals caried ouer sea. **1642** ROGERS *Naaman* 257 The poore shall curse thee, Oh thou regrater, Thou engrosser of corne, and raiser of prises. **1709–10** STEELE *Tatler* No. 118 ¶10 The Scarcity caused by Regraters of Bread-Corn. **1837** CARLYLE *Fr. Rev.* I. I. i, To them the great Sovereign is known mainly as the great regrater of bread. **1870** *Daily News* 3 Sept. 6 A police decree.. preventing regraters from availing themselves of the extraordinary measures taken to provide food for the city [Paris] to make famine prices for their own profit.
fig. **1824** LANDOR *Imag. Conv.*, *Jas. I & Casaubon*, He is ..no forestaller and regrater of manna from heaven, or of palms from paradise.

2. One who collects commodities from the producers and brings to market; a middleman.

(In current use (*c* 1905) in south-western counties.)

1844 LD. BROUGHAM *A. Lunel* II. iii. 57 A middleman between the publisher and the author, like a regrater between the hop-grower and the hop-merchant or the brewer. **1865** *Reader* 26 Aug. 236/2 'Regraters' (as the Devon folk call them..) travel round the villages, and buy up fowls, and cream, and other delicacies.

fig. **1874** T. HARDY *Far fr. Mad. Crowd* xxv, A sort of regrater of other men's experiences of the glorious class.

regrateress: see REGRATRESS.

† **re'gratery.** *Obs. rare.* Also 4 -orie, 4–5 ry(e, 6 -ary. [ad. OF. *regraterie* (1218): see REGRATE *v.*[2] and -ERY.] The practice of regrating.

1362 LANGL. *P. Pl.* A. III. 74 Brewesters, Bakers..recheþ [*v.r.* richen] þorw Regratorie [*v.rr.* regrateryе, regratrye] and Rentes hem buggeþ. **1452** *Cal. Anc. Rec. Dublin* (1889) I. 275 They shulde not go in to the contre to byge corne in regratry of the market. **1581** LAMBARDE *Eiren.* I. ix. (1602) 40 Of cappes and liueries, forestallings, and regrataries, and of extorcions committed by Victualers.

† **re'gratiate,** *v. Obs. rare.* [f. ppl. stem of med.L. *regrātiāre* or *-ārī*, f. *re-* RE- + *grātia* GRACE: cf. *ingratiate* and see also REGRATE *v.*[3], REGRACY *v.*] *trans.* = REGRATIFY *v.* Also *absol.*

a **1619** FOTHERBY *Atheom.* I. iv. §5 (1622) 26 As the Gods haue gratified Men, in receiuing some of them amongst themselues into heauen: so Men haue regratiated them againe, in receiuing of them into their Cities vpon earth. **1657** REEVE *God's Plea* 28 God doth not regratiate, because we cannot ingratiate.

† **re'gratiatory.** *Obs. rare*[−1]. [f. as prec. + -ORY. Cf. med.L. *regrātiātōrie* adv.] Thanks.

1523 SKELTON *Garl. Laurel* 431 So am I preuentid..In rendryng to you thankkis meritory, That welny nothynge there doth remayne Wherwith to geue you my regraciatory.

† **re'gratify,** *v. Obs.* [RE-: cf. REGRATIATE.] *trans.* To gratify in return.

1570 FOXE *A. & M.* (ed. 2) 1131/2 The king to regratifie them agayne, graunted to them a generall pardon of all offences. **1611** SPEED *Hist. Gt. Brit.* IX. xi. §8. 555/2 The decree..was by the king..suffered to passe; and the king was thereupon regratified with a Subsidie of the twentieth part of the subiects goods. **1676** BEAL in *Phil. Trans.* XI. 585 Cherries and Plums make haste to regratify the Planter.

regrating (rɪ'greɪtɪŋ), *vbl. sb.* [f. REGRATE *v.*[2] + -ING[1].] The action of the vb.

a **1550** *Vox Populi* 41 in Hazl. *E.P.P.* III. 269 Suche and suche, That of late are made riche,..By grasyng and regratinge. **1596** SPENSER *State Irel.* Wks. (Globe) 681/2 By such engrossing and regrating we see the dearthe that nowe comonly raigneth heere in England to have bene caused. **1630** BRATHWAIT *Eng. Gentlem.* (1641) 135 In Courts are suits and actions of law;..in the countrey ingrossing and regrating of purpose to oppresse. **1745** *De Foe's Eng. Tradesman* xxxviii. (1841) II. 111 All regrating and forestalling of markets, is accounted so pernicious in trade. **1799** BURKE *Lett., to A. Young* (1844) IV. 453, I was myself the person who moved the repeal of the absurd code of statutes against the most useful of all trades, under the invidious names of forestalling and regrating. **1844** *Act 7 & 8 Vict.* c. 24 (*title*), An Act for abolishing the Offences of forestalling, regrating, and engrossing. **1868** *Daily News* 4 Sept., Theatrical Forestalling and Regrating.—..By buying up the admissions to [Parisian] theatres which dramatic or operatic authors are privileged to sign, and retailing them to the public.

† **re'gratingly,** *adv. Obs. rare*[−1]. [f. REGRATE *v.*[2]] In a regrating manner; after the manner of a regrater.

c **1550** LYNDESAY *Peder Coffeis* 15 He lokis thame vp in to his innis Vnto ane derth, and sellis thair eggis, Regraitandly on thame he wynnis.

regrator (rɪ'greɪtə(r)). Also 4–6 -our. [a. AF. *regratour* = obs. F. *regratteur*: see REGRATER.]

1. = REGRATER 1. Now *rare.*

1362 LANGL. *P. Pl.* A. v. 140 Rose þe Regratour Is hire rihte name; Heo haþ holden hoxterye þis Elleuene wynter. **1429** *Rolls of Parlt.* IV. 349/1 A fals craft of regratouris of ȝern. **1467** in *Eng. Gilds* (1870) 396 That ther be no citezen regratour of see ffysshe. **1500–20** DUNBAR *Poems* xiv. 43 Sic regratouris, the peure men to prevene. **1550** LEVER *Serm.* (Arb.) 130 Take awaye leasmongers, regrators and all suche as by byinge and sellynge make thyngs more dere. **1551–2** [see REGRATE *v.*[2] 1]. **1592** *Sc. Acts Parl.* (1597) c. 148 Quha gettis in his hand by buying, contract or promises, the growand corne on the field, salbe repute a regratour. **1618** DALTON *Countr. Just.* cxv. (1630) 315 Forestallers Regrators and Engrossers..shall be imprisoned. **1697** in Strype *Stow's Surv.* (1754) II. v. xxi. 412/1 That they may sell them in Town dearer to Regrators than those that did bring them in would do. **1772** *Statutes at Large* VIII. 202 An Act for repealing several Laws..against Badgers, Engrossers, Forestallers, and Regrators. **1859** [see REGRATRESS].

2. = REGRATER 2.

1807 VANCOUVER *Agric. Devon* (1813) 107 Some of them become regrators, and attend constantly the Plymouth market. **1884** *Blackw. Mag.* Oct. 502/2 They are thrown into the hands of the regrator, who goes round with a cart and buys their goods dirt-cheap.

regratorie, variant of REGRATERY *Obs.*

re'gratress. *Obs.* exc. *Hist.* Also 7 **regrateress.** [f. REGRATER + -ESS: cf. AF. *regrateresse* (13–14th c.).] A female regrater.

1611 COTGR., *Regratiere*, an Huckstеresse; also, a Regrateresse. **1859** RILEY *Liber Albus* Pref. (Rolls) I. p. lxii, No brewer or brewеress, or regrator or regratress of ale [etc.]. **1877** SKEAT *Notes to Langland's P. Pl.* C. IV. 82 The baker did not sell the bread to the public, but to the regratresses.

regratrye, variant of REGRATERY *Obs.*

† **re'gratulate,** *v. Obs.* [RE- 2 a.]

1. *trans.* To return, make return for, repay.

1615 BRATHWAIT *Strappado* (1878) 8 They'le afterward Regratulate thy loue (paying th' old skore). **1628** FELTHAM *Resolves* I. lxviii. 63 Oh! how should we regratulate his fauours for so immense a benefit..?

2. To make a return to, gratify in return.

1621 G. SANDYS *Ovid's Met.* XIII. (1626) 266 Proue not so ingrate. With slaine Polixena regratulate Our Sepulcher: 'tis she I couet most.

† **regratu'lation.** *Obs. rare.* [RE- 2 a or 5 a: cf. prec.] **a.** *pl.* Thanks, expressions of gratitude. **b.** (See quot. 1678.)

1650 A. B. *Mutat. Polemo* 21 After our most humble regratulations to his Grace for..his affable and noble deportment to us. **1678** PHILLIPS (ed. 4) 2nd Suppl., *Regratulation*, a rejoycing again.

re'grave (riː-), *v. rare*[−0]. [RE- 5 a.] *trans.* To engrave again, re-engrave.

1688 R. HOLME *Armoury* III. 151/2 Grave, or Re-grave, to mend with the Graver those stroaks omitted or not eaten with the Aqua-Fortis.

regreatable, obs. form of REGRETTABLE.

regrede (rɪ'griːd), *v.* [ad. L. *regredī* to turn back, f. *re-* RE- + *gradī* to go: cf. REGRADE *v.* and REGRESS *v.*] *intr.* To retrograde, go back.

1865 *Chambers' Encycl.* s.v. *Perturbation*, The effect of a disturbing force continually directed towards the plane of the ecliptic, is to make the node regrede. **1873** PROCTOR *Moon* 163 Since..the lunar nodes thus regrede, or, as it were, meet the advancing moon.

† **re'gredience.** *Obs. rare*[−1]. [See next and -ENCE.] Regression, return.

1648 HERRICK *Hesper.*, *Aphorism* cxxi, No man comes late unto that place, from whence Never man yet had a regredience.

† **re'gredient.** *Obs. rare*[−1]. [ad. L. *regredient-em*, pres. pple. of *regredī* to REGREDE.] One who retires.

1612 W. PARKES *Curtaine Dr.* (1876) 23 A thousand times more might the pen of his direction discouer, who is the vniversal ingredient and regredient, and Curtaine-drawer of the whole World.

† **re'green,** *v. Obs. rare*[−1]. [RE- 5 a.] *trans.* To make green again.

1598 SYLVESTER *Du Bartas* II. ii. I. *Ark* 66 As the Sommer's sweet-distilling drops..Re-greens the Greens, and doth the Flowrs re-flowr.

† **re'greet,** *sb.*[1] *Obs.* [f. REGREET *v.*] A (return of a) salutation or greeting.

1595 SHAKS. *John* III. i. 241 And shall these hands.. Vnyoke this seysure and this kinde regreete? **1631** BRATHWAIT *Whimzies, Hospitall-man* 44 With a friendly and brotherly regreete one of another,..they betake themselv's to their rest. **1665** —— *Comment Two Tales* 164 A proper Salute, and as mannerly a Re-greet as an old Trot could afford.

b. *pl.* Greetings.

1596 SHAKS. *Merch. V.* II. ix. 89 His Lord, From whom he bringeth sensible regreets. *a* **1639** WEBSTER *Appius & Virg.* III. i, Yet ere my self could reach Virginia's chamber, one was before me, with regreets from him.

† **re'greet,** *sb.*[2] *Obs. rare*[−1]. [perh. a variant spelling of *regrete*: see REGRET *sb.*] ? Protest.

a **1661** FULLER *Worthies, Bucks.* I. (1662) 141 He [Coke] scrupuled to take the oath, pretending many things against it... It was answered, that he had often seen the Oath given to others without any regreet.

re'greet, *v.* Now *rare.* [f. RE- + GREET *v.*[1]]

1. *trans.* To greet again or anew.

1586 MARLOWE *1st Pt. Tamburl.* III. i, And if, before the Sun have measur'd heaven With triple Circuit, thou regreet us not [etc.]. **1611** *Tarlton's Jests* (1844) 27 In the city of Glocester M. Bird of the chappell met with Tarlton, who, joyfull to regreet other, went to visit his friends.

2. To greet (one) in return; also simply, to greet, give salutation to. (Freq. *c* 1600.)

1593 SHAKS. *Rich. II*, I. iii. 67, I regreete The daintiest last, to make the end most sweet. **1607** R. C[AREW] tr. *Estienne's World of Wonders* 119 Neither did he afterwards sticke to regreet me with the said siluer salutation. **1627** DRAYTON *Agincourt*, etc. 107 In like language, this great Earle againe Regreets the Queene. **1864** LOWELL *Fireside Trav.* 89 His hat rose, regreeting your own.

† **b.** To return (a salutation). *Obs. rare*[−1].

1586 WARNER *Alb. Eng.* I. vi, Presently she meetes With Thæseus and pirithous, whose salutings she regreetes.

† **3.** *intr.* To exchange greeting *with* one. *Obs. rare*[−1]. In quot. *fig.*

1604 AN. SC. *Daiphantus* viii. in Arb. *Garner* VII. 388 Unmatched beauty with her virtue meeting: Proud that her lowly 'beisance doth re-greet With her chaste silence.

Hence **re'greeting** *ppl. a.*

1607 DAY *Trav. Eng. Bro.* (1881) 89 Their destinies mutable commandresse Hath never suffer'd their regreeting eyes To kiss each other at an enteruiew.

regreetable, obs. form of REGRETTABLE.

† **re'greeting,** *vbl. sb. Obs.*[−1] [? var. of REGRETTING, or f. GREET *v.*[2]] Complaint, lamentation.

1632 LITHGOW *Trav.* VI. 269 [They] made in the beginning pittifull, and lamentable regreetings.

regress ('riːgrɛs), *sb.* [ad. L. *regressus*, n. of action f. *regredī* to go back: see REGREDE *v.*, and cf. *egress*, *ingress*.]

1. The act of going or coming back; a return or withdrawal; re-entry *to* or *into* the place of issue or origin. Freq. in the phrases (orig. legal) ***egress***, or ***ingress***, ***and regress***.

c **1375** *Sc. Leg. Saints* xxi. (*Clement*) 629 Fra he had to rome regresse [L. *venisset*], & wyst þe tyme cumyne was [etc.]. **1477** *Rolls of Parlt.* VI. 191/1 Afore your moost victorious regresse into this same your Reame. **1515** *St. Papers Hen. VIII*, II. 13 The Deputye, in his progresse and regresse, oppresseyth the Kinges poore comyn folke. **1543–4** *Act 35 Hen. VIII*, c. 10 To haue free ingresse egresse and regresse into all suche places. **1599** HAKLUYT *Voy.* II. I. 177 [The] abouesaid Christians will not quietly suffer their egresse and regresse, into, and out of our dominions. **1632** LITHGOW *Trav.* x. 482, I remarked a perpetuall current, flowing from the Ocean to the Mediterrene Sea without any regresse. *a* **1656** USSHER *Ann.* (1658) 773 Whose progresse and regresse in this journey we here set down out of Strabo. **1696** TRYON *Misc.* i. 2 Where the Air hath not its free egress and regress. **1748** RICHARDSON *Clarissa* (1811) I. xxxv. 259, I have told him that he may indeed watch her egresses and regresses. **1770** LANGHORNE *Plutarch* (1879) I. 192/2 The Lacedæmonians would allow free egress and regress in their city. **1822–56** DE QUINCEY *Confess.* (1862) 182 Every step of my regress..was bringing me nearer to the heath. **1856** STANLEY *Sinai & Pal.* I. i. 38 Early travellers..took one route on their egress and the other on their regress.

fig. **1607–12** BACON *Ess.*, *Great Place* (Arb.) 278 The standing is slipery, and the regresse is either a downefall, or ..an Eclipse. **1656** W. MONTAGUE *Accompl. Wom.* 17 It is necessary, that after we have surveyed many objects, we should make a regress into our selves. **1836–7** SIR W. HAMILTON *Metaph.* xxxviii. (1870) II. 372 We cannot conceive the infinite regress of time. **1866** J. G. MURPHY *Comm., Exod.* xxx. Introd., The progress and regress here are the prophecy and the history of salvation.

2. *Law.* † **a.** = RECOURSE 4 b. *Obs.*

1479 *Act. Audit.* (1839) 94 Becauss þe said henry allegeit he had writtinge..quharthrou he vnderstude he myt saufly Intromet wt the said gudis, pt he haf Regress to him Insafer as law will. **1641** S. SMITH *Herring Buss Trade* 20 The owners shall hold and keep their regresse to the steeres-man, ..for to recover the value..of the Herring so forfeited. **1755** MAGENS *Insurances* II. 99 Which Condition shall preserve to the Owner of the Goods..the Right of having Regress upon the Master.

† **b.** Return to possession; re-entry. *Obs. rare.*

1597 SKENE *De Verb. Sign.* s.v. *Recognition*, The superiour hes entresse & regresse to the property of the lands, and may recognosce the samin. **1628** COKE *On Litt.* 319 Others doe hold it all one in case of a recouery, and a regresse.

† **c.** *Sc.* (See quots.) *Obs.*

1597 SKENE *De Verb. Sign.* s.v. *Reversion*, Ane regresse is giuen bee the superiour of landes to the annalier thereof, quhairby hee promisis to receiue againe him, or his aires to be his vassalles, as they were of before, quhen it sall happen onye of them to redeeme the saidis landes. *a* **1768** ERSKINE *Inst. Law Scot.* II. viii. §18 (1773) 297 Letters of regress were frequently obtained from the superior, by which he became obliged to give the reverser his former vassal full regress to the property, upon his redeeming the lands.

d. *Canon Law.* (See quots.)

1710 tr. *Dupin's Eccl. Hist. 16th C.* I. II. xiv. 75 *note*, Regress is a Term in the Canon Law; It is an Action by which the Resignee may enter upon a Benefice upon a Resignation or upon a Change. **1848** WATERWORTH *Canons & Decrees of Trent* (1888) 261 *note*, *Regress*, right of returning to a benefice vacated in case of death &c., of the actual incumbent.

3. † **a.** Return *to* (or *unto*) a previous state or condition. *Obs.*

1535 STEWART *Cron. Scot.* II. 73 Rome..may neuir regres haif to sic gloir In to oure tyme as that it had befoir. **1610** HEALEY *St. Aug. Citie of God* 398 They love perfect impiety, from which there is no regresse unto piety.

b. The fact of going back from, or in respect of, a state or condition. (Opp. to *progress*.)

1590 LODGE *Rosalind* 56 Thy progresse in loue is a regresse to losse. **1600** W. WATSON *Decacordon* (1602) 218 It is neither the good beginning, nor progresse, nor regresse,.. that notifieth a man to be predestinate, or a reprobate. **1621** H. FARLEY *St. Paul's* E 2, As in Progresse, so in Regresse, O, let vs euer pray, That God will blesse his Maiestie. **1697** G. BURGHOPE *Divine Worship* 138 Let him search into..his progress or regress in piety. **1891** *Nation* (N.Y.) 3 Dec. 423/3 So we will wait and hope, and report progress or regress after our Sicilian tour.

† **4.** Return to a subject. *Obs. rare*[−1].

1578 BANISTER *Hist. Man* IV. 47 But to make regresse, it followeth, yet further..to describe the Muscles.

5. The act of working back in thought from one thing to another, *spec.* from an effect to a cause.

1620 T. GRANGER *Div. Logike* 109 From the priuation of the power or facultie there is no regresse to the habite. **1640** BP. REYNOLDS *Passions* x. 93 There is another Regresse from the Object to the Appetite. **1704** NORRIS *Ideal World* II. vii. 332 If so, then a double absurdity will follow; one by way of direct progress from the cause to the effect, and another by way of regress from the effect to the cause. **1825** COLERIDGE *Aids Refl.* (1848) I. 209 The old axiom..applies with a never-ending regress to each several link, up the whole chain of nature. **1877** E. CAIRD *Philos. Kant* II. xv. 554 An endless regress from reason to reason is no explanation of the world which satisfies the intelligence.

6. *Astron.* = RETROGRADATION.

1642 H. MORE *Song of Soul* II. iii. III. lxxi, In regresse and in progress different Of the free Planets. **1715** tr. *Gregory's Astron.* (1726) II. 534 The Regress of the Nodes is the swiftest when they are in a Quadrature with the Sun. **1750** *Phil. Trans.* XLVII. 71 The regress, in a periodical month, will be 5548″.3, and the progress 16489″.8. **1838** *Penny Cycl.* XI. 383/2 The regress, when the line of apses is perpendicular to the line joining the earth and sun, is about 9°.

regress (rɪˈgrɛs), *v.* [ad. L. *regress-*, ppl. stem of *regredī*: see REGREDE *v.*]

†**1.** *intr.* To recede *from*; to return *to* a subject or place, or *into* a former state. *Obs.*

1552 *Cal. Anc. Rec. Dublin* (1889) I. 428 It redouns to ther owen dishonestie and sham in regressing fro the said order. **1570** FOXE *A. & M.* (ed. 2) 51/2 But this by the waye of digression, now to regresse again to the state of yᵉ first former times. **1593** BILSON *Govt. Christ's Ch.* 329 [This] we haue alreadie seene, and may not now regresse thither againe. **1646** SIR T. BROWNE *Pseud. Ep.* II. i. (1650) 40 All which,..being forced into fluent consistencies, doe naturally regresse into their former solidities.

2. a. To move in a backward direction. Chiefly *Astron.*

1823 WOODHOUSE *Astron.* (ed. 2) II. 660 The node [of the moon] may have regressed through several entire circuits of the heavens. **1838** *Penny Cycl.* XI. 383/1 When the moon is ..near apogee it causes the line of apses to regress. **1896** SETH in *Contemp. Rev.* Aug. 176 Experience itself.. constitutes the premise from which we advance (or rather regress) to its implied condition or explaining cause.

b. *Psychol.* To return in one's mind to an earlier period or stage of life as a result of mental illness or through hypnosis or psychoanalysis. Also *trans.*, to induce regression in (a person). See also REGRESSION 4 d.

1926 J. I. SUTTIE tr. *Ferenczi's Further Contrib.* xi. 137 Now the stage to which these two neurotics regressed seems to be the infantile stage of the first year of life. **1950** *Psychoanalytic Q.* XIX. 501 The immutability of a constant, passive environment forces him to adapt, i.e., to regress to infantile levels. **1956** AMBROSE & NEWBOLD *Handbk. Med. Hypnosis* vii. 146 If a child can be hypnotised and regressed with suitable suggestions, causing him to re-live the actual traumatic episode, much tension can be overcome. **1957** P. LAFITTE *Person in Psychol.* vi. 75 The person changes..for the worse, perhaps regressing directly to infantile behaviour. **1960** *Times Lit. Suppl.* 3 June 356/3 Harry was later hypnotized by a friend of Dr. Puharich and 'regressed' through his life memories to see if he had any knowledge of Egyptian history, language, or religion. **1970** T. X. BARBER *LSD, Marihuana, Yoga & Hypnosis* vi. 259 When regressed hypnotically to the time of the original conditioning, all subjects again manifested the eye-blink response. **1976** F. H. FRANKEL *Hypnosis* v. 67 He was then regressed in time, and referred to business difficulties that he had experienced earlier that day and in recent weeks. **1978** GRIS & DICK *New Soviet Psychic Discoveries* ix. 104 A girl student..insisted that she be regressed by a co-student.

3. *intr. Genetics.* To tend or evolve towards the mean value for the population; to display regression to the mean (REGRESSION 4 b).

1885 *Nature* 24 Sept. 509/2 The type is an ideal form towards which the children of those who deviate from it tend to regress. *Ibid.* 510/1 The stability of a type would, I presume, be measured by the strength of its tendency to regress. **1892** F. GALTON *Finger Prints* i. 21 There is a constant tendency in the offspring to 'regress' towards the parental type. **1909** *Westm. Gaz.* 21 Apr. 5/1 There is a tendency for children of exceptional parents to regress towards the average stock. **1953** SRB & OWEN *Gen. Genetics* xxiii. 497 Instead of showing the average value of their selected parents, the progeny regress from this value toward the original population mean, and in fact average only a little better than the population from which their parents came. **1975** A. SMITH *Human Pedigree* iii. 67 The reason why we have not ended up as uniform as tailor's dummies is that there is only a tendency to regress to the mean... The various genes involved in such a character as weight will combine, from time to time and to confound the general rule, in a manner that is unexceptional [*sic*]. A child will then be heavier than both its parents. It will not have regressed.

4. *trans. Statistics.* To calculate the coefficient(s) of regression of (a variable) *against* or *on* another variable. *colloq.*

1971 *Nature* 8 Oct. 407/1 These parameters were regressed on measurements made of site factors on five sampling sites from the fives dated flows. **1977** D. M. SMITH *Human Geogr.* vii. 170 Katzman..estimated several education production functions by regressing measures of output against measures of school input and local socio-economic status of residents.

regressed (rɪˈgrɛst), *ppl. a.* [f. prec. + -ED[1].] That has regressed or been regressed.

1948 *Jrnl. Nerv. & Mental Dis.* CVII. 443 Lewis's observation goes back to 1926 when he saw a regressed schizophrenic patient reacquire a dorsiflexor response to plantar stimulation. **1965** B. E. FREEMAN tr. *Vandel's Biospeleol.* xxvi. 419 The variations in the regressed eyes of the mole may be noted.

regression (rɪˈgrɛʃən). [ad. L. *regressiōn-em*, n. of action f. *regress-*, *regredī*: see REGRESS *v.*]

†**1.** Return to a subject. = REGRESS *sb.* 4. *Obs.*

c **1520** BARCLAY *Jugurtha* (ed. 2) 20 Nowe wyll I make regression and prosecute my first purposed mater insuing mine authour Salust. **1620** T. GRANGER *Div. Logike* 317 To digression is added also regression, which is a returning back againe to our former speech interrupted by digression.

†**2.** Recurrence or repetition (of a word or statement). *Obs. rare.*

1553 T. WILSON *Rhet.* 109 b, That is called regression, when we repeate a worde eftsones, that hath been spoken, and rehersed before. **1597** J. KING *On Jonas* (1618) 37 His reason of flying to Tarshish, is againe specified, with a regression in the end of the verse, *that he might goe from the presence of the Lord.*

3. a. The action of returning to or towards a place or point of departure.

1597 A. M. tr. *Guillemeau's Fr. Chirurg.* 28 b/1 In such accidents wherin is onlye required a regressione of bloode. **1620** VENNER *Via Recta* viii. 179 Through the regression of the spirits and heat into the interiour parts. **1682** SIR T. BROWNE *Chr. Mor.* (1756) 44 Run not into extremities from whence there is no regression. **1864** BOWEN *Logic* vii. 225 My going upstairs is my progress towards my object, and my coming down is a regression.

b. *Geom.* Return of a curve.

1727–38 CHAMBERS *Cycl.* s.v. *Point*, If the curve turn back again towards the Point whence it first set out, the Point of the Flexure is..called the Point of Regression, or Retrogradation. **1842** DE MORGAN *Calculus* 434 One sound writer..has attempted to translate the words *arête de rebroussement* in English by 'edge of regression'. **1879** THOMSON & TAIT *Nat. Phil.* I. I. §148 When the number is infinite, and the surface finitely curved, the developable lines will in general be tangents to a curve... This curve is called the *edge of regression.*

4. a. Return *to* or *into* a state or condition; relapse; reversion to a less developed form. Cf. REGRESS 3 a.

1646 SIR T. BROWNE *Pseud. Ep.* (1650) 29 That essence, which substantially supporteth them, and restrains them from regression into nothing. **1822–34** *Good's Study Med.* (ed. 4) IV. 285 Dr. Home..completed a radical cure in fourteen of them, no relapse occurring notwithstanding the frequency of such regressions. **1882** *Nature* XXVII. 170 The destructive process is identical. It is a regression from the new to the old. **1917** *Jrnl. Genetics* XXVII. 117 What is frequently called reduction in evolution, or, to use a less ambiguous term, regression. **1950** *Sci. News* XV. 136 They pointed out that the regression of tumours caused by Compound E did not generally last indefinitely. The tumours usually recurred. **1965** B. E. FREEMAN tr. *Vandel's Biospeleology* xxvi. 417 Regression of the eyes is more marked when it is phyletically ancient.

b. *Genetics.* The tendency for the mean value of a partially inherited quantitative character, among any class of relatives of an individual or a group chosen for their values of that character, to lie between the (mean) value for that individual or group and the mean value in the general population. Esp. as ***regression to the mean.***

1885 F. GALTON in *Nature* 24 Sept. 507/1 The experiments showed further that the mean filial regression towards mediocrity was directly proportional to the parental deviation from it. **1889** GALTON *Nat. Inheritance* vii. 103, I trust it will become clear..that the law of Regression in Stature refers primarily to Deviations. **1912** J. A. THOMSON *Heredity* (ed. 2) ix. 321 The amount of the regression affords a useful measure of the intensity of the inheritance. If the regression is slight, it means that the intensity of the inheritance is high. **1952** SRB & OWEN *Gen. Genetics* xxiii. 497 This phenomenon, in which the progeny of selected parents slip back toward the average of the population from which the parents were chosen, has long been known. In this connection the phenomenon was called regression. Today, the term regression has a broader statistical connotation, but it is still applicable in its original sense to the problems we are discussing. **1975** A. SMITH *Human Pedigree* iii. 66 At this stage it is necessary to refer to the phenomenon known as the regression to the mean. Where random mating exists, and where there is no evolutionary pressure favouring any characteristic that is controlled by many genes, the offspring will have a tendency to be nearer average for that characteristic than their parents.

c. *Statistics.* The relationship between the mean value of a random variable and the corresponding values of one or more other variables; **coefficient of regression** = *regression coefficient* in sense 8 below.

1897 K. PEARSON in *Phil. Trans. R. Soc.* A. CLXXXVII. 259 The coefficient of regression may be defined as the ratio of the mean deviation of the fraternity from the mean offspring to the deviation of the parentage from the mean parent. *Ibid.*, From this special definition of regression in relation to parents and offspring, we may pass to a general conception of regression. Let A and B be two correlated organs (variables or measurable characteristics) in the same or different individuals, and let the sub-group of organs B, corresponding to a sub-group of A with a definite value *a*, be extracted. Let the first of these sub-groups be termed an array, and the second a type. Then we define the coefficient of regression of the array on the type to be the ratio of the mean-deviation of the array from the mean B-organ to the deviation of the type *a* from the mean A-organ. **1917** *Phil. Mag.* XXXIV. 205 When the regression of the first variable on the remaining $n-1$ variables is linear, the multiple correlation coefficient measures the dependence of the first variable on the others. **1925** R. A. FISHER *Statistical Methods for Res. Workers* v. 114 The following qualitative examples are intended to familiarise the student with the concept of regression. **1943** M. G. KENDALL *Adv. Theory Statistics* I. xiv. 328 In this chapter we shall mainly be concerned with the case in which regressions are linear or very nearly so. **1952** C. G. LAMBE *Elem. Statistics* vii. 56 This straight line which gives an estimate of the average value of *y* associated with any value of *x* is called the line of regression of *y* on *x* and p/σ_x^2 is called the coefficient of regression of *y* on *x*. **1972** T. H. & R. J. WONNACOTT *Introd. Statistics for Business & Economics* xiii. 287 Multiple regression is the extension of simple regression, to take account of the effect of more than one independent *X* variable on the dependent variable *Y*.

d. *Psychol.* The process of regressing, or a tendency to regress, in the sense of REGRESS *v.* 2 b; *spec.* the tendency of the libido, under the stress of frustration, to return to a simpler and more satisfying stage of development; also, the state of returning mentally to an earlier period, esp. in hypnosis and psychoanalysis.

1910 tr. S. Freud in *Amer. Jrnl. Psychol.* XXI. 214 The flight from the unsatisfying reality into what we call.. disease, but which is never without an individual gain in pleasure for the patient, takes place over the path of regression, the return to earlier phases of the sexual life, when satisfaction was not lacking. **1913** C. G. JUNG *On Psychoanalysis* in *XVIIth Internat. Congr. Med.* §xii. 68 [Freud] called this phenomenon of reactivation or secondary exaggeration of infantile reminiscences 'Regression'. **1920** *Challenge* 21 May 44/3 The *libido*..in its regression to the collective unconscious, gives rise to the similation of archaic psychical adaptations. **1948** *Jrnl. Nerv. & Mental Dis.* CVII. 443 In regression to infantile levels the subject assumed the sleeping posture of an infant. **1961** *Economist* 11 Mar. 962/1 The poor layman who has laboriously got on to nodding terms with infantile sexuality, regression, Oedipal conflicts, displacement and the rest. **1970** T. X. BARBER *LSD, Marihuana, Yoga & Hypnosis* vi. 255 Under regression to infancy, the hypnotized person does not topple from his chair. **1971** *Jrnl. Gen. Psychol.* Apr. 208 In psychology the term 'regression' refers to a primitivization of behavior. **1978** GRIS & DICK *New Soviet Psychic Discoveries* ix. 105 Let me amplify on regressions. Whatever people think, their previous lives are not individual experiences.

5. *Philos.* = REGRESS *sb.* 5.

1637 R. HUMPHREY tr. *St. Ambrose* Pref., The heathen philosopher..holds from privation to habite regression to bee impossible. **1886** A. WEIR *Hist. Basis Mod. Europe* (1889) xii. 472 Truths of science are made contingent on a first cause, or are swallowed up in the mysteries of infinite regression.

6. *Astron.* = REGRESS *sb.* 6.

1823 WOODHOUSE *Astron.* (ed. 2) II. 660 The annual regression of the Moon's node will be found to be 19°.19′.43″. **1839** MOSELEY *Astron.* xxxvii. 121 This annual regression of the equinoctial point..is called the Precession of the Equinoxes.

7. *Geogr.* A retreat or withdrawal of the sea from the land.

1908 W. J. SOLLAS et al. tr. *Suess's Face of Earth* III. 364 Every new transgression (regression), is so far as the encroaching line of breakers itself has not denuded the land, will encounter an altered relief. **1937** *Bull. Amer. Assoc. Petroleum Geologists* XXI. 1436 Rhythmic transgressions and regressions of the sea continued throughout the period of Jackson sedimentation, evidenced by the interwedging of marine and non-marine sediments, as the strand line moved ..back and forth. **1975** *Sci. Amer.* Feb. 90/3 The stratification of sedimentary deposits suggested successive marine transgressions onto the continents and regressions from them. The regressions could be attributed to the subsidence of the ocean basins and the transgressions to the partial filling of the basins with sediment eroded from the continents.

8. *attrib.* and *Comb.*, as (sense 4 c) ***regression analysis, formula, function, theory***; **regression coefficient**, a coefficient in the regression equation; *esp.* the first-order coefficient, which is estimated by the covariance of the two variables divided by the variance of the independent variable; **regression curve**, a graph of the expected value of the dependent variable plotted against the value of the independent variable(s); **regression equation**, an equation which gives the expected value of the dependent variable as a function of the value(s) of the independent variable(s); **regression line** = *regression curve* above.

1948 *New Biol.* IV. 36 We can then use the technique of regression analysis to determine to what extent we can account for the variation in yield in terms of variation in rainfall. **1976** *National Observer* (U.S.) 19 June 18/3 It may seem absurd to label the probability of murder as 'P(M)' and subject it to the technique of regression analysis. **1903** *Phil. Trans. R. Soc.* A. CC. 20 Not only the slope (regression coefficient) of the line, but its position is identical. *Ibid.* 21 If an organ has been modified only by indirect selection, then its partial regression coefficients on any complex of other organs, however large or small, provided it includes all the directly selected organs, will remain unchanged by the selection. **1925** R. A. FISHER *Statistical Methods Res. Workers* v. 114 The regression coefficients are of interest and scientific importance in many classes of data where the correlation coefficient, if used at all, is an artificial concept of no real utility. **1964** R. VON MISES *Math. Theory Probability & Statistics* xi. 576 The correlation coefficient is the geometrical mean of the two regression coefficients. **1905** *Res. Mem. Drapers' Co.* XIV. 21 Yule's method of approaching the problem from the form of the regression curves is..available and capable of very great extension. **1925** R. A. FISHER *Statistical Methods Res. Workers* v. 114 The function which represents the mean height at any age is termed the regression function of height on age; it is represented graphically by a regression curve, or regression line. **1943** M. G. KENDALL *Adv. Theory Statistics* I. xiv. 327 The means of arrays will in general lie more or less closely round smooth curves... Such curves are called regression curves and their equations..are called regression equations. **1972** G. P. BEAUMONT *Elem. Math. Statistics* xii. 152 We begin with a certain minimal property of the regression curves. **1897** *Proc. R. Soc.* LX. 480 The characteristic or regression equations which we have to find. **1943** Regression equation [see *regression curve* above]. **1978** *Nature* 18 May 184/2 The proportion of non-scientific staff [*A*]..is determined largely by the total staff employed (*S*) and the number of addresses amongst which it is dispersed (*D*) according to the regression equation $A = 22{\cdot}23 \log S - 1{\cdot}86D - 8{\cdot}77$. **1971** *World Archaeol.* III. 115 The regression formula predicts that a compound with five adults will have approximately ten huts. **1925** Regression function [see *regression curve* above]. **1904** *Biometrika* IV.

139 The actual degree of resemblance, our brothers being equally variable, is measured by the steepness of this regression line. **1925** Regression line [see *regression curve* above]. **1971** *World Archaeol.* III. 112 Variation away from the regression line is a function of wealth that is not used in this way. **1967** *Times Rev. Industry* Feb. 111/3 The lay reader should not be put off by the complicated language of regression theories, as Professor Kaldor's ideas are fascinating enough, and well enough argued in this lecture to be quite comprehensible to the non-economist.

regressive (rɪˈgrɛsɪv), *a.* [f. REGRESS *v.*]

1. a. Retrogressive; returning, passing back.
1634 T. CAREW *Cœlum Brit.* Wks. (1824) 162 Let those fires..the disorder shew Of thy regressive paces here below. **1728** PEMBERTON *Newton's Philos.* 218 This regressive motion will be greatest, when the nodes are in the quarters. **1759** PULLEIN in *Phil. Trans.* LI. 22 This received a progressive and regressive motion by means of two wheels. **1812** WOODHOUSE *Astron.* x. 79 The equinoctial point would have moved to the west, or have been regressive. **1865** MASSON *Rec. Brit. Philos.* 100 The regressive or contractive movement of the Absolute out of the finite..back into itself. **1888** WRIGHT tr. *Brugmann's Compar. Gram.* §644 Transforming operations are far more frequent in a regressive..than..in a progressive direction.

b. Moving back into an inferior condition; decadent, declining. *rare*$^{-1}$.
1854 DE QUINCEY *Templars' Dial.* Wks. IV. 238 *note*, Agriculture, as an art benefiting by experience, has never yet been absolutely regressive, though not progressive by such striking leaps..as manufacturing art.

c. Acting in a backward direction; retroactive; *spec.* of a tax, that bears proportionately harder on persons with lower incomes.
regressive assimilation, assimilation of a sound to one following it, as in *comp-* from *conp-*.
1888 WRIGHT tr. *Brugmann's Compar. Gram.* §603 If a monophthong arose from two vowels having a different quality, the levelling was sometimes progressive..; sometimes regressive. **1889** R. T. ELY *Pol. Econ.* VI. ii. (1891) 308 Indirect taxes are said to be, in their effect on the citizens, regressive. **1889** *Cent. Dict.*, Regressive assimilation. **1924** F. M. STENTON in Mawer & Stenton *Introd. Survey Eng. Place-Names* ix. 174 Some of these names, which enter into local nomenclature in considerable numbers, may be due to 'regressive assimilation'. **1939** [see PROGRESSIVE *a.* 2 c]. **1964** C. BARBER *Ling. Change Present-Day Eng.* iii. 62 Regressive assimilation..in which the sound exerting the influence comes later in the word than the one influenced. **1976** *Hansard Commons* 9 June 1597 The [licence] fee is a poll tax and it is regressive. It bears very hard on the worse-off.

d. *Psychol.* Of, pertaining, or relating to psychological regression.
1926 J. I. SUTTIE tr. *Ferenczi's Further Contrib.* xi. 137 Besides this regressive trait that fetters the patients to their bed..there may also be at work..the 'secondary' function of the neurosis. **1957** P. LAFITTE *Person in Psychol.* xi. 161 Concentration camp life has plenty of examples of exceptional, as well as of regressive, behaviour. **1969** *Listener* 22 May 736/2 It [sc. *The Boston Strangler*] seeks to entertain by feeding us on clinical information about behaviour of the most regressive kind. **1970** R. F. BALES *Personality & Interpersonal Behav.* iii. 49 To..teach in such a way presumably helps one's normal defenses by providing in one's overt behavior a good example for the more regressive inner self.

2. *Philos.* Proceeding from effect to cause, or from particular to universal.
1836–7 SIR W. HAMILTON *Metaph.* ii. (1877) I. 26 The affirmation of a God being thus a regressive inference, from the existence of a special class of effects to the existence of a special character of cause. **1877** E. CAIRD *Philos. Kant* I. 132 The regressive process whereby science discovers the universal from the particular.

3. *Med.* Tending towards, of the nature of, degeneration or decomposition.
c **1865** *Circ. Sc.* I. 334/2 In the very tissues, a regressive metamorphosis..has already begun. **1898** *Allbutt's Syst. Med.* V. 176 Before the patient's death regressive changes have already set in.

4. *Geogr.* Of, pertaining to, or being a regression of the sea.
1937 *Bull. Amer. Assoc. Petroleum Geologists* XXI. 1436 Near the close of this regressive movement the Loma Novio, Government Wells, and Chernosky Sand members were deposited. **1950** *Ibid.* XXXIV. 284 The regressive type of bioherm or reef may contain within it back-reef types of sediments such as red shale and anhydrite, but the transgressive type does not. **1968** D. L. EICHER *Geologic Time* ii. 49 Transgressive and regressive sequences generally do not contain a complete sedimentary record of all environments that prevailed laterally at the time. **1978** *Nature* 29 June 749/2 There seems little reason to invoke oscillations in sea level..to account for any other transgressive or regressive sequences observed.

Hence **reˈgressively** *adv.*, **reˈgressiveness.**
1853 W. BAGEHOT in *Prospective Rev.* IX. 421 There was a want of prospectiveness and a superfluous amount of regressiveness. **1854** DE QUINCEY *War* Wks. IV. 268 Twenty or thirty years earlier still, they had been ascribed to Voltaire, and so on, regressively, to many other wits. **1856** —— *Confess.* (1862) 233 Moving regressively from the end to the beginning. **1899** G. MATHESON *Stud. Portrait Christ.* I. ix. 108 It has been said that Christianity is a progressive religion; to me its distinctive feature is its regressiveness.

regreˈssivity. [f. REGRESSIVE *a.* + -ITY.] The state of being regressive; regressiveness.
1904 G. S. HALL *Adolescence* I. ii. 55 Retarded development of an organ..is an indication of regressivity. **1972** *Times* 23 Oct. 18/6 VAT will have small regressivity.

regressor (rɪˈgrɛsə(r)). *Statistics.* [f. REGRESS *v.* + -OR.] Any of the independent variables in a regression equation. Also ***regressor variable.***
1956 *Jrnl. R. Statistical Soc.* B. XVIII. 230 Two multiple correlations based on the same numbers of regressors. **1961** KENDALL & STUART *Advanced Theory Statistics* II. xxviii. 355 We understand by 'linear regression' that the conditional mean value of y is a linear function of the regressors $x_1, \ldots, x_p$. **1978** *Jrnl. Econometrics* VIII. 307 (*heading*) Posterior distribution for the multiple correlation with fixed regressors.

regret (rɪˈgrɛt), *sb.* Also 6–7 regrete. [a. F. *regret*, verbal sb. f. *regretter* to REGRET. Adopted earlier in Sc. in the form REGRATE *sb.*[1]]

†**1.** Complaint, lament. *Obs.* = REGRATE *sb.*[1] 1.
1533 BELLENDEN *Livy* (S.T.S.) II. 167 Throw þe miserabil sicht..of þis man, and throw his pietuous regret [*v.r.* regrate], raiss ane huge noyis and clamoure. *a* **1547** SURREY *Æneid* II. 93 With this regrete [*Douglas* regrate] our hartes from rancor moved.

2. a. Sorrow or disappointment due to some external circumstance or event.
1590 SPENSER *F.Q.* I. vii. 20 When her eyes..saw the signes that deadly tydinges spake, She fell to ground for sorrowfull regret. **1662** J. DAVIES tr. *Olearius' Voy. Ambass.* 278 [He had hoped] that our Lives would be an example to the Christians of the Country..; but that, to his regret, he found the contrary. **1759** ROBERTSON *Hist. Scot.* II. Wks. 1813 I. 138 The protestants beheld with regret the earl of Argyll..still adhering to the queen. **1784** COWPER *Task* III. 710 Scenes that I love, and with regret perceive Forsaken, or through folly not enjoyed. **1858** J. B. NORTON *Topics* 192, I concur with the Collector of Moradabad, in thinking that we have not cause to look on the fact with regret.

b. An intimation of regret for inability to do something, *esp.* to accept an invitation.
1851 T. A. BURKE *Polly Peablossom's Wedding* 177 The invitations went out, and strange to say, not a single 'regret' was sent in; but all came. **1859** BARTLETT *Dict. Amer.* 359 *Regret*, a note declining an invitation, and containing an expression of regret for the same; as, 'I can't go to Mrs. Jone's ball next Wednesday, but must send a regret'. A new lady's term. **1896** *Durh. Univ. Jrnl.* 8 Feb. 1 We wonder if it is not possible..for notices of 'regrets' to be posted in the Infirmary as well as at the College... It is rather annoying ..only to find a 'regret' posted in the College.

3. Sorrow or pain due to reflection on something one has done or left undone.
c **1641** CHAS. I *Refl. Strafford's Death* in Somers *Tracts* (1810) IV. 252, I never did bear any touch of conscience with greater regret. **1667** *Decay Chr. Piety* vii. 150 A passionate regret at Sin, a grief and sadness at its Memory, more speciously pretends to enter us into Gods roll of Mourners. **1727** DE FOE *Syst. Magic* I. i. (1840) 17 All wise men looked back with regret upon those actions of their lives which they have been drawn into, and in which they have reason to see themselves mistaken. **1813** SHELLEY *Q. Mab* v. 246 Pining regrets, and vain repentances..pervade Their valueless and miserable lives. **1863** GEO. ELIOT *Romola* xi, A face only a little less bright than usual, from regret at appearing so late.

4. Sorrow at, or *for*, some loss or deprivation or a lost thing or person. Also const. *of*.
1647 CLARENDON *Hist. Reb.* I. §64 And sure never any prince manifested more a most lively regret for the loss of a servant than his majesty did for this great man. **1695** PRIOR *Death Q. Mary* 100 Her piety itself would blame, If her regrets should waken thine. ? **1709** LADY W. M. MONTAGU *Lett., to Mrs. Hewet* Nov. (1887) I. 28 You know people can never leave your company, or writing to you, without regret. **1781** COWPER *Charity* 145 The sable warrior, frantic with regret Of her he loves and never can forget. **1820** SHELLEY *Witch Atl.* xiv, The feeling and sound are fled and gone, And the regret they leave remains alone. **1871** R. ELLIS *Catullus* xcvi. 4 When for a friend long lost wakes some unhappy regret.

†**5.** Dislike, disinclination, aversion. *Obs.*$^{-1}$
1667 *Decay Chr. Piety* vii. 152 Is it a vertue to have some ineffective regrets to damnation, and such a Vertue too, as shall serve to ballance all our vices?

6. a. *attrib.*, with the sense of 'expressing regret'.
1897 *Westm. Gaz.* 26 Aug. 7/3 A sheaf of over seventy 'regret' telegrams. **1898** *Ibid.* 2 Apr. 6/1 Last night the whole of the allotment letters and many of the regret letters were posted.

b. *Comb.*, as ***regret-laden, -worthy.***
1871 H. B. FORMAN *Living Poets* 289 both astonishing and regretworthy. **1873** E. BRENNAN *Witch of Nemi*, etc. 225 As hence we're driven, regret-laden, To that mist-land.

regret (rɪˈgrɛt), *v.* Also 5, 7 regrete. [ad. F. *regretter*, OF. also *regreter* and *regrater*: see REGRATE *v.*[1]

The ultimate origin of the Fr. verb is uncertain; some Romanic philologists are inclined to connect it with the Teutonic stem represented in English by GREET *v.*[2]]

1. *trans.* To remember, think of (something lost), with distress or longing; to feel (†or express) sorrow for the loss of (a person or thing).
13.. *E. E. Allit. P.* A. 243 Art þou my perle þat I haf playned, Regretted by myn one..? **1483** CAXTON *G. de la Tour* C ij, He cam to hym mournyng and weping waylyng and regretyng his wyf. **1611** FLORIO, *Regrettare*, to regret, to condole. **1692** DRYDEN *St. Euremont's Ess.* 104 He died at length regretted of all men. **1735** POPE *Ep. Lady* 234 Sure, if they catch, to spoil the Toy at most, To covet flying, and regret when lost. **1784** COWPER *Task* IV. 777 Sad witnesses how close-pent man regrets The country. **1863** FAWCETT *Pol. Econ.* I. iii. 16 Employers were heard to regret those days when there were no schools to corrupt the industrial virtues of the workmen.

2. To grieve at, feel mental distress on account of (some event, fact, action, etc.).
1553 *Douglas' Æneis* I. iv. 106 Eneas Regrettis oft the hard fortun, and case Of sterne Orontes, now drownyt in the se. **1660** BOYLE *New Exp. Phys. Mech.* Wks. 1744 I 72/2, I shall not regret the trouble my experiments have cost me, if they be found in any degree serviceable to the purposes..to which they were designed. **1671** MACWARD *True Nonconf.* 155 And we have already both acknowledged, and regretted the grievous abuse, occasioned by that latter practice. **1680** COTTON *Death Earl of Ossory*, Ah, cruel Fate, thou never struck'st a blow By all Mankind regretted so. **1732** BERKELEY *Alciphr.* I. §1 What I most regret is the corruption of his mind. **1781** COWPER *Table T.* 176 Poets, of all men, ever least regret Increasing taxes and the nation's debt. **1822** SHELLEY tr. *Calderon* I. 201 Do you regret My victory? Who but regrets a check In rivalry of wit? **1878** LECKY *Eng. in 18th C.* I. i. 124 Alone among the Spaniards the Catalans had real reason to regret the peace.

3. *absol.* or *intr.* To feel regret.
1853 MRS. GASKELL *Ruth* II. x. 281 Those who had umbrellas were putting them up; those who had not were regretting and wondering how long it would last. **1883** 'H. CONWAY' *Called Back* vi. 77 'Do you regret, Mr. Vaughan?' 'No—not if there is a chance.'

Hence **reˈgretting** *vbl. sb.* and *ppl. a.*; **reˈgrettingly** *adv.*
1721 STRYPE *Eccl. Mem.* III. xxvii. 213 The main design ..was to drive on Papal religion and in the mean while to secure the regretting people from rising. **1790** A. WILSON in *Poems & Lit. Prose* (1876) II. 193 Edina's crowd Should never have cost me one regretting sigh. **1826** SCOTT *Jrnl.* 24 Jan., Many were [thinking of me], undoubtedly; and all rather regrettingly. **1837** VERLANDER *Vestal*, etc. 88, I did not think again to feel These vain regrettings of the past. **1907** G. B. SHAW *John Bull's Other Island* IV. 105 No more neglect, no more loneliness, no more idle regrettings and vain-hopings.

regretable, variant of REGRETTABLE.

regretful (rɪˈgrɛtfʊl), *a.* [f. REGRET *sb.* + -FUL.] Full of sorrow or regret. Also const. *of*.
1647 R. FANSHAW tr. *Past. Fido* III. i, Thou art return'd, but nought returns with thee Save my lost joyes regretfull memory. **1743** SHENSTONE *Elegies* xix, Think not regretful I survey the deed. **1791** PAINE *Rights of Man* (ed. 4) 164 The regretful manner in which he expresses himself. **1837** WHEELWRIGHT tr. *Aristophanes* II. 106 Hating the town, regretful of my burgh. **1894** DU MAURIER *Trilby* II. 212 They soon forgot the regretful impressions of the day.

regretfully (rɪˈgrɛtfʊlɪ), *adv.* [f. prec. + -LY[2].]

1. In a regretful manner.
1682 SIR T. BROWNE *Chr. Mor.* 122 Men who dye in deplorable days, which they regretfully behold. **1705** GREENHILL *Embalming* 104 [Man] departs out of this world regretfully. **1872** 'MARK TWAIN' *Innoc. Abr.* xii. 83, I would wake up regretfully. **1880** OUIDA *Moths* I. vi. 179 'She is rude', she added regretfully.

2. It is to be regretted (that); = REGRETTABLY *adv.*
A regrettable use, prob. after HOPEFULLY *adv.* 2.—R.W.B.
1976 *New Statesman* 20 Aug. 237/1 Regretfully, that is no ground for leniency towards him. **1977** *N.Z. Woman's Weekly* 10 Jan. 36/4 Regretfully I'm one of those who suffer from an odd compulsion. **1977** *Times Lit. Suppl.* 15 Apr. 468/4 The investigators, who must regretfully remain anonymous, have produced..a richness of archaeological potential which it will take years to absorb and assess. **1977** *Jrnl. R. Soc. Arts.* CXXV. 336/2 Regretfully, however, the editorial staff may justifiably be thought to stand criticized for what has been omitted.

So **reˈgretfulness.**
1870 E. MULFORD *The Nation* ix. 155 In the strict historical school there is always a regretfulness..that there is now no Hamilton and no Madison.

reˈgretless, *a. rare.* [f. REGRET *sb.* + -LESS.] Feeling no regret.
1858 CARLYLE *Fredk. Gt.* VI. ix. (1872) II. 227 Wilhelmina ..takes charmingly to him..regretless of the Four Kings.

regrettable (rɪˈgrɛtəb(ə)l), *a.* Also 7 regreet-, regreat-, 9 regretable. [a. F. *regrettable*, †*regretable*: see REGRET *v.* and -ABLE.] Deserving of, calling for, regret: **a.** of occurrences, actions, facts, etc. (Common in recent use.)
1603 FLORIO *Montaigne* III. ix. 586, I have seene some.. hate their health because it was not regreetable. *a* **1693** *Urquhart's Rabelais* III. xlviii. 389 The loss of Osyris was not so regreatable in Isis. **1832** CARLYLE *Misc.* (1857) III. 52 The fact of their existence is not the less certain and regretable. **1867** VISCT. STRANGFORD *Selection* (1869) I. 118 It is, therefore, all the more regrettable to come upon the traces of their vitality in French opinion. **1889** *Times* 31 Aug. 5/1 These raids are very regrettable.

b. of what is lost or no longer exists. *rare.*
1835 *Tait's Mag.* II. 454 The custom, we suspect, was one of the few regrettable observances of the feudal era. **1871** EARLE *Philol. Eng. Tongue* (1873) §33 Our loss of this most regrettable old pronoun [man].

Hence **reˈgrettably** *adv.*; **reˈgrettableness.**
1866 *Pall Mall G.* No. 379. 1349/2 As regrettably obvious as ever. **1896** *Naturalist* 50 The writer's correspondence with him (regrettably, yet naturally)..ceased. **1913** *Eng. Hist. Rev.* July 555 The regrettableness of the lapses from what might have been.

regretted (rɪˈgrɛtɪd), *ppl. a.* [f. REGRET *v.* + -ED[1].] Mourned, lamented; viewed, or longed for, with regret.
1781 COWPER *Retirem.* 371 Ah those regretted days, When boyish innocence was all my praise! **1810** CRABBE *Borough* ii. 179 For then she thought on one regretted youth. **1861** tr. *Montalembert's Monks of West* I. 53 One of their most courageous and most regretted defenders.

re'gretter. [-ER[1].] One who regrets.
a **1845** HOOD *Public Dinner* i, The Duke's a regretter, A promise to break it. **1849** MILL *Diss. & Disc.* (1859) II. 341 'The illustrious prince'..has now Lord Brougham for his only, or almost only, regretter and admirer.

regretting, regrettingly: see REGRET *v.*

regrind (riː'graɪnd), *v.* [RE- 5 a.] *trans.* To grind again. Hence **re'grinding** *vbl. sb.*
1859 DICKENS *T. Two Cities* I. v, Samples of a people that had undergone a terrible grinding and re-grinding in the mill. **1885** *Machinery & Engineering* Oct. 89/2 The twist drill..is reground, when blunted, with the greatest accuracy and the least trouble.

regrind ('riːgraɪnd), *sb.* [f. the vb.] An act of regrinding.
1952 L. J. ST. CLAIR *Design & Use of Cutting Tools* x. 187 Tool B_2 would require a metal removal of ·037" from the end per regrind. **1971** *Engineering* Apr. 8/1 (Advt.), You know a Dormer drill right down to the last regrind. **1975** *Drilling Technol. & Collect Chuck* (Bristol Erickson Ltd.) 9 'Stubbing' means that for short holes 3 diameters of drill plus one diameter for chip clearance gives four times more drill life with feeds increased by at least 33⅓%, equals more holes per re-grind.

re'ground, *v.* [RE- 5 c.] *trans.* To furnish with a new ground or basis for etching, painting, etc. So **re'grounding** *vbl. sb.* Cf. GROUND *sb.* 6 and *v.* 8.
1831 J. CONSTABLE *Let.* 4 Dec. (1966) IV. 360, I know very well it can be blotched up, with dry point burr, re-grounding, &c &c, but that is hatefull. **1832** *Ibid.* 28 Feb. (1966) IV. 368 It is necessary..to reground a plate. **1937** *Discovery* Mar. 76/2 To add to the plate he cleans it thoroughly, regrounds it, draws the new work and continues as before.

re'group (riː-), *v.* [RE- 5 a.] *trans.* and *intr.* To group again. Hence **re'grouping** *vbl. sb.*
1885 *Pall Mall G.* 7 Oct. 1/2 Regrouping of parties might begin under much more favourable auspices. **1889** *Spectator* 19 Oct., A happy knack of refurbishing and regrouping the well-known properties. *a* **1944** K. DOUGLAS *Alamein to Zem Zem* (1946) 69 We had all seen the enemy so disorganized that it did not seem possible he could regroup enough to give us much trouble. **1976** *National Observer* (U.S.) 22 May 10/3 It was very important for me to find day care so I could regroup psychologically. **1981** *Times* 25 Apr. 12/3 The host and the other men said their evening prayers. They regrouped around the fire.

re'groupment. [f. REGROUP *v.* + -MENT.] Rearrangement in groups; a rearranged group. Also *attrib.*
1920 *Glasgow Herald* 1 July 6/4 A quiet continuance of the existing regime will allow..a regroupment without any definite break in development. **1961** *Encounter* Jan. 9/2 Villagers from the hills..have been 're-grouped' in new areas where they could be better protected and controlled —but only a third of these re-groupments were economically viable. **1961** *Guardian* 12 May 7/4 Algerians.. who have been herded by the French into 'regroupment centres'. **1963** *Economist* 17 Aug. 562 India is thinking of rounding up the..Nagas into 'regroupment villages'.

re'grout, *v.* [RE- 5 c.] *trans.* To furnish with grouting again.
1967 *Do it Yourself* Nov. 1330/2 The joints between ceramic tiles can be re-grouted with grouting cement. **1974** *Sunday* (Charleston, S. Carolina) 28 Apr. 1-c/2 The tiles will be 'thoroughly cleaned and regrouted and restored to their original newness', he said.

regrow (riː'grəʊ), *v.* [RE- 5 a.] *intr.* and *trans.* To grow again.
1872 W. READE *Martyrdom of Man* 411 The plant or animal grows and re-grows from within by means of a chemical operation. **1920** A. S. PRINGLE-PATTISON *Idea of God* 72 The Tubularia, a kind of sea-anemone, re-grows its flower-like head.
So **re'growth,** the phenomenon of growing or increasing again, *esp.* the renewed growth of vegetation after partial destruction by harvesting, fire, etc.; also *concr.*, the new vegetation that results.
1741 W. ELLIS *Mod. Husb.* May v. 85 Folding Sheep.. will likewise prevent the Regrowth of the Trefoil. **1868** LYELL *Princ. Geol.* III. xliii. (1875) II. 483 The frequent regrowth of supernumerary digits after they have been cut off. **1891** W. K. BROOKS *Oyster* 194 The regrowth of such a bed is, therefore, exactly like the original formation of a natural bed. **1944** *Forestry Terminol.* (Soc. Amer. Foresters) 60/1 *Regrowth*, herbage that grows after grazing or after the plants have gone through a period of dormancy. **1956** PETERSON & FISHER *Wild Amer.* i. 17 Other great stretches, greener and fresher than their surroundings, showed where self-sown regrowth had reclaimed old cleared areas. **1977** J. L. HARPER *Population Biol. Plants* xiv. 438 The sward was then rested from grazing until the regrowth had approached 12.5 cm. *Ibid.* xx. 630 This form of regrowth may be more significant than seedlings as a means of recovery after fire. **1977** *Listener* 2 June 710/3 The National Union of Tailors and Garment Makers..see evidence of the regrowth of the sweat-shop.

†**re'grudging.** *Obs. rare*[−1]. [f. RE-, after *reluctance*, etc.] = GRUDGING *vbl. sb.* 1.
a **1677** MANTON *Exp. Lord's Pr.* Matt. vi. 12 Wks. 1870 I. 188 We may take comfort by this evidence, though there be some reluctances and regrudgings of the old nature.

†**re'guard,** *v. Obs.* Also 7 regard. [RE- 5 a.]
a. *trans.* To guard (a garment) again. Also *fig.*
b. To guard doubly (with pun on prec. sense). Hence **re'guarded** *ppl. a.*
c **1610** BEAUM. & FL. *Philaster* v. iv, Do the lords bow, and the regarded scarlets..cry 'We are your servants'? *c* **1613** ROWLANDS *Paire of Spy-Knaves* 12 Crimson Veluet..All garded and re-garded with gold Lace. **1621** BRATHWAIT *Nat. Embassie* (1877) 106 Pytheas a Lawyer..Garded, regarded, dips his tongue in gold. **1624** HEYWOOD *Captives* III. ii. in Bullen *O. Pl.* IV. 162 We will see his fooles coate guarded, ey and reguarded too from slipping out of our fingers.

reguardant, obs. form of REGARDANT.

†**re'guerdon,** *sb. Obs. rare.* [a. OF. *reguerdon* (Godef.): see next and GUERDON *sb.*] Recompense, reward.
1390 GOWER *Conf.* II. 206 He leith his yerde upon that on, And seith the king hou thilke same Thei chese in reguerdoun be name. **1591** SHAKS. *1 Hen. VI*, III. i. 170 Stoope then, and set your Knee against my Foot, And in reguerdon of that dutie done, I gyrt thee with the..Sword of Yorke.

re'guerdon, *v. rare.* [ad. OF. *reguerdoner*: see RE- and GUERDON *v.*] *trans.* To reward.
1390 GOWER *Conf.* I. 370 And thus was merci reguerdoned, Which he to Theucer dede afore. **1532** *Chaucer's Boethius* IV. pr. iii. Wks. 259b/1 Of what mede shal he be reguerdoned. Certes of right fayre mede and right great, abouen al medes. **1591** SHAKS. *1 Hen. VI*, III. iv. 23 Yet neuer haue you tasted our Reward, Or beene reguerdon'd with so much as Thanks, Because till now, we neuer saw your face. **1814** CARY *Dante, Purg.* xxv. 128 Still we heard The sins of gluttony, with woe erewhile Reguerdon'd.
Hence †**re'guerdonment,** reward. *Obs. rare*[−1].
1599 NASHE *Lenten Stuffe* 34 In generous reguerdo[n]ment wherof he sacramentally obliged himselfe that..he would be the first man should set foot in his kingdome.

reguide, *v. rare*[−1]. [RE-.] To guide back.
a **1618** SYLVESTER *Mayden's Blush* 1685 This urg'd with teares; the Old man, overcome, Cryes, Go on God's name, God re-guide you home.

‖**regula** ('rɛgjʊlə). [L. *rēgula* a ruler, rule, etc., f. *regĕre* to make or lead straight.]
1. *Arch.* A fillet or reglet; *spec.* a short band, with guttæ on the lower side, placed below the tænia in Doric Architecture.
1563 SHUTE *Archit.* C iij, Vnder the Capitall, is made Astragalus, with his Regula..The which Regula, shalbe halfe so much in height as the height of Astragalus. **1598** R. HAYDOCKE tr. *Lomazzo* I. 86 The other must be deuided into three [parts]: give two to torus B: and the other to regula C. **1664** EVELYN tr. *Freart's Archit.* 133 Where they do frequently encounter and meet together with a small Regula between them. **1727–38** CHAMBERS *Cycl.* **1840** PARKER *Gloss. Archit.*; and in mod. Dicts.
†**2.** A rule, norm. *Obs. rare.*
1650 T. GOODWIN *Wks.* (1862) IV. 177 Their punishment is made the regula of all other wicked men's. **1870** S. H. HODGSON *Theory of Practice* II. iv. 255 Logic is the regula of the sequences in meanings..; Grammar the regula of sounds and language.

regulable ('rɛgjʊləb(ə)l), *a.* [ad. L. type **rēgulābilis*, f. *rēgul-āre* to direct; see REGULATE *v.* and -ABLE.] Capable of being regulated.
1660 INGELO *Bentiv. & Ur.* I. (1682) 166 The Soul accomplish'd with many regulable Faculties is the Subject of Vertue. *a* **1688** CUDWORTH *Treat. Morality* (1731) 35 Will ..as consider'd in it self,..hath therefore the Nature of a thing Regulable and Measurable. **1882** PIDGEON *Engineer's Holiday* I. 42 Furnished with coils of hot-water pipes whose temperature is regulable at will.

†**'regulant,** *a. Obs. rare*[−1] [ad. L. *rēgulant-em*, pres. pple. of *rēgulāre* to REGULATE.] Directing, ruling.
1677 GALE *Crt. Gentiles* IV. 351 Libertie in the divine wil is absolute, precedent, regulant: libertie in the human wil is conditionate, subsequent, and regulated.

regular ('rɛgjʊlə(r)), *a.*, *adv.*, and *sb.* Forms: 4–7 reguler, (4 -ere), 6 *Sc.* -ier; 6–7 **regulare**, 5– **regular.** [Orig. a. OF. *reguler* (mod.F. *régulier*), ad. L. *rēgulāris*, f. *rēgula* RULE; in later use re-adopted from, or conformed to, the L. original.]
A. *adj.* **1.** *Eccl.* **a.** Subject to, or bound by, a religious rule; belonging to a religious or monastic order. (Opposed to *secular*.) In early use placed after the sb., esp. in ***canon regular***: see CANON *sb.*[2] 1.
1387 TREVISA *Higden* (Rolls) I. 373 Patrik rered þere a chirche, and dede þere chanouns reguler. **14..** *Why I can't be a Nun* 172 in *E.E.P.* (1862) 142 Thys day schalt thow see An howse of wommen reguler. **1528** ROY *Rede me* (Arb.) 51 Of seculer folke he can make reguler, And agayne of reguler seculer. **1535** STEWART *Cron. Scot.* III. 16 Translatit it fra secular preistis syne To channonis regularis of Sanct Augustyne. **1590** SWINBURNE *Testaments* 64 Of Ecclesiasticall persons there be two sortes, the one Regular, the other Secular. **1631** WEEVER *Anc. Funeral Mon.* 128 These Priests were called Secular, and such as led a Monasticall life Regular. And so Canons were both secular and regular. **1766** BLACKSTONE *Comm.* II. 27 The intrigues of the regular clergy, or monks of the Benedictine and other rules, under arch-bishop Dunstan and his successors. **1836** *Penny Cycl.* VI. 373/2 Besides this auxiliary force, the regular clergy, or monastic orders, take upon them many of these functions. **1884** *Catholic Dict.* (1897) 212/1 The idea of a Regular Clerk is that of a combination of functions.
absol. **1387–8** T. USK *Test. Love* III. i. (Skeat) l. 131 Bothe professe and reguler arn obediencer and bounden to this Margarite-perle.
b. Pertaining to, connected with, a monastic rule or those subject to it. *rare.*
? **1490** CAXTON *Rule St. Benet* 139 He that otherwise dooth shall be correct wyth reguler disciplyne. **1526** *Pilgr. Perf.* (W. de W. 1531) 84 b, All outwarde reguler obseruaunces. **1691** tr. *Emilianne's Frauds Rom. Monks* (ed. 3) 141 Their Churches are more adorned, and their other Regular-places more comporting with the modern way of Building.
2. a. Having a form, structure, or arrangement which follows, or is reducible to, some rule or principle; characterized by harmony or proper correspondence between the various parts or elements; symmetrical.
1584 R. SCOT *Discov. Witchcr.* XIII. xix. (1886) 258 The regular, the irregular, the coloured and the cleare glasses. *c* **1645** HOWELL *Lett.* II. lvi. 79 The English speech though it be rich, copious, and significant,..yet, under favour, I cannot call it a regular language. **1667** MILTON *P.L.* v. 623 Mazes intricate, Eccentric, intervolv'd, yet regular Then most, when most irregular they seem. **1716** LADY M. W. MONTAGU *Let. to C'tess Mar* 14 Sept., I cannot, however, tell you that her features are regular. **1811** *Phil. Trans. R. Soc.* CI. 298 The arguments which I have given in the foregoing article, where only nebulæ of an irregular round figure were considered, need not be repeated when a regular circular form is presented to our view. **1815** J. SMITH *Panorama Sc. & Art* II. 292 In proportion as discoveries were multiplied, the want of a regular and appropriate nomenclature increased. **1840** tr. *Cuvier's Anim. Kingd.* 640 [Sea-urchins] are either regular or irregular,—the regular ones having the mouth in the middle of the underside, and the vent opposite. **1863** GEO. ELIOT *Romola* x, The conjurer ..showed his small regular teeth in an impish..grin. **1922** *Astrophysical Jrnl.* LVI. 164 This state of affairs led Sir John Herschel to avoid the discussion of physical distinctions among nebulae and to elaborate his father's formal classification in an ingenious manner. All nebulous objects were divided into regular and irregular, and the latter alone into nebulae and clusters. **1926** *Ibid.* LXIV. 324 The characteristic feature of extra-galactic nebulae is rotational symmetry about dominating non-stellar nuclei. About 97 per cent of these nebulae are regular in the sense that they show this feature conspicuously. **1973** L. OSTER *Mod. Astron.* xx. 303 We can do little more than speculate at present as to why some spiral galaxies are barred and others are 'regular'.
b. *Geom.* Of curves, figures, and solids: (see quots.).
1665 *Phil. Trans.* I. 105 If curve, whether regular or irregular. **1679** MOXON *Math. Dict.* 130 Regular Figures are those where the Angles and Lines or Superficies are equal. **1704** J. HARRIS *Lex. Techn.* I, *Regular Body*, is a Solid whose Surface is composed of Regular and Equal Figures. *Ibid.*, *Regular Curves*, are such Curves as the Perimeters of the Conick Sections, which are always curved after the same Regular Geometrical manner. **1727–38** CHAMBERS *Cycl.* s.v., All other regular figures consisting of more than four sides, are called regular polygons. **1823** H. J. BROOKE *Introd. Crystallogr.* 137 Distinguishable from regular octahedrons by the unequal inclinations of the plane. **1846** HOLTZAPFFEL *Turning* II. 777 The regular trapezohedron may be sawn from the regular octangular prism.
c. *Bot.* Having all the parts or organs of the same kind normally alike in form and size.
1785 MARTYN *Rousseau's Bot.* iii. (1794) 34 One general division of flowers is into regular and irregular. The first are they whose parts all spring uniformly from the centre of the flower, and terminate in the circumference of a circle. **1807** J. E. SMITH *Phys. Bot.* 256 An equal Corolla is not only regular, but all its divisions are of one size. **1876** HOOKER *Bot. Primer* 49 A regular flower is one in which..the members of each whorl are equal and similar.
d. *Math.* In various senses (see quots.).
1893 A. R. FORSYTH *Theory Functions Complex Variable* i. 12 A function which is monogenic, uniform and, except at poles, continuous, is called a meromorphic function. [*Note*] Sometimes regular, but this term will be reserved for the description of another property of functions. *Ibid.* iii. 52 A point *a* in the plane may be such that a function of the variable has a determinate finite value there, always independent of the path by which the variable reaches *a*; the point *a* is called an ordinary point. [*Note.* Sometimes a regular point.] of the function. *Ibid.* viii. 163 The singularities..in the vicinity of which each branch of the function is uniform. [*Note*] These singularities will, for the sake of brevity, be called regular. **1908** H. HILTON *Introd. Theory Groups Finite Order* ii. 8 A permutation with the same number of symbols in each cycle—such as (1 4 3) (2 5 7) (9 6 8)—is called regular. **1968** P. A. P. MORAN *Introd. Probability Theory* iii. 117 It is convenient to use the words 'regular' and 'positively regular' for the cases where the vector $P^t p(o)$ converges to a vector independent of p(o), and where in addition this vector has all its elements positive. **1972** A. G. HOWSON *Handbk. Terms Algebra & Anal.* xxxi. 154 Some authors weaken the definition of an analytic function on a domain *S* by asking only that the function should be analytic (in the above sense) at all but a finite number of points of *S*. A function which is analytic in the stronger sense would be described by them as being regular on *S*. *Ibid.* xxxvi. 181 Those points..possess a tangent plane..and are called regular points. Points which are not regular are said to be singular. **1978** *Sci. Amer.* Oct. 96/2 A prime is regular if and only if it does not evenly divide the numerator of any of the first $p-3$ numbers in the series of fractions called the Bernoulli numbers... Of the primes smaller than 100 all but 37, 59 and 67 are regular.
3. a. Characterized by the presence or operation of a definite principle; marked or distinguished by steadiness or uniformity of action, procedure, or occurrence.
1594 HOOKER *Eccl. Pol.* I. ii. §1 No certain end could ever be attained, unless the actions whereby it is attained were

regular; that is to say, made suitable..unto their end, by some canon, rule or law. **1607** SHAKS. *Timon* v. iv. 61 Not a man Shall passe his quarter, or offend the streame Of Regular Iustice in your Citties bounds. **1690** STILLINGFL. *Serm.* (1698) III. v. 184 True Courage must be a Regular thing; it must have not only a good End, but a wise Choice of Means. **1722** QUINCY *Phys. Dict.* (ed. 2) 380/2 *Regular*, Constant and Uniform, in opposition to Irregular..; both frequently applied to Diseases. **1761–2** HUME *Hist. Eng.* lxiv. (1806) IV. 720 The English parliament had now raised itself to be a regular check and control upon royal power. **1797** *Encycl. Brit.* (ed. 3) II. 220/1 When it [the light] comes from above, in such a regular, proportioned, and uninterrupted manner. **1867** W. W. SMYTH *Coal & Coal-mining* 249 A bar to the regular working of colliery proprietors. **1871** JOWETT *Plato* III. 133 He supposes the philosopher to proceed by regular steps, until he arrives at the idea of good.

b. Recurring or repeated at fixed times.

1756 *Boston News-Letter* 26 Feb. 1/2 A regular monthly Correspondence between Great Britain and His Majesty's several Colonies. **1781** COWPER *Retirem.* 430 How regular his meals, how sound he sleeps! **1797** *Encycl. Brit.* (ed. 3) IV. 750/1 The lunisolar year..was in use long before any regular intercalations were made. **1844** DICKENS *Chimes* i, 'There's nothing', said Toby, 'more regular in its coming round than dinner-time, and nothing less regular in its coming round than dinner'.

c. Taking place or recurring at short uniform intervals.

1781 COWPER *Table T.* 530 Exact and regular the sounds will be. **1815** SHELLEY *Dæmon* 34 Nor..Doth Henry hear her regular pulses throb. **1824** BYRON *Juan* XVI. cxiii, With awful footsteps regular as rhyme. **1876** T. HARDY *Ethelberta* (1890) 11 Quick regular brushings against the heather.

d. Habitually or customarily used, received, observed, etc.; habitual, constant; *spec.* of a long-standing client or customer.

1797 *Encycl. Brit.* (ed. 3) IV. 746/1 Even in the histories of Herodotus and Thucydides, we find no regular dates for the events recorded. **1838** DICKENS *Nich. Nick.* vii, 'We'll put you into your regular bedroom to-morrow, Nickleby', said Squeers. *Ibid.* xv, It's past my regular time for going to bed. **1841** DICKENS *Barn. Rudge* xi. 296 The regular Maypole customers..each..in..his allotted seat in the chimney corner. **1849** MACAULAY *Hist. Eng.* iii. I. 309 The regular salary, however, was the smallest part of the gains of an official man of that age. **1878** HUXLEY *Physiogr.* xxi. 370 The revolving globe is maintained in its regular orbit. **1885** *Act 48 & 49 Vict.* c. 56 *Preamble*, To permit electors in his regular employ to absent themselves. **1911** G. STRATTON-PORTER *Harvester* vii. 108, I have orders to fill for regular customers. **1966** H. MILLS *In Pursuit of Evil* vi. 59 'Is that a regular customer of yours?' I said to the..woman who owned the shop. **1973** 'H. HOWARD' *Highway to Murder* x. 125 Most of the ladies who patronize my salon are regular clients.

e. orig. *U.S.* Designating size or quality: average, medium; standard. (In quot. 1952 as *sb.*)

1952 *Amer. Speech* XXVII. 266 With regard to sizes of suits there are three basic divisions: regulars—for men of average height and weight; shorts..and longs. **1977** *Guardian* 11 June 14/7 If a Big Mac is too big for you then you might settle for a regular hamburger. **1978** *N.Y. Times Mag.* 23 July 22/2 In gasoline 'regular' has changed from meaning 'without tetraethyl lead' to its opposite—'with lead'.

4. a. Pursuing a definite course, or observing some uniform principle, of action or conduct; adhering to rule; in mod. use *esp.* observing fixed times for, or never failing in, the performance of certain actions or duties.

1602 DANIEL *Ep. Sir T. Egerton* xxiv, Eu'n the Scepter which might all command, Seeing her s' vnpartiall, equall, regular, Was pleas'd to put it selfe into her hand. **1669** J. LEEKE *(title)* The Regular Architect, or the General Rule of the five Orders of Architecture. **1693** DRYDEN *Ep. Congreve* 58 So bold, yet so judiciously you dare, That your least praise is to be regular. **1732** POPE *Ep. Cobham* 209 Nature well known, no prodigies remain, Comets are regular, and Wharton plain. **1883** F. M. CRAWFORD *Dr. Claudius* i, The Herr Doctor was a regular man, and always appeared at his window at the same hour.

b. Orderly, well-ordered, well-behaved, steady.

1705 ADDISON *Italy* (1733) 54 The University of Padua is of late much more regular than it was formerly, tho' it is not yet safe walking the Streets after Sun-set. **1748** *Anson's Voy.* II. vi. 200 Their..behaviour..was much more regular than could well have been expected from sailors..so long confined to a ship. **1779–81** JOHNSON *L.P., Smith* Wks. II. 473 He grew first regular, and then pious. **1800** MRS. HERVEY *Mourtray Fam.* II. 124 Lead a more regular life than you have done since you entered the army. **1879** *Cassell's Techn. Educ.* IV. 22/2 All they intend to send are regular people, neither factious nor vicious in religion.

c. Acting at the proper intervals.

1783 J. HEYSHAM in *Med. Commun.* I. 435 Her belly is regular. **1807** *Med. Jrnl.* XVII. 191 Her tongue was not furred; and her bowels were regular.

5. a. Conformable to some accepted or adopted rule or standard; made or carried out in a prescribed manner; recognized as formally correct.

1647 CLARENDON *Hist. Reb.* VII. §291 That legal regular convention of a sober and modest council. *a* **1680** BUTLER *Rem.* (1759) I. 232 In all Mistakes the strict and regular Are found to be the desp'ratst Ways to err. **1688** NORRIS *Theory Love* II. iii. 117 To make our Self-love Regular and according to order, we must take care not to mistake our true selves. **1731** C. CAMPBELL *(title)* Vitruvius Britannicus,.. containing Plans, Elevations and Sections of the Regular Buildings both Public and Private in Great Britain. **1753** CHAMBERS *Cycl. Supp.* s.v. *Leap*, The difference between the regular and irregular leaps is, that the former are performed by the voice, without any great difficulty or effort. **1797** *Encycl. Brit.* (ed. 3) II. 234/2 There are eight regular mouldings in ornamenting columns. **1802** JAMES *Milit. Dict.* s.v. *Attack*, Regular Attack, is that which is carried on in form, according to the rules of art. **1831** *Society* I. 273 Young ladies making acquaintances so easily, without regular introductions. **1869** OUSELEY *Counterp.* xv. 95 The intervals between the notes remain unchanged by the imitation. When such is the case, the imitation is said to be strict or regular.

b. *Gram.* Of parts of speech, esp. verbs: Following some usual and uniform mode of inflection or conjugation.

1611 FLORIO *Rules Ital. Tongue* in *Dict.* 633 Amongst all the Verbs some are vnder certaine orders, and are called Regular. **1766** DEL PINO *New Sp. Gram.* 38 All Regular Verbs, whose Infinitive is terminated in *-ar*, are conjugated in the same manner. **1824** L. MURRAY *Eng. Gram.* (ed. 5) I. 154 Verbs Passive are called regular, when they form their perfect participle by the addition of *d* or *ed*, to the verb. **1887** ROGET *Introd. Old French* ix. 117 The four conjugations of so-called Regular Verbs.

6. a. Properly constituted; having all the essential attributes, qualities, or parts; normal.

1638 BAKER tr. *Balzac's Lett.* (vol. II) 49 Sir, Expect not from me a Regular Answer to your letters. *a* **1687** PETTY *Pol. Arith.* iv. (1691) 70 Sufficient to victual Nine Millions of Persons, as they are Victualled in Ships, and regular Families. *a* **1708** BEVERIDGE *Wks.* (1846) VIII. 622 It always was, and still is, practised in all regular parish churches. **1886** C. SCOTT *Sheep-Farming* 28 Thus a regular ewe stock consists of four different ages. **1887** MOLONEY *Forestry W. Afr.* 46 The 'regular' oil..is only subject to this allowance if the water and impurities exceed 2 per cent.

b. Of persons: Properly qualified or trained; specially or entirely given up to some occupation or pursuit.

1755 JOHNSON s.v., A regular doctor. **1836** W. IRVING *Astoria* I. 244 Colter, with the hardihood of a regular trapper, had cast himself loose from the party. **1883** 'ANNIE THOMAS' *Mod. Housewife* 46 Having had the strength of mind to abolish the so-called regular 'cook'.

c. *colloq.* Thorough, complete, absolute, perfect.

1821 SHELLEY *Notes to Hellas* Poet. Wks. (1891) 453/1, I could easily have made the Jew a regular conjuror. **1833** R. H. FROUDE in *Newman's Lett.* (1891) I. 438 Perceval is..a regular thoroughgoing Apostolical. **1846** CLOUGH *Let.* in *Poems*, etc. (1869) I. 108 On Wednesday we had a regular flood, and it has been raining more or less ever since. **1885** J. PAYN *Talk of Town* I. 70 It was in this very fireplace I made a regular bonfire of them. **1956** [see BELSEN]. **1960** J. RAE *Custard Boys* II. xiii. 155 You're becoming a regular creeping Jesus. **1977** *Globe & Mail* (Toronto) 2 Mar. 6/6 Here we are today, being urged to go on a regular orgy of appeasement.

d. ***regular fellow*** (or ***guy***), an agreeable, ordinary, or sociable person. Freq. as a term of mild approbation; a 'decent chap'. *colloq.* (chiefly *U.S.*).

A fortuitous juxtaposition in quot. 1840: cf GUY *sb.*[2] 2.

[**1840** BARHAM *Ingoldsby Legends* 1st Ser. 44 Did you see her..With her knees to her nose, and her nose to her chin, Leering up..You'd lift up your hands in amazement, and cry, '—Well! I never *did* see such a regular Guy!'] **1920** F. SCOTT FITZGERALD *This Side of Paradise* ii. 52, I know I'm not a regular fellow, yet I loathe anybody else that isn't. **1924** *Amer. Mercury* Jan. 51/2 He was just one of so many mute and inglorious Babbitts preparing to qualify as regular fellows. **1930** E. H. LAVINE *Third Degree* xiii. 161 So he [*sc.* a policeman] usually decides to become a 'regular guy'. **1936** C. S. LEWIS *Allegory of Love* iv. 173 Chaucer..was not a 'regular fellow', *un vrai businessman*, or a rotarian. He was a scholar, a courtier, and a poet. **1936** H. L. MENCKEN *Amer. Lang.* (ed. 4) 254 When G. K. Chesterton made his first visit to the United States he was much upset when an admiring reporter described him as a regular guy. **1969** P. WILES in Ionescu & Gellner *Populism* 167 W. J. Bryan was to a degree exceptional even in the USA, a 'regular guy'. **1977** ZIGZIG June 17/1 He seems to be a regular, normal guy.

7. *Mil.* Of forces or troops: Properly and permanently organized; constituting the standing army.

1706 LUTTRELL *Brief Rel.* (1857) VI. 44 Squadrons of his regular troops and militia. **1756–7** tr. *Keysler's Trav.* (1760) I. 305 His majesty's regular forces at present consist of about twenty-two thousand men. **1777** WATSON *Philip II*, xv. (1839) 317 A thousand regular troops, together with two thousand of the country people. **1849** MACAULAY *Hist. Eng.* iii. (1890) I. 145 The regular army which was kept up in England at the beginning of the year 1685. **1860** MOTLEY *Netherl.* v. I. 270 Antwerp,..a city in which there was not a single regular soldier.

8. *Astr.* Of a satellite: (see quot. 1951).

1948 D. TER HAAR in *Kgl. Dansk. Vid. Selsk. Mat.-Fys. Medd.* XXV. No. 3. 63 This group has orbits which are all approximately in the equatorial plane of the primary and whose eccentricities are small. We shall call these satellites the 'regular' satellites. **1951** G. P. KUIPER in J. A. Hynek *Astrophysics* viii. 357 The satellite systems vary from the beautifully regular case of Uranus to a completely irregular system like Neptune... 'Regularity' is measured by low relative inclinations, low inclination with respect to the planetary equator, small orbital eccentricities, a common sense of motion—the same as that of planetary rotation—and some degree of regularity in the distances to the planet. **1960** *Jrnl. Brit. Astron. Assoc.* LXX. 35 Regular satellites, eighteen in number, travelling in almost circular orbits in the plane of the equator of the parent planet.

B. *adv.* Regularly, steadily; thoroughly.

1710 PALMER *Proverbs* 3 Another..pursues close and regular. *Ibid.* 82 'Tis impossible to judge well and act regular, when the mind is ruffl'd. **1824** MRS. CAMERON *Marten & his Scholars* iii. 20 Why, my lad, don't you bring home tickets every day when you go regular? **1885** 'F. ANSTEY' *Tinted Venus* 142 Oh, I'm regular jolly, I am!

C. *Comb.*, as ***regular-bred***, ***-built***, ***-growing***, ***-shaped***.

1769 ELLIS in *Phil. Trans.* LIX. 145, I examined this scum .., and could discover it to be full of regular-shaped salts. **1775** SHERIDAN *St. Patr. Day* II. iv, I had rather follow you to your grave than see you owe your life to any but a regular-bred physician. **1802–12** BENTHAM *Ration. Judic. Evid.* (1827) I. 297 The implanting hand of the regular-bred practitioner. **1817** J. K. PAULDING *Lett. from South* I. 105, I can do this without forfeiting my character as a 'regular built' traveller, whose duty it is to tell all he sees, and more besides. **1827** SCOTT *Jrnl.* 31 Jan., English boys..are well-bred, and can converse when ours are regular-built cubs. **1882** *Garden* 23 Sept. 273/2 The blue Ash of Michigan..is a bold, regular-growing tree.

D. *sb.* †**1.** *Sc.* A regulator. *Obs. rare*$^{-1}$.

1513 DOUGLAS *Æneis* I. Prol. 346 Venerable Chaucer,.. Hevinlie trumpat, horleige and reguleir.

2. *Eccl.* **a.** A member of a religious order observing a RULE; one of the regular clergy. (Cf. A. 1.)

1563 FOXE *A. & M.* 593/1 Aboue twenty houses of begging friers besydes a great nomber of regulars and irregulars. **1570** *Ibid.* (ed. 2) 1350/1 Who then folowing ye rule of S. Benet, were called regulars & votaries. **1657** SPARROW *Bk. Com. Prayer* 140 The Regulars and those of the strictest life did fast these weeks. **1683** *Apol. Prot. France* vi. 91 The Cardinals, the Bishops,..all your Regulars, all your Clergy of France. **1767** S. PATERSON *Another Trav.* I. 391 After high mass..the regulars were marshalled in the choir. **1814** DOYLE in Fitz-Patrick *Life* (1880) I. 68 Thus you see how regularly the Regulars are at war. **1871** FREEMAN *Norm. Conq.* IV. xvii. 82 Regulars and seculars strove which should pay the highest honours to the returning hero.

†**b.** One who adheres to the usual religion.

1632 *Star Chamb. Cases* (Camden) 172 If it had beene by a Papist against a Protestant, or by a schismatick against a regular.

†**c.** A properly appointed church-dignitary.

c **1645** HOWELL *Lett.* (1650) II. 49 Bishop Andrews and Sir Henry Martin..declar'd positively that he was not to fall from his dignity or function, but should still remain a regular.

3. A regular noun. *rare*$^{-1}$. (With pun on 2 a.)

1633 B. JONSON *Tale of Tub* III. iv, I hear there's comfort in thy words yet, Canon. I'll trust thy regulars and say no more.

4. a. A soldier belonging to the standing army; a member of the regular forces. Usu. *pl.*

1756–7 tr. *Keysler's Trav.* (1760) I. 305 On these occasions, they [the militia] receive the same pay as the regulars. **1796** STEDMAN *Surinam* I. iv. 85 Both the regulars and the rangers..behaved with unprecedented intrepidity. **1840** DICKENS *Barn. Rudge* lxiii, The regulars and militia.. began to pour in by all the roads. **1870** *Spectator* 20 Aug. 993/1 If he actually declared war with only his regulars in the field, all is explained. **1917** W. OWEN *Let.* 23 Nov. (1967) 509 The C.O. is a terrible old 'Regular'.

†**b.** A regular practitioner. *Obs.*

1764 FOOTE *Mayor of G.* I. Wks. 1799 I. 163 *Lint*... An encourager of quacks, Sir Jacob. *Sir Jac.* Regulars, Lint, regulars. **1795** WOLCOTT (P. Pindar) *Pindariana* Wks. 1812 IV. 204 Nor Quack nor Regular the mark will miss. **1894** 'MARK TWAIN' *Let.* 28 Jan. (1917) II. 606 When the mind-curist is done with you, you *have* to call in a 'regular'.

c. A regular customer, contributor, etc.

a **1852** [see CASUAL *sb.* 3 a]. **1872** 'MARK TWAIN' *Roughing It* xliii. 299, I struck up friendships with the reporters of the other journals, and we swapped 'regulars' with each other and thus encouraged work. 'Regulars' are permanent sources of news, like courts, bullion returns, 'clean-ups' at the quartz mills, and inquests. **1898** *Daily News* 27 Oct. 8/4 You see I has my regulars; mine aint no chance trade. **1902** ELIZ. L. BANKS *Newspaper Girl* xvii. 186 The 'regulars' are engaged on salary, and receive their weekly salaries every Saturday night. **1937** S. L. BERNSTEIN in C. Davy *Footnotes to Film* IV. 229 He can take the risk of alienating his 'regulars' in order to satisfy the requirements of the few. **1949** S. GIBBONS *Matchmaker* xx. 240 Mr. Waite was not a Regular at The Peal of Bells. **1959** 'A. GILBERT' *Death takes Wife* ix. 112 A woman entered his shop... She wasn't one of his regulars. **1970** *Daily Tel.* 28 Sept. 2/2 The Ministry of Technology does not plan at present to introduce coal rationing..but it believes that local coal merchants will limit supplies to 'regulars only'. **1978** *Dumfries Courier* 20 Oct. 16/3 Their popularity with the Edenbank regulars was demonstrated last week when the couple were presented with a framed colour aerial photograph of the hotel.

5. *Cant.* (See quot.) Also in phr. ***to go regulars***, to share profits. Now *Obs.*

1812 J. H. VAUX *Flash Dict.*, *Regulars*, one's due share of a booty &c., on a division taking place. **1840** H. COCKTON *Valentine Vox, Ventriloquist* ii. 5 I'll hire the large concert room upon the Market Hill, and you shall go reg'lars in the profits. **1882** *Sydney Slang Dict.* 7/2 *Regulars*, a thief's share of plunder. *Ibid.* 10/1 A cross-cove, who had his regulars for stalling, cried 'Cop bung', as a pig was marking.

6. In mediæval computation, one of a set of fixed numbers used for ascertaining on which day of the week each month began (***solar regular***), or of a set for finding the age of the moon on the first of each month (***lunar regular***).

1841 HAMPSON *Medii Ævi Cal.* II. Gloss. 331–2. **1973** *Bodl. Libr. Rec.* IX. 11 Lines 1–2 are a list of solar regulars, sometimes called ferial regulars.

regularity (rɛgjʊˈlærɪtɪ). [f. prec. + -ITY, perh. after F. *régularité* (14th c. in Littré).] **1.** The state or character of being regular.

1603 HOLLAND *Plutarch's Mor.* 67 Reason..causeth Morall vertues not to be impassibilities, but rather mediocrities and regularities. **1646** SIR T. BROWNE *Pseud. Ep.* 217 They..conceive a regularity in mutations,..and forget that variety which Physitians therein discover. **1728**

ELIZA HEYWOOD tr. *Mme. de Gomez's Belle A.* (1732) II. 14 He must..have had no knowledge of the Regularity of that Life she led at Rome. **1758** REID tr. *Macquer's Chym.* I. 21 Different methods..have different effects on the figure and regularity of the crystals. **1856** FROUDE *Hist. Eng.* (1858) I. ii. 175 [He was] present at the services in chapel two or three times a day with unfailing regularity. **1884** F. TEMPLE *Relat. Relig. & Sci.* iv. (1885) 99 The regularity of nature is the first postulate of Science.

2. *attrib.*

1925 C. D. BROAD *Mind & its Place* x. 457 The two conditions..are *not* jointly sufficient..to cause a memory even on the most extreme form of the regularity-theory of causation. **1935** *Aristot. Soc. Suppl. Vol.* XIV. 47, I accept the rationalist view, because it seems to me the only alternative to the so-called regularity view—that which reduces causal inference to a mere psychological habit or instinct. **1951** A. C. EWING *Fund. Questions Philos.* (1968) viii. 162 All this should make one hesitate very much before accepting the regularity theory merely because it is the simplest and keeps closest to what is empirically observed. **1954** A. J. AYER *Philos. Ess.* vi. 145 The same is true even on a 'regularity' view of causation. **1965** *Language* XLI. 186 The second breakthrough [in linguistics] was achieved in the 1870's, in the emergence of what I shall call the regularity hypothesis. **1977** M. MANDELBAUM *Anat. Hist. Knowl.* iii. 50 Hart and Honoré drew a sharp contrast between the plain man's notion of causation..and the regularity view, which they accepted as being..applicable in the sciences.

ˌregulariˈzation. [a. F. *régularisation*, or f. next + -ATION.] The act or process of making regular; the state of being made regular.

1853 G. H. LEWES *Comte's Philos. Sci.* 289 The regularization of habitual or continuous intercourse. **1881** *Edin. Rev.* Apr. 360 The regularisation of the right to take water from the irrigation canals. **1892** *Tablet* 23 Apr. 656 He required St. Chad to submit to a process of regularization.

regularize (ˈrɛgjʊləraɪz), *v.* [f. REGULAR + -IZE; cf. F. *régulariser*.] †**a.** (See quot. 1623.) *Obs.* **b.** *trans.* To make regular. (Common in recent use.)

1623 COCKERAM *Eng. Dict.* II, To *Gouerne* or rule, Monarchize, Regularize, Predominate, Magistrate. **1833** MILL *Diss. & Disc.* (1859) I. 64 Philosophy..rarely sets aside the old [classifications], content with correcting and regularizing them. **1882** W. S. BLUNT in *19th Cent.* Sept. 335 It was arranged that he should regularise his position by taking office as Under Secretary for War.

Hence **ˈregularized**, **ˈregularizing** *ppl. adjs.*

1847 GROTE *Greece* II. xi. III. 209 The conception of regularised popular institutions [etc.]. **1850** *Ibid.* lxvii. (1869) VIII. 143 The stirring and regularizing agent. **1872** LIDDON *Elem. Relig.* v. 190 Law is only our way of conceiving of His regularized working.

ˈregularizer. *rare.* [f. REGULARIZE *v.* + -ER[1].] A person or thing that produces regularity.

1921 LD. SHAW *Lett. to Isabel* xvii. 98 'There is a world elsewhere.' That is the secret... That it is which is the great regularizer.

regularly (ˈrɛgjʊləlɪ), *adv.* [f. REGULAR + -LY[2].] In a regular manner.

1. At the proper times; at fixed times or intervals; without interruption of recurrence; constantly.

1526 *Pilgr. Perf.* (W. de W. 1531) 247 Whiche seruyce or houres canonicall, regularly we synge, rede, or saye in the chirche. **1751** JOHNSON *Rambler* No. 141 ⁋10, I regularly frequented coffee-houses. **1788** GIBBON *Decl. & F.* l. V. 246 Till the third day before his death, he regularly performed the function of public prayer. **1802** MAR. EDGEWORTH *Moral T.* (1816) I. ii. 10 He passed through..regularly twice a-day. **1885** *Manch. Exam.* 10 July 5/2 The mine was regularly worked with naked lights.

†**b.** Invariably; in all cases. *Obs. rare*$^{-1}$.

1646 SIR T. BROWNE *Pseud. Ep.* III. xv. 141 Some have foure stomacks..; but for the principall parts, the liver, heart, and especially the braine, regularly it is but one in any kinde or species whatsoever.

c. Steadily, equably.

1825 J. NICHOLSON *Operat. Mechanic* 3 Now as its velocity increases regularly, we may conclude, that [etc.].

2. In accordance with rule or established principles; in a proper or formally correct manner.

1570 FOXE *A. & M.* (ed. 2) 84/1 After his death she is free from the law, to mary to whom she wyll, so it be in the Lord, that is, *regulariter*, regularly. **1611** COTGR., *Regulierement*, regularly, canonically, orderly. *a* **1665** J. GOODWIN *Filled w. the Spirit* (1867) 36 A covenant or deed in writing is made good in law by a seal, regularly affixed to it. **1769** *Junius Lett.* xvi. (1788) 97 It came regularly before the house, and it was their business to determine upon it. **1849** MACAULAY *Hist. Eng.* vii. II. 193 He well knew that, if the crown descended to his wife regularly, all its prerogatives would descend unimpaired with it. **1868** FREEMAN *Norm. Conq.* (1877) II. ix. 351 Spearhafoc..had been regularly nominated to the bishopric.

b. In the usual or customary manner.

1807 *Med. Jrnl.* XXII. 517 One of the men servants..was infected from one of the pustules, and had the disease regularly.

3. In a methodical or orderly manner; with observance of due order or method.

1668 DRYDEN *Dram. Poesy* Ess. (Ker) I. 73 If then the parts are managed so regularly, that the beauty of the whole be kept entire. **1689** BURNET *Tracts* I. 87 There was..an Anthem sung by a set of Musicians very regularly. **1704** HEARNE *Duct. Hist.* (1714) I. 206 During the Life-time of Jehoiada..Jehoaash behaved himself regularly, and governed well. **1810** WELLINGTON 24 Mar. in Gurw. *Desp.* (1838) V. 593 They are bringing a battering train into Spain from France, which looks like an intention to go regularly to work. **1836** SIR W. HAMILTON *Metaph.* i. (1870) I. 9 This question has never, in so far as I am aware, been regularly discussed.

4. In a symmetrical or harmoniously proportioned manner; with proper correspondence of parts, etc.

1695 DRYDEN tr. *Dufresnoy's Art Painting* Observ. (1716) 130 Those great Painters..had indeed made things more regularly true, but withall very unpleasing. **1712** STEELE *Spect.* No. 478 ⁋7 Shelves, on which Boxes are to stand as regularly as Books in a Library. **1719** DE FOE *Crusoe* II. xiii, The city..is regularly built, the streets..straight. **1860** TYNDALL *Glac.* II. xxvii. 379 The whole forming a regularly laminated mass. **1894** DU MAURIER *Trilby* II. 89 Both had regularly-featured faces of a noble cast.

5. *colloq.* Thoroughly, completely. Chiefly with participles.

1789 *Triumphs of Fortitude* II. 4 A young fellow..who is what may be called regularly dissipated. **1832** J. H. NEWMAN *Lett.* (1891) I. 274 Not that I expect to be regularly well as long as I live. **1848** DICKENS *Dombey* xii, Your father's regularly rich, ain't he? **1890** 'R. BOLDREWOOD' *Col. Reformer* (1891) 263 Glad to see you are regularly embarked in squatting life.

So †**ˈregularness**, regularity. *Obs.*

1648 NETHERSOLE *Self-condemned* (1649) 4 The equity and regularnesse of..the said proceedings. **1672** BOYLE *Virtues of Gems* 56 Long Christals..that did emulate native Christal as well in the regularness of the shape as in the transparency of the substance.

ˈregulatable, *a.* [f. REGULATE *v.* + -ABLE.] Capable of being regulated.

1874 MICKLETHWAITE *Mod. Par. Churches* xxv. 210 Fresh air..should be admitted only by pre-arranged and regulatable channels. **1875** KNIGHT *Dict. Mech.* 1914/1 A device for admitting steam in regulatable quantity.

†**ˈregulate**, *ppl. a. Obs.* [ad. late L. *rēgulāt-us*, pa. pple.: see next.] Regulated; regular.

a **1577** SIR T. SMITH *Commw. Eng.* I. viii. (1584) 7 The other they call..the Royall power regulate by lawes. **1603** FLORIO *Montaigne* (1634) 262 Brute beasts are much more regulate than we. **1644** CROMWELL *Let.* 10 Mar. in *Carlyle*, I know you will not think it fit my Lord should discharge an Officer of the Field but in a regulate way.

regulate (ˈrɛgjʊleɪt), *v.* [f. late L. *rēgulāt-*, ppl. stem of *rēgulāre* (5th c.), f. *rēgula* RULE.]

1. a. *trans.* To control, govern, or direct by rule or regulations; to subject to guidance or restrictions; to adapt to circumstances or surroundings.

c **1630** MEAD in Ellis *Orig. Lett.* Ser. II. III. 263 A freind of his sent him two or three Doctors to regulate his health. **1644** MILTON *Areop.* (Arb.) 50 If we think to regulat Printing,..we must regulat all recreations and pastimes. **1682** DRYDEN *Prol. Loyal Brother* 3 Critics would regulate Our theatres, and Whigs reform our State. **1729** BUTLER *Serm.* Wks. 1874 II. 8 Desire of esteem..was given us..to regulate our behaviour towards Society. **1792** *Anecd. W. Pitt* I. iv. 75 Can freedom be regulated without being..in some part destroyed? **1836** J. GILBERT *Chr. Atonem.* ix. (1852) 296 Mercy must be in some way regulated by regard to righteousness. **1877** SPARROW *Serm.* vi. 81 He that reduced the material world to order, can regulate and direct the mind.

refl. **1672** MARVELL *Corr.* Wks. (Grosart) II. 405 Having received your letter.., according to which I shall regulate myselfe upon occasion. **1779** JOHNSON *Let. to Mrs. Thrale* 6 Apr., Does he direct any regimen, or does Mr. Thrale regulate himself?

†**b.** To bring or reduce (a person or body of persons) to order. *Obs.*

1646 FAIRFAX (*title*) Orders Established..for Regulating the Army. **1654** BRAMHALL *Just Vind.* vi. (1661) 127 He might have..called a Councel, regulated him, and reduced him to order and reason. **1685** LUTTRELL *Brief Rel.* (1857) I. 341 In other buroughs..they have new regulated the electors by new charters. **1687** *Ibid.* 421 There are 6 commissioners appointed, who are to inspect all the corporations of England, and regulate them, by turning out such as are against the taking away the penall lawes and test. **1839** *Southern Lit. Messenger* (U.S.) Mar. 220/1 They had dropped hints of their intending, before long, to 'regulate old Jerry Jackson', who, they said, had been stealing corn.

†**c.** To correct by control. *Obs. rare.*

a **1680** BUTLER *Rem.* (1759) I. 218 To regulate the Errors of the Mind. **1682** WOOD *Life* 17 June (O.H.S.) III. 22 The chancellor's letters for regulating the rudeness and miscarriage of the Masters in Convocation.

2. To adjust, in respect of time, quantity, force, etc., with reference to some standard or purpose; *esp.* to adjust (a clock or other machine) so that the working may be accurate.

1662 J. DAVIES tr. *Olearius' Voy. Ambass.* 391 The Persians regulate their Feasts according to the Moon. **1728** R. MORRIS *Ess. Anc. Archit.* 60 Palladio has not been a little assisting to me in regulating the Proportions. **1750** tr. *Leonardus' Mirr. Stones* 33 The heat should be proportioned and regulated by the mineral or effective virtue of the stone itself. **1800** tr. *Lagrange's Chem.* II. 50 Care must be taken to regulate the fire properly. **1812–16** PLAYFAIR *Nat. Phil.* (1819) II. 107 Clocks ought to be regulated by the mean solar time. **1842** *Penny Cycl.* XXII. 485/1 He can..regulate the throttle-valve by hand-gear placed within his reach.

refl. **1776** ADAM SMITH *W.N.* IV. i. II. 9 The quantity of every commodity..naturally regulates itself in every country according to the effectual demand.

†**3.** To make regular or even. *Obs. rare*$^{-1}$.

1649 BLITHE *Eng. Improv. Impr.* (1653) 181 The Corn with much harrowing..will be drawn into wants and uneven places, and much regulated by the Harrow.

4. *intr.* To make regulations.

1895 *Westm. Gaz.* 1 May 2/2 If the Board of Trade has any power to regulate on this point, we trust that it will use it.

5. *refl.*, and *intr.* for *refl. Biol.* To exhibit regulation (sense 1 b).

1902 *Archiv für Entwicklungsmech. der Organismen* XV. 228 Pieces which are more active may be expected to regulate more widely. **1926** J. S. HUXLEY *Ess. Pop. Sci.* 235 The portion of substance which in its normal position would have developed into a half, has the power, if isolated, of regulating itself and its internal structure so as to give rise to a whole. **1971** *Nature* 24 Sept. 233/1 If half the optic tectum is removed and the optic nerve regenerates, the system regulates to preserve a retinotopic projection. **1977** *Sci. Amer.* July 67/1 Parts of the early embryo of various animals can be removed and the remaining parts will embryonically regulate to form a normal whole.

ˈregulated, *ppl. a.* [f. prec. + -ED[1].]

a. Governed by rule, properly controlled or directed, adjusted to some standard, etc. ***regulated tenancy***, a tenancy the rent of which is regulated by the terms of the Rent Acts (see quot. 1965).

Also freq. in combs., as *badly-*, *ill-*, *well-regulated*.

1641 W. T. (*title*) Regulated Zeal, or, An earnest request to all Zealously affected Christians, to seeke the desired Reformation in a peaceable way. **1697** JOS. WOODWARD *Relig. Soc. London* ii. (1701) 19 Those regulated Societies, which are now conspicuous among us for many good works. *a* **1704** T. BROWN *Satire Antients* Wks. 1730 I. 16 These [verses]..had regulated forms, that is regular dances and musick. **1766** *Compl. Farmer* s.v. *Surveying*, Then may you measure all the whole chains by your regulated chain. *a* **1790** ADAM SMITH *W.N.* v. i. III. i. (Bohn) II. 253 When those companies..are obliged to admit any person, properly qualified,..they are called regulated companies. **1828** SPEARMAN *Brit. Gunner* (ed. 2) 336 They are fired with a regulated charge of powder and shot. **1848** ALISON *Hist. Europe* ii. §23 I. 121 Regulated freedom is the greatest blessing in life. **1965** *Act Eliz. II* c. 75 §1 In this Act 'regulated tenancy' means—a) a tenancy to which the Rent Acts apply by virtue of this section; or b) a statutory tenancy arising on the termination of such a tenancy as is mentioned in paragraph (a) of this subsection. **1970** *Internat. & Compar. Law Q.* 4th Ser. XIX. II. 206 Unfurnished tenancies under the Rent Act being either (2) 'controlled' or (3) 'regulated tenancies'.

†**b.** Of troops: Properly disciplined. *Obs. rare*$^{-1}$.

1690 *Lond. Gaz.* No. 2568/3 We hear likewise that the French are in a great Allarm in Dauphine and Bresse, not having at present 1500 Men of regulated Troops on that side.

c. Proverb.

1819 'P. ATALL' *Hermit in America* i. 29 Accidents will happen in the best regulated families. **1850** DICKENS *David Copperfield* xxviii. 291 'My dear friend Copperfield,' said Mr. Micawber, 'accidents will occur in the best regulated families; and in families not regulated by that pervading influence..of Woman.' **1864** C. M. YONGE *Trial* II. iii. 60 Accidents will happen in the best regulated families. **1939** W. S. MAUGHAM *Christmas Holiday* x. 285 Accidents will happen in the best regulated families... If you find you've got anything the matter with you..go and see a doctor right away. **1961** M. KELLY *Spoilt Kill* iii. 159 Foul play... Even in the best regulated families.

†**ˈregulater.** *Obs. rare*$^{-1}$. [f. as prec. + -ER[1].] = REGULATOR.

1654 WHITLOCK *Zootomia* 285 He proceeding therein not by striking of Minutes, but Seasons, as his Regulaters in administration of Remedies.

regulating (ˈrɛgjʊleɪtɪŋ), *vbl. sb.* [f. as prec. + -ING[1].] The action of the vb. REGULATE.

1651 HOBBES *Leviath.* II. xviii. 91 This is not repugnant to regulating of the same by Peace. **1680** BURNET *Rochester* 41 As reasonable for God to prescribe a Regulating of those appetites. **1712** PRIDEAUX *Direct. Ch.-wardens* (ed. 4) 51 He presides for the regulating and directing of this Matter. **1824** W. N. BLANE *Excursion U.S. & Canada* 236 This practice of Regulating seems very strange to an European.

regulating (ˈrɛgjʊleɪtɪŋ), *ppl. a.* [f. as prec. + -ING[2].] That regulates.

1. a. Of principles, persons, etc.

With quot. 1768 compare REGULATOR 1 c.

1710 NORRIS *Chr. Prud.* i. 7 There is therefore a conducting Rule, and a regulating Rule. **1768** *Boston Chron.* 1–8 Aug. 315/1 The reforming or regulating people will not suffer process civil or criminal, to be executed, but where, and against whom they think proper. **1796** *Instr. & Reg. Cavalry* (1813) 27 The commanding officer of the regulating squadron of the line. **1816** J. SCOTT *Vis. Paris* (ed. 5) 185 An attracting and regulating body, that gives compactness and strength to the commonwealth. **1850** McCOSH *Div. Govt.* III. ii. (1874) 364 Besides benevolence, there is needed..a regulating power of justice.

†**b.** ***regulating captain*** or ***judge***: (see quots. 1815–63). *Obs.*

1758 J. BLAKE *Plan Mar. Syst.* 48 The regulating judge to determine how far such man is obliged to serve. **1768** *Woman of Honor* II. 182 Recommended him to a regulating Captain 'as a fit person to serve the King'. **1815** BURNEY *Falconer's Dict. Marine*, *Regulating Captain* is an officer stationed at the different royal ports, in time of war, to examine the seamen intended for the navy. **1863** A. YOUNG *Naut. Dict.* (ed. 2), *Regulating Captain*, in the Navy, 'the Officer appointed to superintend the raising of seamen, and who examines them on their entry'.

2. Of mechanical contrivances.

1825 J. NICHOLSON *Operat. Mechanic* 201 The pipe from the steam-case..has a regulating valve. *Ibid.* 314, *L* is the regulating screw. **1838** *Penny Cycl.* XII. 303/1 The pendulum-spring (also called the regulating-spring and hair-spring). **1877** RAYMOND *Statist. Mines & Mining* 48 The tray which receives the ore..as fast as may be desired, a suitable regulating-gate being employed.

3. *Biol.* Of developing organisms or tissues (cf. REGULATE *v.* 5).

1902 *Archiv für Entwicklungsmech. der Organismen* XV. 231 When a regulating piece is supplied with abundant food, growth and regulation are.. very intimately connected. **1926** J. S. HUXLEY *Ess. Pop. Sci.* 259 This passage from a regulating to a non-regulating condition takes place during gastrulation, before the first structural differentiation, in the shape of the medullary plate, is visible at all.

regulation (rɛgjʊˈleɪʃən). [f. REGULATE *v.*]

1. a. The act of regulating, or the state of being regulated. Also, an instance of this.

1672 EARL ESSEX in *E. Papers* (Camden) I. 27 Till I had them I would not venture one step in yᵉ regulation of Corporacions. **1676** TOWERSON *Decalogue* 501 The whole duty of man.. as concerns the regulation of our manners. **1765** BLACKSTONE *Comm.* I. xviii. 459 The advancement and regulation of manufactures and commerce. **1785** BURKE *Nabob of Arcot's Debts* Wks. IV. 199 For the interiour regulation of India, a minute knowledge of India is requisite. **1849** MACAULAY *Hist. Eng.* viii. II. 334 From the records of the Privy Council it appears that the number of regulations, as they were called, exceeded two hundred. **1885** C. G. W. LOCK *Workshop Receipts* Ser. IV. 316/2 Regulation is effected by raising the pendulum bob to make the clock go faster.

b. *Biol.* The property whereby a living organism can adapt the form of its body to accommodate for changes made or damage done to it, and whereby, in the normal course of development, the nature and growth of the various parts are so inter-related as to produce an integrated whole. Also *attrib.* [a. G. *regulation* (H. Driesch 1898, in *Ergebnisse d. Anat. und Entwickelungsgeschichte* VIII. 718).]

1902 *Archiv für Entwicklungsmech. der Organismen* XV. 187 The term regulation is employed here in the sense given by Driesch as including not only the actual regeneration of organs but any other changes, e.g., changes in the general form or outline and proportions of the body which may accompany or follow the replacement of lost parts. **1928** J. S. HUXLEY *Essays Pop. Sci.* 261 For Haldane, regulation places organisms in a different category from any non-living systems: for Driesch, it demands the intervention of vitalistic 'forces' such as his hypothetical entelechy. *Ibid.* 280 Once the tissues of the organism have become differentiated and it is capable of function, extraordinary powers of regeneration and regulation are developed. **1948** *New Biol.* V. 121 When the two cells resulting from the first cleavage division of a newt's egg are separated, at least one and often both form a complete though half-size individual. And conversely, two two-celled embryo newts can be fused to form a single large individual. This phenomenon of regulation, the adjustment of the entire developmental mechanism to disturbances of this sort, is a characteristic of the early stages of development of many kinds of animals. **1970** AMBROSE & EASTY *Cell Biol.* xiii. 422 Eggs of this type, which have the capacity to redevelop normally after a disturbance, are known as regulation eggs.

2. A rule prescribed for the management of some matter, or for the regulating of conduct; a governing precept or direction; a standing rule.

a **1715** BURNET *Own Time* III. (1724) I. 462 And then several regulations were made, chiefly the famed ones at Clarendon. **1765** BLACKSTONE *Comm.* I. vii. 263 The nature of foreign trade, it's privileges, regulations, and restrictions. **1774** KAMES *Sketches* II. x. (1807) II. 319, I heartily approve every regulation that tends to prevent idleness. **1788** (*title*) A Collection of Regulations, Orders, and Instructions formed and issued for the use of the Army. **1809–10** COLERIDGE *Friend* (1865) 122 The regulations dictated by prudence.. have passed away. **1870** DICKENS *E. Drood* ii, It's against regulations for me to call at night.

3. *Electr.* The degree to which the output (or some other property) of an apparatus remains the same when the load varies, expressed as the percentage change in the former for a given change in the latter.

1899 FRANKLIN & WILLIAMSON *Elem. Alternating Currents* x. 129 A transformer of which the secondary e.m.f. falls off but little with increase of current is said to have good regulation. **1900** M. A. OUDIN *Standard Polyphase Apparatus & Systems* iii. 42 A certain three-phase unitooth machine of large output gave a regulation of 6¼ per cent, from full load to 10 per cent of the load. **1947** *Proc. IRE* XXXV. 444/2 The operations can be performed to any desired degree of precision, providing power supplies of excellent regulation and circuit components of high precision are used. **1975** *Physics Bull.* June 247/2 (Advt.), The 227 output is dependable, too. Excellent regulation of 0·005%, stability to 0·01% and low noise combine to assume high output resolution. **1977** *Design Engin.* July 81/1 Output regulation is specified as less than 0·1% for max to min load and for ±10% line voltage.

4. *attrib.* **a.** That is prescribed by, or in accordance with, a regulation or regulations; such as is required or insisted on under some regulation; hence, regular, usual, ordinary, common.

1836–9 DICKENS *Sk. Boz, Parish* iii, The regulation cap to which the Miss Willises invariably restricted the.. tastes of female servants in general. **1838** —— *O. Twist* xviii, The regulation mode of cutting the hair. **1848** THACKERAY *Bk. Snobs* xxix, He can't afford more than his regulation chargers. **1865** MORLEY *Mod. Charac.* 168 Conversation is, as a rule, reduced to a regulation level of decorous flatness.

b. ***regulation district***, etc. (see quots. 1845). ***regulation movement*** (see REGULATOR 1 c). ***regulation roll***, one of the rolls of the Court of Session, containing a list of those cases in which no appearance has been made for the defender.

1825 *Act 6 Geo. IV*, c. 120 §29 All the Actions above enumerated, originating in the Court of Session, shall be first enrolled in.. the Regulation Roll. **1845** STOCQUELER *Handbk. Brit. India* (1854) 121 The presidency of Bengal is divided into sixteen provinces, in seven of which.. certain regulations prevail... These former are called regulation districts. *Ibid.* 123 Surat [etc.].. constitute the regulation collectorates; Scinde, Sattarah,.. comprise the non-regulation divisions. **1867** A. GREGG *Hist. Old Cheraws* 130 Such, however, was not the history of the Regulation Movement on the Pedee.

Hence **reguˈlationist** *sb.*, one who advocates regulation in some matter. Also as *adj.*

1886 *Pall Mall G.* 2 July 13/2 Several cases where the Regulationist party in America had been circumvented.

regulative (ˈrɛgjʊleɪtɪv), *a.* [f. REGULATE *v.* + -IVE.] **1.** Tending to regulate. Chiefly *Philos.*

1599 BLUNDEVIL *Arte of Logicke* v. i. 116 The principles regulatiue of a Syllogisme be these two phrases of speech. *a* **1834** COLERIDGE *Marginalia* in *Blackw. Mag.* (1882) Jan. 122 Plato had meant something higher and other than regulative. **1847** LEWES *Hist. Philos.* (1867) II. 467 These Ideas are simply regulative: they operate on concepts as the Understanding operates upon sensations. **1874** BLACKIE *Self-Cult.* 9 Logic is not useless; it has a regulative, not a creative virtue.

2. *Biol.* Pertaining to or being regulation (sense 1 b); whose development is guided by regulation; opp. MOSAIC *a.*[1] 5.

1902 *Archiv für Entwicklungsmech. der Organismen* XV. 229 Recognition of the fact that certain regulative processes are wholly or in part mechanical in nature is of importance for the future study of regulation. **1933** [see MOSAIC *a.*[1] 5]. **1933** J. H. WOODGER tr. *L. von Bertalanffy's Mod. Theories Devel.* x. 143 In the regulative eggs cleavage occurs before segregation, so that every blastomere still contains the requisites for the formation of the whole organism. **1936** *Jrnl. Exper. Zool.* LXXIV. 91 The ability of the separated one-half blastomeres following the first cleavage to produce a one-half of normal size—so-called mosaic eggs—or a whole of one-half size—so-called regulative eggs. **1947** L. B. AREY *Developmental Anat.* (ed. 5) ix. 161 All gradations exist between determinative, mosaic eggs and indeterminate, regulative eggs. *Ibid.*, Even the mosaic egg of a tunicate is regulative before fertilization occurs. **1973** R. SEARLS in S. J. Coward *Developmental Regulation* ix. 241 A number of experiments indicate that the limb mesenchyme is completely regulative.

Hence **ˈregulatively** *adv.*

1854 H. L. MANSEL *Man's Concept. Eternity* 10 A conception which is *speculatively* untrue may be *regulatively* true. **1882–3** SCHAFF *Encycl. Relig. Knowl.* III. 1973 It ought not to be hard to answer, whether a belief can be regulatively true, but really false. **1952** *Mind* LXI. 554 Principles which function regulatively in ethical inquiry.

regulator (ˈrɛgjʊleɪtə(r)). [agent-n. f. L. *rēgulāre* to REGULATE; cf. F. *régulateur*, It. *regolatore*.]

1. a. One who regulates.

1655 R. GARDINER *Eng. Griev. Discov.* To Rdr. A iv, Such judges as may be appointed Regulators of the great abuses done thereunto. **1678** CUDWORTH *Intell. Syst.* I. iv. 383 He did not only assert God to be the Cause of Motion, but also the Governour, Regulator and Methodizer of the same. **1765** BLACKSTONE *Comm.* I. 158 Such a spirit.. sets all the wheels of government in motion, which under a wise regulator, may be directed to any beneficial purpose. **1846** ELLIS *Elgin Marb.* I. 179 The directors or regulators of the procession. **1875** HELPS *Soc. Press.* iii. 43 There is great need that the regulator of the machine should be a living, active, forcible creature.

b. *Eng. Hist.* A member of a commission appointed in 1687 to investigate and revise the constitution of various boroughs, for the purpose of influencing the election of members of parliament.

1688 LUTTRELL *Brief Rel.* (1857) I. 460 The regulators are draweing into the several countries to manage the elections. **1690** J. HARRINGTON *Def. Rights Univ. of Oxford* II. 53 Some of them have been ready in surrendering their Charters, and have since been forward Regulators. *a* **1734** NORTH *Lives* (1826) II. 16 There was an itinerant crew of the worst of men... These were termed regulators. **1827** HALLAM *Const. Hist.* xiv. (1876) III. 74 New modelling corporations through commissions granted to regulators. **1861** LD. BROUGHAM *Brit. Const.* xvi. 248 Regulators of Corporations were commissioned to examine all their titles and all their acts.

c. *U.S.* A member of one of the bands formed at various times in wild parts of the country, with the professed object of supplying the want of the regular administration of justice. The earliest and most notable case was in the Carolinas, *c* 1767–71.

1767 LD. MONTAGU in A. Gregg *Hist. Old Cheraws* (1867) 136 Those licentious spirits that have so lately appeared in the distant parts of the Province, and, assuming the name of Regulators, have.. illegally tried, condemned, and punished many persons. **1768** *Boston Chron.* 18–25 July 292/2 We daily hear of new irregularities committed by the people called regulators. **1771** *Chron.* in *Ann. Reg.* 123/2 A letter from.. North Carolina.. says, 'Our Governor, at the head of 2500 men, is going against the Regulators'. **1812** H. WILLIAMS *Hist. N. Carolina* II. 128 The insurgents in North Carolina, who called themselves Regulators, lest they should be called a mob, were in general of the poorest class of citizens. **1824** W. N. BLANE *Excursion U.S. & Canada* 234 On such occasions.. all the quiet and industrious men of a district form themselves into companies, under the name of 'Regulators'. **1847** *Harbinger* (U.S.) 7 Aug. 136/1 The lynchers, or 'regulators' as they are often called, soon find that their foes organize also.

2. *techn.* **a.** A device for controlling machinery in motion, or for regulating the passage of air, electricity, gas, steam, water, etc.

1702 SAVERY *Miner's Friend* 15 The Handle of the Regulator Z must be thrust from you. **1766** *Compl. Farmer* s.v. *Ventilator*, There is an iron regulator.. fixed upright to the end.. of the box. **1778** [W. MARSHALL] *Minutes Agric.* 6 Apr. an. 1775, The drill does its work well.. but the Regulators do not yet please me. **1819** REES *Cycl.* XXIII. s.v. *Mill-work*, For such cases, judicious mechanics have adopted contrivances, or regulators... These regulators are usually termed governors. **1838** N. WOOD *Railroads* 339 The regulator, for increasing or diminishing the supply of steam to the boiler. **1880** LOMAS *Alkali Trade* 312 Preceding this decomposer comes the 'regulator', a brick and iron tower packed with bricks, up which the gases are passed.

b. A device for adjusting the balance of a clock or watch, in order to regulate its speed.

1704 J. HARRIS *Lex. Techn.* I, *Regulator*, a small spring belonging to the Ballance in the new Pocket-Watches. **1793** HOLCROFT tr. *Lavater's Physiogn.* xxxi. 165 Foolish people are like excellent watches which would go well, were the regulator but rectified. **1822** IMISON *Sc. & Art* I. 91 To this balance is fixed a small steel spiral spring, which regulates its motion, and keeps it equable; whence it has its name of regulator.

3. A clock or watch keeping accurate time, by which other timepieces may be regulated.

1758 CLEGHORN in *Phil. Trans.* LI. 258 Mr. Garret keeps his clock very exact, by Glasgow's regulator, Christ-Church. **1804** *Europ. Mag.* XLV. 251/1 Every person to whom minute mechanical accuracy was a matter of importance, was happy to obtain one of these regulators. **1862** *Catal. Internat. Exhib.* II. XIII. 15 A time-keeper, usually termed a regulator..; it has apparatus for transmitting alternate reverse currents of electricity.

4. Something which regulates; a regulating principle or power.

1766 *Compl. Farmer* s.v. *Sheep*, The best regulator for this work.. would be the state of vegetation. **1796** JEFFREY *Let.* in Cockburn *Life* (1852) II. 27 You can have no better regulator than your own successive opinions. **1855** MACAULAY *Hist. Eng.* xx. IV. 437 The weakest Ministry has great power as a regulator of parliamentary proceedings. **1884** H. A. TAINE in *Contemp. Rev.* Oct. 518 The State stands.. as regulator and controller.. of private possessions.

b. *Econ.* A change in the rate of taxation which the Chancellor of the Exchequer may use to manipulate the economy between budgets; the power to operate such an alteration.

1961 *Daily Tel.* 18 Apr. 24/6 (*heading*) Economy 'regulators'. Changes without budget. *Ibid.*, This is the power he is taking to operate two new 'regulators' of the economy at any moment the Government thinks fit. *Ibid.* 7 July 1/8 Labour spokesmen maintained their objection to the Bill mainly on the grounds that excessive 'regulator' powers were left in the hands of the Government. **1968** *Times* 29 Nov. p. iv/4 The activation of the 10 per cent regulator has effectively doubled the tax.. since the spring. **1976** *Daily Tel.* 1 Nov. 16 Full use of the regulator by itself would raise an extra £1,100 million of revenue in a full year and add 2¼ p.c. to prices. The regulator currently permits value added tax to be raised by a quarter and specific duties such as those on drink, tobacco and petrol by a tenth between Budgets.

5. *Comb.*, as ***regulator box***, ***cock***, ***spindle***, ***valve***; also ***regulator-wise*** adv.; **regulator gene** *Genetics* [tr. F. *régulateur* (Jacob & Monod 1959, in *Compt. Rend.* CCXLIX. 1282)], a gene which codes for a polypeptide which can act as an operator to modify the frequency of initiation of transcription, so as to inhibit or stimulate the synthesis of mRNA (and hence of enzyme) on the structural genes of the operon.

1856 CRESY *Encycl. Civ. Eng.* II. xxi. 1274 The Regulator Box.. was first constructed by Mr. Watt. **1875** KNIGHT *Dict. Mech.* 1915/1 The regulator-cock admits oil or tallow for lubricating the faces of the regulator. **1961** JACOB & MONOD in *Jrnl. Molecular Biol.* III. 334 A new type of gene, which we shall call a 'regulator gene'... A regulator gene does not contribute structural information to the proteins which it controls. The specific product of a regulator gene is a cytoplasmic substance, which inhibits information transfer from a structural gene (or genes) to protein. In contrast to the classical structural gene, a regulator gene may control the synthesis of several different proteins: the one-gene one-protein rule does not apply to it. **1969** A. M. CAMPBELL *Episomes* ix. 117 The regulator gene product has since been isolated. **1975** J. B. JENKINS *Genetics* xii. 527 There is some evidence for regulator genes and repressor substances in higher organisms, although their mode of operation appears to be quite different from those discussed under the operon concept. **1840** AIRY in *Mem. R. Astron. Soc.* XI. 252 The inequalities of motion of the regulator spindle. **1850** OGILVIE s.v., Regulator valve. **1663** MRQ. WORCESTER *Water-Comm. Engine* 15 A *Primum Mobile*, commanding both Height and Quantity Regulator-wise.

Hence **ˈregulatorship**.

1837 *Fraser's Mag.* XV. 732 The regulatorship of reason is indispensable. **1899** *Daily News* 28 Sept. 6/3, I am giving up my regulatorship of priestly orders to my son.

regulatory (ˈrɛgjʊlətərɪ), *a.* [f. REGULATE *v.* + -ORY.] **1.** Regulative.

1823 *Blackw. Mag.* XIV. 517 Some such code as I propose —some regulatory system for men to wrong their neighbours by. **1880** W. E. HALL *Internat. Law* I. i. 15 With their definitive failure to establish a regulatory authority international relations tended to drift into chaos. **1977** *Whitaker's Almanack 1978* 354/1, I have decided to use my regulatory powers to increase by 10 per cent. all the revenue duties charged on tobacco and alcoholic drinks.

2. *Biol.* Pertaining to, being, or involving regulation (sense 1 b).

1902 *Archiv für Entwicklungsmech. der Organismen* XV. 217 Morgan has proposed the name 'morphallaxis' for certain regulatory form-changes occurring in..lower animals, in consequence of which a piece gradually assumes more or less exactly the proportions of the whole organism. **1926** J. S. Huxley *Ess. Pop. Sci.* 302 This regulatory function of higher mechanisms is seen also in the domain of pure physiology. *Ibid.* 280 This period of non-regulation not only succeeds one regulatory phase, but precedes another. **1948** *New Biol.* V. 122 Many animals (especially those which undergo spiral cleavage) have little trace of profound regulatory power from the fertilised egg onwards. **1964** *New Perspectives in Biol.* IV. 246 A considerable amount is known about regulatory mechanisms in bacteria. *Ibid.* 259 The regulatory mechanisms that control cell differentiation in multi-cellular organisms may, in the not too distant future, cease to be one of the main unknown areas in biology.

'regulatress. *rare*$^{-1}$. [See regulator and -ess.] A female regulator.

1818 R. P. Knight *Symbolic Lang.* (1876) 99 She equally appeared to be the patroness and regulatress of nutrition and passive generation.

reguline (ˌrɛgjʊlaɪn), *a. Chem.* [f. regul-us + -ine[1]. Cf. F. *régulin*.] Of or pertaining to, of the nature of, regulus.

1669 W. Simpson *Hydrol. Chym.* 6 Antimony and its preparations, viz. the crocus metallorum, or reguline part. **1694** Salmon *Bate's Dispens.* (1713) 432/2 The Reguline or Metalline Part being more weighty, falls down to the bottom. **1754** Huxham in *Phil. Trans.* XLVIII. 834 This reguline substance, or antimony properly so called, is a metallic substance, *sui generis*. **1782** Kirwan *ibid.* LXXIII. 51 Metallic substances, when freest from all foreign mixture, are obtained either in a reguline state, or in that of a calx. **1819** H. Busk *Vestriad* iv. 252 Ah treacherous present of the glittering mine, Fatal as calx, more fatal—reguline! **1884** *Public Opin.* 12 Sept. 336/1 Mr. Dudley.. has succeeded in obtaining a bright reguline deposit of iridium on base metals.

'regulize, *v. rare*$^{-0}$. [f. as prec. + -ize.] *trans.* 'To reduce to regulus or pure metal; to separate pure metal from extraneous matter' (Webster 1828–32).

Regulo ('rɛgjʊləʊ). Also regulo. [a. L. *rēgulō* first pers. sing. pres. indic. of *rēgulāre* to regulate.] **a.** The proprietary name of a thermostatic control for a domestic gas oven.

1922 *Trade Marks Jrnl.* 29 Nov. 2182 Regulo... Taps and valves of ordinary metal... Radiation, Limited,.. Birmingham; manufacturers. **1936** *Economist* 28 Mar. 738/1 The 'New World' cooker, with the 'Regulo'.. revolutionised gas cooking. **1952** F. White *Good English Food* ii. i. 115 The oven..must be the right heat... Gas Companies provide Regulos at the side. **1968** S. E. Ellacott *Everyday Things in England 1914–68* ii. 33 About 1930 an oven-control dial was introduced for gas cookers. This was named 'Regulo'.

b. *attrib.*, esp. followed by a numeral indicating one of a scale of temperature settings marked on a Regulo. Also *fig.*

1926–7 *Army & Navy Stores Catal.* 291 'Regulo-controlled' gas cookers..fitted with the Regulo oven heat controller. **1936** Lucas & Hume *Au Petit Cordon Bleu* 33 Cook in a fairly hot oven (Regulo Mark 6). **1958** *Spectator* 6 June 733/1 There was the Guildhall, where..a temperature approximating to Regulo 7, caused such breathiness among the woodwind. **1958** *Times* 6 Oct. 13/5 Place in well greased roasting-tin and cook for 45–60 minutes, according to size of bird. Regulo Mark 7. **1968** S. E. Ellacott *Everyday Things in England 1914–68* ii. 33 Cookery books..added the appropriate Regulo readings for their recipes. **1971** 'D. Halliday' *Dolly & Doctor Bird* vii. 160 The permanently retired, stultifying in the sunshine at a low regulo setting. **1977** *New Society* 6 Oct. 22/1 The inevitable Tory tactic of keeping things low key by a regulo one campaign, which would let apathy take its toll. We went for regulo nine.

regulon ('rɛgjʊlɒn). *Biol.* [f. regul(ate *v.* + -on[1].] A unit comprising all the genetic material whose transcription is regulated by a single inducer or repressor.

1964 Maas & Clark in *Jrnl. Molecular Biol.* VIII. 365 The term *regulon* is proposed to describe such a system in which the production of all enzymes can be controlled by a single repressor substance. Two types of regulons can be distinguished, those in which the structural genes for the enzymes are adjacent to each other (histidine, tryptophan) and which thus consist of single operons, and those in which they are not (arginine) and which thus consist of several operons. **1976** *Ann. Rev. Microbiol.* XXX. 549 Because a single repressor regulates the specific expression of these operons with G3P as the inducer, the system has been referred to as the *glp* (for glycerophosphate) regulon. **1978** *Jrnl. Molecular Biol.* CXXIV. 359 (*heading*) Dominant constitutive mutations in *malT*, the positive regulator gene of the maltose regulon in *Escherichia coli*.

‖**regulus** ('rɛgjʊləs). Pl. reguli ('rɛgjʊlaɪ). [L., dim. of *rēg-*, *rex* king.]

1. *Astron.* (Now with capital initial.) A bright star (α Leonis) in the constellation Leo, called also *Cor Leonis*.

1559 W. Cunningham *Cosmogr. Glasse* 108 Then I find by that obseruation, the Mone to differ from regulus, j. degree .43. min. **1704** J. Harris *Lex. Techn.* I. **1727–38** Chambers *Cycl.* s.v., The longitude of regulus, as fixed by Mr. Flamsteed, is 25°, 31′, 20″. **1868** Lockyer *Guillemin's Heavens* (ed. 3) 325 It is at the lower extremity..that Regulus, a star of the first magnitude,..shines. **1889** C. L. Markham *Hues' Treat. Globes* 219 The lunar distances of Regulus are given in the Nautical Almanac.

2. *Chem.* †**a.** The metallic form of antimony, so called by early chemists, app. on account of its ready combination with gold. *Obs.* **b.** The purer or metallic part of a mineral, which sinks to the bottom of a crucible or furnace and is thus separated from the remaining matter. **c.** A product of the smelting of various ores, as copper, lead, and silver, consisting of metal in a still impure state.

1594 Plat *Jewell-ho.* ii. 45 Mixed with the Regulus of Antimonie. **1651** Wittie tr. *Primrose's Pop. Err.* 455 The Antimoniall Cup, or the Regulus out of which it is made. **1678** *Phil. Trans.* XII. 953 The first regulus of Gold being separated from the Antimony, both were powdered apart. **1683** Pettus *Fleta Min.* i. (1686) 26 A little Regulus of Lead at the Bottom, which is to be separated. **1709** *Phil. Trans.* XXVI. 379 Iron deprived of this sulphurous part, melts into a Regulus. **1744** Berkeley *Siris* §169 Four ounces of regulus of antimony being calcined by a burning-glass. **1796** Kirwan *Elem. Min.* (ed. 2) II. 105 He places these Reguli under a muffle. *Ibid.* 454 The purest Regulus of Nickel. **1825** J. Nicholson *Operat. Mechanic* 757 There is a great difference in the reguli of iron. **1868** Joynson *Metals* 97 The metal [is] run into pigs, in the state known technically as 'coarse metal', or, more generally 'regulus'. **1874** Raymond *Statist. Mines & Mining* 306 Yielding a regulus assaying 30 per cent. of copper.

attrib. **1859** Sevin in *Jrnl. Geog. Soc.* XXX. 40 The mines produced last year 4,000 quintals of regulus copper. **1868** Joynson *Metals* 107 Then add 8 oz. regulus antimony.

3. A petty king or ruler.

1682 T. A. *Carolina* 36 They are divided into many Divisions or Nations, Govern'd by Reguli, or Petty Princes, which our English call Cacicoes. **1727–38** Chambers *Cycl.* s.v., In the archives of the cathedral of Worcester, Uthredus sometimes styles himself regulus, and sometimes sub-regulus. **1807** G. Chalmers *Caledonia* I. ii. ii. 238 A very strong hill-fort..formed a secure residence for their reguli. **1867** Burton *Hist. Scot.* I. i. 5 Agricola cultivated the acquaintance of a certain Regulus, prince, or chief of Ireland, driven forth by political animosities.

4. The golden-crested (and fire-crested) wren. Cf. kinglet 2.

[**1706** Phillips (ed. Kersey), *Regulus*,..also a little Bird call'd a Wren. **1797** *Encycl. Brit.* (ed. 3) XII. 398/1 The regulus, or gold-crested wren, is a native of Europe.] **1824** Selby in *Mem. Wernerian Nat. Hist. Soc.* V. 400, I have not yet ascertained whether the Reguli of the southern parts of England were likewise observed to migrate. **1842** C. W. Johnson *Farmer's Encycl.* 1036/2 The golden crested regulus or kinglet..is most frequently to be observed in fir plantations. **1851** J. M. Wilson *Rural Cycl.* s.v., The fire-crested regulus, *R. ignicapillus*, is not so common as the preceding species, and is about half an inch longer.

5. *Geom.* A ruled surface; the locus of a singly infinite system of lines, where the consecutive lines do not intersect.

1879 Cayley in *Encycl. Brit.* X. 417/1. **1887** *Ibid.* XXII. 669/2 A quadratic surface is a regulus in a twofold manner, for there are on the surface two systems of lines each of which is a regulus.

regur ('rɛgə(r), 'reɪgə(r)). [ad. Hind. *regaṛ* black soil, ad. Telugu *rē-gaḍa*, *rē-gaḍi* clay.] Rich, dark, calcareous soil rich in clay, formed mainly by the weathering of basaltic rock and occurring extensively on the Deccan Plateau of India. Cf. *black cotton soil* s.v. black *a.* 19. Also *attrib.*

1828 *Edin. New Philos. Jrnl.* VI. 119 Immense deposits of a black alluvial clay are met with in various parts of India. It is denominated cotton ground, from the circumstance of that plant being always cultivated upon it. It is the regur soil of the ryuts. **1838** [see *black cotton ground* s.v. black *a.* 19]. **1879** Medlicott & Blanford *Man. Geol. of India* I. xviii. 429 Regur, in its most characteristic form,..preserves the constant characters of being highly argillaceous and somewhat calcareous, of becoming highly adhesive when wetted,..and of expanding and contracting to an unusual extent under the respective influences of moisture and dryness. **1906** E. W. Hilgard *Soils* xxi. 415 In view of the low rainfall and the closeness of the texture of regur, it is probable that little if any nitrates are currently washed out of the black cotton lands. *Ibid.*, The regur soil-sheet seems to be underlaid over the greater part of its area by a basaltic eruptive sheet. **1965** A. Gourevitch tr. *Gerasimov's Fund. of Soil Sci. & Soil Geogr.* xx. 326 In Asia, tropical black soils (regur) cover much of the Deccan plateau..and are widespread on the islands of Indonesia.

re'gurgitant, *ppl. a. Path.* [See next and -ant[1].] Regurgitating; characterized by regurgitation.

1866 A. Flint *Princ. Med.* (1880) 338 The first symptoms proceeding from mitral obstructive or regurgitant lesions. **1876** Bristowe *Th. & Pract. Med.* (1878) 522 In regurgitant aortic disease the surface..generally presents more or less cicatricial thickening.

regurgitate (rɪ'gɜːdʒɪteɪt), *v.* [ad. med.L. *regurgitāre*, f. *re-* re- + late L. *gurgitāre* (Cassiod.); see gurgitation, and cf. F. *régurgiter* (16th cent.).

Florio (1611) has '*Regorgitare*, to regorge, regorgitate'.]

1. a. *intr.* Of fluids, air, or gases: To gush, rush, or pour back (again).

1653 H. More *Antid. Ath.* ii. xii. §1 (*Schol.*) Nor does it regurgitate into the same Ventricle. **1733** tr. *Belloste's Hospital Surgeon* II. 38 Which afterwards regurgitate in the Veins. **1782** A. Monro *Compar. Anat.* (ed. 3) 60 The bile.. must..regurgitate into it. **1839** Ure *Dict. Arts* 1186 The carbonic acid gas..regurgitates into the apartment through every pore in the stove. **1883** J. W. Clark in *Nature* 22 Mar. 491 A little common air had regurgitated into the whistle when my grasp was relaxed.

fig. **1753** Smollett *Count Fathom* II. lxii. 233 Renaldo's grief seemed to regurgitate with redoubled violence. **1837** Herschel in Babbage *Bridgew. Treat.* App. i. 245 These notions had been fermenting and regurgitating in the cavities of my brain.

b. *transf.* of the containing vessel. *rare*$^{-1}$.

1669 Boyle *Contn. New Exp.* ii. (1682) 87 When my 3 Recievers did this day regurgitate with air produced from the Paste, I kindled a perfumed cone.

2. *trans.* To pour or cast out again from a receptacle, *esp.* from the stomach.

1753 N. Torriano *Gangr. Sore Throat* 5 The Medicine was regurgitated. **1773** T. Percival *Ess.* II. 142 Liquids.. when hastily drunk..were quickly regurgitated. **1816** Kirby & Sp. *Entomol.* xx. (1818) II. 179 When she returns to the hive, she regurgitates it in this form into one of the cells. **1898** *Allbutt's Syst. Med.* V. 975 In cases in which very small amounts of blood are regurgitated into the auricle from the left ventricle the consequences are inappreciable.

absol. **1657** Trapp *Comm. Job* xx. 15 The Whale that swallowed Jonah found him hard meat, and for his own ease was forced to regurgitate.

transf. *a* **1640** Jackson *Creed* xi. xxxvi. §5 Methinks flesh and blood should regurgitate his former murmurings upon this motion made by Jeremiah. **1690** Child *Disc. Trade* x. 174 [They] remove themselves from thence hither, so long, until the City..regurgitates and sends them back.

†**3.** To swallow again. *Obs. rare*$^{-0}$.

1674 Blount *Glossogr.* (ed. 4), *Regurgitate*, to swallow again. **1681** tr. *Willis' Rem. Med. Wks.* Vocab., *Regurgitate*, to swallow up again; or to sup up again what it before had parted with.

Hence **re'gurgitated, re'gurgitating** *ppl. adjs.*

1792 J. Hunter in *Phil. Trans.* LXXXII. 177 Many birds may be called regurgitating animals, and in them it is for the purpose of feeding their young. **1837** Carlyle *Fr. Rev.* III. iv. ix, One regurgitating whirlpool of men and women. **1876** Bristowe *Th. & Pract. Med.* (1878) 395 The entrance..of regurgitated food..into the larynx.

regurgitation (rɪˌgɜːdʒɪ'teɪʃən). [ad. med.L. *regurgitātiōn-em*, n. of action f. *regurgitāre*: see prec. and cf. F. *régurgitation* (16th c.).]

1. The act of pouring or gushing back; the fact of re-issuing or being ejected again from a receptacle. Chiefly *Med.* with reference either to the blood or to food.

1601 Holland *Pliny* II. 148 When the mouth is bitter, by occasion of the regurgitation of choller from liver. **1669** W. Simpson *Hydrol. Chym.* 73 Upon the regurgitation of the menstrues. **1698** Tyson in *Phil. Trans* XX. 131 A Regurgitation of the Fæces into the Stomach. **1747** tr. *Astruc's Fevers* 22 The plentiful regurgitation of the blood on the heart. **1782** A. Monro *Compar. Anat.* (ed. 3) 49 There seems to be no way of the bile getting into the gall bladder but by regurgitation. **1835–6** Todd *Cycl. Anat.* I. 539/1 Regurgitation is prevented by a semilunar valve at the termination of each vein. **1850** *Patents Abridgments, Ice Making Machines* (1877) 13 The valves in the induction pipes of the pumps 'do not close completely but allow a partial regurgitation'. **1880** Garrod & Baxter *Mat. Med.* 402 A patient..who suffered from vomiting or regurgitation after each meal.

transf. **1847** Sir H. Taylor *Notes from Life* (ed. 3) 75 When it begins with passion, there must needs be a period of collapse and regurgitation. **1869** Farrar *Fam. Speech* ii. (1873) 79 In the case of this great Slavonic nation there has been, as it were, a regurgitation of the Aryan wave.

†**2.** The act of swallowing again. *Obs. rare*$^{-0}$.

1658 Phillips, and some later Dicts.

re'gush, *v. rare*$^{-1}$. [re-.] To gush back.

1632 Lithgow *Trav.* x. 467 The water regushed abundantly from my mouth.

regworme: see ringworm.

†**regwort.** *Obs. rare*$^{-1}$. Stinking gladdon.

c **1450** *Alphita* (Anecd. Oxon.) 164 *Spatula fetida*.. regwort.

regyll, variant of regal *sb.*[3], groove.

regyon, -oune, etc., obs. forms of region.

†**re'gyre,** *v. Sc. Obs. rare.* Also reiyre. [ad. L. *regȳrāre* to turn about: see ingyre *v.*[2]] *trans.* To return, retort.

1606 Birnie *Kirk-Buriall* vi. (1833) B iv b, Diogenes.. being admonished,..did reiyre a taunt. *Ibid.* xix. F iij b, But this reason I may rightly regyre.

regyster, obs. form of register.

†**reh, reȝ, rei,** *a. Obs.* Forms: 1 hréo(h), hríoh, 3 reh(ȝ), ræh(ȝ), ræih-; reȝ-, ræȝ-, ræi(ȝ)-, rei(ȝ). [OE. *hréoh* = OS. *hrê*, of obscure etym.] Rough, stormy; fierce, violent; troubled, disturbed (in mind).

Beowulf 548 Hreo wæron yþa. *Ibid.* 1307 Þa wæs frod cyning..on hreon mode. *c* **888** K. Ælfred *Boeth.* xli. §3 Swa swa good scipstiora onȝit micelne wind on hreore sæ ær ær hit ȝeweorðe. *a* **1000** *Boeth. Metr.* i. 71 Wæs him hreoh sefa, eȝe from ðam eorle. *a* **1100** *O.E. Chron.* (MS. D.) an. 1075, Heom on becom swiðe hreoh wæder. *c* **1205** Lay. 4062 Þa oðere weoren ræhere [*c* **1275** reȝere]. *Ibid.* 6388 Ræh he wes on fihte. *a* **1225** *St. Marher.* 13 Þu..art mi broðeres bone, ruffines of helle, þe rehest ant te readwisest of alle þeo in helle. *a* **1275** *Prov. Ælfred* 682 in *O.E. Misc.* 138 Þe luttele mon he his so rei, ne mai non him wonin nei.

Hence †**'rehliche** *adv.*; †**'rehship.** *Obs.*

c **1205** Lay. 8440 Euelin him ræsde to, & hine ræhliche græp. *Ibid.* 9324 Hamun..rehliche fleh, to his Rom-leode. *Ibid.* 24943 Heore ræhscipe scal heom seoluen to reouþe iwurðen.

rehab (ˈriːhæb), *sb. slang.* [abbrev. REHABILITATION.]

1. = REHABILITATION 2 d. Also *attrib. Austral., N.Z.*, and *Canad.*

1948 K. STRONACH in A. E. Woodhouse *N.Z. Farm & Station Verse* (1950) 182 (*title*) Rehab. **1949** L. PETERSON *Chipmunk* 33 The car was completely theirs though; he'd paid cash for it out of his rehab money. **1953** M. SCOTT *Breakfast at Six* i. 12 This block's a Soldiers' Settlement. You know the sort of thing. Under Rehab. *Ibid.* vi. 53 It was the Rehab officer in charge of this settlement and others. **1959** G. C. SLATTER *Gun in my Hand* (1960) xi. 141 Rehab was the caper you jokers. **1964** *Canad. Weekly* 28 Nov. 12/3 By then I had a wife and child and my army rehab allowance was $90 a month. **1965** *N.Z. News* 27 Apr. 9/2 Rehabilitation assistance to returned war servicemen and women, a service known and respected throughout New Zealand as 'Rehab', officially ended on March 31. **1966** G. W. TURNER *Eng. Lang. in Austral. & N.Z.* viii. 172 A house may be bought with a rehab loan or a State advances loan.

2. = REHABILITATION 2 c. Also *attrib. U.S.*

1961 PARTRIDGE *Dict. Slang* Suppl. 1246/2 *Rehab*, a rehabilitation ward or department in a hospital: since ca. 1945. **1970** *New York* 16 Nov. 45/2 The storefront drug-rehab center. **1976** *Amer. Speech 1973* XLVIII. 208 Afterward, alcoholics go to *rehab* 'the rehabilitation center' to readjust to a life free from the use of alcohol. **1977** *Chicago Tribune* 2 Oct. XII. 68/8 (Advt.), Rehab Nurse. Immediate position available in skilled nursing facility for Rehab Nursing Supervisor. **1978** *Tucson Mag.* Dec. 42/3 Hauling young people off to 're-hab' centers against their will may just be illegal.

3. = REHABILITATION 2 a. *U.S.*

1975 R. H. RIMMER *Premar Experiments* (1976) I. 125 If I can persuade him to sell for ten thousand dollars each, I'll toss this house in at ten thousand dollars. That will give us fifteen thousand dollars more for rehab. **1978** *New York* 3 Apr. 36/3 On the one hand, the re-habilitation provided work. Thomas was in touch with Peter Brennan, the building-trades leader, who was quite cooperative. The instructors in the re-hab program were often union members and the young trainees were doing jobs created only because of the program.

Hence as *v. trans.*; also **reˈhabber**.

1977 *Archit. Rec.* Mar. 13/3 We can and should shorten time for developers and rehabbers. **1977** *Sat. Rev.* 23 July 9/2 The rehabilitation, into 28 apartments and several common rooms, of an abandoned tenement at 1186 Washington Avenue... 'rehab-ing' additional tenements in the vicinity of 1186. **1978** *Harper's Mag.* June 43 Solid 1890s structures built practically with slave labor, now rehabbed to perfection. **1979** *Arizona Daily Star* 1 Apr. J1/3 Rehabbing an older city home involves some special problems.

†reˈhabile, *v. Sc. Obs.*$^{-1}$ [var. of REABLE *v.*] *trans.* To rehabilitate.

1535 LYNDESAY *Satyre* 3938 Thay.. Sal be degraithit of thair Nobilitie,.. Vnto the tyme thay by [= buy] thair libertie, Rehabilit be the ciuill magistrate.

rehabilitate (riːhəˈbɪlɪteɪt), *v.* [f. ppl. stem of med.L. *rehabilitāre*; see RE- and HABILITATE *v.*, and cf. F. *réhabiliter* (16th c.; earlier *reabiliter*).]

1. a. *trans.* To restore by formal act or declaration (one degraded or attainted) to former privileges, rank, and possessions; to re-establish (one's good name or memory) by authoritative pronouncement. (In early use only *Sc.*)

1580–1 *Reg. Privy Council Scot.* III. 358 Oure Soverane Lord.. rehabilitattis and restoris the said Robert.. to his gude fame. **1586–7** *Ibid.* IV. 154 Ay and quhill the said James, sumtyme archiebischop of Glasgow, be fullelie restorit and rehabilitat be oure said Soverane Lord. **1633** *Sc. Acts Chas. I* (1814) V. 56/2 His Majestie.. hes rehabilitat the said francis [sometime Earl of Bothwell] his airs and successors againes the act of dishabilitatioun. **1727–38** CHAMBERS *Cycl.* s.v. *Rehabilitation*, The king alone can rehabilitate an officer noted, condemned, and degraded; or a gentleman who has derogated from his rank. **1796** SEWARD *Anecdotes* III. 26 Pope Calixtus the Third.. rehabilitated her memory, declaring her, by a Bull, a martyr to her religion. **1852** MISS YONGE *Cameos* (1877) II. xxxvi. 385 Not only was her name publickly rehabilitated, but the records of the examinations in the archives of France guard her memory for ever. **1875** STUBBS *Const. Hist.* II. xvii. 563 Edward I again seems to have considered that the judges.. were rehabilitated by the payment of a fine.

b. To re-establish the character or reputation of (a person or thing); to clear from unfounded accusations or misrepresentations.

1847 *Blackw. Mag.* LXII. 354 We pass on.. to the chief hero of these peasant wars, whom Mrs. Percy Sinnett under-takes, in the French phrase, to rehabilitate—in other words, to wash a little white. **1862** *Lady Morgan's Mem.* II. 172 Whilst Lady Morgan was rehabilitating the name and character of a man of genius. **1876** F. HARRISON *Choice Bks.* (1886) 396 A great many of these histories are written.. to puff up, or, as it is now the fashion to call it, to 'rehabilitate' a bad man.

refl. **1869** *Latest News* 26 Sept. 9 He hoped to rehabilitate himself; and, if he should ever return here, to continue the fight. **1873** PATER *Stud. Hist. Renaiss.* ii. 19 The older gods had rehabilitated themselves, and men's allegiance was divided.

2. To replace *in* a previous state.

c **1691** SIR G. MACKENZIE *Virtuoso* xiii. Wks. 1716 I. 66 Why may we not say, that Man, if he were rehabilitated in the former State of pure Nature, might.. foresee and prophesy? **1731** *Hist. Litteraria* III. 253 This rehabilitates Dr. Boerhaave in his Name, and Honours.

3. a. To restore to a previous condition; to set up again in proper condition.

1845 CARLYLE *Cromwell* (1871) II. 226 The unwearied Lord Lieutenant.. has been rehabilitating Courts of Justice in Dublin. **1855** BAILEY *Mystic* 23 The fused orb rehabilitated rolls As heretofore upon its cœlar path. **1859** ELLICOTT *Comm. Gal.* Pref. (ed. 2) 15 The very admirable work of Winer has completely rehabilitated the subject. **1875** HELPS *Soc. Press.* vii. 96 That dear boy George Smith had rehabilitated me.

b. To restore (a disabled person, a criminal, etc.) to some degree of normal life by appropriate training.

1944 *New Statesman* 27 May 353/1, I think Dr. Rogerson's Patient would have had a very different outlook, had he been properly Rehabilitated. **1951** *Times* 20 Feb. 4/4 As soon as the wounded were rehabilitated they trained the new men, because of their valuable experience. **1968** *Listener* 19 Dec. 816/1 They want to rehabilitate us, but we think it is the rehabilitation officers who need rehabilitating, not us. **1978** *Lancashire Life* 51/1 The emphasis today is to rehabilitate old folk to enable them to remain active for as long as possible.

c. *absol.* for *refl.* To return from military to civilian status or purpose.

1945 *Daily Tel.* 29 June 4/3 Such assistance will be a precious aid to the first victims of the Axis—a people of 15,000,000 struggling to rehabilitate and develop, despite the grievous loss produced by the systematic murder by the Italians of the trained personnel and educated youth.

Hence **rehaˈbilitated** *ppl. a.*, **rehaˈbilitating**, *vbl. sb.*

1837 CARLYLE *Fr. Rev.* II. I. i, Thither may the wrecks of re-habilitated Loyalty gather, if it will become Constitutional. **1843** MRS. CARLYLE *Lett.* I. 264 For three days his satisfaction over the rehabilitated house lasted. **1924** *Glasgow Herald* 18 Mar. 6/3 The rehabilitating of Austria was carried a stage further.

rehabilitation (ˌriːhəbɪlɪˈteɪʃən). [ad. med.L. *rehabilitātiōn-em*: see prec. and -ATION. In mod. use perh. partly after F. *réhabilitation*.]

1. a. The action of re-establishing (a person) in a former standing with respect to rank and legal rights (†or church privileges); the result of such action; †also, a writ by which such restoration is made. (In early use chiefly *Sc.*)

1533–4 *Act 25 Hen. VIII*, c. 21 §1 Relaxacions, writtes called *Perinde valere*, rehabilitacions, abolitions, and other infinite sortes of buls. **1572–3** *Reg. Privy Council Scot.* II. 174 His Hienes rehabilitatioun to all and sindry thair landis .. as in the same remissioun and rehabilitatioun at mair lenth is contenit. **1633** *Sc. Acts Chas. I* (1814) V. 56/2 The letters of rehabilitatioun of francis Stewart sone to vmquhil francis sometyme Erle of Bothwell. *a* **1639** SPOTTISWOOD *Hist. Ch. Scot.* VI. (1677) 348 A Letter of rehabilitation, whereby he might stand in judgment and plead against his Forfeiture. **1696** PHILLIPS (ed. 5), *Rehabilitation*, an Act whereby the Pope or the King, by Dispensation, or Letters Patents, restores those that are grown low in the World. **1824** ELLIS *Orig. Lett.* Ser. I. I. 212 His remission and rehabilitation under the Great Seal of Scotland was not obtained till April 18th, 1497. **1850** MERIVALE *Rom. Emp.* (1865) I. iii. 95 He pleaded the cause of his wife's brother,.. and obtained his rehabilitation with that of other Marian exiles. **1875** POSTE *Gaius* I. §129 The status of his children is suspended by his right of retrospective rehabilitation, for on escape from captivity a man recovers all former rights.

b. Reinstatement (of a person) in any previous position or privilege.

1831 SOUTHEY in *Q. Rev.* XLV. 173 Having resisted the rehabilitation of the king after his attempted flight. **1841** TRENCH *Parables* (1860) 411 His rehabilitation in his baptismal privileges.

c. Re-establishment of a person's reputation; vindication of character.

1876 *Ch. Q. Rev.* Jan. 337 We live in an age of rehabilitations; but the subjects selected to undergo that process [etc.]. **1879** J. C. MORISON *Gibbon* 160 A rehabilitation of Theodora is not a theme calculated to provoke enthusiasm.

2. a. The action of replacing a thing in, or restoring it to, a previous condition or status.

1858 SPENCER *Ess.* I. 198 Those who look sceptically on this attempted rehabilitation of the earlier epochs of mental development. **1861** *Temple Bar* I. 411 The work of Appuleius is a sort of 'rehabilitation' of the story, with a religious turn given to it. **1973** *Detroit Legal News* 30 Aug. 13/8 Owner or interested party who appeared verbally granted a period of two weeks in which to.. secure a building permit, and to immediately begin rehabilitation.

b. Restoration to a higher moral state.

1868 W. R. GREG *Lit. & Soc. Judgm.* (1869) 379 There are two opposite directions in which the improvement and rehabilitation of the Jamaica peasantry may be sought. **1873** PATER *Stud. Hist. Renaiss.* ii. 29 That rehabilitation of human nature.. which the Renaissance fulfils.

c. Restoration (of a disabled person, a criminal, etc.) to some degree of normal life by appropriate training. Cf. REHABILITATE *v.* 3 b.

1940 M. J. MACDONALD in *Hansard Commons* 17 Oct. 867 There is one.. aspect of the healing of the wounded—.. which I should like to mention,.. it is the secret of the maximum cure possible for the patient. It is the process known as rehabilitation. It is not sufficient that the wound should be healed; the wounded part of the patient must be enabled to function again so that he may once more play his part in society as a worker... I have appointed an adviser on rehabilitation. **1941** *Ann. Reg. 1940* 150 The principal questions for expert study being the.. rehabilitation of men disabled in the war. **1952** *Rehabilitation* July (verso front cover). The British Council for Rehabilitation was founded in 1944... Rehabilitation was defined as 'the whole range of services from the time of the onset of the individuals' disability to the point at which he is restored to normal activity or the nearest possible approach to it'. **1974** *Science* 2 Aug. 423/2 People who are down on jails believe that the institutional setting is too dehumanizing for any meaningful rehabilitation to take place. **1979** *Internat. Rehabilit. Med.* I. 73/1 Mair.. defined rehabilitation as implying the restoration of patients to their fullest physical, mental and social capability.

d. The retraining of a person, or the restoration of industry, the economy, etc., after a war or a long period of military service.

1941 *New Statesman* 15 Feb. 161/1 A military victory would be followed by the economic and democratic rehabilitation of France and Germany. **1941** *Times* (weekly ed.) 30 July 16/2 The possession of these.. assets will ease the task of the Allied Governments when the time comes for the rehabilitation of European finance after the war. **1946** *R.A.F. Jrnl.* May 170 The career-finding agency.. was inaugurated as one of the primary aids for rehabilitation of members. **1950** *N.Z. Jrnl. Agric.* May 458/2 (*heading*) Rehabilitation of Ex-servicemen. *Ibid.*, Land for the rehabilitation of returned servicemen has been.. plentiful in Canada.

3. *attrib.*, as ***rehabilitation area, camp, centre, counselling, grant, officer, programme, studies***. Also **rehabilitation medicine** (see quot. 1971).

1977 *Detroit Free Press* 11 Dec. 18-B/3 Improving city neighborhoods are excellent buys—especially rehabilitation areas where urban pioneers have turned the neighborhood around but buildings are still available at reasonable prices. **1967** W. SOYINKA *Kongi's Harvest* 31 All the prostitutes were sent off to a rehabilitation camp. **1978** R. LUDLUM *Holcroft Covenant* xx. 228 They were shocked beyond anything we can imagine when they learned about the 'rehabilitation camps'. Auschwitz, Belsen—it blew their minds. **1944** *Ourselves in Wartime* iii. 41 The Ministry of Labour.. laid its plans for the rehabilitation of injured citizens. Men and women were trained at one of the Ministry of Labour's rehabilitation centres. **1967** R. RENDELL *Wolf to Slaughter* vi. 64 What d'you do..? Start screaming like an addict in a rehabilitation centre? **1977** *Wandsworth Borough News* 16 Sept. 1/5 Government plans to erect a rehabilitation centre for 125 homeless men on the site of the old Battersea General Hospital. **1976** *Laurel* (Montana) *Outlook* 9 June 13/4 Graduate students received 94 master of science degrees, with 46 being in education, 31 in special education, and 15 in rehabilitation counselling. **1956** T. H. RADDALL *Wings* 30 After I got my discharge from the army I took a forestry course at U.N.B., on my rehabilitation grant. **1969** *Jrnl. Amer. Med. Assoc.* 6 Jan. 137 (*heading*) Rehabilitation medicine's challenge for the 1970's. **1971** *Lancet* 27 Nov. 1207/2 A few years ago the University of New York announced that.. they would no longer use the term 'physical medicine' in the context of rehabilitation but would replace it with the term 'rehabilitation medicine'. *Ibid.*, The following.. relates to a World Congress to be held in Sydney, Australia, in August, 1972: 'Rehabilitation Medicine is a special area of medical practice traditionally concerned with the problems of the severely disabled and with the task of restoring them to a place of independence and dignity in society.' **1977** *Rehabilitation* Jan.–Mar. 8/1 With the recent international tendency to use the term 'Rehabilitation Medicine' instead of 'Physical Medicine' and, therefore, bringing in sociological and psychological factors, the pressing need for coordinated post-graduate study became the Council's challenge. **1979** *Internat. Rehabilit. Med.* I. 44/1 The ultimate goal is to establish rehabilitation medicine alongside diagnosis and treatments, as one of the three activities of all practising doctors. **1968** Rehabilitation officer [see REHABILITATE *v.* 3 b]. **1950** *N.Y. Times* 20 Apr. 1/2 President Truman approved.. a bill authorizing an economic rehabilitation programme for the Navajo and Hopi Indian tribes. **1973** *Brit. Med. Jrnl.* 17 Mar. 687/3 (*heading*) Chair of rehabilitation studies. **1974** *Ibid.* 15 June 622/1 Dr. Cairns Aitken, senior lecturer in the department of psychiatry, Edinburgh University, has been appointed to the newly founded chair of rehabilitation studies at that university.

So **†rehaˈbility**. *Obs. rare*$^{-1}$.

1577 FULKE *Answ. True Christian* 19 And so for all other offences, with dispensations, inhibitions, rehabilities, licences, relaxations, commutations, confirmation.

rehabilitative (riːhəˈbɪlɪtətɪv), *a.* [f. REHABILITAT(E *v.* + -IVE.] Of or pertaining to rehabilitation; designed to rehabilitate.

1958 *Times* 8 Oct. 11/3 The rehabilitative process should begin with a man's arrival and should not stop short at the moment of release. **1963** T. & P. MORRIS *Pentonville* vii. 172 Many inmates are full of ideas about how prison could be improved, both as a deterrent and a rehabilitative technique. **1973** *Black Panther* 22 Sept. 5/2 There are no rehabilitative services offered in the Texas prisons. **1979** *Arizona Daily Star* 8 Apr. (Parade Suppl.) 4/1 This is short-term alimony, where the husband pays his former wife a monthly stipend for a limited period, generally two years, or even a lump sum. The term used by lawyers is 'rehabilitative alimony'. The idea is for the ex-wife to take advantage of the alimony period to return to school, to take a brushup course, or to launch a career. **1979** *Internat. Jrnl. Sociol. of Law* VII. 329 She feels that with the turn away from the rehabilitative model, indeterminate sentences and parole, we may inadvertently end up with a less discriminating system.

rehabilitee (ˌriːhəbɪlɪˈtiː). [f. REHABILIT(ATE *v.* + -EE[1].] One who is (being) rehabilitated.

1972 *Rehabilitation* July–Sept. 7 Only in recent years would government seem to have begun to appreciate the importance of social aspects and the quality of life available for the rehabilitee, as opposed to concentrating on industrial aspects. **1978** *Jrnl. R. Soc. Med.* LXXI. 449 Two beds in the Lonsdale Unit were reserved for rehabilitees.

†rehabiˈtation. *Obs. rare.* [RE- 5 a.] The action of re-inhabiting.

(Florio also gives '*Rihabitare*, to rehabite'.)

1611 FLORIO, *Rihabitanza*, a rehabitation. **1633** BP. HALL *Hard Texts, O.T.* lxv. 367 There shall bee a frequent rehabitation of the whole land of Israel.

†reˈhale, *v. Obs.*$^{-1}$ [RE-.] To drag back.

a **1618** SYLVESTER *Du Bartas, Hymn St. Lewis* 193 Horatius.. Re-heartens His: re-haleth from the Foe Fair Victory, ready with them to goe.

re'hallow, *v.* [RE- 5 a.] To hallow again.
*a*1711 KEN *Psyche* Poet. Wks. 1721 IV. 226 Mind was enlightned, Passions tam'd, My Powers rehallow'd, Will inflam'd. **1809** W. TAYLOR in *Monthly Mag.* XXVIII. 52 The lady, at the ceremony of rehallowing the church, filled all the vessels with water. **1814** *Alonzo & Angioline* (Jod.), A thousand kisses warm and sweet Rehallow this sublime retreat. **1855** LYNCH *Rivulet* XLI. x, Then be my heart, my world, Re-hallowed unto Thee.

re'halogenize, *v. Photogr.* [f. RE- 5 b + HALOGEN + -IZE.] *trans.* To convert the metallic silver in a developed image back to a silver halide (with the silver or the image as obj.). So **re'halogenizing** *vbl. sb.*
1940 F. J. MORTIMER *Wall's Dict. Photogr.* (ed. 15) 549 *Rehalogenising*, the re-conversion of the silver image in a finished print or negative into silver chloride, bromide, or iodide. **1969** M. J. LANGFORD *Advanced Photogr.* xi. 235 This bleach 're-halogenises' the silver image—the ferricyanide oxidises the silver which reacts with the bromide and reverts to a silver halide. **1977** J. HEDGECOE *Photographer's Handbk.* 324 *Bleach*, chemical bath capable of rehalogenizing black metallic silver.

Hence **re,halogeni'zation**, the process of rehalogenizing.
1956 *Focal Encycl. Photogr.* 967/1 *Rehalogenization*, conversion of a silver image back into one of silver halide. **1958** *Newnes Compl. Amat. Photogr.* 323 As this process involves rehalogenisation of the silver image it is essential that the print and utensils used are completely free from hypo. **1967** E. CHAMBERS *Photolitho-Offset* iv. 48 An improvement in the dot etching properties of the positives can be effected by tanning the gelatin in proportion to the silver image, resulting in a greater degree of lateral etching without loss of density. This process is known as rehalogenisation, or metallising.

re'hammer, *v.* [RE- 5 a.] To hammer again.
1884 W. H. GREENWOOD *Steel & Iron* xii. 233 The hollow-fire..employed for reheating the stamps for rehammering and rewelding.

re'handle, *v.* [RE- 5 a.] *trans.* To handle again, in various senses of the verb.
1597 BEARD *Theatre God's Judgem.* (1612) 461 Euen as they dealt with others rigorously and by strength of weapons, so shall they be themselues rehandled and dealt withall after the same measure. **1768–74** TUCKER *Lt. Nat.* (1834) II. 675 Sometimes forced to rehandle my premises to fit them for a further application. **1865** *Cornh. Mag.* May 608 Rehandling the old themes of Jocasta, Thyestes, Œdipus, and Agamemnon. **1879** DOWDEN *Southey* iii. 53 Out of a kind of gratitude he rehandled the *Joan* again and again.

Hence **re'handling** *vbl. sb.*
1885 *Pall Mall G.* 28 May 5 We cannot turn up the originals [of these stories]..so we must take the rehandlings. **1896** *Pop. Sci. Monthly* Feb. 562 The author undertook a thorough rehandling of the work.

re'hang, *v.* [RE- 5 a.] *trans.* To hang again.
1813 ELMES *Dilapidations* (1829) App. 59 Ease and re-hang the sashes, and re-instate the broken glass. **1849** THACKERAY *Pendennis* xxxvii, He hung and re-hung the pictures. **1892** *Pall Mall G.* 6 July 1/2 The Dowdeswells have rehung their gallery partly with pictures of the French school.

re'harden, *v.* [RE- 5 a.]
1. *trans.* To make hard again.
1605 SYLVESTER *Du Bartas* II. iii. III. *Lawe* 473 The King's [Pharaoh's] repentance endeth with his pain. Hee is re-hardned. **1677** MOXON *Mech. Exerc.* No. I. 11 You must.. harden the point of it.., because the heat of the Iron will soften it fast enough,..but then you must re-harden it. **1678** HOBBES *Decam.* Wks. 1845 VII. 131, I conceive now how a body which having [*sic*] been hard and softened again, may be rehardened. **1843** HOLTZAPFFEL *Turning* I. 246 The knife edges..being found too soft..were re-hardened.
2. *intr.* To grow hard again.
1829 J. L. KNAPP *Jrnl. Nat.* 7 That lime rehardens after being made soft, as in mortar, is owing to [etc.].

Hence **re'hardening** *vbl. sb.*
1675 WOODHEAD, etc. *Paraph. St. Paul* 35 That re-hardening still of Pharaoh's heart.

†**re'harm**, *v. Obs. rare*$^{-1}$. [RE-.] *intr.* To do harm in return, to retaliate.
1592 WYRLEY *Armorie, Ld. Chandos* 107 Rare is the vertue hurt not to reharme, Great fortitude offences to remit.

re'harmonize, *v.* [RE- 5 a.] *trans.* To bring again into harmony. Hence **re'harmonizing** *vbl. sb.*
*a*1711 KEN *Hymns Festiv.* Poet. Wks. 1721 I. 193 But Great God-Man Nature re-harmoniz'd, And the lost Grace of Hymning God repriz'd. **1855** BAILEY *Mystic*, etc. 123 The angels would not..From holiest truths eliminate the false, And thus with God's, man's mind re-harmonize. **1855** PUSEY *Doctr. Real Presence* Note Q 215 The re-harmonizing of his being, the restoration of that state in which he was in harmony with God and with himself.
b. *Mus.* (See HARMONIZE *v.* 4.)
1883 *Ch. Praise* Pref. 11 Some tunes have been entirely re-harmonized by him.

re'harness, *v.* [RE- 5 a.] To harness again.
1778 [W. MARSHALL] *Minutes Agric.* 10 Nov. an. 1775, He was three months before he could be re-harnessed. **1853** KANE *Grinnell Exp.* I. (1856) 486 They reharnessed the dogs, and turned to the west.

rehash ('riːhæʃ, riː'hæʃ), *sb.* [f. RE- 5 a + HASH *sb.*[1] 2.] A mere restatement in different words of opinions previously expressed; something served up afresh under a different form or name.
1849 LEWIS *Lett.* (1870) 202 It is merely a re-hash of his old opinions, seasoned with some new abuse of the Colonial Office. **1881** *Gard. Chron.* XVI. 779 That is largely a rehash of what has been oft told in the gardening papers. **1883** *Pall Mall G.* 2 Oct. 3/1 To-day this rehash of the stale commonplaces of last recess is simply unreadable.

re'hash, *v.* [RE- 5 a.] **1.** *trans.* To put into a new form without real change or improvement in the matter; to restate (old ideas or opinions) in new language.
*c*1822 MAGINN *Byron's Werner* II. i. 148 *note*, Ulric is.. the Giaour,..rehashed and served up as a Bohemian. **1884** *Manch. Exam.* 21 May 5/1 All they did was to rehash the old exploded arguments.
2. Chiefly *U.S.* To consider, mull over, discuss (an idea, performance, etc.) afterwards.
1965 MRS. L. B. JOHNSON *White House Diary* 14 Dec. (1970) 340 Our houseguests..were all gathered around Lyndon rehashing the events of the evening. **1974** *Los Angeles Times* 13 Oct. III. 9/1 The Dodgers were anything but downtrodden as they rehashed the game. **1977** *Times* 31 Jan. 48/3 If he meets someone he knows after a session he may stop him on the street to rehash it.

Hence **re'hashed** *ppl. a.*
1827 *Q. Rev.* XXXVI. 127 Great deal of that sort of nonsense—the re-hashed 'grande pensée' of the addle-headed consul of Teflis.

†**re'hator.** *Sc. Obs. rare.* **re-**, **rahatour.** A term of abuse, of obscure origin and meaning. (Cf. REHETOUR.)
1508 DUNBAR *Flyting w. Kennedie* 244 Baird rehator, theif of natour. **1508** KENNEDIE *Flyting w. Dunbar* 401 Rawmowit ribald, renegate rehatour. **1513** DOUGLAS *Æneis* XIII. vi. 117 Now lat that ilk rahatour wend in hy The blak hellis biggyngis to vissy.

†**re'have**, *v. Obs.* [RE- 5 a, after med.L. *rehabēre*, or F. *ravoir*.] *trans.* To regain, to get again. Hence †**re'having** *vbl. sb.*
1472 *Paston Lett.* III. 60, I am in a greet agonye howe is best ffor me to sue to hym ffor rehavyng off my place. **1541–2** *Act 33 Hen. VIII* in Bolton *Stat. Irel.* (1621) 228 Such lessees so rehaving their leases [etc.]. *a*1625 SIR H. FINCH *Law* (1636) 210 So as vpon an appeale the partie shall re-haue them. *c*1640 J. SMYTH *Lives Berkeleys* (1883) I. 91,2000 markes which hee owes the Kinge for the rehaveinge of his Castle and landes. **1658** EARL MONM. tr. *Paruta's Wars Cyprus* 81 By re-having the Kingdom of Cyprus, vpon payment of..great Tribute.

†**re'hayte**, *v.*[1] *Obs. rare*$^{-1}$. (Of obscure origin and meaning; perh. a var. of REHETE *v.*[2])
1526 SKELTON *Magnyf.* 1677 Ye knowe wel, with hym I can not be content..I wyll haue hym rehayted and dyspysed.

†**rehayte**, *v.*[2] *Obs. rare.* Also **-heyte.** [Of obscure origin.] To behave noisily or riotously.
1526 in *Househ. Ord.* (1790) 153 Soe that no man doe rehayte, nor use himselfe otherwise in the chamber than to that place doth accord. *a*1530 HEYWOOD *Weather* 475 (Brandl), What, ye come in reuelynge and reheytynge Euyn as a knaue myght go to a beare beytynge.

rehayte, variant of REHETE *v.*[1] *Obs.*

re'hear (riː-), *v.* [RE- 5 a.]
1. *trans.* To hear again in a court of law or in a judicial manner.
1686, 1702–3 [see REHEARING *vbl. sb.*]. **1756** TOLDERVY *Hist. 2 Orphans* IV. 102 The magistrate..reheard the affair. **1781** S. PETERS *Hist. Connecticut* 145 The first court suspends from the communion; the second re-hears the evidence, and confirms or sets aside the suspension. **1818** CRUISE *Digest* (ed. 2) II. 170 The cause was reheard; and Lord Hardwicke..changed his opinion. **1868** J. H. BLUNT *Ref. Ch. Eng.* I. 261 Delegates named by the Crown to re-hear the cause.
2. To hear (a sound) again.
1799 F. BURNEY *Jrnls. & Lett.* (1973) IV. 297 He has taken the amazing trouble & toil of copying the whole, from the pleasure the interview gave him! though he may always re-hear it *de vive voix*! **1815** HOBHOUSE *Substance Lett.* (1816) II. 47 M. Regnault went on, but, coming to ask 'in whose name shall our negotiators speak?' re-heard the same voices reply, 'in the name of the nation'. **1947** *Observer* 28 Dec. 2/5, I long to rehear such great contrapuntal machines as the *Quoniam* and *Amen* choruses.

re'hearing (riː-), *vbl. sb.* [-ING[1].] A second or subsequent hearing, esp. of a cause or appeal.
1686 EVELYN *Diary* 12 Feb., My greate cause was heard by my Lord Chancellor, who granted me a re-hearing. **1702–3** ATTERBURY *Let.* Misc. Wks. 1739 I. 163 We.. renewed our application for a re-hearing of the matter. **1768** BLACKSTONE *Comm.* III. 391 A new trial is a rehearing of the cause before another jury, but with as little prejudice to either party, as if it had never been heard before. **1831** SCOTT *Abbot* Introd., An author may be justified in using with address, such selection of subject or title as is most likely to procure a re-hearing. **1869** *Athenæum* 27 Mar. 445/3 Each rehearing of 'The Woman of Samaria' deepens our conviction of its high merits. **1885** *Law Times* LXXIX. 156/2 The daughter took out a summons for a rehearing.

rehearsal (rɪ'hɜːsəl). Forms: 4–5 **rehersayle**, **-sail(l(e**, 5 **-sayll**, **-sale**, 5–7 **-sal(l**, 5 **-cel**, 6 **-sell**, **-ceall**, 6– **rehearsal**, (6–7 **-sall**). [f. REHEARSE *v.* + -AL[1].]
1. a. The act of rehearsing; a recounting or recital; a repetition of words or statements; recitation (very common *c* 1430–1650).
*c*1386 CHAUCER *Can. Yeom. Prol. & T.* 299 Forgat I to maken rehersaille Of watres corosif, and of lymaille. *c*1430 LYDG. *Min. Poems* (Percy Soc.) 181 Whilom ther was in a smal village, As myn autor makethe rehersayle [etc.]. *c*1449 PECOCK *Repr.* I. vii. 36 Holi Scripture makith rehercel of many treuthis. **1494** FABYAN *Chron.* I. xxiii. 18 For the more party they..make but a short rehersayll of these .v. Kyngs. **1525** LD. BERNERS *Froiss.* II. ccxxviii. [ccxxiv.] 711 The erle of Derby spake certayne wordes.., wenynge that they shulde neuer haue ben called to rehersall. **1545** BRINKLOW *Compl.* xxv. (1874) 73 A brefe rehersal, conteynyng the somme of all that is hetherto spoken. **1560** DAUS tr. *Sleidane's Comm.* 18 b, The rehersall of every sinne particularly is not necessary. **1599** *Warn. Faire Wom.* I. 682, I can make rehearsal of the words Did pass betwixt you, if I were disposed. **1637** T. MORTON *New Eng. Canaan* (1883) 199 Now that I have made a rehearsall of the birds..I will give you a description of the beasts. **1697** DRYDEN *Virgil, Life* (1721) I. 44 This Poem being now in greatforwardness, Cæsar..would needs be entertained with the rehearsal of some part of it. **1708** DODWELL in Hearne *Collect.* 23 Nov. (O.H.S.) II. 152 His Rehearsals are full of excellent reasoning as well as wit. **1839** YEOWELL *Anc. Brit. Ch.* iii. (1847) 24 His rehearsals of their sayings, and of their accounts of the discourses and miracles of the Lord. **1842** SHERIDAN KNOWLES *Rose of Arragon* II. i, Many..made it a pretext for rehearsal of old grievances. **1870** in Anderson *Missions Amer. Bd.* II. xxiii. 192 The rehearsal of the tragedy of Captain Cook's death.
attrib. **1592** GREENE *Conny Catch.* II. 15 West-ward they goe, and there solemnly make a rehearsall sermon at tiborne. **1709** STRYPE *Ann. Ref.* I. xliii. 432 He made the Rehersal Sermons at Paul's Cross; repeating *Memoriter* the Spital Sermons preached at Easter.
(*b*) In *Psychol.*, the intentional repetition (mentally or verbally) of information in order to keep it temporarily in the memory.
1935 *Amer. Jrnl. Psychol.* XLVII. 66 Reminiscence..has not yet been demonstrated to occur independently of review, either intentional rehearsal or casual revival, during the interval between the two tests of retention. **1951** S. S. STEVENS *Handbk. Exper. Psychol.* xvii. 654/1 Color naming has commonly been used during the rest interval in an attempt to reduce rehearsal. **1960** O. H. MOWRER *Learning Theory & Behavior* x. 365 A telephone number will be 'remembered', without rehearsal, for a short time after it is seen in a directory (or heard spoken), but will then usually be lost quite completely. **1976** [see REHEARSE *v.* 1 d]. **1979** W. A. WICKELGREN *Cognitive Psychol.* viii. 235 The classification of memory into learning, storage, and retrieval leaves the cognitive process of rehearsal somewhat in limbo.
†**b.** A recital in a legal document. *Obs. rare.*
1628 COKE *On Litt.* 19 b, The rehearsall or preamble of a statute is to be taken for truth. **1715** M. DAVIES *Athen. Brit.* I. 308 What opinion my Lord Coke was of, of Divines interfering with Common-Law's rehearsals, is not so certain.
2. a. The practising of a play or musical composition preparatory to performing it in public; a private meeting of actors or performers held for this purpose. Also, the act of practising any ceremony, e.g. a wedding or a state occasion.
1579–80 in Cunningham *Revels Acc.* (1842) 159 Rehersinge of dyvers plaies..and their sondry Rehersells. **1590** SHAKS. *Mids. N.* III. i. 3 Here's a maruailous conuenient place for our rehearsall. **1671** VILLIERS (Dk. Buckhm.) *Rehearsal* II. i, This morning is its last Rehearsal, in their habits, and all that, as it is to be acted. **1728** GAY in *Swift's Lett.* (1766) II. 95 The second part of the *Beggar's Opera*..was almost ready for rehearsal. **1759** JOHNSON *Idler* No. 60 ¶11 By degrees he was admitted to rehearsals. **1811** BUSBY *Dict. Mus.* (ed. 3) s.v., Rehearsals, especially of new music, are indispensably necessary. **1846** DICKENS *Lett.* (1880) I. 165 We have a rehearsal with scenery and band. **1886** MABEL COLLINS *Prettiest Woman* vii, I will call rehearsal for the next day. **1977** *Times* 24 Mar. 2 (*heading*) Ulster trip by Princess becomes rehearsal for Queen's visit.
attrib. **1863** GEO. ELIOT *Romola* lvii, Could he not strip himself of the past, as of rehearsal clothing,..to robe himself for the real scene? **1953** RODGERS & PEARCE *Altar Bound* 45 The rehearsal dinner takes place immediately before or after the rehearsal, and..is given by either the parents of the bride or groom. **1963** A. VANDERBILT *New Compl. Bk. Etiquette* ix. 93 It is becoming more and more popular for the wedding rehearsal to be held in the late afternoon the day before the wedding, followed by a rehearsal dinner, which may be scheduled for six-thirty or seven o'clock. In some sections of the country, mainly the South and Midwest, it is customary for the groom's parents to give the rehearsal dinner.
b. *in rehearsal*, in process of being rehearsed.
1709 STEELE *Tatler* No. 1 ¶6 The Town is at present in very great Expectation of seeing a Comedy now in Rehearsal. **1764** FOOTE *Patron* II. Wks. 1799 I. 349 The piece has long been in rehearsal at Drury-lane playhouse. **1860** F. W. ROBINSON *Grandm. Money* VI. iv, The opera was put in rehearsal, and the most trying time to dramatic or operatic authors succeeded.
3. *attrib.*, as ***rehearsal break***, ***complex***, ***hall***, ***pianist***, ***room***; **rehearsal band**, a band that meets to practise jazz, dance music, etc.; **rehearsal dinner** *U.S.*, a dinner held after a wedding rehearsal (usually in the evening before the wedding); **rehearsal script** (see quot.).
1969 *Down Beat* 17 Apr. 19/3 There have been any number of rehearsal bands around New York in the past 10 years. **1970** *New Yorker* 23 May 78/2 The so-called 'rehearsal' bands of Thad Jones—Mel Lewis, Clark Terry, [etc.]. **1957** *Sentinel* (Milwaukee) 14 Nov. II. 6/3 'That six minutes is beginning to look like an awful long time,' shivered Junie, chewing nonchalantly on a coffee cup during a rehearsal break. **1977** *West Briton* 25 Aug. 10/2 The dawning of a new and promising era for Redruth Amateur Operatic Society... The society took over its new rehearsal complex at Plain-an-Gwarry. **1953, 1963** Rehearsal dinner [see sense 2 a above]. **1974** *State* (Columbia, S. Carolina) 3 & 4 Mar. G8/6 The groom gifts his attendants at the

rehearsal dinner or bachelor dinner. **1960** 'E. McBain' *Give Boys Great Big Hand* x. 107 Unfurnished rehearsal halls and the cubbyhole offices of music publishers. **1976** *Listener* 29 July 121/2 The last 17 hopefuls..gather together in the rehearsal hall. **1977** S. Brett *Star Trap* i. 11 There was a guy..who was rehearsal pianist for the show. **1959** M. Summerton *Small Wilderness* i. 18 Reading a part in a rehearsal room. **1979** *Jrnl. R. Soc. Arts* CXXVII. 500/1 The school housed an excellent theatre, a number of rehearsal rooms, a swimming pool, [etc.]. **1960** Rehearsal script [see *master-scene* s.v. master *sb.*[1] 29].

†**re'hearse**, *sb. Obs.* Forms: 4–6 reherse, 5–6 *Sc.* rehers(s, 5 *Sc.* raherss, -hress, 6 rehears, *Sc.* -heirs, 6–7 rehearse. [f. the vb.]

1. = rehearsal 1. (Chiefly *Sc.*)

c **1375** *Sc. Leg. Saints* xviii. (*Mary Egypt*) 137 þai..passyt, singand, with reherse of þe todyr nocturne þe firste verse. **1423** Jas. I *Kingis Q.* cxxvii, I haue wele herd, and vnderstond, Be thy reherse, the matere of thy gref. *c* **1470** Henry *Wallace* viii. 95 With out raherss off actioun in that tid. *Ibid.* xi. 1134 Litill reherss is our mekill off cair. **1535** Stewart *Cron. Scot.* III. 251 Quhen this rehers befoir the paip wes maid. **1585** T. Washington tr. *Nicholay's Voy.* i. vii. 7 A briefe rehearse of the foundation, force, and situation of the citie of Alger. **1597** Skene *De Verb. Sign.* s.v. *Recordum*, The rehearse, reporte, or testification of the execution of the summondes.

2. = rehearsal 2.

1490 *Coventry Acc.* in Sharp *Diss. Cov. Myst.* (1825) 15 This is the expens of the furste reherse of our players in ester weke. **1584** *Ibid.* 64 Payd ffor ffyve Reherses..v[s].

rehearse (rɪ'hɜːs), *v.* Forms: 4–6 reherce, (5 -cy), rehers, (5–6 *Sc.* rahers), 4–7 reherse, (5 rey-); 6 *Sc.* reheirs, -heirce; 6 reehearce, 6– rehearse. [a. OF. *rehercer*, *-cier* (late AF. *rehearser*), app. f. *re-* re- + *hercer*, *herser* to harrow: see herse *sb.*]

1. a. *trans.* To recite or repeat aloud in a formal manner; to say over, or read aloud, from beginning to end.

c **1375** *Lay Folks Mass Bk.* (MS. B) 152 þi pater noster reherce alwaie, til deken or prest þo gospel rede. *c* **1400** in *Rule St. Benet* 143 þe couent..sall reherce þe same again thrise, and 'Gloria patri'. **1463** *Bury Wills* (Camden) 18 After the gospel to..reherse John Barettys name opynly, saying *De profundis* for me. **1529** More *Dyaloge* i. Wks. 172/1 If we knew them in such wise..as we coulde rehearce them on oure fingers endes. **1590** Shaks. *Mids. N.* v. ii. 404 First, rehearse this song by roate, To each word a warbling note. **1612** Brinsley *Pos. Parts* (1669) 37 Rehearse them Actively and Passively together. **1635** F. White *Sabbath* (ed. 2) 9 Often rehearsing the Lord's-Prayer. **1732** Neal *Hist. Purit.* I. 255 He could readily rehearse in the Greek language all St. Paul's Epistles to the Romans and Galatians. **1781** Cowper *Conversat.* 7, Words learned by rote a parrot may rehearse. **1784** —— *Task* vi. 480 An ancient..tale, By one of sound intelligence rehearsed. **1824** L. Murray *Eng. Gram.* (ed. 5) I. 391 The same composition may be rehearsed in a quicker or a slower time. **1872** Howells *Wedd. Journ.* (1892) 102 Personal histories..which had been rehearsing to those that sat next the narrators.

b. To repeat, say over again (something previously said or heard).

1340 *Ayenb.* 220 þerof anoþre time we habbeþ yspeke..an þeruore hit ne behoueþ naȝt to reherci. *c* **1386** Chaucer *Prol.* 729 Who so shall telle a tale after a man, He moste reherse, as neigh as euer he can, Everich word, if it be in his charge. **1411** *Rolls of Parlt.* III. 650/2 The forsaid Robert schal reherce the wordes that he said to oure forsaide liege Lord. *c* **1489** Caxton *Sonnes of Aymon* x. 265 The proverbe may well be reherced for a trouth, that sayth, Often happeth evill for a good torne. **1535** Coverdale *Ecclus.* xlii. 1 Rehearse not a thinge twyse, and disclose not the wordes, that thou hast herde in secrete. **1577** Hanmer *Anc. Eccl. Hist.* (1619) 28 In the Actes of the Apostles, whence no doubt this is rehearsed. **1634** Sir T. Herbert *Trav.* 110 When these words were rehearsed to the Generall, he was mad with anger. *a* **1704** T. Brown *Dk. of Ormond's Recovery* Wks. 1730 I. 48 The clifts and hills my echo'd thoughts rehearse. **1822** B. Cornwall *Poems, To the singer Pasta*, The critic brings thee praise, which all rehearse. **1875** Jowett *Plato* (ed. 2) IV. 159 Cephalus rehearses a dialogue which is supposed to have been narrated..by Antiphon.

†**c.** To say, utter, speak. *Obs.*

1362 Langl. *P. Pl.* A. iv. 134 Whon Resun to þis Reynkes Rehersede þeose wordes [etc.]. *c* **1400** *Rule St. Benet* 887 On þe last day Sal he reherce & sai vs til: 'þus did þou, & I held me stil'. **1513** Douglas *Æneis* i. ix. 93 Rehersing this, convoyis sche Eneas Towart the place. **1550** J. Coke *Eng. & Fr. Heralds* §151 (1877) 100 Yf you have any more to saye, reherse it, and I voll answere you. **1567** *Gude & Godlie B.* (S.T.S.) 84 Thir wordis to hir he did reheirs, Haill Marie full of grace, The Lord God is with the.

d. *Psychol.* To repeat, either mentally or orally (what it is desired to keep temporarily in the memory).

1917 *Arch. Psychol.* xl. 103 Frequent reviews..throw into relief the portions [of memorised material] that are hazy, inexact and confused..because they fix more clearly in mind the material that is rehearsed. **1964** *Jrnl. Exper. Psychol.* LXVIII. 414/2 The present experiment is designed to investigate the consequences for short-term memory of instructing Ss to rehearse a sequence of digits in groups of one, two, three, four, and five during presentation. **1979** W. A. Wickelgren *Cognitive Psychol.* iii. 84 Time yourself reciting the alphabet verbally. Then time yourself while you go through the alphabet again, this time imaging each letter as if it were projected on a screen. It will take you about three times as long..as it did to rehearse each letter verbally.

2. a. To give an account of; to relate, narrate, recount, describe at length. Now *rare.*

13.. *Seuyn Sag.* (W.) 1147 The tresoun he gan hem alle reherse. *a* **1400–50** *Alexander* 21, I sall rehers..A remnant of his rialte. **1435** *Indenture Fotheringhey* in Dugdale *Monast.* (1846) VI. 1415/1 When alle the werk abof written, rehersyd and devised is fully fynisht. **1483** Caxton *Gold. Leg.* 140b/2 First we shal reherce here the birthe and begynnyng of Iudas. *a* **1533** Ld. Berners *Huon* xlvi. 154 Thou hast so myche to suffer, that therein is none humayne tonge can reherse it. **1577** Vautrouillier *Lutheron Ep. Gal.* 2 There is yet an other righteousnes,..the which we must diligently discerne from the other afore rehearsed. **1620** J. Wilkinson *Coroners & Sherifes* 2 The cause of his not attendance or insufficiencie must be rehearsed. **1712** *Pol. Ballads* (1860) II. 122 But now your last and blackest deed What mortal can rehearse? **1781** Cowper *Table T.* 178 Could you..rehearse The mighty plan, oracular, in verse. **1851** Longf. *Gold. Leg.* iii. *Nativity*, First of all we shall rehearse..The Nativity of our Lord.

†**b.** To relate, state, declare, *how, that, what*, etc. *Obs.*

1362 Langl. *P. Pl.* A. viii. 177 What [*B* how] þou dudest day bi day þe Doom þe wol rehersen. *Ibid.* 186 þat..Dowel reherce þat..we duden as he us hiȝte. *c* **1420** Lydg. *Assembly of Gods* 83, I shall reherse what thys creature Eolus hath doon to me. *c* **1450** *St. Cuthbert* (Surtees) 1559 Bede reherce[s] þat som boke sayes [etc.]. **1477** Norton *Ord. Alch.* iii. in Ashm. (1652) 42 Chaucer reherseth how Titanos is the same. **1539** Bible (Great) *Mark* iv. 15 Some be rehearsed to be by the way side. **1585** T. Washington tr. *Nicholay's Voy.* i. xv. 15b, There was openly rehearsed, how that..the Turkes army hadd taken..the castle. **1633** G. Herbert *Temple, Peace* vi, They that taste it do rehearse, That vertue lies therein.

c. With omission of direct object, usually after *as.*

13.. *K. Alis.* 1664 Herde ye havith, Y wol yow reherce, How messangeris comen from Perce. **1399** Langl. *Rich. Redeles* iii. 315 For, as reson and rith rehersid to me ones [etc.]. *c* **1410** Hoccleve *Mother of God* 125 Right in this wyse, as I reherce can. *c* **1470** Henry *Wallace* v. 124 I bott rahers as my autour will say. **1535** Lyndesay *Satyre* 1696 As efterward, perchance, rehears I sall. **1567** *Gude & Godlie B.* (S.T.S.) 70 Lufe is fulfilling of the Law, as Paull reheirsis in his writ. **1781** Cowper *Charity* 505 Their zeal begotten, as their works rehearse, By lean despair.

3. a. To recount in order; to name or mention one after another; to enumerate, reckon up, †number.

1362 Langl. *P. Pl.* A. i. 22 Heore nomes bed neodful, and nempnen hem I þenke, Bi Rule and bi Resun Rehersen hem her-aftur. **1387** Trevisa *Higden* (Rolls) I. 21 Here I write and reherse þe auctours names of þe whiche þis cronycle is ..i-gadered. *c* **1420** Lydg. *Assembly of Gods* 1518 Whos names reherse I wyll, as I can Bryng theym to mynde in ordre. **1470–85** Malory *Arthur* i. viii. 45 Yrland and Scotland and moo reames than I will now reherce. **1532** Elyot in *Gov.* (1883) I. *Life* 77, I will reherce some other townes as they laye in oure waye. *c* **1580** Sidney *Ps.* xxii. xi, My bones might be rehearsed. **1612** Brinsley *Pos. Parts* (1669) p. ii, I will first rehearse all the seven marks which Socrates giveth. **16..** in Fuller *Ch. Hist.* iii. (1655) 80 In all cases afore rehearsed, the Spiritual Judg shall have power [etc.]. **1738** Gray *Propertius* iii. 1 You ask, why thus my Loves I still rehearse. **1791** Cowper *Iliad* ii. 598, I will rehearse the captains and their fleets. **1864** Pusey *Lect. Daniel* (1876) 320 Rehearsing exclusively the mercies of God to Israel.

†**b.** To mention, make mention of (a person or thing); to cite, quote. *Obs.*

a **1400–50** *Alexander* 329 Noȝt as a prophet ne a prest I prays sall þi selfe, Bot rehers þe as hieȝe gode. *c* **1402** Lydg. *Compl. Bl. Knt.* 99 But this welle, that I here reherce, So hoolsom was that it wolde aswage Bollen hertes. **1471** *Will of T. Clement*, I woll be a brother of the Gray freres and be reherced by name. **1549** Coverdale, etc. *Erasm. Par. 2 Cor.* 55 For this rehearse I the ready mindes of the Macedonians. **1562** Turner *Herbal* ii. 101b, As Plini whome I haue aboue rehersed, teacheth there ryght playnly. **1578** [see rehearsed *ppl. a.*].

†**4.** *intr.* To give an account, or make mention, *of* something. *Obs. rare.*

1483 Caxton *G. de la Tour* E viij b, Of the whiche yf I wold I should reherce you of many of them. *c* **1500** *Lancelot* 2671 Of his manhed war merwell to rahers. **1549** *Compl. Scot.* Ded. 7 The historigraphours rehersis of ane pure man of perse.

5. a. *trans.* To go through or practise (a play, scene, part, etc.) in private, in preparation for a more formal or public performance.

1579–80 [see rehearsal 2]. **1590** Shaks. *Mids. N.* iii. i. 75 Sit downe..and rehearse your parts. *Ibid.* iii. ii. 11 A crew of patches..Were met together to rehearse a Play, Intended for great Theseus nuptiall day. **1728** Gay in *Swift's Lett.* (1766) II. 95 Rich received the duke of Grafton's commands not to rehearse any new play whatsoever, till his grace hath seen it. **1765** Goldsm. *Ess.* vi. Wks. (Globe) 304/2, I..studied the character, which was to be rehearsed the next day. **1820** Shelley *Œd. Tyr.* ii. ii. 72, I have rehearsed the entire scene, With an ox-bladder and some ditch-water. **1865** J. Hatton *Bitter Sweets* xxxii, Let us rehearse a waltz.

fig. **1834** L. Ritchie *Wand. by Seine* 83 The habit of rehearsing virtues in imagination leads us insensibly to practise them in reality.

b. To exercise, train, or make proficient by rehearsal.

1768 [W. Donaldson] *Life Sir B. Sapskull* I. ii. 13 To prepare himself for the change, he had rehears'd his servants in the alteration. **1795** S. Rogers *Words Mrs. Siddons* 58 And, when her shattered nerves forbid to roam, In very spleen—rehearse the girls at home. **1859** Dickens *T. Two Cities* iii. xii, A wood-sawyer..has been rehearsed by Madame Defarge as to his having seen Her..making signs and signals to prisoners. **1898** *Daily News* 12 Mar. 6/3 Dickens rehearsed her in 'Bailey'.

6. To perform, practise, as in rehearsing. *rare.*

1700 Dryden *Cock & Fox* 337 Sometimes we but rehearse a former Play, The Night restores our Actions done by Day. **1825** Coleridge *Aids Refl.* (1848) I. 307 The poor ignorant multitude..rehearsed all the outrages that were acted in our own times by the Parisian populace. **1856** Kane *Arct. Expl.* I. xvii. 212 So he kept on rehearsing his limited solfeggio..and crying and talking by turns.

7. *intr.* To recite; to engage in rehearsal.

1693 C. Dryden in *Dryden's Juvenal* vii. 107 All Rome is pleas'd, when Statius will rehearse, And longing Crowds expect the promis'd Verse. **1739** Cibber *Apol.* (1756) I. 150 When it came to my turn to rehearse, while others read their parts from their books, I had put mine in my pocket. **1765** Goldsm. *Ess.* vi. Wks. (Globe) 304/2 We got together, in order to rehearse. *Ibid.* 305/1, I rehearsed before them. **1819** Shelley *Peter Bell 3rd* vii. xi, Whether he talked, wrote, or rehearsed, Still with his dulness was he cursed. **1886** Mabel Collins *Prettiest Woman* viii, She was perpetually rehearsing to him. **1951** S. S. Stevens *Handbk. Exper. Psychol.* xvii. 654/1, 84 per cent of her younger subjects and 70 per cent of the older ones reported that they had rehearsed in the interval between learning and recall. **1976** G. R. & E. F. Loftus *Human Memory* iv. 56 Rehearsal can do two things: it can keep the information in short-term store for as long as we continue rehearsing, and it can also act as a mechanism by which information is transferred from short-term to long-term store.

Hence **re'hearsed** *ppl. a.*, †(*a*) (also with *afore*) foresaid, afore-mentioned; (*b*) that has been practised beforehand.

1526 *Pilgr. Perf.* (W. de W. 1531) 148b, The trouble and noyse of these rehersed people is so great. **1544** *Exhort. vnto Prayer* A viij, Let vs eschewe in our prayers al the afore rehersed vyces. **1578** Banister *Hist. Man* i. 26 The Cannell bones fastened to the rehearsed Processe named Acromion. **1871** L. Lockhart *Fair to See* I. vi. 167 He turned to confront them, on their entrance, with a carefully rehearsed mien.

rehearser (rɪ'hɜːsə(r)). [f. prec. + -er[1].]

1. One who rehearses, a reciter.

1530 Palsgr. 261/2 Reherser, *recitevr.* **1611** Florio, *Ripitore*, a repeater or relater and rehearser of a matter. **1672** [H. Stubbe] *Rosemary & Bayes* 6 This Rehearser seems of another opinion. **1708** Dodwell in Hearne *Collect.* 23 Nov. (O.H.S.) II. 152 Mr. Rehearser came from the Bath... His Rehearsals are full of excellent reasoning as well as wit. **1775** Johnson *West. Isl.* 261 Nor was much credit due to such rehearsers, who might obtrude fictitious pedigrees.

2. One who conducts rehearsals.

1901 *Scribner's Mag.* XXIX. 462/1 He was not a severe rehearser, as far as long hours went.

rehearsing (rɪ'hɜːsɪŋ), *vbl. sb.* [f. as prec. + -ing[1].] Rehearsal, recital.

a **1300** *Cursor M.* 19882 Saint ambros sais þat we sai thre Rehercing quen child sal houen be. *c* **1385** Chaucer *L.G.W.* Prol. 24 Othere sundery thyngis Of whiche I may nat make rehersyngys. **1388** Purvey *Prol. Bible* iii. ¶5 The fyfthe book..is a rehersyng and confermyng of al the lawe biforegoyng. *c* **1440** *Promp. Parv.* 427/2 Rehersynge, *recitacio.* **1535** Coverdale *1 Chron.* (heading), A rehearsynge of the generacions. *a* **1652** J. Smith *Sel. Disc.* vi. 238 It was not necessary in the rehearsing of every particularity to reiterate that it was in a prophetical vision. **1660** Boyle *New Exp. Phys. Mech.* xliii. 392 As long as was requisite for the rehearsing of a Pater Noster. **1820** Scott *Monast.* xxxv, 'Ill hearing makes ill rehearsing', said the landlady.

re'hearten, *v.* [re- 5 a.] *trans.* To inspire with fresh courage or confidence.

1611 Florio, *Rinfrancare*,..to re-incourage or reharten. *a* **1618** Sylvester *Du Bartas, Hymn St. Lewis* 193 Horatius ..Re-heartens His; re-haleth from the Foe Fair Victory, ready with them to goe. **1883** J. H. Barrows *Serm.* in *Chicago Advance* 5 July, The little company of Christians.. were reheartened by the arrivals from Fort Brady.

re'heat, *v.* [re- 5 a.] *trans.* To heat again. Hence **re'heated** *ppl. a.*; *spec.* in *Aeronaut.*, equipped with or augmented by afterburning. Cf. reheat *sb.* 1 b.

1727 [see reheating *vbl. sb.*]. **1839** Ure *Dict. Arts* 573 In making bottles we should..reheat them as seldom as may be absolutely necessary. **1884** W. H. Greenwood *Steel & Iron* xvi. 357 They are now only very rarely employed for reheating steel ingots. **1886** *Century Mag.* Oct. 941 Our breakfast of reheated coffee and stale bread. **1961** F. K. Mason *Hawker Aircraft since 1920* 74 Work started on a development using a fifty degree swept wing and a re-heated Avon of greatly increased power. **1976** *Farnborough International Exhibition* (Official Programme) 43/1 With a reheated take-off thrust of 38,000 lbs., this engine entered airline service in Concorde.

reheat ('riːhiːt), *sb.* [f. the vb.] **1. a.** The action or an instance of reheating; *spec.* artificial or spontaneous heating of the working fluid in a turbine taking place between stages. Also *attrib.*

1913 [see *reheat factor* below]. **1918** *Engineering* 6 Sept. 245/1 The case of a turbine consisting of two equal stages which, in order to avoid complications due to 'reheat', will be assumed to be operated by water. **1938** *Van Nostrand's Sci. Encycl.* 950/1 Many industrial processes in which heat plays a part, employ reheating, sometimes to the extent of several 'reheats'. **1953** Jennings & Rogers *Gas Turbine Analysis & Practice* iii. 104 One of the factors contributing to this lower efficiency is the..deleterious effect of reheat in the compressor. **1959** *Motor* 27 May 562/3 The resultant gases pass through the high-speed turbine, then a second, 're-heat' combustion chamber followed by the power turbine. **1965** *Economist* 17 Apr. 326/1 The main items needed..are another reheat furnace for the slabbing mill and a cold reduction line. **1966** *McGraw-Hill Encycl. Sci. & Technol.* XI. 425/2 Under suitable conditions of initially high steam pressure and superheat, one or two stages of reheat can be advantageously employed to improve thermodynamic efficiency of the cycle. **1975** J. B. Woodward *Marine Gas Turbines* ii. 44 The reheat step consists of a constant-pressure heating interposed between two expansion processes.

b. *Aeronaut.* = after-burning *vbl. sb.* 2. Also, an afterburner.

1949 [see AFTER-BURNING *vbl. sb.* 2]. **1950** *Engineering* 6 Oct. 295/1 The performance of a jet engine may be changed by 'reheat' i.e., the burning of additional fuel with residual oxygen remaining in the combustion gases after they have passed through the turbine. **1957** *Ann. Reg. 1956* I. 14 The hero of the occasion was Mr. L. P. Twiss flying a Fairey Delta 2 research aircraft, powered by a Rolls Royce Avon turbo-jet fitted with reheat. **1959** *Spectator* 4 Sept. 295/1 A fighter making a 700 mile-an-hour run a few feet from the spectators, with re-heat ablaze, used to be a grand spectacle. **1972** D. HART-DAVIS *Spider in Morning* ii. 21 The reheats were in and burning fuel at a terrifying rate. **1976** *Farnborough Internat. Exhibition* (Official Programme) 11/2 Such is the engines' thrust when reheat is on that fuel is burnt up at an incredible 20 tons an hour.

2. Special Comb.: **reheat factor**, a measure of the performance of a multistage steam turbine, usu. expressed as the ratio of the measured efficiency of the turbine and the (lower) efficiency expected on the assumption of adiabatic expansion of the steam.

1913 H. M. MARTIN *Design & Constr. of Steam Turbines* v. 44 It will be noted that after an expansion of one hundred-fold or so, the ratio ϵ/η becomes practically constant. This ratio..is known as the 'reheat factor'. **1950** J. K. SALISBURY *Steam Turbines & their Cycles* i. 34 The sum of the stage available energies is greater than the turbine available energy by a small amount. The ratio of these two quantities is..the reheat factor. **1961** FOX & MCBIRNIE *Marine Steam Engines & Turbines* (ed. 2) xviii. 438 The significance of the reheat factor is that in a multi-stage steam turbine any particular stage benefits somewhat from the inefficiency of the preceding stages.

reheate, variant of REHETE *v.*[2] *Obs.*

re'heater. [f. REHEAT *v.* + -ER[1].] An apparatus for reheating.

1875 R. F. MARTIN tr. *Havrez' Winding Mach.* 98 Boilers consisting of heaters and reheaters. **1897** *Columbus* (Ohio) *Disp.* 7 Apr. 9/3 The result showed that when the reheater was used a much greater amount of work was performed.

re'heating, *vbl. sb.* [f. as prec. + -ING[1].] The action of imparting heat again to a substance; also, the material by which this is effected.

1727 BRADLEY *Fam. Dict.* s.v. *Garden*, This Reheating will reciprocally be kept up..by the Neighbourhood of the two adjoining Beds; but when the Bed is single, the Reheating should be two Foot broad at least. **1842** *Penny Cycl.* XXIII. 233/1 The principal object of the subsequent reheating in the granulator is to bring it into a favourable state for removal to the moulds. **1884** W. H. GREENWOOD *Steel & Iron* 359 During the reheating of piles or of ingots they are moved about a little.

b. *attrib.*, as ***reheating furnace, oven***, etc.

1839 URE *Dict. Arts* 168 There are two re-heating or annealing furnaces. *Ibid.* 707 In the re-heating ovens, the loss is from 8 to 10 per cent. on the large bar iron. **1884** W. H. GREENWOOD *Steel & Iron* 361 Reheating furnaces burning gaseous fuel.

Reheboth, var. REHOBOTH.

rehed, obs. form of REED *sb.*[1]

reheite, variant of REHETE *v.*[2] *Obs.*

†**re'helm,** *v. Obs. rare.* [RE- 5 a.] *trans.* To supply or cover (one) again with a helmet.

c **1468** in *Archaeol.* (1846) XXXI. 338 Wt out that it lyked him to be rehelmed. **1525** LD. BERNERS *Froiss.* II. clxviii. 189 b/2 But with the crossynge of their speares the erle was vnhelmed. Than he retourned to his men, and incontynent he was rehelmed, and toke his speare.

†**re'het,** *sb. Obs. rare*[−1]. [a. OF. *reheet*, vbl. sb. to *reheter*: see next.] Cheer, entertainment.

a **1400** *Minor Poems fr. Vernon MS.* 490/224 Siþþe was schewed hem bi, Murþe and Munstralsy, And preyed hem do gladly Wiþ Rial Rehet.

†**re'hete,** *v.*[1] *Obs.* Also 4 **rehayte, reheyit.** [ad. OF. *reheter, -heiter, -haiter*, 'to reuiue, reioyce, cheere vp exceedingly' (Cotgr.), the stem of which has been referred to the Teutonic **hait*-HOTE: see Skeat *Notes Eng. Etym.* (1901) 246.]

1. *trans.* To cheer, comfort, or encourage, esp. by kind or friendly words and treatment.

a **1340** HAMPOLE *Psalter* ciii. 17 Þat is, þat man rehete his thouȝt in grace of the holy gost. **13..** *E.E. Allit. P.* B. 127 He wolde..re-hayte rekenly þe riche & þe poueren, & cherisch hem alle with his cher. *c* **1375** *Sc. Leg. Saints* xxix. (*Placidas*) 947 He..gaf hyme mony gyftis gret, hyme & his menȝe to rehet. ?*a* **1400** *Morte Arth.* 221 Thane þe conquerour kyndly carpede to þose lordes, Rehetede þe Romaynes with realle speche. *c* **1400** LOVE *Bonavent. Mirr.* xv. (B.N.C. MS.) 46 b, þei reheteden and conforted her lorde. *c* **1470** *Gol. & Gaw.* 1158 With kynde contenance the renk couth thame rehete.

absol. *a* **1400-50** *Alexander* 3999 Porrus, as a prince suld, ..Turnes him toward his tulkis & titely rehetis.

b. To strengthen (one) *to* do something. *rare*[−1].

a **1340** HAMPOLE *Psalter* xxii. 2 Þe water of grace..makes vs to recouere oure strenght þat we lost in syn, and rehetis vs to doe goed werkis.

2. To refresh (thirst). *rare*[−1].

a **1340** HAMPOLE *Psalter* lxvi. 6 He askis þe watire of godis blissynge, to kole and reheyit his thrist.

3. To entertain with choice food or drink.

c **1470** HARDING *Chron.* CXLII. xv. (1543), Some bookes sayen he poysoned was to dead Of plummes..With whiche a monke there hym did rehete. *c* **1475** *Babees Bk.* 171 Yf.. vnto yow goode mete be brouhte or sente, Withe parte of hit goodely yee theym Rehete.

Hence †**re'heting** *vbl. sb.*[1], refreshing. *Obs.*

a **1340** HAMPOLE *Psalter* xxii. 2 On þe watere of rehetynge forth he me broght. *a* **1400** *Prymer* (1891) 79 He hath browȝte me foorth up on the water of rehetynge.

†**re'hete,** *v.*[2] *Obs.* Also 6 **reheate, reheite.** [Of obscure origin; the relationship, if any, to RAHATE and RATE *v.*[2] is not clear.]

1. *trans.* To assail, attack, persecute. Hence †**re'heting** *vbl. sb.*[2]

14.. *Chaucer's Troylus* III. 349 (Harl. MS. 3943), Al þe rehetyng of his sikes sore, At ones þei fled; he felt of hem no more. *c* **1440** *Partonope* 5197 Grete synne haue ye Thus vngodely to rehete me. *c* **1440** *York Myst.* xxxiii. 364 Rehete hym I rede you with rowtes and rappes. *c* **1470** HARDING *Chron.* CXXXVI. iii. (1543), But then the death hym felly ganne reheate; Wherfoor anone he satte vp in his seate.

b. To annoy, provoke, irritate. *rare*[−1].

1447 BOKENHAM *Seyntys* (Roxb.) 78 Damysel quoth he thou art to blame Thus att the begynnyng me to rehete.

2. To rebuke, rate, scold. Also *intr.* with *at.*

c **1420** *Langland's P. Pl.* C. XIII. 35 To rehercen hit by retoryk to a-rate [*MS. T.* rehete] dedliche synne. **1460** *Paston Lett.* I. 506 My Lord of Salesbury reheted hym, callyng hym knaves son. *Ibid.*, Sir Antony was reheted for his langage. **1509** HAWES *Past. Pleas.* XXIX. (Percy Soc.) 140 If it be knowen, than bothe you and I Shall be reheited at full shamefully.

†**re'hetour.** *Obs. rare.* [Origin and precise meaning obscure.] A servant of some kind.

c **1380** WYCLIF *Serm.* Sel. Wks. II. 229 If men taken hede to þe service of þe Chirche.., it is al turned up so doun, and ypocritis ben maad rehetours. *Ibid.* III. 346 Þis stiward haþ chargid þis hous wiþ newe rehetours, to harm of it.

reheyit, variant of REHETE *v.*[1] *Obs.*

reheyte, variant of REHAYTE *v.*[2] *Obs.*

rehȝe, variant of REIGH *Obs.*

†**rehibit,** *v.* (? Error for EXHIBIT *v.* 1.)

1603 H. CROSSE *Vertues Commw.* E iij b, For the foolish antiquitie honoured men as gods after their deathes; for honour and reuerence is rehibited for some certaine cause.

re'hinge, *v. rare.* [RE- 5 a.] *trans.* To hinge again. (In quot. *fig.*: cf. *unhinge.*)

1660 YEOLSNEY *Sp. to Monk*, col. 2 You have re-hing'd our happynesse.

re'hire, *sb.* [RE- 5 a.] A renewed hiring.

1793 WASHINGTON *Lett.* Writ. (1891) XII. 295 Nor ought there to be any transfer of the Lease, or re-hire of the negroes without your consent first had and obtained in writing.

re'hire, *v.* [RE- 5 a.] *trans.* To hire again. Also *refl.* Hence **re'hiring** *vbl. sb.*

1862 M. HOPKINS *Hawaii* 358 They generally re-hire themselves at the expiration of their engagement. **1891** *Law Times* XCII. 94/1 A sale of its rolling stock and a rehiring of the same rolling stock.

Rehoboam (riːhəˈbəʊəm, riːə-). [f. the name of *Rehoboam*, son of Solomon, King of Judah (I Kings xii–xiv).] †**1.** A shovel hat. *Obs. rare*[−1].

1849 C. BRONTË *Shirley* I. i. 11 A personage of short stature..bearing on broad shoulders a hawk's head,..the whole surmounted by a Rheoboam [**1850** Rehoboam] or shovel-hat, which he did not seem to think it necessary to lift.

2. A large bottle for wine or spirits, bigger than a JEROBOAM and smaller than a METHUSELAH 2.

1895 *Brewer's Dict. Phr. & Fable* (new ed.) 1050/1 A rehoboam of claret or rum is a double jeroboam. **1959** *Gloss. Packaging Terms (B.S.I.)* 28 *Rehoboam*, a wine bottle—capacity 6 reputed quarts. **1960** *Times* 11 Jan. 17/2 A vigorous passing movement across the ground by three Frenchmen with a dummy rehoboam of champagne was ended only by a flagrant knock-on. **1972** [see METHUSELAH 2].

Rehoboth (ˈriːəbɒθ). *S. Afr.* Also erron. **Reheboth.** [a. Heb. *rĕḥōbhōth* wide places.] A Biblical place-name (Gen. xxvi. 22), applied to a river, town, and district in Namibia (South West Africa), and used as the name of a people of mixed African and European descent. Also *attrib.* Hence **'Rehobother.** So **Reho'bothian** *sb.*

1875 C. J. ANDERSSON *Notes of Trav. in S. Afr.* vi. 88 The cattle, etc., might have been retaken had our friends, the Rehobothians, at once accompanied me in pursuit of the marauders. **1926** S. G. MILLIN *South Africans* vii. 198 Today self-governing half-caste tribes like the Bondelswarts and the Reheboths still exist in South-West Africa to trouble the souls of their white neighbours. **1930** C. G. SELIGMAN *Races of Africa* ii. 34 The old Hottentot population of the Cape has become largely absorbed by European admixture with incoming Europeans and East Indian slaves, and has thus constituted the basis of the present ..'Rehoboth' half-breeds. **1935** L. G. GREEN *Great African Mysteries* x. 125 The half-caste Rehoboths..set up nothing less than a civilised republic in a savage land. **1937** *Decisions High Court S.-W. Africa Jan. to Dec. 1936* 59 *Held*, that in this Territory the term 'Baster' when it is ascribed to a person's race is well known to refer to the members of the Reheboth Bastard Community. **1960** *State of Union 1959–60* lxv. 430 The *Rehobothers* whose number is estimated at 8,900 are of mixed origin, having immigrated from the Cape. **1970** *Standard Encycl. Southern Afr.* II. 191/2 The majority are..the descendants of early Basters and they insist on being called Rehoboth Basters, a term they reserve strictly to themselves. **1973** *Observer* (Colour Suppl.) 2 Sept. 56/1 Hereros, Ovambos, Damaras, Kakaovelders, Bushmen and Rehobothers (until recently known as the Bastards).

re'hoist, *v.* [RE- 5 a.] *trans.* To hoist again.

1775 R. CHANDLER *Trav. Greece* (1825) II. 180 We rehoisted our two adventurers. **1790** BEATSON *Nav. & Mil. Mem.* I. 198 Admiral Matthews quitted the Russel, and re-hoisted his flag on board the Namur. **1888** *Times* 20 Nov. 5/1 The Italian consular flag was rehoisted here to-day.

re'honour, *v.* [RE-.] *trans.* To honour again or in return.

1635 *Pref. verse* in J. Hayward tr. *Biondi's Banish'd Virg.*, The guerdon thou do'st merit's sure, for she Whom thou so honoured'st will rehonour thee. **1899** *Westm. Gaz.* 2 Oct. 10/2 Smithfield martyrs' memories rehonoured.

†**re'hope,** *v. Obs.* [RE- 5 a.] To hope again.

a **1618** SYLVESTER *Job Triumphant* 632 If that I say, I will forget my Greife, Forgoe my wrath and yet re-hope Reliefe.

re,hospitali'zation. [f. RE- 5 a + HOSPITALIZATION.] The act or the state of being admitted again to hospital.

1974 M. C. GERALD *Pharmacol.* xvi. 305 The remaining patients retain varying degrees of psychopathology, with many requiring periodic rehospitalization.

re'house, *v.* [RE- 5 a.] *trans.* To house (a person, etc.) again; to provide with other houses. Also *refl.*

1820 COLERIDGE *Lett.* (1895) II. 709 [The suicide] may rehouse himself in a worse hogshead. **1904** G. B. SHAW *Common Sense of Municipal Trading* viii. 75 The municipality bargains with the Local Government Board as to how many people it must rehouse. **1935** *Scrutiny* IV. 134 The problem of re-housing the inhabitants after slum-clearance is at present dealt with unsatisfactorily. **1978** *Lancashire Life* Apr. 105/1 This trolley can be moved freely on its castors, then re-housed in its own base unit. **1980** *Jrnl. R. Soc. Arts* Mar. 186/2, 5½ per cent of London's total built up area was bought and developed for railway use without any statutory responsibility to re-house the displaced residents.

Hence **re'housed** *ppl. a.* (also *absol.* or as *sb.*); **re'housing** *vbl. sb.*

1883 *Fortn. Rev.* Oct. 599 Upon the principles here laid down the rehousing of the poor in towns can be accomplished without expense. **1890** *Spectator* 11 Jan., We must make that inquiry if the question of rehousing is ever to be seriously dealt with. **1904** G. B. SHAW *Common Sense of Municipal Trading* viii. 76 The displaced have solved the rehousing problem by crossing the river into Battersea. **1927** *Scots Observer* 26 Feb. 2/5, I have seen the re-housed in their new environment. **1936** 'G. ORWELL' *Diary* 27 Feb. in *Coll. Essays* (1968) I. 189 The re-housing is almost entirely the work of the Corporation. **1940** HARRISSON & MADGE *War begins at Home* xii. 331 Many of the re-housed families would go back to their old homes if they had not been pulled down. **1966** *Listener* 6 Oct. 511/1 The first few years after the war..saw the re-housing of Turner in the glory that he deserved. **1977** G. SCOTT *Hot Pursuit* iii. 31 Singapore's progressive rehousing policies.

re'humanize, *v.* [RE- 5 a.] *trans.* To humanize again. Also *refl.*

1810 W. TAYLOR in *Monthly Mag.* XXX. 47 The souls of the very bad are forbidden for a time to re-humanize themselves, and become devils. **1847** C. BRONTË *J. Eyre* (1857) 449 It is time some one undertook to rehumanize you. **1876** F. HARRISON *Choice Bks.* (1886) 446 There are forces at work now..to rehumanise the dehumanised members of society.

re'humble, *v. rare.* [RE- 5 a.] *trans.* To humble again.

1598 FLORIO, *Rahumiliare*, to rehumble, to asswage. *a* **1618** SYLVESTER *Mathieu's Tropheis* 65 And had, yer many houres Re-humbled Paris to her Prince's yoake But for Saint Clement's Parricidiall stroake.

rehu'mectate, *v. rare*[−1]. [RE- 5 a.] *trans.* To moisten again.

1686 W. HARRIS tr. *Lemery's Course Chem.* (ed. 2) 138 Continue to rehumectate and rust this matter for twelve several times.

rehumili'ation. *rare*[−1]. [RE- 5 a.] A second or renewed humiliation.

1658 BP. REYNOLDS *Lord's Supper* xiii. Wks. 610 Without any such gross and carnal descent, or rehumiliation of his Glorified Body.

rehy'drate, *v.* [RE- 5 a.] **a.** *intr.* To absorb water again, esp. after dehydration.

1923 J. W. MELLOR *Comprehensive Treat. Inorg. & Theoret. Chem.* III. 763 Crystals of the hemihydrate which practically re-hydrated on cooling. **1968** *Physics Bull.* Dec. 430 Technical advances..have resulted in good products which rehydrate quickly.

b. *trans.* To add water to again after dehydration; *esp.* to restore (dehydrated food) to a palatable state by the addition of water.

1962 F. I. ORDWAY et al. *Basic Astronautics* xiii. 521 The water necessary to rehydrate these processed foods can be recovered. **1965** *Listener* 10 June 875/1 We saw the astronauts learning to rehydrate their plastic bagfuls of strawberry cereal. **1969** *New Scientist* 16 Jan. 128/2 The food was shown to be fully dehydrated; and when later rehydrated it tasted excellent. **1971** *Sci. Amer.* Aug. 18/3 The patient is first rehydrated by intravenous injection, if necessary, and is then fed the oral solution at the rate at which fluid is lost by diarrhea. **1978** *Jrnl. R. Soc. Med.* LXXI. 223 He was given broad-spectrum antibiotics and rehydrated.

Hence **rehy'dratable** *a.*, that may be rehydrated; **rehy'drated** *ppl. a.*

1956 *Nature* 4 Feb. 239/2 When a flake of magnesium vermiculite, which has been partially dehydrated to the phase containing single sheets of interlayer water molecules .., is allowed to become rehydrated, a dark line is observed to enter the flake at the edges and gradually converge on the centre. **1969** *New Scientist* 16 Jan. 128/3 The rehydrated product should as far as possible be identical with the fresh product. **1970** N. ARMSTRONG et al. *First on Moon* vi. 127 U.S. choice beef was better for rehydratable meat cubes than prime, which had too much fat. **1975** *Radio Times* 12–18 July 40 Menu [for U.S. astronauts], rehydratable romaine soup, .. rehydratable coffee. **1975** *Daily Colonist* (Victoria, B.C.) 12 July 1/2 The cosmonauts will dine on steak in plastic pouches, rye bread, cheese spread, rehydrated strawberries and tea with lemon and sugar [etc.].

rehy'dration. [RE- 5 a.] The process of adding or taking up water again, usu. after dehydration.

1866 ODLING *Anim. Chem.* 85 Reconvertible .. by actual or potential rehydration. **1923** J. W. MELLOR *Comprehensive Treat. Inorg. & Theoret. Chem.* III. 763 Special precautions are needed to remove water rapidly before it cools much below 130°, or rehydration sets in. **1936** *Discovery* Oct. 329/1 In summer influenza the protein particles of the blood plasm are subject to hydration, in early winter dehydration takes place while rehydration in late winter is followed closely by an epidemic in February and March. **1947** J. C. RICH *Materials & Methods of Sculpture* iv. 67 The setting of plaster of Paris after it has been mixed with water is also referred to as a *rehydration* and occasionally as a *recrystallization* of the calcined gypsum back to its original hydrated rock form. **1965** *New Scientist* 26 Aug. 498/3 Natural mayonnaise would not be used, since the emulsion separates on freezing giving an oil which, it was feared, would hinder re-hydration. **1979** *Nature* 29 Mar. 389/1 The possibility of oral rehydration has provided Third World health authorities with a very valuable breakthrough in the treatment of diarrhoeal diseases.

rehy'pothecate, *v.* [RE- 5 a.] To hypothecate again. Hence **rehy'pothecating** *vbl. sb.*

1882 OGILVIE. **1883** W. F. CRAFTS *Successful Men* 189 The rehypothecating of trust funds—that is, the secret use of trust funds for speculation. **1884** *Law Times* LXXVIII. 113 The proposed lender had .. never been in a position to make the advance without re-hypothecating the security.

So **rehy'pothecator.**

1883 W. F. CRAFTS *Successful Men* 160 Those rehypothecators of trust funds for private speculations.

rei, sing. of REIS (Portuguese money).

reiate, variant of REALTY[1] *Obs.*

‖**Reich** (raɪç, raɪk). Pl. **Reiche.** [Ger., = kingdom, realm, state: see RICHE, RIKE.] Chiefly during the period 1871–1945, the German state or commonwealth; also, one of a sequence of empires or régimes in Germany, esp. the THIRD REICH.

Apart from *Third Reich*, collocations with an ordinal are rare and do not constitute recognized English historical terminology.

1921 *Times* 19 Jan. 11/2 All the States proclaim .. their loyalty to the Reich. **1924** *Hansard Commons* 16 Jan. 152 We have always pointed out that, .. if any part of the German Reich wished to set up an autonomous area for itself, they must utilise their own constitutional machinery. **1933** *Times* 15 Mar. 15/2 During the past week the Nazi steam-roller has passed over every one of the seventeen Federal States of the Reich. **1946** *Britannica Bk. of Year* (U.S.) 341/2 Germany was deprived not only of all Hitler's annexations of territory, but also of all former German reich territory east of the Oder and western Neisse rivers. **1972** F. FORSYTH *Odessa File* ii. 46, I have commandeered this ship in the name of the Reich. **1973** *Nature* 14 Sept. 107/2 A penetratingly sketched background of the fortunes and misfortunes of the Second and Third *Reiche*. *Ibid.*, The Jews had been emancipated in Prussia in 1812 and .. had come to occupy high places in the Second Reich. **1974** J. WHITE tr. *Poulantzas's Fascism & Dictatorship* VII. v. 338 The dismembering of the State apparatus was also expressed in contradictions between the central authority of the Reich and the provincial authorities. **1976** *New Yorker* 8 Mar. 130/2 The villains here are a secret 'Comrades Organization' of ex-Nazis, who live in Brazil and hope to establish a Fourth Reich.

Also (f. the gen. sing.) **'Reichsbank** [G. *bank* bank], the name of the central bank of the German Reich, 1875–1945; **'Reichsbanner** [G. *banner* banner], a republican para-military organization in Germany from 1924 to 1933; **'Reichsmark** [G. *mark* MARK *sb.*[2]], the monetary unit of the German Reich, replaced in 1948 by the DEUTSCHE MARK; **'Reichs,marschall, -,marshall** [Ger., in full *Reichmarschall des Grossdeutschen Reiches* Marshal of the Greater German Reich], a title bestowed on Hermann Göring (1893–1946) in 1940 by Adolf Hitler; **'Reichsrat** (formerly -rath) (-raːt) [G. *rat(h* council: cf. BUNDESRAT], (*a*) the parliament of the Austrian part of the Habsburg Empire; (*b*) the council of the federated states of Germany between the end of the 1914–18 war and 1933; **'Reichswehr** (-veːr) [G. *wehr* defence], the name of the German army between 1919 and 1935. See also REICHSTAG.

All usu. with capital initial in Eng. as in German.

1879 *Encycl. Brit.* X. 466/1 The Imperial Bank (Reichsbank) ranks far above the others in importance. **1977** *New Yorker* 3 Oct. 85/1 Nazi archives at the Reichsbank .. yielded substantial data. **1924** *Times* 6 Dec. 11/1 Some scattered organizations .. were amalgamated to be the nucleus of a united Republican guard, known as the Reichsbanner Black-Red-Gold .., the 'Great Germany' idea being invariably pushed into the foreground at Reichsbanner demonstrations. **1935** C. ISHERWOOD *Mr. Norris changes Trains* viii. 130 The newspapers were full of death-bed photographs of rival martyrs, Nazi, Reichsbanner and Communist. **1964** *Listener* 25 June 1038/2 The Reich authorities began .. to condemn the Reichsbanner, an organization which existed solely to defend the Republic. **1874** *Anglo-Brazilian Times* (Rio de Janeiro) 23 Dec. 5/3 The business on Hamburg has been done at 448 reis per reichsmark at 90 days and 454 reis for sight drafts. **1924** *Times* 7 Nov. 11/6 The new banknotes of 10, 20, 50 and 100 Reichsmarks, which are part of the reformed and stabilized German currency .. were exhibited at the Reichsbank this morning. **1978** *Time* 3 July 8/1 The old reichsmarks of the Nazi regime had become worthless. **1940** *R.A.F. in Action* 16 On the 20th May, 1940, the Reichsmarshal .. was forced to promise that more guns would be provided immediately. **1976** J. WHEELER-BENNETT *Friends, Enemies & Sovereigns* ii. 36, I have always regretted that I was not present to see his defeat of Goering on that celebrated occasion when the Reichsmarschall had 'made a monkey' out of the chief American prosecutor, Robert Jackson, and David had deflated him. **1858** *New Amer. Cycl.* II. 392/2 The council of state, or *Reichsrath*, composed of 12 members, is a body coördinate to the ministry, and communicating immediately with the emperor. **1905** *Spectator* 11 Feb. 201 Meanwhile the Pan-German delegates in the Austrian Reichsrath are agitating for economic severance from Hungary and alliance with Germany. **1919** *German Constitution* (H.M.S.O.) I. 11 A Reichsrat is formed for the representation of the German States in Federal legislation. **1943** S. H. THOMSON *Czechoslovakia in European Hist.* ix. 180 The Vienna Parliament (Reichsrat) which functioned as the legislative body for the Austrian half of the Empire. **1969** E. WALL *Europe Unification & Law* iii. 72 Though the Reichsrat, representing the federated Länder, could object to a bill, the objection could be overridden by a two-thirds majority of the Reichstag or .. by referendum. **1920** *Times* 30 Oct. 9/3 He depicted the Reichswehr as mainly a Royalist institution. **1934** *Ann. Reg. 1933* 182 A Heimwehr patrol [in Austria] shot dead a German Reichswehr soldier. **1976** J. WHEELER-BENNETT *Friends, Enemies & Sovereigns* iv. 100, I had had first-hand experience of the Seekt and Schleicher periods of the *Reichswehr* and of its brief honeymoon with Hitler which began to wane with the Night of the Long Knives in June 1934.

reich(e, obs. Sc. forms of REACH.

Reichert ('raɪxət). The name of Emil *Reichert* (1838–94), German food scientist, used in the possessive and *attrib.* (freq. in *Comb.* with another name, as *Meissl, Polenske, Wollny*) with reference to standard procedures for determining the proportion of volatile water-soluble fatty acids present in butter, fats, and oils (one of which he published in *Zeitschr. f. anal. Chem.* (1879) XVIII. 68).

1885 *Analyst* X. 103 Reichert's process possesses every advantage over Hehner's, which is becoming replaced by the former. **1887** *Ibid.* XII. 203 (*heading*) On Reichert-Meissl's method of butter analysis. **1892** *Ibid.* VII. 171 Reichert .. proposed to saponify 2·5 grammes of butter with caustic soda and alcohol, evaporate off the alcohol, add 50 c.c. of water and 2 c.c. dilute sulphuric acid, and to distil 50 c.c. in a weak current of air. This method, although Reichert himself calls it Hehner's method, is now known as the Reichert process. *Ibid.* 175 The Reichert-Wollny method is largely adopted in every country except France, and may be considered a standard method. **1894** *Ibid.* XIX. 189 Filtered butter-fat will give a constant Reichert-Meissl number for many weeks. **1901** *Ibid.* XXVI. 71 (*heading*) Note on the Reichert value of butter and other fats. **1906** [see POLENSKE]. **1928** [see KIRSCHNER]. **1936** *Analyst* LXI. 404 As the original Reichert process, using 2·5 g. of fat, and as the Reichert-Meissl process, using 5 g., have been obsolete since Wollny modified the Meissl process nearly 50 years ago, and as the name Reichert is common to the different forms, it may now be used alone in place of the indiscriminate use of the hyphenated forms, Reichert-Meissl, Reichert-Meissl-Wollny, Reichert-Wollny and Reichert-Polenske, when applied to the soluble volatile acids. **1957** *Encycl. Brit.* IV. 469/2 The Reichert-Meissel [*sic*] (Reichert-Wollny) value .. is a valuable characteristic in butterfat analysis. **1973** [see POLENSKE].

Reichian ('raɪxɪən), *sb.* and *a.* [f. the name of Wilhelm *Reich* (1897–1957), Austrian psychologist + -IAN.] **A.** *sb.* A supporter of the theories or practices of Wilhelm Reich, esp. those relating to sexual energy as vital energy (cf. ORGONE), to its effect in determining character and mental health, or to his hypothesis that authoritarian regimes emerge in cultures that are sexually repressive. **B.** *adj.* Of, pertaining to, or following Reich or his theories.

1959 *Partisan Rev.* XXVI. 51 The Reichians want to believe in Socialism again. **1959** N. MAILER *Advts. for Myself* (1961) 295 The Yoga's *prana*, the Reichian's orgone, Lawrence's 'blood'. **1969** P. A. ROBINSON *Freudian Left* I. 10 The true Reichian is convinced that Reich's greatest contributions lay .. in biophysics and astronomy. **1970** R. LOWELL *Notebook* 247 Such cures the bygone Reichian prophets swore to. **1976** *Listener* 8 Jan. 4/2 One of the unique features of present-day Portugal is the concurrence of political and sexual revolution. It provides a laboratory for Reichian radicals who see a causal relationship between sexual repression and totalitarianism, on one side, and sexual liberation and revolution, on the other. **1978** *N.Y. Rev. Bks.* 23 Feb. 29/4 The Victorian idea of TB as a disease of low energy .. has its exact complement in the Reichian idea of cancer as a disease of unexpressed energy.

Reichstag ('raɪçstaːk, 'raɪkstɑːg). [Ger., f. gen. sing. of REICH + *tag* diet: cf. BUNDESTAG.] The diet or parliament of the German Empire (1871–1918) (formerly also, that of the North German Confederation) and of post-Imperial Germany until 1945; the building in Berlin in which this parliament met. Also *transf.*

1867 *Times* 3 Jan. 10/1 It is proposed to exclude Government functionaries, not from the future Diet of the Confederation (Reichstag), but only from the Parliament which is about to assemble. **1870** GEO. ELIOT *Let.* 3 Apr. (1956) V. 87 We went to the Reichstag one morning, and were so fortunate as to hear Bismarck speak. **1889** M. H. VAN DE VELDE *Cosmopolitan Recollections* I. v. 167 Will he attend the Reichstag? **1909** M. A. VON ARNIM *Caravaners* xiii. 220 She began to talk to me .. about .. our Reichstag. **1935** C. ISHERWOOD *Mr. Norris changes Trains* xvi. 263 We ought to be grateful to van der Lubbe, because the burning of the Reichstag had melted the snow. **1944** J. S. HUXLEY *On Living in Revol.* 138 In 1928 .. the Nazis had secured less than 2 per cent. of the seats in the Reichstag. **1975** *Times* 4 Mar. 1/2 From the Tory benches, there was a claim that the Commons was being turned into a Reichstag.

2. *attrib.*, as **Reichstag Fire**, a fire which destroyed the Reichstag building on 27 Feb. 1933, believed to have been engineered by the Nazi party in order to facilitate their seizure of power; **Reichstag Trial**, the subsequent trial of the alleged incendiary, Marinus van der Lubbe, and others; also *transf.*, as the type of a staged trial.

1933 *Times* 1 Mar. 13/2 A communication about the Reichstag fire was issued by the Prussian authorities. **1976** S. HYNES *Auden Generation* v. 143 The Reichstag fire appears as an emblem of public terror. **1968** D. HOPKINSON *Incense Tree* xii. 156 The trial was a travesty in the tradition of the Reichstag Trial at Leipzig. **1970** *Peace News* 17 Apr. 8/1 Bobby Seale has been sentenced to *four years* for contempt of court at Attorney General Mitchell's 'Reichstag Trial' in Chicago.

reick, obs. form of REEK *v.*[2]

†**reid**[1]. *Sc. Obs.* Also 6 reide, reyd. [var. of RAID *sb.* 4, perh. directly a. Du. *reede* or LG. *rêde.*] A roadstead.

1561 *Burgh Rec. Aberd.* (1844) I. 334 Quhat sumewir schip of gudis sellable arrywis to the port, hevin, or reyd. *a* **1578** LINDESAY (Pitscottie) *Chron. Scot.* (S.T.S.) I. 194 His schippis quhilk was lyand in the reid at that tyme. **1596** DALRYMPLE tr. *Leslie's Hist. Scot.* x. 287 Thay ouirthrew in the Reide xvi scotis shipis.

†**reid**[2]. *Sc. Obs.*[−1] (Of obscure origin and meaning: perh. a rendering of eccl. L. *litania major*, the longer litany used on the Rogation days.)

c **1450** HOLLAND *Howlat* 698 Syne all the lentryne but leiss, and the lang reid, And als in the adwent The Soland stewart was sent.

reid(e, obs. ff. READ *sb.*[1] and *v.*, RED *a.* and *sb.*[1], REDE *sb.*[1] and *v.*, REED *sb.*[1]

reidar, obs. Sc. f. READER.

re-identifi'cation. [RE- 5 a.] The action of identifying again.

1882 SPENCER *Princ. Sociol.*, *Pol. Instit.* 564 Where .. military headship becomes in a measure separated from political headship, continued warfare is apt to cause a re-identification of them. **1884** *Manch. Exam.* 29 Feb. 4/6 The re-identification of imported yarns woven into tissues would be impossible.

rei'dentify, *v.* [RE- 5 a.] **a.** *trans.* To identify again or in a new way; also *absol.* **b.** *intr.* To identify oneself with something again.

1934 WEBSTER, Reidentify, v.t. **1959** P. F. STRAWSON *Individuals* i. 32 We cannot attach one occasion to another unless, from occasion to occasion, we can reidentify elements common to different occasions. *Ibid.* 55 A condition .. of the possession of a single, continuously usable framework .. was the ability to *re*identify .. some elements of the framework in spite of discontinuities of observation. **1964** C. M. WISE in D. Abercrombie et al. *Daniel Jones* 208 The second element .. has been reidentified as a voiced postvocalic allophone. **1966** 'HAN SUYIN' *Mortal Flower* xii. 258 Others are longing to go back, to reidentify, but they are afraid of changing.

reif (riːf). Chiefly *Sc.* Forms: 1 réaf, réof, 3 ræf, reue, 5 ref, 5–6 reiff, 6 rieff, reife, reyf, raif, reafe, 7 reaf, 5– reif. [Common W.Germ.: OE. *réaf* = OFris. *râf*, OS. *-rôf* (Du. *roof*), MLG. *rôf* (hence Sw. *rof*, Da. *rov*), OHG. *roub*, *roup* (G. *raub*):—OTeut. **raubo*[m]: see REAVE *v.* The precise relationship of the OE. word to REAF, garment, is not certain.]

†**1.** That which is taken by force or robbery; spoil, plunder, booty. *Obs.*

c **950** *Lindisf. Gosp.* Luke xi. 22 Alla woepeno his ȝenimeð .. & reafo [L. *spolia*] his todælde. *c* **1000** *Ags. Ps.* (Th.) cxviii. 162 Se þe beorna reaf maniȝe [L. *spolia multa*] meteð. *c* **1205** LAY. 8612 [We scullen] ȝemen þes fehtes .. & læten þa ræf liggen. **1375** BARBOUR *Bruce* v. 118 The King gert be departit then All haill the reif amang his men. *a* **1557** *Diurn. Occurr.* (Bannatyne Cl.) 12 The erle of Angus servandis maid ane prey and reif thairof.

2. The act or practice of robbery; spoliation; reavery. *Obs.* exc. *arch.*

a **1250** *Owl & Night.* 458 (Cotton), Ich fare hom & nime leue, Ne recche ich noȝt of winteres reue [*Jesus MS.* teone]. *c* **1400** *Apol. Loll.* 12 For þe sacrilege þat þei do in reif of goodis. **1456** SIR G. HAYE *Law Arms* (S.T.S.) 134 Injure or violence.., as ar thift, ref, or sik thingis. *c* 1470 HENRY *Wallace* XI. 840 Throuch cowatice gud Alexander was lost; And Julius als, for all his reiff and bost. 1500–20 DUNBAR *Poems* ix. 121, I synnit als in reif and in oppressioun, In wranguss gudis taking and posseding. 1546 *Reg. Privy Council Scot.* I. 34 All maner of reiffis, spulȝeis, oppressionis, slauchteris, allegit to haue bene committit. 1585 MONTGOMERIE *Sonn.* xiv. 14 Let richt, not reif, my pensioun bring agane. 1644 *Articles Sc. Commiss.* in Rushw. *Hist. Coll.* III. (1692) I. 366 Whatsoever Thefts, Reifs, Hardships, Oppressions,..or Murther done or committed by them. 1786 BURNS *To James Smith* i, The sleest, pawkie thief, That e'er attempted stealth or rief. 1815 SCOTT *Guy M.* iii, Saint Michael and his spear, Keep the house frae reif and wear.

†**b.** *of reif*, esp. Sc. in *fowl of reif*, bird of prey or plunder. *Obs.*

c 1400 *Apol. Loll.* 104 Þei are maad desseyuable ypocritis, & lurkyng woluis of ref under a schepis flees. *c* 1450 HOLL AND *Howlat* 656 Thus assemblit..All that war fowlis of reif. 1457 *Sc. Acts Jas. II*, c. 32 (1814) II. 51/2 Anentis rukis, crawys and vþer foulys of reif.

reif, reifar, -er, reiffing, obs. Sc. ff. REAVE *v.*[1], REEVE *sb.*[1], REAVER, REAVING.

reification (riːɪfɪˈkeɪʃən, reɪɪf-). [f. L. *rē-s* a thing (cf. REAL *a.*[2]) + -IFICATION.] The mental conversion of a person or abstract concept into a thing. Also, depersonalization, esp. such as Marx thought was due to capitalist industrialization in which the worker is considered as the quantifiable labour factor in production or as a commodity.

1846 GROTE *Greece* (1851) I. 467 *note*, Boiocalus would have had some trouble to make his tribe comprehend the reification of the god Hêlios. 1854 *Fraser's Mag.* XLIX. 74 A process of what may be called reification, or the conscious conversion of what had hitherto been regarded as living beings into impersonal substances. 1882 J. B. STALLO *Concepts & Th. Mod. Physics* 269 The existence, or possibility, of transcendental space is another flagrant instance of the reification of concepts. 1937 T. PARSONS *Struct. Soc. Action* xiii. 476 Positivistic empiricism has been predominantly a matter of the 'reification' of theoretical systems. 1941 H. MARCUSE *Reason & Revol.* II. i. 279 Marx's early writings are the first explicit statement of the process of reification (*Verdinglichung*) through which capitalist society makes all personal relations between men take the form of objective relations between things. 1954 H. J. EYSENCK *Psychol. Politics* viii. 262 Freud's reification of mental mechanisms is a literary rather than a scientific device. 1962 MACQUARRIE & ROBINSON tr. *Heidegger's Being & Time* I. i. 72 The Thinghood itself which such reification implies must have its ontological origin demonstrated. 1971 J. J. SHAPIRO tr. *Habermas's Toward Rational Soc.* iii. 39 The active assault upon culture is based on the same reification as the fetishism of those students who believe that by occupying university classrooms they are taking possession of science as a productive force. 1976 G. THERBORN *Sci., Class & Soc.* i. 26 The ugly consequences, in Friedrich's view, result from a 'reification' of the current epistemological stance of science. 1979 E. H. GOMBRICH *Sense of Order* v. 143 To see the [wavy] line as water, mountains or, perhaps, a fluttering ribbon might be described as 'reification', to see it as a living serpent as 'animation'.

reificatory (riː-, reɪɪfɪˈkeɪtərɪ), *a.* [f. REIFICAT(ION + -ORY[2].] Of, pertaining to, or characterized by, reification.

1951 Z. S. HARRIS *Methods in Structural Ling.* ii. 18 The reificatory question of what parts of human behavior constitute language. 1969 D. TRIESMAN in Cockburn & Blackburn *Student Power* 148 The International Student Conference..coalesced around the fundamental and reificatory tenet that it would only discuss problems of the 'student as such'.

reify (ˈriːɪfaɪ, ˈreɪɪf-), *v.* [f. as REIFICATION + -IFY.] *trans.* To convert mentally into a thing; to materialize.

1854 *Fraser's Mag.* LXIX. 75 The gods of their final and accepted polytheism were, in point of fact, only those sublimer portions of nature which..they had not yet dared to reify. 1882 *Pop. Sci. Monthly* XXI. 151 When people make or find a new 'abstract noun', they instantly try to put it on a shelf or into a box, as though it were a thing; thus they reify it. 1931 M. R. COHEN *Reason & Nature* III. iii. 390 There is..a fundamental philosophic issue: the extent to which the principle of unity should be hypostatized or reified (I wish the use of the word *thingified* were more common). 1953 C. E. OSGOOD *Method & Theory in Experim. Psychol.* xvi. 680 The second hindrance to objectivity is the ubiquitous tendency to reify the word, to assume the word itself some-how carries its own meaning. 1971 *Times Lit. Suppl.* 31 Dec. 1619/3 To look upon them [*sc.* economic laws] as objective necessities, as bourgeois economists do, is to reify them. 1979 E. H. GOMBRICH *Sense of Order* x. 282 The temptation to 'reify' the shield into the open mouth of a gaping mask..proved as irresistible as did the opportunity of turning spiralling volutes into suggestions of eyes.

Hence **'reified** *ppl. a.*, **'reifying** *vbl. sb.* and *ppl. a.*

1941 H. MARCUSE *Reason & Revol.* iv. 115 Lordship and bondage result of necessity from certain relationships of labor, which are, in turn, relationships in a 'reified' world. 1962 MACQUARRIE & ROBINSON tr. *Heidegger's Being & Time* II. vi. 487 Why does this reifying always keep coming back to exercise its dominion? 1965 B. PEARCE tr. *Preobrazhensky's New Economics* 47 One can..understand its laws in the spirit of vulgar economics, that is, by offering in the guise of science mere superficial description, complete with the reified relations of commodity production. 1969 R. BLACKBURN in Cockburn & Blackburn *Student Power* 207 An alienated society naturally encourages a re-ifying vocabulary. 1979 E. H. GOMBRICH *Sense of Order* ix. 242 It is surely not far-fetched to interpret its coiling frame as a reified flourish on a reified support.

†**reigh.** *Obs.* Forms: 1 reoh(c)he, 3 rehȝe, rihȝe, 4 righe, 5 reȝge, reyh(h)e, reygh(e, reigh. [ME. type *reȝe, reyhe*:—OE. **rehhe, reohhe*: the precise relationship to the ME. variant *roȝe* (see ROUGH *sb.*), and to the continental forms answering to this, is not clear.] The fish called the RAY.

c 1050 *Suppl. Ælfric's Gloss.* in Wr.-Wülcker 181/6 *Fannus*, reohhe. [1120 WILL. MALMESB. *De Gestis Pontif.* II. (Du Cange), Ut etiam caudas racharum vestibus eius affigerent.] *c* 1205 LAY. 29557 Heo..nomen tailes of rehȝen and hangede on his cope. *c* 1430 *Two Cookery-bks.* 11 Take Haddok, Pyke, Tenche, Reȝge, Codlynd, an pyke a-way þe bonys. *c* 1440 *Promp. Parv.* 427/2 Reyhhe, fysche, *ragadia. Ibid.* 438/1 Rowhe or reyhe, fishe..*ragadies.* 1480 CAXTON *Chron. Eng.* xcvii, And for more despite they cast on hym the guttes of reighes and of [1520 other] fissh.

attrib. *c* 1205 LAY. 29583 An..þan folke þa þe rihȝen tailes hangede a þan clarkes. *c* 1330 R. BRUNNE *Chron. Wace* (Rolls) 15196 Byhynd hym on his cloþes þey henge, Righe tailles [F. *keues de raies*] on a strenge. 1480 CAXTON *Chron. Eng.* xcvii, The paynyms..hym scorned and cast on hym reigh tailles, so that al his mantel was honged full of reigh tailles.

reiȝhte, obs. pa. t. REACH *v.*[1]

reigle, variant of REGAL *sb.*[3], groove.

reign (reɪn), *sb.* Forms: α. 3–5 reyne, 4–5 reyn, reine; 4–5 regn, 4–7 regne, reigne, (6 riegne), 5–6 reygne, 7– reign; 5 raen 6 raine, rayn(e, raygne, 6–7 raigne, 7 raign, (raighne). β. 3–5 rengne, 5 ryngne. γ. 5, 6 *Sc.* renge, 6 *Sc.* ring, ryng. [a. OF. *regne, reigne, rai(g)ne, rengne*, etc. (10th c.; mod.F. *règne*), ad. L. *regnum* (whence also It. *regno*, Sp. *reino*), f. *regĕre* to rule. The Sc. forms show a normal development of *gn* into *ng*.]

1. a. Royal power or rule; kingdom, sovereignty; also *transf.* power or rule (of persons) comparable to that of a king. Now *rare* (†formerly common without article).

a 1272 *Luue Ron* 71 in *O.E. Misc.* 95 Ector..and cesar.. beoþ iglyden vt of þe reyne. *a* 1300 *Cursor M.* 9318 'Princs o pees' sal man him call, And neuermar es regn fall. *c* 1330 R. BRUNNE *Chron.* (1810) 65 Tille Harald, Godwyn sonne, þe regne wille best falle. *c* 1386 CHAUCER *Monk's T.* 221 King, god to thy fader lente Glorie and honour, regne, tresour, rente. 1450–80 tr. *Secreta Secret.* 6 So that alle tho that ben vndir his regne ben of oon obeyshaunce. 1534 WHITINTON *Tullyes Offices* I. (1540) 12 There is no sure fellowship nor sure trust in hyghe reygne. 1590 SPENSER *F.Q.* III. iii. 40 Then shall Cadwallin die; and then the raine Of Britons eke with him attonce shall dye. 1617 MORYSON *Itin.* I. 246 The English, vnder the Raigne of Queene Elizabeth, obtained like priuiledge. 1656 EARL MONM. tr. *Boccalini's Advts. fr. Parnass.* I. xxiii. (1674) 26 Empires.. which know not how to perfix bounds to their insatiate desire of Reign. 1725 POPE *Odyss.* II. 265 He who like a father held his reign. 1770 GOLDSMITH *Des. Vill.* 288 Some fair female unadorned and plain, Secure to please while youth confirms her reign. 1782 COWPER *Heroism* 90 In Britain's isle, beneath a George's reign. 1813 SHELLEY *Q. Mab* I. 10 The gloomy Power Whose reign is in the tainted sepulchres. 1851 THACKERAY *Eng. Hum.* iii. (1853) 111 In a British drawing-room, under the reign of Queen Victoria.

b. *transf.* Influence, dominion, sway, of something immaterial. † *in reign*, dominant.

c 1402 LYDG. *Compl. Bl. Knt.* 510 So that Dispyt now holdeth forth hire reyne, Through hasty bileve of tales that men feyne. 1567 *Gude & Godlie B.* (S.T.S.) 204 Lyke Prince and King, he led the Regne, Of all Iniquitie. 1596 SPENSER *F.Q.* v. v. 28 She gan to stoupe, and her proud mind convert To meeke obeysance of love's mightie raine. 1656 JEANES *Mixt. Schol. Div.* 20 A soule that is free from both the raigne, or prevalency, and the anxiety of doubts. 1768 *Woman of Honor* III. 131 The allodial sistem was in reign before it was supplanted by the feodal one. 1781 COWPER *Hope* 33 Would age in thee resign his wintry reign. 1821 SHELLEY *Remembrance* 10 The owlet Night resumes her reign. 1867 DK. ARGYLL *Reign of Law* i. 5 The Reign of Law in Nature is..universal. 1883 *Century Mag.* Oct. 804/1 A country where both winter and summer were debarred full reign.

2. †**a.** A kingdom or realm; a territory ruled over by a king; a monarchical state. *Obs.*

a 1300 *K. Horn* 971 Mi Rengne þu schalt welde. *c* 1385 CHAUCER *L.G.W.* 992 *Dido*, This is the reyne of libie there ye bin. 1412–20 LYDG. *Chron. Troy* I. vi. (1555), In your repayre to your fathers reyne..ye shall me with you lede. *c* 1500 *Lay Folks Mass Bk.* 74 Ye sall pray for yᵉ prosperite & wallfare of yᵉ Reygne. 1572 *Satir. Poems Reform.* xxxvi. 51 Dyuers duikis and kingis,..Exylit from þair countreis and thair ringis. 1623 LISLE *Saxon Serm. Easter day*, There was slain on yᵗ night in every house throughout Pharaos reigne the first borne child. 1725 POPE *Odyss.* IV. 12 A gorgeous train Attend the nymph to Phthia's distant reign.

transf. 1340–70 *Alex. & Dind.* 642 þe heie god..þat heuene holdeþ & hap to his hole regne.

†**b.** The kingdom of heaven or of God. *Obs.*

1340 *Ayenb.* 83 þe regne of heuene to wynne, and alle þe dyeuelen..to ouercome. *c* 1386 CHAUCER *Pars. T.* ¶5 Manye been the weyes espirituels that leden folk..to the regne of glorie. 1483 CAXTON *Gold. Leg.* 244 b/2, I shalle drynke it newe wyth you in the regne of my fader. 1532 MORE *Confut. Tindale* Wks. 466/1 They shall..awake at the blast of the trumpe, and euer after liue with yᵉ lorde in his reigne. 1594 CAREW *Tasso* (1881) 29 Th' angels erst banisht from the heau'nly raine.

c. *poet.* A place or sphere under the rule of some specified person or thing, or having a specified character. Now *rare*.

c 1398 CHAUCER *Fortune* 45 Thou born art in my regne of variance. 1590 SPENSER *F.Q.* II. vii. 21 A beaten broad high way..That streight did lead to Plutoes griesly rayne. *Ibid.* III. iv. 49 Like as a fearefull Dove, which through the raine Of the wide ayre her way does cut amaine. 1667 MILTON *P.L.* I. 543 The universal Host upsent A shout that.. Frighted the Reign of Chaos and old Night. 1697 DRYDEN *Virg. Georg.* I. 38 Or wilt thou, Cæsar, chuse the watry Reign..? 1754 GRAY *Poesy* 9 Thro' verdant vales, and Ceres' golden reign. 1817 SHELLEY *Rev. Islam* I. xlviii, The ocean Which girds the pole, Nature's remotest reign.

†**d.** = KINGDOM 5. *Obs. rare.*

1748 THOMSON *Cast. Indol.* II. xi, The vegetable and the mineral reigns. 1781 GIBBON *Decl. & F.* xviii. II. 90 The venom was commonly extracted from the vegetable reign.

3. a. The period of a sovereign's rule.

c 1330 R. BRUNNE *Chron.* (1810) 28 þe ferth ȝere of þe regne..þese þre..Werred on Athelstan. 1389 in *Eng. Gilds* (1870) 121 Of þe regne of þe kyng Richard þe secunde, þe secunde ȝer. 1434 *E.E. Wills* 100 The reyn of our lege lord the kyng Harre the sexte,..the xj yer. 1556 *Chron. Gr. Friars* (Camden) 3 Here beganne the rayne of kyng Henry the third, sonne unto kynge John. 1585 T. WASHINGTON tr. *Nicholay's Voy.* IV. xxix. 149 b, At the time of the deluge..& in the riegne of Ducalion. 1641 J. JACKSON *True Evang. T.* I. 35 In the tenth yeare of his raigne, he sent forth a generall Edict. 1711 STEELE *Spect.* No. 43 ¶9 That Celebrated Poem, which was written in the Reign of King Charles the Second. 1788 GIBBON *Decl. & F.* xlix. V. 130 During the five succeeding reigns,..the contest was maintained with unabated rage. 1833 CRUSE tr. *Eusebius' Eccl. Hist.* I. x. 39 It was about the fifteenth year of the reign of Tiberius. 1841 LANE *Arab. Nts.* I. 106 After a reign of seventy years, he died.

transf. 1500–20 DUNBAR *Poems* xviii. 9 Sum cravis of God to end my ring. 1697 DRYDEN *Virg. Georg.* III. 475 This during Winter's drisly Reign be done. 1812 J. H. VAUX *Flash Dict.*, *Reign*, the length or continuance of a man's career in a system of wickedness, which..is said to have been a long or a short reign, according to its duration.

†**b.** The 'life' of a ship. *Obs. rare*[−1].

1674 PETTY *Dupl. Proportion* 32 If no trading Ship be (one time with another) above 1/10 of her whole reign under sail, or 6 days in 60.

c. *Reign of Terror*: see TERROR.

4. *attrib.*, as **reign mark**, a mark on a piece of oriental ceramic ware indicating in whose reign it was made; **reign name, title**, the symbolic name adopted by a Japanese or (formerly) Chinese ruler, by which his reign is known and dated.

1936 *Burlington Mag.* Jan. 10/2 Distinguished by a reign mark in blue or pink enamel. 1980 *Catal. Fine Chinese Ceramics* (Sotheby, Hong Kong) 6 Where a reign mark is given after the measurement no attribution to the period of this reign is intended unless the words '*and period*' are added. [1834 C. GUTZLAFF *Sketch of Chinese Hist.* I. iv. 89 The Han Dynasty... The characters given after the emperors' names are the kwŏ-haou, 'national designations' of the emperors during their reigns. 1848 S. W. WILLIAMS *Middle Kingdom* II. xvii. 229 Kwoh Hiau, or Reigning Title.] 1935 C. P. FITZGERALD *China* xxiii. 457 Every Ming Emperor retained the same reign title for the full duration of his reign. 1974 *Encycl. Brit. Macropædia* X. 78/1 Mutsuhito, who took the reign name Meiji ('enlightened rule', 1863–1912). 1976 *Times* 10 Nov. 17/1 Reign titles disappeared from China with the fall of the empire in 1911: in Japan they still survive.

reign (reɪn), *v.* Forms: α. 3–6 regn, 4, 6 rein-, 4–6 reygn-, 4–7 reyn-; 5, 6 *Sc.* rigne, 6 ryne; 5–6 rayne, (6 raygne), 5–7 raine, 6–7 raign(e, 7 rain; 4–7 reigne, 6– reign. β. 4–5 rengne, 4, 6 reyngne, 5 reingne. γ. 4 reng, reyng, 4 *Sc.* reinge, 4–7 *Sc.* ring, (5–6 ringe), 4–5 *Sc.* ryng (5 rynge.) *Pa. t.* 5, 6 *Sc.* rang, 6 *Sc.* rong; *pa. pple.* 5 *Sc.* rongyn, 6 *Sc.* rung. [a. OF. *regner* (12th c.; mod.F. *régner*), ad. L. *regnāre*, f. *regnum*: see prec.]

1. *intr.* To hold or exercise the sovereign power or authority in a state; to rule or govern as king or queen; sometimes in restricted sense, to hold the royal office without being actual ruler, to have a limited or nominal sovereignty.

α. *a* 1297 R. GLOUC. (Rolls) 681 After king baþulf leir is sone was king & regnede pritti ȝer. *c* 1325 *Chron. Eng.* 110 in Ritson *Metr. Rom.* II. 274 He reignede after his fader fyn. *c* 1400 *Destr. Troy* 5492 The richest renke, þat reigned in Erthe. 1482 WARKW. *Chron.* (Camden) 10 Kyng Herry schuld..regne as welle as he dyd before. 1523 CROMWELL in Merriman *Life & Lett.* (1902) I. 31 The grete vexacion of his subiectes..by Francoys now raynyng there. 1591 SHAKS. *1 Hen. VI*, I. ii. 31 During the time Edward the third did raigne. 1657 AUSTEN *Fruit Trees* I. 13 This King raigned a long time in Jerusalem. 1738 BOLINGBROKE *Patriot King* (1749) 138 He must begin to govern as soon as he begins to reign. 1788 GIBBON *Decl. & F.* xlix. V. 128 She reigned in her own name and that of her son. 1817 SHELLEY *Rev. Islam* x. xli, But he..The Princess shall espouse, and reign an equal King. 1859 TENNYSON *Guinevere* 519 Worst of the worst were that man he that reigns! 1871 *Daily News* 15 Sept., A Monarch who desired to rule as well as to reign, would soon bring government to a deadlock.

β. *a* 1300 *Cursor M.* 7973 Dauid had rengnd..A-but winters tuelue and mare. 13.. *E.E. Allit. P.* B. 1321 þat ryche in gret rialte rengned his lyue. *c* 1420 *Chron. Vilod.* st. 651 þe fyftenethe ȝere of hurre brother rengnynge. 1534 in *Lett. Suppress. Monast.* (Camden) 18 The rayn of the kyng, how long he shall reyngne, as sayth a prophecy.

γ. *a* 1300 *Cursor M.* 2285 Lang he rengud in þat land. 1375 BARBOUR *Bruce* I. 78 He suld..lat him ryng that had the rycht. *c* 1400 *Sc. Troy-bk.* II. 2164 That Tewtere rengand þare was. 1533 BELLENDEN *Chron. Scot.* I. (1541) Aj, In this tyme rang in Egipt Pharo. *a* 1584 MONTGOMERIE *Misc. Poems* xlviii. 268 God blisse his Grace, and mak him long to ring.

b. Const. *over*, †*upon*, (*on*).

c **1380** WYCLIF *Wks.* (1880) 230 þat he & his children regne long tyme vpon Israel. *c* **1400** *Trevisa's Higden* (Rolls) VI. 151 He regnede over þe West Saxons. **1450** *Rolls of Parlt.* V. 200/2 The honour.. of every Prynce reynyng uppon his people. **1513** BRADSHAW *St. Werburge* I. 297 Wulfere, A noble valyant prynce.. Reygnynge vpon the Mercyens. *a* **1542** WYATT in *Tottel's Misc.* (Arb.) 224 He ruleth not though he raigne ouer realmes. **1591** SYLVESTER *Du Bartas* I. vi. 461 He should have made in vain So great a Prince, without on whom to Reign. **1662** STILLINGFL. *Orig. Sacræ* I. i. §16 They bring the poorer under their power, and reign as Lords over them. **1726** POPE *Odyss.* XVIII. 127 Affright the dogs, and reign A dreaded tyrant o'er the bestial train! **1887** *Times* (weekly ed.) 7 Oct. 2/4 The English Sovereign reigns over one-fifth of the whole human race.

c. *transf.* or *fig.* of God, Christ, etc.

1340 HAMPOLE *Pr. Consc.* 4200 In Capharnaum he [Antichrist] sal regne alswa. *c* **1380** WYCLIF *Serm.* Sel. Wks. I. 258 þei wolden not þat Crist rengnede on hem; and neþeles Crist.. regneþ upon all þis world. *c* **1400** *Apol. Loll.* 2 þe place of hem þat regnun in heuen wiþ Crist. *c* **1450** HOLLAND *Howlat* 474 Our Saluatouris sepultur,.. Quhar he raiss, as we reid, richtuiss to ryng. **1526** *Pilgr. Perf.* (W. de W. 1531) 297 They bothe reygneth holy sayntes before god perpetually. **1567** *Gude & Godlie B.* (S.T.S.) 110 Our God forsuith Ringis in heuin full hie. **1633** P. FLETCHER *Purple Isl.* I. xxxii, Who reigned'st in thy heaven, yet felt'st our hell. **1667** MILTON *P.L.* II. 814 That mortal dint, Save he who reigns above, none can resist. **1788** COWPER *Negro's Compl.* iv, Is there One who reigns on high? **1817** SHELLEY *Rev. Islam* I. xxvii, The Fiend did revel In victory, reigning o'er a world of woe.

d. *fig.* of things (more or less personified).

1362 LANGL. *P. Pl.* A. III. 271 Kuynde wit me tauȝte þat Resun schal regne and Reames gouerne. **1390** GOWER *Conf.* III. 113 Thus the Sonne is overal The chiefe Planete.. And thus betwen hem regneth he. **1553** BECON *Reliques of Rome* (1563) 143b, The Masse rained, ruled, ruffled, and triumphed, as a moste puissant and myghty Queene. **1592** SHAKS. *Ven. & Ad.* 649 Where loue raignes, disturbing iealousie Doth call him selfe affection's centinell. **1637** MILTON *Comus* 334 Disinherit Chaos, that raigns here In double night. **1667** —— *P.L.* IV. 765 Here Love his golden shaft imploies,.. Reigns here and revels. **1782** COWPER *Lily & Rose* vii, The seat of empire is her cheeks, They reign united there. **1817** SHELLEY *Rev. Islam* v. Song vi, While Truth with Joy enthroned o'er his lost empire reigns! **1871** B. TAYLOR *Faust* 2nd Pt. I. i, While.. Reigns in pomp the perfect moon.

2. Of persons: To exercise authority of any kind; to hold sway; to rule.

a **1300** *Cursor M.* 28526 At wrestelyng, at wake, rengd haf i. **1362** LANGL. *P. Pl.* A. II. 35 Alle þis Riche Retenaunce þat Regneden with Fals. *c* **1449** PECOCK *Repr.* III. iv. 299 Than schulde no preest haue immouable godis in lordschip. Forwhi thanne he muste nedis comaunde and regne upon hise tenauntis. *c* **1470** HENRY *Wallace* IX. 1144 The Scottis at large out throu all Fyff thai rang. **1556** LAUDER *Tractate* 374 Quhat plagis.. Sall fall wpon the realmes and kyngis Quharin no faithfull Iugis ryngis. **1597** SHAKS. *Lover's Compl.* 127 He did in the general bosom reign Of young, of old. **1640** BP. HALL *Episc.* I. §16. 67 Saint Paul was the same .. that he was raigning in the Pulpit, or disputing in the Schoole of Tyrannus. **1671** MILTON *P.R.* II. 466 Yet he who reigns within himself, and rules Passions, Desires, and Fears, is more a King. **1819** SHELLEY *Prometh. Unb.* I. 10 Me .. Hast thou made reign and triumph.. O'er mine own misery. **1864** TENNYSON *En. Ard.* 764 [He saw] him, that other, reigning in his place.

transf. *c* **1374** CHAUCER *Compl. Mars* 43 Who reigneth now in blisse but Venus, That hath this worthy Knyght in gouernaunce? **1500–20** DUNBAR *Poems* xlviii. 33 Lord Eolus dois in thy sessone ring. **1784** COWPER *Task* I. 455 The spleen is seldom felt where Flora reigns.

†**b.** To go on or continue *in* some state or course of action. *Obs.*

c **1380** WYCLIF *Wks.* (1880) 68 Also generaly prelatis regnen in symonye. **1442** *Cursor M.* 48 (Bedford MS.), Insampil to hem I may say þat regneþ in her reaut all way. *c* **1470** HENRY *Wallace* VIII. 1359 Than rang I furth in cruell wer and payn. **1556** LAUDER *Tractate* 184 The Liegis of the vngodlie kyng In daylie trubbyll thay sall ryng.

†**c.** To flourish. *Obs. rare.*

? *a* **1450** *Compend. Old Treat.* in Roy's *Rede me* (Arb.) 175 This Bede reygned in the yere off oure lorde god .vij. hundred and xxxij. **1450–80** tr. *Secreta Secret.* 38 In the tyme of this ffysnomyas reynyd the.. doctour ypocras.

†**d.** To flourish *in* some respect. *Obs. rare*$^{-1}$.

1546 tr. *Gasser's Prognost.* d vj, Yet shal thei reigne in large benefites and great renoume.

3. Of things (chiefly immaterial things): To have power, sway, or predominance; to prevail or be prevalent.

a. of qualities, conditions, etc.

a **1340** HAMPOLE *Psalter* ix. 40 When antecrist is distroid all goed sall regne þare in. *c* **1400** *Rom. Rose* 5793 For if.. good love regned over-alle, Such wikkidnesse ne shulde falle. *c* **1440** *Gesta Rom.* I. xlvii. 196 (Harl. MS.), Wher so euer he knewe þat eny discorde or vnrest was Regnynge. **1500–20** DUNBAR *Poems* xxxix. 44 Wirk for the place of paradyce, For thairin ringis no covettyce. **1591** SHAKS. *Two Gent.* I. ii. 15 Lord, Lord: to see what folly raignes in vs. **1616** R. C. *Times' Whistle* IV. 1202 Insatiate Avarice then first began To raigne in the depraved minde of man. **1687** A. LOVELL tr. *Thevenot's Trav.* I. 101 Letters are in no vogue in that Country, and perfound Ignorance reigns among them. **1705** ADDISON *Italy* (1733) 63 The great Secrecy that reigns in their public Councils. **1764** GOLDSM. *Trav.* 239 To kinder skies, where gentler manners reign, I turn. **1818** JAS. MILL *Brit. India* II. v. v. 552 Dissension, improvidence, and pusillanimity reigned at Madras. **1871** JOWETT *Plato* IV. 35 The business of the legislator is to clear up this.. confusion which reigns in the minds of men.

b. of the planets, winds, seasons, etc.

c **1375** *Sc. Leg. Saints* xxi. (*Clement*) 389 Thru þe playnyt þat regnyt þan hyre worthit be ane Il wemane. **1579** E. K. *Gloss.* in *Spenser's Sheph. Cal.* Nov. 16 The sonne reigneth, that is, in the signe Pisces. **1613** SHAKS. *Hen. VIII*, v. iv. 43 Twenty of the Dog-dayes now reigne in's Nose. **1622** BACON *Hen. VII* (1876) 108 Now did the sign reign, and the constellation was come, under which Perkin should appear. **1662** J. DAVIES tr. *Mandelslo's Trav.* 117 The South and Southwest winds reign here [Meliapour] from April to September. **1704** POPE *Summer* 22 In thy heart eternal winter reigns. **1726** SHELVOCKE *Voy. round World* 175 The land winds reign all night. **1821** SHELLEY *I would not be a King*, The path to power is steep and rough, And tempests reign above.

c. of diseases, troubles, etc.

1422 tr. *Secreta Secret., Priv. Priv.* 244 Somyr is hote and dry, and therfor than regnyth reede colere. **1483** CAXTON *Cato* C ij, In that tyme.. reygned a grete pestylence. **1513** DOUGLAS *Æneis* X. xiii. 12 Sik distres rang amang mortale wychtis. **1588** SHAKS. *L.L.L.* IV. iii. 96 A Feuer she Raignes in my bloud, and will remembred be. **1617** MORYSON *Itin.* I. 270 The foule disease of lust, raigning in those parts. **1697** DRYDEN *Virg. Georg.* III. 246 To shun this Ill,.. In Summer's Sultry Heats (for then it reigns). **1845** CARLYLE *Cromwell* (1871) II. 179 Famine has long reigned.

†**4. a.** Of a class or kind of persons: To prevail, to be numerous. *Obs. rare.*

a **1300** *Cursor M.* 2124 It hatt Europe quar mast to day Regns o þe cristen lay. **1560** DAUS tr. *Sleidane's Comm.* 126 They [the Anabaptists] also reigne chiefly in those places, wher the doctrine of the Gospell is prohibited.

†**b.** To range, extend. *Obs. rare*$^{-1}$.

1393 LANGL. *P. Pl.* C. XXIII. 381 Ich wol by-come a pilgryme, And wenden as wide as the worlde regneþ.

†**c.** Of an inanimate thing: To last. *Obs.*$^{-1}$

1691 T. H[ALE] *Acc. New Invent.* 132 A Ship doth commonly Reign about thirty years.

5. To hold a dominant position; to be in the majority.

1715 LEONI *Palladio's Archit.* (1742) I. 94 There might reign a cornice the whole length of it on each side. **1885** *Fortn. in Waggonette* 35 The bank on one side is thickly wooded, the firs chiefly reigning.

6. *trans.* †**a.** To rule, govern (a person, etc.).

c **1374** CHAUCER *Troylus* II. 379 Swich love of freendes regneth al this toun.

b. To put *down* by reigning. *rare*$^{-1}$.

1819 SHELLEY *Prometh. Unb.* II. iv. 100 But who reigns down Evil, the immedicable plague?

†**c.** To live *out* (a specified number of years) as ruler. *Obs. rare*$^{-1}$.

a **1641** BP. MONTAGU *Acts & Mon.* (1642) 136 When he had reigned out forty yeares, he died in winter.

reign, variant of RAIGN *v. Obs.*

†**reignative**, *a. Obs. rare*$^{-1}$. [See REIGN *v.* and -ATIVE.] Ruling, governing.

1387–8 USK *Test. Love* II. ii. (Skeat) I. 83 Right so litel or naught is worth erthely power, but if reignatif prudence in heedes governe the smale.

ˈreigner. *rare.* [f. REIGN *v.* + -ER[1].] One who reigns, a ruler.

1460 CAPGRAVE *Chron.* (Rolls) 52 Here leve we the manere of countyng used befor, where we sette evyr the regner in his last ȝere. **1530** PALSGR. 261/2 Reigner in a kyngdome, *regnatevr*. **1602** CAREW *Cornwall* 144b, Not needing in the Norman Kings new birth to be distinguished with the Raigners number. **1627** SPEED *Eng.* etc. *Abridged* vi. §9 Henry the third, the Normans longest Raigner. **1908** *Daily Chron.* 13 Feb. 4/4 Louis XIV., the record reigner, was never in his life clean all over from the natural exhalations of a monarch's skin.

reigning (ˈreɪnɪŋ), *vbl. sb.* [f. as prec. + -ING[1].] The action of the vb. REIGN.

a **1300** *Cursor M.* 8515 His regnning was wit right resun. *c* **1330** R. BRUNNE *Chron. Wace* (Rolls) 4105 For regnynge of kynges straunge,.. langage men chaunge. **1439** *E.E. Wills* 119 The xviij yere [? of the] Rengnyng of our souereyn lord Kyng Harry. **1633** P. FLETCHER *Elisa* I. xliii, There doth it blessed sit, and looking down,.. Scorns earth, where even Kings most serve by reigning. **1711** in *10th Rep. Hist. MSS. Comm.* App. V. 120 The innocency of James the Second in his reigneing. **1776** GIBBON *Decl. & F.* xiii. I. 394 Of all arts, the most difficult was the art of reigning.

reigning (ˈreɪnɪŋ), *ppl. a.* [f. as prec. + -ING[2].] That reigns, in various senses of the vb.

1. Of persons: Ruling, governing.

1716 LADY M. W. MONTAGU *Let. to C'tess Mar* 17 Oct., I have taken this little fatigue merely to oblige the reigning empress. **1786** JEFFERSON *Writ.* (1859) I. 574 The reigning party in the United Netherlands, and the government of this country. **1828** SCOTT *F.M. Perth* xxxv, He sent him to France to receive his education at the court of the reigning sovereign. **1855** MACAULAY *Hist. Eng.* xx. IV. 444 The Whigs were on principle attached to the reigning dynasty.

b. *transf.*

1705 ADDISON *Italy* 9 Pictures of the reigning Beauties in the Court of France. **1711** STEELE *Spect.* No. 156 ¶ 1 The History of the reigning Favourites among the Women. **1849** THACKERAY *Pendennis* xxxi, The book was daintily illustrated with pictures of reigning beauties.

2. Of things: Prevailing, predominating, chief.

1642 ROGERS *Naaman* 154 The raigning and defiling and deceiving power of it. **1685** EVELYN *Mrs. Godolphin* (1888) 9 The raigneing pestilence of Sixty-fiue. **1711** ADDISON *Spect.* No. 13 ¶6 To show what are at present the reigning Entertainments of the Politer Part of Great-Britain. **1769** FALCONER *Dict. Marine* (1780), *Reigning-winds*, a name given to the winds which usually prevail on any particular coast or region. **1817** CHALMERS *Astron. Disc.* ii. (1852) 63 The reigning principle of this Discourse. **1873** ROGERS *Orig. Bible* ii. (1875) 87 The reigning feature which from first to last distinguishes this book from every other.

reigˈnite, *v.* [RE- 5 a.] *trans.* To ignite again. So **reigˈnition**.

1863 TYNDALL *Heat* iii. 51 The candle is reignited and burns with vivid brilliancy. **1884** *American* VII. 222 The momentary extinction and reignition of the light. **1892** *Pall Mall G.* 21 Apr. 4/3 He.. lit a match, and re-ignited the fuse.

reik, Sc. var. REACH *v.*[1], REAK(s); obs. f. REEK *sb.* and *v.*

reike, obs. f. RICK.

reikie, obs. Sc. f. REEKY.

Reil (raɪl). *Anat.* [The name of Johann Christian *Reil* (1759–1813), German anatomist.] ***island of Reil***: an area of the cerebral cortex which overlies the corpus striatum but is concealed within the lateral sulcus (the fissure of Sylvius).

Described by Reil in 1809 (*Arch. f. Physiol.* IX. 144).

1840 G. V. ELLIS *Demonstrations of Anat.* 31 The fissure [of Sylvius] divides above into two portions, one of which passes before, and one behind some small convolutions which constitute the island of Reil. **1888** W. R. GOWERS *Man. Dis. Nervous Syst.* II. IV. 6 Within the fissure of Sylvius lie the small convolutions of the island of Reil, or insula, four or five in number, which spread out like a fan. **1939** O. LARSELL *Textbk. Neuro-Anat.* XVIII. 219 The lateral fissure (fissure of Sylvius) opens to the hidden cortical surface of the island of Reil. **1961** A. R. BUCHANAN *Functional Neuro-Anat.* xxi. 173 The insular part of the cerebral cortex or island of Reil can be readily exposed by removal of the opercular portions of the frontal, parietal and temporal lobes of the cerebrum.

reil(e, reill, obs. ff. RAIL *sb.*[1], REEL *sb.* and *v.*

reiˈllume, *v.* [RE- 5 a: cf. RELUME.] *trans.* To light up again; to reignite.

1793 WORDSW. *Prose Wks.* (1876) I. 5 To.. reillume the torch of extinguished David. *a* **1822** SHELLEY *Mother & Son* v, The vital fire seemed reillumed. **1848** LYTTON *Harold* v. i, It coils round the dry leaves and sere stalks, and a touch re-illumes it. **1878** SYMONDS *Sonn. M. Angelo* xi, Reilluming memories that died.

reillumiˈnation. [RE- 5 a.] The act of reilluminating; new illumination.

1611 FLORIO, *Ralluminatione*, a re-illumination. **1891** T. HARDY *Tess* xxxv, But reillumination.. returned to him.

reiˈllumine, *v.* [RE- 5 a.] *trans.* To illumine again. Hence **reiˈllumined** *ppl. a.*

1813 SHELLEY *Q. Mab* VII. 180 A smile of godlike malice re-illumined [*later edd.* reillumed] His fading lineaments. **1815** *Zeluca* III. 44 The.. solicitude of his re-illumined mind. **1875** JOWETT *Plato* (ed. 2) III. 145 A single glance at the varying landscape would in an instant revive and reillumine the extinguished spark of poetry.

Reilly, var. RILEY.

reim, var. of RIEM.

re-ˈimage, *v.* [RE- 5 a.] To image again.

1813 SHELLEY *Q. Mab* VI. 8 The stainless mirror of the lake Re-images the eastern gloom. **1814** —— *Ess. & Lett.* (1852) I. 168 He re-imaged with intense thought the minutest recollections of the scene.

†**reimˈbale**, *v. Obs. rare*$^{-1}$. [RE- 5 a: cf. EMBALE *v.*] *trans.* To put up again in bales.

1623 *St. Papers, Col.* 163 Silk came so ill-conditioned for want of reimbaling.

†**reimˈbarge**, *v. Obs. rare*$^{-1}$. [RE- 5 a.] *intr.* To embark again on a barge.

1681 T. JORDAN *London's Joy* 4 With his Retinue he retreats agen To th' Water-side, and.. doth Re-imbarge.

reimbark, -ation, etc.: see RE-EMBARK, etc.

reimˈbibe, *v.* [RE- 5 a.] *trans.* To imbibe (†or soak) again. Also *fig.* Hence **reimˈbibing** *vbl. sb.*

1594 PLAT *Jewell-ho.* I. 57 Let these wast ashes bee reimbibed with more water. **1663** BOYLE *Usef. Exp. Nat. Philos.* II. App. 336 The hot Liquor soon reimbib'd the Salt. **1777** G. FORSTER *Voy. round World* I. 44 The reimbibing of perspired matter. **1823** J. BADCOCK *Dom. Amusem.* 40 The paper has had time sufficient to re-imbibe the moisture. *a* **1960** E. M. FORSTER *Maurice* (1971) iii. 15 Then he would reimbibe the face and the four words.

reimbody: see RE-EMBODY.

†**reimˈbosk**, *v. Obs. rare*$^{-0}$. [RE- 5 a: cf. next.] *trans.* = REIMBUSH *v.*

1659 HOWELL *Vocab.* III. (*Hunting*), The deer is reimboskd,.. *Il s'est rembusché*.

†**reimˈboss**, *v. Obs. rare.* In 7 re-imbosch, -imbosce. [f. RE- 5 a + EMBOSS *v.*[2]: cf. REIMBUSH *v.*] **a.** *refl.* To hide (oneself) again among bushes. **b.** *intr.* (See quot. 1656.)

1640 HOWELL *Dodona's Gr.* (1649) 14 The Ampelonian satyr.. suddenly ran in, and re-imbosch'd himself. **1656** BLOUNT *Glossogr.*, *Re-imbosce*, to lie again in ambush, or return to the Wood.

reimbrace: see RE-EMBRACE.

reimbursaˈbility. [f. REIMBURSABLE *a.*] The quality of being reimbursable.

1978 *Nature* 16 Nov. 201/3 What this means is that Congress is limiting the reimbursability of salaries of the best faculty, the stars, the Nobel Prize winners, those people who make our institutions great.

reim'bursable, *a.* [f. as next + -ABLE, or ad. F. *remboursable*.] That is to be reimbursed, repayable.

1792 HAMILTON *Wks.* (1851) III. 342 Let the sum of 550,000 dollars be borrowed,..reimbursable within five years. **1866** H. MERIVALE in *Life Whately* I. 117 A measure was devised (1835) for the payment of arrears to the clergy by Government, reimbursable by a land-tax.

reimburse (riːɪm'bɜːs), *v.* Also 7 -bourse. [RE- 5 a, perh. after F. *rembourser*.]

1. *trans.* To repay or make up to one (a sum expended).

1611 COTGR., *Rembourser*, to reimburse; to repay, restore, or giue backe, money spent, etc. **1671** EVELYN *Diary* 26 June, The mony we laid out to be reimbours'd out of the contingent monies set apart for us. **1733-4** BERKELEY in Fraser *Life* vi. 218 You will also remember to take bonds for the money, to be reimbursed for the Deanery-house. **1793** SMEATON *Edystone L.* (ed. 2) Pref. 5 It will a good deal fall short of reimbursing my expences. **1839** HALLAM *Hist. Lit.* III. i. §8 The tardy sale of so voluminous a work could not have reimbursed the cost. **1872** YEATS *Growth Comm.* 231 The capital..he reckoned at 10,000,000 guilders, which four prosperous trips would amply reimburse.

†**b.** To refund, disgorge. *Obs. rare*$^{-1}$.

1725 RAMSAY *Gentle Sheph.* v. iii, I'll strip him soon of all to her pertains, And make him reimburse his ill-got gains.

2. To repay, recompense (a person). Also const. *for*, †*of* (the expenditure, etc.).

1637-50 ROW *Hist. Kirk* (Wodrow Soc.) 112 The poore men to be reimbursed. **1669** S. PEPYS in *Pepys' Diary*, etc. (1879) VI. 110, I will see you fully and thankfully reimbursed for what charges shall attend the same. **1672** DRYDEN *Assignation* v. iii, You'll find occasion instantly to reimburse me of my kindness. **1707** FARQUHAR *Beaux' Strat.* I. i, They are willing to reimburse us a little. **1790** BEATSON *Nav. & Mil. Mem.* I. 266 The Colonists were reimbursed by Parliament of all the expences incurred by them in this expedition. *a* **1859** MACAULAY *Hist. Eng.* xxv. V. 251 They had disbursed money largely,..with the certainty that they should never be reimbursed unless the outlay proved beneficial to the public.

b. *refl.* Also in *transf.* uses.

1724 SWIFT *Drapier's Lett.* Wks. 1755 V. II. 47 Hath he saved any other kingdom at his own expence, to give him a title of reimbursing himself by the destruction of ours? **1818** SCOTT *Hrt. Midl.* ii, Wilson felt no scruple of conscience in resolving to reimburse himself for his losses. **1850** GROTE *Greece* II. lxv. (1862) V. 539 Eager to reimburse themselves for this humiliation, they now formed a conspiracy..to seize the government.

3. With double object: (cf. 1 and 2).

1624 CAPT. SMITH *Virginia* Pref. 1 The issue may well reimburse you your summes expended. **1687** A. LOVELL tr. *Thevenot's Trav.* I. 257 Till he be reimbursed the money that he hath laid out. *a* **1745** SWIFT *Story of an Injured Lady* Wks. 1751 XIV. 100 It was but reasonable..to reimburse him some of his Charges. **1803** WELLINGTON in Gurw. *Desp.* (1838) I. 390 If he had consented to be reimbursed this expedition he would have received bonds..for this sum of money. **1841** MACAULAY *Ess.*, *Hastings* (1854) 655 His friends in Leadenhall Street proposed to reimburse him the costs of his trial.

Hence **reim'burser**, **reim'bursing** *vbl. sb.*

1611 COTGR., *Rembourseur*, a reimburser; repayer. *Ibid.*, *Remboursement*,..a reimbursing. **1727-38** CHAMBERS *Cycl.* s.v. *Reimbursement*, Reimbursing is also used for paying the price a commodity costs its owner.

reim'bursement. Also 7 re-em-. [f. as prec. + -MENT, perh. after F. *remboursement*.] The act of reimbursing, repayment.

1611 SPEED *Hist. Gt. Brit.* IX. xiii. §90. 606/2 The King had restored Brest in Britaine to the Duke, vpon reembursements of the money lent. **1662** J. DAVIES tr. *Olearius' Voy. Ambass.* 221 By way of re-emboursement for the charges we had been at. **1762** GOLDSM. *Nash* 9 His scanty commission could never procure him the proper reimbursements. **1790** HAMILTON *Wks.* (1851) III. 9 He..took the risks of reimbursement upon himself. **1837** THIRLWALL *Greece* xxxii. IV. 235 The reimbursement of the 100 talents which they had advanced to the party of the city. **1878** LECKY *Eng. in 18th C.* II. viii. 494 For this expense he promised a parliamentary reimbursement.

reim'bush, *v. rare*$^{-0}$. [RE- 5 a, after F. *rembucher*: cf. REIMBOSK and REIMBOSS.] *trans.* To lodge again among bushes. Also **reim'bushment** (see quots.).

1611 COTGR., *Rembusché*, reimbushed; lodged, or put among bushes... *Rembuschement*, a reimbushment; the place whereat wild beasts enter into a thicket after that they haue preyed, or pastured. **1877** WRAXELL tr. *V. Hugo's Les Misérables* II. c, This manœuvre is peculiar to the tracked deer,..in venery it is called a 'false reimbushment'.

reime, obs. form of REALM.

reim-kennar. *pseudo-arch.* [app. formed by Scott on G. *reim* rhyme + *kenner* knower.] One skilled in magic rhymes.

1821 SCOTT *Pirate* vi, A Norwegian invocation, still preserved in the island of Unst, under the name of the song of the Reim-Kennar. *Ibid.* xxviii, They who speak to the Reim-Kennar must lower their voice.

rei'mmerge, *v.* [RE- 5 a.] To immerge again.

1664 POWER *Exp. Philos.* II. 92 If before the removal of your thumb you reimmerge it again into the vessel'd Quick-silver as before. **1761** *London & Environs* IV. 86 The great increase..re-immerged the survivors into an abyss of horror and despair.

re'immerse, *v.* [RE- 5 a.] *trans.* To immerse again. Also *fig.* So **rei'mmersion**.

1728 DESAGULIERS in *Phil. Trans.* XXXV. 624 Then the Point C being got to H is re-immersed. *c* **1865** G. GORE in *Circ. Sc.* I. 215/2 They..become covered with a film of oxide, which considerably weakens the electric current on their reimmersion. *Ibid.* 222/1 Reimmerse it repeatedly. **1905** *Speaker* 1 Apr. 18/1 It is to the desert that yearly pilgrimages bring hosts of the faithful..to re-immerse themselves in the original enthusiasm.

re'immigrant. [RE- 5 a.] A returning emigrant. So **reimmi'gration**, return.

1864 KINGSLEY *Rom. & Teut.* 27 The Irish have just established popery across St. George's Channel, by the aid of re-immigrants from America. **1894** HUXLEY *Evolution & Ethics*, *Prolegom.* v, They..take measures to defend themselves from the re-immigration of either.

†**rei'mmit**, *v. Obs. rare*$^{-1}$. [RE- 5 a.] *trans.* To insert again.

1669 BOYLE *Contn. New Exp.* II. (1682) 146, I therefore reimmitted the same tube into the same gun.

reim'park, *v. rare*$^{-1}$. [RE- 5 a.] *trans.* To confine again.

1615 J. STEPHENS *Satyr. Ess.*, *Jaylor* (1857) 192 You may ..meet him..riding post in mellancholy to re-impark his wilde runnagates.

reim'part, *v.* [RE- 5 a.] To impart again.

1831 CARLYLE *Sart. Res.* I. ix, Thy unparalleled confession (which we, even to the sounder British world.. grudge to reimpart). **1857** GLADSTONE *Homer*, *Proleg.* (1858) I. 81 In thus reimparting a promiscuous character to the first scenes of Grecian history.

reim'pel, *v.* [RE- 5 a.] To impel again.

1660 BOYLE *New Exp. Phys. Mech.* xxxix. 325 The Water was presently re-impell'd to its former height. **1775** HARRIS *Philos. Arrangem.* Wks. (1841) 331 *note*, The impelling power, for instance, is after a manner re-impelled. **1860** *Cornh. Mag.* II. 71 It repeats..the signals transmitted from London, re-impelling the message to Copenhagen.

reimpje, reimpie, varr. RIEMPIE.

reim'place, *v.* Now *rare*. Also 7 rein-. [RE- 5 a. Cf. F. *remplacer*.] *trans.* To put in place again; to replace.

a **1648** LD. HERBERT *Hen. VIII* (1683) 163 Taking the Canons along with them, [they] reimplaced them, and so departed. **1651** JER. TAYLOR *Serm. for Year* I. xix. 241 For the reimplacing the divine image..God did a greater work then the creation. **1719** LONDON & WISE *Compl. Gard.* 293 You must continue to remove Strawberry Plants out of your Nurserys, to reimplace those Tufts which are dead. **1890** H. M. STANLEY *Darkest Afr.* II. xxvii. 212 If Egypt intended to cast him off..here was this offer of..£1500 salary to reimplace Egypt.

reim'plant, *v.* [RE- 5 a.] *trans.* To implant again. So **reimplan'tation**.

1656 *Artif. Handsom.* 45 How many grave and godly matrons, usually graffe or re-implant on their..browes, the reliques, combings or cuttings of..more youthful hair? *a* **1676** HALE *Prim. Orig. Man.* III. vi. (1677) 281 A Branch torn from a Tree..will resume Life by re-implantation and the Solar Heat. *a* **1891** *Medical News* LII. Advts. I. (Cent.), Reimplantation of a Trephined Button of Bone. **1919** *Jrnl. Amer. Med. Assoc.* 26 July 301/1 Bonnefon's experiences confirm that if a small pathologic process can be cut out completely and then reimplanted in the old site, the environment being normal, it will be invaded by normal cells and lose its pathologic characteristics. **1955** *New Biol.* XVIII. 32 The reimplantation of stored infant tissues into the same animal, and..the observation of the reciprocal influences of host and implant, are technically practicable and established procedures. **1973** *Sci. Amer.* Feb. 28/3 We can transfer the eye into a tissue culture and change its orientation when we reimplant it in a host embryo, and correlate the result with the results of direct-transplantation experiments.

re'import, *sb.* [RE- 5 a.] Reimportation.

1883 *American* VI. 244 The amount available for reimport probably has been returned to us.

reim'port, *v.* [RE- 5 a. Cf. F. *réimporter*.] *trans.* To bring back; *spec.* to import again to the country exporting. So **reimpor'tation**.

1742 YOUNG *Nt. Th.* II. 308 Bid Day stand still,..and reimport The period past. **1776** ADAM SMITH *W.N.* IV. iv. II. 90 In those cases in which the goods..are really exported to some foreign country; and not clandestinely reimported into our own. **1847** LD. LINDSAY *Chr. Art* I. 117 Like the fire of Prometheus, reimported from its sunny fountain in the east. **1853** P. THOMPSON in *Assoc. Archit. Soc. Rep. & Pap.* II. 363 The wool of this country was..dyed, sent abroad, and reimported in the web. **1857** MILL *Pol. Econ.* (ed. 4) II. III. xxiv. 229 The Bank reserves can replenish themselves without any re-importation of the gold. **1883** *American* VI. 244 Making their reimportation illegal.

reim'portunate, *v.*: see next, quot. 1611.

reimpor'tune, *v. rare.* [RE- 5 a.] *trans.* To importune again.

1605 B. JONSON *Volpone* I. i, On first advantage..will I re-importune him Unto the making of his testament. **1611** COTGR., *Reimportuner*, to reimportune, or to reimportunate. **1632** J. HAYWARD tr. *Biondi's Eromena* To Rdr., By.. earnest solicitations to re-importune him to close up what in these two remained unfinished.

reim'pose, *v.* [RE- 5 a. Cf. F. *réimposer*.]

1. *trans.* To impose (a burden, tax, etc.) again.

1611 COTGR., *Reimposer*, to reimpose, to recharge. **1675-6** in J. T. Wheeler *Madras* (1861) III. 418 Pretending to sell the Kings paddy here customs free..and to re-impose an avaldar. **1812** SIR R. WILSON *Priv. Diary* (1862) I. 123 Russia..scarcely even scrupled to re-impose the Turkish yoke upon her allies, the Servians. **1855** BRIGHT *Sp.*, *Russia* 7 June (1876) 262 We have commenced a career of reimposing taxes. **1883** *Manch. Exam.* 26 Nov. 5/2 We ought to..reimpose the sliding-scale duty on corn.

b. To tax again. *rare.*

1776 ADAM SMITH *W.N.* v. ii. I. 463 If they complain and make good their complaints, the whole parish is reimposed next year, in order to reimburse them.

†**2.** To reprint. *Obs. rare*$^{-1}$.

1686 J. ELIOT in *Boyle's Wks.* (1772) I. *Life* 213 My humble request..is, that we may again reimpose the Primer and Catechism; for though the last impression be not quite spent, yet quickly they will.

reimpo'sition. [RE- 5 a. Cf. F. *réimposition*.] The act of reimposing; also, an instance of this, a reimposed tax.

1776 ADAM SMITH *W.N.* v. ii. I. 464 Such reimpositions are always over and above the taille of the particular year in which they are laid on. **1817** J. SCOTT *Paris Revisited* (ed. 4) 25 Abetting the re-imposition of what they know to be imbecile, odious, and unjust. **1860** BRIGHT *Sp.*, *Ch. Rates* 27 Apr. (1876) 540 They would never consent to a reimposition of a Church rate. **1885** *Manch. Exam.* 6 Nov. 5/2 Meditating a reimposition of the tax on corn.

So **reim'posure**.

1855 LYNCH *Lett. to Scattered* viii. 108 The stirrings of a spring life that will shake off old winter's yoke, and make its reimposure impossible.

reim'pregnate, *v.* [RE- 5 a.] *trans.* To impregnate again.

1646 SIR T. BROWNE *Pseud. Ep.* 68 The vigor of the Load-stone is destroyed by fire, nor will it be reimpregnated by any other Magnete then the earth. **1669** WORLIDGE *Syst. Agric.* (1681) 137 That the Sun, Frost, and Rains may.. reimpregnate it again with its former fertile Juice. **1825** J. NICHOLSON *Operat. Mechanic* 340 Iron..can be reimpregnated with carbon, to a certain extent, without materially injuring its malleable properties. **1953** R. LEHMANN *Echoing Grove* 29 But still the stones seemed rocked, the unsterile mounds, reimpregnated, exhaled dust's fever.

reim'press, *v.* [RE- 5 a.] To impress anew.

1667 *Decay Chr. Piety* v. ¶ 13 Every particular command ..tending to re-impress on us some part of that divine image. *a* **1711** KEN *Sion* Poet. Wks. 1721 IV. 380 The lovely Graces on dear Psyche's Breast Macario's Speech so deeply re-imprest. **1779-81** JOHNSON *L.P.*, *Milton* (1868) 63 Religion..will glide by degrees out of the mind, unless it be invigorated and reimpressed by external ordinances. **1838** LYTTON *Alice* II. ii, The whole family were duly impressed and re-impressed with her importance. **1860** PUSEY *Min. Proph.* 192 He reimpresses on them the one simple need of the creature, *seek God*. **1883** V. STUART *Egypt* 217 The deity having the power to reimpress the deceased with life.

reim'pression. [RE- 5 a. Cf. prec. and F. *réimpression*.]

1. The act of reprinting; a reprint of a work.

1616 SPELMAN *De non Temer. Eccl.* (ed. 2) 174, I hitherto by entreaty with-held it from a reimpression. **1684** J. ELIOT in *Boyle's Wks.* (1772) I. *Life* 210 This last gift of 400l. for the reimpression of the Indian Bible. **1787** *Gentl. Mag.* LVII. II. 1053/1, I began to read it as a re-impression of the work which..I had perused and loved. **1816** SINGER *Hist. Cards* 218 Whether this was a re-impression of Murner's book, or a new one on the same model we know not. **1864** F. HALL in *Lauder's Tractate* Pref. 5, I have entered into particulars as to my reimpression of the present poem.

2. A renewed impression.

1665 BRATHWAIT *Comment Two Tales* 23 Fear..wrought strongly enough already on the Carpenter's Imagination, so as it little needed any re-impression. **1924** W. B. SELBIE *Psychol. Relig.* 89 Every one is aware of unaccountable recollections of this kind. Such a reimpression of familiar things may take place even though there is no conscious recollection.

reim'print, *v.* [RE- 5 a.] *trans.* To imprint anew; to reprint. Hence **reim'printed** *ppl. a.*, **reim'printing** *vbl. sb.*

1566 ABP. PARKER *Corr.* (Parker Soc.) 261 The reimprinting of the late Geneva Bible. **1616** SPELMAN *De non Temer. Eccl.* (ed. 2) 173, I haue beene often sollicited within these two yeeres..to reimprint this little Treatise. *a* **1631** DONNE 6 *Serm.* i. (1634) 14 This seal being reimprinted upon us in our second Creation. *a* **1711** KEN *Hymnotheo* Poet. Wks. 1721 III. 77 They inward Joys of Absolution feel, And glory in their re-imprinted Seal.

reim'prison, *v.* [RE- 5 a.] *trans.* To imprison again. So **reim'prisonment**.

1611 COTGR., *Remprisonner*, to reimprison. **1652** J. WRIGHT tr. *Camus' Nat. Paradox* x. 244 If it be your pleasure to re-imprison her in the same Castle. **1798** *Invasion* II. viii. 79, I even could scarcely help regarding my re-imprisonment..as a punishment inflicted upon me, for yielding so inconsiderately. **1837** CARLYLE *Fr. Rev.* I. VI. i, Till..the Uncontrollable be got, if not reimprisoned, yet harnessed.

reim'provement. *rare*$^{-1}$. [RE- 5 a.] A renewed improvement.

1618 BP. HALL *Contempl.*, *N.T.* I. ii. For the childe of a virgin is the reimprovement of that power, which created the world.

reimschoon, var. REMSKOEN.

rein (rein), *sb.*[1] Forms: 4-5 rene, 5 reene, ren, 5-6 rean(e; 4-7 reyn(e, rayne, rain(e, 7-8 reign, 6-7 reine, 6- rein; 5-6 *Sc.* renȝe, rengȝe. [a. OF. *rene* (mod.F. *rêne*), *regne*, *raigne*, *rainne*, etc., earlier *resne* and (AF.) *redne*, usually regarded as repr. a Common Romanic **retina*, f. L. *retinēre* to RETAIN, whence also It. *redina*, *-ine* (Sicil. *retina*), Pg. *redea*, Sp. *rienda*, Prov. and Catal. *regna*; but the divergences in the forms have not been satisfactorily explained, and the correctness of the etym., for OF. at least, is doubtful (see Körting, under *resinum* and *retina*).]

1. a. A long narrow strap or thong of leather, attached to the bridle or bit on each side of the head, by which a horse or other animal is controlled and guided by the rider or driver; any similar device used for the same purpose. (The *pl.* has freq. the same sense as the *sing.*, the two halves being thought of separately.)

For such combs. as *bearing-*, *bridle-*, *check-*, *coupling-*, *curb-*, *gag-rein*, etc., see the first element. *false rein*, 'a lath of leather, passed sometimes through the arch of the banquet to bend the horse's neck' (Chambers *Cycl.* 1727-38).

13.. *K. Alis.* 786 Faste he sat, and huld the reyne. **1375** BARBOUR *Bruce* II. 415 Schir Philip the Mowbray.. Raid till him.. And hynt hys rengȝe. **c1400** *Destr. Troy* 6417 His horse in his hond held by the reyne. **c1450** *Merlin* 407 He hilde the reyne of his bridill in his lefte arme. **c1500** *Lancelot* 2828 Who may he be, ȝhone knycht, So still that hovith and sterith not his Ren? **1592** SHAKS. *Ven. & Ad.* 264 The strong-neckt steed, being tied vnto a tree, Breaketh his raine. **1618** M. BARET *Horsemanship* I. Pref. 2 If they rightly consider the stayd seating of the Horses body, and also the true placing of his head, with the easie cariage of his reine. **1782** COWPER *Gilpin* 88 That trot became a gallop soon, In spite of curb and rein. **1805** SCOTT *Last Minstr.* II. xxxiv, The Dwarf the stirrup held and rein. **1856** 'STONEHENGE' *Brit. Rural Sports* 395/1 For those who ride with a loose rein the snaffle is quite sufficient.

pl. **13..** *Gaw. & Gr. Knt.* 457 With a runisch rout þe raynez he tornez. **c1384** CHAUCER *H. Fame* II. 443 He.. lat the reynes gon Of his hors. **c1450** *Merlin* 493 The horse all quyk with-oute maister her reynes trailinge with the strem. **1484** CAXTON *Ordre of Chyualry* 66 To an horse is gyuen a brydel and the raynes of the brydel ben gyuen in the hondes of the knyght. **1565-6** BLUNDEVIL *Art of Riding* x. 7 When to vse false Reanes, and when to leaue them. **1598** BARCKLEY *Felic. Man* (1631) 177, I have sent thee a paire of reines of Scythia. **1664** BUTLER *Hud.* II. ii. 839 Quitting both their Swords and reigns They grasp'd with all their strength the manes. **1785** G. FORSTER tr. *Sparrman's Voy. Cape G. Hope* I. 53 In this Country they never use reins to their Oxen. **1817** SHELLEY *Rev. Islam* VI. xxi, 'Away! away!' she cried, and stretched her sword,.. And lightly shook the reins. **1875** JOWETT *Plato* (ed. 2) I. 50 If you want to mount one of your father's chariots, and take the reins at a race.

transf. **1660** MRQ. WORCESTER *Exact Def.* 15 A Helm or Stem with Bitt and Reins, wherewith any Child may guide, order, and controul the whole Operation [of an engine].

b. *to give* (a horse) *the rein(s)*, to allow (it) free motion (cf. 2 b). *to draw rein*, to bring one's horse to a stand; to stop riding.

1621 BP. HALL *Heaven upon Earth* §8 Give a free horse the full reins, and he will soon tire. **1834** JAMES *J. Marston Hall* x, We never drew a rein for twenty miles. **1838** LYTTON *Leila* v. i, He spoke, and gave the rein to his barb. **1889** DOYLE *Micah Clarke* xii, We gave rein to our horses.

2. *fig.* **a.** Any means of guiding, controlling, or governing; a curb, check, or restraint of any kind. In later use freq. in ***the reins of government*** (cf. F. *les rênes du gouvernement*).

c1430 LYDG *Reas. & Sens.* 2263, I am guyed by hir reyne, And she as lady souereyne [etc.]. **c1440** CAPGRAVE *Life St. Kath.* v. 1467 What, art thou, dame, led on that rene? Thi witte counte I not worth a beene. **1560** DAUS tr. *Sleidane's Comm.* 134 God.. hath not permitted him to have the reignes at libertie. **1596** DRAYTON *Legends* ii. 119 This held the reines which overrul'd his will. **1638** JUNIUS *Paint. Ancients* 55 Both doe hold the raines of our hearts, leading and guiding our Passions. **1667** MILTON *P.L.* XI. 582 The Men, though grave, ey'd them, and let thir eyes Rove without rein. **1712** POPE *Spect.* No. 408 ¶6 Never too strong for the Reins of Reason and the Guidance of Judgment. **1777** WATSON *Philip II*, XIV. (1793) II. 177 The council of state assumed the reins of government. **1827** HALLAM *Const. Hist.* (1876) III. xvi. 235 Anne herself.. kept in her own hands the reins of power. **1879** FROUDE *Cæsar* v. 44 The Senate had dropped the reins, and no longer governed or misgoverned.

b. In various phrases, esp. *to give (the) rein(s) to*, to allow full course or scope to.

1568 GRAFTON *Chron.* II. 927 A larger reyne of mischiefe geuen to the vulgare people. **1588** SHAKS. *L.L.L.* v. ii. 663 Reine thy tongue. *Lon.* I must rather giue it the reine. **1607** R. C[AREW] tr. *Estienne's World of Wonders* 58 Youth is set at libertie, and haue the reine laid in their neckes to runne at randon. **1611** SHAKS. *Wint. T.* II. iii. 51 When she will take the raine, I let her run. **1638** JUNIUS *Paint. Ancients* 226 Wee must rather give our Invention the full raines. **1667** MILTON *P.L.* x. 674 Som say the Sun Was bid turn Reines from th' Equinoctial Rode.. Up to the Tropic Crab. **1711** 'J. DISTAFF' *Char. Don Sacheverellio* 9 You will find our Knight .. give the Reigns to his Imagination. **1761** GRAY *F. Sisters* 33 We the reins to Slaughter give. **1807** OPIE *Lect. on Art* iv. (1848) 332 No man ever more completely laid the reins on the neck of his inclinations. **1865** M. ARNOLD *Ess. Crit.* ii. (1875) 82 To give it that degree of prominence is to throw the reins to one's whim. **1885-94** R. BRIDGES *Eros & Psyche* Nov. xxi, 'And yet', thus gave she rein to jeer and gibe.

3. *transf.* The handles of a blacksmith's tongs.

1843 HOLTZAPFFEL *Turning* I. 200 Flat-bit tongs.. are.. always parallel; and a ring or coupler, is put upon the handles or reins, to maintain the grip upon the work.

4. *attrib.*, as *rein-knot*, *-ring*, *-rope*; **rein-arm**, **-hand**, that by which the reins are held in driving (also *fig.*); **rein-orchis**, an orchis of the genus *Habenaria*, the Fringed Orchis.

Also in names of mechanical devices attached to or connected with reins, as *rein-holder*, *-hook*, *-slide*, *-snap* (Knight *Dict. Mech.* 1875).

1843 *Ainsworth's Mag.* IV. 436 Our well-fed 'Phaeton' pulled his team together.., dropped his rein-hand, [etc.]. **1844** H. STEPHENS *Bk. Farm* II. 446 Two or three rein-ropes are useful, to fasten to the calf if necessary. **1882** FLOYER *Unexpl. Baluchistan* 60 The probability presents itself that said rein-knot will come out. **1886** *Pall Mall G.* 2 Oct. 2/2 The surveyor.. cannot have his rein hand or his whip hand pulled at, if he is to get over it successfully. **1891** T. HARDY *Tess* viii, She clutched D'Urberville's rein-arm. **1955** E. POUND *Classic Anthol.* III. 188 A leathered front-board with tiger-fell And metal rein-rings as well. **1968** J. ARNOLD *Shell Bk. Country Crafts* xxiii. 267 Attached to the hames are tug-hooks and rein-rings.

rein (reɪn), *sb.*[2] Also 6 **rhen**, 6-7 **reen**. [ad. Da. or Sw. *ren*, †*reen*, Norw. *rein*:—ON. *hreinn*: see REINDEER. Hence also G. *rein(er)*, *renn*, F. *renne*.] The reindeer.

1555 EDEN *Decades* IV. (Arb.) 301 [In Laponia] they tame certeyne wild beastes which they caule Reen. *Ibid.* 331 Hartes.. whiche in the Noruegians tounge are cauled Rhen. **1595** J. DAVIS *Hydrogr. Descr.* Wks. (Hakl. Soc.) 219 The inhabitants.. having the use of a kind of stag, by them called Reen, to drawe those their sleades. **1698** A. BRAND *Embassy into China* 49 Their Cabans or Hutts are generally made of the Skins of the Reens, or some other wild Beasts. **1797** *Encycl. Brit.* (ed. 3) IV. 305/1 They keep immense herds of reins. *Ibid.*, The flesh of the rein is the most coveted part of their food. **1854** A. MURRAY *Geog. Distrib. Mammals* (1866) 150 Some authorities think fossil Rein different from the living. **1896** *Blackw. Mag.* July 91 The Lapps.. are great enemies of the wild rein.

Comb. **1797** *Encycl. Brit.* (ed. 3) IV. 305/1 In summer they [the reindeer] feed on several plants; but during winter on the rein-liverwort.

rein, kidney: see REINS.

rein (reɪn), *v.* Forms: 4, 6-7 **rayne**, 6-7 **rain**, 7 **raign**; 4 **reine**, 5-6 **reyne**, 8 **reign**, 6- **rein**; 5-6 **rene**, 6 *Sc.* **renȝe**. [f. REIN *sb.*[1] Cf. F. *rêner*, which may have existed in AF.]

†**1.** *trans.* To tie (a horse, or its head) *to* something by the rein; to tie up in this way. *Obs.*

13.. *Sir Beues* (MS. A) 1699 He reinede his hors to a chesteine. **c1435** *Torr. Portugal* 149 He Reynyd hys sted vnto a stake. **c1470** *Golagros & Gaw.* 129 The knyght.. Reynit his palfray of pryde, Quhen he ves lightit doune. **1564** in *Child-Marriages* 101 The[y] light both; and ther horse was rayned in the midest of the Lane. **1592** SHAKS. *Ven. & Ad.* 14 Vouchsafe.. to alight thy steed, And rain his proud head to the saddle bow.

2. To fit or furnish with a rein or reins.

1483 *Cath. Angl.* 303/2 To Reyn [*v.r.* Rene], *habenare.* **1598** BARRET *Theor. Warres* 141 A strong bridle, double rayned, wherof one to be of wyer. **1717** POPE *Iliad* v. 448 Beside him stood his lance,.. And, rein'd with gold, his foaming steeds before. **1725** —— *Odyss.* VI. 86 Th' attending train The car prepare, the mules incessant rein. **1795** SOUTHEY *Lett. fr. Spain* (1799) 30 The leaders and the middle pair are without reins, and the nearest [mules] reined only with ropes.

†**b.** *transf.* ? To fasten, make fast. *Obs.*[−1]

1549 *Compl. Scot.* vi. 41 Than the master cryit, and bad renȝe ane bonet.

3. To check or stop, by pulling at the rein.

1530 PALSGR. 678/2 As sone as we mette, he rayned his horse and talked with me a good while. **1622** W. YONGE *Diary* (Camden) 48 The King reined his horse so hard that he came back upon him. **a1713** ELLWOOD *Autobiog.* (1765) 231 Reigning my Horse, to let hers go before me. **1810** SCOTT *Lady of L.* II. xix, Sudden his steed the leader rein'd. **1859** TENNYSON *Enid* 826 When Edyrn rein'd his charger at her side, She shrank a little.

b. *fig.* To put a check or restraint upon (something); to restrain *from* something.

1588 SHAKS. *L.L.L.* v. ii. 662 Sweet Lord Longauill reine thy tongue. **1606** —— *Tr. & Cr.* v. iii. 48 The venom'd vengeance ride vpon our swords,.. reine them from ruth. **1727** GAY *Fables* I. Introd., My tongue within my lips I rein. **1819** SHELLEY *Prometh. Unb.* II. ii. 80 They ride on them, and rein their headlong speed.

4. To govern, control, manage, or direct (also const. *to*), by means of reins. Now *rare*.

1590 SPENSER *F.Q.* I. iv. 9 Like Phœbus fayrest childe, That did presume his fathers fyrie wayne, And flaming mouthes of steedes.. with weaker hand to rayne. **c1611** CHAPMAN *Iliad* x. 341 The horse Pelides raignde, no mortall hand could vse But he himselfe. **1697** DRYDEN *Æneid* VII. 1069 His Son, the Second Virbius, retain'd His Fathers Art, and Warriour Steeds he rein'd. **1735** SOMERVILLE *Chase* I. 108 To rein the Steed Swift-stretching o'er the Plain, to chear the Pack. **1821** SCOTT *Kenilw.* xxx, A milk-white horse, which she reined with peculiar grace and dignity. **1861** CATLIN *Life amongst Indians* 96 We will rein our horses to them—don't be afraid.

b. *fig.* To rule, guide, or govern.

1581 SIDNEY *Apol. Poetrie* (Arb.) 28 They.. range onely rayned with learned discretion. **c1614** SIR W. MURE *Dido & Æneas* I. 659 Lawes and statutes.. Wherby good subjects easily are rain'd. **1663** COWLEY *Verses & Ess.* (1669) 88 Wild Ambition with imperious force Rides, rains, and spurs them like th' unruly Horse. **1801** SOUTHEY *Thalaba* IV. xv, From place to place, As his will rein'd the viewless Element, He rode the Wind.

5. To pull *up* or *back*, to check and hold *in*, by means of the reins.

1552 HULOET, Bridle or rein vp, *fræno.* **1591** PERCIVALL *Sp. Dict.*, *Arrendar*, to rain vp a horse,.. *frænare.* **1827** LYTTON *Pelham* x, I was reining in my horse. **1870** BRYANT *Homer* I. III. 86 They reined their steeds back to the ranks.

fig. **1594** HOOKER *Eccl. Pol.* IV. xi. §8 The cause why the Apostles did thus.. was to rein them in by this mean the more. **1834** MACAULAY *Ess.*, *Pitt* (1851) 299 The influence which had yoked together and reined in so many turbulent and ambitious spirits. **1891** *Tablet* 7 Nov. 743 Principles cannot be reined up short of their logical term.

b. *absol.*

1796 *Instr. & Reg. Cavalry* (1813) 65 When the Regiment or Line wheels into open Column, either by reining back or by wheeling back. **1809** J. MOORE *Campaign in Spain* 173 The Colonel judiciously reined-in to refresh the horses. **1814** SCOTT *Ld. of Isles* VI. xviii, Rein up; our presence would impair The fame we come too late to share. **1832** *Prop. Reg. Instr. Cavalry* II. 20 At the word 'March!' the rear rank reins back. **1888** W. D. LIGHTHALL *Young Seigneur* 20 We reined in at last to a walk.

fig. **1836** MRS. SHERWOOD *Henry Milner* III. vi, None of your practical jokes here,.. rein up, rein up, if you please.

c. To turn a horse by the reins. *rare*[−1].

1897 RHOSCOMYL *White Rose Arno* 277 He had already reined to his right, across the mead.

6. *U.S.* To preserve or keep enclosed *from* stock. Also with *up*.

1799 WASHINGTON *Writ.* (1893) XIV. 230 This field, after the rye has been eaten off by the sheep, is to be reined from stock of all kinds. *Ibid.* 231 The other part.. is to be equally well enclosed, and reined up from stock.

7. *intr.* Of a horse: **a.** To bear, or submit to, the rein; to carry itself in a specified manner when reined. Also *fig.*

1565-6 BLUNDEVIL *Horsemanship* ii. (1580) 4 His long slender head.. which maketh him to reine with the better grace. **1580** LYLY *Euphues* (Arb.) 244 Youth neuer raineth wel, but when age holdeth the bridell. **1601** SHAKS. *Twel. N.* III. iv. 358 Hee will beare you easily, and raines well. **1607** MARKHAM *Caval.* II. (1617) 205 When your horse standeth in his best glory, and reyneth most comely and closest. **1814** SCOTT *Wav.* xlvii, If he had had a wee bit rinnin ring on the snaffle, she wad ha' rein'd as cannily as a cadger's pownie.

b. To move *back*, go backwards, (as) under the influence of the rein. Also *transf.* of persons.

1627 *Lisander & Cal.* IX. 182 Lisander.. rained back a steppe or two. **c1720** GIBSON in *Compl. Farmer* (1766) s.v. *Pleurisy*, Though in the beginning he makes many motions to lie down, yet afterwards he reins back as far as his collar will permit. **1833** *Reg. Instr. Cavalry* I. 73 The horse must be tried to rein back.

rein, obs. form of RAIN, REIGN.

reinable, obs. form of RE-ENABLE.

'**reinage.** *nonce-wd.* [f. REIN *sb.*[1] + -AGE.] Reins collectively.

1863 P. S. WORSLEY *Poems & Trans.* 11 And placed the glittering reinage in his hands, And helped him to his throne upon the car.

Reinald, obs. variant of REYNARD.

†**rei'nanimate**, *v. Obs. rare.* [f. RE- 5 a + IN-[2] + ANIMATE *v.*] *trans.* To reanimate.

1626 DONNE *Serm.* xxi. 212 God.. shall recollect that dust,.. and then re-inanimate that man.

rei'naugurate, *v.* [RE- 5 a.] *trans.* To inaugurate afresh.

1857 MRS. GORE *Castles in the Air* xxx, I had no ambition to reinaugurate myself by another [illness]. **1895** *Current Hist.* (U.S.) V. 298 To re-establish a protective tariff and to reinaugurate a policy of unequal taxation.

reinaugu'ration. [RE- 5 a.] The action of reinaugurating; a fresh inauguration.

1655 FULLER *Wounded Consc.*, *Ornithologie* (1867) 270 The Eagle condescended that the day of his Re-inauguration should not be stained with blood. **1833** I. TAYLOR *Fanat.* i. 9 The great work.., should it be.. the re-inauguration of Christianity among ourselves? **1871** FREEMAN *Hist. Ess.* Ser. I. viii. 214 The re-inauguration of an Emperor whom one Parisian revolution had set up again.

rein-bone, obs. variant of RINGBONE.

†**rein'camerate**, *v. Obs. rare*[−1]. [RE- 5 a: see INCAMERATION.] *intr.* To return to the papal domain.

1672 MARVELL *Reh. Transp.* II. Wks. (Grosart) III. 298 There is some condition annex'd, upon failure of which this fiefe shall reincamerate.

rein'carnate, *a.* [RE- 5 a.] Incarnate again.

1882 MYERS *Renewal of Youth* etc., 213 Re-incarnate, unremembering, tread In the old same footsteps of himself long dead.

rein'carnate, *v.* [RE- 5 a.] *trans.* and *intr.* To incarnate anew.

1858 SEARS *Athan.* III. iii. 272 The Pharisee believed that .. only a part of them [the dead] would be re-incarnated, enter again into their former bodies. **1880** *Contemp. Rev.* Feb. 199 A body which could appear and disappear.. by being, as it were, re-incarnated at one time, and dis-incarnated at another. **1892** *Pall Mall G.* 13 Sept. 3/1 A man dies; his 'Ego' passes to the 'spiritual planes' of nature: after a long interval.. it re-incarnates.

Hence **rein'carnated**, **rein'carnating** *ppl. adjs.*

1883 J. GILMOUR *Mongols* xvii. 199 Buddhism.. with.. its crowds of constantly reincarnating living Buddhas. **1897** MARY KINGSLEY *W. Africa* x. 230 The idea I found regarding reincarnated diseases, existent among the Okÿon tribes.

reincar'nation. [RE- 5 a.] Renewed incarnation; an instance of this.

1858 SEARS *Athan.* III. iii. 273 The Essenes.. rejected totally.. the dogma concerning re-incarnation. **1884**

PEMBER *Earth's Earliest Ages* Pref. 7 Sin must be gradually worn away..in a series of reincarnations upon earth.

b. A fresh embodiment *of* a person.

1884 *St. James's Gaz.* 29 Aug. 5/2 The Imam is supposed to be a reincarnation of a divinity formerly manifest in Mahomet.

Hence **reincar'nationist**, a believer in reincarnation.

1881 *Daily News* 28 Mar. 5/3 The re-incarnationists holding..that there was nothing to prevent Queen Elizabeth becoming Charles Dickens.

reincar'nationism. [f. REINCARNATION + -ISM.] A belief in, or doctrine of, reincarnation.

1907 W. DE MORGAN *Alice-For-Short* viii. 75 This is an entirely unwarranted speculation, based upon no data; a neotheosophical reincarnationism without so much as a single Himalayan Brother to back you up! **1938** *Jrnl. Theol. Stud.* XXXIX. 192 We shall find ourselves emphasizing the subordinationism and the reincarnationism to such an extent that the Origenian theology may well appear to be merely one more form of Gnosticism.

†**rein'cendate,** *a. Obs. rare*$^{-1}$. [f. RE- 5 a + INCEND *v.* + -ATE^2.] Heated again.

1471 RIPLEY *Comp. Alch.* IV. iv. in Ashm. (1652) 145 When the Body with Mercury ys reincendat.

†**rein'cense,** *v.*^{1} *Obs. rare*$^{-1}$. [f. RE- 5 a + INCENSE *v.*^{1}] *trans.* To make a return to (one) with incense.

1654 GAYTON *Pleas. Notes* III. ii. 75 How shall I recompence these high shewn favours? How ever re-incense you for these savours?

rein'cense, *v.*^{2} *rare.* [f. RE- 5 a + INCENSE *v.*^{2}]

1. *trans.* To incense (a person) again.

1592 G. HARVEY *Four Lett.* iii. Wks. (Grosart) I. 182 Sir Iames Croft..was cunningly incensed, and reincensed against mee.

†**2.** To relight (a fire). *Obs. rare*$^{-1}$.

1609 DANIEL *Civ. Wars* VIII. i, She, whose beames do reincense This sacred fire.

reinchain, obs. form of RE-ENCHAIN.

re'incidency. *rare*$^{-1}$. [RE- 5 a.] Relapse.

1622 MABBE tr. *Aleman's Guzman d'Alf.* II. 82, I would haue this re-incidencie and relapse of theirs to be severely punished.

rein'cite, *v.* [RE- 5 a. Cf. F. *réinciter* (Cotgr.).] *trans.* To incite again.

1611 COTGR., *Reinciter*, to reincite. **1645** MILTON *Colast.* Wks. 1851 IV. 361 The deed of procreation..is despis'd, unless it bee cherisht and reincited with a pleasing conversation. **1767** LEWIS *Statius* XII. 1117 He reincites his Band And makes the last Effort. **1801** CHARLOTTE SMITH *Lett. Solit. Wand.* I. 284 The hurricane seemed to have been reincited instead of exhausted.

rein'close, *v.* [RE- 5 a.] To inclose again.

1611 COTGR., *Renclorre*, to reinclose. **1761** MRS. F. SHERIDAN *Sidney Bidulph* III. 89 In this letter I re-inclosed her bill. **1816** KIRBY & SP. *Entomol.* xxv. (1818) II. 419 She ..re-inclosed her brilliant guests in their place of confinement.

rein'clusion. [RE- 5 a.] Renewed inclusion.

1890 *Spectator* 10 May, Reforms which would lead to the re-inclusion of the Free Kirk.

rein'corporate, *v.* [RE- 5 a. Cf. F. *réincorporer* (16th c.).] *trans.* To incorporate again.

1611 COTGR., *Reincorporer*, to reincorporate, reintegrate. **1663** BOYLE *Usef. Exp. Nat. Philos.* II. App. 338 Grind it well again, that..the Sal Armoniack..may be reincorporated with the Colcothar. **1723** *Lond. Gaz.* No. 6152/1 Those Provinces ought..to be deemed reincorporated with the Ottoman Empire. **1774** *Westm. Mag.* II. 327 The King has been pleased..to reincorporate the borough of Saltash. **1777** *Phil. Trans.* LXVII. 62 All seemed to be re-incorporated into the mass. **1860** FROUDE *Hist. Eng.* V. 72 The 'priory and convent of Norwich'.. were reincorporated only with a loss of manors and lands.

So **rein'corporate** *a.*, **reincorpo'ration.**

1685 BAXTER *Paraphr. N.T.*, *Mark* ix. 11 John Baptist was Elias; not the Soul of Elias reincorporate, but [etc.]. **1863** *N. & Q.* 3rd Ser. IV. 12/2 The circumstances which led to the re-incorporation of the English Langue. **1884** *Act 47 & 48 Vict.* c. 65 §2 The dissolution of such district, and..the reincorporation of its area..in the..parishes [etc.].

reincounter, variant of RE-ENCOUNTER.

reincourage: see RE-ENCOURAGE.

rein'crease, *v.* [RE- 5 a.] *trans.* and *intr.* To increase again.

1555 EDEN *Decades* 20 That they myght..apply them selues to reincrease the fruites of theyr countrey. **1596** SPENSER *F.Q.* VI. vi. 15 When they did perceave Their wounds recur'd, and forces reincreast. **1611** COTGR., *Recroistre*, to reincrease; to grow, or spring vp, againe. **1666** G. HARVEY *Morb. Angl.* iii. (1672) 10 A copious afflux of good blood, whereby the preceding diminish'd parts happen to re-increase.

So †**reincrease** *sb. Obs. rare*$^{-0}$.

1611 COTGR., *Recroist*, a reincrease; a new..growth.

†**rein'crew.** *Obs. rare*$^{-1}$. [? f. RECREW after *reinforce*.] Recruit, reinforcement.

1627 D. HOLLES in *Strafford Papers* (1739) I. 41 Young Soldiers for the Reincrew of our Army.

†**reincrudate,** *v. Obs. rare*$^{-1}$. [f. RE- 5 a + **incrudate*.] *trans.* To make crude again.

1670 CLARKE *Nat. Hist. Nitre* 70 That moysture which reincrudates Gold.

reincru'dation. *rare.*

1704 SWIFT *T. Tub* i, This Writer proceeds wholly by Reincrudation or in the *Via humida*. **1894** WAITE tr. *Paracelsus* II. 378 It is also called reincrudation.

†**reincru'descence.** *Obs. rare*$^{-1}$. [Cf. prec.] Recrudescence.

1650 CHARLETON *Paradoxes* Prol. 15 If..there immediately arise a Reincrudescence of the Wound.

'**reinculcate,** *v. rare*$^{-1}$. [RE- 5 a.] *trans.* To inculcate again.

1701 NORRIS *Ideal World* I. Pref. 11 He interposes what was said before, reinculcating that the same was in the beginning with God.

rein'cur, *v.* [RE- 5 a.] *trans.* To incur a second time (Webster 1847).

reindear: see RE-ENDEAR.

reindeer ('reɪndɪə(r)). Forms: 4, 6–7 rayne-, 5 reyn-, 5, 7 reen-, 6 rane-, 7–8 rain-, 8–9 rhen-, 8– rein-. [Ultimately repr. ON. *hreindýri* (mod.Icel. *-dýr*), f. *hreinn* the more usual name for the animal (cf. REIN *sb.*^{2}) + *dýr* DEER: hence also Sw. *rendjur*, Da. *rensdyr*, Du. *rendier*, G. *rennthier*. The immediate source of the comb. in Eng. is not quite clear: in OE. the simple word occurs in the account of Norway obtained by Ælfred from Ohthere.

*c*893 K. ÆLFRED *Oros.* I. i. 18 He hæfde..tamra deora unbebohtra syx hund. þa deor hi hatað hranas; þara wæron syx stælhranas.]

1. a. An animal of the deer kind, *Rangifer tarandus*, having large branching or palmated antlers, formerly common in Central Europe, but now confined to sub-arctic regions, where it is used for drawing sledges, and is kept in large herds for the sake of the milk, flesh, and hides. The caribou of N. America is a variety.

?*a*1400 *Morte Arth.* 922 The roo and þe rayne-dere reklesse thare ronnene. *c*1430 LYDG. *Reas. & Sens.* 3728 To chase at hem and hornes blow,..At reyndere and the dredful roo. *c*1470 HENRYSON *Mor. Fab.* v. (*Parl. Beasts*) xv, The reyndeir ran throw reueir, rone, and reid. **1572** BOSSEWELL *Armorie* II. 57 Tarandrus is a beaste in bodye like a great Oxe... Of some hee is taken to bee a rayne deare. **1632** T. NORTON *New Eng. Canaan* II. v. (1838) 52 A third sorte of deare, lesse then the other (which are a kinde of rayne deare). **1654** WHITELOCKE *Swed. Ambassy* (1772) I. 428 A Laplander and his sledde drawn by a rayne deer. **1712** STEELE *Spect.* No. 406 ¶4 A Song..addressed by the Lover to his Rain-deer, which is the Creature that in that Country supplies the Want of Horses. **1744** A. DOBBS *Hudson's Bay* 47 The Country being mostly rocky, and covered with a white Moss upon which the Rain-Deer or Cariboux feed. **1774** GOLDSM. *Nat. Hist.* (1776) III. 149 Of all animals of the deer kind, the Rein-Deer is the most extraordinary and the most useful. **1835** SIR J. ROSS *N.-W. Passage* xvi. 252 The reindeer all came this way in April. **1863** LYELL *Antiq. Man* 14 With these are mingled bones of the red deer and roe, but the rein-deer has not yet been found.

b. *Her.* (See quot.)

1780 EDMONDSON *Compl. Body Her.* II. Gloss., Reindeer, as drawn in armory, is a stag with double attires, two of them turning down.

2. *attrib.* and *Comb.*, as ***reindeer hair, horn, meat, milk, skin, steak***; **reindeer-fly**, a species of Œstrus which attacks the reindeer; **reindeer lichen, moss**, a species of lichen, *Cladonia rangiferina*, which constitutes the winter food of the reindeer; **reindeer period** (see quot.); **reindeer tongue**, the tongue of a reindeer, usu. smoked, considered as a delicacy; **reindeer tribe**, a tribe using the reindeer, esp. *pl.* certain pre-historic tribes inhabiting France and Belgium.

1759 B. STILLINGFLEET tr. *Gedner's Use Curios.* in *Misc. Tracts* (1791) 165 When our president was gathering, and describing the *rhen-deer-fly. **1896** *Lloyd's Nat. Hist.* 81 The nest is loosely made of dry grass and stalks, and the inside..is lined with willow-down or *reindeer-hair. **1857** DUFFERIN *Lett. High Lat.* (ed. 3) 258 Out of *reindeer horns are made almost all the utensils used in his domestic economy. **1770** G. CARTWRIGHT *Jrnl.* 11 July (1792) I. 8 They [*sc.* caribou] find there many extensive tracts of land destitute of wood, and covered with plenty of *Reindeer Lichen. **1777** LIGHTFOOT *Flora Scot.* II. 880 Brown tipt Rhendeer Lichen. **1891** *Anthony's Photogr. Bull.* IV. 213 Even the grass vanishes, its place being taken by the reindeer lichen. **1926** *Daily Colonist* (Victoria, B.C.) 5 Jan. 2/4 *Reindeer meat was the principal attraction on the menu. **1857** DUFFERIN *Lett. High Lat.* (ed. 3) 258 *Reindeer milk is the most important item in his diet. **1753** CHAMBERS *Cycl. Supp.*, *Reen mossa*, a name used by some for the mountain coralloids, or *rein deer moss. **1830** LINDLEY *Nat. Syst. Bot.* 333 The Rein Deer Moss, which forms the winter food of that animal. **1895** *Outing* (U.S.) XXVII. 16/2 In sheltered places there are surprising growths of reindeer moss. **1881** J. GEIKIE *Prehist. Europe* 101 M. Dupont recognises two stages in the Palæolithic Period, one of which is called the Mammoth period, and the other, which is the more recent, the *Reindeer period. **1797** *Encycl. Brit.* (ed. 3) IX. 569/2 Their shoes [are made] of the *rein-deer skin, with the hair outwards. **1933** [see KAMIK]. **1977** *Country Life* 13 Jan. 80/1 His wife makes..the soft reindeer-skin shoes for winter. **1958** W. BICKEL tr. *Hering's Dict. Class. & Mod. Cookery* 502 **Reindeer steak*,..steak cut from a tender loin, sautéd in butter. **1973** D. FRANCIS *Slay-Ride* v. 67 She gave us reindeer steaks in a rich dark sauce. **1788** *Times* 1 Jan. 4/3 (Advt.), Smoked Salmon and Dutch Herring, Fine New French Olives, and New *Rein Deer Tongues. **1857** J. H. WALSH *Economical Housekeeper* II. iii. 32 Reindeer Tongues, Pork Pies, and a whole host of similar commodities, are sold at the 'sausage shops' in London. **1935** M. MORPHY *Recipes of All Nations* 499 Reindeer are eaten in Norway, and smoked reindeer tongues are considered a great delicacy. **1973** J. FLEMING *You won't let me Finish* xvi. 129 I'm told I am to have some smoked reindeer tongue for my lunch. **1865** TYLOR *Early Hist. Man.* i. 2 The *Reindeer tribes of Central France.

†**rein'dent,** *v. Obs. rare.* [f. RE- 5 a + INDENT *v.*^{1}] *trans.* To provide with fresh teeth.

1611 COTGR., *Rendenter*, to reindent, or set new teeth vnto. **1654** GAYTON *Pleas. Notes* III. v. 101, I will re-indent my mouth, and not see my selfe Tantaliz'd thus to my face, for want of the most necessary Instruments of life.

rein'dict, *v.* [RE- 5 a.] To indict again.

1611 COTGR., *Renditer*, to reindite, or frame a new Indictment against. **1889** *Columbus* (Ohio) *Disp.* 18 Oct., What was your object in having these men re-indicted?

rein'dorse, *v.* [RE- 5 a.] To indorse again.

1884 W. F. CRAFTS *Sabb. for Man* (1894) 385 The Sabbath of the 4th Commandment..was republished by Moses, reindorsed and explained by Christ.

reindow, obs. form of RE-ENDOW.

rein'duce, *v.* [RE- 2 a and 5 a.]

†**1.** *trans.* To bring back, reintroduce. *Obs.*

1595 DANIEL *Civ. Wars* I. xix, But now this great Succeeder, all repaires And reinduc't that discontinued good. **1611** COTGR., *Reinduire*, to reinduce. **1630** W. SCOT *Apol. Narr.* (1846) 287 To reinduce them [the Popish ceremonies] is to disturb the peace of the Kirk. **1655** FULLER *Ch. Hist.* III. i. §20 There was a design..to reinduce Secular Priests into Monks places.

2. To induce anew or again.

1855 SPENCER *Princ. Psychol.* I. IV. ii. §176. 512 The state *a* again induces the state *b*, and is itself once more reinduced. **1876** *Trans. Clinical Soc.* IX. 39 A mixed generous diet.. has not reinduced the disease.

Hence **rein'ducing** *vbl. sb.*

1637 C. DOW *Answ. H. Burton* 36 Their plot..for the reinducing of Popery.

So **rein'duction,** †reintroduction; a fresh induction.

1660 *England's Monarchy* 9 To heal the sores and wasting divisions of the Nation, by a Reinduction of the known ancient and fundamental Laws thereof. **1944** N. MAILER in *Cross-Section* 336 A half-year later, he was made (after reinduction school) a captain.

rein'due, *v.* [RE- 5 a.] *trans.* To put on again.

1884 ALLINGHAM *Blackberries* (1890) 5, I will not re-indue The rags of overnight. **1886** STEVENSON *Dr. Jekyll* x, When I shall again and forever reindue that hated personality.

‖**reine** (rɛn). *Cookery.* [Fr., lit. 'queen'.] Chiefly in phr. *à la reine* 'in the fashion of a queen', used to designate dishes prepared in some special way. Also used alone following the name of the dish.

1845 E. ACTON *Mod. Cookery* i. 37 (*heading*) Rabbit soup a la reine. Wash and soak thoroughly three young rabbits. **1884** MADAME VALERIE *Cookery for Amateurs* ii. 25 *Soups*... *À la Reine*. Although this potage has a fine name it is easily made if you have the remains of cold fowl or turkey. **1930** H. BELLOC *New Cautionary Tales* 13 Turbot à la Reine, and Ices. **1958** W. BICKEL tr. *Hering's Dict. Class. & Mod. Cookery* 254 *Sole..queen style*, à la reine: poached, covered with creamed fish velouté, garnished with truffle slices and small fish dumplings. **1962** *Listener* 26 July 155/3, I had this dish in a tiny restaurant in the Dordogne Valley. It is called plaice *reine*.

reine, obs. form of RAIN, REIGN.

Reinecke ('raɪnɛkə). *Chem.* The name of A. *Reinecke*, 19th-c. German chemist, used in the possessive or *attrib.* to designate (*a*) a red crystalline complex salt, ammonium diamminetetrakis(isothiocyanato)chromate(III), $NH_4[Cr(NCS)_4(NH_3)_2].H_2O$, which is used esp. in *Biochem.* to precipitate large cations, and (*b*) the parent acid of this salt, $H[Cr(NCS)_4(NH_3)_2]$, which can also be isolated as red crystals.

Reinecke described the preparation of the salt in 1863 (*Ann. d. Chem. u. Pharm.* CXXVI. 113).

1892 *Jrnl. Chem. Soc.* LXII. II. 798 Reinecke's salt crystallises in rectangular tables; it is insoluble in absolute ether, but dissolves in water to a ruby-red solution and in alcohol. **1928** *Chem. Abstr.* XXII. 764 The urine is slightly acidified and evapd. to $\frac{1}{5}$ its vol., purified with charcoal, and the creatinine pptd. with Reinecke Salt. **1928** *Brit. Chem. Abstr.* A. 542/2 The mixed potassium ammonium salt of Reinecke's acid, obtained by melting together potassium dichromate and ammonium thiocyanate. **1933** *Biochem. Jrnl.* XXVII. 157 Reinecke's salt, $[(NH_3)_2Cr(CNS)_4]NH_4$, is proving to be a valuable precipitant for a variety of basic substances, and its use is likely to extend. **1935** *Org. Syntheses* XV. 75 The undissolved residue from the second extraction consists chiefly of Morland salt (the guanidine salt of the Reinecke acid). **1965** tr. Hein & Herzog in G. Brauer *Handbk. Preparative Inorg. Chem.* II. xxiv. 1377 The total yield of air-dry Reinecke salt amounts to 250–275 g. *Ibid.* 1378 $H[Cr(SCN)_4(NH_3)_2]$... Synonym: Reinecke acid. **1966** PHILLIPS & WILLIAMS *Inorg. Chem.* II. xxvi. 322 The anion of Reinecke's salt..and that of K_2PtCl_6 are used to precipitate large organic cations.

Hence **reineckate** ('raɪnəkeɪt) [ad. G. *reineckat*: see -ATE[1]], (a salt of) the anion present in Reinecke's salt, $[Cr(NCS)_4(NH_3)_2]^-$.

1928 *Brit. Chem. Abstr.* A. 526/2 The cuprous 'Reineckate' is removed by filtration. **1939** *Thorpe's Dict. Appl. Chem.* (ed. 4) III. 115/1 Reinecke's salt... Its solution gives precipitates with the heavy metals and organic bases, alkaloids yielding characteristic crystalline compounds—reineckates. **1955** J. A. LOVERN *Chem. Lipids of Biol. Significance* ii. 61 Choline is estimated in a variety of ways. The simplest and most frequently used methods depend on the formation of a sparingly-soluble complex with the reineckate radical. **1957** *Jrnl. Antibiotics* X. 188 The antibiotic was..crystallized as its reineckate. **1964** *Oceanogr. & Marine Biol.* II. 152 The reineckate ion is removed with silver nitrate.

‖**Reine Claude** (rɛn klod). [Fr., perh. a. the name of *Claude* (1499–1524), daughter of Louis XII and wife of François I.] = GREENGAGE. Also *attrib.*

1731 P. MILLER *Gardeners Dict.* s.v. Prunus 16. La Reine Claude, i.e. Queen Claudia. This is a small round Fruit, of a yellowish Colour,..and its Juice is richly sugar'd. **1860** R. HOGG *Fruit Man.* 252 Reine Claude. See Green Gage. **1929** E. A. BUNYARD *Anat. Dessert* 118 In France it [*sc.* the greengage] is always known as Reine Claude, and the legend runs that it is thus named after the wife of François I. **1941** MRS. BELLOC LOWNDES *I, too, have lived in Arcadia* xvi. 299 A large old *Reine Claude*, of which the sweet luscious fruit was famed. **1962** *Harper's Bazaar* Aug. 37 Delicious though the *reine claude* can be. **1973** *Guardian* 20 Jan. 3/4 It is the land of..the honeyed Reine-Claude greengages.

reined (reɪnd), *ppl. a.*[1] [f. REIN *v.* + -ED[1].]

1. Furnished with, guided or restrained by, reins. Also *reined-back, -in, -up.*

1483 *Cath. Angl.* 303/2 Renyd, *habenatus.* **1513** DOUGLAS *Æneis* x. v. 95 With renit lyonis ʒokkit to thi chayr. **1740** RICHARDSON *Pamela* (1824) I. 159 He approached me with a sort of reined-in rapture. **1835** W. IRVING *Tour Prairies* xix. (1863) 108 The poor, mutilated, harnessed, checked, reined-up victim of luxury. **1905** W. H. HUNT *Pre-Raphaelitism* II. vii. 174 At first acquaintance with the poet, I thought that later in my knowledge of him I should see some phases of the reined-back pose of Woolner's bust, but this I was unable to do. **1961** *New Statesman* 21 July 92/1 The reined-back rhythms of this verse are especially pleasing.

2. With preceding adv., or in combs., esp. *well reined*, †well broken to the rein.

a **1533** LD. BERNERS *Gold. Bk. M. Aurel.* (1546) Ccvb, Thoughe the knyghte passe his course, yet it is not his faute, yf the horse be not wel reined. **1565–6** BLUNDEVIL *Horsemanship* i. (1580) 3 Vegetius also saith that they [the Parthian horses] be verie well reined. **1598** [see REIN *v.*[2]]. **1767** LEWIS *Statius* XII. 1042 His neat Quiver, Sword, and well-rein'd Steed. **1856** STONEHENGE *Brit. Rural Sports* 395/2 The snaffle..usually called the single-reined bridle.

†**reined**, *ppl. a.*[2] *Obs.*[−1] [f. *rein*, sing. of REINS + -ED[2].] Having reins of a specified kind.

1523 FITZHERB. *Husb.* §78 The fyrst [property] is to be small mouthed, the seconde to be longe rayned.

reines, var. RAINES *Obs.*; obs. f. REINS.

‖**reinette** (reɪ'nɛt). Also 6 reinet, 8 reynette. [F. *reinette*; the more usual form is RENNET, q.v.] A variety of apple, the rennet.

1583 *Rates of Customs* Aiij, Appuls called pippins or reinets the bushel xij*d.* **1706** LONDON & WISE *Retir'd Gard.* x. 43 The Frank Reynette is an old Apple, well known. *Ibid.* 44 Its Juice is very sweet, being more pleasant to the Taste than the Reynette. **1731** MILLER *Gard. Dict.* (1733) s.v. *Apple*, Apples..proper for a Desert,..Golden Reinette,..La Reinette grise. *Ibid.*, Such Apples as are preferr'd for kitchen use,..French Reinette,.. Monstrous Reinette. **1824** LOUDON *Encycl. Gard.* (ed. 2) 691 Rennets, Reinettes or Little Queens. **1862** ANSTED *Channel Isl.* IV. xxi. (ed. 2) 488 The reinettes (or rennets) are a large group.

Hence †**reinetting** = RENNETING *sb. Obs. rare*[−1].

1664 EVELYN *Kal. Hort.* (1729) 191 Apples..Golden Doucet, Apis, Reineting [etc.].

rein'fect, *v.* [RE- 5 a.] *trans.* To infect again. So **rein'fection**; **rein'fectious** *a.*

1611 COTGR., *Reinfecter*, to reinfect. **1696** PHILLIPS (ed. 5), To *Reinfect*, to infect, to give a contagious Disease a second time. **1828–32** WEBSTER, *Reinfectious* (cites VAUGHAN *Med. Repos.*). **1882** *Nature* XXV. 440/1 The disease may break out in a fresh-run salmon without re-infection. **1889** G. A. SMITH *Bk. Isaiah* (ed. 2) I. 422 Not only to find it [*sc.* sin] 'hindering, disturbing, complicating all', but reinfecting with the lust and odour of sin the will which gave it birth. **1897** *Allbutt's Syst. Med.* II. 741 Recurrences are extremely common; and they are not always reinfections. **1928** L. E. H. WHITBY *Med. Bacteriol.* xxi. 210 Finally, the envelope of the corpuscle bursts and the merozoites are set free. These in turn reinfect red corpuscles and develop into trophozoites, thus carrying on the cycle. **1960** *Farmer & Stockbreeder* 12 Jan. 12 Loose smut reinfects growing corn and so perpetuates the disease.

reinfeoff, obs. form of RE-ENFEOFF.

rein'fest, *v.* [RE- 5 a.] To infest again.

1606 G. W[OODCOCKE] *Lives Emperors* in *Hist. Ivstine* Kkj, Vnderstandinge that the Saracens had re-infested Calabria, hee speeded thither.

reinfe'station. [RE- 5 a.] A second or further infestation.

1911 in WEBSTER. **1946** *Nature* 2 Nov. 636/2 One application of 0·5 per cent 'Gammexane' dust has been generally found to..prevent re-infestation for some time. **1968** *Times* 30 Oct. 12/2 A central position of the sewer system was cleared of rats..and no attempt was made to prevent reinfestation.

rein'flame, *v.* Also re-en-. [RE- 5 a. Cf. F. *renflammer* (16th c.), It. *rinfiammare* (Florio).] *trans.* To inflame again.

1611 SPEED *Hist. Gt. Brit.* IX. xvi. §4. 651/2 That the hatreds and enmities..betweene the French and English names, should..be renued, and reinflamed. **1697** DRYDEN *Virg. Past.* VIII. 92 To re-inflame my Daphnis with Desires. **1742** YOUNG *Nt. Th.* IX. 797 Re-inflam'd Thy luminaries triumph. **1842** PARNELL *Chem. Anal.* (1845) 267 Oxygen [and] Nitrous oxide re-inflame a glowing taper.

rein'flate, *v.* [RE- 5 a.] *trans.* To inflate again. So **rein'flation.**

1853 SIR H. DOUGLAS *Milit. Bridges* (ed. 3) 261 The skins may be re-inflated in succession at any time. **1897** *Allbutt's Syst. Med.* II. 245 Reinflation of lung under such conditions ..is often impossible.

rein'flict, *v.* [RE- 5 a.] To inflict again.

1673 *Lady's Calling* I. ii. §10 When a man..reinflicts his miseries upon himself by a grating reflection on his own madness.

re'influence, *v.* [RE- 5 a.] *trans.* To influence again.

a **1711** KEN *Hymns Evang.* Poet. Wks. 1721 I. 169 Our Lord his Dissolution had commenc'd, And Deity his Soul reinfluenc'd.

†**rein'fold**, *v. Obs.* [RE- 5 a.] *trans.* To enfold again. Hence †**rein'folding** *vbl. sb.*

1610 HEALEY *St. Aug. Citie of God* XII. xx. (1620) 437 Admitted to the sight of God..to leaue it againe at length and be re-infolded in mortal misery. **1611** FLORIO, *Rinuolta*, ..re-infolded or re-inwrapped. *Ibid.*, *Ripiegatura*, a reinfolding, a reinwraping.

reinforce (riːɪn'fɔəs), *sb.* [f. the vb.]

†**1.** *Mil.* A reinforcement of troops. *Obs. rare*[−1].

1648 EVELYN *Diary* (1857) III. 29 The general sent to Skippon for a re-inforce of 3000 horse.

2. A part (or one of two parts) of a gun next the breech, made stronger than the rest in order to resist the explosive force of the powder.

1769 FALCONER *Dict. Marine* (1780) s.v. *Cannon*, The first reinforce..includes the base ring. *Ibid.*, The second reinforce begins..where the first terminates. **1797** *Encycl. Brit.* (ed. 3) VIII. 231/2 On the side of the gun upon the first reinforce, are cast two knobs. **1802** JAMES *Milit. Dict.*, s.v., There are generally two in each piece, called the first and second reinforce. **1863** *Sat. Rev.* 12 Sept. 357 The Parrott guns are of cast-iron, with a wrought-iron reinforce. **1881** GREENER *Gun* 26 Other early guns that were mounted were made with a loop underneath the barrel before the reinforce.

b. *attrib.*, esp. **reinforce ring**, a flat ring or moulding round a gun at the points where the reinforces meet or terminate. Also called ***reinforce band.*** (Cf. REINFORCED *ppl. a.*)

1769 FALCONER *Dict. Marine* (1780) s.v. *Cannon*, The first reinforce..includes..the vent-astragal, and first reinforce ring. **1797** *Encycl. Brit.* (ed. 3) VIII. 230/1 At the end of the first reinforce ring. *Ibid.* 233/1 Reinforce-astragal and fillets. **1802** JAMES *Milit. Dict.*, *Reinforce-ring*. There are three in each gun, called the first, second, and third. **1868** *Rep. to Govt. U.S. Munitions War* 130 A smooth-bore cannon. This gun is constructed on the same principles as the others, with steel re-inforce rings.

3. Any thing or part added to an object to strengthen it. Also *attrib.*

1869 BOUTELL *Arms & Armour* x. 204 A remarkable diversity is seen to have existed between the corresponding reinforces or additional defences of the right and left sides. *Ibid.*, When the shoulders were covered by the reinforce-plates, they were distinguished as *pauldrons*. **1875** KNIGHT *Dict. Mech.* 1636/1 A reinforce or strengthening piece on a fabric at a point of wear, or around a hole or eyelet. **1884** *Ibid.* Suppl. 235/1 A cup-shaped reinforce inside the head of a cartridge to strengthen it.

reinforce (riːɪn'fɔəs), *v.* [f. RE- + *inforce*, ENFORCE *v.*; cf. RE-ENFORCE *v.* and RENFORCE.]

I. 1. a. *trans.* To strengthen (a military or naval force) by means of additional men.

1600 E. BLOUNT tr. *Conestaggio* 318 Hauing reinforced the point of his armie with Germaine pikes. **1617** MORYSON *Itin.* II. 204 They neede not reinforce their Companies with the Irish. **1670** COTTON *Espernon* I. I. 40 Seasonably re-inforcing the Garrison, with divers Gentlemen his particular Servants, and a good number of Souldiers. **1725** DE FOE *Voy. round World* (1840) 74 Sending two and thirty of her men on board the great ship, to reinforce the men on board. **1849** ALISON *Hist. Europe* V. xxvii. §48. 40 Fresh troops continually came up to reinforce those who were exhausted with fatigue.

b. To strengthen or increase (a class or party) by fresh additions to the number.

1849 MACAULAY *Hist. Eng.* v. I. 520 The Tory party.. included the whole bench of bishops, and had been reinforced..by several fresh creations. **1874** GREEN *Short Hist.* ii. §1. 60 The middle class, thus created, was reinforced by the rise of a similar class in our towns.

c. To furnish with fresh supplies; to add to, increase, the amount of (something).

1839 DE QUINCEY *Recoll. Lakes* Wks. 1862 II. 210 Some subject of hope..must be called in to reinforce the animal fountains of good spirits. **1856** KANE *Arct. Expl.* I. xix. 230 The bears had..destroyed our chances of reinforcing our provisions.

2. a. To strengthen, make stronger; to furnish with additional support.

a **1635** NAUNTON *Fragm. Reg.* (Arb.) 57 Bashfulnesse, and a naturall modesty..might have hindred his progression, had they not been re-inforced by the infusion of Soveraign favour. **1657** HOWELL *Londinop.* 17 He reinforceth the right of the City by Proclamations. *a* **1676** HALE *Prim. Orig. Man.* (1677) 47 The Memory..by the return of a like Object again is sometimes revived and reinforced. **1805** FOSTER *Ess.* I. ii. I. 20 To reinforce our virtues from the dust of those who first taught them. **1879** W. H. STONE in Grove *Dict. Music* I. 153/2 Bach uses it frequently, sometimes merely to reinforce the basses. **1897** RHOSCOMYL *White Rose Arno* 86 Pengraig recounted what had been agreed upon; reinforcing the whole with evidence and proof.

†**b.** *refl.* To fix (oneself) more firmly. *Obs.*[−1]

1652 COTTERELL tr. *Calprenède's Cassandra* I. 51 The Prince..reinforc'd himselfe all he could in his Saddle.

c. To strengthen (some material thing) by an additional support or added thickness.

1692 RAY *Creation* II. (ed. 2) 119 The side of the Triangle ..was reinforced with a Border. **1729** SHELVOCKE *Artillery* v. 379 These Pipes or Tubes shall be well reinforced with the Sinews of Beasts steeped in Glue. **1769** FALCONER *Dict. Marine* (1780), *Canon renforcé*, a cannon whose breech is reinforced, i.e. thicker than the calibre. **1772** C. HUTTON *Bridges* 87 They must be well reinforced with proper walls or returns. **1890** *Anthony's Photogr. Bull.* III. 185 It is advisable..to re-inforce the punch, with one or more thicknesses of cardboard.

d. *Psychol.* To strengthen (a response), usu. by repetition of a stimulus, esp. one that is painful or rewarding.

1906 C. S. SHERRINGTON *Integrative Action Nervous Syst.* v. 175 These widely separate reflex-arcs therefore reinforce one another. **1927** G. V. ANREP tr. *Pavlov's Conditioned Reflexes* vii. 117 The second method consisted in contrasting the single definite conditioned stimulus..with different neighbouring stimuli which were never reinforced. **1951** S. F. NAGEL *Found. Social Anthropol.* iv. 58 To remain effective, however, the conditioning must be 'reinforced'. **1970** *Jrnl. Gen. Psychol.* July 3 Bugelski..notes that in the orthodox stimulus-response view of learning based on the reinforcement of an instrumental response, it is essential that the behavior appear first and then be..'reinforced by the psychologist (or someone) immediately'. **1973** *Howard Jrnl.* XIII. 281 A points system was used to pay the men for desirable behaviours that would be likely also to be reinforced in life outside the institution.

3. a. To add to the force or strength of; to make more forcible or cogent.

1629 QUARLES *Argalus & P.* II. Wks. (Grosart) III. 265 Give me leave (my Lord) to reinforce A virgin's suit. **1681** H. MORE *Postscr. Glanvill's Sadducismus* 51 Angels..which minister to the Saints, and reinforce the Prayers of good and holy men by joyning thereto their own. **1697** COLLIER *Ess. Mor. Subj.* I. (1709) 9 Since I like the Frankness, and Tendency of your Argument, I'll try if I can Reinforce it. **1843** PRESCOTT *Mexico* II. ii. (1864) 79 It is said, he reinforced the proposal by promising a liberal share of the proceeds of it. **1882** PEBODY *Eng. Journalism* xvi. 123 He liked to reinforce what they said by conveying in anecdote some fragments of that rare knowledge.

b. To increase by giving fresh force to; also simply, to increase, make greater.

1659 *Gentl. Calling* viii. §7 The loud noise of roaring Mirth is re-inforced to drown that poor whisper of Conscience. **1674** PLAYFORD *Skill Mus.* I. ii. 43 Exclamation properly is..but the slacking of the voice to re-inforce it somewhat more. **1684** R. WALLER *Nat. Exper.* 80 We reinforced the Cold by a great quantity of fresh Snow and Salt. **1856** EMERSON *Eng. Traits, Wealth*, They have reinforced their own productivity by the creation of that marvellous machinery. **1865** M. ARNOLD *Ess. Crit.* iv. (1875) 153 Religion had early possessed itself of this force of character, and reinforced it.

4. *intr.* To obtain reinforcements. *rare.*

1611 SHAKS. *Cymb.* v. ii. 18 It is a day turn'd strangely; or betimes Let's re-inforce, or fly. **1811** *Henry & Isabella* I. 133 In the mean while the enemy reinforced, and pursued the English.

II. †**5. a.** To renew or repeat with fresh force.

1603 KNOLLES *Hist. Turks* (1638) 219 Re-inforcing the charge, he with much adoe obtained the victory. **1653** H. COGAN tr. *Pinto's Trav.* xx. 72 Rallying all into one body, they re-inforced the fight. *a* **1662** HEYLIN *Laud* II. (1671) 238 The same offer was reinforced a fortnight after.

†**b.** To direct with renewed force. *Obs.*[−1]

a **1680** BUTLER *Rem.* (1759) V. 4 Cry'd strange!—then reinforced his Light Against the Moon with all his Might.

†**6.** To enforce, or put in force, again. *Obs.*

1640 LENTHALL in Rushw. *Hist. Coll.* III. (1692) I. 19 To manifest to the World, that Our retirements were to reinforce a greater Unity and Duty. **1656** LD. WHITLOCK in *Burton's Diary* (1828) I. 194 Let the old order be reinforced, and Wednesday sennight be the day. **1667–8** MARVELL *Corr.* Wks. (Grosart) II. 239 [To] attend his Majesty, desiring him to reinforce..the laws against Conventicles. **1720** WATERLAND *Defence Div. Christ* Wks. 1823 II. 105 It pleased God..to proclaim the high dignity of God the Son, to reinforce his rightful claim of homage.

†**7.** To constrain or impel afresh. *Obs.*[−1]

1698 FRYER *Acc. E. India & P.* 172 Till young Abdul was reinforced to revenge his Father's Death.

reinforced (riːɪn'fɔəst), *ppl. a.* [f. REINFORCE *v.* + -ED[1]] **1.** That has been reinforced.

1692 *Smith's Seaman's Gram.* II. vi. 94, GH the Reinforced Ring. **1710** J. HARRIS *Lex. Techn.* II, *Re-inforced* Ring of a Cannon, is that which is next after the Trunnions, between them and the Vent, and the Re-inforced part of a Gun, is from the Base Ring to the Re-inforced Ring. **1748** RICHARDSON *Clarissa* (1768) I. 205 The reinforced orders for this hostile apparatus. **1796** *Instr. & Reg. Cavalry* (1813) 172 The reinforced flank or center which is to attack, is then ordered to advance. **1877** *Daily News* 27 Dec. 5/6 The Russian pursuing force..could not possibly assail the reinforced Turkish troops.

2. Special collocations: **reinforced concrete**, concrete with steel bars or network embedded in it to increase its tensile strength; **reinforced plastic**, plastic strengthened by the inclusion of a layer of fibre (esp. glass).

1902 *Min. Proc. Inst. Civil Engineers* CXLIX. 297 Reinforced concrete is extremely economical..where an imposing building is not required. **1906** *Daily Chron.* 27 Apr. 6/2 There is undoubtedly a great future for reinforced concrete. **1910** *Encycl. Brit.* VI. 837/2 The introduction of steel concrete (also known as ferroconcrete, armoured concrete, or reinforced concrete) is generally attributed to Joseph Monier, a French gardener. **1958** *Engineering* 14 Mar. 350/1 A sufficient number of reinforced-concrete buildings have now been in use for more than 50 years to show that, properly designed, reinforced concrete is as durable material as is likely to be required for most purposes. **1966** *McGraw-Hill Encycl. Sci. & Technol.* II. 337/1 Modern bridge abutments are usually made of reinforced concrete. **1974** *Encycl. Brit. Macropædia* III. 184/1 The towers are of reinforced concrete and the cables built up of strands of twisted wire. **1940** *Brit. Plastics* Aug. (Advt. section) 5 Two-piece housing in reinforced plastic material for electric hair drying unit. **1947** W. J. BROWN *Fabric Reinforced Plastics* iv. 76 The increasing use of reinforced plastics for engineering applications. **1959** *Engineering* 16 Jan. 86/1 The principal advantage of the reinforced plastics hull is the much reduced maintenance work and its easy repairability. **1971** *Nature* 30 July 305/1 If the exceptional properties of carbon fibres are to be utilized for engineering purposes they must be fabricated as a 'reinforced plastic'.

reinforcement (riːɪnˈfɔəsmənt). [f. REINFORCE *v.* + -MENT; cf. RE-ENFORCEMENT and F. *renforcement*.]

†**1.** A renewal of force; a fresh assault. *Obs.*⁻¹

1607 SHAKS. *Cor.* II. ii. 117 He..aydelesse came off, And with a sudden re-inforcement strucke Corioles like a Planet.

2. a. The act of reinforcing with fresh troops.

1617 MORYSON *Itin.* II. 187 We haue..commanded..the said Sir Arthur himselfe to march vp with a thousand of the best men to your reinforcement in Mounster.

b. A fresh supply of men to assist or strengthen a military or naval force.

1646 H. LAWRENCE *Com. & Warr. Angels* 187 If souldiers be weake, or succumbe in fight, they send to their Generall for supplies and reinforcements. **1683** TEMPLE *Mem.* Wks. 1731 I. 393 With some of these new Troops, and a Reinforcement from Flanders. **1732** LEDIARD *Sethos* II. IX. 276 He..had just receiv'd..a reinforcement of 30,000 men. **1781** GIBBON *Decl. & F.* xxvi. II. 612 His army was strengthened by a numerous reinforcement of veterans. **1826** SCOTT *Woodst.* xv, The trooper, who goes to Oxford for the reinforcement. **1847** PRESCOTT *Peru* (1850) II. 258 Francisco Pizarro had remained at Lima, anxiously awaiting the arrival of the reinforcements which he had requested.

c. An additional supply or contribution.

1766 *Compl. Farmer* s.v. *Madder*, He was so kind as to make me a present of an hundred sets of them; and this little reinforcement, added to what I had raised of my own [etc.]. **1889** PATER *G. de Latour* (1896) 192 Great reinforcements of sympathy.

3. a. Augmentation of strength or force; the act of strengthening or increasing in any way.

1651 CROMWELL *Let.* 26 July in *Carlyle*, He hath lately gotten great provisions of meal, and reinforcement of his strength out of the North. **1667** MILTON *P.L.* I. 190 What reinforcement we may gain from Hope. **1734** WATERLAND *Doctr. Trinity* vii. Wks. 1823 V. 287 Their faith may be both strengthened and brightened by this additional re-inforcement. **1882** SPENCER *Princ. Sociol., Pol. Inst.* 349 This re-inforcement of natural power by super-natural power.

b. *spec.* Increase in the intensity or amplitude of sound.

1879 PRESCOTT *Sp. Telephone* 51 It was found that each vowel position caused the reinforcement of some particular fork or forks. **1937** A. T. JONES *Sound* viii. 198 When the stem of a vibrating tuning fork is placed on top of a wooden table or other extended wooden surface there is also a reinforcement of the sound. **1959** E. PULGRAM *Introd. Spectrography of Speech* vii. 58 This gain in amplitude is obtained in exchange for loss of duration, for a tuning fork thus placed for reinforcement will cease to operate more quickly than one not so placed. **1969** L. F. YERGES *Sound, Noise, & Vibration Control* 70 Today..deliberate 'electrical' amplification is the more significant means of sound reinforcement. *Ibid.* 145 Reinforcement is usually necessary in the following spaces: 1. Legitimate theaters with more than 1000 seats. 2. Lecture halls with more than 300 seats. 3. Almost all gymnasiums, arenas, and large assembly halls.

c. *Psychol.* (An act of) strengthening or establishing of a response, esp. in learning theory through the repetition of a rewarding or painful stimulus, or the satisfaction of a need; also *attrib.*

1876 W. JAMES *Coll. Ess. & Rev.* (1920) 31 The whole question of its predetermination relates to the intensity of the degree of reinforcement with which the triumphant representation occurs. **1906** C. S. SHERRINGTON *Integrative Action Nervous Syst.* v. 175 This reinforcement is significant of the solidarity of the whole spinal mechanism. **1927** G. V. ANREP tr. *Pavlov's Conditioned Reflexes* vii. 117 The first method consisted in repeating the definite conditioned stimulus a great number of times always accompanied by reinforcement. **1948** E. R. HILGARD *Theories of Learning* iv. 84 Primary reinforcement..is identified with diminution of need. Secondary reinforcement is mediated by a stimulus which has been closely and consistently associated with the need reduction. *Ibid.* xii. 347 Doubts about this basic pattern for reinforcement theory have been expressed frequently throughout the preceding chapters. **1953** C. E. OSGOOD *Method & Theory in Experim. Psychol.* ix. 376 The two crucial conditions for learning [in Hull's system] are thus contiguity and reinforcement. **1960** J. B. CARROLL in Saporta & Bastian *Psycholinguistics* (1961) 333/1 A purely Pavlovian or Watsonian view of language learning has been supplanted generally by some variety of reinforcement theory. **1963** *Listener* 7 Feb. 238/1 The pleasures of gambling, right up to the time the ruined rake rises from the table to shoot himself, are..due to 'the principle of intermittent reinforcement'. **1973** *Howard Jrnl.* XIII. 269 If reinforcement techniques can circumvent this double-bind situation, they may be justified.

4. The act of enforcing anew. Now *rare.*

1641 SMECTYMNUUS *Answ.* ii. (1653) 10 There are two specious Arguments which this Remonstrant brings to perswade this desired re-inforcement. **1657** STALHAM *(title)* The Reviler rebuked: or a Reinforcement of the Charges against the Quakers. **1676** in Marvell *Mr. Smirke* Wks. (Grosart) IV. 75 Openly to break so many known laws of the Land, after so many reinforcements, is not this to be turbulent? **1873** PHILLIMORE *Eccl. Law* I. 649 The following canon, in the main of it, was only a re-inforcement of one of the Lord Cromwell's injunctions.

5. The strengthening structure or material employed in reinforced concrete or plastic.

1905 G. J. FIEBEGER *Civil Engin.* xxi. 405 A beam may have its reinforcement on the tension side only, or on both the tension and compression sides of the neutral axis. **1958** *Engineering* 14 Mar. 350/1 Adequate cover to the reinforcement, including binding wires and stirrups, is essential, as is the elimination of all unnecessary steelwork. **1973** *Materials & Technol.* VI. viii. 521 The resin and the reinforcement, cut to size, are introduced separately into the mould. **1974** *Encycl. Brit. Macropædia* XIV. 519/1 Reinforcements [for plastics] include cotton and asbestos flocks; glass fibres, chopped or in the form of rovings, mats, or monofilaments; carbon fibres; and mineral whiskers.

rein'forcer. [f. as prec. + -ER¹.] **a.** One who or that which reinforces.

1880 EARLE *Philol. Eng. Tongue* (ed. 2) §559 But this signification being lost sight of, we find that *round* comes naturally in as its reinforcer.

b. *Psychol.* That which serves to reinforce or strengthen a response.

1958 L. KRASNER in Saporta & Bastian *Psycholinguistics* (1961) 84/2 'Good' and a head shake were effective reinforcers. **1967** *Listener* 12 Jan. 55/2 By making reinforcers contingent on behaviour we can alter behaviour in a very effective way. **1974** B. F. SKINNER *About Behaviorism* 39 The behavior is said to be *strengthened* by its consequences, and for that reason the consequences themselves are called 'reinforcers'.

rein'forcing, *vbl. sb.* [f. as prec. + -ING¹.]

1. The action of strengthening in some way.

1611 COTGR., *Roboration*, a..reinforcing. **1632** J. HAYWARD tr. *Biondi's Eromena* 26 In reinforcing of the fleete with more men and munition. **1641** SMECTYMNUUS *Vind. Answ.* xiv. 176 Your confident re-inforcing of your comparison. **1868** *Rep. to Govt. U.S. Munitions War* 131 The strongest argument which the advocates of re-inforcing use in their favour is, 'that they prevent the gun from bursting explosively'. **1869** BOUTELL *Arms & Armour* x. 204 The system of adding secondary defences, or reinforcing, appears in active operation.

2. *concr.* = REINFORCEMENT 5.

1966 *McGraw-Hill Encycl. Sci. & Technol.* XI. 426/1 As reinforcing for concrete, steel in several of the following forms may be used.

So **rein'forcing** *ppl. a.*

1848 BUCKLEY *Iliad* 288 Having a reinforcing army. **1869** BOUTELL *Arms & Armour* x. 197 A strong secondary reinforcing plate..was firmly fixed to one side of it. **1906** C. S. SHERRINGTON *Integrative Action of Nervous Syst.* v. 175 Gentle stimuli to the skin of a limb exerted a reinforcing influence on closely following stimuli applied to the limb region of the cortex of the brain. **1938** B. F. SKINNER *Behav. of Organisms* vi. 244 It is possible to show that an emotional or reinforcing stimulus..is effective without regard to various minor properties. **1948** E. R. HILGARD *Theories of Learning* iv. 108 Any stimulus which has been associated with need-reduction may itself serve as a reinforcing agent. **1949** POSTMAN & EGAN *Experim. Psychol.* xiv. 298 The instrumental response and the classical response have both been established through the same reinforcing stimulus—food. **1970** [see *homopolymer* s.v. HOMO-]. **1973** *N.Y. Law Jrnl.* 31 Aug. 1/5 Three major steel companies..were indicted yesterday..on charges of violating anti-trust law in the sale of reinforcing steel bars in Texas. **1973** P. DICKINSON *Gift* v. 75 The men and machines had dug a vast, rectangular wound in the clay;..half was still hummocked mud,..littered with grids of reinforcing rods.

rein'form, *v.* [RE- 5 a.] *trans.* To inform again; to form anew; to invest again with form.

1611 COTGR., *Reinformer*, to reinforme, to present with new informations. **1672** *Phil. Trans.* VII. 5148 Especially such [winds] as are re-inform'd by other auxiliary vapors as they pass. **1687** in Hearne *Collect.* (O.H.S.) IV. 10 Let his Loved Ashes rest, Till reinformed with Light immortall He shall rise. **1887** STEVENSON *Merry Men* v. 202, I but re-inform features and attributes that have long been laid..in the quiet of the grave.

reinfranchise, obs. f. RE-ENFRANCHISE.

†**rein'fund,** *v. Obs. rare*⁻¹. [RE- 5 a.] *intr.* To pour in again.

1704 SWIFT *T. Tub* ix, The best part of his diet is the reversion of his own ordure, which, expiring into steams, whirls perpetually about, and at last re-infunds.

rein'fuse, *v.* [RE- 5 a.] To infuse again. Hence **rein'fusion.**

1660 tr. *Amyraldus' Treat. conc. Relig.* III. ix. 498 To reinfuse decayed strength in a moment. *a* **1677** OLDHAM *Dithyrambick* Poems (1684) 208 We nothing..above our selves produce, Till thou do'st finish Man, and Reinfuse. **1845** MILL *Diss. & Disc.* (1859) II. 248 The chiefs of the barbarians could reinfuse life into a social order to which [etc.]. **1887** BROWNING *Parleyings, C. Avison* ix, To re-infuse..sleep that looks like death With momentary liveliness. **1963** *Lancet* 5 Jan. 61/1 We reviewed the problem of blood-transfusion for Jehovah's Witnesses and discovered that they will accept immediate reinfusion of their own blood.

‖**Reinga** (reˈiŋa). Also **reinga, Re-i-nga;** †**Treaingha.** [Maori, = 'place of leaping'.] In Maori tradition, the place where departed spirits make their way into the next world; hence, the land of departed spirits.

1822 *Proc. Church Missionary Soc.* 364 They say, that, at the death of a Chief, his soul goes to the Treaingha, at the North Cape. **1830** *New Zealanders* x. 236 Reinga signifies, properly, the place of flight; and is said, in some of the accounts, to be a rock or a mountain at the North Cape, from which, according to others, the spirits descend into the next world through the sea. **1884** M. A. MARTIN *Our Maoris* vi. 79 The natives in the north of the island still point out the cliff from which the spirits [of the dead] made their descent into the sea on their way back to the Island of Hawaii, from whence their forefathers came. This cliff was called the Re-i-nga, *i.e.*, the leaping-place. **1938** R. D. FINLAYSON *Brown Man's Burden* 48 Depart, O father, to the Reinga, to the far Hawaiki, to the Lord of the Dead. **1949** P. BUCK *Coming of Maori* IV. iv. 516 Thus death closed the account of the body, and the soul (*wairua*) entered the spirit land (*reinga*) with a clean sheet and without apprehension.

reingage, obs. form of RE-ENGAGE.

reinge, Sc. variant of RINSE *v.*

reingender: see RE-ENGENDER.

rein'gestion. [RE- 5 a.] = REFECTION *sb.* 2 d.

1956 THOMPSON & WORDEN *Rabbit* iii. 27 It is difficult to believe that reingestion has not in fact been observed many times. **1964** H. N. SOUTHERN *Handbk. Brit. Mammals* 254 Utilization of food [by rabbits] assisted by reingestion, or refection, in which soft faecal pellets (mainly from caecum, where microbial digestion occurs) are swallowed. **1964** R. M. LOCKLEY *Private Life of Rabbit* x. 103 Reingestion was observed both out of doors by day and below ground.

reing(n)e, obs. forms of REIGN *v.*

reingorge: see RE-ENGORGE.

†**rein'graff,** *v. Obs.* [RE- 5 a.] = next.

1610 HEALEY *St. Aug. Citie of God* 774 Re-ingraffed into the peace-full stocke from whence his disobedience hath torne him. **1651** BAXTER *Inf. Bapt.* 49 When they are reingraffed into their own Church, their Infants must needs be reingraffed with them. **1659** HOWELL *Lexicon* To tru Philologer, She did reingraffe upon divers words, as chiefly upon chief, faulty upon fault.

rein'graft, *v.* Also 7 re-en-. [RE- 5 a.] *trans.* To ingraft again. Hence **rein'grafting** *vbl. sb.*

1625 DONNE *Serm.* VI. 69 As when my true Repentance hath re-engrafted me in my God and Re-incorporated me in my Saviour. **1752** WESLEY *Wks.* (1872) X. 245 This does not imply the re-ingrafting of these Gentiles. **1885** *Homiletic Rev.* Feb. 106 The re-ingrafting of Israel into their own olive tree.

rein'gratiate, *v.* [RE- 5 a.] *trans.* (chiefly *refl.*) To ingratiate again.

1638 SIR T. HERBERT *Trav.* (ed. 2) 96 Fearing his force, and that..hee would re-ingratiate himselfe. **1669** CLARENDON *Life* III. (1760) I. 119 If He were once re-ingratiated to his Majesty's Trust. *a* **1797** H. WALPOLE *Mem. Geo. II* (1847) I. xi. 357 In order to reingratiate themselves with the mobs. **1882** *Athenæum* 28 Oct. 556/3 Tasso..hoped to re-ingratiate himself with the duke by complimenting him on his third wedding.

re'ingress. [RE- 5 a.] Renewed ingress.

1535 STEWART *Cron. Scot.* I. 224 Auveragus..And his lordis..Saw tha culd nocht haue reingres agane. **1670** EACHARD *Cont. Clergy* 68 Then there was an ingress, an egress, and a regress, or reingress.

rein'gross, *v.* [RE- 5 a.] To engross again. In **rein'grossing** *vbl. sb.*

1679 *Act 31 Chas. II*, c. 3 *(title)* An Act for reingrossing of the Records of Fines burnt or lost in the late Fire in the Temple.

rein'gulf, *v.* [RE- 5 a.] To ingulf again.

1611 COTGR., *Rengloutir*, to reglut, reingulfe, swallow vp againe. **1648** *Petit. Eastern Assoc.* 24 Designes, which have ..reingulfed us in so many new feares. **1828** CARLYLE *Misc.* (1857) I. 126 So long since reingulfed in the silence of the blank bygone Eternity! **1875** E. WHITE *Life in Christ* I. i. (1878) 8 That this intellectual Eye..should then be reingulfed by the dead ruthless force which had given it birth.

rein'habit, *v.* [RE- 5 a.]

†**1.** *intr.* To dwell again. *Obs.*

1538 LELAND *Itin.* (1769) VII. 10 One of the Richards.. broughte the foresayde Monks agayne to Stratford, where amonge the Marsches they reinhabytyd. *a* **1638** MEDE *Daniel* Wks. (1672) 700 A Commission to cause the people to return and re-inhabite. **1736** CARTE *Ormonde* I. 504 They might be able to subsist and re-inhabit in the said kingdom.

2. *trans.* To inhabit (a place, etc.) again.

1600 J. PORY tr. *Leo's Africa* IV. 219 After which time it was reinhabited by certaine people of Granada. **1670** MILTON *Hist. Eng.* III. 130 Towns and Citties were not reinhabited but lay ruin'd and wast. **1825** COLERIDGE *Aids Refl.* 234 The individual soul cannot return to reinhabit the body.

Hence **rein'habiting** *vbl. sb.*; **reinhabi'tation.**

1611 Cotgr., *Rehabitation*, a reinhabitation, reinhabiting. **1613** Purchas *Pilgrimage* vi. viii. (1614) 603 Elmahdi, an hereticall Calipha who procured the reinhabiting thereof.

†rein'hearten, *v. Obs.* [re- 5 a.] *trans.* To give fresh courage to, rehearten.

1652 Earl Monm. tr. *Bentivoglio's Hist. Relat.* 29 The Rebels were afterwards reinheartened by the Queen of Englands protection. **1667** Mrq. Worcester in Dircks *Life* xvii. (1865) 301 To reinhearten my distressed family.

rein'herit, *v.* [re- 5 a.] To inherit again.

1647 Ward *Simp. Cobler* 47 Just it is that such as undersell them, should not re-inherit them in haste. **1895** *St. James's Gaz.* 10 Sept. 12/2 He had been disinherited..; but ..reinherited his patrimonial estate.

reinikaboo: see rannygazoo.

rei'nitiate, *v.* [re- 5 a.] To initiate again.

1652 *Plea for Free State* 4 [They] oppose so obstinately the Publique Establishment, out of no more weighty reason, then to reinitiate splendid Titles. **1866** Mrs. H. Wood *St. Martin's Eve* ii, He..was altogether re-initiated into social life. **1897** *Allbutt's Syst. Med.* IV. 381 The disorder, unless re-initiated by repetition of the cause, may long remain quiescent.

reinjoin, -joy, obs. ff. re-injoin, -joy.

re'ink, *v.* [re- 5 a.] *trans.* To ink again. Hence **re'inking** *vbl. sb.*

1883 *Athenæum* 22 Dec. 815/2 One ribbon will bear re-inking several times. **1937** *Discovery* Oct. 300/2 The stone being kept damp, and re-inked for each print. **1955** J. Ryder *Printing for Pleasure* v. 61 After taking the first print, and without reinking, print onto the top sheet of the platen packing.

reinlarge, obs. form of re-enlarge.

reinless ('reɪnlɪs), *a.* [f. rein *sb.*[1] + -less.]

1. Without a rein or reins: **a.** of a horse.

1559 *Mirr. Mag., Dk. Clarence* xxix, She tearms..A wilfull prince, a raynelesse raging horse. **1591** Harington *Orl. Fur.* xxiv. xxxix, Untill his rainlesse horse bare him away. **1801** Southey *Thalaba* vi. ix, The benignant Power, Who sent the reinless steed. *a* **1881** Rossetti *House of Life* xc, The void car, hurled Abroad by reinless steeds.

b. of a driver or rider.

1873 W. Cory *Lett. & Jrnls.* (1897) 326 If I had been blind and reinless, I should have gone without a bump. **1892** *Daily News* 28 Dec. 5/4 The reinless rider acquires a firmer seat.

2. *transf.* and *fig.* Unchecked, unrestrained.

1566 Drant *Horace, Sat.* i. vi. D iij b, Leuinus..Through lyfe corrupt, and rainlesse youth dyd worke his fames decay. **1772** *Gentl. Mag.* XLII. 240 The reinless fury Of the mad whirlwinds. **1817** Shelley *Rev. Islam* vi. xix, With rein-less speed A black Tartarian horse of giant frame Comes trampling over the dead. **1856** Ruskin *Mod. Paint.* III. iv. vi. §2 The reinless play of the imagination.

†rein'lighten, obs. variant of re-enlighten.

1627 Feltham *Resolves* i. xxviii. 26 Though God depriue me of his presence for a time, he will one day re-inlighten mee.

rei'noculate, *v.* [re- 5 a.] *trans.* To inoculate again. So **reinocu'lation**.

1804 *Med. Jrnl.* XII. 315 The two last children I reinoculated was a few months after vaccination. **1896** *Allbutt's Syst. Med.* I. 652 The occurrence of furuncles in successive crops is due to reinoculation from the surface.

rein'quire, *v.* [re-.] To inquire in turn.

1646 Sir T. Browne *Pseud. Ep.* vii. i. 340 Unto him that demanded on what hand Venus was wounded, the Philosopher thought it a sufficient resolution to reinquire upon what leg King Philip halted.

So **rein'quiry**, renewed inquiry.

1830 *Westm. Rev.* Oct. 437 Re-inquiries and Removals: these, by whatsoever name called—new trials. **1866** *Pall Mall G.* 21 Feb. 1/2 The first returns..were sent back for reconsideration and re-inquiry.

reins (reɪnz), *pl.* Now *arch.* Forms: (1 renys), 4 reenes, -us, 4–7 reynes, (4 reynyez, 5 reynys, 5, 7 reyns), 5–7 raynes, 6–7 raines, (6 rains), reines, 4, 7– reins. Also *sing.* 7 reyn. [a. OF. *reins, rens*, ad. L. *rēnes* pl.]

1. The kidneys.

[*c* **1000** *Sax. Leechd.* III. 140 ᵹif hyt byþ of renys oþþer þan lendene þanne cumþ þæt blod of þara blæddran.] **1387** Trevisa *Higden* (Rolls) VII. 369 He hadde afterward greet penaunce in an evel þat hatte ilium and greveþ faste by þe reynes. *c* **1400** *Lanfranc's Cirurg.* 27 þei hangen & bynden summe membris wiþ oþere as þe reynes to þe rigge. **1450–80** tr. *Secreta Secret.* 31 Disese cometh in thi Reyns. **1586** Cogan *Haven Health* cl. (1636) 147 The Reynes or Kidneys make grosse and ill bloud. **1596** Barrough *Meth. Physick* iii. xxxvii. (1639) 159 The reines are vexed with inflammation for diverse causes. **1667** Milton *P.L.* vi. 346 Spirits..Vital in every part, not as frail man In Entrailes, Heart or Head, Liver or Reines. **1707** Floyer *Physic. Pulse-Watch* 353 So from the Reins the Liver is generated, from that the Heart, from that the Stomach. **1870** Bryant *Homer* II. xxi. 289 Eels and fishes came and gnawed The warrior's reins.

2. The region of the kidneys; the loins.

1382 Wyclif *Ezek.* ix. 2 O man..clothid with lynnen, and an ynkhorn of a wryter in his reynes. **1390** Gower *Conf.* III. 370 Sche hath my wounded herte enoignt, My temples and my Reins also. *c* **1475** *Partenay* 4325 Gaffray gripte he there faste by the raynes, Ech of thaim both suffryng there hug[e] paynes. *c* **1532** Du Wes *Introd. Fr.* in Palsgr. 1068 Gyrte thy raynes as a man. **1572** Walsingham in D. Digges *Complete Ambass.* (1655) 344 The Count de Retz is hurt in the rains of the back with a harquebush shot out of Rochel. **1633** T. Stafford *Pac. Hib.* xiii. (1821) 150 Receeving a blow with a Peece upon the reines of his backe. **1687** A. Lovell tr. *Thevenot's Trav.* i. 168 [The] Rock..bears the marks, as if a Body had been laid on the Back upon it, for the form of the Reins appear there. **1814** Cary *Dante, Inf.* xx. 13 Each.. seem'd to be revers'd At the neck-bone, so that the countenance Was from the reins averted. **1865** Swinburne *Poems & Ball., Song in Time of Rev.* 27 They are girdled about the reins with a curse.

b. *Arch.* (See quot. 1727–38.)

After F. *les reins d'une voûte*.

1727–38 Chambers *Cycl.* s.v. *Vault*, Reins, or fillings up of a Vault, are the sides which sustain it. **1751** Labelye *Westm. Bridge* 21 This upper Arch is..thicker in the Reins, or towards the Bottom, than at the Key or Top. **1872** Shipley *Gloss. Eccl. Terms* 184 The space between the crown and the reins of the arch.

3. In or after Biblical use: The seat of the feelings or affections.

13.. *E.E. Allit. P.* B. 592 For he is þe gropande god,.. Rypande of vche a ring þe reynyez & hert. **1382** Wyclif *Ps.* vii. 10 God serchende hertis and reenes. —— *Wisd.* i. 6 Of the reenus of hym witnesse is God. **1526** *Pilgr. Perf.* (W. de W. 1531) 224, I am nere to theyr mouthes, but I am ferre from theyr raynes [cf. Wyclif *Jer.* xii. 2]. *c* **1580** Sidney *Ps.* vii. x, Thou righteous proofes to hartes and reines dost send. **1603** T. M. *Progr. Jas. I* B 3 b, Griefe seized euery priuate mans raynes. **1659** *Gentl. Calling* To Bookseller, A Manual which..will lively affect, and sit close to the Reins, and penetrate the Heart of the Reader. **1738** Wesley *Ps.* cxxxix. iii. ii, Thy Hand my Heart and Reins possest. **1896** A. E. Housman *Shropshire Lad* xxx, Through their reins in ice and fire Fear contended with desire.

4. *attrib.* and *Comb.*, as †*rein-guard, -gut*; *rein-trying* adj.

1382 Wyclif *2 Sam.* xx. 8 Joab was..gird with a knyif hongynge vnto the reyn gottys in the sheethe. **1823** Crabb *Technol. Dict., Rein-guard* (Mil.), that part of armour which guarded the lower part of the back. **1827** Pollok *Course T.* x, Rein-trying, heart-investigating day.

Reins, variant of Raines *Obs.*

rein'scribe, *v.* [re- 5 a.] *trans.* To inscribe again.

1688 in *Magd. Coll. & Jas. II* (O.H.S.) 260 He gave orders to re-inscribe all the old [names]. **1878** Grosart *H. More's Poems* Mem. Introd. 46/1 To reinscribe the venerable name of Henry More among our real Makers and Singers.

rein'sert, *v.* [re- 5 a.] *trans.* To insert again. Hence **rein'serted** *ppl. a.*

1628 Gaule *Pract. The.* 22 The most compendious Laconicke with a reinserted Parenthesis. **1690** Luttrell *Brief Rel.* (1857) II. 22 The inscription on the monument.., which was defaced in the late kings time, is reinserting again upon it. **1808** Southey *Lett.* (1856) II. 55, I have cut it out of a good book, and shall be glad to reinsert it therein. **1853** Ruskin *Stones Ven.* II. viii. §19. 296 The tablets..have been taken out and reinserted in the newer masonry. **1885** *Manch. Exam.* 21 May 6/3 The clause was therefore not reinserted.

So **rein'sertion**.

1828–32 in Webster. **1885** *Manch. Exam.* 21 May 5/1 Mr. Stuart succeeded in ousting the clause.., and Lord Salisbury has procured its re-insertion.

rein'sist, *v.* [re- 5 a.] *intr.* To insist again.

1775 S. J. Pratt *Liberal Opin.* lv. (1783) II. 162 Reinsisting upon his acceptance as a debt due to him for his civility. **1892** *Pall Mall G.* 30 Mar. 3/3 The Council then proceeded..to reinsist upon its determination [etc.].

reinslave, obs. form of re-enslave.

reinsman ('reɪnzmən). *U.S.*, *Austral.*, and *N.Z.* [f. rein *sb.*[1] + -s- + man *sb.*[1]] One who is skilled in managing the reins; a driver. Also *fig.*

1855 in *Voice* (N.Y.) (1894) 8 Feb., Deeming themselves as skilful reinsmen as those selected by the Boards of Excise. **1872** Talmage *Serm.* 34 The experienced reinsman checks the fiery steed at the first jump. **1904** *N.Y. Times* 13 Dec. 7 A number of well-known amateur reinsmen started from the Harlem River Speedway. **1930** W. Banning in W. & G. H. Banning *Six Horses* 361 A reinsman was a master driver who ..was able to drive each span of his complement wholly independent of the other. **1969** *Sydney Morning Herald* 24 May 27/1 Western Districts reinsman Gordon McWilliam lost a battle of tactics behind the hot favourite, Cocky Raider. **1977** *N.Z. Herald* 8 Jan. 1-9/4 The Cambridge reinsman R. F. Mitchell..had a farewell present at Cambridge last night when he drove Pompano Prince to victory.

†rein'snare, *v. Obs. rare*[−1]. [re- 5 a.] *trans.* To ensnare again.

1624 Quarles *Job* sect. i, He that plants his Engines euery-where..and re-insnares The soule of man.

rein'spect, *v.* [re- 5 a.] To inspect again.

1826 Southey *Vind. Eccl. Angl.* 323 A book that..had been inspected and reinspected by Angels, and approved by God. **1858** Hawthorne *Fr. & It. Note-bks.* II. 95 We went to the Uffizi gallery, and reinspected the greater part of it.

So **rein'spection**.

1828–32 in Webster. **1856** Warter *Southey's Lett.* I. Pref. 13 Possibly he might have found some on reinspection. **1894** *Daily News* 8 June 8/6 A re-inspection had been made of 270 houses in Kensington.

reinsphear, obs. form of re-ensphere.

rein'spire, *v.* [re- 5 a.]

1. *trans.* To inspire again, in various senses.

1624 Heywood *Gunaik.* ii. 65 She renewes and re-inspires the decayed life of a Poet. **1651** Stanley *Poems* 54 This silk-worm (to long sleep retired) The early year hath reinspired. *a* **1711** Ken *Hymns Evang.* Poet. Wks. 1721 I. 172 We oft have heard that great Deceiver say, That he would re-inspire his buried Clay. **1767** Lewis *Statius* v. 514 No Furies were at Hand to reinspire Heroic Thoughts. **1847** Ld. Lindsay *Chr. Art* I. 143 To be modified, filled up and reinspired from their own original resources. **1867** M. Arnold *Rugby Chapel* 199 Ye..recall The stragglers, refresh the outworn, Praise, re-inspire the brave!

b. Const. *with*.

1657 Bp. H. King *Poems* 132 What man then would, who on death's pillow slumbers, Be re-inspir'd with life..? **1697** Congreve *Mourn. Bride* v. xii, O let me..re-inspire thy bosom With the breath of Love. **1718** Pope *Iliad* xv. 65 Phœbus hastes great Hector to prepare.., His lab'ring bosom re-inspires with breath. **1799** *Triumph of Benevolence* II. 371 Mrs. Mannington endeavoured to reinspire him with hope. **1861** J. G. Sheppard *Fall Rome* ii. 67 To re-inspire an effete body with the vitality of youth. **1887** Stevenson *Merry Men* iii. 119 The image of the dead dealer, reinspired with cunning and hatred.

2. To breathe again *into* something. *rare*[−1].

1681 Flavel *Meth. Grace* xxxi. 535 Regeneration..is the life of God reinspired into a soul alienated from it by the power of sin.

Hence **rein'spired** *ppl. a.*

1649 G. Daniel *Trinarch., Hen. IV*, cccxx, The French.. with re-inspired Sayles, Come to ayde Glendoure.

rein'spirit, *v.* [re- 5 a.] *trans.* To inspirit anew. Hence **rein'spiriting** *vbl. sb.*

1659 *Gentl. Calling* viii. §21 When it has despoyled them of that false courage..to permit it to reinspirit them with a true one. **1815** *Zeluca* I. 396 A word was sufficient to reinspirit her. **1885** *Fortn. in Waggonette* 67 Refreshed and reinspirited, on we go. **1889** Pater *Appreciations, Coleridge* 98 That whole episode of the re-inspiriting of the ship's crew.

rein'stall, *v.* [re- 5 a.] To install again.

1597 Beard *Theatre God's Judgem.* (1612) 261 To reinstall him in his kingdome which he was depriued of. **1625** Milton *Ode Death Fair Inf.* 46 Wert thou some Starr.. Which carefull Jove..Took up, and in fit place did re-install? **1671** —— *P.R.* iv. 614 Adam and his chosen Sons, whom thou A Saviour art come down to re-install. **1724** De Foe *Mem. Cavalier* (1840) 88 The king..[did] reinstall his son in the electorate. **1846** Landor *Imag. Conv., Louis XVIII & Talleyrand* Wks. 1853 II. 190/1 Peterborough.. would have reinstalled you at Hartwell. **1870** F. R. Wilson *Ch. Lindisf.* 178 The..east window was first reinstalled.

rein'stalment. [re- 5 a.] Renewed instalment.

1608 Day *Hum. out of Br.* v. ii, We ha yet performd but the least part of duetie, Your reinstalment. **1610** Healey *St. Aug. Citie of God* iii. xvi. 128 The Hetrurians assisted Tarquins endeauours of re-instalment. **1728** Morgan *Algiers* II. v. 317 There is not abundance of Appearance of their Re-instalment in these Realms. **1851** Lytton *Lett. to J. Bull* 2 Its reinstalment to office has not been resuscitation.

reinstamp, obs. form of re-enstamp.

reinstate (riːɪn'steɪt), *v.* [re- 5 a.]

1. *trans.* To reinstall or re-establish (a person or thing) *in* a place, station, condition, etc. Also const. *on*.

1628 in *Crt. & Times Chas. I* (1848) II. 3 The said archbishop is now reinstated in his majesty's favour. **1665** Sir T. Herbert *Trav.* (1677) 156 Such a force as..reinstated him in his own. **1714** R. Fiddes *Pract. Disc.* II. 220 We may reinstate reason in her throne. **1742** Young *Nt. Th.* ii. 318 To..reinstate us on the rock of peace. **1754** Sherlock *Disc.* (1759) I. vi. 209 The Gospel has re-instated Nature in all her hopes..of Immortality. **1835** Lytton *Rienzi* vii. ix, To re-instate him in a power which he evinced the capacity to wield. **1875** McLaren *Serm.* Ser. ii. iv. 60 Before the Apostle can be reinstated in his functions.

b. Without const. Also *absol.*

1599 B. Jonson *Cynthia's Rev.* v. ii, Lady, with the touch of your white hand, let me reinstate you. **1763** Ld. Barrington in Ellis *Orig. Lett.* Ser. ii. IV. 459 Nor is there any appearance that they will ever be re-instated or recompensed. **1835** I. Taylor *Spir. Despot.* ii. §2. 49 The.. intention of the present volume is..not to depress or exclude, but to re-instate and corroborate. **1878** Bosw. Smith *Carthage* 360 The senators could not reinstate him by force.

2. To restore to or in a proper state; to replace.

1793 Smeaton *Edystone L.* §249 Everything being reinstated, it was some time before we met with any but the ordinary interruptions. **1813** Elmes *Dilapidations* (1829) App. 54 Re-instate the skirting, papering &c. where the book-case formerly stood. **1833** *Act. 3 & 4 Will. IV*, c. 46 §110 To reinstate the streets..so opened by them. **1881** *Encycl. Brit.* XIII. 165/1 It is in the power of the company to reinstate property rather than to pay the value of it.

3. To restore to health.

1810 Shelley *Zastrozzi* ii. Pr. Wks. 1888 I. 8 The crisis of the fever..being past, proper care might reinstate him.

Hence **rein'stated** *ppl. a.*, **rein'stating** *vbl. sb.*

1727–38 Chambers *Cycl.*, *Reinstating*, the restoring of a person or thing to its former state or condition. **1766** *Complete Farmer* s.v. *Mole*, To roll those spots after the re-instated turfs are settled. **1890** [see *reinstator*].

rein'statement. [re- 5 a.] **a.** The action of reinstating; restoration, re-establishment.

1797 Holcroft tr. *Stolberg's Trav.* (ed. 2) II. xlvii. 120 The province..was insufficient for the reinstatement of his affairs. **1825–34** B. Montague tr. *Bacon's Wisd. Anc.* (Bohn) 223 The reinstatement and restoration of corruptible things. **1880** Muirhead *Gaius* iv. §57 Nor is there here any room for his reinstatement by the praetor.

b. The restoring or replacing of destroyed or damaged property.

1813 Elmes *Dilapidations* (1829) App. 60 You are hereby required to..perform..the following repairs, and re-instatements of waste. **1881** *Encycl. Brit.* XIII. 165/1 The insured has not the option of requiring reinstatement.

c. *Mil.* Re-establishment of a serviceman in a previously held civilian job after demobilization. Chiefly *attrib.*

1945 *Daily Herald* 17 May 4/3 The Reinstatement Act was working very smoothly—'and I believe I shall have very few cases to go to the reinstatement committees at all.' **1946** *R.A.F. Jrnl.* May 160 With the best will in the world, reinstatement regulations cannot help in such cases.

rein'station. [f. REINSTATE *v.*: see -ATION.] Reinstatement.

1686 F. SPENCE tr. *Varillas' Ho. Medicis* 305 His Ally.. treated with him for his reinstation. **1802** *Noble Wanderers* I. 268 The little plan he had laid for the reinstation of the deposed king. **1879** MEREDITH *Egoist* xxii, The half wager about his reinstation in the service of the Hall.

So **rein'stator**, one who reinstates.

1890 *Sat. Rev.* 2 Aug. 140/2 The reinstating goes on, and Mr. Roden Noel.. is one of the reinstators.

reinstau'ration. *rare*$^{-1}$. [RE- 5 a.] A second instauration.

1610 HEALEY *St. Aug. Citie of God* XV. xxvii. (1620) 536 Could not God, that taught this means of reinstauration, repaire them as he had created them?

†**rein'staure,** *v. Obs. rare*$^{-1}$. [f. RE- 5 a + *instaure* INSTORE *v.*] *trans.* To restore.

1609 HEYWOOD *Brit. Troy* XI. ci, The Greekes to quench theyr fleet themselves dispose And re-instaure their Tents whose spoile was great.

rein'stil, *v.* [RE- 5 a.] *trans.* To instil again.

*a***1711** KEN *Hymnotheo* Poet. Wks. 1721 III. 35 Others they ply'd with doubts,.. Curs'd Infidelity to re-instil.

re'institute, *v.* [RE- 5 a.] *trans.* To institute again. So **reinsti'tution**.

1863 DEUTSCH *Rem.* (1874) 320 Ezra only reinstituted them. **1866** FELTON *Anc. & Mod. Gr.* I. I. iv. 58, 'I reinstituted for the state the sacred chants', says the king. **1867** BUSHNELL *Mor. Uses Dark Th.* 304 There will never again be any re-institution of slavery. **1882** SEELEY *Nat. Relig.* 217 Re-institution of what was obsolete.

†**rein'stock,** *v. Obs.*$^{-1}$ [f. RE- 5 a + IN- + STOCK *v.*] *trans.* To furnish with a fresh stock.

1673 R. HEAD *Canting Acad.* 98 He may rob the Travailer to Re-instock himself.

rein'struct, *v.* [RE-.] *trans.* To instruct again or in turn. So **rein'struction**.

1740 WATERLAND *Regeneration* iii. Wks. 1823 VI. 364 Being reinstructed in the faith and reclaimed in manners. **1862** TROLLOPE *Orley F.* I. 266 He must.. instruct that attorney how to reinstruct him, and how to reinstruct those other barristers who must necessarily be employed. **1888** *Pall Mall G.* 27 Jan. 13/2 A course of reinstruction in the dry rudiments of knowledge.

rein'surance. [RE- 5 a.] A renewed or second insurance; *spec.* one by which an insurer or underwriter secures himself (wholly or in part) against the risk he has undertaken.

1755 MAGENS *Insurances* II. 271 Every Insurer is permitted to take out a Reinsurance on any Insurance he has given. **1802** MARSHALL *Insurance* I. I. iv. §3. 112 The new insurers will be responsible to him in case of loss, to the amount of the re-insurance. **1885** *Law Rep.* 15 *Q. Bench Div.* 11 Notice of abandonment need not be given to the underwriters of a policy of re-insurance.

attrib. **1867** SMYTH *Sailor's Word-bk.* 568 A reinsurance policy made on the same risk.

rein'sure, *v.* [RE- 5 a.] *trans.* and *intr.* To insure again; *spec.* to devolve the risk of an insurance on another insurer. Hence **rein'sured** *ppl. a.*

1755 N. MAGENS *Ess. Insurances* I. 94 Such Insurer, his Executors, Administrators, or Assignees, may re-insure to the Amount of the Sum before insured. **1802** S. MARSHALL *Treat. Insurance* I. 115 At Marseilles.. the insured, in such case, sues the insolvent insurer till he obtains a sentence authorizing him to re-insure at the expense of the insolvent. **1828–32** in WEBSTER. **1859** BARTLETT *Dict. Amer.* 360 It is common with underwriters or insurance companies.. to reinsure a part elsewhere. **1892** *Law Rep., Weekly Notes* 44/2 Before the reinsured obtained the benefit of his reinsurance he must himself have paid on the original insurance.

rein'surer. [-ER^1.] One who reinsures.

1755 MAGENS *Insurances* II. 271 Yet shall he.. truly make known to his Reinsurer all Advices which he.. has received concerning the insured Ship. **1802** MARSHALL *Insurance* I. 113 There is no privity of contract between the original insured and the re-insurers. **1892** *Law Rep., Weekly Notes* 44/1 Payment by the reinsurers to the reinsured.

re'integrate, *pa. pple.* ? *Obs.* [ad. med.L. *reintegrātus*, pa. pple. of *reintegrāre*: see next.] = REDINTEGRATE *pa. pple.*

1508 FISHER 7 *Penit. Ps.* cii. Wks. (1876) 169 That heuenly cyte shall be restored and reintegrate with good crysten people. *a***1648** LD. HERBERT *Hen. VIII* (1683) 412 Our King .. desired to be, if not reintegrate, yet at least in good terms with the Roman Church.

re'integrate (ri:'ɪntɪgreɪt), *v.* [ad. med.L. *reintegrāt-* (Du Cange): see REDINTEGRATE *v.* and cf. F. *réintégrer*, Sp. *reintegrar*, It. *-are*.]

†**1.** *refl.* To reinstate (oneself). *Obs.*

1581 SAVILE *Tacitus, Hist.* III. xxiv. (1591) 128 Here was the fielde where they might reintegrate themselues in their honour again. **1622** J. REYNOLDS *God's Revenge* III. Hist. xiii, He should.. rather seeke to reintegrate himselfe into his Fathers favour. *a***1648** LD. HERBERT *Hen. VIII* (1683) 418 Desiring the King.. to take hold of the present time and to reintegrate himself with the Pope.

2. *trans.* = REDINTEGRATE *v.* 2 b, 2 d. Now *rare.*

1605 BACON *Adv. Learn.* II. vii. §1 Heere I will make a request that.. I may reviue and reintegrate the missapplyed and abused name of Naturall Magicke. *a***1648** LD. HERBERT *Hen. VIII* (1683) 159 That all the followers of the Duke of Bourbon should be reintegrated in their former possessions. **1869** BROWNING *Ring & Bk.* XII. 692 The justice of the Court would presently Confirm her in her rights and exculpate, Re-integrate and rehabilitate.

3. = REDINTEGRATE *v.* 1.

1626 BACON *Sylva* §113 The Falling from a Discord to a Concord.. hath an Agreement with the Affections, which are reintegrated to the better, after some dislikes. **1798** JEFFERSON *Writ.* (1859) IV. 225 The atmosphere alone will reintegrate a soil rested in due season. **1868** SPENCER *Princ. Psychol.* I. v. (1872) I. 86 The disintegrated mass quickly re-integrates itself from the materials brought by the blood. **1898** *Nat. Rev.* Aug. 904 The capital thus sunk will neither yield an income nor be reintegrated.

b. Const. *into, with.*

1855 MISS COBBE *Intuit. Mor.* 174 The Law of Honour, then, merits to be re-integrated into the moral Law. **1881** MORGAN *Contrib. N. Amer. Ethnol.* IV. 10 The eight gentes of the Seneca-Iroquois tribe were reintegrated into two phratries. **1888** J. T. GULICK in *Linn. Soc. Jrnl., Zool.* XX. 231 The vast majority of the divergent forms arising through Local Segregation are reintegrated with the surrounding forms.

reintegration (ri:ɪntɪ'greɪʃən). [a. F. *réintégration* (15th c.), or ad. med.L. *reintegrātiōn-em* (Du Cange), noun of action f. *reintegrāre*: see prec. and REDINTEGRATION.]

†**1.** Renewal of an enterprise. *Obs. rare*$^{-1}$.

1605 BACON *Adv. Learn.* II. xxi. §1 In theyr inceptions, progressions, recoyls, reintegrations, approches and atteynings to their ends.

2. a. = REDINTEGRATION 3. ? *Obs.*

1616 in *Crt. & Times Jas. I* (1848) I. 430 There is no great opinion here of the reintegration of this worthy man into his former honours and brightness. *a***1631** DONNE *Lett.* 3 For re-integration to her Majestie's favour; in comparison whereof, all other Circumstances are but as *atomi*. **1795** in *Ld. Auckland's Corr.* (1862) III. 299 To make a stipulation in favour of the reintegration of the Stadtholder.

†**b.** = REDINTEGRATION 4. *Obs. rare*$^{-1}$.

1656 HEYLIN *Surv. France* 214 During her Sons minority, and after since her reintegration with him, she hath made herself so absolute a mistresse of his mind [etc.].

3. = REDINTEGRATION 1.

It has supplanted *redintegration* as the usual form in this sense.

1818 COLEBROOKE *Obligations* 221 Entire restitution and re-integration in the instance of agreements merely voidable. **1850** *Tait's Mag.* XVII. 701/1 Nothing could appease his remorse but the reintegration of the victim's fame. **1890** MORRIS in Mackail *Life* (1899) II. 241 It is not the dissolution of society for which we strive, but its re-integration. **1973** *Times* 13 Feb. 7/2 Soviet consular officials have told them that their reintegration 'will take time'. **1977** *Sunday Times Mag.* (Perth, Austral.) 4/4 It was not the chattering of birds on the roof that set reintegration in process. **1979** *Internat. Rehabilit. Med.* I. 45/2 Intensive rehabilitation is indicated when.. at least social reintegration into the family can be achieved.

reintegrative (ri:'ɪntɪgrətɪv), *a.* [f. REINTEGRATE *v.* + -IVE: see REDINTEGRATIVE *a.*] Tending to reintegration.

1957 V. W. TURNER *Schism & Continuity in Afr. Society* x. 303 A society continually threatened with disintegration is continually performing reintegrative ritual. **1974** *Gen. Systems* XIX. 67/2 But so brilliantly had Mayan.. societies systematized their communications, that the patient's very gestures ('symptoms') had actuated the reintegrative liturgies. **1981** J. CAREY *John Donne* vii. 221 Donne's interest lies less in resurrection itself than in reintegration. .. His sole intent is to emphasize the power of the reintegrative act.

rein'ter, *v.* [RE- 5 a; cf. F. *renterrer* (16th c.).] *trans.* To inter again.

1611 COTGR., *Renterrer*, to reinterre, to burie againe. *c***1645** HOWELL *Lett.* (1650) II. viii. 10 To Jerusalem.. they convey the bones of their dead friends from all places to be reinterred. **1675** MARVELL *Lett.* Wks. (Grosart) I. 465 The old King's body was to be taken up,.. and to be reinterred with great magnificence. **1849** GROTE *Greece* II. li. (1862) IV. 413 The dead bodies were then exhumed and re-interred.

So **rein'terment**, a second interment.

1815 *Gen. Hist.* in *Ann. Reg.* 66 An official order for shutting up the theatres on the day of re-interment. **1878** BROWNING *La Saisiaz* 614 Just as I could save a root Dis-interred for re-interment when the time best helps to shoot.

rein'terpret, *v.* [RE- 5 a.] *trans.* To interpret afresh.

1611 COTGR., *Reinterpreter*, to reinterpret, reexpound. **1831** CARLYLE *Sart. Res.* III. iii, It needs a scientific telescope, it needs to be reinterpreted and artificially brought near us. **1858** J. MARTINEAU *Stud. Chr.* 151 Revealed religion is ever passing into natural, and natural returning to re-interpret the revealed. **1920** A. S. EDDINGTON *Space, Time & Gravit.* ix. 141 It has been reinterpreted and has finally become merged in the conservation of energy. **1952** B. ULANOV *Hist. Jazz in Amer.* i. 7 The rhythmic base of music has been reinterpreted. **1979** *N.Y. Rev. Bks.* 25 Oct. 11/4 A seasoned cult member is assigned to the nascent convert.. to reinterpret his old life according to the new beliefs.

So **reinterpre'tation**.

1880 *19th Cent.* Aug. 315 These are only specimens of a characteristically commendable reinterpretation. **1956** *Nature* 10 Mar. 443/2 For these reasons there should be a re-interpretation of humanism. **1974** R. A. HALL *External Hist. Romance Langs.* 6 The reinterpretation of an unfamiliar form or part of a form under the influence of another form with which it has been identified.

rein'terrogate, *v.* [RE- 5 a.] *trans.* To interrogate again.

1611 COTGR., *Reinterroguer*, to reinterrogate, reexamine, aske new questions of. **1802–12** BENTHAM *Ration. Judic. Evid.* (1827) II. 214 For interrogated, say re-interrogated: for.. he must always have been interrogated in the first instance. **1815** SCOTT *Guy M.* xxxii, He and Mrs. MacCandlish were then re-interrogated, whether Brown had no arms with him on that unhappy morning.

rein'throne, *v.* [RE- 5 a; cf. RE-ENTHRONE.] To enthrone again. (Common *c* 1630–1750.)

1612 DRAYTON *Poly-olb.* viii. 151 With so effectuall speech imploring their high grace That him they reinthron'd. **1640** HABINGTON *Edw. IV* 59 On this marriage was agreed that King Edward should be deposed, King Henry re-inthrond. **1660** INGELO *Bentiv. & Ur.* II. (1682) 140 They saw Piety re-inthroned, Righteousness restor'd. **1700** TOLAND *Clito* vi, I'll.. Establish Justice, reinthrone the Laws. **1752** YOUNG *Brothers* IV. i, But his confession shall redeem my fame, And re-inthrone me in my princess' smile. **1873** M. ARNOLD *Lit. & Dogma* Pref. 9 To re-inthrone the Bible as explained by our current theology.. is .. impossible.

†**rein'thronize,** *v. Obs.* [RE- 5 a; cf. med.L. *reinthronizāre* (Du Cange).] *trans.* = prec.

1602 WARNER *Alb. Eng.* Epit. 372 The Danes thus outed hence, and the West-Saxon or English blood-royall reinthronized. *c***1645** HOWELL *Lett.* (1650) I. III. xxi, This Mustapha they did reinthronize and place in the Ottoman Empire.

re'intimate, *v.* [RE- 5 a.] *trans.* To intimate again.

1622 WOTTON *Let.* in *Reliq.* (1685) 540 Yet withal, I was not tender to re-intimate unto them, that [etc.].

rein'title, *v.* [RE- 5 a.] To entitle again.

1651 JER. TAYLOR *Serm. for Year* I. xix. 241 For the reimplacing the divine image, for the reintitling it to the Kingdoms of grace and glory.

rein'titule, *v.* [RE- 5 a.] To intitule again.

1600 W. WATSON *Decacordon* (1602) 310 The foresaide claime of heritage,.. whereby.. she is againe reintituled to the same French kingdome and crowne.

rein'tomb, *v.* [RE- 5 a.] To entomb again.

1594 CONSTABLE *Diana* VIII. iv, When reintombing from obliuius ages in better stanzas her surviving wonder.

rein'trench, *v.* [RE- 5 a.] *trans.* To entrench again.

1650 T. BAYLY *Herba Parietis* 22 They saw the prince stand bulwarckt in the midst of so many slaughter'd Moores: and re-intrenched about with his owne dead. **1899** *Rev. of Reviews* Mar. 259 Masses of.. troops reintrenched themselves.

reintro'duce, *v.* [RE- 5 a.] *trans.* To introduce again. Hence **reintro'ducing** *vbl. sb.*

1664 H. MORE *Myst. Iniq.* 281 The Empire which he seduced into Idolatry.. and so re-introduced the Image of the slain Beast by this seduction. **1667** J. CORBET *Disc. Relig. Eng.* 6 A continued succession and series of Treasons, for the re-introducing of Popery. **1728** MORGAN *Algiers* II. v. 316, I may have occasion elsewhere, very probably, to re-introduce the Maltese. **1765** *Museum Rust.* IV. 262 It has been introduced.. for a long series of years; but.. so little noticed, that.. I had much ado to re-introduce it. **1817** COLERIDGE *Biog. Lit.* (Bohn) 77 The very words, objective and subjective,.. I have ventured to re-introduce. **1837** SYD. SMITH *Lett.* Wks. 1859 II. 267/1 Their bills of last year —which Lord John Russell stated his intention of re-introducing at the beginning of this Session. **1869** BROWNING *Ring & Bk.* x. 1855 To shake This torpor of assurance from our creed, Re-introduce the doubt discarded.

reintro'duction. [RE- 5 a.] The action of reintroducing; a renewed introduction.

1661 R. BAILLIE in *Lauderd. Papers* (Camden) I. 95 To countenanc[e] the Reintroduction of bishops and books. **1717** *Wodrow Corr.* (1843) II. 277 They durst not for their lives treat about the reintroduction of Prelacy into Scotland. **1769** BLACKSTONE *Comm.* IV. xxviii. 365 Since the re-introduction of the Jews into England, in the time of Oliver Cromwell. **1830** LYTTON *P. Clifford* xv, During this short conversation the re-introduction of Mr. Clifford.. to Lucy Brandon had been effected. **1863** H. COX *Instit.* I. vi. 55 In order to the reintroduction of the Bill, the session was terminated by a prorogation.

rein'trusion. [RE- 5 a.] The action of intruding again; a renewed intrusion.

1848 LYTTON *Harold.* III. ii, He foresaw the necessary re-intrusion of his wife upon the charm of his.. solitude. **1858** CARLYLE *Fredk. Gt.* II. i. (1872) I. 52 The regress or the re-intrusion of the circumambient hostile populations.

rein'vade, *v.* [RE- 5 a.] *trans.* To invade again or in turn.

1611 COTGR., *Renvahir*, to reinuade. *a***1711** KEN *Hymnotheo* Poet. Wks. 1721 III. 119 Thus I soon felt my flashy Goodness fade, And Sin with greater Force me re-invade. **1895** FARRAR *Gathering Clouds* I. Pref. 7 To show how the world reinvaded.. the nominal Church.

So **rein'vasion**.

1886 STEVENSON *Dr. Jekyll* 40 Lamps, which.. had been kindled afresh to combat this mournful reinvasion of darkness.

rein'vent, *v.* [RE- 5 a.] To invent again.
1686 PLOT *Staffordsh.* 371 This not being the first time, that the same thing has been reinvented. **1870** LOWELL *Among my Bks.* Ser. I. (1873) 180 After Spenser..had reinvented the art of writing well. **1894** *Brit. Jrnl. Photogr.* XLI. 69 This system..has also been reinvented and patented a year or two ago.
absol. **1888** H. S. HOLLAND *Christ or Ecclesiastes* 73 [The mind] invents;..it corrects; it reinvents.
So **rein'vention, rein'ventor**.
1719 *Weekly Medley* 28 Mar., An Art now so long lost, its Loss so lamented, and its re-invention so much coveted. **1852** HAWTHORNE *Wonder-Bk.* (1879) 118 My merit as a reinventor and improver. **1878** NEWCOMB *Pop. Astron.* II. i. 108 He..set himself to the reinvention of the instrument. **1964** W. L. GOODMAN *Hist. Woodworking Tools* 38 It appears to be a re-invention of the Minoan and Roman tool. **1973** *Sci. Amer.* Apr. 85/1 James thought up the idea of the differential gear (actually a reinvention).

rein'version. [RE- 5 a.] The action of inverting again; a second inversion.
1859 PARKINSON *Optics* (1866) 209 The re-inversion of the image is sometimes effected by an eye-piece of three lenses.
So † **rein'verse** *v. Obs.*; **rein'vert** *v.*
1660 BOYLE *New Exp. Phys. Mech.* xvii. 128 By reinverting the Tube you let that bubble return to the open end of it. *c* **1720** S. WESLEY *Hymn of Eupolis* 108 Whether various nature play, Or reinversed, thy will obey. **1907** J. H. PARSONS *Dis. Eye* iv. 43 Just as with a convex lens, the image is inverted. It is re-inverted psychologically in the brain.

reinvest (riːɪn'vɛst), *v.* [RE- 5 a; cf. It. *reinvestire* (Florio) and REVEST.]
1. *trans.* To invest again with or as with a garment. Const. *with*, rarely *in*.
1611 FLORIO, *Reinuestire*, to reinuest. **1629** WADSWORTH *Pilgr.* 12 Then was I reinuested with a Doublet of white Canuas. **1681–6** J. SCOTT *Chr. Life* (1747) III. 533 This Earth, where the old Matter of those Bodies lies, wherein they are to be re-invested. **1837** LOCKHART *Scott* V. ix. 221 That one or two poor half-pay officers..might be..replaced in Highland regiments, and so reinvested with the untheatrical 'Garb of Old Gaul'.
b. To re-endow *with* a possession, power, etc.
1648 MILTON *Tenure Kings* Pr. Wks. 1753 I. 351 Gildas..testifies, that the people, thus reinvested with their own original right [etc.]. *a* **1680** CHARNOCK *Attrib. God* (1834) II. 104 Since they never divested themselves of their original integrity, they could not be re-invested with that which they had never lost. **1738** NEAL *Hist. Purit.* IV. 72 The General and his officers finding themselves reinvested with the Supreme authority [etc.]. **1832** tr. *Sismondi's Ital. Rep.* vi. 131 Galeazzo was recalled, and reinvested with the lordship of Milan. **1863** J. G. MURPHY *Comm., Gen.* iii. 20 To undo what had been done for the death of man, and so reinvest him with life.
2. To replace, re-establish. Const. *in*.
1617 BP. ANDREWES *96 Serm., Holy Ghost* x. (1629) 708 A restitution *in integrum*; a re-investing them in what they were borne to, or were any waies possessed of. **1639** GLAPTHORNE *Argalus* III. Wks. 1874 I. 36 To re-invest blest quiet in his heart. **1686** tr. *Chardin's Trav. Persia* 136 The Vice-Roy..dispoil'd him of his Principality, and reinvested in it Levan's Lawful Heir. **1854** MILMAN *Lat. Chr.* VII. i. (1864) IV. 6 The German line of pontiffs had done much to reinvest the papacy in its ancient sanctity.
† **3.** To vest again *in* a person or body. *Obs.*[−1]
1760 in Picton *L'pool Munic. Rec.* (1886) II. 150 The same land shall..be reinvested in the said Corporation.
4. To invest (money) again.
1848 MILL *Pol. Econ.* III. xiv. §3 (1876) 339 They..save and re-invest their savings because they have nothing on which they care to expend them. **1885** *Law Rep.* 29 *Chanc. Div.* 209 The proceeds of sale have been..reinvested in land.
b. *intr.* To make a fresh investment.
1890 'R. BOLDREWOOD' *Col. Reformer* (1891) 259 To pay off his purchase-money, or re-invest in stores.

rein'vestigate, *v.* [RE- 5 a.] *trans.* To investigate again.
1813 *Gen. Hist.* in *Ann. Reg.* 50 They ought as seldom as possible to re-investigate the evidence. **1856** DOVE *Logic Chr. Faith* I. i. §1. 35 Direct efforts..to re-investigate some ..department of knowledge. **1897** J. HUTCHINSON in *Arch. Surg.* VIII. 240 When I acquainted my friends with these facts he re-investigated the specimen.
So **reinvesti'gation**.
1847 in WEBSTER. **1899** *Allbutt's Syst. Med.* VI. 691 The morbid anatomy demands reinvestigation.

rein'vestiture. [RE- 5 a.] The act of reinvesting; a second investiture.
1815 HOBHOUSE *Substance Lett.* (1816) I. 104 When the people..foresaw the re-investiture of the clergy [etc.]. **1841** TRENCH *Parables* (1860) 401 To trace the steps of his return, from the first beginnings of repentance to his full re-investiture in all the privileges of a son.

rein'vestment. [RE- 5 a.] A fresh investment. Also **rein'vesture.**
1611 COTGR., *Ravestissement*, a readuesting, reinuesture. *Ibid.*, *Revest*, a reinuestment, reinuesture. **1828–32** WEBSTER, *Reinvestment*. **1857** MILL *Pol. Econ.* (ed. 4) I. I. iv. 70 All property..is a part of capital, so soon as it..is set apart for productive reinvestment. **1885** *Law Rep.* 29 *Chanc. Div.* 209 The costs incurred in such reinvestment may be charged for according to the scale. **1931** *Economist* 3 Jan. 25/2 A fair amount of reinvestment business following the heavy dividend disbursements of this week sufficed..to give prices a firm tendency. **1980** W. ASH *Incorporated* vi. 61 Various proposals for the re-investment of the profits.

rein'vigorate, *v.* [RE- 5 a.] *trans.* To give fresh vigour to. Also *absol.*
1658 EVELYN *Fr. Gard.* (1675) 179 When the weather is mild, you may sometimes shew them the air, and reinvigorate with the sun. **1666** BOYLE *Wks.* (1772) I. p. lxxxiii, Restoring the temperament of the debilitated parts, and reinvigorating the blood. **1746** HERVEY *Medit.* (1818) 80 As a spacious field arrayed in cheerful green, relieves and reinvigorates the eye. **1807** G. CHALMERS *Caledonia* I. III. viii. 435 That rational reformer reinvigorated the episcopate. **1862** MRS. S. C. HALL *Can wrong be right?* II. 292 Sometimes his mind would return..and reinvigorate the body.
Hence **rein'vigorated**, *ppl. a.*
1670 G. H. *Hist. Cardinals* II. II. 162 All those reinvigorated Families. **1884** SWINBURNE in T. H. Ward *Eng. Poets* III. 281 The revived and reinvigorated *Lotos-Eaters*.

reinvigo'ration. [RE- 5 a.] A fresh invigoration.
1822–34 *Good's Study Med.* (ed. 4) I. 456 Tonics for that [purpose] of both local and general re-invigoration. **1841** TUPPER *Twins* vii, Volatile salts, a lady's maid, and all that sort of reinvigoration. **1889** *Times* 3 Aug. 9/5 The ideas..of the Anglican Church have undergone..much reinvigoration and development.

rein'vite, *v.* [RE- 5 a.; cf. late L. *reinvītāre*.] To invite again. Hence **rein'viting** *vbl. sb.*
1611 COTGR., *Reinviter*, to reinuite, or bid once more. **1611** FLORIO, *Rinuito*, a re-inuiting. **1624** QUARLES *Sion's Sonn.* xx. 17 Whose beautie reinvites My oft remembrance. *a* **1711** KEN *Christophil* Poet. Wks. 1721 I. 431 Ardent Pray'rs shall re-invite My Jesus to my longing Sight. **1862** LYTTON *Str. Story* xiii, Her sentiment of shame in reinviting your opinion after having treated you with so little respect.
So **reinvi'tation**.
1652 BENLOWES *Theoph.* XIII. (*heading*), The Reinvitation.

rein'volve, *v.* [RE- 5 a.] To involve again.
1641 MILTON *Reform.* II. Wks. 1851 III. 69 To re-involve us in that pitchy Cloud of infernall darknes. **1799** *Phil. Trans.* LXXXIX. 269 The root of any power, being re-involved, returns to the power from which it was extracted.

reioce, -ios(she, -iose, etc., obs. ff. REJOICE.

† **reir**, *v. Sc. Obs.*[−1] [app. aphetic for *arreir* ARREAR *v.* 2.] *intr.* To retire, retreat.
1570 *Henry's Wallace* x. 355 The worthy Scottis, thay reirit [*MS.* weryt] far on bak.

reir, obs. var. of RERE.

reird, common Sc. form of RERD(E.

‖ **reis**[1] (reɪs), *sb. pl.* Now *Hist.* Forms: 6 reyes, 6–7 reys, 8 rayes, 7–9 reis; 7–9 rees, 8 rez, 8–9 res, reas. *Sing.* 8 re, 8–9 ree, 9 rea, rei. [a. Pg. *reis* pl.; the correct sing. is *real* (see REAL *sb.*[1]), of which the normal pl. would be *reaes*.] A former Portuguese money of account of very small value (equal *c* 1906 to about one-twentieth of a penny in Portugal and one-fortieth in Brazil), of which one thousand formed a MILREIS. (In India the *rea* was latterly the four-hundredth part of a rupee.)
1555 EDEN *Decades* 348 Alowynge to hym in pension seuen hundreth reys monethly. *marg.* Seuen hundreth reys are .x.s. **1598** W. PHILLIP tr. *Linschoten* (1864) 165 The Cooper hath three Duckets a moneth, and 3900 Reyes fraught. **1662** J. DAVIES tr. *Mandelslo's Trav.* 107 The Order there is to sell them at 400 Reis. **1691** LOCKE *Lower. Interest* Wks. 1727 II. 59 In Portugal they count their Money by Reys, a very small, or rather imaginary Coin. **1698** FRYER *Acc. E. India & P.* 207, 60 Rees make a Tango. **1720** *Lond. Gaz.* No. 5911/1 The King of Portugal has..laid a Tax of 200 Reas (in English Money about 13 Pence Half-penny) per Pound upon all Sugar. **1727** A. HAMILTON *New Acc. E. Ind.* II. App. 6 Their Accounts [at Bombay] are kept by Rayes and Rupees. [Cf. Yule & Burnell *Anglo-Ind. Gloss.* (1886) s.v., Accounts were kept at Bombay in rupees, quarters, and reas,down at least to November, 1834.] **1872** MARK TWAIN *Innoc. Abr.* v. 35 The Portuguese pennies or *reis* (pronounced rays) are prodigious. It takes one thousand reis to make a dollar.
sing. **1706** PHILLIPS (ed. Kersey), *Ree*, a Portuguese Coin, of which 40 make 1 Ryal or 6 Pence in English Money. **1727–38** CHAMBERS *Cycl.* s.v. *Money*, The good baruco is equal to a Portuguese ree. **1816** 'QUIZ' *Grand Master* v. 100 *note*, A rea is the lowest coin in India. **1875** JEVONS *Money* xiv. 184 The Portuguese unit of account, called the *rei*, is worth only about the nineteenth part of an English penny, and is probably the smallest unit in the world.

‖ **reis**[2], **rais** (raɪs). Also 6 raiz, reiz, 7–8 reys. [a. Arab. *ra*ʼ*is* (also *ra*ʼ*īs* and *rā*ʼ*is*) chief, f. *rās* head: hence also F. *réis*, *raïs*, Pg. *arraes*, *arrais*, Sp. *arraez*.]
1. The captain of a boat or vessel.
1585 T. WASHINGTON tr. *Nicholay's Voy.* I. vii, The Rais and Azappis of the gallies. *Ibid.* xvii, A Raiz of the gallie and a Ianissarie. **1599** HAKLUYT *Voy.* II. I. 291 The Reiz, or Captaines of the Gallies. **1753** *Scots Mag.* XV. 16/1 A rais, that is the captain of a corsair. **1775** R. CHANDLER *Trav. Asia M.* (1825) I. 56 The rais was an obstinate hairy savage. **1845** *Mem. Lady H. Stanhope* I. 269 He then was entitled fully to the rank of Räis Hassan, or Captain Hassan. **1863** PETHERICK *Trav. in Afr.* 4 May (1869) I. 322 The reis of our nugger came overland to the 'Kathleen'. **1886** SIR C. W. WILSON *Fr. Korti to Khartum* 137 The reis or pilot with his assistants, who navigated the ship.
2. A chief or governor.
1678 J. PHILLIPS tr. *Tavernier's Trav.* I. v. 228 In every Village or Borough there is a *Reis*, or chief of the place. **1849** E. B. EASTWICK *Dry Leaves* 62 When he found himself degraded from his position of Rais, or Chief Amir.
b. *Hist. Reis Effendi*, the title of an officer of state in the former Turkish empire, who acted as chancellor and minister of foreign affairs.
1687 *Lond. Gaz.* No. 2301/1 Solyman immediately sent before to Constantinople, the Testerdar and Reys Effendi, with the Seal and Standard of Mahomet. **1753** HANWAY *Trav.* (1762) II. x. iv. 240 The reys effendi represented, that the season was too far advanced. **1819** T. HOPE *Anastasius* (1820) I. iv. 77 The conference between a certain Embassador and the Reïs Effendee would produce a new war.

† **reise**, *sb. Obs.* Forms: 4–5 reys, 5 reyse, 6–7 reise; 5–6 raise. [= OF. *reise*, *raise* (also *rese*, *rase*, etc.) military expedition, raid (13–15th c. in Godef.), a. MDu., MLG. or MHG. *reise* (OHG. *reisa*) in the same sense, f. the stem **rais-*, *rīs-*, to RISE: hence also med.L. *reisa*, *resa*, etc. (see Du Cange).] A journey; *spec.* a military expedition; a hostile incursion or inroad; a raid or foray.
[**1390** *Earl Derby's Exp.* (Camden) 38 Expense hospicii cum prouidenciis factis pro le Reys. *Ibid.* 53 Tempore quo dominus stetit in le Reys.] *c* **1440** *Partonope* 748 This was now a wondyr reys; Whan he woke then fast by bloys Aryued this yong Partanope. **1475** *Bk. Noblesse* (Roxb.) 40 He wanne at the first raise that he made over the see [2,500] townes and castellis. **1494** FABYAN *Chron.* v. cxviii. 94 He lefte not contynually to make reyses and assautis vpon yᵉ Saxons. **1577–87** HOLINSHED *Chron.* II. 48/1 The successe was variable on both sides betwixt the lawfull gouernors and these vsurpers, with dailie raises and skirmishes. **1600** HOLLAND *Livy* II. xlviii. 77 The Latines were much troubled with the reises and rodes of the Aequians. **1609** —— *Amm. Marcell.* 324 Sapor..by way of open reises and raising of booties wasted all Armenia.

† **reise**, *v. Obs.* In 4–5 reyse. [a. MDu., MLG., or MHG. *reisen* (*reysen*) in the same sense, f. *reise*: see prec.] *intr.* To go on a military expedition; to make inroads or raids; to travel, journey. Hence † **'reising** *vbl. sb.*
c **1386** CHAUCER *Prol.* 54 A knyght ther was..In Lettow hadde he reysed and in Ruce. **1387** TREVISA *Higden* (Rolls) VII. 327 Henry..occupied Seynt Michel his mount, and reysed [L. *incursavit*] up eyþer broþer now uppon þat oon, now uppon þat oþer. **1481** CAXTON *Reynard* (Arb.) 43 That men shold saye ye reysed and accompanyed your self with a cursyd and persone agrauate. **1494** FABYAN *Chron.* VII. 388 Sir Rogier Clifford wᵗ other, whiche entended to make a reysyng vpon yᵉ Walshemen.

reise, obs. f. RAISE *v.*, var. of RICE, twig.

reisen, obs. f. RAISE *v.*, RAISIN.

reiskie, -y: see REESKY *a.*

Reisner ('raɪsnə(r)). [f. the name of a German artist in wood, of the time of Louis XIV.] *Reisner-work* (also simply *Reisner*), a method of inlaying in wood of different colours.
1833 LOUDON *Encycl. Archit.* Gloss., *Reisner* [printed *Reigner*] *work*, ornaments made by inlaying wood in the manner of buhl work, with leaves, &c., of different colours. **1846** HOLTZAPFFEL *Turning* II. 732 *note*, Boule work, and reisner work, are considered by the virtuosi to apply exclusively to the two celebrated *ébénistes* of those names. **1875** *Ure's Dict. Arts* (ed. 7) III. 700 *Reisner*, a process of inlaying wood, like Parquetry.

reiso(u)n, obs. ff. RAISIN, REASON *sb.*[1]

reisshe, obs. f. RUSH (the plant).

Reissner ('raɪsnə(r)). *Anat.* The name of Ernst *Reissner* (1824–78), German anatomist, used in the possessive or with *of* to designate a thin vestibular membrane of the internal ear, separating the scala vestibuli from the central duct of the cochlea.
1872 [see SCALA]. **1945** MCNALLY & STUART in C. & C. L. Jackson *Dis. Nose, Throat, & Ear* III. 366 (*caption*) Gross dilatation of the scala media has occurred with displacement of Reissner's membrane on to the wall of the scala vestibuli. **1974** D. & M. WEBSTER *Compar. Vertebr. Morphol.* x. 229 The scala media is separated from the scala vestibuli by a thin, epithelial structure, Reissner's membrane.

re'issuable, *a.* [RE- 5 a.] Of notes, bills, etc.: That may be reissued.
1799 *Act 39 Geo. III*, c. 107 §1 *marg.*, On Promissory Notes payable at the Place where issued and re-issuable, a like Duty of 2*d.* and ½*d.* **1813** *Chron.* in *Ann. Reg.* 250/2 The duties on re-issuable promissory notes. **1897** *Daily News* 3 Feb. 5/3 One indispensable condition of the proposed issue of 1*l.* notes is that..they shall be re-issuable.

re'issue, *sb.* [RE- 5 a.] A second or renewed issue; *spec.* in the book-trade, a republication at a different price or in a different form of part of an impression already placed on the market; also, a reissued gramophone record.
1805 W. TAYLOR in *Ann. Rev.* III. 295 The re-issue could easily be effected from a single centre. **1884** DOWELL *Taxation* IV. iv. I. 70 The fifteenth granted to Henry III.. in consideration of the reissue of the charters. **1937** *Discovery* Oct. 320/1 Apart from this curious re-issue, Godwin's book was reprinted in the Harleian Miscellany in 1746. **1948** *Hansard Commons* 21 Jan. 217 American films.. were good enough to go on attracting cinema-goers even on re-issue. **1966** *Listener* 5 May 664/3 No reservations about a wonderful bargain HMV reissue. **1977** *Rolling Stone* 24

Mar., More people acquaint themselves with Fleetwood Mac and dig back to old reissues.

re'issue, *v.* [RE- 5 a.] To issue again.

a. *intr.* *a* **1618** SYLVESTER *Eleg. Ep. Sir W. Sidney* 124 Heav'n maketh all things to re-issue well. **1786** JEFFERSON *Writ.* (1859) II. 59 It re-issues into the ocean at the northerly end of the Gulf. **1842** TENNYSON *Godiva* 77 Reissuing, robed and crown'd, To meet her lord. **1860** LD. LYTTON *Lucile* II. iv. § I. 77 From the dark tiring-chamber behind straight reissue.. the old mummers.

b. *trans.* **1799** *Act 39 Geo. III*, c. 107 § 1 [A promissory note] which may be re-issued from Time to Time. **1847** LD. LINDSAY *Chr. Art* I. 73 These compositions.. were finally reissued by those masters, more or less modified and improved. **1884** *Law Rep. 12 Q. Bench Div.* 605 The notes, when presented for payment, were cashed by the company, and reissued by them.

Hence **re'issuer**.

1898 GROSART *Pref. Greene's Selimus* 7 The re-issuers may really have known that R(obert) G(reene) was the author.

reist, obs. Sc. form of REST *sb.*

reistafel, var. RIJSTTAFEL.

†**'reister.** *Obs.* Also 6–8 reyster. [ad. obs. F. *reistre* (mod.F. *reître, rêtre*), ad. G. *reiter* REITER *sb.*[1]] = REITER *sb.*[1]

1577 SIDNEY in *Zurich Lett.* (Parker Soc.) II. 293 Offer my services to Butrech, the best doctor among reisters, and the best reister among Doctors. **1594** R. ASHLEY tr. *Loys le Roy* 117b, There is great reckoning made of the Albaneses of Greece.. and of the Reisters of Germanie. **1607** R. C[AREW] tr. *Estienne's World of Wonders* 11 A Scot, who being pursued by certaine Reisters.. leapt with his horse.. into the Sea. **1641** BAKER *Chron.* (1653) 464 The French King sent an Army.. which consisted of nine hundred men at armes.., eight hundred Reysters [etc.]. **1744** OZELL tr. *Brantôme's Sp. Rhodomontades* 208 Now M. de Guise who was a Thorough Soldier, made the Other forget his Lesson, as also all his Reysters.

reisty, variant of REASTY *a.*, rancid.

reisun, obs. form of REASON *sb.*[1]

reisyn(e, obs. forms of RAISIN.

†**reit.** *Obs.* Forms: 6 reyte, 6–7 reite, 7 reet, reit. [Of obscure origin: cf. REEK *sb.*[2]] Chiefly *pl.* Seaweed.

1538 ELYOT *Alga*, reyte [**1548** reites] or wedes in the see. **1555** EDEN *Decades* 343 Weedes of the sea cauled reites or ouse. **1603** HOLLAND *Plutarch's Mor.* 676 It hath gotten about the keele a deale of mosse, reits, kilpe, and tangle. **1610** —— *Camden's Brit.* I. 184 With the Sea weede or reit commonly called Orewood. **1655** BP. RICHARDSON *Obs. O.T., Exod.* 11 Calling it the sea of weeds, or sedge,.. of flag, or rush, tange, rack or reet, in Latin, *alga*,.. which reddish weeds in abundance grew in it. **1661** LOVELL *Hist. Anim. & Min.* Introd. b 7 The Squillae.. live in marine.. places: their meat is oisters, and reites.

reit-buck (riːt-). Also riet-buck, riet-, reit-bok, †ritbock. [ad. Du. *rietbok*, f. *riet* REED + *bok* BUCK.] A South African antelope, *Cervicapra arundinacea* (formerly *Antilope eleotragus*).

[**1785** G. FORSTER tr. *Sparrman's Voy. Cape G. Hope* II. xiv. 222 The riet, or reed ree-bok, I saw but once.] **1795** tr. *Thunberg's Trav.* (ed. 2) II. 44 Rietboks.. and Bonteboks.. frequented much these hilly and verdant fields. **1801** SHAW *Gen. Zool.* II. 348 The female Ritbock resembles the male in colour, but has no horns. **1834** *Penny Cycl.* II. 80/1 The reit bok is not found in the immediate vicinity of the Cape, but farther in the interior of the country it is by no means uncommon. **1850** R. G. CUMMING *Hunter's Life S. Afr.* (1902) 154/1 Here I found reit-buck, which do not frequent the Limpopo in those parts which I have visited. **1889** RIDER HAGGARD *Allan's Wife*, etc. 322 Out bounded a beautiful reit bok which had been lying in the shelter. **1899** —— *Swallow* iv, Up sprang two riet-buck.

reiter (ˈraɪtə(r)), *sb.*[1] Now only *Hist.* Forms: 6–7 reyter, 7 raiter, 8 reitter, 7– reiter. [a. G. *reiter* rider, trooper, f. *reiten* to RIDE. Cf. REISTER.] A German cavalry soldier, *esp.* one of those employed in the wars of the 16th and 17th c.

1584 *Calendar Hatfield MSS.* 85 The repaiement of certaine monney owinge to him for the intelligence of the Reyters. **1591** UNTON *Corr.* (Roxb.) 249 This daye the Kinge departeth towards Gizors,.. to drawe his whole armye of Reyters into those parts. **1617** MORYSON *Itin.* I. 32 When the Fayres of Franckfort draw neere, they send out certaine Reyters, that is Horsemen.. which conduct the Merchants and their goods out of the Frontiers. **1670** COTTON *Espernon* I. II. 46 The Reiters which he had rais'd in Germany could not come to him. **1727–38** CHAMBERS *Cycl., Reitters*, an antient title given the German cavalry. **1820** RANKEN *Hist. France* VII. 19 Not a man of the Reiters or German infantry was spared. **1856** R. A. VAUGHAN *Mystics* (1860) I. 257 A retinue of forty reiters is a moderate attendance for a prelate out on a visitation.

Reiter (ˈraɪtə(r)), *sb.*[2] *Path.* The name of Hans *Reiter* (1881–1969), German bacteriologist, used in the possessive to denote a disease or syndrome first described by him in 1916 (*Deutsche Med. Wochenschr.* 14 Dec. 1535) which is characterized by arthritis, conjunctivitis, and urethritis, typically affects young men, and is usually caused by bacteria of the genus *Chlamydia*.

1923 STEDMAN *Med. Dict.* (ed. 7) 859/2 *Reiter's disease*, a fever of a more or less remittent type, lasting about seventeen days, accompanied with pains in the joints, conjunctivitis, iritis, cystitis, and enlargement of the spleen; it has been observed in the tropics, but its causation is unknown. **1946** *Jrnl. Infect. Dis.* LXXIX. 134 (*heading*) The possible relationship of the pleuropneumonia-like organisms to Reiter's disease, rheumatoid arthritis and ulcerative colitis. **1962** *Lancet* 26 May 1111/1 The symptom-triad of arthritis, conjunctivitis, and urethritis, generally known as Reiter's syndrome, has a striking predilection for young men in military service. **1972** [see *keratoderma* s.v. KERATO-]. **1978** *Jrnl. R. Soc. Med.* LXXI. 335 In Reiter's disease, acute uveitis is usually asynchronous.

†**'reiter**, *v. Obs. rare.* [ad. F. *réitérer* or L. *reiterāre*; cf. ITER *v.*] *trans.* To reiterate.

1577 FRAMPTON *Joyful News* III. 108b, By reiteryng [*printed* reteiryng] the wette Linnen clothe into the Balsamo it will bee healed. **1634** JACKSON *Creed* VII. xxiii, The same practise you have reitered against St. Stephen.

re'iterable, *a. rare*$^{-1}$. [a. F. *réitérable* (16th c.): see REITERATE *v.* and -ABLE.] That may be repeated.

1610 W. FOLKINGHAM *Art of Survey* IV. v. 84 In this Action, sith it is not Reiterable, it is expedient to retriue the vtmost Value and worth.

re'iterance. [ad. L. type *reiterantia: see next and -ANCE.] Repetition.

1872 in Spurgeon *Treas. Dav.* Ps. lxxxviii. 8 (1874) IV. 144 A tedious oft-told tale which comes with something of a dull reiterance. **1880** SWINBURNE *Songs of Spring-t., Thalassius* 213 His heart, Singing, bade heaven and wind and sea bear part In one live song's reiterance.

reiterant (riːˈɪtərənt), *a.* [ad. L. *reiterant-em*, pres. pple. of *reiterāre* to REITERATE.] Reiterating, repeating.

1610 W. FOLKINGHAM *Art of Survey* IV. i. 79 Reiterant Valuation depends vpon the exact knowledge both of the Reuenewes and Reprises. **1850** MRS. BROWNING *Poems* I. 31 In Heaven they said so; and at Eden's gate,—And here, reiterant, in the wilderness! **1898** *Expositor* Oct. 266 It is misleading to speak of the action in the Sacrament as merely symbolical and not reiterant at all.

reiterate (riːˈɪtərət), *pa. pple.* and *ppl. a.* [ad. L. *reiterāt-us*, pa. pple. of *reiterāre*: see next.] Reiterated, repeated.

1471 RIPLEY *Comp. Alch.* VIII. vi. in Ashm. (1652) 172 Than Hevyn uppon Erth must be reitterate, Unto the Sowle wyth the Body be reincorporate. **1561** T. NORTON *Calvin's Inst.* III. 201 Whether repentaunce may be oftentymes reiterate for deadly sinnes. **1644** BULWER *Chiron.* 59 When the voyce is reiterate by conduplication. **1669** W. SIMPSON *Hydrol. Chym.* 105 Much of the blood is taken away, especially by reiterate bloodings. **1711** SHAFTESB. *Charac.* (1737) III. Misc. v. i. 237 It belongs to mere Enthusiasts and Fanaticks to plead the Sufficiency of a reiterate translated Text. **1814** SOUTHEY *Roderick* xxv, Over all predominant was heard, Reiterate from the conquerors o'er the field, Roderick the Goth! **1880** SWINBURNE *Songs of Spring-t., Gard. Cymodoce* 242 Through that steep strait of rock whose twin-cliffed height Links crag with crag reiterate, land with land.

reiterate (riːˈɪtəreɪt), *v.* Also 6 reiterat, reitterate. [f. L. *reiterāt-*, ppl. stem of *reiterāre* to repeat, f. *re-* RE- + *iterāre* to ITERATE. Cf. F. *réitérer* (14th c.).]

1. *trans.* To repeat (an action); to do over again.

1526 TAYLOR in Ellis *Orig. Lett.* Ser. II. I. 335 That he.. shulld within certeyn tyme reiterate and renewe them [acts]. **1563** FOXE *A. & M.* 890/1 The Masse priestes dooe reiterate the sacrifyce of Christ. **1581** J. BELL *Haddon's Answ. Osor.* 421 Then you make him an heretique whatsoever he be that doth reiterate Baptisme. **1609** DANIEL *Civ. Wars* (1717) II. 41 The Ocean.. Reiterates his strange untimely Flows. *a* **1674** CLARENDON *Surv. Leviath.* (1676) 66 Which Sentence was barbarously executed, and afterwards reiterated upon others. **1753** N. TORRIANO *Gangr. Sore Throat* 13 The Bleeding in the Foot was reiterated at Four .. in the After-noon. **1826** SCOTT *Woodst.* xiv, You would have thought the knocking was reiterated in every room of the palace. **1891** S. MOSTYN *Curatica* 91 She had not meant me to reiterate this tribute of respect, but only to offer it once.

absol. **1718** *Entertainer* No. 15. 100 Having once made a Beginning with Success, they easily become prone to reiterate.

†b. To repeat the use or application of (a thing, esp. a medicine). *Obs.*

1580 FRAMPTON *Joyful News* III. (ed. 2) 108b, By reiterating [**1577** reiteryng] the wette Linnen cloth in the Balsamo, it will bee healed. **1600** SURFLET *Countrie Farme* I. xxv. 159 Marle must not be reiterated so oft as dung. **1643** J. STEER tr. *Exp. Chyrurg.* vii. 28 This defensive is to be reiterated two or three times every day. **1771** LUCKOMBE *Hist. Printing* 330 Reiterating these lashes on the middlemost Notch and Plattin hook.

†c. To re-excite (a disease). *Obs. rare*$^{-1}$.

1652 WHARTON *Rothman's Chirom.* Wks. (1683) 627 The Moon.. being here Afflicted by the Quartile of Mars.. often reiterateth small Fevers.

2. To repeat (a request, statement, word, etc.); to give renewed expression to (a feeling).

1560 DAUS tr. *Sleidane's Comm.* 186b, The nobles reiterat their sute. **1599** NASHE *Lenten Stuffe* 36 With what state he hath bene vsed from his swadling clouts, I haue reiterated vnto you. **1622** CALLIS *Stat. Sewers* (1647) 161 By reason this word Payment is reiterated three or four times in this branch of the Statute. **1665** GLANVILL *Def. Van. Dogm.* A 2b, Had I used another style I must have been more diffuse in reiterating what I had said in the opposed Essay. **1728** ELIZA HEYWOOD tr. *Mme. de Gomez's Belle A.* (1732) II. 54 She now reiterated her Prayers, that we would both avoid those dangerous Situations. **1782** MISS BURNEY *Cecilia* x. v, Cecilia re-iterated her assurances. **1815** SCOTT *Guy M.* xxx, My father.. reiterated his orders, that no one should presume to fire until he gave the word. **1876** FARRAR *Marlb. Serm.* i. 2 He reiterated again and again.. the blessings and curses.

†b. To relate (a thing) again. *Obs. rare*$^{-1}$.

c **1650** *Don Bellianis* 91 And so reiterating all his Exploits (as heretofore set down).

†3. To walk over (a place) again. *Obs. rare*$^{-1}$.

1648 HERRICK *Hesper.*, *Teares to Tamasis* (1902) 293 No more shall I reiterate thy Strand.

†4. *intr.* To occur again. *Obs. rare*$^{-1}$.

1733 STACK in *Phil. Trans.* XLI. 141 This having reiterated several times, a Son of hers.. perceiv'd [etc.].

Hence **re'iterating** *vbl. sb.* and *ppl. a.*

1641 SMECTYMNUUS *Answ.* ii. (1653) 12 The often and impertinent reiterating of the Lords Prayer. **1649** MILTON *Eikon.* viii. Wks. 1851 III. 396 It was ill that som body stood not neer to whisper him, that a reiterating Judge is wors then a tormentor. **1694** SALMON *Bate's Dispens.* (1713) a 3 Notwithstanding this seeming Repetition, or reiterating of the very same Thing sometimes.

reiterated (riːˈɪtəreɪtɪd), *ppl. a.* [f. prec. + -ED[1].] Repeated: a. of actions, events, etc.

1643 MILTON *Divorce* I. viii. Wks. 1851 IV. 40 Against reiterated scandals and seducements which never cease. **1678** CUDWORTH *Intell. Syst.* I. iv. 429 The Stoicks.. supposed in the Reiterated Conflagrations, all the Gods to be Melted and Confounded into One. **1768** BOSWELL *Corsica* iii. (ed. 2) 228 The reiterated turmoils, which during a course of ages, have shaken this island. **1827** STEUART *Planter's G.* (1828) 50 At each and all of these reiterated removals, the Roots.. were shortened and pruned. **1872** DARWIN *Emotions* viii. 201 The anthropoid apes utter a reiterated sound, corresponding with our laughter.

b. of words, statements, etc.

1677 HORNECK *Gt. Law Consid.* iv. (1704) 198 A frequent, reiterated, lively representation of the danger of a sinful life. **1795** BURKE *Regic. Peace* iv. (1892) 269 After their reiterated oaths for our extirpation. **1829** SCOTT *Anne of G.* ii, The entreaties and reiterated assurances of his guide induced him to pause. **1868** MILMAN *St. Paul's* v. 105 Such solemn and reiterated appeals to God.

re'iteratedly, *adv.* [f. prec. + -LY[2].] In a reiterated manner; by way of reiteration.

1782 ELIZ. BLOWER *Geo. Bateman* III. 218 In which they had reiteratedly enjoyed their endearing society. **1834** MAR. EDGEWORTH *Helen* (Rtldg.) 332 'Lady Emily Greville's carriage' now resounded reiteratedly. **1866** *Reader* No. 170. 317/2 Reiteratedly dilates upon the diverse doctrines.

So **re'iteratedness**.

1830 BENTHAM *Offic. Apt. Maximized, Further Extr.* 18 Of the assertion, when orally delivered, the probative force is as the loudness and reiteratedness of it.

†**re'iterately**, *adv. Obs. rare.* [f. REITERATE *pa. pple.* + -LY[2].] = REITERATEDLY.

1654–66 EARL ORRERY *Parthen.* (1676) 702 He reiterately vowed.. he would tell. **1794** *St. Papers* in *Ann. Reg.* 222 Apprehensions which his Imperial majesty has reiterately manifested.

reiteration (riːɪtəˈreɪʃən). Also 7–8 ret-. [a. F. *réitération* (16th c.), or ad. L. *reiterātiōn-em*, n. of action f. *reiterāre* to REITERATE.]

1. The (*or* an) act of reiterating, repetition:

a. of actions, etc.

1560 BECON *New Catech.* v. Wks. 1564 I. 459 In thaltare there is no reiteratyon or doing again of (christes) sacrifice. **1604** EDMONDS *Observ. Cæsar's Comm.* 4 When they see their best.. indeuours atchieue nothing, but a reiteration of their labours. **1667** BOYLE in *Phil. Trans.* II. 597 The other .. Experiment.. needed a reiteration to confirm it. **1833** J. H. NEWMAN *Arians* II. iii. (1876) 163 That there is, (so to express it,) a reiteration of the One Infinite Nature of God. **1872** J. G. MURPHY *Comm., Lev.* viii. 35 A sacrifice having atoning validity needs no reiteration.

b. of statements, etc.

1656 BRAMHALL *Replic.* 34 All that followes.. is but a reiteration of the same things, without adding one more grain of reason to enforce it. *a* **1708** BEVERIDGE *Thes. Theol.* (1710) I. 61 Your Baptismal vow and promise, and your many reiterations of it. **1828** SCOTT *F.M. Perth* xxiii, A liar who endeavours by reiteration to obtain a credit for his words. **1875** MCLAREN *Serm.* Ser. II. vi. 96 You will observe the reiteration of the same earnest cry in all these clauses.

2. *Typog.* The action of printing on the back of a sheet; the impression thus made. Also *attrib.*

1683 MOXON *Mech. Exerc.*, *Printing* xxiv. ¶ 15 He folds it again, as before, for a Token-sheet when he works the Reiteration. *Ibid.*, Having now turned the Heap, and made Register on the Reteration Form, he Works off the Reteration. **1727–38** CHAMBERS *Cycl.* s.v. *Printing*, When the sheet is returned for an impression on the other side, called the reiteration. **1771** LUCKOMBE *Hist. Printing* 333.

re'iterative (riːˈɪtərətɪv), *a.* and *sb.* [f. as REITERATE *v.* + -IVE: cf. F. *réitératif, -ive* (16th c.).] a. *adj.* Characterized by reiteration. b. *sb.* A word expressing reiteration.

a **1813** A. MURRAY *Hist. European Lang.* (1823) II. 279 Reiteratives or verbs expressive of repeated or intense action. **1834** *Fraser's Mag.* IX. 76 Do away with the iterative and reiterative plan altogether, and substitute an intellectual one. **1868** LIGHTFOOT *Comm. Phil.* Introd. iv. (1873) 68 He then urges his converts to unity in the strong reiterative language which has been already noticed.

Hence **re'iteratively** *adv.*

1619 *Arraignm. Barnevelt* § 23 Notwithstanding, that by the States of Vtrecht, they were reiteratiuely willed and required to doe it. **1877** *Fraser's Mag.* XVI. 399 The title of 'successor of the successor'.. would soon have become reiteratively inconvenient.

reith, var. RETHE *a. Obs.*

Reithian (ˈriːθɪən), *a.* Also **Reithean.** [f. the name of J. C. W. *Reith* (1889–1971), 1st Lord Reith of Stonehaven, Director-General of the British Broadcasting Corporation (1927–38) + -IAN.] Of, pertaining to, or characteristic of Reith or his principles, esp. relating to the responsibility of broadcasting to enlighten and educate public taste.

1961 *Guardian* 26 Oct. 10/5 The Reithian conception of broadcasting was barely in evidence at the time [*sc.* in 1923]. **1963** *Times* 12 Jan. 4/5 An elaborate compromise between past and present balancing Reithian principles against television's need to survive as show business. **1969** *Observer* (Colour Suppl.) 21 Dec. 38/1 From the great Reithean days the BBC had come to be taken for granted as a pillar of enlightened orthodoxy. **1973** *Times* 9 June 10/4 Nowhere has the Reithian prediction—offer the public what it wants and it will want what it gets—been vindicated more awesomely. **1977** *Punch* 31 Aug.–6 Sept. 327/3 The BBC.. still retains at least something of the old Reithian sobriety or an image of established quality.

reitter, obs. f. REITER *sb.*[1]

reive, reiver, etc.: see REAVE, REAVER.

reiz, obs. f. REIS[2].

‖**reja** (ˈrexa). [Sp.] In Spain, a wrought-iron screen or grille used to protect windows, chapel tombs, etc.

1845 R. FORD *Hand-bk. Travellers in Spain* I. 252/2 The *coro*.. is railed off by a fine *reja*, the work of Sancho Muñoz, 1519. **1870** R. H. BUSK *Patrañas* 147 Then night came: the *maja* stood at her *reja*, looking out for her serenader. **1914** BYNE & STAPLEY *Rejería of Span. Renaissance* p. vii, Renaissance Architecture in Spain could not be fully appreciated without examining the towering wrought-iron grilles, or Rejas, of the period. **1924** J. MASEFIELD *Sard Harker* IV. 289 The windows.. were covered with old iron rejas. **1969** S. SITWELL *Gothic Europe* xii. 139 One remembers Spanish cathedrals very notably on account of their *rejas* or wrought iron screens which are a feature peculiar to Spain.

†**rejag**, *sb. Obs. rare.* [Cf. next and JAG *sb.*[1] 7: see also REJARG.] A sharp retort.

1554 tr. *Latimer's Protest.* in Strype *Eccl. Mem.* (1721) III. App. xxxiv. 92, I coulde.. not be suffered to declare my faithe befor you.. without snakkes, reiagges, revilinges, chekkes, rebukes, and tauntes. **1825** JAMIESON, *Rejag*, a repartee. Loth[ian].

†**reˈjag**, *v. Obs. rare.* [f. RE- 2 a + JAG *v.*[1]] To controvert, refute; to reply smartly.

c **1440** *Promp. Parv.* 427/2 Reiaggyn (or reprevyn), *redarguo*. **1825** JAMIESON, *Rejag*, to give a smart answer.

†**reˈjagged**, *ppl. a. Obs. rare*[−1]. [RE- 5 a.] Jagged or torn repeatedly.

1522 SKELTON *Why not to Court* 603 Ye raynbetyn beggers reiagged, Ye recrayed ruffyns all ragged!

Rejang (reɪˈdʒʌŋ). Also **Redjang.** [Native name.] An Indonesian people of southern Sumatra; a member of this people. Also, their language.

1783 [see BATTA *a.* and *sb.*[3]]. **1839** T. J. NEWBOLD *Straits of Malacca* II. xiv. 227 The Rejangs, a people inhabiting the interior of Sumatra. **1932** W. L. GRAFF *Lang. & Languages* xi. 423 The population of *Indonesian* tongue amounts to about 50 millions... About eight geographical groups can be distinguished... In the *Sumatra* group, *Achinese, Battak, Rejang, Lampong, Malay, Mentaway*. **1955** P. VOORHOEVE *Crit. Survey Stud. Lang. Sumatra* v. 20 We find in the language of Rejang another language which is undoubtedly independent although closely related to Malay.

†**rejarg.** *Obs.*[−1] [? f. JARG v.] = REJAG *sb.*

1534 WHITINTON *Tullyes Offices* I. (1540) 26 Somtyme reiarges and chydynges be specially vsed amonge louers and frendes.

reject (ˈriːdʒɛkt, formerly rɪˈdʒɛkt), *sb.* [orig. an absolute use of next; in later use f. the vb.]

1. †**a.** One who is rejected; a castaway. *Obs.*

a **1555** PHILPOT *Exam. & Writ.* (Parker Soc.) 337 What if that multitude of men were.. not of his elects, but of the rejects? **1622** JACKSON *Judah must into Captivitie* 4 The reject of the Lord.

b. One who is rejected or discarded by others, esp. as unsuitable for some activity (orig. for military service).

1925 *Glasgow Herald* 13 Mar. 8/7 Probably the large proportion of rejects is not so much a symptom of national decadence as a result of the fact that the right sort of men are not coming forward in sufficient numbers. **1942** *Sun* (Baltimore) 4 Nov. 9/4 He said that.. the 'army has been consistently uninterested in taking the rejects into conditioning battalions and reconditioning them'. **1971** *Sunday Express* (Johannesburg) 28 Mar. 17/2 Time and again I have heard members at the turnstiles say that they would prefer to watch South African-born players rather than overseas rejects. **1974** E. TIDYMAN *Dummy* vi. 87 The misborn and the unwanted.. society's rejects. **1979** R. RENDELL *Make Death love Me* ii. 21 He knew someone who .. was also a reject of the University of Kent.

2. A thing rejected as unsatisfactory.

1893 *Nation* (N.Y.) 16 Feb. 125/1 The rough-chipped stones.. are simply 'rejects'. **1935** H. C. BRYSON *Gramophone Record* ix. 234 If rejects are kept below 15 per cent. with rigid examination, then efficiency is high. **1949** J. DEKETH *Fund. Radio-Valve Technique* vii. 61 If this fusing method were applied to values of the dimensions of the A-technique.. there would be a higher percentage of rejects in manufacture. **1952**, etc. [see *export reject*]. **1969** [see CULLER 1 b].

3. *attrib.* **a.** Appositive.

1955 H. KURNITZ *Invasion of Privacy* (1956) ii. 17 This pioneer used a war surplus Eimo camera and 'reject' film which he developed in his bath tub. **1963** R. R. A. HIGHAM *Handbk. Papermaking* ii. 71 The lighter reject materials.. are ejected through a special automatically controlled V-notch slide valve. **1965** *Wireless World* July 22 (Advt.), *Antex* reduces operational fatigue, with resulting drop in reject output. **1977** 'M. YORKE' *Cost of Silence* ix. 69 His friends.. had seen him with Madge and made a few cracks about reject models.

b. General attrib. uses.

1958 *Times* 26 Feb. 8/4 The reject figures of Army recruits has [*sic*] given some cause for concern here. **1963** R. R. A. HIGHAM *Handbk. Papermaking* ii. 71 Heavy material which will not pass through the screen is continuously forced downwards into a reject trough and is removed from a heavy reject box connected to the bottom of the volute trough.

†**reˈject**, *pa. pple.* and *ppl. a. Obs.* [ad. L. *rejectus*, pa. pple. of *reicĕre* to REJECT.] Rejected; cast back or away.

1432–50 tr. *Higden* (Rolls) IV. 283 These childer entendenge the dethe of here fader were reiecte, and putte a wey from hym. **1491** CAXTON *Vitas Patr.* (W. de W. 1495) I. xlii. 68 b/2 By the power of god whyche wythstode her, she was reiecte and caste abacke from the yate. **1556** ROBINSON *More's Utop.* II. (ed. 2) (Arb.) 82 *marg.*, Husbandrie.. now a dayes is reiect vnto a fewe of the basest sort. **1582** BENTLEY *Mon. Matrones* ii. 195 It is a manifest and great token, that man is reiect from the mercie and fauour of God.

reject (rɪˈdʒɛkt), *v.* Also 6 *Sc.* rejekk-. [f. L. *reject-*, ppl. stem of *reicĕre* (*rejicĕre*) to throw back, f. *re-* RE- + *jacĕre* to throw. Cf. also obs. F. *rejecter* var. of *rejetter*, mod.F. *rejeter*: see JET *v.*[2]]

I. 1. a. *trans.* To refuse to recognize, (†allow,) acquiesce in, submit to, or adopt (a rule, command, practice, etc.); to refuse credit to (a statement).

1494 FABYAN *Chron.* VII. 351 Bothe those and other [ordinances] that were right necessary for yᵉ common weale of the cytie were reiected and put of. **1495** *Act 11 Hen. VII*, c. 2 §5 It be laufull to ij of the Justices.. to rejecte and put awey comen ale selling in Tounes. **1563** WINȜET *Four Scoir Thre Quest.* Wks. (S.T.S.) I. 127 Quhy reiect ȝe and dispyssis the samin indifferentlie as superstitious or idolatrical..? **1611** BIBLE *Transl. Pref.* ¶4 It is a manifest falling away from the Faith.. to reiect any of those things that are written. **1654** BRAMHALL *Just Vind.* ii. (1661) 11 The Court of Rome would have obtruded upon us new articles of faith, [but] we have rejected them. **1736** BUTLER *Anal.* Introd., Wks. 1874 I. 8 The whole method of government by punishments should be rejected as absurd. **1784** COWPER *Task* VI. 981 Not that he peevishly rejects a mode Because that world adopts it. **1839** THIRLWALL *Greece* VI. 275 Nor perhaps ought we to reject the farther account .. as a groundless fiction. **1875** JOWETT *Plato* (ed. 2) V. 375 He who rejects the law must find some other ground of objection.

b. *absol.* or *intr.* To be disobedient. *rare*[−1].

1851 MAYHEW *Lond. Labour* II. 349/2 If they resist and reject, in what way do you force them up?

2. To refuse to have or take for some purpose; to set aside or throw away as useless or worthless.

1531 ELYOT *Gov.* II. xxv. 86 b, What is to be effectually folowed or pursued, reiectinge the residue. **1585** T. WASHINGTON tr. *Nicholay's Voy.* Ep. Ded., Aristotle.. reiecteth infantes and olde men as insufficient. **1611** BIBLE *Matt.* xxi. 42 The stone which the builders reiected, the same is become the head of the corner. **1660** BARROW *Euclid* Pref. (1714) 1 Having in a manner rejected and undervalued the other seven [books]. **1697** DRYDEN *Virg. Georg.* III. 598 Reject him, lest he darken all the Flock. **1774** GOLDSM. *Nat. Hist.* (1776) III. 176 The cow.. eats two hundred and seventy-six plants, and rejects two hundred and eighteen. **1813** SHELLEY *Q. Mab* III. 170 Nature rejects the monarch, not the man; The subject, not the citizen. **1828** D'ISRAELI *Chas. I*, II. iv. 87 At the present election, whoever had urged the payment of the loan was rejected.

absol. **1850** BROWNING *Easter-Day* xxx. iii, So I.. Go through the world, try, prove, reject, Prefer.

3. a. To refuse (something offered); to decline to receive or accept.

1671 MILTON *P.R.* II. 457 What if with like aversion I reject Riches and Realms. **1697** DRYDEN *Virg. Past.* VIII. 2 The Love rejected and the Lover's pains I sing. **1766** GOLDSM. *Vic. W.* xxvii, Good counsel rejected, returns to enrich the giver's bosom. **1822** SHELLEY tr. *Calderon* II. 21 Hear'st thou, Hell! dost thou reject it? My soul is offered! **1871** R. ELLIS tr. *Catullus* xxiii. 24 Such prosperity.. Slight not, Furius, idly nor reject not.

†**b.** To refuse *to be* something. *Obs. rare*[−1].

1795 *Fate of Sedley* I. 124 Would you suspect that a little rustic.. could possibly reject to be the wife of a man endowed with rank, fortune and figure?

4. To expel from the mouth or stomach.

1667 MILTON *P.L.* X. 567 Bitter Ashes, which th' offended taste With spattering noise rejected. **1732** ARBUTHNOT *Rules of Diet* in *Aliments*, etc. 294 Tough Phlegm frequently rejected by Vomiting. **1825** LAMB *Elia* II. *Barbara S——*, When he crammed a portion of it [fowl] into her mouth, she was obliged sputteringly to reject it.

b. *absol.* or *intr.* To vomit. *rare.*

1822–34 *Good's Study Med.* (ed. 4) I. 502 As soon as the patient rejects, he may be allowed a little warm water, administered to him sparingly.

†**5. a.** To dismiss (a person) from some relation to oneself; to cast off. Also const. *from. Obs.*

1530 PALSGR. 683/1 He was ones rejected, howe fortuneth it that he cometh thus in favoure agayne? *a* **1548** HALL *Chron.*, *Henry VIII* 200 b, That she should whole .xxij. yeres and more serue him as hys wyfe.. and now to reiecte her, what Princely maner is that. **1611** BIBLE *1 Sam.* xv. 23 He hath also reiected thee from being king. —— *Jer.* vii. 29 The Lord hath reiected, and forsaken the generation of his wrath.

b. To cast off, abandon (a principle or condition). *Obs.*

1587 TURBERV. *Trag. T.* (1837) 127 As hee rejected quight The faith he should have borne Her husband. **1616** CAPT. SMITH *Wks.* (Arb.) 532 At last, reiecting her barbarous condition, [she] was maried to an English Gentleman.

c. To dismiss from one's mind. *Obs.*[−1]

1596 DALRYMPLE tr. *Leslie's Hist. Scot.* III. 180 Casting.. asyd the commoune effairis of the Realme, reiecteng the commoune welth and contemneng the Nobilitie.

6. a. To repel or rebuff (one who makes advances of any kind); to refuse to accept, listen to, admit, etc.

1561 DAUS tr. *Bullinger on Apoc.* (1573) 182 Symon Magus also did couet the same grace: but he was sore reiected of S. Peter the Apostle. **1611** BIBLE *John* xii. 48 He that reiecteth me, and receiueth not my words, hath one that iudgeth him. **1671** MILTON *Samson* 760 Not to reject The penitent, but ever to forgive. **1748** BUTLER *Serm.* Wks. 1874 II. 315 Hospitals are often obliged to reject poor objects which offer.. for want of room. **1788** GIBBON *Decl. & F.* l. V. 205 Whosoever hates or rejects any one of the prophets, is numbered with the infidels.

b. Of a woman: To refuse (a man) as lover or husband. Also with compl., and *absol.*

1581 RICHE *Farewell Mil. Prof.* Iiiij Seyng you haue so scornfully reiected me to be your loiall housbande. **1592** SHAKS. *Ven. & Ad.* 159 Then woo thy selfe, be of thy selfe reiected. **1712–14** POPE *Rape Lock* I. 10 O say what stranger cause, yet unexplor'd, Could make a gentle Belle reject a Lord? *Ibid.* II. 12 Oft she rejects, but never once offends. **1858** LONGF. *M. Standish* VII. 8 Thus to be flouted, rejected, and laughed to scorn by a maiden.

†**c.** To deny (one who makes a request). *Obs.*[−1]

1611 BIBLE *Mark* vi. 26 The king was exceeding sory, yet for his othes sake.. hee would not reiect her.

d. *Psychol.* Of a parent or guardian: to spurn (a child) by denying it the normal emotional relationship between parent and offspring.

1931 *Smith Coll. Stud. in Soc Work* I. 407 Case histories are presented showing the attitude toward their parents.., husbands, and children of twelve mothers who rejected their children. **1932** *Ibid.* II. 237 This type of relationship cannot exist when a mother rejects her child. **1961** H. C. SMITH *Personality Adjustment* xviii. 513 Children raised in negligent and understaffed orphanages are not actively rejected but suffer severe deprivation of warmth and affection. **1973** A. JANOV *Primal Scream* vii. 74 But to feel really rejected means to.. feel utterly alone and unwanted as that child.

7. To refuse to grant, entertain, or agree to (a request, proposal, etc.).

1602 MARSTON *Antonio's Rev.* III. i, She seemeth to reject his suite. *a* **1648** LD. HERBERT *Hen. VIII* (1649) 545 But this [proposal] was rejected; both to exclude the Protestants admittance [etc.]. **1726** SWIFT *Gulliver* III. i, I knew him to be so honest a man, that I could not reject his proposal. **1837** THIRLWALL *Greece* xxxiii. IV. 305 The orders of Cyrus he treated as a suggestion, which he might adopt or reject at his discretion. **1874** GREEN *Short Hist.* iii. §5. 139 The demand was at once rejected by the baronage.

†**8. a.** To refer (a matter or person) *to* another for decision. Also const. *into* a place. *Obs.*

1533 BELLENDEN *Livy* v. x. (S.T.S.) II. 183 Eftir þat þis mater was lang dispute afore þe senate, It was reieckit to þe bischoppis, þat þai mycht decerne þareapoun. **1603** KNOLLES *Hist. Turks* 637 Barbarussa thus rejected into Syria,.. perceived that it tended to his no small disgrace. *Ibid.*, *marg.*, Barbarussa rejected to Abraham the great Bassa.

b. To cast (a fault, etc.) back *upon* a person. Also const. *to. Obs.*

a **1555** PHILPOT *Exam. & Writ.* (Parker Soc.) 402 Either we reject the cause of sin upon God, other else do renew the stoical destiny. **1581** N. BURNE *Disput.* iv. 9 Ane man sould not reiect the caus of his auin euil and vickednes to the prescience of god, bot to him self. **1643** TRAPP *Comm. Gen.* iii. 12 Here he rejects the fault upon the woman, and thorow her, upon God. **1678** MARVELL *Def. J. Howe* Wks. (Grosart) IV. 170 They have found a nudity in the Creator, and did implicitly reject their fault upon Him.

c. To put (a thing) away *into* a place. *Obs.*[−1]

1579 FULKE *Heskins' Parl.* 70 The figures of Manna, and the waters, he reiecteth into the third booke.

9. a. To throw or cast back; †to repel, repulse (an assailant). *rare.*

1603 KNOLLES *Hist. Turks* (1621) 281 Who fighting at too much disadvantage, were by the Turks easily rejected. **1826** [see REJECTED *ppl. a.* b]. **1869** PHILLIPS *Vesuv.* ix. 252 The sea is rejected from the shore, to return in mighty waves. **1889** SYMONDS in *Fortn. Rev.* XLV. 57 We can neither reject ourselves into the past, nor project ourselves into the future, with certainty sufficient to decide [etc.].

†**b.** To cut off (a person) *from* some resource.

1601 in Moryson *Itin.* (1617) II. 181 So [he would] bee utterly rejected from having either credit or aides hereafter from them. **1711** *Fingall MSS.* in *10th Rep. Hist. MSS. Comm.* App. V. 137 His great officers.. would have the Irish ..to be rejected from all expectation of recovering their estates. **1737** WHISTON *Josephus, Antiq.* XVI. iii. §3 The young men were intirely rejected from any hopes of the kingdom.

10. *Med.* To show an immune response to (a transplanted organ or tissue) so that it fails to survive in the body of the recipient. Also *absol.*

1953 *Nature* 3 Oct. 603/1 Embryonic cells transplanted into embryos of different genetic constitutions may survive into adult life, although their hosts would almost certainly have rejected them if transplantation had been delayed until after birth. **1968** *Observer* 7 Jan. 1/1 Although he is now entering the crucial period where his body could begin to reject the implanted heart, today's hospital bulletin said there were no signs of rejection or infection. **1969** *Daily Progress* (Charlottesville, Va.) 12 Jan. A2/3 'The heart rejects like crazy,' Dr Shumway comments. **1974** R. M. Kirk et al. *Surgery* ii. 35/1 A graft that will be ultimately rejected at first appears to be accepted by the host tissues.

II. **11.** The infin. used *attrib.*, designating a part of a record player by means of which the turn table is made to stop (and the pick-up arm usu. returned to its rest) before a side has ended. Also stressed *'reject*.

1947 *Gramophone* Dec. p. xi/2 Automatically plays eight 10-in. or 12-in. mixed records. Repeat and reject switch provided. **1975** J. Grady *Shadow of Condor* ii. 34 Strains from *Carmen* came through the speakers. Malcolm..hit the reject lever. **1976** R. L. Simon *Wild Turkey* xviii. 129 He shuffled over to the turntable and pushed the reject button.

Hence **re'jecting** *vbl. sb.* and *ppl. a.*

1589 Rider *Bibl. Schol.*, A reiecting, *rejectio*. *a* **1653** Gouge *Comm. Heb.* x. 29 This sin is a wilful rejecting of the means, whereby the wounds of sin should be healed. **1931** *Smith Coll. Stud. in Soc. Work* I. 407 The purpose of the study was to test part of the hypothesis..by a comparison of the case histories of a group of rejecting and non-rejecting mothers. **1939** P. M. Symonds *Parent-Child Relationships* i. 24 Attempts to define rejecting behavior are rare. **1970** H. Edelston *Found. & Growth of Character* iii. ii. 117 We hear a great deal of the rejecting mother: not quite so much of the over-demanding child.

rejectable (rɪˈdʒɛktəb(ə)l), *a.* [f. prec. + -able.] That may be, or ought to be, rejected.

1611 Cotgr., *Rebutable*, reiectable, refusable. **1706** in Phillips (ed. Kersey). **1820** W. Tooke tr. *Lucian* I. 229 Do you understand the difference between acceptable and rejectable objects..? **1847** Carlyle in Froude *Life in Lond.* xvii. (1884) II. 18 Melancholy and rejectable spy-glasses.

Hence **re'jectableness**.

1852 Pulsford tr. *Müller's Doctr. Sin* I. 37 That..a strong consciousness is able to be distinctly realized of the rejectableness of evil.

†**re'jectament.** *Obs. rare.* [ad. mod.L. *rejectamentum*: see next.] **a.** Refuse. **b.** One who is rejected.

1653 Sclater *Funeral Serm. 25 Sept.* (1654) 7 That rejectament, which is scraped from the dirty pavement. **1681** Colvil *Whigs Supplic.* (1751) 153 Your majesty's wisdom inherent..Will not disdain to hear complaints Of us though but rejectaments.

‖**rejectamenta** (rɪdʒɛktəˈmɛntə). [mod.L., pl. of *rejectamentum*: see reject *v.* and -ment.]

1. Things rejected as useless or worthless; refuse.

1816 Kirby & Sp. *Entomol.* xxvi. (1818) II. 437 A scavenger, whose business it is to sweep the streets and convey the rejectamenta to one grand repository. **1849** D. J. Browne *Amer. Poultry Yd.* (1855) 201 The rejectamenta of the kitchen..are..accepted with eagerness. **1877** W. H. Dall *Tribes N.W.* 45 Bones, shells, and all varieties of rejectamenta having been deposited here for centuries.

2. Wrack or rubbish cast up by the sea.

1819 Samouelle *Entomol. Compend.* 101 [He] found it.. amongst rejectamenta of the sea. **1856** *Zoologist* XIV. 5309 It had been taken beneath marine rejectamenta at Exmouth. **1866** Tate *Brit. Mollusks* iv. 155 *Pupa badia* is common among the rejectamenta of our tidal rivers.

3. *Phys.* Excremental matter.

1879 Packard *Zool.* ii. (1881) 43 There being many pores or mouths, and but a single outlet for the rejectamenta.

†**rejec'taneous**, *a. Obs.* [ad. L. *rejectāneus* (coined by Cicero to render the Stoic ἀποπροηγμένος), f. *rejicĕre* to reject; cf. *extraneous*, *spontaneous*, etc.] Deserving rejection, rejectable. (Common in H. More's works.)

1657 Farindon *Serm.* Pref. 22 Others are more forced, and therefore Rejectaneous and unprofitable. **1678** Gale *Crt. Gentiles* III. 93 A reprobate, spurious, drossie, vain, adulterine, rejectaneous mind. **1734** Berkeley *Analyst* §28 Supposing the rejectaneous algebraical quantity to be an infinitely small or evanescent quantity.

rejected (rɪˈdʒɛktɪd), *ppl. a.* [f. reject *v.* + -ed[1].] **a.** Refused, repudiated, cast out, etc.; *spec.* in *Psychol.*, refused or denied the normal relationship between parent and child. Cf. reject *v.* 6 d.

1760–72 H. Brooke *Fool of Qual.* (1809) III. 57 The commons can..annex the rejected bills to their bill of aids. **1819** Shelley *Cenci* iv. iv. 151 Stain not a noble house With vague surmises of rejected crime. **1856** Kane *Arct. Expl.* II. xix. 191, I lost some time in collecting such parts of his rejected cargo as I could find. **1931** *Smith Coll. Stud. in Soc. Work* I. 407 The problems for which the rejected child was referred were more frequently of the aggressive, rebellious type. **1961** H. C. Smith *Personality Adjustment* xviii. 513 Such severely rejected children tend to develop a general apathy..to all human relationships.

b. *Ent.* Thrown back; not admitted between other parts.

1826 Kirby & Sp. *Entomol.* xlvi. IV. 332 An insect having a visible Scutellum. *a.* Rejected... When, though visible, it does not intervene between the elytra at their base.

c. Gram. ***rejected condition*** (see quots.).

1947 Partridge *Usage & Abusage* 80/2 Those sentences in which the principal clause speaks of what would be or would have been, and in which the *if*-clause states, or implies, a negative. Grammarians call this: Rejected Condition, as in 'If wishes were horses, beggars would ride'. **1957** R. W. Zandvoort *Handbk. Eng. Gram.* v. ii. 218 Clauses expressing a condition that is not, or is not likely to be, realized [I should not mind so much, if I was not so busy] are called clauses of *rejected condition*.

rejectee (riːdʒɛkˈtiː). *U.S.* [f. reject *v.* + -ee[1], after *draftee*.] One who is rejected as unfit for military service. Also *transf.* Cf. reject *sb.* 1 b.

1941 *Sun* (Baltimore) 18 June 3/1 Twenty-six youths rejected by selective service officials..began taking physical examinations..for admittance to the first camp in the United States to be established for 'rejectees'. **1942** *Nation* 27 Apr. 41 (*heading*) When the draftee becomes a rejectee. **1977** *Time* 20 June 48/2 Determined to become a doctor, Braun did what an increasing number of rejectees do each year: he looked abroad. **1978** J. A. Michener *Chesapeake* 637 'Grandpop, take a look at the kind of boys we want,' and when Cudjo continued pestering him, he pointed to rejectees half the old man's age.

rejecter (rɪˈdʒɛktə(r)). [f. as reject *v.* + -er[1]. Cf. rejector.] One who rejects.

1570 Foxe *A. & M.* (ed. 2) 2134/1 To exhorte..these Agamistes and wilfull reiecters of matrimonie, to take themselues to lawfull wiues. **1675** Brooks *Gold. Key* Wks. 1867 V. 411 However the rejecters of Christ may escape judgment for a time. **1706** Clarke *Let. to Dodwell* (1712) 12 It will follow..that neither Rejecters of the Gospel, nor wicked Christians,..shall be condemned to any other punishment. *a* **1754** Fielding *Conversat.* Wks. 1771 VIII. 115 These rejecters of society borrow all their information from their own savage dispositions. **1830** J. Martineau *Stud. Chr.* (1873) 484 The motive of the rejecter is different.

†**re'jectible**, *a.* and *sb. Obs.* = rejectable.

1702 S. Parker tr. *Cicero's De Finibus* v. 353 Terms Unheard-of and Invented by themselves, *Producta*, for Instance, and *Rejecta* (as if one shou'd say Promotables and Rejectibles). **1748** Richardson *Clarissa* (1811) I. 301 He would be far from being rejectible as a companion for life.

re'jectingly, *adv.* [f. pres. pple. of reject *v.* + -ly[2].] In a rejecting manner.

1832 *Blackw. Mag.* XXXII. 503 He waved his hand rejectingly. **1889** *Daily News* 4 Apr. 5/8 She jerks her handkerchief rejectingly at them until the chosen suitor arrives.

rejection (rɪˈdʒɛkʃən). [a. F. *réjection* (16th c.), or ad. L. *rejectiōn-em*, n. of action f. *rejicĕre* to reject.] **1. a.** The action of rejecting or the state of being rejected.

1552 in Huloet. **1553** T. Wilson *Rhet.* 99 b, Rejeccion is then used when we lay suche faultes from us as our enemies would charge us with all. **1597** Hooker *Eccl. Pol.* v. lxviii. §6 Vtter rejection of the whole Christian faith. **1647** Clarendon *Hist. Reb.* ii. §74 They who were for a rejection of the King's Proposition. **1744** Harris *Three Treat.* Wks. (1841) 86 Were this neglected, what would become of selection and rejection..? **1835** Miss Mitford in L'Estrange *Life* (1870) III. iii. 36 We grieve over the rejection of the Irish Church Bills last year and this. **1856** Froude *Hist. Eng.* (1858) II. ix. 334 The Count..left Paris with a decisive rejection of the emperor's advances.

b. *concr.* That which is rejected; excrement.

1605 Verstegan *Dec. Intell.* iv. (1628) 100 The sand banckes or downes, which the reiection of the sea by little and little hath raised and cast vp. **1839** *Britannia* 13 July, Happy to sun himself and sleep on the basest rejections of the public stable. **1896** *Allbutt's Syst. Med.* I. 898 The later rejections are watery and copious.

c. *Psychol.* The refusal or inability to accept emotionally the fact of being a parent to one's child; the state of rejecting a child or of being rejected by a parent. Cf. reject *v.* 6 d.

1931 *Smith Coll. Stud. in Soc. Work* I. 407 Thirty-five cases of rejection were chosen in which staff members unanimously agreed to that diagnosis. **1939** P. M. Symonds *Parent-Child Relationships* i. 10 Such concepts and terms as rejection and overprotection seem to have emerged into common use out of the child guidance movement. *Ibid.*, Newell..reports on 33 children diagnosed as cases of maternal rejection. **1957** L. C. Steckle *Probl. Human Adjustment* (rev. ed.) vi. 132 Rejection is most effective in building uncertainty. *Ibid.* 133 Parental rejection usually results in aggressively hostile behavior in the child. **1973** A. Janov *Primal Scream* vii. 74 Once that is felt, there are no more feelings of 'rejection'.

2. *Electronics.* The process of attenuating an unwanted electrical signal. Freq. *attrib.*

1940 *Chambers's Techn. Dict.* 712/2 Rejection filter. **1950** Lawson & Uhlenbeck *Threshold Signals* xii. 346 Besides automatic biasing, rejection filters in the i-f amplifier can be used to reduce the effects of c-w interference. **1953** [see detection 3]. **1957** R. W. Landee et al. *Electronic Designers' Handbk.* xvi. 29 If the feedback network by itself does not have a complete null, the depth of the null for the rejection amplifier will be less than the depth of the null for the null network taken by itself. **1967** W. A. Stover *Circuit Design for Audio, AM/FM, & TV* xiii. 227 The IF rejection is enhanced by placing a resonant circuit or filter near the tuner input.

3. *Med.* Failure of transplanted tissue to survive or function in the body of the recipient as a result of the immune response it evokes in the latter.

1954 *Proc. R. Soc.* B. CXLIII. 43 Incompatibilities (falling short of rejection) became apparent when homografts were exchanged between members of separate sublines which..stood only eight to twelve generations apart. **1974** *Times* 5 Apr. 18/3 Professor Shumway believes that heart-transplant patients, like those given kidney transplants, gradually develop a tolerance to the grafted organ and so become less likely to have to cope with severe rejection episodes. **1974** M. C. Gerald *Pharmacol.* i. 7 We are optimistic that..more effective drugs to prevent the rejection of organ transplants will be discovered in the present decade.

4. *Comb.*, as **rejection form** *rare* = *rejection slip* below; **Rejection Front**, an alliance of Arab groups, who refuse to consider a negotiated peace with Israel (see rejectionist); **rejection slip**, a formal notice sent by an editor or publisher to an author with a rejected MS.

1907 Wodehouse *Not George Washington* ii. ii. 42, I papered the walls with editorial rejection-forms, of which I was beginning to have a representative collection. **1917** 'W. N. P. Barbellion' *Jrnl. Disappointed Man* (1919) 296, I used to file..rejection forms and meditated writing a facetious essay on them. **1975** *Financial Times* 23 Dec. 4/8 The 'Rejection Front', which is led by the PFLP, stands strongly opposed to efforts at a Middle East settlement and to conservative regimes in the Middle East, especially in Saudi Arabia and Iran. **1978** *Radio Times* 28 Jan.–3 Feb. 15/4 The Arab 'Rejection Front' nations of Iraq, Algeria, Libya and the People's Democratic Republic of Yemen were prepared to give finance, training facilities and arms to his group. **1906** J. London *Let.* 19 Nov. (1966) 223, I have just received from you, along with a rejection-slip, two poems..which have evidently been submitted to you over my name. **1933** Dylan Thomas *Let.* 9 May (1966) 15 Forget the 'annihilative reverse' of the rejection slip. **1953** H. Miller *Plexus* II. xiii. 217 If they were thin envelopes it meant rejection slips, with a request to forward postage for the return of the scripts. **1978** P. Sutcliffe *Oxf. Univ. Press* iv. i. 108 He, Gerrans, and Doble soon settled upon a formula, a terse but dignified communication that might be a little more comforting to the author than a bare rejection slip, the use of which the Press has always eschewed. **1979** F. Adcock *Inner Harbour* 2 'Please send future work'—Editor's note on a rejection slip.

rejectionist (rɪˈdʒɛkʃənɪst). [f. rejection + -ist.] An Arab who refuses to accept a negotiated peace with Israel. Also *transf.* Also *attrib.* or as *adj.* Hence **re'jectionism**, the policy of a rejectionist.

1976 *Guardian* 2 June 2/2 If Mr Kosygin wants to engineer the format of an Arab 'rejectionist' coalition to confront American penetration of the area, he is unlikely to get much encouragement from President Assad. **1976** *Guardian Weekly* 19 Dec. 8/4 Condemned to death by the mainstream Arafat-led guerrilla leadership—'Fascist' he calls it—Abu Nidal is Palestinian rejectionism at its most uncompromising. **1977** *Time* 10 Jan. 22/1 Last week a prominent member of the rejectionist Popular Front for the Liberation of Palestine..and his wife..were found dead in their West Beirut apartment. **1977** *Listener* 18 Aug. 195/1 If ..the peace moves collapse..he [*sc.* King Hussein] will be ..helpless in a stormy sea of Arab rejectionism. **1977** *Times* 29 Nov. 15/4 It offends no previously declared principles —except those of the 'rejectionists' on both sides. **1979** *Economist* 1 Dec. 14/1 Khomeini would have remained a voice in the wilderness if his austere rejectionist doctrines had not caught the mood of a people whose religion is still young and vigorous.

†**rejec'titious**, *a. Obs.* [ad. late L. *rejectitius*, f. *rejicĕre* to reject: see -itious, and cf. rejectaneous.] Deserving rejection; rejected.

1615 W. Hull *Mirr. Maiestie* 60 The refuse and reiectitious people of Israel. **1642** Cudworth *Disc. Lord's Supper* 43 Those other Feria's, which have been made Rejectitious since, by that Calendar. **1653** Waterhouse *Apol.* 151 Persons spurious and rejectitious, whom their Families and Allies have disowned.

re'jective, *a.* [f. as reject *v.* + -ive.] That rejects, or tends to cast off (Webster 1828–32).

1957 *Publ. Amer. Dial. Soc.* xxviii. 87 The other clause must not be 'rejective' with regard to it [*sc.* the fronted clause]. Examples:..He likes it you think?..Is he coming do you doubt?..(*doubt, forbid, disagree*, etc. are rejective). **1967** *New Yorker* 25 Feb. 108 Besides being called minimal art, it is known as..'reductive art', 'rejective art', [etc.]. **1970** *Britannica Bk. of Year 1969* 798/3 *Rejective art*, a simplified and often depersonalized art (as painting or sculpture) based on the principle of the artist rejecting various options open to him; called also *reductive art, reductivism, rejectivism*.

rejectment (rɪˈdʒɛktmənt). [f. as prec. + -ment. Cf. rejectament.]

†**1.** Rejection. *Obs. rare.*

a **1677** Manton *Christ's Tempt.* Matt. iv. 7 Wks. 1870 I. 299 If Achitophel could not endure the rejectment of his counsel [etc.]. **1690** *Col. Rec. Pennsylv.* I. 338 The Committee of This board presented the Promulgated bills with Amendments and Rejectments.

2. *concr.* Rejected matter, excrement. Also *pl.*

1828–32 Webster (citing Eaton), *Rejectment*, matter thrown away. **1829** J. L. Knapp *Jrnl. Nat.* 107 Originating probably from the rejectments of birds.

rejector (rɪˈdʒɛktə(r)). [a. L. *rejector*, agent-n. f. *rejicĕre* to reject.] **1. a.** = rejecter.

1752 Warburton *Wks.* (1788) IX. 269 The Rejectors of it ..would do well to consider the grounds on which they stand. **1857** Keble *Euch. Ador.* 40 The same sort of trial.. as the Holy Communion has evermore been to rejectors.

b. *Electronics.* = *rejector circuit* below.

1923 *Wireless World* 7 July 441/1 Signals with the frequency of the aerial circuit will pass through the ordinary tuning device, and little will pass through the rejector. **1946** *Electronic Engin.* XVIII. 45/1 Methods of bass compensation in common use involving arrangements of chokes, condensers, tuned acceptors or rejectors..all fail where high fidelity is required. **1977** L. J. Giacoletto *Electronics Designer's Handbk.* (ed. 2) xxiv. 115 (*caption*) Complex frequency characteristic of..the admittance of a single-tuned circuit to which a rejector is coupled.

2. Special Comb.: **rejector circuit**, a circuit consisting of a capacitor and an inductor connected in parallel and having values chosen such that the combination offers a very high impedance to signals of a particular frequency. **1923** *Wireless World* 7 July 441/1 The smaller the damping of the rejector circuit, the better it will perform. **1929** *Daily Express* 7 Nov. 14/3 A rejector circuit, which acts as a by-path for unwanted stations. **1952** *Electronic Engin.* XXIV. 314/1 As the selectivity of the 50 kc/s amplifier is not sufficient to reject the 48 kc/s frequency completely, a separate rejector circuit is used. **1969** NELKON & HUMPHREYS *Electronics & Radio* viii. 170 The parallel *LC* circuit is known as a 'rejector' circuit because the main current is zero at f_0.

rejekk-, obs. Sc. form of REJECT *v.*

†**re'jerk**, *v. Obs.* [RE-.] *trans.* To jerk back. **1605** SYLVESTER *Du Bartas* II. iii. IV. *Captaines* 527 Smarter then Racquets in a Court re-jerk Balls 'gainst the Wals of the black-boorded house.

'**rejig**, *sb.* [RE- 5 c.] Reorganization, rearrangement. **1965** *New Statesman* 23 Apr. 630/1 The *Sunday Citizen*, for all its admitted demerits (which may yet be rectified if still another rejig..is accomplished effectively). **1974** *Guardian Weekly* 10 Aug. 5/1 The idea of the late-night front page rejig is unknown.

re'jig, *v.* [RE- 5 c.] *trans.* To refit or re-equip; to mend. Also *fig.*, to rearrange, refashion, alter. **1948** *Daily Express* 22 Apr. 1/6 Britain will send experts to help rejig French factories. **1958** *Spectator* 2 May 558/1 To alter the period of the action [of *Twelfth Night*], to rejig the entrances and exits of the characters..is really a kind of forgery. **1962** *Economist* 22 Sept. 1084/1 Schemes for rejigging the conditions of press competition. **1972** *Times Lit. Suppl.* 14 Apr. 419/4 Current attempts to rejig Spanish sixteenth and seventeenth-century literature in terms of racial influences, art history, and so on. **1976** A. WHITE *Long Silence* iv. 34 Three [weeks]..he spent with Jean Duclerc, helping re-jig the wireless. **1979** *Economist* 13 Oct. 81/3 Last year, faced with slower-than-expected increases in electricity demand, Hydro-Québec rejigged part of the project to reduce overall capacity.

Hence **re'jigged** *ppl. a.*; **re'jigging** *vbl. sb.* **1960** *Times Lit. Suppl.* 30 Sept. 635/3 The subject is fascinating and the setting never dull, and re-jigged (as the technicians say) it might make an enthralling story. **1969** *Daily Tel.* 6 Oct. 1/1 Whitehall's structure will be considerably changed as a result of the Prime Minister's 'rejigging' of the machinery of government. **1972** *Guardian* 15 June 15/2 Who will take over the re-jigged RIBA? **1977** *New Statesman* 17 June 809/2 His rejigged Radio 4 *Today* programme is now packing the listeners in. **1980** *Jrnl. R. Soc. Arts* Feb. 152/1 This leads me to suggest that the industrial planning process needs re-jigging.

†**re'joice**, *sb. Obs.* Also 5–6 rejoyse, 6–7 rejoyce. [f. the vb.] Joy, rejoicing; a cause of joy. (Common in 16th c.) *c* **1468** in *Archaeol.* (1846) XXXI. 329 He rejoisid, and in his rejoyse in suche case, me thought, as Troylus was in. *c* **1530** L. COX *Rhet.* (1899) 52, I have thought it a synguler reioyse to me if I myght ones se you gadred to-gyther. **1582** BENTLEY *Mon. Matrones* Ep. Ded., To your euerlasting comfort, and the rejoice of christian harts. **1682** SIR T. BROWNE *Chr. Mor.* II. §6 The Angels must not want their charitable Rejoyces for the conversion of lost Sinners.

rejoice (rɪˈdʒɔɪs), *v.* Forms: α. 4–6 reioyse, (5 reioysse, reyjoysse, resjoysse, reyoyse, 5–6 reioys), reioyes-e, (6 *Sc.* -ioyis, -ioiyss); 4–6 reioise, (5 -sse, 6 *Sc.* reiois); 5–7 reioyce, (7–8 rejoyce), 5 rejoice. β. 4 reioische, -sshe, 4–5 reioysche, -sshe; 4–5 reios(c)he. γ. 5–6 reiose, (5 reyose), *Sc.* reios(s, -iosz, 6 reioce. [a. OF. *rejoiss-, resjoiss-*, lengthened stem of *rejoir* (later *rejouir*, mod.F. *réjouir*), f. *re-* RE- + *joir* to JOY *v.*: cf. REJOY. (See also JOISE *v.*)]

†**1.** *trans.* To enjoy by possessing; to have full possession and use of (a thing). *Obs.* **1303** R. BRUNNE *Handl. Synne* 2032 Swyche an eyre y vnderstande Shal neuer wel reioshe hys lande. *c* **1350** *Will. Palerne* 4102 þat here sone..miȝt reioische þat reaume as riȝt eir bi kinde. **1424** in T. A. Beck *Ann. Furnes* (1844) 295 That he have and rejoise iiij.ˣˣ cartfulle of Turfes yerly with in the place forsaide. **1494** FABYAN *Chron.* v. cviii. 82 He reioysed his reygne but shorte whyle. **1525** LD. BERNERS *Froiss.* II. cci. [cxcvii.] 615 The duke of Lancastre is gone into Acquytayne, to reioyce the gyfte that the kynge..hath gyuen hym. **1577** FENTON *Gold. Epist.* 251 Many couetous men do we see..to whom God giues power to get riches..but not libertie to reioyce and vse them.

†**b.** To have (a person) as husband or wife; to have for oneself; to enjoy (a woman). *Obs.* **1430–40** LYDG. *Bochas* III. xxvi. (1554) 97 b, Dary cast..Her to reioyce agein hys father's wyll. *c* **1440** *Generydes* 3696 Sekerly this is the comon voyse, In all the courte that he shall hir reioyse. **1470–85** MALORY *Arthur* VI. xv. 207 [The damsel said] sythen I maye not reioyce the to haue thy body on lyue. *c* **1530** LD. BERNERS *Arth. Lyt. Bryt.* (1814) 417 Who so euer shold haue the chaplet..shoulde in lykewyse reioyse my lady Florence, your doughter.

†**c.** To enjoy (a condition or privilege). *Obs.* **1458** *Pol. Poems* (Rolls) II. 254 God hold hem longe..That Anglonde may rejoise concord and unite. **1485** *Act 1 Hen. VII*, c. 11 §1 They have and rejoice such fredomes and liberties as doth denesyns born within this realme.

2. To gladden, make joyful, exhilarate (a person, his spirits, etc.). *c* **1366** CHAUCER *A.B.C.* 101 We han noon oþer melodye or glee Vs to reioyse in oure aduersitee. **1375** BARBOUR *Bruce* II. 551 Thar cummyng Reiosyt rycht gretumly the king. *c* **1430** LYDG. *Min. Poems* (Percy Soc.) 78 Than I herd a voyce celestialle, Rejoysyng my spirites inwardly. **1513** BRADSHAW *St. Werburge* I. 1724 All these hystoryes noble and auncyent Reioysynge the audyence he sange with pleasuer. **1578** LYTE *Dodoens* II. lxxi. 241 It reioyceth and recreateth the spirites. *a* **1648** LD. HERBERT *Hen. VIII* (1683) 40 This, as it rejoyced the King, so it put him in mind of the Vicissitude of all worldly things. **1712** ADDISON *Spect.* No. 269 ¶8, I love to rejoice their poor Hearts at this season. **1774** KAMES *Sketches* II. viii. (1807) II. 178 It rejoices me, that the same mode is adopted in this island. **1863** COWDEN CLARKE *Shaks. Char.* xvii. 431 His body he rejoices with sack-posset. **1885–94** R. BRIDGES *Eros & Psyche* May vi, Too fair for human art, so Psyche thought, It might the fancy of some god rejoice.

b. In passive. Const. *at*, †*in*, †*of*, etc. **1375** BARBOUR *Bruce* XI. 269 To maynteym weill thair franchiss, He wes reiosit on mony wiss. *c* **1430** LYDG. *Min. Poems* (Percy Soc.) 3 For Davyd aftyr his victory Reyjoyssed whas alle Jerusalem. *c* **1470** HENRY *Wallace* IV. 705 Off his presence scho rycht reiosit was. **1523** LD. BERNERS *Froiss.* I. 275 Of whose comynge the hole courte was greatly rejoysed. **1567** *Gude & Godlie B.* (S.T.S.) 58, I am reioysit at my hart, To se his godlie face. **1666** PEPYS *Diary* 6 June, All the Court was in a hubbub, being rejoiced over head and ears in this good news. **1801** *Lusignan* II. 94 You do not..look half so rejoiced when we meet as I do. **1841** LANE *Arab. Nts.* I. 105 The King was rejoiced at seeing him.

†**c.** *Hunting.* To reward (a hound). *Obs.*⁻¹ *c* **1400** *Master of Game* (MS. Digby 182) x, þenn þe hunter reioyseth his houndes for þe explette of his houndes and also for it is vermynn þat þei renne too.

3. *refl.* To make (oneself) glad or joyful; hence = sense 5. Now *rare*. *c* **1386** CHAUCER *Clerk's T.* 89, I me reioysid of my liberte. *c* **1400** MAUNDEV. (1839) xxxi. 309 Thei reioyssen hem hugely for to speke there of. **1484** CAXTON *Fables of Auian* xv, None oughte to reioysshe hym self of his worship. **1512** *Helyas* in Thoms *Prose Rom.* (1858) III. 91 Every person rejoyced them in theyr degree. **1586** A. DAY *Eng. Secretary* I. (1625) 14 Rejoycing my self on..the hope I have to be returned in safetie. **1876** RUSKIN *Fors Clav.* lxii. 60 Rejoice myself with a glance at the volutes of the Erectheium. *transf.* **1486** *Bk. St. Albans* B iv, Whan yowre hawke hath slayne a fowle, and is rewarded as I haue sayde, let hir not flie in no whise tyll yᵗ she haue Reiosed hir.

†**4.** To feel joy on account of (an event). Also *it is rejoiced*, there is rejoicing. *Obs.* **1468** *Paston Lett.* II. 325 My Lorde coude nat bileve it but if he harde it, how it is rejoysshid in som place that he is nat Chaunceleer. **1505** in *Mem. Hen. VII* (Rolls) 256 They that knowe your grace gretely do rejoyse the maryaje. **1534** MORE *Treat. Passion* Wks. 1279/1 His visitacion thei reioysed not, but were afeard to come nere him. **1556** J. HEYWOOD *Spider & F.* Concl. 24 Let vs rather..Lament their false facktes then reioyce their foule falls. **1611** SHAKS. *Cymb.* v. v. 370 Nere Mother Reioyc'd deliuerance more.

5. *intr.* To be full of joy; to be glad or greatly delighted; to exult. *c* **1374** CHAUCER *Troylus* v. 1165 It is not al for nought That in myn herte I now reioyse thus. *c* **1410** HOCCLEVE *Mother of God* 55 His precious deeth made..cristen folk for to reioisen euere. **1500–20** DUNBAR *Poems* xlviii. 158 Quhairfoir me thocht all flouris did reioss. **1554–9** in *Songs & Ball. Phil. & Mary* (1860) 5 Nothyng shall let us nowe to rejoys and be fayne. **1610** SHAKS. *Temp.* v. i. 206 O reioyce Beyond a common ioy. **1650** JER. TAYLOR *Holy Living* iv. §9 (1727) 281 He once suffered, and for that reason he rejoyces for ever. **1718** *Free-thinker* No. 65. 69 The Nation rejoyces: The Prince is pleased. **1771** *Junius Lett.* lxvii. (1788) 339 They naturally rejoice when they see a signal instance of tyranny resisted with success. **1817** SHELLEY *Rev. Islam* VIII. xxviii, As if the sea, and sky, And earth, rejoiced with new-born liberty. **1859** TENNYSON *Geraint* 771 Never man rejoiced More than Geraint to greet her thus attired.

b. Const. *at*, *in*, †*of*, *over*. Also *to rejoice in*, to have or possess. **1483** LD. DYNHAM in Ellis *Orig. Lett.* Ser. II. I. 157 All the comones of the Contre greitly rejoysshe therof. **1526** *Pilgr. Perf.* (W. de W. 1531) 41 That other gloryed & reioysed in his power. **1530** PALSGR. 683/2, I have reioysed..at his prosperyte. **1535** COVERDALE *Judith* x. 9 That Ierusalem maye reioyse ouer the. **1605** BP. ANDREWES *Serm.* (1841) I. 14 They rejoice of our good. **1628** GAULE *Pract. The.* (1629) 181, I shall once so reioyce in him, that I cannot more reioyce at my selfe. **1726** BUTLER *Serm. Rolls Chap.* v. 80 When we rejoyce in the Prosperity of others. **1784** COWPER *Task* v. 326 Rejoice in him, and celebrate his sway. **1842** MRS. CARLYLE *Lett.* I. 163, I have had a parasol of Mrs. Buller's, who rejoices in two. **1864** TENNYSON *En. Ard.* 127 Rejoicing at that answer to his prayer.

c. Const. with clause, usu. with *that*. **14..** *Tundale's Vis.*, etc. (1843) 112 They in hart rejoysed not a lyte, On hym to loke that they have lybarte. *a* **1530** WOLSEY in G. Cavendish *Life* (Ellis) 184 Lett us all rejoyse and be glade, that [etc.]. **1611** SHAKS. *Wint. T.* v. i. 30 What were more holy, Then to reioyce the former Queene is well? **1667** MILTON *P.L.* XII. 475 Whether I should repent me..or rejoyce..that much more good thereof shall spring. **1784** COWPER *Task* I. 339 Once more I..rejoice That yet a remnant of your race survives.

d. Const. with *inf.* **1508** DUNBAR *Flyting* 106 Quhat ferly is thocht thow reioys to flyte? **1561** WINȜET *First Tract.* Wks. (S.T.S.) I. 8 Vtheris..reioyses to be callit Gospellaris and cunning in Scripture. **1603** SHAKS. *Meas. for M.* III. ii. 249 Reioycing to see another merry. **1819** SHELLEY *Prometh. Unb.* I. 253 Grey mountains, and old woods,..Rejoice to hear what yet ye cannot speak.

Hence **re'joiced** *ppl. a.* **1801** tr. *Gabrielli's Mysterious Husb.* IV. 12 Mrs. Horton flung her arms round the neck of her still more rejoiced husband.

rejoiceful (rɪˈdʒɔɪsfʊl), *a.* Now *rare*. [f. REJOICE *sb.* + -FUL.] Joyful, joyous. **1538** ELYOT, *Lætabilis*, gladde, or reioycefull. **1598** DRAYTON *Heroic. Ep.*, *Alice to Bl. Prince* Annot., Poems (1619) 150 To whose last and lawfull Request, the reioycefull Ladie sends this louing Answere. **1611** SPEED *Hist. Gt. Brit.* IX. xx. §52. 744 In the meane while the King makes a reioicefull entrance into Excester. **1650** *Descr. Fut. Hist. Europe* Pref. 8 The hands of his loving and rejoycefull Subjects. **1890** SARAH J. DUNCAN *Social Departure* 395 Tranquil beyond all telling.., with no rejoiceful tint of rose and gold.

rejoicement (rɪˈdʒɔɪsmənt). [f. REJOICE *v.* + -MENT. Cf. OF. *rejouissement*.] Joy, exultation, rejoicing. **1561** T. NORTON *Calvin's Inst.* II. 70 So hath he ben accepted with the well liking reioycement..of all ages. **1611** SPEED *Hist. Gt. Brit.* IX. xvi. §69. 668 The reioicement caused by this seeming peace..was wonderfully great. **1670** *Conclave wherein Clement VIII was elected Pope* 32 It was rather a stupefaction than a rejoycement. **1837** B. D. WALSH *Aristoph.*, *Acharnians* I. i, What pleasure had I worth rejoicement? **1894** *Catholic News* 8 Sept. 8 His execution took place amidst a scene of popular rejoicement.

rejoicer (rɪˈdʒɔɪsə(r)). [f. as prec. + -ER¹.]

1. One who rejoices. **1610** HEALEY *St. Aug. Citie of God* 720 As if hee were one of the hopefull sufferers, and patient rejoycers. **1648** *Ded. T. Sheppard's Clear Sunshine of Gospel*, England might bee stirred up to be Rejoicers in..these promising beginnings. **1700** SOUTHERNE *Fate of Capua* I. i, A kind Rejoycer in our Growth and Strength. **1845** BROWNING *Soul's Trag.* II. Wks. 1896 I. 476/2 By the side of such a rejoicer. **1882** STEVENSON *Fam. Stud.* Pref. 18, I made haste to rejoice with the rejoicers.

2. One who or that which causes rejoicing. **1612** *Two Noble K.* v. i. 121 Briefe, I am..To those that would, and cannot, a rejoycer. *a* **1834** COLERIDGE *Hymn to Earth* 16 Sister thou of the stars, and beloved by the sun, the rejoicer.

rejoicing (rɪˈdʒɔɪsɪŋ), *vbl. sb.* [-ING¹.]

1. a. The action of the vb. REJOICE; the feeling and expression of joy. **1375** BARBOUR *Bruce* XI. 415 In hert he had gret reiosying. *c* **1468** in *Archaeol.* (1846) XXXI. 331 Wᵗ mellodieus mynstralsye.., castinge out of flowers, rejoising of the people [etc.]. **1484** CAXTON *Fables of Æsop* I. xv, Men ought not to be glad ne take reioysshynge in the wordes of caytyf folke. **1555** EDEN *Decades* 58 Yet receaued they it with muche reioysinge. **1610** SHAKS. *Temp.* III. i. 93 My reioycing At nothing can be more. **1667** MILTON *P.L.* VII. 180 Great triumph and rejoycing was in Heav'n. **1855** MACAULAY *Hist. Eng.* xix. IV. 274 He heard the sounds of rejoicing from the distant camp of the allies.

b. With *a* and *pl.*: An instance, occasion, or expression of rejoicing; a festival. *a* **1540** BARNES *Wks.* (1573) 312/1 Men sit and laugh at them, & haue a great reioysing in them. **1593** SHAKS. *Lucr.* 332 Like little frosts that sometime threat the spring, To ad a more reioysing to the prime. **1707** FREIND *Peterborow's Cond. Sp.* 200 The rejoycings upon this occasion were of short continuance. **1774** BRUCE in Burney *Hist. Mus.* (1776) I. 215 The sixth [instrument] is peculiarly an attendant on festivity and rejoicings. **1864** SKEAT *Uhland's Poems* 91 Who is found to tell to-day What such rejoicings signify?

c. *Rejoicing of* (or *over*, etc.) *the Law* [tr. Heb. *Simchat Torah*, q.v.], the Jewish feast at the conclusion of the Feast of Tabernacles, celebrating the gift of the covenant of the Law. **1861** J. T. BANNISTER *Temples of Hebrews* 390 *Tisri* ..[Day] 23. The rejoicing for the law, a solemnity in memory of the covenant that the Lord made with the Hebrews, in giving them the law by the mediation of Moses. **1892** I. ZANGWILL *Childr. Ghetto* I. 134 It was the Rejoicing of the Law, and the Sons of the Covenant had treated him to rum and currant cake. **1903** W. ROSENAU *Jewish Ceremonial Institutions & Customs* v. 101 On the Day of Rejoicing Over the Law special inducements are held out to the younger members of the congregation to participate actively in the public service. **1925** *Jewish Encycl.* XI. 364/2 *Simhat Torah* ('The Rejoicing over the Law'): Name given to the second day of *Shemini 'Azeret*; it falls on the 23d of Tishri and closes the Feast of Sukkot. **1953** T. H. GASTER *Festivals Jewish Year* vi. 100 Not impossibly, the custom of celebrating the Rejoicing in the Law as a *wedding* was inspired by the idea of sublimating to a more spiritual plane the..staging of a mock wedding at harvest festivals. **1962** B. ABRAHAMS tr. *Life Glückel of Hameln* iii. 52 Her companions were not to return before *Simchat Torah*..Festival of the Rejoicing of the Law, celebrated immediately after that of Tabernacles. **1978** J. SACKS in P. Moore *Man, Woman, & Priesthood* iii. 39 On *Simchat Torah*, the festival of 'Rejoicing in the Law', adults and children forget decorum and dance and sing around the synagogue in celebration of the ending of the yearly cycle of Torah-reading and the beginning of the new.

†**2.** A cause or source of rejoicing or gladness. *c* **1386** CHAUCER *Manciple's T.* 142 To myn hert it was a reioisinge To here thi vois. **1500–20** DUNBAR *Poems* lxxxix. 15 Oure secrete rejoysyng frome the sone beme. *c* **1560** A. SCOTT *Poems* (S.T.S.) viii. 20 Ȝe be, hairt, My hairtis reiosing. **1611** BIBLE *Jer.* xv. 16 Thy word was unto me, the ioy and reioycing of my heart.

3. *attrib.*, as *rejoicing day*, *fire*, *night*, etc. **1611** SHAKS. *Cymb.* III. i. 32 The fam'd Cassibulan.. Made Luds-Towne with reioycing-Fires bright. **1711** ADDISON *Spect.* No. 85 ¶1, I met with several Fragments of it upon the next rejoicing Day. **1760** GRAY *Let. to Wharton* 23 Jan., The first rejoicing night he was terribly frighted, and thought the bonefire was made for him. **1771** LUCKOMBE *Hist. Printing* 269 Sudden commotions of the mind..upon lamenting, or rejoicing occasions. **1885** *Academy* 5 Sept. 147/1 In 1660 he preached a rejoicing sermon on the restoration of Charles II.

re'joicing, *ppl. a.* [-ING².] That rejoices. **1560** BIBLE (Geneva) *Zeph.* ii. 15 This is the reioycing citie that dwelt carelesse. **1700** PRIOR *Carm. Seculare* 192 He.. dictated a lasting peace To the rejoicing world below. **1752** HUME *Ess. & Treat.* (1777) II. 9 To bring light from obscurity..must needs be delightful and rejoicing. **1798**

COLERIDGE *France* i, Thou rising Sun! thou blue rejoicing Sky! **1861** TULLOCH *Eng. Purit.* I. i. 56 An easy and rejoicing hospitality..had reduced the fortunes of the house.

re'joicingly, *adv.* [f. prec. + -LY².] In a rejoicing manner.

1556 J. HEYWOOD *Spider & F.* i. 22 Whiche I (reioysynglie) herde and behelde. **1596** H. CLAPHAM *Briefe Bible* II. 153 Reioycinglie they would suffer any death at the handes of the Romanes. **1652** FRENCH *Yorksh. Spa* iii. 36 A Fountain..doth at the sound of a pipe rejoycingly exult and leap up. **1829** SOUTHEY *Pilgr. Compostella, Legend* x, The Father and Mother were last in the train; Rejoicingly they came. **1885** SWINBURNE *Misc.* (1886) 322 A fact to be thankfully and rejoicingly accepted.

rejoin (rɪ'dʒɔɪn), *v.*¹ Also 5-7 rejoyn, (7 -nd). [ad. F. *rejoin-*, *rejoindre*, f. *re-* RE- + *joindre* to JOIN. The sense, however, is not recorded in F., and was prob. developed in AF. legal use.]

1. *intr. Law.* To reply to a charge or pleading; *spec.* to answer the plaintiff's replication. Hence **re'joining** *vbl. sb.*¹

1456 in W. P. Baildon *Sel. Cas. Chanc.* (1896) 148 This is the reioynyng of Nicholl Marshall vnto the replicacion of Robert Bale. **1530** PALSGR. 683/1, I rejoyne, as men do that answere to the lawe. **1885** L. O. PIKE *Yearbks. 12 & 13 Edw. III* Introd. 110 Hyncley rejoined, again stating matters of fact, which he was again 'paratus verificare'.

†**2.** To answer a reply; also more loosely, to reply. Const. *to*, *with*. *Obs.*

1556 J. HEYWOOD *Spider & F.* lix. 66 In reioyner and reioyning with you, this I saie. **1568** GRAFTON *Chron.* II. 428 To this aunswere the Duke of Orliaunce replyed, and king Henry reioyned. **1646** SIR T. BROWNE *Pseud. Ep.* Pref., Vnto whom..wee shall not contentiously rejoyne. **1665** GLANVILL *Def. Van. Dogm.* 2 Several passages both of the Preface and Body of the Discourse I am rejoyning to.

3. *trans.* To say in answer.

1637 GILLESPIE *Eng. Pop. Cerem.* III. v. 87 Knox rejoyndeth, it is not enough. **1675** R. BURTHOGGE *Causa Dei* 5 You are not to expect Profound, Uncommon, Deep, Elaborate Notions..in what I shall rejoyn to your Letter. **1838** DICKENS *Nich. Nick.* iv, 'If you'll have the goodness', rejoined Squeers. **1859** KINGSLEY *Misc.* II. 99 It will be rejoined, of course, that he was an altogether envious man.

†**4.** To answer (an assertion). *Obs. rare*⁻¹.

1601 BARLOW *Def.* 35 These two last are easily reioyned.

rejoin (rɪ-, riː'dʒɔɪn), *v.*² Also 6-8 rejoyn, (6-7 -joyne). [ad. F. *rejoin-* (see prec.), or f. RE- 5 a + JOIN *v.*]

1. *intr.* Of things: To come together or unite again. Also const. *into*.

1541 R. COPLAND *Guydon's Quest. Chirurg.* L iij b, Whan they be drye sewe them subtylly and the lyppes wyl reioyne togydre. **1606** SYLVESTER *Du Bartas* II. iv. II. *Tropheis* 737 In Soule and Bodie both, Hee cannot come, For they reioyne not till the day of Doom. *a* **1705** RAY *Disc.* II. v. (1713) 293 Several Houses parted from each other, some rejoined, others fell.

2. *trans.* To join again, reunite (persons or things, or one *to* or *with* another).

1570 LEVINS *Manip.* 215/24 To Reioyne, *repangere.* **1591** SPENSER *Ruins Rome* v, Her great spirite, rejoyned to the spirite Of this great masse, is in the same enwombed. **1603** HOLLAND *Plutarch's Mor.* 188 As tin-soder doth knit and rejoyne a crackt peece of brasse. **1642** C. VERNON *Consid. Exch.* 30 Tallies have been counterfeited..which could not bee discovered before they were rejoyned with their foyles. **1707** *Curios. in Husb. & Gard.* 326 If we could rejoin to them the other Principles. **1836** SOUTHEY *Lett.* (1856) IV. 448 The letters were written..to rejoin head, tails, and betweenities, which Hayley had severed.

†**b.** To join, add *to*; to combine *with*. *Obs.*

1582 STANYHURST *Æneis* III. (Arb.) 77 With stincking poysoned ordure Thee ground they smeared, theartoo skriches harshye reioyning. **1791** MRS. RADCLIFFE *Rom. Forest* xviii, Such a proof of regard, rejoined with the entreaties of his own family..was too powerful to be withstood.

c. To reannex. *rare*⁻¹.

1860 GEN. P. THOMPSON *Audi Alt.* cxvii. III. 54 If France could quietly, and with the assent of the in-dwellers, rejoin the Rhenish provinces.

3. To join (a person, company, etc.) again.

1611 FLORIO, *Raggiunto*, reioyned or ouertaken againe. **1737** POPE *Hor. Epist.* II. ii. 209 Thoughts, which..I forgot, Meet and rejoin me. *a* **1769** J. G. COOPER *Estim. Life* iii, Receive the one, and soon the other Will follow to rejoin his brother. **1802** JAMES *Milit. Dict.* s.v., He left his regiment when it broke up camp, but rejoined it again. **1855** BROWNING *Ep. Karshish* 12 Whereby the wily vapour fain would slip Back and rejoin its source.

absol. **1876** VOYLE & STEVENSON *Milit. Dict.* 224/2 If the officer is not likely to rejoin soon.

Hence **re'joining** *vbl. sb.*², †reassembling.

1573 *Nottingham Rec.* IV. 147 The proclamasyon for reioynyng of the Parlament.

rejoinder (rɪ'dʒɔɪndə(r)), *sb.* Also 5-6 reioyner, 6 reioyndre, 7 rijoinder. [a. F. *rejoindre* inf. used as sb. The sense is prob. from AF. usage: see REJOIN *v.*¹]

1. *Law.* The defendant's answer to the plaintiff's replication.

1482 in I. S. Leadam *Star Chamber Cas.* (Selden Soc.) 14 This is the reioyner of John Attwyll..to the replicacion of John Tayllour. **1540** *Act 32 Hen. VIII*, c. 30 §1 Replycacyons, reioynders, rebutters..and other pleadynges. **1588** FRAUNCE *Lawiers Log.* I. ii. 10 In every count, barre, replication, rejoynder, &c. **1649** W. M. *Wandering Jew* (1857) 48 She has Demurs, and Replications, and Rejoynders; but my case hangs. *a* **1683** SCROGGS *Courts-leet* (1714) 168 If they proceed nor further by Replication, Rejoinder, Surrejoinder. **1768** BLACKSTONE *Comm.* III. 310 The rejoinder must support the plea, without departing out of it. **1885** *Law Times Rep.* LIII. 486/1 Rejoinder of issue was made.

2. An answer to a reply (†common in the titles of books and pamphlets); also simply, a reply.

1566 HARDING (*title*) A rejoindre to Mr. Jewels Replie. **1609** R. PARSONS *Quiet Reckoning* title-p., In a large Preamble to a more ample Reioynder promised by him. **1659** BP. WALTON *Consid. Considered* 306, I shall promise to deal in like manner with him, if any rejoinder shall be found needful. **1726** POPE *Odyss.* xx. 231 Rejoinder to the churl the King disdain'd. **1759** FRANKLIN *Ess.* Wks. 1840 III. 232 The assembly took the governor's reply..into consideration, and prepared a suitable rejoinder. **1877** FROUDE *Short Stud.* (1883) IV. I. x. 125 An answer came in a form to which in that age no rejoinder was possible.

b. Without article, in phr. *in rejoinder*.

1556 [see REJOIN *v.*¹ 2]. **1844** DE QUINCEY in 'H. A. Page' *Life* (1877) I. xv. 332 In rejoinder to your note of Wednesday morning, I wrote an answer.

So †**re'joinder** *v. intr.*, to reply. *Obs. rare*⁻¹.

a **1660** HAMMOND *Serm.* xix. Wks. 1683 IV. 604 When Nathan shall rejoynder with a *Thou art the man*,..then their hearts come to the touchstone.

†**re'joindure**. *Obs. rare*⁻¹. [prob. ad. F. *rejoindre* (see prec. and JOINDER), with ending assimilated to -URE.] Reunion.

1606 SHAKS. *Tr. & Cr.* IV. iv. 38 Iniurie of chance..beguiles our lips Of all reioyndure: forcibly preuents Our lockt imbrasures.

†**re'joint**, *v.*¹ *Obs. rare*⁻¹. [Of obscure origin: cf. REJOLT *v.*] *trans.* To upset.

1519 HORMAN *Vulg.* 160, I wyll haue none oyle in my salet for reioyntynge of my stomacke.

re'joint (riː-), *v.*² [RE- 5 a.] *trans.* To join together again; to reunite, or fill up, the joints of.

1677 BARROW *Serm. Creed, Resurrect. Body* Wks. 1686 II. 521 Ezekiel saw dry bones rejoynted and reinspired with life. **1727-38** CHAMBERS *Cycl.*, *Rejointing*, or *Rejoynting*, in architecture, the filling up the joints of the stones in old buildings, etc. when worn hollow by course of time, or by weather. [Hence in Bailey (vol. II), Gwilt, Knight, etc.]

rejois(s)e, obs. forms of REJOICE *v.*

†**re'jolt**, *sb. Obs.* [RE-.] A reacting shock.

1692 SOUTH *Serm., Rom.* i. 32 (1697) II. 201 As long as these inward rejolts and recoilings of the Mind continue. *a* **1711** KEN *Hymnotheo* Poet. Wks. 1721 III. 126 Fond Fool at Death, who his stoll'n Feathers molts, And of his Folly feels the dire rejolts.

re'jolt, *v.* [f. RE- + JOLT *v.*]

†**1.** *intr.* To rise again in the stomach. *Obs.*

1584 COGAN *Haven Health* liii. (1636) 69 As the Country-man said, that had eaten fish fried with Lampe Oyle, they will make the meat eftsoones to rejolt. [Hence in Coles *Adam in Eden* (1657) cli. 231.]

2. *trans.* To jolt again, or back again.

1833 SIR F. B. HEAD *Bubbles fr. Brunnen* 273, I retraced my steps, was rejolted homewards, and..reached my peaceful abode.

‖**rejon** (re'xon). *Bull-fighting.* Pl. **rejones**. [Sp. *rejón* lance, spear, f. *rejo* pointed iron bar, *reja* ploughshare (L. *rēgula* straight piece of wood, f. *regere* to keep straight).] A wooden-handled spear, usu. placed from horseback.

1838 *Q. Rev.* LXII. 397 These noble 'Bestiarii' fought with the '*rejon*', a short projectile spear, about four feet long. **1893** CHAPMAN & BUCK *Wild Spain* v. 57 The knight, mounted on fiery Arab steed, was armed only with the *rejon*, or short sharp lance of those days, five feet in length, and held at its extreme end. **1932** *Times Lit. Suppl.* 7 Jan. 11/1 Nobles and gentlemen, on horseback with long heavy spears (*rejones*)..awaited the bull's attack. **1934** R. CAMPBELL *Broken Record* viii. 184 His *rejon* is nearly always mortal. **1957** A. MACNAB *Bulls of Iberia* x. 99 The *rejón* act..is more popular in Portugal, but is also quite common in Spain. **1967** MCCORMICK & MASCAREÑAS *Compl. Aficionado* i. 19 The rider plays the bull with the horse itself, placing long banderillas, darts known as *rejones*, and killing with a long lance, also called a rejón. **1973** *Times* 5 Dec. 15/1 They attempt to finish him [*sc.* the bull] off with a *rejon*, a long-bladed, wooden-handled spear.

‖**rejoneador** (rexonea'dor). *Bull-fighting.* Pl. **-es**; fem. **-a**. [Sp.] A mounted bull-fighter who places *rejones* (see prec.).

1926 *Blackw. Mag.* Sept. 290/2 No small skill in horsemanship is required to be a successful rejoneador. **1932** E. HEMINGWAY *Death in Afternoon* iii. 31 A man who kills them [*sc.* bulls] on horseback with a javelin, using trained thoroughbred horses, is called a rejoneador or a caballero en plaza. **1957** R. CAMPBELL *Portugal* vi. 114 The great Peruvian horsewoman, the beautiful Conchita Cintron, earned immortal fame as a *rejoneadora*. **1957** A. MACNAB *Bulls of Iberia* x. 100 The *rejoneadores*..are technically deemed amateurs. **1967** MCCORMICK & MASCAREÑAS *Compl. Aficionado* i. 19 Rejoneo has little to do with the true art of toreo on foot; it is too showy, and the danger is risked by the horse, not the man (*rejoneador*). **1973** *Times* 5 Dec. 15/1 Women do fight in Spanish bull rings..but exclusively as *rejoneadoras*, from the backs of..horses.

‖**rejoneo** (rexo'neo). *Bull-fighting.* [Sp.] The art of bull-fighting on horseback with *rejones* (see prec.).

1961 *John o' London's* 609/2 *Rejoneo*, the art of bull-fighting on horseback. **1965** *Pix* (Austral.) 13 Feb. 36/2 Conchita Cintron, first woman to master both rejoneo and the classic Spanish style on foot, was a matadora in her own right. **1967** MCCORMICK & MASCAREÑAS *Compl. Aficionado* i. 19 Alvarez cites further instances of corridas organized to celebrate marriages, all antedating the late mediaeval and renaissance practice of *rejoneo*, or knightly jousting against toros bravos. **1978** *Radio Times* 17-23 June 25/3 In the bull-ring he practises 'rejoneo', the aristocratic form of fighting bulls from horseback.

rejose, obs. form of REJOICE *v.*

†**re'jounce**. *Obs.* Also 6 reiounse. [f. RE- + JOUNCE *v.*] *intr.* **a.** To occur or recur to the mind after the manner of a bump or thump. **b.** ? To be recalcitrant or refractory.

1556 J. HEYWOOD *Spider & F.* lvi. 27 Peace dawpates; while I tell a thing now reiounst In my head, which to vtter I am compounst. **1567** DRANT *Horace, De Arte Poet.* B iij, So that this thing to multiplie still in theire mynde reiounses. *a* **1644** QUARLES *Virgin Widow* IV. i, Poyson doe thy worst. Hah! Dost thou rejounce? Thy Power's curb'd, and cannot work her end.

†**re'journ**, *v. Obs.* Also 6 rejorne, rejurne. [f. RE- + (*ad*)*journ*; cf. med.L. *radjournare*, It. *raggiornare* (Florio), and see READJOURN.]

1. *trans.* To adjourn, postpone, defer, put off.

1513 in Ellis *Orig. Lett.* Ser. I. I. 96, I was..avised by my guyds to have rejorned my purpose. **1556** *Chron. Gr. Friars* (Camden) 66 Item the terme rejurnyd from the Assencion unto Myhylmas. **1598** HARINGTON *Orl. Fur.* XXXI. xxi, Renaldo wisht..the combat might be now rejourn'd, Till Phœbus were about the world return'd. **1617** HIERON *Wks.* III. 84 This dutie..is most vnworthily reiourned into the last place. **1647** MAY *Hist. Parl.* (1854) 229 They cannot lay down arms, nor rejourn the Parliament to any other place.

2. To refer (a person) *to* something. *rare*⁻¹.

1621 BURTON *Anat. Mel.* I. i. II. ix, To the Scriptures themselves I rejourn all such atheistical spirits.

3. *intr.* **a.** To return. *rare*⁻¹.

1533 CRANMER in Ellis *Orig. Lett.* Ser. I. II. 36 This donne, and after our reiornyng home agayne, the Kings Highnes prepared al thynges convenient for the Coronacion.

b. To rejoin, reply. *rare*⁻¹.

a **1641** BP. MOUNTAGU *Acts & Mon.* (1642) 463 Whereto I rejourne, that..the use of Christian Monks..was much more rigid then that of the Essens.

Hence †**re'journing** *vbl. sb. Obs.*

1613 P. FORBES *Comm. Revelation* 36 (Jam.) The answere hath in it a two-fold consolation against the reiourning of the sought vengeance. **1642** (*title*) The Judges' Resolution on the Bench..concerning His Majesties Proclamation for the rejourning of the Michaelmas Term.

†**re'journey**, *v. Obs. rare*⁻¹. [RE-.] *trans.* To journey over again.

1628 FELTHAM *Resolves* II. lxxxvii. 252 Hee that does this, may..rejourney all his voyage, in his Closet.

†**re'journment**. *Obs.*⁻¹ [f. REJOURN *v.* + -MENT.] Adjournment.

1579-80 NORTH *Plutarch, Cicero* (1653) 713 The Prætors ..had made so many rejournments and delayes, that they had driven it off to the last day of hearing.

†**re'joy**, *v. Obs.* Also reioy(e. [ad. OF. *rejoir* (mod.F. *réjouir*): see RE- and JOY *v.*]

1. *intr.* To rejoice, be joyful. Const. *at*, *in*.

c **1315** SHOREHAM III. 169 3yf þy wyl reioyeþ more In enyes kennes þynges..þou ne anourest god ary3t. *c* **1485** *Digby Myst.* (1882) IV. 1321 Therfor in your harte [to] reioye ye may be fayn. **1662** in *Cosin's Corr.* (Surtees) II. 312 He oftens will rejoy and jest at his expressions.

2. *trans.* (and *refl.*). To make joyful or happy; to cause to rejoice. Also const. *of*.

c **1374** CHAUCER *Troylus* v. 395 Let vs speake of lustie life in Troy That we have lad,..And eke of time coming vs rejoy. *a* **1400-50** *Alexander* 3407 3e sall be glad of my degre & gretly reioyd. *c* **1477** CAXTON *Jason* 9 b, Thenne began the ladyes to reioye them silf. *c* **1500** *Melusine* 205 For to make hym to forgete his losse, & forto reioye & haue hym out of melencolye.

3. To enjoy as possessor.

1454 *Paston Lett.* I. 299 So that I may by your frendship the more peasably rejoy my forsaid purchase. **1468** *Ibid.* II. 331 That I and myn assignez may peasseble rejoie theym. *a* **1500** in Arnolde *Chron.* (1811) 39 That they vse hem full and reioye hem for euer.

Hence †**re'joying** *vbl. sb. Obs.*

c **1315** SHOREHAM v. 90 Elyzabet wel þat aspyde, Hou a spylede onder hyre syde, And made hys reioyynge. **1486** *Bk. St. Albans* A v, Ther be ix. inestimable reioyngis in armys. The ix. inestimable reioyngis of armys ben theys. First is a gentilman to be made a knyght in the felde [etc.].

rejoyce, -joyse, etc., obs. ff. REJOICE *v.*

rejoyn(e, obs. form of REJOIN.

re'judge, *v.* [RE- 5 a.] *trans.* To judge again, re-examine, pronounce a fresh judgement on.

1634 SANDERSON *Serm.* II. 286 They that judge others now shall then be re-judged. **1732** POPE *Ess. Man* I. 122 Re-judge his justice, be the God of God. **1769** GOLDSM. *Hist. Rome* (1786) I. p. vii, It appears now too late to re-judge the virtues or vices of those men. **1798** EDGEWORTH *Pract. Educ.* (1811) I. 389 We shall teach them the habit of re-judging flattery. **1880** *Plain Hints Needlework* 12 If, after the first course of judging be done, the best picked out of each class be re-judged a second time.

re'jumble, *v.* [RE-.] †**a.** *intr.* Of food: To rise again, to 'repeat'. (Cf. REJOLT *v.* 1.) *Obs.* **b.** *trans.* To jumble, toss about, again.

1674 RAY *N.C. Words* 38 It rejumbles upon my stomach. **1755** YOUNG *Centaur* v. Wks. 1757 IV. 225 Wouldst thou be rejumbled in this rough Thespian cart..?

re'junction. [RE- 5 a.] Reunion.
1631 CHAPMAN *Cæsar & Pompey* Plays 1873 III. 176 Yet tis free and kept Fit for reiunction in mans second life. **1797** in Nicolas *Disp. Nelson* (1845) II. 333 After a partial cannonade which prevented their re-junction till the evening. **1831** LD. HERTFORD 15 May in *Croker Papers* (1884) II. 126 It did not even secure the rejunction of the Tories.

re'juvenant, *a.* [f. as next + -ANT.] Rejuvenating.
1889 *Pall Mall G.* 22 Nov. 6/3 The stir for Beauty making itself felt..like Nature's rejuvenant spring.

rejuvenate (rɪ'dʒuːvɪneɪt), *v.* [irreg. f. RE- + L. *juvenis* young, perh. after F. *rajeunir*.]
1. *trans.* To restore to youth; to make young or fresh again. Also *absol.*
1807 W. TAYLOR in Robberds *Mem.* (1843) II. 210 It will also rejuvenate the people. **1822** W. IRVING *Braceb. Hall* II. 17 He..had the air of an old bachelor trying to rejuvenate himself. **1862** R. H. PATTERSON *Ess. Hist. & Art* 89 The action of the soul upon its corporeal shrine (rejuvenating it with joy, depressing it with grief). **1881** STEVENSON *Virg. Puerisque* 156 He will pray for Medea: when she comes, let her either rejuvenate or slay.
2. *Geol.* To restore to a condition characteristic of a younger landscape.
1903 H. LE R. FAIRCHILD *Le Conte's Elements Geol.* (ed. 5) ii. 23 If the land area be lifted up the graded streams are rejuvenated—that is, their grade and power are increased. **1944** A. HOLMES *Princ. Physical Geol.* xi. 195 When a river that has already established a flood-plain is rejuvenated, it cuts through its own deposits into the underlying rocks. **1954** W. D. THORNBURY *Princ. Geomorphol.* vi. 143 During the low sea levels on the glacial ages streams presumably were rejuvenated in their lower courses.
Hence **re'juvenated, -ating,** *ppl. adjs.* Also **rejuve'nation; re'juvenator.**
1834 LYTTON *Pompeii* I. vii, All the zest and freshness of rejuvenated life. **1871** NAPHEYS *Prev. & Cure Dis.* I. ix. 305 Rejuvenation in old age. **1880** *19th Cent.* VII. 275, I believe in the rejuvenation of worn-out institutions. **1885** *L'pool Daily Post* 4 Feb. 4/4 The only rejuvenating potion for the country to quaff. **1889** *Lancet* 15 June 1193/2 A great beautifier and rejuvenator of the complexion. **1936** *Geogr. Jrnl.* LXXXVII. 20 Before rejuvenation the river had developed an open mature valley in marked contrast to its present rugged canyon. **1954** W. D. THORNBURY *Princ. Geomorphol.* vi. 142 Mature or old-age topography is likely to have superposed upon it youthful features as a result of rejuvenation. **1969** G. C. DICKINSON *Maps & Air Photographs* xiii. 209 If, for reasons such as rise of the land, fall in sea level, or glacial overdeepening of the main valley, a river begins to cut down into its valley floor, a rejuvenation head will form at the upper limits of this downcutting, working its way progressively upstream. **1970** R. J. SMALL *Study of Landforms* iii. 105 In geologically active areas (such as New Zealand) it is possible that both fault- and fault-line scarps exist together. Indeed, it has been suggested that what are termed 'composite' and 'rejuvenated' scarps may be developed in these circumstances. **1971** *Nature* 19 Feb. 539/1 Further local rejuvenations of the main graben and step faults continued until mid-Pleistocene times, deepening the Lake Naivasha and Lake Natron sectors.

rejuvenatory (rɪ'dʒuːvɪnətərɪ), *a.* [f. REJUVENATE *v.* + -ORY².] Tending to cause rejuvenation.
1971 *Nature* 25 June 530/2 A reverse transcriptase would have 'rejuvenatory' potential if it could restore lost or masked primary information from secondary copies. **1972** *Ibid.* 15 Dec. 414/1 This may represent a special rejuvenatory function of sexual processes.

rejuvenesce (rɪdʒuːvɪ'nɛs), *v.* [ad. late L. *rejuvenesc-ĕre*, f. *re-* RE- + *juvenis* young.]
a. *intr.* To become young again; *spec.* in *Biol.* of cells: To acquire renewed vitality. **b.** *trans.* To impart fresh vitality to (a cell).
1879 tr. *Pasteur's Ferment.* 177 The dark, double-bordered cells are those which were sown but did not rejuvenesce. **1889** GEDDES & THOMSON *Evol. Sex* xii. 163 The only cells capable of being rejuvenesced are the eggs; the only cells capable of rejuvenescing these are the sperms.

rejuvenescence (rɪdʒuːvɪ'nɛsəns). Also 7, 9 -iscence. [f. as prec. + -ENCE.] A renewal of youth, physical, mental, or spiritual. Also *fig.*
a **1631** DONNE *Serm.* lxxix. 815 With a re-juveniscence a new and fresh youth. **1663** BOYLE *Usef. Exp. Nat. Philos.* II. v. viii. 193 Whether Paracelsus and others deservedly call such accidents..a reall renovation or rejuvenescence. **1733** CHEYNE *Eng. Malady* II. i. §2 (1734) 114 If this could be..effected, the Cure would be a true Rejuvenescence. **1779–81** JOHNSON *L.P., Dryden* (1858) I. 285 The works of Chaucer, upon which this kind of rejuvenescence has been bestowed by Dryden, require little criticism. **1813** W. TAYLOR in *Monthly Mag.* XXXV. 426 To restore the circulation of our earlier classics produces, by infusion, a re-juvenescence of the language. **1875** MERIVALE *Gen. Hist. Rome* lxxvi. (1877) 641 The Greek and Roman races..had lost..all power of intellectual rejuvenescence.
b. *spec.* in *Biol.* and *Bot.* The process by which a vegetative cell transforms itself into a new one.
1855 HENFREY *Micrographic Dict.* s.v. *Cell*, Cell-formation also occurs, without division, in cases where the entire contents of a cell separate from the parent, and form a new organism (rejuvenescence). **1875** BENNETT & DYER tr. *Sachs' Bot.* 9 Hence the rejuvenescence of a cell..must be regarded morphologically as the formation of a new one. **1878** BELL *Gegenbaur's Comp. Anat.* p. ix, It results in a simple 'rejuvenescence' of the conjugating individuals.

†**rejuve'nescency.** *Obs.* [-ENCY.] = prec.
a **1661** FULLER *Worthies, Northumbld.* II. (1662) 309 The Poetical fiction of Æson his Re-juvenescency in Medeas Bath. **1666** J. SMITH *Old Age* (1676) 264 The whole Creation now grown old expecteth and waiteth for a certain rejuvenescency. **1755** *Man* No. 23. 1 Spring..gives us a kind of rejuvenescency. **1794** T. TAYLOR *Pausanias* III. 238–9 So the soul acquires rejuvenescency by always descending into generation.

rejuve'nescent, *a.* [f. as prec. + -ENT.]
1. a. Becoming young again.
1807 SOUTHEY *Espriella's Lett.* III. 160 It is a progressive union of minds, for ever rejuvenescent. **1848** THACKERAY *Van. Fair* xlv, The Crawley House in Great Gaunt Street was quite rejuvenescent. **1879** FARRAR *Christ* (1881) 118 Come and see..an aged world rejuvenescent.
b. *spec.* in scientific use.
1859 *Todd's Cycl. Anat.* V. 211/2 The rejuvenescent cell becomes individualised and is transformed into the rudiment of a new plant. **1885–8** FAGGE & PYE-SMITH *Princ. Med.* (ed. 2) I. 114 In young adults..the thymus is often found persistent if not rejuvenescent.
2. Rejuvenating.
1763 LD. BATH in *G. Colman's Posth. Lett.* (1820) 72, I was not a very dangerous man when I left England, but the Waters are rejuvenescent. **1837** HAWTHORNE *Twice-told T.* (1851) I. xix. 278 Though utter sceptics as to its rejuvenescent power, they were inclined to swallow it at once. **1899** R. FRY *Let.* 9 June (1972) I. 173, I have very rarely had a more rejuvenescent visit to Cambridge than this last.

rejuvenize (rɪ'dʒuːvɪnaɪz), *v.* [Cf. REJUVENATE and -IZE.] *trans.* To rejuvenate, make young again. Hence **re'juvenized** *ppl. a.*
1816 T. TAYLOR in *Pamphleteer* VIII. 464 So the divisible life of the soul..is rejuvenized in its subsequent progression. **1849** J. W. DONALDSON *Theat. Greeks* 250 The marvellously rejuvenized Iolaus, the comrade of Hercules. **1877** BLACKMORE *Erema* liii, That ancient and obsolete town, rejuvenized now by its Signor.

rek, obs. form of REEK *sb.*¹

rekand(e, -anth, obs. varr. *reckan* RACKAN.

†**reke,** *sb. Obs. rare.* [? Related to next: cf. ON. *reke*, pursuit of a matter.] Haste, hurry.
c **1320** R. BRUNNE *Medit.* 821 A cumpany..þe whych were sente yn a grete reke, þe dampned mennes legges to breke. *c* **1330** *Arth. & Merl.* 7894 (Kölbing), ʒif we may owhar abreke, Fle we hem wiþ gret reke!

†**reke,** *v.*¹ *Obs. Pa. t.* 4 rak(e. *Pa. pple.* 4 reke. [Of obscure origin: perh. f. *recþ*, *rekþ*, 3 sing. pres. ind. of OE. *reccan* RECCHE *v.*]
1. *intr.* To go, proceed, make one's way, esp. rapidly or in haste; to run.
It is doubtful if the first quot. belongs here.
a **1250** *Owl & Night.* 1606 Myn heorte is neyh alemed þat ic may vnneþe speke, Ac yet ic wile forþurre reke. **13..** *Guy Warw.* (A.) 750 When Gij herd Felice so speke, He tok his leue and gan out reke. **13..** *Sir Beues* 1686 Beues is out of prisoun reke. *Ibid.* 3536 Whan Arondel herde what he spak, Before þe twei kniȝtes he rak. *c* **1380** *Sir Ferumb.* 2177 To þe chambre so harde he rake þat þyderward he ran. *a* **1400** *Octouian* 182 When that sche myght out-breke, To her sone sche gan to reke. *c* **1450** LONELICH *Grail* xxx. 642 Whanne he hadde power forto speke, thanne to his Meyne he gan to reke.
b. Of plants: To shoot up. *rare*⁻¹.
c **1420** *Pallad. on Husb.* I. 194 Deep lond also thou seke, Olyuys grete out of that lond wol reke.
2. *trans.* ? To rule, govern, guide. *rare*⁻¹.
a **1300** *Cursor M.* 11221 [He] þat al wroght and al mai reke, And did þe dumb asse to speke.

†**reke,** *v.*² *Obs. rare. Pa. t.* 3 rack. [? a. ON. *reka* in same senses.] *trans.* To drive; to thrust.
c **1275** LAY. 9320 Hamund..his spere to his heorte rack. **13..** *Guy Warw.* (A.) 2886 ʒif þou miȝt me of hem wreke, & þe felouns out of mi lond do reke.

†**reke,** *v.*³ *Obs.* [= MDu. *reken*, MHG. (and G.) *rechen*, OHG. *rehhan*, Goth. *rikan* to heap up: see RAKE *sb.*¹] *trans.* To cover up in earth or ashes (cf. RAKE *v.* 5); to bury. Also *fig.*
c **1330** *Arth. & Merl.* 1027 (Kölbing), No schal þer neuer no iustise þe bidelue..No in erþe þi bodi reke. **1340–70** *Alex. & Dind.* 594 ȝour bodies..better riht hadde In rouh erþe to be reke to roten hure bonus. *c* **1386** CHAUCER *Reeve's Prol.* 28 Yet in oure Asshen olde is fyr yreke. *c* **1412** HOCCLEVE *De Reg. Princ.* 2408 In swiche lordes is vntrouthe I-reke. [**1530** PALSGR. 684/1, I reke, I cover a thyng with asshes in the fyre (Lydgate).]

reke, obs. f. RAKE, REACH *v.*, RECK *v.*, REEK, RICK.

rekelage, variant of RECOLAGE *Obs.*

rekelness, obs. form of RACKLENESS.

†**'rekels.** *Obs.* Forms: α. 1 récels, (-ils, -eles, rœcels), rícels, rýcels, 3–5 recles, (3 -less, 4 -lis); 3 rekles, 4–5 rekels, (4 -eles, -elis, 5 -ils, -yls), 4 rikels. β. 3 recheles, -is, 5 rychellys, richelle. [OE. *récels* and *rícels* (for **riecels*), f. *récan* to REEK *v.*¹: see -ELS. ON. *reykelse* is from OE.] Incense.
α. *c* **950** *Lindisf. Gosp.* Matt. ii. 11 Gold, cursumbor & recels. —— Luke i. 9 [He] eode þætte [he] rœcels ȝesette. *c* **1000** *Sax. Leechd.* II. 56 Wiþ seaðan, recels lytel, swefl,..weax [etc.]. *c* **1200** ORMIN 1744 Þatt recless þatt te bisscopp þær Biforenn allterr brennde. *a* **1300** *E.E. Psalter* cxl. 2 Mi bede be righted als rekles in þi sight. *c* **1325** *Metr. Hom.* 97 The tother gift..Was rekelis, for wel thai wiste, That rekelis bisend his goddhede. *a* **1400–50** *Alexander* 4977 Rase neuire of Aromitike sike rekils in erthe. *c* **1450** *M.E. Med. Bk.* (Heinrich) 225 Do þer to pouder recles of resyn. **1483** *Cath. Angl.* 302/2 Rekels, *jncensum*.
β. *c* **1200** *Trin. Coll. Hom.* 45 Rechelis for his swetnesse bitocneð inwardliche bede. *a* **1225** *Ancr. R.* 376 Mirre he set biuoren, & recheles kumeð efter. *c* **1440** *Promp. Parv.* 433/1 Rychellys (*K.* richelle), *thus, incensum*.
Hence †**rekel(s)-fat,** censer. *Obs.*
c **1000** *Ælfric Num.* xvi. 46 Nim þin recelsfæ t. *c* **1200** *Trin. Coll. Hom.* 133 Zacharie..gede in þe temple mid his rechel fat. *c* **1200** ORMIN 135 He toc hiss reclefatt onn hand. *c* **1250** *Gen. & Ex.* 3782 For chore wel wiste ðat Gret fier wond vt of is reclefat.

†**'reken,** *a. Obs.* [OE. *recen* = OFris. *rekon* and LG. *reken* (of a street) clear, open, unobstructed (see Richthofen), perh. related to OS. *rekôn* to put in order. In Eng. only as a poetic word of very lax application.]
1. Rapid, violent, terrible. (OE. only.)
c **900** CYNEWULF *Christ* 809 Blac rasetteð recen reada leȝ. *c* **1000** *Ags. Ps.* (Th.) cv. 18 [God] worhte..recene wundur on þam Readan Sæ.
2. Of persons: Ready, prompt; straightforward, upright.
a **1000** *Waldere* ii. 26 Mæȝ siȝe syllan se ðe symle byð recen and rædfest. *c* **1250** *Gen. & Ex.* 3485 Cumeð her forð, and beð alle reken, And lereð wel quat he sal speken. *a* **1310** in Wright *Lyric P.* v. 27 He is..Rekene ase Regnas resoun to rede. **13..** *E.E. Allit. P.* B. 738 If fyue faylen of fyfty þe noumbre, & þe remnaunt be reken, how restes þy wylle? **13..** *S. Erkenwolde* 245 in Horstm. *Altengl. Leg.* (1881) 271, I was ryȝtwis & rekene & redy of þe laghe. ? *a* **1400** *Morte Arth.* 4081 The rekeneste redy mene of þe Rownde Table.
b. Of language: ? Honest, sincere.
13.. *E.E. Allit. P.* B. 756, I schal my þro steke..& my rankor refrayne for þy reken wordez.
3. Smooth, elegant, beautiful, gay.
13.. *E.E. Allit. P.* A. 5 So rounde, so reken in vche araye, So smal, so smoþe her sydez were. *Ibid.* 906, & þou so ryche a reken rose. *Ibid.* B. 1082 Rial ryngande rotes & þe reken fyþel.

reken(en, obs. forms of RECKON *v.*

†**'rekenly,** *adv. Obs.* Forms: 1 (h)recon-, recun-, ricenlice, 4 rekenly, 4–5 rekin-, rekynd-, rakenly. [OE. *recenlice*: see REKEN *a.* and -LY².] **a.** Quickly, immediately, promptly. **b.** Properly, fully.
c **950** *Lindisf. Gosp.* Matt. xxviii. 8 And [hia] eodun hreconlice from byrȝenne mið eȝ e. —— Mark i. 31 And reconlice [*Rushw.* ricenlice] forleort hia hal from februm. **13..** *E.E. Allit. P.* B. 127 He wolde se þe semble..& rehayte rekenly þe riche & þe poueren. **13..** *Gaw. & Gr. Knt.* 251 Þenn Arþour..rekenly hym reuerenced, for rad was he neuer. *a* **1400–50** *Alexander* 2354 Domystyne..rekinly [*v.r.* rakenly] rase & rekyns þire wordis.

rekenth, obs. variant of *reckan* RACKAN.

rekeny, obs. form of RECKON *v.*

rekeouer, rekeu(e)re, etc., obs. ff. RECOVER *v.*

rekil: see RICKLE *v.*

re'kill, *v.* [RE- 5 a.] *trans.* To kill again.
1654 FULLER *Comm. Ruth* (1868) 146 Re-killing him with their torments, fetch him again with comfortable things.

rekils, variant of REKELS *Obs.*

rekin(e, obs. forms of RECKON *v.*

rekindle (riː'kɪnd(ə)l), *v.* [RE- 5 a.]
1. *trans.* To kindle again, set fire to afresh. (Freq. in fig. context.)
1593 NASHE *Foure Lett. Confut.* Wks. (Grosart) II. 212 That thou shouldst..rekindle against him the sparkes of displeasure that were quenched. **1660** BOYLE *New Exp. Phys. Mech.* xi. 79 The Coals began to be re-kindled in several places. *a* **1711** KEN *Urania* Poet. Wks. 1721 IV. 431 Soon as my sight Charissa bless'd, She Fire re-kindled in my Breast. **1797** *Encycl. Brit.* (ed. 3) XIV. 627/1 The phosphorus may be frequently rekindled by means of light. **1862** S. ST. JOHN *Life Forests Far East* II. 98 The ashes of the fires were still warm, and we had no difficulty in rekindling them.
b. *fig.* To inflame afresh, rouse anew.
1652 EARL. MONM. tr. *Bentivoglio's Hist. Relat.* 19 When news was brought that the kings anger was rekindled against the Dutch. **1711** SHAFTESB. *Charact.* (1737) II. 361 Let me advise you..that since you have rekindled me, you do not by delaying give me time to cool again. **1781** GIBBON *Decl. & F.* xxxvi. III. 481 Their ambition was soon rekindled. **1821** SHELLEY *Adonais* ii, One, with soft enamoured breath, Rekindled all the fading melodies. **1860** TYNDALL *Glac.* I. xi. 8 Hirst now undertook the task of rekindling the guide's enthusiasm.
2. *intr.* To take fire again; also *fig.*
1597 BEARD *Theatre God's Judgem.* (1612) 159 So the fire rekindled, and consumed it to nothing. **1829** W. IRVING *Granada* I. vi. 51 All his holy zeal and pious indignation rekindled at the sight. **1878** B. TAYLOR *Deukalion* I. v. 41 No will rekindles, not to war with fate.
Hence **re'kindled** *ppl. a.*, **re'kindling** *vbl. sb.* and *ppl. a.*; also **re'kindlement, re'kindler.**
1660 BOYLE *New Exp. Phys. Mech.* xiii. 85 The re-kindled Match went out again. **1737** THOMSON *To Pr. Wales* ii, Her rekindling eyes resume their fire. **1762–9** FALCONER *Shipwr.* II. 712 Horrors..rous'd to action his rekindling soul. **1838** POE *A. G. Pym* Wks. 1864 IV. 105 All the energy of rekindled hope. **1846** MAURICE *Relig. World* I. iii. (1861) 70 The rekindler of feelings, which had been existing previously. **1855** BAILEY *Mystic* 49 At the great rekindling, when the heavens Shall shine with souls in galaxies. **1883**

Athenæum 24 Feb. 244/3 The occasional rekindlement of the flame by the renewal of 'sight and touch'.

re'king, *v.* [RE- 5 a.] To make king again.
1586 WARNER *Alb. Eng.* III. xvi, You hassard lesse, re-kinging him, Then I vn-king'd to bee.

re'kiss, *v.* [RE- 5 a.] *trans.* To kiss again. Hence **re'kissing** *vbl. sb.*
1588 GREENE *Alcida* Wks. (Grosart) IX. 47 Who receiving it, kissed and rekissed it. **1651** T. STANLEY *Poems* 114 Yet I'le kisse thee dead, Kisse and rekisse thee. **1760–72** H. BROOKE *Fool of Qual.* (1809) I. 112, I..kissed and re-kissed her cold lips. **1885** W. P. BREED *Aboard & Abroad* 156 At Queenstown we..saw the kissings and rekissings..at the separation of parents with daughters.

rekke, obs. f. RACK *sb.*[1], RECK *v.*

rekken(e, obs. ff. RECKON *v.*

rekles, obs. f. RECKLESS; var. REKELS *Obs.*

reknare, -ner, obs. ff. RECKONER.

rekne(n, -nyn, obs. ff. RECKON *v.*

re'knit, *v.* Also 7 **-knette**. [RE- 5 a.] *trans.* To knit (up) again, refasten.
1606 SYLVESTER *Du Bartas* II. iv. II. *Tropheis* 774 What frantick furie art thou mov'd with-all, To now re-knit my broken thred of life? **1616** J. LANE *Contn. Sqr.'s T.* XII. Proem, Canac the Falcon and Tercelets love reknettes. **1850** W. R. WILLIAMS *Relig. Progr.* I. (1854) 200 The renewal of the parental reknits the fraternal tie. **1875** MCLAREN *Serm.* Ser. II. iv. 63 The old bonds are all re-knit.

re'know, *v. rare.* [RE-.] *trans.* †**a.** To know in turn. *Obs.* **b.** To know again.
1606 DRUMM. OF HAWTH. *Answ. to Challenge* Wks. (1711) 233 Most tonitruous, astonishing Chevaliers, Re-know ye, that we..have ecchoed in the Vault of our Understanding, the Volley of your Desires. **1846** BROWNING *Luria* v, Old memories reappear, old truth returns, Our slow thought does its work, and all's re-known.

†**re'knowledge**, *v. Obs.* [f. RE- + KNOWLEDGE *v.*, after L. *recognōscĕre* or F. *reconnaître*: see RECOGNIZE *v.*]

1. *trans.* To acknowledge. (Common in 16th c.)
*c*1440 *Alph. Tales* (E.E.T.S.) 331 þan þis wrichid womman was conpuncte & reknowlegid hur selfe þat sho accusid þis holye man of verray rancor & ill will. **1502** *Ord. Crysten Men* (W. de W. 1506) III. iii. O ij b, A noble man.. vnto his goostly fader reknowleged and confessed vpon the loyalte of his fayth that [etc.]. **1582** BENTLEY *Mon. Matrones* 54 That falling maketh them..to reknowledge the goodnesse of God, and to come to him for..helpe. **1625** PURCHAS *Pilgrims* II. 1129 The new Presbyter receiving of these Jews friendly entertainment and reknowledged for their Lord.

2. *Mil.* To reconnoitre, examine. Also *absol.*
1582 N. LICHEFIELD tr. *Castanheda's Conq. E. Ind.* I. 11 b, The Generall thought it necessarie to reknowledge or haue notice of that Countrie. **1598** BARRET *Theor. Warres* 104 Hee is to reknowledge his quarters very well. *Ibid.*, It then concerneth him to reknowledge, foresee, and to prouide.

3. To recognize (a person). *rare*$^{-1}$.
1611 ASTON *Mann. All Nations* III. xxv. 463 Oftentimes they take the children from their nurses, least mothers should afterwards reknowledge their owne sonnes.

Hence †**re'knowledging** *vbl. sb.*; also †**re'knowledgement**, acknowledgement. *Obs.*
1549 COVERDALE, etc. *Erasm. Par. Thess.* Ded., As a monument and reknowlaginge of my moste bounden duetie. **1579** FENTON *Guicciard.* (1618) 120 The reknowledging of the rights of such as aspired to it. **1598** BARRET *Theor. Warres* 107 He missed and erred in the reknowledging thereof. *Ibid.* IV. i. 118 That the souldiers doe obey their.. officers with great humilitie, and reknowledgement.

rekon, -oun, obs. forms of RECKON *v.*

rekouer(e, -kower, obs. forms of RECOVER *v.*

reky, obs. form of REEKY.

rekyls, variant of REKELS *Obs.*

†**rekyn**, *v. Obs. rare*$^{-1}$. [Of obscure origin.] *trans.* ? To control, keep still.
*a*1400–50 *Alexander* 21, I sall rehers, and ȝe will, renkis, rekyn ȝour tongis, A remnant of his rialte.

rekyng(e, obs. ff. REEKING *vbl. sb.*

rekyuer-, obs. variant of RECOVER *v.*

-rel, or **-erel** (also formerly *-ral, -ril*), a diminutive and depreciatory suffix, in some cases representing OF. *-erel* (mod.F. *-ereau*) or *-erelle*, but in the majority of instances attached to native stems, or occurring in words of obscure origin: see the etym. notes to *cockerel, dotterel, hoggerel, mackerel, pickerel; doggerel; gomerel, haverel, stammerel; bedrel, custrel, gamphrel, gangrel, mongrel, scoundrel, wastrel; costrel, kestrel.*

re'label, *v.* [RE- 5 a.] *trans.* To label again.
1887 *Pall Mall G.* 5 Sept. 11/1 Goods..shipped to Sheffield and then relabelled so as to sell as Sheffield goods. **1896** *28th Rep. Dep. Kpr. Irel.* 36 The Chancery Sealed Depositions in 580 causes have been relabelled.

relace, obs. form of RELEASE *sb.*

‖**relâche** (rəlaʃ). [Fr.] A period of rest, an interval; a break *from* something.
1863 A. J. MUNBY *Diary* 10 Apr. in D. Hudson *Munby* (1972) 155 Caldwell's is one of the few public dancing rooms in London, which is frequented by respectable women... When we arrived, the relâche was begun. **1905** G. BELL *Let.* 24 Oct. (1927) I. xi. 226 Tonight he has asked Yves Guyot to dinner because I said I wanted to see him, so we shall have a little 'relâche' from archaeology. **1910** W. S. BLUNT *Let.* 19 Mar. in R. S. Churchill *Winston S. Churchill* (1969) II. Compan. II. xv. 1159 Wd you rather have a *relâche* from politics?

relacion, -cioun, -cyon, obs. ff. RELATION.

re'lade, *v.* [RE- 5 a.] *trans.* and *intr.* To lade again.
1608 in *Capt. Smith's Wks.* (Arb.) 409 Captaine Smith rather desired to relade her with Cedar. **1632** *St. Papers, Col., E. Indies* 311 A want of stock to relade to the amount aforesaid. **1643** *Declar. Commons, Rebell. Ireland* 48 Two Ships..to relade corn for the reliefe of the Protestant Armie in Vlster. **1722** DE FOE *Col. Jack* (1840) 328 These galleons relade for their return. **1776** PENNANT *Brit. Zool.* III. 174 (Jod.), A Ship of Hull to sail to Iceland, and there relade fish and other goods. **1865** W. G. PALGRAVE *Arabia* I. 8 We were aroused to relade our beasts.

rela'ment, *v.* [RE- 5 a.] *trans.* To lament afresh. Hence **rela'mented** *ppl. a.*
1630 QUARLES *Alph. Elegies* ii, 'Tis knowne, They finde enough to relament their owne [griefs]. **1636** —— *Elegie on Sir J. Cæsar*, He..whose relamented death Estates our griefe.

re'land, *v.* [RE- 5 a.] *trans.* and *intr.* To land again. Hence **re'landing** *vbl. sb.*
a. *trans.* **1710** *Act 8 Anne* Pub. Gen. Acts 217 Great Quantities of such Tobacco..have been Privately Re-landed in this Realm. **1710** *Lond. Gaz.* No. 4701/2 The re-landing of Goods exported. **1759** *Ann. Reg.* 98 The sword-blades appeared, which were ordered to be re-landed at the custom-house. **1836** W. IRVING *Astoria* III. 155 That he should be relanded in October, at Astoria, by the Beaver. **1884** SIR C. BOWEN in *Law Rep.* 13 *Q.B. Div.* 91 On her return thither the cargo was relanded and warehoused.
b. *intr.* **1773** *Life N. Frowde* 39 After they had delivered their Cargo, and re-landed in the Port of London. **1829** H. MURRAY *N. Amer.* I. v. 253 The passengers were obliged to reland.

†**re'lank**, *v. Obs. rare*$^{-1}$. [RE- 5 a.] *intr.* To become lank again.
1545 RAYNOLD *Byrth Mankynde* H h iv, At the last [they] haue voided such like lumps of blud..where withal there bellyes haue relanked and decreased agayne.

re'lapsable, *a.* [f. RELAPSE *v.*] Capable of relapsing or liable to relapse (Ogilvie 1882).

†**relap'sarian**. *Obs. rare*$^{-1}$. [f. RELAPSE *sb.* + *-arian*: cf. INFRALAPSARIAN.] *Theol.* One who believes in the possibility of relapse.
1700 C. NESSE *Antid. Armin.* (1827) 70 The Arminians.. may..also be stiled relapsarians for saying that the elect may totally and finally fall away.

†**relap'sation**. *Obs. rare*$^{-1}$. [app. f. L. *relaps-* (see RELAPSE *v.*) + -ATION, but perh. a mistake for *relaxation*.] ? Falling away.
1569 R. ANDROSE tr. *Alexis' Secr.* IV. III. 36 To heale the relapsation of the gummes.

relapse (rɪ'læps), *sb.*[1] Also 6 **relaps**. [f. the vb.; cf. LAPSE *sb.*]

1. A falling back into error, heresy, or wrongdoing; backsliding.
1533–4 *Act 25 Hen. VIII*, c. 14 §6 Yf they..after abiuracion fall in relapse..they shalbe..burned. **1570** FOXE *A. & M.* (ed. 2) 941/2 Not to departe thence without licence of the Prior for the tyme beyng, vpon payne of relapse. *a*1628 PRESTON *Effect. Faith* (1631) 69 When a sin is committed we should labour to recover our selves out of that relapse. **1667** MILTON *P.L.* IV. 100 Which would but lead me to a worse relapse, And heavier fall. **1713** STEELE *Guardian* No. 19 ⁋3 His mind would be still open to honour and virtue in spite of infirmities and relapses. **1784** COWPER *Task* v. 626 A presage ominous, portending still Its own dishonour by a worse relapse. **1869** J. BALDW. BROWN *Misread Passages* ix. 124 Relapse into idolatry..was a very pressing peril.

2. The fact of falling back again into an illness after a partial recovery; return of a disease or illness during the period of convalescence.
1584 COGAN *Heaven Health* ccxliii. (1636) 317 After that time to sleepe and eat at pleasure, yet measurably for feare of relaps. **1601** HOLLAND *Pliny* II. 391 Those agues which by way of relapse vse often to return againe. **1631** GOUGE *God's Arrows* I. Ded., A very dangerous disease..further increased by two relapses. **1652** GATAKER *Antinom.* B ij, A.. sicknesse, that brought me very low, and some relapses, that kept me down. **1686** LUTTRELL *Brief Rel.* (1857) I. 390 The King of France hath had a relapse of his distemper. *a*1721 SHEFFIELD (Dk. Buckhm.) *Wks.* (1753) I. 36 In love, that languishing disease, A sad relapse we ne'er recover. **1770** BURKE *Corr.* (1844) I. 228 It was a slow fever, with frequent appearances of amendment, and frequent relapses. **1840** DICKENS *Old C. Shop* xi, He was soon led on by the malicious dwarf to smoke himself into a relapse. **1876** BRISTOWE *Th. & Pract. Med.* (1878) 197 A second and perhaps a third relapse succeed.

†**3.** Failure to meet a claim within the proper time. *Obs. rare.*
1593 NASHE *Christ's T.* 47 For a hundred pound commodity..he recouers, by relapse, some hundred pound a yeere. **1631** HEYWOOD *Maid of West* v. Wks. 1874 II. 325 A French merchant runne into relapse And forfeit of the Law.

4. The act of falling or sinking back again.
1876 SWINBURNE *Erechtheus* 1364 The lift and relapse of the wave of the chargers. **1878** BROWNING *Poets Croisic* lxiv, Every dart of every aim..That touches just, then seems, by strange relapse, To fall effectless from the soul.

5. ? A rally, effort at recovery.
1817 SHELLEY *Rev. Islam* XII. xvi, One brief relapse, like the last beam Of dying flames..a blood-red gleam Burst upwards.

relapse (rɪ'læps), *sb.*[2] and *a.* Now *rare.* Also 7 **relaps** (*sing.* and *pl.*). [ad. L. *relaps-us*, pa. pple. of *relābī*: cf. F. *relaps* m., *relapse* f.]

A. *sb.* A relapsed person; one who has fallen again into error or heresy. (Cf. RELAPSER.)
1546 *Reg. Privy Council Scot.* I. 61 The heretikis that ar relapsis. **1592** NASHE *P. Penilesse* (ed. 2) 37 b, When a man is a relapse from God and his Lawes. **1606** WARNER *Alb. Eng.* XIV. lxxxix. 362 Although a Recluse yet to be a Relaps feare thou neuer. **1683** *Apol. Prot. France* iii. 2 The Prisons in France are full of these pretended Relaps. **1699** BURNET *39 Art.* xxv. (1700) 278 They never gave a second Absolution to the Relapse. **1736** CHANDLER *Hist. Persec.* 266 If the Person accused is found a Relapse by his own Confession, he can't escape Death. **1820** RANKEN *Hist. France* VIII. II. ii. 274 They were commanded to receive no converts nor relapses from the Catholic body.

B. *adj.* = RELAPSED *ppl. a. rare*$^{-1}$.
1683 *Apol. Prot. France* ii. 13 What was particular to Ecclesiasticks and Relapse Protestants, is now become universal to all Roman Catholicks.

relapse (rɪ'læps), *v.* Also 6 **relaps**. [f. L. *relaps-*, ppl. stem of *relābī* to slip back: see RE- and LAPSE *v.*]

1. *intr.* To fall back into wrong-doing or error; to backslide; *spec.* to fall again into heresy after recantation. Const. *into, to*; also without const.
1570 FOXE *A. & M.* (ed. 2) 940/2 You be not onely.. impenitent, disobedient,..and relapsed by this your.. hereticall demeanour, but [etc.]. **1639** FULLER *Holy War* II. xxxix. (1840) 102 These Maronites..received the Catholic faith; though soon after..they relapsed to their old errors. **1651** HOBBES *Leviath.* I. xii. 59 The Children of Israel.. relapsed into the Idolatry of the Egyptians. *a*1740 WATERLAND *View Doctr. Justif.* Wks. 1823 IX. 464 Then they enter into the justified state, and so continue all along, unless they relapse. **1773** MRS. CHAPONE *Improv. Mind* (1774) II. 2 When you are your own mistress, you may relapse into..faults. **1824** J. H. NEWMAN *Hist. Sk.* (1873) II. II. i. 247 Cicero..late in life..relapsed into the sceptical tenets of his former instructor Philo. **1855** BREWSTER *Newton* II. xxiv. 357 The tendency of the Church of England to relapse into Romish superstition.

2. To fall back into an illness after partial recovery or from a convalescent state.
1568 GRAFTON *Chron.* II. 858 He should be then cleerely delyuered of his disease: Yet not so cleane rid of it, but that he might shortly relaps. **1655** CULPEPPER, etc. *Riverius* I. ii. 15 They which have been troubled with any of these Diseases..do use many times to relapse and fal into the same again. **1681** *Lond. Gaz.* No. 1586/3 The Prince of Parma is relapsed, and has his Feavor again. **1706–7** FARQUHAR *Beaux' Strat.* IV. i, Your Servant has been telling me that you're apt to relapse if you go into the Air. **1778** JOHNSON *Let. to Mrs. Thrale* 15 Oct., He was mending before he went, and surely he has not relapsed. **1855** KANE *Arct. Expl.* (1856) II. i. 11 Mr. Wilson has relapsed. I..took his place at watch.
transf. **1878** BROWNING *Poets Croisic* xlix, The red fire.. Rallies, relapses, dwindles, deathward sinks!

b. Of stock: To fall again in value.
1896 *Daily News* 15 Dec. 9/1 Home Railway stocks have relapsed to-day.

3. To fall back or sink again *into* (†or *to*) any state, practice, etc.
1593 NASHE *Christ's T.* To Rdr., Into some splenative vaines of wantonnesse, heeretofore have I foolishlie relapsed. **1603** FLORIO *Montaigne* (1634) 300 Our minde doth still relapse into the same depth. **1643** PRYNNE *Sov. Power Parlt.* II. 36 So that..he might more grievously relapse into the said denounced sentence. **1716–7** BENTLEY *Serm.* iii. Wks. 1838 III. 265 He sustains them from relapsing into nothing. **1751** GRAY *Lett.* (1904) II. App. 297 The Chorus..when their vagaries are over, relapse again into common sense and conversation. **1820** W. IRVING *Sketch Bk.* I. 44 When he had relapsed into moody silence, I resumed the subject gently. **1864** D. G. MITCHELL *Sev. Stor.* 55 He relapsed into a musing mood.

†**b.** To fall away *from* a person. *Obs.*
1633 T. STAFFORD *Pac. Hib.* I. v. 35 Hee feared to run into any such inconvenience, as might cause his friends to relapse from him. **1687** DRYDEN *Hind & P.* II. 486 You slip your hold and change your side, Relapsing from a necessary guide.

c. To fall again *under* some one's power. *rare.*
1847 GROTE *Greece* II. xxxv. (1862) III. 251 Salamis relapsed under the sway of its former despot Gorgus.

†**4.** To fall back from a height. *Obs. rare*$^{-1}$.
1638 [see RELAPSING *ppl. a.*].

†**5.** *trans.* To cause to fall back. *Obs.*
1652 COTTERELL tr. *Calprenède's Cassandra* II. 86 Such transportments of passion as were likely to have relaps'd him into his former condition. **1668** H. MORE *Div. Dial.* IV. xxxvii. (1713) 394 Whoever revives to him any hope of recovery, relapses that Kingdom into the state of the first Vial. **1773** J. ROSS *Fratricide* I. 473 (MS.), Some Hellish scheme to still relapse The spleen of Cain.

relapsed (rɪ'læpst), *ppl. a.* [f. prec. + -ED[1].] Fallen back into a previous condition.
1570 FOXE *A. & M.* (ed. 2) 943/1 Asked..why he should not..be pronounced a relapsed hereticke. **1607** TOPSELL

Four-f. Beasts (1658) 145 They..recover for a small time, and then fall into a relapsed malady. **1683** *Apol. Prot. France* ii. 13 The Prisons..are at this present filled with this sort of pretended Relapsed Persons. **1777** WATSON *Philip II*, xx. (1793) III. 49 A relapsed heretic and a determined enemy of their holy faith. **1850** O. WINSLOW *Inner Life* 164 A relapsed state of the spiritual life.

relapser (rɪˈlæpsə(r)). [f. as prec. + -ER[1].] One who relapses, esp. into error or sin.

c **1625** BP. HALL *St. Paul's Combat* I. Wks. 1837 V. 303 Those speculative relapsers that have..abandoned a knowne and received truth. **1636** FEATLY *Clavis Myst.* xl. 610 Back-sliders and relapsers as ye are. **1685** EVELYN *Diary* 3 Nov., Forcing people to the Masse, and then executing them as relapsers. **1745** WESLEY *Wks.* (1872) VIII. 224 The relapsers were often so hardened in sin, that no impression could be made upon them. **1882–3** SCHAFF *Encycl. Relig. Knowl.* I. 182/1 The relapsers, and those who refused to recant, were expelled from the church.

relapsing (rɪˈlæpsɪŋ), *vbl. sb.* [f. as prec. + -ING[1].] The action of the vb. RELAPSE.

1611 SPEED *Hist. Gt. Brit.* IX. xvi. (1623) 834 Conuicted of periurious relapsing. **1648** MILTON *Tenure Kings* Wks. 1851 IV. 477 The Presbyterians..cannot with all their shifting and relapsing, wash off the guiltiness from thir own hands. **1772** PRIESTLEY in *Phil. Trans.* LXII. 194, I had instances of the relapsing of this restored air to its former noxious state. **1865** *Reader* No. 124. 540/3 The relapsings and rallyings of Christendom.

reˈlapsing, *ppl. a.* [-ING[2].] **a.** That relapses.

1638 MAYNE *Lucian* (1664) 211 Forced to roll relapsing stones against steep hills. **1653** G. DANIEL *Idyll., Occas. Refl.* 20 Dead wth ye Terror of relapsing crimes. **1864** PUSEY *Lect. Daniel* vii. 456 God..won Nebuchadnezzar, as he does so many relapsing Christians.

b. ***relapsing fever***, either of two similar kinds of fever characterized by relapses, caused by spirochætes of the genus *Borrelia* and transmitted respectively by lice and by ticks.

1849 *Dublin Q. Jrnl. Med. Sci.* VIII. 50 This fever has been well called a relapsing fever; that is, it was made up of two parts, crisis being very generally present at the termination of each. **1865** *Morn. Star* 20 Apr., Two forms of fever which are known in this country as relapsing fever and typhus. **1877** ROBERTS *Handbk. Med.* (ed. 3) I. 131 Relapsing fever is an acute specific disease,..and it is highly infectious. **1936** *Lancet* 22 Feb. 448/1 Recent investigation of a small outbreak of relapsing fever in Kfar Vitkin, south of Hedera in the coastal plain, showed that all infections could be traced to a cave infested with *Ornithodorus papillipes.* **1966** DUNLOP & ALSTEAD *Textbk. Med. Treatment* (ed. 10) 218 Tetracycline..is the drug of choice, although subsequent relapses of tick-borne relapsing fever due to *Bor. duttoni* may be experienced. **1974** PASSMORE & ROBSON *Compan. Med. Stud.* III. xii. 75/1 The spirochaetes responsible for louse-borne relapsing fever is *Borr[elia] recurrentis* and for the tick-borne form, *Borr. duttoni. Ibid.*, Louse-borne relapsing fever is a disease of cold weather which occurs in epidemic form usually in the wake of disasters such as wars or earthquakes.

†**reˈlasch**, *a. Obs. rare*$^{-1}$. [ad. F. *relâché*, f. *relâcher* to relax.] Relaxed, careless.

1663 HEATH *Flagellum, or O. Cromwell* (1672) 31 Thereby to beget in them a relasch and contemptuous neglect of so base and despicable an Enemy.

relata: see RELATUM.

relatable (rɪˈleɪtəb(ə)l), *a.* [f. RELATE *v.* + -ABLE.] **a.** That may be narrated. **b.** That may be brought into relation with something else. Also, that may be shown to possess mutual relation. Now usu. with *to*. Hence **relataˈbility**.

1825 HONE *Every-day Bk.* I. 1466 The compliments..are not relatable. **1897** *Bookman* Jan. 119/1 He does not seem to have indulged in many relatable amusements. **1937** *Burlington Mag.* July 58/2 The 'relatability' of pictorial forms..follows on the artist's realization of their basis, undifferentiated essentials. **1956** *Jrnl. Theol. Stud.* VII. 88 It is found that 38·5 per cent. of the elements of psalm language is certainly not relatable to psalm contents; the relatability of a large part of the remainder thus becomes questionable. **1964** *Language* XL. 244 A proposal for the relatability of two languages..has been traditionally based on the discovery of systematic sound correspondences between certain of their forms. **1975** T. F. MITCHELL in W. F. Bolton *Eng. Lang.* iv. 165 *Blackboard* is less obviously relatable to *black board* than *blackbird* is to *black bird.*

relate (rɪˈleɪt), *sb.* Also 7 relat. [ad. L. *relātus*, *-a*, *-um*, pa. pple. of *referre*, taken substantively: see RELATE *v.*]

†**1.** A relation, relative. *Obs.*

1651 *Fuller's Abel Rediv., Beza* (1867) II. 218, I am he To whom an infant can no relate be. **1656** S. H. *Gold. Law* 75 Nor were his neer relates, Aaron and Miriam, favoured.

2. *Logic.* One of two objects of thought between which a relation subsists.

1633 AMES *Agst. Cerem.* I. 31 All relates are mutuall causes one of another. **1697** tr. *Burgersdicius' Logic* I. vii. 23 If the Relation..has a Name, one of the two is called the Relate, to wit, that from which the Relation has its name; the other, the Correlate. **1883** GILMAN in *Studies in Logic* 108 The number of instances in which the relation *P'* occurs having a relate which is an object in the universe.

†**reˈlate**, *ppl. a. Obs. rare*$^{-1}$. [ad. L. *relātus*, pa. pple. of *referre*: see next.] Related.

1658 PHILLIPS *Myst. Love* 269 The enunciate of a relate quality is of this kinde, whose conjunction is the relation itself.

relate (rɪˈleɪt), *v.* [f. L. *relāt-*, ppl. stem of *referre* to REFER. Cf. F. *relater* (14th c.).]

I. *trans.* †**1.** In *pass.* **a.** To be borne or thrust in *between* things. *Obs. rare*$^{-1}$.

1490 CAXTON *Eneydos* xxii. 78 The more thicke & depper ben his rotes spred wythin therthe, & related bytwyx the harde roches.

b. To be referred or put *into* a class. *Obs.*$^{-1}$

1542 BECON *Pathw. Prayer* vii. Wks. 1564 I. 64 Who would not haue thought thys holy religious father worthy to be canonised and related into the nomber of Saynctes?

2. a. To recount, narrate, tell, give an account of (actions, events, facts, etc.). †Also with dative pron. (quot. 1652).

1530 PALSGR. 684/1, I wolde nat relate the mater otherwyse than I herde it for all the good in the worlde. **1582** N. LICHEFIELD tr. *Castanheda's Conq. E. Ind.* I. i. 3 b, Letters..wherein hee related and fully declared..what hee had seene in the Indias. **1652** J. WRIGHT tr. *Camus' Nat. Paradox* XII. 328 Hee took the pains to relate him every particular that had pass'd since his imprisonment. **1695** WOODWARD *Nat. Hist. Earth* I. (1723) 1 Observations..both carefully made and faithfully Related. **1749** FIELDING *Tom Jones* VIII. x, If you desire..to hear the story of an unhappy man, I will relate it to you. **1820** W. IRVING *Sketch Bk.* I. 42 He came to me one day and related his whole situation. **1887** BOWEN *Virg. Æneid* II. 548 Take these tidings thou, and relate this news to my sire.

†**b.** With compl.; also const. *inf. Obs. rare.*

1622 DRAYTON *Poly-olb.* xxiv. 593 This man with those before, most worthily related Arch-saints, as in their Sees Arch-bishops consecrated. **1656** STANLEY *Hist. Philos.* v. (1701) 155/1 Plato was out of doubt an Athenian, nor are they to be credited who relate him a Theban. **1660** F. BROOKE tr. *Le Blanc's Trav.* 22 They relate Dalatia in Æthiopia, to be opposite to Meka.

†**c.** To give an account of (a person). *Obs.*

1653 HOLCROFT *Procopius* Pref., Procopius..impartially discoursing of Justinian, and the great ones, doth as much arraign, as relate them to posterity. **1667** MILTON *P.L.* VII. 604 What thought can measure thee or tongue Relate thee.

†**d.** *refl.* To unburden (oneself) *to*. *Obs. rare*$^{-1}$.

1625 BACON *Ess., Friendship* (Arb.) 175 A Man were better relate himselfe, to a Statua, or Picture, then to suffer his Thoughts to passe in smother.

†**3.** To bring back, restore. *Obs. rare*$^{-1}$.

1590 SPENSER *F.Q.* III. viii. 51 Abate Your zealous hast, till morrow next againe Both light of heven and strength of men relate.

†**4. a.** To refer (a person) *to* a book, etc. *Obs.*

1657 J. SERGEANT *Schism Dispach't* 355 Gulling the unwary Reader that all is pure scripture,..relating us to a place where the most important words are wanting.

†**b.** To adduce, cite (an authority). *Obs.*$^{-1}$

1604 T. WRIGHT *Passions* (1620) 311 Galen, to this purpose, relateth Aesop, who said [etc.].

5. a. To bring (a thing or person) into relation *to* another.

1697 J. SERGEANT *Solid Philos.* 455 But so does the Thing infer the Word too, to which we..do relate it. **1833** CHALMERS *Const. Man* I. iii. (1834) I. 139 The law which relates an object, whether present or thought upon, to its appropriate emotion. **1866** HOWELLS *Venet. Life* 176 He pretends to relate the truth you feel to certain moral and religious conditions.

refl. **1856** MASSON *Ess. Biog. & Crit.* 22 How, then, did Shakespeare relate himself to this concrete world of nature? **1879** M. ARNOLD *Mixed Ess.* 187 It is not fully clear how they [words] relate themselves to the context.

b. To connect, to establish a relation between.

1771 LUCKOMBE *Hist. Printing* 267 A Point of more elevation than a Comma, which helps to relate the matter more distinctly. **1846** GROVE *Corr. Phys. Forces* 38 Volta..first enabled us definitely to relate the forces of chemistry and electricity. **1889** E. CAIRD *Philos. Kant* I. I. i. 273 If we hold Kant to the distinction which he makes between perception and conception, it seems impossible to relate them.

II. *intr.* **6.** *Law.* To refer *back*, to have application *to* an earlier date. (Cf. RELATION 4 b.)

1596 BACON *Max. & Use Com. Law* II. (1636) 41 It hath beene much doubted by the law bookes whether the lord's title by escheat shall relate back to the time of the offence done. **1598** *Termes Lawes* 162 Petitions of parlement, to which ye Queene assents on ye last day of parlement shal relate and be of force from the first day of the beginning of the Parlement. **1885** SIR J. F. STEPHEN in *Law Times Rep.* LIII. 781/1 A change of mind after an innocent taking does not relate back to the innocent taking and make it felonious.

7. a. To have reference *to*.

1606 SHAKS. *Tr. & Cr.* I. iii. 323 This challenge that the gallant Hector sends..Relates in purpose onely to Achilles. **1641** HEYLIN *Hist. Episc.* I. (1642) 114 There was nothing left at random which either did relate to government or point of Doctrine. **1711** ADDISON *Spect.* No. 46 ¶5, I shall only give him the Letters which relate to the two last Hints. **1762–71** H. WALPOLE *Vertue's Anecd. Paint.* (1786) III. 26 The following paragraph, relating to Cromwell. **1812** SIR H. DAVY *Chem. Philos.* 12 A great variety of anecdotes relating to the transmutation of metals. **1875** JOWETT *Plato* (ed. 2) V. 499 Old persons are quick to see and hear all that relates to them.

†**b.** To be of interest or important *to*. *Obs.*$^{-1}$

1654–66 EARL ORRERY *Parthen.* (1676) 565 Can you then believe, whilst I have an existence, that your perpetual imprisonment would but relate unto your self?

†**8.** Of persons: To make reference *to*. *Obs.*

1637 HEYLIN *Antid. Lincoln.* Pref. A 7 b, I relate onely in this Antidote to the first Edition. **1655** FULLER *Hist. Cambr.* 2 The Poet, who herein seems to relate to the Hebrew and Greek Professors founded in his dayes at Cambridge.

9. a. To be related, have relation, stand in some relation, *to* another thing (†person or place).

1646 SIR T. BROWNE *Pseud. Ep.* 105 Station is properly no rest but one kinde of motion, relating unto that which Physitians..doe name extensive or tonicall. **1671** in *Cosin's Corr.* (Surtees) II. 266 Be diligent in searching your Audit-books, and inquireing of all persons that related to my predecessor. **1739** CIBBER *Apol.* (1756) II. 140 All who related to the Black-friers..are now dead and almost forgotten. **1742** POPE *Dunc.* IV. 235 The critic Eye..examines bit by bit: How parts relate to parts, or they to whole.

†**b.** Of streams: To be united *to* larger rivers or the sea. *Obs.* (Only in Walton.)

1653 WALTON *Angler* iii. 85 In divers Rivers, especially that relate to, or be near to the Sea. **1676** *Ibid.* I. xvii. (1881) 205 Case-worms, that are to be found..in several little brooks that relate to bigger rivers.

c. To feel affectively involved or connected with someone or something; to have an attitude of personal and sympathetic relationship *to*.

1950 *Childhood Educ.* Nov. 115/1 Group formation such as takes place in the classroom tends to be adult-centered and dependent upon the varying ways children relate to the teacher. **1965** *Listener* 10 June 864/2 Attitudes to other people at the unconscious level appropriate to an early stage of infancy, of the time before we learnt the capacity to relate. to whole persons. **1966** *New Statesman* 14 Oct. 549/1 The Civic Action now begins As friends and former foe relate. **1968** *Globe & Mail* (Toronto) 13 Feb. 33/8 (Advt.), Candidates should..be able to relate to senior officers of the University. **1969** C. DAVIDSON in Cockburn & Blackburn *Student Power* 361 If we only relate to on-campus issues, we run the risk of laying the counter-revolutionary groundwork. **1971** *Guardian* 7 Jan. 8/3 Married people can still relate. **1971** M. SPARK *Not to Disturb* iii. 89 'What do you mean, I don't relate?' she says. 'When you relate you don't ask what you mean. There's such a thing as a trend.' 'Who do you think you are, you—Chairman Mao?' **1977** J. L. HOULDEN *Patterns of Faith* ii. 20 It is possible to relate to him [*sc.* God] and..a Christian is one who finds that the relating is best done in ways that bear on the figure of Jesus.

†**10.** To discourse; to give an account. *Obs.*

1608 SHAKS. *Per.* III. Prol. 55, I nill relate, action may Conueniently the rest conuay. **1667** MILTON *P.L.* VI. 373, I might relate of thousands. *Ibid.* VIII. 51 Adam relating, she sole Auditress. **1747** CHESTERF. *Lett.* (1792) I. cxxviii. 343, I have Arguses..who will watch you narrowly and relate to me faithfully.

†**11.** To treat or negotiate *with* one. *Obs.*$^{-1}$.

1631 WEEVER *Anc. Funeral Mon.* 758 The said Germane Waldgraue related with Waldgraue of Northamptonshire, concerning the marriage of his said daughter.

†**12.** To appear, be evident. *Obs. rare*$^{-1}$.

1668 CULPEPPER & COLE *Barthol. Anat.* Man. I. i. 302 It hath been most clearly manifested..to that most ingenious Venetian Paul Sarpias Fulgentius, as relates from his papers.

related (rɪˈleɪtɪd), *ppl. a.* (and *sb.*) [f. prec. + -ED[1].] **A.** *ppl. a.*

1. Narrated, recited; †referred to. *rare.*

1604 T. WRIGHT *Passions* v. § 4. 191 These twentie places ..they may easily commit..to memorie, therefore I will remit this labour to the related authour. *c* **1611** CHAPMAN *Iliad* X. 291 Base Dolon..neuer turnd to harme The Greeks, with their related drifts.

2. a. Having relation *to*, or relationship *with*, something else. Also *attrib.* without const.

1662–3 PEPYS *Diary* 6 Jan., Saw Twelfth-Night acted well, though it be but a silly play, and not related at all to the name or day. **1728** WOODWARD *Fossils* 33 The same Author treating..of a nearly related Species of Star-Stone.., tells us [etc.]. **1828** CARLYLE *Misc.* (1857) I. 159 These two classes of works stand curiously related with each other. **1846** GROVE *Corr. Phys. Forces* 47 Electricity and magnetism are quantitatively related to them. **1864** BOWEN *Logic* x. 336 Of the countless Relations thus brought to our notice, many are essential to an adequate knowledge of the related object.

b. Having mutual relation or connexion.

1671 MILTON *Samson* 786 Let weakness then with weakness come to parl So near related, or the same of kind. **1690** LOCKE *Hum. Und.* II. xxv. §4 The ideas of relation may be the same in men, who have far different ideas of the things that are related. **1756** BURKE *Subl. & B.* III. xvii, The beauty both of shape and colouring are as nearly related as we can well suppose it possible. **1843** MILL *Logic* I. iii. §10 Whenever two things are said to be related there is some fact or series of facts into which they both enter. **1889** H. PARRY in Grove *Dict. Mus.* IV. 141/1 Even chords belonging to closely related keys are commonly used [etc.].

3. Of persons: Connected by blood or marriage (*to* another, or with each other).

1702 J. PURCELL *Cholick* Ded., It was no sooner known that I had the Honour to be Related to..Your Grace, but [etc.]. **1772** PRIESTLEY *Inst. Relig.* (1782) I. 319 He [John the Baptist]..had no personal knowledge of Jesus, though they were related. **1837** THIRLWALL *Greece* xxxiii. IV. 299 A Persian of the highest rank, related to the royal family. **1845** M. PATTISON *Ess.* (1889) I. 17 Persons related in the degree in which Merovig and Brunchilde were.

†**B.** *absol.* as *sb.* = RELATE *sb.* 2. *Obs.*

1697 tr. *Burgersdicius' Logic* I. vii. 22 Relateds are said either to be Synonimous, or of the same Name; or Heteronymous, *viz.* of a diverse.

Hence **reˈlatedness**, the state or condition of being related.

1865 MASSON *Rec. Brit. Philos.* 114 Theories on the subject of the relatedness or non-relatedness of the Cosmos. **1895** *Dublin Rev.* Apr. 315 The process of amalgamation was favoured by relatedness of race and language.

relater (rɪˈleɪtə(r)). [-ER[1]. Cf. RELATOR.]

1. One who relates; a narrator, historian.

1613 PURCHAS *Pilgrimage* (1614) 398 *marg.*, The Amazons are still on[e] Nation, further then the relaters or their Authors haue trauelled. **1643** MILTON *Divorce* II. xv. Wks. 1851 IV. 100 The divine relater shews us not the least signe of disliking what was done. **1729** BUTLER *Serm.* Wks. 1874 II. 130 This is not founded upon supposition..of a formed design in the relater to deceive. **1740** JOHNSON *Life Drake* Wks. IV. 380 It may easily be concluded that the relaters did not diminish the merit of their attempts. **1818** KIRBY & SP. *Entomol.* xxiv. (ed. 2) II. 384 The relater declares that he had heard it with his ears, and seen it with his eyes. **1863** J. G. MURPHY *Comm., Gen.* xliii. 21 The relater is prone to lump matters in the narration.

†**2.** One who is related *to* a person. *Obs. rare*⁻¹.

1702 *Clarendon's Hist. Reb.* v. §189 Such were continually preferred and countenanced, as were Friends, or Favourers, or Relaters [**1888** related] to the chief Authors and Actors of that Arbitrary Power.

relatif, obs. form of RELATIVE.

relation (rɪˈleɪʃən), *sb.* Also 4–7 relacion, (5 -cioun, 6 -cyon). [a. F. *relation* (14th c.), or ad. L. *relātiōn-em*: see RELATE *v.* and -ION[1].]

1. a. The action of relating in words; narration, recital, account; report. In early use esp. in phr. † *to make relation*.

1390 GOWER *Conf.* III. 77 Nectanabus..relacion Makth to the queene hou sche schal do. *c* **1430** LYDG. *Min. Poems* (Percy Soc.) 36 A riche man who, by commoun relacioun, Had gret power and myhte. **1462** *Paston Lett.* II. 112 Thus it was told me, and..it is my part to geve you relacion thereof. **1555** EDEN *Decades* 65 He knewe by relation of owre men wherof owre swoordes were made. **1578** T. N. tr. *Conq. W. India* 10 He brought perfect relation how the Countrey was riche of gold and silver. **1601** SIR W. CORNWALLIS *Ess.* II. xlvii. (1631) 296, I like no Relation so well, as what mine eye telleth me. **1671** MILTON *Samson* 1595 Give us if thou canst..Relation more particular and distinct. **1725** DE FOE *Voy. round World* (1840) 1 Whatever success they have had in the voyage they have had very little in the relation. **1800** COLERIDGE *Lett.* (1895) I. 337 As to myself, I am doing little worth the relation. **1866** G. MACDONALD *Ann. Q. Neighb.* xii. (1878) 236 The early spring will detain me with the relation of just a single incident.

Comb. **1687** A. LOVELL tr. *Thevenot's Trav.* d ij b, Those who therein are called Relation-makers, nay and the ancient Historians themselves.

b. *Law.* (See quots. and INFORMATION 5 b.)

1632 *Star Chamb. Cases* (Camden) 145 The Kings Attorney generall against my Lord Viscount Savill and others by relation of Sir John Jackson. **1710** *Act 9 Anne* c. 20 §4 Informations..at the Relation of any Person or Persons desiring to sue or prosecute the same. **1798** DALLAS *Amer. Law Rep.* II. 112 There is a distinction between informations filed by the Attorney General, and those filed by him at the relation of a private person. **1885** *Law Rep. 14 Q.B. Div.* 246 A proceeding by way of information by the Attorney-General at the relation of the Board of Works.

2. A particular instance of relating or narrating; a (or one's) narrative, account, statement.

1500–20 DUNBAR *Poems* xxx. 27 My brethir oft hes maid the supplicationis, Be epistillis, sermonis, and relationis. **1560** DAUS tr. *Sleidane's Comm.* 125 The kyng of Englande ..sent thether his Ambassade,..who in the begynning made his relation. **1596** RALEIGH *Discov. Guiana* title-p., A relation of the great and Golden Citie of Manoa. **1653** H. MORE *Antid. Ath.* III. iii. §6, I will only add one Relation more of this nature. **1712** STEELE *Spect.* No. 526 ¶3, I heard this Relation this Morning from a Gentleman who was an Eye-Witness. **1760–2** GOLDSM. *Cit. W.* cviii, Let them but read the relations of their own travellers. **1802** MAR. EDGEWORTH *Moral T.* (1816) I. 216 The countess..related the circumstances... Albert heard her relation with astonishment. **1891** J. WINSOR *Columbus* i. 1 Of such, whether memoirs, relations, or letters, sixty-four are preserved in their entirety.

3. a. That feature or attribute of things which is involved in considering them in comparison or contrast with each other; the particular way in which one thing is thought of in connexion with another; any connexion, correspondence, or association, which can be conceived as naturally existing between things.

1393 LANGL. *P. Pl.* C. IV. 335 Thus ys mede and mercede as two manere relacions. *Ibid.* 344 Knowen ich wolde What is relacion rect. **1413** *Pilgr. Sowle* (Caxton 1483) IV. xxvi. 71 Somme manere of correspondence or relacion must nedes ben bytwene the two that ben y lyke. **1589** PUTTENHAM *Eng. Poesie* III. xxiii. (Arb.) 269 So as there be found a iust correspondencie betweene them by this or that relation. **1597** MORLEY *Introd. Mus.* 76 To make your descant carrie some forme of relation to the plaine song. **1620** T. GRANGER *Div. Logike* 245 It is relation of time, or of the cause. **1690** LOCKE *Hum. Und.* II. xxv. §5 The Nature of Relation consists in the referring or comparing two things one to another. **1730** A. GORDON *Maffei's Amphith.* 328 The Manner how they were placed..has a good deal of relation with the Nature of the internal Form of the Building. **1782** PRIESTLEY *Corrupt. Chr.* I. Pref. 20 Some of my materials bear an equal relation to several..subjects. **1805–17** R. JAMESON *Char. Min.* (ed. 3) 173 The nucleus increases on its part, always preserving the same relation with the entire crystal. **1851** RUSKIN *Stones Ven.* (1874) I. Pref. 8 The relation of the life of the workman to his work. **1879** HARLAN *Eyesight* ix. 131 The size and form of the desk, and its relation to the seat, are not without their effect upon the welfare of the eyes.

b. In phr. *in* or *with relation to.*

1594 HOOKER *Eccl. Pol.* I. viii. §6 The diviner part in relation to the baser of our souls. **1659** *Gentl. Calling* vii. §8 In relation to such his Servants, he is of all other Masters the most bountiful. **1680** MOXON *Mech. Exerc.* No. x. 178 The heighth of the Legs with relation to the intended work. **1724** A. COLLINS *Gr. Chr. Relig.* 184 That proves nothing in relation to the present Samaritans. **1772** MACKENZIE *Man World* II. xi, It is only with relation to those we love that prosperity can produce happiness. **1818** COLEBROOKE *Import Colonial Corn* 7 It is not so in relation to the more distant colonies. **1852** H. ROGERS *Ecl. Faith* (1853) 2 Your nephew..has in relation to religion at least, become an absolute sceptic.

†**c.** *by relation*: by natural consequence, by implication. *Obs. rare*⁻¹.

1680 MORDEN *Geog. Rect., Japan* (1685) 426 They strictly forbid their People to speak of Religion, and by Relation as little to profess it.

d. *Logic.* A constituent of a proposition or propositional function that connects two terms (a dyadic relation) or more (triadic, *n*-adic, etc.).

1870 C. S. PEIRCE *Coll. Papers* (1933) III. iii. §47. 28 *Inclusion in* or *being as small as* is a *transitive* relation. **1885** W. JAMES in *Mind* X. 32 No relation-expressing proposition is possible except on the basis of a preliminary acquaintance with such 'facts'..as this. **1910** WHITEHEAD & RUSSELL *Princ. Math.* I. §30. 245 Functions of this kind always mean 'the term having such and such a relation to *x*'. **1940** W. V. QUINE *Math. Logic* v. 201 Relations in the sense here considered are known, more particularly, as dyadic relations. **1956** H. REICHENBACH *Direction of Time* ii. 26 When the points are in a linear order, or serial order, they are governed by an asymmetrical and transitive relation. **1965** HUGHES & LONDEY *Elem. Formal Logic* xxxix. 272 Such relations are said to be non-symmetrical relations. Examples are: 'implies', 'brother of'... Such relations are said to be non-transitive relations. Examples are: 'one mile distant from', 'first cousin of'. *Ibid.* 274 Every dyadic relation must be either reflexive or irreflexive or non-reflexive. **1978** C. KIRWAN *Logic & Argument* i. 23 A binary relation such as hating, which holds from some but not all things to themselves, is neither reflexive nor irreflexive. Likewise many binary relations are neither transitive nor intransitive and many are neither symmetrical nor asymmetrical.

e. *Philos.*, esp. as ***external relation***, a connection existing between one thing and another which is not intrinsic to the identity of the first; ***internal relation***, a connection between one thing and another which is intrinsic to the identity of the first.

1893 F. H. BRADLEY *Appearance & Reality* iii. 31 Every quality in relation has..a diversity within its own nature, and this diversity cannot immediately be asserted of the quality. Hence the quality must exchange its unity for an internal relation. *Ibid.* iv. 40 This solid unit, existing only by virtue of external relations, is forced to expand. **1922** G. E. MOORE *Philos. Stud.* 288 Yet this last, according to me, is one of the things which the dogma of internal relations denies. **1935** A. J. AYER in *Aristotelian Soc. Suppl. Vol.* XIV. 179 The connexion between the proposition which Mr. Ryle mistakes for the dogma of internal relations and the dogma of internal relations as we understand it, is that they both follow from the proposition that all a thing's characters are intrinsic to it. **1956** R. A. WOLLHEIM in A. J. Ayer *Revolution in Philos.* ii. 22 In logic this view is known as the theory of 'internal relations'. All the relations in which an object stands are rooted in its nature as firmly as triangularity is rooted in the nature of the triangle. **1975** HARGREAVES & WHITE tr. *Wittgenstein's Philos. Remarks* iii. 63 The essential difference between the picture conception and the conception of Russell, Ogden and Richards, is that it regards recognition as seeing an internal relation, whereas in their view this is an external relation.

4. a. *to have* or *make relation*: to have or make reference or allusion *to* something.

1433 *Rolls of Parlt.* IV. 451/2 Yat yis saide worde Cloth.. have relation and understondyng to hole Clothes..and not to other Clothes. **1530** PALSGR. 353 Whan so ever we use in our tonge 'the whiche'..makyng relacion to a substantyve or pronowne spoken of in the sentence next goynge before. **1592** WEST *1st Pt. Symbol.* §23 f, If not certeinly expressed, yet some relation is made to some thing whereby it may be made certein. **1596** DANETT tr. *Comines* (1614) 41 *marg.*, These words haue relation to the Earl of Charolois return into Flaunders. **1611** FLORIO, *Relatizzare*, to haue relation vnto. **1643** TRAPP *Comm. Gen.* l. 2 Some think the Apostle hath relation to this, in that 1 Cor. 15. 29. **1810** BENTHAM *Packing* (1821) 237 Relation being made to the state of the law on one hand. **1818** —— *Ch. Eng., Catech. Exam.* 354 Relation being had to certain inquiries, having for their object [etc.]. **1873** HELPS *Anim. & Mast.* iii. 60 It had relation to horses.

b. *Law* (in phr. *to have relation*). Reference or application *to* an earlier date (cf. RELATE *v.* 6).

1491 *Act 7 Hen. VII*, c. 19 The seid Proviso had relacion to the seid vj day of October the whiche was before the same feoffement. **1642** tr. *Perkins' Prof. Bk.* i. §9. 5 It shall have relation unto the time from the first deliverie. **1766** BLACKSTONE *Comm.* II. 182 The use of the wife's estate.. being then awakened, had relation back, and took effect from the original time of creation.

†**c.** A fiction of law by which two times or other things are identified, and for legal purposes, regarded as one and the same. *Obs.*

1598 *Termes Lawes* 162 The thing subsequent is said to take his effect, by relation, at the time preceding. **1628** COKE *On Litt.* III. xviii. (1648) 70 A relation which is but a fiction in law, shall never make a man a felon. **1749** SALTHOUSE *Wood's Conveyancing* I. vi. §8 (O) 712 In this Case the Dower of the Woman shall be taken away by Relation.

transf. **1605** BACON *Adv. Learn.* I. v. §2 The propositions of Euclyde..being demonstrate, our mind accepteth of them by a kind of relation (as the Lawyers speak) as if we had knowne them before.

5. a. Connexion between persons arising out of the natural ties of blood or marriage; kinship. Cf. RELATIONSHIP.

1660 JER. TAYLOR *Duct. Dubit.* II. ii. rule 3 §40 Affinity makes conjunctions and relations equal to those of consanguinity. **1671** MILTON *P.R.* IV. 519 The Son of God I also am, or was, And if I was, I am; relation stands. **1758** S. HAYWARD *Serm.* xvii. 531 The relation is as real as that of husband and wife. **1818** CRUISE *Digest* (ed. 2) III. 397 In the maternal line, Hannah Willis and Susan Bates stand in the same point of relation with the two above named. **1838** LYTTON *Leila* IV. iii, Their relation almost seemed reversed, and the daughter to be a mother watching over her offspring.

†**b.** Those related to one in this way; one's kindred. *Obs. rare.*

1653 JER. TAYLOR *25 Serm.* vi. 72 He hath need of a great stock of piety, who is first to provide for his own necessities, and then to give portions to a numerous relation. **1702** C. MATHER *Magn. Chr.* VII. (1853) II. 667 Some of them had quite forgot their English tongue, and their Christian name, and their whole relation.

c. A person related to one by blood or marriage; a kinsman or kinswoman; a relative. Also freq. in *pl.*, kinsfolk, relatives.

1502 HEN. VII in *Lett. Kings Eng.* (1846) I. 191 His cousin and relation the king of Spain. **1626** in *Crt. & Times Chas. I* (1848) I. 81 Dr. Smith, a man relation to Audley End.. hath the mastership of Magdalen. **1641** W. HOOKE *New Eng. Teares* 14 The bloody contentions of brethren; and, when relations turn opposites, nothing more opposite. **1697** DRYDEN *Virg. Georg.* IV. 374 Their Friends attend the Herse, the next Relations mourn. **1713** STEELE *Guardian* No. 17 ¶8 He led her to a relation's house. **1773** GOLDSM. *Stoops to Conq.* II. i, I hope, cousin, one may speak to one's own relations, and not be to blame? **1819** SHELLEY *Cenci* I. ii. 69 He might bestow her on some poor relation. **1851** RUSKIN *Stones Ven.* (1874) I. App. 352 In the year 1434, the relations of Churchmen were declared ineligible to the post of Ambassador at Rome. **1870** DICKENS *E. Drood* ix, Rosa had no relation that she knew of.

d. In phr. ***no relation***, denying relationship by blood or marriage despite having the same surname.

1930 E. M. BRENT-DYER *Chalet Girls in Camp* xii. 175 Except..Ruth Wynyard, Lilli van Huysen, and Greta Macdonald—no relation!—all of them had been her [*sc.* Mrs. Macdonald's] pupils. **1977** *Private Eye* 13 May 14/1 We shall see much more of it now that Mr Moss Evans (no relation) has been elected to one of the two highest offices in the land, as General Secretary of the TGWU.

6. a. The position which one person holds with respect to another on account of some social or other connexion between them; the particular mode in which persons are mutually connected by circumstances.

1650 T. B[AYLEY] *Worcester's Apoph.* 63 As it was commonly observ'd by all the Servants, that had nearest relation to him. **1732** LAW *Serious C.* xxiv. (ed. 2) 488 If.. our relation to God be our greatest relation. **1765** BLACKSTONE *Comm.* I. ii. 142 The most universal public relation, by which men are collected together, is that of government. **1849** MACAULAY *Hist. Eng.* i. I. 60 The opinions of the Puritan concerning the relation of ruler and subject. **1867** FREEMAN *Norm. Conq.* (1877) I. iii. 93 The relation of every man to his lord was a relation of homage.

b. *pl.* The aggregate of the connexions, or modes of connexion, by which one person is brought into touch with another or with society in general.

a **1687** WALLER *Epit. Sir G. Speke*, Just unto all relations known, A worthy patriot, pious son. **1745** BUTLER *Serm.* Wks. 1874 II. 276 They ought to be instructed..in what is suitable to the highest relations in which we stand. **1781** GIBBON *Decl. & F.* xliv. II. 670 Our relations to each other are various and infinite. **1796** BURKE *Regic. Peace* iii. Wks. VIII. 278 There was an end of that narrow scheme of relations called our country. **1865** R. W. DALE *Jew. Temp.* xx. (1877) 221 By the death of Christ new relations were established between God and man. **1879** FROUDE *Cæsar* vi. 49 Between mother and child the relations had been affectionate and happy.

c. *pl.* The various modes in which one country, state, etc., is brought into contact with another by political or commercial interests.

1797 ADAMS in *Amer. St. Papers* (1833) I. 40 The minister of foreign relations informed the recalled American minister that [etc.]. **1818** *Parl. Deb.* 18 With respect to our foreign relations, the treaties concluded with Spain and Portugal.. formed a peculiar topic of congratulation. **1827** HALLAM *Const. Hist.* vi. I. 358 His chief praise, however, was his management of continental relations. **1861** M. PATTISON *Ess.* (1889) I. 39 Our commercial relations with the Baltic cities.

7. *Comb.*, as **relation-axis** *adj. phr. Gram.*, involving or consisting of a word expressing a relation and another with respect to which the relation holds; **relation-word** *Gram.*, a word expressing relation between other words or groups of words, e.g. a preposition or conjunction.

1933 L. BLOOMFIELD *Language* 267 They [*sc.* English substantive expressions] occur in the position of axis in the relation-axis construction (*beside John*), with a positional meaning of, say, 'center from which a relation holds good'. **1964** E. A. NIDA *Toward Sci. Transl.* iv. 57 In the phrases *through the house, behind the store*, and *in the shed*, the relationship between the prepositions *through, behind*, and *in* and the following immediate constituents (consisting of the noun with preposed determiner *the*) may be described as 'relation-axis'. **1925** GRATTAN & GURREY *Our Living Lang.* xii. 79 [The work of a preposition] is to show the relation in which a noun stands to some other part of the sentence... For this reason it is also known as a *Relation-word*. **1962** J. SÖDERLIND in F. Behre *Contrib. Eng. Syntax* 117 *Of*-groups where *of* is a pure relation-word.

Hence **reˈlation** *v. intr.*, to form relations.

1862 SPENCER *First Princ.* (1870) 86 Thinking being relationing, no thought can ever express more than relations.

relational (rɪˈleɪʃənəl), *a.* and *sb.* [f. as prec. + -AL[1].]

A. *adj.* **1.** Of or belonging to human relationship.

1662 GURNALL *Chr. in Arm.* verse 18. I. xlix. (1669) 412/1 What thy personal and what thy relational needs are? *a* **1732** T. BOSTON *Crook in Lot* (1805) 17 It may fall in the relational part. Relations are the joints of society. **1799** W. TOOKE *View Russian Emp.* II. 110 One might easily be tempted to take the two nations for relational stems. **1834** J. BROWN *Lett. Sanctif.* vi. 319 Be conscientious in the relational duties to God and man.

2. Of, belonging to, or characterized by relation in general.

1840 *Penny Cycl.* XVI. 336/2 The use of Relational words increases in language in the same proportion as the power of inflection diminishes. **1869** SPENCER *Princ. Psychol.* II. v. (1870) I. 229 The most highly relational feelings are the visual. **1899** C. F. DARCY *Idealism & Theol.* Introd. 6 Its primary qualities..are essentially relational. **1930** J. T. HATFIELD et al. *Curme Vol. Ling. Stud.* 37 The immaterial adnominal cases are the following;..relational—a man *in stature*. **1946** *Language* XXII. 219 A *relational phrase* has two immediate constituents. **1967** *Child Devel.* XXXVIII. 841 This study is concerned with the ability of preschool children to use the relational terms 'more', 'same', and 'less' when comparing the number, length, and weight of objects. **1979** *Trans. Philol. Soc.* 215 The element *-ai/ei-* is also found in association with one of the so-called 'relational particles'.

B. *sb. Gram.* A conjunction or preposition considered as a relation-word; a relational particle.

1964 E. A. NIDA *Toward Sci. Transl.* iv. 62 There are four principal functional classes of lexical symbols: object words, event words, abstracts, and relationals. **1969** *Language* XLV. 485 Relationals are any units which function primarily as markers of relationships between other terms, e.g. *at, by, because, and, or.* **1978** *Ibid.* LIV. 80 Some English prepositions correspond to Japanese genitive constructions with *no* plus relationals.

Hence **relatioˈnality, reˈlationally** *adv.*

1865 BUSHNELL *Vicar. Sacr.* III. iv. (1868) 307 The close relationality of it is cross to our humanly selfish habit. **1867** —— in *Hours at Home* Nov. 6 The objects of nature are relationally..made.

reˈlationary, *a.* [-ARY[1].] Relational.

1847–9 *Todd's Cycl. Anat.* IV. 622/2 To denote that.. arrangement of all the osseous pieces of an animal framework in..relationary order. **1848** R. I. WILBERFORCE *Doctr. Incarnation* v. (1852) 109 Our Lord had an inherent and independent, not merely a conditional and relationary existence.

reˈlationism. *Philos.* [f. RELATION *sb.* + -ISM.] **a.** The doctrine of the relativity of knowledge; relativism. **b.** The doctrine that relations have a real existence.

1858 W. R. PIRIE *Inq. Hum. Mind* iv. 251 The assumption ..necessarily runs into nihilism or relationism. **1885** F. E. ABBOT *Sci. Theism* Introd. ii. 25 Relationism or Scientific Realism..teaches that universals, or genera and species, are, first, objective relations of resemblance among objectively existing things. **1958** W. STARK *Sociol. Knowl.* viii. 338 By the concept of relationism he [*sc.* K. Mannheim] means that if we formulate a truth, we should not do so in abstract and absolute terms, but must always include in the formula the concrete conditions to which it is related. **1975** *Nature* 1 May p. iv (Advt.), The book is concerned with space and time as abstract relations which hold between objects and events (relationism), and as aspects of nature with causal properties of their own (absolutism).

reˈlationist, *sb.* (and *a.*) [-IST.] One who maintains a theory based on a relation between ideas. Also, one who holds that events are connected in a relative way. Also *attrib.* or as *adj.*

1835 J. YOUNG *Lect. Intell. Philos.* xxviii. 281 Dr. Brown says, there must be a feeling of relation in these general ideas,..and says, that were he to take a particular name to himself, he would call himself a Relationist. **1885** W. JAMES in *Mind* X. 31 And may not the 'relationists' be right after all? **1923** C. D. BROAD *Sci. Thought* iii. 89 The former alternative is taken by the Relationist... Time just consists of the relations of before and after among events. **1974** L. SKLAR *Space, Time, & Spacetime* iii. 167 According to the relationist, the postulation of space, time, or spacetime as entities..is simply a confusion. *Ibid.*, The prerelativistic and relativistic versions of the relationist position. **1975** *Nature* 6 Feb. 485/3 Wishing to retain a pure relationist stance, he proposes that the statement 'is absolutely accelerated' is not a relational term, giving it instead the status of a complete assertion.

reˈlationless, *a.* [f. RELATION *sb.* + -LESS.]

a. Having no relations.

1822 LAMB *Elia* Ser. I. *Old Actors*, The survivor stands gaping and relationless as if it remembered its brother. **1873** *Spectator* 15 Feb. 213/2 One of them is a relationless orphan.

b. Bereft of relation in general.

1889 'SCOTUS NOVANTICUS' *Metaph. Nova et Vetusta* (ed. 2) 11. 86 The datum is not atomic or relationless. **1911** *Proc. Mus. Assoc.* May 121 Oneness and homogeneity could be evolved from such apparently relationless short-cut phrases.

relationship (rɪˈleɪʃənʃɪp). [f. as prec. + -SHIP.] The state of being related; a condition or character based upon this; kinship. Also *spec.*, an affair; a sexual relationship.

a **1744** POPE *Dunc.* II. 3 *note*, Our author let it pass unaltered, as a trifle, that no way altered the relationship. **1773** GOLDSM. *Stoops to Conq.* II. i, I want no nearer relationship. **1804** MITFORD *Inquiry* 345 The Welsh themselves have been fond of claiming this relationship [for their language]. **1853** WHEWELL *Grotius* I. 309 Social ties are to be extended more widely by diffusing our relationships. **1880** HAUGHTON *Phys. Geog.* 268 Teeth of a small Marsupial, *Microlestes*,..which show a relationship to Myrmecobius. **1944** M. LASKI *Love on Supertax* viii. 81 'Were you going to marry Lou?' asked Clarissa... 'We hadn't got further than a relationship,' Sid said. **1974** J. GARDNER *Corner Men* v. 41 Bob and I weren't hallo young lovers. We had a relationship, but I wasn't in love with him. **1975** R. RENDELL *Shake Hands for Ever* viii. 76 'Did Mr Hathall have a special friendship with any girl here?'..'Do you mean a relationship? D'you mean, was he *sleeping* with anyone?' **1977** *Rolling Stone* 30 June 62/2 People don't fall in love anymore, they have relationships. **1981** C. R. LAJEUNESSE *Dead Man Running* iii. 11 Rowena and I had a relationship at first, which had been a no-strings-attached affair. Then..she became serious and I had shied away.

†**relatist.** *Obs.*[−1] [f. RELATE *v.*] **a.** A relative, a thing related. **b.** One who relates.

1640 HOWELL *Dodona's Gr.* 10 Which puts so large a distance twixt the tongue and the heart, that they are seldome relatists. **1656** BLOUNT *Glossogr.*, *Relatist*, one that rehearseth or relateth; a reporter.

relatival (rɛləˈtaɪvəl), *a.* Chiefly *Gram.* [f. RELATIVE + -AL[1].] Of or pertaining to a relative or relation.

1869 ABBOTT *Shaks. Gram.* 63 Relatival constructions, —So as; such which; that as. **1879** FARRAR *St. Paul* II. 497 Then follows a chapter of parentheses,..linked together.. by relatival connexions. **1899** *Westm. Gaz.* 21 Mar. 1/2 The new member has a relatival connexion with the House of Lords in the Earl of Portsmouth.

relative (ˈrɛlətɪv), *a.* and *sb.* [ad. F. *relatif, -ive* (13th c.), or L. *relātīv-us*: see RELATE *v.* and -IVE.] A. *adj.*

1. *Gram.* Relating or referring to an antecedent term; esp. ***relative pronoun.***

1530 PALSGR. 81 Of the pronownes relatives *qui*..serveth indifferently for all gendres and nombres. **1552** HULOET, Relatiue or whiche hathe relation to a thynge precedyng, *relatiuus.* **1696** PHILLIPS, *Pronoun*, a Part of Speech..of which there are Four Sorts, Personal,..Relative [etc.]. **1762** KAMES *Elem. Crit.* xviii. (1833) 268 In a natural style, relative words are by juxtaposition connected with those to which they relate. **1845** STODDART *Gram.* in *Encycl. Metrop.* (1847) I. 66/1 The Greek had only the relative Article ὁ, ἡ, τό, and was entirely destitute of our positive Article. **1872** MORRIS *Eng. Accid.* xii. §188 The relative pronouns are *who, which, that, as.* In OE. *who, which, what*, were not relative, but interrogative pronouns.

2. a. Having mutual relationship; related to, or connected with, each other; †correlative.

1594 BLUNDEVIL *Exerc.* I. xvi. (1636) 41 The Relative [numbers] are those which have relation one to another. **1662** HOBBES *Consid.* 21 Protection and Obedience are Relative. **1797** *Encycl. Brit.* (ed. 3) XII. 187/1 The relative modes are such as the composer interweaves with the principal in the flow of the harmony. **1858** HAWTHORNE *Fr. & It. Note-bks.* II. 146 Several different, yet relative designs.

b. Corresponding.

1849 RUSKIN *Sev. Lamps* iii. §9. 71 The square and circle ..with their relative solids the cube and sphere.

c. *Mus.* (See quots. and B. 2c.)

1818 BUSBY *Gram. Mus.* 133 [A transition] from the major scale to its relative minor. **1848** *Mus. Times* II. 104 The signature of *Do* minor is the same as that of *Miƀ* major, which is therefore called its relative major. **1875** OUSELEY *Harmony* v. 69 Every major key has a minor key connected with it, called its 'relative minor'.

3. a. Having relation to the question or matter in hand; pertinent, relevant.

1602 SHAKS. *Ham.* II. ii. 633 Ile haue grounds More Relatiue then this. **1676** I. MATHER *K. Philip's War* (1862) 161 There are judicious persons, who upon the consideration of some relative circumstances,.. have concluded [etc.]. **1734** tr. *Rollin's Anc. Hist.* (1827) II. IV. 272 Giving his answers in such ambiguous terms that let the event be what it would they contained a relative meaning. **1809** SOUTHEY *Lett.* (1856) II. 157 All relative matter, not absolutely essential to the subject, should go in the form of supplementary notes. **1866** *Daily News* 12 Feb. 5/6, I would give no credit to such an assumption without some more relative and positive proof.

†**b.** Of a person: Concerned *in* a thing. *Obs.*[−1]

a **1613** OVERBURY *A Wife*, etc. (1638) 102 She is relative in all; and he without her, but halfe himselfe.

4. a. Arising from, depending on, or determined by, relation to something else or to each other; comparative.

1611 FLORIO *Dict.*, *Rules for Italian Tongue* 641 The second respectiue, relatiue, or limited Preterimperfect tence, which doth euer eyther expressiuely or inclusiuely answere or regard the former. **1673** *S'too him Bayes* 37 No more does it follow that Geneva..must change from North to South, the place of her Relative Situation. **1793** SMEATON *Edystone L.* §235 They were..so marked, that..they could again be restored to the same relative position. **1822** IMISON *Sc. & Art* I. 447 Relative motion is the degree and direction of the motion of one body, when compared with that of another. **1860** TYNDALL *Glac.* II. xv. 308 The point to be decided is the relative importance of his idea. **1881** WESTCOTT & HORT *Grk. Test.* Introd. §39 Relative date affords a valuable presumption as to relative freedom from corruption.

b. Constituted, or existing, only by relation to something else; not absolute or independent.

1704 J. HARRIS *Lex. Techn.* I, *Specifick Gravity*... By some 'tis not improperly called Relative Gravity, to distinguish it from Absolute Gravity. **1763** J. BROWN *Poetry & Mus.* v. 75 Melody therefore is to be considered as a relative thing, founded in the particular Associations and Habits of each People. **1826** COLERIDGE in *Lit. Rem.* (1838) III. 55 Certainty is positive, evidence relative. **1875** JOWETT *Plato* (ed. 2) IV. 238 A votary of that famous philosophy in which all things are said to be relative.

5. a. Of worship: Offered indirectly by means of or through an image.

1660 JER. TAYLOR *Duct. Dubit.* II. ii. rule 6 §41 However any man may intend to pass the relative honour that way, yet no man hath any warrant that God will accept it. **1686** tr. *Chardin's Trav. Persia* 98 They adore 'em not with a Relative Adoration, but pay their Devotion to the Material Substance. **1833** G. S. FABER *Recapit. Apostasy* 14 The Jews and Mohammedans..derived from the Law and the Koran an immortal hatred to graven images and all relative worship. **1884** *Catholic Dict.* (1885) 239/1 The same idea is expressed by Cyril of Alexandria when he speaks of the 'relative veneration and cultus of honour'.

†**b.** (See quot.) *Obs. rare*[−1].

1710 NORRIS *Chr. Prud.* i. 2 Truths of importance are relative Truths, that have an Order or Reference to something farther.

6. Of terms, etc.: Involving or implying relation; depending for meaning or significance upon some relationship of things or persons.

1678 BUNYAN *Come & Welc.* 18 To call God by this relative Title [Father] was rare among the Saints in Old-Testament times. **1696** PHILLIPS s.v., In Logick, Relative Terms are when there is a kind of Opposition, yet such a one, that the one cannot be without the other: as Father and Son, Husband and Wife. **1704** J. HARRIS *Lex. Techn.* I, *Relative Propositions*, are those that include some Comparison, add some Relation, thus: Where the Treasure is, there is the Heart. **1843** MILL *Logic* I. ii. §7 A name is relative when, being the name of one thing, its signification cannot be explained but by mentioning another. **1869** B. HARTE *Tennessee's Part.* Wks. 1880 II. 135 Tennessee's Partner, whom we never knew by any other than this relative title.

7. a. Having, or standing in, a relation *to* something else; correspondent or proportionate *to*.

1660 JER. TAYLOR *Duct. Dubit.* II. ii. rule 6 §65 If it be a reason that is not relative to times and persons. **1732** POPE *Ess. Man* I. 52 Whatever wrong we call, May, must be right, as relative to all. **1793** SMEATON *Edystone L.* §154 The firmness of all the material parts, as relative to the force to be employed. **1866** ROGERS *Agric. & Prices* I. xxiii. 595 The market value will always be relative to its demand. **1877** E. R. CONDER *Bas. Faith* iv. 141 All knowledge must be relative to mind.

b. In relation or proportion *to* something.

c **1789** GIBBON *Autobiog.* (1896) 268 Naples, the most populous of cities relative to its size.

8. a. Having application or reference *to* a thing.

1765 HARRIS *Three Treat.* II. Note 362 Things relative to immediate Want, such as the grinding of Corn by Mills. **1828** STARK *Elem. Nat. Hist.* II. 238 Certain ideas..relative to their wants and the employment of their organs. **1863** H. COX *Instit.* III. v. 658 Powers and duties relative to harbours and navigation.

b. Relating *to* a matter of fact, event, person, etc.; with reference *to.*

1763 HARRIS in *Lett. Lit. Men* (Camden) 401 The letter relative to Charles's death. **1804** NELSON *Lett.* (1814) II. 62, I write to the Admiralty relative to my health. **1853** LYTTON *My Novel* VIII. xiii, A letter to Egerton, with whom he wished to consult relative to a very important point.

c. Conveying a reference or allusion *to* some thing or fact.

1774 J. BRYANT *Mythol.* II. 417 The Ox's head with the Egyptian modius between his horns, relative to the circumstances of his history.

9. Special collocations: ***relative address*** (Computers), an address (sense 7c) which is defined only in relation to some other address; hence ***relative addressing***, the practice of using relative addresses; ***relative density*** = *specific gravity* s.v. GRAVITY 4c; normally defined using water or (for a gas) hydrogen as standard; (cf. quot. 1704 in sense A. 4b); ***relative deprivation*** (Sociol.), deprivation as experienced by a person in respect of opportunities, standard of living, etc., which is relative to the circumstances of the group or society of which he is a member; ***relative humidity*** (Meteorol.): see HUMIDITY 1; ***relative pitch***: (Mus.), the pitch of a note in relation to another; the ability to recognize or reproduce this; also in extended use in *Phonetics*; ***relative sexuality*** (Biol.) [tr. G. *relative sexualität* (M. Hartmann 1909, in *Arch. f. Protistenkunde* XIV. 325)], the phenomenon shown by those species of which an individual or gamete may act as either female or male, according as it is less or more male than its mate.

1956 BERKELEY & WAINWRIGHT *Computers* viii. 352/2 Relative addresses are translated into absolute addresses by adding some specific 'reference' address. **1970** O. DOPPING *Computers & Data Processing* xix. 312 The relative addresses should be tagged to show that they will later have to be modified. **1966** C. J. SIPPL *Computer Dict. & Handbk.* 268/1 Relative addressing is a feature of great significance in multiprogramming, time-sharing, and real time operations. **1967** KLERER & KORN *Digital Computer User's Handbk.* i. 20 Relative addressing is done with addresses that are generated relative to some preset location whose relative address is 0. **1879** J. D. EVERETT *Units & Physical Constants* iv. 30 The relative density of water at various temperatures .., the density at 4°C. being taken as unity. **1892** G. F. BARKER *Physics* III. i. 315 Relative density is the ratio of the absolute density of a gas or vapor to that of air or of hydrogen. **1957** A. EFRON *Basic Physics* I. ix. 105 The relative density of lead is 11·3. **1963** A. F. ABBOTT *Ord. Level Physics* ix. 115 The relative density of a substance is the ratio of the mass of any given volume of it to the mass of an equal volume of water. Numerically, specific gravity and relative density are identical. **1974** FOLIVI & GODMAN *New Certif. Physics* ii. 73/1 The ratio of the density of a substance divided by the density of water is the relative density of the substance. **1949** S. A. STOUFFER et al. *Amer. Soldier* I. iv. 125 To help explain such variations in attitude, by education, age, and marital condition, a general concept would be useful. Such a concept may be that of relative deprivation. *Ibid.* 126 The concept of relative deprivation may seem..not to be applicable to the educational differentials in attitude. **1966** *New Statesman* 8 July 55/2 In the expression 'relative deprivation', as Runciman uses it, the deprivation is largely imaginary and the emphasis..on the relativity. **1972** DOWSE & HUGHES *Polit. Sociol.* xiii. 411 When they cannot achieve these values..dissatisfaction, anger and often aggression occur. This type of situation is a quite usual one in any complex society and is termed 'relative deprivation', which may be defined as 'The tension that develops from a discrepancy between the "ought" and the "is" of collective value satisfaction'. **1926** D. C. MILLER *Sci. of Mus. Sounds* vii. 216 Many writers on the subject have held that the quality of a vowel, as well as that of a musical instrument, is characterized by a particular series of overtones accompanying a given fundamental, the pitches of the overtones varying with that of the fundamental, so that the ratios remain constant; this is the *relative-pitch theory*. **1929** *Melody Maker* Mar. 300/3 A person enjoying the ability to determine the interval between two or more musical sounds is said to possess Relative Pitch. **1933** L. BLOOMFIELD *Language* vii. 117 The Japanese language is said to distinguish two relative pitches, normal and higher. **1949** R-M. S. HEFFNER *Gen. Phonetics* vii. 213 It is the relative pitch of speech sounds which is a linguistic means of differentiation between meanings. **1969** H. L. SMITH in A. A. Hill *Linguistics Today* ix. 94 The four relative levels of stress in English.., the four relative pitch heights.., and the four *junctures* or *transitions*..form three independent but interdependent systems of *prosodic* or *suprasegmental phonemes*. **1977** *Proc. R. Soc. Med.* LXX. 134/1 There is a continuum of skills which ranges from 'tone deafness', through 'relative pitch', to 'absolute pitch'... Most people have relative pitch, in so far as they are able to say, when given a certain reference tone, that a second sound is higher or lower in pitch. **1948** F. E. FRITSCH *Struct. & Reprod. Algae* 327 Relative sexuality, in which one thread [of *Spirogyra*] behaves respectively as male and female to two others, is also on record. **1967** E. STEINER tr. *Esger & Kuenen's Genetics of Fungi* ii. 96 In the light of recent work certain older data are no longer to be interpreted as relative sexuality.

B. *sb.* **1.** *Gram.* **a.** A relative word; *esp.* a relative pronoun. Also *fig.* (quot. 1393).

1388 WYCLIF *Prol.* 57 A relatif, which mai be resoluid into his antecedent with a coniunccioun copulatif. **1393** LANGL. *P. Pl.* C. IV. 357 Man ys relatif rect yf he be ryht trewe. **1520** WHITINTON *Vulg.* (1527) 2 The relatyue of substaunce shall accorde with his antecedent. **1579** FULKE *Heskins' Parl.* 148 He appealeth to the grammarian for the nature of a Relatiue. **1658** EVELYN *Diary* 27 Jan., The government and use of relatives, verbs, substantives. **1762** BP. LOWTH *Introd. Eng. Gram.* 103 *Who, which, what,* and the Relative *that*,..are always placed before the Verb. **1824** L. MURRAY *Eng. Gram.* (ed. 5) I. 194 Relatives are not so useful in language, as conjunctions. **1875** WHITNEY *Life Lang.* v. 96 The relatives ..are an agency we could hardly afford to miss.

†**b.** Applied to a demonstrative pronoun. *Obs.*⁻¹

1677 CARY *Chronol.* 235 Jochanan begat Azariah; he it is that Executed the Priests Office, &c. This Relative [He] may have reference either to Jochanan, or Azariah.

2. a. A thing (†or person) standing in some relation to another.

1426 LYDG. *De Guil. Pilgr.* 3057 Thys..ys the ryght-ful relatyff, To whom, with-oute noyse or stryff, Thow art soget. **1570–6** LAMBARDE *Peramb. Kent* 408 After the husbande and the wife, there followeth..the childe and his Gardein, whom also (since they be Relatiues, as the other be ..) [etc.]. **1606** WARNER *Alb. Eng.* xv. c. 394 Religion and Subiection be each th' others Relatiue. **1660** JER. TAYLOR *Duct. Dubit.* II. ii. rule 1 §11 The band of marriage is Eternal, but it dies with either of the relatives. **1784** J. BARRY in *Lect. Paint.* ii. (1848) 93 The mere..opposition of the several colours, proper to his object, and to the relatives which accompanied it. **1862** SPENCER *First Princ.* I. iv. §24 (1867) 81 An Absolute which existed not alone but along with other Absolutes, would no longer be an absolute but a relative.

b. A relative term. (See A. 6.)

1551 T. WILSON *Logike* 22 b, Relatiues are those, whiche are comprehended with other, or the whiche are named, one with another, and (as a man would say) haue a mutuall respect, one to another. **1588** FRAUNCE *Lawiers Log.* I. xi. 48 Relatiues are contraries,..yet there may bee in other respects a mutuall consent and reciprocall relation betweene them, wherevpon they bee called Relatiues, as father, sonne, husband, wife, &c. **1648** MILTON *Tenure Kings* (1649) 31 We know that King and Subject are relatives, and relatives have no longer being then in the relation. **1697** J. SERGEANT *Solid Philos.* 252 Some Terms which seem Absolute are Relatives. **1855** SIR W. HAMILTON *Metaph.* (1859) II. 536 Thus relatives are severally discriminated; inasmuch as the one is specially what is referred, the other specially what is referred to.

c. *Mus.* (See quots. and A. 2 c.)

1811 BUSBY *Dict. Mus.* (ed. 3) s.v., Every major-key is called the relative of such minor key, and every minor-key the relative of its third above, taken in the major-mode. **1818** —— *Gram. Mus.* 51 Major and Minor keys thus agreeing, are denominated relatives.

3. One who is connected with another or others by blood or affinity; a kinsman. Cf. RELATION 5 c.

1657 GAULE *Sap. Just.* 43 In respect of proximate Parents and of relatives yet living. **1660** JER. TAYLOR *Duct. Dubit.* II. ii. rule 3 §76 Cosens would do better not to marry (says another)..that one person may not be a double Relative. *a* **1703** POMFRET *Prospect Death* 81 Our friends and relatives stand weeping by, Dissolv'd in tears, to see us die. **1793** *Minstrel* I. 24 St. Julian was..a relative to the duchess of York. **1825** THIRLWALL *Crit. Ess.* 125 While he is yet speaking his relatives are announced to him. **1860** TYNDALL *Glac.* I. xvii. 121 He had received intelligence of the death of a near relative.

transf. **1856** KANE *Arct. Expl.* I. xxiii. 305 Flitting and hovering.., like their relatives..Mother Carey's chickens.

†**4.** A relationship. *Obs. rare.*

1657 L. GATFORD in E. D. Neill *Virginia Carolorum* (1886) 278 A practice..abominated of all men that know either what men are,..or what their relatives are, either natural, civil, or Christian. **1675** *Art Contentment* v. vi, We attacque him in all his concerns,..in his honor, in his relatives, nay somtimes in his very essence and being.

5. ***the relative***, that which is relative (in sense 4 b of the adj.).

1856 FERRIER *Inst. Metaph.* xix. 367 Objects, whatever they may be, are the relative in cognition. **1859** J. MARTINEAU *Ess.* (1866) I. 78 We cannot operate backward from the relative to the absolute.

relatively (ˈrɛlətɪvlɪ), *adv.* [f. prec. + -LY².]

1. In a relative manner, in relation to something else; comparatively: **a.** with vbs.

1561 T. NORTON *Calvin's Inst.* I. xiii. (1634) 58 The name of God is there relatively taken, and therefore restrained to the Person of the Father. **1591** PERCIVALL *Sp. Dict.* Eiv, This word *Lo* is often vsed relatiuely, and yet hath no agreement with any antecedent. **1660** R. COKE *Justice Vind.* 49 Here we must look upon Grotius either naturally, or relatively. **1701** NORRIS *Ideal World* I. v. 243 The essence of God may be considered either absolutely or relatively. **1794** PALEY *Evid.* II. ix. §2 (1817) 239 Not only absolutely, but.. relatively, in comparison, that is with those among whom they exercise their office. **1849** MACAULAY *Hist. Eng.* v. I. 585 But, though they have positively advanced, they have relatively gone back. **1861** PEARSON *Early & Mid. Ages Eng.* (1867) I. 15 Arts and sciences can only be talked of relatively among a people such as the Britons were.

b. with adjs. (Sometimes hyphened.)

1825 BENTHAM *Offic. Apt. Maximized, Indications* (1830) 78 *note*, Justice,..denied to the relatively poor,..sold at an enormous price to the relatively rich. **1862** SPENCER *First Princ.* II. xiii. §104 (1867) 301 Parts which..consist of relatively-simple molecules, are seats of but little structure. **1884** L. J. JENNINGS *Croker Papers* I. iii. 85 It was very difficult to induce..the public to regard them as worth the relatively small sum..paid for them.

2. In relation, or with reference, *to* something.

1646 SIR T. BROWNE *Pseud. Ep.* 191 These lateralities in man are not onely fallible, if relatively determined unto each others, but made in reference unto the heavens. **1678** CUDWORTH *Intell. Syst.* I. i. 11 Those Sensible things..are all generated or made Relatively to the Sentient. **1726** BOLINGBROKE *Study Hist.* ii. I. (1752) 38 They saw the measures they took singly, and unrelatively, or relatively alone to some immediate object. **1822** J. H. NEWMAN *Lett.* (1891) I. 69 They know very little of me..who think I do not put a value on myself relatively to others. **1873** MAXWELL *Electr. & Magn.* (1881) I. 47 In a conductor the electrification is free to move relatively to the conductor.

b. In proportion *to*.

1869 TOZER *Highl. Turkey* I. 257 All should be ready to serve, considering the length of the frontier they have to defend relatively to their numbers.

So **'relativeness**, relativity.

1673 H. MORE *App. to Antid. agst. Idolatry* 31 Since this Relative *Latria* (because of its Relativeness) is incompetible to God. **1886** *Amer. Jrnl. Philol.* VII. 444 For a later period ..the expression 'dialect' is one of peculiar relativeness.

'relativism. *Philos.* [f. as prec. + -ISM.]

a. The doctrine that knowledge is only of relations. Also, a name given to theories or doctrines that truth, morality, etc., are relative to situations and are not absolute.

1865 J. GROTE *Exploratio Philosophica* I. xi. 229 The notion of the mask over the face of nature is exactly that which I am sure Dr Whewell does not wish to fall into—it is what I have called 'relativism'. If 'the face of nature' is reality, then the mask over it, which is what theory gives us, is so much deception, and that is what relativism really comes to. **1885** SETH *Scot. Philos.* 183 Hegel alone of all metaphysicians lifts us completely clear of Relativism. **1892** *Athenæum* 20 Aug. 247/1 Many will be pleased with the attack on thoroughgoing relativism. [**1934** C. MORRIS in G. H. Mead *Mind, Self & Society* p. xix, Philosophically the position is here an objective relativism: qualities of the object may yet be relative to a conditioning organism. **1941** H. MARCUSE *Reason & Revolution* II. ii. 353 According to Comte, relativism is inseparable from the conception that sociology is an exact science dealing with the invariant laws of social statics and dynamics. **1959** A. BRECHT *Polit. Theory* v. 172, I do not intend to minimize the extent to which Comte's positivism actually contributed to preparing the ground for modern Scientific Method and Value Relativism. **1976** W. J. STANKIEWICZ *Aspects Polit. Theory* vii. 135 What is logically excluded is relativism as a methodology: a methodology demands fixity of purpose; a fixed purpose excludes relativism.

b. Special collocations: (*a*) ***historical relativism***, the view that there can be no objective standard of historical truth, as the interpretation of data will be affected by subjective factors characteristic either of the historian or of the period in which he lives; (*b*) ***ethical relativism***, the view that there are no universal or objective ethical standards; that each culture develops the ethical standards that it finds acceptable and that these cannot be judged by the ethical standards of another culture; (*c*) ***cultural relativism***, the theory that there are no objective standards by which to evaluate a culture; that a culture cannot be understood except from the point of view of its own values or customs; the practice of studying a culture from such a standpoint.

(*a*) **1937** T. PARSONS *Struct. Soc. Action* xiii. 480 In place of a theory of dialectic evolution on the Hegelian model there emerges a complete historical relativism. **1945** K. R. POPPER *Open Society* II. xxii. 191 But this so-called 'historical relativism' by no means exhausts the historicist character of the Marxist theory of morals. **1956** W. KLUBACK *Dilthey's Philos. Hist.* iii. 58 The value of any age was true for that age but could not with validity be applied to other ages. For Dilthey historical relativism did not imply pessimism. On the contrary, it made man aware of his place in history. **1977** M. MANDELBAUM *Anat. Hist. Knowl.* vi. 150 Some of the conventional arguments for historical relativism, and against the objectivity of historical knowledge, lose much of their force.

(*b*) **1937** T. PARSONS *Struct. Soc. Action* xi. 447 He [*sc.* Durkheim] was forced to define normality with reference to the social type alone, thus ending in a complete ethical relativism. **1944** *Brit. Jrnl. Med. Psychol.* XX. 113/1 This [empirical] point of view is distinct both from ethical absolutism and ethical relativism. **1964** M. RADER *Ethics & Human Community* ix. 236 There is a kind of incongruity in combining the two kinds of relativism. The methodological type requires tolerance..the ethical type condones the most intolerant of societies. **1968** *Internat. Encycl. Soc. Sci.* V. 158 The 'reductionist' form of ethical relativism, which presents the ethical beliefs of a people as functionally dependent on their other beliefs and practices.

(*c*) **1958** F. M. KEESING *Cultural Anthropol.* ii. 47 The scientific habit of looking at each people's standards and values objectively, seeing them as 'relative' to the particular view of life fostered within the culture concerned, has led some thinkers to a philosophic position often called 'cultural relativism'. **1968** *Internat. Encycl. Soc. Sci.* III. 543/2 The methodology of cultural relativism rests on the assumption that the ethnologist is able to transcend, or to eliminate for the moment, his own cultural conditioning and values and to assume the subjective..mentality of an adherent of..the culture. **1976** T. EAGLETON *Crit. & Ideology* iv. 134 Imperialism..bred an awareness of cultural relativism at precisely the point where the absolute cultural hegemony of the imperialist nations needed to be affirmed.

'relativist, *sb.* (and *a.*) [f. as prec. + -IST.]

1. *Philos.* One who holds the doctrine of relativism.

1863 SPENCER *Ess.* III. 302, I diverge from other relativists in asserting that the existence of a non-relative is ..a positive deliverance of consciousness. **1898** *Pop. Sci. Monthly* LIII. 850 Agnostics, relativists, and all others must agree with him. **1935** K. KOFFKA *Princ. Gestalt Psychol.* 347 The relativist's argument rejects in the first place the distinction between the picture as a geographical and a behavioral object. **1953** M. GINSBERG *Ess. Sociol. & Soc. Philos.* I. vii. 124 Relativists generally stress the great diversity of morals. Yet the similarity is much greater. **1967** *Encycl. Philos.* III. 75/1 Writers who call themselves relativists always accept the first and second and sometimes accept the third of the theses. **1976** W. J. STANKIEWICZ *Aspects Polit. Theory* v. 97 If relativists are right in assuming that the analysis of values is complete when the latter are declared to be tastes, wishes or attitudes, it would seem impossible for moral statements to form any kind of pattern for either the individual or society.

2. A student or proponent of the theory of relativity.

1914 [implied in sense 3 below]. **1919** *Nature* 11 Dec. 374/2 The out-and-out relativist will not admit an absolute measure of acceleration any more than of velocity. **1922** A. S. EDDINGTON *Theory of Relativity* 16 The reason why the relativist resurrects this ancient truism is because it is only in this undissected combination of four dimensions that the experiences of all observers meet. **1968** *Amer. Jrnl. Physics* XXXVI. 1109/1 His [*sc.* Einstein's] great passion for the physical explanation of the laws of nature resulted in his abandoning ether and absolute time, thus radically modifying long-established Newtonian space-time. Thus, he was the first true relativist. **1977** *Listener* 24 Mar. 365/2 Newton's definitions of time and space..which were found to be implausible with the coming of the relativists at the end of the 19th century.

3. *attrib.* or as *adj.*

1914 C. D. BROAD *Perception* v. 286 It is no special objection to the relativist theory. **1921** *Nature* 8 Dec. 467/1 The differential equations which the relativist mathematicians use. **1939** V. A. DEMANT *Relig. Prospect* i. 12 Man has no criteria by which to guide himself in the movements of time. He resorts to beating back the forces that oppose what he conceives to be the most advanced phase. This attitude is completely relativist. **1949** *Scrutiny* XVI. I. 26 It is commonly held that the essential point about totalitarian morality is the denial of a universal moral law binding on all mankind and its replacement by a relativist view of morals. **1962** *Listener* 10 May 821/1 We are usually too timid, too relativist, to be so vehement in our defence of righteousness today.

relati'vistic, *a.* [f. RELATIVIST *sb.* + -IC.]

1. Of, pertaining to, or characterized by relativism or relativity.

1886 *Encycl. Brit.* XXI. 382/2 The elaborate presentation of sceptical and relativistic arguments. **1917** A. S. PRINGLE-PATTISON *Idea of God* 212, I applied this specially to the case of the secondary qualities which are usually regarded as the stronghold of the relativistic theory. **1937** T. PARSONS *Struct. Soc. Action* xiii. 480 On the empirical plane one of the first radical representatives of this relativistic view is Dilthey. **1959** A. BRECHT *Pol. Theory* vi. 249 Roscoe Pound ..called it futile to wait for a statement of absolutes, and recommended practical work on the basis of our present civilization—again an activity entirely legitimate from the relativistic viewpoint. **1964** M. JACOBS *Pattern in Cultural Anthropol.* xii. 297 No anthropologist lacks admiration for northwestern art work, no matter how ridiculously relativistic his dogma. **1979** *Sci. Amer.* Mar. 94/2 It seems that a much more relativistic process is going on in the visual system. The boundary between each target square and its immediate background gives only the relation between the light reflected by each of these areas. **1981** *Times Lit. Suppl.* 13 Feb. 176/4 In *Gulliver's Travels* Swift chose the most 'relativistic' form, the travel book, in order to attack the root of relativism.

2. *Physics.* **a.** Pertaining to or based on the theory of relativity; modified or formulated according to the assumptions or consequences of the theory of relativity.

special relativistic, general relativistic adjs.: based on or taking account of the special theory (only) or the general theory, respectively, of relativity.

1914 L. SILBERSTEIN *Theory of Relativity* iv. 94 It requires, according to the relativistic view itself, some essential, though numerically slight, modifications. **1926** *Physical Rev.* XXVIII. 1070 The relativistic theory of the hydrogen atom is apparently incomplete. **1938** *Ann. Reg. 1937* 355 Heitler and Bhabha.. used relativistic quantum mechanics to determine the number of secondary positrons and electrons produced when a fast primary electron passes through matter. **1958** CONDON & ODISHAW *Handbk. Physics* ii. 19 The constancy of v_4 implies a constant ratio between classical time t and relativistic proper time τ. **1970** *Nature* 17 Oct. 273/1 The rectilinear Galilean transformation was discarded by Einstein in favour of the special-relativistic (Lorentz) transformation to a uniformly moving frame. **1972** *Ibid.* 18 Feb. 361/2 The theory of black holes.. may perhaps be considered as one of the aspects of general-relativistic physics which is better understood. **1974** G. REECE tr. *Hund's Hist. Quantum Theory* vii. 99 Sommerfeld applied his theory, which took account of the relativistic correction, to the X-ray term.

b. Characterized by or designating circumstances, esp. those involving speeds approaching that of light or large gravitational potentials, in which discrepancies between the predictions of the theory of relativity and of Newtonian mechanics or classical electromagnetism become significant.

1934 *Discovery* Oct. 285/2 He examined the principles of thermodynamics as they apply in a relativistic universe. **1964** *Astrophysical Jrnl.* CXXXIX. 925 It has been argued in the past that the energy of the relativistic particles associated with the Crab cannot be greater than the kinetic energy of the filaments; otherwise the nebula would expand faster than it is observed to do. This argument is only corrected, however, if the relativistic particles are trapped within the filaments. **1967** *Ibid.* CL. 1005 To extend these results on neutron and supermassive star models to arbitrarily relativistic stars rotating with arbitrary angular velocity is a problem which.. is numerically complicated. **1973** C. W. MISNER et al. *Gravitation* xxiv. 633 The relativistic instability occurs far outside the Schwarzschild radius when the star is very massive... Rotation can stabilize it against relativistic collapse for a while. **1978** *Astrophysical Jrnl.* CCXXIII. 14 Fragmentation of a relativistic shock wave in either the free expansion or the self-similar blast wave solutions probably cannot be avoided.

Hence **relati'vistically** *adv.*

1947 *Physical Rev.* LXXII. 340/1 Relativistically, ν should be replaced by *ca.* **1955** L. D. LANDAU in W. Pauli *Niels Bohr* 52 Perturbation theory has been reconstructed in a relativistically invariant way. **1970** *Nature* 17 Oct. 271/1 To discuss the recoil relativistically we must speak of 4-momentum.

relativitist. [f. RELATIVITY + -IST.] = RELATIVIST *sb.* 2.

1931 *Sci. Progress* XXV. 632 As the relativitist would point out, only the resultant symmetry of our chemical molecules, inspected in the aggregate, is observable. **1939** *Mind* XLVIII. 62 The relativitist, they tell us, has *discovered* that what we think of as a ruler of fixed length, has in fact different lengths according to its position.

relativity (rɛlə'tɪvɪtɪ). [f. as RELATIVIST *sb.* + -ITY. Cf. F. *relativité*.] **1.** The fact or condition of being relative, relativeness.

a **1834** COLERIDGE in *Lit. Rem.* (1839) IV. 223 In every religious and moral use of the word, God,.. a relativity, a distinction in kind.. is so essentially implied [etc.]. **1867** LEWES *Hist. Philos.* (ed. 3) I. p. xxiv, Those who hold the doctrine of the relativity of knowledge. **1889** MIVART *Truth* 258 The relativity of beauty is an accidental relativity.

2. The quantitative dependence of observations on the relative motion of the observer and the observed object; that branch of physics which is concerned with the description of space and time allowing for this dependence.

The modern theory of relativity, developed largely by Albert Einstein (1879–1955), is an extension and generalization of the corresponding principles in classical, or Newtonian, mechanics.

The *principle of relativity*, in its restricted form, is the postulate that the laws of nature have the same form in all inertial reference frames; in its more general form, it states that the laws of nature, when expressed in a suitable ('co-variant') form, have the same form in all reference frames, whether inertial or not.

The *special theory of relativity* (1905), based on the restricted principle of relativity and the hypothesis of the constancy of the speed of light *in vacuo* as seen by observers in any inertial frames, resulted in a theoretical framework for the unification of space and time in a four-dimensional continuum and for the equivalence of mass and energy, and showed how the uniform relative motion of observers affects their measures of length and time.

The *general theory of relativity* (1915), essentially a theory of gravitation, is based on the general principle of relativity, the postulated equivalence of inertial and gravitational mass, and the assumption that the results of the special theory must be valid in the limiting case of zero gravitational potential; it leads to a new set of equations of motion and the result that space-time is curved by the presence of gravitational fields.

1876 J. C. MAXWELL *Matter & Motion* vi. 84 Our whole progress up to this point may be described as a gradual development of the doctrine of relativity of all physical phenomena. Position we must evidently acknowledge to be relative. *Ibid.* 85 (*heading*) Relativity of force. **1882** J. B. STALLO *Concepts & Theories of Mod. Physics* xii. 204 The same considerations which evince the relativity of motion also attest the relativity of its conceptual elements, space and time. **1905** W. J. G. tr. *Poincaré's Sci. & Hypoth.* v. 76 The state of the bodies and their mutual distances at any moment will solely depend on the state of the same bodies and on their mutual distances at the initial moment, but will in no way depend on the absolute initial position of the system and of [*read* on] its absolute initial orientation. This is what we shall call, for the sake of abbreviation, the law of relativity. [**1905** *Sci. Abstr.* A. VIII. 2277 A. Einstein... The relativity of lengths and times.] **1906** J. W. YOUNG tr. H. Poincaré in *Bull. Amer. Math. Soc.* XII. 243 The principle of relativity, according to which the laws of physical phenomena must be the same for a stationary observer as for one carried along in a uniform motion of translation. *Ibid.* 247 Let us consider the principle of relativity; this principle is not only confirmed by our daily experience,.. but it appeals to our common sense with irresistible force. And yet it also is being fiercely attacked. **1912** *Phil. Mag.* XXIII. 375 An acceptance of the Einstein theory of relativity necessitates a revision of the Newtonian system of mechanics. **1916** *Monthly Notices R. Astron. Soc.* LXXVI. 701 These considerations have led Einstein to his postulate of general relativity, which requires the laws of nature to be invariant for *all* transformations of co-ordinates. **1920** R. W. LAWSON tr. *Einstein's Relativity* vii. 20 As a result of an analysis of the physical conceptions of time and space, it became evident that in reality there is not the least incompatibility between the principle of relativity and the law of propagation of light, and that by systematically holding fast to both these laws a logically rigid theory could be arrived at. This theory has been called the special theory of relativity. **1921** *Nature* 1 Dec. 434/2 The result is valid for both the special and the general theory of relativity. **1922** E. P. ADAMS tr. *Einstein's Meaning of Relativity* iii. 68 We shall be true to the principle of relativity in its broadest sense if we give such a form to the laws [of physics] that they are valid in every such four-dimensional system of co-ordinates, that is, if the equations expressing the laws are co-variant with respect to arbitrary transformations. **1928** *Times* 3 Dec. 8/2 The whole point of the theory of relativity is the discovery of invariants, or absolute quantities, the same to all observers, and identical throughout the universe. **1932** W. T. STACE *Theory of Knowl.* xiv. 389 The space-time of modern relativity mechanics. **1959** *Listener* 9 Apr. 631/2 In everyday experience, special relativity gives virtually the same results as Newtonian theory. **1968** *Amer. Jrnl. Physics* XXXVI. 1109/1 Although the principle of relativity is subject to a possible experimental disproof in the future, the importance of the postulational approach is that it freed relativity from electrodynamics as a basis and made special relativity more universal. **1973** L. J. TASSIE *Physics of Elementary Particles* 203 An important result of the theory of special relativity is time dilatation, or the slowing down of moving clocks. **1974** *Encycl. Brit. Macropædia* XV. 584/2 The general theory of relativity derives its origin from the need to extend the new space and time concepts of the special theory of relativity from the domain of electric and magnetic phenomena to all of physics and, particularly, to the theory of gravitation. **1976** M. G. BOWLER *Gravitation & Relativity* p. vii, Einstein's theory of gravitation, general relativity, has been verified at the one per cent level. **1978** *Sci. Amer.* Feb. 131/1 The present understanding of the fundamental laws of nature arose from three principles: special relativity, general relativity and quantum mechanics.

3. The relative grading of posts or salaries, usu. considered within one business (*internal*) or in comparison with others (*external*). Freq. *pl.*

1962 *Rep Comm. Broadc. 1960* 192 The BBC's policy on the payment of its staff takes careful account of internal and external relativities. In assessing internal relativities, the broad aim is to define the difficulty and responsibility of posts at each level over a very wide range of professions... To maintain external relativities, the Corporation draws comparisons with a suitable range of different employment. **1966** *New Statesman* 21 Jan. 71/1 Union A makes a claim in January, on the grounds that they have fallen behind B and C. When A's claim is agreed, B makes a claim in February, because relativity has been destroyed. **1971** *Nature* 20 Aug. 513/1 The institution pressed for the use of internal relativities to determine salaries. **1974** *Times* 9 Feb. 1/2 The new principles and procedures for adjusting wage relativities,.. since the Government agreed to set up machinery inside the Pay Board to examine major relativity claims.

relativization (rɛlətɪvaɪ'zeɪʃən). [f. next + -ATION.] **1.** *Physics.* A relativistic treatment of a problem or theorem. *rare.*

1921 H. L. BROSE tr. *Moszkowski's Einstein the Searcher* vii. 162 Now, the conception of time has been entirely revolutionized by Einstein himself... We thus approach a relativization of causality... Something physiological that ultimately.. resolves itself into a relativization of time.

2. The action of making relative; the fact or process of being made relative. Freq. in *Philos.* and *Linguistics.*

1942 *Mind* LI. 237 This is not exclusive subdivision, but relativization or canalization. **1945** *Polish Sci. & Learning* VI. 19/1 The relativization of the definability of a sign '*a*' to a set of propositions *X* becomes obvious. **1948** L. SPITZER *Linguistics & Lit. Hist.* 73 His [*sc.* Cervantes'] humor, which admits of many strata.. of relativization and dialectics—bears testimony to his high position above the world. **1959** K. R. POPPER *Logic Sci. Discovery* 346, I only learned from Rényi's paper how fertile this relativization could be. **1968** *Language* XLIV. 55 Relativization, Relative reduction and Modifier inversion were set up to handle other constructions. **1977** M. DUMMETT *Elem. Intuitionism* v. 206 The relativization property guarantees that the logical laws which hold good whenever the individual variables are taken as ranging over any admissible domain also hold good when they are confined to some inhabited subdomain which can be characterized by a predicate of the language.

relativize ('rɛlətɪvaɪz), *v.* [f. RELATIVE *a.* + -IZE.] **1.** *Physics.* To render or treat according to the principles and results of the theory of relativity.

1935 J. DOUGALL tr. *Born's Atomic Physics* iv. 84 Before Einstein, no one ever hesitated to speak of the simultaneous occurrence of two events... Einstein proved that this concept must be 'relativized', since two events may be simultaneous in one frame of reference, but take place at different times in another. **1956** E. H. HUTTEN *Lang. Mod. Physics* iii. 108 If we can make a uniform motion into an accelerated one, with a stroke of the pen so to speak, it means that the concept of force becomes relativised.

2. To render relative; to make something relative to, or dependent on, something else. Freq. in *Philos.* and *Linguistics.*

1937 T. PARSONS *Struct. Soc. Action* xi. 447 His [*sc.* Durkheim's] theory of religion, by associating it with the social type, relativized another great body of phenomena. **1948** L. SPITZER *Linguistics & Lit. Hist.* 81 The pun is a bifocal manner of expression which relaxes and relativizes the firmness with which language usually appears to speaking man. **1966** J. J. KATZ *Philos. Lang.* ii. 14 The philosopher of language.. need not restrict his philosophical solutions and claims by relativizing them to the conceptual systems. **1976** *Language* LII. 285 Kuhn proposes to relativize the notion of science. **1978** F. BURTON *Politics of Legitimacy* iii. 87 The raid that evening served to relativize the type of criticism that Jimmy was making.

Hence **'relativized** *ppl. a.*

1972 *Language* XLVIII. 306 This [*sc.* receiving primary stress] should happen, for example, if the relativized NP were the subject of an embedded intransitive sentence. **1977** *Ibid.* LIII. 94 Ross formulates the relativization rule in such a way that it always involves movement of the relativized NP out of the sentence dominating the rest of the relative clause.

relator (rɪ'leɪtə(r)). Also 7 -our. [a. L. *relātor*, agent-n. f. *relāt-*: see RELATE *v.* Cf. F. *relateur*, Sp., Pg. *relator*, It. *relatore*.]

1. a. A relater, narrator. (Common *c* 1600–1750.)

1591 *Garrard's Art Warre* 126 The discription by draught beeing well knowen, accompanied with the liuely voice of the Relator. **1624** F. WHITE *Repl. Fisher* 562 You are an vnfaithfull Relatour of the practise of the Primitiue Church. **1660** BOYLE *New Exp. Phys. Mech.* ix. 72 A faithful Relator of Experiments. **1703** MAUNDRELL *Journ. Jerus.* (1721) 15 The Relators of this Story.. were doubtless fully perswaded of the truth of it. **1759** JOHNSON *Rasselas* xxxvi[i], Imlac.. was not very confident of the veracity of the relator. **1846** TRENCH *Mirac.* iii. (1862) 130 It will cause little wonder that two or three relators have in part seized diversely the culminating points of a story.

†**b.** (One's) informant. *Obs. rare.*

1607 TOPSELL *Four-f. Beasts* (1658) 349 It may be that he or his relator had seen them playing together as Goats do. ?**1610** DONNE *Lett.* Wks. 1839 VI. 338 When this place affords anything worth your hearing, I will be your relator.

†**c.** The historian *of* a place. *Obs. rare*⁻¹.

1691 WOOD *Ath. Oxon.* II. 641 Of that little Parish.. he was in effect the Relator.

2. *Law.* An informer; *spec.* one who supplies the materials for an information by the Attorney General (see RELATION 1 b).

1603 OWEN *Pembrokeshire* i. (1892) 6 Especiallye promoters newelye named Relatours, a generacion hated both of the good and badd people. **1632** *Star Chamb. Cases* (Camden) 96 Sr John Finch for the relator this day replyed. **1674** *N. Riding Rec.* VI. 222 This Court doth approve of, admit, and allow Alex. Dixon to use, exercise and follow the office of a Relator. **1710** *Act 9 Anne* c. 20 §4. **1768** BLACKSTONE *Comm.* III. 427 The attorney general, at the relation of some informant, (who is usually called the relator) files *ex officio* an information in the court of chancery. **1823** *Act. 4 Geo. IV*, c. 76 §23 To the Knowledge or Belief of the Relator or Relators so making Oath. **1865** *Pall Mall G.* 29 May 6 The relator.. is a descendant of a brother of the second wife of the testator.

†**3.** A relative. *Obs. rare*⁻¹. (Cf. RELATER 2.)

1665 SIR T. HERBERT *Trav.* (1677) 246 The Arch-flamen carried the holy Fire, attended by the Priests and three hundred sixty five Youths who were their relators.

4. *Linguistics.* A sentence-element (usu. a preposition) serving to relate one phrase to another.

1933 [see DESCRIPTOR]. **1953** W. J. ENTWISTLE *Aspects of Lang.* v. 157 The *relatum* of a language corresponds to the logical category of substance and finds its pure expression in proper nouns; the *descriptum* corresponds to quantity and has its pure expression in numerals; the *descriptor* with quality and is pure in adverbs; the *relator* with relation and is pure in prepositions. **1965** *Language* XLI. 73 Thus the whole string is a relator-axis phrase of which *on* manifests relator and the rest manifests axis. **1978** *Language* LIV. 353 *Relator* is assigned to constituents that serve to introduce embedded clauses (e.g. *that*), and is thus partially co-extensive with the complementizer of recent TG

re'latrix. [a. late L. *relātrix* (5th c.), female agent-n. f. *relāt-*: see RELATE *v.*] *Law.* 'A female relator or petitioner' (Ogilvie 1882, citing Story).

‖**relatum** (rɪ'lɑːtəm, -'eɪtəm). Pl. -ata. [a. L. *relātum*, neut. pa. pple. of *referre* REFER.]

a. *Logic.* = RELATE. *sb.* 2. **b.** *Linguistics.* (Brøndal's term for) the substantival member of a prepositional phrase (see RELATOR 4).

1872 G. GROTE *Aristotle* iii. 101 Habit, disposition, perception, cognition, position, &c., are all *Relata*. *Ibid.* 102 The *Relatum* and its Correlate seem to be *simul naturâ*. If you suppress either one of the pair, the other vanishes along with it. **1893** W. MINTO *Logic* iii. 118 In mediæval logic the term *Relata* was confined to these perfect cases, but the Category had a wider scope with Aristotle. **1903** B. RUSSELL *Princ. Math.* ii. 24 The class of terms to which some term has the relation *R*.. I call the class of *relata*. Thus if *R* be paternity.. the relata will be children. **1933** [see DESCRIPTOR]. **1946** *Language* XXII. 219 The *relatum* is most commonly a noun or other type of substantive expression. **1953** [see RELATOR 4]. **1974** L. SKLAR *Space, Time, & Spacetime* iii. 167 For temporal and spatiotemporal relata the idealization is that of the instantaneous event.

relaunch (riː-), *v.* [RE- 5 a.] To launch again. Also *fig.*

a **1745** BROOME *Poems, Horace* Ode I The merchant.. soon relaunches from the shore. **1885** WARREN & CLEVERLY *Wand. Beetle* 13 We hauled the boat over, and relaunched her on the other side. **1964** *Yearbk. Astron 1965* 135 The heavier landing vehicle was the penalty to be paid for taking the entire propulsion machinery down on to the lunar surface and re-launching it. **1971** *Daily Tel.* 27 May 1/5 The company was relaunched nearly two years ago... It was originally part of Henry Bowen-Davies' £8m Davies' Investment group which collapsed in 1967. **1980** *Listener* 3 Jan. 6/3 Rupert Murdoch relaunched the *Sun* as a down-market tabloid.

'relaunch, *sb.* [f. the vb.] A renewed launch. Freq. *fig.* of a business or commodity.

1970 *Daily Tel.* 2 Mar. 21/6 The re-launch had the desired effect and Vim's share of the market increased from 33 p.c. to 38 p.c. **1979** *Guardian* 14 Nov. 20/1 (Advt.), The relaunch of Times Newspapers Limited signals the return of the most challenging selling opportunities around.

re'lax, *sb.* [f. the vb.]

1. Relaxation; an instance of this.

1627–77 FELTHAM *Resolves* II. lviii. 282 'Tis not denyed, but labors and cares may have their Relaxes and Recreations. **1643** MILTON *Divorce* II. xiv. Wks. 1851 IV. 97 The first good consequence of such a relaxe will be the justifying of Papal stews. **1733** BUDGELL *Bee* I. 499 Sated Nature crav'd Timely Relax, distent with liquid Pain. **1773** J. ROSS *Fratricide* II. 255 (MS.), Hate now returning With ten-fold force, reliev'd by short relax! **1853** C. BRONTË *Villette* II. xxiii. 141 That bustle and business to which, till five p.m., there was no relax. **1925** A. S. M. HUTCHINSON *One Increasing Purpose* I. xxii. 137 That.. sigh she gave,.. and that relax into his arms. **1961** *Times* 2 Nov. 16/2 Miss Brodie herself, who is always arousing her headmistress's suspicions because of her damning of braces and blessing of relaxes.

†**2.** A device for releasing some part of a machine. *Obs.*

1676 *Phil. Trans.* XI. 716 As the Relax gives way, the Weight will adjust the motion of the hand to the Index E.

re'lax, *a. rare.* [f. the vb., on anal. of LAX *a.*]

1. Lax, wanting in strictness.

1609 BIBLE (Douay) *Judg.* xxi. *comm.*, Lest either justice be over sharpe, or mercie too relaxe. **1790** BEATSON *Nav. & Mil. Mem.* II. 198 He was so relax in discipline, that the garrison.. were seldom in a condition to do their duty properly. **1802** tr. *Ducray-Duminil's Victor* III. 228 We determined first to visit France and to consider Germany, the police of which was more relax than in other countries.

†**2.** Relaxed, slack. *Obs.*

1626 BACON *Sylva* §381 The motion and activity of the body consisteth chiefly in the sinews, which, when the southern wind bloweth, are more relax.

relax (rɪ'læks), *v.* [ad. L. *relaxāre*, f. *re-* RE- + *laxus* LAX *a.* Cf. F. *relaxer* (14th c.).]

I. *trans.* **1.** †**a.** To make (a thing) less compact or dense; to loosen or open up by separation of parts. Also *refl. Obs.*

c **1420** *Pallad. on Husb.* II. 140 Ragston & thinges hard, in cold and hete Relaxed, bereth vyneyerdes grete. **1664** POWER *Exp. Philos.* I. 77 When the Atoms wherewith the Liquor is fully impregnated do relax and open themselves. **1667** MILTON *P.L.* VI. 599 But now Foule dissipation follow'd and forc't rout; Nor serv'd it to relax thir serried files. **1676** CONIERS in *Phil. Trans.* XI. 717 At that time it relaxes or swells the Deal for about two or three hours.

b. To render (a part of the body) less firm or rigid; to make loose or pliable or slack; to enfeeble or enervate (*spec.* in *Ent.*). Also in *fig.* context.

1620 VENNER *Via Recta* iii. 68 It mollifieth and relaxeth the stomacke, taketh away the appetite. **1664** POWER *Exp. Philos.* I. 68 The Optick Nerve being by successful means disobstructed and relaxed. **1781** GIBBON *Decl. & F.* xxv. II. 529 The nerves of discipline were relaxed, and the high-ways were infested with robbers. **1808** *Med. Jrnl.* XIX. 247 The speedy and prompt administration of every remedy tending to relax the surface. **1860** TYNDALL *Glac.* I. xi. 84 The heat relaxed my muscles. **1902** W. J. HOLLAND *Butterfly Bk.* 41 When butterflies or moths have been put up in papers or mounted on pins without having their wings expanded and set it becomes necessary, before setting them, to relax them. **1939** DUNCAN & PICKWELL *World of Insects* xix. 389 Before such stored specimens can be mounted they must be relaxed. **1976** P. W. CRIBB *Lepidopterist's Handbk.* vii. 85, I have just relaxed and set some tortrices without too much trouble.

absol. **1718** QUINCY *Compl. Disp.* 113 They are very mucilaginous, and therefore soften, relax, and heal. **1753** CHAMBERS *Cycl. Supp.* s.v. *Malache*, Such ointments as relax and mollify.

c. To diminish the force or tension of; *esp.* to loosen (one's hold or grasp).

1781 COWPER *Conversat.* 812 Charity may relax the miser's fist. **1790** BURKE *Fr. Rev.* (ed. 2) 93 This distemper .. relaxes and wears out.. the spring of that spirit. **1841** BORROW *Zincali* I. iii. II. 267 Owing to the civil wars, the ties which unite society have been considerably relaxed. **1859** TENNYSON *Guinevere* 454 When.. their law Relaxed its hold upon us. **1866** DK. ARGYLL *Reign Law* vii. (1871) 389 False conceptions of the truth.. may and do relax the most powerful springs of action.

2. a. To make less strict, severe, or rigid; to mitigate, tone down, modify.

1662 GUNNING *Lent Fast* 69 An austerer course of life is relaxed through the frailty of the flesh. **1718** POPE *Iliad* xv. 78 Not till that Day shall Jove relax his Rage. **1769** *Junius Lett.* xii. (1788) 81 We have seen the laws sometimes scandalously relaxed, sometimes violently stretched beyond their tone. **1820** SCOTT *Abbot* ii, The old woman seemed somewhat to relax her tone of severity. **1870** FREEMAN *Norm. Conq.* (ed. 2) I. iv. 173 The rule had clearly been relaxed before the reign of the Great William.

absol. **1768** TUCKER *Lt. Nat.* II. III. xxiv. 39 No man can fix so perfect an idea of that virtue [justice] as that he may not afterwards find reason to add or relax therefrom.

b. To slacken, abate, diminish (an effort, etc.).

1774 GOLDSM. *Nat. Hist.* (1776) II. 64 From the moment the necessity of learning new words ceases, they relax their industry. **1817** SHELLEY *Rev. Islam* VI. xx, [The horse] relaxed its course as it approached me. **1843** BETHUNE *Sc. Fireside Stor.* 29 Having business of importance which demanded his presence elsewhere, [he] began to relax his attention.

c. To cause to abate in zeal or force. *rare.*

1660 SECKER in Spurgeon *Treas. Dav.* Ps. xliv. 17–19 Neither the persecuting hand of men, nor the chastising hand of God, relaxed ancient singular saints. **1824–28** LANDOR *Citat. Shaks.* Wks. 1846 II. 286 Whether we have not.. acted as if we believed that opposition were to be relaxed and borne away by self sufficiency.

d. *refl.* To unbend (oneself); to take relaxation.

1762–71 H. WALPOLE *Vertue's Anecd. Paint.* (1786) V. 135 The philosophic warrior, who could relax himself into the ornament of a refined court. **1772–84** *Cook's Voy.* (1790) IV. 1489 They relax themselves by conversation and other amusements.

3. †**a.** To remit (a rent). *Obs. rare*$^{-1}$.

1528 *Galway Arch.* in *10th Rep. Hist. MSS. Comm.* App. V. 403 It was condessendid by the.. Comens to relax to the said Willam Marten.. the rent that he owith of the tennement to the Comens.

b. To give up, stop (a process).

1883 *Law Rep. 11 Q.B. Div.* 554 He must apply to the Court for an order to release him, and the Court must order the process to be relaxed.

4. a. *Sc.* (now only *Law.*) To free or discharge (a person) from restraint, legal process, or penalty. Also *absol.* To procure a relaxation.

1546 *Reg. Privy Council Scot.* I. 29 Ordanis lettres to be direct to relax James Twedy.. fra the proces of the horne led upon him. *a* **1578** LINDESAY (Pitscottie) *Chron. Scot.* (S.T.S.) I. 26 Quhou schir James Steuart and his brother was put in presoune,.. And hou they war relaxit againe. **1640** R. BAILLIE *Canterb. Self-Convict.* 115 He must have no lesse censure then the great excommunication, from which he must never be relaxed but by the Bishops own mouth. **1752** J. LOUTHIAN *Form of Process* (ed. 2) 141 That.. ye.. relax the said [persons].. from the Process of Denounciation led against them. **1791** KAMES *Dict. Decisions* (ed. 2) II. 329 He who relaxes and registers not, cannot alienate, being still holden and repute rebel. **1838** W. BELL *Dict. Law Scot.* 844 Letters passing the signet whereby a debtor was relaxed from the horn, that is from personal diligence.

b. Of the Inquisition: To hand over (heretics) to the secular power for execution. [Sp. *relaxar.*]

1838 PRESCOTT *Ferd. & Is.* I. vii. I. 377 Those who were to be relaxed, as it was called, were delivered over, as impenitent heretics, to the secular arm. **1853** W. STIRLING-MAXWELL *Cloister Life Chas. V*, 209 Dr. Cazalla was one of fifteen heretics who were 'relaxed', or, in secular speech, burnt in May 1559 at Valladolid.

c. To set free *from* labour. *rare*$^{-1}$.

1762–9 FALCONER *Shipwr.* I. 336 Relax'd from toil the sailors range the shore.

II. *intr.* **5. a.** To become loose or slack; to grow less tense or firm.

1720 POPE *Iliad* XXI. 309 Tired by the tides, his knees relax with toil. **1858** LARDNER *Hand-bk. Nat. Phil.* 128 The piston descends, therefore, and the spring relaxes.

b. Of the features: To become less rigid or stern. Also const. *from, into.*

1797 MRS. RADCLIFFE *Italian* iv, His features relaxed from their first expression. **1832** HT. MARTINEAU *Ireland* iii. 40 Presently the knit brow relaxed, the fierce eye was tamed. **1840** DICKENS *Barn. Rudge* ii, His features would relax into a look of fondness.

6. To abate in degree or force.

1701 ROWE *Amb. Step-Moth.* IV. i, This raging Fit of Honour will relax. **1823** J. BADCOCK *Dom. Amusem.* 47 When our warm weather comes on early, and does not too soon relax. **1834** DISRAELI *Rev. Epick* II. xxiii, This emprise Will not relax until the sun shall rise On men who bless his birth.

7. a. To become less severe, strict, or exacting; to grow milder. Also const. *from.*

1749 H. WALPOLE *Let. to Mann* 4 Mar. (1857) II. 147 The mutinous were likely to go great lengths, if the Admiralty had not bought off some by money, and others by relaxing in the material points. **1789** BELSHAM *Ess.* II. xli. 523 It was hoped.. the Court would relax in its opposition. **1818** JAS. MILL *Brit. India* II. v. ii. 368 The Colonel proposed to relax in the affair of Basslin, and to ask for something else in its stead. **1850** MRS. BROWNING *Prometh. Bound* 216 Thou art, sooth, a brave god, And, for all thou hast borne.., Nought relaxest from scorn!

b. Of persons: To become less stiff or distant; to assume a friendlier manner. Also const. *into.*

1837 DICKENS *Pickw.* ii, He gradually relaxed, and reverted to the subject of the ball. **1837** DISRAELI *Venetia* III. ii, Lady Annabel relaxed into conversation beyond her custom. **1879** HOWELLS *L. Aroostook* (1883) I. 200 It seemed to him as if.. she relaxed towards him as they walked.

c. Of persons: to become less tense or anxious. Freq. imp., 'stop worrying!', 'calm down!'

1935 A. J. POLLOCK *Underworld Speaks* 135/2 *You can relax*, the person playing the hand in contract informing his partner that the contract will be made. **1941** *Men Only* July 70 (*caption*) All right, relax. I'm just watching it [*sc.* the baby] for someone! **1954** T. S. ELIOT *Confidential Clerk* I. 18 As you're here, Eggers, I can just relax. **1959** *Woman* 4 Apr. 48/2, I patted his knee. 'Relax, darling. Our problem is soon to be solved.' **1976** C. WOLFF *Older Love* i. 12, I relaxed over a *crème caramel* and was happy.

8. To slacken in zeal or application (also const. *into*); to seek or take relaxation *from* work or occupation.

1760–2 GOLDSM. *Cit. W.* ix, I once more, therefore, relax into my former indifference with regard to the English ladies. **1774** —— *Retal.* 79 Here Douglas retires from his toils to relax. **1796** C. MARSHALL *Garden.* xxii. (1813) 448 He cannot relax in his duty without his neglect being manifest by serious consequences following it. **1833** CRUSE tr. *Eusebius' Eccl. Hist.* VI. iii. 222 He did not however relax in his perseverance.

†**9.** To slacken in respect *of* something. *Obs.*

1775 *Tender Father* II. 69 No sooner was this effected, than I relaxed of my tenderness and regard. **1797** MRS. A. M. BENNETT *Beggar Girl* (1813) II. 66 The stately brow of Mrs. Buchanan relaxed of its asperity.

10. Chiefly *Physics.* To return towards a state of equilibrium.

1959 G. TROUP *Masers* iii. 45 Interactions occur between the lattice vibrations and the molecules, which enable the molecular system to 'relax' to thermal equilibrium. **1972** *Physics Bull.* Aug. 451/3 The electronic spins, initially unpolarized, relax slowly towards their equilibrium polarization which, in the high field applied and at a very low temperature of 0·4 K, is nearly 100%. **1973** *Nature* 24 Aug. 496/1 We have thus assumed that the observed strains result from a single system which relaxed exponentially after the start of the eruption with a time constant of 7·5 d. **1978** *Sci. Amer.* Sept. 124/2 Regular patterns of differential extinction .. have occurred as the supersaturated faunas of 13 species of small flightless mammals have relaxed toward the smaller number of species that are appropriate to particular mountaintops.

†**re'laxable**, *a. Obs. rare*$^{-1}$. [f. prec. + -ABLE.] Admitting of remission.

a **1677** BARROW *Wks.* (1686) II. 501 Who doth so render himself obnoxious, that if he derogate from a creature, he may not suppose it to be relaxable to him by some pardon?

re'laxant, *a.* and *sb. Med.* [ad. L. *relaxant-em*, pres. pple. of *relaxāre* to RELAX.]

A. *adj.* Causing, or distinguished by, relaxation.

1771 T. PERCIVAL *Ess.* (1777) I. 129 When received into the stomach it is highly debilitating and relaxant. **1822–34** *Good's Study Med.* (ed. 4) I. 309 Where the pain and tension are very distressing, relaxant cataplasms and fomentations are generally advisable. **1977** *Lancet* 24–31 Dec. 1332/1 It may be that these neurons are involved in mediating relaxant effects of the intestine in response to a food bolus.

B. *sb.* A practice or drug serving to produce relaxation.

1832 J. THOMSON *Life W. Cullen* I. 406 He considered the practice of warm bathing the most powerful Emollient and the most considerable Relaxant. **1898** *Allbutt's Syst. Med.* V. 996 In such cases good may result from the administration of arterial relaxants. **1977** *Sci. Amer.* May 99/2 One of its active alkaloids is the basis of drugs that are important in modern surgery as muscle relaxants.

†**re'laxate**, *v. Obs.* [f. ppl. stem of L. *relaxāre*: see RELAX *v.* and -ATE³.] To relax.

1. *trans.* **a.** = RELAX *v.* 1 and 1 b.

1597 A. M. tr. *Guillemeau's Fr. Chirurg.* 40 b/2 We Cauterize alsoe the Eyeliddes which are relaxated. **1655** T. VAUGHAN *Euphrates* 46 The centrall and cælestiall Luminaries have, by their mutuall mixture and conflux of beames relaxated and dilated the Pores of the earth. **1694** MOTTEUX *Rabelais* IV. lxvii. (1737) 275 The retentive Faculty of the Nerve.. was relaxated.

absol. **1657** TOMLINSON *Renou's Disp.* 698 This Unguent .. relaxates, leniates and mollifies.

b. = RELAX *v.* 2 and 2 b.

1664 H. MORE *Myst. Iniq.* vii. 125 What can more relaxate those.. hearty aspirings of our Souls.. then such corrupt conceits as these? **1680** —— *Apocal. Apoc.* 209 The.. zeal.. and strictness of Discipline will be much relaxated.

c. To release, set free (cf. RELAX *v.* 4 a).

1681 H. MORE *Exp. Dan.* 103 Cyrus, King of Persia, will relaxate your Captivity. *Ibid.*, The Messias.. will come to relaxate his people from the Captivity of Sin.

2. *intr.* = RELAX *v.* 5–7.

1597 A. M. tr. *Guillemeau's Fr. Chirurg.* 52 b/2 The face waxeth pale, the Belly relaxateth, and the speach fayleth. **1655–87** H. MORE *App. Antid.* (1712) 218 If they euer relaxate into mirth,.. it is foolishly antick and deformed. **1681** —— *Exp. Dan.* Pref. 68 Our zeal has relaxated against the Church of Rome.

Hence †**relaxating** *vbl. sb. Obs.*

1647 HAMMOND *Power of Keys* iv. 51 The word.. is used again for loosing in our sense, relaxating of, or freeing from a censure of excommunication.

relaxation (ˌriːlæk'seɪʃən). [ad. L. *relaxātiōn-em*, n. of action f. *relaxāre*: see prec. and RELAX *v.*, and cf. F. *relaxation* (1314).]

1. a. Partial (†or complete) remission *of* some penalty, burden, duty, etc.; †also, the document granting such remission.

1526 *Pilgr. Perf.* (W. de W. 1531) 42 The plenary remyssyons ben ever referred communly to relaxacyon of payne. **1533–4** *Act 25 Hen. VIII*, c. 21 §1 Licenses, faculties, grantis, relaxacions, writtes called *Perinde valere*, rehabilitacions, abolitions, and other infinite sortes of buls. **1613** PURCHAS *Pilgrimage* VIII. x. (1614) 792 He..procured a relaxation of tribute from his father in law. **1655** FULLER *Ch. Hist.* III. ii. §3. 19 Others conceive this relaxation indulged in favour to some great offenders. **1727–38** CHAMBERS *Cycl.* s.v., In this sense we say the relaxation of an attachment in the court of admiralty. **1791** BURKE *Corr.* (1844) III. 362 Hitherto all relaxation of penalties proceeded on principles of union. **1844** H. H. WILSON *Brit. India* II. 405 Some relaxation was admitted in regard to the tributes.

b. *Sc. Law.* Release from a judicial penalty, *esp.* from a sentence of outlawry.

1546 *Reg. Privy Council Scot.* I. 59 His grace sall nowther giff respect nor remissioun, suspendere nor relaxatioun, to na maner of persoun..that sal happin to committ slauchter. **1601** *Acts Sederunt* (1790) 34 Na relaxatioun..sall be grantit to ony rebell lawfullie denunceit to the horne. **1752** J. LOUTHIAN *Form of Process* (ed. 2) 140 Follows the Letters of Relaxation on the foresaid Petition and Interlocutor. **1791** KAMES *Dict. Decisions* (ed. 2) I. 262 The Lords found that relaxations must be executed at the head-burgh of that same shire where the denounciation was made. **1838** W. BELL *Dict. Law Scot.* 844 In criminal prosecutions, one who has been outlawed may appeal..for letters of relaxation, reponing him against the sentence.

c. Release from captivity; restoration to freedom.

1609 BIBLE (Douay) *Isa.* xxxii. *comm.*, The fift part. Of the captivitie and relaxation of the kingdom of Juda.

d. (See quots. and RELAX *v.* 4 b.)

1826 *Blackw. Mag.* XX. 84 Relaxation is the act by which the Inquisitors deliver over a person convicted of heresy to the royal judge ordinary, that he may be condemned to a capital punishment. **1894** *Month* Mar. 335 The sentence of 'relaxation' comprised three parts; the judgment of the Inquisition, the verdict of the secular magistrate, and the execution—all this on the same day.

2. a. The action of unbending the mind from severe application; release from ordinary occupations or cares; recreation.

1548 UDALL *Erasm. Par. Luke* ix. 84 b, For of suche sorte ought the pastyme & relaxacion of suche men as are followers of the apostles to bee. **1597** HOOKER *Eccl. Pol.* v. lxx. §3 Those poore and needie,..at these times made partakers of relaxation and ioy with others. **1663** COWLEY *Verses & Ess., Ode Liberty* ii, To thy bent mind some relaxation give, And steal one day out of thy life to live. **1712** ADDISON *Spect.* No. 487 ¶3 In this case Dreams look like the Relaxations and Amusements of the Soul. **1818** HAZLITT *Eng. Poets* ii. (1870) 45 The genius of his poetry..is inspired by the love of ease, and relaxation from all the cares and business of life. **1876** LOWELL *Among my Bks.* Ser. II. 137 It is no marvel when even their relaxations were such downright hard work.

transf. **1756** BURKE *Subl. & B.* IV. x. [The eye] has a sort of relaxation or rest. **1784** COWPER *Task* I. 81 But relaxation of the languid frame..Was bliss reserv'd for happier days.

†**b.** Respite, rest. Const. *of*. *Obs. rare*$^{-1}$.

1728 ELIZA HEYWOOD tr. *Mme. de Gomez's Belle A.* (1732) II. 256 The little Walk would give..Julia some Relaxation of Speech, and the better enable her to continue her Recital.

3. *Path.* A loosening or slackening of the fibres, nerves, joints, etc., of the body; diminution of firmness or tension.

1626 BACON *Sylva* §730 Bathing or Anointing give a Relaxation or Emollition. **1661** LOVELL *Hist. Anim. & Min.* 289 The head is heavy with sleepe, and there is a relaxation of the nerves and ligaments. **1704** F. FULLER *Med. Gymn.* Pref., It [is] impossible to remove some Diseases of the Limbs, without an universal equal Relaxation. **1808** BARCLAY *Muscular Motions* 303 That state of relaxation which a muscle exhibits in the dead body. **1857** BULLOCK *Cazeaux' Midwif.* 129 The relaxation of the pelvic symphyses is a frequent occurrence.

4. a. Diminution of, release or freedom from, strictness or severity.

a **1626** W. SCLATER *Exp. 4th ch. Rom.* (1650) 116, I..can but wonder, How the severity of Laws against Popish Seminaries hath gotten relaxation. **1656** EARL MONM. tr. *Boccalini's Advts. fr. Parnass.* I. v. (1674) 5 Wholesome Institutions, which after a relaxation, are at last quite forgotten. **1772** *Junius Lett.* Pref. (1788) 16 These are not times to admit of any relaxation in the little discipline we have left. **1835** THIRLWALL *Greece* viii. I. 298 The root of the evil lay in the relaxation of the royal authority. **1873** SYMONDS *Grk. Poets* iv. 104 The relaxation of Ionian life..rendered the development of satire in Ionia more natural.

b. Extension of meaning.

1858 GLADSTONE *Homer* III. 20 This relaxation in the sense of *Βασιλεὺς* is no inconsiderable note of change.

5. Abatement of intensity, vigour, or energy.

1695 WOODWARD *Nat. Hist. Earth* III. i. (1723) 142 Relaxation of the Heat. **1756** BURKE *Subl. & B.* IV. xx, Disposing to an universal relaxation, and inducing..that species of it called sleep. *a* **1781** WATSON *Philip III*, III. 244 It might occasion too great a relaxation of the vigour which you have been so long accustomed to exert. **1875** LYELL *Princ. Geol.* (ed. 12) I. II. xx. 514 The grassy covering of the sloping talus marks a temporary relaxation of the erosive action of the sea. **1882** PEBODY *Eng. Journalism* xi. 83 Stuart complains..of his dilatoriness, of his relaxation of energy.

6. *Engin.* and *Math.* A method of solving a set of simultaneous equations (originally *spec.* ones describing the equilibrium of a rigid load-bearing structure) by guessing a solution and successively modifying it to accord with whichever equation or constraint is currently least closely satisfied. Freq. *attrib.*

1935 *Proc. R. Soc.* A. CLI. 60 The method of systematic relaxation... Imagine that one constraint is relaxed, so that one joint is permitted to travel slowly through a specified distance in some specified direction. **1940** R. V. SOUTHWELL *Relaxation Methods in Engin. Sci.* i. 11 The relaxation procedure is a means whereby simultaneous equations may be solved, not exactly, but with steadily increasing approximation. **1957** L. FOX *Two-Point Boundary Problems* iii. 39 In most problems of the type suitable for relaxation the equations can be arranged so that the biggest coefficient in any row lies in the diagonal. **1972** *Physics Bull.* May 273/1 During the war, Southwell and his team had been extending relaxation methods from redundant pin-jointed frameworks to the stress analysis of the continuum.

7. Chiefly *Physics.* The gradual return of a system towards equilibrium; *esp.* the reduction of stress caused by gradual plastic deformation in material held at constant strain. Freq. *attrib.*, as **relaxation time**, the time taken for a system to return to a state of equilibrium; *spec.* (in cases in which the process of return is exponential), the time taken for the deviation from equilibrium to be reduced by a factor *e*.

1867 J. C. MAXWELL in *Phil. Trans. R. Soc.* CLVII. 53 A time T, which may be called the 'time of relaxation' of the elastic force. **1908** J. JEANS *Math. Theory Electricity & Magnetism* x. 349 The time..in which all the charges in the dielectric are reduced to 1/*e* times their original value, is called the 'time of relaxation', being analogous to the corresponding quantity in the Dynamical Theory of Gases. The relaxation-time admits of experimental determination. **1937** *Trans. Amer. Soc. Mech. Engineers* LIX. 451/2 There are many reasons why relaxation tests at constant extension are useful and significant. **1949** *Aircraft Engin.* Jan. 2/1 The field of research offered by the plastic, creep and relaxation properties of metals under general stress systems at high temperatures is yet only partially explored. **1958** *Jrnl. Iron & Steel Inst.* CXC. G3/1 The experiments on relaxation here described based on 10,000 h duration have given some quantitative characteristics for relaxation for 4 types of steel at 410° and 470° C. **1959** G. TROUP *Masers* iii. 35 We shall see that collisions are in fact a form of 'relaxation process' (process tending to restore the system to equilibrium). **1962** CORSON & LORRAIN *Introd. Electromagn. Fields* v. 191 The free charge density ρ therefore decreases exponentially with time at a rate such that after a time..called the relaxation time, it is reduced to 1/*e* or 36·8% of its original value. **1969** C. O. SMITH *Sci. of Engin. Materials* xiii. 367 The relaxation test is usually performed by maintaining total strain (elastic plus plastic) at a constant level and measuring the decrease in load (or stress) as a function of time. **1971** *Nature* 8 Jan. 93/1 Many phenomena, for example, may be assigned their typical relaxation times—the average time for an effect to fade away... Thus, a fit of temper may have a relaxation time of a few minutes, the satiation of hunger by a meal lasts for a few hours. **1972** *Ibid.* 22 Dec. 447/1 Physicists are also interested in such phenomena as the changes in the qualities of the varnish on a Stradivarius violin, these being relaxation phenomena demonstrating both temporal and irreversible properties.

8. Special Comb.: **relaxation oscillator** *Electr.*, a form of oscillator in which the period and resulting waveform are determined by the slow charge and rapid discharge of a resistor-capacitor or inductor-capacitor circuit. See also sense 7 above.

1942 E. WILLIAMS *Thermionic Valve Circuits* v. 128 The simplest relaxation oscillator is perhaps the series connexion of a d.c. supply voltage, a resistance and a condenser, a neon lamp being shunted across the condenser. **1943** *Electronic Engin.* XV. 412 In general the time-base will be derived from a relaxation oscillator producing a 'saw-tooth' wave-form. **1966** *McGraw-Hill Encycl. Sci. & Technol.* XI. 438/2 One of the most widely used forms of relaxation oscillator is the astable multivibrator..which generates a rectangular or square wave.

re'laxative, *a.* and *sb.* [f. RELAX *v.*, after LAXATIVE. Cf. RELAXANT.]

A. *adj.* Tending to relax; of the nature of relaxation. *rare.*

1611 FLORIO, *Rilasciatiuo*, laxatiue or relaxatiue in operation. **1731** *Gentl. Mag.* I. 289 Relaxative diversions, he thinks, fall properly under the considerations of a Saturdays entertainment. **1891** H. C. HALLIDAY *Someone must suffer* III. xi. 197 Grudgingly..has Mrs. Felix ever countenanced these relaxative measures.

†**B.** *sb.* A means of relaxing; *esp.* a relaxing medicine. *Obs.*

1632 B. JONSON *Magn. Lady* III. iv, It is a pursiness, a kind of stoppage..that you are troubled with:..and therefore you must use relaxatives. **1671** L. ADDISON *W. Barbary* 217 The Moresco Festivals seem not so much Commemorative of received Mercies as relaxatives of Corporeal Labors.

So **re'laxatory** *a. rare.*

1581 J. BELL *Haddon's Answ. Osor.* 402 They would graunt plenary remission of Sinnes: and would make out their Bulles relaxatory. **1802–12** BENTHAM *Ration. Judic. Evid.* (1827) V. 430 Two plaintiffs, one of them has been cleared of legal interest..by the relaxatory purge.

relaxed (rɪ'lækst), *ppl. a.* [f. RELAX *v.*]

1. a. Freed from restraint or restrictions; not strict or precise, †esp. in observing a religious rule.

1638–48 G. DANIEL *Eclog.* v. 234 The Florentine prescribes to duller fooles; But Stronger flow from all relaxed Soules. **1671** WOODHEAD *St. Teresa* II. xxxii. 200 He had been Visitor of the Relaxed Fathers of the Province of Castile. **1768** BOYER *Dict. Royal* I. s.v. *Grain*, *Catholique à gros grain*, a relaxed Catholick. **1797** *Encycl. Brit.* (ed. 3) II. 686/1 Augustinians are..divided into rigid and relaxed. **1818** HAZLITT *Eng. Poets* iii. (1870) 74 Shakspeare..is relaxed and careless in critical places. **1855** PUSEY *Doctr. Real Pres.* Note S 704 That ye..may neither yourselves be relaxed, regardless of the fear of God, nor [etc.].

b. Slackened, mitigated, or modified in respect of strictness.

1671 WOODHEAD *St. Teresa* II. xxx. 183 A Monastery of our Lady of Carmel of the Rule relaxed. **1796** MORSE *Amer. Geog.* I. 87 The women wear no more covering than the most relaxed modesty seems absolutely to require. **1858** GLADSTONE *Homer* III. 19 It seems very doubtful..whether ..the relaxed sense ever appears as a title in the singular number. **1881** FROUDE *Short Stud.* IV. II. i. 168 When the law has become relaxed, public opinion takes its place.

2. *Path.* Of parts of the body: Deprived to some extent of the usual firmness; rendered soft or feeble.

1646 SIR T. BROWNE *Pseud. Ep.* 127 This part in Deere.. sometimes becomes so relaxed and pendulous, it cannot be quite retracted. **1733** CHEYNE *Eng. Malady* I. xi. §1 (1734) 99 Those who have weak, loose, and feeble or relax'd Nerves. **1799** *Med. Jrnl.* II. 284 When the body is warm and relaxed, as during sleep, or after fatigue. **1843** LYTTON *Last Bar.* I. iv, His hands were small and delicate, with large blue veins, that spoke of relaxed fibres. **1865** DICKENS *Let.* 6 Nov., I have been unwell with a relaxed throat.

3. In other senses of the vb., esp. (in sense 7) informal, leisurely, at ease; unanxious, free from constraint or tension.

1825 J. NICHOLSON *Operat. Mechanic* 500 The relaxed spring..above lying in a spiral form. **1846** ELLIS *Elgin Marb.* I. 164 Busy movement, and relaxed effort. **1856** KANE *Arct. Expl.* I. vi. 57 There must be either great areas of relaxed ice or open water-leads along the shore. **1958** *Listener* 19 June 1032/2 All the speakers sounded relaxed and informal. *Ibid.* 14 Aug. 249/2 What struck me most was the leisurely, richly human world—'relaxed' we should call it now, when nobody is relaxed—that it evoked. **1961** *Times* 16 Mar. 15/4 'Relaxed' has taken the place of the outmoded 'bronzed and fit'. **1972** M. WOODHOUSE *Mama Doll* ix. 121 He'll be fine, Bottle. Very relaxed character. **1978** *Times* 23 Apr. 12/4 You want a meal at the right price in a relaxed atmosphere.

Hence **re'laxedly** *adv.*; **re'laxedness.**

1818 SHELLEY *Rosal. & Helen* 1170 His mien Sunk with the sound relaxedly. **1855** PUSEY *Doctr. Real Pres.* Note S 704 That ye..may neither..look about hither and thither, nor roll about, relaxedly and vulgarly. **1860** —— *Min. Proph.* 3 An extreme relaxedness, on the borders of further sin. **1952** *Scrutiny* XVIII. IV. 275 What we have here, of course, is not relaxedness or distraction. **1957** Relaxedness [see COMPÈRE *v.*]. **1974** M. Z. LEWIS *Enemies Within* xxxiii. 147, I drove a lot faster and a lot less relaxedly. **1977** *Times* 22 Sept. 8/1 Edward Heath..didn't have anything so relaxedly Edwardian as a confidant.

re'laxer. [f. as prec. + -ER[1].] **1.** One who, or that which, relaxes or loosens. *rare.*

1671 SALMON *Syn. Med.* III. xvi. 361 Relaxers are such as loosen any member distended through cold, dryness, or repletion of wind, &c. **1870** MISS BROUGHTON *Red as Rose* (1878) 229 The pliant relaxer of soft limbs.

2. One who applies the method of relaxation (sense 6).

1957 L. FOX *Two-Point Boundary Problems* iii. 39 There are many tricks a skilled relaxer can use to accelerate the convergence of the process and generally lighten his work. **1959** A. M. OSTROWSKI in R. E. Langer *Numerical Approximation* 4 One of the fields where this difficulty is felt in particularly high degree is that of relaxation. The practical relaxer has it 'in his fingertips' how to steer the successive relaxations.

relaxin (rɪ'læksɪn). *Physiol.* [f. RELAX *v.* + -IN[1].] An ovarian hormone first found in rodents, in which it relaxes the pelvic ligaments and softens the cervix of the uterus.

1930 H. L. FEVOLD et al. in *Jrnl. Amer. Chem. Soc.* LII. 3341 The only physiological property thus far discovered for this hormone is its action on the pelvic ligaments and for this reason we propose the name 'Relaxin'. **1968** PASSMORE & ROBSON *Compan. Med. Stud.* I. xxxvii. 45/2 The polypeptide hormone, relaxin, is probably also produced by the placenta. **1978** *Amer. Jrnl. Obstetrics & Gynecology* CXXX. 473/1 The role of human relaxin in pregnancy has not been determined but relaxin extracted from human luteal tissue is active in the guinea pig public symphysis assay.

relaxing (rɪ'læksɪŋ), *vbl. sb.* [f. RELAX *v.* + -ING[1].] **1.** The action of the vb. RELAX.

1611 FLORIO, *Relasso*,..a relaxing. **1667** LOWER in *Phil. Trans.* II. 545 The Belly falls by the Relaxing of the same [diaphragm]. **1734** WATERLAND *Script. Vindic.* Concl., Wks. 1823 VI. 169 The destroying or relaxing of the other [motives] is so far destroying or relaxing virtue and morality. **1884** *Athenæum* 16 Aug. 204/2 The fourteenth and fifteenth centuries saw a considerable relaxing of the severities of the Cistercian rule.

2. *attrib.* in *Ent.*, applied to containers in which dead insects are relaxed, containing a pad soaked with fluid.

1907 *Yesterday's Shopping* (1969) 699/3 Entomologists' requisites..Killing and relaxing boxes. Each..1/6. **1912** H. ROWLAND-BROWN *Butterflies & Moths* I. v. 53 The nervures and wing-attachments must be softened to permit of their being rearranged. I have not found that the 'relaxing-boxes' are much good for this purpose with other than recently killed specimens. **1952** E. F. DAGLISH *Name this Insect* p. xiii, After some hours in a relaxing chamber the legs and wings will be as easy to arrange as those of fresh-killed specimens. **1963** R. L. E. FORD *Pract. Entomol.* 32 Specimens may be left in a relaxing tin for about twenty-four hours when they will be ready to set. **1976** P. W. CRIBB *Lepidopterist's Handbk.* vii. 84 A relaxing box is a clean plastic box with a layer of clean absorbent material at the bottom.

re'laxing, *ppl. a.* [f. as prec. + -ING².] Causing or producing relaxation; enervating.

1611 FLORIO, *Rilasciante medicina*, a relaxing medicine. **1779** *Gentl. Mag.* XLIX. 79 Ointment of Marsh Mallows, I imagine from its name is understood to be of an emollient relaxing disposition. **1825–9** MRS. SHERWOOD *Lady of Manor* xiii. (1860) II. 120 A climate so peculiarly relaxing as that of Bengal. **1841** JAMES *Brigand* i, All the relaxing joys of an hour's idleness. **1883** 'ANNIE THOMAS' *Mod. Housewife* 95 You will neither go to the bleak Norfolk coast nor to the relaxing air of Bournemouth.

Hence **re'laxingness.**

1883 MISS BROUGHTON *Belinda* II. II. v. 55, I have been advised..to try the effect of a more bracing air, as a corrective to the extreme relaxingness of Oxbridge.

†**re'laxion.** *Obs. rare*⁻¹. [irreg. f. RELAX *v.* + -ION¹.] Remission (of a penalty).

1528 *Galway Arch.* in *10th Rep. Hist. MSS. Comm.* App. V. 403 The which relaxion was gyvin to Willam in recompence of the slaght and saut of Thomas Marten.

re'laxity. *rare.* [irreg. f. RELAX *v.* + -ITY; cf. LAXITY.] Relaxedness, freedom from restraint or tension; the state of being relaxed.

a **1784** S. JOHNSON *Sermons* (1788) I. xiii. 271 Men have ever been persuaded, that by doing something, to which they think themselves not obliged, they may purchase an exemption from such duties as they find themselves inclined to violate: that they may commute with heaven for a temporal fine, and make rigour atone for relaxity. **1908** *Daily Mail* 30 June 9/5 The great secret of voice production is relaxity.

relay (rɪ'leɪ, 'riːleɪ), *sb.*¹ [ad. OF. *relais* (13th c.), hounds or (in later use) horses held in reserve, f. *relayer* to RELAY.]

1. A set of fresh hounds (and horses) posted to take up the chase of a deer in place of those already tired out; †also, the place where these are posted. *Obs.* exc. *arch.*

c **1410** *Master of Game* (MS. Digby 182) Prol., And whan he shall comm ayenn to the semble or metynge, thenn hath he moste to done, forto ordeyne his fynders and the relaies. *Ibid.* xxxiii, And at euery relay suffiseth ii. couple of houndes or iii. atte moste. *a* **1500** *Chaucer's Dreme* 362 A great rout Of hunters, and eke of foresters, And many relaies, and limers. **1575** TURBERV. *Venerie* I. xiv. 36 Then may you choose out a Forest wherein the Relaies be of equall proportion. **1637** B. JONSON *Sad Sheph.* I. ii, *Rob.* What relays set you? *John.* None at all; we laid not In one fresh dog. **1651** DAVENANT *Gondibert* I. II. xxviii, [They] now dispose their choice Relays Of Horse and Hounds, each like each other fleet. **1735** SOMERVILLE *Chase* III. 506 Press'd by the fresh Relay, no Pause allow'd, Breathless and faint, he faulters in his Pace. **1842** SIR H. TAYLOR *Edwin* I. vi, Oh, the best bitch! She holds them all together, Relay or vauntlay, 'tis the same to her.

attrib. **1706** PHILLIPS (ed. Kersey) s.v., The Cry, or Kennel of Relay-Hounds.

2. a. A set of fresh horses obtained, or kept ready, at various stages along a route to expedite travel.

1659 HOWELL *Vocab.* xxix, A horse of relay or return. **1706** PHILLIPS (ed. Kersey), *Relays*, is also sometimes taken for fresh Horses, or the Stage where they are kept. **1713** *Lond. Gaz.* No. 5137/8 [They] came hither..with three Relays of Horses. **1763** SMOLLETT *Trav.* (1766) I. 137 It was as disagreeable to him as to me to wait for a relay. **1843** LYTTON *Last. Bar.* IV. i, Relays of horses are ready, night and day, to bear you to the coast. **1879** A. R. WALLACE *Australasia* xvi. 327 A traveller may have relays of horses to carry him day and night at the rate of ten miles an hour.

transf. and *fig.* **1709** MRS. MANLEY *Secret Mem.* II. 42 It is impossible for Virtue to subsist without the Relay of Vice. **1742** YOUNG *Nt. Th.* II. 250 Who call aloud..For change of follies, and relays of joy, To drag your patient through the tedious length Of a short winter's day. **1860** MAURY *Phys. Geog. Sea* (Low) xii. §552 Thus we are entitled to regard the Mediterranean, the Red Sea, and Persian Gulf as relays, distributed along the route of these thirsty winds..to supply them with vapours.

b. The place where a fresh relay is obtained.

1706 [see above]. **1834** JAMES *J. Marston Hall* xxi, I rode on as fast as possible to the next post relay. **1873** BROWNING *Red Cott. Nt.-cap* IV. 9 How the mind runs from each to each relay, Town after town, till Paris' self be touched.

c. *relay-horse*, a fresh or reserve horse.

1802 JAMES *Milit. Dict.*, *Relay-horses* in the artillery are spare horses that march with the artillery and baggage, ready to relieve others. **1818** JEFFERSON *Writ.* (1830) IV. 447 Couriers and relay-horses by land, and swift-sailing pilot-boats by sea, were flying in all directions.

d. A series of motor vehicles intended to cover a prescribed route (usu. in sequence); an operation involving this.

1942 *R.A.F. Jrnl.* 27 June 6, I chartered a relay of cars which got us to Beirut..up the coast road. **1971** M. TAK *Truck Talk* 129 *Relay*, a procedure commonly used in companies to keep as many trucks as possible moving over the road. **1973** *Amer. Speech 1969* XLIV. 207 *Relay*, driving operation in which the driver takes his unit from one terminal to another, where a new driver takes over to deliver it to the next terminal, and so on. **1975** *Drive* Nov.–Dec. 110/1 The travellers soon continued their journeys—care of AA Relay. *Ibid.* 110/2 Relay's south-east team had to recover a Rolls-Royce..from east London and take it back to..Chelsea.

e. *Bridge.* In full, *relay bid.* (See quot. 1964.)

1959 T. REESE *Bridge Player's Dict.* 183 The relay method is used in some systems played by European teams. In certain sequences the responder does not try to give a picture of his own hand but makes a series of relay-bids at the lowest level so that he can learn more about his partner's hand. **1961** *Times* 30 Aug. 11/5 If the partner responds the minimum in the suit immediately above the opening bid.. his response is either negative (discouraging) or natural (with more than 10 points). In either event it is known as a 'relay' bid and is forcing; it does not indicate a real suit but invites the opener to disclose what values he holds. **1962** *Listener* 27 Sept. 494/2 In this auction North's 1 NT and 2 NT were 'relay bids', just asking partner to describe his hand. **1964** *Official Encycl. Bridge* 452/1 *Relay*, a minimum bid unrelated to the bidder's hand, aimed simply at keeping the bidding open so that the bidder's partner can describe his hand. **1980** *Times* 12 July 7/4 After One Club—One Diamond—One Heart—the usual rebid by responder is One Spade. This is a 'relay' bid, asking opener to clarify his hand.

3. a. A set of persons appointed to relieve others in the performance of certain duties; a relief-gang.

1808 HAN. MORE *Cœlebs* I. 346 Nicholas Ferrar..had relays of musicians every six hours to sing the whole Psalter through. **1840** CARLYLE *Heroes* (1858) 233 They have mosques where it [the Koran] is all read daily; thirty relays of priests take it up in succession, get through the whole each day. **1881** JOWETT *Thucyd.* I. 144 The army was divided into relays, and one party worked while the other slept and ate.

attrib. **1886** *Telegraphist* (Dec.) 14/1, I beg to call your attention to the anomalous position of relay clerks.

b. In full, *relay race.* A race of runners in sequence; *spec.* one run by teams of four athletes, a baton being passed in each team from one runner to the next. Also (in quot. 1920), each of the four sections of a relay race. Also in other sports, e.g. Swimming, where members of a team perform in sequence. Also *attrib.*

1898 M. SHEARMAN *Athletics* x. 301 So popular has this form of racing become that within the last year a number of athletic meetings have been held at which there were a series of these relay races. **1908** T. A. COOK *Olympic Games* 187 Relay Race 1600 Metres... Teams of four with four reserves. **1908** *Daily Chron.* 18 Apr. 5/6 It looked as if its representatives would carry off the prize for the one mile relay race, in which four runners run one lap, carrying a flag each. At the end of the lap the flag is handed to a relay walker, and in his turn the walker hands the flag to a cyclist who completes the race. **1920** *Isis* 13 Oct. 2/2 Ten yards is allotted each side of the starting line in which to pass the baton to the next competitor, for every relay subsequent to the one which begins the race. **1922** F. W. H. NICHOLAS *Handbk. Athletics for Beginner* (ed. 2) x. 44 Relay 100 yards and relay hurdles may be run up and down. **1927** W. DEEPING *Kitty* xxiv. 310 To him life was like a relay-race: you snatched the baton from the failing hand of the past, and sped ahead without looking back till some other racer took the baton from you. **1929** G. M. BUTLER *Mod. Athletics* ii. 8 Names are taken..and made up into senior and junior relay teams of four each. *Ibid.* 9 Juniors are under no circumstances allowed to compete in the senior relays. **1939** *Encycl. Brit. Bk. of Year* 650/2 Peter Fick lowered the world's record for the 400-metre relay..while Ralph Flanagan swam 400 metres free style in 4 min. 46·2 sec. **1950** *Oxf. Jun. Encycl.* IX. 454/1 There are also two kinds of team relay race: the medley, in which there are exponents of all three styles of swimming; and the free-style, in which all members swim the same stroke. **1952** ARMBRUSTER & MOREHOUSE *Swimming & Diving* (ed. 2) x. 201 The types of relays in swimming are usually of two kinds. *Ibid.* 204 The swimming take-off in relay racing differs from that in back relay racing. **1955** R. BANNISTER *First Four Minutes* ii. 18 He had helped Hungary on two occasions to capture the $4\times1{,}500$ metres relay World record. **1958** *Times* 13 Aug. 2/6 The main hopes in this country lie in the men's four by 100 and four by 400 metres relays. **1958** [see BATON *sb.* 2 b]. **1974** *Country Life* 14 Feb. 292/3 The England women's only gold medal in athletics..came in 4×400 metres relay. **1976** *Liverpool Echo* 6 Dec. 18/1 Visibility on the course, however, was too poor to permit the senior relay and a three miles race was substituted. **1978** G. WRIGHT *Illustr. Handbk. Sporting Terms* 150/3 *Relays*, events in which teams of swimmers swim in sequence... A relay team usually consists of four swimmers, but occasionally larger numbers are used.

4. a. An instrument used in long distance telegraphy to enable an electric current which is too weak to influence recording instruments, or to transmit a message to the required distance, to do so indirectly by means of a local battery brought into connexion with it. In mod. use, any electrical device, usu. incorporating an electromagnet, whereby a current or signal in one circuit can open or close another circuit. Also *transf.*

1860 G. PRESCOTT *Electr. Telegr.* 81 The relay is a very essential apparatus in Morse's telegraphic system. **1876** PREECE & SIVEWRIGHT *Telegraphy* 60 The forms of relay more largely used are called polarized. **1907** *Cornhill Mag.* Mar. 363 The difficulty is overcome by using the partly exhausted current to move a special kind of 'switch', or key, called a 'relay'. **1923** E. W. MARCHANT *Radio Telegr. & Teleph.* v. 71 The telephone may be replaced by an ordinary Post Office relay, such as is used for working on the ordinary telegraph line. **1935** MONSETH & ROBINSON *Relay Systems* i. 1 The function of protective relays in modern power systems is to initiate the operation of devices to isolate transmission circuits and apparatus when trouble develops. **1956** G. A. MONTGOMERIE *Digital Calculating Machines* x. 211 For adding numbers, three sets of relays are used, designated as A, B, and C; they are wired together so that, if two numbers are sent respectively to A and B, the sum of the two numbers appears on C. **1969** *Times* 16 Jan. 4/7 Relays are instruments used to switch electrical circuits on and off automatically. They usually consist of an electromagnet which, when activated by an electrical signal, opens or closes a switch in another circuit.

attrib. **1875** KNIGHT *Dict. Mech.* 1915/2 By means of the relay magnet. **1878** STEWART & TAIT *Unseen Univ.* vii. §256. 261 As it were by some relay battery of the universe. **1968** *Brit. Med. Bull.* XXIV. 200/2 The sensory relay region in the thalamus.

b. An installation or satellite which receives, amplifies, and retransmits a radio transmission so that it may be received over a wider area. Freq. *attrib.*

1921 *Wireless World* 10 Dec. 575/1 These men have banded themselves into a relay organisation. They have laid out in definite form certain traffic routes.., and messages.. are broadcasted across the country any time of the night... These relay routes enable the transmission of personal messages from coast to coast, and from the Canadian border to the Mexican border. **1923** *Radio Times* 28 Sept. 26/3 The engineers of the British Broadcasting Company will employ a wireless relay across the Thames. **1945** *Wireless World* Oct. 305 (*heading*) Extra-terrestrial relays. Can rocket stations give world-wide radio coverage? **1962** *Rep. Comm. Broadc. 1960* 257 in *Parl. Papers 1961–2* (Cmnd. 1753) IX. 259 The relay companies are prohibited from originating any programmes of their own. **1966** *McGraw-Hill Encycl. Sci. & Technol.* XIII. 469/2 By far the largest number of television circuit miles is provided by microwave radio relay. **1966** *Electronics* 14 Nov. 47 The company has developed an antenna that allows a plane, say flying over North America, to communicate with a relay satellite orbiting about the equator. **1975** D. G. FINK *Electronics Engineers' Handbk.* XXII. 61 The communications satellite is a radio relay, consisting of a receiver and transmitter, plus a command receiver and transmitter, to control the satellite.

c. A radio transmission or programme which has been relayed.

1929 *Radio Times* 8 Nov. 395/3 We were testing all the arrangements for the Schneider Trophy relay, making sure that the loud-speaker system at various points round the coast could pick up our broadcast. **1929** *B.B.C. Yearbk. 1930* 383 Listeners can..expect to find a number of relays of Central European stations included in the British programmes. **1965** *Listener* 25 Nov. 873/2 *Don Carlos* (Third Programme, November 20) was a direct relay. In spite of all the disadvantages—in timing, indifferent quality of reception, and applause—this kind of broadcast has the incalculable quality of excitement and immediacy that no recording or tape can hope to equal.

5. Special Combs.: **relay rack**, a rack or frame on which relays are mounted, usu. used in a telephone exchange; **relay station**, a radio station that serves as a relay; also *fig.*; **relay valve** *Engin.*, a fluid valve in which the main flow is controlled by a diaphragm actuated by a weep derived from the main flow.

1908 *Daily Chron.* 8 Apr. 3/6 Each girl sits in front of a relay rack, fitted with a bewildering number of small holes, each of which represents a subscriber. **1930** [see RACK *sb.*² 5 g]. **1970** *Jrnl. Gen. Psychol.* LXXXII. 58 A desk-type relay rack with two standard rack panels and an enclosed back stood on a table in the experimental room. **1923** *Radio Times* 28 Sept. 2/2 The proposed relay stations..will have a power of 100 to 150 watts. **1969** *Times* 26 Feb. 8/7 Light..is converted to a train of nervous impulses which are transmitted down the optic nerve to a relay station known as the lateral geniculate body (L.G.B.) and from there to the striate cortex. **1974** *B.B.C. Handbk. 1975* 21/1 Savings on capital expenditure in 1974–5 were achieved through postponement of work on the proposed Caribbean relay station. **1939** R. N. LE FEVRE *Man. Pract. Gas Fitting* xix. 390 The relay valve..is made in a variety of sizes to suit particular gas rates and pipe connections. **1970** MILES & PINKESS *Gas Appliance Control* ii. 41 It is..possible to have a leak in a joint in the weep pipe or in the cover of the relay valve itself which would pass sufficient gas to hold the relay valve open, even if the control were shut. **1977** R. PRITCHARD et al. *Industr. Gas Utilization* ix. 414 Relay valves are used to control gas or air flows using a small actuating valve, which may be a solenoid valve or a thermostat in the weep line.

re-lay (riː-), *sb.*² [RE- 5 a.] A re-laid oyster.

1889 *Pall Mall G.* 18 June 3/1 Not one in twenty knows that the majority of so-called real Whitstable natives are imported relays.

relay (rɪ'leɪ, 'riːleɪ), *v.*¹ [ad. F. *relayer* (13th c.), of obscure origin.]

†**1. a.** *trans.* Of a hunter: To let go (the fresh hounds) upon the track of the deer. Also *absol.* *Obs.*

c **1410** *Master of Game* (MS. Digby 182) xxxiii, He shuld lat þe deere passe and go to þe fues..and relay his houndes vpon þe fues. *Ibid.*, If it so be, þat þe hunter þat haþe relayed, se þat þe deere is lickely to fall in daunger,..he shuld, whan he hath relayed, stonde still in þe fues and halowe þe houndes.

†**b.** To hunt (a deer) with relays. *Obs. rare*⁻¹.

c **1410** *Master of Game* (MS. Digby 182) xxxiii, When he hath be so wele ronne to and enchased and retreved and softe relayed and vanleyed to,..þenne turneth he his heed and stondeth at abaye.

2. To place in relays: to provide with, or replace by, fresh relays.

1788 EARL MALMESBURY *Diaries & Corr.* II. 427 The emissaries of this Cabal had been relayed (if I may use the expression) on the road. **1883** *Pall Mall G.* 18 Dec. 4/2 Our human ponies were not relayed. **1883** *Daily News* 3 Jan. 5/6 Those who watched in the mortuary room were relayed every ten minutes.

3. *intr.* To get a fresh relay.

1829 COL. HAWKER *Diary* (1893) II. 4, [I] relayed with a horse at Winchester that..could only toddle along. *a* **1868** M. J. HIGGINS *Ess.* (1875) 158 He endeavours to make up for the time lost in relaying by what he calls '*pousser les postillons*.'

4. *trans.* **a.** To pass on or retransmit (telephonic or broadcast signals received from elsewhere); *loosely*, to transmit.

1878 *Telegr. Jrnl.* VI. 274/2 They have finally solved the important problem of *relaying* telephone sounds. **1904**

Marconigram July 16/2 With a telegraphone in Chicago, one may telephone from New York, have the telegraphone record his message and repeat it over another wire to St. Louis, where another machine relays it to Denver. **1923** *Glasgow Herald* 22 Mar. 9/2 Little progress has so far been made, as the experiments have only recently been commenced, but last night a Birmingham concert was relayed for London with some success. **1923** *Daily Mail* 14 Aug. 5/3 A special orchestral concert which will be relayed to all the broadcasting stations in Britain. **1958** *Radio Times* 14 Feb. 3/3 The sensitive receiving equipment is also used for relaying programmes from the Commonwealth and the U.S.A. **1969** *Times* 16 July 4/1 The television pictures to be relayed back to earth will be taken by a camera fixed on a special attachment. **1974** *B.B.C. Handbk. 1975* 20/2 Prokofiev's opera *War and Peace* was relayed from the New Sydney Opera House in Australia. **1977** *Rep. Comm. Future of Broadcasting* (Cmnd. 6753) iii. 21 We saw a cable company in Toronto relaying programmes on 24 channels: but several of them were relaying the same programme.

b. *transf.* To pass on (a message or information).

1956 A. H. Compton *Atomic Quest* ii. 117 These men were thoroughly acquainted with our wartime methods of bomb construction and relayed the techniques to Russia. **1974** *State* (Columbia, S. Carolina) 13 Feb. 5-A/1 President Nixon relayed word through a spokesman Tuesday that he has no plans to visit the Middle East.

Hence **'relayed** *ppl. a.*; **'relaying** *vbl. sb.*

1904 *Marconigram* July 16/1 The steel belt machine will transmit a record..by relaying, to great distances. **1949** *Radio Times* 15 July 6/1 [We] presented an electrophone to our aged father on October 5th, 1908... I have a vivid recollection of..listening to a relayed programme.

re-lay (riː-), *v.*[2] Also relay. [re- 5 a.] *trans.* To lay again, in various senses. Also with *out*. Hence **re-'laying** *vbl. sb.*

1590 Sir T. Cokaine *Treat. Hunting* C ij, All Huntsmen are to helpe any hound that is cast out to relay him in againe. **1597** A. M. tr. *Guillemeau's Fr. Chirurg.* 16/2 If the guttes, with these remedyes, will not relaye ther swellinge. **1700** *Providence* (R.I.) *Rec.* (1893) IV. 197 The second part of the said land now relaid out is a peece of swampey land. **1796** W. Brown *Chancery Rep.* III. 91 He alone received the 500*l.*, and..no part of it was relaid out in other securities. **1804** Nelson 18 Apr. in Nicolas *Disp.* (1845) V. 502 Perhaps the hawser-laid rope..may if the hemp is good be relaid and made serviceable. **1858** Greener *Gunnery* 143 This necessitates the relaying of the gun after every discharge. **1894** *Daily News* 1 Sept. 6/1 The re-binding of the volumes, the displacement of 'titles', and their 're-laying', entailed an immense amount of labour.

b. *esp.* To lay or put down again (something previously taken up).

1757 Smollett *Hist. Eng.* iii. xii. (L.), As to damaged pavements,..to cause it to be effectually relayed with good materials at their expense. **1829** Elmes *Dilapidations* (ed. 3) App. 66 Take up and relay the Portland stone coping. **1862** *Catal. Internatl. Exhib.* II. x. 34/2 It is useful..where a main is being re-laid with the gas or water in the same. **1886** Tucker *E. Europe* 185 The cloth was re-laid, and due regard was paid to the cravings of the famished party.

relay, obs. form of rely *v.*[1]

rele, obs. form of reel.

†**re'leage**, *v. Obs. rare*[−1]. [ad. L. *releg-āre* or F. *reléguer*: see relegate *v.*] To banish.

1691 J. Wilson *Belphegor* v. ii, I releage, and confine ye, to your dismal Lake, for a thousand Years, yet more, than were ever decreed ye.

re'learn, *v.* [re- 5 a.] *trans.* To learn again.

a **1711** Ken *Edmund* Poet. Wks. 1721 II. 213 He in Religion nurtur'd from his Youth, In Wisdom's House relearn'd all sacred Truth. **1850** *Westm. Rev.* Apr. 80 The world has never to re-learn its lesson. **1900** Gore *Ep. Romans* II. 100 We must relearn the lesson that St. Augustine is for ever insisting upon.

re'learning, *vbl. sb.* [re- 5 a.] Learning again.

1961 'E. Fenwick' *Friend of Mary Rose* ii. 20 In the new house..he would have an immense amount of relearning to do. **1978** *Dædalus* Fall 33 Nothing is ever learned beyond the need for relearning.

releas, variant of relish *sb.*[2] *Obs.*

re'leasable, *a.* [f. release *v.*[1] + -able.] Admitting of release or dispensation.

1611 Cotgr., *Remissible*, remittable,..releasable. **1612** Selden *Illustr. Drayton's Poly-olb.* xi. 350 He discharged all monasteries and churches of all..taxes,..excepting such as were..not releasable. **1854** *Fraser's Mag.* L. 318 A religious congregation forming simple, i.e. releasable vows. **1936** *Nat. Geogr. Mag.* LXIX. 93/2 Heavy items of apparatus to be carried in releasable form on the outside of the gondola. **1950** *Manch. Guardian* 15 Sept. 7/3 At Church Fenton.., to quote from an Air Ministry News Service message, will be 'a miniature bombing range and miniature aircraft complete with releasable bombs to amuse the children'. **1980** *Nature* 31 Jan. 488/1 The content of LH-RH in the synaptosomal pellet obtained after centrifugation showed a decline with time, indicating depletion of a releasable pool of the neuropeptide.

†**re'leasant**. *Obs. rare*[−1]. [irreg. f. release *v.*[1] + -ant[1].] Release.

1592 *Nobody & Someb.* in Simpson *Sch. Shaks.* (1878) I. 343 What, shall I never from this servitude Receive releasant?

release (rɪ'liːs), *sb.*[1] Forms: 4–5 reles(e, -lees, 5–6 -lesse, (4 -leische, 5 *Sc.* -lesche; 5 -lece, -leese, 6 *Sc.* -leis); 5 releasse, 6 -leace, 6– release. [a. OF. *reles* (12th c.), var. of *relais*, vbl. sb. from *relesser*, *relaisser*: see release *v.*[1]]

1. a. Deliverance or liberation from trouble, pain, sorrow or the like.

c **1315** Shoreham i. 1067 Be nauȝt loþ To do penaunce here; For ȝet þer hys here som reles So nys nauȝt ine þe uere Areyned. *c* **1400** *Rom. Rose* 4440 For Love..Seide, that Hope, wher-so I go, Shulde ay be relees to my wo. *c* **1400** *Chron. R. Glouc.* (Rolls) App. Q. 2 Wo & sorewe to þis lond is cominge..ne worþe neuere reles. *c* **1440** *York Myst.* xxxvii. 288 Nowthir frende nor foo Shulde fynde releis in helle. *c* **1560** A. Scott *Poems* (S.T.S.) v. 48 In May sowld men of amoure go To serf thair ladeis..Sen thair releis in ladeis lyis. **1794** Mrs. Radcliffe *Myst. Udolpho* xxv, Emily had no opportunity of seeking a release from her terrible suspense concerning her aunt. **1819** Shelley *Prometh. Unb.* iii. i. 64 No pity, no release, no respite! **1840** Miss Mitford in L'Estrange *Life* (1870) III. vii. 108 To me individually it would be a great release to be quit of the trouble and expense of the garden. **1878** Browning *La Saisiaz* 330 Death's kindly touch..gave Soul and body both release from life's long nightmare in the grave.

†**b.** Const. *of* (the suffering or its cause). *Obs.*

1340 Hampole *Pr. Consc.* 3565 And what may mak þair payn cees And þam of þair payn to haf relees. **1390** Gower *Conf.* I. 81 Thei that wende pees Tho myhten finde no reles Of thilke swerd which al devoureth. **1423** Jas. I *Kingis Q.* clxxvi, For my reconforting, In relesche of my furiouse pennance. *c* **1430** Lydg. *Min. Poems* (Percy Soc.) 236 For whosoevir unto this name calle, Of cankryd surfetys fynt reles by myracle.

c. *Psychol.* Liberation from emotional or physical tension. Also *attrib.* and in gen. use.

1915 E. B. Holt *Freudian Wish* i. 20 Just what shall happen depends on the relative strengths of the suppressed with and of the censor, and on the amount of release which the joke affords as well as on the degree of violence which it does to the censor. **1933** E. & W. Murphy tr. *Bechterev's Gen. Princ. Hum. Reflexol.* xxv. 272 All processes of release from inhibition are based on the retention—in the centres—of the traces of reflexes. **1934** E. B. Strauss tr. *Kretschmer's Text-bk. Med. Psychol.* i. 12 Are they [*sc.* fits] not really a symptom of cortical paralysis (produced by the lesion) in the sense that they result from a release of sub-cortical activities from cortical control? **1936** P. T. Young *Motivation of Behav.* v. 247 Tension and release occur constantly in the trivial events of daily life. **1948** L. Kanner *Child Psychiatry* (ed. 2) xvii. 245 The term 'release therapy' indicates that the ventilation of specifically oriented feelings of hostility, guilt, and anxiety constitutes a main therapeutic facet. **1954** A. H. Maslow *Motivation & Personality* xi. 187 It is very likely that catharsis, as originally defined by Breuer and Freud, is in essence a more complex variant of release behavior. **1959** *Times* 4 Apr. 7/6 As the American male is said to approach his car as a form of self-expression, so the German sees it as an instrument of release. **1966** *Listener* 4 Aug. 174/1 In some quarters this loss of binding traditions has resulted in the retreat beyond all controls—the anti-culture of 'release'. **1978** M. T. Erickson *Child Psychopathology* vi. 117 The therapeutic effect of release therapy is based on the child's acting out or talking about a traumatic event that is the source of the disturbance.

2. a. The act of freeing, or fact of being freed, from some obligation, duty, or demand; remission; discharge of a person (†or troops).

c **1330** R. Brunne *Chron.* (1810) 185 Bot if þei wille with pes þis lond ȝeld vs alle quite, þei salle þan haf reles, of fayth gode respite. **1362** Langl. *P. Pl.* A. vii. 83 To ha reles and remission on that rental I be-leeue. **1390** Gower *Conf.* III. 373 My will is..that thou make a plein reles To love. *c* **1440** *Promp. Parv.* 428/2 Relece, or for-ȝeuenesse, *relaxacio*. **1530** Palsgr. 261/2 Release, forgyvenesse, *pardon*. **1556** J. Heywood *Spider & F.* lxxi, Bonds of good abearing shall have no release. **1622** Bacon *Hen. VII* (1876) 65 He would not have one penny abated,..because it might encourage other counties to pray the like release or mitigation. **1671** R. Montagu in *Buccleuch MSS.* (Hist. MSS. Comm.) I. 507 His..losing his command by the late release of the levies. **1764** Goldsm. *Hist. Eng. in Lett.* (1772) II. 170 The Spaniards, instead of granting a redress, had rather extorted a release for their former conduct. **1878** Stubbs *Const. Hist.* xix. (1896) III. 362 Henry III..sought in a papal sentence of absolution a release from the solemn obligations by which he had bound himself to his people.

†**b.** Remission *of* a tax, debt, obligation, etc. *Obs.*

1387 Trevisa *Higden* (Rolls) IV. 77 Iosephus..obteynede ..the fauor of the kynge and releische of his tribute. **1502** *Cal. Anc. Rec. Dublin* (1889) I. 389 The sayd James schall hawe reles of the cheff ii.*s.* **1559** *Mirr. Mag., Jack Cade* x, We desired release of subsidies. **1651** Hobbes *Leviath.* i. xv. 75 His Will to have it done being signified, is a release of that Covenant. **1659** Pearson *Creed* (1839) 508 This remission or release of debts hath a great affinity with remission of sins.

c. A written discharge, acquittance, or receipt.

c **1440** *Geste of Robyn Hood* cxvii. in Child *Ballads* III. 62/1 'What wyll ye gyue more', sayd the justice, 'And the knyght shall make a releyse?' **1530** Rastell *Bk. Purgat.* iii. xiv, To make acquitaunces and relesis in his name, and to take bondes. **1611** Cotgr., *Quitance*, an Acquitance, Release, discharge. **1719** De Foe *Crusoe* i. xix, I..caused him to draw up a general release or discharge for the four hundred and seventy moidores. **1809** R. Langford *Introd. Trade* 108 If a Rent be behindhand twenty years, and a release given for the last year, all the rent in arrears is presumed in law to be satisfied.

d. A written authorization or permission for publication, esp. from an owner of copyright or a person depicted in a photograph.

1965 *Tamarack Rev.* Winter 13 Don't touch anything, and be sure to get a release. **1966** K. Giles *Provenance of Death* i. 6 Publishing your photo in an ad. without a release could be libel. **1970** C. Whitman *Death out of Focus* ix. 130 A photographer would be a damned fool to come in here with a print for which he had no release. **1979** R. Cox *Auction* vii. 186 The late Herr Schneider bequeathed it [*sc.* a picture] to me and I was given a release by Herbstein as a result.

†**3.** ***without release*** (tr. OF. *sans reles*), without remission or cessation, continually. *Obs.*

13.. *E.E. Allit. P.* A. 955 In þat oþer is noȝt bot pes to glene, þat ay schal laste with-outen reles. *c* **1400** tr. *Secreta Secret., Gov. Lordsh.* 90 þe wirkere of dissolucioun of waters ys with outen reles. **1566** Whittingham *Ps.* li. 3 My sinne alas doth still remayne Before my face without relesse.

4. *Law.* **a.** The act of conveying or making over an estate or right to another, or disposing of it in some legal fashion (see quot. 1594); a deed or document made for this purpose.

c **1420** *Anturs of Arth.* l, Here I make the relese in my rentis, by þe rode. *c* **1430** Lydg. *Min. Poems* (Percy Soc.) 117 Thus the burges of the borrowe..He endewed into the place wyth dedes of good relese, In fee for ever more. **1487** *Rolls of Parlt.* VI. 389/2 Which Release remayneth with You, Soveraigne Lord; as appereth by the same. **1537** in *Lett. Suppress. Monast.* (Camden) 168 We have taken a releasse and a deade of feofftement of the monasterie of Saint Androse in Northehamptone to the kinges use. **1594** West *2nd Pt. Symbol.* §466 A Release is an instrument, whereby estates, rightes, titles, entries, actions, and other things be sometimes extinguished, sometimes transferred, sometimes abridged, and sometimes inlarged. **1601** *Act 43 Eliz.* c. 4 §4 By any Conveiance, Gifte, Graunte, Lease, Demise, Release, or Conversion whatsoever. **1607** Cowell *Interpr.* s.v., And there is a Release in fact, and a release in lawe. **1743** Viner *Abridgm.* XVIII. 294 If a Man seised of a Rent in Fee grants it for Life, he may enlarge it by Release. **1766** Blackstone *Comm.* II. 324 Releases; which are a discharge or conveyance of a man's right in lands or tenements, to another that hath some former estate in possession. **1844** Williams *Real Prop.* (1877) 135 A release is the proper form of assurance between joint tenants. **1853** T. I. Wharton *Pennsylv. Digest* 470 A release cannot be given in evidence in covenant unless it has been pleaded.

b. ***lease and release***, 'a conveyance of the fee-simple, right, or interest in lands or tenements, under the Statute of Uses, 27 Hen. 8, c. 10, giving first the possession, and afterwards the interest in the estate conveyed' (Tomlins).

1682 Sir O. Bridgman *Conveyances* 185 Lease and Release by the Husband for a Provision for his Wife, and Portions for his Children. **1744** Jacob *Law Dict.* (ed. 5) II. s.v. *Lease & Release*, A Lease and Release made but one Conveyance, being in the nature of one Deed. **1766** Blackstone *Comm.* II. 339 A fourteenth species of conveyance, viz. by lease and release; first invented by serjeant Moore, soon after the statute of uses, and now the most common of any, and therefore not to be shaken. **1841** *Penny Cycl.* XIX. 375/2 In the common conveyance by lease and release, it is usual to give the intended releasee an estate in the land for a year by bargain and sale.

†**5.** The place where fresh hounds are let slip to take up the chase. *Obs.*[−1] (See relay *sb.* i.)

1490 Caxton *Eneydos* xv. 53 [They] assembled theyr rennynge houndes, two and two togyder..; Some wyth the brakkenere, for to be atte the reysynge of the beeest, for to renne after; The other for to be sette atte the relesse.

6. a. The action of setting free, or the fact of being set free, from restraint or confinement; permission to go free; also, a document giving formal discharge from custody.

c **1586** C'tess Pembroke *Ps.* l. viii, In vaine to others for release you flie, If once on you I griping fingers sett. **1610** Shaks. *Temp.* v. i. 11 All prisoners..They cannot boudge, till your release. **1671** Milton *P.R.* i. 409 Who boast'st release from Hell, and leave to come Into the Heav'n of Heavens. **1759** Johnson *Rasselas* xxxviii, I knew no sum would be thought too great for the release of Pekuah. **1847** Emerson *Poems, To Rhea* Wks. (Bohn) I. 403 These presents be the hostages Which I pawn for my release.

b. The act of letting go something fixed or held in a certain position, or confined in some way; also, any device by which this is effected.

1871 *Spons' Dict. Engin.* IV. 1408 Causing the release of the spring-clips to be earlier or later in the stroke. **1882** Ogilvie, *Release*, in the steam-engine, the opening of the exhaust-port before the stroke is finished, to lessen the back-pressure. **1890** *Anthony's Photogr. Bull.* III. 306 The release is pressed too hard and the shutter slips off. **1892** *Pall Mall G.* 10 Sept. 7/2 A little frame carrying five keys. One of these is the release.

attrib. **1884** C. G. W. Lock *Workshop Receipts* Ser. iii. 89/2 The third [hole] is closed by a stopper and capsule, forming a release-valve.

c. *Teleph.* The action of freeing for further use apparatus or circuitry which has been engaged. Freq. *attrib.*

1892 *Pall Mall G.* 10 Sept. 7/2 The subscriber presses the release key. **1919** J. Poole *Pract. Telephone Handbk.* (ed. 6) xxi. 368 Its armature short-circuits the no-voltage release magnet and the switch arm falls back to its open position. **1921** W. Aitken *Automatic Telephone Systems* I. 185 The calling receiver may be replaced just before the register is connected and cause a premature release. **1969** S. F. Smith *Telephony & Telegr. A* ii. 39 If a relay were required to have a high value of release current, it would need as many springs as possible of maximum thickness. **1970** N. N. Biswas *Princ. Telephony* iii. 80 This alarm circuit becomes a necessity in all exchanges where the release of the entire switching stages is controlled by the calling subscriber.

d. *Phonetics.* The action or manner of relaxing or terminating the obstruction involved in articulating a stop consonant.

1920 in Webster. **1951** Z. S. Harris *Methods in Structural Linguistics* 44 In some English dialects perhaps the sequence [tr] (post-dental [t] plus voiceless spirant release), are each composed of smaller segments. **1964** J. C. Catford in D. Abercrombie et al. *Daniel Jones* 34 Variations in vocal fold thickness..produce qualitative variations in..the release-sound of glottal stop. **1969** *English Studies* L. 328 This implies that the difference of total duration between [ptk] and [bdg] is very nearly equivalent to the difference of duration of the release stage. **1978** *Amer. Speech 1975* L. 295 In the style of pronunciation favored by barbershoppers, final voiced stops like those in the key words have a release that gives the impression of an indistinct vowel.

e. *Jazz.* A passage of music that serves as a bridge between repetitions of a main melody. Chiefly *U.S.*

1936 L. Dowling tr. *Panassié's Hot Jazz: Guide to Swing Music* 18 The group of eight measures designated by the letter *b* is called the 'middle part' because it makes the first appearance in the middle of the tune. [*Translator's note*] Also called, quite poetically, 'the release'. **1937** *New Republic* 24 Nov. 69/1 But then the band comes down to the release and Benny holds up one finger and Jess nods. **1946** Mezzrow & Wolfe *Really Blues* (1957) 344 We played a more staccato style on the release. **1949** L. Feather *Inside Be-bop* ii. 67 In the release there is another beautiful sweeping phrase. **1959** Avakian & Prince in M. T. Williams *Art of Jazz* (1960) xvii. 184 Charlie.. develops a series of riffs through the first sixteen bars (tension); then, in the eight-bar release, he contrasts this by playing melodic lines characteristically made up mainly of even eighth notes (relaxation), then returns to eight bars of riffs (tension). **1972** A. Wilder *Amer. Popular Song* ii. 56 The conventional *A-A-B-A* structure (main strain: its virtual repetition: a release, almost always new material: and finally, a literal, varied, or extended restatement of the main strain) was used in *Ol' Man River*.

7. The action of releasing information or other material for publication or public showing; the information or material released.

a. (The releasing of) a news item or official statement, usu. to the press. orig. *U.S.*

1907 *N.Y. Even. Post* (semi-weekly ed.) 15 July 4 The report was given to the press associations.. labelled 'confidential', with a fixed date for 'release', before which no part of it was to be used. **1927** G. Ade *Let.* 31 May (1973) 120, I will be.. up to my eyes in the weekly release grind. **1931** F. L. Allen *Only Yesterday* ix. 276 Press agents distributed their canned releases. **1932** *Atlantic Monthly* Mar. 269/1 The press agents.. did not pour forth their releases to a.. coöperating press. **1957** [see backgrounder]. *a* **1974** R. Crossman *Diaries* (1975) I. 343 The release wasn't ready until a few minutes before I had to deliver the speech.

b. The action of making a film available to cinemas or a gramophone record to purchasers; also, the film or record itself.

1912 *Motion Picture Ann.* 25 An Essanay release called 'Sunshine'. **1927** *Daily News* 8 June 4/4 Some of the recent 'releases' show that Hollywood and Germany are being challenged seriously in the matter of production. **1929** '*His Master's Voice' New Records* Mid-June 13 Theme songs from two great American films that are scheduled for release in the autumn. **1932** *New Yorker* 14 May 57/2, I have not seen it [*sc.* a gramophone record] on any official list and it seems to be a special release. **1949** *St. Paul* (Minnesota) *Pioneer-Press* 19 June 11/3 Busiest year on record for total releases is 1921 when American moviegoers had their choice of 854 different features. **1966** *Illustr. London News* 30 July 31/2 Perhaps this could be quietly excised before the film goes out on general release. **1966** *Guardian* 22 Dec. 4/7 In the pop/folk field the best new release is by The Incredible String Band. **1974** *Times* 19 Oct. 9/1 New Releases... Piano Music by Erik Satie. **1977** *Time* 4 July 4 (Advt.), There's a film to watch—a recent release—8 tracks of stereo to listen to, free naturally, and plenty of room to stretch out or stroll about.

8. Special Combs.: **release agent**, a substance which is applied to a surface in order to prevent adhesion to it, esp. in food packaging and concrete construction; **release date**, a date fixed for the release of information or other material (see sense 7 above); **release group**, a group of servicemen due for release from conscripted service; **release note**, a note authorizing the release of (part of) an aircraft as fit for service; now also in extended use.

1960 A. E. Bender *Dict. Nutrition* 107/2 *Release agents*, substances applied to tinned or enamelled surfaces or plastic films to prevent the food adhering; e.g. fatty acid amides, microcrystalline waxes, petrolatums, starch, methylcellulose. **1965** W. H. Taylor *Concrete Technol. & Pract.* vii. 160 An ideal release agent.. should produce a clean stripping action with a minimum of surface defects on the hardened concrete. **1974** Briston & Katan *Plastics in Contact with Food* iii. 61 Silicone resins are also used as release agents. The baking industry, for instance, uses silicone resins to coat bread baking pans and hundreds of releases from a single coating of resin have been reported. **1910** *Moving Picture World* 26 Mar. 488/1 (*heading*) Independent release dates. **1932** L. C. Douglas *Forgive us our Trespasses* (1937) xv. 306 He decided not to take another look at the gripping letter until he had done at least one essay. He always tried to keep about three weeks ahead of the release date. **1965** *Amer. N. & Q.* Mar. 105/2 Its fine appendix of 'Serials from 1912 to 1930', showing title, director, cast, release date, releasing company. **1945** *News Chron.* 18 Apr. 2/4 We think it would have been much fairer to lower the release group age, such as all men over 45 in Group One and so on, and let some of the youngsters who have been in so-called deferred jobs have a turn. **1946** *R.A.F. Jrnl.* May 149 W.A.A.F. personnel whose release groups have appeared in an advance promulgation are invited to apply for vacancies. **1930** *Air Ann. Brit. Empire* 234 The firm must issue with every consignment they deliver a release note certifying that all inspection has been carried out. **1963** *Times Rev. Industry* Mar. 51/1 When a motor dealer asked a customer from whom he bought a second-hand Wolseley car to sign a 'release note', which turned out to be a guarantee of a third party's commitments under a hire-purchase agreement, the customer was not liable on the guarantee.

† **re'lease**, *sb.*[2] *Obs.* *rare*$^{-1}$. [Later form of reles: cf. release *v.*[2]] Relish.

1604 T. Wright *Passions* v. §4. 189 Things which repugne any way together carrie with them a spice or release of contrarietie.

release (rɪ'liːs), *v.*[1] Forms: 3–5 reles, 4–6 relese, -lesse, -lece, (4 -leese, -leesse, 5 -leece, -lecyn); 4–5 releysche, -lesche, (4 -leische), 5 ralesche, releshe; 5– release, (6 -leace, -lease). [ad. OF. *relesser* (12th c.), *relaiss(i)er* (var. of *relâcher*) :—L. *relaxāre* to relax.]

I. † **1.** *trans.* To withdraw, recall, revoke, cancel (a sentence, punishment, condition, etc.). *Obs.*

1297 R. Glouc. (Rolls) 10297 Þou hast nou.. þe pope bisout, þat he relesi þe entredit. **1387** Trevisa *Higden* (Rolls) V. 371 The kyng hadde relesed [*v.r.* relesched; L. *relaxasset*] and wiþcleped a wel hard avow þat he hadde i-made. *Ibid.* VIII. 233 If that he made eny sentence, the legate.. scholde have releisched hit. **1422** tr. *Secreta Secret.* 128 Al the Cite.. to the Sone relessid the Payne [= penalty] of the eighyn. *c* **1530** *Crt. of Love* 1014 The sixteenth statut doth me grete grevaunce, But ye must that relesse or modifie. **1568** Grafton *Chron.* II. 931 The lyfe was geuen, and the punishment of death releaused. **1629** Milton *Christ's Nativ.* i, For so the holy sages once did sing, That he our deadly forfeit should release. **1671** R. Montagu in *Buccleuch MSS.* (Hist. MSS. Comm.) I. 501 Getting the King here to release that Article of the Treaty.

† **2.** To relieve, alleviate, or remove (labour, pain, etc.). *Obs.*

a **1340** Hampole *Psalter* cxviii. [cxix.] 54 Relesand my trauayls and my noy in þis wrechid life. *c* **1386** Chaucer *Man of Law's T.* 971, I prey yow al my labour to relesse. **1423** Jas. I *Kingis Q.* clxxxiv, Beseching vnto fair venus abufe.. His paine relesch, and sone to stand In grace. **1526** *Pilgr. Perf.* (W. de W. 1531) 99 He begged but one droppe of water, to release his turmentes. **1551** Turner *Herbal* i. B vij b, The iuice that is pressed out, is better & releseth the paine soner. **1597** Daniel *Civ. Wars* vi. lxvi, Would God his blood, and mine had well releast The dangers that his pride is like to breed.

3. To remit; to grant remission or discharge of or for (something); † **a.** a vow or task. *Obs.*

c **1315** Shoreham i. 1790 Relessed Schel hym nauȝt be religioun, þaȝ he be nauȝt professed. *c* **1386** Chaucer *Clerk's T.* 97 But ther as ye han profred me.. To chese me a wyf, I yow relesse That choys, and prey you of that profre cesse.

† **b.** sin or wrong-doing. *Obs.*

c **1380** Wyclif *Serm.* Sel. Wks. I. 77 If preestis have power to relese synne as Cristis vikeris. *c* **1386** Chaucer *Pars. T.* ¶ 508 Thilke synne is so greet that vnnethe may it be releessed. **1422** tr. *Secreta Secret., Priv. Priv.* 134 To a vertues kynge hit appendyth lyghtly to relesse the wronge that is to hym done. **1548** Udall, etc. *Erasm. Par. Mark* iv. 32 Nowe sinnes are not released, but to suche as beleue that sins are freely released. **1574** tr. *Marlorat's Apocalips* 11 Who can release sinnes but onely God?

c. a debt, tax, tribute, etc. Now only *Law.*

c **1386** Chaucer *Frankl. T.* 885 Sire, I releesse thee thy thousand pound,.. I wol nat take a peny of thee. **1387** Trevisa *Higden* (Rolls) IV. 107 He.. relesede.. half þe tribute þat was woned to be payde. *c* **1400** tr. *Secreta Secret., Gov. Lordsh.* 57 And also he vsys þat tyme.. for to reles party of rentys. **1457** *Cal. Anc. Rec. Dublin* (1889) I. 295 That he shall have releshyed to hym during hys live the chef rent of an orchard. *c* **1550** *Disc. Common Weal Eng.* (1893) 27 b, If.. youe should release youre rent.. to the old rate. **1601** R. Johnson *Kingd. & Commw.* (1603) 115 A tribute which Leo the 9. did release to the church of Bamburg. **1647** N. Bacon *Disc. Govt. Eng.* i. lx. (1739) 118 He not only never charged the people with any Tax, but released that of Dane-gelt. **1884** Sir W. B. Brett in *Law Rep. 14 Q.B. Div.* 191 [One] who was competent to do so might have released the debt.

4. a. To give up, resign, relinquish, surrender (*esp.* a right or claim, in favour of another person).

1390 Gower *Conf.* I. 257 In what wise he may relesse His hihe astat, that wot he noght. *Ibid.* 271 Echon.. preiden for this lordes hele, Which hath relessed the querele. *c* **1400** *Destr. Troy* 13626, I releshe þe my ryght with a rank will, And graunt þe þe gouernanse of þis grete yle. **1470–85** Malory *Arthur* x. xxix. 461 Yf that this knyght slee hym, I fully releece my clayme for euer. *a* **1533** Ld. Berners *Huon* liii. 180 As for the wager that I sholde wyn therby, I am content to relese it quyte. *a* **1548** Hall *Chron., Hen. VIII* 172 Whiche of you.. would concent that the kyng shoulde release his Seignioritie or superioritie of Wales, Irelande or Cornewall? **1596** Spenser *F.Q.* iv. ii. 19 Bidding them fight for honour of their love, And rather die then Ladies cause release. **1665** Manley *Grotius' Low C. Warres* 907 As if the Emperor Frederick had released to Philip Duke of Burgundy, all Right of Empire. **1697** Dryden *Virg. Georg.* iii. 346 Nor will the vanquish'd Bull his Claim release. **1775** Johnson *Tax. no Tyr.* 83 That we should at once release our claims. **1841** *Penny Cycl.* XIX. 376/1 An expectant heir cannot release the right which he may have to his ancestor's estate.

b. *spec.* To surrender, make over, transfer (land or territory) to another. Chiefly *Law.*

c **1400** *Rom. Rose* 6999, I quethe hym quyte, and hym relesse Of Egipt al the wildirnesse. **1475** *Bk. Noblesse* (Roxb.) 22 The said Lowes relesid the seide dukedom to the said Richarde. **1593** Shaks. *2 Hen. VI*, i. i. 51 It is agreed.. That the Dutchy of Aniou.. shall be released and deliuered to the King her father. **1664** Anderson *Reports* §83, I release all my Lands, &c. to A. and to his Heirs. **1766** Blackstone *Comm.* II. App. 4 The said Abraham Barker and Cecilia his Wife, Have.. sold, released, and confirmed.. unto the said David Edwards.. all that capital messuage called Dale Hall. **1809** Bawdwen *Domesday Bk.* 620 Colsuan did not release the land of Ingemund and his brother to Earl Alan. **1866** Geo. Eliot *F. Holt* i, I trusted to your getting the estate some time, and releasing it; and I determined to keep it worth releasing.

absol. **1430–1** *Rolls of Parlt.* IV. 386/1 The whech William gave full astate.. of the Burgages, Landes and Tenements aforeseid, and opon that relesed to the seid Suppliant in hir possession. **1462** *Paston Lett.* II. 89 That the seid maner sholde be solde by.. his executours, to whom the seid Sir John hath relesed, as his dute was to do. **1766** Blackstone *Comm.* II. 325 If there be two joint disseisors, and the disseisee releases to one of them [etc.].

c. *spec.* (See quot.)

1876 Digby *Real Prop.* v. §3 (2) 226 When a reversioner desires, not to grant his reversion to a third person, but to convey it to the person who already has the particular estate, he is said to release the reversion.

d. Of a public or military authority: to make available (requisitioned or otherwise withheld items) to the public; to return (land or property) to civilian use.

1917 *Globe* 21 Feb. 4/4 Only this morning a daily paper of some standing remarked that the Government had not 'released' any Colonial mutton.. last week. **1945** *Daily Tel.* 27 July 3/3 (*heading*) R.A.F. & Navy to release houses. *Ibid.*, The Admiralty and Air Ministry are to do all they can to alleviate the housing situation by releasing property.

† **5.** To relax, moderate, mitigate. *Obs.*

1422 tr. *Secreta Secret., Priv. Priv.* 128 So he mayntenyd his lawe, and relessit the duresse of the laue. **1606** G. W[oodcocke] *Hist. Ivstine* xxxvii. 116 The Massilians intreat the Romaines to release their displeasure against the Phocenses. **1677** *Govt. Venice* 207 They released the severity of that Law.

II. 6. a. To set or make free, to liberate, deliver, *of* (now somewhat rare) or *from* pain, bondage, obligation, etc. Also without const.

(*a*) **13..** *Coer de L.* 3034 Ther was no man.. myghte do his sorwe sese, Ne off his paynes hym relese. **1340** Hampole *Pr. Consc.* 3813 For pardon here.. May þam relese of þe dede of payn. **1456** Sir G. Haye *Law Arms* (S.T.S.) 227 He is presumyt ay to be servand quhill he be releschit of his service. *c* **1470** Henry *Wallace* ii. 361 Quhen Wallace was ralesched off his payne. **1509** Hawes *Past. Pleas.* xxix. (Percy Soc.) 138 Ye shall release Me first of my wo and great distresse. **1560** Daus tr. *Sleidane's Comm.* 205 He shall release the people of theyre othe. **1615** G. Sandys *Trav.* 14 They are in a manner releast of their thraldome, in that vnsensible of it. **1870** Tennyson *Pelleas & Ettarre* 290 Let who will release him of his bonds. **1974** *Petroleum Rev.* XXVIII. 675/3 To release the diver of this chore, remote-controlled systems are being developed.

(*b*) *c* **1386** Chaucer *Pars. T.* ¶ 735 Ihesu crist.. relessed vs fro the peynes of helle. **1432–50** tr. *Higden* (Rolls) III. 247 The kynges letters thro whom he scholde releysche the ministres of the temple from every tribute. **1590** Spenser *F.Q.* iii. vii. 1 Long after she from perill was releast. **1666** Marvell *Corr.* Wks. (Grosart) II. 201, I suppose you know that the Duke of Buckingham and Marquesse of Dorchester are again releast from the Tow'r. **1738** Wesley *Ps.* li. xv, Thou only canst release My Soul from all Iniquity. **1781** Cowper *Retirem.* 139 A mind released From anxious thoughts. **1817** Shelley *Pr. Athan.* ii. ii. 66 From death and dark forgetfulness released. **1875** Jowett *Plato* (ed. 2) I. 407 The wicked is not released from his evil by death.

(*c*) *c* **1330** *Assump. Virg.* (B.M. MS.) 529 In what peyne so he be.. I schal hem reles sone anone. **1390** Gower *Conf.* III. 186 So that Athenis, which was bounde, Nevere after scholde be relessed. *c* **1420** Lydg. *Assembly of Gods* 237 Apollo, though Diana hym relese, Yet shall he su to me to haue hys pese. **1560** Daus tr. *Sleidane's Comm.* 176 b, By the kynges authoritie not longe after he was cleane released. **1610** Shaks. *Temp.* v. i. 30 Goe, release them Ariell, My Charmes Ile breake, their sences Ile restore. **1697** Dryden *Virg. Georg.* iii. 101 Six Seasons use; but then release the Cow. **1738** Gray *Propertius* iii. 87 The hand that can my captive heart release. **1818** Shelley *Rosal. & Helen* 908 His foes released him thence. **1860** Tyndall *Glac.* i. xxvii. 198, I recommended him to release the horses and leave the carriage to its fate.

absol. *c* **1440** *Macro Plays* (E.E.T.S.) 67/971 All þe preyer þat seyde be kan, With-owt sorowe of hert, relesyt nought. **1651** Hobbes *Leviath.* ii. xxvi. 138 He that can bind, can release.

b. To unfix, free (a thing) from some fastening.

1833 Tennyson *Two Voices* 403 And I arose, and I released the casement.

c. *U.S.* To make (an employee) redundant. *euphem.*

1976 *National Observer* (U.S.) 24 Jan. 1/4 The two most difficult things I ever had to do were, one: tell 23 teachers we were going to release them [etc.]. **1977** *Time* 12 Dec. 54/2 He closed 1,700 stores, released 10,000 employees, borrowed heavily to revamp and enlarge the remaining 1,932 supermarkets.

7. To make available for publication or public showing; to publish (printed matter, recorded material or the like). orig. *U.S.*

1904 *N.Y. Times* 25 July 5 Chairman Cannon's speech and President Roosevelt's response are completed. The latter is in the hands of the press associations, and will be released Wednesday afternoon. **1912** *Motion Picture Ann.* 42 List of Licensed Pictures. Regularly released during the year 1912. **1916** 'B. M. Bower' *Phantom Herd* v. 71 We've just got to release films the market calls for. **1937** A. Thirkell *Summer Half* xi. 298 If a film gets to Barchester it means it's been released for simply months. **1957** *Essays & Stud.* X. 5 Among words that incur.. reproach are.. *release* (the expression 'to release a film' is denounced by a bishop as 'an abominable Americanism'). **1962** *Sunday Times* (Colour Suppl.) 10 June 7 This is also true of American records, a great many of which are only released because companies have to take them to get some really lucrative artist. **1972** *Daily Tel.* 18 Jan. 9/5 Rehearsals have already started and the record is expected to be released some time in the Autumn. **1980** *Time Out* 21–27 Nov. 49/3 Films considered by their multinational distributors as too 'difficult' to release conventionally.

Hence **released** (rɪ'liːst), *ppl. a.*

1678 Cudworth *Intell. Syst.* i. iii. 165 A Providence perfectly Intellectual, Abstract and Released. **1850** Mrs.

JAMESON *Leg. Monast. Ord.* 25 St. Benedict..beheld the released soul of his sister..flying towards Heaven.

†re'lease, *v.*² [Cf. RELEASE *sb.*²] = RELISH *v.*¹
1604 T. WRIGHT *Passions* v. §2. 167 Some stately maiesticall songs..release I know not what resemblance of action and gesture, consorting with great personages.

re,lea'see. *Law.* [f. RELEASE *v.*¹ + -EE¹. Cf. RELESSEE.] One to whom an estate is released.
1744 JACOB *Law Dict.* (ed. 5) s.v. *Release.* **1818** CRUISE *Digest* (ed. 2) IV. 101 The releasee has an estate actually vested in him at the time of the release. **1886** *Law Rep., Weekly Notes* 56/2 All necessary parties joined in conveying the Neath Abbey Estate to a releasee.

releasement (rɪ'liːsmənt). [RELEASE *v.*¹]
1. The act of releasing, or the fact of being released, from prison, obligation, debt, trouble, etc. (Very common *c* 1550–1800.)
1548 UDALL, etc. *Erasm. Par. Acts* viii. 36 No aunswer made he before him for his realeasement. **1555** HARPSFIELD *Divorce Hen. VIII* (Camden) 130 This releasement is general to all the Jews. **1592** *Nobody & Someb.* in Simpson *Sch. Shaks.* (1878) I. 335 Might not she Make uprors in the land, and raise the Commons, In the releasement of the Captive King? **1603** KNOLLES *Hist. Turks* (1621) 166 He proclaimed unto the people in generall, a releasement of them from all tributes, impositions, and paiments. **1643** MILTON *Divorce* Pref., Wks. 1851 IV. 14 Then mans nature would find immediate rest and releasment from all evils. **1681** LUTTRELL *Brief Rel.* (1857) I. 150 The earl of Shaftsbury, since his releasement, hath been adviseing with councill. **1715** M. DAVIES *Athen. Brit.* I. 63 Leonard Cox.. procur'd his releasement [from the stocks], refresh'd his hungry Stomach, and gave him Mony. **1782** MISS BURNEY *Cecilia* II. iii, [He] went in search of the lady for whose releasement he had fought. **1821** CLARE *Vill. Minstr.* I. 42 His short releasement from his cares and toil. **1855** M. ARNOLD *Balder Dead* 252 Thou hear'st..The terms of thy releasement hence to Heaven. **1887** HALL CAINE *Deemster* xl, To have escaped the peril of it [death] seemed a greater blessing than releasement from this island could ever be.
b. A formal declaration of release.
1771 T. HULL *Sir W. Harrington* (1797) III. 95 Wording what I declared to be a releasement,..more binding than those promises I pretended to absolve you from.
†2. Relaxation, remission, or removal *of* a thing.
1568 GRAFTON *Chron.* II. 109 Before the releasement of the interdiction, the king was..compelled..to geue ouer both his crowne and scepter. **1581** MARBECK *Bk. of Notes* 900 By this it appeareth that saluation falleth vnto men, by releasement of the debt. **1603** KNOLLES *Hist. Turks* (1621) 1051 Wallachia thus impoverished, was not able..to expect any releasement of the evils it was wrapped in. **1647** TRAPP *Comm. Rom.* iii. 25 For the relaxation or releasment of sins, as of bonds or fetters.

releaser (rɪ'liːsə(r)). [f. RELEASE *v.*¹ + -ER¹.]
a. One who, or that which, releases or sets free.
1651 FRENCH *Distill.* Ep. Ded., In the perfection of this Art..is the Sulphur of philosophers set at liberty, which gratifies the releasers thereof with three kingdomes. **1654** GAYTON *Pleas. Notes* III. 125 (Honour'd Releaser,) [he] said, Command what is Fecible. **1828–32** in WEBSTER. **1891** *Blackw. Mag.* CXLIX. 75/2 Till the releaser Death shall come.
b. *Dairying.* A device which removes milk from the vessel in which the output of a milking machine accumulates. Freq. *attrib.*
1950 *N.Z. Jrnl. Agric.* Apr. 378/1 Probably the most important part of any milking shed is the releaser room, as it is here that milk or cream can most easily become affected by unsatisfactory conditions. **1950** *Ibid.* Oct. 369 Up-to-date assembly of releaser, cream separator, skimmed-milk pump, and cream cooler. **1967** HARVEY & HILL *Milk* (ed. 4) xiii. 224 Where milk pipe-lines are provided to transmit the milk directly to the dairy, as in parlours, bails or with milk lines in cowsheds, a releaser is required to remove the milk from the system. Sufficient milk accumulates in the releaser jar which operates valves which seal off the vacuum system and allow the milk to be discharged. **1977** D. N. AKAM in Thiel & Dodd *Machine Milking* iii. 82 A design of diaphragm releaser milk pump that is available in the UK is vacuum driven using a pulsator operating at 50 pulsations/min.
c. *Biol.* [tr. G. *auslöser* (K. Lorenz 1935, in *Jrnl. für Ornithol.* LXXXIII. 143).] A sign stimulus (see SIGN *sb.* 12); restricted by some writers to one that acts between animals of the same species. Freq. *attrib.*
1937 K. LORENZ in *Auk* LIV. 249 All such devices for the issuing of releasing stimuli, I have termed releasers (*Auslöser*), regardless of whether the releasing factor be optical or acoustical, whether an act, a structure or a color. **1953** J. S. HUXLEY *Evol. in Action* iv. 96 The only definite releaser known in man is the pattern made by a mother's smile to her infant. **1953** N. TINBERGEN *Herring Gull's World* xiv. 116 Ritualisation is the result of a secondary evolutionary process which is closely linked to the releaser-function. *Ibid.* xxii. 208 The red patch on the bill seems to be a genuine social releaser. **1962** *Listener* 9 Aug. 207/2 Because animal signal codes are uniform within each species and fixed for long periods, special signal structures may evolve, and these are called releasers. **1971** *Nature* 16 Apr. 432/2 Releaser pheromone effects exist in man, at least in larval forms, and some involve pheromones of other mammals (musk, civetone). **1975** J. ALCOCK *Animal Behavior* vi. 153 The first concept we shall examine is the sign stimulus or releaser, that portion of the total stimulus configuration which acts as the effective cue in releasing a specific behavior pattern. **1980** A. P. BROOKFIELD *Animal Behaviour* vii. 58 Sign stimuli which elicit behaviour in members of the same species are called releasers.

re'leasing, *vbl. sb.* [f. RELEASE *v.*¹ + -ING¹.]
1. The action of the vb. in various senses.
c **1380** WYCLIF *Sel. Wks.* III. 295 Ful absolucion and relessyng of alle peynes in purgatory. **1395** PURVEY *Remonstr.* (1851) 66 The most good pretendid in indulgences is releesinge of peyne enioynid of the chirche. **1466** in *Somerset Medieval Wills* (1901) 209, I bequeithe to the high aulter of the seid church 3*s.* 4*d.* in relesyng of my tithes beyng behynd. *c* **1470** *Golagros & Gaw.* 1358, I mak releisching of thin allegiance. **1544** PHAER *Regim. Life* (1553) I iv b, Thys receit..hath greate vertue..to bring the humoures to equalitie, wyth releasynge of the payne. **1633** P. FLETCHER *Elisa* I. ix, Oh, if confessing Our faults to thee be all our faults releasing. **1692** LUTTRELL *Brief Rel.* (1857) II. 605 To agree about contributing for their duke's releasing.
2. Special Comb.: **releasing factor** *Physiol.*, any of several oligopeptides, released from the hypothalamus into the pituitary portal system, which promote the release from the adenohypophysis into the bloodstream of some specific peptidic hormone.
[**1955** *Endocrinology* LVII. 443 Posterior pituitary extracts contain a corticotropin-releasing factor (CRF) that stimulates the release of ACTH from rat anterior pituitary tissue *in vitro*.] **1965** *Ibid.* LXXVII. 609/1 In 1959, Shibusawa *et al.*..claimed to have prepared a thyrotropin releasing factor (TRF) from dog hypothalamic extracts and from urine. **1966** *Brit. Med. Bull.* XXII. 266/2 On this view, various humoral agents (now called releasing factors) are liberated from nerve-endings (of hypothalamic nerve tracts) into the capillaries (primary plexus) of the portal vessels in the median eminence. **1974** M. C. GERALD *Pharmacol.* xxiii. 413 This supreme command post of the endocrine system directs the activity of the anterior pituitary by neuro-secretory meditator substances called releasing factors. **1977** *Time* 24 Oct. 42/2 Andrew Schally..isolated identified and synthesized three separate hormones—'releasing factors'—by which the hypothalamus directs the release of key hormones from the pituitary.

releasor (rɪ'liːsə(r)). *Law.* [f. as prec. + -OR 2.] One who releases an estate or claim in favour of another. (See RELEASE *v.*¹ 4 and 4 b.)
1628 COKE *On Litt.* 265 The right which the Releasor hath at the time of the Release made. **1775** *Ld. Raymond's Rep.* I. 235 Where there are general words only in a release, they shall be taken most strongly against the releasor.

releave, obs. form of RELIEF *sb.*³

†re-'leave, *v. Obs. rare*⁻¹. [RE- 5 a.] *intr.* To put forth leaves again.
1655 HARTLIB *Ref. Silk-worm* 21 Those trees that have their leaves pull'd off in March, April, and May, do re-leave again, and have new and fresh leaves.

relece, obs. f. RELEASE *sb.*¹ and *v.*¹, RELES.

releckis, obs. pl. form of RELIC.

†re'lect, *pa. pple. Sc. Obs. rare*⁻¹. [ad. L. *relect-us*, pa. pple. of *relegĕre.*] Read again.
1560 HOLLAND *Crt. Venus* III. 298 The Rollis [being] relect quhais tennour ȝe sall heir.

re'lection. [f. L. *relect-*, ppl. stem of *relegĕre* to read again; cf. LECTION *sb.*, PRELECTION.]
†1. The action of reading again; reperusal; also, a correction made upon re-reading. *Obs. rare.*
1600 W. WATSON *Decacordon* (1602) 324 By relection of what hath bene already said there may ynough be gathered sufficient to confirme and demonstrate it against them. **1671** WOODHEAD *St. Teresa* I. Pref. a 4 Without blots, relections, or emendations.
2. The title of the various divisions of a work (*Relectiones Theologicae*) by Franciscus de Victoria.
1630 HAKEWILL *Apol.* (ed. 2) 2 Franciscus de Victoria in his Relection of Temperance. **1839** HALLAM *Hist. Lit.* II. iv. §87 The book..consists of thirteen relections, as Victoria calls them, or dissertations on different subjects.

releef(e, -lef(e, -leff, obs. forms of RELIEF *sb.*

relees(e, obs. forms of RELEASE *sb.*¹ and *v.*¹

releevant, see RELIEVANT.

releeve, obs. form of RELIEVE *v.*

relegable ('rɛlɪgəb(ə)l), *a.* [f. RELEG-ATE + -ABLE.] Capable of being relegated or referred.
1895 *Westm. Gaz.* 25 Feb. 3/1 All such matters as concern the Council as a whole, without being clearly relegable to any one Committee.

†'relegate, *sb. Obs. rare*⁻¹. [ad. L. *relēgāt-us*: see next.] A banished person; an exile.
c **1540** tr. *Pol. Verg. Eng. Hist.* (Camden) I. 186 He banished this springehole [*sic*] as relagate in Fraunce.

relegate ('rɛlɪgeɪt), *v.* Also 7 relig-. [f. ppl. stem of L. *relēgāre*, f. *re-* RE- + *lēgāre* to send.]
1. *trans.* To send (a person) into exile; to banish *to* a particular place. (Cf. RELEGATION 1.) †Also *refl.*, to remove (oneself) to a distance *from* something.
1599 NASHE *Lenten Stuffe* 8 The sands..would no more liue vnder the yoke of the Sea,..but clearely quitted, disterminated and relegated themselues from his inflated Capriciousnesse. **1611** COTGR., *Releguer*, to relegate, banish, exile. **1628** tr. *Mathieu's Powerfull Favorite* 84 That was too gentle to satisfie the cruelty of Tiberius,..onely relegating the culpable out of Rome. **1774** KAMES *Sketches* II. iii. (1807) II. 83 To be relegated to his country-seat, is, to a gentleman of rank, more terrible than a capital punishment. **1862** MERIVALE *Rom. Emp.* lxii. (1865) VII. 407 Nor is it clear that Dion Chrysostomus was actually relegated to the Ister. **1873** TRISTRAM *Moab* xiv. 264 The fortress to which Herod relegated his wife.
2. a. To banish *to* some unimportant or obscure place; to consign *to* a place or position, esp. one of inferiority.
1790 BURKE *Fr. Rev.* (ed. 2) 153 We have not relegated religion (like something we were ashamed to shew) to obscure municipalities or rustick villages. **1865** *Daily Tel.* 16 Nov. 7/7 The various 'bills' that have..been relegated to the dust of official pigeon-holes. **1877** BLACK *Green Past.* xviii. (1878) 147 She would do her best in the sphere to which she had been relegated.
b. To consign (a subject) *to* some province, sphere, domain, etc.
1866 R. W. DALE *Disc. Spec. Occ.* viii. 275 To relegate the intellect to inferior provinces of thought. **1875** JOWETT *Plato* (ed. 2) IV. 406 If occasionally we come across difficulties.. we relegate some of them to the sphere of mystery. **1878** MACLEAR *Celts* iv. 47 To the domain of legend..we must also relegate the tradition.
c. To assign or refer (a thing) *to* a class or kind.
1870 tr. *Pouchet's Universe* 57 Men have never known to what kingdom the sponges should be relegated. **1874** SAYCE *Compar. Philol.* v. 206 The comparative study of the Basque numerals has relegated them to the Finnic family.
d. *Sport.* To reallocate (a team) to a lower division of a league. Cf. RELEGATION 1 c.
1913 *Times* 28 Apr. 12/5 Norwich County..will..be relegated to the Second Division next season. **1934** *Times* 7 May 4/5 Everton, when they were relegated for the first time in their history, climbed back immediately. **1981** *Times* 6 May 10/3 After a trying beginning, that saw the club relegated to the second division.
3. a. To refer (a matter) *to* some authority for decision.
1846 H. ROGERS *Ess.* (1860) I. 180 Affirming that that faith to which the appeal is sure to be ultimately relegated is a faith entirely without reason. **1884** *Law Rep.* 25 *Chanc. Div.* 282 Where there is an agreement, the whole matter ought to be at once relegated to the Taxing Master.
b. To commit, hand over (a thing), *to* another to carry out or deal with.
1864 BOWEN *Logic* ii. 35 The discussion of it is, therefore, relegated to treatises on that science of which it forms a part. **1869** LECKY *Europ. Mor.* iv. II. 43 The later inquisitors, who relegated the execution of the sentence to the civil power. **1872** YEATS *Techn. Hist. Comm.* 427 Men, seeking to escape the drudgery of manual labour, have relegated toil to the captive and the slave.
c. To turn over or refer (a person) *for* something *to* some person or thing.
1870 DISRAELI *Lothair* xli, She would..have been relegated for amusement, during her visit, to the attentions of the dark sex. **1883** *Contemp. Rev.* XLIII. 274 Failing such means of knowledge, we are relegated for information..to incidental statements..of the historians.
Hence **'relegated, 'relegating** *ppl. adjs.*
1611 COTGR., *Relegué*, relegated, banished, exiled. **1692** WOOD *Life* 19 May (O.H.S.) III. 390 Dr. Byrom Eaton resign'd his principality of Gloc. Hall, after it had laid in a religated condition several yeares. **1727–38** CHAMBERS *Cycl.* s.v. *Relegation*, In Rome, relegation was a less severe punishment than deportation, in that the relegated person did not thereby lose the rights of a Roman citizen. **1868** BROWNING *Ring & Bk.* VI. 2076, I am, on earth, as good as out of it, A relegated priest. **1887** H. JAMES *Partial Portraits* (1888) 31 Such a revision of Emerson has no relegating consequences.

relegation (rɛlɪ'geɪʃən). [ad. L. *relēgātiōn-em*, n. of action f. *relēgāre* to RELEGATE.]
1. a. The action of banishing; the state of temporary exile or banishment. In *Roman Antiq.* banishment to a certain place, or to a specified distance from Rome, for a limited time and without loss of civil rights. Also *attrib.*
1586 FERNE *Blaz. Gentrie* II. 128 The King after this repealed the former sentences and procured their relegation. **1605** G. POWELL *Refut. Ep. Puritan-Papist* 112 Banishment ..among the Romanes was 3-fold, Interdiction, Relegation, and Deportation. **1652** J. WRIGHT tr. *Camus' Nat. Paradox* III. 55 Neither the King nor the Queen, who both agreed in this relegation, did communicate to each other their Thoughts. **1684** *Contempl. State Man* II. vi. (1699) 195 Other Banished Persons..within the Isle or Region of Relegation, may go or move whither they please. **1726** AYLIFFE *Parergon* 502 Deportation which is perpetual, and Relegation which is only for a Time. **1856** MERIVALE *Rom. Emp.* xxxviii. (1865) IV. 335 His punishment was not strictly exile, but only the milder form of relegation. **1868** BROWNING *Ring & Bk.* I. 1039 He has been censured, punished in a sort By relegation,—exile, we should say, To a short distance for a little time. **1869** *Ibid.* IX. 1254 The priest, Once fairly at his relegation-place, Never once left it.
b. Banishment or consignment *to* a place.
1829 SOUTHEY *Sir T. More* (1831) II. 190 To consider such relegation to the wilderness as a punishment appropriated for criminals. **1868** GLADSTONE *Juv. Mundi* vii. (1870) 177 The deposition, and relegation to a distance, of the older Gods of the nature system. **1897** P. WARUNG *Tales Old Regime* 192 Instead of..welcoming his relegation to the gaol-cell..he resented his removal.
c. *Sport.* The demotion of a team to a lower division of a league; *spec.* in *Assoc. Football*, the reallocation to a lower division of the Football League of an agreed number of teams scoring the fewest points in a division in the course of a season's play. Also *attrib.*
1924 *Times* 5 May 6/6 Fractions in goal averages decided promotion and relegation. **1928** *Daily Express* 10 Aug. 13/7 Their supporters have recovered from the bitter disappointment felt when relegation became inevitable.

1949 *Times* 9 May 6/5 There was the question about relegation from the Championship. **1951** *Sport* 6–12 Apr. 6/2 Key man in the successful battle now being waged by West Bromwich Albion to steer clear of the First Division relegation zone is Jack Vernon. **1965** [see INJECT *v.* 2]. **1969** *Listener* 1 May 625/3 On Saturday, more than 250 million people are estimated to have watched the ninth club from the bottom of the table beat a relegation candidate by the odd goal. **1977** *Daily Mirror* 12 Apr. 26/4 We are out of the relegation zone now.

2. The action of referring, consigning, etc., a thing *to* others for some purpose.

1844 LD. DUNDONALD *Let.* in *Pearson's 76th Catal.* (1894) 21 The uniform relegation of all my memorials to successive Governments. **1878** *N. Amer. Rev.* CXXVII. 428 The relegation of the government to the mass of the people.

relegioune, obs. form of RELIGION.

releif(e, -leiff, obs. forms of RELIEF, RELIEVE.

releis(che, obs. forms of RELEASE *sb.*[1] and *v.*[1]

releive, obs. form of RELIEF, RELIEVE.

releivo, obs. form of RELIEVO[1].

relek(e, obs. form of RELIC.

re'lend (ri:-), *v.* [RE- 5 a.] To lend again.

1797 W. TAYLOR in *Monthly Rev.* XXIV. 221 The banker ..re-lends to the useful trader, at a high interest, this same deposit. **1884** *Law Rep. 12 Q.B. Div.* 608 The notes in stock were regarded as having been..relent by the firm to the company.

relenquyssh, obs. form of RELINQUISH.

†**re'lent**, *sb. Obs. rare.* [f. the vb.]

1. Slackening of speed.

1596 SPENSER *F.Q.* v. vii. 24 She forward went..Ne rested till she came without relent Unto the land of Amazons.

2. Relenting, giving way.

1590 GREENE *Orl. Fur.* Wks. (Rtldg.) 97/2 Fear of death enforceth still In greater minds submission and relent. **1616** W. FORDE *Serm.* 40 If vertue, if pietie, could worke any relent in death. **1686** GOAD *Celest. Bodies* I. xii. 56 Those [days] which are absolutely Cold and Freezing, without the least Sign of Relent or Yielding.

†**re'lent**, *pa. pple. Obs. rare.* [f. L. *re-* RE- + *lent-us* viscous, soft: see next, and cf. F. *relent* musty.] **a.** Loosened, loose. **b.** Softened.

c **1420** *Pallad. on Husb.* IV. 928 The bee..On titymalle and elmes gynneth pike That bitter be, wherof anoon relent Ther wombes are. *c* **1485** *Digby Myst.* (1882) IV. 620 Who shall gife me water sufficient,..That I may wepe my fill with hart relent..?

relent (rɪ'lɛnt), *v.*[1] Also 5 *pa. pple.* relente. [Ultimately f. L. *re-* RE- + *lent-us* tough, sticky, viscous, slow, etc.; but the immediate source is not clear: cf. L. *relentescĕre* to grow slack (Ovid), F. *ralentir* to slacken (16th c.), †*relentir*, 'to smell mustie, grow fustie' (Cotgr.).]

†**1.** *intr.* To melt under the influence of heat; to assume a liquid form; to dissolve into water. *Obs.*

c **1386** CHAUCER *Can. Yeom. Prol. & T.* 725 He styred þe coles til relente gan The wex agayn þe fuyr. *c* **1410** LYDG. *Reas. & Sens.* 4179 The wexe with hete wil relente. **1471** RIPLEY *Comp. Alch.* II. vii. in Ashm. (1652) 136 Behold how Yse to Water doth relent. **1530** PALSGR. 684/2 Se howe this snowe begynneth to relent agaynst the sonne. *c* **1586** C'TESS PEMBROKE *Ps.* CXLVII. vi, Ice in water flowes,..The streames relenting take their wonted way. **1653** H. MORE *Antid. Ath.* III. xvi. §3 Were those Musical accents frozen there for a time, and..the Air relenting and thawing became so harmoniously vocal? **1670** CLARKE *Nat. Hist. Nitre* 84 The Coal keepeth the Nitre very dry, that it may not relent and moisten by the Air. **1704** POPE *Spring* 69 All nature mourns, the Skies relent in show'rs. **1764** MORRIS in *Phil. Trans.* LIV. 174 On leaving it exposed to the air, the brown matter attracted moisture from it and relented into a thick brown liquour.

fig. *c* **1475** *Lament. Mary Magd.* lxx, Myne herte alas relenteth all in paine, Whiche will brast both senewe and vaine. *c* **1485** *Digby Myst.* (1882) IV. 153 To haue seyn hir, a harte of stone For ruthe wold haue relente. **1784** COWPER *Tiroc.* 112 Preserved from guilt by salutary fears, Or guilty, soon relenting into tears.

†**b.** To become soft or moist; also of colours, to give way, fade. *Obs.*

1531 ELYOT *Gov.* III. xix. (1880) II. 318 The colours beynge nat suerly wrought,..by moystnesse of wether relenteth or fadeth. **1573** TUSSER *Husb.* (1878) 63 Both saltfish and lingfish..from rotting go saue: Least winter with moistnes doo make it relent. **1594** PLAT *Jewell-ho.* II. 32 Keepe these leaues..neere a chimney, or stoue, least otherwise by the damp of the aier they relent again. **1620** MARKHAM *Farew. Husb.* II. xviii. (1668) 95 Beans after they are once dryed..will thaw, give again or relent.

c. To grow less tense or rigid, to relax. *rare*[−1].

1854 S. DOBELL *Balder* xxiv. 172 The painful limbs, contract with pangs, Relented.

2. To soften in temper; to grow more gentle or forgiving; to give up a harsh intention or inclination to severity. †Also const. with *inf.* (quot. 1604).

1526 *Pilgr. Perf.* (W. de W. 1531) 256b, It myght not swage the malyce of the iewes ne cause theyr hertes to relent. **1560** DAUS tr. *Sleidane's Comm.* 163 Nothyng relentynge of their wonted rygour. **1588** SHAKS. *Tit. A.* II. iii. 165, I powr'd forth teares in vaine,..But fierce Andronicus would not relent. **1604** BACON *Apol.* Wks. 1879 I. 436/2 If she once relented to send or visit, those demonstrations would prove matter of substance for my lord's good. **1631** R. BOLTON *Comf. Affl. Consc.* (1635) 232 He seemes now when he sees his misery to relent and to be touched with remorse. **1671** MILTON *Samson* 509 Perhaps God will relent, and quit thee all his debt. **1708** POPE *Ode St. Cecilia* 85 Stern Proserpine relented, And gave him back the fair. **1788** GIBBON *Decl. & F.* xlv. IV. 430 The conqueror paused and relented. **1817** SHELLEY *Rev. Islam* IV. xxii, Her foes relenting turn, And cast the vote of love. **1882** OUIDA *Maremma* I. 25 The carabinier on his right side, relenting, held the wine towards his mouth.

†**b.** To yield, give way; to give up a previous determination or obstinacy. Also const. *to. Obs.*

1528 GARDINER in Pocock *Rec. Reformation* I. 115 We do not yet relent, but stick still to have the Commission after the first form. **1560** DAUS tr. *Sleidane's Comm.* 31 If thou wylte persever thus obstinatlye in thine opinion, and not relent, the Emperour wyll bannishe thee. **1589** PUTTENHAM *Eng. Poesie* III. xxiv. (Arb.) 299 Princes..must be suffred to haue the victorie and be relented vnto. **1624** BURTON *Anat. Mel.* II. iii. VII. (ed. 2) 288 Two refractory spirits will never agree, the onely meanes to ouercome is to relent. **1667** MILTON *P.L.* VI. 790 To convince the proud what Signs availe, Or Wonders move th' obdurate to relent?

†**c.** To slacken, abate; to cool. *Obs. rare*[−1].

c **1560** INGELEND *Disobed. Child* C iij b, As for my loue yt doth neuer relente, For of you I do dreame. **1589** RIDER *Bibl. Schol.* 1206 To Relent as heate, *tepesco*.

†**3.** *trans.* To dissolve, melt, soften. *Obs.*

c **1420** *Pallad. on Husb.* III. 1142 In water first this opium relent, Of sape vntil hit ha similitude. *c* **1450** *M.E. Med. Bk.* (Heinrich) 161 Let do hem to þe fuyre aȝen, tyl þey ben relented. **1509** HAWES *Conv. Swearers* xl, Lyke as Phebus dothe the snowe relente. **1547** BOORDE *Introd. Knowl.* viii. (1870) 147 Butter is good meate, it doth relent the gall. **1612** WOODALL *Surg. Mate* Wks. (1653) 28 This Emplaster.. dissolved or relented with oyl of roses or elders [etc.]. **1661** LOVELL *Hist. Anim. & Min.* 50 Fractures..may be helped by Calves glue, relented in water.

†**b.** To soften (one's heart, mind, etc.); to cause (a person) to relent. *Obs.*

1509 HAWES *Past. Pleas.* XXXII. (Percy Soc.) 159 These men..A maydens herte coude ryght sone relente. **1590** SPENSER *F.Q.* III. vi. 40 Yet pitty often did the gods relent. *c* **1614** SIR W. MURE *Dido & Æneas* II. 543 How dar he this his enterprise reveale To furious Dido? how her minde relent? **1787** BURNS *Young Peggy* iii, Were Fortune lovely Peggy's foe, Such sweetness would relent her.

†**4.** To abate, lessen; to slacken. *Obs.*

1535 LYNDESAY *Satyre* 391, I am bot schent, Without scho cum,..My heauie langour to relent. **1590** SPENSER *F.Q.* II. xi. 27 Oftentimes he would relent his pace, That him his foe more fiercely should poursew. *Ibid.* III. iv. 49 Nothing might relent her hasty flight.

†**b.** To relinquish, abandon, give over. *Obs.*

1556 J. HEYWOOD *Spider & F.* liii. 40 To here him speak, ere he his life should relent. **1565** STAPLETON tr. *Bede's Hist. Ch. Eng.* 54b, After the death of their father they began.. openlie to folowe idolatrie, which while their father liued, they seemed somewhat to have relented. **1586** A. DAY *Eng. Secretary* I. (1625) 142 The disgrace that quickly you shall sustaine, if betimes you relent not these euils. **1684** BUNYAN *Pilgr.* II. 181 There's no Discouragement Shall make him once Relent His first avow'd Intent.

†**c.** To depart this life. *Obs. rare*[−1].

1587 *Mirr. Mag., Albanact* lv, My father..Perceau'd hee must by sicknesse last relent.

†**5.** To repent (an action, etc.). *Obs. rare*[−1].

1590 SPENSER *F.Q.* III. vi. 25 Shee inly sory was, and gan relent What shee had said.

†**b.** *refl.* To repent (oneself) *of* a thing. *Obs.*[−1]

1640 SANDERSON *Serm.* II. 175 We shall not have much cause to relent us of our choice.

†**c.** To pity. *Obs. rare*[−1].

1622 MABBE tr. *Aleman's Guzman d'Alf.* I. 18 Shee that kept the house, seeming to relent her paine, and to be much grieued for it..sorrowfully reply'd.

†**d.** To bewail (a thing) *to* a person. *Obs.*[−1]

1655 tr. *Com. Hist. Francion* III. 74, I could find nothing at all, and relenting my misfortune to my companion [etc.].

Hence †**re'lented** *ppl. a.* Also †**re'lentance**; †**re'lentful** *a.*

c **1420** *Pallad. on Husb.* IV. 105 In the roote Relented dong yputte on, doth hit boote. *a* **1586** SIDNEY *Arcadia* II. (1613) 164 [She] with a relented countenance thus sayd vnto him. **1611** HEYWOOD *Gold. Age* III. i. Wks. 1874 III. 42 The heauens That make me their relentfull minister. **1634** T. JOHNSON *Parey's Chirurg.* XXI. iv. (1678) 465 The relented bloud of such beasts as feed upon Scammony..purgeth violently. **1635** JACKSON *Creed* VIII. xii. §9 This may be the probable reason of his relentance.

†**re'lent**, *v.*[2] *Obs. rare*[−1]. [Of obscure formation.] *intr.* To return.

c **1485** *Digby Myst.* (1882) II. 259 But now, serys, lett vs relente Agayne to caypha and anna, to tell this chaunce.

relenting (rɪ'lɛntɪŋ), *vbl. sb.* [f. RELENT *v.*[1]] The action of the vb., in various senses.

1602 PLAT *Delightes for Ladies* Rec. iii, If you feare their relenting, take the Rose-leaues about Candlemas, and put them once again into a sieue. **1694** KETTLEWELL *Comp. Persecuted* 161 Make it to work..Relenting and remorse in their Persecutors. **1703** ROWE *Ulyss.* IV. i, What means this soft Relenting in my Soul? **1849** MACAULAY *Hist. Eng.* viii. II. 354 The Saturday..passed over without any sign of relenting on the part of the government. **1888** MRS. H. WARD *R. Elsmere* xxxvii, The relenting grew upon him.

b. With *a* and *pl.* An instance of this.

a **1586** SIDNEY (J.), I have marked in you a relenting truly, and a slacking of the main career. **1600** C'TESS ESSEX in Ellis *Orig. Lett.* Ser. I. II. 58 Vouchsafe a relentinge to the not urginge..of that fatell warrant for Execution. **1649** G. DANIEL *Trinarch., Hen. IV*, cccxviii, Strange relentings teare the womb Of Nature. **1709** STANHOPE *Paraphr.* IV. 65 Whose Sins though they be more, yet our Relentings for them are slighter..than Theirs. **1761–2** HUME *Hist. Eng.* lxvi. (1806) V. 37 But Charles next day felt a relenting in this assumed vigour. **1854** EMERSON *Lett. & Soc. Aims, Resources* Wks. (Bohn) III. 203 In the first relentings of March..these osiers hang out their joyful flowers.

re'lenting, *ppl. a.* [f. as prec. + -ING[2].] That relents, in various senses of the vb.

1593 SHAKS. *2 Hen. VI*, III. i. 226 As the mournefull Crocodile With sorrow snares relenting passengers. **1630** PRYNNE *Anti-Armin.* 179 The Scriptures indeed doe binde all faithfull, all relenting sinners to belieue. **1679** J. GOODMAN *Penitent Pard.* II. i. (1713) 142 The first essay of Repentance is a relenting thoughtfulness. **1702** ROWE *Tamerl.* I. i, Like relenting Heav'n He seems unwilling to deface his Kind. **1781** COWPER *Charity* 608 Relenting forms would lose their power, or cease. **1828** D'ISRAELI *Chas. I*, II. vi. 141 The Bishop..had put forth the signs of a relenting sympathy to his former masters.

Hence **re'lentingly** *adv.*

1611 FLORIO, *Rilento*,..relentingly. **1842** MRS. BROWNING *Grk. Chr. Poets* (1863) 56 What if, relentingly, we declare her innocent..? **1845** JANE ROBINSON *Whitehall* xxvii, Ramona..turned relentingly towards the cavalier.

relentless (rɪ'lɛntlɪs), *a.* [f. RELENT *v.*[1] + -LESS.] Incapable of relenting; pitiless.

1592 GREENE *Groat's W. Wit* (1617) 3 Death is relentlesse, and will not be intreated. **1602** MARSTON *Antonio's Rev.* I. iv, Strike me quite through with the relentlesse edge Of raging furie. **1667** MILTON *P.L.* IX. 130 Onely in destroying I finde ease To my relentless thoughts. **1702** POPE *Sappho* 194 In vain he lov'd, relentless Pyrrha scorn'd. **1795** SOUTHEY *Joan of Arc* II. 248 Relentless Henry bade his troops Drive back the miserable multitude. **1798** EDGEWORTH *Pract. Educ.* I. 380 Few things can be more terrific..to the young writer, than the voice of relentless criticism. **1856** EMERSON *Eng. Traits, Times*, A relentless inquisition drags every secret to the day. **1878** LADY BRASSEY *Voy. Sunbeam* xv. 268 An island..which the fiery waves seemed to attack unceasingly with relentless fury.

re'lentlessly, *adv.* [f. prec. + -LY[2].] In a relentless manner; pitilessly.

1815 SHELLEY *Alastor* 292 For sleep, he knew, kept most relentlessly Its precious charge. **1870** ANDERSON *Missions Amer. Bd.* IV. xlii. 417 The Papal ecclesiastics..grew relentlessly cruel where they had power.

re'lentlessness. [f. as prec. + -NESS.] The quality of being relentless.

1808 SOUTHEY *Lett.* (1856) II. 86, I devoted a week to the corrections, weeding them with righteous relentlessness. **1883** H. WACE *Gospel & Witnesses* iv. 86 The relentlessness with which it exposes the fatal vice.

relentment (rɪ'lɛntmənt), *sb.* Now *rare.* [f. RELENT *v.*[1] + -MENT.] The act of relenting; softening of rigour. †Also const. *of* (= on account of).

1628 tr. *Mathieu's Powerfull Favorite* 65 Did he thinke that this Prince who had so little relentment of the death of his sonne, would care for that of his seruants. **1695** J. SAGE *Cyprianic Age* Wks. 1847 II. 71 There should be some relentment of the fury of the persecution. **1793** W. TAYLOR *Goethe's Iph. in Tauris* II. 46 Relentment ceas'd from pity when I came, And Custom whets again the rusted knife. **1825** SINGER *Cavendish's Wolsey* I. 209 *note*, The rejection of the bill may be justly ascribed to the relentment of the king. **1922** JOYCE *Ulysses* 404 The prolongation of labour pains in advanced gravidancy by reason of pressure on the vein, the premature relentment of the amniotic fluid (as exemplified in the actual case) with consequent peril of sepsis to the matrix. **1929** C. E. MONTAGUE *Disenchantment* iv. 65 Great are the forces of decent human relentment after a hearty let-out with the temper.

†**b.** Dissolution. *Obs. rare*[−1].

1658 SIR T. BROWNE *Hydriot.* 9 Some..thought it most equal to submit unto the principle of putrifaction, and conclude in a moist relentment.

†**re'les.** *Obs.* Also 5 relece. [app. a. OF. *reles*, var. of *relais* remainder (see Godef.), f. *relaisser* to leave behind, but the senses of the Eng. word are not recorded in OF. The later form (from the 16th c.) is RELISH.] **a.** ? The sensation or impression left behind by anything. **b.** Taste, aftertaste, or relish. **c.** Odour, scent.

c **1320** *Sir Tristr.* 1356 A maiden of swiche reles Tristrem may to þe bring. *c* **1320** *Cast. Love* 509 Mi word ouȝte ben of good reles, For þou art kyng and prince of pes. **1390** GOWER *Conf.* III. 10, I..take a drauhte of such reles, That al mi wit is herteles. *c* **1400** *Laud Troy Bk.* 11267 Another vessel thenne ther stode, Ful of baume ffresche & gode, And kest vpward his gode reles. *c* **1410** *Sir Cleges* 208 After a chery the reles was The best that euer he ete in place. **1420–22** LYDG. *Thebes* (MS. Laud 557) lf. 64 Nor of þe gvmmes in þe flame spent To make þe eyre swetter of reles As frankensence myrre & aloes. *c* **1440** *Promp. Parv.* 362/1 Odowre, or relece, *odor. Ibid.* 429/1 Reles, tast or odowre, *odor.* **1604** [see RELEASE *sb.*[2]].

reles(e, obs. forms of RELEASE *sb.*[1] and *v.*[1]

†**re'lesch**, *v. Sc. Obs. rare*[−1]. [Of obscure origin: ? cf. RELISH *v.*[2]] *intr.* To sing, carol.

1513 DOUGLAS *Æneis* XII. Prol. 246 The larkis, lowd releschand in the skyis, Lovys thar lege with tonys curyus.

relesche, obs. Sc. f. RELEASE *sb.*[1] and *v.*[1]

relesse, obs. form of RELEASE *sb.*[1] and *v.*[1]

re,le'ssee. *Law. rare.* [RE- 5 a; cf. RELEASEE.] One to whom a release is executed.

1766 BLACKSTONE *Comm.* II. xx. 325 The occupancy of the relessee is a matter of sufficient notoriety already.

re'lessor. *Law. rare.* [RE- 5 a; cf. RELEASOR.] One who executes a release.

1766 BLACKSTONE *Comm.* II. xx. 324 There must be a privity of estate between the relessor and the relessee.

†re'let, *v.*[1] *Obs. rare*$^{-1}$. [app. f. RE- + LET *v.*, perh. after obs. F. *relaisser.*] *trans.* To remit.

1554-9 *Songs & Ball., Phil. & Mary* (Roxb.) 3 What great lovyng kyndnes dyd God show in thys cace?.. That yt so pleased hym to relet owr excyle.

re-'let (riː-), *v.*[2] [RE- 5 a.] *trans.* To let again. Hence **re-'letting** *vbl. sb.*

1780 A. YOUNG *Tour in Ireland* I. 53, I found rents in general at 20s. an acre, with much relet at 30s. **1812** SINCLAIR *Syst. Husb. Scot.* II. 60 To give an industrious.. tenant a preference, when the farm is to be re-let. **1872** *Spectator* 5 Oct. 1267/1 When the landlord relets..those farms on which the old tenants were not willing to pay for the improvement. **1897** *Daily News* 15 Oct. 3/1 The re-letting of premises in Finsbury-circus.

re-let ('riːlɛt), *sb.* [f. the vb.] A property that is let again.

1969 *Guardian* 29 Oct. 1/8 A vast increase in the number of 're-lets' among existing corporation houses. **1971** *Daily Tel.* 5 Aug. 10/7 Relets could be made to young people and earn £40 to £50 a week for the landlord instead of perhaps £10. **1976** *Times* 7 Jan. 13 Even allowing for the substantial numbers of relets from the existing stock, the magnitude of the loss of this source of housing in the new communities is evident.

'relevance. [See next and -ANCE.] Relevancy; *spec.* in recent use, pertinency to important current issues (as education to one's later career, etc.); social or vocational relevancy.

1733 INNES *View Laws Scot.* 11 The Relevance being determined,..the Probation proceeds in the next Place. **1865** LECKY *Ration.* (1878) II. 98 The main principle upon which the relevance of this species of narrative depends. **1890** *Spectator* 19 Apr. 536/2 What relevance had such a fact to the duty of the hour? **1949** *Poetry* (Chicago) Feb. 299 Tate holds that the poem is autonomous, and that the only relevance the subject-ideas have is to each other within the formal meaning of the work itself. **1955** *Bull. Atomic Sci.* Apr. 126/1 Relevance is another one of these non-assessable quantities which circumstances require to be assessed. **1970** *Time* 30 Nov. 40 The impetus came largely from student demands for 'relevance', especially for the overdue admission of more minority-group students. Activism has also done much to curb the old absurdities of trivial research and needless PH.D.s. **1975** *Language for Life* (Dept. Educ. & Sci.) ix. 129 We have heard the case for 'relevance' carried to the point of excluding fantasy or any stories with settings or characters unfamiliar to the pupils from their first-hand experience. **1975** *Times* 12 Feb. 11/7 *Hal* [*sc.* a novel]—while laudable in its social intentions—is little more than a piecing together of stock responses to the current demand for 'relevance'. **1977** *Chem. in Brit.* Mar. 105/3 It may seem anomalous in these days of 'relevance' philosophy in tertiary education that the average student of chemistry gets little inkling from his teachers..of the vast practical importance of disperse systems in industry. **1978** *New Scientist* 21 Sept. 850/2 'Relevance' in research implies both social efficacy and psychic commitment by the research worker.

relevancy ('rɛlɪvənsɪ). Also 6 *Sc.* reliv-. [ad. L. type *relevantia: see next and -ANCY.] **1.** The quality or fact of being relevant: **a.** in *Law*, esp. *Sc. Law.*

1561 *Reg. Privy Council Scot.* I. 173 Of the law it is requirit to the relevancie thairof that ather of the partis..be relevant in the self, utherwyise the haill to be nocht relevant. **1575-6** *Ibid.* II. 487 The relivancy of the said allegeance. **1693** STAIR *Instit.* IV. xxxix. §12 (ed. 2) 665 The meaning of Relevancy (which is more accustomed with us, than elsewhere) imports the Justice of the point, that is alledged to be Relevant. *a* **1715** BURNET *Own Time* VII. (1734) II. 521 Then the Matter of the Charge, which is there called the Relevancy of the Libel, was to be argued by Lawyers. **1746-7** *Act 20 Geo. II*, c. 43 §41 After the debate of the relevancy is ended, the..procurators..shall give in to the clerk informations in writing. **1786** BURKE *Art. agst. W. Hastings* Wks. 1842 II. 107/1 The competence, or credibility, or relevancy of any of the said affidavits, or other attestations. **1818** SCOTT *Hrt. Midl.* xxii, The presiding Judge next directed the counsel to plead to the relevancy. **1838** W. BELL *Dict. Law Scot.* 844 The relevancy of the libel is the justice and sufficiency of the matters therein stated to warrant a decree in the terms asked. **1883** *Law Rep. 11 Q.B. Div.* 594 He failed to satisfy me that in a case in which this strict relevancy could not be proved the advocate would not be protected.

b. in general use.

Now less common than *relevance*.

1826 *Sheridaniana* 49 His answer..would thus come with more relevancy and effect. **1839** HALLAM *Hist. Lit.* II. vii. §3 *note*, It is of no relevancy to the history of literature. **1878** SIMPSON *Sch. Shaks.* I. 95 His Irish enterprise had lost its appositeness and relevancy. **1961** *Jrnl. Physical Chem.* LXV 317/1 We are reporting these investigations..because of their relevancy to problems of the study of apparently simple exchange reactions of chlorine. **1980** *Times Lit. Suppl.* 30 May 609/2 A tendency to confuse relevancy with recency.

2. A relevant remark. (*Nonce use* influenced by IRRELEVANCY.)

1895 'MARK TWAIN' in *N. Amer. Rev.* July 10 Conversations consisted mainly of irrelevancies, with here and there a relevancy, a relevancy with an embarrassed look, as not being able to explain how it got there.

relevant ('rɛlɪvənt), *a.* Also 6 *Sc.* relivant. [ad. med.L. *relevant-em* (1481 in Du Cange), pres. pple. of L. *relevāre* to raise up, etc. (see RELIEVE *v.*): cf. It. *rilevante* 'auailefull, of importance, of worth, of consequence' (Florio), F. *relevant* (17th c. in Littré).]

1. a. Bearing upon, connected with, pertinent *to*, the matter in hand. (Rare before 1800.) Cf. RELEVANCE.

1560 ROLLAND *Crt. Venus* I. 498, I sall the schaw ane answer releuant. **1646** CHAS. I *Lett. to A. Henderson* (1649) 55 To determine our differences, or, at least, to make our Probations and Arguments Relevant. **1646** R. BAILLIE *Anabaptism* (1647) 143 It is very relevant if it were true. **1707** J. FRAZER *Disc. Second Sight* 15 It seems truly to be founded on relevant grounds. **1782** POWNALL *Study Antiq.* 140 A positive regulation respecting marriage, relevant to a like regulation of the institution of the theocracy. **1827** STEUART *Planter's G.* (1828) 78 If we either admit those objections as relevant, or obviate them as unfounded. **1851** GLADSTONE *Glean.* (1879) VI. xxiii. 15 The advantage most relevant of all to the present purpose. **1875** JOWETT *Plato* (ed. 2) IV. 4 Many things in a controversy might seem relevant, if we knew to what they were intended to refer. **1948** D. CECIL *Two Quiet Lives* II. 140 To learn everything that could possibly be thought relevant to the subject. **1969** *Harper's Mag.* Nov. 86 Either we can commit ourselves to changing the institutions of our society that need to be changed, to make them—to use a term which I hate—'relevant'..or we can sit back and try to defend them. **1970** *N.Y. Times* 1 July 44 Museums should have a more involved or relevant public role. **1976** *Listener* 20 May 627/3 The ultimate sin of the broadcaster is to keep off the air, because of his political or social prejudices, subjects which are relevant and significant. **1978** S. BRADEN *Artists & People* p. xvii, What actually makes a work of art relevant to people? It has been said that relevance is achieved when artists meet the real observations of their public.

b. Correspondent or proportional *to* something.

1868 ROGERS *Pol. Econ.* viii. (1876) 76 Population and the supply of food must be exactly relevant. *Ibid.* xiv. 191 The value..is absolutely relevant to the demand for them.

2. *Sc. Law.* Legally pertinent or sufficient.

1561 [see RELEVANCY]. **1644** MAXWELL *Prerog. Kings* 107 If they can make no relevant endictment..against them. **1723** in Maclaurin *Argt. & Decis. Cases* (1774) 70 [They] find the libel relevant to infer the pains of law. **1753** *Stewart's Trial* 149 [They] remit the pannel, with the libel as found relevant, to the knowledge of an assize. **1818** SCOTT *Hrt. Midl.* xxii, The defence, that the panel had communicated her situation to her sister, was a relevant defence. **1838** W. BELL *Dict. Law Scot.* 273 The exception of fraud, or force and fear, is not relevant against all actions.

†3. Relieving; remedial. *Obs. rare.*

1730 BAILEY (folio), *Relevant*, relieving. **1762** ASTON in *Burke's Corr.* (1844) I. 38 They ever pursued vindictive rather than relevant measures.

Hence **'relevantly** *adv.*

1561 *Reg. Privy Council Scot.* I. 180 In respect of the libell relevantlie libellit aganis the said Thomas Kennedy. **1883** *Law Rep. 11 Q.B. Div.* 601 Parties and witnesses who make statements without malice and relevantly.

†'relevate, *v.* (and *pa. pple.*) *Obs.* [f. ppl. stem of L. *relevāre* to RELIEVE; in some cases suggested by F. *relever* or It. *rilevare*, or the pa. pples. of these.]

1. *trans.* To raise the spirits of (a person); to restore to cheerfulness.

1597 A. M. tr. *Guillemeau's Fr. Chirurg.* *iij, Recreate the afflicted, relevate and conforte the depressed and humbled. **1603** *Mirr. Worldly Fame* in *Harl. Misc.* (Malh.) II. 526 Cato, being cumbered with the cares of the commonwealth was wont to relevate his mind with wine. **1708** *Brit. Apollo* No. 72. 2/2 'Tis a place Created Fit To Relevate the Sons of Wit.

2. To raise, elevate. Hence **'relevated** *ppl. a.*

1623 tr. *Favine's Theat. Hon.* I. v. 40 The third [crown] was..releuated with Pales, Piles or Stakes. **1635** J. HAYWARD tr. *Biondi's Banish'd Virg.* 148 Two relevated flanks. **1661** MORGAN *Sph. Gentry* III. v. 45 The Esquires helmet hath the Beaver a little relevated. **1758** *Scots Mag.* XX. 299/1 The upper circle [of the crown] is relevate or heightened with ten crosses florée.

3. *intr.* To rise up. *rare*$^{-1}$.

1661 MORGAN *Sph. Gentry* III. iv. 34 Crowns of Gold, whereof the Navall was made, with a circle of gold relevating like prowes and poupes of Ships.

†rele'vation. *Obs.* [a. OF. *relevacion* (Godef.), or ad. L. *relevātiōn-em*, n. of action f. *relevāre* to RELIEVE.] The action of raising, lifting up, supporting, relieving, etc.

c **1400** *Beryn* 3687 [She] thanked God..Of hir relevacioun from woo into gladness. **1433** *Rolls of Parlt.* IV. 445/1 Yn relevation of that charge. **1451** *Ibid.* V. 222/2 In relevation of oure Navie, and supportation of the grete charges of the same. **1471** in Gross *Gild Merch.* II. 262 Payng for theire stondynge..i. d., in releuacion of the kynges ferme. **1606** J. CARPENTER *Solomon's Solace* xxxiii. 136 The worde which the King here vseth..hath tediousnesse and no releuation, it hath sorrowfull despare. **1658** PHILLIPS, *Relevation*, a raising or lifting up again.

So **'relevator,** one who raises.

1865 NEALE *Hymns Paradise* 32 Thou in fall my Relevator.

†rele'vavith. *Obs. rare.* [ad. L. *relevāvit* 'he has relieved', 3rd sing. perf. indic. of *relevāre*: see RELIEVE *v.* 8.] = RELIEF[2] 1. Also *fig.*

1546 *State Papers Hen. VIII*, I. II. 840, I see not any greate lightlywod, that any good summe will comm in, tyl after Christmas, and then no more then the releuauithes [*printed* relevainthes]. **1562** J. HEYWOOD *Prov. & Epigr.* D iij, The one knaue now croucheth, while thother crauith. But to shew what shalbe his releuauith [etc.].

releve(n, obs. forms of RELIEVE *v.*

relevé (rələve). [Fr., lit. 'raised up'.]

1. = REMOVE *sb.* 2 c.

1825 LADY BLESSINGTON *Jrnl.* Dec. in E. Clay *Lady B. at Naples* (1979) 141 The fragments of *entrées* and *relevés*. **1846** *Jewish Manual, or Pract. Information Jewish & Mod. Cookery* p. xv, *Releves*, or *Removes*, are top and bottom dishes, which replace the soup and fish. **1889** [see *main course* s.v. MAIN *a.* 11]. **1906** *Mrs. Beeton's Bk. Househ. Managem.* lxii. 1668 *Relevé*.., the remove. A course of a dinner, consisting of large joints of meat, four-footed game, and sometimes joints of fish. **1961** FROUD & TURGEON tr. *Larousse Gastronomique* 805/2 Remove. Relevé—Dish which in French service *relieves* (in the sense that one sentry relieves another) the soup or the fish.

2. *Ballet.* (See quot. 1957.)

1930 CRASKE & BEAUMONT *Theory & Pract. Allegro in Classical Ballet* 66 Execute two *Petits Battements* with a *relevé* and *dégagé*. **1953** *Ballet Ann.* VII. 83 That infinitesimal moment of holding the breath in a *relevé* on point in a held pose. **1957** G. B. L. WILSON *Penguin Dict. Ballet* 227 *Relevé* or *temps relevé*, lit. a lifted step. The raising of the body on half- or full-point or points. **1976** *New Yorker* 29 Mar. 92/3 He has an immobile thick torso, a heaviness in plié and relevé.

re'level, *v.* [RE- 5 a.] *trans.* To level again.

1928 *Daily Tel.* 14 Aug. 14/3 Gutters have been filled in, dangerous curb-stones removed, level crossings relevelled. **1975** J. B. HARLEY *O.S. Maps* i. 7 Each area is relevelled in a cyclic system,..the interval depending on the character of the country. Mountain and moorland areas are relevelled every forty years.

†re'levy, *sb.*[1] *Obs. rare.* [ad. med.L. *relevi-um.*] = RELIEF[2] 1.

a **1500** in Arnolde *Chron.* (1811) 214 Yf..yᵉ heir of hym were of full age and owe releuy, haue he his heritage by olde releuy. **1610** HOLLAND *Camden's Brit.* I. 168 Let the Heriots or Relevies be so moderate, as that they may be tolerable.

†re'levy, *sb.*[2] *Obs. rare*$^{-1}$. [ad. It. *rilievi*, pl. of *rilievo* RELIEVO[1].] Relief.

1673 RAY *Journ. Low C.* (1738) II. 433 It is cut smooth and plain, without any sculpture and engraving, or any relevy and imbossment.

†re'levy, *v. Obs. rare*$^{-1}$. [irreg. ad. L. *relevāre* or F. *relever*: see RELIEVE *v.*] *trans.* To raise or set up again.

1622 CALLIS *Stat. Sewers* (1647) 205 If any such annoyance be done, it shall be pulled down, and that he which shall relevy such annoyance..shall incur the penalty.

relewe, obs. Sc. form of RELIEVE *v.*

relewyt, releyit, obs. Sc. pa. pple. of RELIEVE *v.*

relexification (,riːlɛksɪfɪ'keɪʃən). *Linguistics.* [f. RE- 5 a + Gr. λέξι-ς word + -FICATION.] The process of replacing a word or group of words in one language with a corresponding word or group of words from another language, without grammatical adjustment of the items introduced.

1962 W. A. STEWART in F. A. Rice *Stud. Role Second Languages in Asia, Africa, & Lat. Amer.* 46 The vocabulary derived from one source language has been largely replaced ..by a more recent vocabulary derived from another language, while the original grammatical structure is preserved... This process of relexification seems to be the converse of restructuralization. **1965** *Amer. Speech* XL. 172 William Stewart has hypothesized that this Portuguese-based pidgin was re-lexified to yield the English, Dutch, and French pidgins which are the progenitors of the Creoles. This idea of a re-lexification which left the original syntax almost intact is a very attractive one. **1968** *Word* XXIV. 263 The effect of this process is a kind of continuous and massive 'relexification'. **1971** [see INITIATOR]. **1972** J. L. DILLARD *Black English* iii. 121 Within the Negro community, the use of Africanisms has been demonstrably larger in the past; allowing for relexification, we can still see a great deal of indirect influence. *Ibid.* 303 Relexification is the replacement of a vocabulary item in a language with a word from another, without a change in the grammar. If I change the sentence I am very tired to I am très tired I have in a sense relexified the English sentence. A 'Latin' sentence like ego amo tu is of course simply a relexification of I love you with Latin words. **1974** R. A. HALL *External Hist. Romance Lang.* 33 According to certain..theories, these two varieties ..would have been the predecessors of West African Pidgin Portuguese, from which all other modern pidgins and creoles would have sprung by a process of 'relexification'. **1975** *Language* LI. 685 If all of a group of PC's [*sc.* pidgin or creole languages], such as those usually embraced in relexification hypotheses.., have a common ancestor, then the extension of the use of 'mouth' in that ancestor would account for 'mouth' having the added sense in all those PC's.

relexify (riː'lɛksɪfaɪ), *v. Linguistics.* [f. as prec. + -FY.] *trans.* To introduce into (a language) vocabulary taken from another language without grammatical adjustment of the items introduced. Hence **re'lexified** *ppl. a.*

1962 W. A. STEWART in F. A. Rice *Stud. Role Second Languages in Asia, Africa, & Lat. Amer.* 46 If a language A can be shown to derive its vocabulary from language B and its grammatical structure from language C, then language A can be both 'restructured B' and 'relexified C' at the same time. *Ibid.*, It is..possible to consider them all..as relexified forms of some prior language. **1965** *Orbis* XIV. 521 We know that the Philippine creoles were also relexified very rapidly. **1965, 1972** [see prec.]. **1972** J. L. DILLARD *Black English* iii. 122 Hawaiian Pidgin English *pau* (relexified with a Hawaiian word), Melanesian Pidgin English *finish* constitute other relexifications of *cabá*. **1979** *Amer. Speech* LIV. 296 A uniform 'plantation creole'..later 'relexified' into something nearer to the speech of whites.

relȝie, obs. Sc. form of RAIL *v.*[4]

reliability (rɪlaɪəˈbɪlɪtɪ). [f. next + -ITY.]

1. The quality of being reliable, reliableness.

1816 COLERIDGE *Lett.* (1895) II. 667 Either in the taste, courtesy, or reliability of his judges. **1817** —— *Biog. Lit.* iii. (Bohn) 33 Perfect consistency, and (if such a word might be framed) absolute reliability. **1847** in WEBSTER. **1856** GEO. ELIOT *Ess.* (1884) 126 An air of seriousness and reliability. **1860** ADM. FITZROY in *Merc. Marine Mag.* VII. 355 The reliability and the universality of the laws of storms. **1887** *Spectator* 18 June 827/2 We want doctors to bear a stamp of reliability, like the coinage.

2. *Statistics.* The extent to which a measurement made repeatedly in identical circumstances will yield concordant results.

1904 *Amer. Jrnl. Psychol.* XV. 238 The reliability with which any system of measurement represents any particular form of intelligence. **1925** F. C. MILLS *Statistical Meth.* xvi. 561 By the study of successive samples, and by the testing of the subordinate elements in a given sample when broken up into significant sub-groups, much more may be learned as to the reliability of a given measure..than by unquestioning acceptance and uncritical employment of the usual mathematical formulas for probable errors. **1938** A. E. WAUGH *Elem. Statistical Meth.* vii. 138 We can increase the reliability of the mean by studying more cases, and..the reliability is greater also when the variation among the original figures is small. **1950** J. P. GUILFORD *Fundamental Statistics in Psychol. & Educ.* (ed. 2) xvii. 473 Tests of differences and correlation coefficients may often prove to be insignificant merely because the measures used were lacking in reliability. **1978** R. J. JESSON *Statistical Survey Techniques* i. 15 In considering reliability we shall be referring to a measure of the closeness of each observation to its own average over repeated trials.

3. *attrib.*, as ***reliability engineer, race, test, trial***; **reliability coefficient**, any of various measures of statistical reliability; freq. the coefficient of correlation between two sets of measurements made of the same set of quantities.

1910 C. SPEARMAN in *Brit. Jrnl. Psychol.* III. 281 A very convenient conception is that of the 'reliability coefficient' of any system of measurements for any character. By this is meant the coefficient between one half and the other half of several measurements of the same thing. **1930** *Psychol. Rev.* XXXVII. 140 The reliability coefficient of a variable, *X*, is a special type of correlation coefficient which indicates the degree to which individuals systematically differ from each other in the trait as measured. **1954** *Psychol. Bulletin* LI. 229/1 The several types of reliability coefficient do not answer the same questions and should be carefully distinguished. **1972** *Jrnl. Social Psychol.* LXXXVII. 48 The split-half method was employed and resulted in a reliability coefficient for the instrument of ·83. **1969** *Word Study* Apr. 3/2 The reliability engineers, on the other hand, did not want to avoid taboo words; they were chiefly interested in alarming the program to potential failures. **1977** *Chicago Tribune* 2 Oct. XII. 57/4 (Advt.), Reliability Engineer, to direct and perform component reliability studies, coordinate with system requirements, and function as reliability consultant. **1907** *Strand Mag.* Nov. 491/2 A result extraordinarily interesting should be worked out from this thousand-mile [car] reliability race. **1904** *Technics* Aug. 114 As a 'reliability test', the car was driven from London to Newport (Mon.), a distance of about 160 miles. **1929** *Even. News* 18 Nov. 16/4 [He] crashed on his motor-cycle while taking part in a reliability test on Portsdown-hill. **1902** *Car* 3 Sept. 43/1 The cars entered for the Automobile Club's Reliability Trials which are being held this week began to arrive at the Crystal Palace at a very early hour. **1904** *To-Day* 18 May 58/2 The Automobile Club has arranged to hold a reliability trial for motor boats. **1963** P. DRACKETT *Motor Rallying* i. 9 But the true progenitor of the rally was the reliability trial. **1970** *Which?* July 199/1 We have not done any extended reliability trials on the single samples of television sets we tested.

reliable (rɪˈlaɪəb(ə)l), *a.* [f. RELY *v.*[1] + -ABLE.]

1. a. That may be relied upon; in which reliance or confidence may be put; trustworthy, safe, sure.

In current use only from about 1850, and at first perhaps more frequent in American works, but from 1855 freely employed by British writers, though often protested against as an innovaton or an Americanism. The formation has been objected to (as by Worcester in 1860) on the ground of irregularity, but has analogies in *available, dependable, dispensable, laughable* (Webster 1864). The question has been fully discussed by F. Hall in his work *On English Adjectives in -able, with special reference to Reliable* (1877).

1569 *Reg. Privy Council Scot.* I. 667 Thair deliverance..and jugement to be als raliabill..as gif the samyn wer gevin ..be the Lordis of Sessioun. **1624** BP. MOUNTAGU in *Cosin's Corr.* (Surtees) I. 34, I knowe not two honester, abler men, and reliable indeed of their ranke and state. **1792** B. S. BARTON in *M. Cutler's Life*, etc. (1888) II. 288, I have lately used the root, and find it a very reliable medicine. **1800** COLERIDGE *Ess. own Times* (1850) II. 296 The best means and most reliable pledge of a higher object. **1850** W. IRVING in *Life & Lett.* (1864) IV. 70 You have built it up with a care that renders it reliable in all its parts. **1851** HINTON in Hopkins *Life & Lett.* (1878) 87, I think your feelings on subjects of religion are infinitely more reliable than Mr. ——'s views. **1857** GLADSTONE in *Oxford Ess.* 49 He seems to think that the reliable chronology of Greece begins before its reliable history. **1876** TREVELYAN *Life Macaulay* (1883) II. 431 Macaulay may not have been a reliable guide in the regions of high art.

b. *absol.* as *sb.* A reliable person, animal, or thing.

1890 *Anthony's Photogr. Bull.* III. 133 Experiment with all the new things that appear, but do not 'lose your grip' on the old reliables. **1908** [see PEACHERINO]. **1910** W. M. RAINE *Bucky O'Connor* (1920) ii. 20, I hate to have you take that gun, though. I meant to run you down with that same old Colt's reliable. **1911** R. D. SAUNDERS *Col. Todhunter* xii. 171 'You never can tell about these old reliables,' said Tom. 'Solomon might take it into his head to get frisky any minute.' **1950** *Western Folklore* Apr. 138 The cowboy's six-shooter speaks a language universally understood. Familiar epithets for the revolver were *equalizer, shootin' iron,..Old Reliable.* **1970** E. SNOW *Red China Today* (1976) 33 The 'three-way alliance' of mass organizations, Party 'reliables', and army political work teams which had completed the Party purging. **1972** *Village Voice* (N.Y.) 1 June 19/3 One of the Governor's old reliables, Assemblyman Robert Kelly, sponsored the bill in the lower house and told everyone how great it was.

2. *Statistics.* Yielding concordant results when repeated.

[**1892** *Analyst* XVII. 228 When the Babcock test is made according to the instruction given with the machine, strictly reliable results are obtained.] **1932** *Jrnl. Gen. Physiol.* XVI. 23 Under such conditions it might be expected that volumetric measurements be somewhat less reliable than in the simple case first examined. **1942** J. P. GUILFORD *Fundamental Statistics in Psychol. & Educ.* xiv. 273 By a perfectly reliable test, we mean one that is free from errors of measurement. **1970** D. W. MATHESON et al. *Introd. Exper. Psychol.* ii. 26 A sampling technique is reliable if several samples from the same population yield similar data. *Ibid.* vi. 66 If a test is reliable, a subject will receive approximately the same score each time he takes the test.

reˈliableness. [f. prec. + -NESS.] The quality or state of being reliable.

1847 in WEBSTER. **1862** MILL *Logic* II. vii. (ed. 5) I. 303 The number of steps in an argument does not subtract from its reliableness, if [etc.]. **1863** HAWTHORNE *Old Home* (1883) I. 52 There is a certain sturdy reliableness common among them. **1871** SMILES *Charac.* i. 8 Thus reliableness becomes a passport to the general esteem and confidence of mankind.

reliably (rɪˈlaɪəblɪ), *adv.* [f. as prec. + -LY.] In a reliable manner.

1864 in WEBSTER. **1865** *Daily Tel.* 18 Sept. 3/6 The action of the Government is reliably attributed to a note [etc.]. **1876** MILL in W. G. Ward *Ess. Philos. Theism* (1884) I. 304 An intuition..is simply an intellectual avouchment, reliably declaring as immediately evident some truth [etc.].

reliance (rɪˈlaɪəns). [f. RELY *v.*[1] + -ANCE.]

1. The (†or an) act of relying; the condition or character of being reliant; dependence, confidence.

a. Const. *on, upon,* or *in.*

1607 SHAKS. *Timon* II. i. 22 My reliances on his fracted dates Haue smit my credit. **1687** tr. *Sallust* (1692) 241 All these things are their Security and Protection, while my Relyance is only upon my self. *a* **1713** ELLWOOD *Autobiog.* (1714) 33 That my Reliance might be wholly upon him; and not on Man. **1754** SHERLOCK *Disc.* (1759) I. vii. 223 This Reliance on the Promises of God. **1781** JEFFERSON *Corr.* Wks. 1859 I. 291 A private channel on which I have considerable reliance. **1813** SOUTHEY *Nelson* II. 34 A man..upon whose sagacity..he could place full reliance. **1823** —— *Penins. War* I. 216 Don Pedro de Labrador..in whose talents he had great reliance. **1865** TENNYSON *Captain* 57 Those in whom he had reliance..Sold him unto shame. **1877** FROUDE *Short Stud.* (1883) IV. I. viii. 88 In such a labyrinth of lies little reliance can be placed on statements unconfirmed by writing.

b. Without const.

a **1728** WOODWARD (J.), That pellucid gelatinous substance, which he pitches upon with so great reliance and positiveness. **1850** ROBERTSON *Serm.* Ser. III. ii. (1872) 16 Not by merit nor by works, but by trust or reliance only.

2. That on which one relies or depends.

1798 CHARLOTTE SMITH *Yng. Philos.* I. 78 She seemed to have no protection or reliance on earth but him. **1848** W. H. BARTLETT *Egypt to Pal.* iii. (1879) 44 The chief direct reliance is the main river. **1856** KANE *Arct. Expl.* I. xx. 251 The dogs, the indispensable reliance of the party, were in bad working trim.

reliant (rɪˈlaɪənt), *a.* [f. as prec. + -ANT[1].] Having reliance or confidence; confident, trustful. (Cf. SELF-RELIANT.) Also const. *on.*

1856 KANE *Arct. Expl.* II. v. 63 My mind is hopeful and reliant. **1859** GEO. ELIOT *A. Bede* lii, Dinah was too reliant on the Divine will to attempt to achieve any end by a deceptive concealment. **1878** B. TAYLOR *Deukalion* I. v. 41 Seem not reliant,—loose thy clinging hand.

relic (ˈrɛlɪk), *sb.* and *a.* Forms: 3–7 relike, 4–6 relyk(e, relik, 4–7 relicke, (5 -likke, -lykke, 6 realycke), 6–8 relick, 8– relic; 6 rellick, -ycke, *Sc.* -yk, 7 rellike; 4–5 relek, 5 -leck, -leke; 4 reliqe, 5 relyque, 5– relique. [a. F. *relique* (11th c.), ad. L. *reliquiæ* pl., remains: see RELIQUIÆ. OE. had *reliquias* directly from Latin; and the comb. *relic-gong* occurs in a text printed in Cockayne's *Shrine* pp. 74, 79.]

A. *sb.* **1. a.** In religious use, esp. in the Roman Catholic and Greek Churches: Some object, such as a part of the body or clothing, an article of personal use, or the like, which remains as a memorial of a departed saint, martyr, or other holy person, and as such is carefully preserved and held in esteem or veneration.

The plural sometimes denotes the whole remains (i.e. the body or parts of it) of the person in question; see sense 2.

a **1225** *Ancr. R.* 18 A last to þe oðer onlicnesses, & to ower relikes cneoleð, oþer luteþ. *c* **1290** *S. Eng. Leg.* I. 17/567 þe bischop wuste þis holie blod ase relikes riche and guode. *c* **1330** R. BRUNNE *Chron. Wace* (Rolls) 14559 Abbotes þat reliqes had..away þeym lad, & manye in þe erthe þey dalf. *c* **1375** *Sc. Leg. Saints* iv. (*James*) 255 His printes..stal away þe body..and þai aryvyt with þat relik of spanȝe in-to þe kynrik. *c* **1430** LYDG. *Min. Poems* (Percy Soc.) 19 The abbot afftyr..Amonges the relykkes the septure ought he soughte Of Seynt Edward. *c* **1489** CAXTON *Sonnes of Aymon* iii. 112 Bryng afore me your reliques and hallowes, that I shall swere [etc.]. **1532** *Dial. on Laws Eng.* II. xxx. 78 b, Than shal he suspende the churche & take awaye the relikes. **1617** MORYSON *Itin.* I. 175 The Friars keepe for a holy relike the Thorne wherewith Christ was crowned. **1673** RAY *Journ. Low C.* 243 In this City are many..Churches..furnished with rich Altar-pieces, Reliques,..and other Ornaments. **1756–7** tr. *Keysler's Trav.* (1760) IV. 396 The only part wanting in their relic is the middle finger of the right-hand. **1844** LINGARD *Anglo-Sax. Ch.* (1858) II. xiv. 304 A supply of relics for the foundation of churches. **1850** MRS. JAMESON *Leg. Monast. Ord.* 79 His copy of Ambrose,..covered with his blood, was exhibited..as a relic.

transf. **1594** DRAYTON *Idea* 788 You..whose deare remembrance in my Bosome lyes, Too rich a Relique for so poore a Shrine.

†**b.** Applied to the sacred objects of the ancient Jewish and pagan religions. *Obs.*

a **1300** *Cursor M.* 6513 He taght him tables o þe lai,.. Quen he him taght suilk a relik [etc.]. *c* **1374** CHAUCER *Troylus* I. 153 Thei hadde a relyk hight Palladion, That was hire tryst a bouen euerichon. **1513** DOUGLAS *Æneis* XIII. x. 96 O happy cite..With quham sa gret rellykis remane sall. **1582** STANYHURST *Æneis* II. (Arb.) 49 Yf this rellick by you to the cittye were haled, Then, loa, the stout Troians in wars should glorye triumphing. **1606** G. W[OODCOCKE] *Hist. Ivstine* XXIV. 90 The Priests of all the Temples..with..the sacred reliques in their hands.

†**c.** A precious or valuable thing. *Obs. rare.*

c **1385** CHAUCER *L.G.W.* Prol. 321 What dostow here So nygh myn ovne floure so boldely?..Yt is my relyke, digne and delytable. *c* **1400** *Destr. Troy* 13678 He..has riches full ryfe, relikis ynow. *c* **1470** *Gol. & Gaw.* 887 Armyt in rede gold, and rubeis sa round, With mony riche relikis, riale to se.

d. Something kept as a remembrance or souvenir of a person, thing, or place; a memento.

1601 SHAKS. *Jul. C.* II. ii. 89 Great men shall presse For Tinctures, Staines, Reliques, and Cognisance. **1664** MARVELL *Corr.* Wks. (Grosart) II. 145 He, blessed Prince, ..even as to this matter had prepared a Letter which I yet preserve among His other Reliques. **1719** DE FOE *Crusoe* I. xix, When I took Leave of this Island, I carry'd on Board for Reliques the great Goat's Skin Cap I had made, my Umbrella, and one of my Parrots. **1751** JOHNSON *Rambler* No. 83 ⁋9 This regard, which we..pay to the meanest relique of a man great and illustrious. **1838** *Murray's Hand-bk. N. Germ.* 385/1 Luther's..apartment..contains his portrait, bible, and other relics. **1862** STANLEY *Jew. Ch.* (1877) I. vii. 141 Two objects of interest were laid up..in front of it, both relics of Sinai. **1880** *Marine Engineer* 1 July 84/1 A Relic of Her Majesty's Ship 'Orpheus'.

2. a. *pl.* The remains of a person; the body, or part of the body, of one deceased. (Sometimes implying sense 1.)

a **1300** *Cursor M.* 21215 Þ ai did sent andru relikes and him Bring to constantinopolim. **1483** CAXTON *Gold. Leg.* 237/2, I shalle ensigne the of eueriche by symylitude to knowe the tombes and reliques of eche of us. **1596** DALRYMPLE tr. *Leslie's Hist. Scot.* I. 110 The reliques of S. Andro..quhilkes out of Grece he brocht. **1658** SIR T. BROWNE *Hydriot.* Ep. Ded., Men took a lasting adieu of their interred Friends,..having no old experience of the duration of their Reliques. **1691** WOOD *Ath. Oxon.* I. 156 How long he lived after that year, I cannot tell, nor where his reliques were lodg'd. **1718** PRIOR *Solomon* III. 591 Say: shall our Relicks second Birth receive? **1725** POPE *Odyss.* XIV. 156 He..welters on the wave, Or food for fish, or dogs, his reliques lye. **1775** ADAIR *Amer. Ind.* 183 They go along with those beloved relicks of the dead..till they arrive at the bone-house. **1813** SHELLEY *Q. Mab* VII. 188 All around The mouldering relics of my kindred lay. **1854** MILMAN *Lat. Chr.* III. v. I. 381 The reliques of those martyrs whom the Romans burned with fire.

b. *sing.* in the same sense. *rare.*

1635 PAGITT *Christianogr.* III. (1636) 93 The taking up of the Relique of Editha thirteene yeare after her death. **1682** KEN *Serm.* Wks. (1838) 126 This poor relique of clay, which in a few minutes must be restored to its native earth. **1814** MRS. J. WEST *Alicia de Lacy* IV. 258 Those neglects to which this unsepulchred relic of his illustrious father bore a shameful testimony.

c. An old person. *colloq.*

1869 'MARK TWAIN' in *Buffalo Express* 21 Aug. 1/3, I came upon a noble Son of the Forest sitting under a tree, diligently at work on a bead reticule... I addressed the noble relic as follows. **1902** —— in *Harper's Mag.* Dec. 15/1 'How much of it can you two undertake?' 'All of it!' burst from both ladies at once... 'You do ring true, you brave old relics!' **1981** B. HEALEY *Last Ferry from Lido* ix. 161 So far as he's concerned the Ca' Silvestro and the old lady are just a pair of ancient relics.

3. a. *pl.* That which remains or is left behind, in later use esp. after destruction or wasting away; the remains or remaining fragments (of a thing); the remnant, residue (of a nation or people). Also occas. in *sing.* of a single thing or person.

a **1325** *Prose Psalter* xxxvi[i]. 40 [38] Þe vnriȝtful forsoþe shul ben desparplist, and þe relikes of þe wicked shul dien. **1382** WYCLIF *Isa.* xiv. 30 To dien I shal make in hunger thi roote, and thi relikes I shal slen. **1480** CAXTON *Chron. Eng.* ci. 52 b, The reliques of his body shall bene brought fro Rome, and translated in Britaigne. **1568** GRAFTON *Chron.* II. 458 Diuers Frenchmen repayred to the battayle..to take the reliques which the Englishmen had left. **1596** SPENSER *State Irel.* Wks. (Globe) 627/2 Whatsoever relickes there were left of the land-bredd people. **1615** G. SANDYS *Trav.* 194 An hundred paces farther..there are the relikes of a Church. **1656** RIDGLEY *Pract. Physick* 271 The reliques of the Quick-silver will stick to the gold. **1703** POPE *Thebais*

602 Dust yet white upon each altar lies, The relicks of a former sacrifice. **1788** GIBBON *Decl. & F.* xlix. III. 143 After a bloody conflict of eight years.., the relics of the nation submitted. **1817** BYRON *Manfred* III. iv, I stood within the Coliseum's wall, 'Midst the chief relics of almighty Rome. **1851** D. WILSON *Preh. Ann.* III. vi. (1863) II. 152 It is only in this last period..that we find the relics of the war-chariot among the contents of the tomb. **1865** LIVINGSTONE *Zambesi* vi. 148 He brought the relics of our fugitive mail.

sing. *a***1676** HALE *Prim. Orig. Man.* (1677) 298 This Elementary portion of Earth and Water seems to be as it were the sediment and relique of the *Massa Chaotica*. **1774** PENNANT *Tour Scotl. in 1772*, 9 The priory..stood near the bridge, but not a relique exists. **1822** GALT *Provost* xxxii. (1868) 95 He was a relic of some American-war fencibles. **1834** HOGG *Let.* in *Sotheby's Sale Catal.* 22–6 Feb. (1897) 42 He is..the only relic I know of the real intimate acquaintances of Burns.

b. The remains of a meal or of food; remnants, scraps, broken victuals. Now *rare*.

1576 FLEMING *Panopl. Epist.* 75 We would haue had no fragments or broken scraps left. But now..wee haue sore a doo about those reliques. *a***1602** W. PERKINS *Cases Consc.* (1619) 327 Gather vp the broken meate..these reliques and fragments are part of the creatures. **1682** SIR T. BROWNE *Chr. Mor.* I. §4 Treat the poor, as our Saviour did the Multitude, to the reliques of some baskets. **1816** SCOTT *Antiq.* ix, His sister hastened to silence his murmurs, by proposing some of the relics of the dinner. **1830** HERSCHEL *Stud. Nat. Phil.* 2 His food [being] worms..varied with occasional relics, mangled by more powerful beasts of prey.

c. *Biol.* A relict species.

1947 [see EPIBIOTIC *a.* and *sb.* 1]. **1965** B. E. FREEMAN tr. *Vandel's Biospeleology* vii. 70 *Troglochaetus* would seem to be a marine relic. **1974** *New Phytologist* LXXIII. 974 Thistles, mulleins and foxgloves..appear as the stemless relics of the pachycaul inflorescences.

4. a. A surviving trace *of* some practice, fact, idea, quality, etc. In early use chiefly *pl.*

*a***1586** SIDNEY *Arcadia* III. (1622) 259 Doubting some reliks of the late mutiny. **1612** T. TAYLOR *Comm. Titus* i. 13 An infirmitie is a rellike of sinne. **1678** R. BARCLAY *Apol. Quakers* iv. §2. 101 There were some Reliques of the Heavenly Image left in Adam. **1712** BUDGELL *Spect.* No. 365 ¶3 A Relique of a certain Pagan Worship. **1794** PALEY *Evid.* I. vii. (1817) 124 No reliques appear of any story substantially different from the present. **1824** W. IRVING *T. Trav.* I. 349 It is a rich relique of a more poetical age. **1865** TYLOR *Early Hist. Man.* i. 2 A relic of a ruder mental condition.

b. A surviving memorial *of* some occurrence, period, people, etc.

1695 WOODWARD *Nat. Hist. Earth* I. 35 Others..thought that they [shells] were only Reliques of some former great Inundations of the Sea. **1778** PENNANT *Tour Wales* (1883) I. 84 Immense beds of iron-cinders,..the reliques of the Romans. **1791** COWPER *Yardley Oak* 6 Hollow-trunked.. and with excoriate forks deform, Relics of ages! **1832** G. R. PORTER *Porcelain & Gl.* 268 These curious relics of ancient times have also been discovered decorated with coloured glass beads. **1855** MACAULAY *Hist. Eng.* xx. IV. 522 The swords were rusty reliques of Edge Hill and Marston Moor. **1871** FREEMAN *Norm. Conq.* xviii. (1876) IV. 212 Those great roads which abide as the noblest relics of the days of Roman dominion.

c. phr. ***relic of barbarism***, a survival or reminder of bad conditions or practices.

1852 *Harper's Mag.* Dec. 126/2 Railing against the church, against society, against institutions, against 'relics of barbarisms'. **1870** J. H. NEWMAN *Grammar of Assent* iv. 75 When Mr. Wilberforce, after succeeding in the slave question, urged the Duke of Wellington to use his great influence in discountenancing duelling, he could only get from him in answer, 'A relic of barbarism, Mr. Wilberforce'. **1919** W. T. GRENFELL *Labrador Doctor* iv. 68 After giving a talk on psychical influence he had the jacket removed as 'a relic of barbarism'. **1921** T. WOLFE *Let.* 2 Sept. (1956) 16 This 'point system' of selecting teachers is a relic of barbarism.

d. *Linguistics.* The survival of an archaic form; an instance of this. (See also RELICT *sb.* 6.)

1943 *Language* XIX. 257 Nowhere..was there an indication of the genuine vitality of this set of suffixes, which, divested of any specific function, had become mere meaningless relics. **1951** *Amer. Speech* XXVI. 252 The occurrences of *clabbered milk* in the northern counties of the state are probably explained as a sporadic relic. **1962** *Ibid.* XXXVII. 170 In the word *one*, the mid-central vowel is occasionally replaced by /ʊ/—a relic usage evidently related to the pronunciation of *home* as /hʊm/.

5. An object invested with interest by reason of its antiquity or associations with the past.

1596 DRAYTON *Legends* iii. 542 A goodly Table of pure Massie Gold, A Relike kept in Windsor many a day. **1601** SHAKS. *Twel. N.* III. iii. 19 What's to do? Shall we go see the reliques of this Towne? **1632** LITHGOW *Trav.* v. 208 My Interpreter shewed me..one of the doores of the Temple of Salomon,..being indeede a relicke of wonderfull bignesse. **1787** JEFFERSON *Writ.* (1859) II. 317 The good, old and venerable fabric, which should have been preserved even as a religious relique. **1841** SPALDING *Italy & It. Isl.* I. 200 The crowds of reliques which..have reappeared to adorn the modern galleries.

†**6.** An example left by a person. *Obs. rare.*

1610 BOYS *Exp. Domin. Ep. & Gosp.* Wks. (1622) 133 Here then is a notable relique for women to behold. *Ibid.* 555 This her relique is worth our obseruing also.

7. *attrib.* and *Comb.*, as ***relic-box, building, -chest, -hunter, -hunting, -monger, -shrine, -vender, -veneration, -worship***; (in sense 4 d) ***relic form***; ***relic-covered*** adj.; ***relic-like*** adv.; **relic area**, a region noted for the survival of old or otherwise archaic language forms; **relic-knife**, a knife containing in its handle a relic of a saint; †**Relic Sunday**, the third Sunday after Midsummer, on which the relics preserved in a church were specially venerated; †**relic water**, water in which relics have been dipped.

1953 *Language Learning* IV. 104 *Relic areas, on the other hand, are those whose geographical or cultural isolation, and relative lack of prestige, has caused the retention of older forms or prevented the spread of forms characteristic of these areas. **1962** *Amer. Speech* XXXVII. 171 The regional words used by the Ocracokers are the regional words of the North Carolina coast, especially the relic area which lies around Albemarle Sound. **1972** H. KURATH *Studies Area Linguistics* i. 2 He [*sc.* the area linguist] will reserve judgment and recommend further investigation when the linguistic variants exhibit a complicated and apparently erratic dissemination as in certain transition zones or relic areas. **1591** PERCIVALL *Sp. Dict.*, *Relicario*, a *relicke boxe. **1663** GERBIER *Counsel* d iij, The reformation of a Gotis *relick building. *c***1450** *St. Cuthbert* (Surtees) 4248 He vnclosid þe *reliks kyst, And gaf parte to a frende. **1796** *Mod. Gulliver* 2 For want of a cradle, as soon as born, I was popped into a relique chest. **1807** SYD. SMITH *Lett. Catholics* (1808) 28 The *relic-covered jacket of a Catholic. **1933** *Relic form [see *hyperform* s.v. HYPER- IV]. **1951** *Amer. Speech* XXVI. 13 The preservation of relic forms is made possible by geographical or cultural isolation. **1972** M. L. SAMUELS *Linguistic Evolution* vi. 92 The receiving system itself becomes *less* divergent from its neighbour than before, retaining only relic forms from its antecedent. **1797** *Encycl. Brit.* (ed. 3) XVI. 59/1 The..knavery of the Greeks found a rich prey in the stupid credulity of the Latin *relic-hunters. **1893** KATE SANBORN *Truthf. Wom. S. California* 54 The plaster statues have been disgracefully mutilated by relic-hunters. **1891** A. J. FOSTER *Ouse* 139 These were the days of *relic-hunting. **1854** *Jrnl. Brit. Archæol. Assoc.* X. 89 The knife..is of an earlier period, and may perhaps be regarded as a *relic knife. **1593–1602** DONNE *Sat.* II. 84 The snuffe Of wasting Candles..*Relique-like [**1633** reliquely] kept, perchance buyes wedding-geare. **1854** H. MILLER *Sch. & Schm.* vi. (1857) 123 Though not much of a *relic-monger, I would hesitate to exchange it. **1808** SCOTT *Marm.* II. iii, The *relic-shrine of cost, With ivory and gems emboss'd. **1461** *Paston Lett.* II. 28 Wretyn at London, on *Relyk Sonday [12 July]. **1520** in *Arnolde's Chron.* (1811) p. xlvi, On Relyk Sonday, in the aftyr none, was a grete thondre and tempest. **1581** J. BELL *Haddon's Answ. Osor.* 323 b, The feasts..of the patrone of the church, dedication day, and Relicksonday. **1709** *Riders Brit. Merlin*, Fair on Relique-Sunday (being the Sund.-fortnight after Midsum.). **1848** LYTTON *Harold* v. i, Edward was left alone to his monks and *relic-venders. **1848** J. H. NEWMAN *Loss & Gain* II. xix. 284 The doctrine and practice of *relic-veneration. **1562** *Homilies* II. *Idolatry* III. (1859) 236 Our idolaters found too much vantage of reliques and *relique water to follow St. Chrysostom's counsel. **1871** TYLOR *Prim. Cult.* xv. II. 139 The conception..would give a rational explanation of much *relic-worship otherwise obscure.

B. *adj. Geogr., Geol.,* and *Biol.* = RELICT *a.* 4.

1894 J. GEIKIE *Great Ice Age* (ed. 3) xxxi. 488 In many of the Swedish lakes there occur certain forms of life which appear to be a relic-fauna of the Yoldia Sea. **1926** W. H. TWENHOFEL *Treat. Sedimentation* v. 369 The Salton Sink of California is probably an example of a relic sea which appears to have been severed from the Gulf of California in the building of the Colorado River delta. **1940** *Jrnl. Genetics* XL. 72 At this stage it is usual for some or all of the chromosomes to show 'relic' coils or spirals. These coils are to be regarded as the remains of the spirals of the previous division. **1966** MRS. L. B. JOHNSON *White House Diary* 2 Apr. (1970) 379 He described the 'relic forest' of maple, quaking aspen, Douglas fir, and ponderosa pine with huge trunks. By some strange mystery of nature, they have survived from a much earlier time, when the climate was different here. **1976** H. M. FRENCH *Periglacial Environment* v. 95 The presence of obviously relic pingos..in present-day periglacial environments complicates attempts to identify the conditions for present-day pingo growth. **1978** *Nature* 7 Sept. 19/1 Appropriate physical conditions for the origin of life could exist on the relic regolith grains.

ˈrelicary. *rare.* [ad. Sp. *relicario*: see RELIQUARY.] A shrine for relics.

1796 SOUTHEY *Lett. fr. Spain* (1808) I. App. 288 Whatever remains of such Catholic sufferers she could procure she shrined with her own hands,..and she labelled the relicaries in which they were placed. **1829** —— in *For. Rev. & Cont. Misc.* III. 32 Philip II sent for some of the perspiration, to be placed among the other treasures of his relicary.

re-lick, *v.* [RE- 5 a.] *trans.* To lick again.

1607 NORDEN *Surv. Dial.* A vii, This simple rude lumpe, of which, if some more skilfull, will bestow the re-licking, & bring it to his true shape [etc.].

†**ˈrelicly,** *adv. Obs. rare*$^{-1}$. [f. RELIC + -LY².] As a relic; carefully.

1633 [see *relic-like* under RELIC 7].

relict (ˈrɛlɪkt), *sb.* [ad. L. *relict-us, -a, -um*, pa. pple. of *relinquĕre* to leave behind, RELINQUISH; in sense 2 more immediately ad. med.L. *relicta* sb. or OF. *relicte* (14th c.).]

1. = RELIC 1, 1 d, and 5. Now *rare* or *Obs.*

1535 LYNDESAY *Satyre* 2231 Cum, win my pardon; and kiss my relicts, to. *c***1540** in France *Addit. Narr. Pop. Plot* (1679) 36 Steryng them with all perswasions..to dedd Images and counterfeit Relicts. **1632** LITHGOW *Trav.* v. 195 The Apple is..yearely transported for Constantinople.. and there is reserued for a relict of the fruit of the forbidden tree. **1681** R. KNOX *Hist. Ceylon* 80 Each of these Gods hath a Pallenkine..in the which there are several pieces of their superstitious relicts. **1727** A. HAMILTON *New Acc. E. Ind.* I. xxvii. 344 For want of a better Image or Relict to adore, they worship a Monkeys Tooth. **1735** HILD. JACOB *Wks.* 411 In the Statues, Bas-relieves and precious Relicts of the great Masters of old. **1827** MISS SEDGWICK *H. Leslie* (1872) I. 37 The relicts and gifts of a woman whom he had loved. **1884** 'MARK TWAIN' *Huck. Finn* xxxvii. 384 Things that was valuable..on account of them being relicts.

2. a. The widow *of* a man.

1545 *Reg. Privy Council Scot.* I. 9 Dame Jonet Stewart the relict of umquhile Johne Muir of Caldwell and now spous to Thomas Kirkpatrick. *c***1610** SIR J. MELVIL *Mem.* (1735) 256 He married the Earl of March's Relict. *a***1659** OSBORN *Observ. Turks* Wks. (1673) 305 Such cries as are made by the Relicts and Children of slain Souldiers. **1718** HICKES & NELSON *J. Kettlewell* II. xxvii. 129 This Gentle-woman, the Relict of so Worthy a Man. **1776** FOOTE *Bankrupt* III. Wks. 1799 II. 129 There has been..no less than three proposals of marriage already made to my relict. **1804** EUGENIA DE ACTON *Tale without Title* II. 214, I am ordered by the relict of my late master..to inform you that she [etc.]. **1871** FREEMAN *Norm. Conq.* xvii. (1876) IV. 59 Nothing could be further from William's purpose than in any way to disturb the relict of his revered predecessor.

b. Without const. Now *rare*.

1640–1 *Kirkcudbr. War-Comm. Min. Bk.* (1855) 89 To.. confess his fault in declameing, by words, of the gude name and fame of the said relict. **1702** STEELE *Funeral* I. (1734) 15, I never yet could meet with a sorrowful Relict, but was herself enough to make a hard Bargain with me. **1776** T. PERCIVAL *Ess.* III. 347 To the great prejudice of a poor relict and her helpless child. **1873** BROWNING *Red. Cott. Nt.-cap* I. 808 She, sad relict, must drag residue Of days.

†**c.** The surviving partner *of* a person. *Obs.*$^{-1}$

*a***1667** JER. TAYLOR *Wks.* (1835) II. 84 (Cent.), Though the relict of a man or woman have liberty to contract new relations, yet [etc.].

3. a. *pl.* Remains, remnants, residue. Also *sing.* a surviving part; †a survivor.

1598 BARRET *Theor. Warres* IV. i. 116 Hee gathered together the relictes of the defeated armies. **1638** SIR T. HERBERT *Trav.* (ed. 2) 304 In as many places are Christians, or relicts of that holy profession. **1654** R. CODRINGTON tr. *Iustine* XXII. 319 The Carthaginians sent Commanders..to prosecute the relicts of the war. **1728** MORGAN *Algiers* I. i. 10 He there seems to speak of the Relicts of the Pœni. **1817** COLERIDGE *Biog. Lit.* vi. I. 112 The ideas (or relicts of such impression) will exactly imitate the order of the impression itself. **1856** GROTE *Greece* II. xcviii. XII. 638 Isolated relicts of what had once been an Hellenic aggregate.

sing. **1630** B. JONSON *New Inn* Argt., The eldest daughter, Frances,..is the sole relict of the family. **1679** M. RUSDEN *Discov. Bees* 99 The relict of a good Colony that hath had several Hives taken off. **1764** FOOTE *Patron* III. Wks. 1799 I. 359 My Æneas! my precious relict of Troy!

b. A surviving trace, survival. Also *transf.* of a person.

1646 SIR T. BROWNE *Pseud. Ep.* v. xxi. 265 To breake the eggeshell after the meat is out..is but a superstitious relict. **1761** HUME *Hist. Eng.* lxi. III. 320 This parliament took into consideration..the taking away of tithes, which they called a relict of Judaism. **1821** J. Q. ADAMS in C. Davies *Metr. Syst.* III. (1871) 271 The Winchester bushel is the only existing relict of the old English system. **1928** *Daily Express* 3 July 10/2 Our British boards of railway directors are like an ante-room to a museum. They are crowded with relicts of the easy pre-war age for whom the world has never changed.

c. *pl.* The remains of one deceased. *rare.*

*a***1649** DRUMM. OF HAWTH. *Poems* Wks. (1711) 45 The blushing hyacinth and rose Spred on the place his relicts do enclose. **1704** NELSON *Fest. & Fasts* xxxi. (1739) 386 A.. Means to entice the People to..a superstitious Worship of his Relicts. **1807** G. CHALMERS *Caledonia* I. II. vii. 320 *note*, The original church of Dunkeld..was built..for the reception of the relicts of St. Columba.

d. *Biol., Geogr.,* and *Geol.* A relict species, structure, etc.

1905 F. E. CLEMENTS *Res. Methods in Ecol.* 321 *Relict*, a species belonging properly to an earlier type of succession than the one in which it is found. **1950** *Jrnl. Ecol.* XXXVIII. 294 A few relicts of the former open fen are to be seen in the form of scattered plants of *Cirsium palustre*..and *Angelica sylvestris*. **1971** *Nature* 5 Feb. 377/2 Rare plant species are often relicts surviving in restricted ecological niches. The opportunities for these species to spread to other, suitable habitats are minimal. **1977** A. HALLAM *Planet Earth* 17/2 The breccias are revealing to us the relicts of an original lunar crust that formed and was reconstituted several times.

†**4. a.** A deserted or discarded person. *Obs. rare.*

1592 WARNER *Alb. Eng.* VII. xxxvi. 156 Her too much wronged Relict might (as well he might) be greeu'd. **1602** *Ibid.* XI. lxviii. 287 Him blesseth he to whom doth he one of his Relicts gue.

†**b.** *pl.* That which is left behind or rejected; leavings; refuse. *Obs. rare.*

1687 A. LOVELL tr. *Thevenot's Trav.* I. 107 Salt meats are relicts to them, and they feed on nothing but Beans, Pease, Eggs and Bisket. **1748** *Anson's Voy.* II. iv. 167 The broken jars, ashes, and fish-bones..being doubtless the relicts of the cruisers stationed off that Port.

†**5.** A thing left to one by inheritance. *Obs.*$^{-1}$

1726 in H. Campbell *Love-lett. Mary Q. Scots* (1824) 18, I..look on myself but as the steward of a glorious relict.

6. *Linguistics.* Used *attrib.* or in *Comb.* to denote language or vocabulary which is a survival of otherwise archaic or old forms. Cf. also RELIC 4 d, 7.

1934 PRIEBSCH & COLLINSON *German Lang.* vii. 364 Often we find a wedge of linguistic innovation along the rivers and highways with relict-areas preserving ancient forms on the high moors and along the wooded hills. **1947** *Ibid.* (ed. 2) i. 14 The Logudoresian dialect retains certain relict-words with affinities in Basque. **1948** *Trans. Phil. Soc.* 1947 14 It now appears that the original Germanic language of the Low German area was not in any essential matter distinguished from Frisian, but that it was afterwards High Germanized, leaving Frisian as a relict language of its original state. **1963** H. C. DARBY in Brown & Foote *Early English & Norse Stud.* ii. 9 Another example of relict names is found on Dunsmore Heath.

re'lict, *a.* [f. as prec.; cf. DERELICT.] Left, in various senses.

†**1.** Allowed to remain untouched or undisturbed. *Obs.*

c **1420** *Pallad. on Husb.* x. 198 A vyne whos fruyt humour wol putrifie Pampyned is to be by euery side, Relicte on hit oonly the croppis hie. *c* **1450** tr. *De Imitatione* III. lx. 140 In asmuche as his mevinge lafte & relicte to himself drawiþ euere to euel & to lowe þinges.

†**2.** Left by death, surviving. (Cf. RELICT *sb.* 2.) *Obs.*

1649 BP. HALL *Cases Consc.* IV. ii. (1654) 310 If upon the departure of an unbeleeving or hereticall yoke-fellow the relict party must be tyed up. *a* **1661** FULLER *Worthies, Lincolnshire* II. (1662) 159 His Relict Lady..lived long in Westminster.

†**3.** *Obs.* Of lands: **a.** Left by the recess of the sea. **b.** Abandoned, deserted.

a **1676** HALE *De Jure Maris* I. iv. in *Hargrave's Law Tracts* (1787) I. 14 No answer is given to the title of information for lands relict, for these were of several natures. *a* **1687** PETTY *Pol. Arith.* iv. (1691) 68 If the Relict Lands, and the immovables left behind upon them, may be sold.

4. *Geogr.*, *Geol.*, and *Biol.* Surviving from a previous age or in changed circumstances after the extinction or disappearance of related forms or structures.

In origin prob. an *attrib.* use of the sb. rather than a revival of the adj. (cf. quot. 1901).

1898 J. GEIKIE *Earth Sculpture* xvi. 274 The direction, and to a large extent the shape or form of relict mountains, are thus mainly determined by the geological structure. **1901** *Ann. & Mag. Nat. Hist.* VII. 315 Those [animals] remaining in the old place formed a zonally-disposed relict-fauna. **1932** E. W. SINNOTT *Plant Sociology* iv. 63 Besides these characteristic relict species there are others whose fidelity is due to a narrowly specialized adaptation to definite physico-chemical relations of the habitat. **1939** W. H. TWENHOFEL *Princ. Sedimentation* xii. 459 Relict seas are bodies of water that have become separated from the parent body by diastrophic, depositional, or volcanic causes. *Ibid.*, Well-known relict seas are..the Caspian Sea, Lake Nicaragua, and Lake Baikal. **1945** M. J. D. WHITE *Animal Cytol. & Evolution* xiii. 293 [*Saga serrata*] seems to be a 'relict' species, since the localities in which it occurs are very discontinuous and the individual populations of very small size. **1954** W. D. THORNBURY *Princ. Geomorphol.* xvi. 413 Relict features attributable to former existence of periglacial conditions have been described at many places in Europe and North America. **1974** J. D. MILLMAN *Recent Sedimentary Carbonates* I. vii. 221 Coralline algae in continental shelf sediments may be relict but others are modern. **1977** *Birds* Winter 19/1 Fowlmere is a small, relict fen, lying in a hollow of the Gog Magog hills. **1978** *Sci. Amer.* Sept. 111/1 The lobe fins were far less successful as fishes (they survive only as lungfishes and a few relict forms). **1978** T. ROWLEY *Villages in Landscape* ii. 49 Village plans may include relict features of early defensive structures, such as the alignment of Roman town walls.

5. *Astr.* Remaining from the 'big bang'.

1971 *Nature* 3 Sept. 36/2 The discovery in 1965, by Penzias and Wilson, of background radiation which may well be relict radiation from this fireball. **1978** *Sci. Amer.* July 54/3 Encounters between cosmic rays and photons of the relict radiation would severely drain the energy of the cosmic rays above some energy threshold.

So †**re'licted** *a.*; †**re'liction.** *Obs.*

a **1676** HALE *De Jure Maris* I. vi. in *Hargrave's Law Tracts* (1787) I. 31 Custom cannot intitle the subject to relicted lands, or make it part of a manor. *Ibid.* 36 Acquests by the reliction or recess of the sea.

relie, obs. form of RELY *v.*[1]

†**re'lief**[1]. *Obs.* Forms: 3–5 relef, (5 -leff, 6 -leffe), 4–5 relif, -lyf, (4 *pl.* -lyves), releif, 5 relefe, -leue, (*pl.* -leues, -ys), 4–6 releef, (6 -leefe); 5 relyef, 6 relief(e. [a. OF. *relef*, *relief* (also *relie*, *relier*) 'the remnant..of meat left at a meale', also 'rubbidge, or the ruines of ouerthrowne houses' (Cotgr.); cf. Prov. *releu*, Sp. *relieve*, It. *rilevo*, *rilievo*, vbl. sb. corresponding to RELIEVE *v.*, and literally meaning 'that which is lifted or removed'.

The cognate forms appear to establish the connexion of the F. word in sense 2 with *relever*, but the Eng. evidence suggests that OF. (or AF.) had also a form **relif* representing L. *reliqu-um* (compare OF. *antif*:—L. *antiqu-um*) from which the senses placed under 1 are directly derived. The writer of the *Ancren Riwle* clearly associated the word with *relinquĕre*, and in Wyclif and Trevisa it usually renders *reliquiæ* and frequently interchanges with *relic*.]

1. a. That which is left or given up by one.

a **1225** *Ancr. R.* 168 Þe vifte reisun is, noble men & wummen makieð large relef. Auh hwo makien largere relef þene þe oðer? *Ibid.*, Nis þis large relef? Nis þis muchel loaue?

b. The remains of a thing; remainder; residuum.

1382 WYCLIF *Isa.* x. 19 And the releef of the wode of the wilde wode for fewenesse shul be noumbred. **1387** TREVISA *Higden* (Rolls) I. 97 Ierom seiþ þat of þe releef of þis citee were i-buld two grete citees. *Ibid.* IV. 155 Also Silla þe consul..was in Campania forto destroye al þe relif of þe bataille þat heet [bellum] sociale. *c* **1440** *Promp. Parv.* 101/1 *Cracoke*, relefe of molte talowe or grese. *Ibid.* 428/2 *Releef*, or brocaly of mete (or blevynge).

c. The remainder, remnant, or surviving portion of a people or company.

1387 TREVISA *Higden* (Rolls) III. 113 Whan he hadde..i-brouȝt þe relyf of Israel and of Iuda out of Egipte. *Ibid.* V. 251 Þe poure relyf þat was i-left of þe Britouns. **1520** *Maundevil's Chron. Eng.* III. 24/2 [Antiochus] tourned to yᵉ pore releues of yᵉ Jewes. *a* **1548** HALL *Chron., Hen. VIII* 26 b, Wednesday the .xxvj. daye of July the releffe of the speres brought in askry.

d. The remains, or some part of the remains, of a person deceased; a relic. *rare.*

c **1449** PECOCK *Repr.* I. xix. 114 Placis in whiche holi men han lyued..or in whiche the relifis or the relikis of hem abiden. *Ibid.* II. viii. 182 Where the bodi or bonis or eny releef or relik of a Seint mai be had.

2. The remains of food left after a meal; leavings, scraps.

a **1300** *Cursor M.* 13512 Þe releif gadir þai in hepes, And fild þar-wit tuelue mikel lepes. **1382** WYCLIF *Exod.* viii. 3 Froggis that shulen steyn vp..in to the relyues of thi metis. **1426** LYDG. *De Guil. Pilgr.* 4570 Be cause ye Axen the releff Off hys dyner, on & alle. **1483** CAXTON *G. de la Tour* G v b, His wyf brought hym mete whiche she gate and was gyuen to her of the releef of other. **1552** HULOET, Reliefe, or broken meate, *fragmen*, *fragmentum*. **1582** BENTLEY *Mon. Matrones* ii. 10 Pouertie hath taken me,..compelling me to eate the reliefe of swine. **1589** RIDER *Bibl. Schol.* 1206 Reliefe after dinner, *reliquiæ prandij*.

relief[2] (rɪˈliːf). Forms: 4–6 relef, (6 -leffe), relefe, 5–6 releef, 5–7 releefe, -leif, (5 -leyf, *Sc.* raleiff, -leyff, 6 releief), 6–7 releife; 5–6 relyef(e, 5–7 reliefe, 6– relief; 5 relyf, relijf, 6 relyfe. Also 4–6 releue, -leve, (6 *Sc.* -lieve), 5 relyue; *pl.* 5–6 releves, -is, -ys, 5–7 relieves. [a. OF. *relief*, vbl. sb. from *relever* to RELIEVE. The general senses in Eng. are rare in French, and the word had prob. a greater currency in AF. than on the Continent.]

1. a. A payment, varying in value and kind according to rank and tenure, made to the overlord by the heir of a feudal tenant on taking up possession of the vacant estate. Now only *Hist.* except in *Sc. Law.* (Cf. RELIEVE *v.* 8 a.)

So OF. *relief* (Godef.), med.L. *relevium*, *relevamentum*, *relevatio*, etc. (see Du Cange).

c **1330** R. BRUNNE *Chron.* (1810) 214 Of wardes & relefe [F. *gardes et relefs*] þat barons of him held. *Ibid.*, Tille ilk a lordyng suld ward & relefe falle. **1375** BARBOUR *Bruce* XII. 320 Gif ony deis in this battaill, His air, but ward, releif, or taill, On the first day his land sall weild. *c* **1425** WYNTOUN *Cron.* III. v. 782 [He] gert þaim al..halde þar lande of hym in cheyff Fra þine wiþe serwice and raleyff. **1482** *Rolls of Parlt.* VI. 207/2 The Kyng, his heires, and the Quene severally shall have Relieves after the deth of such Auncestres as soo held of thaim. **1503–4** *Act 19 Hen. VII*, c. 15 *Preamble*, Lordes of whom..tenementes be holden in socage [be defrauded] of their releffes. **1597** SKENE *De Verb. Sign.* s.v. *Recognition*, The superiour may recognosce, and reteine the samin [lands] vntil securitie be maid to him for payment of the relieue. **1647** N. BACON *Disc. Govt. Eng.* I. lii. (1739) 91 The Relief of the Country-man is the best Beast that is in his possession; and of him that farmeth his Lands, a year's rent. **1766** BLACKSTONE *Comm.* II. 65 Relief..was before mentioned as incident to every feodal tenure, by way of fine or composition with the lord for taking up the estate. **1776** in Stonehouse *Axholme* (1839) 144 On surrender, the Lord is not entitled to any heriots or reliefs. **1818** CRUISE *Digest* (ed. 2) I. 34 The doctrine of reliefs was also adopted from the laws of Normandy. **1838** W. BELL *Dict. Law Scot.* 844 The casualty of relief is a sum exigible from an heir on his entry with the superior. **1874** STUBBS *Const. Hist.* ix. I. 261 The change of the heriot to the relief implies a suspension of ownership, and carries with it the custom of livery of seisin.

b. *Hist.* Formal acknowledgement of feudal tenure made by a vassal to his lord. *rare.*

c **1330** R. BRUNNE *Chron.* (1810) 202 Merschalle & stiward þerfor about dos sende, & homage & feaute he askes & releue [*rime* chefe]. **1525** LD. BERNERS *Froiss.* II. 295 The bysshop..counsayled that every man shulde be newe sworne, and renewe their releves. *Ibid.* 559 There the erle of Armynake and the Erle of Rodays made their reliefe & homage to the kynge. **1828–40** TYTLER *Hist. Scot.* i. (1864) I. 28 No crown-vassal, widow, orphan, or ward of the crown was to be under the necessity of performing their homage or relief out of the kingdom.

2. a. Ease or alleviation given to or received by a person through the removal or lessening of some cause of distress or anxiety; deliverance from what is burdensome or exhausting to the mind; mental relaxation; †hence also, entertainment, sport (quot. 1575).

1390 GOWER *Conf.* III. 23 Thus for the point of his relief The coc which schal his mete arraie [etc.]. *c* **1400** *Leg. Rood* (1871) 96 Ful grete grace was þore schewd And grete releue to lerd and leude. **1509** HAWES *Past. Pleas.* XXXII. (Percy Soc.) 159 They hoped for to have releve Of theyr imprison which did them so greve. *a* **1547** SURREY in *Tottel's Misc.* (Arb.) 26 That man is farre from blisse, That doth receiue for his relief none other gayn but this. **1575** LANEHAM *Let.* (1871) 18 If he wear taken onez, then what shyft..he woold woork too wynde hym self from them..waz a matter of a goodly releef. **1593** SHAKS. *3 Hen. VI*, III. iii. 20 Tell thy griefe, It shall be eas'd, if France can yeeld reliefe. **1601** ? MARSTON *Pasquil & Kath.* (1878) II. 361 That's the best reliefe To drowne all care, and ouerwhelme all griefe. *c* **1640** MILTON *Sonn.*, *To Nightingale* 12 Thou from yeer to yeer hast sung too late For my relief. **1716–8** LADY M. W. MONTAGU *Lett.* I. xxxi. 107 She is young, and her conversation would be a great relief to me. **1781** COWPER *Truth* 455 The soul, reposing on assured relief, Feels herself happy amidst all her grief. **1818** SHELLEY *Julian* 565, I sought relief From the deep tenderness that maniac wrought Within me. **1857** BUCKLE *Civiliz.* I. vii. 432 It is a relief to turn from so painful a subject. **1876** E. MELLOR *Priesth.* viii. 372 There is..a great relief in unburdening to a friend the sins and sorrows of one's life.

b. Ease from, or lessening of, physical pain or discomfort.

1691 RAY *Creation* I. (1692) 83 The Warming-stone..hath been found to give ease and relief in several Pains and Diseases. **1704** T. FULLER *Med. Gymn.* (1711) 3 Most Men indulge themselves in the Expectation of..sudden Relief. **1789** W. BUCHAN *Dom. Med.* (1790) 451 No lasting relief can be procured till these [humours] are either corrected or expelled. **1820** SHELLEY *Hom. Merc.* ii, Now when..Heaven's tenth moon chronicled her relief, She gave light to a babe all babes excelling. **1879** J. C. MORISON *Gibbon* 172 He underwent another operation and as usual experienced much relief.

c. An agreeable change of object to the mind or one of the senses, esp. that of sight.

1712 ADDISON *Spect.* No. 333 ¶23 He has..interspersed several Speeches, Reflections, Similitudes, and the like Reliefs, to diversify his Narration. **1833** HT. MARTINEAU *Brooke Farm* i. 4 A clump of beeches..were a relief to the eye. **1870** F. R. WILSON *Ch. Lindisf.* 81 The north walls..were built as plain lengths of masonry, without buttresses, windows, mouldings, or relief of any kind.

d. A gradual widening in the bore of a gun-barrel towards the muzzle.

1824 COL. HAWKER *Shooting* (ed. 3) 8 This relief has the effect of making the gun shoot as close as it can do. **1858** GREENER *Gunnery* 306 The relief in the muzzle of a gun has a tendency, by allowing a gradual expansion laterally, to keep the charge of shot better together.

3. a. Aid, help, or assistance given to a person or persons in a state of poverty or want; *spec.* (formerly) assistance in money or necessary articles given to the indigent from funds administered under the Poor Law or from parish doles, or (more recently), financial assistance afforded to those in need by the state under other legislative provisions.

c **1400** *Christ's Compl.* 268 in *Pol. Rel. & L. Poems* (1903) 207 My seruantis suffren hungir & coolde, Releef of þee ȝit haue þei noon. *c* **1412** HOCCLEVE *De Reg. Princ.* 901 If þou heer-after come vn-to swych pref, Thow wolt ful sore triste [*v.r.* thurste] after releef. **1472–3** *Rolls of Parlt.* VI. 48/2 To the verrey honour and worship of God, and grete releif and sustenaunce of pore people. **1548** LATIMER *Ploughers* (Arb.) 23 They woulde bequeth greate summes of money towarde the releue of the pore. **1599** SHAKS. *Hen. V*, I. i. 15 To reliefe of Lazars, and weak age Of indigent faint Soules..A hundred Almes-houses. **1632** SANDERSON *Serm.* 384 The competent releefe of the orderly poore. **1669** W. MONTAGU in *Buccleuch MSS.* (Hist. MSS. Comm.) I. 446 The Church charities and the secular reliefs. **1743** J. MORRIS *Serm.* ii. 47 They..cruelly refuse to the distressed..relief. **1794** BURKE *Lett., to Mrs. Crewe* (1844) IV. 257 In their idea of relief, there is always included something of punishment. **1849** MACAULAY *Hist. Eng.* iii. I. 421 The men, women, and children who receive relief are..one tenth of the inhabitants. **1865** *Pall Mall G.* 13 May 1 If there is to be parochial relief at all..there must be some law to determine the question by whom that relief is to be given. **1921** *Daily Colonist* (Victoria, B.C.) 22 Mar. 1/3 More than $400,000 has now been expended by the city in providing relief, it will be pointed out. **1957** R. HOGGART *Uses of Literacy* ii. 40 At my grandmother's we were not living 'on relief' but, like many around us, we were 'a bit short'. **1965** MRS. L. B. JOHNSON *White House Diary* 12 Aug. (1970) 309 Their world is so narrow, and in their homes—frequently broken homes with one parent or an aged grandparent on relief—the vocabulary is often limited to grunts or profanity. **1966** G. JACKSON *Let.* 3 Mar. in *Soledad Brother* (1971) 95 I've heard men brag about..taking money from black women who are on relief. **1978** S. BRILL *Teamsters* vii. 285 He didn't make a lot... But we never went on relief.

†**b.** Sustenance. *Obs.*

c **1440** *Chron. R. Glouc.* (Rolls) 827 Pur meseise him þuder drof & defaute of biliue [*MS.* δ, relyue]. **1483** *Rolls of Parlt.* VI. 260/1 Greate Games of Swannes of ther owne, by the whiche the greateste parte of their relyf and lyvyng hath be susteyned in longe tyme passed. **1575** GASCOIGNE *Flowers* Wks. 23 With gonnes we kill the Crowe, For spoyling our releefe. **1613** PURCHAS *Pilgrimage* IV. viii. (1614) 382 There is a faire Stone-Hospitall.., allowing three daies reliefe for horse and man freely.

†**c.** Support, sustentation *of* a place. *Obs. rare.*

1463 *Bury Wills* (Camden) 35, [I bequeath] to the nunnys of Thetford, eche nunne vjd. and to the releef and comfort of the place xs. **1464** *Paston Lett.* II. 146 Every man to do his part to the well fare, socour, and releve of our monasteri. **1601** *Act 43 Eliz.* c. 4 § 1 Landes, Tenements, [etc.]..given..for or towardes Reliefe, Stocke or Maintenance for Howses of Correction.

†**d.** A fresh supply or supplies of some article of food or drink. *Obs.*

1575 LANEHAM *Let.* (1871) 45 Cam thear in a too dayz space, from sundry friendz, a releef of a xl. tunn, till a nu supply was gotten agayn. **1613** PURCHAS *Pilgrimage* IX. xiv. (1614) 911 Besides this reliefe of Fowles, they had plentie of Tortoise egges. **1725** DE FOE *Voy. round World* (1840) 108 Frequent relief of fresh water, of plants, fowl, and fish, if not of bread and flesh.

4. a. Assistance in time of danger, need, or difficulty; aid, help, or succour.

c **1500** *Melusine* 270 Many of them for theyre relyf supposed to haue entred into thadmyral shipp & they were drowned. **1529** WOLSEY in *Four C. Eng. Lett.* (1880) 11, I with all myn shal not onely ascrybe thys my relef unto you, but [etc.]. *c* **1586** C'TESS PEMBROKE *Ps.* LXII. ii, To headlong him their thoughtes devise, And past reliefe to tread him down. **1603** R. JOHNSON *Kingd. & Commw.* 3 In sodaine hurliburlies of warre it is commonly seene, that courage affoorde more reliefe then policie. **1659** HAMMOND *On Ps.* cii. 6 For any relief from man, I am as distitute and hopeless of it. **1698** FRYER *Acc. E. India & P.* 184 At night Boats and Pilots went off to her Relief. **1773** GOLDSM. *Stoops to Conq.* v, Prudence once more comes to my relief. **1817** BROUGHAM in *Parl. Deb.* 754 Though the measure did not embrace the relief of the agricultural districts, it was hoped to afford a temporary relief to that species of distress which [etc.]. **1846** J. BAXTER *Libr. Pract. Agric.* (ed. 4) I. 215 The soil is the only resource of permanent relief.

b. Aid or succour rendered to persons or places endangered by war; in later use *esp.* deliverance *of* a besieged town, etc. from the attacking force.

a **1548** HALL *Chron., Hen. VIII* 90 Where as we entended the relief and reskue of you and our sayd subiectes and citie of Turnay. **1596** DALRYMPLE tr. *Leslie's Hist. Scot.* II. 173 Agricola..sayles into Britannie wt a chosen and waled armie, in releife of the Romanis. **1617** MORYSON *Itin.* II. 107 The warre, which is farre from the reliefe of any friend. **1724** DE FOE *Mem. Cavalier* (1840) 27 They had given over the relief of Casal. **1781** GIBBON *Decl. & F.* xxx. III. 165 Stilicho..advanced..to the relief of the faithful city. **1810** WELLINGTON in Gurw. *Desp.* (1838) VI. 257, I..have been prevented from attempting its relief only by the certainty which I had that the attempt must fail. **1869** FREEMAN *Norm. Conq.* xii. (1875) III. 168 He hastened..to the relief of Ambrières.

†**c.** A body of men coming to the relief of a person or place. *Obs. rare.*

1647 N. BACON *Disc. Govt. Eng.* I. lxiv. (1739) 137 [She] retired with the Prince to a relief which they brought from beyond Sea. **1670** COTTON *Espernon* 594 He gave advice to Fight the Relief so soon as ever it began to appear.

†**d.** Assistance towards saving or effecting something. *Obs. rare.*

1659 LEAK *Waterwks.* 26 A rare and necessary Engin, by which you may give great reliefe to Houses that are on Fire. **1662** STILLINGFL. *Orig. Sacræ* I. iv. §3 We are like then to have little relief for finding out of truth in the Poetick Age of Greece.

5. a. Release from some occupation or post of duty; in later use *spec.* of the replacing of a sentinel or watch by a fresh man or body of men. Also *fig.*

1513 DOUGLAS *Æneis* VIII. Prol. 29 Luffaris langis only to lok in thair lace Thair ladeis lufely, and louk but let or releifis. **1602** SHAKS. *Ham.* I. i. 8 For this releefe much thankes. **1633** EARL MANCH. *Al Mondo* (1636) 61 In Warres we often releefe the Watch. Life is a Warfare, yet hath no releefe but Death. **1799** *Instr. & Reg. Cavalry* (1813) 273 The number of men necessary for the relief of the videts (or sentries), are then to be marched off. **1799** WELLINGTON in Gurw. *Desp.* (1838) I. 27 Between foraging parties and outline picquets, we have not men enough left to give a relief. **1847** *Infantry Man.* (1854) 101 All advanced piquets must have three reliefs. **1889** *Infantry Drill* 285 See that the sentries are visited every hour between reliefs.

b. One who relieves another on duty; *esp.* a soldier or body of soldiers relieving another man or company on guard. Also *transf.* of animals.

1709 SWIFT in *Tatler* 10 Sept., Little Parson Dapper, who is the Common Relief to all the lazy Pulpits in Town. **1822** *Regul. & Orders Army* 219 Officers on Guard..are to inspect all Reliefs, both on going out to their Posts, and returning from them. **1826** SCOTT *Woodst.* xv, We are to have a relief from Oxford to-morrow. **1856** KANE *Arct. Expl.* II. i. 19 McGary, my relief, calls me. **1889** *Infantry Drill* 271 The reliefs are kept separated a few yards from the remainder of the piquet, to avoid disturbing them.

transf. **1882** FLOYER *Unexpl. Baluchistan* 145, I gave orders..that the present set [of donkeys] should not be abandoned until their reliefs came.

c. A dish succeeding another.

1788 W. DYOTT *Diary* 1 Sept. (1907) I. 53 We had ninety dishes, fifty-five the first course and relieves, and thirty-five the second course. **1824** BYRON *Juan* xv. lxiii, 'Soupe à la Beauveau', whose relief was dory.

6. a. Deliverance (esp. in *Law*) from some hardship, burden, or grievance; remedy, redress.

1616 in Cary *Rep. Chancery* (1650) 122 The Judges of the common Law..cannot give any remedy or reliefe for the same, either by error or attaint, or by any other meanes. **1670** *Modern Rep.* (1682) I. 305 You give relief every day where there are express Clauses, that there shall be no relief in Law or Equity. **1743** *Viner's Abridgm.* XVIII. 328 Release of all Demands will bar a Demand of a Relief, because the Relief is by reason of the Seigniory. **1761** in Struthers *Hist. Relief Ch.* 287 A presbytery for the relief of Christians oppressed in their Christian privileges. **1771** *Junius Lett.* lix. (1788) 318 No successful attempt has ever been made for the relief of the subject in this article. **1817** W. SELWYN *Law Nisi Prius* (ed. 4) II. 1131 The court refused to grant relief. **1867** *Chambers' Encycl.* s.v. *United Presb. Ch.*, Never were forced settlements more shameless. ..Relief was felt to be a necessity.

b. *Sc. Law.* Release from an obligation; also, a right, under certain circumstances, to reimbursement of expenses incurred by some obligation. Freq. in *bond, claim, clause,* etc. *of relief.*

c **1680** DALLAS *Stiles* (1697) 1 If there be two or moe Cautioners, and that there be a mutual Relief, then the same must be immediatly before the Clause of Registration, and the Clause of mutual Relief conceived as follows. **1797** *Encycl. Brit.* (ed. 3) IX. 692/1 The cautioner, who binds himself at the desire of the principal debtor, has an *actio mandati* or of relief against him. **1838** W. BELL *Dict. Law Scot.* 131 The cautioner's claim is for relief from the principal obligation, with the interest and expenses paid by him.

c. *Church,* etc., *of Relief,* or *the Relief*: (see 9 a).

1764 *Scots Mag.* XXVI. 289/1 The presbytery generally known by the name of the presbytery of Relief. **1766** *Ibid.* XXVIII. 274/2 Now settled minister of the church of Relief at Edinburgh. **1767** *Ibid.* XXIX. 285/2 Another minister, and a preacher,..have..gone into the Relief. **1794** Z. YEWDALL in *Arminian Mag.* Aug. (1795) 371 Here I found a large parish church, two meeting-houses, and a Kirk of relief. **1847** *Mem. Union of Secession & Relief Churches* 7 To begin and maintain a friendly intercourse with the Synod of Relief. *Ibid.*, The overture proposed only intercourse with the Relief as a sister Church.

7. Alleviation *of* some pain, burden, etc.; remission *of* a tax; *spec.* remission of income-tax due on a proportion of earned income.

1526 *Pilgr. Perf.* (W. de W. 1531) 26 b, But also it is relefe and remyssyon of payne to ye soules in purgatory. **1535** in Ellis *Orig. Lett.* Ser. III. II. 340 That I may haue..some releeve of the greate charge wiche the words of the Kyngs Lettres importe. **1667** MILTON *P.L.* x. 976 What thoughts in my unquiet brest are ris'n, Tending to som relief of our extremes. **1860** WHITE *Maltster's Guide* 157 Full directions for applying for relief of malt duty in the case of damage. **1889** A. CHAPMAN *Income-Tax Grievances & their Remedy* i. 9 Appellants who..prove..that their profits have not been equal to the sum at which they were assessed and have paid duty, are entitled to relief and repayment of tax. **1916** [see INCOME-TAX]. **1931** *Economist* 28 Feb. 456/2 A resident British holder of 'Kaffirs' is subject to income tax on dividends at the full rate of British tax (4s. 6d. in the £), less Dominion tax relief (at present 2s. 3d., namely, half the British rate). He is thus liable at the 'reliefed' rate of 2s. 3d. **1969** *Times* 2 May 25 Tax relief can reduce the cost of your investment by up to £16.10.0 per £100 of premium. **1972** *Accountant* 17 Aug. 191/1 The strict ban against relief for part-time directors and employees. **1973** P. O'DONNELL *Silver Mistress* iv. 72 If it's a phony charity account..they probably get tax relief. **1977** *Money Which?* Mar. 123/3 If you become entitled to tax relief on a new outgoing or allowance,..tell the taxman straightaway.

†**8.** *Hunting.* **a.** Of the hare or hart: The act of seeking food; feeding or pasturing. (Cf. RELIEVE *v.* 2 e.) Also *fig.* of persons. *Obs.*

c **1410** *Master of Game* (MS. Digby 182) xxxiv, For gleidly she will not be þere as she hathe pastured, but in tyme of releefe. **1575** TURBERV. *Venerie* 75 He muste take good heede that he come not too earely into the springs and hewtes where he thinketh that the harte doth feede and is at reliefe. *Ibid.* 171 Houndes will haue better sente of an Hare when shee goeth towards the reliefe, than when shee goeth towardes hyr Forme. **1637** B. JONSON *Sad Sheph.* II. vii, A Witch..will be found, or sitting in her fourme, Or els, at releife, like a Hare. **1668** DRYDEN *Even. Love* IV. ii, What, Are you going to reliefe by Moonshine?

†**b.** The giving of food to young hounds after a successful chase. *Obs. rare*⁻¹.

1590 COKAINE *Treat. Hunting* C j, A good Huntsman ought to..carry with him a peece of bread in his sleeue to wet in the bloud of the Hare for the reliefe of his whelps.

†**c.** (See quots.) *Obs. rare.*

1602 *2nd Pt. Return fr. Parnass.* II. v. 854 When you come to your stately gate, as you sounded the recheat before, so now you must sound the releefe three times. *Ibid.* 857 O sir, but your reliefe is your chiefest and sweetest note, that is sir, when your hounds hunt after a game vnknowne.

9. *attrib.* **a.** *Relief Church* (cf. 6 c), a Scottish ecclesiastical body, founded by Thomas Gillespie and others in 1761 in assertion of the right of congregations to elect their own ministers and in protest against the aggressions of the General Assembly; in 1847 it amalgamated with the United Secession to form the United Presbyterian Church. So *Relief minister, presbytery, synod,* etc.

1767 *Scots Mag.* XXIX. 499/1 Three more ministers have been settled in Relief Congregations. *Ibid.*, At the Relief Church at Edinburgh. **1768** *Ibid.* XXX. 277 A sentence was pronounced against Mr. William Cruden,..now Relief minister at Glasgow. **1832** *Church Patronage Reporter* June 20 [A] population of 500,000 belonging to the Secession and Relief Churches alone. **1846** MCCULLOCH *Acc. Brit. Empire* (1854) II. 296 The Relief Synod..now comprises 10 presbyteries, including 109 congregations.

b. In various senses, as *relief agency, bill, boat, committee, duty, fund, guard, line, organization, pallet, party, team, train, valve, work, worker*; **relief road**, a road designed to divert traffic from congested areas; **relief roll** *U.S.*, a list of people receiving state relief; **relief ticket**, a small sum of money given to alleviate hardship; **relief well**, a hole drilled to intersect an oil or gas well in which there is a fire or a blow-out, so as to provide a route for water or mud to stop it.

1951 T. STERLING *House without Door* i. 7 A Jewish *relief agency..which trained refugee Jews in manual skills. **1971** PIVEN & CLOWARD in M. Edelman *Polit. Lang.* (1977) iii. 53 Relief agencies are..compelled to invent rituals of degradation and to subject their clientele to them. **1846** J. BAXTER *Libr. Pract. Agric.* (ed. 4) I. p. viii, His Grace did oppose the *Relief Bill in every stage of its progress. **1897** KIPLING *Captains Courageous* 167 They were turned into *relief-boats to carry fish. **1842** *Picayune* (New Orleans) 23 Jan. 2/5 The *Relief Committee of the Firemen's Charitable Association, will meet..at the Firemen's Insurance Office. **1862** *Times* 14 Apr. 11/4 Proud men..who go before 'relief committees' and submit to be questioned about their wants. **1892** J. C. HARRIS *On Plantation* 139 Where they lived remote from the relief committees, the families of the soldiers were not so well provided for as they had a right to expect. **1838** W. BELL *Dict. Law Scot.* 129 This preference ..extends to non-entry and *relief duties. **1842** S. BAMFORD *Passages in Life of Radical* II. xxi. 104 He had some money in hand belonging to the *relief fund. **1863** *Observer* 26 Apr. 5/4, I cannot..recommend too strongly..to your lady readers' kind consideration, the 'Cracow Ladies' Committee', who are connected with the 'Ladies' Relief Fund Committee' in London. **1877** *Daily News* 1 Nov. 4/6 The relief fund is satisfactorily increasing. **1914** Relief fund [see *flag-day* s.v. FLAG *sb.*⁴ 7]. **1848** BUCKLEY *Iliad* 250 Who had come as a *relief guard from fertile Ascania. **1878** F. S. WILLIAMS *Midl. Railw.* 94 The benefit of a through *relief line for their main traffic to and from the north. **1952** M. MCCARTHY *Groves of Academe* (1953) vi. 120 We're not yet *relief organisations, you must admit. **1974** *Whig-Standard* (Kingston, Ontario) 11 Jan. 7/1 A..graduate..with many years of experience with relief organizations. **1978** *Internat. Relations Dict.* (U.S. Dept. State Library) 15/2 U.S. agricultural surpluses are donated to 'friendly governments' through non-profit relief organizations. **1881** C. A. EDWARDS *Organs* 52 Perhaps the most simple and ingenious of these peculiar pallets is one termed the *relief pallet. **1933** J. BUCHAN *Prince of Captivity* I. iii. 85 Now he has gone and lost himself and..they're talking of a *relief party. **1940** *Gloss. Highway Engin. Terms* (*B.S.I.*) 9 **Relief road*,..a road to enable through traffic to avoid congested areas or other obstructions to movement. **1959** *Oxford Mag.* 26 Feb. 276/1 A relief road is invented, and it must then be guessed how much of the flow along each existing route will be diverted into it. **1960** *Oxford Mail* 10 Oct. 4/6 The idea of relief roads to link the suburbs with the centre is one that deserves to be considered. **1976** *S. Wales Echo* 27 Nov. 5/7 At present it is planned to join the relief road to Hirwaun Road near Tudor Terrace. **1937** C. HIMES *Black on Black* (1973) 127 Remembering suddenly the time the Belle Vernon Milk Company dumped hundreds of gallons of milk into the gutters of Cedar Street when the *relief rolls in Cleveland were the highest they'd ever been. **1938** *Sun* (Baltimore) 16 Apr. 8 The President himself has said that road building will 'take very few people off the relief rolls'. ..Spending should be limited to relief. **1976** *National Observer* (U.S.) 17 Jan. 5/2 Americans who are elderly, blind, disabled, or who have impoverished dependent children—generally, Americans who are on the relief rolls. **1977** M. EDELMAN *Polit. Lang.* v. 80 Social work counseling ..apparently has little or no effect on client satisfaction, behavior, or the size of relief rolls. **1970** *Guardian* 28 Jan. 3/8 *Relief teams are racing against the rainy season, due in the Nigerian delta. **1972** *Ibid.* 22 May 10/6 There is a drought at present in the villages... The relief teams have moved in. **1848** *United Irishman* 20 May 224/2 A beautiful and fertile island..became gradually poorer and poorer... Millions of men, who toiled their lives through from morning to night, found at length they had no *rights* but a right to public alms, and had realized, with all their toiling, nothing but the chance of a *relief-ticket. **1976** J. O'CONNOR *Eleventh Commandment* i. 21 He got a bit of beer money and came away laughing; relief tickets, they call them, and worth a couple of quid... The shops that took relief tickets would always overcharge the working class. **1883** *Leisure Hour* 282/2 The *relief train came up. **1849** WEALE *Dict. Terms*, **Relief-valve*, a valve belonging to the feeding apparatus of a marine-engine. **1925** A. B. THOMPSON *Oil-Field Explor. & Devel.* I. vii. 299 On reaching a rich gas sand the Gleason well ran wild at a rate of about 15,000,000 cub. ft. per day. ..A *relief well failed to effect its object, although sunk only 135 ft. away. **1939** D. HAGER *Fund. Petroleum Industry* ix. 222 The relief well was deflected so that it reached the burning hole at a depth of 7046 ft. **1975** *Petroleum Rev.* XXIX. 238/3 Just one month after the fire had started, the first relief well commenced injecting sea water. **1979** *Tucson* (Arizona) *Citizen* 3 Oct. 3A/3 Two relief wells are being drilled at an angle to Ixtoc 1 in an effort to rechannel the gusher to a controlled well. **1879** *Good Words* 495/2 There is another young engineer superintending his dam, a *relief work about two miles long. *Ibid.* 566/2 A collector, after having tried to induce some Mhars to go to a famine relief work close by, who refused, looking over a wall saw two of them devouring a dead dog. **1895** KIPLING *Day's Work* (1898) 170 They've gone as far as to admit extreme local scarcity, and they've started relief-works in one or two districts. *Ibid.* 202 Then in the evening he pitches in a twenty-page demi-official to me, saying that the people where he is might be 'advantageously employed on relief-work'. **1915** R. FRY *Let.* 28 July (1972) II. 388 I've been a long time in France—went to see the Quaker relief work. **1921** *Daily Colonist* (Victoria, B.C.) 22 Mar. 1/3 At the end of its resources as far as relief work is concerned, the city of Vancouver will urge the Dominion and Provincial Governments to carry a burden which it believes should rightfully be borne by them. **1938** R. D. FINLAYSON *Brown Man's Burden* 16 They were *relief workers and flax-cutters, working hard and making good money. **1973** *Guardian* 9 June 13/4 Latham belongs to that new breed of white man —the relief worker.

relief³ (rɪˈliːf). Also 7 releue, releiue, releave, 7–8 relieve. [Orig. ad. It. *rilievo* 'raised or imbossed worke' (Florio), f. *rilevare* to raise, elevate; afterwards a. the synonymous F. *relief*: see prec. and RELIEVO¹.]

I. a. In the plastic arts, the elevation or projection of a design, or parts of a design, from a plane surface in order to give a natural and solid appearance; also, the degree of such projection; the part which so projects.

high (†or *great*), *low*, and *middle relief*: see the articles ALTO-, BASSO-, MEZZO-RELIEVO, and BAS-RELIEF; also HIGH *a.* 1 b, LOW *a.* 1 b.

α. **1606** B. JONSON *Hymenæi* D iv b, Two great Statues.. bearing vp the Cloudes, which were of Releue, embossed, and tralucent, as Naturalls. *a* **1634** T. CAREW *Coelum Brit.* (1640) 209 A great vaze of gold, richly enchased, and beautified with Sculptures of great Releiue. **1691** RAY *Creation* I. (1692) 82 Pillars and Statues and other carved Works in relieve. **1726** LEONI tr. *Alberti's Archit.* II. 16/2 Mosaic work in relieve.

β. **1662** EVELYN *Chalcogr.* (1769) 107 In bold or faint touches, so as may best express the relief. **1687** A. LOVELL tr. *Thevenot's Trav.* I. 94 The Castle with three Towers, and the Eagle of stone in relief, which are the arms of the Justiniani Genoese Lords. **1702** ADDISON *Dial. Medals* Wks. 1721 I. 539 You find the figures of many ancient Coins rising up in a much more beautiful relief than those on the modern. **1762–71** H. WALPOLE *Vertue's Anecd. Paint.* (1786) II. 243 *note*, A wreath of enamelled flowers in relief, executed by Giles Legare. **1839** URE *Dict. Arts* 215 The face of the block ..is carved in relief into the desired design. **1851** D. WILSON *Preh. Ann.* IV. ii. (1863) II. 247 Floriated patterns in relief. **1879** H. PHILLIPS *Notes Coins* 4 A remarkable difference exists between ancient and modern coins, the former being of extremely bold execution and high relief.

b. A composition or design executed in relief.

α. **1682** WHELER *Journ. Greece* v. 381 In a Relieve below the cornish..is a Triumphal Chariot. **1726** LEONI tr.

Alberti's Archit. II. 15/2 The mold itself is taken..from any relieve, by pouring some liquid plaister over it.

β. **1717** BERKELEY *Jrnl. Tour Italy* 20 Jan., Wks. 1871 IV. 529 The reliefs with which the outside of the Pillar is covered from top to bottom. *c* **1820** S. ROGERS *Italy, Fountain* 3 Richly wrought with many a high relief. **1834** LYTTON *Pompeii* I. i, Upon its surface of bronze were elaborately wrought..reliefs of the Olympian games. **1875** FORTNUM *Maiolica* viii. 68 Some pieces with reliefs and imitation Chinese marks also occur.

2. a. The appearance of solidity or detachment given to a design or composition on a plane surface by the arrangement and disposition of the lines, colours or gradations of colour of which it is composed; hence, distinctness of outline due to contrast of colour.

1789 P. SMYTH tr. *Aldrich's Archit.* (1818) 28 The painted cornices still of a relief that deceived every unapprized spectator. **1797** *Encycl. Brit.* (ed. 3) XVI. 60/1 Relief, in painting, is the degree of boldness with which the figures seem, at a due distance, to stand out from the ground of the painting. **1820** W. IRVING *Sketch Bk.* II. 81 A church with its dark spire in strong relief against the clear cold sky. **1875** CLERY *Min. Tact.* ii. (1877) 21 To prevent their being seen in relief against the sky line.

b. *fig.* Vividness, distinctness, or prominence due to contrast or artistic presentation.

1781 COWPER *Conversat.* 127 His evidence..For want of prominence and just relief, Would hang an honest man. **1839** DE QUINCEY *Recoll. Lakes* Wks. 1862 II. 74 The combination of worldly prosperity..forced into strong relief and fiery contrast this curse written in the flesh. **1878** Bosw. SMITH *Carthage* 53 The horrors perpetrated by the Carthaginians..are brought out into full relief by Diodorus.

3. a. *Fortif.* (See quots.)

1834–47 J. S. MACAULAY *Field Fortif.* ii. (1851) 42 The relief of a work is the height of its interior crest above the bottom of the ditch. **1879** *Cassell's Techn. Educ.* I. 104/2 The relief is the difference of level between the crest of the parapet and the bottom of the ditch.

b. *Phys. Geog.* The contour of some part of the surface of the earth considered with reference to variations in its elevation.

1865 LUBBOCK *Preh. Times* xi. (1878) 373 Assuming the pre-existing relief or excavation rather of the surface. **1878** HUXLEY *Physiogr.* xvii. 299 The observer would find bolder reliefs than he has met with in the Thames valley in the almost mountainous hills of Wales.

4. *attrib.* and *Comb.* (senses 1 and 2), as ***relief-block, -carving, construction, decoration, panel, -plate, -polish*** (sb. and vb.), ***-polishing, portion, -print, -printing, -process, -stamper, -tablet***; **relief map**, a map that indicates the relief of the land, either by the analogous form of its surface or by a system of colouring, shading contour lines, or the like; **Relief nib** [*Relief*, proprietary name], a manufacturer's name for a special kind of nib.

1878 ABNEY *Photogr.* (1881) 183 *Relief-block making is essentially difficult in almost every stage. **1892** E. ROWE *Hints on Chip-Carving* 60 In *relief-carving the teaching must be individual, and consequently fewer students can be taught by one teacher. **1970** *Oxf. Compan. Art* 960/2 Such sculpture is not properly relief carving (e.g. the figures of gods and giants on the Great Altar of Zeus at Pergamum). **1962** *Times* 28 Feb. 5/1 At the same gallery Mr. Michael Rothenstein shows a small collection of his new *relief-constructions. **1960** *Connoisseur's Handbk. Antique Coll.* 236/1 There are various ways of producing *relief decoration: by freehand modelling, free-incising or piercing or, more frequently, by pressing soft clay in plaster moulds. **1960** R. G. HAGGAR *Conc. Encycl. Cont. Pott. & Porc.* 380/1 *Relief decoration*, figures, flowers, and ornamental decoration formed in the mould, or moulded or modelled separately and luted to the ware with slip. **1876** *Nature* 11 May 23/1 *Relief-maps and Models illustrating Geological Phenomena all over the world. **1880** 'MARK TWAIN' *Tramp Abroad* xxxiii. 358 He showed us the whole thing on a relief map. **1934** J. BYGOTT *Introd. Map Work & Pract. Geogr.* vi. 43 After inspecting even a small-scale relief map of Northern England..we realise that the longest rivers flow from the eastern slopes towards the North Sea. **1971** R. W. PURTON *Let's look at Maps & Mapmaking* 16 It is possible to buy relief maps moulded in plastic, on which the physical features are raised as..on a model. [**1908** *Trade Marks Jrnl.* 4 Mar. 347 *Relief..Pens..Esterbrook Steel Pen Manufacturing Company..New York..21st November 1907.] **1920** A. HUXLEY *Limbo* 144 He selected a pen—with a Relief nib he would be able to go on for hours without getting tired—and a large square sheet of writing-paper. **1938** E. BOWEN *Death of Heart* II. iii. 214 Today..she made the following purchases... Half a dozen Relief nibs. **1960** *Twentieth Century* Oct. 343 The pen tray filled with compact sheaves of new relief nibs. **1937** *Burlington Mag.* Feb. 59/2 The *relief-panels of the Pisa pulpit. **1961** *Times* 21 Dec. 3/3 He makes relief-panels and sculpture from charred wood. **1884** KNIGHT *Dict. Mech.* Suppl. 749/2 Joyce's method of producing *relief-plates for printing. **1933** GREAVES & WRIGHTON *Pract. Microsc. Metallogr.* (ed. 2) xiv. 237 *Relief polish is obtained..so that micro-constituents are visible under the microscope. **1968** E. STACH in Murchison & Westoll *Coal & Coal-Bearing Strata* i. 4 Nowadays coals are normally relief-polished and then examined under vertically incident light using immersion objectives. **1902** C. SALTER tr. *H. F. V. Jüptner's Siderology* II. iii. 121 *Relief polishing shows up the hardest constituents, especially cementite, in relief. **1924** GREAVES & WRIGHTON *Pract. Microsc. Metallogr.* vi. 48 Both 'relief polishing' and 'polish attack' may be used to display the microstructure of steels containing cementite. **1839** URE *Dict. Arts* 1162 The protuberant or *relief portion of the die. **1875** tr. *Vogel's Chem. Light* xv. 245 *Relief-prints are much more like photographs than the light-prints. *Ibid.*, It appears that the *relief-printing gives the shades and dark parts better. **1889** *Cent. Dict.*, **Relief processes*, those processes in mechanical or 'process' engraving by which are produced plates or blocks with raised lines. **1940** *Chambers's Techn. Dict.* 713/2 *Relief process* (*Photog.*), any colour process using matrices. **1965** ZIGROSSER & GAEHDE *Guide Coll. Orig. Prints* iv. 53 *Relief processes*, a general term that includes woodcuts, wood engravings, linoleum cuts, [etc.]. **1850** LEITCH tr. *C. O. Müller's Anc. Art* §415 (ed. 2) 579 Larger compositions were introduced..on *relief-tablets.

re'liefer[1]. *rare*$^{-1}$. [f. RELIEF[2], 6 c + -ER[1].] = RELIEVER 1 c.

1798 ALEX STEWART in *Memoir* (1822) 124 Let Churchmen or Dissenters, Reliefers or Seceders be in the right or in the wrong, that can be no rule to us.

reliefer[2] (rɪˈliːfə(r)). [f. RELIEF[2] + -ER[1].] One who receives state relief (sense 3 a).

1936 *Harper's Mag.* Jan. 203/2 Reliefers don't of course live by themselves and form a compact group with relief as their only topic. **1938** *Sun* (Baltimore) 6 Sept. 8/4 Baltimore streets and alleys could do with a little attention from 'grateful reliefers'. **1947** *Ten Eventful Years* IV. 629/1 *Reliefer*, an unemployed person on federal government relief rolls. **1973** B. BROADFOOT *Ten Lost Years* xx. 225 No, we never thought of the poor people. The reliefers.

re'liefful, *a. rare*$^{-1}$. [f. RELIEF[2] + -FUL.] Giving or affording relief.

1748 RICHARDSON *Clarissa* (1768) V. 77 Never was there a more joyous heart..ready to burst its bars for relief-ful expression.

re'liefless, *a.* [f. as prec. + -LESS.] Devoid of relief.

c **1730** SAVAGE *Ep. Sir R. Walpole* 166 The tale pathetic speaks some wretch that owes To some deficient law reliefless woes. **1852** *Meanderings of Mem.* I. 23 Alone reliefless in thy cold distress. **1860** RUSKIN *Mod. Paint.* V. IX. ii. §18. 216 Hopeless, reliefless, eternal, the sorrow shall be met.

relier (rɪˈlaɪə(r)). *rare.* [f. RELY *v.*[1] + -ER[1].] One who relies (*on* a person or thing).

1593 SHAKS. *Lucr.* 639 To thee, to thee, my heau'd vp hands appeale, Not to seducing lust thy rash relier. *a* **1616** BEAUM. & FL. *Woman's Prize* I. iii, My friends [are] no reliers on my fortunes. **1665** J. SERGEANT *Sure Footing* 12 To give the reliers on them all the security [etc.].

relievable (rɪˈliːvəb(ə)l), *a.* [f. RELIEVE *v.*]

1. a. Capable of receiving, admitting of, legal relief; also const. *against.*

1670 *Modern Rep.* (1682) I. 304 A Father may settle his Estate; so as that the Issue shall be deprived of it for Disobedience, and not be relievable in Equity. **1768** BLACKSTONE *Comm.* III. 104 Neither can this court..hold plea of any such word, or thing, wherein the party is relievable by the courts of the common law. **1818** CRUISE *Digest* (ed. 2) IV. 502 If a woman about to marry, gives away a part of her property,..they are relievable against in Chancery. **1827** HALLAM *Const. Hist.* xiii. (1876) III. 22 An original complaint..relievable in the ordinary course of law.

b. That may be relieved or assisted.

1707 NORRIS *Treat. Humility* vi. 252 Being loth to be thought in a releivable condition. **1794–6** E. DARWIN *Zoon.* IV. 79 The maniacal idea is so painful as not to be for a moment relievable by the exertions of reverie. **1893** JOS. STRONG *New Era* xiii. 282 Relievable suffering, wrongs, violations of law, ignorance.

†**2.** Ready to give relief. *Obs. rare*$^{-1}$.

a **1693** AUBREY *Lives* (1898) I. 281 The poor were more relievable, that is, he recieved more kindnesse from them than from the rich.

†**re'lievant.** *Obs. rare*$^{-1}$. [f. as prec. + -ANT[1].] One who receives relief.

1587 in Arber *Eng. Garner* VIII. 345 First 100 Releevants, poor old women, for the most part widows.

relieve, *sb.*, obs. variant of RELIEF[2] and [3].

relieve (rɪˈliːv), *v.* Forms: 4–6 **releue, -leve,** (5 **-levy-e, -levyn,** *Sc.* **-lewe**), 4–7 **releeue, -leeve, -lieue,** (5 **-lyeve**), 6–7 **releiue, -ve,** 4– **relieve**; 5–6 **relyue, -ve,** 6–7 **reliue, -ve;** *Sc.* and *north.* 5 **relef(e, -leff(e, -leef(e,** 5–6 **releife,** 5–7 **releif,** (5 **-ff**), 6 **relyf;** 5 **raleiff,** 6 **-lef.** [ad. OF. *relever* (11th c.), ad. L. *relevāre* to raise again, assist, etc., f. *re-* RE- + *levāre* f. *levis* light (cf. RELEVATE and ELEVATE). The more etymological senses of the word are in Eng. somewhat later, and less usual, than the secondary.]

I. *trans.* **1. a.** To raise (a person) out of some trouble, difficulty, or danger; to rescue, succour, aid or assist in straits; to deliver *from* something troublesome or oppressive. Now somewhat *rare.*

13.. *E.E. Allit. P.* C. 323 Þou schal releue me renk, whil þy ryȝt slepez, þurȝ myȝt of þy mercy. **1377** LANGL. *P. Pl.* B. xv. 592 [The Jews] hopen þat he be to come þat shal hem releue. *c* **1430** LYDG. *Min. Poems* (Percy Soc.) 206 Releeve the porail fro fals oppressioun Of tyrannye. **1500–20** DUNBAR *Poems* xxii. 28 Ȝour legis quhy will ȝe nocht releif, And chereiss eftir thair degre? **1567** *Gude & Godlie B.* (S.T.S.) 113 God..sall releue All Israel of thair distres. **1601** SHAKS. *Twel. N.* III. iv. 395 This youth..I snatch'd one halfe out of the iawes of death, Releeu'd him with such sanctitie of loue. **1632** LITHGOW *Trav.* III. 100 Vpon the fourth day..there came Fisher-boates to relieue vs. **1719** WATERLAND *Vind. Christ's Div.* 195 You are straining hard for some odd, peculiar Sense of the word,..and if this does not relieve you, all is lost. **1813** BYRON *Giaour* viii, The rock relieves him from mine eye. **1836** J. GILBERT *Chr. Atonem.* viii. (1852) 228 No ingenuity, how subtle so ever, can relieve the case from the difficulty. **1841** ELPHINSTONE *Hist. Ind.* II. 131 Who had called in the aid of the king of that country to relieve him from the control of Shir Khán.

absol. *c* **1366** CHAUCER *A.B.C.* 6 Help and releeue, þou mihti debonayre. **1677** OWEN *On Justif.* ix. Wks. 1851 V. 222 It is said that this [argument] will not relieve; for [etc.].

†**b.** To assist or succour in battle. *Obs.*

1375 BARBOUR *Bruce* XI. 347 The kyng, that behynd thaim was, Suld..relief thaim with his baneir. *c* **1400** *Destr. Troy* 9737 Mayntene youre manhode & your men helpe, Faris into fight your folke to releue. *c* **1500** *Lancelot* 3200 Wondir well thai have in armys prewit, And with thar manhed oft thar folk relewit. **1640** tr. *Verdere's Rom. of Rom.* I. 85 [They] could not relive them, being too far engaged in their combat.

c. To bring assistance to (a besieged town, etc.); to free from siege. (Cf. RELIEF *sb.*[2] 4 b.)

1586 EARL LEICESTER *Corr.* (Camden) 259 If he take it [Berges] not in 2 dayes..I will warrant we will relue it well enough. **1617** MORYSON *Itin.* II. 148 The Spaniards attempted againe to relieue the Castle. *a* **1671** LD. FAIRFAX *Mem.* (1699) 82 Soon after Prince Rupert came to relieve the Town We raised the siege. **1781** GIBBON *Decl. & F.* xxxi. III. 259 Arles..must have yielded to the assailants, had not the city been unexpectedly relieved by the approach of an Italian army. **1855** MACAULAY *Hist. Eng.* xii. III. 228 Kirke had arrived from England with troops, arms. ammunition, and provisions, to relieve the city. **1874** GREEN *Short Hist.* v. §1. 221 It was not till Philip had failed to relieve it that the town was starved into surrender.

d. *Law.* To free or clear (one) from an obligation; to give (one) legal relief. Also *absol.*

1562 *Reg. Privy Council Scot.* I. 221 The said William Gordoun [shall be] oblist to releve his said souerte. **1616** in Cary *Rep. Chancery* (1650) 134 Where their case deserveth to be relieved in course of Equity by suit in our Court of Chancery, they should not be abandoned. **1670** *Modern Rep.* (1682) I. 305 You relieve against them, and look upon them to be void. *Ibid.* 306 What if two of the Trustees had died, should she never have married? Surely you would have relieved her. **1838** W. BELL *Dict. Law Scot.* 845 If one of two co-obligants..pay the whole debt, he is entitled to be relieved to the extent of the other's share. *Ibid.*, The obligation to relieve holds in those cases [etc.].

refl. **1655** tr. *Sorel's Com. Hist. Francion* VIII. 28, I will obtain therefore Letters Patents sealed with the great Seal to relieve my self, because I have consented to give six Souses for that which is worth but four.

2. a. To assist (the poor or needy) by gifts of money or necessary articles; to help in poverty or necessity. (Cf. RELIEF[2] 3.)

c **1375** *Sc. Leg. Saints* vi. (*Thomas*) 224 Þe apostile..vith þat tresoure he had tane, pouer men relewit mony ane. *c* **1450** *Knt. de la Tour* (1868) 136 Alle suche pepille..she releued and comforted with almesse. **1491** *Act 7 Hen. VII*, c. 22 *Preamble*, Suche as have no goodes they may comme heder and be releved. **1586** EARL LEICESTER *Corr.* (Camden) 378 He hath had 4,000 florins in monie of me, beside other helps, and, as I am able, I will reliue him. **1653** HOLCROFT *Procopius, Goth. Wars* I. 30 There being no means to releive them; Belisarius..appointed them a daily pay. **1690** CHILD *Disc. Trade* 73 The Poor..will be immediately relieved or set on work where they are found. **1737** POPE *Hor. Epist.* II. i. 226 Behold the hand that wrought a Nation's cure, Stretch'd to relieve the Idiot and the Poor. **1795** *Act 36 Geo. III*, c. 23 §4 All such..Poor..Persons shall be provided for and relieved in..the same Manner as before the..passing of this Act. **1864** *Spectator* 31 Dec. 1489 Lord Wharncliffe's proposal to relieve the Confederate prisoners in the Northern prisons.

absol. **1732** POPE *Ep. Bathurst* 269 Is any sick? the Man of Ross relieves. **1813** SHELLEY *Q. Mab* III. 159 Withered [is] the hand outstretched but to relieve.

fig. *c* **1385** CHAUCER *L.G.W.* Prol. 128 Now hadde the tempre sonne al that releuyd And clothed hym in grene al newe a-geyn.

†**b.** To assist *with* provisions or munitions of war; to furnish *with* fresh troops. Also, to renew the stock of (ammunition). *Obs.*

1375 BARBOUR *Bruce* IV. 456 On this wiss Iames of Douglas,..War weill releyit [*v.r.* relewyt] with armyng, With vittale als, and with clething. **1560** DAUS tr. *Sleidane's Comm.* 255 That he geueth them free and safe recourse throughe hys countrey, and releeue them with victualles. **1568** GRAFTON *Chron.* II. 366 All the Hauens and Portes..were relieued wyth men of armes and archers. **1588** SIR J. HAWKINS in Laughton *Def. Sp. Armada* (1894) I. 359 We spent a great part of our powder and shot, so as it was not thought good to deal with them any more till that was relieved.

refl. **1601** in T. Stafford *Pac. Hib.* II. iv. 150 The Rebels..doe releeue themselves with such warlicke provisions as they need.

†**c.** To provide or furnish *with* something. *Obs.*$^{-1}$

c **1375** *Sc. Leg. Saints* xl. (*Ninian*) 161 He can hym ma bischope with his handis twa..& with relykis cane hym releife.

†**d.** To feed; to supply with food or nourishment. *Obs.*

c **1410** *Master of Game* (MS. Digby 182) i, In the euetyde when thei be releued; in the moruetyde when thei sitte in forme. *c* **1420** *Pallad. on Husb.* XII. 375 Til the lamb be strengthed to pasture, Hym first and last his modir mylk releue. **1590** COKAINE *Treat. Hunting* C ij, Your Hunts-man ..must be very careful that if any of his hounds bee missing, he keepe somewhat to relieue them withall. **1614** RALEIGH *Hist. World* II. (1634) 222 They reserved them, both for the milke to releeve the children withall, and for breed to store themselves.

†**e.** *intr.* Of a hare: To feed. *Obs. rare*$^{-1}$.

1575 TURBERV. *Venerie* 168 An Hare hath greater sent.. when she feedeth and relieueth vpon greene corne, then at any other time of the yere.

3. a. To ease or free (a person, the mind, etc.) from sorrow, fear, doubt, or other source of mental discomfort.

c 1374 CHAUCER *Troylus* v. 1042 And eek, the bet from sorwe him to releve, She made him were a pencel of hir sleve. 1390 GOWER *Conf.* I. 45 Bot so was I nothing relieved, For I was further fro my love. 15.. *Frutefull Treatyse* title-p., Howe they are to be releued and comforted, whose deare frendes ar departed out of thys worlde. 1568 GRAFTON *Chron.* II. 714 King Edward..was releeued of the most part, of his pricking feare, and inwarde suspicion. 1610 SHAKS. *Temp.* Epil. 16 My ending is despaire, Vnlesse I be relieu'd by praier. 1671 MILTON *Samson* 460 This only hope relieves me, that the strife With me hath end. 1746 WESLEY *Princ. Methodist* 50 To think or say, 'There are Demoniacks now, and they are now reliev'd by Prayer', is Enthusiasm. 1801 *Lusignan* IV. 110 Relieve me, I conjure you, from this cruel incertitude! 1847 PRESCOTT *Peru* (1850) II. 336 There was one..who relieved his bosom by revealing the whole plot to his confessor. 1860 TYNDALL *Glac.* II. xxvii. 390 Proofs which should relieve my mind of all doubt upon the subject.

b. To give (a person, part of the body, etc.) ease or relief from physical pain or discomfort. Also *refl.*, to defecate or urinate, and *fig.*

c 1375 *Sc. Leg. Saints* xxxviii. (*Adrian*) 115 þe tyme cumis ..quhene nane sal vthir relefe,..as for to les þame of þar payne. 1548–9 (Mar.) *Bk. Com. Prayer, Visitation of Sick* 141 O Lorde..beholde, visite, and releue this thy seruaunte. 1562 TURNER *Herbal* II. 108 Peares..rosted or sodden, relefe and lighten the stomak. 1595 SHAKS. *John* v. vii. 45 O, that there were some vertue in my teares, That might releeue you! 1746 HERVEY *Medit.* (1818) 80 As a spacious field arrayed in cheerful green, relieves and re-invigorates the eye. 1842 A. COMBE *Physiol. Digestion* (ed. 4) 368 Where ..the bowels are unable to act sufficiently to relieve the system. 1857 BUCKLE *Civiliz.* I. xiv. 825 It is even possible to relieve a function while we continue to employ it. 1931 S. TREMAYNE *Trial A. A. Rouse* 184, I wanted to relieve myself. 1952 BIBLE (Rev. Standard Version) *I Sam.* xxiv. 3 And he came to the sheepfolds by the way, where there was a cave; and Saul went in to relieve himself. 1956 H. GOLD *Man who was not with It* (1965) xii. 99 There's a stomach ache of music..; it churns and stretches, trying to relieve itself. 1960 V. NABOKOV *Invitation to Beheading* xiv. 141 The bliss of relieving oneself, which some hold to be on a par with the pleasure of love. 1961 *Encounter* Feb. 25/1 It [*sc.* a kitten] learned to go down into the alley to relieve itself in the dirt there. 1977 *Sunday Times* 30 Jan. 30/3, I urgently wished to be alone to relieve myself (a serious problem in winter orienteering).

c. To widen or open up; to ease (some mechanical device) by making slacker or wider.

1824 COL. HAWKER *Shooting* (ed. 3) 8 There are two good ways of boring; the one is, to form a cylinder for about three-fourths of the barrel, and let the remaining part be gradually relieved to the muzzle. 1846 HOLTZAPFFEL *Turning* II. 586 The principle of chamfering, or relieving the taps, must not ..be carried to excess.

4. a. To ease or mitigate (what is painful or oppressive); to render less grievous or burdensome.

c 1420 LYDG. *Assembly of Gods* 13 So leyde I me downe my dyssese to releue. c 1500 *Lancelot* 3364 Al perell, al harmys, and myschef, In tyme of ned he can tham al relef. 1567 *Satir. Poems Reform.* vi. 114 Set your cure For till relief the greit penuritie Off laubouraris. 1601 SHAKS. *Twel. N.* II. iv. 4 That old and anticke song we heard last night, Me thought it did releeue my passion much. 1630 BRATHWAIT *Eng. Gentlem.* 149 Would you further the poore mans cause, and see his wrongs releeved? 1660 BLOUNT *Boscobel* II. (1680) 32 Glad to releive the necessities of nature with a messe of milk. 1729 BUTLER *Serm.* Wks. 1874 II. 70 The final cause of compassion is much more to relieve misery. 1788 GIBBON *Decl. & F.* l. V. 197 A wealthy and generous citizen, who relieved the distress of famine. 1843 R. J. GRAVES *Syst. Clin. Med.* xx. 234 Chronic cough and long-continued congestion ..were more effectually relieved by the use of sulphureous waters. a 1862 BUCKLE *Civiliz.* (1873) III. v. 308 To relieve poverty increases it, by encouraging improvidence.

b. To make less tiring, tedious, monotonous, or disagreeable, by the introduction of variety or of something striking or pleasing.

1771 *Junius Lett.* xlix. (1788) 269, I mean now and then to relieve the severity of your morning studies. 1782 G. STUART *Hist. Scot.* vi. II. 211 He relieved..the cares of ambition with the smiles of beauty. 1817 COLERIDGE *Biog. Lit.* (Bohn) 282 The ingredients too are mixed in the happiest proportion, so as to uphold and relieve each other. 1837 DISRAELI *Venetia* I. vi, Large black eyes which.. agreeably relieved a face..somewhat shy and sullen. 1869 J. MARTINEAU *Ess.* II. 303 No great work relieved the barrenness of the time.

5. a. Chiefly *Sc.* To set free, release. Now *rare.*

1554–9 *Songs & Ball. Phil. & Mary* (Roxb.) 3 The rawnsom for ower synns, wherby we ware relyfft. 1572 MORTON in *3rd Rep. Hist. MSS. Comm.* 418/2 The Maister of Forbes..is sa straitlie deteneit captive as upoun na band can he be gottin relevit. a 1657 SIR W. MURE *Sonn.* iv, I expected grace, To snair myselfe in hope to be relíued. 1684 WOOD *Life* (O.H.S.) III. 103 Mr. Sheldon, who would.. releive severall of his books that were then pawned for ale. 1774 MACLAURIN *Argt. & Decis. Remark. Cases* 33 A tuilzie or *rixa*, in which they mixed themselves to relieve a youth in the defunct's grips. 1815 BURNEY *Falconer's Dict. Marine* s.v. *Reliever*, It is used, on searching a gun, to relieve one or other of the springs of the searcher that may have hitched into the cavity.

b. *spec.* To release (one) from guard, watch, or other duty by becoming or providing a substitute.

1601 HOLLAND *Pliny* I. 427 How late soever he sat up.. overnight, he would be sure to relieve the morning watch & sentinell. 1684 tr. *Siege Luxembourg* 9 The Besieged (at the time we went to releive the Trenches) set Fire to the Houses. 1743 BULKELEY & CUMMINS *Voy. S. Seas* 10 At Six, being reliev'd by the Master, he could not see the Commodore's Light. 1823 F. CLISSOLD *Ascent Mt. Blanc* 20 A most laborious employment, in which the guides relieved each other every ten minutes. 1852 THACKERAY *Esmond* I. iv, Her dependants one after another relieved guard..and took the cards turn about. 1856 READE *Never too Late* xi, In an hour another turnkey came and relieved Hodges.

absol. 1788 J. MAY *Jrnl. & Lett.* (1873) 96 In rowing we relieved regularly and frequently.

c. To set (one) free *from*, to ease (one) *of*, any task or burden. Also, *euphem.*, to dismiss *from* a position, to deprive *of* membership.

1671 MILTON *Samson* 5 When any chance Relieves me from my task of servile toyl. 1838 DICKENS *Nich. Nick.* xxii, Let me relieve you of that bundle. 1844 H. H. WILSON *Brit. India* I. 295 General Sir Samuel Auchmuty relieved General Hewett from his duty. 1875 'MARK TWAIN' in *Atlantic Monthly* June 733/1 He was 'relieved' from duty when the boat got to New Orleans. Somebody expressed surprise at the discharge. 1952 E. O'NEILL *Moon for Misbegotten* III. 111 He relieves her of the pitcher and tumblers as she comes down the steps. 1972 *Newsweek* 10 Jan. 11/3 Its present chief..has expelled some 3,000 members (Lascorz was relieved of his membership during a previous clean-up in 1969).

d. To replace (a dish) by another. *rare.*

1741 tr. *D'Argens' Chinese Lett.* xxv. 183 These Dishes are relieved by others, twenty or twenty-four times. 1824 BYRON *Juan* xv. lxiii, Relieved with 'dindon à la Parigeux'.

II. †6. a. To lift or raise up again. *Obs.*

1377 LANGL. *P. Pl.* B. XVIII. 141 And þat deth doun brouȝt deth shal releue. c 1450 *Merlin* 214 Whan the saisnes saugh Sonygreux at erthe, thei..pressed to releve the kynge Sonygreux. c 1477 CAXTON *Jason* 124 The king Eson.. releued her and leyde her on a bed that was there. a 1533 LD. BERNERS *Huon* xx. 56 He knelyd downe..but Huon releuyd hym incontynent. 1575 *Chr. Prayers* in *Priv. Prayers* (1851) 441 Adam, being tumbled down..into the dungeon of shame, was releved and lift up again by thy hand, O Saviour. 1610 SHAKS. *Temp.* II. i. 121 Th' shore, that ore his waue-worne basis bowed As stooping to releeue him.

refl. c 1530 LD. BERNERS *Arth. Lyt. Bryt.* 136 Whan he had thought to have releved him selfe agayne out of the water. a 1533 —— *Huon* xvi. 42 Than venturously they releuyd them with ther swordys in ther handys, & so aprochyd eche to other.

†b. To restore, bring back *into* a state. *Obs.*$^{-1}$

1483 CAXTON *Gold. Leg.* 434 b/2 Alle vi were there by the merites of saynt aulbyn releuyd into their good helthe.

†c. To set up or erect again. *Obs. rare*$^{-1}$.

1464 *Rolls of Parlt.* V. 569/2 He that releeved any such nusaunce and were thereof attaynted, shuld renne in the payne of a c Marc.

†d. *refl.* To essay, presume. *Obs. rare*$^{-1}$.

1390 GOWER *Conf.* II. 215 What man that wole himself relieve To love in eny other wise, He shal wel finde [etc.].

†7. *intr.* **a.** To rise again. Also in *pass.*, to have risen from childbed. *Obs.*

1393 LANGL. *P. Pl.* C. XXII. 161 Thus cam hit out þat crist ouer-cam rekeouered and lyuede [*v.r.* releuede]. a 1450 *Knt. de la Tour* (1868) 125 Bi the praier of the said holy man the child resuscited and releued ayen from dethe to lyffe. c 1450 *Merlin* 397 He ouer-threwe hym a-gein..and at eche tyme that he didde releve, he smote him with his swerde to grounde. c 1500 *Melusine* 103 Whan the lady had ended the terme of her childbed, and that she was releuyd. a 1533 LD. BERNERS *Gold. Bk. M. Aurel.* (1546) C vj, Yf by fortune he falle, he wyll neuer releue agayne.

†b. To return or rally in battle (cf. RELY *v.*[1] 3 a and 3 b). Const. *on, upon, to. Obs.*

c 1400 *Sowdone Bab.* 329 Wenynge it hade be Sauarye, Relevinge fro the hethen stour. c 1400 *Rowland & O.* 1081 Appon hym also relevede a sarazene wighte. c 1450 HOLLAND *Howlat* 523 Feile of the fals folk, that fled of befor, Relevit in on thir twa. 1470–85 MALORY *Arthur* XVIII. xxiv. 769 The knyghtes of the round table releued euer vnto kynge Arthur. 1513 DOUGLAS *Æneis* XI. xiv. 16 Thai that drevyn war abak and chaste Relevis agane to the bargane in haist.

†c. To return *to* a previous state. *Obs. rare*$^{-1}$.

a 1550 *Treat. Galaunt* 219 in Hazl. *E.P.P.* III. 160 O Englonde, remembre thyne olde sadnes; Exyle pryde, and relyeve to thy goodnes.

†8. *trans.* **a.** To take up or hold (a feudal estate) from the superior (cf. RELIEF[2] 1). *Obs.*

c 1489 CAXTON *Blanchardyn* li. 196 The barons of the lande made their homage vnto sadoyne, and toke and releued their lordshippes of hym. 1523 LD. BERNERS *Froiss.* I. 91 He had relyved the duchy of another lorde than of the Frenche kynge, of whom he ought to holde it.

absol. 1525 LD. BERNERS *Froiss.* II. 589 The prince of Wales said to the erle of Foiz that last dyed, that he ought to releve of him.

†b. To recover, regain. *Obs. rare*$^{-1}$.

1596 DALRYMPLE tr. *Leslie's Hist. Scot.* II. 168 Nocht onlie to releiue quhat thair he had loste, bot to subdue quhat was nocht ȝit subduet.

III. †9. To bring (a matter) into prominence; to make clear or evident. *Obs. rare.*

1533 BELLENDEN *Livy* II. i. (S.T.S.) I. 131 For þir ressouns he was constrenit to releve [*v.r.* Reveill] þe mater, quhilk he wald neuer haue done [etc.]. 1566 LETHINGTON in Burnet *Hist. Ref.* (1679) I. Rec. III. 269 An Instrument to relieve the Truth, and to confound false Surmises.

†10. To raise up, make higher. *Obs. rare.*

1661 MORGAN *Sph. Gentry* III. v. 45 The adorning of the Helmet with Crest or Cognizance..being releived and raised up to be known in fight.

11. a. To make (a thing) stand out; to render prominent or distinct; to bring into relief. Also *fig.*

1778 SIR J. REYNOLDS *Disc.* viii. (1876) 485 To Ariadne is given (say the critics) a red scarf, to relieve the figure from the sea which is behind her. a 1797 H. WALPOLE *Mem. Geo. II* (1822) I. 420 The letter..did not want its faults, but he knew not how to relieve them; his awkward acrimony defeated his own purpose. 1838 PRESCOTT *Ferd. & Is.* (1846) I. viii. 372 The style of poetry..must be raised or relieved, as it were, upon the prevailing style of social intercourse. 1851 RUSKIN *Stones Ven.* (1874) I. Pref. 6 The twilight relieving in purple masses the foliage on the Island. 1875 SWINBURNE *Ess. Chapman* 27 To relieve against the broad mass..of outer life the solitary process of that inward.. tragedy.

b. *intr.* To stand out in relief.

1812 *Examiner* 25 May 328/1 Brilliant lights relieving from a large proportion of half tints. 1883 *Harper's Mag.* Aug. 401/1 Relieving dark against their white walls were lines of troops.

Hence **re'lieved** *ppl. a.*

1824 COL. HAWKER *Shooting* (ed. 3) 9 This has not the effect of throwing the shot quite so close as the relieved cylinder. 1869 *Spectator* 26 Jan., If the relieved man earns his relief, he will spend it as well as he does his wages. 1874 H. GARDENER *Unoff. Patriot* 276 One of the relieved pickets.

re'lievedly, *adv.* [f. RELIEVED *ppl. a.* + -LY[2].] In a relieved manner, with relief from anxiety.

1911 R. BROOKE *Let.* 22 Dec. (1968) 327, I rather grasp relievedly at them, after I've beaten vain hands in the rosy mists of poets' experiences. 1925 *Glasgow Herald* 1 Aug. 6/3 The country relievedly witnesses the passing of the crisis. 1951 M. LEINSTER in D. Knight *100 Yrs. Sci. Fiction* (1969) 200 Sometimes he was able to thrust aside..the fact that Jane was dead. Now he grappled relievedly with the question of his sanity or lunacy.

†re'lievement. *Obs.* Also 5–6 releue-, 7 releeue-. [a. OF. *releve-, relievement*, f. *relever* to RELIEVE.] The act of relieving; relief.

1443 *Wars Eng. in France* (Rolls) I. 435 We graunted unto oure saide cousin, in relievement of him..the gavel of ij. m[l]. mewes of salt. 1490 CAXTON *Eneydos* xxix. 113 The falle well vnderstande, well assoylled & deffended may welle haue releuement. 1583 STOCKER *Civ. Warres Lowe C.* IV. 44 All Exceptions, Graces, Priuiledges, Releuements, and generally all other benefites of Lawes. 1613–18 DANIEL *Coll. Hist. Eng.* (1626) 44 To purchase [the Crown]..by large conditions of releeuements in generall, and profuse gifts in particular. 1631 WEEVER *Anc. Funeral Mon.* 278 Hee kept his word with the State, concerning the relieuement of Tributes.

reliever (rɪˈliːvə(r)). Also 6 -or. [f. RELIEVE *v.*]

1. a. One who relieves, in senses of the verb.

1485 CAXTON *Chas. Gt.* 240 Defendour of crysten men.., Releuer of chyrches. 1589 WARNER *Alb. Eng.* Prose Add. (1602) 336 If we should proue so vngratefull as to resist our Relieuors. 1633 T. STAFFORD *Pac. Hib.* II. iii. (1821) 243 It grieved him that the Lord President should suspect him to bee a Releever of James fits-Thomas. 1670 DRYDEN *1st Pt. Conq. Granada* II. i, If there appear relievers from the field, The flag of parley may be taken down. 1776 ADAM SMITH *W.N.* v. i. III. iii. II. 395 The comforters of their distress, and the relievers of their indigence. 1865 DICKENS *Mut. Fr.* IV. vii, Borrowing an hour or so, to be repaid again when he should relieve his reliever.

†b. Among the Brownists, a deacon appointed to administer relief to the poor. *Obs.*

1582 BROWNE *Booke which Sheweth* Def. 54 The Releeuers or Deacons, which are to gather and bestowe the church liberalitie. *Ibid.*, The Releeuer is a person hauing office of God to prouide, gather, and bestowe the giftes and liberalitie of the church, as there is neede. 1610 BP. HALL *Apol. against Brownists* §20 Is there no remedie but you must needs haue such Elders, Pastors, Doctors, Releeuers ..?

c. A member of the Relief Church.

1895 *British Weekly* 7 Feb. 258/1 In this life of yesterday the seceders and 'relievers' were great, though plain. 1897 H. CALDERWOOD in *Mem. Jubilee Synod U.P. Church* 100 Seceders were soon followed by Relievers, and organised Churches grew up.

d. *N. Amer.* A pitcher who relieves the opening pitcher in a baseball match.

1967 *Boston Herald* 8 May 16/2 Fregosi homered in the fifth..off reliever Bob Humphreys. 1976 *Washington Post* 19 Apr. D1/4 Los Angeles chased reliever Roger Moret in the seventh with a five-run explosion. 1979 *Arizona Daily Star* 5 Aug. C2/2 Craig Swan combined with reliever Neil Allen on an eight-hitter as New York stopped Montreal's five-game winning streak.

2. †a. An instrument consisting of an iron ring fixed at right angles to a handle, used in gun testing to release the searcher when fixed. *Obs.*

1800 *Naval Chron.* IV. 54 Take a searcher with one prong, and a reliever. 1802 JAMES *Milit. Dict.*

b. A device to ease the working of a lock.

1801 *Trans. Soc. Arts* XIX. 291 The reliever works so very easy, that the door is made fast.

c. A device for attaching the wire stays of a yacht to the hull in such a way as to lessen the strain on them. (Knight *Dict. Mech.* Suppl. 1884.)

3. *slang.* (See quot.)

1850 KINGSLEY *Cheap Clothes* 11 In some sweating places there is an old coat kept called a 'reliever', and this is borrowed by such men as have none of their own to go out in.

Hence **re'lieveress.** *rare*$^{-1}$.

1631 *Celestina* xi. 127 Thou ease of my passions, thou relieveresse of my paine.

re'lieving, *vbl. sb.* [f. as prec. + -ING[1].] The action of the vb. RELIEVE, in various senses.

a. *trans.* c 1380 WYCLIF *Wks.* (1880) 279 þat þe wast tresour..be wisly spendid in defence of þe rewme, & releuynge of þe pore comouns. 1482 *Monk of Evesham* (Arb.) 91 Sche seyde also that sche hathe resceuyd mekyl releuyng and helpe of her peynys. 1551 GARDINER *Presence in Sacrament* 14 The auctor vttereth a great meny wordes.. declaryng spirituall hungre and thurst, and the releuyng of the same. 1633 P. FLETCHER *Elisa* II. x, To losses old new losse is no relieving. 1724 DE FOE *Mem. Cavalier* (1840) 209 This relieving of Gloucester raised the spirits..of the parliament forces. 1822 *Regul. & Ord. Army* 31 When

General Officers . . pass Guards while in the act of relieving, both Guards are to salute.

b. *intr.* *c* **1530** LD. BERNERS *Arth. Lyt. Bryt.* 424 He fel on his hors necke; and, in the relevynge, he strake at Hector.

re'lieving, *ppl. a.* [f. as prec. + -ING².]

1. That relieves or gives relief.

1681 FLAVEL *Meth. Grace* xv. 291 In him the relieving promises are made to believers. **1788** JOB SCOTT *Jrnl.* (1797) viii. 258 The meeting continued for some considerable time longer, in a very open and relieving manner. **1822–34** *Good's Study Med.* (ed. 4) I. 166 Relieving sweats break forth, sometimes accompanied with an efflorescence. **1897** SIR E. WOOD *Achievements of Cavalry* i. 14 A relieving force coming out, the 'Rally' was sounded.

2. a. ***relieving officer***, an officer appointed by a parish or union to administer relief to the poor.

1836 *Falmouth Pkt.* 23 Sept. 5/2 Application for relief is made to the relieving officer. **1841** *Punch* 23 Oct. 170/2 The family . . told me they were literally dying of hunger, and that they had applied to the vestry, who had referred them to the . . relieving officer. **1850** C. KINGSLEY *Alton Locke* II. xiv. 210 In the midst of all the rout, the relieving officer stood impassive, jotting down scraps of information. **1851** MAYHEW *Lond. Labour* II. 249/2 The relieving officer . . would have given him a pair of shoes and half-a-crown. **1876** *Act 39 & 40 Vict.* c. 61 §19 A . . warrant . . may be issued upon the information of any relieving officer of the guardians stating that relief has been applied for. **1980** G. M. FRASER *Mr American* ix. 167 She has an order for medical attendance from the relieving officer.

fig. **1865** DICKENS *Mut. Fr.* III. viii, She heard the tender river whispering, . . 'I am the Relieving Officer appointed by eternal ordinance to do my work'.

b. *slang.* (See quot. 1881.)

1857 G. LAWRENCE *Guy Liv.* iii, Every one, drawn on by the current, had a stone to throw at his relieving officer. **1881** BLACKMORE *Christowell* xliv, The relieving officer—as the male parent was called in those days at our great universities.

3. *techn.* **a.** ***relieving tackle***: (See quots.).

1769 FALCONER *Dict. Marine* (1780), *Relieving-tackles*, two strong tackles used to prevent a ship from overturning on the careen, and to assist in bringing her upright after that operation is completed... *Relieving-tackle*, is also a name sometimes given to the train-tackles of a gun-carriage. **1815** BURNEY *Falconer's Dict. Marine, Relieving tackles*, are those which are occasionally hooked to the tiller . . in bad weather, or in action, when . . the wheel or tiller-rope is broken or shot away. **1840** R. H. DANA *Bef. Mast* xxv. 84 Once the wheel-rope parted, which might have been fatal to us, had not the chief mate sprung instantly with a relieving tackle to windward, and kept the tiller up till a new one could be rove. **1882** NARES *Seamanship* (ed. 6) 222 The relieving tackles are fitted as luff tackles.

b. ***relieving arch***: (See quots.).

1850 PARKER *Gloss. Archit.* (ed. 5) I. 166 *Relieving Arch*, or Arch of Construction; an arch formed in the substance of a wall to relieve the part which is below it from the superincumbent weight. **1875** KNIGHT *Dict. Mech.* 1916/1 *Relieving-arch*, an arch at the back of a revetment or retaining wall, to relieve the pressure of the bank upon the wall, and act as a tie or interior buttress. **1883** CONDER & KITCHENER *Survey W. Palestine* III. 133 The door of the crypt has a lintel, with a relieving arch above.

Hence **re'lievingly** *adv.*

1793 JOB SCOTT *Jrnl.* (1797) xi. 309 He that speaks . . must feel a door of entrance in the people's minds, or it is very difficult to get safely and relievingly forward. **1858** *Chamb. Jrnl.* IX. 354 Sybil soon relievingly interposed that it was time to dress.

relievo¹ (rɪˈliːvəʊ). Also 7 releuo, 8 releivo, 8–9 rilievo. [ad. It. *rilievo* (riliˈevo): see RELIEF³, and cf. ALTO-, BASSO-, MEZZO-RELIEVO.]

1. = RELIEF³ 1.

1625 SIR T. ROE in *Michaelis' Anc. Marbles* (1882) 189 Twelue tables of fine marble, cutt into historyes, some of a very great releuo. **1641** EVELYN *Diary* 1 Sept., Several rusticall instruments so artificially represented as to deceive an accurate eye, to distinguish it from actual relievo. **1723** CHAMBERS tr. *Le Clerc's Treat. Archit.* I. 79 The Foliages and other Ornaments . . by their Relievo seem to increase its bigness.

transf. **1704** SWIFT *T. Tub* viii, The wind and vapours issuing forth . . distorted the mouth, bloated the cheeks, and gave the eyes a terrible kind of relievo. **1796** W. TAYLOR in *Monthly Rev.* XXI. 491 The comic features have more relievo, than most other productions of the author.

b. ***in relievo***, in relief.

1665 *Phil. Trans.* I. 99 A new kind of Maps in a low Relievo. **1703** MAUNDRELL *Journ. Jerus.* (1721) 137 On that part . . are to be seen Carvings in Relievo. **1789** E. DARWIN *Bot. Garden* II. ii. 177 Round the white circlet in relievo bold A serpent twines his scaly length in gold. **1832** G. R. PORTER *Porcelain & Gl.* 111 In works where different objects appear in relievo, these are made separately. **1847** SMEATON *Builder's Man.* 213 The walls are covered with gigantic figures sculptured in relievo.

transf. **1769** BURKE *Late St. Nation* 60 Two of them stand out in high relievo beyond the rest. The first is a change in the internal representation of this country.

2. = RELIEF³ 1 b.

1627 SIR T. ROE in *Michaelis' Anc. Marbles* (1882) 200 My agent . . hath brought me . . some heads and small releuo's, antient and good worke. **1731** *Gentl. Mag.* I. 499 In one of which [grottos] they found 40 Urns cover'd with Relievos. **1753** HANWAY *Trav.* (1762) I. VII. xcv. 440 The ornaments of the architecture, and the relievo in the frontispiece, are after the chinese and japan manner. **1845** FORD *Handbk. Spain* I. 475/2 Her chapel is very rich in red marbles, Corinthian pillars, and poor sculptured relievos of her history.

3. *Painting.* = RELIEF³ 2.

1685 AGLIONBY *Painting Illustr.* i. 19 To give that Roundness to the Figures, which the Italians call Relievo, and for which we have no other Name. **1738** R. SMITH *Opticks* Pref. 5 The effect of a large concave speculum in heightening the Relievo of Pictures. **1784** J. BARRY in *Lect. Paint.* vi. (1848) 225 The style which Titian afterwards adopted . . was not of so high a relish for relievo and hue.

relievo² (rɪˈliːvəʊ). Also **relievio**. [prob. f. RELIEVE *v.* + -O².] A children's seeking game in which a captured player may be released by another member of his or her side; the call effecting the release.

1888 S. O. ADDY *Gloss. Words Sheffield* 296 *Bedlams* or *relievo*, a game played by boys. *Ibid.* 297 If . . one of the boys out at field runs through the *den* shouting '*Relievo*', without being caught by the *tenter*, the prisoner is allowed to escape. **1912** J. STEPHENS *Crock of Gold* v. 39 'It's a nice game,' said the Leprechaun, 'and so is Cap-on-the-back, and . . Relievo, and Leap-frog.' **1913** —— *Here are Ladies* 261 Tip-and-Tig, Horneys and Robbers, Relievo we played. **1969** I. & P. OPIE *Children's Games* ii. 110 Names which reflect the rescue element are: 'Release', 'Releaster', 'Reliev-i-o', 'Tig and Relievo', [etc.]. *Ibid.* iv. 172 In Scotland, Wales, and the northern half of England, 'Relievo' is the principal seeking game with two sides. *Ibid.* 173 Commonly it is enough for the 'releaser' to shout 'Relievo' or 'Rallio' or perhaps 'Bish-Bash' as he rushes through the den. **1970** *Daily Colonist* (Victoria, B.C.) 19 Aug. 2/1 Summer streets full of youngsters playing Hoist The Sails, Relievo or Giant Step. **1974** *Amer. Speech 1971* XLVI. 83 Line and running games: crack-the-whip, fly-the-whip, follow-the-leader, leap frog, redman, red rover, rolla-rolla, relievio, [etc.].

relif, obs. form of RELIEF¹ and ².

re'lift (riː-), *v.* [RE- 5 a.] *trans.* To lift again. Hence **re'lifting** *vbl. sb.*

1844 H. STEPHENS *Bk. Farm* I. 510 The relifting of a drain that has blown . . is a dirty and disagreeable business for work-people. **1898** T. HARDY *Wessex Poems* 134 The passion . . Her death-rumour smartly relifted To full apogee. **1904** H. BELLOC *Avril* 111 105 The repose and the relifting of musical notes.

'religate, *v. rare.* [f. L. *religāt-*, ppl. stem of *religāre* to bind up or back: see RE- and LIGATE *v.*] *trans.* †**a.** *Surg.* To bind up (a vein). *Obs.*⁻¹ **b.** To bind together or unite (people). **c.** To constrain. Also *absol.* Hence **'religating** *ppl. a.*

1597 A. M. tr. *Guillemeau's Fr. Chirurg.* 17 b/2 The needle wherwith we may stitch, when we desire to religate a Vayne. **1651** C. CARTWRIGHT *Cert. Relig.* I. 36 They are not religated within the same Communion. **1656** BLOUNT *Glossogr., Religate*, to tye hard or again, to binde fast. **1807** COLERIDGE in Cottle *Early Recoll.* (1837) II. 84 It is not even religion, it does not religate, does not bind anew. **1876** GLADSTONE *Gleanings* (1879) III. 130 Religion . . , with a debased worship appended to it, . . but with no religating, no binding power.

religate, obs. form of RELEGATE *v.*

reli'gation. *rare.* [ad. L. *religātiōn-em*, n. of action f. *religāre*: see prec. and -ATION.] The action of tying or binding up (*lit.* and *fig.*).

1617 COLLINS *Def. Bp. Ely* II. ix. 354 Though S. Austen had . . onely told vs of religation, or of binding, it had been enough to shew that S. Austens meaning was, that relligious worship belonged onely to God. **1664** H. MORE *Myst. Iniq.* 21 Origen speaks of the religation of these dæmons near their statues. **1807** COLERIDGE in Cottle *Early Recoll.* (1837) II. 84 If this be not true, there is no religion, no religation, or binding over again.

religeous(e, -eus, obs. forms of RELIGIOUS.

re'light (riː-), *v.* [RE- 5 a.]

1. *trans.* To illumine, kindle, or ignite again.

1645 EVELYN *Diary* [8 Feb.] A torch being extinguished neere it, and lifted a little distance, was suddainely relighted. **1725** POPE *Odyss.* IX. 609 His pow'r can heal me, and re-light my eye. *a* **1802** E. DARWIN in J. G. Strutt *Sylva Brit.* (1822) 2 You, who have seen . . Ten thousand times yon moon relight her horn. **1856** KANE *Arct. Expl.* I. xxxii. 450 Our only hope of heat was in re-lighting our lamp. **1872** AUBREY DE VERE *Leg. St. Patrick, Striving*, Nor of his victory had he joy . . Nor of that heaven relit.

2. *intr.* To take fire again, rekindle. Also *fig.*

1849 C. BRONTE *Shirley* xviii, The desire . . relit suddenly, and glowed warm in her heart. *c* **1865** J. WYLDE in *Circ. Sc.* I. 314/1 It will immediately re-light.

'relight, *sb. Aeronaut.* [f. the vb.] A re-ignition of a jet engine in flight. Usu. *attrib.*

1945 J. GRIERSON *Jet Flight* iv. 101 The fuel should be shut off for a minute or so in order to blow surplus fuel out of the engine before the relight. **1955** MANGHAM & PEACE *Jet Engine Man.* vi. 100 The relight button . . enables the ignition circuit to be energised without the starter motor. **1976** B. JACKSON *Flameout* (1977) II. iv. 69 A thorough examination of the relight systems, every fuel valve, and every fuel feed pipe. **1977** [see RELIGHTING *vbl. sb.*]. **1977** *R.A.F. News* 11–24 May 11/1 Flt Lt Harry Apiafi . . suffered a flame out in the Canberra's starboard engine... While attempting a relight, Harry lost the other engine as well.

re'lighting, *vbl. sb.* [f. RELIGHT *v.* + -ING¹.] The action of the vb.; *spec.* in *Aeronaut.*, the re-ignition of a jet engine in flight.

1955 MANGHAM & PEACE *Jet Engine Man.* v. 98 Relighting is more positive at low engine-windmilling speeds and at lower altitudes. **1960** H. ZEFFER *Princ. & Pract. Aircraft Electr. Engin.* xvii. 517 A typical situation in which re-lighting would be necessary is one where a jet engine has been stopped by an accretion of ice entering the air intake. **1965** *Gloss. Mining Terms* (*B.S.I.*) VII. 10 *Re-lighting station*, a place in a mine at which safety lamps can be relighted under controlled conditions. **1977** *R.A.F. Yearbk.* 34/1 The relighting drills cover three contingencies: the 'hot' relight speaks for itself, the unassisted relight involves diving the aircraft to get the engine rpm sufficiently high for a cold relight attempt, and the assisted relight uses the GTS in exactly the same way as starting the engine.

religieus, obs. form of RELIGIOUS.

‖**religieuse** (rəliʒjøz). Also 8 *erron.* **religieux** (*pl.*). †Also as *pl.* [F. *religieuse* fem. of next.]

1. A woman bound by religious vows, or devoted to a religious life; a nun.

1694 LD. PERTH *Let.* 17 Sept. (1845) 43 Lady Lucy is a most excellent religieuse. **1777** P. THICKNESSE *Year's Journey* II. l. 142 This virtuous, and . . amiable society of *religieux* [ed. 3, 1789, *religieuses*]. **1796** *Mod. Gulliver* 3 That there might be a pair of chaste examples ever before the religieuse, to fix their ideas the right way. **1815** *Chron.* in *Ann. Reg.* 101 During the whole night the religieuses of the hospital prayed near the body. **1847** C. BRONTE *J. Eyre* xiii, A convent full of religieuses. **1893** *19th Cent.* Nov. 754 I had been given to understand that Jane Clermont was a very fervid *religieuse*. **1959** *Times* 25 July 9/1 They [*sc.* béguinages] are communities of *religieuses* who live in separate houses.

2. (See quot. 1968.)

[**1929** E. J. KOLLIST *French Pastry, Confectionery & Sweets* iv. 57 Gâteau Religieuse... Set on clean baking-sheet eclairs from pâte à choux paste... In between each eclair decorate with whipped cream.] **1954** C. TURGEON *Tante Marie's French Cakes & Pastries* 50 Little Nuns. *Religieuses*... This pastry is perhaps the most popular in all France. **1961** A. WESKER *Kitchen* 11 Pastry called 'Religieuse'. **1968** *Guardian* 17 Feb. 9/8 A Religieuses [*sic*] is a gorgeously opulent edifice of éclairs bound with a mortar of chocolate and cream.

‖**religieux** (rəliʒjø). Now *rare* or *Obs.* Also 8–9 *erron.* **religieuse** (*sing.* and *pl.*). [F., ad. L. *religiōsus* RELIGIOUS.] A man vowed to a religious life; a monk.

1654 LD. HATTON in *Nicholas Papers* (Camden) II. 114, I am told . . that the Academy was this day full of the Duke of Glo[ucester's] conversion and being a Religieux. **1719** DE FOE *Crusoe* II. 141 He rather desir'd me to converse with him as a Gentleman, than as a Religieuse [*ed.* **1761** religieux]. **1827** ROBERTS *Voy. Centr. Amer.* 28 Inhabited by the few thousands of Spanish religieuse and Creole descendants of Spanish adventurers.

religio-, mod. combining form of RELIGION or RELIGIOUS, as in ***religio-educational***, ***-ethnic***, ***-historical***, ***-magical***, ***-military***, ***-musical***, ***-mystical***, ***-philosophic***, ***-philosophical***, ***-political***, ***-psychiatric*** (also ***-psychiatry***), ***-scientific***, ***-sexual***, etc.

1966 J. E. HOFMAN in J. A. Fishman *Readings Sociol. of Lang.* (1968) 626 Our hypothesis that whenever *religio-ethnic concentrations and certain other factors coincide, a situation is created which enhances the ideological climate suitable to retentiveness of the ethnic mother tongue. **1953** W. R. TRASK tr. *Auerbach's Mimesis* i. 17 The reader is at every moment aware of the universal *religio-historical perspective which gives the individual stories their general meaning and purpose. **1896** W. ST. JOHN BOSCAWEN *Bible & Monum.* 171 One of the litanies of the *religio-magical creed. **1894** H. SPEIGHT *Nidderdale* 169 There were two orders of the *religio-military brotherhood. **1959** 'F. NEWTON' *Jazz Scene* iii. 45 'Shouting' sects . . have made the most powerful single *religio-musical contribution to jazz. **1976** *Listener* 22 July 92/2 George Sand . . turned *religio-mystical . . with a spate of earnest, spiritual books. **1926** FOWLER *Mod. Eng. Usage* 393/1 We must take account of *religio-philosophic speculations. **1931** *Times Lit. Suppl.* 21 May 408/2 The world-wide religio-philosophical movement known as Theosophy. **1928** *Weekly Dispatch* 3 June 10/5 One of the most remarkable contributions to the *religio-political discussion on record. **1979** M. A. SCREECH *Rabelais* vi. 215 The direct religio-political propaganda. **1964** S. Z. KLAUSNER *Psychiatry & Relig.* i. 1 (heading) *Religio-psychiatry: a social institution. *Ibid.*, The *religio-psychiatric movement is born through several thousand similar encounters. **1968** *Internat. Encycl. Soc. Sci.* XII. 632/2 Religio-psychiatry is a twentieth-century movement whose participants are concerned with the relation between religious and scientific approaches to mental, emotional, or spiritual healing. **1946** D. C. PEATTIE *Road of Naturalist* iv. 49 The Poles snarled back a stream of commingled *religio-sexual obscenity, to show how dirty they could talk if they pleased.

religion (rɪˈlɪdʒən). Forms: 3–4 religiun(e, 4–5 -ioun(e, 5–6 -yon(e, -ione, 7 relligion; 3–6 relygyon, 4 -un, -ioun, 5–6 -ion; 4 riligioun, 6 relegioune; 3– religion. [a. AF. *religiun* (11th c.), F. *religion*, or ad. L. *religiōn-em*, of doubtful etymology, by Cicero connected with *relegĕre* to read over again, but by later authors with *religāre* to bind, RELIGATE (see Lewis and Short, s.v.); the latter view has usually been favoured by modern writers in explaining the force of the word by its supposed etymological meaning.]

1. a. A state of life bound by monastic vows; the condition of one who is a member of a religious order, esp. in the Roman Catholic Church.

c **1200** *Vices & Virtues* 43 Ðo ðe ðese swikele woreld habbeð forlaten and seruið ure drihten on religiun, hie folȝið Daniele, ðe hali profiete. *a* **1300** *Cursor M.* 23049 Þai . . went þaim in to religiun, . . For to beserue vr lauerd dright. **1362** LANGL. *P. Pl.* A. IX. 82 Dobet . . is Ronnen in-to Religiun . . And prechep þe peple seint poules wordes. **1390** GOWER *Conf.* III. 317 In blake clothes thei hem clothe, . . And yolde hem to religion. *c* **1449** PECOCK *Repr.* v. ii. 484 In oon maner religioun is . . a binding vp or a bynding aȝen of a mannys fre wil with certein ordinauncis, . . or with vowis or oothis. *c* **1500** *Lancelot* 1300 Non orderis had he of Relegioune. **1528** ROY *Rede me* (Arb.) 66 Ware thou never in religion?

Yes so god helpe me and halydom, A dosen yeres continually. **1586** A. DAY *Eng. Secretary* I. (1625) 126 Forsweare thou nothing good, but building of Monasteries and entring into Religion. **1663** H. COGAN tr. *Pinto's Trav.* xxviii. 111 Those of the country [China] repute him for a Saint, because he ended his dayes in Religion. **1765** H. WALPOLE *Otranto* iv, My father..was retired into religion in the Kingdom of Naples. **1825** SOUTHEY in *Q. Rev.* XXXII. 364 We must enter into religion and be made nuns by will or by force. **1886** H. N. OXENHAM *Mem. R. de Lisle* 6 The two others..are in religion; the former entered the Order of the Good Shepherd in 1863.

transf. **1535** LYNDESAY *Satyre* 3673 Mariage, be my opinioun, It is better Religioun, As to be freir or Nun.

†**b.** ***man***, etc. ***of religion***, one bound by monastic vows or in holy orders. *Obs.*

c **1200** *Trin. Coll. Hom.* 49 Þis loc ne haueð non to offren bute þese lif-holie men of religiun. *a* **1300** *Cursor M.* 29285 Qua smites preist or clerk,..or ani man of religion,..he is cursd. **13..** *E.E. Allit. P.* B. 7 Renkez of religioun þat reden & syngen. *c* **1380** WYCLIF *Wks.* (1880) 7 ȝif þei seyn þat þei ben most holy and best men of religion. **1426** LYDG. *De Guil. Pilgr.* 3192 Somme folkys of relygyon. **1485** CAXTON *Paris & V.* (1868) 12 To become a man of religion.

†**c.** ***house***, etc. ***of religion***, a religious house, a monastery or nunnery. *Obs.*

13.. *Sir Beues* (MS. A) 4613 An hous he made of riligioun, For to singe for sire Beuoun. **1340** *Ayenb.* 41 Huanne me bernþ oþer brekþ cherches..oþer hous of relygioun. ? *a* **1400** *Arthur* 488 In Abbeys of Relygyoun þat were cristien of name. *c* **1460** FORTESCUE *Abs. & Lim. Mon.* xix. (1885) 155 Oþer kynges haue ffounded byshopriches, abbeys, and oþer howses off relegyon. *c* **1535** in Speed *Hist. Gt. Brit.* IX. cxxi. §95 (1611) 773/1 Spoiled in like maner..as the housys of Religion hath bene. **1568** GRAFTON *Chron.* II. 144 Many houses of relygion within the Citie..were searched for goodes of aliauntes.

2. a. A particular monastic or religious order or rule; †a religious house. Now *rare.*

a **1225** *Ancr. R.* 4 Rihten hire & smeðen hire is of euch religiun, & of efrich ordre þe god, & al þe strengðe. *c* **1290** *S. Eng. Leg.* I. 52/192 Seint Edward cam..To an holi man þat þere was neiȝ in an oþur religion. **13..** *E.E. Allit. P.* B. 1156 His fader forloyne..feched hem wyth strenþe, & robbed þe relygioun of relykes alle. *c* **1400** *Rom. Rose* 6352 Somtyme am I prioresse,..And go thurgh alle regiouns, Sekyng alle religiouns. **1483** CAXTON *Gold. Leg.* 426/1 Saynt Rygoberte..ordeyned a relygyon of chanounes and clerkes. **1528** CROMWELL in Merriman *Life & Lett.* (1902) I. 322 The exchaunge to be made bitwene your colledge in Oxforde and his religion for Saundforde. *a* **1548** HALL *Chron., Hen. VIII* 143 This priest..was receiued into euery Religion with Procession, as though the Legate had been there. **1568** GRAFTON *Chron.* II. 194 This Religion of Saint Iohns, was greatly preferred, by the fall and suppression of the Templers. **1631** WEEVER *Anc. Funeral Mon.* 114 If any professed in the said Religion were negligently forgotten. **1687** A. LOVELL tr. *Thevenot's Trav.* I. 12 A Dagger, which the King of Spain sent as a Present to the Religion. **1769** *Ann. Reg.* 147 Some ships of the religion of Malta. **1858** FABER *Foot of Cross* (1872) 70 There were several false and counterfeit religions, which had troubled the church about this time.

transf. **1497** BP. ALCOCK *Mons Perfect.* B iij, As hymself for his pryde and enuy was cast out of the holy relygyon of heuen.

†**b.** *collect.* People of religion. *Obs.*

1297 R. GLOUC. (Rolls) 2812 Þanne þe religion & holi chirche worþ ef sone ybroȝt al adoun. **1375** BARBOUR *Bruce* xx. 162 Till religioune of seir statis, For heill of his saull, gaf he Siluir in-to gret quantite. *c* **1450** HOLLAND *Howlat* 190 Alkyn chennonis eik of vther ordouris, All maner of religioun, the less and the mair.

†**c.** A member of a religious order. *Obs.*

13.. *Cursor M.* 22001 (Gött), Quatkin man sum euer it es..Or laued or religion. **1303** R. BRUNNE *Handl. Synne* 7557 Specyaly þat comandeþ he..to bysshopes, and persones, To prestys, an ouþer relygyons. *c* **1325** *Chron. Eng.* 527 in Ritson *Metr. Rom.* II. 292 That on partie he sende..To thilke that were povre in londe; That other to povre religiouns; The thridde to povre cleregouns.

3. a. Action or conduct indicating a belief in, reverence for, and desire to please, a divine ruling power; the exercise or practice of rites or observances implying this. Also *pl.*, religious rites. Now *rare*, exc. as implied in 5.

a **1225** *Ancr. R.* 10 Cleane religiun..is iseon & helpen widewen & federlease children & from þe worlde witen him cleane & unwemmed. *c* **1250** *Kent. Serm.* in *O.E. Misc.* 29 Þer were vi. Ydres of stone..wer þo gius hem wesse for clenesse and for religiun. *a* **1300** *Cursor M.* 12676 Þis iacob..was o gret religiun, Hali liue he ladd al-wais. **1382** WYCLIF *Lev.* xvi. 31 The holiday forsothe of restyng it is, and ȝe shulen traueil ȝoure soulis thurȝ perpetuel religioun. **1553** EDEN *Treat. Newe Ind.* (Arb.) 27 They eate that fleshe with great religion. **1577** VAUTROUILLIER *Luther on Ep. Gal.* 151 They that trust in theyr owne righteousnes, thinke to pacifie the wrath of God by their..voluntarie religion. **1613** PURCHAS *Pilgrimage* III. i. (1614) 232 They vsed yet some Religion in gathering of their Cinamon,..sacrificing before they beganne [etc.]. **1667** MILTON *P.L.* I. 372 The Image of a Brute, adorn'd With gay Religions full of Pomp and Gold. **1726** LEONI tr. *Alberti's Archit.* II. 21/2 The Ancients used to found the Walls of their Cities with the greatest religion, dedicating them to some God who was to be their guardian. **1788** GIBBON *Decl. & F.* xlix. V. 89 The public religion of the Catholics was uniformly simple and spiritual. **1900** R. W. DIXON *Hist. Ch. Eng.* xxxvi. (1902) VI. 5 The religions of the religious orders..were swept away under the condemnation of superstition and abuse.

†**b.** A religious duty or obligation. *Obs.*

1537 *St. Papers Hen. VIII*, I. II. 557 Thei thoght a religion to kepe secret, betwene God and them, certayn things. **1549** LATIMER *5th Serm. bef. Edw. VI* (Arb.) 135 The dutye betwene man and wyfe, whiche is a holy religyon, but not religiouslye kepte.

4. a. A particular system of faith and worship.

a **1300** *Cursor M.* 18944 In þat siquar was in þat tun Men of alkin religioun. **1340** HAMPOLE *Pr. Consc.* 4522 Þe Iewes and cristen men,..Sal þan..Assent in Crist als a religion. **1560** DAUS tr. *Sleidane's Comm.* 92 b, They neyther allure nor compelle any man unto their Religion. **1594** HOOKER *Eccl. Pol.* IV. xi. §2 The church of Rome, they say,..did almost out of all religions take whatsoever had any fair and gorgeous show. **1625** B. JONSON *Staple of N.* II. i, I wonder what religion he is of. **1662** STILLINGFL. *Orig. Sacræ* II. vi. §15 Whereby we plainly see what clear evidence is given to the truth of that religion which is attested with a power of miracles. **1732** BERKELEY *Alciphr.* IV. §25 The Christian Religion, which pretends to teach men the knowledge and worship of God. **1791** PAINE *Rights of Man* (ed. 4) 79 If they are to judge of each others religion, there is no such thing as a religion that is right. **1849** MACAULAY *Hist. Eng.* vi. II. 65 All religions were the same to him. **1862** MAX MÜLLER *Chips* (1880) I. ix. 186 All important religions have sprung up in the East.

transf. **1849** LONGF. *Kavanagh* xvi. 78 The memory of that mother had become almost a religion to her. **1872** LIDDON *Elem. Relig.* i. 23 We hear men speak of a religion of art, of a religion of work, of a religion of civilization.

†**b.** ***the Religion*** [after F.]: the Reformed Religion, Protestantism. *Obs.*

1577 *F. de Lisle's Legendarie* G viij, There was a noise raised that the Admiral had endeuoured to expel the Masse, and to plant the Religion in France. **1601** R. JOHNSON *Kingd. & Commw.* 106 They agaiene are deuided into 13 Cantons, 8 whereof are catholike, the residue of the religion. **1642** HOWELL *For. Trav.* (Arb.) 46 They of the Religion, are now Town-lesse and Arme-lesse. *a* **1674** CLARENDON *Hist. Reb.* xv. §153 Those of the Religion possessed them-selves with many arm'd Men of the Town-House.

c. ***religion of nature***: the worship of Nature in place of a more formal system of religious belief.

1902 W. JAMES *Var. Relig. Exper.* iv. 91 In that 'theory of evolution' which..has within the past twenty-five years swept so rapidly over Europe and America, we see the ground laid for a new sort of religion of Nature, which has entirely displaced Christianity from the thought of a large part of our generation. **1961** D. G. JAMES *Matthew Arnold* i. 22 The essay itself is given up chiefly to a warm exposition of her religion of nature.

5. a. Recognition on the part of man of some higher unseen power as having control of his destiny, and as being entitled to obedience, reverence, and worship; the general mental and moral attitude resulting from this belief, with reference to its effect upon the individual or the community; personal or general acceptance of this feeling as a standard of spiritual and practical life.

c **1535** in Burnet *Hist. Ref.* (1679) I. Rec. III. 140 That true Religion is not contained in Apparel,..singing, and such other kind of Ceremonies; but in cleanness of mind [etc.]. **1560** DAUS tr. *Sleidane's Comm.* 46 b, Amonges the Suyces encreased dayly contention for Religion. **1597** HOOKER *Eccl. Pol.* V. lxv. §16 The tribe of Reuben..were..accused of backwardness in religion. **1613** PURCHAS *Pilgrimage* (1614) 20 True Religion is the right way of reconciling and reuniting man to God. **1651** HOBBES *Leviath.* I. xii. 52 There are no signes..of Religion, but in Man onely. **1704** NELSON *Fest. & Fasts* ix. (1739) 587 It keeps a lively Sense of Religion upon our Minds. **1776** ADAM SMITH *W.N.* V. ii. (1869) II. 459 So slender a security as the probity and religion of the inferior officers of revenue. **1832** HT. MARTINEAU *Hill & Valley* iii. 45 The best part of religion is to imitate the benevolence of God to man. **1849** MACAULAY *Hist. Eng.* ii. I. 176 About two thousand ministers of religion..were driven from their benefices in one day. **1877** SPARROW *Serm.* vii. 90 True religion, in its essence and in kind, is the same everywhere.

personified. **1597** SHAKS. *Lover's Compl.* 250 Religious love put out Religion's eye. **1607** —— *Timon* III. ii. 83 Religion grones at it. *c* **1652** MILTON *Sonn. to Sir H. Vane*, Therfore on thy firme hand religion leanes In peace, & reck'ns thee her eldest son. **1717** POPE *Eloisa* 39 There stern Religion quench'd th' unwilling flame. **1781** COWPER *Expost.* 492 Religion, if in heavenly truths attired, Needs only to be seen to be admired. **1844** A. B. WELBY *Poems* (1867) 72 'Tis then that sweet Religion's holy wing Broods o'er the spirit.

b. ***to get religion***: see GET *v.* 12 d.

†**c.** Awe, dread. *Obs. rare*$^{-1}$.

a **1642** BEDELL *Erasmus* in Fuller *Abel Rediv.* (1867) I. 78 He took a general view of most parts of Italy as far as Cumae, where (not without some religion and horror)..he beheld the cave of Sibylla.

6. *transf.* †**a.** Devotion to some principle; strict fidelity or faithfulness; conscientiousness; pious affection or attachment. *Obs.*

1592 SHAKS. *Rom. & Jul.* I. ii. 93 When the deuout religion of mine eye Maintaines such falshood, then turne teares to fire. **1600** —— *A.Y.L.* IV. i. 201 Ros... Keep your promise. *Orl.* With no lesse religion, then if thou wert indeed my Rosalind. **1630** B. JONSON *New Inn* I. i, Out of a religion to my charge, And debt profess'd, I have made a self-decree. **1640** HABINGTON *Edw. IV* 182 The ancient league observ'd with so much Religion betweene England and the Low Countries. **1691** WOOD *Ath. Oxon.* I. Pref., An old Word is retain'd by an Antiquary with as much Religion as a Relick.

b. In phr. ***to make (a) religion of*** or ***to make (it) religion to***, to make a point of, to be scrupulously careful (†not) to do something.

(*a*) **1599** B. JONSON *Cynthia's Rev.* V. ii, Let mortals learn To make religion of offending heaven. **1622** PEACHAM *Compl. Gent.* 44 Nor bee so foolish precise as a number are, who make it Religion to speake otherwise then this or that Author.

(*b*) **1606** SHAKS. *Ant. & Cl.* V. ii. 199 By your command (Which my loue makes Religion to obey) I tell you this. **1869** W. M. BAKER *New Timothy* 199 (Cent.), Its acidity sharpens Mr. Wall's teeth..., yet, under the circumstances, he makes a religion of eating it.

†**7.** The religious sanction or obligation *of* an oath, etc. *Obs.*

a **1619** FOTHERBY *Atheom.* I. vi. §2 (1622) 42 Vnder the religion of an Oath. *c* **1645** HOWELL *Lett.* (1650) II. 117 According to the rules and religion of friendship. *a* **1694** TILLOTSON *Serm.* (1742) II. xxii. 65 If the religion of an oath will not oblige men to speak truth, nothing will. **1704** J. BLAIR in W. S. Perry *Hist. Coll. Amer. Col. Ch.* (1870) I. 107, I shall under the same religion of an oath acquaint your Lordships with..what I remember.

8. *attrib.* and *Comb.*, as ***religion-complex***, ***-dresser***, ***-game***, ***-making***, ***-mender***, ***-monger***, ***-shop***; ***religion-arousing***, ***-infectious***, ***-masked***, ***-raptured*** adjs.; †**religion man** = sense 1 b.

1957 J. S. HUXLEY *Relig. without Revelation* (rev. ed.) vii. 174 Potential *religion-arousing objects. **1922** *Brit. Jrnl. Psychology* Oct. 117 Such complexes clearly exist in the normal mind with perfectly free access to consciousness, *e.g.* the '*religion complex'. *a* **1640** DAY *Peregr. Schol.* (1881) 72 This new vicker was made out of an olde ffrier that had bene twice turnd at a *Religion-dressers. **1961** J. WILSON *Reason & Morals* ii. 120 Thus J. R. Lucas..even puts in a good word for the *religion-game. **1706** A. SHIELDS *Inq. Ch. Communion* (1747) 51 Such as are..*religion-infectious, like to spread and leaven all in communion with such a congregation. **1888** MRS. H. WARD *R. Elsmere* xlix, We are in the full stream of *religion-making. *c* **1430** LYDG. *Min. Poems* (Percy Soc.) 57 *Religioune men alwey wonnyng in the Court,..It may wele ryme, but it accordith nought. **1633** FORD *'Tis Pity* V. iii, Your *religion-masked sorceries. **1824** W. E. ANDREWS *Crit. Rev. Fox's Bk. Mart.* I. 380 The irreligious and blasphemous pretentions of those *religion-menders. **1698** FRYER *Acc. E. India & P.* 366 The Antiquaries..who have searched more narrowly into this up-start *Religion-Monger. **1718** *Entertainer* 253 The Fathers [are represented as]..a Parcel of old passive Religion-Mongers. **1796** SOUTHEY *Lett. fr. Spain* 341 The fervid soul of that blest Maid, *Religion-raptur'd. **1811** MISS HAWKINS *Countess & Gertrude* (1812) II. xxvii. 79 Well may scoffers talk of the *religion-shops of London.

religionary (rɪˈlɪdʒənərɪ), *a.* and *sb.* [f. prec. + -ARY, or ad. F. *religionnaire*, It., Sp. *religionario* sb., Protestant, Calvinist.] **A.** *adj.* Relating to religion; religious. Now *rare.*

a **1691** BP. T. BARLOW *Rem.* 638 His Religionary Professions in his last Will and Testament. **1715** M. DAVIES *Athen. Brit.* I. 219 His Religionary Pamphlets for that purpose were these. **1867** BARING-GOULD *Cur. Myths* I. viii. 164 It is a strange instance of religionary virulence.

B. *sb.* †**a.** A person 'in religion'. *Obs.* **b.** [See etym. note.] A Protestant. ? *Obs.*

1663 H. COGAN tr. *Pinto's Trav.* lxiii. 256 Seven and thirty women, the most of them old, and Religionaries of this temple. **1683** *Apol. Prot. France* iv. 35 The gathering together of the Factions of the Religionaries. **1716** M. DAVIES *Athen. Brit.* III. *Diss. Drama* 6 Those Protestant Religionaries and Popish Sectaries. **1760** *Ann. Reg.* II. 176/1 To distinguish them from the Protestants, who are called Religionaries.

†**re'ligionate**, *v.* *Obs. rare*$^{-1}$. [f. as prec. + -ATE[3].] *trans.* To make religious.

1676 MARVELL *Mr. Smirke* I iij b, There have been Martyrs for Reason,..but how much more would men be so for reason Religionated and Christianized!

religioner (rɪˈlɪdʒənə(r)). [f. as prec. + -ER[1].] **a.** A person 'in religion'. **b.** = RELIGIONIST.

1812 SOUTHEY *Omniana* I. 1 Pope Innocent X appointed a religioner of great virtue, discretion, and experience, secretly to visit the nunneries. *Ibid.* II. 230 All the religioners of both sexes. **1820** SCOTT *Monast.* xxv, These new-fashioned religioners have fast-days, I warrant me. **1852** H. NEWLAND *Lect. Tractar.* 164 Those very externals of divine worship which so many of our..religioners call mummery. **1896** 'Q.' (QUILLER COUCH) *Story of Sea* II. xx. 387 The religioners who embarked for the service of the fleet..were 180, consisting of Augustinians, Franciscans, Dominicans, and Jesuits.

religionism (rɪˈlɪdʒənɪz(ə)m). [f. as prec. + -ISM.] Marked or excessive inclination to religion; exaggerated or affected religious zeal.

1791–1823 D'ISRAELI *Cur. Lit.* (1866) 390/2 The coinage of a novel and significant expression, as this of Professor Dugald Stewart—political religionism. **1817** BP. JEBB *Let.* in C. Forster *Life* lxi. 573 This work has been carried on rather uncouthly: not religion, but religionism, having been the compressing power. **1833** I. TAYLOR *Fanat.* v. 131 The germs of malignant religionism..are not wanting even in Basil. **1856** R. A. VAUGHAN *Mystics* (1860) I. 23 They call in the aid of an imaginative religionism to people their solitude with its glories. **1881** THOROLD *Gospel of Christ* Pref., Surely it is a morose religionism that fears knowledge, or distrusts science.

religionist (rɪˈlɪdʒənɪst). [f. as prec. + -IST.] One addicted or attached to religion; one imbued with, or zealous for, religion. Sometimes in bad sense, a religious zealot or pretender. Also, one professionally occupied with religion; a minister or preacher.

1653 H. MORE *Antid. Ath.* III. i. §3 Religionists having for pious purposes forged so many false Miracles..they have thereby with the Atheist taken away all belief of those which are true. **1671** CROWNE *Juliana* Ded., If I may have leave from our rigid religionists, to prosecute the metaphor. **1697** G. BURGHOPE *Disc. Relig. Assemb.* 4 As for the moderate, rational and intelligent religionists, they are so few. **1711** SHAFTESB. *Charac.* (1737) III. Misc. III. i. 133 He has his private Opinion, Belief, or Faith, as strong as any Devotee or Religionist of 'em all. **1757** HUME *Ess., Nat. Hist. Relig.* (1817) II. 398 These pretended religionists are really a kind of superstitious atheists. **1812** J. HENRY *Camp. agst. Quebec* 214 A dispassionate, placid, and mild religionist. **1843** WORDSW. *Prose Wks.* (1876) III. 169 A Savant, who is not also a poet in soul and a religionist in heart, is a feeble and unhappy creature. **1865** LIGHTFOOT *Comm. Gal.* (1876) 369 The external service of the religionist..is pronounced [by St. James] deceitful and vain. **1870** O. LOGAN *Before Footlights & behind Scenes* xl. 603 While clergymen and religionists, as now, stand afar off and denounce the theatre. **1895** *Wales* Aug. 361/2 The antagonism that some classes of religionists have shown to the pastoral care of the church is to be attributed, most frequently, to one of two things. **1939** WYNDHAM LEWIS *Jews* v. 55 The Jews are..the great religionists of the West. **1958** *New Statesman* 6 Sept. 304/3 Lately in the United States *religionist* has taken on a new and definite meaning. When *religionists* are referred to in the current press, it is clear that this term includes anyone who is professionally occupied with religion, of whatever church, movement or status—that is, anyone from Billy Graham to Reinhold Niebuhr. **1966** *Ibid.* 13 May 683/1 Secularists are not demanding what religionists demand and obtain, namely public subsidy for their own propaganda institutions. They deplore all propagandising of children. **1977** *Private Eye* 1 Apr. 8/1 Mr Arthur Blessit..a Los Angeles religionist, was assaulted by a number of similarly moved but differently associated people.

Hence **religio'nistic** *a.*

1889 BP. W. B. CARPENTER *Perm. Elem. Relig.* v. 192 The religionistic spirit lowers the moral tone.

religionize (rɪ'lɪdʒənaɪz), *v.* [f. as prec. + -IZE.] **a.** *trans.* To imbue with religion, to render religious. **b.** *intr.* To be addicted to, to affect, religion. Hence **re'ligionized, -izing.**

1716 M. DAVIES *Athen. Brit.* III. *Diss. Drama* 32 About every one's Thinking and Religionizing as he will. **1830** I. TAYLOR *Logic in Theol.*, etc. (1859) 104 Our own enlightened and religionized country. **1842** J. H. NEWMAN *Lett.* (1891) II. 384 His great object is the religionizing of the State. **1853** S. H. COX *Interviews Mem. & Useful* 138 (Cent.) How much religionizing stupidity it requires in one to imagine [etc.]. **1869** W. P. MACKAY *Grace & Truth* (1874) 168 The ritualist tells us that man is to be religionised.

religionless (rɪ'lɪdʒənlɪs), *a.* [f. as prec. + -LESS.] **A.** *adj.* Destitute of religion. ***religionless Christianity*** [tr. G. *religionsloses Christentum*], Christianity dissociated from many of the doctrines and practices of conventional religion.

1750 WARBURTON *Julian* II. 192 The gross body of the Jews..returned home religionless as they came. **1829** J. H. NEWMAN *Lett.* (1891) I. 204 The upper classes will be left almost religionless. **1848** THACKERAY *Van. Fair* xiv, A worldly, selfish,..religionless old woman. **1889** J. STRONG in *Minutes Congreg. Council* (U.S.) 364 Teaching a religionless morality. **1953** R. H. FULLER tr. *Bonhoeffer's Lett. & Papers from Prison* v. 123 If religion is no more than the garment of Christianity—and even that garment has had very different aspects at different periods—then what is a religionless Christianity? **1963** *Times* 7 May 13/4 Archbishop Heenan is reported in today's Sunday press to have said that Anglican discussions about religionless Christianity are an embarrassment to Roman Catholics who work for Christian unity. **1969** A. RICHARDSON *Dict. Chr. Theol.* 288/2 It is in the light of Barth's denunciation of religion that Bonhoeffer's plea for 'religionless Christianity', by which he meant unpietistic, unchurchy Christianity, should be understood. **1974** *Oxf. Dict. Chr. Ch.* (ed. 2) 187/1 Though writers of the Death of God school have taken up his [*sc.* Bonhoeffer's] idea of religionless Christianity, his teaching represents a search for the beyond in the midst, and a demand for a radical reform of the Church, which in its existing form he thought to have no message for the present day. **1977** *Church Times* 29 Apr. 6/4 Nor is it one of the newer-style jobs in which the intransigent element in Christian faith is dissolved away in..religionless Christianity.

B. as *sb. collect.*, people without religious belief.

1964 *New Statesman* 14 Feb. 254/3 Literature which Arnold was quite right to suggest would come to occupy the importance of religion for the religionless.

†**re'ligiose**, *sb. Obs. rare*⁻¹. [ad. Sp. *religiosa.*] = RELIGIEUSE I.

1697 tr. *C'tess D'Aunoy's Trav.* (1706) 82 The keeper of the Castle askt me, whether I would see the Religioses, whose Convent is adjoyning thereunto.

religiose (rɪlɪdʒɪ'əʊs), *a.* [f. as RELIGIOUS + -OSE.] Religious to excess; unduly occupied with religion; morbidly or sentimentally religious.

1853 CLOUGH *Let.* in *Poems*, etc. (1869) I. 196 Some of my companions are too much in the religiose vein to be always quite wholesome company. **1885** *L'pool Daily Post* 23 Oct. 4/7 Qualities not specially congenial to the theological or religiose mind. **1932** [see BEGLAMOUR *v.*]. **1966** I. JEFFERIES *House-Surgeon* ix. 168 It was only later, when they were improving, that they would complain about their neighbours, or become religiose, or mutter. **1971** *Times Lit. Suppl.* 22 Oct. 1319/2 Donald's parents—the dying, religiose father and steely, moralizing mother—inhabit an area of real, alarming unsavouriness. **1975** J. NICOLL *Dante Gabriel Rossetti* ii. 48 An unhappy love affair with Rossetti's religiose sister Christina.

religiose, obs. form of RELIGIOUS.

religiosity (rɪlɪdʒɪ'ɒsɪtɪ). [ad. late L. *religiōsitas*: see RELIGIOUS and -ITY. Cf. F. *religiosité* (15th c.), and RELIGIOUSTY.]

1. Religiousness, religious feeling or sentiment.

1382 WYCLIF *Ecclus.* i. 17 The drede of the Lord [is] religiosite of kunnyng. *Ibid.* 18 Religiosite shal kepen, and iustefien the herte. **1483** CAXTON *Gold. Leg.* 245/1 There is treble generacion spirituel of god, that is to saye, of natyuyte, religyosite, and of body mortalite. **1609** BIBLE (Douay) *Ecclus.* i. 17, 18. **1813** *Edin. Rev.* XXII. 222 Their disposition to religious feeling, which they call religiosity, is ..a love of divine things for the love of their moral qualities. **1846** J. MARTINEAU *Misc.* (1852) 188 Our author argues from the religiosity of man to the reality of God. **1887** Z. A. RAGOZIN *Chaldea* iii. 149 Man has all that animals have, and two things which they have not—speech and religiosity.

b. Affected or excessive religiousness.

1799 W. TAYLOR in Robberds *Mem.* (1843) I. 283 Great sticklers for feminine purity, or prudery, or religiosity. **1829** SOUTHEY *Sir T. More* II. 102 A feverish state of what may better be called religiosity, than religion. **1873** MORLEY *Rousseau* I. ix. 317 It is hard to imagine a more execrable emotion than the complacent religiosity of the prosperous.

c. With *pl.* A religious service. *rare*⁻¹.

1834 SOUTHEY *Doctor* ix. (1848) 26 The soporific sermons which closed the domestic religiosities of those..days.

†**2.** = RELIGION I and 2. *Obs. rare.*

c **1449** PECOCK *Repr.* IV. vi. 453 Religiosite of mannys ordinaunce is leeful..and ech such order or dignite and ech such seid religiosite mad bi man [etc.].

‖**religioso** (relidʒi'oso), *adv.*, *sb.*, and *a. Mus.* [It., = religious.] **A.** *adv.* As a direction to the performer: in a devotional manner. **B.** *sb.* A devotional effect; a passage to be played devotionally. **C.** *adj.* Having a devotional quality.

1837 J. A. HAMILTON *Dict. Mus. Terms* (ed. 4) 58 *Religioso, religiosamente* (Italian), with religious feeling, in a devotional manner. **1876** STAINER & BARRETT *Dict. Mus. Terms* 377/1 *Religiosamente, religioso*, in a religious or devotional manner. **1941** W. C. HANDY *Father of Blues* v. 63, I was featuring *The Holy City* as a cornet solo and these saxophones contributed wonderfully to the religioso. **1961** *Times* 4 Dec. 14/5 The tremulous, *religioso* registrations with which the organist coloured the recitatives. **1975** *Sunday Times* 14 Dec. 31/1 In the Prologue to 'The Golden Legend'..Sullivan *religioso* sounded no more inspired than the average Mus.D. exercise of a century ago. **1977** *Gramophone* Apr. 1541/2 In the slow movement there is little sense of *religioso* in the bare chordal writing for strings at the start. **1980** *Country Life* 17 Jan. 177 Even more *religioso* than Gounod at times was the Abbé Lizst.

religious (rɪ'lɪdʒəs), *a.* and *sb.* Forms: 3-5 religius(e, 4-5 -iose, 4-6 -iouse; 4, 6 -eous(e, 5 -eus; 4 -yus, 5 -yous; 4 relygiouse, 6 -i(o)us; 5 -eous; 4-6 -y(o)us, 5 -youx, -yows, 6 -youse; 4 relegiouse; 4- religious, (7 rell-). [a. AF. *religius*, OF. *religious, -eus*, etc. (12th c.; mod.F. *religieux* m., *-euse* f.), or ad. L. *religiōs-us*: see RELIGION and -OUS.]

A. *adj.* **1. a.** Imbued with religion; exhibiting the spiritual or practical effects of religion; pious, godly, god-fearing, devout.

a **1225** *Ancr. R.* 74 ȝif eni weneð þat he beo religius, & ne bridleð nout his tunge, his religiun is fals. **1388** WYCLIF *Dan.* iii. 90 Alle religiouse men, blesse ȝe the Lord, God of goddis. **1398** TREVISA *Barth. De P.R.* XVII. clxxiv. (Bodl. MS.), Holy men & religious þt be nouȝt defouled. **1432-50** tr. *Higden* (Rolls) II. 231 Thei were religious men..hauenge glorious vertues. **1542** BECON *Pathw. Prayer* vii. Wks. 1564 I. 64 Who would not haue thought thys holy religious father worthy to be canonised..? **1599** SHAKS. *Hen. V*, II. ii. 130 Seeme they religious? Why so didst thou. **1642** ROGERS *Naaman* 144 Earthly Selfe so scrues and mixes it selfe with religious, that oft-times the soule markes not the difference. **1667** MILTON *P.L.* XI. 622 That sober Race of Men, whose lives Religious titl'd them the Sons of God. **1715** DE FOE *Fam. Instruct.* I. iv. (1841) I. 81, I think I am religious enough in all conscience. **1787** JEFFERSON *Writ.* (1859) II. 154 He is..very limited in his understanding, and religious, bordering on bigotry. **1841** MYERS *Cath. Th.* IV. §23. 293 A man may be Moral without being Religious, but he cannot be Religious without being Moral. **1877** E. R. CONDER *Bas. Faith* i. 13 The Apostle John and Benedict Spinoza were both intensely religious persons, but it would be difficult to say what their religious feelings had in common.

transf. **1591** SYLVESTER *Du Bartas* I. iii. 254 The Jewes' religious River Which every Sabbath dries his Channell over; keeping his waves from working on that Day.

b. ***most religious***, used as an epithet of royalty. (Cf. CHRISTIAN *a.* 1 b.)

1662 *Bk. Com. Prayer*, We humbly beseech thee..for the High Court of Parliament, under our most religious and Gracious King, at this time assembled. **1820** SHELLEY *Œd. Tyr.* I. 137 The chaste Pasiphae..Wife to that most religious King of Crete.

†**c.** Holy, sacred. *Obs. rare*⁻¹.

1611 CORYAT *Crudities* 77 Pictures of Christ and the Virgin Mary, and many other religious persons.

2. a. Of persons: Bound by monastic vows; belonging to a religious order, esp. in the Church of Rome. (Cf. B. 1.)

a **1300** *Cursor M.* 29374 Þe thrid es men religius, þat has þair ouer man in hus. **1303** R. BRUNNE *Handl. Synne* 7383 Þe fourþe synne ys more perylous, Wyþ man and wommane relygyus. *c* **1400** *Rom. Rose* 6149 Religious folk ben ful covert; Seculer folk ben more appert. **1450-1530** *Myrr. our Ladye* 24 Men & women of holy chyrche, namely relygyous people, oughte to saye theyre seruyce eche howre in hys owne tyme. **1500-20** DUNBAR *Poems* xxxiii. 10 A religious man he slew, And cled him in his abeit new. **1551** ROBINSON tr. *More's Utop.* II. (1895) 145 How ydle a companye ys theyr of prystes, and relygyous men, as they call them? **1599** HAKLUYT *Voy.* II. I. 59 The said city is as big as two of Bononia, & in it are many monasteries of religious persons, al which do worship idols. **1633** T. STAFFORD *Pac. Hib.* I. v. (1821) 73 With a competent number of three thousand Souldiers, Pioners, and religious persons. **1680** DRYDEN *Span. Friar* II. ii, There's a huge, fat, religious gentleman coming up, Sir. **1745** A. BUTLER *Lives of Saints* (1836) I. 192 The superintendency of all the houses of religious women in his kingdom. **1796** SOUTHEY *Lett. fr. Spain* (1799) 415, I remember a religious society was established at Lisbon, calling themselves the Order of Divine Providence. **1810** —— *Kehama* VII. iv, Never yet did form more beautiful.. Bless the religious Virgin's gifted sight.

b. Of things, places, etc.: Of, belonging to, or connected with, a monastic order.

c **1330** R. BRUNNE *Chron.* (1810) 80 Whan þei to Durham com..þer þei bigan a home of religiouse manere. *c* **1375** *Sc. Leg. Saints* iii. (*Andrew*) 864 Ane bischope..religeouse lyf liffand ay. **1470-85** MALORY *Arthur* XIII. viii. 621 Soo had they done had not an old knyghte come amonge them in Relygyous clothyng. **1538** STARKEY *England* I. ii. 43 Settyng themselfe in relygyouse housys, ther quyetly to serue God. **1582** N. LICHEFIELD tr. *Castanheda's Conq. E. Ind.* lxxiii. 151 *note*, An hermitage, or such lyke pore kind of solitary religious place. **1664** DRYDEN *Rival Ladies* II. i, If you will needs to a Religious House. **1674** WOOD *Life* (O.H.S.) II. 301 Those religious places that are neare Oxford. **1711** ADDISON *Spect.* No. 164 ¶4 A shaved Head, and a religious Habit. **1742** CHESTERF. *Lett.* (1792) I. xciii. 262 He dissolved the monasteries and religious houses in England. **1856** FROUDE *Hist. Eng.* x. II. 438 The religious system, in its technical sense, he believed to have become a nursery of idleness. **1888** BERNARD *Fr. World to Cloister* i. 5, I believe ..that the religious life is one..instituted by God, that is substantially in its three vows.

3. a. Of the nature of, pertaining or appropriate to, concerned or connected with, religion.

1538 STARKEY *England* I. ii. 38 Yf his mynd were not ryghtly set wyth relygyouse honour towards God. **1627** MAY *Lucan* III. 447 A sad religious awe The quiet trees vnstirr'd by winde doe draw. **1632** MILTON *Penseroso* 160 Storied Windows richly dight, Casting a dimm religious light. **1651** HOBBES *Leviath.* IV. xlv. 361 They made it for a Religious use. **1715** POPE *Ep. Addison* 12 Some felt..hostile fury, some religious rage. **1769** *Account of Society for promoting Relig. Knowl.* 5 The design of this Society being to promote Religious Knowledge among the Poor. **1788** GIBBON *Decl. & F.* l. V. 202 From his earliest youth, Mahomet was addicted to religious contemplation. **1800** H. MORE *Let.* 11 Sept. (1925) 177, I knew that every Anti-Abolitionist in the world was..an enemy to religious instruction at home. **1809** M. WARING (*title*) A diary of the religious experience of Mary Waring. **1835** J. H. NEWMAN *Par. Serm.* (1837) I. xi. 163 Prayer is the most directly religious of all our duties. **1836** *Introd. Discourse & Lect. Amer. Institute of Instruction 1835* 105 The parent who neglects the religious education of his child might as well suffer him to wander filthy and ragged in the streets. **1850** C. KINGSLEY *Alton Locke* I. xi. 178 'Schooling hasn't made wages, rise, nor preaching neither.' 'But surely..all this religious knowledge ought to give you comfort.' **1853** LYNCH *Self-Improv.* iii. 72 Books least religious in letter and phrase may be most religious in effect. **1858** GEO. ELIOT *Scenes Clerical Life* II. 193 It may be that some of Mr. Tryon's hearers had gained a religious vocabulary rather than religious experience. **1872** *Q. Rev.* CXXXII. 534 The people will have to decide at a general election upon this great question of Religious or Secular Education. **1877** C. GEIKIE *Christ* xlix. (1879) 584 Jerusalem was the religious centre of the Jewish nation. **1914** G. B. SHAW *Parents & Children* p. c, The last ray of art is being cut off from our schools by the discontinuance of religious education. **1960-61** *Where?* Winter 16/2 *Religious instruction* (*RI*), the only subject which state schools are obliged to teach by law. **1961** *Regulations G.C.E. Examinations* (Univ. London) 22 *Religious Knowledge* Ordinary Level. There will be one paper of 2¼ hours. **1968** *Guardian* 28 Nov. 6/3 It is thought that a new attitude in the schools would encourage student teachers to take religious education as a subsidiary subject at colleges of education. **1973** *Listener* 23 Aug. 251/1 To disbelieve in God's existence is..a matter of distrusting the testimony of others or lacking a religious experience oneself.

b. (Chiefly *poet.*) Regarded as sacred.

1618 *Hist. Perkin Warbeck* in *Select. Harl. Misc.* (1793) 59 Even the name of Mortimer and York was sanctified and religious amongst them. **1648** HERRICK *Hesper.*, *To Perilla*, Bring Part of the creame from that Religious Spring. **1700** DRYDEN *Wife of Bath's T.* 212 Lonely the vale, and full of horror stood, Brown with the shade of a religious wood. **1746** COLLINS *Ode to Liberty*, Thy Shrine in some religious wood. *c* **1820** S. ROGERS *Italy, Fire-Fly* 22 Those trees, religious once and always green.

c. Special collocations. ***religious philosophy***: the philosophical study of religion; philosophy that accepts the concept of an omnipotent God; hence ***religious philosopher***; ***religious psychology***: psychology which accepts that a religious context is basic to man's personality and behaviour.

1840 J. S. MILL in *Westm. Rev.* XXXIII. 297 Of Coleridge as a moral and religious philosopher..there is neither room, nor would it be expedient for us to speak more than generally. *Ibid.* 298 We must be looking for a religious philosophy, and our main hope ought to be that it will be such a one as fulfils the conditions of a philosophy—the very foremost of which is, unrestricted freedom of thought. **1902** W. JAMES *Var. Relig. Exper.* iv. 105 An interpretation of Christ's message which in these very Gifford lectures has been defended by some of your very ablest Scottish religious philosophers. *Ibid.* xviii. 431, I doubt if dispassionate intellectual contemplation of the universe, apart from inner unhappiness and need of deliverance on the one hand and mystical emotion on the other, would ever have resulted in religious philosophies such as we now possess. **1912** R. B. PERRY *Pres. Philos. Tendencies* vii. 148 The English school of idealists..has from the outset offered a religious philosophy based on the supremacy of consciousness. **1927** J. S. HUXLEY *Relig. without Revelation* iv. 120 Those who, through study or profession, are brought into contact with religious psychology. *Ibid.* viii. 290 Thouless, who writes on religious psychology from the standpoint of a psychologist who is also a professing Christian. **1951** E. A. BURTT *Types of Relig. Philos.* (rev. ed.) p. vii, An exposition of the main points of view in religious philosophy. *Ibid.* i. 7 What significant comparisons may we make between the religious psychology of individuals who participate in quite different cultures? **1960** D. A. LOWRIE *Rebellious Prophet* xiv. 196 Berdyaev..is inclined to consider him [*sc.* Bulgakov] a religious philosopher rather than a theologian. **1974** B. A. BRODY *Philos. of Relig.* p. vii, For centuries, a principal issue in traditional religious philosophy had been whether one could prove the truth or falsity of a variety of fundamental doctrines.

4. *transf.* **a.** Scrupulous, exact, strict, conscientious. †Also const. *in*, *of*.

1599 PORTER *Angry Wom. Abingd.* (Percy Soc.) 37 A man deuoted to a man, Loyall, religious in loues hallowed vowes. **1601** SHAKS. *Twel. N.* III. iv. 424 A Coward, a most deuout Coward, religious in it. **1618** BOLTON *Florus* To Rdr., Translated..with a religious ayme to his meaning, howsoever it may be many times mist. **1697** DRYDEN *Æneid* I. 769 Religious of his Word. **1711** HEARNE *Collect.* (O.H.S.) III. 109, I must confess that I am so religious in that Affair [of editing], that I transcribe the very Faults. **1760–2** GOLDSM. *Cit. W.* civ, His library is preserved with the most religious neatness. **1798** WELLINGTON in Gurw. *Desp.* (1838) I. 5 On my part, you will always meet with a religious adherence to every article of the treaties subsisting between us. **1856** KANE *Arct. Expl.* I. xvi. 191 We were led to footsteps; and following these with religious care [etc.].

†**b.** Of an oath: solemn. *Obs. rare*$^{-1}$.

1723 STEELE *Consc. Lovers* II. i, The Religious Vow I have made to my Father.

5. Of a horse: **a.** (See quot. 1788.) **b.** *U.S.* 'Having no vicious traits' (D.A.E.).

1788 GROSE *Classical Dict. Vulgar Tongue* (ed. 2) sig. Z4^v, *Religious horse*, one much given to prayer, or apt to be down upon his knees. **1869** *Overland Monthly* III. 127 It is amusing to hear one ask of another, when about to purchase a horse: 'Is he religous?'

6. *Comb.*, as ***religious-mad***, ***-minded***, ***-sane*** adjs.

a **1930** D. H. LAWRENCE *Apocalypse* (1931) vi. 98 Men were religious-mad: not religious-sane. **1888** C. M. YONGE *Beechcroft at Rockstone* II. xx. 153 Thoroughly religious-minded,..his aspirations had been blighted by his father's death. **1954** A. SETON *Katherine* xxvi. 447 Religious-minded Katherine had never been... This strict penitential garb and talk of pilgrimage were surely some passing derangement.

B. *sb.* **1. a.** As *pl.* Those bound by monastic vows or devoted to a religious life according to the principles of the Church of Rome.

a **1225** *Ancr. R.* 10 Gode religiuse beoð i þe worlde, summe nomeliche prelaz & treowe prechures. **1303** R. BRUNNE *Handl. Synne* 8639 Also relygyous are to wyte, þat for maystry wyl gladly smyte. *c* **1380** WYCLIF *Wks.* (1880) 2 ȝif oure newe religious bee in þese same synnys..þei ben cursid of god. *c* **1420** *Sir Amadace* (Camden) xxiv, Go, pray alle the religius of this cite, To morne that thay wold dyne with me. **1483** CAXTON *Cato* G ij b, An abbot..sette and made his relygyous or monkes for to werke. **1546** *Supplic. Poore Commons* (E.E.T.S.) 65 The monkes, friers, and other the supersticious religious. **1597** BEARD *Theatre God's Judgem.* (1612) 405 There grew so great quarrels and discontentments betweene the townesmen and the religious. **1631** WEEVER *Anc. Funeral Mon.* 271 The Religious of those times were as thankfull to their Benefactours. **1674** MARVELL *Corr.* Wks. (Grosart) II. 424 You know the Religious were in that [conspiracy] too with Rohan against the K[ing] of France. **1711** ADDISON *Spect.* No. 164 ¶11 The Letters..are yet extant in the Nunnery where she resided; and are often read to the young Religious. **1768** BOSWELL *Corsica* ii. (ed. 2) 88 They also brought with them some religious, of the order of St. Basil. **1813** HOBHOUSE *Journey* (ed. 2) App. 1123 Those Italian religious who were destined to the service of the mission. **1875** MANNING *Mission H. Ghost* xii. 339 Were these words..spoken to recluses, to men living in a desert, or to religious in cloisters?

b. With reference to other religions.

1585 T. WASHINGTON tr. *Nicholay's Voy.* III. xv. 99 b, These iolly louing religious. **1596** DALRYMPLE tr. *Leslie's Hist. Scot.* III. 179 Ethodie..was brocht vpe amang the religious in the yle of man. **1604** E. G[RIMSTONE] *D'Acosta's Hist. Indies* v. viii. 348 The priests and religious of Mexico (who lived there with a strange observance). **1687** A. LOVELL tr. *Thevenot's Trav.* I. 54 They have several sorts of Religious, among whom the Dervishes are the most familiar and polite. **1738** [G. SMITH] *Cur. Relat.* II. 372 There being great Numbers of those Religious at Ispahan, these Monks go always armed. **1860** PUSEY *Min. Proph.* 152 They had also true Nazarites..; and they felt the weight of these Religious against them.

2. a. A person given up to a religious or monastic life, esp. in the Church of Rome. †In ME. with pl. in *-es*.

c **1330** R. BRUNNE *Chron.* (1810) 136 To þo religiouses þat were in Gascoyne, He gaf a þousand mark. **1340** HAMPOLE *Pr. Consc.* 1888 Dede wil na frendshepe do..til na religiouse, ne til na seculere. **1377** LANGL. *P. Pl.* B. x. 317 Þere shal come a kyng, and confesse ȝow religiouses. *c* **1400** HYLTON *Scala Perf.* (W. de W. 1494) I. lxi, Ryght soo shalte thou stonde as..a relygyous in the sorte of relygyon. **1490** CAXTON *How to Die* 10 These demaundes and questyons ought to be sayd as well to religyouses as to seculers. **1577** HELLOWES *Gueuara's Chron.* (1584) 175 You send him newes as a Chronicler,..and counsel his conscience as a religious. **1600** W. WATSON *Decacordon* (1602) 23 Infamous libels put vp by..one religious against another. **1688** COLLIER *Several Disc.* (1725) 288 Theodoret..at the End of the Life of every famous Religious, desires the Benefit of their Prayers. **1720** DE FOE *Capt. Singleton* xiv. (1840) 249 He met with a kind of religious, or Japan priest. **1765** BLACKSTONE *Comm.* I. 132 A monk or religious was so effectually dead in law, that a lease..determined by such his entry into religion. **1793** W. HODGES *Trav. India* 112 A small district within a larger; it was at this time in the hand of a Gosine, or Hindoo Religious. **1813** EUSTACE *Class. Tour* (1821) III. viii. 311 An Italian Religious, and a Mahometan dervise are..placed by many nearly upon a level. **1888** BERNARD *Fr. World to Cloister* i. 2 The idea of your..adopting the hard life of a religious was one which never occurred to me.

b. A religieuse; a nun.

The form may be intended to represent the F. fem. In recent use not a gallicism.

1491 CAXTON *Vitas Patr.* (W. de W. 1495) I. v. 9/2 There were x. M. men, & xx. M. virgynes in that cite religyous & religiouses. **1512** *Helyas* in Thoms *Prose Rom.* (1828) III. 101, I wyll shortly go and yelde me a nune or religiouse in some nonery. **1651** T. MATTHEW *Life Lady L. Knatchbull* (1931) II. i. 87 Dame Mary Roper..was a much younger Religious. **1922** JOYCE *Ulysses* 706 Anal violation by male religious (fully clothed, eyes abject) of female religious (partly clothed, eyes direct). **1939** R. GODDEN *Black Narcissus* xxx. 273 You've forgotten who you are. You're a religious. A nun. **1948** W. S. MAUGHAM *Catalina* xxix. 189 It behoved Catalina to become a religious. **1980** I. MURDOCH *Nuns & Soldiers* I. 56 When she was being converted she was already purposing to be a religious.

religiousete, -ite, -ity, varr. RELIGIOUSTY.

religiously (rɪˈlɪdʒəslɪ), *adv.* [f. RELIGIOUS *a.* + -LY².] In a religious manner.

1. a. With religious feeling or conduct; in accordance with the principles of religion; piously, reverently, devoutly.

1382 WYCLIF *2 Macc.* xii. 43 Wele and religiously bythenkynge of aȝein rysyng. *c* **1450** tr. *De Imitatione* I. iii. 6 At þe day of dome, it shal not be asked..what good we haue seide, but hou religiously we haue lyued. **1538** STARKEY *England* I. i. 13 They relygyously worschyppyd and honowryd the name of God. **1588** SHAKS. *L.L.L.* IV. ii. 153 Sir you haue done this in the feare of God very religiously. **1613** PURCHAS *Pilgrimage* III. x. (1614) 294 In their Fast or Lent they abstaine very religiously. **1687** BOYLE *Martyrd. Theodora* viii. (1703) 110 The first of those who are recorded to have religiously deceased. **1744** BERKELEY *Siris* §183 In old Rome the eternal fire was religiously kept by virgins. **1853** LYNCH *Self-Improv.* ii. 32 People who would find a religion must seek it religiously.

transf. **1600** *Weakest goeth to Wall* (1618) G iij b, Lady, I affirme it constantly, I love the gentleman religiously.

Comb. **1614** B. JONSON *Barth. Fair* I. i. Wks. (Rtldg.) 312/1, I would be satisfied from you, religiously-wise, whether a widow [etc.].

†**b.** Solemnly, ceremoniously. *Obs.*

1576 FLEMING *Panopl. Epist.* 96, I protest vnfainedly, and promise religiously, that I will be wholy in your iurisdiction. **1595** SHAKS. *John* III. i. 140, I,..from Pope Innocent the Legate heere, Doe in his name religiously demand [etc.]. **1631** GOUGE *God's Arrows* III. §94. 359 Such as would not..by solemne and sacred oath religiously subscribe thereto.

†**2.** In the manner of a 'religious' person, in accordance with a monastic rule. *Obs.*

?*a* **1400** *Plowman's Tale* 23 He n'as not aye in cloister pent, Ne couthe religiousliche lout. **1450–1530** *Myrr. our Ladye* 62 For a relygyous persone oughte to be gouerned relygyously ouer all. **1483** CAXTON *Gold. Leg.* 360/2 A woman which was relygyously clad, whiche was his lauender.

3. Faithfully, strictly, exactly, conscientiously, scrupulously.

1579 E. K. *Gloss Spenser's Sheph. Cal.* June 25 The opinion of Faeries..sticketh very religiously in the myndes of some. **1605** CAMDEN *Rem.* 105 These distinctions of locall names..were religiously observed in Records vntill about the time of king Edward the fourth. **1663** COWLEY *Verses & Ess.* (1669) 106 Duty for Natures Bounty they repay, And her sole Laws religiously obey. **1726** LEONI *Alberti's Archit.* I. 51/1 One thing which I find the Ancients observed very religiously. **1776** GIBBON *Decl. & F.* xiii. I. 385 The image of the old constitution was religiously preserved in the senate. **1846** *Edin. Rev.* LXXXIV. 70 This legend is universally and religiously believed by the Arab Tribes. **1892** G. S. LAYARD *C. Keene* iv. 80 He had religiously tramped all the way home through the deserted streets.

4. In a religious sense; from a religious point of view; with respect to religion.

1833 J. H. NEWMAN *Arians* v. i. (1876) 358 Their own piety enabled them to interpret expressions religiously, which were originally..evasions of the orthodox doctrine. **1834** L. RITCHIE *Wand. by Seine* 90 When the [leper] was thus religiously dead, he was taken out of the town. **1842** J. AITON *Domest. Econ.* (1857) 314 Every minister ought to feel that he stands religiously accountable on this score. **1872** LIDDON *Elem. Relig.* i. 15 The worthlessness, religiously speaking, of unfruitful knowledge.

5. *Comb.*, as ***religiously-minded***.

1935 B. RUSSELL *Relig. & Sci.* vi. 144 The sacred history related in the Bible and the elaborate theology of the ancient and mediaeval Church have become less important than formerly to most religiously minded men and women.

religiousness (rɪˈlɪdʒəsnɪs). [f. as prec. + -NESS.] The state or character of being religious; †religious or careful attention.

1450–1530 *Myrr. our Ladye* 46 Relygyousness shall kepe the harte, and make yt ryghtefull. **1548** UDALL, etc. *Erasm. Par. John* xviii. 105 For all that thei pretende religiousnesse of very feare, lest yᵉ iudge should foorthwith haue punished them. **1561** T. NORTON *Calvin's Inst.* I. v. (1634) 11 In things of so great weight and to which is due a singular religiousnesse. **1599** SANDYS *Europæ Spec.* (1632) 8 What religiousnesse soever is in the peoples minds, may wholy or chiefly be attributed to their Sermons. *a* **1639** W. WHATELEY *Prototypes* I. xi. (1640) 98 A vertue in Abraham was religiousnesse. **1691** WOOD *Ath. Oxon.* I. 154 He could not abide any thing that appertained to a goodly religiousness, or monastical life. **1859** C. S. HENRY *Dr. Oldham's Talks* viii. (1860) 72 He mistakes sanctimony for saintliness, strictness for religiousness. **1877** SPARROW *Serm.* xxii. 292 This religiousness in man is no accident: it comes of his weakness and dependence.

†**reˈligiousty.** *Obs.* In 4–5 -te, 5 -tee, -ete, -ite, 6 -ity. [f. RELIGIOUS + -(I)TY: cf. RELIGIOSITY and obs. F. *religieusité*.]

1. Religiousness; religious life.

1388 WYCLIF *Ecclus.* I. 17 The drede of the Lord is religiouste of kunnyng. Religiouste schal kepe..the herte. *c* **1400** tr. *Secreta Secret., Gov. Lordsh.* 59 In foure maners, þat ys to say [in] religiousite, in Frendschipe, in Curtasye, and reuerence. *c* **1430** HOCCLEVE *New Canterb. T.* (E.E.T.S.) 17/40 Lyuynge in vertuous religioustee. **1475** *Bk. Noblesse* (Roxb.) 82 Men of religiouste and spirituelle.

2. Persons of religion. *rare*$^{-1}$.

c **1530** *Crt. of Love* 686 A figge for all her chastity, Her law is for religiousity.

religius(e, -y(o)us, obs. forms of RELIGIOUS.

relik(e, -likke, obs. forms of RELIC.

reˈlimb, *v.* [RE- 5 a.] *trans.* To provide with new limbs.

1855 SINGLETON *Virgil* I. Pref. 21 An awkward attempt is made to relimb the unhappy trunk.

reˈlimit, *v. Law.* [RE- 5 a.] *trans.* To limit anew. (See LIMIT *v.* 1.) So **relimiˈtation**.

1884 *Law Times* 9 Feb. 262/2 He executed..the resettlement... The estate was thereby re-limited to uses under which the plaintiff took only a life interest. **1886** *Law Rep. 31 Chanc. Div.* 255 Cases of..clerical error, such..as the insertion of a wrong name in a relimitation.

reˈline (riː-), *v.*¹ [f. RE- 5 a + LINE *v.*¹]

a. *trans.* To line again, to provide with a fresh lining.

1851 MAYHEW *Lond. Labour* II. 32/2 A portion of a black silk dress may be serviceable to re-line the cuffs of the better kind of coats. **1894** *Daily News* 17 Sept. 2/7 The blasting-in-stack has been relined with fire bricks. **1976** J. DRUMMOND *Funeral Urn* v. 21 She..asked when she might have the car. He grunted dourly, 'Gotta re-line the brakes.'

b. *spec.* in *Art.* To attach a new backing canvas to (a painting).

1911 M. J. GUNN *Print Restoration & Picture Cleaning* viii. 146 Nothing but re-lining will often save a valuable picture from perishing. **1948** G. L. STOUT *Care of Pictures* v. 96 The painting..had been relined at least once. **1957** *Encycl. Brit.* XVII. 68E/2 *Relining*, the procedure of attaching a new or secondary canvas at the back of a canvas support when that fabric has become too weak to serve its purpose or when the ground or paint has become loosened from it. *Ibid.*, If it [*sc.* the painting] has been relined before, the old relining canvas is removed. **1978** *Daily Tel.* 9 Dec. 14/4 He has cleaned, restored or relined over 85 pictures.

Hence **reˈlining** *vbl. sb.*

1884 W. H. GREENWOOD *Steel & Iron* 488 A stoppage for the relining, drying, and warming-up of a converter. **1921** *Automobile Engineer* XI. 168/1 It is necessary to remove the rear-hubs from their tapers..in order to gain access to the internal brake for relining. **1933** *Radio Times* 14 Apr. 121/2 Have your brakes tested..if they need relining—specify Ferodo... The Ferodo guarantee is tied to the steering wheel of your car when you have the brakes relined with Ferodo.

reˈline (riː-), *v.*² [f. RE- 5 a + LINE *v.*²] *trans.* To mark with new lines; to renew the lines of.

1875 VOYLE & STEVENSON *Milit. Dict.* 330/1 The guns have still to be reamed out preparatory to being relined. **1877** *Academy* 24 Nov. 495/1 It was M. Hopman's late father and himself who relined..Rembrandt's so-called *Night Watch*.

reˈliner. [f. RELINE *v.*¹ + -ER¹.] **1.** A person who provides oil-paintings with fresh linings.

1905 W. H. HUNT *Pre-Raphaelitism* I. 183 The reliner decided that the varnish was neither mastic nor copal. **1911** M. J. GUNN *Print Restoration & Picture Cleaning* viii. 147 In case the services of a picture re-liner and restorer should be needed.

2. Material providing a fresh lining, as for the brakes of a motor vehicle.

1920 *T. Eaton & Co. Catal.* Spring & Summer 395/1 *Tire Reliners* for Ford cars. Made of several layers of heavy tire fabrics. **1945** *Sun* (Baltimore) 8 Nov. 14/3 Motorists could recognize a sound used tire if it had a tread design at least every four inches, no emergency patches on the inside such as boots and reliners, [etc.].

†**reˈlinque,** *v. Obs. rare.* [ad. OF. *relinquir* or L. *relinquĕre*: see RELINQUISH.] *trans.* To leave, abandon. (In Caxton only.)

1483 CAXTON *Gold. Leg.* 423/2, I haue relynqued and lefte my londe and my parentes. **1484** —— *Fables of Æsop* III. iv, They whiche relynquen and leue theyr owne lordes for to serue another straunger..ben wel worthy to be punysshed.

relinquent (rɪˈlɪŋkwənt), *a.* (and *sb.*) *rare.* [ad. L. *relinquent-em*, pres. pple. of *relinquĕre*: see next, and cf. DELINQUENT.] **a.** *adj.* Relinquishing; vanishing. **b.** *sb.* One who relinquishes.

1847 in WEBSTER. **1884** R. BUCHANAN *Foxglove Manor* II. xvi. 48 Knowing something of the relinquent fancies of young vestals, he rejected the idea.

relinquish (rɪˈlɪŋkwɪʃ), *v.* Also 5–6 **relinquys**, **-lynquysshe**, **-lenquyssh**, etc. [ad. OF. *relinquiss-*, lengthened stem of *relinquir*, *relenquir* (12th c. in Godef.):—L. *relinquĕre*, f. *re-* RE- + *linquĕre* to leave.]

†**1.** *trans.* To withdraw from, desert, abandon (a person). *Obs. rare.*

1472–3 *Rolls of Parlt.* VI. 22/1 Yf he wold have relinquyst and departed fro youre most noble persone. *c* **1500** *Melusine* 262 That he was not parfytte frend, who that relenquysshed hys cousyn at hys nede. **1552** *Bk. Com. Prayer, Ordering of Deacons*, I from hencefurth shall vtterlye renounce, refuse, relinquish, & forsake the bishop of Rome.

†**b.** To abandon in fleeing. *Obs. rare*$^{-1}$.

a **1548** Hall *Chron., Edw. IV* 218 The Erle of Warwycke ..was now aduised by the Marques his brother, to relynquishe his horse.

†**c.** To give up as incurable. *Obs. rare*$^{-1}$.

1601 Shaks. *All's Well* ii. iii. 10 To be relinquisht of the artists,..Of all the learned and authenticke fellowes..That gaue him out incureable.

2. To give up or give over, to abandon, desist from (an idea, action, practice, etc.); to cease to hold, adhere to, or prosecute.

1497 Bp. Alcock *Mons Perfect.* D j/2 Who so euer professyth relygyon, & he..not relynquysshyth his owne wyll [etc.]. **1539** in *Lisle Papers* VIII. 41 (MS.), The Bishop of Canterbury..willed him to declare the truth and to relinquish his opinions. **1597** Hooker *Eccl. Pol.* v. lxv. §21 Touching therefore the sign and ceremony of the Cross, wee no way find ourselues bound to relinquish it. **1666–7** Pepys *Diary* 21 Jan., He might be got to our side and relinquish the trouble he might give us. **1766** Fordyce *Serm. Yng. Wm.* (1767) I. i. 39 When will you relinquish delusive pursuits? **1781** Gibbon *Decl. & F.* xviii. II. 109 Alarmed by this intelligence, he hastily relinquished the siege. **1805** *Med. Jrnl.* XIV. 43 Every hope of recovery was abandoned, and her physician relinquished his attendance. **1834** Ht. Martineau *Demerara* ix. 123 The absent brother and sister were less willing to relinquish the hope of return. **1859** Dickens *Lett.* (1880) II. 105, I altogether abandon and relinquish the idea.

†**b.** To leave *to* another to deal with. *Obs.*$^{-1}$

1547 Boorde *Brev. Health* Pref. 5 b, Wherfore I do omyt and leue out manye thynges, relynquyshynge that I haue omytted to doctours of hygh iudgement.

c. To desist from putting forward or supporting for office. *rare*$^{-1}$.

a **1797** H. Walpole *Mem. Geo. II* (1822) I. 388 He.. offered to omit the primate, provided Lord Kildare would.. offer to relinquish the Speaker too.

3. To give up, resign, surrender (a possession, right, etc.). Also const. *to*.

1560 Daus tr. *Sleidane's Comm.* 456 b, They wyll not relinquishe theyr Byshoprike. **1612** Davies *Why Ireland*, etc. 30 The english Lords..placed Irish Tenants vppon the Landes relinquished by the English. **1683** *Brit. Spec.* 129 King Lucius..is said to have relinquished his Crown, and passed over into Bavaria. *a* **1727** Newton *Chronol. Amended* (1728) 36 Sabacon, after a Reign of 50 years, relinquishes Egypt to his son. **1782** Miss Burney *Cecilia* i. i, The Deanery, indeed, she was obliged to relinquish. **1813** Wellington in Gurw. *Desp.* (1838) X. 565 They know my disinclination to relinquish the command. **1849** Macaulay *Hist. Eng.* ii. I. 202 He consented..to relinquish a large part of the territory which his armies had occupied. **1874** Green *Short Hist.* viii. §5. 517 An offer to relinquish ship-money failed to draw Parliament from its resolve.

b. To let go (something held).

1850 Mrs. Jameson *Leg. Monast. Ord.* (1863) 287 St. Antony sustains in his arms the Infant Christ, whom the Virgin, above, appears to have just relinquished. **1865** Dickens *Mut. Fr.* iii. xv, He once more put her hand to his lips, and then relinquished it.

†**4.** To leave behind; also, to leave in a specified condition. *Obs. rare.*

1582 Stanyhurst *Æneis* iii. (Arb.) 79 Thee Pheacan turrets foorth with from sight we relinquish. **1597** A. M. tr. *Guillemeau's Fr. Chirurg.* 51/1 All diseases relinquish some badde reliques in the parte, wherthrough they may the easyer returne agayne. **1679** J. Smith *Narr. Pop. Plot* Ded. B b, To render your People happy while you live, and relinquish them safe when you dye.

†**5.** *intr.* To disappear, pass away. *Obs.*$^{-1}$

1599 B. Jonson *Cynthia's Rev.* iv. i, I'll ensure you they will all relinquish: they cannot endure above another year.

†**6.** *trans.* To cancel, do away with. *Obs. rare.*

1594 West *2nd Pt. Symbol., Chancerie* §118 [He] doth threaten your foresaid Orator, that he may at his pleasure relinquish and disanull the beforesaid last Will and Testament.

†**7.** To release. Const. *of*. *Obs. rare*$^{-1}$.

1671 R. Montagu in *Buccleuch MSS.* (Hist. MSS. Comm.) I. 503 He did relinquish him of his promise of sending any land forces.

Hence **re'linquished** *ppl. a.*, **re'linquishing** *vbl. sb.*[1]; also **re'linquisher.**

1611 Cotgr., *Delaissement*, a..relinquishing, or giuing ouer. *Ibid.*, *Relinqueur*, a relinquisher, leauer, quitter. **1622** Callis *Stat. Sewers* (1647) 9 The Lease expired, C. enters, the Prince ejects him, and the King seizeth this Relinquished ground.

relinquishment (rɪ'lɪŋkwɪʃmənt). [f. prec. + -ment.] The act of relinquishing; abandonment, giving up, surrender (of a practice, possession, attempt, etc.); †renunciation (of a person).

1594 Hooker *Eccl. Pol.* iv. iii. §1 This is the thing they require in vs, the vtter relinquishment of all things popish. **1597** *Ibid.* v. lxiii. §3 Two couenants there are.., the one concerning relinquishment of Satan. **1613–18** Daniel *Coll. Hist. Eng.* (1626) 6 All..from Lucius to Vortigern (who succeeds this relinquishment) were Roman gouernours. **1680** S. Mather *Iren.* 13 If any shall require and insist upon the relinquishment of it. **1796** Morse *Amer. Geog.* I. 584 From this relinquishment by the United States the following tracts of land are explicitly excepted. **1839** James *Louis XIV*, III. 259 The disgrace which might attend the relinquishment of rights which he had asserted. **1867** Freeman *Norm. Conq.* (1877) I. App. 583 The relinquishment of Edinburgh by the English may have been less wholly an act of free will.

b. *U.S.* A tract of abandoned land.

1897 *Outing* (U.S.) XXIX. 570/2 He had come late in the previous summer, bought a relinquishment up the river [etc.].

reliqe, obs. form of relic.

‖**reliquaire** (rɛlɪ'kwɛə(r)). [F.] = reliquary.

1769 H. Walpole *Let. to G. Montagu* 17 Sept., We were shown some rich reliquaires, and the *corpo santo* that was sent to her by the Pope. **1813** Scott *Rokeby* vi. vi, While from the opening casket rolled A chain and reliquaire of gold. **1848** Lytton *Harold* ix. vii, 'In witness of that oath thou wilt lay thine hand upon the reliquaire', pointing to a small box that lay on the cloth of gold.

reli'quarian, *a. nonce-wd.* [f. as reliquary *a.* + -an.] Pertaining to relics.

1884 *Athenæum* 8 Nov. 585 Miss Austen is just the one whose letters might be expected to have a value only (if we may coin a word) reliquarian.

reliquary ('rɛlɪkwərɪ), *sb.* [ad. F. *reliquaire* (14th c.) = Sp. *relicario*: see relic and -ary[1], and cf. It. *reliquiario*, med.L. *reliquiārium*, *-iāre*, f. *reliquiæ*.] A small box, casket, shrine, or other receptacle, in which a relic or relics are kept.

1656 Blount *Glossogr.*, *Reliquary* (Fr. *Reliquaire*), a Coffin, Casket, or Shrine, wherein Relicks are kept. [Hence in Phillips (1658) and Bailey (1721).] **1739** Gray *Let. to West* 12 Apr., We stopt at St. Denis, saw..crucifixes and vows, crowns, and reliquaries of inestimable value. **1841** Bloxam *Gothic Archit.* (ed. 2) 202 A small stone reliquary or shrine of the fourteenth century was discovered a few years ago. **1852** Miss Yonge *Cameos* (1877) I. xv. 108 Then she hung a reliquary round his neck, and sent him to arm for the decisive combat. **1874** Green *Short Hist.* vii. §1. 346 Fresh orders were given to fling all relics from their reliquaries.

transf. *a* **1849** Poe *Coliseum*, Rich reliquary Of lofty contemplation left to Time by buried centuries.

attrib. **1877** W. Jones *Finger-ring* 142 In the possession of Lady Fitz Harding is a remarkable reliquary ring.

'reliquary, *a. rare.* [See prec. and -ary[1].] Belonging to a relic or relics.

1826 G. S. Faber *Diffic. Romanism* (1853) 164 The two most curious specimens of reliquary superstition. **1854** Patmore *Angel in Ho.* i. i. ix, I paced the Close, its every part Endowed with reliquary force To heal and raise from death my heart.

†**reli'quation**[1]. *nonce-wd.* [irreg. f. *relique* relic + -ation.] Devotion to relics.

1617 Collins *Def. Bp. Ely* ii. ix. 367 To resist your Reliquations (the true bankruptures of relligion) is wisdome to Victor, and to the auncient Christians that liued before him.

†**reli'quation**[2]. *Obs. rare.* [ad. L. *reliquātiōn-em* arrears, balance of a debt, n. of action f. *reliquārī* to be in arrears.] Balance, residue, remaining matter.

[**1658** Phillips, *Reliquation*, remains, or a being in arrearage.] *a* **1670** Hacket *Abp. Williams* ii. (1692) 197 The reliquation of that which preceded is, it looks not all like Popery that Presbyterism was disdained by the King.

reli'quation[3] (riː-). Renewed liquation.

1839 Ure *Dict. Arts* 1127, 4. the liquation; 5, the reliquation (*ressuage*).

relique, variant of relic.

†**reliqued**, *a. Obs. rare*$^{-1}$. [f. *relique* relic + -ed, or irreg. f. L. *reliqu-us*.] Remaining, left.

1628 Feltham *Resolves* ii. xix. 60 The Soule hath the reliqu'd Impressa's of diuine Vertue, still so left within her.

‖**reliquiæ** (rɪ'lɪkwiːː), *pl.* [L., f. *reliqu-us* remaining, f. *re-* re- 2 e + *liq-*, *linquĕre* to leave.]

1. Remains of any kind; *spec.* in *Geol.* remains of early animals or plants.

1654 E. Gayton *Pleasant Notes Don Quix.* iii. vii. 114 A sort of these Theeves are now redivivous, (the Reliquiæ I believe of Knight-Errantry) who goe by the name of Spirits. **1840** *Trans. Geol. Soc.* VI. 444 No distinction..can be observed, whereby the human can be separated from the other reliquiæ. **1853** Kane *Grinnell Exp.* xxi. (1856) 165 In a word, the numberless reliquiæ of a winter resting-place. **1867** Murchison *Siluria* xix. (ed. 4) 465 The Drift are simply the reliquiæ of the chief masses of gold. *Ibid.* xx. 485 We have in the Silurian strata fossil reliquiæ of such soft animals as Starfish. **1887** A. M. Brown *Anim. Alkal.* Introd. 15 The ptomaines..are the vital reliquiæ or residue material.. which may become the cause of disease.

2. *Bot.* (See quot.)

1835 Lindley *Introd. Bot.* (1839) 113 The withered remains of leaves, which, not being articulated with the stem, cannot fall off, but decay upon it, have been called *reliquiæ*.

3. Literary remains; unpublished or uncollected writings.

1933 *Times Lit. Suppl.* 2 Nov. 746/2 These reliquiae of Lytton Strachey, collected from periodicals and other sources..belong to all times of his life as a writer. **1948** *Mind* LVII. 517 Scarcely less important..are the Jena manuscripts [of Hegel] published partly by Lasson in 1923 and partly by Hoffmeister in 1931–2. Armed with these *reliquiae* a scholar could approach the making of a commentary with fair confidence.

Hence **re'liquial** *a. nonce-wd.*

1888 G. Macdonald *Elect Lady* xxx. 284 His interest in philology, prosody, history, and reliquial humanity.

†**re'liquian**, *a. Obs.*$^{-1}$ [f. L. *reliquiæ* (see relic) + -an.] Of the nature of a relic or relics.

1629 R. Hill *Pathw. Piety* (ed. Pickering) I. 149 A great ship would not hold the Reliquian peices of Christs Cross, which the Papists have.

†**'reliquies**, *pl. Obs. rare.* [ad. L. *reliquiæ*: see above, and relic.] Relics; remains.

1513 Douglas *Æneis* v. ii. 11 Sen that the reliquies and bonis in feir Of my divyne fadir we erdit heir. **1517** Torkington *Pilgr.* (1884) 7 The Reliquies at Venys canne not be nowmbred. **1563** T. Gale *Inst. Chirurg.* 41 b, The dregges and reliquies of yll, and vicious humours.

'reliquism. *nonce-wd.* [See relic and -ism.] The veneration of relics.

1841 Mackay *Mem. Pop. Delusions* I. 155 The principle of reliquism is hallowed and enshrined by love.

relish ('rɛlɪʃ), *sb.*[1] Also 6–7 **rellish**, 7 **rellice, rallish.** [Later form of reles, with shifting of stress (cf. *rellesde* s.v. relished) and assimilation of the ending to -ish[2].]

1. a. A taste or flavour; the distinctive taste *of* anything.

1530 Palsgr. 261/2 Rellysshe, a sauour, *govst*. **1594** T. B. *La Primaud. Fr. Acad.* ii. 109 God..hath giuen such relishes to meates and drinkes, whereby..all liuing creatures can presently know by their taste what things are good to eate and drinke. **1601** Holland *Pliny* II. 349 As for the cheeses made in France, they taste like a medicine, and haue an aromatical relish with them. **1687** A. Lovell tr. *Thevenot's Trav.* i. 178 We ate Fish..as broad and as thicke as Carpes, and of as good a rellish. **1742** Hume *Ess., Orig. Ideas* (1817) II. 18 A Laplander or Negro has no notion of the relish of wine. **1821** Scott *Pirate* iv, The salt relish of the drift which was pelted against his face. **1842** Tennyson *Will Waterproof* 98 Whether the vintage, yet unkept, Had relish fiery-new.

b. *fig.* or in fig. context.

1592 G. Harvey *New Letter* Wks. (Grosart) I. 266 What pleasanter relish of the Muses, then the Verse of the Other? **1615** Brathwait *Strappado* (1878) 108 If sweet, let th' relish of my poems moue That loue in thee, to thank me for my loue. *a* **1652** J. Smith *Sel. Disc.* ix. viii. (1859) 442 A mind that..hath its inward senses affected with the sweet relishes of divine goodness. *a* **1677** Barrow *Serm.* Wks. 1716 I. 267 Neither indeed hath any thing a more pleasant and savoury relish than to do good. **1723** Waterland *Serm. Eccl.* vii. 14 Wks. 1823 VIII. 459 The fruits of liberty have the more grateful relish after the uneasy hours of a close and tedious confinement.

c. *transf.* A trace or tinge *of* some quality; a suggestion; a sample or specimen; a small quantity.

1597 Shaks. *2 Hen. IV*, i. ii. 111 Your Lordship..hath yet some smack of age in you; some rellish of the saltnesse of Time. **1602** —— *Ham.* iii. iii. 92 Some acte That ha's no rellish of Saluation in't. **1620** E. Blount *Horæ Subs.* 255 The name carried with it a remembrance and rellish of the ciuill warres. **1697** Dryden *Virg. Past.* Pref. (1721) I. 92 The Style..should have some peculiar Relish of the Ancient Fashion of Writing. **1776** Burke *Corr.* (1844) II. 98 Without a shadow, a relish, a smutch, a tinge, anything, the slightest that can be imagined, of anger. **1809** W. Irving *Knickerb.* v. ii. (1849) 265 Let us have a relish of thy art. **1844** H. Stephens *Bk. Farm* II. 702, I never saw a relish of salt produce such an effect.

†**2.** An individual taste or liking. *Obs.*

1607 Shaks. *Cor.* ii. i. 206 We haue Some old Crab-trees here at home, That will not be grafted to your Rallish. **1653** H. More *Antid. Ath.* iii. xvi. §17, I do not here appeal to the Complexional humors or peculiar Relishes of men that arise out of the temper of the Body. **1711** Steele *Spect.* No. 114 ¶7 This Way of Thinking, which is so abstracted from the common Relish of the World. **1758** S. Hayward *Serm.* xvi. 466 Certain austerities in religion which by no means suit their relish.

3. a. An appetizing or pleasing flavour; a savoury or piquant taste. (In quots. chiefly *fig.*)

1665 Boyle *Occas. Refl.* vi. i, To..make his whole Meal of what was meant onely for Sauce, to give a Rellish to what he rejects for it. **1701** W. Wotton *Hist. Rome* i. 7 Rhetoric and Grammar..soon lost their relish with Marcus. **1737** Pope *Hor. Sat.* ii. ii. 32 The tired glutton..finds no relish in the sweetest meat. **1784** J. Barry in *Lect. Paint.* vi. (1848) 225 The style which Titian afterwards adopted..was not of so high a relish for rilievo and hue. **1801** Strutt *Sports & Past.* ii. ii. 68 At the commencement of the seventeenth century, these pastimes seem to have lost their relish among the higher classes of the people. **1868** E. Edwards *Ralegh* I. iv. 73 No amount of favour has relish for the Earl [of Essex], if his rival has favour too.

b. A savoury addition to a meal; an appetiser. Also *attrib.*

1797 W. Priest *Travels in U.S.A.* (1802) 32 About eight or nine in the morning they breakfast on tea and coffee, attended always with what they call *relishes*, such as salt fish, beef-steaks, sausages, broiled fowls, ham, bacons &c. **1798** *Sporting Mag.* XI. 162 To call at a public house..for a relish. **1826** J. F. Cooper *Last of Mohicans* I. vi. 72 Glad to eat their venison raw, and without a relish too. Here..we have plenty of salt. **1831** Mrs. F. Trollope *Dom. Manners Amer.* (1901) II. 41 The herrings..are excellent 'relish', as they call it, when salted. **1851** Mayhew *Lond. Labour* I. 329/1 Beef-steaks, eggs, or something in the shape of a relish. **1875** Jowett *Plato* (ed. 2) III. 28 A relish they shall have—salt and olives and cheese. **1963** R. I. McDavid *Mencken's Amer. Lang.* iii. 120 *Rolliches*, pickled rolls of meat, are still occasionally made in the Hudson Valley, and sometimes anglicized to *relishes*. **1978** *Chicago* June 221/1 The $4.50 to $7.95 dinners include a relish plate (crisp vegetables, cheddar cheese spread, and scoop of homemade liver pâté).

fig. **1841–4** Emerson *Ess., Love* Wks. (Bohn) I. 74 When happiness was not happy enough, but must be drugged by the relish of pain and fear.

4. a. Enjoyment of the taste or flavour of something; the pleasure of tasting or enjoying something agreeable; liking, zest. (In quots. chiefly *fig.*)

1649 Jer. Taylor *Gt. Exemp.* ii. Ad §10. 9 Our relishes are higher after a long fruition, than at the first Essayes. 1667 Milton *P.L.* ix. 1024 Much pleasure we have lost, while we abstain'd From this delightful Fruit, nor known till now True relish, tasting. 1672 Marvell *Reh. Transp.* Wks. (Grosart) I. 42 Ever since their mouths have been so in relish, that the Presbyterians are..the very canibals of capons. 1791 *Gentl. Mag.* LXI. 20/2 The clergy would, from the calls of their profession, if not from natural relish, keep up their classical acquirements. 1833 Ht. Martineau *Vanderput & S.* v. 83 She returned to her spiced baked eels and glass of liqueur with a new relish. 1882 J. H. Blunt *Ref. Ch. Eng.* II. 148 Cranmer pronounced the sentence of deprivation; and..seems to have done this with great relish.

b. Const. *for*, *of* (now rare), †*to*.

1665 Boyle *Occas. Refl.* iv. ix, If we go from God's Ordinances with a love to them, and a rellish of them. 1709 Steele *Tatler* No. 1 ¶6 The true Relish for Manly Entertainment..is not wholly lost. 1713 —— *Guardian* No. 14 ¶1 That which I observe they have most relish to is horses. 1784 Cowper *Task* i. 141 [My years] have not..yet impaired My relish of fair prospect. 1820 Hazlitt *Lect. Dram. Lit.* 14 Our admiration does not lessen our relish for him. 1834 Cary in P. Fitzgerald *Lamb* (1866) 184 Do they gather round and praise Thy relish of their nobler lays? 1872 Morley *Voltaire* 7 A moral relish for veritable proofs of honesty.

5. Sense of taste; power of relishing. *rare*⁻¹.

1774 Goldsmith *Retaliation* 111 Of Praise a mere glutton, he swallowed what came..Till his relish grown callous, almost to disease, Who pepper'd the highest was surest to please.

†**'relish**, *sb.*² *Mus. Obs.* Also 6 relise, releas, 7 rellish. [Of obscure origin: perh. ultimately the same as prec., but the connexion is not clear. See also relish *v.*²] A grace, ornament, or embellishment.

1561 T. Hoby tr. *Castiglione's Courtyer* i. Eiv, A musitien, yf in singing he roule out but a playne note endinge in a dooble relise wyth a sweete tune. 1575 Laneham *Let.* (1871) 61 My doobl releas, my hy reachez, my fine feyning, my deep diapason. 1608 Heywood *Lucrece* Wks. 1874 V. 200, I ha not the power to part from you, without a rellish, a note, a tone. 1616 J. Lane *Contn. Sqr.'s T.* xii. 287 The kinge..sunge so glorious musickes..with relishes and trewe divisions. 1657 R. Ligon *Barbadoes* (1673) 12 A song, which he performed..no Graces, Double Relishes, Trillos, Gropos, or Piano forte's, but plain as a packstaff. 1668 Shadwell *Sullen Lovers* iii, He has the best double Rellish in Gam-ut of any man in England.

relish ('rɛlɪʃ), *sb.*³ *rare.* Also 7 rell-. [ad. OF. *relais* (13th c. in Godef.) a projection of the masonry at the base of a wall.] A projection, now *spec.* in *Joinery* (see quot. 1875).

Cf. also East Anglian *rally* 'a projecting ledge in a wall built thicker below than above, serving the purpose of a shelf' (Forby).

1611 Cotgr., *Forject*, a iutting, or leaning out, or ouer; a rellish, or out-footing. 1679 Moxon *Mech. Exerc.* 171 *Rellish*, see *Projecture*. [*Projecture*, is a jetting over the upright of a Building.] 1875 Knight *Dict. Mech.* 1916/1 *Relish*, (Joinery) the projection of the shoulder of a tenoned piece beyond the part which enters the mortise.

relish ('rɛlɪʃ), *v.*¹ Also 6–7 rellish, 7 rallish. [f. relish *sb.*¹; cf. *disrelish*, and see also release *v.*²]

1. *trans.* **a.** To give or impart a relish to (a thing); to make pleasant to the taste. Also *fig.*

1586 B. Young *Guazzo's Civ. Conv.* iv. 185 So supper began, which was enterchangeablie relished with sundrie sweet and pleasant speeches. 1613 Purchas *Pilgrimage* i. xvi. (1614) 84 Earthly happinesse..is neuer meere and vnmixed, but hath some sowre sauce to rellish it. 1660 Ingelo *Bentiv. & Ur.* i. (1682) 155 Hunger and Thirst are our best sauce..; we still keep some to relish our next meal. c1720 Ramsay *4th Ep. Hamilton* 8 Your herrings, Sir, came hale and feer..; They relish fine Good claret wine. 1791 W. Bartram *Carolina* 349 Excellent coffee, relished with bucanned venison, hot corn cakes, excellent butter and cheese. 1850 Macaulay in Trevelyan *Life & Lett.* (1880) II. 286, I have also a novel.., to relish my wine. 1872 Browning *Fifine* xcii, Gust and smack which relished so The meat o'the meal folks made some fifty years ago.

†**b.** To have a taste, tinge, or trace of (some quality or thing), to partake of. *Obs.*

1604 T. Wright *Passions* v. §4. 192 In amplifications all conceits should relish a certaine greatnesse and carie with them some sort of excesse. a1637 B. Jonson *Discov.* Wks. (Rtldg.) 764/2 This was theatrical wit, right stage jesting, and relishing a play-house. 1656 [? J. Sergeant] tr. *T. White's Peripat. Inst.* 147 But these and many such like seem rather to rellish the nature of vapours. 1702 tr. *Le Clerc's Prim. Fathers* 4 His Style..doth not much relish the Neatness and Elegancy of the Athenian Writers.

c. To provide with something relishing; to please, gratify, delight. ? *Obs.*

1603 Dekker *Wonderful Year* D iv, To rellish the pallat of lickerish expectation..you must belieue [etc.]. 1608 in Capt. Smith *True Relat.* Wks. (Arb.) 103 To make a feast or two with bisket, pork, beefe, fish, and oile, to relish our mouthes. 1626 L. Owen *Running Register* 63 They send her many dainty dishes..to rellish her palate. 1692 Sir T. P. Blount *Ess.* Pref., If it relishes not thy gusto, the only way to be even with me, is for thee to turn Author. 1794 A. Bell in Southey *Life* (1844) I. 470 It relishes me much to listen to your counsel of meeting soon.

†**2.** To taste, take a taste of (also *fig.*); to distinguish by tasting. *Obs. rare.*

1594 Nashe *Unfort. Trav.* K 3b, Strong poyson..so mingled..that when his Grand-sublimity-taster came to relish it, he sunke downe stark dead. 1599 B. Jonson *Ev. Man out of Hum.* iv. iv, Friend! is there any such foolish thing in the world, ha? 'slid, I never relished it yet. 1623–33 Fletcher & Shirley *Night-Walker* i. iv, One that knows not neck-beef from a pheasant, Nor cannot rellish Braggat from Ambrosia.

†**b.** To feel. *Obs. rare*⁻¹.

1610 Shaks. *Temp.* v. i. 23 Shall not my selfe, One of their kinde, that rellish all as sharpely Passion as they [etc.]?

3. To enjoy, take pleasure or delight in.

1605 Shaks. *Lear* i. ii. 51 This policie, and reuerence of Age..keepes our Fortunes from vs, till our oldnesse cannot rellish them. 1633 G. Herbert *Temple, Flower* vi, I once more smell the dew and rain, And relish versing. 1759 Dilworth *Pope* 61 Highly capable of relishing beauties in the performances of others. 1784 Cowper *Task* v. 783 Thine heart, Made pure, shall relish with divine delight,..what hands divine have wrought. 1820 Shelley *Œd. Tyr.* i. 90 January winds, after a day Of butchering, will make them relish carrion. 1837 Hallam *Hist. Lit.* i. i. §92 His fine taste taught him to relish the beauties of Virgil and Cicero. 1861 M. Pattison *Ess.* (1889) I. 46 The German relished for his breakfast the good things..here provided.

refl. 1599 B. Jonson *Cynthia's Rev.* iv. i, O, I am rapt with it,..I never truly relish'd myself before.

b. To like, have a liking for; to care for, be pleased or satisfied with; to approve of.

1594 Drayton *Idea* 338 Foraine Nations rellish not our Tongue. 1632 Sanderson *Serm.* 124 Taxing the Abuses with such Freedome, as (it may be) some will not relish. 1748 *Anson's Voy.* ii. xi. 253 These speculations were not relished [*ed.* 5 adopted] by the generality of our people. 1777 Watson *Philip II*, i. (1793) I. 14 He was too much a Spaniard to relish anything that was not Spanish. 1832 R. & J. Lander *Exped. Niger* III. xviii. 134 This mode of proceeding I did not relish at all. 1865 Dickens *Mut. Fr.* i. ii, It is questionable whether any man quite relishes being mistaken for any other man. 1885 *Manch. Exam.* 11 June 4/7 They do not relish the prospect before them.

c. To take or receive in a particular manner. Now *rare.*

c1600 Drayton *Miseries Q. Margaret* liii, The duke..must cast and cunningly contrive, To see how people relished the same. 1643 Prynne *Sov. Power Parlt.* i. (ed. 2) 17 Which insolent speech the English Bishops relished so harshly, that they [etc.]. 1670 Cotton *Espernon* ii. vi. 245 The Duke of Espernon, whom the King began now much better to relish. 1762 Symmer in Ellis *Orig. Lett.* Ser. ii. IV. 450 How this will be relished at the Prussian Court, I wish I could say, I know not. 1884 *Nonconf. & Indep.* 16 May 469/1 His opening address..was evidently well relished by the audience.

†**d.** To appreciate, understand. *Obs. rare.*

1602 Marston *Ant. & Mel.* i. Wks. 1856 I. 14 Fooles relish not a ladies excellence. 1611 Shaks. *Wint. T.* ii. i. 167 If you, or stupified, Or seeming so, in skill, cannot, or will not Rellish a truth, like vs.

4. *intr.* To have a (or the) taste *of* something; to savour or smack *of*, have a touch or trace *of*.

1602 Shaks. *Ham.* iii. i. 120 For vertue cannot so innocculate our old Stocke, but we shall rellish of it. 1650 Jer. Taylor *Holy Living* (1727) 242 It will make everything relish of religion. 1684 *Scanderbeg Rediv.* i. 3 Streams usually relish of the Fountain whence they proceed. 1703 T. N. *City & C. Purchaser* 84 To be thus affected, would relish too much of a Cynical Humour. 1784 Sir J. Reynolds *Disc.* xii. Wks. 1797 I. 258 Those ideas only which relish of grandeur and simplicity. 1850 L. Hunt *Autobiog.* II. x. 31 His piety..relished of everything that was sweet and affectionate.

5. To taste in a particular way; to have a specified taste or relish. Also in *fig.* context.

1605 Chapman *All Fooles* Wks. 1873 I. 139 Doe not his kisses relish Much better then such pessants as I am? 1654 Fuller *Comm. Ruth* (1868) 101 Afflictions relish sour and bitter even to the palates of the best saints. 1751 *Affect. Narr. of Wager* 97 A Couple of Dogs..relished then as well to our Palates, as the best Mutton we had ever eaten. 1822 Hazlitt *Table-t.* Ser. ii. i. (1869) 1 A glass of old port or humming ale hardly relishes as it ought without the infusion of some lively topic. 1836 W. Irving *Astoria* II. 266 A feast of fish, of beaver, and venison, which relished well with men who had so long been glad to revel on horse flesh. 1866 Whittier *Marg. Smith's Jrnl.* Prose Wks. 1889 I. 13 The supper..relished quite as well as any I ever ate in the Old Country.

b. *transf.* or *fig.* in various contexts (cf. next).

1600 Dekker *Fortunatus* Wks. 1873 I. 92 How sweete your howlings rellish in mine eares? 1652 Needham tr. *Selden's Mare Cl.* 340 These antient Customs seem so to relish, as if those Islands had been subject to our Kings. 1665 Sir T. Herbert *Trav.* (1677) 89 One discommodity it hath, making all the other relish badly. 1719 De Foe *Crusoe* i. (Globe) 219 This Part of Friday's Discourse began to relish with me very well. 1809 Malkin *Gil Blas* xii. i. ¶2 That precaution relished well with his excellency. 1827 Hood *Hero & Leander* ii, Was it that spectacles of sadder plights Should make our blisses relish the more high?

†**6.** *fig.* To be agreeable or pleasant; to find acceptance or favour (*with* one). *Obs.*

1594 Lyly *Moth. Bomb.* i. iii, Nothing can relish in their thoughtes that sauours of sweet youth. 1611 Shaks. *Wint. T.* v. ii. 132 Had I beene the finder-out of this Secret, it would not haue rellish'd among my other discredits. 1649 Bp. Hall *Cases Consc.* (1650) 248 Then will the Christian faith begin to relish with them. 1681 Tate *Lear* Prol., He hopes since in rich Shakespear's soil it grew 'Twill relish yet, with those whose Tasts are true. 1697 Collier *Ess. Mor. Subj.* i. To Rdr. (1709) 182 Indeed, if a Man sets up for a Scepticк, I don't expect the Argument should Relish. 1740 J. Clarke *Educ. Youth* (ed. 3) 33 If that relishes with the Publick.

†**b.** To have a pleasant relish or taste. *Obs.*

1706 Watts *Horæ Lyr.* i. *Remember your Creator* iv, No more the blessings of a feast Shall relish on the tongue. c1728 Earl of Ailesbury *Mem.* (1890) 714 One finds some dishes that relish amongst a quantity of very ill ones.

Hence **'relishing** *vbl. sb.*

1702 *Eng. Theophrast.* 198 Friendship tastes very flat and insipid after the relishing of love.

†**'relish**, *v.*² *Obs.* Also 6 ralish, rellish. [app. f. relish *sb.*², but see also relesch.] *trans.* To sing, to warble.

1591 Shaks. *Two Gent.* ii. i. 20 First, you haue learn'd..to rellish a Loue-song, like a Robin-red-breast. 1593 —— *Lucr.* 1126 Ralish your nimble notes to pleasing eares. 1608 Heywood *Lucrece* Wks. 1874 V. 179 Whils't the King his willful Edicts makes..Hee's in a corner, relishing strange aires.

relish ('rɛlɪʃ), *v.*³ *rare.* [Cf. relish *sb.*³]

†**1.** *intr.* To project, jut out. *Obs. rare*⁻⁰.

1611 Cotgr., *Forjetter*, to iut, rellish, cope, leane out.

2. *trans.* To make shoulders on (wood) in shaping tenons. Hence ***relishing machine*** (Knight).

1884 Knight *Dict. Mech.* Suppl. 749/2 Such stuff is relished at one operation and handling.

'relishable, *a.* [f. relish *v.*¹ + -able: cf. *irrelishable* (1608).] Capable of being relished; enjoyable.

1618 T. Adams *Bad Leaven* Wks. 1862 II. 346 By leeven soured we make relishable bread for the use of man. 1633 —— *Exp. 2 Peter* i. 8 The gospel calls for relishable fruits. 1706 in Phillips (ed. Kersey). 1751 Earl Orrery *Remarks Swift* (1752) 151 Lord Bacon is the first author, who has attempted any style that can be relishable to the present age. 1847 *Blackw. Mag.* LXI. 333 A peculiarly relishable bit of news. 1887 Clark Russell *Frozen Pirate* II. i. 3 Several relishable sea-pies, cakes, and broths.

†**'relished**, *a. Obs.* Also 6 rellesde. [f. relish *sb.*¹ + -ed².] Having a (specified) relish; (well, ill, etc.) tasted or flavoured.

1567 Drant *Horace, Ep.* E vj, Then do I hope to drinke Lyuely and myldlie rellesde wynes. 1594 Carew *Huarte's Exam. Wits* ix. (1596) 123 He could not skil to speake with ornament and sweet and well relished tearms. 1638 Junius *Paint. Ancients* 315 An ill-relished gallamaufrey or hodge-podge. 1653 R. Sanders *Physiogn.* 279, I..have sufficiently waded in this various, yet pleasant relisht Doctrine. 1707 Mortimer *Husb.* (1721) II. 289 The John Apple..is a good relished sharp Apple the Spring following.

'relished, *ppl. a.* [f. relish *v.*¹ + -ed¹.] Liked (as food); enjoyed, appreciated.

1901 *Yearbk. U.S. Dept. Agric.* 1900 433 There was an outbreak of seventeen-year cicadas, which afforded an abundant and greatly relished food supply.

'relisher. *rare.* [f. as prec. + -er¹.] **a.** One who relishes or enjoys. **b.** = relish *sb.*¹ 1 b.

1788 Shirrefs *Poems* (1790) 129 What grand advantages from reading flow None, but the happy relishers, can know! 1888 *Ramsay's Scot. & Scotsmen in 18th C.* II. 82 Salt herrings were set down as a relisher.

'relishing, *ppl. a.* [f. as prec. + -ing².] Having or giving a relish.

1655 Moufet & Bennet *Health's Improv.* (1746) 178 Heath-cocks, whilst they are young, are little inferior to a Pheasant, very well relishing. 1673 Kirkman *Unlucky Citizen* 278 The Hangman had given them a Relishing taste of his Office. 1719 London & Wise *Compl. Gard.* 292 Any Relishing Plants, as Garlick, Onions. 1791–1823 D'Israeli *Cur. Lit.* (1866) 284/2 An experienced caterer of these relishing morsels. 1856 Kane *Arct. Expl.* I. xxix. 395 Our Esquimaux dogs..regarded them with relishing appetite. 1866 Geo. Eliot *F. Holt* (1868) 27 Asking if there were any relishing sauces in the house.

Hence **'relishingly** *adv.*

1698 [R. Ferguson] *View Eccles.* 123 The whole of what is Rellishingly divertive. 1824 *Examiner* 307/1 It savours relishingly of historic feeling. 1880 Meredith *Tragic Com.* iv, She drank her glass relishingly, declaring the wine princely.

†**'relishsome**, *a. Obs. rare*⁻¹. [f. relish *sb.*¹ + -some.] Full of relish.

1593 Nashe *Christ's T.* (1613) 116 So to sweeten the poyson..that it should be more relishsome and pleasant.

'relishy, *a. rare.* [-y¹.] Appetizing.

1864 D. G. Mitchell *Sev. Stor.*, *My Farm Edgewood* 147 Its freshness too, gives it a virtue, and a relishy smack.

re-'listen, *v.* [re- 5 a.] To listen again.

1855 Tennyson *Brook* 18 The brook..seems, as I re-listen to it, Prattling the primrose fancies of the boy.

relivant, obs. Sc. form of relevant.

relive (riː'lɪv), *v.* [f. re- 5 a + live *v.*, in early use on the analogy of *revive.*]

†**1.** *trans.* To raise or restore again to life; to resuscitate. *Obs.*

1548 Udall, etc. *Erasm. Par. Mark* 38b, As thoughe he had not bene able to reliue her, if she had bene deade in deede. 1590 Spenser *F.Q.* iii. iv. 35 Had she not beene devoide of mortall slime, Shee should not then have bene relyv'd againe. 1592 Sylvester *Tri. Faith* iv. xii, By Faith, Saint Paul did Eutichus relive.

2. *intr.* To come to life again; to live anew.

1548 Udall, etc. *Erasm. Par. Mark* 34b, Yf he had sayed that he shoulde shortely haue bene slayne of the Iewes, but woulde anon after reliue. 1579 E. K. *Gen. Argt.* in *Spenser's Sheph. Cal.* §3 The plesaunce thereof, being buried in the sadnesse of the dead winter now worne away, reliveth. 1608 Shaks. *Per.* v. iii. 64 Will you deliuer how this dead Queene relives? 1842 Tennyson *Locksley Hall* 107 Can I but relive in sadness? 1851 C. L. Smith tr. *Tasso* iii. lxviii, Thou, though dead to us, re-liv'st on high.

3. *trans.* To live (a period of time) over again.

a1711 Ken *Hymnotheo* Poet. Wks. 1721 III. 114 O that my mispent Years I might relive. 1797 Southey *Lett. fr.*

Spain (1799) 160 Memory's mystic power Bids me re-live the past. *a*1849 Poe *Marginalia* Wks. 1864 III. 528 It is assumed that the aged person will not re-live his life. **1872** Aubrey de Vere *Leg. St. Patrick, Epil.*, Those blessèd years I would re-live.
refl. **1899** J. Caird *Fundam. Ideas Chr.* II. xix. 239 No other life has so triumphed over death, has so gone on as His has done, reliving itself through the ages.

Hence **re'living** *vbl. sb.*
1548 Udall, etc. *Erasm. Par. Mark* 34 b, The myrthe and ioye whiche was made for her relyuyng.

† **re'liver**, *v. Obs. rare.* [ad. OF. *relivrer* (13th c.): see re- and liver *v.*] *trans.* To give up again, restore.
1456 in W. P. Baildon *Sel. Cas. Chanc.* (1896) 139 That the sayde John be ajugged to relyuere to hym the sayde dedes. **1472–3** *Rolls of Parlt.* VI. 40/2 That then the forseid sommes..be restored and relyvered to the paiers of the same. **1603** Shaks. *Meas. for M.* iv. iv. 6 Why meet him at the gates and reliuer our authorities there?

Hence † **re'livery**, restoration. *Obs.*⁻¹
1464 *Rolls of Parlt.* V. 566/1 To make relyvere of the seid suertees to the seid marchaunt.

rellesde, obs. f. relished.

rellice, obs. f. relish *sb.*[1]

rellick, obs. f. relic.

relligion, -ous, obs. ff. religion, -ous.

rellike, obs. f. relic.

rellish, obs. f. relish.

† **'rell-mouse.** *Obs.*⁻¹ [ad. G. *rellmaus* or Du. *relmuis*, of unknown etym.] The dormouse.
1752 J. Hill *Hist. Anim.* 521 The White-bellied Mus, with a blackish back, and long body. The Rell-Mouse.

rellolacean: see relollacean.

rellycke, rellyk, obs. forms of relic.

re'load (riː-), *v.* [re- 5 a.]
1. *trans.* To make up again as a load; to furnish with a fresh load, etc.
1778 [W. Marshall] *Minutes Agric.* 18 July 1776, Two men would re-load three loads a day. **1841** *Penny Cycl.* XIX. 260/1 [The engine] is thereby prepared for moving the train back again when reloaded. **1872** *Daily News* 1 Aug., The Belgic coal..is perhaps too friable for reloading and despatch by railway. **1884** *Manch. Exam.* 7 Oct. 5/6 Alexandria complains it cannot get trains returned to reload.
2. a. *absol.* To put in a fresh gun-charge.
1784 *Cook's 3rd Voy.* vi. v. II. 306 It is impossible for them to reload, as the animal is seldom at more than twelve or fifteen yards distance, when he is fired at. **1837** W. Irving *Capt. Bonneville* I. 126 In an instant his rifle was levelled and discharged... While he was reloading, he called to Campbell. **1895** Scully *Kafir Stories* 147 He reloaded with some [cartridges] which Langley passed over to him.
b. To load (a fire-arm or cartridge) again. Also, to load (a camera, cassette, etc.) again.
1853 Reade *Chr. Johnstone* 270 Marechal, reload Mr. Gatty's pistol. **1874** J. W. Long *Amer. Wild-fowl* i. 19 The chief superiority of the breech-loader lies in its capability of being so quickly reloaded. **1888** *Judge* Christmas Number 43/1 One Hundred Exposures may be made without 're-loading' the camera. **1892** Greener *Breech-Loader* 176 Cartridge-cases do not pay to reload; it is false economy in England to reload paper cases. **1897** *Sears, Roebuck Catal.* 473/3 The camera..can be reloaded..[in] any place from which the light is excluded. **1940** *Chambers's Techn. Dict.* 713/2 *Reload*, to remove exposed film and insert unexposed film in a camera or magazine in a dark-room or under light-tight conditions (e.g. in a changing bag). **1977** J. Hedgecoe *Photographer's Handbk.* 45 Instead of buying 35 mm film in cassettes you can purchase a bulk length..and then keep reloading cassettes yourself.

Hence **re'loaded** *ppl. a.*; **re'loading** *vbl. sb.* (also *attrib.*).
1822 *Regul. & Ord. Army* (1844) 51 A Salute that may require the reloading of the guns. **1874** J. W. Long *Amer. Wild-fowl* i. 20 The providing or reloading of a sufficient number of metallic shells. **1884** Knight *Dict. Mech.* Suppl. 750/1 *Reloading Tools*, for reloading spent capsules of breech-loading fire-arms. **1892** Greener *Breech-Loader* 157 Use the very best cartridges.., and by no means employ reloaded cases.

reload ('riːləʊd), *sb.* [f. the vb.] That which serves to reload anything, as a film placed in a camera, etc.
1928 *Daily Express* 14 Dec. 14/6 (Advt.), He can use the rod... Shaving Stick as a reload. **1958** *Newnes Compl. Amat. Photogr.* 75, 35 mm. film is also supplied as daylight-loading or darkroom-loading reloads for cassettes. **1961** *Guardian* 16 Mar. 6 He found..a small Minox pocket camera..and, in a brown paper bag, two Minox reloads. **1976** *Shooting Mag.* Dec. 47/2 Despite the budget price it does not make second-quality reloads. **1977** J. Wainwright *Nest of Rats* i. vii. 46 A shooter; a thirty-eight Colt 'Agent' revolver... There was a box of re-loads included in the parcel.

re'loader. [f. reload *v.* + -er[1].] That which or one who reloads.
1909 *Cent. Dict.* Suppl., *Reloader*,..a self-loading conveyer used to collect and transport coal from a coal-storage yard or pocket and to deliver it to railroad-cars or vessels or to place it in other near-by storage-places. **1973** 'A. Hall' *Tango Briefing* vii. 94 This man's forte was fast use of the automatic reloader... He was using something like a ·44 Magnum. **1976** *Shooting Times & Country Mag.* 18–24 Nov., I would very much appreciate advice from reloaders of home made cartridges. **1976** *Shooting Mag.* Dec. 46/2 No reloaders..should have anything to do with powder of unknown vintage that has been subjected to unknown storage conditions.

relo'catable, *a.* [f. relocat(e *v.* + -able.] That can be relocated.
1872 'Mark Twain' *Roughing It* xli. 290 At midnight.. the ledge would be 'relocatable'. **1976** *Milton Keynes Express* 11 June 34/1 (Advt.), Heating Engineer... To initiate sales leads, progress enquiries including those for Intercities Relocatable Boiler House, design systems and negotiate quotations through to acceptance. **1977** *Gloss. Terms Data Processing* (*B.S.I.*) vii. 9/1 *Relocatable program*, a computer program that is in such a form that it may be relocated. **1979** *Personal Computer World* Nov. 69 (Advt.), Relocatable linkable output.

relocate (riː-), *v.* orig. *U.S.* [re- 5 a.]
1. *trans.* **a.** To allocate or assign afresh.
1847 in Webster. **1872** Raymond *Statist. Mines & Mining* 14 The district was located in 1856 for..quartz and placer mining... Since then it has been relocated in 1863. **1879** H. George *Progr. & Pov.* vii. v. (1881) 347 If this work were not done, and one could re-locate the ground [etc.].
b. To locate, find the place of, again.
1885 *Harper's Mag.* May 835/2 Some individuals were able to relocate some of the old diggings.
c. To move to another place; to resettle; to change the location of.
1834 A. Lincoln et al. in I. D. Tarbell *Early Life A. Lincoln* (1896) xvii. 198 To view and relocate a part of the road..we have made the said relocation on good ground. **1866** *Rep. Indian Affairs* (U.S.) 76 If the Indians could be removed to some remote place equally fertile, and there relocated, it would no doubt be to their advantage. **1908** *Pacific Monthly* Feb. 204/2 The section east of here..has been practically all relocated, in places the new track being miles away from the original location. **1936** *Sun* (Baltimore) 21 July 1/3 Families which could not be supported by a shifting of land to moisture-holding grass production for cattle raising..would be 'relocated'. **1956** H. Foster in D. L. Linton *Sheffield* 245 The city does not face what would have been the almost insuperable problem of re-locating its vast heavy industries. **1964** T. W. McRae *Impact of Computers on Accounting* i. 23 This was a somewhat laborious business..causing a whole battery of 'words' to be relocated to different addresses. **1970** *Globe & Mail* (Toronto) 25 Sept. b2/8 Each of the three Canadian companies..has been looking at the possibility of relocating their data centres. **1978** *N.Y. Times* 30 Mar. b3/5 Paving the way for the Nestlé Company to relocate its White Plains headquarters on the property.
2. *intr.* To settle again. Freq. without const.
1841 in Webster. **1851** C. Cist *Cincinnati* 143 [This] determined the company to re-locate on higher ground. **1864** *Congress Globe* 9 Mar. 1018/2 In a larger number of cases these persons having taken homesteads, and again desiring to sell and relocate,..have paid for the lands. **1894** *Chicago Advance* 31 May, The congregation is preparing to re-locate in the north part of the city. **1957** [see runaway *sb.* (and *a.*) 7]. **1964** *New Statesman* 3 Apr. 533/2 It offers an enjoyable evening out in Jaguar-threepointfoursville where the hero has relocated from his Scottish tenement by selling cash registers. **1968** 'E. Lathen' *Stitch in Time* xvi. 134 He was relocating, he explained..because of a sudden desire to specialize in dermatology. **1971** *Daily Mail* 16 Mar. 22/1 (Advt.), Applicants should be prepared to work in our London Office initially, and relocate to new premises in Basingstoke..by 1973. **1978** *New York* 3 Apr. 37/2 The company had to relocate for technical reasons. **1979** *N.Y. Rev. Bks.* 25 Oct. 55/1 (Advt.), Lady author/lecturer who can easily re-locate seeks male counterpart.

relocation (rɛləʊ'keɪʃən, riː-). [In sense 1, f. late L. *relocāre* to relet; cf. F. *relocation* (1585). In sense 2, f. re- 5 a + location (cf. prec.).]
1. *Sc. Law.* ***tacit relocation***, the implied renewal of a lease when the landlord allows a tenant to continue without a fresh agreement, after the original lease has expired.
1746–7 *Act 20 Geo. II*, c. 50 §21 Any lease or tack..made in writing, or by verbal agreement, tacit relocation, or otherwise. **1754** Erskine *Princ. Sc. Law* (1809) 251 In tacks of teinds, as of lands, there is place for tacit relocation. **1838** W. Bell *Dict. Law Scot.* 582 When the term of the lease is expired it is in the power of the landlord and tenant to continue the lease from year to year by tacit relocation. **1886** *Act 49 & 50 Vict.* c. 50 §3 Any lease, tack, or set, whether constituted by writing or verbally, or by tacit relocation.
2. The action of locating afresh; a new allocation.
1837 A. Lincoln Let. 5 Aug. in *McClure's* (1896) Mar. 316/1, I also tacked a provision on to a fellow's bill, to authorize the relocation of a road. **1873** *Trans. Illinois Dept. Agric.* X. 371 The court shall appoint three viewers to examine the necessary re-location. **1877** Raymond *Statist. Mines & Mining* 221 Some relocations have been made under the act of 1872 and its amendments. *Ibid.*, All these relocations and new discoveries. **1901** S. E. White *Claim Jumpers* 232 Under the terms of a relocation, we can use the old stakes and 'discovery'. **1948** *Sierra Club Bull.* Dec. 5/1 A general relocation of the road was thereupon planned, including a higher crossing of Yosemite Creek. **1963** C. R. Cowell et al. *Inlays, Crowns, & Bridges* viii. 89 Re-location of the copper ring may be inaccurate in such an elastic material. **1967** *Boston Sunday Globe* 23 Apr. 9/5 A private company has sponsored refugee relocation. **1973** M. Mann (*title*) Workers on the move: the sociology of relocation. **1979** *Navajo Times* (Window Rock, Arizona) 24 May 1/2 He recognized that relocation would be difficult for the Navajos. **1981** J. Sutherland *Bestsellers* i. 29 A move towards bestsellerism..would seem to presage a general relocation of the bestseller.
3. *attrib.*, as ***relocation allowance, assistance, cost, director, expense, grant***; **relocation centre** *U.S.*, an internment camp to which persons of Japanese birth or origin were committed during the war of 1939–45.
1958 *Observer* 12 Jan. 18/3 (Advt.), Liberal *relocation allowances will be given successful candidates. **1968** *Globe & Mail* (Toronto) 3 Feb. b6/3 (Advt.), Generous relocation allowance. *Ibid.* 17 Feb. b6 (Advt.), Excellent advancement potential and benefits program. *Relocation assistance will be offered. **1976** *Star* (Sheffield) 20 Nov. (Advt.), Relocation assistance will be provided. **1943** S. Menefee *Assignment: U.S.A.* 68 Hearst reporters got anti-Japanese statements from Mayor Fletcher Bowron and other prominent figures in Los Angeles and played up the Dies Committee's 'exposures' of the *relocation centers. **1967** *Economist* 22 Apr. 354/2 In the days just after the bombing of Pearl Harbour, many Americans vented their panic..on the Nisei... The brunt fell most heavily on the large communities on the West Coast... These were evacuated en masse to inland 'relocation centres'. **1970** *Internat. & Compar. Law Q.* 4th Ser. XIX. ii. 237 A sparsely populated Coast where *relocation costs are nominal. **1963** *Freedomways* Summer 425 A *relocation director,..whose job is to help relocate families displaced from areas where new housing is being constructed. **1961** *Times* 27 Jan. 3/3 (Advt.), *Relocation expenses guaranteed for selected Engineers. **1977** *Navy News* July 35 (Advt.), Relocation expenses will be considered where appropriate. **1977** *Times Educ. Suppl.* 21 Oct. 52/3 (Advt.), *Relocation grants available in approved cases.

re'lock (riː-), *v.* [re- 5 a.] To lock again.
1797 Mrs. Radcliffe *Italian* xii, He concluded with a laugh of derision, and was re-locking the door. **1870** Miss Bridgman *R. Lynne* I. xvi. 282 He..relocked the desk.

re'lodge (riː-), *v.* [re- 5 a.] To lodge again.
1805 Southey *Madoc in Azt.* xxii, Till in her mortal tenement relodged Earthly delights might win her to remain.

† **relo'llacean**, *a. Obs. rare*⁻¹. In 7 rellol-. [f. mod.L. *relolleum*, app. invented by Paracelsus, and defined as a 'virtus ex complexione': cf. Waite tr. *Paracelsus* II. 178 ff.] Arising from, or pertaining to, the 'complexion' or natural constitution of things. So also **relo'llaceous** *a.*, **re'lolleous** *a.*
1654 Whitlock *Zootomia* 406 Would we could light on some nobler principles that might sublime us from these Rellolacean Principles,..dead, low, beggarly Elements. **1662** J. Chandler *Van Helmont's Oriat.*, *Premonition*, The ..vital Air of the Body wherein its Diseases Radically dwel, & not in Relolleous qualities, nor in feigned Elementary complexions. **1894** Waite tr. *Paracelsus* II. 180 Here, however, we are speaking of cold and heat in cherionic not in relollaceous matters. *Ibid.* 184 Those things which are not intensified at all, of which kinds are snow and ice, by reason of their relolleous nature.

† **re'long**, *v. Obs. rare.* [ad. OF. *ralonger* (mod.F. *rallonger*), f. *re-* re- + *allonger*: see long *a.*] *trans.* **a.** To extend. **b.** To postpone.
1523 Ld. Berners *Froiss.* I. ccxii[i]. 108/2, I thynke it were good, that the trewce were relonged vnto the fest of saynt John Baptist next folowynge. **1525** *Ibid.* II. lxi. 79/1 Comaundynge that the iourney & batayle..sholde be relonged tyl his comynge to Parys.

re'look, *v.* [re- 5 a.] *intr.* To look again.
1833 S. Austin *Charac. Goethe* I. 186 After looking and re-looking, blinking with one eye and then with the other. **1860** Darwin in *Life & Lett.* (1887) II. 291 Wollaston misrepresents..some passages in my book. He reviewed, without re-looking at certain passages.

† **re'love**, *v. Obs.* [f. re- + love *v.*; cf. L. *redamāre*.] *trans.* and *intr.* To love in return.
*c*1530 tr. *Erasmus' Serm. Child Jesus* (1901) 11 For how many causes Jesus is to be loued of vs; nay to be reloued rather; for he loued vs not yet created. **1604** T. Wright *Passions* v. §4. 211 Love causeth Love, and the beloved reloving augmenteth the originall Love. **1619** W. Sclater *Exp. 1 Thess.* (1630) 236 To reloue [God] is our happinesse. *a*1694 J. Scott *Wks.* (1718) II. 386 This must render his love more valuable and consequently augment our obligation to relove him.

Hence † **re'loved** *ppl. a. Obs.*
1605 A. Wotton *Answ. Pop. Pamph.* 1 Louing and reloued friend, I haue received your courteous letter.

† **re'luce**, *v. Obs. rare.* [ad. L. *relūcēre*: see relucent.] *intr.* To shine back, cast back light.
1413 *Pilgr. Sowle* (Caxton 1483) iv. xxviii. 74 In euery creature..ther relucith a beme of this bryght heuenly myrrour. **1484** Caxton *Fables of Alfonce* ix, The Foxe.. shewed to the wulf the shadowe of the mone whiche reluced in the well.

re'lucence, *sb. rare.* Also † -ency. [See next and -ence, -ency.] The quality of being relucent.
1611 Florio, *Rilucenza*, a shining or relucency. **1717** J. Hog in *E. Fisher's Marrow Mod. Divinity* (1781) Pref. 15 The relucence of gospel-light has been the choice mean.. for the effectuating of great things. **1926** *Spectator* 15 May 849/2 The mystical life..found again and again inspiration and relucence from the poets.

relucent (rɪ'l(j)uːsənt), *a.* Now *rare.* [ad. L. *relūcent-em*, pres. pple. of *relūcēre* to shine back: cf. lucent.] Casting back light; shining, gleaming, bright, refulgent.
*c*1507 *Justes of May & June* 32 in Hazl. *E.P.P.* II. 114 Theyr armure clen relucent without ruste. **1575** Laneham *Let.* (1871) 48 Az it wear the Egiptian Pharos relucent vntoo all the Alexandrian coast. **1626** T. H[awkins] tr. *Caussin's Holy Crt.* 172 Heauen sheweth it selfe wholy relucent in starrs and brightnesse. **1676** Hobbes *Iliad* xxii. 135 As flaming fire relucent was the brass. **1727–46** Thomson *Summer* 142 In brighter mazes the relucent stream Plays

o'er the mead. **1883** *Harper's Mag.* Jan. 182/2 A greater number of relucent points became visible.

transf. and *fig.* **1512** *Helyas* Prol. in Thoms *E. Eng. Prose Rom.* (1858) III. 15 Of such as were relucent in vertuous feates. *a* **1529** SKELTON *P. Sparowe* 1159 Such relucent grace Is formed in her face. **1612** R. SHELDON *Serm. St. Martin's* 17 [He] might contemplate the very diuine attributes, to be in an admirable sort relucent and resplendent, in the very humanitie of Christ. **1671** MACWARD *True Nonconf.* 393 The grace and principle of zeal which..is therein conspicuously relucent. **1897** F. THOMPSON *New Poems* 33 The relucent song take for thy sacred meeds!

reluct (rɪˈlʌkt), *v.* Also 6 reluck-. [ad. L. *reluctārī*, f. *re-* RE- + *luctārī* to struggle: but in later use (see 2 b) prob. a back-formation from *reluctance*, *-ant*.]

†**1.** *intr.* To strive or struggle *to* do something. **1526** *Pilgr. Perf.* (W. de W. 1531) 118 b, The more that ony persone relucketh, wrestleth, or stryues to ouercome these..temptacyons. **1633** EARL MANCH. *Al Mondo* (1636) 72 At that instant [of death] Nature will reluct to keepe still her being, unto which death is repugnant, life pleasing.

2. To struggle, strive, or rebel *against*, to show dislike, to revolt *at*, to offer opposition *to*, a thing.

1547 BOORDE *Brev. Health* lxviii. 19 b, A power of the soule the whiche doth reluct agaynst vyces and synne. **1639** WALTON *Lives, Donne* (1670) 81 He was by nature highly passionate, but more apt to reluct at the excesses of it. **1657** W. MORICE *Coena quasi Κοινὴ* xvi. 262 Infirmities, which he that knows their hearts..may know they reluct against. **1675** *Art Contentm.* XI. x, Our souls will more acquiesce in the accomplishment of the Divine will, then our flesh can reluct to any severe effects of it. *a* **1734** NORTH *Lives* (1826) I. 157 Against which she did not seem to reluct, but held her-self very reserved. **1784** P. OLIVER in T. Hutchinson *Diary* (1886) II. 398, I may possibly create a nausea, which your appetite may reluct at. **1821** LAMB *Elia* Ser. I. *New Year's Eve*, I care not to be carried with the tide,..and reluct at the inevitable course of destiny. **1849** *Escape fr. Toil* 8/2 He is apt to reluct against the oppression of task masters.

b. Without prep.: To offer opposition; to manifest or express reluctance; to object.

1648 *Hunting of Fox* 42 They murther with the Sword of Justice, if in the least we doe reluct. **1671** WOODHEAD *St. Teresa* II. xxxii. 203, I conceived, it would be necessary for me to go there,..though my nature relucted much. **1683** HICKES *Case Inf. Bapt.* 75 They relucted to confess their Sins. **1756** J. ADAMS *Diary* 15 Mar., The girl relucted a little, upon which he gave her three guineas. **1872** M. COLLINS *Pr. Clarice* viii, Clarice wanted to go on the river, but Josephine relucted. **1899** HOWELLS *Ragged Lady* 357, 'I don't know as I should like it very much', his wife relucted.

Hence **reˈlucting** *ppl. a.*

1655 FULLER *Ch. Hist.* III. ii. §38 A few there were, whose relucting Consciences remonstrated against the least Compliance with King Stephen. **1659** *Lady's Call.* II. iii. §7 To wrest the child from the relucting Mother.

reluctance (rɪˈlʌktəns). [f. RELUCTANT: see -ANCE, and cf. F. *réluctance* (rare and objected to by purists), It. *reluttanza*.]

1. a. The act of struggling *against* something; resistance, opposition. (†Also *pl.*) Now *rare*.

1641 M. FRANK *Serm., Call. Peter* (1672) 483 The body itself..by continual reluctances against it [the soul], and perpetually throwing off the commands of it..seems to wish it gone. **1660** MILTON *Free Commw.* Wks. 1851 V. 448 The Reluctance, I may say the Antipathy, which is in all Kings against Presbyterian and Independent Discipline. **1667** —— *P.L.* II. 337 What peace can we return, But, to our power, hostility and hate, Untam'd reluctance, and revenge..? **1764** *Mem. G. Psalmanazar* 68 In spite of all reluctance from pride and self-love. **1882–3** SCHAFF *Encycl. Relig. Knowl.* III. 2094 Thus only can we understand the reluctance of the latter against the traditional system.

b. The property, in a magnetic circuit, of opposing to a certain extent the passage of the magnetic lines of force. (Cf. RESISTANCE.) Also *attrib.*

1888 O. HEAVISIDE in *Electr. Papers* (1892) II. xxxix. 168, I would suggest that what is now called magnetic resistance be called the magnetic reluctance; and when referred to unit volume, the reluctancy (or reluctivity). **1893** A. E. KENNELLY *Electro-Dyn. Machinery* I. iii. 25 Reluctance is thus the analogue, in the magnetic circuit, of resistance in the galvanic. **1896** BEDELL *Princ. Transformer* 249 The co-efficients of induction vary inversely as the reluctance; their ratios are independent of the reluctance. **1967** KURRELMEYER & MAIS *Electricity & Magnetism* xii. 291 An air gap of 0·1 mm has the same reluctance as 1 m of iron of permeability 10,000. **1968** *New Scientist* 11 Jan. 63/2 The reluctance motor is a synchronous machine; its speed is determined entirely by the frequency of the ac supply. **1977** *Gramophone* Aug. 366/1 The moving-iron (variable reluctance) principle is used with a larger than usual fixed magnet.

2. a. Unwillingness, disinclination. Freq. in phr. ***with*** (or ***without***)..***reluctance***. (†Also rarely *pl.*)

1667 *Decay Chr. Piety* viii. ¶50 With what dismal reluctances shall we come to pay for these, of which we have made no advantage? **1710** in Somers *Tracts* II. 247 'Tis not without Reluctance that he consents to part with some Persons. **1712** ADDISON *Spect.* No. 512 ¶1 There is nothing which we receive with so much Reluctance as Advice. *a* **1740** WATERLAND *Wks.* (1823) IX. 383 Lay we aside all inveterate prejudices and stubborn reluctances, as soon as ever we have light enough to see that we have been in an error. **1777** PRIESTLEY *Philos. Necess.* Pref. 31 Like Dr. Hartley, I gave up my liberty with great reluctance. **1825** JEFFERSON *Autobiog.* Wks. 1859 I. 108 This silenced my reluctance, and I accepted the new appointment. **1875** STUBBS *Const. Hist.* xiv. II. 115 Their reluctance delayed proceedings for nearly a year.

b. Const. *at*, *to*, and with *inf.*

1740 CIBBER *Apol.* Ded., Your reluctance to put the vanity of an author out of countenance. **1759** ROBERTSON *Hist. Scot.* v. Wks. 1813 I. 367 He discovered a reluctance at undertaking that office. **1788** MRS. HUGHES *Henry & Isabella* IV. 136 The lady to whom these proposals were directed, appeared to feel no reluctance to the thought of accepting them. **1844** H. H. WILSON *Brit. India* II. 281 The Governor-General's reluctance to the restoration of the Raja. **1871** R. W. DALE *Commandm.* i. 38 Our strange reluctance to have to do with God is not an accident.

c. Recoil *from* something. *rare*$^{-1}$.

1871 HOWELLS *Wedd. Journ.* 110 This absurd reluctance from facts.

†**3.** A struggle or qualm of conscience. *Obs.*$^{-1}$

1666 PEPYS *Diary* (1879) III. 402 My nature..will esteem pleasure above all things, though yet in the middle of it, it has reluctances after my business which is neglected.

¶**4.** Regret, sorrow. (Cf. RELUCTANCY 4.) *Obs.* A misuse, through association with L. *luctus* grief.

1706 HEARNE *Collect.* (O.H.S.) I. 266 His untimely Death happen'd to ye great Reluctance of all good and learned Men. **1710** *Ibid.* II. 369 He died at Rome..to the great Reluctance of all that knew him.

reluctancy (rɪˈlʌktənsɪ). Now *rare*. [See RELUCTANT and -ANCY, and cf. prec.]

†**1.** An internal or mutual struggle or contest; a mental struggle. *Obs.*

1621 BURTON *Anat. Mel.* I. i. II. xi. 45 Lust counsels one thing, reason another, there is a new reluctancy in me. *c* **1645** HOWELL *Vote* in *Lett.* (1650) II. 128 The humors stil are combating for sway (Which wer they free of this reluctancie And counterpoised, man would immortal be). **1651** LILLY *Chas. I* (1774) 219 Also he had many reluctancies in himself, for preferring so unworthy a scornful fellow. **1652–62** HEYLIN *Cosmogr.* To Rdr., I cannot think thereof, without much affrightment; nor intimate thus much of it, without great reluctancies.

†**2.** Resistance or opposition of one thing *to* another. *Obs.*

1640 WILKINS *New Planet* ix. (1707) 250 The Followers of Ptolemy..deny the Heavens to be capable of any reluctancy to Motion. *a* **1665** J. GOODWIN *Filled w. the Spirit* (1867) 247 Nor is there any contrariety, or averseness, or reluctancy to the motion discerned in these fresh waters.

†**b.** Resistance or opposition on the part of persons *against* or *to* something. Also *pl.* *Obs.*

1650 CHARLETON *Paradoxes* Ep. Ded. 5 My obstinate reluctancy, against the Advisoes of my Honoured Friends. *a* **1677** BARROW *Serm.* (1686) II. iii. 43 Notwithstanding our frequent and stiff reluctancies thereto [piety]. **1679** *Hist. Jetzer* 15 Come, come, no more of this reluctancy against the Divine pleasure!

c. = RELUCTIVITY.

1888 [see RELUCTANCE 1 b].

3. Aversion, disinclination, unwillingness. Freq. in phr. ***with*** (or ***without***)..***reluctancy***.

1634 HABINGTON *Castara* (Arb.) 113 For he who suffers want without reluctancie, may be poore not miserable. *c* **1680** BEVERIDGE *Serm.* (1729) II. 545 You must not give your alms with any reluctancy or unwillingness. **1740** CIBBER *Apol.* (1756) II. 80, I yet feel a reluctancy to drop the comparison. **1826** E. IRVING *Babylon* II. VI. 69 The slowness and reluctancy with which errors yield to conviction. **1871** M. COLLINS *Mrq. & Merch.* II. v. 133 Ascribing Amy's reluctancy to her..youth.

¶**4.** Regret. (Cf. RELUCTANCE 4.) *Obs.*

1654 WOOD *Life* 25 July (O.H.S.) I. 186 Hussey &..Peck ..were hang'd in the Castle-yard in Oxon. to the great reluctancy of the generous royalists. **1691** —— *Ath. Oxon.* I. 9 He gave way to fate at Galloway..to the great reluctancy of all learned Men.

reluctant (rɪˈlʌktənt), *a.* [ad. L. *reluctant-em*, pres. pple. of *reluctārī* to struggle against, f. *re-* RE- + *luctārī* to struggle: cf. LUCTATION. Hence also F. *réluctant* (rare), It. *riluttante*.]

1. Struggling; writhing. *rare*.

1667 MILTON *P.L.* x. 515 Down he fell A monstrous Serpent on his Belly prone, Reluctant, but in vaine. **1820** SHELLEY *Liberty* xv, Disdain not thou..To set thine armed heel on this reluctant worm.

b. Offering resistance or opposition *to* something. *rare*.

1726 POPE *Odyss.* XIX. 597 A while, reluctant to her pleasing force, Suspend the restful hour with sweet discourse. **1796** MORSE *Amer. Geog.* I. 382 The soil on the sea coast is hard, and reluctant to the plough.

†**c.** Repugnant, distasteful, *to* one. *Obs.*$^{-1}$

1662 WINSTANLEY *Loyal Martyrol.* (1665) 13 Having eaten up most of the Horses..and whatsoever..could afford them Nourishment, though most reluctant to Nature.

2. Unwilling, averse, disinclined.

1706 J. MATTHEWS *Serm. at Tewkesbury* 8 They must..do some things with a trembling hand, and reluctant heart. **1766** GOLDSM. *Hermit* xvii, From better habitations spurned, Reluctant dost thou rove? **1777** WATSON *Philip II* (1839) 479 Mayenne was now as solicitous to persuade the duke..as he had been formerly reluctant and averse. **1858** LONGF. *M. Standish* II. 91 Taking the hand of his friend, who still was reluctant and doubtful. **1874** GREEN *Short Hist.* iv. §3. 184 Edward was still reluctant to begin the war.

b. *transf.* of things.

1667 MILTON *P.L.* VI. 58 Reluctant flames, the signe Of wrauth awak't. **1712** BLACKMORE *Creation* III. 119 Did not Industrious Man..Extort his Food from the reluctant Soil ..? **1774** PENNANT *Tour Scotl. in 1772*, 306 Here a wet sky brings a reluctant crop. **1796** SCOTT *William & Helen* lix, Reluctant on its rusty hinge Revolved an iron door. **1864** TENNYSON *En. Ard.* 378 [They] bent or broke The lithe reluctant boughs to tear away Their tawny clusters. **1890** 'R. BOLDREWOOD' *Col. Reformer* (1891) 305 The enormous treasure-pile..won from the reluctant earth.

†**c.** Tardy, dilatory, slow. *Obs. rare*$^{-1}$.

1797 HOLCROFT *Stolberg's Trav.* (ed. 2) III. lxxi. 80 The ..bones..may be those of persons who were too reluctant in their flight.

3. Characterized by unwillingness, disinclination, or distaste.

1725 POPE *Odyss.* I. 22 Calypso in her caves constrain'd his stay, With sweet, reluctant, amorous delay. **1786** BURKE *Art. agst. W. Hastings* Wks. 1842 II. 219/2 Which late and reluctant consent and authority were extorted from him. **1849** MACAULAY *Hist. Eng.* ii. I. 171 He had been compelled to give reluctant attendance at endless prayers and sermons. **1856** KANE *Arct. Expl.* I. xiii. 150 Thus fastened to the sledge, he commenced his reluctant journey.

reˈluctantism. *rare*. [f. RELUCTANT *a.* + -ISM.] A reluctant state or condition; reluctance.

1906 *Century Mag.* Feb. 552/2 The incisive coldness of Miss Lamb's demeanor..was sufficient to chill..her youthful admirers into a state of objectified reluctantism.

reˈluctantly, *adv.* [f. RELUCTANT *a.* + -LY[2].] In a reluctant manner; unwillingly.

1678 CUDWORTH *Intell. Syst.* I. v. 866 Not Willingly, but Reluctantly. **1766** GOLDSM. *Vic. W.* xxx, Finding it impossible to resist, he reluctantly complied. **1790** KEIR in *Phil. Trans.* LXXX. 382 A solution of copper..was very reluctantly and slowly precipitated. **1856** FROUDE *Hist. Eng.* ii. (1858) I. 115 A dispensation was reluctantly granted by the pope, and reluctantly accepted by the English ministry. **1875** JOWETT *Plato* (ed. 2) I. 177 To that he very reluctantly nodded assent.

reluctate (rɪˈlʌkteɪt), *v.* [ad. L. *reluctāt-*, ppl. stem of *reluctārī*: see RELUCTANT.]

1. *intr.* To offer resistance; to strive or struggle *against* something; to show reluctance.

1643 T. GOODWIN *Return of Prayers* 109 Halfe thy heart can take pleasure in sinning,..the other halfe reluctates, grieves for it. **1655** FULLER *Ch. Hist.* v. ii. §27 Having.. something within him, which reluctated against those superstitions. **1820** SILLIMAN *Tour fr. Hartford to Quebec* 104 It would be shameful to reluctate at going where a man of seventy-five would lead. **1848** H. ROGERS *Ess.* (1874) I. vi. 325 The sophist..strongly reluctates against..vulgar illustrations of so 'noble' a subject. **1872** H. W. BEECHER in *Chr. World Pulpit* II. 95/1 The child is commanded to do the thing that is right. He reluctates. He is punished.

b. To feel reluctance *to* do something. *rare*$^{-1}$.

1835 I. TAYLOR *Spir. Despot.* IV. 148 Every dispassionate mind reluctates to admit a principle that seems so pregnant with mischief.

c. *U.S.* To recoil *from* a thing. *rare*$^{-1}$.

a **1865** WAYLAND in *Life* (1868) II. x. 239 (Funk), I reluctate from all plans, especially all wise ones.

2. *trans.* To strive against, refuse, reject. *rare*.

1681 FLAVEL *Meth. Grace* i. 12 That man's soul, whose thoughts reluctate, decline, or nauseate so holy and pure an object. *a* **1703** BURKITT *On N.T.* John xxi. 19 Human nature in Christ's ministers, as well as in other men, reluctates sufferings. **1854** HICKOK *Mental Sci.* iii. 101 The mind, that reluctates any emotion, directly evades all occasion for bringing that object into consciousness.

Hence **reˈluctating** *ppl. a.*

1667 *Decay Chr. Piety* xvi. ¶10 Men are fain to devise arguments and colours to delude their reluctating consciences.

reluctation (rɛlʌkˈteɪʃən). [ad. late L. *reluctātiōn-em* (Quicherat); see prec. and -ATION.]

1. Struggle, resistance, opposition, of or in the case of things or persons. Somewhat *rare*.

1605 BACON *Adv. Learn.* I. vi. §6 There being then no reluctation of the creature, nor sweat of the browe, mans employment must..haue ben matter of delight. *a* **1648** LD. HERBERT *Hen. VIII* (1683) 518 He had gotten in the present Parliament, not without much reluctation, one tenth. **1651** BIGGS *New Disp.* ¶210 Impedited in her reluctation and conflict with the forren invasion of the disease. **1794** G. ADAMS *Nat. & Exp. Philos.* IV. xlix. 348 If this fluid resided within bodies in an indolent and passive state, it could exert no reluctation on any mechanical force. **1876** DOWDEN *Poems* 12, I was mingled wholly with the sound Of tumbling billow and upjetting surge, Long reluctation, welter and refluent moan. **1887** E. GURNEY *Tertium Quid* II. 76 The hush and fury, the crises and contrasts, the onsets and reluctations, of musical movement.

†**b.** *Med.* With ref. to the bodily organs. *Obs.*

1632 tr. *Bruel's Praxis Med.* 67 This [motion] is done not without much reluctation and paine. **1650** H. BROOKE *Conserv. Health* 114 The Stomock upon their Ingestion doth not firmly close, but with some sort of Reluctation.

†**2.** Internal or mental struggle; reluctance, unwillingness. Also *pl.* *Obs.* (very common in 17th c.)

1605 BACON *Adv. Learn.* II. xx. §5 In the distinction between vertue with reluctation, and vertue secured. **1611** W. SCLATER *Key* (1629) 265 Because with the whole heart he sinneth not, but hath euer some reluctation against the temptation. **1647** J. VICARS *Coleman-st. Conclave Visited* 28, I for my part..verily hoped (but yet with no little reluctation of spirit, fearing the contrary) he would [etc.]. **1674** J. B[RIAN] *Harv. Home* viii. 51 If still we find a relucation, And that we are loth to depart, as yet.

pl. **1627–77** FELTHAM *Resolves* I. xxv. 44 Those [pleasures] which carry the most pleasing tasts, fit us with the largest reluctations. **1671** FLAVEL *Fount. Life* x. 28 By a sweet and secret efficacy overcome all its Reluctations.

†**b.** Aversion to cruelty. *Obs. rare*.

1618 FLETCHER *Loyal Subj.* III. vi, Thou hast no tendernesse No reluctation in thy heart. **1622** —— *Sea Voy.* IV. i, Turn all those pities, Those tender reluctations that should become your sex, To stern anger.

relucting, *ppl. a.*: see RELUCT *v.*

reluctivity (rɛlʌk'tɪvɪtɪ). [f. as RELUCT *v.* + -IVE + -ITY.] The reciprocal of the magnetic permeability.

1888 [see RELUCTANCE 1 b]. **1896** S. P. THOMPSON *Dynamo-Electric Mach.* (ed. 5) 119 The reluctance or resistance of a circuit in such case is proportional..to the reluctivity or resistivity of the material. **1917** C. M. SMITH *Electr. & Magn. Measurements* x. 277 Reluctance and its reciprocal permeance are characteristics of the circuit. Reluctivity and permeability are characteristic of the given material.

†**re'lue**, *v. Obs. rare.* [ad. L. *reluĕre* to redeem, but in first quot. associated with *luĕre* to wash.] *trans.* To set free again, rescue, deliver.

1413 *Pilgr. Sowle* (Caxton 1483) I. xxvii. 31 He remitted his rigour, descending downe to the erthe, to helpe wesshe and relue his peple. *Ibid.* 54 And why may they not be reluyd by other, which that by other were falsely begyled?

relume (rɪ'l(j)u:m), *v.* [f. RE- + *-lume* (see ILLUME), perh. after late L. *relūmināre* (cf. RELUMINE) or F. *rallumer* (OF. *ralumer*).]

1. *trans.* To relight, rekindle (a light, flame, etc., *lit.* or *fig.*); to cause to burn afresh.

1604 SHAKS. *Oth.* v. ii. 13, I know not where is that Promethean heate That can thy Light re-Lume. **1726–46** THOMSON *Winter* 838 They once relum'd the flame Of lost mankind in polish'd slavery sunk. **1782** V. KNOX *Ess.* xxxiv. (1819) I. 182 To relume the lamp of virtuous love. **1801** SURR *Splendid Misery* I. 84 Oceana..stole from her place of concealment, and relumed the taper. **1864** SWINBURNE *Atalanta* 1590 Flame that once burnt down Oil shall not quicken or breath relume.

b. *fig.* in various applications.

1726–46 THOMSON *Winter* 491 Aratus, who a while relum'd the soul Of fondly-lingering Liberty in Greece. **1758** H. WALPOLE *Let. to Mann* 11 Jan., Sure this is not a reason to relume heats, when tranquillity is so essential. **1831** TRELAWNY *Adv. Younger Son* II. 76 This delicious poison relumed my expiring hopes. **1857–8** SEARS *Athan.* vi. 43 Paul when he wrote to relume the faith of those who wept for them that had fallen asleep.

2. To make clear or bright again.

1746 W. THOMPSON *Sickness* IV. 182 The festers of the wounded soul, Corrupted, black, to pristine white relume. **1814** CARY *Dante, Inf.* x. 77 Not yet fifty times shall be relumed Her aspect, who reigns here queen of this realm. **1829** SOUTHEY *All for Love* IX. v, Pale she was, but faith and hope Had now relumed her eyes. **1860** J. P. KENNEDY *Horse Shoe Robinson* vii. 88 [They] gradually relumed their father's countenance with flashes of cheerful thought.

3. To light up again, to re-illuminate; to shine upon anew.

1786 J. COURTENAY *Poet. Rev. Char. Johnson* 18 And Shakspeare's sun relumes the clouded stage. **1814** SOUTHEY *Roderick* XI, When the sun Relumed the gladden'd earth. **1851** C. L. SMITH tr. *Tasso* I. lxv, Soon as to-morrow's dawn relumes the sky.

fig. **1799** CAMPBELL *Pleas. Hope* I. 267 Lo, nature, life, and liberty relume The dim-eyed tenant of the dungeon gloom. **1831** LANDOR *Misc.* Wks. 1846 II. 619 O when will Health and Pleasure come again,..And wandering wit relume the roseate bowers..?

†**relumi'nation**. *Obs. rare*⁻¹. [ad. late L. *relūminātiōn-em*: see next and -ATION.] Fresh illumination.

1603 HOLLAND *Plutarch's Mor.* 1309 Her [the moon's] ecclipse and defect of light: which the sunne doth remedy by relumination of her streight waies.

re'lumine, *v. rare.* [ad. late L. *relūmināre*: see RE- and ILLUMINE.] *trans.* = RELUME.

1784 COWPER *Task* I. 442 His eye relumines its extinguished fires. **1801** CHARLOTTE SMITH *Lett. Solit. Wand.* I. 161 To relumine the obscured and almost extinguished honours of his family. *a* **1835** HOGG *Tales & Sk.* (1837) II. 23 'She has extinguished our light'... 'We will try to get it relumined'. **1853** TALFOURD *Castilian* III. ii, A lonely throne; whence she shall rise In majesty relumined!

Hence **re'lumined** *ppl. a.*

a **1743** SAVAGE *Recov. Lady of Quality* 40 Each beauty brightens with re-lumin'd fire. **1821** HOOD *Departure of Summer* iv, Time's relumined river. **1822** LAMB *Elia* Ser. I. *Praise Chimney Sweepers*, The expired and not yet relumined kitchen-fires.

†**relusant**, *a. Obs. rare.* Also 5 *Sc.* -and. [a. OF. *reluisant*, pres. pple. of *reluire*: see next.] Relucent.

13.. *E.E. Allit. P.* A. 159, I seȝ by-ȝonde þat myry mere, A crystal clyffe ful relusaunt. **1456** SIR G. HAYE *Law Arms* (S.T.S.) 6 Quhen he sawe him self sa faire sa noble and sa relusand before all the lave he miskend himself.

†**re'luyse**, *v. Obs. rare*⁻¹. [ad. F. *reluis-*, *reluire*:—L. *relucēre*: see RELUCE *v.* and RELUSANT.] *intr.* To shine forth.

1474 CAXTON *Chesse* 141 The royame that reluyseth and shyneth in the kyng and in the quene.

rely (rɪ'laɪ), *v.*¹ Also 4–7 **relie, relye,** 5 *Sc.* **rele-.** [ad. OF. *relier* to bind together, etc.:—L. *religāre*, f. *re-* RE- + *ligāre* to bind: cf. RELIGATE.]

†**1.** *trans.* To gather (soldiers, followers, etc.) together; to assemble, to rally. *Obs.*

c **1330** R. BRUNNE *Chron. Wace* (Rolls) 1001 His folk he relyed [*v.r.* relied þam] hym to, For to assay eft what þey might do. —— *Chron.* (1810) 317 Of knyght & of burgeis an oste he did relie. **1375** BARBOUR *Bruce* III. 34 His men till him he gan rely. *c* **1400** *Laud Troy Bk.* 16889 Pan[ta]salye hir men relies. *c* **1450** *Merlin* 553 The Duke..cried his signe with high voyce, and relyed his peple a-boute hym. **1481** CAXTON *Godfrey* cxxiii. 186 Rogier relyed his lytil felawship And cam deffendyng hym toward the toun. **1591** *Troub. Raigne K. John* I. (1611) E, To armes in hast, K. Iohn relyes his men. **1608** HEYWOOD tr. *Salust's Iug. War* (1609) 50 He gathered his troopes into one battallion, he relieth the rankes and faceth the adverse footmen.

†**b.** *refl.* To come together (again); to rally; also, to betake (oneself) *to* a place (cf. 3 b). *Obs.*

c **1330** [see 1]. *c* **1380** *Sir Ferumb.* 3094 Þe Sarsyns relied hymen ageyn & meteþ with our barouns. **1577–87** HOLINSHED *Scot. Chron.* (1805) II. 238 The manfull courage of the earl of Warwike..whereby he caused them to stay and relie themselves again. **1596** DANETT tr. *Comines* (1614) 44 A few of the Liegeois after they were put to flight relied them-selues together at their cariage. **1641** EARL MONM. tr. *Biondi's Civil Warres* v. 148 The King and Queene were perswaded to relie themselves to Killingworth.

†**2.** *intr.* To assemble, to rally. *Obs.*

c **1330** R. BRUNNE *Chron.* (1810) 224 To Lyncoln þei drowe, & þer þei suld relie. **1375** BARBOUR *Bruce* XX. 440 All the chassaris turnyt agane; And thai relyit with mekill mayne. ? *a* **1400** *Morte Arth.* 1882 Thane relyez the renkez of the Rounde Table. *c* **1450** *Merlin* 393 Whan these saugh hem comynge thei relien and closed hem to-geder.

†**b.** *Hunting.* (Meaning not clear.) *Obs. rare.*

c **1410** *Master of Game* (MS. Digby 182) xxxiii, As ofte as he fyndeth þe fues..he sholde saye lowde: . sy . va . sy . va. sy . va., and relie with his. *Ibid.* xxxiv, If þe houndes fynde what so it be, he shall relye and jopeye, till he haue seen it. *c* **1420** *Anturs of Arth.* 58 And tille þaire riste raches relyes [*v.r.* releues] one þaire raye.

†**3. a.** To rally *to* (attack) an enemy. *Obs.*⁻¹

c **1400** *Laud Troy Bk.* 12620 The Troyens sone that aspied, And to the Gregeis thei sone relied.

†**b.** To rally or retire *to* one's friends or to a certain place. *Obs. rare.*

? *a* **1400** *Morte Arth.* 1391 Than a ryche mane of Rome relyede to his byerns. *c* **1450** *Merlin* 281 And eche hadde a baner wher-to thei sholde relye whan thei were medled with the saisnes. **1600** W. WATSON *Decacordon* (1602) 18 [Priests] destitute of all place of relying vnto [*errata* upon].

†**c.** To trust *to* a person or thing. *Obs.*

1571 CAMPION *Hist. Irel.* (1623) 67 About the young Earle were servants and counsellours..to whom he most relyed. *a* **1604** HANMER *Chron. Irel.* (1809) 335 Cambrensis (herein whom I must relie unto) being then in Ireland. **1616** S. WARD *Balm fr. Gilead* Serm. (1862) 107 Instead of apologies and captation of good will, he relies to this fort, passeth not for man's day.

†**d.** To be devoted *to*, to pertain or belong *to*, a thing or person. *Obs.*

1582 STANYHURST *Æneis* II. (Arb.) 57 A man too pietee, to iustice whoalye relying. *Ibid.* III. 72 Theare stands a plentiful Island Too the dame of myrmayds, too Neptune Princelye relying. *Ibid.* 78 Anchises..On Gods heunlye cryeth, to ther hest with duitye relying.

†**4. a.** (Also *refl.*) To adhere *to*, associate (oneself) *with*, another. *Obs. rare.*

1586 J. HOOKER *Hist. Irel.* in *Holinshed* II. 82/1 Kildare cleauing to Yorke, and Ormond relieng to Lancaster. **1600** HAKLUYT *Voy.* (1810) III. 320 My purpose was to have relied myselfe with Menatouon.

†**b.** To hold *of*, be a vassal or subject *of*, another. (Cf. RELIEVE *v.* 8 a.) *Obs. rare.*

1586 T. B. *La Primaud. French Acad.* (1589) 587 Princes, Dukes..who possesse..Townes, Castels, with vassals holding and relieng of [F. *releuans de*] them by fealtie and homage. **1591** HARINGTON *Ariosto, Life* 418 For countries sake, and of his gratefull nature he was euer relying of the duke of Ferrara.

5. To depend *on* a person or thing with full trust or confidence; to rest *upon* with assurance.

1574 R. SCOT *Hop Gard.* 2, I, for my part, relye not upon other mens opinions. **1596** BP. W. BARLOW *Three Serm.* iii. 102 The Iewes relyed much vpon the prayers of the faythfull. **1638** JUNIUS *Paint. Ancients* 34 Such as relie too much upon them, imitate..what is worst in their workes. **1667** MILTON *P.L.* IX. 373 Go in thy native innocence, relie On what thou hast of vertue. **1697** DRYDEN *Virg. Georg.* II. 452 The tender Twig shoots upward to the Skies, And on the Faith of the new Sun relies. **1748** *Anson's Voy.* III. x. 404 None of the Chinese..employed as Linguists, could be relied on. **1769** *Junius Lett.* xxxv. (1788) 180 Upon what part of your subjects would you rely for assistance? **1837** DICKENS *Pickw.* ii, Can I rely upon your secrecy? **1856** STANLEY *Sinai & Pal.* Advt. (1858) 11 On his accurate observation and sound judgement I have constantly relied. **1885** CLODD *Myths & Dr.* I. iv. 65 The only authority on which the Chroniclers relied was tradition.

b. With reference to facts or statements. (Cf. DEPEND 5 and 5 b.)

1809 GERMAIN LAVIE in *G. Rose's Diary & Corr.* I. 260 You may rely that any communications you may be pleased to make to me shall be held sacred. **1844** GLADSTONE *Glean.* (1879) V. 144 For Mr. Ward may rely upon it that, whether or not he will allow belief to appeal to understanding, unbelief will appeal to it. **1858** DICKENS *Lett.* (1880) II. 83 You and it will travel thither in company, rely upon it.

†**c.** To rest *upon* a support. *Obs.*

1609 J. DAVIES *Holy Roode* E j, Ah see how his most holy Hand relies Vpon his knees, to vnder-prop his Charge. **1631** QUARLES *Samson* xxiii, Two sturdy Pillers..whereon, relied The weighty burthen of her lofty pride. **1683** NORRIS *Wks.* (Grosart) 67 So to th' unthinking boy the distant sky Seems on some mountain's surface to rely.

fig. **1611** SPEED *Hist. Gt. Brit.* IX. xxiii. (1623) 1143 [His] life vntill this time, wee will briefly run ouer—so many dependances of story relying vpon him. **1639** SALTMARSH *Policy* Ded. 6 There your designes, your projects, may rest and relie.

6. To put trust or confidence *in* a person or thing. Somewhat *rare.*

1606 G. W[OODCOCKE] *Hist. Ivstine* v. 24 Those aides and asistances..in which they for the most part trusted and relyed. **1654–66** EARL ORRERY *Parthen.* (1676) 186 Asdrubal placed his Gauls (in whom he least rely'd) in the Left Wing. **1875** DASENT *Vikings* III. 312 If there was anyone in whom he might think he could rely, it was Kark, his thrall.

†**b.** To rest, consist, *in* something. *Obs. rare.*

1594 CAREW tr. *Huarte's Exam. Wits* (1616) 300 The naturall Philosophers..hold, that a man receiueth the conditions of his soule, at the time of his forming..; but not his substance, wherein the whole life relieth. **1642** J. EATON *Honey-c. Free Justif.* 60 Therein relies the very glory of the Godhead of Christ.

†**7.** *refl.* and *trans.* To repose (oneself, one's soul, faith, etc.) *on, upon*, or *in* some person or thing. *Obs.* (freq. in early 17th c. use.)

1598 R. BERNARD tr. *Terence* 194 Who, relying himselfe vpon your judgement, hath made me an actor. **1612** (?) BRETON *Pasquil's Nt.-cap* 96 No faith her husband doth in her relie. **1617** R. FENTON *Treat. Ch. Rome* 38 Should wee relye our soules upon so narrow, so new, and so perplexed a divine? *a* **1641** BP. MOUNTAGU *Acts & Mon.* (1642) 503 Not to rest upon bare words, wee must proceed to enquire what moved them to..rely themselves upon that answer.

†**b.** To rest (a proceeding) *on* something. *Obs.*⁻¹

1627 E. F. *Hist. Edw. II* (1680) 78 A ground work on which he might rely his false proceedings.

Hence **re'lying** *ppl. a.*

1836 BROWNING & FORSTER *Life Strafford* (1892) 155 His more relying friend the archbishop of Canterbury.

†**re'ly**, *v.*² *Obs.*⁻¹ [perh. ad. ONF. **releier*:—L. *relēgāre* to RELEGATE.] *trans.* ? To assign.

a **1400** *St. John* 6 in Horstm. *Altengl. Leg.* (1881) 467 To life ay in lykynge þat lorde þe relyede That in Bedleme was borne.

relyf(e, obs. ff. RELIEF.

relygeous, -ioun, -ious, etc., obs. ff. RELIGION, -IOUS.

relyk(e, -ykke, -yque, obs. ff. RELIC.

relyn, obs. inf. of REEL *v.*¹

rem, *a.* Slang abbrev. of REMANDED *ppl. a.*

1887 [see BUST *sb.*³ d].

rem (rɛm), *sb.*¹ Pl. **rem, rems.** [f. initial letters of *roentgen equivalent man.*] Orig., a quantity of ionizing radiation having the same effect on human tissue as one roentgen of X-rays. The dosage in rems is now calculated by multiplying the dosage in rads by the relative biological effectiveness. Cf. REP⁷.

1947 *Nucleonics* Oct. 38/2 The rep and rem units were introduced by Dr. H. M. Parker. *Ibid.* 39/2 Roentgen-equivalent-man (or mammal), rem... One rem is the estimated amount of energy absorbed in tissue which is biologically equivalent in man to 1 r of gamma- or X-rays. By definition: 1 rem = 83/RBE erg/gm tissue. **1957** *Encycl. Brit.* XVI. 591/1 The biological effects of radiation are not solely dependent on the amount of energy released; it is also a question of how highly localized the energy is. Such considerations have led to another unit, the rem, supposed to be that dose of radiation which has the same biological effect as 1 rad of X-radiation. **1958** W. D. CLAUS *Radiation Biol. & Med.* xviii. 431 The dose in rem is obtained by multiplying the physical dose in rads by the RBE appropriate to the situation. **1958** *Observer* 5 Oct. 15/4 The most active watches..could deliver a dose of five rem (units of radioactive dose measurement) within five years. The International Commission on Radiological Protection has recommended that no one should receive an accumulated dose of more than five rem by the age of 30. **1975** *Nature* 27 Mar. 278/2 Fifteen rem is equivalent to 1·5 rad of alpha radiation (since alpha radiation is considered 10 times as carcinogenic as gamma radiation). **1976** *Sci. Amer.* Nov. 31/2 If the fresh fission products from one megaton of fission were spread uniformly over a perfectly flat area of 1,000 square miles, the gamma-ray dose rate one meter above the ground would be about 250 rems per hour after 10 hours.

REM (rɛm, ɑ:ri:'ɛm), *sb.*² Also **rem.** Abbrev. of *rapid eye movement* (see RAPID *a.* 2 b). Freq. *attrib.*, designating a distinctive type of sleep that occurs at intervals throughout the night and is characterized by such eye movements, more dreaming and bodily movement, an increased pulse rate, and faster breathing.

1957 DEMENT & KLEITMAN in *Jrnl. Exper. Psychol.* LIII. 340/1 In most of the remaining text the following abbreviations will be used: REM's (rapid eye movements) and NREM's (no rapid eye movements). **1969** *Sunday Times* (Colour Suppl.) 16 Feb. 21/3 Subjects regularly deprived of the opportunity to dream by being woken at the onset of REM periods began to show psychological disturbance after a few nights. **1972** F. R. FREEMON *Sleep Research* i. 4 This second type of sleep, called the rem state, has low voltage EEG activity mixed with bursts of theta waves and frequent conjugate eye movements. **1976** SMYTHIES & CORBETT *Psychiatry* xiv. 265 During REM sleep the brain shows intense metabolic activity. **1977** S. DUNKELL *Sleep Positions* ii. 38 As we continue our journey through the night, the duration of each successive REM phase increases.

rem, obs. f. RAVEN *sb.*¹, REAM *sb.*¹, *sb.*², REALM.

re'made (ri:-), *ppl. a.* and *sb.* [RE- 5 a: cf. REMAKE *v.*] Made again or anew. Also *sb.*, an article which has been made over again.

1742 YOUNG *Nt. Th.* IV. 471 The Son of heav'n! The double Son; the Made, and the Re-made! **1897** *Westm. Gaz.* 8 Jan. 10/1 'Remades', or balls that have been played with before,..receive none of his..attentions.

re'magnetize, *v.* [RE- 5 a.] *trans.* To magnetize again. Also **remagneti'zation.**
1839 Advt. in G. S. Haight *George Eliot & John Chapman* (1969) 259 Compasses made to order and remagnatized [*sic*]. **1849** NOAD *Electricity* (ed. 3) 439 The weak needle is then remagnetized by passing a small bar magnet a few times along it from end to end. **1873** MAXWELL *Electr. & Magn.* (1881) II. 85 If the force..acts in the positive direction it will begin to remagnetize the iron. **1876** PREECE & SIVEWRIGHT *Telegraphy* 87 It renders a fresh adjustment or remagnetisation necessary.

remaid, variant of *remeid* REMEDE *Obs.*

†**re'maile.** *Obs. rare*$^{-1}$. [app. a. F. *rimaille* (not found however, before 16th c.), f. *rime* RHYME.] Rhyming, verse.
13.. *Evang. Nicod.* in *Archiv neu. Spr.* LIII. 391 A clerk of yngland In his remaile þus redes.

remain (rɪ'meɪn), *sb.*[1] Forms: 5 *Sc.* re-, ramayn, 6 *Sc.* remane, 6–7 remaine, -mayne, 6- remain. [a. OF. *remain*, vbl. sb. f. *remaindre*: see REMAIN *v.* Now chiefly *pl.*, the singular being common only in sense 4 b.]

I. †**1.** Those left, surviving, or remaining out of a number of persons; the remainder or rest. *Obs.*
c **1470** HENRY *Wallace* VIII. 922 Than thai consent, the ramayn that was thar. **1558** PHAER *Æneid* I. B iv b, O quene that in our woes (alone) such mercy dost extend To vs the poore remayne of Troy. **1617** MORYSON *Itin.* II. 202 Don Iean and the remaine of the Spaniards at Kinsale, were all embarked ready to be gone. **1651** CROMWELL in H. Cary *Mem. Gt. Civil War* (1832) II. 380, I believe the number of these sent will be about a hundred; the remain also being forty or fifty. **1671** EACHARD *Obs. Answ. Cont. Clergy* 102 Thinking themselves the onely poor remain of people, that can dispense the word profitably.

†**b.** The remaining representative of a family.
1592 WARNER *Alb. Eng.* VII. xxxiv. (1602) 165 This Henrie, Earle of Richmond, now poore Lancasters remaine.

2. That which remains or is left (unused, undestroyed, etc.) of some thing or quantity of things; also, that which remains to be done. Now *rare* (common in 16–17th c.).
1529 *Act 21 Hen. VIII*, c. 13 §8 Only the Remain and Overplus above their Expences of their Housholds. **1579–80** NORTH *Plutarch, Theseus* (1676) 9 Those which then returned with Theseus, did seethe in a great brasse pot all the remain of their provision. **1606** SHAKS. *Cymb.* III. i. 87, I know your Masters pleasure, and he mine: All the Remaine is welcome. **1626** in Rushw. *Hist. Coll.* (1659) I. 230, I have been so frugal of making use of the old remain, that there is no need of ammunition, or other necessaries. **1687** *Penal Laws* 32 This..is the antient Remain of the Soveraign Power and Prerogative of the Kings of England. **1716** POPE *Lett.* (1735) I. 290 Chagrins, more than their small Remain of Life seem'd destin'd to undergo. *c* **1825** BEDDOES *Epitaph* Poems (1851) 203 This is the remain Of one best union of that deathless twain.

†**b.** *Arith.* = REMAINDER *sb.* 4 a. *Obs.*
1571 DIGGES *Pantom.* II. xii. N iij, The square of the side *AF* yeldeth 190104, and this diuided by 160 produceth in the quotiente 1188, and the remayne is 24. **1614** T. BEDWELL *Nat. Geom. Numbers* ii. 22 The Remaine or difference of 144, and 148, is 4. **1674** JEAKE *Arith.* (1696) 301 The Greater substracted from the Lesser, the Remain will be so much too short.

†**c.** (Also *pl.*) The balance or unpaid remainder of a sum of money. (Cf. REMAINDER *sb.* 4 b.) *Obs.*
1565 COOPER *Thesaurus* s.v. *Reliquus*, Camillus writeth that he hath receiued the remaines due vnto me. *Ibid.*, *Reliquatio*,..arrearage and remaynes. **1627** EARL MANCH. in *Buccleuch MSS.* (Hist. MSS. Comm.) I. 267 The loans have brought in 240,000*l.* at least; therefore the remain must needs be got up, which is not past 50,000*l.* **1669** *Lond. Gaz.* No. 367/4 The said Officers..shall proceed to the payment of the ensuing Orders, as the remain of that Taxe and the remaines of the [other] Taxe shall come in.

3. A remaining or surviving part or fragment of something. Now *rare.*
1570–6 LAMBARDE *Peramb. Kent* (1826) 143 There standeth yet, upon the high cliffe,..some remaine of a Tower. **1635** PAGITT *Christianogr.* I. ii. (1636) 85 In Hispaniola there were not 300 Natives left, and a very small remaine in the other Ilands. **1665** SIR T. HERBERT *Trav.* (1677) 139 At the stair-head there is some remain of the Gate. **1701** ROWE *Amb. Step-Moth.* III. ii, A large remain of Glory is behind. **1763** MRS. F. BROOKE *Lady J. Mandeville* (1782) II. 53 This sacred deposit, this little remain of what their tender care had left me. *a* **1806** H. K. WHITE *Christiad* I. ix, No sweet remain of life encheers the sight. **1843** KEMBLE *Poetry Codex Vercell.* Pref. 6 A series of publications which..will give to the world of scholars every yet inedited remain of Anglosaxon.

†**b.** A remainder of stock or stores; also, a list or inventory of military stores taken at the appointment of a new storekeeper. *Obs.*
1677 COLLINS in Rigaud *Corr. Sci. Men* (1841) II. 21 A stationer..having bought a remain of above two hundred of Horrox's Astronomy. **1802** JAMES *Milit. Dict.* s.v., In foreign parts a remain is taken only on the appointment of a new storekeeper.

†**c.** A surviving trace *of* some feeling. Also *ellipt.* with adj. *Obs.*
1702 VANBRUGH *False Friend* IV. i, She has still love enough for you, not to be displeas'd with the utmost proofs you can give that you have still a warm remain for her. **1756** BURKE *Subl. & B.* I. iii, When this remain of horror has entirely subsided. **1807** tr. *Three Germans* I. 72 To overcome that small remain of fortitude which yet animated and sustained him.

4. (With *pl.*) **a.** A survival; a relic *of* some obsolete custom or practice; a surviving trait or characteristic. Now *rare.*
a **1641** BP. MOUNTAGU *Acts & Mon.* (1642) 346 And, as a remaine of ancient custome, this continued among Pagans. **1757** MRS. GRIFFITH *Lett. Henry & Frances* (1767) IV. 1 'Tis a Remain of judicial Astrology. **1819** LADY CHARLEVILLE in *Lady Morgan's Autobiog.* (1859) 254 Lady Crewe..had mind and heart, and indeed some fine remains of a race that has passed away. **1883** *Ch. Times* XXI. 333/3 A traditional remain of his office of server.

b. A material relic (*of* antiquity, etc.); an ancient monument, building, or other structure; an object which has come down from past times.
1687 A. LOVELL tr. *Thevenot's Trav.* I. 123 There are such fair remains to be found among the Ruines, as easily show that this has been a..rich..Town. **1691** tr. *Emilianne's Observ. Journ. Naples* 235 The only Remain of Antiquity they shew one is, the Remainder of an Old Steeple. **1769** *De Foe's Tour Gt. Brit.* (ed. 7) I. 161 This ancient Remain is situated about a Quarter of a Mile to the right of the great Road leading from Rochester to Maidstone. **1779** ABERCROMBY *Mirror* No. 52 ¶6 Every remain of Roman greatness attracted my attention. **1848** W. H. BARTLETT *Egypt to Pal.* xvi. (1879) 335 Already we had fallen into the region of ancient remains. **1864** J. H. LUPTON *Wakefield Worthies* 242 The supposition..that Low Hill is a Druidical remain.

†**c.** A literary relic. *Obs. rare.*
1720 STRYPE *Stow's Surv.* (1754) I. I. xxxi. 329/2 Meeting with such a choice remain of this brave London merchant I could not but for his lasting Honour publish it in this place. **1738** WARBURTON *Div. Legat.* I. 128 It is indeed surprizing, that any Man who had attentively considered this admirable Remain, should think it the Forgery of a Sophist.

†**d.** A relic of a person. *Obs. rare*$^{-1}$.
1798 W. FERRIER in A. Ferrier *Mem. & Serm.* (1841) IV. 336 Elisha gathered it up as a precious remain.

II. *pl.* **5.** Surviving members of a company, family, or other body of persons. Also rarely of a single person.
1456 SIR G. HAYE *Law Arms* (S.T.S.) 62 He..ordanyt him to passe in Spayne, for Pompees remaynis of his men maid syk deray thare. **1601** SHAKS. *Jul. C.* V. v. 1 Come poore remaines of friends, rest on this Rocke. **1609** BIBLE (Douay) *Jer.* xi. 23 Their sonnes and their daughters shal die in famine. And there shal be no remaines of them. **1738** C'TESS POMFRET in J. Duncombe *Lett.* (1773) II. 124 There are still some remains of that abdicated court. **1781** JUSTAMOND *Priv. Life Lewis XV*, IV. 9 After having been at once a husband, a brother, and a father, he was the only remains of his family, which was entirely buried in the grave along with him. **1839** YEOWELL *Anc. Brit. Ch.* ix. (1847) 93 The remains of the Druidical order were not persecuted.

†**b.** The remainder; the others. *Obs. rare*$^{-1}$.
a **1649** DRUMM. OF HAWTH. *Hist. Jas. I*, Wks. (1711) 6 Many were executed, the remains in peaceful manner sent home, the king having graciously exhorted them to a life according to the law of God and man.

6. The remaining parts *of* some thing or things; all that is left of something; articles remaining from a store or stock; †the rest *of* a period.
1500–20 DUNBAR *Poems* lxxix. 18, I trowit,..That lang in burgh I sould haue bruikit [the money]; Now the remanes are eith to turss. **1609** BIBLE (Douay) *1 Macc.* vi. 53 They that had remayned in Jurie of the Gentils, had consumed their remaynes, that had bene layd up. **1687** A. LOVELL tr. *Thevenot's Trav.* I. 18 Seven old Galleys..the remains of their Fleet which escaped from the Battel of Lepanto. **1726** CAVALLIER *Mem.* III. 242, I wanted some Rest for the Remains of Winter. **1770** *Junius Lett.* xxxvi. (1788) 190 If you would hope to save the wretched remains of a ruined reputation. **1803** NELSON 3 June in Nicolas *Disp.* (1845) V. 78 You are..on no account..to supply any of his Majesty's Ships..with Naval Stores without being furnished with the Boatswain's and Carpenter's Supplies, Expenses, and Remains. **1855** MACAULAY *Hist. Eng.* xvii. IV. 71 The shop-keepers..stole away with the remains of their stocks to the English territory. **1868** LOCKYER *Elem. Astron.* ii. §9 (1879) 52 Coal is the remains of an ancient vegetation.

b. Const. *of* the destroying force. *rare.*
1715 POPE *Iliad* I. 82 'Tis time to save the few remains of war. **1737** WHISTON *Josephus, Hist.* (1777) Pref. §11 Moreover, what the Romans did to the remains of the war.

c. Const. as *sing.*
1801 *Lusignan* III. 145 Do you then envy me this short remains of happiness? **1833** R. H. FROUDE *Rem.* (1838) I. 286 In one place there is the remains of an Ionic temple. **1874** S. WILBERFORCE *Ess.* (1874) I. 89 The tendency..was really a remains..of the extraordinary and odious instinct which had possessed them.

7. a. The literary works (*esp.* the unpublished ones) left by an author; also, the fragments of an ancient writer.
1652 (*title*) Herberts Remains, or sundry pieces of..Mr. George Herbert, now exposed to publick light. **1681** TATE *Lear* Ded., Nothing but..my Zeal for all the Remains of Shakespear, cou'd have wrought me to so bold an Undertaking. **1724** A. COLLINS *Gr. Chr. Relig.* 172 Celsus, who seems the oldest Heathen author, whereof we have any remains. **1774** J. BRYANT *Mythol.* II. 176 He left behind him many valuable remains, which Bion Proconnesius is said to have translated. **1873** H. ROGERS *Orig. Bible* viii. (1875) 354 The remains of Clement and Polycarp and such fragments of Ignatius as criticism pronounces..genuine.

b. That which is left of a person when life is extinct; the (dead) body, corpse.
1700 DRYDEN *Ovid's Met.* XII. 816 Of all the mighty man the small remains A little urn, and scarcely fill'd contains. *a* **1771** GRAY *Dante* 18, I grop'd About among their cold Remains..often calling On their dear Names. **1797** MRS. RADCLIFFE *Italian* xi, I saw, also, her poor remains laid at rest in the convent garden. **1818** SHELLEY *Rosal. & Helen* 1295 With deep grief and awe The pale survivors followed her remains..Up the cold mountain. **1855** MACAULAY *Hist. Eng.* xviii. IV. 242 The remains of Hastings and Carter were brought on shore with every mark of honour.

c. Substances of organic origin preserved in the earth in a fossilized condition.
1799 KIRWAN *Geol. Ess.* 36 Trees..have been found in great depths in our modern continents,..and often mixed with marine remains. **1840** *Penny Cycl.* XVI. 491/2 Thus employed, 'organic remains' become a clue to many of the darkest pages in the antient history of our planet.

†**re'main,** *sb.*[2] *Obs. rare.* [f. the vb.] Stay.
c **1470** HENRY *Wallace* IX. 615 Laynrik was tayn..; So Lundy thair mycht mak no langar remayn. **1605** SHAKS. *Macb.* IV. iii. 148 A most myraculous worke..Which often since my heere remaine in England, I haue seene him do.

remain (rɪ'meɪn), *v.* Forms: 5–6 **remeyne, -mayne, -mane** (*Sc.* ra-), 6 **remene,** 6–7 **remaine,** 6- **remain.** [a. AF. *remeyn-*, *remayn-*, etc., stressed stem of OF. *remanoir* (also *remaindre*):—L. *remanēre*, f. *re-* RE- + *manēre* to stay.]

1. *intr.* To be left after the removal or appropriation of some part, number or quantity. Also const. *to.*
c **1375** *Sc. Leg. Saints* xxxiii. (*George*) 674 þat þar tempil..sa cleynely suld be distroit, þat na thing suld remayn of It. *c* **1460** FORTESCUE *Abs. & Lim. Mon.* viii. (1885) 126 Yff any parte off þe revenues þeroff remayne ouer the paiement of the same ordynarie chargis, þat so remaynynge is the kynges owne money. **1483** CAXTON *G. de la Tour* G v b, He lost all that he had and no thyng remayned to hym sauf only his body. **1535** COVERDALE *Josh.* x. 40 Thus Iosua smote all the londe.., with all their kynges, and let not one remaine ouer. **1594** BLUNDEVIL *Exerc.* I. iii. (1636) 8 Then I say take 10 out of 17 and there remaineth 7, which I set downe. **1642** tr. *Perkins' Prof. Bk.* ii. §136. 60 But if this part [of the seal] which remaines to the deed hath not any print, then the deed is insufficient. **1697** DRYDEN *Æneid* V. 528 My chill Blood is curdled in my Veins, And scarce the Shadow of a Man remains. **1707** *Curios. in Husb. & Gard.* 53 There is not Sap enough remaining to nourish the Leaves. **1784** COWPER *Task* V. 71 One only care Remains to each, the search of sunny nook. **1821** SHELLEY *Hellas* 83 Freedom so To what of Greece remaineth now Returns. **1859** TENNYSON *Elaine* 594 Now remains But little cause for laughter. **1875** JOWETT *Plato* (ed. 2) V. 68 He is willing to allow himself and others the few pleasures which remain to them.

2. a. To be left over and above what has already been done or dealt with in some way.
c **1375** *Sc. Leg. Saints* xiii. (*Mark*) Prol. 13 Sa remanyt vthire twa [evangelists], of quhame I wel here menyng ma. **1482** *Monk of Evesham* (Arb.) 56 Nowe let vs schewe as we maye thoes thynges that remaynyn of the thyrde place the whyche we sawe and behylde. **1538** STARKEY *England* I. iii. 82 Yet ther ys a nother dysease remenyng behynd, wych gretely trowblyth the state of the hole body. **1600** SHAKS. *A.Y.L.* I. i. 179 Nothing remaines, but that I kindle the boy thither. **1667** MILTON *P.L.* VI. 37 The easier conquest now Remains thee. **1712–14** POPE *R. Lock* V. 29 What then remains but well our pow'r to use..? **1738** GRAY *Tasso* 31 What length of sea remains, what various lands. **1819** SHELLEY *Prometh. Unb.* I. 617 Worse things, unheard, unseen, remain behind.

b. Const. with *inf.* (passive or active).
1538 STARKEY *England* I. ii. 68 Many and grete fautys ther be..wych now remayne..to be sought and tryed out. **1593** SHAKS. *3 Hen. VI*, IV. iii. 60 What now remaines my Lords for vs to do..? **1819** SHELLEY *Cenci* I. i. 100 But that there yet remains a deed to act [etc.]. **1830** TENNYSON *Talk. Oak* 204 A thousand thanks for what I learn And what remains to tell. **1863** FAWCETT *Pol. Econ.* I. vi. 81 The head-lands will remain to be ploughed separately.

c. ***it remains that*** or ***to*** (with *inf.*). Freq. as ***it*** (or ***that***) ***remains to be seen***: it is not yet known or certain.
1540 BIBLE (Cranmer) *1 Cor.* vii. 29 It remayneth, that they whych haue wyues, be as thoughe they had none. **1607** SHAKS. *Cor.* II. iii. 147 Remaines, that in th' Officiall Markes invested, You anon doe meet the Senate. **1611** BIBLE *Transl. Pref.* ¶17 It remaineth, that we commend thee to God. **1772** *Junius Lett.* lxviii. (1788) 362 It remains only to apply the law, thus stated, to the fact in question. **1796** LD. GLENBERVIE *Diary* 16 Oct. (1928) I. 88 It remains, however, to be seen what will be the ultimate result in the present instance of a struggle as yet perhaps but in its infancy. **1811** PINKERTON *Petral.* I. 599 It now remains to attempt a clear classification and description of the Accidential. **1828** *Athenæum* 12 Feb. 103/1 Whether or not the 'Life of Columbus' will restore it, remains yet to be seen. **1859** *Times* 4 Feb. 9/4 That remains to be seen. **1864** J. H. NEWMAN *Apol.* iv. §2 (1904) 133/1 In the interval of which it remains to speak. **1866** MAYNE REID *Headless Horseman* xvi. 88 It remains to be seen how we shall get over it. **1938** H. L. MENCKEN *Let.* 23 Apr. (1961) 427 Whether I'll write anything for publication remains to be seen. **1967** *Listener* 6 July 20/2 How far or how quickly the new government can get anywhere..remains to be seen. **1976** *Southern Even. Echo* (Southampton) 13 Nov. 3/6 It would remain to be seen to what extent it would be practical or desirable to build houses there.

†**3. a.** To fall *to* a person as a REMAINDER. *Obs.*
1439 *E.E. Wills* (1882) 123 Aftir hir discesse, all the saide maners, londes and tenementes, rentes and reuersions, to remayne to his next heire. **1482** WARKW. *Chron.* (Camden) 10 And if it appenede that he disceysed witheoute heyres..thenne schulde the kyngdome..remane unto George, the Duke of Clarence. **1495** *Act 11 Hen. VII*, c. 52 §1 Hereditamentis whiche to him discended, remayned, or reverted.

†**b.** To continue to belong *to* one. *Obs.*
1511 FABYAN *Will* in *Chron.* (1811) Pref. 7 Also I will that my chalice..wt my best aulter clothis and best vestment,..which before daies I gave to my wif, remayn styll to her. *a* **1548** HALL *Chron., Hen. VIII* 185 That the realme of Napels should for euer remain to the Emperour. **1605**

Shaks. *Lear* i. i. 82 To thee, and thine hereditarie euer, Remaine this ample third of our faire Kingdome.

4. a. To continue in the same place (or with the same person); to abide, stay. Also with *on*.

1439 *E.E. Wills* (1882) 124 That thos same maners, londes & tenementes..remayne and abyde in the feefes handes. *c* **1500** *Lancelot* 2347 Bot ȝhit the king hir prayt on sich wyss, That sche remanit whill the thrid day. **1530** Palsgr. 684/2 Suffer no fylthe to remayne on thy nayles. **1560** Daus tr. *Sleidane's Comm.* 7 He was commaunded by his prince to remain at home. **1613** Purchas *Pilgrimage* vi. xi. (1614) 632 Causing (as the Moors report) that the bullets should still remaine in the Pieces when they were discharged. **1671** Milton *Samson* 587 Why else this strength Miraculous yet remaining in those locks? **1769** Robertson *Chas. V*, iii. Wks. 1813 VI. 100 Charles remained six days in Paris. **1776** *Trial of Nundocomar* 68/1 You have for a long time had my money; it shall remain no longer with you. **1841** Lane *Arab. Nts.* I. 97 Thus shalt thou remain in this sea to the end of time. **1890** Gardiner *Hist. Eng.* 13 Aulus Plautius remained in Britain till 47. **1912** J. Joyce *Let.* 23 Aug. (1966) II. 311 Tomorrow I must pawn my watch and chain in order to remain on a little longer. **1939** H. Nicholson *Diary* 11 Apr. (1966) 397 Harold Macmillan is enraged that Chamberlain should remain on.

†**b.** To have one's abode; to dwell. *Obs.*

c **1450** Holland *Howlat* 946 And ilk fowle..Held hame to thar hant, and thar herbery, Quhar thai war wont to remane. **1535** Stewart *Cron. Scot.* II. 226 Within the toun..Ane Brit thair wes remanand in the tyme. **1583** Rich *Phylotus* (1835) 10 In the gallant citty of Naples, there was remaining a young man, called by the name of Alberto. **1611** Shaks. *Cymb.* iv. iii. 14 But for my Mistris, I nothing know where she remaines.

†**c.** To consist; to reside or lie *in* something.

c **1450** Holland *Howlat* 265 Thai weraly awysit..the mater, and how it remanyt. **1559** Abp. Hethe in Strype *Ann. Ref.* (1824) I. App. vi. 399 What..spirituall government is, and in what pointes it dothe cheffely remaine.

5. a. With complement: To continue to be.

1509 Hawes *Past. Pleas.* xxvii. (Percy Soc.) 132, I made mine othe..Unto them all for to remayne full true In stedfast love. **1533** Gau *Richt Vay* (S.T.S.) 32 It sal ewer remane in blyndnes and ingnorance. **1582** N. Lichefield tr. *Castanheda's Conq. E. Ind.* i. xxii. 57 b, Not [to] disclose, that the Factour with the others did remaine prisoners. **1611** Shaks. *Cymb.* i. iv. 173 If shee remaine vnseduc'd, you not making it appeare otherwise [etc.]. **1667** Milton *P.L.* iii. 124, I formed them free, and free they must remain. **1736** Butler *Anal.* i. i. Wks. 1874 I. 20 Men may lose their limbs, their organs of sense,..and yet remain the same living agents. **1791** Cowper *Retired Cat* 66 The sun descended, And Puss remained still unattended. **1822** Shelley tr. *Calderon* i. 188 Which of the two Will remain conqueror? **1875** Jowett *Plato* (ed. 2) IV. 256 Amid the conflict of ideas..the impression of sense remained certain and uniform.

b. *I* (†*will*) *remain*, etc., as the concluding formula of a letter.

1600 C. Percy in *Shaks. C. Praise* 38, I will ever remain Your assured friend Charles Percy. **1634** Strafford in *Strafford Papers* (1739) I. 340, I remain Your Lordship's most humbly to be commanded, Wentworth. **1749** Chesterf. *Lett.* (1792) II. 269 And so I rest or remain, Yours &c. **1793** Cowper *Let. to J. Hall* 10 Dec., I remain, my dear friend, Affectionately yours, W. C. **1873** E. FitzGerald *Let. to F. Kemble* Nov., Here is my Letter done, and I remaining yours always sincerely, E. F. G.

c. To continue in the same state; to lie untouched or undisturbed.

1839 Ure *Dict. Arts* 1268 Draw out the fire, and let it [japan] remain until morning; then boil it until it rolls hard. **1853** Soyer *Pantroph.* 100 Stir this mixture..for three days or more, then let it remain for some time.

6. a. To continue to exist; to have permanence; to be still existing or extant. (Sometimes also implying sense 1 or 2.)

1398 Trevisa *Barth. De P.R.* i. (1495) 3 After the noble..doctryne of wyse..Philosophers lefte and remaynyng wᵗ vs in wrytyng. **1555** Eden *Decades* To Rdr. (Arb.) 49 There remayneth at this daye no token of the laborious Tabernacle which Moises buylded. **1585** T. Washington tr. *Nicholay's Voy.* iv. xiii, Vsing in their fightes many guyles and craftes, which are remained to them from their auncestors. **1638** Junius *Paint. Ancients* 267 The same admiration remaineth from what side soever you doe looke upon her. **1697** Dryden *Virg. Georg.* iv. 304 Th' immortal Line in sure Succession reigns, The Fortune of the Family remains. **1738** Gray *Propertius* iii. 101 A little Verse my All that shall remain. **1781** Cowper *Conversat.* 678 The stench remains, the lustre dies away. **1813** Shelley *Q. Mab* iv. 141 Soul is the only element, the block That for uncounted ages has remained. **1874** Green *Short Hist.* iii. §5. 139 The abbey church of Westminster..remains a monument of his artistic taste.

b. To stick in the mind. Const. *with*.

1607 Shaks. *Timon* iii. vi. 30, I hope it remaines not vnkindely with your Lordship, that I return'd you an empty messenger. **1872** Hardy *Under Greenwood Tree* I. i. vi. 78 The tunes they that morning essayed remained with him for years. **1899** 'Mark Twain' *Man that corrupted Hadleyburg* in *Harper's Mag.* Dec. 30/2 A remark which he made to me has remained with me to this day, and has at last conquered me. *a* **1927** I. Duncan *My Life* (1928) viii. 78 Another, even greater impression, that has remained with me all my life was the 'Rodin Pavillon'. **1977** B. Pym *Quartet in Autumn* vi. 54 She had once noticed an old woman with a lost expression peering through one of the surrounding hedges and that impression had remained with her.

c. To continue with (one). *rare*⁻¹.

1671 Milton *Samson* 1126 In a little time while breath remains thee, Thou oft shalt wish thy self at Gath.

7. †**a.** To be left *with* a responsibility. *Obs.*⁻¹

c **1470** Henry *Wallace* viii. 506 Gyff thow will nocht, ramayne with all the charge.

†**b.** *Sc.* To await *on* (= for) a thing or person.

1513 Douglas *Æneis* i. iv. 84 Be stout, on prosper fortune to remane. **1546** *Reg. Privy Council Scot.* I. 55 That we may provide sum way for our selfis, and ye to remane upoun the finale ansuer. *a* **1557** *Diurn. Occurr.* (Bann. Cl.) 38 The Inglismen past towardis Berwick, and the Governour come to Melross and remanit on his freindis.

c. To await, be left for (one). *rare*.

1579 Spenser *Sheph. Cal.* May 304 And such end, perdie, does all hem remayne, That of such falsers freendship bene fayne. **1590** —— *F.Q.* ii. ix. 6 Were your will her sold to entertaine..Great guerdon, well I wote, should you remaine. **1667** Milton *P.L.* ii. 443 If thence he scape.., what remains him less Then unknown dangers and as hard escape.

d. To be left *with* one in the end, as the result of some action.

1861 Rossetti tr. *Dante's Vita Nuova* (1904) 145 Seeing that in the battle of doubts, the victory most often remained with such as inclined towards the lady of whom I speak.

†**8.** To stay, stop, cease. *Obs. rare*⁻¹.

1480 Caxton *Ovid's Met.* xiv. xi, Som supposed that the warre sholde remayne bycause of this mervayll, but Turnus hade no wylle to leve it.

†**9.** *trans.* To abide, await (an event). *Obs.*⁻¹

1588 Lambarde *Eiren.* iv. xiv. 552 Such persons..must..remayne the comming of the Iustices of Gaole deliuerie.

†**re'mainant,** *a.* and *sb. Obs.* Also 5 **remayand(e,** *Sc.* **ra-),** 6 **remeynant, -maynent.** [Alteration of remenant, after prec., or f. prec. + -ant.] Remaining; remainder; *pl.* remains.

1438–9 *E.E. Wills* (1882) 130 The remaynande of the torgis to x of the nedyest paryschirches. **1456** Sir G. Haye *Law Arms* (S.T.S.) 269 To fornys the remaynand of the bataill. *c* **1470** Henry *Wallace* iii. 401 The ramaynand agayne turnyt that tide. **1523** Fitzherb. *Surv.* xxiv. (1539) 48 Rygge all the remeynant upwarde. ? **1577** *Conuersion Sinner* 5 b, So muche as is remaynent of their mortal life. **1632** Lithgow *Trav.* i. 16 The remainants of that auncient Amphitheatre. **1658** *Virginia Stat.* (1823) I. 466 To the great prejudice and damage to their neighbours and the loss of the remainants cattell.

remainder (rɪ'meɪndə(r)), *sb.*[1] Also 5–6 **-maindre,** (6 **-maender), -mayndre,** (5 **-dore),** 6–7 **-maynder.** [a. AF. *remainder* (sb.) = OF. *remaindre* inf. (:—**remanēre*), var. of *remanoir*:—L. *remanēre*: see remain *v.* and -er⁴.]

1. *Law.* **a.** The residual or further interest remaining over from a particular estate, coming into effect when this has determined, and created by the same conveyance by which the estate itself was granted.

When the residual interest, instead of being devised to another, is reserved by the grantor, it is called a reversion. *contingent remainder*: see contingent A. 9.

1424 *E.E. Wills* (1882) 60 The remaindre of þe maner of Steneby..[I bequeath] to Thomas my son and heir. **1535** *Bury Wills* (Camden) 125 Item I gyve and bequethe vnto my cosyn John Drury..my best gylte goblet, wᵗ the couer as yt ys, the remaynder ther of to be to my godsone, Robert Drury. **1544** tr. *Littleton's Tenures* (1574) 95 b, If a lease bee made to a man for terme of life, the remaynder unto another for terme of life, the remaynder unto the thirde in taile, the remainder unto the fourth in fee [etc.]. **1601** Shaks. *All's Well* iv. iii. 313 Sir, for a Cardecue, he will sell the fee-simple of his saluation, the inheritance of it, and cut th'intaile from all remainders, and a perpetuall succession for it perpetually. **1685** Petty *Last Will* p. vii, I have in Ireland, without the county of Kerry, in lands, remainders, and reversions, about 3100*l.* per ann. **1766** Blackstone *Comm.* II. 164 An estate then in remainder may be defined to be, an estate limited to take effect and be enjoyed after another estate is determined. **1818** Cruise *Digest* (ed. 2) II. 304 Thomas Cary devised to Peter Cary and the heirs male of his body, remainder in the same manner to his other sons. **1876** Digby *Real Prop.* v. 227 A remainder is created by express words at the same time as the particular estate, and is so limited as to come into enjoyment or possession so soon as the particular estate comes to an end.

b. So ***remainder over***. Sometimes = a further remainder.

1544 tr. *Littleton's Tenures* (1574) 13 Yf a man let landes..for terme of yeres, the remainder ouer to an other for terme of lyfe. **1628** Coke *On Litt.* 142 b, If a man..will giue lands in taile, the remainder ouer in fee simple without deed [etc.]. **1766** Blackstone *Comm.* II. 164 This makes A tenant for years, with remainder to B for life, remainder over to C in fee. **1818** Cruise *Digest* (ed. 2) V. 331 Lands were given to an alien in tail, remainder over to another in fee. **1891** *Law Times* XCI. 3/2 Although the deed purported to bar the remainders over, its legal effect was to pass merely a base fee.

c. ***cross remainders***, estates in remainder arising where lands are devised to two or more persons in tail, with remainder to either upon failure of the other's issue.

1766 Blackstone *Comm.* II. 381 Here A and B have cross remainders by implication, and on the failure of either's issue, the other or his issue shall take the whole. **1818** Cruise *Digest* (ed. 2) VI. 435 Cross remainders will not be raised between two persons without words creating a necessary implication. **1858** Ld. St. Leonards *Handy-Bk. Prop. Law* xvii. 110 The common settlement..is..then to the daughters, as tenants in common in tail, with cross-remainders in tail.

d. ***remainder man***, the person to whom a remainder is devised.

1743 *Swinburne's Wills* (ed. 6) 180 Provided that if any of the Remainder Men alien the Land, his Estate shall cease. **1766** Blackstone *Comm.* II. 166 The remainder-man is seised of his remainder at the same time that the termor is possessed of his term. **1818** Cruise *Digest* (ed. 2) VI. 41 It divests the remainder or reversion,..leaving only in the remainder-man or reversioner a mere right of entry. **1881** *Times* 14 Apr. 10/1 With extended facilities and provisions for the security of the remainderman, many encumbered Irish properties would now be willingly disposed of.

e. *transf.* The right to succeed to a title or position on the decease of the holder; *esp.* the right of succession to a peerage expressly assigned to a certain person or line of descent in default of male issue in the direct line.

1809 *Mottos Peers Scotl.* Errata, James, Earl of Hopetoun, was created an English peer..with remainder to the issue male of the body of his father. **1827** Hallam *Const. Hist.* iii. (1876) I. 123 Henry had exercised the power with which his parliament..had invested him, by settling the succession in remainder upon the house of Suffolk. **1893** *Burke's Peerage* 1481 He was advanced to a viscounty 1885, with remainder, in default of his male issue, to his daughter with remainder to her male issue.

attrib. **1893** *N. & Q.* 8th Ser. IV. 461/2 In the event of any future Earl of Cromartie becoming Duke of Sutherland, the Cromartie honours should at once pass to the next remainder heir.

2. a. Those still left out of a number of persons; the remaining ones; the rest (†also in *pl.*).

a **1547** Surrey *Æneid* iv. (1557) E iv b, Troy and the remainder of our folke Restore I shold. **1588** Shaks. *Tit. A.* v. iii. 131 Where you behold vs now, The poore remainder of Andronici. **1656** Heylin *Surv. France* 11 Of the Inhabitants..9000 and upwards are of the Reformation,..the remainders are Papists. **1663** H. Cogan tr. *Pinto's Trav.* i. 2 The remainder of us they left at night in the Road. **1737** [S. Berington] *G. de Lucca's Mem.* (1738) 30 We drove the Remainder headlong off the Deck.

b. That which is left when part has been taken away, used, dealt with, etc.; the residue.

1560 Daus tr. *Sleidane's Comm.* 139 The remainder to be restored when the warre is finished. **1601** Shaks. *All's Well* iv. iii. 272 Not that I am afraide to dye, but that my offences beeing many, I would repent out the remainder of Nature. **1665** Boyle *Occas. Refl.*, *Occas. Medit.* iv. iv, He gave away more out of the Remainder of his Estate, than every liberal Man would have done out of the Whole. **1726** Swift *Gulliver* iii. i, I took out my small Provisions, and, after having refreshed myself, I secured the Remainder in a Cave. **1781** Gibbon *Decl. & F.* xxxi. III. 233 He should be permitted to pass the remainder of his life in..exile. **1836** J. Gilbert *Chr. Atonem.* iii. (1852) 68 Was it not..expected from them, that they should fill up the remainder of the sufferings appointed by their master..? **1875** Jowett *Plato* (ed. 2) IV. 25, I will reserve the analysis of the remainder for another occasion.

3. †**a.** A single person, or a few persons, remaining out of a number. *Obs.*

1579 Fenton *Guicciard.* (1618) 233 In the end..they had recourse to the remainders of the family of the Manfredi their ancient Lords. **1592** Kyd *Sol. & Pers.* ii. i. 303 Ah, Ferdinand, the stay of my old age, And cheefe remainder of our progenie. **1615** G. Sandys *Trav.* 119 That three dayes battell..maintained by a poore remainder of the Mamalucks. **1686** tr. *Chardin's Trav. Persia* 54 Ibrahim that was the only Remainder of the Ottoman Family. **1697** Potter *Antiq. Greece* ii. vi. (1715) 261 After they had utterly routed all the remainders of Xerxes's numerous Army.

b. A remaining (†or still existing) part or fragment; chiefly *pl.* = remains, *esp.* of ancient buildings. (Common in 17th c.)

1604 E. G[rimstone] *D'Acosta's Hist. Indies* vi. xiv. 459 The Edifices and Buildings..were many in number..as doth appeare at this day by their ruines and remainders. **1653** H. More *Antid. Ath.* ii. ii. §2 Seeming Ashes may be no Ashes, that is, no Remainders of any Fewel burnt there. **1702** W. J. tr. *Bruyn's Voy. Levant* iii. 9 With an Intention, as I said before, of visiting all the remainders of Antiquity in that Place. **1872** 'Mark Twain' *Roughing It* l. 357 There'll be a double-barreled inquest here..and your remainders will go home in a couple of baskets. **1878** T. Hardy *Ret. Native* iv. vii, The remainders, being cut into lengths and split open, were tossed into the pan. **1885** —— *Huck. Finn* viii. 62, I was having a good enough time seeing them hunt for my remainders.

c. A remaining trace *of* some practice, quality, feeling, etc. (Cf. remain *sb.*[1] 3 c.) Now *rare*.

1641 Milton *Animadv.* Wks. 1851 III. 211 If you have any remainders of modesty or truth cry God mercy. **1668** Owen in Hearne *Collect.* 26 Nov. an. 1705 (O.H.S.) I. 99 The Remainders of Indwelling-Sin in Believers. **1755** S. Walker *Serm.* 5 Deliver me from the Remainders of Corruption that dwell in me. **1818** Jas. Mill *Brit. India* I. iii. iv. 580 With..a remainder of disgust in the breasts of some of the Omrahs.

4. a. *Arith.* The number which remains after subtraction of a lesser from a greater; the difference between two numbers; the excess after a process of division. (Cf. remain *sb.*[1] 2 b, remainer 2.)

1571 Digges *Pantom.* ii. xxiii. P ij b, The roote quadrate of the remaynder is the perpendiculare falling from the greatest angle to the greatest side. **1594** Blundevil *Exerc.* i. v. (1636) 14 The third number is called the Quotient,..and the fourth number is called the Remainder, if any be. **1656** Hobbes *Six Lessons* Wks. 1845 VII. 231 The remainder after subtraction is the measure of proportion arithmetical. **1696** Bp. Patrick *Comm. Exod.* xxxviii. (1697) 708 Three thousand, dividing 301775 will produce an Hundred and leave 1775 in Remainder. **1798** J. Hutton *Course Math.* I. 12 To prove Subtraction, add the remainder to the less number. **1875** *Encycl. Brit.* II. 528 When the number of times is not exact, the excess of the dividend over the divisor..is called the remainder.

†**b.** = remain *sb.*[1] 2 c. *Obs. rare*⁻¹.

1593 Shaks. *Rich. II*, i. i. 130 My Soueraigne Leege was in my debt, Vpon remainder of a deere Accompt.

5. In the book-trade: A number of copies remaining unsold out of an edition (esp. after the demand for it has fallen off or ceased), and frequently disposed of at a reduced price. Also *transf.*, an unused portion of goods, unused material; = REMNANT *sb.* 4 b.

1757 *Monthly Rev.* Sept., C. Henderson, Bookseller, under the Royal Exchange, having purchased the remainder of the impression of the following very entertaining book.. proposes to sell them for 4s. only. **1854** *Gowans'* (115 Nassau St., N.Y.) *Catal.* No. 13. 6 Remainders of editions by other publishers. **1865** *N. & Q.* VII. 510/2 (Advt.), 'Remainders' of valuable books, all in new condition, at greatly reduced prices. **1873** CURWEN *Hist. Booksellers* 391 Tegg.. visited all the trade sales, and bought up the 'remainders', *i.e.* surplus copies of works in which the original publishers had no faith. **1888** *Athenæum* 22 Dec. 850/2 His main dealings before this having been in 'remainders', and his one solitary publication a failure. **1914** J. LEATHAM *Daavit* 69 My dear good old mother bocht a remander fae Johnnie Hitcheon, and took it an' me ti Saunders ti be mizhur't. **1926** C. N. BENNETT *Photogravure* 121 Paper makers, like drapers, have their remnants, though the name for them in the paper making industry is 'remainders'. **1930** J. H. APPEL *Business Biogr. John Wanamaker* viii. 104 'Bargain Room' opened—'a place where remainders of lots are sold at smaller prices'.

6. *attrib.* passing into *adj.* Remaining, left over; reserve; (sense 5) ***remainder binding, list, -shop***.

1567 LD. HERRIES in Robertson *Hist. Scot.* (1759) II. App. 51 He hoped the remainder noblemen of their party.. would come to the same conformity. **1579** G. HARVEY *Letter-bk.* (Camden) 83 Lett us not be so iniurious to remaender antiquitye as to deprive y[e] fardist of[f] of his due commendation. **1600** SHAKS. *A. Y. L.* II. vii. 39 His braine.. is as drie as the remainder bisket After a voyage. **1824** LAMB *Elia* Ser. II. *Capt. Jackson*, He would sometimes finish the remainder crust, to show that he wished no savings. **1827** HOOD *Mids. Fairies* xxiv, Their memories are dimm'd and torn, Like the remainder tatters of a dream. **1856** KANE *Arct. Expl.* I. xv. 181 All my tired remainder-men were summoned. **1899** *Sketch* 1 Nov. 62/1 The poor evening paper cannot afford this. It must.. be content with the 'remainder biscuit' of the morning's telegrams. **1912** *Chambers's Jrnl.* Dec. 773/2 It is pitiful to see the rows of discarded books in circulating libraries and remainder-shops. **1931** *Times Lit. Suppl.* 10 Sept. 688/2 The unsold sheets of a published book are re-issued with a cancel title or a new preface, or in a remainder binding. **1977** *Gay News* 24 Mar. 21/3, I use anything that's cheap on the remainder list.

7. Special Comb.: **remainder theorem** *Math.*, the theorem that if a polynomial $f(x)$ is divided by $(x-a)$ the remainder will be $f(a)$.

1886 G. CHRYSTAL *Algebra* I. vii. 134 (heading) Results of the application of remainder theorem. **1933** R. W. BRINK *College Algebra* xix. 295 Without performing the divisions, by means of the Remainder Theorem find the remainder after each of the following divisions. **1971** WILLERDING & HOFFMAN *College Algebra* ix. 267 By the Remainder Theorem, the remainder when x^3+7x^2+3x+3 is divided by $x+1$ is 6. As a corollary of the remainder theorem we have the Factor Theorem.

†re'mainder, *sb.*[2] *Obs. rare.* [f. as prec.: cf. REMAIN *sb.*[2]] Stay; time of staying or remaining.

1594 NASHE *Unfort. Trav.* 56 During my remainder there [in Rome]. **1646** SIR T. BROWNE *Pseud. Ep.* 123 The first [reason] is that of Aristotle, drawne from.. the small time of its remainder in the wombe.

re'mainder, *v.* [f. REMAINDER *sb.*[1]] *trans.* To dispose of (an unsold part of an edition of a book) at a reduced price; to treat as a remainder (sense 5). Also *transf.* So **re'maindered** *ppl. a.*, **re'maindering** *vbl. sb.*

1904 *Heffer & Sons' Catal.* 2 As the History of 'Remaindered' Books would almost prove, it might be said that no Book was really great until it had been 'Remaindered'. **1906** *Times* 17 Nov. 9/3 How many books do we see every year produced by publishers who.. 'remainder' them at a few pence a copy? **1907** *Times* 25 Mar. 12/1 There is no doubt now that the boycott is not meant to stop remaindering at low prices. **1910** *Library* I. 46 The plays in question were printed in the years with which they are dated and unsold copies.. remaindered in 1619. *Ibid.* 49 A nineteen-year-old edition was then being remaindered. **1932** *John o' London's Weekly* 25 June 428 He told me he had bought them when they were remaindered by publishers, at 9d. a copy. **1959** *Daily Tel.* 29 Dec. 6/2 Swift turnover for cash, sometimes of goods specially ordered for the sales, and the 'remaindering' of clothes, carpets, furniture and whatnot which might not otherwise be sold so quickly—or even, where fashion is important, at all. **1968** C. M. VINES *Little Nut-Brown Man* x. 155 He liked his books to be in short supply, thus perhaps appearing better sellers than they were; or he disliked the thought of being remaindered. **1981** *Country Life* 1 Jan. 34/1 Picture-books seem to end up by being sold off cheap as remaindered volumes.

remainder-man: see REMAINDER *sb.*[1] 1 d, 6.

re'maindership. *Law.* [f. REMAINDER *sb.*[1] 1.] The possession of a remainder; the fact of there being a remainder.

1865 *Sat. Rev.* 7 Jan. 18/1 The law of entail enables a landowner.. to give to a person yet unborn the remaindership of his estate. **1893** *N. & Q.* 8th Ser. IV. 461/2 This unusual series of remainderships.

So **†re'maindery.** *Obs. rare*[−1].

1490 *Plumpton Corr.* (Camden) 97 A state & feftment.. of lands & tenementes.. for terme of his lyfe, the remaynderie to the ryght heire of William Plompton knight.

†re'maindment. *Law. Obs. rare*[−1]. [irreg. f. REMAINDER *sb.*[1]] A remainder.

1596 BACON *Max. & Use Com. Law* (1635) 52 *marg.*, A recovery barreth an Escheat taile and all reversions and remaindments thereupon.

†re'mainer[1]. *Obs.* Also 5 **remaner**, 5-6 **remayner**, 7 **remainor**. [a. ONF. *remaneir*, = OF. *remanoir* inf.: see REMAIN *v.* and -ER[4].]

1. *Law.* **a.** ? = REMANET 2 a. *rare*[−1].

1454 *Paston Lett.* I. 294 Mastere Pownyngs hath day tille the next terme by a remayner.

b. = REMAINDER *sb.*[1] 1.

1473 *Rolls of Parlt.* VI. 75/2 Nor to oure seid moost derest Wife, nor to her heires or assignes, in, to, or for the remaner.. of the premisses. **1520** SIR R. ELYOT *Will* in *Elyot's Gov.* (1883) App. A, Notwithstanding the said entailles and remayners afore declared.

2. = REMAINDER *sb.* 4 a.

1542 RECORDE *Gr. Artes* (1575) 96 The Remayner is a sum left after a due Subtraction made. **1588** J. MELLIS *Arith.* S iij b, I haue herein alwaies driuen my remayners (or broken partes) into whole numbers. **1669** STURMY *Mariner's Mag.* VI. iii. 106 The Sun enters Gemini May 11; which Substract from 12, the Remainer is 1.

3. = REMAINDER *sb.*[1] 2 b.

1617 *MS. Acc. St. John's Hosp., Canterb.*, The remainor [of the money is] in the boxe. *a* **1625** FLETCHER, etc. *Fair Maid Inn* III. ii, The lesse remainer Is dowry large enough. **1644** NYE *Gunnery* II. (1647) 23 From which stick cut off its just length, the remainer you may use upon the base ring.

re'mainer[2]. *rare.* [f. REMAIN *v.* + -ER[1].] One who remains or stays.

1565 T. STAPLETON *Fortr. Faith* 16, I wil be a remainer in thy tabernacle for euer. **1637** in Cramond *Ann. Banff* (1891) I. 79 Ane daylie remainer fra the Kirk in tyme of dyvyne worschip. **1922** JOYCE *Ulysses* 688 How did the centripetal remainer afford egress to the centrifugal departer?

remaining (rɪˈmeɪnɪŋ), *vbl. sb.* [f. REMAIN *v.* + -ING[1].]

†1. That which remains; a remainder. *Obs.*

c **1375** *Sc. Leg. Saints* viii. (*Philip*) 89 Prestis & deknys þare mad he.. al þe remaynyne to do þat efferyte þare ordyr to. *Ibid.* xviii. (*Mary Egypt*) 855 þe remaynynge þane of þat day I sped me faste one myn way. *c* **1586** C'TESS PEMBROKE *Ps.* LI. i, Clense still my spotts.. Till staines and spotts in me leave noe remaynings. **1621** LADY M. WROTH *Urania* 174 They went to eate that poore remaining that there was left them. **1624** CAPT. SMITH *Virginia* (1629) 212 Such like as they spare of the remainings.

2. The fact of staying or continuing in a place or state; †also, place of staying or residing.

1549 *Compl. Scot.* Prol. 8 The prouest of the prouince quhar ther remanyng vas. **1575** *Reg. Privy Council Scot.* II. 447 The saidis Margaret and Issobell wer in the cumpany and remaning of the said George. **1796** *Instr. & Reg. Cavalry* (1813) 114 Unless the intended and immediate formation of the line requires their remaining where they are. **1855** PUSEY *Doctr. Real Presence* Note A. 31 The remaining, then, of the 'elements in their natural substances' was an open question.

re'maining, *ppl. a.* [f. as prec. + -ING[2].] That remains, in various senses.

1513 DOUGLAS *Æneis* III. ii. 38 We the beseik that.. thou grant ws eik successioun, And for to duell in ane remanand toun. **1645** EVELYN *Diary* 23 Jan., The 3 remaining fountaines which give denomination to this Church. **1683** MOXON *Mech. Exerc., Printing* xxiv. ¶19 He.. doubles the loose half of the Leather over the remaining Nail'd-on half. **1748** HARTLEY *Observ. Man* I. i. §2. 57 These remaining Sensations grow feebler and feebler, till they vanish. **1776** GIBBON *Decl. & F.* xii. I. 334 The remaining actions he intrusted to the care of his lieutenants. **1855** MACAULAY *Hist. Eng.* xv. III. 596 A treason, the consciousness of which threw a dark shade over all his remaining years. **1885** *Athenæum* 4 July 9/1 With.. increasing injuries to the few remaining defences.

re'make (riː-), *v.* Also **re-make**. [RE- 5 a.]

1. *trans.* To make over again, reconstruct. Also *refl.* and *absol.*

a **1635** NAUNTON *Fragm. Reg.* (Arb.) 55 The increasement of Estate and Honour, which the Queen conferred on him, together with the opportunity to remake himself. **1671** WOODHEAD *St. Teresa* II. xxvi. 160 Blessed be thou.. who in an instant destroyest a Soul, and again remakest it. **1799** W. TAYLOR in *Monthly Rev.* XXVIII. 512 It must be re-made over and over again. **1836** J. GILBERT *Chr. Atonem.* ix. (1852) 274 Could not He who first made all creatures perfect, remake us? **1864** BROWNING *Rabbi Ben Ezra* x, Maker, remake, complete,—I trust what Thou shalt do! **1880** MUIRHEAD *Gaius* II. §143 Lest.. a carefully executed testament be set aside when it is no longer possible to remake it.

2. To make again *into* something.

1880 FROUDE *Bunyan* 63 When the law had for a time remade Dissent into a crime.

Hence **re'making** *vbl. sb.*; also **re'maker**.

1778 [W. MARSHALL] *Minutes Agric.* 18 July an. 1776, Re-making in large cock may help hay which is under-made. **1841** EMERSON *Misc.* (1855) 200 What is a man born for but to be a Reformer, a Re-maker of what man has made..? **1889** 'MARK TWAIN' *Yankee at Crt. K. Arthur* 191 If I had the remaking of man, he wouldn't have a conscience.

'remake, *sb.* [f. the vb.] **1.** A second formation of a gold-bearing reef. *Austral.*

1865 *Mining Surveyors' Rep.* (Mining Dept., Victoria) Mar. 74 The lode was however very thin, and ran completely out at 70 feet deep, leaving no track. However a party are now prospecting this ground, to discover if a remake of this reef exists.

2. (Also **re-make.**) A remaking of a film or of a script, usually with the rôles played by different actors; an adaptation of the theme of a film.

1936 *Variety* 24 June 4/4 James Melton assigned the lead in Warners' remake of 'Desert Song'. **1940** *Time* 22 Jan. 76/3 The result is not just another remake, for Director Hawks's weird idea was also to remake the sex of his leading character. **1948** *Sunday Pictorial* 18 July 11/4 'If Winter Comes' (Empire) is a re-make of the famous weepie novel. **1952** *Time* 2 June 92/3 *Lovely to Look at* (M-G-M), a re-make of the old Broadway musical *Roberta* (filmed in 1935 with Fred Astaire and Ginger Rogers). **1957** *Observer* 1 Sept. 11/7 The romance is a remake by director Leo McCarey of his 'Love Affair', which seemed a good film when Irene Dunne and Charles Boyer did it twenty years ago. **1960** *Times* 23 Feb. 4/1 A Hollywood company has undertaken a Western remake of Mr. Akira Kurosawa's famous Japanese costume drama. **1977** *New Statesman* 2 Sept. 312/2 The technicolour remake of the talkie remake of some.. silent Hollywood goodie.

re-'man, *v.* [RE- 5 a.]

1. *trans.* To equip (a fleet, etc.) with fresh men; to man (a gun, etc.) anew.

1666 *Lond. Gaz.* No. 77/3 To Re-man our Fleet,.. resolution is taken of reducing 20, or 25 Companies of Foot. **1804** LARWOOD *No Gun Boats* 11 One will refit, revictual, and re-man his forests of Flotillas. **1823** SOUTHEY *Penins. War* I. 408 For a moment the citizens hesitated to re-man the guns. **1850** GROTE *Greece* II. lxi. (1862) V. 329 These last five [triremes] had been re-manned with Chian crews.

2. To make manly or courageous again; to make again into a man.

1820 BYRON *Mar. Fal.* III. ii. 500 Re-man your breast; I feel no such remorse. **1827** HARE *Guesses* Ser. I. (1873) 181 First unmanning and then re-manning ourselves, each to serve a turn. **1869** BROWNING *Ring & Bk.* XI. 2393 Unmanned, remanned:.. With something changeless at the heart of me To know me by.

remanand, -ant, -aunt(e, obs. ff. REMENANT.

rema'nation. *rare*[−1]. [f. L. *remānāre* (Lucr.) to flow back, after *emanation.*] Flowing back, reabsorption (of a soul in the universe).

1880 S. LANE-POOLE in *Macm. Mag.* Apr. 497 Its pantheistic doctrine of emanation and remanation.

re'mancipate (riː-), *v. Roman Law.* [f. ppl. stem of L. *remancipāre*: see RE- and MANCIPATE *v.*] *trans.* To restore (a thing or person) to the mancipant. Also *absol.*

1656 BLOUNT *Glossogr.*, *Remancipate*, to sell again any-thing to him who first sold it to us. **1880** MUIRHEAD *Gaius* I. §133 When the son has been mancipated the third time, his father ought to take care that the mancipee remancipates to him. *Ibid.* 133 *a*, Unless they have been remancipated by the mancipee to their father or grandfather.

So **remanci'pation.**

1658 PHILLIPS, *Remancipation*, a returning back a commodity into the hands of him of whom it was first bought. **1850** MERIVALE *Rom. Emp.* xxii. (1865) III. 31 Coemption, or the fictitious purchase of the wife from her parents, admitted of remancipation. **1880** MUIRHEAD *Gaius* I. §134 One mancipation is sufficient, which may or may not be followed by remancipation to the parent.

remand (rɪˈmɑːnd, -æ-), *sb.* [f. the vb.]

1. The act of remanding, or the fact of being remanded; now *spec.* recommittal of an accused person to custody (see the vb. 2 b).

1771 MRS. HARRIS in *Lett. Ld. Malmesbury* (1870) I. 211 You will remain at Madrid till the messenger with your remand arrives, and save yourself the fatigue of a double journey. **1852** DICKENS *Bleak Ho.* liv, There was enough against him to make it my duty to take him and get him kept under remand. **1864** *Daily Tel.* 30 Aug., A notorious thief.. brought up on remand. **1884** *Manch. Exam.* 22 May 5/1 Evidence was taken simply to justify a remand.

2. A remanded prisoner.

1888 *Pall Mall G.* 25 Sept. 4/1 It would be more merciful in most cases to order the.. remand a sound birching. **1970** G. F. NEWMAN *Sir, You Bastard* i. 35 The door used by remands, down near the witness box.

3. *attrib.*, as ***remand prisoner, warrant***; **remand centre**, an institution to which young persons between the ages of 14 and 21 years are remanded to await trial or sentence; since 1967, such an institution for a person of any age; *Canad.*, such an institution for adults; **remand home**, an institution to which young persons between the ages of 8 and 14 years are remanded or are committed for detention.

1948 *Criminal Justice Act 11 & 12 Geo. VI* c. 58 s. 48(1)(a) *Remand centres, that is to say places for the detention of persons not less than fourteen but under twenty-one years of age who are remanded or committed in custody for trial or sentence. **1967** *Criminal Justice Act Eliz. II.* c. 80 s. 66(1) Notwithstanding that a remand centre is provided under section 43 of the Prison Act 1952 for the detention of persons of or over the age of fourteen but under the age of twenty-one who are remanded or committed in custody for trial or sentence, any person required to be detained in an institution to which the Act applies may be detained in a remand centre for any temporary purpose or for the purpose of providing maintenance and domestic services for that centre. **1970** G. GREER *Female Eunuch* 180 His impudence in courtrooms and remand centres. **1974** *Globe & Mail* (Toronto) 4 Sept. 1/1 The Calgary remand centre—the first in Alberta—is open for business. The centre will house men held in custody between court appearances pending their trials. **1976** *Southern Even. Echo* (Southampton) 10 Nov. 9/2 A Southampton school-boy was remanded in custody for seven days to Winchester remand centre after the Magistrates decided he was 'unruly'. **1902** *Times* 13 Jan. 9/4 The Children's Committee reported that the three *remand homes at Pentonville-road, Harrow-road, and Camberwell-green were opened for the reception of children on January 1. **1933** *Act 23 & 24 Geo. V* c. 12 s. 108(2) References in any Act to places of detention provided under Section one hundred and eight of the Children Act, 1908, shall be construed as references to remand homes provided under this Act. **1934** 'J. SPENSER' *Limey breaks In* ii. 21 The policeman who took me to the remand home led me into a restaurant and gave me a good feed before he handed me over. **1963** M. DUGGAN in C. K. Stead *N.Z. Short Stories* (1966) 101, I came in for a couple of remand home stares, bread and water and solitary and take that writ on his eyeballs. **1972** G. SERENY *Case of Mary Bell* I. iii. 46 With her father's agreement, she was taken to stay at Fernwood Remand Home, a Newcastle County Council Children's Home for girls. **1897** *Westm. Gaz.* 19 Aug. 2/1 All the men you see in this yard are *remand prisoners. **1977** *Belfast Telegraph* 19 Jan. 4/8 Two visitors to republican prisoners in Crumlin Road jail had been..attacked by loyalist gangs.., a remand prisoner claimed today. **1963** J. N. HARRIS *Weird World Wes Beattie* (1964) i. 12 Wes sits in the Psychiatric Hospital on an attorney general's *remand warrant.

remand (rɪˈmɑːnd, -æ-), *v.* Also 5-6 **-maund.** [ad. F. *remander* (12th c.), or late L. *remandāre* to send back word, to repeat a command: see RE- and MANDATE. Cf. It. *rimandare*, Sp. *remandar*.]

1. *trans.* To send (a thing) back again *to* a place; to reconsign; also, to remit, consign.

1439 *Rolls of Parlt.* V. 30/1 That the saide Rolles..be remaundid and send ayeine unto the saide Places. *c* **1500** *Melusine* 221 They remanded to hym theire wylle with grete yeftes of ryches. **1630** PRYNNE *Anti-Armin.* 276 Let vs once more remaund, adiudge and sinke it to the very depths of Hell. **1653** H. MORE *Antid. Ath.* II. ii. §9 A wonderful Power is required to curb it, regulate it, or remand it back to the Earth and keep it there. **1733** FIELDING *Quix. in Eng.* Pref., Both dissuaded me from suffering it to be represented on the stage; and accordingly it was remanded back to my shelf. **1842** TENNYSON *Love & Duty* 86 Should my Shadow cross thy thoughts..remand it thou For calmer hours to Memory's darkest hold. **1888** BAIN in *Mind* Oct. 536 The ethical writer is not likely to remand to Psychology proper the analysis of Conscience.

†**b.** *Law.* To remit (a prisoner, indictment, record, etc.) back to a court or judge. *Obs.*

1514-5 *Act 6 Hen. VIII*, c. 6 The justices of the Kinges Benche..have full auctoritie..to remaunde and send downe, as well the bodies of all felons and murderers..as their inditements. **1542-3** *Act 34 & 35 Hen. VIII*, c. 27 §88 Which triall so before him had, he shall remaunde with the hole recorde vnto the iustice, before whom yᵉ said plee or voucher was pleaded.

2. To send back (a person); to command or order to go back *to* a place.

1588 in *Harl. Misc.* (Malh.) II. 75 Some came..near London, whom she remanded to their countries, because their harvest was at hand. **1650** FULLER *Pisgah* II. xiii. 273 The Jews were..remanded to wander another way many years, for the punishment of their infidelity. **1677** W. HUBBARD *Narrative* (1865) I. 94 Captain Henchman was sent down to the Governour and Council to know what they should do: they presently remanded him to Pocasset, and ordered him to stay there if there were need. **1712** BLACKMORE *Creation* 306 Where their report the vital envoys make, And with new orders are remanded back. **1771** MRS. HARRIS in *Priv. Lett. Ld. Malmesbury* (1870) I. 214 As you have reason to be fond of Spain and it's inhabitants, you may not be sorry at being remanded. **1802** MAR. EDGEWORTH *Moral T.* (1816) I. 224 If..the prisoner is guilty, I am to remand him to the castle of Spandau.

b. Of a court or magistrate: To send back (a prisoner) into custody, now *spec.* in order that further evidence on the charge may be obtained.

1643 PRYNNE *Sov. Power Parlt.* IV. 27 And if they bring an Habeas Corpus..they shall notwithstanding be remanded and remain prisoners all their dayes. **1748** SMOLLETT *Rod. Rand.* xxx. *heading*, Morgan is sent back into custody, whither also I am remanded, after a curious trial. **1772** *Junius Lett.* lxviii. (1788) 359 If the cause of commitment had been expressed for treason or felony, the court would then have done right in remanding them. **1794** in Bloomfield *Amer. Law Rep.* 29 The said A. is remanded into custody. **1858** A. FONBLANQUE *How we are Governed* 185 The magistrate has the power of remanding him, or sending him back to prison for eight days.

c. To refer (one) back to a passage in a book, or to a period of time. *rare.*

1676 TOWERSON *Decalogue* 50 [On this] I have discoursed already in the foregoing discourse, and must therefore remand you thither. **1866** *Direct. Angl.* (ed. 3) p. vi, We are remanded back to a stated period when the aforesaid 'ornaments' were in use in this Church of England.

3. To call or summon back, to recall. Now *rare* or *Obs.*

1525 LD. BERNERS *Froiss.* II. ccvi, Whan he sawe that he coulde nat atcheue his busynesse, he sygnyfied his estate to the duke of Orlyance, wherevpon he was remaunded, and so he retourned to Parys. **1592** WARNER *Alb. Eng.* VII. xxxvi. 156 With weeping heart he her remands to be with him at one. *a* **1656** USSHER *Ann.* (1658) 569 He remanded his own [men] from the pursuit. **1692** LUTTRELL *Brief Rel.* (1857) II. 482 Captain Wren..can only hear of 2 French men of war there, the rest being remanded home to Brest. *a* **1711** KEN *Hymns Evang.* Poet. Wks. 1721 I. 111 Jealous grown, [he] Remands all Guardians to defend his Throne. **1807** J. BARLOW *Columb.* III. 190 Groan not, my child, thy God remands thee home.

†**b.** To countermand, fetch back. *Obs.*

1676 *Lond. Gaz.* No. 1059/2 Quantities..are already Shipped in parts beyond the Seas for England, and cannot be Remanded without great loss to the Owners thereof. **1772** MRS. SCOTT *Test Filial Duty* II. 171 The baggage was remanded, the captain satisfied for the loss of his passenger [etc.].

†**4.** To demand back from another. *Obs.*

1602 WARNER *Alb. Eng.* IX. xlviii. 224 Each birde shal then remaunde her Plumes. **1649** J. ELLISTONE *Behmen's Epistles* (1886) xxxv. §10 If some Jesuits should come and remand the church from Luther again. **1677** BAKER in Rigaud *Corr. Sci. Men* (1841) II. 29 If after the perusal it may be thought fit to have it printed, I shall remand it from him, and give it another dress.

Hence **reˈmanded** *ppl. a.*, also **reˈmandment**, 'a remandment or ordering back' (Webster, 1847, citing Jefferson).

1888 *Pall Mall G.* 17 Sept. 2/1 He wore the dark-blue dress of remanded prisoners.

remanence (ˈrɛmənəns). [ad. L. type **remanentia*: see REMANENT *a.* and -ENCE.]

1. That which remains; residuum. *rare.*

1666 BOYLE *Orig. Formes & Qual.* 255 To judge of and employ the Remanence of the Amber, after the Distillation is finish'd. *c* **1691** —— *Wks.* III. 81 (R.), This salt..requires no strong heat to make it sublime into finely figured crystals without a remanence at the bottom. **1893** SLOANE *Stand. Electr. Dict.*, *Remanence*, the residual magnetism left after magnetic induction, expressed in lines of force per square centimeter.

2. The fact of remaining; permanence.

1810 COLERIDGE in *Lit. Rem.* (1838) III. 318 Neither St. Augustine nor Calvin denied the remanence of the will in the fallen spirit. **1964** J. STACEY *John Wyclif & Reform* v. 104 The next assertion was a doctrine of Remanence. If annihilation was denied then, in his view, the bread and wine remained bread and wine. **1964** R. H. BAINTON *Hist. Christianity* viii. 238/1 This was not to say..that Christ is not in the sacrament. He is there, in addition to and along with bread and wine, whose substance remains. This doctrine is called remanence. **1974** *Encycl. Brit. Macropædia* XIX. 1051/1 He [*sc.* Wycliffe] sought to replace it [*sc.* the doctrine of transubstantiation] with a doctrine of remanence (remaining).

3. *Physics.* Residual magnetism, *spec.* RETENTIVITY 1 (but see quot. 1962).

1917 G. D. SHEPARDSON *Telephone Apparatus* IV. 279 When the current has been reduced to zero, there still exists a more or less permanent magnetization such as indicated by *OE*, the power of holding this residual magnetization being sometimes called the 'remanence' of the iron, sometimes expressed as a percentage of the maximum magnetization. **1924** C. R. UNDERHILL *Magnets* xxv. 435 The remanence is the structural flux density of a permanent magnet, sometimes called the residual induction. **1947** *Electronic Engin.* XIX. 379/1 The wire originally used..was a medium carbon steel having a remanence of 6,000/7,000 gauss. **1948** [see RETENTIVITY 1]. **1962** M. MCCAIG in D. Hadfield *Permanent Magnets & Magnetism* ii. 26 The hysteresis loop of largest area is known as *the* hysteresis loop. The values of remanent magnetism..and coercive force.. for this hysteresis loop are known as the remanence and coercivity respectively. This definition of remanence conforms with the usage recommended by the British Standards Institution.... In the U.S.A...the same quantity is called residual magnetism, while the word remanence is used to describe the state of an actual magnet after magnetization. Owing to its own self-demagnetizing field such a magnet operates at a point in the top left-hand quadrant of the hysteresis loop. As the British Standard refers to the flux density in such a magnet as 'residual magnetism' there is a complete interchange of meanings of the terms 'remanence' and 'residual magnetism' on the two sides of the Atlantic. **1973** J. G. TWEEDDALE *Materials Technol.* I. iv. 93 When an electromagnetically induced field is changing rapidly, as it might do in a piece of electrical or electronic equipment, it is obvious that a very low remanence is desirable if energy loss and generation of heat is to be avoided. **1976** *Nature* 5 Feb. 381/1 Many of the intrusions have been sampled during our new study and the palaeomagnetism of those possessing stable remanences after a[lternating] f[ield] cleaning is reported here.

So †**ˈremanency.** *Obs.*

1647 JER. TAYLOR *Lib. Proph.* ii. 22 No salvation was consistent with the actuall remanency of that error. **1656** —— *Answ. to Bp. of Rochester* 20 The remanency of concupiscence or Original Sin in the Regenerate.

†**ˈremanent,** *sb. Obs.* [See next.]

1. The remainder, the remaining part, the rest:

a. of a thing or number of things.

1414 *Rolls of Parlt.* IV. 22/2 That ever it stande in the fredom of your hie Regalie to graunte whiche of thoo [things] that you luste, & to wernne the remanent. **1463** in *Somerset Med. Wills* (1901) 199 The remanent restith in the kepyng of thabbat of Glasten. **1582** STANYHURST *Æneis* I. (Arb.) 23 Beholding..yf that knight Antheus haplye Were frusht, or remanent of Troian nauye wer hulling. **1597** A. M. tr. *Guillemeau's Fr. Chirurg.* *vb, I will pursue and addresse the remanent of my studyes. *Ibid.* 23 b/1 We must cut of the threde, and cure the remanent of the wound. **1640-1** *Kirkcudbr. War-Comm. Min. Bk.* (1855) 167 The remanent of hir said husband's rentes and estaite.

b. of a number of persons. (Also *pl.*)

1478 *Liber Niger* in S. Pegge *Cur. Misc.* (1782) 78 The remanent of their servants to be at their livery in the Country. **1509** BARCLAY *Shyp of Folys* (1874) II. 324 The remanent assayle him with envy. **1549** *Compl. Scot.* ix. 76 He sleu men, vemen, ande childir,..the remanent of the pepil var constrenȝeit to fle. **1571** CAMPION *Hist. Irel.* II. iii. (1633) 75 To settle the Realme of Ireland, King Iohn.. banished the Lacyes,..subdued the remanents, tooke pledges [etc.]. **1651** BARKSDALE *Nympha Libethris* (1816) 34 The female remanent, with observant eye, I'd have to learn her mother's housewifery.

2. A remaining part or amount; a remnant; *pl.* remains.

a **1483** *Liber Niger* in *Househ. Ord.* (1790) 58 On the next morning..in every office of household, the remanentes must be taken. **1570** GRINDAL *Let. to Cecil* Wks. (Parker Soc.) 325, I am informed..that among the people there are many remanents of the old [religion]. **1579** FULKE *Heskins' Parl.* 252 Some remanents that were kept to be eaten. **1632** LITHGOW *Trav.* VI. 273 The remanents of that house..is turned ouer for a shelterage to sheepe.

b. A continuation. *rare*$^{-1}$.

1482 WARKW. *Chron.* (Camden) 1 Referre them to my copey, in whyche is wretyn a remanente lyke to this forseyd werke.

3. *Arith.* A remainder.

c **1430** *Art of Nombrynge* (E.E.T.S.) 5 [The number] wherof me shalle with-draw [is] 24. The nombre to be with-draw, 6. The remanent, 18. **1559** W. CUNNINGHAM *Cosmogr. Glasse* 91 The remanent shallbe the iust eleuation of the Pole.

remanent (ˈrɛmənənt), *a.* [ad. L. *remanent-em*, pres. pple. of *remanēre* to REMAIN.]

†**1.** In predicative use: Remaining, staying, abiding; continuing to exist. *Obs.*

1432-50 tr. *Higden* (Rolls) II. 425 Thei were chaungede in to other similitudes,..the mynde of man remanente in theyme. *Ibid.* III. 143 Kynge Astiages toke a grete hoste to this Arpagus, to fiȝhte ageyne men of Persides, hym selfe remanent in Medea. **1513** BRADSHAW *St. Werburge* II. 488 The faith of Christ..In the citie of legions was truely remanent. **1549** *Compl. Scot.* i. 23 Remanent vitht in the plane mane landis far vitht in oure cuntre. **1649** JER. TAYLOR *Gt. Exemp.* Disc. iv. §18 There is no effect remanent upon the body.

2. a. Left behind, remaining, when the rest is removed, used, done, etc. Now *rare.*

1432-50 tr. *Higden* (Rolls) I. 15 Gedrenge the eres of cornes remanent. *Ibid.*, The fragmentes of the cophinnes remanent. **1633** T. ADAMS *Exp. 2 Peter* ii. 7 The very remanent snuff of original goodness must languish out in a stinking dissoluteness. **1651** JER. TAYLOR *Clerus Dom.* 30 This being..the onely remanent expresse of Christs sacrifice on earth. **1715** tr. *Pancirollus' Rerum Mem.* I. I. iv. 12 Its remanent stringy Substance may be so comb'd and teaz'd, as to be weav'd into a Web. **1814** MRS. J. WEST *Alicia de Lacy* IV. 93 Some remanent affections of unsubdued nature carnalized her heart.

b. (Chiefly *Sc.*) Remaining over and above; other; additional. Now *rare.*

c **1449** PECOCK *Repr.* I. viii. 39 Bi an huge gret quantite ouer the remanent parti of the same lawe. **1533** BELLENDEN *Livy* II. ii. (S.T.S.) I. 135 þai and þe remanent conspiratouris..began to commoun of mony hie materis. **1597** A. M. tr. *Guillemeau's Fr. Chirurg.* 53/1 Corrodent bones doe alter and permutate the remanent part of bone. **1682** in *Scott. Antiq.* (1901) July 8 Chancelor of the said wniversaty and..the remanent members of the said facultie. *a* **1691** SIR G. MACKENZIE in *3rd Rep. Hist. MSS. Comm.* 421/1, I have sent your Grace the remanent sheets of the first part of my Criminalls. **1774** in A. MᶜKay *Hist. Kilmarnock* App. iii. 305 Remanent counsellors above named. **1823** M'CLATCHIE *Douglas* III. xvii. 227 The Earl..went out to give the remanent orders of the day to his troops. **1884** *Chr. World* 5 June 426/1 The Moderator, and 'remanent members' of the Assembly.

3. *Law.* = REMANET 2a (see quot. 1829). Hence **ˈremanentcy,** the adjournment of an action. Now *rare.*

1808 BENTHAM *Sc. Reform* 76 By the terrors of remanentcy, as above explained, the plaintiff consents to accept a part of what is his due, giving up the rest.

4. *Physics.* Of magnetism: remaining in a substance or specimen after removal of the magnetizing field.

1866 E. ATKINSON tr. *Ganot's Elem. Treat. Physics* (ed. 2) X. v. 678 The iron used for the electromagnet..must be pure, and be made as soft as possible.... If this is not the case the bar retains, even after the passage of the current a quantity of magnetism which is called the remanent magnetism. **1880** *Nature* XXI. 436/2 The remanent magnetism..seems weakened. **1912, 1931** [see RETENTIVITY 1]. **1939** L. F. BATES *Mod. Magnetism* viii. 258 In general, the remanent magnetism possessed by a ferromagnetic which has been placed in a strong field is sufficient to give satisfactory deflections of a sensitive astatic magnetometer system. **1944** *Proc. IRE* XXXII. 667/2 The remanent flux will go through a series of values corresponding to the sum and difference frequencies between the recording signal and the supersonic signal. **1962** [see REMANENCE 3]. **1971** I. G. GASS et al. *Understanding Earth* xvi. 237/1 The intensity of this remanent or permanent component of magnetisation in basalts is invariably greater than that induced by the present Earth's field.

remaner, obs. form of REMAINER.

remanet (ˈrɛmənɛt). Also 6 **remaneth.** [L., 3rd sing. pres. indic. of *remanēre* to REMAIN.]

1. A remainder.

1511 *Househ. Bk. Dk. Northumbld.* (1770) 2 Divers Vitalls and Stuffs remaynynge.., as it aperith more playnly by a bill of the same Remaneth signed with my hand. **1540** *Churchw. Acc. St. Giles, Reading* (ed. Nash) 58 A remanet for broken plate sold viijs. *c* **1640** J. SMYTH *Hund. Berkeley* (1885) 89 The Remanet paid into the Exchequer is 51s 8d q. by the Collector. **1874** MRS. H. WOOD *Mast. Greylands* xix. 221 The intimacy..must be a sort of remanet of that friendship, meaning nothing. **1891** H. MATTHEWS in *Law Times* XCII. 96/1 Convicts serving remanets of former sentences.

2. *Law.* **a.** A cause or suit of which the hearing is postponed to another day or term.

a **1734** NORTH *Lives* (1826) I. 436 For the causes, left one day, are remanets to the next. **1829** BENTHAM *Justice & Cod. Petit.* 83 The other part [of suits] remain unheard and are called remanets or remanents. **1870** *Daily News* 12 Dec., The list contains 111 cases, 28 of which are remanets.

attrib. **1829** BENTHAM *Justice & Cod. Petit.* 80 If it happens to it to be on the remanet list. **1888** *Evening Post* 23 Nov. 2/6 The remanet witness had been in the box all the morning.

b. A parliamentary bill left over till another session.

1870 *Daily News* 22 July 6 The law on the Press..is impudently made a remanet, and will hang over till next session. **1887** *Edin. Rev.* Jan. 284 The question of 'remanets' at the close of each session.

‖**remanié** (rəmanje), *a. Geol.* and *Geogr.* [a. F. *remanié*, pa. pple. of *remanier* to rehandle, reshape.] Derived from an older stratum or structure.

[**1866** *Q. Jrnl. Geol. Soc.* XXII. 237 If the Diestien beds be divided into upper sandy ooze and lower muddy ooze, the sections show that where the first has been removed and 'remanié', the resulting Scaldésien beds take the form of 'Crag gris'.] **1870** *Ibid.* XXVI. 72 In this 'remanié' deposit there appears to exist an assemblage of species peculiar to two distinct epochs. **1894** J. GEIKIE *Great Ice Age* (ed. 3) xii. 160 The marine organisms.. may indicate an inter-glacial submergence to the extent of 300 or 400 feet, but on the other hand the deposits in which they occur may be *remoniés.* They may well have been dragged forward by the ice from a lower level. **1913** *Rep. Brit. Assoc. Adv. Sci. 1912* 622 Excavation (some 8 feet deep) in 'rubble-drift' material, mostly *remanié* stuff from the Boulder Clay which caps the hill above. **1957** J. K. CHARLESWORTH *Quaternary Era* I. iv. 87 If the lateral glacier is steep it may fall on a trunk glacier as a remanié glacier. **1964** V. J. CHAPMAN *Coastal Vegetation* vi. 137 If a dune undergoing erosion is stabilized, it represents a moderate remanié form. **1969** BENNISON & WRIGHT *Geol. Hist. Brit. Isles* i. 10 A bed may contain fossils of a previous geological age known as derived or remanié fossils. **1978** *Nature* 16 Nov. 258/2 At Hamilton in western Victoria, a bed of calcareous clay containing phosphatic nodules rests unconformably on limestone and clay of early and middle Miocene age and contains abundant *remanié* foraminifera from both formations.

‖**remaniement** (rəmanimɑ̃). [Fr.: see prec.] A rearrangement, a reconstruction.

1920 *Glasgow Herald* 3 Aug. 5 Much more.. needs study in the latest 'remaniement' of the Turkish Ministry... The Grand Vizier.. is determined that the new Cabinet shall be composed of moderate men. **1933** E. K. CHAMBERS *Eng. Folk-Play* 87 The play is said to have been given as far back as 1807, but to me it suggests a literary *remaniement.*

†**re'mansion.** *Obs. rare.* [ad. L. *remansiōn-em*, f. *remanēre* to REMAIN: cf. MANSION.] The act of remaining.

1597 A. M. tr. *Guillemeau's Fr. Chirurg.* 53/1 Corrodent matter or bones, by theire remansione in that place, doe also corrupte the finitimate partes. **1657** TOMLINSON *Renou's Disp.* 67 Because of the discussion of the volatile Sulphur.. and the remansion of the fixed saltness.

remanu'facture, *sb.* [RE- 5 a.] The act, process, or result, of manufacturing again.

1796 W. TAYLOR in *Monthly Rev.* XX. 336 The capture.. of outward-bound.. vessels occasions the re-manufacture or re-exportation of goods like those with which they were freighted. **1851** MAYHEW *Lond. Labour* II. 30/1 These garments are inferior to those woven of new wool..; but in some articles the re-manufacture is beautiful. **1892** *Daily News* 8 Feb. 2/8 Old rails for remanufacture.

So **remanu'facture** *v. trans.*

1825 J. NICHOLSON *Operat. Mechanic* 338 These are sold to the manufacturer to be remanufactured.

re-ma'nure, *v.* [RE- 5 a.] To manure again.

1823 BYRON *Age of Bronze* v, Clashing hosts, who strew'd the barren sand To re-manure the uncultivated land.

remap, re-map (riː-). *U.S.* [RE- 5 a.] = REDISTRICTING *vbl. sb.* Also *attrib.*

1962 *Nashville Tennessean* 2 Sept. 2-B/1 (*heading*) State remap is still issue. **1962** *Economist* 1 Dec. 908/1 Tennessee has approved a constitutional convention on what is called 're-map'. **1974** *State* (Columbia, S. Carolina) 15 Feb. 4-A/3 The department rejected a bitterly disputed remap plan that would have divided the state into 28 districts drawn to maintain the integrity of county lines.

re'march (riː-), *v.* [RE-.] *trans.* and *intr.* To march back or again.

1642 SLINGSBY *Diary* (1836) 88 We remarchd yᵉ first night to Sherif Hutton and there lay 2 nights. **1815** HOBHOUSE *Substance Lett.* (1816) I. 156 Hearing that the Duke of Treviso had remarched the garrison into the town. **1895** *Outing* (U.S.) XXVI. 445/2 Here Cornwallis and Clinton marched and remarched.

So **re'march** *sb.*

1884 *Manch. Exam.* 19 Dec. 5/5 There had been a march and remarch of the Forty Thieves.

re'margin, *v.* [RE- 5 a.] *trans.* To furnish (a leaf of a book) with a fresh margin.

A common term in booksellers' catalogues.

1891 *Kerr & Richardson's Catal.* Nov. 26/1 Some leaves remargined. **1952** J. CARTER *ABC for Book-Collectors* 153 When one or more of the three outer margins of a leaf has been restored, it is said to be re-margined.

remark (rɪ'mɑːk), *sb.*¹ Also 7 **remarke, remarque.** [ad. F. *remarque*, f. *remarquer* to REMARK.]

†**1.** The fact or quality of being worthy of notice or comment. In phr. *of* (..) *remark. Obs.*

1654 H. L'ESTRANGE *Chas. I* (1655) 201 To prepare a charge against the Archbishop of Canterbury, as one of prime remarque in forming of these Canons. **1680** MORDEN *Geog. Rect.* (1685) 410 Some Relations make mention of the Naiques of Madure.. but give us little of Remarque with Certainty. **1702** W. J. tr. *Bruyn's Voy. Levant* lxiv. 237 In which there were three Women, but of no great remark.

2. Observation, notice; comment.

1680 OTWAY *Orphan* II. vi, Pass not one circumstance without remark. **1680** MORDEN *Geog. Rect.* (1685) 123 The Arsenal, the College of the Jesuits.. are worthy of Remarque. **1781** COWPER *Table T.* 205 The cause.. may yet elude Conjecture and remark, however shrewd. **1827** HOOD *Mids. Fairies* lxxvii, Roots, like any bones of buried men, Push'd through the rotten sod for fear's remark. **1830** HERSCHEL *Stud. Nat. Phil.* II. iv. (1851) 132 The grand discovery.. originated in his casual remark of the disappearance of one of the images. **1885** *Manch. Exam.* 15 May 5/3 Lord R. Churchill's latest escapade.. is the theme of general remark.

Comb. **1834** A. CUNNINGHAM *Brit. Lit.* 19 It is remarkworthy that the most natural and impassioned songs in.. our literature were written by a ploughman-lad.

b. Air of observation; look. *rare*⁻¹.

1748 THOMSON *Cast. Indol.* I. lvii, Of all the gentle tenants of the place, There was a man of special grave remark.

3. a. An act of observing or noticing; an observation. Now *rare.* †Also const. *of.*

1660 F. BROOKE tr. *Le Blanc's Trav.* 41 For a clearer intelligence of the worthiest remarkes we made in that great journy. **1676** GREW *Exper. Luctation* iii. §56 If a diligent remarque be made of all those various Colours, Smells [etc.]. **1690** LEYBOURN *Curs. Math.* 448 b, The principal Remarks of this illustrious Planet, made by the Ancients, were these following. **1711** ADDISON *Spectator* No. 50 ¶8 As for the Women of the Country, not being able to talk with them, we could only make our Remarks upon them at a Distance. **1779–81** JOHNSON *L.P., Butler* Wks. II. 188 He had watched with great diligence the operations of human nature... From such remarks proceeded [etc.]. **1855** BROWNING *Fra Lippo* 128, I had a store of such remarks, be sure, Which, after I found leisure, turned to use.

b. A verbal or written observation; a comment; a brief expression of opinion or criticism.

1673 [R. LEIGH] *Transp. Reh.* 4 That we may better understand the pertinency of this Remarque. **1698** NORRIS *Pract. Disc.* IV. 123 This is what I intend; only I have one Remarque to make upon the two other Heads before I proceed to treat of this. **1716** (*title*) Weekly Remarks and Reflections upon the most material news, foreign and domestic. **1791** MRS. RADCLIFFE *Rom. Forest* ii, Which drew from him a remark that the style of this apartment was not strictly Gothic. **1820** B. SILLIMAN *Tour fr. Hartford to Quebec* (1824) 63 The numerous manuscript remarks and annotations on the blank leaves and margins of the books. **1883** F. M. CRAWFORD *Dr. Claudius* iv, He could not bear to hear Mr. Barker's chaffing remarks.

attrib. **1867** SMYTH *Sailor's Work-bk.* 568 *Remark-Book.* This contains hydrographical observations of every port visited, and is sent annually to the admiralty.

†**c.** A mark or record of an observation. *Obs.*⁻¹

1789 G. KEATE *Pelew Isl.* 271 He took a piece of line, which he had brought with him for the purpose of making remarks, and tied a knot thereon as a remembrance of the circumstance.

†**4.** A sign, mark, indication of something notable. *Obs.*

1663 HEATH *Flagellum* (1672) 1 Fate.. brought him [Cromwell] into the world without any terrible remark of his portentuous Life. **1676** I. MATHER *K. Philip's War* (1862) 64 This day deserves to have a Remark set upon it. **1709** STRYPE *Ann. Ref.* I. lii. 520 That which gave a greater Remark to this favourable Providence of God to the Nation.

†**b.** A mark or indication *of* a quality; a remaining trace *of* something. *Obs.*

1667 WATERHOUSE *Fire Lond.* 108 It was not possible almost to wish better or more remarks of Christian Devotion. **1676** WISEMAN *Surg.* I. xxv. 140 She.. is not so freed of that Disease, but that she hath sometimes little Remarques of it. **1686** GOAD *Celest. Bodies* I. iii. 7 God himself hath pleased to give it as a remarque of his power that He causes it to rain on one City, and not on another.

†**c.** A marked physical feature. *Obs. rare.*

1660 WATERHOUSE *Arms & Arm.* 20 So also some have been named from bodily remarks, as.. Fairfax from their faire bush of haire. *c* **1661** *Mrq. Argyle's Will.* in *Harl. Misc.* (1746) VIII. 29/2 Lest the Remarks of his Face should fright fanciful People like a Spectre.

†**d.** A remarkable object. *Obs. rare.*

1675 OGILBY *Brit.* Introd. 1 The more obvious and considerable Remarques of a City. **1678** (*title*) England's Remarques, giving an exact account of the several shires, counties, and islands in England and Wales.

remark (rɪ'mɑːk), *sb.*² Also **re-mark.** Anglicized form of REMARQUE. Also *attrib.*

1880 *Academy* 18 Dec. 449/1 The remark proof carries a very good dry-point portrait of the painter. **1881** *Athenæum* 15 Jan. 100 A new etched plate by Mr. Samuel Palmer, of which a re-mark proof is before us... The re-marks on our impression are [etc.].

remark (rɪ'mɑːk), *v.*¹ Also 7 **remarque.** [ad. F. *remarquer*: see RE- and MARK *v.*]

†**1. a.** *trans.* To mark out, distinguish. *Obs.*

1633 FORD *'Tis Pity* II. v, Thou art a man remark'd to taste of mischief. **1651** JER. TAYLOR *Serm. for Year* II. Ep. Ded., Those blessings and separations with which God hath remarked your family and person. **1671** MILTON *Samson* 1309 His manacles remark him, there he sits.

†**b.** To point out, indicate. *Obs.*

1649 JER. TAYLOR *Gt. Exemp.* Disc. xviii. §5 This effect of power does also remark the Divine wisdom, who hath ordained such symboles. **1660** F. BROOKE tr. *Le Blanc's Trav.* 11 They yet remark the Rock Moses miraculously drew water out of. **1740** tr. *De Mouhy's Fort. Country-Maid* (1741) II. 61 [She] remarked to me a very handsome Man, who had his Eyes continually upon us. **1742** FIELDING & YOUNG tr. *Aristophanes' Plutus* III. iii. *note*, This is literal from the Greek, and the beauty of it need not be remarked.

2. a. To observe, take notice of, perceive.

1675 R. BURTHOGGE *Causa Dei* 35 A Passage in the accurate Pausanias, which I could not but Remarque when I read it. **1718** *Free-thinker* No. 62. 45 It was customary.. to send out a Slave to remark what was said in the Streets. **1765** H. WALPOLE *Otranto* v, Has not your highness remarked it? **1792** CHARLOTTE SMITH *Desmond* III. 156, I remark him every day pass by the windows of the house. **1849** THACKERAY *Pendennis* xx, The looks of gloom and despair which even Mr. Morgan had remarked. **1875** JOWETT *Plato* (ed. 2) V. 120 In the Laws, we remark a change in the place assigned by him to pleasure and pain.

b. With obj. clause.

1768 G. WHITE *Selborne* xxi, I shall be very curious to remark whether they will call on us at their return in the spring. **1832** MRS. F. TROLLOPE *Dom. Manners Amer.* xx. (1839) 184, I remarked that it was not very unusual at Washington for a lady to take the arm of a gentleman.

3. a. To say, utter, or set down, as an observation or comment.

1694 LOCKE *Ess. Hum. Und.* (ed. 2) III. ix. 275 It is easie to observe, what has been before remarked, [etc.]. **1719** WATERLAND *Christ's Div.* ii. Wks. 1823 II. 33, I shall only remark, that when this text is away [etc.]. **1781** COWPER *Hope* 429 The writer well remarks, a heart that knows To take with gratitude.. is all in all. **1826** DISRAELI *Viv. Grey* I. ii, 'Oh, my Lord!' carelessly remarked Vivian, 'I thought it was a mere on dit!' **1849** LYTTON *Caxtons* XI. i, As I have had occasion before to remark, Sphinx and Enigma are nouns feminine. **1875** JOWETT *Plato* (ed. 2) IV. 12 The modern philosopher would remark that the indefinite is equally real with the definite.

b. *intr.* To make a remark *on* a thing. Also without *prep.*, to make remarks.

1845 J. RUSKIN *Let.* 17 June in H. I. Shapiro *Ruskin in Italy* (1972) 118 Perhaps.. it is an English cheesemonger & his wife, who come in, and remark, as happened to me the other day while I was looking at the gates of Ghiberti. **1859** DARWIN *Orig. Spec.* xii. (1901) 313 We can.. understand the singular fact remarked on by several observers that [etc.]. **1861** LEVER *One of Them* xviii, Remarking on a little tinted sketch at the top of the letter.

Hence **re'marking** *vbl. sb.*

1751 HARRIS *Hermes* II. i. (1765) 232 In English likewise it deserves remarking, how the Sense is changed by changing of the Articles. **1854** W. JAY *Autobiog.* ix. 91 Nothing in my estimation and remarkings ever being able to atone for the want of consistency.

re-mark (riː'mɑːk), *v.*² [RE- 5 a.] *trans.* To mark again. Hence **re-'marking** *vbl. sb.*

1611 COTGR., *Renoter*, to renote, remark. **1837** HT. MARTINEAU *Soc. Amer.* III. 220 His works.. are marked, re-marked, and worn. **1870** MISS BRIDGMAN *R. Lynne* II. iii. 55 He insisted on his wife re-marking the whole of the.. wardrobe. **1894** *Daily News* 19 July 8/2 This re-marking is done almost daily at the railway stations and public docks here.

remarka'bility. [f. next + -ITY.] Remarkableness.

1838 MRS. HAWTHORNE in *N. Hawthorne & Wife* (1885) I. 193 He.. said he thought 'women were always jealous of such a kind of remarkability' (that was his word) 'in their own sex'. **1880** *Cornh. Mag.* Feb. 183 The most ordinary of dogs has a sort of remarkability.

remarkable (rɪ'mɑːkəb(ə)l), *a.* and *sb.* Also 7 **remarqueable.** [ad. F. *remarquable* (16th c.): see REMARK *v.* and -ABLE.]

A. *adj.* **1.** Worthy of remark, notice or observation; hence, extraordinary, unusual, singular. Also (*colloq.*) as quasi-*adv.*

1604 R. CAWDREY *Table Alph.*, *Remarkable*, able or worthy to be marked againe. **1606** SHAKS. *Ant. & Cl.* IV. xv. 67 The oddes is gone, And there is nothing left remarkeable Beneath the visiting Moone. **1612** SELDEN *Illustr. Drayton's Poly-olb.* iii. 262 The last and Henry of Huntingdon reckon onely foure remarqueable. **1664** BURNET *Own Time* Suppl. (1902) 91, I heard him preach, and had an interpreter sit by me that explained the remarkablest passages of his sermon. **1705** ADDISON *Italy* 5 The Gulf.. is very remarkable for Tempests and Scarcity of Fish. **1762–71** H. WALPOLE *Vertue's Anecd. Paint.* (1782) I. 227 The next is a very remarkable picture on board at Kensington. **1779** J. WOODFORDE *Diary* 6 Feb. (1924) I. 245 Mr. Ferman and myself went to see a remarkable large Pigg. **1818** W. SEWALL *Diary* 13 Mar. (1930) 39/1 The scholars appeared remarkable well. **1845** CARLYLE *Cromwell* (1871) II. 225 One of the remarkablest State papers ever published in Ireland. **1871** E. EGGLESTON *Hoosier Schoolmaster* iv. 39 He uses sech remarkable smart words. **1880** GEIKIE *Phys. Geog.* iv. 262 The river swells and falls again with remarkable slowness and uniformity. **1890** KIPLING *Barrack-Room Ballads* (1892) 8 We aren't no thin red 'eroes.. But single men in barricks, most remarkable like you.

†**2. a.** Perceptible; admitting of being observed or noted. *Obs.*

1622 MEADE in Ellis *Orig. Lett.* Ser. I. III. 132 The king heard our Comedie on Wednesday, but expressed no remarkable mirth thereat. **1674** FAIRFAX *Bulk & Selv.* 82 Then let us suppose in the stead of an Angel, some remarkable body. *a* **1704** T. BROWN *Two Oxford Scholars* Wks. 1730 I. 5 A demure look, and some other remarkable signs of grace. **1766** *Compl. Farmer* s.v. *Surveying*, Draw a remarkable line with ink, or rather with a black-lead pen quite over your paper.

†**b.** Likely to attract attention; conspicuous, noticeable. *Obs.*

1726 SHELVOCKE *Voy. round World* 97, I sent the pinnace ashore with a bill to be fixed on the door of some remarkable Indian house. **1801** CHARLOTTE SMITH *Lett. Solit. Wand.* II. 212 On the stranger's observing to her that their conference was becoming remarkable.

B. *sb.* A noteworthy thing or circumstance; something extraordinary or exceptional. Chiefly in *pl.* Now *arch.*

1639 FULLER *Holy War* II. xlvi. *heading*, Jerusalem wonne by the Turk, with wofull remarkables thereat. **1653** H. MORE *Antid. Ath.* II. xi. §12 The other Remarkable, and it is a notorious one, is the Cavity on the back of the Male. **1679** MANSELL *Narr. Popish Plot* 102, I was willing to adde a few Remarkables, which I.. purposely reserved for this place. **1741** RICHARDSON *Pamela* (1824) I. lxxxix. 457 The places and remarkables you will see, will be new only to yourself. **1776** J. ADAMS *Wks.* (1854) IX. 395 Be so good as to write me any remarkables in the legislature or the courts of justice. **1817** SCOTT 17 Mar. in *Fam. Lett.* (1894) I. xiii. 421 Two remarkables struck me in my illness. **1856** HAWTHORNE *Eng. Note-bks.* (1870) II. 148 After lunch today we..set forth to see the remarkables of Oxford. **1946** *Richmond* (Va.) *Times-Dispatch* 15 Jan. 10/2 (*heading*) Religious remarkables.

re'markableness. [f. prec. + -NESS.] The fact or character of being remarkable.
c **1658** DURHAM *Exp. Revelation* VI. xiii. (1687) 323 Consider the remarkablenesse of Gods judgements on these persecutors. **1666** J. SMITH *Old Age* (1676) 164 They do agree in their eminency and remarkableness; they are both of them most signal things. **1851** WARDLAW *Zechariah* x. (1869) 191 The remarkableness of the fulfilment of the predictions. **1889** J. M. ROBERTSON *Ess. Crit. Meth.* 12 Fresh literature, of which the remarkableness..will long justify the tribute paid to its less permanently valuable parts.

re'markably, *adv.* [f. as prec. + -LY².]
1. In a remarkable manner; notably, strikingly, conspicuously: **a.** with verbs.
1638 A. READ *Chirurg.* i. 8 If the braine be remarkably wounded, the party remaineth foolish. **1671** MILTON *P.R.* II. 106 Oft to mind Recalling what remarkably had pass'd. **1748** HARTLEY *Observ. Man* I. iii. §5. 387 This agrees remarkably with the perpetual Impressions made upon the optic Nerves. **1817** JAS. MILL *Brit. India* I. Pref. 11 *note*, Those particulars..on which the results in question appeared more remarkably to depend. **1878** LECKY *Eng. in 18th C.* vii. II. 389 The treatment of Bedell..and the Act.. exhibit very remarkably this aspect of the Irish character.
b. with adjs.
1711 ADDISON *Spect.* No. 261 ¶7 If you marry one remarkably beautiful. **1749** FIELDING *Tom Jones* XVIII. xi, He was now as remarkably mean, as he had been before remarkably wicked. **1840** BARHAM *Ingol. Leg.* Ser. I. *Look at the Clock*, [He] had one darling vice; Remarkably partial to any thing nice. **1880** GEIKIE *Phys. Geog.* ii. 84 Hailstorms are sometimes remarkably destructive.
†**2.** In an obvious manner. *Obs. rare*⁻¹.
1666 PEPYS *Diary* 15 Aug., If I do but my duty remarkably from this time forward, I may be as well as ever I was.

remarked (rɪ'mɑːkt), *ppl. a.*¹ [f. REMARK *v.* + -ED¹.] Marked, conspicuous, noted.
1613 SHAKS. *Hen. VIII*, v. i. 33 Now, Sir, you speake of two, The most remark'd i' th' Kingdom. **1771** LUCKOMBE *Hist. Printing* 53 Being remarked for his piety and learning. **1816** 'QUIZ' *Grand Master* I. 13 The captain's clerk..Paid one of them remark'd attention. **1827** DISRAELI *Viv. Grey* v. xi, A man, who..is always a remarkable, and a remarked character, wherever he may be.
Hence **re'markedly** *adv.*
1871 MATEER *Travancore* 363 The discipline and general good deportment which is remarkedly observable in you.

re'marked, *ppl. a.*² [f. REMARK *sb.*² + -ED².] Of an engraving: Characterized by the presence of a remarque.
1883 *American* VII. 120 The work is nearly finished, and a remarked proof is now on exhibition.

remarker (rɪ'mɑːkə(r)). Now *rare.* [f. REMARK *v.* + -ER¹.]
†**1.** One who makes or publishes remarks on a literary work; a reviewer or critic; also, an author of 'Remarks' on some subject. *Obs.* (common *c* 1685–1790).
1684 H. MORE *Answ.* 214 The Remarker had better have let things alone. **1695** in Macfarlane *Genealog. Collect.* (S.H.S.) 425 The Remarker says that the Son of Norman was Simon. **1737** FRANKLIN *Ess.* Wks. 1840 II. 309 To follow the remarker, through all his incoherencies and absurdities, would be irksome. **1756** JOHNSON *Introd. Sir T. Browne's Chr. Mor.* 51 It was observed by some of the remarkers on the *Religio Medici* [etc.]. **1795** BURKE *Regic. Peace* iv. (1892) 326 The Remarker..seems aware that this arrangement..leaves us at the mercy of the new Coalition.
2. One who makes or utters observations; an observer, commenter. Now *rare.*
a **1684** LEIGHTON *Comm. 1st Pet.* Wks. (1868) 197 My remarkers David calls them, they that scan my ways. **1704** STEELE *Lying Lover* III, She pretends to be a Remarker, and looks at every body. **1742** RICHARDSON *Pamela* IV. 271 The Scandal which some severe Remarkers are apt to throw upon the Wives of Parsons. **1788** MME. D'ARBLAY *Diary* Jan., With those keen remarkers..there is a zest in conversing that gives a spirit to every subject. **1810** B. SILLIMAN *Jrnl. Trav.* (1820) III. 35 They are thinking of their dinners (said the remarker) and not of your passports.

‖**remarque** (rəmark). [F.: cf. REMARK *sb.*²] In *Engraving*, a distinguishing feature indicating a certain state of the plate, usually consisting in the insertion of a slight sketch in the margin. Also *attrib.* in ***remarque-proof.***
1882 *Artist* 1 Feb. 58/2 A remarque on a plate is an evidence of the artist's caprice. **1889** *Pall Mall G.* 12 Mar. 3/1 The print-buying world is becoming daily more and more aghast at the encroachments of the remarque. **1890** F. G. KITTON *Charles Dickens by Pen & Pencil* I. iv. facing p. 49 Charles Dickens, his wife and her sister—1843... Remarque: Miss Mary Hogarth. **1925** C. MORLEY *Thunder on Left* vii. 80 If they're girls, how mothers hurry to drill and denature those bright dreaming wits. They love them chiefly because they make so pretty a vignette in the margin of their own self-portrait—like a *remarque* in an engraving.
Hence **re'marque** *v.*, to insert as a remarque.
1884 *Pall Mall G.* 12 Mar. 3/1 Lane's portrait of Dickens and George Cattermole's large portrait so largely 'remarqued' beneath.

remarque, obs. form of REMARK *sb.*¹ and *v.*¹

re'marriage (riː-). Also **re-marriage.** [RE- 5 a.] A second or subsequent marriage.
1620 BP. HALL *Hon. Mar. Clergy* i. §18. 101 The Iewes.. with whom Polygamie and re-marriages, after vniust diuorces, were in ordinarie vse. **1679** EVELYN *Diary* 6 Nov., Was this evening at the re-marriage of the Dutchesse of Grafton. **1815** *Chron.* in *Ann. Reg.* 61 A re-marriage.. between their royal highnesses the duke and duchess of Cumberland. **1856** FROUDE *Hist. Eng.* II. 501 On the death of Jane Seymour, the council urged immediate remarriage on the king. **1892** TENNYSON *Akbar's Dream* note, Akbar ordained that remarriage was lawful.

re'marry (riː-), *v.* Also **re-marry.** [RE- 5 a.]
1. *intr.* To enter again into matrimony.
1525 LD. BERNERS *Froiss.* II. cxi. [cvii.] 320 Thoughe the erle than remary againe the seconde tyme, and haue issue by the seconde wyfe. **1612** WEBSTER *White Devil* v. i, Neere trust them, they'le re-marry Ere the worm peirce your winding sheete. **1673** *Lady's Call.* II. iii. §16 It is not therefore to be expected that many will..be diverted from remarrying. **1752** CARTE *Hist. Eng.* III. 155 The king lost no time in making use of the liberty of remarrying. **1829** SOUTHEY *Sir T. More* (1831) II. 78 It being forbidden by the canon law..to remarry..without a special dispensation. **1879** FARRAR *St. Paul* II. 71 Widows might re-marry if they liked.
b. Const. *to* (now *rare*) or *with.*
c **1630** RISDON *Surv. Devon* §145 (1810) 161 The duchess remarried to sir Thomas St. Leger. **1632** SIR T. HAWKINS tr. *Mathieu's Unhappy Prosperitie* II. 238 Robert remarrying with Sancha. **1709** MRS. MANLEY *Secret Mem.* (1736) I. 174 He re-marry'd to an Heiress. **1895** *Daily News* 14 Nov. 6/2 Upon her mother's remarrying with..an army surgeon. **1901** *Westm. Gaz.* 30 July 4/3 Although she had remarried to a commoner.
2. *trans.* To unite again in marriage. Chiefly *pass.*; also const. *to.*
1523 LD. BERNERS *Froiss.* I. xxi. 12/2 They aduysed by their counsell that the king shulde be remaryed agayne. **1611** SPEED *Hist. Gt. Brit.* VII. xi. 260 After his death..shee was remarried to Egfrid. **1631** WEEVER *Anc. Funeral Mon.* 740 After the death of his wife Elisabeth, hee was remarried vnto Violenta. **1727–38** CHAMBERS *Cycl.* s.v. *Re-marrying*, Uncanonical marriages are deemed null; and the parties are to be re-married in form. **1830** MISS MITFORD *Village* Ser. IV. (1863) 202 She is now, however, re-married to a Mr. Browne. **1853** GROTE *Greece* II. lxxxiv. XI. 119 When his property was confiscated and his wife re-married to another. **1888** BARRIE *Auld Licht Idylls* xii, Tammas had himself married by Jimmy Pawse,..and after that the minister re-married them.
fig. **1647** *Standard of Equality* §9 When the King shall be remarried to the State. *a* **1711** KEN *Hymns Evang.* Poet. Wks. 1721 I. 171 There each good Soul remains in Widdow'd State, In Longings till remarried to its Mate.
3. To take (a person) as a second husband or wife.
1638 FORD *Lady's Trial* v. ii, This gentleman, Benatzi, Disguised as you see, I have re-married. **1859** SALA *Tw. round Clock* (1861) 170 She..had married a very foolish rich old banker, and at his death, remarried a more foolish and very poor duke.
Hence **re'married** *ppl. a.*
1848 *Blackw. Mag.* Apr. 447 *note*, In the middle ages re-married queens lost their title.

re'mass, *v.* [RE- 5 a.] *trans.* To mass together again.
1839–48 BAILEY *Festus* x. 105 The hour..When all shall be remassed in one great creed, All being shall be rebegotten.

remass, variant of RAMASS *v.*¹ *Obs.*

re'mast, *v.* [RE- 5 a.] *trans.* To fit with a new mast or masts.
1781 *Westm. Mag.* IX. 265 While the Bedford was re-masting. **1804** LARWOOD *No Gun Boats* 18 The prefects of the ports will re-ship their rudders, re-mast the Flotilla.

re'master (riː-), *v.* Also **re-master.** [RE- 5 a.] *trans.* To make a new master of (a record); to issue (a recording) from a new master: see MASTER *sb.*¹ 10 a. Hence **re'mastering** *vbl. sb.*
1967 *Punch* 25 Jan. 132/3 Both have been remastered, and only nostalgia entitles you to prefer the original 78s. **1970** *Soviet Weekly* 20 June 4/2 They include speeches which he recorded in the earliest years of Soviet power skilfully re-mastered and transferred to tape. **1975** *Gramophone* Aug. 322/1 They..will be most grateful to A. C. Griffith for the skill with which the transfer and re-mastering has been carried out. **1977** *Rolling Stone* 19 May 23/1 Jeffreys' best-known song (first released in 1973 as a single on Atlantic and now remastered and included on the new LP).

re'masticate, *v.* [RE- 5 a.] *trans.* To masticate again. Hence **re'masticated** *ppl. a.*
1828–32 in WEBSTER. **1840** tr. *Cuvier's Anim. Kingd.* 135 The aliment thus remasticated descends directly into the third stomach. **1843** OWEN *Lect. Compar. Anat.* ix. (1846) I. 105 When it is presented to them in its remasticated state.
So **remasti'cation.**
1828–32 in WEBSTER. **1837** YOUATT *Sheep* 423 After it has been returned for remastication,..and reduced to a pultaceous mass. **1859** *Todd's Cycl. Anat.* V. 538/1 The softened bolus..is destined to receive a thorough.. remastication.

re'match, *v.* [RE- 5 a.] To match again.
1856 MASSON *Ess., Theor. Poetry* 421 Who walks amid Nature's appearances, divorcing them, rematching them, interweaving them. **1871** DARWIN *Desc. Man* II. xiv. (1890) 408 [He] has repeatedly shot..one of a pair of jays,..and has never failed..to find the survivor re-matched.

'rematch, *sb.* [RE- 5 a.] A return match.
1941 *Sun* (Baltimore) 10 Apr. 17/1 Abraham Simon, originally the May opponent in a rematch of a 13-round go with the Bomber in Detroit, in June in New York. **1972** J. MOSEDALE *Football* v. 62 They lost the playoff in a rematch with Los Angeles. **1973** *Times* 15 May 14/8 'I didn't hit out enough,' Mrs Court said, depressed over her showing but willing to play a rematch. **1978** *N.Y. Times* 30 Mar. D22/1 He chose to give Muhammad Ali a rematch before taking on Norton.

ˌrema'terialize, *v.* [RE- 5 a.] *intr.* To materialize again. Hence **ˌrematериali'zation;** **ˌrema'terialized** *ppl. a.*
1898 HOWELLS *Open-eyed Conspir.* 100 Miss Gage rematerialised..after a moment's evanescence. **1907** W. DE MORGAN *Alice-For-Short* xxvii. 280 It was as nothing to Moses to cease to exist when hunted for, and to re-materialize when convenient. **1921** *Glasgow Herald* 29 Jan. 13/1 The fate of the Manchester Repertory and the failure of the Glasgow one to rematerialise warn us [etc.]. **1928** *Sunday Express* 8 Apr. 5/1 He comes back to each of the characters in the way in which they remember him, and.. because of their glimpses of his rematerialised self, [etc.]. **1956** R. M. LESTER *Towards Hereafter* xiv. 169 Levitation, of course, is often a form of dematerialization and rematerialization. **1959** *Times* 13 Oct. 16/4 Their lot is to be transfixed..sawn in half, dematerialized and rematerialized. **1962** *Punch* 26 Dec. 926/3 It's just a simple matter of Rematerialisation. **1978** *Sci. Amer.* Mar. 54/1 The virtual photon rematerializes into any one of a very large number of possible combinations of new particles.

†**remauldit,** *a.* *Obs. rare*⁻¹. [ad. OF. *remauldit*, pa. pple. of *remau(l)dire*: cf. MALEDICT *a.*] Accursed.
1471 CAXTON *Recuyell* (ed. Sommer) 498 O deyanyra ryghte remauldyt vnhappy and moste cursid serpente.

remaynand(e, -ent, varr. REMAINANT *Obs.*

†**re'mayne,** *v.* *Obs. rare.* [ad. OF. *remainer*, *-me(i)ner*, etc., f. *re-* RE + *mener* to lead: cf. mod.F. *ramener.*] *trans.* To lead or bring back.
1481 CAXTON *Myrr.* I. xii. 37 Musyque accordeth alle thinges that dyscorde..& remayne[th] them to concordaunce. *Ibid.* 38.

remaynent, variant of REMAINANT *Obs.*

†**rem'bar,** *v.* *Obs. rare.* [ad. F. *rembarrer*: see RAMBARRE.] *trans.* To shut out, repel.
1588 A. KING tr. *Canisius' Catech.* 53 b, Quha according to thair authoritie suld and may rembar the wolues, defend the sheip. **1600** O. E. [M. SUTCLIFFE] *Repl. Libel* II. Pref. 1 Sufficient hath bin saide..to rembarre the malice of N. D. his encounters.

rembarbe, erron. f. *reubarbe* RHUBARB *sb.*

remberge, variant of RAMBERGE.
1867 SMYTH *Sailor's Word-bk.* 568.

‖**remblai** (rɑ̃blɛ). Also in pl. form **remblais.** [F., f. *remblayer* to embank, f. *re-* RE- + *emblayer* to heap up: see DÉBLAI.]
1. *Fortif.* The earth used to form a rampart, mound, or embankment.
1794 *Amer. State Papers, Mil. Aff.* (1832) I. 99 (Stanf.), The demolition of the old fort very much advanced, and very little remblais made. **1802** JAMES *Milit. Dict., Remblai* (Fr.), earth collected together for the purpose of making a bank, way, &c. **1828** J. M. SPEARMAN *Brit. Gunner* (ed. 2) 215 The earth obtained from the ditch forms the remblai, or elevation. **1876** VOYLE & STEVENSON *Milit. Dict.* 337/1 In general, the number of cubic feet contained in the *remblai* has been furnished by the *deblai*, so as to balance each other.
2. *Mining.* Material used to fill up the excavations made in a thick seam of coal.
1867 W. W. SMYTH *Coal & Coal-mining* 138 The remblais or stowage is found to be so closely packed as to form a very good roof for driving under.

'remble, *v.* *dial.* [Of obscure origin.] *trans.* To move, stir. Hence **'rembling** *vbl. sb.*
1579 W. WILKINSON *Confut. Familye of Loue* 56 They must take heede that in the rembling thereof they crush not all their bones in sunder. **1674** RAY *N.C. Words* 38 To *Remble*: Lincoln, to move or remove. **1864** TENNYSON *North. Farmer* I. viii, I stubb'd 'um oop wi' the lot, an' raaved an' rembled 'um out. *Ibid.* xv, A weänt niver give it ..to Robins—a niver rembles the stoäns.

†**remblere.** *Obs. rare*⁻¹. A puzzle, riddle.
1599 NASHE *Lenten Stuffe* 39 Whiles I am shuffling and cutting with these long coated Turkes, would any antiquarie would explicate vnto mee this emblere, or quidditie..?

rembnand, obs. form of REMNANT *sb.*

‖**remboîtage** (rɑ̃bwataʒ). [Fr., f. *remboîter* to re-case (a book).] (See quot. 1952.)
1952 J. CARTER *ABC for Book-Collectors* 153 *Remboîtage* means the transferring of a book from its own binding to another more elegant, more nearly contemporary, more appropriate—anyway, more desirable; or, alternatively, the transferring into a superior binding of a text more interesting or more valuable than the one for which it was made. **1968** C. P. BRACKEN *Roman Ring* iv. 27, I defy anyone to detect our remboîtages... Many early books were rebound anyway.

Rembrandt ('rɛmbrænt). The name of the Dutch painter *Rembrandt* (1606–69) used *absol.* or *attrib.* to designate a Darwin tulip with streaked or variegated flowers.
1902 *Jrnl. R. Hort. Soc.* XXVI. 975 Tulips, Rembrandt. .. A striped-flowered section raised from the 'Darwin', by MM. Krelage & Son, Haarlem. **1908** *Ibid.* XXXIII. 233 Rembrandts..are broken Darwins, and..often beautifully marked and feathered. **1911** J. WEATHERS *Bulb Bk.* 440/1 What are now known as 'Rembrandt' Tulips are broken or rectified Darwin Tulips. **1929** A. D. HALL *Bk. Tulip* v. 103

The broken forms [of Darwin tulip] are now given a class to themselves and called 'Rembrandts'. **1948** J. C. WISTER *Bulbs for Home Gardens* xi. 122 Rembrandt tulips..are striped varieties, mostly 'rectified' or 'broken' Darwins. **1974** A. HUXLEY *Plant & Planet* xviii. 197 Those tulips called Rembrandts, Bybloems and Bizarres by the fanciers, in which the flowers are streaked or feathered in another colour.

Rembrandtesque (rɛmbrɑːn'tɛsk, -æ-), *a.* [f. the name of *Rembrandt* (see prec.) + -ESQUE.] Resembling the manner or style of Rembrandt.

1863 'OUIDA' *Held in Bondage* I. xi. 242 Look at that little Venus Anadyomene, Arthur, with the fire-light shining on her; quite Rembrandtesque, isn't it? **1879** *Encycl. Brit.* IX. 324/1 Life-size figures full of animation in the faces, 'radiant with Rembrandtesque colour.' **1888** LIGHTHALL *Yng. Seigneur* 121 The windmill was one of those rembrandtesque relics [etc.]. **1934** *Burlington Mag.* May 213/2 The artistic Rembrandtesque pen-and-ink sketches then in vogue. **1952** M. ALLINGHAM *Tiger in Smoke* iii. 55 One of the old naphtha flares..making Rembrandtesque clouds above them. **1976** *Listener* 12 Aug. 174/1 There is not a single illustration from the Book of Job, although one might have expected it to be full of Rembrandtesque motives.

Rem'brandtian, Rem'brandtic, *adjs.* = REMBRANDTESQUE *a.*

1863 *Miss Jemima's Swiss Jrnl.* (1963) i. 8 The white mob-caps of the old women having quite a Rembrandtic effect. **1967** *Listener* 16 Feb. 232/1 He uses a swirl of off-white paint to give the face a Rembrandtian nose.

'Rembrandtish, *a.* [f. as REMBRANDTESQUE *a.* + -ISH.] Somewhat after the style of Rembrandt.

c **1860** STANNARD *Examples Art* 211 Desirous of rescuing ..some Rembrandtish etching. **1880** E. FITZGERALD *Lett.* (1889) I. 459 With some Rembrandtish Light and Shade.

So **'Rembrandtism,** the style of Rembrandt.

1849 RUSKIN *Sev. Lamps* iii. §13. 77 Rembrandtism is a noble manner in architecture, though a false one in painting.

†**rem'bursement.** *Obs.*$^{-1}$ [a. F. *remboursement*: see REIMBURSEMENT.] = REIMBURSEMENT.

1586 BURGHLEY in *Leicester's Corr.* (Camden) 358 The states would not agree to make the rembursement of these things, if your lordships warrant had not past for the same.

†**reme,** *sb.*[1] *Obs. rare.* [ad. L. *rēmus* (It., Sp. *remo*).] An oar.

a **1300** *K. Horn* 1623 (Harl. MS.), Þe see bigan to flowen ant hy faste to rowen, hue aryueden vnder reme in a wel feyr streme. **1511** *Guylforde's Pilgr.* (Camden) 13 Armour was first ther [in Candia] deuysed and founde,..so was yᵉ makyng of remys, and rowynge in bootes.

†**reme,** *sb.*[2] *Obs. rare*$^{-1}$. [? var. of RIM *sb.*[1]; see also RYME.] Surface.

a **1300** *Cursor M.* 4779 He sagh a-pon þe watur reme [*v.r.* reime] Caf flettand dunward [with] þe strem.

R.E.M.E., REME ('riːmiː), *sb.*[3] Also **Reemy.** [Acronym f. initials of *R*oyal (Corps of) *E*lectrical and *M*echanical *E*ngineers.] A Corps of the British Army, formed on 1 June 1942, which handles the repair and maintenance of military machinery. Also *attrib.*

1942 *Daily Tel.* 1 Sept. 4/4 R.E.M.E.—you may pronounce it 'Reemie'—marks an important step forward in Army organisation and a break with a tradition which goes back to Creçy and Poitiers. **1943** HUNT & PRINGLE *Service Slang* 55 *Reemy*, the Royal Electrical and Mechanical Engineers, formed in 1942 for the repair of Army tanks. **1944** A. JACOB *Traveller's War* xiii. 219 It could not have functioned without R.E.M.E. and the enormous industrial undertaking in the rear which this corps operated. **1965** A. NICOL *Truly Married Woman* 16 He had had an outing.. with Higgins, a REME Lieutenant, to see some ruined, Roman fortifications. **1975** C. MOTT-RADCLYFFE *Foreign Body in Eye* xiii. 209 My son is a corporal in the REME and is working as a fitter in one of the ordnance sheds at Tel-el-Kebir. **1978** R. V. JONES *Most Secret War* xlix. 484 We had two other R.E.M.E. officers, Majors K. G. Dobson and R. A. Fell.

†**reme,** *v.*[1] *Obs.* Also 7 reem. [OE. *hréman, hrýman* (for **hrieman*), f. *hréam* REAM *sb.*[1]

Both *hréman* and *hrýman* are normal forms in OE.: the former is distinct from the rarer *hréman* to boast, = OS. *hrômian*, OHG. (*h*)*ruoman* etc. (G. *rühmen*).]

1. *intr.* To cry, call out, shout; also, to cry out in grief or pain, to scream, yell; to lament, weep.

c **897** K. ÆLFRED *Gregory's Past. C.* lv. 429 Se cliopað [L. *cum voce*], se ðe dearninga syngað; ac se hremð [L. *cum clamore*], se ðe openlice..syngað. *c* **950** *Lindisf. Gosp.* John xi. 31 Hia..gaas to ðæm byrȝenne þætte hreme ðer. *c* **1000** ÆLFRIC *Exod.* xxii. 23 ȝif ȝe him deriað, hiȝ hrymað to me, and ic ȝehire hira hream. *c* **1200** *Trin. Coll. Hom.* 89 Þo þe after him comen remden lude stefne. *c* **1275** *Sinners Beware* 167 in *O.E. Misc.* 77 Remen heo schule and grede Deope in helle grunde. **13..** *Sir Beues* (MS. A) 1592 Þe gailers þat him scholde ȝeme, Whan hii herde him þus reme [etc.]. **13..** *E.E. Allit. P.* A. 858 Ʒe remem for rauþe wyth-outen reste. *c* **1400** *Laud Troy Bk.* 2902 Whan that thei herd wymmen so remed, Thei hadde meruayle what it myght be. ?*a* **1500** *Chester Pl.* (Shaks. Soc.) I. 229 This frecke begines to reme and yole. **1674** RAY *N.C. Words* 38 To *Reem*, to Cry: Lancashire.

2. *trans.* **a.** To utter (a shout). **b.** To call out (something). *rare.*

c **1220** *Bestiary* 664 Ðanne remen he alle a rem, so hornes blast oðer belles drem. *a* **1225** *Ancr. R.* 242 Ʒif me remde lude fur! fur! þet te chirche bernde!

†**reme,** *v.*[2] *Obs. rare.* [var. (in SE. dialects) of ME. *ryme*:—OE. *rýman*: see RIME *v.*, and cf. REAM *v.*[3]]

1. *trans.* **a.** To leave, depart from (a land). **b.** To clear (a place) *of* persons.

a **1300** *K. Horn* 1364 (Camb. MS.), Þu makedest me fleme, And þi lond to reme. *c* **1330** *Arth. & Merl.* 4398 (Kölbing), .viii. þousand þo hadde Lot, þat wele him holpe ..þe waies & þe paþes ȝeme, & of þe Sarrains hem reme.

2. *intr.* To clear a way; to make way (for one).

13.. *K. Alis.* 3347 He is the furste with sweord that remith, Thou art the furste with hors that flemeth. *c* **1400** *St. Alexius* (Trin. MS.) 505 Remeþ me [*Laud MS.* ȝiueþ me roum], for godis lone, And leteþ me go to my sone.

reme, obs. form of REALM, REAM *sb.*[2], RIM.

†**'remeable,** *a. Obs. rare*$^{-1}$. [ad. L. *remeābilis*, f. *remeāre* to return.] Capable of returning.

1610 BP. ANDREWES 96 *Serm., Holy Ghost* iii. (1629) 626 So is the Spirit best fitted, made remeable, and best exhibited to us.

remeable: see REMEVABLE.

†**remeal, -mel,** variants of RAMEAL *sb. Obs.*

1622 R. HAWKINS *Voy. S. Sea* (1847) 96 In Brazill..they eate this meale mingled with remels of sugar, or malasses. **1662** *Stat. Irel.* (1765) II. 412 Melasses or remeals the hundred weight.

remeant ('riːmiːənt), *a. rare.* [ad. L. *remeant-em*, pres. pple. of L. *remeāre*, f. *re-* RE- + *meāre* to pass: cf. *permeate*.] Returning.

1848 KINGSLEY *Saint's Trag.* II. ix, Most exalted Prince, Whose peerless Knighthood, like the remeant sun, After too long a night, regilds our clay.

re'measure (riː-), *v.* [RE- 5 a.] *trans.* To measure again, in various senses of the vb.

1590 SPENSER *F.Q.* III. vii. 18 Her wearie Palfrey..she freshly dight, His late miswandred wayes now to remeasure right. **1600** W. WATSON *Decacordon* (1602) 9 With like measure to his brother giuen, it should be remeasured to him againe. **1651** BAXTER *Inf. Bapt.* 238 Their Faith and Integrity in re-measuring (or reforming) the Temple of God. *a* **1711** KEN *Anodynes* Poet. Wks. 1721 III. 396 Assur'd of Supplemental Years, By your re-measuring the Spheres. **1785** G. A. BELLAMY *Apology* II. 204 This obliged me to re-measure back the road I had just come. **1814** SCOTT *Wav.* xv, Measuring and re-measuring, with..tremendous strides, the length of the terrace. **1874** BEDFORD *Sailor's Pocket Bk.* v. 119 The line should be..re-measured in the boat.

So **re'measurement.**

1895 *Daily News* 10 Sept. 3/1 The re-measurement will increase Defender's time allowance by two seconds.

†**'remed,** *v. Obs.*$^{-1}$ [See REMEDE, REMEDY *v.*, and cf. REMEDLESS *a.*] *trans.* To remedy.

1590 FENNE *Frutes*, etc. Gg ij b, And how to remed wrong with right the man had no respect.

remede, remeid (rɪ'miːd), *sb.* Now *arch.* Forms: 5 **remed, remmede, remyde,** 5–6 **ramed(e,** 6 **-meid),** 5– **remeid,** (6 **-meide, -maid),** 6–8 **-mead,** 6–9 **-meed,** 4– **remede.** [a. OF. *remede, remide* (12th c.; mod.F. *remède*), ad. L. *remedium* REMEDY. After the 15th c. only a Sc. form.] Remedy, redress.

remeid of Law (Sc.), the obtaining of justice by appeal from an inferior to a superior court (see Jamieson, s.v.).

c **1374** CHAUCER *Troylus* IV. 889 He desyreth..With yow to been al night, for to devyse Remede in this. *c* **1375** *Sc. Leg. Saints* ii. (*Paul*) 38 Quham it bittis, it mon be ded, þar agane is no remed. **1423** JAS. I *Kingis Q.* cxxxviii, Lat me se Gif thy remede be pertynent to me. **1466** *Plumpton Corr.* (Camden) 17 Therfore provide by your wisdome such remmede in his behalfe, as you semes best. **1549** *Compl. Scot.* Prol. 13 Ane desolat prince, distitute of remeide, ande disparit of consolatione. **1585** JAS. I *Ess. Poesie* (Arb.) 42 Ane greif to them, who mereits it indeid: Yet for all thir appearis there some remeid. **1649** BP. GUTHRIE *Mem.* (1702) 7 They resolv'd upon Application to his Majesty for remeed. **1711** RAMSAY *On Maggy Johnstoun* xiii, We must..when we're auld return to dust, Without remead. **1785** BURNS *Prayer to Sc. Repr.* xviii, Strive, wi' a' your wit and lear, To get remead. **1828** *Blackw. Mag.* XXIV. 915 The matter was ..past all earthly remede. **1868** G. MACDONALD *R. Falconer* I. 306 He made one remorseful dart after the string,..but it was gone beyond remeid.

†**b.** *Coining.* = REMEDY *sb.* 4. *Obs.*

1565 *Act. Dom. Conc.* 22 Dec. in Keith *Hist. Ch. Scot.* (1734) App. 118 That thair be cunzeit ane Penny of Silvir.. of Weicht ane Unce Troce-weicht, with twa Granes of Remeid. **1591** *Reg. Privy Council Scot.* IV. 620 All the saidis assayis keipit the just fynnes..and past nocht beneth the granis of remeid prescrivit in the same Actis.

remede, remeid (rɪ'miːd), *v. Sc. Obs.* exc. *arch.* Forms: 5 **remed,** 6–7 **remeid,** (6 **-maid),** 7–8 **remeed,** 8 **remead,** 5, 9 **remede.** [ad. OF. *remedier*: see REMEDY *v.*] *trans.* To remedy, cure, redress, amend. Also *absol.*

13.. in Wyntoun *Cron.* VII. 3625 Succoure Scotland and remede, That stad is in perplexyte. *c* **1375** *Sc. Leg. Saints* vii. (*James less*) 94 Mannis sonne fra þe ded Is rysine al synnys to remed. *Ibid.* xxxi. (*Eugenia*) 284 Scho..prayt hyme parcheryte to remed hyr Infyrmyte. **1500–20** DUNBAR *Poems* xxii. 56 May nane remeid my melady Sa weill as ȝe. *Ibid.* lxxiii. 5 Remeid in tyme, and rew nocht al to lait. **1579** *Reg. Privy Council Scot.* III. 155 Without his Hienes petifullie considder thair caise and remeid the same. **1596** DALRYMPLE tr. *Leslie's Hist. Scot.* I. 24 It is gude..to kure and to remeid diuers dolouris of the skin. **1640** R. BAILLIE *Canterb. Self-convict.* 103 To remeed their wicked follies, the English expressely ordained their communion Table to stand in the body of the church. **1711** *Countrey-Man's Let. to Curat* 22 They desire him..to remeed the Enormities among the Corrupt Conformists. **1752** E. ERSKINE *Serm.* Wks. 1871 III. 480 What would remead these evils? [**1847** EMERSON *Poems, Monadnoc*, Those dost succour and remede The shortness of our days.]

re'medeless, *a.* and *adv.* In 9 **remead-, remeid-.** [f. REMEDE *sb.*] Remediless(ly).

a **1849** J. C. MANGAN *Poems* (1859) 457 That dusk realm where all is ended, Save remeadless dole. **1850** BLACKIE *Æschylus* I. 231 Spit not your rancour On this fair land remeidless.

†**re'meder.** *Sc. Obs. rare*$^{-1}$. In 6 **remeidar.** [f. REMEDE *v.* + -ER[1].] One who remedies.

1535 STEWART *Cron. Scot.* II. 487, I pray to God, remeidar of all thing, Gif I mycht se in my tyme sic ane king.

re,media'bility. *rare.* [f. REMEDIABLE *a.*: see -ITY.] = REMEDIABLENESS.

1964 A. O. J. COCKSHUT *Unbelievers* 25 Speculations about the remediability of life..are scattered through his writings.

remediable (rɪ'miːdɪəb(ə)l), *a.* Also 5 **-medy-,** 6 **-mede-.** [a. F. *remédiable* (15th c.), or ad. L. *remediābilis* curative, curable, f. *remediāre* to REMEDY: see -ABLE.]

†**1.** Capable of remedying; remedial. *Obs.*

c **1491** *Chast. Goddes Chyld.* 46 Suche medycynes may be spedefull and remedyable. **1596** DALRYMPLE tr. *Leslie's Hist. Scot.* x. 397 Layng medicine remedeable to her warking woundis.

2. Capable of being remedied or redressed.

1570 LEVINS *Manip.* 4/9 Remediable, *recuperabilis.* **1600** E. BLOUNT tr. *Conestaggio* 311 Labouring to remedie that which he thought remediable. **1641** H. AINSWORTH *Orth. Found. Relig.* 37 Mans misery is remediable through the mercy of God. **1707** SLOANE *Jamaica* I. p. lxxxii, They.. were, when remediable, chiefly cured by the infusion of goose-dung. **1758** JOHNSON *Idler* No. 3 ⁋7 This want..may seem easily remediable by some substitute or other. **1828** SOUTHEY in *Q. Rev.* XXXVII. 540 It is an evil..which will be found remediable, if the proper and obvious remedies are ..applied. **1875** JOWETT *Plato* (ed. 2) V. 135 Where injustice, like disease, is remediable, there the remedy must be applied in word or deed.

Hence **re'mediableness** (Bailey, 1727, vol. II); **re'mediably** *adv.* (Webster, 1847).

remedial (rɪ'miːdɪəl), *a.* [ad. L. *remediālis*, f. *remedium* REMEDY: see -AL[1].] **1.** Affording a remedy, tending to relieve or redress.

1651 N. BACON *Disc. Govt. Eng.* II. xviii. (1739) 96 These Laws were but penal, and not remedial for the parties wronged. **1707** CHAMBERLAYNE *Pres. St. Eng.* II. xiv. 189 This Court proceeds..ordinarily..granting out Writs Mandatory and Remedial. **1765** BLACKSTONE *Comm.* I. 55 The remedial part of a law is so necessary a consequence of the former two [etc.]. **1770** BURKE *Pres. Discont.* Wks. 1842 I. 135/1 Every good political institution must have a preventive operation as well as a remedial. **1850** MᶜCOSH *Div. Govt.* IV. ii. (1874) 473 The Gospel professes to be remedial, and remedial of an evil affecting the laws of God. **1862** GOULBURN *Pers. Relig.* III. ix. (1873) 236 That suffering is a medicine, remedial though bitter.

2. *Educ.* **a.** Designating or pertaining to special classes, teaching methods, etc., in basic educational skills to help school-children who have not achieved the proficiency necessary for them to be able to learn other subjects with their contemporaries.

1924 E. M. PAULU (*title*) Diagnostic testing and remedial teaching. **1927** *Psychol. Abstr.* I. 217 A group of 29 teachers ..took a course in remedial reading... They applied to themselves the remedial techniques about which they were studying. **1942** F. SCHONELL *Backwardness in Basic Subj.* x. 204 If remedial work with backward readers is to be effective, a teacher should have..detailed information from a thorough diagnosis... Remedial methods must have therapeutic as well as pedagogical value. **1975** *Language for Life* (Dept. Educ. & Sci.) xviii. 270 Two groups of children were given remedial education, one in the Remedial Centre and one elsewhere. **1977** *Cork Examiner* 8 June 4/9 The most urgent point here was the need to eliminate overcrowded classes by reducing the pupil-teacher ratio to not more than 35 pupils per teacher and the appointment of more remedial teachers. **1978** *Times Lit. Suppl.* 1 Dec. 1394/2 Caught up in the whole nasty mess is the one other child character in the book, Manjit Mirza, a Sikh girl who shares Ronnie's remedial reading lessons.

b. Of a child: receiving or requiring remedial teaching.

1966 *New Statesman* 22 Apr. 575/2 The youngest, according to her passport, is 11 years old. She looks and acts more like a remedial eight-year-old. **1969** *Word Study* Feb. 1/1, I first became aware that something was amiss, neologically, when I heard a teacher refer to one of her students as 'a remedial reader'. **1975** *Language for Life* (Dept. Educ. & Sci.) xxv. 408 The average weekly time lay between 3 hrs. 12 mins. and 3 hrs. 22 mins. for all except the 12 year old 'Remedial' pupils. **1976** *Cumberland News* 3 Dec. 10/2 And then there was the problem of finding somewhere for the remedial children, who need special teaching.

3. Concerned with or aimed at the overcoming of muscular disabilities or postural defects by means of special exercises.

1925 H. E. STEWART *Physiotherapy* xxii. 321 Faulty postures and weight-bearing..will readily deform one [*sc.* a child] whose tissues are subnormal. It is of vital importance to discover these conditions early and institute proper remedial measures. 1943 O. F. G. Smith *Rehabilitation, Re-Education & Remedial Exercises* i. 9 When the patient has learnt to use the appliance,.. whether a piece of needlework or a remedial apparatus, some personal responsibility should be put on him to continue the work in his own time. 1951 F. Charlesworth *Chiropodial Orthopædics* viii. 132 Progressive remedial exercises, Faradism and other form[s] of physiotherapy are a necessary adjunct to the treatment. 1974 *Times* 11 Jan. 15/1 This will be discussed.. at a meeting with the Councils of the Association of Occupational Therapists, the Chartered Society of Physiotherapy and the Society of Remedial Gymnasts. 1975 Arnheim & Sinclair *Clumsy Child* vi. 50/2 The most effective remedial program for the clumsy individual is one founded on the principles of psychomotor development.

Hence **re'medially** *adv.*

1796 Burke *Regic. Peace* i. (1892) 83 It is, preventively, the assertor of its own rights, or remedially, their avenger. 1840 Arnold in Stanley *Life* (1844) II. ix. 175 Before anything is ventured remedially. 1875 E. White *Life in Christ* v. xxxi. (1878) 534 It is God acting, no longer according to the course of law,.. but remedially above law.

re'mediate, *a. arch.* [? f. L. *remediāt*, ppl. stem of *remediāre* to REMEDY.] Remedial.

(Perh. an error for *remedial* or *remediant*.)

1605 Shaks. *Lear* iv. iv. 17 (Qq.), All you vnpublisht vertues of the earth Spring with my teares, be aydant, and remediat [*1st Fol.* -ate] In the good mans distress. 1906 G. G. Coulton tr. *Pearl* 33 And washed me in blood remediate.

re-mediate, *v.*[1] [RE- 5 a.] To mediate again.

a 1652 Brome *Mad Couple* iii. i, I will re-mediate for you to the Widow.

re'mediate, *v.*[2] [Back-formation from REMEDIATION.] *trans.* To remedy or redress.

1969 *Word Study* Feb. 2/1, I encountered the phrase 'teachers *remediating* speech difficulties' (my italics again). Another patent neologism, I thought, derived obviously from a transitive weak verb *to remediate*, itself a back-formation on the analogy of the often-heard *to orientate* 'back-formed' from the noun *orientation*. 1973 *Black World* Mar. 31 Without supportive services to.. remediate their academic deficiencies,.. the students experienced an extremely high failure rate the first year. 1976 *Canad. Jrnl. Linguistics* Spring 92 The effect of expansion was to increase the time allowed for segment analysis, thus remediating such falling behind.

remediation (rɪmiːdɪ'eɪʃən). [n. of action f. L. *remediāre* to REMEDY.] The action of remedying. *Esp.* the giving of remedial teaching or remedial therapy (see REMEDIAL *a.* 2 a, 3). Freq. *attrib.*

1818 Bentham *Ch. Eng.* Pref. 54 On this subject, and on this state of things, remediation.. requires that something should be said. 1826 —— in *Westm. Rev.* VI. 499 Towards remediation, a disposition has of late been expressed by those on whom it depends. 1954 L. J. Cronbach *Educ. Psychol.* vii. 215 (*heading*) Remediation of emotional difficulties. 1969 *Language* XLV. 599 The report was originally designed to provide descriptive information on which to base linguistic retraining or 'remediation' programs. 1970 H. Osser in S. Rogers *Children & Lang.* (1975) v. 304 Most research has been concerned with diagnosis of problems rather than with their remediation. 1975 *Language for Life* (Dept. Educ. & Sci.) xvii. 263 The school psychological service has provided a series of in-service training, workshop courses in the assessment and 'remediation' of specific reading difficulties. 1975 Arnheim & Sinclair *Clumsy Child* vi. 50/1 Because of the inconspicuousness of symptoms and the difficulties inherent in diagnosing clumsiness, delay in remediation has.. been the rule rather than the exception. 1978 M. T. Erickson *Child Psychopathol.* x. 220 Educational remediation is usually conducted by a teacher who has been trained in a special educational program. *Ibid.*, Most remediation teachers are employed by school systems.

remediless ('rɛmɪdɪlɪs, rɪ'mɛdɪlɪs), *a.* (and *adv.*) Forms: 5–7 **remedyless**, (8 **remedie-**), 6 **remeadi-**, 6 (*Sc.*) 7 **remidi-**, 7 **remeedi-**, 6– **remediless**. [f. REMEDY *sb.* + -LESS: cf. REMEDELESS and REMEDLESS. The orig. stressing was *re'mediless*, with the *e* long.]

1. Of persons, etc.: Destitute of remedy; having no prospect of aid or rescue. Now *rare* or *Obs.*

14.. *MS. Cantab. Ff.* i. 6, lf. 131 (Halliw.), Thus welle y wote y am remedyless, For me no thyng may comforte nor amend. 1532 More *Confut. Tindale* Wks. 602/1 He shall for lacke of such preuencion and help, fall into such raylyng and blasphemy, and then is he remedilesse. 1556 J. Heywood *Spider & F.* ii. 158 Being cleare remediles from cure Of all my paines. *c* 1592 Marlowe *Jew of Malta* v. ii, I'll rear up Malta, now remediless. 1621 Donne *Serm.* xv. 149 When the last enemie shall watch my remedilesse body and my disconsolate soule. 1757 W. Thompson *R.N. Advoc.* 21 Poor remediless, aggrieved and tortured Men. 1786 Burke *Charges agst. W. Hastings* Wks. 1813 XII. 243 He demanded these in such a manner that being 'remediless' I was obliged to comply with what he required.

b. Destitute of legal remedy.

1590 Swinburne *Testaments* 169 It seemeth.. vniust also, that they, especially the creditors, should be remedilesse all that while. 1616 in Cary *Rep. Chancery* (1650) 122 Whither the Chancery may relieve B... or else leave him utterly remedilesse and undone. 1667 *Ormonde MSS.* in *10th Rep. Hist. MSS. Comm.* App. V. 59 Your petitioner is herein altogether remedylesse. 1670 in *Phenix* (1721) I. 393 Such Judgments on Jurors leaue them remediless of relief. 1700 *Col. Rec. Pennsylv.* I. 577 Finding yᵉ petitioner to be left remediless by yᵉ Courts.

†c. In quasi-*adv.* use: Without or beyond all remedy. *Obs.* (common in 16th c.)

c 1485 *Digby Myst.* (1882) iv. 1124 It is bot in vayn Thus remedilesse to mak compleyn. 1531 Tindale *Exp. 1 John* (1537) 18 The same synneth agaynste the holye gooste remedylesse. 1542 Udall *Erasm. Apoph.* 82 Sir, ye must remedylesse be obediente to me, and rewled by me. 1567 *Gude & Godlie B.* (S.T.S.) 147 We ar exilit remediles. 1601 Holland *Pliny* I. 46 Whosoever drinketh, is sure to die of it, remedilesse, and yet without paine. 1674 Hickman *Quinquart. Hist.* (ed. 2) 86 They maintain not, that any is left remediless in a state of damnation.

2. Of trouble, disease, etc.: Not admitting of remedy; incapable of being remedied, cured, or redressed. (Very common in 16–17th c.)

1513 Bradshaw *St. Werburge* i. 3160 Alas, remedylesse is our lamentacyon. 1548 Cranmer *Catech.* 115 b, He is able to delyuer us out of al troubles.., although they seme to mans reason remediles. 1581 Mulcaster *Positions* xxxiii. (1887) 119 In all these measure is a mery meane, and immoderatenes a remeadilesse harme. 1640 R. Baillie *Canterb. Self-convict.* Pref. 11 It were better by much, before the remeedilesse stroke be given, to be well advised. 1671 Flavel *Fount. Life* x. 29 This renders their misery the more remediless. 1715 M. Davies *Athen. Brit.* I. 66 Those more inward Resentments.. seem almost remediless and irreconcileable. 1775 Mason *Mem. Gray* in *G.'s Poems* 156 Such persons as die of that most remediless.. of all distempers, a Consumption. 1791 Cowper *Iliad* xvii. 189 So, at once Shall remediless ruin fall on Troy. *a* 1822 Shelley *Prose Wks.* (1888) I. 404 There is no terror in the countenance, only grief—deep, remediless grief. 1875 E. White *Life in Christ* iii. xix. (1878) 254 The law is and will be, that remediless suffering shall follow sin.

†3. Of vices, etc.: Incurable, incorrigible. *Obs.*

1604 T. Wright *Passions* iv. ii. §6. 138, I must say this vice in them to be remedilesse, because it hath bene in euery age.. and neuer amended. 1625 Jackson *Creed* v. xliv. §1 It is the remediless remainder of our first parents' pride. 1675 Baxter *Cath. Theol.* ii. v. 83 We hold also that his vicious necessity of disposition is curable, and not remediless and desperate. 1690 E. Gee *Jesuit's Mem.* 99 Sharp execution of Justice upon the obstinate and remediless.

†4. *adv.* Remedilessly. *Obs. rare*⁻¹.

a 1614 D. Dyke *Myst. Self-deceiving* (ed. 8) 50 It makes him twice, yea, remedilesse miserable.

remedilessly (see prec.), *adv.* Now *rare.* [f. prec. + -LY².] Without or beyond remedy. (Common in 17th c.)

1556 *Olde Antichrist* 74 b, We must remidilesly confesse them to be voide of all charitie. 1596 Drayton *Legends* iii. 409 Like one whose House remedilesly burning [etc.]. 1609 Bp. Hall *Disswas. Poperie* Wks. (1627) 642 A cruell religion, that sends poore infants remedilesly vnto the eternall paines of hell. 1612 Drayton *Poly-olb.* xiv. 30 Remedilesly drown'd in sorrow day and night. 1669 Clarendon *Ess. Tracts* (1727) 126 The government of it is actually and remedilessly altered. 1747 *Col. Rec. Pennsylv.* V. 111 Thus remedilessly exposed to any Attempts the Enemy shou'd be pleased to make. 1808 W. Taylor in *Monthly Mag.* XXVI. 111 Yet to these clerks of the magistrates.. all the objects of national commiseration are thus remedilessly to be consigned. 1868 Miall *Congregationalism Yorks.* 66 My place was remedilessly lost.

remedilessness. Now *rare* or *Obs.* [f. as prec. + -NESS.] The state or condition of being remediless; incurableness.

1601 Dent *Pathw. Heaven* 364 Concerning the torments of hell, I do note three things.. the extremity, perpetuity, and remidilesnesse thereof. 1684 Howe *Redeemer's Tears* Wks. (1846) 88 They show the remedilessness of thy case. *a* 1758 Edwards *Hist. Redemption* ii. i. (1793) 200 The remedilessness of their disease might by long experience be seen.

†**re'mediously,** *adv. Obs. rare*⁻¹. [f. as REMEDY *sb.* + -OUS + -LY².] Remedially.

1659 *Bibliotheca Regia* Pref. 9 His last sleep took from him most remediously all the arts of government.

†**'remedist.** *Obs. rare*⁻¹. [f. REMEDY *sb.* + -IST.] One who seeks out medical remedies.

1716 M. Davies *Athen. Brit.* III. *Diss. Physick* 12 Such were call'd.. Magists.., Prophylactists, Remedists [etc.].

re'meditate, *v.* [RE- 5 a.] *trans.* To meditate (on) again.

1855 Lynch *Rivulet* ix. vii, Let me remeditate the truth, That Christ did for and with us bleed.

So **remedi'tation.** †Const. *of.*

1642 W. Price *Serm.* 28 In a kind of remeditation of what obscenities he hath beene a spectator. 1676 *Life Father Sarpi* in *Brent's Counc. Trent* 26 [He] gave himself to a remeditation of what he had formerly observed.

†**'remedless,** *a. Obs. rare.* [Cf. REMED *v.* and REMEDELESS.] Remediless.

1590 Fenne *Frutes*, etc. Ffiij b, In vaine it is to vexe thy self where cause is remedles. *Ibid.* Gg iij, 'Tis past with us and remedles, wherefore no longer mourne.

remedy ('rɛmɪdɪ), *sb.* Also 6 **remeady.** [a. AF. *remedie, remedy* (= OF. *remede* REMEDE *sb.*), ad. L. *remedium*, f. *re-* RE- + *med-* stem of *medēri* to heal: cf. *medical, medicine.*]

1. a. A cure for a disease or other disorder of body or mind; any medicine or treatment which alleviates pain and promotes restoration to health. †Also without article.

a 1225 *Ancr. R.* 120 Lo her aȝeines wreððe monie kunnes remedies, & frouren a muche vloc, & misliche boten. *a* 1340 Hampole *Psalter* xv. 3 He þat felis him seke he sekis remedy. *c* 1386 Chaucer *Prol.* 475 Of remedies of loue she knew perchaunce. 1398 Trevisa *Barth. De P.R.* vii. lix. (Bodl. MS.), Aȝenste venemouse postemes.. men schal ordeyne a remedy warlich and sone. *c* 1440 *Gesta Rom.* i. 2 (Harl. MS.), I pray þe tell me if þer be ony remedye ayenst my deth. 1484 Caxton *Fables of Poge* x, [He] mynistyred alwey his pylles to euery man that came to hym for ony remedy. 1560 Daus tr. *Sleidane's Comm.* 91 For verely tyme itselfe wyl at laste bring remedy also unto moste daungerous diseases. 1577 B. Googe *Heresbach's Husb.* ii. (1586) 68 b, Nature hath appointed remedies in a readinesse for all diseases. 1651 Wittie tr. *Primrose's Pop. Err.* i. 42 For remedies doe cure without a physician, but not a physician without remedies. 1697 Dryden *Virg. Georg.* iii. 701 This Remedy the Scythian Shepherds found. 1702 J. Purcell *Cholick* (1714) 181 The only Remedy is to lay the Bone open. 1830 Scott *Demonol.* v. (1831) 140 The Scottish law did not acquit those who accomplished.. remarkable cures by mysterious remedies. 1875 H. C. Wood *Therap.* (1879) 688 Whenever it is desired to give a powerful remedy in increasing doses until its physiological effect is produced, it should always be given by itself.

b. *transf.* or *fig.* in various senses.

a 1300 *Cursor M.* 27816 Again þis sin [sloth] remedi es [*v.r.* best medcyn is]—Haf gastli ioi and hope o blis. 1340 Hampole *Pr. Consc.* 3394 Ilk man here lyghtly may Swilk remedys thurgh grace wyn, þat may fordo al venial syn. 1387 Trevisa *Higden* (Rolls) IV. 11 Alisaundre was i-poysoned.. and axede a tool to slee hymself in remedie of sorwe [L. *in remedium doloris*]. 1485 Caxton *Chas. Gt.* 244 For yᵉ remedye of theyr soules themperour gaf.. for almesse xij C vnces of syluer. 1576 Fleming *Panopl. Epist.* 25 Your wisedome and knowledge are remedies available, to cut off the course of suche an infecting canckar. 1607–12 Bacon *Ess., Counsel* (Arb.) 318 For which inconveniences the doctrine of Italy.. hath introduced Cabanett Councelles, a remedy worse than the disease. 1693 Dryden *Juvenal* xvi. (1697) 386 Withdraw thy Action, and depart in Peace; The Remedy is worse than the Disease. 1718 Prior *Solomon* ii. 352 Our griefs how swift! our remedies how slow! 1781 Cowper *Truth* 273 God replies, 'The remedy you want I freely give: The book shall teach you'. 1819 Shelley *Cyclops* 88 Can you show me some clear water spring, The remedy of our thirst? *a* 1862 Buckle *Civiliz.* (1873) II. viii. 582 The only remedy for superstition is knowledge.

†c. ***by remedy of***, by the help or means of. *Obs.*

1398 Trevisa *Barth. De P.R.* xvii. lxi. (Bodl. MS.), A fige tre is made to bere wele frute bi remedie of a tre þat is icleped Caprificus. 1579 Lyly *Euphues* (Arb.) 108 If women be not peruerse they shall reap profite by remedye of pleasure.

2. a. A means of counteracting or removing an outward evil of any kind; reparation, redress, relief.

a 1225 *Ancr. R.* 180 We schulen nu speken of þe uttre vondunge, & techen þe þet habbeð hire, hu heo muwen,.. ivinden remedie, þet is elne, aȝeines hire. *a* 1340 Hampole *Psalter* cxix. 3 þe rightwis man sekis remedy of god, how þere ill lippis may be amendid. 1413 *Pilgr. Sowle* iv. xiii. (Caxton 1483) 63² Now seye me what the semeth in this mater that we may ordeyne a remedy for this grete meschyef. 1483 Caxton *G. de la Tour* C ij, Sith it pleseth yow that I shall dye withoute remedye and withoute mercye. *a* 1500 *Sir Beues* 57/966² (Pynson), Certys, nowe wol he by hyr lye, But if ye fynde some remedy. 1560 Daus tr. *Sleidane's Comm.* 388 He fleeth to the last remeady which untill that time he had purposelye reserved. 1585 T. Washington tr. *Nicholay's Voy.* iv. xxxv. 158 Iupiter was honored amongst them for a remedy of stormes and tempests. 1634 Sir T. Herbert *Trav.* 35 The Nobles, when they saw no remedie,.. submitted to Curroon. 1687 A. Lovell tr. *Thevenot's Trav.* ii. 186 The human remedies which Sea-men use against Spouts, is to furle all the Sails, and to fire some Guns with shot against the Pipe of the Spout. 1747 *Col. Rec. Pennsylv.* V. 93 Such a Defect in the Government as stands in need of the most speedy Remedy. 1774 Burke *Corr.* (1844) I. 473 Popular remedies must be quick and sharp, or they are very ineffectual. 1837 Goring & Pritchard *Microgr.* 168 In this respect.. we have a remedy against those optical deceptions. 1851 Carlyle *Sterling* i. i, It by no means appeared what help or remedy any friend of Sterling's.. could attempt in the interim.

b. ***there is no remedy*** (= way out of it, help for it, alternative) ***but***, etc.

c 1386 Chaucer *Knt.'s T.* 1216 Ther nas noon oother remedie ne reed, But taketh his leue, and homward he him spedde. 1523 Ld. Berners *Froiss.* I. 72 Ther is no remedy but to fight, & to abyde fortune. 1568 Grafton *Chron.* II. 293 There was no remedy but he must fight with him. 1642 Rogers *Naaman* 20 There had beene no remedy, but he must have dyed upon his owne sword. 1719 De Foe *Crusoe* (Globe) 267 We had no Remedy, but to wait and see what the Issue of Things might present.

†c. ***no remedy***, unavoidably. *Obs.*

1538 Bale *Thre Lawes* 1700 Yet must it geue place to Gods worde, no remedye. 1550 Crowley *Epigr.* 242 The vengeaunce of God muste fall, no remedye, Vpon these wicked men. 1598 Shaks. *Merry W.* ii. ii. 127 You must send her your Page, no remedie. 1617 Bp. Andrewes 96 *Serm., Holy Ghost* x. (1629) 706 In default of this (no remedie) the common hammer must come.

†d. ***what remedy?*** what help for it? *Obs.*

1500–20 Dunbar *Poems* xv. 43 The lord sumtyme rewaird will it; Gife he dois not, quhat remedy? 1598 Shaks. *Merry W.* v. v. 250 Well, what remedy?.. what cannot be eschew'd, must be embrac'd. 1608 Armin *Nest Ninn.* (1842) 21 Now you must be hanged says the king... What remedie? sayes hee. 1628 Earle *Microcosm.* (Arb.) 35 He sayes it must not bee so, [y]it is strait pacified, and cryes what remedie.

3. Legal redress.

1450 *Paston Lett.* I. 174, I pray you requyre hym on my Lord ys behalf to compleyn to Justice.. [for a] remedie. 1583 Stubbes *Anat. Abus.* ii. (1882) 10 To go to lawe, and spende all that euer he hath, and yet come by no remedie neither. 1651 Hobbes *Leviath.* ii. xxii. 118 Left to the remedie, which the Law of the place alloweth them. 1766 Blackstone *Comm.* II. 199 Even this right of property will fail, or at least it will be without a remedy, unless I pursue it within the space of sixty years. 1819 J. Marshall *Const. Opin.* (1839) 154 Without impairing the obligation of a contract, the remedy may certainly be modified. 1891 *19th Cent.* Dec. 857 Where injury to character takes the form of aspersion, the primary remedy is in a court of law.

4. *Coining.* The small margin within which coins as minted are allowed to vary from the standard fineness and weight. (Cf. REMEDE *sb.* b.) Also called *tolerance*. Also *attrib.*

1423 *Rolls of Parlt.* IV. 257/1 As touching ye remedie of vid of the pound of Troie, the Kyng will be avised. **1675** R. VAUGHAN *Coinage* 24 The remedies do make so small a difference that it is not considerable. **1805** EARL OF LIVERPOOL *Treat. Coins Realm* 102 They authorised a large remedy to be taken..and did not require the Officers of the Mint to make their coins as perfect as possible, but authorised or suffered them to coin just within the remedy. **1867** *Chamb. Jrnl.* 16 Feb. 106/2 For silver coin, the 'remedy' or margin of error is fixed at one pennyweight per pound Troy. **1875** KNIGHT *Dict. Mech.* 1916/1 The remedy on United States silver coin is $1\frac{1}{2}$ grains to the piece. **1920** *Act 10 Geo. V* c. 3 §1(1), As though for the figure '4' in the column relating to the remedy allowance in respect of millesimal fineness there were substituted the figure '5'.

5. At various schools (as at St. Paul's and Winchester): A time specially granted for recreation; a half-holiday.

1518 COLET *Statute* in Gardiner *Regist. St. Paul's School* (1884) 381, I will also they shall haue noo remedies—yff the maister graunteth eny remedies he shall forfett xls... Except the kyng or a arche bisshopp or a bisshopp..desyre it. **1580** in Boys *Hist. Sandwich* (1792) 228, I ordeine, that the master ..shall not give remedie or leave to plaie aboue once in a week. **1593** *Rites & Mon. Ch. Durh.* (Surtees) 75 To recreat themselves when they had remedy of there master. **1656** in Gardiner *Regist. St. Paul's School* (1884) 382 *note*, [At Newport..it was provided that] each Thursday afternoon.. shall be a remedy or time of recreation. **1860** MANSFIELD *School-Life at Winchester* (1870) 49 Remedies were not a matter of right, but were always applied for..on Tuesday or Thursday. **1893** *Ch. Times* 22 Dec. 1331/2 His lordship afterwards (the *Pauline* reports)..exercised his privilege of desiring a 'remedy' (or half-holiday) on Wednesday.

remedy (ˈrɛmɪdɪ), *v.* Also 6 **remydy**. [a. OF. *remedier* (cf. REMEDE *v.*), or ad. L. *remediāre*, f. *remedium* REMEDY *sb.*]

1. *trans.* †**a.** To grant (one) legal remedy; to right (one) in respect of a wrong suffered. *Obs.*

1414 *Rolls of Parlt.* IV. 57/1 Byfore hene [= any] of the persones that weren..Commissioners upon myn enditement,..I myghte not have been remedied. *Ibid.* To have been remedied of the wronges that we have had. **1454** in Ellis *Orig. Lett.* Ser. II. I. 120 That they shuld be remedyed, and he remedyed them not. **1549** LATIMER *3rd Serm. bef. Edw. VI* (Arb.) 92 There is one [Judge]..wyll remedye you, if you come after a ryghte sorte vnto him. *a* **1662** HEYLIN *Laud* I. (1671) 113 Of which Indignity he complained to the Duke,..and was remedied in it.

b. To bring remedy to (a person, diseased part, etc.); to heal, cure, make whole again. Now *rare*.

1470–85 MALORY *Arthur* XIII. viii. 622 It shal so heuye me at their departynge that..there shal no manere of Ioye remedye me. **1502** *Ord. Crysten Men* (W. de W. 1506) I. iv. E j b, The synner..is fro yͤ moost gretest payne remedyed. **1541** R. COPLAND *Galyen's Terap.* H h iij b, When the party yͭ shulde be holpen & remydyed is hyd in the dypenes of the body. **1590** SPENSER *F.Q.* III. v. 32 Into the woods..shee went, To seeke for hearbes that mote him remedy. **1607** TOPSELL *Four-f. Beasts* (1658) 271 If one Horse do die of it, all his fellows that bear him company will follow after, if they be not remedied in time. **1795** SOUTHEY *Joan of Arc* I. 57 Some pious sisterhood, Who..may likeliest remedy The stricken mind.

2. To cure (a disease, etc.); to put right, reform (a state of things); to rectify, make good.

1412–20 LYDG. *Chron. Troy* I. v. (1555), There is a lawe ysette..that may not be ylette Nor remedyed. *Ibid.* vi, All her ill was holpe and remedyed. **1469** *Paston Lett.* II. 375 With Goddys grace it schall be remedyed well inow. **1509** HAWES *Past. Pleas.* XVIII. (Percy Soc.) 81, I thanke you for your love,..But I your cause can nothing remedy. **1567** MAPLET *Gr. Forest* 37 It being wrought and tempered.. remedieth all kinde of swelling. **1596** DRAYTON *Legends* iii. 389 They tooke up Armes to remedie their wrong. **1651** N. BACON *Disc. Govt. Eng.* II. ii. (1739) 14 The House of Lords shall remedy all offences contrary to the Law of Magna Charta. **1654** BRAMHALL *Just Vind.* ii. (1661) 7 A sharp fit of a feuerish distemper, which a little time..will infallibly remedy. **1754** SHERLOCK *Disc.* I. i. 49 They cannot remedy the Corruption that has spread thro' the Race of Mankind. **1768** GOLDSM. *Good-n. Man* III. i, That shall be remedied without delay. **1814** SOUTHEY *Roderick* XXI. 417 Repentance taketh sin away, Death remedies the rest. **1853** BRIGHT *Sp., India* 3 June (1876) 8 A great deal has been done to remedy the deficiency. **1858** J. H. NEWMAN *Hist. Sk.* (1873) III. v. i. 436 Evils which threaten to continue we try to remedy.

†**3.** *absol.* To provide a remedy. Const. *for*, *of*.

c **1440** LYDG. *Hors, Shepe & G.* 387 For ache of bonys & also for brosoure It remedieth & dooth men ese ful blyve. *c* **1477** CAXTON *Jason* 42 Ye be seke of the maladye of loue wherof no man may remedye but youre lady.

Hence **ˈremedying** *vbl. sb.*

1570 FOXE *A. & M.* (ed. 2) 1221/1 For the remediying and redressyng of those foresayd iniuries. **1597** A. M. tr. *Guillemeau's Fr. Chirurg.* 30 b/2 To the remedyinge and curinge of the which, we ought to tye the Arterye. **1641** WILKINS *Math. Magick* I. iii. (1648) 18 For the remedying of such abuses the Ancients did appoint divers officers.

reˈmeet (riː-), *v.* [RE- 5 a.] **1.** *intr.* To meet again.

1644 QUARLES *Sheph. Orac.* iii, The time will come, wherein We shall remeet, and never part agin. *a* **1657** R. LOVEDAY *Lett.* (1663) 11 When I re-met with them they had been so lost to my memory, that [etc.]. **1859** F. MILLS in *Athenæum* 9 July 49 Ere the shining valves remeet. **1953** J. S. HUXLEY *Evolution in Action* iii. 71 A number of forms.. which then remet when the ice retreated.

2. *trans.* To meet (a person or thing) again.

1928 *Observer* 24 June 8/6 (Advt.), So tersely..does he tell his tale that within 300 pages we re-meet the classical heroes of three generations. **1970** I. PETITE *Meander to Alaska* I. viii. 77 As usual, in travelling north to Alaska, I had the feeling of remeeting spring.

Hence **reˈmeeting** *vbl. sb.*

1648 HERRICK *Hesper., Parting Verse*, 'Tis to be doubted whether I next yeer, Or no, shall give ye a re-meeting here. **1684** *Lond. Gaz.* No. 1994/3 At the remeeting of the said States..these Points will be farther spoken of.

remeeving, -mefe, obs. varr. REMOVING, REMOVE.

remeid: see REMEDE *sb.* and *v.*

remel, see REMEAL and RIMMEL.

remelant, var. REMENANT *Obs.*

reˈmelt (riː-), *v.* [RE- 5 a.] To melt again.

a. *trans.* **1626** BACON *Sylva* §771 The Crude Materialls of Glasse, mingled with Glasse, already made and Remoulten. **1775** R. CHANDLER *Trav. Greece* (1825) II. 180 They re-melted the old dross and scum, and found ore. **1833** LYELL *Princ. Geol.* III. 185 If the lavas could be remelted. **1897** *Allbutt's Syst. Med.* II. 938 Those who remelt the pig brass, and are called 'founders'.

b. *intr.* **1793** SMEATON *Edystone L.* §274 It was perceived to re-melt and unite with the fresh metal. **1865** MASSON *Rec. Brit. Philos.* 78 Into what Empyrean will it remelt when the separating film bursts?

Hence **reˈmelted** *ppl. a.*, **reˈmelting** *vbl. sb.*

1796 PEARSON in *Phil. Trans.* LXXXVI. 431 Perhaps metals in general are rendered purer..by remelting. **1839** URE *Dict. Arts* 1127 The roasting of the mattes..and their treatment by four successive re-meltings. **1861** FAIRBAIRN *Iron* 142 Molten crude iron, or..remelted pig or refined iron.

remember (rɪˈmɛmbə(r)), *v.*¹ Forms: 4–6 **remembre**, (5 **-menbre**), 5–6 **remembyr**, (5 **-bur**, 6 **-bar**, *Sc.* **-bir**), 6– **remember**, (6 *Sc.* **ra-**). [ad. OF. *remembrer* (11th c.), = Prov. and Sp. *remembrar*, It. *rimembrar*:—late L. *rememorārī*, f. *re-* RE- + *memor* mindful: see REMEMORATE *v.*]

I. 1. a. *trans.* To retain in, or recall to, the memory; to bear in mind, recollect (a thing, person, fact, event, saying, etc.). Also *transf.* Cf. MEMORY *sb.* 1 c, d, 2 d.

c **1330** R. BRUNNE *Chron.* (1810) 327 Edward may remembre þe trauaile & þe pyn. **1382** WYCLIF *Tobit* ii. 6 Remembrende that woord, that the Lorde seide by Amos. *c* **1420** LYDG. *Assembly of Gods* 154 Remembre your name was wont to be egall. **1484** CAXTON *Fables of Æsop* I. xviii, Euer I shal remembre the grace whiche thou hast done to me. **1560** DAUS tr. *Sleidane's Comm.* 80 b, They should remembre themselves to be earth and asshes. **1609** HOLLAND *Amm. Marcell.* 217 A thing that no man could remember done since Dioclesian and Aristobulus time. **1678** BUNYAN *Pilgr.* I. (1900) 35 Let this mans misery be remembred by thee. **1750** JOHNSON *Rambler* No. 26 ¶2, I was..left by my father, whom I cannot remember, to the care of an uncle. **1833** TENNYSON *Dream Fair Wom.* xx, The times when I remember to have been Joyful. **1875** JOWETT *Plato* (ed. 2) IV. 130 We must remember the place held by Parmenides in the history of Greek philosophy. **1933** *Boys' Mag.* XLVII. 170/1 If two cars pass over the detectors simultaneously then right of way is given to one and the arrival of the other is 'remembered', the right of way being accorded to it as soon as the first is safely through. **1958** *Engineering* 21 Mar. 358/1 Upon playback the machine 'remembers' the original picture without loss of detail. **1980** 'D. RUTHERFORD' *Turbo* ix. 130 They bend on impact instead of breaking but the material remembers its original shape and goes back to it.

fig. **1732** POPE *Hor. Sat.* II. ii. 73 The stomach.. Remembers oft the School-boy's simple fare. **1833** TENNYSON *Two Voices* 423 My frozen heart began to beat, Remembering its ancient heat.

b. With *inf.* To bear in mind, not to forget, *to* do something.

c **1430** LYDG. *Min. Poems* (Percy Soc.) 12 Remembryng the highe lord to queme. **1461** *Paston Lett.* II. 27 Remembre to take a wryht to chese crowneres in Norffolk. **1535** LYNDESAY *Satyre* 3054 My Lords,..Remember to reforme the consistorie. **1610** SHAKS. *Temp.* III. ii. 99 Remember First to possesse his Bookes. **1733–4** BERKELEY in Fraser *Life* vi. 218 You will also remember to take bonds for the money. **1781** COWPER *Conversat.* 103 But still remember..To press your point with modesty and ease.

†**c.** Const. *with* oneself. *Obs. rare.*

1563 B. GOOGE *Eglogs*, etc. (Arb.) 86 As ofte as I remembre with my self, The Fancies fonde [etc.]. **1613** DAY *Festivals* viii. (1615) 240 That you remember with your selves, who it is that hath made you Fathers of Children.

†**d.** ***remember your courtesy***, be covered. *Obs.*

(The precise origin of the phrase is not clear; compare *leave your courtesy* in *Mids. N.* IV. i. 21, and the following passage: *c* **1560** WEVER *Lusty Juventus* C ij, Well sayd maister doctor... I pray you be remembred, and couer your head.)

1588 SHAKS. *L.L.L.* V. i. 103, I doe beseech thee remember thy curtesie. I beseech thee apparell thy head. [Cf. *Haml.* V. ii. 108.] **1598** B. JONSON *Ev. Man in Hum.* I. i, Pray you remember your court'sy..Nay, pray you be covered.

2. a. To think of, recall the memory of (a person) with some kind of feeling or intention.

1382 WYCLIF *Isa.* lxii. 6 ȝee that remembren the Lorde, ne beth stille. **1490** CAXTON *Eneydos* xix. 69 So shall I remembre elysse as longe as lyffe shall abyde wythin me. **1535** COVERDALE *Eccl.* xii. 1 Remembre thy maker in thy youth, or euer the dayes of aduersite come. **1560** DAUS tr. *Sleidane's Comm.* 314 We must also remember the dead. **1671** MILTON *P.R.* III. 434 Yet he at length..Remembring Abraham by some wond'rous call May bring them back. **1791** BURNS *Lament for Glencairn* x, I'll remember thee, Glencairn, And a' that thou hast done for me! **1841** LANE *Arab. Nts.* I. 111, I will do thee an act of kindness for which I shall be remembered.

b. To bear (a person) in mind as entitled to a gift, recompence, or fee, or in making one's will; hence, to fee, reward, 'tip'.

1470 *Paston Lett.* II. 407 Also my brother Edmonde is not yet remembryd. He hathe not to lyff with, thynk on hym. **1563** BP. SANDYS in Ellis *Orig. Lett.* Ser. I. II. 195 This Contrie..bringith nothing forth fitt to remember youe withall. **1599** *Aberdeen Regr.* (1848) II. 188 The..counsall ..lykvayes ordanis Mr. Peter Blakburne, minister, to be rememberit for the interteneing of the said Mr. George. **1605** SHAKS. *Macb.* II. iii. 23 Anon, anon, I pray you remember the Porter. **1802** MAR. EDGEWORTH *Moral T.* (1816) I. xi. 93 He assured the hostler, that he would remember him the next day. **1871** *Punch* 16 Sept. 113/1 Mr. Keane Hunter is manœuvring to be remembered in Alderman W.'s will.

†**3. a.** To record, mention, make mention of (a thing, person, etc.). *Obs.* (common *c* 1430–1660).

c **1430** LYDG. *Min. Poems* (Percy Soc.) 73 Remembryd by scriptures we fynde and rede, Holsum and holy it is to thynke and pray. **1483** CAXTON *Gold. Leg.* 261/1 Her deth and..her assumpcion wherof the Scripture remembryth no thynge. **1577–87** HOLINSHED *Chron.* III. 963/2 About the same time that the armie before remembred, was set forward into Scotland. **1620–55** I. JONES *Stone-Heng* (1725) 4 History hath not remembred the Ruins of any ancient Buildings digged up in Anglesey. **1652** NEEDHAM tr. *Selden's Mare. Cl.* 62 The Carians possessed the Sea. Their Sea-Dominion is remembred by Diodorus Siculus. **1749** FIELDING *Tom Jones* III. iv, That phenomenon in the face of the former which we have above remembered.

†**b.** To commemorate. *Obs.*

1430–40 LYDG. *Bochas* I. xiv. (1554) 30 This knightly man ..Set up pillers for a memoriall Which remembred his conquests. **1535** COVERDALE *Numb.* v. 15 It is..an offeringe of remembraunce, that remembreth synne. **1610** SHAKS. *Temp.* I. ii. 405 The Ditty do's remember my drown'd father. **1658** *Whole Duty Man* iii. §17 His mercies, especially those remembred in the Sacrament, his giving Christ to die for us.

†**c.** To mention by way of reminder. *Obs. rare.*

1621 ELSING *Debates Ho. Lords* (Camden) 36 L. Ch. Justice moved whether to proceed against Michell,..and remembred the message to the Lower House to sytt as a House this afternoone.

d. To (have mind of and) mention (a person, his condition, etc.) in prayer.

1602 SHAKS. *Ham.* III. i. 90 Nimph, in thy Orisons Be all my sins remembred. **1613** —— *Hen. VIII*, v. i. 73 In thy Prayres remember Th' estate of my poore Queene. **1836** SIMEON in Carus *Life* (1847) xxxiii. 794, I intreat the favour of you to remember at the throne of grace one, who [etc.].

4. a. *absol.* or *intr.* To have or bear in mind; to recall to the mind; also, to exercise or possess the faculty of memory. Also with *about*.

1390 GOWER *Conf.* III. 122 Which yifth men cause to remembre, If any Sor be left behinde. **14..** *Tundale's Vis.*, etc. (1843) 101 In verrey sothe, as I remembur can. **1548** ELYOT, s.v. *Memoria*, Sens any manne coulde remembre. **1588** SHAKS. *L.L.L.* I. i. 258 That shallow vassall..which as I remember, hight Costard. *a* **1631** DONNE *Poems* (1650) 22 So, in forgetting thou remembrest right. **1690** LOCKE *Hum. Und.* I. iv. §20 To remember is to perceive any thing with memory, or with a consciousness, that it was known or perceived before. **1752** GRAY *Lett., to Walpole* (1900) I. 219 As I remember, there were certain low chairs, that looked like ebony. **1812** COLERIDGE *Lit. Rem.* (1836) I. 336 Beasts and babies remember, that is, recognize: man alone recollects. **1819** SHELLEY *Prometh. Unb.* I. 561 Past ages crowd on thee, but each one remembers. **1847** G. P. R. JAMES *Whim* III. ix. 164 Remember about the burning of the will. **1891** W. MORRIS *News fr. Nowhere* ix. 67, I *do* remember about that strange piece of baseless folly. **1919** G. B. SHAW *Heartbreak House* I. 9 *Nurse.* Youve actually remembered about the tea! (*To Ellie*) O, miss, he didnt forget you after all!

b. To have mind, memory, or recollection *of* something. Now *rare* (in later quots. *Sc.* and *U.S.*).

c **1386** CHAUCER *Pars. T.* ¶85 At euery tyme þat I remembre of þe day of doom, I quake. *c* **1440** *Partonope* 3502 Remembring of the Joy he had before. **1523** LD. BERNERS *Froiss.* I. ccxxxvii. 339 Sir Johan Chandos remembred of a knyfe that he had in his bosome. **1613** SHAKS. *Hen. VIII*, I. ii. 190, I remember of such a time, being my sworn seruant, The Duke retein'd him his. **1642** MILTON *Apol. Smect.* Wks. 1851 III. 285 And yet he can remember of none but Lysimachus Nicanor, and that he mislikt and censur'd. **1760–72** H. BROOKE *Fool of Qual.* (1809) II. 54 Among..female fashions..I remember but of one [etc.]. **1808** SCOTT *Mem.* in *Lockhart* i. (1842) 6/1, I remember of detesting the name of Cumberland. **1851** H. STEPHENS *Bk. Farm* (ed. 2) I. 594/1, I remember of another case in which there was no appearance of a lamb. **1862** M. D. COLT *Went to Kansas* x. 150, I then remembered of reading of such a practice among Southern ladies. **1903** *Profitable Advertising* Nov. 500 'Do you remember of ever making a purchase as the result of an advertisement?' asked the writer. **1923** B. HECHT *Florentine Dagger* xiii. 224 She remembers dimly, she says, of striking him with a dagger. **1948** *Amer. Speech* XXIII. 237 Of the two or three thousand local [Pennsylvania Dutch] people whose speech the present writer has heard during the past seventeen years, no native has ever said, 'I remember it', but always, 'I remember of it'.

†**c.** Const. *on* or *upon*. *Obs.*

c **1386** CHAUCER *Nun's Pr. T.* 213 Remembring on his dremes that he mette. **1430–40** LYDG. *Bochas* IX. xiv. (1558) 26 He gan remembre anone..Vpon a verse written in yͤ Sautere. **15..** *Impeachm. Wolsey* in Furniv. *Ballads fr. MSS.* I. 352 Remembyr on Thomas of Canterbury. **1588** A. KING tr. *Canisius' Catech.* 9 b, Remember on me, o lord.

†**d.** To make mention *of* a thing. *Obs. rare*$^{-1}$.

1531 ELYOT *Gov.* II. xiii, Plinie remembreth of a dogge whiche..asaulted the murdrer of his maister.

5. *refl.* **a.** To bethink or recollect, †to think or reflect upon (oneself). Now *rare*.

c **1386** Chaucer *Pars. T.* ¶135, I wol remembre me alle the yeres of my lyf, in bitternesse of myn herte. c **1440** *Generydes* 583, I may not ease my hert.., That doth me harme whanne I remembre me. **1484** Caxton *Chivalry* 10 And thenne he remembryd hym a lytyl and after sayd [etc.]. a **1548** Hall *Chron., Hen. VIII* 194 The Cardinal somewhat remembred hym selfe and sayd, wel my lord I am content to obey. **1592** Shaks. *Rom. & Jul.* i. iii. 9 Nurse come backe againe, I haue remembred me, thou'se heare our counsell. **1605** —— *Lear* iv. vi. 233 Thou old, vnhappy Traitor, Breefely thy selfe remember. **1891** *Illustr. Lond. News* Christmas No. 21/1, 'I long for home'. But she remembered herself. 'That's only a momentary feeling'.

†**b.** Const. *of* or *on*; = 4 b, 4 c. *Obs.*

13.. *E.E. Allit. P.* C. 326 Þenne I remembred me ry3t of my rych lorde. c **1386** Chaucer *Melib.* ¶33 Remembreth yow upon the pacient Job. c **1450** Lonelich *Merlin* 581 (Kölbing), Sche hire remembrid of fadyr and modyr bothe. **1545** *St. Papers Hen. VIII*, I. ii. 806, I cannot remember me of any others [fit to be captains]. **1622** Mabbe tr. *Aleman's Guzman d'Alf.* ii. 308, I remembred my selfe of my Hostesse. **1651** tr. *De-las-Coveras' Don Fenise* 94 Remembring himselfe of the recitall which Rufine had made him. **1760–72** H. Brooke *Fool of Qual.* (1809) III. 88, I remembered me of my gallant messmates. **1890** C. M. Yonge *Slaves of Sabinus* ii. 22 He remembered him of snow-capped Hermon.

c. With obj. clause. (Cf. sense 1.) Now *arch.*

c **1374** Chaucer *Troylus* i. 384 Remembring him, that love to wyde y-blowe Yelt bittre fruyt. **1428** *Lett. Marg. Anjou & Bp. Beckington* (Camden) 43 Treuly, I can not remembre me, that ever I wrote to yow. **1470–85** Malory *Arthur* viii. ii. 275 The kyng merueilled why she dyd soo, and remembryd hym how her sone was sodenly slayne with poyson. **1589** *Hay any Work* 48 O now I remember me, he has also a charge to prouide for. a **1648** Ld. Herbert *Hen. VIII* (1683) 39 Remembring himself, that it was time to visit his Army..he takes leave of the Ladies. **1700** Congreve *Way of World* ii. ix, Now, I remember me, I'm married. **1817** Byron *Manfred* iii. iv. 8, I do remember me, that in my youth..I stood within the Coliseum's wall.

6. a. *impers.* (*it*) *remembers me* [after OF. (*il*) *me remembre*], I remember. Now *arch.*

c **1374** Chaucer *Compl. Mars* 150 What his compleynt was, remembreth me. c **1386** —— *Wife's T.* 469 Whan that it remembreth me Up-on my yowthe. **1484** Caxton *Fables of Æsop* i. iv, I am certayne & me remembreth wel that the dogge lend to her a loof of brede. **1814** Cary *Dante, Par.* xx. 137 It doth remember me, that I beheld The pair of blessed luminaries move. **1831** Scott *Cast. Dang.* i, It may remember you that I undertook..to temporize a little with the Scots.

†**b.** Of a thing: To recur to (one). *Obs.*[−1]

1608 *Yorksh. Trag.* i. ix, When the dread thought of death remembers you.

c. *to be remembered*, to remember; also const. *of*. Now *Obs.* exc. *dial.* (common c 1450–1600).

c **1440** *Generydes* 619 Ther is a land I am remembryd wele, Men call it Perse. **1470–85** Malory *Arthur* ix. xxi. 370 Soo whan the quene loked vpon sir Tristram she was not remembryd of hym. **1509** Barclay *Shyp of Folys* (1570) 46, I am remembred that I haue often sene Great wordly riches ende in pouertie. c **1590** Marlowe *Faust.* x, Are you remembered how you crossed me in my conference with the Emperor? **1605** *1st Pt. Ieronimo* iii. ii. 53 Are you remembred, Don, of a daring message, And a proud attempt? **1828** *Craven Gloss.* s.v., An ye be remembered, i.e. if you remember.

II. 7. a. To remind (a person); esp. to put (one) in mind *of* a thing or person. †Also const. *upon*, *with*. Now *arch.* or *dial.*

c **1386** Chaucer *Frankl. T.* 515 This was as thise bookes me remembre The colde frosty seson of Decembre. c **1449** Pecock *Repr.* i. iv. 22 Thou3 he wolde reherce tho pointis.. of the lawe forto remembre the iugis and the peple ther upon. **1451** *Paston Lett.* I. 190 Item, to remembre T. Denyes of the tale that Fyncheham told. **1530** Palsgr. 685/1, I shal remembre him of it whan he gothe to bedde. **1604** T. Wright *Passions* vi. 320 These..I thought good briefly to set downe..to remember the Reader, that hereafter he may benefit himselfe of them. **1641** R. Marriot *Serm.* 25 The third was a Golden letter, which remembred him with the joyes of Heaven. **1745** *Fortunate Orphan* 68 Emanuel..remember'd Azem of his Promises. **1808** *Edin. Rev.* Jan. 285 He takes care to remember us of Dr. Johnson's saying. a **1850** Rossetti *Dante & Circ.* i. (1874) 98 She remembered me many times of my own most noble lady. **1922** Joyce *Ulysses* 398 Would to God that foresight had remembered me to take my cloak along! **1935** E. R. Eddison *Mistress* (1967) xiii. 229 And while he felt about for firm ground then Lessingham again, most courtly and submissive, remembering Derxis of that former passage with Alquemen.

b. With inf. or obj. clause. Now *dial.* (Very common in 17th c., esp. with *that*.)

c **1449** Pecock *Repr.* i. iv. 21 If a bischop..wolde remembre hem, exorte hem, and stire hem..forto kepe certeyn moral vertues. **1474** *Rolls of Parlt.* VI. 113/1 Remembryng us that it appered unto us [etc.]. **1540–1** Elyot *Image Gov.* (1556) 48 b, Fyrste he wolde remembre hym for what cause he hath called hym. **1596** Nashe *Saffron Walden* 11 Let me remember thee to do this one kindnes more for me. **1638** Chillingw. *Relig. Prot.* i. iii. §77. 177, I am to remember you, that many Attributes in Scripture, are not notes of performance but of duty. **1670** Baxter *Cure Ch. Div.* Pref. 1, I write it to remember the Teachers of the Churches, what principles they have to preach. **1703** J. Savage *Lett. Antients* xxvii. 88 Remembring him that Liberality to Friends is the best way of hoarding Treasure. **1748** Richardson *Clarissa* (1811) II. 239 The edge of the opened door, which he ran against, remembered him to turn his welcome back upon me. **1877–** in dial. glossaries (Lancs., Chesh., Lincs., Warw., Shropsh.).

†**8. a.** To recall (a thing or person) *to* a person. Also with double object, obj. clause, and without const. *Obs.*

1382 Wyclif *John* xiv. 26 He schal..schewe, or remembre, to 3ou alle thingis. c **1440** Capgrave *Life St. Kath.* iii. 1379 Loke on 3our ryng! It wyll remembyr 3ow 3our gloryous weddyng. a **1470** Tiptoft *Tulle on Friendsh.* (Caxton 1481) A ij, Syth my master Seuola remembrid unto me how Lelius hath resouned with him. **1531** Elyot *Gov.* i. iv, Remembryng to hym the daunger of his iuell example. **1617** Wither *Fidelia* in *Juvenilia* (1633) 456 Every severall object that I see Doth severally (methinkes) remember thee. **1649** Milton *Eikon.* Pref., By onely remembring them the truth of what they themselves know to be heer miss-affirmed. **1672** *Mede's Wks.* p. xl, I remembred to him, how often I heard him wonder [etc.].

†**b.** To mention (one's affection, respect, etc.) by way of message *to* another. *Obs.*

1586 A. Day *Eng. Secretary* ii. (1625) 63 Sir, my humble dutie remembred unto you and my good Mistresse, you may please to understand [etc.] **1625** Ussher in *Lett. Lit. Men* (Camden) 132, I pray remember my hearty affeccion unto my Lord of Landaff. **1672** Marvell *Corr.* Wks. (Grosart) II. 408 Pray remember my respects to your Partner.

c. To mention (a person) *to* another as sending a friendly greeting. Also without const.

1560 Gresham in Burgon *Life* I. 302 To whom it may please you, I maye be remembered. **1613** Shaks. *Hen. VIII*, iv. ii. 160 Remember me In all humilitie vnto his Highnesse. a **1674** Clarendon *Surv. Leviath.* (1676) 6 To remember me kindly to Mr. Hobbes. **1713** Steele *Guardian* No. 171 ¶3 Remember me to the lion. **1780** *Phil. Trans.* LXX. 452 He begs to be remembered to you with best compliments. **1804** in *G. Rose's Diaries* (1860) II. 86 Mrs. Tomline desires to be most kindly remembered. **1872** Black *Adv. Phaeton* xxvi. 353 Katty Tatham desires to be remembered to you all.

re-'member, *v.*[2] *nonce-wd.* [re- 5 b.] *trans.* **a.** To put together again. **b.** To supply with a new member.

1871 Spencer *Princ. Psychol.* II. vii. vii. 377 Mind..is a thing we can form no notion of without *re-membering*, *re-collecting* some of our mental acts. **1894** Blackmore *Perlycross* 389 A British tar..a true heart of oak, re-membered also in the same fine material.

re,membera'bility. [f. next + -ity.] The fact of being rememberable.

1839 J. Rogers *Antipopopr.* x. §2. 255 The easy rememberability of the Bible system.

rememberable (rɪ'mɛmbərəb(ə)l), *a.* Also **remembr-**. [f. remember *v.*[1] + -able: cf. obs. F. *remembrable*.] Capable or worthy of being remembered. (Common in 19th c.)

1611 Cotgr., *Memorable*, memorable, remembrable, worthie of memorie. **1800** Hazlitt *Pol. Ess.* (1819) 399 When all is done, nothing rememberable has been said. a **1842** Arnold *Serm. Chr. Life* (1845) 296 A change..of any rememberable kind. **1881** Shairp *Asp. Poetry* v. 143 More rememberable than any blank verse since Milton's.

Hence **re'memberably** *adv.*

1800 Southey *Lett.* (1856) I. 133 The moral features of the people [are] more accurately and rememberably painted. **1809** *Ibid.* II. 157 Say what you have to say as perspicuously ..and as rememberably as possible.

rememberance, obs. form of remembrance.

remembered (rɪ'mɛmbəd), *ppl. a.* [-ed[1].]

†**1.** Already mentioned. *Obs. rare.*

c **1425** *Found. St. Bartholomew's* (E.E.T.S.) 31 Whan the remembrid priour was 3it a-lyue. **1589** Puttenham *Eng. Poesie* (Arb.) 115 Besides all the remembred points of Metricall proportion, ye haue yet two other sorts.

2. Recalled to or kept in memory. Also in combs., as *sad-*, *well-remembered*.

1638 Junius *Paint. Ancients* 17 That the Artificer after a well-remembred knowledge, should invent something of his owne. **1745** *Matrimony pro & con* 3 O! to recall the sad-remember'd Day. **1754** Richardson *Grandison* (1811) I. xxxiii. 253 As dear to me..as her brother from his remembered bravery. **1805** Wordsw. *Prelude* i. 161 No little band of yet remembered names. **1863** Geo. Eliot *Romola* ix, Far in the backward vista of his remembered life.

rememberer (rɪ'mɛmbərə(r)). [-er[1].] One who, or that which, remembers (†or reminds).

c **1449** Pecock *Repr.* ii. vi. 171 Bi this remembraunce the remembrer..schal be the more stirid. a **1542** Wyatt in *Tottel's Misc.* (Arb.) 45 Forgetter of payn, remembrer of my wo. **1579** G. Harvey *Letter-bk.* (Camden) 61 Lett this il-favorid letter suffize for a..remembrer in that behaulfe. **1614** Raleigh *Hist. World* iii. (1634) 89 Artaxerxes called Mnemon, that is to say the Mindful or the Rememberer. **1754** Richardson *Grandison* (1781) IV. vii. 62 What a rememberer, if I may make a word, is the heart! **1809** Syd. Smith *Wks.* (1859) I. 174/1 The maker of verses and the rememberer of words. **1876** F. Harrison *Choice Bks.* (1886) 396 The recollections are very often the inventions of the rememberer.

re'membering, *vbl. sb.* [-ing[1].] The action of the vb. remember; an instance of this. †*in remembering*, in remembrance or memory.

c **1375** *Sc. Leg. Saints* xl. (*Ninian*) 532 Of þat merwale in remembryng. c **1449** Pecock *Repr.* v. xii. 547 Into the remembring of persones not being religiose. **1521** J. T. *Prol. Bradshaw's St. Werburge* 40 Who on this wolde haue remembryng..wolde dispise all thynges..mundayne. **1585** T. Washington tr. *Nicholay's Voy.* Ep. Ded., Doth it not deserue diligent marking and remembring? **1673** *True Worship of God* 51 A Remembring and Renewing of our Baptismal Vow. **1740** J. Clarke *Educ. Youth* (ed. 3) 88 The Matter is well worth the remembring. **1846** Maskell *Mon. Rit.* I. p. clxxxv, Wearying the reader with continued rememberings of much, which we might have wished away. **1918** W. Stevens in *Poetry* (Chicago) May 63 Wait now; have no rememberings of hope, Poor penury. **1969** K. H. Pribram in *Sci. Amer.* Jan. 73 (*title*) The neurophysiology of remembering.

re'membering, *ppl. a.* [-ing[2].] That remembers (†or reminds); †mindful *of* a thing.

c **1449** Pecock *Repr.* v. xii. 546 Wherfore it is resonable, .. that her outward habit be mad to hem into such..a remembring signe. c **1586** C'tess Pembroke *Ps.* cxix. G. i, Grave deeply in remembring mind My trust, thy promise true. **1625** Bacon *Ess., Great Place* (Arb.) 293 Be not too sensible, or too remembring, of thy Place, in Conuersation. a **1676** Hale *Prim. Orig. Man.* (1677) 21 Touching the knowledge of Brutes, touching their remembring Faculty. **1790** Pennant *London* (1813) 498 Death..shaking his remembring hour-glass. **1822** Galt *Provost* xxix, During the remembering prayer, Mr. Pittle put up a few words for criminals under sentence of death. **1886** Swinburne *Death Sir H. Taylor* in *Athenæum* 10 Apr. 488/1 Clothed round with reverence of remembering hearts.

remembir, obs. Sc. form of remember.

remembrance (rɪ'mɛmbrəns), *sb.* Also 4–6 **-aunce**, 5 **-a(u)nse**, **-ans**, 6 **-auns**, 4–8 **remember-**. [a. F. *remembrance* (11th c.; AF. *-aunce*): see remember and -ance, and cf. It. *rimembranza*.]

1. a. (Without article.) Memory or recollection in relation to a particular object, fact, etc. In early use esp. in phrases *to have in r.*, *to call to r.* (see call *v.* 20 b).

13.. *Coer de L.* 6926 Whoso hadde sene hys cuntenaunse, Wolde euer had hym in remembraunse. **1390** Gower *Conf.* I. 5 He schal drawe into remembrance The fortune of this worldes chance. c **1450** *Merlin* 49 The moste remembraunce that I shall haue, shall be vpon yow, and on yowre nedes. **1530** Palsgr. 351 Here is to be called to remembraunce what I sayd afore of *quel*. **1535** Coverdale *2 Macc.* xii. 42 They ..besought God, that the fawte..might be put out of remembraunce. **1611** Bible *Transl. Pref.* ¶7 He hath for euer bound the Church vnto him, in a debt of speciall remembrance. **1667** Milton *P.L.* iii. 704 Worthiest to be all Had in remembrance alwayes with delight. **1725** Pope *Odyss.* viii. 501 This ever grateful in remembrance bear. **1826** J. G. Strutt *Sylva Brit.* (1830) 5 Secured to remembrance by the pencil. **1871** R. Ellis tr. *Catullus* lxiv. 231 Look that..deep-laid in steady remembrance These our words grow greenly.

b. Const. *of*, †inf., or †clause. Formerly freq. in phrases *to have r. of*, *to put* (one) *in r. of*.

c **1386** Chaucer *Knt.'s T.* 188 This maked Emelye han remembrance To do honour to May. —— *Monk's T.* 728 Of honestee yit hadde he remembraunce. **1465** *Paston Lett.* III. 482 This might..put him in remembrance what time he hath lost. **1555** Eden *Decades* 43 You put me so often in remembrance of your departure. **1586** A. Day *Eng. Secretary* ii. (1625) 38 His presence I am resolved shall no more disquiet me, by hearing or remembrance of him. **1623** Bingham *Xenophon* 101 Yet it is honest..that remembrance be had rather of that which is good, than of the bad. **1678** Cudworth *Intell. Syst.* i. v. 693 Though all Learning be not the Remembrance of what the Soul once before actually understood in a Pre-existent State. **1784** Cowper *Task* vi. 252 What he views of beautiful or grand..Prompts with remembrance of a present God. **1816** J. Wilson *City of Plague* ii. ii. 231 Remembrance rises faint and dim Of sorrows suffer'd long ago.

2. a. That operation of the mind which is involved in recalling a thing or fact; recollection. Freq. personified, or in fig. context.

c **1374** Chaucer *Anel. & Arc.* 211 So thirlethe with the poynt of Rememberaunce þe swerde of sorowe..Myn hert bare of blisse. **1500–20** Dunbar *Poems* lxxxii. 105 Than rudelie come Remembrance Ay rugging me, withoutin rest. **1595** Shaks. *John* v. vii. 12 Vnkinde remembrance: thou, & endles night, Haue done me shame. **1671** Milton *Samson* 952 Not for thy life, lest fierce remembrance wake My sudden rage. **1690** Locke *Hum. Und.* ii. xix. §1 The same Idea, when it again recurs without the Operation of the like Object on the external Sensory, is Remembrance. **1785** Reid *Intell. Powers* i. i. 16 When the word perception is used properly..it is never applied to things past. And thus it is distinguished from remembrance.

†**b.** Faculty or power of remembering or recalling to mind. *Obs.* (Cf. next.)

c **1420** Lydg. *Assembly of Gods* 998 To whom Vertew sent embassatours three, Reson, Discresion, & Good Remembraunse. **1509** Fisher *Funeral Serm. C'tess Richmond* Wks. (1876) 291 She was good in remembraunce & of holdyng memorye. **1538** *Bury Wills* (Camden) 133, I, Barbara Mason,..beyng..in hooll mynd and good remembrauns, make this my present testament. **1577** Northbrooke *Dicing* (1843) 143 The witte thereby is made more sharpe, and the remembrance quickened. **1610** Shaks. *Temp.* ii. i. 232 This Lord of weake remembrance. **1631** Widdowes *Nat. Philos.* 52 The wittie excell in remembrance, the dull in memorie.

3. a. With possess. pron. (One's) memory or recollection; also, in later use, (one's) power of remembering (cf. prec.).

c **1374** Chaucer *Troylus* iii. 919 (968) Can I not seyn..If sorow it put out of her remembraunce. c **1410** Hoccleve *Mother of God* 45 Fecche that lady in thy remembrance. **1490** Caxton *Eneydos* xxii. 80 Come to her remembraunce the grete iustyces..vnto her tolde. a **1533** Ld. Berners *Huon* l. 167 Call to your remembraunce how that..Adam & Eue was dyffendyd fro y[e] etinge of fruyte. **1604** E. G[rimstone] *D'Acosta's Hist. Indies* v. xxv. 401 They must confesse themselves of all the sinnes they have committed, to their remembrance. **1660** *Trial Regic.* 44 To the best of my remembrance, he sate there four days together. **1754** Richardson *Grandison* (1781) IV. ix. 87 The obliging wife would banish from his remembrance the petulant mistress. **1819** Shelley *Cyclops* 145 Pour: that the draught may fillip my remembrance. **1864** Skeat *Uhland's Poems* 170 But now is my remembrance weak with eld.

b. The point at which one's memory of events begins, or the period over which it extends.

1565 Cooper *Thesaurus, Memoria patrum*, in the time and remembrance of our fathers. **1601** Shaks. *All's Well* iv. iii.

126 Fro the time of his remembrance to this very instant disaster. **1667** MILTON *P.L.* VIII. 203 Thee I have heard relating what was don Ere my remembrance. **1771** SMOLLETT *Humph. Cl.* 2 June, Let. ii, I know but one other method.., which..has been practised successfully more than once in my remembrance.

4. a. The memory (†or thought) which one has *of* a thing or person.

c **1386** CHAUCER *Pars. T.* ¶157 The fourth point, that oughte make a man have contrition, is the sorweful remembrance of the good dedes that he hath lefte to don here in erthe. **1490** CAXTON *Eneydos* xxii. 78 Anguishe & calamyte,..wherof yᵉ remembraunce greued hym ryght sorowfully. **1551** ROBINSON tr. *More's Utop.* II. (1895) 302 The remembraunce of theire poore indigent and begerlye olde age kylleth them up. **1590** SHAKS. *Mids. N.* IV. i. 164 My loue To Hermia..Seems to me now as the remembrance of an idle gaude. **1655** GURNALL *Chr. in Arm.* verse 11. I. iii. (1669) 27/1 These add to his sin, and the remembrance of his sin..will adde to his torment. **1725** POPE *Odyss.* XIII. 224 Yet had his mind thro' tedious absence lost The dear remembrance of his native coast. **1792** WORDSW. *Descrip. Sketches* 519 Why does their sad remembrance haunt the mind? **1849** MACAULAY *Hist. Eng.* vii. II. 229 Between him and the court was interposed the remembrance of one terrible event.

b. With *a* and *pl.* A recollection, reminiscence.

1601 SHAKS. *All's Well* I. iii. 140 By our remembrances of daies forgon. **1610** —— *Temp.* V. i. 138 How sharpe the point of this remembrance is. [**1706–7** FARQUHAR *Beaux' Strat.* IV. ii, But cussen Mackshane, vil you not put a remembrance upon me?] **1788** GIBBON *Decl. & F.* xlix. V. 158 A faint remembrance of their ancestors still tormented the Romans. **1809** CAMPBELL *Gertr. Wyom.* I. i, Although the wild-flower on thy ruined wall..a sad remembrance bring. **1819** SHELLEY *Peter Bell 3rd* V. x, These obscure remembrances Stirred such harmony in Peter.

c. The surviving memory of a person.

1579 W. WILKINSON *Confut. Familye of Loue, Brief Descr.*, Kyng Edward the vi., a Prince of blessed remembrance. **1611** BIBLE *Exod.* xvii. 14, I will vtterly put out the remembrance of Amalek from vnder heauen. **1698** TATE & BRADY *Ps.* cxii. 6 The sweet Remembrance [1696 Memorial] of the Just Shall flourish when he sleeps in Dust. **1812** SOUTHEY *Omniana* I. 110 He might have secured for himself a lasting and respectful remembrance.

d. *pl.* Greetings expressive of remembrance.

1789 COWPER *Let. to Newton* 1 Dec., With our joint affectionate remembrances to yourself and Mrs. Newton. **1804** in *G. Rose's Diaries* (1860) II. 87 Kindest remembrances to all our good friends. *c* **1850** *Arab. Nts.* (Rtldg.) 528 He bid me also be sure and give his kindest remembrances to you.

5. †**a.** *in* (*into*, rarely *for*) ***remembrance***, as a memorial or record; ***to put in remembrance***, to put on record. *Obs.*

1390 GOWER *Conf.* III. 183 Into remembrance He dede upon him such vengance. *Ibid.* 294 Thei for evere in remembrance Made a figure in resemblance Of him. **1426** LYDG. in *Pol. Poems* (Rolls) II. 132 To put his title in remembraunce, Whiche that he hath to Inglond and to Fraunce. **1490** CAXTON *Eneydos* vi. 24 Of which were fourmed lettres for to write..in remembraunce perpetual þe thinges that [etc.]. **1511** *Guylforde's Pilgr.* (Camden) 27 By token of a fayre stone layde for remembraunce. **1535** COVERDALE *Zech.* xiii. 2, I will destroye the names of Idols out off the londe: so that they shal nomore be put in remembraunce.

b. ***in*** (†***the***) ***remembrance of***, in memory of.

c **1400** MAUNDEV. (Roxb.) xxxiv. 153 Þeroff he drinkez.. in remembraunce of his fader. **1483** CAXTON *Cato* F vij, It is sayd that there is as yet in the same place a pytte in mynde and remembraunce of the sayd myracle. ? *a* **1500** *Wycket* (1828) 6 Do ye this in the remembrance of me. **1581** PETTIE tr. *Guazzo's Civ. Conv.* II. (1586) 105 That the..life of the people of Arpines, should be spared in the remembraunce of Tullie. **1613** PURCHAS *Pilgrimage* I. xiii. 63 The day in remembrance thereof [was] yeerely solemnized with fasting the Euen. **1697** DRYDEN *Æneid* VI. 680 In remembrance of so brave a Deed, A Tomb, and Fun'ral Honours I decreed.

†**6. a.** Mention, notice. *Obs.*

1375 BARBOUR *Bruce* III. 558 Quhen that he herd mak remembrance Off the perellys that passyt war. **1390** GOWER *Conf.* I. 156 As the bok makth remembrance, Alphonse was his propre name. *c* **1440** *Generydes* 2177 Till he was putte [from] his enheritaunce, Wherof be fore was made remembraunce. **1531** ELYOT *Gov.* I. xviii, I can finde no notable remembrance that it was used of auncient tyme. **1607** TOPSELL *Four-f. Beasts* (1658) 497 He saith he found the remembrance of it in the Grecian books. **1631** WEEVER *Anc. Funeral Mon.* 650 This towne..requireth some large remembrance from mee.

†**b.** A commemorative discourse or mention; a memorial inscription. *Obs.*

1509 FISHER *Funeral Serm. C'tess Richmond* Wks. (1876) 289 Here after foloweth a mornynge remembraunce had at the moneth mynde of the noble prynces Margarete. **1598** BARNFEILD *Poems* (Arb.) 119 A Remembrance of some English Poets. **1599** SHAKS. *Hen. V*, I. ii. 229 Lay these bones in an vnworthy Vrne, Tomblesse, with no remembrance ouer them.

†**7. a.** The act of reminding or putting in mind. ***book of remembrance***, a memorandum-book, a record. ***ring of remembrance*** (see quot. 1659). *Obs.*

1461 *Paston Lett.* II. 64 It is not for no lak of remembrans, for I sent to hym thryis or fowyr tymys ther for. **1465** *Ibid.* 202 He sent me word that Wyllyam Worceter had a boke of remembraunce of recaytys. **1535** COVERDALE *Num.* v. 15 It is..an offeringe of remembraunce, that remembreth synne. **1565** COOPER *Thesaurus, Memorialis liber*, a booke of remembrance. **1597** HOOKER *Eccl. Pol.* v. lxv. §4 It serueth, namely, for a signe of rememberance to put vs in minde of our dutie. **1611** BIBLE *Mal.* iii. 16 The Lord hearkened and heard it, & a booke of remembrance was written before him. **1659** HOWELL *Vocab.* xxxiv, A ring of remembrance, viz. two or three interchain'd [cf. COTGR., *Souvenance*,..a Ring with many hoopes, whereof a man lets one hang downe when he would be put in mind of a thing].

attrib. *a* **1626** W. SCLATER *Comm. Mal.* (1650) 186 He hath also, then, his remembrance-book, his register, for the ungodly.

†**b.** ***bill of remembrance***, a royal letter of authority. *Obs.*

1481 in *Muniment. Magd. Coll. Oxf.* (1882) 15 Dayly to atende tyll I myte haue T.S. at leysere and than breke yᵉ matere and schew to hym yᵉ byll of remembranse. **1580** HOLLYBAND *Treas. Fr. Tong, Vn placet*, a bill of remembrance to an Officer from the prince, a bill of processe. **1582** N. LICHEFIELD tr. *Castanheda's Conq. E. Ind.* 69 He gave him other possessions and rents and a bill of remembrance to make him Lorde.

†**c.** ***Clerk of the Remembrance***, = REMEMBRANCER 1 a. *Obs.*

The Act cited by Cowell is one establishing *un Clerc de la remembrancie.*

1607 COWELL *Interpr.* s.v. *Remembrancer*, These [Remembrancers of the Exchequer] anno 37 Ed. 3. Cap. 4. be called clerks of the Remembrance. [Hence in later Dicts.]

d. ***Garden of Remembrance*** (also with small initials), a garden commemorating the dead, esp. those killed in the world wars of 1914–18 and 1939–45.

1954 J. BETJEMAN *Few Late Chrysanthemums* 46 They'll catch me coming..Across the Garden of Remembrance? No, That would be blasphemy. **1959** *Listener* 22 Jan. 166/1 Here is a statue of Byron... Here are cenotaphs commemorating other philhellenes of several nations... The visit to what is now a garden of remembrance was a profoundly moving experience. **1973** J. ROSSITER *Manipulators* iv. 48 With any luck..I'll find the bastard dead and scattered over a garden of remembrance.

†**8. a.** A note or entry serving as a record or reminder; a memorandum. *Obs.*

1430–1 *Rolls of Parlt.* IV. 376/1 Make oute a remembrance under her seall..resityng ye issue yat is joyned. **1465** *Paston Lett.* II. 202 As for such bokys as he hath hyre at hom he wol doo loke yf any remembraunce canne be founde therof. **1586** A. DAY *Eng. Secretary* II. (1625) 63, I haue laden for your account..according to your remembrance sent vnto me for the same,..seuen Buts of Sack. **1601** HOLLAND *Pliny* II. 172 Set down vnder the hand of the sayd prince, in a priuat note-book of remembrances. *a* **1676** HALE (J.), Those proceedings and remembrances are in the Tower, beginning with the twentieth year of Edward I.

†**b.** A reminder given by one person to another; a remark of this nature. *Obs.*

1597 SHAKS. *2 Hen. IV*, V. ii. 115, I do commit into your hand, Th'vnstained Sword..With this Remembrance; That you vse the same [etc.]. **1612** WOODALL *Surg. Mate* Wks. (1653) 1 Brief remembrances touching the particular instruments for the Surgeons Chest. **1638** CHILLINGW. *Relig. Prot.* I. v. §29. 264 But let the understanding Reader, take with him three or four short remembrances.

c. A reminder given by some thing or fact; a thing or fact serving to remind one of something. Now *rare.*

1617 MORYSON *Itin.* I. 107 The Orange trees..are greene in winter, giuing at that dead time a pleasant remembrance of Sommer. **1663** GERBIER *Counsel* 21 To knock their head against that of the doore, for a remembrance, that they were not to passe the threshold. **1739** WESLEY *Wks.* (1872) I. 174, I was not suffered to conclude my subject; a good remembrance that I should, if possible, declare, at every time, the whole counsel of God. **1789** [see REMARK *sb.*¹ 3 c]. **1806–7** J. BERESFORD *Miseries Hum. Life* (1826) I. Introd., What..[are] dressing and undressing but stinging remembrances of the privileged nakedness of the savage?

9. a. An article serving to remind one person of another; a keepsake, souvenir; a token.

1425 *E.E. Wills* (1882) 63, I wil þat Iohn Ondeley haf a coueryd pece of siluer..for a remembraunce of me. **1463** *Bury Wills* (Camden) 34, iij of my beste gownys..for a remembraunce to thinke vpon me. *c* **1532** DU WES *Introd. Fr.* in Palsgr. 1023 Do nat you bryng me some remembraunce or token from them? **1611** TOURNEUR *Ath. Trag.* II. i, Here's the sad remembrance of his life, Which, for his sake, I will for euer weare. **1724** in *Swift's Lett.* (1768) IV. 13, I desire your acceptance of a ring, a small remembrance of my father. **1845** C. DICKENS *Let.* 2 Oct. (1977) IV. 396, I send you the claret jug. But for a mistake, you would have received the little remembrance almost immediately after my return from abroad.

b. A memorial or record of some fact, person, etc. Now *rare.*

c **1470** HENRY *Wallace* XI. 1458 Go nobill buk,..Now byd thi tym, and be a remembrance. *a* **1533** LD. BERNERS *Gold. Bk. M. Aurel.* (1546) G, His wordes and counsels remayne for a remembraunce. **1590** SPENSER *F.Q.* I. i. 2 On his brest a bloodie Crosse he bore, The deare remembrance of his dying Lord. **1607** TOPSELL *Four-f. Beasts* (1658) 192 That figure which is engraven at Rome in a Marble pillar, being a remembrance of some Triumph. **1822** B. CORNWALL *Dram. Scenes, Rape Proserpine*, And is this fountain left alone For a sad remembrance.

†**c.** A heraldic device. *Obs. rare*⁻¹.

1470–85 MALORY *Arthur* IX. xxx. 384 Tristram.. commaunded..his seruaunt to ordeyne hym a blak sheld with none other remembraunce therin.

10. *attrib.* and *Comb.*, as ***remembrance-banquet***, ***wreath***; **Remembrance Day**, the Sunday nearest to 11 Nov., kept in remembrance of those killed in the world wars of 1914–18 and 1939–45, and since 1945 combined with Armistice Day; **Remembrance Service**, a service held on Remembrance Day; **Remembrance Sunday** = *Remembrance Day*; **Remembrancetide**, the period immediately preceding Remembrance Day, considered as if part of the liturgical year.

1930 R. GRAVES *Ten Poems More* 9 A fresh *remembrance-banquet to forestall The Knight turned hermit. **1921** *Times* 11 Nov. 12/2 We have received a number of appeals which may be specially associated with '*Remembrance Day'. **1929** *Radio Times* 8 Nov. 440/2 Remembrance Day, Nov. 11. Wear a Flanders Poppy. **1946** [see *Armistice Day*]. **1974** P. MCCUTCHAN *Call for Simon Shard* i. 5 The old soldiers had brought a Remembrance Day wreath. **1964** L. DEIGHTON *Funeral in Berlin* I. 312 You have an invitation. It's the *Remembrance Service. **1977** *Belfast Tel.* 14 Feb. 4/6 He would like to tell these people who were sniping at the Legion that its Remembrance services would continue. **1942** C. MILBURN *Diary* 8 Nov. (1979) 157 *Remembrance Sunday, and great news today! American troops have landed in North Africa. **1946** *Glasgow Herald* 31 Oct. 4/4 Remembrance Sunday, when Christians gather to remember the young and brave of two generations who died for freedom and the hope of a better world. **1954** R. MACAULAY *Let.* 7 Nov. in *Last Lett. to Friend* (1962) 175 Remembrance Sunday. A poppy on my coat, another on my car. **1977** B. PYM *Quartet in Autumn* v. 42 The only services that drew congregations of any size were Harvest Festival, Remembrance Sunday and the Carol Service at Christmas. **1970** *Sussex Life* Nov. 73/1 *Remembrancetide this year will occupy the period November 2–8. **1977** *Daily Tel.* 5 Nov. 14 The 20th century has seen the creation of new commemorative rituals—and those of Remembrancetide are not the only ones. **1977** *Lancs. Life* Nov. 74/3 They have invited..a local boy who served in the RAF..to place the *remembrance wreath on their memorial.

re'membrance, *v. rare.* [f. the sb.: cf. REMEMBRANCING *vbl. sb.*] *trans.* To remind.

1593 NASHE *Christ's T.* Wks. (Grosart) IV. 261 Let vs looke for the sworde next to remembrance and warne vs. **1656** G. COLLIER *Answ.* 15 *Quest.* Ded., The best return I am able to make you, is, remembrancing you of your duty.

remembrancer (rɪˈmɛmbrənsə(r)). [a. AF. *remembrancer*: see REMEMBRANCE *sb.* and -ER¹.]

1. †**a.** A local official of some kind. *Obs. rare*⁻¹.

1430–1 *Rolls of Parlt.* IV. 386/1 Robt. Holme Esquyer, Remembrauncer of Guyen..suyng for the good of the Corone of oure Soverayn liege Lorde the Kyng, and for the parties of the Duche of Guyen.

b. The name of certain officials of the Court of Exchequer.

(*a*) The ***King's*** (or ***Queen's***) ***Remembrancer***, an officer responsible for the collection of debts due to the sovereign; now an officer of the Supreme Court. (*b*) The ***Lord Treasurer's Remembrancer***. Now only *Hist.* (abolished by Act 3 & 4 Will. IV, c. 99 §41). (*c*) The ***Remembrancer of the First Fruits***, responsible for the collection of all compositions for first fruits and tenths. Now only *Hist.* (abolished by Act 1 & 2 Vict. c. 20 §1).

[**1354** *Rolls of Parlt.* II. 271/2 Que come en l'Eschequer soient diverses offices & places, Gardein de la Pipe, & de la Somons, Remembrancers.] **1455** *Ibid.* V. 342/2 Remembrauncer of the Kynges Eschequier. **1464** *Ibid.* 529/1 The Office of oure Remembrancer in oure Eschequer. **1566** *Act 8 Eliz.* c. 16 §2 Her or their Graces Officers of Remembrauncer and the Treasourers Remembrancer. **1607** COWELL *Interpr.* s.v., Remembrancers of the Exchequer (*Rememoratores*) be three officers, or clerks, one called the Kings Remembrancer... The third is called the Remembrancer of the first fruites. **1662** *Act 14 Chas. II*, c. 21 §3 That the several Remembrancers of the said Court.. make true and perfect Copies of..such other Seizure and Inquisicion. **1724** SWIFT *Drapier's Lett.* Wks. 1755 V. II. 68 The lord Palmerstown is first remembrancer, worth near 2000*l.* per annum. **1797** *22nd Rep. Sel. Committee on Finance* 4 Upon entering into the Details of the Constitution of this Court, the Officers who first present themselves are the Remembrancers. **1838** *Act 1 & 2 Vict.* c. 20 §11 Henry Warre Esquire, the present Remembrancer of First Fruits and Tenths. **1887** POLLOCK *Land Laws* 8 *note*, These rents are now received by the Queen's Remembrancer a few days before the beginning of Michaelmas term.

†**c.** ***Queen's Remembrancer***, an officer having the administration of the Queen Consort's affairs. *Obs.*

[? **1644** *Cal. St. Papers Chas. I, Dom.* (1890) 212 There has always been an officer called the Remembrancer to the Queens of this nation.] **1647** HAWARD *Crown Rev.* 5 Clerke in the Office of the Queenes Remembrancer.

d. An official of the Corporation of the City of London, whose chief duty now is to represent that body before Parliamentary Committees and at Council and Treasury Boards.

'From the records of the City of London, in the Town Clerk's Office, it appears that the office of Remembrancer was instituted in 1570–1' (*Archaeologia*, 1855, XXXVI. 106).

1710 J. CHAMBERLAYNE *St. Gt. Brit.* II. III. 631 Mr. John Johnson, Remembrancer [of the City of London]. **1770** in *Examiner* (1812) 4 May 286/1 Lord Denbigh came up to the City Remembrancer. **1802–12** BENTHAM *Ration. Judic. Evid.* (1827) II. 590 *note*, In the official establishment of the city of London there still exists one officer, the remembrancer [etc.]. **1837** *Municip. Corporations* (Eng. & Wal.) *2nd Rep., London* 45 The Remembrancer is elected by the Common Council. **1882** *Times* 1 Mar. 9/6 Mr. Robarts ..was elected City Remembrancer in 1878, at a salary of 1,500*l.* per annum.

2. One who reminds another; in former use, *esp.* one engaged or appointed for that purpose. (Common in 16–17th c.) Also, a memoirist, a chronicler.

1523 SKELTON *Garl. Laurel* 864 To be your remembrauncer, madame, I am bounde. **1571** GOLDING *Calvin on Ps.* xxxix. 13 God knoweth welynough without a remembrancer, that men have but a short journey to walk upon earth. **1645** DURYE *Israel's Call* 28 You have put me in this place, to be your remembrancer in the name of the

Lord. **1687** R. L'ESTRANGE *Answ. Diss.* 22, I think it would not do Amiss, if the Dissenter should Counter-Advise his Remembrancer upon Two or Three of these Last Points. **1771** SMOLLETT *Humph. Cl.* 28 Apr., Let. ii, If I had not been an ass, I should not have needed a remembrancer. **1835** BROWNING *Paracelsus* II. 42 What does this Remembrancer set down concerning life? **1865** *Examiner* 18 Mar. 161 It is his chosen office to be Remembrancer of all wrongs. **1951** [see CONTINUITY 6]. **1957** *Times* 8 Aug. 8/2 Both [wrote] personal portraits and reminiscences. In both cases Posterity will need to bear in mind that they are not always reliable remembrancers. **1968** G. JONES *Hist. Vikings* IV. ii. 356 Byrhtnoth's brave but..foolhardy stand..found no remembrancer among the victors.

3. *fig.* **a.** of things; also, a thing serving to remind one; a reminder; a memento, souvenir.

1589 G. HARVEY *Pierces Supererog.* Wks. (Grosart) II. 138 Consideration is a good Counsellour: & Reading, no badd Remembrancer. **1594** KYD *Cornelia* III. i. 13 Sweet teares of loue, remembrancers to tyme. **1607** DONNE in *Four C. Eng. Lett.* (1880) 62 No searching vehemencies..made you need so shadowy an example or remembrancer. **1666** J. DAVIES *Hist. Caribby Isles* 297 Their stomacks are their Clocks and Remembrancers. **1778** [W. MARSHALL] *Minutes Agric., Digest* 144 This Diary is the basis of the other accounts, and serves as an almost-infallible Remembrancer. **1809** MALKIN *Gil Blas* x. ii. ¶10, I fell dangerously ill there; and that timely remembrancer was the cause of bringing back your son to you. **1867** HOWELLS *Ital. Journ.* 252 A bit of the sacred wood for a remembrancer.

b. A reminder *of* something.

c **1610** SIR J. MELVIL *Mem.* (1735) 286, I had indited a long Letter..as a Remembrancer of his former Promises. **1682** WHELER *Journ. Greece* III. 263 There are some Remains of noble Structures, Remembrancers of their prosperous State. **1766** GOLDSM. *Vic. W.* iii, Premature consolation is but the remembrancer of sorrow. **1829** SOUTHEY *Sir T. More* (1831) II. 253 You have in them speaking remembrancers of mortality. **1851** HAWTHORNE *Ho. Sev. Gables* v, The..freckles, friendly remembrancers of the April sun and breeze.

c. Used as the title of a book or pamphlet.

1585 HIGINS (*title*) The Nomenclator, or Remembrancer of Adrianus Iunius.., conteining proper names and apt termes for all thinges. **1628** WITHER (*title*) Britain's Remembrancer, containing a Narration of the Plague lately past. **1670** BARKSDALE (*title*) A Remembrancer of Excellent Men. **1749** H. WALPOLE *Lett.* (1846) II. 288 There was a Remembrancer on that subject ready for the press. **1788** (*title*) Egerton's Theatrical Remembrancer, a list of all dramatic performances. **1867** (*title*) The Churchman's Daily Remembrancer, Meditations from Standard Divines.

†**d.** A register or record. *Obs.*

1671 N. PHILIPOT (*title*) Reasons..for a Registry or Remembrancer of all Deeds and Incumbrances of Real Estates.

e. A memorandum-book.

1842 THACKERAY *Fitz-Boodle Papers, Dorothea*, Taking from her waist a little mother-of-pearl remembrancer, she notes them down.

†**4.** One who sends remembrances to another.

1700 PEPYS *Let.* 8 Feb., Captain Hatton, who was my guest to-day and your kind remembrancer.

5. One who seeks to remember.

1798 EDGEWORTH *Pract. Educ.* (1811) II. 245 Here are things mentioned which will much assist the young remembrancer.

Hence **re'membrancership**, the office of remembrancer.

1882 *Times* 1 Mar. 9/6 The Court of Common Council looked upon the Remembrancership as a post given for the term of a year only.

re'membrancing, *vbl. sb.* [See REMEMBRANCE *sb.* and *v.*] The act of remembering or reminding; a reminder.

c **1449** PECOCK *Repr.* II. viii. 188 That men visite and haunte for the seide eende of solempne remembrauncing tho placis and tho ymagis, which it is sure God to chese. **1627** W. SCLATER *Exp. 2 Thess.* (1629) 290 Minding, Remembrancing, putting in minde of dutie. **1800** COLERIDGE *Piccolom.* I. ii. 134 This is no more than a remembrancing That you are now in camp. **1825** LAMB *Elia* Ser. II. *Barbara S——*, [These little books] were precious to her for their affecting remembrancings. **1952** *Essays in Criticism* II. II. 150 Many religious poems in English had a Latin refrain which gave the recurrent gesture of authority and devotional remembrancing.

†**re'membrative**, *a.* and *sb. Obs.* [f. REMEMBER *v.*[1] + -ATIVE: cf. REMEMORATIVE.]

A. *adj.* Mindful; keeping in, or bringing to, mind.

14.. *Pol. Rel. & L. Poems* (1866) 38 Riche is it nat,..Saue an hert [that] is reme[m]bratyf to you in eueri stounde. *c* **1449** PECOCK *Repr.* v. xii. 546 No more conuenient, redier, and ofter seen..remembratijf signe..couthe be founde. **1662** J. CHANDLER *Van Helmont's Oriat.* 269 Where that remembrative memory is not a distinct act.

B. *sb.* A memorial, reminder.

? *c* **1470** G. ASHBY *Active Policy* 11 Ye had lafte to vs..sum remembratife Of a personne lerned & Inuentif.

remembre, -bur, -byr, obs. ff. REMEMBER.

†**re'memorable**, *a. Obs. rare*$^{-1}$. [Cf. REMEMORATE *v.*] Memorable.

a **1641** BP. MOUNTAGU *Acts & Mon.* (1642) 316 Many excellent and rememorable acts.

†**re'memorance.** *Obs.* [a. OF. *rememorance* (13th c.): see next and -ANCE, and cf. It. *rimemoranza* (Florio).] Remembrance.

c **1449** PECOCK *Repr.* II. vi. 171 Bi this rememoraunce the remembrer, if he wole, schal be the more stired to araie and dispose him thidirward. *c* **1470** HARDING *Chron.* LXIII. v, Nowe menne it call, by all rememoraunce, Constantyne noble. **1549** *Compl. Scot.* i. 21 Is nocht that nobil toune extinct furtht of rememorance?

†**re'memorant**, *a. Obs. rare*$^{-1}$. [ad. L. *rememorant-em*, or a. F. *remémorant*: see next and -ANT.] Mindful.

1549 *Compl. Scot.* xx. 175 Than thir tua armes past to githir in gude accord, nocht rememorant of there deidly ald fede that vas betuix them.

†**re'memorate**, *v. Obs.* [ad. ppl. stem of late L. *rememorārī* (Tert., Vulg.), *-āre*: see REMEMBER, and cf. F. *remémorer* (16th c.), It. *rimemorare.*]

a. *trans.* To remind, put in mind (of). Also *absol.* **b.** *intr.* To remember. Hence †**re'memorating** *vbl. sb.*

1460–70 in C. Innes *Sk. Early Sc. Hist.* App. (1861) 506 Pleis it your lordchypis to be remmemorat the vrangous occupatioun of our landis. **1606** BRYSKETT *Civ. Life* 121 Whether our learning be but a rememorating of things which we knew formerly, or else a learning a new. *Ibid.* 128 We shall euer find the like difficulties, whether we rememorate or learne anew. *a* **1670** HACKET *Cent. Serm.* (1675) 691 Ascension-day..rememorates every year that He is gone up into heaven. **1685** *Gracian's Courtiers Orac.* 68 To inform, is far better than to put in mind. Sometimes we are to rememorate, sometimes advise.

rememo'ration. Now *rare.* [ad. late L. *rememorātiōn-em* (Vulg.): see prec. and -ATION, and cf. F. *remémoration* (14th c.).] The action of remembering (†or reminding); an instance of this, †a recalling to mind.

c **1449** PECOCK *Repr.* II. viii. 182 The rememoracioun or the remembraunce of thilk thing..must needis be the febler. **1597** J. KING *On Jonas* (1618) 431 The same word of the Lord agaïne repeated in my text tieth mee to a rememoration of the same particulars. **1624** BP. MOUNTAGU *Gagg* 318 The Protestants..use them for helps of piety, in rememoration, and more effectuall representing of the Prototype. **1654** JER. TAYLOR *Real Pres.* 129 A representing of his body crucified, a rememoration of his crucifixion. **1893** SALTUS *Madam Sapphira* 172 In unconscious rememoration of the famous retort.

†**re'memorative**, *a.* and *sb. Obs.* [f. as REMEMORATE *v.* + -IVE, perh. after a med.L. **rememorātīvus*: cf. F. *remémoratif* (1527).]

A. *adj.* Serving to remind. Also const. *of*.

c **1449** PECOCK *Repr.* II. ii. 136 The setting vp of ymagis in chirchis and the vsing of hem as rememoratijf or mynding signes. **1625** BP. MOUNTAGU *App. Cæsar* 287 Only [a] representative, rememorative, and spirituall Sacrifice. *a* **1641** —— *Acts & Mon.* (1642) 90 'Ιστορικον, Rememorative of actions done.

B. *sb.* A reminder.

1624 BP. MOUNTAGU *Gagg* 315 This Serpent..was a Rememorative of salvation extended by the Sonne of God. **1676** *Life Father Sarpi* in *Brent's Counc. Trent* 39 With little Notes of his own.., but so short,..that one may easily perceive that..he wrote to himself alone for rememoratives.

†**re'memorize**, *v.*[1] *Obs. rare*$^{-1}$. [Cf. REMEMORATE *v.*] *trans.* To recall to mind.

1634 SIR T. HERBERT *Trav.* 110 Melek Bahaman perceives the losse of his liberty when past recovery, rememorizes his sonnes advice [etc.].

re-'memorize (riː-), *v.*[2] [RE- 5 a.] *trans.* To commit again to memory.

1869 A. J. ELLIS *E.E. Pronunc.* II. vi. §3. 618 Even those who employed it would have to re-memorize every word in the language.

†**re'memory**, *sb. Obs. rare*$^{-1}$. [Cf. REMEMORANCE.] Remembrance.

c **1470** HARDING *Chron.* XIV. ii, He made theim wryten, for long rememory, To rule the Isle by theim perpetually.

remen ('rɛmɛn). [Ancient Egyptian.] An ancient Egyptian measure of length (see quots.).

1934 F. PETRIE *Measures & Weights* 5 *Remen* (½ of 29·2 in.). The *Remen* doubled was the diagonal of the square cubit, 29·161 [in.]. **1959** *Chambers's Encycl.* IX. 183/1 The Egyptian royal cubit (20·63 ± 0·2 in. or 524 ± 5 mm)... From this cubit was formed the double remen, the length of the diagonal of a square with sides equal to the royal cubit. Thus, the double remen was equal to $\sqrt{2} \times 20{\cdot}63$ in. (29·16 in., 740·66 mm). This was the basis of the ancient Egyptian land measure. **1969** *Listener* 18 Dec. 859/3 The Royal cubit is $\sqrt{2}$ Egyptian remens, i.e. the diagonal of a 1 × 1 remen square. The 'Megalithic yard' is thus $\sqrt{5}$ remens, or the diagonal of a 2 × 1 remen rectangle.

†'**remenant.** *Obs.* Forms: α. 4–6 **remenant(e, -aunt(e,** (4 **-ont,** 5 **-ent),** 4–5 **-and,** 5 **remunaunde, remynaunte.** β. 4–6 **remanant,** 5–6 **-aunt(e,** 5 *north.* and *Sc.* **-and, -aunde,** (5 *Sc.* **ra-**). γ. 5 **remelant, -aunt, -awnt, remulant.** [a. OF. *remenant, remanant* (AF. *-aunt*), pres. pple. of *remenoir, remanoir* to REMAIN. See also REMAINANT and REMNANT.]

1. The rest or remainder of a number of persons or (rarely) things; the others. Also *pl.*

α. **13..** *K. Alis* 5707 The remenaunt than fleigh on hast, Bisiden into a riche cite. *c* **1385** CHAUCER *L.G.W.* Prol. 304 Fyrst sat the god of loue & thanne this queene..And sithyn al the remenant by & by. *c* **1400** MAUNDEV. (Roxb.) xi. 42 Þe remenaunt he putte in presoun. **1470–85** MALORY *Arthur* I. iii. 39 Kyng Vthers men..slewe many peple & putt the remenaunt to flight. **1546** *Supplic. Poore Commons* (E.E.T.S.) 63 Not withstandynge that the remenaunt of the sturdy beggers..do daylye..stere vs thereunto. *pl.* *c* **1330** R. BRUNNE *Chron. Wace* (Rolls) 3338 Belyn & Brenne..wente..To..take truage of þe remenauntz [*v.r.* heue trewage at Remanans].

β. *c* **1330** *Arth. & Merl.* 6210 (Kölbing), A þousand & mo þai slowen, þe remanant of hors drowen. **1375** BARBOUR *Bruce* VII. 337 Till thar host the remanand fled. *c* **1400** MAUNDEV. (Roxb.) vii. 27 Twa of þam er wonder hie and wyde also, and þe remanand er noȝt so hie. *c* **1470** HENRY *Wallace* III. 185 The ramanand apon thaim folowit fast. **1534** MORE *Treat. Passion* Wks. 1310/2 He myghte thereby haue giuen occasyon of enuye..to Iudas, or peraduenture grefe to the remanant. **1573** J. TYRIE in *Cath. Tract.* (S.T.S.) 17 Ye and the remanant of your propheites ar alluterlie separat from the trew kirk.

2. The rest or remainder of a thing or aggregate of things; that which, or all that, is left over.

α. *c* **1315** SHOREHAM I. 1060 Beter hys þat hy a lyte do her ..And foluelle þat remenaunt Ine purgatoryes tense. ? *a* **1366** CHAUCER *Rom. Rose* 1024 Hir nose, hir mouth, and eye and cheke Wel wrought, and alle the remenaunt eke. *c* **1400** MAUNDEV. (1839) xxi. 230 In alle the remenant of the World, ne myghte a man fynde a more reverent man. **1430** *E.E. Wills* (1882) 87 All the Remenent of my gode & Catell y bequeth to my wif. **1473** in Arnolde *Chron.* (1811) 245 The whiche I reserue to the performyng of the remenaunt off my legates conteyned in this mi testament. **1536** *Act 28 Hen. VIII*, c. 11 §11 Suche rent and seruyces, as for the remenaunt of the sayde yere, shall vppon euery suche lease be due. **1560** DAUS tr. *Sleidane's Comm.* 54 Claude, Duke of Guise..had gathered up the remenaunt of the Frenche armye dispersed at the battle of Pavie.

β. *c* **1375** *Sc. Leg. Saints* xvi. (*Magdalene*) 79 þe remanand dystribut scho to pure mene. **1423** JAS. I *Kingis Q.* clxxi, Spend wele, therefore, the remanant of the day. **1477** EARL RIVERS (Caxton) *Dictes* 68 A wyseman ought..to kepe wele the remanaunt of his good. **1566** in Peacock *Eng. Ch. Furniture* (1866) 88 The Remanaunt to the poore.

γ. *c* **1440** *York Myst.* xxvii. 23 The remelaunt parted schall be. **1462** *Paston Lett.* II. 98, ij c. and l. mark to bene payed at this Estern and the remulant at Mihelmasse. And of the remulant the Kyng shuld be answered.

b. = REMAINDER I. *rare*$^{-1}$.

1544 tr. *Littleton's Tenures* 51 Yf the lorde wil graunt the homage of his lande by his dede to another, sauynge to hym the remenaunt of the seruyces.

3. A remaining thing or part; a remnant.

c **1330** R. BRUNNE *Chron.* (1810) 16 The tothere remenant [F. *le remanaunt*] of the north son salle thei nomen. **1406** *E.E. Wills* (1882) 13 All the remenauntys of my godys, y wyll they be preysyd & parttyd in thre. *Ibid.* 37 Also ij remenauntz of the Lynne bed. **1433** *Rolls of Parlt.* IV. 452/1 The same Clothe to be sold for a remenaunt..and nat for a Clothe.

4. *a remenant*, for the future, henceforward.

c **1330** R. BRUNNE *Chron.* (1810) 115 Ȝe wite wele a remenant [F. *desore*] & forsoth ȝe kenne, þat Inglis & Normant be now ons men.

remenbre, obs. form of REMEMBER.

re'mend (riː-), *v.* [RE- 5 a.] To mend again.

1592 WYRLEY *Armorie, Ld. Chandos* 73 What harme they should His countrie do, that he remend it would.

†**re'mene**, *v. Obs.* [perh. a. OF. *remener* to bring back; but the senses are app. not OF., and may be based upon those of MEAN *v.*[1]]

1. *trans.* To make mention of; to commemorate; to recall to mind.

13.. *Gaw. & Gr. Knt.* 2483 Mony a-venture..þat I ne tyȝt, at þis tyme, in tale to remene. *c* **1400** tr. *Secreta Secret., Gov. Lordsh.* 56 He shal turne hym to þe poeple to prayse hem..and remene [*pr.* remeue] & recomend her gode maneres. *c* **1440** *Macro Plays* (E.E.T.S.) 67/960 Put yt, Lorde, in-to my thowte! Thi olde mercy, let me remene.

2. To compare; to apply by way of comparison or illustration. Const. *to*.

1377 *Pol. Poems* (Rolls) I. 216 This good ship I may remene To the chivalrye of this londe. **1387** TREVISA *Higden* (Rolls) II. 371 þat by þe tale þat is i-feyned þe sooþ by tokenynge may be remened [*printed* remeued: L. *referatur*] to þat þat is soþeliche i-doo in deede. **1390** GOWER *Conf.* I. 51 To thi matiere Of love I schal hem so remene, That thou schalt knowe what thei mene. [Cf. II. 348.] *c* **1440** *York Myst.* xii. 50 þe dewe to þe gode halygaste May be remened [*printed* remeued] in mannes mynde.

3. To interpret, expound, explain. Also *absol.*

1382 WYCLIF *Neh.* viii. 9 Esdras..and the Leuitus, remenyng [1388 expownynge; L. *interpretantes*] to al the puple. *Ibid.* 13 That he remene to them the woordis of the lawe. *c* **1440** CAPGRAVE *Life St. Kath.* IV. 2271 This same figure oure clerkis thus remene.

Hence †**re'mening** *vbl. sb.*; also †**re'menour**, interpreter, translator. *Obs.*

1382 WYCLIF *Ezra* Prol., Leuende the sens of scripture he folewide the errour of eche remenour. —— *Prov.* Prol., The remenyng..of the thre volumes of Salomon. *Ibid.*, The translacioun of the seuenty remenoures. —— *Ecclus.* xlvii. 18 In prouerbis, and comparisouns, and in remenyngus.

remenent, -ont, varr. REMENANT *Obs.*

rement, obs. form of RAIMENT.

†**rementimu'tation.** *nonce-wd.* A second or fresh change of mind.

1650 B. *Discolliminium* 45, I and my Friends shall be allowed the full benefit of all the variations, interpretations, ..mentimutations, rementimutations,..that I and my Mare can devise or possibly imagine.

†**re'merce**, *v. Obs. rare*$^{-1}$. [app. f. RE- + *-merce* as in COMMERCE *v.*] *trans.* To ransom.

1559 BALDWIN *Mirr. Mag., Earl Northumbld.* G v, And that we might this matter set on fyre From Owens iayle, our cosin we remerst.

†**re'merciment.** *Obs. rare.* [a. F. *remercîment*, f. *remercier*: see REMERCY *v.*] *pl.* Thanks.
1654 FLECKNOE *Ten Years Trav.* iv. 8 To whom I answered (after my most humble remerciments for so high a favour) That as I yet wanted nothing [etc.]. **1777** C'TESS OSSORY in Jesse *Selwyn & Contemp.* (1844) III. 189 Begging you to accept our kindest remercimen[t]s for your good company.

†**re'mercy,** *sb. Obs. rare.* [Cf. next and MERCY.] Thanks. Also *pl.*
1542 UDALL *Erasm. Apoph.* 163 b, Persones by hym conquered and subdued, who did..not rendre thankes ne saie remercies for that they had been leat..to escape. **1600** B. JONSON *Cynthia's Rev.* v. ii. Wks. (Rtldg.) 95/2 Remercie, madame, and these honourable censors. **1606** *Sir G. Goosecappe* III. i, Remercy, my more then English pages.

†**re'mercy,** *v. Obs.* [ad. F. *remercier* (15th c.), f. *re-* RE- + *merci* thanks, MERCY.] To thank.
c **1477** CAXTON *Jason* 28 b, Thenne Jason remercyed and thanked the noble Quene Myrro. **1484** —— *Fables of Alfonce* xii, I remercye and thanke yow gretely. **1568** in Maskell *Mon. Rit.* (1846) II. 264 Wyth al my hert I remercye and thanke thee. **1590** SPENSER *F.Q.* II. xi. 16 She him remercied as the Patrone of her life. **1592** WYRLEY *Armorie* 115 With thanks rewards remercied was our paine.

re'merge (riː-), *v.* [RE- 5 a.] To merge again.
1850 TENNYSON *In Mem.* xlvii, That each, who seems a separate whole,..should fall Remerging in the general Soul. **1901** *Spectator* 17 Aug. 221/2 A remoter realm, out of which we emerged, and into which we again remerge.

remeta'morphose, *v.* Also 7 -ise. [RE- 5 a.] *trans.* To change back again.
1598 J. DICKENSON *Greene in Conc.* (1878) 138 When Vlisses mates turn'd from men to beastes..they would in no sort be remetamorphosed. **1636** HEYWOOD *Loves Mistress* I. i. Wks. 1874 V. 92 If men be growne thus savage, oh you powers, Remetamorphise mee into an asse.

re'mete, *v. rare*⁻¹. [RE-] *trans.* To mete out in return.
1647 TRAPP *Comm., Matt.* vii. 2 God delights to give men their own,..to re-mete them their own measure.

remeue, obs. variant of REMOVE *v.*

†**re'mevable,** *a. Obs.* [f. *remeve*, var. REMOVE *v.* + -ABLE.] Capable of being moved; liable to remove, or to be taken away.
1422 tr. *Secreta Secret., Priv. Priv.* 215 Thoures [= towers] of trees reme[v]able thou shalte I-have ouer al, and Knyghtes there-in wel armyd. *c* **1430** LYDG. *Min. Poems* (Percy Soc.) 193 The world so wyd, the air so remevable,.. The fyr so hoot and sotil of nature. **1461** *Rolls of Parlt.* V. 493/2 Afore tyme they were datyf and remevabill.

remeve, obs. variant of REMOVE *v.*

†**re'mevement.** *Obs. rare.* [f. *remeve*, var. REMOVE *v.* + -MENT.] Removal, transference.
1437 *Rolls of Parlt.* IV. 510/1 Withoute eny remevement to be hadde of him into the seid prison. **1439** *Ibid.* V. 29/2 The..delyverance and remevement of the said Recordes.

remewe, obs. variant of REMOVE *v.*; variant of REMUE *v. Obs.*

remex ('riːmɛks). Pl. **remiges** ('rɛmɪdʒiːz). [L. *rēmex*, f. *rēmus* oar.]
†**1.** A rower. *Obs. rare*⁻¹.
1674 PETTY *Disc. Dupl. Proportion* 57 If one Remex or Skuller move [a boat of]..3 inches draught 12000 feet forward in 3600 seconds: then 4 like Rowers [etc.].
2. *Ornith.* One of the principal feathers of a bird's wing, by which it is sustained and carried forward in flight; a wing-quill. Chiefly *pl.*
1767 G. WHITE *Selborne* xii, Peculiar crimson tags..at the ends of five of the short remiges. **1797** *Encycl. Brit.* (ed. 3) XIII. 505/2 The primary and secondary wing-feathers are called *remiges*. **1874** COUES *Birds N.W.* 269 The wings.. have but six remiges, in addition to the ten primaries. **1887** *Athenæum* 16 Apr. 517/3 The absence..of the fifth cubital remex, its coverts only being developed.

remeynant, variant of REMAINANT *Obs.*

remicle ('rɛmɪk(ə)l). *Ornith.* [f. L. *rēmi(g-, rēmex* REMEX: see *-cle* s.v. -CULE.] A smaller outermost primary wing feather in some birds.
1887 R. S. WRAY in *Proc. Zool. Soc.* 344 [In the wild-duck's wing] the distal predigital (11) is always small and is designated the remicle. **1924** *Bull. Amer. Museum Nat. Hist.* L. 316 In the three specimens of *Gavia stellata* seen in the flesh the normal number of quills, ten large ones and the remicle, were present. **1964** A. L. THOMSON *New Dict. Birds* 665/2 In most non-passerine species there are—not counting a remicle, if present..—10 primaries in normal individuals.

remiform ('rɛmɪfɔːm), *a. rare*⁻⁰. [f. L. *rēmus* oar.] Shaped like an oar.
1860 WORCESTER (citing Smart, but app. by mistake for *reniform*): hence in later Dicts.

†'**remigable,** *a. Obs. rare*⁻¹. [f. L. *rēmigāre*: see next and -ABLE.] That one may row over.
1685 COTTON tr. *Montaigne* xxx. (1869) 167 Where steril remigable marshes, now Feed neighb'ring cities, and admit the plough.

'**remigate,** *v. rare.* [f. ppl. stem of L. *rēmigāre*, f. *rēmex* REMEX.] *intr.* To row.
1623 COCKERAM, *Remigate*, to row, or row backe. **1873** LELAND *Egypt. Sketch Bk.* 260 The rascally darkeys.. declined 'tracking' (which is pulling), or remigating (which is rowing).

remi'gation. *rare.* [ad. L. *rēmigātiōn-em*: see prec. and -ATION.] The action of rowing.
Erroneously defined by Cockeram and Blount, through association of the initial letters with the prefix *re-*.
1623 COCKERAM, *Remigation*, a rowing backe. **1656** BLOUNT *Glossogr.*, *Remigation*, a rowing or sailing back again. **1842** *Blackw. Mag.* LII. 726 A man, versed in Latin and Greek, is not, therefore, acquainted with the mechanic laws of remigation or of shipbuilding.

'**remigatory,** *a. rare.* [f. L. *rēmigāt-*, ppl. stem of *rēmigāre* to row + -ORY².] Pertaining to or connected with rowing.
1911 J. MUNRO *F. J. Furnivall: a Record* p. xvii, A special providence seems to have guarded over Furnivall on his remigatory excursions.

re'migial, *a. rare.* [f. L. *rēmigi-um* rowing, or (in mod. use) f. *remig-es* (see REMEX) + -(I)AL.] Serving to propel; now *Ornith.*, of or pertaining to the remiges of a bird's wing.
1592 R. D. *Hypnerotomachia* 21 His hands tooke fast hould upon the remigiall bones of the Eagles pinions. **1879** NEWTON in *Encycl. Brit.* X. 712/1 In this the remigial streamers do not lose their barbs.

†**remigrable.** *Obs. rare*⁻¹. [See next and -ABLE.] Capable of changing back again.
1669 W. SIMPSON *Hydrol. Chym.* 255 They themselves are yet remigrable into a more simple element.

remigrate ('rɛmɪgreɪt, riː'maɪgreɪt), *v.* [orig. (with stress '*remigrate*) f. ppl. stem of L. *remigrāre*; in later use f. RE- 5 a + MIGRATE *v.*]
†**1.** *intr.* To change back again. *Obs.*
1601 CHESTER *Love's Mart.*, etc. (1878) 177 Ought into nought can neuer remigrate. **1651** BIGGS *New Disp.* ¶288 Whatsoever that is truly vital hath once degenerated..never remigrates again from the winter of its privation. **1680** BOYLE *Scept. Chem.* II. 126 The rest, which is incomparably the greater part of the Liquor, will remigrate into Phlegm.
2. To migrate again or back.
1623 COCKERAM, *Remigrate*, to returne vnto his first dwelling. **1790** BEWICK *Hist. Quadrup.* 104 In autumn, the Deer, with the fawns bred during the summer, remigrate northward. **1802** MONTAGU *Ornith. Dict.* (1831) 523 The Turtle [dove]..re-migrates the beginning of September. **1893** F. ADAMS *New Egypt* 40 It is not till..a sultan re-migrated from Tunis to the East, that Egypt once more found herself the seat of empire.

remi'gration. [See prec. and MIGRATION.] The action of remigrating; return.
1608 WILLET *Hexapla Exod.* 35 The Pythagoreans and Platonists..dreame of the remigration and returne of the soule to the bodie. *a* **1676** HALE *Prim. Orig. Man.* II. x. (1677) 233 There was a Return of the Jews under Cyrus, which continued in Partial Remigrations for some time after. **1759** B. MARTIN *Nat. Hist. Eng.* I. 170 *note*, The Time of their Remigration is soon after Harvest. **1859** DARWIN *Orig. Spec.* xii. (1878) 331 The first migration when the cold came on, and the re-migration on the returning warmth.

remile, variant of RIMEL *Obs.*

re'militarize (riː-), *v.* [RE- 5 a.] *trans.* To re-arm (a country or territory that has earlier been disarmed or demilitarized). So **remilitari'zation.**
1937 *Nation* 28 Aug. 215/1 Since the remilitarization of the Reich. **1939** WEBSTER Add., *Remilitarize*.., to prepare or equip again with military forces, defenses, etc. **1944** D. THOMSON *French Foreign Policy* (Oxf. Pamphlets World Affairs LXVII) 5 In 1936..Hitler paved the way for all further aggressions by occupying and remilitarizing the left bank of the Rhine. **1969** *Daily Tel.* 5 Feb. 24/6 The explicit intention to re-militarise Sinai and encourage terrorist groups. **1976** *Survey* Summer–Autumn 13 The status quo ..trend in Soviet policy between 1964 and 1973 was obscured by..remilitarization of the stagnant economy.

re-'mimic, *v.* [RE- 5 a.] To mimic again.
1856 DE QUINCEY *Confess.* 98 The scene in the poem, that had been originally mimicked by the poet from the sky, was here re-mimicked and rehearsed to the life.

remind (rɪ'maɪnd), *v.* Also 7 **re-mind.** [f. RE- 5 a + MIND *v.*]
1. a. *trans.* To recall (a thing) to one's own mind; to remember, recollect. Now *rare* or *Obs.*
1645 WITHER *Vox Pacif.* 189 Let him re-minde, what Attributes were given. **1675** R. BURTHOGGE *Causa Dei* 194 Whosoever seriously Reminds the Circumstance of Time wherein the Apostle wrote..will easily agree that [etc.]. **1706** WATTS *Horæ Lyr.* II. *Victory of Poles over Osman*, This the fierce Saracen wore, (for, when a boy, I was their captive, and remind their dress). **1788** SHIRREFS *Poems* (1790) 167 Ye'll now remind the happy show'r o' rain. **1826** ANDERSON *Poems* 36 (E.D.D.), Their merry homefair I remind. **1859** BARTLETT *Dict. Amer.*, *To Remind*, for remember; as 'the company will please remind'. A New York vulgarism.
†**b.** To bring to mind, to recall to another's mind. *Obs. rare.*
1647 N. BACON *Disc. Govt. Eng.* I. lvii. (1739) 104 The issue whereof may remind, that too much countersecurity from the King to the people, is like so many Covenants in Marriage. **1669** EARL ORRERY *Black Prince* III, O! do not wound me by reminding Things Which rather Trouble than Repentance brings.
2. a. To put (one) in mind *of* something. Also with omission of personal obj., *absol.*, and with direct speech as obj.
1660 JER. TAYLOR *Duct. Dubit.* I. i. rule 1 §16 It hath no other force upon the Conscience but that it re-minds us of a special obligation to thankfulness. **1675** R. BURTHOGGE *Causa Dei* 91 This Re-minds me of the second thing which I propounded to be evinced. **1697** J. SERGEANT *Solid Philos.* C ij, By re-minding them often of such Important Truths. **1751** ELIZA HEYWOOD *Betsy Thoughtless* II. 39, I must intreat you will give me leave to remind you of the consequences. **1791** MRS. RADCLIFFE *Rom. Forest* ix, You do well to remind me of this. **1847** MARRYAT *Childr. N. Forest* xi, They would always have reminded me of such a melancholy accident. **1884** F. M. CRAWFORD *Rom. Singer* I. 19 It reminds me of him and his ways. **1887** *Pall Mall G.* 11 Jan. 14/1 Many of the names remind of celebrated episodes. **1887** E. JOHNSON *Antiqua Mater* 260 Little but the mere name Christus to remind of the current beliefs of Judaism. **1891** KIPLING *Light that Failed* xiv. 291 It will recall and remind and suggest and tantalise, and in the end drive you mad. **1966** D. F. GALOUYE *Lost Perception* ii. 24 'Manuel sent the last two messages,' Gregson reminded. *Ibid.* iv. 44 Forsythe withdrew from his sightless isolation long enough to remind, 'Next week's Thanksgiving.' **1976** B. FREEMANTLE *November Man* vii. 95 'The details..indicated criticism of the Soviet Union,' reminded Kodes.
b. Const. with *inf.* or obj. clause.
1662 H. MORE *Philos. Writ.* Pref. Gen. (1712) 5 That the High Priest..might be re-minded not to do..any thing contrary to the laws thereof. **1670** H. STUBBE *Reply Def. Roy. Soc.* (1671) 14, I must remind this Adversary that the person I designed to accompany..was a Carmelite. **1675** EARL ESSEX *Lett.* (1770) 206, I must also again remind you to advise Mr. Harbord to go more plainly to work. **1741–2** GRAY *Agrippina* Wks. 1884 I. 107, I might remind my mistress that her nod Can rouse eight hardy legions. **1820** SHELLEY *Œd. Tyr.* II. i. 78 Allow me to remind you, grass is green. **1867** DICKENS *Lett.* (1880) II. 287 The time of year reminds me how the months have gone. **1875** JOWETT *Plato* (ed. 2) IV. 408 We may be reminded that in nature there is a centripetal as well as a centrifugal force.
Hence **re'mindal,** the act of reminding.
1883–8 BP. WALSHAM HOW *Comm. N.T.* (S.P.C.K.) Matt. xxii. 3 The remindal and summons to the feast were made by John the Baptist.

reminder (rɪ'maɪndə(r)). [f. prec. + -ER¹.] Something which reminds, or is intended to remind, one; mention made for the purpose of reminding.
1653 H. MORE *Antid. Ath.* I. v. §2 There is an active and actuall Knowledge in a man, of which these outward Objects are rather the re-minders then the first Begetters or Implanters. **1831** ARNOLD in Stanley *Life* (1844) I. vi. 270, I know it is good to have these sobering reminders. **1838** DICKENS *Lett.* (1880) I. 11 Your..reminder of the subject of a pleasant conversation. **1880** MEREDITH *Tragic Com.* (1881) 211 Time passed, whole days: the tender reminder had no effect on him!
b. *Path.* in *pl.* Secondary syphilitic symptoms.
1897 *Allbutt's Syst. Med.* II. 260 They escape the class of phenomena grouped as 'reminders' (the intermediate stage) and are to all appearance cured. **1897** J. HUTCHINSON in *Arch. Surg.* VIII. 230 In 1880 a mild attack of syphilis occurred, not, however, followed by reminders.

re'mindful, *a.* [f. as prec. + -FUL.]
1. Mindful, retaining the memory, *of.*
1810 SOUTHEY *Kehama* XI. i, Remindful of revengeful thoughts. *a* **1845** HOOD *Bianca's Dream* xxxii, Meanwhile, remindful of the convent bars, Bianca did not watch these signs in vain. **1891** MEREDITH *One of our Conq.* III. x. 209 He was in some amazement at himself, remindful of the different nature of our restraining power [etc.].
2. Reminiscent, reviving the memory, *of.*
1864 R. A. ARNOLD *Cotton Fam.* 85 The dropping patter so remindful of their blameless inactivity. **1867** E. YATES *Forlorn Hope* xiv, A thousand little reminiscences..each touchingly remindful of something pleasant.

re'minding, *ppl. a.* [-ING².] That reminds. Hence **re'mindingly** *adv.*
1872 GEO. ELIOT *Middlemarch* II. IV. xxxvii. 271 Even the pale stag seemed to have reminding glances. **1887** A. AUSTIN *Pr. Lucifer* IV. ii, The stroke of the reminding hour when I Should from your voice be willing to depart. **1890** 'ANNIE THOMAS' *On the Children* III. i. 8 'You've forgotten',.. Florence said remindingly.

re'minding, *vbl. sb.* [f. REMIND *v.* + -ING¹.] The act of reminding; a reminder.
1836 J. S. MILL *Let.* Feb. in *Wks.* (1963) XII. 294 The things..were not done even after numerous remindings. **1865** —— *Comte* 129 Everything that he can do without the aid of incessant remindings from other thinkers, is merely provisional, and will require a thorough revision.

†**re'mindless,** *a. Obs.*⁻¹ [-LESS.] Forgetful.
1657 W. MORICE *Coena quasi Κοινὴ* x. 119 Those remindless persons, whom we sometimes see to go about to seek that which they carry in their hands.

†'**reming,** *vbl. sb. Obs.* [f. REME *v.*¹ + -ING¹.] Calling, crying, lamenting, etc.
c **1200** *Trin. Coll. Hom.* 197 Þat hie ne muge heren here remenge, ne here gal. *c* **1220** *Bestiary* 666 For here mikle reming rennande cumeð a gungling. *a* **1400** *Pol. Rel. & L. Poems* (1903) 252 Fletus, *Anglice* Reminge. *c* **1400** *Destr. Troy* 8511 He hade no ruthe of hor remyng, ne þe rank teris. ? *a* **1500** *Chester Pl.* (E.E.T.S.) 448 To..putt them into great Torment, wher Reeminge, Grinninge were fervent.

re'mingle, *v.* [RE- 5 a.] To mingle again.
1853 C. BRONTË *Villette* xxv, That slight rod of Moses could, at one waft, release and re-mingle a sea spell-parted. **1866** FELTON *Anc. & Mod. Gr.* I. I. v. 76 A backward movement commenced by sea, and remingled..Greeks with those from whom they had been severed.

Remington ('rɛmɪŋtən). [The name of Eliphalet *Remington* (1793–1861) and his son Philo (1816–89), gunsmiths of Ilion, New York, the original manufacturers.] A proprietary term for a make of firearms and typewriters.

1865 S. BOWLES *Across Continent* iii. 23 Perhaps he had intuitive knowledge of our brave hearts and our innumerable Colts', Smith and Wessons', Remingtons', Ballards', and double-barreled shot-guns. **1871** W. W. GREENE *Mod. Breech-Loaders* 192 The Remington Rifle... has been extensively used in America, France, Denmark, and Austria. **1888** *Official Gaz.* (U.S. Patent Office) 23 Oct. 350/2 Type-writing machines.—Standard Typewriter Manufacturing Company, New York, N.Y... Used since 1880. 'The word "Remington".' **1895** G. B. SHAW *Let.* 27 Aug. (1965) I. 551, I typewrite on a Bar Lock; but they now all imitate the Remington type so closely that there is no telling. **1895** W. S. CHURCHILL in *Daily Graphic* 27 Dec. 4/3 The rebels, who use Remingtons, fired independently. **1897** *Sears, Roebuck Catal.* 570/2 The Remington Semi-Hammerless Single Barrel Breech Loading Shot Gun... You take no risk in buying the old and reliable Remington. **1906** *Official Gaz.* (U.S. Patent Office) 4 Dec. 1683/1 Remington Arms Company, New York, N.Y... Used ten years. *Remington*... Shotguns, Pistols, Revolvers, and Rifles. **1926** *Trade Marks Jrnl.* 19 May 1177 *Remington*... Typewriters, accounting typewriters and portable typewriters and accessories... Remington Typewriter Company.. New York, U.S.A.; manufacturers. **1935** N. MARSH *Enter Murderer* xvi. 193 'Is there a typewriter?' 'There is. A Remington.' **1949** *Lubbock* (Tex.) *Morning Avalanche* 23 Feb. II. 1/1 Among the rare pistols are an 1850 double-barreled dueling pistol.. and a five-shot Remington pistol. **1959** A. K. LANG in *Alfred Hitchcock's Mystery Mag.* Feb. 77/2 The blonde found herself staring down the muzzle of his Remington. **1973** 'A. HALL' *Tango Briefing* ix. 114 A Remington ·410 across his knees.. just the one shot. **1975** *Country Life* 9 Oct. 920/4 A link between typewriters and women's emancipation. The first Remingtons were produced in 1873.

reminisce (rɛmɪ'nɪs), *v.* [Back-formation from next: somewhat colloquial.]

1. *trans.* and *intr.* To recollect, remember.

1829 [J. R. BEST] *Pers. & Lit. Mem.* 304 Some of my readers may reminisce—the word shall never enter my vocabulary—a political squib, let off towards the conclusion of the American war. **1896** A. LANG in *Longm. Mag.* June 219 She could not have remembered much of Keats... How do people remember anything? How do they reminisce?

2. To indulge in reminiscences. Also with direct speech as obj.

1882 *Pall Mall G.* 8 Sept. 4 There is probably no reason why old Bohemians as well as other people should not 'reminisce'. **1892** M'CRIE *Public Worship Presbyt. Scot.* i. 48 Before his wife's death, so he reminisced, he always went to church. **1961** *Dallas Morning News* 10 Sept. VI. 6 'I bought my first dress from him when I was still a struggling young actress,' she reminisces. **1969** A. GLYN *Dragon Variation* viii. 233 'I remember when the whole thing was eighteenth century,' he reminisced. 'Chandeliers, brocades.' **1978** *Daily Tel.* 28 Aug. 3/1 'I remember the teacher asking what we wanted to be,' Signor Santo Del Bon reminisced.

reminiscence (rɛmɪ'nɪsəns). Also 6 -cens, 7 -cience. [a. F. *réminiscence* (14th c.), or ad. late L. *reminiscentia* (Tert.), f. *reminiscī* to remember, f. *re-* RE- + **men-* (see MIND).]

1. The act, process, or fact, of remembering or recollecting; sometimes *spec.* the act of recovering knowledge by mental effort (cf. *recollection*).

1589 PUTTENHAM *Eng. Poesie* III. xxv. (Arb.) 312 By long and studious obseruation rather a repetition or reminiscens naturall. **1639** N. N. tr. *Du Bosq's Compl. Woman* II. 84 There are those who teach on Plato's grounds, that Inclination comes from a certain Reminiscence. **1655** STANLEY *Hist. Philos.* III. (1701) 78/1 Thus is all her Learning only reminiscence, a recovery of her first knowledge. **1692** SOUTH *Serm.* (1697) I. 361 The other part of memory, called Reminiscence: which is the Retreiving of a thing, at present forgot, or but confusely remembred. **1744** BERKELEY *Siris* §315 The Peripatetics themselves distinguish between reminiscence and mere memory. **1791** COWPER *Four Ages* 23 Knows he his origin? can he ascend By reminiscence to his earliest date? **1867** LEWES *Hist. Philos.* (ed. 3) I. 291 The ingenious doctrine of the soul's reminiscence of a former apprehension of truth. **1879** CALDERWOOD *Mind & Br.* 266 Embryology presents us with a modification of Plato's doctrine of reminiscence.

2. (Chiefly *pl.*) **a.** A recollection or remembrance, as a mental fact.

1813 SHELLEY *Q. Mab* VII. 52 Vague dreams have rolled, And varied reminiscences have waked. **1836** J. GILBERT *Chr. Atonem.* i. (1852) 5 The passive indolence which.. easily mistakes its mere reminiscences for the result of inquiry. **1887** LOWELL *Democr.* 94 Memory which at my time of life is gradually becoming one of her own reminiscences.

b. A recollection or remembrance of some past fact or experience related to others; freq. (in *pl.*), the collective memories or experiences of a person put into literary form.

1811 L. M. HAWKINS *C'tess & Gertr.* I. 96 Till his feelings were ascertained.. his friends were not wanting in these reminiscences. **1843** PRESCOTT *Mexico* (1850) I. 248 As he listened to these reminiscences of the sailors. **1868** FARRAR *Seekers* Introd. 3 Contemporary reminiscences of that day of desperate disaster.

3. An expression, feature, fact, etc., which recalls something else.

1860 PUSEY *Min. Proph.* 153 Other reminiscences of the words of Amos are only a part of the harmony of Scripture. **1873** MIVART *Elem. Anat.* vi. 229 There is a singular and striking reminiscence of vertebræ in the three arches of the bony skull. **1876** HUMPHREYS *Coin-coll. Man.* xxvi. 396 [The Saturnalia] of which the vivid reminiscence still exists in the modern Carnival.

4. *Psychol.* An improvement in the memory or performance of something partially learned, occurring after the learning has ceased.

1913 P. B. BALLARD in *Brit. Jrnl. Psychol.* Monograph Suppl. I. II. 17 As obliviscence is a gradual process of deterioration in the capacity to revive past experiences, so is reminiscence a gradual process of improvement in that capacity. *Ibid.* 31 In the case of very young children the interval which secures maximal reminiscence seems to be three days. **1935** *Amer. Jrnl. Psychol.* XLVII. 89 The results of the two experiments.. indicate that reminiscence.. occurs independently of casual revival or intentional review. **1951** S. S. STEVENS *Handbk. Exper. Psychol.* xvii. 653/1 Although most of the work on reminiscence had used verbal material, the appearance of reminiscence is not restricted to verbal learning. **1978** E. GULIAN et al. in M. M. Gruneberg et al. *Practical Aspects Memory* II. 596 Training sessions following closely together produce no marked improvement in performance and.. clear-cut progress show-ups only after a training gap. This finding is akin to the phenomenon of reminiscence, which is described in a wide range of learning studies.

Hence **remi'niscence** *v.*, to 'reminisce'; **remi'niscenceful** *a.*; **remi'niscencer**.

1888 FRITH *Autobiog.* III. iii. 30 The.. reminiscencer who is fond of talking of matters that can be of no interest to anyone but himself. **1889** *Edin. Rev.* Jan. 64 The reflective reminiscenceful character common to all the writings of the Apocrypha. **1890** SARA J. DUNCAN *Social Depart.* 327 Orthodocia was delightful when she reminiscenced.

†**remi'niscency.** *Obs.* [See prec. and -ENCY.] The faculty of reminiscence.

1655–87 H. MORE *App. Antid.* (1712) 205 If you'll say that Memory is in the Brain, but Reminiscency in the Conarion [etc.]. **1666** S. PARKER *Free & Impart. Censure* (1667) 38 In his Phædo, he fairly argues for the Souls Immortality from its presupposed Reminiscency. **1732** *Hist. Litteraria* IV. 206 The Rules of Reminiscency require, that [etc.].

remi'niscent, *sb.* [f. as next.] A relater or writer of reminiscences.

1822 C. BUTLER *Reminisc.* (ed. 3) I. 4 No one ever discovered a passion for literature at an earlier hour in his life than the Reminiscent. **1837** *Blackw. Mag.* XLII. 76 This reminiscent is not a good converser. **1869** BAGEHOT *Lit. Stud.* (1879) II. 331 It is the excellence of a reminiscent to have a few good stories.

reminiscent (rɛmɪ'nɪsənt), *a.* [f. L. *reminiscent-em*, pres. pple. of *reminiscī*: see REMINISCENCE.]

1. Pertaining to, characterized by, reminiscence.

1765 *Universal Mag.* XXXVII. 356/2 Men, in their sentient, imaginative, and reminiscent part,.. are.. subject to diseases. **1837** SOUTHEY *Doctor* cxxix. (1848) 327 The Biographer, or Historian,.. or rather the reminiscent relator of circumstances. **1855** BAGEHOT *Lit. Stud.* (1879) I. 1 The evident fiction of reminiscent age—striving and failing to remember. **1890** 'R. BOLDREWOOD' *Miner's Right* (1899) 146/2 The most careful reminiscent accuracy.

b. Having reminiscence *of* something.

1830 *Fraser's Mag.* I. 151 A more perfect state of being—a state of which it is reminiscent and anticipant. **1836–7** SIR W. HAMILTON *Metaph.* xxxiv. (1859) II. 278 Some other state of existence, of which we have been previously conscious and are now reminiscent.

2. Of the nature of reminiscence or reminiscences.

1863 *Cornh. Mag.* VII. 391 Some of the charms of youth reminiscent in the grey dignity of acknowledged age. **1883** J. BURROUGHS in *Century Mag.* Nov. 103/2 There is.. a pensive, reminiscent feeling in the air itself. **1892** *Independent* 25 Nov. 220/2 The talk on the way was reminiscent.

3. Evoking a reminiscence *of* a person or thing.

1880 *Academy* 13 Nov. 352 He is strangely reminiscent of Millais. **1891** *Speaker* 2 May 527/2 The verse.. is.. reminiscent of the style of Rowe.

Hence **remi'niscently** *adv.*

1891 COTES *2 Girls on a Barge* 23 'The Cadet', quoth Girton, reminiscently, 'did that rather well'.

remini'scential, *a.* [f. REMINISCENCE: cf. *essential*.] Of the nature of, pertaining to, reminiscence; of a reminiscent character.

1646 SIR T. BROWNE *Pseud. Ep.* Pref. A iij, Would Truth dispense, we could be content, with Plato,.. that Intellectuall acquisition were but Reminiscentiall evocation. **1682** —— *Chr. Mor.* III. §10 Trust not too much unto suggestions from reminiscential Amulets, or artificial Memorandums. **1853** LOWELL *Moosehead Jrnl.* Pr. Wks. 1890 I. 1 At the sound of the name, no reminiscential atoms.. stirred and marshalled in my brain. **1869** MRS. H. WOOD *Roland Yorke* III. 70 Just as Roland Yorke had seen them in his reminiscential visions. **1891** W. C. HUDSON *Man with a Thumb* i. 7 As the old man indulged his reminiscential vein.

Hence **remini'scentially** *adv.* (In recent Dicts.)

remi'niscer. = REMINISCENCER.

1966 *Punch* 30 Nov. 825/1 The revenants and reminiscers: Hearne, Tuckwell, Mozley, Gunning, and the rest—chirpy, inconsequent, lords of anecdote, abbots of unreason.

remi'niscing, *vbl. sb.* [f. REMINISC(E *v.* + -ING[1].] The action of the verb REMINISCE.

a **1910** 'MARK TWAIN' *Autobiogr.* (1924) II. 204 A deal of pretty jolly reminiscing was done. **1929** E. W. SPRINGS *Above Bright Blue Sky* 239 She wanted to do a lot of reminiscing, but I cut her short.

†**remi'niscion.** *Obs. rare.* [irreg. f. L. *reminiscī* + -ION[1].] Reminiscence.

1607 CHAPMAN *Bussy d'Ambois* Plays 1873 II. 85 This strange vision.. stir[s] my thoughts With reminiscion of the Spirits promise. **1688** R. HOLME *Armoury* II. 415/2 Reminiscion is the remembering a thing out of mind.

remi'niscitory, *a.* *rare*$^{-1}$. [f. as prec. + -ITORY.] Of the nature of reminiscence.

1827 LYTTON *Pelham* lxxiii, I still bore a reminiscitory spite against Mr. Job Jonson.

re'mint (ri:-), *v.* [RE- 5 a.] To mint again.

1823 DE QUINCEY *Lett. to Yng. Man* Wks. 1860 XIV. 84 In other cases, when there happen to exist double expressions for the same notion, he called in and reminted them as it were. **1896** SIR R. P. EDGCUMBE *Pop. Fallacies Bimetallism* 121 When the western nations of Europe agree again to remint silver upon a fixed ratio.

remiped ('rɛmɪpɛd), *sb.* and *a.* *Zool.* [ad. F. *rémipède*, f. L. *rēmus* oar + *ped-*, *pēs* foot.]

a. *sb.* One of an order of coleopterous insects having tarsi adapted for swimming (Brande *Dict. Sci.* 1842); also, a crustacean of the genus *Remipes* (Webster 1847). **b.** *adj.* Having feet that are oar-shaped, or used as oars (Webster 1864).

So **'remipede** *sb.*

1826 KIRBY & SP. *Entomol.* xxix. III. 170, I have some suspicion that.. the remipedes, *Notonecta*, *Sigara*, &c. may find their prototypes among the *Crustacea*.

†**re'mise,** *sb.*[1] *Obs.* Also 5 remysse, 7 remyse. [a. F. (in early use prob. AF.) *remise*, vbl. sb. f. *remettre* to remit: cf. late L. *remissa* remission (of sins).]

1. *Law.* A transfer of property.

1473 *Rolls of Parlt.* VI. 75/1 Any Graunte or Grauntes, Ratifications, Confirmations, Remysse or Releases to hym.. made. **1485** *Ibid.* 342/2 Annexions, Remises, Releases or Pardones, to theym.. made or had. **1766** BLACKSTONE *Comm.* II. App. iv. §3. p. xv, This recognition, remise, quit-claim, warranty, fine, and agreement.

2. A remission or cessation of sickness. *rare*$^{-1}$.

1603 FLORIO *Montaigne* III. xiii. 653, I have notwithstanding some remyses or intermissions yet.

3. ? Return, recompense.

a **1578** LINDESAY (Pitscottie) *Chron. Scot.* (S.T.S.) I. 136 We come now.. to thai [= thy] maiestie to gett support, promiss and richt remise [*v.r.* riche revenues] thairfoir.

4. The act of remitting money; a remittance.

1667 TEMPLE *Let.* Wks. 1731 II. 39 They have remitted by this Ordinary to his Excellency a hundred and thirty thousand Crowns, which is the third Remise of about that Sum. **1682** SCARLETT *Exchanges* 16 Its necessary that the Remise be confirmed by the following Post. **1689** *Myst. Iniq.* 38 In order whereunto great Remises of Mony were already ordered him from the French Court.

‖**remise** (rəmiz), *sb.*[2] [F.; see prec.]

1. **a.** A house or shelter for a carriage; a coach-house.

1698 W. KING tr. *Sorbière's Journ. Lond.* 4 Divers of the Citizens Houses, have Port-cochezs to drive in a Coach, or a Cart either, and Consequently have Courts within, and mostly Remises to set them up. **1768** STERNE *Sent. Journ.* I. 62 The Remise Door. *Ibid.* 73 (*The Remise*), Mons. Dessein came up with the key of the Remise in his hand, and forthwith let us into his magazine of chaises. **1841** LADY BLESSINGTON *Idler in France* II. 135 In former days sledges were considered as indispensable in the winter *remise* of a grand seigneur in France.

b. (Ellipt. for *voiture de remise*.) A carriage hired from a livery-stable, of a better class than the ordinary hackney-carriage.

1698 M. LISTER *Journ. Paris* (1699) 142 Many of the *Fiacres* or Hackneys, and all the *Remises*, have one large Glass before. **1753** A. MURPHY *Gray's Inn Jrnl.* No. 45 Without the Expence of a Remise, you may visit Boileau. **1818** LADY MORGAN *Autobiog.* (1859) 200 We got into our *remise*—that special French carriage which never breaks down, drawn by horses that never tire.

2. *Fencing.* A second thrust made after the first has missed and while still upon the lunge; the act of making a thrust of this kind.

1823 ROLAND *Art Fencing* 86 The Remise is made upon your adversary's quitting your blade to make a feint as a return too soon after having parried your attack. **1861** CHAPMAN *Review Art Fencing* I. 20 The remise is provoked by opportunities afforded in the adversary's play, and in that respect differs essentially from the Reprise, a redoubling of the Attack.

3. In some card-games, as quadrille and reversis: **a.** (See quot. 1830.) **b.** A stake in the pool.

1830 'EIDRAH TREBOR' *Hoyle made familiar* 36 Remise is when they who stand the game do not make more tricks than they who defend the pool, and then they lose by remise. *Ibid.* 40 Should.. there be three remises, or stakes, in the pools, then it is at the option of any player to take a card or not. **1850** *Hand-bk. Games* (Bohn) 309 One of the players making the reversis.. would then prevent your having the remises out of the pool.

4. A specially planted shelter for partridges. Also *attrib.*

1905 *Kynoch Jrnl.* Jan.–Mar. 45 An instance where this 'remise' system has been carried out most successfully and on a large scale. *Ibid.* 46 When the natural food is exhausted, in hard weather a few handfuls of small corn.. are scattered about inside the 'remise', which gives employment to many coveys who are hard pressed for food, and they also serve as a sort of headquarters to which all partridges in the neighbourhood can retire if disturbed. **1939** *Country Life* 11 Feb. p. xxii/2 It is this danger which is also one of the dangers of laying out a partridge *remise* as part of a plantation scheme.

†**remise**, *a. Obs.*$^{-1}$ [a. F. *remis(e*, pa. pple. of *remettre*: see next.] Delayed, postponed.
c **1510** Barclay *Mirr. Gd. Manners* (1570) Bv, In sentence remise is lesser iniury, Then in headling sentence pronounced hastely.

remise (rɪˈmaɪz), *v.*[1] Also 5-6 **remyse**. [f. F. *remis(e*, pa. pple. of *remettre*:—L. *remittĕre* to REMIT. Cf. REMISS *v.*]
†**1.** *trans.* To put back again *in* or *into* a place, state, etc.; to replace; to convert again *into*; to send back *to* a place. *Obs.* (freq. in Caxton).
1481 Caxton *Godfrey* Prol. 1 Tadresse and remyse theym in theyr auncyent Fraunchyses and lyberte. **1485** —— *Chas. Gt.* 181 Florypes remysed the relyques in the coffret. *c* **1500** *Melusine* xxvi. 207, I remyse hym in your pocession. **1512** *Helyas* in Thoms *Prose Rom.* (1828) III. 76 They saw the king and the quene remised and set in good love and unite of hert togither. *Ibid.* 82 To five of them he remised the chaynes about theyr neckes. **1598** Sylvester *Du Bartas* I. ii. 164 Yet think not that this Too-too-much remises Ought into noughts; it but the Form disguises. **1623** Bingham *Xenophon* 1 His Mother made intercession for him, set him at libertie, and remised him to his gouernment.
†**b.** To bring *together* again; to lead back again. *Obs. rare.*
c **1500** *Melusine* 134 The king..remysed hys folke togidre, and made to withdraw them al the lytil pas. *Ibid.* 137 He full wel remysed hys folke into the tounne.
2. *Law.* To give up, surrender, make over to another, release (any right, property, etc.).
1487 *Rolls of Parlt.* VI. 390 Ye remysed and relessed..all the residue of the said Fee Ferme. **1491** *Act 7 Hen. VII*, c. 18 Your seid suppliant..them remised and quite claymed..unto the seid late pretended Kyng. **1612** in *O'Flaherty's West Connaught* (1846) 258 Wee..have remised, released, and..quitt claimed..all that our right.., interest, [etc.]. **1655** Fuller *Waltham Abb.* 10 Peter Duke of Savoy remised and quit-claimed from him and his Heirs..the right and claim he had. **1766** Blackstone *Comm.* II. xx. 324 The words generally used therein are 'remised, released, and for ever quit-claimed'. **1841** *Penny Cycl.* XIX. 375/2 The operative words of release are remise, release, renounce, and for ever quit claim.
†**3.** To remit or send (a letter or reply). *Obs.*
1633 T. Stafford *Pac. Hib.* I. viii. 62 Remising therefore onely this Answere, that he despised their Forces. *Ibid.* II. vi. 164 All which may appeare by a Letter remised from the said Iames unto him.

reˈmise, *v.*[2] *Fencing.* [f. REMISE *sb.*[2] 2.] *intr.* To make a remise.
1889 *Fencing* (Badminton Libr.) 96 It is wrong to remise on a riposte made by a disengagement in the low line.

remish (rɪˈmɪʃ), slang abbrev. of REMISSION (sense 4 b).
1958 F. Norman *Bang to Rights* I. 15 That is if I dont get nicked for nothing and get a few days chokey and a few days remish.

†**reˈmiss**, *sb. Obs.*$^{-1}$ [Cf. REMISE *sb.*[1]] Relaxation. (But perh. an error for *remissnes*.)
1589 Puttenham *Eng. Poesie* I. xix. 32 Such manner of men as by negligence of Magistrates and remisses of lawes euery countrie breedeth great store of.

remiss (rɪˈmɪs), *a.* Forms: 5-6 **remys, -ysse**, (6 **-yshe**), 5-7 **remisse**, (6 **-is, isshe**, 7 **-ish**), 6- **remiss**. [ad. L. *remiss-us*, pa. pple. of *remittĕre* to REMIT.]
†**1. a.** Dissolved, liquid. *Obs. rare.*
c **1420** *Pallad. on Husb.* I. 1126 White wax, hard picche, remysse [L. *remissum*] ammonyake—This iij commyxt therefore is good to take. Or thus: ammoniak remysse and figis.
†**b.** *Med.* Weakened in consistency or colour; dilute. *Obs.*
?*a* **1412** Lydg. *Two Merch.* 323 His vryne was remys, attenuat, By resoun gendryd of frigidite. **1547** Boorde *Brev. Health* lxxiii. 25 b, An uryne that is pale of colour..yf it be remyshe, then there is great coldnes in the body. **1625** Hart *Anat. Ur.* II. iv. 69 The vrine became of a remisse and light colour, such as it was wont to be.
†**c.** Of sounds: Weak, soft, low. *Obs.*
1530 Palsgr. Introd. 16 They gyve..unto theyr consonantes but a sleight and remisshe sounde. **1650** Bulwer *Anthropomet.* 203 Instruments which have a more acute or treble sound when the strings are stretched, and a lower and more remisse when they are loosened. **1653** R. Sanders *Physiogn.* 246 The voice acute and smooth, or remiss, with a little trembling.
†**d.** Of taste: Faint, slight. *Obs. rare*$^{-1}$.
1655 Culpepper, etc. *Riverius* v. iii. 126 The Taste..is lessened when it scarce perceiveth remiss savors and strong savors but a little.
2. Of persons: Slack in the discharge of a task or duty; careless, negligent.
c **1450** tr. *De Imitatione* I. xxiii. 20 þou shalt gretly sorwe þat þou hast be so remysse [L. *remissus*] & so negligent. **1472-5** *Rolls of Parlt.* VI. 155/2 If any Custumer or Comptrollour of any Porte, be negligent or remisse in noon pakkyng of the same Clothes. *c* **1510** Barclay *Mirr. Gd. Manners* (1570) Dij, If thou be in office..Be not more remis, do not thy duetie lesse. **1567-8** *Reg. Privy Council Scot.* I. 610 Certifeing the personis..that beis fund remysse or negligent in the premissis. **1602** Warner *Alb. Eng.* XII. lxxi. 296 As well as too remisse in choyce, we may be too precise. **1660** Young *Table of Statutes* 44 Officers remisse to collect rates. **1696** Bentley *Boyle Lect.* ix. (1724) 346 Who can tell, if..they might not in long tract of time have grown remiss in the duties..of Religion? **1776** C. Lee in Sparks *Corr. Amer. Rev.* (1853) I. 158 Though I confess I am naturally remiss, I have not neglected my duty in this point. **1838** Thirlwall *Greece* IV. 55 The satrap..had become as remiss as before in making the stipulated payments. **1893** *Academy* 10 June 497/1 He was a very remiss correspondent.
b. Of conduct, actions, etc.: Characterized by carelessness, negligence, or inattention.
1502 Atkynson tr. *De Imitatione* I. xxiii. 173 Than shalte thou repent full sore of thy remysse and neclygent lyfe. **1509** Barclay *Shyp of Folys* 206 b, Idylnes By wayes remys and dranynge neglygence Of all other synne is rote. **1656** Earl Monm. tr. *Boccalini's Advts. fr. Parnass.* I. xxxviii. (1674) 50, I, in the beginning of my Principality seemed to be of a remiss spirit, and totally incapable of the great affairs of State. **1675** Traherne *Chr. Ethics* 169 To exert almighty power in a remiss and lazy manner, is infinitely base and dishonourable. **1712** Addison *Spect.* No. 471 ¶6 Hope..keeps the Mind awake in her most Remiss and Indolent Hours. **1817** Jas. Mill *Brit. India* II. v. viii. 663 [He] was appointed, under the..expectation that he would supply what had been remiss in the conduct of his predecessor. **1886** *Illustr. Lond. News* 20 Feb. 194/2 It was remiss in Aunt Louisa not to have offered to be her chaperon.
†**c.** Idle; free from labour. *Obs. rare*$^{-1}$.
1566 Adlington *Apuleius* 45 With great lamentation was ordained a remisse time for that day.
3. Characterized by a lack of strictness or proper restraint; lax, loose. ? *Obs.*
c **1450** tr. *De Imitatione* I. xxv. 37 He þat euermore sekiþ þo þinges þat are most laxe and most remisse, shal euer be in anguissh. **1540-1** Elyot *Image Gov.* Pref., By the lasciuiouse and remisse educacion of Varius Heliogabalus, he grewe to be a person moste monstruouse in liuyng. **1583** Stubbes *Anat. Abus.* I. (1879) 76 This ouer great leuitie and remisse libertie in the education of youthe. **1624** in Rushw. *Hist. Coll.* (1659) I. 160 So dangerous it is for Princes by a remiss comportment, to give growth to the least Error. **1651-3** Jer. Taylor *Serm. for Year* (1678) 224 A seldom restraint,—a remiss discipline. **1751** Johnson *Rambler* No. 157 ¶3 Many among my fellow-students took the opportunity of a more remiss discipline to gratify their passions.
†**b.** Not strict or severe in punishing; lenient.
1568 Grafton *Chron.* II. 927 They were gentle and remisse to a great number, and specially to such as offended by cohercion and feare. **1613** *Edict agst. Priv. Combats* title-p., Straitly charging all officers and other His Majestie's subjects to use no conniuencie, or remisse proceedings toward such offenders. **1651** N. Bacon *Disc. Govt. Eng.* II. xxii. (1739) 102 Coming in by the people's favour, he was obliged to be rather remiss than rigorous.
4. Free from vehemence or violence; also, defective or lacking in force or energy.
1550 T. Nycolls *Thucidides* 14 The one is more vehemente for to moue mens hartes, the other more remys and gentle. **1586** B. Young *Guazzo's Civ. Conv.* IV. 189 Euen so after meate,..our will prone to wickednesse, is become more remisse and temperate. **1644** Bulwer *Chiron.* 32 The Hand restrained and kept in is an argument of modesty..sutable to a milde and remisse declamation. **1695** Woodward *Nat. Hist. Earth* IV. (1723) 210 Its Motion becomes more languid and remiss. **1707** Floyer *Physic. Pulse-Watch* 364 A remiss Pulse, is when it is small and slow. **1752** Hume *Ess. & Treat.* (1777) I. 179 The passion must neither be too violent nor too remiss. **1837** Sir W. Hamilton *Metaph.* xlv. (1870) II. 493 Pain or dissatisfaction experienced, when the energy elicited is either inordinately vehement or too remiss.
†**b.** Not intense or strong; moderate, mild. *Obs.* (common in 17th c., esp. of heat and cold).
1573 P. More *Almanack* Evj, But all euills shall seeme more remisse and tolerable than they were the laste yere. **1610** Holland *Camden's Brit.* I. 2 The cold with us is much more remisse than in some parts of France and Italie. **1654** H. L'Estrange *Chas. I* (1655) 123 The King fell sick of the Small-Pocks, but the malignity was very remisse, and gentle. **1686** Goad *Celest. Bodies* I. ix. 28 Her Warmth is so remiss and slack, that she seemeth to befriend a Cold Influence.
†**c.** Moderate, low, slight (degree). *Obs.*
1620 T. Granger *Div. Logike* 104 Note that these middles haue contrariety in them in the remisse, or remote degree. **1657** Austen *Fruit Trees* II. 18 Distinct and severall works of Nature, in moderate and remisse degrees, are all promoted at the same time. **1670** W. Simpson *Hydrol. Ess.* 104 Retaining the same..properties in a remiss degree.
†**5.** Diminished in tension; slack, loose, relaxed.
1623 Jas. I in Rushw. *Hist. Coll.* (1659) I. 115 Not alwayes to use his spurs and keep strait the rein, but sometimes to use the spurs and suffer the reins more remiss. **1644** Bulwer *Chiron.* 37 The turned up Hand, (the Thumbe bent in, and the other Fingers remisse). **1667** Milton *P.L.* VI. 458 What availes Valour or strength,..quelld with pain Which all subdues, and makes remiss the hands Of Mightiest.

remiss (rɪˈmɪs), *v. rare.* [f. L. *remiss-*, ppl. stem of *remittĕre* to REMIT; cf. REMISE *v.*[1]] *trans.*
†**1.** *trans.* To remit; to resolve or dissolve; to mitigate; to let go, pass over. *Obs.*
c **1500** *Melusine* 335 Al that ye shal doo with good wyll I remysse it to your penaunce. **1541** R. Copland *Galyen's Terap.* H hij b, It behoueth asmoche to intende & augment the vertue of the said medycament, as it shulde be remyssed & dymynysshed in ye depth of the body. **1573** P. More *Almanack* Fj b, Oftentymes the drought shall be remyssed and tempered with shoures. **1605** Daniel *Philotas* IV. ii, Words, if they proceed of leuity Are to be skornd,..or of injury To be remiss'd or vnacknowledged. **1656** S. H. *Gold. Law* 103 Once, yea twice have I spoken, but for future wil be wiser, and so compress and remiss it.
†**2.** To assign, adjudge. *Obs. rare*$^{-1}$.
1525 Ld. Berners *Froiss.* II. ccix. [ccv.] 643 The herytage was remyssed and iudged into the handes and possessyon of the Erle of Brayne.
†**3.** To send back (an answer). *Obs. rare*$^{-1}$.
1633 Stafford *Pac. Hib.* I. xix. 113 Answere was remissed by the President, that the State was well perswaded of his loyaltie.
4. *Law.* = REMISE *v.*[1] 2.
1809 R. Langford *Introd. Trade* 108, I, A. B...having remissed, released, and for ever quit claim to C. D...of all ..debts, dues, duties.
Hence †**reˈmissable** *a.*, remissible. *Obs.*$^{-1}$
a **1550** *Image Hypocr.* in *Skelton's Wks.* (1843) II. 425/1 It is..synne..Ageynst the Holy Gost, That is not remissable.

†**reˈmissal.** *Obs. rare.* Forms: 5 **remyssaylle**, (**-moss-**), 6 **-aile, remissaile**, 7 **remissal**. [a. AF. ***remissaille**: see prec. and -AL[1].] *pl.* That which is left over; remains; *esp.* the remains of a meal.
1387-8 T. Usk *Test. Love* Prol. (Skeat) I. 108 The almoigner, that hath drawe up in the cloth al the remissailes, as trenchours, and the relief, to bere to the almesse. *c* **1430** *Stans Puer* 48 Laade nat thy trenchour withe many remyssailes. *c* **1444** Lydg. in *Pol. Poems* (Rolls) II. 220 The poore man stant hungry at the gate, Of remossaylles he wold be partable. *a* **1618** Raleigh *Rem.* (1644) 114 Death hath..left you now to be Lees, and remissalls of your wearyish and dying dayes.

reˈmissful, *a. rare.* [f. REMISS *v.* or *a.*]
†**1.** Full of remission; merciful. *Obs. rare*$^{-1}$.
1603 Drayton *Bar. Wars* I. xi, As though the heauens, in their remissfull doome, Tooke those best lou'd, from worser daies to come.
2. Full of remissness; careless, negligent.
1836 *Tait's Mag.* III. 569 Taking up a vial of physic from the table, he tapped his remissful patient on the shoulder. **1892** *Field* 3 Dec. 880/1 The outlay for road repair under such remissful management.

remissiˈbility. [See next and -ITY.] The state or condition of being remissible.
1698 Norris *Pract. Disc.* IV. 146 Those places of Scripture..must and ought to be understood not of Actual Remission..but of a Remissibility or State of Pardon. **1729** Stackhouse *Body Divin.* IV. i. §2 (1776) II. 423 That which is previous to repentance consists in a bare remissibility of sin. **1780** Bentham *Princ. Legisl.* xvii. §25 The eleventh and last of all the properties that seem to be requisite in a lot of punishment is that of remissibility.

remissible (rɪˈmɪsɪb(ə)l), *a.* [a. F. *rémissible* (15th c.), or ad. L. *remissibilis*; see REMISS *v.* and -IBLE.] Capable or admitting of remission; that may be remitted.
1577 Fulke *Answ. True Christian* 90 Thou wouldest vouche safe to pardon, and to make it remissible. *a* **1594** R. Greenham *Wks.* (1599) 70 If you turne to the Lord..your sin is remissible. **1627-77** Feltham *Resolves* II. ix. 177 Some sins..they allow.. to be such as deserue Punishment, although..remissible. *a* **1703** Burkitt *On N.T.* Heb. ix. 22 Though man had repented,..yet his sins could not have been remitted, had not this blood made it remissible. **1875** Poste *Gaius* III. (ed. 2) 452 An obligation remissible by the private individual whose primary rights are violated.
Hence **reˈmissibleness**, remissibility.
a **1658** O. Sedgwick (*title*), The Anatomy of secret Sins, [etc.],..Together with the remissibleness of all sin.

remission (rɪˈmɪʃən). Also 4 **remis(s)iun**, 4-6 **remissioun, -yssio(u)n**, 5-6 **-issyon, -ys(s)yon**, etc. [a. OF. *remission*, ad. L. *remissiōn-em*, n. of action f. *remittĕre* to REMIT. The order in which the senses appear in English differs widely from their natural development: cf. the note to REMIT *v.*]
1. Forgiveness or pardon *of* sins (cf. 2) or other offences.
a **1225** *Ancr. R.* 346 In remission, & in uorȝiuenesse of alle þine sunnen. *a* **1300** *Cursor M.* 20048 þai sal haue..crist aun beniscun, And o þair sin remisiun. *c* **1380** Wyclif *Sel. Wks.* II. 11 And Joon cam..preching þe baptism of penaunce in remission of synnes. **1447** Bokenham *Seyntys* (Roxb.) 7 Of myn old and newe transgressyoun That I may haue a plener remyssyoun. **1483** Caxton *Cato* 5 Of the sacryfyse that thauncyentes made to god for to haue remyssion of theyr synnes. **1560** Daus tr. *Sleidane's Comm.* 4 If he repent of his owne accorde, and desyre remission of his offence. **1651** Hobbes *Leviath.* III. xxxviii. 245 In..Scripture, Remission of Sinne, and Salvation from Death and Misery, is the same thing. **1788** Gibbon *Decl. & F.* xlix. V. 123 The gift which he had conferred on the Roman pontiff for the remission of his sins. **1846** Browning *Lett.* (1899) II. 212 As naughty children punished by mistake are promised a remission of next offence. **1884** *Catholic Dict.* (1885) 5/1 Absolution from Sin is a remission of sin which the priest..makes in the Sacrament of Penance.
2. (Without *of*.) Forgiveness or pardon granted for sins or offences against divine law; the cancelling of, or deliverance from, the guilt and penalties of sin; †also, power of obtaining such pardon.
c **1325** *Chron. Eng.* 634 in Ritson *Metr. Rom.* II. 296 The spere That Charlemayne was wonet to bere To-fore the holy legioun, That is of gret remissioun. **1362** Langl. *P. Pl.* A. XI. 277 A robbere hadde remission raþere þanne þei alle. *c* **1430** Lydg. *Min. Poems* (Percy Soc.) 239 O blissed Jhesu! do remissioun To alle that axe mercy on ther kne! **1500-20** Dunbar *Poems* viii. 28 Pray now for him..Unto the Lord..To gif him mercie and remissioun. **1579** Lyly *Euphues* (Arb.) 174 Remember..how he sweat water and bloud for thy remission. **1614** Raleigh *Hist. World* II. (1634) 250 Ingratitude and rebellion after his so many benefits, so many remissions, so many miracles wrought. **1685** Baxter *Paraphr. N.T.* Acts ii. 39 The Messiah with his Grace of Remission, and the Spirit, is promised. **1715** De Foe *Fam. Instruct.* (1841) I. 25 He gives repentance and remission.
b. Pardon for a political, legal, or other offence. Now only *Hist.*

1429 *Pol. Poems* (Rolls) II. 145 Be rightful juge, .. Thy right ay sugre with remyssioun. **1535** LYNDESAY *Satyre* 4093 But doubt, ȝe salbe hangit, But mercie or remissioun. **1568** GRAFTON *Chron.* II. 863 Sir Thomas Broughton .. was at hande .. vtterly dispairing of pardon and remission. **1591** SHAKS. *Two Gent.* I. ii. 65 My pennance is, to call Lucetta backe And aske remission, for my folly past. **1613** PURCHAS *Pilgrimage* VIII. xii. 671 If any were found dishonest, they were put to death without remission. **1687** A. LOVELL tr. *Thevenot's Trav.* I. 95 Whosoever are taken stealing of Mastick, are without remission sent to the Galleys. **1864** KIRK *Chas. Bold* I. viii. 376 They entreated, therefore, that letters of remission might be granted to them for this fault.

†**c.** *Sc.* With *a* and *pl.* A formal pardon; a document conveying this. *Obs.*

1456 SIR G. HAYE *Law Arms* (S.T.S.) 52 That all maner of man, that had bene before tyme banist out of Rome, suld cum agayne, and thai suld .. have remissiounes. **1535** LYNDESAY *Satyre* 1132, I dreid, without ȝe get ane remissioun, .. The spirtuall stait sall put ȝow to perditioun. **1546** *Reg. Privy Council Scot.* I. 34 The remissioun grantit to the Capitane of Dumbertane, and all his complices .. sall presentlie be past throw the signet. **1609** SKENE *Reg. Maj.* 158 Gif he quha is accused, alledges ane remission, he sall produce the samine in judgement.

†**d.** An inclination towards pardon. *Obs. rare*$^{-1}$.

1603 SHAKS. *Meas. for M.* v. i. 503, I finde an apt remission in my selfe; And yet heere's one .. I cannot pardon.

†**3. a.** Release from a debt or payment. *Obs.*

1362 LANGL. *P. Pl.* A. VII. 83 To ha Reles and Remission on þat Rental I be-leeue. **1382** WYCLIF *Deut.* xv. 1 To whom is owed eny thing, .. he shal not mowe aȝen aske it, for ȝeer of remyssioun of the Lord it is. **1607** SHAKS. *Cor.* v. ii. 90 Though I owe My Reuenge properly, my remission lies In Volcean brests. **1608** WILLET *Hexapla Exod.* 838 They .. only went vp .. in the seuenth yeare of remission twice.

†**b.** Release, liberation, deliverance, from captivity, etc.; respite. *Obs.*

1432–50 tr. *Higden* (Rolls) II. 291 From whiche victory of Abraham, somme men say the yere of Iubile to haue taken originalle, for that remission of captif men. **1582** N. T. (Rhem.) *Luke* iv. 19 To preach to the captiues remission, .. to dimisse the bruised unto remission. **1635** PAGITT *Christianogr.* I. iii. (1636) 162 For remission of soules the Patriarch graunts no Indulgences. **1761** GOLDSM. *Misc. Wks.* (1837) I. 471 Some remission from the war gave them leisure to form schemes of future prosperity.

†**c.** Release from work or exertion. *Obs. rare.*

1382 WYCLIF *1 Macc.* x. 34 Alle solempne days .. be alle dais of ynmunite .. and of remissioun, to alle Jewis that ben in my rewme. —— *2 Cor.* viii. 13 Forsoth not that it be remyssioun, or slouthe, to othere, .. to ȝou tribulacioun.

4. The action of remitting or giving up partially or wholly: **a.** of a debt, tax, etc.

1382 WYCLIF *Prol. Bible* iii. 6 Also in the vij. ȝeer shal be remissioun of dette to citeseynes and kynnesmen. *a* **1719** ADDISON (J.), Not only an expedition, but the remission of a duty or tax, were transmitted to posterity after this manner. **1841** ELPHINSTONE *Hist. Ind.* II. 491 His remissions [of taxes], as far as they were carried into effect, were productive of great inequality. **1884** *Law Rep. 9 App. Cases 624* He does not ask for any remission of any portion of his obligation.

b. of a penalty or punishment. Also *attrib.*

1736 BUTLER *Anal.* I. iii. Wks. 1874 I. 58 Circumstances of aggravated guilt prevent a remission of the penalties. **1741** BETTERTON *Eng. Stage* II. 51 Queen Mary .. immediately granted .. a Remission of her Father's Execution for that of Transportation. **1797** MRS. RADCLIFFE *Italian* xxvi, The consequence of this confession was a remission of punishment. **1861** PEARSON *Early & Mid. Ages Eng.* 177 This was an illegal remission of an important part of the penalty. **1884** *Catholic Dict.* 442/1 The indulgence .. was no mere remission of canonical penance. **1893** *Daily News* 9 Mar. 6/7 He [a convict] was punished by the forfeiture of remission marks.

†**c.** *Law* = REMISE *sb.*[1] 1. *Obs. rare*$^{-1}$.

c **1450** *Godstow Reg.* (E.E.T.S.) 100 He remytted to them and quyte-claymed... And for þis knowlechyng, remission, fyne, and accorde [etc.].

†**5.** Relaxation; lessening of tension; slackening of energy or application. *Obs.*

1579 LYLY *Euphues* (Arb.) 112 As too much bending breaketh the bowe, so too much remission spoyleth the minde. **1580** *Ibid.* 383 As the Musitians tune their strings, who .. either by intention or remission, frame them to a pleasant consent. **1614** RALEIGH *Hist. World* v. iii. §18. 474 Such accompt of winnings past, is commonly in Gamesters that are at the height of their fortune, a cause of remission and carelessnesse. **1638** JUNIUS *Paint. Ancients* 22 Among the manifold remissions of our minde, among our idle hopes, .. these Images do follow us .. close. **1690** LOCKE *Hum. Und.* II. xix. §4 This difference of intention and remission of the mind in thinking .. every one .. has experimented in himself. **1741** MIDDLETON *Cicero* I. i. 41, I used to speak without any remission or variation.

†**b.** Lowering or humbling (of mind). *Obs. rare.*

a **1628** F. GREVIL *Sidney* (1652) 35 This is that true remission of mind, whereof I would gladly have the world take notice. *Ibid.* 159 So far was his true remission of mind transformed into ejulation.

6. Diminution of force or effect; lowering or decrease of a condition or quality, esp. of heat or cold. (Cf. INTENSION 3.)

1603 HOLLAND *Plutarch's Mor.* 69 Morall vertue .. tempereth the remission and intention, and .. taketh away the excesse and defect of the passions. **1625** N. CARPENTER *Geog. Del.* I. x. (1635) 224 They haue extreame cold Winters, and in stead of Summer a small remission of cold. **1642** HOWELL *For. Trav.* (Arb.) 35 For then when the heate beginneth in Spaine, the violence thereof lasteth a long time without intension, or remission, or any considerable change. **1696** BP. PATRICK *Comm. Exod.* xix. 16 When their trembling was abated, by the Remission .. of the Sound of the Trumpet. **1784** JOHNSON *Let. to Mrs. Thrale* 9 Feb., The remission of the cold did not continue long enough to afford me much relief. **1795–1814** WORDSW. *Excurs.* II. 799 Darkness fell Without remission of the blast or shower. **1879** *St. George's Hosp. Rep.* IX. 14 Marked morning remissions of temperature. **1897** SINGER & BERENS *Unrecog. Laws Nat.* 390 The fundamental belief that gravity admits of neither intension nor remission.

b. *Path.* A decrease or subsidence (esp. a temporary one) in the violence of a disease or pain: also *transf.* of violent emotions.

1685 tr. *Willis' Lond. Pract. Physick* 549 A Continual Fever .. has its times of remission and exacerbation, but none of intermission. **1741–3** WESLEY *Extract of Jrnl.* (1749) 19, I had a clear remission in the morning: but about two in the afternoon, a stronger fit than any before. *a* **1776** R. JAMES *Dissert. Fevers* (1778) 57 In the very worst cases, if it does not effect a cure itself, it generally brings on a remission. **1797** M. BAILLIE *Morb. Anat.* (1807) 59 Empyema may be distinguished .. by rigors having taken place, by a remission of the pain [etc.]. **1849** MACAULAY *Hist Eng.* ii. I. 188 It is the law of our nature that such fits of excitement shall always be followed by remissions. **1899** *Allbutt's Syst. Med.* VIII. 297 One very marked character .. is the tendency of the symptoms to periodicity, remission and relapse.

attrib. **1897** *Allbutt's Syst. Med.* II. 407 This will furnish .. nourishment during the febrile and remission periods.

†**c.** *Gram.* (See quot.) *Obs. rare.*

1797 *Encycl. Brit.* (ed. 3) VIII. 90 Adverbs of intension and remission, or of quantity continuous; as *moderately, vastly, exceedingly*, &c.

7. The action of remitting or sending (back), in various senses; a remittal. *rare.*

1724 SWIFT *Conc. Weavers* Wks. 1841 II. 85/1 The remission of a million every year to England. **1741–2** STACKHOUSE *Hist. Bible* III. i, The Poets' Fiction of the Loss of Eurydice, and her Remission into Hell. **1883** *Law Rep. 8 Probate Div.* 194 A remission under the seal of Her Majesty's Court of Appeals .. commanding the Official Principal .. to resume the cause into his hands.

†**re'missionary.** *Obs. rare*$^{-0}$. [ad. F. *remissionaire*: see prec. and -ARY[1].] One 'whose offence is remitted' (Blount *Glossogr.* 1656).

remissive (rɪˈmɪsɪv), *a.* Also 6 remyssyve. [ad. med.L. *remissīvus* (Du Cange): see REMISS *v.* and -IVE.]

†**1.** Of a letter: Sent in reply. *Obs. rare*$^{-1}$.

1432–50 tr. *Higden* (Rolls) V. 135 Constantyne did write un to his moder a letter remissive.

†**2.** Careless, negligent, remiss. *Obs. rare.*

1514 in *Eng. Gilds* (1870) 146 As aft tymes as the seid Maister and kepers .. shalbe remyssyve, negligent, and forgitt to syng the seid .. obite. **1606** WARNER *Alb. Eng.* xv. c. 396 Taxe England, fertill in good lawes .. For that it so remissiue in their Execution is. **1640** O. SEDGWICK *Christs Counsell* 148 You did fall into your decayed estate by remissive operations or actings.

3. Inclined to, of the nature of, productive of, remission or pardon. Now *rare.*

1611 SPEED *Hist. Gt. Brit.* VI. i. §13. 176 Punishing seuerely the poore Souldier for small offences, but remissiue to the faults of their Captaines and Leaders. **1629** N. CARPENTER *Achitophel* III. (1640) 142 Absolons case was desperate, .. Davids remissive pardon unlikely. **1649** JER. TAYLOR *Gt. Exemp.* Disc. viii. 79 No contrition alone is remissive of sins. **1852** W. ANDERSON *Expos. Popery* (1878) 126, I judicially bestow on thee .. grace remissive of all thy sins.

†**4.** Producing or allowing decrease *of* something.

1686 GOAD *Celest. Bodies* I. xii. 56 Fog .. doth betray a Cause remissive of Cold. **1718** POPE *Iliad* XIII. 887 A train of heroes .. bore by turns great Ajax' sev'nfold shield, Whene'er he breath'd, remissive of his might.

5. Characterized by remission or abatement.

1686 GOAD *Celest. Bodies* II. ix. 285 [They] brought more days of excessive Heat, than of remissive Warmth. **1822** GOOD *Study Med.* III. 585 Remissive lethargy. With short remissions or intervals of imperfect waking.

Hence †**re'missively** *adv.*, leniently; laxly.

1537 BP. LEE in Froude *Hist. Eng.* (1858) III. 417 If your lordship will that I shall deal remissively herein .. I shall gladly follow the same. *a* **1628** PRESTON *Breastpl. Love* (1631) 147 Trust not in Christ by halves, remissively and imperfectly, and weakely, but trust perfectly.

remissly (rɪˈmɪslɪ), *adv.* [f. REMISS *a.* + -LY[2].]

1. In a remiss, lax, or indifferent manner; carelessly, negligently, slackly.

1532–3 *Act 24 Hen. VIII*, c. 11 Them that remisly or insufficiently shall here after mainteyne the same pauement. **1594** HOOKER *Eccl. Pol.* I. xi. §4 It is not in our power not to do the same; how should it then be in our power to do it coldly or remissly? **1628** HOBBES *Thucyd.* (1822) 94 Yet we that live remissly undertake as great dangers as they. **1665** MANLEY *Grotius' Low C. Warres* 613 It is hardly to be believed, how negligently and remissly that Nation .. took these Things. *a* **1715** BURNET *Own Time* III. (1724) I. 425 Lord Danby .. could not give much credit to it, and handled the matter too remissly. **1752** CARTE *Hist. Eng.* III. 423 Presenting the matter at first with a seeming eagerness, but proceeding afterwards more remisly. **1805** WORDSW. *Prelude* III. 322 The months passed on, remissly, .. in vague And loose indifference. **1839** KEIGHTLEY *Hist. Eng.* I. 50 At the same time they acted very remissly against their foreign kinsmen.

†**2.** Faintly, indistinctly. *Obs. rare.*

1530 PALSGR. 24 The consonant shalbe but remissely sounded. **1577** DEE *Relat. Spir.* I. (1659) 95 He pronounceth the i so remissely, as it is scarce heard.

†**3.** Gently, feebly; without vigour. *Obs.*

1642 R. CARPENTER *Experience* v. xviii. 314 And therefore it will worke in them awhile though at length weakly and remissely. **1692** RAY *Disc.* 142 Being very much deaded .. and burning very remisly in Summer time and hot Weather.

†**4.** Moderately, slightly. *Obs. rare*$^{-1}$.

1684 tr. *Bonet's Merc. Compit.* III. 112 In hot Diseases simply Cold things are no way expedient, but things remisly hot.

remissness (rɪˈmɪsnɪs). [f. REMISS *a.* + -NESS.] The quality of being remiss.

1. Carelessness, negligence; laxity.

1570 FOXE *A. & M.* (ed. 2) 2040/1 He litle regarding their inconstancie and remisnes in Gods cause or quarel. **1598** BARRET *Theor. Warres* IV. i. 98 The disorders of souldiers do many times grow through remissnesse .. of officers. **1615** G. SANDYS *Trav.* 7 Encouraged to villanies by the remisnesse of their lawes. **1644** MILTON *Areop.* (Arb.) 51 Impunity and remissenes, for certain are the bane of a Commonwealth. **1685** EVELYN *Diary* 2 Oct., The Reformed Churches in Christendom, now weaken'd and neere ruin'd thro' our remissenesse. **1728** MORGAN *Algiers* II. v. 316 The order [of Knights] rather dreads the Remissness and wonted Luke-warmness of the Catholic Potentates. **1760–2** GOLDSM. *Cit. W.* xl[i], The remissness of behaviour in almost all the worshippers .. struck me with surprize. **1838** THIRLWALL *Greece* xlii. V. 225 This remissness of the Athenians encouraged Charidemus openly to renounce the treaty.

†**b.** Relaxation; ease. *Obs. rare.*

1651 HOBBES *Leviath.* I. viii. 34 In profest remissnesse of mind .. a man may play with the sounds .. of words. **1754** FIELDING *Jonathan Wild* III. xiv, None but the weak and honest can indulge themselves in remissness or repose.

†**2.** Weakening, diminution, decrease or lack of force or intensity. *Obs.*

1608 WILLET *Hexapla Exod.* 259 Nor yet do I consent to them, that thinke Moses still continued his prayers, but that this remisnes was only in his strength. **1659** STANLEY *Hist. Philos.* XIII. (1701) 624/2 The shortness makes amends for the greatness [of the pain], the remissness for its length. **1669** W. SIMPSON *Hydrol. Chym.* 315 According to the intenseness or remissness of the air. **1711** ADDISON *Spect.* No. 249 ¶5 Laughter .. slackens and unbraces the Mind, weakens the Faculties, and causes a kind of Remissness and Dissolution in all the Powers of the Soul.

remissory (rɪˈmɪsərɪ), *a. rare.* [f. as REMISS *v.* + -ORY.] Tending to, of the nature of, remission.

1548 LATIMER *Serm. Ploughers* (Arb.) 33 Propitiatorie, expiatorie, remissorie, or satisfactorie .. signifie all one thynge in effecte. **1592** WEST *1st Pt. Symbol.* §46 f, An Instrument remissory, is an Instrument vnder the parties hand describing & testifying some precedent contract of a debt, duty or fact to be paid, performed, done, released or discharged. **1824** MEYRICK *Antient Armour* II. 4 The use of these thongs we learn from a letter remissory, dated 1358.

remit (ˈriːmɪt, older rɪˈmɪt), *sb.* [f. the vb.]

†**1.** Remission, pardon. Chiefly *Sc. Obs. rare.*

1423 JAS. I *Kingis Q.* cxcv, Quho sal be thare to pray for thy remyt? **1565–6** *Reg. Privy Council Scot.* I. 422 [He] hes alswa obtenit remit and discharge of the said deforcement. **1589** *Ibid.* IV. 388 A remitt for the said cryme.

†**2.** A reference from one part of a book to another. *Obs. rare*$^{-1}$.

1688 DALLAS *Stiles* Index, This Fourth Part is divided in four Branches ..; and when any of them are in the First Part of the Work, there is a Remit to it, and the Page Cited.

3. a. The consignment or reference of a matter to some other person or authority for settlement, *esp.* in *Law*, the transfer of a case from one court or judge to another, or to a judicial nominee. Chiefly *Sc.*

1719 *Wodrow Corr.* (1843) II. 448 This day the Assembly met, and went through their ordinary business; many, many remits to the Commission. **1816** SCOTT *Antiq.* ii, Let there be no remits from the inner to the outer-house. **1833** *Act 3 & 4 Will. IV*, c. 46 §92 The amount .. shall be ascertained by such magistrate .. by means of a remit to persons of skill. **1880** MUIRHEAD *Gaius* II. §278 *note*, The procedure was .. before the consul, .. without any remit to a *iudex*.

b. *N.Z.* An item submitted for consideration at a conference, etc.

1916 *Maoriland Worker* 12 July 4/7 Messrs. Hutchison and Harper moved that the Order Paper Committee put on a remit dealing with Conscription.—Carried. **1918** *Conf. United Federation of Labor* (N.Z.) 4/1 Mr. B. Martin moved the Auckland District Council remit: 'That capitation to the National Executive from the District Councils under clause 12 be reduced to 3d per member.' **1958** *N.Z. Listener* 5 Sept. 8/2 We might see that New Zealand would put a remit up to the International Board and it would be turned down. **1963** *Manawatu Standard* 9 Apr. 12/9 A Canterbury remit that the Government should appoint a Minister of Road Transport .. could not meet with the general approval of the Associated Chambers of Commerce delegates in Rotorua. **1966** G. W. TURNER *Eng. Lang. in Austral. & N.Z.* viii. 174 Policies of influential bodies are a good deal determined by remits from below.

c. A set of instructions, a brief.

1963 *Guardian* 30 May 8/6 The remit given to Sir Gilbert Flemming, who is considering the possibility of the dispersal of Government departments. **1971** *New Scientist* 25 Feb. 407/2 The remit is essentially to produce a scenario of nutritional developments. **1973** M. MACKINTOSH *King & Two Queens* xv. 209 Your self-imposed remit in America was to find out .. what he was covering up. **1977** *Undercurrents* June–July 12/3 The answer lies simply in the fact that the DHSS is a bureaucratic department which does not have the remit to support publications other than official government documents.

remit (rɪˈmɪt), *v.* Also 4–6 remyt, 5–6 -mytte (5 -myght), 5–7 remitt(e. [ad. L. *remitt-ĕre*, f. *re-* RE- + *mittĕre* to send; cf. *admit, commit*, etc. In Eng. use the secondary senses appear earlier and are more prominent than the primary: cf. REMISSION.] I. *trans.*

1. To forgive or pardon (a sin, offence, etc.).

c **1375** *Sc. Leg. Saints* vii. (*James less*) 209 Lord, remyt þis gilt þam to. *Ibid.* xxx. (*Theodora*) 698 He hyr reconsalyt..& remyted hyre al hyr syne. c **1440** *Gesta Rom.* lxxviii. 399 (Add. MS.), Afterwarde the kyng made men to seke the queen,..and all that was done was remytte. **1503–4** *Act 19 Hen. VII*, c. 37 *Preamble*, It pleased your Highnesse..to pardone remitte & forgyve unto your seid Subgiect all the seid Mesprisions. **1535** COVERDALE *John* xx. 23 Whose synnes soeuer ye remytte they are remytted vnto them. **1608** HIERON *Wks.* I. 695 Bee pleased..for His sake to remit my former vngratefulnesse. **1708** J. CHAMBERLAYNE *St. Gt. Brit.* I. III. viii. 254 The English being easily to be reconciled, to pardon and remit Offences. **1823** SCOTT *Peveril* xl, Your Majesty was pleased to remit his more outrageous and insolent attempt upon your royal crown. **1884** A. R. PENNINGTON *Wiclif* ix. 297 It is impossible for the priest to remit the sins of any unless they are first remitted by Christ.

†**b.** To spare, pardon, or forgive (a person).

1526 *Pilgr. Perf.* (W. de W. 1531) 78 He wolde not his prelate to shewe ony mercy on hym, nor to remyt or spare hym in ony thynge. **1549** COVERDALE, etc. *Erasm. Par. John* 44 For God remitteth not hym that forgeueth not his brother. **1583** STUBBES *Anat. Abus.* II. (1882) 13 Can man pardon or remit him whom God doth condemne? **1633** BP. HALL *Hard Texts, N.T.* 79 Bee comforted in God who hath remitted thee.

†**2.** To give up, resign, surrender (a right or possession). *Obs.*

c **1450** *Godstow Reg.* (E.E.T.S.) 42 Milo Basset remitted and furthermore quyte-claymed..to the abbesse of Godestowe.., all the right and clayme that he had. **1472–3** *Rolls of Parlt.* VI. 6/1 That it may please youre seid Highnes ..to remitte and release..to us..all youre right. **1588** SHAKS. *L.L.L.* v. ii. 459 *Qu.* Will you haue me, or your Pearle againe? *Ber.* Neither of either, I remit both twaine. **1647–8** COTTERELL *Davila's Hist. Fr.* (1678) 12 He was led ..to remit his whole authority into the hands of allies. **1654** tr. *Scudery's Curia Pol.* 96 If Queen Elizabeth had not believed..she would not have..remitted her Scepter to my hands. **1670** DRYDEN *Tyran. Love* III. i, Th' Ægyptian Crown I to your hands remit.

3. To abstain from exacting (a payment or service of any kind); to allow to remain unpaid (or unperformed).

1463 *Rolls of Parlt.* V. 498/2 To pardon and remitte unto the seid Commons the seid vi M li. **1560** DAUS tr. *Sleidane's Comm.* 60 It is reason that the lordes remit some part therof [*sc.* rent]. c **1645** HOWELL *Lett.* (1713) 16 All this his Majesty remitted, and only took the Principal. a **1661** FULLER *Worthies* (1840) II. 508 The Queen..rigorously demanded the present payment of some arrears which Sir Christopher did not hope to have remitted. **1701** W. WOTTON *Hist. Rome* vi. 109 She remitted the Arrears that were owing. **1783** BURKE *Rep. Aff. India* Wks. 1842 II. 18/1 They remit, by the like authority, the duties, to which all private trade is subject. **1817** JAS. MILL *Brit. India* I. III. iv. 575 The rents of the husbandman, and other taxes, were remitted. **1863** FAWCETT *Pol. Econ.* III. iii. 323 Let it be assumed that every farmer has the rent of his farm remitted for the next thirty years.

b. To refrain from inflicting (a punishment) or carrying out (a sentence); to withdraw, cancel; to grant remission of (suffering).

1483 *Rolls of Parlt.* VI. 250/2 Oure said soveraigne Lorde ..remitteth and woll forbere the greate punysshement of atteynder. **1553** T. WILSON *Rhet.* 15 b, The whole citie thought to remitte the necessitie of his punishment for the honour of his father. **1616** R. C. *Times' Whistle* IV. 1344 The officer deputed for th' offence Will winck at smale faultes & remit correction. **1693** LUTTRELL *Brief Rel.* (1857) III. 118 The queen remitted the quartering of his body. **1754** SHERLOCK *Disc.* I. i. 46 God may freely forgive the Sins of the World, and remit the Punishment. **1807** CRABBE *Hall of Just.* 3 Remit awhile the harsh command. **1841** JAMES *Brigand* xxxiii, We come to beseech you to remit the sentence of this unhappy young gentleman. **1857** BUCKLE *Civiliz.* I. xii. 673 The exile which followed the imprisonment seems to have been soon remitted. **1868** BROWNING *Ring & Bk.* VI. 127 How does lenity to me Remit one death-bed pang to her?

c. To exempt from confiscation. *rare*⁻¹.

1741 MIDDLETON *Cicero* I. ii. 104 Verres for a valuable consideration sometimes remitted the ship.

d. To allow as a respite. *rare*⁻¹.

1813 BYRON *Corsair* II. xiv, I will, at least, delay The sentence that remits thee scarce a day.

†**4.** To discharge, set free, release, liberate (a person). Also const. *of*, *to*. *Obs.*

1467–8 *Rolls of Parlt.* V. 576/1 To be remitted, acquited or discharged of eny somme or sommes of money. a **1548** HALL *Chron., Hen. VIII* 169 b, Wee clerely remitted, and deliuered hym into his countrey. **1575** R. B. *Appius & Virg.* D j b, If treason none by me be done, or any fault committed, Let my accusers beare the blame, and let me be remitted. **1634** GARRARD in *Strafford's Lett.* (1739) I. 373 Mr. Seldon is remitted of those Fetters that lay upon him. **1647** CLARENDON *Hist. Reb.* VI. §35 His Lordship was committed to the Tower..; and though he was afterwards remitted to more Air, he continued a Prisoner to his death.

II. 5. To give up, lay aside (anger, displeasure, etc.) entirely or in part.

c **1375** *Sc. Leg. Saints* vii. (*James less*) 635 þare-for his malancoly to þat man he remyttyte þare. **1393–4** *Rolls of Parlt.* III. 314/1 Hit forthynketh me, and byseche yowe of your gode Lordship to remyt me your mautalent. **1413** *Pilgr. Sowle* (Caxton 1483) I. xxvii. 31 This blessid lord Ihesu Crist remitted his rigour, descending downe to the erthe. **1560** DAUS tr. *Sleidane's Comm.* 317 b, I beseche him to remit all displeasure. **1577** HANMER *Anc. Eccl. Hist.* (1619) 180 [He] would not thus much have remitted his tyranny, had he not been compelled. **1667** MILTON *P.L.* II. 210 Our Supream Foe in time may much remit His anger. **1761** HUME *Hist. Eng.* I. App. ii. 258 That he would remit his displeasure. **1820** SHELLEY *Œd. Tyr.* II. ii. 99 Remit, O Queen! thy accustomed rage!

b. To give up or give over, abandon, desist from (a pursuit, occupation, etc.).

1587 R. HOVENDEN in *Collect.* (O.H.S.) I. 220 The Ladi Stafford was resolved to remyt hir suite. **1608** WILLET *Hexapla Exod.* 60 They..caused them to remit their workes. **1687** LADY R. RUSSELL *Lett.* I. li. 123 It seems I must remit seeing you, as you once kindly intended. **1726** POPE *Odyss.* XXIV. 286 Who digging round the plant still hangs his head, Nor ought remits the work. **1880** KINGLAKE *Crimea* VI. vi. 159 Engaged..in a siege which they could not remit.

6. To allow (one's diligence, attention, etc.) to slacken or abate.

c **1510** MORE *Picus* Wks. 15/1 Ye shall not think, that my trauaile and diligence in study is any thing remitted or slacked. **1590** MARLOWE *Edw. II*, II. v, He that the care of his realm remits [etc.]. **1742–3** LD. HERVEY in *Johnson's Debates* (1787) II. 409 To make the attainment of it more and more difficult, that they may insensibly remit their ardour. **1780** JOHNSON *Let. to Mr. Thrale* 30 May, Do not remit your care. **1803** MAR. EDGEWORTH *Manuf.* ii. (1832) 101, I have never remitted my attention to business. **1827** HALLAM *Const. Hist.* (1876) I. iii. 143 Nor did the voluntary exiles established in Flanders remit their diligence in filling the kingdom with emissaries.

b. To admit or manifest an abatement *of* some quality. ? *Obs.*

1621 BURTON *Anat. Mel.* I. i. I. i, When he..remembred that he was but a man, and remitted of his pride. **1628** HOBBES *Thucyd.* (1822) 8 To try if the Athenians..would yet in some degree remit of their obstinacy. **1702** *Eng. Theophrast.* 342 The strongest passions sometimes remit of their violence. **1775** S. J. PRATT *Liberal Opin.* v. (1783) I. 84 At the end of about two months, the severity of my fate began to remit of its rigour.

c. To mitigate, diminish, or abate. ? *Obs.*

1615 G. SANDYS *Trav.* 39 Stiffe winter which no spring remits. **1656** RIDGLEY *Pract. Physick* 316 When the heat, pain, Feaver are remitted. **1658** ROWLAND tr. *Moufet's Theat. Ins.* 979 The light by little and little is remitted and slackned. **1750** JOHNSON *Rambler* No. 17 ¶5 Every man has experienced how much of this ardour has been remitted, when a sharp..sickness has set death before his eyes.

†**7.** To relax, relieve from tension. *Obs.*

c **1510** BARCLAY *Mirr. Gd. Manners* (1570) D j, Cease not, perseuer, knock & stande, Remitte not thine armes by knocking fatigate. **1668** CULPEPPER & COLE *Barthol. Anat.* II. iii. 92 When the Breath is drawn in the Midriff is stretched, when it is blowne out, it is remitted or slackned. a **1676** HALE *Prim. Orig. Man.* I. i. (1677) 29 'Tis by this.. the Lungs are intended or remitted. **1711** tr. *Werenfelsius' Logomachys, Disc. Meteors Stile* 192 Let the Judgement.. sometimes remit, and sometimes contract the Reins.

III. 8. To refer (a matter) for consideration, decision, performance, etc., *to* a person or body of persons, now usu. to one specially empowered or appointed to deal with it; also *spec.* in *Law*, to send back (a case) to an inferior court.

c **1400** MAUNDEV. (1839) xxxi. 315 Oure holy Fadir.. remytted my Boke to ben examyned and preved be the Avys of the seyd Conseille. **1455** *Paston Lett.* I. 321 Wheche mater I remytte..to youre ryght wyse discrecion. **1484** CAXTON *Fables of Alfonce* ix, They remytted the cause to be discuted or pleted before the Juge. **1523** FITZHERB. *Husb.* §7 The spirytuall constructyon of this texte, I remytte to the doctours of dyuynitie. **1586** T. B. *La Primaud. Fr. Acad.* I. (1594) 514 Let them remit the judgement and deciding of their controversies to the arbitrement of some good men. **1654** tr. *Martini's Conq. China* 14 He remitted the business to the chief Governors and Commanders. **1762** FOOTE *Orators* I. Wks. 1799 I. 203 We shall..remit the examination of the ignoble ones to the care of subaltern artists. **1863** P. BARRY *Dockyard Econ.* 59 The task and job question was remitted to the Commissioners on the Civil Affairs of the Navy. **1884** *Law Times Rep.* L. 174/1 The defendants gave notice of their motion to set aside and remit the report [of the special referee].

absol. **1838** W. BELL *Dict. Law Scot.* 52 The circuit judge ..may recall the judgment appealed from, and remit to the inferior court with instructions.

b. To send (a person) from one tribunal *to* another for trial or hearing. *rare.*

1538 STARKEY *England* II. ii. 190 At London the jugys schold admyt non in sute, but such only as, for some resonabul cause, were remyttyd to them by the gentylmen of the scyre. **1740** HOWE in *Johnson's Debates* (1787) I. 31 If we remit this offender..to any inferior court [etc.].

†**c.** To commit (a person) *to* the charge or control of another. Also *refl.* *Obs.*

1681–6 J. SCOTT *Chr. Life* (1747) III. 126 God..wholly remitted his People to the Conduct of the Priests and Levites. **1741** RICHARDSON *Pamela* (1883) I. 407 As he knew best what befitted his own rank and condition, I would wholly remit myself to his good pleasure.

†**d.** *refl.* = REFER *v.* 5. *Obs. rare*⁻¹.

1674 *Govt. Tongue* 18, I dare in this remit me to themselves, and challenge..their natural ingenuity to say [etc.].

9. To refer (one) *to* a book, person, etc., for information on some point.

1417 HEN. V in Ellis *Orig. Lett.* Ser. III. I. 62 We remitte hem to have ful declaracion and verrai knaweleche of you in that matere. c **1425** WYNTOUN *Cron.* II. 1346 (Wemyss MS.), Gif ȝe of þat thing mare will wit, To Ovidis buke I ȝow remytt. **1533** MORE *Debell. Salem* Pref., Wks. 931/1 And some suche places yet as I had happed to finde, I haue remitted the reader vnto in myne apologye. **1590** SIR J. SMYTH *Disc. Weapons* 49 To the particularities whereof..I remit those that are disposed to see and consider. **1650** FULLER *Pisgah* II. iv. 113 Well might profane persons be remitted to this river, thereby to be instructed in the Sabbaths due observation. **1714** *Ellwoods' Autobiog.* Pref., Much of this being already done in the ensuing Pages, I chuse to remit the Reader thither. **1769** ROBERTSON *Chas. V*, VII. III. 16 The Emperor..without deigning to answer a single word, remitted him to his ministers. **1835–8** S. R. MAITLAND *Dark Ages* (1844) 156 Let us hear Du Cange, to whom Robertson remits us.

ellipt. c **1410** *Master of Game* (MS. Digby 182) x, Of þe remenaunt of his nature I remytte to Milbournn þe kynges Otyr hunter. **1523** FITZHERB. *Husb.* Prol., I remytte [? to] that boke as myn auctour therof.

†**b.** To direct (one) *to* a task. *Obs. rare*⁻¹.

1544 *Supplic. Hen. VIII* (1871) 51 Remyttynge byshops to attende their offyce and vocacyon by God..appoynted.

10. a. To send (a person) back to prison, or to other custody; to recommit. Now *rare.*

1414 *Rolls of Parlt.* IV. 57/2 Whan I was remitted to the Prison of Flete. **1474** *Ibid.* VI. 103/1 The seid Chaunceller there remitted the seid Thomas Buysshop ageyn. **1653** LD. VAUX tr. *Godeau's St. Paul* 300 The Captain..remitted him, with the rest of his prisoners, into the hands of the Prefect of the Pretorium. **1700** DRYDEN *Sigism. & Guisc.* 287 The prisoner was remitted to the guard. **1827** HALLAM *Const. Hist.* (1876) I. vii. 383 Whether such a return was sufficient in law to justify the court in remitting the parties to custody.

†**b.** To send in return; to send back. *Obs. rare.*

1461 *Paston Lett.* II. 67 Remitte me summe letter, by the bringer her of, of all thes maters. **1660** F. BROOKE tr. *Le Blanc's Trav.* 113 He gave them freedom, and remitted them ransomlesse, sent them all back again.

†**c.** To emit or send out again. *Obs. rare*⁻¹.

1700 DRYDEN *Ovid's Met.* xv. 522 Whether Earth's an Animal, and Air Imbibes; her Lungs with coolness to repair, and what she sucks remits.

11. †**a.** *Law.* To restore to a former and more valid title: see REMITTER² 1. *Obs.*

1544 tr. *Littleton's Tenures* 141 In so much the wyfe is in her remytter, he is remitted to his reuercion. **1632** *Womens Rights* xix. 156 The eldest daughter is remitted, that is remaunded and setled in the ancient estate. **1768** BLACKSTONE *Comm.* III. ii. 21 If the issue in tail be barred by the fine..of his ancestor, and the freehold is afterwards cast upon him; he shall not be remitted to his estate tail.

b. To put back *into*, to admit or consign again *to* a previous position, state, or condition.

1591 SPENSER *M. Hubberd* 1254 He bad the Lyon be remitted Into his seate. **1642** FULLER *Holy & Prof. St.* II. xxii. 142 Thus his indiscretion remitted him to the nature of an ordinary person. **1654** EARL MONM. tr. *Bentivoglio's Warrs Flanders* 186 It was a long while ere it [the city] could be remitted into its former condition. **1671** MILTON *Samson* 687 Nor only dost [thou] degrade them, or remit To life obscur'd which were a fair dismission. **1761** *New Comp. Fest. & Fasts* xxxvi. §2. 353 When death..is making his near approach to..remit us to darkness and oblivion. **1863** BRIGHT *Sp., Amer.* 30 June (1876) 142 You propose to remit to slavery three millions of negroes.

12. To postpone, to put off or defer.

1635 J. HAYWARD tr. *Biondi's Banish'd Virg.* 166 Willingly would hee have knowne then presently the story..but..he remitted it till after supper. **1663** GERBIER *Counsel* 62 Remitting setting of walls untill the next Spring after. **1769** GOLDSM. *Hist. Rome* (1786) II. 25 The conspirators.. remitted the execution of their design to the ides of March. **1786** JEFFERSON *Writ.* (1859) I. 511 We remitted all further discussion till he should send me a copy of his letter. **1836** J. GILBERT *Chr. Atonem.* iii. (1852) 73 We must for the present remit our reply to that part of our subject.

†**b.** To defer the reception of (a person). *Obs.*⁻¹

1663 H. COGAN tr. *Pinto's Trav.* xliv. 175, I hold it fit to remit him unto some other time, when as he may be better acquainted.

13. To refer, assign, or make over *to* a thing or person.

1641 *Vind. Smectymnuus* vi. 78 That which Hierome speakes in the present tense..he would remit to time past. **1720** WATERLAND *Answ. Whitby's Reply* 58 You..object farther..that Christ would not suffer Himself to be called Good, but remitted that Title to the Father only. **1788** REID *Aristotle's Log.* iv. §6. 89 He thinks that the doctrine of modals ought to be banished out of logic and remitted to grammar. **1837** G. PHILLIPS *Syriac Gram.* 9 The vowel in such places is remitted to the preceding letter, if it has been previously without one.

†**b.** To enter or insert *in* (or *into*) a book. *Obs.*

c **1670** WOOD *Life* (O.H.S.) II. 204 This book he gave A. W. because he had, in his great reading, collected some old words for his use, which were remitted therein. **1716** M. DAVIES *Athen. Brit.* II. 219 Which Examinations..were.. remitted by John Fox into his Book of Martyrs.

14. To send or transmit (money or articles of value) *to* a person or place.

1640 HOWELL *Dodona's Gr.* 98 [He] makes one of her proudest Cities his Scale, for remitting his Moneyes to Leoncia. **1690** in J. Mackenzie *Siege London-Derry* 54/1 You are to receive and dispose of the Thousand pounds which shall be remitted to you, to the best advantage. **1758** JOHNSON *Idler* No. 62 ¶4 We parted; and he remitted me a small annuity. **1787** JEFFERSON *Writ.* (1859) II. 149 This has prevented the treasury board from remitting any money to this place. **1840** MACAULAY *Ess., Clive* (1852) III. 61 He had recently remitted a great part of his fortune to Europe, through the Dutch East India Company. **1861** GOSCHEN *For. Exch.* 91 Was it probable..that in a time of great national emergency the New York bankers would remit their capital for employment to Europe..?

absol. **1682** [see *remitted*, below]. **1705** ADDISON *Italy* 471 They oblig'd themselves to remit, after the rate of Twelve Hundred Thousand Pounds Sterling per Annum. **1809** BYRON *Let. to Mrs. Byron* 12 Nov., I expect Hanson to remit regularly.

IV. *intr.* **15.** To abate, diminish, slacken.

1629 *Drayner Conf.* (1647) C, The whole masse of waters continue upon the face of the Fenne till those windes remit. **1643** MILTON *Divorce* (1645) 39 The vigor of his Law could no more remit, then the hallowed fire on his altar could be let go out. **1695** WOODWARD *Nat. Hist. Earth* IV. 198 Till such time as its motion begins to remit and be less rapid.

1770 GOLDSM. *Des. Vill.* 16 How often have I blest the coming day, When toil remitting lent its turn to play. **1850** L. HUNT *Autobiog.* I. viii. 309 The fishermen's wives.. seemed equally determined not to let the intention remit. **1870** BRYANT *Iliad* II. XIII. 23 Meantime the valor of Idomeneus Remitted not.

b. of pain, fever, etc. Also in *fig.* context.

1685 tr. *Willis' Lond. Pract. Physick* 533 If upon sore Lips the Fever does not remit, it will prove of long continuance and severe. **1737** WHISTON *Josephus, Antiq.* II. iii. §4 Neither did his pains remit by length of time. **1747** tr. *Astruc's Fevers* 195 The fever thus treated, remits generally towards the sixth or seventh day. **1783** JOHNSON *Let.* in *Boswell* 30 Sept., I have been.. much harassed with the gout; but that has now remitted. **1887** *Pall Mall G.* 17 Feb. 13/2 The 'Otello' fever at Milan seems at last a little inclined to remit.

16. To relax *from* labour; to give over.

1760–72 H. BROOKE *Fool of Qual.* (1809) I. 84 They remitted from their toil. **1841** EMERSON *Ess., Man the Reformer* Wks. (Bohn) II. 240 Their enemies will not remit; rust, mould, vermin.. all seize their own.

Hence **re'mitted** *ppl. a.*

1682 SCARLETT *Exchanges* 65 Every Remitter that remits not directly, but designs to draw in the remitted Sum again [etc.]. *a* **1700** KEN *Hymnotheo* Poet. Wks. 1721 III. 130 The happy symptons of remitted sin. **1896** DE WINDT *New Siberia* iv. 59 There is also a graduated scale of what are called remitted sentences. **1897** *Westm. Gaz.* 13 Apr. 2/1 But it is not merely in respect of these remitted actions that the County Courts have weighty and important functions.

†**re'mitigate,** *v. Obs. rare*$^{-1}$. [RE-; cf. obs. F. *remitiguer* (Godef.).] *trans.* To mitigate.

1671 MACWARD *True Nonconf.* 387 The apparent singularity of any circumstance remitigated by another extra-ordinary occurrent.

remitless (rɪ'mɪtlɪs), *a. rare.* [f. REMIT *v.* + -LESS.] Without remission; unpardoned; ceaseless.

a **1907** F. THOMPSON *Works* (1913) I. 198 Meek guides and daughters to the blinded heaven In Œdipean, remitless wandering driven.

remitment (rɪ'mɪtmənt). [f. REMIT *v.*]

†**1.** Remission, pardon. *Obs.*

1611 COTGR., *Absoute*, a generall absolution, pardon, forgiuenesse, remitment of offences. **1645** MILTON *Tetrach.* 34 God's Law especially grants every where to error easy remitments. **1670** —— *Hist. Eng.* II. 63 The Procurator endeavour'd to bring all their goods within the compass of a new confiscation, by disavowing the remittment of Claudius.

2. Remitting of money; remittance.

1678 *Trans. Crt. Spain* 109 [He] makes it his business to perswade the people, that Your Majesty has remitted vast sums of money to the Emperour, and hath discovered a great part of the remitment. **1706** PHILLIPS (ed. Kersey), *Remitment* or *Remittance*, a return of Money, &c. **1792** JEFFERSON *Writ.* (1859) III. 419 The debtor who endeavored to make a remitment of his debt, or interest, must have done it three times. **1894** *Columbus* (Ohio) *Disp.* 7 Dec. 1/8 An order.. for the remitment to the township poor fund.. [of] six-tenths of the amount of Dow liquor tax.

†**3.** The act of remitting to custody. *Obs.*

1755 in JOHNSON.

re'mittable, *a. rare.* [f. REMIT *v.* + -ABLE.] Capable of being remitted.

1611 COTGR., *Remissible*, remittable, pardonable, forgiueable. **1844** H. H. WILSON *Brit. India* III. 313 Partly by its discharge, and partly by its transference to a remittable loan, at 5 per cent.

remittal (rɪ'mɪtəl). [f. REMIT *v.* + -AL[1].]

1. Remission *for* sin, or *of* a debt, penalty, etc.

1596 BELL *Surv. Popery* III. vi. 309 Not to procure any remittall for her sins. **1617** MORYSON *Itin.* II. 24 He agreeth to a fine.., yet praying the Lord Liefetenant to be a meanes to her Maiesty for the remittal thereof. *c* **1693** SIR P. PETT in *Lett. Eminent Persons* (1813) I. 60, I should be glad to hear .. that his Lordship shewed any good nature to you in the remittal of the costs you were condemned in. **1854** MILMAN *Lat. Chr.* VII. vi. (1864) IV. 192 A remittal of those acts of penance which the Church commuted at her will.

2. *Law.* The act of referring a case from one court to another.

1808 BENTHAM *Sc. Reform* 107 To regulate concerning the remittal of causes from Division to Division. **1884** *Law Times* LXXVII. 407/1 The option of.. decision by the official arbitrator or remittal to the High Court.

remittance (rɪ'mɪtəns). [f. REMIT *v.* + -ANCE.]

1. A sum of money sent from one place or person to another; a quantity of some article sent in this way; also, the act of sending money, etc., to another place.

1705 ADDISON *Italy* 471 A Compact among private Persons furnish'd out the several Remittances. **1711** *Lond. Gaz.* No. 4808/2 The Swedish Commissary.. has.. received a Remittance of one hundred thousand Crowns. **1769** ROBERTSON *Chas. V*, XI. III. 310 His remittances into England had drained his treasury. **1840** MACAULAY *Ess., Clive* (1852) III. 63 He had invested great sums in jewels, then a very common mode of remittance from India. **1867** SMILES *Huguenots Eng.* xviii. (1880) 328 A distant relative.. took possession of the family estate, and further remittances .. were stopped. **1880** MARKHAM *Peruv. Bark* 408 The Dutch Government bought a portion of the remittance of *C. Calisaya* seeds.

2. ***remittance man***, an emigrant who is supported or assisted by remittances from home (cf. REMITTANCER); also *fig.* So ***remittance-farmer***.

1886 *Pall Mall G.* 10 Feb. 11/1 He was what is called in the colonies a 'remittance man'. **1894** C. L. JOHNSTONE *Canada* 30 The Canadians divide the English gentlemen settlers into 'farmers who work, remittance farmers, and buckboard farmers'. **1897** MISS B. HARRADEN *Remittance-Men* 185 Remittance men never do any good. **1903** [see PALOUSER]. **1959** T. S. ELIOT *Elder Statesman* III. 93 Everyone would sneer at the fellow from London, The limey remittance man for whom a job was made. **1969** *Listener* 9 Jun. 42/2 I'd arrived at the end of the line already: the proclaimed remittance man of an obsolete social system. **1975** C. AIRD *Slight Mourning* vii. 69 'Last heard of in the backwoods of Queensland.'.. 'A remittance man, I'll be bound.'

Hence **re'mittancer,** (*a*) one who sends a remittance; (*b*) a remittance man.

1806 R. CUMBERLAND *Mem.* 435 Your Memorialist was stopped and arrested at Bayonne by order from his remittancers at Madrid. **1849** E. B. HODGE *Keith Kavanagh* p. v, A 'Remittancer' or 'Remittance Man' is, in colonial parlance, a Ne'er-do-well living in the colonies on quarterly remittances received from friends 'at home'.

remittee (rɪmɪ'tiː). [f. REMIT *v.* + -EE[1].] One to whom a remittance is made or sent.

1766 W. GORDON *Gen. Counting-ho.* 339 The porteur or remittee to whom the bill is remitted for acceptance. **1798** W. TAYLOR in *Monthly Rev.* XXVII. 490 A deposit belonging to the drawer, and successively confided to the remittees. **1885** *Law Rep. 14 Q.B. Div.* 612 Remittances are sent.. to cover drafts of the remitter accepted by the remittee.

re'mittence. *rare.* [f. as REMITTENT *a.* + -ENCE; cf. F. *rémittence.*] = REMITTENCY.

1901 *Practitioner* Mar. 311 When the paroxysms return in the evening and are prolonged so that the intermission or remittence takes place in the morning, this fever may be easily mistaken for typhoid.

re'mittency. [See next and -ENCY, and cf. F. *rémittence.*] The quality of being remittent.

1820–6 F. L. GALT in Orton *Andes & Amazons* II. xliv. (ed. 3) 602 The symptoms.. had a remittency about them in most instances. **1898** P. MANSON *Trop. Diseases* ii. 37 The fact of intermittency or remittency being more or less a matter of accident.

remittent (rɪ'mɪtənt), *a.* and *sb.* [ad. L. *remittent-em*, pres. pple. of *remittĕre* to REMIT: cf. F. *rémittent.*]

A. *adj.* That remits or abates for a time: *spec.* in *Path.* of a type of fever, the symptoms of which undergo at intervals a marked abatement or diminution (without disappearing entirely as in the *intermittent* type).

1693 *Phil. Trans.* XVII. 726 The Cortex makes as certain a Cure in the Remittent Fever as in the Intermittent. **1776–84** CULLEN *First Lines Physic* xxvi. Wks. 1827 I. 487 They suffer.. a considerable abatement or Remission... This constitutes what is called a Remittent Fever. **1791** BOSWELL *Johnson* (1831) I. 309 Yet nine years elapsed before it saw the light. His throes in bringing it forth had been severe and remittent. **1804** MITCHILL & MILLER *Med. Repos.* 178 *note*, The more common form of the disease [yellow fever] was the 'bilious' and 'remittent' fever. **1877** ROBERTS *Handbk. Med.* (ed. 3) I. 217 The malarial fevers of hot climates often assume a remittent type.

B. *sb.* **1.** *Path.* A remittent fever.

1693 *Phil. Trans.* XVII. 726 Almost all Epidemical, Autumnal and Camp-Fevers are either Genuine or Spurious Remittents. *a* **1776** R. JAMES *Diss. Fevers* (1778) 96 It would be ridiculous and cruel, if a physician were to refuse the bark to a patient in a genuine remittent or intermittent. *a* **1817** T. DWIGHT *Trav. New Eng.*, etc. (1821) II. 452 The shores of lake Champlain are generally subject to the fever and ague, and to bilious remittents. **1897** MARY KINGSLEY *W. Africa* 53 Fever in Fernando Po.. having periodic outbursts of a more serious type than the normal intermittent and remittent of the Coast.

2. One who remits money.

1855 LORENZ tr. *Van der Keessel's Select Theses* dlxxiv, In that kind of exchange.. there generally are.. four parties; first the person who gives the value or money, and who is called the remittent [etc.].

remitter[1] (rɪ'mɪtə(r)). [f. REMIT *v.* + -ER[1].]

1. One who forgives or pardons. *rare.*

c **1557** ABP. PARKER *Ps.* xli. 120 (*Collect*) Most gentle remitter of sinne, almighty God. **1586** FULKE *Confut. Allen* 143 Not properlie pardoners, forgiuers, or remitters of sinnes.

2. One who sends a remittance.

1682 SCARLETT *Exchanges* 32 The Drawer and Remitter should also.. note the Mackelers or Brogers Name to every Parcel. **1745** *De Foe's Eng. Tradesman* xxviii. (1841) I. 279 It looks like a forwardness to take the remitters money without giving him a sufficient demand for it. **1757** JOS. HARRIS *Coins* 120 *note*, Dealers in bills of exchange are in general terms usually called remitters. **1861** GOSCHEN *For. Exch.* 47 The premium is so high, that remitters will become indifferent whether they buy bills or send gold. **1884** *Law Times Rep.* LI. 390/1 As regards those remittances.. the remitters were entitled to have them specifically appropriated.

remitter[2] (rɪ'mɪtə(r)). [See REMIT *v.* and -ER[4].]

1. *Law.* **a.** A principle or operation by which one having two titles to an estate, and entering on it by the later or more defective of these, is adjudged to hold it by the earlier or more valid one. (Cf. REMIT *v.* 11 a.)

1544 tr. *Littleton's Tenures* 137 Remytter is an auncyent terme in the lawe, & it is where a man hath ii tytles to landes or tenementes.. the lawe adjudgeth hym to be in by force of the elder tytle. **1599** FULBECKE *Prepar. Study of Law* (1620) 57 They wrote of Fines, Vouchers, Remitters. *a* **1625** SIR H. FINCH *Law* (1636) 194 If he.. haue the Freehold cast vpon him by a new title, he shall be in of his ancient title: which is termed a remitter. **1668** HALE *Pref. Rolle's Abridgm.* a ij b, The Titles of Discontinuance and Remitter are great and large Titles, and indeed full of curious Learning. **1768** BLACKSTONE *Comm.* III. ii. 21 The operation of the remitter is exactly the same, after the union of the two rights, as that of a real action would have been before it.

b. The act of remitting a case to another court for decision.

1726 AYLIFFE *Parergon* 78 If the Judge a Quo has once admitted and yielded Obedience unto an Appeal, he cannot afterwards proceed in that Cause without a Remitter. **1808** BENTHAM *Sc. Reform* 106 Cases of remitter excepted,.. no removal of a suit from division to division.

†**c.** Remission, exemption. *Obs. rare*$^{-1}$.

1726 AYLIFFE *Parergon* 267 'Tis a Rule in Law, that in every general Remitter, it is never to be understood, that Fraud and Deceit is thereby remitted.

2. Restoration to rights or privileges, or to a previous state; †a position to which one is restored. Also const. *to. rare.*

1623 in *Crt. & Times Jas. I* (1848) II. 373 The Lord of St. Albans is in his old remitter, and come to lie at his old lodgings in Gray's Inn. **1652** NEEDHAM tr. *Selden's Mare Cl.* 15 The Laws about proclaiming War, Ambassie, Prisoners of War, Hostages,.. Remitter upon return from Captivitie [etc.]. **1663** in *Modern Reports* (1682) I. 132 Confession and promise of future Obedience, ought to precede her remitter, or restitution to the priviledges of a wife. **1857** SIR F. PALGRAVE *Norm. & Eng.* II. 548 Could Louis have recovered the ancient royal residence, such a visible remitter to his pristine royal estate would have been very advantageous.

†**re'mittible,** *a. Obs. rare*$^{-1}$. [f. REMIT *v.* + -IBLE.] Admitting of remission.

1556 J. HEYWOOD *Spider & F.* lxx. 110 Clemencie That doth allway most clementlie encline, To haue regard to remittible disipline.

re'mitting, *vbl. sb.* [f. REMIT *v.* + -ING[1].] The action of the vb. in various senses.

c **1450** *Godstow Reg.* (E.E.T.S.) 42 For this remyttyng and quyte-claymyng the forsaid abbesse.. yaf to hym viij. mark. **1530** PALSGR. 145 Some [adverbs] betoken remytting or slacking of a dede. **1577** HANMER *Anc. Eccl. Hist.* (1619) 506 After the remitting of your faults, there reigned in you no lesse fortitude. **1608** WILLET *Hexapla Exod.* 259 The remitting of his hands. **1651** HOBBES *Leviath.* III. xlii. 274 Eternall life.. is recovered by the Remitting of mens Sins. **1671** R. MONTAGU in *Buccleuch MSS.* (Hist. MSS. Comm.) I. 501 Now is the time of proposing.. the remitting of our levies of four thousand men, to which the treaty binds us. **1849** FREESE *Comm. Class-bk.* 69 To order a sum of money to be received, by sending a Bill of Exchange to another person is called remitting.

re'mitting, *ppl. a.* [f. REMIT *v.* + -ING[2].] That remits or has remission; remittent.

1693 *Phil. Trans.* XVII. 728 When a Remitting Fever is turning Malignant. *a* **1704** T. BROWN *Satire Quack* Wks. 1730 I. 65 [They] never know The least remitting interval of woe. *a* **1776** R. JAMES *Diss. Fever* (1778) 82 Remitting or intermitting fevers may be excited by as many different causes as continual. **1822–34** *Good's Study Med.* (ed. 4) I. 480 Two children who died in a few days of a remitting dyspnœa. **1853** KANE *Grinnell Exp.* xiv. (1856) 103 Against this margin, the great 'drift' through which we had been passing exerts a remitting action. **1899** *Allbutt's Syst. Med.* VII. 72 This chronic progressive mode.. is next in frequency of occurence to the chronic remitting mode.

‖**remittitur** (rɪ'mɪtɪtɜː(r)). *Law.* [a. L. *remittitur*, third pers. sing. pass. of *remittere* to REMIT.] **1.** The remission of excessive damages awarded to a plaintiff, or a formal statement of this.

1770 G. WILSON *Rep. Cases King's Courts, Westm.* I. 30 The court said plaintiff might take judgment *de melioribus damnis* where several damages are given, or enter a *remittitur*. **1792** B. J. SELLON *Pract. Courts King's Bench* I. xi. 500 Where a verdict was given for a greater sum than the amount of the damages laid in the declaration, court will suffer amendment to be made by plaintiff, entering a *remittitur* of the *extra* sum. **1848** J. J. S. WHARTON *Law Lexicon* 579/2 *Remittitur damna*, where a jury gives greater damages than a plaintiff has declared for, it may be rectified be entering a *remittitur* for the excess; or, if a plaintiff have signed judgment for the greater sum, the court will give him leave to amend it, by entering a *remittitur* for the excess.

2. The act of sending the transcript of a case back from an appellate to a trial court for record or further work; a formal notice of this.

1794 W. TIDD *Pract. Court King's Bench* II. xli. 718 Where a writ of error determines in the Exchequer Chamber, by abatement or discontinuance, the judgment is not again in this court, till there be a *remittitur* entered. **1796** B. J. SELLON *Pract. Courts King's Bench* II. xx. 526 On the hearing, the lords either affirm or reverse the judgment on which the clerk of the Parliaments draws a *remittitur*, by which the transcript of the record is remanded into the King's Bench, with the affirmance or reversal to be entered of record. **1820** *Tomlins's Law-Dict.* (ed. 3) II. s.v. Remittitur, In cases of appeal, the Record itself, or a transcript thereof, is sent from the Court of *B.R.* to the Exchequer-Chamber, or House of Lords: when judgment is given in the superior Court, or the Writ of Error abates, or is discontinued, the record or transcript is returned (*Remittitur*, sent back), to the Court of *K.B.*, and the entry of this circumstance is termed a *Remittitur*. **1848** J. J. S. WHARTON *Law Lexicon* 579/2 *Remittitur of record*, formerly when a writ of error, in the Exchequer Chamber, abated, or was discontinued, the transcript must have been remitted, and a *remittitur* entered, before a defendant could sue out execution. **1972** *N.Y. Law Jrnl.* 10 Oct. 2/1 Motion to amend the remittitur granted, the return of the remittitur is requested and, when returned, it will be amended.

re'mix, *v.* [RE- 5 a.] *trans.* To mix again. Hence **re'mixing** *vbl. sb.*

1662 MERRETT *Neri's Art of Glass* I. xxvi, Mix the glasse and powder with diligence, let them stand two hours, then remix them. **1884** L. F. ALLEN *New Amer. Farm Bk.* 80 It may then be overhauled and re-mixed with more earth. **1956** *Nature* 10 Mar. 490/1 The undiminished fertility of the inbred plants when pollinated by bees promotes rapid remixing of genetic material under favourable conditions. **1975** *McGraw-Hill Yearbk. Sci. & Technol.* 256/1 After extraction, the interaction between the feed stream and the enriched product must be such that isotopic remixing, or scrambling, does not occur.

So **re'mixture**.

1801 W. TAYLOR in *Monthly Mag.* XII. 98 After a remixture of the separated clans. **1831** T. HOPE *Ess. Origin Man* I. 164 Those [upper regions] in which electricity, from less interference of and remixture with other forces.., remains most pure.

remlande, -lant, etc.: see next.

remnant ('rɛmnənt), *sb.* and *a.* Forms: α. 4–6 remnaunt, (5 -e), 4 rembnand, 5 remnaund, -ond, 4– remnant. β. 5 remlande, 5, 9 *dial.* remlant, (5 -lawnt, 6 -launte), 9 *dial.* remlin(g, -lit, rimlet. [Contracted form of REMENANT.]

A. *sb.* **1. a.** With *the*. That which remains or is left of a thing or things after the removal of a portion; the remainder, rest, residue. Now applied only to a small remaining part (cf. 2).

α. *c* **1350** *Leg. Rood* iii. 789 Þe thrid part þai hewed oway, And of þe rembnand haue þai made A large cros. **13..** *E.E. Allit. P.* A. 1159 To start in þe strem schulde non me stere, To swymme þe remnaunt. **1411** *E.E. Wills* (1882) 19 Þe remnaund to be payid of my godes þat leuyth. **1469** *Paston Lett.* II. 364 These leud wordds greveth me and her grandam as myche as alle the remnawnte. **1535** COVERDALE *Lev.* xiv. 17 As for the remnaunt of the oyle in his hande [etc.]. **1595** SHAKS. *John* v. iv. 36 Where I may thinke the remnant of my thoughts In peace. **1633** G. HERBERT *Temple, Life* i, Here will I smell my remnant out, and tie My life within this band. **1700** DRYDEN *Pal. & Arc.* I. 27 The remnant of my tale is of a length To tire your patience. **1784** COWPER *Task* v. 36 Smooth as a wall the upright remnant stands. **1838** THIRLWALL *Greece* V. 251 His account of the small remnant of his patrimony which his guardians rendered to him. **1865** GROTE *Plato* I. i. 22 By Ens was understood the remnant in his mind, after leaving out all that abstraction..could leave out.

β. **1434** *Test. Ebor.* (Surtees) II. 41, I will yat all my dettes be payed, and also I will yat ye remlande of my gude be partid in thre. *a* **1460** *How Wise Man taught Son* 32 in Hazl. *E.P.P.* I. 170 This lyfe in mesur that thou lede, And of the remlant thou ne rech.

b. The remainder or rest of a number of persons (or animals). Chiefly, and now only, of a small number (cf. 2 b).

c **1350** *Will. Palerne* 2901 Redli al þo remnant of þe rude bestes for fere be-gunne to fle. *c* **1400** *Destr. Troy* 14000 All the Remnond of Renkes, þat raght fro þe toune, With Eneas afterward etlid to see. **1513** MORE in Grafton *Chron.* (1568) II. 775 She sawe the Lorde Cardinall more redier to depart than the remnaunt. **1535** COVERDALE *Neh.* i. 3 The remnaunt of the captiuyte are there in the londe. **1568** GRAFTON *Chron.* II. 675 The remnaunt returned to the armie with small gaine. **1606** G. W[OODCOCKE] *Hist. Ivstine* XXVIII. 98 Seeing the remnant were few, to whom his mercy might be manifest. **1651** JER. TAYLOR *Serm. for Year* II. xix. 244 Many millions did die accursedly, and the small remnant became vagabonds. **1800** WELLINGTON in Gurw. *Desp.* (1838) I. 181, I wrote to the chiefs of the remnant of Goklah's force. **1862** STANLEY *Jew. Ch.* (1877) I. xv. 301 The remnant of the insurgents takes refuge in the lofty tower.

2. a. With *a* and *pl.* A (small) remaining quantity, part, or piece.

1624 BURTON *Anat. Mel.* I. iv. I. i. (ed. 2) 184 The open parts were cleane, yet there was..in the chinckes a remnant of gold. **1664** POWER *Exp. Philos.* II. 117 The Spontaneous Dilatation..of that little remnant of Ayr skulking in the rugosities thereof. **1697** DRYDEN *Virg. Georg.* III. 474 Where basking in the Sun-shine they may lye, And the short Remnants of his Heat enjoy. **1715** M. DAVIES *Athen. Brit.* I. 14 All which numerous Volumes contain..nothing but little Treatises and small Remnants. **1774** PENNANT *Tour Scotl.* in 1772, 254 A small remnant of the cloister is left. **1825** J. JENNINGS *Obs. Dial. W. Eng.* 177 Wi' remlets o' tha Saxon tongue, That to our Gramfers did belong. **1856** STANLEY *Sinai & Pal.* vi. (1858) 260 Thinly studded with trees, the remnants, apparently, of a great forest. **1888** F. HUME *Mme. Midas* I. Prol., The remnants of their provisions on the voyage.

b. A small remaining number of persons. Also *spec.*, in allusion to Isa. x. 22, a small number of Jews that survives persecution, in whom future hope is vested.

1611 BIBLE *Isa.* x. 22 For though thy people..be as the sand of the sea, yet a remnant of them shall returne. **1613** PURCHAS *Pilgrimage* IX. viii. (1614) 872 Some remnants of them haue been christened. **1630** PRYNNE *Anti-Armin.* 128 They are but a Remnant, a seede, a little flocke. **1713** ADDISON *Cato* I. i, A feeble army, and an empty senate, Remnants of mighty battles fought in vain. **1784** COWPER *Task* I. 340 Once more rejoice That yet a remnant of your race survives. **1814** SCOTT *Ld. of Isles* IV. xx, When, after battle lost, Muster the remnants of a host. **1859** 'L.N.R.' *Missing Link* xiii. 171 The Exiled Remnant..refuse to snuff a candle or poke the fire, but impatiently call, 'Shuboth-guy—Shuboth-guy,' as the stoker passes. **1874** L. STEPHEN *Hours in Library* (1892) I. ix. 314 A few remnants of the aborigines were settled on a township granted by the colony. **1892** I. ZANGWILL *Childr. Ghetto* II. xv. 16 The rest of the 'remant' that was met to save Israel looked more commonplace. **1914** J. HASTINGS *Encycl. Relig. & Ethics* VII. 607/2 The function of Judaism is to fulfil the Isaianic ideal of a missionary 'Remnant'. *Ibid.*, Judaism is to be the religion of a Remnant. **1932** C. ROTH *Hist. Marranos* i. 16 It had been only a weak remnant which had accepted baptism as the alternative to death. **1969** *Guardian* 18 Sept. 8/6 (*heading*) Germany's remnant. *Ibid.*, There are only around 30,000 Jews in Germany today, where once there were 600,000. **1972** C. RAPHAEL *Feast of Hist.* i. 32 In the immediate aftermath of the Holocaust, Jewish history.. seemed to offer a message of bleakness... In the Holy Land, the remnant faced enmity and restriction.

c. Of a single person: A survivor. *rare.*

1594 SHAKS. *Rich. III*, I. ii. 7 Thou bloodlesse Remnant of that Royall Blood. **1642** ROGERS *Naaman* Ep. Ded., The onely remnant of that family. **1804** J. GRAHAME *Sabbath* 464 One hapless man, the remnant of a wreck.

d. *Geomorphol.* = RESIDUAL *sb.* 5.

1893 [see MONADNOCK]. **1896** *Ann. Rep. State Geologist N.J. 1895* 10 This eastern belt of remnants, which are really outliers of the continuous portion of the Pensauken.., runs through Camden..and Salem counties. **1907** *Amer. Jrnl. Sci.* CLXXIV. 470 At the present time there are remaining only few traces of these old bolson surfaces. Most of these remnants have been preserved only on account of being covered by extensive lava sheets. **1942** [see BERM 1 b].

3. a. A remaining trace or survival *of* some quality, belief, condition, or state of things.

1560 DAUS tr. *Sleidane's Comm.* 271 The remnaunt of that doctrine remayned in the mindes of many. **1561** T. NORTON *Calvin's Inst.* III. 173 Thys is not the question among them, whether fayth be yet wrapped with many remnants of ignorance. **1613** PURCHAS *Pilgrimage* I. vii. (1614) 40 The Arke.., the remnant of the elder, and Seminarie of the new world. **1699** BURNET 39 *Art.* xxii. 244 It was a Remnant both of Judaism and Gentilism, that the Souls of the Martyrs hovered about their Tombs. **1703** MAUNDRELL *Journ. Jerus.* (1721) App. 1 This Place has no remnants of its Ancient Greatness. **1813** SHELLEY *Q. Mab* VII. 221 No remnant of the exterminated faith Survived. **1821** J. Q. ADAMS in C. Davies *Metr. System* III. (1871) 127 Every remnant of the original uniformity of proportion has disappeared.

b. *pl.* Traces *of* a fact. *rare*[−1].

1826 SCOTT *Woodst.* i, A jerkin, which..had once been of the Lincoln green, and showed remnants of having been laced.

4. a. A fragment, a small portion, a scrap.

a **1400–50** *Alexander* 22, I sall rehers..A remnant of his rialte. **1592** SHAKS. *Rom. & Jul.* v. i. 47 About his shelues.. Remnants of pack thred, and old cakes of Roses were thinly scattered. **1621** BURTON *Anat. Mel.* III. ii. III. [IV.] i, If he get any remnant of hers, a buske-point, a feather of her fanne. **1766** BLACKSTONE *Comm.* II. 259 Not of any particular estate carved out of it; much less of so minute a remnant as this. **1876** GEO. ELIOT *Dan. Der.* xxxv, That remnant of a human being.

b. *spec.* among drapers and clothiers: An end of a piece of goods, left over after the main portion has been used or sold.

1433 [see REMENANT 3]. **1571** *Wills & Inv. Durh.* (Surtees) I. 362, j. pece of worssett..iiij yeardes in Remlauntes. **1583** STUBBES *Anat. Abus.* II. (1882) 39 They buy remnants of silks, veluets, satins. **1634** FORD *Perk. Warbeck* II. iii, I was ever confident, when I traded but in remnants [etc.]. **1681** *Lond. Gaz.* No. 1665/4 A parcel of Grey Searge, Yard and Nail broad, and two Remnants of strip'd Grape. **1758** JOHNSON *Idler* No. 26 ¶11 A couple that kept a petty shop of remnants and cheap linen. *a* **1845** HOOD *United Family* xix, No remnant can sufficient be For our united family. **1882** CAULFIELD & SAWARD *Dict. Needlework* 421 Remnants of any piece of material, as well as those of ribbon, are always sold at some reduction of the original price.

fig. **1596** SHAKS. *Tam. Shr.* IV. iii. 112 Away thou Ragge, thou quantitie, thou remnant.

†**c.** A scrap or tag of quotation. *Obs. rare.*

1598 B. JONSON *Ev. Man. in Hum.* IV. i, I'll have him free of the wit-broker's, for he utters nothing but stolen remnants. **1609** —— *Sil. Wom.* III. v, Could your grauitie forget so olde and noted a remnant, as, *lippis & tonsoribus notum.*

†**d.** A blow. *Obs. rare*[−1].

1580 LUPTON *Sivqila* 49 Then she reached him suche a remnant, that he had a cause to remember hir.

†**5.** *Law.* A remainder. *Obs. rare*[−1].

1544 tr. *Littleton's Tenures* 10 b, The chylds mother entreth in the remnant, and it occupyeth as gardyne or wardyne in Socage.

6. *attrib.* and *Comb.*

1864 E. G. WHITE *Testimonies* (1871) I. 467 All who have a desire to draw away from God's remnant people..should have the privilege. **1885** —— *Testimony for Church* XXXII. 228 The remnant church will be brought into great trial and distress. **1905** *Westm. Gaz.* 21 Oct. 18/2 'It is not, then, a curious fact,' I said, 'that there should be so many comparatively new books on your remnant stall.' **1905** 'O. HENRY' *Trimmed Lamp* (1907) 115 Did you ever notice me leaning on the remnant counter or peering in the window of the five-and-ten? *a* **1936** KIPLING *Something of Myself* (1937) iii. 75 The *Pioneer* had made as much out of its share in this remnant-traffic as it had paid me in wages. **1972** N. ZNAMIEROWSKI *Rugmaking* 17/1 Remnant counters..are.. excellent sources.

B. *adj.* Remaining.

1550 COVERDALE *Spir. Perle* xii. (1560) 132 The time that is remnant of the flesh. **1594** WILLOBIE *Avisa* 2 Diana deckt the remnant partes, With fewture braue. **1648** DAVENANT *On Death Lady Winchester*, Our remnant love let us discreetly save. **1718** PRIOR *Power* 868 Act through thy remnant life the decent part. **1791** COWPER *Iliad* XIX. 299 Attended laden with the remnant gifts. **1807** J. BARLOW *Columb.* IV. 595 Break those remnant rocks that still impede My current. *a* **1854** H. REED *Lect. Brit. Poets* vi. (1857) 204 His mind held communion with all the remnant glory of classical poetry.

remnantal ('rɛmnəntəl), *a. Geol.* [f. REMNANT *sb.* + -AL.] Of or pertaining to a remnant.

1907 *Amer. Jrnl. Sci.* CLXXIV. 470 Farther south at Paraje..and at El Paso, the same remnantal levels are noted. **1942** [see BERM 1 b].

remobili'zation. [RE- 5 a.] The action of mobilizing again; a further mobilization.

1919 J. L. GARVIN *Econ. Found. Peace* viii. 152 German workers might then have the sympathy of their class in other lands to a degree making quite impossible the effective remobilisation of the Grand Alliance as a debt-collecting agency. **1977** J. L. HARPER *Population Biol. Plants* 392 The demand is met by remobilization of other materials.

re'mobilize, *v.* [RE- 5 a.] *trans.*

1. *Geol.* To make fluid or plastic again.

1954 R. L. PARKER tr. *Niggli's Rocks & Mineral Deposits* xiv. 519 Old deposits may be remobilized in depth and may give rise to solutions that ascend to higher levels. **1965** G. J. WILLIAMS *Econ. Geol. N.Z.* xii. 178/2 Mr Wood's descriptions seem to leave little doubt as to a genetic association of the Moke Creek greenschist and the enclosed copper ore, even though the latter must have been remobilized during metamorphism. **1971** I. G. GASS et al. *Understanding Earth* xxi. 313/1 Continental mountain ranges are..principally composed of original continental crust (in great part remobilised).

2. *Mil.* To recall to active service.

1963 *Times* 26 Feb. 7/7 The prosecutor, M. Gerthoffer, who is a magistrate remobilized with the rank of general, wound up his two-hour final speech.

remocion, variant of REMOTION *Obs.*

re'mock, *v. rare*[−1]. [RE-.] †To mock in turn.

1712 BLACKMORE *Creation* 352 How much the Judge, who does in Heav'n preside, Remocks the scoffer, and contemns his pride!

re'model (riː-), *v.* [RE- 5 a.] *trans.* To model again, reconstruct. (Common in 19th c.)

1789 *Gen. Hist.* in *Ann. Reg.* 9/2 That assembly was wholly incompetent to the task of re-modelling the constitution. **1830** LYTTON *P. Clifford* xix, A stray trinket or two—not of sufficient worth to be re-set or re-modelled. **1849** MACAULAY *Hist. Eng.* i. I. 121 From the time when the army was remodelled to the time when it was disbanded. **1879** M. PATTISON *Milton* 46 All traditions were being questioned, and all institutions were to be remodelled.

Hence **re'modelled** *ppl. a.*, **re'modelling** *vbl. sb.*; also **re'modeller**, **re'modelment**.

1846 GROVE *Corr. Phys. Forces* 4, I will pass to Bacon, the great remodeller of science. **1847** *Blackw. Mag.* LXI. 633 The other remodelments are trash. **1849** MACAULAY *Hist. Eng.* i. I. 119 At Naseby took place the first great encounter between the royalists and the remodelled army. *Ibid.* vi. II. 23 The remodelling might require money. **1869** E. S. FFOULKES *Roman Index* 17 The well-known constitution of Benedict XIV. issued for its remodelment.

'remodel, *sb. Arch.* [f. the vb.] The act of modelling or constructing a building again; a remodelled building.

1956 *Archit. Rev.* CXX. 119/3 Rethinking is needed on the difference between surface grime on a noble building and a cut-rate remodel which might well show a fundamental lack of architectural conviction or emotive power. **1974** R. C. DENNIS *Conversations with Corpse* ii. 15 A house, French Regency, I think... I imagine it's a remodel. **1978** *Tucson Mag.* Dec. 90/3 In a remodel (existing house) we have to be neater, and work slower.

remodifi'cation (riː-). [RE- 5 a.] The action of modifying (again); a further modification.

1831 T. HOPE *Ess. Origin Man* III. 321 Nor from any subsequent difference of situation derives [it] any diversity of remodifications. **1875** RUSKIN *Fors Clav.* lix. 306 The substance of it being in re-modification for Mornings in Florence.

re'modify (riː-), *v.* [RE- 5 a.] *trans.* To modify (again), to make a change in.

1830 LYELL *Princ. Geol.* I. 458 Unless some earthquake shall remodify the surface of the country. **1831** T. HOPE *Ess. Origin Man* II. 407 Before America was remodified by the arts of Europe.

remofe, remoife, obs. Sc. ff. REMOVE *v.*

‖**remolade** (remɔlad). *rare.* [a. F. *rémolade, rémoulade*, ad. It. *remolata*, of obscure origin. Used only in translations of French works.] An unguent used in farriery.

1702 SIR W. HOPE tr. *Solleysell's Compl. Horseman* II. xiii. 267 *marg.*, A Remolade for a Blow. *c* **1720** W. GIBSON *Farrier's Dispens.* III. xiii. (1721) 265/2 Charge the Foot with a Remolade made of half a Pound of Burgundy-pitch [etc.]. **1842** CHERRY tr. *Solleysell's Shoeing Horses* 9 Horses which have feet in which a nail cannot be driven without bending, by reason of their hardness, should have them moistened with remolades or softeners.

remo'lest, *v.* [RE- 5 a.] To molest again.

1611 COTGR., *Rennuyer*, to remolest. *a* **1700** KEN *Edmund* Poet. Wks. 1721 II. 294 The King to martial Business then return'd,..While the fierce Danes his Frontiers remolest.

'remolinite. *Min.* [f. (*Los*) *Remolinos* in Chile, one of its localities.] A former synonym of ATACAMITE.

1852 BROOKE & MILLER *Phillips' Introd. Min.* 619 Analyses of remolinite..from Chile by Klaproth. **1868** WATTS *Dict. Chem.* V. Index 1098/1 Remolinite (s. Atacamite I. 429).

†**re'mollient**, *sb.* and *a. Obs.* [ad. L. *remollient-em*, pres. pple. of *remollīre* to soften (again): see RE- and MOLLIENT.] **a.** *sb.* An emollient. **b.** *adj.* Softening, emollient.

1612 *Enchir. Med.* III. 145 An Incessus may be prepared with the foure remollients, with Camomel, Nasturtium, Penniryoll. **1684** tr. *Bonet's Merc. Compit.* III. 62 Her

Physician..applied remollient, heating and drawing things. **1727** BRADLEY *Fam. Dict.* s.v. *Fat*, Particularly as to anodine and Remollient Fats.

†**remo'llition.** *Obs. rare*$^{-1}$. [ad. L. type **remollītiōn-em*, n. of action f. *remollīre*: see prec. and cf. EMOLLITION.] Softening.

1590 BARROUGH *Meth. Physick* VII. xxi. (1639) 409 In Oedema..it is necessary to have remollition with discussion.

†**re'mollitive,** *a.* and *sb. Obs. rare.* [See EMOLLITIVE and REMOLLIENT.]

a. *adj.* Emollient. **b.** *sb.* An emollient.

1580 *Well of Woman Hill, Aberdeen* A iij b, It is discussiue, laxatiue, remollitiue, and vomitiue. **1590** BARROUGH *Meth. Physick* 384 If the person be strong, take other remollitiues or discussives. *Ibid.* VII. iv. (1639) 386 ℞ the foure kinds of remollitives, or mollificatives.

remolten, pa. pple. of REMELT *v.*

†**re'monarchize,** *v. Obs. rare.* [RE- 5 a.] *trans.* To rule over again as monarch.

1592 WARNER *Alb. Eng.* VIII. xliii. (1612) 206 He that remonarchiz'd our Ile, King Athelstone. **1606** *Ibid.* xv. xcv. 378 Great Britaine, sith a Briton doth remonarchize thy Throne, Remaund thy name.

re'monetize, *v.* [RE- 5 a.] *trans.* To restore (a metal or other substance) to its former use as full legal tender. So **remoneti'zation.**

1877 *Rep. U.S. Monetary Comm. 1876* (44th Congr., 2nd Sess., Senate Rep. No. 703) I. 90 It is not a particular silver coin, the remonetization of which is demanded, but it is the metal silver, in whatever denominations of coin the law may authorize. **1877** *N.Y. Tribune* 16 Nov. 8/1 They regard the ultimate passage of a bill of some kind, remonetizing silver, as a certainty. **1878** *N. Amer. Rev.* CXXVI. 315 If silver is remonetized, for instance, no number of states could nullify the law. **1878** F. A. WALKER *Money* xii. 241 We see..an active agitation for the remonetization of silver in the United States.

†**re'monish,** *v. Obs.*$^{-1}$ [ad. L. *remonēre*: see RE- and MONISH *v.*] *trans.* To admonish again.

1563 NOWELL *Hom. Just. of God* in *Liturg. Serv. Q. Eliz.* (Parker Soc.) 492 When the Jews were monished, remonished, prayed, threatened, so oft by so many prophets.

†**re'monstrable,** *a. Obs.* [See REMONSTRATE *v.* and -ABLE.] Demonstrable.

1604 *Supplic. Masse Priests* §33 If the Church were or could be invisible or not remonstrable. **1618** T. ADAMS *Bad Leaven* Wks. (1629) 712 Was it such a sinne for Adam to eate a forbidden Apple? Yes; the greatnesse is remonstrable in the euent.

remonstrance (rɪ'mɒnstrəns), *sb.* [a. OF. *remonstrance* (15th c.; mod. *remontrance*), = med.L. *remonstrantia*: see REMONSTRATE and -ANCE. In 1609 (sense 3) stressed on first or third syllable.]

†**1.** An appeal, request. *Obs. rare.*

c **1477** CAXTON *Jason* 60 Whan the noble Jason had made his remonstraunce unto the quene Ysiphile..she withdrew her aparte. **1490** —— *Eneydos* xxii. 78 By many exhortacions & pyetous remonstrances excytatiue of all well wyllyng.

†**2.** Demonstration, proof, evidence, manifestation of some fact, quality, etc.; also, a ground *of* some belief. *Obs.* (common in 17th c.)

1597 HOOKER *Eccl. Pol.* v. lxxvi. §6 The manifest oddes..are remonstrances more then sufficient how all our welfare..dependeth wholly vpon our Religion. **1603** BRETON *Packet Mad Lett.* i, The remonstrance of your loue towards me, makes mee glory in so exquisite a friend. **1649** JER. TAYLOR *Gt. Exemp.* I. Ad Sect. vi. 100 The externall and visible remonstrances of religion. **1673** *Lady's Call.* I. i. §19 When the spark [of love] shall be blow'd up by perpetual remonstrances of Passion. **1698** FRYER *Acc. E. India & P.* 61 As a Remonstrance of their Credulity, they bring for proof [etc.]. *a* **1774** GOLDSM. tr. *Scarron's Com. Romance* II. 38 Leander and she caressed only with their eyes, leaving farther remonstrances of kindness to a private meeting.

†**b.** A representation, resemblance. *Obs. rare.*

1640 SHIRLEY *Imposture* I. ii, Our virgins..Shall..make in Each garden a remonstrance of this battle, Where flowers shall seem to fight. **1644** BP. MAXWELL *Prerog. Chr. Kings* xi. 119 If you..parallel them with our times, you will find a full ὑποτύπωσις, remonstrance and resemblance with us.

†**3.** A (written or spoken) demonstration, statement, account, or representation. Usu. const. *of* (the matter declared or brought forward). *Obs.*

1585 T. WASHINGTON tr. *Nicholay's Voy.* I. vii, [I made] vnto them protestations and remonstrances of the wrong and iniurie they did too our Ambassador. **1609** DANIEL *Civ. Wars* IV. xxviii, The King..was glad, Both by his remonstrances well composed, And with his sword..provide To right himselfe. **1609** BIBLE (Douay) *Gen.*, Comm., A briefe Remonstrance of the state of the Church. **1641** HINDE (*title*) A Faithfull Remonstrance of the Holy Life and Happy Death of John Bruen. *a* **1716** SOUTH *Serm.* (1744) IX. iii. 78 The atheist is too wise in his generation, to make remonstrances and declarations of what he thinks. **1760–72** H. BROOKE *Fool of Qual.* (1809) IV. 99 Our remonstrances to my late lord of the..services you had rendered.

b. A formal statement of grievances or similar matters of public importance, *esp.* the ***Grand Remonstrance*** presented by the House of Commons to the Crown in 1641. Now only *Hist.*

1626 in Ellis *Orig. Lett.* Ser. I. III. 236 The Commons had made a Remonstrance to his Majesty, but would not grant him any supply. **1647** CLARENDON *Hist. Reb.* IV. 48 *note*, At the beginning of the Parliament, or shortly after,..a committee was appointed to prepare a Remonstrance of the state of the kingdom. *a* **1674** *Ibid.* XI. §200 Their army, which had merited so much from them by the Remonstrance which they had so lately published. **1770** *Junius Lett.* xxxvii. (1788) 197 The King's answer to the remonstrance of the city of London. **1831** MACAULAY *Ess.*, *Hampden* Wks. 1898 II. 157 That celebrated address to the King..known by the name of the Grand Remonstrance.

c. *Eccl. Hist.* A document presented in 1610 to the States of Holland by the Dutch Arminians, relative to the points of difference between themselves and the strict Calvinists.

a **1662** HEYLIN *Laud* (1668) 81 In the year 1610 the Followers of Arminius address their Remonstrance (containing the Antiquity of their Doctrines, and the substance of them) to the States of Holland. **1674** HICKMAN *Quinquart. Hist.* (ed. 2) 96 Of this Remonstrance..at length a Copy was got, and a Contra-remonstrance made. **1721** tr. *Brandt's Hist. Reform.* II. 79 The Committee of the States, after having duly weighed this Remonstrance and Petition, deputed two of their body to the Classis of Leyden.

4. The action of remonstrating; expostulation.

1603 HOLLAND *Plutarch's Mor.* 10 Children must be trained and brought to their duety in all lenity, by faire words, gentle exhortations, and milde remonstrance. **1748** JOHNSON *Van. Hum. Wishes* 93 Through freedom's sons no more remonstrance rings. **1769** *Junius Lett.* (1788) 173 We should long since have adopted a style of remonstrance very distant from the humility of complaint. **1838** LYTTON *Alice* I. viii, Mrs. Leslie..said nothing, except in kindly remonstrance on the indiscretion of braving the night air. **1874** GREEN *Short Hist.* viii. §2. 465 The book was suppressed on the remonstrance of the House of Commons.

b. With *a* and *pl.* An instance of this.

a **1729** ROGERS (J.), Importunate passions..will not suffer him to attend to the remonstrances of justice. **1774** JEFFERSON *Autobiog.* App., Wks. 1859 I. 132 The remonstrances of the people were disregarded. **1832** LYTTON *Eugene A.* I. vi, The youth..seemed to yield to the remonstrances of his uncle. **1870** DICKENS *E. Drood* viii, We had better not say anything having the appearance of a remonstrance.

5. *R.C. Ch.* A monstrance.

1656 BLOUNT *Glossogr.*, *Remonstrance*,..an instrument so called by the Romanists, and made of silver or gold, to expose the blessed Sacrament on the Altar. **1670–98** LASSELS *Voy. Italy* II. 170 The Remonstrance to expose the B. Sacrament in, is made like a sun. **1846** G. OLIVER *Monast. Dioec. Exon.* 261/1 He bequeathed a remonstrance or ostensoir..to the college. **1873** J. B. BAGSHAWE *Threshold Cath. Ch.* (1883) 211 A vessel called the 'Monstrance' or sometimes, though not so correctly, the 'Remonstrance'.

†**re'monstrance,** *v. Obs. rare*$^{-1}$. [f. prec.] *trans.* To demonstrate.

1621 BP. MOUNTAGU *Diatribæ* 75 To remonstrance the pious disposition of our Saxon Ancestors.

†**re'monstrancer.** *Obs.* [f. prec. sb. or vb. + -ER[1].] One who remonstrates; *spec.* = REMONSTRANT B 1.

1618 *Barnevelt's Apol.* E, The dissensions growing betwixt the Remonstrancers, and Contra-remonstrancers. **1650** R. HOLLINGWORTH *Exerc. Usurped Powers* 32 As the Remonstrancer acknowledgeth. **1716** M. DAVIES *Athen. Brit.* III. *Diss. Drama* 4 The discontented Schematists of all States and Churches; such as Jacobites,..Remonstrancers.

remonstrant (rɪ'mɒnstrənt), *a.* and *sb.* [ad. med.L. *remonstrant-em*, pres. pple. of *remonstrāre* to REMONSTRATE. Cf. F. *remontrant* (1560).]

A. *adj.* **1.** *Eccl. Hist.* (With capital initial.) **a.** Of or belonging to the Arminian party in the Dutch Reformed Church.

This may also be taken as an attrib. use of the sb.

1618 CARLETON in *Hales' Gold. Rem.* III. (1673) 177 Three Remonstrant Preachers..have renounced their Doctrine. **1674** HICKMAN *Quinquart. Hist.* (ed. 2) 2 Whether the Remonstrant or Contra-Remonstrant opinions be most agreeable. **1736** CHANDLER *Hist. Persec.* 335 His Excellency..deposed those Magistrates who were of the Remonstrant Persuasion. **1772** FLETCHER *Logica Genev.* p. v, Giving you a more favorable opinion of your remonstrant brethren. **1840** *Penny Cycl.* XVII. 376/2 The wicked and cruel persecutions to which the Remonstrant party were subjected in consequence of the synod of Dort.

b. ***Remonstrant synod***: (see quot. 1846).

1839 *Penny Cycl.* XIII. 25/1 The synod of Munster and Remonstrant synod, among whom Unitarian opinions are prevalent. **1846** MCCULLOCH *Acc. Brit. Empire* (1854) II. 307 The Remonstrant Presbyterian synod was formed in May, 1830, in consequence of the separation of 17 ministers, with their congregations, from the General Synod of Ulster.

2. That remonstrates or expostulates.

1641 MILTON *Animadv.* Wks. 1851 III. 208 Is it not..to bee wondred that such a weaknesse could fall from the pen of such a wise Remonstrant Man? **1847** LD. J. RUSSELL in Ashwell *Life Bp. Wilberforce* (1880) I. xi. 459, I must repeat the observation I made in my letter to the remonstrant Bishops. **1863** KINGLAKE *Crimea* (1876) I. xiii. 213 The principle of a peaceful coercion applied by the whole of the remonstrant Powers. **1867** TROLLOPE *Chron. Barset* I. xviii. 155 The deep angry remonstrant eyes.

B. *sb.* **1.** *Eccl. Hist.* (With capital initial.) A member of the Arminian party in the Dutch Reformed Church, so called from the Remonstrance of 1610.

1618 CARLETON in *Hales' Gold. Rem.* III. (1673) 177 They did the synod wrong to make this distinction of contra-remonstrants and remonstrants. **1678** R. BARCLAY *Apol. Quakers* V. ix. 129 The Remonstrants (as they are commonly called) do generally themselves acknowledge, that without the outward knowledge of Christ there is no Salvation. **1736** CHANDLER *Hist. Persec.* 335 They were presently suspected..as persons that favoured the Remonstrants. *a* **1819** G. HILL *Lect. Divin.* (1821) III. 192 Grotius favoured the principles of the Remonstrants. **1886** *Encycl. Brit.* XX. 379/2 The Remonstrants are now a small body, but respected for their traditions of scholarship and liberal thought.

2. One who remonstrates; †the author, or a supporter, of a remonstrance (in senses 3 a, 3 b).

1641 MILTON *Animadv.* Wks. 1851 III. 187 Wee had not thought that Legion could have furnisht the Remonstrant with so many brethren. **1672** [see *remonstrating* vbl. sb.]. **1705** T. HEARNE *Collect.* 22 Nov. (O.H.S.) I. 93 He was a feirce Remonstrant. **1755** MAGENS *Insurances* II. 83 The Remonstrants..concluded to apply to Us, praying that we would please to approve and ratify the said Statute. **1800** COLERIDGE *Piccolom.* IV. vii, Necessity, impetuous remonstrant. **1838** DE MORGAN *Ess. Probab.* 171 A want..which no government ever will attempt to supply until increasing knowledge..creates an influential body of remonstrants. **1875** STUBBS *Const. Hist.* II. xiv. 138 If..the king wished to go to Flanders, the remonstrants were of opinion that they were not bound to serve in that country.

Hence †**re'monstrant** *v. intr.*, to protest *against* a thing; †**re'monstranter**, a remonstrant; †**Remon'strantical** *a.*, belonging to the party of the Arminian Remonstrants. *Obs.*

1619 BALCANQUAL in *Hales' Gold. Rem.* II. (1673) 128 It was answered, that both the Consistory and Classis of Camps were altogether Remonstrantical. **1650** R. BAILLIE *Lett. & Jrnls.* (1842) III. 110 If great words would..make them submit to the commands of our Remonstranters [etc.]. **1654** E. JOHNSON *Wond.-wrkg. Provid.* 105* They remonstrant against all Acts of Parliament that passe without their Vote.

re'monstrantly, *adv.* [f. prec. adj. + -LY[2].] In a remonstrant manner.

1872 GEO. ELIOT *Middlem.* IV. lxxvi. 240 'But when she saw the good that might come of staying ——' said Dorothea, remonstrantly. **1876** GEO. ELIOT *Dan. Der.* liii, 'Mother', said Deronda, remonstrantly, 'don't let us think of it'. **1882** C. C. HOPLEY *Snakes* i. 28 Its legs..kicking remonstrantly.

remonstrate ('rɛmənstreɪt, older rɪ'mɒn-), *v.* [ad. med.L. *remonstrāt-*, ppl. stem of *remonstrāre* to demonstrate, f. *re-* RE- + *monstrāre* to show. Cf. OF. *remonstrer* (14th c.; mod.F. *remontrer*).]

†**1. a.** *trans.* To make plain or manifest, demonstrate, exhibit, show. Also const. *to* a person. *Obs.* (common in 17th c.)

1599 B. JONSON *Cynthia's Rev.* v. ii, But I will remonstrate to you the third dor, which is not..indicative, but deliberative. **1604** T. WRIGHT *Passions* II. i. 54 Wee may aptly remonstrate, how inordinate Passions cause and ingenerate in the soul all those vices. **1658** R. FRANCK *North. Mem.* (1821) p. xxvii, Let my writings therefore remonstrate my experiments and my experiments manifest my zeal for solitudes. **1682** H. MORE *Annot. Glanvill's Lux O.* 98 That he may remonstrate the Soul of the Messiah to be his most special Favourite. **1742** YOUNG *Nt. Th.* IX. 1636 With what authority it gives its charge, Remonstrating great truths in stile sublime.

†**b.** To declare or represent *that*, etc. *Obs.*

1647 in Neal *Hist. Purit.* (1754) II. ix. 296 The house of commons having remonstrated..that it was far from their purpose to abolish this government, but only to regulate it. **1680** AUBREY in *Lett. Eminent Persons* (1813) III. 364 Mr. Edw. Wood was the spokes-man: remonstrated that they were Oxon. scholars. **1755** MAGENS *Insurances* I. 164 It was remonstrated to the Assured that it was necessary to see the Invoice of the Cost of..the Cargo.

†**2. a.** To point out (a fault, etc.) to another by way of reproof, disapprobation, or complaint; to protest against (a wrong). Also const. *to*. *Obs.*

1627 *Lisander & Cal.* IV. 75 Shee only gently remonstrated unto her her fault. **1642** FULLER *Holy & Prof. St.* 121 If the conscience of a Counsellour or commander in chief remonstrates in himself the unlawfulnesse of this warre, he is bound..to represent to his Prince his reasons against it. **1709** STANHOPE *Paraphr.* IV. 89 At this Bar..he remonstrated the Illegality of the Violence offered to him. **1723** *Pres. St. Russia* II. 104, I also remonstrated to you the Dissatisfaction your Conduct has given me. **1751** ELIZA HEYWOOD *Betsy Thoughtless* I. 287 Remonstrating to miss Betsy, in the most serious terms, the great error she was guilty of.

†**b.** To point out, state, or represent (a grievance, etc.) to some authority. Also const. *to*. *Obs.*

1647 N. BACON *Disc. Govt. Eng.* I. lxvi. (1739) 156 The Parliament sent but six or seven, to remonstrate their complaints. **1690** J. MACKENZIE *Siege London-Derry* Pref. A iij b, Till they had remonstrated their danger to the Government. **1709** STEELE *Tatler* No. 18 ¶2 The Merchants of Lions have been at Court, to remonstrate their great Sufferings by the Failure of their Publick Credit. **1740–1** in *Johnson's Debates* (1787) I. 189 It is doubtless our duty..to remonstrate to his majesty the distresses of his subjects, and his own danger.

†**3. a.** *intr.* To raise an objection *to* a thing; to address a remonstrance *to* a person. *Obs.*

1666 S. PARKER *Free & Impart. Censure* (1667) 241 You know I have long since remonstrated to these common ceremonies of the World. **1691** BEVERLEY *Thous. Years' Kingd. Christ* 4 The boldness of the Censure of Dissenters..I humbly Remonstrate to in these Particulars. **1749** FIELDING *Tom Jones* I. xiii, The doctor remonstrated to him privately concerning this behaviour. **1792** BUDWORTH *Fortn. Ramble* 93, I in vain remonstrated to the landlord.

†**b.** Const. *inf.* To make a strong request *to* a person *not to* do something. *Obs. rare*$^{-1}$.

1723 *Pres. St. Russia* II. 277 The Ambassadors remonstrated to him not to be so troublesome to the said Persons.

4. To urge strong reasons *against* a course of action, to protest *against*; to expostulate *with* a person, *on* or *upon* an action. Also *absol.*

1695 J. Edwards *Perfect. Script.* Ded., You with the utmost zeal..remonstrated against this practice. **1722** Waterland *Suppl. Arian Subscript. Consid.* 4 It is the proper Business of a Divine..to remonstrate against any growing Corruptions. **1759** Sterne *Tr. Shandy* II. xv, Corporal Trim, by being in the service, had learned to obey,—and not to remonstrate. **1838** Thirlwall *Greece* xxxviii. V. 59 Spartan envoys were sent to Athens, to remonstrate against the proceedings of Timotheus. **1863** Geo. Eliot *Romola* xlvi, Tito and Romola never jarred, never remonstrated with each other. **1899** *Daily News* 20 July 6/3 A friend remonstrated with Mr. W...on his giving up all the proceeds..to a charity.

5. *trans.* To say, assert, or plead in remonstrance. Also const. *to* or *with* a person.

1758–65 Goldsm. *Ess.* v, In spite of what is every day remonstrated from the press—our very nobility..have the assurance to frequent assemblies. **1784** Burns *Prayer Prospect Death* 8 If I have wander'd.., As something, loudly, in my breast, Remonstrates I have done. **1844** Dickens *Christmas Carol* ii, 'I am a mortal', Scrooge remonstrated, 'and liable to fall'. **1845** Miss Strickland *Queens of Engl.* VIII. 33 When those in his household remonstrated with him that this name..had become very unpopular to English ears. **1873** Browning *Red Cott. Nt.-cap* III. 810 Remonstrate to yon peasant in the blouse That [etc.].

6. To persuade (one) *out of* a design. *rare*$^{-1}$.

1817–18 Cobbett *Resid. U.S.* (1822) 144 My men had remonstrated me..out of my design to transplant six acres of Indian Corn.

Hence **remonstrating** *vbl. sb.* and *ppl. a.*; also **remonstratingly** *adv.*

1660 J. Sharp in *Lauderd. Papers* (Camden) I. 57 Most of the remonstrating party pursue the fatal way. **1672** Marvell *Reh. Transp.* I. 144, I do not like this Remonstrating nor these Remonstrants. **1829** *Examiner* 161/2 He remonstratingly exclaimed, 'Too much help!' **1863** J. C. Morison *St. Bernard* III. iv. 348 He wrote a remonstrating letter to Guido. **1882** J. Payn *Thicker than Water* iii, 'Now..do be reasonable', he continued remonstratingly.

remonstration (rɛmənˈstreɪʃən). [a. obs. F. *remonstration*, or ad. med.L. *remonstrātiōn-em*, n. of action f. *remonstrāre* to REMONSTRATE.]

1. The action of remonstrating, remonstrance, expostulation; an instance of this.

The early examples may strictly belong to sense 2.

c **1489** Caxton *Blanchardyn* xvii. 53 How the proude pucelle in amours, after dyuers and many remonstracions made by her maystres vnto her, bygan to wexe moderate. **1491** —— *Vitas Patr.* (W. de W. 1495) II. 180/2 The brother by these remonstracyons toke at his herte so grete contrycyon that he obteyned the mercy of god. **1824** in *Spirit Pub. Jrnls.* (1825) 254 They went down stairs to the bar, and began a remonstration with the landlord. **1828** Landor *Imag. Conv., Victor Saez & Netto* III. 39 Where demonstrations come in the van, remonstrations come in the rear. **1882** *Harper's Mag.* Jan. 243/1 He went many times over the case of his wife,..his own repeated remonstration.

†**2.** Demonstration; an instance of this. *Obs.*

1586 Whetstone *Eng. Mirr.* 116 The remonstration of the civill warres, bloudshed and many grievous calamities, which..afflicted this small kingdome. **1629** Wadsworth *Pilgr.* iii. 12 They begun a remonstration of their rules, and orders, and observations. *a* **1640** Jackson *Creed* x. ii. §3 The deduction, or remonstration of this demonstrative inference is clear to any artist, to any reasonable man.

remonstrative (ˈrɛmən-, rɪˈmɒnstrətɪv), *a.* [f. as REMONSTRATE *v.* + -IVE.] Of or characterized by remonstrance, expostulatory.

1614 Jackson *Creed* III. xxvii. §4 The Churches proposall hath the very remonstratiue roote and Character of the immediat and prime cause. **1647** *Case Kingd.* 16 Puling down al others with Remonstrative or Petitionary Out-cries. **1660** T. M. *Cl. Walker's Hist. Independ.* IV. 63 A remonstrative address from the Army. **1706** in *Pa. Hist. Soc. Mem.* X. 133, I wrote a remonstrative letter to the Governour. **1872** *Yng. Gentleman's Mag.* 114/2 'Another stop for a chimbley' he muttered, with a remonstrative growl. **1882** J. Hawthorne *Pr. Saroni's Wife* (1884) II. 13 Saroni gave a short, remonstrative laugh.

Hence **re'monstratively**, *adv.* (Ogilvie *Suppl.* 1882).

remonstrator (ˈrɛmən-, rɪˈmɒnstreɪtə(r)). [f. REMONSTRATE *v.* + -OR.] One who remonstrates; a remonstrant.

1653 Nicholas in *N. Papers* (Camden) II. 9 The Remonstrators (as I think he calls them) have declared that they will have none of the present Government. **1679** Penn *Addr. Prot.* 64 For Accommodation in some particulars with the Remonstrators or Free-willers. **1736** Carte *Ormonde* II. 419 The Lord Lieutenant was not moved by any thing that could be said in favour of the remonstrators. **1889** *Columbus* (Ohio) *Disp.* 4 Dec., Remonstrators having the privilege of filing their objections and appealing to the courts. **1899** *Daily News* 20 July 6/3 The actor-manager looked at the remonstrator half quizzically.

attrib. **1660** *Lauderd. Papers* (Camden) I. 59 To doe favours to some of the remonstrator way. **1693** *Apol. Clergy Scot.* 16 Severals of the Remonstrator Presbyterians.

re'monstratory, *a.* [f. as prec. + -ORY^2.] Expostulatory.

1823 *Examiner* 790/2 It is right to listen..to all contending and remonstratory interests. **1866** Ruskin *Eth. Dust* (1883) 23, Remonstratory whispers, expressive of opinion that the Lecturer is becoming too personal.

remontant (rɪˈmɒntənt), *a.* and *sb.* [a. F. *remontant*, pres. pple. of *remonter* to REMOUNT.]

a. *adj.* Of roses: Blooming a second time or oftener in a season. **b.** *sb.* A hybrid perpetual rose blooming more than once in a season. Also used (*adj.* and *sb.*) of strawberry plants bearing fruit for a longer period than usual.

1883 *Century Mag.* July 350/1 Beautiful white roses, whose places have not been filled by any of the usurping remontants. *Ibid.* 350/2 The Baronne Prévost..is now the oldest type among hybrid remontant roses. **1901** *Chambers's Encycl.* VIII. 806/1 The Perpetual, or Remontant rose, as the French more correctly term it,..affords a succession, more or less continuous,..of bud and bloom. **1923** J. H. McFarland *Rose in Amer.* ii. 21 The Hybrid Perpetual roses are also called Remontant. Both designations are misnomers so far as bloom is concerned. **1965** E. B. Le Grice *Rose Growing Complete* xii. 170 Single, coarse, once-flowering climbers had, at least a thousand years ago, become many-petalled, or dwarf, or remontant (repeat-flowering). **1968** R. Hay *Gardener's Round* 78 Plant the 'remontant' or perpetual strawberries to have a crop in the autumn. **1969** *Oxf. Bk. Food Plants* 74/2 The perpetuals or remontants are an interesting group [of strawberries], which flower successively during the summer and produce fruit from July till October. **1979** *Guardian* 13 Oct. 15/5 Cover remontant strawberries with cloches.

‖**remontoir** (rəmɔ̃twar). Also -oire. [F., f. *remonter* to REMOUNT.] *Clock-making.* A device by which an exactly uniform impulse is given to the pendulum or balance. Also *attrib.* with *escape(ment)*, *spring*, *wheel*, etc.

1801 *Trans. Soc. Arts* XIX. 335 It requires no more power than any other Remontoire Escapement. *Ibid.* The strength of the remontoire-spring. **1825** J. Nicholson *Operat. Mechanic* 519 A remontoire escape which possesses considerable merit. **1875** J. W. Benson *Time & T.-tellers* (1902) 126 This arrangement, which is called the remontoir, is supplemented in this clock by a double lever escapement. **1878** Lockyer *Stargazing* 322 The remontoire wheel..relaxes its pressure against a friction-wheel.

Hence **re'montoiring** *ppl. a.*, performing the function of a remontoir.

1803 *Trans. Soc. Arts* XXI. 409 Pressed against the teeth of the spring wheel, by remontoiring springs.

re'moor, *v.* [RE- 5 a.] To moor again.

1800 *Hull Pilotage Act* 14 The pilot..shall be paid for..remooring such ship.

re'moot, *v.* [RE-.] *trans.* To moot again or in answer.

1676 *Doctrine of Devils* 172 To that which is said by the Debater..It is remooted, indeed [etc.].

remora (ˈrɛmərə). [a. L. *remora* delay, hindrance (f. *re-* RE- + *mora* delay), also occurring in Pliny *Nat. Hist.* xxxii. 1 as the L. name of the fish called ἐχενηΐς by the Greeks (but modern edd. prefer the reading *mora*): hence It., Sp., and Pg. *remora*, F. *rémora*, *rémore* (16th c.).]

1. The sucking-fish (*Echeneis remora*), believed by the ancients to have the power of staying the course of any ship to which it attached itself.

1567 Maplet *Gr. Forest* 84 The fish Echeneis or Remora, staiship, amazeth also..the beholder by his hid and occult..vertue. **1591** Spenser *Vis. World's Van.* ix, There cloue unto her keele A little fish, that men call Remora, Which stopt her course. **1601** Holland *Pliny* II. 426 The said stay-ship Echeneis or Remora (call it whether you will). **1640** in *Harl. Misc.* (Malh.) IV. 301 With much more likelihood than that the remora stays vessels under full sail. **1666–7** Denham *Direct. Paint.* I. xii, Smith to the Duke doth intercept her way, And cleaves t' her closer than a Remora. **1711** *Phil. Trans.* XXVII. 348 Fig. 12 is a rare sort of Remora, or Stop-Ship, with a very taper Body. **1796** Stedman *Surinam* II. xxx. 385 The remora, or sucking-fish, is frequently found sticking to sharks, and to ships bottoms. **1846** Landor *Imag. Conv., Marcus & Quinctus Cicero* Wks. I. 244 Like the remora, of which mariners tell marvels, it counteracts, as it were, both oar and sail. **1876** *Beneden's Anim. Parasites* Introd. 18 The fish which, through idleness, attaches itself, like the remora, to a neighbour who swims well.

attrib. **1801** *Encycl. Brit.* (ed. 3) Supp. II. 400/2 If the two white fish..be of the remora species, as he is inclined to think [etc.].

b. In fig. and allusive expressions.

1601 B. Jonson *Poetaster* III. ii, 'Death, I am seaz'd on here By a Land-Remora. **1605** Bacon *Adv. Learn.* II. vii. §7 They are indeed but Remoraes and hindrances to stay and slugge the Shippe from furder sayling. **1627** Donne *Serm.* v. 43 This was a Rock in his Sea and a Remora upon his Ship. **1643** Tuckney *Balme of G.* 29 What unhappy remora or Anchor under water not yet seen, hath stopt us in this happy course?

c. *Her.* (See quot.)

1780 Edmondson *Heraldry* II. Gloss. s.v., In blazoning the figure of Prudence, which is represented as holding in her hand a javelin entwined with a serpent proper, such serpent is expressed by the word Remora.

2. An obstacle, hindrance, impediment, obstruction. (Common in 17–18th c.)

1604 Edmonds *Observ. Cæsar's Comm.* 100 That authoritie..was as a Remora to diuers other nations of Gallia from shewing that defection by plaine and open revolt. **1641** H. L'Estrange *God's Sabbath* 59 We have at last shaked off those remora's which retarded our arrivall at the Christian Sabbath. **1672** W. de Britaine *Dutch Usurp.* 19 There is no such Remora to Grandeur, as a coy and squemish Conscience. **1740** Lady M. W. Montagu *Let. to C'tess Pomfret* 4 June, My stay here..shall be as short as these remoras will permit. **1793** Cowper *Let. to Rev. Greatheed* 27 July, These numerous demands are likely to operate as a *remora*, and to keep us fixed at home. **1820** C. Colton *Lacon* cxli. I. 80 The great remora to any improvement in our civil code. **1864** J. H. Newman *Apol.* 407 A sort of remora or break in the development of doctrine.

attrib. *c* **1629** Layton *Syons Plea* (ed. 2) 26 The Remora-Prelats..so blocked up the way, that the said Acts could not pass.

3. *Med.* Stoppage or stagnation. *rare*$^{-1}$.

1782 A. Monro *Compar. Anat.* (ed. 3) 9 Too long a *remora* of the juices might occasion the worst consequences.

4. *Surg.* An instrument used to retain bones or other parts in place. *rare*$^{-0}$.

1688 Holme *Armoury* III. xii. 434/2 A Remora, which is an Instrument used for the helping of a dislocated Shoulder. **1693** tr. *Blancard's Phys. Dict.* (ed. 2), *Remora*, a Chyrurgical Instrument, to reduce a broken Bone. **1875** Knight *Dict. Mech.* 1916/1. **1897** *Syd. Soc. Lex.*

Hence †**'remora** *v.* *Obs. rare*$^{-1}$. To delay.

1686 in *Ellis Corr.* (1829) I. 8 That his Excellency should be remora'd at such a cold harbour.

†**'remoral**, *a.* *Obs. rare*$^{-1}$. [f. prec., or L. *remora* delay + -AL^1.] Given to delay, dilatory.

a **1625** Cope in Gutch *Coll. Cur.* (1781) I. 132 Their private affections do oftentimes yield to their publique judgements, and make them remoral in their friends suits.

re'moralize, *v.* [RE- 5 b.] *trans.* To make moral again; to re-instil with morals. So **re,morali'zation.**

1967 *Guardian* 16 Oct. 6/5 Violence and pain still provide an evil satisfaction which the remoralisation of sex has not yet exorcised. **1974** *Daily Tel.* 21 Oct. 6/8 We are able to remoralise whole groups and classes of people, undoing the harm done..by permissiveness in television, in films, on bookstalls. *Ibid.* 21 Oct. 6/8 We shall need intellectual as well as moral courage to grapple with the dilemmas inherent in the remoralisation of public life.

†**'remorate**, *v.* *Obs. rare.* [ad. L. *remorāt-*, ppl. stem of *remorārī* to hinder, delay, f. *re-* RE- + *morārī* to delay; cf. REMORAL *a.*] *trans.* To detain, delay, obstruct. Hence †**'remorating** *ppl. a.*

1638 Rider *Horace, Odes* III. v, Yet he no otherwise His remorating kindred did adjourne. **1657** Tomlinson *Renou's Disp.* 302 Its long..roots remorate the oxen in ploughing.

remorce, obs. form of REMORSE.

†**re'mord**, *sb.* *Obs. rare.* [a. OF. *remord*, var. of *remors* REMORSE; or independently f. the vb.]

a. An impairment or taint. **b.** Blame, rebuke. **c.** A touch of remorse.

1456 Sir G. Haye *Law Arms* (S.T.S.) 13 The thrid [manner] is carnale..; that takis of the mortell flesch a remorde, sa that it may nocht perfitely understand south-fastnes of haly scripture. *a* **1529** Skelton *Sp. Parrot* 300 But now, for your defence Agayne all remordes arme yow with paciens. **1655** tr. *Sorel's Com. Hist. Francion* II. 50 Their insensibility robs them of Remords, and fils their vaine hearts with joy.

†**re'mord**, *v.* *Obs.* (exc. as *nonce-wd.*) Also 4–5 *pa. t.* and *pa. pple.* **remord(e.** [ad. F. *remordre* (12th c.):—Rom. **remordĕre* = L. *remordēre* to vex, disturb, f. *re-* RE- + *mordēre* to bite, sting, attack, etc.: see MORDANT. In later use chiefly *Sc.*; re-formed by C. Reade in 19th c. (see 2 b).]

1. *trans.* To visit with affliction. *rare*$^{-1}$.

c **1374** Chaucer *Boeth.* IV. pr. vi. 109 (Camb. MS.) God..remordith [L. *remordet*] some folk by aduersite, for they ne sholde nat wexen prowde by longe welefulnesse.

2. To afflict (a person, the mind, etc.) with remorse or painful feelings.

13.. *E.E. Allit. P.* A. 364 My herte waz al with mysse remorde. *c* **1374** Chaucer *Troylus* IV. 1463 (1491) Ye shul dullen of þe rudenesse Of vs sely Troians, but yf rouþe Remorde yow. **1446** Lydg. *Nightingale* i. 190 O synfull man, this oure the aght remord, That standest exiled oute fro charite. **1513** Douglas *Æneis* VII. vii. 140 Geif ony thocht remordis ȝour myndis..Of the effectuus piete maternall. **1567** *Gude & Godlie B.* (S.T.S.) 120 My sinfull lyfe dois me remord. [**1628** Sir W. Mure *Doomsday* 820 A consort sweet..Allayes all mind-remording cares.]

b. To afflict (one's own conscience, oneself, etc.) with remorseful thoughts; also, to unburden with contrition; to examine in a penitent spirit.

c **1450** *Pol. Rel. & L. Poems* (1903) 138 Noght euere-ilke man..sal hafe þi blise, his conscienz bot he remorde. *c* **1470** Henry *Wallace* IV. 590 Wallace to God his conscience fyrst remord. *Ibid.* x. 9 In sum part than he remordyt his thocht, The kingis commaund becaus he kepyt nocht. **1560** Rolland *Crt. Venus* III. 843 That thay wald pance and prent, Considder weill,..Remord thair mindis quhidder gif Chestitie [etc.]. *a* **1578** Lindesay (Pitscottie) *Chron. Scot.* (S.T.S.) I. 406 He began to remorde his conscience. [**1857** Reade *White Lies* III. ix. 124 Others thought he must at some part of his career have pillaged a church;..and now was committing the mistake of remording himself about it.]

3. To recall to mind with remorse or regret.

13.. *Gaw. & Gr. Knt.* 2434 When I ride in renoun, [I shall] remorde to myseluen þe faut & þe fayntyse of þe flesche crabbed. *c* **1470** Henry *Wallace* x. 541 Sadly the Bruce than in his mynd remordyt Thai wordis suth that Wallace had hym recordyt. **1570** *Satir. Poems Reform.* xxii. 94 Remord in mynd thy greit madnes.

b. To recall, remember, record.

c **1450** Holland *Howlat* 654 So mekle was the multitud no mynd it remordis. **1501** Douglas *Pal. Hon.* I. xlv, Diuers vthers quhilks me not list remord. *c* **1507** *Justes May & June* 266 in Hazl. *E.P.P.* II. 130 It was done but onely for the sake

Of kynge Henry..And of the prynce, who lyste it to remorde.

c. To meditate, ponder. *rare*⁻¹.

1535 STEWART *Cron. Scot.* II. 384 He wes nothing content,..And in his mynd remordit oft and knew, Richt suddanelie that he suld him persew.

4. *intr.* To feel remorse.

c **1440** *Alph. Tales* 42 He remordid in his conciens & said; 'Nowder of þies two did itt, I did it my selfe'. **1491** CAXTON *Vitas Patr.* (W. de W. 1495) II. 278/1 A relygyous man ought not to suffre that his conscyence remorde ne grudge of ony thynge. **1531** ELYOT *Gov.* II. v, Beyng meued either with loue or pitie, or other wyse his conscience remording against the destruction of so noble a prince. *c* **1560** A. SCOTT *Poems* (S.T.S.) xiii. 38 Remord & rew, and pondir weill my parte. *c* **1570** *Satir. Poems Reform.* xiv. 73 Quhair thair was mys he gart remorde. **1614** [see *remording*].

b. To awaken remorse. *rare*⁻¹.

1572 *Satir. Poems Reform.* xxx. 210 Trew Preicheours speikis it to ȝow plane, ȝit neuer mercy in your mynd remordis.

5. *trans.* To blame, rebuke.

1523 SKELTON *Garl. Laurel* 86 If so hym fortune to wryte true and plaine, As sumtyme he must vyces remorde. *a* **1529** —— *Col. Cloute* 983 Squyre, knyght, and lorde, Thus the Churche remorde. **1629** SIR W. MURE *True Crucifixe* 624 Yet from his lips not one intemperat word, His mercilesse tormenters doth remord.

absol. **1522** SKELTON *Why not to Court* 1055 Remordynge and bytynge, With chydyng and with flytynge.

Hence †**re'mording** *ppl. a. Obs.*

c **1430** *Pilgr. Lyf Manhode* I. lv. (1869) 33 It is so cruelle, and so prikinge, so remordinge, and so persinge. **1614** EARL STIRLING *Domesday* I. xv, O what a terrour wounds remording soules. *a* **1700** KEN *Hymnotheo* Poet. Wks. 1721 III. 129 The poor Wretch, whose Body shook all o're, While his remording Conscience trembled more.

†**re'mordency.** *Obs. rare*⁻¹. [f. as next + -ENCY.] Compunction, remorse.

1717 KILLINBECK *18 Serm.* 175 This is what the Schools call *Pœna damni*; that remordency of Conscience, that extremity of grief, they feel within themselves.

re'mordent, *a. rare.* [ad. pres. pple. of L. *remordēre*: see REMORD *v.*] Biting in return.

1817 G. S. FABER *Eight Dissert.* (1845) I. 87 A man treading with his heel upon the head of a remordent snake. **1819** —— *Dispensations* (1823) I. 325 That the Seed of the woman should bruise the head of the remordent serpent.

†**re'morder.** *Obs. rare*⁻¹. [f. REMORD *v.* + -ER¹.] One who blames.

a **1529** SKELTON *Sp. Parrot* 368 Wherfor your remorders ar madde..Yow to remorde erste or they know your mynde.

†**re'more,** *sb. Obs. rare.* [Anglicized or Fr. form of REMORA: cf. next. In both examples printed *remove*.] Hindrance, delay.

1627 BEAULIEU in *Court & Times Chas. I* (1848) I. 239 Somewhat stayed him behind,..I think, as I hear, that his true remore hath been want of money. *Ibid.* 260 Want of money is a great remore to our endeavours.

†**re'more,** *v. Obs. rare*⁻¹. [f. L. *remor-ārī*, or perh. f. REMORE *sb.*] *trans.* To hinder, delay.

1641 BROME *Joviall Crew* I. Wks. 1873 III. 370 We have no debt or rent to pay;..Or if we had, should that remore us, When all the world's our own before us.

†**re'morphize,** *v. Obs. rare.* [irreg. f. RE- 5 a, after *metamorphize*.] *trans.* To restore to the original form.

1603 HARSNET *Pop. Impost.* 102 That worthy memorable Story of Saint Macarius..who..did remorphize an olde Woman that had beene turned into a Mare. *Ibid.* 133.

remorse (rɪˈmɔːs), *sb.* Forms: 4-5 remors, (6 remorrs), 5-7 remorce, 4- remorse. [a. OF. *remors* (mod.F. *remords*), ad. late L. *remorsus*, vbl. sb. f. *remordēre*: see REMORD *v.*]

1. *remorse of conscience* (or *mind*) = next. Now somewhat *rare* and *arch.* †Also with *pl.* (cf. 2 b).

c **1374** CHAUCER *Troylus* I. 554 Or hastow som remors of conscience..? **1387** TREVISA *Higden* (Rolls) VII. 171 þis pope..havynge remorse of conscience þat he was somwhat put yn by þe emperoure lefte the popehede. **1483** CAXTON *Cato* D j, He is euer in doubt and in remors of conscience. **1559** SACKVILLE *Induct. Mirr. Mag.* xxxii, And first within the portche and iawes of Hell Sate diepe Remorse of conscience. **1600** E. BLOUNT tr. *Conestaggio* 104 Onely for the remorse of his conscience, preferring the seruice of God before all other respects. **1670** G. H. tr. *Hist. Cardinals* II. I. 110 Perhaps not without some scruples and remorses of Conscience. **1704** *Lond. Gaz.* No. 4029/2 One of these Lieutenants having a Remorse of Conscience, discovered the..Mater. **1729** LAW *Serious C.* xxiii. 467 A man may..go on..without any remorse of mind, or true desire of amendment. **1808** LEMPRIERE *Univ. Biogr.* s.v. *Aunoy*, One of his three accusers afterwards through remorse of conscience confessed the charge to be false.

2. a. A feeling of compunction, or of deep regret and repentance, for a sin or wrong committed. Also const. *at*, *for*, †*of* (the thing done).

c **1400** *Destr. Troy* 1698 þan a sorow full sodenly sanke in his hert, A Remorce of maters, þat hym mys lyket. **1494** FABYAN *Chron.* VII. ccxxix. 260 By this monycion he toke remorce in his conscyence. **1526** *Pilgr. Perf.* (W. de W. 1531) 173 Vndoubted theyr conscyence sholde haue remorse. **1577** VAUTROUILLIER *Luther on Ep. Gal.* 19 The hypocrites..although they feele the remorse of sinne [etc.]. **1597** HOOKER *Eccl. Pol.* v. lxxii. §16 The fruit of our own ill-doing is remorse. **1641** BAKER *Chron.* (1653) 97 The remorse for his undutifulnesse towards his Father, was living in him till he dyed. *a* **1656** BP. HALL *Rem. Wks.* (1660) 162 Another teaches that there..is no hell but remorse. **1719** DE FOE *Crusoe* I. (Globe) 89 When again I was shipwreck'd,..I was as far from Remorse, or looking on it as a Judgment. **1780** COWPER *Progr. Err.* 43 Pleasure brings as surely in her train Remorse and Sorrow and vindictive Pain. **1821** SHELLEY *Fragment on Keats*, Death, in remorse for that fell slaughter,..flew Athwart the stream. **1868** BROWNING *Ring & Bk.* III. 180 We have her own confession at full length Made in the first remorse.

†**b.** With *a* and *pl.* A fit of remorse. *Obs.*

1652 J. WRIGHT tr. *Camus' Nat. Paradox* I. 17 To possess unjustly another's means with continuall Remorses and internall Reproaches. **1702** *Eng. Theophrast.* 123 Our repentances are generally not a remorse for the ills we have done. **1720** MANDEVILLE *Free Thoughts* 126 So at one time or other they are troubled with Remorses. **1761** HUME *Hist. Eng.* II. xl. 399 His remorses gradually diminished.

†**c.** ? Hesitation, scruple. *Obs. rare*⁻¹.

a **1529** SKELTON *Agst. Garnesche* ii. 19 As wytles as a wylde goos, ye haue but small remorrs Me for to chalenge.

†**3. a.** Sorrow, pity, compassion; also *pl.* signs of tender feeling. *Obs.*

a **1547** SURREY *Æneid* IV. 574 This latter grace, Sister, I craue, haue thou remorse of me. **1568** *Jacob & Esau* v. iv, Well, nature pricketh me some remorse on thee to haue. **1590** SPENSER *F.Q.* II. iv. 6 The noble Guyon, mov'd with great remorse, Approching, first the Hag did thrust away. **1639** G. DANIEL *Ecclus.* xii. 54 His Eyes shall be Stor'd wᵗʰ false tears, in remorse of thee. **1667** MILTON *P.L.* v. 566 How shall I relate..without remorse The ruin of so many glorious once..? **1692** DRYDEN *Cleomenes* v. ii, Womanish sighs and tears, and kind adieus, And those ill-timed remorses of good nature. **1700** —— *Pal. & Arc.* II. 345 Curse on th' unpard'ning Prince, whom Tears can draw To no Remorse: who rules by Lions Law.

†**b.** *remorse of equity*, a disposition to relax the strict application of a law. *Obs.*

1597 HOOKER *Eccl. Pol.* v. lx. §6 Remorse of equitie hath moued diuers of the school diuines..ingenuouslie to grant ..that God all-merciful [etc.]. [**1878** PATMORE *L' Allegro*, Those gentle and unsanction'd lines To which remorse of equity Of old hath moved the School divines.]

†**c.** *without remorse*, without mitigation or intermission. *Obs.*

1579 SPENSER *Sheph. Cal.* Nov. 131 The heauens doe melt in teares without remorse. *Ibid.* 171. **1600** SHAKS. *Twel. N.* II. iii. 98 That ye squeak out your Coziers Catches without any mitigation or remorse of voice.

†**4. a.** Regretful or remorseful remembrance or recollection *of* a thing. *Obs.*

a **1529** SKELTON *Knolege, aquayntance*, etc. 29 Remorse haue I of youre most goodlyhod. **1570-6** LAMBARDE *Peramb. Kent* (1826) 295 Sundry of the Noble men, partly upon remorse of their former promise made,..made defection to Maude. **1695** TEMPLE *Hist. Eng.* (1699) 578 Either the Fame of his Forces..or Remorse of his Duty, prevail'd with Duke Robert to offer again his Submissions.

†**b.** Consideration or regard *to* a matter, etc.

1514 in Strype *Eccl. Mem.* (1721) I. App. iv. 8 That it may please his Highness to have Consideration & Remors to this before rehearsed, in considering [etc.]. **1525** *St. Papers Hen. VIII*, VI. 416 The Kinges Highnes hauing most tendre remorce and respect unto the premisses [etc.].

†**c.** A solemn obligation. *Obs. rare*⁻¹.

1604 SHAKS. *Oth.* III. iii. 369 Let him command, And to obey shall be in me remorse, What bloody businesse euer.

†**5.** A matter for regret; a pity. *Obs. rare.*

1548 GEST *Pr. Masse* in H. G. Dugdale *Life* (1840) App. I. 76 Is it not a deadely remorse to respect the worthy Clerkes in thys realme..and yet not one to wryte agaynste hyr? **1576** HUMPHREY in Strype *Ann. Ref.* (1709) I. xliii. 431 That it was a remorse to seem, by sundry apparel, to sunder himself from those brethren.

†**6.** Biting or cutting force. *Obs. rare*⁻¹.

1596 SPENSER *F.Q.* IV. ii. 15 Their speares with pitilesse remorse Through shield and mayle and haberjeon did wend.

7. *Comb.*, as *remorse-smitten*, *-stirred*, *-stricken*, *-stung* adjs.

1777 ELIZ. RYVES *Poems* 60 'Tis not th' accumulated store Of sparkling gems..Can a remorse-stung mind appease. **1826** SCOTT *Woodst.* xiv. *motto*, Be it the working Of the remorse-stirr'd fancy. **1897** MARY KINGSLEY *W. Africa* 514 Over the side the doctor went, to the horror of the remorse-smitten sea-captain. **1973** M. AMIS *Rachel Papers* 56, I couldn't resist taking a certain fascinated pleasure in his remorse-stricken face.

†**re'morse,** *v. Obs.* [f. *remors-*, ppl. stem of L. *remordēre*: see prec. and REMORD *v.*]

1. *trans.* To affect with remorse.

1483 CAXTON *Gold. Leg.* 196 b/2 Her conscience remorsed hir and [she] fyl doun to hir feet in requyryng pardon. **1563** FOXE *A. & M.* 1703/1 Blaxton..fel in such a quake, & shaking (the conscience belyke remorsing him). **1593** NASHE *Christ's T.* (1613) 62 Now (dissemblingly remorsed) they would needs..set vp another [high priest].

2. *intr.* To feel remorse.

1530 PALSGR. 685/2, I have remorced more in my conscyence than all men knewe of. **1557** *Tottel's Misc.* (Arb.) 194 Your hart must nedes remorce of right To graunt me grace. **1690** LOCKE *Hum. Und.* I. iii. §9 They remorse in one place, for doing or omitting that which others, in another place, think they merit by.

Hence †**re'morsed** *ppl. a.*, of the nature of, affected by, remorse. *Obs.*

a **1586** SIDNEY *Arcadia* III. Wks. 1724 II. 691 Wrong stirs remorsed Grief. **1617** J. MOORE *Mappe Mans Mort.* III. viii. 235 They be reputed to come from a remorsed soule for sinne. **1649** BP. HALL *Cases Consc.* III. ix. 334 The soule of the remorsed draweth neare to the grave.

remorseful (rɪˈmɔːsfʊl), *a.* [f. REMORSE *sb.*]

1. Affected with or characterized by remorse; impressed with a sense of, and penitent for, guilt.

1592 *Nobody & Someb.* in Simpson *Sch. Shaks.* (1878) I. 313, I know his penitentiall words proceede From a remorcefull spirit. **1612** W. SCLATER *Sick Souls Salve* 20 An heart of flesh, remorsefull for sinne. **1679** J. GOODMAN *Penit. Pard.* II. iii. (1713) 204 A contrite and remorseful confession of his former sins. *a* **1763** SHENSTONE *Economy* II. 165 From a blacker cause Springs this remorseful gloom? **1828** CARLYLE *Misc.* (1857) I. 223 Many a bitter hour and year of remorseful sorrow. **1881** *Blackw. Mag.* CXXIX. 191 The remorseful philanthropist did all in his power to console him.

†**2.** Compassionate, full of pity. *Obs.*

1591 SHAKS. *Two Gent.* IV. iii. 13 Thou art a Gentleman: ..Valiant, wise, remorse-full, well accomplish'd. **1610** NICOLS *Eng. Eliza* xcvi. in *Mirr. Mag.* 802 The Briton Maid remorsefull of their woes. *c* **1611** CHAPMAN *Iliad* VIII. 208 To this euen weeping king did Ioue remorsefull audience giue.

†**3.** Pitiable. *Obs. rare*⁻¹.

1615 CHAPMAN *Odyss.* x. 331 Eurylochus straight hasted the report Of this his fellowes most remorcefull fate.

Hence **re'morsefully** *adv.*, **re'morsefulness.**

1617 HIERON *Wks.* I. 370 How good in Gods sight was the remorsefulnesse of that poor soule. **1842** TENNYSON *Morte D' Arth.* 171 Him Sir Bedivere Remorsefully regarded thro' his tears. **1887** *Old Man's Favour* I. II. ii. 229 'It might be best for you', muttered her lover in sudden gloomy remorsefulness.

remorseless (rɪˈmɔːslɪs), *a.* [f. as prec. + -LESS.] Devoid of remorse; pitiless, cruel.

1593 SHAKS. *3 Hen. VI*, I. iv. 142 Women are..pittifull..; Thou, sterne, obdurate, flintie, rough, remorselesse. **1612** DRAYTON *Poly-olb.* viii. 349 Whilst we in sundry Fields our sundry fortunes prov'd With the remorseless Pict. **1631** MILTON *Epit. Marchioness Winchester* 29 Atropos..with remorsles cruelty, Spoil'd at once both fruit and tree. **1686** tr. *Chardin's Coronat. Solyman* 31 They are a sort of People endued with savage and remorseless Souls. **1728** MORGAN *Algiers* II. iv. 274 All this the remorseless Basha imputed to obstinacy and guilt. **1812** BYRON *Ch. Har.* I. lxxxvii, So may such foes deserve the most remorseless deed! **1853** J. H. NEWMAN *Hist. Sk.* (1873) II. I. i. 22 They felt..the resistless crushing force of a remorseless foe. **1873** MOZLEY *Univ. Serm.* viii. (1876) 164 The page of history is stained by the dark acts of..remorseless superstition.

b. quasi-*adv.* Without remorse.

1593 SHAKS. *2 Hen. VI*, III. i. 213 As the Butcher takes away the Calfe,..Euen so remorselesse haue they borne him hence. **1742** YOUNG *Nt. Th.* I. 255 Want, and incurable disease,..On hopeless multitudes remorseless seize.

re'morselessly, *adv.* [f. prec. + -LY².] In a remorseless manner; without remorse.

1612 T. TAYLOR *Comm. Titus* i. 6 Such a one.. prostituteth himselfe remorselesly vnto all lewdnes. **1647** TRAPP *Comm. Matt.* vii. 5 Those pollutions he had remorselesly wallowed in. *a* **1716** SOUTH *Serm.* (1744) X. vi. 172 [He] remorselessly and unworthily took his fellow by the throat for an hundred pence. **1814** SOUTHEY *Odes* I. vi, A merciless oppressor hast thou been, Thyself remorselessly oppress'd meantime. **1883** GILMOUR *Mongols* xxix. 242 This religion, which..remorselessly pollutes and crushes man.

re'morselessness. [f. as prec. + -NESS.] The state or quality of being remorseless.

1648 BEAUMONT *Psyche* IX. cxxxix, Never with such fell remorselessness She rag'd in any Breast, as now in His. **1664** H. MORE *Myst. Iniq.* 257 The Remorselesness of Conscience which men easily fall into in both sins. **1834** CAMPBELL *Life Mrs. Siddons* II. ii. 45 The inhuman serenity of her remorselessness. **1855** MILMAN *Lat. Chr.* XIV. v. (1864) IX. 206 He has all the stern remorselessness of an inquisitor.

†**re'morsive,** *a. Obs. rare*⁻¹. [f. as REMORSE *v.* + -IVE.] Remorseful, pitying.

1606 WARNER *Alb. Eng.* XIV. xcii. 371 With ruinating fire and swords remorsiue vnto none.

re'mortgage, *v.* [RE- 5 a.] *trans.* To mortgage anew; to change the terms of a mortgage on (a property). So **re'mortgage** *sb.*; **re'mortgaging** *vbl. sb.*

1960 *Farmer & Stockbreeder* 15 Mar. 125/1, I have tried to raise capital by various means, including re-mortgaging, but without success. **1961** BENJAMIN & ATHOLL *How to borrow Money* vii. 77 A practical alternative to offering a second mortgage as the security may be to re-mortgage the house. *Ibid.*, The probability is that you have had the house for a number of years so that if you could effect the re-mortgage, the amount you would have to repay on your present mortgage would be substantially less. *Ibid.* 78 The comparative costs of re-mortgaging and raising a loan on a second mortgage..should be compared. **1976** *Milton Keynes Express* 25 June 33/5 (Advt.), Deposit loans, personal loans, remortgages, second mortgages, business finance. **1977** *S. Wales Echo* 18 Jan. 11/1 (Advt.), Building society re-mortgages and second mortgages arranged. **1978** *Cornish Guardian* 27 Apr. 34/2 (Advt.), Also available— First mortgages, re-mortgages and personal loans for tenants.

remosion, obs. form of REMOTION.

remote (rɪˈməʊt), *a.* (*sb.*) and *adv.* [ad. L. *remōt-us*, pa. pple. of *removēre* to REMOVE. Cf. obs. F. *remot*, *-mote* (15-16th c. in Godef.).]

A. *adj.* **1.** Placed or situated at a distance or interval from each other; far apart.

c **1420** *Pallad. on Husb.* VI. 47 Yf thaire be treen,..Her oon, ther oon, to leue afer remote I holde hit good. **1601** SHAKS. *Phœnix* 29 Hearts remote, yet not asunder. **1726** LEONI tr. *Alberti's Archit.* I. 16/1 They ought..not..to stand nearer or more remote than Use and Necessity requires. **1776** J. LEE *Introd. Bot.* Explan. Terms 381 *Remota*, remote, placed at some Distance from each other. **1822** IMISON *Sc. & Art* I. 69 The nearer the mill-stones are to each other, the finer the corn is ground, and the more remote from one another the coarser. 1861 J. R. Greene *Man. Anim. Kingd., Cœlent.* 204 In *Aulopora* the somewhat remote corallites are connected by means of a basal creeping cœnenchyma.

Comb. 1867 Sowerby *Eng. Bot.* VII. 163 *Statice Bahusiensis*... Remote-flowered Sea Lavender. 1880 Hogg & Johnson *Wild Fl.* XI. Pl. 871 *Carex remota*... Remote-flowered Sedge.

2. a. Far away, far off, distant *from* some place, thing, or person; removed, set apart. (In *lit.* and *fig.* uses.)

c1586 C'tess Pembroke *Ps.* cv. iv, Soe remote from wrong of meaner hand That kings for them did sharp rebuke endure. 1588 Shaks. *L.L.L.* v. ii. 806 Some.. Hermitage, Remote from all the pleasures of the world. 1602 Marston *Ant. & Mel.* v. Wks. 1856 I. 63 The nigher it is to the flame, the more remote (ther's a word, remote), the more remote it is from the frost. 1664 Power *Exp. Philos.* III. 177 If a Pistol be shot off in a head remote from the eye of a pit, it will give but a little report. 1719 De Foe *Crusoe* I. (Globe) 379 That was the remotest Thing from their Thoughts could be imagin'd. 1770 Goldsm. *Des. Vill.* 143 Remote from towns he ran his godly race. 1797 Mrs. Radcliffe *Italian* xiii, The lake lay so remote from the immediate way to Naples. 1828 D'Israeli *Chas. I*, I. vii. 217 The principle of actions often lies remote from the actions themselves.

b. Widely different or divergent *from* something else. (Cf. 4.)

1659 Hammond *On Ps.* xii. 8 Passing by all these, as remote from the meaning of the place. 1675 Penn *Eng. Pres. Interest* 6 There cannot well be anything more remote from Arbitrariness. 1734 tr. *Rollin's Anc. Hist.* IV. IX. 275 So remote were they in this respect from the character of the ancient Greeks. 1788 Reid *Aristotle's Logic* iv. §5. 89 Conclusions may be drawn very remote from the first principles. 1849 Macaulay *Hist. Eng.* iii. I. 415 That this calculation was not remote from the truth we have abundant proof. 1854 Thoreau *Walden* (1884) 140 These small waves raised by the evening wind are as remote from storm as the smooth reflecting surface.

†**c.** Foreign or alien *to* a thing. *Obs. rare*$^{-1}$.

1719 De Foe *Crusoe* I. (Globe) 34, I was gotten into an Employment quite remote to my Genius, and directly contrary to the Life I delighted in.

3. a. Far-off, far-distant.

1590 Spenser *F.Q.* III. iv. 6 So forth she rode,.. Searching all lands and each remotest part. 1595 Shaks. *John* v. ii. 31 To grace the Gentry of a Land remote. 1632 Lithgow *Trav.* x. 425 By home-bred Robbers, and remote Savages; five times stripd to the skin. 1664 Power *Exp. Philos.* I. 78 Our Posterity may come by Glasses to out-see the Sun, and Discover Bodies in the remote Universe. 1683 *Brit. Spec.* 118 To spread its bright Beams upon this remote and frozen Island of Britain. 1726 Swift (*title*) Travels into Several Remote Nations of the World,.. by Lemuel Gulliver. 1780 Harris *Philol. Enq.* Wks. (1841) 521 Marc Paul.. travelled into those remote regions as far as the capital and court of Cublai Chan. 1818 Shelley *Eugan. Hills* 261 Once remotest nations came To adore that sacred flame. 1838 Prescott *Ferd. & Is.* (1846) I. Introd. 11 Volunteers from the remotest parts of Christendom. 1880 Geikie *Phys. Geog.* Introd. 1 As we gaze into these depths [of space] still remoter and feebler twinkling points appear.

b. Out-of-the-way, retired, secluded.

1611 Shaks. *Wint. T.* III. iii. 31 Places remote enough are in Bohemia, There.. leaue it crying. a1667 Cowley *Agric.* Wks. 1710 II. 725 The Company was gone Into a Room remote. 1719 De Foe *Crusoe* I. (Globe) 266, I sent.. one of the three.. to my Cave, where they were remote enough, and out of Danger of being heard or discover'd. 1784 Cowper *Task* III. 117 With few associates, in remote And silent woods I wander. 1835 Lytton *Rienzi* I. i, The path they had selected was remote and tranquil. 1865 Trollope *Belton Est.* i. 2 The place is remote and the living therefore cheap.

c. In quasi-*adv.* use: At a distance, far off.

1667 Milton *P.L.* II. 477 Thir rising all at once was as the sound Of Thunder heard remote. 1715 Pope *Iliad* IV. 424 Can'st thou, remote, the mingling Hosts descry..? 1765 T. Hutchinson *Hist. Mass.* I. 134 Living very remote at Springfield. 1781 J. Morison in *Sc. Paraphr.* xxi. 1 Attend ye tribes that dwell remote; ye tribes at hand give ear.

d. Distant in (past or future) time.

1712 Addison *Spect.* No. 273 ¶12 Æneas [was] the remote Founder of Rome. 1781 Cowper *Table T.* 492 When remote futurity is brought Before the keen inquiry of her thought. 1823 J. Badcock *Dom. Amusem.* 15 The antiseptic qualities of smoke were known to remotest antiquity. 1875 Jowett *Plato* (ed. 2) III. 165 The inheritance of disease or character from a remote ancestor.

e. (Also in *compar.*) Further.

1814 Scott *Ld. of Isles* III. xxiv, For our separate use, good friend, We'll hold this hut's remoter end. 1862 Spencer *First Princ.* I. iv. §26 (1875) 95 On thinking of a piano, there first rises in imagination its visual appearance, to which are instantly added.. the ideas of its remote side and of its solid substance.

f. Situated, occurring, or performed at a distance (not necessarily great); ***remote control***, control of apparatus, etc., at a distance; also (with hyphen) *attrib.*; so ***remote-controlled*** ppl. adj., ***remote-control*** vb. trans. and intr. (also *fig.*).

1904 L. Andrews *Electricity Control* i. 8 It is probable.. that for installations of a few thousand horse-power only, some simple method of mechanical remote control will be generally preferred. 1920 *Wireless World* 7 Aug. 356/1 Pilot's and mechanic's cockpits are not very roomy compartments and therefore it has become standard practice to employ 'remote control', that is to say the main portion of the wireless apparatus.. are [*sic*] fitted in one or two boxes which can be suspended in any convenient part of the main fuselage of the machine; these circuits being controlled by a small unit.. which may be fitted on the dashboard of the machine. 1933 *Times* 16 May 9/2 A remote control device for the selection of several alternative wireless programmes will soon be made available to the public. 1943 *Gloss. Terms Electr. Engin.* (*B.S.I.*) 84 *Remote-controlled substation*, a substation the operation of which is controlled at a distance. 1956 *Nature* 28 Jan. 160/2 The remote-handling device for removal of the collectors containing the enriched product without exposure to air. 1957 *Economist* 9 Nov. 525/2 Because of their radioactivity, none of the materials can be handled normally. All operations are carried out painstakingly by remote control. 1961 G. Millerson *Telev. Production* iii. 28 (*caption*) Lens turret,.. rotated by rear handle.. or remote switching. 1966 P. O'Donnell *Sabre-Tooth* xv. 203 Two transmitters.. were remote-controlled from the H.Q. section. 1967 Cox & Grose *Organization & Handling Bibl. Rec. by Computer* iv. 95 The use of these direct access devices also paves the way for remote-terminal inquiry. 1970 O. Dopping *Computers & Data Processing* vi. 96 Remote processing of data.. normally requires multiprogramming. In remote processing, input and output goes via communication lines. 1970 'B. Mather' *Break in Line* xv. 187, I wondered if he were still in Calcutta or was remote-controlling from London. 1970 *New Scientist* 6 Aug. 286/1 The study defines remote-access computing as the use of computers where the main computer installation is at a distance from the user, who employs a terminal device to communicate with the computer over telephone or other links. 1972 *Times* 11 Sept. (Botswana, etc., Suppl.) p. vi/2 (*caption*) Remote sensing, a development of aerial photography, can point to possible indications of mineral deposits. 1973 C. W. Gear *Introd. Computer Sci.* iv. 162 Many computer systems have low speed input/output devices, called remote terminals, attached to the central computer. 1974 *Harrods Christmas Catal.* 69/1 Remote-control Gantry Crane, battery operated... 28" high. £8·50. 1977 *Nature* 6 Jan. 34/2 Until this year, the most accurate means of studying the atmospheric pressure at the surface of Mars were provided by remote-sensing from fly-by or orbiting spacecraft. 1978 R. V. Jones *Most Secret War* viii. 68 The German Navy was said to have developed remote-controlled rocket-driven gliders of about three metres span. 1981 *Oxford Jrnl.* 15 May (Advt.), 20" Colour TV. Remote control. *Ibid.*, 14" Colour Portable TV with infra-red remote control hand unit.

4. a. Far off, or distant, in various *transf.* uses: *esp.* not immediately or closely related to, connected with, bearing upon, or affecting something else.

1599 Blundevil *Art of Logike* III. iii, When is a Proposition said to consist of matter remote or vnnatural? When the Predicat agreeth no manner of way with the Subject: as, a man is a horse. 1620 T. Granger *Div. Logike* 104 Note that these middles haue contrariety in them in the remisse, or remote degree. 1679 C. Nesse *Antichrist* 188, I would distinguish them from remoter providences. 1692 Dryden *St. Euremont's Ess.* 357 A Soul that disperses it self upon all remote Actions, and applys it self properly to nothing. 1764 Reid *Inquiry* I. i. 43 The external thing is the remote or mediate object. 1781 Cowper *Conversat.* 154 Their nimble nonsense takes a shorter course,.. And gains remote conclusions at a jump. 1860 Tyndall *Glac.* II. vii. 257 Newton thus applies this apparently remote fact to the blue of the sky. 1869 Ouseley *Counterp.* xxiii. 181 The student is strongly recommended not to modulate.. into extremely remote keys in this style of composition.

b. Of causes, operations, effects, etc.

1620 T. Granger *Div. Logike* 49 Cause, is neere, or remote, *id est*, further of. 1664 Power *Exp. Philos.* II. 192 It is but a sensible expression of Effects, dependent on the same (though more remote) Causes. 1790 Burke *Fr. Rev.* 90 That which in the first instance is prejudicial may be excellent in its remoter operation. 1822–34 *Good's Study Med.* (ed. 4) I. 559 Proximate and remote causes are rather terms of recent, than of ancient writers. 1844 Thirlwall *Greece* VIII. 59 They had not foreseen how the remoter consequences would affect their own safety. 1874 Carpenter *Ment. Phys.* I. ix. (1879) 415 The remoter effects which our actions are likely to have [etc.].

†**c.** Far-fetched; unusual. *Obs. rare.*

1670 Dryden *Tempest* Pref., As his Fancy was quick, so likewise were the Products of it remote and new. 1779–81 Johnson *L.P., Dryden* Wks. II. 386 Words too familiar or too remote, defeat the purpose of a poet.

d. Not closely related by blood or kinship.

1760 Foote *Minor* I. Wks. 1799 I. 239, I will.. trust for the support of my name and family to a remoter branch. 1845 S. Austin *Ranke's Hist. Ref.* I. 421 Family alliances, near or remote, which either already existed, or were now concluded. 1871 Freeman *Norm. Conq.* xvii. (1876) IV. 96 John was a remote kinsman of the Ducal house.

†**5.** Antecedent; ultimate. *Obs. rare.*

1610 B. Jonson *Alch.* II. iii, 'Twere absurd To think that nature in the earth bred gold Perfect in the instant: Something went before. There must be remote matter. 1697 tr. *Burgersdicius' Logic* II. vi. 21 The remote Matter of Syllogism are three Terms, to wit, two Extremes, major and minor,.. and one Middle.

6. Slight, faint. In later use esp. ***not the remotest***, not the slightest, not the least (idea, etc.); also *ellipt.*

1711 Addison *Spect.* No. 119 ¶5 Every thing that had the most remote Appearance of being obscene. 1816 Singer *Hist. Cards* 225 One of the standing figures has no remote resemblance to some of the effigies of Erasmus. 1861 M. Pattison *Ess.* (1889) I. 31 It had a bearing—remote indeed, but real—on what is being done now. 1864 Mrs. Carlyle *Lett.* III. 228 What I have done to deserve all that love I haven't the remotest conception. 1928 D. L. Sayers *Unpleasantness at Bellona Club* xvii. 205 'Was the quantity marked on the bottle?' 'I haven't the remotest. You'd better ask her.' 1969 E. Stewart *Heads* (1970) 94 'Why do you think he was trailing Father Fields?' 'I haven't the remotest,' Greg said.

†**7.** Ulterior. *Obs. rare*$^{-1}$.

1736 Butler *Anal.* I. iii. 74 Good offices will be done him, from regard to his character, without remote views.

B. *sb.* **a.** A remote descendant. **b.** A remote region. *nonce-uses.*

c1653 G. Daniel *Idyll* i. 41 'Twas Shame First taught vs cloths; we peccant, put a blame To each Remote! 1838 S. Bellamy *Betrayal* 15 It was a drear and mountainous remote, as earth's last fugitive retreat it were.

c. *U.S. Broadcasting.* An outside broadcast (see quots.). Cf. nemo.

1937 *Amer. Speech* XII. 100 A *remote pickup* or simply a *remote* means a program brought from some point other than station studios. 1937, etc. [see nemo]. 1947 *Billboard* 1 Nov. 17 First Remote on War Dead's Arrival... What is believed to be the first video broadcast by a remote unit from a moving object will be essayed tomorrow. 1962 *Sat. Rev.* 1 Sept. 17/2 Accent is not only a low-budget show; it is a 'remote'. A 'remote' shoots on location with video-cruiser facilities, as distinct from a studio show. 1967 *Boston Globe* 30 Mar. 3/1 CBS said in future days Cronkite may be seen in some news remotes while Zenker remains at the desk. 1976 *Listener* 15 July 53/1 'Remotes' are what American television technicians call outside broadcasts.

C. *adv.* In comb. with a ppl. forming an adj., = remotely *adv.* 2 b.

1943, etc. Remote-controlled [see sense A. 3 f above]. 1959 H. Barnes *Oceanogr. & Marine Biol.* iv. 200 Various systems could be devised, some complicated and expensive using remote-indicating compasses, but we have merely mounted an ordinary liquid compass in the field of view of the camera. 1976–7 *Sea Spray* (N.Z.) Dec./Jan. 94 The unit is available either directly mounted to a Borg-Warner marine reverse transmission unit or remote mounted and coupled to engine or reverse gear by a universal joint shaft.

†**re'mote,** *v. Obs. rare*$^{-1}$. [f. ppl. stem of L. *removēre*: cf. prec.] *trans.* To remove.

1600 Tourneur *Transf. Metamorph.* xxvi, Because she.. did remote Her heart from heau'n's book, where her name was wrote.

†**re'moted,** *a. Obs.* [f. as remote *a.* + -ed.] Remote, distant; removed.

c1580 Sidney *Ps.* xxii. xvii, From earthes remotedst border. 1607 Heywood *Wom. Killed w. Kindn.* Wks. 1874 II. 152, I must now go and wander.. In forraigne Countries and remoted climes. 1638 Junius *Paint. Ancients* 19 The things.. are full of deformed disproportions, and far remoted from.. true beautie. 1683 Villiers (Dk. Buckhm.) *Rehearsal* III. i. (ed. 4), In a strong Castle, remoted from thee.

remotely (rɪˈməʊtlɪ), *adv.* [f. remote *a.*]

1. In a remote manner; distantly; in a far-off degree.

1598 Florio, *Rimotamente*, remotely, separately. 1617 Moryson *Itin.* II. 51 The Glynnes.. being in the hands of the Obyrnes and O Tooles (and more remotely of the Cauanaghs). a1676 Hale *Prim. Orig. Man.* I. iv. (1677) 104 The most remotely distant Man in that vast Period of Eternity. 1768 Tucker *Lt. Nat.* I. II. 379 We have.. found that all our motives derive either immediately or remotely from our own satisfaction and complacence of mind. 1802 A. Hamilton *Wks.* (1886) VII. 248 Every attempt to do this, is, remotely, a stab at the union of these States. 1875 Whitney *Life Lang.* ii. 8 Among.. remotely kindred or wholly unrelated dialects.

2. †**a.** To, from, or at a (great) distance. *Obs.*

1646 Sir T. Browne *Pseud. Ep.* 294 It is commonly opinioned.. that the Earth was thinly inhabited, at least not remotely planted before the Floud. 1685 Travestin *Siege Newheusel* 27 For this reason, whilst we battered them remotely, they valued us not. 1750 Johnson *Rambler* No. 14 ¶16 Remotely, we see nothing but spires of temples,.. and imagine it the residence of splendor.

b. At or from a distance (not necessarily great). Freq. in comb. with a ppl. forming an adj.

1957 *Railway Mag.* Nov. 758/2 The remotely-controlled signalbox, normally unstaffed, is retained. 1967 *Jane's Surface Skimmer Systems 1967–68* 122 Take-off (4 hp continuous) for remotely-driven accessory box. 1971 *Physics Bull.* July 395/3 The appropriate parts of the projector are light proof and the shutter is operated remotely so that photographic records may be taken in a lit room. 1973 *BBC Handbk. 1974* 246/2 The network control rooms handle.. remotely controlled studios, such as the news studio at Westminster.

remoteness (rɪˈməʊtnɪs). [-ness.] **a.** The state of being remote, in various senses.

a1613 Overbury *Observ. 17 Prov.* (1626) 2 The remotenesse of their Master from them. 1643 Milton *Divorce* 8 The absence and remotenes of a helper. 1666 Dryden *Ann. Mirab.* Let. Sir R. Howard, Anything that shows remoteness of thought or labour in the writer. 1702 Addison *Dial. Medals* ii. 141 His obscurities.. generally arise from the remoteness of the Customs, Persons, and Things he alludes to. 1744 Berkeley *Siris* §25 The timber, by its remoteness from water carriage, is of small value. 1776 Adam Smith *W.N.* v. ii. II. 433 The term.. ought not to be a great deal longer than what was necessary for that purpose; lest the remoteness of the interest should discourage too much this attention. 1830 Herschel *Stud. Nat. Philos.* 279 The same reasoning which places the stars at such immeasurable remoteness, exalts them.. into glorious bodies. 1883 Black *Shandon Bells* xxvi, The papers.. seemed a little sad sometimes... There is a kind of remoteness about them.

b. A remote region; = remote *sb.* b. *nonce-use.*

1880 'Mark Twain' *Tramp Abroad* xxxii. 345 Switzerland, and many other regions which were unvisited and unknown remotenesses a hundred years ago, are in our days a buzzing hive of restless strangers every summer.

remotion (rɪˈməʊʃən). Now *rare*. Also 5 **remosion**, 5–6 **-cion**, **-cyone**, etc. [a. obs. F. *remotion* (15–16th c.), or ad. L. *remōtiōn-em*, n. of action f. *removēre* to remove.]

1. Remoteness. Now *rare*.

1412–20 Lydg. *Chron. Troy* II. xx. (1555), That lande is called inuisyble By cause onely of his remosion. 1625 Brathwait *Five Senses* (ed. 2) Table, He aggravates.. the infelicity of it in her remotion from Sion. 1640 Bp. Reynolds *Passions* xv. 160 To signifie some length, distance, and remotion between a Mans Mind and his Passion. **1731** *Gentl. Mag.* I. 145 To remark their Remotion from, or Proximity to the Earth. **1847** DE QUINCEY *Milton* Wks. 1857 VII. 321 The sense of its utter solitude and remotion from men or cities.

2. The action of removing; removal; putting or taking away.

1449 *Rolls of Parlt.* V. 167/1 As sone as that Office [comes] to your hand..by deth, cession, amocion,..remocion [etc.]. **1464** *Ibid.* 561/2 For the remocion of such ydelnes, and the preferment of labour. **1537** *St. Papers Hen. VIII*, I. 540 We thinke it shalbe mete that some ordre be taken for the remotion of the monkes. **1581** LAMBARDE *Eiren.* II. vii. (1588) 285 The other point..is the carying away, or remotion of the thing that was feloniously taken. **1646** SIR T. BROWNE *Pseud. Ep.* (1650) 12 To conclude..from the remotion of the consequent to the remotion of the antecedent. *a***1676** HALE *Prim. Orig. Man.* (1677) 290 A Conclusion deducible by Reason..by the remotion of all other means as incompatible and insufficient for such a production. **1757** MRS. GRIFFITH *Lett. Henry & Frances* (1767) II. 287 Like ideas, which arise and vanish in the memory, without the mind being able to account for their abduction, or remotion. **1817** COLERIDGE *Biog. Lit.* vii. I. 118 This again is the mere remotion of one absurdity to make way for another. **1830** KATER & LARDNER *Mech.* i. 8 When force is manifested by the remotion of bodies from each other, it is called repulsion. **1895** L. CAMPBELL *Plato's Republic* II. 52 This is in entire keeping with the remotion of the actual from the ideal.

†**b.** *Rhet.* (See quot., and cf. Cicero *De Inventione* ii. 29, 86.) *Obs.*

*c***1530** L. COX *Rhet.* (1899) 82 Remocion of the faute is whan we put it from vs and lay it to another. **1753** CHAMBERS *Cycl. Supp.* App.

†**c.** The process of arriving at some conception (*spec.* that of God) by removal of everything which is known not to be included in it. *Obs.*

1587 GOLDING *De Mornay* iv. 49 That man may bee said to bee most skilfull in that behalfe, which knoweth most Negatiues or Remotions (as they terme them). **1677** GALE *Crt. Gentiles* IV. II. 303 In the consideration of the Divine Essence the way of Remotion is chiefly to be used.

†**3. a.** A motion or inclination *to* something.

*a***1450** *Mankind* 14 (Brandl), I beseche you..with humylite and reuerence to haue a remocyone To þis blyssyde prynce.

†**b.** Commotion, disturbance. *Obs.* *rare*$^{-1}$.

1622 MABBE tr. *Aleman's Guzman d'Alf.* (1630) I. 19 Fearing lest they might cause some remotion [Sp. *remocion*] or alteration in her body, whereby qualmes might arise.

†**4.** The action of removing or departing. *Obs.*

1605 SHAKS. *Lear* II. iv. 115 This act perswades me, That this remotion of the Duke and her Is practise only. *a***1660** HAMMOND *19 Serm.* xi. Wks. 1684 IV. 636 It is the perversest remotion and turning away of the soul from God. **1692** SIR T. P. BLOUNT *Ess.* 165 Those [places] that by the several Remotions and Approaches of the Sun have different Constitutions of Air.

†**5.** Recurrent motion. *Obs.* *rare*$^{-1}$.

1631 CHAPMAN *Cæsar & Pompey* Plays 1873 III. 151 To put them still In motion and remotion, here and there.

re'motivate, *v.* [RE- 5 a.] *trans.* To motivate anew. Hence **re'motivating** *vbl. sb.* and *ppl. a.*

1974 *Listener* 28 Feb. 271/1 They try, in a favourite word of probation officers, to 'remotivate' men who have been through the penal system. **1976** *Archivum Linguisticum* VII. 28 Writers tend to be consistent with themselves if not with each other, although rarer forms are probably remotivated on each occasion. **1977** *Spare Rib* Jan. 8/1 Towards the end of my career, interviewers were invited to a Remotivating Lecture with supervisors and regional controllers. **1977** D. MORRIS *Manwatching* 184 (*caption*) Remotivating Actions succeed by replacing a companion's unwanted mood with a new, more attractive mood.

re'motive, *a. rare.* [f. L. *remōt-* (see REMOTE *v.*) + -IVE.]

†**1.** *Bot.* Characterized by removal of the episperm from the sheath of the cotyledon. *Obs.*

1819 LINDLEY tr. *Richard's Observ. Fruits & Seeds* 69 We may reduce to three principal heads the different modifications of generation in Endorhizæ; 1. Immotive. 2. Admotive. 3. Remotive.

2. That may be removed.

1834 *Gentl. Mag.* June 597 The benefice was formerly vested in the College.., which did not appoint a perpetual Vicar, but only a *clericus conductitius*, or curate remotive.

remou: see REMOUS.

‖**remoulade** (remulad). *Cookery.* Also **ré-**. [a. F. *rémoulade*.] A French salad dressing (see quots.).

1845 E. ACTON *Mod. Cookery* iv. 135 (*heading*) Remoulade. This differs little from an ordinary salad dressing. **1861** MRS. BEETON *Bk. Househ. Managem.* 241 (*heading*) Remoulade, or French salad-dressing. *Ibid.*, 4 eggs, ½ tablespoonful of made mustard, salt and cayenne to taste, 3 tablespoonfuls of olive-oil, 1 tablespoonful of tarragon or plain vinegar... Green remoulade is made by using tarragon vinegar instead of plain. **1877** E. S. DALLAS *Kettner's Bk. of Table* 376 *Remoulade*..may be..described as a Mayonnaise made with hard-boiled yolks of eggs. **1939** A. SIMON *Conc. Encycl. Gastron.* I. 46/1 *Rémoulade*, a salad dressing consisting of the yolks of hard-boiled eggs, oil and vinegar, salt and pepper. Mustard is sometimes added. **1961** *Listener* 20 Apr. 719/2 There is always a little of it [*sc.* tarragon] in smooth French sauces, such as Béarnaise, tartare, and rémoulade. **1966** N. FREELING *Dresden Green* I. 21 He..stopped at the dairy..for a piece of cheese, celery remoulade salad. **1978** G. VIDAL *Kalki* iii. 79 The preparation of a shrimp remoulade.

re'mould (riː-), *v.* [RE- 5 a.] *trans.* To mould again, to fashion or shape anew.

*a***1700** KEN *Hymnotheo* Poet. Wks. 1721 III. 166 This to a God-like Love re-molds the Heart. **1768–74** TUCKER *Lt. Nat.* (1834) II. 400 God..could have remoulded him [man] into a perfect creature. **1790** HAMILTON *Wks.* (1851) III. 31 It is..of the greatest consequence that the debt should..be remoulded into such a shape [etc.]. **1847** HARE *Guesses* Ser. I. (ed. 3) 6 To remould a government and frame a constitution anew are works of the greatest difficulty and hazard. **1876** BLACKIE *Lang. & Lit. Highl. Scot.* ii. 74 The immense mass of traditional materials moulded and remoulded into popular song.

Hence **re'moulding** *vbl. sb.*

1864 PUSEY *Lect. Daniel* vi. 356 The first words..are themselves a re-moulding of a doctrinal statement in the Pentateuch. **1882–3** SCHAFF *Encycl. Relig. Knowl.* 521 The so-called Suabian Concordia—a remoulding of his famous six sermons.

'remould, *sb.* [f. the vb.] A worn tyre on to which a new tread has been moulded. Also *attrib.* Cf. RETREAD *sb.*

1956 C. WILLCOCK *Death at Flight* iii. 35, I asked the firm's transport department to change both front tyres not three weeks ago. And I told them no remoulds. **1960** *Farmer & Stockbreeder* 29 Mar. 21/1 (Advt.), New and remould tyres on terms! Also the new extra grip remould for town and country use. **1972** *Practical Motorist* Oct. 157/1 A remould uses the carcass of a tyre that has already done a lifetime of service. **1973** *Times* 28 Apr. 4/2 Mr Assender claimed yesterday that £6·50 was a fair price for a 'remould quality' 145-13 tyre. **1976** *Drive* Sept.–Oct. 77/1 *Remould* or *remould quality tyres* should by now have disappeared from the forecourt vocabulary, being replaced by the two official designations.

remount (riː-, rɪ'maʊnt), *sb. Mil.* [f. the vb.]

1. a. (See quot. 1802.)

1781 R. F. GREVILLE *Diary* 5 Aug. (1930) 11 This was a favorable opportunity to take a ride, & try a new mare I had lately purchased, & one of a remount, made within a short time of my Appointment. **1802** JAMES *Milit. Dict.*, *A Remount* means a supply of good and serviceable horses for the whole or part of a cavalry regiment. **1810** WELLINGTON in Gurw. *Desp.* (1838) VII. 35, I also beg leave to recommend that about 50 or 60 horses or mares..should be purchased..as a remount for the Officers of the cavalry. **1876** VOYLE & STEVENSON *Milit. Dict.* 413/1 By a late order the name of stud has been changed to that of remount.

b. A horse used to replace another which is worn out or killed.

1829 NAPIER *Penins. War* II. 262 He made every exertion to obtain..remounts for the cavalry. **1876** VOYLE & STEVENSON *Milit. Dict.* 337/1 The general age of remounts varies from 3–5 years old.

2. *attrib.*, as ***remount depot, horse, stable***, etc.

1812 *Examiner* 28 Dec. 822/1 General Bourier has..more than 20,000 remount-horses. **1876** VOYLE & STEVENSON *Milit. Dict.* 191/2 The latter..are offered for sale to the government stud or remount depot. **1880** GILLMORE *On Duty* 26, I visited the camp and remount stable.

remount (riː-, rɪ'maʊnt), *v.* [ad. OF. *remonter*, f. *re-* RE- + *monter* to MOUNT. In later use partly a new formation on RE- and MOUNT *v.*]

I. *trans.* †**1.** To raise or lift up again; to restore to a former state. *Obs.*

*c***1374** CHAUCER *Boeth.* III. pr. i. 49 (Camb. MS.) Thow hast remounted and norysshed me with the weyhte of thy sentenses. **1486** *Bk. St. Albans* C j, Who so puttith hir in mew lene, it will be long or she be remounted. **1530** PALSGR. 685/2, I remounte, I reyse up (Lydgate), *je monte, je eslieue.* **1577** FENTON *Gold. Epist.* 309 If we stumble or fall, he may lend vs his hand eftsoones to remount vs.

b. To set up in place again; *esp.* to mount (a gun) again.

1627 CAPT. SMITH *Seaman's Gram.* ii. 6 Which is the best ..for..remounting any dismounted peece. **1685** TRAVESTIN *Siege Newheusel* 20 This night the besieged..remounted several Cannon upon the new Batteries. **1748** *Anson's Voy.* I. vi. 63 To remount such of their guns as had formerly.. been ordered into the hold. **1794** G. ADAMS *Nat. & Exp. Philos.* II. xvi. 238 The upper ball thus remounted shall roll out of its box.

c. To mount, put together, again.

1888 *19th Cent.* June 853 One man takes to pieces the syringes,..burns the leathers, disinfects the metal parts, and sends them to the instrument-maker to be remounted.

2. a. To replace, to assist or enable (one) to mount again, on horseback.

*c***1400** *Laud Troy Bk.* 6162 His hert gret angur surmounted, That Achilles was remounted. *c***1450** *Merlin* 159 Belias and flaundryns..peyned hem for to remounte hem on her horse. *c***1489** CAXTON *Blanchardyn* xxiv. 86 His men,..wyth right grete peyne,..remounted hym on his hors. *a***1548** HALL *Chron.*, *Edw. IV* 8 b, When he was remounted, he made a countenaunce to assayle hys aduersarie. **1603** KNOLLES *Hist. Turks* (1638) 152 One of his faithfull followers remounted him vpon his owne horse. **1685** TRAVESTIN *Siege Newheusel* 10 The Prince..was in great danger, a Cannon-bullet having taken off one of his Horses legs, but he was presently remounted. **1759** STERNE *Tr. Shandy* II. x, This accident happened so near the house as not to make it worth while for Obadiah to remount him.

b. To provide (cavalry) with fresh horses.

1688 *Lond. Gaz.* No. 2332/3 It is added,..That the Cavalry of Catalogne is to be re-mounted. **1704** *Ibid.* 3987/1, 700 Horses came..to remount the Regiments of Dragoons. **1726** *Ibid.* 6438/1 The King has given Order to the Officers of his Cavalry to remount their Troops. **1816** F. H. NAYLOR *Hist. Germany* II. xxi. 290 This sum..proved of incalculable benefit to the Swedes, because it enabled them to remount their cavalry. **1892** in A. E. Lee *Hist. Columbus* (Ohio) II. 182, I was to make an extensive raid..to capture horses to assist in remounting Grierson's cavalry.

3. †**a.** To rise again to, regain (a state or point).

1486 *Bk. St. Albans* C iij, When ye se yowre hawke may not endew her meete nor remounte her astate. **1647** WARD *Simp. Cobler* (1843) 50 He remounts his proper pitch.

b. To ascend or go up (a place or thing) again.

1621 G. SANDYS *Ovid's Met.* XI. (1626) 233 Iris withdrew;..And by her painted Bow remounts the skies. **1687** DRYDEN *Hind & P.* III. 600 The Sun..That week the virgin balance shou'd remount. *a***1711** KEN *Psyche* Poet. Wks. 1721 IV. 274 Both wing'd and rob'd in Cloud, remount the Skie. **1784** T. HUTCHINS *Descr. Louisiana*, etc. 5 He afterwards remounted that river, and returned to Canada. **1812** W. TAYLOR in *Monthly Rev.* LXVIII. 503 Literature was destined to remount the ladder of instruction..with as gradual and lingering a progression. **1884** *Manch. Exam.* 16 Aug. 4/8 We must beg them to remount the stream to its ancient source.

c. To mount (a horse, etc.) again.

1788 GIBBON *Decl. & F.* l. V. 211 He..descended to Jerusalem, remounted the Borak [etc.]. **1806–7** J. BERESFORD *Miseries Hum. Life* (1826) II. xxvi, Your horse will afterwards keep you dancing for an hour..before he will suffer you to remount him. **1868** Q. VICTORIA *Life Highl.* 38 Albert got off.., walked on a little, and then remounted his poney.

II. *intr.* **4.** To mount, rise, or move upwards again; to make a fresh ascent.

1490 CAXTON *Eneydos* xxiii. 85 She can..tarye & areste sodaynli the flodes & grete ryuers,..and make their bygge stremes rennyng to remounte vpwarde. *a***1533** LD. BERNERS *Gold. Bk. M. Aurel.* (1535) C b, It is necessarie, by time to remount to very hie thinges, lest it bow vnto lowe and yl thinges. **1590** SPENSER *F.Q.* I. i. 44 He backe returning by the Yvorie dore Remounted up as light as chearefull Larke. **1632** J. HAYWARD tr. *Biondi's Eromena* v. 144 Hee gave them no time to remount aboord their Galleyes. **1684** R. WALLER *Nat. Exper.* 93 This Liquor..began to remount in the Neck of the Vessel. **1727** BRADLEY *Fam. Dict.* s.v. *Conserve*, There will stick to the Scummer..a small thread or Filament, which remounts. **1816** BYRON *Ch. Har.* III. lxxiii, To sorrow I was cast, To act and suffer, but remount at last With a fresh pinion.

5. To get on horseback again. †Also const. *to.*

1590 SPENSER *F.Q.* III. ix. 15 Tho hastily remounting to his steed He forth issew'd. **1660** F. BROOKE tr. *Le Blanc's Trav.* 236 Three..of his train alight from horse..and so the Gentlemen remount. **1776** R. CHANDLER *Trav. Greece* (1825) II. 208, I remounted, intending to inquire at Marathon. **1852** GROTE *Greece* II. lxx. (1862) VI. 265 Xenophon then remounted and ascended the hill on horseback.

6. To go back, in the course of an investigation or study, *to* a certain point, period, etc.

1738 BOLINGBROKE *Patriot King* Wks. 1754 III. 44 The shortest and the surest method of arriving at real knowledge is..to remount to first principles. **1776** ADAM SMITH *W.N.* III. iv. (1869) I. 413 Without remounting to the remote antiquities of either the French or English monarchies, we may find in much later times [etc.]. **1837** SIR W. HAMILTON *Metaph.* xlv. (1870) II. 495 In detail, we can rarely account for anything; for we soon remount to facts which lie beyond our powers of analysis and observation. **1884** *Law Times Rep.* LI. 531/2 Without remounting to the Roman law, or discussing the refinements of scholastic jurisprudence.

b. To go back in time *to* a certain date.

1831 BREWSTER *Nat. Magic* xii. (1833) 301 The kindred art of walking on burning coals..remounts to the same antiquity. **1844** LINGARD *Anglo-Sax. Ch.* (1858) I. vii. 301 A practice which remounts to the first ages of Christianity.

c. To go back *to* a source.

1839 tr. *Lamartine's Trav. East* 17/1 This life thus remounts directly to the source from whence it emanates. **1855** W. H. MILL *Applic. Panth. Princ.* (1861) 211 The Mosaic law of levirate or adoption..certifies that all must remount to the same natural parent.

Hence **re'mounting** *vbl. sb.*

1714 *Fr. Bk. of Rates* 208 The bringing in Horses for the remounting of their Troopers.

†**remous** (rəmu). *Aeronaut. Obs.* Pl. **remous** (with *erron. sing.* **remou**). [Fr., = 'eddy, ship's wash'.] (See quot. 1916.)

1911 *Aeroplane* 8 June 8/1 Brooklands has three constant *remous* or eddies, two downward and one upward. *Ibid.*, The only way to get—'s 'bus into the air is to 'taxi' to the sewage farm *remou* and get pulled off the ground by it! **1914** G. HAMEL *Flying* viii. 167 An attempt has been made, by a well known military pilot, to classify remous as 'rollers', 'half-rollers', and 'wulliwas'. **1915** G. BACON *All about Flying* vi. 106 The little eddies known as 'remous' are more entertaining than annoying. **1916** H. BARBER *Aeroplane Speaks* 140 *Remou*, a local movement or condition of the air which may cause displacement of an aeroplane.

re,mova'bility. [f. next: see -ITY.] The state or condition of being removable.

1789 *Deb. Congress U.S.* 16 June (1834) 464, I am not satisfied that removability shall be acquired only by impeachment. *Ibid.* 6 Aug. (1834) 679 The Senate..insisted on the amendment to the Treasury bill, respecting the removability of the Secretary by the President. **1828–32** in WEBSTER. **1836** FONBLANQUE *Eng. under 7 Administr.* (1837) III. 323 The responsibility of Ministers is their removability. **1870** *Pall Mall G.* 3 Sept. 5 The mechanism is now somewhat more exposed to the eye by the removability of the outer mask.

removable (rɪ'muːvəb(ə)l), *a.* (and *sb.*) Forms: 6–7 remoueable, (6 -mooue-), 7–9 removeable; 6 remou-, 6– removable. See also REMEVABLE. [f. REMOVE *v.* + -ABLE.]

1. Subject to removal from an office, jurisdiction, holding, etc.

1534 *Act 26 Hen. VIII*, c. 3 §8 The priours of such celles be named and remouable from time to time. **1574** *Reg. Privy Council Scot.* II. 401 To beir publict office removable of judgement within this realme. **1602** WARNER *Alb. Eng.* XII. lxxiii. 302 In this estate of Consuls (Two remoueable each yeere) Rome flourished. **1679** *Providence Rec.* (1895) VIII. 47 It is generally sayd yᵗ ye Collony would remove such Courts as are remoueable according to Charter. **1726** AYLIFFE *Parergon* 165 Such Curate is removeable at the Will and Pleasure of the Rector of the Mother Church. **1790** BURKE *Fr. Rev.* 41 Servants, the essence of whose situation is to obey the commands of some other, and to be removeable at pleasure. **1855** MACAULAY *Hist. Eng.* xxi. IV. 603 The judges who had laid down this doctrine were removable at the royal pleasure.

b. *sb.* A removable resident magistrate in Ireland.

1888 *Pall Mall G.* 20 Apr. 4/1 Sentences passed by the Removables are being increased on appeal by the county court judges.

2. Capable of being removed (from one place to another, or altogether).

1564 J. RASTELL *Confut. Jewell's Serm.* 162 b, The..table ..was remoueable vpp and downe. **1589** PUTTENHAM *Eng. Poesie* I. xvii. (Arb.) 51 Which carts were floored with bords and made for remouable stages to passe from one streete of their townes to another. **1668** H. MORE *Div. Dial.* III. xl. (1713) 289 All Matter, or whatever else is removeable. *a* **1687** PETTY *Pol. Arith.* v. (1691) 87 That the Impediments of Englands greatness, are but contingent and removable. **1765** BLACKSTONE *Comm.* I. 364 Unless they are..living in an annual service; for then they are not removeable. **1859** LANG *Wand. India* 261 They carried away every marble tablet therein erected, and removeable without much difficulty. **1885** *Spectator* 8 Aug. 1041/2 The evils of a bad system were not removable by attacks upon those who administered it.

Hence **re'movableness**.

1862 F. HALL *Hindu Philos. Syst.* III. ix. 268 The removableness of ignorance by knowledge, &c., would never have been suggested to them.

removal (rɪˈmuːvəl). Also 6–7 -all, 7 remoou(e)all, -moveall. [f. REMOVE *v.* + -AL[1].]

1. a. The act of taking away entirely.

1597 HOOKER *Eccl. Pol.* v. lxv. §19 No redresse can well be hoped for without remouall of that wherein they haue ruined themselues. *a* **1602** W. PERKINS *Cases Consc.* (1619) 67 The remooueall of such reasons and doubts. **1665** MANLEY *Grotius' Low C. Warres* 505 First of all, the Priests and Nobility, intreat the Removal of this miserable Destruction from their Possessions. **1725** N. ROBINSON *Th. Physick* 163 It is a most dangerous Disease, and..demands the best Assistance that can be given..for its Removal. **1745** WESLEY *Answ. Ch.* 43 You look upon both the Disorders and the Removals of them to be supernatural. **1842** J. H. MARKLAND *Remarks Eng. Ch.* 25 Good taste would suggest the removal of the wainscoting altogether. **1890–1** WOODBURY *Encycl. Photogr.* 608 Removal of Film.—The gelatine films may be removed from the glass plate [etc.].

b. The act of 'removing' a person by murder.

1655 *Cal. St. Papers, Dom.* (1881) 355, I think with you that he [Cromwell] will die a violent death,..for his removal is the only way to settle his Majesty in his 3 Kingdoms. **1897** *Hearth & Home* 14 Jan. 378/1 It is true that isolated 'removals' have small apparent effect, but they are invaluable as a demonstration of our power.

2. Dismissal from an office or post; also, transference to another office, etc.

1647 CLARENDON *Hist. Reb.* I. §96 He was advanced to be Keeper of the Great Seal of England..upon the removal of the Bishop of Lincoln. **1661** COWLEY *Cromwell* Wks. 1710 II. 641 Without disputing..the Causes, either of the Removal of the one, or the Preferment of the other. **1743** BULKELEY & CUMMINS *Voy. S. Seas* 3 Captain Norris of the Gloucester having obtained Leave to return to England,.. occasioned the above Removals. **1800** J. ADAMS *Wks.* (1854) IX. 47 When I came into office, it was my determination to make as few removals as possible. **1863** H. COX *Instit.* III. vi. 667 The appointment and removal of magistrates is left to the Lord Chancellor.

3. a. The act of conveying or shifting to another place; the fact of being so transferred.

a **1639** WOTTON in *Reliq.* (1651) 117 Not many minutes after the fall of the body, and removall thereof into the first room. **1690** LOCKE *Hum. Und.* II. xxi. §11 The sitting still even of a paralytic, whilst he prefers it to a removal, is truly voluntary. **1764** BURN *Poor Laws* 108 It hath been generally understood, that removals [of the poor] were first ordained by the 13 & 14 C. 2. **1818** SHELLEY *Julian* 252 He would not bear Removal, so I fitted up for him Those rooms. **1888** F. HUME *Mme. Midas* I. ii, Slivers had pushed all the..loose papers away, and was writing a letter in the little clearing caused by their removal.

†b. *Chess.* A move. *Obs. rare.*

1662 J. DAVIES tr. *Olearius' Voy. Ambass.* 298 Philometer invented the Game of Chesse, which..discover'd to him the duty of a Prince towards his Family and Subjects, by shewing him the removals of the several pieces.

4. The act of changing one's ground, place, or position; *esp.* change of habitation.

1642 MILTON *Apol. Smect.* Wks. 1851 III. 288 All the judicious Panegyricks in any language extant are not halfe so prolixe. And that well appears in his next removall. **1791** MRS. RADCLIFFE *Rom. Forest* i, Such had been the precipitancy of this removal. **1811** MISS MITFORD in L'Estrange *Life* (1870) I. v. 136 This removal will cause you some additional trouble, my dear Sir William. **1899** *Green's Encycl. Sc. Law* XII. 236 Removal from urban tenements is regulated by custom.

attrib. **1881** *Act 44 & 45 Vict.* c. 39 §1 This Act may be cited as the Removal Terms..Act. **1886** W. A. HARRIS *Techn. Fire-Insur. Dict.*, *Removal-damage* is allowed by Offices in cases where their agents authorise such removal. **1939** M. B. LOWNDES *Let.* 23 Oct. (1971) 183 The removal man..told me some interesting things about the art of moving and storing furniture. **1962** J. G. BENNETT *Witness* xviii. 218 One of the removal men asked him if a sofa was to go 'up the apples'. **1973** *Times* 28 Dec. 16/1 (Advt.), Assistance with removal expenses if necessary. **1974** M. GILBERT *Flash Point* xiii. 115 They wore corduroy trousers and jackets belted at the waist.. They looked like removal men. **1979** *Homes & Gardens* June 77/2 They used his pension to buy an old removal van.

removalist (rɪˈmuːvəlɪst). *Austral.* [f. REMOVAL + -IST.] A person or firm engaged in household or business removals.

1959 S. J. BAKER *Drum* (1960) 139 *Removalist*, a person or firm engaging in the shifting of household or business effects. **1966** —— *Austral. Lang.* (ed. 2) i. 4 There is a good deal of evidence to suggest that..*removalist* (a person or firm engaged in moving furniture, etc.)..is an Australian original. **1971** *Classified Telephone Directory* (Brisbane) Pink Pages 251/1 (Advt.), Approved Government contractor for removals and storage. A. F. Palmer Removalists. **1972** D. WILLIAMSON *Removalists* (1973) 61 A self assured removalist in a dust coat enters. The dustcoat is emblazoned with the emblem 'Aussie Removalists'.

remove (rɪˈmuːv), *sb.* Also 6–7 rem(o)oue, -moove, 7 -mouve. [f. the vb.]

1. a. The act of removing a person from a position or office; dismissal. Now *rare*.

1553 [see REMOVE *v.* 3 b]. **1559** *Mirr. Mag.* D iij, The two dukes..On whose remove fro beyng aboute the king We all agreed. **1607** *Statutes* in *Hist. Wakefield Gram. Sch.* (1892) 68 The causes and maner of the ushers remove. *a* **1641** BP. MOUNTAGU *Acts & Mon.* (1642) 341 At length, with much adoe, they procured his remove, and Porcius Festus succeeded. **1712** SWIFT *Wks.* (1883) XV. 486 It is still expected that the duke will be out, and that many other removes will be made. **1799** in *Spirit Pub. Jrnls.* III. 363 We shall find sundry brisk removes of many in public honour.

†b. The act of removing a person by death; murder. *Obs.*

1592 KYD *Sp. Trag.* II. i. 136 Lets goe, my Lord; your staying staies reuenge... Her fauour must be wonne by his remooue. **1602** SHAKS. *Ham.* IV. v. 81 He most violent Author Of his owne iust remoue. **1653** A. WILSON *Jas. I* 89 Intimating..that Overburies untimely remove had something in it of retaliation.

†c. The raising of a siege. *Obs. rare*⁻¹.

1607 SHAKS. *Cor.* I. ii. 28 If they set downe before's, for the remoue Bring vp your Army.

2. †a. The act of taking away, or doing away with, a thing. *Obs.*

1597 BACON *Coulers Good & Evill* Ess. (Arb.) 147 The.. blossome is a positiue good, although the remoue of it to giue place to the fruite be a comparatiue good. **1661** GLANVILL *Van. Dogm.* 71 That which is early received,..as it were grows into our tender natures, and is therefore of difficult remove. **1676** WORLIDGE *Cyder* (1691) 57 A three-fold want of sap..occasioned by the remove of the root.

b. *Farriery.* The act of taking off a horse's shoe in order to dress the hoof and replace the shoe in a proper manner on the same or another foot: hence, an old shoe used over again. Now *dial.*

1594 GREENE & LODGE *Looking Gl.* G.'s Wks. (Rtldg.) 138/2 If you want a shoe, a remove, or the clinching of a nail, I am at your command. **1636** HEYWOOD *Love's Mistress* IV. i, Phœbus fore-horse Must have two new shooes, calk'd, and one remove. **1688** R. HOLME *Armoury* III. 90/1 *A Remove* is, when a shoe is taken off, and set on again with new Nails. **1729** SWIFT *Direct. Serv.* v. Wks. 1751 XIV. 62 His horse wanted two Removes; your Horse wanted Nails. **1821** A. WELBY *Visit N. Amer.* 94 The price I paid to a blacksmith for eight new horse-shoes,..and eight removes. **1880** *Antrim & Down Gloss.*, *Remove*, the re-shoeing of a horse with the old shoes.

c. The act of taking away a dish or dishes at a meal in order to put others in their place; hence, a dish thus removed, or brought on in place of one removed.

1771 B. FRANKLIN in M. Farrand *Benjamin Franklin's Mem.* (1949) 124/1 Every Man at the first Remove, found under his Plate an Order on a Banker. **1773** JOHNSON (ed. 4) *Remove*, a dish to be changed while the rest of the course remains. **1820** *Hermit in London* IV. 161 Two courses and removes, consisting of about 30 dishes. **1828** *Lights & Shades* I. 236 A very genteel dinner,..with a remove, and an excellent dessert. **1852** THACKERAY *Shabby Genteel Story* iii, The maid..brought in that remove of hashed mutton.

3. a. The act of removing or shifting a thing from one place to another.

1582 N. LICHEFIELD tr. *Castanheda's Conq. E. Ind.* I. vii. 17 So as the Moores should not burne them,..which now by their remoue was preuented. **1615** W. LAWSON *Country Housew. Gard.* (1626) 15 This short cutting at the remoue, saues your Plants from winde. **1660** F. BROOKE tr. *Le Blanc's Trav.* 237 Having gotten an Elephant for the remove of our baggage and commodities, we left Moulgas. **1683** MOXON *Mech. Exerc.*, *Printing* xxiv. ¶ 13 Five or six such motions, or rather removes of the Balls. **1791–1823** D'ISRAELI *Cur. Lit.* (1866) 437/1 The birth of the Pretender is represented by the chest.., perhaps alluding to the removes of the warming-pan.

†b. *Fencing.* A thrust made while withdrawing the foot. *Obs. rare.*

1595 SAVIOLO *Practise* H iij, If your enemy be first to strike at you, and if at that instant you would make him a passata, or remoue, it behoueth you to be very ready with your feet and hand.

†c. *Chess.* A move. *Obs.*

1645 *City Alarum* 11 Like two ill Gamesters at Chesse, who make many remooves to little purpose. **1656** BEALE *Chess* A iv b, He which loseth shall have a palpable reason for every remove he maketh.

fig. **1676** MARVELL *Mr. Smirke* 55 Alexander perciev'd by them that this Pawn-bishop had made all his removes right.

†4. a. The act of transferring a person from one office or post to another; the fact of being so transferred. *Obs.*

1610 in *Crt. & Times Jas. I* (1848) I. 107 Upon the remove of the Bishop of Gloucester to Worcester, Dr. Tooker..had thought to have succeeded. **1665** SIR T. HERBERT *Trav.* (1677) 34 By this failer the Master of our Ship had a remove into the Vice-Admiral. **1701** W. WOTTON *Hist. Rome* 270 After a short remove to the Quæstorship of Sardinia, he was appointed to go as Legate. **1751** *Affect. Narr. Wager* 11 His Request being comply'd with, occasioned some Removes: For..our Captain, Kidd, was remov'd to the Pearl.

b. Promotion, at school, of a pupil from a class or division to a higher one.

1747 CHESTERF. *Lett.* (1792) I. xcvi. 272 Every remove, (you know) is to be attended by a reward from me, besides the credit you will gain for yourself. **1768–75** in Maxwell Lyte *Hist. Eton Coll.* (1877) 319 The time allowed for trying boys for their removes is not to be in a school hour. **1857** HUGHES *Tom Brown* I. vii, Tom..was praised, and got his remove into the lower fourth. **1894** WILKINS & VIVIAN *Green Bay Tree* I. 43 Surprising I didn't get my remove this term.

c. At some schools, as Eton and Charterhouse: A certain division of the school.

[**1718** in Maxwell Lyte *Hist. Eton Coll.* (1877) 288 The successive forms were called..First Form, Lower Remove, Second Form,..Fourth Form, Remove, Fifth Form.] **1733** *Ibid.* 305 He has been examined..and is placed in the 4th form, last remove, till further trial. **1844** DISRAELI *Coningsby* I. ix, Some unhappy wight in the remove, wandering about .., seeking relief in the shape of a verse. **1860** *Cornh. Mag.* Dec. 648 To act as policeman to my remove, to mark the boys in and out of chapel, to collect their maps and exercises [etc.]. **1873** E. COLERIDGE in Ornsby *Mem. J. R. Hope-Scott* (1884) I. 20 He was placed in the lower Remove of the Remove in September.

5. a. The (*or* an) act of changing one's place, *esp.* one's place of residence; departure to another place. Now *rare* (very common *c* 1590–1760).

c **1586** C'TESS PEMBROKE *Ps.* CV. xi, Quailes in whole beavies each remove pursue. **1589** PUTTENHAM *Eng. Poesie* III. xix. (Arb.) 240, I call him..the flitting figure, or figure of remoue, like as the other before was called the figure of aboade. **1601** SHAKS. *All's Well* V. iii. 131 Here's a petition from a Florentine, Who hath for foure or fiue remoues come short, To tender it her selfe. **1609** HOLLAND *Amm. Marcell.* 5 Speeding themselves in great hast, for to prevent all rumors of their remove. **1650** S. CLARKE *Eccl. Hist.* I. (1654) 169 Faustus was constrained by frequent removes to hide himself. **1702** C. MATHER *Magn. Chr.* I. vi. 24/1 The next Year there was a great Remove of good People thither. **1757** FRANKLIN *Ess.* Wks. 1840 II. 97 Three removes are as bad as a fire. **1772** PRIESTLEY *Inst. Relig.* (1782) I. 235 Death.. is..a remove for the better. **1820** CLARE *Rural Life* 7 All old favourites..Griev'd me at heart to witness their removes.

†b. A signal for departure. *Obs. rare.*

1581 SAVILE *Tacitus, Hist.* I. lxii. (1591) 35 When al was in order ready to march, they cal to sound the remoue. **1622** F. MARKHAM *Bk. War* V. iii. 171 All things being assured, he may then cause the Drumme-maior to beat a remoue.

†c. A period of absence from a place. *Obs.*⁻¹

1603 SHAKS. *Meas. for M.* I. i. 44 In our remoue, be thou at full, our selfe.

6. a. The space or interval by which one person or thing is remote from another, in time, place, condition, etc.; distance.

1628 FELTHAM *Resolves* II. [I.] xiv. 41 The soules Perspective glasse: whereby, in her long remoue, shee discerneth God. **1686** GOAD *Celest. Bodies* II. xii. 329 A Sign that ♄ is more frigid than ♃, by reason of his greater remove. **1771** WESLEY *Wks.* (1872) V. 385 A giddy, careless temper is at the farthest remove from the whole religion of Jesus Christ. **1845** R. W. HAMILTON *Pop. Educ.* iv. (ed. 2) 66 He would see that scale recede from him to as distant a remove as that where it now stands. **1876** MEREDITH *Beauch. Career* xxxii, As mountains gather vastness to the eye at a certain remove.

b. A step or stage in gradation of any kind; especially in phr. ***but one*** (or ***a***) ***remove from***.

1633 G. HERBERT *Temple, Jordan* ii, Must all be vail'd, while he that reads, divines, Catching the sense at two removes? **1668** R. STEELE *Husbandman's Calling* ix. 225 How can I glorifie my Maker, that am but one remove from a piece of..sinful earth? **1741** RICHARDSON *Pamela* (1824) I. 123 It might be well enough if you were..but a remove or two from the dirt you seem so fond of. **1850** MᶜCOSH *Div. Govt.* (1852) 193 Events are explained by other events separated from them by a thousand removes. **1864** BRYCE *Holy Rom. Emp.* viii. (1875) 126 Yet nascent feudality was but one remove from anarchy.

c. A degree in descent or consanguinity.

1766 GOLDSM. *Vic. W.* i, Our cousins, too, even to the fortieth remove, all remembered their affinity, without any help from the heralds' office. **1789** HUNTER in *Phil. Trans.* LXXIX. 161 These puppies are the second remove from the Wolf and Dog. **1852** DICKENS *Bleak Ho.* i, I am not prepared to inform the Court in what exact remove he is a cousin.

d. *Printing.* The number of sizes by which the type of footnote or side-note is smaller than that of the text; hence, the note itself.

1890 C. T. JACOBI *Printing* v. 70 Footnotes are nearly always set in type two sizes (or removes, as they are called) smaller than text... Side-notes are frequently put into three or four removes smaller. **1898** J. SOUTHWARD *Mod. Printing* I. xxxvii. 224 The usual type for notes is two or three removes from the text. **1934** V. STEER *Printing Design & Layout* xvi. 293 Footnotes are explanatory notes at the foot of the page usually set in type two removes from the size used for the text. **1960** G. A. GLAISTER *Gloss. Bk.* 345/2 *Removes*, quotations or notes set at the foot of a page and in smaller type than that of the text.

7. *attrib.*, as ***remove-ticket***.

1805 NELSON 26 Apr. in Nicolas *Disp.* (1846) VI. 416, I directed Captain Schomberg to make out the proper Remove-Tickets for the wages due to the said men.

remove (rɪˈmuːv), *v.* Forms: *α.* **4–5 remeeve, 4–6 remeue, -meve, (5 -mevyn, -mewe, -mefe, -meff).** *β.* **4–7 remoue, (5 -mouyn), 6–7 remooue, 7 -moove, 5– remove; 4 remo(u(n, remuve (8** *Sc.***),**

4–5 remow(e, 5 *Sc.* ra-), 5 remown(e; also *north.* and *Sc.* 5 remofe, -muf(f, 5–6 -mufe, 6 -moif, 5–6 ramuff, -muif. [a. OF. *remeuv-*, *remouv-* and *remov-*, the stressed and unstressed stems of *remouvoir*:—L. *removēre*, f. *re-* RE- + *movēre* to MOVE. On the variation of form see MOVE *v.*]

I. *trans.* **1. a.** To move or shift from or out of the place occupied; to lift or push aside; to lift up and take away; to take off.

The precise connotation varies to some extent with the nature of the object and the intention of the moving.

a **1300–1400** *Cursor M.* 17288 + 99 (Cott.), Who sal vus helpe to remou þat heuy stone? *c* **1400** MAUNDEV. (Roxb.) xxxiii. 150 Þe tendre erthe was removed fra his place and þare become a valay. *c* **1460** *Towneley Myst.* xxvi. 369 Which shall of us systers thre remefe the stone? **1530** PALSGR. 685/1 Remeve this thynges out of the waye. **1535** COVERDALE *Job* vi. 17 When they be set on fyre, they shalbe remoued out of their place. **1611** BIBLE *Transl. Pref.* ¶5 Translation it is.. that remoueth the couer of the well, that wee may come by the water. **1669** STURMY *Mariner's Mag.* II. vi. 65 On the other Edge make a Line of Equal Parts, with an Ear in like manner to remove at pleasure. **1683** MOXON *Mech. Exerc.*, *Printing* xxiv. ¶19 A Spring in the Tympan removes the Paper in this interval of Time. **1775** S. J. PRATT *Liberal Opin.* lxxxi. (1783) III. 101 Having, as the tea-equipage was removing, some intention to take his leave. **1837** DICKENS *Pickw.* ii, 'What's that?' he inquired, as the waiter removed one of the covers. **1843** YOUATT *Horse* (1848) 313 The shoe having been removed, the smith proceeds to rasp the edges of the crust.

b. To take away, withdraw, from a place, person, etc.; †to raise, abandon (a siege). Also *refl.* to betake oneself away.

c **1425** WYNTOUN *Cron.* III. v. 769 He.. hym ramowit þan in hy, And agane hayme in Medy. **1530** PALSGR. 685/1 Remeve you from thence, my frende. *Ibid.*, I remeve my selfe out of the place I am in. **1560** DAUS tr. *Sleidane's Comm.* 90 So were the warders removed from the gates the same day. **1585** T. WASHINGTON tr. *Nicholay's Voy.* I. xv. 16 They resolued to remoue their siege, and to imbarke themselues with their ordinance. **1648** MILTON *Ps.* lxxxviii. 69 Lover and friend thou hast remov'd And sever'd from me far. **1667** —— *P.L.* VIII. 119 God to remove his wayes from human sense, Plac'd Heav'n from Earth so farr. **1697** DRYDEN *Virg. Georg.* I. 201 Jove.. Remov'd from Humane reach the chearful Fire. **1729** LAW *Serious C.* xv. 273 We can ..remove ourselves from objects that inflame our passions. **1819** SCOTT *Ivanhoe* i, [The swine] made.. no haste to remove themselves from the luxurious banquet of beech-mast and acorns. **1850** MᶜCOSH *Div. Govt.* IV. i. (1874) 464 The Epicureans removed their Gods far above the care and supervision of human affairs.

c. To take or convey away from a place; †to keep apart, separate. Also ***removed***, taken away by death.

1459 *Test. Ebor.* (Surtees) II. 227 Yᵗ thei.. delyuere vn to George Chaworth.. alle his stuffe that he hath at Alfreton, ..he to remeve them at his awne wille. **1596** SHAKS. *1 Hen. IV*, II. ii. 11 That Rascall hath remoued my Horse, and tied him I know not where. **1610** —— *Temp.* II. i. 110 She too, Who is so farre from Italy remoued, I ne're againe shall see her. **1633** P. FLETCHER *Purple Isl.* IV. xi, A border citie these two coasts removing. **1748** *Anson's Voy.* II. vi. 195 Mr. Brett had hitherto gone on in collecting and removing the treasure without interruption. **1816** SOUTHEY *Ess.* (1832) I. 191 The latter was early removed from a world which his Talents.. were.. fitted to adorn. **1850** TENNYSON *In Mem.* Prol. 37 Forgive my grief for one removed, Thy creature, whom I found so fair.

d. To put (a person) out of the way; to assassinate, murder.

1653 A. WILSON *Jas. I* 65 The Prince.. being removed, the Earl of Salisbury (another obstacle) dying six months after the Prince [etc.]. **1655–6** T. ROSS in *Cal. St. Papers, Dom.* (1882) 196, I cannot divine how, except by removing Cromwell, to which one of them had specially devoted himself. **1889** *Times* (weekly ed.) 31 May 6/2 An elaborate article to-day, declares that Dr. Cronin was 'removed' by the Clan-na-Gael after trial and conviction.

e. In *pass.* Of dishes: To be replaced or followed *by*, after removal.

1840 LADY C. BURY *Hist. of Flirt* iv, There was fish and soup, removed by boiled chickens and bacon. **1852** THACKERAY *Shabby Genteel Story* iii, Boiled haddock, removed by hashed mutton.

f. *Cricket.* Of a bowler or ball: to dismiss (a batsman).

1969 *Wisden's Cricketers' Almanack* 300 Underwood.. accounted for Redpath and Walters, each getting an inside edge to the ball that removed him. **1976** *Eastern Even. News* (Norwich) 22 Dec. 14/2 With the fourth ball of his second over Lever removed Venkataraghavan, the ball brushing the batsman's glove before passing through to wicketkeeper Alan Knott. **1977** *Evening Post* (Nottingham) 24 Jan. 16/3 Selvey removed Sivaramakrishnan with his fourth ball.

2. a. To move, shift, transfer or convey from one place to another; to change the place or situation of (†also with *place* as obj.); †to lead (a force) to another place.

13.. *Guy Warw.* (A.) ccxcvi, Lete him be stille, Neuer more remoun him y nille, No do him hennes lede. **1388** WYCLIF *2 Sam.* xx. 12 He remouyde Amasa fro the weie in to the feeld. *c* **1400** *Destr. Troy* 3113 Ho.. beckonet hym boldly.. his place to Remeve. *c* **1420** *Pallad. on Husb.* II. 177 Letuce is to be sette in Ianyueer.., the plantes to remeue In Feueryeer. **1494** FABYAN *Chron.* VI. clxxi. 166 Than he remeuyd his people, and in sondry places faughte with the Danys. **1523** FITZHERB. *Husb.* §129 If thou wylte remoue & set trees gete as many rotes with them as thou can. *a* **1548** HALL *Chron.*, *Edw. IV* 215 He politiquely.. determined in great haste to remove his whole army. **1560** DAUS tr. *Sleidane's Comm.* 301 You ought not to have removed or chaunged the place without the consent of the Emperour. **1613** PURCHAS *Pilgrimage* III. ii. (1614) 234 Their tents, which with themselues, their flockes, and substance, they remoued vp and downe from place to place. **1703** MOXON *Mech. Exerc.* 343 Then removing the string the space of 15 degrees in the Quadrant. **1765** *Museum Rust.* IV. 170 This row being thus planted, the line was removed two feet forwards. **1815** J. SMITH *Panorama Sc. & Art* II. 178 Remove the needle from the situation P to the situation R. **1839** KEIGHTLEY *Hist. Eng.* II. 25 Elizabeth was now removed to Canterbury. **1876** HOLLAND *Sev. Oaks* xi. 151 [He] is about to remove his residence from among us.

refl. *c* **1375** *Lay Folks Mass. Bk.* (MS. B) 301 Þo prest wil after in þat place Remow [*v.r.* remo] him a litel space.

absol. **1615** W. LAWSON *Country Housew. Gard.* (1626) 17 The onely best way.. to haue sure and lasting Sets, is neuer to remoue: for euery remoue is an hinderance.

†**b.** *Law.* To transfer (a cause or person) for trial from one court of law to another. Also *refl.*

1507 *Cal. Anc. Rec. Dublin* (1889) I. 394 Writes of privelage to remowe ple othir ples owte of the cowrt of the citte. **1607** COWELL *Interpr.* s.v. *Habeas Corpus*, is a writ the which a man.. may haue out of the Kings bench, thereby to remooue himselfe thither.. and to answer the cause there. **1627** T. POWELL (*title*) The Attornies Almanacke, provided ..for.. all such as shall have occasion to remove any person, cause or record, from an inferior Court to any the higher Courts at Westminster. **1744** [see REMOVER² 2].

†**c.** *Chess.* To move (a piece). Also *absol.* *Obs.*

1562 ROWBOTHUM *Playe of Cheasts* B ij, Oftentymes the game is lost by remouinge the Rookes Paune or Knyghtes Paune one roume. *a* **1585** MONTGOMERIE *Cherrie & Slae* 215, I gat sik chek, Quhilk I micht nocht remuif nor nek, Bot eyther stail or mait.

3. a. To send or put (a person) away; to compel (one) to go from, or quit, a place.

c **1380** WYCLIF *Serm.* Sel. Wks. I. 401 Ʒif.. þou have a wickide servaunt.., putte him out of his office and remeeve him fer awey. *c* **1425** WYNTOUN *Cron.* II. xvi. 1416 Of neid þaim behuffit to be banyst and ramowyt Fra þar gud, þar kyn, þar kytht. **1432–50** tr. *Higden* (Rolls) VIII. 329 A knyȝhte.. promysede to brynge an hoste of Scottes to remove hym from that sege. **1567** *Gude & Godlie B.* (S.T.S.) 86 From thy face thow sall thame swyith remufe. **1581** *Reg. Privy Council Scot.* III. 396 Thay on nawyse suld ..molest, rais or remove any of the auld tennentis. *c* **1600** SHAKS. *Sonn.* xxv, Then happy I that loue and am beloued Where I may not remoue nor be remoued. **1667** MILTON *P.L.* XI. 96 To remove him I decree, And send him from the Garden. *a* **1768** ERSKINE *Inst. Law Scot.* II. vi. §49 (1773) 273 Warning must be used in order to remove a tenant in a common lease. **1838** W. BELL *Dict. Law Scot.* 848 The tenant is.. entitled to continue his possession.., until legally removed by the landlord.

b. To put (one) away from, or out of, a position or office; to depose, dismiss.

1388 WYCLIF *1 Kings* xv. 13 He remouyde Maacha,.. that sche schulde not be princesse in the solempne thingis. **1433** *Rolls of Parlt.* IV. 477/2 That the seid Sergeauntz be remeved at the ende of every Yere. **1502** ARNOLDE *Chron.* (1811) 36 The Aldermen of the forsayd cite that eueri yere they ben remeued.. and that they so remeued be not chosen ayen the next yere. **1520** *Caxton's Chron. Eng.* III. 20 b/2 The Trybunes were remeved every yere. **1553** in Hakluyt *Voy.* (1886) III. 18 And the person so remoued not to be.. accepted.. from the time of his remoue, any more for an officer. **1775** BURKE *Sp. Conc. Amer.* 87 That the said Chief Justice and other Judges.. shall hold his and their office.. and shall not be removed therefrom but when [etc.]. **1874** STUBBS *Const. Hist.* xii. (1896) I. 511 *note*, None of the sheriffs now removed were employed again.

†**c.** To raise (a siege). *Obs.* (See RAISE *v.* 30.)

1387 TREVISA *Higden* (Rolls) VIII. 329 William de Reeth ..behiȝt þe kyng þat he wolde.. bryng þe oost of Scottes.. to remeve þe seege.. of Berwyk. **1480** CAXTON *Chron. Eng.* ccxxxv. 257 This same yere the king with a grete host entred the see to remeue the sege of rochel. **1586** MARLOWE *1st Pt. Tamburl.* IV. iii, Let us.. hasten to remove Damascus' siege. **1640** YORKE *Union Hon.* 245 He was sent.. to remove the siege of the City of Rochel in France.

†**d.** To clear off, dispose of. *Obs. rare.*

1609 HOLLAND *Amm. Marcell.* 131 In the high tops whereof were balists fitly placed, which removed the defendants that kept lower. **1652** NEEDHAM tr. *Selden's Mare Cl.* 168 Having thus refuted, or upon good ground removed som Opinions of antient Lawyers.

4. a. To take away (*from* a person), to relieve or free one from, some feeling, quality, condition, etc., esp. one of a bad or detrimental kind; †to do away with, put an end to (a practice).

c **1374** CHAUCER *Troylus* I. 691 And for-thy wolde I fayn remeve Thy wrong conceyte. *c* **1400** tr. *Secreta Secret.*, *Gov. Lordsh.* 108 Gouerne hem wel, and.. remowe fro hem all þaire wronges. *c* **1449** PECOCK *Repr.* II. ix. 196 Wherbi is excludid and wilned of Crist to be removed, that eny man schulde worschipe God bi eny outward ymagis. *Ibid.*, Crist in the same chapiter.. removed pilgrimagis. **1567** *Gude & Godlie B.* (S.T.S.) 74 Lord.. Remufe fra me all frawardness. **1596** SHAKS. *Tam. Shr.* I. ii. 72 She moues me not, or not remoues at least Affections edge in me. **1610** —— *Temp.* II. ii. 79 If hee haue neuer drunke wine afore, it will goe neere to remoue his Fit. **1667** MILTON *P.L.* XII. 290 When they see Law can discover sin, but not remove. **1770** *Junius Lett.* xxxix. (1788) 217 In the repeal of those acts.. the parliament have done everything but remove the offence. **1809** *Med. Jrnl.* XXI. 260 That general debility.. which time and attention will in all probability very speedily remove. **1874** GREEN *Short Hist.* vii. §6. 405 The death of Norfolk and Northumberland removed the dread of civil war.

†**b.** To put away (a feeling, thought, etc.) *from* oneself; to set aside. *Obs.*

1388 WYCLIF *Eccl.* xi. 10 Do thou awei ire fro thin herte, and remoue thou malice fro thy fleisch. *c* **1440** *Alph. Tales* 106 It is impossible to remofe ill thoghts fro þe with other mens prayers. **1535** COVERDALE *Eccl.* xii. 1 Put away displeasure out of thy hert, & remoue euell from thy body. [**1611** (xi. 10) Therefore remoue sorrow from thy heart, and put away euill from thy flesh]. **1703** EARL ORRERY *As you Find it* III. i, You had best remove this Scruple quickly.

†**5.** To change, transform, *into* something. *Obs.*⁻¹

c **1430** *Pilgr. Lyf Manhode* I. xli. (1869) 25 And therfore I haue wrethe in myn herte whan ye remeuen [F. *muez*] it in to quik flesh.

†**6.** To go away from, to quit (a place or position). *Obs. rare.*

c **1440** *Generydes* 3223 Too all his ost he gave a speciall charge,.. They shuld remeve that place ij myle large. *c* **1450** *St. Cuthbert* (Surtees) 7514 Ane [bishop] þe whilk by symony þe se gat; with in sex moneths remoued he þat.

†**7.** To move or stir (a part of the body). *Obs.*

1483 CAXTON *Gold. Leg.* 262 b/2 Whan the tyraunte sawe that he remeuyd yet his lyppes.. [he] smote hym wyth hys knyf to the herte. **1523** LD. BERNERS *Froiss.* I. ccclxix. 606 The church that day was so full of noblenesse, that a man might nat a remoued his fete. **1585** T. WASHINGTON tr. *Nicholay's Voy.* II. xxi. 58 b, Pulling and remouing your ioyntes as before is said.

†**8. a.** To move or persuade (one) *out of* or *from* a purpose or resolve. Also without const. *Obs.*

1483 CAXTON *Gold. Leg.* 184/2 He wold haue comen unto our presence but that hys conscyence hath remeuyd hym. **1523** LD. BERNERS *Froiss.* I. ccxxxi. 314 They coude nat remoue him out of that purpose. *a* **1548** HALL *Chron.*, *Edw. IV* 24 b, All the tounes round about, were permanent and stiffe on the parte of kyng Henry, and could not be remoued. **1647** MAY *Hist. Parl.* I. viii. 94 But the King was hard to be removed from his resolution. **1654** tr. *Martini's Conq. China* 167 Nor would he ever be removed from this unhumane sentence.

†**b.** To move, affect (the heart). *Obs. rare*⁻¹.

? **1600** LYLY *Love's Metam.* IV. ii, Men, whose loues are built on truth, and whose hearts are remoued by curtesie.

II. *intr.* **9. a.** To go away or depart from a place; to move off to somewhere else.

α. **13..** *K. Alis.* 7238 He with-seith alle homage.. And bad you remeve out of his lond. *a* **1400–50** *Alexander* 1975 Remefe agayn to þi realm or þou sall it rewe. *c* **1450** *Merlin* 61 They seide 'Sir, we haue no talents to remeve fro hens'. **1495** *Trevisa's Barth. De P.R.* VIII. xviii. xij/2 The mone makyth a man vnstable chaungeable & remeuynge abowte fro place to place.

β. *c* **1375** *Sc. Leg. Saints* xviii. (*Mary Egypt*) 1090 Þu sal na mycht haf to remofe [from the abbey]. *c* **1400** *Rowland & O.* 730 The Oste remowede & forthe thay ȝede,.. To þaire Iournaye þay hye. *c* **1470** HENRY *Wallace* XI. 315 Wallace off France a gudly leiff can tak. The kyng.. Gret langour tuk quhen Wallace can ramuff. **1568** GRAFTON *Chron.* II. 378 From thence they remoued to Saint Albons, and came thether on Christmas Euen. **1585** T. WASHINGTON tr. *Nicholay's Voy.* I. xv. 16 [He] remooued.. to assiege the castle of Tripoli. **1629** J. COLE *Of Death* 51 Hee would rather chuse to stay here, and live in the same [earthly pleasures], then remove to enjoy the heavenly. **1661** GLANVILL *Van. Dogm.* 198 He said, he'd remove into another room. **1706** E. WARD *Wooden World Diss.* (1708) 28 He.. begs a Certificate, when he removes from the Ship. **1796** *Hist. Ned Evans* II. 104 From which few ever remove but to torture.

b. *spec.* To change the place of one's (temporary or permanent) residence; also of a tenant, to quit a house or holding.

1399 LANGL. *Rich. Redeles* III. 301 A new þing þat noyeth nedy men and oþer, Whanne realles remeveth and ridith þoru tounes. **1478** *Paston Lett.* III. 229 My Lord of Suffolk is remevyd in to Suffolk.. and my lady purposed to remeff after on thys day. **1530** PALSGR. 685/1, I remeve, as an armye or the trayne of a prince or gret man removeth from one place to an other. **1555** *Sc. Acts Mary* (1814) II. 494/1 The warning of all tennentis and vtheris to flit and remoue fra landis mylnis fischingis and possessiouns quhat-sumeuer. **1633** FORD *Broken H.* II. i, This house, methinks, stands somewhat too much inward; we'll remove Nearer the court. **1697** DRYDEN *Virg. Georg.* I. 57 Proserpine.. importun'd by Ceres to remove, Prefers the Fields below to those above. **1722** DE FOE *Plague* (1754) 6 This Frenchman.. was one who, having liv'd in Long-Acre.. had removed for fear of the Distemper. **1756** *Act of Sederunt* 14 Dec., Where the tenant hath not obliged himself to remove without warning. **1838** W. BELL *Dict. Law Scot.* 848 In order to authorise judicial removing, the tenant.. must be warned by the landlord to remove. **1855** BREWSTER *Newton* II. xxi. 252 Newton received this letter when he was removing from Jermyn Street to Chelsea.

†**c.** To shift one's place or position. *Obs.*

1340 HAMPOLE *Pr. Consc.* 7365 In helle salle be þan swa gret thrang, þat nane may remow for other ne gang. *c* **1475** *Rauf Coilȝear* 861 The lenth of ane rude braid he gart him remufe. *a* **1533** LD. BERNERS *Huon* lv. 186 He remoued no more for the stroke then it had ben a strong walle. **1562** ROWBOTHUM *Playe of Cheasts* A v b, Their office is not to remoue but in necessitie, and chiefelye for the succoure of theyr kynge. **1595** SAVIOLO *Practise* H ij b, Remoue with your right foot a little back toward his left side. **1656** BEALE *Chess* 8 The King removeth but one house at a time.

10. a. Of things: To change place; to move off or away; to depart, disappear, etc.

1423 JAS. I *Kingis Q.* clxxxviii, In perfyte Ioy, that neuir may remufe. **1481** CAXTON *Myrr.* I. vi. 29 There cheualrye contynued long, And frothens after it remeuid in to Fraunce. **1535** COVERDALE *Isa.* liv. 10 The mountaynes shall remoue, & the hilles shal fall downe. *c* **1586** C'TESS PEMBROKE *Ps.* LII. ix, My trust on his true love Truly attending Shall never thence remove. **1662** STILLINGFL. *Orig. Sacræ* III. ii. §17 Those particles will necessarily remove into that empty space. **1704** POPE *Autumn* 29 Ye trees that fade when autumn-heats remove. *a* **1792** BURNS *Posie* vii, I'll swear.. That to my latest draught o' life the band shall ne'er remove. **1839–48** BAILEY *Festus* xviii. 174 And sigh That truth from that Heaven should ever remove. **1896** A. E. HOUSMAN *Shropshire Lad* xxxvi, But ere the circle homeward hies Far, far must it remove.

†**b.** To change *into* something. *Obs. rare*⁻¹.

1674 PLAYFORD *Skill Mus.* III. 5 That which is an eighth shall remove into a fifth.

†**11.** To move, stir; to be in motion. *Obs.*

a **1400–50** *Alexander* 2943 Sir Dary.. Rerys hym vpp & remevys in hys sete riche. *a* **1450** *Knt. de la Tour* (1868) 37 She might not stere nor remeue more thanne a stone. **1509** HAWES *Past. Pleas.* XXIV. (Percy Soc.) 108 These are the v. wyttes remeuing inwardly. *c* **1555** HARPSFIELD *Divorce Hen. VIII* (Camden) 251 The head thus being above, the body beneath in water, wagging and removing to and fro. **1601** HAKLUYT tr. *Galvano's Discov.* 46 There is further a kinde of herbe there growing, which followeth the sunne, and remooveth after it.

removed (rɪˈmuːvd), *ppl. a.* [f. prec. + -ED¹.]

1. Distant in relationship by a certain degree of descent or consanguinity.

Properly denoting a degree in descent, as ***first cousin once removed*** = a cousin's child; but in later use freq. employed in vague designations of distant relationship, as ***cousin seven times removed***.

a **1548** HALL *Chron., Hen. V* 53 Barbara doughter to therle of zilie cosyn germain removed to kyng Henry. **1594** PARSONS *Confer. Success.* II. iv. 75 Edmond was but nephew remoued, that is to say, daughters sonnes sonne to the said king Richards other uncle. **1611** SHAKS. *Wint. T.* IV. iv. 802 Those that are Iermaine to him (though remou'd fiftie times) shall all come vnder the Hang-man. **1687** MIÉGE *Gt. Fr. Dict.* II. s.v. *Cousin*, A Cousin once removed, *Cousin issu de germain.* **1738** SWIFT *Pol. Conversat.* 62 He's my Cousin-German, quite remov'd. **1748** SMOLLETT *Roderick Random* xviii, My grandfather's brother's daughter.. rabbit it! I have forgot the degree; but this I know that he and I are cousins seven times removed. **1841** LYTTON *Money* I. vii, Cousin to the deceased, seven times removed. **1852** DICKENS *Bleak Ho.* i, He is a cousin, several times removed.

transf. **1600** SHAKS. *A.Y.L.* v. iv. 71 Vpon a lye, seuen times remoued.

2. †**a.** Remote; retired, secluded. *Obs.*

1600 SHAKS. *A.Y.L.* III. ii. 360 Your accent is something finer, then you could purchase in so removed a dwelling. **1609** DOWLAND *Ornithop. Microl.* 54 Imperfection is made not only by the neere part of the Notes, but also by the remoued part. **1632** MILTON *Penseroso* 78 Or if the Ayr will not permit, Som still removed place will fit.

†**b.** Separated by time or space. *Obs. rare.*

1601 SHAKS. *Twel. N.* v. i. 92 His false cunning.. grew a twentie yeeres remoued thing While one could winke. **1628** FELTHAM *Resolves* II. [I.] xxxiii. 105 They haue the aduantage of being beleeued, before a remoued friend.

†**c.** Segregated or set apart. *Obs. rare*⁻¹.

1611 BIBLE *Ezek.* xxxvi. 17 Their way was before me as the vncleannesse of a remooued woman.

d. Lifted or taken away.

1625 [see HARDLY *adv.* 10]. **1683** MOXON *Mech. Exerc., Printing* xxii. ¶8 He removes the other Transpos'd Page into the place of the first remov'd Page. **1688** R. HOLME *Acad.* I. iii. 22/1 If the under Chief had been the colour of the Field, then it had been termed a Chief removed, or fallen out of its place. *a* **1716** SOUTH *Serm.* (1823) V. 281 Nobody.. languishes with the remembrance of a removed sickness. **1748** RICHARDSON *Clarissa* (1768) I. 93 He took the removed chair, and drew it.. near mine.

3. In predicative use: Remote, separated, or distant *from* something, in *lit.* and *fig.* senses.

1617 MORYSON *Itin.* I. 214 He was like neuer to be redeemed, being farre remoued from Christians, who onely trade vpon the Coasts. **1690** LOCKE *Hum. Und.* I. iii. §1 They are farther removed from a title to be innate. **1756** C. LUCAS *Ess. Waters* I. 172 [He] is not, in knowledge or rationality, three degrees removed from the brute. **1864** BRYCE *Holy Rom. Emp.* vi. (1875) 77 A corrupt tongue, equally removed from Latin and from modern French.

Hence **reˈmovedness**.

1604 SHAKS. *Wint. T.* IV. ii. 41, I haue eyes vnder my seruice, which looke vpon his remouednesse. **1845** *Blackw. Mag.* LVII. 147 It has a middle removedness or estrangement from the ordinary speech of men. **1892** *Temple Bar* Jan. 59 The impressions this garden gave were of removedness, of light and shadow, of grass and roses.

†**reˈmoveless,** *a. Obs. rare*⁻¹. [f. REMOVE *sb.* or *v.* + -LESS.] Incapable of being removed.

c **1592** MARLOWE *Massacre Paris* II. iv, As now you are, so shall you still persist, Removeless from the favours of your King.

reˈmovement. [f. REMOVE *v.* + -MENT.]

†**1.** The act of removing from place to place.

1630 *R. Johnson's Kingd. & Commw.* 495 In their travels and removement they are governed by their Stars, and observing the North pole, they settle according to its motion.

2. The act of taking, or the fact of being taken, away; removal.

1845–6 TRENCH *Huls. Lect.* Ser. II. v. 223 All the alleviations and removements of pain and disease. **1862** DARWIN *Fertil. Orchids* i. 48 The derangement in the complex mechanism had hindered the removement of the pollinia.

†**reˈmovent,** *a. Obs. rare*⁻¹. [ad. L. *removent-em*, pres. pple. of *removēre* to REMOVE.] Producing removal.

1625 *Debates Ho. Commons* (Camden) 86 To shew.. the remedyes both removent and promovent.

remover¹ (rɪˈmuːvə(r)). [f. REMOVE *v.* + -ER¹.]

1. One who, or that which, removes or takes away; *spec.* in modern use, a furniture-remover.

1594 SOUTHWELL *M. Magd. Funeral Teares* 56 b, Where the thing remooued was remoouer of it selfe. **1607** HIERON *Wks.* I. 367 If the desirer of our saluation, and the remoouer of all hinderances to it, do yet leaue sinne behind. **1624** T. SCOTT *Vox Regis* 23 Which Court was the onely.. discouerer and remoouer of all such mightie enormities. **1860** GOSSE *Rom. Nat. Hist.* 108 We must see them.. engaged as the scavengers of the forest-wilds of the tropics; the removers of fallen trees. **1861** HUGHES *Tom Brown at Oxf.* III. 264 Grey had discovered a benevolent remover of furniture.

†**b.** *fig.* A poison. *Obs. rare*⁻¹.

1625–6 SHIRLEY *Maid's Revenge* III. ii, *Shar.* A rat! give him his bane... *Ans.* Pray let me see a remover at twelve hours; I would be loth to kill the poor thing presently.

2. One who changes his place; a restless or stirring person. *rare.*

c **1600** SHAKS. *Sonn.* cxvi, Loue is not loue Which alters when it alteration findes, Or bends with the remouer to remoue. **1607–12** BACON *Ess., Fortune* (Arb.) 378 An hastye Fortune maketh an Enterpriser, and Remover (The French hath it better *Entreprenant*, or *Remuant*).

†**b.** A hive from which the bees are made to remove. *Obs. nonce-use.*

1609 C. BUTLER *Fem. Mon.* (1634) 153 Having first placed these two stalls, the Remover (that is driven) and the Receiver, as near as may be to one another.

†**reˈmover².** *Obs. rare.* [f. as prec. + -ER⁴.]

1. The act of moving; movement. *rare*⁻¹.

1663 H. COGAN tr. *Pinto's Trav.* xxv. 95 At the first sight of him, he would have turned back out of the remover of conscience, and true repentance.

2. *Law.* (See quot. and REMOVE *v.* 2 b.)

1744 JACOB *Law Dict., Remover* is where a Suit or Cause is removed out of one Court into another.

removing (rɪˈmuːvɪŋ), *vbl. sb.* [-ING¹.]

1. The action of removing from a place; removal to another place or residence; †also, change, alteration.

1340 HAMPOLE *Pr. Consc.* 6365 Þe son sal þan in þe este stande, With-outen removyng, ay shynande. *c* **1430** *Pilgr. Lyf Manhode* I. xlii. (1869) 25 Many oothere remeeuinges [*F. remuemens*] of which were to longe to holde parlement. **1535** COVERDALE *Ezek.* iii. 11, I herde the noyse of a greate russhinge and remouynge off the most blissed glory off the Lorde out off his place. **1555** EDEN *Decades* 35 In contynual remoouinge as the nature of warre requyreth. **1620** T. GRANGER *Div. Logike* 108 Vegetation, and locomotion are powers of growing, augmentation, mooning, remoouing. **1719** DE FOE *Crusoe* I. (Globe) 268 We waited a great while, though very impatient for their removing. **1750** MRS. DELANY *Life & Corr.* (1861) II. 566, I have not heard from my brother a great while; I suppose his removing has hurried him.

attrib. *a* **1601** LAMBARDE *Dict. Angl. Top.* (1730) 48 Batarsey, the removinge House of the Byshoppes of Yorke. **1684** E. CHAMBERLAYNE *Pres. St. Eng.* I. (ed. 15) 177 There is the Removing Wardrobe, which always attends upon the Person of the King.

2. The action of removing, shifting, taking or putting away; also, an instance of this.

1426 LYDG. *De Guil. Pilgr.* 6372 With-outen any remowyng Off the Eyën in myn hed Into myn Eryn. **1535** COVERDALE *Heb.* xii. 27 No doute that same.. signifieth the remouynge awaye of those thinges. **1563** HYLL *Art Garden.* (1593) 127 The better also they wil prosper, if after euery remoouing.. the blades bee cut. **1642** DRUMM. OF HAWTH. *Skiamachia* Wks. (1711) 193 Such particulars, as.. will much conduce to the removing of all these mistakes. **1712** J. JAMES tr. *Le Blond's Gardening* 116 The Transporting and Removing of Earth is a vast and excessive Charge. **1818** in Willis & Clark *Cambridge* (1886) I. 573 The removing of the present walk with the two trees. **1882** E. C. ROBERTSON in *Proc. Berw. Nat. Club* IX. 507 The removing of the earth brought to view an immense collection of skeletons.

3. *Sc. Law.* The removal of a tenant by, or at the instance of, the landlord; †also, a notice requiring a tenant to remove.

1555 *Sc. Acts Mary* (1814) II. 494/1 Na forther laying furth of stressis and remowing vpone wednisday to be vsit in tyme to cum. **1588** *Reg. Privy Council Scot.* IV. 270 The executioun of ane precept of removing. *Ibid.*, He putt the copy of the removing.. in the said Johnis bosome. **1683** *Acts Sederunt* (1790) 156 Act appoynting Advocations and Suspensions of Decreets of removeing. *a* **1768** ERSKINE *Inst. Sc. Law* II. vi. §51 (1773) 274 A landlord's title to prosecute a removing.. cannot be questioned by a tenant who derives his possession from him. **1838** W. BELL *Dict. Law Scot.* 848 In order to authorise judicial removing, the tenant.. must be warned by the landlord to remove.

So **reˈmoving** *ppl. a.*

1643 [ANGIER] *Lanc. Vall. Achor* 22 Desire to see this Forreiner.. led some of note and worth into a teadious and removing captivitie. **1870** *Daily News* 5 Sept. 6 Sometimes upon a pile of mattresses or bedding.. were to be seen the removing householder himself and his wife and family.

remow, obs. form of REMOVE *v.*

†**remp,** *v. Obs. rare.* [Of obscure origin.] *intr.* To act hastily; to hasten.

c **897** K. ÆLFRED *Gregory's Past. C.* xx. 148 Oft mon bið swiðe rempende, & ræsð swiðe dollice on ælc weorc & hrædlice. *c* **1330** R. BRUNNE *Chron. Wace* (Rolls) 3492 Þe Bretons sawe þer syde ȝede lowe, þey rempede þem to reste a þrowe.

†**remˈpare,** *v. Obs. rare.* Also **renpayre.** [ad. F. *remparer*: see RAMPIRE *v.*] *trans.* To strengthen, fortify. Also *absol.*

1525 LD. BERNERS *Froiss.* II. cxiii. 336 Than he newe renpayred the towne, and furnished it with newe men of warre. **1549** EDW. VI *Jrnl.* (Roxb.) 236 The gates of the hous to be rempared; peple to be raysed. **1581** MULCASTER *Positions* xxxvii. 148 Our state then must reiect the multitude, and rempare with the cunning.

‖**remplaçant** (rɑ̃plasɑ̃). Also fem. **-e.** [Fr.] One who replaces another; a substitute.

1850 LADY EDDISBURY *Let.* 23 Mar. in N. Mitford *Ladies of Alderley* (1938) 280 At 5 Macaulay sent word he was too ill to come, Ed. could get no remplaçant & so at ½ to 8, our dinner having dwindled, we sent for Mama. **1880** E. W. HAMILTON *Diary* 23 May (1972) I. 14 The defence of the Government is.. that as he [*sc.* Sir B. Frere] is more conversant than any '*remplaçant*' could be with the important question of confederation, he had better be left to carry that through. **1915** W. J. LOCKE *Jaffery* xiii. 177 'We've settled nothing about a remplaçante for Mrs. Considine.'.. 'No one can replace Mrs. Considine.'

‖**rempli** (rɑ̃pli), *a. Her.* Also 8 **remply.** [F., pa. pple. of *remplir* to fill up.] (See quots.)

1725 COATS *Dict. Her., Remply*, that is, fill'd up, denoting that all the Chief is fill'd up with a square Piece of another Colour, leaving only a Bordure of the proper Colour of the Chief about the said Piece. **1780** EDMONDSON *Compl. Body Heraldry* II. Gloss. s.v., When a chief is filled with any other metal, or colour, leaving only a border round the chief of the first, it is then called a *Chief Rempli.*

‖**remskoen** (ˈrɛmskʊn). *S. Afr.* Also **reimschoon, remschoen, riemschoen, rimschoen;** pl. also **-e.** [Afrikaans:—Du. *remschoen*, f. *rem* brake + *schoen* SHOE.] = SKID *sb.* 3 a. Also *fig.*

See J. Smuts et al. *Voorloper* (1976) for additional variant forms.

1816 G. BARKER *Diary* 13 Feb. (MS.) in J. Smuts et al. *Voorloper* (1976) 671 My box was set upon the rim-schoen to keep it dry. **1822** W. J. BURCHELL *Trav. Southern Afr.* I. 151 The remschoen (lock-shoe or skid), is a log of wood, generally about eight inches square, and nearly two feet long, having a groove in it to receive the felly of the wheel. **1835** A. STEEDMAN *Wanderings & Adventures in S. Afr.* I. I. ii. 121 On regaining the track, we found the *reimschoon*, or iron slipper, which had fallen from the waggon, lying in the road. **1898** *Cape Argus* 2 Feb. 36, I am pleased to find that my frequent allusion to the backward element in the legislative Council as a *riemschoen party* has gone home. **1912** *East London Dispatch* 2 May 5 Riemschoen Party.—The name applied a few years back to that party in Cape politics which appeared to be averse from progress; the word Riemschoen is applied in other directions with the same meaning, e.g. 'Riemschoen Districts'. **1949** L. G. GREEN *In Land of Afternoon* x. 126 Voortrekker wagons were equipped with wooden axles and the *remskoen* instead of brakes. **1957** *Cape Times* 8 Aug. 9/1 The wagons.. with *remskoene* on, slithered down the steep slopes.

†**remuable,** *a. Obs. rare.* [a. OF. *remuable* (14th c.): see REMUE *v.* and -ABLE.]

1. That may remove (= depart) or be removed; changeable, unstable.

c **1374** CHAUCER *Troylus* IV. 1633 (1682) And this may length of yeres nought fordo, Ne remuable fortune deface. **1390** GOWER *Conf.* III. 256 For where honour is remuable, It oghte wel to ben avised. *c* **1430** LYDG. *Min. Poems* (Percy Soc.) 122 In this world here is none abidyng place, But that it is by processe remuable.

2. Capable of movement.

c **1374** CHAUCER *Boeth.* v. pr. v. 131 (Camb. MS.) The ymaginacion comth to Remuable [L. *mobilibus*] beestis, þat semyn to han talent to fleen or to desiren any thing.

‖**remuage** (rəmɥaʒ). *Wine-making.* [Fr., lit. 'moving about'.] The periodic turning or shaking of bottled wine (esp. champagne) to move sediment towards the cork before disgorgement.

1926 P. M. SHAND *Bk. Wine* v. 154 The bottles are now stacked in wooden racks.. for the delicate operation of *remuage.* **1935** SCHOONMAKER & MARVEL *Compl. Wine Bk.* i. 34 Here takes place the curious process known as the 'shaking', or *remuage.* **1958** D. MORRIS *French Vineyards* ii. 34 When the *remuage* is finished, the bottles are left in darkness. **1967** A. LICHINE *Encycl. Wines & Spirits* 430/2 *Remuage* (moving around) is a term used in the process of making Champagne. Bottles placed in specially built racks are turned or shaken a little every day for about four months before they are shipped, so that the sediment may move down towards the cork. **1977** T. HEALD *Just Desserts* viii. 187 Along the walls were countless bottles top downwards in racks 'Ready for the *remuage*... Gets the sediment down to the cork.'

†**remuant,** *a. Obs. rare.* Also 7 **-ent.** [a. F. *remuant*, pres. pple. of *remuer* to REMUE.] Inclined to remove; restless, changeable.

1625 W. B. *True School War* 12 Those Busibodies, or as the French haue it better, those Remuant spirits, that.. haue rather defaced than built. **1654** *Nicholas Papers* (Camden) II. 92, I protest I am so pationatly troubled for the remuant humour of our frend that I know not what to say. **1659** O. WALKER *Oratory* 66 Fixing his fancy (remuent, and volatile) upon one object.

‖**remuda** (rəˈmuːdə). [Amer. Sp., a. Sp., exchange, replacement.] A herd or collection of saddle-horses kept for remounts.

1892 *Dialect Notes* I. 251 *Remuda*, a 'bunch' of horses, about a score. Usually applied to geldings only. **1903** A. ADAMS *Log of Cowboy* 9 The *remuda*, under Bill Honeyman as horsewrangler, numbered a hundred and forty-two, ten horses to the man. **1907** S. E. WHITE *Arizona Nights* v. 92 In a moment the first of the remuda came into view, trotting forward with the free grace of the unburdened horse. **1924** W. M. RAINE *Troubled Waters* xi. 113 Presently he got up and strolled toward the remuda. **1927** *Blackw. Mag.* Nov. 650/1 In the feeble flare remudas keep on passing. **1955** R. HOBSON *Nothing too Good* vii. 61, I knew this was the horse remuda, the advance guard of the drive. **1972** T. A. BULMAN *Kamloops Cattlemen* ii. 15 They usually brought with them a pretty fair *remuda* of horses.

†**reˈmue,** *sb. Obs. rare*⁻¹. [a. OF. *remue* (Godef.).] Movement forward, advance, progress.

1433 LYDG. *St. Edmund* III. 1217 [They] stood stylle as ston, sore in themsylff amasyd.. Fro ther werk myhte no remews make.

†**reˈmue,** *v. Obs.* Forms: 3–4 **remuwe,** 3–5 **remue,** (4 **-u, -uye**), **remwe;** 3–7 **remew,** 4–5

remewe, (4 -eue). [a. OF. *remuer* (11th c.), f. re- RE- + *muer*:—L. *mūtāre* to change: cf. It. *rimutare*, med.L. *remūtāre* (Du Cange). It is sometimes not clear whether the forms *remeue* and *remewe* belong here, or to *remeve*, obs. variant of REMOVE *v.*]

1. *trans.* To remove, shift, or transfer, to another place; to move from a place.

1297 R. GLOUC. (Rolls) 5522 Remwe in to anoþer stude þi pauilon. *c* **1325** *Chron. Eng.* 744 in Ritson *Metr. Rom.* II. 301 Afterward.. That he hade leyen.. Sixti wynter under molde, An abbot him remue wolde. *c* **1386** CHAUCER *Sqr.'s T.* 172 The hors of bras þat may nat be remewed It stant as it were to the ground yglewed. *c* **1420** *Pallad. on Husb.* II. 280 Sette ek noon almaundes but grete and newe; And hem is best in Feueryeer remewe. **1600** FAIRFAX *Tasso* XIII. lxx, That faith wherewith he could remew The stedfast hils. *refl. c* **1380** *Sir Ferumb.* 77 He stynte & þoȝte noȝt remuye hem [= him] þere til he ha foȝt is fille. **1430–40** LYDG. *Bochas* IX. v. (1558) 23 b/1 And secretly he gan him selfe remue, To be bathed in a preuy stue.

b. To remove to a distance; to put, take, or keep away *from*.

13.. *E.E. Allit. P.* B. 1673 þou, remued fro monnes sunnes, on mor most abide. *c* **1400** tr. *Secreta Secret., Gov. Lordsh.* 93 All þare-by is vnderstandant, and neghys negh, þat þat ys remued of farre. *c* **1420** *Pallad. on Husb.* I. 777 Yet is the chalk or cley lond forto eschewe, And from the rede also thy garth remewe.

2. To remove (a person) from a position or office; to put away, dismiss.

1297 R. GLOUC. (Rolls) 11455 þis tueie erles acorded were þere þat iremewed [*v.r.* yremuwed] al clene þe frenssemen were. *c* **1330** R. BRUNNE *Chron.* (1810) 312 To þe we pleyn vs here, Him for to remue þorgh comon assent. **1390** GOWER *Conf.* I. 318 Witt and resoun conseilen.. that I scholde will remue And put him out of retenue. **1412–20** LYDG. *Chron. Troy* II. xii. (1555) Gvb, She can make a man for his welfare,.. Whan he least weneth, for to be remewed.

b. To raise (a siege). *rare*$^{-1}$.

c **1330** R. BRUNNE *Chron.* (1810) 100 þerfor þe duke him dight, as man of grete value, Roberd Bellyse with myght, þe sege þei wend remue.

3. To remove entirely; to take or clear away.

1297 R. GLOUC. (Rolls) 11613 Bruggen hii breke oueral, hii ne bileuede ssip non.. þat hii ne remuede echon. *c* **1350** *St. Peter* 197 in Horstm. *Altengl. Leg.* (1881) 51 He bad þam stir oway þe stone And remu al þe erth oway. **1390** GOWER *Conf.* III. 21 In no wise The drunkeschipe of love aweie I mai remue be no weie. **1426** LYDG. *De Guil. Pilgr.* 4446, I remewe, in especial, Clene with-outen & with-Inne, The fylthe of euery maner synne.

4. To transfer, translate; to change, alter.

c **1330** R. BRUNNE *Chron. Wace* (Rolls) 164 Geffrey.. fro Breton speche he did remue & made it alle in Latyn. **1340** *Ayenb.* 104 Wyþoute him to chongi, wyþoute him remue ine none manere. *c* **1403** LYDG. *Temple Glas* 1182 Vices eschew, .. And for no tales thin hert not remue.

5. *intr.* To move off or away, to depart, to go.

1340–70 *Alex. & Dind.* 137 (*heading*) How alixandre remewid to a flod þat is called phison. *c* **1400** MAUNDEV. (1839) v. 38 And whan hem lyst, they remewen to other Cytees. *c* **1430** *Hymns Virgin* (1867) 20 þouȝ we wolden from þee remewe, In ech place þou art present. **1482** WARKW. *Chron.* (Camden) 2 Kynge Edwardes hooste.. remewed from the sege, and were affrayed.

6. To stir, to alter one's position, to move.

a **1350** *St. Stephen* 519 in Horstm. *Altengl. Leg.* (1881) 34 þe body remude.. And left to saint Steuen half þe graue. **1390** GOWER *Conf.* II. 316 As if a goshauk hadde sesed A brid, which dorste noght for fere Remue. *c* **1430** *Syr Gener.* (Roxb.) 5559 He hath forbede.. That noon of hem shul remew, Him to help or reskew.

Hence †**re'muing** *vbl. sb.*, removal. *Obs. rare.*

13.. *K. Alis.* 7821 Theo lewed folk prayed theo kyng, Of him to make remuwyng. **1497** *Naval Acc. Hen. VII* (1896) 229 Payed.. to c men.. attendyng about the remewyng of the Regent.

remuent, variant of REMUANT *Obs.*

‖**remueur** (rəmɥœr). *Wine-making.* [Fr., lit. 'mover'.] One who engages in *remuage* (see quots.).

1926 P. M. SHAND *Bk. Wine* v. 154 The *remueur's* task is gradually to work down all the sediment. **1965** O. A. MENDELSOHN *Dict. Drink & Drinking* 279 *Remueur*, the craftsman who daily twists and slightly shakes the bottles containing champagne in the making. **1976** N. ROBERTS *Face of France* xxv. 229 The man who does the tilting and turning [of champagne bottles] is called a *remueur*... He can handle 30,000 bottles a day.

remuf(e, -muff, obs. Sc. forms of REMOVE *v.*

re'mugient, *a.* *rare*$^{-1}$. [f. pres. pple. of L. *remūgīre*, f. *re-* RE- + *mūgīre* to bellow.] Resounding, rebellowing.

1660 H. MORE *Myst. Godl.* III. iii. 63 Trembling and tottering Earth-quakes accompanied with remugient Echoes and ghastly murmurs from below.

remulant, variant of REMENANT *Obs.*

†**remuled**, *a.* *Obs.*$^{-1}$ [ad. OF. *remulé*, found only in the passage here translated.] Mutilated.

1481 CAXTON *Godfrey* li. 93 Atyns was a Greke.. the moost fals, vntrewe man that euer was. And so he wel semed, ffor he had his nosethrellys remuled and tourned.

remunaunde, variant of REMENANT *Obs.*

re'munerable, *a.* *rare.* [See next and -ABLE.] That may be rewarded; deserving of reward.

1593 NASHE *Christ's T.* (1613) 134 Shall he not (of all other) doe him the most remunerablest seruice? **1641** J. JACKSON *True Evang. T.* II. 159 The righteousnesse of the cause.. is an necessary to remunerable suffering, as fuell to make a fire. **1716** M. DAVIES *Athen. Brit.* III. 31 [A neutrality] which how plausible soever to the Commonalty of sure Cards or Self-Interests, is yet scarce sufferable, much less promotable or remunerable *Alibi*.

Hence **remunera'bility**. *rare*$^{-1}$.

1659 PEARSON *Creed* (1816) I. 570 If there were no other consideration, but.. of the liberty and remunerability of human actions.

remunerate (rɪˈmjuːnəreɪt), *v.* [f. L. *remūnerāt-*, ppl. stem of *remūnerārī* (later *-āre*), to reward, f. *re-* RE- + *mūnus* a gift; cf. F. *rémunérer*.]

1. *trans.* To repay, requite, make some return for (services, etc.).

1523 CROMWELL in Merriman *Life & Lett.* (1902) I. 313 Entending to remembre and also remunerate the olde acquayntaunces. **1594** J. DICKENSON *Arisbas* (1878) 37, I will remunerate your kindnesse with most ample recompence. **1607** DEKKER *Sir T. Wyat* Wks. 1873 III. 90 She no doubt, with royall fauour will remunerate The least of your desertes. **1612** T. TAYLOR *Comm. Titus* ii. 13 That was to teach righteousnesse, but this to remunerate it.

2. To reward (a person); to pay (one) for services rendered or work done.

1588 SHAKS. *Tit. A.* I. i. 398 Is she not then beholding to the man..? Yes, and will Nobly him remunerate. **1606** WARNER *Alb. Eng.* XIV. lxxxii. 343 Should Succession fault in not remunerating thee With such a Monument. *a* **1661** FULLER *Worthies* (1840) II. 534 The king remunerated them both, the former with an addition of honour, the latter with an accession of estate. **1849** THACKERAY *Pendennis* xiv, The great Hubbard had acted legitimate drama for twenty nights, and failed to remunerate anybody but himself. **1855** MACAULAY *Hist. Eng.* xx. IV. 526 Dryden.. received thirteen hundred pounds for his translation of all the works of Virgil, and was thought to have been splendidly remunerated. *refl.* **1838** DICKENS *Nich. Nick.* ii, To remunerate themselves for which trouble.., they only charged three guineas each man.

b. Of things: To recompense or repay (one).

1849 COBDEN *Speeches* 34 The principle that our exclusive trade with the colonies remunerates us for the expense of colonial establishments. **1867** H. MACMILLAN *Bible Teach.* ix. (1870) 188 There are few plants that remunerate so largely the labours of the husbandman.

†**3.** To give as compensation. *Obs. rare*$^{-1}$.

1595 *Locrine* II. iii, For your houses burnt We will remunerate you store of gold.

Hence **re'munerated** *ppl. a.*; **re'munerating** *vbl. sb.* and *ppl. a.*; also **re,munera'tee**, one who receives remuneration.

1611 COTGR., *Remuneration*, a remuneration, remunerating. **1816–30** BENTHAM *Offic. Apt. Maximized, Extr. Const. Code* (1830) 14 The benefit of it diffuses itself among any, who.. are in any way connected with the remuneratee. **1825** *Ibid., Observ. Peel's Sp.* (1830) 32 The very field for which it is proposed to engage their remunerated services. **1843** MARRYAT *M. Violet* xliv, Objects that bring no remunerating value. **1846** J. BAXTER *Libr. Pract. Agric.* (ed. 4) I. 272 The farmer.. would get a more remunerating crop from his land than he would obtain under a system of thinner sowing.

remuneration (rɪmjuːnəˈreɪʃən). [a. F. *rémunération*, or ad. L. *remūnerātiōn-em*, n. of action f. *remūnerārī*: see prec.] Reward, recompense, repayment; payment, pay.

1477 EARL RIVERS (Caxton) *Dictes* 6 He shal gyue remuneracion to the goode for theyr goodnesse. *c* **1500** *Melusine* 39 For the salary & remuneracioun of alle the seruyse that euer ye dide vnto his fader. **1590** SWINBURNE *Testaments* 147 So it bee doon in regard of good will, and affection, and not in hope of gaine or remuneration. **1606** SHAKS. *Tr. & Cr.* III. iii. 170 O let not vertue seeke Remuneration for the thing it was. *a* **1653** GOUGE *Comm. Heb.* iii. 5 To be faithfull in the trust that is reposed in one .. deserveth much commendation, and procures also remuneration. **1726** AYLIFFE *Parergon* 188 When such Grant or Donation is liberally and freely bestow'd without any Prospect of an evil Remuneration. **1832** HT. MARTINEAU *Ireland* ii. 26 The rumuneration of the Catholic clergy in Ireland being principally derived from marriage fees. **1853** J. H. NEWMAN *Hist. Sk.* (1873) II. I. ii. 83 The indignant author would accept no remuneration at all.

remunerative (rɪˈmjuːnərətɪv), *a.* [f. as REMUNERATE *v.* + -IVE: cf. mod.F. *rémunératif*.]

†**1.** Inclined to remunerate. *Obs. rare*$^{-1}$.

1626 *Disc. Pr. Henry* in *Select. Harl. Misc.* (1793) 262 That remunerative he was of services, and considerative of those that deserved and needed.

2. That remunerates or rewards.

a **1677** MANTON *Exp. Lord's Pr.* Matt. vi. 11 Wks. 1870 I. 154 Not from his strict remunerative justice, but out of his grace. **1678** CUDWORTH *Intell. Syst.* I. v. 690 Men.. become fit objects for remunerative justice to display itself upon. **1833** I. TAYLOR *Fanat.* ii. 40 Our acquiescence in retributive proceedings as well penal as remunerative.

3. That brings remuneration; profitable.

1859 SMILES *Self-Help* viii. 209 He advanced by degrees to more remunerative branches of employment. **1865** H. PHILLIPS *Amer. Paper Curr.* II. 72 The scheme did not prove remunerative nor a source of revenue. **1880** C. R. MARKHAM *Peruv. Bark.* 334 Although chinchona cultivation is a remunerative public work.. the experiment is still in its infancy.

Hence **re'muneratively**, **re'munerativeness**.

1652 GAULE *Magastrom.* 27 But remuneratively let your starres and planets not onely signe, but cause good fortune or reward. **1877** *Fraser's Mag.* XV. 39 Their time is more remuneratively occupied. **1895** *Manch. Guard.* 14 Oct. 5/5 Of the remunerativeness of the enterprise there can be no doubt, apart from the net gain to the cultivators.

re'munerator. *rare.* [a. late L. *remūnerātor*, or f. REMUNERATE *v.* + -OR. Cf. F. *rémunérateur* (16th c.).] One who remunerates; a rewarder, recompenser.

1688 BOYLE *Final Causes Nat. Things* ii. 84 The children of God will by their most bountiful remunerator be thought fit to inhabit the New world. **1828** LANDOR *Imag. Conv., Rousseau & Malesherbes*, You have no right, sir, to be the patron and remunerator of inhospitality.

re'muneratory, *a.* [f. as REMUNERATE *v.* + -ORY: cf. F. *rémunératoire* (16th c.).] Serving to remunerate; affording remuneration.

1586 A. DAY *Eng. Secretary* I. (1625) 22 Remuneratorie, being a gratefull relation of courtesies, benefits or good turnes receiued. **1617** MORYSON *Itin.* III. 219 The gift of vtensile goods.. is of so little force, as with death it is not confirmed, except it be remuneratory. **1751** JOHNSON *Rambler* No. 145 ¶4 Remuneratory honours are proportioned at once to the usefulness and difficulty of performances. **1765** BLACKSTONE *Comm.* I. 56 Human legislators have for the most part chosen to make the sanction of their laws rather vindicatory than remuneratory. **1844** M. HENNELL *Soc. Syst.* 118 Legislation.. will be remuneratory, and distribute the honour and glory due to pre-eminent virtue.

remurmur (rɪˈmɜːmə(r)), *v.* Chiefly *poet.* [ad. L. *remurmurāre*: see RE- and MURMUR *v.*]

1. *intr.* **a.** To give back or give forth a murmuring sound; to resound with murmurs.

1697 DRYDEN *Virg. Georg.* IV. 667 The Realms of Mars remurmured all around. **1718** MOTTEUX *Quix.* (1733) II. 276 A pleasant Rivulet.. remurmurs over the whitest Pebbles. **1747** T. GIBBONS *Elegy Col. Gardiner* v, Heav'ns high Crystal Domes remurmur with the Sound. **1870** BRYANT *Iliad* II. XXI. 279 The banks around Remurmured shrilly.

b. To answer with murmurs *to* a sound.

1697 DRYDEN *Æneid* XI. 695 A jarring Sound.. Like that of Swans remurm'ring to the Floods. **1703** POPE *Thebais* 166 Eurota's banks remurmur'd to the noise. **1762–9** FALCONER *Shipwr.* I. 34 Yonder cave, Whose vaults remurmur to the roaring wave.

c. Of sounds: To echo in murmurs.

1717 POPE *Iliad* x. 563 A low groan remurmur'd through the shore. **1790** A. WILSON in *Poems & Lit. Prose* (1876) II. 17 Crying and sighing Remurmured through the glen.

2. *trans.* To repeat in murmurs.

1704 POPE *Winter* 64 The trembling trees.. Her fate remurmur to the silver flood. **1789** J. WHITE *Earl Strongbow* I. 202 The woods, the valleys, the mountains around.. daily remurmur the effusions of my misery.

Hence **re'murmuring** *ppl. a.*

1740 SOMERVILLE *Hobbinol* II. 464 While thy remurm'ring Streams Danc'd by, well pleas'd. **1757** DYER *Fleece* I. 608 Deep remurmuring cords Of th' ancient harp.

†**remurmu'ration**. *Obs. rare.* [ad. late L. *remurmurātiōn-em*: see prec. and -ATION.] The action of murmuring or protesting.

1611 W. SCLATER *Key* (1629) 214 So see we many practising vsurie, without any remurmuration of conscience, through errour of iudgement. **1623** R. CARPENTER *Conscionable Christian* 58 To him.. there is no condemnation, or remurmuration of conscience for sinne.

re'muster, *v.* orig. *Services'*. [RE- 5 a.] *intr.* **a.** with pass. sense. To be assigned to other duties. **b.** for *refl.* To assemble again. Hence **re'mustering** *vbl. sb.*

1942 *R.A.F. Jrnl.* 3 Oct. 13 Because Bill Snooks is unfit for air crew duties, he should be allowed to re-muster to.. a sedentary trade. *Ibid.* 14 A.C. 2 So-and-So has certain qualifications which make him suitable for re-mustering or training. **1963** *Times* 5 June 14/1 No. 500 (County of Kent) Squadron, Royal Auxiliary Air Force, disbanded in 1957, will remuster for one day to receive its squadron standard from Lord Avon. **1966** *Punch* 6 July 16 Modern football is a managers' game... Attack is based on the counter which passes the opposing defence before it can remuster after its own attack. **1977** 'J. HERRIOT' *Vet in Spin* (1978) xviii. 166 Normally when an aircrew is grounded he remusters on the ground staff, but yours is a reserved occupation.

remu'tation. *rare*$^{-1}$. [RE- 5 a.] The action of changing back again.

a **1843** SOUTHEY *Doctor* ccxvii. (1848) 584 The mutation or rarefaction of water into air takes place by day, the remutation or condensation of air into water by night.

re'mutiny, *v.* [RE- 5 a.] *intr.* To mutiny again.

1895 HARDY *Jude* I. iii. 20 He anxiously descended.. trying not to think of.. the captain with the bleeding hole in his forehead, and the corpses round him that remutinied every night on board the bewitched ship.

Remy Martin (remi martẽ). Also **Rémy Martin**. [Name of the shippers.] The proprietary name of a cognac; a drink of this.

[**1951** T. E. CARLING *Compl. Bk. Drink* v. 42 Principal Cognac Producers.. Remy Martin.] **1961** C. WILLOCK *Death in Covert* i. 9 A large shot of Rémy Martin in a balloon glass. **1963** *Official Gaz.* (U.S. Patent Office) 26 Feb. TM 137/1 *Remy Martin* for Cognac. First use 1884. **1965** L. MEYNELL *Double Fault* I. iii. 29 Evelyn Barker had a Rémy Martin in front of her. **1965** P. D. WALL *Trio* (1966) iv. 55 He promptly loaded his briefcase with Pernod and Remy Martin. **1975** D. BLOODWORTH *Clients of Omega* xxv. 242 Sipping his Rémy Martin with its lacing of java. **1976** *Trade*

Marks Jrnl. 14 Apr. 783/2 Remy Martin.. Brandy. E. Remy Martin and Co... 29th August, 1973.

remynaunte, variant of REMENANT *Obs.*

remyssale, variant of REMISSAL *Obs.*

remyt, obs. form of REMIT *sb.*

remy'thologize, *v.* [RE- 5 b, after DEMYTHOLOGIZE *v.*] *trans.* To provide with a new mythological system; to reinterpret the elements of (an older mythology) in terms of a newer one. Hence **remythologi'zation**.

1964 K. G. GRUBB *Layman looks at Church* v. 156 The Bible.. has to be 'demythologised' and then remythologised. **1973** R. SLOTKIN *Regeneration through Violence* ii. 36 Both [myth and art] serve as means of ordering and explaining a chaotic and threatening environment. The remythologization of the West began with attempts by French and Spanish Jesuits and English Puritans to order the chaos of the New World. **1974** *Canadian-Amer. Slavic Stud.* VIII. 492 The updating, transformation and 'remythologization' of these legends constituted a form of justification of the validity of their world-view. **1976** H. MONTEFIORE in *Christian Believing* 148, I may expect to 'translate' or 'remythologize' its thought forms and imagery.

†**ren**, *sb. Obs. rare.* [f. *renne*, obs. f. RUN *v.*; cf. Du. *ren*, G. *renn*, ON. *renna*.] A run, course.

c **1250** *Gen. & Ex.* 1 Man og to luuen ðat rimes ren, ðe wisseð wel ðe logede men [etc.]. *c* **1386** CHAUCER *Reeve's T.* 159 The wyf cam lepynge Inward with a ren. *c* **1440** *Promp. Parv.* 429/1 Ren, or rennynge, *cursus*.

†**ren**, *v. Obs.*⁻¹ [? for *rene*:—OE. *rēnian*, *regnian* to set in order.] *trans.* To clear a way for.

a **1340** HAMPOLE *Psalter* lxxxiv. 14 Rightwisnes of penaunce for oure syn sal ga bifor him in vs, that is, it sall ren his cumynge in til vs.

ren, obs. form of RAIN *sb.*¹, REIN *sb.*¹, RUN *v.*

renable ('rɛnəb(ə)l), *a. Obs.* exc. *dial.* Also 5 renabel, -abulle, -abyll, resnabyl, 7 rennible, 9 *dial.* -able, runnable. [a. OF. *renable*, *resnable* (AF. also *rednable*), *reis-*, *raisnable*, etc.,:—L. *ratiōnābil-em* reasonable, RATIONABLE. The sense of 'eloquent' appears to be characteristic of AF. In later use prob. assoc. with *renne* RUN *v.*]

1. Of persons: Ready of speech, eloquent: speaking or reading fluently or distinctly; †esp. in phr. ***renable of tongue***. (Cf. REASONABLE *a.* 3.)

c **1290** *Beket* 1336 in *S. Eng. Leg.* I. 144 Non of heom þar nas, þat he preisede muche þis heiȝe man for he so renable was. **1297** R. GLOUC. (Rolls) 8572 Renable nas he noȝt of tonge, ac of speche hastif. **1377** LANGL. *P. Pl.* B. Prol. 158 A raton of renon most renable of tonge. **1387** TREVISA *Higden* (Rolls) VIII. 25 He was.. resonabel [*v.r.* renable, renabel] of speche [L. *eloquens*], and wel i-lettred. *c* **1400** *Ywaine & Gaw.* 209 Of tong sho was trew and renable, And of hir semblant soft and stabile. *c* **1460** *Towneley Myst.* xxi. 110 Men calle hym a prophete, a lord fulle renabyll. **1781** J. HUTTON *Tour to Caves* (ed. 2) Gloss., *Renable*, loquacious, and never at a stop or inconsistent in telling a story. **1868** SEDGWICK *Mem. Cowgill Chapel* 72 (E.D.D.), Some lassie who was bright and renable was asked to read for the amusement of the party.

b. Of speech, etc.: Ready, fluent, plain.

1387 TREVISA *Higden* (Rolls) I. 11 Noble spekers, þat.. faire facounde and resonable [*v.r.* renable] speche folowed and streynede all her lyf tyme. *c* **1400** tr. *Secreta Secret., Gov. Lordsh.* 103 þe ffyfte [virtue], þat he be curtays.. and ..of renable speche. *a* **1450** MYRC 1008 Hast þou also prowde I-be.. for þow hast a renabulle tonge? **1643** BP. HALL *Devout Soul* ii. (1646) 5 Not [he] that hath the most rennible tongue (for prayer is not so much a matter of the lips, as of the heart). **1674** N. FAIRFAX *Bulk & Selv.* 33 We choose the renablest words belonging to the former, wherewith to set forth the latter. **1895** *E. Anglian Gloss.*, *Rennable*, plain, easy to be understood.

†**2.** Reasonable, moderate. *Obs. rare*⁻¹.

1340 *Ayenb.* 95 þyse þri þinges byeþ nyeduolle to alle þe þinges þet in þe erþe wexeþ. Guod molde, wocnesse norissynde, and renable hete.

'renably, *adv. Obs.* exc. *dial.* Also 4 renab(le)liche, 9 *dial.* runnably. [f. prec. + -LY².]

1. Fluently, readily.

13.. *Sir Beues* (A.) 2974 Forþ þer com on redi reke, þat renabliche kouþe frensch speke. *c* **1386** CHAUCER *Friar's T.* 211 Som tyme we.. speke as renably and faire and wel As to the Phitonissa dide Samuel. **1895** *E. Anglian Gloss.*, *Runnably*, currently; smoothly; without hesitation. Often *Renably* in Suffolk.

†**2.** To a reasonable extent; moderately. *Obs.*⁻¹

c **1315** SHOREHAM III. 19 þou schel haue.. mete and cloþes renableliche, And lyf ine herte blisce.

renagado, obs. form of RENEGADO.

Renaissance (rɪ'neɪsəns, F. rənɛsɑ̃s). Also with small initial. [F., f. *renaître* to be born again, after *naissance* birth: cf. RENASCENCE.]

1. a. The great revival of art and letters, under the influence of classical models, which began in Italy in the 14th century and continued during the 15th and 16th; also, the period during which this movement was in progress.

1845 FORD *Handbk. Spain* II. 745 At the bright period of the *Renaissance*, when fine art was a necessity and pervaded every relation of life. **1854** LOWELL *Keats* Prose Wks. 1896 I. 244 In him we have an example of the renaissance going on almost under our own eyes. **1873** PATER *Renaissance* 2 The word Renaissance indeed is now generally used to denote.. a whole complex movement of which that revival of classical antiquity was but one element or symptom.

b. *ellipt.* The style of art or architecture developed in, and characteristic of, this period.

1840 T. A. TROLLOPE *Summer in Brittany* II. 234 That heaviest and least graceful of all possible styles, the 'renaissance' as the French choose to term it. **1851** RUSKIN *Stones Ven.* I. i. 23 This rationalistic art is the art commonly called Renaissance, marked by a return to pagan systems. **1859** JEPHSON & REEVE *Brittany* 268 The cathedral front is a huge mass of barbarous Renaissance.

c. *attrib.* with *architecture*, *building*, etc.

1842 QUEEN VICTORIA *Jrnl.* 14 Sept. (1980) 37 We.. saw the fine greenhouse the Duke has built, all in stone, in the Renaissance style. **1851** RUSKIN *Stones Ven.* I. App. xi. 370 A choice little piece of description this, of the Renaissance painters. **1857** —— *Pol. Econ. Art* ii. 103 Verona possesses .. the loveliest Renaissance architecture of Italy. **1860** G. A. SPOTTISWOODE in *Vac. Tour* 98 We.. contented ourselves with what we saw of its heavy-looking renaissance buildings. **1882** CAULFIELD & SAWARD *Dict. Needlework*, *Renaissance Braid Work*.—This is also known as Renaissance Lace. **1930** R. FRY *Let.* 12 Sept. (1972) II. 650 [Montrésor] has.. a very ambitious and rather good Renaissance Gothic church. It's odd what a really good and convenient style that makes—in fact it does Gothic much better with less fuss than Gothic itself. **1963** A. LUBBOCK *Austral. Roundabout* 190 Airy, Renaissance-style stucco arches. **1976** *Early Music* IV. 512/2 (Advt.), Renaissance viols from 16th-century models. **1980** I. MURDOCH *Nuns & Soldiers* i. 40 A programme of Renaissance music.

d. Special Combs. **Renaissance humanism** = HUMANISM 4; **Renaissance man**, one who exhibits the virtues of an idealized man of the Renaissance; also *fig.*

1906 W. H. WOODWARD *Stud. Educ. Renaissance* vii. 128 That the Frenchmen in their King's train should be profoundly impressed with the Renaissance man as they found him declared in Rodrigo Borgia, and his enigmatic son, in Ludovico Sforza or Ercole d'Este, is no cause for wonder. **1948** W. K. FERGUSON *Renaissance in Hist. Thought* iii. 71 Bayle.. interpreted Renaissance humanism as an enlightened revolt against barbarism. *Ibid.* v. 128 The discontented rebels against the restrictions of contemporary bourgeois society.. took the lead in the idealization of the Renaissance man, combining the cult of genius with that of free, egoistic personality. **1955** P. O. KRISTELLER *Classics & Renaissance Thought* i. 10 Renaissance humanism was not as such a philosophical tendency or system, but rather a cultural and educational program which emphasized and developed an important but limited area of studies. **1970** E. PACE *Saberlegs* (1971) xiv. 132, I knew your father... A fine man. So many-sided. What I believe you would call a Renaissance man. **1975** *Language* LI. 443 Renaissance humanism was responsible for the most successful system of syntactic analysis to be conceived prior to the advent of explicit syntactic theorizing in the 20th century. **1977** *Time* 8 Aug. 32/3 At 50, Hood is the Renaissance man of sailing; he designed, cut the sails and outfitted *Independence*, the first man in history to control every aspect of a 12-tonner from drawing board to helm.

2. Any revival, or period of marked improvement and new life, in art, literature, etc.

1872 MORLEY *Voltaire* 4 Voltairism may stand for the name of the Renaissance of the eighteenth century. **1882** *Athenæum* 23 Dec. 857/2 The most satisfactory among the signs of a theatrical renaissance. **1925**, etc. [see *Negro Renaissance* s.v. NEGRO 7]. **1969** A. COCKBURN in Cockburn & Blackburn *Student Power* 18 The astonishing works of Mao Tse Tung.. bear witness to the flowering of the May 4 Movement which.. has justly been called the Chinese Renaissance. **1969** *Physics Bull.* June 221/1 The 'renaissance' in optics, one of the oldest disciplines in physics, has been brought about mainly by the advent of the laser. **1973** *Black World* Sept. 95 Arna Bontemps was not of the 'Harlem Renaissance'... His first novel and his poems.. appeared just when.. the Renaissance flopped. **1975** *Nature* 3 Apr. 391/1 A renaissance occurred in 1969 when Adler proved that bacteria have specific chemoreceptors.

Hence **Re'naissancer**, one who participates in a renaissance; = next; **Re'naissancist**, an advocate or student of a renaissance; also *attrib.* or as *adj.*

1895 J. M. FALKNER *Lost Stradivarius* 261 Neo-Platonism .. has enthralled.. many minds from Proclus and Julian to Augustine and the Renaissancists. **1899** G. B. SHAW *Let.* 17 Oct. (1972) II. 113 The mosque [of Sulieman].. is a successful attempt to take St Sophia and give it refined grandeur in the spirit of Brunelleschi and the early dignified Renaissancers. **1949** Renaissancer [see BRAHMSIAN *a.* and *sb.*]. **1973** *Compar. Stud. Soc. & Hist.* XV. 473 That a near-century of scholarship.. should fail indeed to validate even the concept of a Renaissance, would appear to have little if any bearing on.. the prosperity of the guild of Renaissancists in our time. *Ibid.* 478 In characteristic Renaissancist fashion.

Re'naissant, *a. rare.* Also with small initial. [a. F. *renaissant*, pres. pple. of *renaître*: cf. RENASCENT.] **1.** = prec. 1 c.

1864 MISS COBBE *Italics* 14 The great artistic ages, classic and Renaissant. **1886** *Ch. Times* 17 Sept. 686 Gothic is most appropriate for ecclesiastical buildings and Renaissant for gin-shops, theatres and restaurants.

2. = RENASCENT *a.*

1972 *Times* 3 Jan. 15 Rapidly rising output and renaissant business confidence and investment are normally a time at which profits rise. **1972** E. LONGFORD *Wellington* II. xxi. 331 This was all very difficult for a renaissant Tory party which meant to win and win soon.

renal ('riːnəl), *a.* and *sb.* [a. F. *rénal*, or ad. late L. *rēnālis*, f. *rēn* kidney: see REINS.]

A. *adj.* **1.** Of or pertaining to the reins or kidneys.

1656 BLOUNT *Glossogr.* s.v. *Vein*, *Renal veins*, the kidney veins. **1704** J. HARRIS *Lex. Techn.* I, *Renal Artery*, is said by some, to come out of the Aorta, and to enter into the Kidneys. *c* **1720** W. GIBSON *Farrier's Dispens.* i. (1734) 27 By its extraordinary detersive qualities, it scours and cleanses the renal passages. **1788** BAILLIE in *Phil. Trans.* LXXVIII. 357 The renal capsules had undergone no change. **1840** E. WILSON *Anat. Vade M.* (1842) 309 The Renal arteries are two large trunks given off from the sides of the aorta. **1872** HUXLEY *Physiol.* v. 105 The renal excretion has naturally an acid reaction.

2. ***renal colic***, colicky pain caused by obstruction of the outlet of the renal pelvis or that of the ureter, usu. by a calculus (see also quots. 1857, 1901); ***renal dialysis***, dialysis performed artificially as a substitute for normal kidney function; freq. *attrib.* to denote a device to do this; ***renal dwarfism***, ***infantilism***, ***osteodystrophy***, ***rickets***, osteodystrophy due to the failure of the kidneys to convert dietary vitamin D to a more active form.

1857 DUNGLISON *Dict. Med. Sci.* (ed. 15) 222/2 *Colica nephretica*... Renal colic... Acute pains, which accompany nephritis,.. or the passage of a calculus into the ureter. **1865** W. ROBERTS *Urinary & Renal Dis.* III. vii. 405 Neuralgia of the lower intercostal and abdominal nerves.. is distinguished from renal colic by the absence of blood, pus, and transitional epithelium in the urine. **1901** H. MORRIS *Surg. Dis. Kidney & Ureter* II. xxiv. 81 A calculus either may remain fixed in the kidney substance or in a calyx, or may occupy the renal pelvis, within which it can move about, or it may migrate along the ureter towards the bladder. In either of the latter conditions it will probably give rise to renal colic. **1912** O. MAY in *Univ. Coll. Hosp. Mag.* II. 99 (*heading*) A case of 'renal infantilism'. **1920** H. BARBER in *Lancet* 3 Jan. 18/1 Until some standard text-book gives a full account of this condition it is not easy to select a suitable name; but as the kidney disease not infrequently has a very insidious onset, and many of the cases seek advice for the first time for want of development or bone deformity, some name such as renal dwarfism may be used. **1926** G. V. ASHCROFT in *Jrnl. Bone & Joint Surg.* VIII. 279 Renal rickets is a disease not mentioned in medical text-books. *Ibid.* 288 It is to the association of the typical clinical picture, the typical X-ray picture, and deficient renal function that the term Renal Rickets has been applied. **1929** THURSFIELD & PATERSON *Garrod's Dis. Children* (ed. 2) iii. 123 The primary cause of renal rickets is the inability of the diseased kidneys properly to excrete phosphorus. **1930** *Lancet* 10 May 1002/2 Two conditions associated with bone deformities have been differentiated from late rickets—namely, cœliac rickets and renal rickets. *Ibid.*, Cases of cœliac rickets and renal infantilism only occasionally show rickets. *Ibid.*, Rickets occasionally complicates renal dwarfism. **1943** LIU & CHU in *Med.* XXII. 103 The term 'renal osteodystrophy' seems to be a suitable generic name to include cases of osseous disorder associated with renal insufficiency, while the exact nature of the pathological process in the skeleton is still undetermined. **1957** *Brit. Med. Bull.* XIII. 57/2 The terms 'renal dwarfism', 'renal infantilism' and 'renal rickets', although obviously not invariably applicable, were apt in their original use. **1960** *Jrnl. Amer. Med. Assoc.* 24 Dec. 2124/1 Renal dialysis proved successful in treating previously intractable heart failure. **1962** *Lancet* 2 June 1169/1 More common.. is the form associated with renal failure which was at one time called 'renal rickets'.. but which is now more elegantly referred to as 'renal osteodystrophy'. **1963** *Ibid.* 5 Jan. 16/1 Renal-dialysis units mostly use complex and powerful artificial kidneys which require experienced surgical, medical, and biochemical super-vision. **1971** S. MILLIGAN *Adolf Hitler* I. 23 Specialists.. came.. to examine me... Days later a card arrived saying 'Renal Colic'. **1974** *Times* 17 Apr. 2/8 If kidneys for transplant were available many people maintained by expensive renal dialysis machines could be given a fuller life and many of the 5,000 who die each year from kidney failure could be saved. **1982** *Macmillan Guide Family Health* 509/2 Renal colic is usually felt first in the back, just below the ribs.

B. *sb.* A renal artery.

1899 *Allbutt's Syst. Med.* VI. 274 In ten [cases] the upper extremity lay between the inferior mesenteric and the renals.

†**'renaldry**. *Obs. rare*⁻¹. [f. *Renald*, obs. var. REYNARD + -RY: cf. obs. F. *renarderie*.] Guile, cunning, craft.

1612 tr. *Passenger of Benvenuto* I. iv. 269 She vsed all malitious Renaldrie [It. *volpina malitia*] to the end I might stay there this night.

rename (riː-), *v.* [RE- 5 a.] *trans.* To name again; *esp.* to give another or new name to.

a **1660** HAMMOND *Serm.* (1850) 423 By that odious re-naming of sin. **1665** J. WEBB *Stone-Heng* (1725) 62 It is scarcely worth re-naming, much less answering to. **1675** SHERBURNE *Sphere Manilius* 66 [Philippi] afterwards renamed from Philip.. its Reedifier. **1869** TOZER *Highl. Turkey* II. 354 The features of the district were renamed. **1897** *Atlantic Monthly* LXXIX. 36 Then must we have a new vocabulary and re-name the professions.

'Renardine, *a. rare*⁻¹. [f. *Renard* var. REYNARD.] Pertaining to Reynard the Fox. So †**'renardism** = REGNARDISM (Blount 1661).

1886 *Athenæum* 7 Aug. 165/2 There has been much learning expended.. on the question of why the lion was king in the Renardine tales.

renardite (rə'nɑːdaɪt). *Min.* [a. F. *renardite* (A. Schoep 1928, in *Bull. de la Soc. Française de Min.* LI. 247), f. the name of A. F. *Renard*

(1842–1903), of the University of Ghent: see -ITE[1].] A hydrated basic phosphate of lead and uranium, $Pb(UO_2)_4(PO_4)_2(OH)_4.7H_2O$, found as minute, yellow orthorhombic crystals.

1929 *Amer. Mineralogist* XIV. 244 Renardite... Found as minute crystals with quartz, torbernite and clay from the Kasolo Mine, Katanga, Belgian Congo. **1956** [see DEWINDTITE]. **1971** *Mineral Abstr.* XXII. 267/1 The geological, mineralogical, and metallogenic character of the uraniferous schists of the Salamanca province of western Spain are described... Secondary minerals are represented by gummite,.. renardite [etc.].

renascence (rɪˈnæsəns). Also 9 re- (riː-). [See RENASCENT and -ENCE.]

1. The process or fact of being born anew; rebirth, renewal, revival.

1727 EARBERY tr. *Burnet's St. Dead* 187 The Souls have a kind of Renascence, or παλιγγενεσία, a new Life, a new World, and all things new. **1827** COLERIDGE in *Lit. Rem.* (1839) IV. 399 The perpetuity and continued re-nascence and spiritual life of Christ. **1912** E. ST. V. MILLAY in F. Earle *Lyric Yr.* 185 Renascence... O God, I cried, give me new birth, And put me back upon the earth! **1973** *Nature* 20 July 184/3 *The Serengeti Lion*.. has greater significance in that it reflects the renascence of animal study in Africa.

2. = RENAISSANCE 1.

1869 M. ARNOLD *Cult. & An.* 159 The great movement which goes by the name of the Renascence. [*Note*] I have ventured to give to the foreign word *Renaissance* an English form. **1874** GREEN *Short Hist.* vii. 390 Here, as elsewhere, the Renascence found vernacular literature all but dead. *transf.* **1872** MORLEY *Voltaire* 5 The four-score volumes which he wrote, are the monument.. of a new renascence.

†**reˈnascency.** *Obs.* [See next and -ENCY.] = RENASCENCE 1.

1664 EVELYN tr. *Freart's Archit.* Ep. Ded. a4 This [science] of Architecture.. ows her renascency amongst Us to Your Majesties encouragements. *Ibid.* II. i. 91 A renascency from his own Ashes like the Phœnix. **1682** SIR T. BROWNE *Chr. Mor.* III. §25 Job would not only curse the day of his Nativity, but also of his Renascency.

renascent (rɪˈnæsənt), *a.* and *sb.* [ad. L. *renascent-em*, pres. pple. of *renascī*, f. *re-* RE- + *nascī* to be born.] **A.** *adj.* That is being born again, reviving, springing up afresh.

1727 BAILEY (vol. II), *Renascent*, springing up, or being born again. **1747** *Gentl. Mag.* XVII. 212/2 Care must also be taken to prevent any external impression on the renascent bark. **1773** J. ROSS *Fratricide* VI. 552 (MS.) To console her cares, And give renascent vigour to her frame! **1812** SOUTHEY *Omniana* II. 95 These are the first rudiments of the renascent plant. **1849** THACKERAY *Pendennis* lvi, Pen's renascent desire to see his little conquest again. **1883** SYMONDS *Shaks. Predec.* ii. (1900) 22 The genius of youthfulness, renascent,.. was dominant in that age.

B. *sb.* One who takes part in a renaissance.

1898 *Amer. Jrnl. Philol.* Apr. 115 This we owe to the Greek renascents and to their maintenance of the best standards—the three stars of Attic tragedy.

reˈnascible, *a.* *rare*$^{-0}$. [f. L. *renasc-ī* (see prec.) + -IBLE.] Capable of being born or produced again (Johnson 1755). Hence **renasciˈbility** (Bailey 1721); **reˈnascibleness** (Bailey, vol. II, 1727).

†**renash,** *v.* *Obs.* *rare*$^{-1}$. [Of obscure origin.] *intr.* ? To toss the head.

c **1475** in *Archaeologia* (1814) XVII. 293 A rayne of lethir hungry tied fro the hors hede unto the girthis beeneth betwene the ferthir bouse of the hors for renasshyng.

renat(e, obs. forms of RENNET *sb.*[2]

†**reˈnate,** *ppl. a.* *Obs.* *rare.* [ad. L. *renāt-us*, pa. pple. of *renascī*.] Reborn, reincarnate.

1570 LEVINS *Manip.* 39/43 Renate, *renatus.* *c* **1614** FLETCHER, etc. *Wit at Sev. Weap.* I. ii, And to confirm yourself in me renate, I hope you'll find my wits legitimate! **1660** STANLEY *Hist. Philos.* IX. (1701) 428/2 So one man often renate, is named Æthalides, Euphorbus, Hermotimus, Pyrrhus, and lastly Pythagoras.

†**reˈnate,** *v.* *Obs.* *rare.* [f. L. *renāt-*, ppl. stem of *renascī*: see RENASCENT.] **a.** *pass.* To be born again. **b.** *intr.* To form again.

c **1546** JOYE in Gardiner *Declar. Joye* (1546) 91 b, Thus we electe, called & renated of the Spirit, know ye father in Christ. *a* **1548** HALL *Chron., Hen. VII* 32 A pernicious fable and ficcion.. to feyne a dead man to be renated and newely borne agayne. **1578** BANISTER *Hist. Man* VIII. 104 The watrie humor being effused may renate or grow agayne.

reˈnationalization. [RE- 5 b.] The action of removing (a formerly nationalized industry, etc.) from private ownership and bringing it under national control again.

1923 W. P. LIVINGSTONE *Galilee Doctor* IV. ii. 250 It had given them a charter of renationalization. **1957** *Economist* 2 Nov. 437/1 For months the threat of renationalisation kept steel shares subdued and they have been consistent laggards in the market. **1958** *Engineering* 28 Feb. 271/2 Steel leaders are hardening in their opposition to re-nationalisation. **1971** *Guardian* 5 Mar. 13/5 The campaign for 'Renationalisation without compensation'.

reˈnationalize, *v.* [RE- 5 b.]

1. *absol.* To reinvest with national character.

1927 *Scots Observer* 26 Feb. 15/3 Professor M'Fadyen,.. has given us.. a book,.. based on his rich experience as a missionary professor in India... The argument that missions denationalise the native is noted, and reasons are given for the contention that missions really renationalise.

2. *trans.* To transfer (a formerly nationalized industry) from private to national ownership again.

1954 *Ann. Reg. 1953* 22 Steel and transport were to be renationalized. **1959** *Daily Tel.* 13 Mar. 19/7 Its proposals not only to renationalise steel and road transport but also to nationalise by one means or another half of British industry. **1980** *Times* 30 Sept. 4/6 The next Labour Government would renationalize.. transport activity.

renatuˈration. [RE- 5 a.] The process of restoring the nature or properties of what has been denatured.

1940 *Nature* 31 Aug. 301/1 The reversion of heat denaturation in proteins.. has been demonstrated... The present method of renaturation is of interest owing to the well-defined conditions under which the reversion is achieved. **1965** PEACOCKE & DRYSDALE *Molecular Basis Heredity* iv. 37 A quite different approach to this problem has now become available with the discovery that, under carefully chosen conditions, the two strands of DNA of micro-organisms and bacteriophage may be separated and then subsequently reunited to restore the original helical structure and biological activity. This process of 'renaturation' may be followed by centrifugation of DNA. **1978** *Nature* 28 Sept. 352/1 Kunitz demonstrated by enzymatic and physico-chemical methods that renaturation of the inhibitor yielded a product indistinguishable from the original protein.

reˈnature (riː-), *v.* [RE- 5 a.] **a.** *trans.* To restore the nature or properties of (what has been denatured).

1946 *Nature* 30 Nov. 768/2 Some fairly close system of supervision by the international authority will be essential to ensure that the denatured material.. is not being 'renatured' so as to make it suitable for use in a bomb. **1977** *Sci. Amer.* Apr. 44/2 Stewart found that after cooling and the removal of the detergent the interferon recovered its original biological activity: it was renatured.

b. *intr.* To undergo renaturation.

1965 PEACOCKE & DRYSDALE *Molecular Basis Heredity* iv. 38 Such a close correlation clearly has great potentialities in the assessment of the relationship between micro-organisms but cannot be used for higher plants and animals since their DNA are more heterogeneous and do not 'renature'. **1973** *Nature* 11 May 55/2 They demonstrated that the centromeric regions.. renature the most rapidly after denaturation.

Hence **reˈnatured** *ppl. a.*, **reˈnaturing** *vbl. sb.*; also **reˈnaturable** *a.*

1955 *Bull. Atomic Sci.* Jan. 12/1 If reconversion of the denatured nuclear explosives is not a protracted process, the threat of seizure, renaturing, and atomic rearmament would remain indefinitely. **1964** G. H. HAGGIS et al. *Introd. Molecular Biol.* xii. 315 Such a renatured DNA regains its biological activity and can be used to transform bacteria. **1970** *Nature* 26 Sept. 1310/1 Renaturable DNA is defined as DNA that after denaturation.. rapidly reverts to a duplex when the denaturing conditions are removed.

reˈnavigate, *v.* *rare*$^{-0}$. [RE- 5 a.] To navigate again. So **renaviˈgation** (Phillips 1658).

1611 COTGR., *Renaviger*, to renauigate, sayle backe, or sayle ouer againe. **1623** in COCKERAM. **1721-** in BAILEY and later Dicts. **1828–32** WEBSTER s.v., To renavigate the Pacific Ocean.

†**reˈnay,** *sb.* *Obs.* Also reney, renye. [ad. OF. *reneié*, pa. pple. of *reneier*: see next.] A renegade, apostate.

13.. *Coer de L.* 4070 Quod the renay: 'Mercy I crye!' **1340** *Ayenb.* 19 He ys wel renay, þet þet land þet ha halt of his lhorde deþ in-to þe hond of his uyende. *Ibid.*, Ine þri maneres is man ycleped reney and uals cristen. ? *a* **1400** *Morte Arth.* 2795 The renye relys abowte and rusches to þe erthe, Roris fulle ruydlye, bot rade he no more.

†**reˈnay, reˈny,** *v.* *Obs.* Forms: α. 4 renai(e, -aye, 4–6 renay, (5 renn-, reyn-); 4 reneie, 4–6 reney(e, 5 reneyhe. β. 4–6 reny(e, 6 renie. [a. OF. *reneier*, *renier* (*renoier*, etc.):—pop. L. *renegāre*: see RENEGUE, and cf. DENY *v.*]

1. *trans.* To renounce, abjure (one's faith, God, lord, etc.).

α. *a* **1300** *Cursor M.* 8995 Leuedis he luued,.. þat did him drightin to renai. *a* **1330** *Otuel* 524 Me ne stant nouȝt of þe swich awe, þat þou sschalt make me reneie mi lawe. **1377** LANGL. *P. Pl.* B. XI. 121 Though a Crystene man coueyted his Crystenedome to reneye [etc.]. *c* **1400** MAUNDEV. (Roxb.) xi. 42 Þe emperour Iulyan Apostata, whilk reynayd and forsuke Cristen fayth. *c* **1440** CAPGRAVE *Life St. Kath.* IV. 976 We haue heere a mayde whiche with obstinacye Reneyeth [*v.r.* reneyhithe] oure lawes. *c* **1475** *Partenay* 2173 Me moste here-After our lord to renay, And in sarisine lau beleue. **1534** MORE *Comf. agst. Trib.* III. Wks. 1212/1 Hee.. geueth.. parte to suche as willinglye will reney their faith. [**1900** RALEIGH *Milton* 219 He renayed his ancestry.]

absol. **1340** *Ayenb.* 19 Alþaȝ he by be his zigginge cristen, he renayþ be dede. *c* **1380** WYCLIF *Sel. Wks.* III. 371 Lest I .. be drawen to renaye, and sey, Who is Lord?

β. **1375** BARBOUR *Bruce* IX. 739 Thow has a quhill renyit thifay. *c* **1400** *Sowdone Bab.* 1254, I shalle.. make the to renye thy laye. **1483** CAXTON *Gold. Leg.* 20/2 It is redde in thistoryes, whan he renyed and forsoke our Lord [etc.]. **1511** *Guylforde's Pilgr.* (Camden) 44 He shall be compelled incontynentlye to renye his fayth and crystendome. **1579** J. STUBBES *Gaping Gulf* C iv, The king of Nauarre.. had felt the poynt thereof if he had not to hys honour.. renied hys God. **1602** WARNER *Alb. Eng.* XI. lxix. 285 For that thow should'st reny thy Faith, and her thereby possesse, The Soldan did capitulat.

refl. **1549** CHALONER *Erasm. on Folly* M ij b, They dishort vs from sinne, but I renie myselfe, if euer they coulde cunningly diffine, what that should be, we call sinne.

b. To recant (an opinion). Also *absol.*

a **1529** SKELTON *Replyc.* 87 Fayne were ye to reny, And mercy for to cry, Or be brende by and by. *c* **1533** *Song* in Strype *Eccl. Mem.* (1721) I. App. xliv. 121 Which opynions wer good for thee to renay.

2. a. To deny, disown (an utterance). *rare*$^{-1}$.

c **1440** *Partonope* 1835 That I haue sayde In no wyse for me shall be renayed [*printed* remayed].

b. To deny the truth of (a statement).

1510–20 *Compl. too late maryed* (1862) 16 For to saye that therin is servage In maryage, but I it reny, For therin is but humayne company. **1512** *Helyas* in Thoms *Prose Rom.* (1828) III. 66 She blusshed all red,.. but not withstandinge she wende well assuredly to have renied al the case.

3. a. To refuse, decline (a gift). *rare.*

13.. *Gaw. & Gr. Knt.* 1821 Ho raȝt hym a riche rynk [= ring].. Bot þe renk hit renayed, &.. sayde, 'I wil no giftez for gode'.

b. To refuse *to* do something. *rare*$^{-1}$.

c **1489** SKELTON *Death Earl Northumbld.* 78 The commons renyed ther taxes to pay Of them demaunded and asked by the kynge; With one voice importune they plainly sayd nay.

†**reˈnayed, reˈnied,** *ppl. a.* *Obs.* [f. prec. + -ED[1], after OF. *reneié*: see RENAY *sb.*] Apostate, renegade.

a **1300** *Cursor M.* 23111 Wreches mistruand, þat renaid ar traiturs and fals. **13..** *St. Erkenwolde* 11 in Horstm. *Altengl. Leg.* (1881) 266 Þene wos this reame renaide mony ronke ȝeres. *c* **1380** *Sir Ferumb.* 4673 If Fyrumbras may beo taan, þat ilke false reneyed man. *a* **1400** *Pistill of Susan* 198 Þo Ros vp with rancour þe Renkes reneyed. **1585** T. WASHINGTON tr. *Nicholay's Voy.* I. xi. 13 b, This Caddi was a renyed Christian. **1590** SIR J. SMYTHE *Disc. conc. Weapons* 41 b, The Ianissaries.. being Christian mens children renied.

†**reˈnaying,** *vbl. sb.* *Obs.* [f. RENAY *v.* + -ING[1].] The action of renouncing or abjuring.

a **1300** *Cursor M.* 29406 If he in renaiing lijs, efter þat he es monest thris. *c* **1386** CHAUCER *Pars. T.* ¶ 719 Reneying of god and hate of his neighebors. *c* **1440** *Jacob's Well* 131 On .. is renaying; whan a man forsakyth god, & becomyth a iewe or a sarazene. **1529** MORE *Dyaloge* II. Wks. 179/1 It was a plaine renaying of Christes faith to doo anye obseruaunce therto.

†**reˈnayrie, reˈnoyrie.** *Obs.* *rare.* [a. OF. *reneierie*, *renoierie*: see RENAY *v.*] Apostacy.

1340 *Ayenb.* 17 He him to-delþ in þri little boȝes.. þe þridde [is] renoyrye. *Ibid.* 19 Þe þridde ontreuþe þet comþ of prede ys renayrie.

Rence, Sc. variant of RAINES *Obs.*

rence, rench, obs. or dial. forms of RINSE *v.*

rench, obs. form of WRENCH *v.*

†**ˈrencian.** *Obs.* *rare.* [a. OF. *rentien* (Godef.), of obscure origin.] Some kind of cloth.

a **1272** *Luue Ron* 106 in *O.E. Misc.* 96 Ne byt he wiþ þe lond ne leode, Vouh ne gray ne rencyan. *c* **1275** *Serving Christ* 70 in *O.E. Misc.* 92 Ne geyneþ vs.. þe robes of russet ne of rencyan.

rencky: see RENKY *a.*

rencontre (rɛnˈkɒntə(r), F. rɑ̃kɔ̃tr), *sb.* Also 8 -countre, 9 -conter. [a. F. *rencontre* (13th c.), vbl. sb. f. *rencontrer*: see next and cf. RENCOUNTER *sb.*

The form is given by Blount (1656, etc., copying Cotgrave), but later Dictionaries down to the Webster of 1864 recognize only *rencounter*.]

1. a. = RENCOUNTER *sb.* 3.

1619 in *Eng. & Germ.* (Camden) 95 The nice termes his Maty standeth in with the French King.. makes it necessary to acquaint you with a rencontre I had at Antwerp. **1705** VANBRUGH *Country House* I. iv, *Baron.* We have not seen one another since we were schoolfellows before. *Marquis.* The happiest rencontre! **1788** MME. D'ARBLAY *Diary* 2 Aug., One of the letters.. was written just after I had communicated to her my singular rencontre with this lady. **1845** STOCQUELER *Handbk. Brit. India* (1854) 82 The accidental rencontre of a vessel homeward bound awakens family recollections. **1884** 'H. COLLINGWOOD' *Under Meteor Flag* 117 The rencontre was disagreeable, and, to shorten it as much as possible, Isabel.. turned back.

b. *Her.* (See quots.)

The existence of the use in Eng. is doubtful; quot. 1727–38 is ultimately derived from the *Dict. Universel* of Furetière (1690).

1725 COATS *Dict. Her.*, *Rencontre*, or *au Rencontre*, is a French Phrase signifying, that the Face of a Beast stands right forward, as if it came to meet the Person before it. **1727–38** CHAMBERS *Cycl.*, *Rencontre* or *rencontre*, in heraldry is applied to animals when they show the head in front, with both eyes, etc. *Ibid.*, He bears sable, in rencountre, a golden fleece.

c. An organized but informal meeting of scientists.

1975 *Chem. in Brit.* XI. 145/1 One approach is to organize small informal meetings—*rencontres*—at which chemists can meet, be educated by (and educate) representatives from the other sciences. **1975** *Physics Bull.* Dec. 515/3 A few months ago the SRC organized a *rencontre* in Aberdeen on 'Combinatorics' which was a get-together for mathematicians, physicists and chemists. **1977** *Chem. in Brit.* XIII. 105 Theoretical research horizons in colloid science formed the theme of a recent *rencontre* sponsored by the Science Research Council.

2. a. = RENCOUNTER *sb.* 1.

1688 in Ellis *Orig. Lett.* Ser. II. IV. 154 Then had happened a rencontre betwixt a party of his Majesty's Army and that of the Prince of Orange. **1803** MRQ. WELLESLEY in Gurw. *Wellington's Desp.* (1838) II. 609 *note*, I have not yet discovered whether the battle was occasioned.. by an accidental rencontre of the armies before the truce had commenced. **1824** SILLIMAN *Tour fr. Hartford to Quebec* (ed. 2) 157 *note*, Lord Howe..was killed near Ticonderoga ..in a renconter the day preceding the..assault.

b. = RENCOUNTER *sb.* 1 b.

1754 RICHARDSON *Grandison* (1781) III. xxviii. 293, I referred to my known resolution of long standing, to avoid a meditated rencontre with any man. **1772** *Chron.* in *Ann. Reg.* 125/2 A rencontre has just happened..between the Marquis de Fleury..and an officer... They fought with pistols. **1826** SCOTT *Woodst.* xxvii, Perhaps there mingled with his resolution a secret belief that such a rencontre would not prove fatal. **1848** THACKERAY *Van. Fair* lv, The secret of the *rencontre* between him and Colonel Crawley was buried in the profoundest oblivion.

c. = RENCOUNTER *sb.* 1 c.

1666–7 PEPYS *Diary* 18 Feb., He was mighty witty, and she also making sport with him very inoffensively, that a more pleasant rencontre I never heard. **1874** C. GEIKIE *Life in Woods* xxi, I was very much amused at a rencontre between the 'captain'..and one of the passengers, who.. had come on board without having money to pay his fare.

3. = RENCOUNTER *sb.* 2. ? *Obs.*

1677 GALE *Crt. Gentiles* IV. II. ix. I. 476 The affaires of war: wherein oft the most inconsiderable rencontres or occurrences produce the greatest changements. **1770** in Jesse *Selwyn & Contemp.* (1844) III. 3 By the..despair and misery which the poor waggoner testified on this unlucky *rencontre*, I guessed we had done some great mischief.

†**ren'contre**, *v. Obs. rare.* Also 7 -ter. [ad. F. *rencontrer*: see RENCOUNTER *v.*] *trans.*

a. To encounter, to meet with. **b.** To oppose, reverse.

1654 *Nicholas Papers* (Camden) II. 67, I was stoped be the manie disorders and deficulties that I rencontred at my first comming. **1689** HICKERINGILL *Ceremony-Monger* v. Wks. 1716 II. 427 To Ranconter and Ruffle the whole course of Nature, and make Heaven a Pair of Stairs to Hell.

rencounter (rɛn'kaʊntə(r)), *sb.* Also 6 **renconter, -countre,** 7 **rancounter, -tre.** [ad. F. *rencontre*: see prec. and cf. RE-ENCOUNTER *sb.*]

1. An encounter or engagement between two opposing forces; a battle, skirmish, conflict.

1523 LD. BERNERS *Froiss.* I. lxxxiv. 106 At the first rencounter many were ouerthrowen. **1562** J. SHUTE tr. *Cambini's Turk. Wars* 56 Amorathe and Aladino..in the rencountre that they had with Selim [etc.]. **1588** ALLEN *Admon.* 59 Recounte all the..rencounters of a very fewe Catholikes against the heretikes and rebelles in Flanders. **1632** LITHGOW *Trav.* IX. 419 Tartars are not..so manly as the Polonians, who counter-blow them at rancounters. **1682** LUTTRELL *Brief Rel.* (1857) I. 169 There lately happened a rancounter between some forces of the French..and some Spaniards. **1709** STEELE *Tatler* No. 28 ⁋8 There are mentioned several Rencounters between..Detachments of the Swedish and Russian Armies. **1781** JEFFERSON *Corr.* Wks. 1859 I. 288 Three little rencounters have happened with the enemy. **1865** CARLYLE *Fredk. Gt.* XXI. iv. (1872) X. 36 The Russian Armies had only to show themselves to beat the Turks in every rencounter.

b. A hostile meeting or encounter between two adversaries; a duel; †sometimes *spec.* (after French usage) distinguished from a regular duel by being unpremeditated. Also without article.

1590 SPENSER *F.Q.* III. i. 9 He gan to feare His toward perill,..Which by that new rencounter he should reare. **1676** D'URFEY *Mme. Fickle* II. i, Pox on't, a Rencounter is nothing when thou art us'd to't. **1709** STEELE *Tatler* No. 39 ⁋7 A Rencounter or Duel was..far from being in Fashion among the Officers that serv'd in the Parliament-Army. **1753** HANWAY *Trav.* (1762) II. I. i. 3 Duelling is often deemed a rencounter, and as such is pardoned. **1816** SCOTT *Antiq.* xx, We will dine together and arrange matters for this rencounter. I hope you understand the use of the weapon. **1838** PRESCOTT *Ferd. & Is.* (1846) I. viii. 359 The latter were wont to repair to Granada to settle their affairs of honour, by personal rencounter.

transf. **1652** NEEDHAM tr. *Selden's Mare Cl.* Ep. Ded., Our late Wars, wherein the Pen Militant hath had as many sharp rancounters as the Sword. **1665** D. LLOYD *State Worthies* (1766) II. 528 There had been before some rancounters or pen combats betwixt him and Dr. Heylin. **1681** HICKERINGILL *Def. Fullwood's Leges Angliæ* 16 Now for the Rancounter, as thy war-like word is.

c. An encounter or contest of any kind; in early use, esp. a contest in wit or argument.

1632 LITHGOW *Trav.* IX. 386 The Sycilians..are full of witty sentences, and pleasant in their rancounters. **1660** JER. TAYLOR *Duct. Dubit.* I. ii. rule 3 §10 The witty rencounters of disputing men. **1672** MARVELL *Reh. Transp.* I. 166 If so I should, as often it happens in such Rencounters, not onely draw Mr. Bayes, but J. O. too upon my back. **1755** J. SHEBBEARE *Lydia* (1769) I. 47 We have a right to lard our history with rencounters and conquests of these voracious animals. **1830** N. S. WHEATON *Jrnl.* 69 Few quarrels and rencounters happened among the boys. **1880** MEREDITH *Tragic Com.* (1881) 6 That unequal rencounter between foolish innocence and the predatory.

fig. **1785** MME. D'ARBLAY *Let.* 17 Dec., My next business ..was to be presented·[to the king]..I had only to prepare myself for the rencounter.

†**d.** Antithesis. *Obs. rare*⁻¹.

1589 PUTTENHAM *Eng. Poesie* III. xix. (Arb.) 219 Ye haue another figure..which..we may call the encounter [*marg.*, *Antitheton*, or the renconter].

†**2.** The fact of meeting or falling in with something unpleasant; an unpleasant experience. *Obs.*

1609 BIBLE (Douay) *1 Kings* v. 4 But now our Lord my God hath geven me rest rownd about: there is no satan, nor il rencounter. **1632** LITHGOW *Trav.* II. 62 The Turkes.. were mindfull to giue vs the new rancounter of a second alarum. **1682** SIR T. BROWNE *Chr. Mor.* III. §23 Our hard entrance into the World, our miserable going out of it, our ..sad Rencounters in it.

3. A chance meeting of two persons, or of a person with a thing. Also *transf.* (quot. 1685).

1632 LITHGOW *Trav.* x. 488 My formalists durst neuer attempt..any passing countenance in our rancounters. **1685** CROWNE *Sir C. Nice* III. 30 My eyes and the picture had never any rencounter since. **1728** MORGAN *Algiers* II. v. 314 Millions of People dread the Rencounter of an Algerine as they would that of a crew of Dæmons. **1748** SMOLLETT *Rod. Rand.* xvi, I was so well pleas'd with this rencounter..that I forgot my resentment. **1794** GODWIN *Cal. Williams* 46 At sight of Mr. Tyrrel in this unexpected rencounter, his face reddened with indignation. **1816** SCOTT *Old Mort.* iv, The casual rencounter had the appearance of a providential interference. **1876** T. HARDY *Ethelberta* (1890) 408 Perhaps at this remote season the embarrassment of a rencounter would not have been intense.

b. A meeting of two things or bodies; an impact, collision. Also without article, and *transf.* Now *rare* or *Obs.*

1662 STILLINGFL. *Orig. Sacræ* III. i. §8 By their frequent rancounters and justlings one upon another, they at last link themselves together. **1691–8** NORRIS *Pract. Disc.* (1711) III. 38 In the various Rencounter of Bodies knocking and jostling one against another. **1704** SWIFT *T. Tub* xi, My nose and this very Post should have a Rencounter. **1723** CHAMBERS tr. *Le Clerc's Treat. Archit.* I. 67 Projecting Bodies, just at its own height..seem to menace the Eye with a Rencounter. **1779** MANN in *Phil. Trans.* LXIX. 619 When two equal currents of homogeneous fluids meet in opposite directions, there is first a swelling and rising up of them at the point of rencounter. **1794** SULLIVAN *View Nat.* I. 92 In this theory, Doctor Hutton wisely steers clear of a rencounter with the sun.

†**4.** (Also *vessel of rencounter.*) A retort. *Obs.*

1694 SALMON *Bate's Dispens.* (1713) 180/1 Cover the Cucurbit with a Vessel of Rencounter, luting it well. **1727** BRADLEY *Fam. Dict.* s.v. *Age*, Fit a Rencounter to the long Neck, lute the Junctures very close.

rencounter (rɛn'kaʊntə(r)), *v.* Now *rare.* Also 6–8 **rancounter.** [ad. F. *rencontrer*: cf. prec. and RE-ENCOUNTER *v.*]

1. *trans.* To meet or encounter (an army, person, etc.) in hostile fashion; to engage (one) in fight.

1503–4 *Act 19 Hen. VII*, c. 34 *Preamble*, With the Kinges hooste roiall..they were rencountered, vaynquesshed, dispersed. **1590** SPENSER *F.Q.* I. iv. 39 But th' Elfin knight, ..him rencountring fierce, reskewd the noble pray. **1620–55** I. JONES *Stone-Heng* (1725) 31 Boadicia..bearing down all before her till rencountred by Suetonius. **1684** *Scanderbeg Rediv.* iv. 90 Forced him to return back into the Battel, where General Sobieski with a party Rencountred him.

†**b.** *intr.* To encounter each other in battle.

1591 JAS. I *Lepanto* 11 Betwixt the baptiz'd race And circumcised Turband Turkes, Rencountring in that place.

2. *trans.* To meet or fall in with (a person, etc.).

1549 *Compl. Scot.* Ded. 7 The historigraphours rehersis of ane pure man of persie, quha be chance rencountrit kyng darius. **1574** *Reg. Privy Council Scot.* II. 404 A schip of the toun of Tweisk..and ane uther schip..wer in thair dew cours rancounterit and takin be a schip of weare. **1672** SHADWELL *Miser* v. iii, I wonder who those fellows were we rancounter'd last night. **1696** AUBREY *Misc.* 72 A Minister walking over the Park to give Sir John Warre a visit, was rencountred by a venerable old man. **1889** STEVENSON *Master of B.* 97 On the occasion I had the good fortune to rencounter you at Durris-deer.

†**b.** *intr.* Const. *with. Obs.*

1632 LITHGOW *Trav.* VII. 330 To my great contentment, I rancountred here with a countrey Gentleman of mine. *Ibid.* VIII. 373 Vpon the seauenth day, wee rancountred with another soyle. **1644** SIR W. MURE *Let.* Wks. (S.T.S.) Introd. 16 We are now lying before Newcastle engaiged anew to rancounter wᵗ new dangers. **1676** ROW *Contn. Blair's Autobiog.* xii. (1848) 475 The English rencounters with the Dutch Smyrna fleet..and takes some of them.

c. To meet each other.

1802 LD. CAMPBELL *Let.* in *Life* (1881) I. 100 They had arrived before me, but through some misunderstanding we never rencountered.

†**3.** *trans.* To come into contact or collision with.

1671 R. BOHUN *Wind* 38 The Repulse or Antiperistasis, which the hot and dry exhalations meet with by rancountring the cold Clouds. **1685** J. SCOTT *Chr. Life* II. 146 Men wander about in the dark, and justle and rancounter one another. **1695** BLACKMORE *Pr. Arth.* VII. 544 Swords clashing Swords, and Shields rencountring Shields.

b. *intr.* To come together, collide. *Obs.*

1712 BLACKMORE *Creation* I. (ed. 2) 8 Could stupid Atomes..From Regions opposite begin their Flight, That here they might Rencounter, here Unite? **1794** G. ADAMS *Nat. & Exp. Philos.* II. xvi. 239 The balls will seem to rencounter and pass over each other.

†**4.** To move counter *to* something. *Obs. rare*⁻¹.

1689 T. PLUNKET *Char. Gd. Commander* 28 Ran-counter to the counter-part, and you Perchance some un-expected thing may do.

Hence **ren'countering** *vbl. sb.* and *ppl. a.*

1632 LITHGOW *Trav.* x. 505 There is a certaine place of sea, where these destracted tydes make their rancountering Randeuouze, that whirleth euer about. **1720** SWIFT *Mod. Educ.* Wks. 1755 II. II. 35 What a figure he would make at a siege or blockade or rencountering.

†**rencq**, obs. variant of RANK *sb.*[1]

1585 Q. ELIZABETH in *Four Cent. Eng. Lett.* (1880) 29 It becometh, therefor, all our rencq to deale sincerely.

rend, *sb.* [f. the verb: cf. RENT *sb.*]

†**1.** A rent, split, division. *Obs. rare.*

1670 BAXTER *Cure Ch. Div.* 381 O what rends and ruins had it prevented in the Christian world? *a* **1674** CLARENDON *Hist. Reb.* xiv. §99 There appeared such a rend among the Officers of the Army, that the Protector was compelled to displace many of them.

2. *techn.* (Such quots.)

1704 J. HARRIS *Lex. Techn.* I, *Rends* in a Ship, are the same as the Seams between her Planks. *c* **1850** *Rudim. Navig.* (Weale) 140 *Rends*, large open splits or shakes in timber..by its being exposed to the wind and sun.

rend (rɛnd), *v.*[1] *Pa. t.* and *pa. pple.* rent. Forms: 1 **rendan (hrendan),** 3–4 **renden,** 4–5 **rende,** (4 **reende,** 5 **-yn, reynd),** 6– **rend.** *Pa. t.* 3 **rend(d)e,** 3–6 **rente,** 4– **rent.** *Pa. pple.* 3 **i-rend,** 6–7, 9 **rended;** 5–6 **rente,** 4– **rent.** See also RENT *v.* [OE. *rendan* = OFris. *renda, randa* (mod.Fris. *renne, ranne*), not represented in the other Teut. languages.]

1. *trans.* **a.** To tear, to pull violently or by main force, *off, out of,* or *from* a thing or place; to tear *off* or *away.*

c **950** *Lindisf. Gosp.* Mark xi. 8 Oðero..ða twiggo ..ȝebuȝun *vel* rendon of ðæm trewum. *a* **1225** *Ancr. R.* 148 Heo haueð bipiled mine figer—irend of al þe rinde. **13..** *Gaw. & Gr. Knt.* 1332 Syþen rytte þay þe foure lymmes, & rent of þe hyde. *c* **1386** CHAUCER *Wife's Prol.* 635 He smoot me ones..For þat I rente out of his book a leef. *c* **1400** *Destr. Troy* 8518 Þen Andromaca for dol..rent of hir clothis. **1573** TUSSER *Husb.* (1878) 123 Not rend [**1580** rent] off, but cut off, ripe beane with a knife. **1596** SPENSER *F.Q.* v. v. 6 As if she had intended Out of his breast the very heart have rended. *a* **1661** FULLER *Worthies* (1840) III. 94 Being so rudely rent off, it hath..defaced his monument. **1697** DRYDEN *Virg. Georg.* I. 455 The Rocks are from their old Foundations rent. **1760–72** H. BROOKE *Fool of Qual.* (1809) I. 27 He..began to cut and rip and rend away the lacings of his suit. **1807** WORDSW. *White Doe* I. 124 Altar, whence the cross was rent. **1863** HAWTHORNE *Our Old Home* (1879) 362, I seemed to rend away and fling off the habit of a lifetime.

fig. **1613** SHAKS. *Hen. VIII*, I. ii. 93 We must not rend our Subiects from our Lawes, and sticke them in our Will.

b. To take forcibly away *from* a person.

1611 BIBLE *1 Kings* xi. 11, I wil surely rend the kingdome from thee. **1632** LITHGOW *Trav.* IX. 394 This Kingdome after it was rent from the Romanes, remained in subiection vnder the French. *a* **1720** SEWEL *Hist. Quakers* (1795) I. IV. 341 So shall thy government be rent from thee and thy house.

c. *to rap* (or *rive*) *and rend*: see RAP *v.*[3] 1 b and RIVE *v.*

2. To tear, wrench, drag *up* or *down.*

a **1225** *Leg. Kath.* 2152 [He bade] þurhdriuen hire tittes Wið irnene neiles, & renden ham up.. wið þe breoste roten. *c* **1386** CHAUCER *Knt.'s T.* 132 He wan the Citee..And rente adoun bothe wall and sparre and rafter. *c* **1400** *Destr. Troy* 12511 Cut down [were] þere sailes, Ropis al to rochit, rent vp the hacches. *c* **1485** *Digby Myst.* (1882) III. 1083 þe fowle wedes and wycys, I reynd vp be þe rote. **1513** DOUGLAS *Æneis* II. viii. 16 Troianis agane, schaipand defence to mak, Rent turrettis doun. **1650** FULLER *Pisgah* II. 56 God rent them up by the roots in the days of Pekah. **1733** BUDGELL *Bee* IV. 437 Whose daring Sons, by wild Ambition driv'n, Rent up the Hills, and lifted Earth to Heav'n.

3. To tear apart (*asunder*) or in pieces.

c **950** *Lindisf. Gosp.* Luke xiii. 7 Hrendas *vel* scearfað..hia [*Rushw.* ceorfas *vel* rendas; L. *succidite illam*]. **1297** R. GLOUC. (Rolls) 5871 Lute vuel þoȝte he, þo me is wombe rende. *a* **1300** *K. Horn* 727 þe fiss þat þi net rente. **13..** *E.E. Allit. P.* C. 527 For he þat is to rakel to renden his cloþez, Mot efte sitte..to sewe hem togeder. *c* **1350** *Will. Palerne* 1851 þe werwolf..went to him euene, wiþ a rude roring as he him rende wold. *c* **1385** CHAUCER *L.G.W.* 646 *Cleopatra*, He rent [= rendeth] the seyl with hokys lyk a sithe. *c* **1420** *Anturs of Arth.* 317 For him þat rewfully rase, and rente was one rude. *c* **1450** *Merlin* 26 Than Vortiger..made hem to be rente and drawen a-sonder. **1535** COVERDALE *1 Sam.* xv. 27 He gat him by yᵉ edge of his garment & rente it. **1591** SPENSER *M. Hubberd* 1370 Upon those gates..he fiercely flewe, And, rending them in pieces [etc.]. **1645** HOWELL *Twelve Treat.* (1661) 331 The graue Venerable Bishop.. fetcht such a sigh, that would haue rended a rock asunder. **1697** DRYDEN *Virg. Georg.* III. 422 She tears the Harness, and she rends the Rein. **1720** POPE *Iliad* XVI. 363 The Telamonian lance his belly rends. **1784** COWPER *Task* VI. 411 Through generous scorn To rend a victim trembling at his foot. **1820** W. IRVING *Sketch Bk.* I. 17 At times the black volume of clouds over head seemed rent asunder by flashes of lightning. **1860** TYNDALL *Glac.* I. vi. 42 The glacier..is rent by deep fissures. **1872** MORLEY *Voltaire* (1886) 7 A banner that was many a time rent but was never out of the field.

b. To tear (one's clothes or hair) in token of rage, grief, horror, or despair.

a **1225** *Juliana* 70 þa þe reue iseh þis, he rende his claðes. *c* **1330** *King of Tars* 99 Whon the soudan this iherde..His robe he rente adoun. *c* **1385** CHAUCER *L.G.W.* 870 *Thisbe*, Who koude write..how hire heere she rente. *c* **1450** *Merlin* 195 Than a squyer that saugh hym..com cryinge and betynge his hondes to-geder, and rendinge his heer. *a* **1591** H. SMITH *Wks.* (1867) II. 65 The man of Benjamin came.. with his clothes rent, and dust upon his head, in token of heaviness. **1730** YOUNG *Par. Job* 17 His friends..In anguish of their hearts their mantles rent. **1769** SIR W. JONES *Palace Fortune* Poems (1777) 29 She rends her silken robes, and golden hair. *a* **1839** PRAED *Poems* (1864) II. 308 Lo, they will weep, and rend their hair.

c. To wear *out* (clothes) by tearing. *rare*⁻¹.

1596 SHAKS. *Merch. V.* II. v. 5 Thou shalt not gurmandize ..And sleepe, and snore, and rend apparrell out.

d. *techn.* To make (laths) by cleaving wood along the grain into thin strips; also, to strip (trees) of bark.

1688 [Implied in *lath-render*]. **1825** J. NICHOLSON *Operat. Mechanic* 612 The following is the method of rending or splitting laths. **1859** T. L. DONALDSON *Handbk. Specifications* 137 The laths are to be rended out of the best ..fir timber. **1893** BARING-GOULD *Curgenven* xiv, The stools of coppice.. were of some five years' growth since last 'rended' for bark.

4. To tear apart or in pieces, in *fig.* applications; in later use, esp. to split into parties or factions.

c **1380** WYCLIF *Sel. Wks.* III. 441 Fals men multiplien mony bokes of þe Chirche, nowe reendynge byleve, and nowe clowtyng heresies. **1531** ELYOT *Gov.* III. xxii, He therfore was rente with curses and rebukes of the people. **1591** SHAKS. *Two Gent.* v. iv. 47 For whose deare sake, thou didst then rend thy faith Into a thousand oathes. **1610** DONNE *Pseudo-martyr* 285 Hereupon arose such a schisme, as rent that country into very many parts. **1697** DRYDEN *Virg. Georg.* IV. 309 The Commons live, by no Divisions rent. *a* **1715** BURNET *Own Time* II. (1724) I. 274 He saw both Church and State were rent. **1757** BURKE *Abridgm. Eng. Hist.* Wks. X. 421 Popes and anti-popes arose. Europe was rent asunder by these disputes. **1838** PRESCOTT *Ferd. & Is.* (1846) I. v. 246 Navarre.. still continued to be rent with those sanguinary feuds. **1876** HOLLAND *Sev. Oaks* xiv. 195 While men are about to rend each others reputations.

b. Used to denote the effect of sounds, esp. loud noises, on the air.

1602 SHAKS. *Ham.* II. ii. 509 Anon the dreadfull Thunder Doth rend the region. **1667** MILTON *P.L.* XII. 182 Thunder mixt with Haile.. must rend th' Egyptian Skie. **1697** DRYDEN *Virg. Georg.* I. 557 Then, thrice the Ravens rend the liquid Air. **1738** GRAY *Propertius* iii. 47 While the vaulted Skies loud Ios rend. **1844** THIRLWALL *Greece* lxiv. VIII. 318 A shout of joy rent the air.

c. To lacerate (the heart, soul, etc.) with painful feelings.

a **1591** H. SMITH *Serm.* (1637) 614 His heart is not rent, his mind is not troubled. **1666** BUNYAN *Grace Ab.* §104 That Scripture did also tear and rend my soul. **1766** GOLDSM. *Hermit* xl, The sigh that rends thy constant heart Shall break thy Edwin's too. **1877** 'RITA' *Vivienne* III. vii, His strong frame rent and shaken by a storm of emotion. **1891** E. PEACOCK *N. Brendon* II. 87 Her heart was rent by contending emotions.

5. *absol.* To tear; to act by tearing.

c **1250** *Gen. & Ex.* 3506 Ne slo ðu nogt wið hond ne wil, Ne rend, ne beat nogt wið vn-skil. **1388** WYCLIF *Jer.* xv. 3 A swerd to sleeynge, and doggis for to reende. *c* **1400** *Destr. Troy* 10209 He hurlit of helmys, hedis within, Rent thurgh ribbis. **1607** SHAKS. *Cor.* III. i. 248 Whose Rage doth rend Like interrupted Waters. **1641** MILTON *Ch. Govt.* I. vi. Wks. 1851 III. 122 If schisme parted the congregations before, now it rent and mangl'd. **1818** SHELLEY *Julian* 357 The dagger heals not, but may rend again. **1876** BLACKIE *Songs Relig. & Life* 240 Never cast your pearls to swine, Who turn, and rend and trample.

6. *intr.* To burst, split, break, or tear. Also *fig.*

c **1205** LAY. 7849 Scipen gunnen helden, bosmes þer rendden, water in wende. *c* **1470** *Golagros & Gaw.* 691 Ryngis of rank steill rattillit and rent. **1578** T. PROCTOR *Gorg. Gallery* Biij, I should.. heale that hart that rendes. **1589** R. HARVEY *Pl. Perc.* (1590) 25 My shoe shall rend. **1611** BIBLE *1 Sam.* xv. 27 He laid hold vpon the skirt of his mantle, and it rent. **1632** LITHGOW *Trav.* VI. 268 The Rocke, which (as they say) rent at his crucifying. **1705** HICKERINGILL *Priest-cr.* I. Wks. 1716 III. 59 Samuel's Cassock, made of rotten black Cloath, perhaps, or else it would not have rent. **1762** FALCONER *Shipwr.* II. 245 The mizen rending from the bolt-rope flew. **1830** W. TAYLOR *Hist. Surv. Germ. Poetry* I. 277 The veil of the temple rends; an earthquake is felt. **1840** LYELL *Princ. Geol.* II. II. vii. 79 The walls of tenements rending and sinking, until a deep chasm.. was formed.

Hence **'rended** *ppl. a.*[1], torn, rent.

1856 R. A. VAUGHAN *Mystics* (1860) I. 116 Bernard had farther the satisfaction.. of sewing together.. the rended vesture of the papacy. **1872** YEATS *Techn. Hist. Comm.* 305 Straw for plaiting has recently been supplemented.. by the rended leaves of palms.

rend, *v.*[2] *Obs.* exc. *dial.* [f. *rend-*, stem of F. *rendre* RENDER *v.* 17 a: cf. RAND *v.*[4] and RIND *v.*] *trans.* To melt; to produce by melting. Hence **'rended** *ppl. a.*[2]

a **1340** HAMPOLE *Psalter* cv. 19 þe kalfe þai rendid, þe ydol þai made. **1558** *Wills & Inv. N.C.* (Surtees 1835) 167, ij great cakes of rended tallowe xxxiijs. iiijd. **1641** BEST *Farm. Bks.* (Surtees) 30 In makinge of your salve, yow are first to rende or melte your tallowe in a panne.

render ('rɛndə(r)), *sb.*[1] [f. REND *v.*[1] + -ER[1].] One who rends or tears. (Cf. *lath-render*.)

1586 A. DAY *Eng. Secretary* II. (1595) 92 Whie doe you thus vngratefullie.. become.. wretched renders and tearers of your mothers bowels? **1634** CANNE *Necess. Separ.* (1849) 92 The most part of Israel judged them to be renders of the unity of the kirk. **1660** GAUDEN *Brownrig* 240 Our renders will needs be our reformers and repairers.

render ('rɛndə(r)), *sb.*[2] Also 4 rendre, 8 *Sc.* rander. [f. RENDER *v.*]

†**1.** A lesson, repetition. *Obs. rare*$^{-1}$.

c **1325** in *Rel. Ant.* I. 292 Qwan i kan mi lesson [to] mi meyster wil i gon, That heres me mi rendre.

†**2.** The act of rendering up, or making over to another; surrender (of a person or place). *Obs.*

In the *Digby Myst.* (1882) IV. 301 *sure render* is prob. a mistake for *surrender*.

1548 GEST *Pr. Masse* in H. G. Dugdale *Life* (1840) App. I. 98, I meane the applyall and render of the benefyghtes of Christis deth and resurrection. *c* **1600** SHAKS. *Sonn.* cxxv, Take thou my oblacion, poore but free, Which.. knows no art But mutuall render, onely me for thee. **1611** SPEED *Hist. Gt. Brit.* IX. xii. §107. 580/2 Hee also tooke sundry places of speciall importance, some by render, some by assault. **1650** R. STAPYLTON *Strada's Low C. Warres* VIII. 2 The enemies conquest was followed with the present surrender of Middelburg.. By which Render Mondragonio gained such honour as we seldome read parallelled. *c* **1670** HOBBES *Dial. Com. Laws* (1681) 65 If any Man would render himself to the Judgment of the King, where the King hath committed all his power judicial to another, such a render should be to no effect.

3. *Law.* **a.** (Usu. *grant and render*: cf. the vb. 3b.) A return made by the cognizee to the cognizor in a fine; a conveyance of this nature.

For legal details see esp. Cruise *Digest* (1818) V. 107 ff.

[**1581** KITCHIN *Le Covrte Leete*, etc. 153 Fine sur graunt & render, per que le conisee graunt & render al conisour les terres en taile.] **1594** WEST *2nd Pt. Symbol.* §52 A Tenant for life may not without danger to lose his estate, be cognisor in a fine upon grant and render. **1628** COKE *On Litt.* 353 Here it is proved by Littleton, that the grant and render.. is not void. **1651** tr. *Sir J. Davies' Abridg. Reports* II. 41 A fine with grant and render implies a consideration in it selfe. **1727–38** CHAMBERS *Cycl.* s.v., A fine with render is that whereby something is rendered back again by the cognisee to the cognisor. **1773** SALKELD *Reports* s.v. *Fines* 3 G, Fine and Render is a conveyance at Common Law and the Render makes the Conusor a new Purchaser. **1818** CRUISE *Digest* (ed. 2) V. 108 In a fine of this sort, the render must be made of the lands demanded in the original writ, or of something issuing out of those lands.

b. A return in money or kind, or in some service, made by a tenant to the superior.

1647 N. BACON *Disc. Govt. Eng.* I. xxxi. (1739) 47 With a render of rent, which in those days was of Corn or other Victual. **1765** BLACKSTONE *Comm.* I. 221 It is frequent in domesday-book, after specifying the rent due to the crown, to add likewise the quantity of gold or other renders reserved to the queen. **1766** *Ibid.* II. 290 This render.. in socage.. usually consists of money, though it may consist of services still, or of any other certain profit. **1848** PETRIE tr. *A.-S. Chron.* 458/2 They swore.. that they would.. make such renders from the land as had been done before to any other King. **1897** MAITLAND *Domesday & Beyond* 169 Payments in money and renders in kind.

†**c.** *in render*: (see quot. 1607). *Obs.*

1607 COWELL *Interpr.* s.v. *Render*, Also there be certaine things in a maner.. that lie in Render, that is, must be deliuered or answered by the Tenent, as rents, reliefes, heriots, and other seruices. **1741** T. ROBINSON *Gavelkind* i. 3 All Socage Services whatever which lie in Render. **1742** VINER *Abridgment* XIV. 136 If a Thing which lies in Render be granted to another and his Heirs annually, the Non-Payment of it in one Year shall not be any Discharge.

d. The act of performing a service.

1832 AUSTIN *Jurispr.* (1879) I. vi. 325 If each of us promise the other to render the other a service, but the render of either of the services is not made to depend on the render of the other.

†**4.** The act of rendering an account, statement, etc.; an account of expenses. *Obs.*

1611 SHAKS. *Cymb.* IV. iv. 11 Newnesse Of Clotens death.. may driue vs to a render Where we haue liu'd. *Ibid.* v. iv. 17 If of my Freedome 'tis the maine part, take No stricter render of me, then my All. *a* **1734** NORTH *Lives* (1826) III. 177 At the young lord's full age the books themselves, in which stood every farthing accountable in proper place, were exhibited for a render of his accounts. **1768** ROSS *Helenore* 113 The squire ordain'd nae rander to be kept.

5. The first coat of plaster or the like applied to a brick or stone surface.

1833 LOUDON *Encycl. Archit.* 221 One hundred and fifty yards of render and set. **1858** *Skyring's Builders' Prices* 80 Rough render in cement and sand, per yard.

render ('rɛndə(r)), *v.* Also 4–8 rendre, 6–7 *Sc.* rendir, ran(n)der. [a. OF. *rendre*:—pop. Lat. **rendĕre* (also found in med.L.) an alteration, on anal. of *prendĕre*, of class.L. *reddĕre* to give back, f. *red-* RE- + *dare* to give.]

I. †**1.** *trans.* To repeat (something learned); to say over, recite; ? to commit to memory. *Obs.*

In quot. 1362 the reading *rendred* is supported by the alliteration and the later versions: cf. also A. IX. 82.

c **1325** in *Rel. Ant.* I. 292, I donke upon David til mi tonge talmes; I ne rendrede nowt, sithen men beren palmes. **1362** LANGL. *P. Pl.* A. v. 125, I drouȝ me a-mong þis drapers my Donet to leorne.. Among þis Riche Rayes lernde I [*v.r.* I rendrit] a Lessun. **1393** *Ibid.* C. XVIII. 322 Til þei couþe speke and spelle.. Recorden hit and rendren hit. *c* **1400** *Rom. Rose* 4800 It is so writen in my thought,.. That all by herte I can it render. **1530** PALSGR. 685/2, I rendre my lesson, as a chylde dothe. **1560** ROLLAND *Crt. Venus* I. 48 With orisounis.. I randerit ouir to God Omnipotent. **1565** COOPER *Thesaurus*, *Decantare*,.. to render or repete.

†**b.** With *out*: To relate, narrate. *Obs. rare*$^{-1}$.

c **1400** *Beryn* 450 Kit be-gan to rendir out al thing as it was.

2. To give in return, to make return of. Now somewhat *rare*.

c **1477** CAXTON *Jason* 18 He salwed her and she rendrid to him his salewe. **1484** —— *Fables of Æsop* v. iv, Men ought not to rendre euylle for good. **1509** HAWES *Past. Pleas.* XI. (Percy Soc.) 46 In thy youth the scyence engender That in thyne age it may the worship render. *a* **1548** HALL *Chron.*, *Hen. VIII* 171 b, He sheweth himself ingrate and vngentle, and for kyndnes rendereth vnkyndnes. **1582** STANYHURST *Æneis* II. (Arb.) 54 Scant sayd I theese speeches, when woords to me dolful he rendred. **1612** T. TAYLOR *Comm. Titus* i. 8 It is iust with God (saith Paul) to render tribulation to those that afflict his Saints. **1671** MILTON *Samson* 1232 Can my ears unus'd Hear these dishonours, and not render death? **1715** POPE *Iliad* II. 423 Till Helen's woes at full reveng'd appear, And Troy's proud matrons render tear for tear. **1784** COWPER *Task* VI. 959 Receiving benefits and rendering none. **1875** JOWETT *Plato* (ed. 2) III. 15 Ought we to render evil for evil at all..?

b. To return (thanks).

1484 CAXTON *Fables of Æsop* III. i, Al maner of folke ought to rendre and gyue thankynges.. to theyr good doers. *a* **1533** LD. BERNERS *Huon* lxii. 218, I can not render thankes to your holynes for yᵉ good that ye haue done to vs. **1552** *Bk. Com. Prayer, Morn. Prayer*, To rendre thankes for the greate benefytes that we haue receyued at his handes. **1600** SHAKS. *A.Y.L.* II. v. 29 Me thinkes I haue giuen him a penie, and he renders me the beggerly thankes. **1667** MILTON *P.L.* VIII. 6 What thanks sufficient, or what recompence Equal have I to render thee? **1730** A. GORDON *Maffei's Amphith.* 127 The rendering Thanks for the Victory. **1852** TENNYSON *Ode Dk. Wellington* 48 Render thanks to the Giver.

†**c.** To recompense, requite. *Obs. rare.*

1560 BIBLE (Genev.) *Judg.* ix. 56 Thus God rendred the wickednes of Abimelech.. in slaying his seventy brethren.

†**d.** *absol.* To make return or recompense. *Obs.*

1560 BIBLE (Genev.) *Job* xxxiv. 11 For he wil rendre vnto man according to his worke.

3. To give (†or hand) back, to restore. Also with *again* or *back*.

1513 DOUGLAS *Æneis* XII. Prol. 92 Rendryng.. the gers pilis thar hycht Als far as catal.. Had in thar pastur eyt and knyp away. *a* **1533** LD. BERNERS *Huon* lix. 203, I render agayne to you all your londes. **1582** N. T. (Rhem.) *Luke* iv. 20 When he had folded the booke, he rendred it to the minister. **1611** BEAUM. & FL. *King & No K.* III. ii, I beseech your Lordship to render me my knife again. **1667** MILTON *P.L.* x. 749 Desirous to resigne, and render back All I receav'd. **1791** COWPER *Iliad* III. 347 Then Troy shall render back what she detains. **1879** R. T. SMITH *Basil the Great* viii. 99 The Lord.. rendering back to man again the grace which he.. had lost.

absol. **1562** A. SCOTT *Poems* (S.T.S.) i. 146 Reddie ressauaris, bot to rander nocht.

b. *Law* (usu. *grant and render*). Of a cognizee: To make over as a return to the cognizor in a fine. (Cf. the sb. 3 a.)

1594 WEST *2nd Pt. Symbol.* §58 None can take by the first estate granted or rendred by a fine, but some of the parties named in the writ. **1607** COWELL *Interpr.* s.v. *Render*, A fine is either single, by which nothing is graunted, or rendred backe againe by the Cognizee, to the Cognizour: or double. **1653** tr. *Kitchin's Courts Leet*, etc. (ed. 2) 299 A Fine upon grant and render, by which the Conisee grants and renders to the Conisor, the Lands in taile. **1766** BLACKSTONE *Comm.* II. xxi. 354 The cognizee, after the right is acknowledged to be in him, grants back again, or renders to the cognizor.. some other estate in the premises. **1818** CRUISE *Digest* V. 261 They by the same fine granted and rendered the same lands to the use of the said I.S.

c. To give back, return (a sound, image, etc.) by reflection or repercussion. Also with *back*.

a **1600** MONTGOMERIE *Misc. Poems* viii. 30 The roches rings, and rendirs me my cryis. **1606** SHAKS. *Tr. & Cr.* III. iii. 122 Who.. like a gate of steele, Fronting the sunne, receiues and renders backe His figure, and his heate. **1697** DRYDEN *Virg. Georg.* IV. 69 Hollow Rocks that render back the Sound, And doubled Images of Voice rebound. **1822** SHELLEY *When the lamp is shattered* ii, The heart's echoes render No song when the spirit is mute.

fig. **1596** SHAKS. *1 Hen. IV*, III. ii. 82 [They] rendred such aspect As Cloudie men vse to doe to their aduersaries.

4. To reproduce or represent, esp. by artistic means, to depict.

1599 SHAKS. *Hen. V*, I. i. 44 List his discourse of Warre; and you shall heare A fearefull Battaile rendred you in Musique. **1762–71** H. WALPOLE *Vertue's Anecd. Paint.* (1786) IV. 195 Devoid of imagination.. he could render nothing but what he saw before his eyes. **1859** TENNYSON *Elaine* 797 The strange-statued gate Where Arthur's wars were render'd mystically. **1870** MAX MÜLLER *Sc. Relig.* (1873) 276 A name that should approximately or metaphorically render at least one of its most prominent features. **1885** *Truth* 28 May 848/2 The spray is rendered with much lightness and delicacy.

b. To play or perform (music).

a **1676** HALE *Prim. Orig. Man.* (1677) 66 As the Organ or Pipe renders the Tune which it understands not. **1777** SIR W. JONES *Ess. Imit. Arts* Poems, etc. 198 Some intervals, which cannot easily be rendered on our instruments. **1867** FREEMAN in Stephens *Life & Lett.* (1895) I. 381 The services were magnificently done—'rendered' I suppose I should say. **1893** *Daily News* 25 May 5/3 The band and muffled drums rendering the Dead March in 'Saul'.

†**5.** To represent or describe (a person or thing) as being of a certain character or in a certain state; to give or make (one) out to be. *Obs.*

1600 SHAKS. *A.Y.L.* IV. iii. 123 O, I haue heard him speake of that same brother, And he did render him the most vnnaturall That liu'd amongst men. **1601** —— *All's Well* I. iii. 236 There is a remedie.. To cure the desperate languishings whereof The King is render'd lost. **1641** *Vind. Smectymnuus* Pref., He endeavours to render us to the Reader as destitute of all learning. **1705** in *Pennsylv. Hist. Soc. Mem.* X. 81 He has taken the liberty to render thy keeping a coach.. to be not at all with the appearance of a Quaker. **1726** *Col. Rec. Pennsylv.* III. 255 That to do right is not so difficult a Task as some would render it.

†**b.** To show, demonstrate. *Obs. rare*$^{-1}$.

1678 BUNYAN *Pilgr.* I. 205 Thou.. hast such an opinion of thyself, and of what thou doest, as plainly renders thee to be one that did never see a necessity [etc.].

6. To reproduce or express in another language, to translate. Also const. *into*.

1610 T. LORKIN in Ellis *Orig. Lett.* Ser. II. III. 221 Two other houres he spends in French; one in reading, the other in rendring to his teacher some part of a Latine author by word of mouth. **1631** R. BYFIELD *Doctr. Sabb.* 102 That place in Exo. 23. 12.. is abusively rendred by you. **1661** BOYLE *Style of Script.* (1675) 10 A skilful interpreter may happily enough render into his own language a great part of what he translates. **1724** A. COLLINS *Gr. Chr. Relig.* 212 He.. takes them from the Hebrew,.. and not as the Septuagint has rendered it. **1798** FERRIAR *Illustr. Sterne* i. 13 The oldest [edition] which remains was rendered into 'beau langage'. **1855** PUSEY *Doctr. Real Presence* Note S. 338, I have rendered the whole [inscription] without doubt, as addressed to the Christian. **1875** JOWETT *Plato* (ed. 2) I. 3 The word has been rendered in different places either Temperance or Wisdom.

b. To make out, succeed in reading. *rare*$^{-1}$.

1864 EMILY DICKINSON *Lett.* (1894) II. 311 Can you render my pencil? The physician has taken away my pen.

II. 7. To hand over, deliver, commend, or commit, to another; to give, in various senses, †to grant, concede.

c **1375** *Sc. Leg. Saints* xxx. (*Theodora*) 406 þat scho mycht þare resawit be, & tak þe habyt, &..rendryt be to þame as bruthyre. **1547–64** BAULDWIN *Mor. Philos.* (Palfr.) 104 b, By pacience we are rendred unto god and proved amongest men. **1596** SHAKS. *Merch. V.* III. iv. 49 Take this same letter, And..see thou render this Into my cosin's hand. **1607** —— *Cor.* I. ix. 34 Of all the treasure in this field atcheiued..We render you the Tenth. **1616** CHAPMAN *Homer's Hymn Apollo* 117 To render the effect Of mens demands to them, before they fall. **1671** MILTON *P.R.* III. 369 It shall be my task To render thee the Parthian at dispose. **1766** BLACKSTONE *Comm.* II. 450 The contract of sale shall not bind him so as that he shall render the price. **1826** KIRBY & SP. *Entomol.* xl. IV. 101 Organs that secrete the gastric juice and render it to the stomach. **1859** TENNYSON *Geraint* 452 Affirming that his father left him gold..which was not render'd to him.

absol. **1606** SHAKS. *Tr. & Cr.* IV. v. 36 In kissing doe you render, or receiue? *Patr.* Both take and giue.

transf. **1670–98** LASSELS *Voy. Italy* II. 31 These stairs render you up at the Great Hall.

8. To give up, surrender, resign, relinquish. Also with *up*.

c **1400** *Destr. Troy* 13069 Then prinses..Saydon Orestes be right shuld render his londes, And be exilede. **1494** FABYAN *Chron.* VI. ccxvii. 236 Accordynge to his othe, he shulde render the lande, or delyuer it vnto the possessyon of William. **1523** LD. BERNERS *Froiss.* I. ccxii. 258 The frenche kynge..shall rendre and delyuer to the sayde kynge of Englande..the honours, regalities, obeisaunce, homages [etc.]. **1567** *Gude & Godlie B.* (S.T.S.) 162 My spreit I rander in thy handis, Eternal God of veritie. **1590** SHAKS. *Mids. N.* II. i. 185 Ile make her render vp her Page to me. **1606** —— *Ant. & Cl.* IV. xiv. 33 She rendred life, Thy name so buried in her. **1673** *S' too him Bayes* 29, I render my cause, as the sword-men would have it. **1697** DRYDEN *Virg. Georg.* III. 744 The thriven Calves..render their sweet Souls before the plenteous Rack. **1703** ROWE *Ulysses* IV. i, I have learnt to hold My Life from none, but from the Gods who gave it, Nor mean to render it on any Terms. **1820** SHELLEY *Liberty* xiv, Tomb of Arminius! render up thy dead. **1868** GEO. ELIOT *Sp. Gipsy* v. 350 Her Queen Mounted the steps again and took her place, Which Juan rendered silently. **1875** JOWETT *Plato* (ed. 2) I. 216 To this royal or political art all the arts..seemed to render up the supremacy.

b. *esp.* To surrender (a stronghold, town, etc.) to the enemy.

1481 CAXTON *Godfrey* cxliii. 214 They alle shold..bere with them suche goodes as they had, and rendre and gyue ouer the dongeon. *a* **1548** HALL *Chron., Hen. VIII* 84 There was a mutteryng that the toune of Caleys should be rendred into the Frenche kinges handes. **1560** DAUS tr. *Sleidane's Comm.* 90 When the toune was ones rendred, the Byshop of Rome, Clement, chopped of the heades of certen of the Senatours. **1606** SHAKS. *Ant. & Cl.* III. x. 33 To Cæsar will I render My legions and my Horse. **1662** J. DAVIES tr. *Mandelslo's Trav.* 96 After he had held out six dayes, he was forc't to render it and himself up at mercy. **1759** *Hist. War in Ann. Reg.* 42/2 The capital of French America was rendered to the English, after a most severe campaign. **1823** BYRON *Juan* VIII. lxxxvii, The city's taken, but not render'd! **1865** TRENCH *Gustavus Adolphus* ii. 79 In the city rendered by compact, and not taken by storm.

c. *refl.* To give (oneself) up; to surrender.

1549 *Compl. Scot.* xiv. 113 Sa mony castellis and tounis quhilkis hed randrit them be trason to Annibal. **1602** SHAKS. *Ham.* I. v. 4 My hower is almost come, When I to sulphurous and tormenting Flames Must render vp my selfe. *a* **1671** LD. FAIRFAX *Mem.* (1699) 33, I thought it not fit now..to bid the rest to render themselves to me. **1702** *Lond. Gaz.* No. 3885/1 Such Seamen..who..shall Render themselves.., shall not be Prosecuted before a Court Marshal. **1752** J. LOUTHIAN *Form of Process* (ed. 2) 179 Those that are in default till the Exigent in Treason, tho' they render themselves to Justice, forfeit their Chattels. **1821** SHELLEY *Hellas* 386 Then said the Pacha, 'Slaves, Render yourselves—they have abandoned you'. **1863** MRS. A. E. CHALLICE *Heroes*, etc. *Louis XVI*, II. 247 Lord Cornwallis and his army rendered themselves prisoners of War.

†**d.** *intr.* = prec. *Obs.*

1523 *St. Papers Hen. VIII*, VI. 213 They renderyd be such appoinctement, that they went in ther schyrtes with stykkes in ther handes. **1589** *Late Voy. Sp. & Port.* (1881) 85 Upon the first Fire thereof he rendered, and compounded to goe away with his baggage and Armes. **1632** LITHGOW *Trav.* II. 60 The passengers gaue counsell, rather to render, then fight. **1688** SHADWELL *Sqr. Alsatia* IV. i, I am ready to render on Discretion.

†**9.** To send *forth* properly provided. *Obs.*$^{-1}$

1390 GOWER *Conf.* III. 314 Al only at his oghne cost Sche schal be rendred forth with hire.

†**b.** To give out, emit, discharge. *Obs.*

1481 CAXTON *Godfrey* clxxii. 254 Without the toun..ben founden somme fontaynes, but they be but fewe and they rendre but lytil water. **1483** —— *G. de la Tour* H iv, Her holy body rendrid holy oyle. *c* **1500** *Melusine* 317 They al lamented..& rendred teerys in habundance. **1513** DOUGLAS *Æneis* IX. x. 65 Quhayr as the quhissyll rendris soundis seyr. **1607** TOPSELL *Four-f. Beasts* (1658) 80 Although it were a male, yet it did render his urine backward. **1659** LEAK *Waterwks.* 16 A Vessell..to receive the Water..and to render it by the Pipe 7. **1705–30** S. GALE in Nichols *Bibl. Topogr. Brit.* (1790) III. 7 The whole of cedar, which renders a fine fragrancy.

†**c.** To bring forth (young). *Obs. rare*$^{-1}$.

1607 TOPSELL *Four-f. Beasts* (1658) 18 In the twelfe moneth after their copulation, they render their foles.

10. To give (an account, reason, answer, etc.); to submit to, or lay before, another for consideration or approval; also, in mod. use, to send in (an account) to a customer or purchaser.

1481 CAXTON *Myrr.* I. v. 22 And there eche rendred his reson of that he had found and lerned. **1548–9** (Mar.) *Bk. Com. Prayer, Of Ceremonies*, Here be certayne causes rendered, why some of the accustomed Ceremonies be put awaye. **1599** SHAKS. *Much Ado* IV. i. 337, I will challenge him:..By this hand, Claudio shall render me a deere account. **1603** —— *Meas. for M.* I. iii. 49 Moe reasons for this action At our more leysure, shall I render you. **1651** HOBBES *Leviath.* III. xxxiii. 205 There can be rendred no one generall answer for them all. **1662** STILLINGFL. *Orig. Sacræ* III. ii. §14 To see how well he acquits himself in rendring an account of the Origine of the Universe. **1753** JOHNSON *Diary* 3 Apr. in *Boswell*, When I shall render up, at the last day, an account of the talent committed to me. **1795** NELSON in Nicolas *Disp.* (1845) II. 76 It is with the greatest pain I have to render so long a list of killed and wounded. **1838–9** FR. A. KEMBLE *Resid. Georgia* (1863) 42 At the head of each gang [of negroes] is a driver,..who renders an account of each individual slave and his work every evening to the overseer. **1842** TENNYSON *Morte d'Arth.* 74 Thou hast betray'd thy nature and thy name, Not rendering true answer, as beseemed Thy fealty.

†**b.** To declare, state. *Obs. rare.*

1611 SHAKS. *Cymb.* II. iv. 119 Render to me some corporall signe about her More euident then this. *Ibid.* v. v. 135 My boone is that this Gentleman may render Of whom he had this Ring.

11. To pay as a rent, tax, or tribute, or other acknowledgement of dependence. (Cf. the sb. 3 b.)

1526 TINDALE *Prol. Matt.* Wks. (1573) 35/1 The husband-men..would not render to the Lorde of the fruit in due tyme, and therfore [it] was taken from them. **1611** BIBLE *Mark* xii. 17 Render to Cesar the things that are Cesars. **1642** tr. *Perkins' Prof. Bk.* v. §434. 187 If the tenant had been by fealtie and a horse to be rendred yearely. **1727–38** CHAMBERS *Cycl.* s.v. *Render* sb., Other [things] which lie in render, that is, must be rendered or answered by the tenant, as rents, reliefs, heriots, and other services. **1809** BAWDWEN *Domesday Bk.* 317 It is soke, and it is waste, and it renders a pair of spurs. **1874** GREEN *Short Hist.* iv. §1. 158 The successors..swore to observe the old fealty and render the old tribute to the English Crown.

fig. **1588** SHAKS. *Tit. A.* I. i. 160 My tributarie teares, I render for my Bretherens Obsequies.

†**b.** To bring in, yield (a revenue). *Obs.*$^{-1}$

1687 A. LOVELL tr. *Thevenot's Trav.* I. 16 The Jesuites have a Garden, full of Fruit-trees of all sorts, which render them a considerable Revenue yearly.

12. To give, pay, exhibit, or show (obedience, honour, attention, etc.); to do (a service).

1588 J. CRAIG in *Cath. Tract.* (S.T.S.) 249 The honour of God to whilkes al christien men ar oblesed..to rander obedience. **1630** *R. Johnson's Kingd. & Commw.* 123 Fealty and homage;..which he hath ever since the time of Francis the first, denied to render. **1649** BP. REYNOLDS *Hosea* v. 8 Our mouthes wide opened in rendring honour unto him. **1847** MARRYAT *Childr. N. Forest* xvii, I feel indebted to you for the service you have rendered me. **1853** C. BRONTE *Villette* xv, There were personal attentions to be rendered. **1880** L. STEPHEN *Pope* iii. 78 Two friends who were to render him some undefined assistance.

fig. **1599** SHAKS. *Much Ado* v. iii. 33 And Hymen now with luckier issue speeds, Then this for whom we rendred vp this woe.

13. *refl.* To present (oneself), take steps to be *at* (†or *in*) a certain place. Hence *intr.* to be present; to hold, obtain (*rare*).

1619 in *Eng. & Germ.* (Camden) 82 In regard of the great diligence he is to make to render himself in Germany with all speede possible. **1640** tr. *Verdere's Rom. of Rom.* I. 1 All those Princes..rendred themselves at the Tent of the Emperour Amadis of Greece. **1709** MRS. MANLEY *Secret Mem.* II. 79 Rendring himself at the Garden-gate, by Virtue of his Key, he open'd it. **1754** FRANKLIN *Plan of Union* Wks. 1887 II. 361 The most distant members..may probably render themselves at Philadelphia in fifteen to twenty days. **1821** SHELLEY *Sel. Lett.* (1882) 173 The tocsin of the Convent sounded, and it required all the efforts of the Prioress to prevent the Spouses of God from rendering themselves..to the accustomed signal. **1852** MRS. CARLYLE *Lett.* II. 166, I rendered myself at Paddington station on Friday morning. **1874** COUES *Birds N.W.* 374, I believe that some such quality..renders in the whole order.

†**b.** *trans.* in similar use. *Obs. rare.*

a **1637** B. JONSON *Forest* iv, *To World* viii, What bird or beast..That fled his cage,..wull Render his head in there againe! *c* **1645** HOWELL *Lett.* (1650) I. 89 Every soldier..costing him near upon 100 crowns before he could be rendered in Flanders.

c. To infuse (a quality) *into* a thing. *rare*$^{-1}$.

a **1887** R. JEFFERIES *The Open Air* (1893) 243, I wonder the painters..do not sometimes take these scraps of earth and render into them the idea which fills a clod with beauty.

III. 14. To bring (one) *into* a state or condition (*obs.*); also, to cause to be *in* a certain state. *rare.*

1490 CAXTON *Eneydos* ix. 37 That it maye playse the..to rendre theym from theyr lacyuyte in-to..shamefaste chastyte. **1633** FORD *Broken H.* IV. i, Quiet These vain unruly passions which will render you Into a madness. *a* **1676** HALE *Prim. Orig. Man.* (1677) 67 He is rendred into a capacity, 1. Of knowing Him: 2. Of knowing his Will. **1707** *Curios. in Husb. & Gard.* 305 Homberg, whose great Capacity..has render'd him in mighty Esteem with all the Learned. **1810** S. GREEN *Reformist* I. 137 The visionary schemes of fanaticism rendered the thoughts of Percival in continual terror of all worldly pleasure.

†**b.** To present or expose *to*, to bring *under*, something. *Obs.*

1642 FULLER *Holy & Prof. St.* IV. xv. 312 Her private virtues rendring her to the imitation..of all. **1647** N. BACON *Disc. Govt. Eng.* I. xxxviii. (1739) 57 Twelve men enquired of the fame and ground thereof; which if liked, rendred the party under the spot of delinquency. *a* **1661** FULLER *Worthies* (1840) I. 276 His having a prince's mind imprisoned in a poor man's purse rendered him to the contempt of such who were not ingenuous.

15. To make, to cause to be or become, of a certain nature, quality, etc. (Cf. MAKE *v.* 48.)

1560 DAUS tr. *Sleidane's Comm.* 197 It was ones possessed of Englysh men, but it was rendred Frenche, in the tyme of Charles the first. **1596** SHAKS. *Merch. V.* III. ii. 88 These assume but valors excrement, To render them redoubted. **1601** —— *Jul. C.* II. i. 303 O ye Gods! Render me worthy of this Noble Wife. **1654** H. L'ESTRANGE *Chas. I* (1655) 146 That [testimony] once rendred in-valid, the Bishop could easily prognosticate his own ruine. **1671** MILTON *Samson* 1282 He..Thir Armories and Magazins contemns, Renders them useless. **1705** ADDISON *Italy* 2 The Desarts that haue been render'd so famous by the Penance of Mary Magdalene. **1771** *Junius Lett.* lxvii. (1788) 340 *note*, He had a friend..whose advice rendered all their endeavours ineffectual. **1818** CRUISE *Digest* (ed. 2) VI. 357 Cases in which superadded words of limitation may control the word heirs, so as to render them words of purchase. **1844** H. H. WILSON *Brit. India* III. 66 The total silence..rendered it probable, that the Burmas had not awaited the assault. **1860** TYNDALL *Glac.* II. xix. 334 The absorbed heat is expended in rendering the substance viscous. **1886** R. C. LESLIE *Sea-painter's Log* 120 The big hybrid screw liners had already rendered H.M.S. Queen an obsolete type.

refl. **1652** HOWELL *Giraffi's Rev. Naples* II. 85 The Spaniards also having rendred themselves masters of so many Posts. **1698** FRYER *Acc. E. India & P.* 271 From a Salvage Prince [he] rendred himself a tame Follower of the Patriarch.

†**b.** Const. with *as* or *to be*. *Obs.*

1663 GERBIER *Counsel* 51 The Tiler..renders the Noble mans roof, as a beggars Coate. **1665** J. WEBB *Stone-Heng* (1725) 15 So many Segments..as are taken away, renders the Figure inscribed to be a so-many-sided Figure. **1719** W. WOOD *Surv. Trade* 137 By this means we render Foreign Colonies and Plantations, to be in effect the Colonies and Plantations of Great-Britain. **1796** MORSE *Amer. Geog.* II. 81 The great reformations introduced.., as well as the discoveries made, render former accounts to be but little depended on.

†**16.** To cause, produce (a feeling). *Obs. rare*$^{-1}$.

1654 tr. *Scudery's Curia Pol.* 1 This action is of such an..extraordinary nature, as may render astonishment to the..most capeable understandings.

IV. 17. *techn.* **a.** To melt (fat, etc.); to obtain or extract by melting; to clarify. Cf. REND *v.*^{2}

c **1375**- [see RENDERED *ppl. a.*]. **1688** R. HOLME *Armoury* III. 102/2 Render the Tallow, is to poure it through a Strainer, to keep the Dross from the pure Tallow. **1823** J. BADCOCK *Dom. Amusem.* 149 The fat..being rendered, or melted down. **1844** H. STEPHENS *Bk. Farm* II. 243 Hog's lard is rendered in exactly the same manner as mutton suet. **1875** *Ure's Dict. Arts* (ed. 7) III. 453 It is understood that twelve hours suffice to render the oil.

b. *Plastering.* To cover (stone or brickwork) with a first coating of plaster. Cf. RENDER-SET.

1750 *Wren's Parentalia* 309 St. Andrew's Wardrobe Church..was..built of Brick, but finished or rendered over in imitation of Stone. **1756** in Willis & Clark *Cambridge* (1886) II. 530 For rendring the walls of the Stair-cases and ceilings of the same. **1826** GWILT *Rudiments Archit.* Gloss. s.v., The first of three Coat work upon laths, or on brick work, which has been previously rendered. **1843** *Jrnl. R. Agric. Soc.* IV. II. 363 Of outside wall..208 square yards, which must be 'rendered' within if built with stone. **1847** SMEATON *Builder's Man.* 128 Rendering is the first coat upon a naked wall; thus we say, rendered and set... Render, float, and set, is three-coat work.

c. *Naut.* (See quots. and RENDERING *vbl. sb.* 3 b.)

1841 R. H. DANA *Seaman's Man.* 120 *Render*, to pass a rope through a place. A rope is said to render or not, according as it goes freely through any place. **1867** SMYTH *Sailor's Word-bk.* 568 Any rope, hawser, or cable is 'rendered' by easing it round the bitts. *Ibid.*, The rope of a laniard or tackle is said to render when, by pulling upon one part, each other part takes its share of the strain.

renderable ('rɛndərəb(ə)l), *a. rare.* [f. prec. + -ABLE.] Capable of being rendered.

a **1734** NORTH *Lives* (1826) III. 176 So that at all times the books were an account renderable of every branch. **1900** W. W. PEYTON in *Contemp. Rev.* Oct. 528 The word is renderable only by a phrase.

rendered ('rɛndəd), *ppl. a.* [f. RENDER *v.* 17 a + -ED^1.] **1.** Molten, or melted.

c **1375** *Cursor M.* 23314 (Fairf.), In hate brimstane & rendered lede þai salle be sette in þat prisoun. **1541** *Lanc. Wills* (Chetham Soc.) I. 81 Hole cakes of rendred tallow..and oder tallowe unmelted. **1725** BRADLEY *Fam. Dict.* s.v. *Swine*, The Offal of rendred Tallow, which will not melt. **1758** GOLDSM. *Mem. Protestant* (1895) II. 255 The whole Keel is..rubbed with rendered Tallow. **1806** A. HUNTER *Culina* (ed. 3) 94 Fry them with dripping, or rendered suet, until the fish become of a light brown.

2. Of a brick or stone surface: covered with a render (cf. RENDER *sb.*^{2} 5).

1971 *Country Life* 25 Feb. 447 (Advt.), It can be applied to brick, concrete, rendered or roughcast surfaces with equal success. **1973** *Nation Rev.* (Melbourne) 31 Aug. 1450/1 The white rendered, modernised..premises..have been an inconspicuous residential for the past three years. **1978** M. & N. WARD *Home* 90 Stucco-rendered walls.

renderer ('rɛndərə(r)), *sb.* [f. RENDER *v.* + -ER^1.] One who renders, in senses of the vb.

c **1460** *Towneley Myst.* xxx. 146 Here is a bag fulle..Of flytars, of flyars, and renderars of reffys. *a* **1691** BOYLE *Chr. Virtuoso* I. App., Wks. 1772 VI. 679 The Heathen astrologers and renderers of oracles wisely forbore to venture on such predictions. **1695** J. EDWARDS *Perfect. Script.* 528 He is a most exact renderer of the true sense. **1821** SCOTT *Pirate* v, Mrs. Baby, as we have described her, was no willing renderer of the rites of hospitality. **1865** MASSON *Rec. Brit. Philos.* 91 Wordsworth here is but a renderer of the Transcendentalism of Plato.

rendering ('rɛndərɪŋ), *vbl. sb.* [-ING[1].]

1. The action of restoring, surrendering, yielding, giving, etc.; also, that which is yielded or given.

c **1440** *Promp. Parv.* 429/2 Renderynge, *reddicio.* **1474** CAXTON *Chesse* 95 God at the lenyng & the deuyll atte rendryng. **1568** GRAFTON *Chron.* II. 605 To intreate or speake of the rendering of thys towne. **1646** EVANCE *Noble Ord.* 20 The rule of Gods rendrings to the Creature, is according to our workes. *c* **1685** P. HENRY in M. Henry *Wks.* 1853 II. 746/2 Alas! our renderings are nothing to our receivings; we are like the barren field. **1872** RUSKIN *Eagle's N.* §213 Love itself is, in its highest state, the rendering of an exquisite praise to body and soul. **1889** *Times* 10 Dec. 9 The rendering in chromic acid is much higher for the Macedonian mineral.

2. a. Translation, interpretation.

1641 J. JACKSON *True Evang. T.* III. 217 Those.. Translators.. put no more difference betwixt their rendring of Davids Hebrew word, and S. Peters Greek word, but *pursue*, and *ensue*. *a* **1647** FILMER *Patriarcha* ii. §1 (Rtldg.) 22 In the rendering of this place the elder translations have been more faithful. **1774** J. BRYANT *Mythol.* (1775) I. 8 By which is meant the land of Metzor, a different rendering of Mysor. **1863** D. WILSON *Preh. Ann.* II. IV. iv. 286 Some of them are open to conjectural renderings of diverse significance. **1883** M. ARNOLD in *19th Cent.* XIII. 589 Correct rendering is very often conspicuously absent from our authorised version of the Old Testament.

b. Reproduction, representation, performance.

1862 S. LUCAS *Secularia* 67 Almost all the copyists of history hitherto have been more or less mistaken in their rendering of the past. **1881** *Athenæum* 10 Sept. 347/2 The rendering of the cantata.. was excellent. **1893** *Times* 29 Apr. 13/3 The painter has shown himself extremely skilful in his rendering of curious effects of light.

3. *techn.* **a.** The action of plastering with a first coat; the work so done; the plaster thus applied. Also (in Ireland), a coating of mortar used on the underside of slating to keep the slates firm.

1659 HOWELL *Vocab.* li, Lime, oxhair,.. rendring, clear lime. **1663** GERBIER *Counsel* 81 The workmanship only in.. rendering two pence a yard. **1667** PRIMATT *City & C. Build.* 89 For Plaistering, Lathing and Rendring at one shilling a yard. **1707** MORTIMER *Husb.* (1721) I. 383 Rendring on a Brick-wall is Three-pence a Yard. **1798** J. HUTTON *Course Math.* (1828) II. 88 Plasterers' work is of two kinds; namely, ceiling, which is plastering on laths; and rendering, which is plastering on walls. **1825** J. NICHOLSON *Operat. Mechanic* 613 By *set* is denoted a superficial coat of fine stuff or putty upon the rendering. **1889** *21st Rep. Dep. Kpr. Irel.* 18 The dust and broken mortar, which accumulate owing to the fall of the rendering from the roof.

b. Chiefly *Naut.* Yielding, slipping, or running out of tackle or lines.

1769 FALCONER *Dict. Marine* (1780), *Rendering*, as a sea-term,.. is usually expressed of a.. tackle, laniard, or lashing, ..in contra-distinction to sticking or jamming. **1875** KNIGHT *Dict. Mech.* 1916/1 To rack a tackle is to seize the parts together and prevent rendering. **1894** *Outing* (U.S.) XXIV. 227/2 Placing the thumb lightly upon the spool [of the fishing-rod] to control the rendering of the line.

c. Extracting or melting of fat, etc. Also *concr.* and *attrib.*

1792 G. CARTWRIGHT *Jrnl. Labrador* I. p. xiii, *Rendering oil*, a sealer's term for melting fat into oil. *c* **1865** LETHEBY in *Circ. Sc.* I. 94/1 Another mode of rendering, is to submit the melted tallow to the action of steam. **1875** KNIGHT *Dict. Mech.* 1916/2 *Rendering apparatus*, an apparatus for extracting oil or lard from fatty animal matters. **1945** *ABC of Cookery* (Ministry of Food) xii. 46 Rendering means melting to extract the fat from surrounding tissues. **1979** N. & I. LYONS *Champagne Blues* 174 We cook the steak in renderings of pork belly.

'rendering, *ppl. a. rare.* [f. RENDER *v.* + -ING[2].]

†**a.** Giving a reason. **b.** Yielding. *Obs.*

a. 1571 GOLDING *Calvin on Ps.* lx. 13 The copulative (and) is almost by the consente of all men turned here into the rendering particle (for). **1636** B. JONSON *Eng. Gram.* I. xxii, Of Conjunctions.. Rendering are such as yield the cause of a thing going before; as *for, because.*

b. *a* **1600** MONTGOMERIE *Misc. Poems* xxviii. 33 The rendring reid, whilk bouis with euerie blast.

render-set, *v.*, *a.*, and *sb.* [See RENDER *v.* 17 b.]

a. *vb. trans.* To cover (a wall, etc.) with two coats of plaster. **b.** *adj.* Consisting of two coats. **c.** *sb.* Plastering of two coats.

1833 LOUDON *Encycl. Archit.* §80 To lathe.. the ceilings of the kitchen, bed-room,.. render set the walls and partitions. *Ibid.* §89 One hundred and twenty-one and a third yards of render-set plastering. *Ibid.* §246 One hundred and fifty-five yards of floated render set. **1842** GWILT *Archit.* §2248 The following materials are required for 100 yards of render set.

rendezvous ('rɒndɪvu:, 'rɛn-, rɑ̃devu), *sb. Pl.* rendezvous; formerly also rendezvouses. Forms: α. 6–7 **rendez vouz, 7 vous, -vous, -vows, rendesvouz, rendizvouse, 7–8 rendesvous, rendezvouz,** (7 **-vouze,** 8 **-vouse**), 7– **rendezvous;** 6–8 **rendevous, -vouz(e,** 7 **-vouez,** 7 **rendevou, -vow, ren-de-vou.** β. 7 **randez-,** 8 **randizvous;** 6–7 **randevous,** 7 **-vouce, -vouze, -vowes, randivous, -voze, randavus,** 9 *dial.* **randivoose, -vooze;** 7 **randevow, -voo, randavou, -vow,** 9 *dial.* **randivoo, -ibo.** [F., subst. use of *rendez vous* 'present or betake yourselves,' 2nd pl. pres. imper. of *rendre* to RENDER.]

1. *Mil.* **a.** A place appointed for the assembling of troops or armed forces.

1591 CONINGSBY *Siege Rouen* in *Camden Misc.* (1847) I. 22 Our army was marched.. within a myle of Roan, where the rendevous was appoynted. **1600** HOLLAND *Livy* x. xxxiii. 375 He proclaimed the Rendez-vous at Sora, for his Soldiers there to meete. **1625** SIR T. DUTTON in *Fortescue Papers* (Camden) 212 So remote a place as Giteringberke assigned for our randevowes at this tyme of the yeare. **1630** M. GODWYN tr. *Bp. Hereford's Ann. Eng.* 19 Alnewike is appointed the rendez-vous where all the troupes should meete at a set day. **1732** LEDIARD *Sethos* II. VII. 19 It was highly necessary to have a place of arms, a place of defence, and a rendezvous. **1772** SIMES *Milit. Guide* (1781) 11 The order of the march of the troops must be so disposed, that each should arrive at their rendezvous, if possible, on the same day. **1826** SCOTT *Woodst.* xxii, I have.. commissioned arms, levied money, appointed rendezvouses. **1874** FROUDE *Eng. in Irel.* III. x. i. 357 Every man who could shoulder a pike was off to the rendezvous.

b. A place or port fixed upon, or suitable, for the assembling of a fleet or number of ships; also, instructions concerning a rendezvous (quot. 1813).

1600 HAKLUYT *Voy.* (1810) III. 188 Such harbors of the Newfoundland as were agreed for our Rendez-vouz. **1655** *Nicholas Papers* (Camden) II. 180 For the fleet.. Niewport writte that they had their randevous at the Barbados. **1745** P. THOMAS *Jrnl. Anson's Voy.* 65 All the Ships had Orders, in case of Separation, for several Rendezvouses. **1798** NELSON in Nicolas *Disp.* (1846) VII. p. cli, I hope to find all the Frigates on the Rendezvous. **1813** WELLINGTON in Gurw. *Desp.* (1838) XI. 162 It does however appear to me extraordinary that any master of a transport should think of running to any port not in his rendezvous. **1872** YEATS *Growth Comm.* 221 The Dutch West India Company.. found its bay an invaluable rendezvous for the fleet cruising.

†**c.** A station for the supply of men to the navy. *Obs.* Also *attrib.*

1770 *Chron.* in *Ann. Reg.* 169/1 All the rendezvous-lieutenants attended the Lord-Mayor.. in order to have their warrants new backed for pressing. **1771** *Ibid.* 71/2 Hearing he was on board the Oxford at Chatham, she entered at the rendezvous in London, for the same ship.

2. a. In general use: An appointed place of meeting or gathering; a place of common resort.

1594 LYLY *Moth. Bomb.* II. v, A tauerne is the Randeuous, the Exchange, the staple for good fellowes. **1613** OVERBURY *A Wife*, etc. (1638) 297 The bed is the best Rendevou of mankind. **1663** GERBIER *Counsel* 99 Foul creatures, who as soon gotten into a Court make it their randevouze. **1691** WOOD *Ath. Oxon.* I. 500 During his stay in the University of Oxford, his Chamber was the rendezvouz of all the eminent Wits. **1725** POPE *Odyss.* XVIII. 377 Hence to the vagrant's rendezvous repair. **1777** ROBERTSON *Hist. Amer.* (1778) II. v. 110 His quarters became the rendezvouz of the malcontents. **1818** SCOTT *Hrt. Midl.* xi, The place which he had named as a rendezvous.. was held in general to be accursed. **1869** TOZER *Highl. Turkey* I. 308 They have.. the power of meeting on their own account, in which case their rendezvous is a church.

b. *transf.* and *fig.*

1608 E. GRIMSTONE *Hist. France* (1611) A ij b, This citie of Paris,.. the Rendez-vous of the greatest miracles in the world. **1647** HARVEY *Schola Cordis* vii. 8 Thy body is disease's rendevouze. **1679** *Lond. Gaz.* No. 1406/1 Field-Conventicles, those Rendezvouses of Rebellion.

†**3. a.** A place of individual resort; a retreat, refuge. *Obs.*

1596 SHAKS. *1 Hen. IV*, IV. i. 57 A Randeuous, a Home to flye vnto. **1599** —— *Hen. V*, V. i. 88 Newes haue I that my Doll is dead.. and there my rendeuous is quite cut off. **1641** H. THORNDIKE *Govt. Churches* 34 This was a convenient rendez-vous for the Apostle, in the mean while, to preach the Gospel in the parts of Epirus. *c* **1645** HOWELL *Lett.* (1650) I. I. ii, I must make my addresse to you, for I haue no other Rendevous.

†**b.** A last resort or shift. *Obs. rare*[−1].

1599 SHAKS. *Hen. V*, II. i. 18 When I cannot liue any longer, I will doe as I may: That is my rest, that is the rendeuous of it.

†**c.** A depot or store of provisions. *Obs.*[−1]

1608 CAPT. SMITH *True Relat.* 35, 16 daies provision we had.. besides our randevous we could, and might, haue hid in the ground.

†**4. a.** *to make* or *keep* (one's) *rendezvous*, to meet, or be in the habit of meeting, in or at a place. *Obs.*

1599 SANDYS *Europæ Spec.* (1632) 244 Good companions and time-serues, who.. make their Rendez-vows always where the best Cheere is stirring. **1624** GEE *Foot out of Snare* v. 38 The feminine and softer sex.. keep there their Rendeuouz. **1657** *North's Plutarch, Dionysius* 946 To make their rende-vous with their Armes at a day set down at the Towne of the Leontines. **1749** FIELDING *Tom Jones* VIII. xiii, The tavern where we kept our rendezvous.

†**b.** *transf.* of things. *Obs. rare.*

1622 J. REYNOLDS *God's Revenge* III. Hist. xv, The Lake of Geneva.. payes its full tribute, and make[s] its chiefest Rendezvous before that City. **1632** LITHGOW *Trav.* x. 505 There is a certaine place of sea, where these destracted tydes make their rancountering Randeuouze.

5. a. A meeting or assembly held by appointment or arrangement; †also, an assemblage or gathering of persons thus brought together.

1600 FAIRFAX *Tasso* I. xix, The captaines cald foorthwith from euery tent, Vnto the Rende-vous he them inuites. **1628** WITHER *Brit. Rememb.* IV. 211 Her great Hall, wherein So great a Randevow had lately bin. **1672** CAVE *Prim. Chr.* III. ii. (1673) 263 Here was a whole randezvouz of Cripples. **1683** *Brit. Spec.* 78 Here he commands a general Rendezvouz of all his Naval Forces. **1718** BP. HUTCHINSON *Witchcraft* 43 She met a Rendezvous of above Sixty Witches. **1771** SMOLLETT *Humph. Cl.* 17 May, He would not fail to give him the rendezvous at the hour he mentioned. **1819** SCOTT *Ivanhoe* ii, Some rendezvous which had occupied the hours of darkness. **1865** DICKENS *Mut. Fr.* III. vii, As if they had all been out.. and were punctual at a general rendezvous to assist at the secret.

attrib. **1792** A. YOUNG *Trav. France* 57 Music, chess, and the other common amusements of a rendezvouz-room.

†**b.** The assembling, or an assemblage, of things.

1652 J. HALL *Height of Eloquence* p. xxii, It appears not a single passion, but a conflux and general rendez vouz of them all. **1662** STILLINGFL. *Orig. Sacræ* III. ii. §11 All the account we have of the Origine of the world, is from this general Rendes-vous of Atoms in this infinite space. **1680** MORDEN *Geog. Rect.* Introd. (1685) 6 The Ocean is a general Collection or Rendezvouz of all Waters.

c. The pre-arranged meeting (and usu. docking) of two or more spacecraft in space; an instance of this.

1959 *ARS Jrnl.* Aug. 592/1 Many proposed space missions will require achieving rendezvous of two bodies in an orbit about a planet. **1962** F. I. ORDWAY et al. *Basic Astronautics* ix. 385 Orbital operations involving rendezvous with satellites or space stations. **1962** *Listener* 29 Nov. 901/2 The vehicle has to be put into a transfer-orbit which will take it from the Earth inward to the orbit of Venus, meeting the planet at a pre-selected rendezvous. **1965** *Times* 16 Dec. 10/1 The Americans achieved the first rendezvous of man in space today. **1969** *Guardian* 22 July 18/3 About ninety minutes after lift-off Eagle began the complex series of manoeuvres leading to rendezvous. **1973** C. SAGAN *Cosmic Connection* xix. 139 Rendezvous and docking maneuvers are reasonably well developed in manned missions even now.

6. Without article, in *place* (*point, port*, etc.) *of rendezvous.*

1600 J. PORY tr. *Leo's Africa* 45 A place of Rendeuous or meeting for all such as trauell in Carauans from Tombuto. **1658** W. BURTON *Itin. Antonin.* 70 Their place of recourse, or rendezvous, when they acted their seeming extasies. **1711** STEELE *Spect.* No. 49 ¶4 The Coffee-house is the Place of Rendezvous to all that live near it. **1748** *Anson's Voy.* I. vi. 57 The first place of rendezvous should be the bay of port St. Julian. **1833** HT. MARTINEAU *Charmed Sea* vi. 99 The one chosen by the Poles for their point of rendezvous. **1847** DE QUINCEY *Sp. Mil. Nun* x. Wks. 1853 III. 20 St. Lucar being the port of rendezvous for the Peruvian expedition. **1856** R. A. VAUGHAN *Mystics* (1860) II. 101 They themselves indicate neither name nor place of rendezvous.

rendezvous ('rɒndɪvu:, 'rɛn-, -vu:z, rɑ̃devu), *v.* Forms: α. 7 **rendevoze, -vooze, -vouze,** 7–8 **-vouz,** 8 **-vous;** 7–8 **rendes-, rendezvouz(e,** 7– **rendezvous** (7 **-vouse;** *pa. t.* **-voued**). β. 7 **randevous, randezvouse.** [f. prec.]

1. *intr.* To assemble at a place previously appointed; also generally, to assemble, come together, meet: **a.** of troops, fleets, etc.

c **1645** T. TULLY *Siege of Carlisle* (1840) 28 They suborn'd great Companies.. to come and rendevoze at Penrith. **1665** *Surv. Aff. Netherl.* 74, 2800 sail of ships Rendesvouzed in the Sea-towns of Holland. **1678** HICKES in Ellis *Orig. Lett.* Ser. II. IV. 46 Thereupon they resolved to rebel and in order thereto rendezvous this day in the Stewartry of Galloway. **1707** E. CHAMBERLAYNE *Pres. St. Eng.* I. iii. 16 Spithead.. is a Road where the Navy-Royal does frequently Rendevouz. **1780** JEFFERSON *Corr.* Wks. 1859 I. 250 Our new recruits will rendezvous in this State between the 10th and 25th instant. **1817** JAS. MILL *Brit. India* II. IV. i. 38 After rendezvousing at Batavia, the united fleet appeared on the coast of Coromandel. **1885** G. S. FORBES *Wild Life in Canara* 20 They were also instructed to rendezvous promptly.. at any point which might be threatened.

b. of persons in general, animals, or things.

1662 STILLINGFL. *Orig. Sacræ* III. ii. §17 Particles, which will.. never rest till they come to that empty space, where they may again Rendezvous together. **1665** PEPYS *Diary* 13 Sept., Here we rendezvoused at Captain Cocke's, and there eat oysters. **1679** *Establ. Test* 25 In a place remote from his quarter, he rendevouzes with his fellow adventurers. **1700** BLACKMORE *Paraphr., 34th ch. Isa.* 264 The vultures there and all the eagle kind Shall rendezvous. **1771** G. WHITE *Selborne* xlvii, They [swallows] rendezvoused in a neighbour's walnut tree. **1834** MARRYAT *P. Simple* (1863) 46 The Blue Posts, where we always rendezvoused, was hardly opened. **1858** CHAMBERS *Inform.* (ed. 4) I. 709/1 That the herring do not rendezvous even in the deeper parts of our own seas. **1887** STEVENSON *Merry Men*, etc. 285 The fugitives rendezvous'd in the arbour.

c. To band together. *rare*[−1].

1815 MAR. EDGEWORTH *Love & Law* I. ii, They have all rendezvous'd to drive me mad.

d. Of a spacecraft or its crew: to effect a meeting in space, *spec.* to dock with another spacecraft.

1960 *IRE Trans. Aeronaut. & Navig. Electronics* VII. 112/2 The system will eventually rendezvous at R_R. **1966** *Punch* 12 Jan. 68/2 Under bright Uranus We'll rendezvous in space. **1966** *Electronics* 3 Oct. 134, 4 [*sc.* a computer] helped the crew rendezvous and link up with the Agena target on the first orbit. **1969** *Observer* 20 July 7/2 Collins had a difficult time 'space-walking' to an Agena rocket with which they had rendezvoused.

†**2.** Of a commander: To assemble his troops or fleet. *Obs.*

1652 C. B. STAPYLTON *Herodian* 130 There at first he should have rendevoz'd. **1704** HEARNE *Duct. Hist.* (1714) I. 384 Cæsar.. rendevouz'd at Brundusium, shipped off his twelve Legions, and sailed to Epirus. **1745** H. WALPOLE *Lett.* (1846) II. 85 The Duke.. will rendezvous at Stone.

3. a. *trans.* To bring together (troops or ships) at a fixed place. Now only *U.S.*

1654–66 EARL ORRERY *Parthen.* (1676) 672 Having Rendez-vous'd on the Banks of the River Calpes thirty thousand Foot,.. he order'd them to move. *a* **1700** KEN *Edmund* Poet. Wks. 1721 II. 179 Their Naval Strength o'er all their Ports diffus'd, They at a Day appointed rendezvous'd. **1780** JEFFERSON in Sparks *Corr. Amer. Rev.* (1853) III. 11, I think the men will be rendezvoused within the present month. **1895** J. WINSOR *Mississ. Basin* 404

Amherst..had rendezvoused at Oswego about eleven thousand men.

b. To bring together, collect, assemble (persons or things). ? *Obs.*

1670 EACHARD *Cont. Clergy* 34 [He] minces the Text so small, that his Parishioners, until he rendevouz it again, can scarce tell what's become of it. *a* **1680** CHARNOCK *Attrib. God* (1834) II. 371 What legions of angels might he have rendezvoued from heaven. **1719** J. T. PHILIPPS tr. *Thirty-four Confer.* 310 If all Men are to be rendevouz'd in a General Assembly to receive severally every one his Final Doom?

refl. **1674** TILLOTSON *Serm.* i. (1678) 41 How the innumerable blind parts of matter should rendezvous themselves into a world. **1684** T. SMITH in *Phil. Trans.* XIV. 443 The publick Coffee-houses..where the malecontents used to rendezvouz themselves.

†**4.** To crowd *about*, hem in (a person). *Obs.*⁻¹

a **1661** FULLER *Worthies* (1840) II. 326 A gentleman..was so rendezvoused about with beggars in London, that it cost him all the money in his purse to satisfy their importunity.

Hence †**'rendezvouser**, an associate. *Obs.*⁻¹

a **1734** NORTH *Lives* (1826) I. 309 His lordship retained such a veneration for the memory of his noble friend and patron..that all the old rendezvousers with him were so with his lordship.

'rendezvousing, *vbl. sb.* [-ING¹.] The action of the vb. RENDEZVOUS. Also as *ppl. a.*

1679 KING in G. Hickes *Spirit of Popery* 31, I am..far from acknowledging that the Gospel Preached that way, is a Rendezvouzing in Rebellion. **1707** *Vulpone* 22 The rendevouzing Clause of their Act of Security. **1719** *Free-thinker* No. 108. 11, I discovered her, Three Rendezvousing Nights successively, at the Haunted House. **1758** *Descr. Thames* Index 289 Rendezvousing of the Herrings and Cod annually. **1798** *Hull Advertiser* 8 Sept. 2/3 The General was attacked on the very point of rendezvousing. **1965** K. W. GATLAND *Spacecraft & Boosters* II. 90/1 Saint or Satellite Inspector..was intended to provide the capability of rendezvousing with an unidentified satellite orbiting the Earth. **1973** *Daily Colonist* (Victoria, B.C.) 28 Jan. 22/3 Most [clocks] have served rendezvousing couples and time watchers well for many years.

†**'rendible**, *a.*¹ *Obs. rare.* [ad. F. *rendable*: see RENDER *v.* and -ABLE, -IBLE.] That may be given up, or translated.

1611 COTGR., *Rendable*, rendible, renderable, yeeldable, restorable. **1650** HOWELL *Lett.* Addit. xxi. 35 Evry language hath certain Idiomes, proverbs and peculiar expressions of its own which are not rendible in any other but paraphrastically.

'rendible, *a.*² *rare*⁻⁰. [f. REND *v.* + -IBLE.] That may be rent (Worcester 1860).

rending ('rɛndɪŋ), *vbl. sb.* [f. REND *v.*¹ + -ING¹.] The action of the vb.; also with *a* and *pl.*, an instance of this.

c **1400** *Chaucer's Knt.'s T.* 1976 (Harl. MS.), At troye allas þe pite þat was þere, Cracchyng of cheekes, rendyng eek of here. *c* **1440** *Promp. Parv.* 429/2 Rendynge a-sundyr, *laceracio.* **1530** PALSGR. 262/1. **1635** SWAN *Spec. M.* v. §2 (1643) 117 A noise like to the rending of broad cloth. **1651** BAXTER *Inf. Bapt.* 151 The vilest Heresies and rendings of the Church. **1727** BRADLEY *Fam. Dict.* s.v. *Arsenick*, It causes great Pains, Rendings,..violent Vomitings. **1813** BAKEWELL *Introd. Geol.* (1815) 241 Virgil refers to the rending of rocks as one of the common effects of lightning. **1899** *Allbutt's Syst. Med.* VI. 370 The rending or otherwise yielding of the coats of the vessel was accompanied by severe pain.

attrib. **1832** *Quarterly Jrnl. Agric.* III. 651 The next proceeding [in hurdle-making] is rending the different pieces: this is done at the rending frame.

b. A rent piece or fragment. In quot. *fig.*

1859 I. TAYLOR *Logic in Theol.* 234 Men who..bring with them bits and rendings of their academic whims.

'rending, *ppl. a.* [f. as prec. + -ING².] That rends: **a.** In transitive senses.

c **1374** CHAUCER *Boeth.* I. met. i, For lo Rendyng Muses of poetes enditen to me thinges to ben writen. **1683** TRYON *Way to Health* 402 Being of a terrible, rending, tearing, devilish, fierce Nature. *a* **1693** *Urquhart's Rabelais* III. xxxii. 270 Their stinging Acrimony, rending Nitrosity. **1760–72** H. BROOKE *Fool of Qual.* (1809) IV. 79 He speaks peace to the storm of rending passions. **1842** MANNING *Serm.* vii. (1848) I. 101 We have no rending choice to make. **1899** *Allbutt's Syst. Med.* VI. 47 It [anginal pain] may be most acute and agonizing, of a rending character.

b. In intransitive senses.

1718 ROWE tr. *Lucan* I. 289 Darts the swift Lightning from the rending cloud. **1758** BEATTIE *Elegy* 82 O happy stroke, that..Darts through the rending gloom the blaze of day. **1839–52** BAILEY *Festus* 58 The world shall stand still with a rending jar. **1840** R. H. DANA *Bef. Mast* xxxii. 120 With a creaking and rending sound.

rendingly ('rɛndɪŋlɪ), *adv.* [f. RENDING *ppl. a.* + -LY².] In a rending or heart-breaking manner; painfully.

1926 H. CRANE *Let.* 19 Aug. (1965) 273, I have made up a kind of friendship with that idiot boy... He is rendingly beautiful at times.

rendition (rɛn'dɪʃən). [a. obs. F. *rendition* (= Sp. *rendicion*), f. *rendre* to RENDER.]

1. a. The surrender of a place, garrison, possession, etc. (Common in 17th c.)

1601 Q. ELIZ. in Moryson *Itin.* (1617) II. 200 We receiued (with much contentment) the newes of the rendition of Kinsale. **1675** G. TOWERSON *Decalogue* 267 Where the Throne becomes empty, as it is by the Rendition of those that before sate in it. **1691** WOOD *Ath. Oxon.* II. 703 After the rendition of Oxford to the Parliament forces, he lived for some time in the Middle Temple. **1711** *Fingall MSS.* in *10th Rep. Hist. MSS. Comm.* App. V. 169 To freighten..that puissant garrison to a rendition. **1826** SCOTT *Mal. Malagr.* i, Not in right of conquest, or rendition. **1894** *Athenæum* 26 May 678/1 He then discusses..the rendition of Mysore.

fig. **1682** FLAVEL *Fear* 54 Fear..treats with the tempter about terms of rendition.

b. The surrender of a person.

1649 MILTON *Eikon.* Wks. 1851 III. 367 His rendition afterward to the Scotch Army. **1670** TEMPLE *Let.* Wks. 1731 II. 212 Their Answer was, That there was no need of distinguishing the Renditions of the Colony. **1860** S. ELIOT in *Encycl. Brit.* (ed. 8) XXI. 442/2 The rendition of fugitive slaves by the Northern States. **1864** SALA in *Daily Tel.* 13 Sept., Mr. Seward can scarcely place any obstacles in the way of the rendition of this man.

†**c.** The giving up or back of something; return, restoration. *Obs.*

1652 KIRKMAN *Clerio & Lozia* 148 She lost her speech, which love soon made rendition of unto her. **1666** J. SMITH *Old Age* 46 They have assigned unto it [memory] three operations, viz. Reception, Retention, and Rendition.

2. Translation, rendering. Now *U.S.*

1659 PEARSON *Creed* (1839) 231 It is..acknowledged that the most ancient interpreters were divided in their renditions. *a* **1716** SOUTH *Serm.* (1744) VII. 27 The Jews..charge Paul as a perverter of the prophet's meaning, in a false rendition of the sense of the place. **1858** in Bartlett *Dict. Amer.* (1859) 360 The closest possible rendition of the meaning of the original text of the Scriptures into English. **1875** STEDMAN *Victorian Poets* 275, I will not omit mention of Calverley's complete rendition of Theocritus.

3. a. orig. *U.S.* The action of rendering, giving out or forth, acting, performing, etc.

1858 in Bartlett *Dict. Amer.* (1859) 360 On the rendition of the verdict, the large audience present manifested enthusiastic approbation. **1877** H. H. FURNESS *Hamlet* I. Pref. 14 In their rendition of Hamlet by the Messrs. Devrient. **1880** L. WALLACE *Ben-Hur* (1887) 266 When he spoke, the account seemed to have rendition from both of them jointly. **1922** JOYCE *Ulysses* 237 Ben Dollard does sing that ballad touchingly. Masterly rendition. **1939** N. MONSARRAT *This is Schoolroom* III. xvii. 385 No account of twentieth-century culture would be complete without reference to the impact of the dance-band world..as well as strange words and phrases like 'rendition'. **1975** *Radio Times* 3 Apr. 17/1 It's comedian Roy Hudd, strumming the strings..with a rendition of 'Auntie Maggie's Remedy'.

b. Visual representation *of* anything.

1959 E. PULGRAM *Introd. Spectrography of Speech* xiii. 89, I chose a sustained sound... The sketch of Fig. 11 is a complete and exact spectrographic rendition of it. **1972** *Sci. Amer.* Nov. 45/2 (Advt.), If you are interested in additional dimensions of photo-optical performance—rendition of corners,..stray-light shielding—this chart..may provide the detailed answer. **1978** *Amateur Photographer* 2 Aug. 109/2 A polarising filter may be used to darken skies without affecting the rendition of foreground detail.

4. *U.S.* The amount produced or rendered; the yield (of silk).

1889 in *Funk's Stand. Dict.*

rendizvouse, obs. form of RENDEZVOUS *sb.*

'rendles. *Obs.* exc. *dial.* Forms: 5 rennelesse, renlys, 6 renlesse, renels; 5 rendlys, 6–7 -les, 8 -less; 7 rindles, 9 *dial.* rindless, (-lass, -lis). [prob. repr. an OE. **rynels* = Flem. *ren-*, *rin-*, *runsel* (Kilian), Ger. dial. *rensel*, *rinsel* (Diefenbach): see RUN *v.* and -ELS. Palsgrave gives also the form *ronnelles.*] Rennet, runnet.

c **1440** *Promp. Parv.* 429/2 Renlys, or rendlys, for mylke [*K.* rennelesse, *P.* renels], *coagulum.* **1530** PALSGR. 262/1 Rendles for a chese, *presure. Ibid.*, Renlesse to make cheese with, *presure.* **1601** HOLLAND *Pliny* I. 486 As white as milke, and as good as rendles to giue the forme to cheese. *Ibid.* II. 166 It will cruddle milke as wel as rennet or rindles. **1784** TWAMLEY *Dairying* 10 Collecting the Curd at the bottom of the Tub or Pan, after the runnet or rendless has done its duty. **1879** MISS JACKSON *Shropsh. Word-bk.* 352 The *rindless* obtained from a calf whose 'nursing mother' grazes the pasture common to the dairy stock.

rendle-wood. *dial.* [app. f. REND *v.*¹ 3 d.] Barked oak. Also *attrib.*

1887 T. HARDY *Woodlanders* III. iv. 67 A heap of rendle-wood—as barked oak was here called. *a* **1900** —— *Tess* xii, She was kindling 'rendlewood' (barked-oak) twigs under the breakfast kettle.

†**'rendling**, *vbl. sb. Obs. rare*⁻¹. [f. *rendle*, back-formation on RENDLES.] Curdling, setting.

1784 TWAMLEY *Dairying* 33 The rendling of Cheese causeth a very great Fermentation.

rendoun, obs. form of RANDOM.

rendrock ('rɛndrɒk). [f. REND *v.*¹ + ROCK *sb.*] A kind of explosive.

1880 *Libr. Univ. Knowl.* (N.Y.) II. 628 The explosives were dynamite, rendrock and vulcan powder. **1881** LOCK *Spons' Encycl.* III. 901 A number of semi-solid mixtures, such as dynamite,..giant powder, rendrock.

†**'rendry.** *Obs.* [f. RENDER *v.* + -(R)Y: cf. *surrendry.*] Surrender.

1600 HOLLAND *Livy* XXVI. xvii. 596 Touching the rendrie and deliverie of the fortresses in every cittie. **1615** CHAPMAN *Odyss.* XXI. 26 For whose just And instant rendry old Laertes sent Ulysses his ambassador.

rendu (rɑ̃dy), *a.* [Fr., = rendered, delivered.] Of imported goods: designating the price on delivery, including tariffs and delivery costs. Cf. FRANCO *a.*

1957 CLARK & GOTTFRIED *Dict. Business* 275/2 *Rendu price*, one on imported goods meaning that the price includes the cost of the goods themselves, freight insurance, landing fees, tariffs, and the costs of delivering the goods direct to the buyer's place of business. **1959** E. E. NEMMERS *Dict. Econ.* 254 *Rendu price*, an import *delivered price.* The price of imported goods including all charges for tariff and freight. **1962** [see FRANCO *a.*].

†**'rendy.** *Obs. rare.* [app. ad. F. *rendez* in *rendezvous* RENDEZVOUS.] A rendezvous; also, an arrangement or disposal of troops.

1581 STYWARD *Mart. Discipl.* II. 134 Staie thee neere thy trench till thou hast viewed thy selfe and the rendies of the enimies; that is, how manie battailes, how they are placed, of what condition, and where they are disposed to fight. **1596** DRAYTON *Piers Gaveston* Wks. (1748) 212 The Barons then from Bedford setting on, (Th'appointed rendy where they gather'd head).

rendzina (rɛnd'ziːnə). *Soil Science.* [a. Russ. *rendzina*, ad. Polish *rędzina.*] A fertile lime-rich soil which occurs typically under grass or open woodland on relatively soft calcareous bedrock (e.g. chalk and some limestones) and has a dark, friable, humus-rich surface layer above a softer pale calcareous layer formed by the breakdown of the underlying rock. Also *attrib.*

1927 C. F. MARBUT tr. *K. D. Glinka's Great Soil Groups of World* 34 The humus carbonate soils such as the Rendzinas..constitute a good example of the influence of the parent rock on the soil forming process. **1928** C. L. WHITTLES tr. *E. Ramann's Evolution & Classification of Soils* v. 91 Recently under the influence of Russian soil workers the term 'rendzina' has been applied to all soils which have developed from the weathering of calcareous rocks. **1932** G. W. ROBINSON *Soils* xiv. 285 The writer is occupying a debatable position in assigning the chalk soils of England to the rendzina group. **1946** LUTZ & CHANDLER *Forest Soils* xi. 386 Highly calcareous materials frequently give rise to immature soils called rendzinas. **1955** *Proc. Prehistoric Soc.* XXI. 53 Vegetation covering the surface of the loess produced soils due to chemical weathering which can be classified as podsols, chernozems, rendzinas, terra rossas and others. **1971** *Nature* 13 Aug. 453/1 The flora has survived through the post-glacial forest and blanket bog intervals in Teesdale partly on rendzina soils associated with rotted crystalline marble on Widdybank and Cronkley fells. **1973** *Country Life* 29 Nov. 1787/3 *The Rural Landscape of Kent*..is strictly for the diligent reader who can disentangle rendzinas from stagnogley soils. **1976** *Interim* IV. III. 14 Chalk rendzinas go straight from the A horizon to the C.

†**rene**, obs. form of REAN, furrow, balk.

c **1420** *Pallad. on Husb.* I. 61 Withouten moold admyxt, ner sondy lene, Nor hungry cley, ner stonys ful vche rene. *Ibid.* 159 Sette not out thi landis faat or lene To hym whos lond adioyneth on thy rene.

rene, obs. form of RAIN *sb.*¹, REIN *sb.*

reneg, var. of RENEGUE *sb.* and *v.*

renegade ('rɛnɪgeɪd), *sb.* (and *a.*) Also 6 *Sc.* rannu-, rannigard, 7 renegad. [Anglicized form of RENEGADO: see -ADE 3 b.]

1. An apostate from any form of religious faith, *esp.* a Christian who becomes a Muslim.

1583 *Leg. Bp. St. Androis* 10 Ane fals, forloppen, fenyeit freir, Ane rannugard [*v.r.* rannigard] for greed of geir. **1598** BARCKLEY *Felic. Man* (1631) 232 The renegades in place of defending the king joyned with them [the Turks] in the spoyle. **1611** FLORIO, *Ringegato*,..a renegade, a foresworne man, or one that hath renounced his religion or country. **1645** PAGITT *Heresiogr.* (1662) Ep. Ded., Some of the watch-men ought to have been watched themselvs, who..in conclusion run over and turned renegads. **1712** BLACKMORE *Creation* Pref. (ed. 2) 20 Renegades and Deserters of Heaven, who renounce their God for the Favour of Men. **1814** SOUTHEY *Roderick* VIII, How best they might evade The Moor, and renegade's more watchful eye. **1873** SMILES *Huguenots Fr.* I. vii. (1881) 147 Like all renegades, he was a bitter and furious persecutor.

2. One who deserts a party, person, or principle, in favour of another; a turn-coat.

1665 MANLEY *Grotius' Low C. Warres* 127 Not a few English turning Renegades, and being contemned by the Spaniard. **1751** *Affect. Narr. of Wager* 31 For if these Renegades had formed such a Conspiracy, what hindered their accomplishing it? **1817** MOORE *Lalla R.*, *Veiled Prophet* 690 Must he..be driven A renegade like me from Love and Heaven? **1849** MACAULAY *Hist. Eng.* iv. I. 451 The renegade soon found a patron in the obdurate and revengeful James. **1872** C. GIBBON *For the King* ii, The past makes me seem in my own eyes, and in the eyes of others—a renegade.

3. *attrib.*, passing into adj.

1705 ARBUTHNOT *Coins*, etc. (1727) 242 If the Roman Government subsisted now, they would have had renegade Seamen and Ship-wrights enough. **1837** W. IRVING *Capt. Bonneville* II. 6 Kosato, the renegade Blackfoot, had recovered from the wound. **1870** LOWELL *Among my Bks.* Ser. I. (1873) 98 The renegade Christian must forswear the true Deity.

Hence **'renegadism** (renegadeism), the practice of deserting one's religion or party.

1826 B. R. HAYDON *Jrnl.* 25 Feb. in *Autobiogr.* (1853) II. 115 The Academy is certainly modified, but still John Bull never pardons an appearance of renegadeism. **1859** *Blackw. Mag.* Apr. 455/2 We..tacitly acknowledged renegadism..as the standard of moral feeling. **1877** GLADSTONE *Glean.* (1879) IV. 315 This population was liable to be thinned by renegadism and constant war. **1939** A. J. TOYNBEE *Study of Hist.* VI. 104 The..profanity of Jason..gave Hellenism such a vogue and Renegadism such an impetus.

'renegade, *v.* [f. prec.] *intr.* To turn renegade; to go over *from* a religion, party, etc.

1611 COTGR., *Maranisé*, marranized, renegaded. **1716** M. DAVIES *Athen. Brit.* II. 316 Which last [rivalling] both High and Low, do Precaution themselves against..more than against their Converts Renegading or Starving. **1861** MEREDITH *Evan Harrington* III. xv. 236 That was before he renegaded. **1893** LELAND *Mem.* II. 140 Johnson had renegaded from the Confederacy.

renegader ('rɛnɪgeɪdə(r)). [f. RENEGADE *sb.* or *v.* + -ER[1].] = RENEGADE *sb.* 2.

1846 J. R. LOWELL in *Boston Courier* 17 June 2 Haint they cut a thunderin' swarth, (Helped by Yankee renegaders).

renegado (rɛnɪ'geɪdəʊ), *sb.* (and *a.*) Also 6 **renigado,** 7 **rennegado, renegador.** [a. Sp. *renegado*, ad. med.L. *renegatus*: see RENEGATE.]

1. = RENEGADE 1.

1599 HAKLUYT *Voy.* II. I. 186 He was a Renegado, which is one that first was a Christian, and afterwards becommeth a Turke. **1624** BP. MOUNTAGU *Gagg* 238 The body of Babylas made the oracle mute, in despight of Julian that renegado. **1682** LUTTRELL *Brief Rel.* (1857) I. 185 The English renegado, who is interpreter to the Morocco ambassador. **1727** A. HAMILTON *New Acc. E. Ind.* I. vii. 62 This Relation I had from a very old Renegado, who was at the Tragedy. **1755** J. SHEBBEARE *Lydia* (1769) II. 190 A dignified informer, a French refugee, and a renegado to the Church of England. **1814** SOUTHEY *Roderick* IX, Might I meet That renegado, sword to scymitar, In open field. **1850** MRS. JAMESON *Leg. Monast. Ord.* (1863) 348 The last to whom he was sold was a renegado.

2. = RENEGADE 2.

1600 HOLLAND *Livy* II. xi. 39 By the information of a renegado. *a* **1635** SIBBES *Confer. Christ & Mary* (1656) 33 They were renegadoes, having all left him. *a* **1680** BUTLER *Rem.* (1759) II. 408 A Rebel is a voluntary Bandit, a civil Renegado. *a* **1734** NORTH *Exam.* I. ii. §9 (1740) 35 He out of pure Malice to the Government of his Country, prefers that of Holland, and in that Respect writes like a Renegado. **1780** in Sparks *Corr. Amer. Rev.* (1853) II. 437 Many renegadoes from the different Indian nations are collected at the..towns. **1837** CARLYLE *Fr. Rev.* III. III. vii, Federalists in the Senate, renegadoes in the Army, traitors everywhere!

b. *transf.*

1646 J. HALL *Poems* I. 68 A Renegado to all Poetry. **1654** WHITLOCK *Zootomia* 62 A Renegado from some Trade or Profession. **1689** PHILOPOLITES *Grumble. Crew* 2 But our Male-Contents..are such Renagado's from Common Sense, that [etc.]. **1715** M. DAVIES *Athen. Brit.* I. Pref. 43 Even Canus accuses Cajetan for being a Renegado to the Fathers. **1748** J. GEDDES *Composition Antients* 12 The most determined renegado to the interests of society. **1802** MAR. EDGEWORTH *Irish Bulls* 193 To such would be renegadoes we prefer the honest quixotism of a modern champion for the Scottish accent.

†**c.** Used vaguely as a term of abuse. *Obs.*

1611 BEAUM. & FL. *Philaster* II. iv, To bring these Renegados to my Chamber, At these unseason'd hours.

†**3.** A variety of the game of ombre. *Obs.*

1680 COTTON *Compl. Gamester* vii. 69 There are several sorts of this Game called L'Ombre, but that which is the chief is called Renegado, at which three only can play.

4. *attrib.*, passing into adj.

1635 PAGITT *Christianogr.* Ded., The Turkes Janissaries, and Basha's, are most of them renegado Christians. **1653** GREAVES *Seraglio* 96 All the Eunuchs in the Seraglio..are chosen of those Renegado youths. **1677** W. HUBBARD *Narrative* 59 The scouts brought in one Joshuah Tift, a Renegado English-man. **17..** in *Swift's Lett.* (1768) IV. 111 An English renegado slave translated *Effendi Soif* for them. **1798** BRAGGE in *Anti-Jacobin* (1852) 62 The recreant peer to renegado priest. **1829** W. IRVING *Granada* (1850) 154 He singled out a renegado Christian, a traitor to his religion and his king. **1839** JAMES *Louis XIV*, IV. 67 Pelisson..busied himself with renegado zeal in buying proselytes to the faith of the court.

Hence **rene'gado** *v. intr.*, to turn renegado.

1704 J. PITTS *Acc. Mohammetans* ix. (1738) 200 Who after he was ransomed,..renegado'd.

†**renegant,** *a. Obs.* [ad. L. *renegant-em*, pres. pple. of *renegāre*: see RENEGUE *v.*] Renegade.

1549 *Compl. Scot.* viii. 74 The inglis men sal neuyr cal you ane vthir vord bot renegant scottis. **1614** W. PARSONS in *Lismore Papers* Ser. II. (1887) I. 207 This is a soure and renegant tyme. **1615** T. ADAMS *Black Devil* 2 Cast..your minds upon the renegant Jewes.

renegate ('rɛnɪgeɪt), *sb.* (and *a.*) *Obs.* exc. *dial.* Forms: 4 **ranegate, renagat,** 6 **rennagat(e,** *Sc.* **renigat(e, rennigatt,** 6–7 **rennegate,** 4–7 **renegat,** 4–7 (9 *dial.*) **renegate;** 5 **renogat,** 6 **ren(n)ogate.** See also RUNAGATE. [ad. med.L. *renegāt-us*, subst. use of pa. pple. of *renegāre*: see RENAY and RENEGUE, and cf. It. *rinegato*, F. *renégat*, Sp. *renegado* RENEGADO.]

1. A renegade, deserter.

c **1375** *xi Pains Hell* 63 in *O.E. Misc.* 212 Bynd..ranegates with raueners..And cast ham in þe fuyre. *c* **1385** CHAUCER *L.G.W.* Prol. 401, I not where he be now a renagat. *c* **1400** MAUNDEV. (1839) viii. 84 Julianus Apostate..forsoke his Law, and becam a Renegate. **1483** CAXTON *Gold. Leg.* 288/2 Now I shalle be callyd the wyf of a renegate and transgressour. **1535** COVERDALE *1 Macc.* vii. 24 He wente forth..and punyshed those vnfaithfull rennagates. **1565** T. STAPLETON *Fortr. Faith* 123 Whose first Apostles and preachers were al for the most part wicked rennagats. **1600** HOLLAND *Livy* XXIII. xxvi. 491 These fugitiue renegates had first practised to raise troubles and insurrections. **1662** J. DAVIES tr. *Olearius' Voy. Ambass.* 220 *marg.*, Our Persian Interpreter proves a Renegat. **1829** BROCKETT *N.C. Gloss.* (ed. 2), *Renegate*, a reprobate.

2. *attrib.*, or as adj.

c **1485** *Digby Myst.* (1882) III. 238 Alle renogat robber..to put hem to peyn I spare for no pete. **1508** KENNEDIE *Flyting w. Dunbar* 401 Rawmowit ribald, renegate rehatour. **1534** MORE *Comf. agst. Trib.* III. Wks. 1212/2 Manye other contumelies & dispightes, that the Turkes and the false renegate christiens manye tymes dooe. **1593** G. HARVEY *New Lett.* Wks. (Grosart) I. 272 A wilde Asse, of a fugitiue and renegate disposition. **1609** BIBLE (Douay) *Isa.* xxx. 1 Woe unto renegate children, sayth the Lord. **1641** J. TRAPPE *Theol. Theol.* vii. 289 They refused Christ..for the which they are become a renegate people now 1600 years together.

renegation (rɛnɪ'geɪʃən). [ad. L. type **renegātiōn-em*, n. of action f. *renegāre*: see RENEGUE *sb.*] The action of renouncing or renegading.

1615 T. ADAMS *Two Sonnes* 89 Let us reclaime our impudent and refractory renegations by a serious meditation. **1837** CARLYLE *Fr. Rev.* III. v. iv. From far and near..come Letters of renegation. **1896** SAINTSBURY *Hist. 19th C. Lit.* ix. 392 The hour of triumph was the hour..of opposition and renegation.

rene'gotiate, *v.* [RE- 5 a.] *trans.* To negotiate a second or further time. Hence **rene'gotiated** *ppl. a.*

1934 in WEBSTER. **1962** *Economist* 16 June 1096/2 The annexes to these agreements, which determine the air services to be operated, are normally re-negotiated every six months. **1969** *Listener* 26 June 894/3 When you propose to renegotiate housing subsidies, this really means higher rents for a lot of people. **1975** *Times* 19 Feb. 2/8 Mr Crosland.. is expected to support the argument..when Mr Callaghan ..brings back the final renegotiated terms. **1976** *Film & Television Technician* Dec. 1/2 Among the key mechanisms in achieving this, have been the re-negotiated cost of living clauses which the employers have unilaterally abandoned.

renegoti'ation. [RE- 5 a.] A second or further negotiation.

1934 in WEBSTER. **1945** *Britannica Bk. of Year* 771 The renegotiation by the government of original contracts to bring them more in line with actual costs as revealed by experience. **1963** *Ann. Reg. 1962* 274 The renegotiation of the U.S.-Spanish Bases agreement, due for renewal in 1963. **1976** H. WILSON *Governance of Britain* 10 The final Cabinet tally, after the re-negotiations of the terms of entry, was publicly announced to be seventeen in favour, seven against. **1980** *Boston Globe* 30 Mar. 76 Today the 25-year-old.. insists on a renegotiation of his contract.

re'negue, *sb.* Also 7 **-neg,** 9 **-nege.** [f. the vb. (sense 4).] An instance of reneguing at cards.

1654 GAYTON *Pleas. Notes* IV. ix. 235 Now they are for their Tibs who had plaid faire, and made never a Reneg all the time. **1897** *Foster's Complete Hoyle* 622 Revoke, failure to follow suit when able to do so, as distinguished from a renounce or renege.

renegue, renege (rɪ'ni:g, -'nɛg, -'neɪg), *v.* Forms: 6–7, 9 **reneague,** 7–9 **renegue,** (6 **ri-,** 7 **-neigue,** 9 *dial.* **-nague**); 7, 9 **reneg,** (9 *dial.* **-neeg**); 6–7, 9- **renege,** 6–7 **reneage,** 9 *dial.* **rena(i)ge,** 8- *U.S.* **renig.** [ad. med.L. *reneg-āre*, f. *re-* RE- + *negāre* to deny: cf. RENAY *v.*]

1. a. *trans.* To deny, renounce, abandon, desert (a person, faith, etc.). Now *arch.*

1548 UDALL *Erasm. Par. Luke* Pref. 12 Reneague thou and forsake Christ. **1597** J. KING *On Jonas* (1618) 46 That not onely he reneged his obedience in this particular action, but changed the whole trade of his life. **1626** L. OWEN *Spec. Jesuit.* (1629) 62 To blaspheme, and reneage, or denie God. **1657** TRAPP *Comm., Job* xxxiii. 7 Those of this reformed Religion, who will not reneague it. **1691** W. NICHOLLS *Answ. Naked Gospel* 52 Even by those who in other things reneg its Authority. **1817** COLERIDGE *Ess. own Times* (1850) III. 957 He himself retains the opinions and principles which the other had reneged. **1867** MISS BROUGHTON *Not Wisely* (1868) 239 Though he had deserted her and reneged the situation of spiritual guide and teacher. **1914** JOYCE *Dubliners* 163 'There's one of them, anyhow,' said Mr Henchy, 'that didn't renege him.' **1922** —— *Ulysses* 324 We fought for the royal Stuarts that reneged us against the Williamites and they betrayed us.

†**b.** To recant. *Obs. rare*$^{-1}$.

1679 *Hist. Jetzer* 29 He would spend his dearest blood before he would renege one Syllable.

†**2.** *intr.* or *absol.* **a.** To make denial. Also with dependent clause. *Obs.*

1548 UDALL *Erasm. Par. Luke* xxii. 167 b, Whyle Petur reneagueth, while he sweareth naie,..the cocke crewe the secounde tyme. **1575** *Mirr. Mag., King Bladud* lviii, Shall I renege I made them then? Shall I denye my cunning founde? **1605** SHAKS. *Lear* II. ii. 84 Such smiling rogues as these..Renegue [*printed* reuenge], affirme, and turne their Halcion beakes, With euery gall, and vary of their Masters. **1689** HICKERINGILL *Ceremony Monger* i. Wks. 1716 II. 389 But if he reneages..and is forc'd to answer, that he bows to nothing; then beg him for a Fool.

†**b.** To apostatize. *Obs. rare*$^{-1}$.

a **1734** NORTH *Lives* (1826) III. 58 The Turks give all the kindest invitations that can be to Christians to renegue and become Turks.

3. To refuse, decline. *rare.*

1582 STANYHURST *Æneis* II. (Arb.) 64 Too liue now longer, Troy burnt, hee flatlye reneaged. *a* **1734** NORTH *Exam.* I. i. §13 (1740) 21 The Author will needs have..the good King at the head of them by his Reneguing to become the Guarantee. **1757** MRS. GRIFFITH *Lett. Henry & Frances* (1767) IV. 207 Our Postillion, with the thorough Consent of his Horses, renegued going farther. **1866** KENNEDY *Leg. Fictions* 29 How shabby it would look to reneague the adventure.

4. a. *Card-playing.* To refuse or fail to follow suit; to revoke. (But see also the *sb.*, quot. 1897.) Now *local* and *U.S.*

1680 COTTON *Compl. Gamester* x. (ed. 2) 82 Reneging or renouncing, that is, not following suit when you have it in your hand, is very foul play. *Ibid.* 87 You are bound to follow suit, and if you renounce or renege, you lose the whole Game. **1891** *Pall Mall G.* 21 Jan. 2/1 At games of cards renege (spelled renague in Ireland) is almost always used instead of revoke, and bears the same meaning. **1897** *Foster's Complete Hoyle* 277 This privilege of reneging is confined to the three highest trumps.

b. *dial.* (See quots.)

a **1849** J. KEEGAN *Legends & Poems* (1907) 64 Amn't I to undherstand that..Peggy is goin' to ranague you for Micky Gorman? **1872** WHYTE MELVILLE *Satanella* I. i. 12 If iver she schames with ye, renaging [*note* refusing] or such like.. I'll be ashamed to look a harse..in the face again! **1890** *Glouc. Gloss.*, *Reneague*, to renounce a job. **1893** *Wilts Gloss.*, *Reneeg, renegue*, to back out of an engagement, to jilt.

c. To change one's mind, to recant; to break one's word; to go back *on* a promise or undertaking or contract; to disappoint expectations. orig. and chiefly *U.S.*

Now the dominant sense, and freq. in spelling *renege*.

1784 A. ELLICOTT *Diary* 24 Nov. in C. V. Mathews *Andrew Ellicott* (1908) i. 27 The Hussey immediately Reniged and reclaimed the Bed. **1866** C. H. SMITH *Bill Arp* 153 When the Secretary read out my name all mixed up with the Republic, I felt I was obleged to renig. **1906** 'O. HENRY' *Four Million* 123 It might brace her up and keep her from reneging on the proposition to skip. **1917** H. FRANCK *Vagabonding down Andes* 32 Hays renigged at the last moment, but I accepted the invitation issued to the 'general public'. **1935** A. SQUIRE *Sing Sing Doctor* ix. 141, I was afraid our man might renege on his contract. **1936** 'N. BLAKE' *Thou Shell of Death* xiii. 236 She turned very calm and quiet..'I'll never renege. I'll write to Jack... He must come back.' **1946** *Time* 21 Oct. 99/1 The picture begins to renege on its early promise. **1951** A. R. LEWIS *Naval Power & Trade in Mediterranean* v. 150 The naval assault was a success, but Hugh reneged on his side of the bargain. **1962** J. MCCABE *Mr. Laurel & Mr. Hardy* iii. 82 Anderson made a few more films with Stan before he reneged on a contract detail regarding payment. **1968** *Daily Tel.* 13 Dec. 1/2 The Minister is equally annoyed that the National Federation of Building Trade Operatives appears to have reneged on its earlier promise to accept a 1d-an-hour wage cut. **1973** R. LUDLUM *Matlock Paper* v. 43 'You're offering me a chance to renege?' 'Of course. You're under no obligation to us.' **1977** *Time* 7 Mar. 23/1 He was given certain undertakings from other people that they subsequently reneged on. **1981** *Times* 27 Jan. 12/8 Labour's record on immigration has been almost identical to the Conservatives'—it introduced stringent controls and reneged on Britain's commitment to the East African Asians who had United Kingdom passports.

Hence **re'negued** *ppl. a.*, renegade; **re'neguing** *vbl. sb.*; also **re'neguer.**

1594 R. ASHLEY tr. *Loys le Roy* 106 The Mammelvcs, being al Christians reneaged, and of seruile condition. **1597** J. KING *On Jonas* (1618) 187 The relinquisher of his owne life is more to be punished, than a reneger of his seruice in warre. **1600** O. E. (M. SUTCLIFFE) *Repl. Libel* Ep. Ded., Your selfe and other rinegued English, that adhere vnto them. **1632** J. FEATLY *Hon. Chast.* 11 Correct the fury of it by a pious reneaguing. **1659** GAUDEN *Tears Ch.* I. iv. 57 These modern Renegers, Separates, and Apostates. **1921** G. B. SHAW *Back to Methuselah* p. lxv, There was no Prime Minister to whom such renagueing or trafficking would ever have occurred.

renels, obs. variant of RENDLES, rennet.

rener, obs. form of RUNNER.

re'nervate, *v. rare*$^{-1}$. [Cf. next and ENERVATE *v.*] *intr.* To get renewed vigour.

1801 *Lusignan* IV. 129 His strength began to renervate.

re'nerve, *v.* [RE- 5 a.] *trans.* To put fresh nerve into, to strengthen again.

1652 BENLOWES *Theoph.* XII. cxviii, Draught of Promethean fir'd air took Renerves slack joynts, and ransacks each phlegmattick Nook. **1807** J. BARLOW *Columb.* v. 702 War and Washington renerve the soul. **1817** BYRON *Mazeppa* xvii, The sight re-nerved my courser's feet. **1855** LYNCH *Rivulet* I. v, Up from the dust the enfeebled start, Armed and re-nerved for victories.

absol. **1889** SKRINE *Mem. E. Thring* 89 It was a vitalising joy which touched us, not to soothe, but to renerve.

renet, obs. form of RENNET *sb.*[1]

renette, obs. form of RENNET *sb.*[2]

†**re'new,** *sb. Obs.* Also 5 *Sc.* **renewe.** [f. the vb.] Renewal, new invention.

1423 JAS. I *Kingis Q.* cxxv, And there we sawe the perfyte excellence, The said [? *read* sad] renewe, the state, the reuerence..Off hir court. **1615** BRATHWAIT *Strappado*, etc. (1878) 247 That both loue and hate, May make you happy louers by renew. **1631** —— *Whimzies, Exchange-man* 33 Who bray their braines in a mortar, to produce some usefull renew, some gainefull issue for their thriving master.

renew (rɪ'nju:), *v.*[1] Also 4–5 **renuwe,** 4–6 **renewe,** 5 *Sc.* **ranew,** 5–7 **renue,** 7 **reniew.** [f. RE- + NEW *a.*, after L. *renovāre* to RENOVATE. Cf. RENOVEL and RENULE.]

I. *trans.* †**1.** To do over again, revise. *Obs.*$^{-1}$

c **1374** CHAUCER *To Scriv.* 5 So offt a daye I mot þy werk renuwe, It to corect and eke to rubbe and scrape.

2. To make new, or as new, again; to restore to the same condition as when new, young, or fresh.

1382 WYCLIF *Ps.* ciii[i]. 30 Thou shalt renewe the face of the erthe. *c* 1420 *Pallad. on Husb.* I. 770 Let make a stewe With rayn watir, thyn herbis to renewe. 1494 FABYAN *Chron.* II. xxxviii. 27 He renewyd and repayred al olde Temples thorough his Realme. 1535 COVERDALE *2 Chron.* xv. 8 And [Asa] renued the Lordes altare. 1578 TIMME *Calvin on Gen.* 229 Souls are chosen..as a Seed purged from all dross, to renue the Church. 1596 SHAKS. *Merch. V.* v. i. 14 In such a night Medea gathered the inchanted hearbs That did renew old Eson. 1613 PURCHAS *Pilgrimage* (1614) 9 This Light..perfecteth, renueth, and preserueth all things. 1697 DRYDEN *Virg. Georg.* III. 521 The cool Evening-breeze the Meads renews. 1781 COWPER *Charity* 395 The soul whose sight all-quickening grace renews. 1823 S. ROGERS *Italy, Bergamo* 54 His long suit of black Dingy and thread-bare, though renewed in patches Till it has almost ceased to be the old one. 1833 TENNYSON *Miller's Dau.* 27 Would God renew me from my birth I'd almost live my life again. 1866 RUSKIN *Crown Wild Olive* Pref. 29 To dip themselves for an instant in the font of death, and to rise renewed of plumage.

refl. 1490 CAXTON *Eneydos* xv. 54 Alle thynges renewen them at his commynge. 1535 COVERDALE *Lam.* iii. 23 His faithfulnes is greate, and renueth itself as the mornynge. 1607 SHAKS. *Cor.* v. vi. 49 Therefore shall he dye, And Ile renew me in his fall. 1821 SHELLEY *Hellas* 348 Even as that moon Renews itself—Shall we be not renewed!

b. To make spiritually new; to regenerate.

1382 WYCLIF *2 Cor.* iv. 16 That man that is withinne forth [1388 the ynner man] is renewid. —— *Eph.* iv. 23 Be 3e renewid by spirit of 3oure mynde. *c* 1440 *Macro Plays* 73/1142 Ande be renuyde in Gode knowynge a-geyn. 1526 *Pilgr. Perf.* (W. de W. 1531) 1 Man is renewed..by the vij folde graces of the holy goost. 1548–9 (Mar.) *Bk. Com. Prayer, Collect Christmas Day*, Graunt that we..maye dailye be renued by thy holy spirite. 1607 HIERON *Wks.* I. 158 God is strong, able to pardon vs, able to renue vs. 1740 WATERLAND *Regeneration* Wks. 1823 VI. 352 Man renews himself at the same time that the spirit renews him. 1866 NEALE *Sequences & Hymns* 123 The Paraclete that shall renew you.

c. To assume anew, to recover (one's original strength, youth, etc.).

1481 CAXTON *Myrr.* II. vi. 78 Thus [he] reneweth his age as a wyse best that he is. 1560 BIBLE (Genev.) *Isa.* xl. 31 They that waite vpon the Lord, shal renue their strength. *c* 1600 SHAKS. *Sonn.* lvi, Sweet loue renew thy force. 1667 MILTON *P.L.* VI. 783 Heav'n his wonted face renewed. 1821 SHELLEY *Epipsych.* 468 Dew, From which its fields and woods ever renew Their green and golden immortality. 1860 TENNYSON *Tithonus* 74 Thou wilt renew thy beauty morn by morn. 1875 JOWETT *Plato* (ed. 2) V. 236 In age we may renew our youth, and forget our sorrows.

†**d.** To reopen (a wound). *Obs. rare.*

1508 FISHER *7 Penit. Ps.* cxxx. Wks. (1876) 229 His woundes were so renewed that the blode yssued out afresshe. 1541 R. COPLAND *Galyen's Terap.* Cciv b, He estemeth y^t the vlcerate plane must be renewed. Than whan y^t it is made as a fresshe wounde [etc.].

e. *refl.* To refresh (oneself). *nonce-use.*

1858 HAWTHORNE *Fr. & It. Note-bks.* (1871) I. 30 We..renewed ourselves, at the close of the banquet, with a plate of Chateaubriand ice.

3. To restore, re-establish, set up again, bring back into use or existence.

1382 WYCLIF *1 Sam.* xi. 14 Cometh, and goo we into Galgala, and renewe we there the rewme. 1402 *Pol. Poems* (Rolls) II. 75 Josie shal..make an ende of suche fendes, and Cristis reule shal renue. 1480 CAXTON *Chron. Eng.* IV. (1520) 38/2 Crysten men had leve to renewe the servyce of god that was defended afore. 1533 BELLENDEN *Livy* II. xvi. (S.T.S.) I. 191 þe romanis war makand þare provisioun to renew þe grete playis mony 3ere before hantit in þare ciete. 1567 *Reg. Privy Council Scot.* I. 574 The former corruptioun and abuse wes renewit. 1697 DRYDEN *Virg. Georg.* IV. 813 Mighty Cæsar..On the glad Earth the Golden Age renews. 1738 JOHNSON *London* 25 We kneel, and..In pleasing dreams the blissful age renew.

†**b.** To re-enact, put in force again. *Obs.*

1494 in *Eng. Gilds* (1870) 187 Thies ben the ordinaunces, Actes, and Statutes, made..by the Founders of the Gylde ..; nowe renewed, and affermed. 1553 BECON *Reliques of Rome* (1563) 95 b, This decree did Pope Eugenius the third renue.

4. To take up again or afresh; to resume; to begin again, recommence.

c 1400 *Sowdone Bab.* 2200 Laban nolde not forgete The saute to renewe. 1490 CAXTON *Eneydos* xv. 54 The byrdes renewen theyre swete songe gracyouse. 1535 COVERDALE *1 Macc.* xii. 16 We..sente them vnto the Romaynes, for to renue the olde bonde of frendshipe and loue with them. 1560 DAUS tr. *Sleidane's Comm.* 74 They renewe the warres agaïne w^t all their force and power. 1585 T. WASHINGTON tr. *Nicholay's Voy.* I. xix. 22 The Turkes..renued their batterie with great force and 8. peeces at once. 1662 J. DAVIES tr. *Olearius' Voy. Ambass.* 206 We..renew'd among our selves the friendship, which we had before mutually promis'd. 1671 MILTON *P.R.* IV. 19 As..surging waves against a solid rock, Though all to shivers dash't, the assault renew. 1771 *Junius Lett.* lix. (1788) 317 She will be ready to receive him whenever he thinks proper to renew his addresses. 1790 COWPER *Mother's Pict.* 116, I seem..To have renewed the joys that once were mine. 1817 EARL OF DUDLEY *Lett.* (1840) 162, I..was beginning to think that it was high time our correspondence should be renewed. 1821 SHELLEY *Adonais* xviii, The airs and streams renew their joyous tone. 1875 JOWETT *Plato* (ed. 2) I. 112 Socrates renews the attack from another side.

b. To resume (a speech, subject, etc.).

1667 MILTON *P.L.* IX. 1133 Adam..Speech intermitted thus to Eve renewd. *Ibid.* XI. 499 Adam..scarce recovering words his plaint renew'd. 1792 COWPER *Stanza* v. 22 Conscience oft Her tale of guilt renews. 1797 MRS. RADCLIFFE *Italian* xiii, He ventured to renew the subject nearest his heart.

c. To say in resumption.

1687 DRYDEN *Hind. & P.* II. 401 Then thus the matron modestly renewed: 'Let all your prophets and their sects be viewed'. 1853 LYTTON *My Novel* IX. xvi, 'And', he renewed, after a pause,—'and you ascribe this fear of seeing me' [etc.].

5. †**a.** To go over again, to repeat, relate afresh.

14.. *Sir Beues* (MS. M) 868 Iosyan, that was so trewe, Thought she wold her love renewe. *c* 1450 HOLLAND *Howlat* 254 It neidis nocht to renewe all myn vnhele, Sen it was menit to 3our mynd, and maid manifest. [Cf. *ibid.* 708, 872.] *c* 1530 *Crt. of Love* 495 To turn, and sigh and grone,..And eke renew the wordes all that she Bitween you twain hath seid. 1549 LATIMER *5th Serm. bef. Edw. VI* (Arb.) 137 Here I wyll renewe that whyche I sayed before of the styf-necked Iewes. 1596 SPENSER *F.Q.* IV. viii. 64 Then gan he all this storie to renew, And tell the course of his captivitie.

b. To repeat (a promise, vow, etc.); to make or utter again.

1509 FISHER *Funeral Serm. C'tess Richmond* Wks. (1876) 294 She..promysed to lyue chaste,..whiche promyse she renewed after her husbandes dethe. 1596 SPENSER *F.Q.* V. xi. 45 They turne afresh, and oft renew their former threat. 1710 STEELE *Tatler* No. 266 ¶3 The Lady renewed her Excuses. 1817 SHELLEY *Rev. Islam* IV. xxi, Lovers renew the vows which they did plight In early faith.

c. To do over again, to repeat (an action). *rare.*

1599 SHAKS. *Hen. V*, I. ii. 116 Awake remembrance of these valiant dead, And with your puissant Arme renew their Feats. 1781 J. MORISON in *Sc. Paraphr.* xxxv. iii, Oft the sacred rite renew Which brings my wondrous love to view. 1864 TENNYSON *En. Ard.* 161 Many a sad kiss by day by night renew'd.

6. To replace by some new or fresh thing of the same kind; to restore by means of substitution or a fresh supply; to fill (a vessel) again.

1439 in *Ancestor* (1904) July 16, I wol..that the tapres be renewed til the month be endet. *c* 1530 H. RHODES *Bk. Nurture* in *Babees Bk.* (1867) 67 Loke the cup of Wyne or ale be not empty, but ofte renued. 1585 T. WASHINGTON tr. *Nicholay's Voy.* I. xiii. 14 b, We renewed our beuerage out of certaine cesternes. 1586 T. B. *La Primaud. Fr. Acad.* I. (1594) 632 They create the duke and the eight governors of the commonwealth, who are renued from two yeeres to two yeeres. 1687 A. LOVELL tr. *Thevenot's Trav.* I. 157 These Hangings are renewed every seven Years by the Ottoman Emperours. 1726 POPE *Odyss.* XIX. 590 She to the fount conveys the exhausted vase: The bath renew'd [etc.]. 1784 COWPER *Task* I. 434 Beneath the open sky she spreads the feast; 'Tis free to all—'tis every day renewed. *a* 1796 BURNS *You're welcome, Willie Stewart* 6 Come, bumpers high,.. The bowl we maun renew it. 1821 SHELLEY *Hellas* 1062 The earth doth like a snake renew Her winter weeds outworn. 1860 TYNDALL *Glac.* I. xxi. 146 The condensed vapour incessantly got away, but it was ever renewed.

†**b.** To change, make a change in. *Obs. rare.*

c 1530 LD. BERNERS *Arth. Lyt. Bryt.* (1814) 471 Thei wer Sarasyns borne, but as than thei had renewed theyr byleue, and were crystened in Fraunce. *a* 1533 —— *Huon* clxi. 619 Fyrste ye muste renewe your law and byleue in y^e lawe of Mahomet, on whome I do byleue.

c. To repair, make up for. *rare*$^{-1}$.

1768 TUCKER *Lt. Nat.* II. I. 136 Though the corporealists can find nothing to renew the decays of motion.

7. To revive, reawaken (a feeling).

1484 CAXTON *Fables of Alfonce* xi, My fayre Frend, renewe not my sorowe. 1494 FABYAN *Chron.* VI. clxx. 164 The kynge was ascertayned therof; the whiche renued his heuynesse. *a* 1533 LD. BERNERS *Huon* lxx. 238 The auncyent hate..was renewed in his hert. 1615 BRATHWAIT *Strappado*, etc. (1878) 266 Renewing griefe with each renewing morrow. 1697 DRYDEN *Virg. Georg.* III. 509 The Sun's sultry Heat their Thirst renews. 1820 SHELLEY *Let. Maria Gisborne* 174 Quenching a thirst ever to be renewed.

b. To revive, resuscitate, in various uses.

1535 COVERDALE *Ps.* l[i]. 10 Make me a clene hert (o God) and renue a right sprete within me. 1560 DAUS tr. *Sleidane's Comm.* 30 Thou renewest [L. *resuscitas*] the errours therin condemned. 1648 MILTON *Ps.* lxxxv. 28 Thy saving health to us afford And life in us renew. 1660 R. COKE *Power & Subj.* 259 It is his Majesties pleasure to have the memory of things rather buried in oblivion then renued. 1726 ATTERBURY *Serm.* I. vi. 235 [I have] endeavour'd to renew a faint Image of her several Virtues..upon your Minds.

†**c.** To strike afresh. *Obs. rare*$^{-1}$.

1609 BIBLE (Douay) *Ecclus.* xxxviii. 30 [28] The noyse of the hammer reneweth his eare, and his eye is against the similitude of the vessel.

8. To grant anew, *esp.* to grant or give (a lease, bill, etc.) for a fresh period; to extend the period or application of; also, to take afresh, to obtain an extension of.

1617 MORYSON *Itin.* II. 94 His Lordship to settle the Country the better, refused to renew any protections. 1667 MILTON *P.L.* XI. 116 Intermix My Cov'nant in the Womans seed renewd. 1671 —— *Samson* 1357 Shall I..so requite Favour renew'd? 1727–8 BERKELEY *Let. to Prior* 20 Feb., Mr. Petit Rose writes me..about renewing his lease. 1867 MRS. RIDDELL *Far above Rubies* II. xii. 295 Arthur never insisted on a settlement of their accounts, never objected to renew bills. 1887 RUSKIN *Præterita* II. 391 The lease expired..and she did not care to renew it. 1896 *Law Times* C. 488/1 The trustees on its expiration at the end of a year, refused to renew this ticket.

b. *absol.* To give a fresh lease or bill.

1688 WOOD *Life* 19 Nov. (O.H.S.) III. 283 He hath had a good yeare lately for renewing and hath received 800 *li.* 1837 THACKERAY *Ravenswing* i, 'Won't the party renew?' 'Impossible—it's the third renewal'. 1875 W. S. GILBERT *Tom Cobb* I, I suppose I have renewed oftener than any man aloive!

9. *intr.* To grow afresh, become new again.

1414 BRAMPTON *Penit. Ps.* (Percy Soc.) 43 Out of here handys I may no3t fle, But 3yf thi grace in me renewe. *c* 1430 LYDG. *Min. Poems* (Percy Soc.) 243 Whan blood renewyth in every creature, Som observaunce doyng to nature. 1473 *Paston Lett.* III. 103, I praye yow be ware that the olde love of Pampyng renewe natt. 1508 DUNBAR *Tua Mariit Wemen* 116 Quhen that the sound of his saw sinkis in my eris, Than ay renewis my noy. 1549–62 STERNHOLD & H. *Ps.* CIII. v, Like as the Eagle castes her bill, Wherby her age renueth. 1578 LYTE *Dodoens* 310 Causing the heare to renewe and growe againe. 1607 SHAKS. *Timon* IV. iii. 68 Renew I could not like the Moone. 1621 BP. MOUNTAGU *Diatribæ* 299 But come wee to *Primitias*, renuing and growing euery yeere. 1697 DRYDEN *Virg. Past.* x. 106 Gallus, for whom my holy Flames renew Each Hour. 1725 POPE *Odyss.* VIII. 569 Thus while he sung, Ulysses' griefs renew. 1766 *Compl. Farmer* s.v. *Tan*, If the tan is forked up,..the heat will renew again.

†**b.** To change by growth. *Obs. rare.*

1413 *Pilgr. Sowle* (Caxton 1483) IV. ii. 58 These pepyns myght nought kyndely as they shold renewen in to a good Appeltree. *c* 1420 *Pallad. on Husb.* I. 116 Out of their lond eek seedis wol renewe And chaunge hem silf.

†**10.** To begin a fresh attack, to return or come back, *upon* one; to renew the fight. *Obs.*

c 1470 HENRY *Wallace* V. 289 Sad men in deid wpon him can renew. *Ibid.* VII. 707 Ynglis archaris apon thaim can ranew. 1606 SHAKS. *Tr. & Cr.* V. v. 6 Renew, renew, the fierce Polidamas Hath beate downe Menon. *a* 1656 BP. HALL *Rem. Wks.* (1660) 35 My former Complaint renewed upon me.

†**b.** To return (*to* one); to come back. *Obs.*

c 1470 HENRY *Wallace* X. 691 Feill scalyt folk to thaim will son ranew. 1697 DRYDEN *Virg. Georg.* III. 448 Time is lost, which never will renew, While we too far the pleasing Path pursue.

11. To begin again, recommence.

1523 LD. BERNERS *Froiss.* I. cccxxvii. 511 Howe the warre renewed bytwene the french kyng, and the kyng of Nauerre. 1583 STOCKER *Civ. Warres Lowe C.* I. 37 b, This tumult and trouble was supressed, yet renued it agayne. 1640 tr. *Verdere's Rom. of Rom.* III. 223 Whereupon the combat renewed with more cruelty than before. 1744 HARRIS *Three Treat.* III. ii. (1765) 184 Our former Conversation insensibly renewed. 1771 GOLDSM. *Hist. Eng.* II. 62 The battle renewing at the dawn of the ensuing day. 1802 MARIAN MOORE *Lascelles* III. 161 Their intimacy renewed, and Mrs. Carisbrooke was as communicative as [etc.].

†**12.** To resume relations *with* a person. *Obs.*

1768 *Woman of Honor* I. 175 She sincerely detests any thought of renewing with him. *Ibid.* II. 134 If he had seen the least glimpse of an opening to renew with you.

†**renew**, *v.*² *Obs. rare*$^{-1}$. [ad. F. *renouer* (†*-nuer*, *-noer*) to tie again, f. *re-* RE- + *nouer* to tie.] *trans.* To tie (a horse) *to* a thing.

c 1400 *Sowdone Bab.* 1126 Where he was light and toke his rest, His stede renewed til a grene tre.

renewa'bility. [f. next + -ITY.] The quality of being renewable (Worcester 1860).

1976 *Nature* 27 May 350/2 The renewability of forests is a key point in the book.

renewable (rɪ'nju:əb(ə)l), *a.* (*sb.*) [f. RENEW *v.*¹ + -ABLE.] **A.** *adj.* **1.** Capable of being renewed.

1727 BRADLEY *Fam. Dict.* s.v. *Diascordium*, The Colour is indeed renewable by a little fresh Bole. 1779 *Sylph* II. 174 Heaven, who has given us renewable affections. 1817 JAS. MILL *Brit. India* I. II. v. 192 The great estates, in Ireland for example, let under leases perpetually renewable. 1864 BRIGHT *Sp., Permiss. Bill* 8 June (1876) 512 The licence is renewable from year to year. 1874 MOTLEY *Barneveld* xiii. II. 104 A twenty years' peace, renewable by agreement.. had been negotiated.

2. Of a source of energy: not depleted by its utilization.

1971 *Sci. Amer.* Sept. 43/2 (*caption*) Continuous, or renewable, energy supply can be divided into two categories: solar and nonsolar. 1972 ROCKS & RUNYON *Energy Crisis* 8 We have already expanded in numbers and living standard far beyond the capacity of our most accessible and renewable energy source [*sc.* flowing water] to sustain us even in the present. 1975 RUEDISILI & FIREBAUGH *Perspectives on Energy* iv. 295 Geothermal, tidal, and wind energy are three..renewable sources of energy that have been harnessed to a greater or lesser extent. 1978 *Nature* 20 Apr. 661/1 Renewable sources of energy—wind, wave, sun, geothermal heat and the like—are..taken seriously at the United Kingdom Atomic Energy Authority.

B. as *sb.* A renewable source of energy.

1974 *Oceanus* XVII. 20 (*heading*) Using two renewables. 1980 *Times* 22 Aug. 10/2 The CEGB decision to take the first commercial steps for wind-powered electricity makes it easier..to take renewables seriously.

renewal (rɪ'nju:əl). [f. as prec. + -AL¹.]

a. The act of renewing, or the state of being renewed; also, an instance of this.

1681–6 J. SCOTT *Chr. Life* (1747) III. 227 He continued all along in that particular Renewal that was made of it to the People of Israel. 1695 *Eng. Anc. Const. Eng.* 24 A Renewal of this original contract. 1735 BOLINGBROKE *Diss. on Parties* xviii. (ed. 2) 218 The Revolution was..one of those Renewals of our Constitution that We have often mentioned. 1796 C. MARSHALL *Garden.* xii. (1798) 164 A renewal every three or four years will produce finer fruit. 1838 DICKENS *Lett.* (1880) I. 11 Your handwriting came like the renewal of some old friendship. 1874 GREEN *Short Hist.* vi. §2. 277 A return of the King's malady brought the renewal of York's Protectorate.

b. A planned urban redevelopment. Also in phr. ***urban renewal*** s.v. URBAN *a.*

1965 *Economist* 6 Feb. 544/1 For its size Boston is the most renewal-minded city in the country. Mr. Slayton, the federal Urban Renewal Commissioner, recently called its eleven integrated projects..'a laboratory demonstration of renewal techniques'. 1967 *Boston Sunday Herald* 26 Mar. I. 9/6 The BRA leadership is pushing to exempt 'planned unit developments' in renewal areas. 1978 *Jrnl. R. Soc. Arts* CXXVI. 595/2 In urban renewal schemes where roadways and footpaths are altered the lower voltage system usually requires replacement.

c. *attrib.*, as ***renewal premium***, ***shoot***; **Renewal Sunday** (see quot.); **renewal theory**, the branch of probability theory which considers populations of objects which fail and need renewal after randomly distributed intervals.

1862 NEALE *Hymns East. Ch.* 53 St. Thomas's Sunday, called also Renewal Sunday: with us Low Sunday. **1886** W. A. HARRIS *Techn. Dict. Fire Insur.*, Renewal Premiums. **1897** WILLIS *Flower. Pl.* II. 335 In the leaf-axils are formed the 'renewal'-shoots which last over the winter. **1940** G. A. D. PREINREICH *Present Status of Renewal Theory* 25 Lotka has a method of mathematically describing renewal theory, using the Hertz method of approximation to the solution. **1958** *Jrnl. R. Statistical Soc.* B. XX. 243 The study of renewal theory has its origins in the discussion of self-renewing aggregates and the non-stochastic treatment of questions of population growth. **1966** S. BEER *Decision & Control* x. 216 Renewal theory concerns itself with strategies for replacing worn out parts, machines, aircraft or anything else that has to be renewed.

† **reˈnewance.** *Obs. rare*⁻¹. [f. as prec. + -ANCE.] Renewal.

1630 LORD *Banians* 31 Giving a fresh renewance of gladnesse to their parents (when their joy grew stale).

renewed (rɪˈnjuːd), *ppl. a.* [f. as prec. + -ED¹.] Revived, re-established, etc.

a **1400–50** *Alexander* 2819 Rodogars þe riche þat renewid [*v.r.* reuerent] lady þe dere dame of Dari. **1483** *Cath. Angl.* 303/2 Renewyd,..*renouatus.* **1604** SHAKS. *Oth.* II. i. 81 Giue renew'd fire to our extincted Spirits. **1650** FULLER *Pisgah* II. xii. 243 Before his feet (in his renewed kingdome) were firmely fastened on the throne of authority. **1746** HERVEY *Medit.* (1818) 259 Are we become a renewed people,.. zealous of good works? **1781** COWPER *Hope* 35 Renewed desire would grace with other speech Joys always prized. **1821** SHELLEY *Adonais* xix, The beauty and the joy of their renewed might. **1863** GEO. ELIOT *Romola* xxiv, His strong voice had alternately trembled with emotion and risen again in renewed energy.

Hence **reˈnewedly** *adv.*, **reˈnewedness**.

a **1660** HAMMOND *Wks.* (1683) IV. 663 The Apostle..sets up an inward sanctity and renewedness of heart. **1748** RICHARDSON *Clarissa* (1811) II. 336, I declare renewedly my firm resolution to give up the man. **1838** CHALMERS *Wks.* XIII. 115 Renewedness of mind, however awkward a phrase, is perhaps the most nearly expressive of it. **1854** ABBOTT *Napoleon* (1855) II. xii. 200 He was..treated with unblushing perfidy, renewedly assailed without warning.

renewer (rɪˈnjuːə(r)). [f. as prec. + -ER¹.] One who or that which renews, restores, etc.

1398 TREVISA *Barth. De P.R.* x. iv. (Bodl. MS.), Fuyre is iclepid renewer of alle þinges and wardeyne of kinde. *a* **1547** SURREY in *Tottel's Misc.* (Arb.) 14 O place of blisse, renuer of my woes. **1589** COOPER *Admon.* 105 The first renuers and restorers of the Gospell in this latter age. **1615** BRATHWAIT *Strappado* (1878) 179 Protectors of our peace, And sole renewers of our hopes encrease. **1740** WATERLAND *Regeneration* Wks. 1823 VI. 352 He is not his own regenerator..: he is, however, his own renewer. **1861** TRENCH *Ep. 7 Churches Asia* 127 Everywhere setting forth himself as the only renewer of all which sin had made old. **1884** *Western Morn. News* 10 Sept. 4/5 The 'Renewer', that portion of the Electric Telegraph by means of which long cable telegraphy has been made possible.

renewing (rɪˈnjuːɪŋ), *vbl. sb.* [f. as prec. + -ING¹.] The action of RENEW *v.*¹ in various senses; also, an instance of this.

1398 TREVISA *Barth. De P.R.* x. iv. (Bodl. MS.), Fuyre haþ vertu of renewing, for alle þinges eldeþ..ȝif þei beþ nought ikepte..by vertu of fuyre. **1456** SIR G. HAYE *Law Arms* (S.T.S.) 3 The land..is sa turnyt now for the renewing of new lordschip. **1483** *Cath. Angl.* 303/2 Renewynge, *renouacio.* **1526** *Pilgr. Perf.* (W. de W. 1531) 72 In the renewynge of the inwarde man. **1577** B. GOOGE *Heresbach's Husb.* IV. (1586) 190b, Cardamus greatly commendeth this hearbe, for the comforting and renuing of a decayed memorie. **1628** WITHER *Brit. Rememb.* III. 219, I gained some renewings of that rest. **1679** DRYDEN *Pref. to Tr. & Cr.* Ess. (Ker) I. 205 The quarrel..concludes with a warm renewing of their friendship. **1740** WATERLAND *Regeneration* Wks. 1823 VI. 342 The words of the original may be rendered, by the laver of regeneration, and by the renewing. **1892** *Athenæum* 21 May 670/2 [Herbaceous plants] will require much renewing.

reˈnewing, *ppl. a.* [-ING².] That renews.

1602 CAREW *Cornwall* 11 They sink a Shaft downe thither ..to admit a renewing Vent. **1715** CHAPPELOW *Right way to be rich* (1717) 141 You may take t'other look at it..every renewing look enhanses the value and worth of it. **1848** R. I. WILBERFORCE *Doctr. Incarnation* xiv. (1852) 383 These..are the renewing principles of human society.

renewle, variant of RENULE *v. Obs.*

reˈnewment. Now *rare* or *Obs.* [f. RENEW *v.*¹ + -MENT.] Renewal.

1571 GOLDING *Calvin on Ps.* xviii. 44 It was an incredible renewment, that he did not only soodeinly set vp the people agein [etc.]. **1637** R. HUMPHREY tr. *St. Ambrose* Pref., The renewment of the heart is proper to the spirit. **1812** G. CHALMERS *Dom. Econ. Gt. Brit.* 204 The renewment of our commercial treaty with Russia.

reney(e, etc., obs. forms of RENAY.

† **renˈfierce,** *v. Obs. rare*⁻¹. [app. f. FIERCE *a.*, on anal. of next.] *trans.* To render fierce.

1590 SPENSER *F.Q.* II. viii. 45 Whereat renfierst with wrath and sharp regret, He stroke so hugely [etc.].

† **renˈforce,** *v. Obs.* Also 6 renforse, re'nforce, r'inforce, 6–7 r'enforce. [ad. F. *renforcer*: see RE- and ENFORCE *v.*, also RE-ENFORCE *v.*, REINFORCE *v.*]

1. *trans.* To reinforce, strengthen.

1525 LD. BERNERS *Froiss.* II. cxiv. [cx.] 327, I am yet wyllynge to treate of this matter more at lengthe, to renforce this hystorye. **1549** *Compl. Scot.* Ep. Ded. 6 He renforsit the toune vitht victualis, hagbutaris, ande munitions. **1589** PUTTENHAM *Eng. Poesie* III. xxv. (Arb.) 309 Arte is an ayde and coadiutor to nature..by renforcing the causes wherein shee is impotent and defectiue. **1602** SEGAR *Hon. Mil. & Civ.* I. xvi. 23 Having omitted opportunitie to renforce a place of strength called Petra. *a* **1652** BROME *Covent Garden* v. iii, R'enforce the Ranks that are broken.

2. To compel (one) again *to* do a thing. *rare*⁻¹.

1590 SPENSER *F.Q.* II. x. 48 Yet twise they were repulsed backe againe, And twise renforst backe to their ships to fly.

Hence † **renˈforcing** *vbl. sb.*; also † **renˈforcer**.

1566 PAINTER *Pal. Pleas.* I. 92 Erasistratus feling the renforcing of the poulce to proue howe long it would continewe,..still helde his fingers vpon the beating of the poulces. **1589** PUTTENHAM *Eng. Poesie* III. xvi[i]. (Arb.) 194 *marg.*, Emphasis, or the Renforcer. **1604** EDMONDS *Observ. Cæsar's Comm.* 4 The benefite..consisteth chiefly in the renforcing, or..the redoubling of such troupes.

† **renforcee.** *Obs.* Also 7 ranforcee, renforce. [a. F. (*étoffe*) *renforcée*, pa. pple. of *renforcer*: see prec.] A strong make of silk.

1688 *Abridgm. Spec. Patents, Weaving* (1861) 1 Invencion of making, dressing, and lustrateing silke, called black plain, alamodes, ranforcees, and lutestringes. **1698** *Lond. Gaz.* No. 3366/4 A considerable parcel of narrow and broad Allamodes, Renforcees and Lustrings.

ren-forst: see *rain-frost*, RAIN *sb.*¹ 5 a.

reng (rɛŋ). [ad. Pers. *rang*, Skr. *raṅga* colour, hue.] A colouring, esp. a hair-dye.

1929 REDGROVE & FOAN *Blonde or Brunette?* xi. 73 The leaves, dried and powdered, of *Indigofera argentea*, L. ('reng'), cultivated in Persia, constitute the best form in which to employ indigo. **1934** *S.P.E. Tract* XLI. 16 *Reng* is perhaps now in sufficiently common use by hair-dressers to be accorded a place in the national vocabulary. **1966** J. S. COX *Illustr. Dict. Hairdressing* 79/1 *Henna-Reng*, a hair dye consisting of a combination of Henna and Indigo.

reng, obs. f. REIGN *v.*, var. RENGE *sb.*¹ *Obs.*

renga (ˈrɛŋgə). Also renge, renka. [Jap., = linked (verse).] A form of Japanese verse established by the 15th century and consisting of a series of half-tanka, contributed by different poets in turn.

See also note s.v. HAIKU.

1877 W. G. ASTON *Gram. Jap. Written Lang.* (ed. 2) x. 198 *Renka*..is where one person composes part (commonly the second part) of a *tanka*, the remainder being added by some one else. **1890** B. H. CHAMBERLAIN *Things Japanese* 272 A favourite game at these tournaments called *renge*, wherein one person composes the second hemistich of a verse and another person has to provide it with a first hemistich, seems to date from the eleventh century. **1911** —— *Jap. Poetry* IV. 159 This was termed *Renga*, lit. 'linked verses'. **1968** E. MINER *Introd. Jap. Court Poetry* 163 *Renga*... A form dating from about the thirteenth century; several authors would compose a sequence, usually of a hundred sections or stanzas, alternating 5, 7, 5 syllable lines with 7, 7 syllable units, any two of which formed a complete poem.

rengaile, variant of RANGALE. *Obs.*

rengas (ˈrɛŋgəs). [Malay.] Any of several East Indian trees of the family Anacardiaceæ, esp. *Gluta renghas*, containing a sap that often produces allergic reactions in those touching it; the wood or sap of this tree. Also *attrib.*

1836 J. LOW *Diss. Soil & Agric. Penang* iv. 200 *Runggas* —a lofty tree, the juice of which is deleterious to the human frame, creating swellings over the whole body. **1935** I. H. BURKILL *Dict. Econ. Products Malay Penin.* I. 1079 Furniture of 'rĕngas' may certainly be used without inconvenience. **1939** A. KEITH *Land below Wind* xiii. 221 One disadvantage of wearing shorts was the long expanse of leg which was left bare, with the result of..patches of *rengas* poisoning from rubbing against the leaves of the *rengas* tree. **1940** E. J. H. CORNER *Wayside Trees of Malaya* I. 116 Most *Rengas*-trees are large and not a few are among the tallest and finest in the forest. **1956** *Nature* 25 Feb. 366/1 The Colonial hardwood, rengas, has been shown to contain two pigments. **1965** R. MCKIE *Company of Animals* xi. 164 Jim ..confirms the story of the Rengas tree rash. Some people are allergic to this tree.

† **renge,** *sb.*¹ *Obs.* Also 4 reng, rengge, 5 reenge. [a. OF. *renge* (Godef.), related to *renger*, *-ier*, to RENGE. The var. *range* was also adopted in ME., and finally became the standard form: see RANGE *sb.*] A rank, row, line, esp. of fighting men.

13.. *Sir Beues* (A.) 3807 Þe kinges sone of Asie..Out of þe renge he com ride. *c* **1330** R. BRUNNE *Chron. Wace* (Rolls) 5021 Cesar..arraied þem in renges right, & assigned whiche bataille first schold fight. *c* **1386** CHAUCER *Knt.'s T.* 1736 In two renges faire they hem dresse. *c* **1450** *Merlin* 588 Merlin that rode fro oo renge to a-nother ascride hem often 'ore auaunt'. **1481** CAXTON *Myrr.* II. vi. 77 Wythin the ryuer & flode of ynde named Ganges goon the eeles by grete renges whiche ben .c.c.c. feet long. **1530** PALSGR. 262/1 Renge, *rovte, ranc.*

† **renge,** *sb.*² *Obs.* Also 4 reynge. [Of obscure origin; cf. RANGE *sb.*²] A sieve or strainer.

c **1362** *Durham Acc. Rolls* (Surtees) 566 Pro uno reynge emp. pro pistrina xviij *d.* *c* **1430** *Two Cookery-bks.* 38 Þerow a crees bunte syfte hem, & for defaute of a bonte, take a Renge. **1506** *Yatton Church-W. Acc.* (Som. Rec. Soc.) 128 For botomyng of yᵉ clensyng renge..iiij *d.* **1697** G. DAMPIER in *Phil. Trans.* XX. 50 Powder it, and pass it through a Renge or fine Seive.

renge, obs. Sc. f. REIGN *sb.*, obs. f. RING *v.*, var. RINK man. *Obs.*

† **renge,** *v. Obs.* Also 5 rengne. [ad. OF. *renger* to set in rank or line, to roam: see RENGE *sb.*¹ and cf. RANGE *v.*¹]

1. *intr.* **a.** To move hither and thither, roam, stray. **b.** To draw up in line or rank.

a **1225** *Ancr. R.* 164 Þe helle liun rengeð & reccheð euer abuten..soule uorte uorswoluwen. *c* **1330** R. BRUNNE *Chron.* (1810) 40 His Danes wild he venge Ageyn him in bataile, to renne & to renge. *c* **1410** *Master of Game* (MS. Digby 182) xvi, Commonliche þei go byfore her maister rengeynge and playnge with hir taile. *c* **1420** *Avow. Arth.* vii, The raches comun rengnyng him by, And bayet him fulle boldely. *c* **1450** *Merlin* 198 Than thei rode forth and renged close that wey where as the childeren foughten.

2. *trans.* To set in order, put in array.

13.. *Coer de L.* 4443 Her folk wer rengyd in that playn. *c* **1330** R. BRUNNE *Chron.* (1810) 159 Richard was perceyued, þei were renged redie, & how þer pencels weyued. ? *a* **1366** CHAUCER *Rom. Rose* 1380 With many high laurer and pine, Was renged [F. *pueplés*] clene all that gardine. *c* **1410** *Master of Game* (MS. Digby 182) xxiv, Alle þe oþer tyndes gret and longe, wele sette and wele renged. **1475** *Bk. Noblesse* (Roxb.) 70 He had devised and ordeined the herbers to be compassed, rengid, and made. *c* **1489** CAXTON *Blanchardyn* xxix. 105 The two barons..camen to the felde, where they fonden their folke renged to-gydre. **1530** PALSGR. 685/2, I renge, or set in array, or in order one by another, *je arrengie.*

refl. *c* **1330** R. BRUNNE *Chron. Wace* (Rolls) 8257 To renne on þe [pey] schul þem renge. *c* **1450** *Merlin* 127 Than two of hem renged hem and priked after the messagers. *c* **1500** *Melusine* 352 Thenne armed hym euery man, And..came & renged them before the bataylles.

Hence † **renged** *ppl. a. Obs.*

1609 HEYWOOD *Brit. Troy* XIV. xiv, Now mongst their renged Squadrons Troylus flings.

† **ˈrenger.** *Obs. rare*⁻⁰. [Cf. RENGE *sb.*² and RANGER *sb.*] A sieve.

1530 PALSGR. 262/1 Renger for a baker.

rengge, variant of RENGE *sb.*¹ *Obs.*

rengne, obs. f. REIGN *sb.* and *v.*; var. RENGE *v.*

† **renˈgrade,** *v. Obs. rare*⁻¹. [f. *ren-* (as in *renforce*) + *grade*, after DEGRADE *v.*] *trans.* To restore from degradation.

1589 WARNER *Alb. Eng.* v. xxiv, His flight Scotch-qwened his Sister, she rengraded Englands blood.

† **renˈgrege,** *v. Obs. rare*⁻¹. [ad. F. *rengréger* (15th c.): see RE- and ENGREGE *v.*] *trans.* To aggravate.

1600 BP. W. BARLOW *Serm. Paul's Cross* (1601) B viij, Titles, that..imputeth to men faultes which they haue not committed, or doth rengrege or amoinder, that is, make greater or lesse the faults committed.

renguerra (rɛnˈgwɛərə). *Vet. Sci.* Also **renguera**. [S. Amer. Sp. *renguera* limping, lameness, f. *renguear* (Sp. *renquear*) to limp.] = SWAYBACK 2.

1917 S. H. GAIGER in *Jrnl. Compar. Path. & Therapeutics* XXX. 209 Renguera is a new and hitherto undescribed disease of lambs, occurring in the Peruvian Andes. **1938** *Nature* 5 Mar. 400/1 The resulting lesions of demyelination are anatomically related to those observed in the enzootic paraplegia (renguerra) reported to occur among lambs bred in certain areas in the Peruvian Andes. **1966** A. ROBERTSON *Internat. Encycl. Vet. Med.* II. 698 Synonyms [for copper deficiency]. Enzootic ataxia; swayback;..renguerra.

reni-, comb. form of L. *rēn* kidney (see REINS), used in some scientific terms, as *renicapsular*, *-cardiac*, etc.

1858 MAYNE *Expos. Lex.*, *Renifolius*, having reniform leaves,..renifolious. *Renipustulatus*, marked with spots in the form of kidneys: renipustulate.

† **reˈniant.** *Obs. rare.* Also **renyant**. [a. F. *reniant*, pres. pple. of *renier*: see RENAY *v.*] A renegade.

1387–8 T. USK *Test. Love* I. iii. (Skeat) l. 118 A renyant [1560 reniant] forjuged hath not halfe the care. **1674** BLOUNT *Glossogr.*, *Reniant*, a Revolter, a Runnagate.

renicky-boo: see RANNYGAZOO.

renidifiˈcation. [RE- 5 a.] The action of building a nest a second time (Webster 1864, citing Bulwer). So **reˈnidify,** *v.* to make another nest (*Cent. Dict.* 1891).

renierite (rəˈnɪəraɪt). *Min.* [ad. F. *reniérite* (J. F. Vaes 1948, in *Ann. de la Soc. géol. de Belgique* LXXII. B22), f. the name of A. *Renier*, 20th-c. Belgian geologist: see -ITE¹.] A sulphide of copper, germanium, and other metals $(Cu,Fe)_3(Fe,Ge)S_4$, occurring as yellowish tetragonal crystals and granular masses.

1949 *Mineral Mag.* XXVIII. 737 Renierite... Sulphide of Cu, Fe, Ge (7·75%), Zn, As... Named after Prof. Armand Renier, Director of the Geological Survey of Belgium. Near germanite. **1966** *Mineral Abstr.* XVII. 537/2 Germanium-bearing (250 p.p.m. Ge) sphalerite occurring with galena in mineralized Cambrian limestone and dolomite in..southern Sardinia, is found to contain numerous inclusions of renierite up to 10μ in size.

reniew, obs. form of RENEW *v.*¹

reniform ('ri:nɪfɔ:m), *a.* [ad. mod.L. *reniformis*: see REINS and -FORM, and cf. F. *réniforme.*] Having the form of a kidney; kidney-shaped. (Chiefly in scientific use.)

1753 CHAMBERS *Cycl. Supp.* s.v. *Leaf*, Reniform Leaf, one of the shape of a kidney. **1796** KIRWAN *Elem. Min.* (ed. 2) II. 78 [Pyrites is] found reniform. **1819** G. SAMOUELLE *Entom. Compendium* 81 Shell reniform, velvety, and green. **1834** McMURTRIE *Cuvier's Anim. Kingd.* 453 The last joint of the antennæ is either almost globular or reniform. **1861** R. F. BURTON *City of Saints* 570 Three-legged stools with reniform seats. **1880** HUXLEY *Crayfish* v. 237 The corneal substance of the eye is reniform.

Comb. **1847** W. E. STEELE *Field Bot.* 113 Leaves reniform-cordate, glabrous.

renig, U.S. var. RENEGUE *v.*

renigat(e, obs. Sc. forms of RENEGATE.

renin ('ri:nɪn). *Physiol.* [f. L. *rēnes* kidneys + -IN[1].] †**1.** A substance extracted from animals' kidneys and used in medicine. *Obs.*

1894 G. M. GOULD *Illustr. Dict. Med., Biol. & Allied Sci.* 940/2 Extracts have been prepared from nearly every organ in the animal body;..cerebrin, from the brain,..ossin, from bones, renin, from the kidneys. **1900** DORLAND *Med. Dict.* 565/1 *Renin*, a therapeutic extract prepared from the kidneys of animals.

2. A proteolytic enzyme secreted by and stored in the kidneys, which acts in the blood to convert angiotensinogen (hypertensinogen) to angiotensin (hypertensin). [Coined in this sense as G. *renin* (R. Tigerstedt, in *Compt. Rend. 12me Congrès Internat. de Médecine 1897* (1899) II. II. 29).]

1906 *Lancet* 19 May 1375/2 The pressor substance, to which these workers give the name 'renin', is not dialysable. **1938** *Proc. Soc. Exper. Biol. & Med.* XXXIX. 214 Undialyzed renin (0·2 cc) caused moderate vasoconstriction. *Ibid.* 215 Renin is an enzyme-like substance which is activated by a kinase-like material contained in the protein fraction of plasma and whole blood. **1959** [see HYPERTENSIN]. **1965** [see HYPERTENSINOGEN]. **1968** PASSMORE & ROBSON *Compan. Med. Stud.* I. xxxiii. 20/2 Renin is an enzyme which on reaching the blood activates an α_2-globulin called angiotensin formed in the liver, making angiotensin I, a polypeptide containing ten amino acids. Another enzyme converts angiotensin I to angiotensin II by removing two amino acids. This last substance is the most potent pressor agent known. **1977** FREEMAN & DAVIS in J. Genest et al. *Hypertension* vi. 211/1 Renin is synthesized and stored..in the granules of JG [*sc.* juxtaglomerular] cells which are located primarily in the renal afferent arteriole, although these granular cells have also been identified in the efferent arteriolar wall..and in the mesangial cells.

†**re'niously**, *adv. Obs. rare*[−1]. [irreg. f. *reny*, RENAY *sb.* + -OUS + -LY[2].] Like a renegade.

1522 *Stat. Order of Garter* ⁋2 in Ashm. (1672), He that then reniously and cowardly flieth or departith away from thens, ought to be estiemed..never worthi to be electe Knyght, or Felow of the said Company.

'**renish**, *a. Obs.* exc. *dial.* Forms: 4 **renischche**, 4–5 **renysch**, 6 **rhenish**, 7 *dial.* **rennish**, 9 **ran(n)ish**; 4–5 **renyst**, **renisht**, ? 7 **renisht**. [Of unknown origin: cf. RUNISH. The sense in early examples is often obscure.] Strange, uncouth; fierce, wild, etc.

13.. *E.E. Allit. P.* B. 96 We haf broȝt..Mony renischche renkez & ȝet is roum more. *a* **1400–50** *Alexander* 387 Quen he had wroȝt all his will..with a renyst reryd þis reson he said. *Ibid.* 2943 Ser Dary..Rysys him vp renysch & reȝt in his sete. **1596** NASHE *Saffron Walden* Wks. (Grosart) III. 201 Chute,..that bobd me with nothing but Rhenish furie. ? *a* **1600** *King Estmere* viii. in Child *Ballads* II. 52/1 Thus the renisht them to ryde, Of twoe good renisht steeds. **1691** RAY *N.C. Words* (ed. 2) 58 *Rennish*, furious, passionate: a rennish Bedlam. **1866** BROGDEN *Prov. Words Lincs.*, *Ranish*, rash, precipitate, giddy, wild. **1889** *N.W. Lincs. Gloss.*, *Rannish*, rash, violent.

Hence '**renishly** *adv.*, strangely, roughly.

13.. *E.E. Allit. P.* B. 1724 þe fyste with þe fyngeres..þat rasped renyschly þe woȝe with þe roȝ penne. *a* **1400–50** *Alexander* 4931 The renke within þe redell..Rymed him full renyschly & rekind þir wordis.

Renishe, obs. form of RHENISH.

†**reni'tation.** *Obs. rare*[−1]. [irreg. f. L. *renītī* (see next) + -ATION.] = RENITENCY 1.

1597 A. M. tr. *Guillemeau's Fr. Chirurg.* 21 b/1 If there be greate quantitye it causeth such a renitatione or stretchinge out, as a bottle which is full, and closelye stopped.

†**re'nite**, *v. Obs. rare*[−1]. [ad. L. *renītī*, f. *re-* RE- + *nītī* to struggle.] *intr.* To offer resistance.

1647 WARD *Simp. Cobler* 28, I dare say, they that most renite, will least repent.

renitence. *rare.* [a. F. *rénitence* (16th c., Paré): see RENITENT and -ENCE.] = next.

1652 CHARLETON *Darkn. Atheism* 265 An exclusion of all coaction, violence, renitence or imposition. **1676** H. MORE *Remarks* 14 The weight of Lead..had crammed the Sand together..that it stuck by renitence of its irregular parts, one against another. **1743** HON. C. YORKE in *Warburton's Unpubl. Papers* (1841) 140 A man would not do amiss to shut up his books; and without the least renitence roll in the vortex of dulness. **1917** C. R. PAYNE tr. *Pfister's Psychoanal. Method* viii. 168 The result of this renitence consists mostly in the continuance of those symptoms of disease which depend on the repression.

renitency (rɪ'naɪtənsɪ, 'rɛnɪtənsɪ). Now *rare.* Also 7 **-ancie**. [See prec. and -ENCY.]

†**1.** Physical resistance, *esp.* the resistance of a body to pressure. *Obs.*

1613 M. RIDLEY *Magn. Bodies* 2 Freed from all obstacle and renitency. **1634** T. JOHNSON *Parey's Chirurg.* VII. xvii. (1678) 183 The signs of such a Tumour are a certain renitency or resistance. **1681** GLANVILL *Sadducismus* 157 It necessarily and by an insuperable Renitencie expels and excludes all other Matter. **1704** J. HARRIS *Lex. Techn.* I, *Renitency*, is that Resistence which there is in solid Bodies when they press upon, or are impelled one against another.

2. Resistance to constraint or compulsion, opposition, reluctance. Now *rare.*

1626 PRYNNE *Perpet. Regen. Man's Est.* 324 There is a reluctancie, renitancie [*pr.* reuitancie], dislike and hatred of it in his soule. **1668** R. STEELE *Husbandman's Calling* vi. (1678) 157 His oxe..suffers the sharp visits of the goad without renitency or opposition. **1702** C. MATHER *Magn. Chr.* IV. iv. (1852) 96 The obstruction which the renitencies of that gentleman threatened. **1761** STERNE *Tr. Shandy* III. xxxiv, Nature has form'd the mind of man with the same happy backwardness and renitency against conviction. **1802** PALEY *Nat. Theol.* ix. (1819) 129 We have here no endeavour, but the reverse of it; a constant renitency and reluctance. **1844** H. ROGERS *Ess.* (1855) III. 109 This renitency of Mr. Gladstone's to accept..the consequences of his Church Principles.

renitent (rɪ'naɪtənt, 'rɛnɪtənt), *a.* Now *rare.* [a. F. *rénitent* (16th c., Paré), or ad. L. *renītent-em*, pres. pple. of *renītī*: see RENITE *v.*]

1. That offers physical resistance; resisting pressure, hard.

1701 RAY *Creation* II. (ed. 3) 245 An inflation of the Muscles whereby they become both soft, and yet renitent like so many Pillows. **1755** B. MARTIN *Mag. Arts & Sc.* 305 The electrical Matter..can go no further, by Reason of the renitent Quality of the silken Strings. **1889** J. M. DUNCAN *Clin. Lect. Dis. Wom.* xxvii. (ed. 4) 213 The right ovary was swollen, renitent, as big as a walnut.

2. Recalcitrant.

1847 PRANDI tr. *Cantù's Reform. Europe* I. 257 [He] constrained the people to go to mass, and punished the renitent with imprisonment and confiscation. **1882** *Edin. Rev.* July 8 The gaps left by renitent warriors were rapidly filled by intending plunderers.

†**re'nix(e.** *Obs. rare.* [ad. L. type **renixus* (after *nixus*) for actual *renīsus*, f. *renītī*: see RENITE *v.*] A backward effort.

1666 G. HARVEY *Morb. Angl.* iv. 31 The blood by expansion and turgency making a potent renix. **1689** —— *Curing Dis. by Expect.* xxii. 181 A strong pressure upon the Arteria magna, which by a potent renixe did duplicate its force of Pulsation.

†**renk**[1]. *Obs. rare*[−1]. [a. F. *renc.*] = RANK *sb.*[1]

c **1530** LD. BERNERS *Arth. Lyt. Bryt.* xxviii. (1814) 81 As Arthur wente searchynge the renkes [*printed* renkthes; F. *les rencs*] and preses, he encountred the Erle of Foys.

renk[2]. *Coal-mining.* [? var. of RANK OF RINK.] (See quots.)

1851 GREENWELL *Coal-trade Terms, Northumb. & Durh.* 42 *Renk*,..a standard distance of 60 or 80 yards (called the first renk), upon which a standard price is paid for putting a score of coals. **1860** *Mining Gloss.* (Weale) *Renk* (Newc.), The average distance the coals are brought by the putters.

renk, var. RINK man *Obs.*; obs. f. RING *sb.*, RINK course.

renka, var. RENGA.

†**renke**, ? for *renge*, obs. f. REIGN *sb.*

c **1440** *York Myst.* xxix. 17, I haue þe renke and þe rewle of all þe ryall.

†**renkning**, obs. Sc. var. RANKING *vbl. sb.*

1581 *Sc. Acts Jas. VI* (1814) III. 233/1 The samyn was remittit togidder with the renkning and placeing of the haill burrowis within this realme to the commissionaris.

'**renky**, *a. dial.* Also 7 **rencky**, **renty**. [Of obscure origin.] Large and well-made. (See also *Eng. Dial. Dict.*)

1683 G. MERITON *Yorks. Dial.* 11 There is a Rencky Cow, that beats all th' rest. **1691** RAY *N.C. Words* (ed. 2) 58 *Renty*, handsome, well shaped, spoken of Horses, Cows &c.

†**ren'large**, *v. Obs. rare*[−1]. [f. RE- + ENLARGE *v.*; cf. RE-ENLARGE *v.*] *trans.* To set free or open up again.

1616 J. LANE *Cont. Sqr.'s T.* VI. 88 B'entreatinge Manor Lordes, folkes lesse to flize, commons renlarge, restore thold colonies.

renlesse, obs. var. RENDLES rennet.

renlett, obs. f. RUNLET.

renlys, obs. var. RENDLES.

renminbi (rɛnminbi). Also **jenminpi**, **renminpi**, **Renminbi**. [Chinese *rénmínbì*, f. *rénmín* people + *bì* currency.] **a.** The name of the currency introduced in China in 1948. **b.** Occas. used for yuan, the basic unit of this currency.

1957 *Encycl. Brit.* V. 546 B/1 In 1953 the official currency was the jenminpi or People's bank note on the mainland. **1971** [see JIAO]. **1973** *Times* 21 Mar. (China Trade Suppl.) p. iii/6 The basic unit of renminbi—which is abbreviated to RMB—is the yuan. **1974** *China Reconstructs* July 14/3 The Chinese currency, the Renminbi, is stable. **1975** *Ann. Reg. 1974* 320 More than 60 countries were already using the Chinese renminpi as the trading currency with China. **1979** *Fortune* 21 May 110/2 Its young tellers..eagerly explain to a visitor the tax advantages of converting his money into Chinese renminbi and keeping it in Peking.

rennagat(e, obs. ff. RENEGATE.

rennare, obs. f. RUNNER.

renne, obs. f. RUN *v.*

rennegado, -gate, obs. ff. RENEGADO, -GATE.

rennelesse, obs. var. RENDLES rennet.

renner(e, obs. ff. RUNNER.

rennet ('rɛnɪt), *sb.*[1] Also 5 **renniet**, 6 **rennette**, **rennit**, 6–7 **renet**; see also RUNNET. [f. *renne*, obs. form of RUN *v.*, or perh. repr. an OE. **rynet*: cf. RENDLES, EARNING[3], and G. *renne.*]

1. A mass of curdled milk found in the stomach of an unweaned calf or other animal, used for curdling milk in making cheese, etc.; also, a preparation of the inner membrane of the stomach used for this or other purposes.

14.. *Lat. & Eng. Voc.* in Wr.-Wülcker 591/19 *Lactis*, rennet, or rennynge. **1477** NORTON *Ord. Alch.* v. in Ashm. (1652) 79 Milk, & also Blood, And Renniet which for Cheese is good. *c* **1550** LLOYD *Treas. Health* D iij, The rennet of an hare..healith the faulyng Euell. **1562** J. HEYWOOD *Prov. & Epigr.* (1867) 118 It [cheese] is to strong of the rennet, saith hee. **1575** TURBERV. *Faulconrie* 352 Take little sucking whelpes and feede your hawke with the flesh of them stieped in the milk or renet whiche you shall find in the mawes of them. **1620** VENNER *Via Recta* v. 88 That it bee not tart of the rennet, is far wholsomer. **1676** HOBBES *Iliad* (1677) 82 As quickly as the milk is turn'd to curd, When with a proper rennet it is mixt. **1727–38** CHAMBERS *Cycl.* s.v. *Cheese*, Cheese..being a preparation of milk curdled by means of rennet, and afterwards dried, and hardened. **1797** *Encycl. Brit.* (ed. 3) IV. 369/2 No people take less pains with the rennet than the Cheshire farmers. **1845** TODD & BOWMAN *Phys. Anat.* I. 39 Caseine is coagulated very perfectly by the action of rennet aided by heat. **1875** H. C. WOOD *Therap.* (1879) 607 It is customary to place the dried viscus in wine, and to call the liquid thus formed, as well as the prepared stomach, rennet.

fig. **1651** CHARLETON *Ephes. & Cimm. Matrons* II. (1668) 14 The Bawd, who was the very Renet of Concupiscence.

2. Anything used to curdle milk, *esp.* the plant *Galium verum*, Lady's Bedstraw (cf. CHEESE-RENNET).

1577 B. GOOGE *Heresbach's Husb.* II. 109 b, In the Figge tree it [the sap] is milkie, Whiche serueth as a rennet for Cheese. **1578** LYTE *Dodoens* 540 The herbe [Gallion] may serue for Rennet to make Cheese. **1678** SALMON *Pharm. Lond.* 59 Gallium..is used for Rennet or Runnet to make cheese with. **1750** ELLIS *Mod. Husb.* III. I. vii. 110 The Cliver, or Rennet or Curd-wort,..is also pernicious in curdling Milk in the Cow's Bag. **1851** C. A. JOHNS *Flowers of Field* I. 304 The Highlanders use the roots..and the rest of the plant [*Galium verum*] as rennet to curdle milk. **1889** *N. & Q.* 7th Ser. VIII. 231/2 It is likely enough that *Galium*..is still used as rennet in some neighbourhoods.

3. *attrib.*, as ***rennet ferment***, ***gland***; **rennet-bag**, the stomach of a calf used as rennet; **rennet stomach**, the fourth stomach of a ruminant; **rennet whey** (see quot.); **rennet wort**, the plant *Galium aparine.*

1611 COTGR., *Mulette*,..the maw of a Calfe; which being dressed is called the *Renet-bag. **1727** BRADLEY *Country Housewife* (1728) 84 Cheese..may be strengthned, by putting..Spice into the Rennet Bag, as Pepper. **1797** *Encycl. Brit.* (ed. 3) IV. 369/2 The vell, maw, rennet-bag (or by whatever name it is called). **1897** *Allbutt's Syst. Med.* III. 295 The *rennet ferment is the most constant of all the active constituents of the gastric juice. **1872** THUDICHUM *Chem. Phys.* 10 The many little *rennet glands situated in the walls of the stomach secrete a liquid termed the gastric juice. **1889** tr. *Claus' Zool., Mollusca to Man* 317 The food enters the fourth stomach..the longitudinally folded *rennet stomach or *abomasum.* **1855** OGILVIE *Suppl.*, **Rennet-whey*, the serous part of milk, separated from the caseous, by means of rennet. It is used in pharmacy. **1727** BRADLEY *Country Housewife* (1728) 76 To make an artificial Rennet..that is, to boil the Cliver, or as some call it Goose-grass, or others *Rennet-Wort, in Water.

rennet ('rɛnɪt), *sb.*[2] Forms: 6, 8 **runnet**, 6–8 **renate**, 7 **renat**, 7– **rennet**, (8 **ren(n)ette**, 9 **rennett**). [ad. F. *reinette* (see REINETTE), app. f. *reine* queen (cf. QUEEN *sb.* 9 c), but sometimes written *rainette* as if f. *raine* frog, in allusion to the spots which appear on some varieties. Hence also Du. *renet*, G. and Da. *renette*, Sw. *renett*. The obs. Eng. form *renate* was by some writers explained as from L. *renātus.*] One of a large class of dessert apples of French origin, of which the most esteemed varieties are round or flattish in shape, small or medium sized, firm fleshed, and good for keeping; †also formerly applied to a pippin grafted on a pippin-stock (quots. 1612–42).

a **1568** ASCHAM *Scholem.* I. (Arb.) 36 A childe will chose a sweeting..and refuse a Runnet, because it is than grene, hard, and sowre. **1570–6** LAMBARDE *Peramb. Kent* (1826) 223 The sweet Cherry, the temperate Pipyn, and the golden Renate. **1612** DRAYTON *Poly-olb.* xviii. 677 The Renat, which though first it from Pippin came, Growne through his pureness nice, assumes that curious name. **1642** FULLER *Holy & Prof. St.* II. xxiv. 149 When a Pepin is planted on a Pepin-stock, the fruit growing thence is called a Renate, a most delicious apple. **1688** R. HOLME *Armoury* II. 48/1 The

Rennet is a fine lasting Apple,..the Lincoln Rennet is reputed best. **1707** MORTIMER *Husb.* (1721) II. 264 The Golden Runnet is the most certainest Bearer of any Apple I have met with. **1767** ABERCROMBIE *Ev. Man his own Gard.* (1803) 671 English rennet,..Tender rennet,..Spanish rennet [etc.]. **1825** HONE *Every-day Bk.* I. 908 The true 'golden rennet' can only be heard of at great fruiterers. **1843** J. SMITH *Forest Trees* 156, I may observe that all the rennetts are highly flavoured.

attrib. **1712** tr. *Pomet's Hist. Drugs* I. 143 A Fruit of the Size of our Rennet Apple.

† **'rennet**, *sb.*^{3} *Obs. rare*$^{-1}$. [ad. F. *rénette*, *rainette* (1690).] A farrier's tool, used for probing the hoof of a horse.

1725 BRADLEY *Fam. Dict.* s.v. *Retracts*, Then with your Rennet search the Hole, penetrating to the end of it, where the Nail was rivetted to the Hoof.

† **'rennet**, *v. Obs. rare.* [f. RENNET *sb.*^{1}] *trans.* To curdle (milk) with rennet; to supply with rennet.

c **1624** CHAPMAN *Batrachom.* 59 Nor Cheesecakes,.. Lyurings, (white-skind as ladies:) nor the straines Of prest milke, renneted. **1648** HERRICK *Hesper.*, *To his Book*, Come thou not neere those men, who are like Bread O're-leven'd; or like Cheese o're-renneted.

† **'renneting**, *sb. Obs. rare.* Also 8 **rennetting**. [f. RENNET *sb.*^{2} + -ING^{3}; cf. QUEENING *sb.*, and Flem. *renetting* (De Bo).] = RENNET *sb.*^{2}

1707 MORTIMER *Husb.* 595 Ripe pulpy Apples, as Pippins, Rennetings, &c. that are of a syrupy tenacious nature. *Ibid.* Kalendar Jan., Winter Queenings,..Rennetting.

renneting ('rɛnɪtɪŋ), *vb. sb. Cheese-making.* [f. RENNET *sb.*^{1} + -ING^{1}.] The action or process of adding rennet in order to curdle milk. Also *attrib.*

1894 J. OLIVER *Milk, Cheese & Butter* xi. 172 If no other heating than to obtain renneting temperature, this commenced as soon as last milk has arrived. **1917** WALKER-TISDALE & WOODNUTT *Pract. Cheesemaking* xiii. 108 Renneting. Having ripened the milk and regulated it to the renneting temperature, the rennet is added. **1932** R. H. LEITCH *Cheddar Cheese-Making* vii. 41 The standard temperature of renneting Cheddar cheese is 86 degrees Fahrenheit; under average conditions there is no advantage in a higher renneting temperature. **1937** HARVEY & HILL *Milk Products* iv. 200 Renneting is carried out at a temperature of 80°–91° F. **1950** J. G. DAVIS *Dict. Dairying* 100 Renneting. When the correct acidity has been reached rennet is added at the rate of about 1 ml. per gal. of milk... The renneting acidity is one of the crucial points in cheese-making. **1976** —— *Cheese* III. xxi. 498 There are four crucial stages in cheesemaking. These are the acidity at renneting, the stage of pitching, the point at which the whey is removed from the curd, and the time of milling, salting and putting to press.

rennible, obs. form of RENABLE.

renniet, obs. form of RENNET *sb.*^{1}

rennigat(e, -gatt, obs. Sc. ff. RENEGATE.

rennin ('rɛnɪn). *Physiol.* [f. RENN-ET *sb.*^{1} + -IN^{1}.] The specific milk-curdling enzyme of rennet. Hence **re'nninogen**, the zymogen which produces rennin (*Syd. Soc. Lex.* 1897).

1897 *Allbutt's Syst. Med.* III. 287 In addition to pepsin the gastric-juice contains another ferment, namely 'rennin', a milk-curdling ferment.

† **'renning.** *Obs. rare.* [f. *renne* RUN *v.* + -ING^{1}.] = RENNET *sb.*^{1} (See also CHEESE-RUNNING.)

14.. *Lat. Eng. Voc.* in Wr.-Wülcker 573/41 *Coagulum*, rennynge. **1601** HOLLAND *Pliny* I. 348 They vse it in stead of renning, to turn milke and gather curds thereof. **1691** RAY *N.C. Words* (ed. 2) 57 *Race*, Rennet or Renning.

renning, -yng(e, obs. ff. RUNNING.

rennish, *a.*: see RENISH.

rennit, obs. f. RENNET *sb.*^{1}

rennogat(e, obs. ff. RENEGATE.

reno- (riːnəʊ), comb. form of L. *rēnes* kidneys (now more usual than RENI-), as in RENO-PERICARDIAL *a.*, RENOGRAPHY, etc.

† **re'noble**, *v. Obs. rare.* [f. RE- 5 a + NOBLE *a.*] *trans.* To ennoble again.

1607 TOPSELL *Four-f. Beasts* (1658) 266 Neither [will] their books imprinted be any way disgraced or hindered, but rather revived, renobled, and honoured. **1731–2** SAVAGE *On Her Majesty's Birth-Day* 61 Renobled thus by wreaths my queen bestows, I lose all memory of wrongs and woes.

renocero, obs. form of RHINOCEROS.

† **renodate**, *v. Obs. rare*$^{-0}$. [ad. ppl. stem of L. *renōdāre* to untie: see RE- and NODE.] 'To undo, or unknit a knot; also to knit fast or again' (Blount *Glossogr.* 1656). So † **reno'dation** 'an unknitting or undoing of a knot' (Phillips 1658); also † **re'node** *v.*, 'to vnknit' (Cockeram 1623).

renogate, obs. form of RENEGATE.

renogram ('riːnəʊgræm). *Med.* [f. as next + -GRAM.] A graphical record of the varying radioactivity of a kidney into which a radioactive substance has been injected; also, a radiograph or autoradiograph of a kidney.

1954 P. G. SMITH in M. Campbell *Urol.* I. II. ii. 189 The exposure is made as the last few cc. of the contrast medium are being injected. The needle is immediately withdrawn and a second film is made as rapidly as the cassettes can be changed. This last film is known as a renogram or nephrogram. **1964** C. C. WEBSTER in J. F. Glenn *Diagnostic Urol.* x. 190 (*caption*) The radioisotope renogram and blood clearance tracing are produced with three scintillation probes connected through three rate meters and three recorders. **1974** PASSMORE & ROBSON *Compar. Med. Stud.* III. xxii. 16/1 When hippuran (sodium ortho-iodohippurate) labelled with ^{131}I is given intravenously the substance is secreted rapidly into the proximal tubular fluid. Scintillation counters placed over the kidneys measure the radiation emitted by the isotope and the activity/time curve which is recorded is called the renogram. *Ibid.* 16/2 Patients with unilateral disturbances in renal function show differences in the shape and amplitude of the two renograms.

renography (riː'nɒgrəfɪ). *Med.* [f. RENO- + -GRAPHY.] Renal angiography or autoradio-graphy.

1911 *Brit. Med. Jrnl.* 1 Apr. 748 (*heading*) A lecture on renography. **1964** C. C. WEBSTER in J. F. Glenn *Diagnostic Urol.* x. 189 Since its inception in 1955, radioisotope renography has been increasingly utilized for the external measurement of individual kidney function. **1971** *Nature* 17 Sept. p. xi (Advt.), There is an active research programme in renography carried out in conjunction with the renal unit.

Renoiresque (rɛnwɑː'rɛsk), *a.* [f. the name of Pierre Auguste *Renoir* (1841–1919), French painter + -ESQUE.] Of, pertaining to, or characteristic of Renoir or his work.

1958 *Listener* 5 June 934/2 He succeeded in creating a Renoiresque atmosphere of the turn of the century. **1961** *Times* 18 Jan. 15/2 In her Renoiresque paintings Morisot lost a little of her freshness. **1971** R. A. CARTER *Manhattan Primitive* xvi. 150 An oddly put-together woman in a..black scarf top from which her Renoiresque bosom kept emerging.

† **re'nome.** *Obs.* [ad. F. *renom*, later form of *renon* RENOWN *sb.* Earlier examples of the spelling belong to RENOMEE.] Renown.

1523 LD. BERNERS *Froiss.* I. cxlvi. 175 Do nat a thyng that shulde blemysshe your renome. *c* **1557** ABP. PARKER *Ps.* lxxviii. 118 In ages still to come To ryse and sprede..God's actes to hys renome. **1561** T. NORTON *Calvin's Inst.* III. 289 Neither doth Jacob this bicause he is careful for the enlarging of the renome of his name.

† **renomé**, *ppl. a. Obs. rare*$^{-1}$. [OF.] = next.

c **1330** R. BRUNNE *Chron.* (1810) 204 Of Mount Morice Mathi a baron renome.

† **re'nomed**, *ppl. a. Obs.* Also 4 **renumed**, 5–6 **renommed**, (*Sc.* -it, -yt). [ad. OF. *renumé*, *renomé* (later *renommé*), pa. pple. of *renomer*, f. *re-* RE- + *nomer* to name.] Renowned.

13.. *Cursor M.* 13763 (Cott.), þis ilk water..Was mikel renumed in þaa dais. *c* **1374** CHAUCER *Boeth.* III. pr. ii, þat al þing þat is ryȝt excellent..semeþ to be ryȝt clere and renomed. **1390** GOWER *Conf.* I. 131 To him which thenkth his name avance And be renomed of his dede. *c* **1430** LYDG. *Min. Poems* (Percy Soc.) 47 Famous poetis..In Grece and Troye renomed of prudence. **1485** CAXTON *St. Wenefr.* 9 This place as longe as the world shalle endure..shalle be renommed by grete fame. **1523** LD. BERNERS *Froiss.* I. xvii. 19 These two lordes were renomed as chief in all dedis of armes. **1588** A. KING tr. *Canisius' Catech.* 109 Quhat order is maist renommed in the haly kirk?

† **reno'mee.** *Obs.* Also 4–5 **renome**, (5 **-nomme**), **renommee**, 5 **-y(e.** [a. OF. *renomee*, later *renommée*, f. *renomer*: see prec.] Renown. (Very common in Caxton's works.)

c **1386** CHAUCER *Wife's T.* 303 For gentillesse nys but renomee Of thyne auncestres, for hire heigh bountee. **1390** GOWER *Conf.* II. 43 Hire name was Rosiphelee; Which tho was of gret renomee. *c* **1450** *Merlin* 186 Renomee that thurgh alle the worlde renneth yede so thourgh euery londe. **1464** *Rolls of Parlt.* V. 561/1 The fame of renommy of the honour and pollicie therof. *c* **1489** CAXTON *Sonnes of Aymon* xxiv. 521 The renommee therof is flowen over alle the worlde.

re'nominate, *v.* [RE- 5 a.] *trans.* To nominate for a further term of office.

1864 FREMONT in *Daily Tel.* 21 June, If Mr. Lincoln should be renominated. **1899** *Daily News* 17 Apr. 7/2 He stated that Mr. Croker refused to renominate him. **1927** *New Republic* 21 Sept. 122/2 It declares that Mr. Coolidge must, shall and will be renominated. **1975** J. P. MORGAN *House of Lords & Labour Govt.* vii. 180 They illustrated the possible influence of systems of renominating voting Peers at successive General Elections. **1981** *Times* 28 Apr. 15/2 Devices to make it difficult if not impossible for moderate candidates to be renominated.

renomi'nation. [RE- 5 a: cf. prec.]

1. Renewed nomination.

1855 HAWTHORNE *Eng. Note-bks.* (1870) I. 339 He thought the President had a fair chance of re-nomination. **1891** *Times* 11 Feb. 5/2 The gravity of the situation had induced him to accept renomination.

2. A change of name. *rare*$^{-1}$.

1885 *Antiquary* Mar. 96/2 He follows up the intricate history of the companies, and tracks their devious courses through changes, exchanges and renominations.

renommed, renommee: see RENOMED, -EE.

renonse, obs. form of RENOUNCE *v.*

renoperi'cardial, *a. Physiol.* [f. *reno-* as comb. form of L. *rēn* kidney.] Pertaining to the kidneys and pericardium.

1883 E. R. LANKESTER in *Encycl. Brit.* XVI. 676/2 Reno-pericardial orifice placing the left renal sac..in communication with the viscero-pericardial sac.

re'normalizable, *a. Physics.* [f. RENORMALIZ(E *v.* + -ABLE.] That permits of renormalization.

1955 L. D. LANDAU in W. Pauli *Niels Bohr* 66 This phenomenon, not being renormalizable, cannot be considered within the limits of the theory. **1968** D. LURIÉ *Particles & Fields* vi. 266 Such theories, in which all divergences can be absorbed in the coupling-constant and mass renormalizations and thereby ignored, are known as renormalizable field theories. **1978** *Sci. Amer.* Feb. 132/2 For many years it seemed there was no convincing renormalizable theory of the weak interactions.

So **re,normaliza'bility.**

1955 L. D. LANDAU in W. Pauli *Niels Bohr* 54 This renormalizability of the theory is in reality only approximate. **1975** *Nature* 11 Sept. 95/2 In 1971..a Dutch graduate student, 't Hooft, opened the flood-gates by giving convincing arguments for the renormalisability of a rather special type of Yang-Mills gauge theory.

,renormali'zation. *Physics.* [RE- 5 a.] A method used in quantum mechanics of removing unwanted infinities from the solutions of equations by redefining parameters such as the mass and charge of subatomic particles. Freq. *attrib.* Cf. NORMALIZE *v.* 3 a.

1948 *Physical Rev.* LXXIV. 1430/1 The divergent terms in the line shift problem can be thought to be contained in a renormalization of the mass of a free electron. **1954** W. HEITLER *Quantum Theory of Radiation* (ed. 3) vi. 277 What is observable is the total mass and the total charge of the electron and these include the self-mass and self-charge. Although it is still a major unsolved difficulty of the theory that these quantities turn out to be infinite, they should, whatever their value, be combined with the 'original' mass and charge (i.e. the theoretical mass and charge when no interaction with the radiation field existed at all). For the original plus the self-mass and charge the observed finite values of mass and charge should then be substituted. This procedure will be called the re-normalization of mass and charge. *Ibid.* xxx. 310 This is the relativistic form of the 'renormalization terms'. **1954** *Physical Rev.* XCV. 1329/1 Ever since the overwhelming success of the applications of renormalization technique in quantum electrodynamics, the problem of understanding this renormalization procedure without the use of perturbation methods has been of great interest. **1962** N. R. HANSON in A. B. Pippard et al. *Quanta & Reality* v. 88 Theoreticians..invented a technique to diminish the number of possible solutions into something which practising physicists could manage. The result is a rather arbitrary procedure called 'renormalization'. It rejects as physically unpromising most solutions of any wave equation. **1977** L. STREIT in Price & Chissick *Uncertainty Principle & Foundations of Quantum Mechanics* xviii. 353 Virtually every second calculation of quantum electrodynamics included the process of throwing away an infinite term and interpreting the remainder as the 'correct result'. These procedures were formalized in the renormalization theory of Feynman, Dyson and Schwinger. **1979** *Sci. Amer.* Mar. 67/2 In the 1950's it became apparent that the aims of the renormalization procedure can be achieved by a large family of mathematical transformations; these make up the renormalization group.

re'normalize, *v. Physics.* [RE- 5 a.] *trans.* To apply renormalization to.

1955 L. D. LANDAU in W. Pauli *Niels Bohr* 54 The results hereby obtained can be renormalized, that is, if the physical charge of the electron is defined by its interaction with quanta of zero frequency and its mass, as the physical mass of the electron, the undetermined constant Λ disappears from the formulae for the physical effects. **1972** *Sci. Amer.* Nov. 50/1 The second obstacle to a satisfactory theory is that many calculations involving the weak force quickly lead to infinite results. In electromagnetic theory similar divergences are handled by the process called renormalization. Until recently no one could see how to renormalize the divergences presented by the weak force.

So **re'normalized** *ppl. a.*, calculated with the use of renormalization.

1954 *Physical Rev.* XCV. 1329/1 A rather unexpected and quite surprising feature is obtained by comparing the renormalized coupling constant with the unrenormalized coupling constant. **1977** M. E. FISHER in U. Landman *Statistical Mechanics & Statistical Methods in Theory & Application* 17 Renormalized field-theoretic perturbation theory.

renosterbos, -bush, varr. RHENOSTERBOS.

renoume, -noumpne, obs. varr. of RENOWN.

renounce (rɪ'naʊns), *sb.* [ad. F. *renonce*, f. *renoncer* to RENOUNCE.]

1. *Card-playing.* An act or instance of renouncing (see the vb., sense 7).

1747 HOYLE *Quadrille* 33 No person is to be beasted for a Renounce, unless the Trick is turn'd and quitted. **1792** A. THOMSON *Whist* 119 (T.), If with these cards you tricks intend to win, Prevent renounces, and with trumps begin. **1830** 'EIDRAH TREBOR' *Hoyle Made Familiar* 39 If any one renounce, he is basted for each renounce if detected; but a renounce is not made till the trick is turned. **1863** 'CAVENDISH' *Laws of Whist* (ed. 5) 13 If a renounce is corrected after any of the subsequent players have played, they are at liberty to withdraw their cards.

b. A chance of renouncing, by having no cards of a particular suit.

1830 'EIDRAH TREBOR' *Hoyle Made Familiar* 24 Never force your partner but when you are strong in trumps, unless you have a renounce yourself. **1874** GIBBS *Ombre* 82*

He rashly tries, having a renounce already in Diamonds, to clear his hand of Clubs, and so, having a renounce in that suit also, to give himself a better chance.

†**2.** Renunciation. *Obs. rare*$^{-1}$.

1779 BURGOYNE *Maid of the Oaks* v. i, From this moment I renounce it. *Grov.* And you never made a better renounce in your life.

renounce (rɪ'naʊns), *v.* Forms: 4 **renonce**, 4–5 **renonse**, 4–6 **renounse**; 4, 6–8 *Sc.* **renunce**, 5 **renownce**, 4– **renounce**. [ad. F. *renoncer* (OF. also *renuncer*):—L. *renuntiāre* (*-ciāre*) to announce, proclaim, also to disclaim, protest against, f. *re-* RE- + *nuntiāre* to make known, report: cf. *announce*, *denounce*, etc.]

I. 1. *trans.* To give up, to resign (†*to* another), to surrender; *esp.* to give up in a complete and formal manner.

c **1380** WYCLIF *Sel. Wks.* III. 475 Eche of ȝow þat schal not renounce alle þingus þat he has in possessioun may not be my disciple. *c* **1400** *Destr. Troy* 13629 My ryght I renonse to þat rynk sone. **1447** BOKENHAM *Seyntys* (Roxb.) 95 Ther renowncyd he All hys hy astate and eke hys dignyte. **1494** FABYAN *Chron.* v. cxiv. 88 If they wylfully wold renounce the sayd place and put them in his grace, he wolde vtterlye pardon theyr trespace. **1530** PALSGR. 686/1 He hath naught to do withall nowe, no more than you have, he hath renounced his tytle. **1560** DAUS tr. *Sleidane's Comm.* 69 He shall renounce Naples, Milan, Gene, Aste and Flaunders. **1605** in Goudie *Diary J. Mill* (S.H.S.) 193 The said William Bruce..renunceis, quit claimis and dischairgis and ouer gives to the said nobill lord the said twa last of land. **1667** MILTON *P.L.* II. 312 These Titles now Must we renounce, and changing stile be call'd Princes of Hell? **1697** DRYDEN *Virg. Georg.* III. 748 The Victor Horse..The Palm renounces, and abhors the Flood. **1718** LADY M. W. MONTAGU *Lett.* (1887) I. 240 The parents..renounce all future claim. *a* **1768** ERSKINE *Inst. Law Scot.* II. vi. §44 (1773) 270 A tack ceases..if..the tenant renounce his possession to the landlord. **1776** GIBBON *Decl. & F.* xii. I. 333 They soon experienced, that those who refuse the sword, must renounce the scepter. **1856** KANE *Arct. Expl.* I. xxvi. 351, I should require them..to renounce in writing all claims upon myself and the rest. **1875** MANNING *Mission H. Ghost* i. 29 Whatsoever Thou forbiddest I will renounce.

b. *to renounce the world*, to withdraw from worldly interests in order to lead a spiritual life.

c **1450** tr. *De Imitatione* III. xi. 78 þei renounce þe worlde and take a Religious lif. **1494** FABYAN *Chron.* VI. clxiv. 157 Vpon .viii. yeres after that Lothayre..renounsyd the pompe of ye world. **1657** SPARROW *Bk. Com. Prayer* (1661) 290 We renounc'd the world when we were baptized. **1779** COWPER *Love of World* 25 Renounce the world—the preacher cries. **1841** ELPHINSTONE *Hist. Ind.* II. 419 Declaring his own intention of renouncing the world and indulging his love of devotion in retirement at Mecca.

c. To abandon, cast off, repudiate; to decline to recognize, hold, observe, etc.

a **1533** LD. BERNERS *Huon* lxxxii. 253, I shall..renounce his law, and beleue in Mahounde. **1560** DAUS tr. *Sleidane's Comm.* 86 b, He required them to renounce the protestation of the yeare before. *c* **1645** MILTON *Forcers Consc.* 2 You have thrown of your Prelate Lord, And with stiff Vowes renounc'd his Liturgie. **1665** SIR T. HERBERT *Trav.* (1677) 307 After which imprecation the wretch holds up one Finger, thereby renouncing a Trinity. **1713** ADDISON *Cato* I. i, Our father's fortune Would almost tempt us to renounce his precepts. **1757** BURKE *Abridgm. Eng. Hist.* Wks. X. 466 To drive the Pope to extremities by wholly renouncing his authority. **1847** EMERSON *Repr. Men, Napoleon* Wks. (Bohn) I. 368 Napoleon renounced, once for all, sentiments and affections. **1895** SIR N. LINDLEY in *Law Times Rep.* LXXIII. 691/1 It is competent for anybody to renounce or disclaim a trust, and to have nothing to do with it.

†**d.** *refl.* To give up (oneself), esp. in a spirit of resignation. *Obs.*

1588 A. KING tr. *Canisius' Catech.* 96 We confess yat we glaidlie embrace ye Croce of Christ, renuncis our selfs [etc.]. **1594** T. B. *La Primaud. Fr. Acad.* II. 541 Hee must renounce himselfe, and become like to the bruite beast. **1621** T. WILLIAMSON tr. *Goulart's Wise Vieillard* 128 Wee should renounce our selves..because we are not our owne but Gods. **1649** *Bounds Publ. Obed.* (1650) 24 These Authors have read but of few Ionases, who voluntarily renounce themselves to settle a Tempest.

2. To abandon, give up, discontinue (a practice, action, habit, thought, intention, etc.).

1484 RICH. III in Ellis *Orig. Lett.* Ser. II. I. 123 To renounce the wering and usage of the Irisshe arraye. **1508** DUNBAR *Flyting* 54 Renunce, rebald, thy ryming. *c* **1590** MARLOWE *Faustus* vi, I will renounce this magic and repent. **1611** BIBLE *2 Esdras* xiv. 13 Now therefore set thine house in order, and..renounce corruption. **1665** MANLEY *Grotius' Low C. Warres* 463 When the Romans renounced all right and fair dealing, these..opposed them. **1759** DILWORTH *Pope* 73 He renounced all thoughts of paying attendance at Court. **1781** COWPER *Retirem.* 293 That tongue is silent now;..Renounced alike its office and its sport. **1838** THIRLWALL *Hist. Greece* xvii. III. 7 A calamity befel them by which they were forced to renounce this design. **1849** GROTE *Greece* II. xlviii. (1862) IV. 253 He was compelled to renounce the attempt. **1887** BOWEN *Æneid* IV. 319 If a prayer can move thee, renounce this purpose of thine.

b. To abandon or give up (a belief or opinion) by open profession or recantation.

1535 LYNDESAY *Satyre* 1133, I dreid, without ȝe..renunce ȝour new opiniones, The spirituall stait sall put ȝow to perditioun. **1590** SPENSER *F.Q.* II. viii. 51 If thou wilt renounce thy miscreaunce,..Life will I graunt thee. **1769** BLACKSTONE *Comm.* IV. 56 All others must..submit and renounce their errors. **1770** *Junius Lett.* xli. (1788) 224 We ..do not begin to detest him until he affects to renounce his principles. **1841** ELPHINSTONE *Hist. Ind.* II. 87 On his refusing to renounce his tolerant maxims, [he] put him to death. **1860** TYNDALL *Glac.* II. xxvii. 380 Professor Forbes ..renounced the theory, and substituted another.

3. To disclaim or disown obedience or allegiance to (a person). ? *Obs.*

1502 *Ord. Crysten Men* (W. de W. 1506) I. iii. C vij b, And whan one hathe hym named, then he demaundeth him, renouncest thou Sathan. **1500–20** DUNBAR *Poems* xxxiv. 10 Thow art my clerk, the Devill can say, Renunce thy God and cum to me. **1552** *Bk. Com. Prayer, Ordering of Deacons*, I from hencefurth shall vtterlye renounce, refuse, relinquish, & forsake the bishop of Rome. **1593** SHAKS. *3 Hen. VI*, III. iii. 194 To repaire my Honor lost for him, I heere renounce him, and returne to Henry.

b. To cast off, disclaim relationship to or acquaintance with (a person); †also const. *from*.

1582 STANYHURST *Æneis* II. (Arb.) 55 Thee Gods haue flatlye renounst vs, Oure state that whillon preserud. **1594** *1st Pt. Contention* (1843) 24, I here renounce her from my bed and boord. **1602** MARSTON *Ant. & Mel.* IV. Wks. 1856 I. 54, I renounce thy blood, If thou forsake thy valour. **1700** T. BROWN *Amusem. Ser. & Com.* 15 Tho' you presented him in the Morning, he will forget you at Night, and utterly Renounce you the Day following. **1797** MRS. RADCLIFFE *Italian* xiii, I never can renounce you, while you are unchanged. **1838** DICKENS *Nich. Nick.* xxxiii, Your kindred renounce you. **1865** —— *Mut. Fr.* II. xv, My brother has quarrelled with me..and renounced me.

†**c.** In *passive* with complement. *Obs. rare*$^{-1}$.

1661 CRESSY *Refl. Oaths Suprem. & Alleg.* 23 Can the King be acknowledged..a Head of Churches of which he renounces, and is renounced the being so much as a member?

†**4.** To refuse *to* do a thing. *Obs. rare*$^{-1}$.

1582 STANYHURST *Æneis* II. (Arb.) 68 This sayd, shee vannisht, and thogh that I sadlye requyred Too confer further, yeet shee too tarrye renounced.

†**b.** With double obj. To refuse. *Obs. rare*$^{-1}$.

1582 STANYHURST *Æneis* I. (Arb.) 35 On sands they renounce vs an harboure. They doe bid vs battayl.

†**c.** To refuse to carry out; to repudiate (an obligation). *Obs. rare*$^{-1}$.

1617 MORYSON *Itin.* III. 255 Lewis the twelfth, after the league for yeers was expired, renounced the payment of all publike or priuate pensions.

†**5.** To deny (a suggestion or accusation). *Obs.*

1596 HARINGTON *Metam. Ajax* I j b, If you will say there is salte in it, I will acknowledge [= admit] it; but if you will suspect there is gall in it, I renounce it. **1597** BEARD *Theatre God's Judgem.* (1612) 305 When manie were suspected of the murder, and all renounced it [etc.].

6. *intr.* or *absol.* †**a.** To make renunciation. Const. *to* (the thing renounced). Also *Sc.* to dispense *with* (a thing). *Obs.*

c **1375** *Sc. Leg. Saints* xviii. (*Mary Egypt*) 683, I sal renunce but delay to þis fals warld þis ilke day. **1390** GOWER *Conf.* III. 46 Babilla with hir Sones sevene, Which hath renonced to the hevene. **1502** *Ord. Crysten Men* (W. de W. 1506) I. iii. C viij, He renounceth specyally vnto thre synnes. That is vnto pryde, to couetyse, and vnto lechery. **1687** DRYDEN *Hind & P.* III. 147 He of my sons who fails to make it good, By one rebellious act renounces to my blood. **1728** RAMSAY *Last Sp. Miser* xx, I thought..That chiel a very silly dunce, That could not honestly renunce With ease and joys..to win an unce Of yellow boys.

b. *Law.* To make formal resignation of some right or trust, esp. of one's position as heir or executor.

? **1604** in Morison *Dict. Dec.* XXXI. (1806) 13897 The Lords found, That he..might renounce to be heir, albeit he ..were decerned as lawfully charged, not having renounced *debito tempore.* **1695** VENTRIS *Reports* (1701) I. 303 There is no Book which proves the Acts of an Administrator void, where there is a Will and the Executor renounces. **1743** *Swinburne's Wills* (ed. 6) VI. §12. 444 Then two of the Executors of the Son died, and Hay the surviving Executor renounced. **1806** MORISON *Dict. Dec.* XXXI. 13901 [The] Heir, before he renounce, must purge the Estate of his proper debts. **1870** W. D. CHRISTIE *Mem. Dryden* in D.'s Wks. (Globe) p. lxxix, Dryden died without a will, and his widow having renounced, his son Charles administered on June 10.

c. To make a renunciation of something.

1868 GEO. ELIOT *Sp. Gipsy* III. 243 But you, dear Juan, Renounce, endure, are brave. **1872** —— *Middlem.* lxvii, Since providential indications demand a renunciation of me, I renounce.

7. *Card-playing.* To fail to follow suit, to play a card of a different suit from that which has been led; originally implying the *possession* of, but now usually the *want* of, a proper card. In the former case REVOKE is now the current term. (Cf. RENOUNCE *sb.* 1 and RENEGUE *sb.* and *v.* 4 a.)

1656 HOBBES *Lib. Necess. & Chance* (1841) 194 In the same manner as men in playing turn up trump, and as in playing their game their morality consisteth in not renouncing. **1676** WYCHERLEY *Pl. Dealer* v. i, Since my lover has played the card, I must not renounce. **1728** SWIFT *Jrnl. Mod. Lady* Wks. 1755 III. II. 197 Madam, you have no cause to flounce, I swear I saw you thrice renounce. **1747** HOYLE *Quadrille* 33 If any Person renounces and it is discover'd,..all the Parties are to take up their Cards and play them over again. **1787** *Minor* 92 He frequently renounced, and seldom returned her lead. **1830** 'EIDRAH TREBOR' *Hoyle Made Familiar* 41 The player who holds the same has a right to renounce in every suit during the whole game. **1862** 'CAVENDISH' *Whist* (1879) 112 A suit in which he knows that both you and the fourth player renounce.

†**II. 8.** *trans.* To announce, declare, proclaim, pronounce. *Obs.*

a **1450** *Knt. de la Tour* (1868) 97 Tille..that the squier herde of the speche, and how it was renounced that he had leide .v. eggis. **1502** *Ord. Crysten Men* (W. de W. 1506) IV. v. P vij, He [the curate] it ought to renounce unto his souerayne, as is the bysshop of the dyoses. **1596** DALRYMPLE tr. *Leslie's Hist. Scot.* x. 352 Joanna, the Dukes dauchter.., [as] Quene of Jngland al man in publick renunced. **1613** PURCHAS *Pilgrimage* II. xx. 179 They..renounced Anathema to him, that should set downe the time of his [the Messiah's] coming.

Hence **re'nounced** *ppl. a.*

1717 L. HOWEL *Desiderius* 9 Too many of the most renounc'd Asceticks were celebrated for doing what was next to nothing. **1769** *Oxford Mag.* II. 144/1 In her renounced companion's breast. **1781** COWPER *Retirem.* 474 He..feels..A secret thirst of his renounced employs.

re'nounceable, *a.* [f. prec. + -ABLE.] That may be renounced.

1862 CARLYLE *Fredk. Gt.* XIV. viii. (1872) V. 259 She renounces her engagement... Prussian agent answers that it is not renounceable. **1955** *Times* 8 July 14/2 Renounceable allotment letters and application forms for additional shares have been posted. **1979** *Daily Tel.* 19 Jan. 13/2 A three-for-one capitalisation issue will then produce for Midland 86 million renounceable shares which it can sell free of stamp duty.

renouncement (rɪ'naʊnsmənt). [a. F. *renoncement* (15th c.): see RENOUNCE *v.* and -MENT.] The act of renouncing; an instance of this, a renunciation. †Const. *to* (cf. RENOUNCE *v.* 6 a).

1494 FABYAN *Chron.* VII. 547 All though he had and myght ..haue declared his renouncement by the redynge of an other meane persone. **1597** J. KING *On Jonas* (1618) 387 Against sinners past grace, you shall often find renouncements vnto them. **1603** SHAKS. *Meas. for M.* I. v. 34, I hold you as a thing en-skied, and sainted, By your renouncement. **1640** YORKE *Union Hon.* 185 The renouncement of the Titles to the Kingdome of Castile and Leon. **1818** BENTHAM *Ch. Eng., Catech. Exam.* 9 In what condition is he, other than that which he would have been in, had no such renouncement been made? **1865** M. ARNOLD *Ess. Crit.* iv. (1875) 166 The doctrine..of the superiority of renouncement to activity.

renouncer (rɪ'naʊnsə(r)). [f. RENOUNCE *v.* + -ER^{1}.] One who renounces.

1586 A. DAY *Eng. Secretary* I. (1625) 134 Seeing you are in so great an errour..if you become not repentant, and a renouncer betimes [etc.]. **1676** *Doctrine of Devils* 131 Renagadoes, Renouncers, Apostates, from the..Truths of Christian Religion. **1724** SWIFT *Drapier's Lett.* v. Wks. 1755 V. II. 101 He was ready to renounce as much as they pleased. .. I am not so thorough a renouncer. **1841** EMERSON *Misc.* (1855) 200 A Re-maker of what man has made; a renouncer of lies. **1844** DICKENS *Mart. Chuz.* xxi, He renounce me! Cast your eyes on the Renouncer, Pinch, and be the wiser for the recollection!

renounciation, obs. form of RENUNCIATION.

renouncing (rɪ'naʊnsɪŋ), *vbl. sb.* [f. RENOUNCE *v.* + -ING^{1}.] The action of the vb., in various senses; renunciation. Also, an instance of this.

c **1380** WYCLIF *Sel. Wks.* III. 235 How God undirstondes þis renunsynge teches he by lif of Crist. **1494** FABYAN *Chron.* VII. (1516) T t iv/1 The Archebysshop..shewyd vnto them seryously the voluntary renounsynge of the Kyng. **1562–3** *Reg. Privy Council Scot.* I. 230 Befoir the concluding of the caus and renunceing of farther probatioun. **1599** SANDYS *Europæ Spec.* (1605) P iv, Those desperate Atheismes, those Spanish renouncings, and Italian blasphemings. **1660** MILTON *Griffith's Serm.* Wks. 1851 V. 390 To charge him most audaciously and falsly with the renouncing of his own public Promises. **1724** SWIFT *Drapier's Lett.* v. Wks. 1755 V. II. 101 When Sir Charles Sedley was taking the oaths, where several things were to be renounced, he said he loved renouncing. **1897** *Westm. Gaz.* 9 Sept., To this renouncing of the wide sleeve we have been coaxed little by little.

†**re'nounsal.** *Obs. rare*$^{-1}$. [f. *renounse*, obs. f. RENOUNCE *v.* + -AL^{1}.] Renouncement.

1646 EARL MONM. tr. *Biondi's Civil Warres* IX. 188 All France (which falling upon his person by naturall Inheritance; not by anothers Renounsal, was his legal Patrimony).

renounse, obs. form of RENOUNCE *v.*

†**'renovant**, *ppl. a. Obs. rare.* [ad. L. *renovant-em*, pres. pple. of *renovāre*: see RENOVATE *v.*] Renewing; increasing by renewal.

1610 W. FOLKINGHAM *Art of Survey* IV. ii. 81 Perquisites may be diuided into Renouant and Dormant. Renouant Perquisites are Accrewments acquired by Increase and Casualty.

renovascular (riːnəʊ'væscjʊlə(r)), *a. Med.* [f. RENO- + VASCULAR *a.*] Pertaining to the blood vessels of the kidneys.

1961 *Medicine* XL. 347 (*heading*) Functional characteristics of renovascular hypertension. **1974** PASSMORE & ROBSON *Compan. Med. Stud.* III. xx. 8/1 Neutralization of the activity of angiotensin II by specific angiotensin antibodies does not always prevent or reverse hypertension induced by renovascular means.

'renovate, *pa. pple.* and *ppl. a.* [ad. L. *renovātus*, pa. pple. of *renovāre*: see next.] Renewed.

c **1520** BARCLAY *Jugurtha* (ed. 2) 6 The name and glorie of our household by your manhode is renouate and renewed. *a* **1548** HALL *Chron., Hen. VII* 17 b, To shewe that the warre was renovate without hys knowledge and assente. **1568** GRAFTON *Chron.* II. 940 The king openly sware to keepe the new renouate league and amitie. **1873** BROWNING *Red Cott. Nt-cap* I. 744 Of use to the community? I trust Clairvaux thus renovate and regalized..Answers that question.

renovate ('rɛnəʊveɪt), *v.* [f. L. *renovāt-*, ppl. stem of *renovāre*, f. *re-* RE- + *novāre* to make new, f. *novus* NEW.]

†**1.** *trans.* To renew, resume (an action or purpose). *Obs.*

1535 CROMWELL in Merriman *Life & Lett.* (1902) I. 416 That..ye take som occasion at conuenyent tyme..to renovate the saide communycacyon..with the Frensh kyng. **1599** HAKLUYT *Voy.* II. I. 37 Then prince Edward renouating his purpose, tooke shipping againe. **1656** in BLOUNT *Glossogr.* **1796** [see *renovated* below].

†**b.** To renew in effect, to revive. *Obs. rare*$^{-1}$.

1553 LATIMER *Serm. Lord's Prayer* vii. (1562) 51 b, Whosoeuer..wittingly doth the selfe same sin againe: he renouateth by so doyng al those sinnes which before times were forgiuen him.

2. To renew materially; to repair; to restore by replacing lost or damaged parts; to create anew.

a **1522** LELAND *Itin.* (1768) II. 42 Ethelwolde..did clerely renovate and augmentid this Abbay. **1604** R. CAWDREY *Table Alph., Renouate*, to renew, or repaire. **1768** TUCKER *Lt. Nat.* II. I. vii. §8. 140 Secondary qualities..are continually destroyed and renovated according to the changes made in that order by motions of the component parts. **1796** H. HUNTER tr. *St.-Pierre's Stud. Nat.* (1799) I. 213 The ices of the Poles, then, renovate the waters of the Sea, as the ices of mountains renovate those of the great rivers. **1813** SHELLEY *Q. Mab* v. 4 Surviving still the imperishable change That renovates the world. **1857** WOOD *Comm. Obj. Seashore* 11 If he thoroughly renovates his blood by expelling all the impure air. **1878** HUXLEY *Physiogr.* 187 These movements must be of great service in renovating the surface of the earth.

b. To restore to vigour; to refresh.

1671 J. WEBSTER *Metallogr.* viii. 125 It renovateth old Trees that of twenty years have brought forth no fruit. **1794** MRS. RADCLIFFE *Myst. Udolpho* iv, The spirit of St. Aubert was renovated. **1807–8** W. IRVING *Salmag.* xviii. (1860) 408 A little warm nourishment renovated him for a short time. **1837** [see *renovated* below].

c. To renew on a higher level; to regenerate.

1800 COLQUHOUN *Comm. Thames* ix. 281 The great object of renovating the morals of the labouring classes. **1817** CHALMERS *Astron. Disc.* v. (1852) 131 The Gospel..will renovate the soul. **1876** HUMPHREYS *Coin-coll. Man.* xiii. 157 The art displayed on the Persian coinage seems to have been renovated.

3. To restore (a person) to office. *rare*$^{-1}$.

1816 *Gen. Hist.* in *Ann. Reg.* 641 They were also to renovate the members of the councils-general of department.

4. *intr.* To revive, recover. *rare.*

1790 *Bystander* 13 [Like a fountain] scattering its translucent pearls on the drooping flowers, which renovate at their touch. **1812** *Henry & Isabella* II. 258 His exhausted mind and body would here renovate in repose.

Hence **'renovated** *ppl. a.*; ***renovated butter*** = *process butter* s.v. PROCESS *sb.* 13; **'renovater** (Ogilvie *Suppl.* 1855).

1796 BURKE *Regic. Peace* i. (1892) 56 A very active preparation for renovated hostility. **1837** W. IRVING *Capt. Bonneville* II. 217 The travellers now moved forward with renovated spirits. **1843** J. MARTINEAU *Chr. Life* I. ix. 125 Christ..indulging in no dreams of a renovated world without, till [etc.]. **1853** KANE *Grinnell Exp.* xxxviii. (1856) 352 Today..the gulls were flying over the renovated water. **1899**, etc. [see *process butter* s.v. PROCESS *sb.* 13]. **1906** *Daily Chron.* 13 Sept. 5/2 Mr. Hehner went on to explain the nature of American renovated butter. He said that sometimes butter 'went off', and it was then melted down and the sour milk run off and replaced by pure milk and cream. **1937** HARVEY & HILL *Milk Products* iii. 178 Renovated butter. Butter which has become unfit for human consumption is treated in many countries by a process which is said to render it suitable for such consumption. Such methods, however, are not practised in Great Britain.

renovating ('rɛnəʊveɪtɪŋ), *ppl. a.* [f. prec. + -ING².] That renovates.

1641 MILTON *Animadv.* Wks. 1851 III. 219 As if a man should taxe the renovating and re-ingendring Spirit of God with innovation. **1726–46** THOMSON *Winter* 704 All Nature feels the renovating force Of Winter. **1811** W. R. SPENCER *Poems* 39 The world has felt thy renovating rays. **1830** D'ISRAELI *Chas. I*, III. iii. 22 Charles probably meditated to infuse a renovating vigour into his languid administration. **1856** KANE *Arct. Expl.* II. v. 62 The renovating blessings of animal life and restoring warmth.

b. ***renovating spring*** (see REMONTOIR).

1825 J. NICHOLSON *Operat. Mechanic* 519, E is the renovating or remontoire spring, fixed to the same stud.

Hence **'renovatingly** *adv.*

1885 MEREDITH *Diana* xxxix, Her fall had brought her renovatingly to earth.

renovation (rɛnəʊ'veɪʃən). [a. F. *rénovation* (15th c.), or ad. L. *renovātiōn-em*, n. of action f. *renovāre* to RENOVATE.]

1. The action of renovating, or the condition of having been renovated; renewal; restoration; an instance of this, a change effected by renewal.

1432–50 tr. *Higden* (Rolls) III. 117 In whiche yere he see also the renouacion of the temple. **1555** EDEN *Decades* 87 The water therof beinge dronk..maketh owld men younge ageyne. *Marg.* The renouation of age. **1577** tr. *Bullinger's Decades* (1592) 599 They..do hartily reioyce..for the renouation of true religion. **1603** HOLLAND *Plutarch's Mor.* 1301 The dismembring of Osiris, and the resurrection or renovation of his life. **1645** MILTON *Tetrach.* Introd., Wks. 1851 IV. 143 To expect..glorious changes and renovations both in Church and State. **1681** tr. *Belon's Myst. Physick* Introd. 13 Remedies for Conservation and Renovation of Health. **1730–46** THOMSON *Autumn* 1189 How long Shall prostrate Nature groan beneath your rage; Awaiting renovation? **1784** COWPER *Task* VI. 124 The regular return of genial months, And renovation of a faded world. **1834** SOUTHEY *Doctor* (1862) 383 Both the innovations or renovations which Spenser introduced were against the grain. **1875** JOWETT *Plato* (ed. 2) V. 36 To the good man, education is of all things the most precious, and is also in constant need of renovation.

†**b.** Renewal of the body at the resurrection. *Obs.*

1513 BRADSHAW *St. Werburge* I. 3509 Greatter was the hope of the eterne renouacion In her body resolued to naturall consumption. ? **1554** COVERDALE *Hope Faithf.* xxii. Wks. (Parker Soc.) II. 195 Of our bodies The renovation. Therefore is this My expectation. **1667** MILTON *P.L.* XI. 65 Wak't in renovation of the just.

2. *Theol.* Renewal wrought by the Holy Ghost; the creation of a new spirit within one.

1543 *Necess. Doctrine* d iij, In our battaile aforesayde, in.. our dayly spiritual renovation. **1555** EDEN *Decades* 43 To poure vppon his electe the grace of renouation. **1624** GATAKER *Transubst.* 66 The thing that is there wrought, to wit, regeneration and renovation, is a thing intelligible. **1684** BUNYAN *Pilgr.* II. 79 How doth God the Holy Ghost save thee? By his Illumination, by his Renovation, and by his Preservation. *a* **1708** BEVERIDGE *Thes. Theol.* (1711) III. 225 External reformation is nothing without internal renovation. **1841** TRENCH *Parables* (1860) 116 For the true renovation is ever thus from the inward to the outward.

†**b.** Reformation. *Obs. rare*$^{-1}$.

1563 FOXE *A. & M.* 542/2 Concernynge inioynynge of penance I know of none..excepte renouation of liuinge in casting a parte olde vyce, and taking them vnto new vertue.

†**3.** The renewal or resumption of an action, agreement, condition, etc. *Obs.*

1535 COVERDALE *1 Macc.* xii. 17 Oure lettres, concerninge the renouacion of oure brotherhode. **1569** *Reg. Privy Council Scot.* I. 667 Na quietnes bot renovatioun of displesour and troubill may arryise. **1610** HEALEY *St. Aug. Citie of God* 125 Why should I particularize the often renovation of these warres under so many several kings..? **1686** tr. *Chardin's Trav. Persia* 15 To attend the Grand Signior..in order to the Renovation of the Articles. **1774** J. BRYANT *Mythol.* II. 433 The Bull of Perillus was..designed for a renovation of some cruel rites. **1798** W. BLAIR *Soldier's Friend* 77 The renovation of pain that is the necessary consequence of chirurgical treatment.

'renovative, *a. rare*$^{-1}$. [f. as RENOVATE *v.* + -IVE.] Renovating.

1839–52 BAILEY *Festus* 475 A fountain of divine delight, And renovative nature.

renovator ('rɛnəʊveɪtə(r)). [a. L. *renovātor*, agent-n. f. *renovāre* to RENOVATE; cf. F. *rénovateur*.] One who renovates.

1839 I. TAYLOR *Ancient Chr.* I. 367 As often as any stern and fanatical renovator came into the management of these religious houses. **1840** MILL *Diss. & Disc.* (1875) I. 427 The barbarian conquerors were the renovators, not the destroyers of its civilisation.

†**re'nove**, *v. Obs.* [ad. OF. *renover*, *renouver*, or L. *renovāre*: see RENOVATE *v.*] *trans.* and *intr.* To renew.

1422 tr. *Secreta Secret., Priv. Priv.* 243 In that tyme al thynnges begynnyth to renoue and wix newe, and returne Into estate. *c* **1440** LOVE *Bonavent. Mirr.* xliii. (Gibbs MS.) lf. 92 And so he nowe renoued [*v.r.* renewed] þe þrid tyme þe brusures and þe woundes. **1588** A. KING tr. *Canisius' Catech.* 62 b, Be Baptisme we ar regenerat and renouit.

†**re'novel**, *v. Obs.* Also 4–5 renouel. [ad. OF. *renoveler* (mod.F. *renouveler*), f. L. *re-* RE- + *novellus* NOVEL *a.* Cf. RENULE *v.*] To renew.

a. *trans.* *c* **1315** SHOREHAM I. 1826 Þer..Scel be renoueled þet a-gonne hijs, And ayþer folȝy oþer. **1340** HAMPOLE *Pr. Consc.* 7474 And als oft renoueld salle be ilk payne, Als he turned new tylle ilk syn ogayne. *c* **1386** CHAUCER *Melib.* ¶879 To do som thing, by which he may renovele his good name. **1446** LYDG. *Nightingale* I. 23 Meued of Corage be vertu of the seson, In prime-tens renoueled yere be yere. **1473** *Rolls of Parlt.* VI. 65/1 The oold frendelyhode also betwixt theym to be renovelled in such wise, as it may abide. **1537** CROMWELL in Merriman *Life & Lett.* (1902) II. 104 His Maieste hath commaunded you eftsones to renovel the said Ouerture of mediacion vnto him.

b. *intr.* *c* **1374** CHAUCER *Boeth.* III. pr. xi, All things renovelen..with seed imultiplied. *c* **1386** —— *Pars. T.* ¶953 Oones a yer alle thinges in the erthe renovelen.

Hence †**re'novelling** *vbl. sb.*; also †**re'novelance** [OF. *renovelance*], †**re'novelment** [OF. *renovelement*], †**re'novelty** [OF. *renovelté*], renewing. *Obs.*

1413 *Pilgr. Sowle* (Caxton) I. xxii. (1859) 23 The counseyles conteined in the gospels of Criste, whiche ben in a maner renouellynges of the forsayd pertes. *c* **1384** CHAUCER *H. Fame* II. 185 And also moo renoveilaunces Of olde for-leten aqueyntaunces. *c* **1477** CAXTON *Jason* 45 It is a grete abuse to me for to thinke and haue a renouelement of payne. *Ibid.* 123 Peleus..cam unto the kyng in the renouellite of this noble respyrement. **1501** in *Lett. Rich. III & Hen. VII* (Rolls) I. 154 Overture..for the renovelling of the said amitie.

reno-'vesical, *a. Path.* [f. *reno-* as comb. form of L. *rēn* kidney.] Connected with the kidneys and bladder.

1872 ANSTIE in *Practitioner* VIII. 243 Reno-vesical Cantharidism, and the Remedies in General use for its Relief.

renovize ('rɛnəʊvaɪz), *v. U.S. rare.* [A blend of RENOV(ATE *v.* + MODERN)IZE *v.*] *trans.* To restore and modernize.

1933 *Daily Progress* (Charlottesville, Va.) 25 Jan. 3/6 A 'renovize Philadelphia' campaign has met marked success in its early stages. **1935** A. P. HERBERT *What a Word!* ii. 53 A North American warrior tells me that she has seen 'to renovise'! **1965** *Amer. Speech* XL. 303 This suffix has been attached to..verbs (*renovize*, *flavorize*).

renown (rɪ'naʊn), *sb.* Forms: α. 4–7 renoun(e, 5 *Sc.* ra-), 5–6 renovne, 6 -nounn; 4–5 renon(e; 4–7 renowne, (5 *Sc.* ra-), 5 renownn, rennowne, 5– renown. β. 5–7 renoume, (6 *Sc.* -mne), 6 renowm, 6–7 renowme. [a. AF. *renoun*, *renun*, = OF. *renon*, later *renom* (see RENOME *sb.*), f. *renomer* to make famous, f. L. *re-* RE- + *nomināre* to name: cf. RENOMEE. The form *renowme* is prob. an assimilation to the earlier form of the verb, or to later F. *renom*.]

1. ***of renown***, of fame or distinction; widely known or celebrated. †Occas. in *pl.*

α. *a* **13..** *Coer de L.* 689 Sir Foulke Doyly of renoun. *Ibid.* 1682 Hys barouns, Eerles and lordes off renouns. **1377** LANGL. *P. Pl.* B. Prol. 158 A raton of renon most renable of tonge. **1422** tr. *Secreta Secret., Priv. Priv.* 121 The moste wyse clerkes and Maysteris of renoune that haue beyn afor vs in al tymys. *a* **1500** *Bernardus De Cura* 183 That men may say, ȝon man is of renowne. **1535** LYNDESAY *Satyre* 1206 Lo! quhair thair sits ane Priores of renown. **1623** MILTON *Ps.* cxxxvi. 62 In bloody battail he brought down Kings of prowess and renown. **1782** COWPER *Gilpin* 2 John Gilpin was a citizen Of credit and renown.

β. **1560** BIBLE (Genev.) *Gen.* vi. 4 Mightie men, which in olde time were men of renoume. *a* **1592** GREENE *Alphonsus* Wks. (Rtldg.) 228/1 He marcheth on unto our chiefest seat, Naples, I mean, that city of renowm.

b. So ***of great*** (***high***, etc.) ***renown***.

α. **13..** *Seuyn Sag.* (W.) 552 A riche man of gret renoun. *c* **1330** R. BRUNNE *Chron. Wace* (Rolls) 13774 Two þousand of þe Bretouns, Wiþoute men of grete renouns. *c* **1375** *Sc. Leg. Saints* xxx. (*Theodora*) 40 A man of gud renone. *c* **1400** *Melayne* 21 In Tuskayne townnes gon he wyn..This lorde of grete renownn. *c* **1450** *Merlin* 106 Ther was noon but.. seide that he sholde be of high renon. **1551** ROBINSON tr. *More's Utop.* (1895) p. xciv, A prince of much renowne and immortall fame. *a* **1600** *Song* in Shaks. *Oth.* II. iii. 96 He was a wight of high Renowne, and thou art but of low degree. **1784** COWPER *Task* v. 691 As if, like him of fabulous renown, They had indeed ability [etc.]. **1842** TENNYSON *You ask me* 10 A land of just and old renown.

β. **1413** *Pilgr. Sowle* (Caxton) IV. xxxviii. (1859) 63 A noble kynge that hyght Poeticus, of grete power, and wonder grete renoume. **1470–85** MALORY *Arthur* I. xvi. 57 Yonder I see.. the man of the most renoume. **1596** DANETT tr. *Comines* (1614) 263 Which had been of so great estimation and renowme through all Christendome.

†**c.** ***with great renown***, with much distinction or display. Also without adj. *Obs.*

c **1375** *Cursor M.* 14725 (Fairf.) As men dos ȝet in toun þer faire is halden wiþ grete renoun. *c* **1440** *York Myst.* xxv. 207, I rede we make vs redy bowne,..And hym ressayue with grete renowne. *c* **1575** *Raid of Reidswire* iii. in Scott *Minstr. Scot. Bord.* (1802) I. 98 The Rutherfoords, with grit renown, Convoy'd the town of Jedbrugh out. ? *a* **1800** *Lord Saltoun* xi. in Child *Ballads* IV. 348/1 Then out spake her father, he spake wi renown.

2. The fact or condition of being widely celebrated or held in high repute; celebrity, fame, honourable distinction.

α. **1340–70** *Alex. & Dind.* 369 We no recche of no ricchesse no renoun of landus. *c* **1420** *Anturs of Arth.* 293 Ther salle the Rownde Tabille losse the renowne. *a* **1533** LD. BERNERS *Huon* lviii. 197 Huon..had grete desyre too attayne to good renowne. **1600** SHAKS. *A.Y.L.* v. iv. 151 Honor, high honor and renowne To Hymen. **1659** HAMMOND *On Ps.* lxxii. 17 His memory and honour..shall descend upon his posterity, as a mark of renoun. *c* **1683** WALLER *On St. James's Park* 11 'Tis of more renown To make a river, than to build a town. **1751** JOHNSON *Rambler* No. 146 ¶8 Whoever claims renown from any kind of excellence, expects to fill the place which is now possessed by another. **1784** COWPER *Task* III. 59 Forsaking thee, what shipwreck have we made Of honour, dignity, and fair renown! **1821** SHELLEY *Adonais* xlv, The inheritors of unfulfilled renown Rose from their thrones. **1833** TENNYSON *Lady C. V. de Vere* 2 Of me you shall not win renown.

β. **1538** ELYOT s.v. *Celebro*, to celebrate or brynge in renoume. *a* **1583** SIR H. GILBERT *Q. Eliz. Acad.* (1869) 12 Better it is to haue Renowme among the good sorte, then to be lorde over the whole world. **1586** T. B. *La Primaud. Fr. Acad.* I. (1594) 69 Great and proud armies may by notable victories procure to themselves renowm and glorie. **1604** R. CAWDREY *Table Alph., Renowme*, credite, fame.

b. With poss. pron. or genitive: The fame or reputation attaching to a particular person, place, etc.

α. *c* **1374** CHAUCER *Troylus* II. 248 (297), I..love as wele your honour and renoun, As creature in al this world yborn. *c* **1440** *Ipomydon* 1500 Thus Caymys rode toward the towne, Whan he had lost all his renowne. **1508** DUNBAR *Ball. Ld. B. Stewart* 50 Throw Scotland..Fleys on weyng thi fame, and thi renoune. **1580** SIDNEY *Ps.* IX. iii, Their renown, which seem'd so like to last, Thou dost put out. **1638** JUNIUS *Paint. Ancients* 219 Artificers,..if they be not known by the ancient renowne of their shoppes [etc.]. **1726** SWIFT *Gulliver* I. v, The Emperor..the Renown of whose Virtues had..filled the whole World with Admiration. **1849** MACAULAY *Hist. Eng.* vi. II. 123 His renown had spread even to the coffeehouses of London and the cloisters of Oxford. **1874** GREEN *Short Hist.* vii. §6. 403 The renown of the Spanish infantry had been growing.

β. **1455–6** in *Househ. Ord.* (1790) 15 It shold be to his singuler renoume, fame, and laude. **1540–1** ELYOT *Image Gov.* 7 To his most noble and immortall renoume. **1587** GOLDING *De Mornay* Ep. Ded., [To] hold him back from seeking to inlarge his renowme.

†**c.** ***of renown***, in respect of fame or distinction. *Obs. rare.*

c **1330** R. BRUNNE *Chron. Wace* (Rolls) 14753 Westsex [was] þe þrydde of renoun. *c* **1425** WYNTOUN *Cron.* II. xvii.

1664 Off Venes he made þe gret towne þat ȝhit is ryalle of ranowne. **1508** DUNBAR *Gold. Targe* 88 Rich to behald, and nobil of renounn.

†**3.** Report, rumour. (Sometimes implying sense 2.)

c **1330** R. BRUNNE *Chron. Wace* (Rolls) 5003 Renoun ran [*v.r.* tydynges ronne], þat ouer al reches, To ilk a man mad þei speches. *c* **1375** *Sc. Leg. Saints* xii. (*Mathias*) 189 [Of] þat sad ded þe ranowne sowne rane throw al þe towne. *c* **1385** CHAUCER *L.G.W.* 1054 *Dido*, Swich renoun was there sprongyn of hire goodnesse. *c* **1450** *Merlin* 176 And so com the renoun in to the hoste, that thei durste not ride that wey with-oute grete foyson of peple. **1610** SHAKS. *Temp.* v. i. 193 Of whom, so often I haue heard renowne, But neuer saw before.

†**b.** Reputation of a specified kind. *Obs. rare.*

c **1330** R. BRUNNE *Chron.* (1810) 73 Abbot & prioure.. Wer priued of þar office, of woulfes had renoun. **1540–1** ELYOT *Image Gov.* (1549) 12 From that tyme he had the renoume of constance and grauitee. **1603** SHAKS. *All's Well* IV. iii. 19 A young Gentlewoman..of a most chaste renown. **1608** —— *Per.* IV. vi. 42 That dignifies the renowne of a Bawd.

†**c.** Good name, reputation. *Obs. rare*$^{-1}$.

1611 SHAKS. *Cymb.* v. v. 202 To make the noble Leonatus mad, By wounding his beleefe in her Renowne.

†**d.** Commendation *of* a person. *Obs. rare*$^{-1}$.

1631 CHAPMAN *Cæsar & Pompey* Plays 1873 III. 194 His much renowne of you, quit with your utmost.

renown (rɪˈnaʊn), *v.* Also 6–7 **renoume**, (6 **renoumpne**), **renowme**; **renoune**, 6–7 **renowne**. [ad. OF. *renoumer*, var. *renomer*, *-nommer* (see RENOME *v.*); the form *renown* has been assimilated to the sb. See also RENOWNED *ppl. a.*]

1. *trans.* To make famous, spread the fame of; to celebrate. Now *rare*.

α. **1530** PALSGR. 686/1, I renoume one, I gyve hym a renoume, *Je renomme.* **1581** MULCASTER *Positions* xxxix. (1887) 218 Neither take I wealth to be any worthy cause to renowme the owner. **1609** BROUGHTON *Princ. Positions* 25 The third of Esdras was penned to renowme the building of the Temple. **1615** BRATHWAIT *Strappado* (1878) 199 A Prophetesse, Who wrot and spake in verse with such a grace, As she renoumd the Countrey where she was.

β. **1559** MORWYNG *Evonym.* Pref. a j b, I iudge him not to haue bene the first inuentor of this Art, but one that broughte it to lighte and renouned it. **1595** MUNDAY *John a Kent* II. i. (Shaks. Soc. 1851) 20 This resolution dooth renowne ye bothe. **1612** DRAYTON *Poly-olb.* v. 156 That most famous Towne Which her great Prophet bred who Wales doth so renowne. *a* **1639** W. WHATELEY *Prototypes* I. xi. (1640) 142 Those women Gods owne pen hath renowned for gracious and vertuous. **1735** POPE *Prol. Sat.* 179 The Bard whom pilfer'd Pastorals renown. **1743** A. HILL *Wks.* (1753) II. 240, I should feel no inclination to condemn your purpose to renown Strand-green. **1815** W. H. IRELAND *Scribbleom.* 260 As a limb of the Bar, I with honour renown 'em.

refl. **1592** *Nobody & Someb.* in Simpson *Sch. Shaks.* (1878) I. 335 Renowne yourselfe by being kind to her. **1631** MAY tr. *Barclay's Mirr. Mindes* II. 110 They are ambitious to doe strange and wonderfull things, and by them to renowne themselves and their times to Posterity. **1853** JERDAN *Autobiog.* IV. xiv. 255 Being..in the vein to 'renown' myself (using a verb coined at Drummond Castle), I shall [etc.].

†**b.** To report, relate. *Obs. rare*$^{-1}$.

c **1530** LD. BERNERS *Arth. Lyt. Bryt.* 283, I have herd renowned of you, that ye were fre and gentyll of hearte.

†**c.** To celebrate *with* some ceremony. *Obs.*$^{-1}$

1566 ADLINGTON *Apuleius* 28 This day is alwaies renoumpned with some solempne nouell.

2. *intr.* [After G. *renommiren.*] Of German students: To seek notoriety; to make a display; to swagger. Also with *it*.

1825 *Blackw. Mag.* XVII. 331 The Courlanders have been renowning of late. **1839** LONGF. *Hyperion* II. iv. Prose Wks. 1886 II. 92 The student with the sword leaped to the floor. It was Von Kleist. He was renowning it.

Hence **reˈnowning** *vbl. sb.*

1631 MAY tr. *Barclay's Mirr. Mindes* I. 216 To the renowning of their supposed suffrings. **1826** *Blackw. Mag.* XIX. 550 Among many less justifiable pieces of 'renowning' which occurred during my stay, there was one prank [etc.].

renownce, obs. form of RENOUNCE.

†**renowne(e.** *Obs.* Also 4–5 **renoune(e**, **-none**; *Sc.* 5 **ranowne**, 6 **renownye**. [A confusion of RENOMEE and RENOWN *sb.*] Renown.

1375 BARBOUR *Bruce* VIII. 290 Thai suld richt weill revardit be, And gretly ek thair renownee. *c* **1385** CHAUCER *L.G.W.* 1513 *Hypsipyle* (Camb. MS.), Sche knew by folk that in his shepis be That it was Iason ful of renone [*v.r.* renoune, renomee]. **1513** DOUGLAS *Æneis* VIII. xii. 143 The famus honour, and hie renownye, Or glorious gestis of his posterite.

renowned (rɪˈnaʊnd), *ppl. a.* Also 5–7 **renowmed**, etc. [f. as RENOWN *v.* + -ED¹: cf. RENOMED.] Celebrated, famous; covered with renown.

a. In predicative use, or following the sb. †Also with complement (quot. 1456).

α. **1375** BARBOUR *Bruce* II. 32 In fer landis renownyt wes he. ? *a* **1400** *Morte Arth.* 2372 The roy ryalle renownde, with his rownde table. **1456** SIR G. HAYE *Law Arms* (S.T.S.) 141 Sa did he his awin service..to be renouned a worthy man of armes. **1500–20** DUNBAR *Poems* xlviii. 154 Our the laif thy bewty is renownd. **1570** T. NORTON tr. *Nowel's Catech.* (1853) 194 Our prayer is, that the name of God be made renowned and known to mortal men. **1652** MILTON *Sonn.* xvi. *To Cromwell*, Peace hath her victories No less renownd then warr. **1776** GIBBON *Decl. & F.* xi. I. 335 Semno, the most renowned of their chiefs, fell alive into the hands of Probus. **1872** YEATS *Techn. Hist. Comm.* 67 He is also renowned as having well understood the system of turning in wood.

β. **14..** *Pol. Rel. & L. Poems* (1866) 46 Famose poetys of antiquite In grece and troy, renowmyd of prudence. *a* **1533** LD. BERNERS *Gold. Bk. M. Aurel.* (1546) C iv, There haue bene many famous and renoumed by scripture and lerning. **1590** SPENSER *F.Q.* I. x. 3 An auncient house..Renowmd throughout the world for sacred lore. **1621** AINSWORTH *Annot. Pentat.* (1639) *Numbers* 6 The called or, the renowmed:..such as were men of renowne for age and wisdom.

b. In attributive use.

α. **1417** LD. FURNYVAL in Ellis *Orig. Let.* Ser. II. I. 55 The gracious prosperitie and noble health of your renowned person. **1508** DUNBAR *Ball. Ld. B. Stewart* 1 Renownit, ryall, right reuerend and serene Lord. **1573** L. LLOYD *Marrow of Hist.* (1653) 219 The renownedst Oratours in all the world. **1630–1** MILTON *Arcades* 29 That renowned flood, so often sung, Divine Alpheus. **1818** COBBETT *Pol. Reg.* XXXIII. 164 The renowned wisdom of your Honourable House. **1860** TYNDALL *Glac.* I. iv. 33 The Lake of Geneva.., this renowned inland sea.

β. **1470–85** MALORY *Arthur* VIII. iv. 278 One of the famosest and renoumed knyghtes of the world. **1544** LELAND *N.Y. Gift* in *Itin.* (1768) I. p. xxiii, The old Glory of your renowmid Britaine. **1638** BRATHWAIT *Barnabees Jrnl.* III. (1818) 83 Not th' Ephesian Diana Is of more renoumed fam-a.

Hence **reˈnownedly** *adv.*, **reˈnownedness**.

1590 BARROUGH *Meth. Physick* VIII. (1639) 416 To increase and preserve the worthinesse and renownednesse of their good name. **1611** COTGR., *Glorieusement*,.. renowmedly. **1659** BP. WALTON *Consid. Considered* 180 For the honour he bears to the renownedly learned publisher.

renowner (rɪˈnaʊnə(r)). [f. as prec. + -ER¹.]

1. One who celebrates or makes famous. *rare.*

1615 CHAPMAN *Odyss.* XXIV. *ad fin.*, So wrought diuine Vlysses through his woes;..As through his great Renowner I haue wrought. **1642** MILTON *Apol. Smect.* Wks. 1851 III. 270 The two famous renowners of Beatrice and Laura.

2. [After G. *renommist.*] One who seeks notoriety; a swaggerer.

1839 LONGF. *Hyperion* II. iv. Prose Wks. 1886 II. 85 He was a student... In short, he was a renowner and a duellist. **1865** *Pall Mall G.* 7 Dec. 11 Rather..than that the Oxford men are less well behaved than the renowners of Heidelberg.

reˈnownful, *a. rare.* [-FUL.] Renowned.

1606 MARSTON *Sophon.* I. i. Wks. 1856 I. 152 O..Man of large fame, great and abounding glory, Renounefull Scipio. **1892** BROOKE *Hist. E. Eng. Lit.* v. I. 114 Rheda..is the shining and renownful goddess.

reˈnownless, *a. rare.* [-LESS.] Devoid of renown; unrenowned.

1552 HULOET, Renowmles..*ignominis.* **1828–32** in WEBSTER. **1892** *Blackw. Mag.* Mar. 388/2 He grew vexed that a little renownless girl should dare to address a very smart young man like him.

renoyrie, variant of RENAYRIE *Obs.*

renpayre, variant of REMPARE *v. Obs.*

Rens, obs. Sc. form of RHENISH *a.*

rensch, rense, obs. forms of RINSE *v.*

‖**renseignement** (rɑ̃sɛɲəmɑ̃). [Fr.] (A piece of) information; also, a letter of introduction.

1841 E. EVERETT *Let.* 30 Dec. in Dickens *Lett.* (1974) III. 4/1 At Washington you will be able to get abundance of letters & *renseignement* for every part of the interior. *c* **1863** MRS. GASKELL *Lett.* (1966) 931, I am..sending my courier to you in hopes that you will most kindly give him 'renseignements' on one or two points. **1873** W. JAMES *Let.* 25 May in R. B. Perry *Thought & Char. W. James* (1935) I. xx. 346, I take up the pen today mainly on a matter of business, that is, to get at as early a date as possible certain *renseignements* which may affect my choice of how to spend next winter. **1875** LADY C. SCHREIBER *Jrnl.* 20 Nov. (1911) I. 390 Called on the Consul, saw some fine Oriental dishes at his house, got from him various renseignements. **1921** *Glasgow Herald* 17 May 3/8 Given, however, accurate renseignements, properties of high potential value are to be acquired.

Renshaw¹ (ˈrɛnʃɔː). *Tennis.* The name of William Charles *Renshaw* (1861–1904) and his twin brother Ernest (1861–99), used *attrib.* in ***Renshaw smash*** to denote a kind of fast overhead volley with which they were associated.

[**1882**: see SMASH *sb.*¹ 1 b.] **1883** *Field* 7 July 11/1 Deuce was called in five of the games, and the fifth game was won by four of the 'Renshaw smashes'. **1889** W. M. BROWNLEE *Lawn-Tennis* v. 18 This return very soon was called the 'Renshaw smash'. **1975** *Oxf. Compan. Sports & Games* 835/1 He took the ball early—the 'Renshaw smash' was celebrated.

Renshaw² (ˈrɛnʃɔː). *Physiol.* [Name of Birdsey *Renshaw* (1911–48), U.S. neurologist, who investigated such cells.] ***Renshaw cell***: a nerve cell in the spinal cord that is innervated by collaterals from a motor neurone and forms synapses with that and adjacent motor neurones so as to provide an inhibitory feedback path.

1954 J. C. ECCLES et al. in *Jrnl. Physiol.* CXXVI. 533 A detailed study of the interneuronal discharges has established that these interneurones form a specialized group mediating the inhibitory path from motor axons. They may appropriately be given the distinguishing title of 'Renshaw cells'. **1974** M. C. GERALD *Pharmacol.* xv. 277 The Renshaw cells exert an inhibitory influence on the flow of nerve impulses along motor neurons in the spinal cord. **1976** W. R. INGRAM *Rev. Anat. Neurol.* i. 23 Some investigators have questioned the validity of the Renshaw cell concept.

rensselaerite (rɛnsəˈlɛəraɪt, ˈrɛnsələraɪt). *Min.* [Named in 1837 after Gov. Stephen Van *Rensselaer*: see -ITE.] A variety of talc, found in various parts of New York State and Canada, having a fine compact texture which makes it capable of being worked on a lathe and manufactured into various articles.

1860 WORCESTER cites DANA. **1863** DANA *Man. Geol.* 81 Rensselaerite is a kind of Soapstone of compact structure.

†**renˈstall.** *Obs. rare*$^{-1}$. [f. RE- + *enstall* INSTALL *v.*, after *renforce*, etc.] Reinstalment.

1630 J. LANE *Cont. Sqr.'s T.* 195 *note*, Canace tho fore kinge Cambusc did fall, and beggd his grace for Algarsifes renstall [1616 recall].

rent (rɛnt), *sb.*¹ Forms: 2–7 **rente**, (5–6 **rentte**, 5 **rennt**), 4– **rent**. [a. OF. *rente* (12th c.), *rende* = Pr. *renta*, *renda*, Sp. *renta*, Pg. *renda*, It. *rendita*:—pop. L. **rendita* (= class. L. *reddita*), fem. pa. pple. of **rendĕre*: see RENDER *v.* Hence also MDu., MLG., MHG. (also mod.Du., etc.) *rente*, Sw. *ränta*.]

†**1. a.** (In *pl.*) A source or item of revenue or income; a separate piece of landed or other property yielding a certain return to the owner. *Obs.*

c **1154** *O.E. Chron.* (Laud MS.) an. 1137 Martin abbot.. wrohte on þe circe, & sette þar to landes & rentes. *c* **1200** *Vices & Virtues* 77 Ða riche menn ðe laneð here eihte uppe chierches and uppe ða chirch-landes,..oðe uppe oðre þinges þe rentes ȝiueð. *a* **1225** *Ancr. R.* 168 Purses, baggen, & packes, beoð alle eorðliche weolen, & worldliche renten. **1387** TREVISA *Higden* (Rolls) VII. 323 Odo wastede and destroyede the kynges rentes and enchetes. *c* **1410** *Sir Cleges* 94 Whan he thowght..howe he hade his maners sold And his renttes wyde. **1481** CAXTON *Myrr.* I. v, Their Rentes, their tresours or other thinge wherin they delyte them. **1523** LD. BERNERS *Froiss.* I. ccclxxix. 635 This Philip..was abydynge in his mothers house, and lyued honestely on theyr rentes. **1599** SHAKS. *Hen. V*, IV. i. 260 What are thy Rents? what are thy Commings in? **1611** CORYAT *Crudities* 459 A goodly Bishoprick..which he endowed with most ample rents and reuenewes.

†**b.** Revenue, income. *Obs.*

a **1225** *Juliana* 4 An heh mon of cunne ant eke riche of rente. *a* **1300** *Cursor M.* 27248 [Of] ani wrangwis merchandise, Or o wasting of his rent. *c* **1330** R. BRUNNE *Chron.* (1810) 60 þe kyng..granted þam pes to haue, & gaf him ageyn boþe rent & lond. *c* **1386** CHAUCER *Monk's T.* 221 God to thy fader sente Glorie and honour, regne, tresour, rente. **1483** CAXTON *Cato* G iv, Thou oughtest..to holde thyn estate after thy rente and reuenue. **1550** CROWLEY *Last Trumpet* 300 Thou..sekest euer for to fynde wayes to encrease thine yerely rent. **1635** PAGITT *Christianogr.* III. (1636) 43 These Novell Devices brought in a new Rent and great profit to the Clergy. **1687** A. LOVELL tr. *Thevenot's Trav.* I. 166 Palm-Trees, which yield some rent to the Monks. **1708** SWIFT *Abolit. Chr.* Wks. 1755 II. I. 86 To allow each of them such a rent, as..would make them easy. **1783** BURKE *Sp. Fox's E. Ind. Bill* Wks. 1815 IV. 86 Territories yielding a rent of one hundred and forty thousand pounds a year.

fig. **1500–20** DUNBAR *Poems* lxxiv. 39 Rewthe, the frute of nobilnes, Off womanheid the tresour, and the rent.

†**c.** Profit, value. *Obs. rare.*

c **1305** *Land Cokayne* 86 þer beþ iiij willis in þe abbei.. Euer ernend to riȝt rent. **1513** DOUGLAS *Æneis* I. Prol. 82 Set this my werk full feble be of rent.

†**d.** Recompense, reward; a privilege accorded to a person. *Obs. rare.*

a **1300** *K. Horn* 984 Wanne hit is wente, Sire king, ȝef me mi rente. *a* **1300** *Cursor M.* 19593 It fell saint petre als for rent, To call men vnto amendment. **1448–9** J. METHAM *Amoryus & Cleopes* D v (MS.), More Ioy sche had Than Orphe, qwan he hys wyf receyud ayen for yᵉ rent Off his musycal melody.

†**2. a.** A tribute, tax, or similar charge, levied by or paid to a person. ***to hold one's rent***, to succeed in paying a tribute. *Obs.*

c **1290** *Beket* 390 in *S. Eng. Leg.* I. 117 He axede at þe laste Eche ȝere ane certayne rente þoruȝ al engelond wel faste. **1297** R. GLOUC. (Rolls) 5778 þre ȝer he huld is rente ac þe verþe was bihinde. *c* **1380** WYCLIF *Sel. Wks.* III. 87 þe Cherche, þat sellen men leve to synne, and ȝiven hem leve to last þerinne for an anuel rente bi ȝere. *c* **1386** CHAUCER *Man of Law's T.* 1044 Deeth, that taketh of heigh and logh his rente. *c* **1430** LYDG. *Min. Poems* (Percy Soc.) 185 Yf thou wilt..suffre me go frely fro prisoun, Without raunsoun or ony other rent. **1535** STEWART *Cron. Scot.* III. 550 Aganis this erle all Holland did rebell And of thair rentis wald no ansuer mak. **1659** HEYLIN *Examen Hist.* II. 182 That every Minister..may sue for the Recovery of his Tythes, Rents and other duties. *a* **1703** BURKITT *On N.T.* Mark vi. 13 Rather than pay the constant rent of daily relief to their poor parents.

fig. **13..** *Coer de L.* 4028 Kyng Richard hys ax in hond he hente, And payde Sarezynys her rente.

b. The return or payment made by a tenant to the owner or landlord, at certain specified or customary times, for the use of lands or houses; †***rent of assise*** (see ASSIZE *sb.* 2 b, and Blackstone *Comm.* (1766) II. 42). Also, in mod. use, the sum paid for the hire of machinery, etc., for a certain time. ***fair rent***, the amount of rent which a tenant may reasonably be expected to pay for the use of specified land or property; *spec.* that officially registered by a Rent Office for a particular tenancy.

a **1300** *Cursor M.* 28438 Toll and tak, and rent o syse, withalden i haue wit couettise. *a* **1440** *Sir Degrev.* 139 Hys husbondus that yaf rent Was y-hery3ed dounryght. **1480** *Waterf. Arch.* in *10th Rep. Hist. MSS. Comm.* App. V. 316 The rennt of the nexte terme..shall be arrestid in the tennants hands. **1560** DAUS tr. *Sleidane's Comm.* 60 Some of them pay more rent yerely than theyr Fermes be worth. **1607** NORDEN *Surv. Dial.* II. 49, I be Lord of many Mannors, and no doubt I receiue rentes of euery of these kindes. **1653** BROME *City Wit* II. ii, A poor Doctor of Physick..has paid a quarters rent of his house afore-hand. **1707** MORTIMER *Husb.* (1721) I. 391 They commonly allow a Farm to make three Rents, one for the Landlord, one for Charges, and one for the Tenant to live on. **1711** *Lond. Gaz.* No. 4902/4 The Ground Lease expires at Christmas... Rent reserv'd 4*l.* 16*s.* per Annum. **1736** J. MURRAY *Lett.* (1901) 24, I have got a good convenient house on rent. **1766** BLACKSTONE *Comm.* II. 43 Strictly the rent is demandable and payable before the time of sunset of the day whereon it is reserved. **1820** GIFFORD *Compl. Eng. Lawyer* 411 Where the rent is a large sum, the tenant should have it in readiness before sunset. **1865** BARING-GOULD *Werewolves* xiv. 239 Each tenant pays no rent for his cottage and patch of field, but is bound to work a fixed number of days for his landlord. **1886** *Act 49 & 50 Vict.* c. 29 §6 The landlord or the crofter may apply to the Crofters Commission to fix the fair rent to be paid by such crofter to the landlord for the holding. **1891** *Spectator* 18 July 100/2 They include the 'rent' of the engine and trucks, the cost of fuel, and the pay of engine-driver. **1926** *Act 16 & 17 Geo. V.* c. 52 §2 The expression 'full fair rent' in relation to a small holding means the rent which a tenant might reasonably be expected to pay for the holding if let as such and the landlord undertook to bear the cost of structural repairs. **1965** *Act 13 & 14 Eliz. II.* c. 75 §27 In determining..what rent is or would be a fair rent under a regulated tenancy of a dwelling-house regard shall be had,.. to the age, character and locality of the dwelling-house and to its state of repair. *a* **1974** R. CROSSMAN *Diaries* (1975) I. 263, I had to deal with all the questions about rateable value and with the fair-rent clauses. **1976** *Southern Even. Echo* (Southampton) 13 Nov. 6/5 The rent officer in determining fair rents can consider under his brief the property and then fix his figure with reference to similar properties.

†**c.** A piece of property for which rent is received, charged or paid; esp. *pl.* a number of tenements or houses let out to others (and freq. named after the proprietor). *Obs.* except *U.S. dial.*

1466 *Mann. & Househ. Exp.* (Roxb.) 341 It was agreid.. that my said mastyr schal paye hym for the rente that he rentythe to hym for Georges, wyche drawyth be yere iiij. marc. **1491–2** *Rec. St. Mary at Hill* 175 Reparacyons of the new howse in the cherche Rentes. **1517–8** *Ibid.* 299 Ress' of Thomas Clayton for that Remayned in his hondes of the byldyng of Nasynges Renttes next baattes howse xjs. iiij*d.* **1550** CROWLEY *Way to Wealth* A iij b, Whole allyes, whole rentes, whole rowes, yea whole streats. **1732** *Acc. Workhouses* 21 Another workhouse..belonging to the liberty of Hatton-Garden, Saffron-hill, and Ely-Rents. *c* **1847** J. S. COYNE in M. R. Booth *Eng. Plays of 19th Cent.* (1973) IV. 186 You used not to wear such waistcoats as that when you lived in Fuller's Rents. *a* **1902** S. BUTLER *Way of All Flesh* (1903) lv. 254 A rag and bottle merchant in Birdsey's Rents. **1926** *Dialect Notes* IV. 388 *Rent*,.. apartment or rentable house. **1943** [see *rent-hunter* in sense 4 b below].

transf. *a* **1631** DONNE *Elegies* xii. 62 Which haue devided heaven in tenements, and with..theeves, and murtherers stuft his rents soe full.

d. *Pol. Econ.* (See quot. 1817.)

[**1777** J. ANDERSON *Enquiry Nature Corn-Laws* 45 It is not, however, the rent of the land that determines the price of its produce, but it is the price of that produce which determines the rent of the land.] **1815** T. R. MALTHUS *Inquiry Nature & Progress Rent* 1 The rent of land may be defined to be that portion of the value of the whole produce which remains to the owner of the land, after all the out-goings belonging to its cultivation..have been paid, including the profits of the capital employed, estimated according to the usual and ordinary rate of the profits of agricultural stock at the time being. **1817** D. RICARDO *Princ. Pol. Econ.* ii. 49 Rent is that portion of the produce of the earth, which is paid to the landlord for the use of the original and indestructible powers of the soil. **1848** MILL *Pol. Econ.* I. II. xvi. 500 The rent, therefore, which any land will yield, is the excess of its produce, beyond what would be returned to the same capital if employed on the worst land in cultivation. **1884** J. RAE *Contemp. Socialism* ix. 455 No part of Ricardo's theory is more elementary or more unchallenged than this, that the rent of land constitutes no part of the price of bread, and the high rent is not the cause of dear bread, but dear bread the cause of high rent.

e. Money or cash, esp. that acquired by criminal activity or in exchange for homosexual favours; hence *ellipt.* (as quasi-*adj.*), = *rent boy* in sense 4 c below.

1828 W. T. MONCRIEFF *Tom & Jerry* I. 20 Blunt, my dear boy, is..to be able to flash the screens—sport the rhino—shew the needful—post the pony—nap the rent... Money, money, is your universal good. **1925** FRASER & GIBBONS *Soldier & Sailor Words* 242 Rent, money: cash. **1936** J. CURTIS *Gilt Kid* xii. 127, I haven't done anything since I've come out of the nick and the old rent's running a bit low. **1967** A. WILSON *No Laughing Matter* III. 306 I've been rent myself once... I just gave what they paid me for. **1977** *Gay News* 24 Mar. 15/3 A word of warning about the Strand Bar in Hope Street... It's rough and some of the people there are rent.

f. *Econ.* The financial advantage or gain regarded as emanating from a particular skill or ability, *spec.* in phr. *rent of ability* (see quot. 1929).

1879 A. MARSHALL *Econ. Industry* II. xii. 144 Rent of rare natural abilities is a specially important element in the incomes of business men. **1905** G. B. SHAW *Irrational Knot* p. xv, There is an important economic factor, first analyzed by an American economist (General Walker), and called rent of ability. **1929** S. E. THOMAS *Elem. Econ.* (ed. 4) xvii. 261 We may say that there is a rent element in both profits and wages, and that this element depends on the natural or acquired gifts of the employer or worker concerned. Where the differential payment is due to differences of ability, it may be suitably and correctly described as a rent of ability. **1930** *Times* 6 May 12/2 The Fabian Society formerly pleaded for the rent of ability, but the plea fell on deaf ears.

†**3. a.** *Sc.* *on rent*, at interest. *Obs. rare.*

a **1611** *Burgh Rec. Stirling* (1888) I. 126 The soume of ane hundrethe merkis..to be imployed be the toun on rent to the help of the ministrie of this burghe. **1612** *Ibid.* 129 The said soume of five hundrethe merkis salbe imployit on yeirlie rent..for the help and supporte of the ministrie.

†**b.** In France: A sum paid by way of interest upon a public debt. *Obs.*

1689 LUTTRELL *Brief Rel.* (1857) I. 605 He [the King] hath published an edict for a new creation of rents upon the town house of Paris. **1759** *Hist. War* in *Ann. Reg.* 55 *note*, The French court have stopped payment of the following public debts, viz. 1. The three kinds of rents created on the posts.

4. *attrib.* and *Comb.* **a.** Appositive, as *rent-beeves*, *-capon*, *-corn*, *-eggs*, *-geese*, *-hens*, *-oysters*, *-penny*, *-salt*.

1612 DAVIES *Why Ireland*, etc. 17 Such charges as were made vppon ONeale, for *Rent-Beeues. **1634** W. CARTWRIGHT *Ordinary* viii, To screw your wretched tenants up To th' uttermost farthing, and then stand upon The third *rent-capon. **1573** TUSSER *Husb.* (1878) 20 *Rent corne to be paid, for a reasnable rent. **1366** *Durham Acc. Rolls* (Surtees) 45, De cxl *Rent Egges. **1340** *Ibid.* 37 In xl aucis, quarum xiv *Rente ges, vs. vd. **1345** *Ibid.* 41, In cv^xx x gallinis, præter l *Renthennes, xxiiijs. jd. ob. **1611** COTGR., *Ostize*, a rent henne, &c., paid, or deliuered, in lieu of a dwelling house. **1651** *Maldon, Essex, Borough Deeds* Bundle 81 no. 1^v (MS.) For fetching of two bushells of *rent oisters from Tollesbury. *a* **1696** P. HENRY in M. Henry *Life* x. M. H.'s Wks. 1853 II. 737/1 Praise is our *rent-penny, which we pay to our great Landlord. **1399–1400** *Durham Acc. Rolls* (Surtees) 602 Pro cariacione de *rent-salt, xviij*d.*

b. Objective genitive, as *rent-collector*, *-enhancer*, *-holder*, *-hunter* (in sense 2 c), *-master*, *-owner*, *-raiser*, *-raising*, *-raker*, *-receiver*, *-rearer*, *-warner*, *-yielding*.

1875 W. S. HAYWARD *Love agst. World* 9 My agent, who employs the same *rent collector as he does. **1615** BRATHWAIT *Strappado* (1878) 214 Now (*rent-inhauncer) where away so fast? **1657** TRAPP *Comm. Job* xxxi. 39 [I have caused] the poor *Rent-holders..to misse of a subsistence. **1943** *Boston Herald* 28 July 12/1 A recent..cartoon showed two weary *rent-hunters walking past the White House. *c* **1610** SIR J. MELVIL *Mem.* (1735) 373 The *Rent-Masters and their Officers..must be responsible Men. **1844** MILL *Ess. Pol. Econ.* iii. 89 All which is produced beyond this, whether it be in the hands..of any of the numerous varieties of *rent-owners, may be taken for immediate enjoyment. **1549** LATIMER *1st Serm. bef. Edw. VI* (Arb.) 38 You landelordes, you *rent-reisers,..you haue for your possessions yerely to much. **1556** ROBINSON *More's Utop.* (Arb.) 38 *marg.*, Landlordes by the wai checked for *Rent-raisyng. **1611** SPEED *Hist. Gt. Brit.* IX. ix. (1623) 616 The Legate himselfe, whom they tearmed an Vsurer, Symonist, *Rent-raker, Money-thirster. **1549** LATIMER *1st Serm. bef. Edw. VI* (Arb.) 40 Then these grasiers, inclosers, and *rente rearers, are hinderers of the kings honour. **1943** in E. Blunden *Return to Husbandry* 12 The squire has become an absentee landlord, a mere *rent-receiver. **1883** *Standard* 28 May 4 A '*rent warner', in the service of Lord Kenmare. **1848** MILL *Pol. Econ.* I. III. v. 565 Selling at a scarcity value ..never is, nor has been, nor can be, a permanent condition of any of the great *rent-yielding commodities.

c. Miscellaneous, as *rent allowance*, *-arrear(s)*, *assessment*, *book*, *contract*, *control*, (hence *rent-controlled* adj.), *-day*, *-dinner*, *man*, *office*, *officer*, *rebate*, *restriction*, *-scot*, *-suit*, *tribunal*; **rent boy** *slang*, a young male homosexual prostitute; **rent car** *U.S.*, a hire-car; **rent party** *U.S.* = *house-rent party* s.v. HOUSE *sb.*[1] 24; **rent strike**, a refusal to pay rent, usu. by a number of people as a form of protest; **rent table** (see quot. 1952). See also RENT-CHARGE, -ROLL, etc.

1947 *Rep. Assistance Board 1946* iv. 21 The Statutory Regulations provide for the addition of a '*rent allowance' according to the circumstances of each individual case. **1974** COOTE & GILL *Women's Rights* vii. 259 The council gives rent rebates to council tenants and rent allowances to other tenants. **1669** *Ormonde MSS.* in *10th Rep. Hist. MSS. Comm.* App. V. 89 Recovery of *rent-arrears due on lands in the county of Dublin. **1965** *Act 13 & 14 Eliz. II.* c. 75 §25 There shall be constituted *rent assessment committees in accordance with the provisions of Schedule 2 to this Act. **1970** *Internat. & Compar. Law Quarterly* 4th Ser. XIX. II. 208 Generally, the working of the rent assessment committees was commended. **1830** M. EDGEWORTH *Let.* 4 Nov. (1971) 427 The rent to us is to be from his commencement the raised rent. See *Rent book. **1973** *Courier & Advertiser* (Dundee) 1 Mar. 6/4, I haven't seen my rent book for three years. **1978** *Lancashire Life* Apr. 67/1 He inspected Aunt Clara's rent-book and asked her for the names of her grocer and butcher. **1969** *Rent-boy [see KEPT *ppl. a.* 1 a]. **1975** *Daily Tel.* 24 July 3/6 Many of the boys became male prostitutes... They became known as 'rent boys'. **1976** DEAKIN & WILLIS *Johnny go Home* iii. 56 Between the ages of fifteen and twenty he had been a rent boy, a boy prostitute living and working in the West End. **1932** W. FAULKNER *Light in August* xv. 338 They went straight to the garage where Salmon keeps his *rent car. **1970** *Islander* (Victoria, B.C.) 6 Dec. 7/1 Ben quickly turned his machine into a 'rent' car. 'They call them taxis now,' he explained. **1906** *Chambers's Jrnl.* Jan. 118/1 Evidences of the long-continued disturbance of *rent-contracts in Ireland. **1940** W. FAULKNER *Hamlet* I. i. 14 But then I hear tell he always makes his rent contracts later than most. **1931** *Rep. Inter-Departmental Committee Rent Restrictions Acts* (Min. Health) xiv. 46 Some of us, if we had had the task of devising the original system of *rent control..would perhaps have proposed the setting up of rent courts. **1965** *Listener* 20 May 727/1 Local authority subsidies, rent control of private rented houses. *a* **1974** R. CROSSMAN *Diaries* (1975) I. 48, I am engaged on rent controls already. **1946** M. B. LOWNDES *Let.* 9 Jan. (1971) 270 Luckily Susan's flat is *rent controlled. **1971** B. MALAMUD *Tenants* 6 The building was rent-controlled, and from the District Rent Office..Harry had learned he was a statutory tenant. **1978** I. B. SINGER *Shosha* viii. 152 He had a rent-controlled apartment for which he paid no more than thirty zlotys a month. **1616** T. ADAMS *Divine Herbal* 26 If his *rent-day make euen with his Silkeman, Mercer, Taylor, he is well. **1869** MACKAY *Grace & Truth* (1875) 62 Shortly before the rent-day a neighbour comes in. **1837** THACKERAY *Ravenswing* vii, They would invite all farmers to a *rent-dinner. **1943** L. HUGHES in *Poetry* Sept. 312 The *rent man knocked. **1969** *Punch* 1 Jan. 15/1, I do worry about the effect which its long illness is having on its general standing with the butcher, the baker, and the rentman. **1977** COOTE & GILL *Women's Rights* vii. 257 Check the rent register at your local *Rent Office. **1965** *New Statesman* 9 Apr. 561/3 Widely publicised rent scales would..make it easier for *rent officers. **1973** E. BERCKMAN *Victorian Album* 176 Before we ever took this lease, I went to the Rent Officer. **1976** *Southern Even. Echo* (Southampton) 13 Nov. 6/5 The rent officer in determining fair rents can consider under his brief the property and then fix his figure with reference to similar properties. **1926** C. VAN VECHTEN *Nigger Heaven* ix. 150 There were..the modest *rent-parties. **1956** [see *house-party* s.v. HOUSE *sb.*[1] 24]. **1968** P. OLIVER *Screening Blues* vi. 203 One of the most frequently heard songs in the rent-party repertoire was *The Boy in the Boat.* **1936** G. WILSON *Rent Rebates* 10 There is a not inconsiderable body of opinion which has already expressed itself in favour of the adoption of *rent rebate schemes. **1971** *Reader's Digest Family Guide Law* 132/2 To apply for a rent rebate, a tenant must give details of his own income. **1977** *R.A.F. News* 11–24 May 4/6 Some 4,036 soldiers and 59 leading aircraftsmen were on rent rebate. **1921** A. W. BOON *Rent Restriction Act, 1920* 5 The *Rent Restriction Act is very intricate and much involved. **1940** *Economist* 5 Oct. 422/2 Profiteers have been threatened with the Rent Restriction Acts. **1952** A. CHRISTIE *Mrs. McGinty's Dead* ii. 17 Under the Rent Restriction Act the landlord couldn't get the old woman out. **1976** *Evening Post* (Nottingham) 17 Dec. 32/8 Rent increases amounting to £2,025..were not included because of the failure to act on the partial lifting of rent restrictions in November, 1973. **1631** in *Bingham's Reports* V. 341 A grant..of..all rents, revenues, and services, rents-charge, *rents-scot &c...arising in or within the lordships. **1970** *N.Y. Times* 5 Feb. 38/6 The student organization also is lending moral and organizational support to..a widespread local *rent strike. **1973** *Freedom* 26 May 1/2 Let the Trade Union movement now show its regard for the value of education by giving..support to student rent-strikes. **1977** *Transatlantic Rev.* LX. 120 In English class he'd go off on a crusade for Food Co-ops and Rent Strikes. **1883** *19th Cent.* Sept. 439 As regards the procedure in *rent-suits, no material change is made by the Bill. **1927** MACQUOID & EDWARDS *Dict. Eng. Furnit.* III. 241 A..type, known as a '*Rent-Table', was introduced about this time [*sc.* 1750]. **1952** J. GLOAG *Short Dict. Furnit.* 387 *Rent Table*, a type of office table made during the second half of the 18th century, with a round or octagonal top, with drawers immediately below. **1961** 'J. WELCOME' *Beware of Midnight* i. 9 The furniture, too, was solid and respectable. There was an octagonal rent table. **1973** V. CANNING *Finger of Saturn* i. 4 He..set his briefcase on the round rent table. **1945** *Daily Herald* 20 Apr. 4/3 Unanimous proposals of the Committee are: The establishment of 198 *rent tribunals for England and Wales. **1973** E. BERCKMAN *Victorian Album* 28 It means spending half your life before the Rent Tribunal. **1974** COOTE & GILL *Women's Rights* vii. 256 You may be able to recover the extra amount by going to the Rent Tribunal.

rent (rɛnt), *sb.*[2] [f. RENT *v.*[2] Cf. REND *sb.*]

1. The result of rending or tearing apart; a separation of parts produced by tearing or similar violence; *esp.* a large tear in a garment or piece of woven stuff.

1535 COVERDALE *Matt.* ix. 16 Then taketh he awaye the pece agayne from the garment, & the rent ys made greater. **1601** SHAKS. *Jul. C.* III. ii. 179 See what a rent the enuious Casca made. **1623** GOUGE *Serm. Extent God's Provid.* §15 The maine Summier..failed..more shiveringly and with a longer rent in the timber. **1728** YOUNG *Love Fame* II. 98 By night she went, And, while he slept, surpris'd the darling rent. **1798** JANE AUSTEN *Northang. Abb.* (1833) II. xiv. 199 Only think..of my having got that frightful great rent in my best Mechlin so charmingly mended. **1846** A. YOUNG *Naut. Dict., Rents*.., openings or cracks which take place in timber or planks when much exposed to the heat of the sun. **1858** G. MACDONALD *Phantastes* II. xviii. 73 A dark curtain of cloud was lifted up, and a pale blue rent shone between its foot and the edge of the sea.

fig. **1535** COVERDALE *2 Sam.* vi. 8 Then was Dauid sory, because the Lorde had made soch a rente vpon Vsa, and he called the same place Perez Vsa vnto this daye. **1878** J. MILLER *Songs Italy* 64 A gust that made rents Thro' the yellow-sailed fishers.

b. With punning allusion to RENT *sb.*[1]

1616 WITHALS *Dict.* (1634) 166/1 *Pannosus*.., wee say in English 'that hath his rent come in'. **1738** SWIFT *Pol. Conversat.* 56, I have torn my Petticoat with your odious Romping; my Rents are coming in.

2. A breach, split, schism, or dissension in a society or party, or between persons. *rare.*

1608 SYLVESTER *Du Bartas* II. iv. III. *Schism* 14 The rent of th' Hebrew Tribes from th' Ishean's Regiment. **1679** PENN *Addr. Prot.* I. 11 It occasions great Unkindnesses, Rents, Confusions and Divisions in Families. **1719** *Wodrow Corr.* (1843) II. 456 Lest our miserable rents be heightened, and unruly passions be provoked.

3. A cleft or fissure in the surface of the earth; a deep narrow gorge or valley; also, a narrow breach in a wall, etc.

1705 ADDISON *Italy* 283, I believe every one who sees this vast Rent in so high a Rock..must be satisfy'd that it was the

Effect of an Earthquake. *Ibid.* 469 From Lyons there is another great Rent, which runs across the whole Country. **1807** Wordsw. *White Doe* I. 256 Oft does the White Doe loiter there, Prying into the darksome rent. **1848** W. H. Bartlett *Egypt to Pal.* xxiv. (1879) 491 We..could easily have passed through the rents in the walls.

b. *Coal-mining.* A plane of cleavage running across a seam; a back.

1883 Gresley *Gloss. Coal-mining.*

4. The act of tearing or rending; the fact of being rent.

1836 Macgillivray tr. *Humboldt's Trav.* v. 72 The Gulf of Cariaco owed its existence to a rent of the Continent. **1864** Tennyson *Aylmer's F.* 536 [He] read; and tore [the letter] As if the living passion symbol'd there Were living nerves to feel the rent.

rent (rɛnt), *v.*[1] [ad. OF. *renter*, f. *rente*; or directly f. rent *sb.*[1]]

†**1.** *trans.* To provide with revenues; to endow.

1362 Langl. *P. Pl.* A. viii. 35 Treuþe..bad hem..Rule religion and rente [*v.r.* renten] hem betere. *c* **1475** *Partenay* 5300 That place [he] augmented passingly..And rentid gretly to the house encresse. **1485** Caxton *Chas. Gt.* 208 He founded, rented, & releued many & dyuers chyrches.

2. a. To pay rent for (land, houses, etc.); to take, hold, occupy or use, by payment of rent. Also *absol.*

1530 Palsgr. 686/1, I rente, I paye farme hyre. **1603** Shaks. *Meas. for M.* ii. i. 254 If this law hold in Vienna ten yeare, ile rent the fairest house in it, after three pence a Bay. **1622** Mabbe tr. *Aleman's Guzman d'Alf.* i. 196 Such beggers as are so disposed, may rent certaine children. **1671** W. Berkeley in E. D. Neill *Virginia Carolorum* (1886) viii. 335 In Virginia about forty thousand persons..have come to settle and rent. **1716** Addison *Drummer* i. i, I'll e'en marry Nell, and rent a bit of Ground of my own. **1763** Jefferson *Corr.* Wks. 1859 I. 188, I do not know that I shall have occasion to return, if I can rent rooms in town to lodge in. **1885** *Law Rep. 15 Q.B. Div.* 316 The truck in question was rented by the defendant..from the Midland Waggon Co. **1911** M. W. Ovington *Half Man* 44 Not only were they unable to rent in neighbourhoods suitable for respectable men and women. **1979** *N.Y. Rev. Bks.* 17 May 6/2 New Yorkers rent. They don't buy.

b. To obtain money from (someone) by criminal means or in exchange for homosexual favours. *slang.*

1898 O. Wilde *Let.* 11 May (1962) 738 Bosie..is devoted to a dreadful little ruffian aged fourteen... Every time he goes home with Bosie he tries to rent him. **1956** C. Mackenzie *Thin Ice* xiii. 172 'I reckon you thought I was trying to rent Mr. Fortescue, eh?' 'To do what?' I asked in astonishment at such an expression. 'Get money out of him.'

3. To let (*out*) for rent or payment; to hire out. Also *transf.* or *fig.*

1546 *Yorks. Chantry Surv.* (Surtees) II. 323 In the same deanes handes, the Shepgate ther, not rented. **1564** in W. H. Turner *Select. Rec. Oxford* (1880) 307 Sydelyng shalbe taken into the most profytt of this Cytye, and to be rentyd and letten also. **1613** J. Fletcher *Christ's Bloody Sweat* 12 [Soldiers] For prey and spoyle aduenturing to rent Their liues and soules. **1730** A. Gordon *Maffei's Amphith.* 374 Our Community..rents out those Places which otherwise would be useless. **1737** Swift *Let. to J. Barber* 30 Mar., I confess there is no reason why an honourable Society should rent their estate for a trifle. **1817** Paulding *Lett. from South* II. 64 Our guide..was 'rented' out to the King of England, by the legitimate Prince of Hesse Castle. **1895** *Outing* (U.S.) XXVII. 210/1 A few residents, who eke out a meagre existence by renting boats to the occasional sportsman.

†**4. a.** To pay (a sum) as tribute. *Obs. rare*$^{-1}$.

1613 Purchas *Pilgrimage* vi. xi. 524 Muley Hamet..conquered Tombuto and Gago:..Laurence Madoc..saith that Tombuto rented threescore quintals of Golde.

†**b.** To produce or bring in as rent. *Obs. rare*$^{-1}$.

1774 *Ann. Reg.* 150 The estate of Broughton which rents above 700*l.* per annum was..sold for 14,000*l.*

5. *intr.* To let *at* a certain rent. Also const. *for.* Now chiefly *N. Amer.*

1784 G. Washington *Diary* 15 Sept. (1925) II. 292 The Plantation on which Mr. Simpson lives rented well—viz. for 500 Bushels of Wheat. **1805** *New-England Palladium* (Boston) 26 July 3/3 Two convenient Tenaments, for small families, that will rent at 12 pr. cent of what they will be sold for. **1815** Simond *Tour Gt. Brit.* I. 313 Arable land rents at £3 and £4, or even £6 an acre. **1828** P. Cunningham *N.S. Wales* (ed. 3) II. 66 The market-dues for this traffic renting, the present year, at 840*l.* **1947** *Chicago Daily News* 25 Feb. 1/4 (*caption*) 4-room apartment to rent for $120. **1974** *Whig-Standard* (Kingston, Ontario) 11 Jan. 7/2 The smallest 'bedsitter' apartment in central London rents for about $25 per week.

6. *trans.* To charge (a person) with rent; to impose a certain rent on (one).

1881 *Times* 13 Apr. 11/2 Any tenant, however lightly rented, will..have the strongest inducement to bring his landlord before the Court and to get the rent judicially fixed. **1894** *Daily News* 24 Apr. 6/5 It might deprive them of the power..to rent a man upon his own improvements.

7. a. Used (with reference to sense 2) in the form ***rent-a-*** prefixing a noun (usu. with hyphens) to designate the rental of the thing specified, orig. and chiefly a motor vehicle.

Rentacar forms part of a proprietary term in the U.S.

1921 *Chicago Central Business & Office Building Directory* 531/1 *Rent-a-Ford (Inc.)* 1450 S. Michigan av. **1924** *Official Gaz.* (U.S. Patent Office) 19 Feb. 503/1 The Rentacar Company, Toledo, Ohio..Rentacar U-Drive..Automobiles. Claims use since Aug. 6, 1921. **1935** *Arch. Dermatol. & Syphilol.* XXXII. 78 A man..who owned a 'rent-a-car' business. **1963** *Fortune* Sept. 78 (Advt.), Avis is only No. 2 in rent a cars. So we have to try harder. **1966** J. Gardner *Amber Nine* xi. 161 Martin..was at the wheel of the Rent-a-Car Merc. **1969** 'G. Black' *Cold Jungle* ix. 137 The rentacar Zephyr was still waiting on grass. **1971** *E. Afr. Standard* (Nairobi) 13 Apr. 13/6 Rent-a-train and unit-train operations across North America would siphon more than 4 million tons of cargo from the Seaway. **1972** 'G. Black' *Bitter Tea* (1973) ii. 26 The key to my rentacar was in one of my damp pockets. **1976** *National Observer* (U.S.) 21 Aug. 7/1 Rent-a-horse service is available from a riding school next door. **1977** *Rolling Stone* 19 May 11/2 His is a typical L.A. rent-a-home.

b. In various extended and fanciful uses, as ***rent-a-crowd***, ***rent-a-mob***, etc., to denote the spontaneous acquisition or instant availability (usu. for some transitory purpose) of the thing specified. Also *transf.* in *concr.* senses.

1961 *Daily Tel.* 21 Dec. 8/6 Dictators!!! When you liberate a territory or mop up a colonialist enclave, are you disappointed and upset to receive only a tepid welcome from the people? Let *rentacrowd* help you! We can supply cheering crowds for all occasions. **1964** C. Driver *Disarmers* x. 233 The phenomenon which Peter Simple of the *Daily Telegraph* cruelly christened 'Rentacrowd': London's instantly available progressive claque ready..to demonstrate on a whole range of causes. **1968** *Guardian* 22 Aug. 8/6 Ali..is the only man in Britain at the moment who can summon up a sizable Rentacrowd fast. **1970** *Peace News* 5 Sept. 7/1 One of the chief rentacops was reportedly bitten in the genitals by one of his own dogs. **1970** *Guardian* 27 Oct. 11/5 The strategy was based upon a tactic which Oxford students called Rentamob..a hard core of rioters who could turn a demonstration into a confrontation. **1972** M. Jones *Life on Dole* i. 11 In Merthyr Tydfil it was the day for the demonstration against unemployment... There are no professional marchers—no Rentacrowd—here. **1976** *Times* 27 Jan. 4/1 Squatters in London are reported to be using children in a 'rent-a-kid' system, as a means of being rehoused. **1977** *New Society* 7 July 15/1 Trouble was caused not by ordinary workers, still less by management, but by Rent-a-picket... 'There's always the Rent-a-crowd element that hangs on to strikes.' **1979** *Daily Tel.* 17 Nov. 2/1 Sir John denied that the trade union movement was contaminated by the 'rent-a-mob' philosophy.

rent (rɛnt), *v.*[2] *Obs.* exc. *dial.* Also 5–6 rente, (5 rentte). [var. of rend *v.*, after the pa. t. and pa. pple. *rent.*]

1. *trans.* To rend, tear, pull asunder or in pieces.

c **1385** Chaucer *L.G.W.* 843 *Thisbe*, Now what lyoun that be in this forest Myn body mote he renten. *c* **1440** *York Myst.* xxx. 36 All to ragges schall ye rente hym and ryue hym. *c* **1475** *Babees Bk.* 81 Nor thurhe clowyng your flesshe loke yee nat Rent. **1490** Caxton *Eneydos* xxi. 76, I haue not rented, vyolated ne broken, the pyramyde of his faders sepulture. *a* **1548** Hall *Chron., Edw. IV* 191 Rentyng his cote of armes and breakyng his Sword ouer his hed. **1582** Stanyhurst *Æneis* ii. (Arb.) 59 Hudge beams hee brusteth, strong bars fast ioyncted he renteth. *c* **1610** Sir J. Melvil *Mem.* (1735) 92 Then she did rent her angry letter. **1633** Prynne *Histriom.* 4 They would..even stone or rent him all to pieces. **1688** R. Holme *Armoury* iii. 332/1 A Katherine Wheel..is a kinde of Wheel used to rent and tear in peeces grand Malefactors. **1727** Swift *Market-hill Thorn* xvi, Thy confed'rate Dame Shall rent her Petticoats to Rags, And wound her Legs with every Bri'r. **1898** in *Eng. Dial. Dict.*

absol. **1560** Bible (Genev.) *Eccl.* iii. 7 A time to rent, & a time to sowe.

refl. **1603** Knolles *Hist. Turks* (1621) 126 In his madnesse (as some report) renting himself with his teeth. **1613** Purchas *Pilgrimage* viii. iii. (1614) 746 To behold such monstrous Icie Ilands, renting themselues with terrour of their owne massines.

b. To tear (one's face, hair, clothes, etc.) in grief or rage. Cf. rend *v.* 3 b.

? *a* **1366** Chaucer *Rom. Rose* 324 For to rent in manye place Hir clothis,..As she that was fulfilled of ire. **1447** Bokenham *Seyntys* (Roxb.) 70 As a wood womman she ferd Renttyng hir clothis. **1535** Coverdale *2 Sam.* iii. 31 Rente youre clothes, and gyrde sack cloth aboute you, and make lamentacion for Abner. **1591** Sylvester *Du Bartas* i. v. 829 For, finding them by some fell Serpent slain, She rents her brest. **1657** Trapp *Comm. Ezra* x. 1 Of this we read not..but of other effects of his passion, as renting his garments. *c* **1678** *Roxb. Ball.* (1891) VII. 430 My Golden hair I rent and tear like one outragious mad.

c. To rend or tear, in various *fig.* senses.

c **1440** *Gesta Rom.* ii. xvii. 330 (Add. MS.), Lustes of the flessh, that in no maner renten the soule. **1535** Coverdale *Joel* ii. 12 Rente your hertes, & not youre clothes. **1581** Pettie tr. *Guazzo's Civ. Conv.* i. (1586) 27 b, Those who..whet their tongues to rent a sunder..the good name of others. *c* **1586** C'tess Sidney *Ps.* xlvi. iii, The voice of aire his voice doth rent. *c* **1614** Sir W. Mure *Dido & Æneas* ii. 546 In diverse partes his dowbtsome minde he rents. **1681** Colvil *Whigs Supplic.* (1751) 38 Romish craft and policy, Which rents the Dutch and us asunder. **1747** Mrs. S. Fielding *Lett. David Simple* II. 181 A Person, whose every Word and Look can..rent the Heart asunder.

2. To tear *out of*, *from*, or *off*. Also *refl.*

1535 Coverdale *Lev.* xiii. 56 Then shall he rente it out of the clothe. **1539** Bible (Great) *1 Kings* xi. 11, I wyll rent the kyngdome from the. **1627** Hakewill *Apol.* (1630) 169 Wherein nature being but greene and growing, we rent from her, and replant her branches. **1643** Burroughes *Exp. Hosea* i. (1652) 6 These ten Tribes renting themselves from the house of David, did rent themselves likewise from the true worship of God. **1718** J. Fox *Wanderer* 127 To seize upon the..Books, divest them of the..Ornaments, by renting off the..Plates. **1865** Brierly *Irkdale* (1868) 7 Rentin' o' ther clooas off their backs wi' blackberryin'.

3. *intr.* To tear; to give way or separate by tearing or splitting.

1526 *Pilgr. Perf.* (W. de W. 1531) 260 b, Doutlesse his handes & fete dyd rent & teare for the weyght of his blessed body. **1597** A. M. tr. *Guillemeau's Fr. Chirurg.* 10/2 Sometimes onlye the first table of the sculle breaketh and renteth. **1641** J. Jackson *True Evang. T.* ii. 139 The soule grows more when the tabernacle of the body begins to rent. **1695** Blackmore *Pr. Arth.* ii. 828 Though solid Rocks touch'd with Compassion rent, The more obdurate Jew does not relent. **1812–** in *Eng. Dial. Dict.*

fig. **1563** B. Googe *Eglogs* iv. (Arb.) 45 My Harte with this began to rent. **1575** Gascoigne *Herbes* Wks. (1587) 143 My griefe, Whereof to tel my heart (oh) rents in twaine.

rent (rɛnt), *ppl. a.* [pa. pple. of rend *v.*] Torn, in various senses; also, in predicative use, wearing torn or ragged clothing.

c **1375** *Sc. Leg. Saints* xlvi. (*Anastace*) 186 Fra þat place þan vald he ga, raggit & rent & blak alswa. **1382** Wyclif *Josh.* ix. 4 Olde sackis..and rent wyn botels. *c* **1440** *Promp. Parv.* 430/1 Rent, and raggyd, *lacerosus.* **1582** Stanyhurst *Æneis* i. (Arb.) 20 Crash do the rent tacklings. **1597** G. Harvey *Trimming Nashe* Wks. (Grosart) III. 25, I scorne such ragged rent-foorth speech. **1625** Mountagu in *Buccleuch MSS.* (Hist. MSS. Comm.) I. 262 Our rent country cannot be drawn up, but must be torn more [and] more. **1818** Shelley *Rosal. & Helen* 791 Like flowers delicate and fair, On its rent boughs. **1876** Swinburne *Erechtheus* 1345 Earth groans from her great rent heart.

-rent, *suffix* (obs. Sc.): see -red.

rentable (ˈrɛntəb(ə)l), *a.* [f. rent *v.*[1] + -able.]

a. Liable to pay rent. **b.** That may be rented, or let out for rent.

1648 Hexham, *Rentbaer*, He that is subject to pay Rent, or Rentable. **1727** Bailey vol. II, *Rentable*, that may be rented. **1886** *Pall Mall G.* 29 Nov. 3/1 All that is rentable on the..estate is the work of the tenants.

Hence **rentaˈbility**: *spec.* (see quot. 1964).

1818–60 Whately *Commpl. Bk.* (1864) 13 It is the rent (or rather the rentability) that makes the price high. **1922** W. Schlich *Man. Forestry* (ed. 4) I. ii. 107 These changes should not, in the long run, seriously affect the rentability of the forest industry. **1964** *Financial Times* 3 Mar. 5/2 Rentability is the ratio of an undertaking's profits to its capital. **1976** F. Zweig *New Acquisitive Society* ii. iii. 107 Public enterprise..is also supposed to achieve productivity and rentability.

rentage (ˈrɛntɪdʒ). [f. rent *sb.*[1] + -age. Cf. OF. *rentage* (Godef.).] Rent, rental, or renting; also, that which is held for rent.

1633 P. Fletcher *Purple Isl.* vii. ii, All our good we hold from heaven by lease,..Nor can we pay the fine and rentage due. **1888** *Univ. Rev.* Nov. 348 To bring the fact of the rentage of the unfruitful land into harmony with their doctrines. **1892** *Field* 16 July 104/1 The Society's rentage of the Ver lies a few miles south-west of St. Albans.

rental (ˈrɛntəl), *sb.* Also 4–8 rentall, 6 -aill, -ayl. [a. AF. *rental* (Godef.) or ad. Anglo-Lat. *rentale* (Du Cange): see rent *sb.*[1] and -al[1].]

1. a. A list or register of the rents due by tenants to a proprietor; a rent-roll. Now *rare.*

1362 Langl. *P. Pl.* A. vii. 83 To ha reles and remission on þat rental I be-leeue. *c* **1440** *Jacob's Well* 41 3if a styward fynde in þe old court-rollys & rentallys..þat þou art behynde of þi rente to þi lord. **1523** Fitzherb. *Surv.* 12 What rentes..the lorde ought to haue of his tenauntes can nat be knowen but by the..court rolles, rentayles [etc.]. **1584** *Reg. Privy Council Scot.* III. 698 Bringand with thame..ane just and trew inventour and rentall of the convent. **1709** *Lond. Gaz.* No. 4520/3 The two several Demesnes..to be Sold, and a Rental or Proposals thereof is to be had at Mr. Thomas Norton's. **1824** Scott *Redgauntlet* let. xi, I have heard of a thing they call Doomsday-book—I am clear it has been a rental of back-ganging tenants.

b. An income arising from rents received.

c **1395** *Plowman's Tale* i. 474 Her seruauntes be to them vnholde But they can doublin theyr rentall. **1801** *Lusignan* II. 154 Emily's vast rental offered a mark to his ambition. **1878** Lecky *Eng. in 18th C.* II. vii. 239 Prior, in 1730, calculated the rental spent by absentees in England at about 620,000*l.*

2. a. The amount paid or received as rent.

1637–50 Row *Hist. Kirk* (Wodrow Soc.) 42 If any Minister sett his gleib or manse, or any part of the fruits thereof, with diminution of the rentall, that all such tacks be declared null. **1765** Blackstone *Comm.* I. viii. 300 The rental of the kingdom was supposed to be so exceeding low, that one subsidy of this sort did not..amount to more than 70,000*l.* **1844** Disraeli *Coningsby* iii. iii, Lord Everingham..frightened him with visions of rates exceeding rentals.

b. A house, flat, car, etc., let out for rent. Chiefly *N. Amer.*

1952 *Sat. Even. Post* 22 Nov. 25 Sometimes a mob of hoodlums in a rental forced off the road by pursuing police would get tangled up in their own arsenal. **1968** *Globe & Mail* (Toronto) 3 Feb. 3/3 Habitat, Expo's futuristic housing complex, has started a new life as an ordinary rental development. **1970** *New York* 16 Nov. 42/3 They began breaking up the mills and foundries into rentals for small-time manufacturers. **1972** J. Gores *Dead Skip* xi. 76 The house was a rental, and rental properties meant landladies. **1981** *Nordic Skiing* Jan. 47/1 The ski shop carries complete rentals in all sizes and reservations on rental equipment are accepted.

3. *Sc.* A species of lease or 'tack' granted to a 'kindly tenant' (see kindly *a.* 3, quot. 1773).

1565–6 *Reg. Privy Council Scot.* I. 428 Obtenit ane new tak and rentall thairof. **1580–1** *Ibid.* III. 351 They have..had thair rentalis thairof..for ane certane sowme of entrie. *a* **1768** Erskine *Inst. Law Scot.* ii. vi. §38 (1773) 267 Rentals commonly bear a clause, that the rentaller shall neither assign nor subset.

4. The fact or process of renting (in the sense of rent *v.*[1] 3).

1915 *Nat. Real Estate Jrnl.* Nov. 332/2 The duty of the agent to owners whose property he has in charge for rental, requires him to make untiring effort to promptly secure desirable tenants. **1928** *Publishers' Weekly* 12 May 1951 The rental of children's books has not so far been well tested out, as only four of the stores replying have collections of children's books. **1977** *Grimsby Even. Tel.* 31 May 11/2 Advt.), The property is on rental.

5. *attrib.* as ***rental agency, agent, boll, book, car, (feu-)duty, house, land, mail, right, roll***; **rental library** chiefly *U.S.*, a library at which a charge is made for the loan of books.

1947 S. L. McMichael *How to operate Real Estate Business* xxvii. 221 The *rental agency must use considerable tact in fitting tenants into the right locations. **1972** J. Philips *Vanishing Senator* III. iv. 136 Couldn't you try rental agencies? **1978** R. Ludlum *Holcroft Covenant* xiii. 153 The rental agency was not amused, but Holcroft gave them no choice. **1915** *Nat. Real Estate Jrnl.* Nov. 332/2 (*heading*) Duties of *rental agents. **1967** *Boston Sunday Globe* 23 Apr. B43/7 The rental agent is Martin Cerel, Natick realtor. **1979** *N.Y. Rev. Bks.* 17 May 37 (Advt.), Britain's most experienced rental agent is here to give you every assistance with your plans for accommodation. *a* **1768** Erskine *Inst. Law Scot.* II. x. §25 (1773) Sometimes the titular..accepted of a stated quantity of corns yearly, commonly called *rental bolls. **1518–19** *Rec. St. Mary at Hill* 300 Paid for papur for..the *Rentall boke. *a* **1768** Erskine *Inst. Law Scot.* II. vi. §37 (1773) 267 If the proprietor barely inrol a tenant in his rental-book,..the inrolment is sufficient to defend the tenant. **1824** Scott *Redgauntlet* let. xi, I will bear the contents to your credit in the rental-book. **1962** *Time* 7 Dec. 84/3 Cut-rate *rental cars are generally as clean and well-serviced as the big three. **1978** S. Sheldon *Bloodline* xxxiii. 315 It took almost three hours for Max to drive to Lesgets in a Volkswagen, the cheapest rental car he could find. **1640–1** *Kirkcudbr. War-Comm. Min. Bk* (1855) 95 The heritor to pey the tenth and twentieth penny for his *rentall dewtie. **1591** *Reg. Privy Council Scot.* IV. 629 The auld *rentaill few dewitie. **1953** A. Upfield *Murder must Wait* ix. 85 *Rental houses are few ..and the demand for them is heavy. *a* **1768** Erskine *Inst. Law Scot.* II. vi. §38 (1773) 267 A rentaller..by exchanging his *rental lands..incurs the forfeiture of his right. **1928** *Publishers' Weekly* 14 July 169 His basement book-store..is now the home of an unusually successful *rental library. **1934** G. Conklin *How to run Rental Library* i. 11 The rental library..is strictly limited to that type of book-renting business which is organized for the purpose of profit. **1946** R. Chandler *Let.* 9 Jan. (1966) 136 The publishers have co-operated in the rental library swindle over a period of years. **1820** Scott *Monast.* xxxiii, Settling the *rental mails, and feu-duties. **1838** W. Bell *Dict. Law Scot.* 566 The right was not effectual against singular successors, unless the rentaller could show a *rental right. **1433** *Rolls of Parlt.* IV. 479/2 That the rolles of accounte..and the *rentall rolle..be putte and kepte in the cofre.

'rental, *v. Sc. rare.* [f. prec.] *trans.* †**a.** To put in or admit as a 'kindly tenant'. *Obs.* **b.** To let out or hold (land) on a rental.

1565–6 *Reg. Privy Council Scot.* I. 429 Elizabeth allegeit that..scho had broukit the saidis landis, and bene continewalie rentalit thairin fra tyme to time. **1640–1** *Kirkcudbr. War-Comm. Min. Bk.* (1855) 95 It is appoyntit.. that the full worthe of the land be valued as gif the samen were not rentalled. **1818** *Blackw. Mag.* III. 441 Some honest..individual, who rentalled of the Prelate of Glasgow the pendicle of 'Daldue Wester'.

rentaller ('rɛntələ(r)). *Sc.* Also 6 **-alar**, 6–7 **-aler**. [f. prec. sb. or vb. + -ER[1].] One who holds land on a rental; a 'kindly tenant'.

1578 *Exch. Rolls Scot.* (1899) XX. 370 *note*, It will pleis your lordschip resaif this berar as rentalar in our souerane lordes regester. **1597** Skene *De Verb. Sign.* s.v. *Curialitas*, In sik maner as gif he were proprietare, lyfe-rentar, tackesman or rentaller. **1640–1** *Kirkcudbr. War-Comm. Min. Bk.* (1855) 95 It is appoyntit, that all rentallers be valued as weill as the heritores. **1666** in *3rd Rep. Hist. MSS. Comm.* 421/1 That a remedy may be provided wher they have taks or are rentalers. *a* **1768** Erskine *Inst. Law Scot.* II. vi. §37 (1773) 267 It is the most probable opinion, that as rentals were granted from a special regard to the rentaller, they were accounted rights of liferent. **1838** W. Bell *Dict. Law Scot.* 566 The rentallers of Lochmaben, who were formerly servants to the Scottish Kings, have rights which may be transferred to strangers. **1880** *Academy* 8 May 334/1 By virtue of which the widow of a rentaller was entitled to retain possession of the lands during her widowhood.

†**'rentally.** *Obs. rare*$^{-1}$. [? ad. Anglo-Lat. *rentalia*, pl. of *rentale*: see RENTAL *sb.*] Revenues.

1534 in Picton *L'pool Munic. Rec.* (1883) 27 The rentally belonging to the Chantry att the Altar of St. John.

rentalsman ('rɛntəlzmən). *Canad.* [f. RENTAL *sb.* by analogy with OMBUDSMAN.] An official with responsibility for the equitable letting and administration of rented property.

1970 *Deb. & Proc. Legislative Assembly Manitoba* 30 June 3525 In my view, the singularly most unique feature of the proposed amendments is the establishment of the office of Rentalsman. **1971** *Canad. Labour* Mar. 15/3 This rating was based on: a single easy-to-read law, containing a broader statement of tenant rights than the other provinces; appointment of a 'rentalsman' (rental ombudsman); and a public education program on the new legislation. **1974** *Globe & Mail* (Toronto) 13 Apr. 8/2 Ceilings for rent increases..may be breached if the landlord can convince a new Government official called a rentalsman that higher increases are necessary because of costs.

rent-charge. *Law.* Also rent charge. [f. RENT *sb.*[1] + CHARGE *sb.* 11.] **1. a.** A rent forming a charge upon lands, etc., granted or reserved by deed to one who is not the owner, with a clause of distress in case of arrears.

1443 *Test. Ebor.* (Surtees) II. 89 My will ys yat George my son hafe,..a rentcharge of xxvjs viijd issuand owte of my landes and tenementes in Stitnam. **1523** Fitzherb. *Surv.* 21 b, Rent charge is where a man is seased of landes in fee and graunt by poole dede or by dede indented. **1544** tr. *Littleton's Tenures* (1574) 45 Suche rent is rent charge, because such landes and tenementes bee charged of such distres by force of the writinge onelye and not of common right. **1667** Primatt *City & C. Build.* 17 [To] reduce the same to a certain Rent, as if it were an Annuity or Rent-charge. **1712** Steele *Spect.* No. 263 ¶6 Your Father was a fond Fool to give me a Rent-charge of Eight hundred a Year to the Prejudice of his Son. **1818** Cruise *Digest* (ed. 2) III. 282 A rent charge may now be created either by grant, or by the operation of the statute of uses. **1876** Digby *Real Prop.* iv. §5. 204 *note*, Where on a grant in fee simple a rent is reserved to the grantor, this is not a rent service but a rent charge.

b. *transf.* and *fig.*

1668 R. Steele *Husbandman's Calling* v. (1672) 96 The Lord only hath given you an estate: charitable relief of such as are in want, is the Lord's rent-charge which he hath laid upon it. **1726** Pope *Odyss.* xix. 92 A rent-charge on the rich I live; Reduc'd to crave the good I once could give. **1768** *Woman of Honor* II. 175 They become necessarily a rent-charge on the providence of a parish.

2. *attrib.*, as ***rent-charge bank, stock.***

1909 *Daily Chron.* 14 Sept. 5/6 *Rent-charge banks were formed to aid the peasants in redeeming these charges. **1869** *Bradshaw's Railway Man.* XXI. 290 The debenture holders having refused to accept the 4½ per cent. *rent-charge stock at par. **1909** *Gt. Central Railway Co. Rep.* 6 Aug. 13 The South Yorkshire Rent-Charge Stocks.

Hence **rent-charger**, one in receipt of, or who benefits by, a rent-charge.

1870 *Echo* 16 Feb., Fixity of tenure which would make the landlord a pensioner or a rent-charger on his own estate. **1893** Dk. Argyll *Unseen Found. Soc.* xiii. 416 Mere rent-chargers can never have the same motives.

‖**rente** (rɑ̃t). [Fr.] Stock, esp. government stock; the interest or income accruing from such stock. Cf. RENT *sb.*[1] 3 b.

1873 R. Browning *Red Cotton Night-Cap Country* III. 185 Lying stretched on straw, The produce of your miserable *rente*! **1920** J. Galsworthy *In Chancery* III. ix. 283 She had, he knew, but one ambition—to live on her '*rentes*' in Paris. **1926** D. L. Sayers *Clouds of Witness* v. 116 There were substantial dividends from capital invested in French *rentes*. **1927** *Financial Times* 13 July 5/5 French Banks and Rentes hardened, recovering the ground lost recently. **1931** S. Jameson *Richer Dust* xvii. 495, I must find a job... I can't just live on my *rentes*.

rented ('rɛntɪd), *ppl. a.*[1] [f. RENT *v.*[1] + -ED[1].]

†**1.** Possessed of, or endowed with, property yielding a revenue or income. *Obs.*

1393 Langl. *P. Pl.* C. xi. 265 Let hure be knowe For ryche oþer wel yrented [etc.]. **1493** *Festivall* (W. de W. 1515) 7 Lordes and rented men must labour to kepe holy chyrche in rest and peas. **1648** Hexham, *Een Rentenier*,..a Rented man. **1761** *Chron.* in *Ann. Reg.* 107 The jesuits.. demand that the houses of the society may be considered in the same light as the regular abbeys and other rented monasteries.

2. Held, or let, for rent; leased or tenanted.

a **1687** Petty *Pol. Arith.* vi. (1691) 100 Moreover if rented Lands, and Houses, have increased. **1894** H. Gardener *Unoff. Patriot* 60 A nasty little rented house without so much as a garden patch to it.

3. In *Combs.* as ***dear-, high-, low-, lower-rented.***

1801 Jane Austen *Let.* 3 Jan. (1952) 100 It used to be lower rented than any other house in the row. **1818** Fearon *Sk. Amer.* 284 First-rate brick buildings, all new,..and always high rented. **1834** *Tait's Mag.* I. 543/1 His house is, to be sure, dear-rented from its locality. **1886** *Col. Maurice's Let. fr. Donegal* 41 The tenants on that particular estate are remarkably low-rented. **1939** M. S. Rice *Working-Class Wives* viii. 195 The shortage will not have been overtaken by 1941 even if the process of 'filtering-up', (i.e. people who can afford to do so vacating the lower-rented houses and moving into unsubsidized higher-rented houses) were steady and complete.

†**'rented,** *ppl. a.*[2] *Obs.* [f. RENT *v.*[2] + -ED[1].] Torn, lacerated, distracted.

1575 *Mirr. Mag., K. Manlius* L'envoi i Straunge it semes to thee What he that beares this rentid corps should be. **1587** Grove *Pelops & Hipp.* (1878) 78 They royst in silke, when others range the streete in rented rags. **1591** *Troub. Raigne K. John* (1611) 14 Scalding sighes blowne from a rented heart.

Rentenmark ('rɛntənmɑːk). [Ger., f. *renten* securities: see MARK *sb.*[2]] A unit of currency introduced in Germany in November 1923 and tied to the nation's industrial and agricultural resources; in 1924 it was replaced by the *reichsmark* (see REICH).

1923 *Times* 8 Nov. 12/4 The issue of Rentenmarks is to be delayed till it can take place simultaneously throughout the country. **1940** G. Crowther *Outl. Money* i. 19 The Rentenmark note was not itself land, nor was there any method by which the holder of a Rentenmark note could possess himself of the land that was supposed to be behind his note. **1967** T. Stolper tr. *G. Stolper's German Econ.* iv. 91 In the case of the Rentenmark collateral consisted of the 'real-estate debts' of agriculture and of industrial companies. **1974** *Spectator* 21 Dec. 803/1 The Rentenmark was a new unit of currency supposedly backed by the land of the Reich.

renter ('rɛntə(r)), *sb.*[1] [f. RENT *v.*[1] + -ER[1].]

†**1.** One who owns or lets lands or tenements; a proprietor. *Obs. rare.*

1387–8 T. Usk *Test. Love* I. vii. (Skeat) l. 110 Some of hem tooken money for thy chamber, and putte tho pens in his purse, unweting of the renter. *c* **1470** *Gol. & Gaw.* 403 He is the riallest roy, reuerend and rike, Of all the rentaris to ryme or rekin on raw.

†**2. a.** One who collects rents (esp. those belonging to a corporate body), taxes, or tribute. *Obs.*

1557 *Order of Hospitalls* E viij b, The Renters Charge..is, Quarterly to collect and gather..all those Rents that shalbe contayned in a Rentall. **1568** Grafton *Chron.* II. 108 We will..that our speciall renter of our foresaid realmes..paye by yere a thousand mark of siluer. **1762** *Chron.* in *Ann. Reg.* 721 The sieur Massonet, renter of the abbey of St. Antony ..in Viennois, has a son.

b. *attrib.* as ***renter-accompt, -clerk, -warden.***

1708 J. Chamberlayne *St. Gt. Brit.* II. III. (1710) 656 Auditors of the *Renter-Accompt. **1552** in *Vicary's Anat.* (1888) 316 To the *Renterclerk..x.l. **1631** T. Powell *Tom All Trades* (1876) 148 A Bucke at the *Renter Wardens feast. **1903** *Daily Chron.* 20 Jan. 6/7 Mr. Ashby, formerly renter warden of the Armourers and Braziers' Company.

3. A farmer of tolls or taxes. *rare.*

1598 Florio, *Appaltatore*, a hucster, a retailer, a renter.., a farmer of any thing. **1798** *Monthly Mag.* VI. 395 Mr. Rogers, renter of the bridge-tolls [at Worcester]. **1817** Jas. Mill *Brit. India* II. IV. vi. 231 Like other renters of India, [he] had..an inclination to withhold..the sum which he engaged to pay out of the Taxes [etc.].

4. a. A holder of lands, houses, or other property, by payment of rent.

1655 *Boston* (U.S.) *Rec.* (1877) II. 125 A considerable part of the rent due..is nott brought in by the renters of the land according to the contract with the towne. **1766** *Museum Rust.* (ed. 2) I. 96 A renter but of between four and five hundred acres of land. **1831** *Act 1 & 2 Will. IV*, c. 38 §16 The renters of pews in such church or chapel. **1884** *Dickens' Dict. Lond.* 244/1 The renter of a private wire has the.. apparatus entirely under his own control.

b. *spec.* A tenant-farmer.

a **1661** Fuller *Worthies, Essex* (1662) 334 When a Renter [he] impoverished himself, and never inriched his Landlord. **1733** Tull *Horse-hoeing Husb.* Pref. 13 Can we suppose that an English Renter should have more Honour in that Respect than his Roman Holiness..? **1792** Burke *Let. to Sir H. Langrishe* Wks. VI. 313 Substantial renters, opulent merchants..could not easily be suspected of riot in open day. **1882** Sweet & Knox *Sk. Texas Siftings* 51 The joyful glee of farming with negro renters 'on the shares'. **1938** *Mississippi* (Fed. Writers' Project) 104 *Renters*, who hire land for a fixed amount to be paid either in crop values or in cash. **1970** J. Blackburn *Land of Promise* viii. 119 He was on his way to see a renter on one of his farms south of town.

5. A shareholder in a theatre. *rare.*

1807 Janson *Stranger Amer.* 251 The renters who had subscribed to the building of a large theatre in the park of New York. **1893** *Daily News* 30 Jan. 2/1 The 'Renters' of Drury Lane Theatre are rejoicing over a dividend for the past year of 12*l.* 1*s.* per share.

6. A male prostitute. *slang.*

1893 O. Wilde *Let.* Mar. (1964) 336, I would sooner be blackmailed by every renter in London, than have you bitter, unjust, hating. **1895** M. Beerbohm *Let.* 3 May (1964) 103 It was horrible leaving the court day after day and having to pass through a knot of renters. **1969** *Jeremy* I. III. 22/2 *Renter*, male prostitute. **1972** D. Sutton *Lett. R. Fry* I. 5 In many cases 'affairs' were more idealistic than that practised by the 'renters' of Piccadilly.

7. One who organizes the distribution of films to exhibitors.

1908 *Variety* 16 May 11 There are other and larger questions pressing the attention of the exhibitor, renter and manufacturer. **1911** D. S. Hulfish *Cycl. Motion-Pict. Work* II. 112 The film industry is definitely separated into three branches: *manufacturer, renter*, and *exhibitor*. The renter owns the picture films. **1920** I. P. Gore in L. Carson '*Stage' Year Bk. 1920* 52 The success which attended the efforts of the exhibitors, renters, and manufacturers, to combat the peril with which they were confronted. **1927** *Melody Maker* Aug. 820/2 The renters could render far more assistance.. if they would take more interest in the showing of their films at every cinema where they are booked. **1940** *Economist* 13 July 43/1 To ensure that a minimum number of films are made, renters must produce or acquire one British film.

†**'renter,** *sb.*[2] *Obs.* [f. RENT *v.*[2] + -ER[1].] One who rends or tears (chiefly in *fig.* senses).

a **1540** Barnes *Wks.* (1573) 354/1 You may conclude that you bee..vnlearned stockes, peruerters, tearers, renters, of holy scripture. **1651** Baxter *Inf. Bapt.* 196, I was resolved not to engage with a renter of the Church. **1738** W. Wilson *Def. Ref. Prin. Ch. Scot.* Pref. (1769) 6 Are they therefore schismatics, renters and ruiners of the Church? **1784** J. Brown *Hist. Brit. Churches* (1820) II. vi. 297 The public resolutioners persecuted them with manifold reproaches, as ruiners of their king and country,..as renters of the church.

'renter, *v.* [ad. F. *rentrer, rentraire*: cf. RANTER *v.* The entries in Chambers are derived from Furetière's *Dict. Univ.* (1690).]

1. (See quots.) Hence **'rentering** *vbl. sb.* Also *attrib.*

1706 Phillips (ed. Kersey), *To renter*, to sow Cloth after a particular manner, to fine-draw. **1727–38** Chambers *Cycl.*, *Rentering* and *Fine-drawing* in the manufactories, the sewing of two pieces of cloth, edge to edge without doubling them, so that the seam scarce appears at all. **1901** P. N. Hasluck *Tailoring* 21 There are three kinds of absolutely invisible stitches which are used to repair tears... They are stoating, fine-drawing, and rentering. **1921** [see INVISIBLE *a.* 1 f]. **1955** J. E. Liberty *Pract. Tailoring* (ed. 2) iii. 24 Seaming and rentering...this is used in place of stoting when the material does not lend itself to being stoted.

†**2.** (See quot.) Hence †**'renterer.** *Obs.*

1727–38 Chambers *Cycl.* s.v. *Rentering*, To renter in tapestry, is to work new warp into a piece of tapestry.. damaged and on this warp to restore the ancient pattern or design. *Ibid.*, Among the titles of the French tapestry-makers is included that of renterers.

rent-free, *a.* [RENT *sb.*[1]] Exempt from payment of rent. (Usually predicative.)
1631 WEEVER *Anc. Funeral Mon.* 499 Almes-houses for twenty poore widowes to dwell in rent free. **1726** BERKELEY *Let.* Wks. 1871 IV. 130, I prefer his having it rent-free to a rent of twenty pounds. **1866** *Chambers's Encycl.* s.v. *Rent*, Where lands are held rent-free, it is usual for the landlord to reserve some nominal rent. **1883** LD. BLACKBURN in *Law Rep.* 9 *Appeal Cases* 66 It was most reasonable.. that where the salary was partly paid by a rent-free house, the officer should pay the tax on that house.

† **rent-gatherer.** *Obs.* [RENT *sb.*[1]] One who collects rents for or on behalf of another.
1398 TREVISA *Barth. De P.R.* VI. xvi. (Tollem. MS.), The rente gederer was defamid to his lorde þat he hadde wastid his good and catell. **1435-6** in Heath *Grocers' Comp.* (1869) 419 Paid to the rente gaderer ffor ij yeers laboryng abouten .. gaderyng of the seide rente. **1535** COVERDALE *1 Kings* xii. 18 Whan kynge Roboam sent thither Adoram the rentgatherer, all Israel stoned him to death. **1644** VICARS *God in Mount* 135 The Bishop of Winchesters Rent-gatherer and Steward of his Courts.

‖ **rentier** (rɑ̃tje). Also fem. **rentière** (-jɛr). [Fr.] One who makes an income from property or investment. Cf. RENTE.
1847 in WEBSTER. **1885** *Instructions Clerks Classifying Occupations* (Census Eng. & Wales, 1881) 100 Persons without specified occupations.. returned by property, rank, &c... Rentier. **1885** A. EDWARDES *Girton Girl* III. xv. 265 We are private citizens—rentières, living on our means. **1921** R. H. TAWNEY *Acquisitive Society* v. 68 If it [*sc.* a society] is to.. avoid the creation of a class of *rentier*, it must not use for current consumption the whole of the wealth annually produced. **1948** A. HUXLEY *Let.* 25 Jan. (1969) 579 Maria's uncle.. is a rentier, living on an unelastic income. **1954** M. BERESFORD *Lost Villages* II. vi. 205 Any ex-demesne land which *rentier* lords were prepared.. to lease. **1964** T. B. BOTTOMORE *Elites & Society* iii. 45 Pareto's two types of elite.. which he also refers to as the 'speculators' and the 'rentiers'. **1969** *Listener* 6 Feb. 173/2 This grumbling, sinisterly superior *rentière* lived opposite Virginia Lodge, Parkwood Hill, the Dales' suburban residence. **1973** 'D. JORDAN' *Nile Green* xxxi. 145 It's oil sheiks and Latin American generals and Lebanese rentiers who are going to buy your bonds. **1976** M. GREEN *Children of Sun* viii. 316 Brian.. fulminated against *rentiers* and Money Men.. but.. he remained a hedonist and a snob.

'renting, *vbl. sb.*[1] [f. RENT *v.*[1] + -ING[1].]
1. The action of letting or taking at a rent.
1552 in *Vicary's Anat.* (1888) App. xvi. 292 The helpe therunto [repair of houses].. was by the former leases and rentinges preuented. **1591** PERCIVALL *Sp. Dict.*, *Pujamiento*, renting of a commoditie, buying by great. **1946** E. O'NEILL *Iceman Cometh* p. vii, The renting of rooms on the upper floors, under the Raines-Law loopholes. **1974** *Howard Jrnl.* XIV. 41 Renting to the poor became increasingly unprofitable.
2. *slang.* In the sense of RENT *v.*[1] 2 b.
1956 C. MACKENZIE *Thin Ice* xiv. 183 Mr. Jack Shore has done quite a lot of blackmailing, or in his own elegant phraseology a lot of renting, during his inglorious career. **1963** —— *Life & Times* II. 255 At this date [*sc.* 1899] the cant word among homosexuals for their proclivities was 'so'. That seems to have vanished completely from current cant, though 'renting' for male prostitutes and 'camping' to express the way they attract the soliciting male still survive.
3. *attrib.*, as ***renting firm***, ***house***.
1920 I. P. GORE in L. Carson *'Stage' Year Bk. 1920* 52 In the same way the big renting firm came to the rescue of its small rival. **1927** *Melody Maker* Aug. 819/2 Every renting house of any standing requires a capable and experienced cinema musician permanently on its staff.

† **'renting**, *vbl. sb.*[2] *Obs.* [f. RENT *v.*[2] + -ING[1].] The action of rending or tearing.
1426 LYDG. *De Guil. Pilgr.* 2591 My-sylff I may the Rentyng whyte, I knowe yt wel, & the aquyte. **1526** *Pilgr. Perf.* (W. de W. 1531) 254 b, To the rentyng of his handes and fete, that the precyous blode yssued. *a* **1586** SIDNEY *Arcadia* III. (1898) 386 Appalled with the grievous renting of their first combination. **1638** A. READ *Chirurg.* xxv. 191 Cut off the threed hard by the knot, lest the ends.. should cause a renting of that which you did sow. **1688** R. HOLME *Armoury* III. 270/2 There is no sign of a Renting, Tearing, or of a Raggedness of the parts.

† **'renting**, *ppl. a.* *Obs.* [f. RENT *v.*[2] + -ING[2].] That rends or tears, in various senses.
1568 T. HOWELL *Arb. Amitie* (1879) 68 Doth feare the harmes of gaping golfes, and renting rocks doth mone. **1633** P. FLETCHER *Purple Isl.* XI. xii, At length.. A renting sigh way for her sorrow brake. **1687** *Lond. Gaz.* No. 2258/2 Our latent Affections, that kept their Cave during the renting Wind and Earthquake.

'rentless, *a.*[1] [f. RENT *sb.*[1] + -LESS.]
a. Producing no (†interest or) rent. **b.** Rent-free.
1648 HEXHAM, *Rentloos geldt*,.. Rentlesse money that lies still. **1850** BLACKIE *Æschylus* II. 141 A double lodgment for our use, One from the state, the other from the king, Rentless we hold. **1893** DK. ARGYLL *Unseen Found. Soc.* x. 303 There can.. be, therefore, no such thing as rentless land which is at the same time cultivated.

'rentless, *a.*[2] *rare.* [f. RENT *sb.*[2] + -LESS.] Without rents, untorn.
1628 GAULE *Pract. The.* (1629) 228 One shall succeed him, not in a Rentlesse onely, but in a Seamelesse Coat. **1881** NICHOL *Death Themistocles*, etc. 197, I saw the rentless banner wave.

† **rent-rack**, *v.* *Obs. rare.* [f. RENT *sb.*[1] + RACK *v.*[3]] *trans.* = RACK-RENT *v.* Hence † **rent-racked** *ppl. a.*, † **rent-racking** *vbl. sb.* and *ppl. a.*
1612 T. TAYLOR *Comm. Titus* i. 7 From whence are oppressings, rent-rackings, vsuries,.. and murders? **1612** R. CARPENTER *Soul's Sent.* 50 Getting goods wrongfully, as too many rent-racking Land-lords do. **1623** R. CARPENTER *Conscionable Christian* 114 Take not hence liberty, as some doe, to pay no debts, to put money to Vsury, to rent-racke thy Tenants. **1633** MASSINGER *Guardian* II. iv, The rent-racked farmer, needy market folks,.. are privileged.

† **'rentrant**, *a.* *Obs.* $rare^{-1}$. [a. F. *rentrant*, pres. pple. of *rentrer*: see RE-ENTER and RE-ENTRANT.] Re-entering.
1791 NEWTE *Tour Eng. & Scot.* 418 The land.. forming.. three salient, and two great rentrant, or returning angles.

‖ **rentrée** (rɑ̃tre). [Fr.] A return, esp. a return home after an annual holiday.
1892 E. DOWSON *Let.* 22 Aug. (1967) 240 Many thanks for your note, which I found on my rentrée last week. **1896** BEERBOHM in *Yellow Bk.* XI. 20 His *rentrée* into the still silent town strengthened his.. resolves. **1913** —— *Fifty Caricatures*, (*caption*) Rentrée of Mr. George Moore into Chelsea. **1961** *Guardian* 22 Sept. 16/1 The Rentrée is the return to the great cities, the beginning of a new school year. **1977** *Times* 30 Aug. 4/1 Life is about to begin again in France... The word of the moment is *la rentrée*.

rent-roll. [RENT *sb.*[1]] A roll or register of rents; a list of lands and tenements belonging to one, together with the rents paid on them; hence, the sum of one's income as shown by such a list.
1534 *Lett. Suppress. Monast.* (Camden) 280, I have recevyd your rente-rowle, and getheryd up the rent. **1611** COTGR., *Rentier*, a Rent-roll. **1695** CONGREVE *Love for L.* v. ii, No, no, only give you a rent-roll of my possessions. **1781** GIBBON *Decl. & F.* xxxi. III. 204 The ostentation of displaying.. the rent-roll of the estates which they possess. **1827** CARLYLE *Misc.* (1857) I. 31 Where, again we might ask, lay Shakspeare's rent-roll? **1882** BESANT *Revolt of Man* ii. (1883) 37 The holder of a splendid title, the owner of a splendid rent-roll.
attrib. **1842** TENNYSON *E. Morris* 103 The rentroll Cupid of our rainy isles.

rent-seck. *Law.* Also 5-7 sec, 6-7 secke, (6 seeke). [a. AF. *rente secque* lit. dry rent.] A rent reserved by deed in favour of some person, without a clause of distress in case of arrears (and so differing from a RENT-CHARGE).
This distinction in respect of remedy was abolished in 1731 by the statute 4 Geo. II. c. 28 §5.
1472-3 *Rolls of Parlt.* VI. 5/1 Eny persone aforeseid havyng eny Annuite, Office, Fee, Corrodye, Rent Sek, or Pension. **1523** FITZHERB. *Surv.* 21 b, It is called a rent seeke bycause there is no dystresse insedent nor belongyng to the same. **1566** *Act 8 Eliz.* c. 19 §6 All Homages.. Rentes Servyces Rentes Chardges Rentes Seckes, and the Arrerages of the same. **1628** COKE *On Litt.* 143 b, Such rent is rent secke, for that hee cannot come to haue the rent if it be denied, by way of distres. **1676** GEO. DUDE *Law Charitable Uses* vi. 76 Katherine Banne grants, by Deed, a Rentseck out of 208 Acres of Land, for relief of the Poor. **1766** BLACKSTONE *Comm.* II. 42 Rent-seck,.. or barren rent, is in effect nothing more than a rent reserved by deed, but without any clause of distress. **1818** CRUISE *Digest* (ed. 2) II. 454 The law says, that neither the right, before it be reduced into possession, nor the rentseck before seisin had, are assets.

rent-service. [RENT *sb.*[1]] Personal service of various kinds by which lands or tenements are held in addition to, or in lieu of, money payment; tenure of this kind.
1477 *Rolls of Parlt.* VI. 170/1 Discharged of all graunts made of any Offices, Fees or Rents, other than the Rent services. **1523** FITZHERB. *Surv.* 21 Rent seruyce is where a man holdeth his landes of his lorde by fealtie.. or by any other seruice and certayne rent. **1566** [see prec.] **1607** NORDEN *Surv. Dial.* II. 49 Rent seruice, is so called, because it is knit to the tenure, and is as it were a Seruice, whereby a man holdeth his Landes, or Tenements. **1766** BLACKSTONE *Comm.* II. 41 Rent-service is so called because it hath some corporal service incident to it, as at the least fealty, or the feodal oath of fidelity. **1841** *Penny Cycl.* XIX. 394/1 A rent-service reserved out of chattels real will of course belong to the personal representatives of the lessor. **1894** *Daily News* 23 Oct. 7/1 Yesterday.. the last Sheriffs of the City of London were summoned before the Queen's Remembrancer.. to render rent-services to the Crown on behalf of the Corporation of London.

† **'rentual**, *a.* *Obs.* $rare^{-1}$. [f. RENT *sb.*[1], after *censual*, etc.] Containing a list of rents.
1788 *Trans. Soc. Arts* VI. 21 Written in the rentual books of the different estates.

renty, obs. variant of RENKY *a. dial.*

† **'renuence.** *Obs.* $rare^{-1}$. [f. L. *renu-ĕre* to refuse (see next) + -ENCE.] Refusal.
1653 SCLATER *Funeral Serm.* 25 Sept. (1654) 6 He in an humble renuence grew shy, as deeming himselfe unworthy of so great an Honour.

renuent ('rɛnjuːənt), *a.* [ad. pres. pple. of L. *renuĕre*, f. *re-* RE- + *nuĕre* to nod.] 'Employed in drawing back the head for nodding, the epithet of a pair of muscles in the head' (Smart 1840).

renule ('rɛnjuːl), *sb.* *Anat.* [f. L. *rēn* kidney + -ULE.] One of the separate lobules of which the kidneys in some animals are composed.
1847-9 *Todd's Cycl. Anat.* IV. I. 233/2 In many genera the kidneys are composed of a number of separate lobules or renules, each lobe consisting of a cortical and a medullary substance. **1883** FLOWER in *Encycl. Brit.* XV. 366/1 In some cases, as in Bears.., the lobulation is carried further, the whole organ being composed of a mass of renules.

† **re'nule**, *v.* *Obs.* Also **renew(e)le**, **renowle**. [ad. OF. *renuveler* var. *renoveler* to RENOVEL.] *intr.* and *trans.* To renew.
13.. *E.E. Allit. P.* A. 1079 Twelue syþez on ȝer þay beren ful frym & renowlez nwe in vche a mone. *c* **1380** WYCLIF *Serm.* Sel. Wks. II. 105 þe temple was renulid in cloþis and oþer ornamentis. *c* **1380** —— *Wks.* (1880) 315 þe seconde secte is late renewelid in þe tyme of þise newe ordris. **1388** —— *Wisd.* vii. 27 It dwellith in it silf, and renulith alle thingis.

re'number (riː-), *v.* [RE- 5 a.] To number afresh. Hence **re'numbering** *vbl. sb.*
c **1420** tr. *Pallad. Husb.* II. 115 Renombre hem but tymes twyes nyne. **1859** H. COLERIDGE *Gloss. Index* p. vi, Readers are therefore requested to renumber their copies from page 64 onwards. **1881** *Athenæum* 17 Sept. 372/3 The disastrous policy.. carried into effect in the renumbering of the houses in Oxford Street.

† **re'numerate**, *v.* *Obs.* [RE- 5 a.] *trans.* To enumerate again. (See also quot. 1656.)
1656 BLOUNT *Glossogr.*, *Renumerate*, to pay money again that was received; to retell, to recount, to number again. **1657** TOMLINSON *Renou's Disp.* 26, I shall not here renumerate other.. Plants. **1721** PERRY *Daggenh. Breach* 23 These Inconveniences.. need not be further renumerated by me.
So † **renume'ration.** *Obs. rare.*
1596 NASHE *Saffron Walden* Wks. (Grosart) III. 135 Neuer was man so surfetted and ouer-gorged with English as hee cloyd him with his generous spirites, renumeration of gratuities [etc.]. **1658** in PHILLIPS.

renunce, obs. form of RENOUNCE *v.*

re'nunciance. $rare^{-1}$. [See next and -ANCE.] Renunciation.
1837 CARLYLE *Fr. Rev.* II. v. iii, If they two did look into each other's eyes, and each, in silence, in tragical renunciance, did find that the other was all-too lovely.

renunciant (rɪ'nʌnʃɪənt), *a.* and *sb.* [ad. pres. pple. of L. *renunciāre*: see next.]
a. *adj.* Renouncing. **b.** *sb.* One who renounces.
1848 T. ARNOLD *Let.* 2 Jan. (1966) 216 Even now there is a little band of Renunciants scattered over the world. **1872** *Contemp. Rev.* XX. 416 The renunciant's vow is accepted. **1885** PATER *Marius* II. 138 In strong contrast to the wise Emperor's renunciant and impassive attitude. **1931** E. WILSON *Axel's Castle* viii. 257 All were pessimists, renunciants, resignationists, 'tired of the sad hospital' which earth seemed to them.

renunciate (rɪ'nʌnʃɪeɪt), *v.* [f. ppl. stem of L. *renunciāre*: see RENOUNCE *v.*]
† **1.** *trans.* (See quot. and RENOUNCE *v.* 7.) *Obs.*
1656 BLOUNT *Glossogr.*, *Renunciate*, to make relation..; to proclaim or declare openly, to tell what is done.
2. To renounce, give up. *rare.*
1814 MRS. J. WEST *Alicia de Lacy* I. 268 Pray fervently to the Queen of Heaven who will enable you to imitate the renunciating spirit of pious Saint Alexis. **1890** *Pall Mall G.* 30 June 1/3 Mr. Dillon has publicly renunciated the slightest interest in the outlying empire.

renunciation (rɪnʌnsɪ'eɪʃən). Also 5 -nountiacioun, 6 -nunceatioun, 6-7 -nuntiation, 7 -nonciation. [ad. L. *renunciātiōn-em*, n. of action f. *renunciāre* to RENOUNCE. Cf. F. *renonciation* (13th c.).]
1. The action of renouncing, giving up, or surrendering (a possession, right, title, etc.); an instance of this; a document expressing this.
1399 *Rolls of Parlt.* III. 424/1 Uppe the fourme that is contened in the same Renunciation and Cession. **1462** EDW. IV. in Ellis *Orig. Lett.* Ser. II. I. 128 A renountiacioun and relese of the ryght and title that the Corowne of England hathe. **1569** *Reg. Privy Council Scot.* II. 36 The said assignatioun, translatioun, renunciatioun and ourgeving. **1579-80** *Ibid.* III. 256 The renunceatioun of the said reversioun. **1695** *Def. Vind. Deprived Bps.* 16 They desired and procured an express renonciation of their Rights. **1777** PITT in Almon *Anecd.* III. xliv. 196 A renunciation of our own unjust.. claims, must precede even the least attempt to conciliate. **1827** HALLAM *Const. Hist.* xv. (1876) III. 138 The queen's renunciation of her right of succession was invalid in the jurisprudence of his court. **1872** YEATS *Growth Comm.* 244 A compensation being offered to Austria in the renunciation by Spain of all her European dependencies.
b. The action of giving up or resigning something naturally attractive; self-resignation.
1526 *Pilgr. Perf.* (W. de W. 1531) 56 After that foloweth the despisynge & renunciacyon or forsakynge of worldly thynges. **1831** CARLYLE *Sart. Res.* II. ix, It is only with Renunciation (*Entsagen*) that Life, properly speaking, can be said to begin. **1860** TYNDALL *Glac.* I. i. 7 A renunciation of my old and more favourite pursuits. **1876** C. M. DAVIES *Unorth. Lond.* 17 Every prophet has his one distinguishing trait; and that of Buddha was renunciation.
2. The action of rejecting, disowning, or disclaiming; repudiation, formal rejection.
1599 HAKLUYT *Voy.* I. 153 This present renuntiation, reuocation, and retractation of the order and composition

aforesayd, notwithstanding. **1635** PAGITT *Christianogr.* I. iii. (1636) 158 An Adiuration of the Divell and a Renuntiation or renouncing of him. **1675** BAXTER *Cath. Theol.* II. v. 108 You may read the Synod of Dorts express renunciation of it. **1755** YOUNG *Centaur* i. Wks. 1757 IV. 113 Vicious practice is sure to produce..an absolute renunciation of all belief. **1790** BURKE *Fr. Rev.* 26 As solemn a renunciation as could be made of the principles by this society imputed to them. **1870** ANDERSON *Missions Amer. Bd.* I. vii. 137 One cannot but wonder at the rapid renunciation of even the name of Christianity by the people of Jaffna.

b. *spec.* The action of renouncing the devil, the world, and the flesh, at baptism.

1875 SMITH & CHEETHAM *Dict. Christian Antiq.* I. 160/1 The mode of making the Renunciations, and the words employed, are very fully described in the treatise *De Sacramentis*, attributed to St. Ambrose.

†**3.** 'A bringing word back again' (Phillips 1658). *Obs. rare*$^{-0}$.

renunciative (rɪˈnʌnʃɪətɪv), *a.* [ad. med.L. **renunciātīvus*, or f. RENUNCIATE *v.* + -IVE.]

†**1.** Serving to announce or enuntiate. *Obs.*

c **1400** tr. *Secreta Secret., Gov. Lordsh.* 96 þanne he ressayues a stryngthe of vndirstandynge þat ys renunciatyf of ffygures and semblance. **1622** MABBE tr. *Aleman's Guzman d'Alf.* II. 242 Bills, and answers, together with other writings, processiue,..renunciatiue, and infinite other the like.

2. Characterized by renunciation.

1850 MRS. BROWNING *Poems* II. 446 To let thee sit..and hear the sighing years Re-sighing on my lips renunciative. **1880** WARREN *Book-plates* ix. 98 The renunciative mottoes are a somewhat notable class.

So **reˈnunciatory** *a.*

1865 DICKENS *Mut. Fr.* I. iv, A meek renunciatory action. **1898** *Century Mag.* Jan. 463/1 A few big tears—the..outcome of Heaven knows how real a renunciatory struggle.

renuwe, obs. form of RENEW *v.*[1]

†**renverse**, *sb. Obs. rare.* In 7 ran-. [a. F. *renverse*, f. *renverser*: see RENVERSE *v.*]

a. The reverse (of a coin). **b.** The other side (of a case).

1658 OSBORN *Adv. Son* iii. §10 (1896) 67 Policy stamps them with the Image of the Devil, and on their Ranverse, Punishment and Shame. **1679** V. ALSOP *Melius Inquirendum* II. viii. 360 This will more evidently appear if we take the Ranverse of the case, thus.

†**renverse**, *a. Obs. rare*$^{-1}$. [ad. F. *renversé*.] Reversed, turned the wrong way.

1653 A. WILSON *Jas. I* 159 [He] was made to ride Renvers with his face to the horse tail.

†**renˈverse**, *v. Obs.* Also 6-7 renuers(e, 7-8 ranverse. [ad. F. *renverser*, f. *re-* RE- + *enverser* to overturn: see ENVERSED and INVERSE, and cf. RAMVERSE *v.*]

1. *trans.* To reverse (in *lit.* senses); to turn upside down, turn the wrong way, turn back.

1590 SPENSER *F.Q.* I. iv. 41 Whose shield he beares renverst, the more to heap disdayn. **1596** *Ibid.* v. iii. 37 He ..from him reft his shield, and it renverst. **1610** DONNE *Pseudo-martyr* 274 That English Priest Bridgewater, which calls himself Aquipontanus, ouerturning and re-enuersing [*errata* renuersing] his name with his conscience. **1624** SIR T. ROE in *Michaelis' Anc. Marb.* (1882) 188 A halfe lyon of white marble, holding the head of a bull in the pawes, the neck renuersed. **1681** R. FLEMING *Fulfill. Script.* (1800) II. iii. 213 Their darts were ranversed and turned back by the violence of the wind.

2. To overturn or overthrow (*lit.* and *fig.*); to bring to confusion.

α. *c* **1610** SIR J. MELVIL *Mem.* (1735) 61 Thus can God by his Divine Providence renverse the finest Practices and Pretences of mighty Rulers. **1639** DRUMM. OF HAWTH. *Speech for Edinburgh* Wks. (1711) 216 To settle things so.. that they should not vary and change, were to renverse that order which God hath established. **1765** STERNE *Tr. Shandy* VIII. xix, The furious execution of which, renversing everything like thunder before it, has become a new æra to us of military improvements. **1776** MME. D'ARBLAY *Early Diary* Let. Crisp, Sept., In a course of years the commerce of that world commonly renverses all these things topsy turvy.

β. *c* **1645** HOWELL *Lett.* (1650) I. III. xx, God forbid that a business of so high a consequence..should be ranvers'd by differences 'twixt a few privat subjects. **1671** MACWARD *True Non-conf.* 236 Plainly to ranverse both the freedom of making, and necessity of keeping all vowes. **1702** C. MATHER *Magn. Chr.* II. 12 If there were a Town in Spain undermined by Coneys,..a third in Greece ranversed by Frogs. **1728** *Wodrow Corr.* (1843) III. 381 The sentence and decision of the Commission could not be opened and ranversed.

Hence †**renˈversed**, *ppl. a.* (see quot. 1656), †**renˈversing** *vbl. sb.*

1656 BLOUNT *Glossogr.* s.v. *Renversed*, Renversed eyes, are taken for decayed eyes, or those that stand in the head. **1671** [? MACWARD] *Case Accommodation Exam.* 34 The renversings and persecutions of these late times. **1679** J. BROWN *Life of Faith* (1824) II. xx. 364 Esther was employed to effectuate the ranversing of the decree.

‖**renversé**, *a. Her.* [F., pa. pple. of *renverser*: see prec.] Inverted; reversed.

1725 COATS *Dict. Her.* s.v., *Chevron renversé* is a Chevron with the Point downwards. **1868** CUSSANS *Her.* (1893) 130 Renversé or Reversed; turned contrary to the usual direction.

renˈversement. [a. F. *renversement*: see RENVERSE *v.* and -MENT.] The act of reversing or inverting; the result of this. Now *spec.* in *Aeronaut.* (orig. *U.S.*), an aeroplane manœuvre consisting of a half-loop effected simultaneously with a half-turn (see also quot. 1956).

1610 MARCELLINI *Triumphs Jas. I* 87 Their divers Anagrams, Metatheses, and Renversements, according to the Tmurah and Siruphs of the Haebrewes. **1744** FOTHERGILL in *Phil. Trans.* XLIII. 23 This Resin with the Trees which afforded it were buried in the Earth by the Deluge, or by some such violent Renversement. **1763** STUKELEY *Palæogr. Sacr.* 60 'Tis a total renversement of the order of nature. **1954** W. FAULKNER *Fable* 343 The car making the last *renversement* because now it could go no farther. **1956** *U.S. Air Force Dict.* 435/2 *Renversement*,.. any airplane maneuver or performance in which the airplane is made to reverse direction, as in a chandelle, Immelmann turn, or wingover. **1966** E. V. RICKENBACKER *Rickenbacker* (1968) vi. 106, I immediately put my Spad into a *renversement*—pulled the stick straight back to start a loop and simultaneously rolled it over in a half turn. **1973** *Times* 2 Jan. (Forward into Europe Suppl.) p. xii/6 Perhaps the Henry Moore retrospective..and the Francis Bacon exhibition..herald a *renversement*.

‖**renvoi** (rɑ̃vwa). *Law.* [Fr., f. *renvoyer* to send back: cf. RENVOY *sb.*] (See quots.)

1897 J. T. B. SEWELL tr. Labbé in *Outl. French Law as affecting Brit. Subjects* iv. 69 In order to justify the system which repudiates the doctrine of 'renvoi'..it suffices to define exactly what is the intention of the law which authorizes the foreign law to decide. **1898** *Law Q. Rev.* XIV. 231 An English specialist versed in the problems raised by the conflict of laws may well never have heard the name of the *Renvoi*. **1904** J. P. BATE *Doctrine of Renvoi* iv. 53 The basis of the Renvoi-theory is the doctrine that when a conflict-rule refers a matter to a foreign law, the foreign law is referred to *in its totality*. **1905** J. WESTLAKE *Priv. Internat. Law* (ed. 4) ii. 25 In its substance the subject [*sc.* private international law] has been no less deeply affected by the substitution..of political nationality for domicile as the criterion of personal law, and by the controversy which has consequently sprung up about the doctrine called the *renvoi*. **1935** G. C. CHESHIRE *Priv. Internat. Law* vi. 133 The second solution is to give a decision on the assumption that the doctrine of *renvoi* is recognized by English law. This famous doctrine, which presupposes that a reference to the law of the domicil means a reference to the whole of that law, may be explained as follows in connexion with our case of X. The English Court, upon referring to the Private International Law of France, finds that it is referred back to English law as being the law of X's nationality. There is a *renvoi* or a remission to English law. **1959** E. JOWITT *Dict. Eng. Law* II. 1525/1 *Renvoi*, a term employed in private international law to denote the sending, or determination, of a matter to or according to the law of a tribunal outside the jurisdiction where the question arose. **1970** *Internat. & Compar. Law Q.* 4th Ser. XIX. I. 36 The generally accepted English view has been that tort cases are outside the scope of the doctrine of *renvoi*.

†**renvoy**, *sb. Obs.* Also 7 -voie. [a. F. *renvoi*, †*renvoy* (15th c.), vbl. sb. f. *renvoyer*: see next.]

1. The act of sending back; discharge, dismissal.

1600 HOLLAND *Livy* XXXVII. xxxi. 963 When he had rewarded the Rhodian ships with part of the pillage,..he gaue them the renvoie, and sent them home. *c* **1645** HOWELL *Lett.* v. iii. (1655) I. 199 This rupture 'twixt us and France upon the sudden *renvoy* of her Majesties servants. **1654** H. L'ESTRANGE *Chas. I* (1655) 61 King Charles is taxed for violating the Matrimonial Pact by the Renvoy and discarding of the Queens Domestiques.

2. A reference *to* a book or passage. *rare*$^{-1}$.

1650 in *Athenæum* 13 Dec. (1879) 763/2 To which he makes his Marginall Renvoys.

†**renvoy**, *v. Obs. rare.* [ad. F. *renvoyer* (12th c.), f. *re-* RE- + *envoyer*: see ENVOY *sb.*[1]] *trans.* To send back.

c **1477** CAXTON *Jason* 54 b, Wherfore he renuoyed and sente agayn the knight unto the grekes. **1539** CROMWELL in Merriman *Life & Lett.* (1902) II. 229, I doo Renvoye the said palmer thither agayn. **1622** BACON *Hen. VII* (1876) 79 He did continue in his court and custody the daughter of Maximilian,..not dismissing or renvoying her.

reny, var. RENAY *v. Obs.*

renys, obs. f. REINS.

renysch, renyst, varr. RENISH *a. Obs.*

Renyss, obs. f. RHENISH.

reoˈblige (riː-), *v. rare*$^{-1}$. [ad. It. *riobbligare*.] *trans.* To oblige again.

1632 J. HAYWARD tr. *Biondi's Eromena* II. 63 The Prince of Mauritania favours me exceedingly..thereby re-obliging me with the favour of his visits.

reobˈserve (riː-), *v.* [RE- 5 a.] To observe again. So **reobserˈvation**.

1853 LYNCH *Self-Improv.* vi. 148 You must think and observe; re-think and re-observe. **1857** DARWIN in *Life & Lett.* (1887) III. 260, I have, also, lately been re-observing daily *Lobelia fulgens*. **1885** *Athenæum* 5 Dec. 735/2 The principal astronomical work..is the reobservation of the places of the 23,000 stars.

reobˈtain (riː-), *v.* [RE- 5 a.] *trans.* To obtain again; to regain, recover.

1587 *Mirr. Mag., Rich. III*, xiii, I came to reobtaine my dignitie. **1603** FLORIO tr. *Montaigne.* I. xxxvii. 116 The weakest may by occasion reobtaine the place againe. **1643** [ANGIER] *Lanc. Vall. Achor* 23 If you will..endeavour with me to reobtaine the Castle, you shall have all faire usage from me. **1695** *Eng. Anc. Const. Eng.* 90 Since we cannot tell,..if..King James should re-obtain the throne, by what means it may happen. **1701** DE FOE *True-born Eng.* 32 No Merit can their Favour reobtain. **1782** KIRWAN in *Phil. Trans.* LXXIII. 62 If the solution was exposed to nothing from which it could re-obtain phlogiston. **1803** H. K. WHITE *Let. to N. White* 2 May, There remains no way of re-obtaining my volume but this. **1866** ODLING *Anim. Chem.* 62 By treatment with hydrochloric acid we may easily re-obtain the carbonic anhydride.

Hence **reobˈtainable** *a.*; **reobˈtainer**; **reobˈtaining** *vbl. sb.*; **reobˈtainment**.

1598 FLORIO, *Racquistatore*, a recouerer, a repurchaser, a reobtainer. *Ibid.*, *Racquisto*, a recouerie, a repurchase, a reobtaining. **1611** COTGR., *Recouvrable*, recouerable,.. reobtainable. *Ibid.*, *Recouvrance*, a recouerie, reobtainment.

reoccuˈpation (riː-). [RE- 5 a.: cf. F. *réoccupation*.] The action of occupying again; a renewed occupation.

1844 *Lanc. Tracts Civ. War* 140 The 'unkept conditions' [on which Thursland Castle was delivered] appear to relate to the re-occupation of it by Sir John Girlington. **1887** *Spectator* 28 May 722/1 England and Turkey will possess an exclusive right of re-occupation.

reˈoccupy (riː-), *v.* [RE- 5 a: cf. F. *réoccuper*.] To occupy (a place or position) again.

1807 G. CHALMERS *Caledonia* I. I. iv. 182 He reoccupied and refortified such of those posts as promoted his vengeful designs. **1817** COBBETT *Wks.* XXXII. 146 The Bourbons.. have not failed to bring misery in their train in reoccupying the beautiful provinces of Italy. **1841** ELPHINSTONE *Hist. Ind.* II. 177 The former prince..now returned to re-occupy his old possessions. **1875** *Ure's Dict. Arts* (ed. 7) II. 203 A sufficient interval of time had..elapsed to allow the water to re-occupy the space.

Hence **reˈoccupied** *ppl. a.*

1825-9 MRS. SHERWOOD *Lady of Manor* I. viii. 332 They might adorn her grandmamma's reoccupied apartment.

reoˈccur, *v.* [RE- 5 a.] *intr.* To occur again.

1867 ATWATER *Logic* 203 Whenever it is applied in such measure to these several subjects, they will re-occur. **1884** MCCOSH in *Homilet. Monthly* (1885) Jan. 232 In the first chapter of Genesis such passages as this occur and re-occur.

reoˈccurrence. [RE- 5 a.] A further occurrence; a recurrence.

1817 D. O'CONNELL *Let.* 24 June (1972) II. 152 There will not be a reoccurrence even of those wretched squabbles. **1964** B. TRNKA in D. Abercrombie et al. *Daniel Jones* 188 The re-occurrence of voiceless consonants in the same morpheme is found more frequently than that of the corresponding voiced consonants.

†**reod**, *a. Obs.* [OE. *réod* = ON. *rjóð-r*: see etym. note to RED *a.* and *sb.*[1]] Red, ruddy.

a **800** *Erfurt Gloss.* 403 *Flavum vel fulfum*, reod. *a* **900** *O.E. Martyrol.* 25 Dec. 4 þa wæs hire ansyn swa reod & swa fæger [etc.]. *c* **1000** ÆLFRIC *Exod.* xv. 1 þa Moises hæfde ʒefaren ofer þa reodan sæ. *c* **1205** LAY. 3528 Heo iward reod.. swilche hit were of wine scenche. *Ibid.* 19890 Ænne stunde he wes blac..ane while he was reod.

reod, obs. form of REED *sb.*

†**reof**, *a. Obs.* Also 3 ref. [OE. *hréof* rough, scabbed, leprous = ON. *hrjúf-r*.] Rough.

a **1000** *Exeter Bk., Whale* 8 Is þæs hiw ʒelic hreofum stane. *c* **1250** *Gen. & Ex.* 3726 Leateð ben swilc wurdes ref. **1418** *E.E. Wills* (1882) 36, vj. reof quisshens of worsted.

reˈoffer, *v.* [RE- 5 a.] *trans.* To offer again.

a **1618** SYLVESTER *Brief Catech.* iii, Christ our high-priest for ever, Self-offring once to bee re-offred never. *a* **1711** KEN *Hymns Evang.* Poet. Wks. 1721 I. 186 Jesus went..all his Pains God's Anger to atone Re-offering at his Father's awful Throne. **1757** MRS. GRIFFITH *Lett. Henry & Frances* (1767) I. 22, I should be ashamed to re-offer you my love and friendship. **1829** LYTTON *Devereux* IV. ix, I re-offered my arm to the prince.

reolic(h, -liche, var. RULY *a.* and *adv. Obs.*

reome, obs. f. REALM.

reone, var. RYEN *a.*

reopen, obs. form of REAP *v.*

reˈopen (riː-), *v.* [RE- 5 a.]

1. *trans.* **a.** To open again (something that has been closed).

1733 TULL *Horse-hoeing Husb.* i. 8 The weak sorts of Roots can penetrate no farther into it, unless re-open'd by new Tillage. **1814** SCOTT *Wav.* xvii, The eyes of our hero.. gradually closed; nor did he re-open them till the morning sun was high on the lake without. **1816** KIRBY & SP. *Entomol.* xx. (1818) II. 202 In the spring, when it [a window] was re-opened, the bees returned. **1855** BROWNING *Bp. Blougram* 572 He [Luther] comes..Re-opens a shut book. **1865** PUSEY *Truth Eng. Ch.* 16 When the Churches were reopened in Paris after the first revolution.

b. To open up again, to renew.

1848 R. I. WILBERFORCE *Doctr. Incarnation* iv. (1852) 88 In Him intercourse with God was perfectly reopened. **1858** J. MARTINEAU *Stud. Chr.* 140 His..absence reopened their opportunities.

c. To resume the discussion of (something settled or decided).

1851 HUSSEY *Papal Power* ii. 77 Urging him..not to allow questions to be reopened, which had been already fully determined. **1852** DICKENS *Bleak Ho.* xxxiv, After I have finished speaking I have closed the subject, and I won't re-open it.

d. To recommence (firing).

1850 R. G. CUMMING *Hunter's Life S. Afr.* (1902) 41/2 Having loaded, I re-opened my fire. **1881** in Lady Bellairs *Transvaal War* (1885) 136 The rebels then deliberately re-opened fire on the officers carrying the flags.

2. *intr.* and *absol.* To open again.

1830 LYTTON *P. Clifford* xxiii, His warm heart at once reopened to the liking he had formerly conceived for Clifford. **1885** in Lady Bellairs *Transvaal War* 125 Such of the..stores as still held any goods would occasionally reopen.

Hence **re'opened** *ppl. a.*; **re'opening** *vbl. sb.* and *ppl. a.*

1758 J. S. *Le Dran's Observ. Surg.* (1771) 299 A large Quantity of Pus..proceeded from the Re-opening of the Wound. **1818** *Autumn near Rhine* 162 The scene was well calculated to strike re-opening eyes. **1842** PUSEY *Crisis Eng. Ch.* 96 This re-opened intercourse with the East is..a crisis in the history of our Church.

reophore: see RHEOPHORE.

reo'ppose (riː-), *v. rare*⁻¹. [RE- 2a.] *trans.* To oppose in turn.

1646 SIR T. BROWNE *Pseud. Ep.* Pref., Wee shall so farre encourage contradiction, as to promise no disturbance, or reoppose any Penne, that shall Elenchically refute us.

reord, variant of RERD(E *Obs.*

reor'dain (riː-), *v.* [RE- 5a: cf. F. *réordonner* (16th c.), It. *reordinare* (Florio).]

1. *trans.* To ordain, appoint, or establish again.

1611 COTGR., *Re[n]joindre*, to reinioyne, reordaine vnto, reimpose vpon. **1612** DRAYTON *Poly-olb.* xi. 314 Edwyn.. reordained York a Bishop's government. **1882–3** SCHAFF *Encycl. Relig. Knowl.* 1309 Levirate Marriage..an ancient usage of the Hebrews, and re-ordained by Moses.

2. *Eccl.* To ordain (a person) again; to invest afresh with holy orders.

a **1626** BACON *Ch. Controv.* Wks. 1879 I. 347 The re-ordaining of priests, is a matter already resolutely maintained. **1636** PRYNNE *Unbish. Tim.* (1660) 74 Bishop Hall reordained Mr. John Dury, formerly ordained by Presbyters. **1693** *Apol. Clergy Scot.* 57 All of them the greatest men among them are reordained when they come to England. **1732** NEAL *Hist. Purit.* I. 90 Those clergymen who had been ordained by the late Service Book, were to be reordained. **1898** *Westm. Gaz.* 10 Jan. 2/1 There was a widespread opinion among you that our practice of reordaining convert clergymen was an imputation on your Church.

absol. **1661** *Petit. for Peace* 10 A Canon..deposeth those that re-ordain.

re'order (riː-), *v.* [RE- 5a.]

†**1.** *trans.* = REORDAIN *v.* 2. *Obs. rare*⁻¹.

1593 BILSON *Govt. Christ's Ch.* 359 Such as were ordained by Miletius shoulde be reordered.

2. To set in order again; to re-establish, rearrange, etc. Also *absol.*

1609 DANIEL *Civ. Wars* VIII. xliv, Seeking to allay All greeuances; re-order equity. **1656** EARL MONM. tr. *Boccalini's Advts. fr. Parnass.* I. lxxvii. (1674) 100 Whilst powerful men..have disordered the World, men go about to re-order it. **1855** PUSEY *Doctr. Real Presence* 212 The power of the word of God in ordering or reordering as He wills. **1894** HOWELLS in *Harper's Mag.* Feb. 376 Mrs. Campbell runs to the mirror..and hastily reorders her dress.

refl. **1641** EARL MONM. tr. *Biondi's Civil Warres* v. 162 The English this meane while having reordered themselves, set furiously upon them.

3. a. To send again by order.

1799 SICKELMORE *Agnes & Leonora* II. 32, I was therefore re-ordered back to prison.

b. To repeat an order for (a thing).

1810 SOUTHEY in Robberds *Mem. W. Taylor* (1843) II. 300 If it should not reach you in due time after it is advertized, fail not to let me know, that I may re-order it. **1967** COX & GROSE *Organization & Handling Bibl. Rec. by Computer* VI. 162 Not all delayed books are going to be re-ordered.

Hence **re'ordered** *ppl. a.*; **re'ordering** *vbl. sb.*

1595 DANIEL *Civ. Warres* II. lxxii, As seeking but the States reordering. **1600** FAIRFAX *Tasso* XX. lxxxviii, Their Lord in haste To venge their losse his band reordred brings. **1618** WOTTON in *Reliq.* (1672) 485 For the re-ordering of my Exchanges, which have been much incommodated. **1855** PUSEY *Doctr. Real Presence* Note Q. 240 Instances which show how S. Chrysostom speaks of God's 're-ordering nature'. **1938** *New Statesman* 21 May 860/2 Ordered, counter-ordered and reordered machines. **1962** A. BATTERSBY *Guide to Stock Control* v. 42 The boundary between them remains as a mark which indicates the Re-ordering Level (ROL). **1969** *Jane's Freight Containers 1968–69* 416/1 Consistent production rates possible with more frequent reordering cycles.

re-order, *sb.* [RE- 5a.] A renewed or repeated order for goods.

1901 *Scotsman* 8 Apr. 9/7 Current trade is confined to small reorders. **1928** *Publishers' Weekly* 9 June 2376 It is not easy on placing advance orders..to get the full value of the suggestions of the clerks, but on the reorders this is simpler. **1977** *Time Out* 21 Jan. 3/3 The chap behind the counter is often the one who chooses the wine he sells and he is there to take your re-orders when you come back.

†**reordi**, *a. Obs. rare*⁻¹. (Of obscure meaning.)

(*Wel reordi* is perhaps an error for *elreordi* = OE. *elreordiȝ* foreign-speaking, barbarous.)

c **1205** LAY. 25658 He seide þat þer wes icumen a scaðe liðe of westward Spaine, wel reordi [*c* 1275 a wel lopliche] feond.

reordie *v.*: see under RERD(E.

re'ordinate (riː-), *v.* [RE- 5a.] *trans.* To institute or establish again.

1875 BROWNING *Aristoph. Apol.* 202 Had you.., re-ordinating outworn rule, Made Comedy and Tragedy combine.

reordi'nation (riː-). *Eccl.* [ad. med.L. *reordinātio*: cf. F. *réordination* (1575).] The action of ordaining again; the fact of a second ordination.

1597 HOOKER *Eccl. Pol.* v. lxxvii. §3 The reordination of such as others in times more corrupt did consecrate heretofore. **1636** PRYNNE *Unbish. Tim.* (1661) Post. 36 Which..was no reordination of him as a Presbyter, but only a Reconfirmation of him..as a Bishop. **1732** NEAL *Hist. Purit.* (1822) I. 69 There being no dispute about reordination in order to any church-preferment, till the end of queen Elizabeth's reign. **1846** BURN *For. Refugees* 53 The objects of the letters..appear to be the re-ordination of the Rev. John Charpentier [etc.]. **1884** *Catholic Dict.* (1897) 677/1 An imposition of hands, mistaken perhaps for re-ordination.

re,organi'zation (riː-). [RE- 5a: cf. F. *réorganisation* (1812).] The action or process of reorganizing; a fresh organization.

1813 WELLINGTON in Gurw. *Desp.* (1838) X. 149, I have already commenced a re-organization of the cavalry. **1852** GROTE *Greece* II. lxxii. IX. 261 A power of enriching friends or destroying enemies in this universal reorganisation of Greece. **1899** *Allbutt's Syst. Med.* VI. 802 The nerve becomes so irretrievably disorganised as to obliterate all means of reorganisation.

re,organi'zational, *a.* [f. REORGANIZATION + -AL.] Of or pertaining to reorganization.

1972 *Guardian* 26 Jan. 4/3 Yugoslavia's League of Communists united today behind party reorganisational changes.

re,organi'zationist. [f. REORGANIZATION + -IST.] One who favours (political) reorganization; *spec.* a member of a radical Chinese faction (fl. 1930: see quot. 1975). Also *attrib.* or as *adj.*

1930 *Times* 25 Mar. 23/5 Nanking was faced by a revolt from the so-called 'Reorganisationists', a group mainly consisting of the political leaders of the left who had been excluded from office. **1967** J. ISRAEL in A. Feuerwerker et al. *Approaches to Mod. Chinese Hist.* 292 Many Wuhan figures who cast their lot with Wang Ching-wei (exiled leader of the Reorganizationist faction) argued that the revolution remained 'unfinished'. **1975** I. C. Y. HSÜ *Rise Mod. China* (ed. 2) xxiii. 653 Wang and his left-wing followers were out of office. The latter group retaliated by accusing Chiang of betraying the principles and ideas of Sun, and demanded a reorganization of the KMT in the spirit of the 1924 manifesto—hence their nickname 'The Reorganizationists'.

re'organize (riː-), *v.* [RE- 5a: cf. F. *réorganiser* (1812).] *trans.* To organize anew. Also *intr.* for *refl.*

1681–6 J. SCOTT *Chr. Life* (1747) III. 539 By whose omnipotent Agency..the Bodies of his Saints..shall be gathered up, re-united, and re-organized into glorious Bodies. **1813** SIR R. WILSON *Priv. Diary* (1862) II. 258 The news of this failure..obliged him..to reorganise his broken troops. **1850** MRS. BROWNING *Poems* II. 201 Thou shalt yet reorganize Thy maidenhood of beauty. **1857** J. HYDE *Mormonism* vii. 183 They completely reorganized in May, 1857. **1879** FROUDE *Cæsar* viii. 80 He had reorganised the constitution on the most strictly conservative lines. **1972** 'E. LATHEN' *Murder without Icing* i. 14 The time has come for him to reorganize. He will be selling some earlier ventures.

Hence **re'organized** *ppl. a.*; **re'organizer**.

1832–4 DE QUINCEY *Cæsars* Wks. 1859 X. 212 To apply his powers as a re-organizer and restorer to the East. **1870** LOWELL *Study Wind.* (1886) 134 He is a reorganiser of the moral world. **1892** 'MARK TWAIN' *Amer. Claim.* xiv. 129 The rude impact of the thought of these people upon his reorganized condition of mind. **1929** P. HUGHES *Catholic Question, 1688–1829* III. iii. 283 In the re-organised Catholic Committee, O'Connell had from the first been a force.

re'orient (riː-), *a.* [RE- 5a.] Rising again.

1850 TENNYSON *In Mem.* cxvi, The life re-orient out of dust. **1890** F. ST. JOHN THACKERAY *Prudentius* 93 So buried seeds repair our store Reorient from the parched earth.

re'orient, *v.* [RE- 5a.] **1.** *trans.* To rearrange, give a new orientation or direction to (ideas, etc.); to help (a person) to find his bearings again; to redirect (a thing).

1933 *Times Educ. Suppl.* 25 Feb. 57/4 Russia's children are suffering in the grim struggle; but they are not having to be reborn, to reorient their whole lives. **1939** *Sun* (Baltimore) 25 July 8/7 'Britain has *re-Oriented* her China policy.' I don't know whether that pun was Mr. Byas' own. **1951** G. HUMPHREY *Thinking* ix. 306 Psychic 'scaffolding', 'hypotheses', by which the original *Aufgabe* is reoriented. **1956** A. H. COMPTON *Atomic Quest* 32 His [*sc.* Einstein's] quantum and relativity theories were reorienting physics thought. **1966** D. F. GALOUYE *Lost Perception* vii. 74 'I feel so out of touch,..as though I've stood still for two whole years while everything passed me by.' 'We'll reorient you,' Forsythe assured. **1975** *Nature* 10 July 109/1 On day 123 the satellite was reoriented to allow the four Ariel-V experiments which view along the spin axis to observe Cyg X-1, placing it outside the field of view of this experiment. **1977** D. BENNETT *Jigsaw Man* iv. 71 I'll give you a sort of running commentary,' she said. 'Reorient you.'

2. a. *refl.* To adjust (oneself) *to* something; to come to terms with something; to adopt a new direction or relation.

1937 *Jrnl. Compar. Psychol.* XXIV. 296 The animals did recognize a new situation in the tests... Many took much longer about the first jump in the test trials, and appeared to be re-orienting themselves to the whole environment. **1955** M. LOWRY *Let.* July (1967) 381 What with this eye business I have to revise entirely my method of writing and..reorient myself to it. **1962** *Lancet* 8 Dec. 1229/2 Some will reorient themselves in their new surroundings in about three weeks, recognising their new ward as their home. **1963** *Economist* 19 Jan. 232/2 If the railways can really re-orient themselves.

b. *intr.* for *refl.*

1960 C. D. SIMAK in *Mag. Fantasy & Science Fiction* June 104 He had to reorient, he knew. He had to come to..terms ..with this situation. **1974** *Nature* 6 Sept. 16/1 The other spectra are so similar to V that Watkins also assigns them to zinc vacancies. But the V¹ centres do not reorient under uniaxial stress. **1977** *Jrnl. Protozool.* XXIV. 29/2 Some conjugating pairs subjected to antiserum treatment separate belatedly, after a partial cortical fusion has occurred and when the conjugants have reoriented into a heteropolar configuration.

re'orientate, *v.* [RE- 5a.] **1.** *trans.* = REORIENT *v.* 1.

1933 *Planning* 6 June 2 The most urgent necessity..for a common and intensive effort by all parties to reorientate their various points of view. **1958** *Times Lit. Suppl.* 21 Nov. 675/1 How does one re-orientate one's philosophy and economic policy? **1959** B. WOOTTON *Soc. Science & Soc. Pathol.* viii. 267 Glueck's object in treating criminality as a disease is to concentrate attention..on the practical problem of how his [*sc.* the offender's] behaviour may be re-orientated. **1981** P. MCCUTCHAN *Shard calls Tune* xv. 163 [He] came to a small town... He knew where he was... He was re-orientated nicely.

2. *refl.* = REORIENT *v.* 2a.

1940 *Scrutiny* IX. 196 We may perhaps hope that Scotland will be able to reorientate itself with the end of the epoch that has seen its cultural disintegration. **1959** M. SUMMERTON *Small Wilderness* xiv. 174 Struggling to reorientate myself..I tried to place myself in his shoes. **1979** J. WAINWRIGHT *Duty Elsewhere* xvi. 47 Cooke had reorientated himself a little. He was still dizzy.

re,orien'tation. [RE- 5a.] The action or process of reorienting; a fresh orientation.

1920 *Contemp. Rev.* July 6 There will be needed a great collaboration of wisely directed effort at home, combined with an entire reorientation of attitude and policy on the part of the Allies. **1938** *Burlington Mag.* May 248/2 He seems to minimize the imposition of sartorial forms by commercial dictation, surely more often the cunning contrivance of change for change's profitable sake than the concrete expression of social reorientations. **1942** L. B. NAMIER *Conflicts* 16 Far-seeing statesmen discerned the need of such a reorientation. **1951** R. FIRTH *Elem. Soc. Organization* iii. 110 This is represented..by a re-orientation of resources in goods or labour power. **1967** G. STEINER *Lang. & Silence* 83 Many reorientations, many ways of ordering and choosing are available to scholarship and the imagination. **1977** P. BAELZ *Ethics & Belief* vi. 74 Different religions give different answers to this question, all of them involving both a reorientation of insight and understanding and a new pattern of action.

†**reose**, *v. Obs.* Also 3 rese. [OE. *hréosan* = ON. *hrjósa* to shudder.] *intr.* To fall.

Beowulf 1075 Hie on ȝebyrd hruron gare wunde. *Ibid.* 2489 Gomela Scylfing hreas. *c* **825** *Vesp. Psalter* cxliv. 14 Uphefeð dryhten alle ða ðe hreosað. *a* **900** CYNEWULF *Christ* 810 Wongas hreosað, burȝstede berstað. *c* **1000** ÆLFRIC *Hom.* II. 450 þæt hus..hreosende ðine bearn..acwealde. *c* **1205** LAY. 15587 Sæie me wæh hit vælleð þat þe wal reoseð [*c* 1275 fallep]. *Ibid.* 18869 Beornes scullen rusien, reosen [*c* **1275** rese] heore mærken.

reose, var. of REWSIE *Obs.*

reot, obs. f. RIOT.

reoðe, reothe, obs. ff. RUTH.

reother, var. of ROTHER *Obs.*

reou, obs. f. RUE.

reoufulnesse, obs. f. RUEFULNESS.

reouliche, var. of RULY *Obs.*

reounesse, var. of REWNESS *Obs.*

†**'reous**, *a. Obs.*⁻⁰ [ad. L. *reus.*] Guilty.

1623 in COCKERAM.

reousie: see REWSIE *Obs.*

reouðe, reouþe, obs. ff. RUTH.

reouthfully, obs. f. RUTHFULLY.

reouwe, obs. f. RUE *v.*

re-overflow, *v.* [RE- 5a.] To overflow anew.

a **1700** KEN *Hymnotheo* Poet. Wks. 1721 III. 353 All must love God,..Must to the Source of Love re-overflow.

reovirus ('riːəʊvaɪərəs). *Biol.* [mod.L., f. initial letters of *r*espiratory, *e*nteric, *o*rphan (see *orphan virus* s.v. ORPHAN *a.* 2) + VIRUS.] Any of a group of related double-stranded RNA viruses that are sometimes associated with disease in animals, including respiratory and enteric infection in man.

1959 A. B. SABIN in *Science* 20 Nov. 1388/1 Studies..have provided the definitive information required for establishing these strains as members of a new group of viruses, for which I am proposing the name 'reoviruses'. **1970** *Nature* 28 Mar. 1209/1 *Vaccinia* virus and reovirus assemble their mRNA synthesizing enzymes within the mature virion. **1973** R. G. KRUEGER et al. *Introd. Microbiol.* xix. 532/1 Three serological types of reovirus have been identified. The structure of the particles..consists of an RNA core some 40 nm in diameter and an icosahedral capsid 30–50 Å in width. No envelope is present. The 92 capsomeres are closely packed and appear as pentagonal or hexagonal columnar prisms (possibly truncated pyramids) arranged in 5:3:2 symmetry. **1979** *Sci. Amer.* Nov. 65/1 In mice..reovirus attacks the acinar cells of the pancreas.

reowe, obs. f. RUE *sb.* and *v.*, ROW *v.*[1]

reowful(nesse, obs. ff. RUEFUL(NESS.

reowliche, var. RULY *a. Obs.*

reowsunge: see REWSING.

reowthe, obs. f. RUTH.

reowthfulliche, obs. f. RUTHFULLY.

reoxi'dation (ri:-). [RE- 5 a.] The process of oxidizing, or of being oxidized, afresh.

1838 *Civil Eng. & Arch. Jrnl.* I. 162/2 They are then to be ..set fire to,..and afterwards laid by for re-oxidation. **1884** W. H. GREENWOOD *Steel & Iron* vi. 96 The re-oxidation of the carbonic oxide so formed into carbonic anhydride.

re'oxidize, *v.* [RE- 5 b.] **a.** *trans.* To oxidize again.

1940 GLASSTONE *Textbk. Physical Chem.* xii. 1020 The ion, e.g., Ti^{++++}, is first reduced at the cathode, e.g., to Ti^{+++}, which is the active reducing agent; in the process it is re-oxidized to Ti^{++++}, and is again reduced at the cathode and so on. **1957** *Science* 12 Apr. 691/3 Partially reduced ribonuclease..was reoxidized. **1973** *Chem. Soc. Rev.* II. 43 The unwanted epimer can be reoxidized to (78) for recycling.

b. *intr.* To take up oxygen again.

1966 *Economist* 16 Apr. 289/3 The zinc vapour is stripped out of the gases by a spray of molten lead—a vital part of the new process, since it removes the zinc before it can reoxidise. **1976** *Sci. Amer.* July 78/2 The product of the Purofer process is a briquette that does not reoxidize readily because of its small surface area.

So **re'oxidizement**.

1839 *Penny Cycl.* XIV. 56/1 By exposure to the air or other means of reoxidizement.

re'oxygenate, *v.* [RE- 5 a.] *trans.* To oxygenate afresh. Hence **re,oxyge'nation**.

1855 KINGSLEY *Glaucus* 140 Its remaining fresh argued that the coralline had reoxygenated it from time to time. **1884** *Public Opinion* 5 Sept. 306/1 An apparatus for re-oxygenating air that has already been breathed. **1957** G. E. HUTCHINSON *Treat. Limnol.* I. ix. 593 The full reoxygenation of a very deep lake..presents real difficulties.

So **reoxygenize** *v.* (Ogilvie 1882).

rep[1]. Colloq. abbrev. of REPUTATION. Common in early 18th c.; now chiefly *U.S.*

a **1705** SHIPPERY in *Brasenose Ale* (1878) 2 Six go-downs upon rep. to our true English King! **1711** ADDISON *Spect.* No. 135 ⁋10 This Humour..which has so miserably curtailed some of our Words,..as in *mob. rep. pos. incog.* and the like. **1732** FIELDING *Covent Gard. Trag.* II. xiii, Nor modesty, nor pride, nor fear, nor rep, Shall now forbid this tender chaste embrace. **1738** SWIFT *Pol. Conversat.* Introd. 91 Do you say it upon Rep? **1873** J. H. BEADLE *Undevel. West* xix. 367 Of the town proper, a majority of citizens were negroes, with them a few whites of doubtful 'rep', and perhaps a dozen Indians. **1910** E. A. WALCOTT *Open Door* xii. 155 An' me a white man, too, even if me rep. is off color. **1935** 'E. QUEEN' *Spanish Cape Mystery* iii. 68 Got a rep as a bad customer. **1956** 'E. MCBAIN' *Cop Hater* (1958) x. 90 We got a big rep as it is. Ain't nobody in this city who ain't heard of The Grovers. **1978** M. PUZO *Fools Die* iv. 51 He was a legitimate bad guy with an obvious rep in Vegas.

rep[2]. Now *rare.* [Of obscure origin: cf. RIP. The relation to *demi-rep* is not clear.]

1. A man (†or woman) of loose character; a rip.

1747 HOADLY *Susp. Husb.* IV. iv, So many Rivals among your kept Mistresses, and Reps of Quality. **1806** R. CUMBERLAND *Mem.* 474 Old and young, reps and demi-reps flocked to see it. **1886** FARGUS *Living or Dead* II. 169 Now you're about with the biggest uncut rep in town.

2. An inferior or worthless article.

1786 WOLCOTT (P. Pindar) *Lyric Odes* xi. Wks. 1816 I. 117 The fiddle..though what's vulgarly baptiz'd a *rep*, Shall in a hundred pounds be deem'd dog-cheap.

rep[3] (rɛp). Also repp. [ad. F. *reps*, of unknown origin.] A textile fabric (of wool, silk, or cotton) having a corded surface. Cf. REPS.

1860 MRS. GASKELL *Right at Last* 11 What should make you think I care so much for rep in preference to moreen? **1894** BARING-GOULD *Queen of Love* I. 75 Rab..raised the red repp that covered the barrier.

attrib. **1883** *Harper's Mag.* Mar. 538/2 The green rep parlour suites. **1898** G. B. SHAW *Plays* II. *You never can tell* 274 A pair of maroon rep curtains.

rep[4], in school slang, abbrev. of REPETITION.

1864 CREIGHTON in *Life & Lett.* (1904) I. i. 13 It is a very bad sign if fellows talk, or learn rep...during prayers. **1906** [see CON d]. **1930** E. M. BRENT-DYER *Chalet School & Jo* iv. 57 'There's only rep left, and I've arithmetic and French to write!' protested Cornelia.

rep[5]. Abbrev. of REPRESENTATIVE *sb.*; esp. a sales representative.

1896 T. EYTON *Rugby Football* 10 Joe..has annually played and led the Tauranga reps. against the Auckland teams. **1933** L. G. D. ACLAND in *Press* (Christchurch, N.Z.) 18 Nov. 15/7 *Rep.*.. Under the arbitration award it is laid down that 'the shearers shall elect a representative', who deals with the employer..whenever any dispute or question arises. **1938** E. AMBLER *Cause for Alarm* ii. 28 No travellers seen except on Tuesdays and Thursdays... Reps.., Tuesdays and Thursdays. **1959** T. GIRTIN *Unnatural Break* xxviii. 101 The local rep of the League of Empire Loyalists got up in the middle and made a protest. **1959** *New Statesman* 19 Dec. 874/1 One young sales rep, whom I met quite early in the month, was already discovering his soul and finding the process painful. **1969** T. LLOYD in R. Blythe *Akenfield* xiv. 218, I am the only member of this club who isn't a farmer's son..or a rep. **1977** *Jrnl. R. Soc. Arts* CXXV. 679/1 We can have three thousand safety reps for a labour force of thirty five thousand. **1979** *Tucson* (Arizona) *Citizen* 20 Sept. 2A/2 The House turned down an amendment by Rep. Eldon Rudd.

rep[6]. Colloq. abbrev. of REPERTORY 3 (occas. of REPERTOIRE); a repertory company or theatre. Freq. *attrib.*

1925 *Amer. Speech* I. 36/2 A rep show is made up of players with a repertoire of plays. **1929** J. B. PRIESTLEY *Good Companions* II. ii. 283 Each member of the troupe prided himself..on having a large répertoire, known always as a 'rep'. **1933** S. O'CASEY *Let.* 24 Sept. (1975) I. 465 A Rep or a Stage Society production. **1948** H. L. MENCKEN *Amer. Lang.* Suppl. II. 690 *Rep company*, a company presenting a répertoire of plays on the road. **1959** *Times* 5 Jan. 12/2 While the productions are out of Oxford we let the theatre to local societies, visiting reps or small-cost tours. **1959** *Manch. Guardian* 30 Jan. 7/1 She has returned to 'weekly rep.', producing for a sound but as yet undistinguished company which must perform potboilers for most of the year. **1971** *Guardian* 27 Sept. 10/1 Faithful and ageing Rep-goers. **1977** R. BARNARD *Death in High C's* ii. 18 You're back with..the same old rep production. **1977** *Radio Times* 12–18 Nov. 15/1 After the war Major Bates joined Worthing rep as stage manager.

†**rep**[7]. *Obs.* [f. initial letters of *roentgen equivalent physical.*] A quantity of ionizing radiation that will release the same amount of energy in human tissue as one rad (formerly roentgen) of X-rays. Cf. REM *sb.*[1]

1947 *Nucleonics* Oct. 38/2 If the energy lost by ionization in the tissues is the same as the energy loss for one roentgen of gamma radiation absorbed in air, the dose is spoken of as one roentgen-equivalent-physical (abbreviated 'rep'). [*Note*] The rep and rem units were introduced by Dr. H. M. Parker. **1955** *Bull. Atomic Sci.* June 211/1 On a conservative estimate, a dose of 200 reps, such as many Hiroshima survivors must have received, would probably have caused each of their offspring to inherit, on the average, at least one mutation produced by the exposure. **1962** F. I. ORDWAY et al. *Basic Astronautics* xii. 494 The rep or roentgen equivalent physical is the unit that equals the ionization produced by other forms of radiation to that of x-rays and gamma-rays. The rep is defined as the amount of particulate radiation that produces an energy absorption of 93 ergs/g in human tissue.

rep, obs. form of REAP *sb.*[2]

re'pace, *v.* [RE- 5 a.] To pace back or again.

1633 P. FLETCHER *Purple Isl.* IV. xxii, Tritons..who.. speed the rivers flowing race, But strongly stop the wave, if once it back repace. **1729** SAVAGE *Wanderer* IV. 81 Wild beasts to gloomy dens repace their way.

repacifi'cation. *rare.* [RE- 5 a.] The fact of being pacified again.

1665 G. HAVERS *P. della Valle's Trav. E. India* 99 Manifest signes that his re-pacification was rather upon necessity then out of good-will. **1937** *Times* 17 Nov. 17/4 Each costly 'pacification' of Wazirs, Mahsuds, or Mohmands is to be followed by their equally costly repacification at regular and almost predictable intervals.

re'pacify, *v. rare.* [RE- 5 a.] To pacify again.

1604 DANIEL *Civ. Wars* I. xi, His brother Henry..Seeks to re-pacify the people's hate. **1611** FLORIO, *Rappacificare*, to appease or repacifie.

re'pack (ri:-), *v.* [RE- 5 a.] To pack again.

1472–3 [see *repacking* below]. **1611** COTGR., *Remballer*, to repacke, or pack vp againe. **1628–9** DIGBY *Voy. Medit.* (Camden) 69 Repacking our English beefe, wee found it to be verie bad. **1722** DE FOE *Col. Jack* (1840) 328 They were opened, and repacked. *a* **1790** ADAM SMITH *W.N.* IV. v. (1869) II. 94 It is necessary to repack them with an additional quantity of salt. **1813** SIR R. WILSON *Priv. Diary* (1862) II. 121 They had stopped behind to pick up and repack the things which had fallen off one of my led horses. **1896** *Allbutt's Syst. Med.* I. 420 The child is unswathed, rubbed dry, and repacked as before.

Hence **re'packed** *ppl. a.*; **re'packing** *vbl. sb.*; also **re'packer**, one who repacks (Webster 1828).

1472–3 *Rolls of Parlt.* VI. 59/1 [All wools shall] be admytted..and delyvered to the merchaunt biers, withoute any repakkyng therof there to be made. **1615** E. S. *Brittaines Buss* in Arb. *Garner* III. 640 The repacking of the herrings by the sworn Coopers of that place. *Ibid.*, Then will rest to be sold..seventy-five Last full of repacked herrings. **1745–6** in W. Thompson *R.N. Advoc.* (1757) 17 The greatest Part of the Meat by repacking and pickling, will still be fit for Service. **1822** J. FLINT *Lett. fr. Amer.* 76 If I had entertained any doubt..the very repacking of my baggage would at once have removed it. **1842** *Penny Cycl.* XXII. 475/2 These metallic pistons..do not..require the frequent repacking necessary to those with tow or hempen stuffing. **1976** *Shell in Industr. Chemicals* (Shell Internat. Petroleum Co.) 5 Group companies sell Teepol to blenders and repackers.

†**re'paganic**, *a. nonce-wd.* [RE- 5 a: cf. next.] Once more pagan.

1701 BEVERLEY *Apoc. Quest.* 11 In this very Repaganic (if I may so speak) or Repaganiz'd State.

re'paganize (ri:-), *v.* [RE- 5 a.] *trans.* and *intr.* To make or become pagan again. Hence **re'paganized** *ppl. a.*; **re'paganizing** *vbl. sb.* and *ppl. a.*; also **re'paganizer**, **repagani'zation**.

1672 EACHARD *Hobbs's St. Nat.* Lett. 12 An Universal repaganizer, Popeling, a worshipper of the beast [etc.]. **1685** H. MORE *Paralip. Prophet.* xlii. 361 Therefore the Re-paganizing of the Church must be presently after. *Ibid.* 362 If he could not..have turned off Constantine from the Faith or Re-paganized the Christians. **1701** BEVERLEY *Apoc. Quest.* 11 This Empire Repaganizing through Anti-christianism, undermining, and supplanting True Christianity. [See also REPAGANIC.] **1854** MILMAN *Lat. Chr.* IV. v. (1864) II. 292 The chief objects of worship in the re-Paganized land were three statues of gilded brass. **1888** *Outlook & Sabb. Quarterly* (N.Y.) Jan. 457 You have also thought, no doubt, on the repaganization of Christendom.

re'paint (ri:-), *sb.* [RE- 5 a: cf. next.]

1. A substance used in repainting; a layer of colour put on in repainting.

1891 *Portfolio* Mar. 51 There were parts of the surface from which it removed the original fresco-pigments or the tempera repaints. **1901** R. FRY *Let.* 10 Dec. (1972) I. 182, I am at present cutting off the sky with a knife and have found a marvellous landscape underneath, entirely concealed by repaints. **1935** *Burlington Mag.* Nov. 202/1 The picture was ..then almost entirely covered with re-paint.

2. The fact of repainting or being repainted. Also *fig.* and *attrib.*

1893 *Pall Mall G.* 23 Jan. 2/1 Although it has suffered somewhat from repaint..it still remains one of the most beautiful single heads produced by Renaissance painting. **1964** G. MARX *Let.* 27 Oct. (1967) 258, I will be in London in April, doing a repaint job on my old quiz show. **1968** S. JAY *Sleepers can Kill* vii. 74 The car was a black Opel in need of a repaint. **1970** J. WAINWRIGHT *Prynter's Devil* iii. 50 Vac the room first, kiddo. Then start the repaint job.

3. Something repainted, esp. a golf-ball.

1922 WODEHOUSE *Clicking of Cuthbert* i. 16 Why, you are a pearl among women, the queen of your sex... You make the rest look like battered repaints. **1931** M. ALLINGHAM *Look to Lady* xiv. 148 'How's the car business?'.. 'I sold a lovely repaint in Norward last week... We faked it up lovely —registration book and everything.' **1936** *Sun* (Baltimore) 1 Aug. 817, I should like to know whether they [*sc.* golf balls] are new ones or repaints. **1955** *Times* 23 Aug. 4/4 Repaints cost as much as new balls used to.

re'paint (ri:-), *v.* [RE- 5 a.] *trans.* To paint again (*lit.* and *fig.*).

a **1700** KEN *Edmund* Poet. Wks. 1721 II. 159 Till vanishing Sleep Edmund re-possess'd, Repainting it in Dreams upon his Breast. **1761** STERNE *Tr. Shandy* IV. xxv, The coach was re-painted upon my father's marriage. **1815** J. SCOTT *Vis. Paris* Pref. 9 The first thing they do with one of Raphael's pictures is to repaint it. **1830** LYTTON *P. Clifford* xxxiii, A solicitor, the very rails round whose door were so sadly in want of re-painting! **1888** HAVELOCK ELLIS in *Ford's Plays* (Mermaid Ser.) p. xiv, The conflict between the world's opinion and the heart's desire he paints and repaints.

Hence **re'painted** *ppl. a.*, **re'painting** *vbl. sb.*

1864 *Reader* 26 Nov. 667/3 The inferior and repainted works at Fiesole. **1884** *Athenæum* 2 Feb. 157/1 There is much repainting on the faces.

repair (rɪ'pɛə(r)), *sb.*[1] Forms: 4–5 **repeir(e, -eyr(e**; 4–7 **repayr(e**, (5 *Sc.* **rap-**), **-aire, -ar(e**, (7 **-aier**), 4– **repair.** [a. OF. *repeire*, *repaire* (mod.F. *repère*) return, etc., f. *repeirer*, *repairer*, to REPAIR *v.*[1]]

1. (Chiefly in phrases *to make* or *have repair*: cf. 4 b.) **a.** Resort, frequent or habitual going, *to* a place. Now *arch.* or *Obs.*

c **1330** R. BRUNNE *Chron. Wace* (Rolls) 8078 þeyr wonyng ys in þe eyr, [but] Vmwhile to þe erþe þey make repeir. *c* **1375** *Sc. Leg. Saints* xlvi. (*Anastace*) 176 þe prefet yddire had repare. *c* **1425** WYNTOUN *Cron.* I. xvii. 1657 Qwhar common accesse of repayr Men mycht haf to þat figoure fayr. **1456** SIR G. HAYE *Law Arms* (S.T.S.) 190 He saw or persavit him mak grete repaire till his hous. **1570–6** LAMBARDE *Peramb. Kent* (1862) 171 She exhorted repaire to the church. **1581** PETTIE *Guazzo's Civ. Conv.* I. (1586) 38 Flatterers..alwaies make their repaire thether where profite is to be reaped. **1638** HEYWOOD *Wise Wom.* III. i. Wks. 1874 V. 314 By his oft repaire..your good name May be by Neighbours hardly censur'd of. **1691** WOOD *Ath. Oxon.* II. 184 Peter Heylin..was furnished with Books..by his repair to Bodlies Library.

b. *Sc.* Resort (also occas., stay or sojourn) *in* a place or *among* others. Now *arch.* or *Obs.*

c **1375** *Sc. Leg. Saints* xii. (*Mathias*) 292 In þe ayre, quhare þe feyndis has mast repare. *Ibid.* xxxi. (*Eugenia*) 104 A lytil tone..quhar cristine men had repare. *c* **1425** WYNTOUN *Cron.* II. xvi. 1484 In ane ile þai gert þaim ga, Amange þaim na rapayr to ma. *Ibid.* V. iii. 440 Qwhen..þai of Brettane ostagis hade, He gret repayr amange þaim made. **1500–20** DUNBAR *Poems* xliii. 1 Thir ladyis fair, That makis repair, And in the court ar kend. **1535** LYNDESAY *Satyre* 594 ȝit in this Realme I wald mak sum repair. **1812** BYRON *Ch. Har.* I. xxii, On sloping mounds, or in the vale beneath, Are domes where whilome kings did make repair.

†**c.** Chiefly *Sc.* Intercourse or association (*with* others). *Obs.*

c **1450** LYDG. *Secrees* 190 Yiff thou thus doo by vertuous Repeyr, God shal encrese..thy Royal excellence. **1500–20** DUNBAR *Poems* xviii. 17 Ane lady fresche and fair, With gentill men makand repair. **1536** BELLENDEN *Cron. Scot.* (1821) I. p. xxvi, The peple thairof has na repair with marchandis of uncouth realmes. *a* **1653** BINNING *Serm.* (1845) 186 To cleanse even vain thoughts, and shut up, from that ordinary repair, his own heart.

†**d.** Liberty of resort. *Obs. rare*[−1].

1598 MANWOOD *Lawes Forest* xv. ⁋2. 87 In their corne, meadowes, and pastures, the Deere must haue their repaire and quiet feede.

2. The place to which one repairs; *esp.* a haunt, usual abode or dwelling-place.

1375 BARBOUR *Bruce* XVI. 310 The Ersche kyngis than euirilkane Hayme till thar awne repar ar gane. **14..** *Tundale's Vis.*, etc. (1843) 92 To hem that ben in euyle of owtrage Repeyre fynall of hur pylgrimage. **1484** CAXTON

Fables of Æsop v. viii, This labourer passyd before the repayre or dwellynge place of the sayd Serpent. **1616** B. JONSON *Epigr.* I. xxxii, What not the envy of the seas reach'd to,..At home in his repaire Was his blest fate, but our hard lot to find. **1666** DRYDEN *Ann. Mirab.* ccxx, There the fierce winds his tender force assail And beat him downward to his first repair. **1864** *Reader* 2 July 20 When they were the repairs of wild beasts and the sheltering-places of men. **1895** *Harper's Mag.* Feb. 472/2 Converting the hole of the asp into a repair for children.

†**b.** So *place, house,* etc. *of repair. Obs.*

c **1586** C'TESS PEMBROKE *Ps.* XCI. i, Jehova is my fort, My place of safe repaire. **1598** STOW *Surv.* xliii. (1603) 454 The Arch Bishops of Yorke being dispossessed and hauing no house of repayre. **1611** BIBLE *Joel* iii. 17 The Lord will be the hope [*marg.* place of repaire or harbour] of his people.

3. Concourse or confluence of people in or at a place; common or extensive resort of persons *to* a place. Now *rare* or *Obs.*

c **1350** *Ipomadon* 342 The courte was plenere all that day Off worthy lordes,..And other grette repeyre. *c* **1386** CHAUCER *Wife's T.* 368 Or elles ye wol..take youre auenture of the repair That shal be to youre hous by cause of me. **1423** JAS. I *Kingis Q.* lxxvii, Within a chamber..I fand of peple grete repaire. **1482** *Rolls of Parlt.* VI. 224/2 Your true Liege people..wolde there in brief tyme habunde and encrease, by repaire of Merchauntes. **1535** COVERDALE *1 Macc.* ix. 39 There was moch a doo, & greate repayre: for the brydegrome came forth. **1577** FENTON *Gold. Epist.* (1582) 26 He that..holdeth a house of generall repaire, and receyueth the vnthriftie and banished. *c* **1614** SIR W. MURE *Dido & Æneas* II. 875 With earnest repare the paths do seeme to sweate. **1808** JAMIESON s.v., We still say of a street which is retired from the bustle of a town, that there is not much repair in it. **1815** SCOTT *Guy M.* xxxi, The footpath leading there was well beaten by the repair of those who frequented it for pastime.

transf. **1429** *Rolls of Parlt.* IV. 359/2 Touchyng ye repaire of Wolle..to ye said Staple. **1449** *Ibid.* V. 149/2 The..hole repaire of al manere Marchandise to the same Staple.

†**b.** In prepositional phrases, as *among, but, out of, without repair. Obs.* (chiefly *Sc.*).

c **1470** HARDING *Chron.* CXLIII. iii, This earle was then famed amonge repayre The noblest prynce. **1508** DUNBAR *Flyting* 153 In till ane glen thow hes, owt of repair, Ane laithly luge. **1570** *Satir. Poems Reform.* xxviii. 11 Endlang ane Park, I past without repair Be Snawdoun syde. *a* **1585** POLWART *Flyting w. Montgomerie* 196 Where howlring howlets aye doth hant, With robin red-brest, but repaire.

†**c.** Following, retinue, company. *Obs. rare.*

c **1470** HARDING *Chron.* LXXII, The Duke was slayn with all his moste repayre. *a* **1548** HALL *Chron., Hen. VIII* 72 My lorde Cardinall, came to the toune of Douer in hast with a noble repaire.

4. The act of (†returning) going or making one's way *to* a place. Now *rare* or *Obs.*

1375 BARBOUR *Bruce* XVIII. 557 Northwarde tuk thai hame thar way, And destroyit, in thair repair, The vale haly of Beauvare. **1412–20** LYDG. *Chron. Troy* I. v. (1555), In your repayre to your fathers reigne..ye shall me with you lede. **1494** FABYAN *Chron.* v. lxxxiv. 62 When the Lordes of Brytayne sawe..theyr dayly repayre into this lande, they assembled them togyder. **1531** CROMWELL in Merriman *Life & Lett.* (1902) I. 335 At my next repayre thither it pleased his highnes to call for me. **1593** ABP. BANCROFT *Daung. Posit.* I. vi. 23 A repaire of the Kinges faithfull subiectes to his highnesse presence. **1633** FORD *Broken Heart* II. ii, We'll write to Athens For his repair to Sparta. **1666** in *10th Rep. Hist. MSS. Comm.* App. V. 10 His goods [are] like to be spoyled or lost, without his speedy repaire thither. **1698** FRYER *Acc. E. India & P.* p. ii, Our repair aboard Ship, and coming to Fort St. George.

b. in phr. *to make (one's) repair to* (a place or person). Now *arch.*

1500–20 DUNBAR *Poems* xlii. 107 [He] to the court maid his repair. **1568** GRAFTON *Chron.* II. 8 Nothing might lightly happen..by reason whereof he should be compelled to make his repayre thether againe. **1601** HOLLAND *Pliny* I. 118 Diuers kings and princes, who made repaire to Rome with sutes and supplications. **1812** BYRON *Ch. Har.* I. lxix, Then thy spruce citizen, wash'd artisan, And smug apprentice..To Hampstead, Brentford, Harrow make repair. *a* **1850** ROSSETTI *Dante & Circle* I. (1874) 158 A lover..to his lady must make meek repair.

repair (rɪˈpɛə(r)), *sb.*² Forms: 6–7 repaire, 7 -ayre, -are; 6- repair. [f. REPAIR *v.*²]

1. a. The act of restoring to a sound or unimpaired condition; the process by which this is accomplished; the result attained. †Also *pl.*

1595 SHAKS. *John* III. iv. 113 Before the curing of a strong disease, Euen in the instant of repaire and health, The fit is strongest. **1611** —— *Cymb.* III. i. 57 Our Lawes, whose vse the Sword of Cæsar Hath too much mangled; whose repayre, and franchise Shall..be our good deed. **1647** N. BACON *Disc. Govt. Eng.* I. (1739) 203 So must I leave them until some happy hand shall work their repair. **1667** MILTON *P.L.* VIII. 457, I,..Dazl'd and spent, sunk down, and sought repair Of sleep. **1748** CHESTERF. *Lett.* (1792) II. cxli. 1 My health,..for want of proper attention of late, wanted some repairs. **1869** CONINGTON tr. *Horace's Sat.* etc. (1874) 155 After harvest done, they sought repair From toils which hope of respite made them bear. **1876** *Trans. Clinical Soc.* IX. 11 The repair of a wound is less active,..than when other simple or antiseptic dressings are employed.

b. *spec.* Restoration of some material thing or structure by the renewal of decayed or worn out parts, by refixing what has become loose or detached, etc.; the result of this. Also *pl.* (freq. in mod. use). †*upon a repair*, in process of being repaired.

1661 MARVELL *Corr.* Wks. (Grosart) II. 60 A Bill for inabling Churchwardens to rate such monys as are for the repare of the churches, &c. *a* **1676** HALE *Narr. Customes* iii. in S. A. Moore *Foreshore* (1888) 336 As to the care of repayre of ports, this is in a special manner left to the Kinges care and power. **1756** TOLDERVY *Hist. 2 Orphans* I. 60 The school being very old, was at this time upon a repair. **1853** KANE *Grinnell Exp.* xxxvi. (1856) 324 The work of repair was pressed so assiduously, that in three days the stern-post was in its place. **1884** *Rambles around Oxford* (Shrimptons, ed. 2) 86 There appears to have been a large repair of the church in 1668. **1898** *Westm. Gaz.* 9 Nov. 5/2 Whatever be done to the picture, the repair will be clearly noticeable in a few years.

pl. **1677** TEMPLE *Ess. Cure Gout* Wks. 1720 II. 145 Proportioning..the daily repairs to the daily decays of our wasting bodies. **1776** ADAM SMITH *W.N.* II. ii. I. 344 The expence of maintaining the fixed capital in a great country, may very properly be compared to that of repairs in a private estate. **1855** PRESCOTT *Philip II*, I. ii. (1857) 13 The completion of some repairs that were going on in the monastery.

c. Remedy *of* wrong.

1663 BUTLER *Hud.* I. ii. 412 Cerdon the Great, renown'd in Song, Like Herc'les, for Repair of Wrong.

2. a. Relative state or condition of something admitting or susceptible of restoration in event of actual or possible damage or decay; chiefly of buildings or other composite structures and in phr. *in good* (or *bad*) *repair*.

c **1600** SHAKS. *Sonn.* iii, That face..Whose fresh repaire if now thou not renewest, Thou doo'st beguile the world. **1638** SIR T. HERBERT *Trav.* (ed. 2) 114 The castle is yet in good strength and repayre. **1687** A. LOVELL tr. *Thevenot's Trav.* I. 95 One [gate] that was built four hundred years ago, is still in good repair. **1725** SWIFT *(title)* To Quilca, A Country-House in no very good Repair. **1827** SOUTHEY *Penins. War* II. 427 Forty bullock-cars..in such ill repair..that only eleven of them reached Deleitosa. **1845** MCCULLOCH *Taxation* I. i. (1852) 3 To put the roads and bridges into that state of repair which the depressed situation of commerce..seemed to require. **1886** STORY *Fiammetta* 48 The house..was now in very bad repair.

b. *in repair*, in good or proper condition (esp. of structures; so *into repair*). *out of repair*, in bad condition, requiring repairs.

1667 DUCHESS NEWCASTLE *Life of Duke of N.* (1886) II. 134 His two houses..he found much out of repair. **1693** CONGREVE *Old Bach.* IV. iv, I hope nobody will come this way, till I have put myself a little in repair. **1726** SWIFT *Gulliver* III. iv, Houses very strangely built, and most of them out of Repair. **1792** WOLCOTT (P. Pindar) *Odes of Condol.* Wks. 1812 III. 103 Like the Needle, while it wounds the cloth, It puts the rag into repair. **1827** D. JOHNSON *Ind. Field Sports* 4 A sum of money..for keeping the road in repair. **1853** J. H. NEWMAN *Hist. Sk.* (1873) II. I. iii. 129 If a place goes out of repair, the violence of the rain will soon destroy it.

†**c.** *to run to repair*, to require repairing. *Obs.*

1681 OTWAY *Soldier's Fort.* V. i, You shall..not be leaving the house uninhabited, lest it run to repair.

3. *Comb.* as *repair bill, kit, -man* (chiefly *U.S.*), *outfit, -ship, -shop, station, time, work(s)*.

1908 *Westm. Gaz.* 7 Jan. 4/2 The effects of wear and tear would be reduced to a minimum, and the *repair bill..would be kept very low. **1970** *Observer* 1 Feb. 31/6 Ten new pence..now buys a 'Panti-hose and Tights *Repair Kit' from Woolworths. **1975** *Times* 28 Aug. 11/8, I do not regard a song and dance as the infallible, all-purpose dramatic repair kit. **1871** W. S. HUNTINGTON *Road-Master's Assistant* ii. 9 It is a common practice for *repairmen, when replacing mended iron, to squeeze it in perfectly tight. **1928** *Sat. Even. Post* 4 Feb. 140/1 If your car suffers from any of these common motor ills, take it to your car dealer or repairman. **1958** *Times* 13 Sept. 7/7 Such dilemmas as that of the Los Angeles couple whose T.V. stops one night and the husband must go out and find the repairman. **1976** *Washington Post* 19 Apr. A22/4 The tenants refuse to let repairmen into their apartments. **1908** *Sears, Roebuck Catal.* 517/1 Traveler's big complete *repair outfit. **1976** J. R. L. ANDERSON *Redundancy Pay* i. 17 He..bought a pump, repair outfit, and a torch-battery cycle lamp. **1905** *Westm. Gaz.* 16 Nov. 6/2 The King's *repair-ship 'Assistance' was floated off at Tetuan yesterday. **1866** *Harper's Mag.* Sept. 543/1 In the repair-shops of the Columbus and Indianapolis Railroad. **1877** RAYMOND *Statist. Mines & Mining* 447 The company now has its own iron-foundery..and an extensive, well-appointed repair-shop. **1899** J. PENNELL in *Fortn. Rev.* LXV. 118 There the final collapse came, about 100 miles from any reliable repair shop. **1979** *Jrnl. R. Soc. Arts* July 466/1 Somehow the hospital must contrive to be both repair-shop and home. **1906** *Westm. Gaz.* 27 June 7/3 The mechanic..hung on to the radiator from the starting-line to the *repair-station. **1934** *Discovery* Nov. 326/1 Its main depot and repair station is at Lunghwa near Shanghai. **1962** *Autom. Data Proc.* (*B.S.I.*) 52 **Repair time*, time spent outside the periods allocated to routine maintenance and supplementary maintenance in diagnosing and clearing faults, equipment testing and maintenance. **1962** D. R. COX *Renewal Theory* vii. 80 Suppose that a machine is subject to stoppages and call the time necessary to restart a stopped machine a repair-time. **1906** *Westm. Gaz.* 22 Aug. 10/1 Important *repair work is..being undertaken..at the cathedrals of Winchester, Gloucester, York, and Canterbury. **1907** *Ibid.* 21 Mar. 9/1 With no repair works and with insufficient and sometimes incompetent staff, they ran their omnibuses as many hours as they could anyhow be kept on the road. **1969** *Gloss. Landscape Work* (*B.S.I.*) v. 30 *Repair work*, the treatment of incisions, bruises and other wounds or injuries [in trees etc.].

repair (rɪˈpɛə(r)), *v.*¹ Also 4–5 repeire, -eyre, 4–7 repaire, -ayr(e, -ar(e, (5 rap-). [a. OF. *repeirer, repairer*, etc. (mod.F. *repairer, repérer*), for earlier *repadrer*:—late L. *repatriāre* to return to one's country, f. *re-* RE- + *patria* fatherland: cf. REPATRIATE *v.*]

1. *intr.* To go, betake oneself, make one's way, usu. *to* or *from* a place or person. †Also in *pass.*, to have come or arrived.

13.. *Guy Warw.* (A.) 5169 Repeired is þerl sir Tirri..Herhaud of Ardern the gode marchis. *c* **1320** *Sir Tristr.* 2735 Tristrem þou3t repaire, Hou so it euer be. *c* **1384** CHAUCER *H. Fame* II. 247 Thus euery thinge..Hath his propre mansyon To which it sekith to repaire. *c* **1450** *Merlin* 126 Men that repayreden thourgh the Contree to assaye yef thei myght ought wynne vpon the kynge. **1529** WOLSEY in Ellis *Orig. Lett.* Ser. I. II. 2, I beseche yow..repare hyther thys day as sone as the Parlement ys broken up. **1594** KYD *Cornelia* I. 173 Then from her lothsome Caue doth Plague repaire. **1663** BUTLER *Hud.* I. ii. 665 To those Places straight repair Where your respective Dwellings are. **1711** ADDISON *Spect.* No. 123 ¶5 He received a sudden Summons from Leontine to repair to him in the Country the next Day. **1769** ROBERTSON *Chas. V*, v. Wks. 1813 V. 436 The ambassadors of France and England repaired to Spain. **1810** CRABBE *Borough* i. 15, I repair From this tall mansion..Till we the outskirts of the Borough reach. **1849** MACAULAY *Hist. Eng.* v. I. 536 There was no longer any difficulty or danger in repairing to William. **1870** DICKENS *E. Drood* xii, He repairs to Durdle's unfinished house, or hole in the city wall.

transf. **1509** HAWES *Past. Pleas.* XVI. (Percy Soc.) 66 A lady fayre, Whych to love you wyl nothyng repayre. **1549** COVERDALE, etc. *Erasm. Par. Gal.* 9 The Jewes..forsakyng the ceremonies of theyr elders, repayre vnto the spiritual doctrin of the gospel.

b. To resort *to* a place or person; to go commonly, frequently, or in numbers.

1375 BARBOUR *Bruce* X. 556 For I but suspicioun Micht repair till hir preuely. **1390** GOWER *Conf.* III. 123 He harmeth Venus and empeireth, Bot Mars unto his hous repeireth. *a* **1440** *Sir Degrev.* 45 Haukes of nobulle eyre Tylle his perke ganne repeyre. **1470–85** MALORY *Arthur* XIV. ii. 643 Al the world crysten and hethen repayren vnto the round table. **1560** INGELEND *Disobed. Child* in Hazl. *Dodsley* II. 297 Sometimes to the church they do repair. **1600** J. PORY tr. *Leo's Africa* IV. 219 Then they began to repaire vnto this port. *a* **1661** FULLER *Worthies* (1840) III. 208 He used to examine the pockets of such Oxford scholars as repaired unto him. **1691** WOOD *Ath. Oxon.* II. 694 During Mr. Dugdale's stay in London, he repaired sometimes to the Lodging of Sir Hen. Spelman. **1742** FIELDING *J. Andrews* II. iv, It is usual for the young gentlemen of the bar to repair to these sessions. **1809** PINKNEY *Trav. France* 31 In the proper season of the year, the people of Calais repair hither for their evening dance.

transf. **1432** *Rolls of Parlt.* IV. 410/1 Yat all Wolles..and diverses other Merchandises goyng oute of yis Royalme..sholde repaire to ye Staple at Caleis.

c. To betake oneself, resort *to* (a person, place, etc.) *for* something.

1580 SIDNEY *Ps.* IX. v, Thither the world for justice shall repaire. **1655** FULLER *Ch. Hist.* II. vi. §43 If any desire farther Information herein, let him repair to the worthy Work, which..the..Arch-bishop of Armagh, hath written. **1706** E. WARD *Wooden World Diss.* (1708) 62 Sometimes his Captain..repairs to him for a Refitment. **1722** WOLLASTON *Relig. Nat.* vii. 145 No shops to repair to for tools.

†**2.** To return (*again*), to come or go back, *to* or *from* a place, person, etc. Also in *pass.*, to have returned. *Obs.*

In some cases only a contextual sense.

c **1374** CHAUCER *Boeth.* I. met. iii. 5 (Camb. MS.), To myne eyen repeyrede [L. *rediit*] hir fyrst strengthe. *c* **1386** —— *Pard. T.* 550 To hise felawes agayn repaireth he. *c* **1400** *Destr. Troy* 3454 þat Parys in point repairit was home..fayne was þe pepull. **1413** *Pilgr. Sowle* (Caxton) II. lviii. (1859) 56 The spyrites repayred to the bones, soo that they stoden vp. *c* **1450** *Merlin* 150 Ye shall not take it till ye be repeired fro the bateile. *c* **1500** *Lancelot* 1454 Syne to his maister he ayane Reparith. **1590** SHAKS. *Mids. N.* IV. i. 72 That [they]..May all to Athens backe againe repaire. **1633** P. FLETCHER *Purple Isl.* IV. xxxiii, The smoak mounting in village nigh..Begins the night, warns us home repair.

†**b.** Without const.: To return. *Obs.*

c **1374** CHAUCER *Boeth.* III. met. ii. 53 (Camb. MS.) Hyr corage of tyme passed..repeyreth ayein [L. *redeunt animi*] and they roren greuosly. *a* **1400–50** *Alexander* 3751 Quen we repaire with þe palme þan prayses vs oure feris. **1483** CAXTON *Gold. Leg.* 92 b/1 They repayred by amyens and passed by a lytyl vylage named Sayns. **1607** SHAKS. *Timon* III. iv. 69 If I might beseech you Gentlemen, to repayre some other houre.

†**3.** To be present, temporarily or habitually; to have one's resort or abode; to dwell, reside. *Obs.*

13.. *Gaw. & Gr. Knt.* 1017 Trumpez & nakerys, Much pypyng þer repayres. **1375** BARBOUR *Bruce* IV. 477 In-till a stalward place heir-by Reparis all thair cumpany. *c* **1425** WYNTOUN *Cron.* I. xii. 1171 In wildernes, Qwhar na man dar repayr na dwel. **1483** CAXTON *Gold. Leg.* 272/1 Thy blood whiche repayrest in heuenes. **1523** LD. BERNERS *Froiss.* I. xi. 11 Also there was the Erle of Arundell..repayryng about the Kyngis courte. **1560** ROLLAND *Crt. Venus* II. 198 Till he come to quhair the nine [nobles] did repair. [**1585** T. WASHINGTON tr. *Nicholay's Voy.* IV. i. 113 b, Euery one..were by the Lawes constrayned to repayre at a time and houre appointed in his quarters.]

†**4.** *trans.* **a.** To draw *back*, to recover. **b.** To convey. *Obs. rare.*

1596 SPENSER *F.Q.* V. xi. 13 He, ere he could his weapon backe repaire, His side all bare and naked overtooke. **1612** SIR R. BOYLE in *Lismore Papers* (1886) I. 8 This 50li Mr. Eustace delivered Thomas Russell of Ballyea for me who did repair yt unto me.

†**5.** *refl.* **a.** To proceed. **b.** To abide, stay. *Obs.*

1509 HAWES *Past. Pleas.* XXVI. (Percy Soc.) 114 Than on my jorney, my selfe to repayre,..Forthe on I rode. *Ibid.* XXXII. 158 So forth we went unto a chamber fayre, Where many ladies did them selfe repayre. **1588** PARKE tr. *Mendoza's Hist. China* II. vii. 150 They vnderstood..he must abide and repayre himself in some place nigh there aboutes.

repair (rɪˈpɛə(r)), *v.*² Also 4–7 repaire, -ayre, (5 -eyre, 5–6 -are). [a. OF. *reparer* (mod.F. *réparer*) or ad. L. *reparāre* f. *re-* RE- + *parāre* to make ready, put in order: cf. *prepare*.]

†**1.** *trans.* **a.** To adorn, ornament. Also *absol.*

13.. *E.E. Allit. P.* A. 1028 Þe wonez with-inne enurned ware Wyth alle kynnez perre þat moȝt repayre. **1483** CAXTON *G. de la Tour* C. iij, Of them..that so moche waste their good to be jolif and repayre their carayn.

†**b.** To set in order, strengthen. *Obs.*$^{-1}$

1502 ARNOLDE *Chron.* (1811) 162 The Soudan..caused the Holy Lande to be better repared and more suerly kept.

†**c.** To furnish or provide *with* something. *Obs.*

1557 *Will of J. Bowler* (Somerset Ho.), My wif shall kepe maynteyn and repayer all my said children with meate drincke and honnest apparrell. **1616** R. C. *Times' Whistle* v. 1677 What bird doth cut the aire With her swift wing, but that we doe repaire Therwith our tables?

2. To restore (a composite thing, structure, etc.) to good condition by renewal or replacement of decayed or damaged parts, or by refixing what has given way; to mend.

1387 [see REPAIRING *vbl. sb.*^{2} 1]. *c* **1430** LYDG. *Min. Poems* (Percy Soc.) 252 As..an artificeer repaireth a riven cheste. **1494** FABYAN *Chron.* II. xxxi. 23 Whan..Belyn was retourned into Brytayne he repayred olde Cyties. **1560** DAUS tr. *Sleidane's Comm.* 121 He repared his navie and returned to Constantinople. **1617** MORYSON *Itin.* I. 194 The fourth Bridge..being rebuilt or repaired of stone, by King Charles the sixth. **1667** MILTON *P.L.* VI. 878 Disburd'nd Heav'n rejoic'd, and soon repaird Her mural breach. **1703** T. N. *City & C. Purchaser* 71 Houses here and there are always Repairing. **1791** MRS. RADCLIFFE *Rom. Forest* ii, Peter brought materials for repairing the place, and some furniture. **1798** FERRIAR *Illustr. Sterne* iv. 120 When the mutilation of the nose was to be repaired. **1823** LAMB *Elia* Ser. II. *Old China*, While I was repairing some of the loose leaves with paste. **1865** CARLYLE *Fredk. Gt.* XX. x. (1872) IX. 175 A place called Almeida, which Bückeburg had tried to repair into strength.

absol. **1820** GIFFORD *Eng. Lawyer* (ed. 5) 418 The law excuses the lessee, unless there is a covenant to repair and uphold.

b. To heal or cure (a wound). Also *intr.* of a wound: To mend, heal up.

1590 SPENSER *F.Q.* II. i. 43 So well he did her deadly wounds repaire. **1738** GRAY *Propertius* iii. 81 The Melians Hurt Machaon could repair. **1881** *Daily News* 29 Aug. 5/6 The wound was not repairing, and was not better than on Friday.

c. *refl.* To put (oneself) in order again.

1806–7 J. BERESFORD *Miseries Hum. Life* II. xxiii, On arriving, too late to repair yourself, you are obliged to sit down to table..with plastered hair [etc.].

3. To renew, renovate (some thing or part); to restore to a fresh or sound condition by making up in some way for previous loss, waste, decay, or exhaustion. (In later use commonly with approximation to sense 2.)

c **1410** *Master of Game* (MS. Digby 182) iv, Þei burnessh not nor repeireth not hir heere into newe gras tyme. **1526** *Pilgr. Perf.* (W. de W. 1531) 183 b, The fruyte of the tree of lyfe..onely repared & nourysshed yᵉ bodyes of the eaters. **1590** SHAKS. *Com. Err.* II. i. 99 My decayed faire A sunnie looke of his would soone repaire. **1600** E. BLOUNT tr. *Conestaggio* 296 The armie being a little repaired here, the Marques went to the Ile of Coruo to meete with the Indian fleete. **1620** BRINSLEY *Virgil* 103 The way by which Bees may be repaired againe when they shall be vtterly dead and gone. **1637** MILTON *Lycidas* 169 So sinks the day-star in the Ocean bed, And yet anon repairs his drooping head. **1697** DRYDEN *Virg. Georg.* III. 652 While the Southern Air And dropping Heav'ns the moisten'd Earth repair. **1711** ADDISON *Spect.* No. 69 ¶5 We repair our Bodies by the Drugs of America. **1757** GRAY *Bard* 137 Tomorrow he [the sun] repairs the golden flood. **1791** COWPER *Let. to Meriton* 24 June, While your church is undergoing repair, its minister may be repaired also. **1845** BUDD *Dis. Liver* 24 The waste of the tissues which these elements go to repair. **1847** EMERSON *Poems* (1857) 190, I see my trees repair their boughs. **1896** tr. *Boas' Text-bk. Zool.* 32 Mammalia..can, indeed, repair injured epidermis and the like.

b. With immaterial object. Also *refl.*

1398 TREVISA *Barth. De P.R.* II. xvi. (1495) 41 The angels sholde in theimself repare the ymage of god and refourme it and kepe it. **1561** DAUS tr. *Bullinger on Apoc.* (1573) 20 The thyrd day [he] rose agayne from the dead, and repayred life for all belevers. **1598** DRAYTON *Heroic. Ep.* ii. 98 Thy Presence hath repaired in one day, What many Yeeres with Sorrowes did decay. **1611** SHAKS. *Cymb.* II. ii. 14 Mans ore-labor'd sense Repaires it selfe by rest. **1671** MILTON *Samson* 665 Secret refreshings, that repair his strength. **1712–14** POPE *Rape Lock* I. 141 The fair..Repairs her smiles, awakens ev'ry grace. **1789** MRS. PIOZZI *Journ. France* I. 29 The Baths..will, I hope, repair my strength. **1871** PALGRAVE *Lyr. Poems* 95 O love that cannot be repair'd Whate'er the future bring!

absol. **1590** SPENSER *F.Q.* I. vii. 41 'Flesh may empaire', (quoth he) 'but reason can repaire'.

†**c.** To make up (a sum) again. *Obs. rare*$^{-1}$.

1486 *Lichfield Gild. Ord.* (E.E.T.S.) 22 Willing to fulfill, renew, and make hoole the seid summe off xl li. [*marg.* the hole summe of xl li repared.]

†**d.** To revive, recreate (a person). *Obs.*

1591 SHAKS. *Two Gent.* v. iv. 11 Repaire me, with thy presence, Siluia: Thou gentle Nimph, cherish thy for-lorne swaine. **1601** —— *All's Well* I. ii. 30 It much repaires me To talke of your good father.

†**4.** To restore (a person) to a previous state; to reinstate, re-establish, rehabilitate. *Obs.*

1535 COVERDALE *Jer.* xxxi. 4, I wil repayre the agayne (o thou doughter of Israel) that thou mayest be fast and sure. **1646** E. F[ISHER] *Marrow Mod. Divin.* (ed. 2) 25 Such a..person that had..compassion toward man that he might be repaired. **1693** J. EDWARDS *Author. O. & N. Test.* 124 Prometheus is said to have repaired and restored mankind. **1738** WESLEY *Ps.* LI. xix, Then hear the contrite Sinner's Prayer, And every ruin'd Soul repair.

refl. **1614** RALEIGH *Hist. World* II. IV. iv. §4. 207 To repaire himselfe he could finde no way safer, than to put all to aduenture.

†**b.** To remedy, right, or compensate (one). *Obs.*

a **1578** LINDESAY (Pitscottie) *Chron. Scot.* (S.T.S.) I. 129 To be revengit or ellis repairit of all oppressiouns and iniurieis committit. **1647** MAY *Hist. Parl.* II. iii. 52 He accounts himself injured by the Parliament, in not repairing him against Hotham. **1691** BETHEL *Providences of God* (1697) 141, I had great Misfortunes, and..this was a ready way to repair me.

†**c.** *refl.* To recoup (oneself). *Obs. rare.*

1656 EARL MONM. tr. *Boccalini's Advts. fr. Parnass.* I. xc. (1674) 124 The Prince should pay his forfeiture,..of whom he might at his leisure repair himself. *a* **1661** FULLER *Worthies, Cheshire* (1662) 289 He repaired himself by a gainfull composition with the Indians, for the losses he had sustained by the Turkes.

†**d.** To save, deliver *from* something. *Obs.*$^{-1}$

1594 SOUTHWELL *M. Magd. Funerall Teares* (1609) 46 Could thy loue repaire thee from his rage?

5. To remedy, make up (loss, damage, etc.); to set right again.

1533 BELLENDEN *Livy* v. (S.T.S.) II. 231 To repare þe dammaige þat Is hapnit be publict birning. **1601** R. JOHNSON *Kingd. & Commw.* (1603) 93 That losse is not yet repaired, the Emperor not hauing at this time above 5 gallies. **1605** SHAKS. *Lear* IV. i. 79 Ile repayre the misery thou do'st beare With something rich about me. **1667** MILTON *P.L.* VII. 152, I can repaire That detriment. *c* **1710** CELIA FIENNES *Diary* (1888) 128 The one good yeare sufficiently repaires their loss. **1757** BURKE *Abridgm. Eng. Hist.* Wks. X. 168 The Gauls..were altogether unskilful either in improving their victories, or repairing their defeats. **1831–3** E. BURTON *Eccl. Hist.* xii. (1845) 281 They..made Christ..to have been sent into the world to repair the evil, which the Demiurgus had caused. **1849** MACAULAY *Hist. Eng.* vi. II. 67 James..said, with some truth, that the loss of such a man could not be easily repaired.

b. To make good, make up for, make amends for (harm done, etc.).

1562 *Reg. Privy Council Scot.* I. 227 Knawing that the actioun and caus laid to thair charge..is sensyne repairit, dressit and aggreit. **1596** DALRYMPLE tr. *Leslie's Hist. Scot.* I. 123 The rest of the beistes..hald besyd the, in thy power, ay quhil thair maistir repair the skath. **1725** POPE *Odyss.* VIII. 432 A gen'rous heart repairs a sland'rous tongue. **1781** GIBBON *Decl. & F.* xxi. II. 263 The emperor seemed impatient to repair his injustice. **1853** LYTTON *My Novel* VIII. ii, I wish to repair to you any wrong, real or supposed, I may have done you in past times.

c. *intr.* To make reparation *for* something.

1886 FARGUS *Living or Dead* II. 93, I..endeavoured by the warmth of my waved adieu to repair for my show of annoyance.

†**6.** To set straight, make exact. *Obs. rare*$^{-1}$.

1691 T. H[ALE] *Acc. New Invent.* 124 All the forementioned Incurvations are to be trimmed and repaired by reconciled lines.

†**7.** *intr.* To reform. *Obs. rare*$^{-1}$.

1748 RICHARDSON *Clarissa* ci. VII. 399 Marry and repair, at any time; This, wretch that I was! was my plea to myself.

repairability (rɪˌpɛərəˈbɪlɪtɪ). [f. REPAIRABLE *a.* + -ITY: cf. REPARABILITY.] The state or quality of being repairable.

1969 *Jane's Freight Containers 1968–69* 464/1 The ship lines are worried about repairability, particularly in foreign ports.

repairable (rɪˈpɛərəb(ə)l), *a.* [f. REPAIR *v.*^{2} + -ABLE: cf. REPARABLE *a.*] Capable of being repaired; also, that falls to be repaired.

1489 CAXTON *Faytes of A.* I. i. 9 Ther is no faulte made in ony caas lasse repayrable than that whiche is executed by armes. **1598** FLORIO, *Riparabile*, that may be repaired,..repaireable. **1626** BACON *Sylva* §58 The parts in Mans body easily repairable (as Spirits, Blood, and Flesh) die in the embracement of the parts hardly repairable, (as Bones, Nerves, and Membranes). **1691** T. H[ALE] *Acc. New Invent.* p. ci, If a new greater breach came, perhaps it would not be repairable. **1766** ENTICK *London* IV. 9 Part of the nave also being found repairable. **1805** LD. COLLINGWOOD in A. Duncan *Nelson* (1806) 272 Not more than three are in a repairable state. **1884** *Law Rep. 12 Q.B. Div.* 143 The street was a highway repairable by the inhabitants at large. **1890** [see ADOPTION 2 d]. **1936** [see AMENITY 1 a, 3 b]. **1950** [see DILLY *sb.*^{5}]. **1972** *Police Rev.* 10 Nov. 1447/1 There is a reasonable chance that the tyre will be repairable. **1976** *Sci. Amer.* Sept. 73/1 The Shuttle will also provide new capabilities in hauling multiple satellites in a single mission ..performing in-orbit servicing and returning repairable systems.

reˈpairableness. [f. REPAIRABLE *a.* + -NESS.] Capacity for being repaired.

1909 *Daily Chron.* 21 Aug. 6/6 The [hosepipe] tyre succumbed to the superior repairableness of the detachable.

repaired (rɪˈpɛəd), *ppl. a.* [f. REPAIR *v.*^{2} + -ED^1.] Restored to proper condition, mended, etc. Also †*well repaired*, in good repair.

1470–85 MALORY *Arthur* x. ix. 427 They came in to a fayr courte wel repayred. *a* **1547** SURREY in *Tottel's Misc.* (Arb.) 4 The fishes flote with new repaired scale. *a* **1600** HOOKER *Eccl. Pol.* VI. iii. §2 That saving power, which maketh man a repaired Temple for God's good Spirit again to inhabit. **1822** SCOTT *Nigel* ii, His under garments, the looped and repaired wretchedness of which moved at once pity and laughter. **1897** *Daily News* 12 Feb. 9/3 The ring appeared at the repaired parts very common.

reˈpairer^1. *rare.* [f. REPAIR *v.*^{1} + -ER^1.] One who goes or resorts (*to* a place).

1581 MULCASTER *Positions* xxxix. (1887) 215 For reparers from forreine countries into his, whom he will haue well entertained. **1598** STOW *Surv.* x. (1603) 85 The inhabitants and repayrers to this Citie. **1615** HIERON *Wks.* I. 632 Art thou..a reuerent and often repairer to Gods board?

repairer^2 (rɪˈpɛərə(r)). [f. REPAIR *v.*^{2} + -ER^1.] One who or that which restores or mends.

1504 LADY MARGARET tr. *De Imitatione* IV. iv. 266 The defender of my soule and the repayrer of the weykenesse of man. **1513** DOUGLAS *Æneis* XII. Prol. 260 Welcum reparar of woddis, treis, and bewis. *c* **1557** ABP. PARKER *Psalter* Collect 377 The repayrer, upholder and builder of all mansions. **1605** TIMME *Quersit.* II. ii. 110 This vital heate..is the repairer and conseruer of life. **1691–8** NORRIS *Pract. Disc.* (1711) III. 198 He who was to be..the Repairer and Restorer of Human Nature. **1730** A. GORDON *Maffei's Amphith.* 308 The Steps, by the Fault of the Repairers, are hampered at present. **1761** *Misc.* in *Ann. Reg.* 199/1 There is an inferior sort of repairers of wrongs, and reformers of abuses. **1826** SOUTHEY in *Q.R.* XXXIV. 308 He was a great repairer of churches and steeples. **1899** *Fortn. Rev.* Jan. 116 The repairer..alleged that the steel was inferior.

reˈpairing, *vbl. sb.*^{1} *rare.* [f. REPAIR *v.*^{1} + -ING^1.] The fact of going or resorting (*to* a place); †return; †place of repair or resort.

1375 BARBOUR *Bruce* IV. 495 Heir I saw the men..mak luging, Heir trow I be thair reparyng. *c* **1400** *Beryn* 2814 For, when he was go, They had no maner ioy;..For of his repeyryng they had no sikernes. **1632** LITHGOW *Trav.* x. 492 In my repayring diuerse times to the Roade..with my Squadron. **1703** *Lond. Gaz.* No. 3880/1 The exact time of their Repairing respectively on Board.

repairing (rɪˈpɛərɪŋ), *vbl. sb.*^{2} [f. REPAIR *v.*^{2} + -ING^1.]

1. a. The (*or* an) action or process of restoring or mending; reparation, repair.

1387 TREVISA *Higden* (Rolls) V. 129 At þe repayrynge of Seynt Petres chirche he wente to wiþ a mattok, and opened first þe erþe. **1486** *Rec. St. Mary at Hill* 18 The repayryng & renewyng of the vestymentes & Ornamentes belongyng to the awter. **1535** COVERDALE *2 Chron.* xxiv. 13 Yᵉ repairinge in yᵉ worke went forwarde thorow their hande. **1583** STUBBES *Anat. Abus.* II. (1882) 38 A paire of shooes..would haue serued a man almost a whole yeere togither, with a little repairing. **1631** WEEVER *Anc. Funeral Mon.* 565 In all his new buildings or repairings, hee caused the pictures of a Lambe and an Eagle to be thereupon drawne or depicted. **1691** T. H[ALE] *Acc. New Invent.* 28 Their Ransackings, Groundings, Dockings, and Repairings. **1730** A. GORDON *Maffei's Amphith.* 43 This Repairing of it was not perfected by Heliogabalus. **1790** BEATSON *Nav. & Mil. Mem.* I. 58 The repairing of their fleet took them up a considerable time. **1863** H. COX *Instit.* III. viii. 721 The Commissioners are empowered to order the repairing of ships.

†**b.** *spec.* (See quot.) *Obs. rare*$^{-1}$.

1688 R. HOLME *Armoury* III. 259/2 Repairing is to take away the Superfluities of Sodering by Filing, &c.

2. *attrib.* as ***repairing lease, shop, yard.***

1831 A. A. WATTS *Scenes of Life* I. 196 Our tenure was a 'repairing lease'. **1862** *Catal. Internat. Exhib.* II. x. 9 The workshops and repairing-yard. **1863** P. BARRY *Dockyard Econ.* 199 France has no such collection of engine and repairing shops as are to be seen on the Thames. **1935** E. FARJEON *Nursery in Nineties* 522 The house..was on a repairing lease, and some hundreds of pounds were demanded if we left at once. **1972** C. DRUMMOND *Death at Bar* ii. 45 The house agent..rubbed his hands at the prospect of getting some free work done on the place for it was not a repairing lease.

So **reˈpairing** *ppl. a.*

1593 SHAKS. *2 Hen. VI*, v. iii. 22 'Tis not enough our foes are this time fled, Being opposites of such repayring Nature. **1647** CLARENDON *Contempl. on Ps.* Tracts (1727) 505 There is a comforting, relieving, and repairing tongue, as well as a destroying and a devouring tongue.

†**reˈpairment.** *Obs. rare*$^{-1}$. [ad. OF. *repairement*: see REPAIR *v.*^{2} and -MENT.] A renewal.

c **1400** *Lanfranc's Cirurg.* 49 Do þat pece awey & regenere in þe place of þe boon þat was lost a repeirement.

reˈpale (riː-), *v.* [f. RE- 5 a + PALE *v.*^{1}] *trans.* To provide with a new paling.

1667 DUCHESS NEWCASTLE *Life Dk. of N.* (1886) II. 136 He..gave present order for the cutting down of some wood that was left him in a place near adjoining, to repale it.

†**reˈpall,** *v. Obs. rare*$^{-1}$. [f. RE- 5 a + PALL *v.*^{1}] *trans.* To appal, terrify.

1600 FAIRFAX *Tasso* v. xc, Shall vain Reports repall your Courage bold?

†**repalliˈation.** *Obs. rare*$^{-1}$. [RE- 5 a.] ? The result of cloaking or covering up again.

1614 JACKSON *Creed* III. xxxii. §10 Discouering the enemies weakenesse in his new Fortifications, or Repalliations rather of such breaches.

repand (rɪˈpænd), *a.* [ad. L. *repandus* bent backwards, turned up, f. *re-* RE- + *pandus* bent.] *Bot.* and *Zool.* Having an undulating margin, wavy.

1760 J. LEE *Introd. Bot.* III. v. (1765) 181 *Repand*, bending back again; when the Margin is terminated with Angles and interjacent Sinusses, that are both inscribed with the Segments of Circles. **1785** MARTYN *Rousseau's Bot.* xxv. (1794) 374 The leaves also are repand or waved on their edges. **1826** KIRBY & SP. *Entomol.* xlvi. IV. 297 *Repand*, cut into very slight sinuations, so as to run in a serpentine direction. **1845** LINDLEY *Sch. Bot.* vi. (1858) 100 Leaves ovate-acuminate, somewhat repand or sinuated. **1881** *Gard.*

Chron. XVI. 784 It has probably been confounded with Lactarius pyrogatus, but is abundantly different in the larger stature, repand pileus [etc.].

Comb. **1846** DANA *Zooph.* (1848) 295 Teeth short.., often repand-dentate. *Ibid.* 296 The lamellæ are neatly repand-toothed. **1870** HOOKER *Stud. Flora* 294 Leaves repand-crenate.

So †**re'panded** *a. Obs.*

1753 CHAMBERS *Cycl. Supp.* s.v. *Leaf*, Repanded Leaf,.. a leaf, the border of which is marked all round with short lobes, each making a segment of a circle. **1760** P. MILLER *Introd. Bot.* 26 A repanded leaf..is one whose border is indented the whole length [etc.].

re'pandly, *adv. rare.* [f. REPAND *a.* + -LY[2].] In a repand manner.

1852 GRAY in *Smithsonian Contrib. Knowl.* V. vi. 91 The leaves are pale.., thickish in texture,..repandly and sometimes strongly dentate.

re'pando-, combining form of REPAND *a.*, as in ***repando-dentate, -lobate***, etc.

1847 W. E. STEELE *Field Bot.* 128 Leaves lanceolate, repando-denticulate, wavy. *Ibid.* 151 Leaves obovate, repando-dentate, rugose. **1887** W. PHILLIPS *Brit. Discomycetes* 160 Margin deflexed, frequently repando-lobate.

†**re'pandous,** *a. Obs.* [f. as REPAND *a.* + -OUS.] Bent upward or outward.

1646 SIR T. BROWNE *Pseud. Ep.* v. ii. 235 Though they be drawne repandous, or convexedly crooked in one piece, yet the Dolphin that carrieth Arion is concavously inverted. **1654** H. L'ESTRANGE *Chas. I* (1655) 1 He was exceeding feeble in his lower parts, his legs growing not erect, but repandous and embowed. *a* **1682** SIR T. BROWNE *Misc. Tracts* (1684) 20 Round at the bottom, and somewhat repandous, or inverted at the top.

Hence †**re'pandousness,** 'bentness or bowingness backwards' (BAILEY vol. II, 1727). *Obs.*[−0]

re'paper (ri:-), *v.* [RE- 5 a.] *trans.* To paper (a room, etc.) again. Also *absol.* Hence **re'papering** *vbl. sb.*

1854 MRS. GASKELL *North & South* (1855) I. vii. 96 The landlord..had relented from his expressed determination not to repaper. **1857** —— *Life Charlotte Brontë* II. xiii. 313 Some re-papering and re-painting in the Parsonage. **1863** *Sat. Rev.* 17 Jan. 77/2 If it is clearly necessary to repaper the house, we may just as well have the ceilings whitewashed at the same time. **1887** G. R. SIMS *Mary Jane's Mem.* 114 He wouldn't have the wall repapered. **1964** L. DEIGHTON *Funeral in Berlin* xxxvi. 207, I scarcely recognized the office. It had been re-papered. **1974** —— *Spy Story* xiv. 134 You said repapering the sitting-room would be for my birthday.

†**re'par,** *v. Obs. rare*[−1]. [app. f. *re-* RE- + PAR *v.*[1]] *trans.* To shut off, keep back.

13.. *E.E. Allit. P.* A. 611 To hym þat mas in synne no scoghe No blysse bes fro hem reparde.

,repara'bility. [See next and -ITY.] The state or quality of being reparable (Ogilvie 1882).

reparable ('rɛpərəb(ə)l), *a.* [a. F. *reparable* (16th c.), ad. L. *reparābilis*: see REPAIR *v.* and -ABLE. Cf. It. *riparabile*, Sp. *reparable*.]

1. Capable of being repaired, mended, or set right again: **a.** of things. Now *rare.*

1570 LEVINS *Manip.* 4/12 Reparable, *reparabilis.* *a* **1630** EARL PEMBROKE *Poems* (1660) 95 Love grants me then a reparable face, Which, whilst that colours are, can want no grace. **1657–83** EVELYN *Hist. Relig.* (1850) II. 7 Their understandings weakened..reparable, in part only, by much study. **1809** *Naval Chron.* XXI. 332 Twenty reparable..spare wheels. [**1888** R. DOWLING *Miracle Gold* III. xxxvi. 163 'Your clock must have been a terrible loss, but not irreparable'. 'Do you mean that the clock is reparable?']

b. of injury, loss, etc.

1650 JER. TAYLOR *Holy Living* III. iv. §9 An adulterous person is tyed to restitution of the injury, so far as it is reparable. **1779** BURKE *Corr.* (1844) III. 534 The loss of friends (at no time very reparable) is impossible to be repaired at all, at this advanced period. **1824** LANDOR *Imag. Conv., Demosthenes & Eubulides* Wks. 1853 I. 86/2 The mischief is transitory and reparable. **1884** *American* VIII. 356 They inflicted only slight and reparable injuries on those fortresses.

2. Falling to be repaired *by* some one.

1864 R. A. ARNOLD *Cotton Fam.* 438 A vast number of new streets..had not yet been declared public and reparable by the local authorities. **1885** *Law Times* LXXVIII. 299/1 The road should..be declared a highway reparable by the inhabitants at large.

†**3.** Capable of repeating. *Obs. rare.*

After L. *reparabilis echo*, Persius *Sat.* i. 102.

1616–61 HOLYDAY *Persius* (1673) 297 Mœnas..oft did 'Evion' sound; The reparable eccho did rebound. **1624** *Trag. Nero* II. ii. in Bullen *O. Pl.* I. 35 As when the Menades ..Evion do Ingeminate around, Which reparable Eccho doth resound.

Hence '**reparably** *adv.* (Johnson 1755).

reparail(e, -al(e, varr. REPAREL *v. Obs.*

†'**reparate,** *ppl. a. Obs. rare*[−1]. [ad. L. *reparātus*, pa. pple. of *reparāre* to REPAIR.] Repaired.

c **1510** BARCLAY *Mirr. Gd. Manners* (1570) D v, This life is resembled [to] a building ruinate, Nowe shaked with the winde, agayne now reparate.

reparation (rɛpə'reɪʃən). Also 4–7 reparacion, 4 -cyoun, 5 -cioun, 5–6 -cyon; 6 raperecioun, **reperacion, -cyon.** [a. OF. *reparacion* (14th c.; mod.F. *reparation*), ad. L. *reparātiōn-em*, n. of action f. *reparāre* to REPAIR.]

†**1.** A reconciliation. *Obs. rare*[−1].

c **1384** CHAUCER *H. Fame* II. 180 Mo discordes and mo Ielousies,..And moo dissimulacions And feyned reparacions.

2. The action of restoring to a proper state; restoration or renewal (*of* a thing or part); †upholding, maintenance.

1389 in *Eng. Gilds* (1870) 63 He schal payyn, to y[e] reparacion of y[e] lythe, [half a pound of] wax. *c* **1425** *Found. St. Bartholomew's* (E.E.T.S.) 35 Sum man ioyed..for reparacioun of his goyng that he lackyd. **1586** HOOKER *Disc. Justification* Wks. 1888 III. 489 Holy water,..papal salutations, and such like, which serve for reparations of grace decayed. **1605** TIMME *Quersit.* I. xvii. 88 Life..is also conserued by the reparation of natural moysture. **1633** T. ADAMS *Exp. 2 Peter* i. 4 This communication of the Divine nature to us, is by reparation of the Divine image in us. **1659** PEARSON *Creed* (1839) 203 The satisfaction consisteth in a reparation of that honour which by the injury was eclipsed. **1731** ARBUTHNOT *Aliments* (1735) 40 The Fluids and Solids of an Animal Body demand a constant Reparation. **1791** MRS. RADCLIFFE *Rom. Forest* i, To attempt schemes for the reparation of his fortune. **1828** SCOTT *F.M. Perth* xi, You owe me something for reparation of honour. **1888** ROLLESTON & JACKSON *Forms Anim. Life* 608 The Chætopoda appear to have considerable powers of reparation after injury, and the formation of a new head.. has been observed.

†**b.** Spiritual restoration, salvation; also, an instance of this. *Obs.*

1447 BOKENHAM *Seyntys* (Roxb.) 46 In ye ordyr of oure reparacyon Descens it to jacob toknyng supplantacyon. **1560** BECON *New Catech.* Wks. 1564 I. 436 b, Whether it be his..reparation, iustification, glorification, &c., it cometh altogether of the fre grace of god. **1587** GOLDING *De Mornay* Ep. Ded., Let us..busie our selues in the vniuersall table of mans saluation and reparation. *a* **1667** COWLEY *Verses on Virgin* Wks. 1711 III. 54 The Choir of blessed Angels.. wish'd a Reparation to see By him, who Manhood join'd with Deity. **1699** BURNET *39 Art.* ix. 109 This is the Universal Redemption and Reparation that all mankind shall have in Christ Jesus. **1725** tr. *Dupin's Eccl. Hist. 17th C.* I. vi. iii. 247 He speaks at large of our Reparation by Jesus Christ.

†**c.** The restoration of a person. *Obs. rare*[−1].

a **1652** BROME *Love-sick Court* v. iii, Could grief recal Philargus, we would weep A second deluge for his reparation.

3. a. The action of repairing or mending, or the fact of being repaired; repair of material things (as buildings or other structures) by renewal or refixing of decayed or damaged parts. (Now more usually expressed by REPAIR *sb.*[2] 1 b.)

c **1400** MAUNDEV. (1839) xvi. 174 Whan the Mynystres of that Chirche neden to maken ony reparacyoun of the Chirche. **1432–50** tr. *Higden* (Rolls) IV. 231 Herodes.. namede Ascolonita for the reparacion of a cite callede Ascalon. **1495** *Naval Acc. Hen. VII* (1896) 207 Reparacion and Amendyng of certeyne Takle. **1523** FITZHERB. *Husb.* §5 This wayne is made of dyuers peces, that wyll haue a greate reparation. **1541** *Act 33 Hen. VIII*, c. 35 The reparacion and amendment of any the pypes of leade hereafter..broken. **1596** BACON *Max. & Use Com. Law* I. iv. (1636) 23 Stone towards the reparation of such a Castle. **1633** G. HERBERT *Temple, Providence* xxxi, Thorns..make A better hedge, and need lesse reparation. **1665–6** *Phil. Trans.* I. 24 The mines need continual reparation, the Fir-trees lasting but a small time under ground. **1710** *Lond. Gaz.* No. 4643/4 [She] may be fitted to Sea with a moderate Reparation. **1752** JOHNSON *Rambler* No. 192 ¶2 At last the old hall was pulled down to spare the cost of reparation. **1790** BURKE *Fr. Rev.* Wks. V. 436, I would make the reparation as nearly as possible in the style of the building. **1812** SIR J. SINCLAIR *Syst. Husb. Scot.* I. 74 Unless machines are of a strong and powerful construction, they..require perpetual reparation. **1867** FREEMAN *Norm. Conq.* (1877) I. App. 648 The original charter records the reparation of the church.

†**b.** ***in, out of* (..) *reparation,*** in or out of repair or good condition. *Obs.*

1567 in Picton *L'pool Munic. Rec.* (1883) I. 119 Kept in due reparation. **1601** CHESTER *Love's Mart., Dial.* (1878) 26 The newly-builded Minster, Still kept in notable reparation. **1602** MARSTON *Ant. & Mel.* II. Wks. 1856 I. 27 And 'twere not for printing, and painting, My breech and your face would be out of reparation. **1663** GERBIER *Counsel* 92 They..maintain it durable for twenty one years long, in reparation at a yearly small rate.

†**c.** *Sc.* Furniture, furnishings. *Obs. rare*[−1].

1566 KNOX *Hist. Ref.* Wks. 1846 I. 360 The townis..culd nocht be satisfeit, till that the hole repairatioun and ornamentis of the Churche (as thay terme it) war distroyed.

4. a. *pl.* Repairs. Now somewhat *rare.* †Also, in early use, sums spent on repairs.

1439 *E.E. Wills* (1882) 123 The profitz ther-of comyng in the mene tyme, ouer reparacions & expenses, to be keppid to his profite. **1459** *Paston Lett.* I. 447 For the sustentacion of the seyd priour..and for here othyr chargys and reparacionis. **1479** *Bury Wills* (Camden) 51 All reparacyonys of hegges and houses. **1523** LD. BERNERS *Froiss.* I. xlvii. 68 They..bete downe the castell, and bare all the stones into their towne to make reparacyons withall. **1551** ROBINSON tr. *More's Utop.* II. (1895) 150 Their houses continewe and laste very longe with litle labour and small reparacions. **1601** HOLLAND *Pliny* II. 579 One Circamnos.. made some small reparations here about this Labyrinth. **1647** N. BACON *Disc. Govt. Eng.* I. lxvi. (1739) 146 Reparations and adorning of Churches, and Fences of Church-yards. **1656** H. PHILLIPS *Purch. Patt.* (1676) B iij b, Many Tenants would neglect these reasonable and necessary Reparations. **1712** ARBUTHNOT *J. Bull* IV. vi, Do you consider..the expenses of reparations and servants? **1733** NEAL *Hist. Purit.* II. 226 The like reparations of paintings, pictures, and crucifixes were made in the King's chapel at Whitehall. **1775** *Sterne's Sent. Journ.* III. *Contin.* 198 It was written..upon a piece of paper that required some reparations to make it legible. **1818** CRUISE *Digest* (ed. 2) I. 119 He cut them down, and kept them to be used in reparations. **1838** THIRLWALL *Greece* IV. 101 The image of the tutelary goddess was annually stript of its ornaments for the sake of the needful reparations and ablutions.

†**b.** ***in, out of* (..) *reparations.*** = 3 b. *Obs.*

1554 BONNER in Strype *Eccl. Mem.* (1721) III. App. xvi. 41 Whether such as have churches..do kepe their chauncels and houses in good and sufficyent reparacyons. **1563** *Homilies* II. *Repairing Churches* (1859) 276 If his barn..be out of reparations, what diligence useth he to make it in perfect state again. **1588** GREENE *Perimedes* 22 Taking the tongs in hir hand, to keepe the fire in reparations. **1614** RICH *Honest. Age* (1844) 30 The world..is..growne so far out of reparations, that (I thinke) there is no hope of amendment. **1628** COKE *On Litt.* 215 b, Keeping the houses in reparations.

†**c.** ***to keep the reparations,*** to make the necessary repairs.

1577 B. GOOGE *Heresbach's Husb.* I. (1586) 47 b, As long as he payes his rent, and keepes the reparations, it shall not be lawfull to deceiue him. **1591** *Child-Marriages* 144 He was not hable to kepe the reparacions of the said walles.

5. a. The action of making amends for a wrong done; amends; compensation. Also const. *for, of.*

1418 HEN. V in *Proc. Privy Council* (1834) II. 244 For defaulte of reparacioun and restitucion of suche attemptates as be made by certein of oure subgettes. **1487** in *Surrey Archæol. Collect.* III. 163, I will that..reparation be done for any wrong committed by me. **1602** T. FITZHERBERT *Apol.* 4 Their meaning was no other, but only to seek reparation of wrongs done vnto them. **1647** CLARENDON *Hist. Reb.* I. §11 It is thought but a just Reparation for the Reproach that he deserved not, to Free him from the Censure he deserved. **1685** BAXTER *Paraphr. N.T.* Matt. v. 25 If thou have wronged any man, delay not reparation of his wrong. **1706–7** FARQUHAR *Beaux' Strat.* II. i, You were very naught last Night, and must make your Wife Reparation. **1788** REID *Active Powers* v. v. 660 When war is taken for self defence, or for reparation of intolerable injuries, justice authorizes it. **1824** LANDOR *Imag. Conv., P. Leopold & Pres. Du Paty*, The lower courts [of justice], in which the slowness of reparation is the thing most complained of. **1849** MACAULAY *Hist. Eng.* iv. I. 522 The Roman Catholics were in no condition to demand reparation for injustice. **1877** FROUDE *Short Stud.* (1883) IV. I. iii. 33 He..professed himself willing to make reasonable reparation.

pl. **1645** MILTON *Tetrach.* Introd., To defend my self publicly against a printed Calumny..can be no immoderate ..course of seeking so just and needfull reparations.

†**b.** Compensation *for*, remedying *of*, some loss.

1668 CLARENDON *Contempl. Ps.* Tracts (1727) 560 Health is a valuable Reparation for the Diminution of Plenty. **1734** tr. *Rollin's Anc. Hist.* XVII. (1827) VII. 356 Who contributed to the reparation of the losses.

c. Repair of an injury.

1836–9 *Todd's Cycl. Anat.* II. 803/1 Nature had not made the slightest attempt at reparation [of the fracture]. **1881** *Amer. Naturalist* Sept. 709 [It] showed signs of reparation in three days, and in six weeks the injury was completely repaired.

d. *pl.* Compensation for war damage owed by the aggressor.

In the *Treaty of Peace* (1919) the English heading of Part VIII is 'Reparation', but the French is 'Réparations'.

1921 *Glasgow Herald* 28 Oct. 11 The mere purchase of foreign securities to meet reparations..simply means the transference of worthless papers from one body of financiers to another. **1931** F. L. ALLEN *Only Yesterday* ii. 24 Lodge ..wanted Germany to be disarmed, saddled with a terrific bill for reparations, and if possible dismembered. **1947** *Sun* (Baltimore) 2 Apr. 10/2 Reparations to Russia must be paid out of current German production. **1976** C. BERMANT *Coming Home* II. v. 184 Israel..partly with the help of German reparations..was experiencing something of an economic miracle.

†**6.** A preparation for repairing the complexion. *Obs. rare*[−1].

1706 *Closet of Rarities* (Nares), The closet of beauty, or modest instructions for..making..pomatums, reparations, musk-balls [etc.].

7. ***attrib.***, as †***reparation nail, noble*** (see quots.); ***reparation money, payment***, etc.

The sing. and the pl. forms are both found.

1657 *MS. Acc. St. John's Hosp., Canterb.*, This day Margarett Whitmore was admitted an outsister, and paid her reparacon Noble. **1703** MOXON *Mech. Exerc.* 244 Reparation or Lath Nails, which are used for plain Tile Lathing. **1919** J. M. KEYNES *Econ. Conseq. Peace* v. 139 The endless controversy and intrigue between the Allies themselves..culminated in the presentation to Germany of the Reparation Chapter in its final form. **1919** *Treaty of Peace* VIII. Art. 234 The Reparation Commission shall after May 1, 1921, from time to time, consider the resources and capacity of Germany. **1930** *Economist* 4 Jan. 11/2 The British delegation has left for the Hague to attend the resumed Reparations Conference. **1931** *Times Lit. Suppl.* 24 Sept. 717/3 The impossibility of real Reparations payments. **1968** *Tamarack Rev.* Spring 12 'We have restored Jewish pride.' 'By taking German reparation money?' **1977** *Time* 10 Jan. 46/1 More than $20 billion of foreign capital has poured in: mostly gifts from Jews abroad, reparations payments from West Germany and U.S. aid.

Hence †**repa'rationer,** one who repairs; †**repa'rationing,** the act of repairing. *Obs.*

1520 *MS. Acc. St. John's Hosp., Canterb.*, Paied to the ij Reparacioners for ther wagis iijs. vjd. **1536** *Ibid.*, Payd for reparacoening att Rollyng. **1547** *Richmond Wills* (Surtees) 65 Y[e] mendynge and reparacionynge off the hye ways. **1612** STURTEVANT *Metallica* (1855) 59 The repairationers, which maintain and mend the instruments.

reparative (rɪˈpærətɪv), *a.* and *sb.* [See prec. and -ATIVE.]

A. *adj.* **1.** Capable of effecting, or tending to effect, repair; relating to repair.

Common in recent use, esp. with *power* or *process*.

1656 *Artif. Handsom.* 60 These and the like reparative Inventions, by which art and ingenuity studies to help and repair the defects..which God..is pleased to inflict. **1768** [W. DONALDSON] *Life Sir B. Sapskull* I. ix. 99 The barber-surgeons (who in a reparative sense are face painters). **1835–6** *Todd's Cycl. Anat.* I. 448/1 There is scarcely an example..that did not exhibit a considerable display of reparative energy. **1854** OWEN *Skel. & Teeth* in *Orr's Circ. Sc., Organ. Nat.* I. 287 The portions..are soon replaced by the active reparative power of these highly vascular bodies. **1878** T. BRYANT *Pract. Surg.* I. 10 What influence the nerves of the part have upon the reparative process we do not know.

2. Pertaining to the making of amends, or to the remedying of some wrong.

a **1695** KETTLEWELL (J.), Suits are unlawfully entered, when they are vindictive, not reparative. **1795** tr. *Mercier's Fragm. Pol. & Hist.* II. 12 In all these reparative wars..the triumphant party has invariably justice on its side. **1875** POSTE *Gaius* II. §79 It is no bar to a reparative personal action against the thief. **1889** *Times* 31 Aug. 5/1 Having by reparative acts remedied the most pressing evils.

†**B.** *sb.* That which repairs; a reparation.

a **1639** WOTTON *Life Dk. Buckhm.* in *Reliq.* (1651) 112 Whereupon new preparatives were in hand, and partly reparatives of the former beaten at sea.

†**'reparator.** *Obs.* *rare*$^{-1}$. [a. L. *reparātor*, agent-n. f. *reparāre* to REPAIR. Cf. F. *réparateur*.] One who brings about reparation.

1701 NORRIS *Ideal World* I. vi. 355 It is evident that the Christian Religion which proposes to us Jesus Christ as a Mediator and reparator, supposes the corruption of nature by original sin.

re'paratory, *a. rare.* [See prec. and -ORY.] Repairing, reparative.

1852 *Fraser's Mag.* XLV. 325 Does there exist a reparatory reconstructive force to take its place? **1893** STEVENSON *Vailima Lett.* (1895) xxxv. 313 We four begin to rouse up from reparatory slumbers.

†**re'paratrice.** *Obs.* *rare*$^{-1}$. [a. F. *réparatrice*.] A female restorer.

1402 HOCCLEVE *Letter of Cupid* 403 God..of our lady, of lyfe reparatrice, Nolde han be born [etc.].

repare, obs. form of REPAIR.

†**re'parel,** *sb. Obs.* Forms: 5 **reperaylle,** 6 **reparell, -ill, reperell,** 6–7 **reparrel(l.** [f. the vb., or a. OF. *repareil* (Godef.).]

1. Fittings; furniture; apparel.

1466 in *Archaeologia* (1887) I. I. 35 And j nothir basyne of a lampe wᵗoute any Reperaylle ther for. **1517** *Knaresborough Wills* (Surtees) I. 6 The masse booke, portace, chales, vestementt, and all other reparell to oon preiste to say masse with. **1558–9** in *Yorks. Archæol. Jrnl.* LXVII. 366 My best doublet, and my best gowne, and all my other reperell. **1590** GREENE *Never too late* (1600) 98 Trick thy selfe vp in thy best reparell. **1611** BEAUM. & FL. *Knt. Burn. Pestle* Prol., Let them but lend him a suit of reparrel, and necessaries.

2. = REPAIR *sb.*^{2} 2 b.

1550 *Fabric Rolls York Minster* (Surtees) 274 The churche is owte of reparell, so that no man can well abyde in the bodie of the churche..when it is fowle wether.

†**re'parel,** *v. Obs.* Forms: 4–5 **reparail, -ayl,** (5 **-aill, -ayll),** 4 **repayral,** (5 **-yl),** 5–6 **reperal, -el, reparal** (6 *Sc.* **ra-), reparral, -el,** 4–6 **reparel.** (Also 4–6 **-all, -ell,** 5 **-ale, -elle, -yl.**) [ad. OF. *repareiller, -aillier* (14th c. in Godef.), f. *re-* RE- + *apareiller* to APPAREL.]

1. *trans.* To repair (a thing or structure). Also in *fig.* context (quot. *a* 1340).

a **1340** HAMPOLE *Psalter* ii. 9 þai sall be broken in hell, and neuere reparaild. **1388** WYCLIF *Ezek.* xxxvi. 10 Citees shulen be enhabitid, and ruynouse thingis shulen be reparelid. *c* **1400** MAUNDEV. (Roxb.) xi. 42 Adrian..reparailed þe citee of Ierusalem and restored þe temple. *c* **1450** *St. Cuthbert* (Surtees) 4293 þe walles of ȝorke þai reparald. **1490** in Stuart *Cov. Myst.* (1825) 33 These bene the Garments that wer new reparallyd ayaynste Corpus Christi daye. **1513** DOUGLAS *Æneis* IV. vii. 27 His navy lost reparalit I, but faill. **1523** FITZHERB. *Surv.* 39 b, The mylner shall..vpholde and reparell the spindell & the rynde..at his owne proper cost and charge. **1560** *Extr. Burgh Rec. Edinb.* (Rec. Soc.) III. 62 To reparrall the kirk,..mend the glasen wyndokis, and mak settis convenient.

2. To restore *to* some state or condition; to set right again; to recover. *rare.*

a **1340** HAMPOLE *Psalter* xxi. 24 All þat ere born til new life and reparaild til þe sight of god. *c* **1400** tr. *Secreta Secret., Gov. Lordsh.* 112 And make Mercury yn þe fferthe degree, & reparaill þe mone, ffor in holdyng of wayes it ys þe gretteste tokenyng vniuersele. **1435** MISYN *Fire of Love* 52 If þou will entyr to þe kyngdome lost & eft reparayld with cristis blode, þe behouys godis comamentis to kepe.

b. To repair, make good (a loss). *rare.*

c **1430** *Life St. Kath.* (1884) 58 We haue so greet an harm by los of oure wyf þat hit may not be repayreyled aȝeyn. **1450–1530** *Myrr. our Ladye* 175 Knowyng that the falle of theyr felowes shulde be reparelyd by our lady.

3. To devise, contrive. *rare*$^{-1}$.

1434 MISYN *Mending Life* 115 A Ml [= thousand] craftis of feyghtyng he reparells to kest hym from þe luf of god to þe lufe of þe warld.

b. To fit up, to array, to apparel. *rare.*

1501 DOUGLAS *Pal. Hon.* I. xxxiv, Reparrellit was that god-like plesand wone..In richest claith of gold. **1530** PALSGR. 686/2, I reparell, I clothe one, *je habille.* **1534–79** [see REPARELLING *vbl. sb.*].

Hence †**re'parelled** *ppl. a.*; also †**re'pareller,** a repairer. *Obs.*

c **1425** *St. Mary of Oignies* I. iii. in *Anglia* VIII. 136/34 Oure lorde..bihighte þat as reparelde matrymoyne he wolde gyue ageyne to hir in heuene hir felowe. **1546** *Yorks. Chantry Surv.* (Surtees) I. 22 A fre rent of the repareler of the said Bedern.

†**re'parelling,** *vbl. sb. Obs.* [f. prec. + -ING^{1}.] The action of repairing, restoring, fitting out, clothing, etc.; also *Sc.* furnishings, furniture.

a **1340** HAMPOLE *Psalter* ci. 19 Of destruccioun of adam and of reparaylynge thorgh crist. *c* **1400** MAUNDEV. (Roxb.) xix. 87 When þai hafe mister of any monee for reparailyng of þaire kirk. **1497** *Naval Acc. Hen. VII* (1896) 144 The fortyfying Reparalyng amendyng & fynyssyng of the dokke. **1534** in Noake's *Worcester Mon.* (1866) 192 For the rep[ar]ylyng and geryng of yᵉ fyve horses, xijs. **1559** in Knox *Hist. Ref.* Wks. 1846 I. 378 Casting down of kirkis, religious placis, or [the] reparrelling thairof. **1579** in W. H. Turner *Select. Rec. Oxford* (1880) 405 Mʳ Rychard Williams..gave iiijˡⁱ to the repareling of the poore in the almeshowse.

†**reparence.** *Obs.* *rare*$^{-1}$. [irreg. f. F. *reparer* + -ENCE.] Repair, restoration.

1556 *Aurelio & Isab.* H vj, You come to hus for to haue reparence [F. *reparement*] of youre lyfe, and it dothe you ill because that we haue assurede you from the deathe.

†**re'pariment.** *Obs.*$^{-1}$? = REPAIRMENT.

1584 R. WILSON *Three Ladies of London* I. in Hazl. *Dodsley* VI. 361 Must the countenance carry out the knave? Why, then, if one will face folks out, some fine repariment he must have.

†**re'part,** *v. Obs.* [ad. F. *répartir*, f. *re-* RE- + *partir* to PART.]

1. *trans.* To divide or distribute, esp. *among* or *to* a number of persons.

1574 HELLOWES *Gueuara's Fam. Ep.* (1577) 77 To giue the whole heart to one is not much, but howe much lesse, when amongst many it is reparted? **1598** BARRET *Theor. Warres* II. i. 17 He is to repart the victuals..with liberalitie and equalitie vnto euery Camarada. *Ibid.* 20 The..Romanes reparted the people of their Armies into Legions. **1629** J. M. tr. *Fonseca's Dev. Contempl.* 238 Whatsoeuer he gathered [of the manna] ouer and aboue, vnlesse he did repart the same vnto others, it stunke, and did rot and putrifie. **1663** GERBIER *Counsel* 13 The expert Surveyor will repart the Windows..that they may..leave a solid peeres between them. **1681** RYCAUT tr. *Gracian's Critick* 136 Reparting unto every one their peculiar Lessons and Places of Preferment. **1755** MAGENS *Insurances* I. 345 It was approved the same should be reparted as general Average on the Value of the 9600 Mks. given up at Hamburgh.

2. To say in reply. = REPARTEE *v.* 2. *rare*$^{-1}$.

1664 BULTEEL *Birinthea* 102 'Yes', reparted Panthea, 'I will not have you dye'.

3. (See quot.) *rare*$^{-0}$.

The Fr. phrase is *faire repartir un cheval* (see Littré).

1727 BAILEY (vol. II), To *Repart* (with Horsemen) is to put a Horse on, or to make him part the second Time.

Hence †**re'parting** *vbl. sb.*; also †**re'parter.**

1574 HELLOWES *Gueuara's Fam. Ep.* (1577) 152 Of the temporall goods that God giues us, we be not lords but reparters. *Ibid.* 442 Since the riches they onely must get, but the reparting therof is at the will of many. **1588** PARKE tr. *Mendoza's Hist. China* 46 In the meane time that these sixe men be occupied in the reparting of the men, the other sixe doe repart the women in three parts.

repar'take (riː-), *v.* [RE- 5 a.] *trans.* To partake (of) again.

1751 ELIZA HEYWOOD *Betsy Thoughtless* IV. 124 For the sake of re-partaking the remainder of those dainties, which had been so highly praised at dinner.

re'parted, *a. Her.* [RE- 5 a.] Of a shield: Parted a second time.

c **1828** BERRY *Encycl. Her.* I. Gloss., *Recouppé*, French term for reparted per fesse.

repartee (rɛpəˈtiː, rɛpɑː-), *sb.* Also 7 **reparty,** 7–8 **repartie;** 7 **reperte(e, rapartee.** [ad. F. *repartie*, fem. pa. pple. of *repartir* to start or set out again, to reply promptly, f. *re-* RE- + *partir* to PART.]

1. A ready, witty, or smart reply; a quick and clever retort.

c **1645** HOWELL *Lett.* I. I. xviii, He would passe by any thing with some repartie, som witty strain. **1664** DRYDEN *Rival Ladies* Ded., In the quickness of Reparties (which in Discoursive Scenes fall very often) it [rhyme] has so particular a Grace. **1672** VILLIERS (Dk. Buckhm.) *Rehearsal* III. i, First one speaks, then presently t'other's upon him slap, with a Rapartee. **1673** MARVELL *Reh. Transp.* II. 10 This reparty of Theodorus he recommends there for so ingenious. **1712** ADDISON *Spect.* No. 487 ¶4 The Grave abound in Pleasantries, the Dull in Repartees and Points of Wit. **1751** SMOLLETT *Per. Pic.* xxvii, His mistress looked a little disconcerted at this blunt repartee. **1839** HALLAM *Hist. Lit.* IV. vi. §17 The foolish alternation of repartees in a series of single lines will never be found in Racine. **1866** GEO. ELIOT *F. Holt* i, The smiling glances of pretty barmaids, and the repartees of jocose ostlers.

2. Without article: Sharpness or wit in sudden reply; such replies collectively; the practice or faculty of uttering them.

1668 DRYDEN *Even. Love* Pref., As for reparty in particular, as it is the very Soul of Conversation, so it is the greatest grace of Comedy. *a* **1704** T. BROWN *On the Beauties* Wks. 1730 I. 44 Unite two Stocks, to form the witty She, Dorinda's sense, and Flavia's repartee. **1765** GOLDSM. *Double Transf.* 40 Skill'd in no other arts was she, But dressing, patching and repartee. **1829** LYTTON *Devereux* I. iii, Nothing was so favourite a topic as the extent of my rudeness and the venom of my repartee. **1868** FARRAR *Seekers* II. v. (1875) 255 A power of swift repartee is necessary to him.

attrib. **1671** BUTLER *Rem.* (1759) I. 149 [To] speak by Repartee-rotines Out of the most authentic of Romances.

repartee (rɛpəˈtiː, rɛpɑː-), *v.* Also 7 **repartie, -ty, repertee.** [f. prec., or ad. F. *repartir.*]

1. a. *intr.* To make witty or smart replies. Also const. *to.* Now *rare.*

a **1668** DENHAM *Martial* Poems (1668) 80 If wise thou wilt appear, and knowing, Repartie, repartie To what I'm doing. **1676** D'URFEY *Mme. Fickle* IV. ii, I am not so old, but I can Repertee as well as another, if occasion serve. **1689** N. LEE *Princ. Cleve* I. ii, I know how to Repartee with the best. **1710** *Tatler* No. 242 ¶8 Replies, to which all the Malice in the World will not be able to repartee. *a* **1774** GOLDSM. tr. *Scarron's Com. Romance* (1775) II. 32 Perceiving that he has not reparteed to what she has advanced. **1838** *Fraser's Mag.* XVII. 120 He punned not..like Theodore Hook; nor reparteed like George Colman. **1910** G. B. SHAW *Let.* 9 Dec. (1972) II. 957, I spent an hour and a half shouting, bullying ..& reparteeing until I was as one in a Turkish bath.

†**b.** To retort *upon* a person. (Cf. next.) *Obs.*$^{-1}$

1687 SETTLE *Refl. Dryden* 85 Now to repartee upon him in his own beloved style.

†**2.** *trans.* To say by way of repartee or retort. Also const. *upon. Obs.*

1682 *Natural Hist. Coffee*, etc. 30 We cannot but Repartee upon these Alamode Persons, that while they Worship so much only Foreign Creatures, they cannot but be wholly ignorant of those at home. **1686** F. SPENCE tr. *Varillas' Ho. Medicis* 13 Farganaccio reparteed, that he was only his treasurer. *Ibid.* 299 Piero..cou'd not fail of repartying that when the French king was master of Naples [etc.].

†**3.** To answer (a person or something said) with a repartee or retort. *Obs. rare.*

1716 M. DAVIES *Athen. Brit.* II. 72 If Pits had been so Ironically against Bale, he had been deservedly reparteed with his Plagiary Shifts. **1743** G. CARLETON *Mem.* (1809) 29 A piece of raillery..which was as handsomely reparteed.

Hence **repar'teeing** *vbl. sb.*

1680 AUBREY *Lives* (1813) 545 He was incomparably readie at repartying and his witt most sparkling when most sett upon and provoked. **1760** STERNE *Tr. Shandy* III. Auth. Pref., There would be so much..scoffing and flouting, with raillying and reparteeing of it.

†**repartite,** *v. Obs. rare.* [Back-formation from next: cf. REPERTITE *v.*] *trans.* To distribute, place, allot.

1630 LD. DORCHESTER in Ellis *Orig. Lett.* Ser. II. III. 259 The place proves very aggreable to both their Majesties,..for conveniency of lodgings which are well repartited for both. **1642** *Sir E. Harwood's Advice* in *Harl. Misc.* (Malh.) V. 205 For maintenance whereof the charge once arrested, to repartite them on some revenue near adjoining.

repartition (riːpɑː-, rɛpəˈtɪʃən). [ad. L. type **repartitiōn-em*: see RE- and PARTITION *sb.*, and cf. F. *répartition* (1690).]

1. Partition, distribution, allotment (in former use *esp.* of troops or military quarters).

1555 EDEN *Decades* 240 The reparticion and diuision of the Indies and newe worlde betwene the Spanyardes and Portugales. **1598** BARRET *Theor. Warres* IV. iv. 111 Of this repartition he is to giue an order in writing vnto the Captaines of euerie Companie. **1611** G. BLUNDELL in *Buccleuch MSS.* (Hist. MSS. Comm.) 97 If it be possible to get my company upon that repartition, my mind would be very much quieted. **1692** *Lond. Gaz.* No. 2827/1 They..are not like to obtain any alteration in the Repartition that is made of the Winter quarters for the said Troops. **1732** SWIFT *Corr.* Wks. 1841 III. 668 The Irish were parcelled out among the many armies entertained by the French King... This repartition was very mortifying to them. **1755** MAGENS *Insurances* I. 69 This is the Sum, whereon the Repartition ought to be made; all the particular Goods bearing their neat Proportion. **1790** BURKE *Fr. Rev.* Wks. V. 219 No fair repartition of burthens upon all the orders could possibly restore them. **1848** *Tait's Mag.* XV. 828 Property and its follies,..its repartition in the hands of classes. **1861** MILL *Utilit.* v. 87 The standards of justice to which reference is made in discussing the repartition of taxation.

b. With *a* and *pl.* An instance of this.

1656 *North's Plutarch, Tamberlain* 45, I shall omit the several manners of repartitions of his Quarters. **1663** GERBIER *Counsel* 23 The good Surveyour doth contrive the repartitions of his ground-plot, so as most of the necessary Servants may be lodged in the first ground story. **1723** *Pres. St. Russia* I. 53 Each Governor makes Repartitions according to the Number of Farms in his Government. **1849** MILL *Ess.* (1859) II. 394 An adequate amount of the fruits of industry, combined with a just repartition of them. **1882** *Pall Mall G.* 13 Jan. 2/2 To regulate a just repartition of work and salary.

2. A fresh distribution or allotment.

1835 THIRLWALL *Greece* xi. II. 11 The dismemberment of a capital, and its repartition into a number of rural communities. **1861** G. SMITH *Irish Hist.* 25 There was nothing in Kentish gavelkind analogous to the Irish repartition.

re-par'tition (riː-), *v.* *rare*$^{-1}$. [RE- 5 a.] *trans.* To partition afresh.

1816 SOUTHEY in *Q. Rev.* XVI. 241 Witness Germany partitioned and re-partitioned, plundered, ravaged, and insulted.

re-par'titioned, *ppl. a.* [RE- 5 a.] That has been partitioned afresh.

1921 N. ANGELL *Fruits of Victory* iii. 100 The new states of repartitioned Europe seem..either unable or unwilling to help their neighbours.

†**re'partment.** *Obs. rare*$^{-1}$. [ad. Sp. *repartimiento*: see REPART *v.* and -MENT.] Distribution, division.

1574 HELLOWES *Gueuara's Fam. Ep.* (1577) 135 In these repartments of Epaminondas, it apperteyneth not vnto your honour and mee, that we come in a good houre.

reparty, obs. form of REPARTEE *sb.* and *v.*

†**re'pas.** *Sc. Obs. rare*$^{-1}$. [a. F. *repas*: see REPAST.] Repast.

1456 SIR G. HAYE *Law Arms* (S.T.S.) 250 Quhen the prophet was sa wayke that he mycht no mare travaill, he ete and drank his repas.

†**re'pass,** *sb. Obs.* [f. RE- + PASS *sb.*^{2}] The (*or* an) act of passing back again.

c **1557** ABP. PARKER *Ps.* lxxviii. 39 They were like wynde to gesse, that passth wythout repasse. **1607** NORDEN *Surv. Dial.* III. 97 Whether is it as conuenient for passe and repasse for cattle at one little gappe or two..? **1643** TRAPP *Comm., Gen.* iv. 7 The door is for continual pass and repass. **1683** O. U. *Parish Ch. no Conventicles* 14 That Superstition, which the Papists have..been charged with, in such needless Motions, Passes and Repasses.

repass (riː'pɑːs, -æ-), *v.*^{1} [ad. F. *repasser* (13th c.): see RE- + PASS *v.*]

1. *intr.* To pass again in the contrary direction; to return. Chiefly in ***pass and repass***.

1456 SIR G. HAYE *Law Arms* (S.T.S.) 178 Quhen he passis he suld nocht repas agayne till his hame. *c* **1500** *Melusine* 279 Yf there were but I & my peuple only, yet shuld none repasse of them homward. **1533** MORE *Apol.* iii. Wks. 848/1 Because they would..haue their false folies passe and re-passe all vnperceiued. **1562** LEIGH *Armorie* (1597) 40 Messengers..whose office is to passe and repasse on foote. **1600** FAIRFAX *Tasso* XVII. lxxii, But homewards they in armes againe repas. **1671** MRS. BEHN *Forc'd Marr.* I. i, I will pass and repass where and how I please. **1725** POPE *Odyss.* IV. 1094 Swift thro' the valves the visionary fair Repass'd. **1785** J. PHILLIPS *Treat. Inland Navig.* 25 A lawn terminated by water, with objects passing and repassing upon it. **1817** SHELLEY *Rev. Islam* III. xiv, The grate, as they departed to repass, With horrid clangour fell. **1885** *Law Rep. 15 Q.B. Div.* 316 A catch..at the end..which prevented the pin, when passed through a slit, from repassing.

b. To pass again *into* a previous state, *through* a place, etc.

1836–9 *Todd's Cycl. Anat.* II. 767/1 This animal awakes daily,..and re-passes into a state of sleep. **1871** DARWIN *Desc. Man* I. iv. (1890) 113 A man cannot prevent past impressions often repassing through his mind.

2. *trans.* To cross (the sea, a river, etc.) again in the contrary direction.

c **1500** *Melusine* 168 Yf it playse god none of them shal not repasse the see. **1593** SHAKS. *3 Hen. VI*, IV. vii. 5 Wel haue we pass'd, and now re-pass'd the Seas. **1652** COTTERELL tr. *Calprenède's Cassandra* II. 139 Some of them had already repast the Araxis. **1689** *Lond. Gaz.* No. 2494/3 They resolved to return, and had accordingly repassed the Lake. **1725** POPE *Odyss.* I. 378 Homeward with pious speed repass the main. **1776** GIBBON *Decl. & F.* viii. I. 214 In repassing the mountains, great numbers of soldiers perished. **1820** BYRON *Mar. Fal.* V. i. 31 That dread gulf which none repass.

b. To pass again over, through, or by (a way, gate, place, etc.); to go past again.

a **1618** RALEIGH (J.), We shall find small reason to think, that Abraham passed and repassed those ways more often than he was enforced so to do. **1689** *Lond. Gaz.* No. 2491/3 Having..posted themselves in a hollow way which the Enemy were to repass. **1748** THOMSON *Cast. Indol.* I. xxii, They found themselves within the cursed gate; Full hard to be repass'd. **1823** W. TAYLOR in *Monthly Rev.* C. 540 That feeble interest with which we repass a familiar road. **1838** *Penny Cycl.* XII. 303/2 Having a piece cut off..to allow the guard-pin to pass and repass the roller. **1898** WATTS-DUNTON *Aylwin* VI. i, I staggered away from him, and passed and repassed the spot many times.

c. To pass (one) again in a race.

1728 POPE *Dunc.* II. 107 Vig'rous he rises,..Re-passes Lintot, vindicates the race.

d. To pass over (a surface) again in painting.

1784 J. BARRY in *Lect. Paint.* vi. (1848) 215 In repassing those parts with the warm and more oleaginous colours.

3. To cause to pass again; to (†lead over, or) put *through* again.

1565 GOLDING *Cæsar* 164 When he had repassed his army, he cut of the bridge the length of cc. foote. **1613** SACKVILLE in *Guardian* No. 133 Drawing out my sword [I] re-passed it again through another place. **1692** BURNET *Past. Care* vii. 81 One cannot read them too often, nor repass them too frequently in his thoughts. **1701** NORRIS *Ideal World* I. viii. 449 Let him..quietly repass over in his thoughts what has been there discoursed. **1799** G. SMITH *Laboratory* II. 409 Then repass it through a fine linen bag. **1829** CARLYLE *Misc.* (1857) I. 277 Let the distiller pass it and repass it through his limbecs.

b. To pass (a bill, resolution, etc.) again.

1796 MORSE *Amer. Geog.* I. 560 No bill so returned shall become a law, unless it be repassed by two-thirds of both houses. **1812** *Chron.* in *Ann. Reg.* 50 The resolutions agreed to at the last Common Hall, every one of which was unanimously re-passed. **1869** *Spectator* 24 July 861/1 He himself..believed that Mr. Gladstone had repassed the preamble 'in order to give the House of Lords a slap in the face'.

4. *Conjuring.* (See PASS *v.* 6 and 25.)

1589 [see PASS *v.* 25]. *c* **1590** MARLOWE *Faust.* xii, You think to carry it away with your hey-pass and re-pass. **1611** COTGR., *Passe-passée*, Heypasse, repasse; a iugling tricke, or tearme. **1622** FLETCHER *Beggar's Bush* III. i, What a rogue's this juggler! This hey pass, repass! he has repass'd us sweetly. **1627** [see PASS *v.* 25].

Hence **re'passing** *vbl. sb.* and *ppl. a.*; also **re'passable, re'passer.**

1555 EDEN *Decades* 186 In theyr repassynge by the same clyme. **1598** FLORIO, *Ripassata*, a repassing. **1680** COTTON *Comp. Gamester* 28 They dream of nothing but Hazards..of passing and repassing [etc.]. **1697** DRYDEN *Virg. Georg.* I. 323 The torrid Zone Glows with the passing and repassing Sun. **1710** T. FULLER *Pharm. Extemp.* 163 As long as the Matter is repassable. **1746** HERVEY *Medit.* (1818) 223 The city swarmed with passing and repassing multitudes. **1769** *Middlesex Jrnl.* 14–16 Sept. 4/4 A vast passing and re-passing between the parties mentioned. **1800** SOUTHEY *Lett.* (1856) I. 112 This must exclude the great body of passers and repassers. **1849** MACAULAY *Hist. Eng.* iii. I. 376 The constant passing and repassing of traffic.

†**re'pass,** *v.*^{2} *Obs. rare*$^{-1}$. [app. ad. obs. F. *repasser* to cure.] *trans.* To repair, recover from.

a **1631** DONNE *Resurrection*, Sleepe, sleepe, old Sunn, thou canst not have repast As yet the wound thou took'st on Fryday last.

repassage (riː'pæsɪdʒ). Also re-. [a. F. *repassage* (1379): cf. REPASS *v.*^{1} and PASSAGE.]

†**1.** A way of return. *Obs. rare*$^{-1}$.

1413 *Pilgr. Sowle* (Caxton 1483) IV. xxxi. 80 This necke sholde be the passage and repassage fro the hede to the body and ryght so ayeneward.

2. The act of repassing; passage back; liberty or right to repass. Chiefly in ***passage and repassage***.

1433 *Rolls of Parlt.* IV. 425/1 Ye charges of his repassage ayenward. **1444** *Wars Eng. in France* (Rolls) I. 463, lvj. shippes..for the passage and repassage of the quene and of her housholde. **1520** in *Laing Charters* (1899) 82 With free entrie passage and repassage thrughe the sayd west yarde. **1576** FLEMING *Panopl. Epist.* 247 That letters may haue passage and repassage between vs twaine. **1600** HAKLUYT *Voy.* III. 359 Twentie..getting betweene the Fort and them..cut off their repassage. *a* **1618** RALEIGH *Invent. Shipping* (1650) 38 Seeing their passage and Repassage lyes through the British Seas. *a* **1670** HACKET *Cent. Serm.* (1675) 436 The spirits of damnation..are tied in chains of darkness, there is no repassage for them. **1752** CARTE *Hist. Eng.* III. 368 Nor could their passage and repassage be concealed. **1835–6** *Todd's Cycl. Anat.* I. 344/2 A change in the blood..effected by the air of the cells on its re-passage through the bronchial tubes. **1840** POE *Gold Bug* Wks. 1864 I. 53 Facilities of passage and re-passage were very far behind those of the present day.

re'passant, *a. Her.* (See quot.)

c **1828** BERRY *Encycl. Her.* I. Gloss., *Re-passant*, or Counter-Passant, that is, when two lions, or other animals, are borne going contrary ways, one of which is *passant*, by walking towards the dexter side of the shield, in the usual way, and the other *re-passant* by going towards the sinister.

†**re'passion.** *Obs. rare.* [ad. med.L. **repassiōnem*, whence also obs. F. *repassion* (Godef.): see RE- and PASSION.] A counter effect.

1601 GILL *Trinity* 35 This action of God..is not a transeant action, to cause a passion in the subiect, and a repassion in the agent. **1648** HAMMOND *Serm.* Wks. 1684 IV. 485 The Rod itself is smitten whensoever it smites, at every blow wounded and torn by way of repassion.

repast (rɪ'pɑːst, -æ-), *sb.* [a. OF. *repast* (mod.F. *repas*), f. *repaistre* (mod.F. *repaître*):—late L. *repascĕre*, f. *re-* RE- + *pascĕre* to feed: see PASTURE *sb.*]

1. A quantity of food and drink forming, or intended for, a meal or feast; a meal or feast in its material aspect, freq. with reference to the quantity or quality of the food.

13.. *Coer de L.* 3076 Whenne he has..eeten weel a good repast,..Sone he schal be fresch and hayl. **1393** LANGL. *P. Pl.* C. x. 148 He..aspieþ Whar he may raþest haue a repast oþer a rounde of bacon. *c* **1450** LOVELICH *Merlin* 728 (Kölbing) Every fryday thow most faste And to the taken but on repaste. **1494** FABYAN *Chron.* VII. 501 As soone as yᵉ Kyng had there taken a small and short repast, he..rode into a felde. **1542** *Richmond Wills* (Surtees) 37, I wyll yt my freynds and neighbors haue a repayste after my buryall. **1585** T. WASHINGTON tr. *Nicholay's Voy.* III. vi. 79 He is bound to giue a breakefast or repast vnto the Ianissairies. *c* **1656** MILTON *Sonn., to Lawrence*, What neat repast shall feast us, light and choice, Of Attick tast, with Wine..? **1697** DRYDEN *Virg. Georg.* II. 756 The falling Mast For greedy Swine provides a full Repast. **1757** GRAY *Bard* 78 Fill high the sparkling bowl, The rich repast prepare. **1813** BYRON *Corsair* II. iv, Methinks he strangely spares the rich repast. **1870** YEATS *Nat. Hist. Comm.* 78 Bees find a plentiful repast in the myriad flowers.

fig. **1611** SHAKS. *Cymb.* V. iv. 157 If I proue a good repast to the Spectators, the dish payes the shot. **1784** COWPER *Task* IV. 113 He..spreads the honey of his deep research At his return, a rich repast for me. **1820** LAMB *Elia* Ser. I. *Grace bef. Meat*, Why have we none [*sc.* no grace] for books, those spiritual repasts..?

†**b.** ***to take one's repast***, to take one's food, take a meal. *Obs.*

c **1490** CAXTON *Rule St. Benet* 131 What howres..the congregacyon shall take theyr repast and meles. **1528** PAYNEL *Salernes Regim.* (1541) 4 After wee haue dyned or taken our repaste, we muste for a whyle stande vp ryght. **1550** CROWLEY *Epigr.* 42 Suche swyne..That in the filthye puddell take all their repaste. **1585** T. WASHINGTON tr. *Nicholay's Voy.* IV. i. 114 They neuer went to take their repast without leaue. **1725** DE FOE *Voy. round World* (1840) 269 While we were taking our repast it grew quite night.

†**c.** (See quot. 1661.) *Obs.*

1517 [see REPASTER]. **1661** BLOUNT *Glossogr.*, *Repast*,..in the Inns of Court it signifies a single meal taken in the Hall by any one of the Society, who is not in Commons that week.

†**2.** (Without article.) Food, supply of food or victuals. Also *fig. Obs.*

1390 GOWER *Conf.* III. 25 Bot al withoute such repast Of lust, as ye me tolde above,..I faste, and mai no fode gete. **1426** LYDG. *De Guil. Pilgr.* 4618 He gaff hem alderlast Hys owne boody for cheff repast. *c* **1440** *Macro Plays* (E.E.T.S.) 188 Yf a mane ete the flesshe of a gose for his repaste and fedyng. **1577** *Test. 12 Patriarchs* (1706) 91 He was in the pit three days and three nights without repast. **1599** T. M[OUFET] *Silkwormes* 22 What liuing were you then But worms repast, though wise and mighty men? **1613** PURCHAS *Pilgrimage* IX. iii. (1614) 828 They carefully wash the carkasses of their dead, and lay them forth in the night, for repast vnto the Tigres. **1667** MILTON *P.L.* II. 800 They..howle and gnaw My Bowels, their repast. **1698** FRYER *Acc. E. India & P.* p. vii, Monkies the common Repast of the Tygers. **1732** POPE *Hor. Sat.* II. ii. 93 A Buck was then a week's repast.

†**b.** ***to take repast***, to take food. Also *fig.* to associate *with* one. *Obs.*

1526 *Pilgr. Perf.* (W. de W. 1531) 83 It is moche better..to eate euery daye a lytell, than seldome to take repaste, & fede to replecyon. **1574** HELLOWES *Gueuara's Fam. Ep.* (1577) 41 Lying, and cowardnesse, did neuer take repaste with knighthoode. **1590** SPENSER *F.Q.* II. ix. 16 Ne man nor beast may rest, or take repast For their sharpe wounds and noyous injuries.

†**3.** A kind of food or drink. *Obs.*

c **1485** *Digby Myst.* (1882) III. 485 Here, lady, is wyn, a repast, to man and woman a good restoratyff. *c* **1530** H. RHODES *Bk. Nurture* in *Babees Bk.* (1868) 105 Let thy lyuing be of light repaste. **1669** WORLIDGE *Syst. Agric.* (1681) 143 Of the Juice of Goosberries..is prepared a very pleasant cooling Repast.

fig. *a* **1668** DENHAM *A Song*, Sleep that is thy best repast, Yet of death it bears a taste.

4. The action or fact of taking food; the refreshment of food. Now *arch.*

1588 SHAKS. *L.L.L.* IV. ii. 160 (Q.), If (before repast) it shall please you to gratifie the table with a Grace. **1646** SIR T. BROWNE *Pseud. Ep.* 309 The rooms of repast at supper. *a* **1661** FULLER *Worthies* (1840) III. 6 How inconsistent.., to couple a spiritual grace with matters of corporeal repast. **1700** DRYDEN *Theod. & Hon.* 86 The day already half his race had run, And summoned him to due repast at noon. **1859** TENNYSON *Guinevere* 362 The silk pavilions of King Arthur raised For brief repast or afternoon repose.

fig. **1670** BROOKS *Wks.* (1867) VI. 311 Such as make the desolations of their neighbours to be the matter either of their secret repast or open exultation.

b. An occasion of taking or partaking of food; a meal or feast in this sense.

a **1639** WOTTON *Life Dk. Buckm.* in *Reliq.* (1651) 112 The Duke was at breakfast (the last of his repasts in this world). **1644** MILTON *Educ.* 4 After evening repast, till bed time, their thoughts will be best taken up in the easie grounds of Religion. **1732** LEDIARD *Sethos* II. VIII. 157 The approaching night invites us to a repast. **1796** MORSE *Amer. Geog.* II. 569 They eat at their repasts cakes of rice. **1837** DISRAELI *Venetia* I. xi, After their repast, the children went into the garden. **1853** SOYER *Pantroph.* 367 In the 17th century playing fountains were still used at repasts.

fig. **1802** BEDDOES *Hygeia* I. 55 To hang a naked sword..over the head during the repast of life.

†**5.** Refreshment; repose. *Obs.*

1546 *Supplic. of Poore Commons* (E.E.T.S.) 78 One of your Highnes chapplene..when he lusted to ride a brode for his repast. **1590** SPENSER *F.Q.* I. ii. 4 His guest, who, after troublous sights And dreames, gan now to take more sound repast. **1615** BP. HALL *Contempl., O.T.* XI. vi, She that began her prayers with fasting, and heavinesse, rises up from them with chearefulnesse and repast.

repast (rɪ'pɑːst, -æ-), *v.* Now *rare.* Also 6 *Sc.* as *pa. pple.* [ad. L. *repast-*, ppl. stem of *repascĕre* (see prec.), or f. the sb.]

†**1.** *refl.* To refresh (oneself) with food. *Obs.* In latest quots. perhaps *fig.* (cf. prec., sense 5).

1470–85 MALORY *Arthur* VII. xiv, They dranke the wyne, and ete the veneson... And so whan they had repasted hem wel [etc.]. *c* **1530** LD. BERNERS *Arth. Lyt. Bryt.* (1814) 212 Whan that Arthur had well repasted hym selfe and hys horse. **1567** MAPLET *Gr. Forest* 67 In mouing from place to place, with an appetite to repast themselues. **1575** R. B. *Appius & Virg.* in Hazl. *Dodsley* IV. 118 Be of good cheer, Go play and repast thee, man, be merry. **1617** COLLINS *Def. Bp. Ely* I. i. 29 Iohn rested and repasted himselfe on his sacred bosome.

†**2.** *trans.* To feed, supply with food. *Obs.*

1512 *Helyas* in Thoms *Prose Rom.* (1828) III. 34 God allmighty..that..wylled to repast the children of Israel in deserte with manna of heven. **1560** ROLLAND *Crt. Venus* II. 473 So he rais and on his veyage past, Fameist for fude, and richt skarslie repast. **1602** SHAKS. *Ham.* IV. v. 147 Ile ope my Armes, And like the kinde Life-rend'ring Pelican, Repast them with my blood. **1669** EVELYN *Sylva* (1776) 309 The top-leaves and oldest should be gathered last of all, as being most proper to repast the worms with, towards their last change.

absol. **1635** QUARLES *Embl.* I. xii, A mod'rate use does both repast and please.

fig. **1540** TAVERNER *Postils* (Exhort. bef. Communion), So is our soule repasted & nouryshed.

3. *intr.* To feed, feast. Chiefly const. *on, upon.*

1520 WHITINTON *Vulg.* (1527) 41 b, After the ordre, as they be set downe, so repaste vpon them. **1624** QUARLES *Sion's Sonn.* xiv, Refresht with thy delights, I haue repasted Vpon thy pleasures, my full soule hath tasted Thy rip'ned dainties. **1698** FRYER *Acc. E. India & P.* 150 In their Hall where they Repast, at the upper End on the Table is placed a Death's Head. **1720** POPE *Iliad* XXIV. 546 They..found The Guards repasting, while the Bowls go round. **1867** J. B. ROSE tr. *Virgil's Æneid* 296 Birds..Shall on thy huge and bleeding frame repast!

Hence **re'pasting** *vbl. sb.*

1644 MILTON *Areop.* (Arb.) 44 God..left arbitrary the dyeting and repasting of our minds.

†**re'paster.** *Obs.* Also 6 repastour. [f. prec. + -ER[1].] One who takes a repast; *spec.* in the Inns of Court (see REPAST *sb.* 1 c).

1517 *Black Bks. Lincoln's Inn* (1897) I. 182 Who so bryngith any repaster to the Redar's denar or sopar, except the Redar or any of the Benche, schall pay for the Repast. **1566** in Inderwick *Cal. Inner Temple Rec.* (1896) 236 None of this company shall bring any repaster to the reader's drinking or dinner. **1582** STANYHURST *Æneis* I. (Arb.) 24 They doe plye theire commons, lyke quick and greedye repastours.

†**re'pastinate,** *v. Obs.* [f. ppl. stem of L. *repastināre*: see RE- and PASTINE *v.*] *trans.* To dig over again.

1623 COCKERAM, *Repastinate*, to digge againe about a thing. **1656** BLOUNT *Glossogr.* [copying Cooper] *Repastinate*, to dig again about Vines, to alter grounds with often digging and laboring. **1745** tr. *Columella's Husb.* II. xv, Then in the summer months the whole dunghil must be thoroughly mixed and shuffled with spades, in the same manner as if you repastinated it.

†**repasti'nation.** *Obs.* [ad. L. *repastinātiōn-em*: see prec. and -ATION.] The action or process of digging over again.

1569 NEWTON *Cicero's Old Age* 39 The repastinacion or newe digging about the rootes. **1623** COCKERAM *Repastination*, a digging againe. **1675** EVELYN *Terra* (1776) 25 With a slight repastination, one may plant or sow any thing in it freely. **1699** —— *Acetaria* (1729) 118 Composts and Stercoration, Repastination, Dressing and Stoning the Earth and Mould of a Garden.

†**re'pasture.** *Obs. rare.* [See REPAST *sb.* and PASTURE *sb.*] Food; a repast.

1588 SHAKS. *L.L.L.* IV. i. 95 What art thou then? Foode for his rage, repasture for his den. **1614** W. B. *Philosopher's Banquet* (ed. 2) 26 In our meales and repastures.

repat (riːˈpæt), colloq. abbrev. of REPATRIATE *sb.* (also REPATRIATION). Also *attrib.*

1946 BRICKHILL & NORTON *Escape to Danger* xxii. 197 Typical of the repat. boys was 'Chuck' Lark. **1948** *R.A.F. Rev.* June 5/1 (*heading*) Family camp (for repats). **1968** *Punch* 12 June 854/2 The emotions attendant on leaving had the same admixture as before: the expat and the repat were, after all, the same person. **1974** P. FLOWER *Odd Job* iii. 27 He'd got along on a Repat. pension.

†**re'pater,** *v. Sc. Obs. rare*[−1]. [ad. F. *repaître*: see REPAST *sb.*] *trans.* To feed.

1513 DOUGLAS *Æneis* VIII. iv. 70 As all the beistis war Repaterit weyll eftyr thair nychtis lair.

repatriate (rɪˈpeɪtrɪeɪt, riːˈpæt-), *v.* [f. ppl. stem of late L. *repatriāre* to return to one's country, f. *re-* RE- + *patria* native land. Cf. obs. F. *repatrier* (15th c.), F. *rapatrier*, It. *ripatriare*.]

1. a. *trans.* To restore (a person) to his own country. (Common in recent use.)

1611 COTGR., *Repatrier*, to repatriate, or to restore to his owne home. **1619** in *Crt. & Times Jas. I* (1848) II. 143 Tobie Matthew is at Bruxelles, in some hope..to be repatriated, before long. **1880** *Fortn. Rev.* Apr. 508 The number of those finally repatriated appears..to have been 102,000. **1890** *Temple Bar* Oct. 285 The French consul.. repatriated me, sending me home by way of Alexandria. *refl.* **1891** HOWELLS *Imperative Duty* ii. 9 He perceived that the effort to repatriate himself must involve wounds.

b. *transf.* of money.

1909 *Westm. Gaz.* 6 Aug. 10/4 A definite step is about to be taken to repatriate the United States silver coin which circulates in the Dominion of Canada. **1940** *Economist* 13 Jan. 64/2 A considerable amount of French capital remained in London last September and has for the most part been repatriated over the past four months. **1966** *Wall St. Jrnl.* 14 Nov. 24/4 In addition much of their overseas profits are 'repatriated' thus cutting the balance of payments deficit. **1978** *Whig-Standard* (Kingston, Ont.) 19 Jan. 7/7 Unless the province proposes to seize it [*sc.* the Sun Life Building] as a part of the $400 million to be repatriated to Quebec, it has no legal power to do anything.

c. *Canad.* To devolve or return (legislation) to the constitutional authority of an autonomous country. Cf. PATRIATE *v.*

1961 *Ann. Reg. 1960* 73 The Federal Government suggested that the British North America Act should be completely repatriated, making it entirely amendable in Canada rather than on application to the British Parliament. **1968** *Globe & Mail* (Toronto) 5 Feb. 8/5 Federal and provincial governments had been unable..to agree on a formula for repatriating and amending the constitution. **1978** *Independencer* (Ottawa) Jan./Feb. 5/1 Any attempt to repatriate our constitution would be divisive and not help National Unity.

2. *intr.* To return to one's own country. *rare.*

1656 BLOUNT *Glossogr.*, *Repatriate*, to return again to ones Native Country. **1888** GLADSTONE in Morley *Life* (1903) III. 358 When do you repatriate?

Hence **re'patriated** *ppl. a.*

1885 LOWE *Bismarck* II. ii. 148 The re-crowned and repatriated Charles II. **1966** *Wall St. Jrnl.* 14 Nov. 24/4 Pfizer International's repatriated earnings and exports to affiliates have totaled more than $420 million since 1951.

repatriate (riːˈpæt-, riːˈpeɪtrɪeɪt), *sb.* [f. the vb.] A repatriated person.

1921 *Glasgow Herald* 15 Nov. 5/3 The majority of these repatriates have the choice of living on totally inadequate means or entering the workhouse. **1945** *Daily Mirror* 27 Sept. 1/4 Seven ships have been named as bringing repatriates home to Britain. **1973** *Times* 17 Nov. 4/8 Mrs Meir, the Prime Minister, and..the Defence Minister, were among those at Lod airport today to give the repatriates a heroes' welcome.

repatriation (rɪpeɪtrɪˈeɪʃən, riːˈpæt-). [n. of action f. REPATRIATE *v.*: see -ATION.] **1.** Return or restoration to one's own country.

1592 WOTTON in *Reliq.* (1685) 670, I wish your Honour (in our Tuscan Phrase) a most happy Repatriation. **1646** EARL MONM. tr. *Biondi's Civil Warres* VIII. 129 Without Portion or any other thing, save only his re-patriation. **1865** *Pall Mall G.* No. 81. 11/1 The repatriation of the exiled adherents. **1879** *Eastern Question* I. iv. 197 The Porte could not afford the outlay for the repatriation of the refugees. *attrib.* **1882** BRYCE *Manitoba* 144 This repatriation movement from the United States. **1891** *Times* 12 Feb. 5/4 Contributions towards a repatriation fund. **1945** *Daily Mirror* 27 Sept. 1/4 The last batch of liberated prisoners and internees in Singapore boarded a repatriation ship yesterday. **1951** R. CAMPBELL *Light on Dark Horse* I It was through an erroneous repatriation-order that I obtained this last panorama of my early home. **1973** *Bulletin* (Sydney) 25 Aug. 17/3 The Repatriation Commission has amassed a fortune... The Repatriation Act empowers the commissioners to act as guardians of these men's affairs... These pensioners are visited regularly by repatriation officers.

2. *Canad.* Devolution or return of legislation to the constitutional authority of an autonomous country. Also *fig.* Cf. PATRIATION.

1961 *Ann. Reg. 1960* 73 Justice Minister Fulton proposed a two-stage process beginning with repatriation [of the British North America Act] and followed by the working-out of a method of amendment. **1968** *Globe & Mail* (Toronto) 5 Feb. 8/5 Mr. Pearson was asked..why the federal Government had not discussed repatriation of the constitution from Britain. **1976** *Maclean's Mag.* 17 May 45/2 The arguments for and against the repatriation of the Canadian culture take on a national scope.

re'patrioted, *ppl. a. nonce-wd.* [RE- 5 a.] Converted again into a patriot.

1755 H. WALPOLE *Let. to Bentley* 17 Dec., That so often repatrioted and reprostituted Doddington is again to be treasurer of the Navy.

†**re'pause,** *v. Obs. rare*[−1]. [ad. med.L. *repausāre*: see PAUSE *v.* and REPOSE *v.*] *intr.* To repose, rest.

1526 R. WHYTFORD *Martiloge* (1893) 47 Iesu after his deth repaused and rested in his sepulcre.

re'pave (riː-), *v.* [RE- 5 a: cf. F. *repaver* (14th c. Godef.).] *trans.* To pave again or anew.

1611 FLORIO, *Rammattonare*, to repaue with brickes. **1652** BENLOWES *Theoph.* I. l, Blest then who shall..wash the bloody stones With her own cursed Gore; repave them with her Bones. **1868** in Anderson *Missions Amer. Bd.* (1870) IV. xlii. 424 The streets are being repaved and widened. **1886** WILLIS & CLARK *Cambridge* II. 377 Chapel and ante-chapel were..repaved with large squares of stone.

re'pawn, *v.* [RE- 2 d and 5 a.]

†**1.** *trans.* To redeem from pawn. *Obs. rare*[−1].

1641 EARL MONM. tr. *Biondi's Civil Warres* IV. 37 He pawned unto him the two Rubies..which being repawn'd by him and the rest made good out of his own monies, hee return'd into France.

2. To pawn again. Also *absol.*

1858 CARLYLE *Fredk. Gt.* II. xiv. (1872) I. 129 He himself repawned Brandenburg to the Saxon Potentate. **1864** ADDISON *Contracts* II. iii. §3 (1883) 635 If a pawnee repawns, before any default..by the original pawnor [etc.].

So **re'pawn** *sb.*

1866 *Law Rep.* I *Q.B. Cases* 593 A..pawn by the plaintiff to Simpson..and a repawn of them by Simpson as a security for a loan to him by the defendant.

re'pay, *sb.* Now *rare* or *Obs.* [f. next.] Repayment, return.

1593 NORDEN *Spec. Brit., M'sex* I Accept..my willing indeuor, vntill time afforde ablenes to make better repay. **1753** YOUNG *Brothers* I. i, They measure blood by drops And bail not one in the repay. *a* **1810** TANNAHILL *Poems* (1846) 25 He wha deals in scandal only gains A rich repay of scandal for his pains.

repay (rɪˈpeɪ), *v.*[1] [ad. OF. *repaier*, *rapaier*, f. *re-* RE- + *payer* to PAY.]

1. *trans.* To refund, pay back (a sum of money, etc.). Also with double object.

1530 PALSGR. 686/1 What so ever you lay out it shalbe repayed you. **1560** DAUS tr. *Sleidane's Comm.* 74 They require him to repaie the kinge of England his money. **1607** SHAKS. *Timon* I. i. 288 No meede but he repayes Seuen-fold aboue it selfe. **1665** MANLEY *Grotius' Low C. Warres* 401 At the end of the War, whatever was disbursed, should be repaid. **1784** COWPER *Task* III. 364 Human life Is but a loan to be repaid with use. **1818** CRUISE *Digest* (ed. 2) II. 104 It was agreed, that if A. repaid 1000*l.*, &c. borrowed of B.,.. then B. should reconvey to him. **1864** TENNYSON *En. Ard.* 319 Money can be repaid; Not kindness such as yours.

b. To return (a blow, visit, salutation, etc.).

1593 SHAKS. *3 Hen. VI*, II. iii. 3, Strokes receiu'd, and many blowes repaid, Haue robb'd my strong knit sinewes of their strength. **1686** tr. *Chardin's Trav. Persia* 233 According to the Custom of Repaying the Visits of a Person of Quality. **1788** GIBBON *Decl. & F.* I. V. 211 He..received and repaid the salutations of the patriarchs.

c. To give (a thing) in return or recompense (*for* something).

1560 BIBLE (Genev.) *Ecclus.* xii. 6 The moste High..will repay vengeance vnto the vngodlie. **1611** BIBLE *Prov.* xiii. 21 Euill pursueth sinners: but to the righteous, good shall be repayd. **1720** POPE *Iliad* XVII. 38 Come, for my brother's blood repay thy own. **1818** SHELLEY *Eug. Hills* 190 What though thou with all thy dead Scarce can for this fame repay Aught thine own.

†**d.** To avenge (a thing) *on* a person. *Obs. rare*[−1].

1753 YOUNG *Brothers* I. i, Now her eyes repay Her brother's wounds on Philip's rival sons.

2. To make repayment or return to (a person); to pay (one) back in some way.

a **1542** WYATT in *Tottel's Misc.* (Arb.) 71, I was content thy seruant to remain; And not to be repayed after this fashion. **1596** SPENSER *F.Q.* IV. i. 40 Let me now you pray, ..Ye will me now with like good turne repay. **1661** BOYLE *Style of Script.* (1675) 85, I could readily retaliate, and repay them in the same coin. **1748** *Anson's Voy.* I. viii. 82 We should be amply repayed for all our past sufferings. **1791** MRS. RADCLIFFE *Rom. Forest* x, I will repay you for your kindness. **1827** LYTTON *Pelham* ii, He was repaid as such by a pretty general dislike. **1864** TENNYSON *En. Ard.* 309 When Enoch comes again Why then he shall repay me.

3. To make return or recompense for, requite (an action, etc.): **a.** of persons. Also const. *with* (or *by*) and in *pass.* without expressed agent.

1596 SHAKS. *Tam. Shr.* IV. iii. 45 The poorest seruice is repaide with thankes. **1611** BIBLE *Job* xxi. 31 Who shall repay him what he hath done? **1667** MILTON *P.L.* IX. 178 Spite then with spite is best repaid. **1764** GOLDSM. *Trav.* 198 Haply too some pilgrim, thither led, With many a tale repays the nightly bed. **1797** MRS. RADCLIFFE *Italian* i, [She] repaid the fondness of a mother with the affection of a daughter. **1835** SIR J. ROSS *Narr. 2nd Voy.* xxxvii. 513 She repayed her physic by the stone which is used in striking fire. **1869** BROWNING *Ring & Bk.* IX. 1312 Repaying incredulity with faith.

b. of things. Also in *pass.*

1610 HEALEY *St. Aug. Citie of God* XI. xxiii. (1620) 406 That we might know that the spirits merits are not repaid by the bodies qualities. **1781** COWPER *Hope* 771 The abundant harvest, recompense divine, Repays their work. **1809** CAMPBELL *Gertr. Wyom.* I. xi, Her lovely mind could culture well repay. **1860** TYNDALL *Glac.* II. xxix. 399 A series of.. considerations which I think will repay the reader's attention. **1867** LADY HERBERT *Cradle L.* viii. 223 But the view from the summit repays all the toil. *refl.* **1766** *Complete Farmer* s.v. *Drill-rake* 3 A 3/2 Yet even this small work of supererogation repays itself. **1872** MORLEY *Voltaire* (1886) 10 The sacrifice may repay itself a thousand fold.

4. *intr.* To make repayment or return.

1557 N. T. (Genev.) *Rom.* xii. 19 Vengeance is mine: I wil repaye, saith the Lord. **1611** BIBLE *Ecclus.* iv. 31 Let not thine hand bee stretched out to receiue, and shut when thou shouldest repay. **1865** LOWELL *Harvard Commem. Ode* viii, 'Tis not the grapes of Canaan that repay, But the high faith that failed not by the way.

Hence **re'paying** *ppl. a.*; also **re'payal,** repayment; **re'payer,** one who repays.

1650 HUBBERT *Pill Formality* 240 God is..a repaier of the wicked. **1881** MAYNE REID *Free Lances* I. xiii. 139 There could be no mistaking what he meant. Anything but a repayal of friendly services. **1883** *Century Mag.* Oct. 814/1 It is..probably a more repaying industry than orange-growing. **1888** STEVENSON *Black Arrow* 50, I am a good repayer, Jack, of good or evil.

repay (riːˈpeɪ), *v.*[2] [RE- 5 a.] To pay again, or a second time (Ogilvie *Suppl.* 1855).

re'payable, *a.* [f. REPAY *v.*[1] + -ABLE.] That may be, or is to be, repaid.

1828–32 in WEBSTER. **1880** MUIRHEAD *Ulpian* vi. §13 A dowry repayable by instalments. **1890** *Act 54 Vict.* c. i. §3 (1) Such loan shall be repayable by the Guardians to the Board of Works by two equal instalments.

repayment (rɪˈpeɪmənt). Also re- (riː-).

1. The (*or* an) act of repaying; payment back (of money lent, etc.).

1467 in *Eng. Gilds* (1870) 387 Euery man..shalle haue repayment of suche a summe as he hath payde. **1495** *Act 11 Hen. VII*, c. 8 Bondes for suertie perfite and sure repayment of..money lent. **1579** G. HARVEY *Letter-bk.* (Camden) 62, I can forthwith give you my obligation for repayment of the principalls with the loane. **1649** CHAS. II. in Ellis *Orig. Lett.* Ser. I. III. 327, I desire you..to lend me five hundred pounds, whereof I promise you..very faithfull re-payment. **1665** MANLEY *Grotius' Low C. Warres* 90 She promised them both men and money, for their assistance, they giving caution for repayments. **1776** ADAM SMITH *W.N.* II. ii. (1869) I. 297 The easy terms upon which the Scotch banking companies accept of repayment are..peculiar to them. **1818** CRUISE *Digest* (ed. 2) II. 50 Those estates which are held as a security or pledge for the repayment of money. **1885** *Law Rep. 29 Chanc. Div.* 264 Upon Russell's repayment of the same rent to Hampton.

2. Requital, return (of services, etc.).

1574 HELLOWES *Gueuara's Fam. Ep.* (1577) 20 In repayment of my trauell..you commaunded I should dine at your table. **1819** SHELLEY *Julian* 400 Was it I who wooed thee to this breast, Which like a serpent thou envenomest As in repayment of the warmth it lent? **1852** R. S. SURTEES *Sponge's Sp. Tour* (1893) 259 With..the repayment of the kiss Lucy had advanced.

3. *Comb.*, as **repayment mortgage** (see quots.).

1965 *Legal Side of buying House* (Consumers' Assoc.) ii. 31 There are two main differences between a fixed mortgage combined with an endowment policy.., and a repayment mortgage. First, the insurance premiums..are eligible for tax relief... Secondly, if the borrower dies before the mortgage is paid off..the endowment assurance policy.. pays all that is due. **1968** B. D. COLEMAN *Money—How to save it, spend it, & make It* iv. 25 This annuity mortgage (also known as a 'repayment' mortgage),..is simply a mortgage loan on a property to be bought, the principal (or capital borrowed) and interest to be repaid together by means of fixed instalments over a fixed period. **1974** *Listener* 24 Jan. 98/3 A building society prefers its borrowers..to stick to the simple repayment mortgage: paying back the advance over a period by monthly instalments of capital and interest combined.

repayral, -eyl, -yl, varr. REPAREL *v. Obs.*

repayre, obs. variant of REPAIR, RIPPIER.

repayse, variant of REPEASE *v. Obs.*

†**repe,** *v.*[1] *Obs.* Also 3 repie. [OE. *hrepian* var. of *hreppan*, perh. = ON. *hreppa* to get, obtain, OFris. *reppa*, MDu., MLG. *reppen* to move, stir.] *trans.* To touch, lay hold of.

c **1000** *Ags. Gosp.* Matt. viii. 3 Ða astrehte se hælend hys hand & hrepode hyne [*c* **1160** *Hatton* repede]. *a* **1225** *Ancr. R.* 128 Þe uoxes..draweð al into hore holes, þet heo muwen arepen & arechen [*T.* repen & rinen]. *c* **1290** *S. Eng. Leg.* I. 464/89 Heo ne dorste ore louerd repie nouȝht bihinde ne bifore.

†**repe,** *v.*[2] *Obs. rare*$^{-1}$. (Of obscure origin and meaning: cf. OE. *rýpan* to plunder.)

c **1320** *Sir Tristr.* 28 His men he slouȝ among And reped him mani a res.

†**repe,** ? variant of RAPE *adv. Obs.*

c **1380** *Sir Ferumb.* 3583 Þe Sarzyns comeþ after repe [*altered from* rape], Al so harde as þay mowe lepe.

repe, obs. form of REAP.

repeak, obs. form of REPIQUE *v.*

repeal (rɪˈpiːl), *sb.* Forms: 5 repeell, 6 repell(e, repele, repeall, 6–7 repeale, 6– repeal. [a. AF. *repel* = OF. *rapel* (mod.F. *rappel*) a recall, f. *repeler, rapeler*: see next.]

†**1.** Recall, as from banishment. *Obs.*

1483 CAXTON *Gold. Leg.* 117 b/1 Yf they shold assente to your repeell they shold but a whyle dwelle wyth you. **1530** PALSGR. 262/1 Repell, callyng agayne, *repel.* **1590** MARLOWE *Edw. II*, I. iv, I am enjoin'd To sue unto you all for his repeal. **1606** G. W[OODCOCKE] *Hist. Ivstine* XVI. 67 At his repeale and calling home into his Countrey, which he shortly expected. **1612** *North's Plutarch, Dionysius* 1143 The decree of repeale was authorized by the people, and the banished men returned to Syracvsa. **1658** COKAINE *Trappolin* III. i, To petition for the repeal of my dear Trappolin.

2. a. The (*or* an) act of repealing (a law, resolution, sentence, etc.); abrogation.

1503–4 *Act 19 Hen. VII*, c. 28 §1 The seid reversall repelle adnullacion & advoydaunce of this seid Acte. **1525** LD. BERNERS *Froiss.* II. lxxxvi. [lxxxii.] 255 These wrytynges sholde be permanent without ony repell. **1535–6** *Act 27 Hen. VIII*, c. 26 §29 So that every such suspending repeale and revocacion..shalbe made in writing. **1561** T. NORTON *Calvin's Inst.* I. 65 Again there are rehearsed diuerse repelles of his decrees. **1641** *Nicholas Papers* (Camden) I. 5 The said act of Repeale shalbee sent over to bee passed there. **1692** BENTLEY *Boyle Lect.* ix. 335 These Civil Ordinances become obsolete without any repeal. **1710** PRIDEAUX *Orig. Tithes* i. 21 Every part [of that law] had not its particular repeal. **1769** *Junius Lett.* xxxv. (1788) 178 Nothing less than a repeal, as formal as the resolution itself, can heal the wound. **1827** HALLAM *Const. Hist.* xiv. (1876) III. 54 The repeal of the test would not have placed the two religions on a fair level. **1861** TRENCH *Ep. 7 Churches Asia* 11 There was for them no repeal of the sentence of death, but a respite only.

b. *spec.* The cancelling of the Union between Great Britain and Ireland as an Irish political demand, esp. in the agitations headed by O'Connell in 1830 and 1841–6. Also *attrib.*

1831 *Fraser's Mag.* IV. 627/2 The repeal of the Union taking the place which was formerly occupied by the Roman Catholic claims. Repeal immediately became the engrossing topic. **1845** MACAULAY in Trevelyan *Life* (1876) II. 164 Ireland, we fear, is on the brink of something like a servile war—the effect, not of Repeal agitation, but of the severe distress. **1848** W. J. O'N. DAUNT *Recoll. O'Connell* I. i. 3 The champion of Repeal excited my enthusiasm.

†**c.** Revocation, withdrawal. *Obs. rare*$^{-1}$.

1612 DAVIES *Why Ireland*, etc. 203 The Earle of Desmond aboue al men, found himselfe grieued with this resumption, or Repeale of Liberties.

3. Means or possibility of release (*from* punishment). *rare.*

1594 NASHE *Unfort. Trav.* 66 The onely repeale we haue from Gods vndefinite chastisement, is to chastise our selues in this world. **1819** BYRON *Proph. Dante* I. 6 That deep gulf without repeal, Where late my ears rung with the damned cries Of souls in hopeless bale.

4. *Comb.*, as **Repeal Warden** *Irish Hist.*, a local official of the Loyal National Repeal Association. Cf. sense 2 b.

1841 D. O'CONNELL in P. S. O'Hegarty *Hist. Ireland under Union* (1952) xiv. 103 The Office of Repeal Warden.. must be purely ministerial. They must not..be considered, as Representatives or Delegates. **1903** M. MACDONAGH *Life Daniel O'Connell* xx. 392 The article further suggested that the Repeal wardens should be instructed in the military uses and abuses of railways. **1966** L. J. MCCAFFREY *Daniel O'Connell & Repeal Year* ii. 70 The most important cogs in the Repeal machinery on the local level were the priests. They organized and participated in Repeal meetings, and they selected the parish Repeal Wardens.

repeal (rɪˈpiːl), *v.*[1] Forms: 4–5 repele, 5 rappel, rapelle, 5–6 repell, 6 repel, 6–7 repeale, 6– repeal. [ad. AF. *repel(l)er* = OF. *rapeler* (mod.F. *rappeler*), f. *re-* RE- + *appeler* to APPEAL.]

1. *trans.* To revoke, rescind, annul (something determined or appointed, *esp.* a law or sentence).

13.. *Body & Soul* in *Anglia* II. 243 Now I se I am but lorn, þere may no man þis doom repele. *c* **1374** CHAUCER *Troylus* IV. 532 (560) For sen myn fadyr..haþ hire chaunge enseled, He nil not for me his lettre ben repelid. **1427** *Rolls of Parlt.* IV. 322/2 Alle ye Statutes made..and noght repelled. **1474** CAXTON *Chesse* 43 The knyght had leuer to forsake his owne contre and to dye so than to repele his lawes. **1483** —— *G. de la Tour* A viij, Wherfore God took mercy on them and repeled his sentence. **1529** in *Vicary's Anat.* (1888) App. xiv. 257 [To] obserue all the..Rules, and ordynaunces..heretofore made and not Repelled. **1557** N.T. (Genev.) Epistle *iv, Yᵉ Olde [Testament]..was in it selfe infirme and vnperfect, and therfore was abolished and repelled. **1593** SHAKS. *Rich. II*, III. iii. 40 Prouided, that my Banishment repeal'd, And Lands restor'd againe, be freely graunted. **1625** HART *Anat. Ur* II. ix. 110 The Parson repeales his former sentence. **1651** HOBBES *Leviath.* II. xxvi. 138 The Soveraign..having power to make, and repeale Lawes. **1708** SWIFT *Sacram. Test* Wks. 1751 IV. 157, I.. shall give you my Opinion freely about repealing the Sacramental Test. **1781** COWPER *Expost.* 224 Thence date their sad declension and their fall, Their woes not yet repealed. **1827** HALLAM *Const. Hist.* v. (1876) I. 266 It was deemed..expedient to repeal the ancient statute. **1842** BISCHOFF *Woollen Manuf.* II. 75 If the duties upon oil..and dye-wares were repealed.

†**b.** To recall, withdraw (a privilege, grant, etc.).

c **1325** *Song of Yesterday* 177 in *E.E.P.* (1862) 137 Þis poyntes may no mon hym repele He comeþ so baldely to pike his pray. **1454** *Rolls of Parlt.* V. 255/1 That eny auctorite or power..bee..by th' auctorite therof voied, rappelled, revoked. **1525** LD. BERNERS *Froiss.* II. ccxxii. [ccxviii.] 686 Therfore here openly he repelyth agayne all suche graces and grauntes as he hath made to you before this tyme. **1598** DRAYTON *Heroic. Ep.* ix. 43 When first thou didst repeale thy former Grant.

†**c.** To withdraw from use. *Obs. rare*$^{-1}$.

1573 in *Ricart's Kalendar* (Camden) 58 This Maior caused a good reformacion to be made for mesures of barrells and kilderkins which weare made larger..then they weare before, And the old vessels repelled.

†**2.** To recall or retract (a statement); to give up, abandon (a thought, feeling, etc.). *Obs.*

c **1430** *Pilgr. Lyf Manhode* II. civ. (1869) 114 Neuere wolde j repele thing that j hadde euele seid. *c* **1460** ROS *La Belle Dame* 649 Yet may ye wel repeale your bysynesse, And to resoun some-what haue atendaunce. **1596** SPENSER *F.Q.* V. viii. 21 Which my liege Lady seeing, thought it best..all forepast displeasures to repeale. **1642** H. MORE *Song of Soul* II. ii. II. xxiii, Therefore repeal This grosse conceit, and hold as reason doth reveal. **1667** MILTON *P.L.* VII. 59 Adam soon repeal'd The doubts that in his heart arose.

†**3. a.** To recall to a proper state or course; to call upon (one) *to* do something. *Obs. rare.*

1479 in *Eng. Gilds* (1870) 417 Where I may know the kynges rights of his Crowne..conceled or withdrawe, I shall do my trew peyn to repele and reforme it. **1585** *Sc. Acts Jas. VI* (1814) III. 380 Diuerss pairteis intendis..to causs thame be repellit to repay the saides mailes and deweteis.

†**b.** To recall (a person) from exile. *Obs.*

1483 CAXTON *Gold. Leg.* 293/2 This holy man..was exyled and after repeled ageyne. *a* **1548** HALL *Chron., Hen. IV* Introd. a iij b, That Henry duke of Herfford..shal.. departe out of the realme for terme of ten yeres, without returnyng excepte by the kyng he be repealed again. **1590** MARLOWE *Edw. II*, I. iv, Till my Gaveston be repeal'd, Assure thyself thou com'st not in my sight. **1606** G. W[OODCOCKE] *Hist. Ivstine* XVI. 67 They determined to fly for refuge to Clearche who was lately banished his countrey, and [whom they] were constrained to repeale in defence of the same. **1662** COKAINE *Trag. Ovid* IV. iii,[She won] so much upon her Father, That I had been repeal'd if he had liv'd.

refl. **1593** SHAKS. *Rich. II*, II. ii. 49 The banish'd Bullingbrooke repeales himselfe, And..is..arriu'd At Rauenspurg.

fig. **1601** SHAKS. *All's Well* II. iii. 55 This healthfull hand whose banisht sence Thou hast repeal'd. *a* **1625** FLETCHER & MASS. *Cust. Country* II. i, Upon my life this gallant Is brib'd to repeale banished swords.

†**c.** To call or summon back. *Obs.*

1598 SYLVESTER *Du Bartas* II. i. *Eden* 253 Nepenthe, enemy to sadnesse, Repelling sorrows, and repealing gladnesse. **1598** MANWOOD *Lawes Forest* xx. 162 Before that they doe enter the forest, he must repeale and call backe againe his Dogges. *a* **1648** LD. HERBERT *Autobiog.* in *Life* (1886) 225 The effect whereof should be chiefly to complain against me, and to obtain that I should be repealed. **1727** *Philip Quarll* 251 His scar'd Senses returning to their proper Seat, and his stray'd Reason repeal'd.

†**d.** To try to get (one) restored. *Obs. rare*$^{-1}$.

1604 SHAKS. *Oth.* II. iii. 363 Ile poure this pestilence into his eare: That she repeales him, for her bodies Lust.

†**4.** *intr.* To return. *Obs. rare*$^{-1}$.

1596 FITZ-GEFFRAY *Sir F. Drake* (1881) 101 As one,.. Ravisht in Spirite with devoted zeale, Becomes a Priest and will not home repeale.

Hence **re'pealed** *ppl. a.*, **re'pealing** *vbl. sb.* and *ppl. a.*

1444 *Rolls of Parlt.* V. 117/1 All the matiers conteined in this Petition, save onely repellyng of the Statute. **1533** MORE *Debell. Salem* Wks. 1014/1 Where neither the making nor the repelling [of the law] lyeth in neither nother of theyr handes. **1601** SHAKS. *Jul. C.* III. i. 51 For the repealing of my banish'd Brother. *a* **1647** FILMER *Patriarcha* iii. §7 (1884) 52 The repealing or abrogating of any statute. **1647** CLARENDON *Hist. Reb.* v. §148 Any bare votes not grounded upon law or reason, or quotations of repealed statutes. **1735** BOLINGBROKE *On Parties* (1738) 78 His dispensing, or suspending, which was in Effect a repealing Power. **1863** *Sat. Rev.* 11 July 39 The same ignorance or indolence which tempts legislators to introduce sweeping repealing clauses.

†**re'peal,** *v.*[2], obs. variant of REPEL *v.*

1582 STANYHURST *Æneis* II. (Arb.) 58 Soom bands of Troians..Ranck close too geather, thee Greeks most manlye repealing. *Ibid.* III. 89 Night shades moysturs glittring Aurora repealeth.

repealable (rɪˈpiːləb(ə)l), *a.* [f. REPEAL *v.*[1] + -ABLE.] That may be repealed or revoked.

1570 FOXE *A. & M.* (ed. 2) 762/2 All their liberties, which were not repealed, or repealeable by the common law. **1614** BUDDEN tr. *Aerodius' Disc. Parents Hon.* (1616) 11 What he commands is constant and perpetuall, but our lawes bee mutable and repealeable. **1675** *Art Contentm.* VI. ii, Even that decision also would have bin repealable by a greater force. **1843** CARLYLE *Past & Pr.* III. viii, An..act of Heaven's Parliament, not repealable in St. Stephen's or elsewhere! **1888** BRYCE *Amer. Commw.* I. xxxi. I. 479 These rules are sometimes passed by Congress and repealable by Congress.

Hence **repeala'bility** (Webster 1828–32); **re'pealableness** (Webster 1847).

repealer (rɪˈpiːlə(r)). [f. REPEAL *v.*[1] + -ER[1].] One who repeals or advocates repeal.

1765 BLACKSTONE *Comm.* Introd. I. 9 They are..the makers, repealers, and interpreters of the English laws. **1876** BANCROFT *Hist. U.S.* IV. xxix. 46 Grenville heard..one of the repealers of his stamp act propose a revenue from port duties. **1884** *Law Times* LXXVIII. 98/1 If the Corn Law repealers had known of this precedent.

b. *spec.* An advocate of the repeal of the Union between Great Britain and Ireland.

1831 *Fraser's Mag.* IV. 629/1 There were..some little murmurings amongst the more clear-sighted and determined of the repealers. **1848** W. J. O'N. DAUNT *Recoll. O'Connell* I. i. 10 Nor is the injustice of any individual government to Ireland the sole reason why Irishmen are Repealers. **1861** GOLDW. SMITH *Irish Hist.* 180 The Repealers..betray their misgivings as to the soundness of their theory.

So **re'pealist.**

1831 *Fraser's Mag.* IV. 629/1 Such were the murmurings of some of the sterner repealists.

repeall, obs. form of REPEAL *sb.*

re'pealless, *a. rare.* [f. REPEAL *sb.* + -LESS.] Without any cancellation or repeal; from which nothing is erased.

c **1862** E. DICKINSON *Poems* (1955) I. 318 God can summon every face On his Repealless—List.

†**re'pealment.** *Obs.* [f. REPEAL *v.*[1] + -MENT.] Recall from banishment.

? **1605** J. BODENHAM *Wittes' Commw.* 220 Great is the comfort that a banished man takes, at tidings of his repealement. **1627** FELTHAM *Resolves* I. [II.] xii. 38 Though unthankefulnes banisheth love, Gratitude obtaines a repealement.

repear, obs. variant of RIPPIER.

†**re'pease,** *v. Obs.* Also 6 repayse. [ad. OF. *repaiser, rapaiser*, f. *re-* RE- + *-paiser* or *apaiser*: see APPEASE.]

1. *trans.* To appease or pacify again.

1480 CAXTON *Ovid's Met.* XII. ix, He oughte to delyver his doughter to deth, for to repease the goddesse that empesshid their enterpryse. **1523** LD. BERNERS *Froiss.* I. xliv. 61 She had moche a do to repayse hym of his dyspleasure. **1530** PALSGR. 686/2 If he be chaffed ones, we have moche a do to repayse hym.

2. To reassure. *rare*$^{-1}$.

1483 CAXTON *Gold. Leg.* 150 b/1 Whan thangele knewe that for thys salutacion she was tymerous and abasshed anone he repeased her sayeng Marye be nothyng aferd.

repeat (rɪˈpiːt), *sb.* Also 5–6 **repete**, 6–7 **repeate.** [f. the vb.]

1. a. The (*or* an) act of repeating, repetition.

1556 J. HEYWOOD *Spider & F.* lxi. 10 First thants tale told the spiders he did repeate... Then in repeate, the spiders tale he did treate. **1667** MILTON *P.L.* VI. 318 One stroke they aim'd That might determine, and not need repeate. **1855** HOPKINS *Organ* 209 A 'return' or 'repeat' is caused in the series of Pedal sounds. **1869** *Daily News* 20 Aug., A message may be hereafter sent from London to Bombay almost without a repeat.

b. A repetition of a musical piece or performance, or of some part of these.

1853 MISS E. S. SHEPPARD *Ch. Auchester* II. 208 Then burst out a tremendous call for a repeat. **1865** *Morn. Star* 8 Sept., As to the execution of the oratorio..there was one good feature in it—there were no repeats.

c. In *U.S.* phr. ***and repeat***, used to denote the return of a horse or the like back over the distance it has just come. Cf. RETURN *sb.* 1 g.

1819 *Va. Herald* (Fredericksburg) 19 May 4/5 Second day two miles and repeat, free for all ages. **1856** *Trans. Mich. Agric. Soc.* VII. 276 Trotting horses shall be tested in harness, by going at least one mile and repeat. **1903** A. ADAMS *Log of Cowboy* ix. 131 A race horse can't beat an ox on a hundred miles and repeat to a freight wagon.

d. *Broadcasting.* A repetition of a programme which has already been broadcast.

1937 *Printers' Ink Monthly* May 40/3 *Repeat*, a term denoting the second broadcast of a regular studio program broadcast for those stations not served by the original broadcast due to time differences. **1941** *B.B.C. Gloss. Broadcasting Terms* 28 *Repeat*, repetition (as distinct from reproduction) of a programme which has been broadcast, either live or recorded, on one or more previous occasions. **1959** HALAS & MANVELL *Technique Film Animation* xvi. 144 Animation seemed to be too elaborate a process to undertake for the limited number of repeats possible in the television medium. **1965** *Spectator* 5 Mar. 289/2 In the current fortnight no fewer than twenty-seven of the BBC's programmes are 'repeats'. **1973** *Listener* 6 Dec. 798/2 A true interstice piece was the repeat of E. M. Forster's talk on Crabbe, in the interval of *Death in Venice*. **1976** *Weekend Echo* (Liverpool) 4/5 Dec. 2/3 If B.B.C. and ITV have to put repeats on, why don't they show those that were on 15 to 20 years ago.

2. †**a.** A refrain in poetry. *Obs. rare.*

1497 BP. ALCOCK *Mons Perfect.*, The repete of euery balett was this, Englonde may wayle that euer Galand came here. **1589** PUTTENHAM *Eng. Poesie* III. xix. (Arb.) 233 We may terme him the Loue-burden, following the originall, or if it please you, the long repeate.

†**b.** A repeated word or phrase. *Obs.*

1551 T. WILSON *Logike* G j, The third [term] is called the double repeate, which is twise rehersed. *Ibid.* G v, The double repeate which is twise mencioned in both propositions ought to be no doubtfull worde. **1557** N. T. (Genev.) *Matt.* vi. 7 *marg.*, He commandeth vs to beware muche babling and superfluous repetes.

c. *Mus.* A passage repeated or performed twice; the repetition of a passage. Also *fig.*

1663 J. SPENCER *Prodigies* (1665) 3 Similar figures or dispositions..serve as a kind of grateful repeats in the harmony of the world. **1752** AVISON *Mus. Express.* 117 When there are no intermediate notes to introduce the Repeat. **1835** CARRICK *Laird of Logan* 56 She began her complaint against what she called 'these repeats', or singing one line more than once over. **1874** SPURGEON *Treas. David* Ps. xcviii. 5 All repetitions are not vain repetitions, in sacred song there should be graceful repeats. **1884** G. MOORE *Mummer's Wife* (1887) 160 Then there is a repeat, in which the tenors and basses are singing against the women's voices.

d. *Mus.* A sign directing that a passage is to be performed twice.

1667 C. SIMPSON *Compendium* 24 This Mark signifies a Repetition from that place only where it is set, and is called a Repeat. **1706** A. BEDFORD *Temple Mus.* ix. 194 It is.. expressed in our..Anthems by a Mark which we call a Repeat. **1727–38** CHAMBERS *Cycl.* s.v., The great Repeat is only a double bar, dotted on each side. *Ibid.* The small repeat is where only some of the last measures of a strain are to be repeated. **1818** BUSBY *Gram. Mus.* 159 Other abbreviations are also employed under the form of repeats.

†**3.** A recital, account. *Obs. rare.*

1609 MARKHAM *Famous Whore* (1868) 33 Nor will I heere report my foul diseases. For such repeates all modest eares displeases. *c* **1611** CHAPMAN *Iliad* XVI. 57 And so of this repeate enough: Take thou my fame-blaz'd armes [etc.].

4. a. A repetition or duplicate of something.

1842 H. MILLER *O.R. Sandst.* vii. (ed. 2) 144 A doubtful repeat in the strata at one point of junction. **1867** *Sabbath on Rock* ii. 41 The Jewish Sabbath was a repeat of God's seventh day of rest.

b. A device or pattern on cloth, paper, etc., which is repeated uniformly over the surface.

1855 R. N. WORNUM *Anal. Ornament* 19 You have but to design your repeat or unit of repetition; the rest is mere mechanical expansion. **1899** MACKAIL *Life Morris* I. 282 The problem was that..of so arranging the 'repeat' that the pattern should flow continuously over the whole space to be filled, and not fall asunder into patches.

c. *Comm.* A second or fresh supply of goods similar to one already received; also, an order for such a supply, a re-order.

1885 *Pall Mall G.* 14 Nov. 2/1, I ordered patterns and fabrics..only to be disappointed. In short, to use a trade term, I could not be sure of getting a 'repeat'. **1895** *Daily News* 19 Dec. 2/6 We can tell how trade is going by the 'repeats' we get.

5. a. In general *attrib.* (or *adj.*) use, designating a further example or instance of the specified sb.; repeated, occurring again; esp. as ***repeat order, performance.***

1888 *Daily News* 19 Nov. 2/7 There is an encouraging influx of repeat purchases. **1891** *Ibid.* 11 Mar. 2/7 Both new and repeat orders are coming in freely. **1908** A. W. MYERS *Compl. Lawn Tennis Player* xv. 237 'E.R.' comes back in a few minutes for a 'repeat order'. **1935** E. F. BENSON *Lucia's Progress* vii. 206 'Went like hot cakes, ma'am,' said the proprietor, '..and I've just telephoned a repeat order.' **1949** *Radio Times* 15 July 13/4, 9.50 p.m. A repeat performance of *Thaïs* by Massenet. **1961** D. A. BANNERMAN *Birds Brit. Isles* IX. 15 By 10th May all normal clutches have been laid, but repeat-clutches are begun till the last days of May. **1974** J. WAINWRIGHT *Hard Hit* 68 It is a repeat performance of last night; a staring up at the ceiling..a haunting—a remembering. **1978** *Lancashire Life* Nov. 89/1 Postal orders rolled in, followed by repeat orders, together with letters from delighted winners testifying to the efficiency of the pills. **1980** *Times* 6 Sept. 13/5 Last year over half our visitors to London were on repeat visits.

b. Special Combs.: **repeat buying**, the persistent buying of brands with which a shopper is familiar; **repeat fee**, a fee paid to a radio or television artist each time his performance is re-broadcast; **repeat pattern** = sense 4 b; **repeat-sign** *Mus.* = sense 2 d.

1972 A. S. C. EHRENBERG (*title*) *Repeat-buying: theory and applications. **1973** *Nature* 3 Aug. 316/1 A longstanding assumption in the theory of repeat buying has now been explained by results on consumers' brand switching behaviour. **1969** *Daily Tel.* 6 Mar. 18 The principle of the *repeat-fee for the repeated employment of an artistic work has been established in the entertainment world for more than 50 years. **1975** *Broadcast* 21 July 12/2 Repeat fees had to be avoided. **1959** *Listener* 9 Apr. 629/1 There are even numbers of schools where the bastard activity of hand-painted *repeat-pattern-making is still practised. **1967** E. SHORT *Embroidery & Fabric Collage* i. 6 Symmetrical motifs, and repeat patterns, come into their own. **1946** A. L. BACHARACH *Brit. Music of Our Time* iii. 62 *Ostinato* bass-figures..could be indicated by *repeat-signs.

repeat (rɪˈpiːt), *v.* Also 4–7 repete, 6 *Sc.* repit-, 6–7 repeit, 7 repeate; *pa. pple.* 7 repeaten. [ad. F. *répéter* (13th c.), ad. L. *repetĕre* to attack again, do or say again, fetch back, demand the return of, f. *re-* RE- + *petĕre* to attack, make for, demand, seek, etc.]

I. 1. a. *trans.* To say or utter over again (something which one has already said), to reiterate. Also with obj. clause.

c **1375** *Sc. Leg. Saints* vi. (*Thomas*) 77 He can hire pray, In þe sammyne led, fore til repete þai sammyne wordis. **1513** DOUGLAS *Æneis* IV. Prol. 220 By the will I repeit this vers agane, Temporall joy endis with wo and pane. **1597** HOOKER *Eccl. Pol.* v. lxviii. §2 It is true that in sermons we do not use to repeate our sentences seuerally to euery particular hearer. **1617** MORYSON *Itin.* II. 254 We ad nothing more, but doe repeate vnto you, that we then did say in that point. **1667** MILTON *P.L.* IX. 400 Oft he to her his charge of quick returne Repeated. **1719** DE FOE *Crusoe* I. (Globe) 222 He was too earnest for an Answer to forget his Question; so that he repeated it in the very same broken Words. **1780** COWPER *Progr. Err.* 550 His still refuted quirks he still repeats. **1849** MACAULAY *Hist. Eng.* iii. II. 352 The King, as usual, repeated the same words over and over. **1875** JOWETT *Plato* (ed. 2) V. 12 He has repeated his words several times, and yet they cannot understand him.

absol. **1859** TENNYSON *Elaine* 1022 As when we dwell upon a word we know, Repeating, till the word we know so well Becomes a wonder.

b. Used in radio communication, dictation, etc., to emphasize or clarify an important part of the message. Often combined with a negative. Also *transf.*

1938 W. BULLITT Cable 19 Mar. in R. W. Clark *Freud: Man & Cause* (1980) xxiii. 507, I can make available immediately $10,000: but can not (repeat not) be responsible for more. **1943** F. J. BELL *Condition Red* xvi. 259 We are not—repeat—not—a Jap. **1952** *New Statesman* 24 May 612/2 We must not, repeat not, call *Dragon's Mouth*.. a play. **1957** 'J. WYNDHAM' *Midwich Cuckoos* iii. 23 A notification from the R.A.F. was received in Trayne of some unidentified flying object, not, repeat not, a service machine, detected by radar in the Midwich area. **1961** B. PYM *No Fond Return of Love* xi. 104 A notice..which said 'Nobody, repeat *nobody*, is to tamper with the electric heating apparatus in here'. **1973** R. HAYES *Hungarian Game* xxxv. 209 The request was for numbers of people on staff, *repeat*, numbers on staff. **1978** *Guardian Weekly* 8 Oct. 10/2 If—repeat, if—the security forces have been tapping the home telephone of the editor of the Economist.

2. a. To say over, to recite (something previously learned or composed); also, to say or enunciate in a formal manner or in due order; to relate, recount.

1559 W. CUNNINGHAM *Cosmogr. Glasse* 6 You have truly repetyd Ptolomæus wordes. **1560** DAUS tr. *Sleidane's Comm.* 31 b, He wrote to themperour..repeting the whole action at few words. **1597** SHAKS. *2 Hen. IV*, IV. i. 203 And therefore will hee..keepe no Tell-tale to his Memorie, That may repeat and Historie his losse, To new remembrance. **1605** —— *Macb.* IV. iii. 112 These euils thou repeat'st vpon thy selfe, Hath banish'd me from Scotland. **1640** BROME *Antipodes* III. iii, It shall be by posterity repeaten That souldiers ought not to be dund or beaten. **1694** WOOD *Life* (O.H.S.) III. 450 Daniel Stacy..repeated the 4 Easter Sermons at S. Marie's. **1702** ADDISON *Dial. Medals* Wks. 1721 I. 437, I cannot forbear repeating a passage out of Persius..that in my opinion [etc.]. **1754** GRAY *Poesy* 60 She deigns to hear the savage Youth repeat, In loose numbers wildly sweet, Their feather-cinctur'd chiefs, and dusky loves. **1826** SCOTT *Woodst.* xxv, Repeat me these verses again, slowly and deliberately. **1875** JOWETT *Plato* (ed. 2) I. 20 An actor who spoiled his poems in repeating them.

b. *absol.* †Also *spec.* to hear recitations or lessons; to preach as a REPEATER.

1579 *Reg. Privy Council Scot.* III. 244 Mr. Magnus wes placit in the said college be way of interim to repeit with the studentis. **1608** SHAKS. *Per.* I. iv. 74 Thou speak'st like him s [*Q.* himnes] untutered to repeat. **1673** WOOD *Life* (O.H.S.) II. 261 Low Sunday, Samuel Parker of Merton Coll. repeated.

†**c.** To mention, state. *Obs. rare*⁻¹.

1561 DAUS tr. *Bullinger on Apoc.* 19 And first S. Iohn repeteth his name, lest we shuld any thing doubt of thauthour,..But he repeteth not himselfe to be yᵉ seruaunt of God.

†**d.** To celebrate, speak of (as). *Obs. rare.*

1638 BRATHWAIT *Barnabees Jrnl.* III. (1818) 135 Thence to Wenchly, valley-seated, For antiquity repeated. **1671** MILTON *Samson* 645 Reserv'd alive to be repeated The subject of thir cruelty, or scorn.

3. a. To say or utter again after another or others.

1595 SHAKS. *John* III. iv. 95 Greefe fils the roome vp of my absent childe:..Puts on his pretty lookes, repeats his words. **1712** STEELE *Spect.* No. 424 ¶2, I do but repeat what has been said a thousand times. **1754** POCOCKE *Trav.* (Camden) II. 55 Here is an eccho at a well to the Church which repeats seven syllables. **1828** SCOTT *F.M. Perth* xix, With difficulty she forbore from repeating the cries of lamentation and alarm, which were echoed around her. **1874** H. R. REYNOLDS *John Bapt.* I. i. 12 All the writers of the New Testament..do but repeat or transmit the significance of the life and work of Christ.

absol. **1724** RAMSAY *Vision* ix, Eccho answers all; Repetand, and greitand.

†**b.** In *passive.* To be retorted *upon* in the same words. ? *nonce-use.*

1748 RICHARDSON *Clarissa* (1811) VII. 334 *Lovel.* Why so, Sir? *Col.* Why so, Sir ! (angrily)..*Lovel.* (interrupting) I don't choose, Colonel, to be repeated upon, in that accent.

c. With direct speech as obj.: to say or utter again (something that has just been said by oneself or another).

1766 O. GOLDSMITH *Vicar of Wakefield* I. xii. 119 'A groce of green spectacles!' repeated my wife in a faint voice. **1866** C. M. YONGE *Dove in Eagle's Nest* I. ii. 58 'Ah! if the steeple of the Dome Kirk were but finished, I could not mistake it,' said Christina... 'Dome Kirk?' repeated Ermentrude; 'what is that?' **1956** 'C. BLACKSTOCK' *Dewey Death* xii. 278 'He wasn't really bad,' said Barbara... 'Bad!' repeated Mr. Dodds. 'What does that mean?' **1976** H. MACINNES *Agent in Place* xx. 218 'Yes,' Tom repeated, 'he knew he had been tricked.'

II. †**4.** To seek again, return to, encounter or undergo again. *Obs.*

1432–50 tr. *Higden* (Rolls) I. 91 Feynenge oftetymes theym to flee, and after that repetenge fiȝhte. **1645** WALLER *Summer Isl.* III. 106 The pious Trojan so, Neglecting for Creusa's life his own, Repeats the danger of the burning town. **1666** DRYDEN *Ann. Mirab.* cclvii, Others..while through burning labyrinths they retire, With loathing eyes repeat what they would shun. **1697** —— *Virgil* Ded. b iv b, Æneas..having secured his Father and his Son,..repeated all his former Dangers to have found his Wife.

†**5.** *Sc.* To seek in past time; to trace back. *Obs.*

Only in translations, after L. *repetĕre*.

1533 BELLENDEN *Livy* I. Prol. (S.T.S.) I. 8 Þe historie of romanis is of grete besines, becaus It is now to be repetit aboue sevin hundreth ȝeris. **1596** DALRYMPLE tr. *Leslie's Hist. Scot.* I. 68 We think nocht sa far to repeit the beginning athir frome thir..finȝet Goddis, or frome..Gyantes.

6. a. To do, make, perform, or execute over again.

1560 DAUS tr. *Sleidane's Comm.* 382 b, Such thinges.. ought not to have the force of a law, but that all thinges should be repeted from the beginning. **1635** QUARLES *Embl.* II. xiii, He hath ill repented, whose sins are repeated. **1706** *Art of Painting* (1744) 65 There is scarce a painter but has repeated some one of his works. **1727–38** CHAMBERS *Cycl.* s.v., This mark shews, that the particular strain is to be repeated. **1800** tr. *Lagrange's Chem.* II. 104 Add..water to the residuum, boil it a second time, and repeat this operation twice. **1864** BRYCE *Holy Rom. Emp.* v. (1875) 70 He repeats the attempt of Theodoric to breathe a Teutonic spirit into Roman forms.

b. To cause to appear, to bring up or present again. Also freq. in *passive*, denoting recurrence. Also, to broadcast (a radio or television programme) again.

1714 CUNN *Treat. Fractions* Pref. 6 The Reverend Mr. Brown, in his System of Decimal arithmetick, manages such interminate Decimals as have a single Digit continually repeated. **1778** *Encycl. Brit.* (ed. 2) I. 680/2 The second [division of the decimal]..repeats the resulting figure after the dividend is exhausted. **1823** J. MITCHELL *Dict. Math. & Phys. Sci.* 417/2 *Recurring Decimals*, those which are continually repeated in the same order. **1862** STANLEY *Jew. Ch.* (1877) I. viii. 169 Nine times in the course of this single hymn is repeated this most expressive figure. **1923** *Radio Times* 28 Sept. 12/1 Why is it apparently not thought advisable to repeat the 'Request Nights', which..are so popular? **1955** *Ibid.* 22 Apr. 28/3 *Music and Movement*..To be repeated on Friday at 9.55 a.m. **1974** *Listener* 29 Aug. 277/3 There could be no better celebration of the art of standing up and holding forth than the late Dr Bronowski's *The Ascent of Man*, the last episode of which was repeated over the weekend as a tribute.

refl. **1872** FROST *Curve Tracing* 190 The manner in which the curve repeats itself is given in another figure.

c. *intr.* To recur, appear again.

1714 CUNN *Treat. Fractions* 66 If any required Root of some circulating Expression doth not repeat from the Repetend once used, it cannot repeat at all. **1796** HUTTON *Math. Dict.* I. 290/1 That part of the circulate which repeats is called the repetend. **1965** *Listener* 10 June 867/2 A certain rugged, irregular shape tends to repeat throughout the picture. **1967** E. SHORT *Embroidery & Fabric Collage* i. 33 An allover pattern in embroidery differs from one that is printed in that it does not necessarily have to repeat exactly.

d. *trans. Educ.* (orig. *U.S.*). To undertake (a course or period of instruction) again.

1945 C. V. GOOD *Dict. Educ.* 342/2 *Repeater*, a pupil who has repeated or is currently repeating the work of a grade or part of a subject at some designated level of difficulty. **1973** *Sun-Herald* (Sydney) 26 Aug. 83/1 A suggestion has come that he should repeat third year as he is so young. **1976** *National Observer* (U.S.) 28 Aug. 6/3 Make them repeat the course, repeat a year, drop a grade in rank, anything short of expulsion. **1977** *Rolling Stone* 5 May 45/3 Mark had to repeat first and second grades.

7. *spec.* **a.** Of clocks and watches: To strike (the last hour or quarter) again. Also *absol.*

1727–38 CHAMBERS *Cycl.* s.v. *Watch*, Barlow's [watch] was made to repeat, by pushing in two pieces on each side the watch-box; one of which repeated the hour and the other the quarter. **1825** J. NICHOLSON *Operat. Mechanic* 499 A clock..which strikes and repeats, and goes for eight days. **1843** *Penny Cycl.* XXVII. 107/1 The clock would at any time repeat the hour last struck. **1851** *Illustr. Catal. Gt. Exhib.* 1273 Gold watch, striking the hour and quarters, and repeating when wanted.

b. *Naut.* To reproduce (signals made by the admiral). Also *absol.*

1769 FALCONER *Dict. Marine* (1780) s.v. *Signals*, The admiral's signals..are always repeated by the officers next in command; by ships appointed to repeat signals [etc.]. *Ibid.*, To preserve order in the repetition of signals,..the commanders of the squadrons repeat after the admiral. **1809** *Naval Chron.* XXII. 181 Frigates,..To repeat in Admiral Byng's Division. **1867** SMYTH *Sailor's Word-bk.* 568 *To Repeat Signals* is to make the same signal exhibited by the admiral, in order to its being more readily distinguished at a distance.

c. *absol. U.S.* To vote illegally more than once at the same election.

1888 BRYCE *Amer. Commw.* II. III. lxiv. 469 Vagabonds who..are ready to stuff ballot-boxes, to buy votes, to 'repeat', etc.

d. *absol.* Of food: To rise in the gullet, so as to be tasted again.

1879 MISS JACKSON *Shropsh. Word-bk.* **1896** *Mod. Advt.*, Emulsion..does not repeat, which is very much in its favour. **1954** E. B. WHITE *Let.* 28 July (1976) 398 At my age, Miss T., a writer repeats like an onion. **1981** P. HANSFORD

JOHNSON *Bonfire* I. vii. 71, I hope these aren't cucumber sandwiches... Cucumber always repeats.

8. *refl.* **a.** To reproduce or present (oneself) again; to reappear in the same form.

a **1850** JEFFREY (Ogilvie), In personating the heroes of the scene, he does little but repeat himself. **1868** E. EDWARDS *Ralegh* I. xxiv. 561 Biography, like history at large, is apt occasionally to repeat itself.

b. To say again what one has already said. Also *transf.*

1864 FROUDE *Short Stud.* (1867) I. 1 He spoke more than an hour without a note—never repeating himself. **1874** L. STEPHEN *Hours in Library* (1892) I. vi. 220 A man must necessarily repeat himself who writes eighty-five stories.. in less than twenty years. **1965** *Listener* 9 Sept. 393/2 It contradicts most cogently the persistent accusation that Strauss repeated himself.

III. †**9.** Chiefly *Sc. Law.* To ask back, to demand the restitution of (money or goods); to claim, require. Also const. *from. Obs.*

1582 *Reg. Privy Council Scot.* III. 499 All proffite and commoditie quhilk our said Soverane Lord.. mycht ony wyse ask, cleame or repeit fra the saidis pertiners. **1597** *Sc. Acts Jas. VI* §100 *heading*, The maner how gudes taken away, may be repeated. **1609** SKENE *Reg. Maj.* 26 Gif he selles hir dowrie, and she consent thereto after his deceis, she may nocht repete the samine fra the buyer. **1649** JER. TAYLOR *Gt. Exemp.* Disc. x. 136 When a man is in a considerable degree defrauded, then it is permitted to him to repeat his own before Christian arbitrators.

repeatability (rɪpiːtəˈbɪlɪtɪ). [f. REPEATABLE *a.* + -ITY.] Capacity for being repeated; *spec.* the extent to which consistent results are obtained on repeated measurement (cf. REPRODUCIBILITY).

1920 *Music & Lett.* Oct. 289 Repeatability is thus in music an element of the beautiful. **1951** G. HUMPHREY *Thinking* iv. 108 The criterion of repeatability [of experiments] is not fulfilled. **1961** A. FLEUR *Hume's Philos. of Belief* 209 The ultimate warrant for accepting these new scientific ideas lies in their implicit open general challenge to falsification and in their implicit open general promise of repeatability. **1965** *Wireless World* July 338/2 The problems of obtaining good stability and repeatability of resistance value. **1972** *Physics Bull.* May 286/1 By using advanced measurement techniques and controlling the loading procedure a short term repeatability of ± 1 part in 20,000 (± 0·005%) can be achieved. **1976** G. C. SPIVAK in J. Derrida *Of Grammatology* p. lxxxvi, Denying the uniqueness of words, their substantiality, their transferability, their repeatability, *Of Grammatology* denies the possibility of translation.

repeatable (rɪˈpiːtəb(ə)l), *a.* [f. REPEAT *v.* + -ABLE.] Capable of being repeated. *spec.* of a scientific experiment or result.

1802–12 BENTHAM *Ration. Judic. Evid.* (1827) III. 455 Two witnesses and the causes of untrustworthiness repeatable upon each. **1844** *Fraser's Mag.* XXIX. 68 Few see events.. of a more interesting or repeatable description. **1879** MEREDITH *Egoist* xxxvii, To make his home a fountain of repeatable wit. **1935** [see OPERATION 5 a]. **1949** *Monthly Notices R. Astron. Soc.* CXIII. 396 The reason why so many experiments are approximately repeatable is that we take infinite pains to select them from the others. **1955** R. O. KAPP *Facts & Faith* 45 The precision with which experiments are repeatable does not prove that it is in the nature of matter to behave in an orderly manner but only that it is in the nature of scientists to do so. **1969** *Listener* 6 Mar. 301/1 An American botanist.. and his wife.. threw up their careers to devote themselves to evolving a repeatable experiment which could incontrovertibly demonstrate ESP. **1977** *Theology* LXXX. 196 We are here neither in the world of sheer unaccountable miracle nor in that of repeatable experiment.

reˈpeatal. *rare.* [-AL[1].] Repetition.

1891 TALMAGE in *Voice* (N.Y.) 1 Jan., Are there no new lessons from the story, not yet hackneyed by oft repeatal?

repeated (rɪˈpiːtɪd), *ppl. a.* [f. REPEAT *v.*]

1. Reiterated; renewed; frequent.

1611 SHAKS. *Cymb.* I. vi. 4 My supreame Crowne of griefe, and those repeated Vexations of it. **1642** MILTON *Sonn.* viii, The repeated air Of sad Electra's Poet. **1703** DE FOE in *15th Rep. Hist. MSS. Comm.* App. IV. 62 Accept my repeated thanks for the friendship you show. **1764** GOLDSM. *Trav.* 298 The wave-subjected soil Impels the native to repeated toil. **1793** BEDDOES *Calculus* 219 Though I am certain of this increase of weight from repeated experiments. **1855** MACAULAY *Hist. Eng.* xvi. III. 661 The events which were passing.. on the Continent compelled William to make repeated changes in his plans.

2. With advbs. (Well, often, etc.) recited, said over, or related.

1718 PRIOR *Power* 155 The pleasing song, or well repeated tale. **1770** *Junius Lett.* xxxviii. (1788) 202 The cold formality of a well-repeated lesson. **1864** BURTON *Scot Abr.* I. v. 270 An old and oft-repeated tale. **1869** FREEMAN *Norm. Conq.* xiii. (1875) III. 282 They find it much easier to echo some easily repeated formula.

reˈpeatedly, *adv.* [f. prec. + -LY[2].] More than once, again and again, frequently.

a **1718** STEPHENS (J.), And are not these vices, which lead into damnation, repeatedly, and most forcibly cautioned against? **1748** BUTLER *Serm.* Wks. 1874 II. 314 These persons ought repeatedly to be told, how highly blamable they are. **1781** GIBBON *Decl. & F.* xxxi. III. 221 The assurances of.. relief, which were repeatedly transmitted from the court of Ravenna. **1848** W. H. BARTLETT *Egypt to Pal.* xxvi. (1879) 524 On our way to Sidon we repeatedly encountered unknown ruins. **1868** E. EDWARDS *Ralegh* I. xiii. 254 Ralegh.. was repeatedly consulted about Irish affairs.

So **reˈpeatedness.** *rare*[−1].

1664 H. MORE *Myst. Iniq., Apol.* 523 Thus fully have I cleared myself from all general imputations,.. the more industriously, because of the repeatedness of the same.

repeater (rɪˈpiːtə(r)). [f. REPEAT *v.* + -ER[1].]

†**1.** A rehearser, trainer. *Obs. rare*[−1].

1577–87 HOLINSHED *Chron.* III. 920/2 In his chappell he had a deane:.. a subdeane: a repeater of the quire [etc.].

2. a. One who repeats something heard or learned; a relater, reciter.

1598 FLORIO, *Ripitore*; a repeater or relator of a matter. **1656** *Artif. Handsom.* 121 More repeaters of their popular Oratorious vehemencies, than urgers and confirmers of their argumentative strength. **1739** CIBBER *Apol.* (1756) I. 94 Some great author whose sense is deeper than the repeater's understanding. **1797** *Encycl. Brit.* (ed. 3) XVI. 18/2 There is another very peculiar kind of delivery sometimes used in the person of a repeater. **1819** BYRON *Juan* I. xxviii, The hearers of her case became repeaters, Then advocates, inquisitors, and judges. **1893** MAX MÜLLER in Barrows *Parlt. Relig.* II. 936 Thus only can we use the words.. not as thoughtless repeaters, but as honest thinkers and believers.

†**b.** (See quot. 1691.) *Obs.*

1672 WOOD *Life* (O.H.S.) II. 96 Repeaters—1661, Thomas Tomkins, All S[ouls] C[ollege]. **1691** —— *Ath. Oxon.* II. 817 In 1665 he was the Repeater or Repetitioner in S. Maries Church on Low Sunday, of the four Easter Sermons, which being admirably well performed, all to a word *memoriter*, without any hesitation, he obtained a great esteem among the Academians. **1710** HEARNE *Collect.* (O.H.S.) II. 373 The Repeater of the four Easter-Sermons was Mr. Francis Bagshaw. *Ibid.*, Those Privileges that had been granted to former Repeaters.

3. a. A repeating watch or clock. Also *attrib.*

1725 C. MORDAUNT *Let.* in E. Hamilton *Mordaunts* (1965) vii. 141 It [*sc.* a watch] is a silent Repeator. **1766** H. BROOKE *Fool of Quality* I. vii. 290 She did further rob the said right hon. &c. of a large purse of money, his gold repeater, snuff-box, diamond-ring. **1770** *Gentl. Mag.* XL. 438 [To] the four .. [he gave] a gold watch each, one of which was a Paris repeater. **1843** DICKENS *Christmas Carol* ii, He touched the spring of his repeater, to correct this most preposterous clock. **1884** F. J. BRITTEN *Watch & Clockm.* 203 Repeater racks.. should be.. polished underhand. *Ibid.* 224 Repeaters were first made about 1676.

b. *Naut.* A repeating ship.

1782 S. HOOD *Let.* 30 Apr. (1895) 135 Sir George.. took the Eurydice, Admiral Drake's repeater, to carry his *duplicate* despatches. **1829** MARRYAT *F. Mildmay* iii, The signal officers of a repeater had to make out the number of the flag. **1846** YOUNG *Naut. Dict.*, *Repeaters* or *Repeating Ships.*

c. A repeating fire-arm.

1868 *Rep. to Govt. U.S. Munitions War* 27 This rifle is both a breech-loader and a repeater. **1886** *Pall Mall G.* 14 Dec. 7/2 The loading of the repeater can be done in four movements.

d. In *Telegraphy.* A device for automatically retransmitting signals from one circuit to another. Also in *Teleph.*

1859 T. P. SHAFFNER *Telegr. Man.* xxxv. 486 If the line be 600 miles long, and the battery arrangements fail to charge it sufficient for telegraphing, it is the practice to operate it by .. the application of an apparatus called a repeater. **1860** G. PRESCOTT *Electr. Telegr.* 93 A repeater is an apparatus designed for the purpose of duplicating from one electric circuit to another the breaks and completions received from the transmitting station. **1870** POPE *Electr. Tel.* iv. (1872) 45 It was formerly customary to reunite the messages at some intermediate station, but this duty is now usually performed by an apparatus called a repeater. **1923** *Sci. Amer.* Feb. 106/2 The development of the vacuum tube repeaters.. put an entirely different aspect on the problems which have confronted the telephone engineer in the past. *Ibid.* 106/3 These repeaters are placed at regular intervals along the line and as the currents become weakened they pick them up, and.. deliver back into the line a current many times stronger. **1958** *Times* 1 July 8/3 The idea behind the work now in hand is to make possible the inclusion of submerged repeaters at more frequent intervals along the cable, which would proportionately increase the capacity of the communications system. **1972** *Sci. Amer.* Sept. 102/2 Each repeater used in coaxial cables and each relay station used in microwave links adds some noise, mostly from its input circuits.

e. = RELAY *sb.* 4 b. Freq. *attrib.*

1936 *R.C.A. Rev.* I. 26 The modulations are passed on to the distant terminal via the repeater stations. **1940** *Ibid.* V. 36 In order to choose the proper amplifying system it becomes necessary to know the amount of gain to be incorporated in each repeater amplifier. **1946** *Jrnl. Brit. Interplanetary Soc.* VI. 72 Yet three repeater stations circling the Earth could provide a steady, reliable service from Pole to Pole with little more power output than the present London transmitter. **1947** *Proc. IRE* XXXV. 1226/1 In communications systems involving a number of similar repeaters, the distortion permissible in a single repeater is very small. **1959** *Aeroplane* XCVII. 542/1 (*caption*) The 500-lb. repeater satellite proposed by the Space Electronics Corporation. **1965** *New Statesman* 30 Apr. 674/1 Early Bird is an active repeater satellite. That is, it receives signals from powerful ground stations, amplifies them, and rebroadcasts them to the ground. **1972** *Sci. Amer.* Feb. 15/1 Microwaves do not bend with the curvature of the earth, so that for long links it is necessary to use repeaters. **1979** *Ibid.* Jan. 62/3 One example of a 'next generation' circuit that could be built with existing technology is a repeater station in a fiber-optics communication link.

4. *Arith.* A recurring decimal.

1773 *Encycl. Brit.* I. 397/2 Pure repeaters take their rise from vulgar fractions whose denominator is 3, or its multiple 9. **1831** CARLYLE *Sart. Res.* II. iv, Do what one will, there is ever a cursed fraction, oftenest a decimal repeater.

5. Chiefly *U.S.* **a.** One who votes, or attempts to vote, more than once at an election.

1868 [see COLONIST 3]. **1871** *Scribner's Monthly* I. 366 Repeaters changed their coats and hats after every vote. **1884** *Fortn. Rev.* Mar. 389 A leader of a gang of repeaters before the ink on his fraudulent naturalization papers was dry. **1888** BRYCE *Amer. Commw.* II. III. lxiv. 474 [Troy] is full of fellows who go to serve as 'repeaters' at Albany elections. **1904** [see COLONIZER 2].

b. One who is frequently committed to prison. Also, one who repeats an offence; a recidivist.

1884 *Fortn. Rev.* Mar. 389 A repeater before he was of age; a rounder, bruiser, and shoulder-hitter. **1890** *Chicago Advance* 4 Dec., A class of repeaters or rounders, as they are termed, some.. recommitted more than a hundred times to the same prison. **1899** J. FLYNT *Tramping* IV. 386 'Revolver' or 'repeater', is both a tramp and a criminal term for the professional offender, who is continually being brought up for trial. **1938** *Encycl. Brit. Bk. of Yr.* 185/1 These young felons are what prison language describes as 'repeaters', young 'old offenders', who have previously, almost continuously, served prison sentences. **1954** *Daily Mail* 10 Mar. 5/6 As regards the 'repeaters', if a child sees his name in the papers it may well be an incentive.. to future wrongdoing. **1965** MRS. L. B. JOHNSON *White House Diary* 18 July (1970) 303, I asked Nick about repeaters among young criminals. He used some horrifying figure—I believe it was 70 percent. **1977** *Time* 11 July 35/1 After stronger juvenile laws were enacted and violent repeaters were finally jailed in New Orleans, teen-age homicides declined from 29 in 1973 to five in 1975.

c. One who repeats an athletic feat. Also *gen.*, one who repeats an achievement or success.

1895 *Outing* (U.S.) XXVI. 456/2 He is a 'repeater' of the first rank, such performances as winning two three-mile races in the same day.. seeming easy for him. **1944** *Sun* (Baltimore) 13 Jan. 11/2 Mr. Fetterman and Mr. Huffer.. got.. certificates for their suggestions. Mr. Fetterman is a repeater. He.. isn't sure just how many citations have come from the War Production Board for his ideas.

d. *Educ.* A student who undergoes a course or period of instruction again.

1912 *Jrnl. Educ. Psychol.* June 328, 4640 of the children were 'repeaters'... There is nothing to show whether the per cent. thus promoted consists of repeaters regaining their lost grade or of bright children who were skipping a grade. **1945** [see REPEAT *v.* 6 d]. **1976** *National Observer* (U.S.) 6 Nov. 17/3 Repeaters are assigned to schools and remedial classes according to age as well as grade.

e. One who returns repeatedly, esp. to a hotel.

1970 *Globe & Mail* (Toronto) 26 Sept. 31/6 (Advt.), The Bremen probably has the largest number of repeaters on her cruises. **1971** *New Yorker* 4 Dec. 183/2 (Advt.), We're a small hotel... Almost all our guests are repeaters. **1977** *Time* 30 May 21/1 By last week the number of visitors had passed 60,000 (including repeaters), even though news accounts of the 'miracle' cloth have been spotty.

repeatered (rɪˈpiːtəd), *a. Telegr.* and *Teleph.* [f. REPEATER + -ED[2].] Equipped with repeaters.

1932 *Telegraph & Telephone Jrnl.* XVIII. 120/2 The post-war development, as the standard form of trunk line-plant, of repeatered cables which will not carry direct current, drastically limited the progress of further trunk mechanisation. **1964** *Discovery* Oct. 46/1 (*caption*) Repeaters are inserted at intervals along submarine cables to amplify the signal about a million times. A typical trans-oceanic repeatered cable may now carry up to 138 circuits.

repeating (rɪˈpiːtɪŋ), *vbl. sb.* [f. as REPEATER + -ING[1].] The action of the vb. REPEAT in various senses; repetition.

1530 TINDALE *Prol. Deut.* Wks. (1573) 21 The calling to minde, & a repeatyng in the harte of the glorious.. dedes of God. **1595** SHAKS. *John* IV. ii. 19 This acte is as an ancient tale new told; And, in the last repeating, troublesome. **1671** W. MONTAGU in *Buccleuch MSS.* (Hist. MSS. Comm.) I. 500 This.. being the repeating of our dearest Madame's loss by a solicitation relating to it. **1762** FOOTE *Lyar* II. Wks. 1799 I. 294 In common occurrences there is no repeating after him. **1881** MAHAFFY *Old Greek Educ.* xi. 137 The repeating and expounding of the founder's views. **1888** BRYCE *Amer. Commw.* II. III. lxiii. 458 The code.. does not forbid falsehood, or malversation, or ballot stuffing, or 'repeating'.

reˈpeating, *ppl. a.* [f. as prec. + -ING[2].] That repeats, in various senses of the vb.

1. a. Of watches and clocks, or parts of these.

1688 in J. W. Benson *Time & T.-tellers* (1902) 42 His sole making and managing of all pulling repeating pocket-clocks and watches. **1727** GAY *Begg. Op.* I. viii, The gentleman who was here yesterday about the repeating watch. **1764** *Ann. Reg.* 79 A repeating clock which strikes the hours and quarters. **1803** JANE PORTER *Thaddeus* (1826) I. ix. 188 He was pressing the repeating spring, which struck five. **1843** *Penny Cycl.* XXVII. 107/2 Fig. 1 represents the repeating-train between the frames. **1884** F. J. BRITTEN *Watch & Clockm.* 226 Repeating Rack.. [is] a rack in a repeating watch which is shifted one tooth for each blow that is struck.

b. Of ships (see REPEAT *v.* 7 b).

1805 *Naval Chron.* XIII. 466 The *Elven*, a Repeating Sloop. **1844** LD. BROUGHAM *A. Lunel* II. iv. 100 The captain's glass told him that it was only a repeating frigate stationed to windward. **1867** SMYTH *Sailor's Word-bk.* 568 Frigates and small vessels out of the line were deemed repeating ships.

fig. **1810** *Naval Chron.* XXIII. 43 We readily allow the *Naval Chronicle* to serve as repeating frigate. **1824** SCOTT *Redgauntlet* ch. xiii, And you a repeating frigate between Summertrees and the Laird!

c. ***repeating circle***, an instrument for measuring angles, in which accuracy is obtained by repeated measurements on a graduated circle. So ***repeating instrument, theodolet, tripod***, etc.

a **1815** *Brewster's Edinb. Encycl.* VI. 498 The principle to which the repeating circle owes its existence was discovered by Professor Mayer.. in 1758. **1821** TROUGHTON in *Mem. Astron. Soc.* I. (1822) 33 The repeating circle, till within these few years, has been very little used in this country. **1829** PEARSON *Practical Astron.* II. 513 A repeating instrument of the simplest construction. **1841** *Penny Cycl.* XIX. 399/2 A watch telescope can scarcely be applied to a repeating theodolet, and we think that the repeating tripod may be so made as to be free from any objection.

d. Of fire-arms: Capable of firing a number of shots in succession without reloading.

1824 W. N. Blans *Excursion* 47, I saw there several of the celebrated 'repeating swivels.' **1858** Greener *Gunnery* 413 Revolving or repeating pistols have now become as necessary in war as the rifle. *Ibid.* 414 The complicated arrangement of all repeating fire-arms. **1880** *Daily News* 17 Nov., A repeating rifle of novel construction.

e. *Photogr.* ***repeating back***, a form of slide enabling two negatives to be taken on one plate.

1890 Woodbury *Encyc. Photogr.* s.v., There are many forms of studio cameras with repeating backs. **1892** *Phot. Ann.* II. 292 This..possesses the advantage of a repeating back for two cartes..upon one plate.

f. *Telegr.* and *Teleph.* ***repeating coil***, a type of transformer used to transmit a signal from one circuit to another without alteration.

1889 *Telephone* I. 494/2 In connection with one or more of the local circuits on the board are placed repeating coils which terminate in single lines in the local exchanges. **1958** J. R. G. Smith *Elem. Telecomm. Pract.* vi. 105 A repeating coil is a special type of transformer in which the ratio of the windings is equal,..and is used to 'repeat' speech currents from one part of a circuit to another.

2. a. *Arith.* Of decimals: Recurring.

1773 *Encycl. Brit.* I. 397/2 Repeating decimals are of two kinds: viz. some consist only of the repeating figures [etc.]. **1847** De Morgan *Arithm. Bks.* 79 Another tract on repeating decimals.

b. *Math.* (See quot.)

1872 Frost *Curve Tracing* 187 Repeating Curves..whose equations involve trigonometrical functions of the coordinates in the place of the coordinates themselves. The loci of such curves, from the nature of trigonometrical function, are made up of patterns continually repeated in every direction.

3. That repeats a sound.

1709 Mrs. Rowe *Love & Friendship* 43, I..All Day to the repeating leaves complain In mournful Accents. **1839** De Quincey *Recoll. Lakes* Wks. 1862 II. 19 A shout from an aerial height..propagated through repeating bands of men from a distance of many miles.

4. Of a pattern: repeated or recurring uniformly over a surface.

1959 *Listener* 16 Apr. 679/1 Stuffy repeating patterns, 'folksy' craftwork. **1967** E. Short *Embroidery & Fabric Collage* iii. 74 Initials could be designed as a separate motif or incorporated into a repeating design.

†**re'peccating**, *ppl. a. Obs. rare*$^{-1}$. [f. re- + ppl. stem of L. *peccāre* to offend.] = peccant *a.* 3.

1597 A. M. tr. *Guillemeau's Fr. Chirurg.* 49b/1 Only that the repeccating humors be cleanlye purged out.

‖**repêchage** (rɛpəʃɑːʒ, ‖ rəpɛʃaʒ). *Sport* (orig. *Rowing*). Also **repechage**. [a. F. *repêchage*, f. *repêcher* to fish out, rescue; to give an examination candidate a second chance to pass.] An extra contest in which the runners-up in the eliminating contests compete for a place in the final. Also *attrib.*

1928 *Daily Express* 7 Aug. 12 M. Bernasconi, their representative in the single sculls, met Joe Wright..in the repechage—second chance—contests for Saturday's second-round losers. **1948** *Call-Bulletin* (San Francisco) 3 July 5/7 Harvard, upset by Cornell in the first trial heat, got back into the running by the 'repechage' or second-trial system. **1955** *Times* 25 Aug. 2/7 On Friday there will be repechages for teams beaten in the opening heats. **1959** *Times* 20 Apr. 3/1 Those teams knocked out in the first round took part in a *repêchage*. **1976** *Yachts & Yachting* 20 Aug. 375/3 The following day there is a repechage in the same waters. **1978** *Times* 30 June 21/6 The Poles won by virtue of the 'repêchage' principle, which provides for one of the 61 defeated teams to reenter the competition by beating the other defeated teams.

†**repe'dation**. *Obs.* [ad. L. type **repedātiōn-em*, n. of action f. *repedāre* to step back, f. *re-* re- 2 a + *pedāre* to step.] Retrogression, *esp.* of the planets. (Only in H. More.)

1642 H. More *Song of Soul* II. App. lxxvi, Another Adam once received breath, And still another in endlesse repedation. **1653** —— *Antid. Ath.* II. xii. §17 The Directions, Stations and Repedations of those Erratick Lights.

repeell, -peit, obs. ff. repeal *sb.*, repeat *v.*

repel (rɪˈpɛl), *v.* Also 5–6 repelle, 6–7 (9) repell. [ad. L. *repellĕre*, f. *re-* re- + *pellĕre* to drive: cf. *compel*, *impel*, etc.]

†**1.** *trans.* To drive or put away; to remove, extinguish, quench. *Obs.*

1432–50 tr. *Higden* (Rolls) III. 471 Water dothe repelle [L. *extinguit*] oure naturalle thurste, and golde your thurste. **1483** Caxton *Gold. Leg.* 85/2 Thenne was it thyng couenable that he that shold repelle this defaulte shold be born of a vyrgyne. *a* **1586** Montgomerie *Misc. Poems* xvii. 39 Leid, Ane hevy mettall cauld and deid, Repelling loue,.. And quencher of desyre. *c* **1586** C'tess Pembroke *Ps.* cv. xi, [God] their hunger to repel, Candies the grasse with sweete congealed dew.

2. To drive or force back (an assailant or invader, an attack, etc.); to repulse. Also const. *from*, †*out of*, †*into*, †*to*.

c **1450** *Cov. Myst.* (Shaks. Soc.) 106 Hese [Satan's] grete males, good Lord, repelle, And take man onto thi grace. **1500–20** Dunbar *Poems* lxxvi. 5 A pray to deid, quhome vane is to repell. **1566** *Form Com. Prayer* in *Liturg. Serv. Q. Eliz.* (Parker Soc.) 527 The Turks..most fiercely assailing the Isle of Malta..were from thence repelled and driven. **1613** Purchas *Pilgrimage* IX. viii. (1614) 867 They..land in another place, but are repelled to their ships by the Inhabitants. **1678** Wanley *Wond. Lit. World* v. ii. §66. 471/2 Henry, the brother of Baldwin, repelled the Bulgarians out of Greece. **1717** Pope *Iliad* XI. 680 So turn'd stern Ajax, by whole hosts repell'd. **1821–2** Shelley *Chas. I*, IV. 43 Repelling invasion from the sacred towers. **1859** Thackeray *Virgin.* vi, The small body of provincial troops with which he marched to repel the Frenchmen.

absol. **1595** Markham *Sir R. Grenvile* F iv, He repeld them whilst repell he might, Till fainting power was tane from power to fight. **1764** Goldsm. *Trav.* 344 Here..Minds combat minds, repelling and repell'd.

b. To resist, repress (a feeling, incentive, etc.).

1586 A. Day *Eng. Secretary* II. (1625) 37 What sonne will for any zeale or duty once seeke to repell his owne appetite? **1667** Milton *P.L.* VIII. 643 Perfect within, no outward aid require; And all temptation to transgress repel. **1817** Shelley *Rev. Islam* IV. xvii, The hopes which inly dwell, My manners note that I did long repel. **1877** C. Geikie *Christ* I. xxvii. 438 Evil thoughts count as acts with the Eternal, if not at once repelled.

c. *Med.* To force back into the blood or system; to repress (a morbid humour, swelling, eruption, etc.). Now *rare* or *Obs.*

1719 [see repelling *vbl. sb.*]. **1727** Bradley *Fam. Dict.* s.v. *Tumour*, The other [method] is to stop and repel 'em; which is call'd Repercussion, that sends 'em back to their Source. **1753** Bartlet *Farriery* 297 It being thought.. unsafe to repel some of these discharges. **1822–34** [see *Repelled* below].

†**3.** To reject or debar (a person) *from* an office, right, etc. Also without const. *Obs.*

1456 Sir G. Haye *Law Arms* (S.T.S.) 251 Sen women be the law commoun ar repellit, and by put, us think that the quene may nocht be juge in the cas. **1536–7** in Bolton *Stat. Irel.* (1621) 142 By authoritie of this Parliament unhabled and repelled from the exercising, receiving, or occupying of that office for ever. **1566** T. Stapleton *Ret. Untr. Jewel* I. 1 If any coming to the communion duly and semely prepared be repelled of the priest. **1766** Blackstone *Comm.* II. 498 It shall be sufficient to repel the husband from his general right of administring his wife's effects.

†**b.** To stop, hinder, or restrain (a person) *from* an action or manner of acting. *Obs.*

1483 Caxton *Gold. Leg.* 168/2 Many letters by whyche thou repellyd moche folke fro doyng sacrefyse to our goddes. **1609** Bible (Douay) *2 Macc.* v. 18 This man also immediately as he came had bene scourged, and repelled verily from his boldnes. **1617** Moryson *Itin.* I. 262 The Ianizare..repelled him from doing mee any wrong.

†**c.** To put or thrust (one) away. *Obs. rare.*

c **1530** *Pol. Rel. & L. Poems* (1903) 59 Put from the a proude servaunte,..Allso repelle that seruavnte that vsith to blaundysh the. **1540–54** Croke *13 Ps.* (Percy Soc.) 36 For thou art God myne onely strength, Wherfor then doest thou me repell?

4. To turn back, ward off (a weapon, blow or wound). Also in *fig.* context.

1526 *Pilgr. Perf.* (W. de W. 1531) 188 The sheelde of feyth, wherby we may easely resist and repell all such fyry dartes of temptacion. **1594** Hooker *Eccl. Pol.* II. v. §7 Neither doth Tertullian bewray this weakness in striking only, but also in repelling their strokes with whom he contendeth. **1717** Pope *Iliad* XI. 304 But the broad belt.. The point rebated, and repell'd the wound. *c* **1753** Cowper *To Miss Macartney* 42 What though in scaly armour dressed, Indifference may repel The shafts of woe.

b. To ward off, resist (some outward evil).

1600 Holland *Livy* VIII. xxiii. 297 Which contumelie and reprochfull injurie..they would with all their might and maine repell..from them. **1610** Guillim *Heraldry* VI. v. 267 A Military Habit used..to repell the extremity of wet, cold and heate. **1697** tr. *Burgersdicius' Logic* I. xx. 80 House and Clothes [agree] in End; for the End of both, is to repell the Injuries of the Heavens. **1736** Warburton *Alliance betw. Ch. & State* III. iii, Evil which proceeds not from the will is called a mischief; and may be simply repelled. **1780** Bentham *Princ. Legisl.* xiv. § 3 The case in which an individual repels an evil to which the laws do not wish to expose him. **1799** Cowper *Castaway* 40 So long he, with unspent power, His destiny repelled.

5. To drive or force back (something moving or advancing), esp. by physical resistance.

1605 Camden *Rem.* 165 A man ascending a Mountaine, but repelled with contrarie winds. **1657** Trapp *Comm. Job* xxxvi. 19 As the Rocks repel the greatest waves, so doth God his enemies. **1692** Ray *Disc.* (1713) 42 There is very great use of them [mountains], for repelling the vapours..and hindering their Evagation Northward. **1791** Newte *Tour Eng. & Scot.* 153 The waters of both [rivers]..being repelled by the bold and rocky shores of Ross-shire. **1817** Shelley *Rev. Islam* VI. v, I rushed among the rout to have repelled That miserable flight. **1831** Landor *Misc. Poems* Wks. 1846 II. 620 The ebbing sea thus beats against the shore; The shore repels it; it returns again.

b. To force away by the operation of natural laws of matter. (Cf. repulsion.)

1710 [see repelling *ppl. a.*]. **1744** Berkeley *Siris* §237 Why should the particles of common salt repel each other..? **1747** Franklin *Exper. Electr.* (1751) 11 If a cork-ball..be repelled by the tube..'tis surprizing to see how suddenly it flies back. *c* **1790** Imison *Sch. Arts* I. 48 The hairs of his head..will repel one another. **1863** E. V. Neale *Anal. Th. & Nat.* 227 That each particle of matter..repels other particles of matter. **1882** S. P. Thompson in *Nature* XXVI. 554/2 The moving electro-magnets were first attracted towards the opposing poles, and then, as they neared them, were caused to be repelled past.

c. To refuse to mix with (one another), or to admit (moisture).

1744 Berkeley *Siris* §227 Why oil and water, mercury and iron, repel..each other. **1822** Imison *Sc. & Art* I. 23 Oil and water seem to repel each other. **1885** C. G. W. Lock *Workshop Receipts* Ser. IV. 360/2 If the film repel the solution, just run the finger..over the repellent portion.

6. To refuse to accept or receive; *esp.* to reject (a statement, plea, etc.) as unfounded or invalid.

1561 *Reg. Privy Council Scot.* I. 180 The said first exceptioun aucht and suld be repellit. **1573** *Ibid.* II. 260 Quhilk allegeance being repellit be my Lord Regentis Grace and Counsall. **1602** Shaks. *Ham.* II. i. 109, I did repell his Letters, and deny'de His accesse to me. **1852** Mrs. Stowe *Uncle Tom's C.* xxiv. 231 She always repelled quite indignantly any suggestion that anyone around her could be sick. **1873** M. Arnold *Lit. & Dogma* Pref. (1876) 28 The Greek Christianity of the East repelled the Apocalypse, and the Latin Christianity of the West repelled the Epistle to the Hebrews. **1884** *Law Rep.* 9 *App. Cases* 344 It is declared, That the second plea in law of the defenders ought to be repelled.

b. To confute, disprove. *rare.*

a **1634** Chapman *Revenge for Honour* Plays 1873 IV. 293 The kernel of the text enucleated I shall confute, refute, repel, refel. **1794** Paley *Evid.* II. ii. (1817) 26 It is such a morality as completely repels the supposition of its being the tradition of a barbarous age.

7. To drive away or repulse (one who makes advances) with harsh words or treatment, or by denial; to reject (a suit).

1592 Shaks. *Ven. & Ad.* 573 Foule wordes, and frownes, must not repell a louer. **1667** Milton *P.L.* x. 868 Soft words to his fierce passion she assay'd; But her with stern regard he thus repell'd. **1738** Wesley *Ps.* II. x, Whoe'er their Advocate repel, The Anger of their Judge shall feel. **1828** Scott *F.M. Perth* xxv, If I continued to repel his wicked suit. **1860** Tyndall *Glac.* I. xviii. 125 Like suitors that will not be repelled.

b. To affect (one) with distaste or aversion.

1840 Dickens *Old C. Shop* xix, Through this delirious scene, the child frightened and repelled by all she saw [etc.]. **1846** Hare *Mission Comf.* (1850) 276 Such extravagances.. repell minds that have a sense of truth. **1878** R. W. Dale *Lect. Preach.* i. 7 You ought also to remember that for purposes of intellectual discipline, a study which repels you is invaluable.

absol. **1817** Mill *Brit. India* II. v. v. 502 The probability that Hyder would not permit them, unopposed, to pass the river Palâr..was a motive rather to stimulate than to repel. **1821** Shelley *Adonais* liii, What still is dear Attracts to crush, repels to make thee wither. **1847** Emerson *Repr. Men, Swedenborg* Wks. (Bohn) I. 333 Swedenborg..with all his accumulated gifts, paralyzes and repels.

Hence **re'pelled** *ppl. a.*

1822–34 *Good's Study Med.* (ed. 4) III. 197 Repelled gout, and repelled cutaneous eruptions. **1871** Tyndall *Fragm. Sci.* (1879) I. xiii. 374 The attracted end of the needle being nearer to the pole of the magnet than the repelled end.

repel, obs. form of repeal.

†**re'pele**. *Obs. rare.* [? var. of repeal *sb.*; but cf. med.L. *repellus* (Du Cange) as the name of some game.] An additional stake in the Roman game of hucklebones.

1542 Udall *Erasm. Apoph.* 164 The caster..was of force constraigned in the wayе of repele to laie doune to the stake one peece of coyne. *Ibid.* The caster should wynne and take ..all the repeles.

repele, -pell, obs. forms of repeal *sb.* and *v.*

re'pellance, -ancy. [See next and -ance, -ancy.] The act of repelling; a repellent feature or trait.

1860 Ouida *Tricotrin* I. 36 She uttered the words that had wounded her, as though in haughty repellance of their power to sting. **1878** C. Stanford *Symb. Christ* iv. 101 That man in whose conduct grace is scarcely visible through the repellancies of mortal infirmity.

repellant (rɪˈpɛlənt), *a.* and *sb.* [f. repel *v.*]

A. *adj.* **1. a.** = repellent *a.* 2. Also *fig.*

1768–74 Tucker *Lt. Nat.* (1834) II. 317 The repellant quality of external bodies holds their internal parts together in a stronger cohesion. **1877** Sparrow *Serm.* xxiv. 327 Mercy and works of law know not one another; are mutually repellant; refuse to commingle like oil and water.

b. Warding off, defensive.

1839–52 Bailey *Festus* 125 Keep thy spirit pure From worldly taint by the repellant strength Of virtue.

c. = repellent *a.* 2 b.

1897 *Sears, Roebuck Catal.* 274 [Wrap] made of imported black repellant cloth.

d. = repellent *a.* 2 d.

1944 *Living Off Land* v. 111 Repellant cream should be smeared thoroughly on all parts of the skin which are unprotected by clothing.

2. = repellent *a.* 3.

1825 Lytton *Zicci* I. v. His manners were chilling and repellant. **1877** E. Caird *Philos. Kant* Introd. vi 117 The exclusive and repellant conception of individuality given by that philosophy.

B. *sb.* = repellent *sb.*, in various senses.

1689 Moyle *Sea Chyrurg.* II. xiii. 62 Use no repellants, nor anything to cool inflammation. **1794** Anna Seward *Lett.* (1811) IV. 11 May the people, amongst whom I live, be withheld by stronger repellants than their own virtue, from invading my own property. **1805** Luccock *Nat. Wool* 94 The skilful application of tar mingled with butter, which act as repellants to the water. **1860** J. Young *Prov. Reason* 33 To be followed, there is reason to fear, unless some sufficient corrective and repellant be forthcoming, by not less lamentable consequences. **1908** *Jrnl. Econ. Entomol.* I. 83 He had tried repellants against the cotton boll weevil, including lemon, cinnamon, tar and clove oil. **1945** *Tee Emm* (Air Ministry) V. 51 Use the shark repellant sparingly. **1958** Moth-repellant [see moth *sb.*[1] 3]. **1958** *Sunday Times* 20 July 16/5 Simple dressings..and an insect repellant are obvious necessities.

repelle, obs. form of REPEAL *sb.* and *v.*

re'pellence. [See next and -ENCE.] = next.
1866 BUSHNELL *Vicar. Sacr.* II. iv. 159 There have been severities and repellences, and discouraging tokens, blended so continually with the story. **1884** *Pall Mall G.* 8 Oct. 4/2 The armament of the *Rodney*.. is only in strict keeping with his powers of repellence.

repellency (rɪ'pɛlənsɪ). [See next and -ENCY.] The quality of being repellent; repelling power.
1747 FRANKLIN *Exper. Electr.* (1751) 11 You may draw off the electrical fire, and destroy the repellency. **1805** FOSTER *Ess.* I. vii. I. 110 The odious repellency of their example. **1836** J. ABBOTT *Way to do Good* vii. 222 It is this overrated importance which each.. attaches to its own forms.. that constitutes the repellency between the brawlers.

repellent (rɪ'pɛlənt), *a.* and *sb.* [ad. L. *repellent-em*, pres. pple. of *repellĕre* to REPEL.]
A. *adj.* **1.** Of medicines or medical applications: Having the effect of repelling morbid humours, etc. (See REPEL *v.* 2 c.) Now *rare*.
1643 J. STEER tr. *Exp. Chyrurg.* v. 19 It is necessary to use repellent Medicines, to wit, defensives, and clouts wet in Vinegar. **1704** J. HARRIS *Lex. Techn.* I, *Repellent Medicines*, are such things as by stopping the Heat and Afflux of Humors.. decrease the swelling of a part. **1719** QUINCY *Phys. Dict.* (1722) 381/2 All those means are said to be repellent, which check the Growth of the Tumour. **1807–26** S. COOPER *First Lines Surg.* (ed. 5) 62 Every thing wet, whether warm or cold, emollient, repellent or astringent. **1830** LINDLEY *Nat. Syst. Bot.* 39 The leaves [of Sterculia fœtida] are considered repellent and aperient.
2. a. Having the power of repelling other bodies; characterized by repulsion. Also const. *of*.
1744 BERKELEY *Siris* §237 Why should the most repellent particles be the most attractive upon contact? **1794** SULLIVAN *View Nat.* II. 155 Each fragment of a pillar having its attractive and repellent points. **1812** SIR H. DAVY *Chem. Philos.* 136 The different manner.. in which their parts become capable of communicating attractive or repellent powers to other matter. **1864** LOWELL *Fireside Trav.* 47 There are some men.. whose clothes are repellent of dust and mud.
b. Impervious to, not receptive of, moisture.
1805 R. W. DICKSON *Pract. Agric.* I. Pl. 44 A manner of draining where the surface soil and base are repellent. **1885** [see REPEL v. 5 c].
c. Repelling or warding off attack.
1889 PATER *G. de Latour* (1896) 34 He saw the beautiful city.. as if sheathed austerely in repellent armour.
d. Causing certain insects or other animals not to settle or approach.
1971 'G. BLACK' *Time for Pirates* i. 15 The air reeked from ..mosquito-repellent smudge. **1979** D. KYLE *Green River High* x. 131 We were smothered in repellent cream, but that didn't stop them [*sc.* insects].
3. Repelling by coldness of demeanour, or by some disagreeable feature; affecting one with distaste or aversion.
1797 GODWIN *Enquirer* II. xii. 460 Sherlock.. is.. somewhat repellent in his language. **1836** F. MAHONEY *Rel. Father Prout, Songs Horace* i. (1859) 387 Chilled by thy mien repellent and disdainful. **1879** FARRAR *St. Paul* (1883) 519 He overthrew.. the repellent demand that the Gentiles should be circumcised.
B. *sb.* **1.** *Med.* An application serving to repel humours, etc. (see A. 1 above). Now *rare*.
1661 LOVELL *Hist. Anim. & Min.* 431 Fractures.. are cured by repellents hindering inflammation. **1710** T. FULLER *Pharm. Extemp.* 170 Repellents in the Gout are sometimes most exceeding dangerous. **1766** *Compl. Farmer* s.v. *Jardon*, It should be first treated with coolers and repellents, such as hot vinegar, verjuice, &c. **1830** LINDLEY *Nat. Syst. Bot.* 214 The bark of the root and the.. leaves.. are considered by the native Indian doctors as powerful repellents.
†**2.** A repulse. *Obs. rare*⁻¹.
1777 JOHNSON *Let. to Mrs. Thrale* 20 Sept., Did he not hold out against forty such repellents from Mrs. P——?
3. A repelling power or influence.
1802 MRS. E. PARSONS *Myst. Visit* III. 245 All the impediments that act as repellents to your passion. **1802–12** BENTHAM *Ration. Judic. Evid.* (1827) IV. 292 It becomes a perpetual source of disgust, and serves as a perpetual repellent to the eye of scrutiny.
4. A substance that causes certain insects or other animals not to settle or approach. Freq. in *Comb.* preceded by the name of the animal, as ***insect repellent*** (see INSECT *sb.* 4 a), etc.
1908 *Jrnl. Econ. Entomol.* I. 81 (*heading*) Experiments with repellents against the corn root-aphis. **1923** *Ibid.* XVI. 222 A very effective repellent for practical use is a mixture of one part furfural to four parts pine tar oil. **1942**, etc. [see MOTH *sb.*[1] 3]. **1949** *Consumer Reports* July 311/1, 38 brands of insect repellents. **1950** 'N. SHUTE' *Town like Alice* 43 If they were to spend another night upon the veranda she must get hold of some mosquito repellent. **1955** *Sci. Amer.* Aug. 76/3 It is neither an attractant nor a repellent to unconditioned salmon, and would have meaning only to those conditioned to it. **1963** 'F. RICHARDS' *First come, First Kill* v. 60, I probably smell to high heaven of insect repellent. **1968** C. HELMERICKS *Down Wild River North* I. xv. 234 Covering myself.. with canvas against the angry insects blown back from the horses' backs, and bathing my hooded face with repellent. **1979** R. PERRY *Bishop's Pawn* viii. 144 This left the insects free to concentrate on me and the repellent I was using hadn't matured with age.
Hence **re'pellently** *adv.*
1883 TALMAGE in *Chr. Her.* 16 May 272/1 It is religion presented repellently, morning, noon and night. **1885** *Manch. Exam.* 30 Dec. 3/1 They are.. healthy in tone, without being repellently didactic.

repeller (rɪ'pɛlə(r)). [f. REPEL *v.* + -ER[1].]
1. One who repels.
1611 COTGR., *Repoulseur*, a repulser, a repeller. **1832** *Examiner* 805/1 The one pushes the human soul from him—the other, with a bow, consigns it back to its repeller. **1836** LYTTON *Athens* (1837) II. 126 The Athenians.. were the true repellers of the invader. **1875** *Contemp. Rev.* XXV. 701 The apostle of toleration, the impatient repeller of all clerical pretensions.
†**2.** = REPELLENT *sb.* 1. *Obs.*
1661 LOVELL *Hist. Anim. & Min.* 403 The vertigo, is helped by temporal repellers, discutients,.. and quinces. **1710** T. FULLER *Pharm. Extemp.* 43 Repellers mostly have place in the very beginnings of Inflammations. **1753** BARTLET *Farriery* 220 Strains in the hock are to be treated by soaking the parts with coolers and repellers.

†**repelless**, *a.* *Obs. rare*⁻¹. [f. REPEL *v.* + -LESS.] That cannot be repelled.
1595 MARKHAM *Sir R. Grinvile* E vij, Two great Armados ..by assault made knowne repellesse might.

re'pelling (rɪ'pɛlɪŋ), *vbl. sb.* [f. REPEL *v.* + -ING[1].] The action of the vb.; repulse.
1533 BELLENDEN *Livy* II. xiv. (S.T.S.) I. 183 Valerius left þe said auctorite for [þe] Indignacioun þat he tuke in his mynde for þe repelling of his petitiouns. **1611** COTGR., *Repoulsement*, a repulsing, repelling. **1651** HOBBES *Govt. & Soc.* vi. §17. 103 To the repelling of a forraign enemy, they appoint a certain and limited return. **1719** QUINCY *Phys. Dict.* (1722) 381/1 By repelling is meant those Means which prevent such an Afflux of Fluid to any particular part, as would raise it into a Tumour.

re'pelling, *ppl. a.* [f. as prec. + -ING[2].] That repels, in various senses of the vb.
1597 A. M. tr. *Guillemeau's Fr. Chirurg.* 44 b/2 He is called the expulsive or repellinge ligature. **1611** COTGR., *Repercussif*, repercussiue, repelling. **1710** J. HARRIS *Lex. Techn.* II. s.v., In Mechanicks, where Attraction ceases to exert it self, a kind of repelling Force should succeed. **1726** SWIFT *Gulliver* III. iii, When the repelling Extremity points downwards, the Island mounts directly upwards. **1758** J. S. *Le Dran's Observ. Surg.* (1771) 249, I ordered emollient and repelling Cataplasms to be applied. **1841** L. HUNT *Seer* II. (1864) 62 The feeling in the poet's mind changes.. from the repelling to the engaging. **1849** NOAD *Electricity* (ed. 3) 296 When the two repelling poles are brought into contact.
Hence **re'pellingly** *adv.*, **re'pellingness**.
1815 *Zeluca* I. 371 She must behave almost repellingly to the two men of her acquaintance she most esteemed. **1863** THORNBURY *True as Steel* III. 230 The eyes no longer stared repellingly with a fixed and hard glance. **1895** W. S. LILLY *Four Humourists* 66 Despite the repellingness of his style.

repeman, variant of REAPMAN *Obs.*

re-'pen, *v.* [RE- 5 a.] *trans.* To pen again.
c **1616** S. WARD *Coal from Altar* (1627) 77 If Dauid were now to re-pen his Psalme, I think he might alter the forme of his counsell.

†**repend**, *v.*[1] *Obs. rare*⁻¹. [ad. OF. *repenner*, *repesner*, etc. (Godef.).] *intr.* To kick, fling,
?*a* **1400** *Morte Arth.* 2107 Thane riche stedes repende*z*, and rasches one armes.

†**re'pend**, *v.*[2] *Obs. rare.* [ad. L. *rependĕre* f. *re-* RE- + *pendĕre* to pay.] *trans.* To repay.
c **1550** L. WAGER *Life Marie Magd.* 1297 O Lord.. To thee what tong is able worthy thanks to repend. *c* **1557** ABP. PARKER *Ps.* cix. 321 For good they euil agayne requite:.. And so for loue.. whote hate they do repend.

rependant, obs. form of REPENTANT *a.*

†**repen'sation.** *Obs. rare*⁻⁰. [ad. late L. *repensātiōn-em* f. *repensāre*: cf. *compensation*.] 'A making recompense' (Blount 1656).

†**re'pent**, *sb.* *Obs.* [f. the vb.] Repentance; an act of repentance. (Freq. in Greene's works.)
1590 SPENSER *F.Q.* III. xii. 24 Reproch the first, Shame next, Repent behinde. *c* **1590** GREENE *Fr. Bacon* xiv. 15 For this I scourge myself with sharp repents. **1611** in Farr *S.P. Jas. I* (1848) 175 My soule.. In deepe repent, her former folly hates.

repent ('riːpənt), *a.*[1] [ad. L. *repent-*, ppl. stem of *repĕre* to creep.]
1. a. *Bot.* Creeping; *esp.* growing along the ground, or just under the surface, and sending out roots at intervals.
1669 J. ROSE *Eng. Vineyard* (1675) 16 There is no plant whatsoever so conatural to the vine.. as this repent, and humble shrub. **1707** SLOANE *Jamaica* I. 94 This had a small repent root. *Ibid.* 112 This has a crooked repent stem. **1846–50** A. WOOD *Class-bk. Bot.* 74 Holland is said to owe its very existence to certain repent stems, by which its shores are apparently bound together.
b. *Zool.* Creeping, crawling, reptant.
1841 *Penny Cycl.* XIX. 405/1 The third order, *Serpentia*, which are defined as having.. a repent progression.
2. *fig.* Unable to rise to high ideas. *rare*⁻¹.
1684 EVELYN *Let. to Pepys* 8 June, He.. bravely enlarges the empire of our narrow speculations, and repent spirits, whose contemplations extend no further than their sense.

†**re'pent**, *a.*[2] *Obs. rare.* [f. stem of REPENT *v.*; cf. obs. F. *repent* (Godef.).] Repentant.
a **1500** *Chaucer's Dreme* 1694 The queen forthwith hire leue Toke at them all that were present, of hire defaults fully repente.

repent (rɪ'pɛnt), *v.* Also 7 as *pa. pple.* [ad. F. *repentir* (11th c.) f. *re-* RE- + Rom. **penitīre*:—L. *poenitēre*: see PENITENT.]
1. *refl.* To affect (oneself) with contrition or regret for something done, etc. (cf. 3.) Also const. *of*, *for*, *that*. Now *arch.*
c **1290** *S. Eng. Leg.* I. 52/173 Of hire misdedes heo repentede hire sore. *a* **1300** *Cursor M.* 7308 (Cott.), Ful sare yee sal repent yow. *c* **1305** *Pilate* 106 in *E.E.P.* (1862) 114 Longe after þat he [Christ] was ded, he [Pilate] repentede him ilome. *c* **1386** CHAUCER *Pars. T.* ⁋224 Many menne repenten hem neuere of swiche thoghtes. *c* **1400** tr. *Secreta Secret., Gov. Lordsh.* 63 Repent þe noght of þinges passyd. **1484** CAXTON *Fables of Æsop* I. xv, They that be glad.. of the praysynge of flaterers oftyme repente them therof. *a* **1533** LD. BERNERS *Huon* xxiii. 68, I repent me that I hadde not beleuyd you. **1594** SHAKS. *Rich. III* I. iv. 285, I repent me that the Duke is slaine. **1619** LD. DONCASTER in *Eng. & Germ.* (Camden) 207, I now repent me of it, hearing the niewes of Moravia confirmed from all parts. **1682** BUNYAN *Holy War* (Cassell) 157, I was formerly a great companion of his, for the which I now repent me. **1842** TENNYSON *Ed. Gray* 23, I repent me of all I did.
2. *impers.* To cause (one) to feel regret, etc.
13.. *Coer de L.* 324 Hym repented that he cam there. **1390** GOWER *Conf.* III. 270 As he withinne his herte caste, Which him repenteth ate laste. ?*a* **1400** *Morte Arth.* 1391 It salle repent vs fulle sore and we ryde forthire! **1470–85** MALORY *Arthur* VII. viii. 224 Me repenteth, grene knyghte, of your dommage. **1560** DAUS tr. *Sleidane's Comm.* 147 It shall not repent them of y[e] service. **1606** G. W[ODCOCKE] *Hist. Ivstine* XXXVIII. 123 It repented him that he let go Demetrius. **1664** MARVELL *Corr.* Wks. (Grosart) II. 148 This indeed would repent me, for the World will take more notice of it. **1717** *Entertainers* No. 11. 72 It can never repent us to endeavour to tread in the Steps of those bright Examples. **1819** SHELLEY *Prometh. Unb.* I. 303 It doth repent me: words are quick and vain. **1878** SWINBURNE *Tri. Time* xxi, Will it not one day in heaven repent you?
†**b.** In passive. *Obs. rare.*
a **1450** *Knt. de la Tour* (1868) 71 That is to mene, that they that be confession are clensed and repented [etc.]. **1530** *Exam. W. Thorpe* in *Bale's Sel. Wks.* (Parker Soc.) 109, I say to thee, that in the turning about of thy hand such a sinner may be verily repented.
3. *intr.* To feel contrition, compunction, sorrow or regret for something one has done or left undone; to change one's mind with regard to past action or conduct through dissatisfaction with it or its results.
c **1290** *St. Brandan* 104 in *S. Eng. Leg.* I. 222 ȝoure on schal attan ende Repenti er he com aȝe. **1362** LANGL. *P. Pl.* A. v. 186 He þat repenteþ Raþest schulde arysen aftur [etc.]. **1388** WYCLIF *Matt* xxvii. 3 Judas.. repentide, and brouȝte aȝen the thretti pans to the princis of prestis. *c* **1450** *Merlin* 328 So fer haste thow gon that late it is to repente. **1526** *Pilgr. Perf.* (W. de W. 1531) 12 Whan so euer ony synner repenteth, & is sory for his offences towarde god. **1596** SHAKS. *1 Hen. IV*, III. iii. 5 Well, Ile repent, and that suddenly. **1650** T. VAUGHAN *Anthroposophia* 60 This middle-most mansion is appointed for such Soules whose whole man hath not perfectly repent in this world. **1719** DE FOE *Crusoe* II. (Globe) 443 None teach repentance like true penitents. He wants nothing but to repent. **1797** MRS. RADCLIFFE *Italian* xii, If your purpose is evil, pause a moment, and repent. **1859** TENNYSON *Guinev.* 169 No light had we: for that we do repent.
b. Const. *of*, *at* (rare), †*on*.
c **1315** SHOREHAM VII. 536 Wy hy ne moȝe.. Wel repenty of hare mysdede.. þat ich schal segge, ase ich can. *c* **1450** *Merlin* 176 Thei wolde repente with gode will of the stryfe that thei hadde a-gein Merlin, but to late thei were to repente. **1535** COVERDALE *Jonah* iii. 10 He repented on the euell, which he sayde he wolde do vnto them, and dyd it not. **1535** COVERDALE *Jonah* iii. 10 He repented on the euell, which he sayde he wolde do vnto them, and dyd it not. **1662** STILLINGFL. *Orig. Sacræ* II. vi. §1 God doth reserve a liberty to himself, either to repent of the evil or the good that was foretold concerning any people. **1667** POOLE *Dial. betw. Protest. & Papist* (1735) 91 A thousand of their Sins are venial; which, tho' not repented of, will not exclude them from the Favour of God. **1769** *Junius Lett.* xii. (1788) 75 A scene in which a mind like yours will find nothing to repent of. **1818** PARR *Wks.* (1828) VIII. 640, I repent not at the gift. **1875** JOWETT *Plato* (ed. 2) I. 372 Nor do I now repent of the manner of my defence.
†**c.** To be sad, to mourn (for an event). *Obs.*⁻¹
1590 SPENSER *F.Q.* III. viii. 47 Dead.. thou maist aread Henceforth for ever Florimell to bee; That all the noble knights.. may sore repent with mee.
4. *trans.* To view or think of (any action, etc.) with dissatisfaction and regret; to be sorry for.
c **1330** R. BRUNNE *Chron.* (1810) 256 Do ȝit be consaile, þou salle not it repent. *c* **1410** *Sir Cleges* 422, I repent my grauntetynge, That I to the made. **1465** *Paston Lett.* II. 221 For that or for some other cause he repentyth his bargeyn and woll nomore of it. **1542** UDALL *Erasm. Apoph.* 297 b, Yet do I nothyng repente my first aduise & counsaill. **1590** SHAKS. *Mids. N.* II. ii. 111 Content with Hermia? No, I do repent The tedious minutes I with her haue spent. **1617** MORYSON *Itin.* I. 179, I could hardly keepe him from falling down most steepe mountaines.. which made me repent the buying of him. **1640** HABINGTON *Edw. IV* 108 They would sell their lives at so deere a rate, that the King might repent his purchase. **1716** LADY M. W. MONTAGU *Let. to Pope* 14 Sept., I was so much pleased with it, I have not yet repented my seeing it. **1805** T. HARRAL *Scenes of Life* I. 49 The landlord began to repent his kindness. **1821** WHEWELL in Mrs. Douglas *Life* (1881) 65 Hitherto I have had no reason to repent setting off when I did.
b. *esp.* To feel regret, sorrow, or contrition for (something inherently wrong, some fault, misconduct, sin, or other offence).
c **1380** *Sir Ferumb.* 261 Þan he by-gan repentye sare þat he haþ greued his Eem. *c* **1420** LYDG. *Assembly of Gods* 418 She

..in that gret wrethe out of the paleyce went, Seying to herself that chere shuld þey repent. **1537** CRANMER *Let.* in *Misc. Writ.* (Parker Soc.) II. 350 Both you and I may repent our dallying. **1579** FULKE *Heskins' Parl.* 511 To him that intendeth to repent those thinges wherein he hath offended. **1611** W. SCLATER *Key* (1629) 147 If the thing couenanted be lawfull, rashnesse must be repented: but the promise performed. **1697** DRYDEN *Virg. Georg.* IV. 776 The soft Napæan Race will soon repent Their Anger, and remit the Punishment. **1771** GOLDSM. *Hist. Eng.* IV. 95 He declared ..they should one day repent their insolence and presumption. **1807** SOUTHEY *Espriella's Lett.* II. 53 For a few minutes I repented my temerity. **1849** MACAULAY *Hist. Eng.* vii. (ed. 3) II. 187 William declared..that he would make the most Christian king repent the outrage.

†**c.** To regret (a circumstance or event). *Obs.*
1606 G. W[OODCOCKE] *Lives Emperors* in *Hist. Ivstine* Kk iij, The people founde such ease and plenty of all things, that no man repented a womans gouernment. **1631** WEEVER *Anc. Funeral Mon.* 33 Whose death..all the world repented.

†**5.** To live *out* in repentance. *Obs. rare*$^{-1}$.
1601 SHAKS. *All's Well* IV. iii. 272 My offences being many, I would repent out the remainder of Nature.

re'pentable, *a.* [f. prec. + -ABLE.] Capable of being repented of; †repentant.
1571 DK. NORFOLK in *14th Rep. Hist. MSS. Comm.* App. IV. 574 My harty repentable and pytiefull lamentation. *a* **1603** T. CARTWRIGHT *Confut. Rhem. N.T.* (1618) 699 Repentance of all repentable sinne may be in one moment. **1659** GAUDEN *Tears Ch.* 65 It seems scarce pardonable because 'tis scarce a repentable sin or repairable malice.

†**repentaille.** *Obs. rare.* [OF., f. *repentir* to REPENT: see -AL^{1}.] Repentance.
c **1330** R. BRUNNE *Chron. Wace* (Rolls) 11838 Wonder were elles, or art me failles, þey pleye wyþ repentailles. **1390** GOWER *Conf.* II. 356 Thus whan love is evele wonne, Fulofte it comth to repentaile. *a* **1450** *Knt. de la Tour* (1868) 156 Whanne plesaunce is fayled..thanne ofte tymes they falle into repentaille.

repentance (rɪ'pɛntəns). Also 4-6 -aunce, (5 -aunse), 4 -anse, (5 -ans, -once), 6 -ence. [a. F. *repentance* (12th c.): see REPENT *v.* and -ANCE, and cf. OSp. *repentencia* (13th c.).]

1. The act of repenting or the state of being penitent; sorrow, regret, or contrition for past action or conduct; an instance of this.
13.. *Cursor M.* 4958 (Gött.) ȝour repentanse es comen ouer late. **1303** R. BRUNNE *Handl. Synne* 5229 Wyþ sorow of herte and repentaunce þou mayst pay God wyþ lytyl penaunce. *c* **1374** CHAUCER *Troylus* III. 1259 (1308) And at o word with-outen repentaunce Wel-come my knyght. **1447** BOKENHAM *Seyntys* (Roxb.) 9 She steryd the pepyl ever to repentaunce. **1509** FISHER *Serm. C'tess Richmond* Wks. (1876) 300 Wepynges & teares somtyme of deuocion somtyme of repentaunce. *a* **1591** H. SMITH *Serm.* (1637) 220 Repentance is never too late, but it is a true saying, repentance is never too soon. **1601** B. JONSON *Poetaster* v. i, In time [they] should him fear, Lest after they buy repentance too dear. **1682** SIR T. BROWNE *Chr. Mor.* III. §26 What patience could be content to..accept of repentances which must have after penitences, His goodness can only tell us. **1768-74** TUCKER *Lt. Nat.* (1834) II. 65 The Romish doctors reckon three stages in the passage from vice to virtue, attrition, contrition, and repentance. **1813** SHELLEY *Q. Mab* v. 246 Bitterness of soul, Pining regrets, and vain repentances. **1881** BESANT & RICE *Chapl. of Fleet* I. 159 The morning is the time for repentance.

b. *personified.*
1362 LANGL. *P. Pl.* A. v. 43 þenne Ron Repentaunce and Rehersed þis teeme. **1500-20** DUNBAR *Poems* lxxii. 133 Repentence ay with cheikis wait, No..pennence did eschew. **1599** SHAKS. *Much Ado* II. i. 81 Then comes repentance, and with his bad legs falls into the cinque-pace. **1798** WORDSW. *Peter Bell* Prol. xxx, Repentance is a tender Sprite.

2. *stool of* (†or *for*) *repentance, repentance-stool*, a stool formerly placed in a conspicuous position in Scottish churches for the use of offenders (esp. against chastity) making public repentance; also called CUTTY-STOOL. So *repentance-gown*. (Cf. REPENTING *vbl. sb.* b.)
1647 in *Jrnl. Roy. Soc. Antiq. Ireland* (1901) 271 To Adam McNeilis for dressing ye stoole of repentance, 02s. 5d. *a* **1674** CLARENDON *Hist. Reb.* XIII. §48 To stand publickly in the Stool of Repentance, acknowledging their former transgressions. **1690** LUTTRELL *Brief Rel.* (1857) II. 120 They are setting up the stool of repentance in their churches as formerly, where people guilty of incontinency are to doe pennance. *c* **1765** *Collection Scot. Poems* 68 Tague..told him, he behoved to do penance on the repentance stool. **1899** ANDREWS *Church Life* 112 The Synods specially enjoined on all parishes the procuring of a repentance-gown.
fig. a **1704** T. BROWN *Walk round London* Wks. 1709 III. 34 When the Fumes of Melancholy or Wine set them on the Stool of Repentance. **1777** SHERIDAN *Sch. Scand.* II. iii, He has been just half a year on the stool of repentance! **1884** *Christian World* 2 Oct. 737/1 *The Times*..seats itself as it were in shame on the stool of repentance.

3. *Herb of repentance*, the plant rue. (Cf. the etym. note to HERB-GRACE.)
1858-9 *Phytologist* III. 207 This [the Herb-of-Grace] is not a native, but it is well known at the Old Bailey as the Herb-of-Repentance.

repentant (rɪ'pɛntənt), *a.* and *sb.* Also 5 repend-. [a. F. *repentant* (12th c.), pres. ppl. of *repentir*: see REPENT *v.* and -ANT.]

A. *adj.* **1.** Experiencing repentance; sorrowful for past sins, penitent.
c **1290** *S. Eng. Leg.* I. 174/2377 Heo weren echone repentaunt; ne miȝten none men more. *c* **1315** SHOREHAM I. 752 Ryȝt repentaunt and ryȝt deuout Take hys deaþ in þy meende. *c* **1430** LYDG. *Min. Poems* (Percy Soc.) 149 He.. Moost repentaunt for-sook the world. **1495** *Act 11 Hen. VII* c. 57 *Preamble*, Your seid Suppliaunt is as sorrowfull and repentant as any creature may be. **1532** MORE *Confut. Tindale* Wks. 525/2 As those repentaunte sinners bee a parte of the churche predestynate. **1635-56** COWLEY *Davideis* IV. 771 Kind Heav'n..does long since relent, And with repentant Saul it self repent. **1667** MILTON *P.L.* XI. 1 Thus they in lowliest plight repentant stood. **1823** SCOTT *Peveril* xlix, Charles entered, leaning on the shoulder of his repentant peer. **1876** FARRAR *Marlb. Serm.* xxv. 249 He will cleanse from your repentant souls this daily assoilment.
absol. as *pl.* **14..** in *Tundale's Vis.* (1843) 97 Sothfast kyng whos regne is inmutabull To repentaunt by rygour not vengeable. *c* **1430** LYDG. *Min. Poems* (Percy Soc.) 264 It is my guyse, Alle repentaunt to bryng hem to my blys.

b. Const. *of, for.*
1297 R. GLOUC. (Rolls) 5917 Elfred..Of ire trespas biuore ire deþ repentant was. **1387** TREVISA *Higden* (Rolls) I. 363 No man þat dooþ dedelly synne schal be i-saued, but he be verrey repentaunt at his lifes ende of al his mysdedes. *c* **1400** tr. *Secreta Secret., Gov. Lordsh.* 65 Men awe to praye ..and be rependant of hir synnes. **1556** OLDE *Antichrist* 175 b, Them that are hartily repentaunt for their synnes. **1601** HOLLAND *Pliny* II. 550 Penitent also and repentant, for that which he had done in his furious madnesse. **1817** KEATS *Woman! when I*, etc. 4 The downcast eye, repentant of the pain That its mild light creates to heal again.

2. Expressing or indicating repentance.
1594 SHAKS. *Rich. III*, I. ii. 216 After I haue solemnly interr'd..this Noble King, And wet his Graue with my Repentant Teares. **1630** *R. Johnson's Kingd. & Commw.* 87 Some of them have not spared to commit repentant error, to please the Pope. **1717** POPE *Eloisa* 17 Relentless walls! whose darksome round contains Repentant sighs.

B. *sb.* One who repents, a penitent. ? *Obs.*
1532 MORE *Confut. Tindale* Wks. 554/1 Though he haue made a true faithfull promise of pardone, to al true repentauntes and penitentes. **1624** R. SKYNNER in *Ussher's Lett.* (1686) 350 Let not a Man that is a true Repentant think [etc.]. **1657** REEVE *God's Plea* 21 Dumb gestures are fitter for repentants, then high phrased bablings. *a* **1814** *Gonzanga* IV. vi. in *New Brit. Theatre* III. 142 This last design of thy vengeful cruelty has made a sincere repentant of me.
transf. **1589** PUTTENHAM *Eng. Poesie* III. xix. (Arb.) 224, I following the Greeke originall [*metanoia*] choose to call him the penitent or repentant.

repentantly (rɪ'pɛntəntlɪ), *adv.* [f. prec. + -LY^{2}.] In a repentant manner.
1556 J. HEYWOOD *Spider & F.* Ss iij, As that one vnder that one maide did die Repentaunt; so this other repentauntlie Under this other maide. **1634** SIR T. HERBERT *Trav.* 78 To recouer his faith, which he ought to looke after repentantly and with more zeale. **1849** THACKERAY *Pendennis* xxvii, She checked herself repentantly, saying, 'Well, we must not laugh at her [etc.].'

re'pented, *ppl. a.* [f. REPENT *v.* + -ED^{1}.] Regretted; thought of with repentance.
1660 HICKERINGILL *Jamaica* (1661) 59 Till the repented assay of their valour, disciplin'd them into better manners. **1850** MRS. BROWNING *Poems* I. 265 He..sun and moon Perpetual witness made Of his repented humanness.

repenter (rɪ'pɛntə(r)). [f. as prec. + -ER^{1}.] One who repents, a penitent.
1621 CADE *Serm.* 34 Judas..did now repent..much better then the ordinary repenters at shrift. **1681** COLVIL *Whigs Supplic.* (1710) 74 Some say, a Bishop Covenanter, If a Penitent repenter, Causeth more Joy to Sp'rits Divine, Than all the other ninety nine. **1748** RICHARDSON *Clarissa* (1811) II. 371 Having enrolled myself among the too-late repenters, who shall pity me? **1842** G. S. FABER *Prov. Lett.* (1844) II. 101 The repenters..ought forthwith to quit the wicked Church of England.

†**re'pentful,** *a. Obs. rare*$^{-1}$. [f. as prec. + -FUL.] Full of repentance.
1631 *Celestina* VII. 96 An idle and lazy youth, brings with it a repentfull and a painfull old age.

†**repentine,** *a. Obs.* [a. obs. F. *repentin, -ine* (Godef.), or ad. L. *repentīnus*, f. *repent-, repens* sudden: see -INE.] Sudden.
c **1510** BARCLAY *Mirr. Gd. Manners* (1570) B v, Enterprises rashe, hastie and repentine, Are chiefe thinges bringing great workes to ruine. **1597** A. M. tr. *Guillemeau's Fr. Chirurg.* 51 b/1 All repentine and subite permutations are vnto our bodyes very preiudicialle. **1624** BP. ANDREWES *Serm.* (1629) 259 Never trust a repentance repentine; no sodein flash or brunt. **1633** T. ADAMS *Exp. 2 Pet.* ii. 1 Those repentine, serpentine mischiefes sting before they hisse.

repenting (rɪ'pɛntɪŋ), *vbl. sb.* [f. REPENT *v.* + -ING^{1}.] The action of the vb.; repentance.
c **1300** *Cursor M.* 4958 Don yee haue þe sin yee wate, Your repenting es now to late. *c* **1315** SHOREHAM I. 1087 Two þynges her-wyþ-ynne beþ, For-ȝefþe, and repentynge. *c* **1385** CHAUCER *L.G.W.* Prol. 156 Thoo that hadde doon vnkyndenesse..humblely songe hire repentynge. **1530** PALSGR. 262/1 Repentyng, *regret, repentence.* **1599** SHAKS. *Much Ado* II. i. 76 Wooing, wedding, & repenting, is as a Scotch jigge, a measure, and a cinque-pace. *c* **1655** MILTON *Sonn., To C. Skinner* 6 Deep thoughts..to drench In mirth, that after no repenting drawes. **1719** DE FOE *Crusoe* II. (Globe) 444 To talk of my repenting, alas! And with that he fetch'd a deep Sigh. **1851** TRENCH *Poems* 93 Repentings for her quick and angry mood.

b. *attrib.*, esp. *repenting stool*, the stool of repentance (see REPENTANCE 2).
1567 in *6th Rep. Hist. MSS. Comm.* 643/2 He sall.. present him self vpon the Repenting stuill in the parochiall Kyrk of Anstruthair in Repenting maneir. **1721** RAMSAY *Lucky Spence* vii, Whinging fools, That's frighted for repenting-stools. *a* **1722** PENNECUIK *Collect. Scots Poems* (1787) 34 They gave the surplice to the English prelates, And their repenting stools to Scottish zealots.

repenting (rɪ'pɛntɪŋ), *ppl. a.* [f. as prec. + -ING^{2}.] That repents.
1533 FRITH *Answ. More* Wks. (1829) 177 Christ's blood (which must be received with a repenting heart thro' faith). **1618** G. STRODE *Anat. Mortalitie* 145 Vnto the repenting person hee giueth a soft heart. **1666** DRYDEN *Ann. Mirab.* cxcviii, Repenting England..To Philip's manes did an offering bring. **1719** DE FOE *Crusoe* I. (Globe) 7 Like a true repenting Prodigal. **1817** SHELLEY *Rev. Islam* V. v, Tears of repenting joy, which fast intruded, Fell fast.

Hence **re'pentingly** *adv.*
1611 COTGR., *Repentivement*,..repentingly, with repentance. **1642** S. ASHE *Best Refuge* 54 We must repentingly returne unto the Lord. *a* **1774** GOLDSM. *Hist. Greece* I. 134 There were many useful citizens whom they had..sent into banishment, and these they now repentingly wished to restore. **1893** *Daily News* 8 May 5/5 Those who ..repentingly returned to the bosom of the party.

†**repentinous,** *a. Obs. rare*$^{-1}$. [f. as REPENTINE + -OUS.] Sudden.
1651 BIGGS *New Disp.* 147 Grimfac'd repentinous Death.

†**re'pentive,** *a. Obs. rare*$^{-1}$. [f. REPENT *v.* + -IVE: cf. obs. F. *repentif.*] Repentant.
1620 QUARLES *Jonah* (1638) 44 The body must be prostrate; and the minde Truly repentive, and contrite within.

†**re'pentless,** *a. Obs. rare*$^{-1}$. [f. as prec. + -LESS.] Unrepentant.
a **1683** OLDHAM *Poet. Wks.* (1686) 148 Then may the Stupid, and Repentless die, And Heav'n it self forgive no more than I.

repeople (riː'piːp(ə)l), *v.* [ad. F. *repeupler* (13th c.): see RE- and PEOPLE *v.*]

1. *trans.* To people anew; to furnish with a fresh population.
1481 CAXTON *Myrr.* III. xii. 158 After this the world was repeoplyd and made agayn by them that descended of them. **1568** GRAFTON *Chron.* II. 286, I will repeople the towne againe wyth mere Englishe men. **1652** H. L'ESTRANGE *Amer. no Jewes* 10 Noah had so many yeares of his own life to bestow in repeopling and replanting the Earth. **1761** HUME *Hist. Eng.* I. ii. 52 He invited..foreigners to re-people his Country. **1873** GEIKIE *Ice Age* i. 2 We behold.. Britain once more becoming continental, and repeopled.

b. *fig.* To people again in imagination.
1818 BYRON *Ch. Har.* IV. iv, Though all were o'er, For us repeopled were the solitary shore. **1871** MACDUFF *Patmos* v. 56 One can still re-people the solitude with busy life.
absol. **1835** LYTTON *Rienzi* II. iv, I had the power to re-people—to create.

2. *transf.* To restock with bees, fish, etc.
1693 ADDISON *Virg. Georg.* IV. 297 By repeopling their decaying state,..Their ancient stocks eternally remain. **1766** *Complete Farmer* s.v. *Queen-bee*, From the fœcundity of this one female, a whole hive is easily and soon repeopled. **1807** J. BARLOW *Columb.* VIII. 484 Renascent swarms..Re-people still the shoals and fin the fruitful tide. **1862** *Cornhill Mag.* Feb. 201 M. Coste has superintended the laying down of..new oyster beds.., and likewise repeopled a number that had been exhausted.

Hence **re'peopling** *vbl. sb.*
1611 COTGR., *Repeuplement*, a repeopling, repopulating. *a* **1641** BP. MONTAGU *Acts & Mon.* (1642) 125 Presently upon re-peopling of the earth [etc.]. **1798** MALTHUS *Popul.* (1817) I. 466 He..forgets that such a prompt repeopling could not take place without an unusual increase of births. **1863** DANA *Man. Geol.* 203 There was nearly a complete extermination of the species, requiring a repeopling of the seas.

reperal(e, -all, variants of REPAREL *v. Obs.*

reper'ceive, *v. rare*$^{-1}$. [RE- 5 a.] *trans.* To perceive afresh.
1665 J. WEBB *Stone-Heng* (1725) 41 That you may reperceive how little he understands Matters of Antiquity.

†**reper'cuss,** *ppl. a. Obs. rare*$^{-1}$. [ad. L. *repercussus*, pa. pple. of *repercutĕre*: see next.] Beaten upon.
c **1420** *Pallad. on Husb.* XII. 23 When the mone is daies oold xv And so not repercusse [L. *repercussa*] as of the sonne.

repercuss (riːpə'kʌs), *v.* [f. L. *repercuss-*, ppl. stem of *repercutĕre*, f. *re-* RE- + *percutĕre* to PERCUSS.]

1. a. *trans.* To beat or drive back (air, fluids, etc.). ? *Obs.*
1501, 1615 [see *repercussed* below]. **1626** BACON *Sylva* §118 Aire in Ovens, though (no doubt) it doth (as it were) boyle, and dilate it self, and is repercussed; yet it is without Noise. **1669** WORLIDGE *Syst. Agric.* (1681) 297 If the Winds blow directly downward, and..force the dust to arise with the Wind, which is repercussed by the Earth. **1696** SALMON *Fam. Dict.* (ed. 2) s.v. *Redness*, To apply such things to the Eyes, as many repercuss and drive back the Humours offending. **1773** J. ROSS *Fratricide* VI. 389 (MS.), As when the frighted blood through every vein Drives to and fro, propell'd and repercuss'd, By the effluvia of electric fire.
fig. **1601** HOLLAND *Pliny* XXIII. vii, The marrow or pith.. doth repercusse and smite back the said disease, so that it shall not arise and grow. **1603** FLORIO *Montaigne* III. xiii. 610 The said tempestuous rumours did strike and repercusse his thoughts inward.

†**b.** To reflect (beams or rays of light). *Obs.*
1604 STIRLING *Aurora* xxxvii, As the Sunne..darting from aboue, Doth parch all things that repercusse his beames. **1686** GOAD *Celest. Bodies* I. xiii. 73 The Ray, repercussed or reflected in the perpendiculum is redoubled.

†**c.** To return, reverberate (a sound). *Obs. rare.*

a **1585** MONTGOMERIE *Cherrie & Slae* 89 And ay the echo repercust Hir diapason sound. **1626** BACON *Sylva* §245 Whether a Man shall heare better, if he stand aside the Body Repercussing. **1710** [see *repercussing*].

†**2.** Of light: To beat upon (a thing). *Obs. rare*$^{-1}$.

1592 R. D. *Hypnerotomachia* 48 As full of coulers as a Christall glasse, repercust and beaten against with the beames of the sunne.

3. [Back-formation from REPERCUSSION.] *intr.* To cause or admit of repercussions (sense 6 a, *fig.*); to have an unwanted or unintended effect; to reflect or rebound *on* something.

1923 [see *extra-organismal* s.v. EXTRA- 1]. **1969** F. HALLIDAY in Cockburn & Blackburn *Student Power* 323 There are also examples where an initially political campaign by students repercusses back into the campus and detonates an internal revolt within higher education. **1972** *Guardian* 18 Feb. 13/1 The public crucifixion of a mandarin looks likely to repercuss for years. **1975** J. DE BRES tr. *Mandel's Late Capitalism* vii. 243 The tendency towards thorough planning and organization within the companies or enterprises of late capitalism necessarily repercusses on the structure of the bourgeois class. **1976** *Daily Tel.* 1 Dec. 3/3 It is a script which the plaintiffs feel cannot do anything but repercuss poorly on their reputation if it is thought that 'King Kong' is associated with that.

Hence **reper'cussed, reper'cussing** *ppl. adjs.*

1501 DOUGLAS *Pal. Hon.* Prol. iii, Of repercus[si]t air the echo cryis, Amang the branches of the blomed treis. **1615** G. SANDYS *Trav.* 247 The noise that is made by the repercussed waters. **1686** GOAD *Celest. Bodies* I. xiii. 73 The repercussed Heat is sufficient for all Operations Natural to quicken and encourage them. **1710** *Brit. Apollo* No. 9. 1/1 An Eccho..is caus'd by any..Repercussing Body stopping and reflecting the..Sound.

†**reper'cusser.** *Obs. rare.* Also 7 -our. [f. prec. + -ER[1], -OR 2.] *Med.* A repellent.

1634 T. JOHNSON *Parey's Chirurg.* 1032 The immoderate use of repercussers. **1657** TOMLINSON *Renou's Disp.* 29 Others repel by a refrigerating quality..as water and other such repercussours.

repercussion (riːpəˈkʌʃən). Also 6 -par-. [a. F. *répercussion* (14th c.), or ad. L. *repercussiōnem*, n. of action f. *repercutĕre*: see REPERCUSS *v.*]

1. The action of a thing in forcing or driving back an impinging or advancing body; also, the power of doing this. Now *rare.*

1536 BELLENDEN *Cron. Scot.* Cosmogr. xv, This goume is generat of see froith, quhilk is cassin vp be continewal repercussion of craggis aganis the see wallis. **1601** HOLLAND *Pliny* I. 11 The vapor thereof by repercussion, forceth them [the planets] to be evidently retrograde, and goe backward. **1601** BP. W. BARLOW *Defence* 3 A man cannot fasten..any maine stroke and visible vpon soft and yeelding bodies, in that they haue no repercussion. **1662** STILLINGFL. *Orig. Sacræ* III. ii. §17 Because of the repercussion of other Atoms ..they receive such knocks as make them quiet in their places. **1712** BLACKMORE *Creation* IV. (ed. 2) 172 They various Ways recoil, and swiftly flow By mutual Repercussions to and fro. **1799** KIRWAN *Geol. Ess.* 77 From the opposition it must have met in these mountainous tracts, and the repercussion of their craggy sides, eddies must have been formed.

†**2. a.** *Med.* The action of forcing back or driving away by the application of remedies; the operation of repelling (humours, swellings, etc.) from a particular part of the body; also, a medicine or application used for this purpose. *Obs.*

1541 R. COPLAND *Guydon's Form.* R ij b, The seconde [intention]..is fulfilled by repercussyon at the begynnynge. **1612** WOODALL *Surg. Mate* Wks. (1653) 229 Mercurie..For repercussion thou win'st praise. **1663** BOYLE *Wks.* (1772) VI. 372, I should prefer that method in agues before any violent repercussions though it were the famous *febrifuga* called Jesuits' bark. **1671** SALMON *Syn. Med.* I. xlii. 93 The proper..Nourishment of the Similary Parts is done by.. Repercussion not by Attraction. **1727** BRADLEY *Fam. Dict.* s.v. *Tumour*, The other [method] is to stop and repel 'em; which is call'd Repercussion, that sends 'em back to their Source.

†**b.** The forcing back of flame by blowing upon it. Also *fig. Obs. rare.*

1628 BP. HALL *Old Relig.* 9 Like as the repercussion of the flame intends it more. **1633** —— *Occas. Medit.* (1851) 28 O God, if thy bellows did not sometimes thus breathe upon me, in spiritual repercussions.

3. a. Repulse or recoil of a thing after impact; the fact of being forced or driven back by a resisting body.

1553 BRENDE *Q. Curtius* VIII. 174 b, The streame.. apering by the reparcussion of the water in manye places to be ful of great stones in the bottome. **1604** DRAYTON *Owle* (1619) 1137 That (with the Repercussion of the Aire) Shooke the great Eagle sitting in his Chaire. **1672** *Phil. Trans.* VII. 5148 The other Secondary Affections of Winds; as their Undulation, Repercussion from Promontories, Opposition, &c. **1692** RAY *Disc.* II. v. (1693) 205 After much thunder and roaring by the allision and repercussion of the flame against and from the sides of the Caverns. **1760–72** tr. *Juan & Ulloa's Voy.* (ed. 3) I. 371 The waters are violently carried against the rocks: and in their repercussion, form dangerous whirlpools. **1793** A. MURPHY *Tacitus* (1805) VII. 11 By the repercussion bursting out with redoubled force.

b. *fig.* or in fig. context.

1625 JACKSON *Creed* v. xiii. §3 This certainty can never be wrought but by a repercussion of the engraffed notion upon itself. **1639** G. DANIEL *Ecclus.* xxiii. 75 A mighty wall As Diamond Solid, where all Sence must fall With repercussion. **1869** J. D. BALDWIN *Preh. Nations* iv. (1877) 138 Their action..has entered the current of European affairs indirectly only, and by repercussion. **1880** SWINBURNE *Stud. Shaks.* (ed. 2) 79 The injury done her cousin, which by the repercussion of its shock..serves to transfigure..the whole bright light nature of Beatrice.

c. *Med.* = BALLOTTEMENT.

1860 TANNER *Pregnancy* ii. 94 Ballottement, or repercussion, is a valuable means of acquiring information as to the existence of pregnancy. **1889** J. M. DUNCAN *Lect. Dis. Women* vii. (ed. 4) 39 Feeling ballotement or repercussion, hearing the fœtal movements.

4. a. The return or reverberation of a sound; echo, echoing noise.

1595 *Locrine* III. vi, Where every echo's repercussion May help me to bewail mine overthrow. **1630** J. TAYLOR (Water P.) *Sculler* Wks. III. 28/1 The Ecchoes of his groanings seem'd to sound, With repercussion of his dying plaines. **1713** DERHAM *Phys.-Theol.* IV. iii. 119 To bridle the Evagation of the Sound—but not to make a Confusion thereof, by any disagreeable Repercussions. **1760–72** tr. *Juan & Ulloa's Voy.* (ed. 3) I. 95 This dreadful noise is prolonged by repercussions from the caverns of the mountains. **1855** J. H. NEWMAN *Callista* (1890) 309 Like the echo which is a repercussion of the original voice.

transf. **1650** HOWELL *Lett.* III. 4 Let our letters be as eccho's: let them bound back, and make mutuall repercussions. **1750** JOHNSON *Rambler* No. 23 ¶6 Taste and Grace..sounds which..have since been re-echoed without meaning..by a constant repercussion from one coxcomb to another.

b. *Mus.* (See quots.)

1609 J. DOULAND *Ornithop. Microl.* 12 The Repercussion, which by Guido is called a Trope, and the proper and fit melodie of each Tone. Or it is the proper interuall of each Tone. **1727–38** CHAMBERS *Cycl.* s.v., Of these three chords the two extremes, i.e. the final and the predominant one (which are properly the repercussions of each mode). **1872** BANISTER *Music* §391 During the successive entries of the Subject and Answer, the other parts continue with counterpoints,..and this entry of all the parts constitutes the Exposition (or Repercussion), exhibiting the material of which the Fugue is to be formed. **1889** *Grove's Dict. Mus.* IV. 139/1 (*Tonal Fugue*) The alternation of the Subject with the Answer—called its Repercussion..—is governed by necessary, though somewhat elastic laws.

5. a. The action of a substance in reflecting light; †colour resulting from such reflection.

1601 HOLLAND *Pliny* II. 541 A certain blacke vernish which..by the repercussion thereof..gaue an excellent glosse and pleasant lustre to the colors. **1665** MANLEY *Grotius' Low C. Warres* 474 Some thick Clouds received its opposite light, and there dispersed the same by repercussion. **1665** SIR. T. HERBERT *Trav.* (1677) 30 A number of Fish, whose glistering shells made that artificial light in the night, and gave the Sea a white repercussion. **1845** DE QUINCEY *Wordsw.'s Poetry* Wks. 1857 VI. 242 What would the sun be itself,..if its glory were not endlessly ..thrown back by atmospheric repercussions?

b. Reflection *of* beams, rays, etc. Also without *of.* (Common in 17th c.)

1601 HOLLAND *Pliny* II. 110 Certaine buttons..which with the repercussion and reverberation of the Sun-beames, doe shine againe like resplendent gold. **1622** MALYNES *Anc. Law-Merch.* 257 Vpon a house top..where the repercussion of the Sunne did worke vpon them. **1653** MORE *Antid. Ath.* II. xii. §3 That the rays may not be returned; for such a repercussion would make the sight more confused. **1693** J. EDWARDS *Author. O. & N. Test.* 142 By reflection and repercussion of the sun's rays. **1825** COLERIDGE *Aids Refl.* 40 Aph. v, Our election from God is but the repercussion of the beams of his love shining upon us.

†**c.** A reflection *of* something. *Obs. rare*$^{-1}$.

1646 J. HALL *Horæ Vac.* 58 As in a Christall, there is a perfect Repercussion of a Mans visage.

6. a. A blow or stroke given in return; also *fig.* a return of any kind of action, a responsive act, a resulting effect or implication; an unwanted or unintended reverberation. Freq. *pl.*

1603 HOLLAND *Plutarch's Mor.* 188 When our eies be sore ..we turne away our sight unto those bodies and colours which make no reverberation or repercussion backe againe upon it. **1615** H. CROOKE *Body of Man* 611 The bones strike the Nerue,..The same Nerue makes a repercussion vpon the Membrane. **1641** EARL MONM. tr. *Biondi's Civil Warres* v. 92 The subject whereon shee had to worke being hard and apt to resist, made her subject to repercussions. *a* **1684** LEIGHTON *Ps.* xxxix. Wks. (1835) 312 Observing others to improve the good and evil we see in them,..looking on them to make the repercussion stronger on ourselves. **1751** JOHNSON *Rambler* No. 148 ¶5 Tenderness once excited will be hourly increased by the..repercussion of communicated pleasure. **1831** LAMB *Elia*, Ser. II. *Shade of Elliston*, Natural re-percussions, and results to be expected from the assumed extravagances of..mock life. **1906** *Pall Mall Gaz.* 22 Jan. 1 The disasters of Tsardom in the Japanese war have had a repercussion all over Europe. **1935** *Times* 5 July 15/3 The direct effects and indirect repercussions of any projected action. **1948** *Hansard Commons* 26 Jan. 673 All practical measures will be adopted..to minimise repercussions upon other unconvertible European currencies. **1969** T. F. TORRANCE *Theol. Sci.* ii. 85 The inclusion of that fact in the Reformation doctrine of the Grace of God had immense repercussions. **1978** *Lancashire Life* Oct. 96/1 If the strike could be expected to 'bite' anywhere, with anarchic repercussions, Merseyside was the place.

†**b.** The action of returning a blow. *Obs.*$^{-1}$

1608 WILLET *Hexapla Exod.* 480 The law of repercussion and retalion tooke no place.

†**7. a.** A repeated blow. *Obs. rare*$^{-1}$.

1621 G. SANDYS *Ovid's Met.* XII. (1626) 244 Rhœtus.. aggrauates his wound With repercussions of his burning brand.

b. A repeated attack *of* pain. *rare*$^{-1}$.

1796 BURNS *Let. to Thomson* Apr., I have only..counted time by the repercussions of pain.

repercussive (riːpəˈkʌsɪv), *a.* and *sb.* Also 4 -if. [ad. F. *répercussif, -ive* (14th c.): see REPERCUSS *v.* and -IVE.]

A. *adj.* †**1.** Of medicines or medical applications: Serving to repel humours or reduce swellings. *Obs.* Cf. REPELLENT *a.* 1.

c **1400** *Lanfranc's Cirurg.* 210 To enpostyms of blood, þou mi3t do medicyns repercussifs & dissolutiuis sotilly. **1543** TRAHERON *Vigo's Chirurg.* II. i. 14 The inconvenient and untimely application of medicines repercussive. **1601** DOLMAN *La Primaud. Fr. Acad.* (1618) III. 818 The flower thereof is good in repercussiue plaisters. **1657** TOMLINSON *Renou's Disp.* 29 The Greeks call a repercussive Medicament ἀποκρουστικόν. **1694** SALMON *Bate's Dispens.* (1713) 673/1 Besides this, it is very drying, repercussive and anodyn.

2. a. Of sounds: Reverberating or reverberated; echoing, resounding; repeated.

1598 B. JONSON *Case is Altered* I. ii, That word only Hath, with its strong and repercussive sound, Struck my heart cold. **1638** [SHIRLEY] *Mart. Soldier* IV. i. in Bullen *O. Pl.* I. 225 All the Goths and Vandalls shall strike Heaven with repercussive Ecchoes of your name. **1727–46** THOMSON *Summer* 1162 Amid Carnarvon's mountains rages loud The repercussive roar. **1809** MRS. J. WEST *Mother* (1810) 169 The woodland hind Strikes the firm oak with repercussive blows. **1875** SWINBURNE *Ess. & Stud.* 201 *note*, I think now that the fantastic beauty of that single repercussive note would perhaps be out of tune.

b. Of things or places: Returning a sound.

1695 CONGREVE *Taking of Namur* vi, The huge Cyclops did..Massie Bolts on repercussive Anvils beat. **1712** BLACKMORE *Creation* VII. (ed. 2) 358 Ye noise Waves Strike with Applause the repercussive Caves. **1874** HARTWIG *Aerial W.* iv. 39 Echo no longer..confides her sorrows to the remote glen or the repercussive rock.

†**3.** Of light: Reflected. *Obs.*

1604 DEKKER *King's Entert.* Wks. 1873 I. 274 This (the glasse alone) Where the neat Sunne each morne himselfe attires, And gildes it with his repercussive fires. **1701** WATTS *Horæ Lyr., Fun. Poem T. Gunston*, As she labours up to reach her Noon, Pursues her Orb with repercussive Light.

transf. **1598** CHAPMAN *Iliad* XVIII. 192 Their guides a repercussive dread Took from the horrid radiance of his refulgent head. *a* **1639** T. CAREW *To H.D.* 16 Shadowes to delude thine eyes With ayrie repercussive sorceries.

4. a. Of a blow: Causing to rebound. *rare*$^{-1}$.

1712 BLACKMORE *Creation* II. (ed. 2) 69 What vig'rous Arm, What repercussive blow Bandies the mighty Globe still too and fro?

b. *fig.* Of an action, decision, etc.: having repercussions (sense 6 a).

1974 *Daily Tel.* 11 May 17/5 He said that because of the decision to go ahead with the tour he was worried about the repercussive effect on British and international sport. **1975** *Financial Times* 27 Oct. 17/4 Britain will in an important sense continue to be 'reliant' on other sources herself, since she cannot escape repercussive consequences in her own industry and economy whenever Western Europe suffers. **1979** *Jrnl. R. Soc. Arts* CXXVII. 554/2 The repercussive effects of pay policy.

†**B.** *sb. Med.* A repellent. *Obs.*

c **1400** *Lanfranc's Cirurg.* 209 þou must purge þe matere or þou leie þerto ony repercussijf or ony maturatif. **1547** BOORDE *Brev. Health* 75 If the mylke be curded in the brestes, some olde auctours wyll gyue repercussiues. **1601** HOLLAND *Pliny* II. 278 The herbe is..a singular repercussiue in all impostumes and inflammations. **1651** FRENCH *Distil.* v. 135 A plate of the said Mercury laid upon tumours would be a great deale better repercussive then plates of lead, which Chirurgions use. **1725** BRADLEY *Fam. Dict.* s.v. *Tumour*, Repercussives are not used in all sorts of Tumours.

Hence **reper'cussively** *adv.*, **reper'cussiveness** (Bailey, vol. II. 1727).

1831 *Blackw. Mag.* XXX. 874 It did shiver— repercussively broken by gnarled oak.

†**reper'cute,** *v. Obs. rare.* [ad. F. *répercuter* (14th c.), or L. *repercutĕre*: see REPERCUSS *v.*]

a. *absol.* = REPERCUSS *v.* 1. **b.** *trans.* To strike in turn.

1525 tr. *Brunswick's Surg.* xxvi, I did therto leues of iusquiamus sodden..because it repercuteth and resolueth. **1578** BANISTER *Hist. Man* I. 11 When the first bone, percussed by the stroke of the ayre, repercuteth the other in manner of a mallet.

†**reper'cutient,** *a. Obs. rare.* [ad. L. *repercutient-em*, pres. ppl. of *repercutĕre*: see REPERCUSS *v.*] = REPERCUSSIVE *a.* 1.

1684 tr. *Bonet's Merc. Compit.* XIII. 392 The laxity of the part..will not permit us to apply any thing that is violently repercutient or resolvent. *Ibid.* XVII. 592 Cold and very repercutient things must by no means be applied.

†**repercutive.** *Obs. rare*$^{-0}$. [ad. obs. F. *repercutif* (14th c.): see REPERCUTE and -IVE.] = REPERCUSSIVE *sb.*

1611 COTGR., *Repercutif*, a repercutiue; a medicine that repells..paine from the place whereunto it is applyed.

†**repe-refe,** variant of REAP-REEVE *Obs.*

14.. *Voc.* in Wr.-Wülcker 596/7 *Metellus*, a reperefe.

reperel(l, variants of REPAREL *sb.* and *v. Obs.*

reperforator (riːˈpɜːfəreɪtə(r)). *Telegr.* [f. RE(CEIVING *ppl. a.* + PERFORATOR.] A machine which perforates paper tape in accordance with telegraphically received signals.

1916 *Papers Inst. P.O. Electr. Engin.* No. 59. 22 Parment ..proposes re-perforators at the receiver end for *x* messages, receiving a printed slip simultaneously. **1948** *Annals Computation Lab. Harvard Univ.* XVI. 61 The reperforator and the printer operate on a time division basis. **1973**

GOACHER & DENNY *Teleprinter Handbk.* iii. 10/1 Reperforators are used to store teleprinter signals on punched paper tape so that they may be retransmitted later by means of a suitable tape reader.

reper'form, *v.* [RE- 5 a.] To perform again.
1651 BAXTER *Inf. Bapt.* 119 Infant Baptism is God's ordinance, and Baptism not to be reperformed. **1805** W. TAYLOR in *Monthly Mag.* XIX. 219 It rather causes the original organic motion to be re-performed.

reper'fume, *v.* [RE- 5 a.] *trans.* To perfume again. Hence **reper'fumed** *ppl. a.*
1593 DRAYTON *Sheph. Garl.* Ecl. viii, While others..strut the stage with reperfumed wordes. **1888** A. S. WILSON *Lyric Hopeless Love* VI. 19 Thy love Puts music into forest sounds And odours reperfumes.

'reperible, *a. rare.* [ad. L. type **reperībilis*, f. *reperīre* to find: see -IBLE.] Discoverable.
1432–50 tr. *Higden* (Rolls) II. 189 þer is noone ylle thynge but hit is reperible in man. **1875** *N. Amer. Rev.* CXX. 275 We must strip them of their national, local, and personal distinctions, of all, in short, that is not reperible in every one of them.

†**repe'rition**. *Obs. rare*⁻¹. [f. L. *reperīre* to find + -ITION.] Discovery.
1627 SPEED *England* xxxviii. § 1 Neither the reperition nor the repetition thereof shall be accounted impertinent.

re'periwig, *v. rare*⁻¹. [RE- 5 a.] *trans.* To cover again as with a wig.
1608 SYLVESTER *Du Bartas* II. iv. v. *Decay* 815 The Sappy-bloud Of Trees hath twice re-perriwig'd the Wood.

re'perjuring, *vbl. sb. rare*⁻¹. [RE- 5 a.] Repetition of perjury.
1583 STUBBES *Anat. Abus.* I. (1879) 183 What expostulation, railing, scoulding, periuring, and reperiuring is maintained?

reper'mit, *v. rare*⁻¹. [RE- 5 a. Cf. F. *repermettre* (Cotgr.).] *trans.* To permit again.
1611 SPEED *Hist. Gt. Brit.* IX. vi. § 22 Hee..suspended himselfe from vse of his priestly function, till vpon sute he was repermitted.

reper'suade, *v. rare.* [RE- 5 a.] *trans.* and *absol.* To persuade again.
a **1661** FULLER *Worthies, Bedford.* I. (1662) 117 Whereupon for his own preservation he was re-perswaded to return to Pitmister. **1775** S. J. PRATT *Liberal Opin.* vii. (1783) I. 95, I began to re-persuade;..I protested [etc.].

reperté, -tee, obs. forms of REPARTEE *sb.* and *v.*

†**repertible**, *a. Obs. rare*⁻⁰. [a. F. *repertible*, f. L. *repert-*, ppl. stem of *reperīre* to find.] 'Which may be found, gotten, or recovered' (Blount, 1656, from Cotgr.).

†**repertite**, *v. Obs. rare.* [var. of REPARTITE *v.*, with change of vowel as in L. *impertīre*.] *trans.* To quarter in divisions. Const. *upon*.
c **1603** in *Buccleuch MSS.* (Hist. MSS. Comm.) 40 Companies repertited upon Zeeland... These companies were repertited upon Zeeland, but paid hitherto by the generality.

†**reper'tition**. *Obs.* [var. of REPARTITION: see prec.] Division, distribution, allotment.
1578 T. N. tr. *Conq. W. India* 6 It folowed, that in the repertition of yᵉ lands conquered, Iames Velasques gave unto Cortez the Indians of Manicorao. **1635** R. DAFFORNE *Merch. Mirrour* Ep. Ded. a v, The word Repertition is not used in my Booke, as James Peele, and many Merchants doe.

†**reper'titious**, *a. Obs.*⁻⁰ [ad. L. *repertitius*, f. *repert-*, *reperīre* to find.] Found by chance.
1656 BLOUNT *Glossogr.*; hence in later Dicts.

‖**repertoire** ('rɛpətwɑː(r), F. repɛrtwar). Also ré-. [F. *répertoire*, ad. L. *repertorium* REPERTORY.] **a.** A stock of dramatic or musical pieces which a company or player is accustomed or prepared to perform; one's stock of parts, tunes, songs, etc.
1847 *Illustr. Lond. News* 16 Jan. 42/2 The part.., with the exception of the renowned..Robert Macaire, is the best character in his *répertoire*. **1849** THACKERAY *Pendennis* liii, Warrington, who..had but one tune..in his *répertoire*,..sat rapt in delight. **1885** J. K. JEROME *On the Stage* 124, I got hold of the *répertoire* and studied up all the parts I knew I should have to play.
attrib. **1897** *Daily News* 15 Sept. 6/4 A sound repertoire company, where too many plays are not embarked upon, and yet the so necessary variety is not wanting.
b. *transf.*
1872 E. BRADDON *Life in India* vi. 201 A Lascar crossing-sweeper whose native dialect is Bengali or Tamil, and from whose linguistic *répertoire* Oordoo and Hindoo have been wholly omitted. **1959** R. POSTGATE *Good Food Guide* 211 Latest additions to his marvellous repertoire are Honey Duck..and a poussin stuffed with mushroom butter and herbs, encased in a very thin pastry and baked. **1961** WEBSTER, A small but dependable repertoire of jokes designed to amuse the young—Frank Sullivan. **1965** *Listener* 20 May 753/1 Easily reached from Dublin, New Grange itself, with its rich repertoire of geometric art, is the showpiece of Irish prehistory. **1971** *Nature* 13 Aug. 443/2 The most striking aspects of an animal's behavioural repertoire are often the 'displays' it gives in sexual or aggressive encounters. **1973** *Archivum Linguisticum* IV. 55 The analysis of *repertoires*, namely, what that community knows of and does with the languages concerned.

†**re'pertor**. *Obs. rare*⁻¹. [L., agent-noun f. *reperīre* to find.] A discoverer.
1650 FULLER *Pisgah* IV. ii. 31 Let others dispute whether Anah was the Inventour, or onely the Repertour of Mules.

repertorial (rɛpə'tɔərɪəl), *a.* [f. REPERTORY + -AL.] Of or pertaining to (a) repertory.
1898 J. LONDON *Let.* 6 Dec. (1966) 8 Worth far more than five dollars, at the ordinary repertorial rate of so much per column. **1912** G. B. SHAW *Let.* 1 May in *Lett. to Granville Barker* (1956) 181 To follow a year of Shaw with yet another Shaw is not very repertorial. **1928** *Observer* 1 Apr. 15/3 The producer's laudable desire to deliver Ibsen's humour from the old repertorial gloom was most happily realized in some of the minor parts.

repertorily ('rɛpətərɪlɪ), *adv. rare.* [f. REPERTORY + -LY².] In the manner of repertory.
1928 *Observer* 22 Jan. 13/4 Miss Margot Drake's Ann catches fire in the later phases of the play, but some of the other parts are somewhat repertorily done.

‖**repertorium** (rɛpə'tɔərɪəm). [L., f. *repert-*, ppl. stem of *reperīre* to find: cf. next.] †**a.** A catalogue. *Obs.* **b.** A storehouse, repository.
1667 WOOD *Life* (O.H.S.) II. 111 He..shew'd him 'the Repertorium', and spoke to Jennings the reacher of the records, that he should let him have any record that he should point at in the said Repertorium. **1818** LADY MORGAN *Fl. Macarthy* III. i. 17 As for Counsellor Conway Crawley, I look upon him as the very repertorium of the laws. **1866** LIDDON *Bampt. Lect.* ii. § 1 (1875) 45 The Bible is not a great repertorium of quotations.

repertory ('rɛpətərɪ). Also 6 *erron.* **report-**. [See prec. and -ORY.]
†**1.** An index, list, catalogue or calendar. *Obs.*
1552 in *Vicary's Anat.* (1888) 304 The Vse of the first boke called a Repertory. **1588** J. MELLIS *Briefe Instr.* C iv b, Vnto which Leager it shalbe necessary to..make a calender, otherwise called a Reportory or a finder. **1601** HOLLAND *Pliny* II. 372 Hermippus..made besides a Repertorie or Index to euery booke of the said Poesie. **1687** N. JOHNSTON *Assur. Abbey Lands* 179 Whose singular favor I must ever acknowledge..in furnishing me with a Repertory, whereby I am enabled readily to find such Records. **1761** DUCAREL (*title*) A Proposal for Publishing a General Repertory of the Endowments of Vicarages.
attrib. **1773** *Gentl. Mag.* XLIII. 353/2 Quoting a multiplicity of cases from the Repertory [*printed* Ref-] Book.
2. A storehouse, magazine, or repository, where something may be found.
1593 G. HARVEY *Pierce's Super.* Wks. (Grosart) II. 66 As I looke..for his vniuersall Repertory of all Histories, contayning the memorable acts of all ages, all places, and all persons. *a* **1751** BOLINGBROKE *Ess.* II. iii. Wks. 1754 IV. 46 His [Homer's] writings became the sole repertory to later ages of all the theology, philosophy, and history of those which preceded his. **1796** BURKE *Let. Noble Ld.* Wks. 1802 IV. 295 The moral scheme of France..is indeed an inexhaustible repertory of one kind of examples. **1839** HALLAM *Hist. Lit.* III. i. § 14 It is..an immense repertory of unconnected criticisms and other miscellaneous erudition. **1868** MILMAN *St. Paul's* xviii. 456 The established repertory of our statutes and usages.
3. a. = REPERTOIRE.
1845 E. HOLMES *Mozart* 210 The repertory of the German lyric stage was..miserably poor in comic operas. **1866** GEO. ELIOT *F. Holt* xxxi, The tune the most symbolical of Liberalism which their repertory would furnish.
b. A type of theatrical presentation in which the plays performed by a company are changed at regular short intervals; repertory theatres collectively.
1896 [see *repertory theatre* below]. **1910** G. B. SHAW *Let.* 30 Apr. in *Lett. to Granville Barker* (1956) 164 Producing a lot of plays merely to ascertain which draws the most money, and running that and dropping the rest is not Propagandist Repertory. **1926** [see CO-STAR *sb.*]. **1951** *Oxf. Compan. Theatre* 664/2 The pioneer work of all these theatres stimulated an ever-growing interest in Repertory. **1974** *Encycl. Brit. Macropædia* XVIII. 229/1 The change from repertory to the single play and the rise of realistic production also shifted artistic control from the actor to the manager.
c. *ellipt.* for *repertory company*.
1933 P. GODFREY *Back-Stage* ix. 134 The number of small stock companies, calling themselves resident repertories.. continued to consolidate their positions with provincial audiences.
4. *attrib.*, as (sense 3 b) ***repertory acting, actor, actress, company, movement, play, player, system, theatre.***
1917 J. AGATE *Buzz, Buzz!* II. 146 It is in this way that *Repertory acting gets its revenge. **1951** *Oxf. Compan. Theatre* 664/1 Glasgow audiences became acquainted with Repertory acting and production of a high standard. **1917** J. AGATE *Buzz, Buzz!* II. 145 Let us recall the *Repertory actor who, desponding of intellectual success, decided to 'go back to the profession'. **1951** *Oxf. Compan. Theatre* 665/2 John Drinkwater, a Repertory actor and dramatist. **1979** K. O'HARA *Searchers of Dead* vi. 64 Noel was..a sound hard-working repertory actor. **1917** J. AGATE *Buzz, Buzz!* II. 146 The *Repertory actress sometimes succeeds in sending you away from the theatre concerned for the character she has been representing. **1977** 'J. LE CARRÉ' *Hon. Schoolboy* xiii. 290 She frowned..like a repertory actress doing Forgetfulness. **1909** G. B. SHAW *Let.* 29 Dec. in *Lett. to Granville Barker* (1956) 160, I may shortly doubt whether he will throw himself into the *repertory company to be cast for anything you please. **1926** *Scribner's Mag.* Aug. 224/1 Mr. Ames showed what could be done with a first-class repertory company. **1967** *Oxf. Compan. Theatre* (ed. 3) 796/2 There have been many plays, first produced by a repertory company, which have then been transferred to London. **1977** J. AIKEN *Last Movement* i. 13 He was.. highly experienced; he had been in different repertory companies since the age of sixteen. **1951** *Oxf. Compan. Theatre* 663/2 It is impossible to name any one person as the sponsor of the *Repertory Movement in England, but no one can deny that it owes much to the vision and courage of J. T. Grein. **1955** *Radio Times* 22 Apr. 7 The famous Liverpool Playhouse..was founded in 1911 by Miss Horniman, who had started the repertory movement in England. **1974** *Encycl. Brit. Macropædia* XVIII. 231/1 Miss A. E. F. Horniman (pioneer of the British repertory movement). **1903** G. B. SHAW *Let.* 12 Jan. (1972) II. 302 Much Ado..would come in on tour as a Shakespearean *repertory play. **1933** —— in E. J. West *Shaw on Theatre* (1958) 235 All the players in the country, whether they are British Drama League players or Repertory players or regular professional players. *c* **1913** D. MCCARTHY *Drama* (1940) 60 The *repertory system is certainly a means to getting good acting. **1974** *Encycl. Brit. Micropædia* VIII. 514/1 Major English companies using the repertory system include the Royal Shakespeare Theatre in Stratford-on-Avon and London and the National Theatre Company. **1896** W. ARCHER *Theatrical 'World' of 1895* 390 A *repertory theatre, where unbroken runs shall be forbidden by the articles of association. **1897** G. B. SHAW *Our Theatres in Nineties* (1932) III. 273 What we want in order to get the best work is a repertory theatre with alternative casts. **1909** *Times* 9 June 8/6 It may..take a little time for the London public to grow used to the frequent changes of bill which a repertory theatre implies. **1976** E. DEWHURST *After Ball* i. 5 The newly-formed Frensham repertory theatre club had come to the end of its first meeting.

repe'rusal (riː-). [RE- 5 a: cf. next.] A second perusal.
1670 FLAMSTEED in Rigaud *Corr. Sci. Men* (1841) II. 92, I shall be forced to protract the time I had set myself for the reperusal of my papers. **1818** SCOTT *Hrt. Midl.* xviii, On a reperusal, however, he thought that..he could discover something like a tone of awakened passion. **1874** MAHAFFY *Soc. Life Greece* xi. 354 A reperusal discovers to the same mind many things at first overlooked.

repe'ruse (riː-), *v.* [RE- 5 a.] *trans.* To peruse again or repeatedly.
1600 W. WATSON *Decacordon* (1602) 331 If any thinke that this is but a surmise, let them reperuse what here passantly is written. **1742** RICHARDSON *Pamela* IV. 113, I have given myself no Time to re-peruse what I have written. **1820** SCOTT *Monast.* xxiv, This second paper he also perused and reperused more than once. **1862** BUCKLEY *Introd. Partonope* (Roxb.) 24 He reperused with this object in view the legend as narrated by Apuleius.

reper'version. *rare*⁻¹. [RE- 5 a.] Perversion back again.
1716 M. DAVIES *Athen. Brit.* III. *Diss. Drama* 27 Another ..Italian Protestant, Refugee to the Church of England, was still more unfortunate, especially as to his Doubling of his Re-perversion to Popery again.

repet, obs. form of RIPPIT.

repete, obs. form of REPEAT *v.*

repetend ('rɛpɪtɛnd, rɛpɪ'tɛnd), *sb.* [ad. L. *repetend-um* '(that) which is to be repeated', neuter gerundive of *repetĕre* to REPEAT.]
1. *Arith.* The recurring figure or figures in an interminate decimal fraction. (Cf. REPEAT *v.* 6 b.) Also *fig.*
1714 CUNN *Treat. Fractions* 62 The Figure or Figures continually circulating, may be called a Repetend. **1718** MALCOLM *Arith.* Pref. (1730) 12 His [Cunn's] rule for the addition of Circulates having compound Repetends is insufficient for a general rule. **1802–12** BENTHAM *Ration. Judic. Evid.* (1827) III. 198 A chain of character evidence without end; an arithmetical repetend. **1830** *Westm. Rev.* Oct. 442 Think you that this number is the whole? So far from being so, it is a repetend. **1854** B. SMITH *Arith.* 76
2. A recurring note, word, or phrase; a refrain.
1874 HOLLAND *Mistr. Manse* vii. 6 Then [the bells] faltered to their closing toll Whose long, monotonous repetend [etc.]. **1880** *Scribner's Mag.* May 116 In 'The Raven', 'Lenore', and elsewhere, he employed the repetend also. **1895** C. A. SMITH *Repetit. & Parall.* 17 The first 7 stanzas observe alternate initial repetition, '*Puisque*' being the repetend employed.

repetend ('rɛpɪtɛnd), *a. rare.* [ad. L. *repetendus*, gerundive of *repetĕre* to repeat.] That is to be repeated.
1929 R. BRIDGES *Test. Beauty* IV. 181 Taketh repetend life and exuberant difformity of disorder'd growth.

‖**répétiteur** (repetitœr). Also repetiteur. [Fr., = tutor, coach.] **a.** One who teaches musicians and singers, esp. opera singers, their parts.
1938 *Oxf. Compan. Mus.* 792/2 *Répétiteur*.., choirmaster of an opera-house. **1941** L. A. G. STRONG *John McCormack* iv. 70 Covent Garden in those days was blessed by the possession of a master répétiteur at the piano. **1948** *Penguin Mus. Mag.* June 79 He went to his first post as *répétiteur* at Cologne when he was barely 17. **1961** *Times* 13 July 5/3 A stolid arc of singers gathered round the répétiteur. **1970** *Guardian* 24 Apr. 8/2 The opera-house..needed someone to do three jobs; a *repetiteur* was needed, an oboist and an assistant conductor. **1974** *Courier-Mail* (Brisbane) 3 Aug. 15/10 (Advt.), The Australian Opera has vacancies for experienced repetiteurs. **1977** R. BARNARD *Death on High C's* i. 11 Little Mr Pettifer, the repetiteur, was seated at the piano... The cast was bustled into position around him.
b. One who supervises ballet rehearsals, etc.
1952 *Ballet Ann.* 1953 143/1 The Sadler's Wells Ballet... Professor of Dancing and Repetiteur: Harijs Plucis. **1964** W. G. RAFFE *Dict. Dance* 416/2 The *répétiteur* is often a private tutor; but in Theatre he is in charge of..the full preparation for the show; he may also be the ballet-master. **1977** *Times* 16 May 8/6 Then to the Royal Ballet.. eventually becoming..principal *répétiteur*.

repetition[1] (rɛpɪˈtɪʃən). Also 6 -icion, -icyon, *Sc.* -ioun, -itioun. [a. OF. *repeticion* (mod.F. *répétition*) or ad. L. *repetitiōn-em*, n. of action f. *repetĕre* to REPEAT.]

I. 1. a. The action of repeating or saying over again something which one has already said; reiteration; an instance of this.

1526 *Pilgr. Perf.* (W. de W. 1531) 163 b, Of curiosite to saye theyr duty agayne, or to saye it with repeticyons. **1557** BIBLE (Genev.) *Matt.* vi. 7 When ye pray, vse no vaine repetitions as the heathen. **1589** PUTTENHAM *Eng. Poesie* III. xix. (Arb.) 208 Your figure that worketh by iteration or repetition of one word or clause..is counted a very braue figure. **1669** GALE *Crt. Gentiles* I. III. x. 107 The sacred Scriptures abound in elegant Repetitions. **1751** LADY M. W. MONTAGU *Let. to C'tess of Bute* 19 June, When you do not answer any part of my letters, I supppose them lost, which exposes you to some repetitions. **1798** MALTHUS *Popul.* (1878) p. vi, I am fearful that I shall appear..to have been guilty of unnecessary repetitions. **1875** JOWETT *Plato* (ed. 2) I. 485 Let me recapitulate—for there is no harm in repetition.

b. *Rhet.* The use of repeated words or phrases.

1533 T. WILSON *Rhet.* 107 b, Repetition is when we begynne diverse sentencies one after another with one and the same worde. **1585** JAS. I *Ess. Poesie* (Arb.) 65 It is also meit, for the better decoratioun of the verse to vse sumtyme the figure of Repetitioun. **1704** J. HARRIS *Lex. Techn.* I, *Repetition*, (a Figure in Rhetorick) is when a Person thinking his first expression not well understood,..repeats or explains them, another way.

2. a. The action of repeating or saying over something in order to fix or retain it in the memory; †also, the rehearsal of a play.

1581 MULCASTER *Positions* xl. (1887) 231 The morening houres will best serue for the memorie..: the after noone for repetitions, and stuffe for memorie to worke on. **1612** BRINSLEY *Lud. Lit.* xxi. (1627) 246 Once gotten, they were easily kept by oft repetition. **1756** FOOTE *Engl. fr. Paris* II. Wks. 1799 I. 114 It is now in repetition at the French comedy. **1863** GEO. ELIOT *Romola* xxx, Of the new details he learned he could only retain a few, and those only by continual repetition.

b. The action of reciting in a formal manner, *esp.* recitation of something learned by heart; a piece set to be learned and recited.

1597 HOOKER *Eccl. Pol.* v. xl. §1 If the Psalms..deserve to be oftener repeated than they are, but that the multitude of them permitteth not any oftener repetition. **1612** BRINSLEY *Lud. Lit.* vi. (1627) 68 There must be daily repetitions and examinations. **1709** STEELE *Tatler* No. 79 ¶1 A Repetition of the following Verses out of Milton. **1806-7** J. BERESFORD *Miseries Hum. Life* (1826) III. viii, Seeing the boy who is next above you flogged for a repetition which you know you cannot say even half so well as he did. **1864** TREVELYAN *Compet. Wallah* (1866) 129 Seeing that his boys learn their repetitions and get up in time for morning school.

3. Recital, relation, narration, mention.

1594 SHAKS. *Rich. III*, I. iii. 165 *Rich.* Foule wrinckled Witch, what mak'st thou in my sight? *Q.M.* But repetition of what thou hast marr'd. **1607** —— *Cor.* v. iii. 144 A name Whose repetition will be dogg'd with Curses. **1655** STANLEY *Hist. Philos.* III. (1701) 83/1 By repetition of which accident, Charillus often afterwards defended the Dæmon. **1821** BYRON *Mar. Fal.* v. i, Spare us, and spare thyself the repetition Of our most awful, but inexorable Duty.

4. a. The action or fact of doing something again; renewal or recurrence of an action or event; repeated use, application, or appearance.

1597 HOOKER *Eccl. Pol.* v. lxxi. §2 Because by repetition they..confirme the habites of all vertue, it remaineth that we..keep them as ordinances. **1695** DRYDEN tr. *Dufresnoy's Art Painting* Observ. ¶200 The Members would be too naked, if they left not two or three Folds,.. and therefore [they] have us'd those Repetitions of many Folds. **1727-38** CHAMBERS *Cycl.* s.v., Habits are acquired by the frequent repetition of actions. **1781** COWPER *Hope* 22 Pleasure is labour too, and tires as much,..By repetition palled, by age obtuse. **1840** DICKENS *Old C. Shop* i, These glances seemed to increase her confidence at every repetition. **1877** MRS. OLIPHANT *Makers Flor.* v. 148 Genius, getting impatient of universal repetition, strikes out for itself new paths on every side. **1883** *Century Mag.* Oct. 859/2 A notion that architectural beauty is to be attained by an indefinite repetition of ugliness.

b. *Mus.* (See quots. and cf. REPEAT *sb.* 2 c, 2 d.)

1597 MORLEY *Introd. Mus.* 68 When you see this signe :||: of repetition, you must begin again, making the note next before the signe..a semibriefe in the first singing. **1727-38** CHAMBERS *Cycl.* s.v., Repetition..is also a doubling or trebling, etc. of an interval, or a reiteration of some concord or discord. **1881** GROVE *Dict. Mus.* III. s.v., The rapid reiteration of a note is called repetition.

c. The comparative ability of a musical instrument to repeat the same note in quick succession.

1885 C. G. W. LOCK *Workshop Receipts* Ser. IV. 285/1 Another common defect is in the 'repetition': a key will not rise to the level instantly the finger is raised. **1894** ELLISTON *Organs & Tuning* 148 The..repetition is such that the pipes respond to the most rapid staccato passages.

d. The return of a taste. *rare*⁻¹.

1705 JOS. TAYLOR *Journ. Edenborough* (1903) 49 For my part I only drunk one Glass for curiosity, and I am sure, had the repetition of it 20 times in my stomach.

5. A copy or replica of a thing.

1853 KANE *Grinnell Exp.* xxxiv. (1856) 299 We saw a couple of icebergs standing alone in the sky, and at their shadowy tops their phantom repetitions inverted. **1881** *Catal. Nat. Portr. Gallery* 255 A small and highly finished repetition of it was recently sold among the artist's works.

6. *attrib.*, as ***repetition choice, device, phenomenon, rate***; **repetition clock**, a repeating clock; **repetition compound** (see quot.); **repetition compulsion** *Psychoanal.*, a term first used by Freud to describe behaviour that is caused by a more powerful instinct than that of pleasure, whereby a response is repeated regardless of the result; also *transf.*; **repetition sermon** (see quot. 1688); **repetition work**, the occupation of making the same article over and over again.

1934 *Brit. Jrnl. Psychol.* Jan. 254 This difference in *repetition choice correlated with a difference in teachers' ratings on the trait of pride. **1764** *Ann. Reg.* I. 79 The pieces contained in the striking part of the ordinary *repetition clocks. **1957** R. W. ZANDVOORT *Handbk. Eng. Gram.* IX. i. 286 **Repetition Compounds*.., a type of compound which consists in the repetition of the word constituting its first element: *goody-goody, pretty-pretty*. **1925** A. STRACHEY tr. *Freud's The Uncanny* in *Coll. Papers* IV. 391 We are able to postulate the principle of a *repetition-compulsion in the unconscious mind, based upon instinctual activity and probably inherent in the very nature of the instincts—a principle powerful enough to overrule the pleasure-principle. **1941** L. TRILLING in D. Lodge *20th Cent. Lit. Crit.* (1972) 288 [Freud] first makes the assumption that there is indeed in the psychic life a repetition-compulsion which goes beyond the pleasure principle. **1953** A. KOESTLER in *Encounter* I. II. 28/2 British foreign policy.. and French internal politics..seem to be dictated by this kind of repetition-compulsion. **1961** J. A. C. BROWN *Freud* i. 4 This phenomenon, described by Freudians as the repetition compulsion, is met with most frequently clinically..in the choice of a mate where the same personality type is selected each time. **1974** S. ARIETI *Amer. Handbk. Psychiatry* (ed. 2) III. 164/2 In the hyponoic and sometimes..anoetic qualities of the hypnoid state, the dominance of repetition compulsion becomes apparent. **1941** L. MACNEICE *Poetry of W. B. Yeats* 164 The twentieth century suspected most poetic *repetition-devices. **1954** A. H. MASLOW *Motivation & Personality* xi. 188 (*heading*) *Repetition phenomena; persistent, unsuccessful coping; detoxification. **1940** *Chambers's Techn. Dict.* 714/1 **Repetition rate*, the number of times repetition is demanded in a telephone conversation, this being related to the line or transmitter noise, [etc.]. **1948**, etc. [see *pulse repetition rate* s.v. PULSE *sb.*[1] 6]. **1969** *Times* 4 Feb. 13/3 It [*sc.* pulsar NP 0532] has the fastest repetition rate of all known pulsating stars. -**1624** DONNE *Devot.* (ed. 2) 381, I could not heare the Sermon, and these latter Bells are a *repetition Sermon to me. **1688** D. GRANVILLE in *Misc.* (Surtees No. 37) 43 It is a custom in the University of Oxford once in the year in the University Church to have a Repetition-sermon..: that repetition task..is the most difficult employment of the whole year. **1897** *Daily News* 18 Nov. 6/2 Another Manchester firm..discharged a fitter employed on simple *repetition work.

II. 7. (Chiefly *Sc.*) The action of claiming restitution or repayment; a claim of this kind; also loosely, restoration, recovery, repayment.

1533 BELLENDEN *Livy* I. xiii. (S.T.S.) I. 74 This rite of chevelry, and repeticioun of gudis, began first be ane anciant pepil namit equicoli. **1590** *Reg. Privy Council Scot.* IV. 543 But prejudice of his repetitioun of the soume abonewrittin payit be him to the said Sir Robert. **1644** in Spalding *Troub. Chas. I* (Spalding Club) II. 313 Everie vther burghe sall haue repetitioun of the tua pairt of the proportioun of excise furneshit by them. **1649** JER. TAYLOR *Gt. Exemp.* Disc. x. 138 Innocent requiring of my owne, which goes no further than a faire repetition. **1765** *Act 5 Geo. III*, c. 49 §5 Their action..for repetition of any overcharge in such account of expences. **1838** W. BELL *Dict. Law Scot.* 204 A creditor who had obtained a preference in a ranking to which he was not entitled, was found liable to repetition.

repeˈtition[2] (riː-). *rare*⁻¹. [RE- 5 a.] A new petition or request.

1759 FRANKLIN *Ess.* Wks. 1840 III. 240 Repetitions, when they are supported with new reasons,..are justifiable in all cases.

repeˈtitional, *a. rare.* [-AL[1].] = next.

1720 S. PARKER *Biblioth. Bibl.* I. 15 This second, or repetitional Law, being indeed a Recapitulation and Compendium of the first. **1829** BENTHAM *Justice & Cod. Petit., Full Petit.* 117 An interval..between the original series of proceedings, and the repetitional proceedings. **1871** BUSHNELL in *Life & Lett.* xxiv. (1880) 524 Great care to be had of language—no..cantish repetitional stuff. **1965** *Eng. Studies* XLVI. 160 It is..harder to ascertain cases of *amphibolia* than repetitional figures or double constructions.

repetitionary (rɛpɪˈtɪʃənərɪ), *a.* [f. REPETITION[1] + -ARY.] Characterized by, of the nature of, repetition.

1720 S. PARKER *Biblioth. Bibl.* I. 27 Where Moses deliver'd the Second or Repetitionary Law. **1806** R. CUMBERLAND *Mem.* (1807) II. 235 His adoption of a stanza obsolete and repetitionary on the ear. **1891** J. WINSOR *Chr. Columbus* ii. 60 The repetitionary changes of stock sentiment, which swell the body of the text.

†**repeˈtitioner.** *Obs.* [f. as prec. + -ER[1].] The preacher of a repetition sermon.

a **1662** HEYLIN *Laud* (1668) 68 For which he was so ratled up by the Repetitioner. **1691** [see REPEATER 2 b].

repeˈtitionist. *rare*⁻¹. [f. as prec. + -IST.] One who makes a practice of repetition.

1815 *Zeluca* III. 242 'What, another anecdote..!' 'I am a mere repetitionist', cried Medlicott.

repetitious (rɛpɪˈtɪʃəs), *a.* [f. L. *repetīt-*, ppl. stem of *repetĕre* (see REPEAT *v.*) + -IOUS.] Abounding in, or characterized by, repetition, esp. of a tedious kind; tiresomely iterative.

(Noted as common in 19th-c. Amer. use in *N.E.D.*)

1675 PENN *Eng. Pres. Interest* 17 The Great Charter..is comprehensive and repetitious of what I have already been discoursing. **1757** MRS. GRIFFITH *Lett. Henry & Frances* (1767) I. 34 A surprize is an agreeable novelty in this same repetitious world. **1856** HAWTHORNE *Eng. Note-bks.* (1879) I. 136 An English legal document,..very long and repetitious. **1860** HOLLAND *Miss Gilbert* vi. 107 It had been drummed into her ears by the repetitious tongue of her mother.

Hence **repeˈtitiously** *adv.*; **repeˈtitiousness.**

1865 *Sat. Rev.* 14 Jan. 62/1 Man is weak; 'but, more than this, he is wicked—repetitiously and wilfully so'. **1882** P. SCHAFF *Apost. Chr.* (1883) 785 The apparent repetitiousness and dependence of Ephesians on Colossians.

repetitive (rɪˈpɛtɪtɪv), *a.* [f. as prec. + -IVE: cf. *competitive.*] **A.** *adj.* Characterized by, of the nature of, repetition; repetitious.

1839 *New Monthly Mag.* LVI. 51 This little domestic scene was repeated..with just sufficient variation..as might suffice to prevent its appearing stupidly repetitive. **1899** *Allbutt's Syst. Med.* VIII. 211 Observe if there be any alterations or spontaneous repetitive movements of the digits.

B. as *sb.* = *repetition compound* s.v. REPETITION[1] 6.

1961 R. B. LONG *Sentence & its Parts* xvii. 383 The category of repetitives..includes..a few words with components repeated without change. *Poohpooh, tomtom*,.. and *hushhush* are repetitives of this kind.

Hence **reˈpetitiveness.**

1884 *Spectator* 15 Nov. 1509 A sort of patient repetitiveness—there is no such word but there ought to be—which drives onlookers wild.

repetitor (rɪˈpɛtɪtə(r)). [Ger.] A private tutor, esp. in Law, at a German university or college.

1770 *Diary* (MS., Eng. Coll. Rome), Wed 7..in time of Repetition..to yᵉ R.C. [Roman College] a little Theological act perform'd by Padre Angeleni one of yᵉ Repetitors in yᵉ German Colledge. **1886** in WEBSTER. **1895** H. RASHDALL *Universities Europe Middle Ages* I. iv. 250 A *Repetitio* in Medicine and Arts [at Bologna]..was, as a rule, not given by the Master himself but by a 'Repetitor', who attended the lecture and then repeated it to the students afterwards and catechized them upon it. **1968** *Listener* 30 May 699/3 The *repetitor*, a lawyer—not a recognised university teacher and often looked at askance by academic lawyers—sets up house in a university town and acts as a kind of 'crammer', compensating for the frequent lack of suitable classes in the legal faculties and other teaching deficiencies.

repeyle, obs. form of RIPPLE *v.*

reˈphase, *v.* [RE- 5 a + PHASE *v.* 2.] *trans.* To phase again; to readjust the proposed timing of. So **reˈphasing** *vbl. sb.*

1957 *Economist* 2 Nov. 423/2 Rather coyly, the Chancellor added his 1958 and 1959 figures together.., remarking only that the revision 'will mean a re-phasing of the nuclear power programme'. **1957** *New Scientist* 7 Nov. 38/2 It is thought necessary to 'rephase' the plan for modernising the railways. **1970** *Daily Tel.* 22 Jan. 21/3 The CEGB may well rephase the programme to avoid 'bunching' and the 'feast and famine' cycle. **1971** *Nature* 19 Feb. 517/2 BP Chemicals International has announced..the rephasing of the construction of a chemical plant at Baglan Bay, South Wales. *a* **1974** R. CROSSMAN *Diaries* (1976) II. 584 Harold [Wilson] and Peter Shore now feel that the whole closure programme over the next eighteen months should be rephased and slowed down.

reˈphrase, *v.* [RE- 5 a.] *trans.* To put into different words; to express in an alternative way. Also *absol.* and *fig.* Hence **reˈphrasing** *vbl. sb.*

1895 BOYD CARPENTER *Lect. Preaching* 180 The thing.. often needs to be translated and rephrased. **1949** M. MEAD *Male & Female* viii. 176 The extreme ingenuity with which man has rephrased his own physiology. **1952** M. R. RINEHART *Swimming Pool* xi. 103 Perhaps I'd better rephrase the question. **1953** *Essays in Criticism* III. 109 A good opportunity to rephrase and to say more properly what I had to say. **1961** R. B. LONG *Sentence & its Parts* xv. 342 Careful and formal styles..resort to rephrasings that avoid the problem. **1966** OGILVY & ANDERSON *Excurs. Number Theory* i. 5 When somebody else comes along and rephrases the question or perhaps asks a new one, a breakthrough results. **1967** COX & GROSE *Organization & Handling Bibl. Rec. by Computer* IV. 98 The second major objective is to develop a man-machine dialoguing capability which will permit real time rephrasing of input queries. **1981** 'J. ROSS' *Dark Blue & Dangerous* xiv. 80 I'll rephrase what I said. I *know* that you knew Sergeant Proctor.

reˈpick (riː-), *v.* [RE- 5 a.] *trans.* To pick again, in various senses.

1779 [W. MARSHALL] *Minutes Agric., Observ.* 83 The Docks picked out of the Swaths; which were afterwards turned and re-picked. **1818** J. BROWN *Psyche* 116 The same thin Cassius to repick His purpose and to probe his quick. **1830** LYTTON *P. Clifford* viii, Paul hastened to repick his oakum and rejoin his friend.

repicq(ue, obs. forms of REPIQUE *v.*

reˈpicture (riː-), *v.* [RE- 5 a.] *trans.* To picture again.

1847 *New Monthly Mag.* Jan. 14* A full-length portrait of the times..is repictured to the eye. **1875** GEO. JACQUE *Hope: Lights and Shadows* ii. 15 Hopes—Which Fancy with officious art Repictures to the wounded heart.

reˈpiece (riː-), *v.* [RE- 5 a.] *trans.* To piece together again.

1646 in Carte *Ormonde* (1736) II. App. 13 You endeavour what you can to repiece your breach with the Irish. **1825** J. NICHOLSON *Operat. Mechanic* 398 It will..stop the other thread or threads until the broken thread shall be repieced.

repier, obs. variant of RIPPIER.

†**re'pignorate, -erate,** *v. Obs.*$^{-0}$. [ad. ppl. stem of L. *repignorāre, -erāre*: see IMPIGNORATE.] 'To redeem a pledge.' So †**re'pignoration.**

1623 COCKERAM. 1656 BLOUNT *Glossogr.* [from Cooper].

†**re'pike.** *Obs. rare*$^{-1}$. [app. f. REPIQUE *v.*] ? Repercussive or repulsive action.

1687 BEVERLEY *Expos. Song of Songs* Concl., So the Repike Of untun'd Ears its True sounds back do strike With Disacceptance.

repillestok, obs. form of RIPPLESTOCK.

re'pin (riː-), *v.* [RE- 5 a.] To pin again.

1859 READE *Love me* xxvii. Eve slily repinned it on him. 1885 LOCK *Workshop Receipts* Ser. IV. 286/1 The great points in repinning are to drive the pin [etc.].

†**re'pine,** *sb. Obs.* [f. the vb.] The (*or* an) act of repining; discontent, grudge.

1592 SHAKS. *Ven. & Ad.* 490 Were neuer foure such lamps, together mixt, Had not his clouded with his browes repine. 1600 HOLLAND *Livy* 96 Not..iterating still his praises for feare of heaping more matter of envie and repine. 1615 A. STAFFORD *Heav. Dogge* 64 What I must, that I will do, without so much as a repine or a struggle.

repine (rɪ'paɪn), *v.* Also 6–7 repyne. [app. f. RE- + PINE *v.*, but the formation is unusual.]

1. *intr.* To feel or manifest discontent or dissatisfaction; to fret, murmur, or complain. Also const. *against, at,* †*to.*

c 1530 *Crt. of Love* 1262 Enuy will grutch, repining at his wele. 1530 PALSGR. 686/2 Thou repynest agaynst all thynge that I do. 1549 LATIMER *3rd Serm. bef. Edw. VI* (Arb.) 79 It was neuer hard in Ieurye that the people repyned or sayed, The kynge is a child. *a* 1598 ROLLOCK *Lect. Passion* xxvii. (1616) 263 Looke..that thou repine not to this light. 1637 R. HUMPHREY tr. *St. Ambrose* I. 118 One..is repined at, because hee hath some of the inheritance. 1671 MILTON *P.R.* II. 94, I will not argue that, nor will repine. 1728 YOUNG *Love Fame* v. (ed. 2) 97 Repine we guiltless in a world like this? 1771 *Junius Lett.* lvii. (1788) 311 Religious men..make it the last effort of their piety not to repine against Providence. 1820 W. IRVING *Sketch Bk.* I. 185 Through the long and weary day he repines at his unhappy lot. 1878 BROWNING *La Saisiaz* 196 Why repine? There's ever someone lives although ourselves be dead!

fig. 1808 SCOTT *Marm.* IV. x, From pool to eddy..You hear her streams repine.

b. Const. with *that* or inf.

a 1548 HALL *Chron., Hen. VIII* 110 He had repined or disdained, that any man should fare well, or be well clothed, but hymself. 1576 FLEMING *Panopl. Epist.* 66 We ought not to kicke upp the heele, as repining to live in that state, whereunto by birth we were ordeined. 1615 BRATHWAIT *Strappado* (1878) 74 O see how men repine, That you so long conceal'd, should gull the time. 1752 HUME *Ess. & Treat.* (1777) I. 348 We continue still to repine that our neighbours should possess any art, industry, and invention. 1870 BRYANT *Iliad* I. IV. 107, I shall ne'er Contend to save them nor repine to see Their fall.

c. To long discontentedly *for* something. *rare.*

1742 GRAY *Sonn. Death West* 5 These Ears, alas, for other Notes repine. 1827 HALLAM *Const. Hist.* (1876) I. iii. 153 The worship of the church was frequented by multitudes who secretly repined for a change.

†**2.** *trans.* To regard with discontent or dissatisfaction; to fret or murmur at; †to grudge *to* one.

1577 HANMER *Anc. Eccl. Hist.* (1619) 223 So that none in this behalfe can repine or gainsay vs. 1596 SPENSER *F.Q.* VI. vii. 26 In signe Of servile yoke, that nobler harts repine. 1615 T. ADAMS *White Devil* 13 Wouldest thou have permitted this to thy fellow servant, that repinest it to thy master? *a* 1670 HACKET *Abp. Williams* I. (1692) 173 Contented with so much favour as was never repined. 1793 W. ROBERTS *Looker-on* No. 48 (1794) II. 218 She repined, for their own sakes, the malignities of her sex.

Hence †**re'pineful** *a.*, discontented (*obs.*); **re'pinement,** repining, discontent. *rare.*

1655 SHIRLEY *Polit.* III. ii, Most repineful, spleeny. 1743 H. WALPOLE *Lett. to Mann* (1834) I. 301 Now am I relapsed into all the dissatisfied repinement of a true English grumbling voluptuary. 1818 FARADAY in B. Jones *Life* (1870) I. 274 You shall see this man..accompanied by repinement, regret, and contempt, sink into poverty and misery.

repiner (rɪ'paɪnə(r)). [f. prec. + -ER^{1}.] One who repines or is discontented; a grumbler.

1551 ASCHAM *Let. to E. Raven* 23 Feb., He is likely to make..the Germans, of secret repiners, open foes. 1594 T. BEDINGFIELD tr. *Machiavelli's Florentine Hist.* (1595) 91 To occasion these repiners feele the smart of their counsell. 1653 R. SANDERS *Physiogn.* 91 He is a scoffer, derider, and repiner. 1750 BERKELEY *Max. conc. Patriotism* §23 We are not to think..every splenetick repiner against a court is therefore a patriot. 1805 A. WILSON *Epist. to A. Clarke*, Heaven..showers with fury dread, Tormenting ills on the repiner's head. 1854 WHITTIER *Maud Muller* 102 Alas!.. For rich repiner and household drudge!

repining (rɪ'paɪnɪŋ), *vbl. sb.* [f. as prec. + -ING^{1}.] The action of the vb., or an instance of this; discontent, grumbling, fretting.

1550 LEVER *Serm.* (Arb.) 34 It is not therefore repynyng, rebellyng, or resistyng gods ordinance, that wyll amende euyll rulers. 1617 MORYSON *Itin.* I. 266 After some repining he was satisfied therewith. 1663 PEPYS *Diary* 15 May, Which the world takes notice of, even to some repinings. 1712 ADDISON *Spect.* No. 387 ¶2 Repinings, and secret Murmurs of Heart. 1810 CRABBE *Borough* xxi. 342 Let thy repinings cease, Oh! man of sin, for they thy guilt increase. 1867 PARKMAN *Jesuits N. Amer.* i. (1875) 6 Workmen.., who gave him at times no little trouble by their repinings and complaints.

repining (rɪ'paɪnɪŋ), *ppl. a.* [-ING^{2}.] That repines; given to repining; characterized by, or of the nature of, repining.

a 1586 SIDNEY *Arcadia* (1622) 223 One of the repiningst fellowes in the world. *c* 1586 C'TESS PEMBROKE *Ps.* LXXV. ii, No more..Daunce on in wordes your old repyning measure. 1632 LITHGOW *Trav.* x. 432 There was neuer a more repining people. 1702 ROWE *Tamerl.* I. i. 275 Let Bajazet Bend to his Yoak repining Slaves by force. 1782 COWPER *Cricket* 30 Wretched man, whose years are spent In repining discontent. 1877 BRYANT *Voice Autumn* i, There comes, from yonder height, A soft repining sound.

Hence **re'piningly** *adv.*

1571 GOLDING *Calvin on Ps.* xviii. 2 They that..afterward repyningly restreyne his power. *a* 1680 CHARNOCK *Attrib. God* (1834) II. 651 They repiningly quarrelled with him in their wants in the wilderness. 1782 MISS BURNEY *Cecilia* IV. x, She began..repiningly to relate her misfortunes. 1856 *Titan Mag.* Nov. 443/2 Dwelling repiningly on what I have not.

repique (rɪ'piːk), *sb.* Also 7 -peak, peek, -picq(ue. [ad. F. *repic* = It. *ripicco*: see RE- and PIQUE.] In *Piquet*, the winning of thirty points on cards alone before beginning to play (and before the adversary begins to count), entitling the player to begin his score at ninety. Also *fig.*

1668 TEMPLE *Let. Ld. Arlington* Wks. 1731 II. 93 In their Audiences..the Cards commonly run high, and all is Picque and Repicque between them. 1678 PHILLIPS, *Repeak* [1696 *Repeek*],..a term in the Game of Picquet. 1680 COTTON *Compl. Gamester* (ed. 2) 58 The youngers Blank shall bar the former and hinder his Picq and Repicq [*printed* Picy and Repicy]. 1721 CIBBER *School-boy* I, I constantly receive my Rent in nothing but Repiques, Capotts, Gamons, and Doublets. 1771 MACKENZIE *Man Feel.* xxv, His score was 90 to 35, and he was elder hand; but a momentous repique decided it in favour of his adversary. 1830 'EIDRAH TREBOR' *Hoyle Made Fam.* 49 Carte-blanche counts first, and consequently saves piques and repiques. 1859 WRAXALL tr. *R. Houdin* iv. 39 When the cards are dealt out, I will leave you to select the hand you think will enable you best to prevent a repique.

repique (rɪ'piːk), *v.* [f. prec.]

1. *trans.* To score a repique against (the opposing player in piquet).

1659 *Shuffling, Cutting & Deel.* 8, I was Pickquet the last, but am now repickqt. 1709 MRS. MANLEY *Secret Mem.* II. 104 We agreed to play for fifty Pieces the Party; I repiqu'd him eight Times in a dozen. 1755 ED. MOORE in *World* No. 154 (1772) III. 297 He was most cruelly repiqued when he wanted but two points of the game. 1830 'EIDRAH TREBOR' *Hoyle Made Fam.* 49 It also piques and repiques the adversary, in the same manner as if those points were reckoned in any other way.

†**b.** ? To repel, resist. *Obs. rare*$^{-1}$.

1687 BEVERLEY *Exp. Song of Songs* 27 Those enterweaves of Holy Order like The well-curl'd Locks, all falshood that Repique.

†**c.** Used as an imprecation. *Obs. rare*$^{-1}$.

1760 FOOTE *Minor* I. i, Repique the rascal. He promis'd to be here before me.

2. *intr.* To win a repique.

1719 D'URFEY *Pills* V. 278 He piqu'd, and repiqu'd so oft. 1840 LADY C. BURY *Hist. of Flirt* i, He was obstinately bent on repiquing. 1895 SNAITH *Dorothy Marven* vi, The mysteries of sword and musket were discarded for those..of piqueing, repiqueing and capotting.

repit, obs. form of RIPPIT.

replace (rɪ'pleɪs), *v.* [f. RE- 5 a + PLACE *v.*, perh. after F. *remplacer* (1549) or, in late use, *replacer* (17th c.).]

1. *trans.* To restore to a previous place or position; to put back again *in* (or †*into*) a place.

1595 DANIEL *Civ. Wars* III. xxix, A third..Sweares if they would, he would attempt the thing To chaste th' vsurper, and replace their king. 1622 BACON *Hen. VII* 32 This princess..made it her design..to see the majesty royal of England once again replaced in her house. *a* 1674 CLARENDON *Hist. Reb.* XVI. §12 They..replaced Lambert, and all the rest who had been cashiered by Cromwell, into their own charges again. 1749 H. WALPOLE *Corr.* (1846) II. 296 The King has consented to give two earldoms to replace the great families of Somerset and Northumberland. 1838 DE MORGAN *Ess. Probab.* 61 Drawings are made, after each of which the ball is replaced. 1875 KNIGHT *Dict. Mech.* 1918/2 A bridge by which the wheels of cars are replaced upon the track.

refl. 1707 *Curios. in Husb. & Gard.* 352 This Emulation, that Matter always retains, to..replace it self..in the same Figure, which..Nature originally impressed on it.

2. To take the place of, become a substitute for (a person or thing). Freq. in passive, const. *by* (the new person or thing).

1753 A. MURPHY *Gray's Inn Jrnl.* No. 53 Though many have plucked a Branch from it, it is always quickly replaced by another. 1756 LD. BARRINGTON in Ellis *Orig. Lett.* Ser. II. IV. 383 Sir Edward Hawke, and Captain Saunders..went to replace Admirals Byng and West. 1796 H. HUNTER tr. *St.-Pierre's Stud. Nat.* (1799) II. 61 The Moon..goes to replace him [the Sun] there, and appears perpetually above the Horizon. 1823 COLEBROOKE in *St. Cape G. Hope* 346 The paper [money] would be seasonably replaced by a metallic currency. 1862 ANSTED *Channel Isl.* I. iii. (ed. 2) 56 The orchards, also, which in Jersey may be said to replace parks, are not very numerous.

b. *Crystall.* (See quots.)

1847 WEBSTER, *Replaced*, in mineralogy, a term used when a crystal has one or more planes in the place of its edges or angles. 1878 GURNEY *Crystallogr.* 51 A quoin or an edge is said to be replaced, when it is cut off by one or more faces of another simple form.

3. To fill the place of (a person or thing) *with* or *by* a substitute.

1765 *Museum Rust.* IV. 173 You must..replace such as have failed, with the best and most likely plants. 1837 CARLYLE *Fr. Rev.* I. II. iii, Thou wouldst not replace such extinct Lie by a new Lie. 1853 MAURICE *Proph. & Kings* xvi. 269 They talked of replacing buildings of brick with buildings of stone. 1885 WATSON & BURBURY *Electr. & Magn.* I. 262 Let us replace *S* by another closed surface.

b. To provide or procure a substitute or equivalent in place of (a person or thing).

1796 SOUTHEY *Lett. fr. Spain* (1799) 424 A convent, founded for twenty religious, that has thirty now, should not be permitted to replace ten when they died. 1802 MRS. E. PARSONS *Myst. Visit* IV. 144, I pity him for the loss of such a treasure as he will not easily replace. 1856 KANE *Arct. Expl.* II. vi. 71 The natives to the south have lost nearly all their..walrus-lines..and will be unable to replace them till the return of the seal.

4. To return or restore *to* one. *rare*$^{-1}$.

1776 ADAM SMITH *W.N.* II. iii. I. 403 Whatever part of his stock a man employs as a capital, he always expects it to be replaced to him with a profit.

Hence **re'placed** *ppl. a.*; **re'placing** *vbl. sb.*

1865 MANSFIELD *Salts* 241 The belief..that the replaced or conjugated Hydrogen is the whole Hydrogen of a certain proportion of integral water. 1884 *Manch. Weekly Times* 11 Oct. 5/6 The replacing of the tracery of the cloisters..is.. proceeding bay by bay. 1884 KNIGHT *Dict. Mech., Suppl.* 750/2 *Replacing Apparatus*, for the replacing of derailed rolling stock upon the line.

replace (rɪ'pleɪs), *a. rare.* [f. the vb.] Designed to replace something that is worn out or is being discarded.

1927 *Daily Tel.* 10 May 4/5 The life of the first tracks was about 2,000 miles... The replace tracks..embody such obvious improvements that they will undoubtedly give a much longer life.

replacea'bility. [f. REPLACEABLE *a.*: see -BILITY.] The state, property, or condition of being replaceable.

1890 in WEBSTER. 1907 A. W. POLLARD *Bks. in House* 37 As to what should be sold and what kept, the one sovereign test is that of replaceability. 1959 P. F. STRAWSON *Individuals* v. 161 Replaceability by quantifier and variable.

replaceable (rɪ'pleɪsəb(ə)l), *a.* [f. REPLACE *v.* + -ABLE.] **a.** That may be replaced.

1805 W. TAYLOR in *Ann. Rev.* III. 236 The concurring individuals..appear but as insignificant and replaceable instruments. 1871 ROSCOE *Elem. Chem.* 159 The four atoms of hydrogen being replaceable..by metals.

b. *absol.* in *Chem.*, denoting those hydrogen atoms in an acid which may be replaced by base.

1895 W. A. TILDEN *Introd. Study of Chem. Philos.* (ed. 8) xv. 140 Tartaric acid is a case of similar kind. Its molecular formula cannot be less than $C_4H_6O_6$, on account of the existence of the double tartrates, which prove that the acid contains two replaceable basic hydrogen atoms. 1930 W. R. ANDERSON *School Cert. Chem.* iv. 47 With sulphuric acid we can get a salt by turning out half the hydrogen present, but this salt still contains replaceable hydrogen. 1962 PARKES & HARRISON *Basic Physical & Inorg. Chem.* xv. 202 A normal salt is one in which all the replaceable hydrogen of the acid and the hydroxyl (or oxygen) of the base have reacted to form water.

re'placement. [f. as prec. + -MENT.] **1. a.** The act or process of replacing in various senses; the fact of being replaced.

a 1790 ADAM SMITH *W.N.* II. iii, That part of the annual produce destined to the replacement of that capital. 1831 T. HOPE *Ess. Origin Man* I. 45 The word eternal seems only.. to express..a constant replacement of portions of time already gone by. 1875 WHITNEY *Life Lang.* x. 212 There is more wearing-out than replacement by synthetic means.

attrib. 1896 tr. *Boas' Text-Bk. Zool.* 416 Replacement teeth are formed continuously throughout life. 1898 *Allbutt's Syst. Med.* V. 954 A proliferative fibrosis..as opposed to mere 'replacement fibrosis'.

b. *absol.* in *Min.* The dissolution of one mineral and the simultaneous deposition of another in its place. Freq. *attrib.*

1906 *Econ. Geol.* I. 839 As a general term synonymous with 'metasomatism', 'replacement' is preferable to 'substitution'. 1911 *Ibid.* VI. 534 Replacement ore-bodies are generally associated with fissures..capable of conducting solutions from considerable distances. 1928 W. LINDGREN *Min. Deposits* (ed. 3) ii. 27 Metallic ores are often formed by replacement. *Ibid.* xxviii. 739 The quartz monzonite contains a great number of replacement veins carrying much tourmaline. 1965 G. J. WILLIAMS *Econ. Geol. N.Z.* iii. 23/2 The ore-shoots are typical replacement-bodies of quartz, mullock and pug along narrow shears. 1970 K. C. JACKSON *Textbk. Lithol.* iv. 196 Crystal growth, particularly where replacement is important, often results in inclusions of unincorporated minerals in the growing crystal. 1972 M. H. BATTEY *Mineral. for Students* vi. 160/1 Deposition is also influenced by the nature of the country-rocks. The fluids react with these..to produce replacement deposits in the neighbourhood of the vein fissures.

2. Something which or someone who replaces another.

1894 *Q. Jrnl. Geol. Soc.* L. 383 The hypothesis that the rock is a siliceous replacement of a limestone. 1934 H. G. WELLS *Exper. Autobiogr.* I. ii. 62 He..sold little, I think, but jam-pots and preserving jars to the gentlemen's houses round about, and occasional..table glass and replacements. 1944 *Yank* 26 May 3 At the Rapido some replacements couldn't tell the difference between our fire and Jerry's. 1954 W. FAULKNER *Fable* 4 The original regiment had been raised in this district... And most of its subsequent replacements had been drawn from this same district. 1973

Times 15 Feb. 12/6 There are, however, two significant changes in the list of substitutes (whom rugby officials insist on calling 'replacements' to differentiate between them and the fellows used in other sports for tactical reasons without anyone having gone to hospital).

3. *attrib.* and *Comb.*, as ***replacement cost, price, thrust***; **replacement theory** (see quot. 1979); **replacement therapy**, therapy aimed at making up a deficit of a substance normally present in the body.

1928 *Britain's Industrial Future* (Liberal Industr. Inquiry) II. vi. 67 The capital plant of most..undertakings is relatively small, but the roads are an exception, of which the *replacement cost must exceed £1,300,000,000. **1936** J. M. KEYNES *Gen. Theory Employment* xi. 135 The price which would just induce a manufacturer newly to produce an additional unit of such assets, *i.e.* what is sometimes called its *replacement cost*. **1963** *Rep. Comm. Inquiry Decimal Curr.* xiv. 141 The true 'replacement cost' is the present value to the user of the future flow of services he could expect from the old machine were it not prematurely replaced. **1977** *Time* 24 Jan. 44/3 Proponents of replacement-cost accounting argue that the machine should be carried on the books at the price of a new machine. **1974** *Terminol. Managem. & Financial Accountancy* (Inst. Cost & Managem. Accountants) 15 **Replacement price*, the price at which material could be purchased, identical to that which is being replaced or revalued. **1957** C. W. CHURCHMAN et al. *Introd. Operations Research* xvii. 482 (*heading*) Relevant costs in *replacement theory considerations. **1969** J. ARGENTI *Managem. Techniques* 226 (*heading*) Replacement Theory... Problem... When to replace plant, machinery, etc. **1979** *Gloss. Terms Work Study* (*B.S.I.*) 12 *Replacement theory*, a body of mathematical theory connected with the problems of determining the most economical time to replace or repair a piece of equipment. **1962** H. BURN *Drugs, Med. & Man* xiii. 138 In *replacement therapy extracts of glands such as the thyroid gland, the pancreas, the parathyroid gland and the adrenal cortex were prepared from the glands of animals and were given to patients whose own glands were deficient. **1977** *Lancet* 14 May 1048/1 A young woman with von Willebrand disease who asked for a termination of pregnancy and tubal ligation had had..only one bleeding episode in her life requiring replacement therapy. **1971** I. BUTYKAI tr. *Lukovich's Electric Foil Fencing* I. 20 Fencers show a definite preference for angular attacks, *replacement thrusts and ripostes.

replacer (rɪˈpleɪsə(r)). [f. REPLACE *v.* + -ER[1].] A person or thing that replaces another; a substitute. Also *attrib.*

1895 in *Funk's Stand. Dict.* **1913** G. B. DIBBLEE *Newspaper* 110 One may perhaps grumble at the rather obvious significance of the new 'replacers'. **1960** *Farmer & Stockbreeder* 9 Feb. 73/1 Early weaning is done at three weeks, the piglets being moved on to a home mixed replacer meal, compounded for £67 10s a ton. **1965** *Language* XLI. 280 The pronominal replacers are marked for low stress.

reˈplacive, *a.* and *sb.* [f. REPLACE *v.* + -IVE.]

A. *adj.* That replaces something else; substitutive; *spec.* in *Linguistics*, of a morph or morpheme.

1948 *Language* XXIV. 440 Morphemes may be classified ..as (1) additive, (2) replacive, (3) additive and replacive, and (4) subtractive. **1949** E. A. NIDA *Morphology* (ed. 2) 72 In English replacive morphemes are abundantly illustrated in the verbs which undergo a change of syllabic in the past-tense. **1965** *Canad. Jrnl. Linguistics* X. 139 It [*sc.* the Giamina language] became extinct not through replacive bilingualism with Spanish or English but with one of the Yokuts languages. **1974** P. H. MATTHEWS *Morphology* vii. 122 *Men*, for example, would be said to consist of the regular allomorph *man* of the morpheme MAN plus a 'replacive morph' ('replace *a* with *e*' or '*a* → *e*') which was assigned as yet another allomorph of PLURAL. **1977** *Word* 1972 XXVIII. 193 It seems possible to classify Welsh metanalysis into three main types: *additive, subtractive*, and *replacive*.

B. *sb.* Something which replaces or substitutes for something else: *spec.* in *Linguistics*, a replacive morph or morpheme.

1948 *Language* XXIV. 441 The shift of stress in related nouns and verbs in English..is also a type of replacive. **1949** E. A. NIDA *Morphology* (ed. 2) 55 In the example *feet* as a plural of *foot* we may describe the replacement as /iy← u/. Such morphemes are called 'replacives'. **1954** *Word* X. 224 A 'replacive'..is not by any stretch of the imagination composed of phonemic material. **1962** H. A. GLEASON in Householder & Saporta *Probl. Lexicography* 87 The 'replacive'..quite artificially makes an affix out of a process. **1977** *Word* 1972 XXVIII. 203 Complicated series of alterations: some replacives (e.g. *Glama*), but also syncope, assimilation, and so on.

†**reˈplait**, *v.* *Sc. Obs. rare.* Also **resplate**. [f. OF. *replait, repleit* (14th c. in Godef.), rehearing of a plea, f. *re-* RE- + *plait, pleit*: see PLEA *sb.* and PLEAD *v.*] *trans.* To adjourn or remand (a cause or person).

15.. *Chart. Aberdeen* fol. 153 (Jam.), Gif the said serjand hade maid summonds..to this court..of his process resplatit and continewit fra the ferd court [etc.]. **1561** *Reg. Privy Council Scot.* I. 186 Gif the said Lord James thinkis thame to be replaitit, and the executioun thairof to be continewit.., that he continew the samyn.

reˈplan *v.* [RE- 5 a.] *trans.* To plan again. Hence **reˈplanning** *vbl. sb.*

1888 B. W. RICHARDSON *Son of a Star* III. v. 72 He has planned and replanned this day's tactics. **1943** J. S. HUXLEY *TVA* xv. 129 Replanned so as to provide docks and terminals..Guntersville has become transformed. **1946** *Nature* 28 Sept. 438/2 No schemes for reconstructing and replanning London will be satisfactory without drastic adjustments to existing facilities for transport. **1960** *Farmer & Stockbreeder* 22 Mar. 120/3 Farm manager, Frank Stevens, played an important part in replanning the farm. **1976** S. R. SIMPSON *Land Law & Registration* ix. 170 Similar considerations apply to physical planning or replanning and to 'land reform'. **1978** P. BOARDMAN *Worlds of Patrick Geddes* vii. 244 The Viceroy opened a competition with a prize of £500 for the best replanning scheme for the city [*sc.* Dublin].

replant (riːˈplɑːnt, -æ-), *v.* [f. RE- 5 a + PLANT *v.*, perh. after F. *replanter* (1306) = Sp. *replantar*, It. *ripiantare*.]

1. *trans.* To plant (a tree, plant, etc.) again.

1575 FENTON *Gold. Epist.* (1582) 14 A tree..newe replanted..bringeth foorth fruite of farre more sweete and pretious taste than others. **1601** HOLLAND *Pliny* I. 511 All the danger or security of this tree, standeth vpon the choice of that only day wherein it is replanted. **1660** SHARROCK *Vegetables* 33 The roote and cabbage being replanted in the spring. **1712** J. JAMES tr. *Le Blond's Gardening* 179 Plants which rise from Seed..should be taken up..and be replanted. **1763** MILLS *Syst. Pract. Husb.* IV. 33 Some of the..largest and best shaped bulbs should be replanted. **1856** DELAMER *Fl. Gard.* (1861) 40 So it may remain, to be taken up and replanted every third or fourth year.

b. *transf.* To plant (a thing or person) again; to re-establish, resettle, replace. Freq. const. *in*.

1587 [see REPLANTING *vbl. sb.*]. **1593** SHAKS. *3 Hen. VI*, III. iii. 198, I will..replant Henry in his former state. **1605** WINTER in *Gunp. Plot* li b, A Way..to replant againe the Catholicke Religion. **1643** R. BAILLIE *Lett. & Jrnls.* (1841) II. 50 Mr. John Guthrie..could not be replanted in his old church. **1709** STRYPE *Ann. Ref.* I. xix. 221 They have not been able yet to root out the Gospel, since it was in these early Days replanted in the Kingdom. **1837** G. REDFORD *Script. Verif.* vii. 435 Julian..made attempts to re-plant the Jews in their fathers' land.

c. To engraft (teeth) again.

1870 ANSTIE *Practitioner* July 45 The success..obtained by Mr. Coleman in replanting teeth..will be received with unquestionable satisfaction.

2. To plant (ground, etc.) again; to furnish with new plants (or inhabitants). Also *transf.*

1652 H. L'ESTRANGE *Amer. no Jewes* 10 Noah had so many yeares of his own life to bestow in repeopling and replanting the Earth. **1763** MILLS *Pract. Husb.* IV. 435 It is therefore advisable to mark..the hills in which they are, in order to dig them up and replant those spots. **1815** *Chron.* in *Ann. Reg.* 79 The grounds in this quarter must all be replanted. **1887** MOLONEY *Forestry W. Afr.* 235 Where a farm is to be deserted..why cannot it be partially re-planted by those who may have enjoyed its use..?

3. *intr.* To provide and set fresh plants.

1712 J. JAMES tr. *Le Blond's Gardening* 165 The considerable Charge you must be at to replant every Year.

Hence **reˈplantable** *a.* (Cotgr. 1611).

replanˈtation. [RE- 5 a: cf. prec.] **1.** A second or fresh plantation.

1608 H. CLAPHAM *Errour Right Hand* 67 That, and no other, is her Re-plantation. **1682** T. A. *Carolina* 9 Three of which [vines] by Re-plantation..will make very good Wine. **1884** *Pall Mall G.* 9 Sept. 3/2 The only solution of the problem of inundations is 'replantation and canalization'.

2. *Med.* Permanent reattachment to the body of a part which has been removed or severed.

1870 ANSTIE *Practitioner* July 45 Mr. Coleman believes replantation will become the legitimate mode of treatment for chronic periodontitis. **1976** *Daily Tel.* 26 Nov. 17/6 One of the first reports of a successful replantation of a hand is published in the current issue of the *Journal of Bone and Joint Surgery*. **1980** *Times* 12 Aug. 11/5 Microsurgical replantation of limbs is carried out throughout the North American continent, Australia and many European countries.

reˈplanting, *vbl. sb.* [f. REPLANT *v.* + -ING[1].] The action of planting again.

1587 FLEMING *Contn. Holinshed* III. 1383/2 The replanting of religion. **1601** HOLLAND *Pliny* XVII. xi, Hee had thought that it was materiall to the replanting of them. **1827** STEUART *Planter's G.* (1828) 380 In the interval between the removal and the replanting. **1884** *Manch. Exam.* 19 Sept. 8/4 No system of replanting has been properly introduced.

reˈplaster (riː-), *v.* [RE- 5 a.] *trans.* To plaster again.

1849 CLOUGH *Amours de Voy.* I. 152 Strip and replaster and..do what they will with thee. **1895** MRS. WILSON 5 *Years India* 298 The house was replastered from top to bottom.

reˈplate (riː-), *sb.* [f. the vb.] An old plated article which is to be replated.

1851 J. NAPIER *Electro-Metall.* 105 The practical difficulties..when a 'replate' is dipped in the nitric acid. *Ibid.*, The parts of the 'replate' which are sound.

reˈplate (riː-), *v.* [RE- 5 a.] **1.** *trans.* To plate afresh; to renew the plating on.

1851 J. NAPIER *Electro-Metall.* 105 Replating of old articles. **1856** G. GORE in *Circ. Sc.* VIII. 92 Occasionally the depositor has sent to him, to be replated, old worn-out articles formed of Sheffield plate.

2. *trans.* and *intr.* (See quot. 1961.)

1961 H. B. JACOBSON *Mass Communications Dict.* 283 *Replate*, to recast a page of type to insert an important but late story. **1967** *Punch* 18 Jan. 91/1 This..was replated between editions to alter a reference to the *Guardian's* sales. **1967** M. SHULMAN *Kill 3* I. viii. 54 Since it's a London story, let's hold it till as late as possible. The opposition [newspapers] will have to re-plate if they want to pick it up. **1980** 'L. BLACK' *Eve of Wedding* v. 58 'How late will you stay open?' 'Until about three for fudging. We can replate to about two.'

reˈplay (riː-), *v.* [RE- 5 a.] **1.** *trans.* To play (a match, etc.) again.

1884 *Truth* 13 Mar. 369/2 Under these circumstances.. the tie should certainly be replayed. **1898** HOFFMANN *Hoyle's Games Modernized* 100 The hand having been replayed.

2. To play (a gramophone record or a tape) again, or to play back; to reproduce (what has been recorded).

1922 *Daily Mail* 18 Nov. 8 Each instrument is fitted with our special 'Repeater' which automatically replays records when desired without the operator's attention. **1962** A. NISBETT *Technique Sound Studio* 241 Tape which is replayed on the same head as was used for recording does not exhibit faults which would be at once apparent if the tape were replayed on most other machines. **1973** *Sci. Amer.* Jan. 117/1 We could replay the recorded sounds at leisure as many times as necessary to make an accurate comparison with the frequencies of our standard disk. **1973** L. COOPER *Tea on Sunday* xi. 93 He recalled the people... So often by running the first interviews through again as if they were a section of a film being replayed he picked up some clue. **1976** DEXTER & MAKINS *Testkill* 140 One of Byron's cover drives, replayed later on TV in slow motion as a textbook stroke. **1977** *Rolling Stone* 19 May 96/2 The Betamax enables you to record (on tape) your favourite TV programs for replaying later.

Hence **reˈplayed** *ppl. a.*

1892 *Pall Mall G.* 15 Feb. 1/3 Replayed matches will not add to the..list of fixtures.

replay (ˈriːpleɪ), *sb.* **1.** A replayed match.

1895 *Westm. Gaz.* 6 May 7/2 Mr. Tait last week took 83 (on a re-play). **1932** *St. George's Hosp. Gaz.* XXVIII. 25 The re-play took place at Chiswick House, St. Thomas's winning by 7 wickets. **1947** *Sporting Mirror* 7 Nov. p. iii/1 They reached the Junior Cup Final, but after a drawn game at Maidenhead, lost the replay to Reading Albion. **1951** *Sport* 27 Jan.–2 Feb. 4/3 Sunderland were the visitors to St. James' Park in a 6th round replay. **1966** *Listener* 20 Jan. 88/2 The less exhausted players and survivors of replays in the interminable F.A. Cup. **1978** *Morecambe Guardian* 14 Mar. 10/2 In the old days, Chorley were Morecambe's traditional cup rivals and the Shrimps will do well even if they force a replay.

2. The action or an instance of replaying a sound recording, piece of film, etc. Freq. *attrib.*, denoting equipment used for this.

1953 E. S. GARDNER *Case of Green-Eyed Sister* viii. 117 You had insisted on a replay of the tape. **1958** S. ELLIN *Eighth Circle* II. xvii. 132 He put Berrigan's 'I Can't Get Started' on the phonograph and set it for replay. **1962** A. NISBETT *Technique Sound Studio* vii. 130 The facilities for mixing—requiring two replay decks in addition to a mixer and recorder—are generally beyond the scope of the amateur. **1972** *Guardian* 24 Aug. 10/1 It would have been helpful if an echo machine could have produced for the President a replay of his acceptance speech in the same hall four years ago. **1974** *Cleveland* (Ohio) *Plain Dealer* 13 Oct. c. 2/1 The scoreboards will be placed on each side and the instant replay screens at each end. **1975** O. SELA *Bengali Inheritance* xv. 124 Now get the mike connected...He.. pressed the replay tab. **1976** *Daily Tel.* 16 July 3/3 A video-tape machine is to be used by London Transport to run 'replays' of violence at underground stations. **1978** S. BRETT *Amateur Corpse* xv. 137 Gerald spooled through till nearly the end of the tape... The replay button was pressed.

3. *transf.* and *fig.*

1975 P. FUSSELL *Great War* ix. 317 And the economic ruin uncompleted by the Great War was finished by the Second, which necessitated a replay, but much magnified, of immense indebtedness to the United States. **1976** W. H. CANAWAY *Willow-Pattern War* xv. 153, I lay awake..doing an involuntary replay of that horrible dream. **1977** *Time* 30 May 20/2 As Poland approaches the first anniversary of the 1976 riots, an occasion that could invite a replay of last year's protest, the Party Chief is under pressure from Moscow to keep the lid on dissent. **1977** D. ANTHONY *Stud Game* xxiii. 142 Dusty Gordon's party would be a replay of the Hollywood parties Paul Sherwood had dragged me to.

reple, obs. form of RIPPLE *sb.*

reˈplead, *v.* *rare.* [f. RE- + PLEAD *v.*: cf. OF. *repledoier* (13th c.), F. *replaider* (16th c. in Littré).] †**a.** *intr.* To raise a plea. *Obs.* **b.** To plead again. **c.** *trans.* To use as a further plea.

c **1500** *Priests of Peblis* iii. 1244 This officer but dout is callit Deid; Is nane his power agane may repleid. **1540** *Act 32 Hen. VIII*, c. 30 § 1 The same parties haue ben compelled ..to repleade. **1685** *Termes de la Ley* s.v. *Repleader*, The Court makes void all the Pleas which are ill, and awards the Parties to replead. **1748** RICHARDSON *Clarissa* (1768) V. 216, I pleaded my own sake; the Captain, his dear friend her Uncle's; and both repleaded the prevention of future mischief.

reˈpleader. *Law.* [See prec. and -ER[4].] The action of, or right to, a second pleading.

1607 COWELL *Interpr.*, *Repleader* is to plead againe that which was once pleaded before. **1651** tr. *Davies' Abridgm. Coke's Rep.* III. 54 After demurrer no repleader may be without consent of parties. **1768** BLACKSTONE *Comm.* III. 395 Whenever a repleader is granted, the pleadings must begin *de novo*. **1820** TOMLINS *Law Dict.* II. s.v.

reˈpleat (riː-), *v.* [RE- 5 a.] To pleat again.

1695 DRYDEN tr. *Dufresnoy's Art. Paint.* (1716) 143 Raphael also had much of that way in his first works, in which we behold many small Foldings often repleated.

repleat, obs. form of REPLETE *a.* and *v.*

repleave, variant of REPLEVE *v. Obs.*

replecció(u)n, obs. forms of REPLETION.

†**re'pledge**, *sb. Obs.*⁻¹ [f. next.] Replevin.
1631 Brathwait *Whimzies, Undersheriff* 96 A terrible pudder hee keepes with his repledges and distresses.

repledge (rɪ'plɛdʒ), *v.*¹ Also 5 **-plegge**, 6 *Sc.* **-plege**, 7 *Sc.* **-pleadge**. [ad. OF. *repleger*, *-eer*, *-ier* to give or become surety for (a person), f. *re-* RE- and *pleger* to PLEDGE. Hence also med.L. *replegiāre*.]

†**1.** *trans.* To take *out* of pawn again. *Obs.*⁻¹
1479 Sir J. Paston in *P. Lett.* III. 255, I payed v. marke ..to replegge owte my gowne off velwett and other geer.

2. *Sc. Law.* **a.** To withdraw (a person or cause) from the jurisdiction of another court to one's own, upon pledge that justice shall be done. Also *absol.* Now only *Hist.* (abolished in 1747).
1536 Bellenden *Cron. Scot.* v. vii, He..commandit thaim to punis na thing bot small crimes; all hie offencis to be replegit to his gret justice. **1579** *Reg. Privy Council Scot.* III. 241 They and thair brether heraldis hes bene..examit and repledgit fra all maner of inferiour judges to thair awin propir judge. **1609** Skene *Reg. Maj.* II. 158 He quha repledges to his awin Court any man quhom he sould not repledge..sall be in the kings mercie. **1693** Stair *Inst.* (ed. 2) IV. xxxvii. §4 All Sheriffs, Stewarts, Baillies of Royalty [etc.] have criminal Jurisdiction,..but they cannot Repledge. **1746-7** *Act 20 Geo. II*, c. 43 §27 Any power or privilege of repledging from the sheriffs or stewarts court. **1885** W Ross *Aberdour & Inchcolme* i. 22 He could even repledge from the Sheriff and had a right to all the moveables of delinquents.
transf. **1535** Lyndesay *Satyre* 5 His Sone, our Sauiour,.. Repleadgeand his presonaris with his hart-blude.

†**b.** To take back or take over (something forfeited or impounded) on proper security; to replevy. *Obs.*
1597 Skene *De Verb. Sign.* s.v. *Recognition*, To craue and aske fra his superiour the saides landes to him to borgh, that is to repledge them. **1609** —— *Reg. Maj., Stat. David II* 37 b, Gif any man will repledge the poynd within the saidis three dayes; the poynd salbe lettin to borgh.

re'pledge (ri:-), *v.*² [RE- 5 a.] To pledge again.
1751 Smollett *Per. Pic.* xcviii, The jewels were.. purchased, pawned, relieved, and re-pledged by the agent. **1866** *Law Rep.* 1 Q.B. Div. 589 If the pawnee may repledge the pawn, the sub-pledgee may do the same. **1887** *Pall Mall G.* 12 Feb. 6/1 [He] repledged the Liberal party to the fair and just demand for Home Rule.

re'pledger. *Sc. Law.* [f. REPLEDGE *v.*¹] One who repledges. Also *fig.*
1633 W Struther *True Happines* 89 Our Iudge..turneth our repledger, by his mercy rescuing us from Iustice. **1752** J. Louthian *Form of Process* (ed. 2) 31 In which Case, the Repledger, if he failed to do Justice upon him, in due time, tined his Court for Year and Day. **1838** W. Bell *Dict. Law Scot.* 851 On the ground that the alleged offence had been committed within the repledger's jurisdiction.

‖**replegiare.** *Obs. Law.* [med.L.: see REPLEDGE *v.*¹] = REPLEVIN *sb.*
[**1285** *Act 13 Edw. I*, c. 11 (*Stat. Westm.*), Per commune breve quod dicitur Replegiare.]
1483 *Rolls of Parlt.* VI. 252/1 As they should doe in Replegiare bytwene comen persones. **1515** *Act 7 Hen. VIII*, c. 4 Every Advowaunt..that makyth avowre..to any oder person or persons in any replegiare, secound delyveraunce [etc.]. **1529** *Act 21 Hen. VIII*, c. 19 §4 Defendants in the said Writs of Replegiare. **1651** tr. *Kitchin's Jurisdictions* (1657) 284 He cannot take the Distress out of the Pound, but ought to sue a Replegiare.

†**replegi'ation.** *Obs. Sc. Law.* Also 7 **repledg-, repladg-.** [ad. med.L. *replegiātiōn-em*, noun of action f. prec.] The action of repledging.
1574 in Calderwood *Hist. Kirk* (Wodrow Soc.) III. 311 When we sought the priviledge of replegiatioun of the universitie from the civill jugement, yee would not grant it to us. **1609** Skene *Reg. Maj., Stat. Robt. I*, 30 b, At the day of the replegiation: that is, at the day quhen the defender sould haue repledged the lands..and repledged them not. **1641** *Burgh Rec. Peebles* (1872) 101 Ane chartour..off the.. creatioun of burgesses and of the repladgiation of thair comburgessis. **1693** Stair *Inst. Law Scot.* (ed. 2) Index.

†**re'plendish,** *v. Obs. rare.* Also 6 **repplendyssh.** [f. OF. *replendiss-*, *replendir*: see RESPLENDISH *v.*] *intr.* To shine with splendour. Hence †**re'plendishing** *ppl. a.*
1509 Hawes *Past. Pleas.* (Percy Soc.) 213 In his breast there was replendishyng The shinyng Venus. **1517** Watson *Shyppe of Fooles* A ij b, Our auncyent faders here before dyde not lerne theyr repplendysshynge scyence in the multytude of bookes.

So †**re'plendishant** *ppl. a.* [see -ANT.]
1509 Hawes *Past. Pleas.* xxxv. (Percy Soc.) 112 The mone ..is fayre replendysshaunte, In the longe nyght with rayes radyaunte.

re'plenish, *sb. rare.* [f. the vb.] A fresh supply (of money); a refill.
1806 Surr *Winter in Lond.* II. 75, I know you took it queer that I did not stand it, when you wanted a replenish last week. **1881** W. P. Lennox *Plays, Players*, etc. II. i. 9, I gave assent for a replenish of the glass.

replenish (rɪ'plɛnɪʃ), *v.* Forms: 4-5 **replenys**, 5 **-ysch**, 5-6 **-ysh(e**, **-yssh(e**; 4-5 **replenisch**, **-issh**, 6 **-ishe**, 4- **replenish** (also 5 **-esch**, 6 **-esh**; 5 **repleinsch**, **-pleynsch**, 6 ? **replynyssh**). See also REPLESHED and REPLEVISH *v.*² [f. OF. *repleniss-*, lengthened stem of *replenir*: see RE- and PLENISH.]

I. In pa. pple., denoting a condition or state.

1. Fully or abundantly stocked *with* things or animals (†also sometimes extended to persons). ? *Obs.* (very common *c* 1535-1660, in a great variety of contexts.)
1340 Hampole *Pr. Consc.* 8908 Fayr bygyngs on ilka syde, ..with alkyn ryches replenyst. *c* **1400** Maundev. (Roxb.) vii. 25 Þus es all þe cuntree replenyscht with swilk maner of fewles. **1432-50** tr. *Higden* (Rolls) III. 169 When kynge Cirus hade fixede his tentes..repleneschede with victelles [etc.]. **1532** Hervet *Xenophon's Househ.* (1768) 17 That these gardeines maye be..well replenysshed with trees, and all maner of thynges. **1577** B. Googe *Heresbach's Husb.* IV. (1586) 171 b, A Country replenished with Gentlemen of good houses, and good house keepers. **1631** Weever *Anc. Funeral Mon.* 421 This religious house was..replenished with blacke Nunnes. **1696** Whiston *Th. Earth* IV. (1722) 362 The Waters of the Antediluvian Earth were much more replenish'd, nay, crouded with Fish than now they are. **1741** Watts *Improv. Mind* I. (1801) 127 It is probable they are replenished with intellectual beings dwelling in bodies.

b. Provided, furnished, or supplied *with* something. Also without const. ? *Obs.*
1533-4 *Act 25 Hen. VIII*, c. 11 §1 At suche time as the saide olde fowle be mouted and not replenished with fethers to flie. **1588** Shaks. *L.L.L.* IV. ii. 27 His intellect is not replenished hee is onely an animall. **1650** Bulwer *Anthropomet.* 137 Whence Infants speak not before their mouths are replenished with teeth. **1707** Mortimer *Husb.* (1721) I. 266 Cattle and Fowl, wherewith the Country-Farmer is replenished. **1796** Morse *Amer. Geog.* I. 367 These vast and irregular heights, being copiously replenished with water.

†**2.** Filled, fully imbued, pervaded or possessed, *with* some quality or condition. *Obs.*
c **1374** Chaucer *Boeth.* I. pr. iv. 12 (Camb. MS.), They trowen þat I haue had affinite to malefice,..bycause þat I am replenysshed and fulfylled [L. *imbutus*] with thy thechinges. **1483** Caxton *Gold. Leg* 63/1 Iosue the sone of Num was replenyssyd with the spyrite of wisdom. **1502** Atkynson tr. *De Imitatione* I. xxiv. 174 Couetyse persons shalbe replenysshed with all confusyon & penury. **1558** Warde tr. *Alexis' Secr.* I. 44 Death..is..an entring into an eternal life replenished with all joye, solace, and pleasure. **1604** T. Wright *Passions* IV. ii. §1. 127 A soule altogether depriued of vertue, and replenished with vice. **1633** Bp. Hall *Occas. Medit.* 271 How happily is hee replenished with knowledge and goodnesse! **1702** Echard *Eccl. Hist.* (1710) 226 Peter being now replenish'd with the Holy Ghost.

3. Physically or materially filled *with* some thing or things, people, etc. Also (in later use) without const.
1490 Caxton *Eneydos* xiv. 52, I shalle sodaynly make the ayer to wexe obscure..replenysshed with hayle. **1555** Eden *Decades* Pref. (Arb.) 55 Suche owlde caues of the mynes as haue byn dygged, are ageyne replenysshed with vre. **1578** T. N. tr. *Conq. W. India* 74 All the streetes were replenished with people which stoode gaping and wondering. **1612** Woodall *Surg. Mate* Wks. (1653) 221 Generally all the earth is replenished with Brimstone. **1671** J. Webster *Metallogr.* xvii. 246 The Ore of Copper..hath a leaden colour, replenished with certain yellow veins. **1727** Swift *Baucis & Philem.* 33 They found, 'Twas still replenish'd to the top, As if they ne'er had touch'd a drop. **1791** Cowper *Iliad* IV. 308 Thou alone..Drink'st not by measure. No, thy goblet stands Replenish'd still.

†**4.** Full, made full, *of* something. *Obs.*
c **1400** Maundev. (Roxb.) xxi. 93 A gude ile and full replenischt of many maners of ricches. *c* **1450** Lovelich *Grail* l. 695 Every day Repleinsched they were Of the holy gost. **1494** Fabyan *Chron.* v. lxxxii. 60 At sondry tymes whenne the sayd Countre was replenyshed of people. **1568** Grafton *Chron.* II. 684 Of whose valiaunt actes..their eares had manye times bene fylled and replenished.

†**b.** Possessed *of* something. *Obs. rare*⁻¹.
1482 *Rolls of Parlt.* VI. 224/1 Forsomoche that as well the Kyng.., as other Lordes herebefore have ben gretely replenysshed of Markes and Games of Swannes.

II. In ordinary transitive uses.

†**5.** To make full *of*, to fill, to stock or store abundantly *with*, persons or animals. = FILL *v.* 5.
c **1386** Chaucer *Pars. T.* ¶ 846 Trewe effect of mariage.. replenysseth hooly chirche of good lynage. *c* **1400** Maundev. (1839) ix. 102 Thei wolde lye with here Fadre.. for to replenyschen the World aȝen with Peple. **1494** Fabyan *Chron.* VII. ccxxii. 247 This man made the newe forest..and replenysshed it with wylde bestes. **1530** Palsgr. 687/1, I have replenysshed my pastours with catall, and my pondes with fysshe. **1596** Bacon *Max. & Use Com. Law* I. iv. (1636) 23 But [I] am without any remedy except I replenish the ground again with Deere.

†**b.** To provide fully *with* something. *Obs.*
1526 *Pilgr. Perf.* (W. de W. 1531) 4 b, God wrought..the effectes of his mercy in replenysshynge them with his benefytes. **1535** Coverdale *Ecclus.* xxxii. 13 Geue thankes vnto him that hath..replenished the with his goodes. **1582** Bentley *Mon. Matrones* II. 30 His riches doo replenish eurie one with his goods.

†**6.** To occupy (a place) as inhabitants or settlers, to inhabit; to people. *Obs.*
c **1400** *Destr. Troy* 12414 Mony weghes thedur went, & wond in the toune, And Replenisshed the place & the playn londis. **1590** Spenser *F.Q.* III. vi. 36 Daily they grow, and daily forth are sent Into the world, it to replenish more. **1605** Verstegan *Dec. Intell.* i. (1628) 13 They were mightily increased in..Germanie, replenishing euerie quarter and part thereof. **1788** Gibbon *Decl. & F.* lii. V. 460 The vacant habitations were replenished by a new colony.

b. To occupy the whole of (a space or thing); = FILL *v.* 7. Now *rare.*
1563 *Homilies* II. *Idolatry* III. (1859) 216 God is a pure Spirit, infinite, who replenisheth Heaven and Earth. **1593** Shaks. *Lucr.* 1357 The more she saw the blood his cheeks replenish The more she thought [etc.]. **1664** Power *Exp. Philos.* 93 The Quicksilver cannot totally replenish and fill the Tube again. **1675** Traherne *Chr. Ethics* 295 Nothing but honour, and kindness, and contentment would replenish the world. **1829** Landor *Imag. Conv., Scipio Æmilianus*, etc., Wks. 1853 II. 249/2 A light, the pure radiance of which cheered and replenished the whole heart.

†**7.** To fill with food; to satisfy, satiate. Also *transf.* and *fig. Obs.*
c **1450** Lovelich *Grail* xlviii. 377 Nethir mete ne drynk haue we non;..For the vessel vs repleynscheth not here. **1526** *Pilgr. Perf.* (W. de W. 1531) 8 All the appetytes of man shall be replenysshed with all goodnes. **1566** Adlington *Apuleius* x. (1893) 51 When I had wel replenished my self with wine. **1665** Bunyan *Holy Citie* 251 Wherewith she is watered and replenished, as the Earth with rain from Heaven.

†**8.** To fill (a place or space) *with* something. = FILL *v.* 1. *Obs.*
c **1477** Caxton *Jason* 28 Ye are worthy that the ayer be replenisshed with callynges and of voyses. *a* **1548** Hall *Chron., Rich. III* 28 b, With pitefull scriches she repleneshyd the hole mancion. **1613** Purchas *Pilgrimage* IV. vii. (1614) 372 Replenishing the way betweene the Temple and Pallace, with offerings of gold, siluer [etc.]. **1615** G. Sandys *Trav.* 134 They drew out the brains at the nostrils, ..replenishing the same with preseruatiue spices.

†**b.** To fill (a person, the heart, etc.) *with* some feeling or quality. *Obs.*
c **1529** Wolsey in Ellis *Orig. Lett.* Ser. I. II. 7 The delay wherof so replenyssheth my herte with hevynes, that I can take no reste. **1552** *Bk. Com. Prayer, Ordering Deacons*, Replenishe them so with the trueth of thy doctryne. **1635** R. N. *Camden's Hist. Eliz.* I. 68 The immortall joy wherewith shee should replenish all her subjects.

†**c.** To fill (the mind) *with* some occupation.
a **1548** Hall *Chron., Hen. V* 35 b, Thei determined..to replenishe the kynges brayne with some pleasante study.

9. To fill up again; to restore to the former amount or condition.
1612 Drayton *Poly-olb.* ii. 38 The naked Sea Nymphs ride Within the ouzie pooles, replenisht euery Tide. **1666** Pepys *Diary* 19 July, Full of wants of money and much stores to buy, for to replenish the stores, and no money to do it with. **1748** *Anson's Voy.* III. viii. 370 His stores replenished, and an additional stock of provisions on board. **1776** Adam Smith *W.N.* II. ii. (1869) I. 301 The coffers of such a company..must require..a more constant and uninterrupted exertion of expense in order to replenish them. **1832** Ht. Martineau *Homes Abroad* v. 68 Susan was always ready..to replenish the wallets and fill the cans. **1883** C. J. Wills *Mod. Persia* 185 She took the little silver spoon, and replenished my inkstand with water.

†**b.** To fill up (a vacant office). *Obs. rare.*
1632 Sir T. Hawkins tr. *Mathieu's Unhappy Prosperitie* II. 229 Petrus Moronus, whom Charles had drawen from the Cell, to replenish the vacant See. **1651** C. Cartwright *Cert. Relig.* I. 40 Though all vacancies are replenished by Ministers of the Gospel, yet the succession of the Authority was in the Bishops.

III. 10. *intr.* To become filled; to attain to fullness; to increase. *rare.*
1579-80 North *Plutarch* (1676) 76 The City of Athens began to replenish daily more and more, by mens repairing thither from all parts. **1673** H. Stubbe *Further Vind. Dutch War* 80 Her Coffers began to replenish, Her Subjects were rich. **1814** W. Taylor in *Monthly Rev.* LXXIV. 308 He does not luxuriate and replenish, and promise to bloom again.

Hence **re'plenishing** *vbl. sb.*
1528 Paynel *Salerne's Regim.* C ij, The replenisshynge of the stomake by fumes and humidites. **1611** Florio, *Riempitura*, a filling, a replenishing.

re'plenished, *ppl. a. rare.* [f. prec. + -ED¹.] Full; perfect; restored to fullness.
1594 Shaks. *Rich. III*, IV. iii. 18 We smothered The most replenished sweet worke of Nature. **1611** —— *Wint. T.* II. i. 79 The most replenish'd Villaine in the World. **1641** G. Sandys *Paraphr. Song Sol.* VI. iv. 24 More faire then the replenisht Moon.

re'plenisher. [f. as prec. + -ER¹.]

1. One who replenishes or refills.
1599 Hakluyt *Voy.* I. 378 One God euerlasting,.. replenisher of all things euery where. **1864** Pusey *Lect. Daniel* iii. 136 The contribution..in times of peace, of eunuchs and replenishers of the Persian harems. **1892** *Chamb. Jrnl.* 14 May 307/1 The Finisher of delights, and the Replenisher of tombs.

2. *Elect.* A device for increasing or maintaining a charge in certain apparatus.
1867 in Dredge *Electr. Illum.* (1882) I. App. cxxv, An auxiliary generator, termed a replenisher. **1881** Sir W. Thomson in *Nature* XXIV. 435 My 'replenisher' for multiplying and maintaining charges in Leyden jars for heterostatic electrometers.

re'plenishingly, *adv. rare.* [f. pres. pple. of REPLENISH *v.*] In such a manner as to replenish.
1601 Deacon & Walker *Spirits & Divels* 57 The maner of God his being alone is to be in euerie place indefinitiuely, repletiuely, or replenishingly. **1625** Donne *Serm.* Wks. V. 16 God is replenishingly everywhere: but most contractedly and workingly in the temple.

replenishment (rɪ'plɛnɪʃmənt). [-MENT.]

1. The fact of being replenished. *rare*⁻¹.
1526 *Pilgr. Perf.* (W. de W. 1531) 16 b, The fode of aungels is moost perfyte possessyon & replenysshement of all glory.

2. That which replenishes; a fresh supply.
1692 Luttrell *Brief Rel.* (1857) II. 512 Wanting divers necessaries and a replenishment both of seamen and soldiers. **1794** Sullivan *View Nat.* xiv. I. 161 [To] exhaust from the earth the whole of the replenishment which it

received in the day. 1837 T. Hook *Jack Brag* ii, Jack ordered a replenishment of punch.

3. The act or process of replenishing.

1802 Paley *Nat. Theol.* xxvi. (1804) 522 The provision which was originally made for continuing the replenishment of the world. 1862 Lytton *Str. Story* xx, Principles similar to those which Liebig has applied to the replenishment of an exhausted soil.

4. *attrib.*, as *replenishment tanker*.

1963 *Times* 5 Feb. 10/1 The Admiralty had placed an order for three replenishment tankers, to be built on Tyneside. 1976 *Southern Even. Echo* (Southampton) 3 Nov. 2/3 Captain Averill, Master of the RFA replenishment tanker Olwen . . was supporting Royal Navy frigates on duty off Iceland.

†re'plenty, *v. Obs. rare*⁻¹. [f. re- 5 a + plenty *sb.*] *trans.* To return plenteously.

1628 Feltham *Resolves* ii. [i.] lxxxi, She [Hope] blythes the Farmer, does his graine commit To Earth, which with large vse replentieth it.

†re'pleshed, *ppl. a. Obs. rare.* Also replesshyd. [var. of *replenished*, either by further reduction of the form *repleinsched*, or by association with L. *replēre*.] Filled, full.

c1440 Capgrave *Life St. Kath.* iv. 527 The temple-gatis . . Soo ful repleshed no man may entre there. c1450 Lydg. & Burgh *Secrees* 1649 And [when] ful replesshyd I exhorte the [= thee] ffeesshly lustys and bathis to ffle.

replete (rɪ'pliːt), *a.* Also 4–5 repleet, 5–6 -plet, (5 reyplete), 6 *Sc.* -pleit(e, 6–7 -pleate, 6–8 -pleat. [a. F. *replet, replète* (14th c., Oresme), or ad. L. *replētus*, pa. pple. of *replēre* to fill: cf. complete *a.*]

1. a. Physically or materially filled *with* (†or full *of*) some thing or substance. Also without const.

c1386 Chaucer *Nun's Pr. T.* 137 Ware the sonne in his ascencion Ne fynde yow nat repleet of humours hoote. 1432–50 tr. *Higden* (Rolls) I. 135 þro which stoppenge the pleyne growndes of Egipte be replete with water. c1491 *Chast. Goddes Chyld.* 20 The weder is full colde, therfore . . the wycked humours ben styred and make the stomocke replete. 1536 Bellenden *Cron. Scot.* ix. ii, Ane well sprang up . . with sic haboundance of blud, that all the stretis wer repleite thairof. 1599 A. M. tr. *Gabelhouer's Bk. Physicke* 113/2 Infuse theron the expressed oyle, till the glasse be wholy repleate. 1634 Sir T. Herbert *Trav.* 106 Sweet Gardens, repleat with fragrant flowres. 1725 Pope *Odyss.* xv. 149 A golden ewer . . Replete with water from the crystal springs. a1774 Goldsm. *Surv. Exp. Philos.* (1776) II. 3 All places on the surface of the earth are replete with air. 1849 Murchison *Siluria* ii. 30 Much younger rocks replete with organic remains. 1889 Duncan *Lect. Dis. Women* xxiv. (ed. 4) 195 Making the peritonæum to protrude . . as a pouch, which, when replete, resembled a cyst.

b. Filled to satisfaction *with*, full *of*, food or drink; satisfied, sated, gorged.

c1386 Chaucer *Pard. T.* 161 Herodes, . . Whan he of wyn was repleet at his feeste. 1432–50 tr. *Higden* (Rolls) I. 15 Cromes fallenge from the table of lordes, whiche replete lefte fragmente to theire childre. a1533 Ld. Berners *Huon* xxv. 76 They were all satysfyed and replete and had well dynyd. 1704 Swift *T. Tub* Wks. 1760 I. 87 When by these and the like performances they were grown sufficiently replete, they would immediately depart. 1811 *Ora & Juliet* III. 134 So replete was she of the good things of the table, that Zaire stared at her in wonder. 1887 Bowen *Virg. Æneid* iii. 630 With the banquet replete . . he had lain full length in his lair.

†c. Plethoric, fat, stout. *Obs.*

1603 Knolles *Hist. Turks* (1621) 1336 Seeing that the fatnesse of his repleat bodie would not suffer them to take away his life presently. c1645 Howell *Lett.* i. i. xv, They are more plump and replete in their Bodies . . than those that drink altogether Wine. 1758 J. S. *Le Dran's Observ. Surg.* (1771) 12 The Patient being of a strong and replete Habit of Body.

2. a. Filled *with* (†full *of*), abundantly supplied or provided *with*, in various lit. and fig. uses.

1382 Wyclif *Phil.* iv. 18, I am repleet with tho thingis takun of Epafrodite. c1450 Lovelich *Merlin* (E.E.T.S.) 6236 Of alle vertwes sche is Repleet. c1485 *E.E. Misc.* (Warton Cl.) 16 Where is now thy hyȝe palleys, reyplete Of reches . .? 1582 Bentley *Mon. Matrones* ii. 201 Eternall tribulation, and infinite calamitie, repleat with all euills. 1632 Lithgow *Trav.* iv. 132 It is repleate with all the blessings, earth can giue to man. 1704 Swift *T. Tub* Wks. 1751 I. 8 A good sizeable Volume . . replete with Discoveries equally valuable for their Novelty and Use. 1764 Goldsm. *Hist. Eng. in Lett.* (1772) II. 161 Those denunciations of ruin with which their orations are replete. 1847 L. Hunt *Jar Honey* xi. (1848) 149 The very air seems replete with humming and buzzing melodies. 1973 *N.Y. Law Jrnl.* 5 June 4/4 Statutes are replete with misplaced commas.

b. Fully imbued or invested *with* some quality or property.

1432–50 tr. *Higden* (Rolls) II. 217 The lyfe of noon other thynge is more frayle, replete with moste infirmite. 1509 Hawes *Past. Pleas.* xvi. (Percy Soc.) 60, I folowed her into a temple ferre, Replete wyth joy. 1587 Holinshed *Chron.* III. 916/2, I am but a wretch replet with miserie. 1632 Lithgow *Trav.* ix. 409 He was repleate with all abhominable vices. 1671 Salmon *Syn. Med.* ii. xlv. 303 If the Body is repleat with strength, the Sick, without doubt, will escape and not die. 1777 Priestley *Disc. Philos. Necess.* 204, I have shewn . . that the system of immaterialism is replete with absurdity. 1817 Jas. Mill *Brit. India* II. v. vi. 566 The proceedings . . appeared to be replete with irregularity and injustice. 1871 Macduff *Mem. Patmos* xvii. 221 Perspicuous in meaning and replete with practical instruction.

†3. Filled or crowded *with* people. *Obs.*

1533 Bellenden *Livy* iii. iii. (S.T.S.) I. 249 The tempillis war replete with men and women. 1596 *Edw. III*, i. i, The realm of France Replete with princes of great parentage. 1632 J. Hayward tr. *Biondi's Eromena* iv. 122 Don Eulavio's house . . he founde open and repleate with servants.

4. Full, entire, perfect, complete.

1601 Shaks. *All's Well* ii. iii. 183 To whom I promise A counterpoize; If not to thy estate, A ballance more repleat. 1863 Cowden Clarke *Shaks. Char.* xvii. 425 Among the subordinate characters, not one is drawn with more replete originality than that of Owen Glendower.

replete (rɪ'pliːt), *v.* Now *rare.* Also 6–7 -pleat, 6 *Sc.* -pleit. [f. L. *replēt-*, ppl. stem. of *replēre*: see prec.]

†1. *trans.* To fill *with* something; to crowd, stuff, cram. *Obs.*

1432–50 tr. *Higden* (Rolls) IV. 243 The waterleches didde replete the cite of Neapolis with a multitude infinite. 1528 Paynel *Salerne's Regim.* H, Stronge wyne . . vehementlye enflameth a mans body & repleteth the heed. 1567 *Gude & Godlie B.* (S.T.S.) 129 Than Calfis and brint Sacrifice Thy Aulter sall repleit. 1620 Venner *Via Recta* iii. 50 It repleteth their stomackes with crude and phlegmaticke humors. 1669 Cokaine *Poems* 257 They that are gluttons, and love meat, . . The greasy Cook-shops may repleat.

refl. 1636 Quarles *Eleg. Sir J. Cæsar*, Repleat thyself with everlasting Manna.

†b. To fill, stock, or people (a place) *with* things, animals, or persons. *Obs.*

c1540 Boorde *The Boke for to Lerne* B iij b, A fayre gardyn repleatyd with herbes. *Ibid.*, A parke repletyd with dere. 1547 —— *Introd. Knowl.* xxxviii. (1870) 217 Egipt is repleted now with infydele alyons.

†c. To fill (a place) *with* noise, or with a report. *Obs. rare.*

1573 Twyne *Æneid* xi. Gg iv b, With wofull cries and piteous shoutes the town they do repleat. 1694 Motteux *Rabelais* (1737) V. 229 Your placid Life, here inaudite before, Repletes the Town of Lugdun.

†2. To fill (a person, the mind, etc.) *with* some property or quality. Also without const. *Obs.*

1482 *Monk of Evesham* (Arb.) 30 Y felte me repletyd there in the resceyuing of tho discyplynys. 1542 Becon *Pathw. Prayer* xxx. Wks. 1564 I. 83 That thou mayest be repleted wyth the knowledge of spirituall thynges. 1612 R. Sheldon *Serm. St. Martin's* 6 It also repleteth the mind with such a treasurie of discourse. 1658 Cokaine *Obstinate Lady* ii. iii, Ile not desire the Muses to repleat My willing genius with poetick heat.

†b. In *pa. pple.* of a period of time. *Obs.*

a1548 Hall *Chron., Hen. VI* 116 Another sort, adiudged that present time, to be . . moste repleted with perilles. 1589 Ann Dowriche in Farr *S P. Eliz.* (1845) II. 359 Repleated oft with wandring change Recount your life to be.

3. To replenish; to fill again. *rare.*

1704 D'Urfey *Abradatus & Panthea* i, Scarce had the pale Empress of the night . . twice repleted shone serene and bright. 1882–3 Schaff *Encycl. Relig. Knowl.* I. 155 [Hamathites] were transported into Samaria by the Assyrians to replete that depopulated district.

Hence **re'pleted** *ppl. a.*, †well-fed.

1667 *Decay Chr. Piety* viii. ¶34. 282 They preferr'd a repleated slavery, before a hungry freedom.

replete (rɪ'pliːt), *sb.* [f. the adj.] Something that is replete; *spec.* an ant which is distended with food.

1908 W. M. Wheeler in *Bull. Amer. Mus. Nat. Hist.* XXIV. 379 In most cases, as McCook has shown, it is the major workers that most readily tend to become repletes. 1923 *Jrnl. Proc. Roy. Soc. W. Austral.* IX. 47 The impulse to develop repletes is probably due to the brief and temporary abundance of liquid food . . in arid regions. 1929 *Encycl. Brit.* XX. 885/2 Since ants . . have not the art of making receptacles, they [*sc.* honey ants] have adopted the curious method of using the crops of certain workers or soldiers for the purpose of food storage. . . Individuals thus functioning are termed *repletes*. . . When hungry the ants stroke the repletes and receive from them droplets of regurgitated honey-dew collected during times of plenty. 1979 *National Geographic* Nov. 630 The swollen worker ants, called repletes, have been fed by other workers until their abdomens are nearly grape size.

repleteness (rɪ'pliːtnɪs). Also 7 repleat-. [f. replete *a.* + -ness.] The condition of being replete; repletion, fullness, †corpulence.

1603 Florio *Montaigne* ii. xxiii. 393 We are subject vnto a repleatnesse of humours. 1661 K. W. *Conf. Charac., Polititian* (1860) 27 An indicium of . . his repleatnesse of insipid aierial and light whimsies. 1769 *Antiq.* in *Ann. Reg.* 128/1 His age, stature, and repleteness, allowing him but little agility. 1879 Meredith *Egoist* Prel., They tell us that there is a constant tendency in the book to accumulate excess of substance, and such repleteness [etc.].

†re'pletiate, *v. Obs. rare*⁻¹. [irreg. f. replete *a.*] *trans.* To satiate, satisfy.

1665 Sir T. Herbert *Trav.* (1677) 381 Two or three Trees being pierced, in an hours space [they] repletiate the greediest appetite.

repletion (rɪ'pliːʃən). Forms: 4–5 replecioun, 5–6 replecion, -yon, (5 replicion, -ioun, 6 repleacion), 6– repletion; also 4–5 repleccio(u)n, 6 replexion. [a. OF. *repletion* (mod.F. *réplétion*), *replection* (1314), *replexion* (1411), or ad. late L. *replētiōn-em*, n. of action from *replēre*: cf. replete *a.*]

1. The action of eating or drinking to excess; surfeit; the condition of body arising from this; †also, a full plethoric condition or habit of body.

c1386 Chaucer *Nun's Pr. T.* 17 Repleccion ne made hire neuere sik, Attempree diete was al hir phisik. c1410 *Master of Game* (MS. Digby 182) Prol., I pocras tellith: Full repliciouns of metes sleith mo men then ony swerde or knyfe. 1482 *Monk of Evesham* (Arb.) 54 The rednesse and hete the whyche was in my face and in my bodye . . douteles was of the feruent replecyon of wyne dronkyn before. 1542 Boorde *Dyetary* ix. (1870) 250 Replecyon [*v.r.* replexion] or a surfet is taken as well by gurgytacyons, or to moche drynkynge, as . . by epulacyon. 1584 Cogan *Haven Health* cxxxiii. (1636) 135 Kid flesh . . can cause none inflammation nor repletion. 1683 Tryon *Way to Health* 320 All this chiefly proceeds from Repletion, and too much Nourishment, and unconcocted matter. 1748 *Anson's Voy.* iii. ii. 313 We were neither disordered nor even loaded by this repletion. 1837 M. Donovan *Dom. Econ.* II. 329 A sense of heaviness in the stomach, resembling slight repletion. 1863 Mary Howitt *F. Bremer's Greece* I. viii. 254 Everybody goes home to sit at table, and eat to repletion of an abundant repast.

fig. 1603 Florio *Montaigne* ii. xxiii. 393 Of such like repletion are States often seene to be sicke. 1791 Burke *Let. Member Nat. Assembly* Wks. 1792 III. 361 Your malady, in this respect, is a disorder of repletion. 1855 Smedley *Occult Sciences* 289 Our medical authority offers no solution of the difficulty, but sends us straight to the madhouse for a repletion of similar marvels.

2. The fact or condition of being filled up, stuffed full, or crowded.

1398 Trevisa *Barth. De P.R.* v. xiii. (Bodl MS.), þe nose is . . somtyme isette by folnes and replecion of stinkinge and corrupt humours. 1544 Phaer *Regim. Lyfe* (1533) C vj b, If there be replecion of fleum in yᵉ head first ye must purge with pilles of cochie. 1562 Bulleyn *Bulwarke, Dial. Soarnes & Chir.* (1579) 9 b, That in fyne, replecion and tencion of all the course of the vaynes doe come . . by the meanes of the aboundance of bloud. 1791 Bentham *Panopt.* i. I. 49 When the establishment is in this state of repletion. 1870 Anderson *Missions Amer. Bd.* II. xxxviii. 346 The body of the house was filled to repletion by adults.

3. The action of filling up; the filling *of* a cavity or receptacle. ? *Obs.*

1646 Sir T Browne *Pseud. Ep.* 87 Nor is it only the exclusion of ayre by water, or repletion of cavities possessed thereby which causeth a pot of ashes to admit so great a quantity of water [etc.]. 1676 Worlidge *Cyder* (1691) 161 Which vacancy you may again supply . . with other wine . .; which repletion must be reiterated. c1790 Imison *Sch. Art* I. 148 An increase of weight will be found . . from a repletion . . of the vacuities of the fresh water with saline particles.

†b. That which serves to fill. *Obs. rare*⁻¹.

1760–72 H. Brooke *Fool of Qual.* (1809) IV. 116 Father, Son, and Holy Spirit, will then become co-embodied in this divine body; they will be the repletion of it.

4. The satisfaction of a desire or want.

1654 Whitlock *Zootomia* 297 That spendeth through necessity twelve Houres for a course Repletion of his Hunger. 1667 *Decay Chr. Piety* i. ¶5 Projecting the gratifying those desires in whose repletion we placed our happiness. 1690 Norris *Beatitudes* (1692) 95 So [it] prevents and anticipates that Repletion, which our Lord promises. 1836–7 Sir W. Hamilton *Metaph.* xliii. (1870) II. 450 If pleasure be the repletion of a want contrary to nature, that which contains the repletion will contain the pleasure.

Hence **†re'pletional** *a. Obs. rare*⁻¹.

1562 Bulleyn *Bulwarke, Dial. Soarnes & Chir.* 11 b, It is called repleccionall, when the humours increase beyonde their due measure.

†re'pletive, *a. Obs.* [ad. F. *repletif, -ive*, or late L. *repletivus* (Priscian): see replete *a.* and -ive.] Causing repletion, replenishing.

1611 Cotgr., *Repletif*, repletive, replenishing, filling. 1643 Trapp *Comm. Gen.* xlii. 2 And his fulness is not only repletive, but diffusive. a1660 Hammond *Serm.* xix. (1850) 397 Faith . . is repletive in the whole house at once, as in one room, and that a stately palace. 1733 Watts *Philos. Ess., Ontology* (1734) 382 God's Omnipresence . . hath been termed his repletive Presence.

Hence **†re'pletively** *adv. Obs.*

1601 Deacon & Walker *Spirits & Divels* 49 He is able repletiuely and by speciall operation, to dwell in mans spirit for euer. 1621 Lodge *Summary of Du Bartas* 291 Shee [the soul] is not in the body repletiuely, for that appertaineth to him onely who filleth all things.

re'pletory, *a. rare*⁻¹. [f. as replete *v.* + -ory.] Repletive.

1853 Sir W. Hamilton *Discuss* App. iii. C. 774 A University, as an intellectual gymnasium, should consider that its 'mental dietetic' is tonic, not repletory.

†re'pleve, *v. Obs. Law.* Also 6 repleave, 7 replieve. [ad. OF. *replevir* to replevy.]

1. *trans.* To replevy; to bail out. Also *fig.* Hence **re'pleving** *vbl. sb.*

1592 *Termes Lawes* s.v. *Replevin*, Hee shall haue this writ directed to the sherife yᵗ he cause him to be repleued. 1615 Manwood *Lawes Forrest* xxii. §5. 210 b, How many kinds of attachments of the forest there bee: and of Repleuing of persons attached. a1628 Preston *Mt. Ebal* (1638) 23 If a condemned person . . should bee repleeved or ransomed by another. a1644 Quarles *Sol. Recant.* Sol. v. 28 And Grace shall here replieve what Grief distrains.

2. *intr.* To bring an action of replevin.

1638 Earl of Cork in *Lismore Papers* Ser. i. (1886) V. 54 Ned Stowt hath promised me to paie me . . xxiijˡⁱ due unto me for 23 yeares arrears of Rathnolan, for which he was destreigned, and he repleved.

repleven, obs. form of replevin *sb.*

repleviable (rɪ'plɛvɪəb(ə)l), *a. Law.* [f. replevy *v.* + -able.] Replevisable.

1755 in Johnson. 1768 Blackstone *Comm.* III. 7 Such distresses are partly analogous to the antient distress at common law, as being repleviable and the like. 1800

ADDISON *Amer. Law Rep.* 303 Goods are only repleviable when taken by way of distress.

replevin (rɪˈplɛvɪn), *sb. Law.* Also 5 -yn(g, 6 -yne, -en, 6–7 -ine. [a. AF. *replevin(e*, f. OF. *replevir* to REPLEVY: hence also Anglo-L. *replevina* (13th c.). Cf. PLEVIN.]

1. The restoration to, or recovery by, a person of goods or chattels distrained or taken from him, upon his giving security to have the matter tried in a court of justice and to return the goods if the case is decided against him.

[**1347–8** *Rolls of Parlt.* II. 218/2 Que les Baillifs del dit Wapentak denierent la replevine au Baillif le dit Counte de Huntingdon.] **1461** *Paston Lett.* II. 35 That aftir the distresse taken the undirshreve be spoke with all that he make no replevyn with out agrement or apoyntement taken, that the right of the lond may be undirstand. **1471** *Cal. Anc. Rec. Dublin* (1889) I. 345 The Mair and Bailliffes for the tyme beyng make replevyng to every person or persones that will compleyn to them. **1532** *Dial. on Laws Eng.* II. xlvii. 120 b, If a shyryfe by a repleuyn deliuer other beastes than were distreyned [etc.]. **1623** DALTON *Office Sherifs* 165 b, So that by this former statute..the Sherife may breake open a mans castle, or house, to make a Repleuin. **1659** RUSHW. *Hist. Coll.* I. 641 Having sued forth a writ of Replevin, the proper remedy in Law to regain the possession of his Goods. **1768** BLACKSTONE *Comm.* III. 145 The restitution of the goods themselves so wrongfully taken..is effected by action of replevin. **1809** *St. Papers* in *Ann. Reg.* 716/2 Attempts have..been made to wrest from the collectors by writs of replevin..property detained or seized by said collectors. **1863** H. COX *Inst.* II. ix. 522 One remedy for unlawful taking is by action of replevin.

attrib. **1862** *Stat. of Vermont* xv. c. 36 §28 *marg.*, Replevin bond to be sued within one year. *Ibid.* xxx. c. 94 §40 [The liquor] shall be held by such officer until the final determination of the replevin suit.

fig. *a* **1636** LYNDE *Case for Spectacles* (1638) 10 Take therefore from me what learning you will, distraine it, and impound it at your pleasure, I will never trouble you with Replevin. **1684** OTWAY *Atheist* III. (1735) 59 Since I am trapt thus, Like a poor beast that wanted better pasture, There is no Replevin, and I must to pound.

b. Const. *of* the thing distrained.

a **1461** *Rolls of Parlt.* V. 399/1 The owners of the said Catell may never come to have replevyn of thaym. **1529** *Act 21 Hen. VIII*, c. 19 Yf the lorde..dystrayn upon the same maners..for any suche rentes..and replevyne thereof be sued. **1581** LAMBARDE *Eiren.* I. xxiii. 248 In diuerse other cases, as in Repleuine of Cattell vpon a distresse. **1628** COKE *On Litt.* 161 When the Lord hath distrained, and Repleuin is made of the distress by writ or by Plaint. **1738** *Act 11 Geo. II*, c. 19 §23 To prevent vexatious Replevins of Distresses taken for Rent. **1841** *Penny Cycl.* XIX. 400/2 The third form of replevin, and the only one now in use, is replevin of goods.

†**c.** The bailing of, or bail for, a person. *Obs.*

1588 FRAUNCE *Lawiers Log.* I. xii. 55 Bailement, mainprise or manucaption, and replevine..they bee indifferently used to expresse that suretie which the prisoner is to finde. **1618** DALTON *Countr. Just.* 269 Mainprise, or Repleuin, is the sauing or deliuerie of a Man, out of prison,..by finding suerties. **1651** tr. *Kitchin's Jurisdictions* (1657) 524 The said J. was not to be found in my bailiwick, so that I could make no replevin of the said J. by any means.

transf. *a* **1641** BP. MOUNTAGU *Acts & Mon.* (1642) 409 The soules of the wicked..were haled to judgement..without any replevin or manumission for ever.

2. A writ empowering a person to recover his goods by replevin.

1465 *Paston Lett.* II. 191 On Monday next..ther com Pynchemor to Haylesdon with a replevyn, whych was made in Harleston ys name as Understewerd of the Duche. **1592** *Termes Lawes* s.v., Repleuin is a writ, and it lyeth when any man distrayneth an other for rent or other thing... Also if it be in any franchise or bailiwike, the partie shall haue a Repleuin of the Shirife direct to the bailife of the same franchise. **1628** COKE *On Litt.* I. 145 b, If the beastes of diuers seuerall men be taken, they cannot ioyne in a Repleg[iare] but euery one must haue a seuerall Repleuyn. *a* **1683** SCROGGS *Courts-leet* (1714) 83 Replevin ought to be certain in setting forth the Number and Kinds of the Cattle distrained. **1817** W. SELWYN *Law Nisi Prius* (ed. 4) II. 1099 Of the Duty of the Sheriff in the Execution of the Replevin.

3. An action arising out of a case in which goods have been distrained or taken and replevied.

1515 *Act 7 Hen. VIII*, c. 4 As the playntyf shuld have doo yf they had recoveryd in the seid Replevyne. **1532** *Dial. on Laws Eng.* II. xliv. 80 b, Ygnorance shall excuse him of domages in a Repleuyn. **1628** COKE *On Litt.* I. 145 b, And so in a Repleuyn it is a good plea to say that the property is to the Plaintife and to a stranger. **1671** F. PHILLIPS *Reg. Necess.* 331 Most of that little which appears of the use or pleading of Protections in our Law-books or Records..were in Pleas or Actions concerning Lands, or Replevins, &c. but few in personal Actions, or Actions of Debt. **1712** ARBUTHNOT *John Bull* I. vii, He talked of nothing but Actions upon the case, Returns,..Venire facias, Replevins. **1768** BLACKSTONE *Comm.* III. 413 Upon a replevin the writ of Execution is that *de retorno habendo*. **1818** CRUISE *Digest* (ed. 2) V. 444 Where a person brought a replevin for taking his cattle, the defendant avowed [etc.]. **1875** POSTE *Gaius* IV. (ed. 2) 636 In English jurisprudence both parties are said to be equally plaintiffs and equally defendants in the actions called Quare impedit and Replevin.

†**4.** *transf.* The reclaiming of goods. *Obs. rare*$^{-1}$.

1618 BOLTON *Florus* III. xxiii. (1636) 254 When the goods of attainted citizens were adjudged and given away by Sulla unto others,..the replevin of them did doubtlessly endanger the greene raw peace of the state.

replevin (rɪˈplɛvɪn), *v. Law.* [f. prec.]

†**1.** *trans.* = REPLEVY *v.* 1. *Obs. rare*$^{-1}$.

1659 RUSHW. *Hist. Coll.* I. 532 The Statute of Westminster, which saith, That the Sheriffs and others in some cases may not replevin men in Prison.

2. = REPLEVY *v.* 2. Now only *U.S.*

1678 BUTLER *Hud.* III. iii. *Lady's Answ.* 4 That you're a Beast..Is no strange News,..At least to me, who once..Did from the Pound Replevin you. **1711** SWIFT *Jrnl. to Stella* 19 Nov., I hear the owners are so impudent, that they design to replevin them by law. **1751** JOHNSON *Rambler* No. 142 ¶9 To enable her to replevin her only cow, then in the pound by Squire Bluster's order. **1868** M. H. SMITH *Sunshine & Shad. N. York* 703 When goods are seized, an owner appears..to replevin the stock.

†**b.** = REPLEVY *v.* 2 b. *Obs. rare*$^{-1}$.

1720 SWIFT *Let. to Chetwode* 30 Jan., You can pound the Cattle that trespass on your grounds, tho' the next Justice replevins them.

re'plevining, *vbl. sb.* [f. REPLEVIN *v.* + -ING[1].] The action of being replevined. (In quot. *fig.*)

a **1953** H. BELLOC *Farewell to Juliet* in *Sonnets & Verse* (1954) 99 One that was pledged, and goes to his Replevining.

replevisable (rɪˈplɛvɪsəb(ə)l), *a. Law.* Also 6–7 -is(s)h-. [a. AF. *replevis(s)able*: see REPLEVISH *v.*[1] and -ABLE.] That may be replevied.

[**1275** *Stat. Westm.* c. 15 La gent que ne sunt mie replevisables, et..ceaus que estoient replevisables.]

1532 *Dial. on Laws Eng.* II. xlii. 100 b, If he lette any to repleuyn that be nat repleuisshable & thereof be attaynt, he shall lese the office. **1581** LAMBARDE *Eiren.* I. xxiii. 262 It becommeth Iustices of the Peace to be very circumspect in graunting Baile..for feare of wrong by denying it to him that is repleuisable. **1629** in Rushw. *Hist. Coll.* (1659) I. App. 28, I will admit..That a man committed by the King is not replevisable by the Sheriff. **1641** *Ibid.* III. (1692) I. 341 Sir Thomas Trevor..did..Declare the said Chambers his Goods not to be Replevisable. *a* **1683** SCROGGS *Courts-leet* (1714) 92 Cattle taken in Withernam are not replevisable. **1772** *Junius Lett.* lxviii. (1788) 344 In cases not bailable by a justice of peace, nor replevisable by the common writ. **1818** SCOTT *Rob Roy* viii, The felon..not being replevisable under the statute of the 3d of King Edward.

†**re'plevish**, *v.*[1] *Obs. Law.* Also 5 -yssh, 6 -ise. [f. *repleviss-*, lengthened stem of OF. *replevir* to REPLEVY.] *trans.* To replevy.

1433 *Rolls of Parlt.* IV. 478/2 Distresses that been lafte and takyn for the comyn godes, not acquyte ne replevyssbed. **1554–5** *Act 1 & 2 Phil. & Mary* c. 13 §1 Persons, which for any Offence..bee declared not to be replevisable [*v.r.* replevised] or bayled..by the statute of Westminster. **1607** COWELL *Interpr.* s.v., Replevish..is to let one to mainprise vpon Suretie.

†**re'plevish**, *v.*[2] *Obs.* In 5 -issh, -ysh. [var. of REPLENISH *v.*, either by misreading of *n* as *u*, or under the influence of the L. perf. *replēvi*.] *trans.* To replenish.

1426 LYDG. *De Guil. Pilgr.* 23585 Lich a desert or places wilde, wher no man hath lust to bilde, Replevisshed of al ordure. **1447** BOKENHAM *Seyntys* (Roxb.) 24 Fully replevyshed wyth cherytabylnesse. **1450–80** tr. *Secreta Secret.* 29 There are thingis that makith the body fatte..that is, rest and replevisshyng of dyuerse metis.

re'plevisor. [See REPLEVISH *v.*[1] and -OR[1].] 'One who replevies' (Ogilvie 1882).

replevy (rɪˈplɛvɪ), *sb. Law.* Now *rare.* Also 5–7 -ie. [f. next.]

1. A writ of replevin. = REPLEVIN 2.

1451 *Paston Lett.* I. 194 The baly bad hym kete a replevy of his mayster and he wold serve it. **1497** in I. S. Leadam *Sel. Cas. Crt. Requests* (Selden Soc.) 11 Your said oratour sent vnto the Shirif for a replevie..the which replevie was deliuered to the same sir John. **1523** FITZHERB. *Surv.* 10 b, The sherife where the catell is shall make and serue the repleuy. **1554–5** *Act 1 & 2 Phil. & Mary* c. 12 §1 No Cattell ..shalbe impounded in severall places, wherby the Owner ..shalbe constreyned to sue severall Replevis for the delyverye of the said Distresse so taken at one tyme. *a* **1683** SCROGGS *Courts-leet* (1714) 90 The Owner of the Cattle must go to the County Clerk..for a Replevy to be directed to the Bailiffs to replevy them.

2. = REPLEVIN *sb.* 1 and 1 b.

1554–5 *Act 1 & 2 Phil. & Mary* c. 12 §1 Deputies so appointed..shall have auchtorite in the Shiriffes name to make Replevies and Delyverance of suche Distresses. **1584** FENNER *Def. Ministers* (1587) 16 Wee will nowe impounde them and answere them when he bringeth a writte of repleuie to fetche them out. **1628** COKE *On Litt.* I. 145 b, Yet he may haue a Writ of Repleuy to the Sherife. **1647** N. BACON *Disc. Govt. Eng.* I. lxvii. (1739) 162 The Sheriff must grant replevy if it be demanded, although formerly no replevy was without special Writ. **1817** W. SELWYN *Law Nisi Prius* (ed. 4) II. 1099 If the party distrained upon, either sold or eloigned the distress after the replevy [etc.]. **1845** LD. CAMPBELL *Chancellors* lxxiv. III 122 The illegal increase of duties on importations by refusing replevies.

b. = REPLEVIN *sb.* 1 c. Also *transf.*

1607 COWELL *Interpr.*, *Replevie*..is vsed also for the bayling of a man. **1748** THOMSON *Cast. Indol.* II. xxxii, Too late Repentance comes: replevy cannot be From the strong iron grasp of vengeful Destiny. **1772** *Junius Lett.* lxviii. (1788) 348 Coke..accurately distinguishes between replevy by the common writ..and bail by the King's Bench.

replevy (rɪˈplɛvɪ), *v. Law.* Also 6 -ie. [ad. OF. *replevir* (AF. also *replever*), f. *re-* RE- + *plevir* of doubtful origin; see PLEDGE. Hence also med.L. *replevire.*]

1. *trans.* **a.** To bail (a person), or admit to bail.

1554–5 *Act 1 & 2 Phil. & Mary* c. 13 §1 No Justice..shall lett to baile or maineprise any suche person or persons which ..be forbidden to be replevied or bayled by the statute of Westminster. **1615** MANWOOD *Lawes Forrest* xxii. §5. 215 To attach the said warden..to answer wherfore he hath not repleuied him y[t] is so taken. **1651** tr. *Kitchin's Jurisdictions* (1657) 524 The aforesaid D. is conveyed away.., by which means I cannot replevy the said D. **1768** BLACKSTONE *Comm.* III. 129 The writ *de homine replegiando* lies to replevy a man out of prison, or out of the custody of any private person. **1772** *Junius Lett.* lxviii. (1788) 354 The first attempt to reform these various abuses, was by contracting the power of replevying felons.

fig. **1826** SOUTHEY *Vind. Eccl. Angl.* 482 By using the Rosary she had obtained such favour in the eyes of the Virgin, that her soul was replevied.

2. To recover (cattle or goods) by replevin.

1596 BACON *Max. & Use Com. Law* II. (1635) 7 Men.. may have writs for to replevy their cattell distrained and impounded by others. **1623** DALTON *Office Sherifs* 166 It chanceth sometimes that the Tenant after that hee hath Repleuied his beasts, doth sell them away. **1647** N. BACON *Disc. Govt. Eng.* I. li. (1739) 89 If Cattle be taken by Distress, the party that will replevy them shall pay for the return of the Cattle. **1768** BLACKSTONE *Comm.* III. 13 This is for the benefit of the tenants, that they may know where to find and replevy the distress. **1817** W. SELWYN *Law Nisi Prius* (ed. 4) II. 1126 It will follow, that so long as the cause remains in the county court, the plaintiff may replevy the distress after non-suit there. **1875** DIGBY *Real Prop.* vii. §1. 274 *note*, A person whose goods have been distrained seeks to replevy them.

b. Of the sheriff or bailiff: To recover for, or restore to, the owner by replevin. ? *Obs.*

1623 DALTON *Office Sherifs* 166 b, Then the power of the sherife or his bailiffe ceaseth, so as they may not repleuie or deliuer them. **1628** COKE *On Litt.* 145 b, Yet shall the Sherife repleuy the goods distreyned, for it is against the nature of such a distresse to be irrepleuisable. *a* **1683** [see REPLEVY *sb.* 1].

transf. **1596** SPENSER *F.Q.* IV. xii. 31 Yours the Waift by high prerogative. Therefore I humbly crave your Majestie It to replevie, and my sonne reprive.

3. *intr.* or *absol.* To carry out the act of replevin.

1607 COWELL *Interpr.* s.v. *Second deliverance*, After a returne of catel..to him that distreined them, by reason of a default in the party that replevied. **1768** BLACKSTONE *Comm.* III. 13 To replevy..is, when a person distreined upon applies to the sheriff..and has the distress returned into his own possession. **1817** W. SELWYN *Law Nisi Prius* (ed. 4) II. 1100 Although the statute of Westm. 2d. c. 2 is entirely silent as to a bond from the party replevying [etc.]. **1884** *Law Rep. 12 Q.B. Div.* 386 The period of five days is given by the statute to enable the tenant to replevy.

Hence **re'plevying** *vbl. sb.* and *ppl. a.*

1581 LAMBARDE *Eiren.* I. xxiii. 248 Replevijng of the person of a man in case of Villenage. **1607** COWELL *Interpr.* s.v. *Second deliverance*, For the repleuying of the same catell againe. **1648** BP. HALL *Sel. Thoughts* §44 In matter of law, every plain country-man knows what belongs to distraining, impounding, replevying. **1862** *Stat. of Vermont* xxx. c. 94 §40 Any liquor seized..shall not be delivered by the replevying officer to the claimant.

replevyn(e, -yng, obs. ff. REPLEVIN *sb.*

replevys(s)h, variants of REPLEVISH *v. Obs.*

†**re'plial.** *Obs.* Also 6 -iall, -yal(l. [f. REPLY *v.* + -AL[1].] = REPLY *sb.*

1548 GEST *Pr. Masse* D vj, Cocleus..wryteth in hys former replyall to Bullynger. **1593** R. BARNES *Parthenophil* Elegy iv, When for so many lines, I begged replyal. **1594** CAREW *Huarte's Exam. Wits* (1616) 17 God speakes once.. and turnes not to a second repliall.

†**re'pliant.** *Obs. rare.* Also 7 -yant. [a. F. *repliant*, pres. pple. of *replier*: see REPLY *v.*] One who replies or makes a replication.

1594 WEST *2nd Pt. Symbol., Chancerie* §79 And for further replication saith, that the said H. C. late father of this Repliant, was lawfully seised..of the said tenements. **1656** BOURNE *Def. Script.* 52 Mr. John Deacon, a solid and sharp Questionist, Replyant and Demandant.

replica (ˈrɛplɪkə). [a. It. *replica*, f. *replicare*: see REPLY *v.*] **1. a.** A copy, duplicate, or reproduction of a work of art; properly, one made by the original artist.

1824 LADY MORGAN *Salvator Rosa* iii. I. 105 He is said to have reproduced in numerous *replicos* [sic], the scenery of La Cava. **1859** THACKERAY *Virgin.* lxxii, A copy or *replica* of which piece Mr. Warrington fondly remembered in Virginia. **1859** GULLICK & TIMBS *Paint.* 193 The replica in the National Gallery, of 'the Agony in the Garden'. **1887** BLACK *Sabina Zembra* 31 If Miss Zembra would care to have a little replica of it, I should be happy to do that for her.

b. *transf.* A copy, reproduction, facsimile. *spec.* in *Linguistics* (see quots. 1956 and 1966). Also *attrib.*

1865 OUIDA *Strathmore* i, How can they imagine an ill-done replica of ourselves can attract us! **1885** CLODD *Myths & Dr.* II. ix. 205 Such theories..often take the form of belief in the soul as a replica of the body. **1899** KIPLING *Stalky* 71 Each house..was a replica of the rest; one straight roof covering all. **1956** E. HAUGEN in *Publ. Amer. Dial. Soc.* XXVI. 39 The speakers of language B have *borrowed* it from A... The item as pronounced by speakers of A we shall call the *model* and the diffused item as pronounced by speakers of B we shall call the *replica*. **1963** M. FRAYN in Sissons & French *Age of Austerity* xv. 336 The orange-girls, dressed up as replica Nell Gwyns. **1966** R. A. HALL *Pidgin & Creole Languages* i. 5 The European would conclude that it was useless to use 'good language' to the native, and would reply to him in a replica of the latter's incomplete speech.

c. *Mus.* A repeat.

1740 J. GRASSINEAU *Mus. Dict.* 198 *Replica, Reditta*, or *Riditta*, a *repetition*, that is, when one part after a silence repeats or runs over the same notes and intervals, and in fact the same song, which some part had gone over before it, during that silence. **1952** P. A. SCHOLES *Conc. Oxf. Dict. Mus.* 493/1 *Replica* (It.), repeat.

2. *Comb.* **replica method** = *replica technique* below; **replica plate** *Microbiol.*, a plate of culture medium which has been simultaneously inoculated with numerous microbial clones by holding it against a piece of velvet or similar material which has previously had a plate of grown colonies of micro-organisms held against it; so **replica plating**, the technique of making replica plates, usu. with culture media that contain various antibiotics or lack various nutrients, so that unusual clones of micro-organisms can be recognized; **replica technique**, a method of producing a model of an etched metallic surface for subsequent examination in an electron microscope, used when it is impracticable to take a thin slice of the metal.

1941 *Jrnl. Appl. Physics* XII. 695/2 One basic advantage of the *replica methods as compared to the direct methods of surface observation with the electron microscope. **1951** V. E. COSSLETT *Pract. Electron Microscopy* ix. 214 Electron microscopy has to be content with the indirect alternative of replica methods, in which an impression is taken from a surface on to a thin film which may then be examined by transmission in the usual way. **1952** J. & E. M. LEDERBERG in *Jrnl. Bacteriol.* LXIII. 399 (*heading*) *Replica plating and indirect selection of bacterial mutants. *Ibid.* 400 Replica plating is used to facilitate routine tests involving repetitive inoculations of many isolates on different media. **1958** *Times* 31 Oct. 10/7 'Replica plating'..enables strains of bacteria resistant to particular antibiotics, for example, streptomycin, to be quickly isolated. This is a simple and beautiful technique, which has proved of extreme value in research. **1970** D. A. HOPWOOD in Norris & Ribbons *Methods in Microbiol.* IIIA. vi. 404 A particularly interesting application of replica plating is in isolating bacterial variants of changed potentiality for sexual reproduction. **1952** J. & E. M. LEDERBERG in *Jrnl. Bacteriol.* LXIII. 401 A single initial plate may be used to imprint more than one fabric if carry-over from one *replica plate to another vitiates serial transfer. **1977** *Physiologia Plantarum* XXXIX. 140/2 The cells..then grow with the same arrangement on the replica plate as on the master plate. **1943** *Jrnl. Appl. Physics* XIV. 24/1 The direct *replica technique consists in casting a thin film of plastic on the prepared surface. **1955** *Jrnl. Iron & Steel Inst.* CLXXIX. 392/1 A simple two-stage replica technique, using an intermediate dry-stripped Formvar film on to which carbon is evaporated is described. **1966** [see REPLICATE *v.* 2b]. **1966** D. G. BRANDON *Mod. Techniques Metallogr.* 50 Surface replica techniques..increase the resolution available to the metallographer by a factor of 100 over that obtainable by optical microscopy but have a much reduced sensitivity to changes in surface tilt.

replica'bility. [f. next + -ITY.] The state, property, or condition of being replicable.

1957 *Psychiatry* XX. 80/2 Replicability—six investigators can listen to the same tape, and, within the limits of human error, apply the same analytic categories..and come out with the same transcription. **1971** *Jrnl. Gen. Psychol.* LXXXIV. 304 If that were the case, replicability would depend upon the degree that the important personality variables were adequately sampled. **1972** *Nature* 17 Mar. 99/2 Ascites tumours with high replicability are, felt Dr Steel, toys for the experimentalist. **1978** J. DUNN in Hookway & Pettit *Action & Interpretation* 150 Seeking to render human performance in an idiom in which replicability and inter-observer reliabilty are at a premium.

replicable, *a.* [See REPLICATION and -ABLE.]

†**1.** That may be replied to. *Obs. rare*$^{-1}$.

a **1529** SKELTON *Replyc.* 303 Reputyng hym vnable To gainsay replycable Opinyons detestable Of heresy execrable.

2. That may be repeated experimentally.

1953 J. B. CARROLL *Study Lang.* ii. 34 Reasonably consistent and replicable descriptions of the phonemes of a language. **1973** H. J. EYSENCK *Inequality of Man* iii. 108 Even if we regard the observed slight difference as replicable. **1974** *Encycl. Brit. Macropædia* XIII. 1004/2 Replicable phenomena that can be demonstrated with certainty.

So **'replicably** *adv.*

1964 CRYSTAL & QUIRK *Prosodic & Paralinguist. Features in Eng.* iv. 50 Shorter pauses than those of unit length appear to be replicably distinctive.

replicand: see REPLIQUE *v. Obs.*

†**'replicant.** *Obs.* [ad. L. *replicant-em*, pres. pple. of *replicāre*: see REPLY *v.*]

1. A fresh applicant. *rare*$^{-1}$.

1622 MABBE tr. *Aleman's Guzman d'Alf.* 202 Upon the Neck of that comes another replicant, and he laies about him, beseeching him to bestow upon him some old shirt.

2. One who replies.

1631 R. BYFIELD *Doctr. Sabb.* 193 Though this were indeed the divination of the bitter Replicant, and the intention of the Publisher. *c* **1642** *Contra-replicant's Compl.* 2 The next Art of our Replicant is to impose those his nude averments, which are most false and improbable. **1755** CARTE *Hist. Eng.* IV. 55 The ordinary divinity act should be constantly kept with three replicants.

replicase ('rɛplɪkeɪz, -s). *Biochem.* [f. REPLIC(ATE *v.* + -ASE.] An enzyme which synthesizes a complementary RNA molecule on an RNA template.

1963 SPIEGELMAN & HAYASHI in *Cold Spring Harbor Symp. Quantitative Biol.* XXVIII. 162/1 The RNA-dependent-RNA-polymerase which replicates RNA will be called a replicase. **1971** *New Scientist* 20 May 436/3 In making the complementary RNA the replicase observes a strict one-way system; it moves from the so-called 3′ end of the RNA to the 5′ end. **1973** C. WEISSMANN et al. in F. T. Kenney et al. *Gene Expression & its Regulation* ii. 20 Viral replicases show a very high template specificity for the homologous, intact viral RNA.., as well as for the complementary minus strand.., to the exclusion of all other, unrelated viral RNAs and most other RNAs examined.

'replicate, *sb. Mus.* [f. as next.] **1.** A tone one or more octaves above or below a given tone.

1776 BURNEY *Hist. Mus.* (1789) I. i. 5 This system of four sounds is only an octave higher than that of the first tetrachord and..the next is but a replicate of the second. **1846** in *North's Mem. Music* 34 *note*, [Vases] were tuned in harmonical proportions of fourths, fifths, and eights, with their replicates. **1883** W. POLE in Grove *Dict. Mus.* III. 235/2 Replicates of notes in octaves are found to form parts of all musical scales.

2. *Science.* A repetition of an experiment or trial; each of a number of similar parts or procedures which constitute an experiment or trial. Cf. REPLICATION 4c.

1929 *Jrnl. Agric. Sci.* XIX. 213 In the earlier quantitative experiments..the precision of the results left much to be desired, since only four replicates could be used. **1953** *New Biol.* XIV. 85 It was decided that ten replicates, each of 50 ears [of wheat], would probably be sufficient to reveal important changes in population from year to year. **1970** *Sci. Jrnl.* May 65/1 Earliness and qualities of the varieties could always be reproduced, even if many replicates were made. **1976** *Jrnl. Heredity* LXVII. 204/2 The germinability from one microscope field..in each drop constituted one replicate. *Ibid.*, Values given represent data from a single pollen sample germinated in replicates as stated.

replicate ('rɛplɪkət), *a.* [ad. L. *replicāt-us*, pa. pple. of *replicāre*: see REPLY *v.*]

1. *Bot.* Of a leaf, etc.: Folded back upon itself; also, folded so as to form a groove or channel (Ogilvie 1850).

1832 LINDLEY *Introd. Bot.* 410 *Replicate*; when the upper part is curved back and applied to the lower, as in the Aconite. **1870** HOOKER *Stud. Flora* 379 Outer lobes subvalvate with replicate edges. **1876** HARLEY *Mat. Med.* (ed. 6) 394 Stigma simple or triple, minute and replicate.

2. *Entom.* Of the wings of certain insects: Provided with a joint by means of which the outer part folds back on the base.

1891 in *Cent. Dict.*

3. *Science.* Being a replicate (REPLICATE *sb.* 2).

1961 *Lancet* 29 July 231/2 Replicate assays (i.e. repeat assays on different days). **1972** *Science* 26 May 914/3 Three to five replicate chemical analyses were made for each major tissue. **1978** *Nature* 3 Aug. 459/1 The Institute of Petroleum method recommends that 24 replicate runs are carried out to obtain reasonable statistics.

replicate ('rɛplɪkeɪt), *v.* [f. L. *replicāt-*, ppl. stem of *replicāre*: see REPLY *v.*]

1. To answer, reply; to say in answer. *rare.*

1535 STEWART *Cron. Scot.* II. 651 Quhen he had schawin his mynd to him in plane, This ilk Makdufe he replicat agane. **1599** NASHE *Lenten Stuffe* 73 They.., like rattes smothered in the holde, poorely replicated,..'with hunger, and hope, and thirst wee content our selues'. **1820** T. G. WAINEWRIGHT *Ess. & Crit.* (1880) 70 'Anything you please, Sir', replicated the waitère.

2. a. To repeat, reproduce (an action). *rare.*

1607 *Schol. Disc. agst. Antichr.* II. x. 142 Our crosse commemorateth the popish crosse, replicateth in action the popish crossing. **1635, 1857** [see *replicated* below].

b. To make a replica of (a picture, etc.).

1882 W. SHARP *Rossetti* iii. 234 The *Proserpina* has been replicated five or six times. **1964** R. D. HEIDENREICH *Fund. Transmission Electron Microsc.* iii. 71 The intensity distribution bears a close relation to the topography of the surface being replicated. **1966** D. G. BRANDON *Mod. Techniques Metallogr.* 47 The original specimen surface may be preserved and the potential resolution of the carbon and silicon monoxide replica techniques still obtained by replicating the surface with a plastic material and then replicating this plastic negative of the surface with carbon or silicon monoxide. **1973** *Sci. Amer.* Jan. 102/1 The simplest method of studying snow crystals is to replicate them by letting them fall into a thin layer of dilute solution of plastic and solvent. The solvent evaporates rapidly, leaving a thin plastic cast of the snow crystal.

c. *Science.* To repeat (an experiment or trial) and obtain a consistent result.

1923 *Biometrika* XV. 283 We may obtain an estimate of what the variability would be if the conditions of any one trial could be replicated in a number of experiments with the same variety. **1969** *Sci. Jrnl.* Dec. 49/2 Beveridge.. replicated Thouless' experimental finding of differential cultural susceptibility to phenomenal regression. **1970** T. LUPTON *Managem. & Social Sci.* (ed. 2) III. 74 The studies have since been replicated with similar groups and different groups. **1973** J. L. FLEISS *Statistical Methods for Rates & Proportions* iii. 26 One often undertakes a study in order to replicate (or refute) another's research findings.

d. *Biol. intr., trans.*, and *refl.* Of genetic material or a living organism: to reproduce or give rise to a copy of (itself).

1957 J. LEDERBERG in McElroy & Glass *Chem. Basis Heredity* VII. 743 The very interesting statement that the bacterial nucleus apparently does not replicate by a non-dispersive mechanism. **1958** *New Scientist* 10 July 341/1 A characteristic of living matter is its ability to replicate itself. **1960** *New Biol.* XXXI. 20 They [*sc.* the genes] may continue for millions of years exactly replicating their complex structure. **1965** *Listener* 2 Sept. 332/1 It would be fallacious ..to suppose that the major code-bearing molecules, the nucleic acids, can..replicate themselves in isolation. **1968** H. HARRIS *Nucleus & Cytoplasm* i. 7 The other possibility which could account for the persistence of this information in the enucleate cell is that the relevant RNA might be replicated in the cytoplasm. **1969** *Listener* 10 July 34/1 Arthropods survive, replicate, live off their environment. **1972** *Proc. R. Soc.* B. CLXXXI. 29 DNA is replicated at fork-like growing points. **1977** *Sci. Amer.* Nov. 54/3 Attributes by which we identify living things—their capacity to replicate themselves, to repair themselves, to evolve and to adapt. **1979** *Jrnl. R. Soc. Arts* CXXVII. 645/1 The bacterium rapidly divides and replicates.

e. To imitate; to make or be a model or replica of.

1958 *Word* XIV. 365 It is worth considering whether a formalized investigation replicating the game [of 'Twenty Questions'] would not produce a valid and economical description of a vocabulary. **1966** J. J. KATZ *Philos. Lang.* iv. 99 Verbal exchanges between the computers replicate the publicly observable phenomena that occur when human speakers communicate in a natural language. **1967** M. ARGYLE *Psychol. Interpersonal Behaviour* x. 194 Other activities may be used including..setting up groups in cooperation or competition to replicate organizational problems. **1971** *Sci. Amer.* Oct. 53/2 Synthetic melts of lunar composition can replicate the texture seen in the granular moon rocks. **1977** *Times* 19 Nov. 14/4 Striations that could be replicated with modern but not ancient tools. **1979** *Times* 24 Dec. 10/8 The gallery is to have three rooms that replicate rooms at Hutton Castle.

f. To copy exactly.

1970 *Computers & Humanities* IV. 233 The index entries that have been generated in this way, using the computer's ability to replicate strings of characters, are sorted into alphabetic sequence. **1971** *Sci. Amer.* June 88/3 Since binary data are generally consumed within calculation centers, the ability to replicate the data for future manipulations is essential. **1976** *Ibid.* June 63/1 The signal transmitted from the earth is received by the spacecraft's radio system, which faithfully replicates the received phase, increases its frequency by 10 percent and transmits it back to the earth.

3. To fold or bend back. Also *fig.*

1777 [see *replicated* below]. **1880** [see REPLICATION 3c]. **1881** P. ROBINSON *Under the Punkah* 92 Better for him had his arms remained feet, his ears never been replicated.

Hence **'replicated** *ppl. a.*; also **'replicating** *vbl. sb.* (usu. *attrib.*) and *ppl. a.*

1635 J. HAYWARD tr. *Biondi's Banish'd Virg.* 127 Him, who by replicated good-turnes proclaimed..her faults and ingratitude. **1777** PENNANT *Brit. Zool.* (ed. 4) IV. 102 Aperture wrinkled; upper part replicated. **1857** HEAVYSEGE *Saul* (1869) 43 Fire answering to fire as sound to sound, As though to match the replicated peals. **1926** *Jrnl. Min. Agric.* XXXIII. 506 A replicated experiment provides a valid estimate of error. **1957** F. H. C. CRICK in McElroy & Glass *Chem. Basis Heredity* VII. 747 In a replicating structure one expects the bases to pair rather accurately, so that mistakes are rare. **1960** *New Biol.* XXXI. 23 Some persistent change has therefore occurred in the replicating system for proteins. **1961** M. E. HAINE *Electron Microscope* x. 245 The replica.. has one surface flat and the other following the topography of the replicated surface. *Ibid.*, Replicas were formed in plastic and were limited by the large molecular size of the replicating material. **1971** *Nature* 13 Aug. 502/1 Cellulose acetate replicating tape is used to prepare negative replicas of the etched surfaces. **1976** *National Observer* (U.S.) 17 July 15/3 It appears easy to come up with organic compounds and water. But the big gap is, How often do you get replicating organisms? That, if you will, is the missing link in the origin of life. **1977** *Jrnl. Agric. Sci.* LXXXVIII. 127 (*heading*) Response to family selection based on replicated trials. **1978** *Nature* 20 July 212/2 The combined nicking-closing and negative supercoiling activity of gyrase are presumed to act at some site at or beyond the replicating fork to relieve the positive supercoiling strain which builds up during replication and to aid unwinding.

re'plicatile, *a. rare*$^{-0}$. [f. as REPLICATE *a.* + -ILE.] *Entom.* Capable of being folded back.

1825 SAY *Gloss. Entom.* 29.

replication (rɛplɪ'keɪʃən). Also 4–5 replicacioun, 5–6 -cion(e, 6 -cyon; 4 replycasion, etc. [a. OF. *replication, -cion* (also *reppli-*), ad. L. *replicātiōn-em* folding back, repetition, (in legal use) reply, n. of action f. *replicāre* to unfold, reflect on, reply, f. *re-* RE- + *plicāre* to fold.]

1. The action of folding up or back; the result of this; a fold. *rare.*

c **1374** CHAUCER *Boeth.* III. pr. xii. 82 (Camb. MS.), Ne fooldesthow nat to-gydere by replycasion of wordis a manere wondyrful cercle or enuyronynge. **1578** BANISTER *Hist. Man* IV. 45 Sometyme by extension..otherwhiles by replication and enfoldyng therof..the eyes may both open and shut. **1857** FARADAY *Exp. Res.* liii. 399 It..may consist of an infinity of parts resulting from replications.

2. a. Reply, answer, rejoinder. †Also in phr. ***without* (*any*) *replication***, without reply being allowed; without protest or opposition.

c **1386** CHAUCER *Knt.'s T.* 988 My wyl is this for plat conclusion, With outen any repplicacioun, If that you liketh, take it for the beste. **1433** LYDG. *S. Edmund* II. 883 By a maner replicacioun Ech onto other gan crye in ther walkyng. *c* **1485** *Digby Myst.* (1882) III. 203 Thow þes sottes a-ȝens me make replycacyon, I woll suffer non to spryng of þat kenred. **1532** MORE *Confut. Tindale* Wks. 478/1 To minystre mayster Tyndall so muche pleasaunte matter of replicacyon. **1588** PARKE tr. *Mendoza's Hist. China* 88 The sentence pronounced against them..is foorthwith executed without any replication or appellation. **1637** R. HUMPHREY tr. *St. Ambrose* I. 11 To open my mouth by way of replication. **1652** J. WRIGHT tr. *Camus' Nat. Paradox* x. 238 The pitiful Prisoner suffered herself to bee bound..without the least Replication. **1729** GAY *Polly* 11, Such raillery as this, my dear, requires replication. **1784** R. BAGE *Barham Downs* I. 97 But, vanity apart, I am most happy in a promptitude of replication. **1815** *Zeluca* III. 265 This is retort, and replication about a phrase—a word—a nothing. **1876** BANCROFT *Hist. U.S.* III. vii. 105 The 'political adventurer' ..excelled in quick and concise replication.

b. With *a* and *pl.* A reply, answer.

c **1407** LYDG. *Reson & Sens.* 4464, I wil lyke myn oppinioun Make a replicacioun To that ye han rehersed here. **1414** *Rolls of Parlt.* IV. 57/1 Whereby that I myghte have answered in lawe to all maner of persones, that ony Replicacions wolden have maked aȝeyns ony Article of my billes. **1525** LD. BERNERS *Froiss.* II. cci. [cxcvii.] 616 There was no man spake a worde nor made no replycacion. **1535** CROMWELL in Merriman *Life & Lett.* (1902) I. 416 Your Discrete answers and replicacions made in that behalf. **1586** BRIGHT *Melanch.* xvi. 92 A man of hasty disposition.. will make reply.. before the tale be halfe told, whereby he faileth in his replication. **1614** RALEIGH *Hist. World* III. (1634) 37 With which taxation inflamed, he used this replication. c **1670** BUNYAN *Differences Judgm.* Wks. 1737 II. 72, I find yours far short of a candid Replication. **1727** A. HAMILTON *New Acc. E. Ind.* II. liv. 284 The Peasants made solid Replications to the Complaints of the Portugueze. **1798** I. ALLEN *Hist. Vermont* 164 The replication to the foregoing observations was, that the territory of Vermont should be a colony under the Crown. **1830** JAMES *Darnley* xxxvii, An angry replication trembled on the lip of the English captain.

†**c.** An answer to a charge. *Obs. rare.*

1586 J. HOOKER *Hist. Irel.* in *Holinshed* II. 150/1 Upon the replication of the vicount.. knights were appointed to examine all such witnesses. **1647** N. BACON *Disc. Govt. Eng.* I. xxxviii. (1739) 57 A Judge suffered death for passing Sentence upon the Coroner's only Record; unto which a Replication is allowed.

3. *spec.* A reply to an answer.

c **1440** CAPGRAVE *Life St. Kath.* IV. 1508 Therfore I answere to ȝoure replicacion, Seruynge somwhat now ȝoure entent. **1461** *Rolls of Parlt.* V. 465/2 The answeres therunto yeven, and the replications to the same made. **1642** in Rushw. *Hist. Coll.* III. (1692) I. 610 The Petition of the Lords and Commons.. together with his Majesty's Answer thereunto, and a Replication of the said Lords and Commons to the said Answer. **1711** SHAFTESB. *Charac.* (1737) III. 14 Those mighty controversys,.. the subsequent Defences, the Answers, Rejoinders, and Replications. **1732** BERKELEY *Alciphr.* v. §20 Those arguments, answers, defences, and replications.

b. *Law.* The reply of the plaintiff to the plea or answer of the defendant, being the third step in common pleadings. Also without article.

1453 *Paston Lett.* I. 260 To that that he hath aunsuerd y have replyed yn such wyse that y trowe.. that there shall no vayllable thyng be seyd to the contrarie of my seyd replicacion. **1490** *Plumpton Corr.* (Camden) 101 The replycacion of Margaret Scargill to the answere of William Scargill. **1523** FITZHERB. *Surv.* 13 Howe the declaracion, the answere, replicacion, & rejoyndre shulde be made:.. I remyt yᵗ to men of lawe. **1591** HARINGTON *Orl. Fur.* XIV. lxxiii, Her lap was full of writs and of citations,.. Of bils, of answers, and of replications. a **1625** SIR H. FINCH *Law* (1636) 279 Against the plea that the parties to the fine had nothing &c. it is no good replication, that the parties were seised. **1682** LUTTRELL *Brief Rel.* (1857) I. 201 The atturney generall some time since putt in a replication to the plea of the city of London in defence of their charter. **1768** BLACKSTONE *Comm.* III. 310 The plaintiff.. may in his replication, after an evasive plea by the defendant, reduce that general wrong to a more particular certainty. **1817** W. SELWYN *Law Nisi Prius* (ed. 4) II. 759 By the replication it appeared, that the defendant was not charged as a rightful but as wrongful executor. **1865** NICHOLS *Britton* II. 141 Let the objection of bastardy be then determined upon replication.

fig. **1649** W. M. *Wandering Jew* (1857) 48 She has Demurs, and Replications and Rejoinders; but my case hangs, and no order can I get set downe in this tedious Court of Cupid.

c. *Roman Law.* (See quot.)

1880 MUIRHEAD *Gaius* IV. §126 It becomes necessary to introduce yet another clause.. for the pursuer's benefit, which is called a replication, because thereby the force of the exception is replicated and destroyed.

4. †**a.** Repetition. *Obs.*

c **1425** *Orolog. Sapient.* ii. in *Anglia* X. 342/12 He.. ȝafe him to meditacione of þe passione of owre lord Ihesu &.. was.. helede by continuele replicacione þer-of. **1594** CAREW *Huarte's Exam. Wits* (1616) 131 What the things bee.. wee haue heretofore made mention: now we will returne to a replication of them. **1683** TRYON *Way to Health* 642 Those seven Notes are the Basis of all Musical Composition. The Number Eight is a beginning again, or a replication or repetition of the same.

†**b.** *Logic.* (See quot.) *Obs.* *rare*$^{-0}$.

1727–38 CHAMBERS *Cycl.*, *Replication*, the assuming or using the same term twice in the same proposition: otherwise called reduplication.

c. *Science.* Repetition of an experiment or trial so as to test the trustworthiness of its conclusion.

1926 *Jrnl. Min. Agric.* XXXIII. 506 The method adopted is that of replication. **1953** *New Biol.* XIV. 85 More than one sample must always be taken in order to discover the natural variation between individual samples. This is termed 'replication'. **1971** *Jrnl. Gen. Psychol.* LXXXV. 200 The stability of the means can be seen to be high in the replications.

5. Return of a sound; reverberation, echo.

1601 SHAKS. *Jul. C.* I. i. 51 Tyber trembled vnderneath her bankes To heare the replication of your sounds, Made in her Concaue Shores. **1737** GLOVER *Leonidas* VI. 264 The echoes sigh'd In lulling replication. **1850** BLACKIE *Æschylus* II. 250 With replication loud, Leapt the blithe echo from the rocky shore. **1859** FARRAR *J. Home* 206 Heavens! what a melody of replications!

fig. **1678** CUDWORTH *Intell. Syst.* I. iv. §36. 582 Then will the second Hypostasis be look'd upon as the Eccho of an original Voice;.. as if both.. were but certain Replications of the first original Deity with Abatement.

6. a. A copy, reproduction. Also, the action of reproducing.

1692 RAY *Disc.* 209 Every thing that resembles and comes near to it, and is as it were a replication of it. **1859** FARRAR *J. Home* 70 The notes.. mainly consisted of replications of Mr. Grayson's placid physiognomy. **1882** W. SHARP *Rossetti* iii. 179 More fitting for its water-colour stage than for replication in a large oil-painting. **1951** V. E. COSSLETT *Pract. Electron Microscopy* ix. 223 Most materials for replication are initially either too rough or too smooth for the purpose. **1966** D. G. BRANDON *Mod. Techniques Metallogr.* 45 A major advance in replication technique was made when Bradley discovered that an evaporated carbon film was virtually structureless and would faithfully follow surface contours down to a limit of resolution of about 20 Å. **1969** *Computer & Humanities* III. 193 Gutenberg's press in mid-fifteenth century made multiple replication of the visual expression of ideas practicable. **1972** *Language* XLVIII. 346 The vocalic sub-hierarchy assigns markedness values exclusively by means of replication, whereas the consonantal sub-hierarchy assigns markedness values by means of complementation *and* replication, depending on the feature specification. **1975** *New Yorker* 3 Mar. 96/3 The real triumph of 'Female Friends' is the gritty replication of the gross texture of everyday life, placed in perspective and made universal.

b. *Biol.* The process by which genetic material or a living organism gives rise to a copy of itself.

1948 *Nature* 5 June 872/2 Replication seems commonly to mark the end of active cell division and the onset of differentiation. **1955** *Sci. Amer.* Oct. 70/1 Sometimes, because of a mistake in some step of the replication process, a daughter cell gets a gene carrying a garbled message; that is, it does not bear precisely the same information as its original counterpart. **1971** D. J. COVE *Genetics* v. 73 (*caption*) M. Meselson and F. W. Stahl's experiment to demonstrate the semi-conservative replication of DNA. **1972** *Proc. R. Soc.* B. CLXXXI. 29 Replication of chromosomal DNA occurs in sections arranged in tandem. **1977** *Sci. Amer.* Dec. 94/2 In viral replication (and microbial replication in general) mutants appear at a frequency of about one in a million particles, depending on the viral strain and the conditions of culture.

'replicative, *a. Bot.* [f. as REPLICATE *a.* + -IVE. Cf. F. *replicatif*.] **1.** = REPLICATE *a.* 1.

1852 HENSLOW *Dict. Bot. Terms.*

2. *Biol.* Of, pertaining to, or involved in replication.

1960 *New Biol.* XXXI. 130 A hint that some divisions of the plant kingdom have replicative mechanisms that either derange more easily or are more tolerant of novelty than others. **1971** *Sci. Amer.* Aug. 52/1 As has been abundantly demonstrated over the past two decades, DNA is the replicative molecule of the cell. **1975** *Ibid.* May 28/3 We have isolated a structure reflecting that stage: several plus strands of graduated lengths partially bonded to the minus strand on which they are being synthesized; we call such a structure the replicative intermediate. **1976** *Nature* 28 Oct. 731/1 Plasmids can be viewed as primitive bacteriophages that have not yet acquired those specialised functions necessary for a complex replicative cycle.

So **'replicatively** *adv.*

1727–38 CHAMBERS *Cycl.* s.v. *Replication*, The human soul is said to be in a place replicatively, *replicative*, when conceived to be all in the whole, and all in every part thereof. **1957** R. K. MERTON *Student-Physician* App. C. 304 The second criterion is that results must be *replicatively* consistent.

replicator ('rɛplɪkeɪtə(r)). [ad. F. *réplicateur* (Jacob & Brenner 1963, in *Compt. Rend.* CCLVI. 298), f. as REPLICON + *-eur* -OR.]

1. *Biol.* A postulated section of nucleic acid at which replication is initiated and away from which it proceeds in one or both directions.

1963 *Cold Spring Harbor Symp. Quantitative Biol.* XXVIII. 331/1 A unit capable of independent replication or replicon would carry two specific determinants... A structural gene controlling the synthesis of a specific initiator... An operator of replication, or replicator, i.e., a specific element of recognition upon which the corresponding initiator would act, allowing the replication of the DNA attached to the replicator. **1969** A. M. CAMPBELL *Episomes* viii. 107 Effectively, the F factor would have taken over the normal replicator function for the major part of the bacterial chromosome. **1973** *Virology* LIV. 270/1 According to the replicon theory, some replication-deficient mutants should be found in the postulated replicator gene. **1978** *Bull. Amer. Acad. Arts & Sci.* Feb. 17 In cases where more than two X chromosomes were present there were multiple late replicators.

2. That which replicates (in any sense).

1964 *Listener* 15 Oct. 575/1 Looking as far into the technological future as I dare, I would like to describe the invention to end all inventions. I call it the replicator; it is simply a duplicating machine. It could make, almost instantly, an exact copy of anything. **1972** *Science* 27 Oct. 359/1 Adult liver.. has been described as a 'discontinuous replicator'.. that divides at a low 'wear and tear' replacement rate.

'replicatory, *a.* *rare*$^{-1}$. [f. as REPLICATE *a.* + -ORY.] Of the nature of a reply.

1837 *Blackw. Mag.* XLI. 841 A Parliamentary Committee for the reception of testimony on their side, replicatory to that given before Mr. Sadler's Committee.

replicon ('rɛplɪkɒn). *Biol.* [ad. F. *réplicon* (Jacob & Brenner 1963, in *Compt. Rend.* CCLVI. 298), f. *réplic-ation* REPLICATION: see -ON^{1}.] A piece of genetic material which replicates as a unit, beginning at a single site within it.

1963 *Cold Spring Harbor Symp. Quantitative Biol.* XXVIII. 330/2 A genetic element such as an episome or a chromosome (of a bacterium or of a phage) constitutes a unit of replication or replicon. Such a unit can only replicate as a whole... The capacity to behave as a replicon must depend upon the presence and activity of certain specific determinants. In other words, the properties of such units require that they set up specific systems of signals allowing, or preventing, their own replication. **1971** *Jrnl. Molecular Biol.* LVIII. 873 It has been hypothesized that in mammalian cells DNA replication proceeds *via* two replication forks per replicon, which proceed in opposite directions. **1972** *Bacteriol. Rev.* XXXVI. 365/1 The hypothesis was proposed that those DNA molecules that are capable of replication (termed 'replicons') are circular in structure and carry at least two gene loci controlling their replication; at one locus on the replicon is located a regulator gene which produces a diffusible substance (initiator) acting upon the second locus, an operator of replication (replicator), to permit DNA replication to be initiated from that point. **1974** *Nature* 9 Aug. 467/2 Each chromosome contains many tandemly arranged units of replication (replicons), and each replicon is comparable to the whole chromosome of a bacterium or a virus in that its replication is usually bi-directional. **1976** *Ibid.* 29 Jan. 281/1 Each of these components is capable of autonomous replication in certain host strains of bacteria; that is, each is a 'replicon'.

replie, obs. form of REPLY *sb.* and *v.*

replier (rɪ'plaɪə(r)). [f. REPLY *v.* + -ER^{1}.] One who replies or answers; †*esp.* the author of a Reply.

1566 T. STAPLETON *Ret. Untr. Jewel* Pref. to Rdr., I do first laye forthe the wordes of D. Harding, printed in a seueral letter, vpon and aboute the whiche, the Replier hath noted the Vntruthe. **1581** FIELD in *Confer.* II. (1584) K iij b, The Replyers hauing no longer time to prouide their arguments. **1608** WILLET *Hexapla Exod.* 531 Matthias Toring the replier to Burgensis. **1644** HUNTON *Vind. Treat. Monarchy* iii. 13 The Replier vainly carpes at the name, when he cannot denie the thing. **1815** LAMB in Ainger *Life* (1882) 94, I am forced to be the replier to your letter, for Mary has been ill. **1900** *N. & Q.* 9th Ser. V. 312/2 One of the repliers.. adds to his explanation a somewhat amusing supplement.

replieve, variant of REPLEVE *v. Obs.*

re'plight, *v.* [RE- 5 a.] To plight afresh.

1874 HOLLAND *Mistr. Manse* xxi. 96 Hearts and wings again united,.. And their holy troth replighted. **1876** LANIER *Poems, Cent. Medit.* 43 Toil, and forgive, and kiss o'er, and replight.

†**re'plique,** *sb. Obs.* *rare*$^{-1}$. [a. F. *réplique*, f. *répliquer*: see next.] A reply.

1549 SIR W. PAGET in Burnet *Hist. Ref.* (1865) V. 266, I have no commission to make any replique thereto.

†**re'plique,** *v. Obs. rare.* Also 5 replyque; *Sc. pres. pple.* replicand. [ad. F. *répliquer*, ad. L. *replicāre*: see REPLY *v.*] *trans.* and *intr.* To reply (to); to answer; to say in reply.

1456 SIR G. HAYE *Law Arms* (S.T.S.) 167 Than ansueris the baroun, replicand this argument, sayand [etc.]. c **1477** CAXTON *Jason* 44 Iason with these wordes coude nomore replique for he apperceyued that he coude not make his mater good. c **1489** —— *Blanchardyn* xvii. 54 The proude mayden.. wyst nomore what to replyque nor gaynsaye. **1521** *Balade* in *Bradshaw's St. Werburge* (E.E.T.S.) 201 With deth preuent he myght nothyng replique.

reploch, obs. form of RAPLOCH.

re'plot, *v.* [RE- 5 a.] *trans.* To plot or represent again. So **re'plotter; re'plotting** *vbl. sb.*

1896 *Rep. Board of Ordnance & Fortification* (U.S.) 18 A replotting arm for attachment to the Lewis position-finder. **1897** *Ann. Rep. Chief of Ordnance to Sec. of War 1896* (U.S.) 581 A photograph and description of the Lewis replotter. *Ibid.* 582 With this device it is possible to correctly replot the position of a moving target.. at intervals of ten seconds of time without hurry or confusion. **1902** *Encycl. Brit.* XXXI. 367/1 A complete automatic replotter is carried on the table of each instrument, by the use of which the observer can instantly convert the range and direction of the target as read from the instrument into the corresponding range and direction from the gun itself. **1965** PHILLIPS & WILLIAMS *Inorg. Chem.* I. xvii. 633 The change in ease of oxidation down the series is brought out by replotting some of the values. **1968** *Economist* 6 July 54/1 If an essential invention occurs out of order, the time-scale has to be revised and the forecast path of advance replotted.

re'plotment. *rare*$^{-1}$. [f. RE- 5 a + PLOT *v.*] The act of plotting out again.

1701 *Col. Rec. Pennsylv.* XI. 42 Who have gott Double Lotts by my Replotment of the City.

re'plough, *v.* [RE- 5 a.] *trans.* To plough again, *lit.* and *fig.* Hence **re'ploughing** *vbl. sb.*

1733 TULL *Horse-Hoeing Husb.* xi. (Dubl.) 113 This way of Re-plowing the Ridges, moves all the Earth of them. *Ibid.*, That will hinder the Re-plowing of the first Furrows. **1793** tr. *Gresset's Ver-Vert* IV. (ed. 2) 39 The vessel stood Unmoor'd, and ready to replough the flood. **1856** FROUDE *Hist. Eng.* I. 28 The farms were rebuilt, the lands reploughed, the island repeopled.

‖**replum** ('rɛpləm, 'riːpləm). *Bot.* Pl. **repla.** [L. *replum* 'a bolt for covering the commissure of the folding-door' (Lewis and Short).] The central frame or placenta left in certain fruits when the valves fall away by dehiscence.

1830 LINDLEY *Nat. Syst. Bot.* 88 In Carmichælia the valves separate from the suture, which remains entire, like the replum of Cruciferæ. **1849** BALFOUR *Man. Bot.* §534 In Orchidaceæ.. when the valves fall off, the placentas are left in the form of three arched repla or frames. **1861** BENTLEY *Man. Bot.* 319 When the replum extends entirely across the fruit it is two-celled; if only partially, it is one-celled.

re'plumb, *v.* [ad. L. *replumbāre*: see RE- 2 d and PLUMB *v.*] †**1.** To unsolder. *Obs.*$^{-0}$

1623 COCKERAM, *Replumbed*, vnsouldred.

2. [A separate formation on RE- 5 a.] *trans.* To redo or replace the plumbing in (a building). Chiefly as **re'plumbed** *pa. pple.* Also **re'plumbing** *vbl. sb.*

1909 H. G. WELLS *Tono-Bungay* III. ii. 291 My uncle distinguished himself by the thoroughness with which he did the repainting and replumbing. **1973** *Irish Times* 2 Mar. 26/1 (Advt.), Re-roofed, re-wired and re-plumbed in recent years. **1976** *Newmarket Jrnl.* 16 Dec. 39 (Advt.), These properties have been fully modernised including re-roofing, re-wiring, re-plumbing, etc. **1977** [see SEE *v.* 22]. **1978** *Morecambe Guardian* 14 Mar. 23/3 (Advt.), The house has been re-wired, replumbed, had a new bathroom installed, etc.

re'plume, *v.* [RE- 5 a.] To rearrange.

1855 BROWNING *Saul* xv, The right-hand replumed His black locks to their wonted composure.

re'plunder, *v.* [RE- 5 a.] To plunder again.

1655 FULLER *Hist. Camb.* 8 To crie quits with the Barons, William Earl of Sarisbury, and Falk de Brent.. replundred Cambridgeshire.

re'plunge (riː-), *sb.* [f. RE- 5 a + PLUNGE *sb.*] The act of plunging again.

1806 J. GRAHAME *Birds Scotl.* 138 Unless the trout with quick replunge Ruffle the glassy surface. **1869** RUSKIN *Q. of Air* §39 The dolphins' arching rise and replunge.

re'plunge (riː-), *v.* [ad. F. *replonger*: or f. RE- 5 a + PLUNGE *v.*] To plunge again, *lit.* and *fig.*

a. *trans.* *a* **1618** SYLVESTER *Elegie to Marg. Wyts* 92 To be replung'd in Romish superstition. **1719** YOUNG *Revenge* v. ii, Since thou hast replung'd me in my torture, I will be satisfy'd! **1751** *Female Foundling* I. 103 Uneasiness seized me, and I was again replunged into Perplexity and Sorrow. **1801** STRUTT *Sports & Past.* III. vii. 252 She.. dives again, and replunges the owl into the water. **1848** LYTTON *Harold* I. ii, They replunged into barbarism the nations over which they swept. **1863** CONOLLY *Study Hamlet* 25 This replunges Hamlet into his bitterest reflections.

b. *intr.* **1611** FLORIO, *Riprofondare*, to sinke againe, to replunge. **1797** W. TAYLOR in *Monthly Rev.* XXII. 545 Then [he] replunges for six days into the tainted atmosphere of the town in which he dwells. **1844** DISRAELI *Coningsby* VI. i, She.. instantly turned her head and replunged into her conversation.

Hence **re'plunger**.

1882 *Daily News* 7 Jan. 2/1 Signalling lore,.. a language in which 'back-locking', 'slotters', and 'replungers' are important factors.

reply (rɪ'plaɪ), *sb.* Also 6 replie, 7 replye. [f. the vb.]

1. a. An answer or response in words or writing; also *transf.*, a response made by a gesture, act, etc.

1560 in *Jewel's Wks.* (1848) I. 66 The Reply of the Bishop of Sarum to the Letter above written. **1588** SHAKS. *L.L.L.* IV. i. 86 Thus expecting thy reply, I prophane my lips on thy foote. **1602** —— *Ham.* II. ii. 212 How pregnant (sometimes) his Replies are! **1647** CLARENDON *Hist. Reb.* I. §66 The Earl ..without any reply to the particulars, declared 'that he neither cared for his Friendship, nor feared his Hatred'. **1665** GLANVILL *Def. Van. Dogm.* 75, I concluded my Reply with a Brevity that shews I am not fond of an occasion of Disputing. **1737** GLOVER *Leonidas* III. 277 Sparta's king This brief reply deliver'd from his seat. **1781** COWPER *Conversat.* 877 Their wisdom bursts into this sage reply. **1828** SCOTT *F.M. Perth* xxi, The King turned.. with a look of triumph, at the filial affection which his son displayed in his reply. **1833** TENNYSON *Lady Clara V. de V.* 22 You sought to prove how I could love, And my disdain is my reply. **1855** —— *Maud* II. IV. 30 The delight of happy laughter, The delight of low replies.

b. Without article.

1589 PUTTENHAM *Eng. Poesie* III. xix. (Arb.) 209 *Symploche*, or the figure of replie. **1595** SHAKS. *John* III. iii. 49 If that thou couldst.. Heare me without thine eares, and make reply Without a tongue. *c* **1620** A. HUME *Brit. Tongue* I. vii, Quherat al laughed, as if I had bene dryven from al replye. **1667** MILTON *P.L.* II. 467 Thus saying rose The Monarch, and prevented all reply. **1725** POPE *Odyss.* VIII. 167 To whom with sighs Ulysses gave reply. **1751** JOHNSON *Rambler* No. 176 ⁋8 The animadversions of critics are commonly such as may easily provoke the sedatest writer to some.. asperity of reply. **1817** SHELLEY *Rev. Islam* V. xix, At length one brought reply, that she To-morrow would appear. **1859** TENNYSON *Geraint & Enid* 817 That other flush'd And hung his head, and halted in reply.

transf. **1817** SHELLEY *Rev. Islam* II. xvi, All bosoms made reply On which its lustre streamed. **1832** TENNYSON *Œnone* 141 Her full and earnest eye.. Kept watch, waiting decision, made reply.

c. *Mus.* The answer or response in a fugue. (See also quot.)

1597 MORLEY *Introd. Mus.* 105 When the principall (that is the thing as it is firste made) and the replie (that is it which the principall hauing the partes changed dooth make) are sung, changing the partes in such maner, as the highest part may be made the lowest.

d. *attrib.* and *Comb.*, as ***reply-paid*** adj., ***post-card***, ***-signal***.

1884 *Graphic* 30 Aug. 219/3 Reply Postcards can now be sent to Egypt. **1890** *Daily News* 26 Feb. 2/1 The value of a reply-paid voucher will only be refunded to the sender of the original telegram. **1897** P. WARUNG *Tales Old Regime* 101 The reply-signal came up the shaft. **1928** E. WALLACE *Double* xviii. 272 It was evidently, from the indicator, a reply-paid message. **1973** *Times* 14 Mar. 4/6 In the present poll this outcome may well have been achieved by the retiring conservators distributing reply-paid proxy forms.

2. a. A counter-answer, a replication. (In later use only *Sc. Law.*)

1702 COTTON MATHER *Magnalia* VII. 16/2 §5 Unto those Answers the Synod gave Replies; and unto those Replies he gave Returns. **1719** WATERLAND *Vind. Christ's Div.* Pref. A ij, Exchanging Papers, making Answers, Replies, and Rejoinders. **1777** *Acts Sederunt* (1790) 592 Act concerning Replies. **1820** SCOTT *Abbot* i, Answers, replies, duplies, triplies, quadruplies, followed thick upon each other.

b. A pleading by the plaintiff after the delivery of the defence; the final speech of Counsel in a trial.

1837 in Carrington & Payne *Rep. Cases Nisi Prius* VII. 676 The counsel for the prosecution may re-examine the witness, and after the prisoner's counsel has addressed the jury, will be entitled to the reply. **1837** *Rex* v. *Stannard* in *Ibid.* 675 C. Phillips waived his right of reply. **1875** *Act 38 & 39 Vict.* c. 77 Sched. I. §xxiv. 55 A plaintiff shall deliver his reply, if any, within three weeks after the defence or the last of the defences shall have been delivered, unless the time shall be extended by the Court or a Judge. **1898** *Criminal Evidence Act 61 & 62 Vict.* c. 36 s. 3 In cases where the right of reply depends upon the question whether evidence has been called for the defence, the fact that the person charged has been called as a witness shall not of itself confer on the prosecution the right of reply. **1961** L. F. STURGE *Basic Rules Supreme Court* xxiii. 62 The position is further confused by the fact that the Rules give the name 'reply' to what the legal profession is accustomed.. to call a 'defence to counterclaim'... The modern practice is to head the pleading 'Reply and Defence to Counterclaim' and to head each part respectively 'Reply' (meaning the equivalent of the common law replication) and 'Defence to Counterclaim'. **1964** LD. EVERSHED et al. *Atkin's Encycl. Court Forms* (ed. 2) XXXII. 35 Pleadings subsequent to the reply still bear their ancient names: rejoinder, surrejoinder, rebutter and surrebutter, although modern rules do not refer to them by name. **1975** I. H. JACOB *Bullen & Leake's Precedents of Pleadings* (ed. 12) ix. 109 No pleading subsequent to a reply or a defence to counterclaim may be served except with the leave of the court.

†**3.** ? Supply. *Obs. rare*$^{-1}$.

1592 KYD *Sol. & Pers.* II. i. 214 *Guelp.* Feare not for money, man, ile beare the Boxe. *Iul.* I haue some little replie, if neede require.

4. A signal sent by a transponder in response to interrogation. Also *attrib.*, as ***reply pulse***.

1945 [see INTERROGATE *v.* 4 a]. **1947** L. N. RIDENOUR *Radar System Engin.* viii. 263 The replies may be made more complicated in a variety of ways for the purpose either of identifying the beacon or of using it as part of an auxiliary communication system. **1963** R. S. H. BOULDING *Princ. Radar* (ed. 7) xxii. 471 Measurement of the time from the commencement of the interrogating pulse to the receipt of the beginning of the reply pulse enables the distance between the aircraft and the beacon to be determined. **1965** R. S. BERKOWITZ *Mod. Radar* I. ii. 12 When the radar interrogates a beacon and receives a reply whose power is fixed by the characteristics of the beacon transmitter, separate calculations are necessary for the out and back paths.

reply (rɪ'plaɪ), *v.* Also 4 repplye, 4–7 replye, 5–6 replie. [ad. OF. *replier* to fold again, turn back, reply (mod.F. *replier* to fold again, turn, coil):—L. *replicāre*: see REPLICATION.]

I. 1. a. *intr.* To answer or respond in words or writing. Also const. *to*, † *against*.

c **1385** CHAUCER *L.G.W.* Prol. 343 ȝe motyn herkenyn If he can replye A-geyns these poyntys that ȝe han to hym mevid. *c* **1386** —— *Merch. T.* 365 Hym thoughte.. That inpossible it were to repplye Agayn his choys. **1414** *Rolls of Parlt.* IV. 57/1 To the whiche billes myne adversaries repleiden by mouthe and enfourmeden the Kyng.. in that Parlement, how I was outlawed. **1494** FABYAN *Chron.* VII. ccxxxvi. 274 The archebysshop Thomas began to replye agayn the Kynges mynde. **1526** *Pilgr. Perf.* (W. de W. 1531) 173 Here yᵉ enuyous and irous persone maketh sore contradiccyon, & replyeth, sayenge. **1560** DAUS tr. *Sleidane's Comm.* 94 The Protestantes do replie thus. **1597** SHAKS. *2 Hen. IV*, v. v. 59 Reply not to me, with a Foole-borne Iest. **1610** HEYWOOD *Gold. Age* I. Wks. 1874 III. 14 He that next replyes, Mother or friend, by Saturnes fury dyes. **1665** G. HAVERS *P. della Valle's Trav. E. India* 102 His Courtiers seeing him in this mood, would not reply further to him. **1735** POPE *Prol. Sat.* 374 Full ten years slander'd, did he once reply? **1776** HUME *Own Life*, I had fixed a resolution, which I inflexibly maintained, never to reply to anybody. **1797** MRS. RADCLIFFE *Italian* Prol., The friar did not immediately reply. **1855** TENNYSON *Maud* II. III. 7 Or if I ask thee why, Care not thou to reply. **1879** M. PATTISON *Milton* 76 Milton replies to these random charges by a lengthy account of himself.

fig. **1601** SHAKS. *All's Well* II. iii. 87 The honor sir that flames in your faire eyes, Before I speake too threatningly replies. **1714** POPE *Rape of Lock* III. 24 The Nymph exulting fills.. the sky; The Walls, the Woods, and long Canals reply. **1785** COWPER *Task* VI. 231 There is in souls a sympathy with sounds... Some chord in unison with what we hear is touched within us, and the heart replies. **1860** TYNDALL *Glac.* I. xiii. 92 If Nature does not reply to a question we throw it into another form. **1930** R. CAMPBELL *Poems* 9 Clear as a glass the day replies To every feature save her eyes.

†**b.** Const. *upon* a person or thing. *Obs.*

1579 TOMSON *Calvin's Serm. Tim.* 214/1 If a thing be once appointed by him who hath all power, let vs not replie vpon it. **1652** GAULE *Magastrom.* 340 The king replyed upon him again, avouching [etc.]. *a* **1731** ATTERBURY *Serm.* (J.), We should find what reason Castalio's painter had to reply upon the cardinal, who blamed him [etc.].

c. To respond by some gesture, act, or performance; *esp.* to return gun-fire.

1818 SHELLEY *Rosal. & Helen* 9, I see.. thine eyes replying To the hues of yon fair heaven. **1829** SIR W. NAPIER *Penins. War* VIII. v. (Rtldg.) I. 398 The besieged replied.. sharply. **1842** TENNYSON *Audley Crt.* 55 He sang his song, and I replied with mine. **1893** *Daily News* 25 July 4/6 Lancashire.. scored 189 against Somersetshire, who replied with 90 for three wickets. **1894** LD. WOLSELEY *Life Marlborough* II. 175 A battery of eight guns opened on the fleet... The frigates replied.

2. To return a sound; to echo.

In early quots. merely a contextual use of sense 1.

1390 GOWER *Conf.* II. 282 What man that in the wodes crieth, Withoute faile Eccho replieth. **1588** SHAKS. *Tit. A.* II. iii. 18 Whil'st the babling Eccho mocks the Hounds, Replying shrilly to the well-tun'd Hornes. **1712–14** POPE *Rape Lock* III. 100 The nymph exulting fills with shouts the sky; The walls, the woods, and long canals reply. **1809–10** SHELLEY *Bigotry's Victim* i, Whilst India's rocks to his death-yells reply, Protracting the horrible harmony. **1847** TENNYSON *Princ.* III. 358 Blow, let us hear the purple glens replying.

3. To make counter-answer; *spec.* in *Law*, to answer a defendant's plea; to make a replication.

1453 *Paston Lett.* I. 260 To that that he hath aunsuerd y have replyed yn such wyse [etc.]. **1562** WINȜET *Wks.* (S.T.S.) I. 2 Thre wryttingis deliuerit to the said Iohne, quhairin is replyit aganis his ansueris maid to ane part of the said thre questionis. **1768** BLACKSTONE *Comm.* III. xx. 309 The plaintiff may plead again, and reply to the defendant's plea. **1802** JAMES *Milit. Dict.* s.v., After the prisoner's defence before a court-martial the prosecutor.. may reply. **1849** J. L. CAMPBELL *Chief Justices Eng.* II. xxxiii. 401 Lord Mansfield hesitated long about making the right to reply depend upon the giving of evidence by the defendant. **1923** W. G. RUSSELL *Treatise on Crimes* (ed. 8) II. 1835 If the defendant is undefended there is no right to sum up or reply if he calls no witnesses, whether he himself does or does not give evidence: but there is a right to reply if he calls a witness.

4. a. *trans.* To return as an answer; to say in reply. Const. *to*, †*against*, †*upon*.

c **1412** HOCCLEVE *De Reg. Princ.* 1338 Natheless þou maist ageyn me replie, 'To sum folk.. Agayn pouert it is no remedye'. **1526** *Pilgr. Perf.* (W. de W. 1531) 301 b, Nothynge answeryng ne replyenge agaynst theyr wronge and false accusacyons. **1591** SHAKS. *1 Hen. VI*, III. i. 28 Lords, vouch-safe To giue me hearing what I shall reply. **1611** BIBLE *Tobit* ii. 14 But shee replyed vpon me, It was giuen for a gift. **1647** CLARENDON *Hist. Reb.* I. §29 He replyed that he could not think well of it. **1671** MILTON *P.R.* IV. 2 Perplex'd and troubl'd.. The Tempter stood, nor had what to reply. **1751** ELIZA HEYWOOD *Betsy Thoughtless* I. 86 'Ah! madam', replied he,..'where the heart is deeply affected' [etc.]. **1788** GIBBON *Decl. & F.* xlix. V. 123 To the importunities of the Greeks.. he piously replied, that no human consideration should tempt him.. to resume the gift which he had conferred. **1828** SCOTT *F.M. Perth* xxxiv, 'If there be any man willing to fight for honour', replied MacGillie Chattanach, 'the price will be enough'. **1885** JEFFERIES *Open Air* (1893) 157 The man.. replied nothing.

†**b.** To retort *upon* one. *Obs. rare*$^{-1}$.

1513 WEST in Ellis *Orig. Lett.* Ser. I. I. 72 He said.. if ye did any thing to hym then it shuld not be honorable, which I replyed upon hym, sayeng that all the world knew that your Grace went in the Churches cause.

c. To return, re-echo (a cry).

1650 R. BARON *Fortune's Tennis Ball* xviii, The airy Queen.. each yell replies As if another chase were in the skies. **1697** DRYDEN *Virg. Georg.* IV. 764 With his last Voice, Eurydice, he cry'd. Eurydice, the Rocks and River-banks reply'd.

II. †**5. a.** To retract, withdraw. *Obs. rare*$^{-1}$.

1387–8 T. USK *Test. Love* I. vi. (Skeat) I. 181 Whiche thing is wonder, that they knowing me saiyng but soth arne nowe tempted to reply her olde praysinges.

†**b.** To send away, repudiate. *Obs. rare*$^{-1}$.

c **1470** HARDING *Chron.* XVIII. vii, The quene Gwendolyne ..Whome Kyng Locryne forsoke and replyed, And Estrylde weddid againe.

†**6.** To fold back; to double. *Obs. rare.*

c **1450** *Bk. Curtasye* 661 in *Babees Bk.* (1868) 321 Þo ouer nape schalle dowbulle be layde,.. Þo ouer seluage he schalle replye. **1574** BOURNE *Regiment for Sea* xxiii. (1577) 62 b, An instrument shewing you howe many myles of Longitude will answere vnto a degree.. by the replying of a threed.

†**7.** To repeat. *Obs. rare*$^{-1}$.

1576 GASCOIGNE *Philomene* Wks. P j b, Euen so this byrde vppon that name, Hir foremost note replies.

Hence **re'plying** *vbl. sb.* and *ppl. a.*; also **re'plyingly** *adv.*, **re'plyist**.

1548 ELYOT, *Replicatio*, a replyng. **1571** GOLDING *Calvin on Ps.* lxxiii. 1 The Adverbe (Ac).. dooth not simply affirme in this place, but is taken replyingly, (for yit, But yit, yit notwithstanding). **1574** [see REPLY *v.* 6]. **1656** EARL MONM. tr. *Boccalini's Advts. fr. Parnass.* II. xiv. (1674) 156 He without further replying, made all the haste he could out of the Court. **1852** *N. & Q.* 13 Mar. 257 A replyist refers to a work in which is an autobiography. **1871** R. ELLIS *Catullus* lxv. 9 Ah! no more to address thee, or hear thy kindly replying! **1883** GRANT WHITE *Washington Adams* 6 The quick inquiring and replying chat of compatriots who meet unexpectedly in a strange country.

replyal(l, varr. of REPLIAL *Obs.*

replyant, variant of REPLIANT *Obs.*

repman, variant of REAPMAN *Obs.*

†**re'poin,** *v. Obs. rare*$^{-1}$. [a. obs. F. *repoin-*, *repoign-*, stem of *repoindre*:—L. *repungĕre* to prick again: see POIGNANT.] *intr.* To regret, repent.

1523 LD. BERNERS *Froiss.* I. cxxx. 65/1 The knyght retourned again to them, and shewed the kynges wordes, the whiche gretly encouraged them, and repoyned [F. *se repentirent*] in that they had sende to the kynge as they dyd.

re'point (riː-), *v.* [RE- 5 a.] *trans.* To point (a wall, etc.) again. Also *absol.*

1849 *Q. Rev.* Mar. 381 The summer of 1843 was occupied in repointing the joints of the building. **1864** *Daily Tel.* 17 Mar., The shot-holes have all been neatly mended, the shattered bricks re-pointed. **1887** HISSEY *Holiday on Road* 322 It is surely better to retop and repoint than to take away.

repois(e, obs. Sc. forms of REPOSE *v.*²

repolari'zation. [RE- 5 b.] A renewed polarization; the action of repolarizing.

1922 *Public Opinion* 11 Aug. 136/2 What is aimed at is the repolarisation of the individual items of society. **1958** CRANEFIELD & HOFFMAN in *Jrnl. Gen. Physiol.* XLI. 633 (*title*) Propagated repolarization in heart muscle. **1968** *Economist* 20 July 32/1 It also caused him to predict a repolarisation of South African politics. **1973** *Nature* 9 Feb. 400/1 The immediate consequence of contact of ovum and spermatozoon is an action potential, a depolarization and repolarization including a transient reversal of polarity.

re'polarize, *v.* [RE- 5 b.] *intr.* To polarize again.

1958 J. H. BURN *Lect. Notes Pharmacol.* (ed. 5) 37 Normally a second response can be produced when the intra-cellular potential has repolarized to only 2/3 of its full resting negativity. **1965** *Math. in Biol. & Med.* (Med. Res. Council) VI. 262 When curve C is reached the only remaining point at which the ionic current is zero is the new value E_r, so that the membrane repolarizes. **1973** *Nature* 9 Feb. 400/2 The eggs then repolarized, somewhat slowly, to the − 60 mV typical of the end of phase III. **1980** *Sci. Amer.* May 74/3 In an unmyelinated fiber the entire axonal membrane must depolarize and then repolarize.

re'polish (riː-), *v.* [RE- 5 a. Cf. L. *repolīre*, F. *repolir*.] *trans.* (and *absol.*) To polish again, in *lit.* and *fig.* senses.

1590 GREENE *Mourn. Garm.* Wks. (Gros.) IX. 130 Shee infused such interiour and vitall spirits into this carkase, that it seemed repollished with the purity of the senses. **1612** DONNE *A Funeral Elegy* 40 As a sundred clocke is peecemeale laid, Not to bee lost, but by the maker's hand Repolish'd. **1683** DRYDEN tr. *Boileau's Art of Poetry* 11 Polish, repolish, every Colour lay, And sometimes add; but oftner take away. **1793** HERSCHEL in *Phil. Trans.* LXXXIII. 207 These measures were taken with a speculum that has been lately re-polished. **1812** W. TAYLOR in *Monthly Rev.* LXVIII. 253 His silver..requires to be purified and repolished throughout. **1892** GREENER *Breech Loader* 118 Repolishing and browning barrels.

Hence **re'polishing** *vbl. sb.*; also **re'polisher.**

1593 NASHE *Christ's T.* (1613) 153 Thou hast contended, to be a more beautifull Creator and repolisher of thy selfe, then he. **1611** FLORIO, *Ripulimento*, a repolishing. **1624** WOTTON *Archit.* Pref., After the reuiuing and repolishing of good Literature..he was best..vnderstood by Strangers. **1849** NOAD *Electricity* (ed. 3) 300 To render the re-polishing of them unnecessary, M. Haldat tins them.

re'polish (riː-), *sb.* [f. the vb.] A renewed polishing.

1905 *Daily Chron.* 9 Sept. 2/6 The floor is waxed and polished, so only needs dusting and a very occasional repolish.

repo'llute, *v.* [RE- 5 a.] To pollute again.

1645 WITHER *Vox Pacif.* 172 How farre you, in later yeares, have gone To repollute these Islands.

repo'lon. *rare.* Also 6 repolone, 9 repollon. [ad. It. *repolone* or F. *repolon* = Sp. *repelon*, of doubtful origin.] (See earliest quots.)

Cotgr. identifies *repolon* and *passade*, and defines the latter in agreement with Florio; but later French Dicts. explain *repolon* as 'demivolte en cinq temps'.

1598 FLORIO, *Repoloni*..is when a horse doth gallop in a right path, and still returneth in the same, in english it is now called a Repolone. **1727** BAILEY (vol. II), *Repolon* (with Horsemen) is a Demivolt, the Croup inclos'd at five Times. **1753** CHAMBERS *Cycl. Supp.* **1892** LD. LYTTON *K. Poppy* iii. 97 Performing all His volts and demivolts and repollons Among the roaring flames.

†**reponce.** *Obs. rare.* Also -se. [a. F. *reponce*, obs. f. *raiponce*: see RAMPION[1].] A rampion.

1704 *Dict. Rust.* s.v., Reponses, or wild Radishes, are propagated only by seeds. **1706** PHILLIPS (ed. Kersey), *Reponces*, (Fr.) a sort of small wild Radishes, that grow naturally in the Fields, and are eaten in Sallets. **1719** LONDON & WISE *Compl. Gard.* 237.

re'ponder, *v.* [RE- 5 a.] To ponder again.

1613 SHERLEY *Trav. Persia* 96 So that..Your Maiestie may reponder and resolue at leisure of the proceeding of your enterprise. **1863** COWDEN CLARKE *Shaks. Char.* Pref., In pondering and repondering his productions for the chief portion of my life.

reponde'ration. [RE- 5 a.] The action of weighing again.

1664 POWER *Exp. Philos.* I. 29 We then, upon a re-ponderation of it, had lost near two drams of its former weight.

†**repone,** variant of *rebon*, REBOUND *sb.*[1]

c **1440** *Promp. Parv.* 430/1 Repone, of a balle or oþer lyke, *repulsa, repulus.*

repone (rɪ'pəʊn), *v. Sc.* Also 6 repoun. [ad. L. *repōnĕre*: see REPOSE *v.*]

1. *trans. Law.* To restore a person to a position or office previously held; in later use *spec.* to restore to the ministry or to a ministerial charge. Also const. *in*, *to*.

1525 *Sc. Acts Jas. V* (1814) II. 299/1 Reponis, reintegratis, & restoris þe said Jhone till his honour, heretagis, landis, rentis. **1583** in *6th Rep. Hist. MSS. Comm.* 637/1 That he may be reponit and placit in my roume,..landis, honouris and dignitee. *a* **1639** SPOTTISWOOD *Hist. Ch. Scot.* VI. (1677) 445 The desire they had to have their old Ministers repone would make them the more forward. *a* **1670** SPALDING *Troub. Chas. I* (1829) 57 That all ministers deposed since the 1st of February be reponed in their places to their former functions. **1728** *Wodrow Corr.* (1843) III. 398 It's given out..that a design is forming to repone Mr Simson at the next Assembly. **1753** *Scots Mag.* May 253/1 It might please the..Assembly to..repone him again to his ministry. **1838** W. BELL *Dict. Law Scot.* 291 After deposition, the party is not to be regarded as a minister of the church,..even if he should be reponed, unless he is again settled in a ministerial charge.

b. To restore to a certain legal status, to rehabilitate (a person), esp. *against* a decree or sentence, so that the case may be tried afresh. †Also const. with *inf.* and *absol.*

1574 *Reg. Privy Council Scot.* II. 381 To heir and se the said Bischope..reponit to use his lauchfull defenssis. **1671** [? R. MACWARD] *Case Accom. Exam.* 12 As a restitution repones against a discontinuance. **1825** *Act 6 Geo. IV*, c. 120 §29 As soon as the Defender shall enter Appearance and be reponed against the Decree pronounced in Absence. **1838** W. BELL *Dict. Law Scot.* 852 According to the existing form a party may be reponed..by presenting a reclaiming note to the Court. **1850** *Act 13 & 14 Vict.* c. 36 §23 Provided always, that a Pursuer may be reponed against a Protestation. **1896** *Green's Encycl. Scots Law* I. 16 The Sheriff repones the defender.

†**2.** To put (a person or thing) back *in* a place. *Obs. rare.*

1582–8 *Hist. Jas. VI* (1804) 39 That hir majestie should first peaceablie be reponit in the castell of Dumbarton. **1640** R. BAILLIE *Canterb. Self-convict.* 108 The English..removed the prayer it selfe from that place: But our men to shew their Orthodoxie, repone the prayer in the owne old place.

†**3.** To give as a reply; to answer. *Obs. rare.*

1644 J. GOODWIN *Innoc. Triumph.* (1645) 53 In answer to somewhat argued by me..he repones thus. **1671** R. MACWARD *True Non-Conf.* 289 You repone to us the very meanest of their Arguments, not..in the least recocted.

Hence **re'poning** *vbl. sb.* and *ppl. a.*

1753 *Scots Mag.* May 252/2 In relation to the reponing of these brethren. **1896** *Green's Encycl. Scots Law* I. 15 The decree must also not have been recalled under the provisions for reponing. *Ibid.* 16 A defender may be reponed against a decree..by lodging with the Sheriff Clerk a reponing note.

re'pope, *v.* [RE- 5 a.] *trans.* To make (one) pope again.

1869 BROWNING *Ring & Bk.* x. 110 Theodore..convoked a synod, whose decree Did..repope the late unpoped.

re'populate (riː-), *v.* [RE- 5 a.] *trans.* To populate again. Hence **re'populating** *vbl. sb.*

1599 HAKLUYT *Voy.* II. I. 220 This Temiragio returned to the city, and then beganne for to repopulate it. **1611** COTGR., *Repeuplement*, a repeopling, repopulating. **1859** HOLE *Tour Irel.* vii. (1892) 73 Great efforts are being made to repopulate the country. **1881** R. N. BOYD *Chili* 116 The town was..rebuilt and repopulated by emigrants from the province of Biscay.

So **repopu'lation.**

a **1734** NORTH *Lives* (1826) I. 36 That perhaps may tend to some repopulation, which is more needed than any means of extortion. **1832** L. HUNT *Translations* 330 What possible debtor can pay his debts better, Than De-population with Re-population? **1885** *Homilet. Rev.* (U.S.) Feb. 166 Believing that prophecy teaches the repopulation of Palestine by Christianized Jews.

report (rɪ'pɔət), *sb.* Also 6 raport, reaport. [a. OF. *report* (rare) or *raport* (mod.F. *rapport*), vbl. sb. f. *reporter*, *rapporter*: see REPORT *v.*]

1. a. Rumour, common talk. (Sometimes personified.) Now *rare.*

c **1374** CHAUCER *Troylus* I. 593, I haue & schal for trowe or fals report In wrong & ryȝt loued þe al myn lyf. **14..** *Tundale's Vis.*, etc. (1843) 121 The day of trowthe is turned into nyght Thorow wrang report. *c* **1430** LYDG. *Min. Poems* (Percy Soc.) 70 No langage [is] digne thy vertus to expresse, By newe report so clierly they don shyne. *c* **1500** *Lancelot* 777 Arthur by Report hard saye How galiot non armys bur that day. **1559** *Mirr. Mag.*, *Tiptoft* ii, Might report vprightly vse her tong It would lesse greue vs to augment the matter. **1576** FLEMING *Panopl. Epist.* 91 Yet doe the eyes..kindle the more anguishe, whiche see..those thinges, that others heare by reporte. **1600** SHAKS. *A.Y.L.* I. i. 6 My brother Iaques he keepes at schoole, and report speakes goldenly of his profit. *c* **1645** MILTON *Sonn.* x. *To Lady Margaret Ley*, As that dishonest victory..Kil'd with report that Old man eloquent. **1697** DRYDEN *Virg. Georg.* III. 601 'Twas thus with Fleeces milky white (if we May trust Report,) Pan God of Arcady, Did bribe thee. **1784** COWPER *Task* II. 355 Through that public organ of report He hails the clergy. **1797** MRS. RADCLIFFE *Italian* ii, I do not lightly give faith to report.

b. With *a* and *pl.* A rumour; a statement generally made or believed. ***the report goes***: it is commonly said (cf. GO *v.* 13).

c **1412** HOCCLEVE *De Reg. Princ.* 1671 Reportes not so sikyr iuges ben, As man to se þe womannes persone. **1483** CAXTON *Cato* C v, Many euyles comen by wycked and euyl tunges and euyl reportes. **1560** DAUS tr. *Sleidane's Comm.* 52 The report goth that you have conspired to destroy the secte of Luther. **1568** GRAFTON *Chron.* II. 669 The Erle of Warwike..by euill reportes, did as much as in him lay to hinder this mariage. **1613** PURCHAS *Pilgrimage* VI. v. (1614) 587 Baumgarten saith that it was a common report in Cairo when he was there. **1665** BOYLE *Occas. Refl.* IV. xvii. (1848) 274 He will..perhaps Ruine himself..by spreading Reports. *a* **1715** [see GO *v.* 13]. **1781** COWPER *Conversat.* 802, I have lived recluse in rural shades, Which seldom a distinct report pervades. **1828** SCOTT *F.M. Perth* iii, There are bad reports of him among the Dominicans, that is certain. **1848** B'NESS BUNSEN in Hare *Life* (1879) II. iii. 112 The shadow of this..came in the shape of a report from Paris.

c. Repute, fame, reputation. Now only with *good*, etc., as an echo of Biblical passages.

1514 BARCLAY *Cyt. & Uplondyshm.* (Percy Soc.) 28 What thynge is glory,..honour, report, or what is noble name? **1535** COVERDALE *Judith* viii. 13 This Iudith was a woman of a very good reporte with euery one. **1562** *Child-Marriages* 108 The witnes..cold not depose truly that she was of honest name, biecause they hard of her evill Report. **1603** SHAKS. *Meas. for M.* II. iii. 12 A Gentlewoman of mine, Who ..Hath blisterd her report. **1641** J. JACKSON *True Evang. T.* III. 180 Those honest and warrantable recreations, which are of good report among the Saints. **1729** BUTLER *Serm.* Wks. 1874 II. 23 The natural disposition,..to do what is of good report. **1784** COWPER *Task* VI. 813 Her report has travell'd forth Into all lands. **1784** —— *Tiroc.* 459 Of chief and most approved report. **1871** SMILES *Charac.* vii. 195 He had no regard for popularity, but held to his purpose, through good and through evil report.

2. a. An account brought by one person to another, esp. of some matter specially investigated.

c **1410** *Master of Game* (MS. Digby 182) xxxii, EueryChone shall sey his reporte to þe lorde of þat þei haue done and y-founde. *c* **1430** *Syr Gener.* (Roxb.) 5620 Gwynet made noo tariyng But bare the report with glad tithing. **1494** FABYAN *Chron.* V. lxxix. 57 After report to hym brought of the said Espyes that the countre was fertyll and ryche. **1667** MILTON *P.L.* V. 869 This report, These tidings carrie to th'anointed King. **1742** YOUNG *Nt. Th.* II. 377 'Tis greatly wise to..ask them, what Report they bore to Heav'n. **1833** HT. MARTINEAU *Manch. Strike* xi. 120 The messengers appeared..and delivered in their report, which was brief enough.

b. Without article, in phrase ***to make report*** (†also = to make answer).

1534 CROMWELL in Merriman *Life & Lett.* (1902) I. 385 Therof shal I not faile to make true raport to his Highnes. **1560** DAUS tr. *Sleidane's Comm.* 102 b, The Duke and the Lantgrave had made reporte agayne, howe they misliked not the treaty. **1582** N. T. (Rhem.) *Matt.* ii. 8 When you shal finde him, make reporte to me. *c* **1683** WALLER *On St. James's Park* Wks. (1729) 208 Sea-nymphs..From Thetis sent as spies, to make report. **1859** TENNYSON *Marr. Geraint* 756 When Yniol made report Of that good mother making Enid gay.

c. A formal statement of the results of an investigation, or of any matter on which definite information is required, made by some person or body instructed or required to do so.

1661 BLOUNT *Glossogr.* (ed. 2), *Report*, is a Relation of the opinion or judgement of a Referree, upon any case or difference referred to his consideration by a Court of Justice, most commonly the Chancery. *a* **1715** BURNET *Own Time* I. (1715) I. 41 Upon his refusal the rest of the Committee did not think fit to sign the report. **1769** *Junius Lett.* iii. (1788) 47 The reports of the reviewing generals comprehend only a few regiments in England. **1781** *New Ann. Reg.* II. 166/1 The Report of the Commissioners for examining, taking, and stating the Public Accounts of this Kingdom. **1802** JAMES *Milit. Dict.* s.v., Reports of cavalry are given in to the senior generals of cavalry. **1833** *Act 3 & 4 Will. IV*, c. 52 §2 That no Goods shall be unladen from any ship..before due Report of such Ship..shall have been made. **1876** VOYLE & STEVENSON *Milit. Dict.* 89/1 The Queen's Regulations afford..all information as to the preparation of confidential reports.

d. In Parliamentary practice, the account of a bill, etc., given to the House by the Committee appointed to consider it.

1628 [see REPORTER 1 c]. **1724** (*title*) The Report of the Committee of the Lords of..Privy-Council..relating to Mr. Wood's Half-pence. **1817** *Parl. Debates* 1528 The Report of the Committee appointed to inquire into this subject was presented. **1886** *Pall Mall G.* 2 July 11/2 When the bill came down to the House..it should be merely subjected to what is called report—that is, the intermediate stage between the second and third reading.

e. A teacher's official statement in writing about the work and behaviour of a pupil at a school.

1873 C. M. YONGE *Life J. C. Patteson* I. i. 16 The half-yearly reports often lament his want of zeal and exertion. **1906** R. BROOKE *Let.* 1 Apr. (1968) 47 My term's report..has come in, & is very bad. Result: the family are shocked. **1973** 'M. INNES' *Appleby's Answer* ii. 19 It was a mark I'm simply bound in conscience to put into a pupil's report.

3. a. A statement made by a person; an account, more or less formal, *of* some person or thing. Also ***to make report***, to give information.

c **1412** HOCCLEVE *De Reg. Princ.* 1709 þe gipcians faste behelden here, And of hire beaute maden þei report To pharao. *c* **1420** LYDG. *Assembly of Gods* 204 When Apollo had herd the report Of Pluto, in a maner smylyng he seyde. *c* **1475** *Babees Bk.* 203 For the tyme is shorte, I putte theym nouhte in this lytyl Reporte. **1551** BP. GARDINER *Explic. Cath. Faith* 24 b, So as the report made here of the doctrine of the Catholique churche..is a very true reporte. **1591** SHAKS. *Two Gent.* III. ii. 57 We know (on Valentines report) You are already loues firme votary. **1617** MORYSON *Itin.* I. 53, I..mention this from their report, rather then from my iudgement. **1633** BP. HALL *Hard Texts, N.T.* 30 Do not make report of this my glorious transfiguration to any man whomsoever. **1784** COWPER *Task* II. 6 My soul is sick with every day's report Of wrong and outrage.

†**b.** Testimony *to*, or commendation of, a person or quality. *Obs. rare.*

1588 SHAKS. *L.L.L.* II. i. 64 Much too little of that good I saw, Is my report to his great worthinesse. *c* **1600** —— *Sonn.* lxxxiii, And therefore have I slept in your report.

c. *Law.* A formal account of a case argued and determined in any court, giving the important points in the pleadings, evidence, etc. Freq. in *pl.*

'The reports contain a statement of the facts, a short outline of the arguments made use of by counsel, the authorities referred to, and the decision of the court' (McCulloch).

[**1600** ASHE (*title*) Le Table al lievr des Reportes del tresreuerend Iudge Sir Ia. Dyer.] **1617** *Act 15 Jas. I* in Rymer *Fœdera* (1717) XVII. 27 They shall alwaies attend the Judges of such Courts where the Judgments..shall passe with their Reports, to the ende they maie be..reviewed by the said Judges before they be published. **1628**

COKE *On Litt.* 293 Report..in the Common Law.. signifieth a publike relation..[of] Cases iudicially argued [etc.]. **1670** *Moral State Eng.* 59 Every Term bringeth forth a collection of new Reports. *a* **1734** NORTH *Life Ld. Keeper North* (1742) I. 20 Now..every ordinary Practiser publisheth his Reports as he pleaseth..And thus the Shelves are loaded with Reports. **1765** BLACKSTONE *Comm.* I. Introd. 71 The reports are extant in a regular series from the reign of king Edward the second inclusive. **1841** *Penny Cycl.* XIX. 402/2 The earliest reports extant are the 'Year-books'.

attrib. **1650** *Pub. Gen. Acts* 1097 The Parliament have thought fit to..Enact.., That all the Report-Books of the Resolutions of Judges, and other Books of the Law of England shall be translated into the English Tongue.

d. An account, more or less complete, of the statements made by a speaker or speakers (as in a debate, lecture, etc.), of the proceedings at a meeting, or of any occurrence or event, *esp.* such an account noted down with a view to publication in a special form or in the newspaper press.

1812 J. H. LEWIS *Ready Writer* Introd. 16 The art by which they may follow the most rapid speakers, and afterwards read their own reports and memorandums with correctness and facility. **1861** MAY *Const. Hist.* I. 429 When the fear of punishment was abated, the reports became more systematic; and were improved in character and copiousness. **1865** 'OUIDA' *Strathmore* i, Very few of them [*sc.* ladies] would relish the chit-chat about them if they'd correct reports from the club-windows and short-hand notes from the smoking-rooms.

e. A statement in which an accusation is made against (a sailor, etc.); the charge itself; esp. in phr. ***on report***, on a charge.

1850 H. MELVILLE *White Jacket* II. xxxviii. 246 The names of such offenders shall be put down on the report. **1915** *Recruiter's Bull.* (U.S. Marine Corps., N.Y.) June 17/2, I was in that Corps for fifteen years and never saw a man on report. **1948** PARTRIDGE *Dict. Forces' Slang* 154 *In the report*, a colloquial synonym of 'in the *rattle*'. (Navy.) **1963** T. & P. MORRIS *Pentonville* vi. 126 When an officer observes a prisoner committing an offence he must decide whether or not to place the prisoner on Governor's Report. .. Reports are heard on every day except Sundays and public holidays. **1969** *Punch* 5 Mar. 350/2 We're just coming up to the conference point with my sergeant, fifteen hundred hours outside Queensway tube. I'll be on report if he catches me exceeding three miles per hour.

f. ***weather report***: see WEATHER *sb.* 6 a.

†**4.** The act of saying or uttering. *Obs.*⁻¹

1548 GEST *Pr. Masse* B j b, After thee due reporte, and vtterance of thee sayde wordes..they be consecrate.

†**5.** Relation, reference, bearing, connexion. Also const. *to*. *Obs. rare.*

1523 LD. BERNERS *Froiss.* Author's Pref. I. 2, I trust I haue ensewed the true reporte of the sentence of the mater. **1672** EVELYN *Diary* 25 Sept., The kitchen and stables are ill-placed, and the corridore worse, having no report to the wings they joyne to. **1727–38** CHAMBERS *Cycl.* s.v. *Pinion*, Pinion of report is that pinion, in a watch, which is commonly fixed on the arbor of the great wheel.

†**6. a.** *Mus.* A response; a note or part answering to or repeating another; loosely, a note, a musical sound. Also *attrib.* *Obs.*

1502 DOUGLAS *Pal. Hon.* I. xli, Fresche ladyis sang in voice virgineall Concordis sweit, diuers entoned reportis. **1549** *Compl. Scot.* vi. 37 There vas mony smal birdis.. singand melodius reportis of natural music. *Ibid.* 64 In melodius music, in gude accorddis and reportis of dyapason. **1576** GASCOIGNE *Phil.* Wks. K iij b, Hir second note..she did in pleasant wise repeate With sweet reports, of heauenly harmonie. **1592** R. D. *Hypnerotomachia* 37 The aunswerable sounde and delectable report of a warbeling harpe. **1626** BACON *Sylva* §113 The Reports and Fuges, have an Agreement with the Figures in Rhetorick, of Repetition and Traduction. **1646** CRASHAW *Musick's Duell* Wks. (1904) 119 There stood she listning, and did entertaine The musick's soft report. **1662** PLAYFORD *Skill Mus.* I. (1674) 59 This Mood that is so commixt with fancy and Airy reports, one part after other.

attrib. **1600** N. BRETON in *England's Helicon* B b j, A Report Song..betweene a Sheepheard and his Nimph.

†**b.** *Rhet.* = ANAPHORA (see quot.). *Obs.*

1589 PUTTENHAM *Eng. Poesie* III. xix. (Arb.) 208 Repetition in the first degree we call the figure of Report according to the Greeke originall, and is when we make one word begin..many verses in sute.

7. a. A resounding noise, *esp.* that caused by the discharge of fire-arms or explosives.

1590 GREENE *Never too late* (1600) 91 Like lightning, or the flash That runnes before the hote report of thunder. **1623** BINGHAM *Xenophon, Lipsius' Comp.* V iij, They would at the first haue feared the shew and reports of our Peeces. **1660** F. BROOKE tr. *Le Blanc's Trav.* 233 They are.. timorous beyond imagination, trembling at the report of a gun. **1700** DRYDEN *Ceyx & Alcyone* 139 in *Fables* 366 The lashing Billows make a loud report. **1773** COOK *Voy.* (1790) I. 177 They keep time with such exactness, that 60 or 100 paddles..make only a single report. **1820** W. IRVING *Sketch Bk.* II. 254 The report of a distant gun would perhaps be heard from the solitary woodland. **1871** TYNDALL *Frag. Sci.* (1879) I. x. 319 They..exploded with a very loud report in the air.

b. In fire-works, a charge which makes a loud noise when exploded; a case containing this.

1799 G. SMITH *Laboratory* I. 28 You may also glue on every end of the rockets, a report of paper. **1888** W. H. BROWNE *Firework Making* 15 Furnishing the squib with its report is called bouncing.

8. *attrib.* and *Comb.*, as ***report sheet, stage***; **report card**, (*a*) *U.S.*, a document comprising a school report; also *attrib.* and *transf.*; (*b*) *Austral.* (see quot. 1969).

1929 W. FAULKNER *Sound & Fury* 223 But to have the school authorities think that I have no control over her, that ..I didn't even know she had a *report card. **1952** B. ULANOV *Hist. Jazz in Amer.* (1958) xvii. 202 He set up a rating system for bands, based on the report-card letters A to D. **1953** *Manch. Guardian Weekly* 12 Nov. 2/1 The Republicans would be less doleful this morning if they had not seconded so volubly the Democrats' contention that these four elections would constitute 'a report card' on the Eisenhower Administration. **1969** EAGLESON & MCKIE *Terminology Austral. Nat. Football* III. 7 *Report card*, a card on which at the termination of a match, umpires record particulars of any charge(s) they may make against players. **1977** *Time* 22 Aug. 11/3 Carter's early forcefulness..drove six Latin countries..to reject U.S. military assistance rather than agree to prepare 'report cards' for Washington on human rights. **1980** L. ST. CLAIR *Obsessions* xi. 195 Erin's baby bootees, her silver food pusher, her first report card. **1957** C. SMITH *Case of Torches* xiv. 189 He wrote it all down. .. He doodled on his *report sheet. **1966** P. O'DONNELL *Sabre Tooth* i. 7 His report-sheet shows that he was a good man. **1906** FREEMAN & ABBOTT *A.B.C. of Parliamentary Procedure* 74 Reports from Committee of the Whole House. ('*Report Stage'.)—When a Bill is committed *pro formâ* to enable the member in charge to introduce numerous amendments..the Bill so amended is reported and recommitted for a future day. **1976** *Liverpool Echo* 6 Dec. 5/8 We expect concessions to be made during the committee and report stages of the Bill.

report (rɪˈpɔət), *v.* [a. OF. and AF. *reporter*:—L. *reportāre*, f. *re-* RE- + *portāre* to carry. The prominent uses in Eng. however are expressed in OF. by *raporter* (mod.F. *rapporter*): cf. REPORT *sb.*]

I. *trans.* **1. a.** To relate, narrate, tell, give an account of (a fact, event, etc.). Also const. *to* a person. Now somewhat *rare*.

c **1386** CHAUCER *Sqr.'s T.* 64 Ther nys no man that may reporten al. *c* **1386** —— *Epil. Merch. T.* 17 And I sholde rekenen euery vice Which þat she hath,..it sholde reported be And told to hire. *c* **1420** LYDG. *Assembly of Gods* 1486 When I came in I meruelyd gretly of that I behelde & herde there reporte. *c* **1450** LOVELICH *Grail* xlii. 237 Nasciens to hym gan to Reporte In to whiche diuers Contre he gan Resorte. **1500–20** DUNBAR *Poems* xxxii. 69 This report I with my pen, How at Dumfermling fell the cace. **1509** HAWES *Past. Pleas.* XIII. (Percy Soc.) 52, I must procede, and shew of Arismetrik With divers nombres which I must reporte. **1573** G. HARVEY *Letter-bk.* (Camden) 10 If I shuld report and repeat al your wurship miht think me far wurs abusid. **1604** E. G[RIMSTONE] *D'Acosta's Hist. Indies* III. ix. 144 It were a very difficult matter, to report particularly the admirable effectes which some windes cause. **1634** MILTON *Comus* 127 'Tis onely day-light that makes Sin Which these dun shades will ne're report. **1667** —— *P.L.* VI. 21 He.. found Already known what he for news had thought To have reported. **1859** TENNYSON *Elaine* 625 Came the Lord of Astolat out, to whom the Prince Reported who he was. **1883** *Century Mag.* Oct. 927/2 'Outre-Mer', a young poet's sketch-book, reports his first transition from cloister life to travel and experience.

b. Const. *that* or *inf.* Freq. in passive in phr. ***it is reported***, it is commonly said or stated.

1460 CAPGRAVE *Chron.* (Rolls) 139 It is eke reported that Seint Bernard schuld sey the same of this King Henry. **1535** COVERDALE *Ps.* lxxxvi. 5 Of Sion it shall be reported, that he was borne in her. **1542** UDALL *Erasm. Apoph.* 58 There been that reporten hym in this wise to haue aunswered. **1582** N.T. (Rhem.) *Rom.* iii. 8 As we are blasphemed, and as some report us to say. **1606** SHAKS. *Ant. & Cl.* I. iv. 67 On the Alpes, It is reported thou did'st eate strange flesh. **1665** MANLEY *Grotius' Low C. Warres* 431 Both parts reported the number of the slain, to be greater than it was. **1686** tr. *Chardin's Coronat. Solyman* 84 It is reported the Employments which he supply'd..brought into the Chequer a Million sterling yearly. **1819** L. HUNT *Indicator* No. 8 (1822) I. 63 The author says that he has heard it reported..that the fourth Duke of Braganza [etc.]. **1856** FROUDE *Hist. Eng.* (1858) II. vii. 187 The refugee friars.. were reported to be well supplied with money from England.

†**c.** To give an account of (a person), to describe. *Obs.*

1602 SHAKS. *Ham.* V. ii. 350 Report me and my causes right To the vnsatisfied. **1607** —— *Cor.* V. iv. 27 *Men.* He wants nothing of a God but Eternity... *Sicin.* Yes, mercy, if you report him truly. **1635** HEYLIN *Sabbath* I. (1636) 163 Saint Augustine so reports him in his sixt Book *de civitate*.

refl. **1611** SHAKS. *Cymb.* II. iv. 83 The Chimney-peece [is] Chaste Dian, bathing: neuer saw I figures So likely to report themselues.

2. a. To carry, convey, or repeat (something said, a message, etc.) *to* another. Also without const.

a **1400–50** *Alexander* 2414 A lettir he fourmed, In presidine with his awen prince reportand þa wordis. **1490** CAXTON *Eneydos* lii. 146 Nowe goo youre waye, & reporte to the kynge that that I haue saide. **1513** DOUGLAS *Æneis* IV. viii. 61 Hir supplication, with teris full vnglaid, Reportis hir sister, and answere brocht agane. **1560** DAUS tr. *Sleidane's Comm.* 287 b, I wyll reporte this tale unto Duke Maurice. **1667** MILTON *P.L.* XII. 237 The voice of God To mortal eare is dreadful; they beseech That Moses might report to them his will. **1781** COWPER *Truth* 205 Tom.., swift as an express, Reports a message with a pleasing grace. **1870** BRYANT *Iliad* II. xv. 81 Report my words To royal Neptune, and report them right.

b. To repeat (something heard); to relate as having been spoken by another.

c **1440** *Promp. Parv.* 430/1 Reportyn', or bere a-wey thynge þat hathe be seyde or tawȝte, *reporto*. **1530** PALSGR. 687/1, I reporte a thinge agayne, I make rehersall of it, as I herde it, *je fays rapport*. *a* **1548** HALL *Chron., Hen. VIII* 260 b, The kyng hymself made hym answere, as foloweth woorde for woorde, as nere as I was able to report it. **1589** PUTTENHAM *Eng. Poesie* III. xix. (Arb.) 242 We are sometimes occasioned in our tale to report some speech from another mans mouth. **1638** BAKER tr. *Balzac's Lett.* (vol. II) 176 You would aske mee newes, in a time, when reporting it is dangerous. **1671** MILTON *Samson* 1350 He's gone, and who knows how he may report Thy words by adding fuel to the flame? **1845** WHATELY *Rhet.* in *Encycl. Metrop.* I. 296/1 It is desirable that he should deliver them as if he were reporting another's sentiments. **1853** M. ARNOLD *Scholar Gypsy* 90 None hath words she can report of thee.

c. *spec.* To take down (a law-case, speech, discussion, etc.) in writing, now esp. with a view to publication in a newspaper; to prepare a written account of (any meeting, event, etc.). Also *absol.*

1600 ASHE *Table Reportes de Sir J. Dyer* Note, The yeere of the Kings and Queenes raigne in which [the case] is reported. *a* **1617** BACON *Amend. Laws Eng.* Wks. 1730 IV. 6 Cases reported with too great a prolixity, would be drawn into a more compendious report. *a* **1734** NORTH *Life Ld. Keeper North* (1742) I. 34 [He] followed his studies very close, and attended the Courts at Westminster, and reported diligently. **1840** *Penny Cycl.* XVI. 195/2 Others are engaged to report the trials in the courts of law. *Ibid.*, The manner in which the parliamentary proceedings are reported. **1861** *Sat. Rev.* 21 Dec. 631/2 Still less can a country reporter.. accurately report lectures on all subjects indiscriminately. He cannot report, because he does not understand. **1891** *N. & Q.* 26 Dec. 504/1 If Mr. Goschen was correctly reported, ..he spoke thus.

d. To say factually. Also with direct speech as object.

1929 M. A. GILL *Underworld Slang* 15/1 Words that can be used in place of..'said'..Reported. **1977** B. FREEMANTLE *Charlie Muffin* iv. 45 'Completely misread the interview,' he reported.

3. a. To give in or render a formal account or statement of or concerning (some matter or thing); to make a formal report on; to state (something) in such a report. Also with *back*. Phr. ***to report out*** (a bill), of a committee of Congress: to return (a bill) to the legislative body for debate.

1580 *Reg. Privy Council Scot.* III. 280 In cais ony variance result,..than sall they report..the mater and point quhairin the variance standis. **1667** *12th Rep. Hist. MSS. Comm.* App. V. 8 They passed the Bill, as the Committee,..and ordered it to be reported the next day. **1780** *Act* in *New Ann. Reg.* (1781) II. 166/1 That the commissioners..do forthwith report to this house what progress they have made. *a* **1781** in Simes *Milit. Guide* (ed. 3) 9 Taking care to keep an exact roster, that one may not report more than another. **1833** *Act 3 & 4 Will. IV*, c. 52 §2 All goods not duly reported..shall be forfeited. **1855** J. R. LEIFCHILD *Cornwall Mines* 184 The engines which are to be 'reported', that is, to have their duty published once a month. **1863** H. COX *Instit.* I. ix. 167 At the close of a committee of the House of Commons on a bill, the chairman reports the bill forthwith to the House. **1872** RAYMOND *Statist. Mines & Mining* 97 The superintendent reports 24,303 tons of ore taken from the mine during the year. **1883** *Rep. U.S. Bureau Indian Affairs* p. xxiv, The bill as read and referred was reported back by the Senate Committee. **1948** *Sun* (Baltimore) 31 May 8/2 The bill recently was reported out favorably by the House Armed Services Committee. **1965** MRS. L. B. JOHNSON *White House Diary* 10 Apr. (1970) 257 The Committee reported out the Civil Rights Bill, quicker and stronger than ever expected. **1976** *N.Y. Rev. Bks.* 15 Apr. 20/3 The Senate Antitrust Sub-committee may well report out a 'vertical divestiture' bill, which will then go before the full Judiciary Committee. **1976** *Daily Tel.* 25 Sept. 10/4 The society..has arranged for its ticket selling committee to meet next Tuesday to report back their ideas to the society. **1979** *Sci. Amer.* July 68/3 The bill was reported out of committee, but when it was pointed out that enforcing such a statute would cost money and that the bill should be referred to the appropriations committee, support waned and the bill did not come to a vote.

b. To relate, state, or notify (something) as the result of special observation or investigation; to bring in a report of (something observed).

1631 T. POWELL *Tom All Trades* 45 If the Herald report him a Gentleman. **1633** HEYWOOD *Eng. Trav.* II. i, One.. Climbs by the bedpost to the tester, there Reports a turbulent sea and a tempest towards. **1776** *Trial of Nundocomar* 32/1 On my return, I reported to the Chief Justice in court that I did not think it safe. **1781** COWPER *Conversat.* 386 Each individual..Reports it hot or cold, or wet or dry. **1836** MARRYAT *Midsh. Easy* xxxiv, The next morning the packet from England was reported off the harbour's mouth. **1837** W. IRVING *Capt. Bonneville* II. 148 He would..return, and report what he had seen to his companions. **1859** LANG *Wand. India* 275 My friend.. requested the sowars to follow them, and report all they might observe of their actions.

c. To name (a person) to a superior authority as having offended in some way.

1885 *Law Times* LXXX. 4/2 The master..could only report the claimant and could not suspend or dismiss him.

d. *refl.* To make known to some authority that one has arrived or is present at a certain place.

1802 JAMES *Milit. Dict.* s.v., Every officer on his arrival.. must report himself to the governor. **1841** CATLIN *N. Amer. Ind.* xxxvii. (1844) II. 37 Having obtained permission to accompany the regiment..I reported myself at this place. **1867** SMYTH *Sailor's Word-bk.* 569 *To Report one's self*, when an officer returns on board from duty, or from leave of absence.

transf. **1837** CARLYLE *Fr. Rev.* III. I. i, This rising in La Vendée reports itself at Paris on Wednesday the 29th of August. **1876** MELLOR *Priesth.* iv. 174 The miracles..were changes which reported themselves to one sense at least.

II. *intr.* or *absol.* **4.** †**a.** To make a report *of*, to give an account *of*, to speak or talk in a certain way *of*, a person or thing. *Obs.*

1432–50 tr. *Higden* (Rolls) VI. 467 Of whom hit was seide that Kynadius kynge of Scottes scholde reporte in this wise. **1461** *Paston Lett.* II. 30 The seyd Will reportyth of yow as shamfully as he can. **1494** FABYAN *Chron.* 2 Of Fraunce and other I myght lyke wyse reporte To theyr great honour. **1535** COVERDALE *1 Tim.* v. 10 Soch one as was..well reported of in good workes. **1589** PUTTENHAM *Eng. Poesie* III. xix. (Arb.) 233 Many times our Poet is caried by some occasion to report of a thing that is maruelous. **1601** SHAKS. *All's Well* III. v. 60 There is a Gentleman that serues the Count, Reports but coursely of her.

b. To act as a (newspaper) reporter.

1850 in OGILVIE. **1888** L. STEPHEN in *Dict. Nat. Biog.* XV. 21/1 For two sessions he reported for the 'Mirror of Parliament'.

5. a. To make report (*on* a person or thing); †to relate, state.

a **1450** *Knt. de la Tour* (1868) 16 Thei toke her leue and yode into Inglond, and reported as thei hadd founde bi the doughtres. **1533** FRITH *Answ. More* Wks. (1829) 344, I dare say that ye untruly report on us all. *a* **1548** HALL *Chron., Edw. IV* 7 He graunted lycence..for certayn cottesolde sheepe to be transported into..Spayne (as people report). **1596** SHAKS. *1 Hen. IV*, II. iv. 456 This Pitch (as ancient Writers doe report) doth defile. **1607** —— *Cor.* II. ii. 36 To report otherwise, were a Mallice. **1671** J. WEBSTER *Metallogr.* vi. 93 By plowing or accidental digging: as Gold was found in Galecia as Justin reporteth. **1883** GILMOUR *Mongols* xvii. 203 Has any one among us..seen these things, and come back to life to report on them?

b. To make or draw up, to give in or submit, a formal report. Also used in less formal contexts of a journalist or broadcaster. Phr. ***to report back***: to return with a formal report (*to* one's principal).

1628 *Jrnls. Ho. Comm.* I. 905/1 They desire a present Conference..about the great Business... Mr. Glanvyle, Mr. Selden [etc.] to report. **1802** JAMES *Milit. Dict.* s.v., General officers report to the commander in chief only. **1828–32** WEBSTER s.v., The committee will report at twelve o'clock. **1961** *Providence* (Rhode Island) *Jrnl.* 20 July 5 He would study the correct method and report back to the council. **1966** *Rep. Comm. Inquiry Univ. Oxf.* I. 271 An inferior body receives its policy from the superior body and can then be told to do its work and decide within the limits of the policy laid down, only reporting back in cases of real doubt or difficulty. **1968** *Listener* 21 Nov. 667/1 That resolution gave us only 70 hours to report back to the Assembly on the organisation of the force. **1971** *Guardian* 19 Mar. 22/3 The good and bad of compensation: Judy Hillman and Malcolm Stuart report on page six. **1974** *Radio Times* 28 Feb. 35/2 What does a holiday cruise offer you? *Gladys Nicol* reports. *Ibid.* 35/5 The World Tonight: News —Douglas Stuart reporting.

c. To report one's self. (See 3 d.) Also with *in*.

1864 in WEBSTER. **1885** U. S. GRANT *Mem.* I. iii. 45 On the 30th of September I reported for duty at Jefferson Barracks. **1891** *Law Times* XCI. 247/2 The goods were to be applied for within twenty-four hours of the ship's arrival and reporting at the Custom-house. **1969** I. KEMP *Brit. G.I. in Vietnam* viii. 159 'I'm reporting in,' I told him, handing over my orders. **1977** D. BEATY *Excellency* viii. 99 He murmured something about having to report in at the African Airways counter.

III. *trans.* †**6. a.** *refl.* To betake (oneself) for support, to appeal *to* a person or thing. Cf. REFER *v.* 5. *Obs.* (common *c* 1480–1640).

c **1410** *Master of Game* (MS. Digby 182) xxxiii, Of þe whiche y reporte me to þe olde statutes and custumes of þe kynges house. **1450** *Rolls of Parlt.* V. 182/1 As for the Article ..he reporteth hym to the Act that is made theruppon. **1477** EARL RIVERS (Caxton) *Dictes* 23 Reporte the to the moost holsome opynion of all thy counseyllours. **1503** HAWES *Examp. Virt.* VIII. v, She is both good eke fayre and pure As I report me vnto dame Nature. **1579** FULKE *Heskins' Parl.* 405 There is no such Hebrue worde,..as I report mee to all that haue but meane knowledge in the tongue. **1601** HOLLAND *Pliny* II. 297 For farther proofe..I report me to euery mans conscience. **1639** FULLER *Holy War* v. xvii. (1647) 258, I report myself to any that have not the pearl of prejudice in the eye of their judgement.

†**b.** Without const. *Obs. rare.*

c **1485** *Digby Myst.* (1882) IV. 133, I reporte me; your-self behold & see! **1544** BALE *Chron. Sir J. Oldcastle* 51 b, How wele these two wrytynges agre, I report me.

†**c.** To refer *to*, esp. for information. *Obs.*

c **1520** BARCLAY *Jugurtha* 17 b, Touchynge the very credence of the truthe of the mater I reporte that to the authours. **1556** *Aurelio & Isab.* (1608) F j, The merite of this dissimulede annestey unto the feare..oughte to be reportede. **1639** FULLER *Holy War* II. xxxviii. (1647) 94 We report the reader to the character of King Almerick.

†**7. a.** To bring or convey; to carry (news). *Obs.*

c **1489** CAXTON *Blanchardyn* 6 How a knyght wounded cam & reported tydynges to ye kynge of maryenborough. **1590** SPENSER *F.Q.* II. i. 33 Well mote yee thee..That home ye may report thrise happy newes. *Ibid.* x. 3 If some relish of that hevenly lay His learned daughters would to me report To decke my song withall.

†**b.** *Sc.* To bring in, bring in return; also of persons, to obtain, get for oneself. *Obs.*

1508 CADION *Porteous Noblenes* in *Compl. Scot.* (1801) 205 Gudis hid, report bot litill thanke, joy, or pleseir. **1571–2** *Reg. Privy Council Scot.* II. 128 His said schip..wilbe allutirlie wrakkit..; swa that he nor the awnaris of the same will report na commoditie thairby. **1579** *Ibid.* III. 249 Be sic indirect meanis tending to report thankis be making of sum wrang report. **1614** FORBES *Comm. Rev.* Ded., For that of your Maiesties knowne clemencie, I am certaine to report either praise or pardon.

†**8. a.** To utter, pronounce; to bring forward, produce, show. *Obs. rare.*

1548 GEST *Pr. Masse* B j b, The bread & wyne..were profane & vnholy, before the wordes of the institution of the sayd supper were duely reported upon them. *Ibid.* G j b, Thys partecle..as it is a pronone relatyve..therfor reporteth, declareth, & respecteth hys antecedent. **1569** *Reg. Privy Council Scot.* I. 684 Quhill the complenar satisfie the Kirk and report the superintendentis testimoniall thairupoun. *a* **1617** BAYNE *On Eph.* (1658) 64 Honour serveth to report our reverent respect to God.

†**b.** To involve or imply. *Obs. rare*$^{-1}$.

1565 JEWEL *Repl. Harding* (1611) 342 Which maner not reporting any vntruth, S. Basil doth excuse.

†**c.** *intr.* ? To be present. *Obs. rare*$^{-1}$.

1560 *Proude Wives Paternost.* 524 in Hazl. *E.P.P.* IV. 175 Our soules from synne to preserue clere, That the flame of charyte in vs reporte.

†**9. a.** To cause to re-echo or resound. *Obs. rare.*

c **1586** C'TESS PEMBROKE *Ps.* LXXXI. ii, Lett trumpetts tunes report his praise. **1673** [R. LEIGH] *Transp. Reh.* 137 Sighing to the winds, and calling upon the woods, not forgetting to report his mistresses name so often.

†**b.** To send back, re-echo (a sound). *Obs. rare.*

1589 R. ROBINSON *Gold. Mirr.* (1851) 12 The ragged hills and rocky towers reporte, By Ecchoes voyce, the quest of Noble hounds. **1626** BACON *Sylva* §249 If you speak three Words, it will (perhaps) some three times report you the whole three Words.

†**c.** To fire (a gun); to be the cause or occasion of firing. *Obs. rare.*

1592 STOW *Ann.* (1601) 1436 The Castell discharged fiftie canon, and the king of Englands ship lying before the castell, reported as many... Euery health reported sixe, eight, or ten shot of great Ordinance.

10. To fit (a fire-work) with a report.

1873 E. SPON *Workshop Receipts* Ser. I. 133/2 On each of the five spokes tie a case of brilliant fire, reported at its end. **1888** W. H. BROWNE *Firework Making* 43 The saucissons having been all reported, proceed to 'dub in' the ends.

Hence **re'ported** *ppl. a.* Also **re'portedly** *adv.*, according to report.

1812 J. H. LEWIS *Ready Writer* Introd. 12 All the characteristic peculiarities of thought and expression that distinguish the reported speeches of a Chatham and a Tooke. **1846** MCCULLOCH *Brit. Empire* (1854) II. 162 Every year adds three or four more [volumes], exclusively of the reported cases in equity. **1881** BRADLEY *Arnold's Latin Prose* lxv, Reported speeches in *Oratio Obliqua.* **1901** 'LUCAS MALET' *Sir R. Calmady* IV. i, The picture of those reportedly gownless backs had depressed him abominably. **1958** *Times* 28 Nov. 13/6 Some chance remarks reportedly made by Prince Akihito..sent the match-makers searching farther afield. **1959** *Listener* 6 Aug. 199/1 He was..strongly criticized for reportedly kissing an African woman in public. **1972** *New Yorker* 4 Mar. 85/1 What their constituents have said to them since reportedly is not appreciative. **1979** *Time* 2 Apr. 31/1 This probe reportedly is ready to produce indictments against the man that Carter made director of the Office of Management and Budget.

reporta'bility. [f. REPORTABLE *a.*: see -ITY.] The quality or state of being reportable.

1960 BRUNER & KLEIN in J. S. Bruner *Beyond Information Given* (1974) vii. 119 The work of Blackwell in America, and of Dixon in England, suggests strongly that the reportability of a stimulus or awareness of a subject depends upon the nature of response alternatives.

reportable (rɪˈpɔətəb(ə)l), *a.* [f. REPORT *v.* + -ABLE.] **1.** Capable or worthy of being reported.

1858 CARLYLE *Fredk. Gt.* x. v. (1872) III. 251 One of the few reportable points of his Reinsburg life. **1884** *Law Times* LXXVII. 157/1 To distinguish at a glance whether a case is reportable or not.

2. That should or must be reported to some authority.

1942 L. D. KITCHIN *Road Transport Law* 29/1 No notice need be given..for a test and inspection to be conducted within 48 hours of a 'reportable' accident in which the vehicle has been involved. **1976** *Sci. Amer.* Oct. 28/3 Smallpox was made a reportable disease. **1976** G. THURSTON *Coronership* iii. 54 Death in custody in a police station is not, strictly, reportable unless it is unnatural or of unknown cause.

reportage (rɪˈpɔətɪdʒ, ‖ rəpɔrtaʒ). [f. as prec. + -AGE; in sense 2, a. F. *reportage* (Littré *Suppl.*).]

†**1.** Report, repute. *Obs. rare*$^{-1}$.

1612 WEBSTER *White Devil* III. iii, For usurers, That share with scriveners for their good reportage.

2. Reported matter; gossip.

1881 *Academy* 5 Nov. 347/2 He will interest the lovers of personal detail by certain *reportage.* **1892** *Sat. Rev.* 25 June 738/2 Modern reportage-colporting gossips on the stage.

3. The describing of events (usu. by an observer); *spec.* the reporting of events for the press or for broadcasting, esp. with reference to its style; an instance of this, a piece of journalistic or factual writing. Also *transf.* and *attrib.*

1891 E. DOWSON *Let.* 7 Feb. (1967) 184 Howells..writes in dialect, in Yankee and that's not realism (even Zola doesn't go so far) it's reportage. **1931** *Times Lit. Suppl.* 19 Feb. 129/2 Ludwig's works written before the war, plays, novels, *reportage.* **1938** C. CONNOLLY *Enemies of Promise* xvi. 173 The article has a future, especially in the form of the critical essay..and the skilled 'reportage'. **1942** E. PAUL *Narrow St.* xix. 155 What L'Hibou suggested..that Madame Absalom should do with her ears, had best be omitted from this reportage. **1954** KOESTLER *Invisible Writing* xv. 169 Németh's book was planned as a long psychological novel, Kuncz's book as a straightforward reportage. **1959** L.-H. LIANG tr. *Ting Yi's Short Hist. Mod. Chin. Lit.* x. 217 During the early period of the war of Resistance, reportage..became the most popular of all literary forms among both the writers and the broad reading public. **1961** *Listener* 28 Dec. 1125/3 Where *is* your black-and-white photograph without sun and sparkle?.. A big enough limitation, one would think, to render suspect almost any black and white reportage. **1963** *Movie* Apr. 12/1 The makers of documentary and reportage films. **1965** *Listener* 8 Apr. 535/1 In his fourth sonata..there was too little art (and craft) and too much *reportage.* **1969** *N.Y. Rev. Books* 2 Jan. 28/3 Reportages like his account of a journey through the Sudetenland as the Germans entered. **1978** *Poland* May 52/2 Young people need a confirmation of their knowledge about their own country.., and that..is precisely what they find in a realistic reportage. **1979** *London Rev. Bks.* 25 Oct. 8/4 His study of the Hyde Park orators might have been taken as a masterly piece of reportage.

†**re'portary.** *Obs. rare*$^{-1}$. [f. as prec. + -ARY[1].] = REPORTORY.

1594 (*title*) A true reportarie of the..royal accomplishment of the Baptisme of..Prince Frederick Henry.

†**repor'tation.** *Obs. rare*$^{-1}$. [f. L. *reportāre* to REPORT + -ATION. So obs. F. *reportation* (Godef.).] The fact of being carried back.

1647 LILLY *Chr. Astrol.* xlvii. 291 Hippocrates will have Crysis to be an acute or swift reportation in diseases, either to recovery or death.

reportative (rɪˈpɔətətɪv), *a.* [f. REPORT *v.* + -ATIVE.] That presents or introduces reported speech.

1973 *New Society* 6 Sept. 580/2 Containing in fact only one four letter word used in a reportative context. **1975** *Language* LI. 804 Normally, a sentence containing the quotative clitic translates with 'one says', 'they say', or 'it is said', i.e. a reportative verb having an unspecified subject.

reported, -edly: see REPORT *v.*

reporter (rɪˈpɔətə(r)). Also 4–5 -our(e, 6 -ar. [orig. a. AF. **reportour* = OF. *reporteur*, usually *raporteur* (mod.F. *rapporteur*): see REPORT *v.* In later use f. the vb. + -ER[1].]

1. a. One who reports or relates; a recounter or narrator. Now somewhat *rare* (common in 16–17th c.).

c **1386** CHAUCER *Prol.* 814 That he wolde been oure gouernour And of our tales Iuge and Reportour. **1421–2** HOCCLEVE *Dialog* 761 Ther-of was I noon Auctour; I was.. but a reportour Of folkes tales. **1477** EARL RIVERS (Caxton) *Dictes* 16 A reporter or contryuer of talys. **1553** T. WILSON *Rhet.* 63 b, That the reporter with more ease maie remember what he hath to saie. **1599** *Life Sir T. More* in Wordsw. *Eccl. Biog.* (1853) II. 107 The ouer hastie reporter of this blessed newes, repaires with speed to Sir Thomas. *a* **1633** AUSTIN *Medit.* (1635) 2 Saint Luke is the Reporter; and onely he of all the foure records this Story. **1686** WOOD *Life* 6 July (O.H.S.) III. 191 These people..were the chief reporters that the universities were all papists. **1726** SHELVOCKE *Voy. round World* Pref. 9 The malice and dishonest ways that are conceal'd in the breast of the reporter. **1837** HT. MARTINEAU *Soc. Amer.* II. 18 The reporters of this [mission] appear to be peculiarly imaginative. **1952** P. EDWARDS in *Shakespeare Survey* V. 35 If the 1609 Quarto of *Pericles* is reconstructed, or 'reported', we should infer, from the suggestion that two hands are at work on the manuscript, that the text was compiled by two 'reporters'.

b. With adj. denoting the character or intention of the account given.

1400 in *Roy. & Hist. Lett. Hen. IV* (Rolls) 37 Thu hast hadde fals messageres and fals reportoures of us touchyng this matere. **1559** in Strype *Ann. Ref.* (1709) I. viii. 116 Most humbly beseeching the Almighty God..to pardon and forgive our Persecutors and evil Reporters. **1577** PATERICKE tr. *Gentillet* 46 Slaunderers or false reporters, are like secret wounds. **1602** WARNER *Alb. Eng.* XIII. lxxvii. (1612) 318 Their best Reporters say, these Gods were made by men. **1800** HELENA WELLS *C. Neville* (ed. 2) III. 92 In spite of all malignant reporters, be assured [etc.].

c. One specially appointed to make or draw up a report, or to give information of something. Also (*Sc. Law*), one who receives reports (on juvenile offenders).

1625 in *Debates Ho. Comm.* (Camden) 93 A litle forme was left at the upper end of the table for the reporters. **1628** *Jrnls. Ho. Comm.* I. 905 The Report, now made, to be brought in Writing by the Reporters To-morrow Morning. **1796** NELSON 23 Aug. in Nicolas *Disp.* (1845) II. 251, I am in great fear my reporter is taken. **1835** in W. Bell *Dict. Law Scot.* (1838) 853 An accountant, engineer, or other reporter, to whom a remit may hereafter be made by the Court. **1890** 'R. BOLDREWOOD' *Col. Reformer* x, The 'reporter' entered the Garrandilla gate, to give legal notice of the invading army of fleece-bearing locusts. **1968** *Social Work (Scotland) Act* c. 49 s. 36(1) For the purpose of arranging children's hearings and for the performance of such other functions in relation to the children's panel or to children's hearings as may be assigned to him by this Part of this Act, a local authority shall, in accordance with the provisions of this section, appoint an officer, whole-time or part-time, to be known as the reporter. **1976** *Howard Jrnl.* XV. I. 31 The key figure in the new system is the reporter. It is his function to decide, on the basis of reports, whether the child referred to him by the police, social worker or education department is in 'need of compulsory measures of care'.

d. *U.S.* A dog which finds and reports the position of a covey of birds.

1895 *Westm. Gaz.* 12 Dec. 7/2 When a point was obtained, and the birds were fairly located,..the dog took his master right back to where the covey still lay crouched... Such animals are called 'reporters'.

2. a. One who takes down reports of law-cases.

a **1617** BACON *Amend. Laws Eng.* Wks. 1730 IV. 6 It resteth with your Majesty to appoint some sound lawyers.., with some honourable stipend, to be reporters for the time to come. **1617** *Act 15 Jas. I* in Rymer *Fœdera* (1717) XVII. 27 Wee doe ordaine..that, for all times hereafter, there shall be twoe Persons..which shall be Reporters of the Law. **1765** BLACKSTONE *Comm.* I. Introd. 73 Besides these reporters, there are also other authors, to whom great veneration and respect is paid by the students of the common law. **1818** CRUISE *Digest* (ed. 2) III. 383 Confirmed by the three other Justices in separate extrajudicial conferences with the reporter. **1841** *Penny Cycl.* XIX. 403/1 During the reign of Henry VIII.., Dyer, afterwards chief-justice of the Common Pleas, took notes as a reporter.

b. One who reports debates, speeches, meetings, etc., esp. for a newspaper; a person specially employed for this purpose. Also, one who does similar work for other kinds of journal, or for radio or television. Also ***reporter-at-large***.

1798 *Deb. Congress U.S.* 21 Mar. (1851) 1289 The House ought to render the reporters as independent.. as they could be. **1802** *Monthly Magazine* XIV. 160/1 Two cases have recently occurred within the sphere of the Reporter's observation. **1813** LD. MOIRA in *Examiner* 19 Apr. 254/1 The reporters are not allowed to make notes. **1814** J. H. LEWIS *Ready Writer* Introd. 13 The utility of Short-hand to the reporter of debates.. is in itself.. evident. **1832** BABBAGE *Econ. Manuf.* xxviii. (ed. 3) 269 The speeches must be taken down by reporters. **1882** A. W. WARD *Dickens* i. 9 His father .. was now seeking employment as a parliamentary reporter. **1946** M. MCCARTHY *Let.* in *Politics* Nov. 367/1 Mr. Hersey .. is *The New Yorker's* reporter-at-large. **1968** *Listener* 12 Sept. 322/2 Some of the strikers, including some sports reporters, had proposed a return to work... The radio reporters of *France-Inter* returned ten days later.. and TV reporters.. agreed to resume work in mid-July.

appos. **1834** *Tait's Mag.* I. 392/2 Those reporter whelps, I'm told, play the deuce with a new member where they take a spite.

c. In the titles of newspapers and periodical publications.

1797 (*title*) The reporter, or the general observer. **1853** (*title*) St. Helens newspaper and midweek reporter. **1870** (*title*) Cambridge University reporter. **1956** (*title*) Surrey county reporter. **1961** (*title*) Rating and valuation reporter.

†**3. a.** A kind of fire-work. **b.** A pistol. *Obs.*

1688 *Lond. Gaz.* No. 2362/3 Rockets, Runers on the Line, Wheels, Reporters,.. with all manner of other Fire-works were discharged. **1827** SIR J. BARRINGTON *Pers. Sk.* II. 36 Lord C—— had a tolerable chance of becoming acquainted with my friend's reporters (a pet name for hair-triggers). **1865** *Cornh. Mag.* XI. 166 In those days Irish gentlemen always carried their reporters or pistols with them.

4. *Chem.* In full ***reporter group***. A group whose spectroscopic properties are sensitive to its chemical environment and well characterized and which is used as a means of obtaining structural information about a system or molecule in which it occurs.

1970 *Nature* 21 Mar. 1103/1 The method is based on the anisotropy of signals from the nitroxide radical which thus acts as a 'reporter' of molecular motions (for example, whether the spin label is in a region of free or unrestricted movement). **1974** *Sci. Amer.* Mar. 31/1 The method involves attaching a 'reporter' group, usually a nitroxide group that has an unpaired electron, to one of the carbons of a test molecule's fatty-acid tail.

5. *attrib.*, in appositive use, and Comb., as ***reporter-director***, ***-material***, ***-photographer***, ***politician***, ***-researcher***; ***reporter-like*** adj.

1973 C. BONINGTON *Next Horizon* xx. 276 A complete film team of cameraman, sound-recordist, *reporter-director. **1909** C. S. PEIRCE *Let.* 14 Mar. in R. B. Perry *Tht. & Char. of W. James* (1935) II. 440 So it is reported by my rather *reporter-like memory. **1889** 'MARK TWAIN' *Connecticut Yankee* 108 It was my purpose.. to start a newspaper... So I wanted to.. be finding out what sort of *reporter-material I might be able to rake together. **1978** W. F. BUCKLEY *Stained Glass* ii. 15 One *reporter-photographer from *L'Humanité* pressed for admittance. **1894** G. B. SHAW *Let.* 2 Dec. (1965) I. 464 Surely so fine a spirit could have been rescued from the reproach of being.. an ignorantly contemptuous *reporter-politician? **1976** *Time* 27 Sept. 3/1 More than 70 *Time* correspondents, writers, *reporter-researchers and editors set out to assess the South as it is today.

Hence **re'porterize** *v.* (*nonce-wd.*); **re'portership**, the position or office of a reporter.

1881 *Athenæum* 22 Jan. 125/3 His college friendship.. obtained for him a reportership for that paper. **1885** *Law Times* LXXIX. 385/1 Mr. J. H. Fordham.. retired from his reportership in the Rolls Court on the death of his father. **1888** *Harper's Mag.* July 314 Our reporterized press is often truculently reckless of privacy and decency.

reporterage (rɪ'pɔətərɪdʒ). [f. REPORTER + -AGE.] = REPORTAGE 3.

a **1936** KIPLING *Something of Myself* (1937) v. 131 Yet the book was not all reporterage. **1939** JOYCE *Finnegans Wake* (1964) I. 70 Making his reporterage on Der Fall Adams for the Frankofurto Siding.

re'porting, *vbl. sb.* [f. REPORT *v.* + -ING[1].]

a. The action of the verb in various senses.

1460 *Rolls of Parlt.* V. 376/2 Every Lord shuld have his fredome to sey what he wuld sey, withoute eny reportyng or magre to be had for his seiyng. **1603** KNOLLES *Hist. Turks* (1638) 184 Fables, better worth the smiling at, than the serious reporting. *a* **1617** BACON *Amend. Laws Eng.* Wks. 1730 IV. 6 Misprinting, and insensible reporting, which many times confound the students.. will be.. amended. **1738** G. LILLO *Marina* III. ii. 52 Like eyes, disdaining the disguise of truth, And found in the reporting. **1840** *Penny Cycl.* XVI. 195/2 Let us suppose.. that four reporters are engaged.., the process of reporting being the same in each house. **1861** MAY *Const. Hist.* I. 430 No circumstance.. has done more for freedom and good government, than the unfettered liberty of reporting.

b. *attrib.* ***reporting company*** Canad.: (see quot. 1973).

1846 GAWTRESS in Pitman *Reporter* 7 The third style is termed reporting, being Phonography adapted to verbatim reporting. *Ibid.* 15 The writer.. took down a speech, delivered by R. Cobden.., which was set up from his reporting copy. **1871** J. GRANT *Newspaper Press* I. 141 The reporting department.. of our existing morning papers. **1880** *Echo* 23 Nov. 4/6 Shorthand.. with private instruction and reporting classes nightly. **1886** *Encycl. Brit.* XXI. 842/1 Numerous mechanical reporting machines have been invented. **1888** BARRIE *When a Man's Single* iii, I might introduce you.. to the reporting-room. **1973** *Daily Colonist* (Victoria, B.C.) 5 Oct. 9/2 It is a reporting company (new term for what was formerly called a public company) with 5,000 shareholders, mostly in B.C. **1974** *BP Shield Internat.* Oct. 7/3 Prince Philip's masterly handling of the final reporting-back session of the conference.

†**re'portingly**, *adv. Obs. rare.* [f. REPORT *v.*]

a. By report or hearsay. **b.** Correspondently.

1599 SHAKS. *Much Ado* III. i. 116 Others say thou dost deserue, and I Beleeue it better then reportingly. **1611** COTGR. s.v. *Rapporté, Vers rapportez*, Verses whose words reportingly answer one another.

re'portless, *a.* [-LESS.] Unknown, not reported; without repute.

c **1865** E. DICKINSON *Poems* (1955) II. 740 Reportless Subjects, to the Quick Continual addressed—But foreign as the Dialect Of Danes, unto the Rest. *c* **1884** *Ibid.* III. 1120 Still thou art What surgeons call alive—Though slipping—slipping I perceive To thy reportless Grave.

reportorial (rɛpə'təʊrɪəl), *a.* orig. *U.S.* [irreg. f. REPORT *v.* or REPORTER: see -ORIAL.] Consisting of, pertaining to, or characteristic of, reporters.

1858 *82nd Anniv. Amer. Independence* (Boston, Mass.) 6 As far as reportorial observation could extend, the best possible temper prevailed. **1860** in WORCESTER, The reportorial corps of a newspaper. **1883** *Cent. Mag.* July 374 The reportorial method is affecting the younger writers. **1890** *Universal Rev.* Sept. 88 Every petty local occurrence.. is magnified by the reportorial lens. **1926** [see DATED *ppl. a.* 3]. **1949** E. B. WHITE *Let.* 20 Nov. (1976) 315 Boyer wrote ..some reportorial articles that experienced editors.. regarded as thoroughly non-objective. **1955** *Bull. Atomic Sci.* Sept. 249/1 The stifling of routine reportorial inquiry. **1977** M. LIPPER in Bond & McLeod *Newslett. to Newspapers* I. 73 This is especially striking when one keeps in mind.. the role of coffeehouses or clubs as forerunners of modern reportorial staffs.

repor'torially, *adv.* [f. REPORTORIAL *a.* + -LY[2].] In a reportorial manner; as a newspaper reporter.

1862 *N.-Y. Tribune* 22 Apr. 1/4 At headquarters this morning—I mean those of General Heintzelman, to which I am reportorially attached—I found things quiet enough. **1901** *Pop. Sci. Monthly* Feb. 382 Unfortunately, the weather will not let the newspaper alone, and so.. the newspaper must keep pegging away at it, editorially and 'reportorially', until the present anomalous state of things is developed. **1972** J. G. VERMANDEL *Last seen in Samarra* xvii. 114 Safer than admitting to firsthand knowledge, but reportorially a flop, as he kept complaining bitterly to Alex. **1981** *Times Lit. Suppl.* 8 May 512/3 Because Wilkinson remains so reportorially self-conscious,.. he's unable to comprehend the tramps among whom he lives.

†**re'portory.** *Obs. rare*$^{-1}$. [f. REPORT *v.* + -ORY[1]: cf. REPORTARY.] A composition of the nature of a report; an account.

1599 NASHE *Lenten Stuffe* 6 In this transcursiue reportory without some obseruant glaunce, I may not dully ouerpasse the gallant beauty of their hauen.

re'portship. *rare.* [f. REPORT *sb.* + -SHIP.] An instance of reporting for a newspaper.

1912 G. FRANKAU *One of Us* xiii. 129 It was indeed a triumph of reportship: They gave the artiste's *rôles*, her lap-dog's photo.

†**reporture.** *Obs. rare.* [f. REPORT *v.* + -URE.] Report, mention.

c **1485** *Digby Myst.* (1882) III. 2084 To hyr I wyll goo and make reportur. *a* **1500** MEDWALL *Nature* II. 364 (Brandl), Ye can not do hym more dyspleasure, Than therof to make reporture, Therefore let yt rest.

reposal (rɪ'pəʊzəl). [f. REPOSE *v.*[1] and *v.*[2]]

1. The act of reposing (trust, confidence, etc.); †trust or reliance *in* something. *rare.*

1605 SHAKS. *Lear* II. i. 70 Would the reposall [*Q.* reposure] Of any trust, vertue, or worth in thee Make thy words faith'd? **1614** JACKSON *Creed* III. xxiii. §1 What are these then? absolute reposall in his and his Successors infallibility?

†**2.** The fact or state of reposing or resting. *Obs.*

1614 JACKSON *Creed* III. v[i]. §1 After many yeares reposall in the graue. **1642** R. CARPENTER *Experience* II. vii. 161 If they goe on to trouble the peace of my sweet reposall in the bosome of my deare mother, the Church of England.

†**b.** That on which one reposes. *Obs.*

1621 BURTON *Anat. Mel.* I. ii. II. vi, Idleness.. the Divels cushion, as Gualter cals it, his pillow, & chiefe reposall. *Ibid.* III. iv. I. i, It is a Sole Ease, an unspeakable comfort, a sweet reposal.

†**re'posance.** *Obs. rare*$^{-1}$. [f. as prec. + -ANCE.] Repose.

1647 J. HALL *Poems* II. 92 Mount up low thoughts and see what sweet Reposance Heaven can beget.

repose (rɪ'pəʊz), *sb.* Also 6 reposse. [a. F. *repos* (11th c.; OF. also *repaus* = Prov. *repaus*, Sp. *reposo*, Pg. *repouso*, It. *riposo*), vbl. sb. f. *reposer*: see REPOSE *v.*[2]]

1. a. Temporary rest or cessation from activity, in order to refresh or restore the physical or mental powers; *esp.* the rest given by sleep.

1509 HAWES *Past. Pleas.* XXXII. (Percy Soc.) 160, I toke my leve,.. And thanked Correccyon,.. Of my repose and of her lovynge chere. **1590** SPENSER *F.Q.* III. iv. 6 So forth she rode, without repose or rest, Searching all lands. **1610** SHAKS. *Temp.* II. i. 310 Whiles we stood here securing your repose,.. we heard a hollow burst of bellowing. **1635–56** COWLEY *Davideis* II. 3 Up rose the Sun and Saul; Both, as men thought, rose fresh from sweet repose. **1697** DRYDEN *Virg. Georg.* IV. 275 They give their Bodies due Repose at Night. **1738** GRAY *Propertius* ii. 3 Fast by th' umbrageous vale lull'd to repose. **1774** GOLDSM. *Nat. Hist.* (1776) II. 138 The extreme activity of his mind, when awake, in some measure called for an adequate alternation of repose. **1860** TYNDALL *Glac.* I. xxii. 154 Allowing each limb an instant of repose as I drew it out of the snow.

transf. **1862** SIR B. BRODIE *Psychol. Inq.* II. i. 3 A splendid aloe which, after a repose of many years, was again loaded with flowers.

b. In phrases *to* (†*make*) *seek* or *take repose*.

1594 MARLOWE & NASHE *Dido* I. i, Whose weary limbs shall shortly make repose In those fair walls. **1602** MARSTON *Ant. & Mel.* I. Wks. 1856 I. 17 My fathers palace.. will be proud To entertaine your presence, if youle daine To make repose within. **1671** MILTON *Samson* 406 At times when men seek most repose and rest, I yielded. **1697** DRYDEN *Virg. Georg.* IV. 634 Unweildily they.. in the shady Covert seek Repose. **1784** COWPER *Task* IV. 296 'Tis thus the understanding takes repose In indolent vacuity of thought. **1830** TENNYSON *A Spirit Haunts* 14 As a sick man's room when he taketh repose An hour before death.

c. *Eccl.* Death, decease (of a saint). Also ***altar of repose*** (see quot. 1884).

1869 TOZER *Highl. Turkey* I. 59 The festival of the Repose of the Virgin. **1884** *Catholic Dict.* (1897) 445/2 The place to which the Blessed Sacrament is removed—often called the Sepulchre, but properly the altar of repose.

2. Relief or respite from exertion, toil, trouble, or excitement. Also const. *from*, †*of*.

1529 WOLSEY in Ellis *Orig. Lett.* Ser. I. II. 6 Nowe set to your hande that I may come to a laudable ende and repose. **1585** T. WASHINGTON tr. *Nicholay's Voy.* II. v. 34b, [His] repose of his trauailes sustayned on the Seas. **1667** MILTON *P.L.* v. 28 O Sole in whom my thoughts find all repose. **1692** DRYDEN *Eleonora* 243 As swelling seas to gentle rivers glide, To seek repose, and empty out the tide. **1784** COWPER *Task* I. 5, I.. Now seek repose upon an humbler theme. **1821** BYRON *Two Fosc.* II. i, The state had need of some repose. *a* **1854** H. REED *Lect. Eng. Lit.* v. (1878) 171 There was repose from the agony of spiritual persecution. **1855** BAIN *Senses & Int.* II. ii. §9 The eye is fatigued with the glare of sunshine, and is said to find repose in the verdure of the fields.

†**3. a.** A place of rest. *Obs.*

1621 BRATHWAIT *Nat. Embassie* (1877) 139 Seuen fortunate reposes, Ilands, which Fortune fauors. **1628** FELTHAM *Resolves* II. [I.] xviii. 55 The rich lye stoued in secure reposes. **1671** MILTON *P.R.* III. 210 Worst is my Port, My harbour and my ultimate repose.

†**b.** A halt or stay for rest. *Obs. rare*$^{-1}$.

1638 BAKER tr. *Balzac's Lett.* (vol. II) 52 Wee were put in hope.. that here you would make one of the reposes of your Voyage.

†**c.** *Painting.* (See quots.) *Obs. rare.*

The definitions given by Harris and Chambers are based on that of Furetière, *Dict. Univ.* (1690).

1695 DRYDEN tr. *Du Fresnoy's Art Paint.* 161 After great Lights there must be great Shadows, which we call reposes: because.. the Sight would be tired, if it were attracted by a Continuity of glittering objects. **1710** J. HARRIS *Lex. Techn.* II, *Repose*, is a Term in Painting, signifying the Place where the Masses, or great Lights and Shadows are assembled: And this being well understood hinders the Confusion of Objects [etc.]. **1727–38** CHAMBERS *Cycl.*, *Repose*, in painting, is applied to certain masses, or large systems or assemblages of light and shade [etc.].

†**d.** A thing to repose on; a couch or sofa. *Obs.*$^{-1}$

1701 FARQUHAR *Sir H. Wildair* III. iii, There is a repose, I see, in the next room.

4. a. A state of quiet or peaceful inaction or of freedom from disturbing influences; †also, a means of securing this.

1651 HOBBES *Leviath.* I. xi. 47 The Felicity of this life, consisteth not in the repose of a mind satisfied. **1712** M. HENRY *Reform. Serm.* Wks. 1853 II. 487/1 The restraint of the vicious will be the repose of the virtuous. **1769** *Junius Lett.* xxxv. (1788) 179 You relinquish every hope of repose to yourself, and you endanger the establishment of your family for ever. **1811** PINKERTON *Petral.* II. 25 The repose which the waters enjoyed in the inside of these reservoirs. **1871** L. STEPHEN *Playgr. Eur.* iii. (1894) 83 A delicious lazy sense of calm repose was the appropriate frame of mind.

†**b.** Peace of mind. *Obs. rare.*

1712 STEELE *Spect.* No. 527 ¶1 The Repose of a married Woman is consulted in the first of the following Letters, and the Felicity of a Maiden Lady in the second. **1718** LADY M. W. MONTAGU *Let. to C'tess of Mar* 10 Mar., I assured her.. it was absolutely necessary to confine them from public view, for the repose of mankind.

5. a. Quiet, calm or calmness, tranquillity.

1717 POPE *Eloïsa* 166 Black Melancholy.. round her throws A death-like silence, and a dead repose. **1738** GRAY *Propertius* ii. 49 The scenes that hurt the grave's repose. **1819** KEATS *St. Agnes* xxxvi, Like a throbbing star Seen 'mid the sapphire heaven's deep repose. **1846** RUSKIN *Mod. Paint.* II. III. I. vii. §1 As opposed to passion.. Repose is the especial and separating characteristic of the eternal mind and power. **1872** YEATS *Growth Comm.* 48 Just as repose was the ruling principle in Egypt, so restlessness distinguished Greece.

b. *Painting*, etc. Harmonious arrangement of figures or colours, having a restful effect upon the eye.

1695 DRYDEN tr. *Du Fresnoy's Art. Paint.* 23 That.. Majesty, that soft silence and repose, which give beauty to the Piece. **1703** TATE *Her Majesty's Pict.* Notes 22 The Sedateness, and, as Painters call it, the Repose of a Picture, contribute to the Grandeur and Solemnity of the Piece. **1778** SIR J. REYNOLDS *Disc.* (1779) 5 The expression which is used very often on these occasions is, the piece wants repose. **1841** W. SPALDING *Italy & It. Isl.* II. 328 Its faults are many;—an entire absence of beauty and of repose [etc.]. **1909** *Chambers's Jrnl.* Oct. 664/1 The workmen lost the large conception of their ancestors, the patterns [of carpets] lacked repose.

c. Composure, quiet, ease of manner.

1833 TENNYSON *Lady C. V. de Vere* 39 Her manners had not that repose Which stamps the caste of Vere de Vere. **1860** EMERSON *Cond. Life, Culture* Wks. (1889) 531/2 Repose and cheerfulness are the badge of the gentleman—repose in energy.

6. a. Absence of activity (in things); cessation of natural forces; quiescence.

1757 GRAY *Bard* 76 The sweeping whirlwind..hush'd in grim repose, expects his evening prey. **1813** BAKEWELL *Introd. Geol.* (1815) 314 The long intervals of repose appear to characterize volcanoes highly elevated. **1833** LYELL *Princ. Geol.* III. 6 We are also told..of the alternation of periods of repose and disorder, of the refrigeration of the globe [etc.]. **1887** RUSKIN *Præterita* II. 87 Vesuvius was virtually in repose.

b. Undisturbed or unagitated condition.

1855 BAIN *Senses & Int.* II. ii. §4 Hence the natural repose of the eye makes the adjustment for a distant prospect. **1880** MRS. L. B. WALFORD *Troublesome Dau.* II. xxi. 212 Though every feature was now in repose.

c. The fact of being left undisturbed.

1844 G. BIRD *Urin. Deposits* 261 A portion of butter-like fat may form part of the pellicle which forms on the urine by repose.

7. *techn.* **a.** *angle of repose*: (see quots.).

1833 LOUDON *Encycl. Arch.* §805 Where the courses lie at an angle of about thirty-two degrees, or what is called the angle of repose for masonry. **1867** BRANDE & COX *Dict. Sci.*, etc. III. 249/1 In Engineering, the term *angle of repose* is frequently applied to express the angle at which the various kinds of earth will permanently stand, when abandoned to themselves.

b. *Horology.* (See quots.)

1842 *Encycl. Brit.* (ed. 7) VI. 773/1 This contrivance is known by the name of the dead beat, the dead scapement, the scapement of repose; because the seconds index stands still after each drop. *Ibid.* 773/2 The pallet which is called the arch of excursion or arch of repose.

8. Trust, confidence. *rare*$^{-1}$.

c **1800** R. CUMBERLAND *John De Lancaster* (1809) III. 71 If therefore you could bring your mind to put that repose in my honour.

repose (rɪˈpəʊz), *v.*[1] [ad. L. *repos-*, *repōnĕre*, on anal. of *depose*, *dispose*, *suppose*, etc.: cf. REPONE and REPOSIT.]

†**1.** *trans.* To replace; to put back into the same place. *Obs.*

c **1420** *Pallad. on Husb.* II. 334 Her shellis to disclose And write vpon the cornel, hool outake..and so repose [L. *reponas*]. **1544** PHAER *Regim. Lyfe* (1560) U iv, If the gutte hath bene long out, and be so swollen that it cannot be reposed. **1564** HAWARD *Eutropius* VI. 52 He delivered up his crowne into the handes of Pompeius; but Pompeius reposed it again upon his head. **1615** CHAPMAN *Odyss.* IX. 703 Nor think my hurt offends me, for my sire Can soon repose in it the visual fire. **1660** F. BROOKE tr. *Le Blanc's Trav.* 323 Procession ended, they repose the Idols within the same tree.

†**b.** To restore; also *Sc.* = REPONE *v.* 1. *Obs. rare.*

1552 HUTCHINSON *2nd Serm.* Wks. (Parker Soc.) 241 To repose us into his Father's favour again. **1567** *Reg. Privy Council Scot.* I. 526 The persoun of our..Prince [to be] reposit to full suirtie. **1643** R. BAILLIE *Lett. & Jrnls.* (1841) II. 53 The causes of Mr. Gilbert Power's deposition by all were found null, and he ordained to be reposed. *Ibid.* 92 Mr. Andrew Logie..latelie had been reposed to his ministrie.

†**c.** To repress, put down. *Obs. rare*$^{-1}$.

1652 HOWELL *Giraffi's Rev. Naples* II. (1663) 26 A multitude of common people gather'd together..armed with a full..purpose to repose the insolence and pride of the nobility.

2. To place or put; *esp.* to deposit or lay up *in* a place. Now *rare*.

1548 GEST *Pr. Masse* L iij, Iudas reposed in Gods temple an ydoll ymage. **1559** *Mirr. Mag., R. Tresilian* xx, Thynke ther is a treasure..Reposed for all suche as righteousnes ensue. **1576** FLEMING *Panopl. Epist.* 7, I praye you heartily, to repose this in your memorie. **1605** BACON *Adv. Learn.* II. To King §5 Libraries..are as the Shrynes, where all the Reliques of the ancient Saints..are preserued and reposed. *a* **1656** USSHER *Ann.* VI. (1658) 426 They reposed there the spoiles of Jerusalem. **1695** WOODWARD *Nat. Hist. Earth* 29 These Shells were brought out upon the Earth, and reposed therein in the manner we now find them. **1715** M. DAVIES *Athen. Brit.* I. 203 'Twas, as a choice Rarity, repos'd in the Library of the English Benedictines. *a* **1797** H. WALPOLE *Mem. Geo. II* (1847) III. vi. 133 The brass cannon and mortars..were reposed for some days in Hyde Park. **1827** SCOTT *Napoleon* lxxv, The sword was..not to be sheathed or reposed.

†**b.** To station, establish. *Obs. rare.*

1582 N. LICHEFIELD tr. *Castanheda's Conq. E. Ind.* I. xxxix. 92 As for yᵉ bishops they are reposed in cities, as is thought conuenient. **1582** STANYHURST *Æneis* I. (Arb.) 18 Theare Iuno thee Princes her Empyre wholy reposed.

†**c.** To cast or throw *on* something. *Obs.*$^{-1}$

1582 STANYHURST *Æneis* I. (Arb.) 21 Thee southwynd.. Three gallant vessels on rocks gnawne craggye reposed.

3. To set or place (confidence, trust, etc.) *in* a thing or person.

1560 DAUS tr. *Sleidane's Comm.* 98 b, Suche a one as he myght repose his whole truste and confidence in. **1581** J. BELL *Haddon's Answ. Osor.* 240 That man hath the hope of Salvation reposed only in the mercies of God. **1603** KNOLLES *Hist. Turks* (1638) 106 Reposing no great assurance in the prowes of the effœminate Ægyptians. **1607** ROWLANDS *Diogines Lanthorne* 30 Repose not trust in others helpe. **1678** EVELYN *Diary* 16 Oct., Mr. Godolphin requested me to continue the trust his wife had reposed in me. **1753** HANWAY *Trav.* (1762) I. III. xxvi. 110 The governor..charged me..not to repose any confidence in the peasants. *a* **1781** WATSON *Philip III* (1793) I. II. 190 That extraordinary confidence that was reposed in him. **1844** DISRAELI *Coningsby* VII. ii, Herein mainly should we repose our hopes. **1874** GREEN *Short Hist.* iv. §5. 196 In the Baronage the nation reposed an unwavering trust.

b. To place or leave (something) *in* the control or management of another. †Also const. *upon*.

1589 NASHE *Pref. to Greene's Menaphon* (Arb.) 6 This kinde of men that repose eternitie in the mouth of a player. **1666** DRYDEN *Pref. to Ann. Mirab.* Wks. (Globe) 42, I repose upon your management what is dearest to me, my fame and reputation. *a* **1681** WHARTON *Soul of World* Wks. (1683) 668 Therefore our Fate for the most part, and our Power are very much reposed in our Hands. **1884** CHITTY in *Law Times Rep.* L. 389/1 Parliament has reposed in [the Charity Commissioners] a power of authorising a sale.

†**c.** To regard as existing *in* something. *Obs.*

1613 PURCHAS *Pilgrimage* V. xvi. (1614) 529 A certain booke,..wherein they reposed much holines, and worshipped it as a god. *a* **1619** FOTHERBY *Atheom.* I. vi. §2 They reposed great Religion in an oath, in respect of the Actor.

Hence †**re'posed** *ppl. a.*[1], restored. *Obs.*

1657 THORNLEY tr. *Longus' Daphnis & Chloe* 208 They sacrificed to Jupiter Soter, the saviour of the reposed Child.

repose (rɪˈpəʊz), *v.*[2] Also 6–7 *Sc.* repois(e. [ad. F. *reposer*, OF. also *repauser* (10th c.) = Prov. *repausar*, Sp. *reposar*, Pg. *repousar*, It. *riposare*:—late L. *repausāre* (Quicherat): see RE- and PAUSE *v.*]

1. *refl.* To rest (oneself); to lay (oneself) to rest.

1470–85 MALORY *Arthur* X. ii. 416, I wylle repose me here by with a frend of myn. **1509** HAWES *Past. Pleas.* I. (Percy Soc.) 7 Besyde the ymage I adowne me sette, After my laboure my selfe to repose. *a* **1553** UDALL *Royster D.* I. iv. (Arb.) 30 Now may I repose me: Custance is mine owne. **1588** SHAKS. *Tit. A.* I. i. 151 Romes readiest Champions, repose you heere in rest. *a* **1648** LD. HERBERT *Hen. VIII* (1683) 511 This year the Emperor glad to repose himself a while from War, attended his pleasure in Spain. *a* **1700** KEN *Hymnotheo* Poet. Wks. 1721 III. 34 John tenderly repos'd him on his Breast. **1713** DERHAM *Phys.-Theol.* IV. xii. 221 The thick and warm Furrs..are..a soft Bed to repose themselves in. **1806** J. BERESFORD *Miseries Hum. Life* VI. xiii, Being mounted on a beast who..proceeds very coolly to repose himself in the middle of the pond.

b. *fig.* To settle (oneself) with confidence (†*in* or) *on* something. ? *Obs.*

1580 J. HAYE in *Cath. Tract.* (S.T.S.) 67/32 Thou may bawldlie repose thy selfe in the Romain kirk. **1593** SHAKS. *3 Hen. VI*, IV. vi. 47 On thy fortune I repose my selfe. **1759** JOHNSON *Let. to Miss Porter* 1 Mar. in Boswell *Life*, I can repose myself very confidently upon your prudence. **1770** LANGHORNE *Plutarch* (1879) I. 202/2 Fabius having taught the people to repose themselves on acts of religion.

2. *trans.* To lay to rest or repose *on* or *in* something. In later use only *fig.*

1535 LYNDESAY *Satyre* 3577 Iesus..hes nocht ane penny braid Quhairon he may repois his heavinlie head. **1768** GOLDSM. *Good-n. Man* II, I'll go to him, and repose our distresses on his friendly bosom. **1771** MRS. GRIFFITH *Hist. Lady Barton* I. 84 Nor would I..render her wretched, by reposing the distresses of my..mind, in her soft bosom.

b. In *pa. pple.*: Resting, reclining, lying.

1674 MILTON *P.L.* V. 636 On flours repos'd, and with fresh flourets crownd, They eate, they drink. **1727** GAY *Begg. Op.* I. xiii, I could mock the sultry toil When on my charmer's breast repos'd. **1852** M. ARNOLD *Tristram & Iseult* I, The eyes [are] closed—The lashes on the cheeks reposed.

3. To give or afford rest to (one), to refresh by rest.

1549–62 STERNHOLD & H. *Ps.* lxix. 20 O Lord, unto my soule draw nigh, the same with ayde repose. **1581** SAVILE *Tacitus, Hist.* III. vii. (1591) 117 There some fewe daies were spent in reposing the army. **1596** DANETT tr. *Comines* VII. iii. 274 The peace was concluded..whereunto the King of the Romaines agreed, to the end he might repose his subiects. **1632** J. HAYWARD tr. *Biondi's Eromena* II. 51 The time for reposing the Galley-slaves being expired. **1667** MILTON *P.L.* I. 319 Have ye chos'n this place After the toyl of Battel to repose Your wearied vertue..? **1732** POPE *Ep. Bathurst* 260 Whose Seats the weary Traveller repose? **1794** MRS. A. M. BENNETT *Ellen* I. 22 He rose from the bed of down, which for neatness and comfort might repose a Prince. **1876** BANCROFT *Hist. U.S.* VI. xliv. 275 He..halted at Hillsborough to repose his wayworn soldiers.

†**b.** To lodge (one) for the night. *Obs. rare*$^{-1}$.

1725 T. THOMAS in *Portland Papers* (Hist. MSS. Comm.) VI. 132 That apartment where the judges used to be reposed in when they came to this place.

4. *intr.* To take rest; to cease from exertion or travel; to enjoy freedom from disturbance.

a **1548** HALL *Chron., Hen. VIII* 35 [They] desyred him for his pastime after his long trauayle to come and repose in his towne of Lysle. **1585** T. WASHINGTON tr. *Nicholay's Voy.* II. viii. 42 Because the wind was too fresh, we reposed vntil the break of day. **1591** SYLVESTER *Du Bartas* I. vii. 383 Yet must we credit that his hand composed All in sixe Dayes, and that he then Reposed. **1703** MAUNDRELL *Journ. Jerus.* (1732) 25 At Tripoli we repos'd a full week. **1784** COWPER *Task* III. 28 'Twere wiser far For me..to repose Where chance may throw me. **1819** SHELLEY *Prometh. Unb.* II. i. 203 To the rents, and gulfs, and chasms, Where the earth reposed from spasms. **1851** TENNYSON *To the Queen* 26 God gave her peace; her land reposed.

fig. **1856** FROUDE *Hist. Eng.* (1858) I. i. 38 The Justice Shallows were not allowed to repose upon their dignity.

b. To take rest by sitting or lying down; to lie down to rest; also *transf.* to rest in death.

1535 LYNDESAY *Satyre* 934, I will sit still heir and repois. **1610** SHAKS. *Temp.* IV. i. 162 If you be pleas'd, retire into my Cell, And there repose. *a* **1620** SIR W. MURE *Misc. Poems.* xv. 19 Happie nimph, quhoise spreit in peace repoises. **1634** MILTON *Comus* 999 Beds of Hyacinth and roses Where young Adonis oft reposes. **1734** POPE *Ess. Man* IV. 387 When statesmen, heroes, kings, in dust repose. **1742** GRAY *Spring* 22 Still is the toiling hand of Care, The panting herds repose. **1817** SHELLEY *Rev. Islam* IV. xxxiii, At night when I reposed, fair dreams did pass Before my pillow. **1819** —— *Ode* 11 The dust where your kindred repose. **1884** J. COLBORNE *Hicks Pasha* 32 We started at 5 a.m., marched until noon, and reposed.

c. To remain still; to lie in quiet.

1817 SHELLEY *Rev. Islam* VI. xxxiii, Her..eyes, Which, as twin phantoms of one star that lies O'er a dim well, move, though the star reposes. **1842** TENNYSON *Locksley Hall* 13 When the centuries behind me like a fruitful land reposed.

†**5.** To confide or place one's trust *in*, to rely *on*, a thing or person. *Obs.*

Perh. partly derived from sense 3 of REPOSE *v.*[1]

1567 *Gude & Godlie B.* (S.T.S.) 167 We are chosin to repois In faith of Christ. **1591** SHAKS. *Two Gent.* IV. iii. 26, I doe desire thy worthy company, Vpon whose faith and honor I repose. **1629** MAXWELL tr. *Herodian* (1635) 430 There returned also the German auxiliaries, in whose loyaltie he most reposed. **1751** JOHNSON *Rambler* No. 144 ⁋12 His hearers repose upon his candour and veracity. **1781** COWPER *Truth* 455 The soul, reposing on assured relief, Feels herself happy amidst all her grief.

†**b.** To be sure *of* one. *Obs. rare*$^{-1}$.

1569 SIR N. THROGMORTON in Robertson *Hist. Scot.* (1759) II. App. 57 You may repose as well of him in this matter as of the duke of Norfolk.

6. To rest *on* or *upon*, in various senses.

1611 SHAKS. *Cymb.* IV. ii. 212 His right Cheeke Reposing on a Cushion. **1817** SHELLEY *Rev. Islam* III. xxviii, On that reverend form the moonlight did repose. **1819** BYRON *Juan* II. lviii, On such things the memory reposes With tenderness. **1860** TYNDALL *Glac.* II. xiii. 297 Almost every glacier reposes upon an inclined bed. *a* **1862** BUCKLE *Civiliz.* III. iv. 272 Their whole system reposes upon fear.

reposed (rɪˈpəʊzd), *ppl. a.*[2] [f. prec. + -ED[1].] Settled, free from agitation or movement.

a **1533** LD. BERNERS *Gold. Bk. M. Aurel.* (1546) Y viij, To giue contentacion to thy reposed will. *a* **1547** SURREY in *Tottel's Misc.* (Arb.) 29 A mynde With vertue fraught, reposed, voyd of gyle. **1586** B. YOUNG *Guazzo's Civ. Conv.* IV. 228 Embrace this the onelie meane to liue a reposed and contented life. **1610** DONNE *Pseudo-martyr* 281 A law, made by the Popes in reposed & peaceable times. **1664** FLECKNOE *Eng. Stage* in *Love's Kingd.* G vi, Wit being an exuberant thing,..but Judgement a stayed and reposed thing. **1742** YOUNG *Nt. Th.* IX. 1474 Then whence these glorious Forms, And boundless Flights, from Shapeless, and Repos'd?

Hence **re'posedly** *adv.* (Now *rare* or *Obs.*)

1598 FLORIO, *Posatamente*, leisurely, quietly, reposedly. *a* **1615** DONNE *Ess.* (1651) 63 Reposedly, and at home within himself, no man is an Atheist. **1634** TIRWHYT tr. *Balzac's Lett.* I. xvi. 89 Liue hence-forward reposedly, and reconcile your selfe to choice Wits.

reposedness (rɪˈpəʊzdnɪs). [f. prec. + -NESS.] The state or condition of repose or of being in repose.

a **1619** FOTHERBY *Atheom.* II. ii. §8 (1622) 211 Vnder the shadow of Gods wings, the Soule findes her true reposednesse, her refuge. **1634** TIRWHYT tr. *Balzac's Lett.* II. i. 94, I here enioy a reposednesse not vnlike that of the dead. **1884** M. BOOLE in *Jrnl. Educ.* 1 Sept. 342 There is an intelligent and wide-awake reposedness in Jewish girls.

†**re'poseful**, *a.*[1] *Obs.* [f. REPOSE *v.*[1] 3 (or *v.*[2] 4).] In whom confidence is or may be placed: trustworthy, reliable; confidential, responsible.

1627 SIR R. COTTON in Morgan *Phœnix Brit.* (1732) I. 68 Though princes may take..some reposefull friend, with whom they may participate their neerest passions [etc.]. **1640** HOWELL *Dodona's Gr.* 28, I know not, where she can picke out a fast friend, or reposefull confident of such reciprocall interest. **1644** —— *Twelve Treat.* (1661) 28 To another he gave one of the prime and most reposefull Offices about his own Person at Court.

reposeful (rɪˈpəʊzfʊl), *a.*[2] [f. REPOSE *sb.*] Full of repose; having an air of repose; quiet.

1852 READE *Peg Woff.* (1853) 259, I call it beautiful!.. So calm and reposeful; no particular expression. **1869** *Sat. Rev.* 6 Mar. 306/2 That reposeful yet energetic self-reliance, which we justly admire in the ruler. **1879** G. MACDONALD *Sir Gibbie* I. xiv. 198 An attractive expression of reposeful friendliness pervaded his whole appearance.

Hence **re'posefully** *adv.*; **re'posefulness**.

1881 MISS BRADDON *Asph.* II. 311 Seated reposefully in his great red morocco armchair. **1883** G. H. BOUGHTON in *Harper's Mag.* Feb. 392/2 It seems to lack reposefulness.

†**re'posement.** *Obs. rare*$^{-1}$. [f. REPOSE *v.*[1] + -MENT.] Repository.

1586 A. DAY *Eng. Secretary* II. (1625) 103 The Closet in euery house, as it is a reposement of Secrets, so is it onely.. at the owners', and no other commandement.

†**re'poseness.** *Obs. rare*$^{-1}$. = REPOSEDNESS.

a **1592** GREENE *Arbasto* (1617) i, If my presence be prejudiciall to your reposenesse, I hope you will thinke I offended as a stranger.

re'poser. *rare*$^{-1}$. [-ER[1].] One who reposes.

1832 *Blackw. Mag.* XXXII. 600 A steadfast reposer of his fears and anxieties in religious influences.

reposing (rɪˈpəʊzɪŋ), *vbl. sb.* [-ING[1].] The action of REPOSE *v.*[2]; resting, rest.

1565 *Reg. Privy Council Scot.* I. 361 The King and Quenis Majesteis departis this nycht towart Striviling for reposing of thair Hienessis. **1790** R. MERRY *Laurel of Liberty* (ed. 2) 22 Calm reposings in the noontide shade.

attrib. **1594** SHAKS. *Rich. III*, I. iv. 76 Sorrow breakes Seasons, and reposing houres. **1661** *Fasti Aberdonenses* (Spalding Club) 606 For hair to the reposeing bed, and furme in the principle's chamber. **1797** *Monthly Mag.* III. 229 The fiends of lawless pow'r.. Intrude on weary'd toil's reposing hour. **1936** [see *funeral home* s.v. FUNERAL *sb.* 6].

So **re'posing** *ppl. a.*

1797–1803 FOSTER in *Life & Corr.* (1846) I. 220 A neutral reposing state of the passions. **1817** SHELLEY *Rev. Islam* IV. xxviii, I did arise,.. And looked upon the depth of that reposing lake. *Ibid.* XII. iii, Like a reposing child.

re'posit, *sb. rare*[−0]. [f. the vb.] A repository.

1855 in OGILVIE *Suppl.*

reposit (rɪˈpɒzɪt), *v.* Also 7–8 reposite. [f. L. *reposit-*, ppl. stem of *repōnĕre* to REPONE: cf. REPOSE *v.*[1]]

1. *trans.* To put or deposit (a thing) *in* a place; to lay up, store.

a **1641** BP. MOUNTAGU *Acts & Mon.* (1642) 79 Untill he come,.. for whom it is reposited, or laid up. **1664** H. MORE *Myst. Iniq.* vi. 16 Erecting such a Symbol of the Divine presence as was to be afterward reposited in the Ark, namely, the figure of a Cherub. **1695** WOODWARD *Nat. Hist. Earth* I. (1723) 48 These Shells could never possibly have been reposited thereby in the Manner we now find them. **1713** DERHAM *Phys.-Theol.* IV. xiii. 230 Some reposite their Eggs or Young in the Earth. **1779–81** JOHNSON *L.P., Pope* Wks. IV. 29 The original copy of the Iliad, which.. is now .. reposited in the Museum. **1808** G. EDWARDS *Pract. Plan* iii. 23 The valuable riches nature has here reposited for the efforts of human labour. **1864** CARLYLE *Fredk. Gt.* XII. ii. (1872) IV. 138 The King.. handed it.. to a Page to reposit in the proper waste-basket.

2. To replace. *rare.*

1800 C. B. BROWN *Arthur Mervyn*, II. iv. 69 The grave was covered, the spade reposited under the shed, and my seat in the kitchen resumed. **1884** G. H. TAYLOR *Pelv. & Hern. Therap.* (1885) 107 The sphincter appeared to have little power to retain the intestine when reposited.

Hence **re'positing** *vbl. sb.*

1713 DERHAM *Phys.-Theol.* III. ii. 66 A special Providence of God in the repositing of these watery Beds.

repositary (rɪˈpɒzɪtərɪ). [f. prec. + -ARY[1].] = REPOSITORY.

1862 GOULBURN *Pers. Relig.* I. i. (1873) 3 You meet with men who were great repositaries of the literature of the day. **1866** *Cornh. Mag.* Apr. 395 It gratified him to think that she had chosen him for the repositary of her tale.

†**re'positate**, *v. Obs. rare*[−1]. [-ATE.] = REPOSIT *v.* I.

1716 M. DAVIES *Athen. Brit.* III. 104 A Description of the Curiosities repositated in the Cabinet of the Earl of Trautmansdorf.

reposite, obs. form of REPOSIT *v.*

reposition (riːpəˈzɪʃən), *sb.* Also re-. [ad. late L. *repositiōn-em*, n. of action f. *repōnĕre*: see REPOSIT *v.* and -ION[1], and cf. F. *réposition.*]

1. *Surg.* The operation of restoring to the normal position; replacement.

1588 J. READ tr. *Arcæus' Compend. Meth.* 67 Put it in his due place and right order againe... This reposition being made [etc.]. **1661** LOVELL *Hist. Anim. & Min.* 431 *Luxations*,.. it's cured by.. reposition,.. diligent deligation, and soft collocation. **1684** tr. *Bonet's Merc. Compit.* VIII. 288, I place him.. for reposition, binding him fast so that he cannot stir. **1707** SLOANE *Jamaica* II. 151 The leaves.. are laid to broken arms and legs after reposition with great success. **1879** *St. George's Hosp. Rep.* IX. 458 Retroflexion of the uterus discovered, and treated by reposition.

b. Replacement (of a thing), in other senses.

1874 CARPENTER *Ment. Phys.* II. x. (1879) 440 The structure itself is kept up by re-position of new matter.

2. †**a.** Restoration of lands to a forest. *Obs. rare.*

1592 MANWOOD *Lawes Forest* 178 The reposition to the Forest of such landes as were disaforested by the Statute.. is to be done by perambulation and viewe. *Ibid.* Such landes as were disaforested without any reposition.. are called Puralleyes.

b. *Sc.* Reinstatement (of a person) in, or restoration to, a position or office (*esp.* the ministry), or possession of a thing. Now only *arch.*

1643 R. BAILLIE *Lett. & Jrnls.* (1841) II. 53 At the day of reposition a number of gentleweomen and others came to the Church. **1676** W. ROW *Contn. Blair's Autobiog.* (1848) 547 The three suspended conformists.. expecting.. reposition to their charges. **1681** STAIR *Instit.* II. xxiii. §3. 4 Under Assignations are comprehended Translations,.. or Retrocessions,.. which are also called Repositions. **1889** STEVENSON *Master of B.* 276 The Favour of such a Reposition [to the possession of an estate] is too extreme to be passed over.

3. The action of repositing, laying up or aside.

1617 BP. HALL *Quo Vadis?* vi, What can be expected from that age, which is not capable of obseruation, carelesse of reposition? *a* **1653** BINNING *Serm.* (1743) 579 When once a soul apprehends Christ, this is a reposition of all his cares and burdens. **1709** STRYPE *Ann. Ref.* I. xxxv. 365 For reposition and preserving dead mens skulls and bones.

†**b.** *R.C. Ch.* Reservation (of the Sacrament).

1657 W. MORICE *Coena quasi Κοινή* xiv. 183 Protestant Divines condemn the reposition of the Sacrament.

repo'sition, *v.* [RE- 5 a.] **a.** *trans.* To put in a fresh position; to re-state.

a **1859** DE QUINCEY *Posth. Wks.* (1891) I. 278 Shall I revise.. my logic of Political Economy, embodying every doctrine.. which I have amended or re-positioned..? **1959** *Times* 2 Oct. 11/3 Arm rests have been redesigned and repositioned. **1967** COX & GROSE *Organization & Handling Bibl. Rec. by Computer* II. 46 To do so requires that the space left be rapidly and accurately repositioned at the 'exposing' position. **1981** S. BRETT *Situation Tragedy* i. 9 They rearranged their cameras, repositioned their sound-booms.

b. *intr.* To adjust or alter one's position.

1947 A. C. DOUGLAS *Gliding & Soaring* 48 If the tow is to consist of more than two sailplanes the manner in which they shall release or reposition should be decided beforehand. **1977** *Chicago Tribune* 2 Oct. IV. 3/2 The Prisendam will make a second visit in April while repositioning from Singapore to Vancouver.

Hence **repo'sitioned** *ppl. a.*, **repo'sitioning** *vbl. sb.*

1968 P. A. P. MORAN *Introd. Probability Theory* ix. 408 Thus by repositioning there is no restriction in supposing that the distribution of X is confined to the points 0, 1, 2,.., zero being its true left extremity. **1969** *Gloss. Terms Dentistry* (*B.S.I.*) 69 Repositioned flap procedures. (1) Apically repositioned flap operation... (2) Apically displaced flap operation... (3) Laterally repositioned flap operation. **1975** T. ALLBEURY *Special Collection* ix. 60 Air experts had noticed.. the repositioned undercarriage members. **1977** *Proc. R. Soc. Med.* LXX. 432/1 No changes in the surgically repositioned bone. **1980** A. COPPEL *Hastings Conspiracy* xxxviii. 230 A major repositioning of large sections of the Soviet Army.

repositor (rɪˈpɒzɪtə(r)). [agent-n., on L. types, f. REPOSIT *v.*] A replacing instrument.

1884 KNIGHT *Dict. Mech.* Suppl. 750/2 The uterine repositor or elevator. **1895** *Arnold & Sons' Catal. Surg. Instr.* 540 Vulcanite Repositors for inversion of uterus.

repository (rɪˈpɒzɪtərɪ), *sb.* Also 5 reposytorye, 6–7 repositorie. [ad. obs. F. *repositoire* or L. *repositōrium*: see REPOSIT *v.* and -ORY[1].]

1. a. A vessel, receptacle, chamber, etc., in which things are or may be placed, deposited, or stored.

1485 CAXTON *Chas. Gt.* 36 Of the floures charles put a parte in a reposytorye. **1570** LEVINS *Manip.* 105/36 A Repositorie, *repositorium.* **1603** HOLLAND *Plutarch's Mor.* 1200 Many secret monuments, and repositories of demi-gods. **1647** CLARENDON *Contempl. Ps.* Tracts (1727) 514 Those tears.. he keeps in a repository that is never out of his sight. **1698** FRYER *Acc. E. India & P.* 250 On the Outside of this City are Repositories for Snow and Ice. **1712** ADDISON *Spect.* No. 471 ¶2 It is like those Repositories in several Animals that are filled with Stores of their former Food. **1756** C. LUCAS *Ess. Waters* I. 128 At the end of Rathbone-place.. water is.. thrown into an open repository, where it stands. **1806** J. BERESFORD *Miseries Hum. Life* x. xviii, Losing the keys of all your most private repositories. **1862** BURTON *Bk. Hunter* (1863) 56 Stored away in some forgotten repositories, these miscellaneous relics still remain. **1884** *Catholic Dict.* (1897) 305/2 A vase in the form of a dove.. was in the East and France.. used as a repository for the Blessed Sacrament.

b. A place, room, or building, in which specimens, curiosities, or works of art are collected; a museum. Now *rare.*

1658 PHILLIPS s.v., More peculiarly, by the Architects, such places as are built for the laying up of rareties, either in picture or other art are called Repositories. **1667** *Phil. Trans.* II. 486 There being such a stone in their [the Royal Society's] Repository. **1716–18** LADY M. W. MONTAGU *Lett.* I. xvi. 53 The Elector's palace is very handsome, and his repository full of curiosities of different kinds. **1756** P. BROWNE *Jamaica* 39, I have seen a specimen of the red sort .. in the repository of the royal garden at Paris. **1802** JAMES *Milit. Dict.* s.v., The Royal Repository at Woolwich, contains models of every sort of warlike stores, weapons, and fortification. **1876** VOYLE & STEVENSON *Milit. Dict.* 337/2 The repository at Woolwich forms a school of instruction for both officers and men on first joining the artillery.

c. A place where things are kept or offered for sale; a warehouse, store, shop, mart.

1759 A. MURPHY *Let.* 22 July in D. Garrick *Private Corr.* (1831) I. 101 But yours is Beaver's Repository, and there you must judge whether they [*sc.* the horses] are marketable, or likely to tire before they come to the winning-post. **1767** J. WEDGWOOD *Let.* 23 May (1965) 53, I spent a great part of the day in search of a Room for my repository. **1785** GROSE *Class. Dict.*, *Repository*,.. Livery stables where horses and carriages are sold by auction. **1801** MRS. TRIMMER *Oecon. Charity* II. 119 By furnishing different articles for sale at Repositories. **1806** J. BERESFORD *Miseries Hum. Life* XXI. iii, Paying dear for your economy in having made purchases at a 'Cheap Repository'. **1831** [YOUATT] *The Horse* 368 In London, and in most great towns, there are repositories for the periodical sale of horses by auction. *Ibid.* 369 The principal repositories in London. **1848** THACKERAY *Vanity Fair* l, She confides the card to the gentleman of the Fine Art Repository.

2. †**a.** A place where souls are lodged. *Obs.*

1638 FEATLY *Strict. Lyndom.* II. 58 In St. Austines hidden repositories, some soules have ease, and some paine. **1662** H. MORE *Philos. Writ.* Pref. Gen. (1712) 24 Whether the Souls be.. sent from God out of some hidden Repository where they did prae-exist. **1711** ADDISON *Spect.* No. 56 ¶2 There is a Tradition among the Americans, that one of their Countrymen descended in a Vision to the great Repository of Souls.

b. A place in which a dead body is deposited; a vault or sepulchre.

1663 WOOD *Life* June (O.H.S.) I. 476 Buried.. at the high altar in a vault or repository. **1697** POTTER *Antiq. Greece* II. ii. (1715) 196 Women anointed the Balisters of the Churches, and the Repositories of Martyrs. **1774** PENNANT *Tour Scotl. in 1772*, 180 In the middle of these repositories was placed the urn filled with the ashes of the dead. **1807** G. CHALMERS *Caledonia* I. III. vii. 416 Lulach was buried.. in Iona, the accustomed repository of the Scottish kings. **1875** JOWETT *Plato* (ed. 2) III. 305 The ordering of the repositories of the dead.

†**c.** *slang.* 'A lockup or spunging house; a gaol' (Grose, 1785). *Obs.*

3. A place or thing within which something immaterial is thought of as deposited or contained.

c **1645** HOWELL *Lett.* Ep. Ded. Letters can.. be as authentic Registers, and safe repositories of Truth as any Story whatsoever. **1690** LOCKE *Hum. Und.* II. x. §2 This laying up of our Ideas in the Repository of the Memory. **1712–3** POPE *Guardian* No. 4 ¶3, I have found unvalued repositories of learning in the lining of bandboxes. **1788** REID *Aristotle's Log.* ii. §2. 30 A division is a repository which the philosopher frames for holding his ware. **1806** J. BERESFORD *Miseries Hum. Life* I. Introd., What are Theatres but licensed repositories for ill-told lies. **1864** BOWEN *Logic* i. 24 Language is the great repository of thought.

4. A part or place in which something is accumulated or exists in quantities.

1672–3 GREW *Anat. Roots* II. §28 So that the pith is a Repository of better aliment gradually supplied to those Sacciferous Vessels. **1790** UMFREVILLE *Hudson's Bay* 53 He was engaged in.. determining the truth of a copper-mine being up the country. He was two years in search of this valuable repository. **1813** BAKEWELL *Introd. Geol.* (1815) 278 Beside rake veins there are other mineral repositories, called flat veins or flat works, and pipe veins. **1855** J. R. LEIFCHILD *Cornwall* 2 Cornwall is.. an immense subterranean repository of copper and tin.

5. A person to whom some matter is entrusted or confided.

1697 tr. *C'tess D'Aunoy's Trav.* (1706) 25 She made one of her Women, in whom she most confided, the Repository of this Secret. **1773** MRS. CHAPONE *Improv. Mind* (1774) I. 182 Guard against being made the repository of such secrets. **1810** SHELLEY *Zastrozzi* vi, Make me the repository of your sorrows; I would, if possible, alleviate them.

repository (rɪˈpɒzɪtərɪ), *a.* [See prec. and -ORY[2].]

†**1.** Serving for reposition. *Obs. rare*[−1].

1688 BAXTER *Dying Thoughts* (1850) 144 If the bee know .. how to gather her honey and wax, and how to form the repository combs, and how to lay it up [etc.].

2. Pertaining to, of the nature of, replacing heavy ordnance in position after dismounting it.

1876 VOYLE & STEVENSON *Milit. Dict.* 133/2 *Repository exercise*, the mechanical manœuvres with heavy guns. **1890** *Daily News* 21 Aug. 3/2 The Liverpool team.. which took the first prize in the A shift of the repository competition. *Ibid.*, The Liverpool detachment make a point of their repository work.

†**re'positure.** *Obs. rare.* [ad. med.L. *repositūra* (Du Cange): see REPOSIT *v.* and -URE.] Reposition.

1657 TOMLINSON *Renou's Disp.* 489 Bottles.. serving for the repositure of distilled waters. **1661** MORGAN *Sph. Gentry* III. viii. 81 Christians abhorred those obsequies of burning, affecting a repositure into the hands of God, who is able to raise our vile bodies.

†**repo'ssede**, *v. Obs.* Also 6 -seed. [f. RE- 5 a + POSSEDE *v.* Cf. F. *reposséder* (18th c. in Littré).] *trans.* To repossess.

1545 *Lease* in Madox *Formul. Angl.* (1702) 152 It shall be lawfull.. into the said mesuages.. to reentre and the same to repossede. **1600** HOLLAND *Livy* VIII. iv. 283 Doe yee but.. lay claime unto that.., and repossede it at your pleasure. **1606** WARNER *Alb. Eng.* XIV. lxxxv. 353 That Scots and Picts their owne, as earst, should amplie reposseed. [**1616–23** in BULLOKAR and COCKERAM.]

repo'ssess (riː-), *v.* [RE- 5 a: cf. prec.]

1. *trans.* To regain or recover possession of (a place, etc.); to reoccupy. Also *spec.*, to regain possession of or seize (goods being bought by hire-purchase) when a purchaser defaults on his payments.

1494 FABYAN *Chron.* VI. clxiv. 158 After whiche peace concludyd,.. the Kynge repossessyd yᵉ sayd cytie. **1555** W. WATREMAN *Fardle Facions* Pref. 15 Desirous to repossess that, that constrainedly he forsooke. *a* **1586** SIDNEY *Arcadia* (1622) 413 The resolution to dye had repossessed his place in her minde. **1634** FORD *Perk. Warbeck* I. i, Nor doth the house of York decay in honours, Though Lancaster doth repossess his right. *c* **1670** HOBBES *Dial. Com. Laws* (1681) 133 He was received again into Grace, but dyed before he could repossess his benefice. **1742** YOUNG *Nt. Th.* IX. 101 Earth repossesses Part of what she gave. **1782** W. F. MARTYN *Geog. Mag.* I. 34 They affirm, that as soon as the body is deposited in the grave, it is repossessed by the soul. *a* **1821** KEATS *Hyperion* I. 123 Fierce to repossess A heaven he lost erewhile. **1964** *Reading Teacher* Dec. 210/2 One might think.. of a reading program that would enable the children to investigate more widely on their own the worlds of Robin Hood, the cowboys, the spacemen.. when the television is being repaired or repossessed. **1969** *Rolling Stone* 28 June 28/2 The starting point was having their car repossessed in Nashville ten years ago. **1972** *New Society* 12 Oct. 98/3 The record company repossessed the amplifiers and so Bolan, of necessity, switched back to acoustic guitar. **1977** *Field* 13 Jan. 40/1 These committees.. are to consider cases where a farmer needs to repossess a cottage for an incoming employee.

2. *Sc.* To restore (one) †*to*, replace or reinstate *in*, possession of something. †Also without const.

1572–3 *Reg. Privy Council Scot.* II. 195 All personis.. dispossest of houssis.. salbe presentlie repossest to thair houssis. **1574** *Ibid.* 409 To entir and reposses Patrik

Bellenden..in all and sindry [lands]. **1585** *Ibid.* IV. 34 He sall reposses Adam..to the teindis. *a* **1649** DRUMM. OF HAWTH. *Hist. Jas. IV*, Wks. (1711) 67 Kings should repossess kings wrongfully put from their own. **1814** SCOTT *Ld. of Isles* III. ix, They proffer'd aid..To repossess him in his right. **1827** —— *Napoleon* xlii, His son should repossess him in the crown.

3. a. To put (one) in possession *of* something again.

1591 *Acts Privy Council* (1900) XXI. 126 [To] see the supplicant repossessed of his said message, goodes, writings, [etc.] **1622** DONNE *Serm.* 15 Sept. 12 They did scarce know their own title, and yet God repossessed them of it, reinuested them in it. **1660** INGELO *Bentiv. & Ur.* II. (1682) 166 We will endeavour to repossess his Son of his Kingdom. **1728** KENNETT *Register* 323 At length the doctor gets himself re-possessed of his living.

b. *refl.* To regain possession *of* something.

1670 MILTON *Hist. Eng.* Wks. 1851 V. 39 The same Wood, where he had defeated the Britains; who..had now repossess'd themselvs of that place. **1748** *Anson's Voy.* I. v. 48 The Portuguese..soon repossessed themselves of the places the Dutch had taken. **1795** BELSHAM *Mem. Geo. III*, II. 242 Washington..re-possessed himself of his former strong position. **1861** GOSCHEN *For. Exch.* 127 When..the Hamburg banker wishes to repossess himself of his money.

†**4.** To invest again *with* possession of something. *Obs.*

1601 J. WHEELER *Treat. Comm.* 50 To repossesse the Hanses with their old antiquated, and obsolete Priuiledges. **1607** HIERON *Wks.* II. 261 It is Thou only, who art able to repossesse mee with this iewell.

Hence **repo'ssessing** *vbl. sb.*

1633 T. STAFFORD *Pac. Hib.* I. xii. (1821) 140 He would become an humble Suiter to the Lord Deputie (in his behalfe) for the repossessing thereof.

repo'ssessed, *ppl. a.* Chiefly *U.S.* [f. prec. + -ED¹.] That has been regained or seized back, esp. by a vendor; second-hand.

1933 *Sun* (Baltimore) 21 Apr. 19/2 (Advt.), Repossessed Car Corp., 31 W. North Ave. **1936** H. L. MENCKEN *Amer. Lang.* (ed. 4) vi. 293 For the former [sc. *second-hand*] the automobile dealers..have substituted *reconditioned, rebuilt, repossessed* and *used.* **1957** O. NASH *You can't get there from Here* 148 When he was knocked down by a repossessed scooter and the Boy Scouts administered Second Aid. **1974** *Sumter* (S. Carolina) *Daily Item* 24 Apr. 14B/5 (Advt.), Save by getting a repossessed home now. **1977** *Times* 12 Dec. 26/9 (Advt.), Sugar daddy offers—repossessed pastel mink coat ..lynx collar..£2,000.

repo'ssession (riː-). [RE- 5 a: cf. REPOSSESS *v.*]

1. Recovery; renewed possession. Also *spec.*, the recovery of goods being bought by hire-purchase when a purchaser defaults on his payments; legal proceedings to effect this. Also *attrib.*

1582-8 *Hist. James VI* (Bann.) 211 They had the money present to rander to the King and his estaits for laughfull restitution and repossessioun [of Orkney and Zetland]. **1602** WARNER *Alb. Eng.* Epit. (1612) 370 Egelred, now called out of Normandie to the Repossession of his Kingdome. **1652** J. TAYLOR (Water P.) *Journ. Wales* (1859) 34 Meredith.. fought for repossession, and after much bloudshed, lost his labour. **1795** LD. GRENVILLE in *Eng. Hist. Rev.* Apr. (1903) 297 To effect for him the repossession of the territories of which he has been divested. **1853** GROTE *Greece* II. lxxxvi. XI. 305 They had long been anxious for its repossession, and had even besieged it five years before. **1938** *Sun* (Baltimore) 26 Feb. 18/1 Some used-car dealers..employ thugs to beat up customers, if necessary, in repossession activities. **1972** *Mod. Law Rev.* XXXV. I. 24 This balance of power could be achieved if retailers' claims for debt are abolished, leaving repossession or an adverse credit report as the sanctions against non-payment. **1977** *Field* 13 Jan. 40/2 If an occupier refuses an offer of suitable housing, it may provide ground for repossession by the farmer.

†**2.** Restoration, reinstatement. *Obs. rare.*

1598 (*title*) A Briefe Narration of the possession, dispossession and repossession of William Sommers. **1643** R. BAILLIE *Lett. & Jrnls.* (1841) II. 53 Upon the parties humble penitence, and Mr. Gilbert's peaceable repossession, we resolved [etc.].

re'post, *v.*¹ Anglicized form of RIPOST(E *v.*

1730 H. B[LACKWELL] *English Fencing Master* 34 If your Thrust should be parried after drawing your Left-Foot after you, it is impossible you should recover before your Adversary reposts you. **1848** THACKERAY *Van. Fair* li, The little woman..parried and reposted with a home-thrust. **1885** EGERTON CASTLE *Schools of Fence* 138 As the fashion in swords became lighter and shorter, the advantage of parrying first and reposting afterwards became more obvious.

So **re'post** *sb.*

1861 CHAPMAN *Art Fencing* I. 19 The direct return thrust (Repost) or attack after the parry..should be delivered with the greatest rapidity. **1885** EGERTON CASTLE *Schools of Fence* 138 The parry had to be formed in such a way as to act as a repost.

re'post (riː-), *v.*² [f. RE- 5 a + POST *v.*¹] *trans.* To post (a letter, etc.) again.

1963 *Times* 9 Jan. 4/7 Having stolen those postal packets, counsel said, the defendant extracted the passbooks and then reposted them to the building societies. **1977** *Lancs. Life* Nov. 83/3 There were four letters in the box, none of which was addressed to us. Three I re-delivered.., the other I re-posted.

So **re'postage.**

1855 D. G. ROSSETTI *Let.* 23 Jan. (1965) I. 241, I am asked by William to request from you the re-postage of *Athenaeums* when quite done with.

re'posting (riː-), *vbl. sb.* [f. RE- 5 a + POSTING *vbl. sb.*³] Appointment to a new post.

1970 R. WINGATE *Ismay* vii. 159 In India itself regiments with a century or more's traditions of war, service and comradeship had to be split, inevitably reducing their efficiency during the reposting period to zero. **1972** D. BLOODWORTH *Any Number can Play* xix. 200 Pawkinson-Convoy has been recalled for immediate consultation to London and probable reposting. **1981** J. BINGHAM *Brook* 16 He had applied for a re-posting to Melford.

†**re'posure.** *Obs. rare.* [f. REPOSE *v.*² + -URE, after *composure*, etc.] Rest, repose.

1602 MARSTON *Ant. & Mel.* II. Wks. 1856 I. 25 Seat your thoughts In the reposure of most soft content. **1605** [see REPOSAL 1.] **1614** W. B. *Philosopher's Banquet* (ed. 2) 29 Wee may ease our bodies with rest and reposure.

re'pot (riː-), *v.* Also re-. [RE- 5 a.] *trans.* To put (plants) into fresh pots. Also *absol.* Hence **re'potting** *vbl. sb.*

1845 *Florist's Jrnl.* 83 In repotting, the axis..should be raised above the surrounding soil. **1846** J. BAXTER *Libr. Pract. Agric.* (ed. 4) I. 315 After the leaves have attained their growth..the plants should be re-potted. **1858** GLENNY *Gard. Every-day Bk.* 86/2 Market gardeners..disroot their whole stock, and re-pot at one season. **1863** FONBLANQUE *Tangled Skein* II. 181 Superintending the repotting of some choice plants.

re'pour, *v.* [RE- 5 a.] *trans.* To pour back.

1609 HEYWOOD *Brit. Troy* VII. xlv. 150 Some ply the Pompe and..Sea into Sea Repoure. **1610** R. NICCOLS *England's Eliza* ccxlvi, The horrid noise amaz'd the silent night, Repowring downe blacke darknesse from the skie.

‖**repoussé** (rəpuse), *a.* (and *sb.*) [F., pa. pple. of *repousser*, f. *re-* RE- + *pousser*: see PUSH *v.*] **a.** Of metal work: Raised or beaten into relief, ornamented in relief, by means of hammering from the back or reverse side.

1852 *Rep. Juries Exhib.* 1851, 512/2 A candlestick without branches..in *repoussé* work. **1862** *Catal. Internat. Exhib.* II. XXXIII. 5 Stem and base of silver repoussé table. *Ibid.* 24/1 It is made of pure gold, *repoussé* throughout. **1876** OUIDA *Winter City* vii, With firelight on the repoussé gold and silver work of her loose girdle.

b. *ellipt.* as *sb.* Metal-work of this kind; the process of hammering into relief.

1858 QUEEN VICTORIA *Let.* 1 Apr. in R. Fulford *Dearest Child* (1964) 83 A vase by Veité—silver repoussé, really very fine. **1875** *Ure's Dict. Arts* (ed. 7). **1884** KNIGHT *Dict. Mech., Suppl.* 750/2. **1911** [see CRUSTA f]. **1977** *Jrnl. R. Soc. Arts* CXXV. 485/1 The part [of the helmet] which covered the forehead is plain, but above it, in *repoussé*, there is an arched ridge round which curly hair is shown.

‖**repoussoir** (rəpuswar). [Fr., f. *repousser*: see REPOUSSÉ *a.*] An object in the foreground of a painting serving to emphasize the principal figure or scene. Also *transf.* and *fig.*, and *attrib.*

1873 H. JAMES in *Galaxy* Mar. 427 Mr. Casaubon is an excellent invention: as a dusky *repoussoir* to the luminous figure of his wife he could not have been better imagined. **1890** W. JAMES *Princ. Psychol.* II. xxvi. 513 The relative motion felt by the retina is assigned to that one of its components which we look at more in itself and less as a mere repoussoir. **1906** *Westm. Gaz.* 24 Mar. 2/2 A cool, tranquilly pleasing background is degraded to mere dulness in consequence of the gaudy gowns in front of it. Has the word *repoussoir* any meaning to her? **1925** A. HUXLEY *Along Road* III. 169 His exquisitely subtle use of *repoussoirs* and that extraordinary mastery of colour. **1936** *Burlington Mag.* May 208/1 The strong repoussoir character of the trees on the left. **1948** L. SPITZER *Linguistics & Lit. Hist.* v. 235 Since there had to be the Muse..she had to become the *repoussoir*; the personification of the Greek culture which had to be rejected. **1970** T. HILTON *Pre-Raphaelites* v. 150 Brown's..landscapes of the 1850s..shunning the usual devices of *repoussoir* trees and the conventions of aerial perspective. **1974** *Times Lit. Suppl.* 15 Mar. 261/3 The sitter's shoulders sometimes compressed into the narrowing oval of the frame, a *repoussoir* for the all-important face. **1977** 'M. INNES' *Honeybath's Haven* v. 46 The traveller who approaches Hanwell Court by the main drive has the advantage of first viewing the mansion disposed beyond a gigantic *repoussoir* known to art historians as the *Poseidon urging the Sea-Monster to attack Laomedon.*

repp, variant of REP³.

reppe, variant of REPE, to touch. *Obs.*

repped (rɛpt), *a. rare.* [f. REP³ + -ED².] Made like rep; having a surface like rep.

1883 *Cassell's Fam. Mag.* Oct. 696/2 Amazon Soleil is a plain coloured stuff which is repped. **1888** CROSS & BEVAN *Paper-Making* 171 By passing paper between rolls on which devices have been cut, the 'repped' and other papers are produced.

repper ('rɛpə(r)). *slang. rare*⁻¹ [f. REP(UTATION + -ER⁶.] = REPUTATION 4 a.

1910 R. BROOKE *Let.* 7 Nov. (1968) He will find — in his Bed one night: and then she will force him to marry her to save her Repper.

†**'repple.** *Obs.*⁻¹ [Of obscure etym.] ? A staff or cudgel. (Cf. Halliwell, '*Repple*, a long walking staff as tall or taller than the bearer.')

a **1175** *Cott. Hom.* 231 Gief he fend were, me sceolden anon eter gat ȝemete mid gode repples and stiarne swepen.

repple depple ('rɛp(ə)l ˌdɛp(ə)l). *U.S. Mil. slang.* Also **reppo depot.** [f. REPL(ACEMENT + DEP(OT modified by reduplication and rhyme.] A replacement depot (see quot. 1945).

1945 *Amer. N. & Q.* Dec. 136/2 *Repple Depple*, overseas replacement depot where soldiers are assembled before sailing back to the United States. **1945** *N.Y. Times Mag.* 9 Dec. 20/3 One of the last phases of the European war's end —the overseas replacement depot or 'repple depple', where Yanks slated for the long voyage home are gathered together... Repple depples, in short, are dreary places. *Ibid.* He talked out of turn to the repple depple Powers-That-Be. **1947** *Amer. Speech* XXII. 216 *Repple Depple* had a less popular form, *Reppo Depot.* A person who never approached the fighting front was a *Reppo Depot Ranger.* **1973** S. ALSOP *Stay of Execution* (1974) III. 283, I suppose in the American army we would have been sent to a Replacement Depot, or Repple Depple. **1978** J. A. MICHENER *Chesapeake* 771 He was sent to Korea, not with a formed unit but to a replacement depot, a repple depple he explained to his parents.

repplye, obs. form of REPLY *v.*

†**repraise,** *v. Obs.* [RE-] ? To dispraise.

c **1450** *Pol. Poems* (Rolls) II. 227 Justice ne was egaly execute,..Right was repraysede and founde for no repute.

re'pray (riː-), *v.* [RE- 5 a.] To pray again.

1616 J. LANE *Cont. Sqr.'s T.* VIII. 99 Eftsoones repraienge for ann happie end, did to thallmighties will all recommend. **1891** C. E. NORTON *Dante's Hell* xxvi. 142 Much I pray thee, and repray that the prayer avail a thousand.

re'preach (riː-), *v.* [RE- 5 a.] *trans.* To preach again. Hence **re'preaching** *vbl. sb.*

1681 COLVIL *Whigs Supplic.* (1751) 4 Like one of bishop Andrews' sermons, repreached the other day by an expectant in his episcopal trial for the ministry. **1812-29** COLERIDGE in *Lit. Rem.* (1838) III. 110 A beautiful paragraph, well worth extracting, aye, and re-preaching. **1893** FINLAYSON *Ess.* 158 We wish to repreach Isaiah's message.

repre'cipitate (riː-), *v.* [RE- 5 a.] *trans.* To precipitate (a substance) again.

1842 PARNELL *Chem. Anal.* (1845) 293 It is soluble in cold acetic and dilute nitric acids, and is reprecipitated by ammonia. **1881** *Nature* XXIV. 470/1 Bone earth dissolved in acid is reprecipitated by alkalies.

reprecipi'tation (riː). [RE- 5 a: cf. prec.] The action of precipitating, or fact of being precipitated, again.

1869 MRS. OLIPHANT *Hist. Sk. Geo. II* (1879) II. 373 The sudden fall and rising and reprecipitation into the abyss. **1897** *Allbutt's Syst. Med.* III. 176 Reprecipitation of the biurate took place in two or three days.

repreef, -preeve, obs. ff. REPROOF, REPROVE.

repreevable, -prefable, obs. ff. REPROVABLE.

repreeve, obs. form of REPRIEVE.

repreever, obs. f. REPROVER.

repref(e, -preff(e, obs. ff. REPROOF, REPROVE.

reprehend (rɛprɪ'hɛnd), *v.* [ad. L. *reprehendĕre*, f. *re-* RE- + *prehendĕre* to seize: cf. *apprehend*, etc. Hence also F. *reprendre.*]

1. *trans.* To reprove, reprimand, rebuke, censure, find fault with: **a.** a person.

a **1340** HAMPOLE *Psalter* cxxxiv. 15 He scornys þe honurrers of mawmetis and reprehendis þaim. *c* **1374** CHAUCER *Troylus* I. 510 Thow were ay wont eche louere reprehende Of þing fro which þow kanst þe nought defende. *c* **1450** tr. *De Imitatione* II. vi. 46 Thou shalt rest swetly if þyn herte reprehende þe not. **1490** CAXTON *Eneydos* xix. 69 It semeth that thou oughte not in no wyse to reprehende me. **1530** PALSGR. 687/1 He reprehended me afore al the companye. **1578** T. N. tr. *Conq. W. India* 367 Cortes hearing their odious request reprehended them. **1601** F. GODWIN *Bps. of Eng.* 267 For which fact he was bold to reprehend his holinesse sharpely. **1651** HOBBES *Leviath.* II. xxii. 123 Yet was their Assembly judged Unlawfull, and the Magistrate reprehended them for it. **1748** RICHARDSON *Clarissa* (1811) II. xxviii. 179, I severely reprehend him on this occasion. **1828** LANDOR *Imag. Conv.*, *Southey & Porson* ii, If..I am unjust in a single tittle, reprehend me instantly. **1839** YEOWELL *Anc. Brit. Ch.* ix. (1847) 94 Theodoric.., having been reprehended by him, became his enemy.

b. a thing, action, conduct, etc.

a **1340** HAMPOLE *Psalter* xlii. 5 þof men kan fynd noght to reprehend, god kan. *c* **1375** in *Rel. Ant.* I. 39 He that bysyeth hym to lyve piteuosly, he wurchipet God and holy writ, and reprehendet no thing that he undurstondet not. *c* **1380** WYCLIF *Sel. Wks.* II. 201 Whanne a man leeviþ to reprehende an opyn synne. *c* **1475** *Babees Bk.* 29 Therfore I pray that no man Reprehende This lytyl Book. *a* **1529** SKELTON *Agst. Garnesche* iii. 16 Lewdely your tyme ye spende, My lyuyng to reprehende. **1567** *Trial Treas.* (1850) 7 It is an harde thing..For a foolishe man to haue his maners reprehended. **1612** T. TAYLOR *Comm. Titus* ii. 6 This doctrine reprehendeth a common error in the world. **1657** TRAPP *Comm. Job* v. 9 It is extreme folly to reprehend what we cannot comprehend. **1708** J. PHILIPS *Cyder* I. 78, I nor advise, nor reprehend the Choice. **1790** BURKE *Fr. Rev.* 203, I had..much to reprehend, and much to wish changed, in many of the old tenures. **1849** THACKERAY *Pendennis* lxii, I ..most strongly reprehend any man's departure from his word. **1876** E. MELLOR *Priesth.* vii. 313 With a haste and recklessness which cannot be too severely reprehended.

c. *absol.*

1590 SHAKS. *Mids. N.* v. i. 436 Gentles, doe not reprehend. If you pardon, we will mend. **1846** TRENCH *Mirac.* xxx. (1862) 433 The very same who at the first reprehended, will in the end applaud.

†**2.** To refute, prove to be fallacious. *Obs. rare.*

1597 BACON *Coulers Good & Evill* §3 But that denieth the supposition, it doth not reprehend the fallax. *Ibid.* §5 This coulour will bee reprehended or incountred by imputing to all excellencie in compositions a kind of pouertie.

†**3.** *Sc.* To take (one) in wrong doing. *Obs.*[−1]

1538 *Aberdeen Regr.* (1844) I. 156 It selbe lesum to quhatsumever nychtbour that reprehendis the layaris of the said fulze to tak the veschell..quhill thai be punyst.

¶**4.** Misused by ignorant speakers for 'represent' and 'apprehend.'

1588 SHAKS. *L.L.L.* I. i. 184 *Constable,* I my selfe reprehend his owne person, for I am his graces Tharborough. **1714** GAY *What d'ye call it* II. vii, *Constable,* Friends, reprehend him, reprehend him there. [They seize the Sergeant.]

Hence **repre'hending** *vbl. sb.* and *ppl. a.*

1570 FOXE *A. & M.* (ed. 2) 68/2 The cause of whose martirdome was the reprehending of Idolatrie. **1611** RICH *Honest. Age* Epil. (1844) 68 Such a kinde of subiect, as is.. fitting to be roughly rubbed with a reprehending veritie. **1663** GERBIER *Counsel* 60 To shun reprehending of Master workmen openly.

repre'hendable, *a. rare.* [a. obs. F. *reprehendable* (Godef.), or f. prec. + -ABLE: cf. *irreprehendable* (1597).] Reprehensible.

a **1340** HAMPOLE *Psalter* xl. 6 If þai myght fynd any thynge in vs reprehendabile. **1627–77** FELTHAM *Resolves* II. liv. 271 They were reprehendable.

repre'hendatory, *a. rare*[−1]. [f. REPREHEND, after *commendatory*.] Conveying reproof.

1853 *Tait's Mag.* XX. 608 She had given too much occasion for these reprehendatory remarks.

repre'hender. Also 6 -our, -or. [f. as prec. + -ER[1].] One who reprehends or censures.

1555 W. WATREMAN *Fardle Facions* Pref. 20 Let it not moue the,..if any cankered reprehendour of other mens doynges shal saie vnto the [etc.]. **1585** PARSONS *Chr. Exerc.* II. vi. 370 Therefore fell they in fine, to persecute sharply their reprehendors. **1587** FRAUNCE *Amyntas* Ep. Ded., Now for the second sort of reprehenders..mine answere is at hand. **1649** JER. TAYLOR *Gt. Exemp.* I. Sect. viii. 114 He was a severe reprehender of the Pharisees and Sadducees. **1678** R. L'ESTRANGE *Seneca's Mor.* To Rdr., Seneca; the most lively Describer of Publick Vices..and the smartest Reprehender of them.

reprehensible (rɛprɪˈhɛnsɪb(ə)l), *a.* [ad. late L. *reprehensibilis,* f. *reprehens-,* ppl. stem of *reprehendĕre* to REPREHEND: see -IBLE. Cf. F. *répréhensible* (1314).] Deserving of reprehension, censure, or rebuke; reprovable; blameworthy.

1382 WYCLIF *Gal.* ii. 11, I stood aȝens hym in to the face, for he was reprehensyble [*v.r.* repreuable]. **1570** FOXE *A. & M.* (ed. 2) 183/2 Whereby it is to be gathered, that the bishop and deacon are noted infamous and reprehensible. **1589** PUTTENHAM *Eng. Poesie* I. xx. (Arb.) 58 In a meane man prodigalitie and pride are faultes more reprehensible then in Princes. **1651** HOBBES *Govt. & Soc.* i. §7. 10 It is therefore neither absurd, nor reprehensible..for a man to use all his endeavours to..defend his Body. **1665** GLANVILL *Def. Van. Dogm.* 6 To keep such voluminous ado about acknowledg'd uncertainties, is a very reprehensible vanity. **1777** SHERIDAN *Sch. Scand.* III. ii, In my mind, the other's economy in selling it to him was more reprehensible by half. **1831** LAMB *Elia* II. *Ellistonia,* The fault is least reprehensible in players. **1844** LD. BROUGHAM *Brit. Const.* viii. (1862) 104 There is even an irregular, unconstitutional, and reprehensible act done.

Hence **repre'hensibleness** (Bailey vol. II, 1727); **repre,hensi'bility** (*Cent. Dict.* 1891).

repre'hensibly, *adv.* [f. prec. + -LY[2].] In a reprehensible manner or degree.

1637 GILLESPIE *Eng. Pop. Cerem.* II. vii. 27 They who contend..reprehensibly. **1849** MACAULAY *Hist. Eng.* iv. I. 502 Even those laws..were in his judgment reprehensibly lenient. **1885** *Truth* 11 June 932/1 It was reprehensibly foolish and reckless.

reprehension (rɛprɪˈhɛnʃən). Also 4 -cion, 6 -syon, 7 -tion. [ad. L. *reprehensiōn-em,* n. of action f. *reprehendĕre.* Cf. F. *répréhension* (12th c.).]

1. The action of reprehending; censure, reproof, rebuke, reprimand.

c **1374** CHAUCER *Troylus* I. 684 Myn entenciown Nys nought to yow of reprehencion To speke as now. *c* **1477** CAXTON *Jason* 25 Men preyse and alowe moche the fayr Myrro—but I trowe..she sholde be fonden somwhat of Reprehension. **1542** BOORDE *Dyetary* xxxvii. (1870) 299 Vse few wordes to them, excepte it be for reprehensyon or gentyll reformacyon. *a* **1586** SIDNEY *Arcadia* I. (1605) 49 To a heart fully resolute, counsell is tedious, but reprehension is lothsome. **1612** BRINSLEY *Lud. Lit.* xv. (1627) 200 To use sharpe reprehension or correction for that carelessnesse. **1678** R. L'ESTRANGE *Seneca's Mor., Life,* Exhorting them.. sometimes by Good Counsel, otherwhile by Reprehension. **1709** STEELE *Tatler* No. 67 ¶ 12 That when they will not take private Reprehension, they may be tried further by a publick one. **1777** BURKE *Corr.* (1844) II. 194 If they are corrupt, they merit..blame and reprehension. **1801** STRUTT *Sports & Past.* Introd. 41 The evil consequences..have in all ages called loudly for reprehension. **1868** E. EDWARDS *Ralegh* I. xxi. 464 The Dean..had used strong language in reprehension of the Prebendary's acceptance. **1885** *Truth* 28 May 836/1 Such profligate extravagance is deserving of severe reprehension.

b. With *a* and *pl.* An instance of this.

1574 WHITGIFT *Def. Answ.* ii. Wks. 1851 I. 201 What church-discipline would you have other than admonitions, reprehensions, and..excommunications? **1589** PUTTENHAM *Eng. Poesie* I. xvi. (Arb.) 50 To th'intent that such exemplifying..might worke for a secret reprehension to others. **1608** WILLET *Hexapla Exod.* 192 He trieth her with sharpe reprehensions. **1671** FLAVEL *Fount. Life* xxii. 66 He finds them asleep, which occasioned that gentle Reprehension from him. *a* **1704** T. BROWN *Eng. Sat.* Wks. 1730 I. 29 His writings contain'd as severe reprehensions as any others. **1784** COWPER *Tiroc.* 656 An evidence and reprehension both Of the mere schoolboy's lean and tardy growth.

†**2.** Refutation; proof of fallacy. *Obs.*

1531 ELYOT *Gov.* I. xiv, Certayne partes of an oration, that is to say for Narrations, Partitions, Confirmations and Confutations, named of some Reprehensions. **1597** BACON *Coulers Good & Evill* §5 It is not so properly a case or reprehension as it is a counter couler. *Ibid.* §7 An other reprehension is, that things of greatnes and predominancie [etc.]. **1620** T. GRANGER *Div. Logike* 347 Secondly, the solution, or reprehension thereof.

reprehensive (rɛprɪˈhɛnsɪv), *a.* [f. REPREHEND *v.*; cf. *comprehensive,* etc., and obs. F. *reprehensif, -ive* (Godef.).] Of the nature of reprehension; containing reproof. Now *rare.*

1589 PUTTENHAM *Eng. Poesie* I. xiii. (Arb.) 46 The said auncient Poets vsed for that purpose, three kinds of poems reprehensiue. **1592** *Nobody & Someb.* in Simpson *Sch. Shaks.* (1878) I. 299 What I did speake in reprehensive sort. **1609** BP. W. BARLOW *Answ. Nameless Cath.* 22 He answereth by an Interrogation, such as the Rhetoricians call ..a question reprehensiue. **1671** WOODHEAD *St. Teresa* I. Pref. 4 Words consolatory, Instructive, Reprehensive. **1748** RICHARDSON *Clarissa* (1811) III. xl. 231, I give you sincere thanks for every line of your reprehensive letters. **1825** CULBERTSON *Lect. Revel.* xii. 160 The body of this epistle consists of two parts; one of which is commendatory, and the other reprehensive. **1845** A. DUNCAN *Disc.* 159 The benignity of the Deity became a reprehensive witness, reproving and condemning their errors.

Hence **repre'hensively** *adv.*

1631 *Celestina* Ep. Ded. A iij b, Sithence it is written reprehensively, and not instructively. **1678** CUDWORTH *Intell. Syst.* I. iv. 226 Xenophanes..reprehensively admonished the Egyptians after this manner.

reprehensory (rɛprɪˈhɛnsərɪ), *a.* [See prec. and -ORY.] Reprehensive. Now *rare.*

1586 A. DAY *Eng. Secretary* I. (1625) 21 Commendatorie, Monitorie or Reprehensorie. *a* **1614** P. LILIE *Two Serm.* (1619) 56 The words, then, of the angell were not onely reprehensory but consolatory. **1652** URQUHART *Jewel* Wks. (1834) 272 If by mischance..their forwardness in solicitation procure a reprehensory check. **1780** JOHNSON *Let.* 21 Aug., There is no reason for making any reprehensory complaint. **1825** CULBERTSON *Lect. Revel.* xix. 249 The evils specified in the reprehensory part of this epistle.

repreif, obs. Sc. form of REPROOF, REPROVE.

†**re'preme,** *v. Sc. Obs. rare.* [ad. L. *reprimĕre*: for the phonology cf. *exeme, redeem.*] *trans.* To repress.

1549 *Compl. Scot.* xvii. 154 To repreme and distroye the arrogant consait of them that glorifeis & pridis them. *a* **1586** *Satir. Poems Reform.* xxxvii. 23 Sa gude Renoun, quhilk raillaris rage repremis, Advansis moir, þe moir Invyaris wex it.

†**repremi'ation.** *Obs. rare*[−0]. (See quot.)

1611 COTGR., *Repremiation,* a repremiation, a rewarding.

repreofing, obs. form of REPROVING.

repreove, obs. form of REPROVE.

†**repre'sent,** *sb. Obs.* [f. the vb.] A representation; an image.

c **1400** tr. *Secreta Secret., Gov. Lordsh.* 98 Whenne þat vche a wyt hauys in hym [the brain] his represent. **1615** G. SANDYS *Trav.* 82 Their Churches are many of them well set forth and painted with the represents of Saints. **1635** F. WHITE *Sabbath* 163 Resting from servile labour, upon the old Sabbath day, was a figure and represent of spirituall ceasing and abstaining from the servile workes of sin.

represent (rɛprɪˈzɛnt), *v.*[1] Also 6–7 as *pa. pple.* [ad. OF. *représenter* (12th c.) or L. *repræsentāre,* f. *re-* RE- + *præsentāre* to PRESENT.]

†**1.** *trans.* **a.** To bring into presence; *esp.* to present (oneself or another) *to* or *before* a person.

c **1380** WYCLIF *Wks.* (1880) 47 So þat he may not be delyuerid of his hond til he represente hym in his owen persone in þe hondis of his mynystre, and be þe mynystre holden sadly..til þat he represente hym to þe cardynal hostiense. **1413** *Pilgr. Sowle* (Caxton) I. ii. (1859) 8 Representeth your self smartely to this jugement, by ordre, as ye shal be clepyd. *c* **1450** LOVELICH *Grail* lii. 500 He is a manne that ȝow Alle hath taken As presoneres, And to Me Represented now here. **1502** *Ord. Crysten Men* (W. de W. 1506) IV. xxix. 340 She [the soul]..leueth her body and her representeth unto hym unto his blessyd pleasure. **1585** T. WASHINGTON tr. *Nicholay's Voy.* IV. i. 114 In the day time they did represent themselues before the Gouernours. **1649** JER. TAYLOR *Gt. Exemp.* Disc. xii. §7 We are taught to pray not that it be all at once represented or deposited, but that God would minister it as we need it.

†**b.** To bring (one) *to* some privilege or state.

1435 MISYN *Fire of Love* 7 O lufly lufe euerlastynge, þat vs rayses fro þies lawe þinges, &..to þe sight of godis maiestee vs representys. *c* **1450** LOVELICH *Grail* lv. 28 Good Besynesse..schal kepen ȝoure body from Alle torment, and to Endeles blysse ȝow Represent.

†**c.** To render (service); to present (a thing) *to* a person. *Obs. rare.*

c **1425** WYNTOUN *Cron.* v. Prol. 46 Þir ar þe twa gret lichtis ..þat oyssis for to represent And to mynystir þar serwice Tyme be tyme. **1560** ROLLAND *Crt. Venus* IV. 129 Thisbe.. kneilland vpon hir kne, To Rhamnusia the missiue represent Fra the Assise. **1601** HOLLAND *Pliny* II. 493 The Thurines honoured and said Ælius with a statue of brasse, and represented to him a coronet of gold.

†**d.** To produce, give forth. *Obs. rare*[−1].

1601 HOLLAND *Pliny* I. 2 That as the Heauen moueth, it doth represent indeed a pleasant and incredible sweet harmonie both day and night.

2. a. To bring clearly and distinctly before the mind, esp. (to another) by description or (to oneself) by an act of imagination.

1375 BARBOUR *Bruce* I. 18 Aulde storys that men redys, Representis to thaim the dedys Of stalwart folk that lywyt ar. *c* **1392** CHAUCER *Compl. Venus* 58 Whanne I me weel avyse On any estate þat man may represent þane haue yee maked me..Cheese þe best. **1587** GOLDING *De Mornay* xxvii. (1592) 433 The Dreame representeth vs the stone hewen without hand. **1605** BACON *Adv. Learn.* I. To King §2 Wherefore, representing your Majesty many times unto my mind,..I have been..possessed with an extreme wonder at those your virtues. **1638** JUNIUS *Paint. Ancients* 18 The other..studieth also to expresse things prefigured only and represented by the phantasie. **1667** MILTON *P.L.* v. 104 Of all external things, Which the five watchful Senses represent, She forms Imaginations. *a* **1708** BEVERIDGE *Thes. Theol.* (1710) I. 261 Why is God said to have a head and hands? To represent Him the better to our capacities. **1794** PALEY *Evid.* II. ii. (1817) 58 The happiness of the good and the misery of the bad..is represented by metaphors and comparisons. **1856** DOVE *Logic Chr. Faith* Introd. 4 Man may have knowledge which he cannot represent to his formal reason. **1879** *Cassell's Techn. Educ.* IV. 95/1 It remains, therefore, to complete the work by representing the character of the country.

absol. **1692** NORRIS *Curs. Refl.* 27 Our Ideas..are immaterial as to their Representation, that is, they represent after an immaterial manner.

b. To place (a fact) clearly before another; to state or point out explicitly or seriously *to* one, with a view to influencing action or conduct, freq. by way of expostulation or remonstrance.

1582 N. LICHEFIELD tr. *Castanheda's Conq. E. Ind.* I. lxvi. 135 There was represent unto him the great danger which he feared might happen unto him. **1647** CLARENDON *Hist. Reb.* I. §112 The condition of his Son..was argument of great compassion, and was lively and successfully represented to the King himself. **1687** A. LOVELL tr. *Thevenot's Trav.* I. 78 They went..to the Kiaya Bey, and having represented to him how long they had served [etc.]. **1740** LD. CARTERET in *Johnson's Debates* (1787) I. 119 To obviate those dangers from the army which have been so strongly and justly represented. **1794** CHARLOTTE SMITH *Wand. Warwick* 148 He represented to me, that..it would be unworthy of me to assail him with words of reproach. **1829** LYTTON *Devereux* I. ii, I have just represented to my good brother the necessity of sending my sons to school. **1849** MACAULAY *Hist. Eng.* vi. II. 63 It would have been useless to represent these things to James. **1864** D. G. MITCHELL *Sev. Stor.* 79, I represented my official character to the doorkeeper.

c. *absol.* To make representations or objections *against* something; to protest. Now *rare.*

1717 BOLINGBROKE *Let. to Windham* (1889) 23 When the Queen seemed to intend a change in her ministry, they had deputed some of their members to represent against it. **1782** R. CUMBERLAND *Anecd. Painters* II. 81 The Chapter objected to his nomination, and deputed two of their body to represent to Philip against the person of Cano. **1861** LD. BROUGHAM *Brit. Const.* xvi. 248 He..prosecuted seven Prelates for representing against his Declaration appointed to be read in all Churches.

3. a. To describe as having a specified character or quality; to give out, assert, or declare to be of a certain kind. Const. *as,* (†*for,*) *to be,* and with simple complement.

1513 DOUGLAS *Æneis* VII. ii. 53 Picus the king, quhilk dois the represent, Saturnus, for his fader and parent. **1612** E. GRIMSTONE *Heroyk Life* I. 68 Hee did represent it easie, safe, and commodious. **1663** J. SPENCER *Prodigies* Pref. A iv b, Gregory the Great (represented to Posterity as one most studious of the propagation of the Christian Religion). **1685** WOOD *Life* 2 May (O.H.S.) III. 142 Radcliff represented him to be a turbulent man. **1714** POPE *Lett.* (1735) I. 210 May they represent me what they will, as long as you think me what I am. **1764** HARMER *Observ.* I. xviii. 43 The trees are represented..as but just grown green at Jerusalem in March. **1855** MACAULAY *Hist. Eng.* ix. II. 444 Sunderland they represented as the chief conspirator. **1874** L. STEPHEN *Hours in Library* (1892) I. vi. 229 Society is not what Balzac represents it to be.

refl. **1817** JAS. MILL *Brit. India* I. II. ii. 107 The first legislator of the Hindus..appears to have represented himself as the republisher of the will of God.

b. To give out, allege *that,* etc.

1883 [cf. *represented* ppl. adj. below]. **1891** BARBER in *Law Times* XC. 395/1 The defendant did represent that the cow was..sound, when he knew it was not so.

4. a. To show, exhibit, or display to the eye; to make visible or manifest; †to display in one's bearing or air. Now *rare.*

c **1400** *Rom. Rose* 7402 Of her estat she her repented, As her visage represented. **1514** BARCLAY *Cyt. & Uplondyshm.* (Percy Soc.) 32 It is in power of God omnypotent, His very presence to us to represent. **1567** MAPLET *Gr. Forest* 11 Iris ..being..stricken of the Sunne his beames, doth represent and shewe both the figure and colours of the Rainebow vpon the wall next to it. *a* **1578** LINDESAY (Pitscottie) *Chron. Scot.* (S.T.S.) I. 25 He thocht him selff..frie fra the iniuries of all enemyis gif he representit the samyn arrogance that his father did wsse of befoir. **1660** R. COKE *Justice Vind., Arts & Sc.* 2 Neither a right line nor a point can be truly represented to the sense according to the truth of them. **1707** *Curios. Husb. & Gard.* 38 The Root of Fern cut obliquely, represents an Eagle. **1781** COWPER *Hope* 74 But still the imputed tints are those alone The medium represents, and not their own.

b. *spec.* To exhibit by means of painting, sculpture, etc.; to portray, depict, delineate.

c **1400** MAUNDEV. (Roxb.) x. 38 ȝit es þare paynting, whare in þe grete dole þat þai made es representid and purtraid. *a* **1586** SIDNEY *Arcadia* I. (1605) 9 The Painter meaning to represent the present condition of the young ladie. **1661** FELTHAM *Lusoria* in *Resolves*, etc. (1696) 73 They forbad the Holy Ghosts being represented in the form of a Dove. **1663** GERBIER *Counsel* 14 Pilasters, through whose bodies Lions are represented to creep. *Ibid.* 16 To direct the Sculptors how to Represent those Images. **1766** GOLDSM. *Vic. W.* xvi, My wife desired to be represented as Venus. **1821** CRAIG *Lect. Drawing* viii. 422 The subjects for these purposes should always be represented as if placed at a considerable degree of elevation. **1843** RUSKIN *Mod. Paint.* I. I. i. ii. §2 What is commonly considered the whole art of painting, that is, the art of representing any natural object faithfully.

c. Of pictures, images, etc.: To exhibit by artificial resemblance or delineation.

c **1420** LYDG. *Assembly of Gods* 1913 The thyrd wall.. the Tyme representeth of Reuocacion. **1590** SPENSER *F.Q.* III. iii. 29 With thee yet shall he leave.. his ymage dead, That living him in all activity To thee shall represent. **1687** A. LOVELL tr. *Thevenot's Trav.* 94 There is one over the Gate, representing in bas relief our Saviour's riding into Jerusalem upon the Ass. **1711** ADDISON *Spect.* No. 26 ¶5 The Monuments of their Admirals.. represent them like themselves. **1861** M. PATTISON *Ess.* (1889) I. 45 Two allegorical pieces by.. Holbein, representing the Triumph of Riches and the Triumph of Poverty respectively. **1873** BLACK *Pr. Thule* iii, The four walls were.. covered by a paper of foreign manufacture, representing spacious Tyrolese landscapes, and incidents of the chase.

5. a. To exhibit or reproduce in action or show; to perform or produce (a play, etc.) upon the stage.

c **1460** *Play Sacram.* 10 And yt lyke yow to here yᵉ purpoos of yⁱˢ play that [ys] representyd now in yower syght. **1589** PUTTENHAM *Eng. Poesie* I. xv. (Arb.) 49 These matters were also.. represented by action as that of the Comedies. **1615** BRATHWAIT *Strappado* (1878) 161 Saint Bartlemewes, where all the Pagents showne, And all those acts from Adam vnto Noe Vs'd to be represent. **1656** EARL MONM. tr. *Boccalini's Advts. fr. Parnass.* II. xcvii. (1674) 250 Such like Spectacles .. did but little honour to those that caused them to be represented. **1745** P. THOMAS *Jrnl. Anson's Voy.* 203 In China we may.. represent Comedies, and dance Balls in a Lanthorn. **1774** WARTON *Hist. Eng. Poetry* (1775) I. 233 In what manner, if ever, this piece was represented theatrically, cannot easily be discovered. *a* **1822** SHELLEY *Faust* II. 408 Quite a new piece, the last of seven, for 'tis The custom now to represent that number. **1891** *Law Times Rep.* LXIII. 763/1 Any person had a right to dramatise the novel and to represent the drama.

b. To exhibit or personate (a character) on the stage; to act the part or character of (some one).

1662 J. DAVIES tr. *Olearius' Voy. Ambass.* 213 The Physician, a person the fittest in the World to represent a Fool in a play. **1711** STEELE *Spect.* No. 48 ¶5 Persons who represent Heroes in a Tragedy. **1752** BATHURST *Adventurer* No. 3 ¶8 Amazons, to represent whom I have hired all the wonderful tall men and women.. in this town. **1824** SCOTT *St. Ronan's* xx, Oberon, the King of Shadows, whose sovereign gravity.. was somewhat indifferently represented by the silly gaiety of Miss in her Teens. **1888** SHORTHOUSE *Countess Eve* i, He so entirely associated himself with the characters he represented on the stage, that he lost himself in them.

c. *intr.* To appear on the stage; to act, perform.

a **1547** SURREY *Æneid* IV. 622 Like Orestes Agamemnons son In tragedies who represented [*v.r.* -eth] aye Driuen about. **1766** *Char.* in *Ann. Reg.* 7/1, I gave him a taste for.. the 'petits operas' in which I sung and represented myself.

6. a. To symbolize, to serve as a visible or concrete embodiment of (some quality, fact, or other abstract concept). †Also *intr.*, const. *unto.*

c **1380** WYCLIF *Sel. Wks.* III. 462 Ymagis þat representen pompe and glorie of þo worlde. *a* **1483** *Liber Niger* in *Househ. Ord.* (1790) 56 The Steward and Thesaurer in hys absence, within this Courte, represents unto the estate of an Erle. **1508** DUNBAR *Poems* vii. 71 The sueird of conquis.. Be borne suld highe before the in presence, To represent sic man as thou has beyn. **1560** DAUS tr. *Sleidane's Comm.* 25 An Appell of Golde, representynge the shape of the rounde worlde. **1600** E. BLOUNT tr. *Conestaggio* 89 Although the Dutchesse may represent the degree of her Father, .. it were impossible she shoulde represent the qualitie of a male. **1663** BUTLER *Hud.* I. i. 249 This hairy meteor.. With grisly type did represent Declining age of government. **1788** GIBBON *Decl. & F.* xlix. V. 121 The patriciate represented only the title, the service, the alliance, of these distant protectors. **1849** MACAULAY *Hist. Eng.* ii. I. 199 No sovereign has ever represented the majesty of a great state with more dignity and grace. **1866** KINGSLEY *Lett.* (1878) II. 243 The House of Lords seems to me to represent all heritable property, real or personal. **1894** J. T. FOWLER *Adamnan* Introd. 53 Thus the two Finnians represented Welsh and North British traditions respectively.

b. Of quantities: To indicate or imply (another quantity).

1860 TYNDALL *Glac.* I. xxii. 151, I knew the immense amount of mechanical force represented by four ounces of bread and ham. **1878** HUXLEY *Physiogr.* 45 An inch of rain represents about 100 tons of water to the acre.

7. a. Of things: To stand for or in place of (a person or thing); to be the figure or image of (something). Also, with personal subj., to denote *by* a substitute.

c **1430** *Art Nombryng* 5 That vnyte by respect of the figure that he came fro representith an .C. **1432–50** tr. *Higden* (Rolls) VI. 211 Peple honoure noo thynge in theyme [images] but God, or for God and for seyntes, which they represente to us. **1513** DOUGLAS *Æneis* VI. Prol. 91 Ane vthir place quhilk purgatory representis. **1560** DAUS tr. *Sleidane's Comm.* 47 The sacred and holy host that representeth Christes body. **1667** MILTON *P.L.* XII. 255 Before him burn Seaven Lamps as in a Zodiac representing The Heav'nly fires. **1687** A. LOVELL tr. *Thevenot's Trav.* I. 116 This Colossus which represented the Sun, was cast by Chares the Lyndian. **1718** LADY M. W. MONTAGU *Let. to Lady Rich* 16 Mar., I live in a place that very well represents the tower of Babel. **1788** GIBBON *Decl. & F.* xlix. V. 136 His coronation oath represents a promise to maintain the faith. **1830** EIDRAH TREBOR *Hoyle Made Familiar* 2 The inventor [of cards] proposed, by the figures of the four suits,.. to represent the four classes of men in the kingdom. **1856** STANLEY *Sinai & Pal.* xii. (1858) 406 Cyprus thus visible from the mainland, represented to the Hebrew people the whole western world. **1868** LOCKYER *Elem. Astron.* ii. §7 (1879) 39 If we represent the Sun by a globe about two feet in diameter [etc.].

†**b.** To present the figure or appearance of, to resemble. *Obs.*

1551 TURNER *Herbal* I. C vj, Dyll groweth.. wyth a spokye top as fenell hath, whome he doth represent wonders nere. **1615** CROOKE *Body of Man* 855 On their outside they [the valves of the veins] represent the knottes that are in the branches of plants.

c. To be the equivalent of, to correspond to, to replace (*esp.* another animal or plant in a given region).

1855 SMITH & DALLAS *Syst. Nat. Hist.* II. 432 The Llamas, which represent the Camels in the New World. **1879** HARLAN *Eyesight* iii. 34 In the eye, the sides of the box are represented by the sclerotic. **1882** FLOWER in *Encycl. Brit.* XIV. 738/2 The old idea that they in some way 'represented' each other in the two hemispheres of the world was a mere fancy.

8. a. To take or fill the place of (another) in some respect or for some purpose; to be a substitute in some capacity for (a person or body); to act for (another) by a deputed right.

1509 FISHER *Fun. Serm. C'tess Richmond* Wks. (1876) 297 Albeit she dyd not receyue in to her house our sauyour in his owne persone.. she neuertheles receyued theim that dothe represent his persone. *c* **1595** CAPT. WYATT *R. Dudley's Voy. W. Ind.* (Hakl. Soc.) 23 Our Generall sent Cap. Jobson, repræsentinge his person with his authorite, as his Leiftenante Generall. **1651** HOBBES *Leviath.* II. xix. 95 It is manifest, that men who are in absolute liberty may.. give Authority to One man, to represent them every one. **1766** BLACKSTONE *Comm.* II. xiv. 217 All the branches inherit the same share that their root, whom they represent, would have done. **1838** W. BELL *Dict. Law Scot.* 713 When an heir is cited as representing his ancestor, he incurs a passive title if he states a peremptory defence. **1849** MACAULAY *Hist. Eng.* vi. II. 139 During that interval the king was represented by a board of lords justices. **1853** MAURICE *Proph. & Kings* xxvi. 449 There sat upon his soul a weight of sorrow and evil, as if he were representing his whole people.

b. *spec.* To be accredited deputy or substitute for (a number of persons) in a legislative or deliberative assembly; to be member of Parliament for (a certain constituency); hence in *passive*, to be acted for in this respect *by* some one; to have a representative or representatives.

1655 CROMWELL *Sp. to Parlt.* 22 Jan., I have been careful of your safety, and the safety of those that you represented. *a* **1687** PETTY *Pol. Arith.* (1690) 95 May not the three Kingdoms be United into one, and equally represented in Parliament? **1778** BURKE *Corr.* (1844) II. 216, I do not wish to represent Bristol, or to represent any place, but upon terms that shall be honourable. **1780** JOHNSON *Let. to Mrs. Thrale* 9 May, Did I tell you that Scot and Jones both offer themselves to represent the University in the place of Sir Roger Newdigate. **1861** M. PATTISON *Ess.* (1889) I. 47 A committee of nine members, in which every Hanse town was in its turn represented. **1875** JOWETT *Plato* (ed. 2) V. 126 The people and the aristocracy alike are to be represented.. by officers elected for one or two years.

9. a. To serve as a specimen or example of (a class or kind of things); hence, in *passive*, to be exemplified (*by* something).

1858 HAWTHORNE *Fr. & It. Note-Bks.* (1872) I. 25 A soup in which twenty kinds of vegetables were represented. **1868** FREEMAN *Norm. Conq.* (1877) II. x. 489 Both English and Danish blood was represented in the Assembly. **1868** LOCKYER *Elem. Astron.* i. §5 (1879) 34 The spiral or whirlpool nebulæ are represented by that in the constellation of Canes Venatici.

b. In *passive* with personal subject.

1882 *Daily Tel.* 30 Jan., Mr. D. will be represented in the Waterloo Cup by Witchery.

c. *Math.* To act as a representation of (a group).

1897 [see PRIMITIVE *a.* 5 d]. **1971** D. GORENSTEIN in Powell & Higman *Finite Simple Groups* ii. 77 We conclude that $H/O_p(H)$ is faithfully represented as a linear group on the Frattini factor group of $O_p(H)$.

Hence **repre'sented** *ppl. a.*

a **1569** KINGESMYLL *Man's Est.* xi. (1580) 75 This is the true represented Isaac, that humbleth himself to the Aultar. **1822** J. FLINT *Lett. Amer.* 147 His protection is the affection of a free and a represented people. **1836–7** SIR W. HAMILTON *Metaph.* xxiii. (1860) 70 In a representative act.. the represented object is unknown as actually existing. **1883** *Daily News* 11 Oct. 2/2 The auditors were afforded no facilities.. for ascertaining whether the represented securities really existed.

re-pre'sent (ri:-), *v.*² [RE- 5 a.] *trans.* To present again or a second time; to give back.

Early examples (without hyphen) are somewhat doubtful.

1564 PALFREYMAN in Bauldwin *Mor. Philos.* To Rdr., Wee are.. encouraged without feare boldly to represent and returne vnto Him such liuely fruits of His grace. **1633** FORD *Love's Sacr.* v. iii, Thy truth, Like a transparent mirror, represents My reason with my errors. **1654** COKAINE *Dianea* III. 249, I afresh represented her with my love. **1709** STRYPE *Ann. Ref.* I. xxxvii. 380 To represent to the Christian World the Truth founded in the Gospel of Christ. **1810** *Naval Chron.* XXIV. 451 He was first instituted in 1793, and represented in 1799. **1864** BOWEN *Logic* i. 23 The classification of the objects presented and re-presented by the subsidiary powers. **1880** *Athenæum* 24 July 115/2 The Academy of Sciences.. decided to re-present him with the books.

representable (rɛprɪ'zɛntəb(ə)l), *a.* [-ABLE.] Capable of being represented.

1662 EVELYN *Chalcogr.* 123 All the sorts of bodies representable by graving. *a* **1676** HALE *Prim. Orig. Man.* 311 The Perfections of God are not representable by any created Being in a true propriety of their nature. **1704** NORRIS *Ideal World* II. v. 285 God cannot therefore be known by.. any similitude.. because not representable by any image. **1821** *Examiner* 760/1 The best, or at least, the most representable of the tragedies. **1891** *19th Cent.* XXIX. 222, I have spoken of representable, not imitable, truths.

absol. **1828** DE QUINCEY in *Blackw. Mag.* XXIV. 894 Bringing so mysterious a thing as a spiritual nature or agency within the limits of the representable.

b. *spec.* in *Law* (see quot.).

1832 AUSTIN *Jurispr.* (1879) II. xlvi. 807 A fungible or representable thing is a thing whose place, lieu, or room may be supplied by a thing of the same kind or even by a thing not of the same kind, as money in the form of damages.

Hence **representa'bility**.

1879 W. JAMES *Coll. Ess. & Rev.* (1920) 95 The craving for clear representability.. leads often to an unwillingness to treat any abstractions whatever as if they were intelligible. **1977** M. COHEN *Sensible Words* i. 14 What these men share is a confidence in the visual representability of meaning.

representamen (rɛprɪzɛn'teɪmɛn). [f. REPRESENT *v.*: cf. *imitamen.*] The result or product of representation.

1677 GALE *Crt. Gentiles* IV. Proem 5 A singular first notion or idea is the simple imitamen or representamen of some one individual thing in the mind. **1846** SIR W. HAMILTON *Diss.* in *Reid's Wks.* 877 The representation, or, to speak more properly, the respresentamen, itself as an.. object exhibited to the mind.

†**repre'sentance.** *Obs. rare*⁻¹. [f. as prec. + -ANCE: cf. obs. F. *representance* (Godef.).] Representation.

1633 J. DONE *Hist. Septuagint* 94 For they affirme foolishly that the Images.. are the Representances and formes of those who have brought something profitable.

representant (rɛprɪ'zɛntənt), *sb.* [= F. *représentant* (1694), Sp. *representante* (whence quot. 1622), pres. pple. of *représenter* etc.: see REPRESENT *v.* and -ANT¹.]

†**1.** A stage-performer; an actor. *Obs. rare*⁻¹.

1622 MABBE tr. *Aleman's Guzman d'Alf.* I. 175 Hee is but a man, a representant, a poore kinde of Comedian.

2. A person representing another or others; a representative. *rare.*

1651 *Wotton's Panegyrick to K. Chas.* in *Reliq. W.* (1672) 153 As the supreme Character of the Most High is Verity: so what can more become.. his Representants on earth, then Veracity it self? **1651** HOBBES *Leviath.* III. xlii. 300 They that are the Representants of a Christian People, are Representants of the Church. **1831** T. HOPE *Ess. Origin Man* III. 125 *heading*, Representative government.—Control over the representants.

3. An equivalent or counterpart.

1863 TYNDALL *Heat* iv. §144 (1870) 124 This experiment is the microscopic representant of what occurs in Iceland.

So **repre'sentant** *a.*, 'representing, having vicarious power' (Worcester, 1860, citing Latham).

representation (rɛprɪzɛn'teɪʃən). Also 5 -acyon(e, 5–6 -acion. [a. F. *représentation* (1325) or ad. L. *repræsentātiōn-em*, n. of action f. *repræsentāre* to REPRESENT: see -ATION.]

†**1. a.** Presence, bearing, air. *Obs.*

c **1489** CAXTON *Blanchardyn* ix. 37 The knyght sayd vnto Blanchardyn, 'Syre, ye be a right fayre Iouencell, and of noble representacion'. **1598** GRENEWEY *Tacitus, Ann.* II. ix. (1622) 151 This yoong man of a noble birth, of a manly representation. **1640** tr. *Verdere's Rom. of Rom.* II. 136 He espied a Knight of so goodly a representation, that he stayed to observe him.

†**b.** Appearance; impression on the sight. *Obs.*

1489 CAXTON *Faytes of A.* IV. xvii. 279 Amonge the colours is a difference of noblesse for cause of the representacyon that either of hem doon after his nature. **1664** POWER *Exp. Philos.* I. 46 The Weft (being flat wired Silver) that crosses the Warp, it makes a fine Chequered Representation.

2. a. An image, likeness, or reproduction in some manner *of* a thing.

c **1425** *St. Elizabeth of Spalbeck* in *Anglia* VIII. 107 Oure lorde Jhesu.. schewiþ.. þe representacyone of his blyssed passyone in þe persone of the same virgyne. **1542** UDALL *Erasm. Apoph.* 154 Slepe is a certain ymage and representacion of death. **1605** BACON *Adv. Learn.* I. iv. §8 The essential form of knowledge, which is nothing but a representation of truth. *c* **1655** SIDNEY in *19th Cent.* Jan. (1884) 58 Theis kinds of writings which are the representations of the present thoughts. **1687** A. LOVELL tr. *Thevenot's Trav.* I. 102 It seemed to me to be a faint representation of a Town taken by Storm. **1711** STEELE *Spect.* No. 22 ¶3 The Play-House is a Representation of the World in nothing so much as in this Particular. **1746–7** HERVEY *Medit.* (1818) 249 The silent chamber, and the bed of slumber, are a very significant representation of the land where all things are hushed. **1806** A. KNOX *Rem.* I. 28 It is .. the representation of very heaven upon earth. **1875** JOWETT *Plato* (ed. 2) IV. 280 He liked to think of the world as the representation of the divine nature.

b. A material image or figure; a reproduction in some material or tangible form; in later use *esp.* a drawing or painting (*of* a person or thing).

c **1477** CAXTON *Jason* 66 He..swore right solemply tofore the representation of the goddesse pallas..that he sholde retorne. *c* **1489** —— *Blanchardyn* ii. 15 Of Achilles, and of many othre, Of whom he sawe the representacyon in the sayde tappysserye. *a* **1548** HALL *Chron., Hen. VIII* 1 b, Ouer the corps, was an Image or a representacion of the late kyng, laied on Cusshions of golde. **1582** N. LICHEFIELD tr. *Castanheda's Conq. E. India* I. ii. 29 They fell presently downe upon the ground, worshipping that Representation. **1604** E. G[RIMSTONE] *D'Acosta's Hist. Indies* v. vi. 345 They were not content with this Idolatry to dead bodies, but also they made their figures and representations. **1696** BP. PATRICK *Comm. Exod.* xxxii. (1697) 630 They took this opportunity to desire a visible Representation of God among them, as the Egyptians had. **1756–7** tr. *Keysler's Trav.* (1760) III. 215 A representation of the triumphal arch erected by Augustus. **1776–96** WITHERING *Brit. Plants* (ed. 3) IV. 99 This is a good representation, but the leaves are too broad upwards. **1849** MACAULAY *Hist. Eng.* ii. I. 160 The Parliament resolved that all pictures..which contained representations of Jesus or of the Virgin Mother should be burned. **1888** *Athenæum* 3 Mar. 280/1 An inscription.. would explain the scene as an allegorical representation of the triumph of the Cæsarians at Philippi.

c. The action or fact of exhibiting in some visible image or form.

1483 CAXTON *Cato* A iij b, Thymages of sayntes..gyue us memorye and make representation of the sayntes that ben in heuen. **1579–80** NORTH *Plutarch, Numa* (1612) 67 If we consider what Numa ordained concerning images, and the representation of the gods, it is altogether agreeable vnto the doctrine of Pythagoras. **1830** J. G. STRUTT *Sylva Brit.* Pref., Fidelity of representation being..adhered to. **1863** *Sat. Rev.* 6 June 727 Portraits which left on him the irresistible impression of similar..depth of representation.

d. The fact of expressing or denoting by means of a figure or symbol; symbolic action or exhibition. Also *pl.*

1526 *Pilgr. Perf.* (W. de W. 1531) 41 We sholde do as he wolde vs to do by the representacyon or significacyon of ye sayd acte or dede. **1604** E. G[RIMSTONE] *D'Acosta's Hist. Indies* v. xix. 380 The manner of the sacrifice was to drowne them and bury them with certaine representations and ceremonies. *a* **1661** FULLER *Worthies* (1840) III. 317 Superstition.., making piety pageantry, and subjecting what is sacred to lusory representations.

e. *Math.* The image of a homomorphism from a given (abstract) group to a group or other structure having some further meaning or significance; such a homomorphism.

1897 W. BURNSIDE *Theory of Groups of Finite Order* ii. 22 As long as we are dealing with the properties of a group *per se*, and not with properties which depend on the form of representation, the group may, if convenient, be replaced by any group which is simply isomorphic with it. **1908** H. HILTON *Introd. Theory of Groups Finite Order* xv. 180 One and the same group of linear substitutions may give rise to two or more representations of *G*. **1940** D. E. LITTLEWOOD *Theory of Group Characters* iv. 48 To several elements of the group may correspond identical matrices, so that the representation is not simply, but multiply isomorphic with the group. **1949** S. KRAVETZ tr. *Zassenhaus' Theory of Groups* ii. 35 A representation is said to be faithful if the homomorphy induced by the representation is an isomorphy. **1971** D. GORENSTEIN in Powell & Higman *Finite Simple Groups* ii. 76 A faithful, irreducible representation of an abelian group on any vector space is necessarily cyclic. **1974** *Encycl. Brit. Macropædia* I. 752/2 Technically, a representation of a group is a homomorphism of it into another group, most commonly into the group of invertible linear transformations (or matrices) on some linear space. **1980** *Sci. Amer.* May 68/2 The way mathematicians construct a group depends to a large extent on whether the group has a natural representation as the transformations of some geometrical object.

3. a. The exhibition of character and action upon the stage; the (*or* a) performance of a play.

1589 [? NASHE] *Almond for Parrat* Ded. 4 The order and maner of our playes, which he termed by the name of representations. **1663** COWLEY *Cutter Coleman St.* Pref., It met at the first representation with no favourable reception. **1711** STEELE *Spect.* No. 22 ¶1 One of the Audience at Publick Representations in our Theatres. **1756** FOOTE *Eng. fr. Paris* II. Wks. 1799 I. 113 Dramatic things, farcical in their composition, and ridiculous in their representation. **1777** W. DALRYMPLE *Trav. Sp. & Port.* cli, I was told that his theatre was well conducted, but there was no representation during my residence. **1806–7** J. BERESFORD *Miseries Hum. Life* (1826) II. x, The last..scene of the tragedy..is too dreadful for representation. **1849** THACKERAY *Pendennis* vii, Never having been before at a theatrical representation. *a* **1862** BUCKLE *Civiliz.* (1869) III. v. 318 Influence of dramatic representations over opinions.

b. Acting, simulation, pretence. *rare*$^{-1}$.

1805 GODWIN *Fleetwood* I. vii. 156 The inference usually drawn is that his [a widower's] grief was pure mummery and representation.

4. a. The action of placing a fact, etc., before another or others by means of discourse; a statement or account, *esp.* one intended to convey a particular view or impression of a matter in order to influence opinion or action.

1553 BRENDE *Q. Curtius* v. 88 b, When Darius had spoken theis wordes, the representacion of the present perill so amased them all, that they were not able..to shew there aduise. **1662** STILLINGFL. *Orig. Sacræ* III. i. §1 A faithful representation of the State of the case between God and the souls of men. **1666** PEPYS *Diary* 24 July, Drawing up a representation of the state of my victualling-business. *a* **1704** T. BROWN *Praise Drunkenness* Wks. 1730 I. 34 Priests impose no longer on mankind, nor amuse the people with empty representations of what they give no credit to themselves. **1724** A. COLLINS *Gr. Chr. Relig.* 280 A Representation of him, by the said Convocation,..as a person carrying on the cause of irreligion. **1782** PRIESTLEY *Corrupt. Chr.* I. I. 93 There are different representations of the Platonic doctrine. **1853** BRIGHT *Sp., India* 3 June (1876) 4 A fair representation of their views of what was done. **1858** FROUDE *Hist. Eng.* III. xvii. 506 False representations had been held out to bring the lady into the realm.

b. *Insurance.* A special statement of facts relating to the risk involved, made by the insuring party to the insurer or underwriter before the subscription of the policy.

1838 W. BELL *Dict. Law Scot.* 510 Where the representation is untrue, with a fraudulent design to impose on the underwriter, the policy is completely vacated.

5. a. A formal and serious statement of facts, reasons, or arguments, made with a view to effecting some change, preventing some action, etc.; hence, a remonstrance, protest, expostulation.

1679 LONGUEVILLE *Let.* 11 Mar. in *Hatton Corr.* (Camden) I. 182 The King too day, in answer to their Representation (that's ye word now), told them that too much time had been allready lost. **1728** *Col. Rec. Pennsylv.* III. 298 Nothing less than the Preservation of the Rights and Privileges of the Freeman of Pennsylvania could induce us to make the following Representation. **1750** JOHNSON *Rambler* No. 26 ¶7, I resolved..to teach young men, who are too tame under representation, in what manner grey-bearded insolence ought to be treated. **1788** H. WALPOLE *Remin.* i. 14 The minister against the earnest representations of his family..consented to the recall of that incendiary. **1817** JAS. MILL *Brit. India* II. v. i. 307 Mr. Hastings was nominated Governor-General..not to be removed..except by the King, upon representation made by the Court of Directors. **1841** BREWSTER *Mart. Sc.* v. (1856) 69 Ferdinand was enraged..and instructed his ambassador to make the strongest representations to the Pope.

b. *Sc. Law.* 'The written pleadings formerly presented to a lord ordinary in the Court of Session, when his judgment was brought under review' (Bell).

1838 W. BELL *Dict. Law Scot.* 854 Twenty days were allowed from the time of pronouncing the judgment, within which the representation might have been presented.

6. a. The action of presenting to the mind or imagination; an image thus presented; a clearly-conceived idea or concept.

1647 CLARENDON *Hist. Reb.* I. §90 Though he was exceedingly perplexed with the lively representation of all particulars to his memory, he was willing still to perswade himself, that he had only dreamed. **1694** LOCKE *Hum. Und.* (ed. 2) II. xxi. §37 Many..that have had lively representations set before their minds of the unspeakable joys of Heaven. **1727** DE FOE *Syst. Magic* I. iv. (1840) 95 That Canaan, pleased with the lively representation of his grandfather's shame, resolved, if possible, to give himself the satisfaction of bringing it to pass. **1838** SIR W. HAMILTON *Logic* vii. (1860) I. 126 The word representation ..I have restricted to denote..the immediate object or product of Imagination. **1864** BOWEN *Logic* i. 12 The Kantians use Representations to designate the genus which includes..Percepts, Concepts and Ideas. **1885** J. MARTINEAU *Types Eth. Th.* I. I. i. §3. 160 A representation of the imagination is a modification of the mind itself.

b. The operation of the mind in forming a clear image or concept; the faculty of doing this.

1836–7 SIR W. HAMILTON *Metaph.* xxii. (1860) II. 59 The doctrine of representation, under all its modifications, is properly subordinate to the doctrine of a spiritual principle of thought. **1855** H. SPENCER *Princ. Psychol.* §482 It is quite evident that the growth of perception involves representation of sensations.

7. a. The fact of standing for, or in place of, some other thing or person, esp. with a right or authority to act on their account; substitution of one thing or person for another.

1624 GATAKER *Transubst.* 4 The Rocke was Christ onely symbolically and sacramentally, by representation and resemblance. **1660** R. COKE *Power & Subj.* 111 So cannot these Members be formed into a body but by the King, either by his Royal presence or representation. **1671** E. CHAMBERLAYNE *Pres. St. Eng.* I. II. xxii. (ed. 5) 50 No Parliament can begin without the Kings Presence, either in Person, or by Representation by Commissioners. **1838** W. BELL *Dict. Law Scot.* 854 Whatever infers the substitution of one person in the room and place of another..falls under the general denomination of representation.

b. *Law.* The assumption by an heir of the position, rights, and obligations of his predecessor. ***right of representation***, the right whereby the son of an elder son deceased succeeds to his grandfather in preference to the latter's immediate issue (see also quot. 1838).

1693 STAIR *Inst. Law Scot.* III. viii. §32 (ed. 2) 503 The Line of Succession in Moveables, is first, the Nearest Descendents, Male or Female, in the same Degree, equally; whether Sons or Daughters, without Right of Representation. **1766** BLACKSTONE *Comm.* II. 225 The right of representation being thus established, the former part of the present rule amounts to this; that, on failure of issue [etc.]. *a* **1768** ERSKINE *Inst. Law Scot.* III. viii. §11 (1773) 546 There is a right of representation peculiar to heritage, by which one succeeds in heritable subjects, not from any title in his own person, but in the place of, and as representing some of his deceased ascendents. **1838** W. BELL *Dict. Law Scot.* 556 This right of representation takes place in collateral succession to heritage, as well as in that of descendants in the direct line.

8. a. The fact of representing or being represented in a legislative or deliberative assembly, *spec.* in Parliament; the position, principle, or system implied by this.

1769 BURKE *Late St. Nat.* Wks. II. 138 We ought not to be quite so ready with our taxes, until we can secure the desired representation in parliament. **1780** JOHNSON *Let. to Mrs. Thrale* 25 May, It would be with great discontent that I should see Mr. Thrale decline the representation of the Borough. **1802** BOWLES *Th. Gen. Election* 10 A fair and free representation of the people in Parliament was meant to be obtained by means of universal suffrage. **1828** MACKINTOSH *Sp. Ho. Comm.* 2 May, Wks. 1846 III. 489 Neither can it be said, that the Assembly of Canada was so entirely indifferent to its system of representation. *a* **1862** BUCKLE *Civiliz.* (1873) III. i. 33 Down to quite modern times, there was in Scotland no real popular representation.

b. The aggregate of those who thus represent the elective body.

1789 *Constit. U.S.* i. §2 Where vacancies [in Congress] happen in the representation from any state, the executive authority thereof shall issue writs of election. **1790** BURKE *Fr. Rev.* (ed. 2) 60, I found the representation of the Third Estate composed of six hundred persons. **1828–32** WEBSTER s.v., It is expedient to have an able representation in both houses of congress. **1883** *Manch. Guard.* 22 Oct. 5/3 A fresh method of election, by which the representation shall be made to reflect with greatly increased accuracy the wishes and opinions of the whole of the electors.

re-presen'tation (riː-). [RE- 5 a.] A renewed presentation or presentment.

1805 EUGENIA DI ACTON *Nuns of Desert* II. 196 Mr. Veerman made his atonement in a re-presentation of Miss Blenheim. **1817** COLERIDGE *Biog. Lit.* (Bohn) 118 In order to discriminate it..from mere reflection and re-presentation. **1857** LEWES *Hist. Philos.* Introd. 29 If all reasoning be the re-presentation of what is now absent. **1899** *Allbutt's Syst. Med.* VII. 313 The fact..seems to show that visual re-presentation is in this respect like auditory re-presentation.

representational (rɛprɪzɛn'teɪʃənəl), *a.* [f. REPRESENTATION + -AL^1^.] **a.** Pertaining to, or of the nature of, representation; also, holding the doctrine of representationism.

1855 in OGILVIE *Suppl.* **1858** PIRIE *Inq. Hum. Mind* ii. 46 The representational school of the Greek philosophers. **1867** BUSHNELL in *Hours at Home* Nov. 5, I speak of the representational office they are designed to fill. **1876** FAIRBAIRN in *Contemp. Rev.* June 134 If..religion exist only in the relative and representational form.

b. *spec.* in *Art.* (See quots. 1961, 1962.)

1923 [see *non-representational* s.v. NON- 3]. **1934** C. LAMBERT *Music Ho!* II. 115 The repetitions of..[an] underlying curve in an abstract or representational picture have no dramatic content. **1956** R. MACAULAY *Towers of Trebizond* xxii. 256, I could see he [*sc.* an ape] was going to be a painter of the abstract type... I thought Suliman ought to try and be a little representational too. **1959** HALAS & MANVELL *Technique Film Animation* 12 Though there is still ..some useful place in normal draughtsmanship and painting for the exactly representational illustration as against a good photograph, there would seem to us to be no argument in favour of an exactly representational animated picture. **1961** M. LEVY *Studio Dict. Art Terms* 96 *Representational art*, that kind of painting or sculpture which tries..to reproduce the physical appearance of objects, persons, or other subjects. As distinct from non-representational art where the interest in surface appearances is of little or no account. **1962** R. G. HAGGAR *Dict. Art Terms* 286/2 *Representational*, describes art in which figures and objects are depicted as they appear to the eye, or as they are known to be, in contradistinction to abstract or non-representational art. **1965** *New Statesman* 9 Apr. 566/2 The academy is now positively soliciting exhibits from Pop artists and abstractionists. However,..there's no cause for alarm. The R[oyal] A[cademy] will continue to show the best of British representational art, but it aims, also, to provide an annual cross-section of everything which is being done by British artists.

Hence **represen'tationalism**; **represen'tationalist** *a.* and *sb.*; **represen'tationally** *adv.*

1846 J. D. MORELL *Hist. View Philos.* I. ii. 232 The great aim of Reid's philosophy..was..to controvert the representationalist hypothesis. **1867** BUSHNELL in *Hours at Home* Nov. 6 The objects of nature are relationally or representationally made. **1899** HALDANE *Ferrier* ii. 52 This system of 'representationalism', of representative ideas, necessarily leads to scepticism. **1921** A. HUXLEY *Crome Yellow* xii. 115 One could admire representationalism in the Old Masters... But in a modern? **1934** C. LAMBERT *Music Ho!* II. 113 It is all very well to hammer out a theory, however mistaken, that applies to an art functioning in space: it is quite another matter to apply this to an art that functions in time. Most of the modern fallacies about abstraction, literary sentiment, representationalism, romantic contamination, etc. in music are due to ignoring this elementary distinction. **1937** R. I. AARON *John Locke* II. iii. 121 These accounts would have been the same if Locke had never adopted the representationalist position... Though nominally Locke remains representationalist in his explanation of the knowledge we have of our minds, actually he proceeds as if we know ourselves and our operations directly. **1976** *Jrnl. R. Soc. Arts* CXXIV. 567/1 The Brocks were among the last great representationalists, preservers of a world of recognizable human types in clearly defined historical settings. **1978** *N. & Q.* Feb. 91/2 He felt attracted to this best ally of representationalism.

represen'tationary, *a.* *rare*$^{-1}$. [f. as prec. + -ARY.] Representative.

a **1860** YOUNG (Worcester), An hereditary, associated, representationary system.

represen'tationism. [f. as prec. + -ISM.] The doctrine that the immediate object of the mind in perception is only a representation of the real object in the external world.

1842 SIR W. HAMILTON *Diss.* in *Reid's Wks.* II. 817/2 If the immediate, known, or representative, object be regarded as a modification of the mind or self, we have one variety of representationism. **1847** *Blackw. Mag.* LXII. 243 Representationism declares, that the perception is the proximate and that the matter is the remote object of the mind. **1885** SETH *Scot. Philos.* 145 The Representationism of the present day has its roots almost entirely in the Kantian theory.

represen'tationist. [f. as prec. + -IST.] An adherent of the doctrine of representationism.
1842 SIR. W. HAMILTON *Diss.* in *Reid's Wks.* II. 817/2 The Representationists, as denying to consciousness the cognisance of aught beyond a merely subjective phænomenon, are likewise Idealists. **1847** *Blackw. Mag.* LXII. 242 Reid, so far from having overthrown the representative theory, was himself a representationist. **1885** SETH *Scot. Philos.* 145 Kant is, indeed, the very prince of Representationists.

representative (rɛprɪ'zɛntətɪv), *a.* and *sb.* [ad. F. *représentatif*, *-ive* (1330), or med.L. *repræsentātīv-us*: see REPRESENT *v.* and -ATIVE.]
A. *adj.* **1. a.** Serving to represent, figure, portray, or symbolize. Also const. *of* (the thing figured, etc.).
1387-8 T. USK *Test. Love* II. xiii. (Skeat) l. 41 Also, in good by participation, and that is i-cleaped 'good' for far fet and representative of godly goodnesse. **1589** PUTTENHAM *Eng. Poesie* I. xvii. (Arb.) 51 They playing places, and prouisions which were made for their pageants and pomps representatiue before remembred. **1609** BIBLE (Douay) *Ezek.* ix. *comm.*, Which signe..is representative and commemorative of our Redemption. **1634** SIR T. HERBERT *Trav.* 69 They take vp the representative Bodie, intimating thereby his Resurrection. **1711** SHAFTESB. *Charac.* (1737) II. 395 You are sure never to admire the representative-beauty, except for the sake of the original. *a* **1740** WATERLAND *Def. Queries* Wks. 1823 I. II. 32 Not merely as representative of God the Father..but as strictly and truly God. **1844** W. H. MILL *Serm. Tempt. Christ* iii. 66 The prophet Ezekiel..is required to bear for forty days the representative penalty of his people's sins. **1851** MANSEL *Proleg. Log.* (1860) 12 That sensitive perception takes place through the medium of a representative idea. **1867** HOWELLS *Ital. Journ.* 179 The group of statuary.. representative of the Maremma and family returning thanks to the Grand Duke.
†**b.** Apparent, seeming. *Obs. rare*$^{-1}$.
1646 SIR T. BROWNE *Pseud. Ep.* 82 That the bodies of Flies, Pismires and the like, which are said oft times to be included in Amber, are not reall but representative.
c. Presenting, or capable of presenting, ideas of things to the mind.
1753 CHAMBERS *Cycl. Supp.* App., *Representative power*, in metaphysics, a term introduced by Leibnitz, to signify that power of the human soul, by which it represents to itself the universe. **1814** W. TAYLOR in *Monthly Mag.* XXXVIII. 211 The representative memory must be exercised. **1836-7** SIR W. HAMILTON *Metaph.* (1877) II. xx. 13 We have thus a Representative Faculty; and this obtains the name of Imagination. **1842** —— *Diss.* in *Reid's Wks.* II. 822/1 The distinction between perception as a presentative, and Memory,..as a representative, cognition.
d. Relating to mental representation.
1847 *Blackw. Mag.* LXII. 242 It is the very essence..of the representative theory to recognise, in perception, a remote as well as a proximate object of the mind. **1934** A. C. EWING *Idealism* vi. 283 By the term 'representative theory of perception' I mean to cover *any* theory of perception which admits the existence of physical objects in the realist sense but is not a direct theory.
e. *representative fraction*: the ratio of a distance on a map to the distance it represents on the ground. Cf. *R.F.* s.v. R II. 2 a.
1886 H. D. HUTCHINSON *Mil. Sketching made Easy* i. 2 If the Representative Fraction is marked on a sketch, the scale can be understood, and the sketch can be used, by anyone, even though it be a foreign one. **1969** G. C. DICKINSON *Maps & Air Photographs* vii. 99 Whether written as a fraction or a ratio, this means of expressing the scale is called the representative fraction (R.F. for short) of the map.
2. a. Standing for, or in place of, another or others, *esp.* in a prominent or comprehensive manner.
c **1624** LUSHINGTON *Recant. Serm.* in *Phenix* (1708) II. 494 The number is universal; not collective, but representative for the whole primitive church. *a* **1715** BURNET *Own Time* I. (1715) I. 80 The Nation, of which the King was only the representative head. **1856** DOVE *Logic Chr. Faith* VI. §4. 356 The disobedience of our representative father entailed..a fallen nature. **1861** TRENCH *Comm. Ep. 7 Churches Asia* 3 A king or queen, as representative persons in a nation.
b. *spec.* Holding the place of, and acting for, a larger body of persons (*esp.* the whole people) in the work of governing or legislating; pertaining to, or based upon, a system by which the people is thus represented.
1628 A. LEIGHTON in *Camden Misc.* VII. 7 An indelible dishonour it will be to you, the state representative. **1643** CHAS. I *Conc. Treaty at Oxford* Wks. 1662 II. 330 The two Houses of Parliament being the Representative Body of the Kingdome. **1769** *Junius Lett.* xxxv. (1788) 185 A question of right arises between the constituent and the representative body. By what authority shall it be decided? **1819** MACKINTOSH *Parl. Suffrage* Wks. 1846 III. 206 The representative assembly must therefore contain some members peculiarly qualified for discussions of the constitution and the laws. **1844** LD. BROUGHAM *Brit. Const.* vi. (1862) 89 We mean by a Representative Government one in which the body of the people..elect their deputies to a chamber of their own. **1879** GLADSTONE *Gleanings* I. viii. 214 We have, *proh pudor!* found no better method of providing for peace and order in Jamaica..than by the hard and vulgar, even where needful, expedient of abolishing entirely its representative institutions. **1921** H. SAMUEL *Let.* 8 May in M. Gilbert *Winston S. Churchill* (1977) IV. Compan. III. 1461 The very early establishment of representative institutions. **1975** J. PLAMENATZ *K. Marx's Philos. Man* xv. 464 How..would they [*sc.* the workers] ensure that this system was not as much of a sham as bourgeois representative government was, according to Marx?
c. Connected with, or based upon, the fact of one person representing another.
1766 BLACKSTONE *Comm.* II. 225 The issue or descendants..are severally called to the succession in right of such their representative proximity. **1845** STEPHEN *Comm. Laws Eng.* (1874) II. 663 By inheritance or other such representative title as in the Act specified.
3. Typical of a class; conveying an adequate idea of others of the kind.
1788 GIBBON *Decl. & F.* xlix. V. 165 The college of princes and prelates..reduced to four representative votes the long series of independent counts. **1853** DE QUINCEY *Autobiog. Sk.* Wks. 1853 I. 8 So representative are some acts, that one single case of the class is sufficient to throw open before you the whole theatre of possibilities in that direction. **1869** TYNDALL in *Fortn. Rev.* 1 Feb. 238 This experiment is representative, and it illustrates a general principle. **1873** SYMONDS *Grk. Poets* xi. 391 Amid this multitude of poems it is difficult to make a fair or representative selection.
4. Taking the place of, replacing, other forms or species (cf. quot. 1863).
1845 DARWIN *Voy. Nat.* iii. (1879) 53 This close agreement in structure and habits, in representative species ..always strikes one as interesting. **1863** BATES *Nat. Amazon* xiii. (1864) 430 Many of these were 'representative forms' (species or races which take the place of other allied species or races) of others found on the opposite banks.
B. *sb.* **1. a.** A person (or thing) representing a number or class of persons (or things); hence, a sample or specimen.
1647 CLARENDON *Hist. Reb.* I. §119 All which drew the eyes of most..towards him, as the Image and Representative of the Primitive Nobility. **1676** TOWERSON *Decalogue* 10 Noah and his sons..were..the representatives of all mankind. **1693** J. EDWARDS *Author. O. & N. Test.* 110 They were punish'd for what Adam their representative did long ago. **1712** ADDISON *Spect.* No. 457 ⁋2, I have two Persons, that are each of them the Representative of a Species. **1824** LAMB *Elia* Ser. II. *Blakesmoor in H——shire*, A few bricks only lay as representatives of that which was so stately and so spacious. **1848** R. I. WILBERFORCE *Doctr. Incarnation* viii. (1852) 191 Through the indwelling of Deity, the representative of mankind was viewed with favour. **1873** TRISTRAM *Moab* vi. 104 Three terebinth trees, the solitary representatives of timber we met with. **1896** LYDEKKER *Brit. Mammals* 62 Since the sole British representative of this Family is the Common Mole [etc.].
b. A typical embodiment *of* some quality or abstract concept.
1715 ADDISON *Freeholder* No. 27 ⁋7 Among other statues he observed that of Rumour whispering an ideot in the ear, who was the representative of Credulity. **1743** BULKELEY & CUMMINS *Voy. S. Seas* 208, I don't believe there ever was a worse Representative of Royalty upon the Face of the Earth. **1809-10** COLERIDGE *Friend* (1866) 124 Providence..had marked him out for the representative of reason. **1845** MAURICE *Mor. Philos.* in *Encycl. Metrop.* (1847) II. 622/1 The person who always stands as the type and representative of the..scepticism of this period is Pyrrho. **1865** R. W. DALE *Jew. Temp.* x. (1877) 103 He [Christ] is the great Representative of our religious life.
2. a. One who (†or that which) represents a number of persons in some special capacity; *spec.* one who represents a section of the community as member of a legislative body; a member of Parliament or (*U.S.*) of the House of Representatives.
1635 *Essex Inst. Hist. Coll.* (1862) IV. 93/1 By the towne rep[re]sentative, 22 of the 12th moneth. **1658** *Stat. Virginia* (1823) I. 502 Wee find..the present power of government to reside in such persons as shall be impowered by the Burgesses (the representatives of the people). **1660** R. COKE *Power & Subj.* 109 We will therefore enquire..whether a House of Commons, as it now stands, can be their Representative. **1671** E. CHAMBERLAYNE *Pres. St. Eng.* I. II. ii. (ed. 5) 37 The Clergy of England had antiently their Representatives in the Lower House of Parliament. **1713** STEELE *Englishm.* No. 10. 67 The Elected became true Representatives of the Electors. **1769** *Junius Lett.* xxxv. (1788) 184 The English nation declare they are grossly injured by their representatives. **1787** *Consititution U.S.* I. §2 No person shall be a representative who shall not..be an inhabitant of that state in which he shall be chosen. **1809** KENDALL *Trav.* I. v. 27 The deputies are now frequently denominated representatives. They were anciently called committee-men. **1863** H. COX *Instit.* I. iii. 13 The election of representatives of the Commons. **1977** *Time* 18 July 10/3 Young proved himself a sensible and reasonable Representative—and also an independent one. **1979** *Daily Tel.* 8 Jan. 8 Members of Parliament are representatives and not delegates.
b. *House of Representatives*, the lower or popular house of the United States Congress or of a State legislature. Also, similar legislative bodies in Australia and New Zealand.
1789 *Constit. U.S.* I. §1 A congress of the United States, which shall consist of a Senate and House of Representatives. **1852** *Act 15 & 16 Vict.* c. 72 §32 There shall be within the Colony of New Zealand a General Assembly, to consist of the Governor, a Legislative Council, and House of Representatives. *Ibid.* §40 For the Purpose of constituting the House of Representatives of New Zealand it shall be lawful for the Governor,..to summon and call together a House of Representatives in and for New Zealand. **1861** LD. BROUGHAM *Brit. Const.* App. ii. 410 The House of Representatives is chosen every two years by each of the States of the Union electing Deputies. **1891** *National Australasian Convention Debates* 23/1 This Convention [of Sydney, March 1891] approves of the framing of a federal constitution, which shall establish,—1. A parliament, to consist of a senate and a house of representatives. **1930** L. G. D. ACLAND *Early Canterbury Runs* 1st Ser. ii. 27 He was a member of the House of Representatives and of the Provincial Council. **1965** *Austral. Encycl.* VII. 9/1 The Speaker's chair in the House of Representatives is also of interest.
†**3.** A representative body or assembly. *Obs.*
1648 ASHHURST *Reasons agst. Agreement* 1 The people who shall subscribe this paper shall agree..to choose an equall Representative consisting of 300 men. **1651** N. BACON *Disc. Govt. Eng.* II. xvi. (1739) 83 Such are the ways of debate in the Grand Representative of the Kingdom. **1726** SWIFT *Gulliver* III. vii, I desired that the Senate of Rome might appear before me in one large Chamber, and a modern Representative in Counterview, in another. **1761** HUME *Hist. Eng.* III. lx. 292 They pretended to employ themselves entirely in adjusting the laws, forms, and plan of a new representative.
4. a. One who represents another as agent, delegate, substitute, successor, or heir; also *spec.* a person specially appointed to represent his sovereign or government in a foreign court or country.
1691 D. GRANVILLE *Lett.* (Surtees No. 37) 121, I cannot.. cease to charge the guilt of soe great a sin upon you my representative in my parish. **1751** EARL ORRERY *Remarks Swift* (1752) 212 From hence perhaps, kings have thought themselves representatives of God. **1765** BLACKSTONE *Comm.* I. xiii. 398 About the reign of king Henry the eighth ..lord lieutenants began to be introduced, as standing representatives of the crown. **1766** *Ibid.* II. xiv. 210 Whenever a right of property transmissible to representatives is admitted. **1828** SCOTT *F.M. Perth* iv, Are we not representatives and successors of the stout old Romans..? **1864** PUSEY *Lect. Daniel* 154 Perdiccas, Antipater..were..guardians of the weak or infant representatives of Alexander. **1957** CLARK & GOTTFRIED *Dict. Business & Finance* 299/1 *Representative*, in selling, a salesman, either one employed by the seller or operating as an agent. **1961** P. F. PAYNE *Brit. Commercial Institutions* v. 70 The manufacturer's agent carries out functions similar to those of the wholesaler's representative. **1976** *Gramophone* June 37/3 Raymond Cooke and Robert Cox of KEF demonstrated the excellence of their loudspeakers and there were recitals by record industry representatives.
b. One who or that which in some respect represents another person or thing.
1691-8 NORRIS *Pract. Disc.* (1711) III. 184 A Good man is the greatest Representative of God upon Earth, he represents the best and greatest of his Perfections. **1788** PRIESTLEY *Lect. Hist.* III. xv. 122 Money is only a commodious représentative of the commodities which may be purchased with it. **1824** L. MURRAY *Eng. Gram.* (ed. 5) I. 30 Every simple sound would have its distinct character; and that character be the representative of no other sound. **1856** KANE *Arct. Expl.* II. ix. 94 The veritable sugar has been long ago defunct; but we have its representative molasses. **1896** LYDEKKER *Brit. Mammals* 62 The arm-bone, or humerus, in the True Moles is almost square, and..unlike its representative in ordinary Mammals.
†**5.** Representation. *Obs. rare.*
1688 *Col. Rec. Pennsylv.* I. 238 He had used means to have a due representative of ye attending there, according to ye Charter. **1760-72** H. BROOKE *Fool of Qual.* II. 63 A family picture, the representative of a brother.

repre'sentatively, *adv.* [-LY².] In a representative manner; in respect of representation.
c **1430** *Pilgr. Lyf Manhode* I. lxxxvii. (Roxb.) 49 Vertualliche j vnderstonde summe,..and representatyfliche summe, of the thinges j vnderstonde. **1599** SANDYS *Europæ Spec.* (1632) 214 By generall consent of the Prince and whole Realme representatively assembled in solemne Parliament. **1608** WILLET *Hexapla Exod.* 33 The name Iehouah is..not communicable to any angel either properly or representatiuely. **1673** HICKMAN *Quinquart. Hist.* Ep. A 7 b, He thought the Bread was the Body of Christ Representatively. **1704** NORRIS *Ideal World* II. iii. 181 Tho' all Ideas are spiritual and immaterial, really and essentially, yet they are not all so representatively. **1792** *Gentl. Mag.* LXII. I. 118 Though he offered himself representively in the Eucharist, the Eucharist is a real sacrifice. **1855** W. H. MILL *Applic. Panth. Princ.* (1861) 192 It is equally clear.. that the title of the Branch in Zechariah's prophecy was only representatively his.

repre'sentativeness. [f. as prec. + -NESS.] The character of being representative.
1664 H. MORE *Myst. Iniq.* 226 Observing what Reason will..spy out concerning their significancy and representativeness of things. **1684** T. BURNET *Th. Earth* I. 302 In a thought there are two things, consciousness, and a representation... Now what hath local motion to do with either of these two, consciousness, or representativeness? **1704** NORRIS *Ideal World* II. xi. 418 The possibility of this like-wise appears from the essential representativeness of their nature. **1842** MRS. BROWNING *Grk. Chr. Poets* 21 No ancient could be missed in the all-comprehensive representativeness of the Laodicæan writer. **1887** *Pall Mall G.* 2 June 5/2 A critical analysis reveals a..weakness in the display, from the point of view of just 'representativeness'.

†**repre'sentativer.** *Obs. rare*$^{-1}$. [f. as prec. + -ER¹.] A representative.
1676 MARVELL *Mr. Smirke* 8, I mean of the humor of this *Parliamentum Indoctum*, this single Representativer.

repre'sentativeship. [f. REPRESENTATIVE *sb.* + -SHIP.] The office of representative.
1845 in B. Gregory *Side Lights Confl. Meth.* (1898) 429 His report of his representativeship to Canada. **1854** D. KING *Presb. Ch. Gov.* 171 What becomes of the special representativeship of elders?

representativity (ˌrɛprɪzɛntə'tɪvɪtɪ). [f. REPRESENTATIVE *a.* + -ITY.] Representative character; representativeness.
1901 *N. Amer. Rev.* Apr. 632 By far the most signal instance of Professor Wendell's open-mindedness is his

recognition of Mark Twain's..representativity as a Westerner.

representator (rɛprɪzɛn'teɪtə(r)). [a. late L. *repræsentātor* (Tertull.), agent-n. f. *repræsentāre* to REPRESENT.]

†**1.** A representative or representer. *Obs. rare.*

1607 *Schol. Disc. agst. Antichr.* I. ii. 58 He [the cross] becommeth a representator of Christes death worthy to bee adored. **1638** SIR T. HERBERT *Trav.* (ed. 2) 162 They adored the Sunne..a representator of a more powerful Diety. **1650** BULWER *Anthropomet.* 11 Gallants, whose geometrical pates would not well square with these times, which have cap'd their grave Representators.

2. One who gives a representation. *rare*$^{-1}$.

1816 M. G. LEWIS *Jrnl. W. Ind.* 6 Jan., The negroes.. afterwards share the money collected from the spectators, allotting one share to the representator himself.

†**repre'sentatory**, *a. Obs. rare*$^{-1}$. [Cf. prec. and -ORY.] Representative.

1674 OWEN *Holy Spirit* (1693) 223 They were Representatory, or..introductory of Christ and the Gospel.

represen'tee. [f. REPRESENT *v.*]

†**1.** One who is represented. *rare*$^{-1}$. *Obs.*

1624 BP. MOUNTAGU *Gagg* 309 You honour the Image with the same honour that the Representee is honoured withall.

†**2.** A (parliamentary) representative. *Obs.*

1644 HEYLIN *Stumbling-bl.* Tracts (1681) 727 The highest Judicatory, consisting of the Kings most excellent Majesty, the Lords Spiritual and Temporal, and the Representees of the Commons. **1648** E. BOUGHEN *Geree's Case Consc.* 43 The Parliament, that is, of the Peers and Commons, representees of the people met in a lawfull and free Parliament. **1659** GAUDEN *Tears Ch.* 448 By their proxyes and representees chosen and sent from their severall distributions.

3. *Law.* One to whom a representation is made.

1911 G. S. BOWER *Law Actionable Misrepresentation* 1 A representation is a statement made by, or on behalf of, one person (hereinafter called 'the representor') to, or with the intention that it shall come to the notice of, another person (hereinafter called 'the representee'), which relates, by way of affirmation, denial, description, or otherwise, to a matter of fact. **1971** R. A. PERCY *Charlesworth on Negligence* (ed. 5) ii. 34 In *Jones* v. *Still* an honest misrepresentation, even if negligent, was held to give no cause of action, since no duty to take care in making the statement arose because there was no contract, fiduciary relationship or reliance by the representee upon the special skill, knowledge or training possessed by the representor.

representer (rɛprɪ'zɛntə(r)). [f. as prec. + -ER[1]. Cf. also REPRESENTOR.]

†**1.** One who presents or offers. *Obs. rare*$^{-1}$.

1483 CAXTON *Gold. Leg.* 307 b/1 They ben our kepars, oure mynystres.., the berers of our sowles in to heuen and representers of our prayers vnto god.

2. †**a.** One who or that which exhibits, shows, or makes manifest; an exhibitor. *Obs.*

1570 FOXE *A. & M.* (ed. 2) 1246/1 As touchyng Images, ..that they be representers of vertue & good example. **1605** WILLET *Hexapla Gen.* 166 This representer and foreshewer of Christs euerlasting priesthood. **1635** *Sheph. Holiday* II. v. in Hazl. *Dodsley* XII. 393 This mirror here, the faithful representer Of that which I adore, your beauteous form. **1685** CROWNE *Sir C. Nice* III. 30 Diving into my pocket, to present the representer with a gratification.

b. One who represents by acting; one who performs, plays, or impersonates; †an actor.

1591 PERCIVALL *Sp. Dict.*, *Representador*, a representer, a plaier of comedies, actor. **1638** MAYNE *Lucian* (1664) 377 Though they plainly saw not the madnesse of Ajax, but of the representer acted. **1651** HOBBES *Leviath.* I. xvi. 80 Any Representer of speech and action, as well in Tribunalls, as Theaters. **1863** COWDEN CLARKE *Shaks. Char.* iv. 100 Theatrical conceit was never better impersonated than by the great representer of Pyramus.

3. One who makes a representation, or states a matter in a certain light. Now *rare* or *Obs.*

1647 JER. TAYLOR *Lib. Proph.* Ep. Ded. 35 It is farre more unlikely that after Ages should know any other truth, but such as serves the ends of the representers. **1686** W. SHERLOCK *Papist not Misrep.* 21 The difference between the Mis-representer and Representer in this article is no more but this. **1703** SAVAGE *Lett. Antients* xlix. 116 The Representers have not only an interest in Falshood, but likewise an Art to make it pass for Truth. **1741** WARBURTON *Div. Legat.* v. iv. II. II. 440 One singular Circumstance in Favour of the Character of the Representers.

b. *spec.* The authors of the Representation presented to the General Assembly of the Kirk of Scotland in 1721 in connexion with the Marrow Controversy. (See MARROW *sb.*[1] 2 e.)

1722 *Wodrow Corr.* (1843) II. 644 The second part of the Marrow was published on Saturday, with a long preface and appendix, which is confidence enough in the Representers. **1848** A. THOMSON *Hist. Secession Ch.* 24 Meanwhile, the Representers are summoned to appear before the Commission.

†**c.** An exponent *of* some thing or person. *Obs.*

1760–72 H. BROOKE *Fool of Qual.* (1809) II. 9 Lawyers.. are equally the..representers and misrepresenters, explainers and confounders of our laws. **1766** *Museum Rust.* IV. 121 Mr. Mills gives, as his authority.., Mr. Miller's Gardener's Dictionary..and he does him no honour as his representer.

†**4.** A representative of a thing or person. *Obs.*

a **1586** SIDNEY *Arcadia* v. Wks. 1724 II. 813, I am but the representer of all the late flourishing Arcadia. **1663** BOYLE *Usef. Exp. Nat. Philos.* I. iii. 58 Man.., if not as a resembler, yet as a representer of the Macrocosme or Great World [etc.]. **1691** BAXTER *Nat. Ch.* viii. 31 His Honour as Gods chief Officer, and in a sort representer.

†**b.** *spec.* = REPRESENTATIVE B. 2. *Obs.*

1652 *Observ. Forms Govt.* Pref. 6 The people have not the power of choosing Representers to govern, if Governours must be sent of God. **1678** MARVELL *Growth Popery* 24 It is to be confessed, that the Knights, Citizens and Burgesses there assembled, are the Representers of the People of England. **1726** SWIFT *To a Lady* Wks. 1751 XIV. 227 When my Muse officious ventures On the Nation's Representers.

repre'senting, *vbl. sb.* [-ING[1].] The action of the vb. REPRESENT in various senses; representation.

c **1440** CAPGRAVE *Life St. Kath.* IV. 1502 These fayre riche sepultures Whiche be-tokene in her representyng That there is beryed duke or ellis kyng. **1581** SIDNEY *Apol. Poetrie* (Arb.) 26 Poesie..is an arte of imitation,..that is to say, a representing, counterfetting, or figuring foorth. **1643** MILTON *Divorce* II. xvii, He who understands not after all this representing, I doubt [etc.]. **1666** PEPYS *Diary* 8 Aug., The representing of our want of money being now become useless. **1693** DRYDEN *Juvenal* Ded. (1697) 71, I..apply'd my self to the representing of Blindsides, and little Extravagancies.

b. *attrib.* in ***representing days*** (see REPRESENTATION 5 b, and RECLAIMING *vbl. sb.* b).

1790 *Acts Sederunt* Index, Representing Days. **1838** W. BELL *Dict. Law Scot.* 852 If the reclaiming, or representing days, against an interlocutor of a Lord Ordinary, had.. expired, without a petition or representation [etc.].

repre'senting, *ppl. a.* [-ING[2].] That represents; representative.

1681–6 J. SCOTT *Chr. Life* (1747) III. 286 It is usual in Sacraments to call the representing Signs by the Names of the things which they represent. **1704** NORRIS *Ideal World* II. v. 289 All knowledge of him by the mediation of any representing image..being both needless and impossible. **1786** A. GIB *Sacr. Contempl.* II. I. v. 178 Of Him the first man was a figure, a representing type.

†**repre'sentively,** *adv. Obs. rare*$^{-1}$. = REPRESENTATIVELY.

1650 R. HOLLINGWORTH *Exerc. Usurped Powers* 17 The body of the kingdom..either collectively or representively.

representment[1] (rɛprɪ'zɛntmənt). [-MENT: cf. obs. F. *représentement* (Godef.).]

1. The act of representing in some form or figure; the fact of being so represented, or the result of such representation. Now *rare* (very common in 17th c.).

1594 DANIEL *Cleopatra* v. ii, Which Representments seeing, worse than Death She deem'd to yield to Life. **1625** BP. MOUNTAGU *App. Cæsar* 253 In rememoration, and for more effectuall representment of the Prototype. **1642** JER. TAYLOR *Episc.* (1647) 288 The Church is in the Bishop (viz. by representment) and the Bishop is in the Church (viz. as a Pilot in a ship). **1675** CAVE *Antiq. Apost.* (1702) 30 By this symbolick representment..God was teaching a new lesson. **1825** COLERIDGE in *Lit. Rem.* (1836) II. 355 This secret Jove would extort from the *Nous*, or Prometheus, which is the sixth representment of Prometheus. **1877** E. R. CONDER *Bas. Faith* iv. 162 All those immediate judgments which the intellect passes on the presentments of sense, or the representments of memory [etc.].

†**2.** Representation by discourse or argument.

1640–1 LD. J. DIGBY *Sp. in Ho. Com.* 9 Feb. 11 Representment of inconvenience may bee made. **1653** MILTON *Hirelings* Wks. 1851 V. 337 So far approv'd, as to have bin trusted with the representment and defence of your Actions to all Christendom. **1680** H. DODWELL *Two Lett.* (1691) 58 You cannot expect to prevail on men's interests, and inclinations, by a bare representment of the unreasonableness of their actions.

re-pre'sentment[2] (riː-). [RE- 5 a: cf. REPRESENT *v.*] Renewed presentation.

1822 LAMB *Elia* Ser. I. *Dream Children*, The soul of the first Alice looked out at her eyes with such a reality of representment. **1866** CRUMP *Banking* v. 133 There being sufficient funds to meet the bill, and before the representment of the bill the funds disappeared.

repre'sentor. [-OR.] = REPRESENTER. *spec.* in *Law*: one by or on behalf of whom a representation is made.

1553 BALE tr. *Gardiner's De Vera Obed.* d vij b, In that place he hath set princes whom as representours of his image vnto men, he wolde haue to be reputed [etc.]. **1643** HERLE *Answ. Ferne* 30 Their consents..should oblige the Commonalty as consenting in their Representors. **1646** SIR T. BROWNE *Pseud. Ep.* 262 Art being but the Imitator or secondary representor, it must not vary from the verity of the example. **1653** *Clarke Papers* (Camden) III. 7 Colonel Pride is chosen one of the Representors for..London. **1911**, **1971** [see REPRESENTEE 3].

†**re'press,** *sb. Obs.* [f. the vb.] Repression.

c **1440** *Gesta Rom.* xv. 51 (Add. MS.), Here housbond and she helde hym in so grete vyolete [? *read* vylete] and represse. *Ibid.* lxi. 378 Wenyng that they were comyn in represse of Cristen feithe. **1533–4** *Act 25 Hen. VIII*, c. 14 For the represse of heretikes, and such erronious opinions in tyme cominge, be it established [etc.]. **1586** J. HOOKER *Hist. Irel.* in *Holinshed* II. 153/1 A reasonable and a vsed cesse was to be set and leuied..for the represse of their enimies.

repress (rɪ'prɛs), *v.*[1] [f. L. *repress-*, ppl. stem of *reprimĕre*: see RE- and PRESS *v.*, and cf. REPREME and REPRIME.]

1. a. *trans.* To check, restrain, put down or keep under (something bad or objectionable).

c **1374** CHAUCER *Troylus* III. 1033 Whanne cause is & somme swych fantasye With pite so wel repressed is That it vnneþe doth or seyth amys. **14..** in *Tundale's Vis.*, etc. (1843) 93 The fyre hit quencheth also of envy And represseth the bolnyng eke of pryde. *c* **1430** LYDG. *Min. Poems* (Percy Soc.) 70 O loode-sterre of al goode governaunce! Alle vicious lustes by wisdom to represse. **1526** *Pilgr. Perf.* (W. de W. 1531) 44 Whiche vertue represseth the sensuall appetyte. **1553** T. WILSON *Rhet.* 14 To represse this rage..God hath lightened man with knowledge. **1596** LODGE *Marg. Amer.* 15 Thy nying grave remember, Which if thou dost, thy pride shall be repressed. **1626** T. H[AWKINS] *Caussin's Holy Crt.* 337 Chastity, is a uertue, which represseth the impure lusts of the flesh. **1709** POPE *Ess. Crit.* 682 Thus long succeeding Critics justly reign'd, Licence repress'd, and useful laws ordain'd. **1751** JOHNSON *Rambler* No. 159 ⁋10 [When] this troublesome instinct..instead of repressing petulance and temerity, silences eloquence. **1774** GOLDSM. *Nat. Hist.* (1776) I. 363 Those terrible tempests that deform the face of nature, and repress human presumption. **1817** SHELLEY *Rev. Islam* IV. xxii, While o'er the land is borne Her voice, whose awful sweetness doth repress All evil. **1849** MACAULAY *Hist. Eng.* vi. II. 89 He was authorised by law to repress spiritual abuses. **1875** JOWETT *Plato* (ed. 2) V. 155 Let there be a general law which will have a tendency to repress actions of impiety.

b. To check by some special treatment; to make less troublesome; to cure, stanch.

1493 *Petronilla* 48 (Pynson), Ye alas hir langoure to represse Lyst nat onys byd hir arise. **1601** HOLLAND *Pliny* II. Index, Hungrie worme in the stomacke, how to be repressed and cured. **1622** DRAYTON *Poly-olb.* xiv. 176 When in her pride..she nourish'd goodly vines, And oft her cares represt with her delicious wines. **1715** POPE *Iliad* I. 612 When now the rage of hunger was represt. **1805** W. SAUNDERS *Min. Waters* 34 A few drops of strong nitrous acid, poured into this hepatic water, at once represses the offensive smell. **1807–26** S. COOPER *First Lines Surg.* (ed. 5) 360 The bleeding may be repressed by means of a piece of fine sponge.

2. a. To check or withstand (some passion, feeling, etc.) in another by opposition or control.

c **1385** CHAUCER *L.G.W.* 2591 *Hypermnestra*, His maleyce is hym be-raft; Repressid hath Venus his crewel craft. **1430–40** LYDG. *Bochas* VIII. xvii. (1558) 11 b, Chastice tyrantes and their malice represse. **1555** EDEN *Decades* 20 He went aboute to represse theyr outragiousenes. **1560** DAUS tr. *Sleidane's Comm.* 4 He of a fatherly love desyrous to represse his rashenes. **1603** KNOLLES *Hist. Turks* (1638) To Rdr., They might long since..haue repressed his fury, and abated his pride. **1660** R. COKE *Power & Subj.* 146 To repress their insolence, the yearly return of Danegelt was enacted. **1678** WANLEY *Wond. Lit. World* v. ii. §17. 469/2 Tiberius..repressed the daring boldness of the proud Persian Cosroes. **1828** D'ISRAELI *Chas. I*, II. viii. 185 While this minister lived, he repressed the dark passions of Tiberius. **1856** FROUDE *Hist. Eng.* I. i. 66 This vigorous arming to repress the self-seeking tendencies in the mercantile classes.

b. To keep or hold back, to restrain or check (a person) from action or advance.

1638 JUNIUS *Paint. Ancients* 103 He did represse the one ..and he did prick on the other. **1726–46** THOMSON *Winter* 979 Armies stretch Each way their dazzling files, repressing here The frantic Alexander of the north. **1819** SHELLEY *Prometh. Unb.* I. i. 328 Who are those with hydra tresses.. Whom the frowning God represses..? **1823** LAMB *Elia* Ser. II. *Poor Relations*, He may require to be repressed sometimes..—but there is no raising her. **1865** KINGSLEY *Herew.* vi, The men, mistaking his intent, had to be represt again by Hereward.

3. a. To keep down, suppress (one's desires, feelings, etc.), to keep under control; to restrain, refrain from (an action).

1390 GOWER *Conf.* III. 166 He scholde his vanite represse With suche wordes as he herde. *a* **1556** CRANMER *Wks.* (Parker Soc.) I. 34 In all matters of our christian faith..we must repress our imaginations. **1583** GOLDING *Calvin on Deut.* xvii. 97 Wee must bee earnest in repressing our desires, and in bridling them. **1621** BURTON *Anat. Mel.* I. ii. III. iii, They..are so far from repressing rebellious inclinations, that they giue all encouragement vnto them. **1671** MILTON *Samson* 543 Desire of wine..Thou couldst repress. **1716** POPE *Iliad* VIII. 573 The prudent goddess yet her wrath repress'd. **1719** YOUNG *Busiris* IV. i, Turn, turn, blasphemer, and repress thy taunts. **1748** JOHNSON *Van. Hum. Wishes* 95 Our supple tribes repress their patriot throats. **1810** SCOTT *Lady of L.* II. xii, The ancient bard his glee repress'd. **1823** —— *Peveril* xlix, The Countess,.. unable to repress her curiosity, placed herself near Fenella. **1865** TROLLOPE *Belton Est.* i, It was her duty to repress both the feeling of shame and the sorrow.

b. *refl.* To contain (oneself) from speaking.

1876 T. HARDY *Ethelberta* (1890) 335 Mrs. Doncastle seemed inclined to make no remark..and at last Menlove could repress herself no longer.

c. *Psychol.* [tr. G. *verdrängen* (used in this sense by Breuer & Freud 1893, in *Neurol. Centralbl.* XII. 10).] In *Psychoanalysis*, of a patient or person who is the object of study: to keep out of the conscious mind, or suppress into the unconscious (unacceptable memories or desires). Also *absol.*

1909 A. A. BRILL tr. *Freud's Sel. Papers on Hysteria* i. 7 The patient has not reacted to psychic traumas because the nature of the trauma..concerned things which the patient wished to forget and which he therefore intentionally inhibited and repressed from the conscious memory. **1919** M. K. BRADBY *Psycho-Analysis* III. vii. 82 He believes the unconscious to be exclusively composed of contents repressed from the conscious. **1920** *Discovery* Mar. 69/2 The motive for repression is one's personal comfort. One represses to preserve one's peace of mind. **1943** J. S. HUXLEY *Evolutionary Ethics* ii. 15 The impulses whose thwarting generated the guilty hate may themselves become coloured with guilt, or be repressed. **1977** R. A. BARON et al. *Psychol.* x. 337 This unconscious mechanism can begin to create new problems... The individual loses some control over the situation when he represses his awareness of it.

4. a. To reduce (troublesome persons) to subjection or quietness; to put down by force, suppress; †to subdue (a town).
1390 GOWER *Conf.* III. 197 God schal hise foomen so represse, That thei schul ay stonde under foote. **1413** *Pilgr. Sowle* (Caxton 1483) IV. xxx. 78 They haue comaundement for to repressen aduersaryes and enemyes that besyen them to destroyen the countrey. *c* **1460** FORTESCUE *Abs. & Lim. Mon.* vii. (1885) 125 The Kynge shall often tymes sende his comissioners.. to represse and punysh riatours and risers. **1533** MORE *Apol.* xii. Wks. 870/2, I woulde wyshe the spiritualtye and temporaltye.. to represse and keepe vnder those euyll and vngracious folke. **1582** STANYHURST *Æneis* II. (Arb.) 61 This was Prince Priamus last ende and desteny final, Who saw thee Troians vanquisht, thee cittye repressed. **1605–6** *Act 3 Jas. I*, c. 4 (*title*) An Acte for the better discovery and repressing Popish Recusants. **1769** *De Foe's Tour Gt. Brit.* (ed. 7) III. 55 Dunstable.. was.. rebuilt by Henry I. to repress a vast Number of Robbers which infested the Country. *a* **1862** BUCKLE *Civiliz.* (1873) III. i. 20 It would have been a hopeless undertaking for any king to try to repress such powerful subjects.

b. To put down, quell (a rebellion, riot, etc.).
1475 *Rolls of Parlt.* VI. 144/2 Which Troubles, Commotions, and other offenses above named.. been nowe repressed. **1533** BELLENDEN *Livy* II. xxvi. (S.T.S.) I. 236 The sedition rising be mocioun of þe law foresade was suddanlie repressit be þir novellis. **1603** KNOLLES *Hist. Turks* (1621) 255 Amurath to repress this.. rebellion sent Bajazet Bassa.. with a strong armie into Europe. **1858** FROUDE *Hist. Eng.* III. xiii. 107 The duty of repressing riots .. in England lay with the nobility in their several districts. **1874** GREEN *Short Hist.* v. §4. 244 The royal commissioners sent to repress the tumult were driven from the field.

†c. To suppress (a book). *Obs. rare.*
In first quot. intended also for *re-press* = reprint.
1615 *Band, Ruffe & C.* (Halliw.) 7 Thus to please both, and grant them their request, My sentence is—the booke shall be represt. *c* **1645** HOWELL *Lett.* (1650) II. 2 You shall do well to repress any more copies of the satyr.

5. To keep under, check, curb, prevent from natural development, manifestation, etc.
c **1557** ABP. PARKER *Ps.* xxxviii. 106 There is no helth in all my flesh, Thy wrath my wealth doth so represse. *c* **1620** A. HUME *Brit. Tongue* (1865) 3 Amang quhom James the first, .. houbeit repressed be the iniquitie of the tyme, deserved noe smal praise. **1750** GRAY *Elegy* 51 Chill Penury repress'd their noble rage. **1796** H. HUNTER tr. *St.-Pierre's Stud. Nat.* (1799) I. 384 An unnatural constraint is used to repress a period of life all fire and activity. **1830** J. W. CROKER in *C. Papers* (1884) II. xv. 83 The essential spirit of opposition was so strong that it often repressed or fettered those sentiments. *a* **1862** BUCKLE *Civiliz.* (1873) III. iv. 269 The fairest and most endearing parts of our nature being constantly repressed, ceased to bear fruit.

†6. In *lit.* use: To force or drive back. *Obs.*
1623 BINGHAM *Xenophon* 89 Some of the light-armed of the enemy ran forth..; which quickly were repressed by our Archers & Peltasts. **1662** HOBBES *Seven Prob.* ii. (1682) 12 If two bodies cast off the Air, the motion of that Air will be respress'd both ways, and diverted into a course towards the Poles on both sides.

re'press (riː-), *v.*^{2} [RE- 5 a.] To press again.
1875 KNIGHT *Dict. Mech.* 1918/2 A machine for repressing brick after being partially dried. *Ibid.* 1919/2 The repressing press may be of any suitable form and construction. **1892** in Lee *Hist. Columbus* II. 539 Finely ground clays, pressed with heavy presses and repressed into uniform shape and compactness.

†re'pressal. *Obs. rare*$^{-1}$. [-AL^1.] Repression.
1593 BILSON *Govt. Christ's Ch.* 1 God ordaining powers and deliuering the sword for the defence of the simple and innocent, and repressall of the wicked and injurious.

repressed (rɪ'prɛst), *ppl. a.* [f. REPRESS *v.*^{1} + -ED^1.] Restrained, checked, suppressed: *esp.* in *Psychol.* (cf. REPRESS *v.*^{1} 3 c). Also *absol.*
1665 MANLEY *Grotius' Low C. Warres* 439 When the Besiegers had stopped it up behind also, first throwing fire therein, the repressed force thereof at length burst out. **1764** GOLDSM. *Trav.* 346 Repress'd ambition struggles round her shore. **1876** T. HARDY *Ethelberta* (1890) 135 'Yes—you are quite right', said the repressed young painter. **1904** *Psychol. Bull.* I. 357 The theory of Freud, that dreams are disguised realizations of repressed desires. **1919** M. K. BRADBY *Psycho-Analysis* I. iii. 34 It [*sc.* the unconscious] also contains the repressed. **1923** J. S. HUXLEY *Ess. Biologist* v. 187 The publication of Darwin's *Origin of Species* was to them what psycho-analysis is (or may be) to a patient with a repressed complex. **1954** D. RIESMAN *Individualism Reconsidered* (1955) xxii. 336 It was not easy to find convincing evidence for the existence of repressed Oedipal desires in every adult whom he analyzed. **1960** M. SPARK *Bachelors* vi. 81 Repressed homosexuality is a meaningless term because no one can prove it. **1973** J. G. STARKE *Validity of Psycho-Anal.* ii. 14 For psycho-analysts, perhaps the most important component is *repressed* material.

Hence **re'pressedly** *adv.*
1858 G. MACDONALD *Phantastes* viii, Her forehead was high, and her black eyes repressedly quiet.

re'presser. *rare.* [f. as prec. + -ER^1: cf. REPRESSOR.] **1.** One who, or that which represses.
c **1449** PECOCK *Repr.* I. xx. 130 The Book clepid The Represser of over moche wijting the Clergie. **1526** *Pilgr. Perf.* (W. de W. 1531) 56 b, A conquerour of his owne wyll, a represser of Ire, and a pure louer of his ennemy. **1630** BRATHWAIT *Eng. Gentlem.* (1641) 26 To speake generally of Action, as it is the represser, so Idlenesse is the producer of all vice. **1951** *Jrnl. of Personality* XIX. 472 Repressers.. are patients who avoid contact with such emotional material. They are apt to block in the presence of sexual or aggressive stimuli.

2. = REPRESSOR 2.
1957 [see REPRESSOR 2]. **1971** *New Scientist* 22 July 182/1 Two classes of DNA-switching molecules are known so far in bacteria, one class acts negatively—repressers—and one acts positively, but indirectly—sigma factors.

re'pressful, *a. rare*$^{-1}$. [-FUL.] Repressive.
1893 F. MOORE *Gray Eye* III. 51 A responsible official.. whose chastely-braided uniform looked repressful of tips.

re'pressible, *a.* [-IBLE: cf. *irrepressible.*] **1.** Capable of being repressed (Ogilvie 1882). *rare*$^{-0}$. Hence **re'pressibly** *adv.* (ibid.).
2. *Biochem.* That may be inhibited by the action of a repressor; susceptible to the action of a repressor.
1957, 1964 [see REPRESSOR 2]. **1974** *Nature* 10 May 110/1 The interactions which control repressible and inducible operons in bacteria are now well understood in principle.

re'pressing, *vbl. sb.*^{1} [f. REPRESS *v.*^{1} + -ING^1.] The action of the verb; checking, restraint, subjugation.
c **1340** HAMPOLE *Prose Tr.* 13 Anoþer es restreynynge or repressynge of ill styrrynge. *c* **1449** PECOCK *Repr.* Prol. 4 In the firste of whiche parties schal be mad in general maner the seid repressing. *c* **1460** FORTESCUE *Abs. & Lim. Mon.* vi. (1885) 123 It shalbe nescessarie þat the kynge haue alway some ffloute apon the see, ffor the repressynge off rovers. **1521** *Carew MSS.* (1867) I. 20 For the repressing of whose malice I assay all the friends I can. **1583** STUBBES *Anat. Abus.* II. (1882) 41 Good lawes there are, both for the repressing of these and al other enormities whatsoeuer. *c* **1630** SANDERSON *Serm.* II. 273 For the.. repressing and discountenancing of insolency. *a* **1715** BURNET *Own Time* III. (1724) I. 517 In it the repressing of tyranny is reckoned a duty incumbent on good subjects. **1884** *Athenæum* 16 Feb. 210/2 The record of a despot of genius.. meeting savage uprising by equally savage repressing.

repressing (riː'prɛsɪŋ), *vbl. sb.*^{2} Also re- (with hyphen). [f. RE- 5 a + PRESSING *vbl. sb.*^{1}: cf. REPRESS *v.*^{2}] **1.** A new impression made from an old matrix of a sound recording.
1960 'I. T. ROSS' *Murder out of School* iv. 38 Old records .. collectors' items now, that had somehow never come out as well in the long-playing repressings the companies had issued. **1975** *Daily Tel.* 17 Mar. 10/3 If you can only afford one of the three recent issues, it must be 'Chopin 3' of RCA's collection of re-pressings.

2. The action of pressing again.
1967 M. CHANDLER *Ceramics in Mod. World* v. 142 Shaping methods for fireclay bricks include extrusion and wire-cutting (often followed by re-pressing).

re'pressing, *ppl. a.* [f. REPRESS *v.*^{1} + -ING^2.] That represses. So **re'pressingly** *adv.*
1872 GEO. ELIOT *Middlem.* II. III. xxxii. 152 Solomon put his hand before her repressingly. **1909** A. A. BRILL tr. *Freud's Sel. Papers on Hysteria* vii. 161 What becomes conscious as an obsession and obsessive affect and substitutes the pathogenic memory in the conscious life, are compromise formations between the repressed and the repressing ideas. **1951** *Jrnl. of Personality* XIX. 472 We hypothesized that intellectualizing patients.. would show higher accuracy for threatening material than the repressing type of patient. **1975** I. M. BLANCO *Unconscious as Infinite Sets* vi. 82 The unrepressed unconscious of the ego is, in the Freudian conception, the *repressing* aspect of the ego.

repression (rɪ'prɛʃən). [ad. L. type **repressiōn-em*, n. of action f. *reprimĕre*: see REPRESS *v.*^{1} and cf. F. *répression* (15th c.).]
†1. Capability or power of repressing. *Obs.*$^{-1}$
c **1374** CHAUCER *Troylus* III. 1038 And some so ful of furye is and despit That it sourmounteth his repressioun.

2. a. The action of repressing, in senses of the verb; also, an instance of this.
1533 MORE *Apol.* xlix. Wks. 927/1 Any new order concerning heresies, with yᵉ chaunge of lawes before deuised for the repression of them. **1553** in Burnet *Hist. Ref., Rec.* II. I. No. 56 Do such things for the Advancement of Justice, and for the repression and punishment of Malefactors. *c* **1611** CHAPMAN *Iliad* XI. 472 But Ioue (that weighs aboue All humane pow'rs) to Aiax breast diuine repressions droue, And made him shun who shunn'd himself. **1648–9** *Eikon Bas.* 21 No declaration.. from My self could take place, For the due repression of these Tumults. **1818** BENTHAM *Parl. Reform* 62 Repression of insolence is, therefore, in his situation prescribed by considerations [etc.]. **1860** TYNDALL *Glac.* I. xvi. 109 That eastern religion whose essence is the repression of all action.

†b. *Med.* (See quot.) *Obs. rare*$^{-1}$.
1582 HESTER *Secr. Phiorav.* I. xxvii. 30 The Feuer of Repression.. is an alteration of the bloud, whiche is caused of beeyng ouer hott, and then colde.

c. *Psychol.* The action, process, or result of suppressing into the unconscious or keeping out of the conscious mind unacceptable memories or desires. Also *attrib.*
1909 A. A. BRILL tr. *Freud's Sel. Papers on Hysteria* iv. 88 If I could now make it probable that the idea became pathogenic in consequence of the exclusion and repression, the chain would seem complete. **1910** S. FREUD in *Amer. Jrnl. Psychol.* XXI. 193, I called this hypothetical process 'repression' (*Verdrängung*), and considered it was proved by the undeniable existence of resistance. *Ibid.*, One of my cases, in which the conditions and the utility of the repression process stand out clearly enough. **1930** R. LEHMANN *Note in Music* VII. 274 Gerald was not free, not calm and balanced: quite the reverse—a tangle of passionate conflicts and repressions. **1939** T. S. ELIOT *Family Reunion* I. 40, I always said his Lordship Suffered from what they call a kind of repression. **1954** R. F. C. HULL tr. *Jung's Devel. of Personality* in *Coll. Wks.* XVII. iv. 115 No breaking down of repressions can ever destroy true creativeness. **1973** J. G. STARKE *Validity of Psycho-Anal.* ii. 14 In essence, repression is the mental process of rejecting and excluding material from consciousness.

3. *Biochem.* The inhibition of enzyme synthesis by the action of a repressor on an operon.
1957 [see REPRESSOR 2]. **1959** *Jrnl. Molecular Biol.* I. 176 It now appears to be a general rule, for bacteria, that the formation of sequential enzyme sequences involved in the synthesis of essential metabolites is *inhibited* by their end product. The convenient term 'repression' was coined by Vogel to distinguish this effect from another, equally general, phenomenon: the control of enzyme *activity* by end products of metabolism. **1973** R. G. KRUEGER et al. *Introd. Microbiol.* xv. 437/2 Repression is distinct from feedback inhibition in that the former results in the cessation of enzyme synthesis whereas the latter leads to inactivation of an existing enzyme.

Hence **re'pressionist,** one who advocates repression or repressive measures.
1875 *Good Words* 266 The people, he said, did not take strong drinks, although they seemed to have no objection to them when they had an opportunity of receiving them—an argument for repressionists. **1888** *Chicago Advance* 9 Aug., Even political repressionists are practically turning moralists.

repressive (rɪ'prɛsɪv), *a.* [f. REPRESS *v.*^{1} + -IVE: cf. F. *répressif, -ive*, and med.L. *repressīvus.*] Having the nature of, or tending to, repression.
1597 G. HARVEY *Wks.* (Grosart) III. 9 Goe to the Apothecarie, and fetch mee some represiue *Antidotum* to put into the bason, to keep downe the venemous vapors. **1731** in BAILEY (vol. II). **1749** SMOLLETT *Regicide* v. i, The successive pangs Of fond impatience and repressive fear. **1797** GILLIES *Aristotle* II. 233 Although our republic rejects the community of goods as repressive to exertion. **1830** LYELL *Princ. Geol.* I. 392 Beds of solid travertin.. must often.. obstruct the vent, and thus increase the repressive force. **1876** FARRAR *Marlb. Serm.* x. 91 This repressive education is the very reverse of that which for centuries has been carried on at our public schools. **1921** R. MACAULAY *Dangerous Ages* xii. 234 His phrases drifted over Mrs Hilary's head. '.. a deterrent force residing in the ego and preventing us from stepping outside the bounds of propriety .. conflict with the progress of human society.. inhibitory and repressive power of the censor.' **1944** J. S. HUXLEY *On Living in Revolution* 57 It is much harder to feel strongly about social problems such as malnutrition or unemployment, because the connection with the repressive mechanism is not so automatic. **1968** A. HERON *Towards Quaker View of Sex* i. 7 This still repressive and inhibited outlook towards sex.. has brought difficulties to the serious student of human behaviour. **1970** *Nature* 26 Sept. 1371/2 Whose tortured minds are nourished by absurd slogans such as 'creative vandalism' and 'repressive tolerance'.

Hence **re'pressively** *adv.* (Worcester 1846, citing Allen); **re'pressiveness.**
1878 SEELEY *Stein* I. 408 Countries which, owing to the jealousy and repressiveness of the government, are entirely devoid of political culture. **1884** CATH. L. PIRKIS *J. Wynne* II. vi. 68 A repressiveness.. which would have utterly frozen anyone susceptible of the process.

re'pressor. Also 8 -our. [a. L. *repressor*, agent-n. f. *reprimĕre* to REPRESS: cf. REPRESSER.] **1.** One who, or that which represses. *rare.*
1611 FLORIO, *Ripressore*, a repressor. **1676** TOWERSON *Decalogue* 416 No furtherer of uncleanness but on the contrary the repressor of it. **1725** J. LEWIS *Life Pecock* (1744) 62 An account of a book published by the bishop, entituled, The repressour [etc.]. **1860** (*title*) The repressor of over much blaming of the clergy, by Reginald Pecock.

2. *Biochem.* A substance which by its action on an operon can inhibit the synthesis of a specific enzyme or set of enzymes.
1957 H. J. VOGEL in McElroy & Glass *Chem. Basis Heredity* ii. 286 In order to facilitate further discussion, the following terminology will be used hereafter: a relative decrease, resulting from the exposure of cells to a given substance, in the rate of synthesis of a particular apoenzyme is termed 'enzyme repression'; the substance thus decelerating enzyme synthesis is a 'represser' ('repressor'); an enzyme-forming system that can be antagonized by a represser is 'repressible'; and, under conditions of repression, the formation of the enzyme is 'repressed'. **1964** G. H. HAGGIS et al. *Introd. Molecular Biol.* x. 273 Either inducible cells contain built-in repressors, which are inactivated by added inducers, or repressible enzyme synthesis depends on intracellular inducers inactivated by external repressors. There is evidence that the first of these alternatives is the correct one. **1971** J. Z. YOUNG *Introd. Study Man* iii. 54 The repressor is produced by a regulator gene. **1973** B. J. WILLIAMS *Evolution & Human Origins* vi. 91/1 Diffusable repressor substances that form complexes with specific operator regions prevent the mRNA transcription.

repressory (rɪ'prɛsərɪ), *a.* [f. REPRESS *v.*^{1} + -ORY^2.] Having the qualities of a repressor; designed to repress.
1905 W. J. LOCKE *Morals M. Ordeyne* (1906) xi. 117 But what do I know of the repressory methods employed in seminaries for young ladies? **1954** D. RIESMAN *Individualism Reconsidered* xxii. 347 The repressory forces must draw their energies from the great energy reservoir of the id.

re'pressure. *rare*$^{-1}$. [RE- 5 a.] Repeated or renewed pressure.
1811 PINKERTON *Petral.* I. 444 Saussure concludes that these dislocations of beds are produced by a *refoulement*, or repressure, which has folded them over each other.

re-'pressuring, *vbl. sb.* [f. RE- 5 a + PRESSURE + -ING^1.] The pumping of fluid into an oil well so as to increase or maintain the pressure in the oil-bearing strata, allowing more oil to be extracted.

1929 *Jrnl. Inst. Petroleum Technologists* XV. 430 If a flush field is produced inefficiently and re-pressuring is left until the field is almost commercially exhausted the ultimate yield of the pool must be very considerably less than when properly controlled back-pressures have been used from the beginning and re-pressuring operations commenced in the early life of the field. **1940** *Sun* (Baltimore) 24 Sept. 6/8 An oil field at Walters, Okla., has been revived by a method known as repressuring. **1961** *Economist* 2 Dec. 955/2 This pipeline..will eventually carry..salt water in the opposite direction, to be pumped into the underground structure in order to keep up underground pressure and keep the oil flowing up and out to the coast. This 're-pressuring' project is one of the largest ever undertaken outside the United States.

re'pressurize, *v.* [RE- 5 a.] *trans.* To pressurize again; to renew pressure in.

1953 *Jrnl. Inst. Electr. Engineers* C. II. 646/2 After completion of the modifications, the system was repressurized, but when the routine 66-kV d.c. 15-min test was applied, failure occurred on two phases. **1962** J. GLENN in *Into Orbit* 41 You have one large handle for repressurizing the cabin with oxygen in case of a bad leak. **1971** *Daily Tel.* 26 July 22/5 He and Irwin will then repressurise their cabin, take off their spacesuits..and then get seven hours rest.

repreuable, obs. f. REPROVABLE.

repreuar, obs. f. REPROVER.

repreue, -preve, -prewe, obs. ff. REPROOF, REPROVE.

repreuendeli, obs. f. REPROVINGLY.

repreve, obs. f. REPRIEVE *v.*

†**re'preyn**, *v. Obs. rare.* [ad. OF. *repreigne*, *repregne*, etc., pres. subj. of *reprendre* to REPREHEND.] *trans.* To reprove, rebuke. Hence **re'preyning** *vbl. sb.*

a **1380** *St. Ambrose* 440 (Vernon MS.) in Horstm. *Altengl. Leg.* (1878) 15 He nolde not suwe hem in no vice, But he wolde in certeyne Wiþ opene vois him wel repreyne. *Ibid.* 857 He hem wolde blame..And repreyne hem of wikkednesse. *a* **1380** *Minor Poems fr. Vernon MS.* 529/112 He wol þe ȝelde for þi gode dede ffoul repreynynge [*printed* repreyuynge] to þi mede.

reprice, obs. form of REPRISE *sb.*

repricing (riː'praɪsɪŋ), *vbl. sb.* [RE- 5 a.] The act of changing, usually by increasing, a price.

1959 *Times* 1 June 11/2 If anomalies are to be avoided..this 'repricing' should be undertaken systematically. **1974** *Daily Colonist* (Victoria, B.C.) 8 Sept. 7/7 There would be re-pricing, probably several times, during the model year.

re'prick (riː-), *v. rare.* [RE- 5 a.]

†**1.** *intr.* Of a hare: To 'prick' in a reverse direction. *Obs. rare*$^{-1}$.

1602 *2nd Pt. Return fr. Parnass.* II. v. 937 By that I knewe that they had the hare and on foote, and by and by I might see him sore and resore, prick and reprick.

2. *trans.* To prick again.

1611 FLORIO, *Ripunto*, repricked.

reprie, obs. form of REPRIEVE *v.*

reprief(e, obs. ff. REPRIEVE *sb.*, REPROOF, and REPROVE.

reprieval (rɪ'priːvəl). Also 6–7 reprivall(l. [f. REPRIEVE *v.* + -AL.] = REPRIEVE *sb.* in various senses. Now *rare* (common in 17th c.).

α. *a* **1586** SIDNEY *Arcadia* (1598) 352 Gynecia, to whom the fearefull agonies shee still liued in, made any small repriuall sweete. *c* **1595** SOUTHWELL *St. Peter's Compl.* 31 Senses and soules repriuall from all cumbers. **1669** in *10th Rep. Hist. MSS. Comm.* App. V. 98 Wee..ordered that the reprivall of the said Walter..should be continued untill the next Summer Assizes. *a* **1684** LEIGHTON *Comm. 1 Pet.* Wks. (1859) 220/2 These reprivals and prolongings of this present life.

β. *a* **1613** OVERBURY *Characters* (1615) D vj b, His [the sailor's] sleepes are but repreeuals of his dangers. **1656** HEYLIN *Surv. France* 25 The Baron was again committed to prison, till the Queen Mother had wooed the people..to admit of his reprievall. **1675** BAXTER *Cath. Theol.* II. VIII. 156 Is not the very reprieval of the World from deserved ruine and misery so many thousand years an Act of Grace? **1821** SOUTHEY *Vis. Judgm.* iv, Change of place to them brought no reprieval from anguish. **1874** BARING-GOULD *Yorksh. Odd.* (1875) II. 242 The Parliament having remonstrated at the reprieval of Popish recusants, the King reluctantly signed the warrant for their execution.

reprieve (rɪ'priːv), *sb.* Also 6–7 repreeue, 7 reprive, (7 repriefe, 9 reprief). [f. the vb.]

1. The act of reprieving; the fact or favour of being reprieved.

1607 SHAKS. *Cor.* v. ii. 53 You are condemn'd, our Generall has sworne you out of repreeue and pardon. **1623–4** MIDDLETON & ROWLEY *Span. Gipsy* v. i, Promise me you'll get reprieve For the condemned man. **1671** MILTON *Samson* 288 So many dy'd Without Reprieve adjudg'd to death, For want of well pronouncing Shibboleth.

b. An instance of this; a formal suspension of the execution of a sentence upon a condemned person; a respite from a penalty imposed; a remission or commutation of a capital sentence.

1598 SHAKS. *Merry W.* II. ii. 6, I haue grated vpon my good friends for three Repreeues for you, and your Coach-fellow Nim. **1603** —— *Meas. for M.* IV. ii. 140 His friends still wrought Repreeues for him. *a* **1680** BUTLER *Rem.* (1759) I. 210 Like Princes had Prerogative to give Convicted Malefactors a Reprieve. *a* **1721** SHEFFIELD (Dk. Buckhm.) *Wks.* (1753) I. 290 All we could give was but a poor reprieve, A hardship worse than death to minds resolv'd. **1789** *Constit. U.S.* II. §2 The president shall have power to grant reprieves and pardons for offences against the United States. **1843** LEVER *J. Hinton* xxii, Like the felon, that feels there is no chance of a reprieve, I could look my fate more steadily in the face. **1874** L. STEPHEN *Hours in Library* (1892) I. vi. 231 A reprieve is granted at the last moment.

transf. **1676** D'URFEY *Mme. Fickle* v. ii, *Tob.* Methinks I cou'd beat this Drawer into a Wicker Bottle. *Zech.* Sirra, as a Reprieve for Life, bring out the Butt.

†**c.** The time during which one is reprieved.

1603 SHAKS. *Meas. for M.* II. iv. 39 That in his Reprieue (Longer, or shorter) he may be so fitted That his soule sicken not.

2. A warrant granting or authorizing the suspension or remission of a capital sentence.

1602 *Life T. Cromwell* v. v, Here is a kind reprieve come from the king To bring him straight unto his majesty. **1603** SHAKS. *Meas. for M.* IV. ii. 74, I hope it is some pardon, or repreeue For the most gentle Claudio. *a* **1674** CLARENDON *Hist. Reb.* VIII. §283 The very morning that Sir John Hotham was to die, a reprieve was sent from the House of Peers to suspend his execution for three days. **1758** *Ann. Reg.* I. 100/2 A reprieve was brought to Newgate for Dr. Hensey, respiting his sentence for a fortnight. **1781** GIBBON *Decl. & F.* xix. II. 136 The second messenger entrusted with the reprieve, was detained by the eunuchs. **1820** BYRON *Mar. Fal.* I. i, The ducal table, cover'd o'er With..Despatches, judgments, acts, reprieves, reports. **1841** *Penny Cycl.* XIX. 403/2 If the reprieve is sent by the secretary of state, it is under the sign manual of the king.

3. *transf.* Respite from a natural or violent death.

a **1633** AUSTIN *Medit.* (1635) 276 Hee..was made an end of. And so must all men, be the time of their Reprieve never so long. *a* **1677** BARROW *Serm.* Wks. 1716 II. 35 He liveth only by reprieve from that..sentence, the day thou sinnest thou shalt die. **1712** STEELE *Spect.* No. 498 ⁋2 If you would but bestow a little of your wholesome Advice upon our Coachmen, it might perhaps be a Reprieve to some of their Necks. **1784** JOHNSON *Let. to Mrs. Thrale* 20 Mar., God has in his mercy granted me a reprieve; for how much time his mercy must determine. **1816** SCOTT *Antiq.* vii, The sense of reprieve from approaching and apparently inevitable death had its usual effect. **1870** BRYANT *Iliad* I. v. 161 With those who flee Is neither glory nor reprieve from death.

b. A respite, or temporary escape, from some trouble, calamity, etc.

1635 QUARLES *Embl.* IV. xiv. 3, I search'd the Shades of Sleep, to ease my day Of griping sorrowes with a nights repriefe. **1655** FULLER *Ch. Hist.* I. vi. §2 Perceiving his Countrey condemned by Gods Justice to Ruine, he could procure a Reprieve, though not prevail for the Pardon thereof. **1733** CHEYNE *Eng. Malady* II. ix. §1 (1734) 206 It is absolutely necessary..to gain a Reprieve from these Symptoms. **1782** MISS BURNEY *Cecilia* v. iv, Cecilia..contrived..to keep her maid in the room. Miss Belfield, supposing this to be accidental, rejoiced in her imaginary reprieve. **1821** CLARE *Vill. Minstr.* I. 133 The moth, for night's reprief, Waited safe and snug withal 'Neath the plantain's bowery leaf. **1851** GALLENGA *Italy* 381 The people..were only allowed a choice between the instant surrender of their rights, and a short reprieve, which entitled them to call themselves their own masters till the end of the war.

reprieve (rɪ'priːv), *v.* Forms: α. 5–6 repry, 6 reprie. β. 6–7 reprive. γ. 7 repre(e)ve, 7– reprieve. [First in pa. pple. *repryed*, app. ad. AF. *repris*, pa. pple. of *reprendre*: see REPRISE *v.* 3. The insertion of the *v* and the later change of vowel are difficult to account for.]

†**1.** *trans.* To (take or) send back *to* prison; to remand; to detain on remand. *Obs.*

α. **1494** FABYAN *Chron.* VII. 389 They were repryed, and sent vnto the Toure of London, where they remayned longe after. *Ibid.* 672 [They] were brought vnto Guyldehalle, and there areygned; but the sayd Turbyruyle was repryd to pryson. **1542–3** *Act 34 & 35 Hen. VIII*, c. 27 §84 The said Iustices..maie reprie the prisoner, til they haue aduertised the Kinges maiestie of the matter. **1556** J. HEYWOOD *Spider & F.* lxxviii. 158 Whervpon they repryede me to prison cheynde. **1588** LAMBARDE *Eiren.* IV. xiv. 563 Iustice Welsh thought it meete to reprie the prisoner, without giuing iudgement upon him.

β. **1571** CAMPION *Hist. Irel.* II. ix. (1633) 116 Of this Treason he was found guilty, and reprived in the Towre a long time. **1587** FLEMING *Contn. Holinshed* III. 952/2 His moonks garment was plucked from his backe, and he repriued [*Hall* repried], till the king were informed of his malicious obstinacie.

†**b.** To remit for trial. *Obs. rare*$^{-1}$.

1556 J. HEYWOOD *Spider & F.* xxiv, The faughter..apealth to be repride, From London to Louane, there to be tride.

†**2.** To postpone, delay, put off. *Obs. rare.*

1548 ELIOT s.v. *Amplio*,..to deferre or delai a thyng in iugement, to repry. **1567** R. MULCASTER *Fortescue's De Laud. Leg.* (1672) 128 It was in the Judges power to have reprived or respected the woman's arraignment till the end of the year. **1628** FORD *Lover's Mel.* I. i, I repriev'd Th' intended execution with entreaties And interruption. **1630** MAY *Contin. Lucan* VII. 533 Not one dayes absence can preuent, Nor scarce repriue my Fate. **1664** KATH. PHILIPS *Death* v, in *Poems* 233 Since we cannot Death reprieve, Our Souls and Fame we ought to mind, For they our Bodies will survive.

†**3.** To bring back, redeem. *Obs. rare*$^{-1}$.

c **1557** ABP. PARKER *Ps.* cxxvi. 375 What tyme the Lord shall backe repry Hard Sions thrall to death so nye [etc.].

4. To respite or rescue (a person) from impending punishment; *spec.* to suspend or delay the execution of (a condemned person).

β. **1596** SPENSER *F.Q.* IV. xii. 31, I humbly crave your Majestie It to replevie, and my sonne reprive. **1600** DEKKER *Fortunatus* Wks. 1873 I. 170 Untie their bands. Vice doth reprive you both, I set you free. **1655** *Clarke Papers* (Camden) III. 38 Three executed at Salisbury, the rest reprived and pardoned.

fig. **1648** CRASHAW *Delights Muses* Wks. (1904) 152 Those sweet Aires that often slew mee Shall revive mee Or reprive mee. **1675** BAXTER *Cath. Theol.* II. VI. 115 Nature is reprived and continued by some degree of Grace.

γ. **1647** C. HARVEY *Sch. of Heart* xii. 24 Justice condemnes; let mercy, Lord, reprieve me. **1695** BLACKMORE *Pr. Arth.* I. 451 Her Power can sentenc'd Criminals reprieve. **1749** FIELDING *Tom Jones* Wks. 1775 VII. 209 He who escapes from death is not pardoned, he is only reprieved, and reprieved to a short day. **1809** KENDALL *Trav.* I. 21 He may reprieve a condemned malefactor till the next meeting of the general assembly; but he can grant no pardon. **1892** ZANGWILL *Bow Mystery* 180 'Pending further inquiries into this', said the Home Secretary,..'I have reprieved the prisoner'.

fig. **1648** BOYLE *Seraphic Love* Wks. (1744) I. 163/2 Her afflictions torment him, whilst his own reprieve him. **1655** FULLER *Ch. Hist.* IV. ii. 174 Let her Memory therefore be reprieved till the day of Judgement.

b. Const. *from* the penalty, punishment, etc.

β. **1592** NASHE *Four Lett. Confut.* D, Maister Birdes Letter shall not repriue you from the ladder. **1632** BROME *North. Lasse* II. iv, Then Sir for this time you shall be repriv'd, From further penance.

absol. **1674** BREVINT *Saul at Endor* 229 No Indulgence can reprive from any Punishments that we can see.

γ. **1601** SHAKS. *All's Well* III. iv. 30 He cannot thriue, Vnlesse her prayers..repreeue him from the wrath Of greatest Iustice. *c* **1660** SOUTH *Serm.* (1715) I. 31 Company, though it may reprieve a Man from his Melancholy, yet it cannot secure him from his Conscience. **1717** POPE *Iliad* X. 236 When night descending, from his vengeful hand Reprieved the relics of the Grecian band. **1770** GOLDSM. *Des. Vill.* 238 Reprieve the tottering mansion from its fall.

†**5.** To pardon, forgive. *Obs. rare*$^{-1}$.

1629 SHIRLEY *Wedding* I. iii, I hope your worship will reprieve my boldness; tis out of love to your daughter.

Hence **re'prieved** *ppl. a.*, **re'prieving** *vbl. sb.*

1633 P. FLETCHER *Elisa* II. x, Teares are most due, when there is no reprieving. **1664** H. MORE *Myst. Iniq.* 111 To enclose him in a Pyx like a reprieved prisoner. **1758** *Ann. Reg.* I. 81/2 The reprieved were turned over to the Grafton and Sunderland. **1868** E. EDWARDS *Ralegh* I. xxi. 457 A fortnight after the return of the reprieved prisoners to the Tower of London.

reprieve, obs. form of REPROOF, REPROVE.

†**re'prievement.** *Obs. rare.* [f. prec. + -MENT.] The action of reprieving; a reprieve.

1633 T. ADAMS *Exp. 2 Peter* ii. 3 Thou art one of those scape-goats in whose temporary reprievement the Judge of all flesh doth but represent the necessity of his last assizes. **1647** T. HILL *Paul* (1648) 5 Like to obtain mercy, at least a reprievement, as to the execution of the judgement.

re'priever. *rare*$^{-1}$. [f. as prec. + -ER^{1}.] One who reprieves.

1685 BAXTER *Paraphr. N.T.* John i. 9 As the Repriever and Restorer of blinded Intellects.

reprife, obs. form of REPROOF.

reprimand ('rɛprɪmɑːnd, -æ-), *sb.* [ad. F. *réprimande*, earlier *reprimende* (= Sp. *reprimenda*), f. *réprimer* to repress, reprove.] A sharp rebuke, reproof, or censure, esp. one given by a person or body having authority, or by a judge or magistrate to an offender.

1636 in *Crt. & Times Chas. I* (1848) II. 258 Crofts..got committed to my Lord Dorset, and Apsley to his chamber with a sharp admonition and reprimand. **1681** in Somers *Tracts* (1748) I. 138 The Person who made such an Inference deserved a Reprimand in the open Court. **1707–8** WYCHERLEY *Let. to Pope* 28 Feb., A friend's reprimand often shews more friendship than his compliment. **1732** LEDIARD *Sethos* II. VIII. 162 A grave reprimand from the senate. **1788** H. WALPOLE *Corr.* (1820) 128 Probably even they who might be corrected by his reprimand adopted some new distinction as ridiculous. **1838** DISRAELI in *Corr. w. Sister* 1 Mar. (1886) 97 Yesterday O'Connell received his reprimand in one of the most crowded houses I remember. **1854** MACAULAY *Biog.* (1860) 61 Goldsmith gave his landlady a sharp reprimand for her treatment of him. **1896** LELY *Stat. of Pract. Util.* 38 *note*, The penalty for a first offence being only a reprimand and costs.

reprimand (rɛprɪ'mɑːnd, -æ-), *v.* Also 7 **-man.** [ad. F. *réprimander*, †*reprimender* (1642), f. *réprimande*: see prec.]

1. *trans.* To rebuke, reprove, or censure (a person) sharply or severely.

1681 PRIDEAUX *Lett.* (Camden) 102 In the same manner he proceeded to repriman them for their unworthy behavior both to his Majesty and us. **1687** H. HOLDEN in *Magd. Coll. & Jas. II* (O.H.S.) 124 The Bishop..in a large speech..reprimanded the Fellows of their disobedience. **1727** SWIFT *Poisoning E. Curll* Wks. 1755 III. I. 149 This gentleman..reprimanded Mr. Curll for wrongfully ascribing to him the aforesaid poems. **1748** *Anson's Voy.* I. iii. 30 The Boatswain immediately reprimanded them, and ordered them to be gone. **1770** *Junius Lett.* xxxviii. (1788) 205 The lofty terms in which he was persuaded to reprimand the city. **1835** W. IRVING *Tour Prairies* 203 The Captain..reprimanded the sentinel for deserting his post, and obliged him to return to it. **1875** JOWETT *Plato* (ed. 2) I. 137 In such cases any man will be angry with another, and reprimand him.

absol. **1856** Kane *Arct. Expl.* I. xvi. 195 It was in vain that I..argued, jeered, or reprimanded: an immediate halt could not be avoided.

†**b.** To censure, find fault with (an act). *rare*$^{-1}$.

1722 Waterland *Arian Subscript.* Suppl., Wks. 1823 II. 380 Lord Burghley..reprimanded the warm proceedings of the Heads against him.

†**2.** To repress, restrain. *Obs. rare*$^{-1}$.

1710 T. Fuller *Pharm. Extemp.* 116 It [i.e. the electuary] reprimands the Animal Spirits when too furious.

Hence **repri'mander**; **repri'manding** *vbl. sb.* and *ppl. a.*; **repri'mandingly** *adv.*

1748 Richardson *Clarissa* (1811) II. 315 Giving a hint, which perhaps..you will reprimandingly call, 'Not being able to forego the ostentation of sagacity.' **1851** J. Hamilton *Royal Preacher* xvii. (1854) 220 A long lecture of rough reprimanding and perverse faultfinding. **1867** *Quiver* II. 186 Then said the owl unto his reprimander—'Fair sir, I have no enemies to slander.' **1899** *Westm. Gaz.* 2 Aug. 10/3 The cleric found his Bishop in a reprimanding mood.

†**reprimate**, *pa. pple. Obs. rare*$^{-1}$. [irreg. f. L. *reprim-ĕre* (see next) + -ate, perh. after F. *reprimé*.] Deprived *of* an attribute.

1579 Baker *Guydon's Quest. Chirurg.* 51 Those [cauters] that blyster, make no scarre, which muste be well applyed, correct, and reprymate of theyr malyces.

re'prime (rɪ-), *v.*¹ *rare*. [ad. L. *reprimĕre*: cf. repreme.] *trans.* To repress.

1819 W. Tennant *Papistry Storm'd* (1827) 8 But hoolie, Muse! reprime your haste, Descrybe mair gently a' the matter. **1898** Meredith *Odes Fr. Hist.* 74 Are we of worth amid our satanic excrescences..this, for the less than a call, Will Earth reprime, man cherish.

re'prime (riː-), *v.*² [re- 5 a.] **a.** To prime again.

1830 Marryat *King's Own* lii, The guns were primed and reprimed, without the fire communicating to the powder. **1836** —— *Pirate* xvi, Hawkhurst had reprimed his musket.

b. *absol.*

1976 *Shooting Mag.* Dec. 65/1 (Advt.), Lee Load-All 12 G... 2nd Station reprimes with a push from inside the shell to prevent concave heads.

Hence **re'primer**, an instrument for repriming a spent cartridge.

1884 Knight *Dict. Mech.* Suppl. 750/1 A complete set for rifle cartridges consists of primer, extractor, charger, loader, and reprimer.

†**'repriment**¹. *Obs. rare*$^{-1}$. [ad. obs. F. *reprimende*.] A reprimand.

1652 Evelyn *State France* Misc. Writ. (1805) 44 That repriment which Socrates once gave to a young man who would render him no accompt of his long absence.

†**'repriment**². *Obs. rare*$^{-1}$. [ad. L. *repriment-*, ppl. stem of *reprimĕre* to repress.] *Med.* A repressive application.

1684 tr. *Bonet's Merc. Compit.* xiv. 508 The difficulty about the use of Repriments [in pleurisy]..is very great.

†**re'prinse.** *Obs. rare.* Also 6 reprince. [a. F. *reprinse*, obs. var. of *reprise* reprise *sb.*]

1. A step in dancing (cf. reprise *sb.* 5).

1531 Elyot *Gov.* i. xxiv, Comunely nexte after sengles in daunsing is a reprinse, whiche is one mouing only, puttynge backe the ryght fote to his felowe.

2. Recapture, recovery.

1592 Wyrley *Armorie, Ld. Chandos* 96 To armed knights and squiers..Bout this reprince I secretly do send.

re'print (riː-), *sb.* [f. the vb.]

1. a. A reproduction in print of any matter already printed; a new impression of a work previously printed, without alteration of the matter.

1611 Florio, *Ristampa*, a reprint, a reprinting. **1822** Moule *Bibl. Heraldica* 11 Mr. Haslewood paid seven guineas for a copy..to assist him in the reprint. **1837** Lockhart *Scott* lxxiv, An uniform reprint of the Novels. **1841** W. Spalding *Italy & It. Isl.* III. 198 He had just been made aware of a Milanese reprint of his book. **1883** *Law Times* 20 Oct. 425/2 The second edition is not, however, a simple reprint of the first.

b. *attrib.*

1928 *Publishers' Weekly* 30 June 2603 Bookstores have in a new form a problem that confronted them twenty-five years ago when the reprint fiction began to appear in cloth binding. **1951** A. C. Clarke *Sands of Mars* xi. 135 She immediately sold the second reprint rights of Gibson's latest series. **1951** M. McLuhan *Mech. Bride* (1967) 23/2 The current effort to make almost every reprint cover look lustier than the next has brought them all to a dead level of fleshliness. **1952** E. Mannin *Let.* in *Manch. Guardian Weekly* 16 Oct. 13/1 May I, as an English author who is a victim of the deplorable American publishing habit of farming-out their cheap editions to what are called 'reprint houses', be allowed to point out some important points. **1961** T. Landau *Encycl. Librarianship* (ed. 2) 323/1 *Reprint series*, a number of publications, being reprints, not necessarily related in subject or treatment, issued by a publisher in uniform style and assigned a collective series title. **1964** F. Bowers *Bibliogr. & Textual Crit.* vi. i. 163 The normal reprint transmission of variants is disrupted by the annotator's correction of error. **1981** J. Sutherland *Bestsellers* i. 14 The [American] bookclubs..have in the past been much less reprint affairs than in the UK.

2. *Typog.* Printed matter used as copy to be set up and printed again.

1824 J. Johnson *Typogr.* II. xviii. 578 Without making any distinction between manuscript and reprint. **1888** *Century Mag.* Dec. 303/1 'How are ye off for copy, Mike?' 'Bad', answered the old printer, 'I've a little reprint, but no original matter at all'.

re'print (riː-), *v.* [re- 5 a.]

1. a. *trans.* To print (a work) again in a new edition; to print (matter) a second time. Also *absol.*

1551 in *Udall's Royster D.* (1847) p. xxx, To preynt, repreynt, utter, and sell, that the worke of Peter Marter. **1624** Gataker *Transubst.* 38, I hope when this Bishop of Flanders booke cometh to be reprinted againe [etc.]. **1676** Ray *Corr.* (1848) 123, I have been lately solicited to reprint my Catalogue of English Plants. **1712** Hearne *Collect.* (O.H.S.) III. 479 He is reprinting your Letter to Sʳ. Chr. Wren. **1752** Berkeley *Tar-water* Wks. 1871 III. 498 Accounts of the effects of tar-water were reprinted in America. **1849** Macaulay *Hist. Eng.* vii. II. 176 His History of his own Times, his History of the Reformation,..are still reprinted. **1891** *Law Rep., Weekly Notes* 44/1 It was his practice to reprint from time to time articles which had previously appeared in his newspaper. **1934** H. G. Wells *Exper. Autobiogr.* II. ix. 646 Macmillan's, my English publishers, were caught unawares by the demand and had sold out the first edition before they reprinted.

b. To print again in a different form.

1693 Luttrell *Brief Rel.* (1857) III. 139 The Gazet was printing with the Satturday's account, but this relation being brought on Sunday, it was wholly reprinted.

2. To impress or stamp again. *rare.*

1662 South *Serm., Gen.* i. 27 (1727) I. 75 To rub over the defaced Copy of the Creation, to reprint God's Image upon the Soul. **1683** Moxon *Mech. Exerc., Printing* xxiv. ⁋ 19 The hindside of the Plattin by the Second Pull reprints part of the First Pull.

3. *intr.* for *pass.*

1821 R. Southey *Let.* 11 Jan. in *N. & Q.* (1975) Sept. 402/1 Do not bind your set, till I send you some corrections and additions for the first volume, which is now reprinting. **1942** *World Rev.* Apr. 17 In this war he is a Home Guard officer and the author of four training manuals, which, despite the paper shortage, reprint every few months. **1967** *Listener* 12 Jan. 68/3 It will be for these [colour photographs] that *Slowly Down the Ganges* has to reprint. **1980** *Daily Tel.* 21 Aug. 14 The book has sold 10,000 copies since May. It is now reprinting.

Hence **re'printed** *ppl. a.*; **re'printing** *vbl. sb.*

1575 Jugge in *Cal. Script.* Printer to Rdr., The trauayle I haue in hand in the reprintyng of oour English Byble. **1605** Stow *Ann.* 1438 My worke was preuented by Printing and reprinting..of Raigne Wolfes collection. **1708** in Watts *Gram. made Easy* (1742) a j b, To Import re-printed Copies from any Place. **1878** Roffe *Handbk. Shaks. Mus.* 76 One of the reprintings is in the Musical Library. **1885** *Athenæum* 19 Dec. 803/1 It is better work than..the reprinted works of the late Albert Smith.

re'printer (riː-). [f. prec. + -er¹.] One who reprints, or who publishes a reprint.

1689 D. Granville *Lett.* (Surtees No. 37) 82 The ingenious reprinter of the late edition. **1765** H. Walpole *Let. to Earl of Hertford* 14 Feb., Williams, the reprinter of the *North Briton*, stood in the pillory to-day in Palace Yard. **1866** *Athenæum* 17 Nov. 644/2 A very large reprinter of English tales and novels. **1892** in *Critic* (U.S.) 12 Mar. 162/1 The absence of international copyright and competition among rival reprinters has helped this.

reprisal (rɪ'praɪzəl), *sb.* Forms: 5 **reprisail**, 5, 7 **-sale**, 6–7 **-sall**, (6 **-soll**), 7 **represal**, 7– **reprisal**; also 7–8 **reprizal**, (6 **-zall**, 7 **-zeal**). [a. OF. *reprisaille* (found in AF. in 1352): see reprise *v.* and -al¹. The mod.F. *représaille* (recorded in 15th c.) is ad. It. *ripresaglia* (f. *ripreso*), or med.L. *reprœsalia* (see Du Cange), whence also Sp. *represalia, -aria.*]

I. 1. (Without article or plural.) The act or practice of seizing by force the property (or persons) of subjects of another nation, in retaliation for loss or injury suffered from these or their countrymen. Now only *Hist.*

reprisal implied the refusal of the offending nation to grant redress for the injury done, but did not itself create a state of war between the two countries.

a. ***letters*** (or ***commission***) ***of reprisal***, an official warrant authorizing an aggrieved subject to exact forcible reparation from the subjects of another state: see marque¹ 1 and 2. †Also *ellipt.* in same sense (quot. 1472).

1447 *Rolls of Parlt.* V. 135 To graunte to youre saide Besechers, letters of Marc and Reprisail. **1472** *Ibid.* VI. 65/1 Any Sentence, Jugement, Margue or Reprisale yeven..by his Highnes and his Counseill. **1591** *Art. conc. Admiralty* 21 July §56 All such that contrary to their Commissions of reprisall, haue caried any prizes by them taken into Barbary, Fraunce [etc.]. **1619** Sir R. Naunton in *Fortescue Papers* (Camden) 88 They have bene forced to sue for lettres of reprisal, and have obteined leave under the Great Seale to repaire theyr losses from the subjects of those nacions by whom they were formerly spoiled. **1680** *Lond. Gaz.* No. 1573/4 A Vessel fitted out as a Privatier..boarded her and took her (pretending they had Letters of Reprizall). **1765** Blackstone *Comm.* I. vii. 250 In this case letters of marque and reprisal..may be obtained, in order to seise the bodies or goods of the subjects of the offending state, until satisfaction be made, wherever they happen to be found. **1789** *Constit. U.S.* i. §8 Congress shall have power..to..grant letters of marque and reprisal. **1839** Keightley *Hist. Eng.* I. 450 The king of Scotland..having granted letters of reprisal against the Portuguese to three brothers.

b. In phrases, as ***to make reprisal***; ***by way of***, ***by***, or ***in reprisal*** (passing into 4 c); and in other contexts.

1687 A. Lovell tr. *Thevenot's Trav.* 277 When the Ambassadours of the Franks complain.., all the answer they have is, that they must make reprisal upon them. **1725** De Foe *Voy. round World* ii. 28 The [Spanish] Doctor..desired..That none of our Men..would ever come so much in Reach of the Spaniards on Shore, as to put it into their Power to seize upon them by Reprizal. **1727–38** Chambers *Cycl.* s.v., This merchant has seized the effects of the Spaniard don—by way of reprisal, because the Spaniards had seized his, and no redress could be had at the court of Madrid. **1803** Wellington in Gurw. *Desp.* (1838) II. 418 You will do well to bring away with you all the principal shroffs and soucars, by way of reprisal for the injuries..done by the enemy to the Soubah's country. **1819** Jefferson *Autobiog.* App., Wks. 1859 I. 117 Our first overt act of war was Mr. Henry's..making reprisal on the King's treasury at the seat of government, for the public powder taken away by his Governor. **1839** Hallam *Hist. Lit.* ii. iv. §88 He treats of the general right of war, the difference between public war and reprisal. **1867** Burton *Hist. Scot.* (1873) III. 68 When Scotland, in reprisal for injuries committed by England on her shipping, seized an English vessel.

c. *attrib.* as †***reprisal goods***, ***office***.

1645 in *Cal. State P., Dom., Chas. I* 168 My said brother, who is collector for Reprisal goods. *Ibid.* 285 Prays that you will order her payment of this..out of the Reprisal office.

2. a. An act or instance of seizing property or persons belonging to another state by way of indemnity or recompense for loss sustained. ***letters of reprisals***: (see 1 a.) †Also const. *of.*

1611 Cotgr. s.v. *Represaille, Lettres de represailles*, Letters (Patents) of Mart or Marque; letters authorizing reprisalls. **1614** Selden *Titles Hon.* 210 The lawes of Marque or Reprisales. [Cf. *Rolls of Parlt.* II. 250/1 (anno 1352) La Lei de mark et de reprisailles.] **1641** Baker *Chron.* (1653) 565 Sundry quarrells and complaints arose between the English and the French, touching reprisals of Goods taken from each other by Pirates of either Nation. **1669** R. Montagu in *Buccleuch MSS.* (Hist. MSS. Comm.) I. 456 Letters of reprisals against the Dutch..should be granted. **1765** Blackstone *Comm.* I. vii. 251 And indeed this custom of reprisals seems dictated by nature herself. **1790** Beatson *Nav. & Mil. Mem.* I. 40 Letters of marque, or general reprisals, against the ships, goods, and subjects of the King of Spain, were ready to be issued. **1839** Hallam *Hist. Lit.* iii. iv. §129 If justice is refused to us by the sovereign, we have a right to indemnification out of the property of his subjects. This is commonly called reprisals. **1863** *Sat. Rev.* 13 June 745 The Admiral..was then instructed to put the necessary pressure on the Government by proceeding to reprisals. He accordingly detained five vessels.

b. In phr. ***to make reprisals*** (cf. 4 b). Also *fig.*

1663 Cowley *Verses Sev. Occas., Adv. Five Hours* 26 They all shall watch the Travels of your Pen, And Spain on you shall make Reprisals then. **1761** Hume *Hist. Eng.* (1806) III. xl. 352 The queen..gave all the English liberty to make reprisals on the subjects of Philip. **1777** Watson *Philip II*, x. (1839) 179 Not receiving satisfaction, she proceeded to make reprisals, and seized effects, belonging to Spanish and Flemish merchants. **1802** James *Milit. Dict.* s.v. *Marque*, Granting the subjects of one prince or state liberty to make reprisals on those of another. **1872** Yeats *Growth Comm.* 279 As soon as England was able to protect her merchant-shipping and to make reprisals at sea, piracy declined.

transf. **1774** Pennant *Tour Scot. in 1772*, 221 The loss sustained by the sea..which, we know, makes more than reprizals in other places. **1818** Scott *Hrt. Midl.* ii, He considered himself as robbed and plundered; and took it into his head, that he had a right to make reprisals. **1849** Lyell *2nd Visit U.S.* II. 55 In the winter, when the sea is making reprisals on the delta.

3. †**a.** The taking *of* a thing as a prize. *Obs.*

c **1595** Capt. Wyatt *R. Dudley's Voy. W. Ind.* (Hakl. Soc.) 6 Our Generall..plied..to the rock, wheare wee had the first chase that wee might justlie auer the reprisoll of. **1596** Nashe *Saffron Walden* 62 Whiles..there be any reprisalls of purses twixt this and Cole-brooke.

†**b.** A prize. *Obs. rare.*

1596 Shaks. *1 Hen. IV*, iv. i. 118, I am on fire, To heare this rich reprizall is so nigh, And yet not ours. **1611** Florio, *Ripresaglia*, All maner of reprisals, prises, pillage, luggage.

c. Regaining, recapture; recaption. ? *Obs.*

1660 Hickeringill *Jamaica* (1661) 58 To whom our Nation in some measures stands indebted for the Reprizal of that Honour at Rio-Novo, which was so shamefully lost..in Hispaniola. **1726** J. M. tr. *Trag. Hist. de Vaudray* ii. 130 The Enemy..open'd the Campaign with the Siege of St. Omer. The King, endeavouring to repair that Loss by the Reprizal of St. Valery, narrowly escaped [etc.]. **1768** Blackstone *Comm.* III. 4 Recaption or Reprisal is another species of remedy by the mere act of the party injured. **1867** Smyth *Sailor's Word-bk.* 569 *Reprise*, or *Reprisal*, is the retaking a vessel from the enemy before she has arrived in any neutral or hostile port.

4. a. An act of retaliation for some injury or attack; *spec.* in warfare, the infliction of similar or severer injury or punishment on the enemy, e.g. by the execution of prisoners taken from them. Also *attrib.*, as ***reprisal attack***, ***raid***.

1710 *Lond. Gaz.* No. 4726/1 The Garrison..was detained in Reprisals for the following Injuries. **1788** Gibbon *Decl. & F.* l. V. 185 If he falls by their hands, they are exposed in their turn to the danger of reprisals, the interest and principal of the bloody debt are accumulated. **1797** Godwin *Enquirer* i. xi. 101 Their children attempt a reprisal. **1855** Brewster *Newton* II. xv. 43 He..deserved those severe reprisals which doubtless embittered the rest of his days. **1874** Green *Short Hist.* x. §4. 791 Lord Cornwallis..found more difficulty in checking the reprisals of his troops..than in stamping out the last embers of insurrection. *c* **1945** *Hutchinson's Pict. Hist. War* XII. 157/1 The vicious battering of the industrial and military bases of Germany provoked none of the great so-called 'reprisal' raids which characterised April and May. **1947** R. W. Cooper *Nuremberg Trial* 81 Everything was to be prepared to carry out reprisal attacks on London. **1956** H. Nicolson *Diary* 29 Oct. (1968) 311 Israel has launched against Egypt an attack that seems more serious than a reprisal raid.

b. In phr. ***to make reprisals*** (cf. 2 b).

1710 Shaftesb. *Charac.* (1737) I. ii. iii. 268 In case of violence offer'd 'em..there are Hands ready prepar'd to make sufficient Reprisals. **1756** C. Lucas *Ess. Waters* III. 215, I mean not to make reprisals upon these unkind, mistaken gentlemen. **1778** Miss Burney *Evelina* xx, He had studied this address by way of making reprisals for my conduct at the ball. **1813** Shelley *Notes to Q. Mab* Wks. (1891) 43/2 She must be the tame slave, she must make no reprisals. **1878** Bosw. Smith *Carthage* 169 Hamilcar was driven to make reprisals for the barbarities of the Libyans by throwing his prisoners to be trampled to death.

c. Without article (cf. 1 b).

1839 James *Louis XIV*, II. 92 A prompt and decided measure of reprisal immediately put a stop to this kind of slaughter in detail. **1859** Thackeray *Virgin.* lii, Who might give me up to the Indians in reprisal for cruelties practised by our own people.

II. †5. = reprise *sb.* 2. *Obs. rare*$^{-1}$.

1647 N. Bacon *Disc. Govt. Eng.* i. lxx. (1739) 184 All such as had Lands worth 20*l.* yearly besides Reprizals.

6. (Chiefly *pl.*) A return or compensation; a sum or amount paid or received as compensation. (Cf. reprise *sb.* 3 a.) Now *rare.*

1668 *Ormonde MSS.* in *10th Rep. Hist. MSS. Comm.* App. V. 60 An addresse from the Commissioners.. concerning reprizeals. **1668** Clarendon *Vindic.* Tracts (1727) 64 By increasing the stock for reprisals to such a degree, that all men's pretences might in some measure be provided for. **1704** Swift *Mech. Operat. Spirit* Misc. (1711) 276 Since that Arabian is known to have borrowed a Moiety of his Religious System from the Christian Faith, it is but just he should pay Reprisals. **1715–20** Pope *Iliad* xi. 834 My sire three hundred chosen sheep obtain'd. (That large reprisal he might justly claim, For prize defrauded, and insulted Fame). **1866** Geo. Eliot *F. Holt* ix, He was able to refund, to make reprisals, if they could be fairly demanded. **1878** Lecky *Eng. in 18th C.* II. vi. 177 This restitution was to be postponed until reprisals had been made for the adventurers and soldiers who had got possession of their estates.

†7. = reprise *sb.* 4. *Obs. rare*$^{-1}$.

a **1797** H. Walpole *Mem. Geo. II*, III. 62 Speaking to him at different reprisals with kindness to mark his satisfaction.

8. *Arch.* (See reprise *sb.* 6, quot. 1888.)

Hence **†re'prisal** *v. intr.*, to make reprisal.

1593 Nashe *Christ's T.* (1613) 93 What is left for a man to do,.. but either to hang at Tiborne, or pillage and reprizall where he may.

†re'prisary, *a. Obs. rare*$^{-1}$. [See next and -ary.] Authorizing reprisals.

1544 in *Lett. & Pap. Hen. VIII*, XIX. ii. 466 The merchants here.. require letters reprisaries against our merchants.

reprise (rɪ'praɪz; now (chiefly in sense 7) rə'pri:z), *sb.* Also 6 **repryse, -pryce, -price,** 7–8 **reprize.** [a. F. *reprise* (13th c.), f. *repris*, pa. pple. of *reprendre* to take back, resume, etc. (see next); cf. Sp. and Pg. *represa*, It. *ripresa.*

The renewed influence of Fr. *reprise* is apparent in the modern pronunc. and development of sense 7.]

I. †1. The fact of taking back something for one's own advantage or profit; an amount taken back from one in this way; hence, loss, expense, cost. *Obs.* (in Gower only).

1390 Gower *Conf.* I. 153 Al the world ne may suffise To stanche of Pride the reprise. *Ibid.* 157 Humblesce is al otherwise, Which most is worth, and no reprise It takth ayein. *Ibid.* II. 285 Love is evere of som reprise To him that wole his love holde.

2. a. A deduction, charge, or payment (such as a rent-charge or annuity) falling to be made yearly out of a manor or estate. Chiefly *pl.* in phrases ***above, besides, beyond,*** or ***†over, reprises.***

[**1414** *Act 2 Hen. V* Stat. ii. c. 3 Si mesme la persone neit terres ou tenementz de annuell value de quarant souldz outre les reprises dicelles.]

1433 *Rolls of Parlt.* IV. 476/2 Uchon of hem may spende ..yerely, over the reprise, of londe or rente in fee. **1435** *Ibid.* 486/2 The yerely value..overe the reprises and charges. **1484** *Lett. Rich. III & Hen. VII* (Rolls) I. 82 Alle the revenues,..with there reprises and deduccions therof. **1509–10** *Act 1 Hen. VIII* c. 8 Hereditamentes of the yerely value of xl markes above all charges and repryces. **1546** *Yorks. Chantry Surv.* (Surtees) II. 518 In reprises yerely going forth of the same. **1656** Bramhall *Replic.* vi. 235 All charges damages and reprises must first be cast up and deducted, before one can give a right estimate of benefit or losse. **1687** *Royal Proclam.* 4 Nov. in *Lond. Gaz.* No. 2298/1 A Lease-hold Estate of Fifty pounds per Annum above all Charges and Reprizes. **1704** in Picton *L'pool Munic. Rec.* (1886) II. 35 Being in yᵉ whole of yᵉ yearly value of Twelve Pounds beyond Reprises. **1728** *Act 18 Geo. II* Preamble, A Lease-hold Estate of Fifty Pounds per annum above all Charges and Reprizes. **1831** *Act 1 & 2 Will. IV*, c. 45 §1 The clear yearly Value above all Reprises of the Rectory.

†b. A charge, duty, or tax. *Obs. rare*$^{-1}$.

1645 Evelyn *Diary* 30 July, My *Matricula* contained a clause, that I, my goods, servants, and messengers, should be free from all toll and reprises.

†3. a. A return or compensation received or paid. (Cf. reprisal *sb.* 6.) *Obs.*

c **1570** *Pride & Lowl.* (1841) 66 Let no man it dispise, Or him that wrot it for no recompence, Save labour for his paine without reprice. **1662** *Irish Act 14 & 15 Chas. II*, c. 2 §17 Whatsoever adventurer..shall be removed from his present possession,..shall forthwith have a reprize of equal value.. in other forfeited lands. **1665** in *17th Rep. Dep. Kpr. Irel.* 21 The Court is of Opinion that it is a Deficiency, and that the reprize ought to be to the heir of Alexander Pymme. **1736** Carte *Ormonde* II. 242 It appeared that one interest or other must suffer for want of reprizes.

†b. Reprisal; the act of taking something by way of retaliation. *Obs.*

1667 Dryden *Maid. Q.* v. i, By Force retake it from those tyrant Eyes, I'll grant you out my Letters of Reprize. **1687** —— *Hind & P.* iii. 862 If so, a just Reprise would only be Of what the Land usurp'd upon the Sea. **1700** —— *Ovid's Met.* xii. 319 We rise Mad with revenge to make a swift reprise.

†c. The act of recapturing a vessel taken by the enemy; also, the vessel so taken. *Obs. rare*$^{-0}$.

1727–38 Chambers *Cycl.* s.v., If the reprize have been made within 24 hours, the vessel is to be restored to the proprietor. *Ibid.*, If the reprize have been abandoned by the enemy. [Hence in Falconer *Dict. Marine* (1769).]

4. a. A resumption or renewal of an action; a separate occasion of doing something. Chiefly in phr. ***at*** or ***in..reprises.*** Also ***†by reprises,*** alternately. Somewhat *rare.*

1685 Dryden *Albion & Alb.* i. i, The two last Lines are sung by Reprises, betwixt Aug[usta] & Tham[esis]. **1711** Shaftesb. *Charac.* (1737) III. Misc. ii. i. 30, I am led to write on such Subjects as these, with Caution, at different Reprises, and not singly, in one Breath. *Ibid.* v. iii. 303 The most refractory and obstinate Understandings are by certain Reprises or Returns of Thought..necessitated..to acknowledg the actual Right and Wrong. **1713** Earl Cromarty *Acc. Gowrie Conspir.* 14 The unhappy Condition wherein the Church and State of Scotland were plunged.. not once or twice, but in frequent Reprises. **1895** M. R. James *Abbey St. Edmund* 122 The western tower fell, not all at once, but in two reprises.

b. *spec.* (See quots.)

1727 Bailey vol. II, *Reprise* (with Horsemen) is a lesson repeated, or a manage recommenced. **1850** *Bohn's Handbk. Games* 228 (*Quadrille*) Reprise and Report, are synonymous with Party. [*Ibid.* 227 Party, is the duration of the Game, according to the number of tours agreed to be played.] **1861** Chapman *Review Art Fencing* i. 20 The remise..differs essentially from the Reprise, a redoubling of the Attack.

II. †5. *Dancing.* (See quot. and reprinse 1.)

1521 R. Copland *Introd. Frenche, Maner of dauncynge* 16 b, A repryse alone ought to be made with the ryght fote in drawynge the ryght fote bakwarde a lytyll to the other fote. The seconde repryse ought to be made..with the lyft fote in reysynge the body in lyke wyse.

6. *Arch.* (See later quots.)

Cotgr. (1611) gives '*Reprises de pierre*, denting peeces of stone'. See also Godefroy *Dict.* X. 552/1.

1501 Douglas *Pal. Hon.* iii. xvii, Pinnakillis, fyellis, turnpekkis money one,..Skarsment, reprise, corbell, and battellingis. **1850** Ogilvie, *Reprise*, a term used by masons to denote the return of mouldings in an internal angle. **1888** C. C. Hodges *Hexham Abbey* 30 *note*, A reprise or reprisal is the foot of a window mullion or jamb, which is worked on the same stone as the sills.

7. *Music.* **†a.** A refrain. *Obs.*$^{-0}$ **b.** A cadence. ? *Obs.* **c.** The resumption or recurrence of the first theme or subject of a movement after the close of the development.

1702 Boyer *Dict. Royal* i. s.v., *La Reprise* (*le Refrain*) *des Ballades, des chansons*, the Reprise, repetition, upholding, or burden of Ballads and Songs. **1811** Busby *Dict. Mus.* (ed. 3), *Cadence*, or *Reprise*, a pause or suspension at the end of an air, to afford the performer an opportunity of introducing a graceful extempore close. **1879** in Grove *Dict. Mus.* I. 472 That portion of the first movement of a sonata or symphony —or other movement in similar form—which occurs between the double bar and the reprise of the first subject.

d. *transf.* in *Linguistics.* The repetition of a word or word-group occurring in a preceding phrase; a restated element. Also *attrib.* as ***reprise construction.***

1950 *Archivum Linguisticum* II. 144 The aim of this article is to establish the frequency with which reprise constructions occur in *Chanson de Roland.* **1955** [see grammaticalization]. **1959** M. Schlauch *Eng. Lang. in Mod. Times* iv. 99 Reprise constructions (called resumptions by Partridge) in formal discourse employed the appositional pronoun to recall a noun separated from its verb by a long series of interrupting modifiers. **1963** F. T. Visser *Hist. Syntax Eng. Lang.* I. i. 53 Type 'He, Alexander, cwæð.'.. The following 'reprise construction' is remarkable for the subject's being expressed four times. **1971** *Catholic Biblical Q.* XXXIII. 218 This structure makes sense out of *didaskalos* (vs. 10) as a reprise, for, far from ending the preceding unit (as it would as an inclusion), it introduces the theme of vss. 9–15, *Jesus as teacher.*

e. The repetition of a theatrical performance; a restaging or rewriting of a play (esp. for television), a repeated showing of a (piece of) film; a rerun, a replay. Also in extended use, a further performance of any kind; a reconstruction, a repeat.

1953 *Sun* (Baltimore) 9 Oct. 10/2 Mr. Moore came on the screen bubbling over with a joke which he was eager to share with the viewers. It required a reprise from the previous week's performance. **1955** *Times* 20 May 3/4 It is the season for *reprise* at this club theatre. Formerly, in shows of this kind, the menu has included so many delightful dishes of the past served cold by inexpert chefs as to be somewhat gruesomely indigestible. **1961** *Guardian* 1 Feb. 9/4 A polished reprise of his campaign sermons. **1968** *Globe & Mail* (Toronto) 17 Feb. 39 Nancy last night watched a television reprise of her dramatic victory in amazingly fast time in the Olympic giant slalom. **1972** *Publishers' Weekly* 11 Sept. 51/1 The author spins a good tale on the level of a reprise of what life was like for a young girl in a small town 30 years ago. **1977** *Time* 30 May 25/1 Carter headed next to the studios of KNXT-TV for a locally televised reprise of his successful national call-in program.

re'prise, *v.* Also 5–6 **repryse,** 6–7 **reprize.** [f. F. *repris*, pa. pple. of *reprendre*, f. *re-* re- + *prendre* to take: related to ***reprehend*** as ***comprise*** to ***comprehend.*** For pronunc., see sense 1 f.]

I. 1. †a. *intr.* To begin again, start afresh. *Obs. rare*$^{-1}$.

c **1450** Lovelich *Grail* xvi. 462 But the blood cowde he staunchen in non wise But every day newe it gan for to reprise, As long as with-inne was the hed.

†b. *trans.* To recommence, resume. *Obs.*

1481 Caxton *Myrr.* i. xv. 50 Hym behoueth to come doun as sone as a stone tyl that he come in to thayer where he may repryse his fleyng. **1483** —— *Gold. Leg.* 315 b/2 Anone they reprysed their songe after theyr customme. **1491** —— *Vitas Patr.* (W. de W. 1495) i. xlii. 70 a/2 The holy Egypcyen reprysed his worde and sayde [etc.]. **1603** Florio *Montaigne* iii. xiii. 650 By advertisements & instructions, reprised by intervalles: entermixing certaine pawses of rest.

†c. To take up again, to reassume. *Obs. rare*$^{-1}$.

1481 Caxton *Godfrey* clxxxiii. 269 They that..laye in theyr beddes sprange vp anon and reprysed theyr harnoys and armes.

†d. To take anew, gain afresh. *Obs. rare*$^{-1}$.

1590 Spenser *F.Q.* ii. xi. 44 That dead-living swayne, Whom still he marked freshly to arize From th' earth, and from her womb new spirits to reprize.

†e. ? To take separately. *Obs.*

a **1641** Bp. Montagu *Acts & Mon.* (1642) 133, 62. weeks and 7. weeks, in fractions reprised, must first be accomplished.

f. (With pronunc. (rə'pri:z).) To repeat (a theatrical performance, song, etc.); to restage or rewrite. Cf. reprise *sb.* 7 e.

1965 *Observer* 5 Dec. 24/3 The theatre rocks as Dolly reprises more times than is artistically justifiable the chorus of this..infectious title-song. **1970** *Ibid.* 29 Nov. 29/1 The song is tearfully reprised off-screen. **1975** *Listener* 5 June 735/1, I decided that..it would be necessary to reprise this scene in a heightened form.

2. a. To take back again, esp. by force; to recapture (a thing or person), to recover; also, to buy back. (Freq. in 17th c.) *Obs.* (exc. *arch.*)

1481 Caxton *Godfrey* xxiv. *heading*, How Solyman.. reprised and toke agayn the castel. **1596** Spenser *F.Q.* iv. iv. 8 He now begunne To challenge her anew, as his owne prize, ..And proffer made by force her to reprize. *c* **1611** Chapman *Iliad* xvii. 130 Now ye might reprise the armes, Sarpedon forfeited,..would you but lend your hands. **1654** H. L'Estrange *Chas. I* (1655) 57 Lewes brake furiously in upon..the chief Rebel,..reprizeth many ships formerly taken by him. **1676** Otway *Don Carlos* iv. i, Th'adst better meet a lion on his way, And from his hungry jaws reprize the prey. *a* **1711** Ken *Preparatives* Poet. Wks. 1721 IV. 6 Time which when once away it flies, I never, never can reprise. **1780** Burke *Econ. Reform* 241 Buckingham-house was reprised, by a bargain with the publick, for one hundred thousand pounds.

†b. *intr.* To make reprisals. *Obs. rare*$^{-1}$.

1552 in Strype *Eccl. Mem.* (1721) II. x. 331 To permit indirectly our merchants to reprize upon the French.

†3. To withdraw from trouble or punishment; to reprieve. *Obs. rare.*

c **1557** Abp. Parker *Ps.* xciv. 266 As carefull thoughtes in store dyd ryse,.. Thy comfort so dyd me repryse, My soule to scape the foyle. *c* **1586** C'tess Pembroke *Ps.* cvi. xi, Phinees, justice done, their lives repris'd.

†4. To take or hold back out of a sum. *Obs.*

1559 Abp. Parker *Corr.* (Parker Soc.) 99 Item, that fees to keepers of parks and woods not yet valued be not reprised out of the value of the manors. **1707** Fleetwood *Chron. Prec.* 172 That Man has not an Estate of 8*l. ultra Reprisas*, because there is 13*s.* 4*d.* to be reprized or taken back again, which is, I think, the meaning of the word.

5. a. To compensate (a person). Cf. reprise *sb.* 3 a. *Obs.* (exc. *arch.*)

1662 *Irish Act 14 & 15 Chas. II*, c. 2 §18 All such..who have been..dispossessed of their estates..shall be forthwith reprized in forfeited lands. **1668** in *10th Rep. Hist. MSS. Comm.* App. V. 60 The Lord Lieutenant and Counsel's advice to the Commissioners to spend some of their remaining time to reprize Protestants. **1705–6** Penn in *Pa. Hist. Soc. Mem.* X. 111 Now know that to reprise or pay you, I have money in the hands of the executors. **1736** Carte *Ormonde* II. 242 He was misled to think there were lands enough to reprize such of the Adventurers and Soldiers as were to be dispossessed. **1878** Lecky *Eng. in 18th C.* II. vi. 177 The adventurers and soldiers who were removed were at once reprised.

†b. *refl.* To recoup (oneself). *Obs. rare*$^{-1}$.

1677 *Govt. Venice* 319 Having lost..the Honour he bore, ..to reprize himself, he assumed the Title of that Kingdom.

II. †6. To reprehend, reprove (a person). *Obs. rare.*

a **1450** *Knt. de la Tour* (1868) 113 Atte the dredfulle day he wolle axe acomptes..wherof y doubte that mani shalle be reprised. **1474** Caxton *Chesse* 161 He shold correcte and reprise the Kyng of his euyl vices. **1483** —— *G. de la Tour* D vij b, How a hooly bisshop reprysed and taught many ladyes.

Hence **†re'priser,** one who receives a reprise; **†re'prising** *vbl. sb.* = reprise *sb.* 4.

1603 Florio *Montaigne* ii. x. (1632) 226 We are taught to cast our eyes over it, in running it over by divers glances,.. and reiterated reprisings. **1630** Dodridge *Principality Wales* 76 With the ordinary deductions and Reprizes taken out of it..in charges, fees, to officers, and other reprizers.

reprisoll, obs. form of reprisal.

re'pristinate, *v.* [f. re- + pristine *a.*] *trans.* To restore to the original condition or position; to revive. Hence **re'pristinated** *ppl. a.*

1659 H. L'Estrange *Alliance Div. Off.* 480 It will not be amiss to enquire..by what degrees they were repristinated and rendered in their former state. **1869** Shedd *Homilet.* 372 The practice of catechising children and youth should be repristinated in the American Churches. **1969** R. H. Bainton *Erasmus of Christendom* (1970) i. 14 The glory of Greece, the grandeur of Rome, the grace of Galilee should repristinate society and revivify the Church. **1970** *Jrnl.*

Ecumenical Stud. VII. 804/1 The disavowal of the doctrine ..and its displacement by the repristinated authorities of Scripture and Christian experience. **1977** *Theology* LXXX. 200 The power exercised by the remembered and interpreted past has been deliberately conserved and repristinated by methods which have not excluded secular rituals.

repristi'nation. [f. prec.] The action of restoring to a pristine condition; restoration, rehabilitation.
1838 Cdl. Wiseman *Ess.* (1853) II. 32 That same 'Reformation' signifying a repristination of primitive Christianity. **1868** Browning *Ring & Bk.* I. 23 But his work ended, once the thing [is] a ring, Oh! there's repristination!

reprival(e, obs. forms of REPRIEVAL.

†**repri'vation.** *Obs. rare*⁻¹. [irreg. f. *reprive*, obs. var. REPRIEVE *v.* + -ATION.] Reprieve.
1583 Stubbes *Anat. Abus.* II. (1882) 13 [He] being found gilty,..is presently, without any further imprisonment, repriuation or delay,..committed to the sword.

re'privatize, *v.* [RE- 5 b; cf. G. *reprivatisieren.*] *trans.* To make private again; to denationalize. Also *absol.* Hence **reprivati'zation**.
1950 Webster Add., Reprivatize v.t. **1959** *Economist* 4 Apr. 53/1 A whole series of political and legal hurdles will have to be taken before the way is clear to denationalise, or reprivatise, in earnest. **1963** *Ibid.* 12 Jan. 136/3 He has promised to continue the work of 'reprivatisation' (denationalisation). **1980** *Evening News Mag.* 18 Jan. 22/1 The ugliest word yet coined by Whitehall is its latest—'reprivatisation', meaning the selling back to private enterprise of parts of nationalised industries. **1980** *Economist* 6 Dec. 18/2 Reprivatisation of the profitable naval yards.

reprive, obs. f. REPRIEVE.

reprizal(l, obs. ff. REPRISAL.

reprize, obs. f. REPRISE *sb.* and *v.*

repro ('riːprəʊ). [Colloq. abbrev. of REPRODUCTION.] **1.** *Printing* and *Photogr.* = REPRODUCTION 1 e. Chiefly *attrib.* in, or *ellipt.* for, ***repro proof*** = *reproduction proof* s.v. REPRODUCTION 3.
1946 Melcher & Larrick *Printing & Promotion Handbk.* 247/1 The offset or other printer..should..be encouraged to reject any proofs..of poor quality and ask for better 'repros'. **1948** R. R. Karch *Graphic Arts Procedures* viii. 231 Care must be taken to see that repro proofs are well printed. **1952** R. W. & E. W. Polk *Practice of Printing* (ed. 4) viii. 62 There are two kinds of reproduction proofs (commonly known as repros) used for the making of plates for letterpress, offset, and gravure. **1967** E. Chambers *Photolitho-Offset* iii. 31 Reproduction proofs on paper can be transferred into same-size negatives... The process.. consists in making a repro-proof and covering with a sheet of special film. **1972** *Screw* 12 June 28/4 What's the chance of getting a repro of that shot? **1973** D. A. Spencer *Focal Dict. Photogr. Technol.* 528 Repro pulls can be made on baryta coated paper, or ink-accepting transparent or translucent film. **1977** J. Hedgecoe *Photographer's Handbk.* 17 (*heading*) A repro copy stand.
2. A reproduction or copy, usu. of a piece of furniture (cf. REPRODUCTION 2 a). Chiefly *attrib.* or as *adj.* Also *Comb.*
1958 *Spectator* 8 Aug. 193/1 Her Tudorbethan villa, with its Repro-Jaco interior. **1967** *House & Garden* Mar. 79/1 Good traditional design (*not* 'repro') marries brilliantly with good contemporary. **1967** *Sunday Times* 14 May 12/7 The total environment is compromised..by the 'repro' furniture introduced into the flats. **1970** 'D. Halliday' *Dolly & Cookie Bird* ii. 13 We have a workshop of our own for repairs and a bit of repro work. **1973** *Daily Tel.* (Colour Suppl.) 16 Mar. 41/3 You may ask what is the difference between a fake and a 'repro'. **1976** *New Society* 13 May 363/1, I can't imagine..a Rembrandt on the wall opposite, even if it were an unframed repro. **1978** *Morecambe Guardian* 14 Mar. 27/8 (Advt.), Good antique and repro furniture.

reproach (rɪ'prəʊtʃ), *sb.* Also 5-8 **reproch(e**. [a. F. *reproche* (12th c.), vbl. sb. f. *reprocher* (see next), = Prov. *repropche*, Sp. and Pg. *reproche*, It. *rimproccio*. The OF. variants *reproce* and *repruce* were also adopted in ME. (see these forms).]
1. A source or cause of disgrace or shame (*to* a person, etc.); a fact, matter, feature or quality bringing disgrace or discredit upon one.
c **1420** Lydg. *Assembly of Gods* 71 Thys traytour Eolus.. dayly me manaces..Whyche to my name a reproche syngler Shuld be for euer. **1494** Fabyan *Chron.* I. xvii. 16 Some.. sayd, that to hym it was great reproche and dishonoure,.. that he had nat the rule of al yᵉ lande. *a* **1548** Hall *Chron. Hen. VI* 169 It was not honorable, but a reproche and infamy to the Kyng, to have one to bee a Protector and governor of hym. **1617** Moryson *Itin.* I. 240 They thinking it a reproch that we should ride ouer their graues, did with inraged countenances fling stones at vs. **1671** Milton *Samson* 353, I pray'd for Children, and thought barrenness In wedlock a reproach. **1785** Reid *Intell. Powers* II. xx. 278 It is no wonder that..others..spurn at a knowledge they cannot account for, and vainly attempt to throw it off, as a reproach to their understanding. **1818** Hallam *Mid. Ages* (1872) I. 135 Can it be an excessive reproach that the citizens fled from their dwellings. **1888** Bryce *Amer. Commw.* I. I. ix. 116 The conduct of Indian affairs..has always been a reproach to the United States.
b. A thing, animal, or person forming a source of disgrace or discredit.
1712 Blackmore *Creation* (ed. 2) 139 The noxious Plant, and savage Animal, Which you the Earth's reproach and blemish call. **1751** Johnson *Rambler* No. 136 ⁋11 Wretches, whom all but their dependents numbered among the reproaches of the species.
2. Shame, disgrace, opprobrium, or blame, incurred by or falling upon a person or thing. †***in reproach***, blamed, censured.
1484 Caxton *Fables of Æsop* III. ix, The woman whiche lyueth in this world without reproche or blame is worthely to be gretely preysed. **1490** —— *Eneydos* xi. 42 God forbede that it may be sayd of Eneas..to haue reproche by ony of our sayd wordes. **1523** Ld. Berners *Froiss.* I. clxii. 200 Many good knyghtes and squyers..hadde rather a dyed, than to haue had any reproche. **1534** Whitinton *Tullyes Offices* I. (1540) 28 Of the hye pride of herte which is in reproche, and maye be called mad hardynesse. **1591** Spenser *M. Hubberd* 222 Shame light on him, that..that, which is the noblest mysterie, Brings to reproach and common infamie! **1643** Sir T. Browne *Relig. Med.* II. §3 There is no reproach to the scandal of a Story; it is such an authentick kind of falshood. **1751** Johnson *Rambler* No. 154 ⁋9 We may with as little reproach borrow science as manufactures from our ancestors. **1855** Macaulay *Hist. Eng.* xii. III. 232 He tried gentler means than those which had brought so much reproach on his predecessor. **1875** Jowett *Plato* (ed. 2) V. 490 These are the sort of practices..which cast a reproach upon the succour of adversity.
b. With poss. pron. (One's) shame or disgrace.
1513 More in Grafton *Chron.* (1568) II. 768 All the worlde shall to our honour and her reproche, perceyue [etc.]. **1579** Gosson *Sch. Abuse* (Arb.) 20 If you..pul off the visard that Poets maske in, you shall disclose their reproch. **1611** Bible *Gen.* xxx. 23 And shee..bare a sonne, and said; God hath taken away my reproch. **1671** Milton *P.R.* III. 66 As thou to thy reproach mayst well remember.
†**c.** ***to a reproach***, to a disgraceful extent. *Obs.*⁻¹
a **1715** Burnet *Own Time* II. (1724) I. 158 They were ignorant to a reproach: And many of them were openly vitious.
3. Blame or censure directed against a person, sometimes implying abusive or opprobrious language, but also (esp. in mod. use) applied to mild upbraiding or rebuke. ***term*** etc. ***of reproach***, one expressing strong censure or condemnation.
c **1477** Caxton *Jason* 21 If he..cometh to suche felicite and gothe to chaunge certes he is worthy of reproche. **1513** Douglas *Æneis* I. Prol. 74 That na lovingis ma do incres thi fame, Nor na reproche diminew thi guid name. **1560** Daus tr. *Sleidane's Comm.* 197 They..drove awaye with reproche the kinges officers. **1590** Spenser *F.Q.* II. iv. 5 Ever as she went her toung did walke In fowle reproch, and termes of vile despight. **1666** Pepys *Diary* 27 Nov., I was sorry to see this way of reproach taken against us. **1712-14** Pope *Rape Lock* v. 3 In vain Thalestris with reproach assails. **1791** Cowper *Iliad* III. 72 Such is thy dauntless spirit, whose reproach Perforce I own, nor causeless nor unjust. **1849** Macaulay *Hist. Eng.* vi. II. 1 The name of Whig was never used except as a term of reproach. **1880** Mrs. Forrester *Roy & V.* I. 6 The look of reproach deepens in Viola's eyes.
†**b.** ***in reproach of***, in scorn of. *Obs. rare*⁻¹.
1494 Fabyan *Chron.* VI. clxii. 155 All was doon in reproche of Ethelburga, whiche slewe hir lorde Brigthricus.
4. †**a.** An insult in act or deed. *Obs. rare.*
1494 Fabyan *Chron.* VII. 374 For the Cristen hoost shuld be assuryd from the sodayne and vnware assautes and reprochis of the infidelles, therfore he closyd theym within a strength of dyche and pale. **1565** Cooper *Thesaurus* s.v. *Contumelia*, To doe one many injuries and reproches. **1600** Sir W. Cornwallis *Ess., Prayse Rich. III* (1617) D iij, The reproch offered his body.
b. An expression of disapproval, censure, reproof, or upbraiding; †a verbal insult, an opprobrious expression or epithet.
1548 Elyot, *Contumelia*,..a reproche, a rebuke, a checke, a taunte. **1560** Daus tr. *Sleidane's Comm.* 33 b, Stoutly contemnyng al the reproches of the adversaries. **1597** Beard *Theatre God's Judgem.* (1612) 492 Calling him make-bate and seditious villaine, with other opprobrious reproches. **1611** Bible *Transl. Pref.* ⁋14 Fearing no reproche for slownesse, nor coueting praise for expedition. **1671** Milton *Samson* 393 Thrice she assay'd with..amorous reproaches to win from me My capital secret. **1732** Lediard *Sethos* II. IX. 315 The justice of the reproaches..drove Anteus into despair. **1788** Gibbon *Decl. & F.* xlviii. V. 27 She neither heard nor regarded the reproaches of mankind. **1819** Shelley *Cenci* v. i. 98 Have I not the power to fly My own reproaches? **1834** James *J. Marston Hall* viii, Every time he opened his mouth his words were drowned in murmurs and reproaches.
c. *pl.* A series of antiphons and responses, in which Christ is represented as reproaching his people, sung in Roman Catholic (and sometimes in Anglican) churches on Good Friday.
1884 *Catholic Dict.* 405/1 These 'reproaches' are addressed in dramatic form by Christ to the Jewish people. **1897** *Westm. Gaz.* 15 Apr. 6/3 Early services..consisting sometimes of the Litany or Morning Prayer,..and occasionally the singing of the Reproaches. **1900** *Daily News* 14 Apr. 8/4 No words were used during the service, beyond those given in the Book of Common Prayer and the Reproaches.
†**5.** An object of scorn or contempt. *Obs.*
1560 Bible (Genev.) *Neh.* ii. 17 Let vs buylde the wall of Ierusalem, that we be no more a reproche. —— *Ps.* lxxix. 4 We are a reproche to our neighbours.

reproach (rɪ'prəʊtʃ), *v.* Also 5-7 **reproch(e**. [ad. F. *reprocher* (OF. also *reprochier*) = Prov. *repropchar*, Sp. and Pg. *reprochar*, It. *rimprocciare*, referred by Diez to a Rom. **repropiāre*, f. L. *prope* near (the phonology of the stem being as in F. *approcher*: see APPROACH *v.*), but by Caix to a **reprobicāre* from *reprobus* or *reprobāre*. The similarity of the senses to those of F. *reprouver*, to REPROVE, is somewhat in favour of the latter suggestion. Earlier forms of the verb in English are REPROCE and REPRUCE.]
1. a. *trans.* To object or cast up (a thing) *to*, or bring (up) *against*, a person as a reproach or fault. Also const. *on.* Now *rare.*
c **1489** Caxton *Sonnes of Aymon* vi. 141 It shall not be reproched to me that ye fyghte me a fote & I on horsbacke. *a* **1648** Ld. Herbert *Hen. VIII* (1683) 561 He failed not to reproach unto the Pope his assisting of Francis. **1654-66** Earl Orrery *Parthen.* (1676) 18 Ah, Madam (said I) reproach me not the crime you yourself made me commit. **1668** Dryden *Dram. Poesy* Ess. (ed. Ker) I. 61 The French writers..do not burden themselves too much with plot, which has been reproached to them..as a fault. **1830** W. Taylor *Hist. Surv. Germ. Poetry* II. 60 Lichtenberg.. reproached to the rude polemic his ingratitude. **1845** E. B. Barrett *Lett. R. Browning & E. B. B.* I. 69 Jealousy of contemporaries, which we hear reproached..on men of letters. **1870** *Daily News* 25 Oct., The mere fact of their frequenting cafés should not be reproached against them.
†**b.** To recall with reproaches. *Obs. rare*⁻¹.
1533 Bellenden *Livy* II. xii. (S.T.S.) I. 173 Þe pepill.. ran with grete cumpanyis to seruilius Consull, Ilkane reprocheand þe promisses maid be him.
2. a. To upbraid, reprove, or rebuke (a person); †to revile, abuse. Const. *for* (†*of*) something.
1513 Douglas *Æneis* I. Prol. 504 Gif I haue failȝeit, baldly repruif my ryme, Bot..Reproche me nocht quhill the work be oursene. **1533** Bellenden *Livy* II. xxv. (S.T.S.) I. 233 He began to reproche þame of þare fleing. **1586** A. Day *Eng. Secretary* II. (1625) 31 That I should be occasioned thus to reproch you as I do, is..vnto me no great contentment. **1611** Bible *Job* xxvii. 6 My heart shall not reproach me so long as I liue. **1662** J. Davies tr. *Olearius' Voy. Ambass.* 10 Our Musketteers..reproach'd him for having communicated too much to us. **1797** Mrs. Radcliffe *Italian* vi, She gently reproached him for doubting the continuance of her regard. **1815** Shelley *Lett.* Pr. Wks. 1880 III. 347 Your letter has lain by me for last week, reproaching me every day. **1877** Froude *Short Stud.* (1883) IV. I. x. 124 He reproached Fitzurse for ingratitude for past kindness.
absol. **1611** Bible *Ps.* xliv. 16 For the voice of him that reproacheth, and blasphemeth. *Ibid.* lxxiv. 10 O God, how long shall the aduersarie reproach? **1961** B. Fergusson *Watery Maze* xv. 364 Like the good soldier he was, he never reproached or repined.
refl. **1727** De Foe *Syst. Magic* I. iv. (1840) 99 How would they have reproached themselves. **1841** Lane *Arab. Nts.* I. 100 As she sat reproaching herself, she beheld the Wezeer standing at her hand. **1870** Dickens *E. Drood* iv, I will not say that I have reproached myself.
b. To upbraid (one) *with* something.
1725 De Foe *Voy. round World* (1840) 45, I would reproach them with what had past. **1772** *Junius Lett.* xxiii. (1788) 133 *note*, The Duke..reproached him in plain terms with his duplicity. **1838** Lytton *Alice* I. xiii, Lady Vargrave's heart reproached her with not having..loved this sweet girl as she deserved. **1855** Macaulay *Hist. Eng.* xiii. (1899) II. 10 He was reproached with this misfortune as if it had been a crime.
refl. **1855** Ld. Houghton in *Life* (1891) I. xi. 527 It is one of those inconsideratenesses with which I am continually reproaching myself.
c. To censure or reprove (a thing, act, etc.).
1660 Heylin *Hist. Quinquart.* (title-p.), The five Controverted Points, Reproached in these last times by the Name of Arminianism. **1697** Dryden *Æneid* x. 974 Mezentius with his ardour warm'd His fainting friends, reproach'd their shameful flight. **1748** Johnson *Van. Human Wishes* 120 His last sighs reproach the faith of Kings. **1813** Shelley *Q. Mab* VI. 93 Their everlasting and unchanging laws Reproached thine ignorance.
†**3.** To reject, reprobate. *Obs. rare*⁻¹.
1534 Whitinton *Tullyes Offices* II. (1540) 75 What..may lette me to folowe those thynges whiche be laudable semynge to me, and to reproche such as be contrarye?
4. To bring (a thing) into reproach or discredit; to be a reproach to (a person).
1593 Nashe *Christ's T.* 46 Riches as they haue renowned, so they haue reproched London. **1603** Shaks. *Meas. for M.* v. vi. 426 Imputation, For that he knew you, might reproach your life, And choake your good to come. **1823** J. Badcock *Dom. Amusem.* 152 Successful competition in the show of cotton goods for many years reproached the British manufacturer. **1886** *Daily Tel.* 21 June (Cassell), The Inner Temple Hall, reproached with..Smirke's poverty-stricken perpendicular Gothic.

reproachable (rɪ'prəʊtʃəb(ə)l), *a.* Now *rare.* [a. F. *reprochable* (13th c.), or f. prec. + -ABLE.]
1. a. Deserving of, or liable to, reproach; censurable.
1531 Elyot *Gov.* I. iv, Suche companions and playfelowes, whiche shal nat do in his presence any reprocheable acte. **1542** Udall *Erasm. Apoph.* 216 That [which] this kyng iudged contrarie to all reason and reprocheable.., the same nowe..is accumpted an high pointe & royall thing. **1603** Holland *Plutarch's Mor.* 191 Silence (a thing more often praise-worthy than reprochable). **1657-83** Evelyn *Hist. Religion* (1850) I. 166 Nor, in the mean time, is our ignorance reproachable. **1710** Steele *Tatler* No. 199 ⁋4 This has given Way to such unreasonable Gallantries, that a Man is hardly reproachable that deceives an innocent Woman, tho' she has never so much Merit, if she is below him in Fortune. **1779** G. Keate *Sketches fr. Nat.* (ed. 2) I. 58 A brother, whose conduct towards her had been in the highest degree reproachable. **1823** *Ann. Reg.* 158 It was reproachable with fewer excesses. [**1892** Zangwill *Bow Mystery* 56 His linen was reproachable, his dingy boots were down at heel.] **1972** *Sunday Tel.* 30 Apr. 14/2 It is here that 'The Green Flag' is reproachable. The history of a rebellion is incomplete if it

gives hardly a clue as to the nature and attitudes of the power at which the rebellion was directed.

†**b.** Involving reproach *to* one. *Obs. rare.*

1634 W. Tirwhyt tr. *Balzac's Lett.* 391, I have now no other pretention, but to follow such [studies] as can be no way reproachable unto me. 1767 S. Paterson *Another Trav.* I. 205 A different way, less shocking and less reproachable to our nature, might..answer the end as well.

†**2.** Conveying or implying reproach; reproachful. *Obs.*

1531 Elyot *Gov.* iii. ii, He also prohibited that any thinge shuld be radde or spoken, reprocheable or blasphemous to god. 1576 *Tyde taryeth no man* in Collier *Illustr. E.E. Pop. Lit.* xvi. 16 The preacher brake out with reprocheable talke, Saying that we cittizens were all to bad.

Hence **re'proachableness, -ably.** *rare*$^{-0}$.

1648 Hexham, *Lasterlicken*, Reproachably, or Blameably. [1847- in Webster and later Dicts.] 1727 Bailey vol. II, *Reproachableness*, capableness, etc. of being reproached. [Hence in Jodrell, Webster (1847) and later Dicts.]

re'proacher. [f. reproach *v.* + -er[1].] One who reproaches (†or reviles).

1566 T. Stapleton *Ret. Untr. Jewel* Epist., That Rude Reprocher Diogenes. *c* 1586 C'tess Pembroke *Ps.* cxxiii. 248 Scorn of proud scorners, reproach of mighty reprochers. 1660 Ingelo *Bentiv. & Ur.* ii. (1682) 13, I accuse thee..as a..Reprocher of our most Excellent Constitutions. 1693 Mather in Owen *Holy Spirit* Pref. 1 Virulent Reproachers of the Operations of the Spirit. *a* 1832 Bentham *Deontol.* (1834) II. 101 It is only a pain planted in the mind of the reproacher. 1841 D'Israeli *Amen. Lit.* (1867) 229 Our reproachers fortunately possessed the arts, and even the learning, which we were willing..to acquire.

reproachful (rɪˈprəʊtʃfʊl), *a.* [-ful.]

†**1.** Full of reproach or shame; shameful, disgraceful. Also, deserving of reproach or censure; blameworthy. *Obs.* (common in 17th c.).

1549 Coverdale, etc. *Erasm. Par. 1 Cor.* 5 By the vyle, lowe and reprochefull crosse of Christe. *Ibid.* 31 Well maye she be coumpted reprochefull, yf she..shewes her owne unshamefastenesse. 1590 Spenser *F.Q.* iii. i. 9 Full of disdainefull wrath he fierce uprose For to revenge that fowle reprochefull shame. 1606 Bryskett *Civ. Life* 87 Esteeming more an honest and a glorious death then a naturall and reprochfull life. 1666 Bp. S. Parker *Free & Impart. Censure* (1667) 238 He yielded himself up to a most reproachful death. 1681 R. L'Estrange *Tully's Offices* 9 To be Ignorant, and to be deceived, we look upon as a wretched, and a reproachful thing. 1737 Whiston *Josephus, Hist.* Pref. §5 It must be reproachful to write lies when they must be known ..to be such. 1796 Morse *Amer. Geog.* I. Pref. 3 It would be reproachful for them to suffer this ignorance to continue.

†**b.** Discreditable, disreputable. *Obs. rare.*

1581 Savile *Tacitus, Hist.* (1591) 104 Thither resorted also of the baser sort certaine well knowen to Vitellius..with which kinde of reprochfull acquaintance he was delited wonderfully. 1655 tr. *Sorel's Com. Hist. Francion* xii. 38 Hortensius..advised him to take heed how he adventured again to see for Forrage in such reproachfull places.

†**c.** Const. *to* a person, etc. *Obs.*

1584 Cogan *Haven Health* (1636) 276 *Inhærere libris*, which never yet was reproachfull to a student. 1670 G. H. *Hist. Cardinals* iii. ii. 262 A subject indeed too scandalous and reproachfull to the whole Colledge. 1765 Burke *Corr.* (1844) I. 77 His conduct in public affairs has been very reproachful to himself and extremely disgustful to me.

2. Full of reproach, reproof, or censure; upbraiding, †abusive.

1548 Elyot, *Contumeliosus*,..spitefull, reprochfull. 1565 Cooper *Thesaurus* s.v. *Contumelia*, To rate with reprochfull woordes. 1588 Shaks. *Tit. A.* ii. i. 55 Not I, till I haue.. Thrust these reprochfull speeches downe his throat. 1648 Milton *Observ. Art. Peace Ormond* Wks. 1851 IV. 561 A long digression of evill and reproachfull language to the Parlament and Army of England. *a* 1656 Hales *Gold. Rem.* (1673) i. 98 He is rewarded with no less reproachful a name then that of Satan. 1769 Blackstone *Comm.* IV. xviii. 252 Neither are mere reproachful words, as calling a man knave or liar, any breach of the peace. 1832 Lytton *Eugene A.* i. viii, Walter, your voice is reproachful! 1866 Mrs. Gaskell *Wives & Dau.* I. 296 'It's Lady Harriet', said Mrs. Gibson ..in reproachful dismay.

absol. 1589 Puttenham *Eng. Poesie* iii. xix. (Arb.) 218, I choose to name him the Reprochfull or scorner.

†**3.** Derogatory *to* a person, etc. *Obs. rare.*

1570-4 G. Scott *Treat. Errors Rom. Ch.* in Farr *S.P. Eliz.* (1845) II. 522 Accursed is the worke, Reprochefull unto God. 1645 Pagitt *Heresiogr.* (1662) 140 That assertion is reproachfull to the wisedome of God.

reproachfully (rɪˈprəʊtʃfʊlɪ), *adv.* [-ly[2].]

1. In a reproachful, reproving, (†opprobrious or abusive), manner.

1548 Elyot, *Contumeliose*, spitefully, reprochfully. 1567-9 Jewel *Def. Apol.* (1611) 29 What hath the people so much offended you, that you should..so reprochfully report of them..? 1596 Spenser *F.Q.* vi. xii. 27 Most of them..spake reprochfully, not caring where nor when. 1617 Moryson *Itin.* iii. 83 They cannot speake more reprochfully of any Host, then to say;..I did not eate my belly full there. *a* 1714 Sharp *Serm.* (1754) III. xi. 199 To speak a word against him, will be to talk slightly and reproachfully of him; as calling him a glutton, or a wine-bibber. 1838 Lytton *Alice* i. iii, Why does she look reproachfully at me..if I attempt to draw her to the past? 1867 Mrs. H. Wood *Orville Coll.* ix, George..glanced reproachfully at her as he turned.

2. Shamefully, disgracefully, contumeliously.

1593 Shaks. *2 Hen. VI*, ii. iv. 97 Shall I then be vs'd reproachfully? 1641 Baker *Chron.* (1653) 125 William Bussey..is committed to the Tower of London, and most reprochfully used. 1668 Clarendon *Vindic.* Tracts (1727) 49 Publickly and reproachfully executed and put to death. 1713 Birch in *Guardian* No. 36 ¶2, I do not know any sort of Wit that hath been used so reproachfully as the Pun.

re'proachfulness. [f. as prec. + -ness.] The condition or quality of being reproachful (in senses of the adj.).

1548 Udall *Erasm. Par. Luke* vii. 73 b, This mannes humanitee and curteous behaueour..ye turne into an occasion of slaundreous reprochefulnesse. 1583 Golding *Calvin on Deut.* cxxiv. 762 To the end that Justice should bee had in honour, and that we should not surmise any reprochefulnesse in it [etc.]. 1644 Quarles *Barnabas & B.* 291 The reproachfulness of that death which thy Son suffered. 1853 Kane *Grinnell Exp.* xxvii. (1856) 221 And looked toward me with a sort of startled reproachfulness. 1882 Miss Braddon *Mt. Royal* II. v. 96 'You would leave me..', said Mrs. Tregonell, with mild reproachfulness.

re'proaching, *vbl. sb.* [f. reproach *v.* + -ing[1].] The action of reproving or upbraiding.

1542-3 *Act 34 & 35 Hen. VIII*, c. i, Songes and plaies and enterludes..for the rebuking and reproching of vices. 1611 Bible *Ecclus.* xxix. 28 These things are grieuous to a man of vnderstanding: the vpbraiding of house-roome, and reproching of the lender. 1648 Milton *Observ. Art. Peace Ormond* Wks. 1851 IV. 572 For the reproaching, let them answer that are guilty. 1656 *Artif. Handsom.* 66 These..fall ..to bitter and scurrilous reprochings.

re'proaching, *ppl. a.* [f. as prec. + -ing[2].] That reproaches; upbraiding.

1742 Richardson *Pamela* III. 169 My Lady said, None of your reproaching Eye, Pamela; I know what you hint at. 1795 Southey *Joan of Arc* iv. 465 She look'd at him With a reproaching eye of tenderness. 1817 A. Bonar *Serm.* II. xv. 319 The cruel desertions of reproaching kindred.

Hence **re'proachingly** *adv.*, in a reproaching manner; reproachfully.

1791 Charlotte Smith *Celestina* (ed. 2) I. 27 [His mother], who seemed to look at him reproachingly. 1826 *Chron.* in *Ann. Reg.* 136/2 She..looked upon him so reproachingly, that he shrunk from his purpose. 1880 'Ouida' *Moths* ix, 'Unless she be really ill'..said her mother reproachingly.

re'proachless, *a.* [f. reproach *sb.*] Irreproachable.

1826 K. Digby *Broadst. Hon.* I. *Godefridus* 85 He appeals ..to those who..could bear testimony to his reproachless fame. 1892 *Pall Mall G.* 20 Sept. 6/2 The unfortunate army ..fought with reproachless courage to the very last.

Hence **re'proachlessness.**

1856 Masson *Chatterton* i. iii. (1874) 89 Evidence in favour of Chatterton's punctual conduct..has been strained into a testimony to his moral reproachlessness.

†**re'proachment.** *Obs. rare*$^{-1}$. [f. reproach *v.* Cf. obs. F. *reprochement* (Godef.).] Reproach.

c 1585 *Faire Em* iii. 1102 In limiting your love so unorderly, for which you rashly endure reproachment.

†**reprobable,** *a.* *Obs. rare.* [ad. med.L. *reprobābilis*, f. L. *reprobāre*: see reprobate *v.*, and cf. obs. F. *reprobable* (Godef.).] Deserving or worthy of rejection or reproof; reprobate.

1432-50 tr. *Higden* (Rolls) VIII. 151, I schalle divide the chosen peple of God from peple reprobable [L. *a reprobis*], as ly3hte from derkenesse. 1523 in W. H. Turner *Select. Rec. Oxford* (1880) 42 To your reprobable dishonesties and rebuke. 1528 Roy *Rede me* (Arb.) 44 No thynge ther in was reprobable, But all to gedder true and veritable.

'reprobacy. [f. reprobate *a.*: see -acy.] The state or condition of being reprobate.

1594 O. B. *Quest. Profit. Concern.* 17 There is also a certaine sparke or seed of vertue euer remaining in man.. vnlesse reprobacie haue ouer-run all. 1647 Trapp *Comm. Heb.* vi. 8 God..smiteth these sinners..with blindenesse and reprobacy of minde. 1760-72 H. Brooke *Fool of Qual.* (1809) II. 156 The length to which human nature can go in reprobacy. 1819 *Metropolis* II. 203 With..all the appearance of reprobacy in their dress and in their deportment. 1873 Symonds *Grk. Poets* viii. 242 The extravagancies..were committed defiantly, in open reprobacy, in scorn of the acknowledged law.

So **'reprobance.** *rare* (only in allusive use of quot. 1604).

1604 Shaks. *Oth.* v. ii. 209 This sight would make him do a desperate turne: Yea, curse his better Angell from his side, And fall to Reprobance [*Qq.* reprobation]. 1878 Swinburne *Poems & Ballads* 2nd Ser. 213 Like Absalom with locks luxurious, Or like Judas fallen to reprobance.

†**reproba'tarian,** *sb.* and *a.* *Obs. rare.* [f. reprobate *sb.* or *v.*] **a.** *sb.* One who professes the doctrine of reprobation. **b.** *adj.* Relating to reprobation.

1657 Pierce *Div. Philanthr.* 13 What Tertullian speaks against Marcion, might very well be repeated against the Absolute Reprobatarians. 1676 Glanvill *Ess.* vii. 22 By such Principles..they undermined..the fierce and churlish Reprobatarian Doctrines.

reprobate (ˈrɛprəbeɪt), *sb.* [ad. L. *reprobāt-us*: see next.]

1. One rejected by God; one who has fallen away from grace or religion; one lost in sin.

1545 Bale *Image Both Ch.* ii. (1550) 41 The wyse menne of this worlde, the verye reprobates from God, all drye without the true faythe, dranke vp this fylthye water. 1557 N.T. (Genev.) *2 Cor.* xiii. 5 Knowe ye not your owne selues, how that Iesus Christ is in you, except ye be reprobates? 1630 Prynne *Anti-Armin.* 103 Mr. Bradford speakes this onely to silence Reprobates and damned men. 1678 R. Barclay *Apol. Quakers* vii. §8. 225 We must know Christ in us, except we be Reprobates, or unjustified Persons. 1728 Morgan *Algiers* I. vi. 179 His People were become perfect Reprobates, quite devoid of all Religion. 1851 Longf. *Gold. Leg.* v. i. 232 A hopeless reprobate, a hardened sinner, Must be that Carmelite now passing near.

2. An abandoned or unprincipled person; one whose character is utterly bad; a scamp.

1592 Nashe *Four Lett. Confut.* D iij, Thy pen is in state of a Reprobate with all men of iudgement and reckoning. 1603 Shaks. *Meas. for M.* iv. iii. 78 What if we do omit This Reprobate,..til he were wel enclin'd. 1607 Heywood *Fayre Mayde Exch.* Wks. 1874 II. 80 Come from him, hee's a reprobate. 1706 E. Ward *Wooden World Diss.* (1708) 15, I am far from drawing him a downright Reprobate. 1715 De Foe *Fam. Instruct.* i. i. (1841) I. 12 They always grow worse and worse, till they grow mere reprobates. 1829 Lytton *Disowned* I. iii. 33 At the age of thirteen [I] was as thorough a reprobate as the tribe could desire. 1840 Macaulay *Ess., Clive* (1887) 526 The general opinion seems to have been that poor Robert was a dunce, if not a reprobate. 1879 Froude *Cæsar* xv. 226 He saw himself driven into banishment by an insolent reprobate, a patrician turned Radical and demagogue.

reprobate (ˈrɛprəbət), *a.* [ad. late L. *reprobāt-us*, pa. pple. of *reprobāre*: see next. Most of the senses are based upon Biblical passages.]

1. Rejected or condemned as worthless, inferior or impure. Now *rare.*

1545 Bale *Image Both Ch.* ii. (1550) 105 Declare them first of all to the worlde, to be the reprobate veselles of dishonour, which of wylfulnesse contempneth my eternall veryte. 1560 Bible (Genev.) *Jer.* vi. 30 Thei shal call them reprobate [L. *reprobum*] siluer, because the Lord hathe reiected them. 1582 N.T. (Rhem.) *Heb.* vi. 8 The earth.. bringing forth thornes and bryers, it is reprobate [L. *reproba*]. 1665 J. Spencer *Vulg. Proph.* 1 There is a great deal of reprobate Silver which carries the image of the King and looks like Sterling. 1737 Cruden *Concordance* (1845) 395 This word among metallists is used to signify any metal that,..when tried,..betrays itself to be adulterate or reprobate. 1827 Pollock *Course T.* ii. 69 Creeds.. unsanctioned.., And reprobate in heaven.

†**2.** Depraved, degraded, morally corrupt. *Obs.*

1550 Crowley *Way to Wealth* A vj b, God hath geuen the vp in to a reprobate minde [*Rom.* i. 28]. 1557 N.T. (Genev.) *2 Tim.* iii. 8 Men of corrupte mindes, reprobate concerning the faith. 1588 Shaks. *L.L.L.* i. ii. 64 If drawing my sword against the humour of affection, would deliuer mee from the reprobate thought of it, I would take Desire prisoner. 1593 —— *Lucr.* 300 By reprobate desire thus madly led, The Romane Lord marcheth to Lvcrece bed. 1656 Cowley *Pindar. Odes, Isa.* xxxiv, *note* iii, Some men are so given up even to the most reprobate sense of Aristotle, that not so much as the Divine Authority can draw them from it. 1671 Milton *Samson* 1685 Insensate left, or to sense reprobate, And with blindness internal struck.

†**b.** Const. *to* (= with respect to, in respect of).

1557 N.T. (Genev.) *Tit.* i. 16 Thei..are abominable and disobedient, and vnto euerie good worke reprobate [L. *reprobi*]. 1760 C. Johnston *Chrysal* (1822) II. 86 Something so grossly reprobate to every sense of real virtue.

3. Rejected by God; lost or hardened in sin.

1561 T. Norton *Calvin's Inst.* i. 2 Those men that are in themselues reprobate and accursed. 1651 Hobbes *Leviath.* iii. xxxvii. 235 The end of Miracles, was to beget beleef, not universally in all men, elect, and reprobate; but in the elect only. 1667 Milton *P.L.* i. 697 Thir..Strength and Art are easily outdone By spirits reprobate. 1852 Mrs. Stowe *Uncle Tom's C.* xxxv. 314 Hard and reprobate as the godless man seemed now [etc.]. 1878 Stewart & Tait *Unseen Univ.* i. §44. 61 Others cannot admit the eternity of misery, but believe the most reprobate will ultimately be reclaimed and elevated into the regions of bliss.

b. Of abandoned character; lost to all sense of religious or moral obligation; unprincipled.

1660 F. Brooke tr. *Le Blanc's Trav.* 3 The greatest part of our company were reprobate persons, and absolute Atheists. 1719 De Foe *Crusoe* ii. (Globe) 531 She was not built for a Privateer, but was run away with by a reprobate Crew. 1766 [Anstey] *Bath Guide* v. 47 'Twas shocking to hear The Oaths of that reprobate gouty old Peer. 1884 *Illustr. Lond. News* 25 Oct. 387/3, I have known persons so utterly reprobate and abandoned as to order 'sherry and angostura' ..as a whet before dinner.

4. *absol.* Those who are rejected by God, and thus excluded from participation in eternal life with Him. (Opposed to *the elect.*)

1563 Foxe *A. & M.* 1141/2, I beleue yt we al shal rise again in these our bodies. The elect..to liue wt Christ for euer: the reprobate..to liue wt ye deuil and his angels. 1594 T. B. *La Primaud. Fr. Acad.* ii. 7 It is said of the reprobate and of them that are hardened, of which sort are all Atheists, that [etc.]. 1651 Hobbes *Leviath.* iii. xxxviii. 244 Wee do not read, that to any of the Reprobate is promised an Eternall life. 1675 R. Burthogge *Causa Dei* 66 Thus it is in the Elect and Reprobate. 1833 J. Waterworth tr. *Veron's Rule Cath. Faith* 144 Can the predestinate be lost, or the reprobate saved?

†**5.** Implying or involving something disgraceful or discreditable. *Obs.*

1589 Puttenham *Eng. Poesie* iii. xxiii. (Arb.) 279 This word *Cheuaucher* in the French tongue hath a reprobate sence, specially being spoken of a womans riding. 1612 Naunton in *Buccleuch MSS.* (Hist. MSS. Comm.) I. 118 My mediation to bring Sir F. Gr[eville] and him to meet.. was, I know not how, turquesed into a reprobate sense.., as if I were too suspiciously inward with Sir F. Gr.

†**6.** Deserving or worthy of condemnation or reproof; appropriate to reprobates. *Obs.*

1601 ? Marston *Pasquil & Kath.* i. 21 Reprobate fashion, when each ragged clowt..Reekes in the face of sacred maiestie His stinking breath of censure! 1645 Milton *Colast.* Wks. 1851 IV. 374 Who would have deny'd it, but one of a reprobate ignorance in all hee meddles with. 1768 Sterne *Sent. Journ.* I. 135 (*Amiens*), There was nothing wrong in the sentiment; and yet I instantly reproached my heart with it in the bitterest and most reprobate of expressions. 1771 Mrs. Griffith *Hist. Lady Barton* III.

171 The following part of my unhappy story..impels me to wild distraction, or to reprobate despair.

reprobate ('rɛprəbeɪt), *v.* Also 5–7 as *pa. pple.* [f. L. *reprobāt-*, ppl. stem of *reprobāre*, f. *re-* RE- 2 d + *probāre* to PROVE: cf. REPROVE *v.*]

1. *trans.* To disapprove of, censure, condemn.

1432–50 tr. *Higden* (Rolls) VI. 407 Sergius..beynge a cardinalle diacon, and reprobate by Formosus the pope, wente to Fraunce. *Ibid.* VIII. 259 Gregory the x^the^.. approbate certeyne of the ordres of beggers..; somme he reprobate, as frers Saccines. **1607** J. CARPENTER *Plaine Mans Plough* 36 So those Scribes..were rejected..and their workes reprobated. **1671** [R. MACWARD] *True Nonconf.* 145 It was not only not introduced, but plainly reprobate by our Lord and his Apostles. **1752** LAW *Spirit Love* II. (1816) 129 For nothing is reprobated in Cain, but that very same which is reprobated in Abel. **1787** WINTER *Syst. Husb.* 205 His neighbours reprobated his method of proceeding. **1850** W. IRVING *Mahomet* vii. (1853) 36 He reprobated what he termed the heresies of his nephew. **1882** J. B. STALLO *Concepts Mod. Physics* 57 The 'assumption' of universal attraction is reprobated as an 'absurdity' by James Croll.

†**b.** To abhor *to* do a thing. *Obs. rare*$^{-1}$.

1779 EARL MALMESBURY *Diaries & Corr.* I. 236 His Prussian Majesty has..perhaps employed means we should reprobate to make use of.

2. Of God: To reject or cast off (a person or persons) from Himself; to exclude from participation in future bliss. (Cf. REPROBATION 3.)

1526 *Pilgr. Perf.* (W. de W. 1531) 24 b, For theyr synne they be reprobate & forsaken of god. **1646** SIR T. BROWNE *Pseud. Ep.* 340 That the Thiefe on the right hand was saved, and the other on the left reprobated..we are ready to admit. *a* **1711** KEN *Psyche* Poet. Wks. 1721 IV. 294 Paternal God, though it is just To reprobate infected Dust [etc.]. **1751** LAVINGTON *Enthus. Meth. & Papists* III. (1754) 3 Persons of weak Spirits..will naturally..look upon themselves as reprobated, and forsaken of God. **1783** COWPER *Let. to Newton* 21 Apr., Such a man reprobated in the great day, would be the most melancholy spectacle. **1847** J. KIRK *Cloud Disp.* xi. 164 Proof that God has reprobated from eternity a certain part of mankind.

3. To reject, refuse, put away, set aside. (Sometimes with suggestion of sense 1.)

1609 BIBLE (Douay) *Gen.* xxv. *comm.*, The younger is elected, the elder reprobate. *a* **1661** FULLER *Worthies* (1840) III. 130 Pole being reprobated, Julius the Third..was chosen in his place. **1773** JOHNSON *Let. to Mrs. Thrale* 20 Sept., I think the resolution both of my head and my heart engaged, and reprobate every thought of desisting from the undertaking. **1782** PRIESTLEY *Matt. & Spir.* (ed. 2) I. Pref. 30 Mr. De Luc..will see this opinion..reprobated with contempt. **1850** NEALE *Med. Hymns* (1867) 116 Reprobated and rejected Was this Stone.

b. *Law.* To reject (an instrument or deed) as not binding on one. (Chiefly in *Sc. Law*, as opposed to APPROBATE.) Also *absol.*

1726 AYLIFFE *Parergon* 305 An Exception lies against the Tenor of an Instrument by other Proofs and Evidence in Writing: and this Method (among others) is the best way of reprobating an Instrument. *a* **1768** ERSKINE *Inst. Law Scot.* III. iii. §49 (1773) 465 The grantee does not in such case approbate and reprobate the same deed. **1836** *Blackw. Mag.* XXXIX. 662 You cannot approbate and reprobate the same instrument. **1899** *19th Cent.* May 734 The clerical objector cleaves to the one set of laws and rejects the other. He seeks to approbate and reprobate.

†**c.** To repudiate, cast off, disown. ? *Obs.*

1748 RICHARDSON *Clarissa* (1811) I. xxv. 179, I beseech him not to reprobate his child for an aversion which it is not in her power to conquer. **1780** *Newgate Cal.* V. 154 The seduction was followed by very disagreeable consequences: the father reprobated his daughter.

†**4.** *intr.* To employ reproaches. *Obs. rare*$^{-1}$.

1698 *Christ Exalted* 100 He reprobated exceedingly against Israel.

Hence '**reprobated** *ppl. a.* Also *absol.*

1535 JOYE *Apol. Tindale* (Arb.) 16 Where the state of the electe and of the reprobated immediately after their deth is described. **1647** WITHER *Carmen Expost.* B iij, God hath, for that offence, Expos'd you to a reprobated sense, Believing lies. **1668** CLARENDON *Contempl. Ps.* Tracts (1727) 571 It is not possible for the most reprobated sinner to believe [etc.]. **1782** COWPER *Table-T.* 459 Callous and tough, The reprobated race grows judgment-proof. **1790** HAN. MORE *Relig. Fash. World* (1791) 197 This reprobated strictness therefore..is in reality the true cause of actual enjoyment.

'**reprobateness.** *rare*$^{-0}$. [f. REPROBATE *a.* + -NESS.] The state of being reprobate.

1611 FLORIO, *Reprobaggine*, reprobateness, reprobation. **1731** BAILEY vol. II, *Reprobateness*, the state of a reprobate; wickedness, impiety.

'**reprobater.** *rare.* [f. REPROBATE *v.* + -ER[1].] One who reprobates.

1806 M. NOBLE *Contn. Granger's Hist. Eng.* III. 490 John, duke of Argyle, the patriotic reprobater of French modes. **1822** T. TAYLOR *Apuleius* 310 A reprobater of what is evil.

'**reprobating,** *ppl. a.* [f. as prec. + -ING[2].] That reprobates or condemns.

a **1660** HAMMOND *Serm.* (1850) 359 In passing judgments upon men's future estates, the censorious reprobating spirit. **1690** NORRIS *Beatitudes* (1692) 103 A good way to counterballance the Severity of their Reprobating Decrees. **1847** KIRK *Cloud Disp.* xi. 164 He carries out his reprobating decree.

reprobation (rɛprə'beɪʃən). Also 5–6 -cio(u)n. [ad. late L. *reprobātiōn-em*, noun of action f. *reprobāre*: see REPROBATE *v.* and -ATION, and cf. F. *réprobation* (14th c.).]

†**1.** Reproof, shame. *Obs. rare*$^{-1}$.

1436 *Libel Eng. Policy* in *Pol. Poems* (Rolls) II. 165 They that the see shulde kepe are moche to blame..And Seynt Malouse turneth hem to reprobacioun.

2. The action of raising objections or exceptions (*against* a thing or person); a legal objection or exception. *rare.*

c **1485** *Digby Myst.* (1882) II. 46 We know your trewe delygens To persue all tho that do reprobacion A-gayns owur lawes by ony redarguacion. **1681** STAIR *Inst. Law Scot., Form of Process* 43 The Lords will supersede to advise the Testimonies..till the Reprobation be first advised. **1856** BOUVIER *Law Dict., Reprobation*, The propounding of exceptions either against facts, persons or things, as to allege that certain deeds or instruments have not been duly or lawfully executed.

3. *Theol.* Rejection by God; the state of being so rejected or cast off, and thus ordained to eternal misery. (Opposed to *election* in the Calvinistic doctrine of predestination: cf. REPROBATE *a.* 4 and *v.* 2.)

1532 MORE *Confut. Tindale* Wks. 815/1 To fall in dispicions vpon Gods eleccion,..and eternall sentence of reprobacion. *a* **1569** KINGESMYLL *Confl. Satan* (1578) 16 Is it then such a note of reprobation as that a man may say.. we are not Gods children? **1628** WITHER *Brit. Rememb.* VIII. 533 They Reprobation otherwhile confound With our Predestination. **1651** C. CARTWRIGHT *Cert. Relig.* I. 222 Austine doth call reprobation predestination to destruction. **1699** BURNET *39 Art.* xvii. (1700) 167 Those who do once persuade themselves that the Doctrine of Reprobation is false. **1753** SMOLLETT *Cnt. Fathom* (1784) 51/2 He would have left the whole species in a state of reprobation, rather than redeem them at that price. **1813** SHELLEY *Q. Mab* VII. 149 These in a gulf of anguish and of flame, Shall curse their reprobation endlessly. **1860** PUSEY *Min. Proph.* 30 To sin on without punishment is a sign of reprobation.

4. Rejection of a person or thing; condemnation as worthless or spurious.

1582 N.T. (Rhem.) *Heb.* vii. 18 Reprobation certes is made of the former commandment. **1607** TOPSELL *Four-f. Beasts* (1658) 232 It is good also to set down the faults and signes of reprobation in Horses. **1693** DRYDEN *Disc. Satire* Ess. (ed. Ker) II. 23 You are empowered to..set a brand of reprobation on clipt poetry, and false coin. **1805** FORSYTH *Beauties Scotl.* II. 443 The out-field land remained in a state of utter reprobation. No dung was ever spread on any part of it.

b. Disapproval, censure, reproof.

1727 POPE & GAY *Punning* Swift's Wks. 1751 VI. 247 The Lord mercifully spared his Neck, but as a mark of Reprobation wryed his Nose. **1797** MRS. RADCLIFFE *Italian* xi, She proceeded to speak of Ellena with the caustic of severe reprobation. *a* **1848** R. W. HAMILTON *Rew. & Punishm.* vii. (1853) 330 The history unfolded by Scripture is one series of reprobations against sin. **1883** SPENCER in *Contemp. Rev.* XLIII. 15 The fear of public reprobation affects men more than the fear of divine vengeance.

†**c.** Token of condemnation; disfigurement.

1774 GOLDSM. *Nat. Hist.* I. 381 There is scarce a limb of the body, or scarce a feature of the face, that has not suffered some reprobation, either from art or nature.

Hence †**repro'bationer**, a believer in the doctrine of reprobation. *Obs. rare*$^{-1}$.

1692 SOUTH *Serm.* (1727) III. 431 Any of the Geneva, or Scotch Model, (which sort of sanctified Reprobationers we abound with).

reprobative ('rɛprəbeɪtɪv), *a.* [f. REPROBATE *v.* + -IVE.] Conveying or expressing disapproval or reprobation.

1835 I. TAYLOR *Spir. Despot.* III. 109 Nor has ever a public reprover employed language more stern and reprobative. **1856** C. J. ELLICOTT in *Cambr. Ess.* 155 Even a collector like Fabricius..felt himself obliged to disclaim any, save a reprobative interest in these poor gospels. **1872** *Contemp. Rev.* XXI. 75 Infants and men are alike fit subjects of the elective or reprobative decree.

Hence '**reprobatively** *adv. rare*$^{-1}$.

1846 MRS. GORE *Eng. Char.* (1852) 149 He displaces the centurion, of whom the private secretary spake reprobatively over-night.

reprobator[1] ('rɛprəbeɪtə(r)). *Sc. Law.* [ad. med.L. (*actio*) **reprobātōria*: see REPROBATE *v.* and -ORY[2].] An action for the purpose of proving a witness to be liable to valid objections or to a charge of perjury.

1666–88 DALLAS *Syst. Stiles* 900 Not admitted to be added after a Reduction was Filled up,..but reserved a special action of Reprobator. *Ibid.*, Reprobators found Relevant upon Libelling of Corrupting of Witness. **1681** STAIR *Inst. Law Scot., Form of Process* 43 Even after Sentence, Reprobators are Competent. *a* **1768** ERSKINE *Inst. Law Scot.* IV. ii. §29 (1773) 678 The party objecting may..protest for a reprobator, *i.e.* protest that he may be allowed afterwards to bring evidence of the witness's enmity to him, or of his partial counsel in some other article. **1838** W. BELL *Dict. Law Scot.* 854 The ground of reprobator might have been proved both by the oath of the party who had adduced the witness objected to, and by the testimony of other witnesses. *Ibid.* There is no recent example of an action of reprobator.

†'**reprobator**[2]. *Obs. rare*$^{-1}$. [a. L. type *reprobātor*, agent-n. f. *reprobāre* to REPROBATE.] = REPROBATER.

1684 T. HOCKIN *God's Decrees* 260 God himself.. becomes the absolute Reprobator of men.

'**repro,batory,** *a.* [f. as REPROBATE *v.* + ORY[2].] Reprobative, condemnatory.

1823 *New Monthly Mag.* VIII. 559 The fate of Sir Charles Vernon afforded an ample field for reprobatory exclamation. **1831** SCOTT *Jrnl.* (1890) II. 381, I drew up, with much anxiety, an address reprobatory of the Bill.

†**reprobature.** *Obs. Sc. Law.* [f. as prec. + -URE.] The course or procedure of taking exception to a witness (cf. REPROBATOR[1]).

1681 STAIR *Inst. Law Scot., Form of Process* 43 Prompting, and instructing witnesses how to depone, or threatning them,..are pregnant grounds of Reprobature.

†**re'probitant,** *a. Obs. rare*$^{-1}$. (Formation and meaning obscure.)

a **1529** SKELTON *Sp. Parrot* 436 Grete reysons with resons be now reprobitante, For reysons are no resons, [etc.].

†**re'probrious,** *a. Obs. rare*$^{-1}$. [irreg. f. L. *reprobāre*, on analogy of *opprobrious.*] Reproachful, abusive.

1585 in G. Tolstoy *40 Yrs. Interc. Eng. & Russ.* (1875) 266 One of your people..wrote letters to his countrie with many reprobrious inventions to the infamy of our kingdome.

†**re'proce,** *sb. Obs. rare*$^{-1}$. [a. AF. (and OF.) *reproce*, var. of *reproche* REPROACH *sb.* See also REPRUCE *sb.*] Reproach.

a **1325** *Prose Psalter* lxviii. 10 For ich suffred for þe reproces, confucioun couerd my face.

†**re'proce,** *v. Obs. rare.* [ad. AF. (and OF.) *reprocer*, var. of *reprocher* to REPROACH. See also REPRUCE *v.*] *trans.* and *absol.* To reproach. Hence †**re'procing** *vbl. sb.*

a **1325** *Prose Psalter* xliii. 18 Fram þe voice of þe reproceand and þe ozains spekand. *Ibid.* lxxiii. 11 Þing to witen, God, þat þyn enemy shal reproce þe. *Ibid.* lxxviii. 4 We ben made in reprocing to our nezburзs.

re'process, *v.* [RE- 5 a.] *trans.* To subject (something) to a special process again. So **re'processed** *ppl. a.*; **re'processing** *vbl. sb.*

1939 *Sun* (Baltimore) 21 Feb. 14/4 'Reprocessed'..should be applied to wool made into a fibrous state for reuse. **1944** *Richmond* (Va.) *Times-Dispatch* 16 Jan. 9/1 A 'reprocessing' routine has been made an important part of the discharge procedure. **1948** *News Chron.* 15 Jan. 2/2 Production can be increased by reprocessing what we used to throw away. **1956** *Nature* 3 Mar. 400/1 The United Kingdom is likely..to reprocess the burnt elements from reactors. **1962** E. GODFREY *Retail Selling & Organization* xix. 190 When an item is sold, the punched ticket is returned to the warehouse, where it is re-processed for sales records to be made. **1977** *New Yorker* 9 May 142/2 The Japanese are..troubled..by our objections to the use of reprocessed nuclear fuel. **1979** *Bull. Amer. Acad. Arts & Sci.* May 44 Participants discussed the time necessary for a nation to convert a reprocessing plant to weapons production and how that time might be lengthened without giving up nuclear energy.

repro'claim (riː-), *v.* [RE- 5 a.] *trans.* To proclaim again.

1591 *Troub. Raigne K. John* (1611) 61 It resteth we throughout our territories Be reproclaimed and inuested King. **1638** RIDER *Horace, Odes* I. xii, What persons name Shall the deluding Echo reproclaime. **1816** COLERIDGE *Lay Serm.* (Bohn) 329 Whoever should have the hardihood to reproclaim its solemn truths must commence with a glossary. **1862** M. HOPKINS *Hawaii* 264 Protestantism was re-proclaimed as the religion of the government.

So **reprocla'mation.**

1883 *American* V. 403 A formal..reproclamation of their principles. **1885** J. BROWN *Bunyan* 133 All the country through there were proclamations and reproclamations.

repro'cure (riː-), *v.* [RE- 5 a.] *trans.* To procure again.

1591 SYLVESTER *Ivry* 317 If it [the Church] may ever hope to reprocure A holy and a happy Peace. **1679** KID in G. Hickes *Spirit of Popery* 12 The reprocuring of the Lords fallen work. **1815** JEFFERSON *Writ.* (1830) IV. 263 The means of reprocuring some part of the literary treasures which I have ceded to Congress. **1840** POE *W. Wilson* Wks. 1864 I. 432 Lights were immediately reprocured.

Hence **repro'curable** *a.*

1866 ODLING *Anim. Chem.* 91 Acetic acid is reprocurable from alcohol by oxidation.

reproduce (riːprə'djuːs), *v.* [f. RE- 5 a + PRODUCE *v.*, prob. after F. *reproduire* (16th c.).]

1. a. *trans.* To bring again into material existence; to create or form anew; *spec.* in *Biol.* to form (a lost limb or organ) afresh; to generate (new individuals).

1611 COTGR., *Reproduire*, to reproduce, to yeeld or bring forth againe. *a* **1676** HALE *Prim. Orig. Man.* II. vii. 193 Which..if they had been the Product of the Plastick power of the Earth, would have been Annually re-produced. *a* **1700** KEN *Hymnotheo* Poet. Wks. 1721 III. 85 God's Voice departed Souls shall re-instate, And reproduce Men easier than create. **1753** CHAMBERS *Cycl. Supp.* App. s.v. *Reproduction*, Some of these worms have..then begun to reproduce a head or a tail, or both. **1800** FELLOWES *Chr. Philos.* (ed. 3) 227 Man..reproduces his kind; and he vanishes into darkness. **1848** W. H. BARTLETT *Egypt to Pal.* x. (1879) 225 We gathered the seed of some of these,.. hoping to reproduce them at home. **1870** ROLLESTON *Anim. Life* Introd. 67 Some Amphibia possess a great power of repairing injuries, and of reproducing destroyed or amputated organs.

b. With immaterial object.

1776 ADAM SMITH *W.N.* II. ii. (1869) I. 293 Industrious people, who re-produce, with a profit, the value of their annual consumption. **1818** COBBETT *Pol. Reg.* XXXIII. 372 The great prosperity, which the industry and energy of the nation soon re-produced. **1863** FAWCETT *Pol. Econ.* I. iv. 28 A man may spend capital on productive wealth; then capital is..reproduced.

refl. **1842** MANNING *Serm.* i. (1848) I. 6 As sin, through the power of death, withers off..it perpetually reproduces itself. **1877** *Nature* 30 Aug. 360/1 It is evident..that the sounds would reproduce themselves with the same pitch in the scale.

c. *absol.* To multiply by generation.

1894 *Times* (weekly ed.) 31 Aug. 689/2 It [the bacillus] reproduces at the rate of hundreds per day. **1896** tr. *Boas' Text-bk. Zool.* 38 Among those animals which reproduce only by fertilised ova, successive generations are almost always alike.

2. To produce again by means of combination or change.

1666 BOYLE *Orig. Formes & Qual.* Wks. 1772 III. 61 If we could reproduce a body which has been deprived of its substantial form. **1704** NEWTON *Optics* (1721) 134 Whenever all those Rays..are mix'd again, they reproduce the same white Light as before. **1839** G. BIRD *Nat. Philos.* 325 A convex lens..will bring all the rays to a focus, and reproduce white light. **1878** HUXLEY *Physiogr.* 116 When the vapour of water is condensed it reproduces pure water.

3. a. To bring about again; to effect, exhibit, or present anew; to repeat in some fashion.

1688 DRYDEN *Brit. Rediv.* 217 His inborn courage.. Might reproduce some second Richard's reign. **1830** HERSCHEL *Stud. Nat. Phil.* 119 Whenever we notice a remarkable effect of any kind, our first question ought to be, Can it be reproduced? **1860** TYNDALL *Glac.* II. xiv. 307 Rendu affirmed..that all the phenomena of a river were reproduced upon the Mer de Glace. **1877** *Nature* 6 Sept. 403/2 He has rendered it possible to reproduce the human voice with all its modulations at distant points.

refl. **1870** ROGERS *Hist. Gleanings* Ser. II. 52 History is apt to reproduce itself.

b. To repeat in a more or less exact copy; to produce a copy of (a work of art, picture, drawing, etc.), now *esp.* by means of engraving, photography, or similar processes.

1850 LEITCH tr. *C. O. Müller's Anc. Art* §83 (ed. 2) 50 In colonies the form of the images in the metropolis was faithfully reproduced. **1868** FREEMAN *Norm. Conq.* (1877) II. ix. 400 The rude art of English masons strove to reproduce the campaniles of Northern Italy. **1892** *Photogr. Ann.* II. 238 The diagrams reproduced on the adjoining pages.

absol. **1849** LYTTON *Caxtons* I. v, I already began to imitate, to reproduce.

c. *intr.* To turn out (well, etc.) in a copy.

1891 *Pall Mall G.* 2 Dec. 3/2 The drawings..reproduce in monochrome-plate process with greater strength than might be expected.

d. *trans.* To cause to be heard (sound originating elsewhere or on another occasion); also *absol.* Freq. with advbs.

1899 *T. Eaton & Co. Catal.* Spring & Summer 191/1 A graphophone..a perfect machine, reproduces perfectly. **1924** *Radio Times* 19 Dec. 620/1 (Advt.), He can 'pick' up the entertainment being sent out from any British or Continental Station and reproduce it at Loud Speaker strength. **1961** G. A. BRIGGS *A to Z in Audio* 21 If you can reproduce the bottom note of a double bass properly, you are not doing badly. **1978** *Gramophone* July 272/1 Totally enclosed headphones..can usually reproduce extreme bass frequencies more easily.

4. To present again in writing or print.

1860 TYNDALL *Glac.* I. xxv. 178 A letter..so interesting that I do not hesitate to reproduce it here. **1885** *Spectator* 25 July 977/1 The legends..here reproduced were well worth reproducing.

5. To create again by a mental effort; to represent clearly to the mind.

1869 TOZER *Highl. Turkey* II. 201 These scenic edifices.. enable our mind's eye to reproduce the people.. congregated together. **1870** ROGERS *Hist. Gleanings* Ser. II. 199 The novels of the eighteenth century enable us to reproduce the parson of the time with ease.

6. To bring out again.

1835 G. HOGARTH *Mus. Hist.* (1838) II. 158 He also remodelled his opera of *The Wood Girl*, and reproduced it under the title of *Sylvana*.

Hence **repro'duceable** *a.*, reproducible; **repro'duced, repro'ducing** *ppl. adjs.*

1832 HT. MARTINEAU *Hill & Valley* vi. 87 The second and third..constituted the reproduceable capital of the concern. **1882** SEELEY *Nat. Relig.* 103 A sort of reflected or reproduced eternity. **1892** *Photogr. Ann.* II. 106 Dispositives and reproduced negatives. **1893** *Athenæum* 30 Sept. 452/1 His adoption of his master's [style] is that of a student..not that of a mere reproducing copyist. **1941** *B.B.C. Gloss. Broadcasting Terms* 28 *Reproducing desk*, table carrying one or more turn-tables and other equipment for playing gramophone records, disc recordings, or pressings. **1946** *Penguin Music Mag.* Dec. 93 Reproducing instruments are improving as much as recording has improved. **1964** *Listener* 17 Sept. 442/2 Recordings made for the reproducing piano by Josef Lhévinne. **1970** J. EARL *Tuners & Amplifiers* iii. 69 Power so liberated..detracts from the reproduced signals.

repro'ducer (riː-). [f. prec. + -ER[1].]

1. One who or that which reproduces.

1774 BURKE *Amer. Tax.* Wks. 1792 I. 565 You understand ..that I speak of Charles Townshend, officially the re-producer of this fatal scheme. **1841** GLADSTONE *State in Rel. Ch.* iv. §100 (ed. 4), Not as a creator, or an inventor, or even a reproducer, of a system. **1876** *Contemp. Rev.* XXVII. 968 A timid, dependent, incoherent reproducer, whose plagiarisms his old pupil amused himself by detecting.

2. *spec.* In the phonograph, the part by which the sound is reproduced. Also, any device for reproducing recorded sound.

1888 *Nature* 29 Nov. 108/1 Consequently, there are two diaphragms, one a recorder and the other a reproducer. **1899** *T. Eaton & Co. Catal.* Spring & Summer 191/3 The price of the Universal Graphophone, with a long run clockwork motor recorder, reproducer, hearing, speaking tubes and horn, is $50. **1937** *Jrnl. Soc. Motion Picture Engineers* XXIX. 218 With a high-quality microphone, a high-quality reproducer, and a suitably corrected amplifier, the response curve can be made uniform. **1961** G. A. BRIGGS *A to Z in Audio* 169 The console includes a tape reproducer with 7½", 15" and 30" speeds. **1978** *Gramophone* Aug. 399/3 The Stanton 681EEE, which continues in production, is already a very fine reproducer.

3. *Computers.* A machine for making copies of punched cards or tape.

1940 W. J. ECKERT *Punched Card Methods* ii. 20 The High Speed Reproducer. This machine is used to transfer information from one card to another. **1949** [see INTERPRETER 5 a]. **1964** F. L. WESTWATER *Electronic Computers* vi. 100 A machine called a reproducer.. automatically reproduces the information in a pack of old cards into new ones. **1970** A. CHANDOR et al. *Dict. Computers* 291 *Paper tape reproducer*... Also known as a reperforator.

reproducibility (ˌriːprədjuːsɪˈbɪlɪtɪ). [f. next + -ITY.] The capacity to be produced again; the quality of being reproducible; the extent to which consistent results are obtained when produced repeatedly. Cf. REPEATABILITY.

1936 H. J. PATON *Kant's Metaphysic of Experience* I. xix. 371 Kant assumes that experience presupposes the reproducibility of appearances. **1939** *Jrnl. Amer. Chem. Soc.* LXI 3336/2 The agreement between two such sets of points indicates the reproducibility. **1946** *Nature* 7 Sept. 347/2 In many circuits increased reproducibility of electrical conditions does not indicate an increased reproducibility of light-emitting characteristics. **1953** *Industr. & Engin. Chem.* Feb. 465/ [illegible]ithin the reproducibility of the data, no effect of change [illegible] catalyst quantity or flow rate was noted. **1962** *Listener* 6 Dec. 952/1 This accuracy, and the reproducibility that goes with it, lies at the heart of mass production. **1969** *Physical Rev. Lett.* XXIII. 1402/2 The accuracy obtained for the energy is better than ±0·1% and the reproducibility is about ±0·05%. **1977** J. D. DOUGLAS in Douglas & Johnson *Existential Sociol.* i. 54 This oversimplifies the problem of objectivity by assuming that reproducibility constitutes objectivity and that providing a record of research makes it possible to reproduce results. **1981** *Times Lit. Suppl.* 13 Feb. 169/4 The illustrations to Milton.. might suggest that one thing Blake liked about printmaking was the sheer fact of reproducibility, for a surprising proportion of the Milton pictures exist in two or more copies.

repro'ducible (riː-), *a.* [f. as REPRODUCER + -IBLE.] That may be reproduced; admitting or susceptible of reproduction.

1834 HT. MARTINEAU *Moral* I. 4 The first constitutes fixed capital; the second and third reproducible capital. **1883** *Fortn. Rev.* 1 Aug. 275 The results of scientific discoveries ..are, as a rule, reproducible at will. **1949** E. P. ABRAHAM et al. in H. W. Florey et al. *Antibiotics* II. VIII. xv. 637 The initial experiments were concerned with finding reproducible conditions for obtaining penicillin. **1972** *Physics Bull.* Jan. 15/1 Atomic clocks now provide a unit of time reproducible to 1 part in 10^{12}.

Hence **repro'ducibly** *adv.*

1961 *Jrnl. Physical Chem.* LXV. 317/2 The round cells were reproducibly positioned in the light beam which entered the thermostated mineral oil-bath through a window. **1974** *Nature* 13 Dec. 589/1 A survey of various brain regions of the rat revealed that cell-free fractions from the corpus striatum contained adenyl cyclase which was reproducibly activated by low concentrations of D-LSD.

reproduction (riːprəˈdʌkʃən). [f. REPRODUCE, after *production*; cf. F. *reproduction* (1690).]

1. a. The action or process of forming, creating or bringing into existence again.

1659 PEARSON *Creed* (1839) 361 Things immaterial and incorruptible cannot be said to rise again; resurrection implying a reproduction. **1666** BOYLE *Orig. Formes & Qual.* Wks. 1772 III. 61 The experiment recorded by our author about the reproduction of salt-petre. **1776** ADAM SMITH *W.N.* II. v. (1869) I. 368 No equal quantity of productive labour employed in manufactures can ever occasion so great a reproduction. **1845** H. ROGERS *Ess.* (1874) I. iii. 107 We shall as soon see the reproduction of an Aristotle as of a Demosthenes. **1845** McCULLOCH *Taxation* Introd. (1852) 6 A system of taxation acting on capital..destroys alike the desire and the means of reproduction.

b. The process, on the part of certain animals, of reproducing parts of the organism which have been destroyed or removed. (Now freq. called *regeneration* to distinguish it from next.)

1727–38 CHAMBERS *Cycl.* s.v., The reproduction of several parts of lobsters, crabs, etc. makes one of the great curiosities in natural history. **1774** GOLDSM. *Nat. Hist.* VIII. 172 We owe the first discovery of this power of reproduction in animals to Mr. Trembley, who first observed it in the polypus. **1840** tr. *Cuvier's Anim. Kingd.* 18 Organized beings have even the faculty of reproducing.. certain of their parts of which they may have been deprived. This has been named the power of reproduction. **1884** *Mind* July 415 The question of the Reproduction of Lost Parts is interesting from several points of view in biology.

c. The process of producing new individuals of the same species by some form of generation; the generative production of new animal or vegetable organisms by or from existing ones; also, power of reproducing in this way. Also *attrib.* as ***reproduction rate***.

1782 J. WESLEY in *Arminian Mag.* Oct. 545 He [*sc.* Buffon] substitutes for the plain word *Generation*, a quaint word of his own, *Reproduction*, in order to level man not only with the beasts that perish, but with nettles or onions. **1785** SMELLIE tr. *Buffon's Nat. Hist.* (1791) II. 16 And, without limiting our research to the generation of man, or of any particular animal, let us contemplate the general phænomena of reproduction. **1835–6** *Todd's Cycl. Anat.* I. 145 When we examine animals in the next grade, we find reproduction taking place by the concurrence of sexes. **1861** BENTLEY *Man. Bot.* 749 Much difference of opinion has arisen..as to the mode in which reproduction takes place in the different divisions of the Vegetable Kingdom. **1883** WALLEM *Fish Supply Norway* 10 (Fish. Exhib. Publ.), The reproduction of the cod is extraordinarily great. **1928**, etc. Reproduction rate [see GROSS *a.* 6 a]. **1936** *Discovery* Sept. 298/1 It is the net reproduction rate which measures whether the population is maintaining itself or not.

d. The action or process of bringing again before the mind in the same form.

1800 FELLOWES *Chr. Philos.* (ed. 3) 232 *note*, I suppose ideas to be..capable of excitement and reproduction. **1836–7** SIR W. HAMILTON *Metaph.* (1877) II. xx. 13 By reproduction..I strictly mean the process of recovering the absent thought from unconsciousness. **1884** T. SULLY *Outlines Psychol.* 477 Fear and anger have their rise in the mental reproduction of some organic pain.

e. The action or process of repeating in a copy. Also *attrib.*

1856 KAY & JOHNSON *Rep. Cases in Chancery* II. 285 Having regard to the international treaties, the Plaintiff reserves his right of reproduction, which is a sufficiently apt word in this case. **1870** W. A. COPINGER *Law of Copyright in Works of Lit.* vi. 101 Copyright may be infringed..by reproduction under an abridged form. **1883** HALDANE *Workshop Receipts* Ser. II. 181/1 Autographs for reproduction must be written with ink or pencil. **1890** *Anthony's Photogr. Bull.* III. 247 For the photographer who is exclusively occupied with reproduction photography, this is fully satisfactory. **1923** H. CRANE *Let.* 21 June (1965) 137 He is offering..$25.00 for the original, and the reproduction rights without any payment. **1967** KARCH & BUBER *Offset Processes* iv. 71 The cost of reproduction (photographable) proofs..brought about the obvious question.

f. *Econ.* In Marxist theory, the process by which given capital is maintained for further production by the conversion of part of its product into capital; ***simple reproduction***, reproduction in which the amount of capital remains constant, any surplus value being consumed; ***enlarged, expanded*** (etc.) ***reproduction***, reproduction in which the amount of capital is increased by conversion of part of the surplus value into additional means of production. Also *attrib.*

1887 MOORE & AVELING tr. *Marx's Capital* II. xxiii. 578 The conditions of production are also those of reproduction. *Ibid.* 579 If this revenue serve the capitalist only as a fund to provide for his consumption..then..simple reproduction will take place. *Ibid.* 582 The value of the capital advanced divided by the surplus-value annually consumed, gives the number of years, or reproduction periods [etc.]. **1939** *Rev. Econ. Stud.* VII. 32 According to Marx's analysis, in the case of enlarged reproduction, if gross investment..is not larger than $c_1 + c_2$..there would be no net accumulation of capital at all. **1955** M. DOBB *Econ. Theory & Socialism* xvi. 266 These examples were designed to show the relations which would need to hold for expanded reproduction (i.e. a process of annual net investment) to take place and continue of its own momentum. **1965** B. PEARCE tr. *Preobrazhensky's New Economics* 62 The consciously adopted economic policy of the State is quite often not a reaction to the difficulties encountered in practice in developing socialist reproduction. **1970** B. BREWSTER tr. *Althusser & Balibar's Reading Capital* III. iii. 266 The analysis of reproduction destroys the appearance..of a 'free' contract between the worker and the capitalist. **1975** *Chinese Econ. Studies* VIII. IV. 79 In the course of reproduction, the scale of operation would not have expanded... This reproduction based on the original scale is called simple reproduction.

g. The process of reproducing sound; the degree of fidelity with which this is done.

1908 *Sears, Roebuck Catal.* 195/2 The Type FH Harvard Disc Talking Machine... Perfectly uniform speed, essential to perfect reproduction, is obtained. **1924** *Radio Times* 19 Dec. 619/2 (Advt.), Sound reproduction that is very near perfection. **1946** *Penguin Music Mag.* Dec. 93 The standard of reproduction with which people appear to be content, even very musical people, is far from satisfactory. **1962** *Times* 5 July 15/4 It would be foolish to assume that sound reproduction has reached a stage of ultimate perfection;.. research is constantly in progress both on ways of improving reproduction from discs and on alternative means of reproduction. **1978** *Gramophone* July 275/1 If headphones are what you want, you will not be disappointed. The reproduction of classical music or pop, piano, voices, orchestra—all are splendid.

2. a. A copy or counterpart; in recent use *esp.* a copy of a picture or other work of art by means of engraving or some other process. Also, in more recent use, an article of furniture, etc., in a style reproduced from an earlier period. Freq. *attrib.*

1807 J. BARLOW *Columb.* II. 88 More perfect some, and some less perfect yield Their reproductions in this wondrous field. **1853** J. H. NEWMAN *Hist. Sk.* (1873) II. I. i. 23 The Huns were but reproductions of the ancient Scythians. **1892** *Photogr. Ann.* II. 111 The hypothesis as to the nature of heliochromic reproductions. **1925** C. CAMP in *Scribner's Mag.* Sept. 318 People who call your best pieces reproductions when you know that they are not. **1925** *Scribner's Mag.* Oct. 15 (Advt.), A reproduction whale-oil lamp which measures 18½ inches to the top of the bulb. **1964** *Times Rev. Industry* Mar. 37/3 Sales [of furniture] are growing (unfortunately, almost entirely of 'reproduction' styles, which do not help our attempts to project an image of a new Britain). **1975** M. KENYON *Mr Big* xx. 190 Some reproduction Chippendale dining-chairs. **1977** *Whitaker's Almanack 1978* 887/1 The footwear industry is based on Florence, reproduction furniture at Cascini and Poggibonsi. **1981** J. B. HILTON *Playground of Death* vi. 71 There were one or two expensive reproduction pieces—a corner cupboard (for drinks) and a Jacobean footstool.

b. A representation in some form or by some means of the essential features of a thing.

1844 EMERSON *Nature, Commodity* Wks. (Bohn) II. 144 The useful arts are reproductions or new combinations by the wit of man, of the same natural benefactors. **1856** STANLEY *Sinai & Pal.* Pref. 22 The Bedouin tents are still the faithful reproduction of the outward life of the patriarchs. **1879** FARRAR *St. Paul* (1883) 71 St. Luke's dramatic reproduction of the vague murmurs of a throng.

3. Special Combs.: **reproduction constant** or **factor** *Nuclear Physics* = *multiplication constant* or *factor*; **reproduction proof** *Printing*, a printed proof for use as an original for further, photographic, reproduction.

1962 *Newnes Conc. Encycl. Nucl. Energy* 729/1 **Reproduction constant.* This is an alternative, and less-frequently used, name for the multiplication factor..of a reactor. **1945** H. D. SMYTH *Gen. Acct. Devel. Atomic Energy Mil. Purposes* iv. 35 The whole success or failure of the uranium project depended on the multiplication factor k, sometimes called the *reproduction factor. **1947** *Science* 10 Jan. 28/1 Usually, *k* is called the 'reproduction factor' of the system. A self-sustaining chain reaction evidently is possible only when $k > 1$. **1952** GLASSTONE & EDLUND *Elem. Nucl. Reactor Theory* iv. 79 A multiplication factor or reproduction factor, defined as the ratio of the number of neutrons of any one generation to the number of corresponding neutrons of the immediately preceding generation. **1948** R. R. KARCH *Graphic Arts Procedures* 370/1 (Index), *Reproduction proofs. **1949** MELCHER & LARRICK *Printing & Promotion Handbk.* 246/2 Reproduction proofs must be perfect—if anything, more perfect than would be acceptable in finished copy, since every slightest flaw will be duplicated in the whole run. **1967** Reproduction proof [see REPRO 1].

reproductive (riːprəˈdʌktɪv), *a.* [f. REPRODUCE, after *productive*.]

1. Of the nature of, pertaining to, or effecting, reproduction.

1753 CHAMBERS *Cycl. Supp.* App. s.v. *Reproduction*, What is said of the want of the reproductive power of these parts, relates only to the head and tail ends. **1830** LYELL *Princ. Geol.* I. 200 We might divide the consideration of springs.. into their destroying and reproductive agency. **1865** MERIVALE *Rom. Emp.* VIII. lxviii. 335 The slave population was not reproductive; it was only kept at its level by fresh drafts from abroad. **1890** 'R. BOLDREWOOD' *Col. Reformer* (1891) 241 Plans of reproductive outlay, certain to pay cent per cent.

2. *spec.* in *Biol.* Connected with or effecting generative reproduction in animals or plants.

1836–9 *Todd's Cycl. Anat.* II. 412/1 This type of the reproductive apparatus extends through a wide range of animals. **1859** *Ibid.* V. 220/1 Reproductive organs of the red Algæ. **1870** ROLLESTON *Anim. Life* Introd. 47 The reproductive system has furnished a basis for the division of the Class Mammalia. **1888** ROLLESTON & JACKSON *Anim. Life* 208 Ordinary nephridia, which take on a sexual function at the reproductive season.

Hence **repro'ductively**, **repro'ductiveness**, **reproduc'tivity**.

1860 PUSEY *Min. Proph.* 167 Moab..had the degrading worship of Baal-peor, re-productiveness. **1873** SYMONDS *Grk. Poets* viii. 240 A profound sympathy with nature in her large and perpetual reproductiveness. **1881** *Academy* 30 Apr. 322 The common impressionability and reproductivity of nervous tissue. **1883** *Chicago Advance* 3 May, None can ..have been so reproductively fruitful as that first one.

reproductive (riːprəˈdʌktɪv), *sb. Zool.* [f. the adj.] A reproductive insect.

1934 C. A. KOFOID *Termites* i. 8 The alates become functional reproductives only after they leave the parent colony and, in isolation, start a new one. **1971** E. O. WILSON *Insect Societies* (1972) xix. 370/2 Some of the workers are inseminated and serve as the usual reproductives. **1977** *Nature* 2 June 395/3 At a critical time..approximately one generation time before the season ends, the entire effort is thrown into producing reproductives (queens and males).

repro'ductor. *rare*⁻¹. [f. REPRODUCE *v.*] An animal used for reproducing its species.

1888 W. WILLIAMS *Princ. Vet. Med.* (ed. 5) 264 A Ministerial Order in Prussia prohibits the removal or use, as reproductors, of affected stallions.

repro'ductory, *a. rare.* [Cf. prec. and -ORY².] 'Pertaining to or used in reproduction' (Webster 1847).

1962 *Sci. Survey* XIX. 289 Reproductory behaviour and its approximate synchronisation depend to a large extent on the action on the central nervous mechanisms of hormones.

repro'fane, *v.* [RE- 5 a.] *trans.* To profane afresh.

1614 SYLVESTER *Bethulia's Rescue* I. 194 If this thine Altar ..Be re-profan'd with Heathen Hecatombs.

reproffe, obs. form of REPROOF.

†**re'proffer**, *v. Obs. rare.* [RE- 5 a.] *intr.* Of a stag: To turn back into the water again.

1486 *Bk. St. Albans* E vij, Therfore it is (Profre) as thyse hunters sayne And (Reprofre) yf the same waye he torne agayne. **1602** *2nd Pt. Return fr. Parnass.* II. v. 907 The Hart presently discended to the Riuer, and being in the water, proferd, and reproferd, and proferd againe.

re'profile, *v.* [RE- 5 c.] *trans.* To give a new profile to; to reface. So **re'profiled** *ppl. a.*; **re'profiling** *vbl. sb.*

1963 *Times* 24 May (London Underground suppl.) p. xii/5 Wheels where the steel 'tyres' are worn away may be changed for 're-profiling'. *Ibid.*, A worn pair of wheels is readily replaced by a newly reprofiled (or refaced) pair. **1964** J. SUMMERSON *Classical Lang. Archit.* iv. 29 The Mannerist idiom of Vignola whose famous cornice—re-profiled—you will at once recognize.

re'program, re'programme, *v.* [RE- 5 a.]

1. *trans.* To program differently; to supply with a new program. Also *transf.* and *fig.*

1963 [implied in REPROGRAMMING *vbl. sb.* below]. **1964** *Ann. Reg. 1963* 390 If any alteration had to be made to the map this could be done simply by re-programming the tape instead of having to redraw the map. **1972** *Listener* 6 July 13/2 A small clockwork mouse..[has] been very fully wound up and pointed in a certain direction, but there doesn't seem to be any means of re-programming it on the way. **1973** *Publishers Weekly* 18 June 9 (Advt.), Shows the hitherto unsuccessful dieter how to 'reprogram' himself for lifetime slimness. **1974** *News & Courier* (Charleston, S. Carolina) 21 Apr. C-10/2 The birds were taken from their nests as babies and were raised as pets. Ben David now is trying to reprogram the birds to fly free and kill to eat and live. **1977** D. RAMSAY *You can't call it Murder* I. 63 He resumed..questions. Bam, bam, bam. As if he were re-programming a computer.

2. To allocate to different spending programmes.

1971 *Hearings Comm. Armed Services, U.S. Senate 92nd Congress 1st Sess.* (S. 939) III. 2093 Fiscal year 1967 Navy funds were reprogramed to match maritime administration funds for program initiation.

So **'reprogramming** *vbl. sb.*; also **re'programmable** *a.*

1963 *Rep. Comm. Inquiry Decimal Currency* xiv. 138 in *Parl. Papers 1962–3* (Cmnd. 2145) XI. 195 Ancillary machine costs:..re-programming of computers. **1971** J. Z. YOUNG *Introd. Study Man* xxii. 302 This reprogramming of the read-out of the DNA may serve to bring into play a new complex of enzyme systems. **1974** *Jrnl. Politics* XXXVI. 77 One instrument for executive spending flexibility is 're-programming' of funds within an appropriation. **1978** *Sci. Amer.* Feb. 72/2 Since the machines are reprogrammable, it is feasible to apply them to the assembly of products manufactured in families of models.

reprographer (rɪˈprɒgrəfə(r)). [f. as next + -ER¹, as *photographer*, etc.] One who makes facsimile copies of documents.

1967 *Britannica Bk. of Year* 804/1 *Reprography*,.. facsimile reproduction (as by photocopying) of graphic matter (as documents); *reprographer*,..*reprographic, adj.* **1969** S. CUADRA *Ann. Rev. Information Sci.* IV. vi. 178 Old-style reprographers not only mixed their own 'soup', but they also made their own work schedules. **1972** *Libr. Resources* Spring 150 The education of library reprographers is a permanent concern.

reprographic (riːprəˈgræfɪk), *a.* and *sb.* [f. as next + -IC: see -GRAPHIC.] **A.** *adj.* Of or pertaining to reprography.

1961 *Engineering* 17 Nov. 633 Development to improve the efficiency of reprographic services. **1963** *Ibid.* 3 May 606 'Reprographic' has become recognized as the omnibus adjective for the many processes and methods now used to produce copies of documents of all kinds. **1966** *Times* 11 May 17/3 Admel International, of Weybridge, Surrey, a leading maker of what is called reprographic equipment,.. is to be sold to an American group. **1973** *Nature* 31 Aug. 535/3 As reprographic technology progresses, interlibrary affiliates grow, and..publishers are likely to find the economic realities of their business approaching prohibitiveness. **1977** *Times* 24 Oct. 3/3 Its [*sc.* HMSO's] empire includes printing presses, binderies, warehouses, bookshops, reprographic units and laboratories.

B. *sb. pl.* (const. as *sing.*) = next.

1967 *Financial Times* 15 Mar. 21/2 The expansion in reprographics has had to call on many branches of technology to cope with the demand for better machines. **1969** *Daily Tel.* (Colour Suppl.) 31 Jan. 13/1 (Advt.), Reprographics: a word coined little over five years ago to describe the means used to reproduce the enormous volumes of drawn, typed and written material which has to be circulated in industry, commerce and government today. **1975** B. J. PERRY in Barr & Line *Ess. Information & Libraries* 119 Information science research is a complex area that requires the application of skills from many different disciplines, including..reprographics. **1980** *Financial Rev.* 5 Mar. 21/4 A 30 per cent drop in world demand for reprographics products.

reprography (rɪˈprɒgrəfɪ). [ad. G. *reprographie*, f. *repro-duktion* REPRODUCTION + *photo-graphie* PHOTOGRAPHY.] The branch of technology concerned with the copying and reproduction of documentary and graphic material.

1961 *Bibliogr., Documentation, Terminol.* I. 105 The term 'reprography' is today used to cover all processes for the photographic reproduction and multicopying of documents. **1962** *Archives* V. 235 *Reprography.* This new and convenient, though not very likeable, word is a collective term for the processes of facsimile reproduction of documents, whether by means of photographic, electronic or other methods. **1963** *Special Libraries* Dec. 646/1 The term 'reprography', coined about ten years ago, is intended to describe all methods of facsimile reproduction of documentary materials with the exception of conventional printing. Although little used in the United States, the term is achieving considerable popularity in Europe. **1967** *Financial Times* 15 Mar. 21/1 The almost unpronounceable word 'reprography' is in. It covers a field with ill-defined boundaries, edging at its simplest into pencil-making and at its most sophisticated into desk-top photosetting. **1977** *Author* Summer 67 Cassettes and other forms of electronic storage are examples of what is becoming known as reprography.

repro'ject, *v.* [RE- 5 a.] To plan again.

1795 WOLCOTT (P. Pindar) *Hair Powder* Wks. 1812 III. 301 Where thou, and honest Rumbold-hunting Harry Project and reproject and oft miscarry.

re'promise, *sb. rare*⁻¹. [RE- 5 a.] A renewed or further promise.

1750 HODGES *Chr. Plan* (1755) 171 This repromise supposes plainly, that there was one prior to any, that is mentioned by the prophets.

†**re'promise**, *v. Obs.* [ad. L. *reprōmittĕre*: see next and PROMISE *v.*] *trans.* To promise in return. Hence **re'promised** *ppl. a.*

1526 *Pilgr. Perf.* (W. de W. 1531) 231 The..crowne of lyfe whiche god hath repromysed to all them that loueth hym. *a* **1618** SYLVESTER *Job* II. 175 How shall that Hap appear, Which you yer-while did so re-promise, hear? **1620** T. GRANGER *Div. Logike* 219 Whereby God promiseth his grace, and loue vnto men, and men repromise constant obedience due to him. **1633** BP. HALL *Hard Texts, N.T.* 496 The extending of the bounds of this repromised land towards the north.

†**repro'mission.** *Obs.* Also 4 -myscioun, -miscioun, 4–5 -myssioun, 6 -myssyon. [a. OF. *repromission*, or ad. L. *reprōmissiōn-em*, f. *reprōmittĕre*: see next.] A counter-promise, a promise made in return. *land of repromission*, the promised land.

1382 WYCLIF *Heb.* vi. 15 So he longe suffringe gaat repromyscioun, or biheeste aȝen. *c* **1400** MAUNDEV. (Roxb.) Pref. 1 Þe land of repromission, þat men calles þe Haly Land. **1526** *Pilgr. Perf.* (W. de W. 1531) 1 The passage of the chyldren of Israel..through the reed see towarde the lande of repromyssyon. **1642** CHAS. I. *Let.* 14 June, The humble Repromission and Resolution of the Captains and Souldiers. **1659** R. GELL *Amendm. Bible* 85 Repromission or answering by promise to God's stipulation. **1692** *Covt. Grace Conditional* 29 By Conditions I understand the restipulation or repromission in a Covenant.

†**repro'mit**, *v. Obs. rare*⁻¹. [ad. L. *reprōmittĕre*, f. *re-* RE- + *prōmittĕre* to promise. Cf. obs. F. *repromettre*.] To promise in return.

1637–50 ROW *Hist. Kirk* (Wodrow Soc.) 26 A faire ansuer ..was returned by the Queen, and the Assemblie repromitts to be loveing,..and obedient subjects to hir Majestie.

re'promulgate (riː), *v.* [RE- 5 a.] *trans.* To promulgate again.

1847 in WEBSTER. **1866** *Macm. Mag.* Feb. 273 The fundamental principle of persecution has been distinctly repromulgated. **1871** FARRAR *Witn. Hist.* iii. 117 The tenth Lateran Council found it necessary to repromulgate the doctrine of immortality.

So **repromul'gation.**

a **1754** MᶜLAURIN *Serm. & Ess.* (1755) 243 The clear repromulgation of that law..has far superior effects.

reproof¹ (rɪˈpruːf). Forms: α. 4 reproef, 4–5 reprof, 4–6 reprofe, 5–6 reproffe, 5–7 reproofe, (6 -proufe), 5– reproof; 4–6 reproue, (4 -pruve, 5 -prowe), 5–6 reprove; also 5–6 *Sc.* repruf(e, -pruff, (5 -prwfe, -prwe), 6 repruif. β. 4–5 repref, (5 -preff, -preffe), 4–6 reprefe, -preef, (6 -fe), 5–6 *Sc.* repreif(e, 6 reprief(e, -prife, reypriff; 4–6 repreue, -preve, 6 repreeve, -prieve, -prive. [a. OF. *reprove*, *-prouve* (AF. also *repreove*), vbl. sb. f. *reprover* to REPROVE. On the variation in the forms see PROOF *sb.*]

†**1.** Shame, disgrace, ignominy or reproach, adhering or resulting to a person in consequence or by reason of some fact, event, conduct, etc. (Occas. with *a* and *pl.*) *Obs.*

α. **13..** *Seuyn Sag.* (W.) 2871 Methink thou wirkis, to thi reproue, Onence thi son that thou sold loue. **1340** HAMPOLE *Pr. Consc.* 5555 Thurgh defaute of hym er þai In grete reprove. *c* **1400** LOVE *Bonavent. Mirr. Life Xt.* (B.N.C.) lf. 14 It is abhomynable þynge and a grete reproofe to a mayden ..to be a grete iangelere. *c* **1500** *Lancelot* 1252 Madem, I wot that for to loue yone knycht,..It war to yow no maner of Reprwe. **1569** *Reg. Privy Council Scot.* II. 56 Under the pane of repruif, infamy, and perjurie. **1590** SHAKS. *Com. Err.* v. i. 90 She did betray me to my owne reproofe. *a* **1631** DONNE *Serm.* (1640) 360 If..thou return..to the Repursuite of those half-repented Sins..: This is a Reproofe.

β. *c* **1380** *Sir Ferumb.* 404 Ne were it for repreue, By Mahoun, þat ys my vowee of þyn heued y wolde þee reue. *c* **1386** CHAUCER *Pard. T.* 595 It is repreeue and contrarie of honour For to ben holde a commune hasardour. **1430–40** LYDG. *Bochas* v. xxxii. (1554) 141 b, Bochas list not expresse More of his life fulfilled of all repreues. **1513** DOUGLAS *Æneis* I. Prol. 435 That war repreif to thair diuinite, And na reproche vnto the said Enee. **1567** *Lucres & Eur.* H iv b, Yf I shoulde carye thee about wyth me,..what reprefe and shame shulde it be both to the and me?

†**b.** One who, or that which, is a disgrace or discredit to something. *Obs. rare.*

c **1436** *Pol. Poems* (Rolls) II. 148 Thow Phellippe, foundour of new falsehede, Distroubar of pees,..reprof of alle knyghthode. **1501** DOUGLAS *Pal. Hon.* I. i, Schaw now thy schame,..schaw thy endite reprufe of rethoryis.

†**2.** Insulting or opprobrious language or action used against a person; insult, contumely, scorn. *Obs.*

α. *a* **1340** HAMPOLE *Psalter* xiv. 4 Reprofe that was sayd agayns men he accept it noght. *c* **1380** WYCLIF *Sel. Wks.* III. 336 More men wondren whi þei cursen..not for reprofe don to Crist and his majeste. *a* **1400** *Prymer* (1891) 97 (Ps. cxix. 22), Bere awey fro me reprof and despyt. **1596** DALRYMPLE tr. *Leslie's Hist. Scot.* x. 284 Lenox selfe thay cast doune to the Inglis schipis farr of with gret reprofe.

β. *c* **1380** WYCLIF *Serm.* Sel. Wks. I. 34 To þe repreef of Crist þei clepide him a Samaritan. *c* **1460** *Play Sacram.* 456 As he was on yᵉ rode that he was on don wᵗ grett repreue.

c **1510** MORE *Picus* Wks. 15/2 God had accepted them as worthy to suffer wronge and repriefe for his sake.

†**b.** With *a* and *pl.* An instance of this; an insult in word or deed. *Obs.*

α. a **1340** HAMPOLE *Psalter* cxxii. 4 Oure saule trauayls in reprofis and oure body in passiouns. *c* **1400** MAUNDEV. (Roxb.) Pref. 1 He sufferd many reprufes and scornes by vs. **1480** CAXTON *Chron. Eng.* cxcviii. 176 They cast vpon hym many snowe balles and many other reproues dyd him.

β. c **1330** R. BRUNNE *Chron. Wace* (Rolls) 7996 Bytwyxt to þer a stryf þey herde, Of grete reprefs ilk oþer onswerde. **1382** WYCLIF *Ecclus.* xxix. 9 And repreues and cursis he shal ȝelde to hym. *c* **1450** tr. *De Imitatione* II. i. 40 Crist was.. in his grettist nede among repreues forsaken of his frendes. **1549** CHALONER *Erasm. on Folly* B ij b, Euen these sage Stoikes dooe not in deede so greatly despise pleasure, as outwardly thei dissemble, and afore folks dooe baite hir with a thousand repreues. **1597** *Guistard & Sismond* B ij, As to the great repreeve also contrived, which alder first ayen me ye object.

†**c.** An object of scorn or contempt. *Obs.*

a **1340** HAMPOLE *Psalter* xxi. 5, I am a worm and noght man, reproue of men & outkastynge of folke. **1382** WYCLIF *Judith* vii. 16 Betere it is.. than wee die, and be repref to alle flesh. **1535** COVERDALE *Ps.* xxx. 11, I am become a very reprofe amonge all myne enemies.

3. Censure, rebuke, reprimand, reprehension.

α. c **1350** *Will. Palerne* 652 Alisandrine.. bi-þouȝt hire ful busily howe best were to werche,.. properly vnparceyued for reproue after. **1422** tr. *Secreta Secret., Priv. Priv.* 189 Reprowe was founde for amendement of hym that Is reprowid. **1538** STARKEY *England* I. iv. 139 They may abase themselfe in al vayn lustys & vanyte, wythout punyschement or reproue of any degre. **1568** GRAFTON *Chron.* II. 662 In reproofe of Jasper Erle of Penbroke, he created William Lord Herbert Erle of the same place. **1607** SHAKS. *Cor.* II. ii. 37 A Mallice, that.. would plucke reproofe and rebuke from euery Eare that heard it. **1611** BIBLE *Prov.* xv. 5 A foole despiseth his fathers instruction: but hee that regardeth reproofe, is prudent. **1709** POPE *Ess. Crit.* 583 Those best can bear reproof, who merit praise. **1848** DICKENS *Dombey* ii, Mrs. Chick contented herself with a glance of reproof.

β. **1382** WYCLIF *Matt.* xi. 20 Thanne Jhesus began for to seie repreue to citees. *c* **1400** *Rom. Rose* 7240 Men.. holden us for so worthy, That we may folk repreve echoon, And we nyl have repref of noon. *a* **1548** HALL *Chron., Hen. IV* 7 He .. suffered them to robbe and pill without correction or reprefe. **1600** FAIRFAX *Tasso* XVI. xlv, I thee enchanted and allur'd to loue, Wicked deceit, craft worthie sharpe repriefe.

Comb. **1382** WYCLIF I *Esdr.* Prol., The studies of enuyouse men.. that alle thing that we wryten, weenen repref wrthi.

b. With *a* and *pl.* A censure, rebuke, etc.

α. **1513** DOUGLAS *Æneis* I. Prol. 452 Of resoun me behuvis Excuse Chaucer fra all maner repruvis. **1548** UDALL, etc. *Erasm. Par. Matt.* ix. 41 Unto this manifest and false reprofe .. Jesus aunswered verey gentelye. **1794** MRS. RADCLIFFE *Myst. Udolpho* xii, How have I deserved these reproofs? **1879** FARRAR *St. Paul* I. VI. xxiii. 445 A reproof is intolerable when it is administered out of pride or hatred.

β. **1549** CHALONER *Erasm. on Folly* L ij, What maistrie is it for them to set light store by two or three of those learned mens reprives. **1596** DALRYMPLE tr. *Leslie's Hist. Scot.* IV. 238 Pape Honorie, throuch scharpe writeings, accused his wickednes wᵗ a sour repreife.

†**4. a.** The condition of being under censure or disapproval. *Obs. rare.*

c **1374** CHAUCER *Troylus* II. 370 (419), Ye nold han had no mercy ne mesure On me, but alwey had me in repreue. *c* **1420** *Pallad. on Husb.* II. 151 Ther as wrecchid greues, Sour lond, to weet, or salt is, neuer delue; And alwey thristy dri lond in repreue is.

†**b.** Cause for censure; fault, blame. *Obs.*

c **1375** *Sc. Leg. Saints* x. (*Matthew*) 367 Matrimone he can commend, gyf þat it will anowrnyt be.. & but reprufe kepit alsa. **1413** *Pilgr. Sowle* (Caxton) IV. xxix. (1859) 62 All thyng .. shold ben.. good, and commendable, that noo repreef were founden therin. **1567** *Gude & Godlie B.* (S.T.S.) 31 Do gude for euill, and leid ȝour lyfe Without reprufe.

5. Disproof, refutation. Now *rare* or *Obs.*

1529 MORE *Dyaloge* IV. Wks. 272/1 There were shewed vnto hym manye thynges for the reproofe of that vnresonable and detestable heresye. **1664** JER. TAYLOR *Dissuas. Popery* II. title-p., In.. reproof and conviction of Roman Errors. **1739** LABELYE *Short Acc. Piers Westm. Bridge* 38 As to the many false Reports.. I leave the Piers of Westminster-Bridge, to give them the strongest Reproofs. **1814** CARY *Dante, Parad.* III. 3 By proof of right, and of the false reproof.

Hence †**re'proofful** *a.*; **re'proofless** *a.*

1609 *Ev. Woman in Hum.* IV. i. in Bullen *O. Pl.* IV, This critique is hoarsh, unsaverie, and reproofeful. **1827–35** WILLIS *David's Grief for Child* 18 The rapt wires of his reproofless harp.

re-proof[2] (riː-). [RE- 5 a.] A second proof.

c **1825** CAMPBELL in *New Monthly Mag.* (1847) May 74, I must leave you to correct this dull essay on the London College, yet if I could have a re-proof it would be desirable.

repro'pitiate, *v.* (and *pa. pple.*). *rare.* [ad. L. *repropitiāre* (Tert. and Vulg.).] *trans.* †To make propitiation for (a thing or person) again; to restore to favour. So **repropiti'ation**.

1582 N.T. (Rhem.) *Heb.* ii. 17 That he might repropitiate the sinnes of the people. **1617** BP. ANDREWES 96 *Serm., Holy Ghost* x. (1629) 708 Accepted to repropitiation, that is ἱλασμός, to as good grace, and favour as ever. *Ibid.*, [Absalom was] repropitiate, when he was admitted to the king's presence and kissed him.

repro'posal. [RE- 5 a.] A fresh proposal.

1650 B. *Discolliminium* 44 In his Reproposalls he tenders a faire Treaty.

re'prosecute (riː-), *v.* [RE- 5 a.] *trans.* To prosecute again.

1701 NORRIS *Ideal World* I. iii. 175 To unstring my instrument for a while, and reprosecute our theory.

reprovable (rɪ'pruːvəb(ə)l), *a.* ? *Obs.* Forms: *α.* 4–6 **reprouable**, (4–5 **-abil**), 6 **reproueable**, (6–8 **-veable**), 6–7 **reprooueable**, 4– **reprovable**. *β.* 4–5 **repreuable**, 5 **-v(e)able**, **repreev-**, **reprefable**, 6 **repryuable**. [f. as REPROVE *v.* + -ABLE, after med.L. *reprobābilis* (Du Cange): cf. F. *réprouvable* (14th c., Oresme).] Deserving of reproof or censure; blameworthy, reprehensible.

In common use (in the *α*-forms) from *c* 1380 to 1650.

α. a **1340** HAMPOLE *Psalter* xxxviii. 2, I sett kepynge til my mouth.. þat nane reprouabil word withpassid me. *c* **1380** WYCLIF *Wks.* (1880) 292 Also seynt poul iugiþ of petris synne, and aȝen-stoode him for he was reprouable. *a* **1471** FORTESCUE *Wks.* (1869) 490, I se the naughty and reprovable people helped with richesses. **1589** PUTTENHAM *Eng. Poesie* I. xxvi. (Arb.) 65 The ancient guise in old times vsed at weddings (in my simple opinion) nothing reproueable. **1660** JER. TAYLOR *Worthy Commun.* i. §5. 101 Thy faith was not only little but reprovable. **1746** WESLEY *Princ. Methodist* 3 Those.. who may be hinder'd, by their Prejudice in my Favour,.. from observing what is reproveable.

β. **1382** WYCLIF *Prov.* xxv. 10 The whiche kepe thou to thee, lest thou be maad repreuable. *c* **1400** tr. *Secreta Secret., Gov. Lordsh.* 66 In þayre secretz and writynges no fals þynge ne repreuable ys founden. *c* **1460** SIR R. ROS *La Belle Dame* 512 Yit atte lest y am nat repreuable. **1526** SKELTON *Magnyf.* 1436 That I shall suffer none impechment.. nor losse repryuable.

Hence †**re'provableness** (Bailey vol. II, 1727); †**re'provably** *adv.*

c **1449** PECOCK *Repr.* I. x. 50 Wherfore folewith that he vnresonabili and reprouabili askith.

reproval (rɪ'pruːvəl). [f. next + -AL[1].] The act of reproving; reproof.

1846 WORCESTER cites *Gentl. Mag.* **1872** *Athenæum* 28 Dec. 845/3 To.. expiate their enthusiastic adherence by an equally enthusiastic reproval. **1895** *Chicago Advance* 20 June 1353/1 The reproval and stultification of the Christian communities.

reprove (rɪ'pruːv), *v.*[1] Forms: *α.* 4–7 **reproue**, (4 **reproeve**, **-pruue**), 6–7 **reprooue**, **-ve**, 4– **-reprove**; 5 **reprof(f**, also *Sc.* **reprow**, **-pruff**, 5–6 **-prufe**, 6 **-proif**, **-prw**. *β.* 4–6 **repreue**, **-ve**, (4 **repreove**), 5–6 **repref(e**, 6–7 **reprieve**, **-prive**; also *Sc.* 5 **rapreiff**, 5–6 **reprew**, (6 **ra-**), 6 **repreif**, **-prief**. [ad. OF. *reprover* (AF. also *repruver*; mod.F. *réprouver*):—L. *reprobāre*: see REPROBATE *v.* The *β*-forms are from those parts of the verb in which the stem had stress (AF. *repreov-*, OF. *repreuv-*): see PROVE *v.*]

†**1.** *trans.* To reject. *Obs.*

a **1340** HAMPOLE *Psalter* xx. 12 Amange þe deuels of hell, þe whilke þou has forsaken and reproued. **1382** WYCLIF *Luke* xx. 17 The stoon whom men bildinge reproueden [**1388** repreueden], this is maad in to the heed of the corner. *c* **1450** *Mirour Saluacioun* 3474 The stone whilk the biggers reproved in the heved is made angulere. **1526** TINDALE *Heb.* vi. 8 That grounde which beareth thornes and bryars is reproved and is nye vnto cursynge. **1582** BENTLEY *Mon. Matrones* 69 It seemeth to them God is parciall, bicause he hath elected some, and some reproued. **1604** E. G[RIMSTONE] *D'Acosta's Hist. Indies* II. xii. 109, I am almost ready to follow the opinion of such as reproove the qualities .. which Aristotle gives vnto the Elements, saying they are but imaginations.

†**b.** *Sc.* To set aside as invalid. *Obs. rare*[−1].

1480 *Act. Dom. Conc.* (1839) 52/1 þat þe saidis provost, chanonis, & chapelanis, sall brouke & Joyse þe said landis.. quhil þe said lettre be Repreifit & declarit of na vale.

2. To express disapproval of (conduct, actions, beliefs, etc.); to censure, condemn. Now *rare.*

α. **1340–70** *Alex. & Dind.* 220 þat non haþel.. mihte alegge any lak our lif to reproue. **1432–50** tr. *Higden* (Rolls) III. 401 Thyne arte is to be reprovede that schewede not this to the before. **1483** CAXTON *Cato* F viij, Tho ben fooles that blamen and reprouen the tyme, sayeng that the tyme is cause of theyr sekenesse. **1579** GOSSON *Sch. Abuse* (Arb.) 54 If he come to our stall, and reproue our ballance when they are faultie. **1615** J. STEPHENS *Satyr. Ess.* 20 Envy loves That humor best, which bitterly reproves All states. **1658** EVELYN *Fr. Gard.* (1675) 58, I do not utterly reprove the graffing of the wood, though but of one year. **1770** GOLDSM. *Des. Vill.* 169 He tried each art, reproved each dull delay. **1820** SHELLEY *Fiordispina* 40 Lulled by the voice they love, which did reprove The childish pity that she felt for them.

β. c **1380** WYCLIF *Wks.* (1880) 9 ȝif þei haten.. trewe men to techen frely holy writt and repreuen synne. *c* **1450** tr. *De Imitatione* II. ii. 42 Oþir men knowe oure defautes & repreue hem. **1513** DOUGLAS *Æneis* I. Prol. 106 My werk or ȝe repreif Considdir it warlie, reid oftair than anis. **1567** *Satir. Poems Reform.* vii. 82 Quhat preachour this repreif, I pray ȝow, durst?

3. To reprehend, rebuke, blame, chide, or find fault with (a person). Also const. *for*, †*of.*

α. a **1325** *Prose Psalter* xlix. 9 Y ne shal nouȝt repruue þe in þy sacrifices. **1340** HAMPOLE *Pr. Consc.* 5314 Alle þis sall he do þos openly To reprove þe synful men þar-by. *c* **1400** MAUNDEV. (Roxb.) xv. 70 Me thoȝt grete schame þat Sarzenes.. schuld þus reproue vs of oure inperfiteness. *c* **1450** LOVELICH *Grail* xxxvi. 8 [For] On thyng that he dyde At Rome, Reproved he was be Clergies dome. **1568** GRAFTON *Chron.* II. 729 Reproouing and reuiling him with such yll wordes.. that all the hearers abhorred it. **1667** MILTON *P.L.* x. 761 What if thy Son Prove disobedient, and reprov'd retort, Wherefore didst thou beget me? **1727** DE FOE *Syst. Magic* I. iv. (1840) 95 Others suggest, that Noah having reproved and reproached Canaan for some crime,.. the Devil took hold of his resentment. **1855** TENNYSON *Maud* I. xx. i, Was it gentle to reprove her..? **1871** B. TAYLOR *Faust* (1875) II. I. iii. 27 You praise us—reprove us, It doesn't move us.

β. **1303** R. BRUNNE *Handl. Synne* 37223yf þou for wraþþe madyst chydyng, Or repreuedyst a man of vyle þyng. **1377** LANGL. *P. Pl.* B. x. 261 God in þe gospel grymly repreueth Alle þat lakken any lyf. **1483** CAXTON *Cato* 4 Of Saynt Ambrose that repreuyed openly themperour of his synne. **1549** *Compl. Scot.* xv. 123 Thou repreifis & accusis me of the faltis that my tua brethir committis daly. **1596** SPENSER *F.Q.* V. vi. 24 Nor suffering the least twinckling sleepe to start Into her eye..; But if the least appear'd, her eyes she streight reprieved.

†**b.** To accuse or convict. *Obs. rare.*

c **1380** WYCLIF *Wks.* (1880) 30 þer-for crist seiþ to þe iewis who of ȝou schal repreue me of synne. **1382** —— *John* xvi. 8 He schal repreue the world of synne. *c* **1440** *York Myst.* xxxii. 241 Oure poynte expresse her reproues þe Of felonye falsely and felle.

†**c.** To reproach, taunt. Const. *of.* *Obs. rare*[−1].

c **1330** R. BRUNNE *Chron. Wace* (Rolls) 11665 þey repreue vs of our auncessours þat þey ouer-cam þem wyþ harde stours; Of pouerte þey make vmbreyd.

4. *absol.* To employ reprehension or rebuke.

a **1340** HAMPOLE *Psalter* xiii. 6 þaire mouth is ay redy to myssay and repreue. **1382** WYCLIF *Prov.* xxv. 10 Lest perauenture he asaile to thee, whan he shal heren, and to repreuen cese not. **1533** GAU *Richt Vay* 29 Al the writ quhilk is inspirit.. is profetabil to tech, to reprw, to correk. **1611** BIBLE *2 Tim.* iv. 2 Reprooue, rebuke, exhort with all long suffering & doctrine. **1766** FORDYCE *Serm. Yng. Wom.* (1767) I. i. 36 Reprove only when you must. **1821** SHELLEY *Epipsych.* 603 The troop which errs, and which reproves. **1876** MISS BRADDON *J. Haggard's Dau.* I. 11 He came to the water-side tavern to reprove and exhort.

†**5.** To disprove; to prove (an idea, statement, etc.) to be false or erroneous. *Obs.*

c **1374** CHAUCER *Boeth.* V. met. iv. 130 (Camb. MS.), Whan it retorneth in to hym self it reproeueth and distroyet the false thinges by the trewe thinges. **1377** LANGL. *P. Pl.* B. x. 345 'Contra', quod I, 'bi cryste þat can I repreue'. *c* **1430** *Pilgr. Lyf Manhode* I. lxxxv. (1869) 49 For to assoile better þine argumentes þat seist j haue falsed and repreved þi gretteste principle. **1538** BALE *God's Promises* II, All thys is true, Lorde, I cannot thy wordes reprove. **1593** SHAKS. *2 Hen. VI*, III. i. 40 Reproue my allegation, if you can, Or else conclude my words effectuall. **1691** RAY *Creation* I. (1692) 25 This confident Assertion of DesCartes is fully examined and reproved by.. Mr. Boyl.

†**b.** To refute or confute (a person). *Obs.*

1563 WINȜET *Four Scoir Thre Quest.* Wks. (S.T.S.) I. 101 Men in this vocatioun.. suld.. be.. potent to repreue and conuict the gainsayaris of the samin. **1585** T. WASHINGTON tr. *Nicholay's Voy.* II. ix. 42 b, Where he sayth the second to lye on the North part, he may by the view & eisight onely be reproued, being in deed towards the East. **1601** HOLLAND *Pliny* XVI. xxxi, Deceived they are, and may be reproved by the instance of fig-trees.

†**6.** To impair, diminish. *Obs. rare.*

1450–80 tr. *Secreta Secret.* 9 Kepe euyr temperaunce in largete.., ne neuer repreue thi yeftis with ayentakyng. **1576** FLEMING *Panopl. Epist.* 403 Hee sheweth that his loue is so farre from being reproued, that it is augmented. **1590** GREENWOOD *Collect. Sclaund. Artic.* G ij b, This is hit that.. maketh all the syluer saints.. to bestur them, least their portions should be reproued; They would gladly haue their portions improued.

re-prove (riː-), *v.*[2] Also 6 reprove. [RE- 5 a.] *trans.* To prove again.

1529 MORE *Dyaloge* III. Wks. 209/2 An infidell whom thei haue proued and reproued fals in his faith to God. **1572** J. JONES *Bathes Buckstone* Pref. 3 Proving & reprovinge, by most waighty arguments & best authorities al that he did. **1881** GREENER *Gun* 290 The bulges are knocked down.. and the barrel re-proved until it either bursts or stands proof. **1891** *Nature* 25 June 179/2 He re-proved the complete identity of the electricity of lightning.

reproved (rɪ'pruːvd), *ppl. a.* [f. REPROVE *v.*[1] + -ED[1].]

†**1.** Rejected; reprobate. Also *absol.* *Obs.*

c **1400** HYLTON *Scala Perf.* (W. de W. 1494) I. lxv, All other yeftes.. are com in to good & to bad, to chosen & to reproued. **1435** MISYN *Fire of Love* 6 Als chosyn, god noȝt displesys.. so repreuyd, god noȝt plesys. *c* **1450** *Mirour Saluacioun* 3462 The forsaide beelders.. Callid it be propre name the reproved stone. **1450–1530** *Myrr. of our Ladye* 143 Not amongest the reproued, but amongest hys chosen. **1523** FITZHERB. *Husb.* §144 Ydle folke shall.. sorowe with the reproued and forsaken folkes in hell.

2. Rebuked, reprehended.

1821 SHELLEY *Adonais* xlv, Oblivion as they rose shrank like a thing reproved.

†**re'provement.** *Obs. rare*[−1] [f. as prec. + -MENT.] Reproof, rebuke.

1675 COCKER *Morals* 39 Nothing can more to my improvement tend, Than the reprovement of a loving Friend.

reprover (rɪ'pruːvə(r)). [f. REPROVE *v.*[1] + -ER[1].] One who or that which reproves.

α. **1422** tr. *Secreta Secret., Priv. Priv.* 189 Whan a man Is ouer-harde reprouet, he hatyth his reprowere. *c* **1532** DU WES *Introd. Fr.* in *Palsgr.* 1017 An answere to the correcters and of all workes reprouers. **1591** HARINGTON *Orl. Fur.* Pref. ¶ ij b, But now because I make account I haue to deale with three sundrie kindes of reproouers. **1681** FLAVEL *Meth. Grace* xxviii. 474 A wise and faithful reprover is of singular use. **1741** MIDDLETON *Cicero* II. x. 362 Sulpicius was.. a reprover of the insolence of his own times. **1833** I. TAYLOR *Fanat.* i. 3 If Religion be deemed by these sarcastic reprovers altogether an illusion. **1868** SWINBURNE *Ess. &*

Stud. (1875) 342 One kneeling as reproved..; the reprover, an erect ascetic figure, stands over him.
β. **1382** WYCLIF *Prov.* xxvii. 11 Studie to wisdam,.. that thou mowe to the repreuere answern a wrd. **1435** MISYN *Fire of Love* 69 þerfore I haue þoght sum maner of answer to schew, & to repreuars fully not gyffe steed. **1570** DEE *Math. Pref.* b iij, If I would say.. that it [music] were to be otherwise vsed, then it is, I should finde more repreeuers, then I could finde.. skilfull of my meaning.

reproving (rɪˈpruːvɪŋ), *vbl. sb.* [f. as prec. + -ING¹.] The action of the verb in various senses; reproof.
a. *c* **1380** WYCLIF *Wks.* (1880) 47 It is a remembraunce, amonestynge, a reprouynge. *c* **1440** *Jacob's Well* 6 þe more þe cursed man is styred.. wyth þe wynd of techyng & of reprovyng. **1535** COVERDALE *Ecclus.* xlviii. 10 He was ordeyned in the reprouynges in tyme. **1593** SHAKS. *Lucr.* 242 The worst is but deniall and reproouing. *a* **1791** WESLEY *Serm.* Wks. 1811 IX. 265 A spirit of reproving. **1850** W. C. BENNETT *Baby May* Poems 12 Tiny scorns of smiled reprovings That have more of love than lovings.
β. *c* **1325** *Chron. Eng.* 850 Bituene Edrich ant the kyng Aros a repreofing. *c* **1400** MAUNDEV. (1839) Prol. 1 There it lykede him to suffre many Reprevinges and Scornes for us. *c* **1450** tr. *De Imitatione* II. ii. 42 The meke men receiuyng repreuinges.. is in pes wel ynowe. **1567** *Gude & Godlie B.* (S.T.S.) 152 Thay lykit not my.. Praying, fasting, nor repreuing.

reˈproving, *ppl. a.* [-ING².] That reproves.
1382 WYCLIF *Amos* v. 10 Thei hadden in hate the repreuynge man in the ȝate. **1795** SOUTHEY *Joan of Arc* IV. 343 Then the Maid Fix'd on the warrior her reproving eye.

reˈprovingly, *adv.* [f. prec. + -LY².] In a reproving manner.
1382 WYCLIF *Wisd.* ii. 12 The riȝtwis man.. repreuendeli puttith to vs the synnes of lawe. **1456** SIR G. HAYE *Law Arms* (S.T.S.) 30 Thai.. will bakbyte behynd bakkis, and reprovandly lak that thai before had lovit. **1829** SOUTHEY *Young Dragon* Epil. 4 That smile I read aright, for thus Reprovingly said she. **1885** *Harper's Mag.* Mar. 567/2 She .. shook her head reprovingly.

reproˈvision (riː-), *v.* [RE- 5 a.] **a.** *trans.* To supply with a fresh stock of provisions. **b.** *absol.* To lay in fresh provisions.
1895 *Daily News* 21 Oct. 5/7 Porters.. are effecting the re-provisioning of the town. **1898** *Westm. Gaz.* 30 June 7/1 Ships of war.. will not be able in the Canal.. to revictual or reprovision.

† **reˈpruce,** *sb. Obs. rare.* Also repruse. [a. AF. *repruce*, var. *reproce*: see REPROCE and REPROACH *sb.*] Reproach.
a **1325** *Prose Psalter* xliii. 16 þou settest us repruse to our neȝburs. *Ibid.* lxxiii. 23 Be þou þenchand of þyn repruces. *c* **1400** *Laud Troy Bk.* 7673 Ector sayde, 'whan I schal thole .. Suche vilony and suche repruse' [etc.].
So † **reˈpruce** *v. trans.*, to reproach. *Obs. rare.*
a **1325** *Prose Psalter* vi. 1 Lord, ne repruce me nouȝt in þy vengeaunce; ne reproue me nouȝt in þyn yre. *Ibid.* lxxviii. 13 ȝelde to our neȝburs seuen double in her bosme her lackinge wich, Lord, hij repruced þe.

reprune (riː-), *v.* [RE- 5 a.] To prune again.
1664 EVELYN *Kal. Hort.* July (1729) 209 Re-prune now Abricots and Peaches. **1742** YOUNG *Nt. Th.* IX. 1219 In Mid-way Flight Imagination tires; Yet soon re-prunes her Wing to soar anew.

reprw, obs. Sc. form of REPROVE.

repry, obs. variant of REPRIEVE *v.*

repryuable, obs. form of REPROVABLE.

reps (rɛps). [a. F. *reps*: see REP ³.] = REP³.
1867 *Art Jrnl.* XXIX. 228/3 The reps has this objection, that it is so susceptible and tenacious of odour. **1877** A. B. EDWARDS *Up Nile* iii. 59 A cushioned divan covered with a smart woollen reps ran along each side.

repselver: see REAP-SILVER.

† **ˈrepster.** *Obs. rare*⁻¹. [f. *rep-* REAP *v.* + -STER.] A reaper.
c **1430** LOVE tr. *Bonavent. Mirror Life Christ* xv. (MS. e Musæo) lf. 59 And abacuk anoþer prophete bare mete to his repsteres on þe felde.

rept, obs. pa. pple. of REAP *v.*

reptant (ˈrɛptənt), *a.* [ad. L. *reptant-*, pple. of *reptāre* to creep.] Creeping, crawling, repent.
1657 TOMLINSON *Renou's Disp.* 297 Its roots are round.. and reptant like grass roots. **1835** KIRBY *Hab. & Inst. Anim.* II. xxiv. 489 Its four legs, and reptant motions show that it is most nearly connected with the Reptiles. **1853** MACDONALD & ALLEN *Botanist's Word-bk.* **1888** ROLLESTON & JACKSON *Anim. Life* 482 The majority are reptant, but of these some few can swim.

reptation (rɛpˈteɪʃən). [ad. L. *reptātiōn-em* (Quintilian), n. of action f. *reptāre* to creep.] The action of creeping or crawling.
1842 BRANDE *Dict. Sc.*, etc., *Reptation*, a mode of progression by advancing successively parts of the trunk, which occupy the place of the anterior parts which are carried forwards, as in serpents. **1947** R. L. G. IRVING tr. *Casteret's My Caves* iii. 54 Reptation involves an attitude so seldom adopted by the human race that it appears to be the fate allotted to a few inferior creatures.

† **ˈreptatory,** *a. rare*⁻⁰. [f. *reptāt-*, ppl. stem of L. *reptāre* to creep + -ORY.] 'Having the character of reptation' (Mayne 1859); 'creeping; as, reptatory animals' (Webster 1864, citing Dana).

† **ˈreptible.** *Obs. rare*⁻¹. [ad. late L. *reptibilis* (Boethius): cf. REPTILE *sb.*¹ and -IBLE.] A reptile.
1655 M. CARTER *Hon. Rediv.* (1660) 151 Reptibles, and Insects, all manner of Flyes and Grasshoppers.

reptilarium: see REPTILIARY.

reptile (ˈrɛptaɪl, formerly ˈrɛptɪl), *sb.*¹ Also 4, 7 reptil, 6 -yll. [ad. late L. *reptile* (Vulg.), neut. of *reptilis*: see REPTILE *a.*, and cf. F. *reptile* (1314).]
1. A creeping or crawling animal; *spec.* an animal belonging to the class REPTILIA. †Also *collect.*
1390 GOWER *Conf.* III. 118 Every neddre and every Snake And every Reptil which mai moeve. *c* **1532** DU WES *Introd. Fr.* in *Palsgr.* 1053 All beestes, byrdes, fyshes, reptyll them movyng from place to other. **1634** R. H. *Salernes Regim.* Pref. 2 We observe in Reptiles and other Creatures, that they most incline to that which most consorts with their Nature. **1667** MILTON *P.L.* VII. 388 God said, let the Waters generate Reptil with Spawn abundant. **1735** POPE *Prol. Sat.* 331 Eve's tempter thus the Rabbins have exprest, A Cherub's face, a reptile all the rest. **1774** GOLDSM. *Nat. Hist.* (1776) IV. 172 When the animal is obliged to move, it drags itself forward like a reptile. **1863** DANA *Man. Geol.* 5 Of existing Vertebrates the number of species of Fishes is about 10,000; of Reptiles, 2000;.. of Mammals, 2000. **1894** J. T. FOWLER *Adamnan* Introd. 33 The former immunity of Ireland from reptiles.
2. *transf.* A person of a low, mean, grovelling, or repulsive character.
1749 FIELDING *Tom Jones* X. i, For a little reptile of a critic to presume to find fault with any of its parts.. is a most presumptuous absurdity. **1751** JOHNSON *Rambler* No. 170 ¶ 12 Reptiles whom their own servants would have despised, had they not been their servants. **1825** W. COBBETT *Rur. Rides* (1885) II. 93 These reptiles publish.. a newspaper. **1834** HT. MARTINEAU *Farrers* iv. 74 Those who shrink from looking fully and kindly even upon those who may be the reptiles of their race. **1974** WODEHOUSE *Aunts aren't Gentlemen* v. 45 She spoke as follows, her manner and diction similar to those of a sergeant-major addressing recruits. 'What's the matter with you, you poor reptile?'
3. *attrib.* and *Comb.*, as ***reptile house, -man, oil; reptile-like, -spawning*** adjs.
1834 *Tait's Mag.* I. 232/1 A new marriage of reptile-spawning fraud and time. **1845** G. MURRAY *Islaford* 57 Feelings foreign to the throng Of reptile-men that walk in slime. **1873** W. CARLETON *Farm Ballads* (1893) 119 Some reptile-like deed that coils plain in our sight. **1876** GOODE *Anim. Resourc. U.S.* in *Smithson. Coll.* XIII. VI. 52 Extraction of Bird and Reptile Oils. **1883** *Nature* 3 May 17/1 The most important work undertaken in the Gardens during the past year had been the new Reptile House. **1975** J. MCCLURE *Snake* v. 64 The reptile man at the museum.. said.. that method of preservation had been abandoned.

reptile (ˈrɛptaɪl), *sb.*² *Math.* Also rep-tile. [f. *rep(licating) tile* with a pun on REPTILE *sb.*¹] A two-dimensional figure of which two or more can be grouped together to form a larger figure having the same shape.
1966 S. W. GOLOMB in *Jrnl. Combinatorial Theory* I. 281 Certain polyominoes are 'rep-tiles', i.e., they can be used to tile enlarged scale models of themselves. **1972** C. S. OGILVY *Tomorrow's Math* (ed. 2) iv. 73 The following are unproven conjectures... Every rep-tile also tiles a parallelogram... A rep-tile with five or more sides cannot be convex. **1977** *Sci. Amer.* Jan. 110/3 Another kind of nonperiodic tiling is obtained by tiles that group together to form larger replicas of themselves. Solomon W. Golomb calls them 'reptiles'.

reptile (ˈrɛptaɪl, formerly ˈrɛptɪl), *a.* [ad. late L. *reptilis* (Sidonius), f. *rept-*, ppl. stem of *repĕre* to creep (cf. REPENT *a.*¹) + *-ilis* -ILE. In later examples to some extent an attrib. use of REPTILE *sb.*¹]
1. a. Of animals: Creeping, crawling; reptant.
1607 TOPSELL *Four-f. Beasts* (1658) 388 Some.. think that they were so called, because their outward forme representeth some such reptile creature. **1720** GAY *Rural Sports* I. 168 Cleanse them from filth, to give a tempting gloss, Cherish the sully'd reptile race with moss. **1727–46** THOMSON *Summer* 241 Wak'd by his warmer ray, the reptile young Come wing'd abroad. **1795** SOUTHEY *Joan of Arc* IX. 183 Feel thine own worthlessness, A reptile worm.
transf. **1742** YOUNG *Nt. Th.* I. 158 Wrapt round and round In silken Thought, which reptile Fancy spun!
†b. Of plants: Repent. *Obs. rare.*
1727 BRADLEY *Fam. Dict.* s.v., *Capreolus*, the.. tendril by which the Vines and such like reptile plants fasten themselves. **1727–38** CHAMBERS *Cycl.* s.v., Reptile is likewise used, abusively, for plants which creep on the earth, or on other plants.
2. Of the nature of, characterized by, pertaining to, the action of creeping or crawling.
1727–38 CHAMBERS *Cycl.* s.v., Its reptile motion may also be explained by a wire wound on a cylinder. **1774** GOLDSM. *Nat. Hist.* (1776) VII. 322 There they continue in a reptile state for a year.
3. *transf.* Having the characteristics of reptiles; grovelling, mean, low, malignant.
1654 Z. COKE *Logick* p. (a), On the raised wings of whose perfections, the prone and Reptile soul soars a pitch. **1661** BLOUNT *Glossogr.*, *Reptile* or *Reptitious*, that creeps; or, by privy means, gets to high estate. **1664** EVELYN tr. *Freart's Archit.* Pref. 3 These low and reptile Souls. *a* **1734** NORTH *Lives* (1826) III. 382 He was forced to deal in low concerns and reptile conceits that scarce rose from the ground. **1818** BYRON *Ch. Har.* IV. cxxxvi, The small whisper of the.. paltry few, And subtler venom of the reptile crew. **1849** ROBERTSON *Serm.* Ser. I. viii. (1866) 134 He will creep and crawl before you to submit to any reptile meanness. **1889** *Times* 23 Nov. 5/3 The semi-official and reptile press.. employed to insinuate charges against the Chief of the Staff.

‖**Reptilia** (rɛpˈtɪlɪə). *Zool.* [L., pl. of *reptile* REPTILE *sb.*¹] *pl.* Those animals which creep or crawl; *spec.* in mod. use, that class of vertebrate animals which includes the snakes, lizards, crocodiles, turtles and tortoises.
1627–77 FELTHAM *Resolves* I. lxxxviii. 137 The Beasts, Fishes, and the reptilia, which are of grosser composition. **1660** R. CRANE *Strict Acc. Bab. Merch.* 9 Like the Insects, and the Reptilia of the Earth. **1835–6** *Todd's Cycl. Anat.* I. 90/2 These characters, by many of which the amphibia are distinguished from the reptilia [etc.]. **1878** BELL *Gegenbaur's Comp. Anat.* 415 In the Reptilia indications of the vertical dermal fringe can sometimes be just made out.

reptilian (rɛpˈtɪlɪən), *a.* (and *sb.*). [See prec. and -AN.]
1. Resembling a reptile; having the characteristics of the Reptilia.
1846 WORCESTER cites SILLIMAN. **1863** DANA *Man. Geol.* p. ix, The.. reptilian Bird of Solenhofen. **1865** *Englishman's Mag.* Nov. 388 It was then that the ocean swarmed with reptiles and reptilian fish. **1881** LUBBOCK in *Nature* No. 618. 403 The profound break once supposed to exist between birds and reptiles has been bridged over by the discovery of reptilian birds and bird-like reptiles.
b. Consisting or composed of reptiles.
1851 RICHARDSON *Geol.* viii. (1855) 294 The Sauria.. may be regarded as the true type of the Reptilian Class. **1876** GOODE *Fishes Bermudas* 61 *note*, These, with a small Saurian,.. make up the reptilian fauna of the Bermudas.
c. *sb.* A member of the class Reptilia.
1847 WEBSTER cites LYELL.
2. Of or pertaining to, characteristic of, a reptile or the Reptilia.
1849 H. MILLER *Footpr. Creat.* iv. (1874) 60 It might be regarded, found detached, as at least a reptilian, if not mammalian, bone. **1860** GILLMORE tr. *Figuier's Rept. & Birds* Introd. 3 Exhibiting.. closer approximation to the reptilian structure than any existing bird. **1893** NEWTON *Dict. Birds* I. 16 The presence of the Ambiens Muscle is a Reptilian feature.
3. *transf.* Mean, malignant, underhand.
1859 GEO. ELIOT *A. Bede* xii, He had an agreeable confidence that his faults were all.. impetuous,.. leonine; never crawling, crafty, reptilian. **1888** *Pall Mall G.* 5 Nov. 4/2 His dead father is fair game for Reptilian slanderers.

reptiliary (rɛpˈtɪlɪərɪ). [f. REPTILE *sb.* + -ARY¹, after *aviary*.] A building or enclosure in which reptiles are kept, as for display. Also **reptiˈlarium** [-ARIUM]; **repˈtillery** [-ERY].
1928 *Daily Tel.* 11 Sept. 14 This is the new open-air reptiliary. **1938** *Times* 30 Apr. 9/4 Before long a reptilarium would be installed at Whipsnade. **1976** *Southern Even. Echo* (Southampton) 10 Nov. 1/4 A reptillery has been in existence at Holiday Hill, near Lyndhurst, for about 15 years. **1978** *Autoworld* No. 68. 23/1 You can visit a wild goat park.., a butterfly reserve,.. a reptiliary in the New Forest.

reptiliferous (rɛptɪˈlɪfərəs), *a.* [f. REPTILE *sb.*¹ + -FEROUS.] Containing fossil reptiles.
1858 MURCHISON *Siluria* (1859) App. Q. 572 Those fishes which characterize the Uppermost Old Red or yellow sandstone of the South of Scotland have not been found in the Reptiliferous Sandstones of Elgin. **1885** JUDD in *Nature* 28 Jan. (1886) 310 On the Relation of the Reptiliferous Sandstone of Elgin to the Upper Old Red Sandstone.

reptiliform (ˈrɛptɪlɪfɔːm), *a.* and *sb.* [f. as prec. + -FORM.] **a.** *adj.* Having the form of a reptile. **b.** *sb.* An animal of this kind.
1835–6 *Todd's Cycl. Anat.* I. 101/2 In this they are also imitated by the tadpole state of the higher reptiliform groups. **1890** COUES *Ornith.* 92 This group is called *Sauropsida* or reptiliforms.

reptilious (rɛpˈtɪlɪəs), *a. rare.* [f. REPTILE *sb.*¹ + -IOUS.] Resembling a reptile.
1879 MEREDITH *Egoist* xxi, The advantage taken of it by Willoughby.. made her feel abject—reptilious. **1936** L. C. DOUGLAS *White Banners* xv. 317 Considering with what reptilious patience she had waited.

ˈreptilism. *rare.* [-ISM.] Reptilian nature.
1821 *Blackw. Mag.* X. 698 The vulgar vocabulary of rottenness and reptilism. **1843** *Ibid.* LIV. 211 That reptilism which lurks in every corner of public life.

repˈtility. *rare.* [-ITY.] †**a.** The habit of creeping. *Obs.* **b.** Reptilian character or conduct.
1657 TOMLINSON *Renou's Disp.* 349 Knot-grasse.. called Serpinaca from its reptility. **1745** A. HILL *Wks.* II. 250 One might pronounce him fallen below contempt, but that he aims to heave, in his reptility.

reptiˈlivorous, *a.* [f. REPTILE *sb.*¹, after *carnivorous*, etc.] Devouring reptiles.
1858 MAYNE *Expos. Lex.* 1079/2. **1885** *Field* 4 Apr. 453/3 The other bird is piscivorous and reptilivorous, and destroys no end of frogs, lizards, and the like. **1886** WALLACE in *Fortn. Rev.* Sept. 305 A triangular head and short tail which sufficiently marks out the tribe of viperine poisonous snakes to reptilivorous birds and mammals.

reptillery: see REPTILIARY.

ˈreptiloid, *a.* [f. REPTILE *sb.*¹ + -OID.] Reptiliform.
1888 *Pop. Sci. Monthly* May 75 The thrushes.. are farthest removed in structure from the early reptiloid forms.

†**rep'titious**, *a. Obs.* [f. L. *reptitius*, for which *repertitius* is now read.] (See quots.)

1656 BLOUNT *Glossogr.* [from Cooper], *Repititious* [**1661** *Reptile* or *Reptitious*], that creeps; or by privy means gets to high Estate. **1658** PHILLIPS, *Reptitious*, stealing or creeping on by degrees. **1742** C. OWEN *Serpents* I. i. 2 Some Serpents are reptitious, creep on the Belly, and some have Feet.

reptyme: see REAP-TIME.

republic (rɪ'pʌblɪk), *sb.* (and *a.*) Also 7 -ique, -ike, 7–8 -ick; 7 rei-. [ad. F. *république* or L. *rēspublica* (abl. *rēpublicā*), f. *rēs* thing, affair + *publicus* PUBLIC *a.*]

†**1.** The state, the common weal. *Obs.*

1603 DRAYTON *Bar. Wars* II. x, Neither yet thinke, by their vnnaturall Fight What the republique suffred them among. **1651** HOBBES *Govt. & Soc.* v. §5. 78 Those men are of most trouble to the Republique, who haue most leasure to be idle. **1684** *Scanderbeg Rediv.* iii. 41 The Republick might be highly endangered by an Inter-Regnum.

2. a. A state in which the supreme power rests in the people and their elected representatives or officers, as opposed to one governed by a king or similar ruler; a commonwealth. Now also applied loosely to any state which claims this designation.

1604 R. CAWDREY *Table Alph.*, *Republike*, a Commonwealth. *a* **1626** BACON *Ch. Controv.* Wks. 1879 I. 347 It may be, in civil states, a republic is a better policy than a kingdom. *a* **1674** CLARENDON *Hist. Reb.* XI. §155 The Army..would depose the King, change the Government, and settle a Republick by their own Rules. **1727** COLDEN *Hist. Five Ind. Nat.* p. xv, Each Nation is an absolute Republick by its self, govern'd in all Publick Affairs of War and Peace by the Sachems or Old Men. **1771** *Junius Lett.* lix. (1788) 316 When I impute to him a speculative predilection in favour of a republic. **1841–4** EMERSON *Ess.*, *Heroism* Wks. (Bohn) I. 110 Whatever outrages have happened to men may befal a man again; and very easily in a republic. **1884** *Q. Rev.* CLVII. 2 The success of the United States has sustained the credit of Republics—a word..which has lately come to have the additional meaning of a government resting on a widely-extended suffrage. **1947** E. WAUGH *Scott-King's Mod. Europe* 4 Out of it [*sc.* history] emerged the present republic of Neutralia, a typical modern state, governed by a single party, acclaiming a dominant Marshal, supporting a vast ill-paid bureaucracy whose work is tempered and humanised by corruption. **1976** *Whitaker's Almanack 1977* 829/2 Republic of Burundi... Burundi became independent as a Constitutional monarchy but this was overthrown on November 28, 1966. The Constitution and Parliament were also abolished. The President rules through a Cabinet of Ministers and the UPRONA party apparatus. Burundi is a one-Party State.

b. Applied to particular states having this form of constitution.

1631 HEYLIN *St. George* 349 The publike honours done unto him, by the greatest Princes and Republicks in the Christian world. **1632** LITHGOW *Trav.* I. 25 The Reipublicks of Pisa and Siena. **1654** tr. *Scudery's Curia Pol.* 26 Were it not much better for the Republique of Venice..? **1726–46** THOMSON *Winter* 505 Servius, the king who laid the solid base On which o'er earth the vast republic spread. **1790** BURKE *Fr. Rev.* Wks. V. 110 These commonwealths will not long bear a state of subjection to the republick of Paris. **1833** *Penny Cycl.* I. 447/2 The republic of the United States of America..consists of twenty-four states, and three territories. **1882** HINSDALE *Garfield & Educ.* II. 359 The Republic has the right to call on all her children for service.

c. Without article: Republican constitution or government. *rare*$^{-1}$.

1791 BURKE *Let. Member Nat. Assembly* Wks. 1792 III. 340 The existence of such an executive officer, in such a system of republic..is absurd in the highest degree.

3. *fig.* and *transf.* **a.** Any community of persons, animals, etc., in which there is a certain equality among the members.

1750 JOHNSON *Rambler* No. 77 ¶8 He..may be considered as not unprofitable to the great republic of humanity. **1789** WASHINGTON in Eliot *Hist. Harvard Coll.* (1848) 152 It gives me sincere satisfaction to learn the flourishing state of your literary republic. **1818** KIRBY & SP. *Entomol.* xviii. (ed. 2) II. 114 The large females, like the female wasps, are the original founders of their republics. **1869** J. MARTINEAU *Ess.* II. 15 Our nature is a republic of equal principles.

b. *the republic of letters*, the collective body of those engaged in literary pursuits; the field of literature itself.

1702 ADDISON *Dial. Medals* i. 19 Pray consider what a figure a man would make in the republick of letters [etc.]. **1739** HUME *Hum. Nat.* I. vii. (1874) I. 325 One of the greatest..discoveries that has been made of late years in the republic of letters. *a* **1808** BP. HURD *Notes Addison's Tatler* No. 159, The satire contained in this paper..I doubt, has done no small hurt in the republic of letters. **1870** BURTON *Hist. Scot.* (1873) VI. lxvi. 63 There was another field of exertion..in the republic of letters.

4. *attrib.* (passing into *adj.*) Of the nature of, characteristic of, pertaining to, a republic or republics; republican. Now *rare* or *Obs.*

1638 MAYNE *Lucian* (1664) A iv, Who..do defile the English Tongue with their Republick words, which are..scarce significant to a Monarchicall understanding. **1654–66** EARL ORRERY *Parthen.* (1676) 787 The Republick Cities and Countries of Greece. **1687** DRYDEN *Hind & P.* III. 1251 To Crows..And Choughs and Daws, and such republic birds. **1710** E. WARD *Brit. Hud.* 2 When our Good Sov'reign Lords the People Were Crown'd by a Republick Cripple. **1755** *Monitor* No. 13 I. 111 Let the republic German Princes..unite for their common safety!

†**re'publical**, *a. Obs.* [-AL[1].] = next.

1656 in *Eng. Hist. Rev.* (1902) XVII. 438 The Presbyterians and the Republicall party are desirous he [Cromwell] should take uppon him that title. **1660** BURNEY *Κέρδ. Δῶρον* (1661) 103, I equally favour your Lordships, and the lowest member of the body, which is truly Republical. *a* **1674** CLARENDON *Hist. Reb.* XVI. §93 The governor was their friend, and devoted to the Presbyterian republical party.

republican (rɪ'pʌblɪkən), *a.* and *sb.* [f. REPUBLIC + -AN, prob. after F. *républicain.*]

A. *adj.* †**1.** Belonging to the commonwealth or community. *Obs. rare*$^{-1}$.

1691 *Address Publicans New-Eng.* in *Andros Tracts* (1869) II. 234 The Agents..brought back word, That the People of New-England were possest of great quantities of Republican Money.

2. a. Of or belonging to a republic; having the form or constitution of a republic; characteristic of a republic or republics.

1712 ADDISON *Spect.* No. 269 ¶10 To vent among them some of his Republican Doctrines. **1771** *Junius Lett.* lix. (1788) 316, I would have the manners of the people purely and strictly republican. **1844** THIRLWALL *Greece* VIII. 463 The change from republican to monarchical institutions was in general beneficial to the provinces. **1863** MARY HOWITT tr. *F. Bremer's Greece* II. xv. 117 There prevails..a republican equality and disorder, which the republican American would be extremely astonished at. **1864** [see B. 2].

b. Of persons or parties: Favouring, supporting, or advocating the form of state or government called a republic.

1793 BP. HORSLEY *Serm.* 30 Jan. 13 *note*, It has been a great point with Republican Divines to explain away the force of this text [Rom. xiii. 1]. **1848** W. H. KELLY tr. *L. Blanc's Hist. Ten. Y.* I. 411 The leaders of the republican party did not share the mistake.

c. *republican calendar*, the calendar adopted for a short time (see quot.) by the French Republic; so *republican era*, dating from 22 Sept. 1792.

1839 *Penny Cycl.* XIII. 173/1 The republican kalendar was first used on the 26th of November, 1793, and was discontinued on the 31st of December, 1805.

3. a. In *U.S. politics* (with capital) as the distinguishing epithet of a special party, its principles, measures, etc.

Originally applied to the Anti-Federal party which latterly became the DEMOCRATIC; but subsequently a party opposed to this (formed in 1854 to resist the extension of slave territory), which favoured liberal interpretation of the constitution, extension of the central power, and a protective tariff.

The Republican party formed in 1854 is now a predominantly conservative party, favouring agricultural, commercial, and financial interests and a limited central government (see M. M. Mathews *Dict. Americanisms*, 1951, and Sperber & Trittschuh *Amer. Polit. Terms*, 1962, for further details of the development of this sense).

1806 TALLMADGE in *M. Cutler's Life*, etc. (1888) II. 326 Our exclusive republican Brethren, those dear Lovers of the people. **1839** [see FEDERAL *a.* 3]. **1854** A. E. BOVAY *Let.* 26 Feb. in F. Curtis *Republican Party* (1904) I. vi. 177 Urge them..to band together under the name I suggested to you at Lovejoy's Hotel in 1852. I mean the name 'Republican'. **1856** *Porter's Spirit of Times* 4 Oct. 71/1 New Jersey..[was] discovered by the late Republican Convention, in their explorations for a candidate for Vice President. **1862** J. M. LUDLOW *Hist. U.S.* 61 The other party, then [1793] called the Republican party (a name, you must observe, which has entirely changed in modern days, and is now applied to a party the true successor of the old Federal one). **1866** *Chambers' Encycl.* s.v., The Federalist, National Republican, Whig, and Republican party has been essentially the same. **1905** *Baltimore Amer.* 7 Mar. 4/1 Republican Senators..cannot find desks on the Republican side, as there are more Republicans in the Senate than there are desks for Republican Senators. **1976** *Columbus* (Montana) *News* 1 July 6/3 Charles Eckels attended the Republican Convention in Helena last week as chairman from this District.

b. Used as a distinguishing epithet by political parties outside U.S.

1958 *Listener* 27 Nov. 865/1 One [new French party] is the Republican Centre. **1975** *Financial Times* 31 Oct. 6/8 Mr Ecevit, chairman of the main Opposition, the Republican People's Party (RPP). **1980** S. J. BURKI *Pakistan under Bhutto* ii. 22 The formation of the landlord-dominated Republican Party.

4. *Ornith.* Living, nesting, or breeding, in large flocks or communities, esp. the N. American *republican swallow*, and the S. African *republican grosbeak* or *weaver-bird*.

1829 AUDUBON *Amer. Ornith.* Pl. 68 Republican [or] Cliff Swallow, *Hirundo Fulva*. **1839** —— *Ornith. Biogr.* V. 415. **1855** SMITH & DALLAS *Syst. Nat. Hist.* II. 266 The most remarkable nest, however, is that made by the Social or Republican Grosbeak (*Philetærus Socius*). **1868** *Chambers' Encycl.* s.v. *Weaver-bird*, The Social or Republican Weaver of South Africa..constructs a kind of umbrella-like roof, under which 800 or 1000 nests have been found.

B. *sb.* †**1.** One attached to the interests of the commonwealth or community. *Obs. rare*$^{-1}$.

1691 *Address Publicans New-Eng.* in *Andros Tracts* (1869) II. 233 A Place where there still dwelt..some Men of Conscience, and shrewdly suspected to be Republicans.

2. a. One who believes in, supports, or prefers a republican form of government. *red republican* (see quot. 1864 and RED *a.* 9 b).

1697 VANBRUGH *Relapse* Epil. 22 I'm very positive you never saw A through republican a finish'd beau. **1705** ADDISON *Italy* 405 Such a Chimerical Happiness is not peculiar to Republicans. **1735** BOLINGBROKE *On Parties* 54 The Whigs were not Dissenters, nor Republicans, though They favour'd the former. **1829** LYTTON *Disowned* I. xiv, His evident attention flattered the fierce republican. **1864** WEBSTER s.v., *Red republican*, one bent on maintaining extreme republican doctrines, even at the expense of blood. **1876** RUSKIN *Fors Clav.* VI. lxiii. 92, I hate republicans, as I do all other manner of fools.

b. *transf.* Cf. REPUBLIC *sb.* 3 b.

1816 I. D'ISRAELI *Inquiry Lit. & Polit. Char. James I* 3 His other brothers, the republicans of literature, want a heart to admire the man.

3. a. *U.S. politics.* A member of the Republican party (see A. 3 a). *Black Republican* (see quot. 1866).

1782 J. ADAMS *Diary* 26 Dec., Vaughan has a brother in Philadelphia, who has written him a long letter about the Constitutionalists and the Republicans. **1808** —— *Wks.* (1854) IX. 602 The federal administration lasted twelve years. The republicans..have ruled eight years. **1866** *Chambers' Encycl.* s.v., The Whig party..adopted the name of Republicans, and were called by their opponents Black Republicans, from their anti-slavery tendencies.

b. *U.S.* (See quot.)

1832 FERRALL *Ramble thro' U.S.* 88 The stumps..and 'republicans' (projecting roots of trees, so called from the stubborn tenacity with which they adhere to the ground..), rendered the difficulties of traversing this forest..great.

4. *Ornith.* A republican weaver-bird or swallow.

1801 *Encycl. Brit.* Suppl. II. 400/2 *Republicans*, the name given by Vaillant..to a kind of birds..in South Africa.

re'publicanism. [f. prec. + -ISM: cf. F. *républicanisme* (18th c.).]

1. Republican spirit; attachment or adherence to republican principles; republican government or institutions, etc.

1689 D. GRANVILLE *Lett.* (Surtees, No. 37) 71 The contagion of the age, the spirit of popularity and republicanisme. **1715** ADDISON *Freeholder* No. 29 ¶6 For with some of these men, at present, loyalty to our king is Republicanism, and rebellion Passive-obedience. **1779–81** JOHNSON *L.P.*, *Milton* (1868) 63 Milton's republicanism was, I am afraid, founded in an envious hatred of greatness. **1800** SYD. SMITH *Six Serm.* 110 There are many men of..approved integrity, who have unjustly incurred the charge of republicanism. **1845** DARWIN *Voy. Nat.* vii. 129 Tyranny seems..better adapted to these countries than republicanism. **1853** J. H. NEWMAN *Hist. Sk.* (1873) II. I. iv. 180 England herself once attempted the costume of republicanism.

2. Something having a republican character or tone; a republican term or phrase.

1863 HAWTHORNE *Our Old Home* (1879) 49 With..kindly endurance of the many rough republicanisms wherewith I assailed him.

re,publicani'zation. [f. next + -ATION.] The action of republicanizing.

1798 W. TAYLOR in *Monthly Rev.* XXVI. 527 To impassion the French for the epuration of morals and the republicanization of governments. **1970** R. A. H. ROBINSON *Orig. Franco's Spain* i. 53 'Republicanisation' of local councils took place on a large scale; possibly this was as much the result of voluntary changes of allegiance..as of arbitrary measures.

re'publicanize, *v.* [ad. F. *républicaniser* (Littré): see REPUBLICAN and -IZE.]

1. *trans.* To render republican in principles or character; to convert into a republican form.

1797 W. TAYLOR in *Monthly Rev.* XXIII. 559 The first public measure which tended avowedly to republicanise France. **1813** WELLINGTON in Gurw. *Desp.* (1838) X. 516 They have a Board of Officers now sitting to consider of a military constitution for the army, which it is intended to republicanize. **1849** MILL *Ess.* (1859) II. 362 Their great task was to republicanize the public mind. **1871** *Standard* 5 Jan., Agents commissioned—according to the expression of the day—to republicanise the country.

b. *transf.* To treat, alter, or re-cast, on republican principles.

1797 SOUTHEY *Let. to J. May* 26 June, The French never can have a good epic poem till they have republicanised their language. **1858–9** MARSH *Eng. Lang.* xxx. (1860) 676 Let us not, with malice prepense, go about to republicanize our orthography and our syntax.

2. *intr.* To show republican tendencies.

1834 *New Monthly Mag.* XLII. 42 Even the peerage of France was beginning to republicanize.

Hence **re'publicanized** *ppl. a.*; **re'publicanizer**; **re'publicanizing** *vbl. sb.*

1812 SHELLEY in Dowden *Life* (1887) I. 337 It develops the..actual state of republicanized Ireland. **1840** THACKERAY *Catherine* i, After a deal of republicanising,..Stuartising, and Orangising. *c* **1871** SHERMAN in *Critic* 29 Sept. (1894) 198/1 We will welcome you back as the 'republicanizer' of the worst anarchy on the globe.

re'publicanly, *adv. rare.* [f. REPUBLICAN *a.* + -LY[2].] In a republican manner.

1659 *Eng. Monarchy freest State* 9 The general peace either altogether unsetled, or done Republicanly, and so slightly, infirmly and not lastingly. **1837** J. S. MILL *Let.* June in *Works* (1963) XII. 339 Twelve pages on the *immediately present* state of French politics..written republicanly by Thibaudeau.

†**republi'carian**, *a.* and *sb. Obs.* = REPUBLICAN.

1682 *Lond. Gaz.* No. 1727/6 The pernicious Artifices..of turbulent Republicarian and Antimonarchical Spirits. **1689** EVELYN *Diary* 15 Jan., There were Republicarians who would make the Pr. of Orange like a Statholder.

†**re'publicate**, *v.* [? f. REPUBLIC + -ATE.] *trans.* ? To make popular.

a **1670** HACKET *Abp. Williams* I. (1692) 137 The Cabinet-men at Wallingford-House, set upon it to consider, what Exploit this Lord should commence, to be the Darling of the Commons, and as it were to re-publicate his Lordship.

republication (riːpʌblɪˈkeɪʃən). [RE- 5 a.]

1. A fresh promulgation *of* a religion or law.

1730 M. TINDAL (*title*) Christianity as old as Creation, a republication of the Religion of Nature. **1763** STUKELEY *Palæog. Sacra* Pref., Christianity is a republication of the patriarchal religion. **1854** MILMAN *Lat. Chr.* IV. i. (1864) II. 168 Mohammedanism, in more respects than one, was a republication of Mosaic Judaism. **1865** R. W. DALE *Jew. Temp.* xxii. (1877) 250 Every holy life is a visible republication of the Divine law.

2. A fresh publication *of* a will.

1743 *Swinburne's Testaments* (ed. 6) VII. §14. 524 That this Republication of the first Will was a Revocation of the last. **1766** BLACKSTONE *Comm.* II. xxxii. 502 The republication of a former will revokes one of a later date, and establishes the first again. **1818** CRUISE *Digest* (ed. 2) VI. 168 The devisor knew of the death of the devisee,.. after which she made a codicil that operated as a republication of her will. **1858** LD. ST. LEONARDS *Handy-Bk. Prop. Law* xvii. 128 You should inquire whether the conveyance renders a republication of your will necessary.

3. The action of republishing (a work), or the fact of being republished.

1789 H. WALPOLE *Let. to C'tess Ossory* 4 Aug., I did see, and wondered.. at the republication of the long-forgotten verses on the 'The Three Vernons'. **1841** KEBLE in *Hooker's Wks.* (1888) I. p. cxv, It is hoped that this republication of his remains.. will cause them to become more generally read. **1868** G. DUFF *Pol. Surv.* 150 Much of the correspondence would bear republication in a permanent form.

b. A fresh publication *of* a literary work; a work published again.

1796 WITHERING *Brit. Plants* (ed. 3) I. Pref. 5 This may rather be regarded as a new work than as a re-publication of an old one. **1856** DE QUINCEY *Confess.* 142 As a 'Reader' to the Press in the field of Greek re-publications. **1892** *Bookman* Nov. 57/1 As the volume is so much of a republication it does not claim.. detailed criticism.

Republicrat (rɪˈpʌblɪkræt). *U.S. politics.* Also **Republocrat.** [Blend of REPUBLI(CAN *sb.* 3 + DEMO)CRAT 2.] A member of a political faction that includes both Republicans and Democrats. Also, a conservative Democrat with Republican sympathies.

1940 *Better Eng.* Oct. 55/1 A republocrat, as 'Time' uses it, is a republican or a democrat who will have anyone but Mr. Hoover. **1944** *N.Y. Post* 24 Apr. 19/4 The 'Republicrats', meaning reactionary Democrats in league with the Republicans, want to discredit F.D.R. **1946** *Time* 22 Apr. 11/1 Would you be good enough to give us the names of the 'republocrats' in the House and Senate who have organized for the purpose of defeating President Truman's legislative program? **1949** *Southern Farmer* July 3 All we ask is that the Hindu philosophers tell us how to make the Southern Republicrats climb up a rope and disappear.

Hence **Republi'cratic** *a.*

1944 *New Republic* 19 June 801/1 The Republicratic gang engineering the supposed Southern 'revolt' against the New Deal appears well satisfied with the results of the Mississippi convention.

republish (riːˈpʌblɪʃ), *v.* [RE- 5 a.]

1. *trans.* To publish again:

a. a book or other work, a statement, etc.

1625 BP. MOUNTAGU *App. Cæsar* 31 The Booke is extant (published by warrant, and re-published by command this present year). **1644** MILTON *Jdgm. Bucer* Postscr., If these their books.. shall for the propagating of truth be publisht and republisht [etc.]. **1815** *Old Eng. Plays* IV. 223 They who republish such dramas as have hitherto only been printed from.. the prompter's books are entitled to much indulgence. **1840** in Sturgeon *Annals Electr.* IV. 374 We have been induced to republish the principal facts. **1862** S. LUCAS *Secularia* 272 He laid down a principle, to which he adhered.., to the extent of republishing it without comment or qualification.

b. a declaration, law, etc.

1688 LUTTRELL *Brief Rel.* (1857) I. 438 His majestie hath been pleased to republish his declaration for liberty of conscience.

c. a will or deed.

1766 BLACKSTONE *Comm.* II. xxiii. 379 No after-purchased lands will pass under such devise, unless.. the devisor republishes his will. **1837** *Act 7 Will. IV & 1 Vict.* c. 26 §34 Every Will re-executed or republished, or revived by any Codicil. **1858** LD. ST. LEONARDS *Handy-Bk. Prop. Law* xvii. 128 Perhaps it would be better to re-publish your will without inquiry.

2. To revive, bring into use again. *rare*$^{-1}$.

1840 *Penny Cycl.* XVII. 142/2 John van Eyck may be said to have 'republished', though he probably did not invent painting in oil.

Hence **re'published** *ppl. a.*

1884 RUSKIN *In Montibus Sanctis* Pref., In order not to add to the expense of the republished text.

re'publisher (riː-). [f. prec. + -ER[1].] One who republishes.

1752 WARBURTON *Serm. Nat. & Rev. Relig.* Wks. 1788 V. 90 He who considers Jesus only in the light of a Republisher of the Law of nature [etc.]. **1817** JAS. MILL *Brit. India* I. II. ii. 107 The first legislator of the Hindus.. appears to have represented himself as the republisher of the will of God. **1868** *Daily News* 22 July, The re-publishers of Cobbett's 'History of the Reformation'.

re'publishment. [f. as prec. + -MENT.] The act of republishing.

1854 in *Allibone's Dict. Authors* (1877) I. 39 The fact of the profitable republishment of the old English classics.

re'pudiable, *a. rare.* [See REPUDIATE *v.* and -ABLE.] That may be repudiated.

1611 COTGR., *Repudiable*, repudiable, refusable [etc.]. **1647** JER. TAYLOR *Lib. Proph.* v. 96 The reasons.. make the Authority it selfe the lesse authentick and more repudiable. *Ibid.* vi. 117. [**1656** in BLOUNT *Glossogr.*, from Cotgr.]

repudiant (rɪˈpjuːdɪənt), *a. rare.* [See REPUDIATE *v.* and -ANT[1].] Characterized by repudiation; = REPUDIATIVE *a.*

1954 W. FAULKNER *Fable* 144 The owner.. still.. invincibly repudiant.

†**re'pudiate,** *ppl. a.* and *sb. Obs.* [ad. L. *repudiāt-us*: see next.]

A. *ppl. a.* **1.** Of a woman: **a.** Rejected or put away by her husband; divorced.

1548 UDALL, etc. *Erasm. Par. Matt.* xix. 94 The wyfe oughte not to be repudiate and cast of. **1596** DRAYTON *Leg.* iv. 876 His former Wife being repudiate. **1640** YORKE *Union Hon.* 136 He married Isabel,.. being repudiate wife of King John. **1660** R. COKE *Power & Subj.* 175 Nor his gossip, nor a Vestal nun, nor one repudiate, let no Christian man marry.

b. Rejected after betrothal or engagement.

1568 GRAFTON *Chron.* II. 879 Margaret which was affied to Charles the seuenth French king and by him repudiate. **1627** DRAYTON *Mis. Q. Margaret* xliii, That great Earle.. tooke in high disdayne, To haue his Daughter so repudiate.

c. *transf.* of a river.

c **1630** in Risdon *Surv. Devon* §225 (1810) 238 All discontent, and thus repudiate, Unto the southern coast her course doth [Tamar] take.

2. In general use: Rejected, set aside.

a **1548** HALL *Chron., Hen. IV* 9 b, Edmond was.. for his deformitee repudiat and put by from the croune royall. **1603** DRAYTON *Bar. Wars* I. xxx, To be debarr'd of that Imperial State.. Basely reiected, and repudiate.

B. *sb.* The (*or* a) divorced wife.

1611 SPEED *Hist. Gt. Brit.* IX. xxiv. §54 Dominions.. which they claimed by our Elenor, the repudiate of the King of France. **1665** SIR T. HERBERT *Trav.* (1677) 321 Zaynib (the repudiate of Ben-Harkah) was his fourth and last Wife. **1727** BAILEY vol. II, *A Repudiate*, a divorced woman, one put away.

repudiate (rɪˈpjuːdɪeɪt), *v.* [f. L. *repudiāt-*, ppl. stem of *repudiāre* to divorce, reject, etc., f. *repudium* REPUDY *sb.*]

1. *trans.* **a.** Of a husband: To put away or cast off (his wife); to divorce, dismiss.

1545 JOYE *Exp. Dan.* xi. 185 This Antiochus repudiated his own wyfe called Laodice. **1597** BEARD *Theatre God's Judgem.* (1612) 414 Hugh Spencer.. was he that first persuaded the king to forsake and repudiate the queene his wife. **1663** H. COGAN tr. *Pinto's Trav.* lx. 245 He had repudiated a daughter of his, which he had married three years before. **1716** BOLINGBROKE *Refl. upon Exile* Wks. 1754 I. 112 His separation from Terentia, whom he repudiated not long afterward, was perhaps an affliction to him at this time. **1850** W. IRVING *Mahomet* vii. (1853) 37 Abu Lahab and his wife.. compelled their son, Otha, to repudiate his wife. **1870** EDGAR *Runnymede* xxxv. 202 The pope forced her husband to repudiate her.

b. To cast off, disown (a person or thing).

1699 BENTLEY *Phal.* 316 Other Writers; who being Dorians born, repudiated their vernacular Idiom for that of the Athenians. **1844** DICKENS *Mart. Chuz.* xvi, He felt it necessary.. to repudiate and denounce his father. **1855** PRESCOTT *Philip II*, I. I. iii. 31 England, after repudiating her heresies, was received into the fold of the Roman Catholic Church. **1873** *Daily News* 12 Sept. 4/4 M. de Mahy .. called upon the Ministers to repudiate the document.

2. To reject; to refuse to accept or entertain (a thing) or to have dealings with (a person).

a **1548** HALL *Chron., Hen. VII* 1 b, The damosell dyd not alonly disagre and repudiate that matrimony, but abhorred .. his.. desyre. **1674** *Govt. Tongue* 100 O let not those that have repudiated the more inviting sins, show themselves philtr'd and bewitch'd by this. **1837** LOFFT *Self-form.* II. 63 Gladly would we have repudiated the property.. so heavily bestowed upon us. **1862** BEVERIDGE *Hist. India* II. VI. viii. 802 If they repudiated the empire placed within their reach, some other power would certainly seize it. **1879** M. ARNOLD *Mixed Ess.* 32 Not only did the whole repudiate the physician, but also those who were sick.

b. To reject (opinions, conduct, etc.) with condemnation or abhorrence.

1824–9 LANDOR *Imag. Conv., Lucian & Timotheus*, You have acknowledged his eloquence, while you.. repudiated his morals. **1840** HERSCHEL *Ess.* (1857) 109 A doctrine which .. we must repudiate. **1865** R. W. DALE *Jew. Temp.* viii. (1877) 85, I repudiate the dreams of Pantheism.

c. To reject (a charge, etc.) with denial, as being quite unfounded or inapplicable.

1865 DICKENS *Mut. Fr.* III. i, The old man shook his head, gently repudiating the imputation. **1874** GREEN *Short Hist.* viii. §6. 525 Politically it repudiated the taunt of revolutionary aims.

3. To reject as unauthorized or as having no authority or binding force on one.

1646 SIR T. BROWNE *Pseud. Ep.* 42 He hath obtained with some to repudiate the books of Moses. **1692** BENTLEY *Boyle Lect.* ix. 304 Repudiating at once the whole Authority of Revelation. **1837** LOFFT *Self-form.* II. 174, I had repudiated the second hand faculty as vain.. and delusive. **1852** H. ROGERS *Ecl. Faith* (1853) 74 You would repudiate at once his claims.. to be your infallible guide. **1879** FROUDE *Short Stud.* (1883) IV. v. 350 They were ready.. to repudiate the authority of the Pope.

b. To refuse to discharge or acknowledge (a debt or other obligation). Chiefly of (American) states disowning a public debt, and freq. *absol.*

1837 LOFFT *Self-form.* I. 249 If a man.. repudiate the care of his wife or children, villain is a word not villanous enough for him. **1847** WEBSTER s.v., The state has repudiated its debts. **1863** H. SPENCER *Ess.* II. 228 Sir Robert Inglis.. hinted that the national debt would not improbably be repudiated if the proposed measure became law.

absol. **1843** SYD. SMITH *Wks.* (1859) II. 331/2, I am accused of applying the epithet repudiation to States which have not repudiated. **1862** J. SPENCE *Amer.* 74 In each of the States that has repudiated there was a large majority of men thoroughly honourable in their private affairs.

Hence **re'pudiated** *ppl. a.*, **re'pudiating** *vbl. sb.* and *ppl. a.*

1635 J. HAYWARD tr. *Biondi's Banish'd Virg.* 143 My first businesse was to hasten the repudiating of the Queene. **1788** H. WALPOLE *Remin.* ii. 24 Eldest daughter.. of the repudiated wife of the earl of Macclesfield. **1843** SYD. SMITH *Wks.* (1859) II. 328/1 Persons who.. are inclined to consider the abominable conduct of the repudiating States to proceed from exhaustion. *Ibid.* 329/1 This swamp we gained.. by the repudiated loan of 1828. **1880** DIXON *Windsor* III. xiii. 124 Henry allowed her to live with his repudiated daughter.

repudiation (rɪpjuːdɪˈeɪʃən). [ad. L. *repudiātiōn-em*, n. of action f. *repudiāre*: see prec. and -ATION, and cf. F. *répudiation* (15th c.).] The action of repudiating or fact of being repudiated.

1. Divorce (of a wife).

1545 JOYE *Exp. Dan.* xi. 185 This Antiochus repudiated his own wyfe.. Which.. repudiacion or diuorce from his firste wyfe was the occasion of greate mischeif. *a* **1635** NAUNTON *Fragm. Reg.* (Arb.) 26 Upon repudiation of the Lady, he clapt up a marriage for his Son. **1686** tr. *Chardin's Trav. Persia* 332 They must return the Portion they had, upon the Repudiation. **1727** A. HAMILTON *New Acc. E. Ind.* I. iii. 26 They allow of Repudiation, but neither Party can marry again, till the Term of three Years be expired. **1803** *Edin. Rev.* I. 491 She does not appear even to have understood what they meant by repudiation. **1867** FREEMAN *Norm. Conq.* (1877) I. vi. 473 If the repudiation of Estrith was accompanied.. by the assertion of the claims of the Æthelings to her brother's crown.

2. The action of rejecting, disowning, disavowing, etc.; spec. in *Canon Law* (see first quot.).

1848–56 BOUVIER *Law Dict.* s.v., In the canon law, repudiation is the refusal to accept a benefice which has been conferred upon the party repudiating. **1858** FROUDE *Hist. Eng.* III. xvii. 495 His denial was.. not like the broad, absolute repudiation of a man who was consciously clear of offence. **1877** BLACK *Green Past.* iii. (1878) 21 A murmur of indignant repudiation nerved him to a further effort.

b. *spec.* of a debt. (Cf. the vb. 3 b.)

1843 [see REPUDIATE *v.* 3 b]. **1862** J. SPENCE *Amer.* 74 Repudiation has not been the course of those who could not, but of those who, having the means, would not pay. **1868** ROGERS *Pol. Econ.* xi. (1876) 143 This country ran considerable risk of repudiation after the close of the great continental war.

Hence **repudi'ationist** *sb.* and *a.*, (one) advocating repudiation; *spec.* in *U.S.*, one who advocates the repudiation of a public debt.

1867 *Nation* (N.Y.) No. 127. 446/1 The repudiationists are undoubtedly strong. **1883** *American* VI. 387 More honorable than alliances with the whiskey interest or the repudiationists of the South. **1930** *Times* 11 Nov. 15/4 That is the most effective way in which he can support the Government and repudiate the repudiationists. **1931** *Star* 8 May 16/1 The small Lang 'Repudiationist' rump came to Mr. Scullin's assistance. **1932** *New Statesman* 16 Jan. 53/2 Germany is repudiationist to a man.

repudiative (rɪˈpjuːdɪətɪv), *a.* [f. REPUDIATE *v.* + -IVE.] Characterized by repudiation or rejection *of* something.

1860 J. WHITE *Hist. France* (ed. 2) 3 An island.. generally unapproachable, and at all times utterly repudiative of a permanent bridge. **1870** BURTON *Hist. Scot.* (1873) VI. lxxi. 243 There were Lowland families.. repudiative of any other leader but the great marquis.

repudiator (rɪˈpjuːdɪeɪtə(r)). [a. L. *repudiātor*, agent-n. f. *repudiāre* to REPUDIATE.] One who repudiates; *spec.* one who advocates the repudiation of a public debt.

1843 SYD. SMITH *Wks.* (1859) II. 331/1, I see now.. a whole army on the plains of Pennsylvania.., battalions of repudiators, brigades of bankrupts. **1852** H. NEWLAND *Lect. Tractar.* 107 The great repudiator of Chinese exactness. **1870** *Daily News* 16 Apr., Despisers and repudiators of anti-slavery men and their opinions.

re'pudiatory, *a. rare.* [f. REPUDIATE *v.* + -ORY.] Favouring repudiation (of debts).

1882 *American* IV. 67 They refused to admit.. a delegate who was of known repudiatory principles.

†**re'pudious,** *a. Obs. rare.* [ad. L. *repudiōs-us* (Plautus): see next and -OUS.] **a.** = REPUDIATE A. 1. **b.** (See quot. 1656.)

1558 FORREST *Grysilde Sec.* (1875) 90 Grysilde to Walter repudius Because she was not pleasinge to his iye. **1656** BLOUNT *Glossogr.*, *Repudious*, villainous, dishonest, reproachful, that one refuseth and abhors much.

†**'repudy,** *sb. Obs. rare.* [ad. L. *repudium.*] Divorce; rejection, repulse.

1432–50 tr. *Higden* (Rolls) VI. 381 The qwene.. takynge a libelle of repudy, of repulsion, entrede a monastery. *c* **1480** HENRYSON *Test. Cres.* 74 Upon ane uther he set his haill delyt, And send to hir ane lybel of repudy. **1560** ROLLAND *Crt. Venus* IV. 68 Thay wald not thoill Venus haif lichtlines, Nor repudie, rebuik, nor ȝit distres.

†**repudy**, *v. Obs. rare.* [ad. F. *repudier* (15th c.) or It. *ripudiare*, L. *repudiāre*, f. *repudium*: see prec.] = REPUDIATE *v.*

c **1477** CAXTON *Jason* 119 Ye wylle now leue and repudye me in all poyntes. **1483** —— *Gold. Leg.* 410/1 Eche man myght haue foure wyues..and refuse and repudye thre tymes. **1635** J. HAYWARD *Banish'd Virg.* 141 An inkling of either repudying or making away of his present wife.

repugn (rɪ'pjuːn), *v.* Also 4–7 **repugne**, (6 **-pougne**), 4–6 **repungne**, 5–6 **repung(e**. [ad. F. *répugner* (14th c.), or L. *repugnāre*, f. *re-* RE- + *pugnāre* to fight: cf. *impugn*.]

†**1.** *intr.* To be contradictory or inconsistent. *Obs.*

c **1374** CHAUCER *Boeth.* v. pr. iii. 119 (Camb. MS.), It semyth quod I to repugnen and to contraryen gretly þat god knowit byforn alle thinges, and þat ther is any freedom of liberte. **1432–50** tr. *Higden* (Rolls) IV. 259 Hit repugnethe not that the chirche holdethe..Adam to haue be made of therthe the x kalendes of Aprile, and Criste to haue be incarnate the viij. kalendes of Aprile. *c* **1449** PECOCK *Repr.* III. xix. 408 If thei be considerid, tho chapitres schulen be seen forto not repugne bitwixe hem silf. **1533** MORE *Answ. Poysoned Bk.* Wks. 1121/1 Be content to knowe that goddes will, his worde, and his power, bee all one, and repugne not. **1576** GRINDAL *Wks.* (Parker Soc.) 384 Sixthly, places in the scriptures, seeming to repugn, are reconciled. **1654** Z. COKE *Logick* 68 Inseparable which is not easily separated from the subject, though to be separated nothing repugneth.

†**b.** To be contrary or opposed *to* something. *Obs.*

1395 PURVEY *Remonstr.* (1851) 131 When they ben certeyne that it repugnith to holy scripture..refuse it vtterly. **1457** *Lichfield Gild Ord.* (1890) 21 All other ordinaunces..which do not repunge to this ordinaunce. **1533** FRITH *Answ. More* (1548) D iv b, I see that sainct Thomas which felt Chrystes woundes..called hym his Lorde and God, and that no texte in scripture repugneth vnto yͤ same. **1586** T. B. *La Primaud. Fr. Acad.* (1589) 546 A corrupt common-wealth is that which repugneth and is directly contrarie to that which is good and just. **1673** H. STUBBE *Further Vind. Dutch War* App. 73 By sundry circumventions, and such proceedings as repugned to the Union of the Provinces.

†**c.** To stand *against* something. *Obs.*

1540–1 ELYOT *Image Gov.* 112 The detestable practice of usurie, which utterly repugneth against all humanitee. **1571** GOLDING *Calvin on Ps.* lxxiv. 5, I (although the accent repugn against it) doubte not, but that the sence which I have set down is the native sence.

†**d.** To be at variance *with* something. *Obs.*

1563 *Homilies* II. *Alms-deeds* III. (1859) 399 It is contrary to God's Word, it repugneth with his promise. **1609** BIBLE (Douay) *Ezek.* xviii. *comm.*, It is expressly affirmed that God would have al sinners to repent,..which semeth to repugne with the former doctrin. **1662** H. STUBBE *Ind. Nectar* Pref., What seemed..conformable to God's word, and the primitive practise: both which..did not repugn with my designed Speculations.

†**e.** To differ or vary *from* something. *Obs.*⁻¹

1600 W. WATSON *Decacordon* (1602) 285 It doth repugne from the very nature of all religious profession.

2. To offer opposition or resistance; to resist; to be recalcitrant; to object. Now *rare.*

1382 WYCLIF *1 Sam.* xv. 23 For as synne of deuynynge [*printed* denyynge] bi deuelis is to repugne. **1393** LANGL. *P. Pl.* C. I. 136 Ac of the cardinales at court, that cauȝt han Such a name,.. repungen [1377 inpugnen] ich nelle. **1531** ELYOT *Gov.* I. xiv, Wherfore they can nat resorte unto passetyme;..for nature repugnyng, they unneth taste anything that may be profytable. **1567** *Triall Treas.* (1850) 42 Yet will I prouoke, spurne, and pricke, Rebell, repugne, lashe out and kicke. **1596** DALRYMPLE tr. *Leslie's Hist. Scot.* III. 184 Finding na man to repugne, [he] ascriues vnto him selfe the dignitie of the king. **1646** OWEN *Country Ess.* Wks. 1851 VIII. 62 If any should dissent..I would entreat him to lay down some notes..and he shall not find me repugning. **1837** CARLYLE *Fr. Rev.* II. I. x, On the motion of Lameth,.. and other Patriot Nobles, let the others repugn as they will.

b. To fight, strive, or contend *against* a person or thing. Now *rare.*

1382 WYCLIF *Ezra* Prol., Other while concience repugnende aȝen hemself opinli thei to-tern that thei reden priueli. **1432–50** tr. *Higden* (Rolls) VII. 209 Wymundus..a man of noble eloquence, repugnede ageyne his erroures. **1483** CAXTON *Gold. Leg.* 65/2 For it is a synne to withstande and to repugne ayenst his lord. **1549** COVERDALE, etc. *Erasm. Par. 1 John* 47 Therfore like as he resisteth the sonne, euen so doethe he repugne agaynste the father. **1596** L. PIOT tr. *Silvayn's Orator* 346 Who then will judge you to be such a one, if you repugne against the will of the gods? **1675** tr. *Camden's Hist. Eliz.* I. (1688) 19 Against these Statutes nine Bishops in the Higher House..stifly repugned. **1858** CARLYLE *Fredk. Gt.* III. iii. (1872) I. 148 A Bund, or general Covenant for complaining; to repugn..against a domineering Ritterdom.

†**c.** To object or offer resistance *to* a thing.

1494 FABYAN *Chron.* I. xiii. 14 To yͭ repugnyth Wyllyam de Malmesbury, sayeng [etc.]. **1568** GRAFTON *Chron.* II. 404, I sweare that..I shall neuer repugne to thys resignation. **1581** SAVILE *Tacitus, Hist.* I. lxxx. (1591) 45 First they murder..the seuerest of the Centurions repugning to their seditious attempts. **1644** DIGBY *Nat. Bodies* vii. (1658) 62 Bodies which repugn to the dilatation of flame, may neverthelesse have much fire enclosed in them.

†**d.** Const. *at* a thing. *Obs.*

1529 *State Papers Hen. VIII* (1830) I. 339 His Grace repugned not therat, but herkened wel to it. **1586** BRIGHT *Melanch.* xvi. 97 It [the heart] repugneth oft times at the strong conclusions..reason can make.

3. *trans.* †**a.** To fight or contend against, to resist or repel (a person). *Obs.*

c **1380** WYCLIF *Serm.* Sel. Wks. II. 68 Who þat fallith upon þis stoon, repungning Crist or his lawe, shal be broken in his conscience. *c* **1470** HARDING *Chron.* CXVII. iv, With speare and swerd eyther other so repugned With axe and dagger. **1485** CAXTON *Chas. Gt.* 225 He aroos a lytel, & myghtyly repugned the geaunte. **1549** COVERDALE, etc. *Erasm. Par. 1 Tim.* 7 Therefore Prynces are neyther vnhonestly to be flattered, nor sediciously repugned. **1609** HOLLAND *Amm. Marcell.* XIV. ix. 19 A man gainesaying and repugning the flatterers that by whole troupes barked at him. **1635** QUARLES *Embl.* III. vi. 147 It is just that thy enemy should be my enemy, and that he who repugnes thee, should repugne me.

b. To oppose, resist, or contend against (something); to repel or reject; to refute, etc. Now somewhat *rare* (common in 16–17th c.).

c **1400** *Destr. Troy* 2670 þai..repugnet þo pointtes with a proude wille. **1496** *Dives & Paup.* (W. de W.) IV. xx. 184/2 It is full peryllous to the suget to repugne the dome of his souerayn. *a* **1533** LD. BERNERS *Gold. Bk. M. Aurel.* (1546) P viij, The olde Camyll repugned the counsell of his frendes. **1578** BANISTER *Hist. Man* I. 25, I meane not hereby to repugne altogether yͤ doctrine of so worthy a man. **1651** WITTIE tr. *Primrose's Pop. Err.* 329 Why the use thereof should be repugned, I see no reason. **1731** *Hist. Litteraria* II. 577 The very nature of his Subject..repugns any such Suspicion. **1780** EARL MALMESBURY *Diaries & Corr.* I. 273 Enervated to a degree, she repugns everything which bears the features of activity or exertion. **1833** SARAH AUSTIN *Charact. Goethe* I. 301 The sound mind of the German nation repugned these pernicious vagaries. **1878** COOTE *Romans of Brit.* Pref. 6 A homogeneity of race in England which truth plainly repugns.

†**c.** To deny *that*, etc. *Obs. rare*⁻¹.

1555 EDEN *Decades* 84 Yet doo I not repugne that in sume caues of mountaynes, water is turned into ayer.

†**4.** To be contrary or opposed to (a thing). *Obs.*

1387–8 T. USK *Test. Love* III. ii. (Skeat) l. 158 So me thinketh truly, that free choice fully repugneth Goddes forweting. **1545** JOYE *Exp. Dan.* vi. K viij b, So that their constitucions and actes repugne not the gospell of Christ. **1587** HOLINSHED *Chron.* (1807–8) IV. 592 To doo two things which seeme to repugne ech other. **1654** VILVAIN *Theol. Treat.* ii. 77 Absolut Reprobation repugns right reason, and begets absurdities. **1681** WHARTON *Apotolesma* Wks. (1683) 37 Some being utterly lost in conceipts that repugn Philosophy.

5. a. *intr.* To be repugnant *to* (the mind). *rare*⁻¹.

1831 T. HOPE *Ess. Origin Man* II. 15 Where..we have only the option to believe what repugns to our intellect, or what seems..to glide most easily into the same.

b. *trans.* To affect (one) with repugnance or aversion. Also *absol.*, to cause repugnance.

1868 J. H. STIRLING in *N. Brit. Rev.* XLIX. 358 Browning has a flavour of his own, of which, in the first taste, the newness repugns. **1890** —— *Philos. & Theol.* ii. 28 To attempt to philosophize the Christian Godhead would only repugn. **1890** *Harper's Mag.* Nov. 875/1 She seemed to be afraid of saying nothing: no term repugned her.

†**re'pugnable**, *a. Obs.* [f. prec. + -ABLE: cf. obs. F. *repugnable* (Godef.).] **a.** Capable of being repugned or refuted. **b.** Contrary, opposed.

1579–80 NORTH *Plutarch, Marcellus* (1612) 315 The demonstration prouing it so exquisitely, with wonderfull reason and facilitie, as it is not repugnable. **1632** LITHGOW *Trav.* IX. 398 No such..repugnable Currents, as be in the firths of Stronza and Westra. **1655** M. CARTER *Hon. Rediv.* (1660) 88 That what Laws should be Enacted, might be answerable to the Will of God, and not repugnable to the Customs of the Land.

repugnance (rɪ'pʌgnəns). Also 5–6 **repung-**. [a. F. *répugnance* (13th c.), or L. *repugnantia*: see REPUGN *v.* and -ANCE.]

1. Contradiction, inconsistency; contradictory opposition or disagreement of ideas or statements. Also with *a* and *pl.*

1387–8 T. USK *Test. Love* III. iv. (Skeat) l. 42 It is open at the ful, that without al maner repugnaunce god beforn wot al maner thinges ben don by free will. *c* **1449** PECOCK *Repr.* V. ii. 489 So the same secte schulde be good and badde, leeful and vnleeful, which is repugnaunce. **1533** MORE *Answ. Poysoned Bk.* Wks. 1123/2 He sheweth that it implieth repugnaunce, and that therefore God cannot do it. **1568** GRAFTON *Chron.* II. 211 The Copie [of the letter] that came to my hande seemed to conteyne diuerse repugnaunces. **1630** PRYNNE *Anti-Armin.* 147 These seuerall Answers..will reconcile all seeming repugnances of Scripture. **1678** GALE *Crt. Gentiles* IV. iii. 79 In the words of Hosea c. 8. 4. there appears a kind of repugnance. **1755** B. MARTIN *Mag. Arts & Sc.* I. iv. 17 You will observe..a palpable Absurdity and Repugnance in the one, and..a perfect Consistency and Agreement in the other. **1824** MACKINTOSH *S. Amer. States* Wks. 1846 III. 474 In it there is more than the usual repugnance between the title and the purport. **1888** BRYCE *Amer. Commw.* I. I. App. 542 Care is taken in preparing the draft, in seeing that it is free from errors or repugnances.

†**2.** Resistance or opposition offered to a thing or person. *Obs.*

14.. in *Tundale's Vis.* (1843) 129 Nature withowtt any stryff Of repugnaunce or any recystence Gaff thys meyde a specyall prerogatyf. **1430–40** LYDG. *Bochas* XI. xxxi. (1554) 211 b, Christes martirs..List agein tirauntes make no repugnance. **1523** SKELTON *Garl. Laurel* 211 To make repugnaunce agayne that ye haue sayde. **1547** *Homilies* I. *Charity* I. (1859) 68 So went he unto his death without any repugnance or opening of his mouth to say any evil.

†**b.** Opposition or contrariety between or of things. *Obs.*

c **1400** tr. *Secreta Secret., Gov. Lordsh.* 78 þe kyndly comyth of repugnance of contrarious qualytez and contradiccioun. **1538** STARKEY *England* I. iv. 108 Ther ys no repugnance betwyx your opynyon and myne in thys grete mater. **1555** EDEN *Decades* 269 By the commixtion and repugnance of fyre, could, and brymstone greate stones are here throwne into the ayer. **1654** Z. COKE *Logick* Pref., Whereof..after long Exagitations and Repugnance of Affairs, we have gotten more then a (glad) glimpse.

†**c.** Disagreement in feelings or tastes. *Obs. rare.*

1531 ELYOT *Gov.* II. xi, Where is any repugnaunce, may be none amitie, sens frendshippe is an entier consent of willes and desires.

†**d.** A mental struggle. *Obs. rare*⁻¹.

1538 STARKEY *England* I. ii. 29 Ychone in hym selfe, when he doth nough[t], felyth a gruge in conscyence and repugnance in mynd.

3. Strong dislike, distaste, antipathy, or aversion (*to* or *against* a thing). Also *pl.*

1643 SIR T. BROWNE *Relig. Med.* II. § 1, I feel not in myself those common antipathies..: those national repugnances do not touch me. **1665** GLANVILL *Def. Van. Dogm.* p. v, I confess I addrest myself unwillingly and not without repugnance to the performance. **1765** H. WALPOLE *Otranto* v. 172 If I were sure Isabella would have no repugnance. **1796** BURNEY *Mem. Metastasio* I. 90 It is terrible that..he should have no repugnance to injuring numbers. **1854** MILMAN *Lat. Chr.* VI. iii. III. 76 A deep repugnance against ecclesiastical tyranny may have taken root within his heart. **1874** GREEN *Short Hist.* vii. § 3. 370 No marked repugnance to the new worship was shown by the people at large.

repugnancy (rɪ'pʌgnənsɪ). [See -ANCY.]

1. Contradiction, inconsistency, etc. = REPUGNANCE 1. Now *rare* (common *c* 1560–1800).

1560 BECON *New Catech.* Wks. (1564) I. 464 b, Whiche are two suche repugnauncies and contraries, as darkenes is not more contrary to lyght, nor death to lyfe. **1589** PUTTENHAM *Eng. Poesie* I. i. (Arb.) 20 Without any repugnancie at all, a Poet may in some sort be said a follower or imitator. *a* **1625** SIR H. FINCH *Law* (1636) 391 This carrieth a repugnancie in it, inasmuch as the house and the wall are all one thing. **1681** GLANVILL *Sadducismus* I. (1726) 78 Both the Hypotheses do entangle..the Doctrine..with greater Difficulties and Repugnancies. **1785** PALEY *Mor. Philos.* (1818) II. 31 If these..serve to remove the apparent repugnancy between the success of prayer and the character of the Deity, it is enough. **1822–34** *Good's Study Med.* (ed. 4) II. 610 From the number and repugnancy..there is no small difficulty in reducing them to anything like an intelligible classification. **1865** *Daily Tel.* 21 Oct. 3/4 Even Sir James Stephen.. acknowledged that he could not render the exact legal idea of 'repugnancy' more intelligible.

†**b.** The opposite *of* something. *Obs. rare*⁻¹.

1586 A. DAY *Eng. Secretary* I. (1625) 3 The repugnancy hereof is when either with too much curtalling our arguments..or with too many or ouer-often repetitions,.. wee abbreuiate or amplifie our Epistles.

2. Opposition or resistance of mind or feeling. In later use = REPUGNANCE 3.

1557 N.T. (Genev.) *1 Cor.* i. 10 *note*, Dissention of mynde, wherof procedeth repugnancie of iudgement, which is the mother of schisme and heresie. **1577** tr. *Bullinger's Decades* (1592) 302 Yet is that repugnancye still in theyr heartes. **1642** ROGERS *Naaman* 131 Such an horrible repugnancie of heart against this way. **1681** BELLON *Myst. Physick* 64 If the Sick has a repugnancy against so frequently taking of the Drink, it may be given less often. **1742** FIELDING *J. Andrews* (1815) Pref. 6 It hath not that violent repugnancy of nature to struggle with, which that of the hypocrite hath. **1839** KEIGHTLEY *Hist. Eng.* II. 52 Pole's strong repugnancy to accept the highest dignity. **1868** MILMAN *St. Paul's* 316 He treated the Puritan divines with more and more determined repugnancy.

†**b.** Dislike or aversion on the part *of* one. *Obs.*

1702 ECHARD *Eccl. Hist.* (1710) 399 Scarce any man arrived at the Empire with a more sullyed reputation, or a greater repugnancy of the people.

†**3.** Opposition or resistance to action; tendency to oppose. *Obs.*

1587 HOLINSHED *Chron.* III. 979/2 His too much repugnancie..in matters of councell to the residue of the councellors about the king. **1602** WARNER *Alb. Eng.* Epit. 385 King Henrie the sixth was triumphantly crowned.. mauger the Dolphins then repugnancie. *a* **1635** NAUNTON *Fragm. Reg.* (Arb.) 42 He was sent Lord Deputy into Ireland, (as it was thought) for a kind of haughtinesse of spirit, and repugnancy in Councels.

repugnant (rɪ'pʌgnənt), *a.* and *sb.* [a. F. *répugnant* (1372) or ad. L. *repugnant-em*, pres. pple. of *repugnāre* to REPUGN.]

A. *adj.* **1.** Contrary or contradictory *to*, inconsistent or incompatible *with*, †divergent *from*, †standing *against*, something else.

1387–8 T. USK *Test. Love* III. i. (Skeat) l. 128 All lawes, or custome,..that contrarien law of kinde, vtterly ben repugnaunt and aduersary to our godds wil of heuen. **1461** *Rolls of Parlt.* V. 467/1 Repugnaunt or contrarie to the seid right. **1477** in *Eng. Gilds* (1870) 307 All thinges not repugnant to the premisses. **1534** WHITINTON *Tullyes Offices* I. (1540) 5 Whan that thynge semeth to be repugnaunt with honestye, that semeth profytable. **1551** T. WILSON *Logike* 17 b, Obey the higher power in all things that are not directly repugnant from the will of God. **1590** C. S. *Right Relig.* 24 Repugnant plainely against the law of Moses. **1660** R. COKE *Power & Subj.* 140 If the Laws..do command things repugnant to Gods word. **1685** H. MORE *Paralip. Prophet.* xlix. 459 Not at all repugnant with our Hypothesis. **1748** *Anson's Voy.* II. iv. 165 The coming in sight of that Island was directly repugnant to the Merchant's instructions. **1818** CRUISE *Digest* (ed. 2) V. 28 The clause was void, because it was repugnant to the body of the act. **1864** BOWEN *Logic* iv. 91 The number of attributes in the universe not logically repugnant to each other is infinite.

b. Without const., *esp.* of two or more things in relation to each other.
1387–8 T. USK *Test. Love* III. iii. (Skeat) l. 32 To euery wiȝt..is seen these thinges to be repugnaunt. *c* **1449** PECOCK *Repr.* III. xix. 408 Therfore tho chapitres ben not bitwixe hem silf repugnant. **1528** GARDINER in Pocock *Rec. Ref.* I. 118 In hurts done and taken on either party there is many times tidings repugnant. **1590** SWINBURNE *Testaments* 122 Those conditions which by reason of contraritie or repugnant perplexitie be impossible, or incompatible. **1614** RALEIGH *Hist. World* II. (1634) 372 There being found three places of Scripture touching this point, seeming repugnant or disagreeing. **1660** BARROW *Euclid* I. xxvii, The outward angle AEF will be greater than the inward angle DFE, to which it was equal by Hypothesis, which is repugnant. **1766** BLACKSTONE *Comm.* II. 157 A condition either impossible, illegal, or repugnant. **1800** *Med. Jrnl.* IV. 213 When these are..variously combined with no properties chemically repugnant. **1864** BOWEN *Logic* iv. 65 Considered in relation to each other Marks are either Congruent or Repugnant.

†**c.** Diverse, different. *Obs. rare*⁻¹.
1544 tr. *Littleton's Tenures* (1574) 99 Yᵉ cause of the diversity betwene these two cases is repugnant ynough.

2. Making or offering resistance (*to* a person or thing); opposing, resisting, hostile, antagonistic, refractory.
c **1460** G. ASHBY *Dicta Philos.* 1029 Suche folk as be conversant With goode men and wise, to Il repugnant. **1494** FABYAN *Chron.* VII. 436 But to all this was the towne of Gaunt repugnaunt, in so moche yᵗ mortall warre beganne. **1533** BELLENDEN *Livy* III. xvi. (S.T.S.) II. 11 Sum tyme (becaus he was repugnant) he bad tak him perforce. **1581** PETTIE tr. *Guazzo's Civ. Conv.* II. (1586) 102 b, He ought to be called ignorant, whose minde is repugnant to knowledge. *c* **1595** CAPT. WYATT *R. Dudley's Voy. W. Ind.* (Hakl. Soc.) 35 To which proceedings above all others Captain Jobson.. was much contradictorie and repugnante. **1627** MAY *Lucan* III. (1631) 592 As when strong windes with tydes repugnant meet, One way the Sea, the waues another go. **1818** BYRON *Ch. Har.* IV. lxxv, I abhorr'd..The drill'd dull lesson, forced down word by word In my repugnant youth. **1875** BROWNING *Aristoph. Apol.* 5 Never again may these repugnant orbs Ache themselves blind.

†**b.** Of medicines: Operative *against*, counteractive *to*, something. *Obs. rare.*
1559 MORWYNG *Evonym.* 148 It is repugnant against all kinds of worms within the body. **1568** SKEYNE *The Pest* (1860) 23 Quhilk is repugnant to all vther kynd of poysone.

3. Distasteful or objectionable *to* one.
1777 WATSON *Philip II*, XIV. (1793) II. 210 The limitations..imposed upon the sovereign's authority were utterly repugnant to Philip's temper. **1825** LAMB *Elia* Ser. II. *Stage Illusion*, Characters in comedy..which involve some notion repugnant to the moral sense. **1869** FREEMAN *Norm. Conq.* (1875) III. xi. 57 A step likely to be in many ways repugnant to Northumbrian feeling.

b. Exciting distaste or aversion; offensive, loathsome, repulsive.
1879 tr. *De Quatrefages' Hum. Spec.* 49 The flesh also assumes a repugnant appearance.

†**B.** *sb.* **1.** A recusant or resister. *Obs. rare*⁻¹.
1625 BP. MOUNTAGU *App. Cæsar* 143 What..Edict did ever command it to be professed, or..imposed penaltie upon repugnants, or non-consentients unto it?

†**2.** *Logic.* A term or proposition forming the contrary or contradictory of another. *Obs.*
1654 Z. COKE *Logick* 169 One of the contradicents and repugnants being put, the other is removed. **1697** tr. *Burgersdicius his Logic* II. x. 44 Seek first the Consequences of the Predicate,..then the Repugnants.

re'pugnantly, *adv.* [f. prec. + -LY.] †In a contrary, contradictory, or inconsistent manner.
1556 J. HEYWOOD *Spider & F.* xcii. 139 Whose deede and his thought repungnantlie varie, His woord and his thought iar likewise contrarie. **1586** HOOKER *Disc. Justif.* (1618) 59. Works of righteousnesse therefore are not so repugnantly added in the one proposition; as in the other, Circumcision is. **1668** H. MORE *Div. Dial.* I. xxviii. (1713) 58 That is again spitefully interposed,..and yet repugnantly to your own admired Oracle.

So **re'pugnantness**, 'repugnancy; contrary nature or quality' (Bailey 1727, vol. II).

repugnate (rɪˈpʌgneɪt), *v. rare.* [f. ppl. stem of L. *repugnāre*: see REPUGN *v.*] *trans.* and *intr.* To oppose, resist.
1829 I. TAYLOR *Enthus.* vii. (1867) 169 A feeling.. repugnates and subdues those self-gratulations. **1849** —— *Loyola & Jes.* (1857) 278 Nor can it be but by a sort of force that the will continues long to follow where the judgment repugnates.

repugnatorial (rɪˌpʌgnəˈtɔərɪəl), *a. Zool.* [f. L. *repugnātōri-us* + -AL¹.] Serving for defence; applied to certain glands or pores in *Diplopoda*, from which a malodorous fluid can be emitted.
1898 PACKARD *Textbk. Entomol.* 372 Certain beetles are endowed with repugnatorial glands.

†**re'pugnatory**, *a. Obs. rare.* [ad. F. *repugnatoire*: see prec.] Defensive.
1737 OZELL *Rabelais* III. Prol. III. p. vii, Others made ready Bows..and others Warlike Engines, repugnatory and destructive. *Ibid.* 211 *note*, He calls 'em Repugnatory Weapons, not Expugnatory as our Translator [*sc.* Urquhart] inadvertently turns it.

re'pugner. *rare.* [f. REPUGN *v.* + -ER¹.] One who repugns.
c **1449** PECOCK *Repr.* II. xi. 208 The repungners aȝens the ..afore tretid gouernauncis. **1570** FOXE *A. & M.* (ed. 2) 369/1 Excommunicatyng all repugners and rebellers agaynst the same.

repugning (rɪˈpjuːnɪŋ), *vbl. sb.* [f. as prec. + -ING¹.] Opposition, resistance.
1395 PURVEY *Remonstr.* (1851) 131 Where they be vncertain of such founding eyther repugning, put it aback, neyther take it as beleue. **1555** W. WATREMAN *Fardle Facions* I. v. 60 Sondry Kynges by the repugnynges of the people haue lien untoombed. **1596** DALRYMPLE tr. *Leslie's Hist. Scot.* III. 197 He gaue her landes and steddings.., nocht respecteng the scharpe repunging of the Pechtes. **1630** G. WIDDOWES *Schysmatical Puritan* Pref., A dispising of Canonicall obedience; a repugning against our Reformed Church.

repugning (rɪˈpjuːnɪŋ), *ppl. a.* [f. as prec. + -ING².] That repugns; †*esp.* contrary or opposed *to* something. *Obs.*
c **1440** CAPGRAVE *Life St. Kath.* v. 1406 This vengeauns is repugnynge to your deyte. **1509** BARCLAY *Shyp of Folys* (1570) 3 Unkindnes..is repugning to reason and iustice. **1577** tr. *Bullinger's Decades* (1592) 251 God..cannot any time either erre, or conceiue any false opinions, or repugning counsels. **1586** A. DAY *Eng. Secretary* I. (1625) 67 Actions of such kinde are alwayes vnto the noble and best endued mindes vtterly repugning. *a* **1602** W. PERKINS *Cases Consc.* (1619) 28 When a thing is done with a repugning or gain-saying conscience.

repuit(e, obs. Sc. forms of REPUTE *v.*

re'pull, *v.* [RE- 2 a.] To pull *back* again.
1632 LITHGOW *Trav.* IX. 404 Forthwith his Master repulling him backe, cast him [a dog] in the Lake.

repullulate (rɪˈpʌljʊleɪt), *v.* [f. ppl. stem of L. *repullulāre* (Pliny): see PULLULATE.]
1. *intr.* To bud or sprout again. Also *fig.* Hence **re'pullulating** *ppl. a.*
1623 in COCKERAM. **1637** GILLESPIE *Eng. Pop. Cerem.* Ep. A iij, The repullulating twigges and sprigges of Popish superstition. **1674** *Phil. Trans.* IX. 110 These Tufts did as often repullulate, as they were struck and wiped clean off. **1716** M. DAVIES *Athen. Brit.* III. 85 Soon after the Gothick Barbarity repullulated again. **1822** MRS. E. NATHAN *Langreath* III. 290 Whose branches I fear are withered, never to repullulate again.
2. *Path.* Of diseases: To start afresh; to recur.
1762 R. GUY *Pract. Obs. Cancers* 14 The Disease is apt to repullulate, and speedily prove fatal. *a* **1776** R. JAMES *Dissert. Fevers* (1778) 84 Such [fevers] as are symptomatic, and repullulate constantly from a permanent cause.

repullulation (rɪpʌljʊˈleɪʃən). [f. prec.]
1. The action or fact of sprouting again.
1622 DONNE *Serm.* Wks. (1839) VI. 89 He would haue left no seed or he would not have admitted such a repullulation. **1668** H. MORE *Div. Dial.* v. xiv. II. 327 That inmost..sense of the Soul, which is the Repullulation of the pure Love. **1771** *Misc. Ess.* in *Ann. Reg.* 172/2 Analogous to the repullulation of trees after lopping.
2. *Path.* Recurrence of a disease; return of a morbid growth.
1725 HUXHAM in *Phil. Trans.* XXXIII. 389 In a Case or two I observ'd a Repullulation of Pustules. **1862** GROSS *Syst. Surg.* (1872) I. 229 If the least germ of morbid product be left, repullulation will be almost inevitable.

re'pullulative, *a.* [f. REPULLULATE *v.* + -IVE.] Having the faculty of sprouting again.
1825 COLERIDGE *Lett.* (1895) II. 743 Nature is..divisible as the polyp, repullulative in a thousand snips and cuttings.

re,pullu'lescent, *a.* [f. pres. pple. of L. *repullulescĕre*: cf. REPULLULATE *v.*] Reviving, springing up afresh.
a **1734** NORTH *Lives* (1826) II. 113 One would have believed this expedient..calculated to obviate the ill use a repullulescent faction might make.

re'pulpit (riː-), *v.* [RE- 5 a.] *trans.* To restore to the pulpit.
1875 TENNYSON *Q. Mary* I. v, You have ousted the mock priest, re-pulpited The shepherd of St. Peter.

repulse (rɪˈpʌls), *sb.* [ad. L. *repulsus* or *repulsa*, f. *repuls-*, ppl. stem of *repellĕre* to REPEL. Cf. obs. F. *repulse*, *-poulse* (Godef.).]
1. The act of repelling an assailant or hostile force; the fact of being driven back in an engagement or assault.
c **1540** tr. *Pol. Verg. Eng. Hist.* (Camden) I. 190 Thei pursewed the repulse and committed great slaughter. **1577–87** HOLINSHED *Chron.* I. 25/1 If the enimies were put to the repulse, they would easilie escape the danger with swiftnesse of foot. **1603** KNOLLES *Hist. Turks* (1638) 25 He notwithstanding the former repulse, the next yeare..laid hard siege again to Ptolemais. **1667** MILTON *P.L.* VI. 600 What should they do? if on they rusht, repulse Repeated. **1821** SHELLEY *Hellas* 988 Repulse, with plumes from conquest torn, Led the ten thousand..Through many an hostile Anarchy. **1879** H. PHILLIPS *Addit. Notes Coins* 3 A grand silver medal commemorates the repulse of the Turks before the City of Zenta.
†**b.** An act or mode of repelling an injury. *Obs.*
1590 SEGAR (*title*) The Booke of Honor and Armes, wherein is discoursed the causes of Quarrell, and the nature of Iniuries, with their repulses. *Ibid.* I. 14 Hee vnto whom the Lie is giuen for a repulse of iniurie ought to be the Challenger.
2. Refusal (of a request, suit, etc.); denial, rejection, rebuff.
1533 BELLENDEN *Livy* II. vi. (S.T.S.) I. 152 Þocht þe said porsena desirit þe tarquinis to be restorit, he knewe na thing bettir þan repulss of sic desiris. **1592** NASHE *Four Lett. Confut.* 43 Many followers, whose dutifull seruices must not bee disgrac'd with a bitter repulse in anie suite. **1601** F. GODWIN *Bps. of Eng.* 5 He gaue not ouer with one repulse, but..procured a second conference. **1654** BRAMHALL *Just Vind.* vii. (1661) 165 This was the second repulse, yet the Popes were not so easily shaken off. **1712** ADDISON *Spect.* No. 457 ¶3 Applications for Places, with their respective Successes or Repulses. **1759** ROBERTSON *Hist. Scot.* v. Wks. 1813 I. 376 Upon this repulse, Mary's commissioners withdrew. **1782** MISS BURNEY *Cecilia* IX. v, The rigour of your repulse aiarmed me. **1853** C. BRONTË *Villette* xxxvii, I went on, gaining courage on finding that I met attention rather than repulse.
†**b.** In phrases *to take* or *have* (*the*) *repulse*, *to give* (one) *the repulse*. *Obs.*
1603 HOLLAND *Plutarch's Mor.* 431 Pavlvs Aemilivs making sute for his second Consulship, was rejected and tooke repulse. **1611** CORYAT *Crudities* 31, I went to the Dominican Monastery, and made suit to see it, but I had the repulse. **1644** BULWER *Chirol.* 54 Shaking his head, [he] gave him the repulse. **1692** R. L'ESTRANGE *Josephus, Antiq.* IV. viii. (1733) 96 Her Husband's Brother had given her the Repulse.
3. The act of forcing or driving back; the fact of being forced back. Now *rare* or *Obs.*
1578 BANISTER *Hist. Man* I. 24 By their meanes, eche sodaine..stroake of the brest hath an easie repulse, in their yelding from it. **1615** W. LAWSON *Country Housew. Gard.* (1626) 28 That saues a second wound, and a second repulse of sap. **1710** J. HARRIS *Lex. Techn.* II. s.v., It is one of the laws of Nature..that Repulse or Reaction is always equal to Impulse or Action. **1776** G. SEMPLE *Building in Water* 145 And, in the Repulse, think what a most powerful Suction that Repulse will create.
†**b.** A check in growth. *Obs. rare*⁻¹.
1657 AUSTEN *Fruit Trees* I. 87 Stocks removed have so great a wound and repulse by removing only, that they cannot well beare another so soone after.

Hence **re'pulseless** *a.*, 'that cannot be repelled' (Webster 1847).

repulse (rɪˈpʌls), *v.* [f. L. *repuls-*, ppl. stem of *repellĕre* to REPEL; cf. also obs. F. *repulser* (mod. *repousser*), ad. L. *repulsāre*.]
1. *trans.* To drive or beat back (an assailant); to repel by force of arms.
1533 BELLENDEN *Livy* II. vi. (S.T.S.) I. 147 Porsena, repulsit of his first assalt, set him be prudent counsell to sege þe ciete. *a* **1548** HALL *Chron., Hen. VII* 34 b, The Easterlynges had muche a do to withstande and repulse them oute of their gates. **1617** MORYSON *Itin.* II. 192 If wee had beene repulsed with any blow giuen vs,..all the Irish.. would haue turned their swords against vs. **1697** DRYDEN *Virg. Georg.* III. 620 Thy faithful Dogs..who, for the Folds Relief,..Repulse the prouling Wolf. **1788** GIBBON *Decl. & F.* l. V. 244 His valour withstood and repulsed the superior numbers of the Christians. **1841** ELPHINSTONE *Hist. Ind.* II. 623 Even then he was more than once repulsed before the city fell into his hands. **1865** *Reader* 4 Mar. 246/1 These sorties..were made with vigour, and not repulsed quite so easily as he would have us believe.
absol. **1489** CAXTON *Faytes of A.* I. ix. B iv, To come hand to hand for to repulse or shoue forth with sperys. **1585** JAMES in Motley *Netherl.* v. (1860) I. 223 The enemy pursued very hotly; the Englishmen stood to repulse, and are put most to the sword.
†**b.** To repel or ward off (an injury). *Obs.*
1590 SEGAR *Book of Honor* I. 4 Whosoeuer being offered iniurious speach, shall say to the offerer therof Thou liest,.. doth therby repulse the iniurie, and force the Iniurer to challenge. **1606** BRYSKETT *Civ. Life* 82 It is lawfull for a man to repulse an iniury, and to defend himselfe.
†**c.** To force back (a thing). *Obs. rare.*
1601 DOLMAN *La Primaud. Fr. Acad.* (1618) III. 738 Hotte and dry exhalations..being repulsed backe by the beames of the stars into the cloudes. **1664** POWER *Exp. Philos.* III. 157 Being repulsed by the ambient Ayr, they recoyl again, and return in a Vortical Motion.
2. To repel with denial; to reject, refuse, rebuff. †Also const. *from*.
1533 BELLENDEN *Livy* II. xiv. (S.T.S.) I. 182 Becaus his petitiouns war repulsit afore þe senate, he said in þis wise. **1577** PATERICKE tr. *Gentillet* (1602) 165 These embassadours seeing themselves repulsed from their demaund, returned to Capua. **1602** SHAKS. *Ham.* II. ii. 146 He repulsed, A short Tale to make, Fell into a Sadnesse. **1667** MILTON *P.L.* x. 910 Eve Not so repulst..at his feet Fell humble. **1766** GOLDSM. *Vic. W.* xxxi, Mr. Thornhill..was going to embrace his uncle, which the other repulsed with an air of disdain. **1859** TENNYSON *Geraint & Enid* 834 Being repulsed By Yniol and yourself, I schemed and wrought Until I overturn'd him. **1894** J. T. FOWLER *Adamnan* Introd. 26 They were repulsed with laughter.
†**b.** Const. with *inf.* *Obs. rare*⁻¹.
1590 SEGAR *Book of Honor* IV. 57 A Gentleman that is knowne a Spie for the Enemie..may be repulsed to fight with euerie other Gentlemen of good fame and reputation.
†**c.** To rebuke, reprove. *Obs. rare*⁻¹.
1746 in W. Thompson *R.N. Advoc.* (1757) 24 The O——s of the Flesh Branch..frequently repulsed their Men for refusing to..salt what was not fit for Service.
†**3.** To shut out, exclude *from* something. *Obs.*
1548 UDALL, etc. *Erasm. Par. Matt.* xviii. 76 Lorde..how often shal I pardon my brother..and after what numbre of faultes shall he be repulsed from pardone? **1602** FULBECKE *1st Pt. Parall.* 26 Then the children only..are repulsed from the inheritance, and then it goeth to them of the kinred which are nearer in degree.
4. To affect with repulsion. *rare*⁻¹.
1845 LUNDIE *Missionary Life in Samoa* ix. 52 Many things [in Australia] shocked and repulsed his feelings.

Hence **re'pulsed** *ppl. a.*, repelled, †conveying a repulse; **re'pulser**, one who repels; †a repelling medicine. Also **re'pulsing** *vbl. sb.* and *ppl. a.*
1490 CAXTON *Eneydos* xxvii. 102 The ryuages & portes.. be to them repulsyng, contrare & rebel, euer more. *a* **1578** LINDESAY (Pitscottie) *Chron. Scot.* (S.T.S.) II. 93 The governour..was nocht content heirof and gaif nothing againe bot ane repullsit ansuer. [Also *Ibid.* 146.] **1590** SIR J.

SMYTH *Disc. Weapons* 4b, To the repulsing either of horsemen or footemen. **1611** COTGR., *Repoulseur*, a repulser, a repelier. **1632** tr. *Bruel's Praxis Med.* 113 In the increase [of the disease] repulsers must be aboue resoluers. **1711** in *10th Rep. Hist. MSS. Comm.* App. V. 163 By this repulseing of the enemy to his own side of the river. **1889** *Pall Mall G.* 4 Jan. 3/3 In the repulsed attack the Guards lost about that proportion in a very few minutes.

repulsion (rɪˈpʌlʃən). [ad. late L. *repulsiōn-em*, n. of action f. *repellĕre*: cf. REPULSE *sb.* and *v.*, and F. *répulsion* (1450 in Godef.).]

†**1.** Repudiation, divorce. *Obs. rare.*

1412-20 LYDG. *Chron. Troy* V. xxxvi. (1555), He..The Kinges doughter hath vtterly forsake And in all haste did a libell make And forge a writ of repulsyon. **1432-50** tr. *Higden* (Rolls) VI. 381 The qwene..takynge a libelle of repudy, of repulsion, entrede a monastery.

2. a. The action of forcing or driving back or away.

1547 *Acts Privy Council* (1890) II. 534 A violent and tumultuous repultion of the watchmen of the cittie, from and out of their said liberties. **1624** WOTTON *Archit.* in *Reliq.* (1672) 38 Then there is a repulsion of the Fume, by some higher Hill or Fabrick that shall overtop the Chimney. **1631** *Celestina* VI. 75 Shee hath eyes which let flye darts of repulsion. **1736** WARBURTON *Alliance betw. Ch. & State* III. iii, Evil which proceeds not from the will is called a mischief; and may be simply repelled; and this repulsion is called restraint. **1788** *Trifler* No. 19. 259 Whatever has tended to the repulsion of barbarity, and the improvement of civilization, is an object on which panegyric can never be exhausted. **1817** JAS. MILL *Brit. India* I. II. vi. 256 The sacred lamp was lighted for the repulsion of evil spirits. **1820** RANKEN *Hist. France* VII. I. ii. 80 The repulsion of the Spanish army under the Archduke Albert from Picardy.

b. *Med.* The action of repelling humours, eruptions, etc., from the affected parts; †a means of effecting this.

1725 BRADLEY *Fam. Dict.* s.v. *Wounds*, A Repulsion must be made in the beginning, that is, you must divert the Course of the Humours, and prevent their falling upon the Wound: Bleeding is the best Repulsion. **1773** T. PERCIVAL *Ess.* II. 214 Complaints, which had succeeded the sudden repulsion of an eruption on his foot, by means of an astringent bath. **1822-34** *Good's Study Med.* (ed. 4) IV. 433 There is also a greater tendency..to a sickness, or some other disorder of the stomach, upon repulsion by cold.

3. a. *Physics.* The action of one body in repelling another; tendency of bodies to increase their mutual distance. (Opposed to ATTRACTION.)

1725 N. ROBINSON *Th. Physick* Pref. 9, I have often thought all the several Principles of Philosophy might be comprehended under the two distinct Terms of Attraction and Repulsion. **1797** *Encycl. Brit.* (ed. 3) XVI. 85/2 Repulsion, as well as attraction, has of late been considered as one of the primary qualities of all matter. **1830** HERSCHEL *Stud. Nat. Phil.* 297 The production of motion by the mutual attractions and repulsions of distant or contiguous masses. **1850** DAUBENY *Atom. The.* iv. (ed. 2) 125 The force of repulsion..tends to keep the particles of an aëriform fluid at a certain distance apart. **1866** R. M. FERGUSON *Electr.* (1870) 7 We may conclude that magnetic attraction and repulsion takes place only between magnets temporary or permanent.

attrib. **1882** S. P. THOMSON *Electr. & Magn.* 212 Repulsion Electrometers. **1891-** *Electrom.* 288 Repulsion Apparatus.

b. *transf.* Tendency to separate or put further apart, to introduce division or difference, etc.

1843 GLADSTONE *Glean.* (1879) V. i. 59 Where their influence..is necessarily at an end.., nay rather, where it is converted into a force of absolute, of most powerful repulsion. **1876** DOUSE *Grimm's L.* 78 What we are here concerned with is the process of ethnic and linguistic repulsion.

c. *Genetics.* The condition of two genes, in an individual heterozygous at each of two linked loci, when the dominant allele of each occurs on the same chromosome as the recessive allele of the other. Opp. COUPLING *vbl. sb.* 6e.

[**1908** *Science* 15 May 786/1 When in F_1 the two dominants, femaleness and the *grossulariata* factor coexist, there is a repulsion between them, such that each gamete takes one or other of these two factors, not both. **1911** *Proc. R. Soc.* B. LXXXIV. 3 We were therefore led to recognize—A. A system of partial coupling under which two factors are generally associated. B. A system of complete repulsion (or as we have sometimes called it 'spurious allelomorphism') under which two factors are never associated in the same gamete.] **1926**, **1970** [see COUPLING *vbl. sb.* 6e]. **1977** MATHER & JINKS *Introd. Biometrical Genetics* viii. 203 The associated distribution will lead to coupling linkage in F_1 and so may be denoted by C, while the dispersed distribution will give repulsion linkage and so may be denoted by R.

4. Influence tending to repel one from a person or thing; dislike, aversion, repugnance.

1751 JOHNSON *Rambler* No. 160 ¶5 There are many natures which..seem to start back from each other by some invincible repulsion. **1847** EMERSON *Poems, Visit*, If Love his moment overstay, Hatred's swift repulsions play. **1863** GEO. ELIOT *Romola* xv, There was an unconquerable repulsion for her in that monkish aspect. **1871** B. TAYLOR *Faust* (1875) II. III. i. 169 Strong repulsion written on thy brow I see.

5. *attrib.* **repulsion motor** *Electr.*, an a.c. commutator motor for single-phase operation in which current is supplied to the stator only, the armature being short-circuited through the brushes and its current induced from the stator winding.

1904 E. B. RAYMOND *Alternating Current Engin.* iv. 187 The repulsion motor..can be used as an electric brake. **1920** *Whittaker's Electr. Engineer's Pocket-bk.* (ed. 4) 229 The repulsion motor is the simplest and commonest of all a.c. commutator motors. **1972** C. C. BARNES et al. *Electrics* 72/73 148 A repulsion motor has a single-field winding and a wound rotor with a centrifugal device to short-circuit the commutator.

repulsive (rɪˈpʌlsɪv), *a.* and *sb.* [a. F. *répulsif*, *-ive* (14th c.), or f. REPULSE *v.* + -IVE.]

A. *adj.* **1.** Having the character of repelling; driving or forcing back; returning a sound; resisting moisture, etc.

c **1611** CHAPMAN *Iliad* XVI. 66 For the repulsiue hand of Diomed doth not spend His raging darts there. **1744** AKENSIDE *Pleas. Imag.* I. 111 To the quivering touch Of Titan's ray, with each repulsive string Consenting. **1791** E. DARWIN *Bot. Gard.* I. 560 To..bathe unwet their oily forms, and dwell, With feet repulsive on the dimpling well. **1810** CRABBE *Borough* i. 132 Fences are..placed around, (With tenters tipp'd) a strong repulsive bound. *c* **1815** MOORE *Irish Melodies* Poet. Wks. II. 146 And with rude repulsive shock Hurls her from the beetling rock.

b. Const. *of* or *to* (the thing repelled).

1720 POPE *Iliad* XXI. 192 Repulsive of his might the weapon stood. **1791** MRS. RADCLIFFE *Rom. Forest* ii, The desolation of the spot was repulsive to his wishes. **1828** *Blackw. Mag.* XXIV. 32 The spiritual and temporal authorities are distinct,..and both repulsive of European intercourse.

2. *Physics.* Of the nature of, characterized by, repulsion. (Opposed to ATTRACTIVE.)

1704 NEWTON *Optics* (1721) 363 A repulsive Force by which they fly from one another. **1770** PRIESTLEY in *Phil. Trans.* LX. 198 The balls separated..; and, continuing in a repulsive state, appeared to be electrified negatively. **1830** KATER & LARDNER *Mech.* vi. 69 The space around each atom of a body, through which this repulsive influence extends, is generally limited. **1885** WATSON & BURBURY *Math. The. Electr. & Magn.* I. 46 If the mutual force had been attractive instead of repulsive..the expression for the work done would be the same as that for the repulsive force, but with reversed sign.

3. Repellent; intended or tending to repel by denial, coldness of manner, etc.

1598 CHAPMAN *Blinde Beg. Alexandria* Wks. 1873 I. 22 Be not discouraged that my daughter.., Like a well fortified and loftie tower, Is so repulsiue and vnapt to yeelde. **1792** BURKE *Corr.* (1844) III. 414 Nothing could be more completely cold, distant, and even repulsive to me, than the conduct and manner of ministers in this and in every other point. **1794** MRS. RADCLIFFE *Myst. Udolpho* xx, She suddenly raised herself, and with a repulsive gesture and a countenance of forced serenity, said [etc.]. *c* **1815** JANE AUSTEN *Persuas.* vi, Mary was not so repulsive and unsisterly as Elizabeth. **1843** S. WILBERFORCE in Ashwell *Life* (1879) I. vi. 233, I could not..receive it in silence, because this would seem cold, unfriendly and repulsive. **1863** R. QUEEN *Heather Lintie* (ed. 2) 43, I ne'er wi' ither bairns gallanted Wha looks repulsive on me slanted.

4. Repellent to the mind; disgusting.

1816 BENTHAM *Chrestom.* 314 Presenting itself to the eye of the mind in the repulsive character of an absolutely dark spot. **1838** EMERSON *Addr., Lit. Ethics* Wks. (Bohn) II. 211 The repulsive plants that are native in the swamp. **1866** G. MACDONALD *Ann. Q. Neighb.* xv. (1878) 317 There was something so repulsive about the woman. **1874** L. STEPHEN *Hours in Library* (1892) I. vi. 199 Balzac..is often repulsive, and not unfrequently dull.

Comb. **1855** WHYTE MELVILLE *Gen. Bounce* ix. 125 A hard-featured and repulsive-looking woman.

B. *sb.* †**1.** A repelling medicine or application.

1656 RIDGLEY *Pract. Physick* 17 Whether repulsives may be used? **1671** SALMON *Syn. Med.* III. xvi. 363 Repulsives or Repellers..are opposed to Attractives.

†**2.** A repelling or counteracting force. *Obs. rare.*

1667 WATERHOUSE *Fire Lond.* 59 God having..placed in nature ballances and repulsives as well as insolences and pestilences of assaults on harmony.

Hence **reˈpulsively** *adv.*, in a repelling manner.

1748 RICHARDSON *Clarissa* (1811) III. vii. 54 She.. repulsively, as I may say, quitting my assisting hand, hurried into the house. **1840** *New Monthly Mag.* LVIII. 58, I was prevented by the lady, who, putting out her hand repulsively, said, 'Oh! don't send him to me'.

repulsiveness (rɪˈpʌlsɪvnɪs). [f. REPULSIVE *a.* + -NESS.] The state or quality of being repulsive or disagreeable.

1820 HAZLITT *Lect. Dram. Lit.* 179 The repulsiveness of the story is what gives it its critical interest. **1841** D'ISRAELI *Amen. Lit.* (1867) 116 Printing ancient writers with all their obsolete repulsiveness in orthography and type. **1875** MAINE *Hist. Inst.* i. 17 The difficulty of mastering the contents has..been aggravated by the repulsiveness of the form.

†**reˈpulsory**, *sb.* and *a.* [f. as REPULSE *v.* + -ORY, or ad. late L. *repulsōrius.*] (See quots.)

1611 COTGR., *Repoussoir*, a repulsorie; a thing that repulseth, driueth backe, or pusheth out. **1727** BAILEY vol. II, *Repulsory*, fit to repel, or pull back.

repulveˈration. *rare*$^{-1}$. [RE- 5a.] A second or subsequent pulverizing.

1740 TULL *Horse-Hoeing Husb.* (ed. 2) Addend. 260 This present growing Crop will thereby have the Benefit of..the Repulveration of that Earth afterwards.

†**reˈpumicate**, *v. Obs. rare.* [ad. L. **repūmicāre* (cf. next), f. *pūmex* PUMICE.] (See quots.)

1623 COCKERAM, *Repumicate*, to plaine a thing. **1647** R. BARON *Cyprian Acad.* 11 She that wanteth a sleekestone to repumicate her linnen, will take a pibble. **1656** BLOUNT *Glossogr.* [copying Cooper], *Repumicate*, to raze with a Pumice, to make slick or smooth.

So †**repumiˈcation** [L. *repūmicātio*, Pliny]. *Obs.*

1623 COCKERAM II, Smoothnes, *Repumication.* **1658** PHILLIPS, *Repumication*,..a slicking, or raizing with a pumice.

reˈpump (riː-), *v.* [RE- 5a.] To pump again.

1753 N. TORRIANO *Gangr. Sore Throat* 85 Lest..the gangrenous Matter be repumped back thro' the Mouths of the newly abraded Vessels. **1903** *Motoring Ann.* 296 If upon re-pumping, a tyre be found not to hold air properly,..it must be removed for repair.

reˈpun (riː-), *v.* [RE-.] *intr.* To pun again or in return.

1721 AMHERST *Terræ Fil.* No. 39 (1726) 212 They would pun and repun, in several languages, upon each other.

reˈpunish (riː-). [RE-.] To punish again or in return. So **reˈpunishment.**

1549 *Latimer's 2nd Serm. bef. Edw. VI* To Rdr. (Arb.) 49 When he comes he wil..recompence his long sufferaunce wyth greuous repunishmentes. **1612** *Proc. Virginia* 89 in *Capt. Smith's Wks.* (Arb.) 157 Some of the baser sort that we haue..punished for their villanies, would hire vs that we should not tell it to their kings or countrymen, who would also repunish them.

reˈpurchase (riː-), *sb.* [RE- 5a.] The act of buying back. (Common in late 19th-c. use.)

1611 FLORIO, *Ricompra*, a repurchase or bying againe. **1863** *Sat. Rev.* 16 May 631 He promised to give an option of repurchase at a future time. **1875** JEVONS *Money* xviii. 233 Independently, however, of repurchase, stamps are so continually being cancelled [etc.].

reˈpurchase (riː-), *v.* [RE- 5a.] *trans.* To purchase again, to buy back.

1592 *Nobody & Someb.* 1940 in Simpson *Sch. Shaks.* (1878) I. 353 Leases, likewise forfeited, By him repurchast. **1593** SHAKS. *3 Hen. VI*, V. vii. 2 Once more we sit in Englands Royall Throne, Re-purchac'd with the Blood of Enemies. **1671** WOODHEAD *St. Teresa* I. xiv. 90 This soul.. which thou hast so often repurchased again and again. **1713** C'TESS WINCHELSEA *Misc. Poems* 115 Repurchases in time th' abandon'd Sheep. **1796** BURKE *Let. Noble Ld.* Wks. VIII. 46 Every day he lived he would have re-purchased the bounty of the crown. **1870** E. PEACOCK *Ralph Skirl.* I. 213 It was a cherished whim of the Squire to repurchase this fragment.

absol. **1858** LD. ST. LEONARDS *Handy-Bk. Prop. Law* vii. 43 If you sell out stock..and then you re-purchase at a loss, you are not entitled to any allowance on that account.

Hence **reˈpurchased** *ppl. a.*; **reˈpurchaser.**

1598 FLORIO, *Racquistatore*,..a reobtainer, a repurchaser. **1652** J. WRIGHT tr. *Camus' Nat. Paradox* XII. 342 Miestas besides his re-purchased Liberty was ravisht to see so many Laurells shadowing his Son's Temples.

†**reˈpure**, *v. Obs. rare.* [RE- 5a.] *trans.* To purify again. Hence **reˈpured** *ppl. a.*

1606 SHAKS. *Tr. & Cr.* III. ii. 23 What will it be When that the watry pallats taste indeede Loues thrice repured Nectar? **1611** BARKSTED *Hiren* (1876) 85 No, no, nor state, nor honor can repure Dishonor'd sheets. **1635** SHIRLEY *Lady of Pleas.* V. i, The winds shall..breathe rich odours to re-pure the air.

†**reˈpurgate**, *v. Obs.*$^{-1}$ [f. ppl. stem of L. *repurgāre*: cf. REPURGE *v.*] *trans.* To purge anew.

1664 H. MORE *Myst. Iniq., Apol.* 553 Other Reformed Churches, which also are so laudably repurgated from the grosser corruptions of the great Babylon.

†**repurˈgation.** *Obs.* [f. as prec., or ad. late L. *repurgātiōn-em.*] Renewed purgation.

1612 WOODALL *Surg. Mate* Wks. (1653) 273 Repurgation is, whereby metals and other substances are purged from superfluities of another nature, adhering to them. **1637** GILLESPIE *Eng. Pop. Cerem.* II. iii. 17 Who promised some Reformation and Repurgation of superstitious worships.

repurge (riːˈpɜːdʒ), *v.* [f. RE- 5a + PURGE *v.*, after L. *repurgāre*, Sp. *repurgar*, F. *repurger*, etc.] *trans.* To purge or cleanse again. Also *refl.*

1560 DAUS tr. *Sleidane's Comm.* 437 Whether the soules of the godly not yet repurged, be relieved with Masses..and almose dedes. **1575** FENTON *Gold. Epist.* (1582) 220 The spot in a house can not be repurged with all the treasures in a kingdome. **1645** PAGITT *Heresiogr.* (1661) 36 That God had commanded him to destroy all the ungodly, and to repurge the Church. **1753** N. TORRIANO *Gangr. Sore Throat* 23 Monday she was repurged with Success. **1862** R. H. PATTERSON *Ess. Hist. & Art* 235 The Chinese Empire..has purged and repurged itself again and again.

Hence **reˈpurged** *ppl. a.*, **reˈpurging** *vbl. sb.*

1606 KING *Serm.* Sept. 26 So many repurged Churches of Christendome. **1611** FLORIO, *Repurgatione*, a repurging.

reˈpurify (riː-), *v.* [RE- 5a.] To purify again. Hence **reˈpurified**, **reˈpurifying** *ppl. adjs.*

1575 FENTON *Gold. Epist.* (1582) 116 A puddle that can not eftsoones be repurified. **1599** NASHE *Lenten Stuffe* 70 Absolute, essentiall alterations of metalles there may bee made by an artificiall repurified flame. **1615** CHAPMAN *Odyss.* VI. 49 Let's to the river, and repurify Thy wedding garments. **1630** J. TAYLOR (Water P.) *Praise Clean Linen* Ded., Wks. II. 164 The Most Mondifying, Clarifying, Purifying and Repurifying, Cleanser.

reˈpurple, *v. rare.* [RE- 5a.] *trans.* To make purple again.

1591 SYLVESTER *Ivry* 28 Neither shall my Pen Re-purple Lisle. **1606** J. DAVIES *Sir T. Overbury* Wks. (Grosart) 17 The purple robe is oft re-purpelled With royal blood.

repurˈsuit. [RE- 5a.] Renewed pursuit.

a **1631** DONNE *Serm.* xxxvi. (1640) 360 If..thou return to thy vomit, to the re-pursuite of those halfe-repented sins.

† **repurveance.** *Obs.*$^{-1}$ = PURVEYANCE.
a **1440** *Sir Degrev.* 1146 He had y-made repurveaunce For al hys retenaunce Fourty days and mare.

re'push, *v.* [RE-.] *intr.* To push in return.
1616 J. LANE *Contn. Sqr.'s T.* IX. 177 Pusshinge, repusshinge, vibratinge agen, as valient mortal and immortal men.

re'put, *v. rare.* [RE- 5 a.] To put (*on*) again.
1673 R. HEAD *Canting Acad.* 127 He reputs on his Doublet.

reput, obs. Sc. form of REPUTE.

,reputa'bility. [See next and -ITY.] The state or quality of being reputable.
1846 WARRINGTON in *Builder* 25 July, Upon my reputability, experience, and judgment, . . I pronounce on this work . . its utter condemnation. **1894** *Westm. Gaz.* 3 June 2/2 Order and reputability may create cogent reasons.

reputable ('rɛpjuːtəb(ə)l), *a.* [f. REPUTE *v.* + -ABLE. Cf. obs. F. *reputable* (Godef.).]
†**1.** Capable of being regarded or taken into account. *Obs. rare*$^{-1}$.
1611 SPEED *Hist. Gt. Brit.* VII. xliii. §1. 354 Disauowing Prince Edward as illegitimate, and therefore not reputable for succession.
2. Having a good reputation; of good repute; estimable, honourable, respectable: **a.** of acts, employments, circumstances, etc.
1674 *Govt. Tongue* 206 Faults . . exemplified to us in common practice, (nay some of them as reputable and ingenious). **1699** BENTLEY *Phal.* Pref. 29 His Imployment, as a Book-seller, I think a very reputable one, if He himself be not a Disgrace to't. **1742** RICHARDSON *Pamela* III. 365 To find . . that you would have been led beyond what was reputable. **1825** LAMB *Elia* Ser. II. *Barbara S*——, The parents of Barbara had been in reputable circumstances. **1878** SIMPSON *Sch. Shaks.* I. 109 To reveal matters in which his share had not been very reputable.
b. of persons or their character.
1692 DRYDEN *St. Euremont's Ess.* 34 If so be the reputable Men of the latter time, had existed in that of Fabricius [etc.]. **1728** MORGAN *Algiers* II. i. 212 Rakik, the most reputable of all the African Chronologists. **1761** HUME *Hist. Eng.* lxix. (1806) V. 195 The jury were men of fair and reputable characters. **1837** J. D. LANG *New S. Wales* I. 172 A grant of land belonging to a reputable Scotchman. **1858** GREENER *Gunnery* 330 Certain men who set themselves up for reputable gunmakers.
Hence '**reputableness,** 'being of good Repute' (Bailey vol. II, 1727).

reputably ('rɛpjuːtəblɪ), *adv.* [f. REPUTABLE *a.* + -LY.] In a reputable or respectable manner.
1738 NEAL *Hist. Purit.* IV. 241 He could not so reputably do it. **1748** RICHARDSON *Clarissa* (1811) II. xxxv. 254 Hers is a protection I could more reputably fly to, than to that of any other person. **1832** HT. MARTINEAU *Homes Abroad* ii. 34 Ready to establish themselves reputably in society. **1860** HOLLAND *Miss Gilbert* iii. 35 He had lived comfortably and reputably.

† '**reputate,** *pa. pple.* and *v. Obs. rare.* [f. ppl. stem of L. *reputāre* to REPUTE.] **a.** *pa. pple.* Considered. **b.** *v.* To consider.
1432-50 tr. *Higden* (Rolls) I. 141 To the mownte of Taurus from the costes of Ynde, where the hille callede Taurus and Caucasus be reputate [L. *reputatur*] oon. **1570** LEVINS *Manip.* 41/9 To Reputate, *æstimare.*

reputation (rɛpjuː'teɪʃən). Also 4-6 **reputacion(e,** 4-5 **-cioun,** 5 **-syoun,** 6 **-cyon;** 4-6 **reputatioun,** 6 **-tyon,** etc. [ad. L. *reputātiōn-em* computation, consideration, n. of action f. *reputāre* to REPUTE. Cf. F. *réputation* (15th c.).]
†**1. a.** Opinion, supposition; also, the opinion or view *of* one about something. *Obs. rare.*
c **1380** WYCLIF *Sel. Wks.* III. 255 ȝif þei seie þat þei assoyle, þei speke by reputacioun, and nouȝt bi wytynge ne bi trowynge. **1533-4** *Act 25 Hen. VIII*, c. 12 They . . traytorously beleeued in their hartes, that the kinge . . was no lenger rightfull king of this realme, in the reputacion of almightie god.
†**b.** Account or estimation *of* a thing. *Obs. rare.*
1563 *Homilies* II. *Idolatry* III. (1859) 253 They seem to take the multitude for 'vile souls' . . of whose loss or safeguard no reputation is to be had. **1613** PURCHAS *Pilgrimage* III. v. (1614) 264 Such reputation haue they of this forme, which they call a Prayer . ., That [etc.].
2. The common or general estimate of a person with respect to character or other qualities; the relative estimation or esteem in which a person or thing is held. In phrases:
†**a.** *in* (or *of*) *reputation.* In later use applied to titles given by courtesy. *Obs.* (Cf. 3 b.)
c **1386** CHAUCER *Pard. T.* 274 He is, as by commune opinion, Yholde the lasse in reputacion. *c* **1440** *Partonope* 7370* What they be of condicioun And how they be of reputacioun. *c* **1440** *Gesta Rom.* xlv. 176 (Harl. MS.), He shall be in Reputacion as a fool. **1602** SHAKS. *Ham.* II. ii. 344 How chances it they trauaile? their residence both in reputation and profit was better both wayes. **1642** W. BIRD *Mag. Honor* 165 There are other Lords in reputation and appellation, who neverthelesse are not *de jure*. **1677** LOGAN in *Blome's Guillim* (1679) II. 75 Ladies in Reputation.
b. *to be* (*have, hold,* or †*take*) *in* (or †*at*) *no, great,* etc., *reputation.* Now *rare.*
c **1386** CHAUCER *Pard. T.* 298 For which he heeld his glorie or his renoun At no value or reputacioun. **1432-50** tr. *Higden* (Rolls) V. 451 Wherefore ȝitte . . the consuetude of Britons is to have as in noo reputacion the promise of Ynglische men. **14..** *Why I can't be a nun* 216 in *E.E.P.* (1862) 143 There was a lady, that hyȝ[t] dame pride; In grete reputacion they her toke. **1535** COVERDALE *1 Sam.* xviii. 30 Dauid behaued him selfe more wysely . .: so that his name was in greate reputacion. **1542** UDALL *Erasm. Apoph.* 264 b, As for the saied Cilicians, he had [them] in so vile reputacion, that [etc.]. **1690** LOCKE *Hum. Und.* III. x. §34 Since rhetoric . . is publicly taught, and has always been had in great reputation. **1704** SWIFT *T. Tub* ii, They . . fell in love with the Ladies, but especially three, who about that time were in chief Reputation. **1788** REID *Aristotle's Log.* ii. §2. 31 The Ramean divisions were in no small reputation about two hundred years ago.
c. *of no, great, small,* etc., *reputation.*
1413 *Pilgr. Sowle* (Caxton 1483) IV. xxxvii. 84 Oftyme suche maystres as ben of lest reputacion ben mooste necessary. **1494** FABYAN *Chron.* VII. 458 The realme of Fraunce that day susteynyd such confusyon . . by people and men of no reputacion as archers. **1553** LATIMER *Serm. Lord's Prayer* Wks. (Parker Soc.) II. 3 It is a word of much importance and great reputation. **1591** SHAKS. *Two Gent.* I. iii. 6 While other men, of slender reputation Put forth their Sonnes, to seeke preferment out. **1656** EARL MONM. tr. *Boccalini's Advts. fr. Parnass.* I. x. (1674) 13 That trade was . . but of small reputation to him that used it. **1827** SCOTT *Surg. Dau.* i, He was a man . . of such reputation in the medical world, that [etc.]. **1886** RUSKIN *Præterita* I. 427 Of some literary reputation.
3. The condition, quality, or fact, of being highly regarded or esteemed; credit, note, or distinction; also, respectability, good report.
a. *of reputation.* (Usually attached to a sb.)
c **1375** *St. Augustin* 1020 in Horstm. *Altengl. Leg.* (1878) 79/1 Rihtwys men in þis liuyng Schul not beo of reputacion But raþur euer beo put adoun. **1581** MARBECK *Bk. of Notes* 661 *Ish*, signifieth a man of reputation. **1585** T. WASHINGTON tr. *Nicholay's Voy.* II. vii. 37 The women of reputation weare . . damask or other rich silkes. **1773** GOLDSM. *Stoops to Conq.* II. i, But in the company of women of reputation I never saw such an idiot. **1784** J. POTTER *Virtuous Villages* II. 58 My honest endeavours to live a life of reputation. **1851** HUSSEY *Papal Power* iii. 124 This . . was answered by a writer of reputation at that time. **1875** JOWETT *Plato* (ed. 2) I. 368, I have seen men of reputation . . behaving in the strangest manner.
b. In other prepositional phrases, esp. *in reputation.* (Cf. 2 a.)
a **1533** LD. BERNERS *Gold. Bk. M. Aurel.* (1546) B iij b, The auncient sages were holden in reputacion, bycause there were fewe teachers and many lerners. **1567** *Triall Treas.* (1850) 35 If you desire to enjoy me at your will, My sister you must haue in reputation still. **1662** EVELYN *Chalcogr.* Table, When they began to be in reputation. **1741** *Col. Rec. Pennsylv.* IV. 543 They carried on the Publick affairs with Reputation. **1799** S. TURNER *Anglo-Sax.* (1836) I. IV. v. 295 He is represented to have . . passed the remainder of his life in reputation and justice. **1817** JAS. MILL *Brit. India* II. v. i. 307 Mr. Hastings had ascended with reputation through the several stages of the Company's service. **1858** BUCKLE *Civiliz.* (1869) II. v. 219 Morellet who was then high in reputation.
c. In other constructions.
1549 CHALONER *Erasm. on Folly* F iij, Shame, reproch, losse of reputacion, . . maie do the as much hurt as thou felist theim. **1598** BARCKLEY *Felic. Man* (1631) 623 Some hunt after honour, others after riches and reputation. **1654** WHITLOCK *Zootomia* 21 The living may be Tenants at will to reputation; but it is the possession of the dead. **1690** LOCKE *Hum. Und.* III. x. §6 To this Abuse . . Logick and the liberal Sciences . . have given reputation. **1728** YOUNG *Love Fame* III. 197 Some nymphs sell reputation; others buy. **1781** COWPER *Table-t.* 520 Thus reputation is a spur to wit. **1822** HAZLITT *Table-t.* Ser. II. xvi. (1869) 340, I have said all reputation is hazardous, hard to win, and harder to keep. **1861** GEO. ELIOT *Silas M.* i, If he had any reputation for knowledge or showed any skill in handicraft.
d. With *a* and *pl.* Also, †a source of honour and credit (*obs.*); a person of note or distinction.
1653 NICHOLAS in *N. Papers* (Camden) II. 26 The cheerfull contribution of the Emperor . . is of excellent Example . . and a very great honour and reputation to his Majesty's cause. **1685** *Gracian's Courtier's Orac.* 162 Nothing but truth can give a true Reputation. *a* **1704** T. BROWN *Eng. Sat.* Wks. 1730 I. 25 The Reflections are beautiful and give a just reputation to their Author. **1748** *Anson's Voy.* II. vi. 200 It was . . no small reputation to the men, that they should in general refrain from indulging themselves. **1826** MISS MITFORD in L'Estrange *Life* (1870) II. x. 234 A real impression has been made, and a reputation of the highest order established. **1852** THACKERAY *Esmond* III. ii, To achieve a great reputation for learning. **1870** DISRAELI *Lothair* xxxi, That is Baron Gozelius, one of our great reputations.
4. The honour or credit *of* a particular person or thing; one's good name, good report, or fame in general. † *on reputation*: see GO-DOWN I.
1553 EDEN *Treat. Newe Ind.* (Arb.) 9 To recouer theyr honour and reputacion diminished by the same. **1617** MORYSON *Itin.* I. 148 The yong man . . to save the reputation of the Virgin, confessed, that he came to rob the house. **1674** *Govt. Tongue* 40 This Vice . . seems to have maintained not only it's Empire, but it's reputation too. **1739** DUNKIN *Let.* 25 Apr. in *Swift's Lett.* (1768) IV. 229 His gracious endeavours to raise my reputation and fortune. **1769** *Junius Lett.* iii. (1788) 44 You feel, as you ought to do, for the reputation of your friend. **1842** MISS MITFORD in L'Estrange *Life* (1870) III. ix. 132 The young artist who under the name of 'Phiz' has so much aided Mr. Dickens's reputation. **1858** BUCKLE *Civiliz.* (1869) II. i. 31 The reputation of the state was the first consideration.
b. With *a* and *pl.* Someone's good name, etc.
1712-14 POPE *Rape Lock* III. 16 A third interprets motions, looks, and eyes; At ev'ry word a reputation dies. **1781** COWPER *Truth* 163 She . . Laughs at the reputations she has torn. **1841** EMERSON *Turner* Ess. (1904) 43/2 The reputations that were great and inaccessible change and tarnish.
5. The estimation, credit, or ascription *of* being or possessing something.
1570-6 LAMBARDE *Peramb. Kent* (1826) 253 That Chylham Castle had aunciently the reputation of an Honour, appeareth by a Note. **1651** HOBBES *Leviath.* I. xii. 58 That which taketh away the reputation of Wisedome. *a* **1679** —— *Rhet.* I. v. (1681) 9 Glory, Which is the reputation of Vertue. **1711** ADDISON *Spect.* No. 117 ¶4 The Knight told me, that this very old Woman had the Reputation of a Witch all over the Country. **1832** HT. MARTINEAU *Hill & Valley* iii. 48 It will do no good to remove the chest, now that I have the reputation of having one. **1873** BLACK *Pr. Thule* xxi, He had the reputation of being able to get through his work thoroughly.

reputational (rɛpjuː'teɪʃənəl), *a.* [f. REPUTATION + -AL.] Of or pertaining to reputation.
1921 G. B. SHAW *Lett.* 22 Dec. in *B. Shaw & Mrs. Campbell* (1952) 217 It maddens me to see people blundering away . . the reputational chances of their lifetime. **1967** *Listener* 19 Jan. 103/3 [T. F.] Powys is now at the nadir of the twenty-year reputational trough that follows death.

reputative (rɪ'pjuːtətɪv), *a.* [ad. L. type **reputātīv-us*: see REPUTE *v.* and -IVE.] Considered or regarded as such; putative.
a **1656** VINES *Lord's Supp.* (1677) 263 There are many reputative members that are in the visible society. **1675** BAXTER *Cath. Theol.* II. x. 212 The Covenants Action is physically none, but only such as some call a Reputative Act. **1721** SIR J. PALMER *Rep. Cases King's B.* 375 A joint occupation for five or six years is sufficient for to make reputative appurtenances. **1837** G. S. FABER *Prim. Doctr. Justif.* 52 Certain it is, that our eleventh Article puts forward the reputative idea.

re'putatively, *adv.* [f. prec. + -LY^{2}.] By repute or reckoning, reputedly; putatively.
1615 CHAPMAN *Odyss.* Ep. Ded., This Prozer Dionysius, and the rest of these graue and reputatiuely learned. **1658** BAXTER *Saving Faith* v. 34 A Belief and Love indeed he hath, but morally and reputatively it is as none. **1702** C. MATHER *Magn. Chr.* v. iii. (1852) 296 They have this also reputatively by divine appointment. **1837** G. S. FABER *Prim. Doctr. Justif.* 17 A Righteousness, reputatively made his, through Faith.

repute (rɪ'pjuːt), *sb.* [f. the vb.]
†**1.** Opinion, estimate. *Obs. rare.*
1551 T. WILSON *Logike* (1580) 74 One . . saied thus after other mennes judgement, and repute given. **1674** W. TOMLINSON *Epistle to Flock* 3 Their judgment and repute of thee is true. **1707** E. CHAMBERLAYNE *Pres. St. Eng.* I. III. ii. 265 The Common Repute is, that a Gallon of Wheaten Meal weighs 7 Pound Avoirdupois. *a* **1711** KEN *Hymns Evang.* Poet. Wks. 1721 I. 162 One act intense, may in God's mild repute, For a whole Age of Penances commute.
2. Reputation of a specified kind.
1551 T. WILSON *Logike* (1580) 88, I desire of all men . . to give me none evill repute for my well meanyng. **1588** SHAKS. *L.L.L.* I. i. 72 Let them be men of good repute and carriage. **1667** MILTON *P.L.* II. 472 Winning cheap the high repute Which he through hazard huge must earn. **1771** *Junius Lett.* l. (1788) 273 In what repute can he conceive that he stands with his people? **1819** SHELLEY *Cenci* v. ii. 36 You have a good repute for gentleness. **1879** DIXON *Windsor* II. i. 7 Boasting of no small repute in arms and of a great repute in verse.
†**b.** The reputation *of* (having or being) something. *Obs.*
1651 *Fuller's Abel Rediv., Scaliger* 499 He wrote much . .; but to avoid the repute of ambition would not suffer them to be Printed. **1683** KENNETT tr. *Erasm. on Folly* 82 Only to such as challenge the repute of Wisdom. **1699** LD. REAY in *Pepys' Diary* (1879) VI. 189 Who had then the repute of an honest man.
†**3.** Relative estimation; rank or position. *Obs.*
1615 G. SANDYS *Trav.* 48 A place of high trust, and the third in repute through the Empire. *c* **1645** HOWELL *Lett.* I. xxxviii. (1650) I. 57 All these Cardinals have the repute of Princes. **1659** PHILIPOTT *Kent* 139 An ancient Farme, which formerly had the Repute of a Mannor. **1700** DRYDEN *Ovid's Met.* XII. 246 O father, first for prudence in repute.
4. Reputation, distinction, honour, credit.
1615 G. SANDYS *Trav.* 23 Ceremony which giueth repute vnto things in themselues but triuiall. **1716** ATTERBURY *Serm.* (1737) III. 223 These ungodly . . set up for a repute by disbelieving everything. **1781** COWPER *Conversat.* 818 That fables old . . Revived are hastening into fresh repute. **1817** JAS. MILL *Brit. India* III. ii. 68 This is a rule . . one would not be surprised at finding in force and repute. **1875** JOWETT *Plato* (ed. 2) V. 106 A man of repute will desire to avoid doing what is ludicrous.
5. The reputation of a particular person.
1662 PEPYS *Diary* 23 Dec., Mr. Edward Montagu is quite broke at Court with his repute and purse. **1683** D. A. *Art Converse* 16 Omitting nothing that rage can invent to black his repute. **1784** COWPER *Tiroc.* 461 Our public hives of puerile resort . . To such base hopes . . Owe their repute in part. **1882** SPURGEON *Treas. Dav.* Ps. cxx. 2 Lips should never be red with the blood of honest men's reputes.
b. In phr. *by repute.*
1838 JAMES *Robber* ii, I know him well, by repute.

repute (rɪ'pjuːt), *v.* Also 5 **repotten.** [ad. F. *réputer* (1294 in Godef.), or L. *reputāre*, f. *re-* RE- + *putāre* to reckon, think, etc.]
1. *trans.* To consider, think, esteem, reckon (a person or thing) to be, or as being, something.
a. with simple complement.
c **1460** G. ASHBY *Dicta Philos.* 1107 Sum men reputen of consuetude Euery thinge goode. **1483** CAXTON *Cato* B j b, To thende that they may be reputed and holden sage and wyse. **1568** GRAFTON *Chron.* II. 829 The enterprise . . was of him reputed of no regarde or estimacion. **1612** T. TAYLOR *Comm. Titus* i. 9 If any shall deeme and repute it an impotent

meanes to raise men to the grace of life. **1678** Cudworth *Intell. Syst.* I. i. §17. 17 The glory of being reputed the First Inventors or Founders of the Atomical Philosophy. **1718** *Free-thinker* No. 62. 46 The Morning-Sneezings..were not reputed Good. **1825** Jefferson *Autobiog.* Wks. 1859 I. 66 As to this they shall be reputed at peace. **1859** Tennyson *Guinev.* 379 Lancelot came, Reputed the best knight and goodliest man.

b. with infinitive, esp. *to be* or *to have*.

1483 Caxton *Gold. Leg.* 219b/1 Why reputest thou the dedes of my merytes to be unworthy? **1523** Ld. Berners *Froiss.* I. cxxxi. 159 They reputed themselfe to haue the vyctorie. **1588** Shaks. *Tit. A.* I. i. 448 Ingratitude, which Rome reputes to be a hainous sinne. **1656** Bramhall *Replic.* v. 209 How he reputes their sufferings..to be his own. **1711** in *10th Rep. Hist. MSS. Comm.* App. V. 193 Reputeing what was don to his great friend to be don to himself. **1832** R. & J. Lander *Exped. Niger* II. xi. 136 His soldiers..are reputed to be brave, bold, and enterprising men. **1875** Jowett *Plato* (ed. 2) V. 29 Rhadamanthus..is reputed among us to have been the justest of men.

†**2. a.** To take (one) *for* something. *Obs.*

1477 Earl Rivers (Caxton) *Dictes* 38 As a leche is not reputed nor taken for goode nor connying that..can not hele him selfe. **1483** Caxton *G. de la Tour* B ij, Who that spekeih ouermoche is not reputed for wyse. **1568** Grafton *Chron.* II. 718 King Lewys, whom he reputed for his mortall enemie. **1615** Jackson *Creed* IV. xi. §1 Dost thou imagine that he reputes Christ for the Son of God..? **1670** H. Stubbe *A Reply* 71 He..is content to repute me for Pious.

†**b.** To regard, reckon, account *as* something.

1483 Caxton *Gold. Leg.* 376/2, I repute alle erthelye thynges as donge and fylthe. **1535** Stewart *Cron. Scot.* (1858) I. 37 All ȝour injure we repute as our awin. *a* **1548** Hall *Chron., Hen. VIII* 105b, They yt fle be worthy to be reputed as traitors to ye king. **1615** G. Sandys *Trav.* 49 The rest reputed as naturall Turks. **1654** Bramhall *Just Vind.* vi. (1661) 140 The Barons of the kingdom reputed him as a Traytor.

†**c.** To consider to be *in* a person or thing. *Obs.*

1477 Earl Rivers (Caxton) *Dictes* 35 A wys man reputeth not the worship of god in wordes but in dedes. **1525** Ld. Berners *Froiss.* II. xxvi. 73 Sir, ye repute but small honour in the kyng of Nauar. **1533** Cromwell in Merriman *Life & Lett.* (1902) I. 353 His highnes doth not onlie repute moche honour in your grace [etc.].

†**d.** To account oneself *to have* something. *Obs.*$^{-1}$

1539 Tonstall *Serm. Palm Sund.* (1823) 27 By pride reputynge to haue them of hym selfe, and not of god.

†**e.** To consider *that* or *how*. *Obs. rare.*

1549 Chaloner *Erasm. on Folly* G ij, I would my Maisters ..shoulde repute with theym selues, how on all sydes theyr myndes are vexed continually. **1623** Bingham *Xenophon* 63 Xenophon reputing in his minde, that..the enemie..might distresse the cariage in passing by [etc.].

†**3.** To assign, attribute, impute, or reckon *to* a person. Also const. *for* or *to* something. *Obs.*

1432 *Rolls of Parlt.* IV. 406/1 Yat men mowe repute and cast the defaute, if eny be, there it aught. **1483** Caxton *Gold. Leg.* 388/2 Theffusyon of our blood shal be reputed to you for baptesme. **1523** Ld. Berners *Froiss.* I. clxv. 202 It ought nat to be reputed to me any prowes. **1550** J. Coke *Eng. & Fr. Heralds* §9 (1877) 60 This Clowes is the fyrst kyng of Fraunce to whom I repute honoure. **1582** N.T. (Rhem.) *Rom.* iv. 9 For we say that unto Abraham faith was reputed to justice. **1659** Hammond *On Ps.* cvi. 31 It was reputed to him for righteousness.

†**b.** To regard, take into account. *Obs.*$^{-1}$

c **1450** Lovelich *Grail* li. 50 That he ne wolde for myn hygh falsnesse My synnes to Repotten In this distresse.

†**4.** To have or hold (one) in repute or esteem; to think (well, etc.) of; to value. Also, to hold equal in worth *to* something. *Obs.*

1444 *Rolls of Parlt.* V. 73/2 To repute, accept,..and take my said Lord..to his goode and benygne grace and favour. **1485** Caxton *Chas. Gt.* 30 He was byloued & dere reputed of euery body. **1535** Coverdale *1 Sam.* xxvi. 24 As thy soule hath bene greatly reputed in my sighte this daye, so let ye Lorde repute my soule in his sighte. **1571** Campion *Hist. Irel.* xii. (1633) 38 Conill Lord of Connaght..honourably reputed him, and with all his people was converted. **1579** Lyly *Euphues* (Arb.) 48 Is there any thing in the world to be reputed (I will not say compared) to friendship? *c* **1665** Mrs. Hutchinson *Mem. Col. Hutchinson* (1846) 37 Their generous..inclinations..had made the family continue as well beloved and reputed as any of the prouder houses in the country.

†**5.** *intr.* To think (highly, etc.) *of* a thing or person. Also with omission of adv. *Obs.*

1593 Shaks. *2 Hen. VI*, III. i. 48 He..By reputing of his high discent,..Did instigate the..Duchesse. **1599** B. Jonson *Cynthia's Rev.* v. ii, I can allow..you should repute highly..of your own endowments. **1634** Sir T. Herbert *Trav.* 42 The Priests are singularly reputed of. **1634** W. Tirwhyt tr. *Balzac's Lett.* (vol. I) 14, I doe therefore account myselfe very happy to be reputed of, by a person who is able to give a value to things of themselves worthless. **1698** Potter *Antiq. Greece* (1715) II. *Index*, Adultery, how reputed of, and punish'd.

repute (rɪ'pjuːt), *pa. pple.* Chiefly *Sc.* [irreg. f. OF. *reputé* or L. *reputātus* (see prec. and the etym. note to depute *ppl. a.*), perh. partly by assimilation to such forms as *execute*.] Reputed, considered, reckoned. ***habit and repute***: see habit *ppl. a.*

c **1375** *Sc. Leg. Saints* xxxi. (*Eugenia*) 278 Scho herd tel þat in sic ane abbay can duel..a man reput of gud fame. **1442** *Rolls of Parlt.* V. 59/1 That the seide declaration..be not hadde, repute ner takyn for accompte. **1456** Sir G. Haye *Law Arms* (S.T.S.) 152 Gude will..is repute till a persone for gude dede. **1500–20** Dunbar *Poems* xxxix. 3 Fredome, honour and nobilnes..Ar now in cowrt reput as vyce. **1567** *Gude & Godlie B.* (S.T.S.) 43 Princes ar repute Nobilest, The quhilk rewlis moste awfullie. **1639** Drumm. of Hawth. *Consid. to Parlt.* Wks. (1711) 185 He shall still..be repute, holden, and decerned legitimate. **1685** *Scotch Proclam.* 28 Apr. in *Lond. Gaz.* No. 2032/3 Under the pain of being Repute and esteemed Art and Part with them all in their wicked Deeds and Practices. **1753–1861** [see habit *ppl. a.*].

reputed (rɪ'pjuːtɪd), *ppl. a.* [f. repute *v.*]

1. Held in repute. Now used after an adverb, as ***internationally reputed***, etc. (not often found in good sources).

1549 Chaloner *Erasm. on Folly* 8 He preferred also the Ideote, and simple vulgars, before other learned and reputed persons. **1613** Beaum. & Fl. *Captain* v. i, Am I at length reputed? *a* **1641** Bp. Mountagu *Acts & Mon.* (1642) 245 So grave and reputed an Historian as is Iosephus. **1928** *Daily Express* 8 Aug. 15/3 Dr. Hanslick, the universally reputed professor of musical history. **1969** *Daily Tel.* 4 Aug. 17/6 An internationally reputed geologist.

2. a. Supposed, accounted, reckoned (to be something specified); *spec.* in *Law*, as ***reputed manor*** (see manor 3 b), ***owner***, etc.

1576 *Act 18 Eliz.* c. 3 §2 The Mother and reputed Father of such Bastard Child. **1595** Shaks. *John* I. i. 136 The reputed son of Cordelion. **1672** Sir T. Browne *Let. Friend* §24 He had no opinion of reputed felicities below. **1755** Young *Centaur* iii. Wks. 1757 IV. 174 A wretch, almost smothered with all the reputed means of happiness. **1832** R. & J. Lander *Exped. Niger* II. ix. 83 Owing to the reputed badness of the path, that..was rejected for a more northerly one. **1838** W. Bell *Dict. Law Scot.* 854 The creditors of the apparent or reputed owner. *Ibid.* 855 The doctrines of reputed ownership. **1890** Sir F. Pollock *Oxford Lect.* 114 A 'reputed manor' will serve as well as a real manor for most purposes.

b. ***reputed pint, quart***, etc.: (see quot. 1904). Also, the amount of liquid contained by such a measure.

1904 Makins & Lambert *Licensed Victuallers' Handbk.* (rev. ed.) xiii. 216 Reputed quart means a bottle containing the sixth of a gallon, and a reputed pint a bottle containing the twelfth of a gallon. An Imperial Pint is an eighth part of a gallon. **1935** [see Methuselah 2]. **1959** *Gloss. Terms Packaging* (B.S.I.) 29 The normal bottle of wine should contain ⅙ of a gallon..and is known as a 'reputed quart'... Variants of the above are known as 'mock quarts'..and may be of less capacity.

re'putedly, *adv.* [f. prec. + -ly².] By repute or common estimation.

1687 Boyle *Martyrd. Theodora* xi. (1703) 157 A reputedly infamous Death. **1804** Southey in *Ann. Rev.* II. 64 A lesson, says the author, to countries that are reputedly so civilized. **1884** M. E. Wilkins in *Harper's Mag.* June 26/1 Mrs. King was reputedly a sharp woman at a bargain.

†**re'puteless**, *a. Obs. rare*$^{-1}$. [f. repute *sb.* + -less.] Devoid of repute; inglorious.

1596 Shaks. *1 Hen. IV*, III. ii. 44 Opinion..Had still kept loyall to possession, And left me in reputelesse banishment.

re'qualify (riː-), *v.* [re- 5 a.] *trans.* and *intr.* To qualify again.

1570 Foxe *A.& M.* (1596) 259/1 Þe pope, to requalifie againe ech part with some retribution for their monie receiued, tooke this order indifferentlie betweene them. **1814** Mrs. J. West *Alicia de Lacy* II. 306 He must do his duty,..requalify himself for the calls of his high station. **1883** *Standard* 18 June 3/4 Charles W. Dickinson, to the Excellent, to requalify in gunnery.

re'quarrel, *v. rare*$^{-1}$. [re- 5 a.] †To assail or attack again.

1592 Warner *Alb. Eng.* IX. xlvii, By this drink I sweare (Requarreling the cup) we and her lippes imparted weare.

reque, variant of *reke* reach *v.*

requeer, -queir, obs. forms of require *v.*

requeist, obs. Sc. form of request.

†**requel**, variant of recueil *sb.* 2. *Obs.*

1527 Hacket *Let. to Wolsey* (MS. Cott. Galba B. IX. lf. 94b), Yesterday my lord Cardenal..prayd me to dynner with hym, of whom I had ryght honorable and good requel.

†**requensance**, obs. f. recognizance *sb.* 1.

1481 in *Eng. Gilds* (1870) 322 They were bond, in a requensaunce of xxti *li.*, to abyde the awarde.

requere, obs. form of require.

request (rɪ'kwɛst), *sb.*¹ Also 4–5 requeste, 5 *Sc.* raquest, 6 *Sc.* requeist, requeast. [a. OF. *requeste* (12th c.; mod.F. *requête*) = Prov., Sp., and Pg. *requesta*, It. *richiesta*: see quest *sb.*¹ and require *v.*]

I. 1. The act, on the part of a specified person, of asking for some favour, service, etc.; the expression of one's desire or wish directly addressed to the person or persons able to gratify it: **a.** in phr. *at* (one's) *request*.

c **1330** R. Brunne *Chron.* (1810) 266 Þise kynges stille þei left at þe pape's request. *c* **1398** Chaucer *Fortune* 76 At my requeste..releue hym of hys peyne. *c* **1420** Lydg. *Assembly of Gods* 573 Wyll ye your rancour sese at my request? **1470–85** Malory *Arthur* III. iv. 103 He hadde made hym knyght at the request of the Cowherd. **1535** Lyndesay *Satyre* 3388 ȝe sall, at Chastities requeist, Pas and examine ȝon thrie. **1600** Shaks *A.Y.L.* II. v. 23 *Iaq.*..Wil you sing? *Amy.* More at your request, then to please my selfe. **1687** A. Lovell tr. *Thevenot's Trav.* I. 228 At my request..they let her go a drift. **1821** Shelley *Ginevra* 102 Her maidens.. left her at her own request to keep An hour of quiet.

b. in other contexts. Also (esp. with verbs of giving, refusing, obtaining, etc.), the matter or subject of the asking; that which one asks for.

Usually differing from next only by the use of the possessive pronoun.

c **1410** Hoccleve *Mother of God* 95 Our Lord god nat list to werne thee Of thy requeste. *c* **1420** Lydg. *Assembly of Gods* 215 That I may, by your request, her good grace gete. **1447** Bokenham *Seyntys* (Roxb.) Introd. 6 Whos request to me is a comaundement. **1513** Douglas *Æneis* IV. viii. 59 With siclik wordis hir request scho maid. **1542** Udall *Erasm. Apoph.* 295b, Alexander could in no wyse abyde to haue any nay in his requestes. **1607** Shaks. *Timon* I. i. 279 No I will doe nothing at thy bidding: Make thy requests to thy Friend. **1667** Milton *P.L.* VII. 111 This also thy request with caution askt Obtaine. **1714** Pope *Imit. Hor.* II. vi. 77 Consider, 'tis my first request. **1827** Pollok *Course T.* x, Thus have I sung beyond thy first request. **1875** Jowett *Plato* (ed. 2) IV. 427, I fear that I may seem ungracious if I refuse your courteous request.

2. a. An act or instance of asking for something; a petition or expressed desire; a writing or document of this nature; also, that which is asked for.

c **1374** Chaucer *Troylus* III. 99 (148) Lo here an hard request, A resonable lady for to werne. *c* **1460** Sir R. Ros *La Belle Dame* 146 Of his yen the shot y knewe anon, Which federid was with right humble requestis. **1484** Caxton *Fables of Æsop* II. i, They alle to gyder..maade a request to Jupiter that he wold gyue them a kynge. **1563** Winset *Wks.* (S.T.S.) II. 33 It is a iust requeist. **1611** Shaks. *Cymb.* I. vi. 181, I had almost forgot T'intreat your Grace, but in a small request. **1668** Denham *Passion of Dido* Poems 136 Ask him to lend To this, the last request that I shall send, A gentle Ear. **1781** Gibbon *Decl. & F.* xvii. II. 67 In a poetical request, addressed to one of the last..of the Roman Princes who reigned in Gaul. **1838** Miss Mitford in L'Estrange *Life* (1870) III. vi. 88 The request made in the foregoing letter was conceded. **1876** G. D. Ham *Revenue Vade-m.* 567 The conditions under which the request is granted..are to be written or printed on the request.

b. *spec.* A letter, etc., asking for a particular record, song, etc., to be played on a radio programme, often accompanied by a personal message; a record played or a song, etc., sung, either over the radio or to a live audience in response to a request.

1928 *Radio Times* 12 Oct. 79/3 The B.B.C. can never promise to comply with requests, for..suitable opportunities may not arise for weeks or even months. **1949** *Ibid.* 15 July 24/3 Listeners' requests played by Sandy Macpherson at the BBC theatre organ. **1966** *Listener* 4 Aug. 181/3 Judging by the requests, the classical and pre-classical composers are out. **1977** *Zigzag* Mar. 8/2 My sister..saw Roy Eldridge..playing requests in a bar.

3. Without article. †**a.** ***to make request***, to ask or beg. *Obs.*

13.. *E.E. Allit. P.* A. 281 To be excused I make requeste. *c* **1440** *Partonope* 4971 God..I now Reney Yf for hym make I request To yow. *c* **1470** Henry *Wallace* XI. 351 Quhat gestis he had; to tell thai mak raquest. **1560** Daus tr. *Sleidane's Comm.* 370 Theyr adversaries had made request to be heard in these thinges only. **1611** Bible *Neh.* ii. 4 Then ye king said.., For what doest thou make request? **1700** Dryden *Sigism. & Guisc.* 390, I neither am disposed to make Request for life, nor offered life to take.

Comb. *a* **1598** Rollock *Wks.* (Wodrow Soc.) II. xxvi. 306 The request-maker was one Joseph.

b. The act of asking or fact of being asked (to do something). Chiefly in prepositional phrases, now esp. ***by request***, in response to an expressed wish (†so ***at request***).

c **1460** Sir R. Ros *La Belle Dame* 122 For the compleynt ..Cam to his voyce alway with-out request. **1560** Rolland *Crt. Venus* IV. 741 With all requeist excuse that ȝe wald me. **1589** R. Humston (*title*) A Sermon preached at Reyfham.. and eftsoones at request published. **1607** Shaks. *Cor.* II. iii. 150 The Custome of Request you haue discharg'd. **1683** Sir H. Grimstone tr. *Croke's Rep.* I. 548 Where one is bound to levy a Fine upon Request. **1727–38** Chambers *Cycl.* s.v., For the relief of petitioners, who..should address themselves, by way of request, to his majesty. **1818** Cruise *Digest* (ed. 2) IV. 486 That then the said R. Booth, his heirs, &c. upon request,..should grant and execute..a new lease. **1841** tr. *Anc. Laws & Inst. Wales* XIII. 632/2 There are three motes of request: for tillage; festal games; and the burning of woods. **1976** *Daily Tel.* 20 July 2/7 A list should be provided on request.

†**4.** A knightly quest. *Obs. rare.*

1470–85 Malory *Arthur* III. v. 105 Thenne were they called al thre..., and euerych of hem..armed them surely. But sir gauayne had the fyrst request, and therfore we wille begynne at hym.

†**5.** *Math.* A postulate. *Obs. rare.*

1551 Recorde *Pathw. Knowl.* II. xxii, [Because] all ryghte angles bee equall togyther (by the fourth request). **1570** Billingsley *Euclid* I. Postul. 6 Peticions or requestes. **1709–29** Mandey *Syst. Math., Arith.* 5 Requests or Petitions. 1. That to any Number we may take a greater.

6. The fact, state, or condition of being asked for or sought after; demand; †vogue, fashion. Chiefly in phrases (*a*) ***in*** or ***into request***, † (*b*) ***of request***, † (*c*) ***out of request***. †Also *pl.*

a. **1586** T. B. *La Primaud. Fr. Acad.* (1589) 753 We shall see cleerely enough that the faithful ought to have that in great request. **1594** Nashe *Unfort. Trav.* 15 My gowne and attyre according to the custome then in request. **1611** Bible *Transl. Pref.* ¶3 To bring his abridgements into request. **1667** Pepys *Diary* 2 Sept., The only fruit in request..was the Katharine payre. **1711** Addison *Spect.* No. 47 ¶2 Idiots are still in Request in most of the Courts of Germany. **1822** Hazlitt *Table-t.* Ser. II. iii. (1869) 71 It may perhaps come into request at some future period. **1871** Smiles *Charac.* ii. (1876) 55 Human intelligence, which is in constant request in a family, needs to be educated.

b. **1599** H. Buttes *Dyets drie Dinner* C iij, Both these, are of last and least request. **1613** Purchas *Pilgrimage* ii. iii. 100 Gilgal was a place of request in this kinde. **1632** Lithgow *Trav.* iv. 145 The colour of greatest request among them is greene. **1655** Moufet & Bennet *Health's Improv.* 167 Shrimps were of great request amongst the Romans.

c. **1592** G. Harvey *Four Lett.* Wks. (Grosart) I. 191 Even Guicciardines siluer history, and Ariostos golden cantoes, grow out of request. **1622** Malynes *Anc. Law-Merch.* 78 All these stones being out of request with vs, are to be bought for Russia and other places. **1635** R. N. tr. *Camden's Hist. Eliz.* ii. 167 These books..were often read untill..being contemned they grew out of request.

d. **1601** Shaks. *All's Well* i. i. 169 Off with't while 'tis vendible. Answer the time of request. **1690** Temple *Ess., Poetry* Wks. 1731 I. 249 While this World lasts, I doubt not but the Pleasures and Requests of these two Entertainments will do so too.

†**7.** ***in the request of***, in search of. *Obs. rare*$^{-1}$.

1759 Goldsm. *Polite Learn.* ix, I have seen these harmless reptiles..ply busily about, each in request of a shell to please it.

II. 8. ***Court of Request(s)***: †**a.** A former court of record, technically forming part of the king's council, held by the Lord Privy Seal and the Masters of Requests for the relief of persons petitioning the king; also, in later use, the hall at Westminster in which the court was held. *Obs.*

On the origin and history of the court see Leadam *Select Cases in the Court of Requests* (Selden Soc. 1898).

1516 *Fabyan's Chron.* vi. cliii. 82 A court or counceyll,..lyke vnto the court of requestys, nowe at this day holden in Englonde. **1529** in Leadam *Sel. Cases Crt. Requests* (1898) Introd. 14 Hereafter folowe the names of such Counseillours as be appoynted for the heryng of power mennes causes in the Kynges courte of Requestes. **1591** Lambarde *Archeion* (1635) 22 The Court of Requests that specially heareth the suits of poore men, and of the Princes servants. **1640–4** in Rushw. *Hist. Coll.* iii. (1692) I. 1 The King..came Accompanied with his Nobles through Westminster-hall and the Court of Requests, to the Abbey. **1669** E. Chamberlayne *Pres. St. Eng.* xii. (ed. 2) 217 He [the Lord Privy Seal] is by his Place of the Kings Privy Council, and Chief Judge of the Court of Requests, when it shall be re-continued. **1680** Dryden *Prol. Lee's Cæsar Borgia* 23 One theatre there is of vast resort, Which whilome of Requests was called the Court. **1735** *Court Mercury* (*title-p.*), In the Passage leading from Westminster-Hall to the Court of Request. **1766** Entick *London* IV. 421 A kind of hall.., called the Court of Requests, used chiefly by those who attend the parliament to walk in.

b. A local court for the recovery of small debts.

The constitution and practice of these courts varied in different localities; for the most part they have been merged in the County Court system established in 1847.

1603–4 *Act 1 James I*, c. 14 §1 The Court of Requestes comonlie called The Courte of Conscience, in the Guild Hall of the same Citie. **1707** E. Chamberlayne *Pres. St. Eng.* iii. x. 355 There is a Court of Request or Conscience, so call'd, because medling with nothing above 40s. value. **1749** *Act 22 Geo. II*, c. 47 §1 Such Commissioners are hereby constituted a Court of Justice, by the Name of The Court of Requests for the Town and Borough of Southwark. **1798** [see court *sb.*[1] 11 c]. **1837** *2nd Rep. Munic. Corporations Eng. & Wales* 12 There are two Courts of Requests within the limits of the Corporate jurisdiction; one for London..and the other for Southwark. **1845** *Act 8 & 9 Vict.* c. 127 §10 Every Judge of any such Court of Requests, or Conscience..shall be removable by the Lord Chancellor for Misbehaviour or Incapacity.

c. In India: A small-debt court composed of military officers, held in districts which are outside the jurisdiction of any ordinary court of this kind.

1876 Voyle *Milit. Dict.* 338/1 In each military cantonment a court of request is assembled monthly, and all persons are amenable to it except soldiers in the ranks. **1879** *Act 42 & 43 Vict.* c. 33 §142 Courts of request under this Act shall in all practicable cases consist of five officers.

†**9.** ***Master of (the) Request(s)***: **a.** One of the leading officers of the Court of Requests. Hence ***Mastership of Requests***. *Obs.*

1553 *Cal. St. Papers, Domestic* (1856) 51 All such private suits as are customably brought to the King or his Council, and delivered to the Masters of Requests. **1579** *Ibid.* 637 Signified by letter of Mr. Sec. Wylson to the Masters of Requests. **1625** Bacon *Apophth.* lxxxiv. 110 Sackford, Master of the Request to Queen Elizabeth, had diuerse times moued for audience, and been put off. **1675** *Lond. Gaz.* No. 977/4 This day His Majesty was graciously pleased..to cause him [Thomas Povey, Esq.] to be Sworn one of the Masters of Request. **1691** Wood *Prop. for Printing Ath. Oxon.* 4/2 He had refused a Mastership of the Requests. **1716** M. Davies *Athen. Brit.* II. 316 Nothing but a great Pension for Life and a Master of Requests place, were thought encouragement enough for it.

†**b.** In France: One of a number of officials forming an advisory and judicial body with a variety of functions. *Obs.*

1560 Daus tr. *Sleidane's Comm.* 174 In the moneth of August, ended his lyfe at Paris William Budey, maister of the requestes. **1611** Cotgr. s.v. *Requeste, Maistres des requestes*, the Masters of Requests; at first there were but two,..afterwards they came to be fiue [etc.]. **1727–38** Chambers *Cycl.* s.v. *Request*, In France..they have eighty masters of requests to take cognizance of causes between the officers of the crown, the servants of the houshold, &c.

†**c.** In Scotland. Also ***Office of Requests***. *Obs.*

1561 *Reg. Privy Council Scot.* I. 159 Gif ony letter..be direct fra the Quenis Grace to the Lordis of Counsale, that the maister of Requeistis present and deliver the samyn to the Chancellar. **1582** *Ibid.* III. 529 To promote him to the office of Requeistis; quhairin he continewit weill neir the space of thre yeir. **1607** *Ibid.* XIV. Addenda 472 Mr. Peter Rollok, the Maister of Requeistis. **1633** *Ibid.* Ser. ii. V. 107 Sir James Galloway, Maister of Requeists.

10. ***Letters of Request***: †**a.** A note addressed by a ruler or government to a foreign power, requesting compensation for injury done to a subject, or a proper consideration of his claims. *Obs.*

1442 *Rolls of Parlt.* V. 64/2 Of the whiche Wronges..satisfaction is not made; notwithstanding that divers your Letters of request have been delivered to the high Maister of Pruse,..for the reformation of the same. **1676** Molloy *De Jure Marit. & Nav.* i. ii. §8. 18 Nor should the Prince or State of the Person injur'd, value his misfortune at so low a rate as to deny him Letters of Request. *Ibid.* §11. 19 This will be no cause for Letters of Reprizal, though perhaps it may occasion Letters of Request..to have a rehearsing of the cause. **1752** Beawes *Lex Mercat. Rediv.* 204.

b. *Eccl.* A documentary request sent by the judge of one ecclesiastical court to another, esp. to desire that a case may be withdrawn from his own jurisdiction to that of a superior court.

1840 *Act 3 & 4 Vict.* c. 86 §13 It shall be lawful for the Bishop of the Diocese..to send the Case by Letters of Request to the Court of Appeal of the Province. **1873** Sir R. Phillimore *Eccles. Law* II. 1278 It has been said that the Arches Court may take original cognizance by Letters of Request of all causes which may be brought in a Diocesan Court of the Province. *Ibid.* 1279 Letters of request are sometimes issued for other purposes than for sending the cause to another court.

11. *attrib.* as, ***request item, night, number, programme, session, week***; **requestman** *Naut.*, a seaman who makes a written request to an officer; also *pl.*, applied to the occasion appointed for the presentation of such requests; **request note**, a note addressed to a revenue officer requesting permission to remove excisable articles; †**request place**, a place at which horses and guides might be requisitioned; **request stop**, a stop at which a bus will halt only on request from a passenger or intending passenger.

1923 *Radio Times* 28 Sept. 17/1 Special *Request Items. **1972** P. Black *Biggest Aspidistra* i. iii. 29 The pluggers kept the initiative by inventing the request item. **1916** 'Taffrail' *Pincher Martin* vii. 116 '*Request-men an' defaulters—'shun!' bawled the master-at-arms. **1951** H. Hastings *Sea Gulls over Sorrento* in J. C. Trewin *Plays of Year* IV. 75 You'd better write out a request... You know the routine... Requestmen is at 0900 tomorrow morning and not before! **1961** *Times* 27 Feb. 14/6 Shortly after breakfast C.P.O. Coleshill knocked on my cabin door and entered with his list of requestmen and defaulters. **1923** *Radio Times* 28 Sept. 12/1 Why is it apparently not thought advisable to repeat the '*Request Nights', which..are so popular? **1856** Bouvier *Law Dict.* (ed. 6) *Request Notes. **1876** G. D. Ham *Revenue Vade-m.* 567 The entries for all goods, except cattle, delivered on a request note, are to be passed within three days. **1971** 'D. Halliday' *Dolly & Doctor Bird* iii. 37 The small coloured orchestra..suddenly broke..into a *request number for jiving. **1827** G. Thompson *Trav. in S. Africa* (ed. 2) I. 261 After a sharp ride we reached Jakhal's-Fonteyn, the first '*request place' in a district called the Winterveld. **1889** *Cent. Dict.*, *Request-program, a concert program made up of numbers the performance of which has been requested by the audience. **1955** *Radio Times* 22 Apr. 10/2 A request programme of records. **1976** *Times* 4 Aug. 12/3 On the radio, request programmes for 'troopies' in the operational areas aim to keep spirits high. **1959** M. Shadbolt *New Zealanders* 76 The crackling voice of the *request-session announcer. **1943** G. Greene *Ministry of Fear* iv. i. 223 Buses slid quickly past the *Request stops. **1955** O. Lancaster in *Daily Express* 25 Nov. 1/2 (*caption*) Five years' continuous service without once stopping at a request stop. **1973** *Times* 15 Oct. 17/5 Hiding behind another bus at a request stop so as to avoid seeing the uplifted hand. **1928** *Radio Times* 7 Dec. 649/2 (*heading*) Children's Hour *request week... The Fourth Request Week will begin on January 7, 1929.

re'quest, *sb.*[2] *rare*$^{-0}$. [ad. F. *requête*: see prec.] (See quot., which is translated from Furetière *Dict. Univ.* 1690.)

1727–38 Chambers *Cycl.* s.v., *Request*, in hunting, is when the dogs have lost the quest or track of the beast, and must request, or quest it again... They say, to call to the request, come to the request, &c.

request (rɪ'kwɛst), *v.*[1] Also 7 as *pa. t.* [ad. OF. *requester*, f. *requeste*: see request *sb.*[1]

In the *Wars Alex.* 3443 *request* is probably a scribal error for *reknest* or *rekenest*, superlative of reken *a.*]

1. With *infin.* To express a wish or desire *to* have, hear, etc.; to ask or beg the favour or permission to be allowed *to* do something.

1565 Stapleton tr. *Bede's Hist. Ch. Eng.* 181 He requested farder to haue instructions by his letters what maner of tonsure the clergy should vse. **1596** Shaks. *Tam. Shr.* iv. iii. 122 But did you not request to haue it cut? **1641** T. Hayne *M. Luther* 29 He requested to heare Erasmus judgement concerning Luther. **1760–72** H. Brooke *Fool of Qual.* (1809) III. 133 [He] requested to speak with him apart. **1784** *Laura & Augustus* III. 117, I requested to place down my own name for two chances. **1800** Helena Wells *Constantia Neville* (ed. 2) III. 193 To that village I requested to go. **1818** G. S. Faber *Horæ Mosaicæ* I. 217 He again and again requests to be excused from the ungrateful task. **1853** Cayley *Las Alforjas* II. 55 We had requested to sleep in the straw-loft, but our host absolutely refused.

b. Similarly with *that* or obj. clause.

1611 Bible *1 Kings* xix. 4 Hee requested for himselfe that hee might die. **1797** Mrs. Radcliffe *Italian* i, He then summoned courage enough to request he might be allowed to inquire after her health.

2. *trans.* To ask, or ask for (something).

1594 Willobie *Avisa* xlvii, Let sighes and sobbes request her grace. **1635** Quarles *Embl.* v. xi. 285 The drooping Crests of fading Flowres Request the bounty of a morning Raine. **1654** Gataker *Disc. Apol.* 30 Reqesting my Readers patience and pardon, if I shal seem to detain him over-long. **1725** Pope *Odyss.* iv. 856 My ship equip'd within the neighb'ring port, The Prince..Requested for his speed. **1772–84** *Cook's Voy.* (1790) V. 1564 Captain Cook's company was requested. **1819** Shelley *Cenci* iv. iv. 79 Favour me, Sir,..to tell the ladies That I request their presence. **1855** Brewster *Newton* II. xiv. 25 Leibnitz requested farther information respecting the..discoveries.

b. With *that* or inf. clause.

1766 Goldsm. *Vic. W.* xxxii, I requested that the table might be taken away. **1832** Southey *Hist. Penins. War* III. 437 Requesting that he would endeavour to form a cabinet. **1850** Mrs. Jameson *Leg. Monast. Ord.* 424 Ivo..requested of him to send some of the brethren of his Order to preach the Gospel in his distant..diocese.

3. To ask (one) *to* do something.

1533 Bellenden *Livy* v. xxiii. (S.T.S.) II. 227 Þe senate requeistit him to leif nocht þe public weill in trubill. **1535** Lyndesay *Satyre* 93, I thee requeist..Me to defend from the deids of defame. **1585** T. Washington tr. *Nicholay's Voy.* ii. v. 34 b, Requesting him to take the same for his lodging. **1609** W. M. *Man in Moone* B iv b, He..brought him to an alehouse, and request him to alight, and enter with him. **1671** Milton *Samson* 1630 He his guide requested..As over-tir'd to let him lean a while. **1791** Boswell *Johnson* an. 1738, Pope..requested Mr. Richardson..to endeavour to find out who this new author was. **1818** Scott *Hrt. Midl.* vii, Butler requested them to open the gate. **1859** Darwin in *Life & Lett.* (1887) II. 170, I request you, after you have finished, just to re-run over the heads.

absol. **1580** Lyly *Euphues* (Arb.) 278 My Father placed vs all in good order, requesting eyther by questions to whette our wittes, or by stories to trye our memoryes.

†**b.** With double object. *Obs. rare.*

1563 Winȝet *Four Scoir Thre Quest.* Wks. (S.T.S.) I. 60 Quhilk thing we requeist thee, gentill Reidar. *c* **1592** Marlowe *Jew of Malta* iii. iii, Let me request thee this; Go to the new-made nunnery.

†**c.** *ellipt.* To ask (one) to act *against* another, to come or go *to* a place, etc. *Obs. rare.*

1582 N.T. (Rhem.) *Rom.* xi. 2 Know you not in Elias..how he requested God against Israel? **1598** B. Jonson *Ev. Man in Hum.* i. iv, I was requested to supper last night. *Ibid.* iv. iv, I pray you, sir, let me request you to the Windmill. **1606** Shaks. *Ant. & Cl.* ii. vii. 127 Pompey, goodnight. Good Brother, Let me request you of[f]. **1613** Purchas *Pilgrimage* ix. iv. (1614) 838 He was requested to their warres against the Tapwees.

†**d.** To win over by entreaty. *Obs. rare*$^{-1}$.

1632 Lithgow *Trav.* vii. 302, I intreated them to forbeare, but they would not be requested.

Hence **re'quested** *ppl. a.*, **re'questing** *vbl. sb.* Also †**re'questant**, a requester.

1561 Preston *K. Cambyses* C ij b, In stead of his requested life, pleaseth Your grace take mine. **1577** Hellowes *Gueuara's Chron.* 51 In his commaundements hee was uerie wise, and in requesting uerie humble. **1582** Stanyhurst *Æneis*, etc. *Ps.* iv. (Arb.) 132 The lord therefor, when I pray, wil harcken Too mye requesting. **1634** Sir T. Herbert *Trav.* 161, I dare not goe about to trouble you..without a requested pardon. **1660** *New Haven Cal. Rev.* (1858) II. 338 Concerning yᵉ sale of a certaine vessell..then sould by yᵉ requestants vnto one Mʳ. Rich: Raymond. **1884** Tennyson *Becket* ii. ii, If you, At my requesting, will but look into The wrongs you did him. **1892** *Athenæum* 1 Oct. 454/1 To supply the requested particulars with regard to the stops and other details.

re'quest, *v.*[2] *rare*$^{-0}$. [ad. F. *requêter*: cf. prec. and request *sb.*[2]] (See quot.)

1727–38 Chambers *Cycl.* s.v., To request the game is chiefly used, when, after having run it down the night before, they seek it again the next morning with the bloodhound, or the like.

requester (rɪ'kwɛstə(r)). [f. request *v.*[1] + -er[1].] One who requests.

1564 Abp. Parker *Corr.* (Parker Soc.) 209 Doubtful it is to me by what authority these requesters do exercise their conference. **1625** Ussher *Answ. Jesuit* 406 The requester is oftentimes superiour to him whose prayers hee desireth. **1647** Herrick *Noble Numb., Gods Gifts not soone granted*, Though a while He makes requesters stay, With princely hand, He'l recompence delay. **1754** Richardson *Grandison* (1781) IV. xvi. 128 Thus..can he..send away a requester so much delighted with him, as to forget what her request was. **1796** Jane Austen *Pride & Prej.* x, A regard for the requester would often make one readily yield to a request. **1973** *Nature* 13 Apr. 485/2 How many requesters, before writing, saw my paper?

‖**requeté** (reke'te). *Hist.* Also **Requeté**. [Sp.] A member of a Carlist militia that took the Nationalist side during the Spanish Civil War of 1936–39.

1936 *Times* 26 Aug. 12/4 The troops engaged on the insurgent side have consisted of *requetes*, Navarrese volunteers almost to a man. **1938** *Times Lit. Suppl.* 27 Aug. 558/3 The first, longer and better of the two stories..describes how a Carlist *requeté* in North Spain deserted his side to secure the reprieve of his father. **1944** Wyndham Lewis *Let.* 5 Jan. (1963) 374, I was glad to learn from Augustus that he had exchanged his requeté uniform for that of the Home Guard. **1957** P. Kemp *Mine were of Trouble* ii. 21 The Requeté movement drew its main strength from the Basque provinces, especially from Navarre. **1979** D. Robinson *Eldorado Network* xvii. 129 The Requetés..were a sort of Basque militia... Fought for Franco.

requicken (riː'kwɪk(ə)n), *v.* [re- 5 a.] To quicken again, reanimate, revive.

a. *trans.* **1592** G. Harvey *Four Lett.* iii. Wks. (Grosart) I. 197 Sweet Musike requickneth the heauiest spirites of dumpish Melancholy. **1607** Shaks. *Cor.* ii. ii. 121 Then straight his doubled spirit Requickend what in flesh was fatigate. *a* **1693** *Urquhart's Rabelais* III. xxv. 210 Which Body so raised up and requicknd, will tell us the Sum of all you shall require of him. **1822–34** *Good's Study Med.* (ed. 4) I. 114 The organs of assimilation..if once requickened are very apt to be unduly excited. **1879** CHR. ROSSETTI *Seek & F.* 216 Our Redeemer bought with a great price His right to re-quicken us.

b. *intr.* **1611** SPEED *Hist. Gt. Brit.* IX. xiii. §9. 715 Neither was the spirit of the English (after it began to requicken) idle elsewhere. **1618** BOLTON *Florus* Pref. Biij, Vnder the gouernment of Traian, their sinewes requicken. **1878** SWINBURNE *Poems & Ball.* Ser. II. *Inferiæ* 2 Spring, and the light and sound of things on earth Requickening.

Hence **re'quickened** *ppl. a.*; **re'quickening** *vbl. sb.* and *ppl. a.*

1617 HIERON *Wks.* II. 226 A renuing and a requickning of that heauenly life. **1850** O. WINSLOW *Inner Life* v. 156 What will be some of the effects of a revived, requickened state of the spiritual life? **1861** LYTTON & FANE *Tannhäuser* 11 Awake Starts the requicken'd soul with all her powers. **1891** *Edin. Rev.* July 212 A requickening form of Christian belief and practice.

requiem ('rɛkwɪəm, 'riːkwɪəm), *sb.*¹ [L. *requiem*, acc. of *requiēs* 'rest', the first word of the Introit in the Mass for the Dead, 'Requiem æternam dona eis, Domine', etc.]

1. *R. C. Ch.* A special mass said or sung for the repose of the souls of the dead. Also ***Mass of Requiem*** (common in early use).

1303 R. BRUNNE *Handl. Synne* 2615 'Requiem' ne shulde be note be sunge Ne seyde for hym, wyþ mannys tunge. *a* **1380** *St. Bernard* 1105 in Horstm. *Altengl. Leg.* (1878) 59/2 Whon seint Malachi ded was, Bernard for him song an heiȝ mas—Of Requiem i trowe hit were. *c* **1430** LYDG. *Min. Poems* (Percy Soc.) 72 The tone had ever right grete devocioun, Of requiem his masse to syng or say. **1470–85** MALORY *Arthur* XXI. viii. 853 An the morne al the preestys and clerkys..were there & sange masse of requyem. **1553** BECON *Reliques of Rome* (1563) 204 Sensyng of the altare when Masse of Requiem is songen. **1591** SPENSER *Ruins of Time* 196 Scarse anie left vpon his lips to laie The sacred sod, or Requiem to saie. **1668** R. L'ESTRANGE *Vis. Quev.* (1708) 26 The Apothecary's Mortar Rings the Passing-Bell, as the Priest's Requiem finishes the business. **1766** BLACKSTONE *Comm.* II. 495 A use more truly pious, than any requiem, or mass for his soul. **1794** MRS. RADCLIFFE *Myst. Udolpho* viii, She heard, at a distance, the monks chanting the requiem for his soul. **1805** SCOTT *Last Minstr.* v. xxx, Behind, four priests, in sable stole, Sung requiem for the warrior's soul. **1884** *Cath. Dict.* (1897) 612/2 There are special rules on the relations of Office and Conventual Mass, Mass of Requiem, etc., in the rubrics of the Missal.

attrib. *a* **1529** SKELTON *P. Sparowe* 401 He shall be the preest The requiem masse to synge. **1559** *Mirr. Mag., Dk. Suffolk* xvi, The Queene did moue me..To helpe to bring him to his Requiem Masse. **1861** *Times* 21 Aug., A solemn requiem mass was celebrated..at the Catholic Chapel. **1882** ROSSETTI *Ballads & Sonn.* 154 The slain king's corpse on bier was laid With chaunt and requiem-knell.

b. A musical setting of a mass for the dead.

1789 BURNEY *Hist. Mus.* IV. 563, I am in possession of a *Te Deum*, and a *Requiem*, of his composition. **1842** BRANDE *Dict. Sci.*, etc. s.v., The requiems composed by Mozart, Jomelli, and Cherubini are well known. **1845** E. HOLMES *Mozart* 345 Mozart began to speak of death, and said that he was writing this 'Requiem' for himself.

2. Any dirge or solemn chant for the repose of the dead. (Chiefly *poet.*)

1611 BEAUM. & FL. *Philaster* v. i, I'll provide A masque shall make your Hymen..sing sad Requiems to your departing Souls. **1633** COWLEY *Elegy on Mr. R. Clarke*, Him to Elysium's lasting Ioyes they bring, Where winged Angels his sad Requiems sing. *a* **1700** KEN *Edmund* Poet. Wks. 1721 II. 39 That they with Joy might their own Requiem sing, And close their Eyes. **1797** MRS. RADCLIFFE *Italian* iii, That solemn and peculiar kind of recitative which is in some parts of Italy the requiem of the dying. **1830** SCOTT *Demonol.* x. 386 Three ladies were seen, who sung a solemn requiem. **1876** BANCROFT *Hist. U.S.* II. xl. 492 The requiem [had been] chanted by the women in mournful strains over their bones.

b. *transf.* of birds, the sea, etc.

1640 HABINGTON *Castara* III. (Arb.) 142 Spring..Whose fether'd Musicke onely bring Caresses, and no Requiem sing On the departed yeare. **1788** BURNS *To Miss C[ruikshank]* 18 While all around the woodland rings, And ev'ry bird thy requiem sings. **1809** CAMPBELL *Gertr. Wyom.* III. xxvi, And for the business of destruction done Its requiem the war-horn seem'd to blow. **1869** C. GIBBON *R. Gray* v, The sea was murmuring a doleful requiem over the mischief of the previous night.

†**3.** An invitation to rest or repose. *Obs.*

1607 HIERON *Wks.* I. 432 We dwell carelesse, quiet and sure in our owne opinion. Euery man sings a requiem to his own heart. **1668** BP. HOPKINS *Serm. Vanity* (1685) 70 It was but small comfort, when the rich man sung his Requiem, Soul take thine ease, thou hast goods laid up for many years. **1684** CHARNOCK *Wks.* (1865) IV. 488 Our deceitful heart may sing a requiem to us while we are fools.

4. Rest, repose, peace, quiet.

1616 BULLOKAR *Eng. Exp.*, *Requiem*, Rest: ceasing from labour. **1638** G. SANDYS *Paraphr. Job* iii, Else had I an eternall Requiem kept, And in the armes of Peace for ever slept. **1665** GLANVILL *Def. Vanity Dogm.* 50 Though the first of their respective solutions is pleasant and encouraging, and seems to promise my mind a requiem. **1790** G. WALKER *Serm.* II. xxii. 140 In his presence alone is to be found the requiem of their troubled souls. **1816** BYRON *Death Sheridan* 67 Repose denies her requiem to his name, And Folly loves the martyrdom of Fame.

Hence **'requiem** *v. intr.*, to quieten down.

1838 ELIZA COOK *Song of Mariners* iv, We know each blustering gale that blows May requiem to a last repose.

†**requiem**, *sb.*² *Obs.* Also 8 requien. [= F. *requiem* (1690), *requien* (1578), but usually *requin* (1539), Pg. *requeime*, prob. a native name assimilated to prec.] The white shark.

1666 J. DAVIES *Hist. Caribby Isles* 102 The Requiem otherwise called the Shark-fish is a kind of Sea-dog or Sea-wolf. *Ibid.* 103 The French and Portuguez commonly call it Requiem, that is to say Rest, haply, because he is wont to appear in fair weather. **1696** tr. *Duquesne's Voy. E. Indies, Canary Isl.* 61 The Requiem, the Monster of the Sea, that's shap'd like a Sea-Dog, is in length from three or four Foot to eight. **1705** tr. *Bosman's Guinea* 281 Hayes or Requiens, by some (though utterly wrong) named Sea-Dogs,..are very thick as well as very long, some of them betwixt twenty and thirty foot.

‖**requiescat** (rɛkwɪ'ɛskæt). [L., the first word of *requiescat in pace* 'may he (or she) rest in peace'.] A wish for the repose of the dead.

1824 WIFFEN *Tasso* III. lxxii, Many a tuneful tongue Sweet in the solemn march his requiescat sung. **1852** THACKERAY *Esmond* II. xiii, A thousand such hillocks lay round about..each bearing its cross and requiescat. **1860** LD. LYTTON *Lucile* I. vi, That emotion! I bury it here by the sea,..And a heart's requiescat I write on that grave.

†**requi'esce**, *v. Obs. rare*⁻¹. [ad. L. *requiēscĕre*, f. *requiēs* rest.] *intr.* To rest, repose.

1677 GALE *Crt. Gentiles* IV. I. 24 The mind, when it acts, must requiesce in the love, not of the Creature, but of God.

requiescence (rɛkwɪ'ɛsəns). [f. L. *requiēscĕre* (see prec.), after QUIESCENCE.] A state of quiescence, rest, repose.

1654 FLECKNOE *Ten Years Trav.* 91, I am now arrived at Bruxelles..wanting nothing of that requiescence which every thing enjoys in that which it most desires. **1775** WRAXALL *Tour N. Europe* 216, I threw myself on the bed,..glad to retire to silence and requiescence. **1837** CARLYLE *Fr. Rev.* I. III. viii, Such bolts..shall strike agitated Paris if not into requiescence, yet into wholesome astonishment.

†**re'quietory.** *Obs. rare*⁻¹. [ad. L. *requiētōrium*, f. *requiēs* rest.] A sepulchre.

1631 WEEVER *Anc. Funeral Mon.* 419 The bodies..are not onely despoiled of all outward funerall ornaments, but digged vp out of their requietories.

†**requile**, obs. form of RECOIL *v.*

1573 TWYNE *Æneid* XI. I. i. 4 Lyris while His bridell raignes he raught from horse to ground he doth requile.

†**re'quirable**, *a. Obs.* Also 4 requer-. [orig. a. OF. *requerable* (1275 in Godef.); in later use f. REQUIRE *v.* + -ABLE.] Capable of being required; that may properly be asked for.

c **1374** CHAUCER *Boeth.* II. pr. vi. 41 (Camb. MS.), But which is thilke yowre dereworthe power þat is so cleer and so requerable [L. *expetibilis*]. **1576** FLEMING *Panopl. Epist.* 5 Looke what dutie and seruice is requireable of a friende to a friende. **1634** SIR T. HERBERT *Trav.* 133 Nor wants this Towne any fruit requirable for the Zone tis placed in. *a* **1676** HALE *Prim. Orig. Man.* (1677) 136 It contains..all Circumstances requirable in a History to inform.

†**re'quiral.** *Obs. rare*⁻⁰. [-AL¹.] Demand.

1611 COTGR., *Requisition*, a requisition, requirall.

†**re'quirance.** *Obs. rare.* [-ANCE; cf. OF. *requerance* (Godef.).] The fact or condition of requiring something; requirement.

1662 J. CHANDLER *Van Helmont's Oriat.* 34 Therefore, besides the ignorance of Nature in its Root,..the Schooles have not known the causes, number, requirance of things. *Ibid.* 280 Marking, that the sensitive soul doth not govern man according to the requirance of our Species.

†**re'quirant.** *Obs.* [-ANT: cf. F. *requérant* (14th c.).] One who makes a request or demand; a wooer or suitor.

a **1467** *Gregory's Chron.* (Camden) 155 For the surplus of the tyme that the saudyers shalle serve, the requyrant shalle ben holdyn to sendyn hem at hys propyr dysposycyon. **1566** PAINTER *Pal. Pleas.* (1890) III. 329 A fayththfull Louer and deuout requirant to this Iolly dame. **1755** MAGENS *Insurances* I. 294 The Cargo of Wheat arrived from London..consigned to the said Requirants. **1812** in G. E. Cory *Rise of S. Afr.* (1910) I. vii. 213 The R.O. Requirant feels himself obliged to declare that he has not any ground for further action against the defendant.

re'quire, *sb. rare.* [f. the verb.] Demand, requisition.

1502 *Ord. Crysten Men* (W. de W. 1506) IV. xxvi. Ffj b, They be not bounde after the requyre of commaundement. **1611** H. BROUGHTON (*title*) A Require of Agreement to the Groundes of Divinitie studie. **1843** E. JONES *Poems, Sens. & Event* (1879) 13 When suddenly, with intenser utterance, scream'd The music's wild require.

require (rɪ'kwaɪə(r)), *v.* Also 5 requer (*Sc.* ra-), requeere, 5–7 requere, *Sc.* requeir; 4–7 requyre, 6 reqwy(e)r, 7 reqire. [a. OF. *requer-*, *requier-*, stem of *requerre* (mod.F. *requérir*) = Prov. *requerre*, *-querer*, *-ir*, Sp. *requerir*, Pg. *requerer*, It. *richiedere*:—L. *requīrĕre*, f. *re-* RE- + *quærĕre* to seek, ask: see QUERE *v.* The form *require* may be directly from L.: cf. INQUIRE.]

I. † **1.** *trans.* To ask (one) a question; to inquire of (one) *why*, *if*, etc. *Obs. rare.*

13.. *Gaw. & Gr. Knt.* 1056 For-þy, sir, þis enquest I require yow here, þat ȝe me telle with trawþe [etc.]. **1548** UDALL, etc. *Erasm. Par. Matt.* xx. 99 She..being required what she would, sayeth [etc.]. *a* **1578** LINDESAY (Pitscottie) *Chron. Scot.* (S.T.S.) II. 47 Thairfor he spak the mair scharplie in his cause and requyrit the cardinall quhy he keipit nocht promise into him. **1578–9** *Reg. Privy Council Scot.* III. 76 He wes..required gif he wald retene the said charge.

†**b.** To question (one) *of* something. *Obs. rare*⁻¹.

1535 STEWART *Cron. Scot.* II. 527 How Culenus..requyrit the Kirkmen of the Takynis in the Sky, and of thair Ansuer.

†**2.** To ask or request (one) for something. Usu. const. *of* (rarely *for*). *Obs.*

c **1375** *Sc. Leg. Saints* iii. (*Andrew*) 972 Þane sad scho: 'lord, lat be! of sic thinge requere nocht me!' *c* **1400** *Rom. Rose* 5233 He shulde not bide so long, til he Of his helpyng hym requere. *a* **1450** *Knt. de la Tour* (1868) 7 He..sware to her that he wolde neuer requere her of no suche materes. **1483** CAXTON *G. de la Tour* F vij b, He..enhaunceth the meke and humble that requyreth hym of mercy. **1500–20** DUNBAR *Poems* xvi. 16 Sum is for gift sa lang requyrd. **1523** LD. BERNERS *Froiss.* I. ix. 7 Than yᵉ quene..required hym all wepyng of his good counsaile. **1583** STOCKER *Civ. Warres Low C.* III. 106 b, They had the night before, requyred the Leydens of certaine horsemen, to discouer the enemie.

†**b.** With double obj. To ask (one) for (a thing); also, to request or command (one) to do (something). *Obs.*

c **1386** CHAUCER *Wife's T.* 1052 He plighte me his trouthe there, The firste thyng I wolde hym requere, He wolde it do. *c* **1430** *Pilgr. Lyf Manhode* I. cxxxiii. (1869) 70 Wherto hast þou required me þe armures, whan þou..wolt not bere hem? **1573** L. LLOYD *Marrow of Hist.* (1653) 241 My son, said he, this I charge and require thee.

†**3.** To ask, request, or desire (one) to do something. With various constructions: **a.** With *that* (sometimes omitted). *Obs.*

1375 BARBOUR *Bruce* XII. 263 Quharfor I ȝow requeir and pray, That..ȝhe pres ȝow at the begynnyng. **1483** CAXTON *Gold. Leg.* 196 b/1 Requyryng our lord with salte teris that ..he wold delyuer them of this pestylence. **1560** DAUS tr. *Sleidane's Comm.* 26 b, He requireth them therefore that they woulde not deale after this sorte. **1613** SHAKS. *Hen. VIII*, II. iv. 144 In humblest manner I require your Highnes, That it shall please you [etc.].

†**b.** With infinitive. *Obs.*

1412–20 LYDG. *Chron. Troy* I. vi. (1555), First I the requere..Not to arrecte as to presumption [etc.]. **1470–85** MALORY *Arthur* III. xi. 112, I requyre the as thow arte a true knyght to gyue me my yefte. **1559** W. CUNNINGHAM *Cosmogr. Glasse* 83, I muste earnestly require you, to teach me some way [etc.]. **1600** E. BLOUNT tr. *Conestaggio* 323 Being required by the kinsemen of the dead, to take it from thence. **1640–1** *Kirkcudbr. War-Comm. Min. Bk.* (1855) 75 Gif they be not requyerit by you to come so prepared, the blame shall be imputed to you.

†**c.** With imperative. *Obs.*

c **1450** *Merlin* 74, I pray yow and requyre telle me of that ye knowe my herte desireth so. **1500–20** DUNBAR *Poems* lxix. 32 Cum neir, And be nocht strange, I the requeir. *c* **1530** *Pol., Rel. & L. Poems* (1866) 41 Humbly also y you Requer, ..Reffuse me nat oute of your Remembraunce. *a* **1533** LD. BERNERS *Huon* lix. 205 Syrs, I requyre you arme you quyckely. **1584** HUDSON *Du Bartas' Judith* III. 84 Defend vs mighty Lord wee thee require.

†**d.** With ellipse (usu. of the infin.). *Obs.*

c **1400** *Rule St. Benet* 1053 Vs aw to ȝem our tong And spek not bot we be requerde. *a* **1450** *Knt. de la Tour* (1868) 5 It is an higher..thinge forto praise and thanke God, thanne to requere hym. **1485** CAXTON *Paris & V.* (1868) 35 Many tymes he had ben requyred of many noble prynces. **1561** T. HOBY tr. *Castiglione's Courtyer* II. (1577) K v b, The poore naked soule..that requireth hir with such passion & so instantly. **1586** A. DAY *Eng. Secretary* I. (1625) 66 Longer could I occupie my selfe to trauell in this action with you, but that I deeme it more then impertinent any further therein to require you. **1607** SHAKS. *Cor.* II. ii. 160 He wil require them, As if he did contemne what he requested, Should be in them to giue. **1611** BIBLE *2 Macc.* vii. 10 When he was required, he put out his tongue.

†**e.** To invite, call, summon *to* something. *Obs.*

1513 DOUGLAS *Æneis* XII. viii. 54 And hym allane,..He askis and requiris into melle. **1600** HAKLUYT *Voy.* (1810) III. 233 Thus the poore king..being required thither to a banquet, was traiterously caryed away. **1665** J. SPENCER *Vulg. Proph.* 59 If the inspired man required them to a faith of some Prediction or Doctrine.

4. To demand of (one) *to* do something.

1751 JOHNSON *Rambler* No. 163 ¶13 It was his practice to impose tasks upon me, by requiring me to write upon such subjects. **1867** FREEMAN *Norm. Conq.* (1877) I. App. 662 The government required each county to find its quota of ships. **1882** J. H. BLUNT *Ref. Ch. Eng.* II. 11 The Judges were required to give their opinion.

II. 5. a. To ask for (some thing or person) authoritatively or imperatively, or as a right; to demand, claim, insist on having.

c **1380** WYCLIF *Serm.* Sel. Wks. I. 336 Þe blood of just Abel shal be requyrid of Cayn. **1432–50** tr. *Higden* (Rolls) II. 97 Lestage, that is a thynge required [L. *exacta*] in feires. **1490** CAXTON *Eneydos* viii. 34 [They] notefyden vnto the quene, how the sayd kyng had requyred her in maryage. **1526** *Pilgr. Perf.* (W. de W. 1531) 28 b, Of all these benefytes ..he wyll requyre streyte accountes. **1535** COVERDALE *Gen.* xliii. 9, I wyll be suertye for him, of my handes shalt thou require him. **1581** SAVILE *Tacitus, Hist.* III. x. (1591) 119 His death was now violently required. **1610** SHAKS. *Temp.* v. i. 132, I..require My Dukedome of thee, which, perforce I know Thou must restore. **1667** MILTON *P.L.* v. 529 Our voluntarie service he requires. *a* **1720** SEWEL *Hist. Quakers* (1722) I. III. 80 Oliver Cromwell..requir'd, both of the Soldiers and others, the Oath of Fidelity. **1856** FROUDE *Hist. Eng.* II. ix. 347 The royal commissioners appeared at the Charterhouse to require the submission of the brethren.

b. To ask for (something) as a favour; to beg, entreat, or request (†*of* one). Now *rare.*

c **1430** LYDG. *Min. Poems* (Percy Soc.) 247 Thy feet embracyng..Mercy requeeryng, thus I wyl begynne. *c* **1477** CAXTON *Jason* 12 b, Peleus promised to Jason that he sholde accomplisshe..al that he had required of him. **1542** UDALL in *Lett. Lit. Men* (Camden) 7, I shall not require of your maistership any thing, but oonly that without which noo man can live. **1590** SPENSER *F.Q.* I. iii. 12 Dame Una, weary Dame,..entrance did requere. **1655** STANLEY *Hist. Philos.* I. (1701) 58/1 Being thirsty he required Water of one of his Scholars. **1697** DRYDEN *Æneid* VII. 209 They go commission'd to require a Peace. **1788** COWPER *New Year's Gift* 10 What favour then not yet possessed Can I for thee require..? **1842** TENNYSON *Gardener's Dau.* 224 Requiring at her hand the greatest gift, A woman's heart.

c. *intr.* To make request or demand.

1423 JAS. I *Kingis Q.* cxcv, To quham for me thou pitousely requere. **1430–40** LYDG. *Bochas* V. xii. (1558) 122 b, Mekely requiryng vnto Scipion To receyue them in thys mortall rage. **1556** in *Ripon Ch. Acts* (Surtees) 361 Also I will that myn executors reqwyer on sute for my twentie nobles. **1582** N. T. (Rhem.) *Mark* xv. 8 And when the multitude was come vp, they began to require [L. *rogare*] according as alwaies he did vnto them. **1734** POPE *Ess. Man* IV. 123 Shall burning Ætna, if a sage requires, Forget to thunder, and recall her fires? **1819** KEATS *St. Agnes* vi, They must..require Of Heaven with upward eyes for all that they desire.

d. To ask or request *to* have, etc. Now *rare* (common 1550–1640).

1542 UDALL *Erasm. Apoph.* 233 When Achilles was slain, Aiax required to haue his harnesse and weapen. **1560** DAUS tr. *Sleidane's Comm.* 322 b, Thambassadors require [L. *petunt*] to have the conditions mitigated. **1582** STANYHURST *Æneis* II. (Arb.) 68, I sadlye requyred, Too confer further. **1622** S. WARD *Life of Faith* (1627) 12 When hee should haue been tyed to the stake, he required to stand untyed. **1640** tr. *Verdere's Rom. of Rom.* II. 123 He..was informed by his Squire, that a man..required to speak with him. **1821** SCOTT *Kenilw.* xiv, The Earl's chamberlain..informed Tressilian that his lord required to speak with him.

6. To demand as necessary or essential on general principles, or in order to comply with or satisfy some regulation.

1415 *Crowned King* 37 A..subsidie..To be rered in the reaume as reson requyred. **1477** *Sc. Acts Jas. III*, parl. x. c. 73 That ilk heck of the said cruves be three inch wide, as the auld statute requiris. **1515** BARCLAY *Egloges* iv. c iv b, If thou wilt haue of mine Then right requireth that I haue part of thine. *a* **1548** HALL *Chron., Hen. VIII* 82 The kinges rode about the felde as honor of armes required. **1562** *Reg. Privy Council Scot.* I. 223 To wair thair lyfes as thair dewetie and detfull obedience requyris. **1682** DRYDEN *Religio Laici* 201 If the Gentiles, whom no law inspired, By nature did what was by law required [etc.]. **1708** J. C. *Compl. Collier* (1845) 51 All is for want of such Admeasurement as the Act required. **1770** *Junius Lett.* xxxviii. (1788) 204 The spirit of their present constitution requires that the king should be feared. **1847** TENNYSON *Princ.* IV. 317 Public use required she should be known.

b. To demand or call for as appropriate or suitable in the particular case; to need for some end or purpose. †*required to*, requisite for.

c **1386** CHAUCER *Clerk's T.* 374 Whan that the cas required it, The commune profit koude she redresse. *c* **1420** *Pallad. on Husb.* II. 359 Their magnitude a larger lond requyreth. **1526** *Pilgr. Perf.* (W. de W. 1531) 1 The condicyons requyred to a pilgrym that entendeth to go to the erthly Jerusalem. **1560** DAUS tr. *Sleidane's Comm.* 13 Howe can men discerne such vertues in him as be required in a mightye prynce? **1601** SHAKS. *All's Well* IV. iii. 108 If the businesse bee of any difficulty,..it requires hast of your Lordship. **1668** WILKINS *Real Char.* Ep. Rdr., That great Industry, or Accurate judgment,..required to such a Work. **1687** A. LOVELL tr. *Thevenot's Trav.* I. 123 Every one of these Towers..required an Army to take them. **1723** CHAMBERS tr. *Le Clerc's Treat. Archit.* I. 2 A Computation of the expences of the Building, and of the time required to go through with it. **1759** BROWN *Compl. Farmer* 110 An acre of ground will require ten pound of seed. **1795** *Gentl. Mag.* July 581/2 Irony, like Satire, is one of those edged tools which require skilful handling. **1810** CRABBE *Borough* i. 8 Cities and towns, the various haunts of men, Require the pencil; they defy the pen. **1868** LOCKYER *Elem. Astron.* ii. §7 (1879) 39 More than 1,200,000 Earths would be required to make one Sun.

c. To demand as a necessary help or aid; hence, to stand in need of; to need, want.

c **1420** *Pallad. on Husb.* IV. 53 In grauel wole thei growe But moist bothe erthe & ayer they ther require. *c* **1430** LYDG. *Min. Poems* (Percy Soc.) 46 Trewe metalle requeryth noon allay. **1538** STARKEY *England* I. i. 15 In many thyngys, ..nature requyryth the dylygence of man. **1563** WINȜET *Four Scoir Thre Quest.* Wks. (S.T.S.) I. 61 The defence of fraud and falset necessarlie requeris a cloke of finȝeit eloquence. **1638** JUNIUS *Paint. Ancients* 46 So doth one of these two alwayes require the others helpe. **1671** MILTON *P.R.* II. 412 Great acts require great means of enterprise. **1770** GOLDSM. *Des. Vill.* 60 Light labour..Just gave what life required, but gave no more. **1849** M. ARNOLD *To Republican Friend*, For such doing they require not eyes. **1875** JOWETT *Plato* (ed. 2) I. 62 The body which is in health requires neither medical nor any other aid.

d. *it requires*, there is need for, it is necessary to have, etc. (Usually const. with *inf.*)

1820 W. IRVING *Sketch Bk.* I. 44 Surely it does not require a palace to be happy with Mary. **1845** M. PATTISON *Ess.* (1889) I. 18 It required all the personal influence of the king to check..his irritated followers. **1895** *Law Times* XCIX. 476/2 It requires the talents of a Boileau..to play the part of a *flâneur* with any success.

7. *intr.* To be requisite or necessary. Now *rare*.

c **1500** *Lancelot* 1962 And pwnice them quhar pwnysing Requeris. **1523** LD. BERNERS *Froiss.* I. ccxxxvi. 334 Ye shall fynde the men of warr suche as to dedes of armes requyreth. **1547** *Homilies* I. *Reading Script.* I. (1859) 8 If it shall require to teach any truth or reprove false doctrine. **1802** BEDDOES *Hygëia* VIII. 168 It does not require to be professionally conversant with the sick to be sensible, that [etc.]. **1862** SPENCER *First Princ.* I. iv. §24 (1875) 79 To produce that orderly consciousness..there requires the assimilation of each impression to others.

8. a. To feel, or be under, a necessity *to* do something.

1805 tr. *Lafontaine's Hermann & Emilia* I. 161 'Louisa', said he to her, 'I require to behold you a wife'. **1853** G. J. CAYLEY *Las Alforjas* II. 58 The wise man..requires to be engaged in deeper and more perplexing matters. **1879** B. TAYLOR *Stud. Germ. Lit.* 104 This is all of the great migratory movement which we require to know.

b. To fall necessarily, to need, *to be* done, etc.

1842 WHEWELL in *Life* (1881) 259 It is a task which requires to be performed. **1857** MAURICE *Ep. St. John* xvii. 277 In speaking of the state of mankind..two facts require to be explained. **1875** JOWETT *Plato* (ed. 2) III. 253 The wicked are miserable because they require to be punished.

III. †**9.** *trans.* To seek after, search for. Also, to inquire after; to call upon, summon. *Obs.*

c **1450** *Merlin* 218 These fledde till thei come be-fore the yate;..and these other come vpon hem that right straytly hem required. **1582** STANYHURST *Æneis* I. (Arb.) 24 They theire lost feloes with long talck greedye requyred. **1609** BIBLE (Douay) *Ecclus.* xxxix. 13 The memorie of him shal not depart, and his name shal be required [L. *requiretur*] from generation to generation. **1642** H. MORE *Song of Soul* I. III. xxiv, Though the glory of the Lord ore-flow The earth, ..Yet waters he in waters doth requere. **1666** DRYDEN *Ann. Mirab.* cclvi, Those who have none sit round where once it was And with full eyes each wonted room require. **1697** —— *Virg. Georg.* III. 160 In vain he burns..And in himself his former self requires. **1715** POPE *Iliad* II. 945 But the brave chiefs..wandering o'er the camp, required their lord. **1742** GRAY *West* 6 A different Object do these Eyes require. **1797** *Monthly Mag.* III. 548 The sheriff is to cause the defendant to be required at five successive county-courts.

†**b.** To search into, investigate, pursue. *Obs.*⁻¹

1563 MAN *Musculus' Commonpl.* 16 It is needeful also for some places of Scripture, that this question bee required.

required (rɪ'kwaɪəd), *ppl. a.* [f. REQUIRE *v.*]

a. That is required, in the various senses of the vb.; requisite.

1601 SHAKS. *All's Well* II. v. 65 The ministration, and required office. **1604** —— *Oth.* II. i. 234 Now for want of these requir'd Conueniences, her delicate tendernesse wil finde it selfe abus'd. *a* **1720** SEWEL *Hist. Quakers* (1722) I. III. 80 Some of the Soldiers..took the requir'd Oath. **1849** HERSCHEL *Astron.* §198 Then will the final arc A. B. C. D. read off on the circle be ten times the required angle. **1885** LEUDESDORF *Cremona's Proj. Geom.* 291 The points *H* and *K* will lie on the required conic.

b. *required reading*, literature which one is required to read for an educational course or which must be read in order to gain an understanding of some subject.

1921 H. J. LASKI in *Holmes-Laski Lett.* (1953) I. 370 They are quite intolerable—pushing little professors full of pedantic details, nosing into the dull routine of unimportant matters, pushing their little quack remedies, interested in getting the wrong books on to lists of required reading. **1930** *Publishers' Weekly* 15 Mar. 1547/1 Some of the important courses in our colleges and universities cannot be taught successfully..because of the lack of a sufficient number of books for required reading. **1954** *N.Y. Times Bk. Rev.* 31 Jan. 1/1 Here is a book that should be required reading for Democrats in 1954. **1962** *Listener* 17 May 873/2 They genuinely stimulate thought and thus become required reading for social critics, amateur and professional. **1976** J. WAINWRIGHT *Walther P. 38* 62 The usual sort of stuff which ..was 'required reading' for any moderate education.

Hence **re'quiredness**, the fact or quality of being required.

1938 W. KÖHLER *Place of Value in World of Facts* ii. 35 At the bottom of all human activities are 'values', the conviction that some things 'ought to be' and others not. Science, however, with its immense interest in mere facts seems to lack all understanding of such 'requiredness'. **1946** C. MORRIS *Signs, Lang. & Behavior* iii. 63 A command such as 'Come here!' may signify with high constancy the requiredness of the response which it prescribes. **1977** A. ECCLESTONE *Staircase for Silence* iv. 78 Péguy spoke often of it as invincible anxiety; while Abraham Heschel called it a sense of requiredness, in the language of the Bible: what is required of me?

requirement (rɪ'kwaɪəmənt). [-MENT.]

†**1.** The act of requiring; a requisition, request.

1530 GARDINER in Froude *Hist. Eng.* (1881) I. 290 My Lord Cardinal, that obtained his legacy by our late Sovereign Lord's requirements at Rome.

†**2.** The fact of being requisite; necessity. *Obs.*⁻¹

1658–9 in *Burton's Diary* (1828) III. 248 Mr. Speaker would not without requirement mention the name Danvers.

3. That which is required or needed; a want, need.

1662 GLANVILL *Lux Orient.* xiii. 125 For this Justice is but the distributing to every thing according to the requirements of its nature. **1727** BAILEY vol. II, *Requirement*, the Thing required. **1856** KANE *Arct. Expl.* II. vii. 79 We must prepare beforehand the entire daily requirements of the sick. **1878** LECKY *Eng. in 18th C.* II. vii. 422, £15,000 would have amply met the requirements of the county.

b. That which is called for or demanded; a condition which must be complied with.

1841 MYERS *Cath. Th.* III. §39. 144 Has any individual, or church, or nation, ever yet come up to their [the Scriptures'] generally acknowledged requirements? **1868** M. PATTISON *Academ. Org.* iv. 106 The other professors are under more stringent requirements to teach.

re'quirer. Now *rare*. [f. REQUIRE *v.* + -ER¹.] One who requires.

1525 LD. BERNERS *Froiss.* II. xxxiii. 98 They said, they had sene and herde dyuers ensamples of requyrers and nat requyrers. **1587** GOLDING *De Mornay* xxiii. 395 The requirers of those playes, are honored; and why then are the plaiers of them reproched? **1611** FLORIO, *Richieditore*, a requirer, a requester. **1681** STAIR *Instit.* I. xx. §22 Wodsets are also taken off by Premonition or Requisition,..yet so that the requirer may pass from his requisition. **1860** PUSEY *Min. Proph.* (1885) I. 71 Christ..a Requirer of mercy, a Praiser of purity of heart.

re'quiring, *vbl. sb.* [f. as prec. + -ING¹.] Request, demand; requisition.

1387 TREVISA *Higden* (Rolls) VI. 313 At þe prayer and requirynge of pope Gregory, Gy of Marchia..chasede him out of þat londes. *c* **1470** *Gol. & Gaw.* 1330 Schir Gawane the gay, throu requiring, Gart the souerane..Cary to the castel. **1579** W. WILKINSON *Confut. Familye of Loue, Heret. Affirm.* b j b, The letter according to the requiring of Christ, ..leadeth us to the death of Sin. **1617** HIERON *Wks.* II. 358 The matter may be so handled, as that He may take no delight in His owne requirings. **1687** in *Magd. Coll. & Jas. II* (O.H.S.) 139 A requiring of him to deliver up his office. **1727** BAILEY vol. II, *Requirement*,..a requiring. **1785** PALEY *Mor. Philos.* III. xx, The oath lays a snare..and I do not perceive, that the requiring of it..produces any good effect. **1871** B. TAYLOR *Faust* (1875) II. II. iii. 128 Hear the requiring, Bring wood for firing.

†**re'quiry.** *Obs. rare.* [f. as prec. + -Y: cf. *inquiry*.] Request, demand.

1598 FLORIO, *Requisitione*, requisition, requirie. **1641** EARL MONM. tr. *Biondi's Civil Warres* IV. 40 To doe homage to King Henry..requiring but 3. monthes space after requiry. **1667** WATERHOUSE *Fire Lond.* 117 Answer God, O England! Prince and people, in this requiry of his.

†**requise(d,** *pa. pple. Obs. rare.* [ad. F. *requis(e*, pa. pple. of OF. *requerre*: see REQUIRE *v.*] Required.

a **1548** HALL *Chron., Edw. IV* 227 The forme and maner, that in suche a case is requise and accustumed to be done. **1557** N. T. (Genev.) Ep. *iv, To drawe as wel the Iewes as Gentils to God, it was requised that a newe Couenant shulde be made.

requisite ('rɛkwɪzɪt), *a.* and *sb.* Also 5–6 requysite, -yte, (6 -ytt), requisyte, (5 -ques-), 6–7 requisit, etc. [ad. L. *requīsīt-us*, pa. pple. of *requīrĕre* to REQUIRE.]

A. *adj.* **a.** Required by circumstances or the nature of things, necessary, indispensable.

1472–3 *Rolls of Parlt.* VI. 38/2 Asmany and such Writtes ..as to hir shal be requisite in that partie. **1522** MORE *De quat. Noviss.* Wks. 102 There are ye wote well two poyntes requisite vnto saluacion. **1592** KYD *Sp. Trag.* III. xii. 97 If he be thus helplessly distract, Tis requisite his office be resignde. **1611** SHAKS. *Wint. T.* IV. iv. 687 A good Nose is requisite also, to smell out worke for th'other Sences. **1659** THORNDIKE *Wks.* (1846) II. 504 Supposing the belief of Christianity to be a condition requisite to the having of God's Spirit. **1761** HUME *Hist. Eng.* III. l. 97 Martial law, so requisite to the support of discipline, was exercised upon the soldiers. **1836** KINGSLEY *Lett.* (1878) I. 36 One is expected to have obtained all requisite classical knowledge at school. **1878** JEVONS *Prim. Pol. Econ.* 28 We can hardly say that capital is as requisite to production as land and labour.

b. *requisite variety*, the variety necessary in a system for it to be able to control another system in which there is variety.

1956 W. R. ASHBY *Introd. Cybernetics* xi. 207 This is the law of Requisite Variety. To put it more picturesquely: only variety in R can force down the variety due to D; only variety can destroy variety. **1966** S. BEER *Decision & Control* xii. 281 But however many interacting sub-systems of preys and predators, big fleas and little fleas, are invoked, it is none the less evident that the balance of animal populations would be grossly upset very rapidly unless the law of requisite variety held in general throughout nature. **1975** R. M. GLORIOSO *Engin. Cybernetics* v. 72 As a minimum requirement, the number of different possible states of the system must equal the number of possible states of the environment, although the proper states of the system must be available as well. Thus, to reduce the variety in the environment, the system must be capable of achieving the 'requisite variety'.

B. *sb.* That which is required or necessary; something indispensable.

1602 *Archpriest Controv.* (Camden) II. 224 They doe whollye reste for meate, drinke, and other requisits to lyfe, upon the providence of God. **1665** GLANVILL *Def. Van. Dogm.* p. viii, You think it more suitable to the requisites of the present Age, to depress Scepticism. **1750** JOHNSON *Rambler* No. 71 ¶5 Till all the requisites which imagination can suggest are gathered together. **1810** CRABBE *Borough* xxiii. 76 Alas! he wants the requisites to rise, The true connexion, the availing ties. **1880** C. R. MARKHAM *Peruv. Bark* 315 The form of febrifuge which combines..the two requisites of efficacy and economy.

†**requisite,** *v. Obs. rare*⁻¹. [f. as prec.] *trans.* To request or require.

c **1450** *Godstow Reg.* I. 147 Paying there-of ȝerly to hym & to his eyeris or to his assynys oon rose..whenne þey been conueniently requisityd or Axid.

'requisitely, *adv. rare.* [f. REQUISITE *a.* + -LY².] Necessarily.

1656 EARL MONM. tr. *Boccalini's Advts. fr. Parnass.* I. xlv. (1674) 60 Learning, which is born and bred in poverty, was requisitely to live therein, as in her particular Element. **1683** E. HOOKER *Pref. Pordage's Mystic Div.* 65 Properly præliminari, antecedaneous and very requisitly assistent to the advance of the inquisitiv Readers judgment. **1976** *Daily Tel.* (Colour Suppl.) 13 Feb. 29/2 Neither in England nor

America could Jack Scalia expect to rise to the top earning bracket until he is over 30 and projects the requisitely aggressive and reliable image.

requisiteness ('rɛkwɪzɪtnɪs). [f. as prec. + -NESS.] The state of being requisite or necessary; needfulness, necessity.
1600 SURFLET *Countrie Farme* v. xxiii. 726 Which they steepe in the decoction of the seed or flowers of hops.. greatly standing vpon the requisitenes of their hops thereunto. **1663** BOYLE *Usef. Exp. Nat. Philos.* II. v. xx. 303 In some few cases the requisiteness and danger of destructive valour may make its Actions become a vertuous Patriot. **1764** HARMER *Observ.* iii. §11. 104 An additional proof of the requisiteness of attending to the customs of the East. **1843** MILL *Logic* III. v. §3 That particular condition.. whose requisiteness..we happen to be insisting on at the moment. **1876** BANCROFT *Hist. U.S.* IV. xxvii. 20 The general reported the ensuing quarrel as a proof of..the requisiteness of troops for the support of 'the laws'.

requisition (rɛkwɪ'zɪʃən), *sb.* [a. F. *réquisition* (12th c.), or ad. L. *requīsītiōn-em*, n. of action f. *requīrĕre* to REQUIRE.]
1. a. The action of (†requesting or) requiring; a (†request or) demand made by a person.
1503 in *Lett. Rich. III & Hen. VII* (Rolls) I. 201 [Our] instaunt petition to make an instrument..and the noble men standing about to be witnes[ses, as] we made like requisition. **1566** *Reg. Privy Council Scot.* I. 485 Quhais requisitioun being bayth ressonabill, and honorabill [etc.]. **1620** in *Reliq. Wotton* (1672) 533 Neither of them ought to deny it: provided the same requisition be seasonably made, not upon rash and precipitate advice. **1752** CHESTERF. *Lett.* (1792) III. cclxxiv. 253, I am sure you would have written, according to your engagement and my requisition. **1777** ROBERTSON *Hist. Amer.* II. v. 66 With this requisition.. Montezuma was so obsequious as to comply. **1797** MRS. RADCLIFFE *Italian* xxxii, I obey your requisition and inquire the purpose of it. **1856** MERIVALE *Rom. Emp.* xlii. (1865) V. 143 The legatus was compelled to send his son to Rome as the bearer of these requisitions.
b. A requirement, necessary condition.
1836 J. GILBERT *Chr. Atonem.* vii. (1852) 196 How gloriously does the Christian atonement meet this requisition! **1839** HALLAM *Hist. Lit.* II. viii. §59 It would be ..a great mistake to imagine that the requisitions for academical degrees were ever much insisted on. **1856** FERRIER *Inst. Metaph.* Introd. 7 It is to be accounted for.. by that neglect of the chief requisition of philosophy which has been already pointed out.
2. a. The (*or* an) action of formally requiring or calling upon one to perform some action, discharge some duty, etc.; †the fact of being so called upon. Also, a written demand of this nature.
In earlier use chiefly a Sc. (legal) term (cf. 2 b).
1553 *Reg. Privy Council Scot.* I. 149 Quhairof as yit thair can be na redress had for na requisitioun that the Wardane of Scotland can mak. *Ibid.* II. 192 Alexander..requirit and desyrit him to entir the said maister Thomas to the said Alexander within sex dayis efter his requisitioun. *a* **1648** LD. HERBERT *Hen. VIII* (1683) 117 If either of the two recover from France, Places belonging to the other, he shall, upon requisition, restore them within a month. **1747** in Kames *Dict. Decis.* (1797) IV. 161 A tenant..having affirmed, that he made requisition to the heritor for that purpose, it was questioned, if he could be allowed to prove the requisition by witnesses. **1780** BURKE *Sp. Bristol* Wks. 1792 II. 315 The reasons for taking away the penalties..and for refusing to establish them on the riotous requisition of 1780. **1840** MACAULAY *Ess., Clive* (1887) 558 According to the by-laws of the Company, there can be no ballot except on a requisition signed by nine proprietors. **1892** *Daily News* 5 Apr. 3/7 He stated that during his lesseeship of the Lyceum he had spent 45,000*l.* on the house..some of this voluntarily and some under 'requisitions'.
b. *Sc. Law.* 'A demand made by a creditor that a debt be paid, or an obligation fulfilled.'
1681 STAIR *Instit.* I. xx. §22. 410 Requisition requires also the same solemnities that Premonition requires. **1693** *Ibid.* II. i. §4 (ed. 2) 162 But even compleat Heretable Rights themselves, containing personal Clauses of Requisition, become Moveable by the Requisition or Charge. *a* **1768** ERSKINE *Instit. Law Scot.* II. ii. §16 (1773) I. 175 Requisition used by a creditor upon a right of wadset. **1838** W. BELL *Dict. Law Scot.* 855 In certain cases, requisition is necessary to put the debtor *in mora*; and then the proper way of proving requisition is by a notarial instrument.
3. The action of requiring a certain amount or number of anything to be furnished; a demand or order of this nature, *esp.* one made upon a town, district, etc., to furnish or supply anything required for military purposes.
1776 ADAM SMITH *W.N.* IV. vii. (1869) II. 201 It has been proposed..that the colonies should be taxed by requisition. **1790** BEATSON *Nav. & Mil. Mem.* I. 171 A requisition was made of the six thousand auxiliaries, which the States General were..obliged to furnish. *c* **1806** SIR R. WILSON *Cape Gd. Hope* in *Life* (1862) I. App. ix. 391 The cavalry was mounted by requisition on the best horses of the country. **1860** WOOLSEY *Introd. Internat. Law* §129 After the battle of Jena..the requisition upon humbled Prussia was more than a hundred millions of francs. **1876** VOYLE & STEVENSON *Milit. Dict.* 338/1 Supplies are now..stored in magazines in rear of an army, and a requisition is made on them for the daily wants of the troops. **1897** *Cavalry Tactics* xxii. 141 When the inhabitants are hostile, and refuse to comply with the requisition, an intimation that..they will be taken by force, usually has the desired effect.
attrib. **1806** SIR R. WILSON *Jrnl.* 11 Feb. in *Life* (1862) I. v. 307, I..have been on several committees to fix the price of requisition horses.
4. The state or condition of being called or pressed into service or use. In phrases: **a.** *to put* (*place, call*) *in* (or *into*) *requisition.*
1796 CHARLOTTE SMITH *Marchmont* IV. 56 His eldest son ..having been put in requisition: he was himself, he said, too old for a soldier. **1815** HELEN M. WILLIAMS *Narr. Events France* xi. 244 As the carriages arrived near the bridge, they were immediately put in requisition [to transport the wounded]. **1827** SOUTHEY *Penins. War* II. 477 He placed all horses and mares above a certain height in requisition for the French armies. **1831** W. GODWIN *Thoughts Man* 84 When the first novelty of his pieces was gone, they were seldom called into requisition. **1877** GLADSTONE *Glean.* (1879) I. 152 The old terrors, the old bugbears, were at once put in requisition.
b. (*to be*) *in* (constant, etc.) *requisition.*
a **1817** W. BELOE *Sexagenarian* I. 333 The guillotine was (to use their abominable jargon) in constant requisition. **1838** LYTTON *Alice* I. iii, That duty done, once more the straw hat and Sultan were in requisition. **1868** T. H. KEY *Philol. Ess.* 204 The words..are with them in constant requisition.
5. *attrib.*, as ***requisition form, note, notice, paper, slip.***
1929 T. H. BURNHAM *Engineering Econ.* xv. 206 Tools may only be issued against a *requisition form signed by a duly authorized official. **1916** G. FRANKAU *Poetical Wks.* (1923) I. 226 A faked *requisition note. **1974** P. GORE-BOOTH *With Great Truth & Respect* 150 We..were alarmed by the appearance of *requisition notices on the doors of adjoining houses. **1911** *Daily Colonist* (Victoria, B.C.) 23 Apr. 1/7 Burns said he would start tonight for Los Angeles.. Governor Marshall having honored *requisition papers. **1938** L. BEMELMANS *Life Class* III. ii. 221 A stack of *requisition slips, for the carpentry department, for the painters,..for the printer.

requisition (rɛkwɪ'zɪʃən), *v.* [f. prec. Cf. mod.F. *réquisitionner* (Littré *Suppl.*).]
1. *trans.* **a.** To require (anything) to be furnished for military purposes; to put in requisition.
1837 CARLYLE *Fr. Rev.* III. I. viii, Such hundredfold miscellany of teams, requisitioned or lawfully owned, making way,..rolled here to right and to left. **1870** *Daily News* 8 Dec., The Government authorised the prefects and sous-prefects to requisition such horses as might be needed. **1881** HENTY *Cornet of Horse* viii. (1888) 74 A considerable portion of the allied army were quartered..in large convents requisitioned for the purpose.
b. To make demands upon (a town, etc.).
1870 *Daily News* 14 Dec., The French Army of the North, after permitting Amiens and Rouen to be..requisitioned by the enemy [etc.]. **1897** *Cavalry Tactics* xxii. 141 When it is intended to requisition a village or town, all the outlets should be guarded.
2. To make requisition for; to demand, call for, request to have or get.
1874 BURNAND *My Time* xiv. 113 Everything necessary for his departure..had to be requisitioned hastily. **1882** BESANT *Revolt of Man* xii, They..drove about the country requisitioning provisions. **1887** *Pall Mall G.* 6 Oct. 11/1 May I requisition your fairness to a political opponent to be allowed to point out [etc.]. **1892** *Ibid.* 3 Aug. 3/3 He gets a weekly list of all new publications, and requisitions what he thinks he will be able to sell.
b. To press into service; to make demands on.
1879 BLACK *Macleod of D.* xxxiii, And so the hospitalities of the little inn were requisitioned to the utmost.
c. To call upon, call in, for some purpose.
1887 *Times* (weekly ed.) 14 Oct. 7/4 The military had to be requisitioned. **1893** EARL DUNMORE *Pamirs* II. 292 Seven men with shovels were requisitioned.
Hence **requi'sitioning** *vbl. sb.* Also *attrib.*
1871 *Daily News* 19 Sept., In our camp..we are discussing the requisitioning capabilities of London... In these latter days we do not call it plunder, we call it requisitioning.

requi'sitionally, *adv. rare*$^{-1}$. [f. REQUISITION *sb.*] By means of military requisitions.
1796 *Campaigns 1793-4* II. xii. 101 So wonderful are the resources of France when requisitionally called forth.

requisitioner (rɛkwɪ'zɪʃənə(r)). [f. REQUISITION *v.* + -ER[1].] = REQUISITIONIST.
1968 M. GUYBON tr. *Solzhenitsyn's First Circle* lxii. 392 After Christmas they were made to give up half of it for the cities, and the requisitioners were never satisfied.

requi'sitionist. [f. as REQUISITION *sb.* + -IST.] One who makes a requisition.
1819 *Edin. Rev.* XXXII. 442 To make each sturdy requisitionist repent of having set his hand to the call. **1852** J. H. NEWMAN *Scope Univ. Educ.* 67 They call the demand tyrannical, and the requisitionists bigots or fanatics. **1865** *Sat. Rev.* 4 Feb. 135 There were pledges sufficient..to satisfy the most rigorous requisitionists.

requisitionize (rɛkwɪ'zɪʃənaɪz), *v. rare.* [f. REQUISITION *sb.* + -IZE.] *trans.* To request or require (one to do something) by written requisition.
1845 J. KEBLE *Let.* 6 Feb. in G. Battiscombe *John Keble* (1963) xiii. 254 If it is thought well to requisitionize the Proctors to veto the affair..you may put my name down to it.

†re'quisitive, *a.* (and *sb.*) *Obs. rare.* [f. as next + -IVE.] Expressing a request; of the nature of requiring. Also *ellipt.* as *sb.*
1751 HARRIS *Hermes* I. viii. (1765) 143 If we interrogate, 'tis the Interrogative Mode; if we require 'tis the Requisitive. *Ibid.* 154 The Requisitive or Imperative has no first Person of the singular.

requisitor (rɪ'kwɪzɪtə(r)). *rare.* [f. *requīsīt-*, ppl. stem of L. *requīrĕre* + -OR.] One who makes a requisition or requisitions.
1790-93 HELEN M. WILLIAMS *Lett. France* (1796) IV. 18 (Jod.), It was now decreed..that the property, which each individual possessed, should be at his own disposal, and not at that of any publick requisitors. **1894** H. FISHWICK *Lancashire* 279 The result was that the requisitors themselves summoned the meeting.

†requisi'torial, *a. Obs. rare.* [a. F. *réquisitorial* (Littré).] = REQUISITORY *a.* 1.
1716 *Lond. Gaz.* No. 5491/2 M. Manteuffel..has.. presented Requisitorial Letters.., for the Passage of the Saxon Troops through the King of Prussia's Dominions. **1755** MAGENS *Insurances* 270 Upon Receipt of a requisitorial Order from the..Honourable Regency at Oldenburg.

re'quisitory, *sb. rare.* [ad. F. *réquisitoire*: cf. next.] In French legal practice, the demand made by a public prosecutor for the punishment of the accused on the charges stated.
1824 *Examiner* 494/2 The requisitory or charge was then read, and..the Crown lawyer prayed for a very moderate penalty. **1890** *Harper's Mag.* Nov. 938/1 What rendered his requisitory still more interesting..was the relationship of the orator to the hapless Bompard.

requisitory (rɪ'kwɪzɪtərɪ), *a. rare.* [ad. med.L. *requisitōri-us* (see REQUISITE and -ORY), or obs. F. *réquisitoire* (1403).]
1. a. Of the nature of, expressing or conveying, a request or requisition.
1447 *Rolls of Parlt.* V. 135/1 Havyng the King oure Soveraigne Lordes gracious Letters of prive seal requisitorie unto the Duc. **1449** *Ibid.* 150/2 Wherfore the Kyng..do write his letters requisitorie, and sende his mesages for due reformation to have be hadde in this behalve. **1855** MOTLEY *Dutch Rep.* II. 305 Upon the 18th March, 1570, the Duke addressed a requisitory letter to the alcades, corregidors, and other judges of Castile, empowering them to carry the sentence into execution.
b. Capable of making a requisition.
1825 JEFFERSON *Autobiog.* Wks. 1859 I. 78 Their power.. was only requisitory, and these requisitions were addressed to the several Legislatures.
†2. Sought on purpose. *Obs. rare*$^{-1}$.
1621 LODGE *Summary of Du Bartas* II. 27 There are two sorts of these dreames, the one, which are called curious or requisitory, to which are referred the dreams sought out.. and obteyned, by wicked vowes and profane sacrifices.

re'quit, *sb. rare*$^{-1}$. [Cf. next and QUIT *sb.*] Requital.
1786 BURNS *To J. Smith* vi, The star that rules my luckless lot, Has fated me the russet coat,..But in requit, Has blest me wi' a random shot O' countra wit.

†re'quit, *v.*[1] *Obs.* [f. RE- + QUIT *v.*] *trans.* To repay, requite.
Requit in *Morte Arth.* 1680 is prob. a scribal error for *reknit* 'reckoned'.
a **1553** UDALL *Royster D.* III. iv. (Arb.) 52 If ye can this remitte, This gentleman other wise may your loue requitte. **1582** N. LICHEFIELD tr. *Castanheda's Conq. E. Ind.* I. xlviii. 104 In the which thou shalt not onely shew me pleasure, but also binde me to requit thy good will. **1607** SHAKS. *Cor.* IV. v. 76 The droppes of Blood Shed for my thanklesse Country, are requitted.

re-quit (riː-), *v.*[2] [RE- 5 a.] To quit again.
1855 LYNCH *Rivulet* LXIV. iii, Home flies the bee, then soon re-quits the hive.

re'quitable, *a.* Now *rare* or *Obs.* [f. REQUITE *v.* + -ABLE.] Capable of being requited.
1610 HOLLAND *Camden's Brit.* I. 578 Good turnes are so long acceptable, as they may be requitable. **1648** BOYLE *Seraph. Love* xiv. (1700) 89 God's Favours.., how little they are requitable, for we can give him nothing but his own.

requital (rɪ'kwaɪtəl). [f. REQUITE *v.* + -AL[1].]
1. Return for some service, kindness, etc.; recompense or reward for action or exertion. †Also, power of making a return.
1579 G. HARVEY *Letter-bk.* (Camden) 62 To minister superabundant matter of sufficient requitall. **1582** STANYHURST *Æneis* I. (Arb.) 35 First begin a freendshippe, for he wyl make fullye requital. **1639** FULLER *Holy War* III. i. (1840) 115 So unwelcome are courtesies to them whose above their requital. **1651** HOBBES *Leviath.* I. xi. 48 To receive benefits..as long as there is hope of requital, disposeth to love. **1815** W. H. IRELAND *Scribbleomania* 175 Whose bold perseverance at length reap'd requital. *a* **1871** GROTE *Eth. Fragm.* i. (1876) 11 Such and such behaviour [is] to be rendered on his part, such and such sentiments to be manifested as requital on theirs.
b. In phr. *in* (†rarely *for*) *requital* (*of*).
1590 GREENE *Never too late* (1600) 37 Ready for requitall of such gracious countenance, to vnsheath my sword. **1591** SHAKS. *Two Gent.* I. i. 153 In requital whereof, henceforth, carry your letters your selfe. **1627** SANDERSON *Serm., ad Clerum* ii. (1681) 25 Giving such constructions to Gods truth as will for Requital give largest Allowance to their Practices. **1634** MILTON *Comus* 626 He..Would sit, and hearken even to extasie, And in requitall ope his leather'n scrip [etc.]. **1697** POTTER *Antiq. Greece* I. v. (1715) 22 In requital of all his former Kindnesses, they basely deserted him. **1817** JAS. MILL *Brit. India* II. IV. v. 172 Requesting a sum of money..and offering in requital to withdraw from the province. **1839** CARLYLE *Chartism* iv. (1858) 16 There is not a horse willing to work but can get food and shelter in requital.
c. With *a* and *pl.* A return or repayment (*for* or *of* something).

a **1591** H. Smith *Wks.* (1867) II. 360 The best requital that we can make for our good cheer. **1613** Wither *Epigr.* xvi. *To School-master*, Your love doth well deserve to have Better requitalls than are in my power. **1648** Boyle *Seraph. Love* xiv. (1700) 90 All the Duties we can pay our Maker, are less properly Requitals than Restitutions. **1732** Lediard *Sethos* II. ix. 285 He fear'd he should have but a poor requital from the king. **1844** H. H. Wilson *Brit. India* III. 559 It might seem to be an ungrateful requital of the unquestioned services of the Company.

2. Return or repayment of an injury, etc.; retaliation, revenge. Const. *of*, *for*.

1582 Stanyhurst *Æneis* II. (Arb.) 62 Doubting thee Troians blooddye reuengment, And also fearing thee Greekish fyrie requital. **1597** Hooker *Eccl. Pol.* v. xxxii. §3 If..we should take the quarrel of sermons in hand, and revenge their cause by requital. *a* **1602** W. Perkins *Cases Consc.* (1619) 200 Men are content to lay aside all hatred and requitall of euill. **1641** Milton *Animadv.* Wks. 1851 III. 189 Remember how they mangle our Brittish Names abroad; what trespasse were it, if wee in requitall should as much neglect theirs? **1869** Farrar *Fam. Speech* iii. (1873) 106 In requital it may be, for many injuries. **1885** *Manch. Exam.* 30 Mar. 5/1 In requital of that shameful act of perfidy.

3. Compensation *for* a want. *rare*.

1885 *Manch. Weekly Times* 7 Feb. 5/5 The common sense which, in requital for the want of more showy qualities, we may claim as the attribute of Englishmen.

re'quitative, *a. rare.* [f. requite *v.* + -ative.] Serving to requite.

1862 F. Hall *Hindu Philos. Syst.* 150 The pandits.. allege, that there is produced, in the soul, by good or by bad works, the quality denominated requitative efficacy.

re'quite, *sb. rare.* [f. the vb.] Requital.

1561 Preston *Cambyses* Dj, For councel giuen vnto the King is this thy iust requite? **1862** Hislop *Prov. Scot.* 3 A drap and a bite's but a sma' requite.

requite (rɪ'kwaɪt), *v.* Also 6 -quyte, -quight. [f. re- (as in *repay*) + *quite*, var. of quit *v.*]

1. *trans.* To repay, make return for, reward (a kindness, service, etc.).

1529 Wolsey in *Four C. Eng. Lett.* (1880) 11 So I shal not fayle to requyte your kyndnes. **1597** Morley *Introd. Mus.* Ded., There be two whose benifites to vs can neuer be requited: God, and our parents. **1639** Fuller *Holy War* II. xlvi. (1840) 114 They requited Christ's passion, and died for him who suffered for them. **1683** J. Gadbury *Wharton's Wks.* Pref., He served his Soveraign faithfully, the King as bountifully requites his Services. **1778** Cowper *Let.* 1 Jan., The pleasure of requiting an obligation has always been out of my reach. **1819** Shelley *Cenci* II. ii. 34 Requiting years of care with contumely. **1854** Macaulay *Biog.* (1867) 16 His servility was requited with cold contempt.

refl. **1711** Pope *Temp. Fame* 363 To conceal from sight Those acts of goodness, which themselves requite.

b. To repay, make retaliation or return for, to avenge (a wrong, injury, etc.).

1555 Eden *Decades* 131 With so gentell a reuenge requitynge thingratitude of hym. **1596** Spenser *F.Q.* iv. vi. 9 Let me this crave,.. That first I may that wrong to him requite. **1611** Bible *Gen.* l. 15 Ioseph..will certainely requite vs all the euill which we did vnto him. **1654** Bramhall *Just Vind.* vi. (1661) 153 To requite their invectives, he made the statutes of provisors. **1820** Shelley *Hom. Merc.* lxv, I will requite..His cruel threat. **1874** Green *Short Hist.* vii. §6. 409 Drake..had requited the wrongs inflicted by the Inquisition on English seamen.

absol. **1611** Bible *Jer.* li. 56 The Lord God of recompenses shall surely requite.

2. To repay, make return to (one) for some service, etc.

1560 Daus tr. *Sleidane's Comm.* 275, I am fully determined to requite your Prince with lyke thankefulnes. **1611** Middleton & Dekker *Roaring Girle* D.'s Wks. 1873 III. 164, I am so poore to requite you, you must looke for nothing but thankes of me. **1656** Stanley *Hist. Philos.* vi. (1701) 228/1 This place, to which Aristotle owed his Birth, he afterwards requited with extraordinary Gratitude. **1725** De Foe *Voy. round World* (1840) 244, I was as well able to requite him for a large present as he was to make it. **1790** Cowper *Mother's Pict.* 86, I should ill requite thee to constrain Thy unbounded spirit into bonds again. **1864** Skeat *Uhland's Poems* 163 [He] Expects from him some tale or minstrel-lay, And afterward requites him with the like.

b. To pay back, make retaliation on (one) for some injury, etc.

c **1590** Marlowe *Faust.* x, Not so much for the injury.. hath Faustus worthily requited this injurious knight. **1627** Capt. Smith *Seaman's Gram.* xiii. 61 Hee payes vs shot for shot; Well, wee shall requite him. **1656** Bramhall *Replic.* 47 It is hard when they come to accuse us of blood guiltiness, I could requite him with a black list of murthers and Massacres. **1819** Shelley *Prometh. Unb.* I. 392 He but requites me for his own misdeed. **1852** Miss Yonge *Cameos* (1877) II. xxx. 313 The lady had the last word, but was requited with a blow.

†**c.** *refl.* To avenge (oneself). *Obs. rare*$^{-1}$.

1613 Purchas *Pilgrimage* vii. iii. (1614) 669 The Indians ..slew many Tartars, who could not see to requite themselues thorow the smoke.

†**3.** To repay with the like; to return (a visit).

1548 Udall, etc. *Erasm. Par. Matt.* xxi. 102b, Jesus.. requited their question with an other. *a* **1648** Ld. Herbert in *Life* (1886) 202, I spent my time much in the visits of the princes,..who did ever punctually requite my visits.

†**b.** To salute (one) in return. *Obs. rare.*

1590 Spenser *F.Q.* i. x. 49 They him saluted, standing far afore; Who, well them greeting, humbly did requight. **1591** —— *M. Hubberd* 587 Lowly they him saluted in meeke wise; But he..scarce vouchsafte them to requite.

4. To make return of; to give or do in return *for* something. †Also with double obj.

a **1547** Surrey *Æneid* ii. 185 If I speake truth, and..For graunt of life requite thee large amendes. **1555** Eden *Decades* 7 They serue them with lyke sause, requitinge deathe for deathe. **1581** Marbeck *Bk. of Notes* 779 They are iustified freely, because working nothing, and requiting nothing, they are iustified by onely faith. **1631** Gouge *God's Arrows* iii. §60. 296 In case of *talio*, or requiting like for like. **1877** C. Geikie *Christ* xxxvi. (1879) 431 To requite like for like was assumed as both just and righteous.

†**5.** To take the place of, to make up for, to counterbalance or compensate. *Obs.*

1603 Owen *Pembrokeshire* (1892) 5 Pembrokshere reacheth to the Ryver Taf, and then Carmarthenshere requiteing it, reaches to the Ryver Cledde. **1646** Sir T. Browne *Pseud. Ep.* ii. iii. (1672) 80 Which is a way of intelligence very strange, and would requite the lost Art of Pythagoras, who could read a reverse in the Moon. **1680** H. More *Apocal. Apoc.* 184 From whence will naturally flow.. scarcity and poverty to requite their luxury before. **1697** Dryden *Virg. Past.* iv. 76 Thy Mother well deserves that short delight, The nauseous Qualms of..Travel to requite.

Hence **re'quited** *ppl. a.* (only in *ill-* or *well-requited*); **re'quiting** *vbl. sb.* Also †**re'quite-ful** *a.*, making due return; †**re'quiteless** *a.*, unrequited, without requital; **re'quitement**, requital, revenge.

1730–46 Thomson *Autumn* 899 Wallace.., Great patriot hero! ill *requited chief! **1828** Scott *F.M. Perth* xv, There is enough of employment for them; well requited employment, too. **1607** Middleton *Five Gallants* ii. i, Yet were you never that *requiteful mistress That grac'd me with one favour. **1607** Norden *Surv. Dial.* v. 227 It would not beare a crop of requitefull increase. **1603** J. Davies *Microcosmos* (Grosart) 68 For this, his loue *requitelesse doth approue, He gaue her beeing, meerly of free grace. **1606** Chapman *Gentl. Usher* iii. i, Why fayth, deare friend, I would not die requiteless. *a* **1548** Hall *Chron., Hen. IV*, 17b, The erle Douglas sore beyng greued with the losse of his nacion and frendes, entendyng a *requitement if it were possible of the same..did gather a houge armie. **1893** *Strand Mag.* V. 347/2 Dark deeds of requitement. **1553** T. Wilson *Rhet.* 18b, Thankefulnesse is a *requityng of loue, for loue. **1578** Golding tr. *Seneca's Benef.* (title-p.), The Dooing, Receyving, and Requyting of Good Turnes.

requiter (rɪ'kwaɪtə(r)). [f. requite *v.* + -er[1].] One who requites.

1595 *Quest of Enquirre* (1881) 19 Bee of good cheare, Brother, you are not the first that hath trauild for an vnkinde requiter. *c* **1611** Chapman *Iliad* Pref. A 4b, For which.. God made me amply his requiter. *a* **1677** Barrow *Serm.* iv. Wks. 1700 I. 41 Honour..is a virtue which renders a man.. a grateful resenter and requiter of courtesies. **1710** Hearne *Collect.* 7 Mar. (O.H.S.) II. 356 His grand Patron and.. bounteous Requiter. **1881** *American* III. 182 The ungrateful requiter of the kindness of such friends.

requotation. [re- 5a.] A new or revised quotation (of the price of a share).

1964 *Economist* 29 Aug. 848/1 A requotation for their shares. **1973** *Daily Tel.* 14 Feb. 1/6 Pergamon Press..is back in profit and looking for an early requotation on the Stock Exchange.

re'quote (riː-), *v.* [re- 5a.] To quote again. Also, to quote a new price for (a share).

1817 Hazlitt *Pol. Ess.* (1819) 217 Mr. Southey requoted Mr. Canning's quotation. **1889** Child *Ballads* III. 305/1 Sidney's words, though perhaps a hundred times requoted since they were cited by Addison, cannot be omitted here. **1967** *Economist* 27 May 946/4 The shares were requoted after the financial troubles.

requovir, obs. form of recover *v.*

requoyle, obs. form of recoil *sb.* and *v.*

rer, obs. form of rear *v.*[1]

re-'radiate, *v.* Also reradiate. [re- 5a.] *trans.* To radiate again (what has been absorbed or received). Also *absol.*

1913 F. W. Raynes *Heating Systems* xv. 184 The arrangement and grouping of the heating surfaces affect the radiant heat transmitted, in that a more or less percentage is rendered ineffective through being simply re-radiated from surface to surface. **1928** *Daily Tel.* 10 Jan. 16 A short-wave receiver of a sensitive type which will not re-radiate, and so interfere with neighbouring receivers. **1942** J. D. Stranathan *Particles Mod. Physics.* vi. 255 Electrons of the scattering material are supposed to be set into vibration by the varying electric field. These..are then supposed to re-radiate the energy in all directions. This re-radiated energy represents the scattered X-rays. **1952** *Archit. Rev.* CXI. 18/2 Any type of screen will itself be heated by the sunshine falling upon it, and will re-radiate this heat into the building. **1976** *Sci. Amer.* Sept. 75/3 The earth intercepts a vast amount of solar energy... About 60 percent is reflected without interacting further and most of the remainder is absorbed by the atmosphere or by oceans and landmasses and is promptly reradiated as heat.

Hence **re-'radiated** *ppl. a.*

1942 [see above]. **1974** Harvey & Bohlman *Stereo F.M. Radio Handbk.* vii. 155 This reradiated signal is picked up by the dipole. **1978** R. V. Jones *Most Secret War* xxi. 175 We could in principle re-radiate this already re-radiated signal back to the aircraft.

,re-radi'ation. [re- 5a.] The action of re-radiating; also *concr.*

1881 *Nature* XXV. 15 The re-radiation which the strip almost instantaneously exerts. **1915** W. H. Eccles *Wireless Telegr.* 132 The Joulean wastage in the surrounding ground is usually so great that it is well to limit the re-radiation, and to seek rather to transfer the collected energy somewhat rapidly to the detector. **1924** *Times* 17 Jan. 8/5 The first intelligible programmes began to come through in time for successful re-radiation here before the close of the old year. *Ibid.*, A large number of letters have been received..from listeners..commenting on the surprisingly good quality of the re-radiation. **1976** *Nature* 2 Sept. 15/2 Solar radiation is absorbed in ground energy levels of atoms or molecules, producing excitation. Fluorescence or reradiation then follows.

†**'rerage.** *Obs.* Also 5 rereage, 6 rearage, 7 reradge. [Aphetic f. OF. *arerage*: see arrearage.] Arrears of payment; the state of being in arrears, etc. (Common *c* 1400–1550.)

1377 Langl. *P. Pl.* B. v. 246, I haue mo maneres thorw rerages than thorw *miseretur et commodat.* ? *a* **1400** *Morte Arth.* 1680 He wylle gyfe a rekenyng that rewe salle aftyre, ..Or þe rereage be requit of rentez þat he claymez. *c* **1440** *Jacob's Well* 128 So slyly, þat þe lord is in þi dette, þere þou schuldyst ben in reragys. **1530** *Proper Dyaloge* in *Roy's Rede me*, etc. (Arb.) 139 Wherby the comones sufferinge damage The hole lande is brought in to rerage. *c* **1550** Bale *K. Johan* 1752 Shall they pay no tribute yf the realme stond in rerage? **1636** Heywood *Challenge* iv. i. Wks. 1874 V. 50, I needs most freely must acquit all debts 'Twixt you and mee, and there Ingeniously Confesse my selfe in reradge.

re'rail (riː-), *v.* [re- 5a.] *trans.* To replace (railway engines, etc.) upon the rails. Also *fig.* So **re'railing** *vbl. sb.*

1888 *Lockwood's Dict. Mech. Terms* 283 Rerailing..is done with screw jacks and timber blocking, or with ramps. **1889** *Scribner's Mag.* Sept. 346/2 They are supposed to.. have made possible the rerailing of the engine. **1895** *Funk's Stand. Dict.*, *Re-rail*.., to put on the track again; to cause to take the rails again, as derailed rolling-stock. **1914** W. de Morgan *Ghost meets Ghost* ii. iii. 455 'And where else did you go?' said the Earl, to re-rail the conversation. **1967** G. F. Fiennes *I tried to run Railway* ii. 6, I learned how to re-rail wagons and engines without sending for the crane.

re'raise (riː-), *v.* [re- 5a.] To raise again. Hence **re'raising** *vbl. sb.*

1683 Moxon *Mech. Exerc., Printing* xix. ¶2 This must be mended in the Matrice by re-raising it to its due Thickness. **1863** H. Spencer *Ess.* III. 34 Subsequently he reraises this apparent anomaly when saying [etc.]. **1884** *Law Times* LXXVII. 411/2 Not only would this..re-raise the question as to the power of the committee, but [etc.]. **1937** *Jrnl. Eng. & Germanic Philol.* XXXVI. 2 The raising (resp. re-raising) of *ǣ* (< *ē*) > *ē*. **1937** *Times* 31 Dec. 12/1 The object of making it impossible for such points of friction to be reraised in future.

rerd(e, *sb. Obs.* exc. *dial.* Forms: 1–3 reord(e, 3 rorde, 4–5 rurd(e, ruerde, rewerd; 3–4 rerde, 3–6 rerd, 5 rerid, reryd, 6 (8–9) reird, 8–9 reerd; 4 rearde, 6, 9 reard, 8 raird. [OE. *reord* voice, cry, = OHG. *rarta* voice, melody, Goth. *razda* voice, speech, language, ON. *rödd*, *radd-* voice, song: the further etym. is uncertain. After 1400 almost exclusively Sc., usually in senses 2b and 3.]

†**1.** Voice, utterance, cry. *Obs.*

Beowulf 2556 Hordweard oncniow mannes reorde. *a* **900** Cynewulf *Christ* 510 Englas tweʒen..cleopedon..ofer wera menʒu beorhtan reorde. *c* **1000** *Ags. Ps.* (Th.) cxxxvii. 5 Eorðan kyningas..ʒehyrdan hlude reorde, þines muðes.. word. *c* **1200** Ormin 16664 Þu mahht herenn gastess rerd Wiþþ erþliʒ flæshess ære. *a* **1250** *Owl & Night.* 311 ʒet thu ..telst that ich ne can noʒt singe, Ac al mi rorde [*v.r.* reorde] is woning. *a* **1300** *Vox & Wolf* 114 in Hazl. *E.P.P.* I. 61 He com to the putte, thene vox i-herde; He him kneu wel by his rerde. **1340** *Ayenb.* 211 Lhord god yhyer mine bene and mine rearde þet ich grede to þe. *a* **1400–50** *Alexander* 387 With a reryst reryd þis reson he said.

2. A loud or noisy cry; noise or din made by crying or roaring; †a noisy tongue.

13.. *Seuyn Sag.* (W.) 910 He criede and makede rewli rerd. **13..** *E.E. Allit. P.* B. 390 Summe..Rwly wyth a loud rurd rored for drede. *c* **1400** *Ywaine & Gaw.* 2073 Than kest he up so lathly rerde, Ful mani folk myht he have ferde. *c* **1425** Wyntoun *Cron.* i. ix. 804 þa bestis..oyssis wiþ gret rerde to rare. *c* **1480** Henryson *Mor. Fab.* v. 23 Ryfand his hair, he cryit with ane reird. **1721** Kelly *Scot. Prov.* 44 A house with a Reek, and a Wife with a Reerd will soon make a Man run to the Door. **1819** Hogg *Jacobite Relics*, *Q. Anne* vi, Then she ga'e a reirde, Made a' the smiths to glower.

b. Uproar or clamour made by a number of persons (or animals).

1500–20 Dunbar *Poems* xxxiii. 94 Thik was the clud of kayis and crawis,..The rerd of thame raiss to the sky. **1536** Bellenden *Cron. Scot.* (1821) II. 34 Na man wist quhat wes to be done, throw reird of men and beistis. *a* **1578** Lindesay (Pitscottie) *Chron. Scot.* (S.T.S.) I. 86 [They] brak about him witht sic ane reird and clamour. **1718** Ramsay *Christ's Kirk Gr.* iii. xix, Sic a reird ran thro' the rout. **1791** J. Learmont *Poems* 167 Their raird rang rudely owr the lift. **1822** Scott *Nigel* ii, Then the reird raise, and..murdered I suld hae been, without remeid. **1894** *Northumbld. Gloss.*, *Reard*, *Reerd*, riot, confusion.

3. Noise or din of any kind.

c **1400** *Destr. Troy* 12697 þe remnond..Herd þe rurde & þe ryfte of þe rank schippis. *c* **1470** Henry *Wallace* viii. 208 Gret rerd thar rais all sammyn quhar thai ryd. **1508** Dunbar *Gold. Targe* 241 For reird it semyt that the raynbow brak. **1536** Bellenden *Cron. Scot.* (1821) I. 75 Sa huge nois rais be reird and sowne of bellis. **1585** Jas. I. *Ess. Poesie* (Arb.) 13 With threatning thunders, making monstrous reard. **1715** Ramsay *Christ's Kirk Gr.* ii. xiii, Back gate..she loot a fearfu' raird. **1806** R. Jamieson *Pop. Ballads* I. 243 Till far and near, wood, rock and cave, The thunderin' reird return.

rerd(e, *v. Obs.* exc. *Sc.* Forms: 1 (riord-), reordian, 2 -ien, 5–6 rerde, reird, 6 reard, 6 (9) raird. [OE. *reordian*, f. *reord*: see prec.]

†**1.** *intr.* To speak, discourse. *Obs.*

Beowulf 3025 Sceal..se wonna hrefn..fela reordian. *a* **900** Cynewulf *Christ* 196 Þa seo femne..þus reordode.

a1000 *Genesis* 1253 þa reordade rodera waldend..& þa worde cwæð. c1205 LAY. 22173 He reordien gan and þas word sæide.

2. To make a noise; to roar, resound, etc.

c1425 WYNTOUN *Cron.* lxxvii. 608 (Wemyss), Syne efter it begouth to wax, And within him rerd and rax. c1470 *Gol. & Gaw.* 914 The rochis reirdit vith the rasch, quhen thai samyne rane. 1513 DOUGLAS *Æneis* VIII. v. 68 The wod resoundis schill,..The hillis reirdis. 1535 STEWART *Cron. Scot.* III. 233 With buglis blast quhill rairdit all the ryce. 1585 MONTGOMERIE *Sonnets* xii, Can thunder reird the higher for a horne? 1824 MACTAGGART *Gallovid. Encycl.* 403 Ice is said to be rairding, when it is cracking.

Hence **ˈrerding** *vbl. sb.* and *ppl. a.* Also †**ˈrerdour**, clamour, tumult. *Obs. rare*$^{-1}$.

1535 STEWART *Cron. Scot.* I. 277 Sic reirdour raiss amang thame vp and doun. *Ibid.* II. 462 Quhill all the rochis with thair reirding rang. 1591–1603 JAS. I *Sonett, Poet. Exercises,* The rearding thunders, and the blustering winds.

†**rere**, *v.*[1] *Obs. rare.* [Aphetic for *arere*: see ARREAR *v.* and cf. REIR *v.*] *intr.* or *trans.* To retreat, or cause to retreat.

The sense in the second quot. is not quite clear, but connexion with OE. *hréran* to move, stir, seems unlikely.

c1330 R. BRUNNE *Chron.* (1810) 71 Non stode Harald dynt, þat bifor him kam. Þe rouht of þare rascaile he did it rere & ryme. ?a1400 *Morte Arth.* 2810 Alle that rewlyde in the rowtte they rydene awaye, So rewdly they rere theys ryalle knyghttes.

†**rere**, *v.*[2] *Sc. Obs. rare.* [Of obscure origin; app. related to REERE *sb.*] *intr.* To resound; to cry, roar.

c1450 HOLLAND *Howlat* 13 Throw thir cliftis so cleir,..I raikit till ane Reveir, That ryallye reird [*v.r.* apperd]. *Ibid.* 638 Thai come.., Thir fowlis of rigour, With a gret reir. Than rerit thir Merlȝeonis that mountis so hie. 1508 DUNBAR *Flyting* 236 Cry grace, tykis face, or I the chece and sley; Oule, rere [*v.r.* rare] and ȝowle.

rere, *adv. rare*$^{-1}$. [var. REAR *a.*[1]] Rearwards.

1814 CARY *Dante, Inf.* xx. 43 Aruns, with rere his belly facing, comes.

rere, obs. form of REAR *sb.*[3], *a.*[2], and *v.*; var. REERE noise. *Obs.*

rere-, comb. form: see REAR-.

†**rere-account.** *Obs. rare.* Also 5 -accompt. [RERE-.] A subsequent account or reckoning.

1486 *Naval Acc. Hen. VII* (1896) 19 Rendered in the rereaccompt of stuff. 1639 FULLER *Holy War* III. xxii. 149 Such reckonings without the host are ever subject to a rere-account. 1650 —— *Pisgah* II. I. v. 357 This insinuates that at this rere-account, the Talents were Talents indeed.

re-ˈread (riː-), *v.* [RE- 5 a.] *trans.* To read over again; to peruse a second time. (Common in 19th c.)

1782 MISS BURNEY *Cecilia* VII. i, Cecilia read and re-read this letter. 1794 ANNA SEWARD *Lett.* (1811) III. 347, I am too busily employed in more necessary concerns to re-read ..his works. 1848 THACKERAY *Let.* in *Scribner's Mag.* I. 398, I have been re-reading the *Hoggarty Diamond* this morning. 1876 F. HARRISON *Choice Bks.* (1886) 78 The immortal..poets of our race are to be read and re-read.

Hence **re-ˈread** *ppl. a.*; **re-ˈreading** *vbl. sb.*

1881 *Nation* (N.Y.) XXXII. 386 Perhaps a rereading of 'Lear'. 1893 W. C. ROBINSON tr. *Ten Brink's Hist. Eng. Lit.* I. 80 The often re-read work of the Roman philosopher. 1898 R. F. HORTON *Commandm. Jesus* vi. 85 These five re-readings of the Mosaic regulations.

ˈreread, *sb.* [RE- 5 a.] An instance of reading again.

1973 M. AMIS *Rachel Papers* 185 Finally, I belaboured one of Gerard Manley Hopkins's sleazier lyrics, implying (a last-minute reread made clear) that it was high time we burned all extant editions of the little fag's poetry. 1977 T. ALLBEURY *Man with President's Mind* ii. 13 The report got a routine re-read.

re-ˈreadable, *a.* [RE- 5 a.] Capable of being re-read; capable of being read about for a second time with pleasure.

1948 F. R. LEAVIS *Great Tradition* i. 9 His books..have a permanent life as light reading—indefinitely re-readable. 1967 *Punch* 22 Feb. 282/3 He makes the Paris of the 'twenties, Joyce and Fitzgerald re-readable, something of a feat.

re-reader. [RE- 5 a.] One who re-reads.

1957 'O. EDWARDS' *Talking of Books* 190 It can be argued that all these are specialists or exceptional classes of re-readers. 1965 K. TILLOTSON *Mid-Victorian Stud.* xxiv. 309 Dickens..is perhaps chiefly a re-reader—going back and back to that shelf of boyhood favourites lovingly enumerated in *David Copperfield.*

rere-arch, variant of REAR-ARCH.

†**rere-ban(d.** [a. OF. *rereban* (Wace, etc.).] obs. var. ARRIÈRE-BAN.

13.. *Guy Warw.* (A.) 3685 Þi rereban þou do of-sende; To awreke [þe] þou haue in mende. 1523 [see ARRIÈRE-BAN]. a1533 LD. BERNERS *Huon* ciii. 341 Then he sent for his rerebande, as farre as his empyre stretched.

†**rere-banquet.** *Obs.* Also 6–7 reere-, 7 reer-, rear-. [Cf. RERE-SUPPER.] A 'banquet' or collation taken after dinner or supper.

1530 PALSGR. 262/1 Rere banket, *ralias.* 1584 R. SCOT *Discov. Witchcr.* III. xvi. (1886) 52 The fairies or witches being at a reere banket. 1589 PUTTENHAM *Eng. Poesie* III. xxiv. (Arb.) 288 He came..in the after noone, and finding the king at a rere-banquet,..turned back againe. 1606 HOLLAND *Sueton.* 235 He devided repast into three meales every day at the least, and sometime into foure, to wit, Breakefast, Dinner, Supper and rere-bankets. 1620 tr. *Boccaccio's Decam.* 26 b, Being disposed to a rere-banquet after dinner. 1631 BRATHWAIT *Eng. Gentlew.* (1641) 286 Accoutred with a reere-banket to belull the abused soule with the sleepe of an incessant surfeit. 1659 *Lady Alimony* Cj, Balls, Treats, Reer-Banquets, Theatral Receipts To solace tedious hours.

fig. 1602 FULBECKE *2nd Pt. Parall.* Introd. 6 The booke of Littletons tenures is their breakfast, their dinner, their boier, their supper, and their rere-banquet.

rere-brace. *Obs.* exc. *Hist.* Also rer(e)bras. [a. AF. **rerebras*, f. *rere-* back + *bras* arm: cf. VAMBRACE.] Armour for the upper arm from the shoulder to the elbow (originally a plate protecting the back of the arm only).

c1330 R. BRUNNE *Chron. Wace* (Rolls) 10030 Hym self was armed..Wyþ..Vaumbras & rerbras. ?a1400 *Morte Arth.* 2566 An alet enamelde he oches in sondire, Bristes þe rerebrace with the bronde ryche. 1411 *E.E. Wills* (1882) 19 A pare of vambrace and rerebrace, a pare of legge herneys. 1441 *Plumpton Corr.* (Camden) p. liv, Like men of were, with brest plate, vambrace & rerebrace. 1496 *Dives & Paup.* (W. de W.) x. vi. 379/2 We sholde take with us rerebras and vanbras & gloues of plate.

1824 *Archaeologia* XX. 503 In later times the armour for the arm was distinguished into the vambrace, elbow-piece, brassart (the same as rerebrace) and pauldron. 1830 SKELTON *Meyrick's Antient Rome* Pl. IX. 5 The rere-brace with its long armed gauntlet for the bridle arm.

†**rere-brake.** *Obs.*$^{-1}$ (Meaning uncertain.)

'Probably the projection put on the crupper to prevent the horseman being pushed over the horse's tail by the thrust of a lance' (Meyrick).

1422–61 *Treat. Peaceable Joust.* in Meyrick *Antient Armour* (1824) III. Gloss. s.v., A rerebrake with a roule of lethir well stuffid.

†**rere-cord**, *sb. Obs. rare.* (Meaning uncertain.)

1334–5 *Durham Acc. Rolls* (Surtees) 526 In 1 Rerecord et reparacione dicte carecte, 3*d.* 1353–4 *Ibid.* 554 Et in.. Whypcord et rerecordes empt., 5*s.* 3*d.*

re-reˈcord, *v.* Also rerecord. [RE- 5 a.] *trans.* To record again. Also *absol.*

1930 *Proc. IRE* XVIII. 1335 Before sound film can be rerecorded a matched print must be made. 1932 *Times Educ. Suppl.* 17 Dec. p. ii/2 The records made by the great tenor ..have been re-recorded by the Company. 1955 L. FEATHER *Encycl. Jazz* 25 He..restored him to the music world by rerecording *Honky Tonk Train Blues.* 1964 *Oceanogr. & Marine Biol.* II. 429 The background characteristics of low speed recordings may be somewhat improved by re-recording at higher speeds. 1977 *New Yorker* 29 Aug. 67/1 The music of long-dead musicians long ago re-recorded for in-flight listening. 1978 W. F. BUCKLEY *Stained Glass* xii. 110 It was recorded and rerecorded that in her youth she had actually studied under Clara Schumann.

Hence **re-reˈcorded** *ppl. a.*, **re-reˈcording** *vbl. sb.*

1930 *Proc. IRE* XVIII. 1333 Once it was discovered that re-recording was practical a great many other reasons for its use were discovered. 1962 A. NISBETT *Technique Sound Studio* v. 104 It is now possible to compare the original and re-recorded signals directly. 1975 P. G. WINSLOW *Death of Angel* ix. 186 It seems to be a re-recording of another tape. 1977 *Gramophone* Aug. 357/2 The incredibly high copying speeds needed to make the exercise economically viable (32 or 64 times normal speed) put severe limits on the re-recorded sound quality.

†**rere-county.** *Obs. rare.* [ad. AF. *rerecounté* (Anglo-L. *retro-comitatus*): see COUNTY[1] 4.] A subsidiary county-court, held by the sheriff on the day after the regular one.

[1285 *Act 13 Edw. I*, c. 39 (*Stat. Westm.*) In pleno Comitatu, vel in retro Comitatu, ubi fit colleccio denariorum Domini Regis. c1290 *Fleta* II. lxvii. §18 (1647) 151 In pleno Comitatu, vel saltem in crastino die post Comitatum, qui quidem dies dicitur Retro-comitatus. 1328 *Act 2 Edw. III*, c. 5 Que ceux que livrer volent lour briefs as viscountes, les livrent en plein Counte, ou en rerecounte.] 1641 *Termes de la Ley* 241 b, Rere county..seemes by those statutes to bee some publike place which the Sheriffe appointed for the receiving of the kings mony after that his county court was done. [1810 *Stat. Realm* I. 258/2 That they which will deliver their Writs to the Sheriff, shall deliver them in the full County, or in the Rere County.]

re-reˈdelve, *v. rare*$^{-1}$. [See RE- 4 b.] *trans.* To delve a third time.

1598 SYLVESTER *Du Bartas* II. ii. I. *Ark* 532 In March he delves them, re-re-delves, and dresses.

†**rere-demain.** *Obs. rare.* In 6 -mayne, -maine. [Later form of RERE-MAIN; the reason of the *de* is not clear.] A back-handed stroke.

a1548 HALL *Chron., Rich. III* 35 b, But al such plagues, calamities and troubles..I shall with a reredemayne..make them rebounde to our commen enemye. 1591 HARINGTON *Orl. Fur.* XVI. l, Such a blow he lent him as he past, Vpon his shoulders, from the reredemaine. *Ibid.* XLII. xlvii, Right blowes and reardemaine he striketh many.

rere-ˈdorter. *rare.* Also 6 -our. [RERE-.] A privy situated at the back of the dormitory in a convent or monastery.

?a1500 *MS. Arundel* 146 (Halliw.), If any suster in the rere-dortour, otherwyse callyd the house of esemente, behave her unwomanly. 1891 W. H. ST. J. HOPE in Venables *Chron. de Parco Lude* Introd. 55 This communicated directly at its southern end with the reredorter. 1900 —— in *Yorks. Archæol. Jrnl.* XV. 354 The rere-dorter built after the fire was 92 feet long.

reredos (ˈrɪədɒs). Forms: 4–5 rerdos(e, 5 -doos(e; 5–6 reredosse, (5 -doos, -dose, -doce, -des, 6 -doyse, 6–7 -dorse), 4– reredos; 6 reyredewse; 6 reerdos, rardros, (7 -dess); 7 reardashe, -dorse; 5 redoce, 6 -doss, -dorse, -drosse; 5 reddos. [a. AF. **reredos* (cf. *areredos*, 1399 in *Rolls of Parlt.* III. 431/2), f. *rere-* RERE- + *dos* back: see DOSS *sb.*[1] and DORSE *sb.*[1] Also in Anglo-L. as *retrodorsorium* (14th c.).

In eccl. use the word is common during the 15th cent., rare in the 16th, and from about 1550 appears to have been practically obsolete until revived in the 19th c. The earliest dictionaries which give it are those of Craig (1848) and Ogilvie (1850). In a number of early examples it is impossible to determine the precise sense intended.]

1. *Eccl.* **a.** An ornamental facing or screen of stone or wood covering the wall at the back of an altar, frequently of ornate design, with niches, statues, and other decorations.

1372–3 *Durham Acc. Rolls* (Surtees) 180 In contr. facta pro le Rerdose ad magnum altare in ecclesia (de Merington). 1376–7 *Ibid.* 585 In exp...pro cariacione del Rerdos. 1419 *Test. Ebor.* (Surtees) I. 396 In ornamentum summi Altaris dictæ ecclesiæ Cath. Ebor., videlicet Reredose. 1448 *Will of Hen. VI* in Willis & Clark *Cambridge* (1886) I. 355 Fro the reredos atte the high auter vnto the quere dore. 1463 *Bury Wills* (Camden) 19 [I bequeath] x. marks to the peyntyng rerdoos and table at Seynt Marie avter of the story of Magnificat. 1519 *Fabric Rolls York Minster* (Surtees) 267 The goodly reyredewse is so full of dust and copwebbes that by lyklyode it shalbe shortly lost. c1541 in *Archaeologia* (1821) XIX. 272 The Reredose at the highe Altar..ys excellently well wrought and as well gylted.

1836 PARKER *Gloss. Archit.* (1850) I. 384 At Bampton, Oxfordshire, a very perfect reredos remains in the east wall of the north transept, where an altar has stood. 1843 *Ecclesiologist* II. 22 The reredos is richly arcaded. 1879 SIR G. G. SCOTT *Lect. Archit.* I. 181, The remarkably ancient retable or movable reredos formerly belonging to the high altar.

b. A choir-screen.

1446 in *Hist. Dunelm. Script. Tres* (Surtees) p. cclxxiii, Novum opus vocatum le Rerdoose, ad ostium chori. a1490 BOTONER *Itin.* (Nasmith 1778) 290 Et a porta chori vocata le reredos usque orientem continet 47 gressus. 1861 *Morning Post* 24 Oct., The five remaining bays [of the choir]..have been restored; only three of them, though, will be within the reredos.

†**2.** A hanging of velvet or silk for covering the wall at the back of an altar. *Obs.*

Usually named together with a *dos, dorse,* or *vant dorse*: the precise distinction from these is not clear.

1381 in *Hist. Dunelm. Script. Tres* (Surtees) p. cliii, Unum rerdose broudatum cum crucifixo et imaginibus. 1482 *Will Ld. Beauchamp* (Somerset Ho.), An aulter cloth doce & redoce of the same [red velvet]. a1524 *Will Sir R. Sutton* in Churton *Life* (1800) 521 A Dorse and Redorse of Crymsyn Velvet with Flowres of Golde, in length, two yards three quarters. 1552 *Inv. Ch. Goods* (Surtees, No. 97) 74 A redrosse and vendrosse of yalowe and greine saye and curteyns to the same. *Ibid.* 163 One rardros and vandros for th'alter.

†**3.** A wooden panelling attached to a wall behind a seat. *Obs.*

1396 *Mem. Ripon* (Surtees) III. 123 Et in iij vayneschotes emp. pro j selour, et j reredos facta in camera capituli, 18*d.* 1452–3 *Durham Acc. Rolls* (Surtees) 277 Pro le Sylarynge domus rasturæ et le Rerdose ibidem. [1842 GWILT *Archit.* §415 The rere-dos was a sort of framed canopy hung with tapestry, and fixed behind the sovereign or chieftain.]

4. The brick or stone back of a fire-place or open hearth; an iron plate forming a fire-back. *Obs.* exc. *arch.*

1392 *Earl Derby's Exp.* (Camden) 219 Item pro factura de ij rakks..Item pro factura j reredos pro eisdem. 1486 *Nottingham Rec.* III. 258 Breke for to make þe reredose of þe same chymney with. a1500 in Arnolde *Chron.* (1811) 92 Also ye shall enquire..yf ther be ony chemeny yᵗ hath a reerdos made vncumly oder wise than it ought to be for perill of fire. a1548 HALL *Chron., Hen. VIII* 74 By Ouens, harthes, reredorses, Chimnayes, Ranges, and such instrumentes that there was ordained. 1577 HARRISON *England* II. xii. (1877) I. 240 Ech one made his fire against a reredosse in the hall, where he dined and dressed his meat. 1657 HOWELL *Londinop.* 394 All Armorers and other artificers..which have or use any Reardorses, or any other places dangerous for fire. 1720 STRYPE *Stow's Surv.* (1754) II. IV. ii. 34/2 In London, by the law no man may build or make a Reredorse for the fire of Charcoals within any house. 1836 J. DOWNES *Mt. Decam.* I. 308 The 'reredoss' or antique ironback of the chimney place, still used in the Welsh farm of older fashion. 1843 LYTTON *Last Bar.* I. v, There was no rere-dosse, or fire-place. 1861 *Our Eng. Home* 127 The billets were heaped against the reredos, or plate of iron fixed against the back of the chimneys.

¶**b.** A brazier. *rare*$^{-1}$.

1859 PARKER *Dom. Archit.* III. iii. II. 57 The reredos, or brazier for the fire of logs, in the centre of the hall, continued in use.

†**5.** The back or rear. *Obs. rare*$^{-1}$.

1480 CAXTON *Chron. Eng.* ccxiv. 200 The forsaid erle marchal was all arayed with his batayll at the reredoos of the erle of lancastre.

†**6.** A piece of armour for the back; a backplate. *Obs. rare.*

1405 *Fabric Rolls York Minster* (Surtees) 9 *note*, A breast-plate with 'rerodos' [*sic*], a pair of 'rerebraces', and a pair of 'sabatons'. 1412–20 LYDG. *Chron. Troy* III. xxii. (MS. Digby 230) lf. 102 b, And some chose of the newe entaille.. An hole breste plate with a rere doos.

re-re'duce, *v. rare*$^{-1}$. [RE- 5 a.] *trans.* To bring back again to a former condition.
a **1676** HALE *Prim. Orig. Man.* II. vii. (1677) 191 Some great Continents.. were anciently firm Land,.. and yet were afterwards reduced again into the Dominion of the Ocean, and after all that re-reduced into firm Land.

re-'reel, *v.* [RE- 5 a.] *trans.* To wind again on to a reel, or from one reel to another. Hence **re-'reeling** *vbl. sb.*; **re-'reeler** (see quot. 1964).
1906 R. W. SINDALL *Paper Technol.* vi. 75 (*caption*) Double-Drum Reeler. The reels from the paper-machine are re-reeled, slit, and finished off on this machine. **1929** CLAPPERTON & HENDERSON *Mod. Paper-Making* xvi. 246 (*caption*) Four-drum winder for re-reeling newsprint. **1937** E. J. LABARRE *Dict. Paper* 211/1 *Re-reeling machine*, the apparatus on which the web of paper is re-reeled after passing through the operations of tub-sizing.. and drying. **1964** *Gloss. Letterpress Rotary Printing Terms* (*B.S.I.*) 17 *Re-reeler*, an auxiliary unit to rewind the web or webs for subsequent operations. **1967** E. CHAMBERS *Photolitho-Offset* xv. 237 The paper can be either cut into sheets or re-reeled for finishing elsewhere.

re-'reference. *rare*$^{-1}$. [RE- 5 a.] A second reference.
a **1734** NORTH *Lives* (1826) I. 429 His lordship set his face also against the infinite delays by re-hearings, re-references, and new trials.

rere-fief. [a. OF. *rerefief* (Godef.).] Var. *arrière-fief*: see ARRIÈRE.
1766 BLACKSTONE *Comm.* II. 57 These inferior feudatories (who held what are called in the Scots law 'rere-fiefs').

re-re'fine (riː-), *v.* [RE- 5 a.] To refine again. Hence **re-re'fined** *ppl. a.*; **re-re'finer**; **re-re'fining** *vbl. sb.*
1631 MASSINGER *Emperor East* I. ii, I re-refine the court, and civilize Their barbarous natures. **1678** *Yng. Man's Call.* 383 Gods mingled service I did re-refine From Romish rubbish, and from humane dross. **1882** ROMANES in *Nature* XXV. 335 We may try in thought to refine this relation, and to re-refine it again and again. **1971** *Daily Colonist* (Victoria, B.C.) 10 Feb. 21/5 The re-refined oil sells for 26 cents a quart. **1973** *Sci. Amer.* Feb. 48/3 Today only 100 to 150 million gallons of the 500 million gallons of oil annually drained from the nation's crankcases are re-refined. **1975** *Conservation of Energy* (Shell Internat. Petroleum Co.) 12 Shell companies are examining the most effective means of collecting and re-conditioning used lubricating oils, including re-refining. *Ibid.*, It is possible that 10 per cent of the world demand for lubricants will be met by re-refined oils in the early 1980s. **1977** *Laconia* (New Hampshire) *Evening Citizen* 21 July 5/5 Your car's dirty motor oil might soon be 'rerefined' through an environmentally safe process which will help conserve.. crude oil. *Ibid.*, A lot of rerefiners' raw material is being burned as fuel. **1977** *Lubricants Business* (Shell Internat. Petroleum Co.) 8 Re-refining is likely to be primarily attractive in a number of developing countries where savings in foreign exchange could be an important factor.

re-re'form, *v.* [RE- 5 a.] To reform again.
1705 *Double Welcome* xliii, To Re-reform us all from bad to worse. **1858** BUSHNELL *Serm. New Life* 417 Converted, reformed and re-reformed in religion. **1884** *Chicago Advance* 3 Jan., Born where people were in the midst of re-reforming the Reformation.
So **re-refor'mation.**
a **1631** DONNE in *Select.* (1840) 265 God continue to us the light of this Reformation,.. and we shall not need any such re-reformation, or super-reformation. **1691** BEVERLEY *Mem. Kingd. Christ* 7 The Antichristian, and Turkish Tyranny shall Fall, and a Great Re-Reformation Ensue.

re-'reft, *pa. pple.* [RE- 5 a.] Torn away again.
1623 COCKERAM, *Rereft*, tane away again. **1632** LE GRYS tr. *Velleius Paterc.* 171 Syria and other provinces which he had seized upon, being rereft him, were part restored to the people of Rome.

rerefy, obs. form of RAREFY.

reregard, obs. form of REARGUARD.

re-'register, *v.* [RE- 5 a.] To register again. So **re-'register** *sb.*; **re-regi'stration.**
1858 COX in *Key to Law Rep., List of Chancery & Common Law Forms* 11 Registers of Judgment and Copies. Re-registers of do. **1883** *Law Times Rep.* XLIX. 151/1 The Imperial Hotel Company.. was re-registered with fresh articles of association. **1894** *Westm. Gaz.* 7 July 7/1 However, re-registration is cheap and easy.

re-re'hearing, *vbl. sb.* [RE- 4 b.] A third hearing.
1674 STAVELEY *Rom. Horseleach* (1769) 208 A certain case .. received a hearing, rehearing and re-rehearing before it had its final resolution.

re-'reign, *v.* [RE- 5 a.] To reign again.
1589 WARNER *Alb. Eng.* VI. xxxi, They A People shall remaine.. and of that Streene Shall Fiue at length re-raigne.

re-re'iterated, *ppl. a.* [RE- 5 a.] Again reiterated or repeated.
1859 TENNYSON *Vivien* 203 Yield my boon,.. And grant my re-reiterated wish.

re-re'joinder. [Cf. RE- 2 a.] A surrejoinder.
1884 SPENCER in *Contemp. Rev.* XLVI. 30 A very reasonable rejoinder this seems until there comes the re-rejoinder.

re-re'lapse, *sb.* [RE- 5 a.] A second or further relapse.
a **1618** SYLVESTER *Miracle of Peace* xxxv, Our sins (I feare) will work worse afterclaps, And there's most danger in a re-relapse.

re-re'late, *v.* [RE- 5 a.] To relate again.
1782 ELIZ. BLOWER *Geo. Bateman* II. 210 To whom Mrs. Mabberly re-related Cecilia's misadventure. **1899** *Review of Rev.* Mar. (U.S. ed.) 332 As related and rerelated at soldiers' reunions.

re-re'lease, *v.* [RE- 5 a.] *trans.* To release (a film, record, etc.) again. So **re-re'lease** *sb.*; **re-re'leasable** *a.*; **re-re'leased** *ppl. a.*
1948 *Daily Mail* 7 Feb. 2/5 'Mrs. Miniver'.. turned up.. on 're-release', and lasted only seven days. **1968** *Listener* 26 Sept. 416/2 The Disney product had to be aimed at all ages, it had to be 'endlessly re-releasable'. **1975** *N.Y. Times* 4 Mar. 38/1 The new D. W. Griffith Theater, which has re-released Cocteau's 'Les Enfants Terribles'. **1977** *It* May 28/1 There are the re-released 'Jimmy Weatherspoon and Ben Webster' 'Stitt Palysbird'. **1977** *Guardian Weekly* 28 Aug. 20/1 There are currently 38 Presley albums available in this country.. and, with re-releases, he has had 117 singles on sale here.

†**rere-main.** *Obs. rare*$^{-1}$. [a. AF. *reremain (= *arere-main*, OF. *ariere-main*: see Littré, s.v. *arrière-main*), f. *rere-* RERE- + *main* hand.] = RERE-DEMAIN.
13.. *K. Alis.* 7395 Wel they foughte in the playn, With target, and with reremayn, With overhed, and with stoke.

reremouse: see REARMOUSE.

re-'render, *v.* [RE- 5 a.] *trans.* To render or return again.
1627–47 FELTHAM *Resolves* 201, I would not if I could, receive favours of my friends, unless I could re-render them. **1857** HEAVYSEGE *Saul* (1869) 406 Before the sun sets 'neath the sea Again to Zaph re-render me.

re-re'peat, *v.* [RE- 5 a.] *trans.* To repeat again. Hence **re-re'peated** *ppl. a.*
1629 GAULE *Holy Madn.* 154 How it tickles him to re-repeat the Line. **1761** MRS. F. SHERIDAN *Sidney Bidulph* II. 151 He explained them.. to Rachel in English, who re-repeated them to her lady within her curtains. **1815** *Zeluca* II. 67 He read the accompanying note again and again, with .. re-repeated wonder. **1882** E. P. GOODWIN *Serm. to Amer. Board For. Missions* 30 An era of Pentecosts to be repeated, and re-repeated with every widening range.

re-re'port, *v.* [RE- 5 a.] To report again.
1599 R. LINCHE *Fount. Anc. Fiction* I iv, Joying to re-report the least-heard noise. **1748** RICHARDSON *Clarissa* (1811) V. 71 This fellow reported the following particulars, as they were re-reported to me.

re-represen'tation. [RE- 5 a.] A second representation.
1679 LUTTRELL *Brief Rel.* (1857) I. 10 The house.. having made a representation and a re-representation to his majestie of the priviledge of the house in chusing their speaker. **1932** *Brain* LV. 459 These impulses.. may be.. passed on to the main part of the lateral nucleus by short inter-nuclear connections where they acquire a re-representation.

rere-rib, -shaft, varr. REAR-RIB, -SHAFT.

re-re'solve, *v.* [RE- 5 a.] To resolve again.
1742 YOUNG *Nt. Th.* I. 422 Man.. In all the Magnanimity of Thought Resolves; and re-resolves. **1762** GOLDSM. *Cit. W.* xxvii, So after resolving, and re-resolving, I had courage enough to tell her my mind. **1830** W. TAYLOR *Hist. Surv. Germ. Poetry* I. 15 The senseless indecisive man Ponders and re-resolves all night.

re-resti'tution. [RE-.] Restitution made in return.
1729 JACOB *Law Dict.*, *Re-restitution*, is where there hath been a Writ of Restitution before granted: And Restitution is generally Matter of Duty; but Re-restitution is Matter of Grace.

rere-supper. *Obs.* exc. *arch.* Also 4–5 -soper(e, 4–6 -souper; 6–7 reare-, 7 rear-, reer-supper. (Written indifferently with or without hyphen and as one word.) [a. AF. *rere-super*: see RERE and SUPPER.] A supper (usually of a sumptuous nature) following upon the usual evening meal, and thus coming very late at night. (App. in use down to the early part of the 17th c.)
1303 R. BRUNNE *Handl. Synne* 7260 Rere sopers yn pryuyte [F. *les rere supers en priuité*]. *Ibid.* 7268 Ȝyt are þere ouþer rere sopers Wyþ men þat serue knyȝtys and squyers. **1390** GOWER *Conf.* III. 32 Thanne is he redy in the weie Mi reresouper forto make. *c* **1430** LYDG. *Min. Poems* (Percy Soc.) 90 He fonde up first ryot and dronkennesse.. Fonde reresoupers and fetherbeddis softe. *a* **1450** *Knt. de la Tour* (1868) 8 Also she wold haue rere sopers whanne her fader and moder was a-bedde. **1509** FISHER *Serm. C'tess Richmond* Wks. (1876) 294 Eschewynge banketres, reresoupers, ioncryes betwyxe meales. **1553** T. WILSON *Rhet.* 110 b, With banquetyng from daie to daie, with sumptuous reare suppers. **1606** G. W[OODCOCKE] *Hist. Ivstine* XII. 55 Immediatly vpon a banket, the Physician Thessalus made a reare-supper. **1665** BRATHWAIT *Comment Two Tales* 50, Reer Suppers were my Solace: I suited my youthful Fancy to jovial Company. [**1826** SCOTT *Woodst.* xvi, He was guilty of the enormity of rere-suppers. **1830** JAMES *Darnley* xxvi, Prognostications of a rere supper.]

re-re'turn, *v.* [RE- 5 a.] To return again.
1609 ROWLEY *Search for Money* (Percy Soc.) 9 Ale, though kept awhile in the clouds of the body, yet may againe perfectly and providently returne to the fatte, and so re-returne to the body. **1887** *Echo* 21 June 3/2 The cheers were now returned and re-returned with increasing volume.

re-re'veal, *v.* [RE- 5 a.] To reveal again.
a **1631** DONNE *Poems* (1635) 367 Davids Successors, in holy zeale, In formes of joy and art doe re-reveale To us so sweetly and sincerely too, That I must not rejoyce as I would doe. **1830** SOUTHEY in *Corr. w. C. Bowles* (1881) 194 His dreams were old patriarchal truths, long forgotten, and now re-revealed. **1894** *Forum* (U.S.) May 306 [The Bible] is now being re-revealed as man's great text-book in psychology.

re-re'vise, *sb.* [RE- 5 a.] A second revise.
1858 O. W. HOLMES *Aut. Breakf.-t.* 54, I require to see a proof, a revise, a re-revise.. of all my productions, especially verse. **1895** *Daily News* 27 May 8/3 Balzac literally re-wrote his works on proofs, and on revises, and re-revises.

re-re'vise, *v.* [RE- 5 a.] *trans.* To revise again. Hence **re-re'vised** *ppl. a.*
1786 COWPER *Let. to Lady Hesketh* 3 Apr., I thought of detaining the third, fourth, and fifth books till I should have re-revised the first. **1806** SOUTHEY *Let. to G. C. Bedford* 17 June, What with revising and re-revising over and over again, they will amount to something like it at last. **1864** *Realm* 16 Mar. 2 We have had a code, a revised code, and a re-revised code, each more in advance than its predecessor.
So **re-re'vision,** further revision.
1823 J. BADCOCK *Dom. Amusem.* p. iv, The new articles.. stood particularly in want of re-revision. **1881** *Athenæum* 28 May 713/2 The result of ten years' revision and re-revision ..could hardly be other than emendation.

re-revo'lution. [RE-] A counter-revolution. So **re-revo'lutionize** *v.*
1778 H. WALPOLE *Lett., to Mason* Wks. 1846 V. 490 A re-revolution was so probable. **1800** SOUTHEY *Lett.* (1856) I. 89 Italy may very likely be re-revolutionised.

rereward, variant of REARWARD.

†**rerewarder.** *Obs. rare*$^{-1}$. [f. RERE- or REARWARD.] (See quot.)
1589 PUTTENHAM *Eng. Poesie* III. xii. (Arb.) 176 But if such supplie be placed after all the clauses,.. then is he called by the Greeks *Hypozeugma*, and by vs the Rerewarder.

rere-winter. *rare*$^{-1}$. [RERE-.] A late spell of winter.
1841 KEMBLE in Garnett *Phil. Ess.* (1859) p. xii, This rere-winter troubles me: I was beginning to think of.. migrating, when lo! frost and snow forbid me.

re-'ride, *v.* [RE- 5 a.] *trans.* To ride (a route, contest, etc.) again. Hence **'reride** *sb.*
1884 *Cyclists' Touring Club Monthly Gaz.* Nov. 335/2 Favourable stretches of high-way are ridden and re-ridden with wearying iteration upon safety bicycles, which are 'safe' only in name. **1903** *Daily Chron.* 28 Sept. 8/7 The tie will have to be re-ridden. **1976** *Billings* (Montana) *Gaz.* 17 June 1-H/3 Judges gave one cowboy a fourth reride.

rerify, obs. form of RAREFY.

re-'ring, *v.* [RE- 5 a.] To ring again.
1805 SOUTHEY *Madoc in Azt.* xxiv, Hark! from the towers of Aztlan, how the shouts Of clamorous joy re-ring!

re-'rise, *v.* [RE- 5 a.] To rise again.
1798 W. TAYLOR in *Monthly Mag.* V. 208 If thrice by Phœbus' toil re-rose its wall Of molten brass. **1839–48** BAILEY *Festus* xxxiv. 360 To seize the nascent souls Of men as they rerose from death to life. **1855** TENNYSON *Brook* 169 We.. Arrived, and found the sun of sweet content Re-risen in Katie's eyes, and all things well.
Hence **re-'risen** *ppl. a.*, **re-'rising** *vbl. sb.* and *ppl. a.*
1814 SOUTHEY *Ode to Alex. I*, iv, Moscow's re-rising walls Had rung with glad acclaim. **1816** —— *Lay of Laureate* Proem xiv, When that last and most momentous hour, Beheld the re-risen cause of evil yield. **1839–52** BAILEY *Festus* xix. 290 Some thought the gates of Heaven were sealed to all Until the great re-rising.

re-'rivet, *v.* [RE- 5 a.] *trans.* To rivet again. Hence **re-'riveted** *ppl. a.*
1869 SIR E. J. REED *Shipbuild.* i. 11 A stream of water was then thrown upon the re-riveted parts. **1898** *Daily News* 20 Aug. 7/2 It will be necessary to re-rivet at least twelve feet of the plating.

re'robe, *v.* [RE- 5 c.] *trans.* To dress in a fresh robe; to clothe in a robe again. So **re'robing** *vbl. sb.*
1849 C. BRONTË *Shirley* II. v. 126 She immediately took the book from her and, with her own hands, commenced the business of disrobing and rerobing her. **1934** DYLAN THOMAS *18 Poems* 32 Second Rise of the skeleton and Re-robing of the naked ghost.

re-'roll, *v.* [RE- 5 a.] *trans.* To roll again. Hence **re-'roller,** one who or that which rolls iron or steel again; **re-'rolled** *ppl. a.*
1846 GREENER *Sci. Gunnery* 125 The frequent welding and re-rolling of iron is of the most beneficial tendency. **1868** *Q. Rev.* July 299 About 250,000 tons [of rails] require to be taken up, re-rolled, and re-laid. **1891** *Pall Mall G.* 29 May 6/2 The gelatine strip is unrolled from one spindle and re-rolled upon another. **1931** *Times* 16 Mar. 19/7 The re-rollers are feeling the pinch. **1955** *Times* 14 July 15/3 Difficulties were experienced due to the national shortage of re-rolled steel products. **1963** *Punch* 13 Feb. 242/1 It is one of the largest 're-rollers' in the industry. **1967** KARCH &

BUBER *Offset Processes* viii. 357 Reroll the screens and reassemble them on the pump. **1976** *Woman's Day* (N.Y.) Nov. p. H/1 On lightly floured surface roll out each half 3/16 inch thick. Cut in 3-inch squares (reroll scraps).

re-'romanize, *v.* [RE- 5 a.] To make Roman-Catholic again. So **re-romani'zation.**
1606 SYLVESTER *Du Bartas* II. iv. *Tropheis* 163 Re-Romaniz'd, so (say they) Heav'n [he] conjures; His errours at Saint Denis hee abjures. **1882-3** SCHAFF *Encycl. Relig. Knowl.* I. 307/1 Immediately after the battle of Mühlberg Ferdinand I sent the Jesuits into Bohemia to re-romanize the country. *Ibid.*, Ferdinand II..now carried through what his ancestor, Ferdinand I, had only attempted,—the re-romanization of Bohemia.

re-'roof, *v.* [RE- 5 a.] To furnish with a new roof.
1867 A. BARRY *Sir C. Barry* viii. 280 To re-roof and re-light them. **1875** ALEX. SMITH *Aberdeenshire* II. 1155 The church was repaired and reroofed in 1829.

re-'route, *v.* [RE- 5 a.] *trans.* To set upon a new route; to re-direct. Also *fig.* So **re-'rout(e)ing** *vbl. sb.*
1929 *Daily Express* 5 Jan. 2/1 Post Office officials..said that it was the first move in a general 're-routing' of mails. **1936** J. STEINBECK *In Dubious Battle* xiii. 203 The police stood, re-routing the traffic. **1961** 'E. LATHEN' *Banking on Death* xi. 94 Arthur was on a Chicago-Boston flight which was rerouted to Washington because of the blizzard. **1971** *Daily Tel.* 21 Oct. 14/5 A council is to spend £250 on re-routeing a drainpipe to save an asparagus bed. **1978** S. HERZEL in P. Moore *Man, Woman, & Priesthood* viii. 108 Any real understanding of sexuality and spirituality must be re-routed through a new awareness of the metaphoric and personal character of language itself.

re-'row, *v.* [RE- 5 a.] *trans.* To row (a race) again. Also *absol.* Hence **'re-row** *sb.*
1892 *Pall Mall Gaz.* 13 June 3/2 The C.U.B.C. had the race re-rowed this morning. **1901** *Daily Chron.* 19 July 8/3 Kingston and London were ordered to re-row. *Ibid.* 12 Aug. 8/2 After a foul and a re-row the Senior Pairs fell to H. U. Gould and C. M. Steele. **1979** *Oxford Mail* 31 May 16/8 Division II (6–10): Subject to rerow 11.45 today.

†**rert.** *Obs. rare*$^{-1}$. (Origin and meaning obscure: perhaps an error for *cert*, certain, sure.)
13.. *E.E. Allit. P.* A. 590 Goddez ryȝt is redy & euer more rert, Oþer holy wryt is bot a fable.

re-'rubber, *v.* [RE- 5 c.] *trans.* To provide (a tyre) with a fresh covering of rubber. So **re-'rubbering** *vbl. sb.*
1908 *Westm. Gaz.* 2 June 4/2 At the end of three months ..the first set are sent to be re-rubbered... Re-rubbering [costs] £30. **1923** *Daily Mail* 16 Feb. 5 (Advt.), Tyre re-rubbering and general Tyre repairs. **1973** *Times* 28 Apr. 4/2 A wornout tyre that has been rerubbered with a new tread.

re-'ruminate, *v.* [RE- 5 a.] *trans.* To ruminate again.
1591 HORSEY *Trav.* (Hakl. Soc.) 213 When you [? *read* we] meet in Polland we shall reruminat our aquaintaince merily. **1617** COLLINS *Def. Bp. Ely* II. x. 531 Thus does he ruminate and re-ruminate his cud againe.

re-'run, *v.* [RE- 5 a.] To run (*over*) again; *spec.* to show (a motion picture) again (also *fig.*); to subject again to an experimental or computational procedure.
1804 LARWOOD *No Gun Boats* 8 We must re-run the gantelope of our Bounties and Recruitings. **1859** DARWIN in *Life & Lett.* (1887) II. 170, I request you, after you have finished, just to re-run over the heads. **1962** 'D. SHANNON' *Extra Kill* vii. 103 There was a picture Fox made... Last week I saw it's being rerun at a neighborhood house. **1967** E. CHAMBERS *Photolitho-Offset* XV. 239 The product cannot be re-run through the machine. **1971** J. B. CARROLL et al. *Word Frequency Bk.* p. xxxvii, The discrepancy was caused by technical problems in making final corrections..in the computer tape... Discrepancies in individual subject categories were so small..that it was not considered worthwhile to rerun the distributions. **1973** *Sci. Amer.* Dec. 45/2 Our entire simulation of the Antennae (with $n = 350$) could be rerun in less than five minutes on any fast modern computer. **1976** M. MAGUIRE *Scratchproof* viii. 115 Re-run it... Slow down the projection speed. **1976** E. MACLAREN *Nature of Belief* ii. 16 You can't re-run a piece of history with different variables the way you can repeat a chemistry experiment without the chlorine. **1977** *Virology* LXXVIII. 207/2 The DNA isolated by this procedure was then rerun in a CsCl density gradient.
Hence **re-run** *ppl. a.*
1929 *Amer. Speech* IV. 386 The term *smoke* is comparatively new..and means an inferior grade of whitish, cloudy alcohol, usually *re-run alky* at that. **1968** A. DIMENT *Gt. Spy Race* vii. 94 The excuses running through their minds like re-run television shows.

re-run, *sb.* [f. the vb.] **1.** A repeat showing of a motion picture; also, the film itself; also *transf.*, of broadcast or printed material. Also *fig.*
1934 in WEBSTER. **1955** *Times* 28 July 9/7 Film costs rather more than 'live' television, but it has a great advantage for re-run purposes. **1965** *Times Lit. Suppl.* 25 Nov. 1070/4 Re-runs of old silent films. **1968** *Guardian* 22 Mar. 10/6 *Around the World in 80 Days* starts a rerun in 70 millimetre at the Coliseum Cinerama Theatre. **1968** P. MARLOWE *Hire me a Hearse* ix. 137 It didn't take very long for Hazard to run the spools through again. In the rerun some of it sounded repetitious. **1971** *Wall St. Jrnl.* 22 July 1/5 Liberty magazine, which was around from 1924 until 1950, makes a comeback with reruns of its old articles. **1978** G. VIDAL *Kalki* vi. 151 On the wall opposite the window a row of TV monitors showed us..a rerun of *I love Lucy.* **1979** *Dædalus* Summer 15 The current quarrel..is just the latest rerun of that earlier script.

2. The repeated performance of a computation or computer program. Usu. *attrib.*
1946 J. B. CONANT *Man. Operation Automatic Sequence Controlled Calculator* ii. 50 Starting, stopping and rerun instructions. **1958** [see GENERATOR 4 c]. **1980** R. LONGBOTTOM *Computer Syst. Reliability* vii. 105 A further category of rerun time is incurred when it is found that previously created files have been lost... The time to restore files is again application dependent.

3. A repeated occurrence or attempt.
1976 H. WILSON *Governance of Britain* iii. 65 A tendency developed in the 1960s for a defeated minister almost automatically to seek for a re-run at Cabinet. **1977** *Daily Tel.* 17 Mar. 1/1 The Left-wing appeared to be in no mood to have a re-run of last year's rebellion, when the Government was defeated by 28 votes.

res[1] (reɪz). Pl. res. [L., = thing.] **1.** orig. in *Law* (see quots. 1851, 1854); hence *gen.*, the condition of something; the matter in hand, the point at issue, the crux.
[**1684** G. MACKENZIE *Institutions Law of Scotland* I. ii. 10, I do resolve, first, to lay down what concerns the Persons of whom the *Law* treats: *Secundo*, what concerns the things themselves treated of, such as rights, obligations &c. *Tertio*, the actions whereby these rights are pursued, which answers to the Civilians, *objecta juris, viz. Personae, res, & Actiones.*] **1851** P. COLQUHOUN *Summary Roman Civil Law* II. 1 *Res*.. is used in contradistinction to *persona*... In another and more restricted sense it signifies those objects of rights which are neither *personae, actiones*, nor *facta*. **1854** P. CUMIN *Man. Civil Law* 59 *Q.* Define *Res*. *A.* All physical and metaphysical existences, in which persons may claim a right. **1923** *Law Rep. King's Bench Div.* II. 439 If the res —the thing actually and directly in dispute—has been already adjudicated upon, of course by a competent Court, it cannot be litigated again. **1947** WODEHOUSE *Full Moon* vi. 126 Do you mind if we get back to the *res*. Time presses. **1949** W. STEVENS in *Trans. Connecticut Acad. Arts & Sci.* Dec. 166 The poem is the cry of its occasion, Part of the res itself and not about it. **1966** WODEHOUSE *Plum Pie* i. 23, I saw that I had better come to the *res* without delay.

2. Used in a number of Latin (*esp.* legal and philos.) phrases, as: **res 'cogitans** *Philos.*, the concept of man as that of a thinking being.
[**1641** DESCARTES *Meditationes* ii. 23 Sed quid igitur sum? res cogitans: quid est hoc? nempe dubitans, intelligens, affirmans, negans, volens, nolens, imaginans quoque, & sentiens.] **1904** J. IVERACH *Descartes, Spinoza & New Philos.* iii. 63 It is not possible to take the mind as a thing among other things; a mere *res cogitans* can apprehend nothing but thoughts or ideas. **1962** M. MCLUHAN *Gutenberg Galaxy* 247 The mental *res cogitans* and the material *res extensa*. **1972** Z. VENDLER (*title*) Res cogitans: an essay in rational psychology.
res co'mmunis *Law*, common property; something incapable of appropriation.
[*a* **1259** BRACTON *De Legibus* (Rolls Ser., 1878) I. 54 Extra patrimonio autem dicuntur res sacræ, et religiosæ, et communes.] **1704** T. WOOD *New Institute Imperial or Civil Law* II. i. 65 *Res communes* are those in which no Person has a Property, neither can any one be Master of them, or deprive others of the use of them. **1854** P. CUMIN *Man. Civil Law* 65 *Q.* When an island rises in the Sea, who is proprietor?.. *A.* The first occupier: until occupation, no one, it is a *res communis*. **1923** W. S. HOLDSWORTH *Hist. Eng. Law* (rev. ed.) II. III. iii. 273 He [*sc.* Bracton] then discourses upon..res publicæ and res communes. In his treatment of the latter topic there are traces that he had read Azo hastily. **1970** *Internat. & Compar. Law Q.* XIX. 237 It has been suggested that Antarctica has, in fact, become *res communis*.
res ex'tensa *Philos.*, a material thing considered as extended substance.
1940 *Philos. & Phenomenol. Res.* I. 181 This cosmos of meaning and unmeaning into which man is born, this rich structure of all kinds of relationships, is levelled down to the status of *res extensa*. **1962** [see *res cogitans*].
res 'gestæ, (an account of) things done, achievements; an account of a person's career; events in the past; in *Law*, the facts of a case, used esp. with reference to evidence that includes spoken words; also in *sing.* **res gesta.**
1616 G. CAREW *Let.* 24 Jan. (1860) 27 In this gazette you may not expect any more than *res gestae*. **1696** W. NICOLSON *Eng. Historical Libr.* I. 213 The like Scruples I have upon me as to some other *Res Gestæ* of this King, which are said to have been written by Robert Bale, sometime Recorder of London. **1794** *Trial of J. H. Tooke* in *T. B. Howell's State Trials* (1818) XXV. 440 That letter your lordships have received, and, I believe, without any objection from this side of the table, probably upon the ground, that as it is an answer to an act which is charged against the prisoner, it is fit to be received as part of the *res gesta* upon the subject. **1815** S. M. PHILLIPPS *Treat. Law of Evidence* I. vii. 202 Hearsay is often admitted in evidence, as part of the *res gestae*; the meaning of which seems to be, that where it is necessary, in the course of a cause, to inquire into the nature of a particular act and the intention of the person who did the act, proof of what the person said at the time of doing it is admissible evidence, for the purpose of shewing its true character. **1930** BURROWS & CAHN *S. L. Phipson's Law of Evidence* vi. 54 Acts, declarations, and incidents which constitute, or accompany and explain, the fact or transaction in issue, are admissible, for or against either party, as forming parts of the *res gesta*. **1936** *Mind* XLV. 518 Signor Gentile..roundly denies any distinction between *res gestae* and *historia rerum gestarum*, maintaining that all history is contemporary history. **1951** S. F. NADEL *Foundations Social Anthropol.* i. 14 Events in the past, which, being as it were closed chapters, *res gestae*, and having had their particular consequences, exemplify more typically the just-so happenings which limit our search for regularities. **1959** A. G. WOODHEAD *Study of Greek Inscriptions* 56 Cross-references concerning offices held or *res gestae* in general. **1969** *N. Dakota Law Rev.* Winter 208 Children talk best in their native habitat. What they say when pressures of emotion and strangeness are absent is more apt to be true, somewhat analogous to *res gestae*.
res 'integra *Law* (see quot. 1959); also *transf.*
1754 in F. Vesey *Reports* (1814) I. 11, I confess, if this had been *res integra*, I should doubt, whether the testator's declaration is a proper execution within the fifth clause.. but I find myself bound by such a number of former precedents, that I must give way to their superior weight. **1760** G. GILBERT *Cases in Law & Equity* 250 And if the Matter had been *res integra* and undetermined, he should have held it ill if it had been brought by the other Name. **1834** J. RAM *Science of Legal Judgment* xiv. 126 If the matter were entire.., *res integra*, a new case or point.., it might admit of difficulty. *a* **1873** MILL *Three Ess. Relig.* (1874) 203 The question whether it is so or not is *res integra*, untouched by any of the results of human knowledge and experience. **1959** JOWITT *Dict. Eng. Law* II. 1533/2 *Res integra*, a point governed neither by any decision nor by any rule of law, which must therefore be decided upon principle. **1961** *Times* 15 Feb. 15/3 If the matter were *res integra*, his Lordship saw great force that in 1843 the words 'voluntary contribution' would be understood as intended to cover an annual subscription.
res 'ipsa 'loquitur *Law*, a principle that the proven occurrence of an accident implies the negligence of the defendant unless he provides another cause; also *transf.* and *attrib.*
1659 H. GRIMSTON tr. *Croke's Reports King James* 508 It is apparent, that the money was lent for Interest, and is more than the Statute permits; Wherefore being usury apparent, the Court shall adjudg it accordingly: And..if the corrupt agreement be not expressed in the verdict, and the matter is apparent to the Court to be usury, there the Jury needs not to shew that it was corruptly, for *res ipsa loquitur*. **1864** in Hurlstone & Coltman *Exchequer Reports* II. 725 There are certain cases of which it may be said res ipsa loquitur, and this seems one of them. **1872** *Wharton's Law-Lexicon* (ed. 5) 846/1 *Res ipsa loquitur* (the thing speaks for itself), a phrase used in actions for injury by negligence where no proof of negligence is required beyond the accident itself, which is such as necessarily to involve negligence. **1908** *Times Law Rep.* XXIV. 551/2 *Res ipsa loquitur* does not mean, as I understand it, that merely because at the end of a journey a horse is found hurt, or somebody is hurt in the streets, the mere fact that he is hurt implies negligence. **1927** LD. HEWART in A. P. Herbert *Misleading Cases* p. v, '*Res ipsa loquitur*', as the man in the street said when a sack of flour, in the best manner of the attic declension, fell upon him from an upper room. **1954** *Cambr. Law Jrnl.* Apr. 132 In *Ybarra* v. *Spangard*..the Californian District Court of Appeal held that the plaintiff might sue all the defendants and recover a joint judgment in a *res ipsa loquitur* situation. **1965** *Mod. Law Rev.* XXVIII. v. 623 When a textbook attains an eighteenth edition surely the maxim *res ipsa loquitur* could hardly boast a better exemplification. **1973** *N.Y. Law Jrnl.* 19 July 12/3 At the new trial plaintiff shall be permitted to produce an expert to establish a case under the doctrine of res ipsa loquitur.
res judi'cata *Law*, a matter that has been adjudicated by a competent court.
[*a* **1259** BRACTON *De Legibus* (Rolls Ser., 1881) IV. 266 Item cadit assisa, si petens petat per assisam quod per judicium amisit, quia cadit assisa propter exceptionem rei judicatæ, & agat si voluerit de falso judicio.] **1693** LD. STAIR *Inst. Law Scot.* (ed. 2) IV. xl. 675 *Res Judicata* is Relevant, not only being a Decreet between the Pursuer and the Defender; But it is sufficient, if it was between their Predecessors or Authors. **1867** *Wharton's Law-Lexicon* (ed. 4) 830/1 *Res judicata*, a point decided by authority. **1927** C. K. ALLEN *Law in Making* iii. 109 It was a commonplace with the Orators, and especially with Cicero, that the *res iudicata*, or *iudicatum*, was an integral part of the civil law. **1955** *Times* 14 July 11/3 All too often he spoke of *res judicatae* as if they were mere *obiter dicta*. **1972** *Mod. Law Rev.* XXXV. i. 96 The husband's solicitor maintained that the issue of cruelty was *res judicata*.
res non 'verba, 'things not words'; material fact or concrete action as opposed to mere talk.
1949 E. POUND *Pisan Cantos* lxxxii. 116 And for all that old Ford's conversation was better, Consisting in *res* non *verba*. **1961** *Times* 26 Apr. 20/2 The strapping muleteer who saves every situation by his guiding principle of *res non verba*.
res 'nullius *Law*, no one's property; strictly, a thing or things that can belong to no one.
[*a* **1259** BRACTON *De Legibus* (Rolls Ser., 1878) I. 60 Res quidem nullius esse dicuntur pluribus modis, natura sive jure naturali, ut feræ bestiæ, volucres, et pisces... Item tempore dicunter res in nullius bonis esse, ut thesaurus.] **1704** T. WOOD *New Inst. Imperial or Civil Law* II. i. 67 *Res nullius* (or things which are not the Goods of any Person or number of Men) are those that are of a *divine* Right. **1833** J. S. MILL in *Jurist* IV. 24 It matters not that the property has now become *res nullius*, and is therefore, properly speaking, our own. **1951** F. SCHULZ *Classical Roman Law* IV. i. 361 Wild animals (game, fishes, birds) were *res nullius* as long as they enjoyed their natural freedom. **1977** *Times Lit. Suppl.* 28 Jan. 110/2 To the South African government, South West Africa had fallen into a state of *res nullius*, and sovereignty was acquired by virtue of her occupation.

res[2] (rɛz). Abbrev. of RESIDENCE *sb.*[1]
1882 W. WHITMAN *Daybks. & Notebks.* (1978) II. 288 Sam Long 614 Sansom St—res: 3210 Race. **1972** *Guardian* 17 Feb. 11/1 Her own little bijou res in Chelsea. **1972** J. GORES *Dead Skip* x. 68 I've got a res add on Hemovich 5-0-7 Nevada Street.

res, variant of RESE *sb.*

re'saddle (riː-), *v.* [RE- 5 a.] To saddle again.
1856 V. LUSH *Jrnl.* 17 Jan. (1971) 174 Giving them strict injunctions to take care of Rollo I left them to resaddle. **1857** DUFFERIN *Lett. High Lat.* (ed. 3) 50 The horses were resaddled; and..we took leave of our courteous entertainers. **1897** *Harper's Mag.* Apr. 754/2 Diaz..stood off the attack till his cavalry could resaddle.

resaf, obs. Sc. form of RECEIVE *v.*

resagar, -gor: see RESALGAR.

resai(ee, variants of REZAI.

resaif(f, obs. forms of RECEIVE *v.*

re'sail (riː-), *v.* [RE- 5 a.]

1. *intr.* To sail (back) again; to set sail again.
1586 WARNER *Alb. Eng.* III. xvi, The Dane inraged sayled thence.., And did with Brenn, resayling home, at great aduantage meete. **1725** POPE *Odyss.* IV. 931 From Pyle resailing and the Spartan Court. **1780** FAWKES & MEEN *Rhodius' Argonautics* IV. 1565 Discharge this duty, and resail to Greece. **1898** *Daily News* 25 Oct. 6/2 The San Nicholas resailed, followed by the American cruiser.

2. *trans.* To sail (a race) again.
1895 *Daily News* 16 Sept. 3/3 We beg to state.. the reason why the last two races were not ordered to be resailed.

'resail, *sb.* [f. the vb.] A race sailed again.
1947 *Sun* (Baltimore) 8 Sept. 14/6 In the resail, sailed Saturday, the breeze barely let the racers finish within the time limit. **1970** *Cape Times* 28 Oct. 25/8 Experience has shown that resails of cancelled races are not always successful.

†**resaille**. *Obs. rare*⁻¹. (Meaning obscure.)
c **1450** LYDG. & BURGH *Secrees* 2279 [A counsellor ought] Off thyn Rentys knowyn the Resaylle.

resaitter, obs. Sc. form of RESETTER.

resaive, obs. form of RECEIVE *v.*

re'salable (riː-), *a.* [RE- 5 a.] Capable of being resold.
1866 A. L. PERRY *Elem. Pol. Econ.* (1873) 85 Personal services, unlike material products, are not commonly resalable by the purchaser.

resale (riː'seɪl, 'riːseɪl), *sb.* [RE- 5 a. Cf. RESELL *v.*] **1.** The act of selling again (something bought).
1625 BACON *Ess., Riches* (Arb.) 239 Monopolies, and Coemption of Wares for Resale..are great Meanes to enrich. **1816** M. GREENLEAF *District of Maine* 71 The remainder [is held] by different individuals, who have purchased solely with a view to the profit of resales. **1852** GROTE *Greece* II. lxxiii. IX. 365 It was difficult to keep.. what was bought and opportunity for resale did not seem at hand. **1890** GROSS *Gild Merch.* I. 46 This enactment is particularly directed against buying for re-sale.

2. *attrib.* **a. resale price**, the price at which a commodity is sold again; **resale price maintenance**, the determination by a manufacturer of a minimum price at which his goods may be sold to the consumer or ultimate user.
1919 C. T. MURCHISON *Resale Price Maintenance* x. 159 The rights of a patentee, by conditions of sale, to control the use of his article even after it has passed from him and is in the hands of the vendee, is..unqualifiedly upheld and the *dicta* of the Court are certainly not hostile to the idea of resale price maintenance. **1929** *Congress. Rec.* LXX. 2431 A communication from the chairman of the Federal Trade Commission, transmitting a report of that commission on Resale Price Maintenance. **1936** *Publishers' Weekly* 12 Dec. 2298/2 Compare report of the Federal Trade Commission on resale price maintenance, 70th Cong. 2d Sess. H. Doc. No. 546. **1940** *Economist* 14 Sept. 332/1 Most newspapers were generally in favour of resale-price agreements with boycotting clauses. **1945** *Economica* XII. 228 The trading stamp is primarily the product of resale price maintenance. **1967** *Listener* 27 July 104/3 Price-cutting of chocolate and sweets begins following abolition of resale price maintenance. **1973** *Guardian* 1 June 12/1 Mr Heath..made his reputation at the Board of Trade partly on the abolition of resale price maintenance.

b. In sense 'second-hand'.
1960 *Farmer & Stockbreeder* 29 Mar. (Suppl.) 13/2 Every one of your surplus jute sacks has a good re-sale value. **1967** *Boston Sunday Herald* 26 Mar. I. 38/8 The offices opposite Fisherman's Beach, Swampscott, will specialize in both new and resale homes. **1970** *Globe & Mail* (Toronto) 26 Sept. B2/3 The supply of money is good for conventional mortgages on resale houses. **1975** M. BRADBURY *History Man* iii. 40 It's a very sound residential area.., you'd keep your resale value. **1977** *New Yorker* 24 Oct. 39/2 I'm conducting here a gents' resale business. *Ibid.* 40/3 You were in a gentlemen's resale shop.

†**re'salgar**. *Obs.* Also 4–5 reys-, rysalgar; 5 rys-, rosalgere; 5 ras-, 7 resalger; 6 resagar, -gor. [ad. Arab. *rahj al-ghār* (see REALGAR), the *j* being represented by *s*, as in It. *risigallo*, med.L. *risigallum*, *resegale*. The form *rosalger* appears later as *rosager* ROSAKER.] Realgar, disulphide of arsenic.
c **1386** CHAUCER *Can. Yeom. Prol. & T.* 261 Oile of Tartre, Alum glas, berme worth, and argoille, Resalgar, and oure matires enbibyng. [Thynne's ed. *resagor*; hence in R. Scot *Disc. Witchcr.* (1584) XIV. i. 354; also in Lyly *Galathea* (1585) II. iii. as *resagar*.] **14..** *Stockholm Med. MS.* II. 559 in *Anglia* XVIII. 321 Hys jows, medelyd with rosalgere.. wyll ben howndys bane. **14..** in Ashm. *Theat. Chem. Brit.* (1652) 271 Alume, Atriment, alle I suspende, Resalgar and Arsnick I defende. [**1584–5**, see above.] **1607** TOPSELL *Four-f. Beasts* (1658) 327 Then it is good to eat out the core with the powder of Resalgar. **1610** MARKHAM *Masterp.* II. vi. 228 You shall neuer apply..Resalger, Arsnicke, Mercury sublimate, nor any such violent corrosiue.

re'salient (riː-), *a. rare*⁻¹. [RE- 5 a.] Of angles: Issuing again after re-entering.
1879 SCOTT *Lect. Archit.* II. 142 This..suggests the idea ..of reducing the lower range to a smaller width, thus breaking the arch section into resalient angles.

re'salt (riː-), *v.* [RE- 5 a.] To salt again.
1850 O. WINSLOW *Inner Life* iv. 134 Jesus speaks of the salt being re-salted. **1895** *Daily News* 5 June 5/5 The heads were in bad condition..and were re-salted.

†**resalue**, *v. Obs. rare*⁻¹. [a. F. *resaluer*: see RE- and SALUE *v.*] *trans.* To resalute.
1481 CAXTON *Godfroy* cxix. 180 Emyrferius put out his heed & salewed them, & they resalewed hym.

†**resalu'tation**. *Obs. rare.* [ad. L. *resalūtātiōn-em*: see next and -ATION.] The return of a salutation.
1548 ELYOT, *Resalutatio*.., a resalutacion. **1603** HOLLAND *Plutarch's Mor.* 437 Popilius without any resalutations or greeting againe, delivered him the letter. **1655** tr. *Sorel's Com. Hist. Francion* IV. 24, I did salute them,..and the proud resalutation did come with an ill will from them.

resa'lute (riː-), *v.* Now *rare.* [ad. L. *resalūtāre*, or (in sense 2) f. RE- 5 a + SALUTE *v.*]

1. *trans.* To salute in return.
1493 *Festivall* (W. de W. 1515) 110b, Let us ofte and devoutly say..this salutacyon & we may be sure yᵗ she wyl resalute us agayne. **1581** PETTIE tr. *Guazzo's Civ. Conv.* I. (1586) 13b, If through heedlesnesse you resalute not a friend, he will speake no more to you. **1631** HEYWOOD *Eng. Eliz.* (1641) 164 She was not behind in courtesie, but lovingly resaluted them again. **1697** *State Philadelph. Soc.* 21 The People resalute the Minister with a 'Lord be with thy Spirit'. **1762** *Ann. Reg.* I. 126/1 The knights..made their reverences to his majesty, who..re-saluted them.

2. To salute again or anew.
a **1586** SIDNEY *Arcadia* (1622) 332 Hee felt his breast beat, and thereafter saw his vnclowded eyes weakely striue to shine againe; thus first resaluting the light. **1627** DRAYTON *Agincourt*, etc. 187 Those Birdes we see, that leaue vs in the Prime, Againe in Autumne re-salute our Clime. **1667** MILTON *P.L.* XI. 134 Mean while To re-salute the World with sacred Light Leucothea wak'd.

Hence **resa'luted** *ppl. a.*, **resa'luting** *vbl. sb.*
1598 FLORIO, *Risaluto*, a resaluting or greeting againe. **1615** CHAPMAN *Odyss.* XII. 8 We drew her vp to land, And trod our selues the resaluted sand.

resam (rɛ'sæm). [Malay.] A Malaysian tropical fern, *Gleichenia linearis*, which has creeping rhizomes and leathery pinnate leaves. Also *attrib.*
1902 H. N. RIDLEY *Malay Plant Names* 219 Resam. *Gleichenia linearis*..A common fern. **1939** J. D. GIMLETTE *Dict. Malayan Med.* 200/1 *Rĕsam* leaves are used by Malays in making internal and external medicines for fever. **1964** M. E. D. POORE in Wang Gungwu *Malaysia* I. ii. 51 If the frequency of cultivation increases, the land deteriorates seriously..and forest is replaced by unproductive lallang.. or resam (*Gleichenia* spp.).

†**resanate**, *v. Obs. rare*⁻¹. [f. ppl. stem of late L. *resānāre*, f. *re-* RE- + *sānāre* to heal.] *trans.* To heal again, to cure. So †**resa'nation**.
1597 A. M. tr. *Guillemeau's Fr. Chirurg.* 46b/1 How necessarye these operationes are to the resanation of the disseases. **1599** —— tr. *Gabelhouer's Bk. Physicke* 83/2 This gargarisme is of admirable operatione, and resanatione of the diseases of the throte. *Ibid.* 110/1 For the vngula caballina hath a divers vigor of resanatinge the Lunges.

resanctifi'cation. [RE- 5 a.] A second or further sanctification.
1897 'MARK TWAIN' *Following Equator* xlix. 473 The Fort was built three centuries ago by a Mohammedan Emperor —a resanctification of the place in the interest of *that* religion.

re'sanctify (riː-), *v.* [RE- 5 a.] *trans.* To sanctify again.
1675 WOODHEAD, etc. *Paraphr. St. Paul* 82 All things.. unclean before God, if they are not resanctified in Christ. **1847** BUSHNELL *Chr. Nurt.* viii. (1861) 218 He will reclaim and resanctify the great principle of reproductive order.

†**re'sarce**, *v. Obs. rare*⁻¹. [ad. obs. F. *resarcir* or L. *resarcīre*, f. *re-* RE- + *sarcīre* to patch.] *trans.* To patch up, mend.
1524 *St. Papers Hen. VIII*, VI. 366 That the Kinges Grace studieth not a litle, howe to resarce and supplie on his side al maner of defaultes and errours.

re,sarce'lée, re'sarcelled, *a. Her.* [See SARCELLED *a.*] (See quots.)
1586 FERNE *Blaz. Gentrie* 176 A crosse resarcelled is, as if a crosse were sewed or set againe to the other. **1725** COATS *Dict. Heraldry* 298. **1727** BAILEY (vol. II), *Resarcelee*, as a Cross Resarcelée signifies one Cross, as it were, sewed to another, or one Cross placed upon another, or a slenderer Cross charged upon the first. **1780** EDMONDSON *Compl. Body Heraldry* II. Gloss., *Resarcelée*, a Cross Resarcelée..is a cross voided and open at each end.

†**re'sarciate**, *v. Obs.* Also -tiate. [irreg. f. L. *resarci-re* (see RESARCE) + -ATE.] *trans.* To mend, amend.
a **1656** VINES *Lord's Supp.* (1677) 234 To resarciate the damage or injury done to thee. **1657** TOMLINSON *Renou's Disp.* 57 We resartiate their native humidity.

resat, obs. Sc. pa. pple. of RECEIVE *v.*

resaunt, variant of RESSANT.

resave (riː-), *v. rare*⁻¹. [RE- 5 a.] *trans.* To save again.
1581 RICH *Farew.* (1846) 107 How greate the joye of the mother was when she sawe the honestie of her daughter, (as it were) resaved out of this yong princes handes.

resave, obs. form of RECEIVE *v.*

resaw ('riːsɔː), *sb.* [f. RE- 5 a + SAW *sb.*¹ See also RESAWING *vbl. sb.*] **a.** A machine used for the further cutting of sawn wood. **b.** Wood cut by such a machine. Also *attrib.*
1915 *Saw in History* (Henry Disston & Sons) iii. 36 Boards and thin Cants, or Planks, made by the log saw are run through the Resaws and are manufactured into two or more thin boards. **1958** R. H. HORDERN *Woodworking Machinist* I. i. 7 The band mill to achieve the preliminary breaking-down and squaring, and the band or circular resaw to carry out the final resawing. **1971** *Timber Trades Jrnl.* 21 Aug. 38/1 The first band resaw machine to be installed in the district is a Stenner type VHM 36in. *Ibid.* 11 Sept. 43/1 The new production line was so successful that the additional machines were installed. These are a VHS slab resaw followed by an EDS double edger. **1972** J. MINIFIE *Homesteader* viii. 63 Re-saw is a half-inch board with little to recommend it but ductility and ease of handling.

resawe, obs. Sc. form of RECEIVE *v.*

re'sawing (riː-), *vbl. sb.* [RE- 5 a.] The action of sawing again. Also *attrib.*
1611 FLORIO, *Risegatione*, a resawing, a clipping. **1875** KNIGHT *Dict. Mech.* 1920/1 *Resawing-machine*, a machine for cutting up squared timber into small stuff or boards. **1881** FRANKLYN *Glance at Australia* 369 One of Fay's large re-sawing machines.

resay (riː-), *v. rare*⁻¹. [RE-.] *trans.* To say again or in reply.
1610 MARCELLINE *Triumphs Jas. I* B ij, Heresy findeth daily something to re-say and to confound Paper withall.

resayfe, -sayff, -sayve, etc., obs. ff. RECEIVE.

resayt(e, obs. ff. RECEIPT *sb.*

†**resbon**. *Obs. rare*⁻¹. [Corruptly for *reston*, var. of OF. *raston*: see RASTON and RATTOON¹.] A cheese-cake.
1585 T. DAWSON *Good Huswiues Jewell* I. (1596) E4 To make good Resbones. Take a quart of fine flower [etc.].

rescaille, obs. form of RASCAL.

rescaive, obs. form of RECEIVE *v.*

†**rescat**. *Obs. rare*⁻¹. [a. Sp. *rescate*: cf. REESCATE *v.*] Ransom.
1588 T. HICKOCK tr. *C. Frederick's Voy.* 11b, Euery day we were taken prisoners,..and euery morning at our departure we must pay rescat 4. or 5. Pagies a man.

rescayve, obs. f. RECEIVE *v.*

resceant, -sceaunte, varr. of RESIANT *Obs.*

resceipte, -ceit(e, obs. ff. RECEIPT *sb.*

resceive, obs. f. RECEIVE *v.*

rescent, obs. f. RESENT *v.*

rescet, -cett(e, obs. ff. RESET *sb.* and *v.*

resceve, obs. f. RECEIVE *v.*

rescew, obs. f. RESCUE.

resceyt(e, obs. ff. RECEIPT *sb.*

resceyve, -schave, -schayfe, obs. ff. RECEIVE *v.*

resche, obs. f. RUSH.

reschebusk, obs. f. RUSHBUSH.

re'schedule, *v.* [RE- 5 a.] *trans.* To replan in accordance with a different timetable; to change the time of (a planned event or activity); *spec.* to arrange a new scheme of repayments of (an international debt).
1966 A. BATTERSBY *Math. in Managem.* viii. 198 It can be ..used to prepare an amended input for re-scheduling the product launch. **1968** *Economist* 17 Feb. 40/1 Requests to reschedule the country's debts for just one more year. **1970** *Daily Tel.* 14 Apr. 5/6 Fords will try to avoid lay-offs by re-scheduling production. **1973** *Times* 14 Dec. 4/5 Programmes will have to be rescheduled, and both ITV and BBC were working on that yesterday. **1977** P. WAY *Super-Celeste* 18 We may be rescheduling the flight. **1978** *N.Y. Times* 30 Mar. A3/3 The United States was prepared to.. reschedule outstanding loans to developing countries. **1980** *Daily Tel.* 3 Sept. 19 The task of rescheduling the Brazilian debt will present international banks with their biggest challenge yet.

Hence **re'scheduled** *ppl. a.*, **re'scheduling** *vbl. sb.*
1968 S. E. VARNER *Rescheduled School Year* 6 One plan for a rescheduled school year—the all-year school or rotating four-quarter plan—has been discussed. **1973** 'D. JORDAN' *Nile Green* iv. 23 There's this debt rescheduling problem still unsolved... But..we could talk with the [World] Bank and do a joint deal. **1976** P. R. WHITE *Planning for Public Transport* vii. 145 By slight rescheduling of existing runs, a fairly fast direct journey can be provided from the larger village(s)..into the market town.

†**reschette**, *v. Obs. rare.* [OE. *ræscętan*, f. *ræscan* vb. or *ræsc* sb. (in comb. *líȝ-ræsc*).] *intr.* To crackle.

a **1000** *Gloss.* in *Wr.-Wülcker* 215/16 *Crepitat*, *i. resonat*, scylþ, cyrmþ, ræscetteþ. *a* **1000** *Be Domes Dæȝe* 152 Đonne fyren liȝ blawað and braslað,.. ræsct and efesteð. *Ibid.* 165 Đæt reðe flod ræscet fyre. *c* **1200** *Marherete* 18 The hude.. swartete as hit snarchte and barst on to blemen that hit aras up oueral ant here leofliche lich reschte of þe leie.

reschew, obs. f. RESCUE *sb.*

rescheyve, obs. f. RECEIVE *v.*

reschowe, obs. f. RESCUE *v.*

†**re'scide**, *v. Obs. rare.* [irreg. var. of next, or for *recide*, ad. L. *recīdĕre*.] *trans.* To cut.

1597 A. M. tr. *Guillemeau's Fr. Chirurg.* 54/2 The sagittalle suture was rescided cleane overthwarte. *Ibid.* 54 b/1 His Parietale was clean rescided throughe.

rescind (rɪ'sɪnd), *v.* [ad. L. *rescind-ĕre*, f. *re-* RE- + *scindĕre* to split, divide, etc. Cf. F. *rescinder* (1422).]

1. *trans.* To cut off, take away, remove. (In *fig.* uses.) †Also ***rescinding***, taking away, leaving out.

1643 PRYNNE *Sov. Power Parl.* App. 168 His unnecessary expences are rescinded, his superfluous cut off. **1664** H. MORE *Myst. Iniq.* xvi. 58 The introduction thereof into the Church of Christ is the rescinding so many Souls from the body of the Church. *a* **1687** PETTY *Pol. Arith.* iv. (1691) 69 England it self rescinding Wales, hath but Three Acres to every Head, according to the present State of Tillage and Husbandry. *a* **1734** NORTH *Lives* (1826) I. 376 It proved that which they call an hemiplegia, which rescinded the chief use of one leg and one arm. **1788** V. KNOX *Winter Even.* III. IX. ix. 280 He who resolves not to be entertained.. will rescind a copious source of soothing satisfaction. **1812** WOODHOUSE *Astron.* xxxiii. 315 In order.. to rescind the occasion of ambiguity which might be attached to the phrase of constant parallax.

†**b.** To deprive (one) *of* a thing. *Obs. rare*$^{-1}$.

1718 *Entertainer* No. 42. 297 He that dares not speak like an Englishman.. deserves to be rescinded of his Birthright.

†**2.** To cut through, sever. *Obs. rare*$^{-1}$.

1651-3 JER. TAYLOR *Serm. for Year* (1678) 224 To rescind the fatal chain, and break in sunder the line of God's anger.

3. To abrogate, annul, revoke, repeal, cancel.

1637-50 ROW *Hist. Kirk* (Wodrow Soc.) 492 He answered, He could grant neither the one nor the other till first they should rescinde.. their subscryved Covenants. **1690** LUTTRELL *Brief Rel.* (1857) II. 38 The parliament.. past an act for rescinding the kings supremacy over the church. **1776** ADAM SMITH *W.N.* I. x. (1869) I. 126 It required a particular Act of Parliament to rescind this bye-law. **1818** HALLAM *Mid. Ages* (1872) I. 461 The council of ten had.. power over the senate and other magistrates, rescinding their decisions. **1846** BATEMAN *Law of Auctions* (ed. 3) 91 *note*, The vendor shall have the power of rescinding the contract. **1877** FREEMAN *Norm. Conq.* (ed. 3) II. App. 594 The monks petitioned, and the vote was rescinded.

Hence **re'scinder**; **re'scinding** *ppl. a.* Also **re'scindable** *a.*, **re'scindment** (Worcester, 1846, citing Story).

1876 BANCROFT *Hist. U.S.* IV. xli. 161 Of the ninety-two who voted not to rescind, eighty-one.. were re-elected; of the seventeen rescinders, only five. **1887** *Pall Mall G.* 9 Nov. 14/2 The rule that a rescinding resolution requires a majority of two-thirds.

†**re'scindent**, *a. Obs. rare.* [f. pres. pple. of L. *rescindĕre*: see prec.] Cutting.

1597 A. M. tr. *Guillemeau's Fr. Chirurg.* lf. xiv b/2 A rescindente Instrumente, the one end wherof serveth for a rasore. **1772** NUGENT tr. *Hist. Fr. Gerund* I. 532 And taught man the manuduction of the rescindent spade.

rescission (rɪ'sɪʒən). Also 7 **rescision**. [ad. late L. *rescissiōn-em*, n. of action f. *rescindĕre* to RESCIND. Cf. F. *rescision* (1517).]

†**1.** The action of cutting off. *Obs. rare.*

1611 COTGR., *Recision*, a rescission; a cutting, or paring off. *a* **1626** BACON *Holy War* (1629) 124 The words of the Prophet.. which declare this Reiection, and, to vse the words of the Text, Rescision of their Estate to haue been for their Idolatry.

2. The action of annulling or abrogating.

1651 JER. TAYLOR *Serm. for Year* I. iv. 43 No ceremonial and pompous rescission of our Fathers' crimes can be sufficient. **1695** H. DODWELL *Def. Vind. Deprived Bps.* 97 This therefore would allow the Church.. a perfect rescission of such a Contract. **1727-38** CHAMBERS *Cycl.* s.v., A thing's being found damaged, or sold at above double the just value, is a good cause of rescission. **1776** JOHNSON *Let. to Taylor* 17 Feb., The Case which you sent me contains such vicissitudes of settlement and rescission. **1844** H. H. WILSON *Brit. India* I. 281 Several.. counselled the rescission of the obnoxious orders. **1875** POSTE *Gaius* I. (ed. 2) 142 A power of cancellation and rescission. **1931** *Daily Express* 16 Oct. 14/6 Rumours regarding bond interest, caused a sharp rise.. in the Four per Cent. Rescission issues. **1964** *Mod. Law Rev.* XXVIII. III. 269 Keeping the contract alive for as long as the employers would tolerate the breach without exercising their right of rescission. **1976** *Evening News* (Newburgh, N.Y.) 12 Sept. 12A/1 The rescission of funds in no way affects the proposed federal prison.

†**resci'ssorian**, *a. Obs.*$^{-0}$ [-AN.] = next.

1658 PHILLIPS s.v. *Rescind*, A Rescissorian Act, is that which makes void a former Act, or Law.

rescissory (rɪ'sɪsərɪ), *a.* Also 7 rec-. [ad. late L. *rescissōri-us*, f. *resciss-*, ppl. stem of *rescindĕre* to RESCIND. Cf. F. *rescisoire* (1579).]

1. Of the nature of, or having the effect of, rescinding or revoking; connected with, or characterized by, rescission:

a. of legal actions, etc. (Chiefly *Sc. Law.*)

'Rescissory actions are those actions whereby deeds, &c. are declared void' (Bell).

1605 DANIEL *Queen's Arcadia* III. i, I ouerwhelme My practise too, with darknes, and strange words;.. Conditions, Codicilles, Acceptilations, actions recissorie. **1754** ERSKINE *Princ. Sc. Law* (1809) 442 Rescissory actions are divided, 1. Into actions of proper improbation. 2. Actions of reduction-improbation. **1818** COLEBROOKE *Obligations* I. 222 Every person who apprehends himself hurt or affected by a deed is entitled to a rescissory action for setting it aside. **1838** W. BELL *Dict. Law Scot.* 829 The action of simple reduction and the action of reduction-improbation, are the two varieties of the rescissory actions of the law of Scotland. *Ibid.*, In the simple reduction the summons, like all rescissory summonses, commences with the Will. **1846** BATEMAN *Law of Auctions* (ed. 3) 65 The first of this class of conditions is called rescissory; the second compensatory.

b. of legislative measures, etc.; *spec.* of the act passed by the Scottish Parliament in 1661, by which the acts of all the parliaments held from 1633 were rescinded.

See Burnet *Own Time* II. (1724) I. 117-119.

1640 in Rushw. *Hist. Coll.* II. (1659) II. 1007 It is impossible, without passing the Rescissory Act,.. to have a valid Parliament. **1654** H. L'ESTRANGE *Chas. I* (1655) 161 Next they fell upon forming an Act Rescissory, whereby former Acts.. should be nulled. **1671** [R. MACWARD] *True Nonconf.* 378 Say not that the first part of the abovementioned rescissory clause, relative to the Act. 1592. Is simple. **1754** ERSKINE *Princ. Sc. Law* (1809) 57 This act, though falling under the act rescissory of Charles II, seems to have been considered as still in force by 1663, *c.* 21 which [etc.]. **1861** BUCKLE *Civiliz.* II. 283 The parliament.. consented to what was termed the rescissory act. **1894** *Daily News* 5 Mar. 5/8 The rescissory power wielded by the non-elective peers over the legislative acts of the.. House of Commons.

†**2.** Asking for rescission. *Obs. rare*$^{-1}$.

1610 SELDEN *Duello* iv. 14 S. Lewis and the rest were constrained.. to yeeld to the rescissory petitions of their subjects.

†**re'sconse**, *v. Obs. rare.* Also **-sconce**. [ad. obs. F. *resconser* to hide, etc. (Godef.).] *intr.* To set. Hence **re'sconsing** *vbl. sb.*

1618 *Kalender of Sheph.* xxxv. *heading*, Of the rising and resconsing of the signes in the Orison. *Ibid.* xxxv, Thus orison [neither] riseth ne resconceth. Meridian also riseth not ne resconseth.

resconter, -tre: see RESCOUNTER *sb.* and *v.*

re'score, *v. Mus.* [RE- 5 a.] *trans.* To score (a piece of music) again. Hence **re'scored** *ppl. a.*; **re'scoring** *vbl. sb.*, the action or an instance of scoring again; a rescored version.

1890 *Daily News* 16 Aug. 5/4 Bizet.. once undertook the task of re-scoring Bellini's 'Norma'. *Ibid.* He had thrown the re-scored MS. into the fire. **1926** WHITEMAN & MCBRIDE *Jazz* xi. 227 Most of the rehearsing and discussing and rescoring was done in consultations outside. **1955** G. ABRAHAM in H. Van Thal *Fanfare for E. Newman* 22 Small details and large patches of drastic rescoring alike show Wagner's finer mastery of the orchestra in the 1860s. **1962** *Times* 8 Oct. 16/5 Sir Malcolm Sargent has rescored the music. **1976** *New Yorker* 9 May 129/1 Whether they were played in Arne's own orchestration or in the rescoring by Charles Edward Horn.. was not stated. **1981** P. DICKINSON *Seventh Raven* iv. 47 He met this guitarist and rescored the whole bloody thing.

rescouh, obs. form of RESCUE *v.*

†**re'scounter**, *sb. Obs.* Also 6 **-contre**, 7 **-conter**. [ad. It. *riscontro* (Sp. *rescuentro*) recounter, comparison, balancing, etc., f. *ri-* RE- + *scontro* (:—**ex-contra*) encounter.]

1. Encounter, hostile meeting. *rare*$^{-1}$.

1543 HARVEL in *State Papers Hen. VIII*, IX. 537 Somme thinkith that Barbarossa wil go to Alger, or infest the cost of Spaine, not finding other rescontre.

2. Balancing of contra-accounts; settlement or payment of differences on accounts, in later use *spec.* on the Stock Exchange. Also *pl.*, and *attrib.* as ***rescounter-day***, ***-settlings***.

1622 MALYNES *Anc. Law-Merch.* 421 Which according to the said computation is all one in effect betweene them, and might by way of rescounter answere each other in account. **1682** SCARLETT *Exchanges* 222 If any Payments cannot be made exactly by Resconter for the just Sum,.. they give and take from one another.. a Note for the Value that one or the other must pay. **1753** A. MURPHY *Gray's Inn Jrnl.* No. 57 Tickets—India-Bonds—Rescounters—Consolidate. **1774** COLMAN *Man of Business* IV. i, You know the rescounter day, sir; and if Mr. Beverley does not pay his differences within these four-and-twenty hours, the world cannot hinder his being a lame duck. **1775** T. MORTIMER *Every man his own Broker* 39 These are called, in 'Change Alley, the Rescounter Settlings. **1796** *Grose's Dict. Vulgar T.* (ed. 3), *Rescounters*, the time of settlement between the bulls and bears of Exchange-alley, when the losers must pay their differences, or become lame ducks.

3. An engagement to pay the sum due on a balance of accounts. Also *attrib.* in ***rescounter-book***.

1682 SCARLETT *Exchanges* 222 In other Fairs the Resconters must be clearly exprest on Paper, written with Ink, in Books for that purpose, called Resconter-Books,.. and when the Resconter is once made, its as effectual as if the Bill were paid with ready Cash.

†**re'scounter**, *v. Obs. rare.* Also 6 **-contre**. [ad. It. *riscontrare* (Sp. *rescontrar*) to meet with, encounter, to compare or collate, etc.: cf. prec.]

1. *intr.* To meet or encounter *with* an enemy. (Cf. RECOUNTER *v.* and RENCOUNTER *v.*)

1543 HARVEL in *State Papers Hen. VIII*, IX. 424 Andrea Doria issuid owt of Geane incontinently with 48 galeis,.. to rescontre with the French navye. *Ibid.* 537 It hath ben raportid that Barbarossa was departed from Tolon with 30 galeis, to rescontre, as men thinke, with Janetin Doria.

2. *trans.* To balance or settle in the way of business. Hence **re'scountering** *vbl. sb.*

1606 *Cæsar Papers* in *Lansdowne MSS.* (Brit. Mus.) CLII. fol. 211 The Statute provided for all Straungers dealing by waie of merchaundize.. for the rescountring or ballancing of such trade as.. they bringe into this kingdome. **1622** MALYNES *Anc. Law-Merch.* 156 That Merchants assuring each to other, may rescounter their *Premios*, in the accounts kept thereof betweene them.

†**re'scoure**, *v. Obs. rare*$^{-1}$. [ad. OF. *rescoure*, *-cure*: see RESCUE *v.*] *trans.* To rescue.

c **1400** *Laud Troy Bk.* 8645 Thre thousand knyȝtes.. called he forth,.. Fro men of armes hem to rescouere, For thei were most with-oute Armure.

†**re'scours**, *sb.*[1] *Obs.* Chiefly *Sc.* Also 5 **reskowrs**. [Alteration of RESCOUS, prob. influenced by *cours* COURSE *sb.*] Rescue.

c **1330** R. BRUNNE *Chron. Wace* (Rolls) 2939 Bot þou come, rescours to make, Neuere in armes schalt þou me take. **1375** BARBOUR *Bruce* XIII. 369 Thar sall nane of all Yngland To mak ȝow rescours tak on hand, And but rescours may no castele Be haldin lang. **1439** *Rolls of Parlt.* V. 16/2 John Forman.. was lawefully arrested;.. and as they were going to bringe hym [to Tutbury].. cometh one Piers Venables.. and made a rescours, and toke awey the saide John Forman fro theym. **1536** BELLENDEN *Cron. Scot.* (1821) II. 478 Thus had the castel bene left desert, war not the Governour declarit to pas.. to the rescours thairof.

†**re'scours**, *sb.*[2] *Sc. Obs. rare*$^{-1}$. In 6 **resk-**. [Alteration of *recourse*, after prec.] Recourse.

1533 BELLENDEN *Livy* I. xi. (S.T.S.) I. 65 Þai were constrenit to haue þare vtir reskours to þe samyn.

†**re'scours**, *v. Sc. Obs. rare.* [Cf. RESCOURS *sb.*[1]] *trans.* To rescue.

1533 BELLENDEN *Livy* II. xiii. (S.T.S.) I. 177 The consulis send ane burreo to tak him; bot he was haistelie rescoursit be þe pepill. **1536** —— *Cron. Scot.* (1821) I. p. xl, This man, that rescoursit the king, wes callit Turnbull.

†**rescous**, *sb. Obs.* Forms: α. 4-7 **rescous(e**, **rescouss(e**, 4-5 **rescus(e**, 5 **reskuse**, 6-7 **rescusse**. β. 5 **rescues**, **reschewes**, **-scowes**, 6 **reskues**. [a. OF. *rescous(s)e*, *rescusse*, etc. (It. *riscossa*; Rom. type **re-ex-cussa*), vbl. sb. to OF. *rescourre* to RESCUE. The β-forms may in some cases be taken as plurals of *rescue*.]

1. Rescue, assistance, aid.

α. *c* **1330** R. BRUNNE *Chron. Wace* (Rolls) 5406 Wyder.. Wyþ twenty þousand mad hem rescus. **1390** GOWER *Conf.* II. 73 In rescouss of the toun aboute, Which with the Gregois was belein. **1412-20** LYDG. *Chron. Troy* I. ix. (1555), Of which slaughter the grekes wer confuse, Tyll Pelleus came to their rescuse. *c* **1477** CAXTON *Jason* 39 b, The whiche.. assembled them for to come to the rescousse of theyr lord. *a* **1548** HALL *Chron., Hen. IV* 23 Fortifiyng the same for fere of rescous that might issue from Caleis. **1602** CAREW *Cornwall* 125 b, For want of timely rescouse, the breath poasted out of his body.

β. ? *a* **1400** *Morte Arth.* 433 Byde hy[m] make reschewes for menske of hyme selvene. *c* **1430** *Pilgr. Lyf Manhode* IV. xxv. (1869) 189 Driveth hire fro me, j prey yow, and beth me a rescues for hire. **1470-85** MALORY *Arthur* I. xiv. 55 And whan Gryflet sawe rescowes, he smote a knyght on the tempils. **1568** GRAFTON *Chron.* II. 318 The Captaine.. having no comfort to have any quick reskues, yeelded.

2. *Law.* = RESCUE *sb.* 2.

1451 *Paston Lett.* I. 195, I told Gonnor that I shuld certifie a rescuse, and prayd the baly of the hundred that he wold record the same. **1485** *Act 1 Hen. VII*, c. 7 If any Rescous or Disobeysance be made to any Person having Authority to do Execution.. by any such Warrant. **1530-1** *Act 22 Hen. VIII*, c. 12 If any person.. make rescous agayne any Mayre .. or other person. **1581** LAMBARDE *Eiren.* II. vii. (1588) 231 Offence and felonie.. in him that helpeth the prisoner to get away, which is commonly termed Rescusse. **1618** DALTON *Countr. Just.* lxxvii. (1630) 196 Every disseisin rescous and trespasse implieth a force. **1632** *Star Chamb. Cases* (Camden) 137 The Lord Chiefe Justice found very much fault with Casen about Jenner's oppression, and his multiplicitie of suites upon the rescusse. **1690** *Act 2 Will. & Mary* I. c. 5 §4 Upon any Pound-breach or Rescous of Goods or Chattels distrained for Rent. **1768** BLACKSTONE *Comm.* III. 146 Being thus in the custody of the law, the taking them back by force is looked upon as an atrocious injury, and denominated a rescous.

†**rescous**, *v. Obs.* Also 4 **rescouse**, 5 **reschewse**, 6-7 **rescusse**. [a. OF. *rescouser*, *-cuser*, f. *rescouse*: see prec.] *trans.* (and *refl.*) To rescue. Hence **rescousing** *vbl. sb.*

c **1330** R. BRUNNE *Chron. Wace* (Rolls) 13039 Þe Romayns Petron wilde rescouse, But Bretons a-geyn þem faste gan brouse. *c* **1400** *Rowland & O.* 1536 Sir Otuell hase thre kynges slone & reschewsede hym with honour. **1581** LAMBARDE *Eiren.* II. vii. (1588) 232 If a stranger doe.. rescusse such an one as is under arrest for Felonie, then is it Felonie.. in the straunger. **1605** BACON *Adv. Learn.* II. xxiii §32 A readye rescussing of a mans selfe from scornes. *a* **1625**

Sir H. Finch *Law* (1636) 355 Here for contempts a Capias lyeth against Peers of the Realme, as for rescousing of one arrested by the course of the Law.

rescow(e, obs. forms of rescue.

re-scream, *v.* [re- 5 a.] To scream again.
1849 Clough *Amours de Voy.* II. 161 While men and women and papers Scream and re-scream to each other the chorus of victory.

re-'screen, *v.* [re- 5 a.] *trans.* To screen again. So **re-'screening** *vbl. sb.*
1950 *Hansard Commons* 7 Nov. 770 In view of the replies made yesterday by colleagues of the right hon. Gentleman that the main screening took place in 1943, when circumstances were very different, would he look into the question of whether re-screening, now that circumstances have changed, should be instituted? 1957 Manvell & Huntley *Film Music* iii. 97 Creating the score by screening and rescreening each sequence where music is required. 1967 E. Chambers *Photolitho-Offset* xi. 160 These Canon optical tone filters..eliminate moiré by diffusing the screen pattern through interference effects during rescreening. 1967 Karch & Buber *Offset Processes* ii. 12 Letterpress printed halftones (pictures) in books can often be 'picked up' as line shots, or rescreened for printing by the offset-lithographic process. 1979 *Listener* 29 Nov. 739/1 The Mudd documentary, which CBS will not re-screen, will gradually recede in memory.

rescribe (rɪ'skraɪb), *v.* [ad. L. *rescrībĕre*, f. *re-* re- + *scrībĕre* to write. Cf. obs. F. *rescripre*, *rescrire* (mod.F. *récrire*).]
†**1.** To write back, write in reply. *Obs.*
1462 J. Paston in *P. Lett.* II. 89, I preie yow hertili that ye feithfully and truly rescribe to me..what ye knowe in this mater. 1494 Fabyan *Chron.* vii. 453 It was not longe after, yt the Frenshe kyng hadde thus rescrybed vnto Kynge Edwarde [etc.]. 1523 Cromwell in Merriman *Life & Lett.* (1902) I. 313 Wher as I accordinglye haue not in lyke wise remembrid and rescribid [etc.]. 1600 W. Watson *Decacordon* (1602) 31 The Author..being friendly admonished in a letter..rescribing backe in a most saucie and peremptorie manner. 1661 J. Stephens *Procurations* 21 The said Pope rescribes thus. 1726 Ayliffe *Parergon* 220 Whenever a Prince on his being consulted by any one rescribes or writes back in this manner [etc.].
2. To write again or anew; to rewrite. Now *rare.* Hence **re'scribed** *ppl. a.*
1565 Jewel *Repl. Harding* (1611) 235 Therefore to conclude, I must subscribe, and rescribe, euen as before. 1588 J. Mellis *Briefe Instr.* F ij, Than first rescribe the opposite of the error..and then the same rescribe againe in the proper place. 1640 Howell *Dodona's Gr.* 67 This did not a whit stirre him, but calmely called for more Paper, to rescribe them. 1852 T. L. Peacock *Horæ Dramaticæ* II. *note* Wks. 1875 III. 356 A careful search will probably discover many more than two rescribed leaves. 1854 S. Dobell *Convalescent to Physic.*, Friend, by whose cancelling hand did Fate forgive Her debtor, and rescribe her stern award.

†**rescribendary.** *Obs. rare*⁻⁰. [ad. med.L. *rescribendāri-us* (Du Cange).] (See quot.)
1656 Blount *Glossogr.*, *Rescribendary*, an Officer in some of the Courts of Rome, who taxeth or valueth supplications.

rescript ('riːskrɪpt). Also 7 *pl.* rescrips. [ad. L. *rescriptum*, pa. pple. neut. of *rescrībĕre* to rescribe. Cf. F. *rescrit*, †*rescript* (13th c.).]
1. a. A decretal epistle from the Pope in reply to some question or difficulty referred to him; also, any Papal decision, decree, or edict.
1528 Gardiner in Burnet *Rec. Ref.* (ed. Pocock) I. 95 All such rescripts, breves, and bulls, as might conduce to the effectual definition..of the matter. 1574 Hellowes *Gueuara's Fam. Ep.* (1577) 287 With a rescript from Rome, they take degree of Bachelers, Licentiats, and Doctors. 1635 Pagitt *Christianogr.* II. vi. 41 The summes of money which the Pope receiveth for first fruits, Palls, Indulgences, Bulls, ..Rescrips,..cannot be counted. 1726 Ayliffe *Parergon* p. xvi, These Determinations [of the Popes] were stiled Rescripts or Decretal Epistles, having the Force of Laws. *c*1750 Shenstone *Ruin'd Abbey* 136 The French tyrant, by the futile grant Of papal rescript, claim'd Britannia's throne. 1825 Syd. Smith *Wks.* (1867) II. 199 Let him read the rescript of pope Pius VI, of the 17th of June, 1791. 1868 Freeman *Norm. Conq.* (1877) II. x. 511 The rescript of Pope Leo required Eadward either to found a new, or to enlarge an old, monastery.
b. (The original sense.) The reply sent by a Roman emperor to a magistrate or other person consulting him on a doubtful point of law or as to the action to be taken in particular circumstances.
1605 Camden *Rem.* 121 Men were not forbidden to change name or surname, by the rescript of Dioclesian. 1685 Stillingfl. *Orig. Brit.* ii. 56 Eusebius saith..That Hadrian, in his Rescript to Minutius..forbad a General Persecution of any as Christians. 1765 Blackstone *Comm.* I. 5 We must not prefer the edict of the praetor, or the rescript of the Roman emperor, to..the sanctions of an English parliament. 1827 Hare *Guesses* Ser. I. (1873) 118 In their rescripts and other ordinances, the Roman emperors spoke in the plural number. 1862 Draper *Intell. Devel. Europe* x. (1864) I. 309 On the arrival of the rescript of Theodosius the pagans laid down their arms.
2. Any edict, decree, order, or formal announcement made by a ruler or governing body, or having an official character. (Common in 19th c.)
1545 Joye *Exp. Dan.* vi. 94 The kinge with publyk rescript and open recantacion confessinge his synne setteth forth the glory of god. 1610 Willet *Hexapla Dan.* 325 Artashasht.. sent a rescript to hinder the building of the citie. 1652 Needham *Selden's Mare Cl.* 144 He would by no means determine ought contrary to those Laws by any Rescript of his own. 1716 J. Chamberlayne *St. Gt. Brit.* I. III. x. 249 The two Senior Advocates..present him, with a short Latin Speech, and the Rescript of the Archbishop. 1765 Sterne *Tr. Shandy* VII. xxxiii, It was a commissary sent to me from the post-office, with a rescript in his hand, for the payment of some six livres. 1790 Beatson *Nav. & Mil. Mem.* I. 56 They prevailed on the Court of Versailles to publish their sentiments and intentions, which they did in a rescript. 1858 *Times* 29 Nov., The leaders obeyed the rescript, but punctuality is impossible to an Asiatic. 1870 *Pall Mall Budget* 27 Aug. 31/2 The Bavarian bishops have been forbidden by a rescript from the Minister of Public Worship to promulgate the dogma in any way.
3. Something written over again; a rewriting.
1820 Lamb *Elia* Ser. I. *Oxford in Vac.*, In the line just above that in which he is about to print his second name (his re-script). 1853 C. Bronte *Villette* xxxiii, I wrote it three times..subduing the phrases at every rescript. 1870 Swinburne *Ess. & Stud.* (1875) 88 Those glorious rescripts ..which Surtees of Mainsforth passed off even upon Scott as genuine.
b. *Law.* A duplicate or counterpart.
1843–56 Bouvier *Law Dict. U.S.* (ed. 6).
4. A palimpsest writing.
1817 W. Taylor in *Monthly Mag.* XLIV. 326 The poetry was a rescript, and the parchment had originally served for a Cicero.

†**re'scription.** *Obs.* [a. F. *rescription* (13th c.), or ad. late L. *rescriptiōn-em*, n. of action f. *rescrībĕre* to rescribe.]
1. A rewriting, writing over again.
1588 J. Mellis *Briefe Instr.* F j b, And [on] this rescription into a new leafe, ye shall sald [= balance] the former accompt in that place. 1674 Jeake *Arith.* (1696) 271 The Figural Names.., to avoid prolixity in the often rescription ..are usually expressed by Marks or Characters. 1697 Luttrell *Brief Rel.* (1857) IV. 230 Unless they would ratifye every article..without any exception or rescription, they might prepare to depart.
2. The action of replying in writing; a written reply.
1597 A. M. tr. *Guillemeau's Fr. Chirurg.* *iij, Certayne rescriptions and memorialles..touchinge the manuall operations of Chyrurgerye. 1598 Drayton *Heroic. Ep.* i. Argt., In this Epistle doth her Griefe complaine; And his Rescription tells her his againe. 1627 —— *Agincourt*, etc. 190 If you vouchsafe rescription, stuffe your quill With naturall bountyes. *a*1657 R. Loveday *Lett.* (1663) 31 You cannot oblige me more then to be punctual in rescription.
3. [After F. *rescription.*] An official order for payment of a certain sum of money; a promissory note issued by a Government.
1796 *Ann. Reg., Hist.* 155 A paper, known by the name of rescriptions, had been given for advances to government, and made payable in specie at a fixed period. 1798 —— *St. Papers* 307 A purchase of thirty-two millions of Dutch rescriptions.

re'scriptive, *a. rare*⁻⁰. [f. as rescript + -ive.] 'Pertaining to, or answering the purpose of a rescript; deciding; settling' (Webster 1864).
So **re'scriptively** *adv.*, 'by rescript' (Webster 1828–32, citing Burke).

†**rescrite.** *Obs.*⁻¹ [a. OF. *rescrit.*] Rescript.
1382 Wyclif *1 Macc.* xii. 7 For ȝe ben oure bretheren as the rescrite conteyneth, that is vndirput.

†**rescry**, *v. Obs. rare*⁻¹. [a. OF. *rescrier*: see re- and escry *v.*] *trans.* To call back.
*c*1450 Lovelich *Grail* xiv. 136 At that word his Ax he took In honde, His Meyne to Rescrye, ȝif he myhte fonde.

'rescuable, *a.* [f. rescue *v.* + -able.] Capable of being rescued. Hence **rescua'bility.**
1611 Cotgr., *Recouable*, rescuable, recouerable, redeemeable. 1654 Gayton *Pleas. Notes* III. viii. 116 Every thing under force is rescuable by my Function. 1975 *Sci. Amer.* Dec. 34/2 The transition from Stage I (rescuable) to Stage II (killed) is a first-order, or 'one hit', reaction, whose rate is directly proportional to the amount of colicin. 1976 *Listener* 3 June 693/1 Men had taken the most obvious solace in alcohol, about the only rescuable commodity from many of the ruins. 1979 *Nature* 22 Nov. 382/2 The lack of rescuability of focus-forming activity from transformants caused by MSV DNA fragments remains to be resolved.

rescue ('rɛskjuː), *sb.* Forms: 4–5 rescowe, 6 -cow; 5–6 rescew(e, reskew, (7 reschew); 5–6 rescu, (6 -ku), 5– rescue. [f. the vb., in place of the earlier rescous.]
1. a. The (*or* an) act of rescuing (esp. persons) from enemies, saving from danger or destruction, etc.; succour, deliverance.
13.. *Gaw. & Gr. Knt.* 2308 No meruayle þaȝ hym myslyke, þat hoped of no rescowe. *c*1440 *Generydes* 2549 Ther fought thei still & reskew was ther non. *c*1450 *Merlin* 156 Thider preced bothe partyes to the rescowe. 1475 *Bk. Noblesse* (Roxb.) 28 At the rescue of the cite [of] Averaunces. *a*1533 Ld. Berners *Huon* lx. 207 They can not scape..and they are without hope of any rescue. 1582 N. Lichefield tr. *Castanheda's Conq. E. Ind.* I. ix. 25 b, They of the shippe Raphael, came presentlye to their succour and rescew. 1642 Rogers *Naaman* 19 What rescue hath the dry stubble against the advantage of fire? 1653 Milton *Ps.* vii. 6 Least as a Lion..He hast to tear my Soul asunder Tearing and no rescue nigh. 1738 Wesley *Ps.* XVIII. iv, He heard me from his glorious Throne, And sent the timely Rescue down. 1820 Byron *Mar. Fal.* IV. ii, The Genoese are come—ho! to the rescue! 1860 Tyndall *Glac.* I. xviii. 127 Rescue would be out of the question, should the climber go over the edge.
b. *Bridge.* = *rescue bid* in sense 3 c below.
1917 [see overbid *v.* 2 c]. 1932 H. Phillips *One Hundred Contract Bridge Hands* 114 West's double is for 'business'. .. North does not attempt a 'rescue'.
2. *Law.* **a.** The forcible taking of a person or goods out of legal custody; forcible recovery (by the owner) of goods distrained.
*c*1450 *Godstow Registers* (1905) 332 If hit happun þe foreside sir Richard..to deliuer þe distres..or to make rescu with þreteninge [etc.]. 1496 *Rolls of Parlt.* VI. 516/1 Any suche Shire..or Toune, where any persone make suche rescue of any distres to be takyn by suche Collectour. 1590 Shaks. *Com. Err.* IV. iv. 114, I am thy prisoner, wilt thou suffer them to make a rescue? 1597 —— *2 Hen. IV*, II. i. 61 *Fal.* Keepe them off, Bardolfe. *Fang.* A rescu, a rescu. *Host.* Good people bring a rescu. 1768 Blackstone *Comm.* III. i. 17 In case the distress was taken without cause, or contrary to law..the tenant may lawfully make rescue. 1769 *Ibid.* IV. 131 Rescue is the forcibly freeing another from an arrest or imprisonment. 1818 Scott *Hrt. Midl.* iii, Precautions.. justifiable..from the apprehensions so generally entertained of an expected rescue. 1841 *Penny Cycl.* XIX. 412/2 An indictment for a rescue must set out the circumstances under which the person, &c. was arrested, and the rescue effected. *Ibid.* 413/1 Upon rescue of goods distrained for rent.
b. A person rescued from custody.
1888 M. Morris *Claverhouse* 131 [They] marched victoriously off with such of their rescues as would go with them.
3. *attrib.* **a.** Connected with the rescue of property or persons, as ***rescue-appliance, bell, boat, capsule, car, company, co-ordinator, cradle, dinghy, man, mission, operation, party, race, service, ship,*** †**-*shot*** (= fee), ***squad, station, team, tube, work.***
1898 *Engineering Mag.* XVI. 154/2 New *Rescue-Appliances and Their Use in Mines. 1939 *Sun* (Baltimore) 26 May 8/6 The *rescue bell was plunged down to be attached to one of the aft hatches. 1960 W. O. Shelford *Subsunk* vii. 80 *Squalus* sank in an area where there were no appreciable tides to delay the divers or the functioning of the rescue bell. 1941 *Sun* (Baltimore) 12 Aug. 17/2 They had in storage enough Dorchester county white oak to construct keels and frames for all the *rescue boats. 1978 *Lochaber News* 31 Mar. 4/6 At the same time the rescue boat from Dochgorroch sped to the scene. 1977 *Sunday Times* 24 Apr. 1/5 We just dropped everything we had in our hands and ran to the *rescue capsules, which were closed and lowered down to the sea. 1911 *Chambers's Jrnl.* Nov. 747/2 Half-a-dozen *rescue-cars, fitted with life-saving apparatus and carrying a crew of trained men..will be allocated to certain districts. 1975 *Irish Times* 30 May 14/8 Foir Teoranta, the State *rescue company, has exercised its right to appoint its nominee. 1963 G. Moffat *Lady with Cool Eye* vi. 70 As *rescue co-ordinator..shouldn't you know who's operating in your area? 1977 *N.Z. Herald* 5 Jan. 1-1/1 The fishermen fastened the rope to a bollard and fitted a *rescue cradle to run along the rope to the comparative safety of the rocks. 1972 *Police Rev.* 10 Nov. 1444/1 Fluorescent pigments..put to good practical effect in painting *rescue dinghies. 1921 *Dict. Occup. Terms* (1927) §47 **Rescue man*, a member of colliery rescue team, called upon in cases of fire, explosions, etc., in mine to go underground in an attempt to rescue workers. 1940 *New Statesman* 9 Nov. 465/1 The rescue men had blue overalls and white steel helmets. 1977 *R.A.F. News* 11–24 May 2/5 Peter Pitcher rang up his 200th *rescue mission when he joined in a flight to pick up three boys from ..a mudbank in the Mersey. 1960 *Council Brit. Archaeol. Rep.* x. 41 While excavations as such are excluded from this *Report* it is difficult to omit all reference to the *rescue-operations which must follow when attempts to preserve a site have failed. 1975 *Country Life* 3 Apr. 825/1 [Augustus] John himself despised the idea of a 'rescue operation', as he called it, where his reputation was concerned. 1892 Zangwill *Bow Mystery* 153 Somehow he had become the leader of the *rescue party. 1937 *Ann. Reg. 1936* 17 At the same time local authorities were advised to organise rescue parties of six or eight men each for action after air attack. 1897 *Daily News* 6 July 5/3 There were *rescue races, more diving,..and water polo. 1976 *Northumberland Gaz.* 26 Nov., Bill Hardcastle opened the *rescue service's first harbour fete. 1941 *Sun* (Baltimore) 12 Aug. 17/2 Officials of the Cambridge Shipbuilders, Inc., today pushed plans for eight more *rescue ships to be built for the quartermaster. 1944 M. Horton *Let.* 1 Mar. in Schofield & Martyn *Rescue Ships* (1968) viii. 136 The introduction and work of Rescue Ships during phases of the Battle of the Atlantic when the U-boats were on the offensive did a tremendous lot towards maintaining the high morale of the Merchant Navy. *a*1802 *Jamie Telfer* xlix. in Child *Ballads* IV. 8/2 He has paid the *rescue-shot, Baith wi gowd and white monie. 1954 'M. Cost' *Invitation from Minerva* 176 He headed the *Rescue Squad, saw the German shepherd dogs drawn up, the blazing torches. 1973 *N.Y. Law Jrnl.* 2 Aug. 13/5 The defendant..was taken to the hospital. This was done by a rescue squad. 1979 *Arizona Daily Star* 1 Apr. (Advt. Section) 1/1 Memorials may be made to the Gila County Sheriff's Dept. Rescue Squad. 1908 *Westm. Gaz.* 2 Apr. 7/2 A well-equipped *rescue-station and experimental gallery, established by the leading Lancashire coalowners, was opened to-day. 1976 *Cumberland News* 3 Dec. 11/6 Rescue station, Derwentwater Boat Club, Portinscale, Peter Fry Rescue Trust. 1956 M. Stewart *Wildfire at Midnight* ix. 79 The night had been black and wild... Bill Persimmon had telephoned for the local *rescue team. 1973 *Guardian* 13 Apr. 24/5 At 11.29, the rescue teams were alerted. 1980 G. Greene *Dr. Fischer* xiii. 88 By the time I reached the ski-lift the rescue team was already on the way up. 1977 *N.Z. Herald* 5 Jan. 1-3/2 The two lifesavers on the helicopter, Mr. M. Lawson and Mr. T. Radonich, jumped into the water with a *rescue tube, which was used to fly Mr. Stewart back home. 1946 R. J. C. Atkinson *Field Archaeol.* ii. 67 On *rescue-work sites, where the archaeological material is in any case eventually to be destroyed, the question of restoration does not arise. 1962 D. Lessing *Golden Notebk.* III. 402 The pleasure of recognition, of a bit of rescue-work, so to speak, rescuing the formless into form.

b. Directed to, aiming at, the raising of fallen or degraded women, as ***rescue home, shelter, society, work, worker***, etc.

1890 W. Booth *In Darkest England* I. vi. 51 The records of our *Rescue Homes abound with life-stories..which prove..the existence of numbers of innocent victims. **1894** *Daily News* 13 Sept. 2/6 Offshoots of the first rescue home have been planted in many directions. **1927** E. C. Trenholme *Rescue Work* iii. 21 It was through this venture failing that one of them came into a rescue home. **1981** C. Scott *Heavenly Witch* ix. 136 At Nîmes the first rescue home was opened, the start of a chain of rescue homes. **1889** L. Ridding *Woman's League* 12 An Industrial Training Home, Temperance Work, a *Rescue Shelter..these various efforts are inspired by the starting of the League. **1869** (*title*) Licensing prostitution; reprinted (with permission) from the Report for 1869 of the *Rescue Society, London. **1981** F. K. Prochaska *Women & Philanthropy* vi. 188 The dramatic growth in rescue societies and Magdalene homes. **1884** H. Brown *Is it Nothing to You?* iv. 87 The objects of this society are to promote—(1) Purity among men. (2) A chivalrous respect for womanhood. (3) The preservation of the young from contamination. (4) *Rescue work. **1896** Mrs. Caffyn *Quaker Grandmother* 297, I hope you enjoyed your first taste of—rescue-work—that's the word, isn't it? **1911** G. B. Shaw *Doctor's Dilemma* p. lxxvi, The morbid interest in misery and vice which turns some others to philanthropy and 'rescue work'. **1977** Rowbotham & Weeks *Socialism & New Life* 13 This tendency was reinforced by rescue work and the moral shock with which the middle-class reformers encountered, amidst poverty and overcrowding, the complexities and ambiguities of working-class family patterns. **1898** *Times* 16 Dec 7/6 During the year 218 women and girls have been dealt with by our lady *rescue worker. **1930** G. B. Shaw *Wks.* VII. 180 The only logical conclusion apparent is that the White Slave traffickers are in complete control of our picture theatres, and can close them to our Rescue workers as effectively as they can reserve them for advertisements of their own trade.

c. Special Combs., as **rescue archæology**, emergency excavation of archæological sites in the face of projected building or road development; hence **rescue archæologist**; similarly ***rescue dig, excavation***; **rescue bid** *Bridge*, a bid made to rescue one's partner from what seems a difficult position, as when his or her bid has been doubled; **rescue breathing**, mouth-to-mouth resuscitation; **rescue circle** *Spiritualism* (see quot. 1961); **rescue mission** *U.S.*, a mission established to help those in need of moral or spiritual rehabilitation; **rescue opera**, an opera, often based on real events, in which the hero or heroine is rescued after great tribulations.

1969 I. N. Hume *Historical Archaeol.* ii. 43 There are no rules that exist specifically to guide *rescue archaeologists. **1972** *Rescue News* Autumn 1/1 For some years rescue archaeologists have been worried that the finds from the increasing number of emergency excavations are not receiving proper treatment. [**1966** *Council Brit. Archaeol. Rep.* xvi. 51 The 'rescue' aspect of archaeology has nowadays become particularly important.] **1969** I. N. Hume *Historical Archaeol.* ii. 43 The only recourse is to resort to what is euphemistically known as **rescue archaeology*... Rescue archaeology occurs when time has almost run out. **1978** *Sci. Amer.* Jan. 111 An international campaign of rescue archaeology at the ruined city. **1913** F. Irwin *Auction High Lights* 261 The forcing-bids, the doubles and redoubles, the '*rescue'-bids had just this result, that A's hand brought him 604 instead of 299. **1973** *Times* 10 Nov. 10/5 He had been invited to partner a beginner who had no suspicion of the dangers..from uninvited rescue bids. **1961** *Sunday Times* 17 Sept. 4/5 Scandinavian countries have a long lead on Britain in training in '*rescue breathing'. **1968** W. Warwick *Surfriding in N.Z.* 18/2 Attempt rescue breathing as soon as you can reach the victim's face. **1921** A. Conan Doyle *Wanderings of Spiritualist* iv. 93 He has run a *rescue circle for the instruction of the lower spirits who are so material that they can be reached more easily by humanity than by the higher angels. **1961** R. Crookall *Supreme Adventure* III. i. 105 At 'Rescue Circles' where 'earthbound' men (who have shed the Physical Body without being aware of the fact, and whose Soul Body is still enveiled by the vehicle of vitality) are made to realise their condition—that they have 'died'. **1973** *Light* Spring 10 Visitors, or clients, of a rescue circle are more demanding. **1962** *Daily Tel.* 9 July 10/2 '*Rescue digs' of this kind have now become one of the principal antiquarian activities of the Ministry of Works. **1957** G. Clark *Archaeol. & Society* (ed. 3) ii. 57 *Rescue-excavations, organized in Britain by the Ministry of Works, when known ancient monuments had to be flattened. **1902** S. H. Hadley *Down in Water St.* ii. 39 The first *Rescue Mission in the world..was started by Jerry McAuley, October 8, 1872, at 316 Water Street, New York. **1912** P. I. Roberts *Dry Dock of Thousand Wrecks* vi. 93 He has displayed all along the earmarks of a rescue mission worker. **1972** *National Observer* (U.S.) 27 May 7/5 The camp's food..was below rescue-mission fare. **1943** A. Loewenberg *Ann. Opera 1597–1940* 280 Dalayrac: Léhéman ou La Tour de Newstadt... More successful in Germany where it was one of the favourite '*rescue operas' of that period. **1959** *Listener* 25 June 1128/2 *Les deux Journées* (1800) and *Fidelio* (first version 1805) have a great many features in common: their theme ('rescue opera'), its source in an actual event.

rescue ('rɛskjuː), *v.* Forms: 4–7 rescow(e, 4 -coue, 5 -cove, 5 -chow(e, -kowe; 4–6 reskew(e, (5 -chew), 5–7 rescew(e; 4 rescuwe, 4– rescue, (7 reskue). [a. OF. *rescou-, reskeu-*, etc., stem of *rescoure, -cure, -keure, -corre*, etc. (F. *recourre*), = It. *riscuotere*:—Rom. type **reex-cutĕre*: see re- and excuss *v.*]

1. a. *trans.* To deliver (a person) from the attack of, or out of the hands of, assailants or enemies.

13.. *Guy Warw.* (A.) 2031 With that com his folk prikeinde And her lord rescowed there. **13..** *Coer de L.* 4002 Prove we thys toun to wynne, Rescue thys folk that be withinne. *c* **1350** *Will. Palerne* 1226 þe ȝong kene kniȝtes.. rescuede him rediliche for rinkes þat him ladden. *c* **1400** *Destr. Troy* 6838 Let vs reskew the Renke, refe hym his fos! *c* **1500** *Lancelot* 2701 Sir gawan thar reskewit he of fors, Magre his fois, and haith hyme set one hors. **1533** Bellenden *Livy* II. vii. (S.T.S.) I. 153 Of þe remanent plegeis be hir reskewit he tuke litill force. *a* **1548** Hall *Chron., Edw. IV* 190 She made hym capitain of Alnewike Castle, whiche he with his freshe men kept till thei wer rescowed. **1643** Whitelock *Mem.* (1853) I. 248 He took.. many horse and arms, and rescued all their prisoners. **1719** De Foe *Crusoe* I. (Globe) 256, I wish'd..that I had any way to have come undiscover'd within shot of them, that I might have rescu'd the three Men. **1819** Scott *Ivanhoe* xvi, How thou wilt rescue her afterwards from the clutches of Bois-Guilbert seems considerably more doubtful. **1934** G. B. Shaw *Too True to be Good* III. 95 You were sent out here to rescue my daughter from these dreadful brigands. **1969** I. & P. Opie *Children's Games* iv. 163 Here the seeker is at almost greater disadvantage than in 'Buzz Off', for a hider can rescue a prisoner merely by getting in sight of the den.

b. To liberate by unlawful force from legal custody. Also in *fig.* context.

1600 E. Blount tr. *Conestaggio* 143 Had not Damain D'Aguiar..had the charge thereof,..there was so great a concourse of people..that the offender had been easily rescued. **1680** Lady Chaworth in *12th Rep. Hist. MSS. Comm.* App. V. 55 Two Jesuits goeing to prison..were rescued and taken quit away out of the officers hands. *a* **1703** Burkitt *On N.T.* Luke vii. 17 The Lord of life arrests the serjeant death, and rescues the prisoner out of his hand. **1769** *Junius Lett.* xxx, They..rescue the general, and drive away the sheriff's officers. **1818** Scott *Hrt. Midl.* iii, When ..Wilson..had arrived at the scaffold.., there appeared no signs of that attempt to rescue him.

2. a. To deliver (a castle, town, etc.) from siege.

c **1330** R. Brunne *Chron.* (1810) 275 To þe Baliol suld þei send, þer Castelle to rescue. **1375** Barbour *Bruce* xi. 67 Gif our fayis assay To reskew Strewilling. **1435** in *Wars Eng. in France* (Rolls) II. 584 A castel..that myghte be hastelie rescowed. **1480** Caxton *Chron. Eng.* ccl. 320 The duke of gloucestre wente ouer the see to Caleys for to rescue the toune. **1560** Daus tr. *Sleidane's Comm.* 54 After he recovereth Wireiburge and reskeweth the castel beseged. **1591** Shaks. *1 Hen. VI*, I. vi. 2 Rescu'd is Orleance from the English Wolves.

b. To recover, take back by force.

c **1450** *Merlin* 586 Thei were com oute to hem to bateile for to rescowe the pray. **1568–9** *Act 11 Eliz.* in Bolton *Stat. Irel.* (1621) 328 Until he or they pay to the..seyser of the said hogges..the value and price of the swine so rescowed. **1590** Spenser *F.Q.* I. iv. 39 But th' Elfin knight,..him rencountring fierce, reskewd the noble pray. **1628** Coke *On Litt.* 160 b, If the Tenant rescue the distres [etc.]. **1643** Whitelock *Mem.* (1853) I. 239 The Scots took Coquet Island.., and rescued and restored to the owners a great herd of cattle taken away by the king's forces. **1768** Blackstone *Comm.* III. 12 They may be rescued by the owner, in case the distress was taken without cause. **1867** Smyth *Sailor's Word-bk.* 569 There is no rule prescribed by the law of England in the case of foreign property rescued.

3. To deliver or save (a person or thing) *from* some evil or harm. Also freq. without const. *spec.* in *Bridge*, to make a rescue bid (see rescue *sb.* 3 c); also *absol.*

c **1330** R. Brunne *Chron. Wace* (Rolls) 5255 While þat y haue..myght..þat hym for deþ [*v.r.* fro dede] y may rescuwe. *c* **1374** Chaucer *Troylus* III. 808 (857) Whan a chaumber a-fyr is,..Wel more nede is, it sodeynly rescowe Than to dispute. **1390** Gower *Conf.* I. 64 As he al one alle othre myhte Rescowe with his holy bede. *c* **1450** Holland *Howlat* 433 To the Dowglas that senȝe was send,..all Scotland fra scaith to reskewe. **1483** Caxton *Cato* A vij, He supposed that it had be his wyf and fayne wold haue rescued hir. *c* **1560** A. Scott *Poems* (S.T.S.) xiii. 42 Gif ȝe knew my mynd as it is plicht, ȝe wald..me reskew. **1581** Mulcaster *Positions* xii. (1887) 61 Whether ye meane to reskew the patient from the headache. **1615** G. Sandys *Trav.* 29 Which set accidentally on fire, Lucius Metellus..did rescue with the loss of his eyes. **1678** Lady Chaworth in *12th Rep. Hist. MSS. Comm.* App. V. 52 They saw a man drownding, and she made her boat make up to rescue him. **1718** *Free-thinker* No. 65. 70 It..is sufficient to rescue Mankind from Tyranny and Oppression. **1791** Cowper *Yardley Oak* 58 Thou..art become (Unless verse rescue thee awhile) a thing Forgotten. **1819** Shelley *Cenci* III. i. 376 Some accident might interpose To rescue him from what is now most sure. **1874** Green *Short Hist.* ii. §7. 99 England was rescued from this chaos of misrule by the efforts of the Church. **1921** F. Irwin *Compl. Auction Player* x. 133 It is seldom wise to attempt to 'rescue' your partner from a double. **1958** *Listener* 13 Nov. 805/3 In a match-pointed pairs contest I might consider rescuing to Two Clubs.

4. *refl.* To save or deliver (oneself) in some respect.

c **1330** R. Brunne *Chron. Wace* (Rolls) 8878 (Petyt MS.), How þei were raised þei had wondere,.. With þat worde þei þam rescued, þei ne wist how þei suld [be] remued. **1390** Gower *Conf.* III. 4 The knihtli David him ne mihte Rescoue, that he with the sihte Of Bersabee ne was bestad. *c* **1460** Sir R. Ros *La Belle Dame* 91 þat in noo wyse I couthe my selfe rescow, But nede I must cum In, and se þe fest. **1567** Maplet *Gr. Forest* 71 Men at the firste were faine to rescue them selues in iourneying, by setting thereon. **1610** Bp. Carleton *Jurisd.* 27 That he appealed from the high Priest, reskuing himselfe from his iudgement,..is euident. **1775** Johnson *Tax. no Tyr.* 9 The traders of Birmingham have rescued themselves.

5. *absol.* To afford deliverance or safety. *rare.*

1390 Gower *Conf.* II. 195 Riht so no lawe mai rescowe Fro him that wol no riht allowe. *c* **1500** *Lancelot* 517 Thar is no thing sal sucour nor reskew, Your worldly honore nedis most adew. **1611** Bible *Dan.* vi. 27 He deliuereth and rescueth. *a* **1700** Dryden (J.), Riches cannot rescue from the grave, Which claims alike the monarch and the slave.

rescued ('rɛskjuːd), *ppl. a.* [f. prec. + -ed[1].] Saved, delivered, liberated. Also *absol.*

1667 Milton *P.L.* xii. 199 The Sea..Aw'd by the rod of Moses so to stand Divided, till his rescu'd gain thir shoar. **1719** De Foe *Crusoe* I. (Globe) 246 As soon as I had secur'd my two weak rescued Prisoners. **1781** C. Johnston *Hist. J. Juniper* II. 202 Then turning to the rescued guest, [he] invited him politely to breakfast. **1814** Southey *Carmen Triumph.* xiv, Raise now the song of joy for rescued Spain! **1869** Freeman *Norm. Conq.* (1875) III. xiv. 364 To enjoy the congratulations of a rescued people.

rescuee (rɛskjuːˈiː). [f. rescue *v.* + -ee[1].] One who is rescued.

1950 O. Nash *Family Reunion* (1951) I. 32 In case of fire, no hero he; Merely a humble rescuee. **1954** I. Murdoch *Under Net* xii. 171 The simultaneous sight of so many eligible rescuees was too much for him. **1979** C. Kilian *Icequake* v. 75, I don't feel much like a rescuer just now. Much rather be a rescuee.

ˈ**rescueless**, *a. rare*$^{-1}$. [f. rescue *sb.* + -less.] Without rescue.

1586 Warner *Alb. Eng.* II. xii, He topled ore his side The Monstrous King, that resculesse to flying people cride.

rescuer ('rɛskjuːə(r)). [f. rescue *v.* + -er[1].] One who rescues.

1535 Stewart *Cron. Scot.* II. 114 This is the man we traist this tyme salbe The haill reskewar of oure libertie. **1553** *Act 1 Mary* Sess. II. c. 3 §7 The said Rescuers and Disturbers shall suffer like Imprisonment. **1614** Bp. Andrewes *Serm.* (1841) IV. 79 The rescuer and the revenger of David. **1665** Pepys *Diary* 5 Aug., Colonel Danvers..was rescued from the captain of the guard, and carried away; one only of the rescuers being taken. **1856** Kane *Arct. Expl.* I. xvii. 200 Nearly all our party, as well the rescuers as the rescued, were tossing in their sick bunks. **1884** *Manch. Exam.* 16 July 5/2 The rescuer was a volunteer.

rescuing ('rɛskjuːɪŋ), *vbl. sb.* [f. as prec. + -ing[1].] The action of the verb; deliverance, help.

1375 Barbour *Bruce* v. 419 He na hop had of reskewing. *c* **1386** Chaucer *Pars. T.* ¶731 He delitith him..nat in the rescowynge ne releeuynge of his euene cristene. **1545** (*title*) The Rescuynge of the Romishe fox. **1711** Shaftesb. *Charac.* (1737) I. 20 The crusades, the rescuing of holy lands, and such devout gallantrys are in less request than formerly. **1867** A. J. E. Wilson *St. Elmo* viii. 101 If it be Thy will, make her the instrument of rescuing.

ˈ**rescuing**, *ppl. a.* [-ing[2].] That rescues.

1880 *Daily News* 17 Sept. 5/2 The rescuing girl was nearly as much exhausted as the rescued. **1893** *Athenæum* 4 Nov. 631/3 The vessels..are drawn with..just feeling for the buoyancy of the rescuing craft.

rescu'ssee. *Law. rare*$^{-0}$. [f. *rescus* rescous *v.* + -ee[1].] 'The party in whose favour the rescue is made' (Crabb, 1823).

ˈ**rescusser.** *Law. rare.* Also 8–9 -or. [f. as prec. + -er[1], -or.] One who makes a rescue.

1632 *Star Chamb. Cases* (Camden) 130 He is charged..for suinge the rescussers, and for suing the Sheriffes bondes of appearance upon some of them. **1704** J. Harris *Lex. Techn.* I, *Rescussor*, is he that commits such a Rescous.

rescyve, obs. form of receive *v.*

resdue, obs. form of residue.

†**rese**, *sb. Obs.* Forms: 1, 3 ræs, (1 hræs), 3–5 res(e, 3, 5 rease, 4 ras), 4–6 resse, rees(e, 5 reess, reys, 6 reece). [OE. *rǽs* masc. = ON. *rás* fem. (whence race *sb.*[1]), MLG. *râs* current:—OTeut. **rǣs-*, of uncertain relationship. In ME. chiefly a poetic word (very common in the 14th c.), used with considerable laxity of meaning.]

1. A rush or run; a swift course or rapid onward movement; the act of running or moving rapidly or impetuously.

a **900** Cynewulf *Crist* 727 Wæs se þridda hlyp, Rodorcyninges ræs, þa he on rode astaȝ. *c* **950** *Lindisf. Gosp.* Matt. viii. 32 Mid hræs ȝe-eade all suner..in sæ. —— Luke viii. 23 Ofduna astaȝ hræs windes on luh. *c* **1000** Ælfric *Hom.* II. 514 He het hwilon ða hundas ætstandan, þe urnon on ðam ræse, deorum ȝetenge. **13..** *E.E. Allit. P.* A. 873 Lyk flodez fele laden, runnen on resse. **1340–70** *Alisaunder* 1189 The steede straught on his gate & stired hym under, And wrought no wod res but his waye holdes. **1398** Trevisa *Barth. De P.R.* xvi. i. (Tollem. MS.), Also þe rees of þe see is let with multitude of grauell and sonde. *c* **1420** *Anturs of Arth.* 112 He rayked oute at a res, for he was neuer rad. **1483** Caxton *Gold. Leg.* 256 b/2 The deuylle cam wyth a grete Rese to the place.

b. The act of running or rushing against or upon others; a rush in (or to) battle; an onset, assault, attack, sally.

[*Beowulf* 2357 Syððan ȝeata cyning guðe-ræsum swealt.] *c* **1000** Ælfric *Exod.* 329 þraca wæs on ore,..beadumæȝnes ræs,..þær Judas for. *c* **1205** Lay. 21367, I þan uormeste ræse fulle fif hundred. *c* **1325** *Poem Times Edw. II* 248 in *Pol. Songs* (Camden) 334 Hii sholde gon to the Holi Lond and maken there her res. *c* **1330** *Arth. & Merl.* 7152 (Kölbing), He bihinde to ben bi cas, To susten þe paiems ras. **1387** Trevisa *Higden* (Rolls) VIII. 348 þere Edward dwelled al a ȝere wiþ oute eny reese of enemyes. **1425** *Rolls of Parlt.* IV.

298/1 By ye Rees of a Spaynell, yere was on a nyght taken.. a man. 1494 FABYAN *Chron.* VII. 646 Certayne knyghtes.. dyuerse and sondry tymes brake out by sodeyne resys, and skyrmysshed with the lordes people.

2. *in* (or *on*) *a rese*: **a.** In a rush or run; hence, in haste (to get from one place to another).

a 1300 *Cursor M.* 6550 Quen þai war war o moyses þai fled a-wai, als [*v.r.* al] in a res. 13.. *E.E. Allit. P.* B. 1782 þenne ran þay in on a res, on rowtes ful grete. 13.. *Gaw. & Gr. Knt.* 1164 Rachches in a res radly hem folȝes. c 1374 CHAUCER *Troylus* IV. 322 (350) For wo he nyste what he mente, But yn a res to Troylus he wente. a 1400–50 *Alexander* 2979 þai russhyn vp in a reys, rynnyn into chaumbres. c 1460 *Towneley Myst.* iv. 255, I wille ryn on a res, And slo hym here, right as he lyse.

b. In a hurry, in haste (to do something). So *with..rese.*

a 1300 *Cursor M.* 25433 þof adam rap him in a res.. vs all for to spill. c 1330 *Arth. & Merl.* 3990 (Kölbing), King Nanters, king Lot, king Karodas, þis men armed wiþ gret ras. a 1400–50 *Alexander* 1996 He þam redis in a rese & reches to þe sedis.

3. Action proceeding from sudden or violent impulse; wantonness, recklessness, rashness.

a 1250 *Owl & Night.* 512 Hit nys for luue noþeles, Ac is þeos cherles wode res. a 1310 in Wright *Lyric P.* xxxvi. 100 Unbold icham to bidde the bote, Swythe unreken ys my rees. c 1330 R. BRUNNE *Chron.* (1810) 169 To maynten þe pes, þe foles forto felle, þat rise wild in res. 1413 *26 Pol. Poems* 50 God sende vs pes! þerto eche man be boun: To letten fooles of here res [etc.].

b. *to rue one's rese*, to repent of an act or course of action. Cf. RACE *sb.*[1] 1 b.

a 1300 *Cursor M.* 4325 Reu his res þan sal he sare. c 1330 R. BRUNNE *Chron.* (1810) 237 þe Walssh wer alle day slayn, now rewes þam þer res. a 1375 *Joseph Arim.* 491 He arayes his riche men.. þat þorw him reowen no res, þat his red wrouȝten. c 1400 *Song Roland* 370 Thoughe Roulond rew þat rese. c 1420 *Avow. Arth.* xxii, Ȝette Menealfe, or the mydnyȝte, Him ruet alle his rees.

c. Hot or hasty temper; impatience, anger.

c 1330 R. BRUNNE *Chron. Wace* (Rolls) 4815 þe kyng was of so felon rees, He ne wolde here of preyere ne pes. 1387 TREVISA *Higden* (Rolls) IV. 99 Emila.. wolde nouȝt diffame here lord.. by wymmen rees and anger. c 1400 *Gamelyn* 101 Than bispak his brother that rape was of rees.

d. Natural impulse to something. $rare^{-1}$.

1398 TREVISA *Barth. De P.R.* VII. vii. (Bodl. MS.), [The sick man] liþe vpright and if he yturned is for a tyme to ligge on his side, bi his owne rees he turneþ hym silfe efte and liþe vpright.

4. A sudden or violent impulse; a fit or paroxysm; an attack of distraction or frenzy.

c 1275 *Luue Ron* 10 in *O.E. Misc.* 93 þis worldes luue nys bute o res.. vikel & frakel & wok and les. c 1350 *Will. Palerne* 439, I mase al marred for mournyng neiȝh hondes, but redeliche in þat res þe recuuerere þat me falles [etc.]. 1387 TREVISA *Higden* (Rolls) IV. 149 Lucrecius.. wroot som bokes bytwene þe reses of his woodnesse. 1390 GOWER *Conf.* III. 3 Halfdrunke in such a res With dreie mouth he sterte him uppe. c 1400 *Arth. & Merl.* 820 (Kölbing), þeo hore start vp in a res And.. Smot hire in þe visage.

b. A rash or violent act.

c 1330 R. BRUNNE *Chron.* (1810) 267 To while þise Cardinals trauaild for þe pes, Here of a wikhals how he bigan a res. c 1400 *Gamelyn* 547 Gamelyn and Adam haden doon a sory rees, Bounden and y-wounded men ayein the kinges pees.

5. A short space or point of time, a moment.

a 1300 *Cursor M.* 8878 (Cott.), Vte o þat tre it brast a blese þat brent þam al wit-in a rese. c 1370 *Clene Maydenhod* 26 For monnes loue ȝif þou beo-holde Hit lasteþ but a luytel res. c 1460 *Towneley Myst.* xxii. 62 Make rowme in this rese I byd you, belyfe. *Ibid.* xxiii. 481 Thou shall haue drynke within a resse.

†**rese**, *v.*[1] *Obs.* Forms: 1 **ræsan**, 3 **ræsen**, 3–5 **rese**, 4 **reese** (? **rise**). [OE. *rǽsan* = ON. *rása* to rush, MDu. *râzen* (Du. *razen*), MLG. *râsen* (G. *rasen*) to rage, storm, f. the stem **rǽs-*: see prec.]

1. *intr.* To rush *on* or *upon* a person, etc.; to make a rush, attack, or assault *on* one.

Beowulf 2691 Fyr-draca.. ræsde on ðone rofan. a 900 *O.E. Martyrol.* 21 Jan. 28 þæs burhȝerefan sunu wolde ræsan on hi.. & hi bysmrian. 971 *Blickling Hom.* 181 þa færinga coman þær hundas forþ.. & ræsdon on þone apostol. 1387 TREVISA *Higden* (Rolls) VI. 477 It semede as þeyȝ sche schulde have i-resed on þe rebel kyng. 1398 —— *Barth. De P.R.* XII. Introd. (Tollem. MS.), Som [birds] takeþ here pray fleyinge in þe eyer, and reeseþ neuer up on pray on þe grounde. c 1450 *Mirour Saluacioun* 377 No beest nor bridde cruwell shuld neuer on man hafe resed.

transf. c 1400 *Melayne* 1305 The Bischoppe es so woundede that tyde With a spere.. That one his ribbis gan rese.

b. So with *to*.

c 1205 LAY. 1679 Ældai heo ræmden & resden to þan castle. c 1275 *Ibid.* 6496 þat deor vp astod and resde to þan stede. c 1400 *Chron. R. Glouc.* (Rolls) App. H. 55 O dur.. resede to þe folc & slou ham in o stunde.

2. To make a rush or run; to spring or start.

c 1205 LAY. 1004 þe riche haueð muchel rum to ræsen biforen þan wrecchan. 1387 TREVISA *Higden* (Rolls) I. 231 þan Marcus resede too, and.. kauȝte hym wiþ his honde. *Ibid.* III. 211 þe nyȝt to fore his deth his chambre wyndowes were so griselich.. i-oponed, þat Iulius resede out of his bedde. 1495 *Trevisa's Barth. De P.R.* XVIII. xliv. 806 The elyphaunt hath large eeres.. and reesyth and smyteth therwyth ful sore whan he is wrathe.

3. To show excitement; to rage.

a 1225 *Ancr. R.* 326 Ure Louerd weop.. and grisbatede, and meingde his blod [*var.* & resede & mengde him seluen]. c 1440 *Ipomydon* 1831 (Kölbing), He sterte up in a brayde And bygan for to rese, As he wold take hyr by the nese.

†**rese**, *v.*[2] *Obs.* Forms: 1 **hrisian**, **hrysian**, 2 **hresien**, 3 **risien**, 3–4 **rusien**, 4 **resye**, **rese**. [OE. *hrisian* = OS. *hrisian* to shake, tremble. Goth. *-hrisjan* to shake. The phonology of the Eng. forms is not quite clear.]

1. *trans.* To shake; to cause to shake or tremble. Also *absol.*

c 825 *Vesp. Psalter* cviii. 25 [Hia] ȝeseȝun mec & hrisedon heafud heara. c 1000 *Ags. Ps.* (Spelman) xxviii. 7 Stefn drihtnes hrysiendis westen. 13.. *Sir Beues* (A.) 1818 Whan he com of þat wilde brok, His gode stede him resede & schok. 1340 *Ayenb.* 116 þervore bit sainte Pawel his deciples þet hi by yzet ase tours yroted ase trawes ine love, zuo þet non vondinge him ne moȝe resye [*printed* refye] ne rocky. 1377 LANGL. *P. Pl.* XVI. 78, I had reuth whan Piers rogged [*R.* þat Piers rused (*sc.* the tree)], it gradde so reufully.

2. *intr.* To shake, in various senses.

Beowulf 226 Wedera leode on wang stiȝon, sæwudu sældon, syrcan hrysedon. a 1000 *Andreas* 127 (Gr.) Hæðne hildfrecan heapum þrungon, guðsearo gullon, garas hrysedon. c 1160 *Hatton Gosp.* Mark i. 30 Soðlice þa sæt symones sweȝer hresiȝende [*earlier MSS.* hriðiȝende]. c 1205 LAY. 18868 Scullen stan walles biuoren him to-fallen. Beornes scullen rusien. *Ibid.* 26917 þa riden Rom-leoden, riseden burnen [c 1275 rusede wepne]. 1340 *Ayenb.* 23 þe grete wynd.. þe greate helles makeþ to resye. c 1386 CHAUCER *Knt.'s T.* 1128 Ther-out cam a rage and such a vese, That it made al the gates for to rese.

rese, obs. form of RAISE *v.*

rese, late variant of REOSE, to fall. *Obs.*

re'seal (riː-), *v.* [RE- 5 a.] *trans.* To seal again. Hence **re'sealing** *vbl. sb.*

a 1700 KEN *Hymnotheo* Poet. Wks. 1721 III. 77 The Faithful.. Re-seal'd for Bliss with the Triunal Name. 1820 SCOTT *Abbot* xxxiii, 'Let Auchtermuchty carry this packet' (which he had resealed with his own signet) 'to my father'. 1884 *Pall Mall G.* 10 June 10/2 Judge Warren ordered the resealing of the probate. 1884 *Manch. Exam.* 26 Nov. 4/6 His letters.. were found opened and officially re-sealed.

reseant, variant of RESIANT *Obs.*

research (rɪ'sɜːtʃ, 'riːsɜːtʃ), *sb.*[1] Also 7 **-serch**. [ad. obs. F. *recerche* (1539; mod.F. *recherche*): see RE- and SEARCH *sb.*]

1. The act of searching (closely or carefully) *for* or *after* a specified thing or person.

1577 *F. de Lisle's Legendarie* G iv b, Being deliuered of that which they most feared, which was the researche for the Princes imprisonment. 1794 GODWIN *Cal. Williams* 210, I carefully avoided the habitation.. lest it should.. furnish a clue to the researches of my pursuers. 1799 SICKELMORE *Agnes & Leonora* II. 190 His father.. was making every possible research after us. 1827 DISRAELI *Viv. Grey* VI. iii, Fortune has not favoured me.. in my researches after a bed. 1847 C. BRONTE *J. Eyre* xxxiii, She had left Thornfield Hall in the night; every research after her course had been vain. 1889 *Nature* 19 Sept. 493/2 Constant explorations are being carried out.. chiefly in researches after gold and other precious metals.

2. a. A search or investigation directed to the discovery of some fact by careful consideration or study of a subject; a course of critical or scientific inquiry. (Usu. in *pl.*)

a 1639 WOTTON *Surv. Educ.* in *Reliq.* (1672) 85 There must go before a main research, whether the Child that I am to manage, be of a good nature or no. 1675 L. ADDISON *Pres. St. Jews* 237 Waving all Critical reserches into the word Talmud. 1728 YOUNG *Love Fame* VI. 413 Ye men of deep researches, say, whence springs This daring character, in tim'rous things? 1752 HUME *Ess. & Treat.* (1777) II. 9 These researches may appear painful and fatiguing. 1799 J. ROBERTSON *Agric. Perth* 290 Our most profound researches are frequently nothing better than guessing at the causes of the phenomena. 1830 D'ISRAELI *Chas. I*, III. iii. 26 Such ambiguous facts.. often baffle the researches of the historian. 1850 SIR B. BRODIE *Psychol. Inq.* I. i. 12 Cuvier was usually engaged for seven hours daily in his scientific researches. 1870 YEATS *Nat. Hist. Comm.* 5 Fresh necessities have led continually to fresh researches.

b. Without article: Investigation, inquiry into things. Also, as a quality of persons, habitude of carrying out such investigation.

1694 W. HOLDER *Princ. Harmony* Introd., The Matter lies deep in Nature and requires much Research into Natural Philosophy to unfold it. 1729 BUTLER *Serm.* Wks. 1874 II. 208 Men of deep research.. should just be put in mind, not to mistake what they are doing. 1809 W. IRVING *Knickerb.* Acc. Author (1849) 19 He found Mr. Cook a man.. of great literary research, and a curious collector of books. 1861 M. PATTISON *Ess.* (1889) I. 30 A writer of painstaking research, who goes.. to original and documentary authorities. 1892 *Photogr. Ann.* II. 161 Spectrum photography for the purposes of photographic research.

c. ***research knee-jerk***, a knee-jerk requiring special means to elicit it.

1899 *Allbutt's Syst. Med.* VI. 521 Sternberg.. found that the research knee-jerk is hardly ever.. really absent in healthy people.

3. Investigation or pursuit *of* a subject. *rare.*

1701 NORRIS *Ideal World* I. vii. 396 A thing.. happily performed in that admirable one the Research of Truth. 1759 DILWORTH *Pope* 53 His thoughts being quite weaned from Parnassus to the research of truth.

4. *Mus.* (See quot.) $rare^{-0}$.

1727–38 CHAMBERS *Cycl.* [from the *Dict. de Trévoux*], *Research*, in music, is a kind of prelude or voluntary.. wherein the composer seems to *search* or look out for the strains and touches of harmony, which he is to use in the regular piece to be played afterwards. 1876 STAINER & BARRETT *Dict. Mus. Terms.*

5. *attrib.* and *Comb.*, as ***research assistant, building, bureau, council, degree, department, doctorate, fellow, fellowship, grant, lab, laboratory, library, officer, personnel, post, programme, project, room, scholarship, station, student, unit, vessel, work, worker; research-minded*** adj.; **research and development**, in an industrial context, work directed on a large scale towards the innovation, introduction, and improvement of products and processes; freq. as *attrib. phr.*; abbrev. *R and D* s.v. R II. 2 a.

1923 *Industr. & Engin. Chem.* (News ed.) 20 Jan. 10/1 (Advt.), Professorship or assistant professorship in first class college or university desired by chemist, Ph.D., with seven years' experience in university teaching and six years' practical experience in *research and development work. 1935 *Chem. & Engin. News* 10 Jan. 15/1 Arthur R. Hitch has resigned from the Ethyl Gasoline Corp. to accept the position of director of research and development with the Nelio-Resin Corp. and the Southern Pine Chemical Co., Jacksonville, Fla. 1946 *Happy Landings* July (verso front cover), It is the latter type of accidents.. with which the research and development branches of M.S.A.P. is [*sic*] primarily concerned. 1968 J. SANGSTER *Touchfeather* xv. 182 Research and development is a notoriously difficult thing to budget for. 1979 *Arizona Daily Star* 5 Aug. B 4/5 The research-and-development costs of a new product, when funded by government, artificially reduce the price of the product. 1914 *Leeds Univ. Tenth Rep., 1912–13* 41 Two *Research Assistants in Botany. 1977 D. MACKENZIE *Raven & Kamikaze* xi. 128 I've been a senior research assistant for three and a half years. 1934 H. G. WELLS *Exper. Autobiogr.* ix. 815 It is the least grandiose and most practicable group of *research buildings in the world. 1925 *Scribner's Mag.* Oct. 404/1 The trade-union congress decided to open an 'official' *research bureau of its own. 1934 *Amer. Speech* IX. 113/1 *Traffic counts* are made by men from the *research bureau* of a *tourist organization*. 1920 *Brit. Med. Jrnl.* 27 Mar. 447/2 The Committee will come to life again as the Medical *Research Council and will act under the direction of a Committee of the Privy Council. 1971 *Nature* 5 Mar. 23/1 Rather more than £100 million are spent through the research councils. 1903 *Encycl. Brit.* XXXV. 788/1 *Research degrees. 1960 EELLS & HASWELL *Academic Degrees* ii. 27 Second in importance as a research degree and much more recent is the Doctor of Education. 1920 M. BEER *Hist. Brit. Socialism* II. xiv. 290 The Fabians have long felt the need for a special *research department. 1964 Research department [see *experiment station* s.v. EXPERIMENT *sb.* 7]. 1902 *Encycl. Brit.* XXXI. 397/1 The B.Lit. and B.Sc. (founded in 1895, and completed in 1900 by the institution of *research doctorates), have attracted graduates from.. other countries. 1899 *Research fellow [see FELLOW *sb.* 7 a]. 1966 *Rep. Comm. Inquiry Univ. Oxf.* II. 387 There are two broad classes of research fellow in the colleges. 1921 *Leeds Univ. Sixteenth Rep., 1919–20* 76 Mr. T. Hanby resigned the Gas *Research Fellowship. 1946 [see GRANT-IN-AID]. 1971 *Daily Tel.* 16 June 10/3 An IBM Research Fellowship has been awarded at Oxford University to Mr. M. R. Topp. 1930 *Univ. Sheffield Ann. Rep., 1929–30* 37 Mrs. May Mellanby.. has been appointed a member of the *Research Grants' Committee. 1940 H. G. WELLS *Babes in Darkling Wood* II. ii. 150 His income, derived from research grants, scientific writing, a small parcel of investments and gifts from his brother, was precarious. 1949 *Spectator* 18 Nov. 665/1 What the subject really needs.. is field-workers and a research grant. 1980 M. BOOTH *Bad Track* iv. 77 Thank God for research grants. 1973 D. FRANCIS *Slay Ride* xiii. 162 It's a *research lab job. 1914 *Leeds Univ. Tenth Rep., 1912–13* 43 A considerable sum of money was raised by public subscription for the establishment of an International *Research Laboratory. 1922 *Sci. Amer.* Aug. 100 Long before so-called industrial research laboratories were established in any country, there existed a very thorough international cooperation in scientific research. 1957 C. SMITH *Case of Torches* xi. 130 How often do you send reports to the Research Laboratories? 1962 Y. MALKIEL in Householder & Saporta *Probl. Lexicogr.* 3 Numerous *research-library catalogues make it a point to distinguish between mono-, bi-, tri-lingual and polyglot dictionaries. 1978 *Amer. N. & Q.* XVI. 141/1 During the 1950s a familiar sight at the loading dock of research libraries was the van of Hacker Art Books. 1959 *Times* 27 Apr. (Rubber Industry Suppl.) p. xii/7 *Research-minded graduates with high academic qualifications.. have excellent opportunities with some of the larger companies. 1971 HALSEY & TROW *Brit. Academics* xii. 291 There are more research-minded lecturers than senior lecturers. 1914 *Oxf. Univ. Calendar 1915* 74 *Research Officer in Diseases of Trees. 1972 *Classification of Occupations* (Dept. Employment) II. 47/2 Other titles include Research officer (Foreign and Commonwealth office). 1939 R. V. JONES *Most Secret War* (1978) ix. 73 The only method of dealing with the former is direct espionage, or the observation of indiscretions by *research personnel concerned. 1972 *Lebende Sprachen* XVII. 47/1 *Research personnel*, Forschungspersonal. 1966 *Rep. Comm. Inquiry Univ. Oxf.* II. 252 Included as full-time are all those with a university and/or college teaching or *research post. 1950 *N.Z. Jrnl. Agric.* June 514 (*caption*) The Rukuhia Soil Research Station (Hamilton).. carries out a *research programme in soil physics. 1958 *Bull. Amer. Assoc. Petroleum Geologists* XLII. 701 Some years ago the Field Research Laboratory of the Magnolia Petroleum Company began a Recent sediments research program in the Gulf of Mexico. 1977 *Sci. Amer.* Dec. 15/1 He now.. carries on a research program in the behavioral ecology of ants. 1949 *Radio Times* 15 July 23/2 Mrs. Proudfoot is engaged on a *research project for Nuffield College. 1977 *Canad. Jrnl. Linguistics 1976* XXI. 196 Throughout a good part of his career he has been associated, directly or indirectly, with research projects concerned with the description of corpora of recorded language. 1922 *Leeds Univ. Seventeenth Rep., 1920–21* 75 Honour Students now have the advantage of a separate laboratory, one of the old *Research Rooms having been specially equipped for the purpose. 1933 [see CARREL(L b]. 1949 J. ROUTH in *Granta* (Christmas ed.) 43/2 Then he takes them to the research room where the research workers take down their case histories. **1907** G. B. SHAW *Let.* 21 Mar. (1972) II. 675 Can't you get a *research scholarship, and travel for a year or so on that? **1937** *Granta* 3 Feb. 218/2 On graduating he was awarded the Earl of Derby Research Scholarship in History. **1917** *Rep. Fuel Research Board* 10 The *Research Station, as planned, will be capable of any extensions which will be required for future researches. **1974** 'E. FERRARS' *Hanged Man's House* v. 42 A lot of scientists in a research station. **1924** *Univ. Sheffield Ann. Rep., 1923–24* 36 There were 8 Post-Graduate *Research Students in the Session 1923–24. **1934** H. G. WELLS *Exper. Autobiogr.* II. ix. 815 Five hundred..research students from abroad were always to be working there. **1976** R. BARNARD *Little Local Murder* x. 129 Why don't you try a research student? **1937** *Whitaker's Almanack* 344/1 Clinical *Research Units. **1941** C. MORGAN *Empty Room* I. 5 Duck-boards stretched across..muddy gravel from the small square Lodge, where, he presumed, Research Unit Seven had their living quarters. *a* **1974** R. CROSSMAN *Diaries* (1976) II. 192 To try to get them a medical school for Warwick University and a motor research unit. **1977** *Guardian* 27 Apr. 6/2 Two *research vessels from the Institute of Marine Research at Bergen headed for the area yesterday. **1903** J. B. TOMLINSON (*title*) *Research work on popular and general subjects. **1935** *Burlington Mag.* Aug. 90/2 Most of the research-work..has already been undertaken. **1950** *Univ. Nottingham Ann. Rep.* 12 The staffing of departments needs to be reviewed in the light of the amount and kind of teaching required and of the research work in progress. **1917** *Jrnl. Soc. Automotive Engineers* Oct. 262/1 He was an experimental rather than an analytical *research worker. **1950** *Univ. Nottingham Ann. Rep.* 12 In many departments the work is seriously hampered simply by lack of space for research workers. **1969** I. & P. OPIE *Children's Games* p. vi, The research-worker..blessed with an unending flow of information can be in as embarrassing a position as he whose sources are limited.

re'search (riː-), *sb.*[2] *rare.* [RE- 5 a.] A second or repeated search.

1746 *Ascanus* 272 Those Parts having already been thoroughly ransack'd, and in all Probability would not be exposed to a Re-search. **1878** SPURGEON *Treas. Dav.* Ps. cvii. 4 They wandered up and down in vain searches and researches.

research (rɪ'sɜːtʃ, 'riːsɜːtʃ), *v.*[1] [ad. obs. F. *recercher* (mod.F. *rechercher*) = It. *ricercare* (med.L. *recercāre*): see RE- and SEARCH *v.*]

1. a. *trans.* To search into (a matter or subject); to investigate or study closely. Also, to engage in research upon (a subject, a person, etc.).

1593 G. HARVEY *New Letter* C iij, Some that haue perused eloquent bookes, and researched most curious writinges. *a* **1639** WOTTON in Gutch *Coll. Cur.* I. 216 To research with freedom..all their proper characters, and endowments. **1665** WALTON *Life Hooker* Introd., It must prove..a work of much labour to inquire, consider, research, and determine, what is needful to be known concerning him. **1786** MRS. A. M. BENNETT *Juvenile Indiscr.* I. 103 He had employed himself..in researching history. **1942** R. CHANDLER *High Window* (1943) xxxiii. 219 Some I was told, some I researched, some I guessed. **1959** *Encounter* Dec. 32/2 I'll author an article about it after I've researched the matter further. **1965** *New Statesman* 23 Apr. 642/1 Bryan Magee must have worn cosy blinkers when he researched lesbianism for his TV programme. **1971** D. POTTER *Brit. Eliz. Stamps* xv. 180 Collect, study and research your stamps. **1978** S. SHELDON *Bloodline* xiv. 175 She researched the guests, found out their likes and dislikes, what they ate and drank, and what type of entertainment they enjoyed. **1980** *Times* 1 Oct. 1/4 Union leaders..said they wanted time to 'research' the company's case before the next meeting.

b. *intr.* To make researches; to pursue a course of research. Also const. *in(to)*, *on*.

1781 H. WALPOLE *Let.* 27 Jan. (1858) VII. 505, I know, as Gray would have said, how little I have *researched*, and what slender pretensions are mine. **1801** SOUTHEY *Let. to John Rickman* 20 Nov. in *Life* (1850) II. 175 On these three subjects he is directed to read and research—corn-laws, finance, tythes, according to their written order. **1811** MOORE *Mem.* (1856) VIII. 97 When you write, or rather when you research, do not forget [etc.]. **1867** J. MACFARLANE *Mem. T. Archer* vi. 135 He travelled with the tourist—researched with the historian. **1935** D. L. SAYERS *Gaudy Night* i. 23, I believe she's researching on the Bacon family. **1958** *Times Lit. Suppl.* 14 Nov. 653/2 The *Savage Affair* is about one Michael Savage..researching into Commonwealth Drama. **1975** *Nature* 6 Nov. 27/3 He is a biochemist who has researched in many areas. **1977** *Navy News* July 12/3 Former lieutenant-commander, John Winton has researched into sea ballads, ships' logs, and sailors' personal writings and reminiscences to produce the latest of his works. **1977** K. O'HARA *Ghost of T. Penry* xv. 142 If you'd ever learn to research properly..you'd know you're always civil.

c. *trans.* To engage upon research for (a book or the like).

1965 *Listener* 4 Mar. 343/3 The book has been thoroughly and conscientiously 'researched', as the Americans say. **1973** *Which?* Dec. 367/1 This continued to research monthly features for sale to the mass-circulation *Daily Mirror.* **1975** *Publishers Weekly* 2 June 49/3 Barbara Villet, ex-*Life* reporter, researched her book in five big New York hospitals.

†**2.** To seek (a woman) in love or marriage. *Obs.*

1622 J. REYNOLDS *God's Revenge* I. Hist. ii, Because he seeth it labour lost, to research Christeneta, he will not bee obstinate in his suite. *Ibid.* iv, He is not capable to bee dissuaded from researching his Mistresse. **1649** *Alcoran* 23 You will not offend God in speaking a word in secret to women that you research in marriage.

Hence **re'searching** *vbl. sb.* and *ppl. a.*

1611 FLORIO, *Ricerca*, a search, a researching. *a* **1639** WOTTON in *Reliq.* (1672) 351 Your Style, which seemeth unto me..full of Sweet Raptures, and of researching Conceits. **1887** *Charity Organis. Rev.* Nov. 408 A stranger would be introduced, who by his questioning compelled researching of principles. **1930** J. B. PRIESTLEY *Angel Pavement* viii. 393 He wants to come along early next week and bring his researching friend Jiggs or Hoggs or something. **1981** J. SUTHERLAND *Bestsellers* xiii. 145 The most respected researching novelist in Britain is probably Len Deighton.

re'search (riː-), *v.*[2] [RE- 5 a.] *trans.* and *intr.* To search again or repeatedly.

1760–72 H. BROOKE *Fool of Qual.* (1809) II. 76, I searched and researched my memory. **1804** EUGENIA DE ACTON *Tale without Title* II. 246, I have searched and researched every corner of the house. **1861** O'CURRY *Lect. MS. Materials* 434 To search and research through the ancient MSS. themselves. **1876** 'MARK TWAIN' *Tom Sawyer* xxxii, The lads searched and re-searched this place, but in vain.

researchable (rɪ'sɜːtʃəb(ə)l), *a.* [f. RESEARCH *v.*[1] + -ABLE.] Worthy of being researched; suitable for methodical investigation.

1967 L. VON BERTALANFFY *Robots, Men & Minds* II. 86 There is a wealth of researchable and fascinating problems which..will open new perspectives and bring evolution into the framework of organismic and systems thinking. **1977** A. GIDDENS *Stud. in Social & Polit. Theory* iv. 169 Ordinary language is not therefore just a topic that can be made available for analysis, but is a resource that every sociological or anthropological observer must use to gain access to his 'researchable subject-matter'.

re'searched, *ppl. a.* [f. RESEARCH *v.*]

†**1.** Refined; recondite. *Obs.*

1654 H. L'ESTRANGE *Chas. I* (1655) 137 Men of the most re-searched nations are not usually the best qualified for Government. **1676** *Phil. Trans.* XI. 639 The clear and distinct neatness of its ratiocinations alwaies discovers to it the shortest way of researched Truths.

2. That has been subjected to research; that is the result of research.

1956 C. W. MILLS *Power Elite* ii. 33 The old southern aristocracy, in fictional image and in researched fact, is indeed often in a sorry state of decline. **1966** *New Society* 31 Mar. 25/3 This is a thorough, well researched, and authorised biography. **1978** *Jrnl. R. Soc. Arts* CXXVI. 737/2 The project teachers were involved in researched teaching about race relations. That is to say, the majority were either tape-recording their work or teaching with observation by colleagues.

re'searcher. [f. RESEARCH *v.*[1] + -ER[1].] One who researches; an investigator, inquirer.

1615 MAXWELL (*title*) Admirable and Notable Prophecies, ..by Iames Maxwell, a Researcher of Antiquities. **1670** W. SIMPSON *Hydrol. Ess.* 120 Whether by chymical researchers it was ever found. **1776** HAWKINS *Hist. Music* I. III. i. 253 The more sober researchers into antiquity. **1802** J. RITSON *Anc. Eng. Metr. Rom.* I. p. cxlii, Thomas Tyrwhitt, so ardent a researcher into ancient poetry. **1833** WHITTIER *Pr. Wks.* (1889) I. 292 The researchers of the bosoms of men. **1879** T. H. S. ESCOTT *England* II. 412 He is followed by the more thoughtful researcher, who goes beneath the surface.

b. One who devotes himself to scientific or literary research (esp. as contrasted with one whose time is chiefly occupied in teaching or directly remunerative work).

1883 E. R. LANKESTER in *Times* 21 Sept. 5 Teaching here appears to be producing an income which may support a researcher. **1883** *Pall Mall G.* 29 Sept. 12/2 By what means are we to decide whether the money paid to the researcher is being spent upon research? **1894** *Westm. Gaz.* 4 Dec. 2/1 The statute under which degrees are to be conferred on researchers.

c. *Psychical Researcher*, a member of the Society for Psychical Research; one who investigates psychical phenomena.

1885 *Daily News* 14 Feb. 5/2 It..will sum up the aspirations of Theosophists and Psychical Researchers. **1888** *Pall Mall G.* 24 Oct. 4/1 Psychical Researchers and other students of the supernatural.

re'searchful, *a.* [f. RESEARCH *sb.*[1] + -FUL.] Devoted to, characterized by, replete with, research.

1819 COLERIDGE in *Rem.* (1836) II. 129 Pity that the researchful notary has not..told us in what century..he was a writer. **1866** *Reader* No. 171. 342/1 The researchful sketches of Professor Wilson. **1875** M. A. LOWER *Eng. Surnames* (ed. 4) I. p. xxvi, A more erudite and researchful book.

researchist (rɪ'sɜːtʃɪst). [f. RESEARCH *v.*[1] + -IST.] = RESEARCHER.

1923 *Chambers's Jrnl.* Feb. 95/1 In an age when the superstitious seek eagerly for a sign..House of Clays would have disappointed a psychical researchist. **1961** D. ANGUS *Descent of Venus* v. 106 He claims to be a researchist in human relationships.

reseat (riː'siːt), *v.* [RE- 5 a.]

1. *trans.* To seat again, or replace, (a person) in a former abode, dignity, or position.

1637 SALTONSTALL *Eusebius' Constantine* 35 Those that have bin restored to those offices which had beene taken from them, being recalled and reseated in their places. **1654–66** EARL ORRERY *Parthen.* (1676) 615 The Generals re-seated them in those Thrones, of which they had been deprived. **1795** SOUTHEY *Lett. fr. Spain* (1808) I. 153 This morning Manuel was re-seated behind the coach. **1814** SIR R. WILSON *Priv. Diary* (1862) II. 343 This the pope, however, would not do..until he was reseated in the papal chair. **1859** TENNYSON *Guinev.* 521 Better the King's waste hearth and aching heart Than thou reseated in thy place of light.

fig. *a* **1690** E. HOPKINS *Serm.* Wks. 1809 IV. 486 When they are most calm..and their reason..again reseated upon its throne. **1810** CRABBE *Borough* v, If we could..that old ease and harmony re-seat, In all our meetings.

b. *refl.* To seat (oneself) again.

1818 SCOTT *Hrt. Midl.* xxi, 'True, true',—said the Monarch, reseating himself. **1838** LYTTON *Alice* III. vii, Evelyn, having risen to shake hands with Mrs. Hare, did not reseat herself. **1897** MARY KINGSLEY *W. Africa* 384, I reseat myself in the bottom of the boat.

2. To provide with a fresh seat or seats.

1851 MAYHEW *Lond. Labour* II. 29/2 Trousers are reseated and repaired where the material is strong enough. **1871** *Echo* 11 Feb., It has been decided to reseat the choir of Canterbury Cathedral as a memorial to the late Dean.

Hence **re'seating** *vbl. sb.*

1827 MALCOLM *Sk. Persia* ix. I. 120 The regulations of our risings and standings, and movings and reseatings.

‖**réseau** (rezo). Also †6 *Sc.* **rasour**; **reseau.** Pl. **-x.** [Fr., = net, web, etc.] **1. a.** A plain net ground used in lace-making.

1578 *Inv. R. Wardr.* (1815) 218 Aucht small peces of rasour of quhite silk. *Ibid.* 222 Ane lang taillit gowne of rasour of quhit silk. **1578** in F. B. Palliser *Hist. Lace* (1865) xxxiii. 395 Fyve litell vaills of wovin rasour of threde. **1865** F. B. PALLISER *Ibid.* vii. 105 There were two kinds of ground used in Brussels lace, the bride and the réseau. **1911** *Encycl. Brit.* XVI. 41/2 To the period from 1620 to 1670 belongs the development of long continuous scroll patterns with *réseaux* and *brides.* **1953** M. POWYS *Lace & Lace-Making* v. 40 The laces of Louis XVI have a lighter design, finally becoming little more than a border to the Réseau or net grounds on which are sprinkled small sprays. **1959** *Chambers's Encycl.* VIII. 294/1 Later, in the 18th century, Milan lace adopted the *réseaux* made popular in northern Europe. **1975** *Oxf. Compan. Decorative Arts* 524/1 Sometimes the *réseau* was bobbin-made and the threads attached to the open edges of the *toilé*, following the pattern.

b. With qualifying adjective or phrase, as ***réseau à l'aiguille*** (a lɛgɥij) [Fr. *aiguille*, needle], hand-made net ground; ***réseau ordinaire*** (ɔrdinɛr) [Fr., ordinary], standard machine-made net ground; ***réseau rosacé*** (rozase) [Fr., rosaceous] a mesh ground with a flower pattern.

1865 F. B. PALLISER *Hist. Lace* vii. 106 Since machine-made net has come into use the 'réseau à l'aiguille' is rarely made, save for royal trousseaux. *Ibid.*, Machinery has now added a third [way of making the réseau], the tulle or Brussels net, 'réseau ordinaire', made of Scotch thread. **1900** E. JACKSON *Hist. Hand-Made Lace* 218 *Réseau Rosacé*, the name given to the réseau ground in Argentan lace. **1911** *Encycl. Brit.* XVI. 41/2 Grounds composed entirely of varieties of *modes* as in the case of the *réseau rosacé*..were sometimes made then [*sc.* about 1700 to 1760]. **1953** M. POWYS *Lace & Lace-Making* iv. 14 The ground is the Réseau Ordinaire and the central filling the Mignon.

2. A network or grid, esp. one superimposed as a reference marking on photographs in astronomy, surveying, etc.

1902 *Nature* 5 June 140/1 The réseau is hinged in front of the plate, its correct register being determined by geometrical contacts. **1906** *Athenæum* 27 Jan. 111/1 Prof. Turner showed specimens of photographic reproductions of *réseaux* for stellar photography made by M. H. Bourget. **1940** C. A. HART *Air Photogr. applied to Surveying* ix. 245 Extreme accuracy of recording on a stereoscopic instrument becomes of value only when there is provided a stable basis of measurement, such as a reseau, a device commonly used in astronomical measurements from photographs. **1963** W. K. KILFORD *Elem. Air Survey* i. 19 A squared réseau is also sometimes engraved on the plate. This will make apparent any distortions of the negative due to non-flatness in the focal plane. **1976** J. B. GARNER et al. *Surveying* xiii. 228 The Principal Point is engraved on this glass, as are a number of small crosses, conventionally at 10mm centres in either direction, all of which are imaged at every exposure. These crosses form a reseau grid and enable the user to determine any subsequent distortion of the film to considerable accuracy.

3. A spy or intelligence network, esp. in the French resistance movement.

1960 G. MARTELLI *Agent Extraordinary* v. 82 This arrangement..enabled him to devote more time..to the running of the *réseau.* **1966** M. R. D. FOOT *SOE in France* ix. 258 Various intelligence réseaux in Paris. **1973** L. SNELLING *Heresy* II. i. 62 These agents made no connection between Graham and the escape *réseau.* **1974** T. ALLBEURY *Snowball* vii. 37 Paul Loussier had been an active member of one of the SOE *réseaux* in Paris when the Resistance was only measured in hundreds.

†**'resecate,** *pa. pple. Obs. rare.* Also 6 *Sc.* resecat. [ad. L. *resecāt-us*, late pa. pple. of *resecāre* to cut back: see RESECT *v.*] Cut off or away.

1530 in Strype *Eccl. Mem.* I. xv. 118 Superfluities, if any such should be thought and found, may be resecate; but to destroy the whole, it were great pity. **1536** BELLENDEN *Cron. Scot.* (1821) I. 54 The cursit pepill war, in thay dayis, resecat fra al gud cumpany.

†**rese'cation.** *Obs. rare.* [ad. late L. *resecātiōn-em*, n. of action f. *resecāre*: see prec.] The action of cutting off or away.

1607 TOPSELL *Four-f. Beasts* (1658) 476 The Holy Fire which the shepheards call 'the pox'..neither admitteth medicine nor resecation by knife. **1625** JACKSON *Creed* v. l. §6 Fulness of felicity did immediately result from these moral abstractions or resecations of superfluities.

rese'crete (riː-), *v.* [RE- 5 a.] *trans.* To secrete again.

1859 CORNWALLIS *New World* I. 131 Which store [of gold] is always quietly re-secreted under the ground of the tent or elsewhere. **1876** *Trans. Clinical Soc.* IX. 3 A linear incision in the iris, which when the aqueous humour was resecreted, gaped sufficiently to form the required pupil.

So **rese'cretion.**

1869 G. LAWSON *Dis. Eye* (1874) 6 Some astringent lotion to arrest the resecretion of the purulent matter. **1900** J. HUTCHINSON in *Arch. Surg.* XI. 215 The wound had simply healed and re-secretion had taken place.

†**re'sect**, *pa. pple. Obs. rare.* [ad. L. *resect-us*, pa. pple. of *resecāre*: see next.] Cut off or away; removed by cutting.

1545 RAYNOLD *Byrth Mankynde* 99 These partes beynge once resecte and cutte from the bodye, then turne the reste. **1642** H. MORE *Song of Soul* II. i. II. xlvi, I ought reject No soul from wished immortalitie, But give them durance when they are resect From organized corporeitie.

resect (rɪ'sɛkt), *v.* [f. L. *resect-*, ppl. stem of *resecāre* to cut off, f. *re-* RE- + *secāre* to cut.]

†**1.** *trans.* To cut off or away; to remove. *Obs.*

1653 R. BAILLIE *Dissuas. Vind.* (1655) 87 You will take yourself here to the whole Assembly at Westminster, resecting both their Directory and Confession. **1686** HORNECK *Crucif. Jesus* xvii. 421 He means no more than that the sins should be resected which cleave to it.

2. *Surg.* To cut or pare down; to remove a portion of (bone, cartilage, nerve, etc.) in this way; to cut out (in part).

1846 BRITTAN tr. *Malgaigne's Man. Oper. Surg.* 183 Others have proposed to..resect the bones of the fore-arm without disarticulating the humerus. **1879** *St. George's Hosp. Rep.* IX. 656 The whole of the bones which form the ankle-joint had been resected. **1894** *Lancet* 3 Nov. 1033 A portion of the sixth rib was resected. **1924** R. HOWARD *Surg. Emergencies* iv. 71 The portion of the gut to be resected is brought well out of the wound. **1976** *Nature* 25 Mar. 351/1 Two weeks after the initial operation the correct nerve to the anconeus muscle was crushed, or cut and resected.

absol. **1897** *Trans. Amer. Pediatric Soc.* IX. 91 In a tuberculous case you may resect repeatedly and yet the child will not get well.

3. *Surveying.* To map by resection.

1888 W. H. RICHARDS *Textbk. Mil. Topogr.* (ed. 2) iv. 38 Having determined stations by intersection, as described, the surveyor may, by reference to them, resect or find the point on his survey which corresponds to his position on the ground. **1931** M. HOTINE *Surveying from Air Photographs* vi. 92 The problem is..to resect the position of the perspective centre in space.

Hence **re'sected** *ppl. a.*

1897 *Syd. Soc. Lex.* s.v. *Resection*, The partially resected bone is replaced at the termination of the operation. **1913** A. R. HINKS *Maps & Survey* v. 108 Round about the intersected and resected points, the detail is sketched in by eye estimation.

resection (rɪ'sɛkʃən). [ad. L. *resectiōn-em*, n. of action f. *resecāre*: see prec. and cf. mod.F. *résection*.]

†**1.** The action of cutting off or away. *Obs.*

1611 COTGR., *Resection*, a resection; a cutting, paring, or shredding off. **1650** BULWER *Anthropomet.* 237 Without resection of the same [band], speech would become lame and imperfect. **1662** J. CHANDLER *Van Helmont's Oriat.* 163 Galen..knew that cutting off or resection was privately opposite to a Being that is born.

2. *Surg.* The operation of cutting or paring away a portion of bone or other structure, esp. the articular ends of bones.

1775 GOOCH in *Phil. Trans.* LXV. 375, I have been informed..that a resection of the bone is no uncommon practice at Paris. **1846** BRITTAN tr. *Malgaigne's Man. Oper. Surg.* 178 Partial and complete resection of the bones of the upper limbs. **1879** *St. George's Hosp. Rep.* IX. 317 Compound fracture about the elbow-joint, which rendered primary resection of the articulation necessary. **1881** *Amer. Jrnl. Med. Sci.* LXXXII. 263 (*heading*) Resection of about six and a half feet of the small intestine, with recovery. **1926** *Jrnl. Amer. Med. Assoc.* 20 Nov. 1728/2 Prostatic resection is applicable to a large number of cases of prostatic hypertrophy commonly subjected to prostatectomy. **1944** W. W. BABCOCK *Princ. & Pract. Surg.* xxxiii. 650 Avulsion of the entire ganglion has been supplanted by resection or division of the posterior sensory root. **1967** H. S. K. SINGHA *Pocket Surg.* viii. 131 Treatment consists in the resection of all visible tumour together with a wide margin of normal tissue. **1980** *Brit. Med. Jrnl.* 29 Mar. 882/1 Some surgeons can produce primary union of the bowel anastomosis in all but 5–10% of patients..even for anterior resection of the rectum.

attrib. **1884** KNIGHT *Dict. Mech.*, Suppl. 751/2 Resection Instruments. **1895** *Arnold & Sons' Catal.* 104 Six Resection Knives.

3. *Surveying.* The process of determining the position and orientation of a plane table from bearings of points already mapped, prior to mapping surrounding detail in relation to it.

1888 W. H. RICHARDS *Textbk. Mil. Topogr.* (ed. 2) iv. 38 Finding the place by resection with the magnetic needle. **1923** D. CLARK *Plane & Geodetic Surveying* I. 212 Resection is usually confined to small scale work. **1976** M. GILBERT *Night of Twelfth* vii. 86 He demonstrated on the map, 'that brings you into an area roughly here. You can't do an exact resection, of course.'

Hence **re'sectional** *a.*

1888 MASSEY *Electr. in Dis. Women* i. 2 A symptom that prompts most of the plastic and resectional operations.

resectionist (rɪ'sɛkʃənɪst). *Surg.* [f. prec. + -IST.] One who carries out resection.

1934 *Jrnl. Amer. Med. Assoc.* 24 Feb. 648/1 Transurethral resection..can be done by competent resectionists in more than 95 per cent of obstructions [of the prostate]. **1972** J. P. MITCHELL *Princ. Transurethral Resection & Haemostasis* xxvii. 225 This cumbersome attachment to the normal resectoscope impedes the resectionist.

resectoscope (rɪ'sɛktəskəʊp). *Med.* [f. RESECT *v.* + -O + -SCOPE.] A surgical instrument for transurethral resection.

1926 M. STERN in *Jrnl. Amer. Med. Assoc.* 20 Nov. 1726/2 It has been possible to reduce the problem to a mere cystoscopic procedure by the evolution of a cutting current capable of operating in a water medium, and a cystoscopic instrument for its application. This instrument is provided with a small movable ring or loop of tungsten wire which, when actuated by a suitable current, is capable of removing longitudinal spaghetti-like sections of tissue... Of these instruments I have named..the latter the resectoscope. **1951** M. CAMPBELL *Clin. Pediatric Urology* i. 74 Miniature resectoscopes are now available for transurethral removal of vesical neck obstruction..uretocele or small intra-vesical growths. **1962** *Lancet* 28 Apr. 914/1, I must admit to a certain amount of fear of producing incontinence in using the resectoscope on the female bladder neck, and prefer to use fulguration first, even if resection is necessary later. **1974** J. D. MAYNARD in R. M. Kirk et al. *Surgery* viii. 180 Provided IVP shows some renal function, treatment [of bladder neck obstruction] consists of posterior bladder neck resection per urethra with a resectoscope.

‖**reseda** (rɪ'si:də). Also *erron.* resida. [L. *resēda*, acc. to Pliny f. the imperative of *resēdāre* to assuage, allay (the words *resēdā morbis* having been used as a charm when applying the plant to the reduction of tumours).]

1. *Bot.* An extensive genus of herbaceous plants (typical of the order *Resedaceæ*), common in the Mediterranean region. The best known species are the Mignonette (*R. odorata*) and the Dyer's Weed (*R. luteola*).

1753 CHAMBERS *Cycl. Supp.* s.v., The species of reseda enumerated by Mr. Tournefort are these. 1. The common reseda [etc.]. **1754** *Catal. Seeds* in *Fam. Rose Kilravock* (Spald. Club) 427 Sweet-scented resida. **1785** MARTIN *Rousseau's Bot.* xx. (1794) 280 Sweet Reseda or Mignonette has oblong leaves some of which are entire. **1797** *Encycl. Brit.* (ed. 3) XVI. 87/1 Reseda, Dyer's-weed, Yellow-weed, Weld, or Wild-woad. **1875** BENNETT & DYER tr. *Sachs' Bot.* 177 Distinctly successive formation of the members of a whorl (as in..flowers of Reseda, &c.).

2. [orig. in French form *réséda*.] A pale green colour similar to that of mignonette.

1883 *Contemp. Rev.* Sept. 424 Réséda,..a pretty pale green which came in some seven years ago.., the soft tint of mignonette. **1889** *Pall Mall G.* 28 Feb. 4/1 Réséda has been all the rage this season, and réséda it was in the streets till you got quite..tired of seeing it. **1968** E. BRILL *Old Cotswold* v. 85 Its tall spires can sometimes be seen on the banks of newly-widened roads, the pale reseda of its leaves conspicuous among the darker greens of coarser herbage.

attrib. and *Comb.* **1873** *Young Englishwoman* Mar. 130/1 A costume of réséda-coloured poplinette is composed of a skirt rasterre, and a redingote tunic. *Ibid.* Apr. 182/2 A dress of réséda grosgrain silk. **1884** *Pall Mall G.* 8 Apr. 4/2 A réséda skirt. **1902** *Westm. Gaz.* 23 Oct. 3/1 One sees..dark blue and reseda-green and some red frocks and costumes. **1927** F. B. YOUNG *Portrait of Clare* 25 She forced herself to dwell upon the vision of the reseda shantung dress designed by Liberty. **1977** *Western Morning News* 30 Aug. 9/2 (Advt.), 1977 BMW 528. Manual. Reseda Green. Sunroof. Tint.

resede, obs. variant of RESIDE *v.*

resedew, obs. form of RESIDUE.

ˌ**resedimen'tation.** *Geol.* [ad. It. *risedimentazione* (C. I. Migliorini 1950, in *Atti Soc. Tosc. di Sci. nat., Mem.* A LVII. 83): see RE- 5 a.] Movement of previously deposited sediment from one location to another by marine currents. So **re'sediment** *v. trans.*; **re'sedimented** *ppl. a.*

1957 *Jrnl. Geol.* LXV. 231/1 Migliorini coined the term 'resedimented rocks' which is not entirely unambiguous but is nevertheless useful as a short way of referring to the deposits of turbidity currents. *Ibid.*, Various types of markings on the sole of the graywackes..explaining them on the basis of resedimentation by turbidity currents. **1973** *Nature* 26 Jan. 267/2 Because most coarse material resedimented from modern stable continental shelves passes down submarine canyons we interpret major occurrences of coarse resedimented material down slope of the Cambro-Ordovician shelf break as evidence of submarine canyon activity. *Ibid.* 268/1 Episodes of resedimentation occurred from soon after the inception of the miogeocline in Lower Cambrian times to the changes in sedimentary polarity..in Middle and Upper Ordovician times. **1978** [see *resuspension* s.v. RE- 5 a].

re'see (ri:-), *v.* [RE- 5 a.] To see again.

a **1618** SYLVESTER *Mathieu's Mem. Mort.* II. xcii, For a short time Thy Sun is over-cast: But, thou shalt once re-see't more bright than ever. **1658** J. WEBB *Cleopatra* VIII. I. 52, I made a strong resolution never to re-see that unfaithfull man whilst I lived. **1798** JANE AUSTEN *Northang. Abb.* v, Catherine was disappointed in her hope of re-seeing her partner. **1846** TENNYSON in *Mem.* (1897) I 236 Your friends here, who live in the hope of re-seeing you.

re'seed (ri:-), *v.* [RE- 5 a.] *trans.* To sow again. Also *absol.* Occas. as *sb.*, an area which has been reseeded. Hence **re'seeded** *ppl. a.*, **re'seeding** *vbl. sb.*

1888 *Voice* (N.Y.) 6 Sept., The meadow will need reseeding much sooner if seeded with grain. **1891** *Daily News* 25 June 5/4 As the seasons have been moist very few acres have required re-seeding. **1940** R. G. STAPLEDON *War Food Production Advisory Bull. No. 1* 26 The field was twenty-five acres, of which fifteen were re-seeded. *Ibid.*, The re-seeded portion of the field had the best grass. *Ibid.* 27 By 1938 we considered the area..to be in a sufficiently good condition to plough and re-seed. **1945** 'G. ORWELL' *Animal Farm* viii. 72 The pasture was exhausted and needed re-seeding. **1946** *Nature* 26 Oct. 587/1 Reseeded grassland. **1960** *Farmer & Stockbreeder* 5 Jan. 94/2 During the past 20 years vast acreages of old grassland..have been ploughed and re-seeded on official advice. **1966** *Economist* 24 Sept. 1208/3 Your attack on crofting ignores the remarkable Lewis reseeding schemes. **1970** *Watsonia* VIII. 193 A large area where the *Cerastium* used to grow had been re-seeded. **1973** *Stornoway Gaz.* 2 June 4/3 Maybe you're sleeping soundly o' nights, dreaming of all your frisky lambs and ewes on the surging reseeds. **1981** *Times* 11 Feb. 8/4 The reseeding of rubber plantations in southern Thailand.

re'seek (ri:-), *v.* [RE- 5 a.] To seek again.

a **1812** BARLOW (cited by Webster). **1830** LYTTON *P. Clifford* vii, Anticipating the time when Paul..would gladly and penitently re-seek the shelter of her roof. **1855** BAILEY *Mystic*, etc. 132 In loving God the soul reseeks its source. **1892** A. DE VERE *Leg. St. Patrick, Epil.*, I, bondsman in this land, re-sought this land.

†**resegall.** *Obs. rare*$^{-1}$. [ad. It. *risigallo* (†*risa-*), or med.L. *risigallum*.] = RESALGAR.

1610 MARKHAM *Masterpiece* II. lxxx. 359, I am to giue you this for a rule, that by no meanes you vse to a wind-gall, either arsnike, or resegall.

re'segregate, *v.* [RE- 5 a.] *trans.* To segregate again. So **resegre'gation**.

1923 *Daily Mail* 24 May 6 As travelling facilities improved these races began to resegregate themselves. *Ibid.*, With the upheaval of the war, when..the population was in a state of flux, resegregation probably became more rapid and accentuated. **1954** *Newsweek* 27 Sept. 59/2 (*heading*) Now resegregation. *Ibid.*, In this fashion were Greenbrier County's desegregated schools resegregated. **1970** *Washington Post* 22 Jan. A20/1 'Resegregation' is what may occur when a formerly *de jure* segregated school system complies with the order to desegregate and..people move around in such a way as to 'resegregate' the schools—only on a *de facto* basis this time. **1976** *Time* 27 Sept. 57/3 Another pattern of resegregation occasionally takes place within desegregated schools when students are simply assigned to segregated classes.

reseight, obs. form of RECEIPT *sb.*

†**re'seiser.** *Obs. rare.* Also **-sir.** [See RESEIZE and -ER[4].] The act, on the part of an overlord, of resuming possession of estates, property, or privileges, upon failure of the holder to carry out or comply with the required conditions.

1559 in Strype *Ann. Ref.* (1709) I. App. viii. 23 The Meanes how the Bisshoppe after his Consecration comyth to his Temporalties; And of the Reseiser therof, if the Bisshoppe procede not therin in due Order. **1567** STANFORD *Exposicion* 80 Reseisir lieth where a general liuere or *ouster le main* is missued by any person or persons vnduely and not according to the forme and order of the law. *Ibid.* 83 b, Whether in this case yᵉ missuing of yᵉ same shal be a cause of reseiser or not.

reseit(e, obs. forms of RECEIPT *sb.*

reseize (ri:'si:z), *v.* Forms: 5 **receyse**, 6–7 **reseise**, 6– **reseize**, 7– **re-seize**; 5 **recease**, 6 **-sease**, 7 **-seaze**. [ad. OF. *resaisir* (mod.F. *ressaisir*; med.L. *resaisīre*, etc.): see RE- and SEIZE *v.*]

†**1.** *trans.* To invest or endow (one) again *with*, put again in possession *of*, something; to replace *in*, or restore to, a former position or dignity. *Obs.*

1413 *Pilgr. Sowle* (Caxton 1483) v. ix. 100 Full soone he shall be fette oute of thy hand Receysed shalle he be with paradys. **1562** *Burn. Paules Ch.*, Because the kinge hais reuested and reseased me of the whole archbishopricke. **1590** SPENSER *F.Q.* II. x. 45 He..therein reseized was againe, And ruled long with honorable state. **1607** BP. ANDREWES *Serm.* (1841) II. 219 We..need to be consecrate anew, to re-seize us of the first fruits of the Spirit again. **1647** N. BACON *Disc. Govt. Eng.* I. xlvi. (1739) 76 By this means he re-seized and reassumed the English, in partnership with the Norman in their ancient right.

2. To seize, take hold or possession of, (some thing or person) again.

1567 STANFORD *Exposicion* 82 b, To come & shew why the land should not bee reseised. **1599** *Death Philip II* in *Harl. Misc.* (Malh.) II. 285 The goute reseasing him, accompanied with a fever, made him far sicker than before. **1602** WARNER *Alb. Eng.* IX. xlviii. 222 The rightfull heire of Portugale his Empyre shall re-seaze. **1666** *Ormonde MSS.* in *10th Rep. Hist. MSS. Comm.* App. V. 21 His Grace re-seized the lands. *a* **1700** KEN *Hymnotheo* Poet. Wks. 1721 III. 105 In his Cell his Sorrow him reseiz'd. **1768** BLACKSTONE *Comm.* III. x. 187 The sheriff is commanded to reseise the land and all the chattels thereon. **1817** JAS. MILL *Brit. India* I. III. iv. 608 When the opposing army was obliged to retrace its steps, they immediately reseized the country. **1845** LD. CAMPBELL *Chancellors* lii. (1857) III 28 A motion about re-seizing the lands of a relapsed recusant.

absol. **1567** STANFORD *Exposicion* 82 The kinge may reseise wᵗout a *Scire facias*. *Ibid.* 83 b, Whether the king shal reseise in that case.

Hence **re'seizer**, 'one that seizes again.'

1755 in JOHNSON; hence in later Dicts.

re'seizure (ri:-). ? *Obs.* [RE- 5 a: cf. prec.] The action of seizing or taking back again.

a **1626** BACON *Holy War* (1629) 122 Here we haue the Charter of Foundation: It is now the more easie to iudge of the Forfeiture, or Reseisure. **1647** N. BACON *Disc. Govt. Eng.* II. xxviii. (1739) 132 This was one great Windfal which the Parliament had from the ruins of Rome, not by way of Usurpation, but by re-seizure. *a* **1683** SCROGGS *Courts-Leet* (1714) 107 The Defendant..before this Reseizure laboured the said Gelding, riding upon him, and drawing with him.

rese'lect, *v.* [RE- 5 a.] *trans.* To select again. So **rese'lection**.

1940 F. D. DAVISON *Woman at Mill* I. 83 Lot 32..had been forfeited and was available for re-selection. **1953** *New Biol.* XIV. 47 In Peru a special type [of cotton] of *barbadense* has been acclimatized and reselected. *Ibid.* 58 In Egypt we attempted also a further refinement of purity, and even improvement, by continued reselections of single-plant origin. **1979** *Guardian* 5 July 24/3 The NEC..agreed to put reselection of MPs back on the agenda. **1981** *Observer* 31 May 12/3 One left wing MP..said after last week's National Executive had voted against MP's being reselected unopposed [etc.].

re'sell (riː-), *v.* [RE- 5 a.] To sell again.

1574 *Galway Arch.* in *10th Rep. Hist. MSS. Comm.* App. V. 424 Fleash..to be sold and bought at the first hand only without to shell or reshyll it again. **1755** MAGENS *Insurances* I. 401 [They] cannot know what Profit or Loss they are to have on what they have so bought untill they resell. **1771** BURROW *Rep.* III. 1921 The Defendant..had bought Goods at an Auction, which were..put up again and resold. **1816** SCOTT *Antiq.* iii, Osborne resold this..windfall to Dr. Askew for sixty guineas. **1863** FAWCETT *Pol. Econ.* I. iii. 16 The company has commenced reselling the land to its original proprietors.

Hence **re'seller**.

1896 *Daily News* 28 Jan. 8/7 For American mixed [maize] re-sellers are asking more money.

†**re'semblable**, *a. Obs.* [a. OF. *resemblable* (14th c.): see RESEMBLE *v.* and -ABLE.] Capable of being compared or likened; comparable, similar (*to* some person or thing); like.

? *a* **1366** CHAUCER *Rom. Rose* 985 These arowis..Were alle fyve on oon maneere, And alle were they resemblable. **1390** GOWER *Conf.* I. 35 For man of Soule resonable Is to an Angel resemblable. *c* **1407** LYDG. *Reson & Sens.* 2137 They be nat resemblable To my beaute nor comparable. **1429** *Pol. Poems* (Rolls) II. 143 That thow mayst be resemblable founde,..Liche themperour worthy Sygesmounde. *c* **1530** LD. BERNERS *Arth. Lyt. Bryt.* (1814) 201 He should haue the fayre Florence, to whome the ymage was resemblable. **1665** SIR T. HERBERT *Trav.* (1677) 253 Thales Milesius was of opinion that the Earth floated and was aptly resemblable to a ship swimming in the Water.

resemblance (rɪˈzɛmbləns), *sb.*[1] [a. AF. *resemblance* (*a* 1300 in *Manuel de Peches* 4035) = mod.F. *ressemblance*: see RESEMBLE *v.* and -ANCE.]

1. a. The quality or being like or similar; likeness or similarity in appearance or any other respect; the fact of some likeness existing or being present. Freq. const. *to*, *between*, or †*with*; †also in phr. *by* or *with resemblance*.

1390 GOWER *Conf.* III. 122 Libra..hath figure and resemblance Unto a man which a balance Berth in his hond. *c* **1430** LYDG. *Min. Poems* (Percy Soc.) 58 This world is ful of stabilnesse,..Verraily by resemblaunce, So as the crabbe gothe forwarde. *c* **1475** *Lament. Mary Magd.* xxxiii, The speare with euery naile Thirled my soule by inwarde resemblaunce. **1509** HAWES *Past. Pleas.* XIII. (Percy Soc.) 51 So is enprynted in his propre mynde Every tale wyth hole resemblaunce. **1598** R. HAYDOCKE tr. *Lomazzo* I. 61 Anie other Goddesse, which hath any kinde of resemblance with the Earth. **1607** TOPSELL *Four-f. Beasts* (1658) 95 Either sex loose every year their hoofs..that nature may show their resemblance in their feet to a Hart. **1648** BOYLE *Seraph. Love* xvi. (1700) 98 This other Resemblance, betwixt God's Work on us, and the load-stones on the Iron. **1651** HOBBES *Leviath.* II. xxiv. 130 In this also, the Artificiall Man maintains his resemblance with the Naturall. **1718** *Free-thinker* No. 63. 54 There is not the least Resemblance between Words and Colours. **1771** *Junius Lett.* lxii. (1788) 331 A vague comparison between two things which have little or no resemblance to each other. **1820** W. IRVING *Sketch Bk.* I. 189 There are always general features of resemblance in the works of contemporary authors. **1855** PRESCOTT *Philip II*, II. vii. I. 222 The cap, being red, was thought to bear much resemblance to a cardinal's hat. **1871** JOWETT *Plato* IV. 4 These differences are accompanied by resemblances..to passages in other Platonic writings.

Comb. **1748** RICHARDSON *Clarissa* xciv. VII. 364 My resemblance-forming fancy immediately made it to be him.

†**b.** Const. *of* = to. *Obs.* (freq. in 17th c.)

1601 HOLLAND *Pliny* I. 79 The rocke into which there goeth a tale, that the ship of Vlysses was turned, for the resemblance it hath of such a thing. **1638** JUNIUS *Paint. Ancients* 21 An image wherein there might be perceived some resemblance of Pallas. **1690** LOCKE *Hum. Und.* II. viii. §15 The Ideas, produced in us by these secondary Qualities, have no resemblance of them at all. **1793** COWPER *Mary* 50 Should my future lot be cast With much resemblance of the past.

†**c.** Congruity, suitability. *Obs. rare*⁻¹.

1715 LEONI *Palladio's Archit.* (1742) I. 64 The Pillars are ..coarsly wrought, as seems to become a Country-house, to which nice and finish'd Works bear not so true a resemblance as plain and natural ones.

†**d.** *to make resemblance*, to appear about *to* do something. *Obs. rare*⁻¹.

1634 *Malory's Arthur* (1816) I. 231 And therewith he made resemblance [*Malory* semblaunt] to strike off his head.

e. *Biol.* An evolved similarity in appearance between organisms of different species.

1862 H. W. BATES in *Trans. Linn. Soc.* XXIII. 502 Mimetic analogies..are resemblances in external appearance, shape, and colours between members of widely distinct families. **1902** *Encycl. Brit.* XXVII. 149/2 Mimetic resemblance is far commoner in the female than in the male, a fact readily explicable by selection, as suggested by Wallace. **1912** *Proc. Zool. Soc.* 361 Some of the cases of resemblance [of Blattidæ to Coleoptera] are so detailed and close that it is impossible to regard them as anything but examples of true mimicry. **1931**, **1951** [see MIMICRY 2]. **1968** R. D. MARTIN tr. *Wickler's Mimicry* ii. 22 One of the most astonishing cases of one species resembling another (interspecific resemblance) occurs in a butterfly of the swallowtail family (Papilionidae) in the species *Papilio dardanus.* **1974** *Encycl. Brit. Macropædia* XII. 214/1 In mimicry the animate agent of selection..interacts directly with at least two of the similar forms and is deceived by their similarity... A convergent resemblance, on the other hand, results from the action of similar forces of natural selection ..on unrelated organisms, which may be geographically or temporally isolated from each other.

2. a. The external appearance, or characteristic features, peculiar to an individual or a class of persons or things.

1390 GOWER *Conf.* I. 366 Solyns..seith of fowhles ther is on, Which hath a face of blod and bon, Liche to a man in resemblance. **1483** CAXTON *Cato* A iij, His sone..did do make an ymage to the resemblaunce of hys fader. **1594** SHAKS. *Rich. III*, III. vii. 11 His resemblance being not like the Duke. **1596** SPENSER *F.Q.* IV. viii. 32 Beautie, which was made to represent The great Creatours owne resemblance bright. **1610** GUILLIM *Heraldry* II. v. (1611) 49 In ancient roles I find the Bend drawne somewhat Archwise or after the resemblance of the Bent of a Bow. **1636** BRATHWAIT *Rom. Emp.* 339 Very able of body, of a beautifull resemblance. **1697** DRYDEN *Virg. Georg.* III. 96 She..in her Face a Bull's Resemblance bears. **1712** ADDISON *Spect.* No. 351 ¶7 [Satan] gliding through the Garden, under the resemblance of a Mist. **1781** COWPER *Charity* 396 The soul, whose sight all-quickening grace renews, Takes the resemblance of the good she views. **1870** DISRAELI *Lothair* iv, A garden..which ..had the resemblance of a vast mosaic.

†**b.** *in resemblance of*, after the likeness or fashion of. *Obs. rare.*

1390 GOWER *Conf.* III. 294 Thei for evere in remembrance Made a figure in resemblance Of him. **1775** ADAIR *Amer. Ind.* 216 Four other religious places, in resemblance of the Jewish synagogues. *Ibid.* 217 [Benzo] says, they wash their new born infants, in resemblance of the Mosaic law.

†**c.** A specific character or attribute. *Obs. rare.*

1622 BACON *Hen. VII* (1876) 22 It did refresh and reflect upon the King a most odious resemblance, as if he would be another King Richard. **1686** tr. *Chardin's Trav. Persia* Ep. Ded., None of those Magnificent Images of Divinity, are equal to Your Majesty in the Divine Resemblances of Affability, Courtesie, Vigilance..and Constancy.

†**3. a.** A thing having similarity or likeness to another. *Obs. rare.*

c **1386** CHAUCER *Wife's Prol.* 368 Been ther none othere maner resemblances That ye may likne your parables unto, But-if a sely wyf be oon of tho? **1413** *Pilgr. Sowle* (Caxton 1483) V. xi. 101 Though the dede were nowhere nyghe soo grete, yett is hit a manere of resemblaunce. **1477** EARL RIVERS (Caxton) *Dictes* 7 And sayd Sedechias, commonely euery resemblance delyteth other.

†**b.** A symbol or figure *of* something. *Obs.*

1561 DAUS tr. *Bullinger on Apoc.* (1573) 144 b, Oyle is a resemblaunce of the Holy Ghost. **1597** HOOKER *Eccl. Pol.* V. lvii. §5 We take not baptisme nor the Eucharist for bare resemblances..of things absent. **1659** HAMMOND *On Ps.* lxii. 3 So is [it] a fit resemblance to signify him that is ready to kill another. **1669** GALE *Crt. Gentiles* I. I. x. 52 Names are but pictures, shadows, or ressemblances of things.

†**c.** A simile or comparison; a thing compared to another. (Cf. 5.) *Obs.*

1624 BEDELL *Lett.* viii. 118 Consider those resemblances taken out of the holy Scripture, wherein that godly Father is frequent. *a* **1653** GOUGE *Comm. Heb.* xi. 25 These and other like resemblances are fit..in regard of the uncertainty of life; it may on a sudden vanish, as soon as the foresaid resemblances. **1694** W. HOLDER *Princ. Harmony* 77 For, (to use a homely resemblance) That our Food..may not cloy the Palate..the Cook finds such kinds..of Sawce, as.. please the Palate.

4. a. A likeness, image, representation or reproduction of some person or thing.

1390 GOWER *Conf.* II. 83 After what forme that hem thoghte, The resemblance anon thei wroghte. **1604** F. G[RIMSTONE] *D'Acosta's Hist. Indies* V. xix. 420 The idoll.. which they called the resemblance of their God. **1631** WEEVER *Anc. Funeral Mon.* 812 A marble, vpon which is the resemblance of a man crosse-legged, all in male armour. **1667** MILTON *P.L.* IX. 538 Fairest resemblance of thy Maker faire, Thee all things living gaze on. **1697** BP. PATRICK *Comm. Exod.* xxii. 18 If a Man see any where Waxen Resemblances, made and set either at their Doors [etc.]. **1777** SIR W. JONES *Ess. Imit. Arts* Poems, etc. 204 What is an imitation, but a resemblance of some other thing? **1802** MAR. EDGEWORTH *Moral T.* (1816) I. 252 One of these words was an exact resemblance of the word tyrant. **1833** N. ARNOTT *Physics* (ed. 5) II. 235 We now understand how an admirable miniature resemblance of the objects before us is produced upon the retina of the eye.

†**b.** An appearance or show *of* some quality; a demonstration of affection; a likelihood or probability. *Obs.*

1561 T. NORTON *Calvin's Inst.* I. Pref., A certaine vaine resemblance of righteousnesse doeth abundantly content vs in stede of righteousnesse in dede. **1590** SPENSER *F.Q.* III. vii. 16 He ween'd that his affection entire She should aread; many resemblaunces To her he made, and many kinde remembraunces. **1603** SHAKS. *Meas. for M.* IV. ii. 203 *Pro.* But what likeliehood is in that? *Duke.* Not a resemblance, but a certainty.

c. A person resembling another in some way; (one's) like. *rare*⁻¹.

1794 MRS. RADCLIFFE *Myst. Udolpho* ix, I shall never meet with his resemblance.

†**5.** *Rhet.* The action or fact of comparing one person or thing to another. (Cf. 3 c.) *Obs.*

1589 PUTTENHAM *Eng. Poesie* III. xix. (Arb.) 250 When we liken an humane person to another in countenaunce, stature, speach or other qualitie, it is not called bare resemblance, but resemblaunce by imagerie or pourtrait.

†**re'semblance**, *sb.*[2] *Obs. rare*⁻¹. [See RESEMBLE *v.*[2]] Assembly.

1662 HOBBES *Considerations* 14 You were also assisting to the Resemblance of Divines that made the Directory.

†**re'semblance**, *v. Obs. rare.* [f. *sb.*[1]] *trans.* To resemble. Hence **re'semblancing** *ppl. a.*

1652 GAULE *Magastrom.* 141 They must needs be taking speciall notice of it..for..a resemblancing configuration, or a prodigious wonder. **1652–62** HEYLIN *Cosmogr.* III. (1673) 24/2 Such a noise..as resemblanceth at a great distance a clap of Thunder.

resemblant (rɪˈzɛmblənt), *a.* and *sb.* [a. OF. *resemblant* (mod.F. *ressemblant*), pres. pple. of *resembler* to RESEMBLE: cf. SEMBLANT.]

A. *adj.* **1.** Similar, having resemblance or likeness, *to* something. †Also const. *of* (quot. 1786).

1390 GOWER *Conf.* II. 85 Gold and selver..To whiche alle othre be degres Of the metalls ben acordant, And so thurgh kinde resemblant. **1571** DIGGES *Pantom.*, *Math. Treat.* xxv. Ff iv b, In sundry proportions and proprieties so agreable and resemblante to those regulare solides, whose names they beare. **1586** FERNE *Blaz. Gentrie* 173 Some Painims did beare the like signe in Armes, very resemblant to the playne crosse. **1607** J. CARPENTER *Plaine Mans Plough* 14 That part of the land of Israel right resemblant to the field of the foolish. **1741–2** STACKHOUSE *Hist. Bible* (1767) IV. VI. iv. 134 A passage very resemblant to what we read here. **1786** BIGLAND *Hist. Mon. & Gen. Coll. Gloucester* I. 439 This Figure, which is very resemblant of those in the Temple Church. **1816** SINGER *Hist. Cards* 215 The figures in Mexican hieroglyphical paintings also afford objects very resemblant to those on our court cards. **1857** *Fraser's Mag.* LVI. 599 In no work..is there such a gallery of portraits, and so resemblant to what they were in..the flesh.

2. Characterized by resemblance or similarity; similar, like.

1581 PETTIE tr. *Guazzo's Civ. Conv.* I. (1586) 31 The most naturall and resemblant picture of a Gentleman. **1797** *Philanthrope* 263 Presenting to the eye the resemblant signs of its objects. **1835** SOUTHEY *Doctor* lxxix. (1848) 178 Resemblant therefore as the features were, the dissimilitude of expression was more apparent. **1882–3** SCHAFF *Encycl. Relig. Knowl.* I. 450 The single features are often strikingly resemblant.

3. Aiming at the production of resemblances.

1870 RUSKIN *Aratra Pentel.* iv. (1872) 117 The object of the great Resemblant Arts is..to resemble as closely as possible.

B. *sb.* †**1.** A semblance; a show. *Obs. rare.*

1470–85 MALORY *Arthur* XIV. vi. 649 The lyon sawe that he made no resemblaunt to fyghte with hym. **1546** LANGLEY tr. *Pol. Verg. De Invent.* VII. iii. 133 After his example other counterfeicted a resemblant of perfeccion namyng themselfes Hieronomians.

2. A counterpart, analogue. *rare*⁻¹.

1893 *Sat. Rev.* 25 Feb. 204/2 Forms or scraps or resemblants of it belong..to Lorch, Brandenburg, and Ispahan.

resemble (rɪˈzɛmb(ə)l), *v.*[1] [ad. OF. *resembler* (12th c.; mod.F. *ressembler*), f. *re-* RE- + *sembler*:—L. *similāre*, *simulāre*, f. *similis* like: cf. It. *risim-*, *risomigliare.*]

1. *trans.* To be like, to have likeness or similarity to, to have some feature or property in common with (another person or thing).

1340 *Ayenb.* 61 Hi resembleþ an eddre þet hatte serayn. **1377** LANGL. *P. Pl.* B. XVI. 214 Þe sone, if I it durst seye, resembleth wel þe wydwe. *c* **1420** LYDG. *Assembly of Gods* 1572 Mathew in hys mood, Resemblyd an Aungell with wynges gloryously. **1530** PALSGR. 688/1 It is nat he but he resembleth hym moche. **1585** T. WASHINGTON tr. *Nicholay's Voy.* II. vi. 36 These trees doe properly resemble the Lentiscus. **1605** SHAKS. *Macb.* II. ii. 13 Had he not resembled My Father as he slept, I had don't. **1665** BOYLE *Occas. Refl.* III. i. 241 A sort of vain and flanting Grandees, who..do but too much resemble these painted Clouds. **1718** *Free-thinker* No. 75. 142 Cunning resembles Prudence, as an Ape resembles a Man. **1771** *Junius Lett.* lxvii. (1788) 339 The unhappy Baronet has no friends, even among those who resemble him. **1830** D'ISRAELI *Chas. I*, III. vi. 114 There was no Stuart whose countenance resembled that of Charles the First. **1896** *Law Times* C. 466/2 The coronet..did not so closely resemble a Royal Crown as to be likely to be taken for it.

2. To compare or liken (a person or thing) *to* another. Now *arch.*

1377 LANGL. *P. Pl.* B. XII. 265 To lowe lybbyng men þe larke is resembled. **1390** GOWER *Conf.* II. 135 The maladie Which cleped is ydropesie Resembled is unto this vice. **1477** EARL RIVERS (Caxton) *Dictes* 16 Lyff may be resembled unto the fleyng of an arowe. **1509** FISHER *Funeral Serm. C'tess Richmond* Wks. (1876) 303 This noble prynces whome we dyde resemble vnto the blessyd woman Martha. **1539** TAVERNER *Erasm. Prov.* (1545) 93 Ydle personnes whiche flee paynes, who be very well resembled to cattes by the englysh prouerbe. **1604** T. WRIGHT *Passions* II. iii. §3. 72 We may resemble our Passions to men affected with the dropsie. **1678** CUDWORTH *Intell. Syst.* I. iv. §25. 425 As Jupiter and the world may be resembled to a man, so may Providence be to the soul. **1711** ADDISON *Spect.* No. 160 ¶4 Thus Solomon resembles the Nose of his Beloved to the Tower of Libanon. **1774** GOLDSM. *Nat. Hist.* (1862) I. ii. 9 The ships..may be resembled to two men. **1825** COLERIDGE *Aids Refl.* (Bohn) I. 131 At the date of St. Paul's Epistles, the Roman world may be resembled to a mass in the furnace in the first moment of fusion. **1887** *Athenæum* 31 Dec. 897/3 Mars, the red planet to which that star [Antares] was thus resembled, is in Virgo.

†**b.** To compare together, or *with* another thing. Also *ellipt. Obs.*

1533 MORE *Debell. Salem* Wks. 984/1 How goeth nowe.. thys aunswere of this good man..touchyng the point that I resemble theim for? **1599** J. RAINOLD *Overthrow Stage-plays*

(1629) 78 A marvellous case, that I should compare and resemble plaiers together so absurdly. **1622** CALLIS *Stat. Sewers* (1647) 153 And if one would resemble this case with other authorities, and with the reason of other Book cases of the Law, it will be made thereby apparant, that [etc.]. **1673** MARVELL *Reh. Transp.* II. 203 The Power of Princes is not improperly resembled and derived down by Paternal Authority.

†**c.** To explain (a thing) *in* a certain way.

1592 BABINGTON *Comf. Notes Gen.* xxxii. 11 Jacobs halting some haue resembled..in this sorte. First that it should betoken an halting posterity.

†**3.** To represent, depict, make an image or likeness of (a person or thing); to figure, typify. *Obs.*

1390 GOWER *Conf.* III. 125 This Signe is verraily resembled Lich to a man, which halt assembled In eyther hand a water spoute. **1562** LEIGH *Armorie* (1597) 70 b, There are nine rebatings of Armes, which..are resembled, as hereafter followeth. **1579–80** NORTH *Plutarch, Alexander* (1612) 674 Lysippus..hath perfectly drawne and resembled Alexanders manner of holding his necke. **1613** PURCHAS *Pilgrimage* IV. xviii. 437 The Chinians,..if they would resemble a deformed man, they paint him with short habite ..and a long nose. **1638** JUNIUS *Paint. Ancients* 53 Painters and Carvers..when they were to resemble the Gods, departed not one inch from the Poets. **1705** STANHOPE *Paraphr.* I. 25 Admitting the Ignorance..of former Ages to be well resembled by the Darkness of the Night.

†**b.** To imitate or copy. *Obs. rare*$^{-1}$.

1613 B. JONSON *Challenge at Tilt* Wks. (1616) 998 In what shape soeuer I present my selfe, thou wilt seeme to be the same? Not so much as my chariot but resembled by thee?

4. To make like *to* some person or thing. Also in *pa. pple.*, made like, similar. Now *rare*.

c **1460** FORTESCUE *Abs. & Lim. Mon.* ii. (1885) 112 Thair kyngdomes bethe than most resembled to the kyngdome of God. **1565** COOPER *Thesaurus* s.v. *Abripio*, Although nature hath not resembled him, or made him like vnto his father. **1586** MARLOWE *1st Pt. Tamburl.* II. vi, I hope we are resembled, Vowing our loves to equal death and life. **1665** BOYLE *Occas. Refl.* I. vi. 175 Outward Accidents, and Conditions, whose restless Vicissitudes but too justly and too fitly resemble them to Wheels. **1865** BUSHNELL *Vicar. Sacr.* III. iii. 241 A want of system..too closely resembled to a want of truth to allow any solid title to respect.

†**5.** *intr.* To seem, to appear. *Obs.*

c **1375** *Sc. Leg. Saints* xxv. (*Julian*) 503 He resemblyt fore to be worthy and gud. *c* **1400** MAUNDEV. (1839) xix. 210 And thei seyn, that theise Bestes ben Soules of worthi men, that resemblen in lyknesse of the Bestes, that ben faire. **1453** *Rolls of Parlt.* V. 270/2 Come unto theym resemblyng to be theire grettest frendes. *c* **1475** *Partenay* 4521 An huge tablet this fair lady bar..Resembling to be fourged all of-new. *c* **1477** CAXTON *Jason* 56 b, They..resemble well by theyr countenaunce and habylemens that they ben departed from noble and goode hous. *c* **1510** BARCLAY *Mirr. Gd. Manners* (1570) D iij, Reputing in his thought By suche maner giftes thee greatly to content, Because thou resembled as poore and indigent.

6. To be like in some respect *to* another person or thing. Now *rare*.

1429 *Pol. Poems* (Rolls) II. 144 God graunt the grace for to resemble in al Unto these noble worthy conquerours. *a* **1471** FORTESCUE *Wks.* (1869) 485 Suche a compassion resembleth rather to cruelte than to pyte. **1530** PALSGR. 134 Participles.., in some accidentes, resemble unto their verbes. **1584** COGAN *Haven Health* i. 8 That which resembleth vnto cleare water, betokeneth [etc.]. **1715** M. DAVIES *Athen. Brit.* I. 328 Fortescue's Fate..resembles something to Chancellor Bacon's Misfortunes. **1836** LYTTON *Athens* (1837) I. 52 The Persian Creed derived from Zoroaster resembled the most to that of Christianity.

b. To have mutual likeness; to be like or similar to each other.

1751 *Female Foundling* II. 6 Few Characters could resemble more, than the Characters of these two Women. **1817** JAS. MILL *Brit. India* I. II. x. 431 In one feature or two, nations resemble, which are placed at stages considerably remote. *a* **1871** GROTE *Eth. Fragm.* ii. (1876) 31 Wherein they resemble and wherein they differ.

Hence **re'sembled** *ppl. a. rare*.

1575–85 ABP. SANDYS *Serm.* v. 84 So in this resembled bodie, and ciuil societie, there must be diuersitie as of members so of functions.

†**re'semble**, *v.*^{2} *Obs.* [f. RE- + SEMBLE *v.*: cf. REASSEMBLE and F. *rassembler*.]

1. *intr.* To assemble, collect, come together.

c **1450** LOVELICH *Grail* xiv. 713 With an horn he gan to blowe, And made his meyne to resemble aȝen. **1513** BRADSHAW *St. Werburge* I. 3210 Than shortly resembled vnto that sayd place The people of Hamburgens, a great company. **1533** in W. H. Turner *Select. Rec. Oxford* (1880) 117 Resemblinge in a great multitude together. **1596** LODGE *Marg. of America* D 3 b, Thither likewise resembled the flower of the nobilitie and Ladies.

2. *trans.* To bring together or collect.

c **1477** CAXTON *Jason* 143 In this estate was I..till that the goddes haue resemblid this lady and me by your grete defaute. **1494** FABYAN *Chron.* VI. clxx. 165 Wherfore ye Danys resembled theyr people, and gaderyd a newe hoost.

resembler (rɪ'zɛmblə(r)). [f. RESEMBLE *v.*^{1} + -ER^1.] One who or that which resembles some other person or thing; †a representative, type.

1581 MULCASTER *Positions* xxxviii. (1887) 173 Apollo..to haue the presidencie ouer nyne wymen, the resemblers of learning. **1587** GOLDING *De Mornay* vi. (1592) 82 The said Prouidence..is the euerlasting vnderstanding of God,..and the resembler of his goodnesse. **1601** HOLLAND *Pliny* x. li. I. 297 Surely it was no delight and pleasure that he sought herein to content the tooth, but only that he would have the name to eat the resemblers of mans voice. **1654–66** EARL ORRERY *Parthen.* (1676) 808 Those Happinesses the gods deny me in length, their perfectest Resembler confers on me in Weight. **1680** BOYLE *Scept. Chem.* III. 188 A body by it self, that has few resemblers in the World. **1716** SWIFT *Corr.* Wks. 1841 II. 531 Until Curll and his resemblers are hanged. **1824** LANDOR *Imag. Conv., Southey & Porson* I. Wks. 1846 I. 18 Your attempt to prove Wordsworth shall I say the rival or the resembler of the ancients? **1893** *Chicago Advance* 16 Mar., We have been upborne, while our Southern resemblers are waiting still the stirring of their nest.

†**re'sembling**, *vbl. sb. Obs.* [f. as prec. + -ING^1.] A likeness; resemblance; comparison.

1480 CAXTON *Trevisa's Higden* III. xviii. 133 b, þe men of Athene..maden an ymage of gold, resemblyng and remembraunce of socrates. **1513** DOUGLAS *Æneis* VI. Prol. 156 Set thow to Vulcane haif full gret resembling,..Thow art bot Jovis smyth. **1533** MORE *Debell. Salem* Wks. 986/2 His not putting to answer maketh ye mater of my resemblyng muche the more strong for me. **1611** COTGR., *Resemblement*, a resembling, representing. **1691** RAY *Creation* I. (1692) 172 A resembling of God to a proud Man.

re'sembling, *ppl. a.* [f. as prec. + -ING^2.]

1. That resembles or corresponds to some other thing specified or implied; similar, like.

1561 DAUS tr. *Bullinger on Apoc.* (1573) 184 b, The high Bishop and King of Rome hath in his resemblyng Empire obedient children. **1645** MILTON *Tetrach.* Wks. 1851 IV. 155 In most resembling unlikenes, and most unlike resemblance. **1654–66** EARL ORRERY *Parthen.* (1676) 496 'Twas by many resembling expressions that the generous Zenophon evinc'd to me his fidelity. **1694** R. BURTHOGGE *Reason* 265 Schenckius..Reports another but resembling story. **1710** NORRIS *Chr. Prud.* ii. 92 Policy or Cunning comes a great deal nearer to Prudence, than Wit, as being the most resembling Imitatour. **1813** W. TAYLOR in Robberds *Mem.* (1843) II. 414 It is not so resembling a parody.

†**b.** In pred. use, const. *to* or with direct obj. *Obs.*

1654–66 EARL ORRERY *Parthen.* (1676) 188 His resolutions and flame were resembling unto mine. *Ibid.* 293 My reception was much resembling my fathers.

2. Similar to each other; mutually like.

a **1586** SIDNEY *Arcadia* I. (1605) 33 The hounds were.. many of them in colour and markes so resembling, that it shewed they were of one kind. **1716** LADY M. W. MONTAGU *Let. to Mrs. S. Chiswell* 13 Aug., No two places were ever more resembling. **1762** KAMES *Elem. Crit.* XVIII. ii. (1774) II. 34 In describing two resembling objects a resemblance in the two members of the period ought to be studied. **1847** H. MILLER *Test. Rocks* (1857) 492 They have in several respects a resembling structure.

Hence †**re'semblingly** *adv. Obs. rare*.

1661 BOYLE *Style of Script.* 253 Resemblingly transported with a like motive. **1687** N. JOHNSTON *Assur. Abbey Lands* 203 Which I can compare to nothing more resemblingly, than the difficulties [etc.].

re'seminate, *v. rare*. [ad. L. *resemināre* (see SEMINATE *v.*); in both quots. after Ovid *Met.* xv. 392.] *refl.* To reproduce as from seed.

1646 SIR T. BROWNE *Pseud. Ep.* 134 Concerning its generation, that without all conjunction, it begets and reseminates it selfe. **1866** J. B. ROSE tr. *Ovid's Met.* 446 One bird there is, himself reseminates, The Phœnix of Assyria.

resen, obs. form of REASON *sb.*^{2}

re'send (riː-), *v.* [RE- 5 a.] *trans.* To send back or again.

1554 BRADFORD *Lett.* Wks. (Parker Soc.) II. 116 My book ..I did give unto you; howbeit, if you be weary of it, you may re-send it again. **1575** G. HARVEY *Letter-bk.* (Camden) 96, I resende you a furlonge of salutations. *c* **1624** BP. H. KING *Surrender*, Thou in another [kiss]..resend The truest heart that Lover ere did lend. **1661** in *Cosin's Corr.* (Surtees) II. 312, I would..returne your civility of sending me one.. by re-sending one inclosed in yours. **1829** LAMB *Let. to Procter* in *Final Mem.* xvii. 156 If you have not burned your returned letter, pray resend it me. **1894** GLADSTONE *Sp. Ho. Com.* 1 Mar., This operation of sending and re-sending.. between the two Houses, this particular Bill,..has continued long enough.

absol. **1866** R. M. FERGUSON *Electr.* (1870) 245 It would be advisable to..resend at the mid-station by translation.

†**re'sengle**, *v. Obs. rare*$^{-1}$. [ad. OF. *resengler* (mod.F. *ressangler*): see RE- and CINGLE.] *trans.* To refasten the girths of (a horse).

1485 CAXTON *Chas. Gt.* 158 [He] descended fro hys hors for to vngyrde and lose hys sadle and after resengled hym.

re'sensitize, *v.* [RE- 5 a.] *trans.* To sensitize again.

1951 M. HYNES *Med. Bacteriol.* (ed. 5) vii. 91 After an interval..antibodies are formed again in sufficient amounts to resensitize the animal. **1967** E. CHAMBERS *Photolitho-Offset* i. 3 If additions are required to the image, it is necessary to 'resensitise' the stone by eliminating from it the insoluble products originating from the gum, which stop penetration by any greasy substance.

†**re'sent**, *sb. Obs. rare*. Also 7 rescent. [f. the vb.] **a.** A trace or flavour. **b.** A grateful feeling. **c.** Resentment.

1610 HOLLAND *Camden's Brit.* I. 324 The country people and towne-dwellers of Kent, aboue all other Englishmen retaine still the resent of their ancient worthinesse. **1663** GERBIER *Counsel* f 5 Its but to expresse the rescents of my Obligation. **1686** tr. *Chardin's Coronat. Solyman* 60 The secret hatred which he bare them..gave him a plausible pretence to shew his resent.

resent (rɪ'zɛnt), *v.* Also 7 ressent, rescent, recent; ris(s)ent. [ad. F. *ressentir*, †*resentir* (13th c.), = Sp. *resentir*, It. *risentire*, f. L. *re-* RE- + *sentire* to feel.]

I. †**1.** *refl.* [= F. *se ressentir*, It. *risentirsi*.] To have a feeling *of* pain; to feel pain or distress; to regret, repent. *Obs.*

1605 *Gunp. Plot* E 2 b, How infinitely greater cause haue wee to feele and ressent our selues of the smart of that wound. *a* **1637** N. FERRAR tr. *Valdes' 110 Consid.* (1638) 49 They sin against God, when they resent themselves, and are grieved touching that which God doth. **1654** EARL MONM. tr. *Bentivoglio's Warrs Flanders* 145 At the hearing whereof the mutiners began to rescent themselves, and to be inraged both with anger and shame.

†**2.** *trans.* To feel (something) as a cause of depression or sorrow; to feel deeply or sharply. *Obs.* (common *c* 1645–1660).

1620 SHELTON *Quix.* II. xliv. 288 Tis said then, that Sancho was scarce departed, when Don Quixote resented his solitarinesse. **1644** CHAS. I in Ellis *Orig. Lett.* Ser. I. III. 303 The misfortune of our forces in the north wee know is ressented as sadly by you. **1661** FELL *Life Hammond* 222 To be absent from any part of publick Worship he thus deeply resented. **1670** G. H. *Hist. Cardinals* II. III. 200 The death of this Cardinal was not so resented by the Court, because he was not of any extraordinary parts. **1728** MORGAN *Hist. Algiers* I. vi. 170 He so resented the Insolence of that.. Rebel that he sickened and died.

†**b.** To repent, regret (an action). *Obs.*

1622 MABBE tr. *Aleman's Guzman d'Alf.* I. 173 How much did I then risent my former follies? **1630** B. JONSON *New Inn* Argt., He..began, though over-late, to resent the injury he had done her. **1676** *Life Father Sarpi* in *Brent's Counc. Trent* 16 Because he had formerly cut in pieces a number of living creatures..he seemed to resent it with a kind of compassionate displeasure.

†**3.** To feel or experience (joy, sorrow, pain, etc.). *Obs.* (common *c* 1650–1680).

1640 tr. *Verdere's Rom. of Rom.* I. 87 Not leaving him without resenting the griefe which he saw him endure. **1648** BOYLE *Seraph. Love* iv. (1700) 32 God resents an infinite satisfaction in the Accomplishment of his own Will. **1682** CREECH *Lucretius* (1683) 183 For these can reap no joy, no more content Than what these Earth-born Swains did first resent. *a* **1734** NORTH *Lives* (1826) I. 167 He had so much good nature as to resent all her pains as if they were personally his own.

†**4.** To perceive by smell. (Only in Fuller, and in *fig.* contexts.) *Obs.*

1642 FULLER *Holy & Prof. St.* V. iv. 371 This bird of prey resented a worse then earthly savour in the soul of Saul. **1655** —— *Ch. Hist.* IV. iv. §6 The dullest nostrils resenting it done, not for love of vertue, but his own security.

†**b.** To smell out (in *fig.* sense); to perceive.

1641 BAKER *Chron.* (1653) 80 King Henry..apprehending the danger, and then resenting the mischief of falling into his enemies hands. *a* **1656** BP. HALL *Rem. Wks.* (1660) 403 Let fooles be mocked with these fancies, but you whom God hath indued with singular judgment..will easily resent the fraud. **1665** SIR T. HERBERT *Trav.* (1677) 73 Jangheer had immediate notice of his Sons flight, and resenting how dangerous it might prove [etc.].

II. †**5.** *refl.* (Cf. I.) **a.** To express one's resentment *of* some act. *Obs. rare*$^{-1}$.

1617 MORYSON *Itin.* II. 122 His Lordship shortly after, wrote a letter to him, resenting himselfe in very high tearmes, of the wrong he conceiued to be offered him.

†**b.** To show one's resentment by some act of revenge; to revenge oneself. *Obs. rare*.

1618 in *Camden's Lett.* (1691) 216 The disgrace lately done to the French Ambassadour..maketh them cry here upon a *bellum piraticum*: but they..will be much troubled how to resent themselves. **1656** EARL MONM. tr. *Boccalini's Advts. fr. Parnass.* II. xciii. (1674) 246 [He] hath not heart enough..to resent himself.

†**6.** *intr.* To manifest resentment *at* something.

1625 BACON *Ess., Friendship* (Arb.) 169 When he [Pompey] had carried the Consulship for a Friend of his, against the pursuit of Sylla, and that Sylla did a little resent thereat..Pompey..bad him be quiet.

7. *trans.* To feel oneself injured or insulted by (some act or conduct on the part of another); to show that one is displeased or angry at (some wrong, injury, etc. sustained).

1628–9 DIGBY *Voy. Medit.* (Camden) 33 Rissenting my going out of their port to inuade any shippes that came thither. **1667** MILTON *P.L.* IX. 300 Thou thy self with scorne And anger wouldst resent the offer'd wrong. **1697** DRYDEN *Virg. Georg.* III. 350 He with a gen'rous Rage resents his Wounds. **1729** BUTLER *Serm.* Wks. 1874 II. Pref. 20 Men do not in fact resent deliberately any thing but under this appearance of injury. **1781** COWPER *Hope* 354 The screaming nations, hovering in mid air, Loudly resent the stranger's freedom there. **1828** SCOTT *F.M. Perth* xxix, It is best to be plain at once—resent my refusal as you will. **1875** JOWETT *Plato* (ed. 2) V. 50 The second capture of Troy was deeply resented by the Assyrians.

absol. **1717** POPE *Eloïsa* 199 How often must it..hope, despair, resent, regret, Conceal, disdain—do all things but forget. **1759** ADAM SMITH *Mor. Sent.* II. ii. 203 That the gods neither resent nor hurt, was the general maxim of all the different sects of the ancient philosophy. *a* **1814** *Hortensia* II. iii. in *New Brit. Theatre* IV. 164, I charge thee by that heaven, Not to resent for me—O hear me, Leopold!

b. With *inf.* as object. *rare*.

1704 SWIFT *Batt. Bks.* To Rdr., The town highly resented to see a person of Sir William Temple's character and merits roughly used. **1884** W. C. SMITH *Kildrostan* 72 She'll think It is her place to keep me company, And will resent to see another here.

†**8. a.** To take or receive *as* or *for* something.

1642 *Declar. Lords & Comm.* 2 Sept. 2 The Lords and Commons doe declare, that they resent the aforesaid expressions of the people,..as a testimony of..dutifull affection. **1642** *Lancash. Tracts Civil War* (Chetham Soc.)

41 It will..be taken and recented by the House for an acceptable service in a time of great need.

†**b.** To take or receive in a certain way or with certain feelings; to take *well* or *ill*. *Obs.* (common *c* 1655–85).

1654 *Message fr. Ld. Protector to Gt. Turk* 3 This message was resented with so much terrour and astonishment. **1658–9** in *Burton's Diary* (1828) IV. 223 This was presently noised abroad, and very ill resented by the army. **1669** PEPYS *Diary* 13 Feb., It was mighty well resented and approved of. **1678** W. MOUNTAGU in *Buccleuch MSS.* (Hist. MSS. Comm.) I. 327, I confess it's a tender point, and I long to know how it was resented. *a* **1734** NORTH *Lives* (1826) III. 136 They came only to spy how his lordship (their grandee) was resented among us.

†**c.** To take favourably, to approve of. Also *intr.* To meet with acceptance. *Obs. rare.*

a **1646** J. GREGORY *Postuma, De Æris et Epochis* (1649) 168 Mahomet having introduc'd a new Superstition, which the men of Mecha..resented not, was forced to flie that place. **1650** *Descr. of Fut. Hist. Eur.* To Rdr. 1 There are several passages in it, which (I know) will not resent with our Great Ones.

†**9.** To appreciate, to be sensible of, to feel grateful for (a kindness, favour, etc.); to remember with gratitude. *Obs.* (common *c* 1665–90).

1647 CHAS. I in *Clarendon St. Pap.* (1773) II. 365 Let the army know, that we highly resent this their expression to us: And..we shall auspiciously look upon their loyal intentions. *a* **1677** BARROW *Serm.* (1683) II. xxvi. 373 Should we not be monstrously ingratefull if we did not deeply resent such kindness? **1702** C. MATHER *Magn. Chr.* III. I. iii. (1852) 309 If she gratefully resented that small thing for the sake of the hand it came from. **1765** WARBURTON in W. & Hurd *Lett.* (1809) 360, I was sure that this instance of his friendship to you would ever be warmly resented by you. [**1829** WEBSTER *Lett.* (1902) 617, I shall resent through life (to use an expression of Boyle's) your unwearied and affecting kindness to me.]

III. †**10.** To give forth, exhale (a perfume), to have an odour or suggestion of, to show traces of (some quality, etc.). *Obs. rare.*

1622 DRAYTON *Poly-olb.* XXV. 221 Where doth the pleasant air resent a sweeter breath? *c* **1630** DIGBY *Cure Wounds by Symp.* (1669) 2 The said fright..makes the Ligaments, and other parts of his body the more supple to runne; insomuch, that he resents it all his life afterwards and becomes a good courser. **1633** DONE *Hist. Septuagint* 37 Herein you shall doe us contentable pleasure, and courtesie resenting amitie.

†**11.** To savour *of*, to have a touch or taste *of*; to be characteristic or suggestive *of* (a person or thing). *Obs.* (common *c* 1640–65).

1638 W. SCLATER *Serm. Experimentall* To Rdr., They.. seeme by reason of their long lodging in the dust, to resent something of the earth. **1654** FULLER *Ephemeris* Pref. 3 Some works resent too much of their authour. **1668** M. CASAUBON *Credulity* (1670) 34 O, that the Tragedies..had somewhat that resented of piety in them. **1826** SOUTHEY *To Mem. Yng. Officer* 20 Therefore doth the draught Resent of comfort in its bitterness.

resenter (rɪˈzɛntə(r)). [f. prec. + -ER[1].]

†**1.** One who has a feeling or appreciation *of* something. *Obs.*

1651 *Wotton's Reliq.* (1672) 175 The Earl was the worst Philosopher, being a great Resenter, and a weak Dissembler, of the least disgrace. *a* **1657** R. LOVEDAY *Lett.* (1659) 212 Mention me to my Cousin E. as I am a grateful resenter of their last excellent entertainment. **1664** H. MORE *Myst. Iniq.* Pref. 8 A due resenter of the common Rights and just Security of Mankind.

2. One who feels or shows resentment. *rare*$^{-1}$.

1825 SCOTT 28 Nov. in *Fam. Lett.*, In such cases there are usually some private motives of the resenters' own.

reˈsentful, *a.* [f. RESENT *sb.* or *v.* + -FUL.]

†**1.** Expressive of feeling; appreciative. *Obs.*$^{-1}$

1654–66 EARL ORRERY *Parthen.* (1676) 672 This was the civilest, shortest, and resentful'st answer I could give her.

2. Full of, inspired by, resentment.

1656 EARL MONM. tr. *Boccalini's Advts. fr. Parnass.* 413 And growing into great choler, the Spaniards said that the Medici should do well to be once quiet... Lorenzo, without any the least alteration, reply'd to these resentful words. **1726** POPE *Odyss.* XVII. 436 His soul, resentful as humane, Dooms to full vengeance all the offending train. **1751** *Affecting Narr. of Wager* 145 On this he..put on a terribly fierce Aspect, and dropt some resentful Expressions. **1782** MISS BURNEY *Cecilia* III. v, With a look of resentful mortification. **1841** W. SPALDING *Italy & It. Isl.* III. 255 The present charge arises from the undeniably resentful temper of the Italians. **1874** MOTLEY *Barneveld* (1879) II. 239 He was at that moment resentful..against the whole party.

Hence **reˈsentfully** *adv.*; **reˈsentfulness**.

1836 CHALMERS *Mor. Philos.* Wks. 1849 V. 340 Grim resentfulness of aspect. **1856** FROUDE *Hist. Eng.* II. vii. 177 All..inheriting the pride of their birth, and resentfully conscious of their fallen fortunes. **1867** MRS. H. WOOD *Orville Coll.* x. 141 'He wants to stay here', she resentfully cried. **1878** T. HARDY *Ret. Native* III. vii, His colour rose in a quick resentfulness frequent with him.

†**reˈsentient.** *Obs. rare*$^{-1}$. [ad. L. *resentient-em*, pres. pple. of *resentīre* to RESENT.] That which causes a change of feeling.

1655 VAUGHAN *Silex Scint.*, *Timber* (1858) 156 What resentient can work more within, Than true remorse, when with past sins at strife?

†**reˈsentiment.** *Obs. rare.* [a. F. *resentiment*, vbl. sb. f. *resentir* to RESENT: cf. *sentiment*.] = RESENTMENT, in various senses.

1595 DANIEL *Civ. Wars* IV. 5 Though this King might haue resentiment And will t'auenge him of this iniury [etc.]. **1651** EVELYN *Diary & Corr.* (1852) III. 57 The grateful resentiments of your Ladyship's favour. **1661** —— *Fumifugium* Misc. Writ. (1805) I. 211 We have..a parliament whose decrees and resentiments take their impression from his Majesties great genius.

reˈsenting, *vbl. sb.* [f. RESENT *v.* + -ING[1].] The action of the vb., in various senses.

1632 J. L. *Womens Rights* 231 An elephant in whom..is.. a wonderfull memorie and recenting of things past. **1635** PERSON *Varieties* I. viii. 31 A perpetuall resenting of a good turn received. *a* **1716** SOUTH *Serm.* (1744) XI. 158 Despair ..supposes..the resentings past, and the day of grace spent.

reˈsenting, *ppl. a.* [f. as prec. + -ING[2].] That resents, in various senses of the vb.; that conveys or implies resentment; resentful.

1656 EARL MONM. tr. *Boccalini's Advts. fr. Parnass.* I. xxxv. (1674) 46 [He] in a resenting manner told Buonfadio, That..he had deserved to be treated as he had been. **1693** TATE in *Dryden's Juvenal* xv. (1697) 375 Can Men, or more resenting Gods, invent, Or Hell inflict proportion'd Punishment..? **1695** J. SAGE *Cyprianic Age* Wks. 1847 II. 74 He wrote in a yet more resenting strain. **1709** ADDISON *Tatler* No. 133 ¶2 The Dignity and Disdain of a resenting Lover. **1761** MRS. F. SHERIDAN *Sidney Bidulph* III. 125, I have no more ill in my heart than one of your children; but I am a little resenting may be.

Hence **reˈsentingly** *adv.*

1611 FLORIO, *Risentitamento*, resentingly, feelingly. **1668** H. MORE *Div. Dial.* I. xiii. (1713) 28 Hylobares..does thus judiciously and resentingly recapitulate your main Reasonings. **1791** CHARLOTTE SMITH *Celestina* (ed. 2) II. 89 Montague..was piqued extremely, and would resentingly have answered.

†**reˈsentive,** *a. Obs.* [f. RESENT *v.* + -IVE.] Apt or inclined to resent, in various senses.

1662 H. STUBBE *Ind. Nectar* Pref. 5 Those returns, that the..Prince may exspect from an ingenuous and resentive Servant. **1709** MRS. MANLEY *Secret Mem.* (1720) III. 183 She had so totally subverted..the resentive faculty in him, that [etc.]. **1735** THOMSON *Liberty* IV. 1016 From the keen resentive North,..The Guardian Army came.

†**reˈsentless,** *a. Obs. rare*$^{-1}$. [f. RESENT *v.* + -LESS.] Destitute of feeling or affection.

a **1649** DRUMM. OF HAWTH. *Poems* Wks. (1711) 33 The dove the dove, the swan doth love the swan, Nought so resentless unto man as man.

resentment (rɪˈzɛntmənt). Also 7 rec-, ress-. [ad. F. *ressentiment* (16th c.), or It. *risentimento*, f. F. *ressentir*, It. *risentire*: see RESENT *v.*

The first occurrence of the word in English appears to be in Florio (1611) prob. in sense 4.]

1. An indignant sense *of* injury or insult received, or *of* wrong or affront done to some person or thing to which one is attached. Now *rare.*

1619 in *Eng. & Germ.* (Camden) 99, I had no will..to shew any ressentment of this neglect in publike, and therefore resolved to swallow it for a while. **1641** BAKER *Chron.* (1653) 145 Some years after..King Edward begun to show his resentment of the stubborn behaviour of his Nobles towards him. **1706** STANHOPE *Paraphr.* III. 351 Zeal ..appears in his Resentment of the Profanations committed upon the Temple. *a* **1754** CARTE *Hist. Eng.* (1755) IV. 183 They brought with them into the house of commons very keen resentments of their confinement. **1781** COWPER *Expost.* 328 In just resentment of his injured laws, He pours contempt on them and on their cause.

2. a. A strong feeling of ill-will or anger against the author or authors of a wrong or affront; the manifestation of such feeling against the cause of it. Also in *pl.*, and const. *against*, *at*.

1634 W. TIRWHYT tr. *Balzac's Lett.* 335 But I would you knew, I haue no resentments against forcelesse enemies. **1638** R. BAKER tr. *Balzac's Lett.* (vol. III) 149 The wretched man..was not worthy of so noble a Resentment as yours. **1675** H. MORE in R. Ward *Life* (1710) 313 Several excellent Passages.., that are very expressive of a vigorous Resentment. **1706** ESTCOURT *Fair Example* III. i, Rather than be subject to her Resentments, I'll compound the matter, and give 'em her my self. **1759** ROBERTSON *Hist. Scot.* IV. Wks. 1813 I. 301 Her resentment against the king seems not to have abated. **1760–62** GOLDSM. *Cit. W.* x, The Daures..feel no resentment at these injuries. **1828** D'ISRAELI *Chas. I*, II. ii. 29 The war with France has been traced to the personal resentments of Buckingham. **1848** LYTTON *Harold* IV. vii, A victorious effort of justice over resentment. **1883** FROUDE *Short Stud.* IV. III. 263 The shocked conscience of mankind..was already kindling into resentment.

†**b.** *pl.* Remarks expressive of ill-feeling. *Obs.*$^{-1}$

a **1715** BURNET *Own Time* III. (1724) I. 579 Armstrong took this heavily: and in one paper which I saw, writ in his own hand, the resentments upon it were sharper than I thought became a dying penitent.

†**c.** A cause of resentment; a grievance. *Obs.*$^{-1}$

1683 *Agathocles* 5 The first Resentments that provoke their Cries Are Heavy Loans, and frequent Subsidies.

d. *Social Psychol.* A term introduced by Nietzsche (as G. *ressentiment*) to describe an attitude which arises, often unconsciously, from aggressive feelings frustrated by the sensed inferiority of one's situation or personality and freq. results in some form of self-abasement. Cf. RESSENTIMENT.

1899 HAUSSMANN & GRAY tr. *Nietzsche's Geneal. Morals* i. 33 The slave-revolt in morality begins by resentment itself becoming creative and giving birth to values—the resentment of such beings, as real reaction, the reaction of deeds, is impossible to, and as nothing but [*sic*] an imaginary vengeance will serve to indemnify. **1911** A. M. LUDOVICI tr. *Nietzsche's Ecce Homo* in *Compl. Wks.* XVII. 20 Freedom from resentment and the understanding of the nature of resentment—who knows how very much..I am indebted to my long illness for these two things. *Ibid.* 21 Nothing on earth consumes a man more quickly than the passion of resentment. **1943** G. A. MORGAN *What Nietzsche Means* vi. 150 At bottom, Nietzsche thinks, resentment is caused by a desire to stun pain. It differs from healthy revenge particularly in that, being impotent to express itself by immediate action, it poisons and consumes within. **1957** H. E. BARNES tr. *Sartre's Being & Nothingness* ii. 47 Others so as to make the Not a part of their very subjectivity, establish their human personality as a perpetual negation. This is the meaning and function of what Scheler calls 'the man of resentment'. **1974** B. F. SKINNER *About Behaviorism* x. 154 The controlling measures used by an authority make it more likely that a person will escape or counter-attack, and relevant conditions may be felt as resentment; at the same time the measures may generate compliant behavior.

†**3. a.** A (sorrowful) feeling or sense *of* some trouble, loss, fault, etc. *Obs.*

1632 SIR T. HAWKINS tr. *Mathieu's Unhappy Prosperitie* I. 135 Hearts being ever tender in the ressentment of calamities. **1655** STANLEY *Hist. Philos.* I. (1701) 38/2 The Advice he gave concerning equal Marriage..was out of resentment of his own Troubles. **1698** TUTCHIN *White-Hall in Flames* Ded. 2 From a just Resentment of this great Loss ..did I attempt the following Poem.

†**b.** A (pleasant) sense *of* something enjoyed. *Obs. rare.*

1660 INGELO *Bentiv. & Ur.* II. (1682) 146 They were expressing their mutual Resentments of their Common Felicity. **1682** H. MORE *Annot. Glanvill's Lux O.* 79 It naturally enhances all the enjoyments..and makes them for ever have a more deep and vivid resentment of them.

†**4. a.** A feeling of emotion of any kind. Also without article. *Obs.* (common *c* 1650–1700).

1632 SIR T. HAWKINS tr. *Mathieu's Unhappy Prosperitie* I. 96 Could he thinke, that a Prince who had so little resentment in the death of a sonne, would care for the losse of his servants. **1658** R. FRANCK *North. Mem.* (1821) 275 Deep impressions, and ravishing refreshing resentments. **1676** OTWAY *Don Carlos* II. i, One so accomplish'd, and that lov'd you too, With what Resentments must he part with you? **1705** STANHOPE *Paraphr.* I. 71 The different Resentments, with which the Approach of this Judgment will be entertained. **1748** HARTLEY *Observ. Man* I. iii. §3. 373 There generally remains a pleasing or displeasing Recollection or Resentment.

†**b.** A feeling *of* sorrow, joy, etc. Also, a trace *of* some feeling. *Obs.*

1632 SIR T. HAWKINS tr. *Mathieu's Unhappy Prosperitie* I. 34 In so just a resentment of sorrow. **1638** R. BAKER tr. *Balzac's Lett.* (vol. III) 129 The victorious and triumphant newes..gives me some resentment of joy. **1652** J. WRIGHT tr. *Camus' Nat. Paradox* IV. 87 Merinda..had very reall Resentments of Affection for Almeria. **1683** FELL in *Hatton Corr.* (1878) II. 26 [You] who know how solicitous the resentments of friendship are. **1757** SHERLOCK *Disc.* (1764) II. 333 Some Resentments of the same Spirit of Joy and Gratitude.

†**c.** A natural or spontaneous feeling, disposition, or inclination (*towards* something). *Obs.*

1654–66 EARL ORRERY *Parthen.* (1676) 133 As thou art Heir to our Blood, be so also to our generous resentments. **1675** R. BURTHOGGE *Causa Dei* 81 Nor are we able to defend ourselves against so Good, so Pious a Resentment. **1690** NORRIS *Beatitudes* (1694) I. 106 'Tis not enough to have.. some kind resentments towards Righteousness.

†**d.** A feeling or sentiment towards another.

1675 R. BURTHOGGE *Causa Dei* 107 Mr. Hobbs, for whom you manifest no good Resentment. **1682** PEPYS 26 May in *Diary* (1879) VI. 146 The satisfaction of understanding your healths, and the kind resentments you had upon the notice of mine. **1705** STANHOPE *Paraphr.* II. 28 Professing the kindest Resentments, and most impatient Wishes for the Safety and Happiness of their Souls.

†**5.** Feeling or sensation; susceptibility to sensuous or mental impressions. *Obs.*

1653 *Nissena* 12 It was impossible for him..without the resentments of a thousand deaths. **1661** GLANVILL *Van. Dogm.* 94 Our Eyes mis-inform us not, but faithfully transmit their recentment to the mind. **1704** J. TRAPP *Abra-Mulé* Ded., Men are generally less capable of those tender Impressions, which the Ladies (who are form'd with finer Resentments) more easily receive.

†**6. a.** An appreciation or understanding *of* something. *Obs.*

1638 MEDE *Wks.* (1672) 7 As they might have known, had they had a true resentment of Morality. **1651–3** JER. TAYLOR *Serm. for Year* I. xxiii. 304 Sadnesse does in some cases become a Christian, as being an Index of a..wise proper resentment of things. **1678** CUDWORTH *Intell. Syst.* 25 Expressing such a hearty Resentment of the Excellency of Piety, and the wretchedness and sottishness of Atheism.

†**b.** Interest in a thing; regard *for*, care *of*, something. *Obs. rare.*

1654 Z. COKE *Logick* Pref., Which humble attempt my Lords, here Imploreth both your Resentment and Patronage. **1664** H. MORE *Myst. Iniq.* 546 Who has so deep a resentment for Order and Unity in the Church [etc.]. **1751** HUME *Princ. Mor.* v. ii. 83 They ask'd if it was possible we could have any general Concern for Society, or any disinterested Resentment of the Welfare or Injury of others.

†**7.** Grateful appreciation or acknowledgement (*of* a service, kindness, etc.); a feeling

or expression of gratitude. *Obs.* (common *c* 1650–1750).

1651 CROMWELL *Let.* 4 Feb. (Carlyle), A Testimony.. which deserves a fuller return, of deep resentment, value, and acknowledgement, than I am any ways able to make. **1672** CAVE *Prim. Chr.* I. xi. (1673) 348 What more fit than thankfulnes to God and a high resentment of such favours and blessings. **1714** H. GROVE *Spect.* No. 588 ¶2 Nothing renders a Person more unworthy of a Benefit, than his being without all Resentment of it. **1762** BP. FORBES *Jrnl.* (1886) 233, I think myself obliged to testifie a grateful Resentment of that particular Place in your Regard. **1772** *Rec. Old Colony Club*, The most grateful resentments for the immerited honor. **1849** *N. Amer. Rev.* July 104 A farmer in .. New England, who had recently lost his wife, called upon a lawyer..remarking that 'he wished to make a proper resentment on the occasion'.

†**8. a.** Reception in a particular way. *Obs. rare*$^{-1}$.

1655 CROMWELL *Sp.* 22 Jan. (Carlyle), I have troubled you with a long Speech; and I believe it may not have the same resentment with all that it hath with some.

†**b.** A particular idea, opinion, or view *of* or *upon* something. *Obs. rare.*

1675 J. SMITH *Chr. Relig. App.* II. 18 Has one man (in all this tract of time) had other Resentments of this thing, than such as have been expressed. **1688** LUTTRELL *Brief Rel.* (1857) I. 429 On the late proceedings of the pope..have been very ill resentments taken in France. **1748** RICHARDSON *Clarissa* (1811) IV. 194, I have great temptations..to express my own resentments upon your present state.

†**9.** Change of mind; retractation *of* something; regret for past conduct. *Obs. rare.*

1646 J. GREGORY *Notes & Obs.* (1650) 75 But for late resentments they are not much to be valued. **1684** in Hay Fleming *Six Saints* (1901) I. App. 229, I, Arthour Cunghame, adheres to the resentment of my given consent to banishment. **1705** in Hutchison *Hist. Ref. Presb. Ch.* (1893) 149 'He declared his resentment'—his regret for having so acted.

resequent ('riːsɪkwənt, rɪ'siːkwənt), *a.* (*sb.*) *Geomorphol.* [f. RE- + *-sequent* in CONSEQUENT, SUBSEQUENT *adjs.*] **a.** Designating, or characterized by the presence of, a stream or streams having a course which follows the dip of strata in the manner of a consequent stream but is stratigraphically at a lower level than the original surface of the underlying geological formation. Hence as *sb.*, a resequent stream.

1906 W. M. DAVIS in *Bull. Amer. Geogr. Soc.* XXXVIII. 608, I suggested a few years ago that streams which, after spontaneous development aside from an original consequent course, come again to follow it, should be called resequent streams. *Ibid.*, In the third stage..a new series of similar streams—lateral resequents—is beginning to be developed on the crown of the then newly-uncovered hard-rock anticlines. **1937** WOOLDRIDGE & MORGAN *Physical Basis Geogr.* xv. 212 A good example is afforded by the Central Weald of Kent and Sussex, where there are many good examples of synclinal valleys for which resequent origin must be deemed probable. **1954** W. D. THORNBURY *Princ. Geomorphol.* v. 114 Resequent valleys drain in the same direction as the original consequent drainage but are at lower topographic levels and have developed with respect to new base levels of erosion. **1970** R. J. SMALL *Study of Landforms* iii. 91 Where inversion of relief has once been achieved, continued erosion can lead to a restoration of the original structure-relief relationship; the synclinal valleys and anticlinal ridges are then, strictly speaking, 'resequent'. *Ibid.*, vii. 235 Synclinal streams may even be 'resequents', which are traditionally regarded as the eventual outcome of drainage development in areas of folded rocks.

b. Of a fault-line scarp or a related feature: having a relief similar to that originally produced by the faulting; freq. *spec.* where such relief results from erosion of an obsequent scarp.

1913 W. M. DAVIS in *Bull. Geol. Soc. Amer.* XXIV. 198 If this change of form is a slope, more or less perfectly graded, descending to the relatively depressed side, it may be called a resequent scarp. **1941** C. A. COTTON *Landscape* xxiii. 265 Fault-line scarps are of two kinds, resequent and obsequent, according as they face in the direction the initial fault-scarp faced on the same line of fault or in the opposite direction. *Ibid.*, Resequent fault-line scarps..are commoner than obsequent. **1970** R. J. SMALL *Study of Landforms* iii. 105 It will be seen that consequent and resequent scarps are very similar, and indeed many would argue that to make a distinction between them is purely academic, on the grounds that it is invariably impossible to decide in actual cases whether or not an obsequent scarp has previously existed along a fault-line (and thus whether the scarp in question is resequent or not).

rese'quester (riː-), *v.* [RE- 5 a.] *trans.* To sequester again. So **re,seque'stration.**

1649 *Nicholas Papers* (Camden) I. 133 To compound, if by employment you are reingaged, is to be resequestred againe. **1649** *Com. Advance Money* II. 1156 Last August a re-sequestration was laid on Branton Sheaf... [Mr. Bassett] applies to know the cause of his re-sequestration.

†**reserate,** *v. Obs.* [f. ppl. stem of L. *reserāre* to unbar, unbolt, open, f. *re-* RE- 2 d + *sera* bar, bolt.] *trans.* To open up. Hence †**reserating** *vbl. sb.* and *ppl. a.*

1597 A. M. tr. *Guillemeau's Fr. Chirurg.* 49/1 We must gentlely and easilye reserate the same [humors], least that in reseratinge of the same you increase the ague. **1657** TOMLINSON *Renou's Disp.* 179 One made of solid matter which serves to open, reserate and dilate..the uterus. **1689** G. HARVEY *Curing Dis. by Expect.* v. 34 A Medicine.. agreeing with all Temperaments, where reserating Oppilations is the indication. **1710** T. FULLER *Pharm.* 224 Its use is to reserate the too close compages of the Blood.

†**rese'ration.** *Obs.* [See prec. and -ATION.] The action of opening; that which opens up.

1597 A. M. tr. *Guillemeau's Fr. Chirurg.* 49/1 We must, before the reseratione, administer an ounce of Cassie. **1627** FELTHAM *Resolves* II. [I.] xxix. (1677) 220 Wine is the Reseration of the Soul and Thoughts. **1633** HART *Diet of Diseased* III. xvii. 296 A temperate warme bath..by reseration of the pores of the body refresheth and cooleth.

†**rese'rene** (riː-), *v. Obs. rare*$^{-1}$. [f. RE- 5 a + SERENE, after It. *rasserenare.*] *trans.* To make serene again.

1755 TEMPLE *Orl. Fur.* XXXII. xv, She thinks that this may be her wished Ruggier, And re-serenes her brow, and eyes.

reserpine (rɪ'sɜːpiːn). *Pharm.* [ad. G. *reserpin* (J. M. Müller et al. 1952, in *Experientia* VIII. 338), f. initial letter of RAUWOLFIA + *-e-* + L. *serp-entina* (see below), fem. of *serpentinus* SERPENTINE *a.*: see -INE[5].] A colourless crystalline alkaloid $C_{33}H_{40}N_2O_9$, which is obtained from the roots of several plants of the genus RAUWOLFIA, notably *R. serpentina*, and is used to treat hypertension and as a sedative.

1952 [see CHLORPROMAZINE]. **1954** *Jrnl. Amer. Med. Assoc.* 20 Mar. 1040/1 It seems that reserpine reduces the blood pressure by exerting an effect on the central nervous system. **1958** *Observer* 30 Nov. 12/4 New drugs such as chlorpromazine and reserpine make the minds of the mentally ill more accessible. **1966** *New Scientist* 24 Nov. 430/3 Reserpine interferes with the retention, mainly in the hypothalamus.., of a number of amines. **1973** *Sci. Amer.* Sept. 121/1 Once widely used, reserpine has been replaced by the phenothiazines because of the greater frequency of reserpine's serious side effects. **1974** *Times* 20 Sept. 3/7 There seems little doubt that this link between regular use of reserpine and an increased cancer risk is genuine.

Hence **re'serpinized** *a.*, treated with reserpine; **re,serpini'zation**, the process of, or condition resulting from, treatment with reserpine.

1960 *Federation Proc.* XIX. 266/1 (*heading*) LSD-25 and brain serotonin in reserpinized rat. **1962** *Lancet* 22 Dec. 1330/2 The accumulation and retention of ^{14}C from the blood-glucose in vivo are greatly diminished in the heart of 'reserpinised' rats. **1963** *Federation Proc.* XXII. 364/2 The animal was 5 to 10 times more sensitive to these substances after reserpinization than before. **1973** *Nature* 13 Apr. In the absence of endogenous catecholamines (that is reserpinization) the transient contractile tension response to the ionophore was attenuated, but elevation of resting tension persisted. **1975** *Pediatric Res.* IX. 463 (*heading*) The chronically reserpinized rat as a possible model for cystic fibrosis.

reservable (rɪ'zɜːvəb(ə)l), *a.* [f. RESERVE *v.* + -ABLE.] That may be reserved.

1665 *Irish Act 17 & 18 Chas. II*, c. 2 §13 A certificate.. containing the lands allotted..with..the number of acres.. and the rents reservable. **1756** AMORY *Buncle* (1770) I. 226 Acquiescing in every obstruction, as ultimately reservable to divine providence. **1971** *Daily Tel.* (Colour Suppl.) 29 Oct. 7/1 There were three seat prices—50p, 80p and £1.10. But only the most expensive were reservable in advance.

reserval (rɪ'zɜːvəl). *rare.* [f. as prec. + -AL[1].] †**a.** Reserve. *Obs.* **b.** Reservation.

1647 W. BROWNE tr. *Polexander* II. 195 His troupes were ..appointed to make a body for their last Reservall. **1895** R. L. DOUGLAS in *Bookman* Oct. 22/2 The reserval of the rights of Philip V. to the French throne.

†**re'servance.** *Obs. rare.* [f. RESERVE *v.* + -ANCE: cf. OF. *reservance*, It. *riserbanza.*]

1. Reservation. *rare*$^{-1}$.

1550 in Burnet *Hist. Ref.*, *Rec.* II. I. l. (Pocock) V. 302 We are pleased, that the reservance of our rights and titles, mentioned in our former articles sent to our said commissioners, be in general words.

2. Capacity of retaining. *rare*$^{-1}$.

1646 SIR T. BROWNE *Pseud. Ep.* 131 The eares implying attention,..the hooked bill, reservance and tenacity.

3. Reserve. (Also in *comb.*)

1631 BRATHWAIT *Whimzies, Questman* 125 Her foote most gingerly paced, for more state-reservance. **1635** —— *Arc. Pr.* Opinion etc., He demeaned himselfe with such cautious reservance and judicious prudence, as [etc.].

†**re'servancy.** *Obs. rare.* [f. as prec. + -ANCY.] **a.** Inclination to retain unchanged; conservatism. **b.** Reservation.

1630 BRATHWAIT *Eng. Gentlem.* (1641) 9 It may appeare with what reservancie they continue their ancient habit: loth ..to introduce any new custome. *Ibid.* 76, I doe think it fitting, that gentlemen should be sociably affected, ever with a reservancie, with whom they keep company.

reservation (rɛzə'veɪʃən). Also 4 -cioun, 5 -cion. [a. OF. *reservation* (14th c.), or ad. late L. *reservātiōn-em*, n. of action f. *reservāre* to RESERVE.]

I. 1. *Eccl.* **a.** The action of reserving as a tithe.

c **1380** WYCLIF *Last Age Ch.* (1840) 23 þei [priests] make reseruacions, þe whiche ben clepid dymes, ffirst fruytis, oþer pencions. **1645** PAGITT *Heresiogr.* (1661) 265 The reservation of Tythes is set down in expresse words, Levit. 27. 30.

b. The action, on the part of the Pope, of reserving to himself the right of nomination to a vacant benefice, or the fact of this being reserved to him by some rule or constitution of the Church. (Usually in *pl.*)

1480 CAXTON *Chron. Eng.* VII. 130 b, The kynge send.. ambassatours to yͤ pope pryenge hym yͭ he sholde leue of & medle not in his courte of yͤ kepynge & reseruacions of benefyces in Englande. **1560** DAUS tr. *Sleidane's Comm.* 365 b, Bishops of Rome..by reservations and graces expectative, as they name them, have derived all the gaine to Rome. **1725** tr. *Dupin's Eccl. Hist. 17th c.* I. II. iii. 46 Benedict XII made a general Reserve of all the Benefices *in Curia*;..Innocent VI was oblig'd to revoke all the Reservations by a Bull. **1845** S. AUSTIN *Ranke's Hist. Ref.* I. 493 That the prerogatives of the papal months,.. reservations, and of course, annates, should be abolished. **1884** *Catholic Dict.* 716/1 Reservations..which depend only on a rule of the Chancery, and not also on a Papal constitution.

c. The action or fact, on the part of a superior, of reserving to himself the power of absolution in certain cases. (Cf. RESERVED *ppl. a.* 5.)

1608 WILLET *Hexapla Exod.* 279 The papall reseruation of cases..to the pope. **1884** *Catholic Dict.* (1897) 786/2 The object of the reservation is to increase the shame of the penitent. *Ibid.*, This power of reservation, however, is given for edification, not destruction.

2. *Law.* The action or fact of reserving or retaining for oneself some right or interest in property which is being conveyed to another; an instance of this; a right or interest so retained; the clause or part of a deed by which something is thus reserved.

1487 *Rolls of Parlt.* VI. 390/2 That..all other Actes..be as to the said Fee Ferme onely,..except the said reservation of xviii *li vs.* **1532** *Dial. on Laws Eng.* II. xxii. 43 b, If a man make a feffement and reserue the profites.., that reseruacion is voyde in the lawe. **1579** W. RASTELL *Termes Lawes* 167 b/2 Reseruation, is taken diuers waies, and hath diuers natures... Sometimes a reseruation doth get and bring forth an other thing which was not before... And dyuers other such reseruations there be. **1596** BACON *Max. & Use Com. Law* II. (1635) 30 He reserved some retribution of rents, or services, or both, to him and to his heires: which reservation is that, which is called the tenure of land. **1642** tr. *Perkins' Prof. Bk.* v. §431. 186 When shee had the third part of the land out of which the reservation was made, it is reason [etc.]. **1766** BLACKSTONE *Comm.* II. 290 The *reddendum* or reservation, whereby the grantor doth create or reserve some new thing to himself out of what he had before granted. **1776** ADAM SMITH *W.N.* I. v. (1869) I. 35 When a landed estate, therefore, is sold with a reservation of a perpetual rent [etc.] **1818** CRUISE *Digest* (ed. 2) IV. 223 The reservation was in the same terms with the power, and consequently was pursuant to it. **1872** YEATS *Growth Comm.* 295 A reservation was made of a royalty of 20% on all silver produced.

3. a. The action or fact of reserving (for oneself or another) some right, power, privilege, etc.; a right, etc., thus reserved.

1605 SHAKS. *Lear* II. iv. 255, I gave you all..But kept a reseruation to be followed With such a number. **1622** MALYNES *Anc. Law-Merch.* 429 His estate onely is liable.. and yet with reseruation of such necessarie things, as Honestie, Honour, Humanitie, and Christianitie doth challenge. *a* **1683** SIDNEY *Disc. Govt.* III. xiv. (1704) 284 There was therefore a reservation of the supreme Power in the People, notwithstanding the creation of Magistrats without Appeal. **1714** SWIFT *Public Spir. Whigs* Wks. 1751 VIII. 28 These are the Opinions which Steele and his Faction..are endeavouring..to propagate..; with what Reservation to the Honour..of the Queen, I cannot determine. **1790** BURKE *Fr. Rev.* 18 Whilst our government is soothed with a reservation in its favour, to which it has no claim, the security..is taken away. **1848** MILL *Pol. Econ.* II. xii. §2 The labourers..have always done so, with the reservation of a power to tax those superfluities for purposes of public utility.

b. Orig. in the U.S., a tract of land set apart by Government for some special purpose, or for the exclusive use of a native people, esp. North American Indians. (Cf. RESERVE *sb.* 5 b.)

1789 *Deb. Congress U.S.* 25 May (1834) 41 The reservation,..of six miles square round the fort at Oswego, is within the territory of the State of New York. **1792** *Mass. Hist. Soc. Coll.* (1806) 1st Ser. I. 287 The whole Six Nations live on grounds, called the State Reservations, and are intermediate spaces settled on both sides by white people. **1830** GALT *Lawrie T.* IV. xii. (1849) 186 Without touching the reservation round Jadiville. **1841** CATLIN *N. Amer. Ind.* (1844) II. 102 In these states, their reservations became surrounded by white people. **1859** MARCY *Prairie Trav.* vi. 216 A reservation of land upon which the government designed to establish the Comanches. **1859** *Native Voice* (Vancouver) (1959) Feb. 5/4 Has the Government of this Island the power to remove the Indians (by purchase) from that piece of outside Victoria Harbour known as the Indian Reservation? **1883** *Century Mag.* June 218/1 Between these two lines was a Government reservation. **1953** D. CUSHMAN *Stay away, Joe* 22 Won't have anything to do with the Injuns off the reservation. **1957** M. BANTON *W. Afr. City* i. 15 A tangle relating to the ownership of land in the Kru Reservation. **1965** *Austral. Encycl.* I. 88/2 Western Australia maintains 167 native reservations. **1970** *Times* 24 Mar. 6/6 Port Elizabeth is close enough to the Transkei Bantustan (African reservation) to be affected by the complex restrictions designed to stop industry from attracting Africans out of the reservations. **1971** D. HEFFRON *Nice Fire & Some Moonpennies* ii. 18 He told me to remember that when you're off the Reservation, people take you not as an individual but as an Indian. **1973** *Black Panther* 8 Sept. 8/2 The Apaches, originally from Arizona, New Mexico and parts of Mexico, were sent to Florida by the U.S. Army after they refused to remain on a reservation in Arizona.

attrib. **1866** *Rep. Indian Affairs* (U.S.) 100 The reservation Indian is under the protection of the general government. **1887** *Pall Mall G.* 31 Oct. 7/1 It is acknowledged on all sides..that the reservation policy is a failure. *Ibid.*, The reservation Indians in that State. **1946** G. FOREMAN *Last Trek of Indians* 260 Eighty of them came to their agency and enrolled with the reservation Indians. **1977** *Listener* 13 Oct. 462/1 In the 1950s..a whole generation of reds..was squashed... A few of us survivors are kept on like reservation Indians to remind the winners of how tolerant they've become.

c. orig. *U.S.* The action or fact of engaging seats, rooms, places, etc., or of hiring a vehicle, in advance; something reserved in advance. Also *attrib.*

1906 F. LYNDE *Quickening* xiii. 118 That sleeping-car reservation for Thomas Gordon—have you secured it? **1907** *Springfield* (Mass.) *Weekly Republican* 19 Dec. 16 A considerable number of New York and Boston people have made reservations at the Curtis hotel in Lenox for the holiday season. **1925** *Scribner's Mag.* July 32/1 (Advt.), Reservations for 1925–26 should be made as soon as possible to insure entrance. **1935** R. MACAULAY *Personal Pleasures* 18 Do tickets, passports, money, travellers' cheques, packing, reservations, boat trains, inns, crouch and snarl before you like those surly dragons that guard enchanted lands? **1949** *Skyline Trail* (Montreal) Mar. 14/2 It is most important that hikers procure their hotel reservations well in advance. **1968** *Globe & Mail* (Toronto) 17 Feb. 35 (Advt.), For reservations, call or write Atlantic Car & Truck Rental. **1971** *Financial Mail* (Johannesburg) 26 Feb. 656/2 When his travel agent phoned the Cape Town reservation centre about that day's 19.15 flight to Johannesburg, a reservation clerk said: 'We have no idea how many seats are left.' **1977** E. LEONARD *Unknown Man No. 89* xx. 207 Ryan kept going, ..past the reservation desk to the foyer.

d. Exemption from military service because of an important civilian occupation. Also *attrib.*, as ***reservation age***, etc.

1916 *List of Certified Occupations* (Local Government Board) 4 The *only* ground for making these reservations is that the men protected are engaged on work of national importance. **1940** *Economist* 20 July 73/2 He [*sc.* Ernest Bevin]..is transferring persons to war work by pressure and persuasion rather than by compulsion. An early example of this was the raising of the reservation age in certain industries while postponing the date, so that men below the new age limit could..transfer into war jobs where they would still be reserved. **1941** *Manch. Guardian Weekly* 26 Sept. 194 The test of reservation should be the work a man is actually doing, not his declared occupation. *Ibid.*, The reservation system cannot be said to operate fairly in our present critical state unless its categories are tightened. **1942** *Ann. Reg. 1941* 27 Hitherto all men above the reservation age had been exempted, whether they were actually occupied or not. **1944** *Manpower* (Ministry of Information) 11 Each occupation had its own age of reservation. The more important the job, the lower the age of reservation. The skilled tradesmen in the Armed Forces were drawn from men below the age of reservation in corresponding civilian occupations.

e. = RESERVE *sb.* 5 e. In full, ***central reservation***.

1937 *Memorandum on Lay-Out & Construction of Roads* (Ministry of Transport) 15 Gaps for vehicles in the central reservation should in no case be formed opposite the exits from the minor roads. *Ibid.* 17 The separation of dual carriageways should be effected by a reservation of the greatest width practicable. **1959** *Highway Code* 16 Do not reverse or turn in the carriageway or cross the central reservation. **1972** *Times* 10 June 2/2 Police are to investigate why a new M1 crash barrier near the Toddington service area failed to stop a lorry from crossing the central reservation. **1977** *Oxford Mail* 20 Apr. 1 Oxfordshire's ambulance chief has called for safety barriers down the central reservation of the new Witney Bypass before there is a serious crash.

4. a. An expressed or tacit limitation or exception made with regard to something; the action of making an exception of this kind.

1614 RALEIGH *Hist. World* II. (1634) 189 Such fables argue that Josephus is not to be believed, but with discreete reservations. **1676** TOWERSON *Decalogue* 525 The same school hath admitted tacite interpretations and reservations. **1713** STEELE *Guardian* No. 57 ¶3 The Father's close Equivocal Management, so as always to keep a Reservation to use upon Occasion, when he found himself prest. **1719** D'URFEY *Pills* (1872) II. 75 Dearest, believe without a Reservation. **1788** GIBBON *Decl. & F.* xlix. V. 161 Frederic subscribed, with some reservations, the freedom of four-and-twenty cities. **1794** BLOOMFIELD *Rep.* 30 A Bill of Sale, without any Condition or Reservation, was drawn up. **1849** MACAULAY *Hist. Eng.* ii. I. 157 With this highly important reservation, it had been resolved to set up in England a hierarchy closely resembling that which now exists in Scotland. **1856** FROUDE *Hist. Eng.* vi. (1858) II. 11 The lay lords replied without reservation that they would support the crown. **1891** —— *Divorce Cath.* xviii. 326 The Abbots and Priors had sworn to the supremacy, but..with secret reservations to save their consciences.

b. ***mental reservation***, a qualification tacitly introduced in making a statement, taking an oath, etc., when it is thought inexpedient or unnecessary to speak or dissent openly; also, the fact or practice of making such qualifications.

1606 WARNER *Alb. Eng.* xv. xcv. 380 Tongues-Othes, Harts-Thoughts, Disiunctiues, by a Mentall reseruation. **1629** WADSWORTH *Pilgr.* ii. 10 They did it with a mentall reseruation. **1690** LEE *Massacre of Paris* II. i. 12 Without the smallest Mental Reservation, Equivocation, or the least Reserve. **1716** ADDISON *Freeholder* No. 6 ¶5 We expressly disavow all evasions and mental reservations whatsoever. **1824** SCOTT *Redgauntlet* ch. xvii, A devout belief in whatever had been said of the punic faith of Jesuits, and of the expedients of mental reservation. **1888** J. RICKABY *Mor. Philos.* 233 This looks very much like lying, but..it is speaking the truth under a broad mental reservation.

†5. a. The action of keeping back or concealing from others; something thus kept back or concealed; a secret; a deceptive answer or excuse. *Obs.*

1598 B. JONSON *Ev. Man in Hum.* III. ii, He will not swear, he has some reservation, Some conceal'd purpose, and close meaning sure. **1601** SHAKS. *All's Well* II. iii. 260, I most vnfainedly beseech your Lordshippe to make some reseruation of your wrongs. **1612** NAUNTON in *Buccleuch MSS.* (Hist. MSS. Comm.) I. 113 His Majesty's reservations having too many occasions in this undermining age of the world. *c* **1645** HOWELL *Lett.* I. IV. xxi, The French is..not so full of scruples, reservations, and jealousies as the Spaniard, but deals more frankly, and with a greater confidence and gallantry.

†b. The fact or habit of being reticent; reservedness in discourse. *Obs. rare.*

1649 JER. TAYLOR *Gt. Exemp.* II. §12. 40 His disciples wondred to see him alone talk with a woman, besides his custome, and usuall reservation. *a* **1674** CLARENDON *Hist. Reb.* x. §115 Persons of all conditions repaired to his Majesty of those who had serv'd him; with whom he conferr'd without reservation.

†c. Reserved conduct, reserve. *Obs. rare.*

1655 tr. *Sorel's Com. Hist. Francion* II. 37 You could feign Chastity and Reservation to intrap me. **1658** PHILLIPS s.v., Also Reservation, or Reservednesse, is used in Romances for that distance and state, which Ladies observe in their behaviour toward those that Court them.

II. 6. *Eccl.* The action or practice (in the Roman Catholic, Greek, and other churches) of retaining or preserving for some purpose a portion of the eucharistic elements (esp. the bread) after the celebration of the sacrament; †also, a part of the elements thus reserved.

a **1551** GARDINER in Cranmer *Answ. Gardiner* (1551) III. 165 Justine the Martyr..testifieth a reseruacion to be sent to them that were sycke. **1577–87** HOLINSHED *Chron.* III. 1003/1 Item, we will haue in our churches reseruation. *a* **1626** BP. ANDREWES *Answ. Perron* 6 So that Reservation needeth not; the intent is had without it. **1832** W. PALMER *Orig. Liturg.* II. viii. 229 It is true, that this reservation has been the most usual, and, perhaps, the most ancient, practice of the Church. **1862** *Union* 11 Apr. 226 Another sufficient reason for reservation would be an improved liturgical arrangement for Good Friday.

†7. a. The action or fact of keeping back a matter for further action or later decision. *Obs.*

1590 SWINBURNE *Testaments* 260 Where the testator.. reserueth somewhat to be done at another time,..euen by the ciuill law in this case the testament is perfect, notwithstanding such reseruations. **1659** PEARSON *Creed* (1839) 417 Which..signifieth a reservation of his sin unto the judgment of the world to come.

†b. The action or fact of keeping back something from others or for one's own use. *Obs.*

1601 SHAKS. *All's Well* I. iii. 231 He wil'd me In heedefull'st reseruation to bestow them. **1607** HEYWOOD *Fayre Mayde Exch.* H 2 b, My aduise in the reseruation of those Letters, Which I will haue you hide from eie of day. **1633** BP. HALL *Occas. Medit.* §18 O God, thou distillest thy graces upon us, not for our reservation, but conveyance. **1634** —— *Contempl.*, *N.T.* IV. v, That in the distribution of our goods, we should expect his blessing, not in their entireness and reservation.

†c. Preservation of a thing. *Obs. rare.*

1637 R. HUMPHREY tr. *St. Ambrose* Pref., It was the vanity of Democritus to promise the reservation of the bodyes of men. **1641** HINDE *J. Bruen* xxx. 93 This commemoration of Saints, and Martyrs, did breed and bring forth reservation of their Reliques.

reservationist (rɛzəˈveɪʃənɪst), *sb.* (and *a.*) *U.S.* [f. RESERVATION + -IST.] One who makes reservations (senses 3 c and 4 a). Also *attrib.* or as *adj.*

1920 *Glasgow Herald* 18 Mar. 9 The reservationist Senators are..too much attached to their limitations and qualifications to abandon them for anything. **1933** W. S. HOLT *Treaties defeated by Senate* x. 296 The reservationists did not constitute a majority. **1978** *N.Y. Times* 30 Mar. B20/1 (Advt.), Reservationist... 2 yrs ticketing exp.

†reˈservative, *a.* *Obs. rare.* [a. obs. F. *reservatif, -ive* (Cotgr.), or ad. med.L. **reservātīvus*: see RESERVE *v.* and -ATIVE.] Having the quality of preserving or retaining.

1497 BP. ALCOCK *Mons Perfect.* A iij/2 Medycynes reseruatyf agayn all mortall syknesse. **1541** R. COPLAND *Guydon's Quest. Chirurg.* E j b, And in the hynder ventrycle [of the brain] is put the vertue reseruatyfe or memoratyfe. **1611** COTGR., *Reservatif*, reseruatiue, reseruing.

†reˈservatory, *sb.* *Obs.* [ad. med.L. *reservātōrium* store-house, f. *reservāt-*, ppl. stem of *reservāre*: see RESERVE *v.* and -ORY[1].]

1. A receptacle for food; a cupboard; a store-room or store-house.

1662 J. DAVIES tr. *Olearius' Voy. Ambass.* 179 Under their [Cormorants'] Bills, they have a great bag of shrivell'd skin, ..and they make use of it as a reservatory for the fish they take. **1691** tr. *Emilianne's Frauds Rom. Monks* (ed. 3) 36 Every Religious has in his own Apartment a Reservatory, stor'd with Fruit and other Necessaries. **1807** ROBINSON *Archæol. Græca* I. xxiii. 101 The Acharnensian parasites were to deposit an hecteum of their dole in the reservatory of Apollo, to whom they were to offer sacrifices.

2. A vessel for liquids. *rare.*

1666 J. DAVIES *Hist. Caribby Isles* 195 There must also be a very great care taken, that the Reservatory into which the squeezed juice falls..be often wash'd. **1720** MRS. MANLEY *Power of Love* VI. (1741) 314 A little Reservatory, in Case of extream Sickness and Distress, of some of the Vaudois Wine, and a few Conserves.

3. A reservoir for water, etc. (In common use *c* 1670–1740.)

1666 J. DAVIES *Hist. Caribby Isles* 8 Pools and Reservatories of fresh water, which supply the scarcity of Springs and Rivers. **1680** MORDEN *Geog. Rect.*, *Spain* (1685) 177 Bringing the Water from great Reservatories which they made in the Mountains. **1704** *Collect. Voy. & Trav.* III. 4/1 The Snow..remains as it were in Wells and Reservatories. **1719** QUINCY *Phys. Dict.* (1722) 39/2 The most convenient Springs or Reservatories of cold Water to wash in. **1747** *Act 21 Geo. II*, c. 8 Any of the watercourses, canals, reservatories, or pipes.

b. A receptacle for fluids in animals or plants.

1692 RAY *Creation* II. (ed. 2) 125 The Reservatories, where Pliny says, that Camels do a long time keep the Water which they drink. **1713** DERHAM *Phys.-Theol.* (1727) 422 Their leaves are channelled fit to catch and convey Water down to their Reservatories. **1731** *Hist. Litt.* I. 30 The Milk, ..rarifying with the Heat, is no longer to be contain'd in its small Reservatories.

reˈservatory, *a.* *rare.* [f. as prec. + -ORY[2].] Of or belonging to reservation.

1654 GAYTON *Pleas. Notes* III. v. 100 An excellent bugbeare..to set in one of Cloacina's reservatory, or privie Chambers. **1693** EVELYN *De la Quint. Compl. Gard.* I. 182, I keep in a leaning posture in the Reservatory Baskets those Trees that are designed for the Wall.

reserve (rɪˈzɜːv), *sb.* [a. F. *réserve*, f. *réserver* to RESERVE.]

I. 1. a. Something stored up, kept back, or relied upon, for future use or advantage; a store or stock; an extra quantity.

a **1658** CLEVELAND *Poems* (1677) 72 Cavalier buds, whom Nature teems, As a Reserve for England's Throne. **1691** T. H[ALE] *Acc. New Invent.* 44 Not only for their present use.. but for a Reserve to answer accidents during their Voyages. **1705** ADDISON *Italy* 147 The hidden Reserves and secret Magazines of the Church. **1719** LONDON & WISE *Compl. Gard.* 107 How to order Trees planted for Reserves. **1785** BURKE *Sp. Nabob Arcot* Wks. 1842 I. 321/1 Being made acquainted that they must again exert their influence for a new reserve of the happy parsimony of their servants. **1806–7** J. BERESFORD *Miseries Hum. Life* (1826) IV. x, A drunken sailor who..ejects his reserve of tobacco against the lady's drapery. **1868** ROGERS *Pol. Econ.* ix. (1876) 103 It is a maxim in business that a man..should have a hoard or reserve from which he can draw, when the times are untoward. **1876** VOYLE & STEVENSON *Milit. Dict.* 339/1 In the artillery, there are three reserves of ammunition.

b. The amount of capital kept on hand by a banker, insurance company, etc., in order to meet ordinary or probable demands. Also *pl.* Also, that part of the profit of a joint stock company which is not distributed to shareholders. ***hidden reserve***: see HIDDEN *ppl. a.* 1 d.

1866 CRUMP *Banking* ix. 184 The enormous subsidies.. had caused an immense drain upon the metallic reserves of the Bank for the last year or two. **1880** B. PRICE in *Fraser's Mag.* May 675 The banker does not lend all he receives. The difference is called his reserve. **1885** *Jrnl. Inst. Actuaries* Apr. 141 On a new method of comparing the Reserves for Policies. **1930**, etc. [see HIDDEN *ppl. a.* 1 d]. **1940** *Economist* 25 May 936/1 This has..involved a redefinition of reserves. In former years this item in our figures was a repository for a mixture: reserves provided against specific assets, and other items properly chargeable against profits were combined with 'free reserves' which were, in effect, merely undivided profits. Now the line is more tightly drawn to include the latter and exclude the former. **1974** *Terminol. Managem. & Financial Accountancy* (Inst. Cost & Managem. Accountants) 63 *Reserves*, undistributed or surplus profits. The creation and distribution of certain reserves are affected by company policy and legal considerations, e.g. the provisions of the Memorandum and Articles of Association of the company.

c. The amount of a mineral, or of oil or natural gas, which is known to exist in the ground in a particular region and to be capable of exploitation. Usu. *pl.*

[Cf. quot. 1860 in sense 5.]
1912 M. H. BURNHAM *Mod. Mine Valuation* i. 66 Ore in a developed mine lying below that which the engineer is willing to class as a reserve, and pay for, is 'possible' only. [*Note*] The above table classes as reserves only the ore lying above the deepest level. **1922** *Bull. Amer. Assoc. Petroleum Geologists* VI. 444 Within the last few years the necessity has developed for estimating recoverable reserves on oil and gas properties. **1945** J. A. BROWN in L. M. Fanning *Our Oil Resources* i. 6 In the Maracaibo basin of Venezuela alone there are proved reserves of at least 5 billion barrels of crude oil. **1969** *Australian* 24 Oct. 18/2 Ore reserves fall into four general categories—proven, profitable, possible and indicated. Proven is ore that has been blocked out on four sides; probable is ore that has been opened on two or three sides, while possible ore has been opened on one side only; indicated ore is ore that has been outlined by diamond drilling but which has not been opened by underground work. **1979** *Nature* 26 July 261/1 What the board is actually talking about if it uses the word 'proven' is 'reserves': materials that have been mapped out sufficiently well that they can be the subject of mining by known methods.

d. *spec.* Extra energy; a supply of energy or resilience. Usu. *pl.*

1929 H. CRANE *Let. c* 23 Oct. (1965) 347, I feel quite rested already, but I know that I need a little 'reserve'. **1934** H. G. WELLS *Exper. Autobiogr.* I. vi. 369 Dr. Collins heard of my plight and wrote also. I detected a helpful motive and wrote among other things to assure him that I had 'reserves' for a year or so. **1941** *Lilliput* Mar. 206/1 We had lovely weather all the time. I was so glad. Most children don't feel it, but Jonathan is such a fragile little thing, no reserves at all.

2. *Mil.* **a.** *pl.* Those troops or portions of an army which are withheld from action in order to serve as a reinforcement, or, in case of retreat, as cover to the main body. Also *sing.* in the same sense. (Cf. also 4 b.)

1648 HEYLIN *Relat. & Observ.* I. 32 All the Sectaries of England are invited to be Reserves to this Army. **1670** COTTON *Espernon* I. I. 7 At the Battel of Dreux, where he fought at the head of the Reserve. *a* **1671** LD. FAIRFAX *Mem.* (1699) 84, I had the right wing, with some Scots horse, and lances for my reserves. **1796** *Instr. & Reg. Cavalry* (1813) 191 If a line with reserves, finds it necessary to retire in face of an enemy; the alternate squadrons and reserves will retire two or three hundred paces, and then front. **1844** H. H. WILSON *Brit. India* II. 25 The troops had been distributed in four columns of attack and a reserve. **1859** JEPHSON *Brittany* xii. 193 Charles now ordered up his reserve. **1863** *Sat. Rev.* 10 Oct. 491 The Federal reserves under the command of Generals Palmer and Negley came into action. *fig.* **1863** TREVELYAN *Compet. Wallah* (1866) 315 The time will surely come when we may bring up our reserves with happy effect.

b. That portion of the military or naval forces of a state which is maintained as a further means of defence in addition to the regular army and navy, and is liable to be called out in time of war or emergency; also, in recent use, a member of this force, a reservist. Also *attrib.*

1866 *Chambers's Encycl.* VIII. 204/2 The reserve of the British possessions abroad amounts nominally to 90,780 men. **1876** VOYLE & STEVENSON *Milit. Dict.* 338/2 In the British army this force consists of the auxiliary forces, as well as the army reserves, the militia reserve, or any other reserve and land forces. **1891** PATTERSON *Naut. Dict.* 368 State naval reserves are on about the same footing as the militia. **1898** *Daily News* 30 Mar. 5/3 Recruits.. will be enlisted for three years' army and nine years' reserve service.

c. In games, an additional player kept in readiness to take the place of another if required. Also *pl.*, the reserve or second team.

1900 UPWARD *Eben. Lobb* 71, I have so many to select from... But.. I can put you down as a reserve. **1961** *Daily Express* 14 Jan. 10 Aston Villa assistant manager Dick Taylor.. saw 19-year-old Cheung bamboozle Villa reserves. **1976** E. DUNPHY *Diary* in *Only a Game?* v. 147 All you have got to look forward to is Aldershot reserves away next Wednesday. **1976** *Evening Post* (Nottingham) 14 Dec. 18/5 The England reserve, who injured his back against East Midlands last week, is replaced by Nottingham Casuals' Ian Henry. **1977** *Belfast Tel.* 22 Feb. 29/3 He played for the reserves last night and if there is no reaction, he will be in the Thistle first team tonight.

†**3. a.** A certain amount *of* some quality, feeling, etc., still retained or remaining. *Obs. rare.*

1646 SIR T. BROWNE *Pseud. Ep.* I. vi. (1686) 18 A reserve of Puerility we have not shaken off from School. **1647** CRASHAW *Poems* (1858) 176 Their deadly hate lives still, and hath A wild reserve of wanton wrath. **1714** POPE *Epil. Rowe's J. Shore* 20 Still hoarding up, most scandalously nice, Amidst their virtues, a reserve of vice.

†**b.** A place or thing in which something is preserved or stored. *Obs.*

1644 DIGBY *Nat. Bodies* xxiv. §2. 214 How can one imagine that such iuice should circulate the whole body of an animall,.. and retire to the reserue where it is kept for generation. **1655** MRQ. WORCESTER *Cent. Inv.* §17 A reserve for Snow to keep wine in. **1659** LEAK *Water-wks.* 30 The Reserve must be alwaies full of Water a foot high. *Ibid.* 32.

†**c.** A thing or means to which one may have recourse; a refuge. *Obs. rare.*

1673 *Lady's Call.* I. v. ¶28 'Tis.. thought to be but the effect of destitution and secular wants, a reserve rather then a choice. **1699** BENTLEY *Phalaris* Pref. 51 The only reserve then that I had left was to write to Mr. Græevius. *a* **1715** BURNET *Own Time* II. (1724) I. 320 So he thought, he had a sure reserve to gain England at any time over to them.

4. a. *in reserve*, kept or remaining unutilized; still available.

1691 T. H[ALE] *Acc. New Invent.* 91 The only Method in reserve.. is this of Lead. **1692** BENTLEY *Boyle Lect.* v. 153 Still he hath another Expedient in reserve. **1814** CHALMERS *Evid. Chr. Revel.* i. (ed. 5) 13 There is still a second argument in reserve. **1858** FROUDE *Hist. Eng.* xiii. III. 163 He had a force in reserve with which he could.. crush them. **1887** IRVINE *Football* 125 The tactics of keeping the wing players in reserve.

b. *of reserve*, acting as, or destined for, a support or recourse. Chiefly *Mil.* in *army, body* or *corps of reserve*, after F. *armée* or *corps de réserve*.

1693 *Mem. Ct. Teckely* II. 151 Some pierced even to the Body of Reserve. **1719** LONDON & WISE *Compl. Gard.* 107 That we may always have some [trees] as 'twere in a Body of Reserve for that purpose. **1763** MILLS *Pract. Husb.* IV. 340 The weakest of the two shoots.. they called the shoot of reserve. **1802** JAMES *Milit. Dict.* s.v. *Army*, An army is.. generally.. formed into three lines; the first of which.. forms the van-guard.. and the third, the rear-guard or corps of reserve. **1844** H. H. WILSON *Brit. India* I. 199 An army of reserve.. was prepared to support the advance. **1866** *Chambers's Encycl.* VIII. 204/2 The Army of Reserve is a force incorporated under the act 22 and 23 Vict. c. 42 (1859).

II. 5. a. Something reserved or set apart for some reason or purpose. In later use also in technical applications (see quots.).

1649 JER. TAYLOR *Gt. Exemp.* III. ad Sect. xiv. (1667) 428 Either they that remain are sealed up to a worse calamity, or left within the reserves and mercies of Repentance. **1679** C. NESSE *Antichrist* 146 Besides the reserve of 45 y. hereafter to be spoke of. **1695** KENNETT *Par. Antiq.* Gloss. s.v. *Chirch-Scot*, A reserve of Corn rent paid to Secular Priests, or to the Religious. **1710** PRIDEAUX *Orig. Tithes* ii. 72 They were Maintained out of the Sacrifices, that were offered, and.. had every time they officiated a reserve over and above for the support of their Families also. **1799** *Hull Advertiser* 28 Dec. 2/1 The Earl of Breadalbane's woods.. contain about two thousand chosen reserves, from 40 to 100 years old. **1808–25** JAMIESON, *Reserve*, the designation given to a tree reserved in a hag. **1860** WORCESTER (citing ANSTED), *Reserve*, a part of a lode laid bare by the exploring and regular work of a mine, from which the ore can be at any time removed.

b. A district or place set apart for some particular use, or assigned to certain persons. (Cf. RESERVATION 3 b.) Also as the final element in *Combs.*: see GAME *sb.* 16 a, NATIVE *a.* 15, NATURE *sb.* 15 a.

1805 *Statutes at Large U.S.A.* (1846) VII. 98 The latter [Indian] reserve to be subject to the same laws and regulations as may be established in the circumjacent country. **1832** T. BAILLIE *Acct. Province N. Brunswick* 79 The Richibucto River is also well and thickly settled, to the head of the tide excepting in a large tract reserved for Indians, which reserve is a great drawback on the prosperity of the place. **1852** GODLONTON & IRVING *Kaffir War* III. xvii. 232 They fell upon two Fingo kraals in the 'Reserve'.. and completely destroyed them. **1853** MOODIE *Life in Clearings* 50 The fever of the 'Clergy Reserves question' was then at its height. **1867** PARKMAN *Jesuits in N. Amer.* xxxii. (1875) 426 The government of the United States at length removed them [the Indians] to reserves on the western frontier. **1882** *St. James's Gaz.* 15 Mar. 6/1 Other dangers of the oyster in the shallow waters of the reserves are heat and cold. **1890** 'R. BOLDREWOOD' *Col. Reformer* (1891) 251 A reserve for travelling stock. **1892** *Pall Mall G.* 21 Apr., Each monk's 'reserve' contains a passage.. which serves as his exercise ground. **1908** C. MAIR *Through Mackenzie Basin* 57 These reserves are holdings you can select when you please, subject to the approval of the Government. **1928** J. D. TAYLOR *Christianity & Natives of S. Afr.* 6 The Adequacy or Inadequacy of the Existing Native Reserves begins to be recognised as the crux of the Native question. **1953** P. ABRAHAMS *Return to Goli* IV. ii. 106 At the moment the Blacks of the Reserves have only about 10 per cent of the total land area of the Union. **1965** *Austral. Encycl.* I. 88/2 Southern Australia.. has allocated a large part.. of the western desert in the north-west of the State for aboriginal reserves. **1973** *Black World* June 46/1 Australia, for over 30,000 years a Black man's country, has for the past 200 years been dominated by white western-europeans, and the original inhabitants.. have been murdered, poisoned, rounded up and confined on Reserves. **1977** *Belfast Tel.* 22 Feb. 2/7 The two men were working in a reserve containing eight tigers.

attrib. *a* **1843** SOUTHEY *Comm.-pl. Bk.* Ser. II. (1849) 627 The Indian Reserve-lands at Gay Head. **1880** E. KIRKE *Garfield* 12 The old gentleman, a robust specimen of a Western Reserve Yankee. **1911** W. H. KOEBEL *In Maoriland Bush* xix. 253 An occasional small patch of 'reserve' bush throws its long shadow down the steep hillsides.

c. A distinction given to an animal or other exhibit at a show, indicating that it will receive a prize in the event of another being disqualified.

1867 [used at the Royal Agricultural Society's Show at Bury St. Edmunds]. **1895** *Daily News* 25 June 3/3 The Duke of York had a reserve for a red-polled cow.

d. In textile or pottery decoration: an area which is left the original colour of the material or the colour of the background. Also phr. *in reserve*.

1876 HAMERTON *Etching & Etchers* 281 Reserves of pure white amidst dark shading may be made anywhere. **1910** *Burlington Mag.* XVII. 284/1 [In these early Mohammedan textiles] for the most part the surface is covered by circular reserves in which.. figures.. are placed in pairs symmetrically confronted. **1957** K. M. KENYON *Digging up Jericho* v. 79 A design in a dark red slip applied.. in a series of diamonds or triangles, often so arranged that the underlying cream slip forms a series of chevrons in reserve. **1971** *Cambr. Anc. Hist.* (ed. 3) I. II. xxiv. 689 The pottery is painted in a brown or blackish paint on a buff to yellow slip. Designs are simple but very distinctive, consisting of horizontal bands with zigzags, triangles, or multiple chevrons, often left 'in reserve'. **1980** *Catal. Fine Chinese Ceramics* (Sotheby, Hong Kong) 166 With reserves of emblems and precious objects alternating with trellis diaper panels around the rim.

e. In full, *central reserve*. A central area separating lanes of a dual carriageway or motorway.

1937 *Sunday Times* 10 Jan., Nearly all the new roads have broad central 'reserves' and broad grass verges on each side. **1968** *Highway Code* 15 When crossing a dual carriageway, treat each half as a separate road. Wait at the central dividing strip (the central reserve) until there is a safe gap in the traffic. **1969** *Times* 21 Apr. 7/1 By-passes, some with dual carriageways and central reserves, present a greater inconvenience.

6. a. An expressed limitation, exception, or restriction made concerning something; †a condition of this nature. Now *rare.*

1654 tr. *Scudery's Curia Pol.* 109 With this reserve and difference, that she shall receive that illustrious honour from my hands, and not I from hers. **1671** MILTON *P.R.* IV. 165, I give to whom I please,.. yet with this reserve, not else, On this condition [etc.]. **1699** BENTLEY *Phalaris* 258 It is at his Service: but with this reserve, that he shall not abuse me for Lending it. **1729** *Wodrow Corr.* (1843) III. 432 All his declarations seemed to be yet consistent with some favourite scheme.. he had taken up, and that led him into his reserves as to the personal property. **1865** M. ARNOLD *Ess. Crit.* viii. (1875) 319 How many reserves must be made in praising either his poetry, or his criticism!

b. A mental limitation or qualification of the adherence one gives to some principle, article of belief, etc.

a **1679** W. OUTRAM *Serm.* (1682) 304 To evade and escape the plainest truths by some reserves. **1690** LEE *Massacre of Paris* II. i. 12 Without the smallest Mental Reservation, Equivocation, or the least Reserve. **1716** ADDISON *Freeholder* No. 53 ¶7 However any one may concur in the general scheme, it is still with certain reserves and deviations, and with a salvo to his own private judgment. **1771** FLETCHER *Checks* Wks. 1795 II. 23 Their secret reserves evidence them to be only such believers as Simon Magus. **1859** MILL *Liberty* i. 19 In the minds of almost all religious persons.. the duty of toleration is admitted with tacit reserves. **1874** L. STEPHEN *Hours in Library* (1892) I. vi. 200 The.. story.. is to be received with a certain reserve.

c. *without reserve*, without limitation or restriction of any kind. In modern use chiefly with reference to sales by auction.

1700 WELLWOOD *Mem.* 239 His Subjects were obliged to obey him without Reserve. **1751** JOHNSON *Rambler* No. 162 ¶4 He that trusts without reserve will at last be deceived. **1794** PALEY *Evid.* (1825) II. 16 It [Christianity] denied without reserve the truth of every article of heathen mythology. **1799** *Times* 1 June 1/1 (Advt.), The beautiful Collection of paintings.. now exhibiting, and selling off without reserve. **1805** *Times* 7 Nov. 4/2 The whole of the above are in prime condition, and will be sold without reserve. **1846** BATEMAN *Law Auctions* II. ii. (ed. 3) 152 Where, after a sale has been declared to be without reserve, a single private bidder is employed, such bidding will not, under any circumstances, be justifiable.

d. = *reserve price.*

1854 D. G. ROSSETTI *Let.* c 26 June (1965) I. 203 The rest he put into a sale at Christie's, after taking my advice as to the reserve he ought to put on the Hunt, which I fixed at 500 gs. It reached 300 in real biddings, after which Mac's touters ran it up to 430, trying to revive it, but of course it remains with him. **1911** R. FRY *Let.* 4 Feb. (1972) I. 340 It [*sc.* a picture] was valued by Berenson.. at £6,000 but I don't think.. that the reserve will be nearly so high as that. **1977** *Irish Press* 29 Sept. 15/5 Fastest trial winner of the day, in 29.87, The Best Band, went to 1,025 guineas, but this was a long way short of the reserve.

7. *Eccl.* **a.** = RESERVATION 1 b. *rare*$^{-1}$.

1725 tr. *Dupin's Eccl. Hist. 17th C.* I. II. iii. 46 Benedict XII made a general Reserve of all the Benefices *in Curia*.

b. = RESERVATION 1 c.

1884 *Catholic Dict.* 718/1 He quotes.. from Constitutions of Richard, bishop of Salisbury, clear cases of Papal reserve.

8. *Techn.* **a.** A preparation used to prevent or modify, in those places to which it is applied, the action of colouring matter upon textile fabrics; a resist. Also *attrib.*

1836 *Penny Cycl.* VI. 156/1 Coloured reserves, capable of communicating different colours in the course of their application; and.. mordant reserves. **1839** URE *Dict. Arts* 224 The reserve style, where the white cloth is impressed with figures in a resist paste. *Ibid.* 228 A chrome orange reserve may be made by introducing a larger proportion of sub-acetate of lead. **1875** *Ure's Dict. Arts* (ed. 7) I. 641 Another way of combining madder or garancin colours with steam colours is by blocking on the dyed object.. a reserve paste.

b. A preparation used for similar purposes in electro-plating. Also *attrib.*

1873 SPON *Workshop Rec.* Ser. I. (1885) 217/2 By reserves, certain parts of a metallic article.. are coated with another metal. *Ibid.*, Make a gold reserve, and use a silver reserve. *Ibid.* 218/1 Resist or Reserve Varnishes.

III. 9. a. Self-restraint; self-control; imposition of some limit to one's action.

1665 BOYLE *Occas. Refl.* Pref. a 5 b, That noble Figure.. I should be loath to use.. with no more Reserve than those great Orators Tully and Isocrates have Sometimes done before me. **1760** *Hist.* in *Ann. Reg.* 29/1 Notwithstanding this reserve of the king.. the victory was compleat. **1821** SHELLEY *Hellas* 540 He crouches, watching till the spoil be won, And must be paid for his reserve in blood. **1860** RUSKIN *Mod. Paint.* V. VIII. iv. 184 Reserve.... I mean by it the power which a great painter exercises over himself in fixing certain limits.. which he will not transgress.

b. Abstention from giving a full explanation or expressing one's mind freely; reticence; also *spec.* in casuistry, an intentional suppression of truth in cases where it might lead to inconvenience.

1704 NORRIS *Ideal World* II. xii. 512 The reserve of a theory; which.. ought not to attempt to explain everything, but to have some clouds mingled with its light. **1725** POPE *Odyss.* XIV. 220 On dark reserve what better can prevail, Or from the fluent tongue produce the tale? **1751** JOHNSON *Rambler* No. 176 ¶2 A furious critic, whose age, rank, or fortune gives him confidence to speak without reserve. **1794** PALEY *Evid.* II. ii. (1817) 58 As to the rest a solemn reserve is maintained. **1815** ELPHINSTONE *Acc. Caubul* (1842) I. 71 The King.. said he had sent for us that we might converse without reserve. **1864** NEWMAN *Apologia* App. 67 It was a duty.. to observe a great reserve and caution in communicating to them the knowledge of 'the whole counsel of God'.

c. Avoidance of too great familiarity; want of cordiality or open friendliness.

a **1721** PRIOR *Celia to Damon* 16 My soul surpris'd,.. Left all reserve, and all the sex behind. **1728** YOUNG *Love Fame* VI. 45 There is no woman, where there's no reserve. **1751** JOHNSON *Rambler* No. 163 ¶5 This frigid reserve somewhat disgusted me. **1810** CRABBE *Borough* xxiii, Her trembling joy appears, Her forced reserve, and his retreating fears. **1838** LYTTON *Alice* II. v, On the whole, they made just allowance for his habits of distant reserve. **1879** MRS. A. E. JAMES *Ind. Househ. Managem.* 79 English people in England are too apt to wrap themselves up in what they think is a dignified reserve.

†**d.** *on* or *upon the reserve*: (*a*) in a waiting attitude; (*b*) reserved; reticent. *Obs.*

1655 *Nicholas Papers* (Camden) II. 161, I cannot make any conjecture of Cromwells busines with his parliament, but think he lyes upon the reserve. **1701** W. WOTTON *Hist. Rome* 336 This made them keep themselves upon the Reserve. **1740** tr. *De Mouhy's Fort. Country-Maid* (1741) II. 352 She took me in her Arms, and express'd a Regret for being upon the Reserve, declaring an entire Confidence in me. 1771 T. Hull *Sir W. Harrington* (1797) III. 159 He really of late has been very much upon the reserve, seldom caring..to go on with the discourse. 1809 Malkin *Gil Blas* vii. i. ¶7, I shall..disclose a secret to you; though men in our profession cannot be too much on the reserve.

†10. An instance of keeping some knowledge from another person; a fact or item of information kept back or disguised; a secret. *Obs.*

1680 Burnet *Rochester* Pref. (1692) 4 He used very few reserves with me. 1714 Swift *Pres. St. Aff.* Wks. 1751 IV. 260 Thus he grows to abound in Secrets and Reserves, even towards those, with whom he ought to act in the greatest Confidence. 1768 Sterne *Sent. Journ., Character*, He insisted I had a reserve, and that I would speak my opinion frankly. 1795 Burke *Corr.* (1844) IV. 296 Consult Mr. Grattan, with whom I have no reserves, and I wish you to have none. 1797–1805 S. & H. Lee *Canterb. T.* V. 264 Thrown wholly off his reserves by surprise and vexation.

IV. 11. a. *attrib.* or as *adj.* Kept in reserve, constituting a reserve. Also, pertaining to, designed for, or used by reserves.

1719 London & Wise *Compl. Gard.* v. viii. 108 This Transporting of Reserve-Trees may be done 'till Midsummer. 1720 De Foe *Capt. Singleton* v. (1840) 94 Our reserve men advancing, we resolved to fire. 1828 J. M. Spearman *Brit. Gunner* (ed. 2) 13 No reserve waggons. 1853 Stocqueler *Milit. Encycl.* 231/1 The depôt companies left at home by infantry regiments embarking for foreign service are now called the Reserve companies. 1853 Mrs. Gaskell *Cranford* xv. 228 Miss Matty would be perplexed as to her duty if she were aware of any little reserve-fund being made for her while the debts of the bank remained unpaid. 1875 Bennett & Dyer tr. *Sachs' Bot.* 627 Every cell, tissue, or organ in which assimilated substances are stored up for subsequent use is called a Reservoir of Reserve-material. 1876 Voyle & Stevenson *Milit. Dict.* 339/1 The reserve ammunition of a regiment is carried in carts. 1916 'Boyd Cable' *Action Front* 125 Men who live month in month out in a narrow territory, bounded on the east by the forward firing line and on the west by..the villages of the reserve billets. 1923 Kipling *Irish Guards in Gt. War* I. 128 They took over reserve-billets. 1928 [see dog-fight 2]. 1959 N. Mailer *Advts. for Myself* (1961) 50 In early 1941 he wrote to his father that he would like to take advantage of his reserve commission to enter the army. 1974 D. Kyle *Raft of Swords* x. 97 In Vancouver..there are a great many British immigrants. Some..are ex-service, still on the reserve list. 1976 *Leicester Advertiser* 26 Nov. 1/4 He was..reserve champion at the East of England [Show]. 1976 M. Butterworth *Remains to be Seen* iv. 54 His eye was immediately taken by the fuel warning light. He switched to the reserve tank.

b. Special Combs.: **reserve bank**, a central bank holding currency reserves (chiefly *Austral.* and *N.Z.*); **reserve buoyancy**, bouyancy available to a craft in excess of its weight; **reserve cell** *Med.*, a cell whose further differentiation constitutes the renewal of immediately adjacent tissue; freq. *attrib.*; **reserve currency**, a currency widely used in international trade and held in reserves by foreign banks; **reserve price** (see quot. 1957).

1905 C. A. Conant *Princ. Money & Banking* II. vii. 292 The essential requirement..is an ultimate source of credit which shall be strong enough to inspire confidence in its ability both to redeem its circulating notes and to grant discounts. A central *reserve bank, whose credit is unquestionable, is then enabled to meet the demand for credit from private bankers by redistributing the paper in their hands. 1965 *Austral. Encycl.* I. 414/1 At the apex of the structure is the central bank, the Reserve Bank of Australia, which is a government-owned institution established by Act of the Commonwealth Parliament in 1959. 1966 *Encycl. N.Z.* I. 149/2 The extent to which a bank can extend credit which, when used by its customers, will cause it to lose funds to other banks, is determined by the amount of cash it holds at the Reserve Bank and its ability to borrow at the Reserve Bank's discount rate. 1976 *Eastern Even. News* (Norwich) 13 Dec. 1/1 The Reserve Bank in Sydney said the Australian dollar was being revalued by 1.28 per cent. 1904 A. C. Holms *Pract. Shipbuilding* vi. 65 *Reserve buoyancy may be defined as the lifting power, and is measured by the volume of the hull above the load-line. 1951 D. H. C. Birt *Sailing Yacht Design* vi. 99 There is no reserve buoyancy forward on heeling to balance that in the after-sections. 1975 W. Muckle *Naval Archit. for Marine Engineers* i. 3 It [*sc.* freeboard] provides reserve buoyancy which can enable it to float in the event of damage. 1909 *Amer. Jrnl. Physiol.* XXV. 181 Lymphocytes may be '*reserve cells' kept on hand to immediately combat injury to the tissues. 1930 C. Bloom in Maximow & Bloom *Textbk. Histol.* xxxiv. 693 Most of the chromophobe cells [of the hypophysis], the so-called chief or principal or reserve cells, have relatively small amounts of cytoplasm. 1940 *Amer. Jrnl. Cancer* XL. 214 (*heading*) Reserve-cell carcinomas. *Ibid.* 216 They appear to be the only epithelial cells in the mucous membrane of the bronchial tree which are concerned with cell division and cell differentiation. It seems reasonable, therefore, to look upon them as the reserve cells from which the ciliated columnar cells and goblet cells are replenished. 1952 *Amer. Jrnl. Obstetr. & Gynecol.* LXIV. 268 Adenomatous hyperplasia and epidermization [in the cervix] seem to be related to activity of a multipotential cell termed the 'reserve cell'. 1975 L. Foulds *Neoplastic Devel.* II. iii. 111 Convincing photomicrographs of a layer of small cuboidal cells [in cervical epithelium] have been published and these cells have been identified as the basal cells or reserve cells from which the layer of overlying columnar cells is renewed. *Ibid.* 112 Reserve cell hyperplasia without metaplasia consists, as a rule, of not more than five or six layers of cuboidal cells similar to normal reserve cells, covered by an intact layer of columnar cells. 1967 *Listener* 26 Jan. 116/3 Britain, in or out of the Common Market, should maintain sterling as a *reserve currency. 1971 *Daily Tel.* 10 May 14/3 The special kind of foreign exchange held in official reserves is called..a *Reserve Currency*. 1978 *Time* 3 July 8/1 The D-mark is being pushed more and more into the role of an international reserve currency. 1919 W. F. & G. D. Nokes *Auctioneer's Man.* (ed. 8) i. 11 A short time before the date of the sale the auctioneer should ascertain the *reserve price for the property. 1935 *Chambers's Encycl.* I. 569/1 Where, under the conditions, a sale by auction is subject to a reserve price, no contract is concluded..if the highest bid is lower than the reserve price. 1957 Clark & Gottfried *University Dict. Business & Finance* 275/2 *Reserve price*, at a public auction, the lowest price which a seller is willing to accept; the price below which he reserves the right to withdraw the goods from sale. 1977 D. Clark *Gimmel Flask* iv. 74 The vendors..are entirely at the mercy of the ring unless the articles have reserve prices put on them.

reserve (rɪˈzɜːv), *v.*[1] Also 4 rec-, 5 ress-, 4–5 *Sc.* reserwe. [ad. OF. *reserver* (mod.F. *réserver*), ad. L. *reservāre*, f. *re-* re- + *servāre* to keep, save: cf. *preserve*.]

1. a. *trans.* To keep for future use or enjoyment; to store up *for* (†*to*) some time or occasion; to refrain from using or enjoying at once.

1340 Hampole *Pr. Consc.* 3928 þus pardon in purgatory availles,..bot som clerkes counsailles þat we it spare and reserve haly, Until we com til purgatory. c1400 Love *Bonavent. Life Christ* (B.N.C.) lf. 60 It is leuefulle to goddis seruauntes forto haue money and reserue it to hir nede. 1621 T. Williamson tr. *Goulart's Wise Vieillard* 123 Pleasure seemes to reserue her dainties to the last, and for the last seruice and messe. 1667 Milton *P.L.* viii. 50 Such pleasure she reserv'd, Adam relating, she sole Auditress. 1709 Swift in *Lett. Lit. Men* (Camden) 340, I shall reserve the rest of my threatnings till further provocation. 1718 Lady M. W. Montagu *Let.* 31 July, I..have reserved my thanks to the conclusion. 1824 J. H. Newman *Hist. Sk.* (1873) II. ii. xi. 294 The appeal to the gentler emotions of the soul is reserved..for the close of his oration. 1841 Lane *Arab. Nts.* I. 100, I have not reserved my tear but for the time of my difficulty.

b. To keep back or hold over to a later time or place or for further treatment; to postpone the discussion, decision, or declaration of (a matter). Const. *for*, *to*, etc., and †with infin. as obj.

1382 Wyclif *Jude* i. 6 Aungels that kepten not his princehed..he reserude in to the doom of greet God, in euerelastinge boondis vndir derknesse. 1456 Sir G. Haye *Law Arms* (S.T.S.) 74 God reservis till his jugement all secrete misdedis. 1535 Coverdale *2 Pet.* ii. 9 How to reserue the vniust vnto the daye of iudgment for to be punyshed. 1581 Pettie *Guazzo's Civ. Conv.* ii. (1586) 52 It shall suffice for this time to discourse onelie of publike Conuersation, and the other wee will reserue for tomorrow. 1602 Shaks. *Ham.* i. iii. 69 Take each mans censure; but reserue thy iudgement. 1634 W. Tirwhyt tr. *Balzac's Lett.* 53, I will reserve to speak as I ought of this rare vertue, till my great work come to light. 1687 A. Lovell tr. *Thevenot's Trav.* i. 231 They..add every day part of that which they have reserved to the real growth of that day they cry it on. 1714 Addison *Spect.* No. 556 ¶2, I shall reserve for another time the History of such Club or Clubs. 1838 Thirlwall *Greece* V. 217 The great rebellion.., as it is not immediately connected with the affairs of Greece, we reserve for more particular notice in another place. 1878 Huxley *Physiogr.* 72 Its full discussion must be reserved for the next chapter.

c. *refl.* To keep (oneself) in reserve *for* some occasion, etc.

1605 Bacon *Adv. Learn.* i. vii. §6 Adrian..desired to comprehend all things, and not to reserve himself for the worthiest things. c1645 Howell *Lett.* II. 76 (Cent.), Farewel, my noble Friend, cheer up, and reserve yourself for better Days. 1876 J. Parker *Paracl.* i. v. 56 Little natures reserve themselves for great occasions: majestic natures make all occasions great.

†d. *refl.* To restrain (oneself) from action or participation in some affair. *Obs. rare.*

1586 Jas. VI in Ellis *Orig. Lett.* Ser. i. III. 14 Reserve up youre self na langer in the earnist dealing for my Mother. 1670 G. H. *Hist. Cardinals* i. i. 16 It is the custom of the Italians, to constrain and reserve themselves as much as possibly.

2. a. To retain as one's own; to keep *to* or *for* oneself.

c1375 *Sc. Leg. Saints* xxxiv. (*Pelagia*) 274 Scho..hale hyr gud to-gyddir brocht, reseruand til hyr richt nocht. c1425 Wyntoun *Cron.* v. x. 1935 God has reserwit til hym all [þe] wit of þat þat is to fal. 1464 *Mann. & Househ. Exp.* (Roxb.) 187 The bayles and al hoder thenges resservede to myselfe as they ware befor. 1490 Caxton *Eneydos* xviii. 67 In suche a wyse that no thynge I haue reserued for my selfe but that it was alle habandouned vnto the. 1530 Palsgr. 688/1 It is good to be lyberall but ever reserve somwhat to your selfe. 1596 Spenser *State Irel.* Wks. (Globe) 611/1 [They] acknowledged King Henry for theyr soverayne lord, reserving yet..unto themselves all theyr owne former priviledges. 1613 Heywood *Silver Age* i. i. Wks. 1874 III. 95 Onely the Darreine tower I still reserue In that to pennance me a life retir'd. 1667 Milton *P.L.* xii. 71 Man over men He made not Lord; such title to himself Reserving. 1783 Pennant *Tour Chester to Lond.* 76 It is conjectured, that the king at that time reserved this manor to himself. 1824 *Excursion U.S. & Canada* 408 They are induced to sell their lands..although they generally reserve a small tract for themselves. 1877 Froude *Short Stud.* (1883) IV. i. iii. 35 Every question..in which an ecclesiastic was a party, the Church courts had endeavoured to reserve for themselves.

†b. To keep (a matter) from the knowledge of others. *Obs.*

1719 De Foe *Crusoe* ii. (Globe) 322 The Ideas of Things which we form in our Minds, perfectly reserved, and not communicated to any. 1725 Pope *Odyss.* iii. 107 Of all the chiefs, this hero's fate alone Has Jove reserved, unheard of, and unknown. 1727–38 Chambers *Cycl.* s.v. *Reservation*, A proposition which,..if qualified with something reserved or concealed in the mind, becomes true.

3. a. To set apart, keep (†*to* or) *for* another. Also occas. without const.

1382 Wyclif *Gen.* xxvii. 36 Whethir thow hast not reseruyd, he seith, to me thi blissyng? 1382 —— *2 Pet.* ii. 17 To whom the thicke mijst of derknessis is reserued. c1400 Gower *Addr. Hen. IV* in *Pol. Poems* (Rolls) II. 12 So schal thin highe mede be reserved To him which al schal qwiten ate laste. c1420 Lydg. *Assembly of Gods* 2088 Then shall ye haue the triumphall guerdoun That God resereueth to euery creature. 1494 Fabyan *Chron.* i. xiv. 15 The Fader..for the thirde, Cordeilla, resorued no thynge. a1547 Surrey in *Tottel's Misc.* (Arb.) 23 And that I haue deserued..Is to his handes reserued That neuer felt the smart. 1584 Powel *Lloyd's Cambria* 101 After the death of Edward to reserue the crowne to the dukes use. 1605 Shaks. *Macb.* iii. iv. 46 *Macb.* The Table's full. *Lennox.* Heere is a place reseru'd Sir. a1648 Ld. Herbert *Hen. VIII* (1683) 234, I pray you give me by writing, that you deny it, reserving me yet your safe Conduct to return. 1667 Milton *P.L.* ix. 768 Was..to us deni'd This intellectual food, for beasts reserv'd? 1766 Goldsm. *Vic. W.* xxviii, Happiness, I fear, is no longer reserved for me here. 1810 Scott *Lady of L.* ii. xxxv, Thy churlish courtesy for those Reserve, who fear to be thy foes. 1874 Green *Short Hist.* ii. §7. 95 [He] exacted from him..a humiliation which men reserved for the deadliest of their foes.

b. In *passive* with reference to discoveries or important achievements.

1732 Berkeley *Alciphr.* ii. §1 This discovery was reserved to our times. 1833 N. Arnott *Physics* (ed. 5) II. 100 It was reserved for Mr. Dalton to make the admirable discovery [etc.]. 1864 Bryce *Holy Rom. Emp.* xiii. (1875) 205 The third and crowning triumph of the Holy See was reserved for the thirteenth century. 1894 J. T. Fowler *Adamnan* Introd. 56 It was reserved for Columba to evangelize the Northern Picts.

4. *Eccl.* **a.** To set apart, keep back (cases for absolution) to be dealt with by a superior authority. Const. *to*, *for*. (Cf. reservation 1 c.)

c1357 *Lay Folks' Catech.* (T.) 257 Yit may we noght be assoiled of our false athe, Bot of our bisshop or him that has his power, For swilk cas is riuely reserved til him seluen. 1727–38 Chambers *Cycl.* s.v. *Reserve*, Certain cases,..called reserved cases, as being reserved to the bishop. 1846 W. Maskell *Mon. Rit.* (1882) I. 97 In the Constitutions published in 1367 by Thoresby, archbishop of York, thirty-seven cases are reserved to the archbishop himself. 1876 *Mr. Gray & Neighb.* I. 97 It would be a difficult case of conscience..that he should feel bound to 'reserve' for his bishop. 1884 *Catholic Dict.* (1897) 786/1 Papal cases are reserved to the Pope—episcopal cases to the bishop.

b. To set apart (benefices) for presentation by the Pope. *rare*$^{-1}$. (Cf. reservation 1 b.)

c1380 Wyclif *Last Age Ch.* (1840) 24 For no more schulde fatte beneficis be reserved þanne smale, ȝif no pryuy cause of symonye were tretide.

5. a. To retain or secure (some right or profit) for oneself or another by formal stipulation; †to provide or stipulate *that*. (Chiefly in legal use.)

c1407 Lydg. *Reson & Sens.* 1665 And specialy to be reserved That peyse and novmbre be observed, Throgh rethoryke, as in sentence. 1442 *Rolls of Parlt.* V. 57/2 Reservyng to the seide Feffeez iiᵐ *li* yerely. 1532 *Dial. on Laws Eng.* ii. xxii. 43 b, If a man make a feffement and reserue the profites..that reseruacion is voyde in the lawe. 1570 *Act 13 Eliz.* c. 8 §5 Contracts..whereupon is not reserved..to the Lender..above the Sum of ten Pound. 1609 Skene *Reg. Maj.* 35 Bot gif he hes na wife, the time of his deceis, the ane just halfe of the gudes, is reservand to him, to be disponed as he pleases. 1641 *Termes de la Ley* 242 b, If a lease bee mad for yeares of ground, reserving the great trees growing upon the same,..the lessee may not meddle with them. 1791 Kames *Dict. Decis.* (ed. 2) I. 292 A father having reserved a faculty to burden the estate with wadsets,..this was found not a real burden. 1818 Hallam *Middle Ages* (1872) I. 195 Military service does not appear to have been reserved in the beneficiary grants made to cathedrals. 1883 *Law Rep. 11 Q.B. Div.* 575 The tenant is not concluded by the amount of rent which may have been reserved on the premises.

b. To set apart (a portion of rent) for payment *in* corn, etc.

1575–6 *Act 18 Eliz.* c. 6 §1 That thone thirde parte at the leaste of tholde Rente be reserved and paide in Corne for the saide Colleges. 1766 Blackstone *Comm.* II. xx. 318 Antiently the greater part of rents were reserved in provisions. 1776 Adam Smith *W.N.* i. v. I. 40 The rents which have been reserved in corn have preserved their value much better than those which have been reserved in money.

6. a. To set (a thing) apart for some purpose or with some end in view; to keep *for* some use.

1415 *E.E. Wills* (1882) 23, I woll that Isabell my wyfe haue..all my corne..oute take xl quarters of wete reserued to fullfell with my wille. 1463 *Bury Wills* (Camden) 31, I wil mine ffeffes and executours, so it hurte not the sale, reserve the gardyn that it may longe to the longe tyled hous. 1596 Spenser *State Irel.* Wks. (Globe) 612/1 They use to place him that shalbe theyr Captayne, uppon a stone allwayes reserved for that purpose, and placed commonly upon a hill. 1637 *Decree Star Chamb.* §33 in Arber *Milton's Areop.* 23 Euery Printer shall reserue one Book..and shall..deliuer it to the Officer..to be sent to the Librarie at Oxford. 1697 Dryden *Virg. Georg.* iii. 253 Distinguish all betimes,..Whom to reserve for Husband of the Herd. 1788 Gibbon *Decl. & F.* l. V. 175 Their powers are reserved for the moments of flight and pursuit. 1817 Jas. Mill *Brit. India* II. iv. v. 162 Jaffier..offered to accept of his mediation; reserving in his mind the use of every clandestine effort to accomplish his own designs. 1892 S. C. Scrivener *Our Fields & Cities* 112 The 300 acres reserved (for poor men's gardens).

b. To set (a person) apart *for* some fate, destiny, end, etc. †Also const. *to*. Now *rare*.

1387 Trevisa *Higden* (Rolls) VII. 95 He wasted þe south marche, sleynge þe males, reservynge þe females to his lust. 1432–50 tr. *Higden* (Rolls) VI. 477 Canutus..revivynge, was gladde that he was reservede to lyfe that he myȝhte do penaunce. **1513** DOUGLAS *Æneis* v. xi. 52 O pepill vnhappy, to quhat mischevous end Fortoun reservis ȝow of this warld to wend? **1566** PAINTER *Pal. Pleas.* II. 130 The Gods having made all thynges mortall, so have they reserved onely themselves to bee immortall. **1595** DANIEL *Civ. Wars* I. cix, Now reserued in our age, To home confusion and disordered rage. *c* **1645** HOWELL *Lett.* (1650) I. I. xxvi. 42, I hope God hath reserv'd me for a better destiny. **1667** MILTON *P.L.* II. 161 We are decreed, Reserv'd and destin'd to Eternal woe. **1826** SCOTT *Woodst.* xix, Good God! for what am I reserved! *a* **1873** LYTTON *Pausanias* I. i, Worthy of the destinies for which I foresee that the son of Miltiades is reserved.

†**c.** To make an exception of, or in favour of (a thing or person); to except or exempt (one) *from* something. *Obs.*

1523 LD. BERNERS *Froiss.* I. ccclxxxvi. 656 For they knowe well ynoughe howe ye were in Scotlande, wherfore they shulde haue reserued you. **1534** MORE *Comf. agst. Trib.* II. Wks. 1204/2 There be very few..reserued also, but that they set theyr heart verye sore theron. **1613** PURCHAS *Pilgrimage* IX. ix. 725 The old Men, Women, and sick Folks were reserued from this Tribute. **1635** QUARLES *Embl.* I. i. 5 Our great Creator did Reserve this Tree, and this alone forbid. *a* **1806** HORSLEY *Serm.* xxii. (1816) II. 211 In this same decree, which so remarkably reserves the abstinence from blood, the Sabbath is not at all reserved as a thing either of necessity or expedience.

d. In pottery decoration, etc.: to leave in the original colour of the material or the colour of the background. Usu. as *pa. pple.*

1875 *Ure's Dict. Arts* (ed. 7) I. 641 In the white spaces reserved are now blocked steam colours. **1885** L. M. SOLON *Art Old Eng. Potter* (ed. 2) iii. 86 A space was reserved between the two ridges, leaving a hollow to be filled in by slips of divers colours. **1908** J. F. BLACKER *ABC of Collecting Old Eng. China* (ed. 2) 41 Rich ground colours were successfully employed... Panels were reserved in white for painting. **1972** *Trans. Oriental Ceramics Soc.* XXXVIII. 123 Round the sides are six small landscapes in panels reserved in red and gilt trellis-diapered ground.

e. To exempt (a person) from military service because he is engaged in an important civilian occupation. Also, to class (a civilian occupation) as high-priority, thereby exempting many of those employed in it from military service.

1915 *Local Govt. Board Circular No. R.4: 1st Suppl.* 1 Mechanics and electricians engaged in the maintenance and repair of tools and machinery, engine men and stokers.. have already been reserved in all trades. **1915**, etc. [implied in *reserved occupation*]. **1922** *Encycl. Brit.* XXXI. 705/2 In a public announcement the list of starred occupations subsequently reserved was set out as follows: [etc.]. **1940** [see RESERVATION 3 d]. **1941** *Illustrated* 13 Sept. 9/1 Farm workers are reserved at twenty-five, but I knew many of the farm-hands had already joined up. **1950** O. BLAKESTON *Pink Ribbon* ii. 27 Then..along came the war... I was 'reserved' because of my occupation.

7. a. To retain or preserve alive; to exempt from slaughter; to save *from* death. Now *rare.*

1382 WYCLIF *Gen.* xii. 12 Thei shal slee me, and thee thei shall reserue. **1483** CAXTON *Gold. Leg.* 215/1 Thou hast power ouer my flesshe but cryst reserueth my soule. **1555** EDEN *Decades* Pref. to Rdr., Reseruynge such as were ouercome in the warres and conuertynge them to a better mynde. **1592** KYD *Sp. Trag.* I. ii. 104 Men of warre, Such as warres fortune hath reseru'd from death. **1603** SHAKS. *Meas. for M.* v. i. 472 One in the prison That should by priuate order else haue dide, I haue reseru'd aliue. **1625** BACON *Ess., Viciss. Things* (Arb.) 569 In the other two Destructions,..the Remnant of People, which hap to be reserued, are commonly Ignorant and Mountanous People. **1848** MRS. JAMESON *Sacr. & Leg. Art* (1850) 101 The legend which supposes St. John reserved alive has not been generally received in the Church.

†**b.** To leave untouched or intact; to refrain from removing or destroying. *Obs.*

1634 SIR T. HERBERT *Trav.* 46 Some reserue a locke vpon the top of the head. *a* **1679** W. OUTRAM *Serm.* (1682) 304 These men must find out some distinctions whereby they may..reserve that hand.

†**8. a.** To keep or maintain (a person or thing) in a certain state or condition. *Obs.*

1514 BARCLAY *Cyt. & Uplondyshm.* (Percy Soc.) 12 But suche as were fayre, and of theyr stature ryght As wyse and subtyle reserved she in syght. **1526** *Pilgr. Perf.* (W. de W. 1531) 144 He was euer more quyet and restfull in hymselfe, and reserued his spiryt euer at liberty. **1590** C'TESS PEMBROKE *Antonie* 1353 You euer-liuing Gods..which.. subiect to no chaunge Chaunge all, reseruing nothing in one state. **1632** LITHGOW *Trav.* II. 73 He reserueth vnder his command, fourty thousand..Horse-men. **1633** HEYWOOD *Eng. Trav.* II. i, Till that day come, you shall reserve yourself A single man.

†**b.** To retain (a person) in one's service. *Obs.*

1526 SKELTON *Magnyf.* 1723 Thynke you with Magnyfycence I shal be reserued?

†**c.** To retain (a thing) unaltered. *Obs. rare*$^{-1}$.

1597 MORLEY *Introd. Mus.* 95 *Phi.* You blamed my beginning, yet haue you altred it nothing. *Ma.* I haue indeede reserued your beginning.

†**9. a.** To keep in store; to lay up as a store or stock; to deposit for preservation. *Obs.*

1480 in Gross *Gild Merch.* (1890) II. 70 Ye shall see that all dutis that lengithe to the yelde of the Trynnytie be trewly rerit and reservit by yowr powers. **1538** STARKEY *England* II. i. 151 A certayn summe..the wych..schold ever be reseruyd in a commyn place. **1553** EDEN *Treat. New Ind.* (Arb.) 25 Palaces in which the artillery or armure of the cytie is reserued. **1613** PURCHAS *Pilgrimage* VII. xii. (1614) 707 Their water is raine water, reserued in Cisternes. **1657** S. PURCHAS *Pol. Flying-Ins.* 205 If wee negligently reserved hens, or other food, in the morning, wee should have onely bones. **1692** RAY *Creation* I. (ed. 2) 200 Stagnating Water, reserved in Pools and Cisterns.

†**b.** To keep, preserve (things liable to decay or destruction). *Obs.*

1555 EDEN *Decades* 57 Certeine fruites..whiche they reserue for store as wee doo chestnuttes. **1585** T. WASHINGTON tr. *Nicholay's Voy.* III. i. 69 b, The snow.. being reserued in these colde places serueth in whotte weather too refreshe..his drinke. **1605** CAMDEN *Rem., Epitaphs* 27 The Ægyptians embalmed and filled them with odoriferous spices, reseruing them in glasse or coffins. **1658** EVELYN *Fr. Gard.* (1675) 248 Pull as many of them out of the ground, as you desire to reserve. **1750** JOHNSON *Rambler* No. 51 ¶6 The best methods of conserving, reserving, and preserving fruits.

†**c.** *intr.* To remain, to continue in existence or in a certain state. *Obs.*

1529 MORE *Dyaloge* II. Wks. 179/2 Yf theyr opinions hadde any where continuallye endured there woulde theyr bokes haue continually reserued. **1632** LITHGOW *Trav.* VI. 258 The water of Iordan..will reserue vnspoiled, both moneths and yeares. **1641** H. L'ESTRANGE *God's Sabbath* 26 Because it [manna] tainted against nature, and miraculously reserved upon other dayes.

†**10. a.** To keep in one's possession. *Obs.*

1533 MORE *Apol.* v. Wks. 851/1 The copye that was deliuered me (which copy I reserue and kepe for my declaracion). *c* **1600** SHAKS. *Sonn.* xxxii, Though they be out-stript by every pen, Reserue them for my loue, not for their rime. **1604** —— *Oth.* III. iii. 295 She so loues the Token,..That she reserues it euermore about her.

†**b.** To keep, preserve (antiquities, relics, etc.).

1570–6 LAMBARDE *Peramb. Kent* (1826) 169 They do yet reserve..a Mace and a Horne, assured badges of an incorporation. **1605** VERSTEGAN *Dec. Intell.* iv. (1628) 106 The head whereof which is yet reserued, myselfe haue seen. **1648** J. RAYMOND *Il Merc. Ital.* 93 In the next Church the Pillars are reserv'd in wodden cases, which Saint Peter and Saint Paul were tyde too. *a* **1653** GOUGE *Comm. Heb.* xiii. 7 An Idolatrous practise of..offering oblations unto them, and of reserving their Reliques. **1708** BURNET *Trav.* (ed. 3) 225 The vast Vaults..and the Remains of Antiquity, that are reserved in them.

†**c.** Of places: To contain, retain (things) in or on themselves. *Obs. rare.*

1632 LITHGOW *Trav.* VI. 255 [The Dead Sea] breedeth nor reserueth no kinde of fishes. *Ibid.* x. 447 The Snowy Alpes..reserue continually Snow on their tops.

11. *Eccl.* To retain or preserve (a portion of the consecrated elements) for certain purposes. (Cf. RESERVATION 6.)

1548–9 *Bk. Com. Prayer, Communion of Sick,* And if the same day there be a celebracion of the holy communion in the Churche, then shal the priest reserue (at the open communion) so muche of the Sacrament..as shal serue the sicke person. **1571** *Thirty-nine Art.* xxviii, The Sacrament of the Lordes Supper was not, by Christes ordinaunce reserued, caryed about, lyfted vp, or worshipped. *a* **1626** BP. ANDREWES *Answ. Perron* (1854) 19 Against the time of extremity it was thought not amiss to have it reserved. **1832** W. PALMER *Orig. Liturg.* II. viii. 229 The custom of the Christian Church has been to reserve the sacraments of Christ's body and blood from the public liturgy, and not to consecrate them in private. **1849** ROCK *Ch. of Fathers* III. II. xi. 41 A portion of the eucharist, under one kind alone, was always reserved in the church, from each mass to the other.

absol. **1900** DIBDIN *Reserv.* 4 Do you reserve in both kinds?

†**12.** To retain or preserve, to continue to have, possess, or show (a characteristic, quality, mark, etc.). *Obs.* (common *c* 1585–1635.)

1570 BUCHANAN *Chamæleon* Wks. (S.T.S.) 53 [He] threatenit schamefullie (gif he had reservit any schame) the quenis maiestie of Ingland. **1585** T. WASHINGTON tr. *Nicholay's Voy.* IV. xx. 134 Armenia the greater, nowe called Turcomania, and Armenia the lesser, which yet reserueth his name. **1632** LITHGOW *Trav.* IX. 405, I had done that.. which neuer man had done before me reseruing life. **1665** SIR T. HERBERT *Trav.* (1677) 305 The Persians had this Character of old,..of all men the most civil; which disposition they reserve unto this day. **1726** LEONI *Alberti's Archit.* I. 45/2 A liquid..substance, which..when harden'd ..reserves in the mass the original figure of its parts.

13. = BOOK *v.* 4 a, b. Also *absol.*

1935 R. MACAULAY *Personal Pleasures* 20, I never reserve seats in advance, it is quite too much trouble... If a railway ticket does not get me on to a French train, then France is not the land of liberty, equality or fraternity. **1936** G. B. SHAW *Simpleton* II. 70 There are such a lot of priests in the world, Iddy. It would be impossible to reserve seats for them all. **1967** L. DEIGHTON *Expensive Place* iii. 23 What say to La Coupole? It's one of the few places..where we don't have to reserve.

re-serve (riː-), *v.*² [RE- 5 a.] *trans.* To serve again, in various senses.

1866 *Lond. Rev.* 2 June 609/2 The papers..were obliged to re-serve the former dishes which had pleased their patrons. **1884** *Law Rep.* 14 *Q.B. Div.* 190 The petition when amended must be re-served within a week.

reserved (rɪˈzɜːvd), *ppl. a.* [f. RESERVE *v.*]

†**1. a.** Excepted. Chiefly in prepositional use: With the exception of, except, save. *Obs.*

1474 CAXTON *Chesse* (Axon) 108 Alle worldly thynges ben mortifyed and appetissid in olde men reseruyd auaryce only, whiche alleway abideth wyth hym. **1481** —— *Godfrey* cxxxii. 196 They haue taken it entierly, Reserued a dongeon. **1531** ELYOT *Gov.* II. vi, All men were abashed, reserued the chiefe Justice. **1556** *Aurelio & Isab.* (1608) L vij, Soddaineley..was Isabell..stripede of her attire (reservede a riche smocke). **1579–80** NORTH *Plutarch, Pyrrus* (1612) 405 And the Sea being high wrought..made shipwrackes of them, the Admirall onely reserued. **1591** SHAKS. *1 Hen. VI,* v. iv. 167 Onely reseru'd, you claime no interest In any of our Towns of Garrison.

†**b.** With due respect for; duly regarded. *Obs.*

1526 SKELTON *Magnyf.* 1680 Yet, syr, reserued your better aduysement, It were better he spake with you or he wente. **1577–87** HOLINSHED *Chron.* III. 1010/1 But the reuerence of these writers reserued, this cannot be true concerning the church.

†**2.** Preserved; remaining undestroyed. *Obs.*

1555 EDEN *Decades* 52 They lerned by the reserued chyldren. **1667** WATERHOUSE *Fire Lond.* 100 Dwelling and Trading in the remains of the Freedom, and in the reserved Suburbs.

3. Averse to showing familiarity, or to open expression of thought or feeling; cold or distant; reticent, uncommunicative.

a. Of conduct, character, disposition, etc.

1601 SHAKS. *All's Well* III. v. 65 All her deseruing Is a reserued honestie. *a* **1661** FULLER *Worthies* (1840) III. 386 Such was brave Monck in his reserved mind, A riddle to his foes he did appear. **1691** WOOD *Ath. Oxon.* II. 196 Men of the Presbyterian perswasion..generally are morose, clownish, and of sullen and reserved natures. **1749** FIELDING *Tom Jones* XIII. xi, 'Pursuit of whom?' said Sophia, a little recollecting herself, and assuming a reserved air. **1780** BURKE *Econ. Reform* Wks. III. 336 The judges are, or ought to be, of a reserved and retired character. **1813** *Sketches of Character* (ed. 2) I. 211 [He] was of a reserved disposition. **1872** RUSKIN *Eagle's Nest* §92 The reserved and proud imagination of the master-schools.

b. Of persons.

1612 BACON *Ess., Seeming Wise* (Arb.) 214 Some are so close, and reserved, as they will not shewe their wares, but by a darke light. **1660** F. BROOKE tr. *Le Blanc's Trav.* 251 His wife being very reserv'd and discreet in her husband's presence, but in his absence more free and jolly. **1685** CROWNE *Sir C. Nice* I. 6 We are the most reserved family in the world. There were fourteen sisters of us, and not one of us married. **1746** COLLINS *Ode Evening* 5 Thy springs, and dying gales, O Nymph reserv'd. **1782** COWPER *Friendship* 188 The man I trust, if shy to me, Shall find me as reserv'd as he. **1806** SURR *Winter in Lond.* III. 76 [They] are certainly queer, stiff, reserved sort of people. **1877** FROUDE *Short Stud.* (1883) IV. I. xii. 146 As a statesman he was reserved, seldom showing his own thoughts.

transf. **1622** WITHER *Philarete* (1633) K 4 Let who will praise and behold The reserved Marigold.

absol. **1692** DRYDEN *St. Euremont's Ess.* 92 So difficult is it in the most reserved, not to forget themselves in a great Fortune. **1728** YOUNG *Love Fame* IV. 255 Fame is a bubble the reserv'd enjoy; Who strive to grasp it, as they touch, destroy.

†**c.** Retired, secluded. *Obs. rare*$^{-1}$.

1653 WALTON *Angler* xi. 205 They will usually lye..in one reserved place, where the water is deep, and runs quietly.

4. Restrained or restricted in some way.

1654 BRAMHALL *Just Vind.* ii. (1661) 26 It is good to be sparing and reserved in censuring hereticks for obstinacy. **1724** SWIFT *Drapier's Lett.* Wks. 1755 V. II. 120 It hath been the wisdom of the English parliaments to be very reserved in limiting the press. **1860** GEN. P. THOMPSON *Audi Alt. Part.* cxxxiv. III. 101 The early Protestants, from whom the Anglican Church makes a reserved and cautious profession of being descended.

5. a. Set or kept apart; specially retained for some person or purpose, etc. (See the verb.)

1616 T. GODWIN *Moses & Aaron* I. (1641) 30 The chiefe Rabbies sate in reserved chaires, these are those chiefe seats in the Synagogues. **1625** B. JONSON *Staple of News* IV. i, With all your..reseru'd Questions, and Answers that you game with. **1727–38** CHAMBERS *Cycl.* s.v. *Case,* At the article of death,..all reserved cases are absolvable by the ordinary. **1791** KAMES *Dict. Decis.* (ed. 2) I. 291 In a question, how far a reserved faculty..accresced to a creditor whose debt was contracted before that faculty? **1798** HUTTON *Course Math.* (1806) I. 153 Divide the reserved quotient by the square of *s*, and reserve this quotient. **1838** W. BELL *Dict. Law Scot.* 858 Reserved powers are of different sorts; as a reserved power of burdening a property, or a reserved power to revoke or recall a settlement or other deed. **1867** T. C. ANSTEY *Notes Repr. People Act* 54 Those 'antient rights'.. are sometimes called 'reserved rights' also, from the circumstance of the Reform Act of 1832 having expressly reserved them. **1884** *Catholic Dict.* (1897) 786/2 Absolution from a reserved sin may be given by the superior who reserves it. **1897** W. WALSH *Secr. Hist. Oxf. Movem.* x. (1898) 342 The ostensible reason for restoring the Reserved Sacrament is that it is then always ready to be given to the sick.

b. *reserved seats*, those seats (at a public entertainment or meeting, or on a train etc.) which may be specially engaged beforehand. Also *fig.* and in *sing.*

1858 LYTTON *What will He do* I. iii, Happy to see any of your friends in the reserved seats. **1860** in M. W. Disher *Cowells in Amer.* (1934) 194 Most of the Audience were 'reserved seat' people, and pleasant. **1873** HAMERTON *Intell. Life* VIII. ii. 288 Reserved seats in the great assemblage of the world. **1889** J. HATTON *Reminisc. J. L. Toole* I. i. 19, I glance at the house from the wings, find it crammed, the reserved seats filled with aristocratic and fashionably-dressed people. **1916** G. B. SHAW *Androcles & Lion* Pref. p. xciv, An insane conceit of being the elect of God, with a reserved seat in heaven. **1935** R. MACAULAY *Personal Pleasures* 19 Now for the train;..Second-class... No, nothing else about it matters, and I have no reserved seat. **1980** D. WILLIAMS *Murder for Treasure* v. 50 He too could have travelled in a reserved seat, untroubled, unmolested and delivered on time.

c. *Reserved List*, a list of naval officers removed from active service but kept in reserve in case of being required. So *reserved officer, pay*, etc.

1851 *Lond. Gaz.* No. 21222. 1673/1 These officers will be placed on reserved Half-pay. *Ibid.* 1673/2 In case of War, or of emergency,..to call such Officers from the Reserved List into Active Service. **1866** *Chambers' Encycl.* s.v. *Reserved List,* In the remote contingency of the Active List being exhausted,..these 'reserved' officers would be liable to be called upon to serve.

d. In pottery decoration, etc.: left in the original colour of the material or the colour of the background.

1895 in *Funk's Stand. Dict.* **1930** *Discovery* Aug. 255/2 From the fourth level [of the excavations at Ur] came a peculiar form of painted pottery that has been termed 'Reserved slip-ware', the paint being applied to the whole body of the pot and then wiped off at intervals so as to produce a series of striations. **1934** [see *high-lying* s.v. HIGH *adv.* 10 a]. **1954** M. RICKERT *Painting in Brit.: Middle Ages* 231 *Reserved edges*, spaces left around a painted ornament exposing the vellum of a manuscript page. In Hiberno-Saxon decoration the reserved edges aid in clarifying a complicated pattern of spirals or interlace. **1960** K. M. KENYON *Archaeol. in Holy Land* iii. 62 This slip in turn is partially covered by a red slip, so that the reserved portions of the cream slip form a pattern, usually in some combination of chevrons or triangles. **1977** *Sci. Amer.* Mar. 122/2 (*caption*) Pot *d* carries a 'reserved' design, produced by applying a red slip over an orange underslip.

e. ***reserved occupation***, a high-priority civilian occupation, most of those employed in which are exempted from military service.

1915 *Local Govt. Board Circular No. R.2* 2 A list has been prepared..of still further occupations (to be known as 'reserved occupations'), to which, in the public interest, from the point of view of the export trade or for other reasons, it is desirable to extend some measure of protection, either because the persons included in them..are engaged in work which could not be interrupted without serious dislocation or because the industries affected are such that it would be unwise to take more men from them without special investigation. **1940** M. NICHOLSON *How Britain's Resources are Mobilized* 21 A Schedule of Reserved Occupations, designed to ensure that work of national importance should not be endangered through losing too many men to the armed forces. **1944** A. THIRKELL *Headmistress* iv. 79 Her girls wished to go straight into the Forces..while their parents wanted them to..get a job in a reserved occupation. **1960** G. BUTLER *Death lives Next Door* i. 36 Never left England, not me. In a reserved occupation. **1972** M. JONES *Life on Dole* viii. 61 Mining was a reserved occupation, and even young men who wanted to get into uniform found themselves directed to the pits.

reservedly (rɪˈzɜːvɪdlɪ), *adv.* [f. prec. + -LY[2].] In a reserved manner; with or in reserve.

1611 FLORIO, *Riserbatamente*, reseruedly, sparingly. **1638** BAKER tr. *Balzac's Lett.* (vol. II) 130 You should goe more reservedly to worke, and retaine more providence for the future. **1679** *Animadv. Sp. Five Jesuits* 6 He might use another reserve with respect to the words private persons, understanding reservedly, persons that have no authority from the Pope. **1710** STEELE *Tatler* No. 213 ¶1 They are so reservedly complaisant till they have learned to resign their natural Passions. **1748** RICHARDSON *Clarissa* (1811) IV. 27, I could not have behaved more reservedly to Mr. Solmes. **1835** I. TAYLOR *Spir. Despot.* III. 106 Never are such reforms recorded otherwise than in terms of commendation; never are they reservedly mentioned as [etc.]. **1892** *Welsh Rev.* I. 718 Take note of the sentence reservedly kept by me to frustrate man's design.

reservedness (rɪˈzɜːvdnɪs). [f. as prec. + -NESS.] The state or quality of being reserved; reserve, reticence, caution.

1609 DANIEL *Civ. Wars* VIII. lii, Her lookes, not let abrode (but carefully Kept in, restraind) held their reservednesse. **1624** BEDELL *Lett.* iii. 71 It is a wise reseruednesse in them, not to intermedle with that wherein they might easily fault. **1676** TOWERSON *Decalogue* 396 They shall..at all times use ..that reservedness and modesty in their outward deportment. **1711** ADDISON *Spect.* No. 57 ¶6 A Woman is too sincere to..act with that Caution and Reservedness which are requisite in our Sex. **1753** RICHARDSON *Grandison* (1781) II. ix. 123 Sir Charles's reservedness..may not let them know the secrets of his heart in this particular. **1797** JANE AUSTEN *Sense & Sens.* xviii, The reservedness of his manner towards her contradicted one moment what a more animated look had intimated the preceding one. **1873** M. ARNOLD *Lit. & Dogma* 58 Is this reservedness of affirmation about God less worthy of him, than the..licence of affirmation of our dogmatists..?

reˌserˈvee. *rare.* [f. RESERVE *v.* + -EE[1].] 'One to whom something is reserved' (Worcester, 1860, citing Story).

reˈserveful, *a.* *rare*$^{-1}$. [f. RESERVE *sb.* + -FUL.] Full of reserve or restraint.

1886 *Q. Rev.* Apr. 468 The reserveful simplicity with which he comments upon his own [services].

reˈserveless, *a.* *rare*$^{-1}$. [f. as prec. + -LESS.] Without a reserve, having no reserve in hand.

1882 *Pall Mall G.* 15 Nov. 5/2 Were the stroke delivered suddenly, it could not fail to have a terrific effect, or to teach our reserveless bankers a very wholesome lesson.

reserver[1] (rɪˈzɜːvə(r)). [f. RESERVE *v.* + ER[1].]

1. One who reserves. *rare.*

1612–28 BP. HALL *Contempl., O.T.* VIII. v. (1820) I. 336 Either Israel wanted skill, or our reservers honesty. *a* **1639** WOTTON in *Reliq.* (1672) 370, I am in this likewise no reserver of my good will till the last. **1755** in JOHNSON. **1966** *Punch* 7 Dec. 841/2 The room has the great advantage of being changed every day, so that no one except the reserver and his guest know exactly which floor the room is on at any given time.

†**2.** = RESERVOIR *sb.* 1. *Obs.*

1670–98 LASSELS *Voy. Italy* II. 192 Spouts of stone, by which they used to let the water from above into the vast Reserver. **1683** *Weekly Memorial* 31 The Reserver of St. Ferreol is above 2000 Toises in Circumference. **1718** OZELL tr. *Tournefort's Voy.* II. 357 The Reserver, which is of Marble, wherein they bathe.

reˈserver[2]. *rare*$^{-1}$. [-ER[4].] A reservation.

1807 BENTHAM *Let. to Romilly* Wks. 1843 X. 425 As to everything else, I have no reservers.

reservery (rɪˈzɜːvərɪ). *nonce-wd.* [f. RESERVE *sb.* + -ERY.] The occupation of serving as a reservist; the system of reserve forces.

1878 STEVENSON *Inland Voy.* (1896) 177 'Reservery', said he, 'seems a pretty mean way to spend one's autumn holiday'. *Ibid.* 181 Reservery and general militarismus (as the Germans call it) was rampant.

reserving (rɪˈzɜːvɪŋ), *vbl. sb.* [f. RESERVE *v.* + -ING[1].] The action of the vb., or an instance of this; reservation.

1532 *Dial. on Laws Eng.* II. xxii. 43 b, It semeth that the reseruynge of suche vse is prohibit by the lawe. **1542–3** *Act 34 & 35 Hen. VIII*, c. 5 §9 The sauinges reseruinges and prouisions..of the saide former act. **1551** GARDINER in Cranmer *Answ. Gardiner* III. 165 Touching reseruyng, whiche Clement might seme to denye. **1598** FLORIO, *Riserue*,..reseruings, sparings, hoordings. **1841** TUPPER *Twins* xxx, There were no concealments now between them, no reservings.

reˈserving, *ppl. a.* [-ING[2].] †**a.** Except (for), saving. *Obs.* **b.** Containing a reservation.

1540–1 ELYOT *Image Gov.* 13 He commaunded that no man shoulde write unto hym in any other fourme, than shoulde bee written to a private person, reservyng the name of Emperour. **1670** MARVELL *Let.* Wks. (Grosart) II. 319 The Lords..have added a reserving clause for his Majestie's ancient prerogative in all ecclesiastical things.

reservist (rɪˈzɜːvɪst). [f. RESERVE *sb.* + -IST; cf. F. *réserviste*.] One who belongs to or serves in the reserve forces.

1876 *World* V. 14 The 'Reservists' of our army put in a most creditable appearance when called out at the late manœuvres. **1883** *Spectator* 19 May 636 A French regiment is composed of men actually with the colours, and of the reservists. **1895** *Daily Tel.* 13 Aug. 5/1 The mobilisation of the Spanish reservists..continues.

reservoir (ˈrɛzəvwɑː(r)), *sb.* Also 8 -oire. [a. F. *réservoir*, f. *réserver* to keep, RESERVE + *-oir*: see -ORY[1].]

1. a. A more or less capacious receptacle (of earthwork, masonry, or the like), specially formed or constructed to contain and store a large supply of water for ordinary uses.

1705 ADDISON *Italy* 273 A Set of Galleries that are hewn into the Rock... Some will have 'em to have been a Reservoir of Water. **1756** C. LUCAS *Ess. Waters* I. 136 Water is conveyed from the reservoirs at Islington to many different parts of our capital. **1788** GIBBON *Decl. & F.* l. V. 177 The towers of Saana, and the marvellous reservoir of Merab, were constructed by the kings of the Homerites. **1841** ELPHINSTONE *Hist. India* II. 121 He was constantly taken up with aqueducts, reservoirs, and other improvements. **1871** TYNDALL *Fragm. Sci.* (1879) I. v. 173 At Canterbury there are three reservoirs covered in and protected.

b. A tank or cistern for water.

1727–38 CHAMBERS *Cycl.* s.v., The reservoir in a building is a large bason, usually of wood, lined with lead, where water is kept to supply the occasions of the house. **1771** J. ADAMS *Diary* 4 June, Wks. 1850 II. 268 They have built a shed over a little reservoir made of wood,..and into that have conveyed the water from the spring. **1787** M. CUTLER in *Life*, etc. (1888) I. 206 A large reservoir of water is placed in the third loft of the house. **1930** *Daily Express* 6 Oct. 3/7 They were..lying in their bunks... Above them were water reservoirs. The force of the explosion burst the water tanks.

c. A place or area in which water naturally collects in large quantities.

1730–46 THOMSON *Autumn* 821, I see the rocky siphons stretch'd immense, The mighty reservoirs. **1756** C. LUCAS *Ess. Waters* I. 32 Temporary springs..have no reservoir or considerable receptacle in the bowels of the earth. **1784** BELKNAP in *B. Papers* (1877) II. 185 These Mountains, then, are the grand reservoir of water for many parts of New England. **1822** J. FLINT *Lett. Amer.* 290 The lake, forming an extensive reservoir, greatly equalizes the discharge of water. **1866** BAKER *Albert N'yanza* II. 95, I looked down.. upon that vast reservoir which nourished Egypt.

d. *fig.* A place or sphere where something is collected or tends to collect, after the manner of water.

1690 TEMPLE *Ess., Learning* Misc. II. 9 The Ancient Colledges, or Societies of Priests, were mighty Reservoirs or Lakes of Knowledge. **1728** YOUNG *Love Fame* VI. 323 Grand reservoirs of public happiness, Through secret streams diffusively they bless. **1839** THIRLWALL *Greece* l. VI. 233 This had been the principal reservoir..into which the tribute of the East had flowed. **1882** FARRAR *Early Chr.* II. 307 Rome—the reservoir, as Tacitus says, into which all things infamous and shameful flowed.

e. A body of porous rock holding a large quantity of oil or natural gas.

1912 E. H. C. CRAIG *Oil-Finding* iii. 47 In the case of calcareous rocks it is probably merely because the limestone affords a porous reservoir that it is found impregnated with oil. **1938** D. HAGER *Pract. Oil Geol.* i. 34 In Mexico the most productive oil reservoirs of the Golden Lane were the reef limestones in the Tamasopa formation. **1951** K. K. LANDES *Petroleum Geol.* iii. 101 The escape of gas to the surface in disproportionate amounts to the oil produced will result in more and more sluggish oil being left behind in the reservoir. **1970** W. G. ROBERTS *Quest for Oil* ii. 16 The first known deposits of mineral oil, or petroleum, were found because they showed themselves as seepages from underground reservoirs. **1980** *Times* 15 May 19/2 British Petroleum has discovered a second, deeper reservoir on its onshore field at Kimmeridge.

2. a. A part of an animal or plant in which some fluid or secretion is collected or retained.

1727–38 CHAMBERS *Cycl.* s.v. *Receptaculum*, A reservoir or cavity near the left kidney, into which the lacteal vessels do all discharge their contents. **1741** MONRO *Anat. Bones* (ed. 3) 24 Such Bones are said to have a large Reservoire of Oil. **1849** BALFOUR *Man. Bot.* 10 The cavities..are denominated cysts, reservoirs of oil, and receptacles of secretions. **1855** T. R. JONES *Anim. Kingd.* (ed. 2) 513 A large central nervous ganglion, and on each side of this there is a minute round reservoir. **1884** BOWER & SCOTT *De Bary's Phaner.* 431 The primary arrangement of the secretory reservoirs presents little of interest.

b. A part of some apparatus in which a fluid or liquid is contained. *spec.* in a closed hydraulic system, a tank containing fluid that can be supplied to the system when needed to compensate for small losses.

1784 M. CUTLER in *Life*, etc. (1888) I. 106 Some particles of mercury had exuded through the leather of the reservoir [in a thermometer]. **1793** BEDDOES *Let. Darwin* 46 It was inhaled through a tube, and in consequence of pressure on the reservoir, a strong current set into the mouth. **1830** HERSCHEL *Stud. Nat. Phil.* III. i. (1851) 229 The pressure of the external air on the surface of the mercury in the reservoir. **1859** HAWTHORNE *Marb. Faun* xliv, The lamp required to be replenished.., though its reservoir of oil was exceedingly capacious. **1875** KNIGHT *Dict. Mech.* 1920/2 The reservoirs of ranges are usually vertical iron boilers, connected by pipes with the water supply of the city. **1946** W. H. CROUSE *Automotive Mech.* xxv. 550 The master cylinder includes a reservoir or supply tank that contains an additional quantity of brake fluid. **1966** HILLIER & PITTUCK *Fund. Motor Vehicle Technol.* XVI. 418 The flow of fluid from the reservoir to the main chamber is controlled by a compensating valve, which is set to open when the piston is in the fully returned position. **1970** K. BALL *Fiat 600, 600D Autobook* x. 117/2 Normal maintenance of the hydraulic system is confined to checking the level of the brake fluid in the reservoir at regular intervals.

c. In the organ. (See quots.)

1835 *Penny Cycl.* IV. 198/1 In the organ, the air is condensed into a reservoir called the wind-chest, which supplies the pipes. **1840** *Ibid.* XVI. 492/2 The registrars, by which the equal rising of the reservoir is ensured. **1881** C. A. EDWARDS *Organs* 41 Bellows consist of two parts, termed respectively the 'Feeder' and the 'Reservoir'.

3. a. Any receptacle for fluids (or vapours).

1774 J. BRYANT *Mythol.* I. 194 Ætna..being a reservoir of molten matter. **1774** GOLDSM. *Nat. Hist.* (1776) IV. 307 It has a fifth stomach, which serves as a reservoir, to hold a greater quantity of water than the animal has an immediate occasion for. **1792** J. BELKNAP *Hist. New Hampsh.* III. 114 Large troughs or vats..to serve as reservoirs for the sap when collected. **1808** *Phil. Trans.* XCVIII. 125 The gas.. is conveyed by iron pipes into large reservoirs, or gazometers. **1854** BREWSTER *More Worlds* iii. 49 The fluid matters which produced external volcanoes, exist in internal reservoirs of limited extent, forming subterranean lakes. **1880** HAUGHTON *Phys. Geog.* ii. 68 If there were any communication between their respective reservoirs of molten lava.

†**b.** A receptacle or repository for things or articles; a place where things are laid up or stored. *Obs.*

1739 R. BULL tr. *Dedekindus' Grobianus* 114 Down to its Reservoir the Meat's convey'd And due Digestion is the better made. **1769** FALCONER *Dict. Marine* (1780) s.v. *Basin*, A wide and spacious reservoir for shipping. **1786** tr. *Beckford's Vathek* (1868) 115 Every reservoir of riches was disclosed to their view. **1803** *Censor* 1 Nov. 126, I thrust my sweetheart into the coal-cellar... I flattered myself that he could remain unseen in some corner of that large reservoir. **1836** *Backwoods of Canada* 216 The inner lining of birch-bark being drawn between the poles so as to form hollow pouches all round; [many articles occupied] these reservoirs.

c. A store or collection, a reserve supply, *of* something. Also, a reserve supply of people.

1784 COWPER *Task* II. 201 What is His creation less Than a capacious reservoir of means..? **1813** SIR H. DAVY *Agric. Chem.* (1814) 215 In the production of a plant from a seed, some reservoir of nourishment is needed before the root can supply sap. **1837** DICKENS *Pickw.* iv, The labours of others have raised for us an immense reservoir of important facts. **1860** MAURY *Phys. Geog.* vii. §359 There is in the upper regions of the air a great reservoir of positive electricity. **1875** BENNETT & DYER tr. *Sachs' Bot.* 627 The organs of assimilation..stand at a distance from the reservoirs of reserve-material. **1941** *Illustrated* 13 Sept. 12/2 Inside six months he has raised, clothed, equipped, and put into training on a voluntary basis a reservoir of 200,000 young men as potential air crews for the R.A.F. **1943** W. WILLKIE *One World* x. 131 There exists in the world today a gigantic reservoir of goodwill toward us, the American people. **1973** *Computers & Humanities* VII. 166 Concordances can contribute to linguistic studies as reservoirs of meanings and usages. **1979** *Wichita* (Kansas) *Eagle* 23 May 3c/6 A potential reservoir of additional workers for Wichita manufacturing has been created by McDonnell Corp., which is laying off workers in St. Louis.

d. *Med.* A population which is chronically infested with the causative agent of a disease and can infect other populations. Also *transf.*

1913 [see sense 5 a below]. **1939** C. F. CARTER *Microbiol. & Path.* (ed. 2) xxiv. 253 For the continuous existence of a disease there must be some reservoir of infection. *Ibid.*, The most important reservoirs of infection are human or animal cases or carriers. Plants may be the reservoir of infection in some of the mycoses. **1947** *Ann. Rev. Microbiol.* I. 353. A precise demonstration of the mechanisms through which the reservoir of the disease functions would constitute a great advance in constructing the biological pattern of influenza. **1965** B. E. FREEMAN tr. *Vandel's Biospeleol.* xv. 246 It would be possible that bats serve as a reservoir of histoplasmosis. **1977** *Sci. Amer.* Mar. 61/2 When no human being harbours the [smallpox] virus, there should remain only one reservoir: the stocks in research and diagnostic laboratories.

4. ¶ ***au reservoir***: see AU REVOIR.

5. ***attrib.*** **a.** Having or containing, fitted with, serving as, a reservoir or receptacle of any kind.

1797 *Encycl. Brit.* (ed. 3) XI. 199/2 The operator in general carries the matter about with him on what is called a reservoir lancet. **1845** STIMPSON *Organ in Town Hall B'ham* 6 The Bellows of the Great Organ have also what are termed Reservoir Bellows. **1875** KNIGHT *Dict. Mech.* 1920/2 *Reservoir-stove*, one having a large boiler attached. **1884** *Ibid.* Suppl. 751/2 *Reservoir Battery*, one having a reserve of material. *Ibid.*, Reservoir blow-pipe, with air chamber. **1884** *Pall Mall G.* 4 Oct. 4/2 The liquid contained in the so-called reservoir-cells on the walls of the first stomach [of the camel]. **1884** *Queen* 16 Feb. (Advt.), The 'Victor' reservoir pen can be used with any good fluid ink, and any ordinary nib... Price 3s.6d. **1889** *Pall Mall G.* 1 Jan. 1/3 Reservoir pens capable of deluging an opponent with ink. **1913** *Trans. Soc. Trop. Med. & Hygiene* VI. 269 The monkey is most probably the normal 'reservoir host' [for *Physaloptera mordens*].

b. Of the nature of, pertaining to, connected with, a water-reservoir.

1839 *Civil Eng. & Arch. Jrnl.* II. 169/2 Reservoir-locks will be found very useful on slack water navigation. **1884** KNIGHT *Dict. Mech.* Suppl. 752/1 An electrical reservoir level recorder, used at Nottingham. **1890** *Engineering* 16 May 596/2 The reservoir gauge went back from 15 in. to 10 in. **1894** *Daily News* 31 July 5/3 The construction of the reservoir dam at Assouan.

c. Special Combs.: **reservoir engineering**, the study and exploitation of natural oil and gas reservoirs; so **reservoir engineer**; **reservoir rock**, rock (capable of) forming a reservoir for oil or natural gas.

1949 M. MUSKAT *Physical Princ. Oil Production* i. 28 While..the.. properties of the reservoir will determine its inherent potentialities as an oil-producing system, there is still much left to the choice of the *reservoir engineer with regard to the actual exploitation program to be undertaken. **1973** *Mod. Petroleum Technol.* (Inst. Petroleum) (ed. 4) v. 172 The primary aim of a reservoir engineer is to obtain maximum recovery at minimum cost. **1946** *Petroleum Engineer* Jan. 51/1 The war..has led to a greater realization than ever before of the need for applying the most advanced *reservoir engineering principles of production and oil conservation to obtain maximum economic recoveries. **1954** *Mod. Petroleum Technol.* (Inst. Petroleum) (ed. 2) iv. 122 A balanced view of production operations calls for some knowledge of the fundamentals of reservoir engineering as well as of the more purely mechanical methods employed. **1977** *Times* 2 Nov. 3 (Advt.), Reservoir engineering is largely an art... Our job is to get information about..oil-bearing rock..below the sea bed. **1912** E. H. C. CRAIG *Oil-Finding* iii. 46 The relative porosity of strata is one of the determining factors in the movements of oil, and the selection of a *reservoir rock. **1951** K. K. LANDES *Petroleum Geol.* vii. 191 Throughout the world, sandstone is by far the most important reservoir rock. **1975** G. ANDERSON *Coring* i. 18 Permeability normally varies from one location to another vertically as well as horizontally in a reservoir rock.

reservoir ('rɛzəvwɑː(r)), *v.* [f. the sb.] *trans.* To store up, keep in or as in a reservoir. Hence **'reservoired** *ppl. a.*

1858 H. W. BEECHER *Life Thoughts* (1859) 65 A reservoired state of feeling out of which the various parts of life ought to flow. **1866** ALGER *Solit. Nat. & Man* III. 156 Mental force is..reservoired, subject to the summons of the will. **1887** *Pall Mall G.* 24 Dec. 10/1 Millions of poods of oil have been lost, owing to the inefficient way in which it is reservoired and stored. **1896** L. ABBOTT *Chr. & Soc. Prob.* vi. 175 These men are making available to the community the reservoired resources of the globe.

re'servor. *Law.* [f. RESERVE *v.* + -OR.] 'One who reserves' (Worcester, 1860, citing Story).

reset (rɪ'sɛt), *sb.*[1] Forms: 3-5 **recet**, 4-5 **recett(e**, **rescet**, 4-6 **resset(te**, 4-7 **resett** (5 **reyset**), 4- **reset**. [a. OF. *recet*:—L. *recept-um*: see RECEPT *sb.*[1] and cf. RECEIPT *sb.*]

†**1.** The opportunity, advantage, privilege, etc., of being received or sheltered in a place; refuge, shelter, harbour, succour. Chiefly in phrases *to have* (*get, take*) *reset*. *Obs.* (latterly *Sc.*)

1297 R. GLOUC. *Chron.* (Rolls) 8385 Sire Reinaud..þen toun wuste bihinde, þat hor men ȝif hii nede adde recet miȝte vinde. *a* **1300** *Cursor M.* 5299 To mi lauerd yee com wit me..; I sal askin yow sum recett. *c* **1330** R. BRUNNE *Chron. Wace* (Rolls) 920 He was on þat wolde þem saue, & at his castles recet [*v.r.* rescet] to haue. **13..** *E.E. Allit. P.* A. 1066 Þer entrez non to take reset. *c* **1380** *Sir Ferumb.* 1021 In his pauillouns to haue recet piderward gan he drawe. **1450** *Rolls of Parlt.* V. 213/2 In the same Shires were such recette or comfort shall be hadde. **1535** STEWART *Cron. Scot.* I. 297 Sailland to seik quhair tha mycht get resset, In other land sum duelling place to get. **1685** *Scot. Proclam.* in *Lond. Gaz.* No. 2032/3 To the end the said..Rebels may have no Reset, Harbour, Comfort or Refuge from any of the Subjects of this Our Realm.

†**b.** A place of reception, refuge, shelter, or accommodation; an abode, haunt, usual residence or retreat. *Obs.* (latterly *Sc.*)

1297 R. GLOUC. (Rolls) 2175 Scotlond aþ euere ybe a luþer recet [*v.r.* rescette] ylome. **13..** *Coer de L.* 3156 At even, whenne the sunne was sette, Every man drewe to his recet. *c* **1350** *Will. Palerne* 2801 To recuuer sum resset þere we vs rest miȝt. *c* **1400** tr. *Secreta Secret., Gov. Lordsh.* 74 Alle Bestes drawyn to her resset, and neddrys to her holys. **1424** *Sc. Acts Jas. I* (1814) II. 6/2 þ[t] in all burowis townys.. quhar comon passages ar þat þar be ordanyt hostilaris and resettis, haifande stabillis and chalmeris. *c* **1470** *Gol. & Gaw.* 38 Resset couth thai find none That suld thair bute bene. **1513** DOUGLAS *Æneis* XIII. vi. 190, I, Troian, for me vp in this feild, Ane new resset and wycht wallys sall beild. **1582** *Reg. Privy Council Scot.* III. 557 That the samin [houses] be not a resset to thevis and fugitives thairefter.

†**c.** (Chiefly *Sc.*) One who receives or shelters another; *esp.* a resetter (of a thief or criminal).

c **1440** *Bone Flor.* 1746 A burges that was the thefys reyset, At the townes end he them mett. *c* **1470** HENRY *Wallace* II. 17 This gentill man was full oft his resett. **1552** *Reg. Privy Council Scot.* I. 130 Gif he beis fugitive and passis to his nychbour.., the resett of him sall pay the xx lib. **1570** *Satir. Poems Reform.* xi. 97 Lat all that fische be trapt in net, Was counsall, art, part, or reset,..Or ȝit with helping hand him met. **1641** *Sc. Acts Chas. I* (1814) V. 501/1 That circuit courts of justiciaire also be establisched..yeirlie for tryell and punisching of all theiffis, sorneris, robberis, and ressetts þairof.

2. *Sc.* (*Law*). **a.** Reception or shelter given to another, *spec.* to a thief, criminal, or proscribed person; the act or practice of receiving or harbouring such persons. Now *arch.*

1456 SIR G. HAYE *Law Arms* (S.T.S.) 246 Ony man that gevis outhir resset or favoure to Goddis inymyes. *c* **1470** HENRY *Wallace* IV. 715 Than thai..Accusyt hir sar of resset in that cas. ? **1572** *Satir. Poems Reform.* xxxvi. 48 Our antecessoris..oft tymes baid þe hasard of þe weir, For þe resset and succouring of straingeris. **1603** *Reg. Privy Council Scot.* VI. 526 The ressett of the personis quha laitlie maist shamefullie and barbarouslie slew the Laird of Mellestanes. **1679** *Royal Proclam.* in *Spirit of Popery* (1680) 64 We have ..prohibited the reset of these Murtherers. **1717** *Wodrow Corr.* (1843) II. 298 In several of the noted processes before the Justiciary, as in the case of torture, that of reset and converse. **1818** SCOTT *Rob Roy* xxvi, There is nae laws now about reset of intercommuned persons, as there was in the ill times o' the last Stuarts.

b. The act or practice of receiving stolen goods.

a **1768** ERSKINE *Inst. Law Scot.* IV. iv. §63 (1773) 723 The crime of reset of theft consists either in harbouring the person of the thief after the goods are stolen, or in receiving or disposing of the goods. **1838** W. BELL *Dict. Law Scot.* 858 *Reset of Theft*; is the offence of receiving and keeping goods, knowing them to be stolen, and with an intention to conceal and withhold them from the owner. **1863** *Glasgow Her.* 15 Apr., Theft and Reset.

†**3.** A receptacle. Also *transf. Obs. rare.*

c **1380** WYCLIF *Sel. Wks.* III. 390 Freris ben ressett, and a swolowhe of symonye, of usure, of extorsiouns. **1388** —— *Ecclus.* xxxix. 22 As resettis [L. *exceptoria*] of watris in the word of his mouth.

†**4.** *Sc.* The act of receiving; receipt *of* something. *Obs. rare.*

1533 BELLENDEN *Livy* IV. xiv. (S.T.S.) II. 95 Quhiddir the tovne of fidena Or þe toun of veos war mare ganand for resett of þare battell. *c* **1590** *Hist. Jas. VI* (1804) 229 The ambassador, eftir the ressett of this answere, returnit to the Regent, quhair they consultit togidder for a..remeid.

†**5.** *Med.* A receipt or recipe. *Obs. rare*$^{-1}$.

1564-78 BULLEYN *Dial. agst. Pest.* (1888) 21 If this purging were not, we would clense and expulse with our resettes that whiche should serue our tourne well enough.

†**6.** *Hunting.* = RECEIPT *sb.* 14. *Obs. rare*$^{-1}$.

1616 SURFL. & MARKH. *Country Farme* VII. xxv. 686 A quarter of a myle before them..you shall place your Reset, which would be a brace of greyhounds somewhat stronger than the former.

reset (riː'sɛt), *sb.*[2] [f. RESET *v.*[2]] **a.** 'Among printers, matter reset' (Webster, 1847). **b.** 'The act of resetting' (Ogilvie, 1882).

reset (rɪ'sɛt), *v.*[1] Forms: 3-6 **recette** (5 **recepte**), 4-6 **resette**; 4 **rescet**, 4-6 **resset** (6 **-ett**), 5- **reset** (7 **-ett**). Also as *pa. pple.* (and *pa. t.*). [ad. OF. *receter*, *recetter*:—L. *receptāre*, f. *recept-*, ppl. stem of *recipĕre* to receive: cf. RECEIPT *v.*[1]]

1. *trans.* To receive, harbour, or shelter (a person, *esp.* an offender against the law). Now *arch.*

1297 R. GLOUC. (Rolls) 4635 Þe kunde men of þis lond recetted were þere. **1375** BARBOUR *Bruce* IX. 282 Schir Iohne Mowbray is vith him gane, And war resettit with the king. **1393** LANGL. *P. Pl.* C. IV. 501 Ac he þat receyueþ oþer recetteþ hure ys recettor of gyle. **1436** *Rolls of Parlt.* IV. 511/1 They herber and reset alle maner of myslyvers. **1456** SIR G. HAYE *Law Arms* (S.T.S.) 246 He dois again the precept of the kirk..to favour na resset inymyes of the faith. **1512** *Act 4 Hen. VIII*, c. 20 Preamble, John Tayler felonsly and traytoursly resetted one Archbold Armestrong wich was proclaymed a Rebell. **1577-87** HOLINSHED *Chron.* III. 842/2 The manslaiers, spoilers, robbers, & violaters of the same truces and safe conducts..haue beene recetted..by diuerse of the kings liege people upon the coasts. **1640-1** *Kirkcudbr. War-Comm. Min. Bk.* (1855) 87 William Gordone in Nether-corsock resset the said runaway. **1681** *Scot. Act* in *Lond. Gaz.* No. 1648/4 If any Man shall Resett..any Servant, Tennant or Cottar who is so put away, he shall be lyable to pay three years Fee to the Master who did put him away. **1752** J. LOUTHIAN *Form of Process* (ed. 2) 158 Resetting Traitors, or those who lay at the Horn for treasonable Practices. **1816** SCOTT *Old Mort.* viii, You knew, that, as a loyal subject, you were prohibited to reset, supply, or intercommune with this attainted traitor.

b. As *pa. pple.* (Chiefly *Sc.*)

c **1470** HARDING *Chron.* CXCIV. iii, He..rode on alwaye Vnto Paris, wher he was faire recepte [*rime* mette]. **1513** DOUGLAS *Æneis* VI. x. 81 That sic forloppin Troianis..Suld thankfully be resset in that ring. **1570** *Satir. Poems Reform.* xxvi. 127 He was reset by his command.

2. To receive (stolen goods) from a thief with intent to cover or profit by the theft. Also *absol.*

1609 SKENE *Reg. Maj.*, *Stat. Alex. II*, xxi. (1774) 336 Quha resets theift stollen fra anie man; he sall be estemed as ane common theif. **1625** in Ferguson & Nanson *Rec. Carlisle* (1887) 280 She did recett Michaell Blaklocke sheats that were stollen. **1817** *Lintoun Green* IV. 51 Twa tinkler-gangs, here ither met,..To sorn, reeve, steel, lift, and reset. **1863** *Glasgow Her.* 15 Apr., A woman, named Mary Arnot, was convicted of having resetted the stolen property.

reset (riː'sɛt), *v.*[2] Also **re-set**. [RE- 5 a.] *trans.* To set again, in various senses of the verb.

I. 1. a. To replace (*esp.* gems) in a (former or new) setting.

1655 FULLER *Ch. Hist.* V. iv. §7 Elizabeth,..finding so fair a flower..fallen out of her Crown, was careful quickly to gather it up again, and get it re-sett therein. **1684** R. WALLER *Nat. Exper.* Pref., For a time they fall out of their Collets.., and [are] worth nothing till..they are again reset in their proper places. **1830** LYTTON *P. Clifford* xix, A stray trinket or two—not of sufficient worth to be re-set. **1883** HALDANE *Worksh. Rec.* Ser. II. 371/2 The hair can be again reset as firmly as it was before [etc.].

b. *Surg.* To set (a broken limb) again.

1884 'H. COLLINGWOOD' (W. J. C. Lancaster) *Under Meteor Flag* 114 We succeeded in getting the limb reset, and the wound properly attended to.

2. To plant again, replant.

1716 M. DAVIES *Athen. Brit.* III. 85 Soon after the Gothick Barbarity repullulated again, and was re-set.

3. To set again in a different way or position.

1776 BURNEY *Hist. Mus.* I. 171 The plays of Shakespeare might be reset. **1882** HOLLAND *Logic & Life* (1885) 268 The life of an entire people is shifting and resetting..its landmarks.

4. To put a new edge on; to sharpen again.

1823 BYRON *Juan* XIV. liii, Reset it: shave more smoothly. **1885** *Lock's Worksh. Rec.* Gen. Index, Resetting bandsaws.

5. *Typog.* To set up (type) again; to recompose.

1847 in WEBSTER. **1884** *L'pool Mercury* 14 Feb. 5/6 Practical printers are already moving to see whether they cannot save the cost of re-setting old editions. **1896** DE VINNE *Moxon's Mech. Exerc., Printing* 420 The compositor ..undertook to reset this book in modern style.

6. To set up or fix in proper order again.

1829 ELMES *Dilapidations* (ed. 3) App. 66 Take down and re-set the chimney-pots. **1844** H. STEPHENS *Bk. Farm* II. 35 Such an occurrence will create the trouble to the shepherd of resetting the whole net. **1860** *Merc. Mar. Mag.* VII. 114 The sail can be reset. **1880** CARNEGIE *Pract. Trapping* 8 Should they be rained upon, they will all require re-setting or re-covering.

7. a. To cause (a device) to return to a former state, esp. a condition of readiness.

1919 R. MORDIN *Strowger Automatic Telephone Exchange* iii. 64 When the release magnet armature knocks the double dog out of engagement with the shaft it also, by means of the lever shown, re-sets the side switch. **1931** *Proc. R. Soc.* A. CXXXII. 301 The mechanical relay M_R is used only for extinguishing or resetting thyratron Q. **1977** D. ANTHONY *Stud Game* xxv. 160, I..reset the burglar alarm.

b. *Computers.* To set (a binary cell) to zero; to return (a counting device) *to* a specified value, esp. zero.

1947 *Proc. IRE* Aug. 759/1 The triggered flip-flop is the only one to respond..; as it is reset it gives out a positive pulse. **1956** G. A. MONTGOMERIE *Digital Calculating Machines* iii. 47 If the wheels are left in engagement on the return stroke they are reset to the previous values. **1971** J. H. SMITH *Digital Logic* i. 12 A binary divider is a modified toggle which has only one input. If electrical pulses are applied to this input the unit will 'set'. The second pulse will 'reset' the circuit.

8. To set (hair) again.

1932 E. BOWEN *To North* xii. 120 She..had had, since lunch, her hair shampooed and re-set.

II. 9. a. *intr.* for *refl.* **b.** Of a device: to return to an initial state.

1895 W. J. LOCKE *Gate of Samaria* xvi. 194 She..noticed a look upon Thornton's face,—the after-light, as it were, of a sneer, before the features had time to reset. **1971** *Gloss. Electrotechnical, Power Terms (B.S.I.)* I. iii. 13 A relay resets when it returns to its initial position. **1980** *Sci. Amer.* May 49/1 When both currents are removed, the switched junction automatically resets, closing the loop.

Hence **re'setting, re-'setting** *vbl. sb.*

1846 HOLTZAPFFEL *Turning* xxii. II. 471 The resettings by which the same superficies is repeated. **1861** WYNTER *Soc. Bees* 74 What advantage does this method present over a resetting of the page in the usual manner? **1882** *Spon's Encycl.* s.v. *Leather*, The next step is re-setting (*retenage*)... This is another setting out with the sleeker. **1897** *Daily News* 3 May 8/5 A publication..containing excellent new tunes and re-settings.

†**re'setment.** *Obs. rare.* In 5 **recettement.** [a. AF. *recettement* (Britton): see RESET *v.*[1] and -MENT.] The act or practice of unlawful receiving or harbouring. (Cf. RECEPTMENT.)

1449 *Rolls of Parlt.* V. 151/1 Such takyng or takynges, recettements, abettementes..of such misdedes aforesaide. **1450** *Ibid.* 213/2 That the same recettours and Comfortours appere before you..to answer..of the same recettement and comfort.

re'settable (riː-), *a.* [f. RESET *v.*[2]] Capable of being reset. Hence **resetta'bility.**

1879 TENNYSON *Lover's Tale* IV. 198 Some with gems Moveable and resettable at will. **1971** *Physics Bull.* July 390/1 The smooth tunability and resettability (1:3 × 10^4 which is an instrumental limitation) is not understood. **1973** G. J. KING *Newnes Colour T.V. Servicing Man.* I. i. 35/1 Not all models employ a resettable cut-out. **1975** *Gramophone* June 118/2 Resetability [*sic*] of the slider controls could be improved if a cursor line were engraved on the rectangular knob. **1979** *Sci. Amer.* Aug. 131/1 A system of this type can be viewed as a mathematical strongbox with a resettable combination lock.

resetter (rɪ'sɛtə(r)). Forms: *α.* 4, 6 **ressettour**, 4, 7 **recettor**, 5 **-our**. *β.* 5 **resettyr**, 6 **resettar**, 7 ressettare, -er, recetter, 6- resetter. [a. OF. *recetour*, *-eur*: see RESET *v.*[1] and -OR 2, -ER[1].] One who resets. †**a.** A harbourer of criminals, thieves, etc. *Obs.* **b.** A receiver of stolen goods.

α. *c* **1380** WYCLIF *Sel. Wks.* III. 318 Alle ressettours and meynteneris of siche witingly ben cursed. **1393** LANGL. *P. Pl.* C. IV. 501 Ac he þat receyueþ oþer recetteþ hure ys recettor of gyle. **1449** *Rolls of Parlt.* V. 151/1 To enquere.. of all such misdoers, ther abbettours and Recettours. **1576** *Reg. Privy Council Scot.* II. 573 The resettouris..salbe usit and demanyt as the rebellis thame selffis. **1632** SANDYS *Ovid's Metam.* XIV. Notes 481 A pilfering thiefe confessed ..how by the aduice of one of his recettors he compassed this hearb.

β. *c* **1440** *Alph. Tales* 73 Commonlie þe lytle þieff is hanged, Bod his resettyr & his mayntynnur is savid. **1525** *St. Papers Hen. VIII*, IV. 418 *note*, Togither with yair part takaris, assistaris, supplearis, wittandlie resettaris of yair personis [etc.]. **1590** in Noake *Worcestersh. Relics* (1877) 61 Divers of them are common locksters and resetters of yarne and will pilfer from the owners thereof. *a* **1639** SPOTTISWOOD *Hist. Ch. Scot.* VI. (1677) 375 A Proclamation was likewise renewed against the Jesuites, and their ressetters. **1675** J. SMITH *Chr. Relig. App.* II. 23 Let us think that both Thief and Recetter, the Reporter and Believer of such Stories are grievous offenders. *a* **1768** ERSKINE *Inst. Law Scot.* IV. iv. §63 (1773) 724 Such as sell goods belonging either to thieves, or to other lawless persons.., may be justly considered..as resetters of the goods. **1833** *Act 3 & 4 Will. IV*, c. 46 §52 Being proceeded against as receivers or resetters of stolen goods. **1889** *Standard* 9 Nov. 5/2 Their credit with the resetter is exhausted.

re'settle (riː-), *v.* Also re-settle. [RE- 5 a.] To settle again, in various senses.

1. a. *trans.* To settle (a thing or person) again *in* a place; to replace, re-establish. Also without const. Also, to settle again in another place; *spec.* to establish (a homeless or evicted person, etc.) again in a house or community, or (*S. Afr.*) in another area. Cf. RESETTLEMENT 1 c.

1545 RAYNOLD *Byrth Mankynde* 65 So that the hand may be resetteled in his place. **1611** SPEED *Hist. Gt. Brit.* IX. vi. §28. 491 To resettle peace in Gods Church, which he seemed onely to desire. **1654–66** EARL ORRERY *Parthen.* (1676) 627 He appointed Curio to resettle Nicomedes in Bithynia. **1696** WHISTON *Th. Earth* III. (1722) 277 This upper Earth..was..not only the old one dissolv'd, and resettled in its ancient place again. **1728** ELIZA HEYWOOD tr. *Mme. de Gomez's Belle A.* (1732) II. 110 Peace and Security thus resettled in Constantinople, the victorious Emperor sent word [etc.]. **1750** CARTE *Hist. Eng.* II. 118 They..gave out publickly that he was bringing over with him his half-brothers, in order to resettle them by force in England. **1937** [implied s.v. RESETTLED *ppl. a.*]. **1951** R. FIRTH *Elem. Social Organiz.* iv. 142 In the olden days in Ireland a working team ..was drawn from the community..to resettle an evicted family. **1965** *Listener* 30 Sept. 482/2 About 1,500 [old people]..require something between forty and fifty days to be resettled back in the community. **1972** *Stand. Encycl. S. Afr.* V. 379/1 A total of 115 000 Bantu from the western areas of Johannesburg and elsewhere were resettled in new homes in new Bantu towns. **1978** C. A. BERRY *Gentleman of Road* ix. 74 You're in a bad state and I'd like to resettle you. **1978** A. BRINK *Rumours of Rain* 105 'How many hundreds and thousands of 'exceptions' do you think there are?' he asked angrily. 'Whole societies uprooted and resettled.' **1981** *Eastern Province Herald* (S. Afr.) 2 June 5/6 This will cause friction between those who are resettled and those who were there before.

b. *refl.* To reseat (oneself) *in* or *on* something; to settle again in one's seat.

1821 SCOTT *Kenilw.* xxiv, Resettling himself in the saddle. **1835** LYTTON *Rienzi* II. ii, The Bishop, resettling himself on his saddle, ambled solemnly on. **1857** HUGHES *Tom Brown* I. viii, They..heard the supper-party resettle themselves.

c. *intr.* To settle down again.

a **1680** CHARNOCK *Attrib. God* (1834) I. 695 That mud,.. when it is resettled at the bottom,..is not so much in quantity as it was before. **1794** LD. AUCKLAND *Corr.* (1862) III. 262 We are going to town for three or four days, and shall then resettle here. **1835** LYTTON *Rienzi* II. i, They ever and anon lifted..their several goblets, and then..re-settled to their contemplations.

2. a. To bring into order again; to restore to a settled state or condition.

1611 FLORIO, *Ricomporre*, to recompose, or resettle. **1640** tr. *Verdere's Rom. of Rom.* III. xix. 72 All things thus well resetled, Rozanel and Tristor prevailed..with Clarisel. **1687** *Lond. Gaz.* No. 2301/2 His Majesties next concern and application, has been to re-settle those distracted Countries. **1725** G. SMITH *Distill.* 14 You will have no occasion to meddle with the same, lest they be disturbed and want to be resettled. **1773** FOOTE *Bankrupt* III. Wks. 1799 II. 125, I have the means in my power to resettle all our matters again. **1899** *Daily News* 13 July 6/3 The impulses which unsettle and resettle public opinion.

b. To settle over again; to make a new settlement of or in (something).

1859 LANG *Wand. India* 216 Why not make it expedient to do away with the perpetual settlement of Lord Cornwallis, and resettle the whole of Bengal? **1888** BRYCE *Amer. Commw.* I. xxx. (1893) I. 350 Similar suggestions..have been made for re-settling the relations of Ireland to Great Britain.

refl. **1857** SPENCER *Progress* (1864) 441 Things from time to time re-settle themselves in a way that best consists with national equilibrium.

3. To settle (a country) again.

1714 *Fr. Bk. of Rates* 241 This present Favour..will not contribute at all to the resettling the said Colony with Success,..unless the ancient Inhabitants will return.

4. To assign by a new settlement.

1858 LD. ST. LEONARDS *Handy-Bk. Prop. Law* xvii. 121 Powers..to lease the estate..; to sell it, and buy another estate with the money, to be re-settled.

Hence **re'settled** *ppl. a.*; **re'settling** *vbl. sb.*

1626 BACON *Sylva* §417 Some time will be required after the Remove, for the Resetling, before it can draw the Juyce. *a* **1758** EDWARDS *Hist. Redemption* (1793) III. 419 After the flood what great things did God work for the resettling of the world. **1898** *19th Cent.* Apr. 521 The world just now is busy with a general resettling of its map. **1937** *Sun* (Baltimore) 25 May 12/2 Nobody in Washington is able to indicate the means by which resettled farmers and sharecroppers can pay rent on these expensive houses. **1977** *Time* 4 Apr. 21/1 When Sanjay and his elder brother Rajiv visited a community of resettled slumdwellers, they were given a tumultuous welcome. **1981** *Eastern Province Herald* (S. Afr.) 2 June 5/4 The synod..urged the Diocesan Council to create a committee to co-operate with other concerned groups, and resettled people themselves, in planning a strategy to cope with the problems brought about by forced removal.

re'settlement. [RE- 5 a.]

1. a. The act of resettling; a fresh settlement.

a **1639** WOTTON in *Reliq.* (1672) 103 Whenceforth we may account a full Re-settlement of Lordship and propriety through the Realm. **1660** INGELO *Bentiv. & Ur.* II. (1682) 194 Necessary for the Re-settlement of the Affairs of the Kingdom. **1744** WARBURTON *Occas. Refl.* Wks. 1788 VI. 334 The Return from the great Captivity, and Resettlement in the Land of Judæa. **1859** LANG *Wand. India* 217 It is a great mistake to suppose that the whole of the land-holders in Bengal would cry out against a resettlement of that province. **1878** MORLEY *Diderot* i. 3 The resettlement of Europe by Charlemagne.

attrib. **1897** *Daily News* 8 Feb. 2/1 'Resettlement Day' is a Jewish celebration,..commemorating the return of the Jews to England in the time of the Commonwealth.

b. *spec.* The act of resettling demobilized servicemen into civilian life.

1918 *Labour Gaz.* May 175/1 (*heading*) Resettlement of officers and professional men... The report of the Committee appointed to consider the resettlement of officers has been approved by the Minister of Reconstruction. **1920** *Brit. Med. Jrnl.* 4 Sept. 340/1 Many doctors who served long with the forces have found the period following demobilization a time of uncertainty and financial stress. For them 'resettlement' has proved an uphill business. **1922** *Encycl. Brit.* XXX. 821/2 (*heading*) The first two years of resettlement. The success of the preparations which had been made..is indicated by the figures of re-absorption of men demobilized. **1945** *Yorkshire Post* 19 Apr. 3/2 The Minister of Labour has provided several admirably chosen lecturers..to tell Servicemen of the plans made for their release and resettlement when their term of service comes to an end.

c. *S. Afr.* The act of resettling Blacks in their supposed homelands.

In South Africa resettlement involves the enforced removal of Blacks from one area, often followed by a period in temporary resettlement camps, before their removal to the 'homelands'.

1954 *Bantu* Nov. 11 (*caption*) Compare these neat little houses with the unhygienic tin and brick shacks of Sophiatown..and you would understand why the resettlement of the Bantu had become imperative. **1976** A. LEMON *Apartheid* viii. 153 The further resettlement of up to half the existing number of Africans in white areas is being seriously contemplated. **1981** *Observer* 31 May 12/4 About four million have been moved since 1948 and at least another million are marked down for 'resettlement'.

2. The process of settling down again; the result of a resettling.

1675 J. ROSE *Eng. Vineyard Vind.* 44 Others, roll their Casks about the Cellar to blend with the Lees, and after few daies resettlement rack it off. **1839** DE LA BECHE *Rep. Geol. Cornwall*, etc. viii. 257 The white clay there situated might be a resettlement of the Bovey clay.

3. *attrib.* and *Comb.*, as ***resettlement area, board, camp, centre, grant, office, officer, plan, programme, project, scheme, village.***

1971 *Progress* (Cape Town) May 7/4 The *resettlement areas..to which so many African urban people have been endorsed. **1954** *Bantu* Nov. 4 The views expressed in this article are personal and in no way bind the Department or the Natives *Resettlement Board. **1973** Resettlement board [see *resettlement programme* below]. **1971** *Progress* (Cape Town) May 7/5 The valiant attempts of the women of these missions and *resettlement camps to make some sort of living for themselves and their families. **1972** *Times* 19 Dec. 3/1 There are events planned in all the 14 resettlement camps. **1973** *Resettlement centre [see *resettlement programme* below]. **1977** *R.A.F. News* 11–24 May 7/1 Even the *resettlement grant does not sweeten the bitter pill. **1945** *Daily Tel.* 17 May 3/3 They would be welcomed at the employment exchanges and the *resettlement offices if they had not got a job. **1922** *Encycl. Brit.* XXX. 821/1 A number of officers known as *Resettlement Officers were appointed .., whose business was to travel the country and investigate the causes which impeded the turnover from war to peace. **1946** *Lancet* 2 Feb. 177/1 Our resettlement officer almost got the job, but like me he didn't have the Finnish, or the Norwegian, Swedish, or Danish, without which, out there, the execution of big business is apparently impossible. **1974** 'J. LE CARRÉ' *Tinker, Tailor* xxxii. 286 The first person..to visit him was the resettlement officer, talking about a friendly teaching agency. **1945** *Daily Tel.* 17 May 3/3 (*heading*) Mr. Bevin explains *resettlement plans. **1973** *Guardian* 16 Apr. 20/1 No more Uganda Asians will be allowed into the resettlement centres. An announcement.. by the Home Office..marks the first stage in the *resettlement programme and has the full backing of the Uganda Resettlement Board. **1973** J. HOAGLAND *South Afr.* xi. 299 The Portuguese moved quickly to establish the resettlement program in Mozambique. **1936** *Sun* (Baltimore) 28 Jan. 8/7 The Government's *resettlement project at..Reedsville. **1921** W. SHERREN *Rights of Ex-Service Man & Woman* iii. 23 The Civil Liabilities *Resettlement Scheme of 1918 was instituted to provide assistance to ex-officers and men who had suffered serious hardship by reason of their military service. **1954** *Bantu* Sept. 44 Throughout the ages various Resettlement Schemes have been undertaken similar to the Scheme of the Western Areas of Johannesburg. **1952** *Times* 22 Sept. 5/1 Volunteer teams..after receiving a short course of instruction in spoken Malay..live in the new *resettlement villages. **1973** J. HOAGLAND *South Afr.* xi. 299 There were 433,000 Africans living in resettlement villages.

reseve, obs. form of RECEIVE.

re'sew (riː-), *v.* [RE- 5 a.] To sew again. Hence **re'sewing** *vbl. sb.*

1597 A. M. tr. *Guillemeau's Fr. Chirurg.* 14/1 In the resowinge of a wounde, we must note [etc.]. *Ibid.* 16/1 We coulde not easyly resowe them agayne. **1896** *Daily News* 23 May 6/3 There are fewer stitches to give way and need resewing.

resew, reseyve, obs. forms of RECEIVE.

reseyt, obs. form of RECEIPT *sb.*

†**resgat.** *Obs.* [ad. Pg. *resgate*, = Sp. *rescate*, f. *resgatar*, Sp. *rescatar*: see REESCATE.] Ransom.

1582 N. LICHEFIELD tr. *Castanheda's Conq. E. Ind.* I. 27 b, Promising also that..he would giue for his resgat, Christian Pilots. **1625** PURCHAS *Pilgrims* II. 864 The first had his resgat thrice sent for, to ransome him out of the E. Indies.

resh, obs. form of RUSH (the plant).

re'shape (riː-), *v.* [RE- 5 a.] To shape anew.

1827 CARLYLE *Misc., Richter* (1869) 11 The character is as it were forcibly crushed into some foreign mould, in the hope of being thereby reshaped and beautified. **1875** WHITNEY *Life Lang.* iv. 48 It has been reshaped to suit better the convenience of those who used it. **1895** *Thinker* VIII. 252 The Church..reshapes its architecture to accommodate these agencies. **1916** JOYCE *Portrait of Artist* (1969) 67 The change of fortune which was reshaping the world about him into a vision of squalor and insincerity. **1951** E. E. EVANS-PRITCHARD *Social Anthropol.* v. 86 The theories have been shaped and reshaped by this steady growth of knowledge. **1960** *Farmer & Stockbreeder* 29 Mar. 17/1 British economic policy has had to be reshaped to deal with an adverse trend in the balance of payments.

refl. **1837** CARLYLE *Fr. Rev.* III. II. i, The wreck and dissolution must reshape itself into a social Arrangement as it can and may. **1897** BARING-GOULD *Bladys* Pref. 7, I allowed [the idea] to re-shape itself, in fresh scenes, with fresh developments, and fresh incidents.

Hence **re'shaping** *vbl. sb.* and *ppl. a.*

1882 *Athenæum* 7 Jan. 27/3 A reshaping of a comedietta of Haynes Bayly. **1897** WATTS-DUNTON *Aylwin* XIII. iii, Not even the reshaping power of memory would suffice to appease my longing. **1951** R. FIRTH *Elem. Social Organiz.* iii. 89 This has been particularly marked with the coming of industrialism, foreshadowing the destruction or radical re-shaping of their social structure. **1964** F. L. WESTWATER *Electronic Computers* iv. 89 The pulse train is fed back into the tube after amplification and re-shaping. **1969** *Gloss. Landscape Work* (*B.S.I.*) v. 30 *Reshaping*, a pruning operation directed to improving the shape of a tree.

re'shaper (riː-). [f. RESHAPE *v.* + -ER[1].] One who or that which reshapes.

1961 WEBSTER, *Reshaper*, one that reshapes something; *esp.* a worker who does the final blocking of hats. **1964** F. L. WESTWATER *Electronic Computers* iii. 49 The effect of passing through a gate causes a deterioration in the pulse shape. This can be corrected by some non-logical element such as an amplifier or reshaper.

re'share (riː-), *v.* [RE- 5 a.] To share again.

1603 J. DAVIES (Heref.) *Microcos.* Wks. (Grosart) I. 66/2 Semiramis..lusting to reshare Hir Sonne, her Sonne her Threed of Life did share.

re'sharpen (riː-), *v.* To sharpen again.

1884 *Machinery & Engineering* I. 90/1 A small special.. machine is made, which resharpens the milling cutter. **1889** *Pall Mall G.* 21 Jan. 6/3 The cutting knife is moveable, and can be resharpened.

re'sheathe (riː-), *v.* To sheathe again.

a **1700** KEN *Edmund* Poet. Wks. 1721 II. 189 God, at their Pray'rs, his naked Sword re-sheath'd.

Resh Galuta (ˌreɪʃ gəluːˈtɑː). Also **Resch Glutha** and with small initials. [Aramaic, lit. 'chief of the exile'.] = EXILARCH. Also *transf.*

1829 H. H. MILMAN *Hist. Jews* III. XIX. 160 Babylon, where, during his days of splendour, the Resch-Glutha fixed his residence. *Ibid.* 162 The Court of the Resch-Glutha is described as equally splendid; in imitation of his Persian master, he had his officers, counsellors, and cupbearers. **1867** C. M. YONGE *Pupils of St. John* x. 159 A stately personage..known as the Resch Glutha, or Chief of the Captivity. **1903** *Jewish Encycl.* V. 293/1 This last story indicates that the resh galuta had by that time become the subject of Mohammedan legend. **1931** C. ROTH *Jewish Bk. of Days* 6 Huna Mari, Prince of the Captivity, executed, 470. This high office (otherwise known as that of Exilarch—*Resh Galutha*) was enjoyed by the secular head of the 'exile' in Babylonia in virtue of his descent from the house of David. **1971** *Encycl. Judaica* VI. 1031/2 During subsequent periods the *nesi'im* of Yemen were referred to as *resh galuta*, although they had no connections with the Babylonian exilarch or the House of David.

re'shift (riː-), *v.* [RE- 5 a.] To shift again, in various senses.

1599 SANDYS *Europæ Spec.* (1632) 238 They have also a mystery in shifting and reshifting in one and the same Masse from one Alter to another. **1665** PEPYS *Diary* 9 July, So back again home and reshifted myself.

re'shine (riː-), *v.* [RE- 5 a.] *intr.* To shine again. Hence **re'shining** *ppl. a.*

1582 STANYHURST *Æneis* III. (Arb.) 87 Thee stars are darckned, glittring Aurora reshined. **1592** G. HARVEY *Four*

Lett. Sonn. xi, Mirrours.. That radiantly display their beauteous beames Of glistring Vertue, and reshining Witt. **1610** HOLLAND *Camden's Brit.* (1637) 461 So brightly reshine in his English verses, all the pleasant graces.. of speech. **1662** J. CHANDLER *Van Helmont's Oriat.* 173 Let it be an Analogy, or proportionable resemblance re-shining.. in their effects.

re'ship (riː-), *v.* [RE- 5 a.]
1. *refl.* and *intr.* To take ship again.
1654-66 EARL ORRERY *Parthen.* (1676) 656 A couple of ordinary men who had re-ship'd themselves again for Asia. **1801** *Dundee Advertiser* 27 Feb., Richardson further adds he saw his vessel in a wrecked state before he reshipped.
2. *trans.* To put into, or on board of, a ship again; to transfer to another ship.
1714 MANDEVILLE *Fab. Bees* (1733) I. 113 The merchants in general must lose much more by this half that is reshipp'd, than they got by the half that is consumed here. **1790** BEATSON *Nav. & Mil. Mem.* I. 376 Several days were employed in reshipping the cannon, mortars, and heavy stores. **1828** SOUTHEY *Ess.* (1832) II. 257 When any of these outcasts are reshipped from one port, they make their way back to another as speedily as possible. **1874** WALFORD *Insurance Cycl.* III. 568 The wool at the time of the fire was about to be re-shipped.
3. To set in position, fix up, again.
1875 BEDFORD *Sailor's Pkt. Bk.* viii. (ed. 2) 285 The apparatus.. may.. be altogether and at once unshipped, and re-shipped again at pleasure.

re'shipment (riː-). [RE- 5 a.]
1. The act of reshipping.
1796 MORSE *Amer. Geogr.* I. 636 The inconveniences and expenses of reshipment at New Orleans. **1861** GOSCHEN *For. Exch.* 15 Produce, on which the charges of shipment or re-shipment are infinitely heavier. **1885** *Law Rep. 10 App. Cases* 419 The cost of transhipment or reshipment, as the case may be, should be general average.
2. The quantity reshipped.
1887 *Pall Mall G.* 8 Feb. 12/1 The reshipments are larger by about 2 per cent.

re'shoe (riː-), *v.* [RE- 5 a.] *trans.* To shoe (a horse) again. Hence **re'shoeing** *vbl. sb.*
1856 'STONEHENGE' *Brit. Rural Sports* 668/1 The want of re-shoeing is more likely to prevent contraction than to cause it. **1892** *Daily News* 16 Nov. 5/5 No aluminium shoes broke, and they were used over again for re-shoeing.

re'shoot (riː-), *v.* [RE- 5 a.] To shoot again.
a **1618** SYLVESTER *Job Triumphant* I. 884 Though a Tree be felled; from the Root, Yet is there hope that Branches will re-shoot. **1900** G. B. SHAW *Let.* 4 Nov. (1972) II. 194 He has .. become too curious to see how their marriage will turn out to reshoot himself more efficiently. **1900** *Law Rep. Appeal Cases* 429 No doubt the action of the current upon the net is calculated more or less to shift the position of it, and so from time to time to make it necessary to gather it up and reshoot it, to restore it to its perpendicular position. **1955** H. KURNITZ *Invasion of Privacy* (1956) xiv. 88 It's a hundred-to-one he'll.. reshoot the picture so that not a speck of what you want in it remains. **1956** *Nature* 21 Jan. 120/1 The information can be conveniently stored against the day when better interpretation methods allow one to make the fullest use of the recordings, without having to reshoot in areas which are often exceedingly difficult of access. **1975** R. L. SIMON *Wild Turkey* (1976) xi. 72 *Badass* has had a change in shooting schedule... We're going to have to reshoot two days. **1976** A. DAVIS *Television* 28 Plays were still recorded in sequence... The maxim otherwise was to stop the tape and reshoot only for technical mishaps.

re'shooting, *vbl. sb.* [f. prec. + -ING¹.] The action of the verb RESHOOT.
1960 L. COOPER *Certain Compass* 121 There was some re-shooting we could do. **1975** [see RE-EDIT *v.*, RE-EDITING *vbl. sb.*]. **1978** *Times* 26 Aug. 7/2 We had another preview. The picture was obviously better... He did not think any reshooting was necessary.

†**re'shore** (riː-), *v. Obs. rare*⁻¹. [RE- 5 a.] *trans.* ? To return to the shore of.
1632 LITHGOW *Trav.* x. 495 Hauing agayne re-shoared the Maine, I coasted Galloway.

re'shrine, *v.* [RE- 5 a.] To enshrine again.
1878 GROSART *Ded. Sonn.* in *H. More's Poems*, More, in this living now I would re-shrine for homage.

Resht (rɛʃt). The name of a province and town in north-west Iran, used *attrib.* to designate patchwork made there.
1888 A. S. COLE *Descr. Catal. Coll. Tapestry & Embroidery S. Kensington Mus.* 314 Patchwork of cloth of various colours... Resht work. *Persian.* **1923** *Daily Mail* 26 Feb. 15 There is also a kind of Persian patch-work called 'Resht'. It is really an amazingly ingenious mosaic of cloth, only *one* thickness being used, and was generally arranged in four colours—red, green, grey, and white. **1960** H. HAYWARD *Antique Coll.* 237/1 *Resht patchwork*, a type of mosaic patch-work produced at Resht, Persia, during the 18th and 19th cent. for covers and prayer-rugs. The designs are inlaid in coloured felts with outlines and details worked in coloured silks in chain-stitch and couched-work. Inferior examples are often not true patchwork, as the small pieces are applied to the ground and not inlaid.

reshta, var. RISHTA.

re'shuffle (riː-), *v.* [RE- 5 a.] *trans.* To shuffle (cards, etc.) again; also, to redistribute (posts within a cabinet, organization, etc.).
1830 'EIDRAH TREBOR' *Hoyle Made Familiar* 65 The cards must be re-shuffled. **1875** 'CAVENDISH' *Round Games at Cards* 8 If a card is exposed in cutting,.. the pack must be re-shuffled. **1899** *Westm. Gaz.* 13 June 1/2 You just defeat the Ministry, reshuffle the Portfolios, find a new head. **1963** *Ann. Reg. 1962* 117 Chief Akintola proposed to reshuffle the Western Nigeria Development Corporation's management. **1973** A. MANN *Tiara* iii. 18 The London correspondent of *Messaggero* thought the British Cabinet would be reshuffled.

reshuffle (riː'ʃʌf(ə)l, 'riː-), *sb.* [f. the vb.] The act of reshuffling. Used *esp.* to denote a redistribution of posts within a government or cabinet, etc.
1897 *Daily News* 19 July 3/1 Queensland has been content with only seventeen shuffles or re-shuffles. **1922** L. WOOLF *Downhill all Way* (1967) i. 37, I feel that this is no time for a mere reshuffle of the ancient Conservative and Liberal Pack and for entrusting power to one or other of the two parties whose political principles and practice are directly responsible for the disastrous situation in which the country finds itself today. **1931** A. L. ROWSE *Politics & Younger Generation* x. 272 It [*sc.* the Tyrol] should be returned to Austria.. at the first reshuffle in Europe. **1940** H. NICOLSON *Diary* 3 Apr. (1967) 65 We get over the telephone the final text of the Government reshuffle. **1947** *New Secondary Education* (Ministry of Educ.) 10 Such reorganisation as could be effected in existing buildings by a 'reshuffle' of the children. **1953** E. SIMON *Past Masters* IV. i. 211 Nothing was ever done about the dry rot... Two rooms are involved... So another grand re-shuffle is at hand. **1955** *Daily Express* 14 Oct. 1/5 (*caption*), I *do* wish the P.M. would make up his mind about the Cabinet reshuffle. **1965** *Listener* 17 June 884/2 A reshuffle in the Fund's liabilities among the various depositors. **1976** *Liverpool Echo* 22 Nov. 17/2 Moore went off injured.. and it took them a good quarter of an hour to adjust to the enforced reshuffle. **1978** J. R. L. ANDERSON *Death in Greenhouse* ii. 32 [He] was given his present job at the Foreign Office in the Government re-shuffle.. last year.

re'shuffling, *vbl. sb.* [f. RESHUFFLE *v.* + -ING¹.] The action of the verb.
1883 E. W. HAMILTON *Diary* 28 May (1972) II. 440 His having to quit the Government would be a loss in itself, but what is worse it would involve a reshuffling of the cards. **1926** J. S. HUXLEY *Ess. Pop. Sci.* 28 Sexual reproduction means first a reshuffling of the factors, and then a recombination of them in new arrangements. **1934** *Mind* XLIII. 525 The mere repetition and reshuffling of changeless entities to which, according to M. Bergson, we should be condemned if we did not have intuition to tutor us. **1937** *Sun* (Baltimore) 7 Dec. 9/2 The proposed 'reshuffling' of operations and routes of American lines.

re'shut (riː-), *v.* [RE- 5 a.] To shut again.
a **1618** SYLVESTER *Maiden's Blush* 1569 He will'd That each man's money should again be put Into his Sack, and then the Sack re-shut. **1774** GOLDSM. *Nat. Hist.* (1776) II. 149 Reshutting the other eye, we shall find that part of the room visible.

†**'resiance.** *Obs.* [ad. obs. F. *res(s)eance*: see RESIANT and -ANCE.] Abode, residence.
1577 HARRISON *England* II. iv. (1877) I. 99 Through his personall resiance, if he happen to dwell and be resident in the same. **1605** M. SUTCLIFFE *Brief Exam.* 145 The world knoweth, how they haue domineered in the places of their resiance. **1632** HOLLAND *Cyrupædia* 172 Intending to keepe resiance in a Citie. [**1658** in PHILLIPS. **1704** in HARRIS *Lex. Techn.* I. **1867** T. C. ANSTEY *Notes Repr. People Act* 47 The Franchise in all and each was the same. It was a simple 'Resiance' (or Residency) Franchise.]
So †**'resiancy** (also 7 resc-). *Obs.*
1580-1 *Act 23 Eliz.* c. 15 §13 Upon Certificate made to the saide Courte of Exchequer.. testyfieing suche his most Resyauncy. **1588** LAMBARDE *Eiren.* IV. xix. 606 So much of this Statute.. as doth concern the resiancie of those Iustices of the Peace. **1622** CALLIS *Stat. Sewers* (1647) 191 This Statute requireth an actual habitation or resciancy, and not a Mathematical or Imaginary resciancy. **1673** *MS. Declaration* (Yorksh.), Inhabitants within the said Duchy do suit of resiancy unto the tourne and court leet. [**1867** ANSTEY *Notes Repr. People Act* 51 The antient 'common right' of Universal, or 'Resiancy' Suffrage.]

resiant ('rɛzɪənt), *a.* and *sb.* Now *arch.* Forms: 5 receande, resceant, -aunte, resseaunt, 5-6 (9) reseant (7 ree-); 5 ressi-, 5-7 resiaunt (6 -aunte, resyant, -aunt(e), 6 resiant (6 -ante, 7 -ent, resciant, -ent). [a. OF. *reseant* (*rec-*, *resc-*, *resseant*, etc.), pres. pple. of *reseoir*:—L. *residēre*: see RESIDE *v.*¹]
A. *adj.* †**1.** Resident, dwelling; abiding. In predicative use, or placed after the sb., sometimes in *pl.* form. *Obs.* (Common *c* 1450-1650.)
a. Of persons.
c **1450** *St. Cuthbert* (Surtees) 7544 In durham mynster þare he fande Certayn seculers receande. **1482** *Rolls of Parlt.* VI. 198/1 The persone.. with whom they were dwellyng, reseant or resortyng. **1542** UDALL *Erasm. Apoph.* 140 In whatsoeuer place of the worlde he is resyaunte or maketh his abode. **1584** R. SCOT *Discov. Witchcr.* XVI. iv. 401 Certaine divells speake onelie the language of that countrie where they are resiant. **1611** B. JONSON *Catiline* IV. iv, I have already Dealt, by Umbrenus, with the Allobroges Here resiant in Rome. **1670** *Cosin's Corr.* (Surtees) II. 242 The names of all the convicted women recusants.. who were resiant in Durham. **1752** J. LOUTHIAN *Form of Process* (ed. 2) 178 If any Person so outlawed for High Treason shall.. be Resiant or Inhabitant out of the Limits of the Kingdom. [**1865** NICHOLS *Britton* II. 224 If the lord is sure that the proof will be made against the villain, that he was his astrer, reseant in his villenage.]
pl. **1491** *Act 7 Hen. VII*, c. 5 §1 They and their successours and their tenauntes and servauntes Resceauntes uppon their londes. *c* **1530** in Burnet *Hist. Ref.* II. 189 That the said Prelates.. continually should be abiding and Reseants upon their said Promotions within this Realm.
b. Of things.
1581 MULCASTER *Positions* xxxvii. (1887) 153 The plat for the monarchicall learner being alwaye reseant in the chusers head. *a* **1624** BP. SMITH *Serm.* (1632) 189 A King.. that hath the Spirit of the liuing God resiant in him. **1681** T. FLATMAN *Heraclitus Ridens* No. 15 (1713) I. 101 The People .. would have been apt to believe a certain Sovereignty even Paramount to the Kings, to be resiant in the House of Commons.
†**c.** Settled, occupied. *Obs. rare*⁻¹.
1583 STUBBES *Anat. Abus.* (1882) 140 Wee must refrain all bodily labours, to the end that wee may the better be resiant at these spirituall exercises vppon the Sabaoth day.
†**2.** In attributive use: **a.** Of residence or stay. **b.** = RESIDENT *a.* 2. *Obs. rare.*
1593 NASHE *Christ's T.* 61 Is a Monarche no Monarch, because hee reareth not his resiant Throne amongst his vtmost Subiects? **1600** HOLLAND *Livy* I. xx. 14 To the end they should attend continually about the church, as resiant chaplaines.
B. *sb.* A resident. Now *rare.*
1433 *Rolls of Parlt.* IV. 476/1 The most true and indifferent Commoners, Burgeys, Resceantz, continuell Hous-holders. **1533** MORE *Apol.* xxxv. Wks. 900/2 In the cytye selfe, eyther of resiauntes therin, or of resorters thereto. **1587** FLEMING *Contn. Holinshed* III. 1308/1 Desirous to be a dweller and resiant in his countrie where he was borne. **1624** BP. MOUNTAGU *Immed. Addr.* 103 Being Resiants in those heauenly habitations. **1641** HEYLIN *Hist. Episc.* I. vi. (1657) 179 [189], A thing which could not possibly be supposed.. had he beene here a resiant. **1738** *Hist. View Crt. Excheq.* i. 4 All Quarrels that were moved between the Resiants there. **1787** HAWKINS *Life Johnson* 455 To his villa at Streatham, in Surrey; Johnson was invited not as a guest, but as a resiant. **1839** STONEHOUSE *Axholme* 133 This John granted the famous deed.. to his tenants and resiants in the Isle of Axholme. [**1867** T. C. ANSTEY *Notes Repr. People Act* 49 Sometimes even in exclusion of the 'common right of all the Resiants'.]
Comb. **1753** CHAMBERS *Cycl. Suppl.*, *Resiant rolls*, are rolls wherein the resiants of a tithing, &c., are set down.

†**resianty.** *Obs. rare*⁻¹. In 5 **reseantee.** [f. prec. + -Y.] = RESIANCE.
1467-8 *Rolls of Parlt.* V. 630/2 [This being] caused be reseantee of all the Kynges Courtes holden and abidyng at Westm[inster].

†**resiccate,** *v. Obs. rare*⁻¹. [f. L. type **resiccāt-*, f. *re-* RE- + *siccāre* to dry: cf. *desiccate.*] *absol.* To have a drying effect.
1657 TOMLINSON *Renou's Disp.* 338 It calefies moderately, resiccates manifestly, and is somewhat astrictive.
So †**resi'ccation,** drying up. *Obs. rare.*
1615 CROOKE *Body of Man* 267 The shutting vp and resiccation of these vessels within a few dayes after the birth.

†**re'side,** *sb. Obs. rare.* [f. the vb.] Residence, sojourn. (Only in Brathwait.)
1630 BRATHWAIT *Eng. Gentlewom.* (1641) 293 Make no reside there where the least occasion of lightnesse is ministred. **1635** —— *Arcad. Princ.* **3 In the time of his reside at Court, there were no Transcripts held so precious as his Poems.

reside (rɪ'zaɪd), *v.*¹ Also 5 resyde, 7 recide, 6 resede, -cede. [ad. F. *résider* (= Sp. and Pg. *residir*, It. *risedere*) or L. *residēre* to remain behind, rest, etc., f. *re-* RE- + *sedēre* to sit.]
†**1. a.** *intr.* To settle; to take up one's abode or station. *Obs. rare.*
c **1460** *Maitl. Cl. Misc.* (1855) III. 37 Thai came in Navarn and Wisbayn, and resydit on the ryver of Hyber. **1490** CAXTON *Eneydos* xix. 70 It sholde be a shame to me.. to reside in this land of lybie, wythoute to accomplishe my wyage. *a* **1657** W. BURTON *Itin. Antonin.* (1658) 250 This Legion.. was taken into Britain by Claudius Cæsar, and planted here, where.. it recided against the Silures.
†**b.** To rest or rely *upon* oneself. *Obs. rare*⁻¹.
1610 HEALEY *St. Aug. Citie of God* XII. vi. (1620) 423 The iust cause of the bad Angels misery is their departure from that high essence to reside vpon themselues.
2. a. To dwell permanently or for a considerable time, to have one's settled or usual abode, to live, *in* or *at* a particular place.
1578 T. N. tr. *Conq. W. India* 135 Nor yet ever any hath come so neare Mexico where Mutezuma dooth reside. **1585** T. WASHINGTON tr. *Nicholay's Voy.* II. xviii. 51 The Sarail, where ordinarilie the great lord Turk doth resede. *Ibid.* IV. xxxvi. 159 b, The second [patriarch] recedith at Caire. **1603** SHAKS. *Meas. for M.* III. i. 277 There at the moated-Grange recides this deiected Mariana. **1651** HOBBES *Leviath.* III. xlii. 290 To appoint his successour in that place, in which he last resided and dyed. **1697** DRYDEN *Virg. Georg.* IV. 610 Secure within resides the various God, And draws a Rock upon his dark Abode. **1740** LADY M. W. MONTAGU *Lett.* xii. III. 22, I purpose to set out for Naples. I am told by every body that I shall not find it agreeable to reside in. **1838** LYTTON *Alice* I. ii, His father resided in the next county. **1873** RUSKIN *Fors Clav.* V. lviii. 279 Those of the Companions who could reside on the lands would, each on their own farm, establish [etc.].
transf. **1610** SHAKS. *Temp.* III. i. 65 The verie instant that I saw you, did My heart flie to your seruice, there resides To make me slaue to it. **1815** SHELLEY *Alastor* 512 Where these living thoughts reside, when.. my bloodless limbs shall waste I' the passing wind. **1973** C. SAGAN *Cosmic Connection* xiii. 88 Such a solution is liquid at the temperatures and pressures at which the Venus clouds reside.
b. Of persons having some special status or position. Hence, to live (at a place) for the discharge of official duties; to be 'in residence'.
1456 SIR G. HAYE *Law Arms* (S.T.S.) 146 In distribucioun of wagis in collegis, is nocht gevin bot to thame that resydis. *c* **1530** in Burnet *Hist. Ref.* I. Rec. II. xxiii. 62 You Sir Gregory being his Ambassadour there continually residing. ? **1667** in Pettus *Fodinæ Reg.* (1670) 39 One Vnder-Steward to reside at the Mines. **1715** *Lond. Gaz.* No. 5324/3 James Jefferyes, Esq., to reside for His Majesty's Service with the King of Sweden. **1860** *Bentley's*

Quarterly I. 528 A clergyman resides on his living; a cabinet-minister resides (if he does reside) in Downing Street.

c. Of animals. (Not now in serious use.)

1748 *Anson's Voy.* II. iv. 157 This place..abounds with goats... These animals reside here in great tranquillity. **1794** S. WILLIAMS *Vermont* (1809) I. 108 The Woodchuck..resides in a hole which he digs in the ground.

3. a. Of power, rights, etc.: To rest or be vested *in* a person, etc. †Also const. *with*.

1607 *Stat.* in *Hist. Wakefield Sch.* (1892) 59 That the election..alwaies reside and remayne with themselves. *a* **1674** CLARENDON *Surv. Leviath.* 122 Let us suppose this Soveraignty to reside, and be fixed in an assembly of men. **1736** BERKELEY *Disc.* Wks. 1871 III. 416 Power—physical power—resides in the people. **1791** PAINE *Rights of Man* (ed. 4) 21 When despotism has established itself for ages..it is not in the person of the King only that it resides. **1832** AUSTIN *Jurispr.* (1879) I. xii. 354 Rights are exercised by persons, or if not exercised by persons reside in persons. **1874** GREEN *Short Hist.* i. §1. 4 The actual sovereignty within the settlement resided in the body of its freemen.

b. Of qualities, attributes, etc.: To be present or inherent *in* a person or thing.

1611 SHAKS. *Wint. T.* I. ii. 272 Cogitation Resides not in that man, that do's not thinke. **1692** BENTLEY *Boyle Lect.* iv. 140 The meanest Plant cannot be rais'd without Seed by any Formative power residing in the Soil. **1720** WATERLAND *Eight Serm.* 199 Attributes and Powers must have something to reside and inhere in. **1784** COWPER *Tiroc.* 373 Resides such virtue in that air, As must create an appetite for pray'r? **1828** CARLYLE *Misc.* (1857) I. 200 A man in whose heart resides some effluence of Wisdom. **1843** MILL *Logic* I. ii. §5 The meaning resides not in what they denote, but in what they connote. **1871** MOZLEY *Univ. Serm.* vi. (1876) 127 The glory of nature in reality resides in the mind of man. **1972** *Incorporated Linguist* XI. 30 The significance of linguistic theorizing resides..in the fact that it provides intellectual training while..introducing the learner to problems of the functioning of linguistic systems.

c. To be physically present *in* a thing. Now *rare*.

1620 VENNER *Via Recta* vii. 117 Corrupt humors, that reside in the body. **1758** REID tr. *Macquer's Chym.* I. 277 He concluded that in this Saline matter resides the true Acid. **1823** J. BADCOCK *Dom. Amusem.* 18 The acid which was long known to reside in wood. **1846** TIZARD *Brewing* (ed. 2) 548 The rich nectarium residing in the lupuline is prevented by the dense worts from exuding.

†**4. a.** To remain or continue *in* a certain place or position. *Obs.*

1620 VENNER *Via Recta* viii. 175 The third is, that they reside not in the chaire of intemperance, that is, prolong not the time in eating and drinking superfluously. **1775** R. CHANDLER *Trav. Asia M.* (1825) I. 100 In Scio, it was well known, the distemper had resided for some time.

†**b.** Of things: To lie, be placed or stationed, somewhere. *Obs. rare.*

1633 T. STAFFORD *Pac. Hib.* II. viii. (1821) 319 Her Majesties Magazines of Victualls, Munition, and Treasure residing there in great quantities. **1725** POPE *Odyss.* I. 237 Far from your Capital my ship resides At Reithrus, and secure at anchor rides. **1742** GRAY *Propertius* ii. 9 Let on this head unfadeing flowers reside.

†**re'side**, *v.*[2] *Obs.* [ad. L. *residēre*, f. *re-* RE- + *sidĕre* to sink.]

1. *intr.* To sink down, to subside.

c **1586** C'TESS PEMBROKE *Ps.* LXXXIX. iv, Thy lordlie check the seas proud courage quailed, And highly swelling, lowly made reside. *a* **1702** CONGREVE *Birth of Muse*, Every rolling surge resides in peace.

2. To sink or settle down as a deposit.

1605 TIMME *Quersit.* I. xiii. 56 The matter of meane substance, which is sulphurus, oylely, & apt to burne, resideth in the bottome of the glasse. **1660** SHARROCK *Vegetables* 93 The mixt earth that was carryed in the flood being apt to reside to the bottom. **1676** *Phil. Trans.* XI. 620 The sulphurs and Bitums are alwaies obvious to be discerned in the waters wherein they are, because they reside in them, or swim on them.

3. To alight. *rare*−[0].

1616 BULLOKAR *Eng. Expos.*, *Reside*, to alight. **1623** COCKERAM II. A ij, To Alight from a horse, *reside*.

residence ('rɛzɪdəns), *sb.*[1] Forms: 4 **residense**, 5 **resydennce**, 6 **reci-**, **resi-**, **resydens**, **reci-**, **resydence**, 4- **residence**. [a. F. *résidence*, = Prov. *residensa*, Sp. and Pg. *residencia*, It. *residenza*, *-zia*, ad. L. *residentia*: see RESIDE *v.*[1] and -ENCE.]

1. a. *to have* (†*hold*, *keep*, or *make*) *one's residence*, to have one's usual dwelling-place or abode; to reside. *to take up one's residence*, to establish oneself; to settle.

c **1386** CHAUCER *Can. Yeom. Prol. & T.* 107 In lanes blinde, Wher as these robbours and these theves by kynde Holden here prive ferful residence. **1535** LYNDESAY *Satyre* 574, I haue maid my residence With his Princes of greit puissance. **1585** *Reg. Privy Council Scot.* III. 747 The parrochynnis quhair they wer borne or had thair cheiff residence. **1649** *Alcoran* 405 The Heaven, where God kept his residence. **1667** MILTON *P.L.* I. 734 Many a Towred structure high, Where Scepter'd Angels held thir residence. **1788** PRIESTLEY *Lect. Hist.* v. xxxvi. 263 The arts and sciences took up their residence..at Rome. **1794** S. WILLIAMS *Vermont* (1809) I. 98 In these [forests] a great variety and number of animals had their residence. **1833** CRUSE tr. *Eusebius* IV. xi. 139 He also had his residence at Rome.

b. So *to have* (etc.) *residence*.

c **1430** LYDG. *Min. Poems* (Percy Soc.) 138 Whan foure steedys of Phebus goldene chare, List in this regioun holde residence. **1432-50** tr. *Higden* (Rolls) I. 179 Hit was not conueniente an Emperoure to kepe residence where thapostles crownede kepede the principate. **1508** DUNBAR *Poems* vii. 30 Welcum..Withe us to liue, and to maik recidence. **1592** SHAKS. *Rom. & Jul.* II. iii. 24 Within the infant rind of this weake flower Poyson hath residence, and medicine power. **1622** FLETCHER *Sea-Voy.* II. ii, What place is this? Sure something more than human keeps residence here. **1667** MILTON *P.L.* II. 999, I upon my Frontieres here Keep residence. **1833** CHALMERS *Const. Man* (1835) I. 72 Virtue..has had everlasting residence in the nature of the Godhead.

c. The circumstance or fact of having one's permanent or usual abode in or at a certain place; the fact of residing or being resident.

1480 *10th Rep. Hist. MSS. Comm.* App. V. 315 No manere freman..shall dwell..without the citie by no contynuell resydennce. **1500-20** DUNBAR *Poems* lvii. 4 Men makis in court thair solistationis:..Sum be continewale residence. **1602** SHAKS. *Ham.* II. ii. 343 How chances it they trauaile? their residence both in reputation and profit was better both wayes. **1652** NEEDHAM tr. *Selden's Mare Cl.* 479 Then they were glad to invite our Merchant's Residence with what privileges they would desire. **1714** R. FIDDES *Pract. Disc.* II. 341 There was one special and standing monument of his residence among them. **1790** in Dallas *Amer. Law Rep.* I. 243 There is an essential difference between residence and abiding in a particular place. **1821** SCOTT *Kenilw.* vii, That he should move their sovereign to honour Woodstock occasionally with her residence during her royal progresses. **1860** WOOLSEY *Introd. Internat. Law* iv. (1879) 132 Ambassadors in ancient times were sent on special occasions by one nation to another. Their residence at foreign courts is a practice of modern growth. **1883** *Cent. Mag.* Oct. 858/1 The next center of fashionable residence was Blucker street.

transf. **1695** WOODWARD *Nat. Hist. Earth* I. (1723) 74 Those Parts..had been formerly in the Possession of the Sea, and the Place of its natural Residence. **1830** LYELL *Princ. Geol.* I. 43 The marine shells..demonstrate the former residence of the sea upon the mountains.

d. *Anthrop.* The place in which it is customary for a couple to settle after marriage, according to the prevailing kinship system. Also *attrib.* Cf. MATRILOCAL *a.*, NEOLOCAL *a.*, etc.

1865 J. F. MCLENNAN *Primitive Marriage* viii. 154 Teadhloch and cuedichc.., Gaelic names for family, mean the first having a common residence; the second those who eat together. **1889** E. B. TYLOR in *Jrnl. Anthrop. Inst.* XVIII. 247 Now, on looking out from the schedules the adhesions of this avoidance-custom, a relation appears between it and the customs of the world as to residence after marriage. **1924** W. H. RIVERS *Social Organisation* v. 90 The last aspect of father-right and mother-right to be mentioned ..is one with which perhaps I ought to have dealt in the second chapter, namely, the place of residence in case of marriage. **1938** G. A. RIECHARD in F. Boas *Gen. Anthrop.* ix. 421 Among primitives residence is of even greater importance. **1968** JACOBSON & SCHOEPF tr. *Levi-Strauss's Structural Anthrop.* xv. 309 The impact of residence on descent. **1972** E. A. HOEBEL *Anthrop.* (ed. 4) xxi. 427/2 There are, then, five basic varieties of residence. *Ibid.*, It is not a simple..matter as to whether a given household represents one kind of residence pattern or another.

2. The fact of living or staying regularly at or in some place for the discharge of special duties, or to comply with some regulation; also, the period during which such stay is required of one. Now freq. in phrase *in residence*.

a. *Eccl.*, with ref. to the presence of incumbents in their benefices, canons in their cathedrals, etc.

c **1380** WYCLIF *Sel. Wks.* III. 493 No persone ne vicare ne prelate is excusud fro personele residense to be made in þer beneficys. *c* **1444** LYDG. in *Pol. Poems* (Rolls) II. 217 Avaunsyd personwys holde residence Among ther parysshens. *c* **1449** PECOCK *Repr.* III. xix. 406 In the oold tyme the bischop and hise preestis..helden residence in the modir chirche. *a* **1548** HALL *Chron.*, *Hen. VIII* 188 For lacke of residence..all y[e] parishioners lacked preaching. **1570** FOXE *A. & M.* (ed. 2) 1664/2 He departed from Lichefield to a benefice in Leycester shyre,..wherupon he keepyng residence, taught diligently. **1632** *Star Chamb. Cases* (Camden) 105 With the Spanish Divines he holdeth residence *de jure divino*, but if they erred in anything it was about personall residence. **1699** GALE *Let.* in *Pepys' Mem.* (1828) V. 255 My residence determines tomorrow, because my last sermon could not be made till then, though the eating residence terminated a few days ago. **1803** SYD. SMITH *Wks.* (1867) I. 48 As exceptions to the general and indisputable principle of residence. **1845** WILBERFORCE in Ashwell *Life* (1879) I. vii. 283, I wish I was in residence to play the host to you. **1892** KITCHIN *Compotus Rolls St. Swithun's Priory* Introd. 3 The Canon in Residence.. actually gave orders that the Rolls..should be thrown into the fire.

fig. **1647** FULLER *Good Th. in Worse T.* (1841) 150 It were liberty enough, if for the next seven years all sermons were bound to keep residence on this text: Brethren, love one another.

b. In other connexions, as with ref. to colleges or universities, electoral rights, etc. Used *spec.* with reference to a residential post held by an artist, poet, sculptor, writer, etc., within a community or institution for the purpose of teaching his craft or influencing communal life. Also *transf.* (freq. *joc.*). Cf. also *poet-in-residence* (POET 1 e).

1584-5 *Extr. Burgh Rec. Glasgow* (1876) I. 116 The tuelf puir men of the said hospitall sall mak residence.

1849 MACAULAY *Hist. Eng.* viii. II. 275 The connection between the scholar and the school did not terminate with his residence. **1867** T. C. ANSTEY *Notes Repr. People Act* 66 'Residence' was required in certain cases, but not in others. **1868** M. PATTISON *Academ. Org.* iv. 109 The head is usually bound to residence during term. *Ibid.* v. 315 The 'residence' of an undergraduate student is now considered to be 168 days out of 365. **1896** *Academy* 18 Jan. 56/1 At Oxford residence will not be resumed until the end of next week. **1954** R. JARRELL *Pictures from Institution* iii. 94 How glad Dr. Rosenbaum was that he was only a Composer in Residence. **1965** *Economist* 30 Oct. 499/2 Its money will also be used..to help symphony orchestras and support artists-in-residence at universities. **1968** MRS. L. B. JOHNSON *White House Diary* 30 Apr. (1970) 667 He [*sc.* Eric Hoffer] said, 'I call myself a conversationalist in residence.' **1970** *Times* 16 Apr. 8/5 No girls throwing smoke in our eyes at last night's Gold Leaf concert..instead a tame composer, a 'composer in residence'... Peter Patterson..is the lucky man commissioned to write pieces. **1972** W. KING *Black Short Story Anthol.* 133 She [*sc.* Alice Walker] is presently writer-in-residence at Tougaloo College,..Mississippi. **1975** *New Yorker* 5 May 45/3 An artist-in-residence at WNET's Television Laboratory and a consultant on television to the Rockefeller Foundation. **1976** C. BERMANT *Coming Home* I. v. 70 A few weeks later, a Jewish boy was billeted on us... I'm not sure if I welcomed it, for I had begun to enjoy my role as Jew in residence. **1979** *Guardian* 27 June 8/3 (Advt.), Photographer in Residence required... There are no specific teaching commitments but the photographer will be expected to participate in the life of the centre and be available to students and others on an informal basis. **1980** *Early Music Gaz.* Apr. 8 (Advt.), Lessons in solo and ensemble performance are conducted by an artist-in-residence each semester.

†**3.** Continuance in some course or action. *with residence*, with insistence. *Obs.*

c **1430** LYDG. *Min. Poems* (Percy Soc.) 164 The chief of foolis,..And able in his foly to hold residence. *c* **1450** *St. Cuthbert* (Surtees) 862 In þe bischope presence þus cuthbert prayed with residence. *a* **1602** W. PERKINS *Cases Consc.* (1619) 23 Men are not simply condemned for their particular sinnes, but for their continuance and residence in them. **1609** TOURNEUR *Funeral Poem Sir F. Vere* 137 And in the due performance of her Lawes His favours had their constant residence.

†**4. a.** *to make residence*, to stay at or in a place for a certain time. *Sc. Obs.*

c **1470** *Gol. & Gaw.* 503 In his avne presence Heir sall I mak residence. *c* **1500** *Lancelot* 670 If that I mak abid or resydens In to o place langar than o nycht. **1571** *Reg. Privy Council Scot.* II. 81 The Lordis of Counsell makis na residence in Sessioun for deciding upoun the saidis lettres of advocatioun. **1596** DALRYMPLE tr. *Leslie's Hist. Scot.* IX. 206 Quhen the king thrie days thair had maid recidence.., the fourt day he returnis quhairfra he cam.

†**b.** *without residence*, without delay or tarrying. *Obs. rare.*

c **1500** *Lancelot* 2359 Sche gart bryng, withouten Recidens, With grete effere this knycht to hir presens. **1560** ROLLAND *Crt. Venus* II. 976 Thay bad me pas withoutin residence, Vnto the ten Sibillais of science. **1584-7** GREENE *Carde of Fancie* Wks. (Grosart) IV. 24 He trauailed by the space of seauen weekes without anie residence, vntill he came to a Citie called Barutta.

5. a. The place where one resides; one's dwelling-place; the abode *of* a person (esp. one of some rank or distinction). (*of*) *no fixed residence* = (*of*) *no fixed abode* s.v. ABODE *sb.*[1] 5. ? *Obs.*

[**1508** KENNEDIE *Flyting w. Dunbar* 424 Quhen that the ravyns sall ryve out bath thine ene, And on the rattis salbe thy residence.] **1595** SHAKS. *John* II. i. 284 All those soules, That to their euerlasting residence, Before the dew of euening fall, shall fleete. **1634** MILTON *Comus* 947 Not many furlongs thence Is your Fathers residence. **1654-66** EARL ORRERY *Parthen.* (1676) 31 That place, the then Residence of Altezeera. **1705** ADDISON *Italy* 251 Caprea,..a Place that had been the Retirement of Augustus for some time, and the Residence of Tiberius for several Years. **1781** GIBBON *Decl. & F.* xxxi. III. 199 One thousand seven hundred and eighty houses, the residence of wealthy and honourable citizens. **1848** W. H. BARTLETT *Egypt to Pal.* iv. (1879) 67 His residence was both Palace and Temple. **1859** *Times* 1 Feb. 9/5 Robert Murry, 35, and Johanna Murry, 28, described as husband and wife, and travelling ventriloquists of no fixed residence, were charged with attacking and robbing Robert Hobbs on the highway of a purse containing a 5*l*. Bank of England note. **1863** W. HARDMAN *Let.* (1925) ? 24 Aug. 72 His books were curious, inasmuch as the customers had no fixed residences. **1897** MARY KINGSLEY *W. Africa* 513 Every dangerous place in West Africa is regarded as the residence of a god.

transf. **1593** SHAKS. *Rich. II*, II. i. 119 Chasing the Royall blood With fury, from his natiue residence. **1615** CROOKE *Body of Man* 429 The vpper Region or the Head wherein the soule hath her Residence of estate, guarded by the Sences. **1667** MILTON *P.L.* VIII. 346 Understand the same Of Fish within thir watry residence. **1863** E. V. NEALE *Anal. Th. & Nat.* 196 The regulative will, or soul,..has no special residence within the brain.

b. A dwelling, abode, house, *esp.* one of a superior kind; a mansion.

1603 SHAKS. *Meas. for M.* V. i. 13 It deserues..A forted residence 'gainst the tooth of time. **1784** COWPER *Task* v. 157 Nor wanted aught within, That royal residence might well befit, For grandeur or for use. **1794** MRS. RADCLIFFE *Myst. Udolpho* i, Considerable additions were necessary to make it a comfortable family residence. **1844** H. H. WILSON *Brit. India* II. 365 A residence was assigned him at Bithur.

†**c.** A settlement (of traders). *Obs. rare.*

1634 SIR T. HERBERT *Trav.* 36 At the North-west end the English Merchants haue a residence. [**1890** GROSS *Gild Merch.* I. 156 In 1687 one of the principal 'residences' or marts of the Company was at Hamburgh.]

d. = RESIDENCY 3.

1889 *Dublin Rev.* Jan. 166 The inhabitants dress differently in this residence from what they do in other parts of Java.

e. [tr. Russ. RESIDENTURA.] A group or organization of intelligence agents in a foreign country.

1969 H. H. COOPER *Cave with Two Exits* I. 69 In Rome he was met by a young man from the Residence... The Resident himself..was extremely secure... His cover was strictly diplomatic.

6. *fig.* The (*or* a) seat *of* power, liberty, etc.

1642 MILTON *Apol. Smect.* Wks. 1851 III. 297 To call that inviolable residence of justice and liberty, by such an odious name. **1781** COWPER *Truth* 387 The blest residence of truth divine. **1789** BRAND *Hist. Newcastle* II. 218 The free cities of Italy; the very early residences of trade and manufactures. **1827** SCOTT *Napoleon* xlvi. Wks. 1870 XIII. 138 The residence of the supreme authority,..the..Junta.

7. a. The time during which one resides in or at a place.

1683 DRYDEN *Life Plutarch* in *P.'s Lives* (1700) I. 66 He was intrusted also with the management of publick affairs in the empire during his residence in the metropolis. **1777** W. DALRYMPLE *Trav. Sp. & Port.* cli, There was no representation during my residence. **1841** MYERS *Cath. Th.* III. 67 The Jews lost..their spoken language..during their comparatively short residence in Babylon.

b. A period of residing; a stay.

1686 tr. *Chardin's Trav. Persia* 378 During a residence of four months that I stay'd at Court. **1857** GEN. NICHOLSON in Smiles *Charac.* iii. (1876) 73, I was always the better for a residence with him and his wife. **1871** HARE *Walks in Rome* I. Introd. 11 It must not..be supposed that one short residence at Rome will be sufficient to make a foreigner acquainted with all its varied treasures.

8. *attrib.*, as ***residence address, house, part, permit, room, time***, etc.; **residence city** [tr. G. *residenzstadt*], a seat of a royal or princely court; cf. RESIDENZ; **residence counsellor** *U.S.*, a psychiatric adviser attached to a residential block in a university; **residence général** [tr. F. *résidence générale*], the official residency of the senior French representative in a French protectorate.

1890 'MARK TWAIN' *Lett. to Publishers* (1967) 264, I do not know your *residence-address or Whitford's. **1961** L. MUMFORD *City in Hist.* xiii. 386 The chief new cities built from the sixteenth to the nineteenth century were '*residence cities' for kings and princes, like Versailles, Karlsruhe, and Potsdam. **1973** *Pennsylvania Voice* 10 Oct. 5/1 A *residence counselor who has been dealing with a student may feel that he is not properly equipped to help the student resolve his problem. **1955** *Times* 9 May 8/4 The crowd..had tried to break into the *residence-general. **1838** *Act 1 & 2 Vict.* c. 23 §7 Where the *Residence House.., and Appurtenances belonging to any Benefice shall be inconveniently situate [etc.]. **1889** *Cent. Mag.* July 374/2 The *residence parts of the town. **1962** *Guardian* 14 Aug. 1/7 Bishop Roseveare was given the letter informing of the cancellation of his *residence permit. **1977** *Times* 16 Apr. 12/7 Herr Klee got a job..which clinched his residence permit. **1887** *Pall Mall G.* 19 July 16/1 The *residence rooms will be so designed and furnished as [etc.]. **1895** *Outing* XXVII. 183/2 She led him by the most imposing buildings and through the finest *residence streets. **1962** A. BATTERSBY *Guide to Stock Control* viii. 76 With an average stock of 200 tons and annual sales of 1,200 tons, the *residence time is 2 months. The more commonly used 'turnover' is 6 times a year, which is the reciprocal of the residence time. **1969** *Gloss. Terms Vacuum Technol. (B.S.I.)* 13 *Residence time*, the average time for which a molecule is bound to a surface in a state of sorption. **1977** *Sci. Amer.* May 23/2 The period of time a particular amount of water spends in its cycle is termed its residence time... Deep in the oceans the residence time of a body of water may be more than 1,000 years. **1978** *Nature* 20 July 246/1 The concept of oceanic residence time has been used widely in marine chemistry; element residence times range from 10^8 to < 100 yr, and provide a useful measure of the reactivity of an element in the ocean. **1883** *Cent. Mag.* July 335/2 Titusville ..is the favourite *residence town of prosperous brokers.

† **residence**, *sb.*² *Obs.* Also 6 resyd-, 7 recid-. [ad. L. type **resīdentia*, f. *resīdĕre* RESIDE *v.*²: see -ENCE.]

1. That which settles as a deposit; sediment. (Very common in 17th c.)

1541 ELYOT *Cast. Helthe* IV. i, Whan there appereth in the uryne a resydence lyght and whyte. **1594** PLAT *Jewell-ho.* 32, I may not here omit to commend the..residence and groundes of all Channels,..Rivers and Ditches. **1646** SIR T. BROWNE *Pseud. Ep.* (1650) 132 Wherein beside a terreous residence some salt is also found. **1684-5** BOYLE *Min. Waters* 71 The Spontaneous residence, if I may so call it, that the Liquor lets fall by meer standing.

pl. **1662** MERRETT tr. *Neri's Art of Glass* xxxviii, Powder the dregs and residences of the Aqua-fortis. **1684-5** BOYLE *Min. Waters* 90 To take notice of the Residences of many of the Mineral Waters of France.

b. The residuum or deposit left after any chemical process.

1560 WHITEHORNE *Ord. Souldiours* (1588) 30b, If the pouder bee good, you shall see them all to fire at ones; so that there shall be no residence remaining. **1658** R. WHITE tr. *Digby's Powd. Symp.* (1660) 122 Cause it to be boyled untill it come to an evaporation and see its residence.

c. Remains, leavings. *rare*⁻¹.

c **1550** H. RHODES *Bk. Nurture* in *Babees Bk.* (1868) 80 Put you your trenchour in the same, and all your resydence.

2. The settling of sediment in liquids.

1600 SURFLET *Countrie Farme* VI. iv. 734 Vntill such time as the earth haue made his perfect residence and setling in the bottome of the glasse. **1626** BACON *Sylva* §302 Separation..is wrought by Weight; as in the ordinary Residence or Settlement of Liquors. **1684** tr. *Bonet's Merc. Compit.* VIII. 303 Boil the Colature, defæcated by residence to half.

† **'residence**, *v. Obs. rare.* [f. RESIDENCE *sb.*¹] (Meaning obscure.)

1608 W. SCLATER *Malachy* (1650) 47 Wherein the Prophet even residenceth the speeches of these hypocriticall Jews. **1611** —— *Key* (1629) 229 He shewes that these things were, in many, but vaine bragges; residencing their vaine boasting fitly to the fashion of our people.

† **resi'dencer, -ier**, *a.* and *sb. Obs. rare.* [a. AF. *residencer* (1430 in Godef.), ad. med.L. *residentiārius*: see RESIDENTIARY¹.]

A. *adj.* Residentiary. (Also in *pl.* form.)

1428 in *Surtees Misc.* (1890) 7 Maistre John Selow chanon residencier of ye kyrk of Yorke. *c* **1460** J. RUSSELL *Bk. Nurture* in *Babees Bk.* (1868) 189 Alle prechers residencers and persones þat ar greable. **1486** *Lichfield Gild Ord.* (E.E.T.S.) 18 Ioan Herwood and..George Radclyf, somtime chanons residencyeres in the seid cathedral church.

B. *sb.* **1.** A canon, incumbent, etc., in residence.

1522 *Stat. Ord. Garter* xx, The Dean or Register, or the most ancient Residencer of the said College. **1628** EARLE *Microcosm., Singing-men* (Arb.) 52 Their humanity is a leg to the Residencer.

2. A resident representative.

1541 WYATT *Declaration* Wks. (1816) 283 A Prince were as good send naked letters, and to receive naked letters, as to be at charge for residencers.

residenciarie, -y, obs. ff. RESIDENTIARY.

residency ('rɛzɪdənsɪ). [f. as RESIDENCE *sb.*¹: see -ENCY.]

1. a. = RESIDENCE *sb.*¹ in various senses. Also *attrib.* Now chiefly *N.Amer.*

1579 FENTON *Guicciard.* I. 1 It was..greatly honored.. with the seate and residencie of the throne of Religion. *Ibid.* 13 Constantinople, the soueraigne residencie of that Empire. **1604** *Const. & Canons Eccl.* xliv, All those..shal after the dayes of their Residencie..presently repaire to their Benefices. **1654** COKAINE *Dianea* II. 114 Constancy may have residency in all things but the minds of lovers. **1670** MAYNWARING *Vita Sana* xvi. 148 Fear..chaseth the spirits to and fro from their residency and faculties. **1966** *Publ. Amer. Dial. Soc. 1964* XLII. 35 *Shanty-..Irish*, i.e., those who remain in the lower-class communities near the center of the city (or, irrespective of residency, preserve the social traits of the shanty Irish). **1970** *Daily Colonist* (Victoria, B.C.) 2 Apr. 30/1 The controversial [abortion] measure contains no residency requirement and would allow a pregnancy to be terminated at any time. **1981** *Times* 16 Feb. 15/7 Degrees for people who want to be more effective and secure in their Jobs or Professions... No residency required. (Advt. by an Amer. university.)

† **b.** *Eccl.* = RESIDENCE *sb.*¹ 2 a. *Obs.*

1590 *Humble Motion with Submiss.* 27 There wanteth residensy in many able men; there is no practise of preching in many resident. *c* **1613** *Soc. Condit. People Anglesey* 55 Of these that keep true residency, some keep indifferent houses, others deserve no great commendation. **1651** N. BACON *Disc. Govt. Eng.* II. xxviii. (1739) 139 Residency, and Non-residency, was a Theme formerly learned from the Canon Law, in which, as also in the thing it self, the Clergy were the only skilful men.

c. Of a musician or a band: the state of being permanently or regularly engaged at a club, etc.

1966 *Melody Maker* 7 May 5/3 Colin Smith..has left to take up a residency at London's Georgian Room. **1968** *Ibid.* 30 Nov. 6/1 The Nice..used to have a residency there. **1971** *Ibid.* 4 Sept. 21 She moved back to Chicago and played long residencies there..as a pianist vocalist. **1975** *Evening Herald* (Dublin) 8 May 12/4 (Advt.), *Popular vocalist*..seeks position with musicians..; preference for residency in lounge.

2. a. The official residence of a representative of the Governor-general (formerly the East India Company) at an Indian native court. Also *transf.* (in sense of RESIDENT *sb.* 2 d) and *attrib.* Now only *Hist.*

1800 *Asiatic Ann. Reg.* II. 19/1 The revenues and charges of Fort Marlbro', the chief Residency of Bencoolen. **1845** STOCQUELER *Handbk. Brit. India* (1854) 306 'The Residency'..containing the establishment of the Company's Resident at the court of his Highness the Nizam. **1877** *Scribner's Mag.* Sept. 601/2 We steam slowly along, past the English Residency with its beautiful gardens. **1958** L. VAN DER POST *Lost World of Kalahari* v. 90, I spent the evening and night with the Resident and his wife..in the ample Residency. **1980** J. HONE *Flowers of Forest* I. 8 The annual reception for the Queen's Birthday at the old British Residency on the Nile.

attrib. **1844** H. H. WILSON *Brit. India* II. 238 The Mahrattas entered the Residency grounds. **1971** R. RUSSELL tr. *Ahmad's Shore & Wave* xv. 159, I once met Lord Mountbatten myself in Kashmir at a Residency lunch.

b. = RESIDENCE *sb.*¹ 5 e.

1970 K. BENTON *Sole Agent* xviii. 199 [He is]..supplied by the Soviet Illegal Residency here, in Lisbon, to help Rogov to get rid of the body. **1977** 'J. LE CARRÉ' *Hon. Schoolboy* iii. 53 What did he do up there..his networks blown to smithereens? His foreign residencies, his reptile fund frozen solid by the Treasury—they meant his operational accounts..and not a friend in Whitehall or Washington to call his own? **1981** J. SIMPSON *Moscow Requiem* II. vi. 177 The KGB resident in Riyadh..made his last radio contact with the KGB Residency in Aden.

3. An administrative division in the Dutch East Indies. Also *attrib.*

1814 RAFFLES *Java* (1817) I. 289 In the different residencies were provincial courts, styled *landraads*. **1861** J. W. B. MONEY *Java* I. 197 As president of the landraad, and as judge of the residency court. **1863** *Chambers's Encycl.* V. 691/2 The island is divided into East, West, and Middle Java, containing 22 subdivisions, called Residencies.

4. *N. Amer.* The position or station of a resident (RESIDENT *sb.*¹ 3); the period during which one holds this position.

1924 *Mod. Hospital* XXIII. 422/1 Residencies should also be offered in general hospitals. **1933** *Southern Med. Jrnl.* XXVI. 773/2, I am not in sympathy with the prolonged residency extending over more than two years. **1949** G. D. WOLF *Physician's Business* (ed. 3) i. 10 A promising young doctor, following a year's internship, could receive an assistant residency for two years. *Ibid.*, The ideal residency is one in which all phases of the specialty are stressed. **1958** F. G. SLAUGHTER *Daybreak* I. i. 9 They were also competing for a residency on the Neurosurgical Service—a vitally important stepping-stone for an ambitious doctor on the last lap of his training. **1975** R. H. RIMMER *Premar Experiments* i. 66 I've got a friend who's an MD... He's doing his residency at Boston City Hospital. **1977** *Washington Post* 24 May 1/2 Georgetown University Medical School and Providence Hospital have announced their joint development of a residency program in..general, or family, practice. **1979** *Sci. Amer.* Oct. 16/3 After an internship and residency at the Hospital of the University of Pennsylvania he was Special Projects Associate in epidemiology at the Mayo Graduate School of Medicine in Rochester, Minn.

residens(i)ary, obs. forms of RESIDENTIARY.

resident ('rɛzɪdənt), *a.* and *sb.*¹ Also 5-6 **resydent** (5 **-dentt**), **residente**, 6 **reasident**. [ad. L. *resident-em*, pres. pple. of *residēre* to RESIDE: cf. F. *résident* sb. (13th c.), Sp., Pg., and It. *residente*, It. *risedente*.]

A. *adj.* **1.** Residing, dwelling, or having an abode in a place. **a.** In predicative use.

1382 WYCLIF *2 Macc.* xii. 2 These that dwelten, or wern resident, Tymothe, and Appollonye. **1423** JAS. I *Kingis Q.* cxv, Say to the men that there bene resident, How long think thay to stand in my disdeyne. *c* **1485** *Digby Myst.* III. 467 We xal do your intente, in thys place to be resydent whyle þat ȝe be absent. **1530-1** *Act 22 Hen. VIII*, c. 14 He or she..shall nat be taken out of the saintuary, wherein the same person shall then be resydent. *a* **1592** GREENE *Orpharion* Wks. (Grosart) XII. 13 Tell mee whether Venus is resident about this mount of Erecinus, or no. **1634** SIR T. HERBERT *Trav.* 19 In no other part are those Birds resident. **1686** tr. *Chardin's Trav. Persia* 40 The Christian Princes that were then resident at the Port. **1726** AYLIFFE *Parergon* 15 He is not said to be resident in a Place, who comes thither with a Purpose of retiring immediately from thence. **1792** CHIPMAN *Rep.* (1871) 25 D. was resident at Bennington, but not an inhabitant. **1860** MOTLEY *Netherl.* i. (1868) I. 5 The inhabitants of each [country], whether resident in France.. or Flanders.

fig. **1784** COWPER *Task* IV. 594 Authority herself not seldom sleeps, Through resident, and witness of the wrong. **1876** J. WEISS *Wit, Hum. Shaks.* v. 179 Ophelia..is always more resident in his soul than maintained within a palace.

b. In attributive use.

1817 *Parl. Deb.* 1343/2 He considered resident country gentlemen the greatest blessing of this country. **1845** STOCQUELER *Handbk. Brit. India* (1854) 134 Its resident population does not much exceed two hundred and twenty thousand, comprised within the..limits of the city.

c. Of animals or birds: Remaining in one place or country throughout the year; non-migratory.

1828 FLEMING *Hist. Brit. Anim.* p. xiii, The Resident Animals are such as can accommodate themselves to all the changes of this variable climate. **1856** KANE *Arct. Expl.* I. xxxi. 427 The same sagacity that has taught them the habits of the resident animals. **1899** EVANS *Birds* 17 There are many Birds which, though resident as species, are migratory as individuals.

2. a. Staying in or at a place in discharge of some duty or in compliance with some regulation. (Cf. RESIDENCE *sb.*¹ 2.)

1426 AUDELAY *Poems* 33 Curatus resident thai schul be And ald houshold oponly. **1456** SIR G. HAYE *Law Arms* (S.T.S.) 146 Wagis are nocht ordanyt to be gevin to persounis nocht resident. **1538** STARKEY *England* I. iv. 133 A nother yl custume, that prestys be not resydent apon theyr bunfycys. **1560** DAUS tr. *Sleidane's Comm.* 390 That every man be resident in his own church, and that eche man shuld have one benefice. **1617** MORYSON *Itin.* II. 131, I am come to Kilkenny..without any one Commander or Captaine of the Army, hauing left them all with commandement to be resident on their charge. **1669** STURMY *Mariner's Mag.*, *Penalties & Forfeitures* 8 If any Customer, Comptroller, or Searcher be not resident upon his Place and Office. *a* **1790** WARTON in *Boswell* an. 1754, There was only one other Fellow of Pembroke now resident. **1800** COLQUHOUN *Comm. Thames* 200 A Marine Police..under the particular direction of the Superintending and Resident Magistrate. **1803** *Med. Jrnl.* IX. 195 Mr. Wachsell, the resident surgeon. **1812** *Laws & Ordinances City of New-York* 202 It shall be the duty of the said resident physician and health commissioner, to meet daily at the health office, from the thirty-first day of May to the first day of October. **1844** [see *grave-trap* s.v. GRAVE *sb.*¹ 6]. **1874** *Chambers's Encycl.* V. 544/1 Resident political agents are appointed by the British government at the courts of the native princes. **1899** SOMERVILLE & 'ROSS' *Some Experiences Irish R.M.* i. 10 You wouldn't meet a Christian out of doors, unless it was..a resident magistrate. **1902** *U.S. Laws & Statutes* (1903) XXXII. I. 694 With the first meeting of the Philippine legislature..there shall be chosen, by the said legislature.. two resident commissioners to the United States. **1919** *Bull. Johns Hopkins Hospital* XXX. 191/2 The assistant residents, even those who did not become chief resident physicians, often continued in office for several years. **1931** V. PALMER *Separate Lives* 40 I'm a Resident Magistrate now, you know. One of the biggest stations in the Territory. **1952** GRANVILLE *Dict. Theatrical Terms* 151 *Resident manager*, the manager of the theatre as distinct from the acting manager of a visiting company. He handles all the local business. **1962** PLANO & GREENBERG *Amer. Polit. Dict.* iii. 38 *Resident commissioner*, a delegate elected by the people of a territory to represent them in the House of Representatives. He may speak in the House and serve on committees, but he may not vote... Only Puerto Rico has a resident commissioner. **1963** J. JOESTEN *They call it Intelligence* II. viii. 73 Abel..held the post of 'resident officer'... His job was to recruit and organize local spies. **1974** P. GORE-BOOTH *With Great Truth & Respect* 364 On 16 May 1967, at about 6.00 in the morning, my bedside telephone rang. The Resident Clerk at the Foreign Office said that President Nasser had ordered the United Nations Expeditionary Force to leave the Egyptian frontier with Israel. **1976** *National Observer* (U.S.)

22 May 22/1 The resident correspondent can suggest people to interview. **1977** *Belfast Tel.* 19 Jan. 3/9 The resident band ..will be George Chambers and the Apex.

†**b.** Continually present *in* an assembly. *Obs.*

1658 OSBORN *Adv. Son* II. xxiii. Wks. (1673) 181 Mr. Hampden, Mr. Pim, &c. were resident in all Parliaments, their age gave them opportunity to assist in.

3. Of qualities, powers, etc.: Abiding, present, inherent, prevalent, established.

1525 LD. BERNERS *Froiss.* II. cxxix. [cxxv.] 367 It wyll be very harde to make peace in that place, where as great hatered and warre is resydent. **1576** FLEMING *Panopl. Epist.* 44 Let this thought be alwayes resident in your mind. **1610** HEALEY *St. Aug. Citie God* (1620) 225 One ignorant of him would not have thought any effeminat sparke resident in him. **1668** CULPEPPER & COLE *Barthol. Anat.* II. vi. 101 The Pulse, which is..raised by the influent Blood, and the Pulsifick or Pulsative faculty, there resident. **1791** PAINE *Rights of Man* (ed. 4) 9 It exists in the whole;..it is a right resident in the nation. **1831** BREWSTER *Optics* xvi. 138 Some have thought that the particles of light are..turned aside by the forces resident in the particles. **1863** BP. EWING *Past. Let.* 25 There the belief and practice we adhere to is most fully resident.

4. a. Of things: Situated, lying. ***resident site*** (see quot. 1610).

1571 DIGGES *Pantom.* IV. xxv. Gg iij b, This Figure also receyueth the Cube, with his 8 solide angles residente in the 8 centers of his Hexagonall playnes. **1610** W. FOLKINGHAM *Art of Survey* II. i. 47 Situation may be said to be Resident, and Respicient. Resident Site depends vpon the setling, laying and lying of the grounds. **1695** WOODWARD *Nat. Hist. Earth* III. i. (1723) 130 The Water..of the Globe, as well that resident in it, as that which floats upon it. **1971** *Nature* 12 Mar. 91/1 The non-polar amino-acids, for example in myoglobin and haemoglobin, are resident in the interior of the protein molecule, out of contact with the aqueous environment.

†**b.** Remaining still; firm, abiding. *Obs. rare.*

1653 JER. TAYLOR *Serm. for Year* I. xi. 139 The watry pavement is not stable and resident like a rock.

B. *sb.* **1. a.** One who resides permanently in a place; sometimes *spec.* applied to inhabitants of the better class. Also, a guest staying one or more nights at a hotel or boarding-house.

1487 *Rolls of Parlt.* VI. 404/1 To any Inhabitauntes, residentes or dwellers in any Cite. **1833** HT. MARTINEAU *Loom & Lugger* I. iii. 35 It was yet more that he had been a long resident with his family. **1844** H. H. WILSON *Brit. India* I. 523 It was agreed that no persons, except those in the Company's employ, should be allowed to go to India as residents. **1890** *Spectator* 5 Apr., In Ireland..'residents' will soon grow as numerous as in the thinner 'residential districts' of Great Britain. **1956** M. STEWART *Wildfire at Midnight* xii. 103 A little sitting-room beside the residents' lounge. **1969** 'L. BRUCE' *Death with Blue Ribbon* vii. 71 Carolus ordered three doubles. He had stayed in the Residents' Lounge too long.

fig. **1830** HERSCHEL *Study Nat. Phil.* III. iii. (1851) 289 The pursuits of the enlightened resident or traveller in every department of science. **1865** MOZLEY *Mirac* iii. 70 What can be..a more ghostly resident in nature than the sense of right and wrong?

b. A resident incumbent.

1812 *Chron.* in *Ann. Reg.* 85 The number of non-residents exceeds the number of residents. **1873** SIR R. PHILLIMORE *Eccles. Law* II. 1145 The bishop shall provide, that in every church there shall be one resident.

c. A bird belonging to a species that does not migrate but is found all the year round in a particular area.

1896 KIRKALDY & POLLARD tr. *Boas's Text Bk. Zool.* 465 Woodpeckers..are 'residents', or wander about in a limited locality. **1920** H. F. WITHERBY *Pract. Handbk. Brit. Birds* I. 18 After nesting our residents [*sc.* rooks] are subject to partial and irregular movements—some probably emigrating to Continent. **1978** *Ibis* CXX. 496 In West Africa..residents and migrants overlap throughout the dry season.

2. a. A diplomatic representative, inferior in rank to an ambassador, residing at a foreign court. Now only *Hist.* (Common in 17th c.)

1650 MILTON *Lett. State* Wks. 1851 VIII. 268 They..give out threatning language in a most despiteful manner against our Resident. **1654** WHITELOCKE *Swed. Ambassy* (1772) II. 231 It might be supposed, that..he should understand the difference between a resident and an ambassador extraordinary. **1739** GRAY *Let. to Mother* 19 Dec., Mr. Mann, the resident, had sent his servant to meet us at the gates. **1761** HUME *Hist. Eng.* II. xliv. 494 Sir Henry Nevil, the English resident in France. **1849** MACAULAY *Hist. Eng.* vi. II. 101 The resident of the Elector Palatine..fitted up a chapel in Lime Street.

transf. **1663** COWLEY *Cutter Coleman St.* I. vi, He's shrewdly wrong'd if he be n't Cromwel's Agent for all the Taverns between Kings-street and the Devil at Temple-bar, indeed he's a kind o' Resident in 'em. **1684** OTWAY *Atheist* III. i, You keep Company with the Devil's Resident.

b. A representative of the (†East India Company or) Governor-general of India residing at a (†commercial station or) native court. Now only *Hist.* **c.** The governor of a residency in the Dutch East Indies. Now only *Hist.* **d.** An agent or representative of the British government in a semi-independent native territory. Now only *Hist.*

1786 BURKE *Art. agst. W. Hastings* Wks. 1842 II. 108 The mischiefs likely to happen to the said country from the establishment of a resident. **1793** HODGES *Trav. India* 43 A factory belonging to the English company, where a commercial resident is constantly stationed. **1814** RAFFLES *Java* (1817) I. 292 In criminal [cases], the jurisdiction and authority of the Resident has been considerably extended. **1839** T. J. NEWBOLD *Pol. & Statistical Acct. Straits of Malacca* I. iv. 126 The public property there was estimated ..by the British resident. **1844** H. H. WILSON *Brit. India* II. 273 The Resident consented..to the Raja's request for a suspension of hostilities. **1861** J. W. B. MONEY *Java* I. 196 The resident is the first local European authority. **1863** *Chambers's Encycl.* V. 545/1 The Administration of the Native States is generally vested in an hereditary..prince, ..controlled in some degree by a British resident. **1884** *Nonconf. & Indep.* 29 May 529/2 The Resident in Bechuanaland is the right man in the right place. **1958** [see RESIDENCY 2 a]. **1965** A. NICOL *Truly Married Woman* 88 Ride to the white man who is Resident. **1971** R. RUSSELL tr. *Ahmad's Shore & Wave* i. 13 The British Resident was confiding to the Finance Minister his distrust of the Prime Minister.

3. *N. Amer.* A medical graduate who has completed an internship and is engaged in specialized practice under supervision in a hospital, usu. as training for independent specialization. Also *attrib.* Cf. REGISTRAR 3.

1892 *Rep. Johns Hopkins Hospital* III. 21 Dr. William Osler [gave]..Books for Resident's Reading Room. **1914** *Mod. Hospital* II. 30/2 The sixth floor is primarily for residents' quarters. The chief resident will have his study, bed room, and private bath. **1931** E. G. REID *Great Physician* vi. 116 Long term residents took the place of the usual short term internship. His first Resident Physician had under him three assistant residents. **1938** [see INTERN *sb.*]. **1970** *Globe & Mail* (Toronto) 26 Sept. B8/4 (Advt.), Hospital approved for interne and resident training, nursing school, [etc.]. **1977** 'E. TREVOR' *Theta Syndrome* vi. 85 Never..disturb the senior resident when he's on his rounds, unless the place is on fire.

4. [tr. Russ. *rezidént.*] An intelligence agent (in a foreign country). Cf. also REZIDENT.

1963 'J. LE CARRÉ' *Spy who came in from Cold* viii. 74 The Resident in a particular country would make a requisition. .. The Resident could draw it [*sc.* money] himself and hand it to the agent. **1968** A. DIMENT *Bang Bang Birds* v. 63 Of course this Agency has a resident in Stockholm. **1975** *Times* 16 Dec. 7/5 Herr Guillaume soon became a 'resident'—the head of a group of spies.

†**resident,** *sb.*[2] *Obs. rare.* [ad. L. *resīdent-*, ppl. stem of *resīdēre* to RESIDE *v.*[2]]

1. Deposit or sediment.

1625 HART *Anat. Ur.* I. v. 47 The next vrine was of a pale straw coloured yellow, with some whitish residents. **1655** CULPEPPER, etc. *Riverius* I. ii. 13 Shaking it..that it may have some of the fecies or residents of the Pouder in the bottom to make it more strong. **1666** BOYLE *Formes & Qual.* 129 As much as one Ounce of dry Residents, whether Saline or Earthy.

2. Residue, remainder.

a **1610** HEALEY *Cebes* (1636) 130 After a little toile, the whole resident of their life shalbe topt with..tranquility.

resi'dental, *a. U.S.* [f. RESIDENT *a.* or *sb.*[1] + -AL[1].] Residential.

1875 H. JAMES *Transatlantic Sketches* 303 The beautiful residental apartments of the Pitti Palace. **1884** *American* VIII. 238 The Pope has decided to create a residental archbishopric at Carthage.

†**residen'tarian.** *Obs. rare*$^{-1}$. [f. as prec. + -ARIAN.] One given to remaining at table.

1680 T. LAWSON *Mite into Treas.* 23 The daily Feaster, such as the Residentarians, whose Legs can scarce bear about his gross Corpulent Body.

†**residentary,** *a. Obs. rare.* [f. as prec. + -ARY.] = RESIDENTIARY *a.*[1]

1686 J. S[ERGEANT] *Hist. Monast. Convent.* 112 The Cardinals Residentaries in the Court of Rome. *a* **1693** *Urquhart's Rabelais* III. l. 404 Some Residentary Kings in Capadocia.

residenter ('rɛzɪdɛntə(r), *Sc.* rɛzɪ'dɛntə(r)). Also 5 resedenter, 7 recidentor. [f. RESIDENT.]

†**1.** *Eccl.* A residentiary. *Obs. rare.*

1455 *Test. Ebor.* (Surtees) II. 191 Sir John Bernyngham, tresorer of York mynster, and Maister John Marsshall, resedenter of the same mynster. **1719** *Brit. Compend.* (ed. 2) 239 The present Dean, and Residenter of St. Paul's.

2. *Sc.* and *U.S.* A resident, inhabitant. ***old residenter***, a pioneer in the U.S.

1678 SIR G. MACKENZIE *Crim. Laws Scot.* II. viii. §i, The Justice-deputs were not ordinar Residenters in Town. **1746–7** *Act 20 Geo. II*, c. 43 §3 The inhabitants and residenters within the same. **1765** *Phil. Trans.* LV. 194 The total of residenters..being 15,734. **1812** BRACKENRIDGE *Views Louisiana* (1814) 127 They were ceded by the Spanish government, as an appendage to the possession of every residenter in the village. **1827** *Western Monthly Rev.* I. 70 Hence arose a feud and a collision of authorities between the old and the new 'residenters'. **1844** H. STEPHENS *Bk. Farm* I. 221 The obligations incumbent on him as a residenter of the parish. **1875** W. MCILWRAITH *Guide Wigtown.* 57 In the memory of some not very aged residenters. **1880** W. H. PATTERSON *Gloss. Words Antrim & Down* 82 *Residenter, sb.* an old inhabitant. **1898** E. N. WESTCOTT *David Harum* 253, I ain't what ye might call an old residenter. **1967** *Buchan Observer* 5 Sept. 7 Residenters..are becoming greatly concerned. **1975** *New Yorker* 29 Dec. 36/3 Well, here's an old guy in the audience—an old residenter, that's what they called them—with a long grey beard.

transf. **1882** *Chamb. Jrnl.* XIX. 89 Nor did the birds come merely as stray visitors, but as actual residenters. **1921** H. GUTHRIE-SMITH *Tutira* xxii. 212 Such residenters are attracted..by the influx of sparrows, rats, and mice. **1971** M. TAK *Truck Talk* 130 *Residenter*, any old tractor still used over the road.

residential (rɛzɪ'dɛnʃəl), *a.*[1] and *sb.* [See RESIDENCE *sb.*[1] and -AL[1]. So Sp. *residencial*, It. *-enziale*.]

A. *adj.* **1. a.** Serving or used as a residence; in which one resides.

1654 GAYTON *Pleas. Notes* IV. 213 Let him see The Residential Court of Chastity. **1690** NORRIS *Beatitudes* (1692) 163 To his fix'd Dwelling and Residential Abode among us. **1718** J. FOX *Wanderer* No. 8. 43 The residential Palace of a Monarch, beautify'd with a delightful Park. **1740** WATERLAND *Regeneration* 13 In Baptism, the same Spirit fixes, as it were, his Dwelling, or residential Abode. **1886** *Fortn. Rev.* XXXIX. 24 It [*sc.* a medical college for women] has no residential hall, nor is it desirable perhaps that it should have any. **1910** *Bradshaw's Railway Guide* Apr. 1009 Imperial Hotel. First-class family and residential. **1923** W. J. LOCKE *Moordius & Co.* xxiii. 308 An untidy boarding-house in Torrington Square, Bloomsbury, which called itself a Residential Hotel. **1943** [see *neighbourhood unit* s.v. NEIGHBOURHOOD 7]. **1960** *Times* 21 Mar. 8/5 Oxford, Cambridge and the other residential universities enjoy special prestige compared with the civic universities. **1963** *Specification & Recommendations for Permanent Residential Caravans* (B.S. 3632) 4 The term 'Permanent residential caravan' means a structure with a wheeled chassis.. designed for use as a permanent dwelling..and so constructed as to be movable by towing or other methods of transport. Hereinafter the term 'residential caravan' will be used for brevity. **1969** *Sunday Times* (Colour Suppl.) 9 Nov. 85/4 The residential towers in flat units will next year house only 400 students. **1977** *Times Educ. Suppl.* 21 Oct. 56/2 (Advt.), Required..a head teacher for this newly opening.. residential school for maladjusted boys of secondary age. **1981** J. CAREY *John Donne* i. 23 The Inns of Court.. operated like residential clubs or hotels.

b. Adapted or suitable for the residence of those belonging to the better class; characterized by houses of a superior kind.

1878 F. S. WILLIAMS *Midl. Railw.* 219 The landowner alleged that the line would injure a considerable residential estate. **1882** *Nature* XXVII. 70 Sixty to be residential districts, and sixty..comparatively poor neighbourhoods. **1900** H. A. JONES *Mrs. Dane's Defence* III. 49 My dear Sir Daniel, we live in a residential neighbourhood..and what possible occupation is there..except to discuss scandal. **1922** JOYCE *Ulysses* 647 A phenomenally beautiful tenor voice like that..could easily..procure for its fortunate possessor..an *entrée* into fashionable houses in the best residential quarters. **1981** J. B. HILTON *Playground of Death* iv. 46 Below was the black tumour of a residential area.

2. Connected with, pertaining or relating to, residence or residences (in general or specific sense).

1856 *Illustr. Lond. News* XXIX. 172/1 It is thought that the locality will be much sought after for villa residences, and thus obtain a residential traffic. **1857** SMILES *Stephenson* (1859) 172 Witnesses were called to prove residential injury which would be caused by the..smoke and fire from the locomotives. **1869** *Bradshaw's Railway Man.* XXI. 298 The moderate advance of rates..did not affect the 'residential' or periodical and season tickets. **1881** *Nation* XXXII. 178 Fixing the residential qualification of voters. **1934** WEBSTER, Residential zone. **1952** *Density of Residential Areas* (Ministry of Housing & Local Govt.) 1/1 The term 'residential density'..signifies the degree of closeness with which dwellings, and hence the people occupying them, are arranged in the residential areas of towns and villages. **1961** E. A. POWDRILL *Vocab. Land Planning* v. 97 The residential zone will become an industrial and commercial zone and so creating [*sic*] new problems. **1974** *Drive* Autumn 110/2 Disc parking and residential parking schemes, plus a maze of one-way streets, make life harder for motorists. **1977** *Age* (Melbourne) 18 Jan. 8/3 Parents doing residential adoptions (i.e. going to the country of the child's origin) are approved by the host country.

3. Of or belonging to a Resident. *rare.*

1885 *Glasgow Her.* 4 Dec. 6/3 A British Resident—or, to speak correctly, a British official endowed with Residential powers, has been established in Mandalay.

B. as *sb.* A residential hotel.

1953 K. TENNANT *Joyful Condemned* xxxvi. 351 Margot took down from Stella the address of the residential where she and Dorsie were staying. **1954** J. SYMONS *Narrowing Circle* xxix. 129 She had a connection with the Gongora Residential. **1973** *Nation Rev.* (Melbourne) 31 Aug. 1450/1 The..premises..have been an inconspicuous residential for the past three years.

†**resi'dential,** *a.*[2] *Obs. rare.* [f. RESIDENT *sb.*[2]] Left as a residuum.

1651 BIGGS *New Disp.* ⁋213 As if the whole heap of evill were taken away at once,..but the good had been residentiall about the parenchymatick Laboratorie of the Liver.

resi'dentially, *adv.* [f. RESIDENTIAL *a.*[1] + -LY[2].] As a residence; according to residence; with the provision of residential accommodation.

1913 *Chambers's Jrnl.* Jan. 51/2 London contains no single palace residentially associated with our long line of sovereigns. **1922** *Daily Mail* 1 Dec. 8 It is sufficiently developed to be comfortable residentially. **1974** *Sci. Amer.* Sept. 125/1 The American high school has all the requisites of an institution designed to promote mating: single males and females are assembled in substantial and equal numbers, are residentially selected for social homogeneity, [etc.]. **1978** *Daily Tel.* 24 July 13/2 The conference was being held residentially at Lambeth.

residentiary (rɛzɪ'dɛnʃərɪ), *sb.* and *a.*[1] Also 6 -sary, -siary, -ciarie, 7 -ciary. [ad. med.L. *residentiārius*: see RESIDENCE *sb.*[1] and -ARY.]

A. *sb.* **1.** An ecclesiastic who is bound to official residence, *esp.* a canon of a cathedral or collegiate church.

c **1525** in Ellis *Orig. Lett.* Ser. III. II. 65 Also Dr Barrye late residenciary of Southwell is deceased. **1570** FOXE *A. & M.* (ed. 2) 1218/1 Last of all came ye queere of Paules, with their residensaries. *c* **1630** RISDON *Surv. Devon* §107 (1810) 109 Being.. residentiaries, their livings be so much the more increased. **1676** MARVELL *Mr. Smirke* 2 They cannot transmit it..to their most Domestick Chaplain, or to the closest Residentiary. **1713** *Guardian* No. 80 ¶4 One of the Vergers came to the Residentiary in waiting. **1766** ENTICK *London* IV. 30 Which aforetime had been a house for a residentiary of St. Paul's. **1837** SYD. SMITH *Wks.* (1850) 633 The Bishop of London says, there were more Residentiaries before the Reformation. **1861** BERESF. HOPE *Eng. Cathedr. 19th C.* 55 What need have the dean and the residentiary.. of any great superfluity of sitting room?

2. One who or that which is resident.

1615 T. ADAMS *Black Devil* 44 The inmate and residentiary of their hearts is that uncleane vulture. **1664** POWER *Exp. Philos.* I. 11 A wise and prudent Animal, and therefore a fit Residentiary in the Court of Kings. **1691** NORRIS *Pract. Disc.* 331 The Stationary Angels that wait upon the Throne of God, the Residentiaries of Heaven. **1825** COLERIDGE *Aids Refl.* (Bohn) I. 324 The residentiary, or the frequent visitor of the favoured spot.

b. *transf.* and *fig.*

c **1620** T. ADAMS *Black Saint* Wks. (1629) 367 Faith, temperance, patience,.. are perpetuall Residentiaries in the Temple of their Soules. **1641** HINDE *J. Bruen* xl. 124 These [Bibles] hee placed to be continuall residentiaries, the bigger in the Parlour, and the lesse in the Hall.

†**3.** A Jesuit house. *Obs. rare*$^{-1}$.

1626 L. OWEN *Spec. Jesuit.* (1629) 29 They haue..eight Seminaries and 1010 Residenciaries.

B. *adj.* **1. a.** ***canon residentiary***, a canon of whom residence is required.

1632 in J. Crosse *York Mus. Festiv.* (1825) App. 2 Precentor and canon residentiary of the same church. **1706** HEARNE *Collect.* 3 Apr. (O.H.S.) I. 217 He..was made Canon Residentiary. **1847** T. DALE (title-p.), The Golden Psalm. Being an Exposition..of Psalm xiv. By the Rev. Thomas Dale, M.A., Canon Residentiary of St. Paul's. **1870** *Daily News* 11 Feb., He was nominated by his father to a canon residentiary in Ely Cathedral.

b. Involving, relating or pertaining to, official residence.

a **1662** HEYLIN *Laud* (1668) 86 A Prebend and Residentiary place in the Cathedral Church at Lincoln. **1721** BAILEY, *Residentiary*, belonging to a Resident. **1841** *Act 4 & 5 Vict.* c. 39 §5 The holding of a Canonry Residentiary, Prebend, or Office. **1886** *N. & Q.* 7th Ser. II. 447/2 Dr. John Taylor died 1766, at his residentiary house.

2. Residing or resident in a place.

1640 HOWELL *Dodona's Gr.* 73 When hee was Residentiarie upon the skirts of the Ampelona. **1658** SLINGSBY *Diary* (1836) 208 Whether he be residentiary in a Wilderness or in the World. **1668** H. MORE *Div. Dial.* I. xix. (1713) 41 The same Christ, who was the Conductor of the Israelites into the Land of Canaan, and the Residentiary Guardian of that People. **1818** W. TAYLOR in *Monthly Rev.* LXXXVII. 532 Those trades which are commonly exercised by settled and residentiary Christians. **1889** C. EDWARDES *Sardinia & the Sardes* 90 We may..excuse the barons of Sardinia, whether residentiary or absent.

b. Connected with residence.

1871–2 *Act 34 & 35 Vict.* c. 117 Sched. §1 The rights and interests, pecuniary or residentiary, of the..pensioners.

†**resi'dentiary**, *a.*[2] *Obs. rare*$^{-1}$. [f. RESIDENCE *sb.*[2]] Residual; of small value.

1774 *Projects* in *Ann. Reg.* 117/2 We might, likewise, make it..into flower-pots, and even other less residentiary vessels, for gardens and parterres.

resi'dentiaryship. [f. RESIDENTIARY *sb.*] The office of a (canon) residentiary.

1624 LAUD *Diary* 6 Dec. 155 A matter of difference in the church of Hereford, concerning a Residentiaryship. **1691** WOOD *Antiq., Fasti* (1815) I. 329 The rectory of Waldgrave, ..a Residentiaryship in the church of Lincoln [etc.]. **1751** T. SHARP in *Lett. Lit. Men* (Camden) 375 Dr. Tillotson obtain'd his residentiaryship of St. Pauls. **1768** WARBURTON in W. & Hurd *Lett.* (1809) 422 His Residentiaryship (half the Deanship) is said to be destined for Dr. Egerton's commendum. **1831** *Examiner* 601/2 The residentiaryship of St. Paul's..is bestowed on the Rev. Sidney Smith.

†**'residenting,** *ppl. a. Obs. rare.* [f. RESIDENT *a.*] Residing, resident.

1717 *Wodrow's Corr.* (1843) II. 339 Those who are complete members of a congregation, residenting heritors, and the elders, in a special manner, are to be regarded.

†**'residently,** *adv. Obs. rare*$^{-1}$. [f. RESIDENT *a.*] With continuance; steadfastly.

1609 TOURNEUR *Funeral Poem Sir F. Vere* 324 He..did residently dwell Upon the purpose of a true intent.

'residentship. [f. RESIDENT *sb.*[1] + -SHIP.]

1. The office or post of a Resident.

1583 STOCKER *Civ. Warres Lowe C.* IV. 5b, All.. ecclesiasticall parsons whose Abbaies, Monasteries, Foundations, and Residentships..lye without the Countries of Holland and Zealand. **1691** WOOD *Ath. Oxon.* II. 643 He, loving Solitude, declined..the Residentship at London for the City of Hamburgh. **1710** SHAFTESB. *Charac.* (1737) III. Misc. v. iii. 337 If there be any such Residentship or Agentship now establish'd; 'tis not immediately from God himself. **1794** BURKE *Sp. agst. W. Hastings* Wks. XV. 387 When first the forced loan was levied upon them, under his residentship. **1835** *Fraser's Mag.* XI. 251 The prebends of Westminster are good; so are the residentships of St. Paul's. **1890** *Daily News* 21 June 5/6 The Residentship at Hyderabad, the 'blue ribbon' of the Indian political service.

2. The district under the control of a Resident.

1805 tr. *Lafontaine's Hermann & Emilia* IV. 44, I.. entreated you to confer upon me an employment in the residentship.

‖**residentura** (rɛzɪdɛn'tʊərə). Also **rezidentura.** [Russ. *rezidentúra*: cf. RESIDENT *sb.* 4.] A group or organization of intelligence agents in a foreign country.

1963 A. DULLES *Craft of Intelligence* viii. 102 Within the embassy there would still be intelligence officers, but they would restrict themselves, except in emergencies, to 'clean' operations... This unit the Soviets call the 'legal *residentura*'. Outside the embassy..perhaps in a bookstore or a photography shop..was headquarters of the 'illegal' *residentura*. **1969** A. MARIN *Rise with Wind* i. 8 He wouldn't like to be a Russian *Kaygaybehnik* confronted with Clay... The man was capable of bursting into any accessible *residentura* and slaughtering the comrades. **1977** 'R. ROSTAND' *Killing in Rome* i. 5 Chief of the entire *rezidentura* [in Rome] was the first secretary himself, a KGB colonel. **1979** *Daily Tel.* 15 Oct. 5/2 The deputy chief of the KGB Rezidentura in Tokyo..maintains numerous contacts among the staff and research fellows.

‖**Residenz** (rezɪ'dɛnts). Also **residenz.** [Ger., lit. 'residence'.] The building in which a German princely court resided before 1918; a town which was the seat of a princely court. Hence **Residenzstadt** (-ʃtat) [G. *stadt* town], the seat of a court.

1840 THACKERAY in *Fraser's Mag.* Aug. 151/2 Twice as many people in the streets as you see at midday in a German *residenz* or an English provincial town. **1848** —— *Van. Fair* lxiii. 570 Troops of people..flock to the Residenz and share in the pleasures of the fair and the festivities there. **1915** F. H. BURNETT *Lost Prince* xxii. 215 But I want to know who lives at the Residenz? **1961** L. MUMFORD *City in Hist.* Note to plate 4. These royal tomb cities were thus the earliest form of permanent Residenzstadt, like Versailles or Karlsruhe. **1965** *Observer* 9 May 40/7 The State apartments in the old Kings' Residenz..are being repainted. **1973** *Country Life* 15 Nov. 1542/1 The two vases in the Residenz in Munich. **1980** *Times* 9 Aug. 8/7 The Residenz, the baroque palace of the Von Schönborns.

re'sider. [f. RESIDE *v.*[1] + -ER[1].] A resident.

1632 LITHGOW *Trav.* x. 506 [He is] a Resider in Edenburgh. **1724** SWIFT *Drapier's Lett.* Wks. 1755 V. II. 35 We,..being persons of considerable estates in this kingdom, and residers therein. **1789** MME. D'ARBLAY *Diary* June, The amazing quantity of indigenous residers; old women and young children. **1852** LD. COCKBURN *Circuit Journ.* (1887) 279 The resider in a good London house.

re'siding, *vbl. sb.* [f. RESIDE *v.*[1] + -ING[1].] Residence; †dwelling-place.

c **1586** C'TESS PEMBROKE *Ps.* LXIX. x, Lett not one be left abiding Where such rancor had residing. **1606** SHAKS. *Ant. & Cl.* II. ii. 37 *Ant.* My being in Egypt Cæsar, what was't to you? *Cæs.* No more then my reciding heere at Rome Might be to you in Egypt. **1627** SPEED *England* v. §7 [Lambeth] euer since hath beene the residing of all those worthy Prelates of our Church. **1711** ADDISON *Spect.* No. 123 ¶2 Since my residing in these Parts I have seen and heard innumerable Instances. **1865** D. SMITH *Serm. & Lett.* (1869) 216 It is a temporary residing in order to a permanent residing.

residiuacion, residivation, obs. forms of RECIDIVATION.

residual (rɪ'zɪdjuːəl), *sb.* [See next.]

1. *Math.* **a.** A residual quantity.

1557 RECORDE *Whetst.* V j b, We maie comprehende vnder the same name..all other residualles Cossike, whiche be made by subtraction. *Ibid.* P p 4, The nombers..that be compounde with − be named Residualles. **1673** KERSEY *Algebra* II. ix. I. 239 When the Root of a Residual is to be added unto, or subtracted from the Root of its correspondent Binomial. **1764** LANDEN *Residual Analysis* Pref. 3 Such quantities, and algebraic expressions, as by Mathematicians are denominated residuals. **1796** STOKES in *Trans. R. Irish Acad.* (1797) VI. 229 It is expedient to remove the surds out of the denominator by multiplication; this is usually done by the multiplication of the denominator taken as a binomial or residual. **1841** *Penny Cycl.* XIX. 413/1 *Residual*, an expression which gives the remainder of a subtraction.

b. (See quots.)

1867 SYLVESTER in *Educ. Times* May 42 A residuum of the second or any even order in such series, may be made to consist of a single point, which I call residual of the original μ points. **1873** SALMON *Higher Plane Curves* (ed. 2) 136 If two systems of points α, β, together make up the complete intersection with the cubic of a curve of any order, one of these systems is said to be the residual of the other.

c. The difference between an observed or measured value of a quantity and its true, theoretical, or notional value.

1868 J. C. WATSON *Theoret. Astron.* vii. 370 In the case of a limited number of observed values of x, the residuals given by comparing the arithmetical mean with the several observations will not..give the true errors. **1872** *Mem. R. Astron. Soc.* XXXIX. 100 The usual treatment of equations, by rendering a minimum the sum of the squares of the residuals, not only assumes equal weights for the observations, but also that positive and negative errors are equally probable. **1906** WRIGHT & HAYFORD *Adjustment of Observations* (ed. 2) ii. 12 The sum of the positive residuals is equal to the sum of the negative residuals. **1923** GLAZEBROOK *Dict. Appl. Physics* III. 647/2 The distribution of 174 residuals in a certain case is shown in Fig. 1. The residuals are the differences between observed and calculated monthly sea levels at three tidal observatories. **1932** *Human Biol.* IV. 478 Departures from the average arm girth and calf girth of children of the given four skeletal dimensions, we have termed residuals and have regarded them as indices of muscular development. **1967** *Oceanogr. & Marine Biol.* V. 12 When the residuals at a port are evaluated at say hourly intervals and then plotted against time, a graphical representation of the variations in the surge component at that port is obtained. **1972** *Nature* 17 Mar. 96/1 A major contribution to understanding of the seismic velocity variation necessarily comes from travel time residuals (these are differences between observed arrival times of P-waves at seismometers and the theoretical arrival time from a standard set of tables).

2. a. A remainder; an amount still remaining after the main part is subtracted or accounted for.

1860 MAURY *Phys. Geogr.* ix. §445 These feeble forces in the water received one of the quantities of small value—residuals of compensation—with which the astronomer has to deal. **1878** NEWCOMB *Pop. Astron.* III. iv. 338 The moon ..is always held in that position by a minute residual of the earth's attraction. **1967** *Economist* 28 Oct. p. xxxiii/2 According to the recorded items on the balance of payments Sweden should by now be dead broke. The one thing that has kept it afloat is an unexplained positive 'residual' in the balance of payments. **1973** 'E. MCBAIN' *Let's hear It* iii. 42 His first impression was one of total harmony... Her face and figure came as residuals to his brief course in art appreciation.

b. The part of a gravity anomaly or magnetic anomaly that remains after subtraction of the regional. Also *attrib.*

1949 *Geophysics* XIV. 45 Since the density of salt is less than that of the surrounding sediments, its residual is negative. *Ibid.* 516 Residual maps have been used extensively by geophysicists to bring into focus local features which tend to be obscured by the broad features of the field. **1965** KRUMBEIN & GRAYBILL *Introd. Statistical Models in Geol.* xiii. 325 Many residual maps contain geological information of value in exploration for natural resources. **1978** *Nature* 13 July 146/1 After removing the mean values we projected the residuals on to profiles transverse and parallel to the plate motion and averaged the values over 0·5° intervals.

3. A substance or product of the nature of a residuum. Also *transf.*

1885 G. H. TAYLOR *Pelv. & Hern. Therap.* 29 The blood, with its residuals and products of waste. **1886** *York Her.* 6 Aug. 3/4 Gas-lime was another residual, and when used properly was a most valuable fertiliser. **1899** *Daily News* 24 June 4/1 The casual docker is often a residual—the driftwood of society.

4. A royalty paid to an actor, musician, etc., for a repeat of a play, television commercial, etc.

1966 *Guardian* 14 May 7/1 The 'residuals', or BBC fringe benefits, lie chiefly in adoption by the Transcription Service. **1971** *Daily Tel.* 25 Mar. 21/4 He [*sc.* Frank Sinatra] will continue to receive money from..record royalties, residuals of his television programmes and a share in the profits of his films. **1972** D. RAMSAY *Little Murder Music* 78 'What makes a jingle date such an important affair?.. The money?' 'And how. I could wind up making more in residuals alone.' **1977** *Rolling Stone* 13 Jan. 19/1, I love doing jingles because I get residuals.

5. *Geomorphol.* A portion of rocky or high ground remaining after erosion.

1968 R. W. FAIRBRIDGE *Encycl. Geomorphol.* 587/1 Normal fluvial erosion begins to be established, and eventually, only residuals of limestone..are left standing. **1970** R. J. SMALL *Study of Landforms* v. 162 Above the peneplain, a few isolated hills..would remain. Such residuals were referred to by Davis as 'monadnocks'.

residual (rɪ'zɪdjuːəl), *a.* [ad. med. or mod.L. **residuāl-is*, f. *residuum*. Cf. It. *residuale*, F. *résiduel*.]

1. *Math.* **a.** Resulting from, formed by, the subtraction of one quantity from another.

1570 BILLINGSLEY *Euclid* x. prop. 73. 283 If from a rationall line be taken away a rationall line commensurable in power onely to the whole line: the residue is an irrationall line, and is called a residuall line. **1673** KERSEY *Algebra* II. i. I. 138 The Powers from the Residual Root $a - e$ differ only in the signs + and − from like Powers formed from the Binomial Root $a + e$. **1700** MOXON *Math. Dict.* 142 *Residual Figure*, the remaining Figure after Subtraction of a less from a greater. **1704** J. HARRIS *Lex. Techn.* I, *Residual Root*, in Mathematicks, is one composed of two Parts or Members only connected together with the Sign −. **1734** J. WARD *Introd. Math.* (ed. 6) 172 From thence will arise Surds either Binomial, or Residual. **1798** HUTTON *Course Math.* (1827) I. 167 A Residual Quantity, is a binomial having one of the terms negative. As $a - 2b$.

b. ***residual analysis*** or ***calculus*** (see quots.).

1758 LANDEN *Disc. Residual Analysis* 5 Which method I call the Residual Analysis; because, in all the enquiries wherein it is made use of, the conclusions are obtained by means of residual quantities. **1801** *Encycl. Brit.* (ed. 3) Suppl. II. 401/1 *Residual analysis*, a calculus proposed by the inventor, Mr. Landen, as a substitute for the method of fluxions. [Account follows.] **1890** *Cent. Dict.* s.v., *Residual calculus*, the calculus of residuals or residues.

2. a. Remaining; still left; left over. ***residual legatee*** = ***residuary legatee*** s.v. RESIDUARY *a.* 1 b; also *fig.*; ***residual powers*** = ***residuary powers*** s.v. RESIDUARY *a.* 2 b.

1609 [BP. W. BARLOW] *Answ. Nameless Cath.* 73 Whose Manes, that is, whose residuall memorie, will both *Manare* and *Manere* by diffusion and duration. **1801** W. TAYLOR in *Monthly Mag.* XII. 576 It becomes the few residual friends of toleration and humanity to rally with closer union. **1822** T. TAYLOR *Apuleius* 172 The remaining space of the year is completed by the residual months. **1860** TYNDALL *Glac.* 124 The sky was now for the most part overcast, but through the residual blue spaces the sun at intervals poured light. **1881** WESTCOTT & HORT *Grk. N.T.* Introd. §184 The residual Pre-Syrian text which is neither Western nor Alexandrian. **1919** G. B. SHAW in *Irish Statesman* 25 Oct. 428/1 When the enfranchisement of the Dominions began with Canada, the question on which freedom depends: namely, which party is to have residual powers, was hardly raised. Those were early days for democracy; and the residual powers were left technically to England. **1963** *Listener* 21 Feb. 334/1 The Liberals cash in..by claiming to be the residual legatees of the radical tradition. **1967** *Boston Sunday Herald* 30 Apr. III. 10/1 A specially interesting use of this guide's table of 'Life Expectancy' and 'residual values' of textiles is in evaluating garments and other textile items donated to charity. **1969** F. HALLIDAY in Cockburn & Blackburn *Student Power* 296 The dominant 'mainstream' faction.. was labelled as 'Trotskyite', a residual term meaning that the group was Marxist but opposed to the official Japan Communist Party line. **1976** *National Observer* (U.S.) 3 July 8/6 'There shouldn't be any wholesale dumping of what we think are good risks into the residual market,' says the Insurance Information Institute spokesman. **1979** *Jrnl. R. Soc. Arts* Jan. 97/2 Alice was the residual legatee and executrix.

b. In the physical sciences: Left as a residuum, *esp.* at the end of some process.

1757 *Phil. Trans.* L. 351 These.. serve to bring back the residual blood from the tumors. **1799** SIR H. DAVY in Beddoes *Contrib. Phys. & Med. Knowl.* 187 More hydrogen and residual carbon. **1807** *Phil. Trans.* XCVII. 252 The united quantities give the sum of the residual gas. **1871** B. STEWART *Heat* (ed. 2) §387 The pressure of the residual air which remained in the vacuum chamber. **1896** *Pop. Sci. Jrnl.* L. 242 The heat referred to is mainly.. the residual heat of a cooling globe.

c. Left unexplained or uncorrected.

1830 HERSCHEL *Study Nat. Phil.* II. vi. §158 Leaving, as it were, a residual phenomenon to be explained. *Ibid.*, The residual facts are constantly appearing in the form of phenomena altogether new. **1867** J. HOGG *Microsc.* I. ii. 58 There will always be residual terms in the general expression for the aberration. **1871** B. STEWART *Heat* (ed. 2) §141 These irregularities.. are merely due to the residual error in our observations.

d. Applied to magnetism which is retained after the removal of the magnetizing force or in the absence of a magnetizing current.

1837 *Phil. Mag.* X. 195 If the interrupted keeper be applied to a compound magnet, it will be attracted only with a force equal to the quantity of residual magnetism, which being very small the attraction will be comparatively feeble. **1874** *Tyer's Block Telegraph & Electric Locking Signals* (ed. 5) 14 There is also.. an electro-magnet fitted with 'horns' or 'keepers'.., so arranged as to.. retain for an indefinite period the residual magnetism produced on the passage of each signal. **1886** [see RETENTIVENESS 6]. **1902** *Encycl. Brit.* XXX. 430/2 If a bar of hard steel is placed in a strong magnetic field, a certain intensity of magnetization is induced in the bar, but when the strength of the field is afterward reduced to zero, the magnetization does not entirely disappear. That portion which is permanently retained, and which may amount to considerably more than one-half, is called the residual magnetization. **1912**, etc. [see RETENTIVITY 1]. **1917**, etc. [see REMANENCE 3].

e. Applied to the small charge which some capacitors remain capable of delivering after 'discharge'.

1838 FARADAY in *Phil. Trans. R. Soc.* CXXVIII. 24 It is the assumption for a time of this charged state of the glass between the coatings in the Leyden jar, which gives origin to a well-known phenomenon, usually referred to the diffusion of electricity over the uncoated portion of the glass, namely, the residual charge. **1878** *Encycl. Brit.* VIII. 39/2 Kohlrausch called attention to the close analogy between the residual discharge and the 'elastic recovery'.. of strained bodies... The instantaneous strain which follows the application of a stress is analogous to the initial charge of the jar, and the gradually increasing strain which follows to the gradual formation of the latent or residual charge. **1921** T. F. WALL *Electr. Engin.* iv. 62 The successive charges after the first discharge are known as residual charges. **1938** H. G. MITCHELL *Textbk. Electr.* iv. 64 The residual discharge of the condenser can easily be explained if we assume that the charge penetrates the glass and cannot all reach the conducting plates when these are connected.

f. *Physical Geogr.* Applied to a deposit or feature formed *in situ* by the weathering of rock, and to a soil largely composed of such material.

1895 *Geogr. Jrnl.* V. 140 Most of the peneplains that I have examined.. still possess residual elevations,.. evidently to be regarded as unconsumed remnants of the denudation of the former cycle. **1906** E. W. HILGARD *Soils* i. 11 When soils have been formed without removal from the site of the original rock, by simple weathering, they are designated as sedentary, or residual soils. **1933** [see PENEPLAIN *sb.*]. **1937** WOOLDRIDGE & MORGAN *Physical Basis Geogr.* xi. 150 While its origin has given rise to considerable controversy, all are agreed that it [*sc.* laterite] is essentially a residual deposit. **1944** A. HOLMES *Princ. Physical Geol.* viii. 119 Ultimately the angular block is transformed into an onion-like structure of concentric shells of rusty and thoroughly rotted residual material. **1954** W. D. THORNBURY *Princ. Geomorphol.* iv. 74 Soils were commonly divided into two major groups, residual and transported. Residual soils were classified according to the type of rock from which they were derived. **1972** J. G. CRUICKSHANK *Soil Geogr.* ii. 57 Parent materials may be classified by their mode of formation as follows: 1 Weathered rock in place which produces residual soils.

g. ***residual stress***, stress present in an object in the absence of any external load or force.

1931 A. NÁDAI *Plasticity* xxxviii. 259 Stresses of this kind, remaining after partial plastic flow, may be called residual stresses. **1958** *Engineering* 18 Apr. 498/1 The operation of welding gives rise to residual stresses, i.e. stresses which exist independently of the external loading. **1976** LINDBERG & BRATON *Welding & Other Joining Processes* xii. 454 A weldment heated to a temperature at which the yield strength is low.. will relieve the residual stresses and increase fatigue life.

residuary (rɪˈzɪdjuːərɪ), *a.* and *sb.* [ad. L. type **residuāri-us*: see RESIDUUM and -ARY.]

A. *adj.* **1.** *Law.* **a.** Of the nature of the residue of an estate. Also *transf.*

1726 AYLIFFE *Parergon* (J.), 'Tis enough to lose the legacy, or the residuary advantage of the estate left him by the deceased. **1743** *Swinburne's Testaments* I. (ed. 6) 40 The Testator devised the residuary Part of his Estate to two Executors. **1827** JARMAN *Powell's Devises* II. 102 A residuary bequest.. operates upon all the personal estate, of which a testator is possessed at the time of his death. **1859** MILL *Diss. & Disc.* (1875) II. 210 The labourer,.. a mere bought instrument in the work of production, having no residuary interest in the work itself.

b. ***residuary legatee*** or ***devisee***, one to whom the residue of an estate is left. Also *transf.*

1743 *Swinburne's Testaments* VI. (ed. 6) 415 Where an Executor and residuary Legatee dies before Probate, his Executor shall have the Administration. *a* **1794** LD. CAMDEN in *Powell's Devises* (1827) II. 45 Where the intention of a testator is to devise the residue exclusive of a part given away, the residuary devisee shall not take that part in any event. **1838** W. BELL *Dict. Law Scot.* 858 He is in effect a residuary legatee since he is entitled to the whole estate after paying the testator's debts and legacies. **1858** LD. ST. LEONARDS *Handy-Bk. Prop. Law* xx. 154 Where a gift is to a charity of an estate, which is void, the estate will go to the residuary devisee. **1865** DICKENS *Mut. Fr.* I. ii, If the son had not been living, the same old servant would have been sole residuary legatee. **1962** S. E. FINER *Man on Horseback* viii. 123 The Justice party.. in a sense was the residuary legatee of the old Democrats. **1967** E. RUDINGER *Wills & Probate* 11 The wife is probably the residuary legatee.

c. ***residuary clause***, a clause by which a residue is devised.

1818 CRUISE *Digest* (ed. 2) VI. 226 In the residuary clause, the testator had made use of the most expressive and comprehensive words.

2. Of the nature of a residuum or remainder of any kind: **a.** With reference to chemical processes, scientific observations, etc.

1793 BEDDOES *Obs. Obesity* 97 The oils, ammoniac, and carbone appear to be formed from the residuary azote and carbone. **1800** *Phil. Trans.* XC. 197 The residuary gas being transferred into another tube. **1858** BUSHNELL *Serm. New Life* 378 Mere residuary substances of a dry and fruitless life. **1881** *Nature* XXIV. 515/1 The haze observed in miniatures examined by high magnifying power is an invaluable indication of spherical residuary aberration.

b. In general use. spec. ***residuary powers***, powers remaining with one political group after other powers have been allocated to another group, e.g. as between a federal government and a province.

1798 J. ADAMS in Ludlow *Hist. U.S.* (1862) 64 Immediately we shall see a Pennsylvania party and a Virginia party arise in the residuary confederacy. **1833** CARLYLE *Misc.* (1857) III. 185 Picking up a few residuary snips. **1853** KANE *Grinnell Exp.* xxxii. (1856) 275 We celebrated it by an extra dinner.. and a couple of our residuary bottles of wine. **1881** WESTCOTT & HORT *Grk. N.T.* Introd. §2 A small fraction of the whole residuary variation. **1919** G. B. SHAW *Let.* in *Irish Statesman* 22 Nov. 536/2 The meaning of residuary powers and the importance of the Australian precedent in their bearing on the Irish national question. **1950** THEIMER & CAMPBELL *Encycl. World Politics* 163/2 In some federations.. the powers of the federal government are named in the constitution and all other powers (the residuary powers) belong to the regions.

3. Applied to the Established Church of Scotland after the Disruption in 1843. *Obs.* or *arch.*

1843 *Witness* 19 May 2/7 (*heading*) Residuary Assembly. .. After the Evangelical Party had left the House [etc.]. **1845** J. BRIGHT in *Hansard Commons* 16 Apr. 882/2 Even in Scotland.. there were the Secession Church, the Relief Church, and the Free Church; that which the State upheld being called by the complimentary name of the Residuary Church. **1883** R. CLELAND *Inchbracken* iii. 22 The 'Residuary' Presbytery, as you are pleased to denominate the church of your fathers.

B. *sb.* A residuary legatee. *rare.* Also *fig.*

1817 LAMB *Let. to Field* in *Final Mem.* x. 102 Of course you have heard of poor Mitchell's death, and that G. Dyer is one of Lord Stanhope's residuaries. **1920** E. GOSSE in *Edin. Rev.* Jan. 47 He was the residuary of his own temperament.

†**residu'ation**[1]. *Obs. rare.* [Erroneous for RECIDIVATION. Cf. RESIL(I)UATION.] Relapse.

1534 MORE *Comf. agst. Trib.* II. Wks. 1195/2 Far from occasion geuing of new residuacion into his former sinne.

residu'ation[2]. *Math.* [f. RESIDU-AL: see -ATION.] (See quot. 1880, and RESIDUAL *sb.* 1 b.)

1873 SALMON *Higher Plane Curves* (ed. 2) 134 Prof. Sylvester's remarkable theory of residuation. **1880** SYLVESTER in *Amer. Jrnl. Math.* III. 60 The theory of residuation, in its simplest form,.. teaches us that the rule of the older chemistry known by the name of double decomposition, viz. that (a, b), (c, d) = (a, c), (b, d) is applicable to the same symbols regarded as points of a cubic curve.

residue (ˈrɛzɪdjuː), *sb.* Also 4–7 **resydue** (6 **reasi-**), 5–7 **-dew(e**, 6 **-du**; 5–6 **resedew(e** (6 **resi-**); 6 **resideu.** [ad. F. *résidu* (14th c.), ad. L. *residuum* RESIDUUM.]

1. The remainder, rest; that which is left.

a. Of things.

Method of Residues: see Mill *Logic* (1843) III. viii. §5.

1362 LANGL. *P. Pl.* A. v. 240 With þe Residue and þe remenaunt [of my living].. I schal seche seynt Treupe. **1426** LYDG. *De Guil. Pilg.* 17024 To Acomplysshe.. the Resydue in effect, that Folweth in the same vers. **1484** CAXTON *Fables of Poge* viii, After this.. the sellar demaunded of the byar the resydue. *a* **1533** LD. BERNERS *Huon* lxvii. 231 In grete payne & mysery we must vse the resydew of our lyues. **1616** R. C. *Times' Whistle* v. 1716 If with moderate fare they were contented They might.. save the residue of all their wealth. **1656** SANDERSON *Serm.* (1689) 537 In the residue of the fifth verse. **1718** *Free-thinker* No. 7. 47 Nothing farther could be done unless the Residue was forthcoming. **1780** S. J. PRATT *Emma Corbett* (ed. 4) II. 41 If you looked him in the face, or, more properly,.. in the residue of his face. **1826** FARADAY *Exp. Res.* (1859) 218 The residue supported combustion a little better than common air. **1878** HUXLEY *Physiogr.* 199 Others assume that it is.. the residue of the heat which the earth originally possessed.

b. Of persons.

1382 WYCLIF *Zeph.* ii. 9 The residues of my folc shuln welde hem. **1475** *Rolls of Parlt.* VI. 139/1 The said Henry Bodrugan.. the residue of the same Britons yet kepeth in prisone. **1526** *Pilgr. Perf.* (W. de W. 1531) 266 b, On this maner the poore vnlerned fysshers Peter, John, Andrewe & James were taught, & the resydue of yᵉ holy couent. **1575** TURBERV. *Trag. Tales* (1837) 40 Both.. promist not to faile Themselves to come, and bid the residue. **1610** HOLLAND *Camden's Brit.* (1637) 113 The residue of Britans remaining alive, withdrew themselves. **1719** DE FOE *Crusoe* II. (Globe) 367 The Residue of the conquer'd People fled to their Canoes. **1836** W. IRVING *Astoria* III. 7 A number of men mounted guard,.. while the residue.. employed themselves below in dragging up the barges and canoes.

†**c.** The leavings *of* a destructive agent. *Obs.*

1560 BIBLE (Genev.) *Joel* i. 4 The residue of the canker-worm hathe the caterpiller eaten.

†**d.** Phr. ***in***, or ***for, the residue***, for the rest, as to the remainder. *Obs.*

1548 BODRUGAN *Epit.* 249 In the residue it was not my mynde to trifle with the fine flowers of Rethorike. **1560** DAUS tr. *Sleidane's Comm.* 111 b, For the residue they committe all that ever they have unto the Emperour.

e. *Sociol.* A term used by Vilfredo Pareto (1848–1923) for fundamental impulses which motivate human conduct, and which are not the product of rational deliberation.

1933 *Harper's Mag.* CLXVII. 573 In each of these two groups of phenomena we have found a constant element, the sentiment out of which both the actions and the explanations rise. The *expression* of such a sentiment is what Pareto calls a 'Residue'. **1935** BONGIORNO & LIVINGSTON tr. *Pareto's Mind & Society* II. vi. 508 It might perhaps be advisable to give word-names to the things we have been calling *a*, *b*, and *c*... Suppose we call the things *a*, *residues*, the things *b*, *derivations*, and the things *c*, *derivatives*. *Ibid.* 509 Residues correspond to certain instincts in human beings, and for that reason they are usually wanting in definiteness, in exact delimitation. **1935** L. J. HENDERSON *Pareto's Gen. Sociol.* v. 23 Theology and metaphysics and parts of law consist, in great measure, of systematic and extensive derivations from certain very important residues like those involving the words justice, duty, sanctity, and absolute. **1939** F. CREEDY *Human Nature writ Large* xix. 400 Public documents which have won high praise and wide acceptance.. owe their acceptability to the fact that their Residues or fundamental assumptions coincide with those of the crowd. **1958** W. STARK *Sociol. of Knowl.* viii. 320 These residues or drives determine all the comings and goings on the stage of life. The 'derivations', or thoughts and beliefs which, objectively speaking, derive from the residues, but which subjectively appear to the people who harbour them as 'their ideas', 'their convictions', 'their philosophies'. **1966** S. E. FINER *V. Pareto: Sociol. Writings* 38 Thus, if you strip from the theory its variable part you are left with a residuum. This is the constant element and Pareto therefore calls it a *residue*.

2. *Law.* That which remains of an estate after all charges, debts, and bequests have been paid.

1411 *E.E. Wills* (1882) 20 þᵉ residue of alle my godes. **1454** *Ibid.* 134 Yf my seide goodes, Residues, and dettis may not suffice. **1529** CROMWELL *Will* in Merriman *Life & Lett.* (1902) I. 63 The residue of all my goodes, catalles, and debttes not bequethed.. I will shalbe sold. **1590** SWINBURNE *Testaments* 115 He to whom all or the residue is bequeathed, is thereby vnderstood to be made executor. **1766** BLACKSTONE *Comm.* II. 492 Then the residue of the goods shall go to the executor to perform the will of the deceased. **1818** CRUISE *Digest* (ed. 2) V. 499 It was still the same residue remaining in the wife, which she had not disposed of before. **1865** DICKENS *Mut. Fr.* III. vii, He, John Harmon, .. gives the whole rest and residue of his property to the Crown. **1967** E. RUDINGER *Wills & Probate* 9 After disposing of specified items and sums of money, you give the remainder—the residue, lawyers call it—to some named person... You could, of course, provide that your residue should be divided.. among a number of people.

attrib. **1838** W. BELL *Dict. Law Scot.* 585 Legacy and Residue Duties.

3. †**a.** *Math.* = REMAINDER 4 a. *Obs.*

c **1430** *Art Nombryng* 17 Thow shalt fynde the same figures that thow haddest before; And so that nought be the residue. And yf thow have any residue [etc.]. **1570** BILLINGSLEY *Euclid* v. prop. 19. 146 If the whole be to the whole, as the part taken away is to the part taken away: then shall the residue be vnto the residue, as the whole is to the whole. **1636** MELLIS *Recorde's Gr. Artes* 154 From the last subtract the first, and the residue diuide by a number lesse by 1, then the number of the places.

b. *Number Theory.* A remainder left when a given number is divided into some integer; also, a number congruent to a given number modulo a third number; ***quadratic, cubic,*** etc., ***residue***, a remainder left when a given number is divided into the square, cube, etc., of some integer; ***residue class***, the class of integers congruent to one another modulo a given number (e.g. 2, 5, 8, 11, etc., are members of a residue class modulo 3).

1860 *Rep. Brit. Assoc. Adv. Sci. 1859* I. 231 The set of numbers 0, 1, 2...P − 1 (or any set of P numbers respectively congruous for the modulus P to those numbers) is termed a complete system of residues for the modulus P. **1899** *Q. Jrnl. Math.* XXX. 363 The same representation of the coefficients also determines the residue when the coefficient is not a multiple of the modulus. **1939** USPENSKY & HEASLET *Elem. Number Theory* vi. 134 Of two numbers congruent for the modulus *m*, each is called a 'residue' of the other modulus *m*. *Ibid.* x. 270 A number *a* is said to be a quadratic residue of another number *m* if the congruence x^2

= *a* (mod *m*) can be satisfied by some integer *x*. **1948** O. ORE *Number Theory & its Hist.* ix. 214 Since these are the numbers that correspond to the same remainder *r* when divided by *m*, we say that they form a residue class (mod *m*). There are *m* residue classes (mod *m*). **1963** W. W. R. BALL *Math. Recreations & Ess.* (ed. 12) ii. 60 There is an arithmetic of residues, closely analogous to the arithmetic of ordinary numbers. **1966** OGILVY & ANDERSON *Excursions in Number Theory* iv. 43 If we identify every integer, positive, negative, or zero, with its remainder modulo *m*, we thus have all the integers partitioned into congruence classes, or residue classes, modulo *m*. **1977** *Sci. Amer.* July 127/2 Gauss used complex numbers of the form $a + bi$..to formulate and prove a version of the law of quadratic reciprocity for biquadratic residues. The number *k* is said to be a biquadratic residue of another number *m* if *k* is congruent modulo *m* to the fourth power of an integer. Thus the biquadratic residues of 10 are 0, 1, 5 and 6.

c. *Theory of Functions.* (See quots.)

1893 A. R. FORSYTH *Theory of Functions* x. 223 The sum of the residues of a doubly-periodic function relative to a fundamental parallelogram of periods is zero. **1957** T. M. APOSTOL *Math. Analysis* xvi. 524 In many cases it is relatively easy to evaluate the residue at a point without the use of integration. **1959** G. & R. C. JAMES *Math. Dict.* 334/1 If $f(z)$ is an analytic function of the complex variable z in the 'deleted' neighbourhood consisting of all z satisfying $0 < |z - z_0| < \epsilon$, then the residue of $f(z)$ at z_0 is

$$\frac{1}{2\pi i}\int_C f(z)dz,$$

where C is a simple closed rectifiable curve about z_0 in the 'deleted' neighbourhood. The value of the residue is..the coefficient of $(z - z_0)^{-1}$ in the Laurent expansion of $f(z)$ about z_0. **1973** RAUCH & LEBOWITZ *Elliptic Functions, Theta Functions, & Riemann Surfaces* i. 19 A differential of the *first kind* is one whose set of Laurent expansions has no poles. Differentials of the *second kind* have poles but with zero residue at each pole while differentials of the *third kind* allow poles with non-vanishing residues.

4. = RESIDUUM 3. Also *atttib.*

1807 T. THOMSON *Chem.* (ed. 3) II. 357 The liquid being now filtered, boiled, and evaporated to dryness, left a residue, which may be considered as tannin. **1838** —— *Chem. Org. Bodies* 287 The aqueous residue was decanted off a resinous precipitate. **1887** A. M. BROWN *Anim. Alkaloids* 82 The tissue-residue is then retreated with alcohol at 99°; this when evaporated gives a new residue. **1899** tr. *Jaksch's Clin. Diagn.* (ed. 4) 418 Inflammatory fluids are comparatively rich in fibrin..and in dry residue products.

5. *Chem.* (See quot. 1873.) In mod. use applied to any molecule when incorporated without major alteration in a larger one; *esp.* in *Biochem.*, an amino-acid, sugar, or other molecule incorporated in a polymer such as a protein, carbohydrate, etc.

1852 H. WATTS tr. *Gmelin's Hand-bk. Chem.* VII. 76 The compound thus formed by substitution contains therefore the residues of the two compounds united, that is to say, the first compound + the second, *minus* an equal number of H- and O-atoms. *Ibid.* 77 Oxamide..may be regarded as a compound of the two residues, $C^4H^2O^4$ and 2NH. **1873** —— *Fownes' Chem.* 251 Suppose one or more of the component atoms of a fully saturated molecule to be removed: it is clear that the remaining atom or group of atoms will no longer be saturated... Such unsaturated groups are called residues or radicals. **1886** E. F. SMITH tr. *V. von Richter's Org. Chem.* 30 Ordinarily, radicals are groups containing carbon, while all others, like OH, SH, NH_2, NO_2, are residues or groups. **1903** *Jrnl. Chem. Soc.* LXXXIV. I. 214 The (albumin) molecule may be regarded as made up of 125 groups or residues. **1934** W. R. FEARON *Introd. Biochem.* xv. 231 The test is believed to depend on the hydrolytic unmasking of an aldehyde group in the hexose residue. **1955** H. R. DOWNES *Chem. Living Cells* v. 186 In one sample of lactoglobulin, for example, there were found 20 serine residues, 36 from aspartic acid, and 50 from leucine. **1975** *Nature* 27 Feb. 694/2 Even the smallest protein (say 50 residues) is extremely complicated.

†'**residue**, *a.* *Obs. rare.* [ad. L. *residuus*: see prec.] Remaining, surviving.

1382 WYCLIF *I Macc.* iii. 37 The kyng toke to a part of the residue oost. **1382** —— *I Thess.* iv. 14 We that lyuen, that ben residue, or left [L. *qui residui sumus*], in the comynge of the Lord. **1432-50** tr. *Higden* (Rolls) I. 29 Þat the weye may be patente to the residu peple of God.

residuous (rɪˈzɪdjuːəs), *a.* Now *rare.* [ad. L. *residuus*: see next and -OUS.] Remaining.

1626 BP. H. KING *Serm. Deliverance* 76 In bedding or garments infected there is *Contagio residua*, a lurking, residuous contagion. **1677** R. CARY *Chronol.* I. II. 77 That Difference or Residuous Number is to be sought out in the third Table. *a* **1711** KEN *Hymnarium* Poet. Wks. 1721 II. 12 Devoutly numb'ring my residuous Days, Not by the Minutes, but by Songs of Praise. **1789** KEIR *Dict. Chem.* 117/2 The purity of the residuous or burnt air. **1829** LANDOR *Imag. Conv., Dante & Beatrice* Wks. 1853 II. 154/2 All that is residuous of a wasted world.

residuum (rɪˈzɪdjuːəm). Pl. **residua** (rɪˈzɪdjuːə); also 8 **residuums**. [a. L. *residuum*, neut. of *residuus* remaining, f. *residēre* to remain, RESIDE *v.*¹]

1. That which remains; a residue. (Chiefly of immaterial things, and often with more or less direct allusion to sense 3.)

1672 T. JACOMBE *Serm. Rom.* (1868) 126/1 (Stanf.), God ..lets out so much of these corruptions.., and the residuum or overplus he keeps in. **1765** BLACKSTONE *Comm.* I. 93 That residuum of natural liberty. **1802** JEFFERSON *Writ.* (1830) III. 489 The residuum of money remaining in the treasury. **1848** H. ROGERS *Ess.* (1874) I. vi. 287 His reasonings..are not, therefore, vitiated by the residuum of error which we reject. **1875** JOWETT *Plato* (ed. 2) IV. 136 To us there seems to be no residuum of this long piece of dialectics.

b. Applied to persons of the lowest class.

1867 BRIGHT in *Times* 27 Mar. 7/4, I call this class the residuum, which there is in every constituency, of almost hopeless poverty and dependence. **1888** BRYCE *Amer. Commw.* (1888) III. 71 The ignorant masses of such great cities as New York, Brooklyn, Philadelphia, Chicago,.. answer better to what is called in England 'the residuum'.

2. *Law.* = RESIDUE *sb.* 2.

1743 *Swinburne's Testaments* I. (ed. 6) 40 One of the Daughters of the Testator sued for her distributive Part of the Residuum. **1766** BLACKSTONE *Comm.* II. 514 When all the debts and particular legacies are discharged, the surplus or *residuum* must be paid to the residuary legatee. **1842** STEPHEN *Comm. Laws Eng.* II. 250 In relation to the *residuum* which may be in the hands of the administrator.

3. *spec.* That which remains after a process of combustion, evaporation, etc.; a deposit or sediment; a waste or residual product.

1756 C. LUCAS *Ess. Waters* II. 52 The residuum of Tinemouth sea water was some degrees brighter. **1779** *Phil. Trans.* LXIX. 433 The residuums of air that remained unabsorbed were more or less phlogisticated. **1839** URE *Dict. Arts* 822 The residuum of the pyrites is turned to account in Sweden. **1887** A. M. BROWN *Anim. Alkaloids* p. xv, Of all the extractive composite residua the alkaloids of animal origin..are worthy of the deepest interest.

fig. **1850** ROBERTSON *Serm.* Ser. III. i. (1872) 4 You could not evaporate the truth..and then show the residuum of falsehood glittering and visible.

resiege, *v.* 'To seat again. Obsolete', Johnson, quoting Spenser *F.Q.* II. x. 45, where the true reading is RESEIZE.

Corrected by Todd (1818), but retained in some later Dicts.

resiente, obs. form of RESIANT.

re'sift (riː-), *v.* [RE- 5 a.] To sift again.

1834 G. BENNETT *Wand. N.S.W.* II. 212 It is then resifted at another bench and rebaked. **1870** ANDERSON *Missions Amer. Bd.* II. xix. 152 They were sifted and re-sifted, with every effort to separate the precious from the vile.

re'sign, *sb. rare.* [f. the vb.] Resignation.

1639 CHAPMAN & SHIRLEY *Chabot* v. sig. H3ᵛ, My free Resigne of title, office,..would buy my poore lives safety. **1640** SHIRLEY *Constant Maid* I. i, To delay The free resign of that your worth may challenge. **1640** —— *Coronation* IV. i, You have gain'd more in a royall brother Then you could lose by your resigne of Epire. **1971** J. V. ALLEN *Cowboy Lore* IV. 159 It was a pistol shot that laid Pete out, It was his last resign.

resign (rɪˈzaɪn), *v.*¹ Forms: 4-6 **resygn(e**, 6 **reasygne**, 4- **resign**; 5 **resyne**, 5-6 **resine**; 5 **res(s)yng(e**, 6 *Sc.* **resing**. [ad. OF. *resigner* (13th c.), †*resiner* (= Sp. and Pg. *resignar*, It. *ri-*, *rassegnare*), ad. L. *resignāre* to unseal, cancel, give up, f. *re-* RE- 2 d + *signāre* to SIGN.]

I. *trans.* **1.** To relinquish, surrender, give up, or hand over (something). Also with *up* (now *rare*) and const. *to* a person, *into* one's hands.

a. an office, position, right, claim, etc.

c **1380** WYCLIF *Wks.* (1880) 64 Þei..resignen not here benefis goten þus by symonye. **1387** TREVISA *Higden* (Rolls) IV. 415 He resignede his dignite to Linus. *c* **1400** *Brut* cl. 162 Here y resyngn op þe crone of þe reaume of Engeland into þe Popis Hande. *c* **1440** CAPGRAVE *St. Kath.* IV. 93 But these same..leften here honour and resigned her right. **1544** *Supplic. Hen. VIII* (E.E.T.S.) 33 If he repent not, and reasygne vp hys offyce, which he can not execute. **1591** SPENSER *M. Hubberd* 573 To whom their living they resigned quight For a few pence. **1631** WEEVER *Anc. Funeral Mon.* 767 Sigebert..resigned vp his kingdome. **1671** MILTON *P.R.* I. 27 The Baptist..would have resign'd To him his Heavenly Office. **1731** FIELDING *Lottery* Air xx, Resign over all pretensions in her to me. **1768** STERNE *Sent. Journ., Paris*, I..should have resigned all my places one after another. **1818** CRUISE *Digest* (ed. 2) VI. 348 Upon his resigning the great seal. **1839** KEIGHTLEY *Hist. Eng.* I. 92 The see of York, the ancient claims of which to equality with Canterbury he was forced to resign. **1876** VOYLE & STEVENSON *Milit. Dict.* 339/2 Non-commissioned officers are not allowed to resign their situation to escape trial by court-martial.

fig. **1592** SHAKS. *Ven. & Ad.* 1039 Her eyes..resign their office and their light To the disposing of her troubled brain. **1781** COWPER *Hope* 33 Would age in thee resign his wintry reign, And youth invigorate that frame again.

b. something pertaining to one or in one's possession or charge.

The uses in quots. 1600 and 1615 are uncommon.

c **1450** *Godstow Reg.* 202 Elenore..resinid & quiet-claimyd..to þe house of seint Iohn baptiste of Godestowe.. iiij. *d* of rente. **1535** STEWART *Cron. Scot.* II. 713 That all Northumberland And Cumbria he sould frelie resing, Into the handis of this Dauid king. **1593** SHAKS. *Rich. II*, I. i. 176 Take but my shame, and I resigne my gage. **1600** E. BLOUNT tr. *Conestaggio* 207 The Duke exhorted Tristan Vaz with many reasons to resigne the forte. **1615** BRATHWAIT *Strappado* (1878) 4 Resigne then what thou owest, or forbeare To taxe our credits when our skore's not cleere. **1667** MILTON *P.L.* x. 749 Desirous to resigne, and render back All I receav'd. **1731** SWIFT *Consid. Two Bills* Wks. 1751 XII. 103 The late Archbishop..stipulated with the Tenant to resign up twenty or thirty Acres to the Minister of the Parish. **1788** GIBBON *Decl. & F.* xliv. IV. 347 The divorced wife resigned the bunch of keys, by the delivery of which she had been invested with the government of the family. **1838** LYTTON *Alice* I. i, You resigned all that would have attracted others. **1839** THIRLWALL *Greece* xlvi. VI. 73 The commonwealth was required..to resign a great part of its foreign possessions.

transf. *a* **1823** MRS. RADCLIFFE *Moonlight* in *Gaston de Blondeville* (1826) IV. 251 Who, silent, watch the bark the coast resign, The Pharos lessen, and the mountains fade.

c. a task, charge, etc.

1513 DOUGLAS *Æneis* IV. Prol. 211 All sic crymes in luffis caus I resing To the confessioun of morall Ihon Gower. **1667** MILTON *P.L.* III. 688 Suspicion sleeps At wisdoms Gate, and to simplicitie Resigns her charge. **1715** POPE *Iliad* IV. 378 To you the glorious conflict I resign. **1784** COWPER *Tiroc.* 551 Then why resign into a stranger's hand A task as much within your own command?

d. one's life, being, soul, etc.

1588 SHAKS. *Tit. A.* I. i. 191 What should I d'on this Robe ..to day, To morrow yeeld vp rule, resigne my life? **1646** MILTON *Sonn.* xiv. 3 Meekly thou didst resign this earthy load Of Death, call'd Life. **1665** DRYDEN *Ind. Emp.* v. ii, If Blood you seek, I will my own resign. **1711** STEELE *Spect.* No. 133 ¶5 Noble and Heroick Minds that have resigned this Being. **1796** MORSE *Amer. Geogr.* I. 317 *note*, He resigned a life, which had been singularly devoted to the welfare of his country. **1819** SHELLEY *Cenci* IV. i. 63 That done, My soul, which is a scourge, will I resign Into the hands of him who wielded it.

e. something aimed at or desired.

1697 DRYDEN *Virg. Past.* VII. 33 The praise of artful Numbers I resign. **1736** GRAY *Statius* i. 23 The palm despair'd resign. **1849** M. ARNOLD *Resignation* Poems (1906) 76 Be passionate hopes not ill resign'd For quiet, and a fearless mind.

2. a. To give up, make over, abandon, consign *to* a person, thing, or condition.

c **1386** CHAUCER *Man of Law's T.* 682 And therfor to the feend I the resigne, Let him endyten of thi treccherie. **1589** [? NASHE] *Almond for Parrat* 11 Whether he would haue the care of the commonwealth..resigned to the retorting of T.C. his unreuerent railings. **1667** MILTON *P.L.* XII. 301 So Law appears..but giv'n With purpose to resign them in full time Up to a better Cov'nant. **1697** DRYDEN *Virg. Georg.* I. 124 The light Stubble, to the Flames resign'd, Is driv'n along, and crackles in the Wind. **1704** SWIFT *T. Tub* vi, His two Brethren..for ever discarded from his House, and resigned to the wide World. **1766** GOLDSM. *Vic. W.* viii, Mr. Burchell..resigned her up to the chaplain. **1791** MRS. RADCLIFFE *Rom. Forest* viii, Had I resigned you to his will I should have remained secure. *c* **1860** BRYANT *A Sick-bed* xi, Then to the sleep I crave Resign me.

b. To yield up (oneself, etc.) with confidence *to* another for care or guidance.

c **1366** CHAUCER *A.B.C.* 80 Myn hele in-to thyn hand al I resigne. *c* **1430** *Syr Gener.* (Roxb.) 1886 With louyng chere ..Hir hert to him she did resigne. *c* **1450** tr. *De Imitatione* III. xlii. 113 Forsake þiself, resigne up þiself, & þou shalt fruisshe gret pes. **1642** ROGERS *Naaman* 130 [She] will not ..resigne up her selfe to God. **1667** MILTON *P.L.* x. 148 Was shee made thy guide,..that to her Thou did'st resigne thy Manhood? **1751** DODDRIDGE in *Paraph. Ch. Scot.* xliv. 5 To thee, as to our cov'nant God, We'll our whole selves resign. **1869** J. MARTINEAU *Ess.* II. 79 He..vows to resign himself to her direction.

c. To make surrender of (one's will, reason, etc.), in reliance upon another.

1585 JAS. I *Ess. Poesie* (Arb.) 29 Amongst our hands, he must his witts resing, A holy trance to highest heauen him bring. **1647** COWLEY *Mistr., The Soul* iii, If my Will do not resign All her Liberty to thine. *c* **1698** LOCKE *Some Thoughts on Conduct of Understanding* (1881) 61 Those who always resign their judgment to the last man they heard or read. **1781** COWPER *Retirem.* 130 To..Resign our own and seek our Maker's will.

d. To give (oneself, one's mind, etc.) up *to* some emotion, condition, or state. Also const. with *inf.*

1718 POPE *Iliad* XIII. 590 Æneas..for a space resign'd To tender pity all his manly mind. **1738** tr. *Guazzo's Art Convers.* 16 They did not so absolutely resign themselves up to a solitary Life, as to be entirely regardless of their neighbours. **1791** COWPER *Retired Cat* 61, I will resign myself to rest. **1815** SHELLEY *Alastor* 628 Yet a little, ere it fled, Did he resign his high and holy soul To images of the majestic past. **1898** G. B. SHAW *You never can Tell* II. 265 She smiles in spite of herself, and resigns herself to indulge him a little. *a* **1953** E. O'NEILL *More Stately Mansions* (1964) I. ii. 39 Resign myself to be a grandmother!

†**3.** To give over, desist or refrain from. *Obs.*

c **1374** CHAUCER *Troylus* III. 25 Thei dredyn shame, and vices thei resigne. *c* **1440** *Partonope* 3413* Of this and more ..Myne autor seyth which shall not fyne. Hem to reherse I will resyne. **1492** RYMAN *Poems* xlix. I. in *Archiv Stud. neu. Spr.* LXXXIX. 215 Now is tyme for to inclyne To vertue, and synne to resyne. **1590** SPENSER *F.Q.* III. xi. 5 Whom when the Gyaunt saw, he soone resinde His former suit, and from them fled apace.

†**4.** To cause (a person) to give up his place.

1674 *Essex Papers* (Camden) I. 286 That party made their braggs that they would resigne Arlington at his Returne.

II. *intr.* **5. a.** To give up an office or position; to retire; †to abdicate.

c **1450** *St. Cuthbert* (Surtees) 8289 At laste to reule it him thoght herd. He resygned and went away. *a* **1470** GREGORY *Chron.* in *Hist. Coll. Cit. Lond.* (Camden) 76 And that yere ..he resynyd, and Edwarde his sone..was crounyd. **1530** PALSGR. 688/1 He is contented to resyne, but he demaundeth to great a pencyon. **1593** SHAKS. *Rich. II*, IV. i. 190, I thought you had been willing to resigne.

1744 H. WALPOLE *Lett.* II. 3 Lord Granville has resigned: that is the term. **1818** CRUISE *Digest* (ed. 2) III. 37 Where a clerk..entered into a general bond to the patron, to resign whenever the patron should require him. **1860** WARTER *Sea-board* II. 7 If my Lord bishop wants to resign. **1876** VOYLE & STEVENSON *Milit. Dict.* 339/2 Non-commissioned officers..can resign when they find themselves unequal to perform the duties of their rank.

b. orig. *U.S.* Const. *from.*

1885 J. HAWTHORNE *Love or a Name* 95 Is it true..that you have resigned from the Compensation Fund Commission? **1905** 'M. E. WILKINS' *Debtor* 171 You would say at once they ought to be forced to resign from their offices. **1926** G. B. SHAW *Translations & Tomfooleries* 235

My brothers said I ought to resign from my clubs. **1959** *Chambers's Encycl.* II. 68/1 In 1922 he resigned from office and was raised to the peerage as earl of Balfour. **1973** HOWAT & TAYLOR *Dict. World Hist.* 1619/2 In April 1951 he resigned from the government..in protest against an increase in social service charges. **1980** *Times* 20 Aug. 1/2 Mr A. J. P. Taylor resigned from the British Academy over what he described as a witch hunt by some members to remove Professor Anthony Blunt.

6. To submit, to yield, *to* a person or thing. Now *rare*.

c **1450** tr. *De Imitatione* III. xlii. 113 Somme resigneþ, but with som excepcion, for þei trust not fully to god. **1592** SHAKS. *Rom. & Jul.* III. ii. 59 Vile earth to earth resigne, end motion here. **1701** COLLIER *M. Aurel.* (1726) 19 That we should..resign to his wisdom, and adore his goodness. **1742** RICHARDSON *Pamela* IV. 173, I will hope still the best, and resign to God's Will and his. **1805** EUGENIA DE ACTON *Nuns of Desert* I. 288 Sophia and Emily Selwyn endeavoured to resign to their destiny. **1827** *Examiner* 325/2 The sun is resigning to the softer sway of the moon. **1861** FLOR. NIGHTINGALE *Nursing* ii. (ed. 2) 23 People..take every disease as a matter of course, to be 'resigned to'.

7. To make surrender or relinquishment.

1738 WESLEY *Ps.* CXXXIX. ii, Thy Voice would break the Bars of Death, And make the Grave resign. **1871** R. ELLIS tr. *Catullus* viii. 9 Now she resigns thee; child, do thou resign no less. *a* **1964** in *Penguin Bk. Austral. Ballads* (1964) 75 'Die or resign, Jack Donahoe!' they [*sc.* police] shouted in their joy.

† **re'sign**, *v.*[2] *Obs. rare*[−1]. [ad. L. *resignāre* to unseal: see prec.] *trans.* To disclose, reveal.

1595 B. BARNES *Div. Cent. Sonn.* xxi, Whome with thine angels manna thou didst feede,..When Moyses first thy statutes did resigne.

re-sign (riː-), *v.*[3] [RE- 5 a.] **a.** *trans.* To sign again.

1805 W. TAYLOR in *Monthly Mag.* XX. 111 A monarch signs and resigns his name so often. **1855** PUSEY *Doctr. Real Pres.* i. (1869) 155 The German copy of the Confession was ..formally re-signed at subsequent periods.

b. *intr.* Of a sportsman, performer, etc.: to sign a contract for a further period. Also *trans.*, to renew the contract of (a person).

1938 C. E. SUTCLIFFE et al. *Story of Football League* iii. 19 The player claimed from the club a sum of £250 which.. had been promised him..on re-signing in June. **1951** *People* 3 June 8/3 We are urging players not to re-sign for next season until we have consulted the Ministry. **1976** *Jrnl.* (Newcastle) 26 Nov., Berwick Rangers have re-signed centre-forward Billy Laing..who has been on a month's trial at Shielfield. **1977** *Rolling Stone* 21 Apr. 5/1 (*caption*) The Rolling Stones re-sign with Atlantic.

† **re'signal**, *sb. Obs. rare*[−1]. [f. RESIGN *v.*[1] + -AL[1].] Resignation.

1634 SANDERSON *Serm.* II. 283 A bold and just challenge of an old judge, made before all the people, upon his resignal of the government into the hands of a new king.

re-'signal (riː-), *v.* [RE- 5 c.] *trans.* To refurnish with railway signals. Hence **re-'signalling** *vbl. sb.*

1928 *Observer* 10 June 5/4 (*heading*) Re-signalling London Bridge. **1970** *Railway Mag.* Oct. 577/1 A further stage of the resignalling of the Bristol region..was completed in mid-August.., following which the London—Reading—Bath —Bristol route is now entirely controlled by colour-light signals. **1977** *Modern Railways* Dec. 469/1 However, until the Victoria and Brighton area resignalling projects are completed..the practical scope for a general speed-up of train services is minimal.

† **re'signant**, *sb. Obs. rare.* [a. F. *résignant*, or ad. L. *resignant-*: see RESIGN *v.*[1] and -ANT[1].] One who resigns.

1597 *Lawes Parlt. Scot.* Table, s.v. *Resignation*, The procuratorie suld be sealed and subscrived be the resignant. **1620** BRENT tr. *Sarpi's Hist. Counc. Trent* VIII. 792 The better sort were excluded by resignation, and hee onely preferred who pleased the resignant. **1693** HACKETT *Life Abp. Williams* II. 27 The good News came together, very welcome to the Resignant, that Sir Thomas Coventry should have that Honour.

resignant, *a. Her.* ? *Obs.* [a. F. *résignant*: cf. prec.] (See quots.)

1572 BOSSEWELL *Armorie* II. 42 Their tayles forked,.. resignante, reuerberante..and countercoloured. **1688** HOLME *Armoury* II. vii. 138/2 The tail resignant, is when the same is lost or gone, hath no tail, or maketh no shew of a Tail. *c* **1828** BERRY *Encycl. Herald.* I. s.v., This term is sometimes applied to the tail of the lion when it is hid, as tail resignant.

re'signatary. [ad. F. *résignataire*: see next and -ARY[1].] One in whose favour something is resigned.

a **1768** ERSKINE *Inst. Law Scot.* II. vii. §18 Upon this act a notarial instrument is taken by him in whose favour resignation is made, called the resignatary. **1884** *Catholic Dict.* (1897) 788/1 A conditional resignation..is of five kinds,..(3) with the right of resumption, if the resignatary should die before the resigner.

† **resignate**, *v. Obs.*[−1] [f. L. *resignāt-*, ppl. stem or *resignāre*: see RESIGN *v.*[1] and -ATE[3].] To resign. In *ppl. a.* **resignating**.

1692 W. MARSHALL *Myst. Sanctif.* vi. (1764) 91 Their salvation is by faith, because sincere obedience is wrought in them.., and some call it the resignating act of faith.

resignation (rɛzɪgˈneɪʃən). Also 4–5 -cio(u)n, 6 -tioun; 5–6 resygnacyon. [a. F. *résignation*, †-*acion* (14th c.), = Sp. *resignacion*, It. *risegnazione*, med.L. *resignation-em*: see RESIGN *v.*[1] and -ATION.]

1. The (*or* an) action of resigning an office, etc.

a. *Eccl.* (See quots. 1598 and 1680.)

1387 TREVISA *Higden* (Rolls) VIII. 309 Also he reserved to hym self þe first benefice þat voyded by deeþ, by resignacioun, oþer by translacioun. **1467–8** *Rolls of Parlt.* V. 591/2 What so ever Prebende, that..by deth, resignation, dymyssion, or eny other cause..happeth to fall voide. **1562** *Bk. of Presidentes* 152 b, An Indenture vpon the resignacion of a benefice. **1598** [RASTELL] *Termes Lawes* 173/1 Resignation, is where an incumbent of a Church resigneth or leaueth to the Ordinarie, which did admit him to it, or to his successours, and that differeth from surrender. **1611** COTGR., *Regrés*, a resignation of a Benefice, vpon condition, that if during the Resignors life it become voyd by the resignation or death of the Resignee, it shall returne..vnto him. **1680** GODOLPHIN *Rep. Can.* (ed. 2) xxv. §3. 284 Resignation is *Juris proprii spontanea Refutatio*, or the voluntary yielding up of the Incumbent (into the hands of the Ordinary) his interest and right, which he hath in his Benefice. **1706** tr. *Dupin's Eccl. Hist. 16th Cent.* II. v. 91 That Resignations into the Pope's Hands are null, if the Resigner does not outlive his Resignation Twenty Days. **1765** BLACKSTONE *Comm.* I. 476 Archbishopricks and bishopricks may become void..by resignation. All resignations must be made to some superior. **1818** CRUISE *Digest* (ed. 2) III. 38 It was contended on the part of the bishop, that although there were several adjudged cases upon the subject of general bonds of resignation [etc.]. **1873** PHILLIMORE *Eccl. Law* I. II. xiii. 517 In this chapter the grave subject of the resignation of an office or benefice by a priest is considered.

attrib. **1680** GODOLPHIN *Rep. Can.* (ed. 2) Index, Resignation-Bonds, whether good in Law.

b. In general use.

1412–20 LYDG. *Chron. Troy* I. 126 For whiche he made a resygnacion To his brother, next heyr by degre. **1494** FABYAN *Chron.* VII. 547 And for the sayde resygnacyon shuld haue his full force and strengthe, he..redde the scrowle of resygnacyon hymselfe. **1593** SHAKS. *Rich. II*, IV. i. 179 The Resignation of thy State and Crowne To Henry Bullingbrooke. **1601** R. JOHNSON *Kingd. & Commw.* (1603) 101 Immediately vppon this resignation, with a loude voice he nominateth the partie, whome in his iudgement hee thinketh woorthy to succeede in his place. **1658–9** *Burton's Diary* (1828) IV. 237 Henry II. went thither and they made a resignation of their power to him. **1756** NUGENT *Gr. Tour, Netherlands* I. 217 The chair of leather gilt, in which Charles V. performed the ceremony of his resignation. **1789** *Constitution U.S.* i. ¶3 If vacancies [in the senate] happen by resignation or otherwise, the executive may make temporary appointments. **1848** W. H. KELLY tr. *L. Blanc's Hist. Ten Yrs.* I. 481 When..the ministers learned the step that had been taken.., they..gave in their resignation. **1898** *Green's Encycl. Sc. Law* X. 317 Resignation of Trustees.

c. In *Chess*.

1969 A. GLYN *Dragon Variation* ix. 271 One or two of the inexpert protested at the resignation. ('He hasn't been mated, has he? Why does he give up? Why doesn't he play on?')

2. *Sc. Law.* 'The form by which a vassal returns the fee into the hands of a superior' (Bell).

1555 *Sc. Acts Mary* (1814) II. 494/1 All resignatiounis to be maid be vassallis..of thair propirteis in the superiouris handis. **1569** *Reg. Privy Council Scot.* I. 670 To dispone heretablie the landis of Strathnaver..for payment of the sowme of four thowsand markis, be resignatioun, to be haldin of the King. *a* **1768** ERSKINE *Inst. Law Scot.* II. vii. §17 The proper symbols of resignation are staff and baton. **1814** SCOTT *Wav.* lxxi, It will cost but a charter of resignation *in favorem*. **1838** W. BELL *Dict. Law Scot.* 858 Resignation is made in virtue of a procuratory of resignation.

3. A giving up *of* oneself (to God).

c **1450** tr. *De Imitatione* III. xlii. 112 Of pure resignacion of a mannys self. **1504** ATKYNSON tr. *De Imitatione* III. xlii. 231 If they make a hole resygnacyon & a dayly oblacion of them selfe. *a* **1664** FRANK *Serm.* (1672) 212 A voluntary resignation of our selves and all that is ours to his choice, order, and disposing.

4. The fact of resigning oneself or of being resigned; acquiescence, submission, compliance.

1647 CLARENDON *Hist. Reb.* I. §106 Though he was not superiour to all other men in the affection, or rather resignation of the King,..he had a full share in his Master's esteem. **1736** BUTLER *Anal.* I. v. Wks. 1874 I. 109 The proper discipline for resignation is affliction. **1781** GIBBON *Decl. & F.* xxxi. (1787) III. 243 Proba supported, with Christian resignation, the loss of immense riches. **1838** LYTTON *Leila* II. ii, 'Our day is come' said the good knight Villena, with bitter resignation. **1881** BROOKS *Candle of Lord* 98 You want to show him the possibility of a resignation and delight in suffering.

b. Const. *to* a person, his will, etc.

1663 COWLEY *Cutter Colman St.* IV. iv, The same Obedience and Resignation to a Father's Will I found in my Aurelia. **1690** LOCKE *Hum. Und.* IV. xvi. §4 A blind resignation to an authority which the understanding of man acknowledges not. **1711** STEELE *Spect.* No. 153 ¶1 An abandoned Resignation to their Appetites. **1736** BUTLER *Anal.* I. v. 141 Passive submission or resignation to his will. **1812** KNOX & JEBB *Corr.* II. 89 Resignation to God, whether in the way of obedience or of suffering, can be substantial, only so far as it grows out of knowledge and love.

5. *attrib.*, as ***resignation letter, rally, speech.***

a **1974** R. CROSSMAN *Diaries* (1976) II. 713 When the word didn't come he was compelled to write his resignation letter. **1961** *Economist* 2 Dec. 906/1 Democrats are beginning to repudiate their party at public 'resignation rallies'. **1938** H. NICOLSON *Diary* 3 Oct. (1966) 374 It begins by Duff Cooper making his resignation speech.

Hence **resig'nationism** (see quot.).

1898 *Contemp. Rev.* May 736 Nietzsche..distinguishes between the 'romantic pessimism'..and the 'Dionysiac pessimism'... He brands the former as Resignationism.

resig'nationist. *rare.* [f. RESIGNATION + -IST.] One who follows a philosophy of resignation, a believer in resignationism.

1931 [see RENUNCIANT *sb.*].

resigne, obs. form of RAISIN.

† **re'signe**, *a. Obs. rare*[−1]. (See quot.)

14.. *Le Venery de Tuety* in *Rel. Ant.* I. 151 When he [the hart] goth wexyng tyl he come to .xxxij. yere, than is he callyd an hert resygne, for cause his hed aftir that tyme wexith no furthere.

re'signed, *ppl. a.* [f. RESIGN *v.*[1] + -ED[1].]

† **1.** With *up*. Given up, abandoned, surrendered.

1654–66 EARL ORRERY *Parthen.* (1676) 221 The receiving a resign'd up Mistriss, is like losing a life for a Friend. *Ibid.* 638 He shipt his Army for Italy in the resigned-up Fleet of the Pontick King.

2. Full of resignation; submissive, acquiescent.

1699 COLLIER *Def. Short View* 44, I wonder at his being so Resign'd. What, not care to have stark Nonsense found upon him! **1757** GRAY *Mrs. Clarke* 7 In agony, in death resign'd. **1812** J. WILSON *Isle of Palms* III. 276 Though ever lost to human kind And all they love, they are resign'd. **1855** MACAULAY *Hist. Eng.* xviii. IV. 170 Anne..assumed the interesting character of a meek, resigned sufferer. **1894** WOLSELEY *Marlborough* I. 284 Sufficiently philosophical to be resigned, he was yet too ambitious to be contented.

Comb. **1856** MRS. CARLYLE *Lett.* II. 294 A sad, grey, resigned-looking, suffering woman.

b. Const. *to*.

1747 *Mem. Nutrebian Crt.* II. 91 Resigned to death with the heroick firmness of a primitive christian. **1781** COWPER *Charity* 151 To deep sadness sullenly resign'd. **1820** BYRON *Mar. Fal.* I. ii. 43 Calm, but not overcast, he stood resign'd To the decree. **1838** LYTTON *Alice* II. ii, Evelyn..had grown in some measure reconciled and resigned to her change of abode.

c. Characterized by resignation.

1749 FIELDING *Tom Jones* VI. iii, He should insist on the most resigned obedience from his daughter. **1833** TENNYSON *Two Voices* 98 Thought resign'd, A healthy frame, a quiet mind. **1885** J. K. JEROME *On the Stage* 111 A limp horse that..looked the picture of resigned misery.

3. That has retired from a position.

1896 *Daily News* 11 Mar. 4/7 A major..has threatened an action for libel against one of the resigned officers.

re'signedly, *adv.* [f. prec. + -LY[2]] In a resigned manner; with resignation; submissively.

1671 WOODHEAD *St. Teresa* I. Pref. 19 She advised them, patiently, and resignedly, to bear this Cross. *a* **1700** KEN *Hymnotheo* Poet. Wks. 1721 III. 386 Lovers in their Arms resign'dly died. *a* **1721** SHEFFIELD (Dk. Buckhm.) *Wks.* (1753) I. 79 Will any dog..Resin'dly leave his bitches and his bones, To turn a wheel? **1857** W. COLLINS *Dead Secret* (1861) 251 To face resignedly the duties and the sacrifices which the discovery of it imposed on them. **1887** *Cornh. Mag.* Mar. 277 The sports of the season..pass slowly and resignedly.

re'signedness. [-NESS.] Resignation.

a **1664** FRANK *Serm.* (1672) 212 We begin our Christianity with the same resignedness. *a* **1695** KETTLEWELL *Chr. Obed.* (1715) 533 Our trust and dependence, submission and resignedness. **1748** RICHARDSON *Clarissa* (1811) I. 139 The example which my mother sets of meekness, and resignedness to the wills of others. **1859** GEO. ELIOT *Adam Bede* xxxix, The man..going forth with sad blind resignedness to an unreal sorrow.

resignee. [f. RESIGN *v.*[1] + -EE[1].]

1. One to whom anything is resigned. ? *Obs.*

1611 COTGR. s.v. *Survivance*, That the Resignor may.. otherwise dispose of it if he happen to suruiue the Resignee. **1642** tr. *Perkins' Prof. Bk.* i. §47. 22 An infant may be Grantee, Lessee, Obligee, Resignee.

2. = RESIGNER.

1761 *Second Let. to Earl of Bxxx* 1 A right honourable resignee. **1973** *Times* 15 May 17/3 The only resignee that Mr Nixon chose to criticize.

re'signer. [-ER[1].] One who resigns.

1555 *Sc. Acts Mary* (1814) II. 494/1 That the Instrument thairof be seilit with the seill of the resignar. **1611** FLORIO, *Risegnatore*, a resigner. **1706** [see RESIGNATION 1]. *a* **1768** ERSKINE *Inst. Law Scot.* II. vii. §20 In resignations *ad remanentiam* made..by the resigner himself a special solemnity is introduced. *a* **1797** H. WALPOLE *Geo. II* (1820) I. 157 Of all the resigners, the Duke of Grafton had treated his master with the greatest decency. **1806** W. TAYLOR in *Monthly Mag.* XXII. 32 The resigners of livings, to be consistent, must maintain [etc.]. **1884** [see RESIGNATARY].

re'signful, *a. rare.* [f. RESIGN *v.*[1] + -FUL.] Expressing resignation.

1876 MRS. WHITNEY *Sights & Ins.* II. 419 The faint, tender little face, the sweet mouth, the resignful eyes.

resigning (rɪˈzaɪnɪŋ), *vbl. sb.* [f. RESIGN *v.*[1] + -ING[1].] Resignation.

1395 PURVEY *Remonstr.* (1851) 144 Bi merciful dispensacioun aftir wilful resigning. *c* **1450** *Godstow Reg.* 202 Þat hir resininge & quite claiminge sholde be sure, she strengthid hit with þe puttinge to of her seele. **1482** *Caxton's Chron. Eng.* ccliii. X 5 b, The peple wondred of the ceesing and resignyng of Felix to hym. **1530** PALSGR. 262/1 Resyning of a thyng. **1743** *Buccleuch MSS.* (Hist. MSS. Comm.) I. 407 His Lordship's resigning is of no loss to the service.

re'signing, *ppl. a.* [-ING[2].] That resigns.

1703 COLLIER *Ess. Mor. Subj.* II. 99 Neither ought we to be too Implicit or Resigning to Authorities. **1710** STEELE *Tatler* No. 198 ¶2 The peaceful, mild, resigning, humble

Inhabitant, that animated her beauteous Body. **1894** R. BRIDGES *Humours Crt.* I. 109 The still fresh air of this October morning, With its resigning odours. **1899** J. W. S. SIMPSON *Mem. W. S. Simpson* 100 This resigning Choir found a home in the Church of St. Vedast.

re'signment. Now *rare.* [f. as next + -MENT.] The act of resigning; resignation.

c **1470** HARDING *Chron.* CLVII. iv, Then his title he sought By resignement and renunciacion. **1592** *Nobody & Someb.* in Simpson *Sch. Shaks.* (1878) I. 330 Give up thy state to these two princely youthes, And thy resignment shal preserve thy life. **1606** G. W[OODCOCKE] *Hist. Ivstine* XVII. 69 With his life [he] made resignement of the kingdome of Macedon. **1648** BOYLE *Seraph. Love* (1660) 8 That Love.. which results from an entire Resignment to..the Lov'd Party. **1729** BUTLER *Serm.* Wks. 1874 II. 70 Time..begets in us that resignment of temper, which ought to have been produced by a better cause. **1825** SOUTHEY *Tale Paraguay* Poet. Wks. VII. 22 In this resignment to their hopeless case. **1891** *Q. Reg. Current Hist.* (Detroit) Feb. 10 It was feared that the Chancellor's resignment portended a precipitation of the inevitable war.

†**re'signor.** *Obs. rare.* [f. RESIGN *v.*[1] + -OR.] One who resigns.

1611 COTGR. s.v. *Regrés,* If during the Resignors life it become voyd by the resignation or death of the Resignee.

resile (rɪˈzaɪl), *v.* [ad. obs. F. *resiler, resilir,* or L. *resilīre* to jump back, recoil, f. *re-* RE- 2 a + *salīre* to jump, leap: see SALIENT *a.*]

In senses 1–3 chiefly in Scottish use.

1. *intr.* To draw back *from* an agreement, contract, statement, etc.

1529 *State P. Hen. VIII,* I. 343 If the Quene wold herafter resile and goo back from that, she semeth nowe to be contented with. **1671** [R. MACWARD] *True Nonconf.* 231 Dare you..say, that the King and Parliament had power, either to resile, or to loose others, from the Bonds, which they themselves had thus established? *a* **1676** BP. GUTHRIE *Mem.* (1702) 46 The next day he resiled from the Writ he had sign'd. **1830** SCOTT *Demonol.* ix. 293 Much pains was taken on her that she might resile from that confession. **1884** *Law Times Rep.* L. 643/1 Neither the company nor the landowner can, without the consent of the other, resile from the..contract.

b. Without const.: To retract, draw back.

1662 J. ELLIS *Retract.* 18, I was so weak as to resile and recal what I had said. **1754** ERSKINE *Princ. Sc. Law* (1809) 67 The party resiling is liable in damages to the other. **1814** SCOTT *Wav.* lxvi, A 'sma' minute, to prevent parties frae resiling'. **1845** CAMPBELL *Chancellors* III. 565 But he thought it was too late to resile.

2. To draw back *from* a course of action, attitude of mind, etc.

1637 GILLESPIE *Eng. Pop. Cerem.* Epist. B, Let them resile from their violent proceedings. **1676** ROW *Contn. Blair's Autobiog.* xii. (1848) 465 It has been said that I have resiled from my wonted zeal for Presbyterial Government. **1813** *Examiner* 22 Feb. 126/2 The noble family had too much real love of their country to resile from her service.

3. To shrink, recoil, retreat, *from* something with aversion or non-acceptance.

1697 CLELAND *Poems* 79 (Jam.), Read Duram and Calvin well; If from their reasons you resile, I'le count you sots. **1776** HUME *My own Life* in *Ess.* I. 6 The more I resiled from their excessive civilities, the more I was loaded with them. **1813** COLLINSON *Key* iii. 60 Other persons resiling with abhorrence from unbelief. **1825** C. BUTLER *Bk. R.C. Ch.* 131 The pope resiled from the salutation. **1873** J. HALL *Questions of Day* viii. 101 So far from resiling from the prophecies,..we regard the volume of evidence furnished by them as ever accumulating with the lapse of time. **1892** BRUCE *Apologetics* II. iii. 201 The modern mind has resiled from the pessimistic views of ethnic religions.

4. Of material things: To recoil or rebound after contact. Also const. *from.*

1708 KEILL *Anim. Secretion* 43 The Particles which hit against one another do not resile, but unite together. **1738** BAYNE *Gout* 102 An unequal velocity of particles will hinder and disturb their attractions, and by resiling from one another, cause an intestine motion which prevents their union. **1805** *Edin. Rev.* VII. 81 The one by impinging on the other must be made to resile, according to the common laws of motion.

b. Of elastic bodies: To return to their original position after being stretched or compressed.

1709 *Phil. Trans.* XXVII. 81 There needs no more for stretching forth the Proboscis thus contracted, but the Fibres to resile to their former Position. **1853** URE *Dict. Arts* (ed. 4) I. 362 The cake of caoutchouc, after being so condensed, resiles much more considerably than after the compressing action of the screw. **1898** MANSON *Trop. Dis.* xxiii. 374 The drainage tube is allowed slowly to resile towards the fixed end.

5. a. To turn back from a point reached.

1887 FERGUSON *Ogham Inscriptions* 97 Reading up to this digit..and resiling thence.

b. To return to one's original position.

1889 *Ch. Q. Rev.* XXVII. 351 It is impossible to specify any body of men of which so large a percentage has resiled as that of those who have become Roman Catholics during the period of which we are now speaking.

Hence **re'siling** *vbl. sb.* Also **re'silement.**

1644 MAXWELL *Prerog. Chr. Kings* 102 The resileing of one partie contractor is not sufficient to void the contract. **1724** *Wodrow's Corr.* (1843) III. 146 A resiling from the declaration made by the Non-subscribers in the Synod. **1822** C. BUTLER *Reminisc.* (ed. 3) 181 Mr. Pitt's resiling from the coalition..will be mentioned in the pages of history with universal commendation. **1884** OGILVIE s.v. *Back* adv. 7, In withdrawal or resilement from an undertaking.

re'siliate, *v. rare*[−1]. [ad. F. *résilier.*] *trans.* To annul, cancel.

1881 *Daily News* 7 Mar. 6/1 Resiliating, at great cost to the State, the contracts with Heilbronner and other houses.

resilience (rɪˈzɪlɪəns). [ad. L. type **resilientia*: see RESILIENT and -ENCE, and cf. It. *resilienza.*]

1. a. The (*or* an) act of rebounding or springing back; rebound, recoil. (See also quot. 1656.)

1626 BACON *Sylva* §245 Whether there be any such Resilience in Eccho's. **1656** BLOUNT *Glossogr., Resilience,* a leaping or skipping back, a rebounding; a going from ones word. ?**1799** COLERIDGE *Hymn to Earth,* Mightier far was the joy of thy sudden resilience. **1843** CARLYLE *Past & Pr.* (1858) 79 The Heaviest..has its deflexions..nay at times its resiliences, its reboundings. **1866** J. MARTINEAU *Ess.* I. 41 The heart does not always propel without resilience.

b. Revolt, recoil *from* something.

1858 SEARS *Athan.* III. ii. 267 Those smaller sects whose fierce resilience from Catholicism isolates them from the common reason. **1890** GARNETT *Milton* 38 Nor can we doubt that the old Puritan fully approved his son's resilience from a church defined by Arminianism and prelacy.

c. Repugnance, antagonism.

1882 MOZLEY *Reminisc.* I. xii. 85 It was possibly a mutual resilience between him [Hartley Coleridge] and people of more orderly ways that prevented him from standing at Oriel till some years after.

2. Elasticity; the power of resuming the original shape or position after compression, bending, etc.; *spec.* the energy per unit volume absorbed by a material when it is subjected to strain, or the maximum value of this when the elastic limit is not exceeded.

1824 TREDGOLD *Cast Iron* 82 The term modulus of resilience, I have ventured to apply to the number which represents the power of a material to resist an impulsive force. **1834** *Good's Study Med.* (ed. 4) I. 530 The natural elasticity or resilience of the lungs. **1867** C. T. F. YOUNG *Fouling Iron Ships* 164 To bend back again.., if the metal possesses sufficient resilience to do so. **1897** *Allbutt's Syst. Med.* IV. 470 [The skin] giving a sensation of the loss of all elasticity or resilience. **1908** E. S. ANDREWS *Theory & Design of Structures* i. 27 The work done per unit volume of a material in producing strain is called resilience. **1965** J. A. CORMACK *Definitions Strength of Materials* iii. 67 Show that resilience per cubic inch in direct tension or compression may be expressed in the form $f^2/2E$, where f is the intensity of stress induced and E is the modulus of elasticity. **1978** B. I. SANDOR *Strength of Materials* iv. 79 The maximum value of the elastic strain energy in a unit volume that has not been permanently deformed is called the modulus of resilience. *fig.* **1893** *Independent* (N.Y.) 19 Oct., The resilience and the elasticity of spirit which I had even ten years ago.

resiliency (rɪˈzɪlɪənsɪ). [Cf. prec. and -ENCY.]

1. Tendency to rebound or recoil.

1668 H. MORE *Div. Dial.* III. xxiv. (1713) 238 There is the more strong and peremptory Resiliency from this sordid Region of Misery and Sin. **1676** —— *Remarks* 143 The resiliency of the Quick-silver against the top of the Tube. **1751** JOHNSON *Rambler* No. 110 ¶7 The common resiliency of the mind from one extreme to another. **1826** [J. R. BEST] *Four Yrs. France* 78 Disgusted with these appearances of distrust and resiliency.

2. Tendency to return *to* a state.

1778 *Phil. Surv. S. Ireland* 144 Such is the resiliency of all nature to its original state.

3. = RESILIENCE 2.

1835–6 *Todd's Cycl. Anat.* I. 511/2 The resiliency by which the skin recovers itself after pressure. **1863** WYNTER *Subtle Brains* 33 The process of vulcanization that gives such extraordinary resiliency to the material. **1890** W. J. GORDON *Foundry* 191 The advantage of combining the softening influence of the saccharine with the resiliency of the colloid.

4. Buoyancy, power of recovery.

1857 R. TOMES *Amer. in Japan* xvi. 379 Notwithstanding the calamities caused by the earthquake, there was shown a resiliency in the Japanese character which spoke well for their energy. **1888** *Leeds Mercury* 24 Feb. 4/7 The active properties of resiliency possessed by the Russian rouble.

resilient (rɪˈzɪlɪənt), *a.* [ad. L. *resilient-em,* pres. pple. of *resilīre* to RESILE.]

1. Returning to the original position; springing back, recoiling, etc. Also, looking back.

1644 BULWER *Chiron.* 43 The hand resilient or leapeing back to the Northward of the Body. **1706** PHILLIPS (ed. Kersey), *Resilient,* leaping back, rebounding, or recoiling. **1822–34** *Good's Study Med.* (ed. 4) III. 191 Absorbing what he calls the resilient pulsations of sound. **1839–48** BAILEY *Festus* xxx. 345 The soul in death resilient Looks back to whence its impulse came. **1880** BLACKMORE *Mary Anerley* III. iv. 60 Never yet looked horse through bridle, without at least one eye resilient towards the charm of headstall.

b. *resilient escapement,* a form of lever escapement used in watches.

1879 *Cassell's Techn. Educ.* IV. 369/2 Another modification, called 'Cole's resilient', consists in the bending of the extreme points of the teeth back [etc.]. **1884** F. J. BRITTEN *Watch & Clockm.* 150 Mr. J. F. Cole devised a resilient escapement without any banking pins.

2. Resuming the original shape or position after being bent, compressed, or stretched.

1674 PETTY *Disc. Roy. Soc.* 122, I think it easiest to consider Elastic, Springing, or Resilient Bodies, as Laminæ, Laths, or Lines. **1767** GOOCH *Treat. Wounds* I. 89 The fibrils of the resilient part of the nerve. **1859** *Todd's Cycl. Anat.* V. 287/2 The power of the heart is materially reinforced by the resilient structure which composes the parietes of the aortic bulb. **1873** *Contemp. Rev.* XXII. 181 His conscience consolidates itself, the original fibres grow firmer, more massive, and more resilient.

b. *resilient stricture* (see quot.).

1874 VAN BUREN *Dis. Genit. Organs* 102 A resilient stricture is one which..is elastic, India-rubber like, contracting quickly after being dilated. **1891** MOULIN *Surg.* II. xxiii. 1273.

3. *fig.* Of persons, their minds, etc.: Rising readily again after being depressed; hence, cheerful, buoyant, exuberant.

1830 *Fraser's Mag.* II. 90 One vast receptacle for the abode of resilient and noisy saints like unto himself. **1859** S. R. HOLE *Tour Irel.* 30 Nothing but..the resilient spirit of roving Englishmen could have induced us to sally forth. **1870** J. HAMILTON *Moses, Man of God* viii. 150 Resolute and resilient is the stout heart of the sinner.

Hence **re'silientness,** 'rebounding Quality, Resiliency' (Bailey, vol. II, 1727).

re'siliently, *adv.* [f. RESILIENT *a.* + -LY[2].] In a resilient manner, esp. such that the original position is resumed after bending or other shock.

1946 *Jrnl. Inst. Electr. Engineers* XCIII. IIIA. 330/2 The components were insulated from mechanical shock by mounting them on a tray resiliently supported within the frame. **1977** *BSI News* Oct. 8/3 A straight extension of ISO 2373 for the larger machines is not necessarily possible because of the difficulty of resiliently mounting them.

resilin (ˈrɛzɪlɪn). *Biol.* [f. L. *resil-īre* to jump back, recoil, RESILE + -IN[1].] An elastic material formed of cross-linked protein chains that is found in the cuticles of many species of insect, notably forming the hinges and ligaments of wings.

1960 *New Scientist* 14 July 104/1 Resilin is a protein of a new kind in which the protein chains are cross-linked by means of bonds of a new sort which are resistant to tryptic digestion. **1960** T. WEIS-FOGH in *Jrnl. Exper. Biol.* XXXVII. 889 The main conclusion is that the characteristic elasticity is caused by a peculiar protein, called resilin, which differs from other structural proteins also in respect of amino acid composition. **1961** BAILEY & WEIS-FOGH in *Biochimica & Biophysica Acta* XLVIII. 453 We therefore propose to name it resilin, derived from the Latin resilire, *i.e.* to spring back (pronounced rez'ilin). (We are indebted to Professor D. S. Robertson, Cambridge, who suggested the name.) **1969** R. F. CHAPMAN *Insects* xxii. 435 Resilin contains various amino acids including two previously unknown ones which provide the links between the protein chains. **1970** *Nature* 26 Dec. 1338/1 Resilin is a significant structural component of the sucking pump in many different insects. **1973** *Sci. Amer.* Nov. 92/3 The flea's leap is powered not by muscle alone but is assisted by the elastic protein resilin.

†**resi'lition.** *Obs.* [f. RESILE *v.* + -ITION.] The (*or* an) act of springing back; recoil, rebound, resilience.

1658 PHILLIPS, *Resilition,* a rebounding, or leaping back. **1671** R. BOHUN *Wind* 10 By Descension or Resilition, from the Middle Region. **1708** KEILL *Anim. Secretion* 22 The greater their Elasticity, their Concursions and Resilitions will be the more sensible. **1727–38** CHAMBERS *Cycl., Recoil,* or *Rebound,* the resilition of a body, chiefly a fire-arm.

†**resil(i)u'ation.** *Obs.* [Erroneous for RECIDIVATION. Cf. RESIDUATION *sb.*[1]] Relapse.

1513 MORE in *Grafton's Contn. Harding* (1812) 488 There is, as phisicians saie, and as we also finde, double yͤ perell in the resylynacion [*sic*; **1543** resiliuacion] yᵗ was in the firste syckenesse. **1577–87** HOLINSHED *Chron.* I. 178/2 The English kingdome.., as it had beene falne into a resiluation, came to extreame ruine. **1580** LYLY *Euphues* (Arb.) 316, I see now that as the resiluation of an Ague is desperate, and the second opening of a veyne deadly [etc.].

resilium (rɪˈzɪlɪəm). *Conch.* [mod.L., f. as RESILIN + *-ium,* neut. ending.] The resilient central part of the 'hinge' of a bivalve, which tends to force apart the two valves.

1906 G. BOURNE tr. *Pelseneer's Mollusca* in E. R. Lankester *Treat. Zool.* V. v. 213 The ligament finally becomes external..or internal; in the latter case it is a 'resilium'. **1926** *Proc. Malacol. Soc.* XVII. 44 Nacreous shells..possess glutinous hinge-joints consisting of conchyolin disposed in a dual fashion as 'resilium'—more or less in the centre of the hinge base—and 'ligament' to the right and left of it. **1962** *Science* 29 June 1121/3 (*heading*) Aragonite in the resilium of oysters. **1973** R. T. ABBOTT *Kingdom of Seashell* 16/1 These valves are brought together by one or two strong adductor muscles and forced ajar by a rubberlike wedge, or resilium, which acts much the same way as a rubber wedge placed in the hinged side of a closing door.

re-'silver (riː-), *v.* [RE- 5 a.] *trans.* To silver again; to replate with silver or quicksilver.

1839 in G. S. Haight *Geo. Eliot & J. Chapman* (1969) 259 Sextants, Quadrants, &c., re-silvered and repaired. **1856** *Orr's Circ. Sci., Pract. Chem.* 92 Re-silvering old articles. **1873** *Young Englishwoman* Jan. 52/1 Whether looking-glasses can be re-silvered... A very good furniture dealer will re-silver this for you. **1875** BEDFORD *Sailor's Pkt.-bk.* v. (ed. 2) 152 Directions for re-silvering sextant glasses when injured by damp or wet. **1973** W. H. HALLAHAN *Ross Forgery* iii. 40 The mirror must have been resilvered not too many years ago.

†**resimated,** *ppl. a. Obs.*[−1] [f. L. *resīm-us,* f. *re-* RE- + *sīmus* snub-nosed.] Turned up.

1681 GREW *Musæum* I. 73 These five Bones are resimated or bended upward, with some resemblance to a Saddle.

resin, obs. f. RAISIN; var. REASON *sb.*[2]

resin (ˈrɛzɪn), *sb.* Forms: 4 recyn(e, reysen, 4–6 resyn, 6–8 resine, 8– resin (9 rezin). [ad. F.

résine, ad. L. *rēsīna* (Sp., Pg., and It. *resina*), cogn. with Gr. *ῥητίνη*. See also ROSIN.]

1. a. A vegetable product, formed by secretion in special canals in almost all trees and plants, from many of which (as the fir and pine) it exudes naturally, or can be readily obtained by incision; various kinds are extensively used in making varnishes or adhesive compositions, and in pharmacy. (Cf. GUM-RESIN and OLEO-RESIN.)

1388 WYCLIF *Jer.* viii. 22 Whether resyn is not in Galaad? *Ibid.* li. 8 Take ȝe recyn to the sorewe therof. *c* **1450** *M.E. Med. Bk.* (Heinrich) 225 Do þer to pouder recles, of resyn, & a party of virgyne wex, & boile hyt wel. **1538** LELAND *Itin.* (1769) V. 91 The Wood of them in Burning savorith of Resine. **1744** BERKELEY *Siris* § 18 A good pine might be made to yield resin every year. **1807** J. E. SMITH *Phys. Bot.* 27 Here we find in appropriate vessels the resin of the Fir and Juniper. **1843** HOLTZAPFFEL *Turning* I. 30 In many of the more dense woods, we..find an abundance of gum or resin. **1876** HARLEY *Mat. Med.* (ed. 6) 409 Resin possesses the valuable quality of adhesiveness, and it is also slightly stimulant.

b. With *a* and *pl.* A particular kind of resin.

1801 *Med. Jrnl.* V. 366 Benzoic acid has been hitherto found in no other vegetable substance, except resins and balsams. **1837** M. DONOVAN *Dom. Econ.* II. 349 The aromatic portion of ginger is a resin, which constitutes about one tenth of the whole root. **1884** BOWER & SCOTT *De Bary's Phaner.* 185 Resins are abundant, e.g. in the Euphorbias, and in Opium.

2. A resinous precipitate obtained by special treatment of certain vegetable products; a similar substance obtained from the bile of animals.

1681 tr. *Willis' Rem. Med. Wks.* Vocab., *Resine*, a chymical extraction of several druggs so called, being in substance like to rosine or resine. **1712** tr. *Pomet's Hist. Drugs* I. 29 The Resin or Magistery of Jalap is made with Spirit of Wine. **1826** HENRY *Elem. Chem.* I. 401 The resin of bile may be obtained by the following process... Berzelius, however,..denies that it is a true resin. **1880** J. W. LEGG *Bile* 2 He also separated a resin or fat, to which he attributed in chief the colour and taste of the bile.

3. Any synthetic material resembling a natural resin; now usu. any of a large and varied class of synthetic organic polymeric materials (solid or liquid) that are thermosetting or thermoplastic (see also quot. 1934) and are used esp. as plastics or their chief ingredients. Freq. with qualifying adj. or sb., esp. *synthetic*.

1883 *Amer. Chem. Jrnl.* V. 338 Concentrated sulphuric acid on a mixture of benzoic aldehyde and resorcin gave a reddish resin. **1909** *Chem. Abstr.* III. 1818 Process of manufacturing synthetic resins as substitutes for shellac, consisting in treating *o*-cresol with formaldehyde in the presence of an acid. **1934** *Chem. Rev.* XV. 123 The resinous plastic field may well be divided into two main divisions dependent upon properties which find reflection in use. (1) The resins, which are melted for flow and cooled for hardening into the finished shape... (2) The resinoids, which in molding are heated for flow and also heated for hardening effect. **1937** *Discovery* Jan. 27/2 A new series of synthetic resins, claimed to be as clear as optical glass and to be..non-shattering,..is being marketed in the United States. **1943**, etc. [see ION EXCHANGE]. **1951** *Engineering* 20 Apr. 469/3 The setting of synthetic-resin glues by high frequency heating. **1957** *Which?* Autumn 20/2 The actual processing of these fabrics consists of various ways of putting the resin in under heat and pressure. **1970** GAIT & HANCOCK *Plastics & Synthetic Rubbers* iii. 60 Production of phenolic resins is still increasing. **1973** *Materials & Technol.* VI. i. 86 Much imported and all British-made plywood is manufactured with synthetic resin adhesives of one type or other. **1976** *McGraw-Hill Yearbk. Sci. & Technol.* 182/1 Probably the cheapest resin to use for plastic bottles is polystyrene.

4. a. *attrib.* and *Comb.*, as *resin acid, candle, †gum, lac, -oil, -pot, soap, -wax*; *resin-based, -bonded, -finished, -scented, -tipped, -treated* adjs.; **†resinasphalt**, = RETINASPHALT; **resin-bush**, a South African shrub (see quot.); **resin-flux**, an excessive flow of resin, occurring as a disease in pine-trees; **resin gas**, illuminating gas made from resin; **resin opal**, a variety of opal (see quot.); **resin-plant** (see quot.); **resin-weed**, = *rosin-weed*.

1892 *Photogr. Ann.* II. 77 Rectified turpentine should always be used, since the crude oil contains *resin acids, formic acid, etc. **1811** PINKERTON *Petral.* I. 595 In the strata of this substance, Mr. Hatchet also observed small masses approaching to the nature of the lignite of Cologne, and which he called *resinasphaltum*, or *resinasphalt. **1959** *Times* 3 Mar. 7/7 *Resin-based paint. **1940** 'PLASTES' *Plastics in Industry* x. 147 Not only have a number of private houses been built of *resin-bonded plywood, but also several garages and petrol stations. **1959** *Engineering* 16 Jan. 86/1 This year there are in evidence still more hulls either moulded or sheathed in resin-bonded glass fibre. **1978** *Lancashire Life* Oct. 125/2 Birchwood ply used for work tops, resin-bonded and waterproofed particle board, steel runners with nylon bearings, [etc.]. **1866** *Treas. Bot.* 479/2 *Euryops speciosissimus* is called *Resin-bush by the colonists, because of a gummy exudation often seen on the stem and leaves. **1849** JAMES *Woodman* vii, Neither lamp nor taper, nor even a common *resin candle, gave light within. **1963** A. J. HALL *Textile Sci.* v. 231 It also has the effect of making the *resin-finished fabric tear more easily. **1887** GARNSEY & BALFOUR tr. *De Bary's Comp. Morph. Fungi* 384 The symptoms of disease which precede death in fir-trees are known as '*resin-flux' ('Harzsticken, Harzüberfülle'). *Note*, The word resin-flux is therefore introduced as indicating a prominent symptom of the disease, although it is not an exact rendering of the German terms. **1836–41** BRANDE *Chem.* (ed. 5) 556 *Resin Gas. **1856** *Orr's Circ. Sci., Pract. Chem.* 516 The liquor which is produced by the compression of resin-gas. **1382** WYCLIF *Jer.* li. 8 Taketh *recyne gumme to his sorewe. **1839** URE *Dict. Arts* 1097 The Hindus from time immemorial have possessed the *resin lac. **1856** *Orr's Circ. Sci., Pract. Chem.* 518 Seven and a quarter gallons of *resin-oil. **1868** DANA *Min.* (ed. 5) 198 *Resin opal (Wachsopal, Pechopal, *Germ.*), wax-, honey- to ochre-yellow, with a resinous lustre. **1884** MILLER *Plant-n.* 115/1 *Resin-plant, Carana, *Bursera acuminata*. **1890** E. H. BARKER *Wayfaring France* 40 The earthen *resin-pots fixed to the pines. **1937** J. BETJEMAN *Continual Dew* 11 Drained dark the pines in *resin-scented rain. **1875** *Ure's Dict. Arts* III. 850 Manufacture of Yellow or *Resin Soap. **1922** JOYCE *Ulysses* 653 A pyre of crosslaid *resintipped sticks. **1962** J. T. MARSH *Self-Smoothing Fabrics* i. 5 It was soon observed that the *resin-treated fabrics possess certain properties in addition to 'crease-resistance'. **1891** *Anthony's Phot. Bull.* IV. 299 Bringing their undersides in contact with the *resin-wax cement. **1852** L. B. MACKINNON *Atlantic & Transatlantic Sk.* I. 268, I found that he had spoken the truth, and that the *resin grass, or weed, had peculiar leaves which always grew in the same direction. **1869** PARKMAN *Discov. Gt. West* xvii. (1875) 206 The meadows..spangled with the yellow blossoms of the resin-weed and the Rudbeckia.

b. *attrib.*, in terms denoting vessels in plants that contain resin secreted by cells lining them, as ***resin canal, duct, passage, reservoir***.

1854 *Q. Jrnl. Geol. Soc.* X. II. 4 In form the amber is either like drops,..or as the casts of resin-ducts and cavities. **1875** BENNETT & DYER tr. *Sach's Bot.* 77 The origin of resin and gum passages depends also on the formation of inter-cellular passages. **1884** BOWER & SCOTT *De Bary's Phaner.* 357 In the angle of the Y lies a resin-canal. *Ibid.* 441 Among the *Coniferæ* all investigated species..have resin-passages or resin-reservoirs. **1896** W. R. FISHER tr. *Schlich's Man. Forestry* V. 14 Turpentine is chiefly found in the resin-ducts. **1924** W. S. JONES *Timbers* iv. 24 The presence of resin canals in dicotyledonous woods is, as in the case of Conifers, of considerable diagnostic value. *Ibid.* v. 30 Resin ducts are usually absent from the wood of many genera of Conifers. **1938** H. E. DESCH *Timber* ii. 20 Resin canals run vertically in the stem and horizontally in the rays, and are just large enough to be seen with the naked eye. **1967** N. T. MIROV *Genus Pinus* vii. 486 When the pine is wounded, the resin canals are severed. The oleoresin, squeezed from the epithelial cells into the resin canals, may be gathered in receptacles attached below the wound.

resin (ˈrɛzɪn), *v.* [f. prec.] *trans.* To rub or treat with resin.

1865 *Spohr's Autobiog.* II. 69 The bow, which she had previously resined. **1899** BEATR. HARRADEN *Fowler* 225 He resined his bow, and began.

resinaceous (rɛzɪˈneɪʃəs), *a. rare.* [ad. L. *rēsīnāceus*: see RESIN *sb.* and -ACEOUS.] That yields resin; resinous.

1669 WORLIDGE *Syst. Agric.* 275 *Resinaceous*, rosenny, or yielding Rosin. **1674** BLOUNT *Glossogr.* (ed. 4), *Resinaceous*, of or belonging to Rozen. **1879** LEWIS & SHORT *Lat. Dict.*, *Resinaceus*, resinous, resinaceous.

resinate (ˈrɛzɪnət), *sb. Chem.* [f. RESIN *sb.* + -ATE[4]. Cf. F. *résinate*.] A salt formed by the action of a resinous acid on a base.

1838 T. THOMSON *Chem. Org. Bodies* 530 The resinate of ammonia is easily formed... The resinates of the earths and metallic oxides are powders, insoluble in water, alcohol, and ether. **1868** WATTS *Dict. Chem.* V. 79 *Resinates*, a general name for the salts of the acids obtained from turpentine.

resinate (ˈrɛzɪneɪt), *v.* [f. RESIN *sb.* + -ATE[3].] *trans.* To flavour with resin; to impregnate with resin or synthetic resin.

1891 in *Cent. Dict.* **1945** C. S. FORESTER *Commodore* xviii. 198 The Governor had taken advantage of the campaigns in which he had served to study the foods of the different countries. Vienna and Prague had fed him during the Austerlitz campaign; he had drunk resinated wine in the Seven Islands. **1966** *New Scientist* 22 Sept. 667/2 One of the drawbacks in resinating cloth is the tendency to reduce the durability of garments by making fibres more brittle.

resine, obs. f. RESIGN *v.*; obs. Sc. f. *risen*, pa. pple. of RISE *v.*

ˈresined, *ppl. a.* [f. the vb.]

a. Treated with resin.

1884 DANIELL *Princ. Physics* xiv. 395 A glass rod..rubbed longitudinally by a resined cloth..will produce a shrill sound.

b. Of wood: from which resin has been extracted or collected.

1926 *Contemp. Rev.* May 640 Resined wood lasts better than wood not resined, or wood from the same tree above the limit of the cuts.

reˈsinein(e. *Chem.* [a. F. *résinéine* (Fremy): see RESIN *sb.* and -IN(E.] (See quots.)

1855 OGILVIE *Suppl.*, *Resineine*, an oil yielded by colophony. **1868** WATTS *Dict. Chem.* V. 79 *Resineïn*, or *Resinone*; this name is given by Frémy to a hydro-carbon (probably impure colophene..) obtained by the dry distillation of colophony.

†ˈresing, *vbl. sb. Obs.* [f. RESE *v.*[1] + -ING[1].] An attack, assault.

1387 TREVISA *Higden* (Rolls) III. 257 Half þe peple stood i-armed..for resynge and stekkynge of straunge naciouns. *Ibid.* V. 299 Seint Mammertus..ordeyned..letanyes..aȝenst erþe schakynge..and peril of resynge of wylde bestes.

reˈsing (riː-), *v.* [RE- 5 a.] *trans.* To sing again. Hence **reˈsinging** *vbl. sb.*

1618 MYNSHUL *Charac. Prison* Ep. Ded. 1, I come not now to re-sing, but to re-cant the errours both of my pen and iudgment. **1687** BEVERLEY *Expos. Song of Songs* 54 That Song, that sprung In those first Times, is now, as new, Resung. *a* **1700** KEN *Hymns Festiv.* Poet. Wks. 1721 I. 209 Re-sing this Day the same Angelick Strain. **1885** *Manch. Exam.* 15 Apr. 3/1 *Apollo and Marsyas*..is..an imaginative resinging of the contending chants.

resing, obs. Sc. form of RESIGN *v.*

resinic (rɛˈzɪnɪk), *a.* [f. RESIN *sb.* + -IC.] Of, belonging to, or derived from resin.

1895 in *Funk's Stand. Dict.*

resiniferous (rɛzɪˈnɪfərəs), *a.* [f. RESIN *sb.* + -(I)FEROUS. Cf. F. *résinifère*, Sp., Pg., and It. *resinifero*.] Yielding or containing resin.

1673–4 GREW *Anat. Pl.*, *Anat. Trunks* (1684) 110 The utmost are not Milk-Vessels, but Gum-Vessels, or Resiniferous. **1676** —— *Anat. Fl.* 156 As in Box, and Yew, as also Fir, and all Resiniferous Plants. **1797** *Encycl. Brit.* (ed. 3) XV. 3/2 The outmost are gum or resiniferous vessels, destined for the secretion of turpentine. **1881** *Scribner's Mag.* XXII. 834 The fragrance of wild honeysuckle and resiniferous trees.

resinifiˈcation. [a. F. *résinification*: see RESIN *sb.* and -(I)FICATION.] **1.** The act or process of making resinous; the fact of becoming resinous.

1800 tr. *Lagrange's Chem.* II. 249 There is still a fourth operation in resinification. **1856** *Orr's Circ. Sci., Pract. Chem* 493 Its liability to smoke..may arise..from a resinification of the camphine. **1875** *Ure's Dict. Arts* III. 448 The resinification of the drying oils may be effected by the smallest quantities of certain substances, which would act in the manner of ferments.

2. A reaction in which a synthetic resin is formed; conversion into a synthetic resin.

1913 *Chem. Abstr.* VII. 1484, H_2O inhibits polymerization and resinification, but favors the production of larger quantities of AcOH and HCO_2H. **1928** *Industr. & Engin. Chem.* Aug. 796/1 If a mixture of phenol and formaldehyde is heated, with or without a catalyst, resinification occurs. *Ibid.*, When a certain degree of resinification is reached, the process is usually interrupted. **1938** *Jrnl. Physical Chem.* XLII. 351 A more active catalyst in the resinification might be expected to increase the number of cross linkages. **1973** *Materials & Technol.* VI. viii. 587 If phenol is added in excess monomethylol phenol ..is mainly formed and this, in a secondary condensation or resinification reaction, is converted into polynuclear methylene phenols.

†resinifluous, *a. Bot. Obs.* [f. RESIN *sb.*, after *mellifluous*.] Producing resin.

1657 TOMLINSON *Renou's Disp.* 388 The Pine-trees..are all tall, coniferous, resinifluous.

resiniform (ˈrɛzɪnɪfɔːm), *a.* [ad. F. *résiniforme*: see RESIN *sb.* and -FORM.] Having the character of resin.

1811 PINKERTON *Petral.* II. 467 If I may be allowed to use the expression, it is what Dolomieu has called resiniform lava. **1852** TH. ROSS tr. *Humboldt's Trav.* I. vi. 214 A resiniform matter, soluble both by alcohol and by water.

resinify (ˈrɛzɪnɪfaɪ), *v.* [ad. F. *résinifier*: see RESIN *sb.* and -FY.]

1. *trans.* To change (into) natural or synthetic resin.

1816 TINGRY *Varnisher's Guide* (ed. 2) 21 What is called frankincense is gallipot resinified. **1882** *Athenæum* 7 Oct. 469/2 Oxidized or resinified by the influence of the air. **1933** *Chem. Abstr.* XXVII. 4110 The disaggregated mass may be resinified more deeply with CH_2O.

2. *intr.* To become resinous; to become a (natural or synthetic) resin.

1856 *Orr's Circ. Sci., Pract. Chem.* 476 Common nut oil..is more apt to resinify and clog the wick than linseed. **1887** A. M. BROWN *Anim. Alkaloids* 31 Parvoline resinifies readily on exposure to the air. **1920** *Chem. Abstr.* XIV. 3672 The Na salt of the 163° acid completely resinified on illumination in H_2O. **1963** F. M. DEAN *Naturally Occurring Oxygen Ring Compounds* i. 2 Naturally occurring furans generally resinify in these conditions.

Also **ˈresinified** *ppl. a.*, **ˈresinifying** *vbl. sb.*

1928 *Industr. & Engin. Chem.* Aug. 798/1 Refractive indices of very highly resinified mixtures. **1933** *Ibid.* June 646/1 Like all resinifying reactions, that which forms vinyl resins is imperfectly understood. **1936** *Trans. Faraday Soc.* XXXII. 388 For the resinifying reactions we refer again to the scheme given earlier.

resinite (ˈrɛzɪnaɪt). *Min.* [f. RESIN *sb.* + -ITE[1].] Retinasphalt.

1849 DANA *Geol.* x. (1850) 542 Some of the wood is beautifully opalized, though the greater part has the pitchy lustre of resinite.

resinize (ˈrɛzɪnaɪz), *v.* [f. RESIN *sb.* + -IZE.] To treat with resin. Hence **ˈresinized** *ppl. a.*, treated with or containing resin.

1878 ABNEY *Photogr.* (1881) 145 Another mode of producing a dull surface..is to use resinised paper. **1908** W. R. FISHER tr. *Schlich's Man. Forestry* (ed. 2) V. 706 Resinised wood, owing to its easy combustibility, is excellent for kindling purposes, and in mountain districts abroad is still employed for torches.

reˈsink (riː-), *v.* [RE- 5 a.] To sink again.

1612 J. DAVIES (Heref.) *Muse's Sacrifice* Wks. (Grosart) II. 29/2 Though there I vow'd.., I brake my vow and me re-suncke in sinne.

resino-, combining form of RESIN *sb.*, as in **resino-electric** *a.*, containing or exhibiting resinous or negative electricity (Webster,

1828–32, citing Ure); **resino-extractive** *a.*, designating extractive matter in which resinous matter predominates (*ibid.*); **resino-vitreous**, partaking of the characters of resin and glass.
1839 Ure *Dict. Arts* 40 The texture of amber is resino-vitreous, its fracture conchoidal, and lustre glassy.

resinography (rɛzɪ'nɒgrəfɪ). [f. resin *sb.* + -ography.] The study of the morphology, internal structure, and related properties of synthetic resins. Hence **resi'nographer**, one who practises resinography; **resino'graphic** *a.*, of or pertaining to resinography; **resino'graphically** *adv.*, by means of resinography.
1946 Rochow & Gilbert in J. J. Mattiello *Protective & Decorative Coatings* V. v. 476 Resinography, as the name implies, is the graphic study of resins. The term is proposed by the authors to serve as an analogue of metallography and mineralography. *Ibid.* 484 The resinographer must explain that the effect of magnetite on electrical and other properties should be considered. *Ibid.* 485 Resinographic methods, employing the optical microscope and reflected light, are designed for those large classes of resinous materials which are too opaque for examination by transmitted light. *Ibid.* 503 So much information about the fillers can be gathered quickly from a molding..that Stafford and Williams.. usually briquet a portion of the sample and examine it resinographically. **1949** *Analytical Chem.* XXI. 461/1 A resinographic examination of this type of plastic reveals the number of phases, their mode of association; particle sizes and shapes, and relative reflectivity. **1961** G. L. Clark *Encycl. Microscopy* 527/1 Demonstration of macromolecular boundaries is the least developed and most difficult part of resinography. **1970** *Encycl. Polymer Sci. & Technol.* XII. 81 Usually there is enough reflectivity in the surface of a resinographic specimen to reveal the topography. **1976** T. G. & E. G. Rochow *Resinography* i. 14 Besides information from these four levels of study,..the resinographer must make his own examination and arrive at his own conclusions about the identity and utility of a plastic or fiber.

resinoid ('rɛzɪnɔɪd), *a.* and *sb.* [f. resin *sb.* + -oid. Cf. F. *résinoïde.*]
A. *adj.* Resembling resin.
1830 Lindley *Nat. Syst. Bot.* 232 A bitter resinoid matter, slightly soluble in water. **1894** *Westm. Gaz.* 18 June 8/1 Cyona Tincture is an alcoholic extract which has been found to contain a resinoid substance.
B. *sb.* **1.** A resinous substance.
1880 *Libr. Univ. Knowl.* VIII. 818 The resinoid extracted from it has the name of *leptandrin.* **1894** *Times* 11 Aug. 11/2 The woody fibre disappears first, leaving a residue richer in resinoids.
2. A synthetic resin; *spec.* one that is thermosetting, or is not permanently soluble and fusible.
1925 Baekeland & Bender in *Industr. & Engin. Chem.* Mar. 225 The resinous products..are..decidedly infusible. Furthermore, they are insoluble in ordinary solvents and are incomparably stonger and more resistant to chemical and physical agents than the natural resins or the artificial resins of the Novolak type; in order to differentiate them from all these, we feel warranted in designating them more accurately under the name of 'phenol resinoids'. **1934** [see resin *sb.* 3]. **1935** C. Ellis *Chem. Synthetic Resins* I. i. 14 The term 'resin' is restricted by some to thermoplastic resins, and the word 'resinoid' is used to designate the heat-hardening resins. **1936** H. W. Rowell *Technol. Plastics* i. 12 Phenolic and other synthetic resinoids now have an increasing use in the varnish industry. **1949** B. L. Davies *Technol. Plastics* xi. 188 The three stages in the polymerization [of phenol with formaldehyde] were first recognized by Baekeland,..all being called resinoids to distinguish them from the permanently soluble, permanently fusible, resins. **1959** *Times* 18 Nov. 12/5 The diamonds produced in the laboratory consist, in effect, of abrasive grit suitable for use in resinoid-bonded grinding wheels.

†**resinophore**, *a.* (*sb.*) *Chem. Obs.* [ad. G. *resinophor* (W. Herzog 1921, in *Österr. Chem.-Zeitung* XXIV. 77): see resin *sb.* + -phore.] ***resinophore group***, a group whose presence in a molecule was considered to be responsible for resinous properties or resin formation. Also *ellipt.* as *sb.*
1922 *Chem. Abstr.* XVI. 1671 The 'resinophore group', formed from ureas capable of being converted into resinous substances, is the complex −N=C=N−. **1935** C. Ellis *Chem. Synthetic Resins* II. xxv. 562 An investigation of the effect of heat on several mono- and di-arylidene ketones showed that the grouping −CH=CHCO− was responsible for resinification; that is, this group is a 'resinophore'. **1937** R. S. Morrell et al. *Synthetic Resins & Allied Plastics* xv. 375 Comparison between Herzog and Kreidl's resinophore groups and Standinger's chain theories shows that preference must be given to the latter in any explanation of the causes of resinification.

†**resinose**, *a. Obs.*$^{-1}$ [ad. L. *rēsīnōs-us*: see resinous *a.* and -ose.] Resinous.
1712 Petiver in *Phil. Trans.* XXVII. 424 A Milk, which smells Resinose.

resinosis (rɛzɪ'nəʊsɪs). *Forestry.* [f. resin *sb.* + -osis.] The excessive production of resin (in conifers).
1922 F. Dorrance tr. *Sorauer's Man. Plant Dis.* I. xvi. 716, I have had the opportunity to observe resinosis as a contitutional disease, i.e. as the manifestation, even in old trees, of a tendency throughout the whole plant body, to form resin excessively. **1968** F. G. Browne *Pests & Dis. of Forest Plantation Trees* ii. 950 In New Zealand the species [sc. *Pythium undulatum*] is closely associated with a virulent resinosis of the roots, root collars, and stems of *Larix decidua* and *L. leptolepis.*

resinous ('rɛzɪnəs), *a.* [ad. L. *rēsīnōs-us*: see resin *sb.* and -ous. So F. *résineux*, Sp., Pg., and It. *resinoso.*]
1. Of the nature of resin.
1646 Sir T. Browne *Pseud. Ep.* 51 As all resinous bodies, Turpentine, Pitch, and Frankincense. **1694** Salmon *Bate's Dispens.* (1699) 229/1 This Tincture is only the resinous Parts of the Balsam dissolv'd in the Spirit of Wine. **1791** Hamilton *Berthollet's Dyeing* I. i. i. i. 15 It has been proposed to divide the colouring particles into extractive and resinous. **1838** T. Thomson *Chem. Org. Bodies* 288 Sulphuric acid..dissolves the corydalina, and leaves the green resinous matter. **1878** A. H. Green, etc. *Coal* i. 21 The resinous character also prevents the spores from being wetted.., and tends to preserve them from decay.
2. Of plants or their parts: Containing resin.
1656 Blount *Glossogr.*, *Resinous*, full of rozen or gum. **1673–4** Grew *Anat. Pl.*, *Anat. Trunks* (1684) 110 The Barque of Oak it self is also somewhat Resinous. **1712** tr. *Pomet's Hist. Drugs* I. 146 The Fruit..more resinous, and falls easily when ripe. **1797** *Encycl. Brit.* (ed. 3) XVII. 692/2 Made of the most porous and resinous wood to be found. **1811** A. T. Thomson *Lond. Disp.* (1818) 35 The root is biennial, thick, fleshy, and resinous. **1858** Carpenter *Veg. Phys.* §51 A peculiar form of woody fibre is found in the stems of resinous woods.
3. Of properties, etc.: Properly belonging to, or characteristic of, resin.
1811 A. T. Thomson *Lond. Disp.* (1818) 217 It is in brittle fragments of an almost black colour, having a shining, resinous fracture. **1838** T. Thomson *Chem. Org. Bodies* 550 Has a resinous and aromatic smell. **1884** Mrs. C. Praed *Zero* xiii, The atmosphere was pungent with a resinous odour.
4. Made or compounded of resin; affected or produced by the burning of resin.
1808 S. Young in *Med. Jrnl.* XIX. 567 A convenient slip of firm linen, uniformly covered by a resinous plaster. **1862** Dickens *Uncomm. Trav.* xxviii, I can smell the heavy resinous incense as I pass the church. **1871** B. Taylor *Faust* (1875) II. ii. iii. 140 The resinous atmosphere Gives hint of pitch. **1871** Tyndall *Fragm. Sci.* (1879) I. iv. 122 The resinous fumes slowly diminished.
5. *Electr.* = negative *a.* 7. Now *Obs.*
1742 J. T. Desaguliers *Diss. Electr.* 41 The Air being electrical of a vitreous Electricity, and sulphur of a resinous Electricity. **1756** *Phil. Trans. R. Soc.* XLIX. 152 Some writers on electricity have said, that there were two kinds of electrical fire, the one resinous, and the other vitreous. **1797** *Encycl. Brit.* (ed. 3) VI. 421/2 Mr. Du Fay discovered the difference between positive and negative, or, as they were for some time called, the vitreous and resinous electricities. **1840** Carlyle *Heroes* (1858) 198 Thunder was not then mere Electricity, vitreous or resinous. **1860** Emerson *Cond. Life, Wealth*, The genius of reading and of gardening are antagonistic, like resinous and vitreous electricity. **1885** Watson & Burbury *Math. The. Electr. & Magn.* I. 94 A superficial electrification on the inner surface, the total amount of which will be resinous.
6. *Comb.*, as ***resinous-like***, ***-looking*** adjs.
1807 T. Thomson *Chem.* (ed. 3) II. 449 It converts the drying oils into a yellow resinous-like mass. **1832** Brewster *Nat. Magic* xiii. 339 The dense fluid..quickly hardens into a transparent and yellowish resinous-looking substance.
Hence **'resinously** *adv.*, (*a*) with 'resinous' electricity; (*b*) with an impregnation of resin. Also **'resinousness**, 'resinous or rosiny quality' (Bailey, vol. II. 1727).
1794 G. Adams *Nat. & Exp. Phil.* IV. xlvi. 264 Bodies electrified resinously repel each other. **1830** Lindley *Nat. Syst. Bot.* 53 Shrubs with alternate, toothed, resinously glandular, exstipulate leaves. **1873** Maxwell *Electr. & Magn.* (1881) I. 32 All electrified bodies are found to be either vitreously or resinously electrified.

resiny ('rɛzɪnɪ), *a.* [f. resin.] Resinous.
1576 Newton *Lemnie's Complex.* (1633) 234 It is blacke like pitch, and shineth like to feat,..and as certaine resiny stuffe. **1847** in Webster. **1893** *Times* 13 Dec. 3/5 Shellac.. resiny blocky.

resipiscence (rɛsɪ'pɪsəns). [a. F. *résipiscence*, or ad. L. *resipiscentia*, f. *resipiscĕre* to recover one's senses, come to oneself again, f. *re-* re- + *sapĕre*: see sapient.] Repentance for misconduct; recognition of errors committed; return to a better mind or opinion.
1570 T. Norton tr. *Nowel's Catech.* (1853) 177 Sinners.. have need of repentance, which some like better to call resipiscence or amendment. **1606** in Spottiswood *Hist. Ch. Scot.* vii. (1677) 499 Nothing had appeared in them but an obdured obstinacy, without any token of resipiscence. **1657** W. Morice *Coena quasi Κοινὴ* xxiii. 231 If their return be upon the score of resipiscence, far be it from me to be such an one as Beza complains of.
1827 Hallam *Const. Hist.* (1876) II. viii. 67 They drew a flattering picture of the resipiscence of the Anglican party. **1864** Merivale *Conv. Rom. Emp.* 37 Full of horror at his own backsliding, full of hope for his tardy resipiscence. **1881** Saintsbury *Dryden* vi. 127 These prefaces and dedications show an ever-growing command of prose style, and, very soon, the resipiscence of Dryden's judgement.
So †**resi'piscency**. *Obs.*
c **1540** tr. *Pol. Verg. Eng. Hist.* (Camden No. 36) 122 [Gildas] somtimes gentlie exorting them to goodnes and resipiscentie. **1672** Sir T. Browne *Let. to Friend* §40 So closely shut up within the holds of vice and iniquity, as not to find some escape by a postern of resipiscency.

resipiscent (rɛsɪ'pɪsənt), *a.* [ad. L. *resipiscent-em*, pres. pple. of *resipiscĕre*: see resipiscence.] Returning to a sound state of mind.
1872 F. Hall *False Philol.* 67 Grammar,..resipiscent and sane as of old. **1880** *Sat. Rev.* 26 June 821/2 Mr. Martin, at last resipiscent, and even like 'a prophet new inspired'.

resist (rɪ'zɪst), *sb.* [f. the vb.]
†**1.** Resistance. *Obs.*
1535 Stewart *Cron. Scot.* III. 411 Makand heirschip fra blude and fyre also, Without resist quhair euir tha list till go. **1584** Lodge *Forbonius & Prisc.* H j b, I make no resist in this my louing torment. **1608** Day *Hum. out of Breath* v. ii, Proud his assault, as proud be our resist. **1630** J. Lane *Contn. Sqr.'s T.* x. 437 (Ashm. MS.), Camball tooke (without resiste) the town.
2. In calico-printing, a preparation applied to those parts of the fabric which are not to be coloured, in order to prevent the dye from affecting them. Also *attrib.*
1836 *Penny Cycl.* VI. 156/1 White resist for deep blue, to be applied by the cylinder. *Ibid.*, After printing on the resist pastes, the goods should be hung up. **1860** Smiles *Self Help* ii, The process for producing what is called resist work in calico printing. **1890** W. J. Gordon *Foundry* 175 A style where a 'resist' is printed on the blank cloth, the 'resist' being a substance that is unaffected by the dye.
3. a. Any composition applied to a surface to protect it in part from the effects of an agent employed on it for some purpose (also ***resist-varnish***); *spec.* such a composition used to provide protection against the etchant or solvent in photo-engraving, photogravure, or photo-lithography.
1839 Ure *Dict. Arts* 218 The copper is covered by a resist varnish while being heated by the transmission of steam through its axis. **1873** Spon *Worksh. Rec.* Ser. i. 199/1 [Steel] requires to be preserved against the action of the cleansing acids and of the graining mixture, by a composition called resist. **1886** W. T. Wilkinson *Photo-Engraving on Zinc & Copper* v. 34 When it is judged that the etching has proceeded far enough, the resist of ink and resin is removed by the copious use of turpentine. **1890** *Pall Mall G.* 20 Feb. 3/1 When the 'resist' has been sufficiently applied, the instrument is again passed over the plate. **1933** T. S. Barber *Photo-Engraving, Electrotyping & Stereotyping* i. 17 The portions of the bichromated surface which were exposed to light, and already made insoluble, acted as an acid resist. **1960** [see *micro-machining* s.v. micro- 2 a]. **1967** V. Strauss *Printing Industry* v. 213 Polyvinyl alcohol..can be dissolved in water and sensitized with bichromates. Such a solution..can serve as a photomechanical coating resulting in an acid resist. Coating, exposure, and development of polyvinyl alcohol resists do not differ from other resists. But polyvinyl alcohol resists have the advantage that they need not be heated as high as glue-enamel resists in order to make them sufficiently acid-resistant. **1975** Fink & McKenzie *Electronics Engineers' Handbk.* viii. 6 The [semiconductor] wafer surface to be masked is coated with a photosensitive coating known as photoresist, or resist. The masking plate is then..exposed with ultraviolet light... The photo-masking step is followed by an etching step. **1978** *Sci. Amer.* Nov. 63/1 The wafer is first coated with an X-ray-sensitive organic polymer called an X-ray resist.
b. *Pottery.* A material (usu. wax-based) which is applied to pottery in order to prevent glaze or lustre from adhering to certain parts and is removed before or during firing. Orig. and freq. *attrib.*
1904 A. Hayden *Chats on Eng. China* xii. 231 The.. method, with the design left in white, was produced in handsome and highly artistic styles, and there is a pattern, known as the 'Resist' pattern, which is much sought after. **1910** J. F. Blacker *ABC of Collecting Old Eng. Pott.* xxiii. 214 The commonest application of silver resist is used on a white or ivory ground. **1933** W. B. Honey *Eng. Pott. & Porc.* iv. 59 Designs of formal flowers and inscriptions.. were also done in darker brown or in 'resist' so as to appear of a lighter colour. **1957** Mankowitz & Haggar *Encycl. Eng. Pott. & Porc.* 189/2 The decoration is painted upon the glazed surface of the ware in a 'resist', covered with metallic solution and fired, the infusible resist portion firing away during the process leaving a white decoration reserved against a bright metallic background. **1967** M. Chandler *Ceramics in Mod. World* iii. 108 (*caption*) The water-soluble resist is washed off before the plates are fired. *a* **1977** *Harrison Mayer Ltd. Catal.* 19/1 Wax resist decoration is very frequently used both under and over a glaze and in combination with stain decoration.

resist (rɪ'zɪst), *v.* Also 5 *Sc.* rasyst, 5–6 resyst(e. [ad. F. *résister*, †*resistir* (= It. *re-*, *risistere*, Sp. and Pg. *resistir*), or L. *resistĕre*, f. *re-* re- + *sistĕre*, redupl. form of *stāre* to stand.]
1. *trans.* Of things: To stop or hinder (a moving body); to succeed in standing against; to prevent (a weapon, etc.) from piercing or penetrating.
c **1374** Chaucer *Boeth.* i. met. vii. (1868) 29 þe fletyng streme..is arestid & resisted ofte tyme by þe encountrynge of a stoon. *a* **1533** Ld. Berners *Huon* lv. 186 Sorbryn.. strake..such a stroke that the buckles nor ony thynge elles coude resyste the stroke. **1658** Phillips s.v. *Resistence*, A solid body, which resisteth and opposeth whatsoever comes against it. **1667** Milton *P.L.* xii. 491 Spiritual Armour, able to resist Satans assaults. **1727–38** Chambers *Cycl.* s.v. *Respiration*, The air presses the lungs as much as the thorax resists them. **1797** *Encycl. Brit.* (ed. 3) VII. 363/1 They made the towers round instead of square, imagining this figure to be the strongest to resist the battering engines. **1860** Tyndall *Glac.* ii. xix. 332 It quite resisted the edge of a knife. **1894** H. S. Maxim in *Daily News* 4 June 5/7 It is quite true that I used a steel plate to resist my projectiles.

b. To withstand the action or effect of (a natural force or physical agency).

1567 MAPLET *Gr. Forest* 2 b, It maketh it able to resist fire. **1687** A. LOVELL tr. *Thevenot's Trav.* I. 6 A white soft Rock .. does not long resist the Sea Winds .. that eat it away. **1766** *Compl. Farmer* s.v. *Madder* 5 G 2/1 That which was dyed with the madder .. resisted during thirty minutes a boiling which the other could not bear during ten. **1784** COWPER *Task* III. 465 The stable yields a stercoraceous heap, .. potent to resist the freezing blast.

c. Of immaterial things.

1726–31 TINDAL *Rapin's Hist. Eng.* (1743) II. XVII. 51 If the interest and sollicitations of the King her Husband had not strongly resisted her zeal for her Religion. **1856** EMERSON *Eng. Traits, Race* Wks. (Bohn) II. 21 But whilst race works immortally to keep its own, it is resisted by other forces.

2. Of persons: To withstand, strive against, oppose: **a.** a person, his will, etc.

1432–50 tr. *Higden* (Rolls) III. 333 This philosophre Demostines resistede the legates of the Molosynes commen to Athenes. *c* **1460** FORTESCUE *Abs. & Lim. Mon.* (1885) 115 Wherfor thai ben myghty, and able to resiste the aduersaries of this reaume. **1530** PALSGR. 688/1 He intendeth to take possessyon here agaynst my wyll, but he shall be resysted. **1593** SHAKS. *3 Hen. VI*, II. v. 79 Thou that so stoutly hath resisted me, Giue me thy Gold. **1651** HOBBES *Leviath.* II. xxi. 110 Their Representative had the Libertie to resist, or invade other people. **1672** PETTY *Pol. Anat.* (1691) 47 This Force I take to be sufficient to resist any number of men. **1717** POPE *Iliad* XI. 955 Shall Greece yet stand? Resists she yet the raging Hector's hand? **1771** *Junius Lett.* xliv. (1788) 248 They knew, that the present house of commons .. were likely enough to be resisted. **1817** SHELLEY *Rev. Islam* X. xxviii, O King of Glory! thou alone hast power! Who can resist thy will? **1864** BRYCE *Holy Rom. Emp.* xiii. (1875) 211 The Lombard league had successfully resisted Frederick's armies.

b. an attack, invasion, blow, or hostile action of any kind.

1533 BELLENDEN *Livy* III. ii. (S.T.S.) I. 247 Þe Inemyis .. assaleȝet .. Þe Romane pussance, as Insufficient to resist þare Invasions. **1535** COVERDALE *Matt.* v. 39, I saye vnto you: that ye resist not euell. **1585** T. WASHINGTON tr. *Nicholay's Voy.* II. xiii. 48 Constantine .. seeking to resist the courses and robberies which the Parthes dayly vsed towards the Romains. **1610** SHAKS. *Temp.* I. ii. 465, I will resist such entertainment, till Mine enemy ha's more pow'r. **1667** MILTON *P.L.* II. 814 That mortal dint, Save he who reigns above, none can resist. **1840** THIRLWALL *Greece* VII. 355 He felt himself unable to resist the attack. **1874** GREEN *Short Hist.* iv. §3. 184 Pardon was freely extended to all who had resisted the invasion.

c. a moral or mental influence or suggestion.

1483 CAXTON *G. de la Tour* f iij b, Be ye thenne strong .. to resist and ouercome them [temptations]. **1529** MORE *Dyaloge conc. Heresyes* I. Wks. 153/2 So muste reason not resyste faithe but walke with her. **1577** NORTH *Gueuara's Diall Pr.* 37 The favour that God wil geve you .. no man can resist it. **1656** JEANES *Fuln. Christ* 112 His grace .. can resist the strongest, and most restlesse temptations. **1670** COTTON *Espernon* III. x. 522 With all these advantages he was not able to resist four words. **1717** LADY M. W. MONTAGU *Lett.* II. 35 The Greeks .. resist, with incredible fortitude, the Conviction of their own eyes. **1786** BURNS *To unco Guid* viii, What's done we partly may compute, But know not what's resisted. **1817** KEATINGE *Trav.* I. 81 It is hard to resist the surmise that Cæsar's account is drawn up with quite as much regard to effect as to reality. **1875** JOWETT *Plato* (ed. 2) V. 33 Those who had never been taught to resist pleasure would be equally at the mercy of those who could.

d. something proposed to be done or likely to happen, a law or command, etc.

1593 SHAKS. *Rich. II*, IV. i. 148 It will the wofullest Diuision prove... Preuent it, resist it, and let it not be so. **1607** —— *Cor.* III. i. 267 He hath resisted Law And therefore Law shall scorne him further Triall. **1771** *Junius Lett.* xliv. (1788) 254 If the process of the courts of Westminster-hall be resisted. **1781** COWPER *Expost.* 540 Thy parliaments .. Whate'er was asked, too timid to resist, Comply'd with. **1810** in Craufurd *Gen. Craufurd* (1891) 108 This arrangement .. had before now been proposed to me, and I had resisted it. **1837** DICKENS *Pickw.* v, The dismal man, .. resisting Mr. Pickwick's invitation to breakfast .., walked slowly away. **1844** H. H. WILSON *Brit. India* II. 403 The disinclination of the native Princes to submit to, or their ability to resist, its dictation.

e. a natural force, weakness or disease, etc.

1593 SHAKS. *3 Hen. VI*, IV. iii. 59 It boots not to resist both winde and tide. **1596** SPENSER *F.Q.* IV. v. 43 Fleshly weaknesse, which no creature may Long time resist. **1806** *Med. Jrnl.* XV. 545 A case .. where the inoculation was resisted till the twenty-ninth time.

†**3.** To prevent. Const. with inf. or *from*. *Obs.*

1500–20 DUNBAR *Poems* xxvii. 105 To put this in rememberance, Mycht no man me resist. *a* **1586** SIDNEY *Arcadia* II. (1605) 139 Beautifull trees, which resisted the sunnes darts from ouer-much piercing the naturall coldnesse of the River.

†**4.** To repel, affect with distaste. *Obs. rare*$^{-1}$.

1608 SHAKS. *Per.* II. iii. 29 These cates resist me, she but thought upon.

5. *intr.* †**a.** To stand *against*, to make opposition *to*, a person or thing. *Obs.*

c **1375** *Sc. Leg. Saints* xxii. (*Laurence*) 16 It has vertu .. fore to resyst a-gane fyre-slacht. *Ibid.* xxxiii. (*George*) 12 To resyst ay to sathane & to lordis of mykil mycht. *c* **1425** WYNTOUN *Cron.* v. xi. 3548 Bot Valentynyane Þe emperoure Resistyt ay til his erroure. **1483** CAXTON *Cato* b ij b, Thou oughtest .. to haue strengthe for to resiste ageynst alle aduersytees. **1538** STARKEY *England* II. i. 165 Except man wyth cure, .. & labur, resyste to the same, they ouer-run reson. **1563** *Mirr. Mag., Blacke Smyth* 175 b, That no man should resist agaynst his kyng. **1609** BIBLE (Douay) *Deut.* ix. 2 A great people and tal, .. against whom no man is able to resist. **1651** tr. *De-las-Coveras' Don Fenise* 274 She forced herselfe to resist against the excesse of her affliction.

b. Without const. To offer resistance.

a **1547** SURREY *Ecclesiastes* iv. 31 What can he doo but yeld, that must resist aloone? **1582** STANYHURST *Æneis* I. (Arb.) 21 Thee storme dyd conquoure, thee ships scant weaklye resisted. **1604** SHAKS. *Oth.* I. ii. 80 Lay hold vpon him, if he do resist Subdue him, at his perill. **1653** HOLCROFT *Procopius, Goth. Wars* I. 30 The Horse-men, .. having nothing to resist with, are easily shot. **1771** *Junius Lett.* lxiii. (1788) 332 That the counsel did not resist, is true. **1822** SHELLEY tr. *Calderon's Mag. Prodig.* III. 125 How wilt thou then Resist, Justina? *a* **1862** BUCKLE *Civiliz.* (1873) II. viii. 573 The nation not daring, and what was still worse, not wishing, to resist, gave way.

†**c.** To refuse *to* do something. *Obs. rare*$^{-1}$.

1539 *Act 31 Hen. VIII*, c. 4 In case it happen the Mayer .. make defaulte of paymente of the saide recompence & satisfaction, and resiste to paye the same.

†**6.** To stop; to rest. *Obs.*

c **1470** HENRY *Wallace* VIII. 1090 Bot I rasyst [*v.r.* desist] throw chargis off our consaill, The southmaist part off Ingland we sall se. **1556** *Aurelio & Isab.* (1608) O v, In yowere hande the goode and the ill of the ladies resistethe.

Hence **re'sisted** *ppl. a.*

1713 M. HENRY *Folly Despising* Wks. 1853 I. 179/1 The rejected Saviour and the resisted Sanctifier. **1753** CHAMBERS *Cycl. Suppl.* s.v. *Resistance*, When the compression of the fluid is just sufficient to prevent a vacuum behind the resisted body. **1842** GWILT *Archit.* 1024 The resisting and resisted parts are not only contiguous, but cohere.

†**re'sistable**, *a. Obs.* [f. RESIST *v.* + -ABLE. Cf. RESISTIBLE *a.*]

1. That may be resisted; resistible.

1608 TOPSELL *Serpents* (1658) 601 The Serpents of Europe are .. more resistable for their weakness and strength. **1689** *Thoughts Gentlemen's Undertaking at York* 16 The Chimney-man that is Irresistable in his Office, is Resistable if he gather the Corn in the Town-fields. **1752** CARTE *Hist. Eng.* III. 71 Henry thought Charles's power .. scarce resistable by the rest of Europe.

2. Capable of resisting. Const. *of*. *rare*$^{-1}$.

1670 PETTUS *Fodinæ Reg.* Introd., I speak of Fire, I might also Discourse of the strange nature of Bone-Ashes, .. so resistable of that Element.

Hence †**resista'bility; re'sistableness.** *Obs.*

1622 *K. Jas. Direct. conc. Preachers* in Rushw. *Hist. Coll.* (1659) I. 65 The Universality, Efficacy, Resistability [1642 Resistibility], or Irresistibility of Gods Grace. **1784** J. BROWN *Hist. Brit. Ch.* (1820) I. 205 The universality, efficacy or resistableness of God's grace.

†**re'sistal.** *Obs. rare*$^{-1}$. [f. as prec. + -AL[1].] Resistance.

1631 T. HEYWOOD *Fair Maid of West* II. IV. i, All resistals, Quarrels, and ripping-up of injuries, Are smothered in the ashes of our wrath.

resistance (rɪ'zɪstəns). Also 6 -aunce, 6 resystaunce. [a. F. *résistance*, later form of *resistence* RESISTENCE: see RESIST *v.* and -ANCE.]

1. a. The act, on the part of persons, of resisting, opposing, or withstanding. Const. *to*, †*of*.

1417 in Ellis *Orig. Lett.* Ser. II. I. 59 To putt therwith a greate fortificacion aboute the same for resistance of the sayd enimies. **1535** COVERDALE *Eccl.* iv. 12 One maye be ouercome, but two maye make resistaunce. **1560** DAUS tr. *Sleidane's Comm.* 72 They tende to a publique peace, and to the resistaunce of Christes ennemies. **1651** HOBBES *Leviath.* II. xxx. 175 Such is all resistance to the essentiall Rights of Soveraignty. **1687** A. LOVELL tr. *Thevenot's Trav.* I. 229 They met with a stout resistance. **1729** BUTLER *Serm.* Wks. 1874 II. 95 Cases .. in which sudden resistance is the only security. **1769** *Junius Lett.* xvi. (1788) 99 There is yet a spirit of resistance in this country, which will not submit to be oppressed. **1827** SOUTHEY *Hist. Penins. War* II. 596 The efforts .. for organizing a civic and national resistance. **1874** GREEN *Short Hist.* viii. §5. 499 The threat, however, failed to break the resistance of the Commons.

b. *passive resistance*: see as a main entry.

c. Organized covert opposition to an occupying or ruling power; *spec.* (usu. with def. article and capital initial) in the war of 1939–45, the underground movement formed in France in June 1940 with the object of resisting the authority of the German occupying forces and the Vichy government; any organization of this type with similar ends.

1939 *War Illustr.* 28 Oct. 217/1 Underground resistance to Hitler has been organized amongst the workers in all the big industrial centres of Germany. **1940** *Times* 19 June 6/3 General de Gaulle .. broadcast from London a message to the French nation last night. The text of his speech .. is as follows: .. Whatever happens the flame of French resistance must not and shall not be extinguished. **1946** A. HUXLEY *Let.* 28 Mar. (1969) 541, I was sent a number of French books recently... Novels about the Resistance— half heroism, half unutterable moral squalor. **1959** *Listener* 17 Sept. 454/3 To judge by the atmosphere of this tale the resistance in Denmark must have been a less desperate affair than it was in many parts of Europe. **1967** *Freedomways* VII. 143 The men and women who have been notable in African history—not only the rulers and statesmen, but also the educators and scholars, writers and artists, religious leaders, heroes of resistance. **1976** H. TRACY *Death in Reserve* xxii. 170 In this area, *Sanglier* had been an important man in the Resistance. **1981** *Guardian* 2 June 6/7 In the many rural areas [of Afghanistan] under the control of the resistance and unchallenged by the Russians, the insurgents impose their own curfew.

2. a. Power or capacity of resisting.

1590 SIR J. SMYTH *Disc. Weapons* 4 b, If they were of diuerse lengths .. and thereby .. of lesse force and resistance. **1667** MILTON *P.L.* VI. 838 They astonisht all resistance lost, All courage. **1703** MOXON *Mech. Exerc.* 256 When the Earth on which we would make Pillars or Piers is of [un]equal resistance, that is to say, not good. **1753** CHAMBERS *Cycl. Suppl.* s.v., In the comparing together the resistances to all velocities. **1894** H. S. MAXIM in *Daily News* 4 June 5/7 Provided he can produce something which has greater resistance for its weight than steel or copper bronzes. **1897** MARY KINGSLEY *W. Africa* 637 Not that these good people have a greater resistance to the fever than the Jamaica Christians. **1953** *Sun* (Baltimore) (B ed.) 9 Sept. 3/4 How germs develop resistance to the drugs. **1968** [see RESISTANT *a.* 2].

b. *Psycho-anal.* Opposition, freq. unconscious, to allowing memories or desires which have been repressed as unacceptable or disruptive to emerge into the conscious mind.

1905 *Psychol. Bull.* II. 256 Resistance (in the form of indifference, etc.), would greatly delay the inquiry. **1909** A. A. BRILL tr. *Freud's Sel. Papers on Hysteria* vii. 167, I started with the presupposition that .. this paranoia must contain unconscious thoughts and repressed reminiscences which have to be brought to consciousness .. by overcoming a certain resistance. **1913** E. JONES *Papers on Psycho-Anal.* i. 6 Whenever an individual considers a given process as being too obvious to permit any investigation into its origin, and shows resistance to such an investigation, we are right in suspecting that the actual origin is concealed from him. **1924** J. RIVIERE tr. *Freud's On Psychotherapy* in *Coll. Papers* I. 254 It [*sc.* a technique of suggestion] does not permit us .. to recognize the *resistance* with which the patient clings to his disease and thus even fights against his own recovery. **1936** M. M. GREEN tr. *Reik's Surprise & Psycho-Analyst* iv. 52 We have discovered resistance in analysis as the emotional expression of this opposition. **1951** P. M. SYMONDS *Ego & Self* xii. 175 In order to defend the ego against anxiety, resistances are built up against the recognition of these unconscious impulses. **1964** E. KRAPF tr. *Caruso's Existential Psychol.* III. i. 150 Placing the burden of resistance on the patient alone provides a good excuse for one's own incapacity and totalitarian one-sidedness. **1977** C. F. MONTE *Beneath Mask* ii. 53 Resistance to recall is one evidence of motivated forgetting or repression.

c. In *Comb.* with a preceding sb., as ***crease resistance***, resistance to creasing, etc.

1932 [see *drug-resistance* s.v. DRUG *sb.*[1] 3]. **1947** [see CREASE *sb.*[2] 5]. **1959** *Times* 12 Jan. 11/4 Gives shrink, stretch, and rot-resistance. **1959** [see *flame-resistance* s.v. FLAME *sb.* 10]. **1966** *Economist* 8 Jan. 113/1 There are now two processes .. for giving man-made fibre garments a permanent press. This builds up crease resistance in normal wear. **1973** R. G. KRUEGER et al. *Introd. Microbiol.* xv. 422/1 Transmissible drug resistance was discovered .. around 1960.

3. a. Opposition of one material thing to another material thing, force, etc.

1625 N. CARPENTER *Geogr. Del.* I. iv. (1635) 80 The Heauens in their motion find no resistance. **1645** WALLER *My lady Isabella*, Musick so softens and disarms the mind, That not an arrow does resistance find. **1659** HAMMOND *On Ps.* lxxxix. 13 Above all the oppositions and resistances in nature. **1715** GREGORY *Elem. Astron.* (1726) II. 710 They are stopp'd and repell'd by the Resistance of the neighbouring Vortices. **1838** *Civ. Eng. & Arch. Jrnl.* I. 374/2 Whereby he imparts great additional strength or power of resistance to the said metal rails and bars. **1880** GEIKIE *Phys. Geogr.* iv. 284 The rocks offering many varying degrees of resistance to erosion, they are worn down unequally.

b. *esp.* in the physical sciences, the opposition offered by one body to the pressure or movement of another.

1656 tr. *Hobbes' Elem. Philos.* (1839) 211, I define resistance to be the endeavour of one moved body .. contrary to the endeavour of another moved body. **1690** LOCKE *Hum. Und.* II. iv. §3 All the Bodies in the World, pressing a drop of Water on all sides, will never be able to overcome the Resistance it will make. **1710** J. CLARKE *Rohault's Nat. Philos.* (1729) I. 123 If I put my Finger to any of its Parts, I ought to feel the Resistance. **1777** PRIESTLEY *Matt. & Spir.* (1782) I. ii. 16 The cause of all resistance is repulsive power. **1831** LARDNER *Hydrost.* ix. 192 The resistance of different fluids will be different according to their specific gravities. *c* **1860** FARADAY *Forces Nat.* i. 41 The resistance of the air having been avoided. **1883** *Encycl. Brit.* XV. 751/1 Where the line representing the total resistance exerted at that joint intersects the joint.

pl. **1753** CHAMBERS *Cycl. Suppl.* s.v., Though the hypothesis of a fluid .. be of great use in explaining the nature of resistances. **1797** *Encycl. Brit.* (ed. 3) XVI. 92/2 Of all the resistances of bodies to each [other], there is .. none of greater importance than the resistance or reaction of fluids. **1840** *Civ. Eng. & Arch. Jrnl.* III. 89/2 To overcome what are called the friction and resistances of the engine. **1855** J. R. LEIFCHILD *Cornwall* 186 A steam pressure of 150 lbs, exclusive of engine resistances.

c. Hence ***line of resistance***.

1851 *Catal. Gt. Exhib.* 374 Forming a diagonal line of traction in the direct line of resistance. **1851** RUSKIN *Stones Ven.* (1874) I. x. 122 This moral character of the arch is called by architects its 'Line of Resistance'.

d. ***line***, etc., ***of least resistance***: (see quot. 1871); also *fig.*, the easiest method or course of action.

1865 MILL *Auguste Comte* 101 In the play of antagonistic forces, the path it [*sc.* our intelligence] points out is (in scientific phraseology) the direction of least resistance. **1871** G. E. VOYLE *Dict. Artillery Terms* (ed. 2) 185/2 *Line of least resistance*, in blasting or mining, is a line drawn from the centre of the charge perpendicular to the surface of the ground. *Ibid.* 213/1 By taking 1/10 of the cube of the line of least resistance in feet, the proper charge of powder .. is given in pounds. **1903** G. B. SHAW *Man & Superman* III. 134 This Life Force says to him 'I have done a thousand wonderful things unconsciously by merely willing to live and following the line of least resistance: now I want to know myself and my destination, and choose my path.' **1908** W. McDOUGALL *Introd. Social Psychol.* vii. 179 He often seems to act, not in the line of least resistance, but in the line of greatest resistance. **1923** W. G. BOULTON *Blasting with High Explosives* xv. 45 L = Line of least resistance in feet... The line of resistance is the shortest distance from the chamber to the surface. **1931** *Economist* 7 Feb. 300/2 This was no doubt the line of least resistance, when money had to be found. **1954** M. SHARP *Gipsy in Parlour* xxiv. 233 He took by nature the line of least resistance. **1967** C. V. BARK *See Living Crocodiles* xi. 184 It is taking the line of least resistance. It saves trouble.

4. a. Non-conductivity in respect of electricity, magnetism, or heat; *spec.* resistance to an unvarying electric current.

1760 J. WESLEY *Desideratum* 17 While the electric fire, which is in all bodies, is left to itself, undisturb'd by any external violence, it is more or less dense... And there is some resistence to every endeavour of altering its density... This resistence is least in metals, minerals, water, quicksilver, animals and vegetables... In these bodies the resistence is greater, when their surface are polish'd. **1767** J. PRIESTLEY *Hist. Electricity* 116 The difference between electric and non electric bodies was owing to the different resistance..to the passage of the electric fluid. **1860** G. PRESCOTT *Electr. Telegr.* 279 A conductor, in fact, whose resistance is nothing. **1871** B. STEWART *Heat* (ed. 2) §282 To determine the thermal resistance of various liquids. **1888** *Philos. Mag.* XXV. 422, I will now for a moment compare the case of magnetic resistance with a natural case of ordinary resistance. **1963** A. F. ABBOTT *Ordinary Level Physics* xxxvii. 479 The resistance of a wire depends on its dimensions and the material from which it is made. **1975** [see RESISTOR].

b. A part of an electrical apparatus used to offer a definite resistance to a current, a resistor.

1878 *Encycl. Brit.* VIII. 45/2 In the quicksilver agometer of Müller..the resistance is formed by a column of mercury of variable length. **1894** *Daily News* 6 Sept. 6/2 Lowering electric lights after the manner applied to gas, and without the use of resistances.

5. ***piece of resistance***, = F. *pièce de résistance* (see PIÈCE b).

1797 BURKE *Regic. Peace* iv. Wks. IX. 7 Our appetite demands a *piece of resistance*. **1858** HOGG *Life Shelley* I. 459 The good girl liked a piece of resistance, a solid tome. **1894** DU MAURIER *Trilby* I. 239 The pieces of resistance and plum-pudding and mince-pies.

6. *attrib.* and *Comb.*, as ***resistance-attribute, pile***; (sense 1 c) ***resistance cell, club, fighter, figure, forces, group, hero, man, movement, network, plan, work, worker***; (sense 4 a) ***resistance-capacitance, -capacity*** (both used *attrib.*), ***-coupling; resistance-coupled*** adj.; **resistance-box**, *Electr.*, a box containing one or more resistance coils (Knight *Dict. Mech.* 1875); also *transf.*; **resistance coil** (see quot. 1873); so ***resistance helix***; **resistance furnace**, an electric furnace which is heated by passing a current through elements of high resistance; **resistance-piece**, = sense 5; **resistance pyrometer**, a form of resistance thermometer suitable for use at high temperatures; **resistance thermometer**, a temperature-measuring device in which the change in electrical resistance with temperature of a platinum or other metallic wire is measured; **resistance transfer factor** *Biol.*, a plasmid that promotes the transfer from one bacterium to another of a genetic determinant for drug resistance; **resistance welding**, a method of welding in which the heat to cause fusion of the metals is produced by the passage of an electric current through the contact resistance between the two surfaces, these being held together by mechanical pressure.

1862 H. SPENCER *First Princ.* II. iii. §48 (1875) 166 The *resistance-attribute of matter must be regarded as primordial. **1899** *Allbutt's Syst. Med.* VII. 250 The great splanchnic area forms the *resistance box of the circulation. **1942** E. WILLIAMS *Thermionic Valve Circuits* iii. 33 The condenser, C_2, is therefore omitted and the circuit becomes the orthodox *Resistance-capacitance Coupling circuit. *Ibid.* 69 Consider the resistance-capacitance coupled circuit. **1962** SIMPSON & RICHARDS *Physical Princ. Junction Transistors* ix. 208 A resistance-capacitance coupled amplifier. **1924** P. J. RISDON *Wireless* xxvii. 221 In the case of resistance or *resistance-capacity coupling, instead of an inductance coil, a high resistance is employed for establishing the necessary differences of potential. **1962** SIMPSON & RICHARDS *Physical Princ. Junction Transistors* v. 88 Many audio and low radio-frequency amplifiers, having resistance-capacity coupling between stages. **1972** D. RAMSAY *Little Murder Music* 139, I succeeded in making my way to a resistance cell. **1945** *Sun* (Baltimore) 6 Oct. 2/5 German underground units, composed chiefly of Hitler youth and former prisoners of war, were springing up in all parts of Germany, with some secret '*resistance clubs' reviving the worst of Nazism. **1862** *Catal. Internat. Exhib., Brit.* II. No. 2867 *Resistance Coils, for testing the position of a fault in telegraph conductors from a distant station. **1873** MAXWELL *Electr. & Magn.* (1881) I. 429 A Resistance Coil is a conductor capable of being easily placed in the voltaic circuit, so as to introduce into the circuit a known resistance. **1931** MOYER & WOSTREL *Radio Handbk.* xiii. 684 *Resistance-coupled amplifiers. A typical circuit in which the amplifier is connected by the method of resistance coupling. **1962** SIMPSON & RICHARDS *Physical Princ. Junction Transistors* ix. 219 A relatively heavily loaded resistance-coupled stage operating over a reasonably long range of ambient temperature. **1921** J. SCOTT-TAGGART *Thermionic Tubes* vi. 207 A form of coupling between successive valves in an amplifier which has been of considerable use is that known as '*resistance coupling'. **1963** *Listener* 14 Feb. 304/2 He joins up with various bands of multi-racial *resistance fighters. **1976** H. TRACY *Death in Reserve* xxii. 172 The local *gendarmerie*, guided by the old Resistance fighters,..covered the flanks. **1958** *Times Lit. Suppl.* 21 Mar. 149/1 The sexual fantasies of various *Resistance and non-resistant figures. **1944** *Resistance forces [see *E.A.M.* s.v. E. III]. **1959** *Listener* 16 Apr. 674/3 Fighting between Tibetan resistance forces and the Chinese. **1904** M. MACLEAN *Mod. Electr. Pract.* V. 239 To prevent more or less arcing in what is ostensibly a *resistance furnace. **1928** *Jrnl. Iron & Steel Inst.* CXVII. 853 Materials of construction for electric resistance furnaces, and the advantages of the latter over fuel-fired furnaces, are described. **1957** *Resistance group [see COURIER *sb.* 1 b]. **1974** J. THOMSON *Long Revenge* ii. 22 For reasons of security, Mercer wasn't put in direct touch with the local Resistance group. **1884** KNIGHT *Dict. Mech.* Suppl. 752/2 Such unequal action is remedied by the provision of a high *resistance helix shunting the arc. **1975** N. FREELING *What are Bugles blowing For?* vii. 45 Was he a *Resistance hero then? **1945** *Daily Herald* 8 May 4/8 The Germans..started shooting at Dutch *Resistance men. *Ibid.* 28 May 4/2 Armed forces of the Danish *resistance movement have passed a resolution..demanding the arrests [*sic*] of all collaborators. **1953** *Encounter* Nov. 6/2 The rising sales of even the most expensive Japanese garments..were taken to be a kind of resistance-movement against Western-style attire. **1978** R. V. JONES *Most Secret War* xxiii. 189 It would be some time before the Resistance movements began to operate coherently. **1969** F. HALLIDAY in Cockburn & Blackburn *Student Power* 317 Students also provided the cadres for the various *resistance networks..which channelled arms, funds and information to the FLN. **1895** C. SCOTT *Apple Orchards* 87 The *resistance piece was in the wicker basket. **1838** *Civil Eng. & Arch. Jrnl.* I. 374/1 What is called a *resistance pile, with one of the patentee's blocks or chairs. **1944** *Daily Tel.* 15 May 4 Mr. Wareing reveals.. the existence of a *Resistance plan to seize power. **1899** *Physical Rev.* VIII. 197 The failure of Siemens' *resistance pyrometer was simply due to faulty construction. **1920** *Whittaker's Electr. Engineer's Pocket-bk.* (ed. 4) 290 Resistance pyrometers. For exact readings when temperature is steady... Range: minus 200° up to 1000° C. **1959** *Jrnl. Iron & Steel Inst.* CXCIII. 318/3 He then describes the four main types of pyrometer, namely, the optical pyrometer, the resistance pyrometer, the thermocouple, and the radiation pyrometer. **1887** *Phil. Trans. R. Soc.* A. CLXXVIII. 164 In comparing the platinum *resistance thermometer with other instruments, it will be seen that it is essentially practical. **1920** *Whittaker's Electr. Engineer's Pocket-bk.* (ed. 4) 286 The Callendar compensated resistance thermometer consists of a pure platinum wire wound on a mica or fireclay frame and connected by stout copper or platinum leads to terminals in the thermometer head. **1959** Resistance thermometer [see CONDUCTIVITY 2]. **1960** WATANABE & FUKASAWA in *Biochem. & Biophys. Res. Communications* III. 664 Each resistance factor is not a transmissible factor in itself but..the resistance factors are carried by some transmissible factor. .. We propose to refer to this factor as '*resistance transfer factor (RTF)' tentatively. **1965** *Times* 26 Feb. 15/3 The resistance transfer factor, like the sex factor, may stimulate conjugation—so that resistance can sweep rapidly through a colony. **1970** PASSMORE & ROBSON *Compan. Med. Stud.* II. xviii. 57/2 Resistance transfer factors represent a world-wide problem which is becoming increasingly serious. **1914** *Proc. Inst. Mech. Engin.* 170 The best, the most controllable and the least likely method of injuring the material, which gave the most uniform satisfactory results, was electric *resistance welding. **1927** [see METALLIC *a.* 1 h]. **1975** BRAM & DOWNS *Manuf. Technol.* ii. 61 Resistance-welding techniques are characterised by the absence of flux or filler. **1959** *Listener* 17 Sept. 454/3 They are engaged in sabotage and *resistance work. **1962** L. DEIGHTON *Ipcress File* 221 Grenade was a *resistance worker in 1940 when..every one else in France was rooting for Marshal Pétain. **1974** J. THOMSON *Long Revenge* ii. 23 A suspected French Resistance worker.

resistanceless (rɪˈzɪstənslɪs), *a.* [f. RESISTANCE + -LESS.] Marked by a total lack of (electrical) resistance.

1968 *Physics Bull.* Dec. 410/2 The Meissner effect provided an important clue to the understanding of superfluidity, by showing that it was more than resistanceless flow. **1969** [see EXCITONIC *a.*]. **1978** *Sci. Amer.* Apr. 88/2 Certain properties of the glassy superconductors, such as the transition temperature where resistanceless flow begins, are significantly different from those in crystalline materials.

†reˈsistancy. *Obs. rare*[−1]. [f. as RESISTANCE: see -ANCY and cf. RESISTENCY.] Resistance.

1656 JEANES *Fuln. Christ* 88 If we take the word (irresistably) in opposition unto a final, complete, and victorious resistancy.

resistant (rɪˈzɪstənt), *a.* and *sb.* [a. F. *résistant*, pres. pple. of *résister* to RESIST. Cf. RESISTENT.]

A. *adj.* **1.** That makes resistance or opposition.

1610 GUILLIM *Heraldry* III. xvii. (1611) 159 The rending and ruine of all that were resistant. **1668** HOWE *Bless. Righteous* (1825) 52 There is no resistant principle remaining, when the love of God is perfected in it. **1768–74** TUCKER *Lt. Nat.* (1834) II. 462 It is the essence of matter to be solid, that is, resistant and moveable. **1840** *Tait's Mag.* VII. 389 The aristocratic..elements..are become resistant, conservative, or inactive. **1860** TYNDALL *Glac.* II. v. 252 Each portion of the ice is surrounded by a resistant mass. **1884** *Contemp. Rev.* Oct. 528 The pressure of resistant wills now becomes incalculable.

2. That is not overcome by some disease or drug. Const. *to*.

1897 MUIR & RITCHIE *Man. Bacteriol.* 291 An animal is shedding into the air..myriads of bacilli which may rapidly spore, and thus arrive at a very resistant stage. **1898** *Yearbk. U.S. Dept. Agric. 1897* 399 The..cross yielded the Golden Clairette, a valuable new sort [of vine], apparently highly resistant to Phylloxera. **1925** *Scribner's Mag.* July 1/1 Genetics has made possible better strains of livestock... Disease is less to be feared because of resistant stocks. **1968** *New Statesman* 5 Jan. 10/3 A germ which normally inhabits the intestines of a cow, for instance, but which normally doesn't harm man, could be rendered resistant, perhaps, to a whole group of antibiotics, and could then escape from the animal, and pass that resistance on to another type of germ which *was* dangerous to man.

3. In *Comb.* with preceding sb.

1902 [see *fire-resistant* adj. s.v. FIRE *sb.* B. 2]. **1932** [see *drug-resistant* adj. s.v. DRUG *sb.*[1] 3]. **1936** [see CREASE *sb.*[2] 5]. **1947** [see *flame-resistant* adj. s.v. FLAME *sb.* 10]. **1959** *Times* 12 Jan. 11/4 Porous, crush-proof, stress and tear-resistant and washable. **1963** *B.S.I. News* June 8/2 Bad news for burglars was the announcement in May of a BSI specification for thief-resistant locks. **1968** *Times* 12 Oct. 18/8 One of the organisms sometimes responsible for travellers' diarrhoea is now sulphonamide-resistant. **1978** *Cornish Guardian* 27 Apr. 34/6 (Advt.), White Ceiling Tiles all with F.R.A. (Fire Resistant Additive).

B. *sb.* **a.** One who or that which resists; a resister; *spec.* a member of a resistance movement. Cf. RÉSISTANT.

1600 W. WATSON *Decacordon* (1602) 2 The thunder-bolt fell vpon the afflicted Priests.., striking all resistants with Ecclesiasticall censures. **1659** PEARSON *Creed* VI. 577 According to the degrees of power in the Agent and the Resistant, is an action perform'd or hindered. **1828–32** in WEBSTER. **1884** *Health Exhib. Catal.* p. liii/1 The most powerful resistant of acids or acid gases. **1903** *Westm. Gaz.* 3 June 7/1 To issue summonses against Nonconformist passive resistants. **1944** *Ann. Reg. 1943* 172 To the injury of the United Nations and the French resistants. **1948** W. FORTESCUE *Beauty for Ashes* xxxv. 273 *Mademoiselle*..had been one of the true Resistants, refusing even in the blackest hours of the war to admit even the possibility of defeat, or to allow pessimism among the peasants. **1959** *Sunday Times* 22 Mar. 23/7 A disguised and wounded Hungarian resistant.

b. In calico-printing, = RESIST *sb.* 2.

1879 *Spons' Encycl. Manuf.* I. 50 The first crops of citric acid crystals..are used largely by the calico-printer as a 'resistant' for iron and alumina mordants.

Hence **†reˈsistantly** *adv.*, resistingly. *Obs.*[−1]

1611 SPEED *Theat. Gt. Brit.* x. (1614) 19/1 Brightrik..sent the Steward of his house to know their intents, whom resistantly they slew.

‖résistant (resistɑ̃). Also *fem.* **résistante.** [Fr.] A member of the French Resistance (see RESISTANCE 1 c).

1966 M. R. D. FOOT *SOE in France* vii. 175 Mathilde Carré..proclaimed herself already an ardent résistante. **1967** *Listener* 16 Mar. 370/3 Pierre d'Harcourt was twenty-six when, after Dunkirk, he shed his cavalry uniform to become a pioneer *résistant*. Maybe the cavalry discipline helped to restrain his impetuosity. **1978** *Dædalus* Fall 29 Everyone in France was a 'résistant'.

†reˈsistence. *Obs.* Also 5–6 **-ens, resyst-, recistence, -ens.** [a. OF. *resistence*, = Sp. and Pg. *resistencia*, It. *re-, risistenza*, ad. late L. *resistentia* (Augustine), f. *resistĕre* to RESIST: see -ENCE.] = RESISTANCE. (In common use to c 1530.)

c **1374** CHAUCER *Troylus* III. 990 Loue, a-yeyns þe which þat no man may Ne oughte ek goudly make resistence. *c* **1386** —— *Can. Yeom. Prol. & T.* 356 Thise metales ben of so gret violence, Our walles may not make hem resistence. **1450** *Rolls of Parlt.* V. 200/2 For suche distres takyng, and yn resistens therof, ther is grete assembles. **1494** FABYAN *Chron.* VI. clxxi. 165 After many resistences by hym doon, to auoyde yᵉ temptacion therof. **1512** *Act. 4 Hen. VIII*, c. 20 Preamble, Theire adherentes made extreme resistens ayenst your said Beseecher. *a* **1548** HALL *Chron., Hen. VIII* 176 The Spaniardes so defended them with ordinaunce & resistences that they slew .v. or vi. M. Frenchmen. **1596** SPENSER *F.Q.* VI. xi. 43 Where the bold knight Encountring him with small resistence slew. **1704** J. HARRIS *Lex. Techn.* I, *Resistence of the Medium*, is the opposition against, or hindrance of the Motion of any Body moving in a Fluid. **1727–38** CHAMBERS *Cycl.* s.v., A greater weight is required to overcome their united resistence, than to overcome their several resistences one after another.

†reˈsistency. *Obs.* [ad. late L. *resistentia*: see prec. and -ENCY.] Resistance, repulsion.

1640 WILKINS *New Planet* ix. (1707) 250 It will easily follow, that these Bodies have resistency from one another. *a* **1688** CUDWORTH *Immut. Mor.* (1731) 77 We feel things at a Distance in the dark, by the Resistency which they make upon the further end of the Staff that we hold in our hands.

resistent (rɪˈzɪstənt), *a.* and *sb.* [ad. L. *resistent-em*, pres. pple. of *resistĕre* to RESIST.]

A. *adj.* = RESISTANT *a.*

1640 G. WATTS tr. *Bacon's De Augm. Sci.* III. iv. 149 A Pestilentiall aire seizeth on bodies more open and lesse resistent. **1860** TYNDALL *Glac.* II. xxvii. 377 The more resistent ones [*sc.* laminæ] stand out in ridges after the softer parts between them have been eaten away. **1887** W. G. PALGRAVE *Ulysses* 255 Native Indian tribes..resistent to the last..against every Argentine attempt at civilising..them.

†B. *sb.* = RESISTANT *sb.* *Obs.*

1600 W. WATSON *Decacordon* (1602) 15 The foresaid resistance was not schisme in the Resisten[t]s. **1644** DIGBY *Nat. Bodies* xiii. §5 The resistance..weakned by the thinnenesse of the resistent there.

resister (rɪˈzɪstə(r)). Also 5 **resistour.** [f. RESIST *v.* + -ER[1].]

1. a. One who resists. Cf. also *passive resister* s.v. PASSIVE RESISTANCE.

1375 BARBOUR *Bruce* XVIII. 214 Quhen the feld wes clengit cleyne, Sa that na resisteris wes seyne. **1459** *Rolls of Parlt.* II. 370/1 Lyve and dye with the said Erle, ayenst his resistours. **1558** GOODMAN *How to Obey* 176 To counte your selues therin no rebells, but lawfull resisters. **1579** W. WILKINSON *Confut. Fam. Love* Heret. Affirm. biijb, Disputation..with the unwillyng ones and resisters. **1611** SPEED *Hist. Gt. Brit.* IX. xxiv. (1623) 1158 [They] slew no small numbers of their resisters. *a* **1656** HALES *Gold. Rem.* (1677) 29 To resist the truth which is..believed by the resister himself is a direct contradiction. **1710** A. B. *Answ. to Argts. Bp. Oxford's Resistance* 18 That they never consider'd the Matter at all, and therefore assisted these

Resisters. **1832** *Examiner* 97/1 The resisters of an exaction. **1873** SMILES *Huguenots France* vi. (1881) 100 The resisters of the policy were in both cases Calvinists.

b. *spec.* A member of a resistance movement; a resistant. Also with capital initial.

1952 *Chambers's Jrnl.* Feb. 66/2 But all three of them, when they were drunk, believed themselves to have been the most stout-hearted Resisters, members of the Underground. **1959** *Encounter* Aug. 45/1 The treatment accorded to the records of the *Résistance* is especially entertaining.. Thousands of Resisters wrote their personal recollections. **1966** M. R. D. FOOT *SOE in France* vi. 129 In Greece and in Yugoslavia SOE sought to back any anti-German bodies of resisters.

2. That which resists; a resisting body or force.

*a***1586** SIDNEY *Arcadia* III. (1724) II. 575 Philoclea's shamefacedness and humbleness were as strong resisters as choler and disdain. **1596** T. JOHNSON *Cornucopiæ* B j b, Organy and Rue are great resisters of poyson. **1656** [? J. SERGEANT] tr. *T. White's Peripat. Inst.* 73 If a Moveable be struck violently against a hard resister. **1686** GOAD *Celest. Bodies* I. ix. 28 If Warmth be the producer of Moisture, Cold must be the Resister. **1759** *Phil. Trans.* LI. 84 You see, that animal, vegetable, and metallic bodies.. are easily changed into resisters or non-conductors.

re'sistful, *a.* [f. as prec. + -FUL.] Capable of, or inclined to, resistance.

1614 C. BROOKE *Rich. III*, Poems (1872) 132 The wrong-incensed peeres, augment his band, And giue his weakenes, a resistfull force. **1846** HAWKSLEY in Helps *Friends in C.* (1847) I. 134 The human constitution becomes gradually more resistful and.. hardened. **1870** J. HAMILTON *Moses, Man of God* vii. 120 The resistful only supplied victims.

resisti'bility. [f. as next + -ITY. Cf. F. *resistibilité*.]

1. The quality of being resistible.

1617 DONNE *Serm.* cxxxii. Wks. 1839 V. 365 Resistibility and Irresistibility of Grace, which is every Artificers wearing now. **1642** [see RESISTABILITY]. *a***1656** HALES *Gold. Rem.* (1688) 510 The Bremenses who handled the Head *de gratia, & libero arbitrio* in general, and in particular overthrew resistibility of Grace. **1850** J. BROWN *Disc. & Sayings Our Lord* (1852) II. xx. 300 This character of resistibility the evidence in favour of Christianity possesses. **1974** *Times* 4 Feb. 8/2 Irresistibility is simply not borne out by statistics. A survey conducted in 1965 showed not only that 81 per cent of Italian males objected to the closing of licensed brothels but that nearly three quarters made use of prostitutes, which suggests a high degree of resistibility.

2. Power of offering resistance.

1646 SIR T. BROWNE *Pseud. Ep.* 3 Whether the resistibility of his reason did not equivalence the facility of her seduction. **1690** LOCKE *Hum. Und.* IV. vii. §13 The complex Idea of Extension and Resistibility, or Solidity. **1820** *Blackw. Mag.* VIII. 251 Such was its innate and surpassing resistibility of temperament, that it could not be overwhelmed.

resistible (rɪ'zɪstɪb(ə)l), *a.* [f. RESIST *v.* + -IBLE. Cf. F. *résistible*, Sp. *resistible*.] Capable of being resisted; to which resistance can be made.

1643 PRYNNE *Sov. Power Parl.* III. (ed. 2) 121 Our Opposites must.. make Kings as resistible, censurable, deprivable,.. as far forth as they. **1675** BAXTER *Cath. Theol.* II. I. 172 They make Gods Grace a resistible thing, which Man can frustrate. **1759** JOHNSON *Rasselas* xxxi, Earthquakes themselves, the least resistible of natural violence. **1813** SIR R. WILSON *Priv. Diary* (1862) II. 235 A tempting booty, but I feel confident resistible, if not tangible with honour. **1884** *Ch. Times* 14 Nov. 858/4 A genuine outbreak.. would be no more resistible than James II found it. **1903** G. B. SHAW *Man & Superman* III. 134 As to your Life Force, which you think irresistible, it is the most resistible thing in the world for a person of any character. **1966** *Listener* 9 Nov. 597/3 The most resistible of the new MPs.. his voice, as usual, half-way between a splutter and a jeer. **1979** *Financial Times* 14 Apr. 21/3 The water babies themselves are frightful infants.. given to singing resistible underwater ditties.

Hence **re'sistibleness; re'sistibly** *adv.*

1674 HICKMAN *Quinquart. Hist.* (ed. 2) 125 God by his Spirit shall only resistibly, indifferently and remotely.. regenerate and renew our selves. **1847** WEBSTER, *Resistibleness.* **1888** J. MARTINEAU *Study Relig.* II. III. ii. 272 A dynamical resistibleness to a numerical law.

resisting (rɪ'zɪstɪŋ), *vbl. sb.* [f. RESIST *v.* + -ING[1].] The action of the vb. RESIST.

1482 *Monk of Evesham* (Arb.) 89 Chesyng rather to dyssymylle.. than by her blamyng and resysting stere and moue agenste hem the wrathe.. of suche euyl dysposyd persons. **1558** GOODMAN *How to Obey* 123 There is nothing in this saying.. which can condemne lawfull resisting of vngodlie Rulers. **1614** DONNE *Biaθanatos* (1648) 110 The Devill is overcome by Resisting, but the World and the Flesh by running away. **1742** RICHARDSON *Pamela* III. 86 This Passion had been heighten'd by my resisting of it. **1760–72** H. BROOKE *Fool of Qual.* (1809) IV. 91 Here has been a large body of the gens d'armes sent for them, so that there was no resisting.

re'sisting, *ppl. a.* [f. RESIST *v.* + -ING[2].] That resists or offers resistance. ***resisting medium*** (see MEDIUM *sb.* 4).

Freq. in modern use as the second element in *Combs.*, as *cold-, disease-, dust-, fire-resisting*, etc.

1593 Q. ELIZ. *Boeth.* II. 25 These be not yet remedyes for thy disease, but serues for bellowes against the cure of thy resisting sorowe. **1595** SHAKS. *John* II. i. 38 Against the browes of this resisting towne. **1625** K. LONG tr. *Barclay's Argenis* I. xx. 60 Neither did lesse feare invade his resisting thoughts. **1694** SALMON *Bate's Dispens.* (1699) 402/1 It would be presently dull'd.. by the resisting Sulphur. **1743** EMERSON *Fluxions* 288 The Resistance of a Globe moving in a resisting Medium. **1798** HUTTON *Curs. Math.* (1807) II. 357 The resisting force is equal to the weight that urges it. **1862** SPENCER *First Princ.* II. v. §56 (1875) 182 Uniform motion in a straight line, implies the absence of a resisting medium. **1863** GEO. ELIOT *Romola* xl, But the resisting thoughts were not yet overborne. **1898** *Allbutt's Syst. Med.* V. 329 Anything which.. tends to diminish the resisting power of the individual.

Hence **re'sistingly** *adv.*

1548 UDALL *Erasm. Par. 1 John* ii. 46 b, Doth not he, that lyueth after such sorte, resistingly denie Christ? **1905** *Westm. Gaz.* 1 July 17/2 The mob.. fell back slowly and resistingly before the rifle volleys of the troops.

resistive (rɪ'zɪstɪv), *a.* [f. RESIST *v.* + -IVE.] **1.** Capable of or inclined to resistance.

1603 B. JONSON *Sejanus* II. i, Resistiue 'gainst the sunne, the raine, or wind. **1646** SIR T. BROWNE *Pseud. Ep.* IV. v. 191 The most vigorous part protecting it selfe, and protruding the matter upon the weaker and lesse resistive side. **1837** CARLYLE *Fr. Rev.* III. VII. iii, Pardoning the submissive, cutting down the resistive. **1870** E. L. HULL *Serm.* Ser. II. 153 Every dark temptation makes us strong in resistive might. **1897** *Allbutt's Syst. Med.* III. 271 One man is more resistive than another, according to his strength of constitution.

2. *Electr.* Pertaining to, possessing, or resulting from electrical resistance; *spec.* in connection with resistance as a component of impedance (in this sense opp. REACTIVE *a.* 6 a and b).

1929 *Wireless World* 30 Jan. 116/2 The reactive component in each case is drawn at 90° to the resistive component. **1937** A. V. EASTMAN *Fund. Vacuum Tubes* v. 153 Since power considerations in a voltage amplifier are minor, the output load may be partly reactive instead of resistive. **1947** R. LEE *Electronic Transformers & Circuits* i. 6 With many sine wave electronic transformers, the transformer load is resistive. **1958** *New Scientist* 21 Aug. 658/3 The Stellarator uses resistive heating only in the first stage, to bring the plasma into the million degree region. **1964** R. F. FICCHI *Electr. Interference* 217 Resistive coupling is the association of two or more circuits with one another by means of resistance mutual to the circuits. **1969** L. E. C. HUGHES et al. *Dict. Electronics & Nucleonics* 231/1 Reactive loads are made entirely resistive by adding inductors or capacitors in series or shunt. **1980** *Times* 23 June 18/7 He used the equations for capacitative and resistive loss in electric cables.

Hence **re'sistively** *adv*; **re'sistiveness.**

1803 W. TAYLOR in *Monthly Mag.* XIV. 491 Resistiveness, or the capability of becoming an object of sensation. **1864** A. LEIGHTON *Myst. Legends Edin.* (1886) 238 Persistiveness draws, as it were, a power from the wearing out of resistiveness. **1887** *Buck's Handbk. Med. Sci.* IV. 649/1 Flexion and extension of the leg at the knee, either passively or resistively.

resi'stivity. [f. RESISTIVE *a.* + -ITY.] **1.** *Electr.* The specific resistance of a substance, now usu. defined as the resistance of a conductor of unit length and unit cross-sectional area.

1885 O. HEAVISIDE in *Electrician* 4 Sept. 311/1 'Specific resistance' may well be called 'resistivity'. **1890** *Nature* 9 Oct. 577/2 The.. diameter of any of the conductors.. divided by its electric resistivity. **1895** [see -IVITY]. **1943** C. L. BOLTZ *Basic Radio* i. 26 Anyone capable of working out a formula can therefore find the resistance of any conductor by looking up the tables for specific resistance or resistivity. **1962** *Newnes Conc. Encycl. Electr. Engin.* 658/1 Copper of the highest purity has a resistivity lower than that of any other known material except silver. A standard value for the resistivity of annealed copper was established in 1913 by the International Electrotechnical Commission as 0·017 241 Ω per m length and mm² section. **1975** *Country Life* 6 Feb. 331/3 The scientific techniques used by the archaeologists, such as the resistivity meters used to detect areas where the soil is broken up by the tops of mine shafts. **1975** G. ANDERSON *Coring* vii. 121 The porosity of the sand is above 20% and the resistivity ranges from 0.3 ohm-m for saltwater sands to several ohm-meters for oil-saturated sands.

2. Special Combs.: **resistivity surveying,** measurement of the current passing between electrodes embedded in the ground at a series of positions over a given area, in order to identify regions of differing resistivity and hence locate buried structural features; so **resistivity survey,** a set or programme of such measurements.

1927 *Terrestrial Magnetism* XXXII. 49 The Department of Terrestrial Magnetism of the Carnegie Institution of Washington has undertaken a series of resistivity surveys in regions where records of earth-current potential gradient are being obtained. **1952** M. B. DOBRIN *Introd. Geophysical Prospecting* xvi. 298 The interpretation of the actual data obtained in field resistivity surveys is usually a highly empirical and generally unreliable process. **1966** *McGraw-Hill Encycl. Sci. & Technol.* XI. 22/2 Electromagnetic and electrical resistivity surveys are used to locate deposits of metallic sulfides, which, except for sphalerite, are good electrical conductors. **1931** *Engin. & Min. Jrnl.* CXXXI. 325 *(heading)* Earth resistivity surveying. **1953** R. J. C. ATKINSON *Field Archaeol.* (ed. 2) i. 38 Resistivity surveying requires at least two operators, one at the instrument and one to move the electrodes. **1963** *Times* 3 June 6/2 Resistivity surveying has been conducted by Mr. Whybrew, of the Ministry's test branch, and buried features have been detected.

resistless (rɪ'zɪstlɪs). [f. RESIST *v.* + -LESS.]

1. That cannot be resisted; irresistible.

1586 MARLOWE *1st Pt. Tamburl.* V. ii, So.. Must Tamburlaine by their resistless powers.. Conclude a league of honour. **1638** MAYNE *Lucian* (1664) 390 It must be of a strong and resistlesse vertue. **1656** JEANES *Fuln. Christ* 112 It can subdue the most raging, and resistlesse lusts. **1693** S. HARVEY in Dryden *Juvenal* ix. (1697) 237 Try to Imprison the resistless Wind. **1748** JOHNSON *Van. Hum. Wishes* 137 Resistless burns the fever of renown. **1813** PARR *Let.* Wks. 1828 VIII. 496 So peerless, so resistless, and upon this occasion so guileless an advocate.. as Mr. Burke. **1874** GEO. ELIOT *Coll. Breakf. P.* 114 That resistless weight Obstinate, irremovable by thought.

2. Powerless to resist; unresisting.

1591 SPENSER *Muiopot.* 436 He seized greedelie On the resistles pray. **1612** W. PARKES *Curtaine-Dr.* (1876) 44 Vpon whose breasts are charactred and insculpt the ensignes of weaknesse and resistlesse impotency. **1818** KEATS *Endym.* III. 266 O misery of hell! resistless, tame, Am I to be burnt up? **1892** *Cornh. Mag.* May 559 She was quite resistless, quite gentle.

re'sistlessly, *adv.* [f. prec. + -LY[2].] In a resistless manner; irresistibly.

1727 BLACKWALL *Sacr. Class.* (1740) I. 61 'Tis resistlessly plain, that the divine writers do not always confine themselves to plain and common grammar. **1813** T. BUSBY *Lucretius* II. 24 *note* (Jod.), He.. displays to us in colours resistlessly strong one of the most dreadful instances of human affliction. **1852** MRS. STOWE *Uncle Tom's C.* xl. 346 Had not this man braved him—steadily, powerfully, resistlessly? **1890** 'R. BOLDREWOOD' *Col.-Reformer* (1891) 103 The chestnut.. dropped with his mouth wrenched resistlessly from the rider's hold.

So **re'sistlessness.**

1870 *Echo* 5 Dec., The self-confidence and resistlessness of the men in the road.

†re'sistment. *Obs. rare*[−1]. [f. RESIST *v.* + -MENT.] Resistance.

1605 *Answ. Discov. Romish Doctr.* 39 The resistment of this present King of that countrie, the Bull of Pius Quintus against Queene Elizabeth.

resistor (rɪ'zɪstə(r)). *Electr.* [f. RESIST *v.* + -OR.] A passive device which impedes the flow of an electric current, used to develop a voltage drop across itself or to limit current flow.

[**1759**: see RESISTER 2]. **1905** *Sci. Amer. Suppl.* 27 May 24586/1 The resistance medium or 'resistor', when solid, usually consists of a core of carbon, coke, or graphite. **1930** *Engineering* 31 Jan. 128/3 A higher-temperature zone heated by non-metallic resistor rods. **1947** R. LEE *Electronic Transformers & Circuits* vi. 181 Tubes may require resistors in the plate and grid leads to damp out parasitic oscillations. **1965** *Wireless World* July 329/2 To monitor this current a 50 Ω resistor is inserted in the earthed lead of the recording head. A 1 kc/s signal source is then injected into the radio input of the recording amplifier and the voltage across the resistor measured with a valve voltmeter or oscilloscope. **1975** FINK & MCKENZIE *Electronics Engineers' Handbk.* vii. 4 Wire-wound resistors usually exhibit an increase in resistance with higher frequencies because of skin effects.

re'sit (riː-), *v.* [RE- 5 a.] *trans.* and *intr.* To sit (an examination) again, usu. after failing at a previous attempt; to retake (an examination), e.g. in order to improve one's grade.

1959 *Chambers's 20th Cent. Dict.* 1380/2 *Resit,.. v.i.* to sit an examination again after failing. —— *n.* an opportunity or act of resitting. **1968** *Sunday Times* 30 June 15 So many students resit the engineering examination each year that an eventual pass rate of 80 percent.. may occur. **1974** A. FOWLES *Pastime* i. 6 He'd had to re-sit English to get the minimum the library required. **1979** *Jrnl. R. Soc. Arts* Dec. 9/1 The candidates for this session's examination were exclusively restricted to those who had been referred in a previous examination or who were resitting in order to obtain higher grades.

resit ('riːsɪt), *sb.* [f. the vb.] The act of resitting an examination; also, an examination held specifically to enable candidates to resit. Also *attrib.*

1959 [see RESIT *v.*]. **1972** D. HASTON *In High Places* ii. 30 For once he'd passed his exams in June and didn't have any resits in September. **1973** *Guardian* 14 June 7/2 Resit school breaks its 11-plus record. Out of 50 pupils.. who had to resit their 11-plus examination.. 31 have passed. **1977** *Belfast Tel.* 19 Jan. 3/4 One wonders how your recent correspondents, who feel that an Eleven-Plus resit is unnecessary, can accept the position arising as a result of the supplementary test which has not been held.

resite ('rɛzaɪt), *sb. Chem.* [ad. G. *resit* (H. Lebach 1909, in *Zeitschr. f. angew. Chem.* XXII. 1601), f. L. *rēs-ina* RESIN *sb.* + *-it* -ITE[1].] Any of the insoluble, infusible resins that are the final products of phenol-aldehyde copolymerizations.

1913 H. LEBACH in *Jrnl. Soc. Chem. Industry* XXXII. 559/2 For the final product, whether it be called Bakelite 'C', Resinite, Condensite, or by some other name, I suggest the name 'Resite'. **1935** C. ELLIS *Chem. Synthetic Resins* I. xiv. 307 Resites (C stage) are branched-chain macro-molecules. **1950** *Thorpe's Dict. Appl. Chem.* (ed. 4) X. 24/2 The resin hardens on further heating and becomes insoluble and infusible. This is the 'C' or resite stage and consists of macromolecules with numerous branched and cross-linked chains. **1973** [see RESITOL].

re-'site (riː-), *v.* [RE- 5 a.] *trans.* To place on another site; to relocate. Hence **re-'siting** *vbl. sb.*

1955 *Times* 19 July 9/7 Many argue that the bridge will still be needed even when the tunnel has been built; then the question of re-siting it may arise. **1967** E. CHAMBERS *Photolitho-Offset* viii. 106 These cameras.. have facilities for the exact siting of films, plates, transparencies and masks with three-point lay and location pins for accurate re-siting and register of copy. **1969** *Jane's Freight Containers 1968–69* 555/1 They are completely mobile and can be pushed or towed for re-siting. **1976** P. R. WHITE *Planning for Public Transport* x. 213 In so far as population re-sited from existing industrial cities is located in new or expanding towns of about 100 000 population, similar improvements could occur.

resitol ('rɛzɪtɒl). *Chem.* [a. G. *resitol* (H. Lebach 1913, in *Chem.-Zeitung* 19 June 734/1), f. *resit* RESITE *sb.* + *res-ol* RESOL.] Any of the rubbery, insoluble resins produced in phenol-aldehyde copolymerizations at a stage intermediate between resol and resite.
1913 H. LEBACH in *Jrnl. Soc. Chem. Industry* XXXII. 559/2 Besides these products, Baekeland distinguishes an intermediate polymerisation product, which he terms 'Bakelite "B"'... This intermediate condensation product I would suggest to call 'Resitol'. **1950** *Thorpe's Dict. Appl. Chem.* (ed. 4) X. 24/2 When heated at temperatures above 100° c. it melts and froths, becoming more viscous and eventually reaching the rubbery stage, the 'B' or resitol stage. **1973** *Materials & Technol.* VI. viii. 588 Phenol resins evolve in three stages, which are connected with the degree of condensation: 1. Resol or A-stage (beginning of condensation): the resin is fluid, soluble, and still contains much water. 2. Resitol or B-stage (continued condensation, slight cross-linking): insoluble, rubbery. 3. Resite or C-stage (final condition of the cured product): infusible and insoluble.

re'sitting (riː-). [RE- 5 a.] A second sitting.
1661 J. DAVIES *Civ. Warres* 367 Lenthalls legal and conscientious objections against their re-sitting were never answered. **1754** H. WALPOLE *Lett.* (1846) III. 38 The grand juries are going to petition for the resitting of the Parliament. **1889** *Anthony's Photogr. Bull.* II. 385 The cost of the merchandise used in a resitting.

re'situate (riː-), *v.* *N. Amer.* [RE- 5 a.] = RELOCATE *v.* 1 a. Also *refl.*
c **1865** E. DICKINSON *Poems* (1955) II. 734 Bore Death from Passion All His East He—sovreign as the Sun Re-situated in the West And the Debate was done. **1974** D. RICHARDS *Coming of Winter* i. 6 He could feel sharp blades of undergrowth so he resituated himself once or twice.

re'sizer (riː-). [f. RE- 5 a + SIZE *v.* + -ER¹.] 'A tool for restoring an object, as a cartridge-shell, to its original size' (*Funk's Stand. Dict.* 1895.) So *resizing-tool*.
1882 *Worc. Exhib. Catal.* III. 57 Rifle with..resizing tools.

† **reskippeson**: see SKIPPESON.

reskus(e, variants of RESCOUS *sb. Obs.*

re'slash (riː-), *v.* [RE- 5 a.] To slash again. Hence **re'slashing** *vbl. sb.*
1718 OZELL tr. *Tournefort's Voy.* II. 184 Leaves..slash'd into three principal parts, and reslash'd again almost like the other leaves. **1970** J. FORD et al. in H. W. Mulligan *African Trypanosomiases* xxvii. 548 He [*sc.* Morris]..checked regeneration by stumping and burning, and not by annual reslashing. **1973** J. J. MCKELVEY *Man against Tsetse* iii. 162 Unpaid community labor, which was recruited under the provisions of the 1937 Sleeping Sickness Ordinance, accomplished almost all of the subsequent slashing and reslashing of regrowth over the years.

re'slay (riː-), *v.* [RE- 5 a.] To slay again.
1791 ANNA SEWARD *Lett.* (1811) III. 49, I am not at all tempted..to..re-slay the already slain. **1839** *Standard* 24 Aug., Lord B—— re-slew the slain in a speech of great brilliancy and sarcasm.

re'slide (riː-), *v.* [RE-.] *intr.* To slide back.
1592 WYRLEY *Armorie, Ld. Chandos* 29 Slow Lidian brooke,.. Staying in doubt th'ocean t'enter in, Or to reslide where first it did begin.

reslush (riː'slʌʃ), *v.* *Paper-making.* [RE- 5 b.] *trans.* To convert (dry or semi-dry paper stock) into slush by the addition of water.
1963 *Economist* 11 May 555/2 Drying the pulp for shipping and then 're-slushing' it. **1967** E. CHAMBERS *Photolitho-Offset* xvi. 247 A few mills in this country make pulp from waste paper by 'reslushing'.

re'smelt (riː-), *v.* [RE- 5 a.] To smelt again. Also *fig.* Hence **re'smelting** *vbl. sb.*
1839 URE *Dict. Arts* 1248 Those of the third class c.. are set apart, and re-smelted. **1858** GREENER *Gunnery* 103 Thousands of tons have been..re-smelted by two adjoining iron-works. **1875** STEDMAN *Victorian Poets* (1887) 453 That magic transmutation which alone justifies a resmelting of the antique.

resmethrin ('rɛzmiθrɪn). [-*ethrin* f. PYR)ETHRIN.] A synthetic pyrethroid employed as an insecticide in the form of a spray.
1971 *Pesticide Sci.* II. 16/1 (*table*) 5-Benzyl-3-furylmethyl (±)-*cis-trans*-chrysanthemate (Resmethrin). **1971** *Bull. World Health Org.* XLIV. 329/1 Resmethrin was superior to the other synthetic pyrethroids and to the natural pyrethrins against all insects tested. **1975** *Daily Tel.* 25 Oct. 8/2 The answer is to keep a bottle of resmethrin..handy and give any new plants a going over with it.

re'smile (riː-), *v.* [RE-.] To smile back.
1708 OZELL tr. *Boileau's Lutrin* (1730) III. 38 The smirking Barber brandishes on high A Bumper, which re-smiles with mutual Joy.

re'smooth (riː-), *v.* [RE- 5 a.] *trans.* To smooth again.
1830 LYTTON *P. Clifford* iii, The treasury of Mrs. Lobkins resmoothed, as it were, the irritated bristles of his mind. **1847** TENNYSON *Princ.* III. 225 And thus your pains May only make that footprint upon sand Which old-recurring waves of prejudice Resmooth to nothing.

resnabel, -yl, obs. forms of RENABLE.

re'snub (riː-), *v.* [RE- 5 a.] To snub again.
1735 HERVEY *Mem.* II. 35 And then carried the Queen to walk and be resnubbed in the garden.

Resochin ('riːsəʊkɪn). *Pharm.* Also resochin. [a. G. *resochin*, f. *reso-rcinol* RESORCINOL + *chin-olin* QUINOLINE.] A proprietary name for CHLOROQUINE.
1946 *Trans. R. Soc. Trop. Med. & Hygiene* XL. 170 Atebrin, sontochin, resochin and quinine were observed to cause arrest of development and degeneration of ring and amoeboid forms. **1947** [see CHLOROQUINE]. **1951** *Trade Marks Jrnl.* 12 Dec. 1135/1 *Resochin*... Pharmaceutical preparations. Farbenfabriken Bayer..; Manufacturers and Merchants. **1955** *Official Gaz.* (U.S. Patent Office) 19 July TM 157/1 Farbenfabriken Bayer Aktiengesellschaft, Leverkusen-Bayerwerk, Germany. Filed Dec. 15, 1954. *Resochin.* Applicant claims ownership of German Reg. No. 602,220, dated Nov. 2, 1950. **1958** J. H. BURN *Lect. Notes Pharmacol.* (ed. 5) 105 Chloroquine was also discovered by the Germans as resochin, but was tested and developed in America during the last war. **1970** W. PETERS *Chemotherapy & Drug Resistance in Malaria* i. 5 From the time of its synthesis by Andersag..in 1934, chloroquine, or Resochin as it was first known to the German workers, faced a precarious existence.

resociali'zation (riː-). *Social Psychol.* [RE- 5 b.] The action or process of (re)inducing conformity to accepted standards of social behaviour. Also *attrib.*
1964 M. ARGYLE *Psychol. & Social Probl.* i. 20 When we come to consider the re-socialization, or indoctrination, of adults, we shall introduce two further principles of learning: cognitive learning and learning by means of emotional arousal. **1970** P. MAYER *Socialization* p. xiii, Major social changes, such as ongoing urbanization or industrialization, involve the resocialization of people of all ages. **1974** M. C. GERALD *Pharmacol.* xii. 232 Some view their program [*sc.* of Alcoholics Anonymous] as a resocialization process attempting to develop individual maturity. **1976** *Guardian* 23 July 15/5 The regular presence of women in the unit, unthinkable in the old isolation system, is seen as an essential part of the resocialization process by staff and psychiatrists alike. **1977** F. MUSGROVE *Margins of Mind* ix. 196 A period of 'desocialization' may be an important preliminary to the effective resocialization of adults.

re'soften (riː-), *v.* [RE- 5 b.] To soften again. Hence **re'softening** *vbl. sb.*
1611 FLORIO *Worlde of Wordes* 439/3 *Rimollire*,..also to remollifie, to resoften or asswage. **1889** P. N. HASLUCK *Model Engin. Handybk.* 136 By the appearance of the colours we are informed of the temperature of the steel, or in other words, how far, or to what extent the resoftening has progressed. **1894** DUKE OF ARGYLL *Burdens of Belief* 90 Come burnished autumn with thy wealth of flame,.. Come leaves with tints too blended for a name, And lakes resoftening lights that come from you. **1963** J. OSBORNE *Dental Mech.* (ed. 5) i. 16 The impression is taken, chilled, the surface resoftened by flaming and the impression re-inserted.

† **re'soign**, *v. Obs. rare*⁻¹. In 5 resoyngne. [ad. OF. *resoignier*, etc., f. *re-* RE- + *soigner* to be anxious, careful, f. *soin* care.] *intr.* To fear.
c **1500** *Melusine* 140 Our enmys..are come to assayll vs without cause vnto our right herytage and also we ought not to resoyngne ne dylaye therfore.

re'soil (riː-), *v.* [RE- 5 a and 5 c.]
1. *trans.* To soil or dirty again.
1591 SYLVESTER *Du Bartas* I. *Ivry* 29 Neither shall my Pen Re-purple Lisle; nor with dead Grease agen Re-soile the Soile at Courtras.
2. To cover again with soil. Hence **re'soiling** *vbl. sb.*
1842 *Civil Eng. & Arch. Jrnl.* V. 85/2 The top surface of cuttings and the seat of embankment are usually uncallowed for the purpose of resoiling the slopes. **1852** WIGGINS *Embanking* 117 For soiling and re-soiling, 1*d.*

re'sojourn (riː-), *v.* [RE- 5 a.] *intr.* To sojourn again.
1648 HERRICK *Hesper., To Dean-bourn*, A people..rude (almost) as rudest Salvages, With whom I did, and may re-sojourne when Rockes turn to Rivers.

resol ('rɛzɒl). *Chem.* Also **-ole** (-əʊl). [a. G. *resol* (H. Lebach 1909, in *Zeitschr. f. angew. Chem.* XXII. 1601), f. L. *rēs-īna* RESIN *sb.* + *-ol* -OL.] Any of the alcohol-soluble, usu. fluid resins formed as the first stage in phenol-aldehyde copolymerizations and often prepared as precondensates in the manufacture of plastic.
1913 H. LEBACH in *Jrnl. Soc. Chem. Industry* XXXII. 559/2 These initial stages of Bakelite have received various names... Four years ago I proposed to call the whole of this class 'Resoles'. **1933** *Ibid.* LII. 420T/2 Similar *o*-hydroxy-substituted substances are supposed to represent molecules of Bakelite A (resole). **1935** C. ELLIS *Chem. Synthetic Resins* I. xiv. 306 The resols, or initial products of alkaline condensation are mono- or poly-alcohols. **1956** J. N. ANDERSON *Appl. Dental Materials* xxi. 260 The resin is in the 'resole' state and is modified by adding fillers and colouring matter. **1973** *Materials & Technol.* VI. viii. 590 Resols used as starting materials have a very limited storage life owing to the presence of reactive groups.

re'solder (riː-), *v.* [RE- 5 a: in early examples after F. *resouder*, †*resoder*, It. *risaldare*.] *trans.* To solder again. Also *absol.* and *fig.* Hence **re'soldering** *vbl. sb.*
1598 FLORIO, *Risaldatura*, a resoldring, a refastning. **1605** SYLVESTER *Urania* lxx, I'ld rather sing..the Bethanian Lazarus reuiuing, Then valiant Theseus Sonnes re-sodering. **1847** TENNYSON *Princ.* v. 45 We twain, with mutual pardon ask'd and given For stroke and song, resolder'd peace. **1900** HASLUCK *Model Engineer's Handybk.* 75 Turn the outer end of the cylinder true,..then reverse and resolder on the chuck.

re'sole (riː-), *v.* [RE-.] **a.** *trans.* To furnish (a boot, shoe, etc.) with a new sole.
a **1853** ROBERTSON *No Church* iv, His boots had come home, resoled and heeled. **1863** W. C. BALDWIN *Afr. Hunting* iii. 65 A day employed in re-soling shoes.
b. *intr.* To admit of being resoled. *rare.*
1922 *Daily Mail* 24 Nov. 11 (Advt.), You can get 'cheap' shoes which look worse every day you wear them, and won't re-sole once.

re'solemnize (riː-), *v.* [RE- 5 a.] *trans.* To solemnize again.
1621 G. SANDYS *Ovid's Met.* XIV. (1626) 283 His fathers funeralls re-solemniz'd, He puts to Sea, with ships well-nigh surpriz'd By Iris flames. **1654–66** EARL ORRERY *Parthen.* (1676) 617 The Nuptials were re-solemnized.

reso'licit (riː-), *v.* [ad. It. *risollecitare*, = F. *ressolliciter*.] *trans.* To solicit again.
1641 EARL MONM. tr. *Biondi's Civ. Wars* III. 117 The second messengers, who with a herald were sent to resollicite him.

† **reso'licitude.** *Obs. rare*⁻¹. [From the Fr. original.] Renewed solicitude.
1490 CAXTON *Eneydos* xxvi. 92 Thou hast broughte me from solysitude, & remysed into resolysitude.

† **re'solidate**, *pa. pple. Obs.*⁻¹ [ad. med.L. *resolidātus*, pa. pple. of *resolidāre* to strengthen again.] Made solid again; reunited.
1485 CAXTON *St. Wenefryde* 4 In the place of her necke where as her heede was smyten of and after by dyuyne operacion was sett on ageyn & resolydate.

reso'lidify (riː-), *v.* [RE- 5 a.]
1. *intr.* To become solid again.
1861 *Chambers's Encycl.* II. 546/1 The C[amphor] sublimes and resolidifies in the interior upper part of the flask. **1875** CROLL *Climate & T.* xxxi. 523 The moment that it parts with the heat received, it will of course resolidify.
2. *trans.* To make solid again.
1898 *Westm. Gaz.* 12 Dec. 9/2 Improving low grade butters by washing them in a melted state and then resolidifying them with buttermilk.
So ,**resolidifi'cation**.
1871 TYNDALL *Fragm. Sci.* (1879) II. v. 66 Watch its subsequent resolidification.

resolu'bility. [f. as next + -ITY. Cf. F. *résolubilité*.] The quality of being resoluble.
1855 H. J. S. SMITH in *Oxford Ess.* 123 In assigning reasons for his disbelief of the universal resolubility of nebulae. **1879** *Encycl. Brit.* X. 48/1 Researches on the resolubility of algebraic equations by radicals.

resoluble ('rɛzəljuːb(ə)l), *a.*¹ [ad. late L. *resolūbilis* (4th c.): see RE- and SOLUBLE, and cf. F. *résoluble* (1577).] Capable of being resolved, in various senses; resolvable.
1602 FULBECKE *2nd Pt. Parall.* 62 Though the sale be pure and vnconditionall, yet it is resoluble and defeasible. **1660** R. COKE *Justice Vind.* 5 We see all things are in their individuals resoluble into their first composition. **1665–6** *Phil. Trans.* I. 204 The two first sorts are made of a matter easily resoluble. ? **1705** BERKELEY in Fraser *Life* (1871) 421 Qu. if extension be resoluble into points it does not consist of? **1871** EARLE *Philol. Eng. Tongue* §649 The distinctiveness of all that which we call brogue, accent, &c. is ultimately resoluble into a speciality of modulation. **1871** *Daily News* 30 June, One of those mysteries resoluble only by a knowledge of the fact that [etc.].
Hence '**resolubleness**.
1670 BOYLE *Tracts, Temp. Subterr. Reg.* ix. 34 Many of them may be wrought on,..even by moist Air, which argues the resolublenesse of their Constitution.

re-soluble (riː'sɒljuːb(ə)l), *a.*² [RE- 5 a.] Capable of being dissolved again.
1839 URE *Dict. Arts* 541 A solution that lets fall, with caustic soda, a precipitate partly re-soluble in carbonate of ammonia. **1846** POE *Willis* Wks. 1865 III. 30 All which claims to be new..is re-soluble into the old.

resolucion, obs. form of RESOLUTION.

† **resolutative**, error for RESOLUTIVE *a.*
1582 HESTER *Secr. Phiorav.* I. xliv. 54 The [remedy].. hath a penetratiue vertue and resolutative.

'**resolute**, *sb. rare.* [See next.]
† **1.** A payment. *Obs.*
1534 *Yorks. Chantry Surv.* (Surtees) II. 512 In Resolutes yerely going forthe of the same vˢ ijᵈ. **1573** ABP. PARKER *Corr.* (Parker Soc.) 455 Subsidies, free rents, new-year's gifts, and other such resolutes ccccˡ. **1610** W. FOLKINGHAM *Art of Survey* IV. iv. 84 In this Rancke may be Marshalled al Resolutes, Dechashes, Decrements.
2. A resolute or determined person.
1602 SHAKS. *Ham.* I. i. 98 Young Fortinbras..Hath.. Shark'd vp a List of Landlesse Resolutes. **1799–1800** COLERIDGE tr. *Schiller's Piccolomini* I. iii. 62 Many a resolute, who now appears Made up to all extremes.

resolute ('rɛzəl(j)uːt), *a.* (and *pa. pple.*) [ad. L. *resolūtus*, pa. pple. of *resolvĕre* to RESOLVE. So It., Sp., Pg. *resoluto*, F. *résolu*.]
I. † **1.** Dissolved. *Obs. rare*⁻¹.
c **1420** *Pallad. on Husb.* I. 1119 For bathis hoot, ammoniak is tolde Right good, with brymstoon resolute.
† **2.** Of loose texture; friable. *Obs. rare.*
c **1420** *Pallad. on Husb.* III. 12 Now wold also thi puls be sowen there As thynne, & resolute..hit were. *Ibid.* IV. 51 Panyk & mylde in hoot & drie is sowe As now. Light resolute lond they desire.

†3. Morally lax, dissolute. *Obs. rare*$^{-1}$.

1432–50 tr. *Higden* (Rolls) III. 191 He wente to the cite of Crotines, resolute moche in vertues and in honeste, techenge men, women, and childer vertuous life.

†4. Relaxed, weak, infirm. *Obs. rare*$^{-1}$.

1607 TOPSELL *Four-f. Beasts* (1658) 148 The weak, resolute, or paralytike members being therewith anointed, they are much eased, if not recovered.

II. †5. Of rents: Paid, rendered. *Obs.*

c **1466** in *Bedfordsh. N. & Q.* (1886) I. 361 Rent resolute to our..lord the kyng, as to his manor of Bycleswade. **1534** *Liber Regis* (1786) p. ix, What annuell..rents..and Fees..ben yerly accustumed to be resolute and paid. **1670** *Act. 22 Chas. II*, c. 6 §9 Allowances to be made of divers Pensions, Portions, Rents Resolute, or other Things of the like Nature.

III. †6. Determinate, decided, positive, absolute, final. *Obs.*

1501 *Lett. Rich. III & Hen. VII* (Rolls) I. 169 The same commissioners..promysid us..to shewe us the resolute mynde of the said king. **1532** MORE *Confut. Tindale* Wks. 524/2 Wherin what hys finall and resolute sentence is, ye shall..very scantly perceiue. **1597** HOOKER *Eccl. Pol.* v. xlix. §3 The answere of God was a resolute denyall of favour to them for whom supplication was made. **1606** BRYSKETT *Civ. Life* 122 His resolute opinion in that matter cannot be picked out of his writings.

†b. Esp. ***resolute answer***. (Common in 16th c.)

1513 MORE *Rich. III*, Wks. 66/1 If he woulde geue them a resolute aunswere to the contrarye. **1581** J. BELL *Haddon's Answ. Osor.* 503 To satisfie this place of S. Paule, here is an easie and a Resolute aunswere. **1629** MASSINGER *Picture* IV. i, I expect now Your resolute answer: but advise maturely Before I hear it. *a* **1656** HALES *Gold. Rem.* (1688) 420 The Præses eagerly urged them to give their resolute answer.

†7. Of persons: Decided with regard to matters of doubt or opinion. *Obs. rare.*

1581 N. BURNE *Disput.* in *Cath. Tract.* (S.T.S.) 148 Sua [they] vald be na mair resolut be the iudgement of the bellis, nor thay var befoir. **1631** WEEVER *Anc. Funeral Mon.* 797 He ..got the surname *Doctoris resoluti*, of Resolute or Resoluing Doctor.

8. Of persons, their minds, etc.: Determined, having a fixed resolve, constant, firm: **a.** Const. *against*, *for*, *in*, †*to*, †*upon*, and with inf.

1533 BELLENDEN *Livy* II. vii. (S.T.S.) I. 155 Þai war all resolute of ane mynde, to put ane end als sone to þare ciete as to þare liberte. **1579** LYLY *Euphues* (Arb.) 134 They would neuer haue ben so dissolute in their life, or so resolute in their owne conceipts. **1634** W. TIRWHYT tr. *Balzac's Lett.* 187, I am determined to continue resolute in well doing. **1670** COTTON *Espernon* I. I. 20 His Majesty..conceiv'd a mortal animosity against him, and was resolute to his ruine. **1715** DE FOE *Fam. Instruct.* I. iv. (1841) I. 93 Are you so resolute against yourself? **1719** —— *Crusoe* II. (Globe) 519 Seeing they were resolute for Mischief. **1838** WORDSW. *Blest Statesman He*, Him who holds his ministry, Resolute, at all hazards, to fulfil Its duties. **1874** GREEN *Short Hist.* vii. §6. 406 If the Queen was resolute for peace, England was resolute for war.

b. Without const., in predicative or attrib. use.

1579–80 NORTH *Plutarch, Agis & Cleomenes* (1657) 666 Agis..shewed himself in his counsell then, no rash, but a resolute and valiant man. **1588** SHAKS. *L.L.L.* v. ii. 705 *Clo.* Ile do it in my shirt. *Dum.* Most resolute Pompey. **1604** T. WRIGHT *Passions* III. ii. 84 In most vehement passions the resolutest minds are best prooued. **1652** J. WRIGHT tr. *Camus' Nat. Paradox* 337 Liante..placed himself at the head of this resolute Party. **1729** BUTLER *Serm.* Wks. 1874 II. 100 A certain determination, and resolute bent of mind, not to be convinced or set right. **1817** SHELLEY *Rev. Islam* IX. ix, They were few, but resolute. **1863** GEO. ELIOT *Romola* xxix, The simple, resolute man looked round him with grave joy.

9. Of actions, etc.: Characterized by determination or firmness of purpose.

1603 SHAKS. *Meas. for M.* II. i. 12 That the resolute acting of [y]our blood Could have attain'd th' effect of your owne purpose. **1632** LITHGOW *Trav.* II. 65 After a most resolute deliberation. **1784** COWPER *Task* v. 619 His master-lust Falls first before his resolute rebuke. **1813** SHELLEY *Q. Mab* III. 153 He..leads Invincibly a life of resolute good. **1874** GREEN *Short Hist.* ii. §8. 101 Young as he was, Henry mounted the throne with a resolute purpose of government.

resolute ('rɛzəl(j)u:t), *v.* Now *U.S.* [orig. f. *resolūt-*, ppl. stem of L. *resolvĕre* to RESOLVE, but in mod. use a back-formation from *resolution*.]

†1. *refl.* To resolve, decide (oneself) *upon* a person. *Obs. rare*$^{-1}$.

a **1548** HALL *Chron., Hen. VIII* 184b, After long debate the kyng resoluted him selfe vpon sir Thomas More [to be his Chancellor].

†2. *trans.* To resolve, dissolve *into* something.

1727 BRADLEY *Fam. Dict., Hail*, a cloudy Vapour resoluted into Water which in the Fall through..the Air is congealed, and so made Hail.

3. *U.S. intr.* To draw up or pass resolutions.

1860 in De Vere *Americanisms* (1871) 655 When you have done resoluting, you will only have lost your time. **1888** BRYCE *Amer. Commw.* v. xc. III. 233 The discontented.. flocked every Sunday afternoon to cheer denunciations of corporations and monopolists, and to 'resolute' against the rich generally.

resolutely ('rɛzəl(j)u:tlɪ), *adv.* [f. RESOLUTE *a.* + -LY^2.] In a resolute manner.

†1. Determinately, positively, definitely. *Obs.*

a **1548** HALL *Chron., Hen. VIII* 258 He tolde them resolutely that onelesse thei would yelde vp the toune franckly [etc.]. **1617** MORYSON *Itin.* II. 225 Hee resolutely beleeuing they were intended for Ireland. **1661** BOYLE *Spring of Air* III. xxxi, Possibly he would have spoken less resolutly if he had made all the trials.

2. With fixed purpose, boldly, determinedly.

1596 SHAKS. *1 Hen. IV*, I. ii. 38 A purse of Gold most resolutely snatch'd on Monday night, and most dissolutely spent on Tuesday Morning. **1647** CLARENDON *Hist. Reb.* I. §40 Frankly and resolutely to enter into a war with Spain. **1728** MORGAN *Algiers* II. iv. 271 He may be said to have deported himself rather resolutely than prudently. **1833** I. TAYLOR *Fanat.* vi. 183 *note*, To deny all connexion of causation is to be resolutely incredulous. **1868** E. EDWARDS *Ralegh* I. i. 9 Traditions which are resolutely..upheld by the inhabitants of the village.

resoluteness ('rɛzəl(j)u:tnɪs). [f. as prec. + -NESS.] The fact or character of being resolute; firm determination.

1593 G. HARVEY *Pierce's Super.* 38 Pollicy deemeth that vertue a vice,..that resolutenes, dissolutenes. **1599** SANDYS *Europæ Spec.* (1605) F iv, Men who with incessant industry and resolutenes incredible..leave no exploite.. vnattempted. **1675** BROOKS *Gold. Key* Wks. 1867 V. 169 A willingness and resoluteness to suffer for him when we are called to it. **1840** ARNOLD *Hist. Rome* II. 375 The plain resoluteness of his character..caused him to be elected tribune of the commons. **1890** *Spectator* 25 Jan., To make his resoluteness serve the purpose of extricating the great German from..a difficult and ambiguous crisis.

resolution^1 (rɛzə'l(j)u:ʃən). Also 4–6 -cioun, 5–7 -cion, 5–6 -cyon. [a. OF. *resolucion*, *-tion* (14th c.; mod.F. *résolution*, = Sp. *resolucion*, It. *re-*, *risoluzione*), or ad. L. *resolūtiōn-em*, n. of action f. *resolvĕre* to RESOLVE.]

I. †1. a. = DISSOLUTION 8. *Obs. rare.*

1382 WYCLIF *2 Tim.* iv. 6 The tyme of my resolucioun [L. *resolutionis*], or deeth, is nyʒ. *c* **1449** PECOCK *Repr.* I. xi. 57. **1582** N. T. (Rhem.) *2 Tim.* iv. 6 The time of my resolution is at hand.

†**b.** A state of dissolution or decay. *Obs.*$^{-1}$

1533 BELLENDEN *Livy* II. xiv. (S.T.S.) I. 184 Þe membris ..brocht baith þame self and all þe body to extreme resolucioun [L. *tabem*].

2. a. The process by which a material thing is reduced or separated into its component parts or elements; a result of this. Also *attrib.*

1412–20 LYDG. *Chron. Troy* IV. xxxv, The flawme.. queynt, that they ne myght se Nought but smoky resolucions. **1513** BRADSHAW *St. Werburge* I. 3327 Our sauiour..preserued her body..Both hole and sounde from naturall resolucion. **1555** EDEN *Decades* (Arb.) 239 It dooth preserue the same from resolution & putrefaction. **1626** BACON *Sylva* §400 The Immediate Cause of Death, is the Resolution or Extinguishment of the Spirits. *a* **1676** HALE *Prim. Orig. Man.* III. vi. (1677) 278 The Resolution or Maceration of Frogs and Worms will reproduce Individuals of the same species. **1707** *Curios. in Husb. & Gard.* 230 By their Resolution, or the true Anatomy I made of them, I found them to be compos'd of much Sulphur, a little Mercury, and less Salt. **1794** HUTTON *Philos. Light*, etc. 297 The decomposition or resolution of phlogistic substances.. is now well understood. **1822–34** *Good's Study Med.* (ed. 4) I. 12 The high temperature in the stomach produces a concretive resolution. **1881** *Nature* XXIV. 397/2 A simpler or fundamental group being the resolution product.

transf. **1856** EMERSON *Eng. Traits, Race*, All our experience is of the gradation and resolution of races.

b. Const. *to*, *into*. Also, conversion *into* something else, or *into* a different form.

1519 *Interl. Four Elem.* in Hazl. *Dodsley* I. 12 Corruption of a body..Is but the resolution..Of every element to his own place. **1659** HAMMOND *On Ps.* xc. 3 The resolution of the body to dust, may be fitly exprest. **1812** SIR H. DAVY *Chem. Philos.* 51 Their resolution into the supposed elements of the chemists of those days. **1867** H. MACMILLAN *Bible Teach.* vii. (1870) 134 Instances of the resolution of the stem into a rolled and compressed leaf may be seen in grasses and bulbous plants.

c. Orig., the effect of an optical instrument in making the separate parts of an object (*esp.* the stars of a nebula) distinguishable by the eye. Now more widely, the act, process, or capability of rendering distinguishable the component parts of an object or closely adjacent optical or photographic images, or of separating measurements of similar magnitude of any quantity in space or time; also, the smallest quantity which is measurable by such a process.

1860 *Olmsted's Mech. Heavens* 396 The resolution of this nebula. **1867** J. HOGG *Microsc.* I. ii. 72 *Resolution*, or the power of showing clearly minute details. **1868** LOCKYER *Guillemin's Heavens* (ed. 3) 396 Each new triumph of optical skill results in a resolution of some nebulæ, before irreducible. **1902** *Encycl. Brit.* XXXII. 776 A resolving power of 100,000 would suffice for the resolution of the closest lines in the spectrum. **1931** *Proc. R. Soc.* A. CXXXII. 307 The 'resolution' (*i.e.*, the smallest interval of time by which two impulses could be separated and still be separately recorded) of the relay ring..was between 1/100th and 1/200th second. **1935** *Nature* 12 Oct. 592/2 The remarks on numerical aperture may give rise to confusion, as the term 'definition' is used, instead of the correct one, 'resolution'. **1958** *Engineering* 28 Mar. 389/2 The accuracy and resolution of the equipment are both equal to one digit in the fourth significant place. **1962** *Which?* Mar. 70/1 We measured the resolution. This is the ability of the projector to reproduce fine detail. **1968** *Brit. Med. Bull.* XXIV. 255/1 This provides 8-bit resolution for the input samples. **1971** J. Z. YOUNG *Introd. Study Man* ii. 20 As they examine the world more and more minutely with instruments of ever higher resolution they come upon phenomena not previously described. **1972** *Sci. Amer.* July 19/3 A 1,000 kilohertz..sonar would provide a resolution of 30 centimeters on a target 200 meters away. **1973** *Ibid.* June 47/1 The time resolution of the shutter is about a nanosecond. **1978** *Ibid.* Mar. 144/2 (Advt.), A usable resolution of 0.001° C makes the HP 2804 an excellent choice for measuring minute temperature differences. **1978** *Nature* 18 May p. xviii/1 By means of a selector key the weighing range of 200 g, resolution to 0·01 g, or of 2 kg, resolution to 0·1 g, can be selected.

3. *Med.* †**a.** Dissolution or dispersion of humours or of morbid matter in the body. *Obs.*

1398 TREVISA *Barth. De P.R.* XVIII. lxxxvii. (Bodl. MS.), In somer [though] þere be grette resolucion of humours þer is grete wastinge þereof. *c* **1400** *Lanfranc's Cirurg.* 353 It wole make þe mater mollificatif, & make þe poris open to resolucioun. **1543** TRAHERON *Vigo's Chirurg.* II. 65 It causeth the humours to breath out wyth gentyll resolution, and sedation of payne. **1620** VENNER *Via Recta* viii. 190 Through paruity of exercise, and resolution of superfluous matter by the pores many crude..humours are bred. **1778** *R. James' Diss. Fevers* (ed. 8) 7 To bring about a concretion or resolution of the humours which excited the fever.

†**b.** Conversion into purulent matter. *Obs.*

1597 A. M. tr. *Guillemeau's Fr. Chirurg.* 17b/1 The suppuratione, or resolution to matter, beinge finished. **1676** WISEMAN *Surg. Treat.*, If..the Strumæ [be] recent and but moderately hard, the Resolution or Suppuration of them is seizable.

c. Disappearance of inflammation without coming to suppuration.

1783 W. CULLEN *First Lines* §249 Wks. 1827 II. 8 If an inflammation be cured while the state and texture of the part remain entire, the disease is said to be terminated by Resolution. **1833** *Cycl. Pract. Med.* II. 790/2 Resolution is not only the most favourable, but the most common termination of inflammation. **1853** MARKHAM tr. *Skoda's Auscult.* 286 When resolution of the inflammation commences,..the bronchial respiration returns.

†4. Conversion to a liquid state. *Obs.*

1644 DIGBY *Treat. Bodies* I. x. 77 In the hoat springes of extreme cold countries, where the first heates are vnsufferable, which proceede out of the resolution of humidity congealed. **1686** GOAD *Celest. Bodies* II. ii. 174 It must be caused by the resolution of the Snow which was dissolved the Week before.

5. Relaxation or weakening of some organ or part of the body. Now *rare.*

1547 BOORDE *Brev. Health* cclxxi. 90b, A palsey doth come..by resolucion or els compression of the nervous or sinewes. **1558** BP. WATSON *Sev. Sacram.* xvi. c, What resolution, and as it were a meltinge of his bodie and bowelles. **1601** HOLLAND *Pliny* II. 49 Those that haue the palsie or resolution of the nerues. **1661** LOVELL *Hist. Anim. & Min., Isagoge*, Fear..causeth loosenesse, resolution of the muscles, and sometimes death with a small pulse. **1708** *Brit. Apollo* No. 45. 2/1 A Resolution of the Nerves may ensue, and this faltring of the Tongue be..caused. **1779** JOHNSON *Let. to H. Thrale* 23 June, Weariness is itself a temporary resolution of the nerves. **1899** *Allbutt's Syst. Med.* VII. 618 Owing to the complete muscular 'resolution' the cheeks will be flaccid.

II. 6. a. The process of resolving or reducing a non-material thing into simpler forms, or of converting it into some other thing or form.

With quots. 1662 and 1677 compare 1656 in b.

1388 *Prol. Wyclif Bible* xv. (1850) 57 In translating into English, manie resolucions moun make the sentence open. *Ibid.*, I Englishe it thus bi resolucioun. **1570** BILLINGSLEY *Euclid* I. prop. I. 9 The first principles and grounds, which are indemonstrable, and for theyr simplicity can suffer no farther resolution. **1662** STILLINGFL. *Orig. Sacræ* II. iii. §3 The infallible veracity of God in the Scriptures, as the last resolution of faith. **1677** J. OWEN *Reason of Faith* Wks. 1852 IV. 114 Those of the Roman church who are the most averse from that resolution of faith which most Protestants acquiesce in. **1786** H. TOOKE *Purley* (1829) I. 96 Though your method of resolution will answer with most sentences, yet I doubt much whether it will with all. **1797** *Encycl. Brit.* (ed. 3) X. 193/2 Of the Composition and Resolutions of our Ideas, and the Rules of Definition thence arising. **1845** *Proc. Philol. Soc.* II. 167 This form furnishes a complete and intelligible resolution of the phrase. **1893** CHASE in *Archiv Stud. neu. Sprache* C. 252 Resolution of contractions is denoted by italics.

b. Const. *into* or †*in*.

1530 PALSGR. 79 The pronownes derivatyves have thre accidentes,..by whiche their gendre and nombre is expressed, and resolucyon in to their primityves. **1597** MORLEY *Introd. Mus.* Annot., Black or halfe black ligatures, ..with the resolution of the same in other common notes. **1656** BRAMHALL *Replic.* vii. 44 What that Catholick Church is, into the authority whereof they make the last resolution of their Faith. **1660** R. COKE *Justice Vind.* Pref. 12 This sensless resolution of all things into Reason. **1706** W. JONES *Syn. Palmar. Matheseos* 51 The Resolution of Powers into their Roots is called Evolution or the Analysis of Powers. **1837** WHEWELL *Hist. Induct. Sci.* (1857) I. 140 The Resolution of the apparent motions of the heavenly bodies into an assemblage of circular motions. **1875** JOWETT *Plato* (ed. 2) III. 14 The resolution of justice into two unconnected precepts.

c. In prosody, the substitution of two short syllables in the place of a long one.

1884 HADLEY & ALLEN *Grk. Gram.* §1080 A tribrach stands by resolution in place of the first trochee.

7. †**a.** *Math.* and *Logic.* (See quots. and ANALYSIS 7, 8.) *Obs.*

1557 RECORDE *Whetst.* Cc. ij, Proue theim bothe by resolution: and then shall you knowe, the reason of their agremente. **1570** BILLINGSLEY *Euclid* I. prop. I. 9 A demonstration *a posteriori*, or resolution is, when contrariwise in reasoning, we passe from the last conclusion made by the premisses..til we come to the first principles and grounds. *Ibid.* XIII. prop. 5. 396 Resolution, is the assumption or taking of the thing which is to be proued, as graunted, and by things which necessarily follow it, to passe vnto some truth graunted. **1704** J. HARRIS *Lex. Techn.* I, *Resolution* (in Mathematicks) is a Method of Invention, whereby the Truth or Falshood of a Proposition..is discover'd, in an Order contrary to that of Synthesis, or Composition. **1727–38** CHAMBERS *Cycl.* s.v., The business of resolution is, to..examine the truth or falshood of a proposition, by ascending from some particular known truth,..by a chain of consequences, to another more general one in question.

b. *Logic.* (See quot.)
1855 ABP. THOMSON *Laws Th.* §71 (1860) 118 Resolution, where the marks of the definitum are made its definition: as in 'a pension is an allowance for past services'.

8. *Mus.* †**a.** (See quots.) *Obs. rare.*
1727-38 CHAMBERS *Cycl.*, *Resolution*, in music, is when a canon or perpetual fugue is not written all on the same line, or in one part; but all the voices that are to follow the guida, or first voice, are written separately. **1811** BUSBY *Dict. Mus.* (ed. 3) s.v., Formerly also, a Canon was said to be resolved, or written in Resolution, when instead of being comprised in a single stave, all the parts were given on separate staves.

b. The process by which a discord is made to pass into a concord.
1727-38 CHAMBERS *Cycl.* s.v. *Discord*, These discords.. must be succeeded by concords: which is commonly called the resolution of the discord. **1760** STERNE *Tr. Shandy* IV. vi, The preparation and resolution of the discord into harmony. **1838** *Penny Cycl.* XII. 50/1 Sometimes the resolution is brought about by the base, as in the instance of the discord of the 2nd. **1889** PROUT *Harmony* ix. §198 The interval of a seventh is always a dissonance, and therefore requires resolution—that is, to be followed by a consonance.

9. *Mech.* (See quots. 1798 and 1830.)
1785 T. PARKINSON *Syst. Mech.* iv. 78 (*heading*) Composition and resolution of forces. **1798** HUTTON *Course Math.* (1807) II. 137 The Resolution of Forces is the finding of two or more forces which, acting in any different directions, shall have the same effect as any given single force. **1830** KATER & LARDNER *Mech.* v. 52 It is frequently expedient to substitute for a single force two or more forces, to which it is mechanically equivalent, or of which it is the resultant. This process is called 'the resolution of force'. **1882** MINCHIN *Unipl. Kinemat.* 124 The equations.. expressing the components of the given strain with reference to a new set of axes.. constitute the resolution of strain.
fig. **1852** MRS. STOWE *Uncle Tom's C.* xxxii. 292 Legree.. governed his plantation by a sort of resolution of forces.

III. 10. a. The answering *of* a question; the solving *of* a doubt or difficulty. †Also, the supplying *of* an answer. Now *rare.* (Freq. in 17th c.)
1548 GESTE *Pr. Masse* 103, I wyl addresse me to the ful answere and resolution of the same. **1577** HANMER *Anc. Eccles. Hist.* v. xii. (1619) 85 Rhodion promised also to publish the resolutions of his Problemes. His Commentaries upon the six daies works are at this day extant. **1604** E. G[RIMSTONE] *D'Acosta's Hist. Indies* II. xi. 106 Whoso woulde neerely consider the causes.. shall finde them insufficient for the full resolution of this point. **1651** BAXTER *Inf. Bapt.* 275 In resolution of the question of universall Redemption. **1705** STANHOPE *Paraphr.* I. 350 For a resolution of this enquiry, the case of Abraham will be of great use to us. **1758** JOHNSON *Idler* No. 24 ¶2 Of this question.. we must be content to live without the resolution. **1845** LEWES *Hist. Philos.* III. ii, The resolution of that problem.. had left him unsatisfied. **1847** MILLER *First Impr. Eng.* x. (1857) 164 Several antagonist theories have been promulgated in attempted resolution of the puzzle.

b. The solution *of* an arithmetical or mathematical problem. Now *rare* or *Obs.*
1579-80 NORTH *Plutarch* (1676) 20 [He] gathered it out by certain accidents, as they do in the resolutions of certain Geometrical questions. **1636** MELLIS *Recorde's Gr. Artes* 160 For the resolution whereof, and of all such other like, reduce 23 pound 8 shillings, all into shillings. **1715** tr. *Gregory's Astron.* (1726) I. 317 Concerning the Resolution of the most considerable Problems of the First Motion by Calculation. **1797** *Encycl. Brit.* (ed. 3) I. 431/2 Of the Resolution of Equations. **1817** H. T. COLEBROOKE *Algebra* 207 The resolution of these equations is so named, because it is in general effected by making the middle term.. disappear from between two square terms. **1845** *Encycl. Metrop.* I. 543/1 The resolution of this equation gives the solution of the proposed problem. **1875** *Encycl. Brit.* I. 517/1 A problem subservient to the resolution of indeterminate problems of the first degree.

†**c.** Without const. An answer or solution. *Obs.* (Freq. in 17th c.)
a **1542** WYATT in *Tottel's Misc.* (Arb.) 50 It liketh me (quod she) to haue hard your question, But, lenger time doth ask a resolucion. **1581** PETTIE *Guazzo's Civ. Conv.* I. (1586) 6 Your resolutions, doe me content so well, That I delight.. to aske. **1643** SIR T. BROWNE *Relig. Med.* I. §9, I can answer all the objections.. with that odde resolution I learned of Tertullian, *certum est quia impossibile est.*

†**d.** In phr. *of.. resolution*, (hard or easy) to resolve. *Obs. rare.*
1658 SIR T. BROWNE *Hydriot.* I. (1736) 11 How the Romans left so many Coins seems of hard Resolution. **1675** BAXTER *Cath. Theol.* I. I. 110 A strange dispute, and of most easie resolution.

11. a. A statement upon some matter; a decision or verdict on some point. Now *rare* or *Obs.*
1581 MARBECK *Bk. Notes* 1055 The Lord hath giuen a generall resolution, that no man can enter into the kingdome of heauen, vnles [etc.]. **1588** FRAUNCE *Lawiers Log.* I. iv. 25 Which last resolution of his I follow at this present. **1601** HOLLAND *Pliny* I. 143 He speaketh so confidently thereof, as I will not altogether discredit his resolution in this behalfe. **1646** SIR T. BROWNE *Pseud. Ep.* I. i. (1686) 3 He hath reserved many things unto his own resolution. **1674** *Essex Papers* (Camden) I. 197 [He] promiseth to give his resolution about ye petitioners before his departure.
1818 CRUISE *Digest* (ed. 2) VI. 506 The established law in cases of this nature was according to the resolution in the Duke of Norfolk's case.

b. A formal decision, determination, or expression of opinion, on the part of a deliberative assembly or other meeting; a proposal of this nature submitted to an assembly or meeting.
1604 *Jrnls. Ho. Comm.* 28 June, No Resolution or further Speech in it [a question] at that Time. **1651** HOBBES *Leviath.* II. xxii. 119 Present at all the Deliberations, and Resolutions of the Body. *a* **1715** BURNET *Own Time* (1897) I. 98 When these resolutions were passed with this protestation, a great many.. met, and formed an association apart. **1771** *Junius Lett.* xlviii. (1788) 264 Yet now you confess that parliaments are fallible, and that their resolutions may be illegal. **1833** HT. MARTINEAU *Manch. Strike* iv. 41 To hold a meeting.. in order to prepare resolutions to be laid before the masters. **1872** FREEMAN *Eng. Const.* iii. 155 The passing by the House of Commons of such a resolution as this.

c. A solution or settlement *of* a dispute.
1890 *Spectator* 15 Mar., The Italian Government, though it is strong, hardly hopes to see a resolution of its quarrel with the Papacy.

†**12.** An explanatory account *of* something. *Obs.*
1582 *Reg. Privy Council Scot.* III. 536 [The safeconduct had been obtained, and directed to him] togidder with a resolution of the forme and tyme appointit for his departing. **1658** SIR T. BROWNE *Hydriot.* 19 We much deplore the loss of that Letter which Cicero expected or received from his Brother Quintus, as a resolution of Brittish customes.

IV. †**13. a.** The removal of doubt on some point from a person's mind. *Obs. rare.*
1578 LYTE *Dodoens* To Rdr., For thy instruction and resolution in these matters I referre the to the same Authors. **1635** PAGITT *Christianogr.* III. (1636) 73 A German Monke adviseth him that doubteth of Purgatory, for his resolution to make his iourney into Scotland the greater. **1644** J. COTTON *Keyes Kingd. Heaven* iv. 18 The Church of Antioch sent messengers to Ierusalem for resolution and satisfaction in a doubt that troubled them.

†**b.** Confidence; conviction, certainty, positive knowledge. *Obs. rare.*
1590 GREENE *Never too Late* Wks. (Grosart) VIII. 98, I haue such resolution in thy constancie, that [etc.]. **1605** SHAKS. *Lear* I. ii. 108, I would vnstate my selfe, to be in a due resolution. *a* **1637** HOLLAND (Webster), Little resolution and certainty there is as touching the islands of Mauritania.

14. a. The (*or* an) act of resolving or determining; anything resolved upon; a fixed determination.
1590 GREENE *Orl. Fur.* (1599) 15 Trust me.. I will sacke it, or on this Castle wall Ile write my resolution with my blood. **1617** MORYSON *Itin.* I. 55 Suddenly al the passengers resolued to leaue the ships..; at which resolution the Masters of the ships stormed. **1647** CLARENDON *Hist. Reb.* III. §30 Mr. Pimm was looked upon as.. not of those furious resolutions against the Church as the other leading men were. **1709** STEELE *Tatler* No. 7 ¶24 He hopes they will come to a Resolution to send for no more Bulls to Rome. **1752** JOHNSON *Rambler* No. 193 ¶3 To be praised then every man resolves; but resolutions will not execute themselves. **1817** JAS. MILL *Brit. India* II. IV. v. 202 The Nabob,.. fully persuaded of the resolution of the Council to depose him [etc.]. **1874** GREEN *Short Hist.* II. §8. 104 Neither warning nor desertion moved the resolution of the Primate.

b. Const. *for, of.*
1633 FORD *Broken Hrt.* I. i, A resolution for a lasting league Betwixt your families, was entertained. **1647** CLARENDON *Hist. Reb.* III. §42 A sincere resolution of amity and unity between the two nations.

15. Determination; firmness or steadiness of purpose; unyielding temper.
1588 SHAKS. *Tit. A.* III. i. 239 Thy griefes [are] their sports: Thy resolution mockt. **1592** —— *Lucr.* 352 My will is back'd with resolution. **1636** E. DACRES tr. *Machiavel's Disc. Livy* II. 329 On each part he makes the Armyes equall for their order, valour, resolution, and number. **1667** MILTON *P.L.* VI. 541 He comes, and settl'd in his face I see Sad resolution and secure. *a* **1703** BURKITT *On N.T.* Matt. iv. 10 A great temptation must be withstood with great resolution. **1754** JOHNSON in *Boswell*, He was.. a coward, because he had not resolution to fire it off himself. **1819** SHELLEY *Cenci* I. iii. 173 Be thou the resolution of quick youth Within my veins. **1870** DICKENS *E. Drood* vii, You seem to have resolution and power enough to crush me.

†**16.** A resolute person. *Obs. rare*$^{-1}$.
1643 SIR T. BROWNE *Relig. Med.* I. §3 Those desperate Resolutions, who had rather venture at large their decayed bottome then bring her in to be new trim'd in the dock.

re-solution² (riːsəˈl(j)uːʃən). Also **resolution**. [RE- 5 a.] Renewed or repeated solution.
1802 *Phil. Trans.* XCIII. 14 On re-solution in water, and crystallization, this saline matter proved to be.. vitriol of zinc. **1850** ROBERTSON *Serm.* Ser. III. v. (1872) 61 There are questions which, having been again and again settled, still from time to time present themselves for re-solution. **1874** GARROD & BAXTER *Mat. Med.* (1880) 132 The former is dissolved out and crystallized, and purified by re-solution and crystallization. **1957** G. E. HUTCHINSON *Treat. Limnol.* I. xi. 708 Evaporation to dryness and resolution liberates some of the previously unreactive iron.. in a reactive form. **1966** PHILLIPS & WILLIAMS *Inorg. Chem.* II. xxxii. 524 A second factor controlling the re-solution of the hydroxide in alkali would appear to be the ease of change of coordination number. **1968** R. W. FAIRBRIDGE *Encycl. Geomorphol.* 1051/2 In southern England, many large speleothems are today being destroyed by drips from the original formative source ('re-solution').

resolutioner (rɛzəˈl(j)uːʃənə(r)). [f. RESOLUTION + -ER¹.]
1. *Hist.* (With capital initial.) A member of that party in Scotland which accepted the resolutions passed in 1650 for rehabilitating those persons who had not taken part in the struggle against Cromwell.
1693 *Apol. Clergy Scot.* 78 The Publick Resolutioners had made defection. *a* **1715** BURNET *Own Time* I. (1897) I. 97 Those who adhered to these resolutions were called the Public Resolutioners. *Ibid.* 111 The Resolutioners were known to have been more in the king's interests: so they were not so kindly looked on as the Protestors. **1816** SCOTT *Old Mort.* v, They had parted in some unkindness at the time when the kingdom of Scotland was divided into Resolutioners and Protestors. **1872** *Contemp. Rev.* XXI. 76 Resolutioners like Dickson and Protesters like Patrick Gillespie.

2. One who joins in or subscribes to a resolution.
1816 SOUTHEY *Ess.* (1832) I. 364 They say,.. the said resolutioners of Bishopsgate-ward,.. 'We claim.. a constitutional voice in the House of the people'. **1854** H. MILLER *Sch. & Schm.* xxiv. (1858) 535 The parochial resolutioners, amounting in all to ten.

resolutionist (rɛzəˈl(j)uːʃənɪst). [f. as prec. + -IST.] One who makes, or joins in, a resolution.
1846 *Life Guthrie* in *Lives Henderson & G.* 145 This attack was unpalatable both to the courtiers, and the Resolutionist Presbyterians. **1856** *Chamb. Jrnl.* V. 136 [They] had declared their high resolves to confront the superstition... Simon.. was the loudest among these resolutionists. **1891** *Daily News* 1 Jan. 3/4 My directors are as anxious as the resolutionists can be to secure for those in their service equitable conditions of labour.

resolutive (ˈrɛzəl(j)uːtɪv), *a.* and *sb.* [ad. med.L. **resolūtīv-us* (see RESOLUTE *v.* and -IVE), whence also It. and Sp. *resolutivo*, F. *résolutif.*]
A. *adj.* **1. a.** Having the power to dissolve.
c **1400** *Lanfranc's Cirurg.* 334 þan leie þervpon þe medycyn resolutif. *Ibid.*, Of medicyns resolutiuis, summe ben simple. **1528** PAYNELL *Salerne's Regim.* dd iij, The .iiij. is baynyng specially resolutive, for that letteth bloud lettyng. **1566** WARDE tr. *Alexis' Secr.* III. I. (1568) 49 A Repercussiue and Resolutiue oyntment against the Canker. **1601** HOLLAND *Pliny* II. 557 Astringent it is, and yet resolutiue. **1651** BIGGS *New Disp.* ¶133 There ariseth from the bottome a resolutive power. **1712** tr. *Pomet's Hist. Drugs* I. 196 Gum Tucamahaca is digestive, resolutive, neurotick. *a* **1774** GOLDSM. tr. *Scarron's Com. Rom.* (1775) I. 309, I just now applied to him an anodyne and resolutive cataplasm on a livid tumour. **1873** R. BARNES *Dis. Women* xl. 517 So-called resolutive pessaries of iodine, made up into conical balls, with cocoa-nut butter or other ingredients.

b. *Path.* Terminating by resolution.
1861 BUMSTEAD *Ven. Dis.* (1879) 544 The tubercular syphilide.. disappears by interstitial absorption; hence, it has been called non-ulcerative or resolutive.

2. *Law.* **a.** ***resolutive condition***, a condition by the happening of which a contract or obligation is terminated.
a **1623** SWINBURNE *Spousals* (1686) 138 Forasmuch as this Condition is not suspensive, but resolutive or extinctive. *Ibid.* 144 [He] adviseth his Pupil to contract Matrimony conditionally,.. under some like Resolutive Condition. **1832** AUSTIN *Jurispr.* liii. (1879) II. 899 Rights subject to a contingency or condition resolutive. **1875** POSTE *Gaius* III. 384 Conditions are Suspensive or Resolutive.

b. ***resolutive clause***, in *Sc. Law*, a clause extinguishing the right of the person who contravenes the conditions laid down in the deed.
1765 *Act 5 Geo. III*, c. 26 Preamble, [They] should convey, settle, and intail the lands.. with all the proper, prohibitive, irritant, and resolutive clauses. **1838** W. BELL *Dict. Law Scot.* 164 By the resolutive clause, the right of the person contravening is resolved and extinguished. **1868** *Act 31 & 32 Vict.* c. 101 §9 It shall not be necessary.. to insert .. prohibitory, irritant, or resolutive clauses.

3. *Logic.* Analytical. ? *Obs.*
1654 Z. COKE *Logick* 4 It is delivered by an Analytical and Resolutive method, proceeding from the object and end foreknown. **1656** tr. *Hobbes' Elem. Philos.* (1839) 66 There is therefore no method, by which we find out the causes of things, but is either compositive or resolutive... And the resolutive is commonly called analytical method, as the compositive is called synthetical.

B. *sb.* A medical application or drug which serves to resolve or disperse morbid matter.
c **1400** *Lanfranc's Cirurg.* 234 Rasis forbediþ þat þou schalt leie þerto no repercussiuis, ne noon resolutiuis but if þe mater be avoidid tofore. **1562** BULLEIN *Bulwarke, Dial. Sorenes & Chir.* 13 b, Whose cure must be in drawing forthe from the matter, with resolutiues, or softening medicenes. **1725** BRADLEY *Fam. Dict.* s.v. *Tumour*, You must neither use Convulsives nor Repercusives, but only gentle Resolutives. **1756** P. BROWNE *Jamaica* (1789) 121 The root is warm, and may be successfully administered as a resolutive, sudorific, or diaphoretic. **1873** R. BARNES *Dis. Wom.* xl. 519 It has been recommended to establish a seton in the vaginal-portion as a derivative and resolutive.

ˈ**resolutory**, *a. rare.* [ad. late L. *resolūtōri-us* (cf. prec. and -ORY). Hence also Sp. and Pg. *resolutorio*, F. *résolutoire* (15th c.).]
†**1.** Explanatory, enlightening. *Obs.*
1609 DOULAND *Ornith. Microl.* 45 A Resolutorie Table, shewing the value of the Signes, by the beholding of every figure. **1669** HOPKINS *Serm.* (1685) 24 Out of these distinctions, I shall form several propositions, resolutory, as I hope, to my subject in hand.

2. *Law.* = RESOLUTIVE 2 a.
1818 COLEBROOKE *Oblig. & Contr.* 10 If an agreement bear, that the obligation shall have present operation and effect, but cease upon a certain event, that is a subsequent and resolutory condition; and the conditional obligation is called a resolutory one. **1875** POSTE *Gaius* III. 384 Tradition, coupled with a Resolutory condition, operates two transfers of ownership.

resolvaˈbility. [f. next + -ITY.] The capability of being resolved into parts.
1845 HERSCHEL *Ess.* (1857) 661 The character of easy resolvability into separate and distinct stars. **1865** MASSON *Rec. Brit. Phil.* 36 The resolvability of all Truth, or

Knowledge..into Experience. **1871** *Schellen's Spectr. Anal.* §41. 163 The D-line..is separated into two lines and shows besides a cloudy line of still further resolvability.

resolvable (rɪˈzɒlvəb(ə)l), *a.* Also 7–8 -veable. [f. RESOLVE *v.* + -ABLE. Cf. RESOLVIBLE.] Capable of being resolved, in various senses of the verb.

1646 SIR T. BROWNE *Pseud. Ep.* 316 The causes [are] surely best resolvable from observations made in the Countries themselves. **1688** NORRIS *Love* I. v. 60 All Love is not, as some pretend, resolvable into Self-love. **1755** YOUNG *Centaur* ii. Wks. 1757 IV. 159 Want of faith. All is resolveable into that alone. **1770** *Phil. Trans.* LX. 435 The force of every particle, which impinges obliquely, is resolvable into two. **1816** GILCHRIST *Philos. Etym.* p. xxi, All words are resolvable into a few primitives. **1877** E. R. CONDER *Bas. Faith* ii. 55 Bold surmise..asks whether atoms may not themselves be resolvable into force.

b. ***resolvable nebula***, a nebula which admits of resolution by a powerful telescope.

1785 HERSCHEL in *Phil. Trans.* LXXV. 251 Clusters of stars also may become resolvable nebulæ. **1853** WHEWELL *Plur. Worlds* 90 When we have thus to reckon as many galaxies as there are resolvable nebulae. **1870** PROCTOR *Other Worlds* xii. (1872) 291 The stellar nebulæ—resolvable and irresolvable.

Hence **reˈsolvableness** (Bailey, vol. II, 1727).

†**reˈsolvance.** *Obs. rare*⁻¹. [f. RESOLVE *v.* + -ANCE.] Resolve, decision.

1603 in *Lismore Papers* Ser. II. (1887) I. 45 To vnderstand their resoluance what they ment to do therin.

resolvancy (rɪˈzɒlvənsɪ). *rare.* [f. RESOLVE *v.* + -ANCY.] An outcome or solution.

1930 G. GREENE *Two Witnesses* 84 How utterly grown-up we then become, and the crowded confused days have to be made to clear, have to reach their own resolvancies.

†**reˈsolvative,** *a. Obs. rare*⁻¹. [f. RESOLVE *v.* + -ATIVE.] = RESOLUTIVE *a.* 1 a.

1577 FRAMPTON *Joyful News* II. (1596) 2 Copall..is resoluatiue, and softneth by some watrish partes that it hath.

resolve (rɪˈzɒlv), *sb.* [f. the vb.]

1. A determination or resolution.

1592 SHAKS. *Rom. & Jul.* IV. i. 123 Get you gone, be strong and prosperous In this resolue. **1600** W. WATSON *Decacordon* (1602) 350 A catholike resolue for our Romane faith. **1667** WATERHOUSE *Fire London* 135 The common affection of Countrymen soders them into a common resolve of kindness each to other. **1700** DRYDEN *Cymon & Iph.* 526 Speak thy resolves; if now thy courage droop, Despair in prison. *a* **1794** GIBBON *Misc. Wks.* (1814) I. 125 My private resolves were influenced by the state of Europe. **1847** HELPS *Friends in C.* (1851) I. 43 Mere stoicism, and resolves about fitting fortune to one's self. **1889** JESSOPP *Coming of Friars* ii. 78 She made up her mind never to marry again, and she kept her resolve.

2. Firmness or steadfastness of purpose.

1591 SHAKS. *1 Hen. VI*, V. v. 75 A Lady of so high resolue, (As is faire Margaret). **1602** MARSTON *Antonio's Rev.* IV. v, We must be stiffe and steddie in resolve. **1789** BURNS *To Dr. Blacklock* viii, Come, Firm Resolve, take thou the van. **1813** SHELLEY *Q. Mab* IV. 155 Man is of soul and body, formed for deeds Of high resolve. **1873** SYMONDS *Grk. Poets* ix. 296 We find in them no hesitancy and difficult resolve.

3. A determination of a deliberative body; a formal resolution. Now *U.S.*

1656 *Burton's Diary* (1828) I. 270 A short vote or resolve of this House..would haply give satisfaction for the present. **1657** *Ibid.* II. 94 The several resolves of Parliament touching the matter. **1713** ADDISON *Cato* II. i, Cæsar's approach has summon'd us together, And Rome attends her fate from our resolves. **1775** FRANKLIN in *Burke's Corr.* (1844) II. 28, I hear your proposed resolves were negatived by a great majority. **1794** S. WILLIAMS *Vermont* 296 That part of the resolves in which the state was threatened. **1859** BARTLETT *Dict. Amer.* (ed. 2) 362 Resolves are usually private acts, and are often passed with less formality. **1865** H. PHILLIPS *Amer. Paper Curr.* II. 55 These resolves were ordered to be published.

†**4.** Answer, solution. *Obs.*

a **1625** *Faithf. Friends* II. ii, I crave but ten short days to give resolve To this important suit. **1643** MILTON *Divorce* I. viii, In hope to give a full resolve of that which is yet so much controverted. **1670** W. SIMPSON *Hydrol. Ess.* 25 If you consult what I say..you may find a sufficient resolve thereof.

†**5.** *Mus.* (See quot.) *Obs. rare*⁻¹.

1721 BRADLEY *Philos. Acc. Wks. Nat.* 160 The progressive Tones from that Ground-Note to the Octave, which is the Resolve of the Ground-Note, declares the Key.

resolve (rɪˈzɒlv), *v.* Also 4–7 resolue. [ad. L. *resolvĕre*, f. *re-* RE- + *solvĕre* to loosen, dissolve. Cf. It. *re-*, *risolvere*, Sp. and Pg. *resolver*, obs. F. *resolver*, *-vir* (mod.F. *résoudre*).]

I. †**1.** *trans.* To melt, dissolve, reduce to a liquid or fluid state. *Obs.*

For examples with const. *into*, *to*, see 6 and 9.

c **1374** CHAUCER *Boeth.* IV. metr. v. (1868) 133 No man ne wondreþ whan þe weyȝte of þe snowe yhardid by þe colde is resolued by þe brennynge hete of phebus. **1388** WYCLIF *Job* xxviii. 2 A stoon resolued, ethir meltid, bi heete, is turned in to money. *c* **1420** *Pallad. on Husb.* XII. 526 Whit wex is to resolue In fynest oil. **1530** PALSGR. 688/1 This metall can nat be resolved without a marvayllous sharpe fyre. **1555** EDEN *Decades* (Arb.) 141 Cleopatra resolued a pearle in vineger & drunke it. **1609** HOLLAND *Amm. Marcell.* 117 Euphrates was risen by reason of snow newly thawed and resolved. **1678** DRYDEN *All for Love* III. i, He could resolve his Mind, as Fire does Wax, From that hard rugged Image, melt him down [etc.]. **1732** ARBUTHNOT *Aliments*, etc. I. 270 Soaps which resolve solid Substances.

transf. **1582** BATMAN *Barth. De P.R.* XI. iii. 159 And the west winde..resolveth and unbindeth winter. **1638** RAWLEY tr. *Bacon's Life & Death* (1650) 5 The Drying caused by Cold, is but weak, and easily resolved.

2. a. To disintegrate; to break up or separate into constituent or elementary parts. Now *rare* or *Obs.*

1398 TREVISA *Barth. De P.R.* III. xix (1495) 65 The smoke that is resoluyd and comyth from the thynge that is smellyd. *c* **1400** tr. *Secreta Secret., Gov. Lordsh.* 68 Þe bodyes [of men]..ar resoluyd by kyndly hete, þat makes drye þe moystnes of þe body. *c* **1420** *Pallad. on Husb.* I. 365 The see grauel is lattest for to drye,.. The salt in hit thi werkis wol resolue. **1577** B. GOOGE *Heresbach's Husb.* (1586) 17b, A mellow ground that is fat, and will soone be resolved. **1584** COGAN *Haven Health* ccxviii. (1636) 251 The fumes and vapors of ale..cannot bee so soone resolved as those that rise up of wine. **1620** VENNER *Via Recta* iii. 52 They will too soon resolue the iuyce of lighter meats. **1633** EARL MANCH. *Al Mondo* (1636) 94 It is well for man that his bodie by death becomes putrid, resolved and crumbled to nothing. **1776** BOWDEN *Farmer's Director* 18 By the assistance of alternate rain and drought, to resolve and break the hard clods.

†**b.** To analyse, examine (a statement). *Obs.*

1594 HOOKER *Eccl. Pol.* II. vii. §9 Examine, sift, and resolve their alledged proofs, till you come to the very root whence they spring.

†**c.** *Math.* To solve (an equation). *Obs.*

1743 EMERSON *Fluxions* 36 Then we had been obliged to substitute $a + z$ or $a - z$ for x in the given Equation before it could be resolved. **1798** HUTTON *Course Math.* (1827) I. 269 The form that a cubic equation must necessarily have, to be resolved by this rule.

d. To analyse (a force or velocity) into components. (Cf. RESOLUTION 9.)

1785 T. PARKINSON *Syst. Mech.* iv. 80 One force..may be resolved into any number, either in the same, or different planes, producing the same effect with it. **1825** J. NICHOLSON *Operat. Mechanic* 5 Each of those portions may, by a similar process, be again divided, resolving the original force to infinity. **1866** HERSCHEL *Fam. Lect. Sci.* 90 This force then being resolved in radial and tangential directions [etc.].

e. Orig. of optical instruments (or persons using them): To separate, break up (an object) into distinguishable parts. Now more widely, to distinguish (things similar in magnitude or close together in time). Cf. RESOLUTION 2 c.

1785 HERSCHEL in *Phil. Trans.* LXXV. 219 When he resolves one nebula into stars, he discovers ten new ones which he cannot resolve. **1868** LOCKYER *Elem. Astron.* §77 Star-clusters..so distant that even in telescopes of great power they could not be resolved. **1870** EMERSON *Soc. & Sol.* Wks. (Bohn) III. 3 The remoter stars seem a nebula of united light; yet there is no group which a telescope will not resolve. **1932** *Proc. R. Soc.* A. CXXXVI. 313 Two particles separated by as little as 1/500th second could be 'resolved' and correctly recorded.

3. *Med.* **a.** To soften (a hard tumour); to disperse or dissipate (humours, swellings, etc.). ? *Obs.*

c **1400** *Lanfranc's Cirurg.* 210 If þou miȝt not wiþ repercussiuis do awei þe enpostym ne resolue him. *Ibid.* 353 Whanne þe mater þat þou wolt resolue is swiþe hard. **1541** COPLAND *Galyen's Terap.* Hh iv, When ecchymosis is all dygested & resolued, than it is parmytted to drye the broken flesshe. **1601** HOLLAND *Pliny* II. 274 Those plasters which resolue or maturat any impostumed place. **1683** SALMON *Doron Med.* II. 427 For it resolves all hard humors. **1748** HARTLEY *Observ. Man* I. ii. §1. 127 Embrocations are of Use in resolving Obstructions. **1786** J. HUNTER *Ven. Dis.* IV. vi. 404 This method of resolving buboes occurred to me at Belleisle in the year 1761.

absol. **1562** TURNER *Herbal* II. (1568) 117 Oyl that is made of vnrype oliues..doth myghtely resolue. **1610** MARKHAM *Masterp.* II. clxxiii. 483 It burneth, draweth, and resolueth, and is goode for scurfe. **1708** *Brit. Apollo* No. 93. 2/2 Green Tea..Resolves, and Attenuates.

†**b.** To dissipate or allay (pain, etc.). *Obs. rare.*

1573 *Treas. Hid. Secrets* xix, Oyle of Rue is hot, resolving pain. **1600** SURFLET *Countrie Farme* II. xlviii. 306 An oyle.. which hath power to resolue, soften, and appease the griefe of colde rheumes or distillations. *a* **1617** BAYNE *On Eph.* (1658) 130 Fire..hath not onely heat resolving numbnesse, ..but it hath light.

c. To remove (inflammation) by resolution.

1732 ARBUTHNOT *Rules Diet* in *Aliments*, etc. 321 Such a Fever is often resolv'd by a bleeding at the Nose. **1898** *Allbutt's Syst. Med.* V. 361 When empyema follows upon pneumonia, the pulmonary inflammation sometimes is never resolved.

†**4. a.** To slacken, relax (the limbs, etc.); to weaken. *Obs.*

1483 CAXTON *Fables of Æsop* 3 By cause the water was hote and their stomake [was] resolued by the water. **1540–1** ELYOT *Image Gov.* (1556) 30 Lyke as by the other the strengthe of bodie is resolvyd. **1588** KYD *Househ. Phil.* Wks. (1901) 248 The night..[in which] we may sufficiently restore our bodies resolued with the..heate of the day. **1644** BULWER *Chiron.* 35 The Hand collected, the Fingers looking downewards, then turned and resolved. **1715** ROWE *Lady Jane Grey* II, Every moving accent that she breathes Resolves my courage, slackens my tough nerves.

†**b.** To render lax in feeling or conduct. *Obs.*

c **1550** H. RHODES *Bk. Nurture* in *Babees Bk.* (1868) 106 It is a very hard work of continence to repell the paynting glose of flatterings whose words resolue the hart with plesure. **1611** B. JONSON *Catiline* III. iii, Each house [being] Resolved in freedom.

†**c.** To relax or withdraw (a law). *Obs.*

1537 *State Papers Hen. VIII*, VII. 706 The act made for money by exchange, the wiche,..onles it be resolvid, wilbe a great ocacion..to cawse a stey for salis of wolen clothis.

5. †**a.** To cause (discord) to pass away. *Obs.*

1526 *Pilgr. Perf.* (W. de W. 1531) 282b, It resolueth discorde, reconsyleth ennemyes, & maketh them frendes.

b. *Mus.* To cause (a discord) to pass into a concord. (Cf. RESOLUTION 8 b.)

1727–38 CHAMBERS *Cycl.* s.v. *Discord*, The discord is resolved by being immediately succeeded by a concord. **1797** *Encycl. Brit.* (ed. 3) XVI. 125/1 There is no possible manner of resolving a dissonance which is not derived from an operation of cadence. **1838** *Penny Cycl.* XII. 50/1 Most discords require to be prepared, and all must be resolved. **1868** OUSELEY *Harmony* ii. (1875) 20 When the discords have thus been rendered agreeable to the ear, they are said to be resolved.

II. 6. a. To separate (a thing) *into* its component parts or elements; to dissolve *into* some other physical form. †Also const. *in.*

c **1430** *Life St. Kath.* 99 My body whyche aftur þe inevitable lawe of nature abydeth to be resolued into deþ. **1477** NORTON *Ord. Alch.* v. in Ashm. (1652) 79 Liquors departeth Qualities asunder, Substance resolving in Attomes. **1533** BELLENDEN *Livy* I. xv. (S.T.S.) I. 85 Becaus þe stoupis and pillaris þareof war all of tre, they war haistelie brynt and resoluit in powder. **1598** BARCKLEY *Felic. Man* (1631) 706 God will rayse up His worke that is resolved into dust. **1635** SWAN *Spec. M.* v. §2 (1643) 138 Green clouds.. are altogether watery, and as it were resolved into water. **1668** CULPEPPER & COLE *Barthol. Anat.* I. xxvii. 65 The sooty Vapors are condensed, and being resolved into water, are [etc.]. **1781** COWPER *Charity* 562 He ordains things..To be resolv'd into their parent earth. **1817** JAS. MILL *Brit. India* I. II. x. 446 The Empire of the Mahrattas..would have been resolv'd..into its primitive elements. **1891** *Spectator* 4 July 5/2 A..campaign intended to break up Italy, or to resolve the German Empire back again into its elements.

b. In figurative contexts.

1526 *Pilgr. Perf.* (W. de W. 1531) 60 His herte shall yerne and melte,..& be hole resolued in to teares. **1568** WILMOT *Tancred & Gismonda* II. iii, A resolution that resolues my bloud Into the Ice-sie drops of Lethes flood. **1607** SHAKS. *Timon* IV. iii. 442 The Seas a Theefe, whose liquid Surge, resolues The Moone into Salt teares.

c. To convert, transform, alter (a thing) *into* some other thing or form.

1570–6 LAMBARDE *Peramb. Kent* (1826) 327 A Towne called Horsmundene, which name (resolved into Saxon Orthographie) is [etc.]. *a* **1623** SWINBURNE *Spousals* (1686) 27 By the same means..are those Spousals by them contracted in their Minority..resolved or turned into Matrimony. **1641** *Jrnls. Ho. Comm.* 31 Dec., That the House be resolved into a Committee, to take into Consideration the Militia of the Kingdom. **1743** TOMLINSON *Prot. Birthright* 13 Into whose Authority all Christians have resolved their Faith and Obedience. **1861** DICKENS in *All Year Round* 1 June 221 The spectral figure ..seemed all resolved into a ghastly stare. **1889** *Standard* 9 Apr., Emin..has seen islands resolved into headlands.

7. a. To reduce by mental analysis *into* more elementary forms, principles, or relations. †Also const. *in.*

1388 *Prol. Wyclif Bible* xv. (1850) 57 An ablatif case absolute may be resoluid into these thre wordis. **1570** BILLINGSLEY *Euclid* I. prop. 32. 42 Euery right lined figure is resolued in two triangles. **1628** T. SPENCER *Logick* 284 When the causes doe argue the effect, the effect is resolued into the causes. *a* **1674** CLARENDON *Surv. Leviath.* (1676) 8 He resolv'd all Wisdom and Religion itself into a simple obedience and submission to it. **1719** DE FOE *Crusoe* I. (Globe) 204 After I had entertain'd these Notions, and, by long musing, had as it were resolv'd them all into nothing. **1774** PENNANT *Tour Scotl. in 1772*, 233, I was for resolving this phænomenon into Ship-wrecks. **1841** MYERS *Cath. Th.* IV. §2. 184 Why may we not..resolve Christianity into a system of practical Morality? **1875** JOWETT *Plato* (ed. 2) IV. 239 All sensation is to be resolved into a similar combination of an agent and patient.

†**b.** To reduce or convert (a quantity) *into* some other denomination. *Obs.*

1571 DIGGES *Pantom.* I. xxi. Gj b, Then resolue 20 foote into inches. **1669** STURMY *Mariner's Mag.* II. vi. 66 The Degrees resolved into Hours and Minutes, is 1 Hour 49 Min. **1672** PETTY *Pol. Anat.* (1691) 352 The victuals.., resolved into money, may be estimated 3*s.* 6*d.* per week.

8. *refl.* **a.** Of things: To pass, by dissolution, separation, or change, *into* another form or *into* simpler forms.

1602 SHAKS. *Ham.* I. ii. 130 Oh that this too too solid Flesh, would melt, Thaw, and resolue it selfe into a Dew. **1614** RALEIGH *Hist. World* I. i. §7 (1634) 9 The Waters.. resolved their thinner parts into Aire. **1799** SOUTHEY *Cool Refl. during Midsummer Walk*, For the flesh upon them; It hath resolved itself into a dew. **1814** CHALMERS *Evidences* ii. 46 The argument..resolves itself into four parts. **1868** HERSCHEL in *People's Mag.* Jan. 63 Its pileus..has the singular property of resolving itself..into a black liquid. **1879** LUBBOCK *Addr. Pol. & Educ.* iii. 44 His complaint resolves itself into two parts.

b. Of a deliberative body: To convert (itself) *into* a committee.

1710 *Lond. Gaz.* No. 4699/3 The House resolved it self into a Committee of the whole House. **1753** [see COMMITTEE 3]. **1818** *Parl. Debates* 1422/1 The house then resolved itself into a committee on the bill. **1885** *Manch. Exam.* 7 Oct. 5/3 The meeting unanimously resolved itself into a committee.

9. To reduce, transform, or change (a thing) *to* something else. Also *refl.* Now *rare.*

1538 STARKEY *England* I. i. 16 Yf ther be any cyuyle law ordeynyd wych can not be resoluyd therto, hyt ys of no value. **1593** NASHE *Christ's T.* Wks. (Grosart) IV. 67 The Snow on thy Mountaines, by the Sunne is resolued to water. **1633** BP. HALL *Hard Texts, N.T.* 321 O ye my faithfull ones who are now resolved to the very dust of the earth. **1665** DRYDEN *Ind. Emp.* II. i, Ye Immortal Souls, who once were Men, And now resolv'd to Element agen. **1799** SOUTHEY *Minor Poems* Poet. Wks. II. 202 Earth, air, and water's ministering particles Now to the elements Resolved, their uses done. **1856** LEVER *Martins of Cro' M.* xxiii, All resolves itself to some question of a harm to one side. **1875** STEDMAN

Victorian Poets 387 The succeeding chorus..resolves attention to enchantment.

III. †10. To untie, loosen. *Obs. rare.*

1558 Phaer *Æneid* vii. 155 Resolue [L. *solvite*] your heades attyre, & celebrate this daunce with me. **1609** Bible (Douay) *Dan.* v. 16 Thou canst interpret obscure things, and resolve [L. *dissolvere*] thinges bound.

11. a. To answer (a question, argument, etc.); to solve (a problem of any kind).

1577 tr. *Bullinger's Decades* (1592) 458 Mee thinketh therefore that this question canne bee none otherwise resolued. **1581** J. Bell *Haddon's Answ. Osorius* 212 Least he exclayme agayne that his argumentes are not throughly resolved, I will answere in few wordes. **1647** Sprigge *Anglia Rediv.* ii. i. (1854) 72 This resolved the question at the council of war without putting it. **1685** Baxter *Par. N.T.* Matt. xxii. 18 He answered so cautelously as not to resolve the third question. **1750** Johnson *Rambler* No. 19 ¶15 After a great part of life spent in enquiries which can never be resolved. **1793** Smeaton *Edystone L.* §219 A curious question, which being myself unable to resolve, I must leave to the learned. **1830** Sir J. Herschel *Study Nat. Phil.* iii. i. (1851) 221 We are called upon to resolve the important and difficult problem. **1975** *New Yorker* 17 Nov. 94/2 Bress proposed the questions to be resolved by the jury—whether the subpoenas were properly served on the McSurelys, whether they refused to comply with a lawful command of Congress, and whether their refusal was willful. **1976** *Amer. Speech 1973* XLVIII. 248 Nor can *Atlas* materials resolve Kypriotaki's basic question of lexical or environmental control of initial syllable deletion.

refl. **1800** Stuart in Owen *Wellesley's Desp.* (1877) 576 This question of war will soon resolve itself.

b. With double object.

1588 Shaks. *Tit. A.* v. iii. 35 Resolue me this, Was it well done..To slay his daughter? **1596** —— *Tam. Shr.* iv. ii. 7 What Master reade you first, resolue me that? **1687** T. Brown *Saints in Uproar* Wks. 1730 I. 75 Resolve me a question or two. **1706** Estcourt *Fair Example* i. i, Pray will you resolve me one Question? **1781** Mrs. Inchbald *I'll tell you what* iv. i, If you can resolve me that..I have no censure for you.

c. To explain; to make clear.

c **1585** *Faire Em* i. 314 In friendship then resolue What is the cause of your unlookt for stay? **1633** Ford *'Tis Pity* i. ii, What's the ground? *Sor.* That, with your patience, signiors, I'll resolve. *a* **1661** Fuller *Worthies* (1840) III. 424 Some resolve all this passion on a point of mere revenge. **1718** Prior *Solomon* iii. 838 The Man who would resolve the Work of Fate, May limit Number, and make Crooked Strait. **1821** Wordsw. *Eccl. Sonn.* i. xxix, The full-orbed Moon..doth appear Silently to consume the heavy clouds; *How* no one can resolve. **1866** Bushnell *Vicar. Sacr.* Introd. 14 Attempts have been made, in all ages,..to assert what is called 'the moral view' of the atonement, and resolve it by the power it wields in human character.

12. a. To remove, clear away, dispel (a doubt, difficulty, or obscurity).

1571 Digges *Pantom.* i. xix. Fij, Small practize will resolue all doubtes. **1593** Shaks. *3 Hen. VI*, iv. i. 135 But ere I goe, Hastings and Mountague, Resolue my doubt. **1643** Sir T. Browne *Relig. Med.* 48 Myself can shew a catalogue of Doubts which are not resolved at the first hearing. **1666–7** Marvell *Corr.* Wks. (Grosart) II. 210 If you find any thing perplext in it, I shall..resolve any scruple that you may have of its exposition. **1706** Vanbrugh *Mistake* ii. Wks. 1893 II. 254 You must resolve one doubt, which often gives me great disturbance. **1776** Gibbon *Decl. & F.* xvii. I. 464 He was frequently requested to resolve the doubts of inferior judges. **1817** Jas. Mill *Brit. India* II. iv. v. 165 All doubts might be resolved by the interrogation..of the commander. **1873** Black *Pr. Thule* xiii. 198 She had bravely resolved her doubts and made up her mind.

†b. To dissipate, dispel (fear). *Obs. rare.*

1595 Shaks. *John* ii. i. 371 Kings of our feare, vntill our feares resolu'd Be..purg'd. *c* **1605** ? Rowley *Birth of Merlin* v. ii, Speak, learned Merlin, and resolve my fears.

†c. To satisfy (a person's curiosity). *Obs.*⁻¹

1749 Fielding *Tom Jones* vii. iii, Indeed we cannot resolve his curiosity as to this point.

13. a. To decide, determine, settle (a doubtful point).

1612 T. Taylor *Comm. Titus* i. 9 Resoluing all doubtful cases. **1662** Playford *Skill Mus.* ii. (1674) 110 Which of these two is the best way, may easily be resolved. **1704** Swift *Mech. Operat. Spirit* Misc. (1711) 274, I have been perplex'd for some time to resolve what would be the most proper Form to send it abroad in. **1749** Fielding *Tom Jones* iv. xii, Whether Mrs. Honour really deserved that suspicion ..is a matter which we cannot indulge the reader's curiosity in resolving. **1842** Cole *Westm. Abbey* 107 Whether or not they [*sc.* mandates] were executed, our antiquaries have not yet resolved.

b. With dependent clause (or equivalent) expressing the decision arrived at.

1586 Leicester *Corr.* (Camden) 401 The surgion doth fully resolue..he is without danger for this blowe. **1621** Lady M. Wroth *Urania* 40 They all beheld this place with great wonder, Parselius resoluing it was some Enchauntment. **1642** J. M[arsh] *Argt. conc. Militia* 18 It is resolved by the Judges that the King may hold his Parliament without the Spirituall Lords. *a* **1719** Rogers (J.), Happiness, it was resolved by all, must be some one uniform end. **1818** Cruise *Digest* (ed. 2) II. 309 It was resolved, that the remainder limited to B. was good.

†c. To set down decisively as being of a certain character. *Obs. rare.*

1609 B. Jonson *Sil. Wom.* iv. ii, But he loses no reputation with us, for we all resolu'd him an asse before. **1625** Bp. Mountagu *App. Cæsar* 2 All things..so Delivered..are Errors actuall in themselves; and so stand resolved and accounted of in the Doctrine of the Church.

†d. To conclude, to settle (a thing) in one's mind. *Obs.*

a **1618** Raleigh *Rem.* (1644) 237 He left me so weak that he resolved not to find me alive. **1658–9** *Burton's Diary* (1828) IV. 55, I was some days since to seek what to resolve in this great debate. **1702** J. Logan in *Pennsylv. Hist. Soc. Mem.* IX. 122 Having solicitously resolved several things in my thoughts relating to it, I endeavoured to stave them off.

†e. To fix on, choose (a person). *Obs.*⁻¹

1709 Mrs. Manley *Secret Mem.* (1736) 3 She had.. resolved him for her peculiar Pleasures.

14. a. To determine or decide upon (a course of action, etc.). Also, *with* oneself.

Const. with direct object, or with (*that* and) clause.

1523 Hen. VIII in *Lett. Kings Eng.* (Halliw.) I. 284 We.. have resolved and determined that..ye shall then have your letters of discharge. **1588** Shaks. *Tit. A.* ii. i. 105 So must you resolue, That..You must perforce accomplish [it] as you may. **1609** B. Jonson *Sil. Wom.* iii. i, It shall be done, that's resolved. **1667** Milton *P.L.* i. 662 Warr Open or understood must be resolv'd. *Ibid.* ix. 830 Confirm'd then I resolve, Adam shall share with me in bliss or woe. **1682** Bunyan *Holy War* (1905) 198 Wilt thou..suffer thy priviledges to be invaded and taken away? or what wilt resolve with thy self? **1699** Bentley *Phal.* Pref. p. iii, 'Twas very well resolv'd of them, to make the Preface and Book all of a piece. **1710** Shaftesbury *Charac.* (1737) I. *Advice* i. i. 153, I have resolv'd with myself, that the maxim might be admitted. **1781** Gibbon *Decl. & F.* xxix. III. 125 As soon as they had resolved his death, they condescended to flatter his pride. **1819** Shelley *Cenci* iii. i. 169 All must be suddenly resolved and done. **1842** R. I. Wilberforce *Rutilius & Lucius* 265 He had seen enough of the Christians to resolve that nothing should induce him to stain his hands with their blood.

b. To adopt or pass as a resolution.

1590 Cartwright in Fuller *Ch. Hist.* ix. (1655) 201 At some of such meetings..it was resolved..that such.. conferences in severall Shires should be erected. **1604** *Jrnls. Ho. Comm.* 26 June, Resolved, upon further Motion, That Mr. Speaker..should present Thanks to his Majesty [etc.]. **1806** *Med. Jrnl.* XV. 253 Resolved unanimously, that this meeting..entertains the most firm conviction that [etc.]. **1849** Macaulay *Hist. Eng.* ii. I. 175 The Commons began by resolving that every member should, on pain of expulsion, take the sacrament [etc.]. **1866** Lowell *Seward-Johnson Reaction* Prose Wks. 1890 V. 288 The Convention might almost as well have resolved the multiplication table article by article.

c. To put (a person) *out of* a condition by a resolution.

1798 I. Allen *Hist. Vermont* 237 The inhabitants of Vermont had lived in a state of independence.., and could not now submit to be resolved out of it.

†15. a. To free (one) from doubt or perplexity; to bring to certainty or clear understanding. *Obs.* (Common in 17th c.)

1548 Geste *Pr. Masse* 81 The broken bread and blessed wyne is institute purposely to resolve and ascertayn our senses. **1570–6** Lambarde *Peramb. Kent* (1826) 360 If you yet doubt, conferre (I pray you) his report with theirs, and it shall resolve you. **1603** Shaks. *Meas. for M.* iv. ii. 225 Yet you are amaz'd, but this shall absolutely resolue you. **1649** Jer. Taylor *Gt. Exemp.* ii. Ad Sect. xii. 98 To strengthen the weake, to resolve the scrupulous, to teach the ignorant. **1719** De Foe *Crusoe* i. (Globe) 305 We knew not what Course to take, but the Creatures resolv'd us soon.

†b. Const. *of* or *in* the matter of doubt. *Obs.*

1567 *Reg. Privy Council Scot.* I. 515 That thai being certifiit of the veritie may be resolvit of all doubt. **1583** Stubbes *Anat. Abus.* ii. (1882) 68 Ask..and I will doe the best I can, to resolue you in anything you shall demand. **1648** Gage *West. Ind.* 6 To resolve the Pope himself of whatsoever difficult points in Divinity may be questioned. **1651** Culpepper *Astrol. Judgem. Dis.* (1658) 6, I know you would be resolved in one particular. **1767** S. Paterson *Anoth. Trav.* II. 23 You may ask whatever questions you please, and you shall be resolved of everything within my power.

†c. With dependent clause introduced by *where, which, why*, etc. (Passing into 17 b.) *Obs.*

1593 Shaks. *3 Hen. VI*, ii. i. 9, I cannot ioy, vntill I be resolu'd Where our right valiant Father is become. *a* **1648** Ld. Herbert *Hen. VIII* (1683) 582 He sent to Spain to be resolv'd..which of the two Marriages were most convenient. **1690** Locke *Govt.* i. xi. §147 It will always remain a Doubt..till our A. resolves us, whether Shem.. had right to Govern. **1720** De Foe *Capt. Singleton* xvi. (1840) 276 Whether we..may come off any better.., I cannot resolve thee. **1756** Washington *Lett.* Writ. 1889 I. 253, I wish your Honor would resolve me, whether the militia..must be supplied out of the public stocks of provisions.

†16. a. To convince (one) *of* something. *Obs.*

1576 Fleming *Panopl. Epist.* 403 For, thus bee you fully resolved of my nature, that with such reverence I remember you. **1591** Shaks. *1 Hen. VI*, iii. iv. 20 Long since we were resolued of your truth. *a* **1604** Hanmer *Chron. Irel.* (1633) 159 This Lacy behaved himselfe so discreetly..that the King was resolved of his truth and fidelity. **1744** Fielding *Tumble-down Dick* Argt., She advises him to go to the Roundhouse,..and there be resolved from his own mouth of the truth of his Sire.

†b. To assure (one) *that*. Also with *of*. *Obs.*

1590 Webbe *Trav.* To Rdr., They doubtles will resolue them that it is true which is here expressed. **1594** Hooker *Eccl. Pol.* ii. iv. §2 Nothing but only the word of God can.. resolue us that we do well. **1642** Rogers *Naaman* 830 It is said of Hanna, that ere Eli had resolved her from God of a sonne, shee was full of trouble. **1650** R. Stapylton *Strada's Low C. Wars* viii. 30 And, when they resolved him no danger should accrue to either [etc.].

†17. a. To inform, tell (a person) *of* a thing. *Obs.*

1568 *Reg. Privy Council Scot.* I. 629 It is thocht convenient to resolve all personis of the same, that nane heireftir sall pretend occasioun of ignorance. **1594** Shaks. *Rich. III*, iv. v. 19 My Letter will resolue him of my minde. **1632** Lithgow *Trav.* x. 451 He went back, resoluing them of my stiffe denyall.

†b. With dependent clause. *Obs.*

1592 Marlowe *Massacre Paris* iii. iv, The wound, I warrant you, is deep, my lord. Search, surgeon, and resolve me what thou seest. **1601** B. Jonson *Poetaster* iv. ii, Pray you, resolue mee, why giue you that heauenly prayse, to this earthly banquet? **1690** Locke *Govt.* ii. ii. §9, I desire them to resolve me, by what Right any Prince..can put to death ..an Alien. **1697** Dryden *Æneid* viii. 150 Resolve me, Strangers, whence and what you are.

†c. With direct question, or *ellipt.* Chiefly in imperative, asking for an answer. *Obs.*

1607 Norden *Surv. Dial.* ii. 56, I pray thee, if thou canst, resolue me. Whether is the heriot payd [etc.]? **1687** T. Brown *Saints in Uproar* Wks. 1730 I. 76 Who was your father? Come, resolve me immediately. **1709** Prior *Mezeray's Hist.*, Can Sense this Paradox endure? Resolve me, Cambray, or Fontaine. **1772** Wesley *Jrnl.* 31 Oct., They asked me, 'whether they were good or bad spirits?' But I could not resolve them. **1819** Scott *Ivanhoe* xvii, Resolve me, Holy Clerk, hast thou never practised such a pastime?

†d. To answer (one); to make answer to. *Obs.*

1586 Young *Guazzo's Civ. Conv.* iv. 219, I resolue thee (faire Ladie) thus, that many times I tried [etc.].

18. †a. To advise (one) to a decision. *Obs.*

a **1648** Ld. Herbert *Hen. VIII* (1683) 458 He was resolv'd by his Council rather to weary and famish the Emperors Army. **1656** *Burton's Diary* (1828) I. 32, I would have the Committee to resolve you how you will proceed.

b. To determine (a person) *on* a course of action. Also with inf.

1836 Browning & Forster *Life Strafford* (1892) 15 The events of the interim had resolved the leaders of the house on abandoning the terms proposed. **1890** Sir C. Russell in *Daily News* 24 July 2/7 The knowledge of this marriage resolved Lord and Lady C...to send their son abroad.

19. *refl.* **†a.** To make up one's mind. *Obs.*

a **1528** Fox *Let. to Wolsey* in Strype *Eccl. Mem.* V. 406 Of whom his ho. wil resolve hymself, we cannot yet tell. **1587** Fleming *Contn. Holinshed* III. 1351/1 Resolue your selfe my lord, you haue a goodlie soule. **1600** E. Blount tr. *Conestaggio* 25 Solliciting Sebastian to resolue himselfe either to enter or be excluded. **1626** Fletcher *Noble Gent.* iv. iv, Tell me, have you resolv'd yourself for court?

†b. To join oneself *to* another's opinion. *Obs.*⁻¹

1568 Grafton *Chron.* II. 648 The Erle of Salisbury and other his friendes, seyng his courage, resolued themselues to his opinion.

†c. To free (oneself) *of* a doubt. *Obs. rare.*

1580 Lyly *Euphues* (Arb.) 418 If thou resolue thy selfe of a doubt, I cannot thinke thee very sharpe. **1597** Morley *Introd. Mus.* 4 If you remember that which before you tolde mee you vnderstood: you would resolue your selfe of that doubt.

d. To assure, satisfy, or convince (oneself) on some point.

1593 Lodge *William Longbeard* C 3 In youth be true, and then in age resolve thee, Friends will be friends. *a* **1618** Raleigh *Rem.* (1644) 237 If I live to return, resolve your self that it is the care for you that hath strengthened my heart. **1657** S. Purchas *Pol. Flying-Ins.* 74 If you taste it, you will easily resolve your self. **1710** Shaftesb. *Charac.* (1737) II. ii. iii. 276 We apprehend a larger Scheme, and easily resolve our-selves why Things were not compleated in this State. **1814** Cary *Dante, Par.* xxviii. 7 [As one who] turneth to resolve him, if the glass Have told him true. **1869** Goulburn *Purs. Holiness* vi. 48 He must resolve himself on the question.

IV. *intr.* **†20.** To take rise. *Obs. rare*⁻¹.

c **1374** Chaucer *Boeth.* v. metr. i. (1868) 151 Tigris and eufrates resoluen and spryngen of a welle in þe kragges of þe roche of þe contre of achemenye.

21. To melt, dissolve, become liquid. ? *Obs.*

c **1400** tr. *Secreta Secret., Gov. Lordsh.* 72 In þis tyme..þe wyndes blowyn, þe snow resoluys. *c* **1440** *Alph. Tales* 443 þis yse resoluyd into watir. **1536** Bellenden *Cron. Scot.* (1821) I. p. xxxiii, Ony frosin thing that is cassin in it, meltis and resolvis hastilie. **1595** Shaks. *John* v. iv. 25 Euen as a forme of waxe Resolueth from his figure 'gainst the fire. **1611** B. Jonson *Catiline* iii. iii, May my brain Resolve to water, and my blood turn phlegm. **1665** *Phil. Trans.* I. 106 After a while it resolves again, and grows dilute. **1731** Arbuthnot *Aliments* iv. 104 When the Blood stagnates in any part of the Body, it first coagulates, then resolves, and turns alkaline. **1759** B. Martin *Nat. Hist. Eng.* I. 19 Congealed (as it were) in Clusters, which resolve, and the frozen Swallows revive by the Warmth.

fig. **1696** Southerne *Oroonoko* v. v, Our honours, interests resolving down, Run in the gentle current of our joys.

22. a. To undergo dissolution or separation into elements; to pass *into*, return or change *to*, some form or state.

c **1400** tr. *Secreta Secret., Gov. Lordsh.* 68 It ys to wete þat mannys body..continuely er dimunisshed and resoluyn aȝeyn. **1509** Fisher *Serm. C'tess Richmond* Wks. (1876) 304 Fyrst it [*sc.* the body] anone begynneth to putrefye & resolve in to foule corrupcyon. **1589** Greene *Menaphon* (Arb.) 58 Pleusidippus eyes at this speach resolued into fire. **1649** G. Daniel *Trinarch., Hen. IV* lxxvii, This Insect..Resolues to dirt againe in the next Storme. **1655** T. Stanley *Hist. Philos.* (1701) 5/1 He conceived Water to be the first principle of all natural Bodies, whereof they consist, and into which they resolve. **1715** Pope *Iliad* ii. 44 The phantom ..Resolves to air, and mixes with the night. **1716** *Ibid.* vii. 113 Go then, resolve to earth, from whence ye grew. **1847** C. Bronte *J. Eyre* xxvii, The roof resolved to clouds, high and dim. **1878** M. A. Brown tr. *Runeberg's Nadeschda* 66 The marble then In transformation dire into speech resolved.

b. Of non-material things.

1679 Dryden *Troil. & Cress.* i. i, Then every thing resolves to brutal Force, And headlong Force is led by hoodwink'd Will. **1711** Shaftesb. *Charac.* (1737) II. iii. i. 345, I..celebrate the Beautys which resolve in Thee, the Source..of all Perfection. **1752** Hume *Ess., Balance Trade* (1817) I. 315 These cases, when examined, will be found to resolve into our general theory. **1818** Scott *Br. Lamm.* xv, It would resolve into an equitable claim. **1852** Sir W. Hamilton *Discuss.* 533 What would otherwise resolve into a conscious outrage of the most sacred obligations.

c. *Path.* To undergo resolution.
1822–34 *Good's Study Med.* (ed. 4) II. 285 Regular fit of gout..gradually resolving, and leaving the constitution in its usual or improved health. **1898** P. MANSON *Trop. Diseases* xxvii. 434 These drugs have undoubtedly the power of causing the eruption in yaws to resolve.

d. *Law.* To lapse; to become void.
1838 W. BELL *Dict. Law Scot.* 695 On his failure to pay within the time limited, the sale resolves, and the property ..returns to the seller.

e. *Mus.* To change from discord to harmony.
1889 PROUT *Harmony* xiv. §332 All chords of the ninth can resolve upon their own generator. **1898** STAINER & BARRETT *Dict. Mus. Terms* 310/2 The note on which the suspension resolves is not heard with the suspension.

23. a. To come to a determination; to make up one's mind; to take a firm purpose or decision.
1590 SIR J. SMYTH *Disc. Weapons* Ded. 8 To know, how of himselfe..with valour to resolue and performe. **1597** BACON *Coulers Good & Evill* Ess. (Arb.) 143 As he sayth well, Not to resolue, is to resolue, and many times it.. ingageth as farre in some other sort as to resolue. **1622** FORD, etc. *Witch of Edmonton* I. i, Upon what certainty shall I resolve? **1667** MILTON *P.L.* IX. 97 Thus he resolv'd, but first ..His bursting passion into plaints thus pour'd. **1748** THOMSON *Cast. Indol.* II. lxii, Resolve! resolve! and to be men aspire! **1760–2** GOLDSM. *Cit. W.* xxvi[i], So after resolving, and re-resolving, I had courage enough to tell her my mind. **1832** AUSTIN *Jurispr.* (1879) I. xxi. 452 When such expressions as 'resolving' and 'determining' are applied to a present intention to do a future act.

b. Const. with inf.
1570–6 LAMBARDE *Peramb. Kent* (1826) p. vi, I resolved (for sundrie iust respectes) to begin first with that Shire. **1588** SHAKS. *L.L.L.* IV. iii. 371 Shall we resolue to woe these girles of France? **1613** PURCHAS *Pilgrimage* VIII. iii. (1614) 744 He..committed many errours, especially in resoluing to winter in that desolate place. **1719** DE FOE *Crusoe* I. (Globe) 45, I resolv'd to hold fast by a Piece of the Rock. **1856** FROUDE *Hist. Eng.* (1858) I. iii. 252 At one time he had resolved..to give way.

c. With *on* or *upon*; also †*of*, †*in*.
1586 MARLOWE *1st Pt. Tamburlaine* II. vi, Since..He dares so doubtlessly resolve of rule. **1606** SHAKS. *Ant. & Cl.* III. xi. 9, I haue my selfe resolu'd vpon a course, Which has no neede of you. **1659–60** PEPYS *Diary* 23 Jan., This day the Parliament..resolved of the declaration to be printed for the people's satisfaction. *a* **1715** BURNET *Own Time* I. (1724) I. 36 The course they all resolved on was, that [etc.]. **1782** MISS BURNEY *Cecilia* VIII. iv, Cecilia..had still the..good sense..to resolve upon making the best use [etc.]. **1809** *Susan* II. 103 Mrs. Howard..immediately resolved in going with him. **1863** GEO. ELIOT *Romola* xx, The ceremony had been resolved upon rather suddenly.

†**d.** To decide on setting out *for* a place. *Obs.*
1597 SHAKS. *2 Hen. IV*, II. iii. 67, I will resolue for Scotland. *a* **1643** CARTWRIGHT *Ordinary* V. v, Let's swear Fidelity to one another, and So resolve for New England. **1734** tr. *Rollin's Anc. Hist.* XVII. vii. (1827) VII. 204 He resolved for Sicily which would open him a passage into Africa. **1760** *Impostors Detected* IV. iii. II. 189 We were obliged to separate, and every one take his chance... As for me I resolved for Lisbon.

†**24. a.** To be satisfied or convinced. *Obs.*
1585 T. WASHINGTON tr. *Nicholay's Voy.* I. xx. 24 The Gouernor by the counsell of those that had perswaded him too surrender, resolued vppon so small an assurance of the Bascha. **1591** SHAKS. *1 Hen. VI*, I. ii. 91 Resolue on this, thou shalt be fortunate, If thou receiue me for thy Warlike Mate. **1598** B. JONSON *Ev. Man. in Hum.* I. v, *Bob.* For doe you see, sir,..I could not extend thus farre. *Mat.* O Lord, sir, I resolue so. **1659** HAMMOND *On Ps.* 610, I have allwayes, since I knew any thing of thee, resolved of the truth of it.

†**b.** To consult, take counsel. *Obs.*
1591 SPENSER *M. Hubberd* 123 It behoves, ere that into the race We enter, to resolve first hereupon. **1641** HINDE *Life J. Bruen* xviii. 56 He made them sometimes as his counsellours, to advise, conferre, consult, and resolve with them, in matters of conscience. **1719** DE FOE *Crusoe* I. (Globe) 260 Let us retreat out of their View or Hearing, least they awake, and we will resolve further.

resolved (rɪˈzɒlvd), *ppl. a.* [f. prec. + -ED¹.]
1. Of persons: Determined, decided, settled in purpose. Also const. with inf., *that*, etc.
1520 HEN. VIII in *Lett. Kings Eng.* (Halliw.) I. 246 Whereunto..none of our..ancestors were ever so.. determinate resolved as we be at this time. **1560** DAUS tr. *Sleidane's Comm.* 6 He was fully resolved to stire up no further disputation. **1611** BIBLE *Luke* xvi. 4, I am resolued what to doe. **1687** T. BROWN *Saints in Uproar* Wks. 1730 I. 83, I am resolved to undeceive mankind. **1737** BERINGTON *Mem. G. de Lucca* (1738) 51 These Considerations made me as good as resolv'd to go along with him. **1760–2** GOLDSM. *Cit. W.* xxvii, He was resolved they should have learning. **1819** SHELLEY *Cenci* III. i. 341 That word parricide, Although I am resolved, haunts me like fear. **1847** C. BRONTË *J. Eyre* xxxv, He was in deep earnest, wrestling with God, and resolved on a conquest.

b. Const. with *for*, †*against*, †*from*, †*of* (= on).
1582 T. WATSON *Cent. of Love* xcvi, I liue secure,.. Fully resolu'd from louing any more. **1639** FULLER *Holy War* IV. xvii. 198 About this time many thousands of the English were resolved for the Holy warre. **1641** W. MOUNTAGU in *Buccleuch MSS.* (Hist. MSS. Comm.) I. 289 The Temple is resolved of a Christmas. **1659** HAMMOND *On Ps.* 610 My enemies are maliciously resolved against me.

†**2.** Convinced, satisfied. *Obs.*
1577 WHETSTONE *Gascoigne* ii, Yet trust me frends.., I am resolu'd, I neuer liu'd til now. **1595** RALEIGH *Discov. Guiana* (1887) 106 For mine own part I am resolved it is true. **1608** MIDDLETON *Trick to catch Old One* III. i, Since you are so well resolved of my faith toward you. **1719** D'URFEY *Pills* (1872) III. 97 Being well resolved that none Could see her Nakedness.

3. †**a.** Of the mind, etc.: Freed from doubt or uncertainty; fixed, settled. *Obs.*
1497 *Lett. Rich. III & Hen. VII* (Rolls) I. 110 Our fynal and resolved mynde is that ye obteyne al thes articles comprised in the second parte. **1578** BANISTER *Hist. Man* v. 82 To passe this point with a cleare resolued mynde. **1643** SIR T. BROWNE *Relig. Med.* I. §3, I could never perceive.. that a resolved conscience may not adore her Creator anywhere. **1660** INGELO *Bentiv. & Ur.* II. (1682) 76 It is difficult to suppose that he hath any resolved thoughts concerning God.

b. Of actions, states of mind, etc.: Fully determined upon, deliberate.
1595 SHAKS. *John* II. i. 585 From a resolu'd and honourable warre, To a most base and vile-concluded peace. **1638** A. READ *Chirurg.* xxxi. 230 A doubtfull hope is better than a resolved despaire. **1694** KETTLEWELL *Comp. for Penitent* 92 Confess them to him with a resolved aversion: being resolved in heart to forsake all. *a* **1716** SOUTH *Serm.* (1744) X. 185 A settled, constant, resolved living in sin. **1890** 'R. BOLDREWOOD' *Miner's Right* (1899) 13/1 A great and often resolved scheme.

†**c.** Deliberately adopted or accepted. *Obs.*
1659 RUSHW. *Hist. Coll.* I. 176 They shew that some of the Opinions which offended many, were no other then the resolved Doctrine of this Church.

d. That has been decided *on*.
1748 RICHARDSON *Clarissa* (1811) VIII. 273 Not a resolved-on case.

4. Of persons, the mind, etc.: Characterized by determination or firmness of purpose; resolute.
1586 MARLOWE *1st Pt. Tamburl.* I. ii, What strong enchantments tice my yielding soul To these resolved, noble Scythians. **1612** DRAYTON *Poly-olb.* viii. 272 Brave Voadicia made with her resolued'st men To Virolam. **1681** H. MORE *Postscr. to Glanvill's Sadducismus* (1726) 17 Of whom he is sworn Advocate and resolved Patron, right or wrong. **1749** FIELDING *Tom Jones* XVI. iv, Here stands your resolved daughter. **1816** SCOTT *Antiq.* i, The hat pulled over his resolved brows. **1856** FROUDE *Hist. Eng.* (1858) I. iii. 207 Men of..broad resolved temper.
Comb. **1890** 'R. BOLDREWOOD' *Col. Reformer* (1891) 202 A subdued, bronzed, resolved-looking man.

†**b.** Confirmed (in some practice or course). *Obs.*
1614 RALEIGH *Hist. World* II. (1634) 183 A nation of valiant and resolved Idolaters. **1692** BENTLEY *Boyle Lect.* ii. 32 No wonder the resolved Atheists do so labour and bestir themselves to fetch Sense and Perception out of the Power of Matter.

†**c.** Openly or sincerely attached to some party or body. *Obs.*
1647 CLARENDON *Hist. Reb.* VI. §261 Which drove all resolved men from their houses into York, where they only could be safe. **1657** BAXTER *Present Thoughts* 33 The one sort were never hearty resolved Christians. **1732** NEAL *Hist. Purit.* I. 55 A yoke which some of the most resolved Protestants could not bear.

†**5.** Melted, dissolved. *Obs.*
1582 T. WATSON *Cent. of Love* lxxvii, Time brings a fludd from newe resolued snowe. **1666** BOYLE *Orig. Formes & Qual.* 300 Dropping a little resolv'd salt of Tartar upon the solution of common Sublimate.

†**6.** Of parts of the body: Soft, relaxed. *Obs.*
1576 BAKER *Jewell of Health* 162 The extenuation of resolved and weake members. **1650** BULWER *Anthropomet.* 182 Lips are soft and resolved.

7. Separated, broken up, analysed.
1812 WOODHOUSE *Astron.* xxxiii. (1832) 682 One effect, from a resolved part of the Sun's disturbing force. **1818** T. BUSBY *Gram. Mus.* 429 There is the resolved Canon, the unresolved Canon. **1868** LOCKYER *Guillemin's Heavens* (ed. 3) 397 Another point of resemblance between the resolved globular clusters, and the nebulæ of the same form.

re'solvedly, *adv.* [f. prec. + -LY².]
†**1.** Definitely, determinately. *Obs.*
1611 BEAUM. & FL. *King & No King* III. ii, All the kindness I can shew him, is to set him resolvedly in my rowle, the two hundred and thirteenth man. **1646** S. BOLTON *Arraignm. Errors* 353 Who is it that saith resolvedly, we must be one, we cannot live without you? **1677** GILPIN *Demonol.* (1867) 55 The will doth not resolvedly embrace any object till the light of the understanding hath made out..the goodness or conveniency of the object.

2. In a determined manner; resolutely.
1595 MUNDAY *John a Kent* 19 But when no answere either could receive, Resolvedly thus we set downe our rest. **1636** SANDERSON *Serm.* II. 49 The greatest blame must remain upon the untowardness of the will, resolvedly bent upon the evil. **1689** *Lond. Gaz.* No. 2484/1 We..do most heartily and resolvedly offer, and engage our Lives and Fortunes to Your Service.
1826 SCOTT *Woodst.* iv, The young commonwealth's-man turned and walked sternly and resolvedly forth. **1876** BANCROFT *Hist. U.S.* V. xlix. 79 Resolvedly blind to consequences, George III. scorned to dissemble.

re'solvedness. [f. as prec. + -NESS.] Resolution, determination; firmness, fixedness of purpose.
1611 W. SCLATER *Key* (1629) 219 In things substantiall, I loue resoluednesse. **1686** HORNECK *Crucif. Jesus* xxii. 680 How mightest thou have shamed the devil by a continued resolvedness!
1856 RUSKIN *Mod. Paint.* IV. v. App. ii, This resolvedness to break into shell-shaped fragments..is only characteristic of the rock at this spot. **1872** BUSHNELL *Serm. Living Subj.* 60 What can he do by mere will-force and resolvedness, when the heavenly trust is wanting?

resolvend (rɪˈzɒlvənd), *sb. Arith.* [ad. L. *resolvend-um*, neut. gerundive of *resolvĕre* to RESOLVE.] The number formed by extending the remainder after subtraction in the process of extracting the square or cube root.
1675 COLLINS in Rigaud *Corr. Sci. Men* (1841) I. 215 Offering any resolvend..whatever, he could by direct operations give the logarithm of the root sought. **1709** J. WARD *Introd. Math.* I. xi. (1734) 128 It very often happens that the Resolvend is not a true Figurate Number. **1798** HUTTON *Course Math.* (1827) I. 88 From the resolvend take the subtrahend, and to the remainder join the next period of the given number for a new resolvend. **1811** *Self Instructor* 165 Bring down the next point, 57, which call the resolvend.
So †**re'solvend** *a.* (See quot.) *Obs.*
1694 OUGHTRED *Key to Math.* [161 The (Power to be resolved or) *Potestas Resolvenda. Ibid.*] 164 All the punctations..must be made in the Potestas Resolvend.

resolvent (rɪˈzɒlvənt), *a.* and *sb.* [ad. L. *resolvent-em*, pres. pple. of *resolvĕre* to RESOLVE.]
A. *adj.* **1.** Chiefly *Med.* Having the power to resolve; causing solution. Also const. *of*.
1676 WISEMAN *Surg. Treat.* I. xix. 94, I..applied the milder resolvent Emplaster. **1732** ARBUTHNOT *Rules of Diet in Aliments*, etc. I. 249 A Juice..resolvent of the Bile. **1762** R. GUY *Pract. Obs. Cancers* 75 The resolvent Applications taking no effect. **1822–34** *Good's Study Med.* (ed. 4) II. 463 All the chylific organs secrete an unusual quantity of resolvent juices. **1866** ODLING *Anim. Chem.* 158 The so-called resolvent action of alkalies upon the animal economy.

2. Of a proposition: That merely asserts what is already included in the conception of the subject.
1856 FERRIER *Inst. Metaph.* (ed. 2) 25 *note*, The proposition adds nothing to our knowledge: it is merely explicative, or resolvent.

3. *Math.*, in ***resolvent equation, product***, etc.
1859 R. HARLEY in *Mem. Lit. & Phil. Soc. Manchester* (1860) XV. 173 The product..which may be called the symmetric or resolvent product, according as it is or is not symmetric. **1861** CAYLEY in *Phil. Trans.* (1862) CLI. 263 Then..$f\omega$ is the root of an equation of the order 24 called the Resolvent Equation. **1882** —— in *Quart. Jrnl. Math.* XVIII. 60 Transformation of the Jacobian Sextic into the Resolvent Sextic of a special quintic equation.

B. *sb.* **1.** *Med.* A medicine or application to cause the resolution of a swelling; a discutient.
1676 WISEMAN *Surg. Treat.* I. xix. 92 Young people.. require to be treated with milder Resolvents then those who live a labouring life. **1758** WOOD *Farriery* 16 As soon as Resolvents take effect [etc.]. **1797** *Encycl. Brit.* (ed. 3) XVII. 567/2 Soap is also externally employed as a resolvent. **1834** J. FORBES *Laennec's Dis. Chest* (ed. 4) 193 Blood-letting, derivatives, and resolvents or stimulants of the absorbent system,..retard the progress of the disease. **1883–4** *Med. Ann.* 9/2 He believes the drug to be an aplastic or resolvent of great energy.

2. Something capable of resolving; a solvent.
1706 PHILLIPS (ed. Kersey), *Resolvents*, in Chymistry, certain Liquors that are us'd for the dissolving of Metals, or Minerals. **1708** J. KEILL *Anim. Secretion* Pref. xv, Different Substances require different Resolvents. **1900** *Q. Rev.* July 55 The whole earth, the one disinfectant and resolvent of death and decay.

3. A means of removing difficulties, settling problems, etc. Const *of*.
1851 WILLMOTT *Pleas. Lit.* ii. 6 The harsher resolvents of digamma and allegory. **1880** R. G. WHITE *Every-Day English* 142 A coin which would serve as a common resolvent of all accounts. **1892** *Critic* (U.S.) 1 Oct. 186/2 But those who know the man..scarcely look for such a resolvent of Samoan troubles.

4. *Math.* A resolvent equation, function, etc. ***Galois resolvent***: see GALOIS.
1859 *Phil. Mag.* XVIII. 54 One of the roots of its resolvent ..is a rational function of another. **1860** *Rep. Brit. Assoc.* (1861) 147 Let us consider the function F(a, x), which is a particular case of the resolvent [etc.].

resolver (rɪˈzɒlvə(r)). [f. RESOLVE *v.* + -ER¹.]
†**1.** A resolvent substance. Also with *of*. *Obs.*
c **1400** *Lanfranc's Cirurg.* 6 Cap. ij. of resolueres.
1632 tr. *Bruel's Praxis Med.* 92 Heere strong resolvers are requisite..because the Impostume cannot by other meanes be resolued. **1663** BOYLE *Usef. Exp. Nat. Philos.* II. v. xviii. 276 Opium..proves sometimes a great resolver, and commonly a great Sudorifick. **1756** BURKE *Subl. & B.* IV. xxi, Water..is found when not cold to be a great resolver of spasms.

2. One who, or that which, answers a question, solves a doubt or difficulty, etc.
1609 [BP. W. BARLOW] *Answ. Nameless Cath.* 27 Hee is a sound Resoluer. **1683** E. HOOKER in *Pordage's Mystic Div.* 88 A better Resolver thereof in all cases England never saw. *a* **1715** BURNET *Own Time* (1766) II. 116 It was said, that the serving an end was a good resolver of all cases of conscience. **1775** *Chron.* in *Ann. Reg.* 82/2 A woman applied to a resolver of lawful questions..to be satisfied in relation to some future events.

3. One who makes a resolve; one who supports a resolution.
1749 LAVINGTON *Enthus. Meth. & Papists* (1752) 18 Though from human Infirmity the Resolver himself has sometimes forgot his vow. **1839** *Fraser's Mag.* XIX. 757 All these addressers and resolvers were taken in. **1894** WOOLLEY in *Voice* (U.S.) 13 Sept., It improves a resolution to have the resolver mean it.

4. *Electr.* An electromechanical device which transforms the representation of an electric vector from polar to Cartesian coordinates (see quot. 1956); also, more widely, an electronic device which resolves an input signal into components.
1952 G. A. & T. M. KORN *Electronic Analog Computers* vi. 283 A special rotatable transformer called a resolver. **1956**

BERKELEY & WAINWRIGHT *Computers* iii. 101 A special form of transformer known as a resolver..built something like an electric motor... Turning of the rotor varies the coupling between the windings so as to produce the sine and cosine functions. *Ibid.* viii. 353/1 Resolver..a device for resolving a vector into two mutually perpendicular components. **1975** *Daily Tel.* (Colour Suppl.) 24 Oct. 29/1 Many find that they can get a very pleasant 'surround' effect by using a pair of modest rear speakers coupled to a simple unit called a resolver. The Neal resolver, for example, sorts out the signals from a stereo amplifier and passes to the rear loudspeakers the out-of-phase information—the peripheral elements of the sound. **1976** *Sci. Amer.* Feb. 78/1 The addition of servo control calls for feedback from sensors such as potentiometers, encoders and resolvers, which measure the position of each joint.

re'solvible, *a.* [f. RESOLVE *v.* + -IBLE.] Capable of being resolved; resolvable.

1691 NORRIS *Pract. Disc.* (1711) III. 118 The whole misery of man is resolvible into Pain and Grief. **1701** —— *Ideal World* I. ii. 43 This is the first of those principles into which the deficiencies of nature are resolvible. **1816** tr. *Lacroix's Diff. & Integr. Calc.* 102 This equation..is resolvible, both with respect to *x* and to *y*. **1869** F. W. NEWMAN *Misc.* 14 We may construct some Geometrical propositions which are purely Verbal, resolvible by a comparison of Definitions.

resolving (rɪ'zɒlvɪŋ), *vbl. sb.* [f. as prec. + -ING[1].] **1.** The action of the verb in various senses.

c **1400** *Lanfranc's Cirurg.* 209 A resoluyng in an vnclene bodi drawiþ more matere þerto þan it resolueþ. **1513** BRADSHAW *St. Werburge* I. 130 But after the resolving of his blessed body He raised deed men to lyfe agayne truely. **1609** *MS. Acc. St. John's Hosp., Canterb.*, Layd owt to John Kevell towardes his resollving of him at the court, ijs.

1659 HAMMOND *On Ps.* Pref. 9 Sufficient to recommend it to the Readers most diligent resolving. **17..** RAMSAY *Coalier's Daughter* iii, After mature resolving..He tenderly thus tell'd her. **1889** *Pall Mall G.* 16 Jan. 6/2 It is strange that all the Unionist speaking and resolving beforehand was in opposition to them.

2. *Comb.* **resolving power**, the capability of an optical or photographic system to separate or distinguish closely adjacent images; also, the similar capability of a radio telescope; **resolving time**, the interval from the start of a counted pulse in a pulse counter to the time when another pulse can be detected and counted separately.

1879 *Lond. &c. Phil. Mag.* VIII. 262 The resolving-power of a telescope on a double star. **1887** *Encycl. Brit.* XXII. 374/1 While the resolving power of a spectroscope with grating..is independent of the wave-length for each order, the resolving power of a spectroscope with prism will vary inversely as the third power of the wave-length. **1955** *Sci. Amer.* Mar. 38/1 The resolving power is measured by the sharpness of the peak; it is usually expressed as the 'half-power beam width', which means the width of the arc along which the antenna receives half or more of the maximum signal power. **1977** J. NARLIKAR *Struct. Universe* iv. 107 Because visual wavelengths are considerably shorter than radio wavelengths.., the optical telescope can achieve a better resolving power with an aperture of a few centimetres than the radio telescope can with an aperture of several metres. **1942** W. B. LEWIS *Electr. Counting* viii. 83 The anode potential rises more rapidly after extinction and the resolving time is reduced. **1948** *Jrnl. Sci. Instruments* XXV. 37/1 The resolving time of the input circuit of the scaler was measured directly by feeding into the scaler pairs of pulses of variable separation. **1963** B. BROWN *Experimental Nucleonics* 175 Due to the short resolving time much higher count rates are possible.

re'solving, *ppl. a.* Chiefly *Med.* [f. as prec. + -ING[2].] That resolves.

c **1400** *Lanfranc's Cirurg.* 230 þou schalt do þerto sumtyme mollificatiuis & sumtyme resoluyng þingis. **1563** T. GALE *Antidot.* I. 3 Of resolving medicines: Symple and compounde. **1639** LD. DIGBY *Lett. conc. Relig.* (1651) 43 For either of us there is no resolving evidence to be taken from the Fathers. **1663** BOYLE *Usef. Exp. Nat. Philos.* II. xiv. 247 Unlesse they be of such a resolving and abstersive nature, as to be able to make way for themselves into the recesses of the body. **1758** J. S. tr. *Le Dran's Observ. Surg.* (1771) 259, I prescribed resolving Fomentations.

resommon, obs. form of RESUMMON.

reson(e, obs. forms of RAISIN, REASON *sb.*[1]

† **reson**, obs. form of REASON *sb.*[2]

1449 in *Cal. Proc. Chanc. Q. Eliz.* (1830) II. Pref. 54 The which flores wt þe resons above shullen accord in heith wt the flores and resons of an other hous there.

resonance ('rɛzənəns). Also 5 resonn-. [a. OF. *resonance, resonnance* (15th c.; mod.F. *résonance*), = It. *risonanza*, Sp. and Pg. *resonancia*, ad. L. *resonantia* echo (Vitruvius), f. *resonāre* to resound: see -ANCE.]

1. a. The reinforcement or prolongation of sound by reflection, or *spec.* by synchronous vibration.

1491 CAXTON *Vitas Patr.* (W. de W. 1495) I. xlviii. 92/1 Merueyllous howlynges and waylynges.., wherof the resonnaunce or sonne was soo horryble that it semyd it wente vppe to heuen. **1502** *Ord. Crysten Men* (W. de W. 1506) v. vii. PP ij, For the beaute, for the force and for the resonaunce. **1603** HOLLAND *Plutarch's Mor.* 67 Let us see (I say) what resonance and melodie bare wood may yeeld. **1608** HEYWOOD *Lucrece* I. i, Ther's no resonance In a bare stile: my title beares no breadth. **1776** BURNEY *Hist. Music* (1789) I. viii. 149 Resonance is but an aggregate of echos or of quick repetitions and returns of the same sound. **1833** *Cycl. Pract. Med.* I. 219/1 If percussion be practised on a soft and inelastic surface, the impulse..will elicit no resonance from it. **1876** tr. *Blaserna's Sound* ii. 41 A room in which sound shall be considerably strengthened without degenerating into resonance.

b. *Path.* The sound heard in auscultation of the chest while the person is speaking, or that elicited by percussion of various parts of the body.

1822-34 *Good's Study Med.* (ed. 4) II. 526 [Auscultation] affords, under different circumstances, four different kinds of measure, as that of its degree of intensity, which M. Laennec has denominated resonance. **1845** P. M. LATHAM *Lect. Clin. Med.* I. i. 15 There are other sounds..entirely produced by our percussion of the præcordial region. These should rather be called resonances than sounds. **1897** *Allbutt's Syst. Med.* IV. 655 When the alveoli are filled with coagulum, although the bronchi still contain air, the resonance is completely lost.

c. *Electr.* The phenomenon of an oscillating signal (as an electric current or electromagnetic radiation) producing an effect upon an oscillating current of the same frequency; the condition in which a circuit or device produces the largest possible response to an applied oscillating signal, *esp.* when its inductive reactance balances its capacitative reactance.

1886 *Electrician* 20 Aug. 296/2 By this to-and-fro reflection, or electrical reverberation or resonance, the amplitude of the received current may be made far greater than the strength of the steady-flow current from the same impressed force. **1889** FLEMING *Altern. Current Transf.* I. 420 In order to determine whether..the oscillations were of the nature of a regular vibration, he availed himself of the principle of resonance. **1893** SLOANE *Electr. Dict.* 470 When exposed to electric resonance, or to a sympathetic electric oscillatory discharge, a spark passes from across the gap. **1897** A. HAY *Princ. Alternate-Current Working* xii. 159 This phenomenon of the neutralisation of an inductance by means of a capacity is generally referred to as electrical resonance. **1920** E. W. STONE *Elem. Radiotelegr.* i. 22 When these two reactances are equal, a state of resonance is said to obtain. **1920** *Whittaker's Electr. Engineer's Pocket-bk.* (ed. 4) 446 Resonance is rarely established with the fundamental frequency of the supply, but is generally due to harmonics. **1943** C. L. BOLTZ *Basic Radio* viii. 129 The phenomenon of a circuit responding most to one frequency is called resonance. **1959** K. HENNEY *Radio Engin. Handbk.* (ed. 5) vi. 46 It was realized that a hollow closed conducting box of arbitrary shape possessed electrical resonance properties similar to the conventional coil and capacitor circuit. **1964** R. F. FICCHI *Electr. Interference* v. 48 Past the point of resonance, the inductive reactance continues to increase and the capacitor is no longer effective as a bypass filter. **1975** D. G. FINK *Electronics Engineers' Handbk.* xv. 30 One type of forced commutation uses resonance to generate an alternation which brings the current in a conducting thyristor to zero.

d. *Physics* and *Chem.* (i) Generally, a condition in which a particle is subjected to an oscillating influence (as an electromagnetic field or another particle) of such a frequency that a transfer of energy occurs or reaches a maximum; an instance of this; an exchange of energy occurring under such conditions.

1895 *Abstr. Physical Papers* (Physical Soc.) I. 355 It is thus impossible that resonance should obtain between the electric waves of Hertz and the molecules of a body, and consequently impossible for an ordinary prism to disperse electric waves. **1902** *Phil. Mag.* III. 396 A new type of light absorption, which it may be possible to refer to the electrical resonance of small metallic particles for waves of light. *Ibid.* IV. 428 The variable nature of the colour..makes it appear improbable that the action is similar to that of aniline dyes; namely, a resonance within the molecule. **1931** *Proc. R. Soc.* A. CXXX. 477 The possibility of the occurrence of line spectra due to a resonance between the α-particle and the nucleus. **1935** *Physical Rev.* XLVII. 751/2 The large cross sections [for neutron scattering] may thus be called a resonance effect, but the 'resonance' is very unsharp. **1959** *Physical Rev. Lett.* II. 427/1 Quite a narrow resonance (half-width ≤ 20 Mev) appears in these cross sections just below this threshold. **1966** WILLIAMS & FLEMING *Spectrosc. Methods Org. Chem.* iv. 78 Since different protons in an organic molecule have varying electronic environments, the precise value of the magnetic field required to bring any one into resonance at constant frequency will vary slightly from proton to proton. **1970** I. E. MCCARTHY *Nuclear Reactions* I. i. 6 The reaction occurred preferentially at four different energies between about 4 MeV and 5·3 MeV. Resonance was said to occur in the α, Al^{27} system at these energies. **1974** *Accounts Chem. Res.* VII. 341/2 The Raman spectra are dominated by the porphyrin vibrational modes which are enhanced by resonance with the allowed electronic transitions in the visible and near-ultraviolet region. **1976** *Sci. Amer.* Jan. 50/2 The method of detection employed is an application of Werner Heisenberg's uncertainty principle and it consists in searching for an enhancement at a particular energy in the probability of interaction between known particles. Such an enhancement is called a resonance.

(ii) *Chem.* = MESOMERISM b.

1927 *Sci. Abstr.* A. XXX. 84 (*heading*) The problem of several bodies and resonance in quantum mechanics. [Abstr. of paper by W. Heisenberg in *Ztschr. f. Physik* (1926) XXXIX. 499.] **1931** *Physical Rev.* XXXVII. 489 In some cases there may be several ways of drawing valence bonds in a given compound. In such cases, the real situation is again a combination of the various possibilities, and on account of resonance the energy is lower than it would otherwise be. **1939** L. PAULING *Nature of Chem. Bond* ii. 35 In case that the extreme covalent structure A:B and the extreme ionic structure A^+B^- correspond separately to the same bond energy value, then the two structures will contribute equally to the actual state of the molecule, and the actual bond energy will be greater than the bond energy for either structure alone by an amount equal to the interaction energy of the two structures; that is, resonance between the two structures will stabilize the molecule. *Ibid.* xii. 408 A substance showing resonance between two or more valence-bond structures does not contain molecules with the configuration and properties usually associated with these structures. **1950** N. V. SIDGWICK *Chem. Elements* I. 525 From the crystal structure of sodium formate Zachariasen has shown that in the ion there is complete resonance between the two C—O groups. **1968** *Nature* 24 Aug. 801/2 This departure from planarity, by interfering with resonance, was expected to make the molecule so unstable that one hardly expected to find it. **1978** P. W. ATKINS *Physical Chem.* xv. 494 These structures are less stable than the Kekulé forms, because the A—D bonds, etc., are long and weak; therefore, although they must be allowed to take part in the resonance they contribute more weakly.

(iii) *spec.* (also ***magnetic resonance***) the transition of a particle possessing a magnetic moment between different quantum states in the presence of a magnetic field and electromagnetic radiation of the appropriate frequency; a spectroscopic technique (as ***electron spin resonance, nuclear magnetic resonance***, etc.) in which such phenomena are observed.

1938 *Physical Rev.* LIII. 318/2 The experimental procedure is to vary the homogeneous field for some given value of the frequency of the oscillating field until the resonance is observed by a drop in intensity at the detector and a subsequent recovery when the resonance value is passed. **1942** Nuclear magnetic resonance [see NUCLEAR *a.* 4]. **1952** *Physical Rev.* LXXXVIII. 951/1 We have observed conduction electron spin resonance absorption in fine particles of metallic sodium. **1957** *Endeavour* Oct. 185/1 When atomic nuclei are placed in a constant magnetic field of high intensity and subjected at the same time to a radio-frequency alternating field, a transfer of energy takes place between the high-frequency field and the nucleus. This phenomenon is known as nuclear magnetic resonance. **1965** R. N. DIXON *Spectroscopy & Structure* viii. 182 Electron spin resonance spectrometers usually use fields of the order of 3000 G, and the resonance is then at microwave frequencies of about 9000 Mc/sec. **1967** ATKINS & SYMONS *Struct. Inorg. Radicals* i. 7 Signals can be detected by nuclear magnetic resonance under conditions where lines are too broad to detect by electron spin resonance. **1977** *Nature* 17 Nov. 272/2 The spectrum of the enriched pigment contains one additional resonance at approximately 130·8 p.p.m. downfield from TSP-d_4.

(iv) *spec.* in *Nuclear Physics*, a short-lived particle, or an excited state of a particle, manifested as an increase, at certain well-defined energies, in the probability of interaction of other particles.

1964 *Physical Rev. Lett.* XIII. 64/2 We have searched for a possible spin alignment of the resonance by analyzing the strong decay into Ξ^* (1530) + π. **1965** *Science* 10 Sept. 1183/2 When the nucleon is exposed to any kind of high-energy beams, it is transformed into short-lived states of higher energy, which are known under various names, such as 'hyperons' or 'resonances'. **1969** *Times* 5 Feb. 13/7 The Xi resonances belong to the heavier class of nuclear particles known as baryons. **1972** G. L. WICK *Elem. Particles* iv. 60 Analyses of particle tracks also helped to reveal numerous short-lived particles called resonances. **1975** *Physics Bull.* Dec. 537/3 Excited states of the nucleons, so called resonances, can be produced by inelastic electron scattering.

e. *Mech.* (i) A condition in which an object or system is subjected to an oscillating force having a frequency close to that of a natural vibration of the object or system; the resulting amplification of the natural vibration.

1899 FRANKLIN & WILLIAMSON *Elem. Alternating Currents* v. 59 Mechanical resonance. If a periodic force of given maximum value and given frequency acts upon the body..the body will be set vibrating at the same frequency as that of the force, and the violence of the motion will be greatest, for the given value of the periodic force, when the frequency of the force is equal to the proper frequency of the body. **1913** *Phil. Mag.* XXVI. 125 If the lower bob is of solid metal..its damping coefficient will be small and the resonance in consequence probably inconveniently sharp. **1935** J. E. YOUNGER *Struct. Design Metal Airplanes* xv. 272 In the prevention of dangerous structural vibration, the first principle is to avoid resonance. **1952** D. E. CHRISTIE *Intermediate College Mech.* xii. 306 In practical engineering it is frequently desirable to keep forced oscillations well away from resonance. **1959** *Listener* 5 Feb. 252/1 Where the lengths of waves and ship are almost equal, we experience severe pitch and heave motions... This 'resonance' can be destroyed in two ways. **1974** *Encycl. Brit. Micropædia* VIII. 525/1 Mechanical resonance..is known to have built up to such large proportions as to be destructive, as in the case of the Tacoma Narrows Bridge.

(ii) Amplification of wave or tidal motion in a body of water when this motion has the same frequency as a natural vibration of the body of water.

1955 P. H. KUENEN *Realms of Water* ii. 37 Lake Baikal..has..no resonance whatever and the tide is less than one inch. *Ibid.* 42 In the Malay Archipelago..resonances in the separate basins with natural periods of oscillation. **1975** *New Yorker* 12 May 94/2 Certain harbors sometimes have problems with a phenomenon known as resonance, wherein waves that might be, say, two feet high on the outside build up energy within the harbor until waves in there stand ten feet high or higher.

f. *Astr.* The circumstance or phenomenon of the periods of revolution of two bodies about a single primary being, exactly or approximately, in the ratio of two small integers.

1923 *Astron. Jrnl.* XXXV. 70/2 From the mechanical point of view, the chief feature of the motion of an asteroid of the Trojan group is due to resonance. **1928** *Bull. Amer. Math. Soc.* XXXIV. 283 Here the millions of 'stones' or 'rocks' which must constitute those rings revolve round Saturn and resonances are caused by the action of its larger satellites. **1968** R. A. Lyttleton *Mysteries Solar Syst.* vii. 229 The adopted value implied a period of the unknown planet of some 218 years, which is not very different from three times the period of Uranus, namely 84 years. It would be sufficiently near in fact to give a mild resonance, because of the approximate 3:1 ratio. **1979** *Science* 5 Oct. 39/1 Mimas has been implicated because it orbits Saturn in exactly twice the time that any particles happening to orbit within the Cassini division would. This whole-number relationship of orbital periods is called resonance.

g. *fig.* and other *transf.* uses.

1607 R. C[arew] tr. *Estienne's World of Wonders* 298 So ought our hearts..to haue no other resonance but of good thoughts. **1828** Carlyle *Misc.* (1857) I. 207 He has a resonance in his bosom for every note of human feeling. **1876** Geo. Eliot *Dan. Der.* II. xvii, Hints of this, intended to be complimentary, found an angry resonance in him. **1892** J. Sully *Human Mind* II. xiv. 58 That the corporeal resonance does form an essential ingredient in emotion is abundantly proved by a variety of facts. **1925** J. Laird *Our Minds & Their Bodies* I. 21 It is the commonest thing in the world to say that we are 'not ourselves' when our bodies, so to say, ring differently to us from their normal resonance. **1939** *Scrutiny* VII. 441 In particular, his temperament was painfully out of resonance with his father's. **1956** Day & de la Warr *New Worlds beyond Atom* v. 34 A part of the wave-form emitted by the drug forms a discord with the radiations of the disease while another part of it is in resonance with the organ which is being treated. **1962** E. F. Haden et al. *Resonance-Theory for Linguistics* 48 Resonance in Linguistics is a bond, imagined as a hybrid or a wave, linking two language entities. **1965** J. M. Stephens *Psychol. of Classroom Learning* vii. 176/2 In real life many problems have been solved by this seemingly mysterious, unconscious 'resonance'. **1967** E. H. Lenneberg *Biol. Foundations Lang.* ix. 378 Perhaps a better metaphor still is the concept of resonance... Exposure to adult language behavior has an excitatory effect upon the actualization process much the same way a certain frequency may have..upon a specific resonator; the object begins to vibrate in the presence of the sound. In the case of language onset, the energy required for the resonance is, in a sense, supplied by the individual himself. **1976** *Southern Even. Echo* (Southampton) 16 Nov. 3/5 For much of the piece there is an extra resonance and significance about Gray's otherwise-familiar anti-hero. **1977** A. Sheridan tr. *J. Lacan's Écrits* iii. 86 What is redundant as far as information is concerned is precisely that which does duty as resonance in speech.

2. a. The quality of reinforcing or prolonging a sound by vibration.

1669 Boyle *Physiol. Ess., Absol. Rest* §7 Some famous Lutes..attained not their full seasoning and best resonance, till they were about fourscore year old. **1835–6** *Todd's Cycl. Anat.* I. 481/1 Intended for the reception of the sounds produced by the resonance of the bony case just described. **1875** Ellis tr. *Helmholtz' Sensat. Tone* I. v. §7 The investigation of the resonance of the cavity of the mouth is of great importance.

b. The enhancement of one colour by its proximity to another or others. Cf. resonant *a.* 2 b.

1933 *Burlington Mag.* Jan. 3/1, I knew that Titian was a master of rich and sumptuous colour. I knew how splendidly he could evoke from his blues and crimsons their fullest and deepest resonance.

3. *attrib.*, as ***resonance apparatus, box, frequency, particle, vibration***, etc.; **resonance absorption** *Nuclear Physics*, absorption of energy or of a particle under conditions of resonance; *spec.* = next; **resonance capture** *Nuclear Physics*, absorption of a particle by an atomic nucleus which occurs only for certain well-defined values of particle energy; **resonance chamber** = resonator 2; **resonance energy**, (*a*) an energy value at which resonance occurs; (*b*) *Chem.*, the extent of stabilization of a molecular structure attributed to mesomerism; **resonance fluorescence**, fluorescence in which the light emitted has the same wavelength as that which excites the emission; **resonance hybrid** *Chem.*, a molecular structure which is a mesomeric combination of a number of forms; **resonance radiation**, (the radiation emitted in) resonance fluorescence; **resonance Raman spectrum** [Raman], a Raman spectrum excited by light having a frequency equal to that of a band in the absorption spectrum of the scattering substance (see quot. 1975[1]); so ***resonance Raman effect, spectroscopy***, etc.; **resonance scattering** *Nuclear Physics*, elastic scattering of a particle by an atomic nucleus at an energy of the incident particle for which the scattering cross-section is large compared with that for adjacent values of the energy (cf. *potential scattering* s.v. potential *sb.* 4 c); **resonance stabilization** *Chem.* = *resonance energy* (*b*).

1945 H. D. Smyth *Gen. Acct. Devel. Atomic Energy Mil. Purposes* iv. 24 The term '*resonance absorption' is used to describe the very strong absorption of neutrons by U-238 when the neutron energies are in certain definite portions of the energy region. **1952** [see sense 1 d (iii) above]. **1961** G. R. Choppin *Exper. Nuclear Chem.* viii. 114 In indium a resonance absorption occurs for neutrons with a kinetic energy of 1·44 ev. *a* **1879** Randegger *Singing* 11 The chest, mouth, or head..only act respectively as the '*resonance apparatus' of the voice. **1873** S. Taylor *Sound & Music* (1896) 85 This convenient adjunct to a tuning-fork goes by the name of a *resonance-box. **1937** G. Gamow *Struct. Atomic Nuclei* xi. 224 We may have here a case of *resonance-capture. **1964** M. Gowing *Britain & Atomic Energy 1939–45* i. 40 Various other ways of reducing the capture of neutrons by resonance capture..were considered. **1896** Curtis *Voice Building* (1901) 74 The condition and shape of the *resonance cavities..give to the human voice a peculiar beauty and timbre. **1919** D. Jones *Outl. Eng. Phonetics* vi. 15 The effect of a *resonance chamber in modifying quality of tone may be illustrated experimentally. **1962** A. Nisbett *Technique Sound Studio* iii. 59 The mouth, nose and throat cavities act as resonance chambers for sound coming from the vocal cords. **1931** *Jrnl. Amer. Chem. Soc.* LIII. 1368 The energy of the bond is largely the *resonance or interchange energy of two electrons. **1941** in M. Gowing *Britain & Atomic Energy 1939–45* (1964) 430 Neutrons of certain critical, or resonance, energies are strongly absorbed by uranium without causing fission. **1965** Phillips & Williams *Inorg. Chem.* I. iii. 75 The difference between the computed binding energy of a hypothetical structure and that computed using all possible structures, i.e. the actual binding energy of the real molecule, is called the resonance energy. **1925** *Sci. Abstr.* A. XXVIII. 121 In the case of *resonance fluorescence the re-emitted line possesses a greater Doppler width than the incident line. **1977** I. M. Campbell *Energy & Atmosphere* viii. 260 (*caption*) Schematic diagram of apparatus for the resonance fluorescence detection of hydroxyl radicals in air. **1921** W. H. Eccles *Continuous Wave Wireless Telegr.* iii. 172 When an external sine force acts upon a vibrator, whether at the *resonance frequency or not, it gradually builds up a vibrating motion to a definite final amplitude. **1974** *Encycl. Brit. Macropædia* XIX. 101/2 Wind supplied the power causing the bridge to vibrate at one of its torsional resonance frequencies without sufficient damping. **1939** L. Pauling *Nature Chem. Bond* xii. 407 Each of these tautomers in its normal state is represented..by a *resonance hybrid of this structure and others. **1964** N. G. Clark *Mod. Org. Chem.* xxv. 525 The true structure of benzene is..a resonance hybrid, to which the two Kekulé formulae..contribute equally. **1975** *Sci. Amer.* May 43/2 Other *resonance particles decay by the 'strong' interaction in about 10^{-23} second. **1905** R. W. Wood in *Phil. Mag.* X. 514 Repeated efforts have been made..to detect a lateral emission of yellow light by sodium vapour when in the act of absorbing sodium light... This seems to be the first case found of the phenomenon, which it may perhaps be well to style *resonance radiation, to distinguish it from fluorescence. **1928** [see quench *v.* 3 d]. **1963** R. W. Ditchburn *Light* (ed. 2) xvii. 661 Sodium absorbs and re-emits as resonance radiation the two well-known yellow lines at wavelengths 5890 Å. and 5896 Å. **1960** tr. Shorygin & Krushinskii in *Soviet Physics Doklady* V. 793 The possibility of observing *resonance Raman spectra is limited to a considerable degree by the loss of light due to absorption. **1962** *Pure & Appl. Chem.* IV. 87 The study of the resonance Raman effect can contribute not only to the extension of the technique of Raman spectroscopy, but also to an investigation of the nature of the interaction of light with matter. **1975** *Jrnl. Chem. Soc.: Dalton Trans.* 381/1 When a molecule..is excited with a laser beam whose wavenumber corresponds or closely corresponds with the band maximum of a strongly allowed electronic transition of the molecule, then a rigorous resonance Raman (r.r.) spectrum may be obtained. Such spectra are normally characterised by an enormous increase in the intensity of a totally symmetric fundamental of the molecule together with the appearance of long overtone progressions in this same fundamental. **1975** *Nature* 25 Dec. 770/1 The results of Lewis and Spoonhower using resonance Raman spectroscopy imply the existence of a strong complex between retinal and a tryptophan residue in rhodopsin. **1937** Bethe & Placzek in *Physical Rev.* LI. 462/1 Near resonance, the *resonance scattering σ_2 must be added to the potential scattering. **1955** A. E. S. Green *Nuclear Physics* xiii. 456 These deviations are attributed to the interference between the potential and resonance scattering associated with the *l*th partial wave. **1978** *Nature* 26 Oct. 730/1 Resonance scattering of light from a beam of free atoms is an ideal technique for making precise absolute measurements of the shift in wavelength of the light relative to the reference wavelength of the beam atoms. **1939** L. Pauling *Nature Chem. Bond* i. 10 Because the resonating system does not have a structure intermediate between those involved in the resonance, but..a structure which is further changed by the *resonance stabilization, I prefer not to use the word 'mesomerism'..for the resonance phenomenon. **1952** [see oxyanion]. **1978** K. Yates *Hückel Molecular Orbital Theory* iii. 118 In order to evaluate the resonance stabilization of benzene, as represented by the formulation (XI), a comparison should be made with cyclohexatrienes possessing the benzene geometry. **1909** *Westm. Gaz.* 4 Sept. 10/1 If the period of vibration of the two parts is the same '*resonance vibrations' are set up.

So **'resonancy**. *rare*⁻¹.

1681 H. More *Expos. Dan.* Pref. 10 There might be a Paronomasticall Resonancy of words in his mind.

resonant ('rɛzənənt), *a.* and *sb.* [ad. pres. pple. of L. *resonāre* to resound. Cf. F. *résonnant* (†*resonant*), Sp. and Pg. *resonante*, It. *risonante*.]

A. *adj.* **1. a.** Of sounds: Re-echoing, resounding; continuing to sound or ring.

1592 *Conspir. Pretended Ref.* Pref. iv, An heape of earnest and resonant, but vndigested wordes. **1667** Milton *P.L.* xi. 559 His volant touch..Fled and pursu'd transverse the resonant fugue. **1860** W. J. C. Muir *Pagan or Christian?* 105 The clear dignity of its resonant expression [is] becoming a feeble whisper. **1873** S. Taylor *Sound & Music* (1896) 80 A column of air is easily set in resonant vibration by a note of suitable pitch. **1877** Black *Green Past.* iv, Although he had never made the gallery of the Union tremble with resonant eloquence.

fig. **1842** Mrs. Browning *Bk. Poets* Wks. (1904) 641/2 Massinger's more resonant majesty. **1883** Tyndall in *Contemp. Rev.* XLIV. 38 The name and fame of Rumford..were resonant in Europe at the beginning of this century.

b. *Phonet.* Of consonants: liquid or nasal. Cf. the sb.

1943 K. L. Pike *Phonetics* vii. 144 The *sonorants* are nonvocoid resonants and comprise the lateral resonant orals and resonant nasals (e.g. [m], [n], and [l]). **1948** W. F. Twaddell in *Language* XXIV. 141 Before the resonant consonants, only /e/, /a/, and /u/ occurred regularly.

2. a. Of bodies: Causing reinforcement or prolongation of sound, esp. by vibration.

1685 Boyle *Effects Motion* vii. 87 The peculiar kind of tremulous motion into which the parts of the resonant body are put. **1850** Mrs. Browning *Poems* II. 98 The resonant steam-eagles Follow far on the direction of her..hand. **1871** Tyndall *Fragm. Sci.* (ed. 6) I. iii. 81 Mounted thus upon their resonant cases, you hear them loudly sounding the same musical note. **1897** *Allbutt's Syst. Med.* IV. 655 The lungs remain resonant when the larger bronchial tubes are filled with gelatine.

b. Of colours: emphasizing each other by contrast.

1887 *Portfolio* XVIII. 233/2 His painting has ever become slighter, higher in tone and less full and resonant in colour.

3. Of places: Echoing or resounding *with* something.

1813 Shelley *Q. Mab* viii. 103 Fertile valleys, resonant with bliss. **1872** Yeats *Techn. Hist. Comm.* 194 As the Greek and Roman music passed away, the sombre groves of ancient Germany became resonant with sound.

4. a. Involving, exhibiting, or bringing about electrical resonance (resonance 1 c).

1888 *Electrician* 28 Sept. 663/2 Drawing the micrometer terminals so far apart that sparks can only be made to pass by means of resonant action. **1925** Resonant frequency [sense 5 below]. **1938** *Jrnl. Appl. Physics* IX. 654/2 Such a resonator may often be equivalent to a conventional resonant circuit. **1947** R. Lee *Electronic Transformers & Circuits* vii. 192 The heights of resonant peaks and frequency distance between peaks depend upon circuit *Q* and coefficient of coupling *k*. **1959** K. Henney *Radio Engin. Handbk.* (ed. 5) v. 27 Multiple resonance imposes practical limits on the way in which resonant circuits may be combined. **1964** R. F. Ficchi *Electr. Interference* v. 56 The isolation offered by the turns eliminates resonant effects. **1966** *New Scientist* 15 Dec. 627/1 The device, known as a resonant-gate transistor, was developed by a team of scientists in..Pittsburgh.

b. *Physics* and *Chem.* Pertaining to, involving, exhibiting, or taking part in any other kind of resonance.

1934 Resonant frequency [sense 5 below]. **1944** L. F. & M. Fieser *Org. Chem.* xx. 523 Results of the ozonization experiments cited above accord with the concept of two resonant Kekulé forms contributing in an equal extent to the structure. **1960** Dicke & Wittke *Introd. Quantum Mechanics* xvi. 291 When the energy of the incoming particles corresponds to such a state, a resonant condition is said to occur, in which the scattering cross-section is markedly greater than for nonresonant energies. **1965** *Physics Lett.* XIV. 159/1 The enhancement observed [in pion-nucleon interaction] need not necessarily be identified with a resonant state. **1973** *Sci. Amer.* Nov. 125/3 The reason is that one second is about the period at which a 10-inch pendulum vibrates naturally, that is, one second is the frequency of vibration to which the pendulum is resonant. **1976** *Chem. Physics Lett.* XLI. 292/1 The resonant electronic transition is the axial $d_z{}^2 \leftarrow d_z{}^2$ transition at 17450 cm^{-1}.

5. Special collocations: **resonant cavity**, a cavity resonator (see resonator 3 b); **resonant frequency**, a frequency at which resonance (of any kind) takes place; **resonant scattering** *Nuclear Physics* = *resonance scattering* s.v. resonance 3.

1945 *Nature* 15 Sept. 323/1 Dr. J. T. Randall applied the resonant-cavity technique to the relatively ineffective magnetron of pre-war days, and made of it a radically new and immensely powerful device which remains the heart of every modern radar equipment. **1955** *Science* 9 Dec. 1132/3 The deuteron beam..then enters the first of two 48-megacycle resonant-cavity accelerator sections. **1925** W. Greenwood *Text-bk. Wireless Telegr. & Teleph.* i. 19 The resonant frequency is..equal to the natural frequency when the damping is negligible. **1934** J. P. Den Hartog *Mech. Vibrations* ii. 52 The forced frequency coincides exactly with the natural frequency... This important phenomenon is known as 'resonance', and the natural frequency is sometimes called also the 'resonant frequency'. **1964** R. F. Ficchi *Electr. Interference* v. 49 The smaller the total inductance, the higher the resonant frequency. **1948** *Physical Rev.* LXXIV. 926/1 The present work was begun with the object of detecting nuclear resonant scattering from Mg^{24} nuclei which are excited by resonant radiation from the radioactive Na^{24} nuclei. **1955** [see *potential scattering* s.v. potential *sb.* 4 c]. **1963** W. E. Burcham *Nuclear Physics* xiii. 484 From the observed cross-section for the resonant scattering effect, with appropriate account taken of the thermal broadening,..a total width of $(2{\cdot}1 \pm 0{\cdot}4) \times 10^{-5}$ eV for the 412 keV level of ^{198}Hg was found.

B. *sb.* A liquid or nasal consonant.

1875 Whitney *Life Lang.* iv. 63 The result is the class of nasals (or 'resonants'), m, n, and ng (as in *singing*). **1899** *Allbutt's Syst. Med.* VII. 449 Voiced Nasal Resonants. **1948** W. F. Twaddell in *Language* XXIV. 141, /i/ before resonants was at best very rare. **1956** J. Whatmough *Language* 37 Thus we have the class known as resonants (e.g. *l, m*). **1970** B. M. H. Strang *Hist. Eng.* ix. 406 The third sub-system consists of resonants, i.e. sounds which may or may not have syllabic function (thus corresponding to approximants, liquids and nasals in P[resent-day] E[nglish]). **1976** *Archivum Linguisticum* VII. 167 The gemination becomes an additional argument for the reconstruction of laryngeals next to a resonant or *s*.

Hence **'resonantly** *adv.*

1685 Boyle *Effects Motion* vii. 88 To which note it answered very resonantly, and not sensibly to others, which we made trial of. **1865** *Daily Tel.* 28 Oct. 3/5 Now shrilly ringing, now resonantly surging through nave and aisle. **1880** L. Wallace *Ben-Hur* 426 To get to the Praetorium, as the Romans resonantly styled the palace of Herod on Mount Zion. **1971** *Nature* 15 Oct. 469/2 From the observational viewpoint the soft X-ray enhancement..can be interpreted in terms of solar X-rays resonantly scattered in the Earth's atmosphere. **1977** *Gramophone* May 1737/2 Here if anything he is even more resonantly impressive than he was for Klemperer. **1978** *Sci. Amer.* June 124/1 The audio oscillator was tuned to resonantly oscillate the water.. so as to cause vibrational standing waves to form on the surface.

resonate (ˈrɛzəneɪt), *v.* [f. L. *resonāre* to resound: see -ATE[3].] **1.** *intr.* To produce or exhibit resonance. Also *fig.*

1873 S. TAYLOR *Sound & Music* (1896) 117 The wires of the corresponding note will of course resonate with it. **1896** CURTIS *Voice Building* (1901) 140 In exit the tone should be allowed to resonate in all the natural acoustic cavities. **1946** *Physical Rev.* LXIX. 37 It [*sc.* a resonant cavity] was adjusted to resonate at about 30 mc/sec. **1955** R. S. H. BOULDING *Radar Pocket Bk.* vi. 72 An artificial line can be charged from an a.c. supply without a rectifier by making a choke in the charging circuit resonate, at the supply frequency, with the capacitance of the line. **1956** *Jrnl. Chem. Physics* XXIV. 468/1 In NMR spectra nuclei which give signals at the same applied field or resonate with the same Larmor frequency may be considered magnetically equivalent. **1976** *Publishers Weekly* 27 Sept. 80/1 Prose.. resonating with the illustrations.

b. *spec.* in *Chem.* To exhibit mesomerism (cf. RESONANCE 1 d(ii)). Const. *among* or *between* different structures, as if a real physical alternation were occurring.

1933 PAULING & WHELAND in *Jrnl. Chem. Physics* I. 369 In the first step the C—C bond breaks and there are formed two phenyl-methyl radicals, which however can resonate between only the structures A and B of Fig. 3. **1957** G. E. HUTCHINSON *Treat. Limnol.* I. iii. 196 The molecule resonates between the following structures. **1965** G. W. WHELAND *Resonance in Org. Chem.* i. 7 Only by exercising the utmost care in the choice of words can one avoid the appearance of implying that the molecules.. are oscillating back and forth among the several structures, and hence that these structures must possess real physical significance... The common statements that the hybrid *resonates* among the structures and that the structures *resonate* with one another almost unavoidably give this quite erroneous impression. **1976** *Sci. Amer.* Nov. 59/1 Perhaps the baryon resonates between these configurations, much as the benzene ring resonates between its various possible structures.

2. *trans.* To act as a resonator for; to amplify by resonance.

1904 *Physical Rev.* XVIII. 231 Having the radiating aërial resonating the primary circuit, it is now necessary to have a second primary circuit in tune with the first. **1975** *Sci. Amer.* July 48/2 Signals become convolved when sounds are reverberated or resonated or, in the case of photographs, when images are blurred.

Hence **ˈresonating** *ppl. a.*; ***resonating chamber*** = RESONATOR 2.

1873 S. TAYLOR *Sound & Music* (1896) 135 A reed does not need to be associated with a resonating column in order to produce a musical sound. **1912** *Chem. Abstr.* VI. 3220 An extensive research on the properties and behavior of resonating gas mols. **1933** *Jrnl. Chem. Physics* I. 611 A negative carbon atom, with one unshared and three shared electron pairs, occurs rather often in resonating structures, as in carbon monoxide, [etc.]. **1938** Resonating chamber [see RESONATOR 2b]. **1959** E. PULGRAM *Introd. Spectrogr. Speech* vii. 55 The resonating tuning fork continues to operate for a while after the struck fork has been stopped. **1968** B. M. H. STRANG *Mod. Eng. Structure* (ed. 2) 35 The character of the sound produced can be varied over a considerable range by changing the shape of the resonating chambers. **1974** D. M. ADAMS *Inorg. Solids* vii. 230 In PbI_2, with its inert pair of *s*-electrons, bonding is via two resonating *p*-electrons. **1974** R. C. HIBBELER *Engin. Mech.* xxii. 958 Resonating vibrations can cause tremendous stress and rapid failure of parts.

resonator (ˈrɛzəneɪtə(r)). [Agent-noun, on L. types, f. *resonāre* to resound.]

1. An instrument responding to one single note, and used for its detection when combined with other sounds.

a **1869** DONKIN *Acoustics* I. (1870) 92 In order to distinguish the higher and fainter ones [*sc.* harmonic tones], it is necessary to put the ear in communication with resonators. **1876** tr. *Blaserna's Sound* viii. 171 The apparatus.. is composed of 8 resonators adapted to the harmonic series of the fundamental note C. **1898** *Allbutt's Syst. Med.* V. 467 It has been shewn.. by means of resonators that the normal heart-sound consists of two notes.

2. a. An appliance for increasing sound by resonance; a body or object which produces resonance.

1871 DARWIN *Desc. Man* II. xiii. (1890) 376 The œsophagus.. becomes much swollen; and this probably acts as a resonator. **1873** S. TAYLOR *Sound & Music* (1896) 120 The sound-board of the pianoforte.. is in fact a solid resonator. **1894** BOTTONE *Electr. Instr.* 176 A paper resonator.. greatly reinforces the sound when the phonograph is speaking.

b. *spec.* (See quot. 1888.)

1888 *Pall Mall G.* 4 May 1/3 These primary or laryngeal vocal tones are reinforced by the resonators, that is, by the portion of the larynx above the vocal cords, the upper throat or pharynx, the nose, and the mouth. **1938** *Oxf. Compan. Mus.* 994/2 The frontal sinuses.. have apparently considerable value as resonators: it is said that the Australian natives have a great want of resonance in their speech due to the small size of these sinuses. All the resonating chambers or passages mentioned above.. are in direct communication with the air which has passed through the vocal cords. **1970** A. C. GIMSON *Introd. Pronunc. Eng.* (ed. 2) 11 These cavities [*sc.* pharynx, mouth, nasal cavity] function as the principal *resonators* of the note produced in the larynx. *Ibid.* 19 The way in which the speaker's vibrator and resonators function together.

3. *Electr.* **a.** An apparatus used for the detection of radio waves; also, any device which displays electrical resonance.

1889 *Phil. Mag.* XXVIII. 125 For this proof we must give somewhat different dimensions to our apparatus in order to be able to introduce electric resonators into its interior. **1893** SIR R. BALL *Story of Sun* 121 A photographic plate, or a Hertzian resonator, to astonish us. **1898** *Edin. Rev.* Oct. 301 With a 'resonator' of similar construction.. he was able to detect answering sparks. **1943** *Proc. IRE* XXXI. 448/1 The simple circuit of Fig. 14(a) is well known as the Hertzian oscillator and is readily recognized as a lumped capacitance associated with a single-turn inductor. At frequencies up to several hundreds of megacycles such a resonator is quite practical.

b. *spec.* (in full *cavity resonator*), a hollow enclosure with conducting walls which is capable of containing electromagnetic fields having particular frequencies of oscillation, and of exchanging electrical energy with them; such devices are used esp. for the amplification or detection of microwaves.

1936 *Proc. IRE* XXIV. 1320 [All of these terminals may act as more or less sharply resonant systems... They may.. be thought of as electromagnetic analogues of the Helmholtz resonator.] *Ibid.* 1324 A cylindrical resonator attached to the hollow tube system. **1943** *Ibid.* XXXI. 447/2 The flexibility of the Klystron is seriously limited by the fact that cavity resonators are permanently attached to the grids and thus form an integral part of the tube itself. **1952** REINTJES & COATE *Princ. Radar* (Mass. Inst. Technol. Radar School Staff) (ed. 3) ix. 613 Cavity resonators are hollow metal-walled chambers fitted with devices for admitting and extracting electromagnetic energy. **1956** *Nature* 10 Mar. 470/2 During the past four or five years,.. the Radiation Laboratory has concentrated much effort.. on the construction of a linear accelerator of the cavity-resonator type. **1966** *McGraw-Hill Encycl. Sci. & Technol.* II. 577/2 Coaxial cavity resonators are often used as wavemeters, particularly for lower than microwave frequencies. **1975** D. G. FINK *Electronics Engineers' Handbk.* IX. 29 In the reflex Klystron a single resonator is used to modulate the beam and extract of energy from it, making the tube simple and easy to tune.

4. An object or system which resonates, in any other sense.

1897 *Abstr. Physical Papers* (Physical Soc.) III. 356 Next a resonator of a perfectly-conducting material is imagined to be introduced. This resonator, while absorbing energy from the incident radiation and radiating it again without loss, will, in general, change the character of the radiation, either in its frequency, the law of its damping, or both. **1914** J. H. JEANS *Rep. Radiation & Quantum Theory* ii. 9 Planck.. supposed that the emission and absorption were accomplished by 'resonators' of perfectly definite periods. **1949** KOESTLER *Insight & Outlook* p. ix, The theory of memory traces as selective resonator systems suggested in various forms by Jacques Loeb.. and others. **1959** E. PULGRAM *Introd. Spectrogr. Speech* vii. 55 This effect of sympathetic vibration is called resonance, and the object activated by it is a resonator. **1974** G. REECE tr. *Hund's Hist. Quantum Theory* ii. 24 He [*sc.* Planck] constructed a model for the emission and absorption of radiation at the walls of a black body by assuming the presence of resonators. **1979** *Sci. Amer.* Mar. 81/1 It was soon learned that a particular wavelength could be selected by designing an optical resonator that will allow only the chosen wavelength to pass repeatedly through the amplifying dye cell... The resonator consisted of a partially reflecting glass plate at one end of the laser and a diffraction grating at the other.

ˈresonatory, *a. rare.* [See RESONATE *v.* and -ORY.] Producing resonance.

1879 SAYCE *Sci. Lang.* (1881) I. iv. 231 The partial tones .. may be.. detected by the help of resonatory instruments. **1961** L. F. BROSNAHAN *Sounds of Language* i. 2 The process of vocal sound production in language appears on analysis to consist basically of the production of an airstream, the conversion of some of the kinetic energy of this airstream into acoustic energy in the form of a complex of sound waves, and the subsequent resonatory modulation of that complex.

resonn, obs. form of RAISIN.

resorb (rɪˈsɔːb), *v.* [ad. L. *resorbēre*, f. *re-* RE- + *sorbēre* to drink in. Cf. F. *résorber*, Sp. and Pg. *resorber*, It. *risorbire*.] To absorb again; *esp.* in *Physiol.*, to absorb into the circulation (material already in the body, esp. material that has been digested or broken down).

1640 R. BAILLIE *Canterb. Self-conv.* Postscr. 20 Their.. aspersions, which yet ye have a stomach to resorbe, to spew them out once againe. **1730** SHORT *Diss. Tea* 57 The Liquids .. are neither exhaled nor resorbed by the Veins. **1772** PRIESTLEY in *Phil. Trans.* LXII. 190 The generation of air, .. except what might be absorbed by quicksilver or resorbed by the substance itself. **1826** SOUTHEY *Vind. Eccl. Angl.* 177 Human souls, which like sparks.. were borne aloft, and then .. were resorbed into the pit. **1876** SWINBURNE *Erechtheus* 1563 [The host] Drew seaward as with one wide wail of waves Resorbed with reluctation. **1901** J. S. MARSHALL *Princ. & Pract. Operative Dentistry* iv. 76 The absorbent organ secretes.. a digestive fluid or soluble ferment which dissolves or digests the dental tissues and alveolar walls, and prepares them to be resorbed. *Ibid.* xxxiv. 509 Bone is resorbed through the action of the osteoclast cells. **1902** *Brit. Med. Jrnl.* No. 2154. 918 The extravasated blood was resorbed. **1928** MOORE & KEY tr. *Leriche & Policard's Normal & Path. Physiol. of Bone* iv. 71 If.. one brings about increase of circulation, bone in the epiphyses is resorbed to the extent of detaching itself from the investing cartilage and becoming very friable. **1967** M. E. HALE *Biol. Lichens* viii. 118 The acids are not resorbed by the hyphae. **1968** R. D. MARTIN tr. *Wickler's Mimicry in Plants & Animals* xi. 107 The flea will resorb its eggs if the female host miscarries.

Hence **reˈsorbed** *ppl. a.*; **reˈsorbing** *ppl. a.*, undergoing resorption. Also **reˈsorbable** *a.*, that may be resorbed; **reˈsorbence**, reabsorption, backward flow; **reˈsorbent** *a.*, absorbing again.

a **1800** WODHULL (T.), Again resorbent ocean's wave Receives the waters, which it gave. **1803** *Med. Jrnl.* IX. 95 Digitalis.. augments the oscillation of the resorbent vessels. **1881** W. CORY *Lett. & Jrnls.* (1897) 472 The forward plunge and resorbence of a wave. **1889** *Science* 29 Mar. 232/2 Not until the silicates are developed, and the granitic quartz begins to form, does the resorbent action discontinue. **1910** J. P. BUCKLEY *Mod. Dental Materia Medica* II. 315 (*heading*) Resorbed root. **1928** MOORE & KEY tr. *Leriche & Policard's Normal & Path. Physiol. of Bone* iv. 85 In resorbing callus the cells were hypertrophied. **1962** K. F. LAGLER et al. *Ichthyology* viii. 257 When the fish descends.. the resorbent capillary network collapses so as to enlarge the area of contact of the gas gland for rapid secretion of gases into the bladder. **1967** *Archivum Immunol. et Therapiae Exper.* XV. 809 (*caption*) Section through a resorbable 256 Walker tumor. **1973** *Nature* 9 Mar. 135/2 Seven [voles] were pregnant but four had resorbing embryos. **1976** *Biomed.* XXV. 131/1 Porous resorbable ceramics have been found to be most suitable [as bone substitutes] since they encourage replacement of resorbed ceramic with new bone.

resorcin (rɪˈzɔːsɪn). *Chem.* Also **-ine.** [f. RES(IN) + ORCIN.]

1. = RESORCINOL.

1868 WATTS *Dict. Chem.* V. 82 *Resorcin*, $C_6H_6O_2$, a compound homologous with orcin.. produced by the action of potash on galbanum. **1880** *Jrnl. Soc. Arts* Apr. 446/2 The same body will act on resorcine to produce a colour only differing from the last in that it contains hydroxyl instead of amido groups. **1899** *Allbutt's Syst. Med.* VIII. 517 Sulphur has a peculiar action of its own, but allied to it are ichthyol and perhaps resorcin.

2. *attrib.* and *Comb.*, as ***resorcin-ammonia, -sulphonic***, etc.; ***resorcin brown, green.***

1872 WATTS *Dict. Chem.* 1st Suppl. 993 Resorcin-ammonia.. is formed by passing dry ammonia gas into a solution of resorcin in anhydrous ether. **1881** *Nature* XXIV. 48 The salts of resorcinsulphonic acid. **1897** *Allbutt's Syst. Med.* III. 558 Boas' resorcin test is also useful. **1899** *Ibid.* VIII. 705 Resorcin pastes.. are excellent, if temporary, remedies. **1905** CAIN & THORPE *Synth. Dyestuffs* 42 The fast green or Resorcin green is.. produced by the action of nitrous acid on resorcinol. *Ibid.* 62 The first.. disazo-dye stuff was the Resorcin brown discovered by Wallach in 1881.

resorcinol (rɪˈzɔːsɪnɒl). *Chem.* [f. RESORCIN + -OL.] A dihydric phenol formerly obtained from galbanum or other resins but now made synthetically, and used as a dye, in the manufacture of phenol-formaldehyde resins, etc.; = RESORCIN.

1881 WATTS *Dict. Chem.* 3rd Suppl. 1747 Resorcinol introduced into the animal organism is converted into a sulphonic acid. **1892** *Phot. Ann.* II. 94 A small proportion of resorcinol greatly increases the stability of the solution. **1949** *Thorpe's Dict. Appl. Chem.* (ed. 4) IX. 476/1 Of the dihydric phenols, resorcinol is industrially second to hydroquinone in importance, and is used in considerable amount. **1964** N. G. CLARK *Mod. Org. Chem.* xxi. 439 The three dihydroxybenzenes are called catechol, resorcinol, and hydroquinone (quinol).

attrib. **1892** *Phot. Ann.* II. 108 Derivatives in which a halogen is substituted in the resorcinol residue [etc.]. **1959** *Times* 27 Apr. (Rubber Industry Suppl.) p. vii/3 In this country all tire cord is impregnated by an aqueous process.. using the mixed latices and resorcinol-formaldehyde resin. **1972** *Materials & Technol.* V. iv. 95 Resorcinol adhesives, with the added advantage of being neutral or nearly so, are superior to all others as adhesives for wood, giving exceptional durability.

resorcylic (rɛzɔːˈsɪlɪk), *a. Chem.* [f. RESORC-IN + -YL + -IC.] Pertaining to, derived from, resorcinol.

1894 MORLEY & MUIR *Watt's Dict. Chem.* IV. 400/2 Resorcylic acid. *Ibid.*, Resorcylic aldehyde.

†**reˈsore**, *v. Obs. rare.* (See quot. 1486.)

1486 *Bk. St. Albans* E viij b, And after when he dowblith and turnyth agayne Then he resoorth as goode hunteres saynne. **1602** *2nd Pt. Return fr. Parnass.* II. v. 937 By that I knewe that they had the hare and on foote, and by and by I might see him sore and resore, prick and reprick.

†**resorp**, variant of (or error for) RESORB *v.*

1656 FLECKNOE *Ten Years Trav.* 119 These must unsay what they have said, and like venomous Beasts, resorp their own poyson.

resorption (rɪˈsɔːpʃən). [Noun of action, on L. types, f. L. *resorbēre* RESORB *v.* So F. *résorption*.] The fact or process of reabsorption, *spec.* of an organ, tissue, or excretion. Cf. RESORB *v.*

1818–20 E. THOMPSON tr. *Cullen's Nosology* (ed. 3) 239 Scrophula fugax: very simple.., generally occurring on resorption from ulcers of the hand. **1876** DUHRING *Dis. Skin* 66 It may terminate either in resorption, suppuration, or hypertrophy. **1889** *Science* 29 Mar. 232/2 While the silicates are crystallizing in a molten mass, if porphyritic quartz is present it undergoes resorption. **1902** *Brit. Med. Jrnl.* No. 2154. 918 App. 12 Resorption of body cells (liver, kidney, &c.) frequently takes place. **1910** LAKE & RASTALL *Textbk. Geol.* xiii. 232 These phenocrysts have often undergone a certain amount of corrosion, or resorption. **1928** MOORE & KEY tr. *Leriche & Policard's Normal & Path. Physiol. of Bone* iv. 71 When osteoclasts are present there is resorption. **1962** BLAKE & TROTT *Periodontology* viii. 82 In other cases there is resorption of the apices of vital teeth. **1962** K. F. LAGLER et al. *Ichthyology* viii. 247 In many rayfishes.. gas resorption is also performed by.. the oval organ situated in the posterior portion of the gas bladder. **1974** *Nature* 22

Mar. 343/1 This is accomplished by inhibition of bone resorption, of the tubular reabsorption of calcium, and of the intestinal absorption of calcium.

re'sorptive, *a.* [Cf. prec. and -IVE.] Pertaining to, of the nature of, resorption.

1886 *Philadelphia Med. Times* XVI. 490/2 The removal of such substances is dependent upon the action of specialized cells, called resorptive or giant cells, and the process is physiological. **1889** *Science* XIII. 232 The resorptive phenomena of porphyritic quartz and other minerals in eruptive rocks. **1951** *Jrnl. Bone & Joint Surg.* A. XXXIII. 936 All resorptive processes occur principally in relation to calcified matrices and not to osteoid or uncalcified cartilage. **1978** *Sci. Amer.* Feb. 112/3 My own observations of such 'flypaper' trappers as butterworts and sundews suggest that these plants have secretory and resorptive mechanisms that are quite different from the ones likely to operate in pitcher plants.

resort (rɪ'zɔːt), *sb.* Also 4–6 resorte. [a. OF. *resort*, *ressort* resource, aid, spring, etc., f. *resortir*: see next.]

I. 1. a. That to which one has recourse for aid or assistance, or in order to accomplish some end.

c **1374** CHAUCER *Troylus* III. 134 In trowth alway to don ȝow my seruyse, As to my lady right, and cheif resorte. **1433** *Rolls of Parlt.* IV. 441/2 He ne kan..other resort have for salvation. **1691** T. H[ALE] *Acc. New Invent.* 43 Nor..do we offer this as a new Resort whereto this Report..may be thought to have driven us. **1781** COWPER *Hope* 378 Between justice, as my prime support, And mercy, fled to as the last resort, I..steal along with heav'n in view. **1840** R. H. DANA *Bef. Mast* xxiii, A knowledge of the expedients and resorts in times of hazard, which was remarkable. **1860** TYNDALL *Glac.* I. xxvii. 196 A fit one [*sc.* sledge] was not to be found, and a carriage was therefore the only resort.

†**b.** Means or way of escape. *Obs. rare*⁻¹.

1422 tr. *Secreta Secret., Priv. Priv.* 153 Al men hit [*sc.* death] haue in mynde, Of that there is noone resorte.

2. †**a.** The right or privilege of having final decision or appeal vested in one. *Obs.*

1475 *Bk. Noblesse* (Roxb.) 22 To holde frely in souvereinte and resort of none creature but of God. **1523** LD. BERNERS *Froiss.* I. ccxii. 257 His eldest son, shulde renounce all maner of soueraynte, resorte, and rightes, that he shulde haue of any of theym.

b. Recourse *to* some person, thing, or expedient, for aid or assistance, for the settlement of some difficulty, or the attainment of some end.

1474 *Rolls of Parlt.* VI. 117/2 The same persones..to have resort unto the collectours of the same x^{th} part,..to understond..in whoos kepyng the same sommes..resten. **1659** HAMMOND *On Ps.* lxi. 1 O Gratious God, to thee is my only resort. **1668–9** STILLINGFL. *Serm.* (1673) I. vii. 123 For the design that was laid for that,..we must have resort to the account that is given of it. **1710** PRIDEAUX *Orig. Tithes* ii. 73 The constant resort which is had unto them..is not without its expence. **1818** CRUISE *Digest* (ed. 2) V. 572 For the true idea of seisin, resort must be had to the ancient system of feudal tenures. **1884** *Manch. Exam.* 19 June 5/1 It will be impossible to close the Committee to-night without resort to a sitting of unusual length.

c. ***in the last resort*** [after F. *en dernier ressort*], orig. as a judge or court from which there is no appeal; hence, as a last expedient, in the end, ultimately. (Cf. DERNIER b and RESSORT 2.)

1672 TEMPLE *Ess., Gov.* Wks. 1720 I. 97 All Government is a Restraint upon Liberty; and under all, the Dominion is equally Absolute, where it is in the last Resort. **1727–38** CHAMBERS *Cycl., Presidial*, a tribunal, or bench of judges, established..to judge ultimately, or in the last resort, of the several cases brought before them by way of appeal from the subaltern judges. **1765** BLACKSTONE *Comm.* I. 11 Arbiters of the property of all their fellow-subjects, and that in the last resort. **1858** J. MARTINEAU *Stud. Chr.* 352 Life, indeed, is just the one thing..on whose disposability in the last resort..the very existence of society depends. **1884** tr. *Lotze's Metaph.* 121 If in the last resort it is the greatest perfection which determines the divine choice [etc.].

d. ***without resort***, without appeal. *rare*⁻¹.

1827 SCOTT *Napoleon* Introd., Wks. 1870 IX. 10 The people were judges without resort.

e. ***court of first resort*** (cf. 2 c).

1863 H. COX *Instit.* II. ii. 308 Parliaments relinquished much of their wonted authority as a court of first resort.

†**3. a.** Opportunity for repair or access *to* a place. **b.** Return. *Obs. rare.*

c **1420** LYDG. *Assembly of Gods* 68 So that the deere shall haue no resort Withyn short tyme to no maner shade. **1430–40** —— *Bochas* VIII. viii. (1494) C vij, In this resort [he was] receyued..In greate noblesse by cause of that viage.

4. General or habitual repair of persons to some place or person.

a. In phr. ***to make*** (or ***have***) ***resort***.

1432–50 tr. *Higden* (Rolls) IV. 427 In suche festes peple of alle the Iewery hade resorte un to hit. **1473** *Rolls of Parlt.* VI. 66/1 The same Marchauntes have be encoraged to make and contynue their resort unto this his Lande. **1565** *Reg. Privy Council Scot.* I. 353 Intending thair to mak thair resort and residence. **1577** HARRISON *England* II. i. (1877) I. 6 Great resort also was made unto them from all places of the realme. *c* **1611** CHAPMAN *Iliad* XI. 723 To th' Altars of the Gods they made diuine resorts. **1662** STILLINGFL. *Orig. Sacræ* II. iv. §8 Many other Prophets and Seers..to whom the people made their resort.

b. Const. *of* (the persons resorting). †Also *pl.*

1470–85 MALORY *Arthur* XVIII. i. 725 Syre Launcelot had many resortes of ladyes and damoysels that dayly resorted vnto hym. **1531–2** *Act 23 Hen. VIII*, c. 12 Those townes.. where there is moste resorte and repaire of people. **1579** SPENSER *Sheph. Cal.* Aug. 157 Resort of people doth my greefs augment. **1630** PAGITT *Christianogr.* I. ii. (1636) 58 In which are many languages spoken, by reason of the resort of abundance of merchants. *a* **1682** SIR T. BROWNE *Tracts* (1683) 139 By frequent resort of the French, who to the number of some thousands came over. **1766** in Ellis *Orig. Lett.* Ser. II. IV. 485 Where was a great resort of French company. **1817** JAS. MILL *Brit. India* I. III. i. 491 He patronized learning and encouraged the resort of learned men. **1844** H. H. WILSON *Brit. India* I. 543 An unrestrained and unregulated resort of persons to India for religious purposes.

c. In phr. ***of*** (***great, public***, etc.) ***resort***, applied to places.

1585 T. WASHINGTON tr. *Nicholay's Voy.* II. xi. 45 b, A towne of great resort aswel from the firme land as the sea. **1603** SHAKS. *Meas. for M.* I. ii. 104 But shall all our houses of resort in the Suburbs be puld downe? **1683** *Brit. Spec.* 104 Encouraging..to build Houses, Temples, and Places of Publick Resort. **1709** STEELE *Tatler* No. 83 ¶1 It is my frequent Practice to visit Places of Resort in this Town. **1725** THOMAS in *Portland Papers* VI. (Hist. MSS. Comm.) 113 There is a large colliery of great resort. **1849** MACAULAY *Hist. Eng.* vii. II. 214 The Five Mile Act had banished him ..from almost all places of public resort. **1853** KANE *Grinnell Exp.* x. (1856) 76 Their seats of favorite resort, in the early part of the season.

5. †**a.** Concourse or assemblage of people. *Obs.*

1470–85 MALORY *Arthur* VI. xvi. 209 Syre launcelot gate al his armour..and put hit vpon hym for drede of more resorte. **1513** MORE in Grafton *Chron.* (1568) II. 777 The Protector had the resort, and the King in maner desolate. **1577** B. GOOGE *Heresbach's Husb.* IV. (1586) 191 b, The Lorde Cobham (whose house you shall seeldome see without great resort). **1634** MILTON *Comus* 379 Her wings That in the various bussle of resort Were all to ruffl'd. **1700** DRYDEN *Ajax & Ulyss.* 320 Secure, I enter'd through the hostile Court, Glitt'ring with steel and crowded with resort.

b. An assemblage, gathering, throng, crowd.

c **1550** CHEKE *Matt.* ix. 8 And when yᵉ resort saw this yei marveild. **1597** J. PAYNE *Royal Exch.* 9 The greate resorte to that..Edifice are of sundrie titles and degrees. **1628** WITHER *Brit. Rememb.* IV. 370 Gaming-houses whither great resorts Were wont to come. **1698** FRYER *Acc. E. India & P.* 55 For a long time the Portugals..drew a great resort hither. **1703** PRIOR *Erasm. Imit.* 9 Folly with her wild Resort Of Wit and Jest disturbs the solemn Court. **1760–72** H. BROOKE *Fool of Qual.* (1809) I. 94, I daily frequented Markham's coffee-house, amidst a promiscuous resort of swords-men, literati, beaus, and politicians. **1806** R. CUMBERLAND *Mem.* 286 A great resort of men of talents now flocked around him.

†**6. a.** Repair of one person with others or to some place. *Obs.*

1535 LYNDESAY *Satyre* 242 And out of Rome hes baneist Chastity, Quha with our Prelats can get na resort. **1607** SHAKS. *Timon* I. i. 127 Ioyne with me to forbid him her resort, My selfe haue spoke in vaine. **1635** HEYLIN *Sabbath* II. (1636) 18 Calvin..makes this the speciall cause of Saint Pauls resort unto the places of assembly. **1671** MILTON *P.R.* I. 367 Nor from the Heav'n of Heav'ns Hath he excluded my resort sometimes.

†**b.** Those with whom one associates. *Obs.*⁻¹

1579 LYLY *Euphues* (Arb.) 42 As touching my residence and abiding heere in Naples,..my resorte and companye [etc.].

7. A place to which persons repair.

Now freq. in comb. with *health, holiday, seaside*, etc.

1754 YOUNG *Centaur* II. Wks. 1757 IV. 140 This intellectual cloud, which hangs, like a fog, over every gay resort of our moral invalids. *a* **1796** BURNS *Caledonia* 15 Chiefly the woods were her fav'rite resort. **1856** STANLEY *Sinai & Pal.* I. i. (1858) 18 Wherever these springs are to be found, there..must always have been the resort of wanderers in the Desert. **1883** *Harper's Mag.* Sept. 521/1 The bustle of arrival and departure..[animates] the village in the way peculiar to American towns near a 'resort'. **1885** *Manch. Exam.* 10 Sept. 5/3 The houses licensed were the resort of thieves. **1893** K. D. WIGGIN *Polly Oliver's Problem* (1894) ii. 30 She would become the head of a summer resort, with a billiard-room and a bowling-alley. **1909** 'O. HENRY' *Roads of Destiny* xviii. 294 He was manager at different times of..a dozen hotels and summer resorts, an insurance company, and a district leader's campaign. **1936** [see *holiday resort* s.v. HOLIDAY 4]. **1976** *Morecambe Guardian* 7 Dec. 14/4 The man behind the proposal described Carnforth as 'a poor little town that could never become a health resort'.

II. †**8.** ? A channel or arm (of the sea). *Obs.*⁻¹

c **1477** CAXTON *Jason* 68 By this yle is a resorte of the see unto an other litill yle.

†**9.** *Mus.* (Meaning uncertain.) *Obs. rare*⁻¹.

1501 DOUGLAS *Pal. Hon.* I. xli, Duplat, triplat, diatesseriall, Sesqui altera, and decupla resortis, Diapason of mony sindrie sortis.

†**10.** A mechanical spring. *Obs.* (Cf. RESSORT 1.)

1597 A. M. tr. *Guillemeau's Fr. Chirurg.* 17 b/2 A resorte, or springe, because it [*sc.* forceps] might allwayes be aperte. **1662** J. BARGRAVE *Pope Alex. VII* (1867) 130 The hand.. returned to its place with force, as if it had a resort or spring to force it to its proper place. **1714** MANDEVILLE *Fab. Bees* (1733) II. 177 The motion of the hands, what number of resorts soever it is communicated by, is originally owing to something else that first moves within.

fig. **1666** DRYDEN *Ann. Mirab.* cc, Pathless destiny; Whose dark resorts since prudence cannot know, In vain it would provide for what shall be. **1676** —— *State Innoc.* Pref., If you can enter more deeply..into the causes and resorts of that which moves pleasure in a reader.

III. 11. *attrib.* and *Comb.*, as (sense 7) ***resort city, cottage, estate, hotel, -motel, -motor hotel, railroad station, town***; **resort clothes, -wear**, clothes suitable for wearing at a holiday resort.

1974 *Sumter* (S. Carolina) *Daily Item* 20 Apr. 1A/5 Police mounted a room-by-room sweep of hotels in this *resort city. **1978** R. LUDLUM *Holcroft Covenant* viii. 93 In every resort city there was always one major shop that catered to the reading requirements of a specific nationality. **1974** *Country Life* 2 May 1097/2 Their Côte d'Azur collection of women's *resort clothes. **1977** N. FREELING *Gadget* I. 24 Bring more than resort clothes... Evening things, feminine. **1971** *Jamaican Weekly Gleaner* 3 Nov. 3/1 A long debate on the merits or otherwise of licensing *resort cottages. **1975** *New Yorker* 19 May 115 (Advt.), The Mountain View House is a *resort estate with a charm only a century of family ownership can achieve. **1919** E. HOUGH *Sagebrusher* 49 A few passengers from the *resort hotel back in the town began to appear. **1977** *Whitaker's Almanack 1978* 778/2 Tourism is the most important industry, with a good choice of resort hotels. **1963** *New Yorker* 1 June 123/1 (Advt.), America's most *funderful* *resort-motel. *Ibid.* 8 June 58 (Advt.), America's 3 great new resort-motor hotels. **1928** *Publishers' Weekly* 3 Nov. 1868/1 The..delay involved when a package must change trains in a *resort railroad station. **1970** *Southerly* XXX. 124 Occasionally a car hummed along the bitumen..making..for one of the string of *resort towns further along the coast. **1972** D. E. WESTLAKE *Cops & Robbers* (1973) xvi. 243 You could always tell a resort town, it ran much heavier to neon. **1965** *Punch* 10 Mar. p. xvi/2, Harvey Nichols's spring collection, which includes Italian and French *resort-wear, can be seen on Mar 15. **1975** *Harper's & Queen* June 69 The latest collection of resort wear.

resort (rɪ'zɔːt), *v.*¹ Also 5–6 resorte, 6 reasorte. [ad. OF. *resortir* (mod.F. *ressortir*) to rebound, retire, etc., f. *re-* RE- + *sortir* to issue, go out, etc., of obscure etymology.]

†**1.** *intr.* To issue, to come out, again. *Obs. rare.*

c **1400** MAUNDEV. (1839) xiii. 148 That Ryvere comethe towardes Ynde, undre Erthe, and resortethe [*F. ressortist*] in to the Lond of Altazar. **1480** CAXTON *Ovid's Met.* XII. x, The stronge poynte of his darte folded and resorted agayn.

†**2. a.** To return *to* oneself; to revert *to* a former condition or custom. *Obs.*

c **1400** *Destr. Troy* 3553 When he past of his payne..And resort to hym selfe.., He plainted full pitiously. *c* **1420** LYDG. *Assembly of Gods* 63 Where any wood ys, he [Eolus] shall make hyt pleyn, Yef he to hys lyberte may resorte ageyn. **1441** *Plumpton Corr.* (Camden) p. lxi, He was long tyme afterward in dispare of his life, & shall now never resort to the bodyly strength & heale of his person that he was in before. **1589** PUTTENHAM *Eng. Poesie* III. xxiv. (Arb.) 290 All such persons as take pleasure to shew their limbes..should be inioyned either to go starke naked, or else to resort backe to the comely and modest fashion of their owne countrie apparell.

†**b.** To return (*to* a place, or *home*). *Obs.*

c **1430** LYDG. *Min. Poems* (Percy Soc.) 186 He is a fole that scaped is daunger,..and fled is fro prisoun, For to resorte. *c* **1450** LOVELICH *Grail* xiv. 583 Whanne that Alle I-taken they were..He gan to Resorte to that bataylle There Seraphe fawht. *a* **1529** SKELTON *Sp. Parrot* 281 Go, litell quayre,..Home to resorte Jerobesethe perswade.

†**c.** To return *to* a subject or matter; also, to go back in a discourse or in time. *Obs.*

c **1430** LYDG. *Min. Poems* (Percy Soc.) 140 But to resorte ageyn to my mateere. *c* **1450** —— *Secrees* (E.E.T.S.) 10 Here the Translator resortith ageyn to set in a prologe. *c* **1460** FORTESCUE *Abs. & Lim. Mon.* xiv. (1885) 142 It be houyth þat we nowe resorte to the poynte in wich we lafte. **1547** J. HARRISON *Exhort. Scottes* in *Compl. Scot.* (1872) 216 Bvt to resort to our purpose, how can it stand with reason [etc.]? **1654** G. GODDARD *Introd. Burton's Diary* (1828) I. 42 Some would have resorted back again to the business of the Council, and put a full period to that. **1749** FIELDING *Tom Jones* XI. vii, He was obliged to resort above a year..back, to find any object for this unwarrantable passion.

†**d.** To revert or fall *to* one's lot or share. *Obs.*

1430 LYDG. *St. Margaret* 361 Whan it falleth thei haue of me mastrie, Ageyn to me resorteth al the wrak. **1492** in *Somerset Med. Wills* (1901) 299 If hit so happe that Johanne my doughter fortune to deye..then I will that the 40 *li* before to her bequeithen resorte and turne to the use and profit of all my next children then living. *a* **1676** HALE *Hist. Common Law* vi. (1713) 122 The Rule of Descents in Normandy was..That the Descent of the Line of the Father shall not resort to that of the Mother.

†**e.** To retire or retreat. *Obs. rare.*

c **1450** *Merlin* 391 Thei dide presse to the rescowe..and made hem resorte bakke more than a bowe draught.

†**3.** To turn, direct one's attention, *to* a subject.

c **1450** LYDG. *Secrees* 308 Till I abrayde, in purpoos to Resorte To hym that drough this processe moost devyne. **1494** FABYAN *Chron.* 2 Of Fraunce and other I myght lyke wyse reporte.., But to Englande if I shall resorte, Ryght mysty storyes [etc.]. **1534** MORE *Comf. agst. Trib.* I. Wks. 1149/1 This first kinde of tribulacion haue you to my minde opened sufficiently, & therfore I pray you resort now to the second. **1581** LAMBARDE *Eiren.* II. v. (1588) 183, I will leave them, and resort to those other.

4. To betake oneself, to repair or go, *to* a person for aid. (Now only as in c.)

c **1460** *Wisdom* 942 in *Macro Plays* 66 Wyche be owur selff neuer may be a-mendyde With-owt Gode..; Therfor to hym let vs resort. **1494** FABYAN *Chron.* II. xxx. 22 Brenne.. nat hauynge any comfort how he myght attayne to his former dygnyte, lastly resorted..vnto the Duke. **1535** COVERDALE *Ps.* cxlii[i]. 9 Delyuer me (o Lorde) fro myne enemies, for I resorte vnto the. **1579** TOMSON *Calvin's Serm. Tim.* 930/2 If we will profit in the holy scripture, let vs learne to resort to our Lord Iesus Christ. **1667** POOLE *Dial. betw. Protest. & Papist* 25 Not so much as giving notice to his people who they were to whom they must resort for justice.

†**b.** To refer or turn *to* a document, book, author, etc., for information or guidance. *Obs.*

1439 *E.E. Wills* (1882) 128 If ther be eny clause or matier in his olde will..to the wich it shall seme to the saide executours..for to be necessary to resorte, and to take remembraunce of. **1571** DIGGES *Pantom.* I. xxxv. L ij b, Now it behoueth you to resorte to your plattes, searching out as nigh as you can by estimation the middlemost place. **1613** PURCHAS *Pilgrimage* I. vii. (1614) 40 If any would entertaine longer dispute about this, he may..resort vnto Geropius Becanus his Gigantomachia. **1728** MORGAN *Algiers* I. Pref. v, This gentleman, to whom I often resort, has only saved me so much labour.

c. To have recourse *to* something for assistance or furtherance of an object.

1647 CLARENDON *Hist. Reb.* II. §21 The King thought it time to resort to other counsels. **1754** SHERLOCK *Discourses* (1759) I. i. 14 Men should have other Helps to resort to, besides their own Strength and Reason. **1790** BURKE *Fr. Revol.* 84 The Revolution which is resorted to for a title, on their system, wants a title itself. **1817** JAS. MILL *Brit. India* III. ii. 67 The evidence to which the nature of the circumstances compelled the complainants..to resort. **1860** TYNDALL *Glac.* II. ix. 270 At length we resort to actual experiment. **1875** JOWETT *Plato* (ed. 2) V. 55 The Persian kings..resorted to mercenaries as their only salvation.

5. To repair, to make one's way, to come or go *to* a person.

1447 BOKENHAM *Seyntys* (Roxb.) 101 Of thi lyfe here in the last our..My sustrys and I shul to the resorte. **1470–85** MALORY *Arthur* VI. i. 183 Thenne alle the knyghtes of the table round resorted vnto the kyng & made many Iustes & turnementes. **1530** PALSGR. 688/2, I wyll resorte to hym to morowe for your cause. *c* **1595** CAPT. WYATT *R. Dudley's Voy. W. Ind.* (Hakl. Soc.) 39 He approched our bote in the night, which our Captaine would in noe wyse permitt, but willed that they shoulde resorte unto him the next daie. **1637** *Prynne Papers* (Camden) 67 The persons and dispositions of those that resorted to the said Prynne and Burton in their way to their said imprisonment. **1871** R. ELLIS tr. *Catullus* lxviii. 137 What, to Catullus alone if a wayward fancy resort not? **1878** SIMPSON *Sch. Shaks.* I. 54 On his arrival Stucley resorted to him to congratulate him.

b. To repair *to* one frequently or habitually.

1470–85 MALORY *Arthur* XVIII. i. 725 Thenne..syr launcelot beganne to resorte vnto quene Gueneuer ageyne. **1535** COVERDALE *Ps.* cxli[i]. 7 Which thinge yf thou wilt graunte me, then shal the rightuous resorte vnto my company. **1591** SHAKS. *Two Gent.* III. i. 110 No man hath accesse by day to her. *Val.* Why then I would resort to her by night. **1607** ROWLANDS *Diogines Lanth.* (Hunt. Cl.) 25 Crowes will to carrion still, Like euer vnto like resort, The bad embrace the ill. **1617** MORYSON *Itin.* III. 48 To her that at the drinking bench challengeth loue, the Dutch resort.

†**c.** To consort or associate *with* others. *Obs.*⁻¹

1585 T. WASHINGTON tr. *Nicholay's Voy.* IV. i. 114b, They resorted with the elders and were no more subiect to goe vnto the warres.

6. To repair ordinarily or frequently *to* a place.

1432 *Rolls of Parlt.* IV. 405/1 Certaines..charges to be..payed, unto the sustenyng of ye saide warkes, of every Shipp and Boote resortyng thider. **1509** FISHER *Funeral Serm. C'tess Richmond* Wks. (1876) 295 At nyght before she wente to bedde, she faylled not to resorte vnto her chappell. **1563** *Child-Marriages* (1896) 67 The banes were not askid in the church wherto he doth resort. **1611** BIBLE *Ps.* lxxi. 3 Bee thou my strong habitation, whereunto I may continually resort. **1633** G. HERBERT *Temple, Ch. Porch* lxix, Resort to sermons, but to prayers most: Praying's the end of preaching. **1842** TENNYSON *Will Waterpr.* 210 Head-waiter of the chop-house here, To which I most resort.

b. With plural subject.

1479 in *Eng. Gilds* (1870) 424 And that the Bakers lak no stuffe..at suche tymes as many straungers resortith to the towne. **1521** *State P., Carew MSS.* (1867) I. 20 This is the very land of refuge that English pirates resort most unto. **1585** T. WASHINGTON tr. *Nicholay's Voy.* I. viii. 7b, They haue two market dayes.., to the which resort an infinite number of people. **1613** PURCHAS *Pilgrimage* V. v. (1614) 473 Emanuel Pinner at Cambaia obserued many to resort thither on pilgrimage. **1669** GALE *Crt. Gentiles* I. I. ii. 12 When Plato was in Egypt, the Iews resorted thither. **1712–14** POPE *Rape Lock* III. 9 Hither the heroes and the nymphs resort To taste awhile the pleasures of a Court. **1782** PRIESTLEY *Corrupt. Chr.* II. VI. 29 The churches could not contain those that resorted to them. **1867** SMILES *Huguenots Eng.* iv. (1880) 59 The heads of the Reformed party..resorted to Paris in large numbers. **1894** J. T. FOWLER *Adamnan* Introd. 33 A cave in an island..whither Irish pilgrims still resort.

7. To proceed or go *to* (or *towards*) a place; to respond *to* a call or summons. †Also without const.

c **1450** LOVELICH *Grail* lv. 46 Aleyn Remevede from that plas,..and his bretheren with hym gonnen Resort. **1496** *Naval Accts. Hen. VII* (1896) 167 Proclamacion to cause the maryners that hade takyn wages to Resorte to the Ship. **1509** HAWES *Past. Pleas.* XXIX. (Percy Soc.) 139 On a day, for hys owne dysporte, To the court of Rome he gan to resorte. **1568** GRAFTON *Chron.* II. 677 After this battaile the Northren men resorted towarde Warwike. **1613** PURCHAS *Pilgrimage* I. vii. 33 Noah..entered the Arke at Gods appointment, to which by Diuine instinct resorted both birds and beasts. **1667** MILTON *P.L.* XI. 81 The Sons of Light Hasted, resorting to the Summons high, And took thir Seats. **1703** POPE *Thebais* 668 To Argos' realms the victor god resorts, And enters old Crotopus' humble courts. **1774** GOLDSM. *Nat. Hist.* (1776) V. 203 The number of females that, on this occasion, resort to his call, is uncertain. **1804** LAUDERDALE *Publ. Wealth* (1819) 357 The advantages..are at once suggested, by resorting to the drawing-rooms..even of the British West India planter. *a* **1859** OLMSTED *Mech. Heavens* xxii. (1860) 241 At the age of twenty-five years, he resorted to Italy, for the purpose of studying astronomy, where he resided a number of years.

†**b.** Of blood: To flow *to* some part. *Obs.*

1531 ELYOT *Gov.* II. xii, The quicke bloode somwhat resorted unto his visage. **1566** DRANT *Horace, Sat.* I. viii. D viij b, The blood resorted to an hole, purple, and smoking new. **1607** TOPSELL *Four-f. Beasts* (1658) 273 The other Authors..say, that the madness of a Horse cometh..by some hot bloud resorting to the panicles of the brain.

†**c.** Of a stream, etc.: To flow *to* (another stream). *Obs.* (Common in Leland.)

1538 LELAND *Itin.* (1745) I. 99 Ther cam doun a Broke from West, resorting, as one said, to Wilebek streme.

†**d.** Const. with inf. *Obs.*

1460 *Pol., Rel., & L. Poems* 194 In connaunt, wreche, þou art one-trewe, And Redy also to Resorte, To folowe vyces and sle vertu. *c* **1471** *Pol. Poems* (Rolls) II. 279 O that nobill prynce and emperour flouere, To sitt at Londone resorte he than. **1509** FISHER *Funeral Serm. C'tess Richmond* Wks. (1876) 296 The straungers of honeste, whiche of theyr curtesy resorteth for to vysyte the soueravne, must be consydered. **1560** DAUS tr. *Sleidane's Comm.* 54 Mo Bowres resorted to aide yᵉ others.

†**e.** Without const. To come. *Obs. rare.*

1550 BALE *Image Both Ch.* III. Kkvb, For whan I shal resorte, be certaine and sure of it, mi iuste rewarde shal come with me. *a* **1553** UDALL *Royster D.* II. iii, When wil our new master come?.. I would it were to morow: for till he resorte Our mistresse being a Widow hath small comforte.

†**f.** To retire or withdraw *into* (a place). *Obs.*

1535 COVERDALE *2 Sam.* xvii. 13 But yf he resorte in to a cite, then shal all Israel cast roapes aboute the same cite. **1560** DAUS tr. *Sleidane's Comm.* 341 They resort every man with his family into his owne chamber.

8. To have repair, to stay, in a place.

1453 *Rolls of Parlt.* V. 230/2 Repairyng or resortyng by the space of vi wokys withinne youre said Reaume. **1523** FITZHERB. *Husb.* §10 If it be very ranke grounde,.. where catel doth resort, plowe not that lande, tyll ye wyll sowe it. **1590** SHAKS. *Com. Err.* v. i. 28 'Tis pitty that thou liu'st To walke where any honest men resort. **1632** LITHGOW *Trav.* III. 85 His Nauy which sometimes resort in the Leuante. **1727** *Philip Quarll* (1816) 14, I..believe, that..these habitations belong to their captain, and that the company resort in caves up and down these rocks. **1773** HAN. MORE *Search aft. Happiness* ii. 138 A court, Where pleasures, dress'd in every shape, resort.

†**9.** *trans.* To frequent, to haunt (a place). *Obs.*

1575 *Gamm. Gurton* III. iii. 76 Seeke him at Hob Fylchers shop, for, as charde it reported, There is the best ale in al the towne and now is most resorted. **1640** BROME *Sparagus Garden* II. ii, A pallace of pleasure, and daily resorted and filled with Lords and Knights, and their Ladies. **1756** C. LUCAS *Ess. Waters* I. 35 Our Thames..is tainted with..the scarce numerable ships and other vessels that resort her port.

re-sort, *v.*² [RE- 5 a.] To sort afresh.

1889 *Pall Mall G.* 25 Nov. 2/2 She re-sorts the various loving couples, makes every one..happy.

resorter (rɪˈzɔːtə(r)). [f. RESORT *v.* + -ER.]

1. One who resorts (*to* a place or person); a frequenter or visitor.

1533 MORE *Apol.* xxxv. Wks. 900/2 All that hathe bene punished in this diocise..or in the cytye selfe, eyther of resiauntes therin, or of resorters thereto. **1575** BARET *Alv.* s.v. *Smell*, A common resorter to euery mans table: a smell feast. **1648** C. WALKER *Hist. Independ.* I. 134 How to carry himselfe in his charge towards the Kings, His Servants and all Resorters to Him. **1798** ANNA SEWARD *Lett.* (1811) V. 148 Of absurdity and bad taste, the politer resorters to Matlock cannot surely be acquitted. **1812** COLMAN *Br. Grins, Low Amb.* lxvii, A pasteboard elephant..was formed to..charm the sage theatrical resorters.

2. One who runs a business in a resort. *U.S.*

1927 *Scribner's Mag.* Apr. 383/2 Take me along on a Southern trip to see what the rich resorters are wearin'? **1978** *Minneapolis Tribune* 4 Apr. 6A/1 The severe reduction of motorized opportunities..would devastate the resorters and outfitters of northeastern Minnesota.

†**re'sortible**, *a. Obs. rare*⁻¹. [f. as prec. + -IBLE.] Open or possible *to* one.

1586 FERNE *Blaz. Gentrie* 314 Anye trade of life, misterye, or facultye which is not resortible ne conuenable to a gentleman.

re'sorting, *vbl. sb.* [f. as prec. + -ING¹.] The action or fact of having repair or recourse (*to* some place or thing, etc.); an occasion of this.

1490 CAXTON *Eneydos* lxv. 164 Ascanyus buylded firste the towne or cyte of Albe in lombardye. And there was his resortynge. **1530** PALSGR. 262/1 Resortyng to, *actraict, recours*. **1579** NORTHBROOKE *Dicing* (1843) 89 Let the people, and especially women, giue eare to Pagan Ouid,.. speaking of those common resortings vnto playes. **1660** A. BROME *Songs* II. xiv. 7 We'l in our own faces our colours display, And hallow our yearly resorting. **1887** *Pall Mall G.* 2 Aug. 7/1 There has been no rough horse-play, and no resortings to election irregularities.

attrib. **1540** PALSGR. *Acolastus* II. iv, Howe mete or howe redy (at hande) a resortynge place,..haue I gotten me.

resoun, obs. form of REASON *sb.*¹

†**re'sound**, *sb. Obs.* [f. the vb.] A returned or re-echoed sound; a resonance.

a **1586** SIDNEY *Arcadia* IV. Ecl. iv, And you, O trees,.. receaue The strange resound of these my causeful cryes. **1615** JACKSON *Creed* V. xx. Wks. IV. 177 The pleasant spectacle and sweet resounds which woods and shady fountains afford. **1682** SIR T. BROWNE *Chr. Mor.* (1716) 40 Virtuous actions have their own trumpets, and without any noise from thy self will have their resound abroad. **1701** BEVERLEY *Praise Glory* 53 The whole State of that Kingdom, shall be fill'd with the Highest Resounds of that Perfected New Song. **1835** H. EVANS in *Mississippi Valley Hist. Rev.* (1927) XIV. 213 Distinctly..the resound of guns was heard in quick succession.

resound (rɪˈzaʊnd), *v.*¹ Forms: 4–6 **resoun**, **resown(e**; 6 **resounde**, **resownd**, 6– **resound**. [f. RE- + *soun(e* SOUND *v.*, after F. *resonner* (OF. *resoner*), or L. *resonāre* (Sp. and Pg. *resonar*, It. *risonare*).]

I. *intr.* **1.** Of places: To ring or re-echo *with* (or †*of*) some sound. Also with *to*.

c **1386** CHAUCER *Sqr.'s T.* 413 There sat a faukoun..That with a pitous vois bigan to crye, That al the woode resowned of hire cry. **1508** DUNBAR *Gold. Targe* 240 Thay fyrit gunnis wyth powder violent,..The rochis all resownyt wyth the rak. *a* **1547** SURREY *Prisoner Windsor Castle*, The secrete groues which oft we made resounde, Of pleasaunt playnt, and of our ladies' praise. **1610** HOLLAND *Camden's Brit.* (1637) 51 Their Theatre resounded with hideous howlings. **1671** MILTON *P.R.* II. 290 A pleasant Grove, With chaunt of tuneful Birds resounding loud. **1697** DRYDEN *Virg. Ecl.* v. 90 For this, with chearful Cries the Woods resound. **1788** GIBBON *Decl. & F.* xlix. V. 135 The dome resounded with the acclamations of the people. **1812** COMBE *Syntax, Picturesque* II. 44 While ev'ry hedge and ev'ry tree Resound with vocal minstrelsy. **1861** F. O. MORRIS *Rec. Animal Sagacity & Character* 121 He..lies buried..in those very shrubberies which had so often resounded to his joyous cries. **1867** SMILES *Huguenots Eng.* vii. (1880) 128 They daily made the vaults resound with their prayer and praise.

b. Without const.

c **1450** *Merlin* 274 The nyghtingale and these other briddes songen so lowde that the wode and the river resovned. *c* **1500** *Lancelot* 3436 Hornys, bugillis blawing furth thar sownis, That al the cuntre resownit hath about. **1591** SPENSER *Ruins of Time* 597 When all his mourning melodie He ended had, that both the shores resounded. **1605** SHAKS. *Macb.* IV. iii. 6 New sorowes Strike heauen on the face, that it resounds As if it felt with Scotland. **1667** MILTON *P.L.* VI. 218 Together rush'd Both Battels maine..; all Heav'n Resounded. **1784** COWPER *Task* I. 586 Yet even these..can..with dance, And music of the bladder and the bag, Beguile their woes, and make the woods resound. **1848** BUCKLEY *Iliad* 28 The waves..roar against the lofty beach, and the deep resounds.

2. Of things: To make or produce an echoing sound.

1530 PALSGR. 688/2 Harke howe this horne resoundeth. *c* **1586** C'TESS PEMBROKE *Ps.* CXXVI. ii, Tongues with gladdnes lowdly resounded. **1610** HOLLAND *Camden's Brit.* (1637) 306 Hammer milles, which beating upon the iron resound over all the places adjoyning. **1718** POPE *Iliad* XIII. 470 His arms resounded as the boaster fell. **1784** COWPER *Task* I. 357 Thump after thump resounds the constant flail. **1810** SCOTT *Lady of L.* I. x, Then through the dell his horn resounds. *c* **1850** *Arab. Nts.* (Rtldg.) 187 Instruments of music resounded through the building. **1873** S. TAYLOR *Sound & Music* (1896) 86 The air contained in the ball resounds very powerfully to a single note of different pitch.

3. a. Of sounds: To echo, to ring.

a **1547** SURREY *Æneid* II. 383 Lowder more and more The din resounded with rattling of armes. **1590** SPENSER *F.Q.* III. viii. 30 When those pittifull outcries he heard Through all the seas so ruefully resownd. **1626** T. H[AWKINS] tr. *Caussin's Holy Crt.* 75 Strooken with the hammer, the noyce wherof will resound, through all the earth. **1667** MILTON *P.L.* VIII. 334 The rigid interdiction, which resounds Yet dreadful in mine eare. **1781** COWPER *Heroism* 62 And echoing praises..resound at your return. **1828** SCOTT *F.M. Perth* iv, These words, which resounded far through the streets, were accompanied by as many fierce blows. **1849–50** ALISON *Hist. Europe* VIII. lii. §64. 365 The sound of these cannon resounded from one end of the Peninsula to the other.

b. To be much mentioned or repeated; to be celebrated or renowned.

1578 BANISTER *Hist. Man* VIII. 110 Many..whose names on earth resounde as ecchoes from the rockes. **1667** MILTON *P.L.* I. 579 And what resounds In Fable or Romance of Uthers Son. **1836** THIRLWALL *Greece* xii. II. 163 The fame of Croesus resounded through Greece. **1864** TENNYSON *Milton* 4 Milton, a name to resound for ages.

†**c.** To answer to something. *Obs. rare.*

1560 ROLLAND *Crt. Venus* III. 328 Bot to ressoun that ȝour Sermone resound. **1741** MIDDLETON *Cicero* (ed. 3) III. xii. 305 The consenting praise of all honest men,..which resounds always to virtue, as the eccho to the voice.

II. *trans.* **4.** To proclaim, repeat loudly (one's praises, etc.); to celebrate (a person or thing).

1561 in Googe *Eglogs* (Arb.) 8 If Homere here might dwell, whose praise the Grekes resounde. **1615** G. SANDYS *Trav.* 19 Happie, that had such a trumpet as Homer, to resound his vertues. **1633** G. HERBERT *Ch. Milit.* 64 The Warrier his deere skarres no more resounds. **1697** DRYDEN *Virg. Georg.* II. 543 To Bacchus..let us tune our Lays, And in our Mother Tongue resound his Praise. **1725** POPE *Odyss.* I. 2 The man..Long exercised in woes, oh Muse! resound. **1856** MERIVALE *Rom. Emp.* xli. (1871) V. 118 Horace resounds the praises of Italy in strains not dissimilar to those of Virgil.

†**b.** With complement. *Obs. rare.*

1600 ABBOT *Jonah* 615 Their owne stories resound them to have bene exceeding filthie. **1667** MILTON *P.L.* III. 149 Th' innumerable sound Of Hymns and sacred Songs, wherewith thy Throne Encompass'd shall resound thee ever blest.

5. a. To repeat or utter (words, etc.) in a loud or echoing manner. Now *rare*.

1594 SPENSER *Amoretti* xix, The quyre of Byrds resounded Their anthemes sweet. **1659** HAMMOND *On Ps.* xx. 9 Let all the congregation resound Amen. **1715** E. SMITH *Serm. at Wisbeech* 15 As soon as the sound is out of your ears, to graft the profitable sense upon your hearts and resound it at home in your conscience. **1742** YOUNG *Nt. Th.* VII. 176 Tho' nations, which consult Their gain, at thy expence, resound applause. **1810** SCOTT *Lady of L.* III. xv, The.. matrons round The dismal coronach resound. **1882–3** SCHAFF *Encycl. Rel. Knowl.* II. 1326 They repeat aloud the *oratio dominica* (the Lord's Prayer), they resound the creed and the doxology.

†**b.** To sound or din *into* one's ears. *Obs.*⁻¹

1641 SIR S. D'EWES in Rushw. *Hist. Coll.* (1692) I. III. 312 They resound nothing into the Ears of the old Emperor Matthias, but his Cousin Ferdinand's high Merits.

6. a. Of places: To re-echo, to give back or repeat (a sound) again.

1579 SPENSER *Sheph. Cal.* Aug. 159 The forest wide is fitter to resound The hollow Echo of my carefull cryes. **1594** MARLOWE & NASHE *Dido* IV. ii, Whose hideous echoes make the welkin howl, And all the woods Eliza to resound! **1630** DRUMM. OF HAWTH. *Flowers Sion*, Many an Hymne they..

Teacht Groues and Rocks, which did resound their Layes. 1667 MILTON *P.L.* II. 789 Hell trembl'd at the hideous Name, and sigh'd From all her Caves, and back resounded 'Death!' 1741 MONRO *Anat. Nerves* (ed. 3) 86 Serving as.. Vaults to resound the Notes. 1809 WORDSW. *Sonn. Liberty* II. x, Cliffs, woods and caves, her viewless steps resound. 1821 CLARE *Vill. Minstr.* II. 37 Fancy's echo still yon field resounds With noise of blind-man's buff.

†**b.** To return in response or answer *to* something. *Obs. rare.*

a 1617 BAYNE *Lect.* (1634) 100 The faithfull heart resoundeth to Gods command an answer of desire. 1681-6 J. SCOTT *Chr. Life* (1747) III. 544 To which welcome Sentence they will doubtless all immediately resound a joyful Choir of Hallelujahs.

7. To cause (a thing) to sound again.

1775 S. J. PRATT *Liberal Opin.* xxiii. (1783) I. 158 The coachman.. resounded the whip, and drove us upon the full trot to the door.

re-sound, *v.*² [RE- 5 a.] To sound again.

1897 *Daily News* 5 May 3/1 Soon the alarm was sounded, and re-sounded, and sounded again all over Aouri. 1899 *Westm. Gaz.* 5 Aug. 1/3 Every available chair was utilised as a temporary rest ere the bells sounded and re-sounded.

†**re'soundable,** *a. Obs. rare*⁻¹. [f. RESOUND *v.* + -ABLE.] Capable of resounding.

c 1485 *Digby Myst.* (1882) III. 904, I be-seche thyn hey paternyte, that my prayour be resowndable to þi fathyrod In glory, to opyn þeyn erys to þi son.

re'sounding, *vbl. sb.* [f. as prec. + -ING¹.] The action of the vb. RESOUND.

c 1374 CHAUCER *Boeth.* III. met. xii. (E.E.T.S.) 107 þere he temprede hys blaundissyng songes by resounyng of hys strenges. 1483 CAXTON *Cato* a vj b, Whan the husbond herde the noyse and resownyng of the stone within the water [etc.]. 1611 CORYAT *Crudities* 27 Vpon the resounding of the Eccho there seemed three to sound together. 1626 BACON *Sylva* §817 The Resounding of the Sea vpon the Shoare, And the Murmur of Winds in the Woods, without apparent Wind; shew Wind to follow.

re'sounding (rɪ'zaʊndɪŋ), *ppl. a.* [f. as prec. + -ING².] That resounds or re-echoes; sonorous. Also *fig.*

c 1374 CHAUCER *Boeth.* III. met. xii. (Chaucer Soc.) 15 There he temprede hise blaundyssynge songes by resownynge strenges. 1412-20 LYDG. *Chron. Troy* Prol. 49 The werbles of his resownyng harpe Appese dyde the bitter wyrdys scharpe. 1601 HOLLAND *Pliny* XI. xix, They feare mightily that resounding noise, comming with a double stroke. 1634 MILTON *Comus* 243 So maist thou be translated to the skies, And give resounding grace to all Heav'ns Harmonies. 1733 POPE *Ess. Man* III. 155 In the same temple, the resounding wood, All vocal beings hymn'd their equal God. 1794 T. J. MATHIAS *Purs. Lit.* (1798) 429 In the resounding language of the poet of Panopolis. 1860 TYNDALL *Glaciers* II. xxv. 362 A perpendicular shaft.. into which a resounding cataract discharged itself. 1897 MARY KINGSLEY *W. Africa* 542 A village that enjoyed the spacious and resounding name of Rumpochembo, from a celebrated chief. 1977 *Guardian Weekly* 4 Sept. 16/1 The Federal Energy Administration.. says that in the month ending in mid-August, American oil consumption was up a resounding 8 per cent over the same time last year.

Hence **re'soundingly** *adv.*

1611 COTGR., *Resonnamment*, resoundingly, lowdly,.. melodiously. 1885 D. C. MURRAY *Rainbow Gold* III. VI. ii. 196 He suffered both hands to fall resoundingly upon his thighs. 1889 HERRING & ROSS *Irish Cousin* III. i, She also began by kissing it resoundingly.

resoune, obs. form of REASON *sb.*¹

†**resour.** *Obs. rare*⁻¹. (App. a variant of or error for *reson, resun*, REASON *sb.*²)

1493 in Chandler *Life Waynflete* 369, vi coople refters in oon bay wt dooble syde resours.

resource (rɪ'sɔəs, rɪ'ɔːs). Also 7 ress-. [ad. F. *ressource*, †*ressourse*, f. OF. *re(s)sourdre* to rise again, f. *re-* RE- + *sourdre*:—L. *surgĕre* to rise.]

1. a. A means of supplying some want or deficiency; a stock or reserve upon which one can draw when necessary. Now usu. *pl.*

sing. 1611 COTGR., *Ressource*, a resource, new spring. *c* 1650 DENHAM *Of Old Age* 107 For whatsoever from our hand she [*sc.* the earth] takes, Greater, or less, a vast return she makes. Nor am I only pleas'd with that resource. 1760 *Hist.* in *Ann. Reg.* 10/1 Out of the general want a resource arose to their armies, who were the more readily recruited, because the scanty pay.. of a soldier became an object of envy to the wretched peasantry. 1849-50 ALISON *Hist. Europe* I. iv. §96. 534 The treasure of the Hotel de Ville presented an immediate resource. 1965 H. I. ANSOFF *Corporate Strategy* i. 6 A large majority of decisions must be made within the framework of a limited total resource. 1969 *Nature* 20 Dec. 1233/1 Satisfactory land use—that is, one that will provide a sustained yield of a resource—must take full account of the ecology. 1978 *Sci. Amer.* Nov. 82/3 The very best of them, such as W. F. Leopold's classic *Speech Development of a Bilingual Child*, continue to be a rich resource for contemporary investigators.

pl. 1797 BEWICK *Brit. Birds* Introd. 9 The Ostrich.. runs with amazing rapidity, and consequently requires similar resources of air. 1800 COLQUHOUN *Comm. Thames* vi. 237 It was limited with respect to pecuniary Resources. 1874 GREEN *Short Hist.* vii. §5. 392 The new resources of thought and language which literature felt to be at its disposal.

b. *pl.* The collective means possessed by any country for its own support or defence. See also *natural resources* s.v. NATURAL *a.* 6 e.

1779 BURKE *Corr.* (1844) II. 302 The first thing to be done for the defence of a country, is to have its resources and its arms in honest and able hands. 1818 COLEBROOKE *Import Col. Corn* 124 That period.. when.. the country shall be reduced to its own insulated resources. 1870 YEATS *Nat. Hist. Comm.* 2 In speaking of the natural resources of any country we refer to the ore in the mine, the stone unquarried, the timber unfelled [etc.].

2. a. Possibility of aid or assistance. (Chiefly in phr. ***without resource***, after F. *sans ressource.*)

1697 DRYDEN *Æneid* XI. 477 Vanquish'd without resource; laid flat by fate. 1749 SMOLLETT *Regicide* II. iv, Nor by an oath precipitate, involve Thy fate beyond resource. 1796 MORSE *Amer. Geogr.* II. 322 'Geneva', says the historian of this revolution, 'is lost without resource, in respect to religion, to morals'. 1819 SHELLEY *Cenci* III. i. 204 For we cannot hope That aid, or retribution, or resource Will arise thence. 1854 J. S. C. ABBOTT *Napoleon* (1855) II. xxiv. 442 The flower of the French army was lost without resource.

†**b.** Recourse *to* one for aid. *Obs. rare*⁻¹.

1720 MRS. MANLEY *Power of Love* 236 But Hymen was his first Relief, he had no resource to any other Deity.

3. a. An action or procedure to which one may have recourse in a difficulty or emergency; an expedient, device, shift.

1697 DRYDEN *Æneid* X. 512 [He] Us'd threatnings, mix'd with pray'rs, his last resource. 1748 *Anson's Voy.* (ed. 4) III. ii. 426 We had no other resource left than chincing and caulking. 1781 GIBBON *Decl. & F.* xxvi. II. 12 Many are the resources of courage and poverty. 1790 BURKE *Fr. Rev.* 44 A revolution will be the very last resource of the thinking and the good. 1853 MACAULAY *Biogr.*, *Atterbury*, A mind inexhaustibly rich in all the resources of controversy. 1863 GEO. ELIOT *Romola* xxix, Tito began to think that flight was his only resource.

b. Applied to persons or places. *rare.*

1734 tr. *Rollin's Anc. Hist.* (1827) II. II. 46 Taking Syphax himself prisoner who was the most powerful resource the Romans had. 1802 tr. *Ducray-Duminil's Victor* IV. 222 This holy mansion was the resource of young lovers, and the terror of parents.

4. A means of relaxation or amusement.

[1752 CHESTERF. *Lett.* cclxxiv. (1792) 255 Sloth, indolence, and *mollesse* are pernicious and unbecoming a young fellow; let them be your *ressource* forty years hence at soonest.] 1776 GIBBON *Decl. & F.* xiii. I. 394 The amusements of letters and of devotion, which afford so many resources in solitude. 1837 DISRAELI *Venetia* I. iii, Reading had been her chief resource. 1853 J. H. NEWMAN *Hist. Sk.* (1873) II. I. i. 3 He has a resource in the chase, an occupation, ever ready at hand. 1890 'R. BOLDREWOOD' *Col. Reformer* (1891) 221 We are not over supplied with resources.. as yet.. I have sent for some books and ordered the weekly papers.

5. Capability in adapting means to ends, or in meeting difficulties.

1853 KANE *Grinnell Exp.* xxii. (1856) 171 They are a gentlemanly, well-educated set of men.., full of personal resource. 1877 MRS. OLIPHANT *Makers Flor.* v. 143 He was a man of a keen and bitter wit, full of resource and readiness. 1879 FROUDE *Cæsar* xxii. 371 Resource in difficulties is the distinction of great generals.

6. *attrib.* and *Comb.*, as (sense 1 a) ***resource allocation, base, limit, zone***; ***resource-based, -bound, -intensive, -limited, -poor, -supplying, -wasteful*** adjs.; **resource aggregation** (see quot. 1968); **resource centre**, a library or other centre which houses a collection of *learning resources* (LEARNING *vbl. sb.* 4); such a collection itself; also *attrib.*; **resource industry**, an industry of which the raw materials occur as natural resources; **resource profile** (see quot. 1967); **resource time**, the length of time a resource is required for a specific project.

1967 A. BATTERSBY *Network Analysis* (ed. 2) ix. 144 When Esso Petroleum transferred their accounts to a computer, they recognized 20 categories of clerical staff for *resource aggregation. 1968 *Gloss. Terms Project Network Anal.* (*B.S.I.*) 9 *Resource aggregation*, the summation of the requirements of each resource, for each time period, calculated according to a common decision rule. 1964 K. G. LOCKYER *Introd. Critical Path Anal.* viii. 70 The name given by Production Controllers to this aspect of their work is *Loading*; regrettably, new names have been devised by some of the earlier CPA workers, amongst them *Manpower Smoothing*, and **Resource Allocation*. 1965 H. I. ANSOFF *Corporate Strategy* i. 6 A resource-allocation pattern which will offer the best potential for meeting the firm's objectives. 1977 P. JOHNSON *Enemies of Society* vi. 80 Classical economics had dealt with scarcity, value, choice, resource-allocation and efficiency. 1974 *Times* 8 Jan. (Europe Suppl.) p. xvi/5 How do you regard that oil? Is it British or is it European or is it just Shell's? I regard it as part of the *resource base. 1967 *Times* 28 Feb. (Canada Suppl.) 32 *Resource-based industries.. have been characteristic of the economy. 1977 *Bull. Amer. Acad. Arts & Sci.* Oct. 18 Doubts about the continuity of past, present, and future.. are expressed in current *resource-bound models of growth. 1968 *Globe & Mail* (Toronto) 3 Feb. 47/1 (Advt.), The School has a gymnasium and central library with *resource centre. 1971 in T. D. F. Barnard *New Directions in Librarianship* 44 There are new trends towards treating the library as a nexus for resource centre development. 1976 *Ann. Rep. Manpower Services Comm. 1975-76* ii. 20/1 The report therefore recommended that a resource centre should be established so that any organisation wishing to mount industrial relations training could be directed to appropriate sources of advice and teaching material. 1968 *Globe & Mail* (Toronto) 13 Jan. B5/1 Long on *resource industry and lean in secondary industry, British Columbia continues to be especially vulnerable to the fluttering of foreign economies and markets. 1970 *Toronto Daily Star* 24 Sept. 1/8 This list.. is likely to be lengthened to include some resource industries, pipelines, and possibly steel. 1976 *Conservation News* Sept.-Oct. 20/2 A planned transition to a less *resource-intensive economy. 1970 S. L. BARRACLOUGH in I. L. Horowitz *Masses in Lat. Amer.* iv. 132 In many regions there is a sharp *resource limit that would permit at most a doubling in the amount of productive land available. 1967 A. BATTERSBY *Network Analysis* (ed. 2) xii. 208 Before running the programme a 'duration limited' run or a '*resource limited' run must be specified. 1977 *Jrnl. R. Soc. Arts* CXXV. 389/1 The processing of many materials could.. become energy-limited rather than resource-limited. 1969 *New Scientist* 2 Oct. 18/1 The flow of food and raw materials to the developed nations (almost all of which are *resource-poor) will slowly dry up. 1973 *Listener* 20 Dec. 846/2 The resource-poor countries. 1967 A. BATTERSBY *Network Analysis* (ed. 2) ix. 141 Fig. 9.1 is called a '*resource profile' of a project, and it is obtained by 'resource aggregation'. The resources required by each job are specified when its duration is calculated; then when the scheduled starting times have been decided, the requirements are totalled over concurrent jobs for each discrete time period. 1969 R. B. FULLER *Operating Man. Spaceship Earth* ii. 27 They had to control various *resource-supplying mines, forests, and lands with which and upon which to build the ships and establish the industries. 1973 *Bulletin* (Sydney) 25 Aug. 50/2 Australia has no idea of proposing the formation of a consortium of resource-supplying countries. 1964 K. G. LOCKYER *Introd. Critical Path Anal.* viii. 72 It is necessary to know the amount of work available—that is, the capacity available. This, too, must be specified in *resource-time. 1976 *Carn* Feb. 20/2 It is easy to demonstrate that a *resource-wasteful and energy-intensive lifestyle is very damaging to the environment. 1965 *New Statesman* 12 Nov. 732/1 We should select important amenity '*resource zones' such as the Broads and, rather than trying to stop all industrial development in them, get all interested parties to hammer out ways of developing them for all-round use—with recreation taking a high priority.

Also as *v. trans.*, to supply (a person, etc.) with resources; hence **re'sourced** *ppl. a.*; **re'sourcing** *vbl. sb.*

1975 *Listener* 27 Mar. 398/1, I would have gone in for smaller [school] units.. resourced from some central agency. 1975 *Library Assoc. Rec.* LXXVII. 258 The policy of the Association.. must be against diminished resourcing of libraries. 1975 *Language for Life* (Dept. Educ. & Sci.) ix. 133 These and many other devices ensure that all the non-specialist teachers of English are fully resourced. 1979 *Observer* 23 Sept. 4/8 Social workers have been inadequately trained and inadequately resourced to meet the expectations upon them.

re'sourceful, *a.* [f. prec. + -FUL.]

1. Full of resource; fertile in expedient.

1851 D. G. MITCHELL *Fresh Glean.* 67 What is five francs a day to a man of such resourceful spirit? 1868 GLADSTONE *Juv. Mundi* x. (1869) 389 His distinguishing intellectual endowment is to be.. resourceful, elastic, versatile. 1891 E. PEACOCK *N. Brendon* I. 12 She was a strong-willed, resourceful woman.

2. Rich or abounding in resources.

1880 SIR R. TEMPLE *India in 1880*, 95 The Government, again, finding the money market in London so conveniently resourceful, resorted to it. 1888 BRYCE *Amer. Commw.* v. xcvi. III. 346 The economical conditions of a new and resourceful country, with an abundance of unoccupied land and mineral wealth.

Hence **re'sourcefulness.**

1869 FARRAR *Fam. Speech* i. (1873) 35 With all our energy and resourcefulness. 1899 *Allbutt's Syst. Med.* VIII. 942 Experiments characterized by a sagacity, a resourcefulness, and a perseverance rarely excelled.

re'sourceless, *a.* [f. as prec. + -LESS.] Without resource; destitute of resources.

1787 *Generous Attachm.* IV. 113 The resourceless Mr. Traffic, confounded and silent, is the picture of despair! 1826 W. JAY *Chr. Contempl.* vi. 197 He is laid waste, but he is not resourceless. 1886 A. WEIR *Hist. Basis Mod. Europe* (1889) 540 Resourceless youths who managed to exist.. on the patronage of the public.

Hence **re'sourcelessness.**

1827 A. W. FONBLANQUE *Eng. under 7 Administr.* (1837) I. 84 We are only to look around us, and wonder at our utter resourcelessness. 1866 *Contemp. Rev.* II. 202 Poverty,.. thinking on her own resourcelessness, sought his company. 1897 WESTCOTT *Chr. Aspects of Life* 413 The temptations and resourcelessness of the poor.

†**resourd,** *v. Obs. rare.* Also **resword, resourdre.** [ad. OF. *resourdre*: see RESOURCE.] *intr.* To rise or spring up again.

c 1440 MYRC *Festial* 203 Scho.. dyde penawnce for her synnes, and soo reswordyd agayne to grace. *c* 1477 CAXTON *Jason* 27 Yf a herte infortunate.. may resourdre whan fortune wyll fauoure and ayde. 1481 —— *Myrr.* II. iii. 67 Gyon or nylus.. renneth vnder the erthe so ferre that it resourdeth in to the longe see whiche enuyronneth alle Ethiope. 1483 —— *Gold. Leg.* 290/1 From whens that the dethe grewe, from thens the lyf resourded.

†**re'souvenance.** *Obs. rare*⁻¹. [a. F. *resouvenance.*] Recollection, memory.

c 1430 *Pilgr. Lyf Manhode* II. cxxvii. (1869) 123 This mirrour is resouenaunce and acordaunce to that that men seyn.

resow (riː-), *v.* [RE- 5 a.] To sow again.

1611 FLORIO, *Riseminare*, to resowe, to sowe againe. 1626 BACON *Sylva* §669 They are forced to Resow Summer-corn where they Sowed Winter-corn. 1766 *Compl. Farmer* s.v. *Rye* 6 M 2/1 The chief use of this sort is to re-sow lands where the autumnal crop has failed. 1778 [W. MARSHALL] *Minutes Agric., Observ.* 78 Resowing Clover, when the Oats were in Haw, was of no perceptible service. 1859 DARWIN *Orig. Spec.* iii. 75 If several varieties of wheat be sown together, and the mixed seed be resown [etc.].

resowne, obs. form of REASON *sb.*¹

resoyngne: see RESOIGN.

resp, *sb. dial.* Also 8 respe. [Of obscure origin. Connexion with G. *räspe, raspe* (hence Da.

raspe, Sw. *rasp*), malanders, is very doubtful.] A distemper in sheep, the red-water.

1789 *Trans. Soc. Arts* VII. 77 The disorder..resembles what is termed in Lincolnshire, amongst the sheep, the Resp. **1799** A. YOUNG *Agric. Linc.* 376 About Louth, the loss in feeding rape, by the respe is very great. **1805** R. W. DICKSON *Pract. Agric.* II. 1169 The Resp or Red-water is another disorder to which sheep are exposed.

Hence ˈ**respy** *a.*, afflicted with the resp.

1856 P. THOMPSON *Hist. Boston* 720 Respy mutton.—The flesh of respy sheep.

resp (rɛsp), *a.* *nonce-wd.* Abbrev. of RESPECTABLE *a.* 4 a.

1922 JOYCE *Ulysses* 158 Resp girl (R.C.) wishes to hear of a post in fruit or pork shop.

resp, Sc. var. RASP *sb.*[1] and *v.*[1]; var. RASP *v.*[2]

†**respair**, *v.* and *sb.* *Obs. rare.*

Rendering L. *spem habere*, and so app. intended as the converse of *despair*, but other MSS. have *respire*.

c **1425** WYNTOUN *Chron.* IV. xvi. 1590 (Cotton), Sa Rome, befor dispayrit, þan Respayr in gud hope began [*Edinb.*[2] Respair hade in gude hope agane].

reˈsparkle, *v.* [RE- 5 a.] To sparkle again.

1708 OZELL tr. *Boileau's Lutrin* 52 Your Eyes resparkle with their wonted Fires.

respass, obs. f. RASPIS[1], variant of RASPIS[2].

reˈspeak (riː-), *v.* [RE- 5 a.]

1. To re-utter, re-echo, resound.

1602 SHAKS. *Ham.* I. ii. 128 The Kings Rouce, the heauens shall bruite againe, Respeaking earthly Thunder. **1855** SINGLETON *Virgil* I. 64 We sing not to the deaf: respeak the forests all. **1898** *Longm. Mag.* Jan. 226 Every meanest mound Respeaks the word that cries To Lazarus, Arise!

2. To speak again or further.

1620–6 QUARLES *Feast for Worms* 1665 The Lord to Ionah thus respake.

respect (rɪˈspɛkt), *sb.* Also 3–6 **respecte**; *Sc.* 5, 9 **respek**, 9 **respeck**. [ad. L. *respect-us*, f. ppl. stem of *respicĕre*: see next. Hence also F. *respect*, Sp. *respecto*, *respeto*, It. *re-*, *rispetto*, Pg. *respeito*.]

I. In phrases (usually) without article.

These are chiefly direct adoptions of L. uses, as *habere respectum*, *respectu*, *sine respectu*.

1. ***to have respect to***: **a.** To have regard or relation *to*, or connexion with, something.

c **1391** CHAUCER *Astrol.* I. §21 Euerich of thise 12 Signes [of the zodiac] hath respecte to a certein parcelle of the body of a man and hath it in gouernance. **1398** TREVISA *Barth. De P.R.* XIX. vi. (Bodl. MS.), For euen fernes haþ alwey respect to ye vttermoste parties. **1541** ELYOT *Cast. Helthe* K vj b, Sanguyne and fleumatyke men have more respecte unto drythe; coleryke and melancolye, unto moysture. **1551** WILSON *Logicke* (1580) 12 b, The ground of every thyng, and the ende whereunto it hath respecte or consideracion. **1652** EARL MONM. tr. *Bentivoglio's Hist. Relat.* 8 Other such like important affairs, all which have respect to the Generall Union. **1699** SALMON *Bate's Dispens.* (1713) 134/2 This Spirit is opening, and has Respect to the Head and Womb. **1759** SARAH FIELDING *C'tess of Dellwyn* II. 37 Perhaps Lady Dellwyn's restless..Movement might have more Respect to the shewing of her Shadow, than even herself. *a* **1842** ARNOLD *Lect. Mod. Hist.* (1845) 125 The limits..have, often, respect to no natural boundaries, but are purely arbitrary. **1877** M. ARNOLD *Last Ess. on Church* 105 They all have a useful end to serve, and have respect to that end solely.

b. To have reference, to refer, *to* something.

1542 UDALL *Erasm. Apoph.* 243 This latine diccion, *præsens*,..hath respecte vnto three tymes. **1584** R. SCOT *Discov. Witchcr.* 551 This name hath not alwaies a respect unto the generation of the sonne of God. **1608** W. WILKES *Sec. Mem.* 13 Those rules..have respect more to your owne private, then reference to the publicke, good. **1641** L'ESTRANGE *God's Sabbath* 126 The truth is, all ceremoniall laws have respect to the latitude of Jury. **1724** A. COLLINS *Gr. Chr. Relig.* 49 The expressions..have only in a secondary sense a respect to that destruction. **1819** G. S. FABER *Dispens.* (1823) I. 167 We may be sure, that it had respect to some special point of doctrine. **1849** S. R. MAITLAND *Ess.* 19, I will here offer only a single remark, which has respect to the use [etc.].

2. ***to have respect to***: †**a.** To turn *to*, refer *to*, for information. *Obs.*

1432–50 tr. *Higden* (Rolls) I. 115 As for other meruayles of the temple haue respecte to the bokes of Kynges.

†**b.** To have an eye *to*, to give heed *to*, by looking at. *Obs.*

a **1483** *Liber Niger* in *Househ. Ord.* (1790) 45 This maistyr sittith in the halle, next unto these Henxmen, at the same boarde, to have his respecte unto theyre demeanynges. **1535** COVERDALE *Gen.* iv. 4 The Lorde had respecte vnto Abell and to his offerynge. — *Eccles.* xi. 4 He that regardeth ye wynde, shal not sowe: and he that hath respecte vnto the cloudes, shal not reape. **1611** BIBLE *Isa.* xvii. 7 At that day shall a man looke to his Maker, and his eyes shall haue respect to the Holy one of Israel.

c. To give heed, attention, or consideration *to* something; to have regard *to*; to take into account. Also const. ellipt. with *that*. (Cf. 13.)

1483 *Lett. Rich. III & Hen. VII* (Rolls) I. 45 To endent with his grace as it shall mowe be best accorded betwene thaim, havyng respecte as well to the ease of this tymes as to othere presidentes. *c* **1500** *Lancelot* 381 To dremys, sir, shuld no man have Respek. **1584** R. SCOT *Discov. Witchcr.* (1886) 7 Whosoever shall onllie have respect to the constancie of their words uttered, would easilie beleeve they were true indeed. **1625** PURCHAS *Pilgrims* II. VII. vi. 1125 But hauing respect that night began to come on,..we tooke in our sailes. **1688** HOLME *Armoury* III. 339/1 Of Weights, I have had respect to that of Troy only. **1864** J. H. NEWMAN *Apol.* App. 84 In an oath one ought to have respect to the intention of the party swearing.

d. To have in view; to allude *to*.

1542 UDALL *Erasm. Apoph.* 59 To this had the poete Horatius respecte, in thus saiyng. **1583** FULKE *Def. Trans. Script.* (Parker Soc.) 566 What folly it is to think our translators had respect to your popish devotions, by the name of 'devotion'! **1824** HEBER *Life Jer. Taylor* p. cxxxviii, He tells us that Balaam, when he prayed to die the death of the righteous, had only respect to length of days. **1873** J. H. NEWMAN *Idea Univ.* 328 When I speak of the formation of a Catholic school of writers, I have respect principally to the matter of what is written.

3. †**a.** ***in respect of***, in comparison with. *Obs.*

Common in the 16th and 17th centuries.

13.. *E.E. Allit. P.* A. 84 Þe sunne bemez [were] bot blo & blynde, In respecte of þat adubbement. **1432–50** tr. *Higden* (Rolls) VII. 149 Brennynge flammes.., in respecte of [L. *respectu*] the heete of whom this fyre materialle is but as warme warm water unto scaldynge water. **1526** *Pilgr. Perf.* (W. de W. 1531) 14 Fewe of them or none in respecte of the hole miscaryed. **1588** SHAKS. *L.L.L.* v. ii. 639 Hector was but a Troyan in respect of this. **1621** LADY M. WROTH *Urania* 85 His spirit is so much greater, as commonly a mans is, in respect of a womans. **1687** A. LOVELL tr. *Thevenot's Trav.* I. 152 A well of indifferent good Water, at least in respect of the other Waters of Mecha. **1749** LAVINGTON *Enthus. Meth. & Papists* II. (1754) 14 Their respect to him, he says, is nothing in respect of what they ought to shew. **1751** R. PALTOCK *P. Wilkins* xxii, What can she bring from it, says I to myself, in respect of what must be left behind?

†**b.** So ***in*** (or ***to***) ***the respect of***. *Obs.*

1432–50 tr. *Higden* (Rolls) I. 77 That the altitude and eminence scholde be schewede excellente, and incomparable in the respecte of [L. *respectu*] oure places habitable. *a* **1533** LD. BERNERS *Gold. Bk. M. Aurel.* (1546) 4 b, I write to thee but littell to the respecte of that I would write. **1550** CRANMER *Defence* 87 He is but a yonge newe author in the respect of those which we haue brought in for our party.

c. Also ***in respect to***.

1526 *Pilgr. Perf.* (W. de W. 1531) 7 Englande, whiche is but a small yle and a lytell corner in respecte to ye hole worlde. **1690** CHILD *Disc. Trade* (1698) 218 The productions of the Spanish-West-India commodities are so inconsiderable in respect to the English. **1771** LUCKOMBE *Hist. Print.* 130 Printing at this city was early, in respect to other places in this kingdom. **1904** H. JAMES *Golden Bowl* I. i. 11 She had struck him, in respect to the beautiful world, as one of the beautiful, the most beautiful things.

†**d.** ***in respect***, in comparison. *Obs.*

1542 UDALL *Erasm. Apoph.* 148 Bondemenne are in respecte and comparison, the feete of their maisters. **1591** SYLVESTER *Du Bartas* I. iii. 513 What will remaine? Ah! nothing (in respect). **1621** BURTON *Anat. Mel.* II. iii. III. (1651) 326 That all-commanding country is possessed by petty Princes, Rome a small Village in respect.

4. ***in respect*** (***of***): **a.** With reference to; as relates to or regards. †Also with *the*.

1530 TINDALE *Answ. More* (Parker Soc.) 175 The axe doth nothing in respect of the hand that heweth, save receive. **1591** SHAKS. *Two Gent.* III. i. 327 Item, shee is not to be fasting in respect of her breath. **1620** BRATHWAIT *Five Senses* in *Archaica* (1815) II. VI. Table, He aggravates..the misery of this life in respect of Sin. **1654** R. CODRINGTON tr. *Iustine* IX. 139 This day did set a period to all Greece, in the respect of their antient liberty. **1748** HARTLEY *Observ. Man* I. Pref., The great Freedom which I have used in respect of all Orders of Men. **1792** OSBALDISTON *Brit. Sportsman* 51 Bedding in respect of horses and other cattle, denotes straw or litter spread under them to lie on. **1825** MOORE *Sheridan* I. 236 In respect of mere style, too, the workmanship of..Sheridan is well worth..attention. **1868** VISCT. STRANGFORD *Select.* (1869) II. 240 These letters are undated both in respect of time and place.

†**b.** In view *of*, by reason or because *of*. *Obs.*

1583 FULKE *Def. Trans. Script.* xviii. 473 Oecumenius,..a Doctour of as little authoritie, as anye other, in respect of the late season, in whyche he liued. **1632** LITHGOW *Trav.* II. 75 Serigo..was anciently called..Schotera, in respect of the fine Marble that is got there. **1669** STURMY *Mariner's Mag.* II. vi. 68 This Quadrant..I hold to be as necessary an Instrument as Seamen can use, in respect of its plainess, and brevity. **1738** tr. *Guazzo's Art Convers.* 132 Their Juniors do them Honour in Respect of their being older.

c. Considering, seeing, since (*that*).

1580 FULKE *Dang. Rock* xii. Wks. (Parker Soc.) II. 319 Rather in respect that he had greater cause to love Christ. **1600** SHAKS. *A.Y.L.* III. ii. 17 In respect it is in the fields, it pleaseth mee well. *a* **1641** BP. MOUNTAGU *Acts & Mon.* (1642) 105 Nor was it conferred upon him by..Darius Histaspes, in respect that he was heire apparant unto the former Kings of Judah. **1649** EVELYN *Diary & Corr.* (1852) III. 53 How to prevent future ruin, in respect some of us are for an universal toleration: others, for English freedom only? **1876** GLADSTONE *Glean.* (1879) II. 350 To a bad clergyman this may be an advantage, in respect that it allows him to remain bad, and to grow worse with impunity.

†**d.** In case. *Obs. rare*$^{-1}$.

1597–8 BACON *Ess.*, *Of Expense*, Some forbeare it not vpon negligence alone, but doubting to bring themselues into Melancholy in respect they shall finde it broken.

e. With respect *to* something. (Cf. 7 b.) *rare.*

1841 LATHAM *Eng. Lang.* II. x. 178 Unless we admit the supposition in respect to *g*, that has been indicated in respect to *c*. *Ibid.* 184.

†**5.** ***for*** (***the***) ***respect of***: **a.** For the sake of, because of. **b.** In respect of. *Obs.*

1542 UDALL *Erasm. Apoph.* 95 To geue a mocke to the feloe that stood so highly in his owne conceipte for the respecte of suche trifleyng bagguage. **1549** LATIMER *Ploughers* (Arb.) 25 Who wyll susteyne any damage for the respecte of a publique commoditie? **1566** PAINTER *Pal. Pleas.* II. 315 And verily his prophecy was to true for respect of that which followed.

6. ***without respect***: †**a.** Without discrimination or consideration. *Obs.*

c **1540** tr. *Pol. Verg. Eng. Hist.* (Camden Soc. No. 36) 211 Thus the barbarus people, withowte respecte, polluted bothe thinggs divine & humaine. **1594** BEDINGFIELD tr. *Machiavelli's Florentine Hist.* (1595) 203 Murthering both guiltie and unguiltie people without respect.

b. Without consideration *of*, or regard *to*, something. Also const. ellipt. with *what*.

1549 LATIMER *Ploughers* (Arb.) 19 A fayth that maketh a man rightuous wythout respecte of workes. **1590** SPENSER *F.Q.* III. ii. 7 Onely for honour and for high regard, Without respect of richesse or reward. **1603** KNOLLES *Hist. Turks* (1621) 38 The Emperour..adventured his owne person, without respect what danger might thereof ensue. **1651** JANE *Image Unbr.* 59 Iconoclastes heapes up untruths without respect to the apparence of their detection.

7. ***with respect***: †**a.** Relatively; in due proportion. *Obs. rare.*

1597 J. KING *On Jonas* (1618) 224 In part, not wholly; with respect, not absolutely. **1646** EARL MONM. tr. *Biondi's Civ. Wars* IV. 3 Their governours..ought to make use thereof alternatly, and with respect, but not excesse.

b. With reference or regard *to* something.

1719 DE FOE *Crusoe* II. (Globe) 409 After this, the Colony enjoy'd a perfect Tranquillity with Respect to the Savages. **1765** A. DICKSON *Treat. Agric.* (ed. 2) 32 With respect to the first of these questions, there are three opinions. **1824** SIR J. MACINTOSH *Sp.* 15 June, Wks. 1846 III. 439 With respect..to the State Papers laid before us, I see nothing in them to blame or to regret. **1871** B. STEWART *Heat* (ed. 2) §12 A body ..changes its state with respect to heat.

†**c.** In regard *of* something. *Obs. rare*$^{-1}$.

1642 EATON *Honey-c. Free Justif.* 472 Not drawne thereto with the terrours of the Law, or hireling-like with respect of our owne profit. **1721** BRADLEY *Philos. Acc. Wks. Nat.* 162 At a vast Distance from one another, with respect of Magnitude.

II. 8. †**a.** An aspect of a thing; a relative property or quality; a relationship. *Obs.* (Common in 17th c.)

1495 *Trevisa's Barth. De P.R.* (W. de W.) III. v. 52 The soule that is one is callyd by dyuers names in dyuers respectes and highte anima while he is in the body and yeuyth it lyfe. **1586** A. DAY *Eng. Secretary* II. (1625) 104 [The secretary] is at the pleasure and appointment of another to be commanded, and being in a second respect as a friend [etc.]. **1599** B. JONSON *Ev. Man out of Hum.* IV. v, Things of consequence must haue their respects, where, how, and to whom. **1653** H. MORE *Conject. Cabbal.* (1662) 3 The logos,..in which all ideas and their respects are contained. *a* **1670** RUST *Disc. Truth* (1682) 157 If there be no immutable respects in things, but Just and Unjust..are respects made be meer arbitrarious Will. **1748** G. WHITE *Serm.* (MS.), Doth Relation to us alter the Case, and that Respect alone impart worth? **1753** JOHNSON *Adventurer* No. 107 ¶5 Whatever has various respects, must have various appearances of good and evil, beauty or deformity.

b. A particular, a point, a detail. Only in phrases with *in*, as ***in all***, ***many***, or ***some respects***, ***in this respect***, etc.

1581 J. BELL *Haddon's Answ. Osorius* 179 Let us compare with this blynd Philosophy of Cicero, the Divinity of Osorius in all respectes as bussardlyke. **1583** STUBBES *Anat. Abus.* II. (1882) 76 Dooing the dutie of a good shepheard in euerie respect. **1611** BIBLE *Transl. Pref.* ¶15 Neuer scorne those that be not in all respects so complete as they should bee. **1671** MILTON *P.R.* IV. 521 Yet thee I thought In some respect far higher so declar'd. **1736** BUTLER *Anal.* I. i. Wks. 1874 I. 30 Death may, in some sort, and in some respects, answer to our birth. **1777** SHERIDAN *Sch. Scand.* IV. iii, She shall..be her own Mistress in that Respect for the future. **1800** COLQUHOUN *Comm. Thames* Pref., The Subject is in many respects new. **1875** JOWETT *Plato* (ed. 2) I. 463, I should like to know in what respect the argument is not sufficient.

9. A relationship of one person or thing to another; a reference *to* some thing or person.

a. In phr. ***to have a*** (..) ***respect to***.

1551 T. WILSON *Logike* (1580) 12 Relatives are those whiche.., as a man would saie, have a mutual respect one to an other. **1587** GOLDING *De Mornay* xvi. (1617) 286 Punishment and sin haue a mutuall respect one to another, as a sore and a salue. **1681** BELON *New Myst. Physick* 12 The Fourth thing to be observed, has a Respect to the certainty of the Cure. *a* **1706** EVELYN *Hist. Relig.* (1850) II. 29 The observance of the seventh day had a peculiar respect to the Israelites. **1710** BERKELEY *Princ. Hum. Knowl.* I. §140 It having a like respect to other spirits that blueness or heat by me perceived has to those ideas perceived by another. **1816** FABER *Orig. Pagan Idol.* II. 288 The pretended nurses of Jupiter have all a similar respect to the deluge. **1850** McCOSH *Div. Govt.* III. i. (1874) 322 A worldly morality which has no respect to God.

b. In other uses. Also with *betwixt*.

1607 J. NORDEN *Surv. Dial.* I. 12 An indifferent Surueyor, namely, such a one as carieth equall respects to Lord and Tenant. **1644** DIGBY *Nat. Soul* 359 We shall find, that all they do consist *in*, or *of* certaine respects betwixt two things. **1729** BUTLER *Serm.* Wks. 1874 II. 13 The very terms..imply a relation or respect of parts to each other. **1748** G. WHITE *Serm.* (MS.), To be careful of our respects to him and careless of those to men, is to be defective in one half of our Religion.

†**10. a.** Relationship; reference. *Obs.*

1596 SHAKS. *Merch. V.* v. i. 99 *Ner.* It is your musicke Madame of the house. *Por.* Nothing is good I see without respect, Methinkes it sounds much sweeter then by day! **1621** BURTON *Anat. Mel.* III. iv. I. iii, Whether he can produce respect without a foundation or terme. **1662** PLAYFORD *Skill Mus.* III. (1674) 34 Relation, or reference, or respect not harmonical.

†**b.** Bearings, results. *Obs. rare*$^{-1}$.

1692 DRYDEN *St. Euremont's Ess.* 14 The First Wars of the Romans were of very great Importance in their respect, but little remarkable.

III. †**11.** A respite. *Obs.* Cf. RESPET(T *sb.*

c **1440** *Alph. Tales* 221 And þan sho askid of þe law a respecte, & had it grawntid. **1533** in Marsden *Sel. Pl. Crt.*

Admiral. (Selden Soc.) II. 65 All other letters of grace, respectes, and other impetracions of favour. **1567** *Reg. Privy Council Scot.* I. 540 Eschetis of gudis,..respectis, remissionis, supersedereis.

†12. a. Appearance, aspect. *Obs. rare.*

1582 BATMAN *Barth. De P.R.* IV. x, There is holownes of eyen with moyst respect [L. *cum humido aspectu*]. **1615** SANDYS *Trav.* (1627) 216 Tyrus, is now no other than an heape of ruines; yet have they a reuerent respect.

†b. A view; a backward survey. *Obs. rare.*

1542 BOORDE *Dyetary* ii. (1870) 235, I had rather not to buyld..a howse, than to buylde one without a good respecte in it, to it, and from it. *a* **1661** FULLER *Worthies, Wales* IV. (1662) 7 The Welsh travailers, when they have climed up a hill,..rain their horses backward, and stand still a while, taking a prospect (or respect rather) of the Country they have passed.

13. a. Regard, consideration. Const. *of* or *to*.

c **1530** *Crt. of Love* xxiii, No respecte hauyng what was beste to done. **1551** ROBINSON tr. *More's Utopia* II. (1895) 305 The respecte of euery mans priuate commoditie. **1593** SHAKS. *Lucr.* 275 Then, childish fear, avaunt!.. Respect and reason, wait on wrinkled age! **1605** A. WOTTON *Answ.* 118 They will do nothing, but with especial respect to themselves. **1606** G. W[OODCOCK] *Hist. Ivstine* v. 25 The Athenians..tooke more respect to their safety, then care of their honour. **1652** NEEDHAM tr. *Selden's Mare Cl.* 25 Wee shall next see what respect hath been had unto the Sea, either in the very first or any more antient Distribution or Division of things. **1791** COWPER *Iliad* XIX. 314 For no respect of amorous desire, Or other purpose, have I lay'd mine hand On fair Brisëis. **1814** CARY *Dante, Par.* XXII. 35, I will make answer even to the thought, Which thou hast such respect of. *a* **1834** COLERIDGE *Lit. Rem.* (1839) IV. 396 Have no respect to what nation a man is of.

b. Discrimination, partiality, or favour in regard *of* persons or things. (Cf. PERSON *sb.* 13.)

1535 COVERDALE *Prov.* xxiv. 23 It is not good, to haue respecte of any personne in iudgment. **1558** GOODMAN *How to Obey* 170 Gods vengeance, which he with out respecte of persones wil powre..vpon all transgressors. **1601** SHAKS. *Twel. N.* II. iii. 98 Is there no respect of place, persons, nor time in you? **1641** THORNDIKE *Govt. Ch.* 38 We see the reason why there is no respect of Timothy, in his instructions to the elders of Ephesus. **1837** HT. MARTINEAU *Soc. Amer.* III. 33 Those who are brought up to have any respect of occupations,—to regard a grocer as beneath a banker. **1874** SIDGWICK *Meth. Ethics* III. v. 239 It is of the highest importance that judges and administrators should never be persuaded by money or otherwise to shew 'respect of persons'.

†c. Heed, care, attention. *Obs.*

1557 NORTH *Gueuara's Diall Pr.* (1568) 23 Women must take great respect, least they geve straungers occasion to speake of them. **1596** BACON *Max. & Use Com. Law* Pref., When men shall carry a respect not to descend into any course that is corrupt. **1615** W. LAWSON *Country Housew. Gard.* (1626) 22 At the setting of your plants you must haue such a respect, that the distance of them [etc.]. **1647** LILLY *Chr. Astrol.* clxvii. 723 Having care and respect to give February 29. dayes in the Leap-yeer.

†d. *pl.* Attention or consideration given to more than one point or matter. *Obs.*

1612 BACON *Ess., Of Ceremonies & Respects*, It is losse also in businesse to be too full of respects, or to be to curious in obseruing times and opportunities. **1640** E. DACRES tr. *Machiavelli's Prince* 205 We see that men..proceed therein diversly; some with respects, others more bold. **1656** EVELYN *Mem.* (1857) III. 73, I shall,..I hope, prevail with you that I may have the honour to see you again at my poor villa, when my respects are less diverted.

†e. An opinion or view. *Obs.*

1662 GERBIER *Princ.* 28, I must proceed and conclude with my humble respects concerning Palaces of..Princes.

14. a. A consideration; a fact or motive which assists in, or leads to, the formation of a decision; an end or aim. (Very common in 17th c.)

1549 LATIMER *Ploughers* (Arb.) 37 He was not moued wyth these worldlie respectes, with these prudente considerations. **1595** SHAKS. *John* III. i. 318, I muse your Maiesty doth seeme so cold, When such profound respects doe pull you on. **1632** BROME *Northern Lass* I. vii, What Respect Moves you to make this strong disswasion? **1673** TEMPLE *Observ. United Prov.* Wks. 1720 I. 26 These Respects gave the first Rise to a Treaty of Peace. **1705** ADDISON *Italy* 511 The same Respect that made him quit this Government, might at another time tempt him to give up that of Neuf-Chatel. **1760–72** H. BROOKE *Fool of Qual.* (1809) IV. 64 All the honours and worldly respects, for which I formerly risked my life. **1846** TRENCH *Mirac.* i. (1862) 105 Higher respects than those of flesh and blood moved Him to the choosing of the present moment.

b. With *for*. (Common *c* 1550–1650.)

1536 CROMWELL in Merriman *Life & Lett.* (1902) II. 16 Whiche..compelled his Maiestie to staye in the graunting of any contribucion for the respectes expressed. **1570–6** LAMBARDE *Peramb. Kent* (1826) p. vi, I resolved (for sundrie iust respectes) to begin first with that Shire. **1632** LITHGOW *Trav.* v. 221 He saw the guide..send a Moore before him, for what respect he knew not. **1662** BARGRAVE *Pope Alex. VII* (1867) 36 At his return he was for several respects promoted to a Cardinal's cap.

IV. †15. ? Dread, fear. *Obs.*

1432–50 tr. *Higden* (Rolls) VII. 147, Y lawde and commende thy manhode that thou dredes God moore then me, and the respecte of hevyn moore then thy cuntre.

16. a. Deferential regard or esteem felt or shown towards a person or thing.

1586 T. B. *La Primaud. Fr. Acad.* I. (1589) 680 We have the temples in great respect and reverence. **1596** SHAKS. *1 Hen. IV*, I. iii. 8 That Title of respect, Which the proud soule ne're payes, but to the proud. **1611** BIBLE *Transl. Pref.* ¶1 Zeale to promote the common good..deserueth certainly much respect and esteeme. **1690** TEMPLE *Ess., Heroic Virtue* Wks. 1720 I. 205 So great a Respect, or rather Veneration, is paid to this wise and admirable Constitution. **1712** STEELE *Spect.* No. 406 ¶1 A Friend, for whom he has a very great Respect. **1788** GIBBON *Decl. & F.* xlii. IV. 220 Some voluntary respect was yielded to age and valour. **1839** KEIGHTLEY *Hist. Eng.* II. 35 Her character remains the object of respect to all parties. **1878** R. W. DALE *Lect. Preach.* viii. 222 There is a certain measure of respect due from the people to their pastor.

b. The condition or state of being esteemed or honoured.

1597–8 BACON *Ess., Of Ceremonies & Respects*, Not to vse Ceremonies at all, is to teach others not to vse them againe, and so diminish his respect. **1633** BP. HALL *Hard Texts, N.T.* 32 For they are in so high and deare respect with God. **1655–60** STANLEY *Hist. Philos.* (1701) 78/2 What wants reason, wants respect. **1772** *Junius Lett.* lxviii. (1788) 343 You stand degraded from the respect and authority of your office. **1820** BYRON *Mar. Fal.* v. iii, Youth without honour, age without respect. **1865** M. ARNOLD *Ess. Crit.* ii. (1875) 83 By which he may be..held in respect when he himself is inclined to take liberties.

†c. Rank, standing; station in life. *Obs.*

1601 HOLLAND *Pliny* I. 106 The townes of any respect be Dædala and Crya, peopled onely with banished persons. **1601** SHAKS. *Jul. C.* I. ii. 59, I haue heard, Where many of the best respect in Rome..Haue wish'd, that Noble Brutus had his eyes. **1651** tr. *De-las-Coveras' Don Fenise* 295 Although it was night, I saw that which made me judge her to be a person of respect.

transf. **1652** CULPEPPER *Eng. Physic.* (1656) 83 The greater wild Daisie is a Wound Herb of good respect.

†d. ***a coach*** (or ***litter***) ***of respect***, ? one used on occasions of state. *Obs.*

1676 LADY FANSHAWE *Memoir* (1829) 281 Then a coach of respect, lined with cloth of gold, mixed with green. Then a litter of respect, lined with the same stuff.

e. ***with*** (***all due***) ***respect*** and varr.: a polite phr. expressing proper deference, freq. used before stating (with some insistence) disagreement with another person's views. Also const. *to*.

1826 M. R. MITFORD *Our Village* II. 207 [My greyhound] is sliding her snake-like head into my hand, at once to invite the caress which she likes so well, and to intimate with all due respect that it is time to go home. **1923** C. MACKENZIE *Parson's Progress* xviii. 257 With all respect to the gentleman at the back of the hall who passed that remark, I tell him that if you think you can do anything with your review.., you're mistaken. **1977** *Belfast Tel.* 28 Feb. 6/4 With respect, I feel that the views expressed by Lord MacDermott are unbalanced from the very isolated position of a judge who, by necessity of office, must lead a somewhat cloistered life. **1977** *Church Times* 22 July 10/1 It is, with the greatest respect to His Grace, very little use to say that the book has 'caused more hubbub than it is worth'. **1978** *Ibid.* 25 Aug. 11/3 With all due respect to your three correspondents, I do not think they have answered M. J. Feaver's question (August 11). **1978** *Times* 13 Mar. 19/4 With great respect, this well-intentioned suggestion seems almost wholly devoid of merit. **1980** J. FOLLETT *Churchill's Gold* II. i. 86 With respect, admiral, we should not be building boats for any other purpose than for sinking enemy shipping.

17. *pl.* **†a.** Deferential or courteous attentions; actions expressive of respect for a person; politenesses, courtesies. *Obs.*

1612 BACON *Ess., Of Praise*, Some praises come of good wishes and respects, which is a forme due in ciuility to Kings and great persons. **1648** GAGE *West Ind.* 25 We..gave hearty thanks to the Indians for their kind respects unto us. *a* **1656** BP. HALL *Rem. Wks.* (1660) 46 The Promoters of the petitions were entertained with great respects. **1707** *Refl. upon Ridicule* 352 The Science of Respects, is, as I may say, the Soul of Society.

†b. Deferential salutations. *Obs. rare*$^{-1}$.

a **1674** CLARENDON *Hist. Reb.* XII. §101 When they had made their several respects, and came to the King, he lightly moved his hat, and bade them cover.

c. In complimentary formulæ, usually conveying a message expressive of regard or esteem.

c **1645** HOWELL *Lett.* IV. xxvi, So with my very kind respects to my Sister, I rest Your loving brother, J. H. *a* **1657** R. LOVEDAY *Lett.* (1663) 35, I pray do my due respects to those you think my friends. **1729** SWIFT *Let. to Gay* 19 Mar., You are the first to present my most humble respects to the duchess of Queensberry. **1780** in Nichols *Anecd.* (1815) IX. 263 The Lord Chancellor presents his best respects to Mr. Thicknesse. **1782** MISS BURNEY *Cecilia* VII. ix, Pray give my respects to him. **1833** HT. MARTINEAU *Loom & Lugger* II. iv. 77 And give my respects to the Lieutenant's lady. **1894** RAYMOND *Sam & Sabina* x, 'Here's luck!' said Ashford. 'My respects!' drank Christopher.

d. ***to pay one's respects***, to show polite attention *to* a person by presenting oneself or by making a call.

1668 ETHEREDGE *She wou'd if she cou'd* I. i, If I can I will slip away, and pay my respects to your lady. **1734** tr. *Rollin's Anc. Hist.* (1827) V. 2 The Gauls..came to pay their respects to that general. **1771** SMOLLETT *Humph. Cl.* (1815) 188 When he came home, he expressed great eagerness to pay his respects to his master. **1833** HT. MARTINEAU *Brooke Farm* i. 2, I generally choose this road, and pay my respects to the rookery before doing the same to the lady. **1886** W. J. TUCKER *E. Europe* 116, I came out here the day before yesterday to pay my respects to the Count.

V. 18. *Comb.*, as ***respect-inspiring***, ***-worthy*** adjs.

1876 MRS. OLIPHANT *Phœbe, Junior* xxxviii, His clergyman,..an awful and respect-inspiring personage. **1833** CARLYLE *Diderot, Misc. Ess.* (1888) V. 9 In this French Sheffield, Diderot's father was a cutler,..a much respected and respect-worthy man. **1889** 'MARK TWAIN' *Connecticut Yankee* xiii. 154 They were about all that was useful, or worth saving, or respectworthy. **1915** A. QUILLER-COUCH *Nicky-Nan* xxiii. 296 A neighbours' quarrel, and between folks I know to be so respectworthy. **1973** *Times Lit. Suppl.* 7 Sept. 1024/4 Horatio Parker (who was none the less respect-worthy, never mean or petty).

respect (rɪˈspɛkt), *v.* [f. L. *respect-*, ppl. stem of *respicĕre* to look (back) at, regard, consider, or ad. the frequentative of this, *respectāre*. Cf. F. *respecter* (16th c.), Sp. *respe(c)tar*, Pg. *respeitar*, It. *rispettare*.]

†1. *trans.* To respite; to put off, neglect. *Obs.*

1542–3 *Act 34 & 35 Hen. VIII*, c. 16 § 2 Soondrye soomes of money been respected to many persones, whiche haue ben Shirieffes..vpon theyre accomptes. **1549** DK. SOMERSET in Strype *Eccl. Mem.* (1721) II. 292 We..addressed our letters to you for due execution to be don..upon Paget..: which, as we be informed, is not don but respected. **1613** PURCHAS *Pilgrimage* 194 If he respect washing after these, if he be learned, he shall forget his learning. **1620** J. WILKINSON *Coroners & Sherifes* 10 There they respected execution of him to the intent they might procure his pardon.

†2. To regard, consider, take into account. *Obs.* (In common use *c* 1560–1660.)

1548 GESTE *Pr. Masse* 76 Is it not a deadely remorse to respect the worthy clerkes in thys realme and ye greate number of them and yet not one to wryte agaynste hyr? **1581** J. BELL *Haddon's Answ. Osorius* 139 Not bycause it is of itselfe nothyng (if you respect the substaunce of it). **1606** G. W[OODCOCK] *Hist. Ivstine* II. 13 For if ye respect the king, he had a great deale more wealth then valour. **1668** CULPEPPER & COLE *Barthol. Anat.* I. xvii. 45 The Kidney is shaped..like an Asarum leaf, if you respect the plane surface.

†b. To heed, pay attention to; to observe carefully. *Obs.* (Frequent *c* 1575–1630.)

1560 DAUS tr. *Sleidane's Comm.* 317 b, I respected nothinge els, than that..I might enjoy the inheritance of the heavenly kingdome. **1579** W. WILKINSON *Confut. Fam. Love* 16 b, The cunnyng Archer respecteth more to hitte the marke, than the curious watchyng of the clouen ayre. **1614** MERITON *Chr. Mans Assuring-ho.* 34 He little respecteth where he clappes himselfe downe. **1662** PLAYFORD *Skill Mus.* (1674) 29 Respect not the fourth below, but look to your fifth above.

†c. To regard, consider, look upon, as being of a certain kind, etc. *Obs. rare.*

1592 MARLOWE *Massacre Paris* II. v, Her gory colours of revenge, Whom I respect as leaves of boasting green. **1598–9** B. JONSON *Case Altered* IV. ii, To whom my father gave this name of Gasper, And as his own respected him to death. **1602** WARNER *Alb. Eng.* XIII. lxxviii. 322 Corruption not Production should we Euelnesse respect.

3. To be directed to; to refer or relate to; to deal or be concerned with.

1563 *Homilies* II. *Fasting* I. (1859) 284 For, when it [*sc.* fasting] respecteth a good end, it is a good work. **1598** BACON *Sacr. Medit., Miracles*, His doctrine respected the soule of man. **1663** PATRICK *Parab. Pilgr.* xxviii. (1668) 323 The greatest wits want perspicacity in things that respect their own interest. **1704** HEARNE *Duct. Hist.* Pref., The two parts of Knowledge which in a more eminent degree respect the Common Good and Convenience of Mankind. **1759** JOHNSON *Rasselas* xxx, Even love and hatred respect the past, for the cause must have been before the effect. **1819** G. S. FABER *Dispens.* (1823) I. 183 The primary question..would obviously respect the nature of that serpent. **1866** *Reader* July 676 The remaining part of the book respects man's position.

b. In *pres. pple.* With reference or regard to.

1732 POPE *Ess. Man* I. 51 Respecting Man, whatever wrong we call, May, must be right, as relative to all. **1782** PAINE *Let. Abbé Raynel* (1791) 73 Respecting Canada, one or other of the two following will take place. **1802** MAR. EDGEWORTH *Moral T.* (1816) I. xii. 95 He could not agree with him respecting the price. **1874** GREEN *Short Hist.* II. §8. 103 The legislation respecting ecclesiastical jurisdiction.

†c. To resemble. *Obs. rare*$^{-1}$.

1604 T. WRIGHT *Passions* (1620) 219 The heart..of man triangularly respecteth the blessed Trinitie; every corner a Person, and the solide substance your common essence.

†d. To relate to, as regards the effect or result produced. *Obs.*

1614 LATHAM *Falconry* (1633) 95 This scowring..resisteth rottennesse, also it greatly respecteth the head. **1655** CULPEPPER, etc. *Riverius* Printer to Rdr., For the use of these Books respects chiefly the Poor of this Nation. **1700** FLOYER *Cold Baths* I. ii. 36 Moistening respects the Skin, but heating and cooling shews the Effects it has on the Humours.

4. To treat or regard with deference, esteem, or honour; to feel or show respect for.

1560 DAUS tr. *Sleidane's Comm.* 34 b, He did not one whit respecte the highnes or dignitie of any parson. **1595** DANIEL *Civ. Wars* III. xxxviii, Which meaner wights of trust, and credit bare Not so respected could not looke t' effect. **1612** BACON *Ess., Fortune*, Fortune is to bee honoured and respected, and it be but for her daughters, Confidence and Reputation. **1657** W. RAND tr. *Gassendi's Life Peiresc* II. 181, I can truly bear him witness, that he most dearly respected them all. **1727** SWIFT *Let. to Gay* 27 Nov., I always loved and respected him very much. **1780** COWPER *Nightingale & Glow-worm* 33 Respecting in each other's case The gifts of nature and of grace. **1828** D'ISRAELI *Chas. I*, II. 298 Who could imagine that such a patriot would not be respected even by his enemies? **1879** R. K. DOUGLAS *Confucianism* iv. 96 If he should be unable to govern with dignity, the people will not respect him.

refl. **1784** COWPER *Task* II. 377 To such I render more than mere respect, Whose actions say that they respect themselves. *a* **1862** BUCKLE *Misc. Wks.* (1872) I. 112 When any class of men cease to be respected by the nation, they soon cease to respect themselves.

†b. To esteem, prize, or value (a thing). *Obs.*

1591 SHAKS. *Two Gent.* I. ii. 134 Shall these papers lye, like Tel-tales here? If you respect them; best to take them vp. **1613** PURCHAS *Pilgrimage* VII. xii. (1614) 712 Iron they had not: Gold they respected not. **1638** JUNIUS *Paint. Ancients* 177 They did respect gemmes more than to mangle them with cutting.

c. To treat with consideration; to refrain from injuring or interfering with; to spare.

1621 T. WILLIAMSON tr. *Goulart's Wise Vieillard* 146 Death respects neither babe, young nor old, man nor woman, rich nor poore. *a*1721 SHEFFIELD (Dk. Buckhm.) *Wks.* (1753) I. 4 Who..respectest none, And neither spar'st the laurel, nor the crown! 1745 POCOCKE *Descr. East* II. 152 In the excursions which they make for pleasure they are commonly respected by the Arabs. 1849 MACAULAY *Hist. Eng.* vi. II. 17 Lewis had, like James, repeatedly promised to respect the privileges of his Protestant subjects. 1877 A. B. EDWARDS *Up Nile* xii. 316 A dynasty that not only lightened the burdens of the poor but respected the privileges of the rich.

†**d.** To toast; to drink the health of. *Obs. rare.*
1708 J. PHILIPS *Cyder* I. 519 Whoever tastes, let him with grateful Heart Respect that ancient loyal House. 1766 A. NICOL *Poems* 50 (E.D.D.), Good ale and usque ga'd about In healths, as they respected Their friends that day.

†**5.** To expect, anticipate, look (for). *Obs. rare.*
1560 DAUS tr. *Sleidane's Comm.* 285 b, He would in no wyse assente to that,..& herein respected no daunger. 1601 B. JONSON *Poetaster* II. i, Gaine sauours sweetly from any thing; He that respects to get, must relish all commodities alike. 1623 PEMBLE *Wks.* (1635) I, I verily suppose there is none among you, who respects to heare his owne praises; if there be, I come not hither to give satisfaction to such.

6. a. *Her.* Of charges: To look at, face (*esp.* each other).
1562 LEGH *Armory* (1597) 46 A Lyon..is returned from his pray and taketh his rest, respecting his enemies. 1610 GUILLIM *Heraldry* III. xxii. (1611) 169 Fishes are borne hauriant, both respecting each other and also endorsed. 1688 HOLME *Armoury* III. 28/2 A Philip and Mary shilling hath a Man and Womans head respecting each other. 1780 EDMONDSON *Heraldry* II. Gloss. s.v., When beasts, birds or fish, are placed in armory to face each other, they are, by some mod. Heralds, termed respecting each other. 1847 [see RESPECTANT I].

†**b.** To regard; to look upon. *Obs.*
1567 *Trial Treas.* (1850) 28 God doth so guide the hartes of the juste, That they respect chiefly the celestiall treasure. 1596 *Thanksgiving* in *Liturg. Serv. Q. Eliz.* (1847) 668 Graciously respecting us in the merits of thy dear Son. 1620 E. BLOUNT *Horæ Subs.* 115 Wise men will not view such persons but with scorn, nor respect them but with disesteem.

†**c.** To look towards (a certain direction); to face (a specified place). *Obs.*
1583 STUBBES *Anat. Abus.* II. (1882) 4 Upon the south side it respecteth Germanie. 1603 KNOLLES *Hist. Turks* (1621) 795 That side of Malta which respecteth Sicilia, hath in it many good harbours. 1668 CULPEPPER & COLE *Barthol. Anat.* I. xvii. 47 With their sharp and lunary part they respect the kidneys. 1707 MORTIMER *Husb.* (1721) I. 374 The Rooms that respect each particular Coast,..as those Rooms..that regard the East. *a*1734 NORTH *Lives* (1826) II. 104 The latter stands on a sharp cliff respecting the north.

d. *intr.* To face or look *to* or *towards. rare.*
1585 T. WASHINGTON tr. *Nicholay's Voy.* I. iv, These Ilands by a small diuision of the Sea, respect towardes the South and North. 1612 BREREWOOD *Lang. & Relig.* (1635) 96 The..east side, that respecteth toward Europe. 1864 BOUTELL *Her. Hist. & Pop.* xxxii. (ed. 3) 470 An eagle rising and respecting to the sinister.

respectability (rɪspɛktəˈbɪlɪtɪ). [f. RESPECTABLE *a.* + -ITY. Cf. mod.F. *respectabilité.*]
1. a. The state, quality, or condition of being respectable in point of character or social standing. Also with a somewhat derogatory implication of affectation or spuriousness.
1785 TRUSLER *Mod. Times* I. p. vi, He is very sensible that there are in all classes of life, men of honour and respectability. 1802 MRS. J. WEST *Infidel Father* II. 157 He is said to have passed through the ordeal of a military life with high respectability. 1847 C. BRONTË *J. Eyre* x, A model of elderly English respectability. 1898 G. B. SHAW *You never can tell* II. Stage-direct., The excellent quality and condition of these garments, the gold-rimmed folding spectacles,..all testify to his respectability. 1907 G. B. SHAW *Major Barbara* III. 281 The seven deadly sins!—Yes, the deadly seven... Food, clothing, firing, rent, taxes, respectability and children. 1969 *Listener* 3 Apr. 443/1 The social cost was high: hypocrisy;..the substitute of 'respectability' (spurious morality) for thought-out morals. Now that couples who aren't ready to support them needn't have children at all, marriage is redundant. 1978 P. BAILEY *Leisure & Class in Victorian England* viii. 178 We approach respectability as a role rather than as an ideology... The myth of substantial working-class respectability.

b. *concr.* Those who are respectable.
1808 *Spirit Public Jrnls.* XII. 327 All the weight, talent, and respectability of the country. 1891 S. C. SCRIVENER *Our Fields & Cities* 87 Respectability pooh-poohs, but 'Respectability' does not visit the north-east corner of the cemetery Père la Chaise at Paris.

c. *transf.* Of things.
1903 G. B. SHAW *Man & Superman* p. xxviii, He and I and Mr. Sidney Webb were sowing our political wild oats as a sort of Fabian Three Musketeers, without any prevision of the surprising respectability of the crop that followed. 1976 *Times* 21 May 1/4 The alleged smear campaign against the Liberal Party..gained new respectability yesterday when the Prime Minister confirmed..that attempts were indeed being made to discredit individual members of the Liberal Party.

2. a. A person of respectable character.
1840 CARLYLE *Heroes* (1858) 342 Smooth-shaven Respectabilities not a few one finds, that are not good for much. 1888 *Times* 20 Sept. 7/2 Irishmen..laugh in their sleeve when the dull respectabilities of the Gladstonian party take the thing seriously.

b. *pl.* Those features of life and conduct which are regarded as respectable.
1843 CARLYLE *Past & Pres.* I. v. 41 With his cash-accounts and larders dropping fatness, with his respectabilities, warm garnitures, and pony-chaise. 1875 JOWETT *Plato* (ed. 2) I. 191 Out of a regard to the respectabilities of life.

3. Importance. *rare.*
1817 T. DWIGHT *Trav. New Eng.*, etc. (1821) II. 241 The District of Maine is fitted to derive its respectability especially from fishing, and commerce. 1824 L. MURRAY *Eng. Gram.* (ed. 5) I. 223 The diversity of sentiment on this subject, and the respectability of the different opponents, will naturally induce the readers to pause and reflect, before they decide.

reˈspectabilize, *v.* [f. next + -IZE.] *trans.* To render respectable.
1843 *Blackw. Mag.* LIV. 529 It took a long time to respectabilize its neighbourhood. 1879 MISS BRADDON *Clov. Foot* xxvii, Mr. Desrolles left the Manor House a new man. .. He was respectabilised by a full purse. 1933 G. STEIN *Autobiogr. Alice B. Toklas* v. 119 Uhde wished to respectabilise himself and she wanted to come into possession of her inheritance, which she could only do upon marriage. 1940 C. P. SNOW *Strangers & Brothers* xliv. 318 But the café had been respectabilized since then. There were now two floors, and neat waitresses. 1977 *Daily Tel.* 30 Apr. 13/4 Journalists are urged not to 'respectabilize' racist organizations.

respectable (rɪˈspɛktəb(ə)l), *a.* and *sb.* [f. RESPECT *sb.* + -ABLE. Cf. F. *respectable*, Sp. *respetable*, It. *rispettabile, -evole*, Pg. *respeitavel.*]
A. *adj.* †**1.** Worthy of notice, observation, or consideration. *Obs. rare.*
*a*1586 SIDNEY *Arcadia* III. Wks. 1724 II. 598 This unexpected adventure, or vehemently respectable misadventure. 1605 VERSTEGAN *Dec. Intell.* i. (1628) 10 It is also respectable that the most antient Germans being pagans ..ordained [etc.].

2. a. Worthy or deserving of respect by reason of some inherent quality or qualities.
1599 SANDYS *Europæ Spec.* (1605) F ij, The prince in maiesty..; and the people in their multitude are respectable and honourable.
1750 CHESTERF. *Lett.* ccxv. (1792) II. 326 Your studies, the respectable remains of antiquity. 1781 GIBBON *Decl. & F.* xxvii. III. 42 The wisdom of his laws, and the success of his arms, rendered his administration respectable in the eyes both of his subjects, and of his enemies. 1801 ELIZ. HELME *St. Marg. Cave* II. 56 His sorrows appear to me not only respectable but sacred. 1817 JAS. MILL *Brit. India* II. v. iv. 430 He had a personal antipathy to Hyder Ali, which in a mind like his was capable of weighing down more respectable motives. *a*1859 MACAULAY *Hist. Eng.* xxiii. V. 28 There might be a large respectable minority whose recollections might materially differ from the recollections of the majority.

b. Considerable in number, size, quantity, etc.
1755 MAGENS *Insurances* II. 475 They see a respectable Marine kept up in their Country ready to succour each other in Case of War. 1780 S. J. PRATT *Emma Corbett* (ed. 4) II. 44 He has the good fortune to conceal under his hat..a respectable contusion. 1840 BARHAM *Ingol. Leg.* Ser. I. Pref., A beautiful green lane..will carry them..to the foot of a very respectable hill. 1869 TOZER *Highl. Turkey* II. 337 Modern authorities—whose writings amount to a respectable literature.

c. Of comparative excellence; tolerable, fair.
1775 J. JEKYLL *Corr.* ii. (1894) 49 At five the spectacles commence; and first the comedy, which is very respectable. 1799 MRS. J. WEST *Tale Times* I. 155 He was said to possess very respectable literary talents. 1824 DIBDIN *Libr. Comp.* p. xv, The typographical execution..is delightful, and the engraved frontispieces are very respectable. 1858 HAWTHORNE *Fr. & It. Note-bks.* I. 155 It is at best but a respectable production. 1903 *Athenæum* 24 Oct. 552/1 Other places have had respectable weather.

d. Of writers, in respect of authority or literary merit.
1781 C. JOHNSTON *Hist. J. Juniper* II. 100 A question, both sides of which are supported by such respectable authorities. 1796 H. HUNTER tr. *St.-Pierre's Stud. Nat.* (1799) II. 436 An anonymous English Author, highly respectable for the soundness of his judgment. 1824 L. MURRAY *Eng. Gram.* I. 277 The practice of many writers, and some even of our most respectable writers, appears to be erroneous. 1866 FITZGERALD *Lamb* (ed. 2) 193 The complete collection of the more respectable English essayists.

3. a. Of persons: Worthy of respect, deserving to be respected, by reason of moral excellence.
1755 J. SHEBBEARE *Lydia* (1769) II. 436 An example to be followed by no man who would appear respectable in the great world. 1770 LANGHORNE *Plutarch* (1879) I. 179/2 Thucydides was a great and respectable man. 1816 COLERIDGE *Lett.* (1895) II. 665 If a balance and harmony of powers..render womanhood amiable and respectable. 1831 SIR J. SINCLAIR *Corr.* II. 236 The inhabitants of Norway are a most respectable race of people.

b. Used as a commendatory epithet.
1755 *Man* No. 9. 4 We shall endeavour..to ingratiate this respectable order [the clergy] with the people. 1780 S. J. PRATT *Emma Corbett* (ed. 4) II. 152, I caught the..affection ..from the respectable authors of my being. 1804 PARR in Barker *Life* (1829) II. 560, I am now on a visit to my respectable friend, Mr. Rye. 1815 *Paris Chit-chat* (1816) II. 174 Nor would the painter fail to give a conspicuous place to the respectable sister Bignan.

†**c.** As a term of address. *Obs.*
1768 *Woman of Honor* I. 205 My ever respectable Aunt. 1808 *Mem. Female Philos.* I. 72 My respectable, my tender mother.

4. a. Of persons: Of good or fair social standing, and having the moral qualities regarded as naturally appropriate to this. Hence, in later use, honest and decent in character or conduct, without reference to social position, or in spite of being in humble circumstances.
1758 MRS. LENNOX *Henrietta* v. viii. (1761) II. 260 It will be more for your reputation to have it known that you lived in such a respectable society. 1771-2 *Ess. fr. Batchelor* (1773) I. 120 His secretary,..the Provost, and many other respectable persons came to consult with him. 1806 R. CUMBERLAND *Mem.* (1807) II. 338 Visitors so respectable as the Lord Chief Justice Mansfield, the Ex-Premier Lord North. 1845 FORD *Handbk. Spain* I. 54 The best plan for those who want to buy a horse is to apply to some respectable private person. 1879 FROUDE *Cæsar* viii. 86 He expressed the opinions of the respectable middle classes, who had no sympathy with revolutionists.

b. So of appearance, character, institutions, etc.
1760-72 H. BROOKE *Fool of Qual.* (1809) IV. 4 A man..of a very respectable appearance. 1788 *Trifler* No. II. 140 He sent us to the most respectable schools he could select. 1803 MARY CHARLTON *Wife & Mistr.* IV. 32 The loss of the provision which might have afforded you a respectable maintenance. 1834 HT. MARTINEAU *Moral* I. 3 All labour for which there is a fair demand is equally respectable. 1889 A. LANG *Lett. Lit.* i. (ed. 2) 7 The 'Idyls'..are full of a Victorian respectability, and love of talking with Vivien about what is not so respectable.

c. Of decent or presentable appearance.
1775 S. J. PRATT *Liberal Opin.* lv. (1783) II. 154, I believe I have a pair of respectable metal buckles in the house. 1855 DICKENS *Dorrit* I. xxxv, It will be necessary to find a milliner, my love... Something must be done with Maggy too, who at present is..barely respectable. 1974 A. PRICE *Other Paths to Glory* I. iv. 41 Make us all a lot of hot, strong coffee while I get myself respectable. 1978 K. ROYCE *Satan Touch* v. 77 Herb Stahm knocked on Ashley's bedroom door. 'It's me, Herb.' 'Come on in.' That meant they were respectable.

†**d.** Creditable; of a good or superior kind.
1775 S. J. PRATT *Liberal Opin.* lxxxv. (1783) III. 126 It will not..redound much to my credit, or inspire..any respectable ideas of my understanding. 1786 MRS. A. M. BENNETT *Juv. Indiscr.* III. 188 Of whom he entertained a very respectable opinion. 1800 *Asiatic Ann. Reg.* III. 18/1 Judging that a respectable address of congratulation on the occasion will be becomingly proper, as well as dutiful from us.

†**5.** Convenient, suitable. *Obs. rare*$^{-1}$.
1773 J. WENTWORTH in Chase *Hist. Dartmouth Coll.* (1891) I. 440 An advertisement in your name, notifying a meeting on the day of your appointment, and at a place and spot most respectable to the College.

6. *Comb.*, as ***respectable-looking, -tawdry.***
1808 COLERIDGE in *Edin. Rev.* XII. 370 A very respectable-looking man had been up these rivers. 1820 SCOTT *Abbot* xx, He then addressed, by the title of Sir Robert, an elderly and respectable-looking gentleman. 1874 J. W. LONG *Amer. Wild-fowl* ix. 153 That makes quite a respectable-looking flock. 1916 E. POUND *Lustra* 112 A quiet and respectable tawdry trio.

B. *sb.* A respectable person.
1814 MOORE *Mem.* (1853) II. 23 We have been visited by some of the respectables in this neighbourhood. 1841 J. T. HEWLETT *Parish Clerk* I. 293 To show his respect for the respectables by touching his hat. *c*1890 *Fred Wilson's Fate* 97 It was an assembly of the respectables, and they were not his 'crowd'. 1940 E. GILL *Autobiogr.* vii. 262 With the *young* snobs and the *young* sycophants, the *young* hangers-on of the academies and, above all the young *respectables* there is nothing to be done. 1966 *Guardian* 15 June 9/8 Middle aged respectables here tend to shy away from discussion. 1978 P. G. WINSLOW *Coppergold* 142 You think I'm rotten, don't you?.. You're like Daddy and all the old respectables.

Hence **reˈspectableness.**
1760-72 H. BROOKE *Fool of Qual.* Ded., May it please your Respectableness. 1771 WHITAKER *Hist. Manch.* I. 165 The pencil of Age may justly be allowed to throw a shade of respectableness..over the productions of very antient Art.

respectably (rɪˈspɛktəblɪ), *adv.* [f. prec. + -LY².] In a respectable way or manner; to a respectable degree.
1775 S. J. PRATT *Liberal Opin.* xlii. (1783) II. 210 On the credit side of his books, where, no doubt, the silver buckles figured respectably. 1790 *Bystander* 286 The author of that piece can write respectably, but not for the stage. 1805 EMILY CLARK *Banks Douro* I. 74 The business by which he so respectably supported himself. 1850 SMEDLEY *F. Fairleigh* xlix, I rang for breakfast, and set resolutely to work to demolish it, in which I succeeded very respectably. 1882 MRS. RIDDELL *Prince of Wales's Garden-p.* 146 What a mother she was!.. Through what troubles she struggled to bring up her children respectably.

†**reˈspectance.** *nonce-wd.* = RESPECT *sb.*
1820 T. MITCHELL *Aristoph.* I. 230 Your snug coffer to fill, Undisturb'd by respectance or pity.

reˈspectant, *a. rare.* [-ANT.]
1. *Her.* Of animals: Facing each other.
1688 HOLME *Armoury* II. xix. 470/2 He beareth Argent, two Snakes in Salter respectant. *c*1828 BERRY *Encycl. Her.* I. s.v., Respectant, in triangle. Three birds, or other animals, with their beaks, or heads, meeting in triangle. 1847 *Gloss. Heraldry* 267 Respectant, or Respecting each other: terms used in describing two animals face to face. Rampant beasts of prey so borne, are said to be combatant.

2. Looking backward.
1830 TENNYSON *Poems* 99 Three shadows, fronting one, One forward, one respectant, three but one.

reˈspected, *ppl. a.* [f. RESPECT *v.* + -ED¹.] Held in respect.
In Shaks. *Meas. for M.* II. i. 169 misused for *suspected.* *a*1586 SIDNEY (J.), There is nothing more terrible to a guilty heart, than the eye of a respected friend. 1878 SEELEY *Stein* III. 344 The part which is..unruly, can only be restrained by the power of a respected Government.

respecter (rɪˈspɛktə(r)). [f. RESPECT *v.* + -ER¹.] One who respects: **a.** In phr. ***respecter of persons*** (see PERSON *sb.* 13).

1611 BIBLE *Acts* x. 34 Of a trueth I perceiue yᵗ God is no respecter of persons. *a* **1715** BURNET *Own Time* III. (1900) II. 457 He was going to be judged by one that was no respecter of persons. **1802** MAR. EDGEWORTH *Moral T.* (1816) I. xix. 166 The law..is no respecter of persons. **1871** FREEMAN *Norm. Conq.* (1876) IV. 128 To teach them that their King was no respecter of persons.

b. In general use.

1670 EACHARD *Cont. Clergy* 104 Whereby they may become his diligent attenders, and hearty respecters. **1797** MRS. RADCLIFFE *Italian* xvii, This accusation is brought against you by a respecter of truth. **1801** HELEN M. WILLIAMS *Manners Fr. Repub.* I. iii. 25 This venerable respecter of the rights of man. **1853** HERSCHEL *Pop. Lect. Sci.* iii. §7 (1873) 99 They are no respecters of boundaries.

respectful (rɪˈspɛktful), *a.* [f. RESPECT *sb.*]

†**1.** Mindful, heedful, careful (*of* something). *Obs.*

1598 CHAPMAN *Iliad* I. 151 O thou impudent! of no good but thine owne, Euer respectfull. *c* **1611** *Ibid.* XXIII. 63 Being aliue, I found thy memorie Euer respectfull. **1650** VENNER *Via Recta* 280, I aduise all such as are respectfull of their health. **1663** GERBIER *Counsel* (1664) 34 All those who have made..their respectfull observations of the Dimensions the Creatour hath been pleased to give to..Man.

†**b.** Considerate (*to* something). *Obs. rare.*

1650 EARL MONM. tr. *Senault's Man bec. Guilty* 372 It is the most perverse and least respectful punishment of all those that befall sinfull man. *a* **1665** GOODWIN *Filled w. Spirit* (1867) 225 If..God were so far indulgent or respectful to the zealous desires of men.

†**2.** Worthy of, or commanding, respect. *Obs.*

1650 GENTILIS *Consid.* 64 Alcibiades..strives to become great and make himselfe respectfull by contending with great ones. **1659** FULLER *App. Inj. Innoc.* II. x. 94 The like is frequent in many respectfull Families in England. **1702** C. MATHER *Magn. Chr.* III. Introd. Rem. 7/1 Both of these [persons] have a respectful Character in the Churches of this Wilderness.

3. Full of, exhibiting, or marked by respect.

1687 A. LOVELL tr. *Thevenot's Trav.* I. 87 The People with a low and respectful Voice, wished him all Happiness and Prosperity. **1707** NORRIS *Treat. Humility* vi. 244 Humility is the most respectful inferiour, and the most obedient subject in the world. **1737** [S. BERINGTON] *Mem. G. de Lucca* (1738) 60, I..stood gazing, tho' at a respectful Distance, at the Bassa's beautiful Daughter. **1794** MRS. RADCLIFFE *Myst. Udolpho* xliv, Ludovico received the sword with a respectful bow. **1830** MISS MITFORD in L'Estrange *Life* (1870) II. xiii. 296 The funeral was, of course, quite private—only ourselves, in a mourning coach—but handsome and respectful. **1875** JOWETT *Plato* (ed. 2) III. 7 The respectful attention shown to him by Socrates.

b. Const. *of.*

1846 D. JERROLD *Chron. Clovernook* Wks. 1864 IV. 444, I must..above all make it respectful of money. **1892** *Harper's Mag.* Sept. 504/2 A moderate man, respectful of tradition and of the established order of things.

respectfully (rɪˈspɛktfʊlɪ), *adv.* [f. prec. + -LY².] **a.** In a respectful or deferential manner.

a **1586** SIDNEY *Arcadia* I. ii. (1891) 8b, Kalander soone iudged that his guest was of no meane calling; and therefore the more respectfullie entertaining him. *a* **1667** COWLEY *Ess., Of Avarice,* These really Poor men, who are (methinks) to be respectfully treated in regard of their quality. **1687** A. LOVELL tr. *Thevenot's Trav.* I. 53 So soon as the Grand Signior perceives him, he rises up,..and salutes him very respectfully. **1766** GOLDSM. *Vic. W.* xiv, A youth, who, entering the room, respectfully said something softly to the old stranger. **1791** MRS. RADCLIFFE *Rom. Forest* xii, She returned his compliment respectfully. **1842** MIALL in *Nonconf.* II. 1 Grateful acknowledgements are respectfully tendered. **1885** S. COX *Expos.* xiii. 160 He was..respectfully familiar with Moses and the prophets.

b. ***Yours respectfully***: a conventional formula used in the subscription of letters.

1812 'L. IRVING' *Let.* 11 Jan. in C. Mackenzie *My Life & Times* (1963) I. 51 Your early reply through the post office will oblige. Yours respectfully, Leathley Irving. **1859** MRS. GASKELL *Let.* 10 Nov. (1966) 592 Believe me to remain, Yours respectfully E C Gaskell. **1885** R. D. BLACKMAN *Letter-Writer's Vade-Mecum* (ed. 9) 42 In addressing a stranger, the proper salutation is 'Sir', ..and the letter may be concluded..'Yours respectfully'. **1907** F. CROCKER *Let.* July in T. H. Baynes *Early Hist. St. Andrew's Church, Oxford* (1973) 14 On behalf of my fellow-workmen I respectfully beg to solicit from you a donation towards the Fund. Yours respectfully. **1960** J. STROUD *Shorn Lamb* v. 56 'Dear mr mall,' it said '..if she says she don't want donald, we will have him, yours respectfully.'

reˈspectfulness. [f. as prec. + -NESS.] The fact of being respectful.

1626 in Rushw. *Hist. Coll.* (1659) I. 239 He hath also heard with what duty and respectfulness to his Majesty their Lordships have proceeded therein. **1676** TOWERSON *Decalogue* 240 From respectfulness in our language pass we to respectfulness in our actions. **1748** RICHARDSON *Clarissa* (1811) III. 325 Her respectfulness seems too much studied. **1832** L. HUNT *Sir R. Esher* (1850) 386, I took the opportunity of kissing her hand with a respectfulness which I felt at the bottom of my heart. **1892** *Daily News* 8 Nov. 6/8 Respectfulness towards those to be ruled was nine-tenths of effective administration.

†**reˈspection.** *Obs.* Also 5 respeccioun, 6 respeccyon. [ad. late L. *respectiōn-em*, n. of action f. *respicĕre* to RESPECT.] Sight; aspect; regard; respect (of persons).

c **1400** *26 Pol. Poems* 133, I may nat from thy respeccioun By no way, lorde, hyde now me. *c* **1500** *Melusine* 319 Melusyne in her lamentable place..was vpon the wyndowe hauyng respection toward Lusynen. **1509** HAWES *Past. Pleas.* XIII. (Percy Soc.) 50 For it behoveth to have respeccyon Unto the tale. **1527** TINDALE *Wks.* (1573) 78/2 Then sayd Christ, goe thou and do likewise, that is, without difference or respection of persons.

respective (rɪˈspɛktɪv), *a.* [ad. late L. *respectīv-us*: see RESPECT *v.* and -IVE. Hence also F. *respectif*, Sp. and Pg. *respectivo*, It. *ri-, respettivo.*]

†**1.** Of persons: Regardful, attentive, considerate, careful. *Obs.* (Very common 1600–30.)

1525 BP. CLERK *Let. to Wolsey* (MS. Cott. Vit. B. VII. fol. 168), His Holynes semyd to be v[ery] respective and waare lest he shold speke to farre. **1596** SHAKS. *Merch. V.* v. i. 156 Though not for me, yet for your vehement oaths, You should haue beene respectiue and haue kept it. **1603** *Buccleuch MSS.* (Hist. MSS. Comm.) I. 237 Wishing you both to be respective that..you raise as small numbers as may be. *a* **1643** J. SHUTE *Judgem. & Mercy* (1645) 206 Thus respective the children of God have ever been to bring Glory to God in all their Actions.

b. Careful or regardful *of* something. Now *rare.*

1599 *Warn. Faire Wom.* I. 249 He's very wise, she very circumspect, Very respective of her honest name. **1620** VENNER *Via Recta* iv. 79, I aduise all such as are respectiue of their health, vtterly to abandon the vse of them. **1651** CARTWRIGHT *Cert. Relig.* I. 314 Bellarmine was more curious and criticall,..then..tender and respective of the credit of these antient Doctours.

1847 EMERSON *Repr. Men, Swedenborg* Wks. (Bohn) I. 316 But Swedenborg is systematic, and respective of the world in every sentence.

†**c.** Attentive *to* a person or thing. *Obs.*

1600 ABP. ABBOT *Jonah* 222 So respective is the Lord to those who fly to him. **1632** LITHGOW *Trav.* x. 459 Hauing no more Religion (and lesse respectiue to deuotion) than an externall presumptuous show. **1644** VICARS *God in Mount* 177 The inhabitants..were very kind and respective to the Souldiers. **1705** *Lawyer's Fortune* III. ii, I grant that a man with no estate would be more respective to her than he that has.

2. Of conduct, etc.: Marked by regardful care or attention; heedful. Now *rare.*

1598 R. HAYDOCKE tr. *Lomazzo* II. 65 To be very pleasant, but with such respectiue moderation, that their laughter exceed not. **1600** HOLLAND *Livy* XXVI. xlix. 623, I would..haue a respectiue consideration, that no one thing among us should suffer abuse. **1609** HEYWOOD *Brit. Troy* v. xviii, Then view that Saturne with Respective Eies. **1652** COTTERELL tr. *Calprenède's Cassandra* II. 23 The most holy zeal, and the most respective passion that ever was.

1854 PATMORE *Angel in Ho.* vii. 98 How spoil'd the bread and spill'd the wine, Which, spent with due, respective thrift, Had made brutes men and men divine.

†**b.** Discriminating; partial. *Obs.*

1592 SHAKS. *Rom. & Jul.* III. i. 128 Away to heauen respectiue Lenitie, And fire and Fury, be my conduct now. **1608** WILLET *Hexapla Exod.* II. Ded., Your lordships respectiue care in preferring men of desert. **1643** SIR T. BROWNE *Relig. Med.* I. §47 The day that must..reduce those seeming inequalities, and respective distributions in this world, to an equality..in the next.

†**3.** Respectful, courteous, civil (*to* or *towards* one). *Obs.* (Very common 1600–50.)

1579 FENTON *Guicciard.* I. 32 They were told with wordes reuerent and respectiue, with what naturall deuocion the people of Florence honored the house of Fraunce. **1599** SANDYS *Europæ Spec.* (1632) 19 Being a people for the most part of a grave and stayed behaviour, very respectiue and courteous. **1628–9** DIGBY *Voy. Medit.* (Camden) 34 He desired me, in a faire and respectiue manner, to make what hast I could to be gone from thence. **1648** GAGE *West Ind.* 148 But above all unto their Priest they are very respective. **1709** MRS. MANLEY *Secr. Mem.* (1736) II. 234 He enter'd the Chamber with a respective Boldness becoming the Character of a Servant, faithful to his Master. **1785** T. POTTER *Moralist* II. 33, I veiled these shining talents under the mask of a most respective politeness.

†**4.** Worthy of respect or deference; respectable.

1591 SHAKS. *Two Gent.* IV. iv. 199 What should it be that he respects in her, But I can make respectiue in my selfe? **1611** SPEED *Hist. Gt. Brit.* VI. iii. §6. 53 This Prince to make his estate more respectiue, caused his owne Image to bee stamped thereon. **1633** GERARD *Part. Descr. Somerset* (1900) 3 The ancient and respective family of Wrothe Knights who till this day live at Durants.

5. †**a.** Having relationship or reference *to* something; correspondent. *Obs.*

1589 PUTTENHAM *Eng. Poesie* II. xiii. [xviii.] (Arb.) 145 The monosillable *me* being respectiue to the word *others*.., ought not to haue the same accent, as when he hath no such respect. **1600** HOLLAND *Livy* IV. xlviii. 170 Some speech..framed rather to the time and present occasion, than respective to their owne high place and dignitie. **1697** J. SERGEANT *Solid Philos.* 127 To which are Respective..one way or other, all our other Notions of the Thing which we have, or can have.

b. Without const. Relative. Now *rare.*

1599 BLUNDEVIL *Logicke* I. xi. 33 Which are said to be relatiue or respectiue? Those that cannot be well understood of themselues without hauing relation to some other thing. **1620** T. GRANGER *Div. Logike* 12 Respectiue apprehension is of things relatiuely. **1668** CULPEPPER & COLE *Barthol. Anat.* I. iii. 5 The Cause Efficient..is the coldness of the Membranes, not simple but respective.

1865 PUSEY *Truth Eng. Ch.* 185 But this adoration is not absolute,..but diminished, participated, and respective.

†**c.** Proper, due, fitting. *Obs. rare.*

1605 CAMDEN *Rem.* 195 The Northerne people brought to the field the Earl of Albemarle the only respective heire of those partes. **1612** T. TAYLOR *Comm. Titus* ii. 9 When occasion of speach is offred, as by questions asked, they must make respectiue answers.

6. Properly pertaining to, or connected with, each individual, group, etc., of those in question; separate, several, particular.

a. With possessive pronoun, usually *their.*

1646 (*title*), An Ordinance of the Lords..for the Ordination of Ministers..within their respective Bounds. **1663** BUTLER *Hud.* I. ii. 666, I charge ye all..to those places straight repair Where your respective dwellings are. **1696** WHISTON *The. Earth* IV. (1722) 323 The Waters under the heavens were now gathered together into their respective and distinct places. **1743** EMERSON *Fluxions* 100 Taking..each of the Terms in the Quantity..and multiplying each by its respective Coefficient.., you will at last obtain this Form. **1774** GOLDSM. *Nat. Hist.* (1776) VII. 277 All these live upon their respective plant. **1844** STEPHENS *Bk. Farm* II. 289 Those pannels..may be permanently fixed in their respective places. **1864** BRYCE *Holy Rom. Emp.* vi. (1866) 85 The practical sovereignty of all three brothers was admitted in their respective territories.

b. With *the*, †*every*, †*a.*

1647 CROMWELL in *Carlyle* App. C. ix, After..a Copy of the Votes [had been] delivered to the Chief Officer of every respective Regiment..we desired [etc.]. **1678** CUDWORTH *Intell. Syst.* 863 This seeming very absurd, that the Souls of Brutes also should..subsist after the Deaths of the Respective Animals. **1694** SALMON *Bate's Dispens.* (1713) 87/1 There is no reason, that Metals and Minerals should be exempted from being repleat with a respective Oil also. **1701** LUTTRELL *Brief Rel.* (1857) V. 45 In boroughs where are not fifty electors the respective hundred is to join in chusing members. **1776** ADAM SMITH *W.N.* I. xi. III. (1869) I. 221 These will always be nearly in proportion to the respective produce of different years. **1833** HT. MARTINEAU *Charmed Sea* i. 2 To distinguish the respective rank and quality of those who externally so nearly resembled each other. **1866** FREEMAN *Hist. Ess.* (1872) 25 We cannot fix the respective amounts of truth and falsehood from direct evidence.

†**7. a.** Looking, facing *to* a certain quarter. *Obs.*

1601 HOLLAND *Pliny* I. 501 Virgill condemned altogether the planting of any trees, respective to the West.

†**b.** ***respective point, line***: (see quots.). *Obs.*

1581 R. NORMAN *New Attractive* 15 This poincte Respectiue, is a certaine poincte, whiche the touched Needle doeth alwaies Respecte or shewe. *Ibid.* 20 The other [line] crossyng the line Respectiue at right angles is the false East and West that the varying Needle..sheweth. **1625** CARPENTER *Geogr. Del.* I. ii. 25 The center of the Earth is not an Attractiue, but a meere Respectiue point. *Ibid.*, A Respectiue point is that, which the Bodies in their motions doe respect and conforme themselues vnto.

†**reˈspective,** *adv. Sc. Obs.* [Prob. a. L. *respective.*] Respectively.

1547 *Reg. Privy Council Scot.* I. 76 Tak diligent inquisitioun of the personis..that rannderis nocht agane the said taxt to the saidis tennentis respective. **1565** *Ibid.* 328 Takand the burding upoun us.., ilkane of us for oure awin part respective. **1634** in Cochran-Patrick *Rec. Coinage Scot.* (1876) Introd. 37 As gif the samyn gifts and ilk ane of thame respectiue wer herein..incorporat. **1642** DRUMM. OF HAWTH. *Skiamachia* Wks. (1711) 193 The Peace..which..we enjoy; and have established unto us..by the Laws Ecclesiastical, & Civil Laws of this Kingdom, respective.

respectively (rɪˈspɛktɪvlɪ), *adv.* [f. RESPECTIVE *a.* + -LY². Cf. F. *respectivement.*]

†**1. a.** Carefully, attentively. *Obs.*

1556 OLDE *Antichrist* 24 In case we marke respectiuely the apostles tymes,..it shall..appeare, that..many rose [etc.]. **1589** *Late Voy. Spain & Portugal* (Grosart) 71 Which good example..caused the commandement to be more respectiuelie regarded all the iourney after. **1614** LATHAM *Falconry* x. 38 She will be as soone reclaimd and made a certaine hawke,..if she be well vsed, and respectiuely handled. **1620** tr. *Boccaccio's Decam.* (1625) II. 157 They quickly caught great store of fish to the King's high contentment, who observed their behaviour very respectively.

†**b.** With due consideration of facts or circumstances. *Obs.*

1607 in *Harington's Nugæ Ant.* (1804) II. 216 Which text he handled so well, so learnedly, and so respectively. **1612** T. TAYLOR *Comm. Titus* iii. 1 The second part of the Chapter warneth Titus, how to carrie himself more respectiuely..in contentious questions. *a* **1677** BARROW *Wks.* (1686) I. 281 The decision of such matters is to be reserved to those who, by study and experience, have attained peculiar faculties to doe it respectively.

2. Respectfully; with becoming respect, deference, or courtesy. Now *rare.* (Common in 17th c.)

1583 FOXE *A. & M.* (1684) III. 929/1 The Kings will was that none of the Religion should be molested, but respectively used. **1593** G. HARVEY *Pierce's Super.* II. Wks. (Grosart) II. 291 Might I respectiuely presume to intimate my slender opinion, without flattery, or other vndecency. **1607** MIDDLETON *Five Gallants* II. i, Gentlemen, you are all most respectively welcome. **1649** in *Def. Rights Univ. Oxford* (1690) 9 Towards whom we ever have and shall respectively comport ourselves. **1720** MRS. MANLEY *Power of Love* 142 Persons began to think and speak less respectively of that Passion, than in Days of their Forefathers. **1962** *John o' London's* 25 Jan. 82/2 The magistrate is the *Beak* or, less respectively, the *Old Tosser*.

†**3. a.** Relatively; comparatively. *Obs.*

1570 FOXE *A. & M.* (ed. 2) 1470/2 After numbryng of the Articles, then come they and say that some be respectiuely hereticall, some erroneous, and some offensiue. **1587** GOLDING *De Mornay* vi. (1592) 74 They must differ respectiuely and not essentially. **1635** SWAN *Spec. M.* v. §2 (1643) 80 It is not absolutely cold, but respectively. **1664** POWER *Exp. Philos.* I. 47 Its exiguity is to be respectively understood, of such Seeds as extend to large productions.

†**b.** Const. *to* something. *Obs.*

1601 BP. W. BARLOW *Defence* 167 Austen concludeth that hee is called the sonne respectively to his father. **1656**

BRAMHALL *Replic.* iii. 129 They neither say nor intend this absolutely, but comparatively; not universally but respectively to some particular controverted points. **1759** B. STILLINGFLEET *Misc. Tracts* (1762) 349 But this is only respectively to the species of animals.

4. Relatively to each of several persons or things; individually, singly, separately; each to each, severally.

1626 BACON *Sylva* §228 The Impressions from the Objects of the Senses, doe mingle respectiuely, euery one with his kinde. **1688** HOLME *Armoury* III. 322/1 Into [these] Grooves the taps or screw-pins respectively fit. **1736** BUTLER *Anal.* I. iii. 68 Virtue and vice are naturally rewarded and punished as beneficial and mischievous to Society; and rewarded and punished respectively as such. **1779** FORREST *Voy. N. Guinea* 218 Hospitality must prove similar in countries and times, that respectively could never hear of each other. **1854** RONALDS & RICHARDSON *Chem. Technol.* (ed. 2) I. 167 The parts of the furnaces from which the gases should be taken are respectively 20 ft. above the blast in the former, and 22 ft. in the latter. **1891** *Law Rep.* Weekly Notes 79/2 Of the three defendants.., two were respectively president and secretary of the..Society.

re'spectiveness. Now *rare* or *Obs.* [f. as prec. + -NESS.]

†**1.** Consideration of circumstances; care, attention, heedfulness. *Obs.*

1598 R. HAYDOCKE *Lomazzo* To Reader iiij b, So that hee shall find neither a Paraphrasticall, Epitomized, or meere Verball translation,..but such a mixed respectiuenesse, as may shewe I indevoured nothing more, then the true vse, benefit, and delight of the reader. **1601** YARINGTON *Two Lament. Trag.* V. i. in Bullen *O. Pl.* IV, It shall be done with all respectivenesse; Have you no doubt of that, my gratious Lord. **1616** LD. BUTTEVANT in *Lismore Papers* Ser. II. (1887) II. 16 Not doubting of youre discreet Respectyvnes herin, I betake youe to God.

†**2.** Deference, respect; respectfulness. *Obs.*

1609 ABP. ABBOT *Exam. Sprot* 38 The minister of the Gospell, who..is made to teach obedience and respectivenesse unto Kings. **1645** RUTHERFORD *Tryal & Tri. Faith* Ep. Ded., I rest, Your Honours at all Obliged Respectivenesse in the God of Grace, S.R. **1709** MRS. MANLEY *Secr. Mem.* (1736) I. 111 The Respectiveness of his Flame and unwearied Silence.

†**3.** Relationship. *Obs.*

1650 O. SEDGWICK *Christ the Life* 14 All this hath a special and peculiar Respectiveness and Serviceableness to your Good. **1686** W. DE BRITAINE *Hum. Prud.* xxxii. 122 Another Mans too much Sufficiency..is a diminution of their Respectiveness, and therefore dangerous.

4. The condition or fact of being relative; relativity. *rare*$^{-1}$.

1659 H. L'ESTRANGE *Alliance Div. Off.* 267 The Absoluteness, or Respectiveness of Gods Decrees.

†**re'spectivist.** *Obs. rare.* [f. RESPECTIVE *a.* 3 + -IST.] One who uses the term 'respectively'.

1570 FOXE *A. & M.* (ed. 2) 1473/2, I aske of you, good Maisters Respectiuistes, whiche make these Articles respectiuely, some to be hereticall, some erroneous. *Ibid.*, But what haue these our respectiuistes to do with the Apostle Paul.

respectless (rɪ'spɛktlɪs), *a.* [f. RESPECT *sb.* + -LESS. Very common in 17th cent.]

†**1.** Regardless; heedless, reckless; unheeding, careless. *Obs.*

a **1542** WYATT *Ps.* li. in *Anglia* XIX. 436 He knowth well to mercy is ascrybid respectles labour. **1598** B. JONSON *Ev. Man in Hum.* I. i, He thats so respectlesse in his course, Oft sels his reputation vile and cheape. *a* **1639** BURTON *Anat. Mel.* I. ii. III. xv. (1651) 132 'Tis the common fortune of most Scholars to be servile and poor.., and lay open their wants to their respectless Patrons.

†**b.** Const. *of.* (Passing into 2 a.) *Obs.*

1607 T. WALKINGTON *Optick Glasse* Ep. Ded. 3, I might seeme..respectlesse, both of mine owne good name, and your better desert. **1621** BURTON *Anat. Mel.* III. i. III. i. 526 Wee are so vncharitable one towards another, so respectlesse of God. **1643** MILTON *Divorce* I. x. (1645) 24 The sixt place declares this prohibition to be as respectlesse of humane nature as it is of religion.

†**c.** With dependent clause, or inf. *Obs.*

1592 WYRLEY *Armorie, Ld. Chandos* iv. 31 Tossing light things subiected to great might, Respectles where or when so ere they light. **1611** TOURNEUR *Ath. Trag.* III. iv, I am as much respectlesse to enjoy Such pleasure as ignorant what it is. **1620–6** QUARLES *Feast for Wormes* 1120 Dauntlesse he his dreadfull voice extends, Respectlesse whom his bolder cry offends.

2. a. Devoid of respect or deference; discourteous, disrespectful. Also const. *of.* Now *rare.*

1591 FLORIO *2nd Fruites* 109 [The] cittie of Genoua... Where you shall haue..men respectles, and women gracelesse. **1617** ASSHETON *Jrnl.* (Chetham Soc.) 13 This fellow being in drinke, gave us manie insolent respectless speeches. *a* **1656** HALES *Gold. Rem.* I. (1673) 28 To prevent all inconvenience, that might arise out of disdainful and respectless carriage.

c **1825** BEDDOES *Poems, Second Brother* IV, The unfashionable worm, Respectless of the crown-illumined brow,..creeps courtier-like..to his food.

†**b.** Unworthy of respect. *Obs.*$^{-1}$

1621 HAKEWILL *David's Vow* 96 How shall the people reuerence him, whom his owne family respects not, and his owne behaviour therein makes him respectless?

†**3.** Impartial, unbiassed. *Obs. rare.*

1598 MARSTON *Sco. Villanie* II. vi. 201 Oh indignity To my respectless free-bred poesie. *Ibid.* III. viii. 211 The stroaks Of my respectlesse rude Satyrick hand. **1612** W. PARKES *Curtaine-Dr.* 59 Respectlesse death, what may thy dwelling be, That equals all?

†**4.** Devoid of limitation; unrestricted. *Obs.*$^{-1}$

a **1660** HAMMOND *Serm.* Wks. 1684 IV. 569 All our tenure or plea, to grace or glory, to depend not on any absolute, respectless, though free donation.

Hence †**re'spectlessly** *adv.*; †**re'spectlessness.**

1612 SHELTON *Quix.* IV. vi. (1620) I. 358 Desiring Camila to beare with his respectlessnesse therein. **1627** DOUGHTY *Serm. Div. Myst.* (1628) 12 How respectlessely doe they thrust into the most hidden secretes? **1668–9** PEPYS *Diary* 4 Jan., They do carry themselves very respectlessly of him.

†**re'spectuous,** *a. Obs.* [f. RESPECT *sb.* + -(U)OUS, perh. after F. *respectueux*, Pg. *respect-, respeituoso*, Sp. *respet(u)oso*, It. *rispett(u)oso.*]

1. Worthy of respect.

1603 KNOLLES *Hist. of Turks* (1621) 1217 Neither is it to be maruelled..if they [*sc.* princes] become respectuous and admirable in the eyes and sight of the common people. **1686** F. SPENCE tr. *Varillas' Ho. Medicis* 151 He endeavoured to evade it, by shewing that it departed from a more mean, and less respectuous hand.

2. Respectful, deferent.

1603 HOLLAND *Plutarch's Mor.* 62 A certaine respectuous reverence which they bare unto their Reader and Doctour. **1673** S. C. *Art of Complaisance* 167 They are also modest and respectuous. **1683** D. A. *Art Converse* 35 Our superiours we ought to reverence by a respectuous silence.

re'spell (riː-), *v.* [RE- 5 a.] To spell again, *esp.* according to some phonetic system. Hence **re'spelling** *vbl. sb.*

1806 W. TAYLOR in *Ann. Rev.* IV. 613 Yuhidthiton might be respelt into the familiar English phrase 'You hit the tone'. **1859** WORCESTER *Dict.* Pref. p. xxiii/2 In giving the authorities for pronunciation.., neither the respelling nor the notation of the orthoepists cited has generally been exhibited. **1865** *Philol. Soc. Trans.* 254 Each word is respelt in such a manner as to represent what the author supposes to be the correct pronunciation.

†**re'sperse,** *v. Obs.* [f. L. *respers-*, ppl. stem of *respergĕre* to besprinkle, f. *re-* RE- + *spargĕre* to sprinkle, scatter.]

1. *trans.* To sprinkle, spot, stain. *rare*$^{-1}$.

1482 *Monk of Evesham* (Arb.) 89 He was right feyre and sembly in whyte clothyng thawghe they were resperste and had on hem a few spottys.

2. To asperse, accuse. *rare*$^{-1}$.

1563 FOXE *A. & M.* 865 b, A man..not excommunicated, nor interdicted,..noted, respersed, or conuicted.

3. To scatter, disperse. (Only in Jer. Taylor.)

1649 JER. TAYLOR *Gt. Exemp.* Pref. ¶47 Those excellent ..discourses which..we find respersed and thinly scattered in all the Greeke and Roman Poets. **1654** —— *Real Pres.* x. 187 As appears in the instances above reckoned and in others respersed over this Treatise.

Hence †**re'spersed** *ppl. a. Obs.*

1649 JER. TAYLOR *Gt. Exemp.* II. Disc. viii. 67 This we gather, as fragments are gathered, by respersed sayings.. recorded in holy Scripture.

†**re'spersion.** *Obs.*$^{-1}$ [ad. L. *respersiōn-em*, n. of action f. *respergĕre*: see prec.] The action of sprinkling.

1649 JER. TAYLOR *Gt. Exemp.* I. Ad Sect. 7. 109 All the joyes which they should have received in respersion and distinct emanations.

re'spersive, *a. rare*$^{-1}$. [f. as RESPERSE *v.* + -IVE.] Tending to scatter.

1898 MEREDITH *Odes Fr. Hist.* 74 Our nature arises rejuvenescent from Earth, However respersive the blow.

†**respet(t,** *sb. Obs.* Also **respete.** [An intermediate form between RESPECT *sb.* (sense 11) and RESPITE *sb.*] A respite.

14.. *Customs of Malton* in *Surtees Misc.* (1890) 59 The sayd Burgese schall haffe hys viij days respett. *c* **1440** *York Myst.* x. 285 Do with me what ȝe will... I aske no more respete. **1512** *Nottingham Rec.* III. 338 That he mey not hafe a respette till his offeyce. **1581** *Reg. Privy Council Scot.* III. 395 He dispensit with the passing of ane respett cravit to Thomas Ker. *c* **1639** SIR W. MURE *Ps.* cii. 5 By reason of my groans, Whose noise no respett gives.

Hence †**respet(t,** *v.* (*a*) *intr.*, to pause, stop speaking; (*b*) *trans.*, to put off, reserve. *Obs.*

1561 T. HOBY tr. *Castiglione's Courtyer* I. (1577) D. iv b, Here the Count respeting a while, M. Bernard Bibiena saide merely [etc.]. **1588** R. HOVENDEN in *Collect.* (O.H.S.) I. 227, I maye respett my answeare till I maye confer with my companye.

re'spew, *v. rare*$^{-1}$. [RE- 5 a.] *trans.* To vomit back again.

1608 SYLVESTER *Du Bartas, Vocation* 412 Because the flood..Re-spews them still into themselves.

re'sphere (riː-), *v.* [RE- 5 a.] *trans.* To replace in the proper sphere.

1835 J. HARRIS *Gt. Teacher* (1837) 43 Principles, which had faded,..as stars are said to have become extinct, he rekindled and resphered. **1861** LYTTON & FANE *Tannhäuser* 36 What now re-spheres, After deflection long, our errant orb.

respice, obs. form of RASPIS[1].

†**re'spicient,** *a. Obs. rare.* [ad. L. *respicient-em*, pres. pple. of *respicĕre* to RESPECT.] Having respect to something outside.

1610 W. FOLKINGHAM *Art of Survey* II. i. 47 Situation may be said to be Resident, and Respicient. *Ibid.* ii. 49 Respicient Situation hath dependance upon Boundage and Neighbourage.

respies, variant of RASPIS[2].

respight, obs. form of RESPITE.

re'spin (riː-), *v.* [RE- 5 a.] To spin anew. Hence **re'spinning** *vbl. sb.*

1608 SYLVESTER *Du Bartas* II. iv. *Schisme* 490 That fruitfull Worm, Which (of it selfe) fine shining Sleaves doth form,..Re-spins a-fresh [etc.]. **1611** FLORIO, *Refilare*, to spin, to respin. **1846** MCCULLOCH *Acc. Brit. Empire* (1854) I. 685 The waste of the finer numbers is re-spun into a second quality. **1880** L. WALLACE *Ben-Hur* 401 With the spinning and re-spinning of this slender thread.

respira'bility. [f. next + -ITY.] The quality of being respirable (Webster, 1847).

respirable (rɪ'spaɪərəb(ə)l, 'rɛspɪrəb(ə)l), *a.* [a. F. *respirable* (16th c.), or ad. late L. *respīrābilis* (Boeth.): see RESPIRE and -ABLE.]

1. Capable of, or fit for, being respired.

1779 *Phil. Trans.* LXIX. 343 Into this tube..I introduce two measures of respirable air. **1807** T. THOMSON *Chem.* (ed. 3) II. 138 Though this gas be respirable, it is much less so than common air. **1863** *Pilgr. over Prairies* I. 254 The air became every moment less respirable. **1898** *Allbutt's Syst. Med.* V. 7 Irritant gases have been classified as non-respirable and respirable.

2. Capable of respiring.

1822–34 *Good's Study Med.* (ed. 4) I. 471 In both diseases the nerves of the respirable organ are alone in a morbid condition. **1862** WRAXALL tr. *Hugo's Les Misérables* IV. xxii, All of us, whoever we may be, have our respirable beings.

Hence **respirableness** (Webster, 1847).

†**respiracle.** *Obs. rare*$^{-1}$. [ad. late L. *respīrāculum* respiration, breathing, f. *respīrāre* to RESPIRE.] A breathing-place.

1555 EDEN *Decades* (Arb.) 362 Except it receaue the ayer by sum respiracle or breathynge place.

†**respirant,** *a. Obs. rare*$^{-1}$. In 6 **-aunt.** [ad. L. *respīrant-em*, pres. pple. of *respīrāre* to RESPIRE.] Respiring, breathing.

1575 LANEHAM *Let.* (1871) 50 The sweetnes of sauoour on all sidez, made so respiraunt from the redolent plants and fragrant earbs.

respirate ('rɛspɪreɪt), *v.* [Back-formation from RESPIRATION.] *trans.* To subject to artificial respiration.

1968 *Exper. Neurol.* XX. 416 The animals were artificially respirated by a Harvard 670 D pump. **1971** *Nature* 28 May 263/2 Trackers were cannulated and the animals were respirated artificially with a Harvard respirator.

'respirating, *ppl. a. rare.* [f. **respirate*, ad. L. *respīrāt-*, ppl. stem of *respīrāre* to RESPIRE + -ING[2].] Respiring.

1649 J. ECLISTON tr. *Behmen's Epist.* vi. (1886) 66 A former of the re-expressing or re-spirating Will. **1839** J. E. READE *Deluge*, etc. 145 The respirating breath withheld, On which she lived. **1887** *Homeop. World* 1 Nov. 507 In the bronchitis of typhus when the respirating muscles seemed to be paralyzed.

respiration (rɛspɪ'reɪʃən). Also 5 **-cioun,** 6 **-cion.** [ad. L. *respīrātiōn-em*, noun of action f. *respīrāre* to RESPIRE. So F. *respiration* (15th c.), Sp. *respiracion*, It. *re-, rispirazione.*]

1. a. The action of breathing (†out); the inspiration and expiration of air. ***artificial respiration***: see ARTIFICIAL *a.* 5.

c **1430** LYDG. *Min. Poems* (Percy Soc.) 196 Ayer of nature yevith inspiracioun,..Off kyndly heete gevyth respiracioun. **1543** TRAHERON *Vigo's Chirurg.* 95/1 It swageth payn, and clenseth the place, and aydeth respiration, or breathing. **1577** HARRISON *England* III. ix. (1877) I. 65 Liuelie creatures shut vp in the hard stones, and liuing there without respiration or breathing, as frogs, todes, &c. **1615** CROOKE *Body of Man* 793 Life cannot bee maintayned without Respiration, neither can Respiration bee performed without motion. **1665–6** PEPYS *Diary* 22 Jan., What, among other fine discourse, pleased me most, was Sir G. Ent about Respiration. **1710** J. CLARKE tr. *Rohault's Nat. Philos.* (1729) I. 77 The sucking in of Air through a Quill is done in the same manner as Respiration. **1774** GOLDSM. *Nat. Hist.* (1776) VI. 171 Though this be the general method of explaining respiration in fishes [etc.]. **1826** S. COOPER *First Lines Surg.* (ed. 5) 422 Unless he bend his body very much forwards, in order to facilitate respiration. **1878** HUXLEY *Physiogr.* 80 The respiration of animals depends upon the presence of oxygen.

transf. a **1649** CRASHAW *Carmen Deo Nostro* Poems (1904) 289 A long and dayly-dying life, which breaths A respiration of reviving deaths. **1684** *Contempl. St. Man* II. vi. (1699) 196 That Fire of Sulphur, being pent in without vent or respiration, shall send forth a poysonous scent. **1814** WORDSWORTH *Excursion* VIII. 365 Sails Which..Pass with the respirations of the tide. **1878** LONGF. *Birds of Passage* v. *Vittoria Colonna* viii, The respiration of the sea, The soft caresses of the air.

b. A respiratory murmur.

1834 J. FORBES *Laennec's Dis. Chest* 475 In the same place imperfect pectoriloquy, and also cavernous respiration, existed.

c. *Bot.* The process by which a plant absorbs oxygen from the air, and gives out carbon dioxide.

1831 BURNETT in *Jrnl. R. Institution* I. 100 This function, which is performed chiefly by the leaves and petals,..is attended with..the conversion of oxygen into carbonic acid;

it is the respiration of plants. **1849** J. H. BALFOUR *Man. Bot.* §282 The changes which are produced in the atmosphere by living plants have been included under the title of Vegetable Respiration. **1882** VINES tr. *Sachs' Bot.* 717 The dried weight of the plant is very small..because a portion of the substance has been destroyed in the process of respiration.

d. *Biochem.* and *Biol.* The biochemical and cellular processes by which absorbed oxygen is combined with carbon in the organism to form carbon dioxide and generate energy; more widely, any metabolic process in which energy is produced by the net transfer of electrons from a substrate to an external oxidant (usu. called ***anærobic respiration*** when this is not free oxygen); also extended to include energy-producing metabolic processes (fermentations) not involving a separate oxidant.

1856 J. C. MORRIS tr. *Lehmann's Man. Chem. Physiol.* 272 This exchange of oxygen and carbonic acid, which we improperly call respiration, is not confined to any single spot of the organism. **1880** A. GAMGEE *Text-bk. Physiol. Chem. Animal Body* I. ix. 366 The respiration of muscles during contraction. **1900** A. J. EWART tr. *Pfeffer's Physiol. Plants* I. ix. 546 (*heading*) The relationship between aerobic and anaerobic respiration. *Ibid.* 549 The actual anaerobic respiration (or fermentation) continues unchecked. **1908** HALL & DEFREN tr. *Aberhalden's Text-bk. Physiol. Chem.* xviii. 412 It [*sc.* the blood] takes the oxygen from the lungs and gives it up to the tissues. The first gas-exchange is commonly spoken of as external respiration, and the latter as internal respiration. **1929** R. A. GORTNER *Outl. Biochem.* viii. 386 In the dark the respiration of cells is inhibited by carbon monoxide. **1934** A. T. HENRICI *Biol. of Bacteria* xi. 174 Those processes which yield energy for the organism are respiration. *Ibid.* 184 A great many, probably all, microörganisms capable of growing either as strict or facultative anaerobes..may obtain energy by this intermolecular respiration, by a simultaneous oxidation of one compound and reduction of another. **1949** KELLY & HITE *Microbiology* xiv. 175 The phenomenon of 'life without air' has since [Pasteur's time] been explained by the study of anaerobic respiration or fermentation. **1965** G. A. STRAFFORD *Essent. Plant Physiol.* viii. 131 Fermentation is the form of anaerobic respiration carried out by some fungi and bacteria. **1970** AMBROSE & EASTY *Cell Biol.* vi. 183 The pyruvic acid is used for respiration (oxidation of carbon to CO_2) in the mitochondria. **1974** *Nature* 13 Dec. 579/1 The enzymes responsible for the first step in nitrate assimilation and for nitrate respiration are the nitrate reductases, both these processes involving the conversion of nitrate to nitrite.

2. A single act of breathing.

c **1611** CHAPMAN *Iliad* XXII. 413 When again her respirations found Free pass. **1648** WILKINS *Math. Magic* II. v. 184 In an hower a man will need at least 360 respirations. **1707** FLOYER *Physic. Pulse-Watch* 431 Measuring the Number of Pulses by the Number of Respirations. **1836** LANDOR *Imag. Conv., Pericles & Aspasia* Wks. 1846 II. 393 These are not regrets, Cleone; they are respirations, necessary to existence. **1876** BRISTOWE *Th. & Pract. Med.* (1878) 186 The respirations are generally slightly increased in number during the earlier period of the disease.

3. Opportunity for breathing again (cf. RESPIRE *v.* 3); a breathing-space; a respite. ? *Obs.*

1611 BIBLE *Esther* iv. 14 Then shall there enlargement [*marg.* respiration] and deliuerance arise to the Iews. **1649** BP. HALL *Cases Consc.* IV. vi. (1654) 348 Some meet respiration of a more full triall and inquiry into each others condition. **1696** S. PATRICK *Comm. Exod.* xxiii. (1697) 448 God now gave them some rest, and respiration..from their employments. **1752** JOHNSON *Rambler* No. 205 ¶13 Such were the days which Seged of Ethiopia had appropriated to a short respiration from the fatigues of war.

†**4.** An inspiration. *Obs. rare*$^{-1}$.

1622 DONNE *Serm.* cliv. Wks. 1839 VI. 184 Sometimes it is hard to distinguish between a Respiration from God and a Suggestion from the Devil.

5. *attrib.*, as ***respiration rate***.

1929 R. A. GORTNER *Outl. Biochem.* viii. 242 The sudden rise in respiration rate may be due to the fact that at, or below, 14·75 per cent moisture all, or practically all, of the moisture in the wheat kernel is in the form of bound water. **1970** AMBROSE & EASTY *Cell Biol.* ii. 89 An apparatus originally designed by Warburg can be used to measure respiration rates.

Hence **respi'rational** *a.*, relating to respiration (Ogilvie *Suppl.* 1855).

†**respirative**, *a. Obs. rare*$^{-1}$. [See RESPIRE *v.* and -ATIVE.] Respiratory.

1578 BANISTER *Hist. Man* IV. 53 Not naturall but voluntary (sayth Galen) is the respiratiue motion.

respirato-, used as a comb. form, with the sense of 'respiratory as well as', etc.

1835 KIRBY *Hab. & Inst. Anim.* II. xvii. 104 Whenever the animal is alarmed it withdraws this gorgeous apparatus of respirato-prehensory organs within its tube.

respirator ('rɛspɪreɪtə(r)). [a. L. type **respīrātor*, agent-n. f. *respīrāre* to RESPIRE. Cf. F. *respirateur*.]

1. *Chem.* An apparatus used for testing the composition of exhaled air. ? *Obs.*

1792 A. YOUNG *Trav. France* 153 A respirator, with vital air in a jar on one side, and lime-water in another.

2. A device of gauze or wire covering the mouth, or mouth and nose, and serving to warm the inhaled air or to prevent the inhalation of dust, smoke, or other noxious substances; also, a gas mask, or any mask for providing protection against noxious substances in the air.

The earliest form of respirator was invented by Julius Jeffreys in the autumn of 1835.

1836 JEFFREYS *Patent Specif.* No. 6988. 5 The above is a description of the instrument which is adapted to the mouth alone, and which may be named the oral respirator. **1838** MRS. CARLYLE in *New Lett. & Mem.* (1903) I. 72 A thing made of black silk with a quarter of a mile of brass wire in it. .. They call it a respirator. **1872** *Chem. News* 17 May 239/1 The charcoal respirators invented by me in 1854 are now coming into general use, especially in manufactories and laboratories. *Ibid.*, The respirator is suspended for ten or fifteen minutes over some strong solution of ammonia in a large beaker; in this way the charcoal absorbs a very large amount of ammoniacal gas... The wearer can remain for a considerable time in an atmosphere containing chlorine without suffering any inconvenience. **1875** KNIGHT *Dict. Mech.* 1923/1 Respirators are used by cutlers and other grinders to exclude the dust from the lungs. **1898** *Allbutt's Syst. Med.* V. 232 Respirators worn over the mouth are not now so much in vogue as formerly. **1915** MRS. BELLOC LOWNDES *Diary* 26 Apr. (1971) 61 The [German] soldiers.. had their noses plugged with cotton wool and respirators over their mouths, but even so, 1000 perished by their own gas. **1915** *Sphere* 7 Aug. 146/1 Respirators for the use of the Russian soldiers, who have been attacked by gas bombs. **1938** *Ann. Reg. 1937* 25 Not a little of the increase was due in reality to military reasons, the Home Office being assigned some £4,000,000 for the provision of respirators and the development of emergency fire brigade services for protecting the civil population in the event of war. **1971** *Brit. Med. Bull.* XXVII. 75/2 The use of..air-fed respirators..could greatly reduce the future incidence of asbestos-related cancers in this work. **1978** CADOGAN & CRAIG *Women & Children First* x. 219 Forbidden to play with his gas mask, he muses bitterly on the 'jolly good times' that should result from unrestricted access to respirators.

3. *Med.* An apparatus for maintaining artificial respiration.

1929 DRINKER & MCKHAN in *Jrnl. Amer. Med. Assoc.* 18 May 1659/2 (*caption*) The mechanical respirator, showing patient ready to be pushed into the tank. **1932**, **1938** [see IRON LUNG 1]. **1966** DUNLOP & ALSTEAD *Textbk. Med. Treatm.* (ed. 10) 941 The action of all positive pressure respirators (or ventilators, as they are more correctly described) is to produce inflation of the lungs at a rate of 14 to 20 cycles per minute, expiration being allowed to occur passively. **1967** SLONIM & CHAPIN *Respiratory Physiol.* iv. 48/2 Drinker-type 'iron lung' respirators are devices built to enclose all the body below the neck. **1977** C. STORR *Tales from Psychiatrist's Couch* xi. 118 His respiratory muscles were working again and he was out of the respirator for large parts of the day.

Hence **'respiratored** *ppl. a.*, provided with, or wearing, a respirator.

1887 *Story of a Kiss* I. xi. 171 A wan, yellow lady, closely veiled and respiratored.

respiratory (rɪ'spaɪərətərɪ, 'rɛspɪrətərɪ), *a.* [ad. mod.L. *respīrātōrius*, or F. *respiratoire* (Sp. and It. *-orio*).] **1.** Of, pertaining to, or serving for respiration.

1790 SMELLIE *Phil. Nat. Hist.* I. 124 The stigmata, or respiratory organs, of caterpillars and other insects. **1816** KIRBY & SP. *Entomol.* iv. (1818) I. 140, I could discover, in this animal, no respiratory plates. **1834** J. FORBES *Laennec's Dis. Chest* 425 The respiratory sound became much more perceptible at the roots of the left lung. **1881** MIVART *Cat* 278 The external respiratory nerve of Bell.

2. Special collocations: ***respiratory centre***, a region of the brain which exercises control over respiration; ***respiratory pigment***, a protein molecule with a pigmented prosthetic group, involved in the transfer of oxygen or electrons within living systems; ***respiratory quotient***, the ratio of the volume of carbon dioxide evolved to that of oxygen consumed; ***respiratory syncytial virus***, an RNA virus that causes disease of the respiratory tract; ***respiratory therapy*** (U.S.), the management of patients receiving artificial respiration or ventilation and of the apparatus involved; so ***respiratory therapist***, one trained in this; ***respiratory tract***, the passages through which air passes in respiration; ***respiratory tree***, a branched system of respiratory passages.

1883 *Encycl. Brit.* XX. 480/1 The *respiratory centre must be regarded as the seat of origin of the impulses which cause the muscular movements of inspiration and expiration. **1948** A. BRODAL *Neurol. Anat.* xi. 391 The existence of a respiratory centre is generally admitted in the medulla. **1896** *Q. Jrnl. Microsc. Sci.* XXXIX. 3 A *respiratory pigment of a kind unusual in the Chætopoda. **1933** *Biol. Bull.* LXIV. 233 In several of the invertebrates also, respiratory pigments, either hemoglobin or hemerythrin, are found within special cells of the circulating blood or body fluids. **1968** PASSMORE & ROBSON *Compan. Med. Stud.* I. viii. 7/1 Cytochromes. These are respiratory pigments found in all cells. **1890** BILLINGS *Med. Dict.* II. 453/1 **Respiratory quotient*, the relation of the inspired free oxygen to that expired in the form of carbonic acid. **1900** W. S. HALL *Text-bk. Physiol.* iv. 218 The respiratory quotient varies considerably in different *species*, and in the same animal under different conditions. **1968** PASSMORE & ROBSON *Compan. Med. Stud.* I. xxxi. 7/1 Ketosis is associated with a low respiratory quotient (RQ), below 0·75, which reflects a predominance of fat metabolism. **1961** *New Eng. Jrnl. Med.* CCLXIV. 1174/1 The present report presents convincing evidence for the etiologic role of the *respiratory syncytial virus in acute respiratory illnesses among children. **1968** *New Scientist* 15 Feb. 368/1 Respiratory syncytial virus (RSV) is now the most dangerous of the respiratory pathogens that affect young children. **1965** P. SAFAR (*title*) *Respiratory therapy. **1973** D. A. HOLADAY in Caldwell & Moya *Adv. Respiratory Care & Physiol.* vi. 85 Their duties include..administration of other categories of respiratory therapy to patients in intensive care units, post-anesthesia recovery rooms, and other areas..where continuous ventilators are in use. **1974** TYLER & NETT in T. L. Petty *Intensive & Rehabilitative Respiratory Care* (ed. 2) vi. 79 The patient with acute respiratory failure is being cared for by both nursing and respiratory therapy staffs. *Ibid.* 98 The nurse, *respiratory therapist, and, where available, the physical therapist have vital roles in the successful care of any patient from the onset of acute illness throughout the convalescent and rehabilitative phases. **1978** *Detroit Free Press* 16 Apr. (Parade Suppl.) 5/3 Alice Gaul, a former U.S. Navy nurse, and Mary Masal, a respiratory therapist, managed to keep that man alive through the eight-hour flight. **1936** *Discovery* July 206/2 It has not appeared to produce the usual irritative effects of ether on the *respiratory tract. **1977** *Chest* LXXI. 346/1 Aerosol topical anesthesia for instrumentation of the respiratory tract was first described in 1949. **1932** BORRADAILE & POTTS *Invertebrata* xviii. 575 Finally there is a short, wide cloaca. Into the latter usually open two long, branched *respiratory trees, whose ramifications end in thin-walled ampullae through which water, when pumped in by contractions of the cloaca, passes into the body cavity, carrying oxygen to the coelomic fluid, and so to the organs. **1970** W. H. PARKER *Health & Dis. in Farm Animals* iii. 35 The respiratory tree is an apt phrase used to describe the continuous sub-division of the bronchi.

†**re'spire**, *sb. Obs. rare*$^{-1}$. [f. next.] A respiration; a breath.

1645 G. DANIEL *Poems* Wks. (Grosart) II. 68 My close-breathing tires My Lungs, in oft respires.

respire (rɪ'spaɪə(r)), *v.* Also 5–6 **respyre**. [ad. F. *respirer* (13th c.), or L. *respīrāre*, f. *re-* RE- + *spīrāre* to breathe. So Sp. and Pg. *respirar*, It. *re-*, *rispirare*.]

I. *intr.* †**1.** To come up to the surface to breathe. *Obs. rare*$^{-1}$.

1387–8 T. USK *Test. Love* I. v. (Skeat) l. 35 He..in-to water entreth and anon respireth.

2. a. To breathe; to inhale and exhale air.

1592 DAVIES *Immort. Soul* XXIV. ii. (1714) 80 This makes the Pulses beat, and Lungs respire. **1599** A. M. tr. *Gabelhouer's Bk. Physicke* 40/1 Impose that into the Nose of the Patient, but not to close, because he might respire. **1603** T. DAVIES (Heref.) *Microcos.* Wks. (Grosart) I. 24/1 Man, and Beast, and what doth els respire. **1692** BENTLEY *Boyle Lect.* vii. 224 The ordinary Air in which we live and respire. **1721** BRADLEY *Philos. Acc. Wks. Nat.* 105 It respires by the Gills, which are Lungs peculiar to Fishes. **1769** E. BANCROFT *Guiana* 192 This Fish frequently respires. **1803** *Med. Jrnl.* X. 251 The patient appearing..to have much difficulty in respiring. **1835–6** *Todd's Cycl. Anat.* I. 143/1 Quadrupeds and birds respire universally by means of lungs. **1882** SWINBURNE *Tristram of Lyonesse* 10 These.. Saw love and wrath and light and night and fire Live with one life and at one mouth respire.

fig. **1805** WORDSW. *Prelude* III. 132 All That I beheld respired with inward meaning.

b. To draw breath, to live. *rare*$^{-1}$.

1619 DRAYTON *Bar. Wars.* II. 55 Yet the braue Barons, whilst they do respire, With Courage charge.

†**c.** To breathe a word *against* something. *Obs.*

1621 QUARLES *Argalus & P.* (1678) 26 Parthenia should obey, and not respire Against their sacred counsels, or withstand The plot.

d. To carry out or exhibit the biochemical processes of respiration.

1927 M. BODANSKY *Introd. Physiol. Chem.* viii. 200 A tissue that has been washed until it no longer 'respires' will, upon the addition of glutathione, again take up oxygen and yield carbon dioxide. **1951** M. ABERCROMBIE et al. *Dict. Biol.* 197 Many organisms (or parts of them) respire anaerobically for some time when their supply of oxygen is insufficient for aerobic respiration. **1976** *Sci. Amer.* Feb. 68/2 When the crop is ensiled, the plant cells continue to respire for a period of time and the aerobic bacteria on the plant increase in number.

3. *fig.* To breathe again, after distress, trouble, etc.; to recover hope, courage, or strength.

c **1425** WYNTOUN *Cron.* IV. xvi. 1587 (Royal MS.), Sa Rome before dispayrd than Respyre in to gud hope began. **1525** *St. Papers Hen. VIII*, VI. 430 He shalbe able to do no feate on the see, ne so sone to respire and inquiet thEmperour. **1535** STEWART *Cron. Scot.* II. 92 Syne at the last thair spreitis did respyre. **1590** SPENSER *F.Q.* III. iii. 36 Then shall the Britons..From their long vassalage gin to respire. **1673** TEMPLE *Obs. on United Prov.* Wks. 1720 I. 29 The Arch-Duke, newly respiring from so long a War. **1717** POPE *Iliad* XI. 424 Stern Hector's conquest in the middle plain Stood check'd awhile, and Greece respired again. **1807** J. BARLOW *Columb.* IV. 242 Quell'd by his fame, the furious seeks accord, Europe respires beneath his guardian sword. **1816** WORDSW. *Siege Vienna raised*, The Imperial City stands released From bondage threatened by the embattled East, And Christendom respires.

4. To take breath; to rest or enjoy relief from toil or exertion.

1590 SPENSER *F.Q.* I. ix. 8 Ah, Love! lay down thy bow, the whiles I may respyre. **1633** P. FLETCHER *Purple Isl.* XI. l, But here I feel amends..; here leave me to respire. **1742** YOUNG *Nt. Th.* IX. 1741 Pause, then; and, for a moment, here respire.—If human thought can keep its station here. **1769** WILKIE *Epigoniad* III. 39 The Spartan bands..The fight maintained; nor from their toils respired. **1819** SHELLEY *Prometh. Unb.* II. v. 2 On the brink of the night and the morning My coursers are wont to respire.

†**5. a.** Of wind: To blow. *Obs. rare.*

1432–50 tr. *Higden* (Rolls) I. 59 The wyndes respirenge and restenge in the profundite of hit. **1597** A. M. tr. *Guillemeau's Fr. Chirurg.* 51 b/1 If there respire a south-west wind, with warmishe showres of rayne. **1762** HOOLE tr. *Tasso* XIII. 401 Alone the wind from Libya's sands respires.

†**b.** Of smell or vapour: To exhale, transpire. *Obs.*

c **1460** *Bk. Quintessence* 4 þe seel of lute of wijsdom, maad of þe sotillest flour,..ymeyngid so þat no þing respire out. **1526** *Pilgr. Perf.* (W. de W. 1531) 34 b, To whome the ennemy caused oftentymes whan he was at masse a meruaylous swete sauour to respyre and smell aboute his fyngers.

II. *trans.* **6.** To breathe; to inhale and exhale (air, etc.).

1548–77 Vicary *Anat.* v. (1888) 42 The ayre is respyred and drawen to the lunges. *a* **1618** Sylvester *Hymn of Alms* 276 A sighfull Air (though Soule-less) to respire. **1651** T. Stanley *Poems* 172 O'erjoyd are they To breathe the air which she respires. **1711** Gay *Rural Sports* i. 12, I.. Long in the noisy Town have been immur'd, Respir'd its smoke. **1784** Cowper *Task* i. 138 That play of lungs, inhaling and again Respiring freely the fresh air. **1827** D. Johnson *Ind. Field Sports* 238 The dogs received the poison.. by respiring the effluvia arising from them. **1853** W. Gregory *Inorg. Chem.* 154 The air will certainly destroy life if respired.

fig. **1601** B. Jonson *Poetaster* iv. viii, Mee thinkes, now I come neere her, I respire Some aire of that late comfort I receiu'd. **1824** W. Irving *T. Trav.* II. 11, I seemed to respire hope and comfort with the free air. **1829** Lytton *Devereux* iv. iii, The very breath which a literary man respires is hot with hatred.

7. To breathe or give out, to exhale (an odour, etc.). Chiefly *fig.*

1577 Frampton *Joyful News* iii. (1596) 88 The selfesame [cinnamon].. being ground, respiring out from it the same smel which the most fine Cinamon hath. **1601** B. Jonson *Poetaster* i. iii, The ayre respires the pure elyzian sweets, In which she breathes. **1669** Gale *Crt. Gentiles* i. i. 6 Every Art doth respire a sweet science to the glasse of our understanding. **1794** Colebrooke *Asiatic Res.* VIII. (Cent.), From this great being were respired the Rigveda, etc. **1807** J. Robinson *Archæol. Græca* iii. xix. 310 Men who, armed with lances and bucklers, seemed only to respire war. **1841** L. Hunt *Seer* (1864) 74 In the south of Europe, where every thing respires animal sensibility.

8. To breathe (a thing) *into* a person's ear.

1846 Landor *Imag. Conv., Dante & Beatrice*, Are you willing that the Tempter should intercept it [love], and respire it polluted into your ear?

Hence **re'spired** *ppl. a.*; **re'spiring** *vbl. sb.* and *ppl. a.*

1597 A. M. tr. *Guillemeau's Fr. Chirurg.* 10/1 Beinge smitten [she] without anye respiringe, is fallen into a Vertiginem. *c* **1611** Chapman *Iliad* xvi. 102 He wrought it out With short respirings, and with sweate. **1697** Congreve *Mourn. Bride* ii. ix, When I.. felt the balm of thy respiring lips. **1822** Good *Study Med.* I. 447 The diminution in the bulk of respired air.. may be accounted for.

†**re'spirement.** *Obs. rare*$^{-1}$. [a. obs. F. *respirement* (Godef.).] Recovery.

c **1477** Caxton *Jason* 123 Peleus.. cam unto the kyng in the renouellite of this noble respyrement.

re'spirer. *rare*$^{-0}$. One who respires.

1611 Cotgr., *Respireur*, a breather, a respirer.

re'spirit (riː-), *v. rare.* [re- 5 a.] *trans.* To inspire with fresh spirit or courage.

1609 Heywood *Brit. Troy* xiv. ix, When Re-spirited Greece had Domineer'd And brav'd the Sieged Troians. **1890** *Illustr. Lond. News* 15 Nov. 618/1 These cool influences somewhat respirited me. **1929** R. Bridges *Testament of Beauty* iii. 84 All his Knights cleansed and respirited, reclothed as might be.

respirometer (rɛspɪˈrɒmɪtə(r)). [f. L. *respīrāre* to blow, breathe out + -ometer.]

1. *Med.* A device which measures the quantity of air expired, so that the condition of the lungs may be studied; = spirometer.

1889 *Cent. Dict.* 5111/1 *Respirometer*, an instrument which is used to determine the condition of the respiration. **1907** *Arch. Otology* XXXVI. 401 A person afflicted with pulmonary tuberculosis.. so weakened by his disease that he can raise the water only six inches in the 'Respirometer'. **1964** Bates & Christie *Respiratory Function in Disease* ii. 6 For bedside use, the Wright Respirometer, a pocket-sized instrument, is preferable.

2. *Physiol.* A device which measures the rate of consumption of oxygen by a living or organic system.

1915 *Jrnl. Physiol.* XLIX. p. xxiv, (*heading*) A quantitative respirometer. **1923** *Jrnl. Agric. Res.* XXIII. 101 (*heading*) A new and efficient respirometer for seeds and other small objects. **1948** *Jrnl. Exper. Med.* LXXXVII. 177 (*caption*) Details of respirometer chamber to hold twenty eggs. **1969** *Sci. Jrnl.* Nov. 19/2 A simple fully automatic respirometer which measures organic pollution in sewage has been developed.

Hence **respi'rometry**, the measurement of rates of oxygen consumption; **ˌrespiro'metric** *a.*, by means of or pertaining to the respirometer.

1932 *Jrnl. Gen. Physiol.* XVI. 5 (*heading*) Studies in respirometry. **1960** *Antibiotics Ann.* VII. 563 (*heading*) Respirometric assay of nystatin in animal tissue. **1972** *Ann. Rep. Freshwater Biol. Assoc.* XL. 41 Dr Jones has continued to use respirometric techniques.. to study the factors that cause inhibition of bacterial and other biological activity. **1977** A. G. Callely et al. *Treatm. Industr. Effluents* xvii. 278 Biological test methods applied to this type of waste include respirometry, aeration flask tests, and continuous treatment tests.

respis, variant of raspis^{2}.

respite ('rɛspɪt), *sb.* Forms: 3–7 respit, 6 -itt(e; 4–6 respyt(e, 5– respite; 4 respiȝt, 7–8 respight. See also respet(t. [a. OF. *respit* (mod.F. *répit*):—L. *respect-us* respect *sb.*]

I. 1. Delay, or extension of time, asked or granted for some reason (orig. for further consideration of a matter). Also in phr. ***to put in respite***, = respite *v.* 4.

c **1290** *Beket* 631 in *S. Eng. Leg.* I. 124 So þat respit was þar-of I-nome, and ech wende In his side. *a* **1300** *Cursor M.* 21508 Heri þe higt Of a dai respit and a night. *c* **1325** *Song of Merci* 185 in *E.E.P.* (1862) 124 Graunt vs repentaunce, and respiȝt, And schrift and hosel, or we day. *c* **1386** Chaucer *Pars. T.* ¶ 104 Iob preyde respit a while to biwepe and waille his trespas. *c* **1420** Lydg. *Assembly of Gods* 211 Yef I had respyte, Her to an answere cowde I counterfete. **1494** Fabyan *Chron.* vii. 471 To assygne certayne indyfferent persones to agre the sayd erles, and they to haue halfe a yere of respyte for to quyet ye matyer. **1560** Daus tr. *Sleidane's Comm.* 112 b, The Prince called them before hym, geving them two monethes respite to deliberate. **1591** Spenser *M. Hubberd* 326 The Foxe then counsel'd th' Ape for to require Respite till morrow t' answere his desire. **1622** Malynes *Anc. Law-Merch.* 94 Vpon proofe made, that he did will another to craue the said respite of time for the paiment. **1676** Dryden *Aurengz.* v. i, Give me some Respight, I'll discharge the Debt. **1768** Blackstone *Comm.* III. App. ii. p. x, The process therein.. is put between them in respite.. untill the day of Easter in fifteen days. **1770** *Junius Lett.* xxxvi. (1788) 189 If I had followed the dictates of my own opinion, I should never have allowed you the respite of a moment. **1856** Froude *Hist. Eng.* (1858) I. iv. 288 The authorities of the church.. were now allowed a respite of two years. **1875** Stubbs *Const. Hist.* II. xiv. 21 The articles that concerned the debts of the Jews, the right of entering and leaving the kingdom.. were likewise put in respite until fuller counsel could be had.

†**b.** ***respite of homage***, the postponement of the act of personal homage, for which a small sum was paid at intervals into the Exchequer. *Obs.*

1541 *Act 33 Hen. VIII*, c. 22 Euerie person.. suing for any generall liuerie.. shall paie.. for the respite of homage in the hanaper.. viii.*d.* **1621** Abp. Williams in *Fortescue P.* (Camden) 169 Soe I may be restored to my temporalties with a respite of homage (which the King grants every day to laymen). [**1656** Blount *Glossogr.*, *Respite* or *Respight of Homage* was the forbearing of Homage which ought first of all to be performed by the Tenant, that held by Homage; which Respite was paid upon divers good reasons.]

c. Delay specially granted in the carrying out of a capital sentence; a reprieve.

1722 De Foe *Moll Flanders* (1840) 342 A poor convict ordered to be transported in respite from the gallows. **1777** Johnson in *Boswell* 28 June I obtained.. an account of the disposition of the court towards him, with a declaration that there was no hope even of a respite. **1861** Trench *Comm. Ep. Churches Asia* 11 There was for them no repeal of the sentence of death, but a respite only. **1869** Browning *Ring & Bk.* xi. 474 Much respite did I grant! Why grant me respite who deserve my doom?

transf. **1703** Prior *Ode to Col. Villiers* 30 Wisdom and Eloquence in vain would plead One Moment's Respite for the learned Head. **1784** Cowper *Task* ii. 67 But grant her end More distant, and that prophecy demands A longer respite. **1879** Froude *Cæsar* xiii. 180 The annihilation of those hordes had given Rome a passing respite.

d. One who is respited or reprieved. *rare.*

1774 *Ann. Reg.* 169 The following capital respites in Newgate have received his majesty's mercy on condition of transportation.

2. Temporary cessation of labour, suffering, war, etc.; (an) interval of rest.

13.. *Coer de L.* 5433 He doos hymself gret dishonour, That he schal Sarezynes respyt gyve. **13..** *E.E. Allit. P.* A. 644 To dyȝe.. & syþen wende to helle hete, þer-inne to won with-oute respyt. *c* **1430** *Syr Gener.* (Roxb.) 5343 Litle respite at mych nede Falleth som tyme wele to spede. *c* **1481** Caxton *Dialogues* 29 He sayde to me That it shall be respyte Bitwene the englisshmen And the scottes. **1513** Douglas *Æneis* xi. iii. *heading*, Quhow Eneas onto the Latynis gave Twelf days of respyt the deid corps to grave. **1573** Tusser *Husb.* (1878) 162 Some respit to husbands the weather may send. **1641** J. Jackson *True Evang. T.* i. 22 The short respite the Church had between the second and third Persecution. **1677** Lord Danby in *Buccleuch MSS.* (Hist. MSS. Comm.) I. 523 Our master will take the two months' respite of arms.. as an act of pure kindness to himself. **1726** Leoni *Alberti's Archit.* I. 49/2 When you think it time for a respite, cover the top of the Wall over with Straw. **1790** Burke *Fr. Rev.* Sel. Wks. II. 84 The king and queen.. lay down.. to indulge nature in a few hours of respite, and troubled, melancholy repose. **1856** Emerson *Eng. Traits, Religion*, The clergy obtained respite from labour for the boor on the Sabbath. **1873** W. Mathews *Getting on in World* xvi. 285 When shall we learn.. that frequent respites from toil are the very safety-valves of professional men?

†**3.** Delay in action; stay. *Obs.*

1375 Barbour *Bruce* viii. 344 Quhen thai of the reirward saw Thair vawarde be sa discomfit, Thai flede vithouten mair respit. **1390** Gower *Conf.* III. 220 The god bad make no respit, That he ne scholde him slen anon. *c* **1430** *Syr Gener.* (Roxb.) 3147 Therfor send him hir without respit, Thou shalt it finde for thi profit. *c* **1477** Caxton *Jason* 42, [I] wolde that I were there.. withoute ony respyte. **1591** Shaks. *1 Hen. VI*, iv. i. 170 Our Selfe, my Lord Protector, and the rest, After some respit, will returne to Calice.

†**4.** Leisure; opportunity for doing something.

1509 Barclay *Shyp of Folys* (1874) II. 316 The payne were longe, and great sholde be the charge, And to the same I haue to small respyte. **1577** *Test. 12 Patriarchs* (1604) 62 We fell upon the men of Jobel.., so as we gave them no respite to return again upon us. **1611** Bible *1 Macc.* xii. 25 Hee.. met them in the land of Amathis: for he gaue them no respite to enter his countrey.

†**5.** Time granted to one until the coming *of* a certain date. *Obs. rare*$^{-1}$.

1667 Milton *P.L.* xi. 272 Where I had hope to spend, Quiet though sad, the respit of that day That must be mortal to us both.

6. *Mil.* (See quot. and cf. respite *v.* 6 b.)

1823 Crabb, *Respite*.. signifies, in military accounts, a certain sum of money, which is directed to be withholden from the issue of pay, in order to make up the several stoppages in regimental distributions.

II. †**7.** Respect; regard; comparison. *Obs.*

c **1374** Chaucer *Troylus* v. 137 Not I nat whi, but out of more respit, Myn herte hath for tamende it grete delit. **1382** Wyclif *Ps.* lxxii. 4 For ther is not respit to the deth of hem. —— *Ecclus.* xxxiv. 14 In respyt of hym it shal be blissid. *c* **1400** *26 Pol. Poems* 132 Mennes dayes ben shorte,.. For in respyte of tyme euermare They beth nothyng equipolent.

respite ('rɛspɪt), *v.* Forms: 4–5 respiten, 4– respite, 5–7 respyt(e, 6 *Sc.* resput, 7–8 respit(t; 6 respyght, 7 respight. Also 5 *pa. pple.* respite. [a. OF. *respiter*, *respoitier*:—L. *respectāre* to respect.]

I. 1. *trans.* To grant a respite to (one).

c **1386** Chaucer *Frankl. T.* 854 But wolde ye vouche sauf vp on seuretee Two yeer or thre for to respiten me. *c* **1400** *Rom. Rose* 6084, I have fele dyverse wonyng, That I kepe not rehersed be, So that ye wolde respiten me. **1430–1** *Rolls of Parlt.* IV. 385/2 The saide tenantz.. be respitid as wele of the taxe. *c* **1500** *Lancelot* 1162 Wharfor, me think It best is to delay, And resput hyme for a tuelmoneth day. **1530** Palsgr. 688/2, I maye well respyte hym for a whyle but he shall paye it every penny. **1622** Malynes *Anc. Law-Merch.* 94 To desire the creditor to respit him some time for the paiment of it. **1768** Blackstone *Comm.* III. xxiii. 354 The entry therefore on the roll or record is, 'that the jury is respited, through defect of the jurors, till the first day of the next term'.

b. *esp.* from death or execution.

13.. *Seuyn Sag.* (W.) 1005, 'I schal him respite,' saide th' emperour. **1390** Gower *Conf.* I. 77 And be this cause he was respited, So that the deth him was acquited. *c* **1450** *Merlin* 39 When they herde hym sey that thei sholbe respited fro deth thei were gladde. **1474** Caxton *Chesse* 11 Thus he respited hym of his deth by his debonayrte. **1533** Ld. Berners *Huon* lxxxiv. 264 All the golde that is in the worlde shall not respyte them fro the deth. *c* **1586** C'tess Pembroke *Ps.* xlix. iii, Tell me whome, but longer time hee [death] leaves Respited from the tombe for treasures meed? **1608** Shaks. *Per.* i. i. 116 Forty days longer we do respite you. **1648** Bp. Hall *Breathings Devout Soul* (1851) 163 It is for something, sure, that thou hast thus long respited me from my grave. **1704** Prior *Let. to Boileau Despreaux*, Alcides respited by prudent Fate, Sustain'd the Ball. **1814** Scott *Ld. of Isles* ii. v, As some poor criminal might feel, When, from the gibbet or the wheel, Respited for a day. **1869** Browning *Ring & Bk.* xi. 360 Respite me, save a soul. then, curse the world!

transf. **1748** Hartley *Observ. Man* ii. iv. 369 All Bodies Politic seem.. to be respited for certain Intervals by partial, imperfect Reformations. **1866** Crump *Banking* ix. 189 It was deemed wise to respite the small notes till 1833.

absol. **1788** Priestley *Lect. Hist.* v. xlvii. 350 Our mode of respiting for the sake of benefiting the souls of the criminals. **1841** Lane *Arab. Nts.* I. 98 He respiteth, but suffereth not to escape.

†**c.** To save or prolong (one's life). *Obs.*

1474 Caxton *Chesse* 64 Put hym self in parelle of deth for to respyte hys maysters lyf. **1483** —— *G. de la Tour* N iij b, I neuer shold respyte ne saue to no man hys lyf, which hade deserued to deye. **1603** Shaks. *Meas. for M.* ii. iii. 41 Oh iniurious Loue That respits me a life, whose very comfort Is still a dying horror.

†**2.** To relieve by an interval of rest. *Obs.*

1563 Golding *Cæsar* v. (1565) 115 In doyng herof he spent ten dayes, not respityng hys souldiers from their labour so muche as the nyght tyme. **1615** Crooke *Body of Man* 40 Then all the faculties are respited and cease from their functions. **1667** Milton *P.L.* v. 232 From the heat of Noon retir'd, To respit his day-labour with repast, Or with repose. **1670** —— *Hist. Eng.* ii. 43 With a dreadful industry of ten days, not respiting his Souldiers day or night.

II. 3. To grant delay or postponement of (a sentence, punishment, obligation, etc.).

1390 Gower *Conf.* I. 116 Thus be we come forto preie That ye mi worldes deth respite. *c* **1440** *Generydes* 1641 Thanne to the Sowdon furth with all they went,.. And prayed hym to respite the Iugement. **1450** *Knt. de la Tour* (1868) 143 For to respite her dethe and aquite her of alle shame. **1577** Grindal *Let.* Wks. (1843) 395 By that occasion my appearance was respited; and I now remain as a man in suspense. **1621** Elsing *Debates Ho. Lords* (Camden) 79 The Kinge hathe respyted his going to the Tower in this tyme of his greate sicknes. **1668** J. Owen *Expos. Ps.* cxxx. Wks. 1851 VI. 481 The full and final punishment of these angels is reserved and respited unto the appointed season. **1758** *Ann. Reg.* i. 100/2 A reprieve was brought to Newgate for Dr. Hensey, respiting his sentence for a fortnight. **1760** T. Hutchinson *Hist. Mass.* (1765) 343 The execution was only respited a few months. **1818** Cruise *Digest* (ed. 2) II. 541 The conveyances to be made in pursuance of the partition, are respited, till the infant comes of age. **1885** *Daily Tel.* 3 Feb., The recognisances of the witnesses for the prosecution were respited sine die.

†**b.** To remit (a penalty). *Obs. rare.*

1489 Caxton *Faytes of A.* iii. xvii. 207 The law ought to be respited to hym, and the lyf saued. *a* **1533** Ld. Berners *Huon* xxxi. 95 Thou shalt neuer departe hense alyue, I shall neuer respyght thy dethe.

†**c.** To allow to remain unpaid for a time. *Obs.*

1640 *Recorde's Gr. Artes* 609 By this Table you may know what any Annuitie being respited or forborn for any number of yeers.. will come unto. **1647** Clarendon *Hist. Reb.* iv. §1 They were promised payment upon the public faith in November following; till which time they were to respite it. **1757** Burke *Abridgm. Eng. Hist.* Wks. X. 213 The taxes.. extorted without mercy, and even, when respited, made utterly ruinous by exorbitant usury.

4. To delay, postpone, put off.

c **1430** *Syr Gener.* (Roxb.) 1851 No lenger put ye in delay His desire to Respite. *c* **1450** *Merlin* 105 Thei seide, 'We wolde that his sacringe and coronacion be respite to Penticoste'. **1521** *St. Papers* I. 33 Ye mowght have respytyd the directyng of your letters. **1610** Donne *Pseudo-martyr* Advt. to Rdr., To giue my Reasons, why I respited the handling of the two last Chapters. **1683** Pettus *Fleta Min.* Ded., I must respit that intention, for I have not done with this Subject. **1707** J. Stevens tr. *Quevedo's Com. Wks.* (1709) 5 If you please, Reader, to respit your other Business, .. I will relate some Passages that will not be unpleasant.

1761 HUME *Hist. Eng.* (1806) IV. lv. 269 He had not now leisure to consider a matter of so great importance, and must therefore respite his answer till his return. **1834** WORDSW. *Even. Volunt.* iv, Care may be respited, but not repealed. **1865** BUSHNELL *Vicar. Sacr.* II. iv. (1868) 203 His whole feeling is now loose upon him, respited by no occupation.

5. To cease from, give up (*obs.*); to suspend.

c **1374** CHAUCER *Anel. & Arc.* 259 Your manly Rayson aught it for to Respite To slee your frende. *c* **1430** *Syr Gener.* (Roxb.) 3101 More worship ye mighte Acheve To respite youre wilfulnes, And by youre counsel you redres. *c* **1460** SIR R. ROS *La Belle Dame* 409 But þat sykenes will sone be remedyde. Respyte your thought, and put all þis a-syde. **1570** T. NORTON tr. *Nowel's Catech.* (1853) 129 That, after respiting their work awhile, they may return more fresh and lusty to it again. **1726** LEONI *Alberti's Archit.* I. 49/2 At what distances it is proper to respite the Work, we may gather from the thickness of the Wall. **1817** T. SCOTT *Paris Revisit.* (ed. 4) 83 As if all the common rules of intercourse had been respited, and the usual calls of industry..overpowered by more inspiring invitations.

6. *Mil.* **a.** To suspend (one) from pay.

1705 *Lond. Gaz.* No. 4106/3 Our Officers are all commanded to repair..to their respective Posts, on pain of being Respited. **1708** *Ibid.* No. 4419/6 Such as shall not then appear will be Respited, and receive no more Pay from that time. **1802** JAMES *Milit. Dict.* s.v., To be respited on the muster roll, to be suspended from pay, &c. during which period all advantages of promotion, pay, &c. are stopped.

b. To keep back, withhold (pay).

1802 JAMES *Milit. Dict.* s.v., The money which is respited upon the muster-roll is accounted for by the muster master general. **1844** *Regul. & Ord. Army* 87 The Pay of all Officers, who do not join their Regiments on the expiration of their Leave of Absence, is to be withheld,..and the pay so respited is not to be issued to them [etc.].

†**7.** *intr.* **a.** To refrain, desist. *Obs. rare.*

1390 GOWER *Conf.* I. 91 Men schal respite As now to take vengement. *Ibid.* 369 Thelaphus..preith his fader to respite. Achilles tho withdrowh his hond.

†**b.** To rest; to recover *from* something. *Obs.*

1575 TURBERV. *Trag. T.* (1837) 28 For I and mine will respite here a space, I like the seate, and fancie well the place. **1769** GOLDSM. *Hist. Rome* (1786) I. 390 It was hoped ..that the commonwealth would have time to respite from the calamities it had sustained.

'respiteless, *a.* [f. RESPITE *sb.*] Without respite or relief (Webster, 1864, citing Baxter).

†**resplaid,** *pa. pple. Sc. Obs.* [App. f. RE- + SPLAY *v.*] ? Embroidered.

1560 ROLLAND *Crt. Venus* I. 121 His hois thay war of the reid Skarlet maid,..Of nedill wark richt richelie all resplaid.

†**resplait,** *v. Sc. Obs.* Also **resplate, resplete.** [a. ONF. *respleiter*, OF. *resploit(i)er*, f. *re-* RE- + *esploit* EXPLOIT *sb.* 5.] *trans.* To adjourn; to defer consideration or payment of.

1448 *Burgh Rec. Aberdeen* (Spalding Cl.) I. 401 The quhilk avisit,..resplaitit this quhil thai be forthir avisit with men of law. **1456** *Ibid.* 404 Thai resplatit the said soume of gold to the nowmer of vi nobillis, till thai spek with Androw Child. *a* **1557** *Diurn. Occurr.* (Bann. Cl.) 41 In this Parliament wes foirfaltit the erle of Lennox,..and the laird of Tulibarden wes respletit.

So †**resplait (respliet)** *sb.*, adjournment. *Obs.*

1609 SKENE *Reg. Maj.* 110 Gif any judgement for any cause before ane Judge be asked..[to] be put to the next Court in respliet, because of better advisement.

resplend (rɪ'splɛnd), *v.* [ad. L. *resplendēre*, f. *re-* RE- + *splendēre* to shine. So F. *resplendir*, It. *risplendere.*] *intr.* To be resplendent or radiant; to shine brightly.

1492 RYMAN *Poems* cii. 3 in *Archiv Stud. neu. Spr.* LXXXIX. 276 This sterre bright..is shynyng With beames of light resplending. **1560** ROLLAND *Crt. Venus* I. 103 Ane Charbukill sa cleir Quhilk did resplend as the sterne M[atutine]. **1622** REYNOLDS *God's Revenge* II. 57 He sees Berinthia's modesty resplend and shine in her affection. **1688** *Lond. Gaz.* No. 2343/1 And the Glory of Your Majesty's Favours so much the more resplends towards us. **1852** THACKERAY *Esmond* II. xv, The dowager..resplended in velvet and gold lace. **1890** STEVENSON *Vailima Lett.* 29 The house was a picture: it resplended of propriety.

Hence **re'splending** *ppl. a.*

1632 LITHGOW *Trav.* I. 30 That resplending Image.

†**re'splendant,** *a. Obs.* [a. OF. *resplendant*: cf. prec. and -ANT.] = RESPLENDENT.

1509 BARCLAY *Shyp of Folys* (1570) 245 Pure and resplendaunt is all thy apparayle. **1589** GREENE *Menaphon* (Arb.) 68 The radiant glory of this resplendant face. **1627** E. F. *Hist. Edw. II* (1680) 1 In the most resplendant pride of his age..crowned King of England.

resplendence (rɪ'splɛndəns). [ad. late L. *resplendentia* (Aug.): see RESPLEND *v.* and -ENCE.] Brightness, brilliance, lustre, splendour.

1432-50 tr. *Higden* (Rolls) II. 7 The chere of theyme dothe ȝiffe grete resplendence lyke to an angelle. *Ibid.* VI. 91 Etheldreda..ȝafe grete resplendence thro miracles. **1555** EDEN *Decades* (Arb.) 367 When also it [silver] is founde lyinge..amonge certeine scales or cloddes of earth, they saye that it is perfecte, although it haue not to the eye suche resplendence. **1561** —— *Art Nauig.* I. ii, The resplendence or shining of the sonne. **1609** HOLLAND *Amm. Marcell.* 163 It discoloureth and diminisheth his [the sun's] most pure resplendence. **1676** MARVELL *Mr. Smirke* 34 [He] shuts his eyes as not being able to indure the resplendence of those evident Truths. **1794** G. ADAMS *Nat. & Exp. Philos.* II. xx. 382 A hue and resplendence similar to that of white metals. *c* **1850** NEALE *Hymns East. Ch.* 134 Fill'd with celestial resplendence and light. **1878** BAYNE *Purit. Rev.* i. 19 The lighting up of the soul with the very resplendence of heaven.

re'splendency. [See -ENCY.] = prec.

1611 COTGR., *Resplendeur*, resplendencie,..brightnesse. *a* **1618** SYLVESTER *Panaretus* 830 Nay nothing, nothing under Heav'n, may misse The Minds-guide rayes of my Resplendencies. **1661** BURNEY *Κέρδιστον Δῶρον* 26 The resplendencie of all Scepters was at the coming of Shiloh. **1737** BP. BROWN *Proc. Understanding* I. ix. (ed. 3) 140 Light in its greatest Resplendency is Material, and an Object of Sensation. **1760** SARAH FIELDING *Ophelia* I. vii, I could not help being struck at the resplendency of all the ornaments. **1856** KANE *Arct. Expl.* I. iii. 37 Making the ice around us one great resplendency of gemwork. **1878** BROWNING *La Saisiaz* 78 Any more than thy resplendency, Jean-Jacques.

resplendent (rɪ'splɛndənt), *a.* [ad. L. *resplendent-em*, pres. pple. of *resplendēre* to RESPLEND. So obs. F. *resplendent*, It. *risplend(i)ente.*] Shining, brilliant, splendid.

1448 *Craft of Lovers* v. in *Stowe's Chaucer* (1561) 341 O Courfin figure, resplendent with glory. **1500-20** DUNBAR *Poems* lxxxvii. 25 Roys red and quhit, resplendent of colour. **1513** BRADSHAW *St. Werburge* I. 659 This fayre prynces, resplendent in vertue. **1593** G. HARVEY *Pierce's Super.* II. Wks. (Grosart) II. 266 The resplendentest mirrour of Feminine valour. **1638** SIR T. HERBERT *Trav.* (ed. 2) 36 All now adding lustre to the Moguls rich resplendent diadem. **1669** GALE *Crt. Gent.* I. I. i. 7 A more resplendent and bright beam of Divine Revelation. **1709** MRS. MANLEY *Secret Mem.* (1736) II. 271 The most resplendent Sight upon Earth. **1784** COWPER *Task* v. 743 His are the mountains.. And the resplendent rivers. **1820** HAZLITT *Lect. Dram. Lit.* 145 If I have done them injustice, the resplendent passages I have to quote will set everything to rights. **1883** J. GILMOUR *Mongols* xviii. 211 A temple..resplendent from afar in colours and gold.

re'splendently, *adv.* [f. prec. + -LY[2].] In a resplendent manner; brilliantly.

1736 BAILEY (fol.), *Resplendently*, shiningly, brightly. *c* **1800** FOSTER *Life & Corr.* (1846) I. 174 A still pool.. shining resplendently in the morning sunshine. **1859** SALA *Tw. round Clock* (1861) 160 Miserable dogs mostly, for all their fine clothes—always resplendently, though dirtily, attired. **1875** W. S. HAYWARD *Love agst. World* 4 With the squire's red coat shining resplendently on the box.

So **re'splendidly** *adv. rare*$^{-1}$.

1796 *Campaigns* 1793-4, I. I. iii. 23 So in arms has desert been resplendidly crown'd.

†**re'splendish,** *v. Obs.* Also 5 **resplendis, -issh,** 5-6 **-yssh,** 6 **rysplendyssh.** [ad. F. *resplendiss-*, lengthened stem of *resplendir* to RESPLEND.] *intr.* To be resplendent. Also *fig.*

c **1475** *Partenay* 1196 As shinyng fire his uisage semynge be, With wonder rednesse so resplendising. *c* **1500** *Melusine* 230 Helmets & salades wel garnysshed with fyn gold & syluer, which resplendysshed full clere. **1540-1** ELYOT *Image Gov.* 149 Some most do resplendishe in actes that bee honest, other seme quickest in malice. **1549** CHALONER *Erasm. on Folly* I j, Good folkes in whom the image of the sprite of God resplendisheth.

†**re'splendishant,** *a. Obs.* Forms: 5 **resplendisant, -isshaunt,** 5-6 **-ys(s)haunt(e,** 6 **-isaunt, -izaunt.** [ad. F. *resplendissant*, pres. pple. of *resplendir*: see prec.] Resplendent.

c **1477** CAXTON *Jason* 101 The riche..shepe of gold which was so resplendisant that it rejoyced all the yle. **1509** HAWES *Past. Pleas.* 79 In the myddle there was resplendyshaunte A dulcet spring..Of golde and asure. *Ibid.* (Percy Soc.) 57 The golden rayes..Through windowes was resplendyshaunt. **1581** J. BELL *Haddon's Answ. Osor.* 331 b, The resplendizaunt, and most orient excellency of his Majesty.

So †**re'splendishent** *a. Obs. rare.*

1586 FERNE *Blaz. Gentrie* 48 The charge of the feeld being gold maketh a most resplendisent and glorious shew.

†**re'splendishing,** *vbl. sb. Obs.* [-ING[1].] Splendour.

1612 J. DAVIES (Heref.) *Muse's Sacr.* Wks. (Grosart) II. 7/2 So, your cleare Eyes doe giue resplendishing to all their Obiects be they ne'er so vile.

†**re'splendishing,** *ppl. a. Obs.* [-ING[2].] Resplendent.

1483 CAXTON *Gold. Leg.* 348/1 Crowned with a ryght resplendysshyng crowne. **1489** —— *Faytes of A.* IV. xvii. 279 Gold of his nature is veray clere and resplendishyng. **1567** MAPLET *Gr. Forest* 5 b, The Diamond is..in colour almost Christallike, but somewhat more resplendishing. **1593** G. HARVEY *New Letter* Wks. (Grosart) I. 268 Like the shining Sun in his resplendishing Chariot.

†**re'splendishure.** *Obs.* In 5 **-ysshour.** [ad. OF. *resplendissour, -issur*, etc.] = next.

1483 CAXTON *Gold. Leg.* 281/3 By the resplendysshour of his grete and many myracles and vertues.

†**re'splendour,** *sb. Obs.* Also 5 **-eur,** 7 **-or.** [a. OF. *resplendor, -ur, -eur*, = Sp. and Pg. *resplendor*, It. *risplendore*: cf. RESPLEND *v.* and SPLENDOUR.] Splendour, brightness.

c **1477** CAXTON *Jason* 20 Your resplendour is clere among the women as the sonne is among the sterres. **1483** —— *Gold. Leg.* 422/3 In resplendour or lyghte of alle good vertues. **1560** ROLLAND *Crt. Venus* II. 575 Of phebus the.. resplendour Refreschit him. **1582** N. LICHEFIELD tr. *Castanheda's Conq. E. Ind.* I. 79 b, Out of it there came such a resplendour or brightnes, that it blinded mens eyes. **1622** MABBE tr. *Aleman's Guzman d'Alf.* II. 2 Reaching forth such a Resplendour and fullnesse of light unto us. **1646** SIR T. BROWNE *Pseud. Ep.* VI. xi. (1686) 270 The resplendor and ray of some interior..Beauty.

Hence †**re'splendour** *v.*, to make resplendent.

1632 LITHGOW *Trav.* x. 500 Soiles so abundant in all things, fit to illustrate greatnesse, Resplendour Gentry, and succour Commons.

resplete, variant of RESPLAIT *v. Obs.*

re'splice (riː-), *v.* [RE- 5 a.] *trans.* To splice (a rope or yard) again.

1834 M. SCOTT *Cruise Midge* (1863) 15 The large lateen sail..with its long elastic spliced and respliced yard. **1875** MARTIN *Winding Mach.* 69 The practice in Belgium is to cut and resplice the thickest section of the rope.

respliet: see RESPLAIT *sb. Obs.*

responaut ('rɛspəʊnɔːt). [Irreg. f. RESPIRATOR + Gr. *ναύτ-ης* sailor, after *astronaut*, etc.] A person dependent upon a mechanical respirator to maintain breathing.

1964 *Sunday Times* 12 Jan. 18/5 The story of the 'responaut' Ann Armstrong as told by Moira Keenan was an enthralling one. **1964** *Med. Officer* 7 Aug. 97/2 A new group of severely disabled people. This group, calling themselves Responauts (because they share similar problems with astronauts and oceanauts in establishing and maintaining communications and vital air supplies) are young people whose lives have been saved through the invention and use of the first artificial organ—an iron lung or mechanical respirator—following a severe attack of respiratory polio. **1965** *Daily Mirror* 30 Dec. 12/2 The Responaut..—a quarterly magazine Ann edits for people like herself who need a breathing machine to keep alive. People the doctors call 'responauts'. **1969** *Guardian* 22 Sept. 7/2 Responauts don't have to be chained to their apparatus in a hospital ward. **1979** *47th Ann. Rep. Pilgrim Trust 1977* 23 The Refresh Trust was formed in 1972..for the purpose of building and equipping a place where a few responauts could safely have a holiday.

respond (rɪ'spɒnd), *sb.* Also 4-6 **responde.** See also RESPOUN(D, *sb.* [a. OF. *respond* (Godef.), f. *respondre*: cf. next and RESPONSE *sb.*]

1. *Eccl.* **a.** = RESPONSORY *sb.* 1 a. (See also quot. 1710.)

1387 TREVISA *Higden* (Rolls) VII. 39 He made in preysinge of oure lady þe respondes [L. *responsoria*] 'Stirps Iesse' and 'Solem iusticie'. *c* **1394** *P. Pl. Crede* 377 A ribaut ..þat can nouȝt wel reden His rewle ne his respondes but be pure rote. *c* **1431** *Rec. St. Mary at Hill* (1905) 16 To go on procession to the tombe..syngyng a Respond of Seynte Stephen with the prose therto. **1494** FABYAN *Chron.* VI. cciii. 213 He made dyuers impnes, sequenses, and respondes. **1547** *Injunct. Edw. VI* in Cardwell *Doc. Ann.* (1839) I. 14 When ix lessons should be read in the church, three of them shall be omitted, and left out with the responds. **1579** FULKE *Refut. Rastel* 743 The very sound and sense of the Anthemnes, Respondes, and Versicles, declare whence they proceeded. **1662** *Bk. Com. Prayer* Conc. Service Ch. ¶2 This godly..Order of the ancient Fathers hath been so altered..by planting in uncertain stories, and Legends, with multitude of Responds, Verses, vain Repetitions [etc.]. **1710** WHEATLEY *Bk. Com. Prayer* (1759) iii. 128 *note*, A Respond is a short Anthem, interrupting the middle of a chapter, which is not to proceed till the Anthem is done. The long Responses are used at the close of the Lessons. **1855** PROCTER *Hist. Bk. Com. Pr.* 167 *marg.*, The Respond and Anthem. **1888** *Tablet* 9 June 932 Consecutive readings of Holy Scripture, instead of fractional portions interrupted by incongruous responds.

b. A response to a versicle.

c **1555** BRADFORD *Hurt Hearing Mass* (Copland) D iiij, The clarke answering in the name of al, *Et cum spiritu tuo*, and other respondes. **1627** *Cosin's Corr.* (Surtees) I. 111 Doth he begin with the Lord's Prayer; orderly proceeding with the Verses and Responds, so that the Clark and people may answere him? **1659** H. L'ESTRANGE *Alliance Div. Off.* 76 These versicles with their Responds are pure Canonical Scripture. **1861** TULLOCH *Eng. Purit.* 289 They went to church, and would answer the parson in responds. **1862** GOULBURN *Pers. Relig.* II. x. (1870) 139 The audible respond is valuable.

transf. **1613** PURCHAS *Pilgrimage* VIII. vii. (1614) 773 The King and his Magician stand neerest the tree and begin, all the people following with their Responds.

2. An answer, a response. Now *rare.*

1600 HOLLAND *Livy* XXXVIII. xiii. 990 The priests and prophets there deliuer the reponds and answeres of the Oracle in uerses. **1675** J. SMITH *Chr. Relig. App.* II. 45 The same Platonick introduceth Apollo, giving Responds against the hair. **1868** J. K. HUNTER *Retrospect Artist's Life* xxvi. 248 A grand respond to my appeal.

†**b.** A part in singing. *Obs. rare*$^{-1}$.

1601 HOLLAND *Pliny* I. 286 Of late we haue known many of them taught..to sing..and keepe their responds in course after others, in good consent and harmony.

3. *Arch.* A half-pillar or half-pier attached to a wall to support an arch. Cf. RESPOUN(D *sb.* 2.

1448 HEN. VI *Will* in Willis & Clark *Cambridge* (1886) I. 354 The same Quere shal conteyne in brede from side to side within the respondes .xxxij. fete. *Ibid.*, The yle..fro respond to respond .xv. fete.

1838 BRITTON *Dict. Archit.* 393 From these..passages it appears that a half column, or a pilaster attached to a wall, or to a pillar, and responding, or corresponding, to another on the opposite side of the building, was called a respond. **1851** TURNER *Dom. Archit.* II. ii. 29 There are no responds, the arches at the ends springing from corbels. **1881** FREEMAN *Subj. Venice* 208 The four responds have the four evangelistic symbols.

attrib. **1847** HADFIELD *Eccl., Castell., & Dom. Archit.* 5 The respond-corbel at the west end of the north side. **1886** WILLIS & CLARK *Cambridge* II. 119 The respond-shafts and wall-ribs still adhere..to the sides of that noble quadrangle.

respond (rɪ'spɒnd), *v.* [ad. L. *respondēre*, f. *re-* RE- + *spondēre* to pledge, promise, warrant. So OF. *respondre* (mod.F. *répondre*), Sp. and Pg.

responder, It. *re-*, *rispondere*. For early forms in Eng. see RESPOUN(D *v.*]

†**1.** *trans.* To provide with a corresponding entry. *Obs. rare.*

1588 J. MELLIS *Briefe Instr.* D viij, That each parcell both in your Debitor and Creditor be orderly noted and responded in your Journall.

2. a. To answer or correspond to (something); to reciprocate. Now *rare* or *Obs.*

1600 FAIRFAX *Tasso* x. xl, His great deedes respond his speeches great. *Ibid.* XIV. x, The water..Which sea sometime is call'd, sometime the maine, Yet nought therein responds a name so great. **1642** J. M[ARSH] *Argt. conc. Militia* 4 The king should not be denied the means, by which he may respond the great confidence placed in him. **1804** *Something Odd* III. 99 The sweet smiles she bestowed on him, were now responded by each countenance.

b. *U.S.* To answer, satisfy.

1890 *Cent. Dict.* s.v., The prisoner was held to respond the judgment of the court.

c. *Bridge.* To make (a bid) in reply to a partner's opening (or subsequent) bid. Cf. RESPONDER 1 b.

1958 *Listener* 16 Oct. 611/2 East should have responded Two Hearts. **1959** T. REESE *Bridge Player's Dict.* 158 If one diamond were opened and partner responded two clubs, there would not be a sound rebid. **1976** *Times* 1 May 12/6 To partner's opening One Heart it is dangerous to respond Two Clubs.

3. *intr.* **a.** To correspond *to* something. *rare.*

1591 SPARRY tr. *Cattan's Geomancie* I. xxviii. 41 The principall pointes..do diuide the Zodiacke into foure partes or quarters, responding to the foure parts and seasons of the yeare. **1838** [see RESPOND *sb.* 3].

b. To make answer, to give a reply, in words. Also *fig.*

1719 WATERLAND *Vind. Christ's Div.* 7 Your Business was not to oppose, but to respond. *a* **1734** OLDISWORTH in Johnson *L.P.*, *Smith*, I remember him in the divinity school responding and disputing with a perspicuous energy. **1816** SHELLEY *Daemon* I. 51 When west winds sigh and evening waves respond In whispers from the shore. **1832** PALMER *Orig. Liturg.* II. 21 A long litany, in which the deacon directed the people to pray for many different objects and the people responded. **1878** BROWNING *La Saisiaz* 24 Mine is but man's truest answer—how Were it did God respond?

c. To answer by some responsive act; to act in response *to* some influence.

1726 W. BROOME *To Pope*, Poems (1727) 97 To every Theme responds thy various Lay. **1791** MRS. RADCLIFFE *Rom. Forest* i, Her mind responded but too easily to the apprehension of new misfortunes. **1862** SPENCER *First Princ.* I. iv. §25 (1875) 83 Chemical actions responding to the co-existence of light, heat, water, and carbonic acid around it. **1872** HUXLEY *Physiol.* ix. 221 A defect in the retina, which renders that organ unable to respond to different kinds of luminous vibrations. **1876** *Jrnl. Soc. Telegr. Engin.* V. 514 We wish to construct a receiver to respond to a tone made by 128 vibrations per second. **1910** J. ERSKINE-MURRAY *Wireless Telephones* vii. 51 An electric circuit will respond most readily to impulses which come timed to its own natural rate of vibration. **1939** N. DE V. HART *Bridge Players' Bedside Bk.* xii. 57 North responded to the Forcing Two in Diamonds with Two Hearts. **1952** A. GRIMBLE *Pattern of Islands* 233 One or two cases had begun to respond to gynocardate injections. **1954** G. I. M. SWYER *Reproduction & Sex* xv. 203 More of the women..had responded until they were in their fifties or sixties. **1967** M. KENYON *Whole Hog* xx. 195 You could have responded to my three clubs, you could have said something.

d. *U.S.* To give satisfaction.

1890 *Cent. Dict.* s.v., The defendant is held to respond in damages.

‖**responde** (rɪˈspɒndiː). *Sc. Law.* [L., 2 sing. imp. of *respondēre*. Cf. RESPONDIE.]

a. (With *book.*) 'A book kept by the Directors of Chancery, in which are entered all non-entry and relief duties payable by heirs who take precepts from Chancery' (Bell). †**b.** A single entry in this book. †**c.** The amount of the duties specified in any entry.

1587 *Act Jas. VI*, Parl. xi. c. 73 In case Schireffes, Stewardes and Baillies, make not their compts, at the ordinar time of checker..That vpon the sight of the buik of Responde, letters be directed, to charge the persons, to quhome precepts of seasing hes bene granted..To pay the summes conteined in the Respondees. **1597** SKENE *De Verb. Sign.* s.v., *Responde*, or the buike of Responde... It is called 'responde', quhilk is the first worde of ilke artickle of the said buike. *Ibid.*, He suld come again to the Chancellarie, and raise ane new precept,..and ane new memorial or 'responde' is maide thereof. **1676** LAUDER *Decisions* Suppl. III. (1826) 109 Because the sheriff must be answerable for the respond[e] contained in these precepts. **1687** *Acts Sederunt* 30 June, The responde-book shall make mention of the date of the decreet extracted, as the same stands in the minut-book. *a* **1768** ERSKINE *Inst. Law Scot.* II. v. §50 The sums due to the crown for the nonentry and relief duties, which are all stated in the responde book.., and are chargeable upon the sheriff, who must account..for them to the exchequer. **1838** W. BELL *Dict. Law Scot.* 859.

‖**respondeat superior** (rɛˈspɒndeɪæt suːˈpɛrɪɔə(r)), *phr. Law.* [L., 'let the principal answer'.] A maxim embodying the rule of vicarious liability (see quots.).

[**1601** W. FULBECKE *Parallele or Conference Civill Law, Canon Law & Common Law* I. x. f. 76 A plea in Abatement of a writte bee not peremptorie, but a *respondeat vlterius*.] *a* **1634** E. COKE *Fourth Part Inst. Lawes Eng.* (1644) xi. 114 Now it is good to know, how the law commonly called *Respondeat superior*, holdeth in this Court and in other Courts. **1848** W. HARTON *Law Lexicon* 587/2 *Respondeat superior*, (let the superior answer). If a coroner of a county is insufficient, the county, as his superior, shall answer for him. **1903** *Automobile & Carriage Builders' Jrnl.* May 133/2 The maxim *respondeat superior*. **1965** *Mod. Law Rev.* XXVIII. 584 It is trite learning that civil responsibility could in general be imposed *respondeat superior*. **1976** *Billings* (Montana) *Gaz.* 6 July 3-A/2, I have no trouble with the concept of accepting responsibility for one's actions. It's called 'respondeat superior'. That is, the principal is liable for the actions of his agent which are authorized. It was what the Nuremberg trials were all about.

respondence (rɪˈspɒndəns). [a. obs. F. *respondence*, = Sp. and Pg. *respondencia*, It. *rispondenza*: see RESPOND *v.* and -ENCE.]

1. †**a.** ? Responsibility, liability. *Obs. rare*$^{-1}$.

1586 BURGHLEY in *Leicester's Corr.* (Camden) 358 The states commissaries haue not been made privie to our musters and paiements, whearebie the issue will be, respondence for repaiment to bee made hereafter to hir majesty.

b. (See INTENDENCE.)

†**2.** Answer, response, to a sound. *Obs.*

1590 SPENSER *F.Q.* II. xii. 71 Th' Angelicall soft trembling voyces made To th' instruments divine respondence meet. **1600** FAIRFAX *Tasso* XI. v, With sweet respondence in harmonious kinde Their humble song the..aire doth beat.

3. Correspondence, agreement, concord.

1598 BP. HALL *Sat.* v. i. 57 His rent in faire respondence must arise. **1633** T. ADAMS *Exp. 2 Peter* i. 21 In fit respondence to the work of our redemption. **1673-4** GREW *Anat. Pl.*, *Anat. Roots* vii. 140 The suitableness and respondence betwixt the several Parts of the Stock and Cyon. **1794** ANNA SEWARD *Lett.* (1811) III. 381 With such a guest, the respondence of intellect..must have added zest to the delight of gazing on scenery so lovely. **1863** NEALE *Ess. Liturg.* v. 125 The five great epochs of the Church..bear no mutual respondence.

b. Response *to* some stimulus.

1867 MAUDSLEY *Physiol. Mind* 92 The act is consensual, or..instinctive, in respondence to a visual sensation or picture. **1874** CARPENTER *Ment. Phys.* I. ii. (1879) 44 Movements in respondence to the impressions made by external agencies.

re'spondency. [See prec. and -ENCY.] Correspondence, congruence.

1603 DANIEL *Panegyric to King* lxvi, To stand Against all th' interplaced respondencies Of combinations. **1629** T. ADAMS *Fool & his Sport* Wks. 774 Thus you see the respondencie of the spirituall to the naturall Foole, in their qualities. **1826** E. IRVING *Babylon* VI. II. 111 We begin to observe the respondency of this to the former parts of the prophecy. **1833** CHALMERS *Const. Man* (1834) II. ix. 91 He whose hand did frame our internal mechanism, has attuned it in the most correct and delicate respondency.

respondent (rɪˈspɒndənt), *sb.* [f. as next: so obs. F. *respondant* (mod.F. *répondant*).]

1. a. One who answers; *spec.*, one who defends a thesis against one or more opponents; also in recent use (chiefly *U.S.*), one who supplies information for a survey.

1528 TINDALE *Obed. Chr. Man* Wks. (1573) 171/2 *Ego nego, Domine Doctor*, said the respondent. **1536** *Act 28 Hen. VIII*, c. 13 §2 Suche beneficed persons..shall..be apponent and respondent in the same [disputations]. **1603** FLORIO *Montaigne* I. xx. (1632) 45 Magitians are but ill respondents for me. **1648** JENKYN *Blind Guide* iii. 43 Are you not respondent? Was it not your part to answer what was brought against your wicked Position? **1721** AMHERST *Terræ Fil.* No. 20 (1726) 103 The respondent sits over-against the opponent, and is prepared to deny whatever he affirms. **1753-4** RICHARDSON *Grandison* (1781) III. 119 Take care, Charlotte, that you make as free a respondent.. as you are a questioner. **1816** COLERIDGE *Lay Serm.* (Bohn) 336 Each person must be herein querist and respondent to himself. **1875** JOWETT *Plato* (ed. 2) III. 8 When Thrasymachus has been silenced, the two principal respondents..appear on the scene. **1955** *Bull. Atomic Sci.* 175/2 Almost one-third of the respondents said they were upset by witnessing the casualties. **1961** *Technology* Feb. 34/1 The respondents were not asked how often they had applied each technique, if more than once, since many would probably have no accurate record of this. **1968** *Amer. Jrnl. Public Health* LVIII. 327/1 The questionnaires were unsigned on their return and were thrown into a large pile at the front of the room in such a manner that no one from the military hierarchy could identify the responses of any respondent. **1970** D. GOLDRICH et al. in I. L. Horowitz *Masses in Lat. Amer.* v. 176 The interviewers selected respondents randomly from the household. **1975** *Amer. Speech 1973* XLVIII. 22 Recent behavioral tests..have shown that respondents are capable of identifying informants as black or white from auditory cues only.

†**b.** One who makes himself answerable for another. *Obs. rare*$^{-1}$.

1672 R. MONTAGU in *Buccleuch MSS.* (Hist. MSS. Comm.) I. 517, I shall come away with so good a character from this place, that I shall not have shamed my respondent.

c. A rhyme-word. *rare*$^{-1}$.

1804 CHARLOTTE SMITH *Conversat.*, etc. II. 137 Some word of great force to close his couplet, to which there are not, perhaps, above two or three respondents.

2. A defendant in a lawsuit; now *spec.* in a divorce case.

1562 *Child Marriages* (1897) 73 This respondent sais, that he & Margaret Alat were maried in Weuerham church. **1651** G. W. tr. *Cowel's Inst.* 224 If we respect the persons, they are both complainants, and respondents. **1752** J. LOUTHIAN *Form of Process* 250 The said A.B. Appellant to make Payment to the said D.E. and H.I. Respondents. **1857** *Act 20 & 21 Vict.* c. 85 §28 The Court..may direct that the Person with whom the Husband is alleged to have committed adultery be made a Respondent. **1871** B. TAYLOR *Faust* (1875) I. xxiii. 205 To crush to pieces the innocent respondent—that is the tyrant-fashion of relieving oneself in embarrassments.

3. *Math.* (See quot.)

1888 *Encycl. Brit.* XXIII. 7/1 In any table the results tabulated are termed the 'tabular results' or 'respondents', and the corresponding numbers by which the table is entered are termed the 'arguments'.

4. *Psychol.* The result of, or response to, a specific stimulus (see quot. 1937).

1937 B. F. SKINNER in *Jrnl. Gen. Psychol.* XVI. 274 It is a necessary recognition of the fact that in the unconditioned organism two kinds of behavior may be distinguished. There is, first, the kind of response that is made to specific stimulation... I shall refer to such a reflex as a *respondent* and use the term also as an adjective in referring to the behavior as a whole. **1940** HILGARD & MARQUIS *Conditioning & Learning* iii. 66 Respondents..are movements elicited by recognized stimuli.

respondent (rɪˈspɒndənt), *a.* [ad. L. *respondent-*, pres. pple. of *respondēre* to RESPOND. So obs. F. *respondent*, *-ant* (mod.F. *répondant*), Sp. *respondiente*, It. *rispondente*.]

†**1.** Correspondent (*to* something else). *Obs.*

1533 BELLENDEN *Livy* II. xxi. (S.T.S.) I. 213 þai thocht na thing mare respondent to resson and equite. *Ibid.* 215 þat þe end of þare vayage mycht be respondent to þare begynnyng. **1588** PARKE tr. *Mendoza's Hist. China* 24 The which.. seemeth somwhat to be respondent to our holy sacred and christian religion. **1671** GREW *Anat. Pl.* (1682) 9 Seeing the even verges of the Lobes of the Seed hereto respondent. **1672** FLAMSTEED in Rigaud *Corr. Sci. Men* (1841) II. 128, I shall not fail..to do my endeavour to make respondent observations. **1726** POPE *Odyss.* XVII. 315 Well may this Palace admiration claim, Great, and respondent to the master's fame!

2. Answering; making reply. Also, having the position of defendant in an action.

1726 AYLIFFE *Parergon* 67 It is necessary, That the Party Respondent should be present in Court. *a* **1797** H. WALPOLE *Mem. Geo. III* (1845) I. vi. 87 To hear the King's Speech, and the respondent Address read. **1802-12** BENTHAM *Ration. Judic. Evid.* (1827) I. 502 Either amicable or adverse in relation to such respondent witness. **1899** *Daily News* 7 Jan. 4/5 Counsel representing the respondent magistrate.

3. a. Responsive *to* some influence.

1766 GOLDSM. *Vic. W.* xxviii, My heart is respondent only to softer emotions. **1792** CHARLOTTE SMITH *Desmond* II. 143 Her heart finds respondent sentiments only in yours. **1867** MAUDSLEY *Physiol. Mind* 147 Many of the remaining actions ..are really respondent to an idea or emotion. **1874** CARPENTER *Ment. Phys.* (1879) 81 Sensations are excited by impressions,..and respondent motions are called forth.

b. *Psychol.* Responsive, or that occurs as a reflex, to some specific stimulus; esp. as ***respondent conditioning***, the conditioning of an organism to a particular response through the controlled use of a stimulus.

1937 B. F. SKINNER in *Jrnl. Gen. Psychol.* XVI. 274 The distinction between operant and respondent behavior. **1940** HILGARD & MARQUIS *Conditioning & Learning* iii. 72/1 Respondent behavior, like ordinary spinal reflexes, is elicited by specified stimuli. **1966** I. G. SARASON *Personality* iv. 75 The actual role played by reinforcement has been studied intensively in..experimental situations, one involving classical or respondent conditioning. **1974** H. W. BERNARD *Personality* x. 241 Respondent conditioning can also be used as a therapeutic approach.

‖**respondentia** (rɛspɒnˈdɛnʃ(ɪ)ə). [mod.L.] A loan upon the cargo of a vessel, to be repaid (with maritime interest) only if the goods arrive safe at their destination. (Cf. BOTTOMRY.)

1727 A. HAMILTON *New Acc. E. Ind.* II. xxxiii. 14 There was one Captain Perrin Master of a Ship, who took up about 500£ on respondentia.., payable at his Return to Bengal. **1755** MAGENS *Insurances* II. 353 Merchants and other Traders frequently lend Money on Bottomree or at Respondentia and cause their Vessels with their Cargoes to be insured. **1803** *Ann. Rev.* I. 382/2 He begins money with Homer's oxen, and respondentia-bonds in the Cimmerian Bosphorus. **1867** SMYTH *Sailor's Work-bk.* 570 Upon respondentia the lender must be paid his principal and interest, though the ship perish, provided the goods be safe. **1898** *Green's Encycl. Law Scot.* X. 323 It is essential to the validity of a bond of respondentia that it should have been granted for the benefit of the cargo.

re'sponder. [f. RESPOND *v.* + -ER^{1}.]

1. a. One who responds or replies; a respondent.

1879 *Daily News* 19 Sept. 2/1 A reference which was very gratefully recognised by one of the responders [to the toast]. **1894** *Forum* Aug. 710 Imaginary responders were set up if there were no real ones.

b. *Bridge.* The partner of the opening bidder.

1932 *Daily Tel.* 8 Oct. 15/5 The partner of the opening bidder is known as the responder. **1952** I. MACLEOD *Bridge* iv. 49 If the responder raises the opener's suit, it is a quantitative bid only. **1966** *Listener* 13 Jan. 78/2 What happens..if the responder has only sufficient high card strength to raise One No Trump to Two No Trumps as an invitation to game? **1976** *Times* 1 May 12/7 When there is opposition bidding the responder's duty is to show the strength of his hand.

2. †**a.** An early, electrolytic, form of radio receiver. *Obs.*

1901 *Western Electrician* 27 July 49/1 To the new receiving device its inventors [*sc.* De Forest and Smythe] have applied the name 'responder', a term first suggested by the London Electrician as one suitable for any resistance device sensitive to electric radiations. **1904** *Electr. Rev.* 3 Sept. 330 The principle of this receiver or 'responder', is based upon the fact that the Hertzian oscillations produce sudden electrolytic action in a cell containing certain electrodes and solutions. **1915** W. H. ECCLES *Wireless*

Telegr. 246 In one type of electrolytic detector, now merely of historic interest, the processes of electrolysis are employed to form fine threads of metal across the gap or gaps, and these threads are destroyed by the oscillations to be detected. The consequent alteration of resistance is observed by telephone or galvanometer. Of this type is..the 'responder' of de Forest and Smythe.

b. A device which automatically retransmits a pulse or signal on receiving one from an interrogator. Also ***responder beacon***.

1945 *Nature* 15 Sept. 323/2 *A* and *B* are pulse-interrogator stations, the aircraft has a responder of constant and accurately known delay-time... 'G-H' and 'Babs'.. utilize coded responses sent back by a ground responder-beacon in reply to pulses from an airborne or shipborne interrogator. **1945** *Electronic Engin.* Oct. 735 Vehicles could now carry small questioning transmitters ('interrogators') and obtain replies from 'responder' beacons on land or sea. **1957** *Encycl. Brit.* XVIII. 873 Y/1 Beacons of the synchronous sort just described are variously called radar beacons, responder beacons, racons, or transponders, there being no important distinction among these terms. **1966** D. TAYLOR *Introd. Radar & Radar Techniques* iv. 45 A responder beacon..is a 'repeater', in the sense that it would retransmit after a very short time-interval any pulse signal received. **1977** *Offshore Engineer* Aug. 46/2 The remote vehicle's depth, horizontal range, slant range and relative bearing can all be determined by using this single responder in conjunction with Wesmar's new SS400TS sonar tracking system. The responder acts as a transmitter/receiver, receiving electronic signals through an umbilical.

3. *Biol.* and *Med.* An individual, structure, etc., that responds or reacts to some stimulus or treatment.

1963 *Jrnl. Exper. Med.* CXVIII. 954 Responders showed both Arthus and delayed allergic skin reactions to the immunizing conjugates. **1973** *Nature* 30 Nov. 245/1 Cells were classified as either β^+ or β^- (responders and non-responders to β-adrenergic stimulators) or P^+ or P^- (responders and non-responders to prostaglandin E_1). **1976** *Lancet* 30 Oct. 928/1 A further analysis was made into responders and nonresponders... The responders were defined as patients in whom the number of ulcers decreased by more than 50% over 2 or more months.

†**re'spondie.** *Sc. Obs.* (See RESPONDE.)

1645 *Sc. Acts Chas. I* (1814) VI. 180/1 To call for payment and compt of all Respondies and Debts addebted..to the publike. *Ibid.* 181/1 The Clerk..shall have the trust and keeping of the Respondie-Books, and of all the Accompts.

re'sponding, *ppl. a.* [f. RESPOND *v.* + -ING.] Corresponding; responsive.

1683 MOXON *Mech. Exerc., Printing* xxii. ¶7 He.. removes them to the responding Quarter of the Form Imposing, into the responding places. **1819** T. CHALMERS *Serm.* (1836) I. 232 A responding affection can be deposited in the heart of man. **1863** GEO. ELIOT *Romola* xxiv, A loud responding sob rose at once from the wide multitude. **1921** G. CECIL *Life Ld. Salisbury* II. vi. 219 His action was generally attributed to the decision to call out the Reserves ..and Lord Beaconsfield implied as much in his responding speech. **1933** C. VANDYCK *Contract Contracted* 21 As the Playing Trick count is not used until the Trump Suit has been decided upon the Responding Hand is obviously the first one to use it. **1952** I. MACLEOD *Bridge* vi. 73 The responding hand..never assumes, at least until the second trial bid, that the opener is slamming. **1965** in J. Money *Sex Research* 107 Seldom does the responding female directly manipulate the clitoris through an entire sexual response cycle. **1968** R. KYLE *Love Lab.* (1969) xviii. 210 Data on several hundred responding individuals has more scientific validity than data on one.

responsa: see RESPONSUM.

†**re'sponsable,** *a. Obs. rare.* [= F. and Sp. *responsable*, It. *responsabile*, med.L. *responsābilis*, f. *responsāre*.] Responsible.

1641 'SMECTYMNUUS' *Answ.* xviii. (1653) 76 But now since Episcopacy comes to be challenged as a Divine Ordinance, how shall wee be responsable to those Texts. **1648** ASHHURST *Reasons agst. Agreemt.* 11 Men that can neither write, read, nor have any estates responsable.

†**re'sponsal,** *sb. Obs.* Also 5–7 responsall(e, 6 *Sc.* responsaill. [ad. med.L. *responsālis* (see next), used as sb. in various senses.]

1. A response, reply.

1432–50 tr. *Higden* (Rolls) V. 395 The tenors of whiche letters.., with the responsalles [L. *responsis*] of Gregory,.. were putte in the registre of Gregory. *c* **1480** HENRYSON *Test. Cres.* 127 Ye gave me anis ane devine responsaill That I suld be the flour of luif in Troy. **1609** ARMIN *Maids of More-Cl.* (1880) 96 T'would allay his hot endeauours with a cold responsall. **1624** F. WHITE *Repl. Fisher* 241 The determination..is like Apollo his riddles and responsalls. **1652** N. CULVERWEL *Lt. Nature* I. xiii. (1661) 109 How cautelous they were in their Oracular Responsals.

b. A liturgical response or respond.

a **1652** J. SMITH *Sel. Disc.* iv. 123 The responsals or antiphons wherein each of them catcheth at the other's part. **1688** *Answ. Dissenter's Objections to Bk. Common Prayer* 11 The Responsals of the Congregation are Matters of Offence to some. **1753** CHAMBERS *Cycl. Suppl.* s.v. *Antiphony*, St. Ambrose [calls antiphony] *responsoria*, or singing by responsals. [**1893** J. CHRISTIE *Acc. Parish Clerks* 15 Ability to read the Epistles and Lessons, to sing Responsals, Grails, and other parts of the Service.]

2. The respondent in a disputation. Also *attrib.*

c **1500** in Peacock *Stat. Cambridge* (1841) App. p. xxxviii, The Responsall shall have a Deske ordeyned for hym byfore the Father. *c* **1551** BP. GARDNER *Explic. Cath. Faith* 130 One was answered at Cambridge when he pressed the responsall, what saye ye to myne argumente. **1574** in Peacock *Stat. Cambridge* (1841) App. p. xi, A Sophister provided by the Proctour shall knele before the Responsall sett [= seat].

3. One appointed by a prelate to give or send replies to questions; an apocrisiary.

1570 FOXE *A. & M.* (ed. 2) 308/2 The Archbyshop receauyng this appellation, and saying that he would aunswere to the same either by him selfe or by his responsall. **1610** DONNE *Pseudo-martyr* 23 He suspended him vntill he might vnderstand from his Responsall with the Emperor, whether that pretended Commandement..were not subreptitious.

†**re'sponsal,** *a. Obs.* Also 4 -aill. [ad. late L. *responsālis* (6th c.), f. *responsāre* to reply. Cf. OF. *responsal, -el.*]

1. Answerable, responsible.

c **1400** *Beryn* 2623 Such answers vs purvey, þat þey..shull be responsaill For of [*sic*] wele. **1550** *Reg. Privy Council Scot.* I. 106 Giff he be nocht responsall for the said sowme, that the Schereff..putt him in the irnis. **1587** *Ibid.* IV. 192 His complices nawayes being responsall in law to answer for thair deid. **1641** HEYLIN *Hist. Episc.* II. (1657) 442 The Presbyters..in the Countrey villages, should be responsall to the Bishop. **1653** *Consid. Dissolving Crt. Chanc.* 44 [They] will want that wisdom and estates, which the other have to make them responsal.

2. Responsive; of the nature of responses.

1607 S. COLLINS *Serm.* (1608) 25 They should haue beene like an Oracle responsall, without any Philippizing. **1653** R. LOVEDAY *Lett.* (1663) 45 'Tis but an easie task for your Pen, and will engage mine to be responsal. **1680** BAXTER *Cath. Commun.* (1684) A 2 That the Primitive Churches had some Responsal Forms..I shall recite an evidence out of Chrysostom. **1738** NEAL *Hist. Purit.* IV. 416 The Liturgy to be abbreviated..by omitting all the Responsal prayers.

3. Correspondent, appropriate. *rare*$^{-1}$.

1647 SPRIGGE *Anglia Rediv.* III. vi. (1854) 168 Would thou hadst took that leisure time To visit some responsal clime.

re'sponsary. *rare.* [ad. med.L. *responsārium.*] = RESPONSORY *sb.*

c **1557** ABP. PARKER *Ps.* G ij, And after that..make a great noise by the responsaries..of the Psalmes. **1715** M. DAVIES *Athen. Brit.* I. 256 The Pagans had not only such certain forms of Prayer, but also Repetitions and Responsaries. **1866** *Liturgy Ch. Sarum* 88 The Ten Commandments, and their responsaries.

response (rɪ'spɒns). Forms: 4 respouns(e, 4, 6 respons, 5–6 responce, 7– response. [In ME., a. OF. *respuns, respons* (mod.F. *répons*) masc. or *response* (mod. *réponse*), fem. In later use directly ad. L. *responsum* neut. (also late L. *responsus* masc.), f. *respondēre* to RESPOND.]

1. a. An answer, a reply.

c **1300** *Beket* 825 In a chambre faste iloke alle hi were ibrouȝt, That hi ne scholde ascapie noȝt er hi respounse sede. *c* **1330** R. BRUNNE *Chron. Wace* 11924 Þe chartre þey schewed þer barouns, & seide, 'swich ys Arthures respouns'. **1338** —— *Chron.* (1810) 98 What was his respons writen, I ne sauh no herd. **1533** BELLENDEN *Livy* I. xix. (S.T.S.) I. 109 It is said þat Turnus was na thing satifyit on his respons. **1589** PUTTENHAM *Eng. Poesie* III. xix. (Arb.) 214 Ye haue a figuratiue speach which the Greeks cal Antipophora, I name him the Responce. **1604** R. CAWDREY *Table Alph.* (1613), *Responses*, answers. **1673** CAVE *Prim. Chr.* I. vii. 192 The Author of the Questions and Responses. **1675** BAXTER *Cath. Theol.* I. 113 He..needeth no more of mine for the confutation of his vain responses. **1712** STEELE *Spect.* No. 266 ¶4, I heard an old and a young Voice repeating the Questions and Responses of the Church-Catechism. **1751** HARRIS *Hermes* Wks. (1841) 161 With respect to the interrogative, the return is necessarily made in words.. which are called a response or answer. **1798** COLERIDGE *Anc. Mar.* 411 But..speak again, Thy soft response renewing. **1869** A. HARWOOD tr. *E. de Pressensé Early Yrs. Chr.* III. iii. 404 We know the response of ancient philosophy to this question.

b. *transf.* and *fig.* An action or feeling which answers to some stimulus or influence; *spec.* in *Psychol.* (freq. opposed to *stimulus*), an observable reaction to some specific stimulus or situation; the fact of such reaction.

1815 SHELLEY *Alastor* 564 A pine,..to each inconstant blast Yielding one only response. **1860** TYNDALL *Glac.* I. §15. 103 A joyous rush was the creature's first response to the signal. **1875** JOWETT *Plato* (ed. 2) IV. 130 Something which found a response in his own mind seemed to have been lost. **1908** E. L. THORNDIKE in *Ess. Philos. & Psychol. in Honor W. James* 597 A situation arouses a response which brings an annoying state of affairs. The probability of a similar response in the future is lessened. **1919** J. B. WATSON *Psychol.* i. 16 Having now examined at some length into the general nature of both stimulus and response, we should be prepared to understand the object of a psychological experiment. **1934** H. DAVIS in C. Murchison *Handbk. Gen. Exper. Psychol.* 983 They..constitute an objective response of great value for analyzing the activities of the cortical tissue. **1948** A. C. KINSEY et al. *Sexual Behav. Human Male* v. 159 Evidence of minimal psychic components with good enough physical responses. **1952** FORD & BEACH *Patterns Sexual Behav.* xii. 239 Her capacity for complete response returned. **1957** B. F. SKINNER in Saporta & Bastian *Psycholinguistics* (1961) v. 228/1 Semantic theory is often confined to the relation between response and stimulus which prevails in the verbal operant called the tact. **1965** in J. Money *Sex Research* 101 Three women were able to achieve orgasmic response by breast manipulation alone. **1976** SENTER & DIMOND *Psychol.* vi. 102 Relaxation and anxiety are competing responses. You must behave in one way or the other.

c. The way in which an apparatus responds to a stimulus or range of stimuli.

1911 H. M. HOBART *Dict. Electr. Engin.* II. 630/1 The receiver must be sharply tuned so that the variations of frequency may be sufficient to make an appreciable difference in the strength of its response. **1915** W. H. ECCLES *Wireless Telegr.* 245 Fig. 176 shows the response of the detector (change of *I*) at various values of the intensity of magnetism *I* and the field *H*, for four different magnetic cycles. **1926**, etc. [see *frequency response* s.v. FREQUENCY 6 a]. **1958** O. R. FRISCH *Nuclear Handbk.* XIV. 16 In designing a scintillation counter the spectrum of the fluorescent radiation must be marked as far as possible with the spectral response of the multiplier. **1961** G. MILLERSON *Television Production* iii. 41 Where the tube's response to red is excessive, this may be held back with an appropriate green or blue filter. **1970** J. EARL *Tuners & Amplifiers* iii. 68 The latest 'quality' amplifiers..boast a power response which is almost as good as the frequency response.

d. *Bridge.* A reply to a partner's opening (or subsequent) bid.

1939 N. DE V. HART *Bridge Players' Bedside Bk.* x. 52 South's response of Six Clubs showed first round control of clubs. **1947** S. HARRIS *Fund. Princ. Contract Bridge* I. iv. 35 It sometimes happens that South is able to make a positive response. **1958** *Listener* 16 Oct. 611/2 West makes her natural response of Three Diamonds. **1967** P. ANDERTON *Play Bridge* iii. 28 The negative response is 2 N.T. in which case the hand will probably be played in 3 H. **1976** *Times* 1 May 12/6 A minimum response can be shown only by a rebid of the suit.

2. *Eccl.* **a.** = RESPONSORY *sb.* 1.

1450–1530 *Myrr. our Ladye* 107 After lessons foloweth Responces. *Ibid.*, Thys fyrste responce ys songe in faythe and in praysynge of the blyssed Trynyte. **1592** tr. *Junius on Rev.* xix. 3 The song of the Antiphonie or response. **1811** BUSBY *Dict. Mus.* (ed. 3), *Response*, or *Responso*. The name of a kind of anthem sung in the Roman church after the morning lesson. **1836** *Tracts for Times* No. 75, Lesson 8. (Homily continued.)..Response 8 (used on the Sundays after Trinity). **1879** SIMMONS *Lay Folks Mass Book* 200 The laity..were not allowed to read the lessons in church, nor to say the *Alleluia*, but only the psalms and the responses (*responsoria*), without the *Alleluia*.

b. A part of the liturgy said or sung by the congregation in reply to the priest. (Correlative to VERSICLE.)

1659 HAMMOND *On Ps.* xxxi. 6 Observing their responses most superstitiously. **1710** STEELE *Tatler* No. 213 ¶2 [He] was seen soon after reading the Responses with great Gravity at Six of Clock Prayers. **1797** MRS. RADCLIFFE *Italian* xi, Again he fancied her voice spoke in a part of the plaintive response delivered by the nuns. **1810** CRABBE *Borough* ii. 16 Where priest and clerk with joint exertion strive..; That, by his periods eloquent and grave; This, by responses, and a well-set stave. **1886** RUSKIN *Præterita* I. 354 The responses of the morning prayer.

3. An oracular answer.

1513 DOUGLAS *Æneis* X. i. 76 Sa feyll responsis of the goddis abufe. *a* **1660** HAMMOND (J.), The oracles,..from giving responses in verse, descended to prose. **1687** A. LOVELL tr. *Thevenot's Trav.* I. 37 He that demands the response, roles it [*sc.* a piece of wood] three times. **1762** WARBURTON *Doctr. Grace* I. v, In the Mosaic dispensation .., where the church was conducted in every step, at first by oracular responses, and afterwards by..Prophets. **1822** SHELLEY tr. *Calderon's Mag. Prodig.* I. 138 Consider the ambiguous responses Of their oracular statues. **1869** TOZER *Highl. Turkey* II. 219 The ancient oracle..from which..the Greeks of his time used to seek responses.

4. *Mus.* 'In a fugue, the repetition of the given subject by another part' (Busby).

1797 *Encycl. Brit.* (ed. 3) VII. 491/2 Every fugue finds its response in the part immediately following that which commenced. **1854** CHERUBINI *Counterp. & Fugue* 63 It may be said that the Response decides the particular kind and nature of the fugue.

5. *pl.* = RESPONSION 3.

1810 *Oxford Univ. Cal.* p. ii, Feb. 21, Responses commence.

6. *attrib.* and *Comb.*, as ***response function***, ***rate***; esp. in *Psychol.*, as ***response bias***, ***-movement***, ***pattern***, ***probability***, ***set***; ***response-contingent*** adj.; **response time** *Electr.*, the time taken for a circuit or measuring device, when subjected to a change in input signal, to change its state by a specified fraction of its total response to that change.

1970 *Jrnl. Gen. Psychol.* LXXXII. 63 These findings appear to be incompatible with the notion that both scales measure '*response bias'. **1958** B. FLANAGAN et al. in Saporta & Bastian *Psycholinguistics* (1961) 415 (*title*) The control of stuttering through *response-contingent consequences. **1972** *Sci. Amer.* May 97/1 The results of such analyses produce response functions..which can be plotted to show the mean responses of different species of trees to conditions of temperature, precipitation and prior growth. **1975** D. G. FINK *Electronics Engineers' Handbk.* xxv. 25 The antenna and receiver are configured to match a target signal at a particular angle, delay, and frequency. The radar will respond with reduced gain to targets at other angles, delays, and frequencies. This *response function can be expressed as a surface in a four-dimensional coordinate system. **1892** VAN LIEW & BEYER tr. *Ziehen's Introd. Physiol. Psychol.* i. 14 Goltz has termed the automatic movements '*response-movements'. **1936** J. KANTOR *Objective Psychol. of Gram.* xx. 290 For objective psychology, moods are nothing but particular *response-patterns or speech-community styles of utterance. **1965** *Brit. Jrnl. Psychol.* LVI. 217 (*heading*) Response patterns and strategies in the dynamics of concept attainment behaviour. **1966** W. N. DEMBER *Psychol. of Perception* (1970) viii. 287 All of the word-recognition experiments can be interpreted in terms of *response-probability. **1946** *Jrnl. Amer. Statist. Assoc.* XLI. 522 The number of mail questionnaires and field interviews required to achieve a specified precision will vary with the *response rate. **1966** *Rep. Comm. Inquiry Univ. Oxf.* II. 351 The figures for Great Britain are from a survey (with a response rate of 53 per cent.) of those university teachers who responded to the inquiry by the Robbins Committee in 1961–2 (in which the response rate was 86 per cent.). **1970** *Jrnl. Gen. Psychol.* LXXXII. 64 '*Response set' is a generalized tendency to be agreeable. **1972** D. P. CAMPBELL in J. N. Butcher *Objective Personality Assessment* vi. 119 Response set, acquiescence and social desirability, are currently popular.. even though the data in support of them [as concepts] are will-o'-the-wispy, at best. **1958** R. B. HURLEY *Junction Transistor Electronics* xix. 364 Output *response times are reduced by a factor of 2·5. **1970** WILLARDSON & BEER *Semiconductors & Semimetals* V. i. 7 The response time is determined by the rate at which the [infrared detector] element warms and cools. **1975** D. G. FINK *Electronics Engineers' Handbk.* XVII. 49 Performance specifications usually include the response of the system to a step input, measured in terms of response time, rise time, delay time, settling time, and overshoot.

Hence **re'sponseless** *a.*, giving no response or reply; **re'sponser**, one who makes response.

1845 *Blackw. Mag.* LVIII. 36 The base, cold crowd.. Stood round, responseless to his fire. **1845** JANE ROBINSON *Whitehall* xix. 221 Mistress Chaloner looked at him.. to ascertain who this lively responser was.

responsi'bility. [See next and -ITY. So F. *responsabilité*, It. *-ita*, Sp. *-idad.*]

1. The state or fact of being responsible.

1787 HAMILTON *Federalist* No. 63 II. 193 Responsibility in order to be reasonable must be limited to objects within the power of the responsible party. **1796** BURKE *Regic. Peace* iii. Sel. Wks. (1892) 258 Where I speak of responsibility, I do not mean to exclude that species of it [etc.]. **1827** SOUTHEY *Hist. Penins. War* II. 746 He was made to understand that any risk which he incurred would be upon his own responsibility. **1874** SAYCE *Compar. Philol.* viii. 305 It is only when the conception of the individual has been reached that the idea of responsibility begins. **1973** *Black Panther* 17 Nov. 3/1 The attack was deliberate and appears to be associated with the letter from the 'Symbionese Liberation Army' claiming responsibility. **1974** *Oxford Mail* 26 Oct. 1/4 Four explosions shook New York's business and financial districts within a few minutes today and a self-styled Puerto Rican liberation movement claimed responsibility.

b. Const. *of* the thing done or to be done.

1840 DICKENS *Old C. Shop* xvii, Then the entertainment began..; Mr. Codlin having the responsibility of deciding on its length. **1847** PRESCOTT *Peru* (1850) II. 137 He still shrunk from the responsibility of the deed. **1881** W. COLLINS *Black Robe* viii, I took the responsibility of leaving him undisturbed.

c. Const. *for*.

1903 G. B. SHAW *Man & Superman* I. 17 Mamma knows that she is not strong enough to bear the whole responsibility for me and Rhoda without some help and advice. **1928** E. O'NEILL *Strange Interlude* II. 66 Looks damnably upset... Wants to evade all responsibility for her, I suppose. **1971** G. K. ROBERTS *Dict. Polit. Analysis* 190 The individual responsibility of British ministers for the actions of their civil servants. **1974** *Black Panther* 19 Jan. 3/1 A communique signed by the Symbionese Liberation Army claimed responsibility for the attack. **1975** *Times* 20 Aug. 13/1 Just as one was wondering who would 'claim responsibility' for spoiling the Headingley wicket—Saór Eire, the Women's Liberation Army..—up popped the Campaign to Free George Davis. **1981** M. SPARK *Loitering with Intent* ii. 32, I can't take responsibility for your mother this afternoon.

2. a. With *a* and *pl.* A charge, trust, or duty, for which one is responsible.

1796 BURKE *Regic. Peace* iii. Sel. Wks. (1892) 258 That confidence.. fixes a responsibility on the Ministers entire and undivided. **1847** C. BRONTE *J. Eyre* iv, Anxious to be relieved of a responsibility that was becoming irksome. **1880** *19th Cent.* Apr. 687 As the responsibilities became greater and warfare more scientific.

b. A person for whom one is responsible.

1832 MARRYAT *N. Forster* xxxvi, [He] would hand over to Newton's charge any one of the unmarried responsibilities.

c. A person to whom one is responsible; a person in authority. *nonce-use.*

1893 E. DOWSON *Let. c* 22 Mar. (1967) 275, I have to let the responsibilities know exactly how many people I have invited.

3. *U.S.* 'Ability to answer in payment; means of paying contracts' (*Cent. Dict.* 1890).

responsible (rɪ'spɒnsɪb(ə)l), *a.* (and *sb.*) [a. obs. F. *responsible* (1502), f. L. *respons-*, *respondēre* to RESPOND. Cf. RESPONSABLE.]

A. *adj.* †**1.** Correspondent or answering *to* something. *Obs.*

1599 B. JONSON *Ev. Man out of Hum.* II. i, The admiration of your Forme; to which (if the bounties of your minde be any way responsible) [etc.]. **1629** MAXWELL tr. *Herodian* (1635) 140 If you expect a Doome, or Death, responsible to your blacke deeds, and detestable Villanies; the World cannot afford it. **1698** FRYER *Acc. E. India & P.* 14 The Mouth large, but not responsible to so large a Body.

†**2.** Capable of being answered. *Obs. rare*$^{-1}$.

1647 LILLY *Chr. Astrol.* lviii. 383 This is a difficult Question, and yet by Astrologie responsible.

3. a. Answerable, accountable (*to* another *for* something); liable to be called to account.

1643 PRYNNE *Sov. Power Parl.* III. App. 12 To hold this Popish erronious opinion, that they are in no case responsible to their whole Kingdomes or Parliaments for their grossest exorbitances. **1662** J. DAVIES tr. *Olearius' Voy. Ambass.* 405 Being responsible to the King for what might happen to us. **1720** WATERLAND *Doctr. Trin.* v. Wks. 1823 V. 115 Willing or not willing, every man is responsible, at last, for the doctrines he teaches. **1790** BURKE *Fr. Rev.* 42 Our constitution has made no sort of provision towards rendering him, as a servant, in any degree responsible. **1850** MCCOSH *Div. Govt.* III. i. (1874) 278 Man is a free agent and morally responsible to his Governor. **1868** FREEMAN *Norm. Conq.* (1877) II. 321 The country was left.. without any single responsible chief.

b. Morally accountable for one's actions; capable of rational conduct.

1836 J. GILBERT *Chr. Atonem.* ii. (1852) 50 The great God has treated us as responsible beings. **1858** FROUDE *Hist. Eng.* IV. xviii. 35 James arrived at an age when he could be treated as responsible. **1875** BAIN *Mental & Mor. Sci.* 396 In criminal procedure, a man is accounted responsible if motives still continue to have power over him.

c. *responsible government*: (see quot. 1910); also in extended use (esp. under influence of sense 5).

1839 LD. DURHAM *Rep. Affairs Brit. N. Amer.* 142 By creating high prizes in a general and responsible Government, we shall immediately afford the means of pacifying the turbulent ambitions, and of employing in worthy and noble occupations the talents which now are only exerted to foment disorder. **1865** EARL RUSSELL *Essay on Hist. Eng. Govt. & Constitution* p. lxviii, Others said, 'the grant of what is called "responsible government" [in Canada] is a grant of independence. It must be resisted.' **1906** W. S. CHURCHILL in R. S. Churchill *Winston S. Churchill* (1969) II. Compan. I. 506 We are not, of course, confined to any particular form of Responsible Government. **1910** *Colonial Office List* v. i. 633 The colonies possessing responsible government, in which the Crown has only reserved the power of disallowing legislation and the Secretary of State for the Colonies has no control over any public officer except the Governor. **1930** G. B. SHAW *Apple Cart* I. 33 The people have found out long ago that democracy is humbug, and that instead of establishing responsible government it has abolished it. **1957** *Encycl. Brit.* XII. 174/2 The device known as dyarchy, or double government,.. was intended to train Indians for responsible government.

4. *U.S.* Answerable to a charge.

1650 in T. Hutchinson *Hist. Mass.* (1765) 452 You are required to attach the goods or lands of William Stevens to the value of one hundred pounds, so as to bind the same to be responsible at the next court at Boston.

5. a. Capable of fulfilling an obligation or trust; reliable, trustworthy; of good credit and repute. Also in *Comb.*

1691 LOCKE *Consid. Money* Wks. 1714 II. 12 Not knowing that the Bill or Bond is true or legal, or that the Man bound to me is honest or responsible. *a* **1817** JANE AUSTEN *Persuasion* iii, Could not be a better time, Sir Walter, for having a choice of tenants, very responsible tenants. **1853** C. BRONTE *Villette* xiv, There was about him a manly responsible look, that redeemed his youth. **1884** J. QUINCY *Figures of Past* 345 The collection and delivery of parcels.. might be undertaken by one responsible person. **1896** H. JOHNSTON *Dr. Congalton's Legacy* ix. 103 Responsible land-owners, bonnet-lairds, farmers, otherwise a nondescript crowd.

Comb. **1852** DICKENS *Bleak Ho.* xxviii, A responsible-looking gentleman dressed in black. **1891** MOSTYN *Curatica* 57 When the meeting was dissolved, I joined myself to a responsible-looking brother, and.. begged an explanation. **1960** *Times* 7 Mar. 13/5 Are publishers responsible-minded parents?

b. Of respectable appearance.

1780 S. G. PRATT *Emma Corbett* (ed. 4) I. 98 A new wig.. to be made so as to resemble a responsible head of hair. **1852** DICKENS *Bleak Ho.* lviii, His linen is arranged to a nicety, and he is wrapped in a responsible dressing-gown.

6. Involving responsibility or obligation.

1855 PRESCOTT *Philip II*, I. I. ii. 12 He selected two persons for the responsible office of superintending his education. **1880** *19th Cent.* Apr. 707 Native officers so appointed to high and responsible positions.

B. *sb. pl.* An actor who undertakes to play any part which may be temporarily required.

1885 JEROME *On the Stage* 80 In the provinces, thirty shillings is a high figure for a good all-round 'responsibles'. *Ibid.* 121 Hearing that one of their 'responsibles' had just left, I went straight to the manager,.. and was accepted.

Hence **re'sponsibleness**.

1727 in BAILEY (vol. II). **1812** G. CHALMERS *Dom. Econ. Gt. Brit.* 138 At this crisis.. every bill was suspected, as being of doubtful responsibleness. **1856** EMERSON *Eng. Traits* v. *Ability*, They have solidarity, or responsibleness, and trust in each other.

re'sponsibly, *adv. rare.* [f. prec. + -LY[2].] In a responsible manner.

1847 in WEBSTER. **1891** KIPLING *Light that Failed* (1900) 240 Mr. Beeton stood by with the air of an ambassador and breathed responsibly.

responsion (rɪ'spɒnʃən). Also 6 -cion. [a. F. *responsion* (†*responcion*), = Sp. *responsion*, It. *re-*, *risponsione*, or ad. L. *responsiōn-em*, n. of action f. *respondēre* to RESPOND.]

1. An answer or reply; a response. Now *rare*.

1502 ARNOLDE *Chron.* (1811) 10 By ony responcions or peticions of them in parlement. **1509** HAWES *Past. Pleas.* XI. (Percy Soc.) 42 Seven sophyms.. Thys ydre used.. Unto the people, and was full rigorious To devoure them, where lacked responsion. **1555** W. WATREMAN *Fardle Facions* Pref. 13 By obscure and doubtfully attempred Responcions, and voices of spirites. **1656** S. HOLLAND *Zara* (1719) 123 To the first he yielded a ready responsion, but to the other he answered in very obscure terms. **1677** GALE *Crt. Gentiles* III. 99 To confer among themselves by Questions and Responsions or Answers. **1802–12** BENTHAM *Ration. Judic. Evid.* (1827) II. 10 Fourth point—responsion performed in the presence of the judge. **1880** *Cent. Mag.* XIX. 294 (Cent.), Everywhere in nature, Whitman finds human relations, human responsions.

†**2.** A sum falling to be paid; *esp.* an annual payment which was required from knights of the military orders. *Obs.*

c **1470** EDW. IV in Ellis *Orig. Lett.* Ser. II. I. 143 A Lumbard.. shalbe bounde.. in the said somme, to be paied .. to such as the saide Bisshopp.. wol assigne to receyve the same, be it for the responsion of the Commandeur of Torfischyn. **1480** *Acta Dom. Conc.* (1839) 50 þe soume of vj^{xx} pund, of þe Responsioune of þe said Trestramys landis, aucht to our souuerain lorde. **1540** *Act 32 Hen. VIII*, c. 24 Commanderies, preceptories, contribucions, responsions, rentes.. which appertained.. to the priours. [**1706** PHILLIPS (ed. Kersey), *Responsions*, a Word us'd among the Knights of St. John of Jerusalem, for certain Accounts made to them, by such as held their Lands, or Stocks. **1727–38** CHAMBERS *Cycl.* s.v., Such a knight Templar paid a responsion of fifty pounds per annum to his order, on account of such a commandery.]

3. *pl.* The first of the three examinations which candidates for the B.A. degree at Oxford were required to pass. (Responsions were ended by statute in 1960.)

1813 *Oxford Univ. Cal.* p. ii, Feb. 17, Responsions commence. **1845** WILLIAM GRESLEY *Frank's Trip to Continent* 2 He had just come home from Oxford after having.. passed his responsions. **1881** *Truth* 6 Oct. 443 The new examination in lieu of responsions at Oxford, which has just been instituted.

4. A public university disputation.

1841 PEACOCK *Stat. Cambr.* 9 When they had kept two responsions.. under the regency of a master of arts.. they were presented.. as candidates for admission.

responsive (rɪ'spɒnsɪv), *a.* and *sb.* [a. F. *responsif*, *-ive*, = Sp. and It. *responsivo*, or ad. late L. *responsīv-us*, f. *respons-*, *respondēre*: see RESPOND *v.* and -IVE.]

A. *adj.* **1.** Answering, responding; making answer or reply. †**a.** Of letters or epistolary replies. Also in pl. form. *Obs.*

1529 WOLSEY in Burnet *Hist. Ref.* (1679) I. Rec. II. xxiii. 62 Shewing unto the same how ye have received Letters from the King's Highness and me, responsives to such as ye wrote. *c* **1560** A. SCOTT *Poems* (S.T.S.) ix. 3 Suppois I am not eloquent To wryt ȝow answer responsyve. **1620** BRENT tr. *Sarpi's Counc. Trent* II. (1676) 126 When there shall be occasion to write some Letter, missive, or responsive. **1726** AYLIFFE *Parergon* 157 A Certificate.. is a Responsive Letter, or Letter by way of Answer.

b. In other uses. Also const. *to*.

1667 MILTON *P.L.* IV. 683 Celestial voices.. Sole, or responsive each to others note. **1715** POPE *Odyss.* I. 200 High strains responsive to the vocal string. **1747** COLLINS *Passions* 37 A soft responsive voice was heard at every close. **1781** COWPER *Charity* 177 Responsive to the distant neigh he neighs. **1802–12** BENTHAM *Ration. Judic. Evid.* (1827) III. 48 By the responsive testimony of the defendant, the existence of the criminative fact cannot be established. **1850** BLACKIE *Æschylus* I. 26 There the grey heath lit the responsive fire. **1889** *Daily News* 25 July 7/2 The proctors for the Bishop of Lincoln were assigned to bring in their responsive allegation within a fortnight.

c. *Bridge.* Of a double: used to invite a change to an unbid suit in response to a partner's take-out double.

1959 *Listener* 12 Mar. 489/3 His double would be 'responsive'. *Ibid.* 30 July 190/1 The responsive double is a double intended to give information when partner has already made an informatory double. **1964** *Official Encycl. Bridge* 456/2 The minimum strength for a responsive double varies slightly with the level of the auction. **1973** REESE & DORMER *Compl. Bk. Bridge* viii. 120 Responsive doubles are usually played up to the level of three spades.

2. Correspondent or corresponding. *rare.*

1602 SHAKS. *Ham.* v. ii. 159 Three of the carriages in-faith are.. very responsiue to the hilts. **1634** CANNE *Necess. Separ.* (1849) 34 The bishops.. do not maturely consider the responsive conclusions which follow upon their principles. **1867** MACFARREN *Harmony* i. 17, He extended it by the addition of four responsive or relative modes.

3. Responding readily to some influence.

1762 FALCONER *Shipwr.* II. 45 Thus, and so quick, the helm responsive flew. **1792** A. YOUNG *Trav. France* 205 The vibrations of pleasurable emotions seemed more responsive than common. **1841** D'ISRAELI *Amen. Lit.* (1867) 584 The imaginative critic has described the excursions of our muse with responsive sympathy. **1868** DICKENS *Let.* 29 Jan., They are a bright, responsive people here. **1871** HOLME LEE *Miss Barrington* II. xv. 232 Felicia seemed attentive and responsive.

b. Const. *to*.

1768 BEATTIE *Minstr.* I. lv, Responsive to the sprightly pipe, when all In sprightly dance the village youth were join'd. **1793** *Minstrel* II. 55 The heart of Eleanor did not beat responsive to his warm attachment. **1850** MCCOSH *Div. Govt.* II. ii. (1874) 210 There is no living being to feel responsive to his feelings. **1884** J. M. MATHER *Life & Teaching Ruskin* (ed. 2) 5 His nature was responsive to the influences brought to bear upon it.

4. Characterized by the use of responses.

1778 BP. LOWTH *Transl. Isaiah* xxvii. 2 In that day, To the beloved Vineyard, sing ye a responsive song. **1848** R. I. WILBERFORCE *Doctr. Incarnation* xii. (1852) 326 Where this responsive system of worship is lost, the nature of a public service will soon be forgotten. **1882** J. H. BLUNT *Ref. Ch. Eng.* II. 565 The alternation of the responsive system of prayer into that of prayer by the minister alone.

†**5.** Responsible, answerable. *Obs. rare.*

1642 JER. TAYLOR *Episc.* (1647) 371 For all of it, he is responsive to God Almighty. **1646** —— *Apol. Liturgy* §133 Such persons.. for whom the Church her selfe may safely be responsive, that is, to men learned and pious.

B. *sb.* †**1.** An answer, a response. *Obs.*

1683 CAVE *Ecclesiastici, Epiph.* 429 In answer to both he wrote Ἀντεπιστολή.. a large Responsive, wherein he particularly opens the Doctrine of the Catholick Church.

2. A responsory. *rare*$^{-1}$.

1855 MILMAN *Lat. Chr.* XIV. iv. (1864) IX. 178 *note*, The mixture.. of Latin Responsives and Sequences with the chief passages in the dialect of Thuringia.

Hence **re'sponsively** *adv.*

1778 BP. LOWTH *Transl. Isaiah* Notes vi. 3 This hymn, performed by the seraphim, divided into two choirs, the one singing responsively to the other. *a* **1851** MOIR *Bass Rock* iii. Wks. 1852 I. 204 And linnets from each brake responsively Piped to each other. **1866** LIDDON *Div. Our Lord* vii. (1875) 391 The primitive Christians sang among themselves responsively a hymn of praise to Christ as God.

re'sponsiveness. [f. prec. + -NESS.] The state or quality of being responsive.

1847 in WEBSTER. **1877** E. R. CONDER *Bas. Faith* ii. 89 Without dulling their responsiveness to each new impression. **1882** A. W. WARD *Dickens* vii. 205 A swift responsiveness to the impulses of humour and pathos.

So **respon'sivity.**

1866 DORA GREENWELL *Ess.* 132 This responsivity within the human Soul. **1901** *Ann. Rep. Board of Regents Smithsonian Inst. 1899–1900* 68 A principle of knowledge which may appropriately be styled the responsivity of mind. **1942** *Amer. Jrnl. Physiol.* CXXXV. 721 Suppression [of cortical response] is a decrease of responsivity of a certain area.. caused by previous stimulation of specific cortical regions. **1976** *Lancet* 30 Oct. 953/2 Responsivity to change in America is remarkable.

Responsivist (rɪ'spɒnsɪvɪst), *sb.* (and *a.*) *Indian Hist.* [f. RESPONSIVE *a.* + -IST.] One who advocated working within the diarchical administrative system introduced in Indian provinces during British rule. Also *attrib.* or as *adj.*

1927 *Glasgow Herald* 1 Feb. 8 Agitation is afoot in Calcutta against the acceptance by Mr Ghuznavi of one of the two Bengal transferred portfolios with Mr Chakra Varti, the Responsivist leader, as his Hindu colleague. **1927** *Observer* 27 Mar. 11/2 The third general election, held at the end of last year, when the Swarajists, as distinct from the Responsivists, lost ground. **1936** J. NEHRU *Autobiogr.* xlviii. 387, I remember a frequent complaint of my father's that his Responsivist friends had no sense of humour. **1950** L. FISCHER *Life Mahatma Gandhi* xxvii. 234 A dissident group, headed by M. R. Jayakar and N. C. Kelkar, who believed in still more co-operation with the British, but less with the Moslems, split off from the Swarajists and formed the Responsivist party. **1951** D. G. TENDULKAR *Mahatma* II. 307 The Responsivists joined hands with the Independents in Bombay and formed the Indian National Party. **1969** D. DAS *India from Curzon to Nehru & After* xi. 122 The dissidents met at Akola and formed the Responsivist Party. **1970** J. S. SHARMA *India since Advent of British* IV. 271 The Conference of the Responsivists cooperation party which was held at Akola adopted its Manifesto.

responsor (rɪ'spɒnsə(r)). [f. RESPONSE + -OR.] A device that receives and processes the reply from a transponder, being usu. incorporated in the same unit as the interrogator.

1945 *Army & Navy Jrnl.* 18 Aug. 1534/4 *Responsor*, receiver used specifically in IFF system to receive the reply to a challenge. **1947** A. ROBERTS *Radar Beacons* xviii. 388 A simple responsor using a lamp to locate a beacon in range. **1976** P. HONOLD *Secondary Radar* v. 208 *Responsor*, the receiver of responses.

† **re'sponsor,** obs. var. RESPONSORY *sb.* 1 b.

a **1649** CRASHAW *Poems* (1904) 218 The Versicle... The Responsor. *Ibid.* 219–229.

respon'sorial, *sb.* [a. med.L. *responsoriāle*, f. *responsōria* RESPONSORY *sb.* So F. *responsoriale* (Godef.).] A book of responsories.

1853 ROCK *Ch. of Fathers* III. II. xi. 18 Out of the Antiphoner.. came forth the full song-book.. for the canonical hours,.. the responsorial or book of responses.

respon'sorial, *a.* [See RESPONSORY *sb.* and -AL[1].]

1. Making answer or reply; responsive.

1820 SOUTHEY *Wesley* I. 204 *note*, Rimius's Narrative of the Rise and Progress of the Herrnhuters, and the Responsorial Letters of the Theological Faculty of Tubingen, annexed to it.

2. Pertaining to, of the nature of, responses.

1842 J. H. NEWMAN *Ch. of Fathers* 23 A peculiar kind of singing—the antiphonal or responsorial. **1872** *Contemp. Rev.* XXI. 132 The responsorial portions of Morning and Evening Prayer.

respon'sorially, *adv. Eccl.* [f. RESPONSORIAL *a.* + -LY[2].] In a responsorial manner; with responses.

1901 PROCTER & FRERE *New Hist. Bk. Common Prayer* xi. 406 The Arians.. went through the city.. to their places of worship, singing responsorially all the way. **1929** E. C. THOMAS *Lay Folks' Hist. Liturgy* II. v. 186 On these occasions the processional chant, or Rogation psalm, was sung responsorially. **1978** P. G. COBB in C. Jones et al. *Study of Liturgy* II. III. v. 186 It is not until the fourth century that there is clear evidence of psalms being sung responsorially.

responsory (rɪ'spɒnsərɪ), *sb.* [In sense 1, ad. late L. *responsōria* pl. (in med.L. also sing. *-ōrium* neut., *-ōria* fem.), f. *respons-*, *respondēre* to RESPOND: see -ORY. Cf. F. *responsoire* (Godef.).]

1. *Eccl.* **a.** An anthem said or sung after a lesson by a soloist and choir alternately.

Often applied to the gradual (which follows the epistle at mass).

1432–50 tr. *Higden* (Rolls) VII. 39 [He] made in the lawde of that blissede virgyn,.. these ij. responsoryes, Stirps Jesse, and Solem justitiæ. **1526** *Pilgr. Perf.* (W. de W. 1531) 248 In matyns communly be iii orbes,.. of ye whiche euery orbe conteyneth iij psalms, iii lessons, and iii responsories. **1563** FOXE *A. & M.* 895/2 The Responsorie, which is called the Gradual (being wont to be songe at the steps going vp), with alleluya. **1638** MEDE *Wks.* (1672) 60 The Jews in their Divine Lauds were wont to praise God after this manner, in Antiphons or Responsories. **1688** HOLME *Armoury* III. 190/2 The Responsory being sung, and some Prayers said, they return from Church. **1763** BURN *Eccles. Law* I. 38 The invitatories, responsories, verses, collects, and whatever is said or sung in the quire. **1844** LINGARD *Anglo-Sax. Ch.* (1858) II. App. A. 332 The responsories.. indicated by the initial words of each versicle. **1877** J. D. CHAMBERS *Div. Worship* 90 The Clerks ought continually to stand unless when a Responsory is sung.

transf. **1649** MILTON *Eikon.* xxiv. Wks. 1851 III. 491 Which if I should repeat again, would turn my answers into Responsories, and begett another Liturgie. **1684** *Contempl. St. Man* II. ii. (1699) 144 What shall it be to be celebrated by all the Angels and Saints in Celestial Responsories?

† **b.** A response to a versicle. *Obs. rare.*

a **1649** CRASHAW *Poems* (1904) 217 The versicle... The responsory.

† **2.** An oracle. *Obs. rare*[−1].

1677 GALE *Crt. Gentiles* III. 58 The ephod of the Idolatrous Iews which they consulted as their Responsorie.

† **re'sponsory,** *a. Obs.* Also 7 -ary. [ad. med.L. *responsōrius*: see prec.]

1. Of the nature of an answer or reply; relating or pertaining to answering.

1586 A. DAY *Eng. Secretary* I. (1625) 22 To these and to many others.. are many Epistles Responsorie. **1602** FULBECKE *1st Pt. Parall.* 58 Before.. the libel [is] exhibited in Court, & notice taken thereof by the def. by some responsory acte. **1638** MEDE *Wks.* (1672) 791 Divers other Letters Responsory to Beverovicius have been long expected. **1652** URQUHART *Jewel* Wks. (1834) 292, I could have inserted dialogismes, displaying their interrogatory part.. and that part which concerns the responsory. **1737** L. CLARKE *Hist. Bible* (1740) I. I. 106 Job.. maintains his virtue in responsory speeches successively to every one of theirs.

b. (Cf. RESPONSORY *sb.* 1.)

1641 R. B. K. *Parall. of Liturgy w. Mass-bk.* 28 The Versicle responsory to this is the fourth verse. **1659** H. L'ESTRANGE *Alliance Div. Off.* 146 The first part of it, whose responsory terminations are 'Have Mercy upon us'.

2. Responsive, grateful.

1641 J. SHUTE *Sarah & Hagar* (1649) 57 The dull earth is responsory for that it receiveth: onely men are unthankful. *a* **1643** —— *Judgem. & Mercy* (1645) 202 He thinks not himself so obliged to.. be responsary for such a favour.

‖ **responsum** (rɛ'spɒnsəm). Pl. **responsa.** [L., = answer, response.] **1.** A reply by a rabbi or Talmudic scholar to an inquiry on some matter of Jewish law.

1896 S. SCHECHTER *Studies in Judaism* 1st Ser. xi. 330 The greatest part of the literary activity of the Gaonim consists in their Responsa, in which they gave decisions on ritual questions, or explanations of difficult passages in the Talmud. *Ibid.* 331 The titles borne by the various collections of those Responsa belong to a period later than the author's. **1932** C. ROTH *Hist. Marranos* viii. 201 The responsa of the Levantine rabbis of the period are filled with discussions relating to the position of the Marranos in Jewish law. **1941** G. G. SCHOLEM *Major Trends in Jewish Mysticism* ix. 340 You find Zaddikim who write rabbinical responsa. **1962** B. ABRAHAMS tr. *Life Glückel of Hameln* iii. 66 Good Rabbi Asher.. wrote a great responsum in my husband's favour. **1968** *New Scientist* 23 May 385/3 The team is investigating the responsa written by Jewish legal experts in Medieval Spain... A responsum.. consists of a judgement usually revolving around a concrete problem in the commercial, social, moral or religious sphere. **1977** *N.Y. Times* 11 Jan. 30/1 Responsa.. are fundamental in the evolution of Jewish law. Altogether, there are approximately 500,000 responsa written by 5,000 different authorities.

2. responsa prudentum (pruː'dɛntəm) *Law* [L., = the answers of the learned], in Roman Civil Law: the opinions and judgements of learned lawyers, variously forming part of this law (cf. Justinian *Inst.* I. ii. §8). Also *transf.* in modern use.

In cl. Lat. *responsa prudentium* is the usual form, but most of the legal sources cited below have *prudentum* following the example of Blackstone (1765).

1681 LD. STAIR *Institutions Law Scotl.* I. i. 3 And so many times these *responsa prudentium*, have been received with as much Authority, and more heartiness for Laws, than the Dictates of Soveraigns. **1765** BLACKSTONE *Comm. Laws Eng.* I. 80 The *responsa prudentum* or opinions of learned lawyers. **1859** T. C. SANDARS *Institutes Justinian* 13 The *responsa prudentum* came to be enumerated among the direct sources of law. **1877** *Law Rep. Exchequer Division* II. 70 Of course the value of these responsa prudentum is affected by various circumstances. **1883** J. B. MOYLE *Imperatoris Justiniani Institutionum* I. 50 The establishment of the empire brought with it a considerable change in respect of the responsa prudentum.

† **re'sponsure.** *Obs. rare*[−1]. Response.

1600 TOURNEUR *Transf. Metam.* lxxvii. 537 To whom they moue, black todes give responsure.

† **resport.** *Obs. rare.* [a. OF. *resport* (Godef.).] Regard.

c **1374** CHAUCER *Troylus* IV. 86 (Campsall MS.), Hauyng vn-to my tresour ne my rente Right no resport. *Ibid.* 850 Whi ne hastow to þi-seluen som resport?

† **respost,** obs. form of REPOST, RIPOST(E.

1692 SIR W. HOPE *Fencing Master* 7 Respost is when a Man hath given in a Thrust,.. then he is said to receive a Thrust upon the respost or back of the Parrade.

† **respoun(d,** *sb. Obs.* Also respun, -on, -owne, -ownd. [ad. OF. *respuns* RESPONSE, or f. OF. *respundre*: see next.]

1. = RESPOND *sb.* 1 a.

c **1400** *Rule St. Benet* (Prose) 16 By-tuixe þe lescuns þre respuns; and eftir þe þridde respun þe vers. *Ibid.*, Foure lescuns red wid respuns. *c* **1440** *Promp. Parv.* 431/1 Respowne (*K.* respounde, *P.* respon), *responsorium.* **1466** in *Archæol.* L. (1887) 45 The responnys of the trinite.

2. = RESPOND *sb.* 3.

1435 *Indent. Fotheringhey Ch.* in Dugdale *Monast.* (1830) VI. III. 1414/2 The cler-story.. shal be made of clene asheler growndid upon ten mighty pillars, with four respounds. *Ibid.*, To the two respownds of the sayd qwere shal be two perpeyn-walls.

† **respoun(d,** *v. Obs.* [a. OF. *respundre*, repr. L. *respondēre* to RESPOND.] To reply.

a **1300** *Cursor M.* 12181 Maister leui.. Teched him a letter þan, And badd him þar-to respond [*rime* stund; *Fairf.* respounde]. *c* **1325** *Song of Yesterday* 81 in *E.E. Poems* (1862) 135 þe most fool, i herde respounde, Is wysore, whil he lyue may, þen he þat.. was buried ȝusterday. *c* **1330** R. BRUNNE *Chron. Wace* 4238 By letteres woly hem first somoune, To here þer wyl, what þey respoune.

re'spray, *v.* [RE- 5 a.] *trans.* To spray (esp. with paint) again. Hence **re'sprayed** *ppl. a.*; **re'spraying** *vbl. sb.* Also **'respray** *sb.*, the action or fact of spraying again.

1934 *Webster*, Respray, *v.t.* **1959** *Listener* 16 Apr. 657/2 The car had been re-sprayed. **1962** *Law Rep. 1961* 26 July 35 The defendant appealed against so much of the decision as ordered him to pay for the respray. *Ibid.* 40 The defendant should be taken to have injured a motor-car that was already in certain respects (that is, in respect of the need for respraying) injured. **1968** 'D. RUTHERFORD' *Skin for Skin* ii. 16 The engine's nearly perfect but she does need a re-spray. **1975** G. SEYMOUR *Harry's Game* iii. 46 The stolen and resprayed Cortina. **1976** M. GILBERT *Night of Twelfth* vii. 65 A car which.. was resprayed. First with a light grey undercoat, then with a dark grey finish.

re'spread, *v.* [RE- 5 a.] To spread anew.

1651 *Fuller's Abel Rediv., Luther* 53 He, by Gods Word and Spirits inspiration, The Gospels Light re-spred, for every Nation. *a* **1711** KEN *Psyche* Poet. Wks. 1721 IV. 293 Primeval Night and Chaos would re-spread Nature untun'd, should Love continue dead. **1868** H. LAW *Beacons Bible* (1869) 129 The old temptation respreads its wily bait. **1879** MRS. A. E. JAMES *Ind. Househ. Managem.* 67 We.. had the floor respread with mud.

re'spring, *v.* [RE- 5 a.] To spring up again. Hence **re'springing** *vbl. sb.*

1617 HIERON *Wks.* II. 233 The seasonable falling of raine furthereth the re-springing of the languishing corne. **1816** SOUTHEY *Poet's Pilgr.* Proem 13 Yet at the present object love re-springs.

† **resprise,** variant of REPRISE *v.*, to recover.

1491 CAXTON *Vitas Patr.* (W. de W. 1495) I. xlvii. 83/1 The lordes.. were incontynent moeuyd to wepynge & waylynge; And a lytyll after that they had resprysed theyr spyrytes, the emperour desyred [etc.].

† **'respuate,** *v. Obs. rare*[−1]. [irreg. f. obs. F. *respuer* or L. *respuĕre*: see next.] To reject.

1657 TOMLINSON *Renou's Disp.* 418 Another stone.. which repels and respuates Iron.

re'spue, *v. rare.* [ad. L. *respuĕre.*] *trans.* To reject strongly.

1818 *Blackw. Mag.* IV. 329 These I failed not to reject and respue with indignation. **1823** T. L. BEDDOES *Poems* (1851) 224 Teaching him to 'respue' this effeminate style of versification.

respun, var. RESPOUN(D *sb.*

respy, *a.*: see RESP *sb.*

respyce, obs. f. RASPIS[1]; var. RASPIS[2].

ress(e, obs. ff. RUSH *sb.*

ressaif, -aive, obs. Sc. ff. RECEIVE.

ressait, obs. f. RECEIPT *sb.*

‖ **ressalah** (rə'sɑːlə). Also 8 **rissalla,** 9 **risalah, russala(h), rusala.** [ad. Urdū (Arab.) *risālah*, f. Arab. *arsala* he sent.] In India, a squadron of native cavalry.

1758 W. HASTINGS *Let.* in Gleig *Mem.* (1841) I. 70 Shokum Sing and Harroon Cawn (formerly of Roy Doollub's Rissalla). **1800** WELLINGTON in Gurw. *Disp.* (1844) I. 147 Charged with having endeavoured to seduce from the service of.. the Rajah of Mysore a russalah of horse. **1849** EASTWICK *Dry Leaves* 89 Four days later came two Risālahs of Bengal Irregular Cavalry. **1862** BEVERIDGE *Hist. India* III. VIII. iv. 366 Ghuznee to be garrisoned by the 16th native infantry, a ressalah of Skinner's horse [etc.].

ressaldar, var. RISSALDAR.

'ressant. *Arch.* Also 5 **res(s)aunt.** [Of doubtful origin; adopted in 19th cent. from quot. 1478.] An ogee moulding.

1478 BOTONER *Itin.* (Nasmith, 1778) 220 A felet. A double ressaunt. A boutel. *Ibid.* 269 A resaunt lorymer. **1844** WILLIS *Archit. Nomen.* 42 *note*, The ogee or ressant-shaped arch. **1860** *Handbk. Ludlow* (1865) 17 A moulding peculiar to the East of England, the double ogee or double resaunt.

ressate, -ayt, obs. ff. RECEIPT.

ressave, -awe, -ayf, etc., obs. ff. RECEIVE.

resseaunt, obs. f. RESIANT.

resseit, -eyt(e, obs. ff. RECEIPT *sb.*

ressent, obs. variant of RESENT *v.*

‖**ressentiment** (rɛsɑ̃timɑ̃). [Ger., a. F. *ressentiment*, f. *ressentir* to RESENT: cf. RESENTIMENT.] = RESENTMENT 2 d.

1943 G. A. MORGAN *What Nietzsche Means* vi. 151 Nietzsche illustrates the second type, which directs *ressentiment* outward, by anarchists, socialists and communists, who make 'society' to blame for their misery. **1949** R. K. MERTON *Social Theory* iv. 145 We must distinguish it [*sc.* rebellion] from a superficially similar but essentially different type, '*ressentiment*'. Introduced in a special technical sense, by Nietzsche, the concept of *ressentiment* was taken up and developed sociologically by Max Scheler. **1958** F. HEIDER *Psychol. of Interpersonal Relations* xi. 291 For Scheler, as for Nietzsche, '*ressentiment*' is an envy combined with a feeling of impotence to attain the value that another person has. **1968** *Internat. Encycl. Social Sci.* XII. 27/2 Scheler conceives of *ressentiment* as a complex syndrome involving conscious attitudes, feelings, and moral judgments as well as unconscious defenses and wishes. The ressentiment-laden person tends to devaluate authoritative persons and groups. **1975** W. S. SAHAKIAN *Hist. & Syst. Psychol.* i. 31 Nietzsche termed *ressentiment* that form of behaviour arising out of repressed hostility.

ressett, obs. Sc. pa. pple. of RECEIVE *v.*; obs. f. RESET *sb.*[1] and *v.*[1]

resseve, -eyve, obs. ff. RECEIVE.

resshe, resshy, obs. ff. RUSH(Y.

ressiaunt, obs. f. RESIANT.

resson(e, obs. ff. REASON *sb.*[1]

resson, obs. Sc. f. REASON *v.*

re'ssort. Now *rare.* [a. F. *ressort.*]

†**1.** A mechanical spring. (Cf. RESORT *sb.* 10.)

1658 R. WHITE tr. *Digby's Powd. Symp.* (1660) 144, I see wheels, ressorts, and counterpoises. **1676** TEMPLE *Let. to Sir J. Williamson* Wks. 1720 II. 391 This..might be very material for his Majesty and Ministers to know, as the main Ressort of the present Government. **1692** M. MORGAN *Late Victory over French Fleet* Ded. iii, They who are behind the Curtain, and play the Ressorts of the Machine, laugh at the Easiness of their Votaries.

2. = RESORT *sb.* 2 c.

[**1727–38** CHAMBERS *Cycl.* s.v., Presidials judge in the last ressort of all criminals prosecuted by the provosts of the marshals.] **1878** STEVENSON *Inland Voy.* 170 Every man is his own doctor of divinity in the last ressort.

ressoun, obs. form of REASON *sb.*[1]

ressyng, obs. variant of RESIGN.

rest, *sb.*[1] Forms: 1 ræst(e, hræst), 1, 4- rest, 1-6 reste; 4-5 rist, ryst, 5 riste, ryste, ruste. [OE. *ræst(e, rest(e* fem., = Fris. *rest(e, rêst, ræst*, MDu. *reste (erste)*, OS. *resta* bed, MLG. *reste*, OHG. *resta, restî* (MHG. *reste*) rest. It is possible that the OE. form *ræst* corresponds more directly to OS. *rasta*, MHG. *raste, rast* (G. *rast*; hence also in Sw. and Da.), which agree in form with Goth. *rasta* mile, OHG. *rasta* (MHG. *raste, rast*) league, ON. *rǫst* (pl. *rastir*, Norw. *rast, rost*, Sw. *rast*) league, app. = 'a distance after which one rests'. Another set of forms appears in MDu. *ruste* (Du. *rust*), MLG. *roste, ruste*, G. *rüst(e, rust*, etc., which seem to imply an ablaut-series *rest-, rast-, rust-*.

The usual form in ME. is *rest(e*, but some texts have *rist, ryst*. This change of vowel is found also in other words ending in *-est*, as *lest, (be)quest*, so that there is no direct connexion with Da. *rist*, which is prob. from LG. *reste*.]

I. †**1.** A bed or couch. *Obs.* (OE. only.)

a **900** *O.E. Martyrol.* 4 Mar. 34 Þa ȝenam heo sancte Adrianes hand..& asette æt hire heafdum on hire ræste. *c* **950** *Lindisf. Gosp.* Matt. xxiii. 6 [Hia] lufað..ða formo resto *vel* ðæ foresedlo in farmum. **971** *Blickl. Hom.* 11 Salomones reste wæs mid weardum ymbseted. **1054** *O.E. Chron.* (MS. C) an. 1054, Þy ylcan ȝeara swealt Osgod..swa swa he on his reste læȝ.

2. a. The natural repose or relief from daily activity which is obtained by sleep.

c **825** *Vesp. Psalter* cxxxi. 5 Ȝif ic sellu slep eȝum minum, ..oððe reste ðunwengum minum. *c* **960** *Rule St. Benet* (Schröer) 47 Be muneca reste. Ænlypiȝe munecas ȝeond ænlypiȝe bed restan. *c* **1200** ORMIN 6492 Þeȝȝ tokenn nihhtess resste þær. **13..** *K. Alis.* 5338 (Weber), Thoo was the folk to rest-ward. Ac now hem cometh a wonder hard. *c* **1350** *Ipom.* 7220 (Kölbing), Goo to thy bedde, I comaunde the, And lett me haue my reste. *c* **1400** *Destr. Troy* 9213 Þen he rose fro his rest in a Rad hast. **1470–85** MALORY *Arthur* x. xxix. 461 Thus they fought tyl it was nyghte and.. eueryche party drewe to their reste. **1513** T. MORE in Grafton *Chron.* (1568) II. 765 His maister gaue him in charge not to forebeare his rest. **1560** DAUS tr. *Sleidane's Comm.* 130 b, John Leidane gave him self to reste, & slepeth thre whole daies together. **1611** SHAKS. *Cymb.* II. ii. 12 The Crickets sing, and mans ore-labor'd sense Repaires it selfe by rest. **1697** DRYDEN *Virg. Georg.* III. 793 No dreadful Dreams awak'd him with affright; His Pains by Day secur'd his Rest by Night. **1719** DE FOE *Crusoe* II. (Globe) 577 The People seemed to be all at their Rest. **1761** GRAY *Odin* 36 Who is he..That calls me from the bed of rest? **1833** HT. MARTINEAU *Loom & Lugger* I. iv. 62 Nicholas was permitted to depart to his rest. **1896** BADEN-POWELL *Matabele Campaign* xv, Overhead, in the darkening sky,..the matron evening star beams calmly on our rest.

b. In phr. *to go to* (one's) *rest*, to betake oneself to repose for the night. Also *transf.* of the sun (sometimes with other verbs), etc.

c **900** tr. *Bæda's Hist.* III. ii. 156 Þa he to reste eode, þa forget he [etc.]. **1205** LAY. 28328 To reste eode þa sunne. *a* **1300** *Cursor M.* 6317 Þat night yod moyses to rest. Onslepe he lai in þat forest. *c* **1385** CHAUCER *L.G.W.* Prol. 198 This floure gan close, and goon to rest For derknesse of the nyght. *Ibid.* 201 Home..I me sped To goon to reste and erly for to ryse. *a* **1400–50** *Alexander* 686 Quen þe son is to reste [*v.r.* rist]. *c* **1420** *Anturs of Arth.* xxxvi, Whene the ryalle renke was gone to his ryste. **1535** LYNDESAY *Satyre* 3967 That beand done, I hauld it best That everie man ga to his rest. **1585** T. WASHINGTON tr. *Nicholay's Voy.* II. xi. 46 Euery one had prepared himselfe too goe to his rest. **1614** BP. HALL *Recoll. Treat.* 118 An other..goes to his rest, not breaking an houres sleepe for that which would break the heart of some others. **1678** BUNYAN *Pilgr.* I. (1900) 52 This done, they went to their rest again. **1848** *Scottish Jrnl. of Topogr.* II. 13/2 The sun had been lang to rest before John thocht aboot steerin'.

c. In phr. *to take* (one's) *rest.*

c **1375** *Sc. Leg. Saints* xxv. (*Julian*) 744 Quhen Iulyane In-to þe oste his rest had tane. *c* **1386** CHAUCER *Merch. T.* 1856 My reste wol I take Now day is come, I may no lenger wake. **1490** CAXTON *Eneydos* xxiv. 89 The tyme after the daye is paste and goon is couenable..for the bodyes humayn that haue traueylled, to take rest. **1535** COVERDALE *Matt.* xxvi. 45 Then came he to his disciples, and sayde vnto them: Slepe on now, and take youre rest. **1610** SHAKS. *Temp.* II. i. 197 We two..will guard your person, While you take your rest, and watch your safety. **1820** KEATS *Eve St. Agnes* xxxviii, Here will I take my rest After so many hours of toil and quest.

†**d.** In phrases wishing one good repose. *Obs.*

14.. *Guy Warw.* 6687 (Cambr. MS.), Also so god geue yow reste, Fylle the cuppe of the beste. **1535** LYNDESAY *Satyre* 4628, I will..pray to God omnipotent, To send ȝow all gude rest. **1590** SHAKS. *Com. Err.* IV. iii. 33 One that thinkes a man alwaies going to bed, and saies, God giue you good rest. **1599** —— *Pass. Pilgr.* 181 Good night, good rest. Ah, neither be my share.

3. a. Intermission of labour or exertion of any kind; repose obtained by ceasing to exert oneself. *day of rest*, the Sabbath. In later use also with *a* and *pl.*

c **888** K. ÆLFRED *Boeth.* xxxiv. §8 Þæt is sio an ræst eallra urra ȝeswinca. *c* **1000** ÆLFRIC *Exod.* xvi. 23 Sæterndæȝes rest ys drihtne ȝehalȝod. *c* **1200** ORMIN 4169 Þe sefennde, þe lattste daȝȝ, he sette þeȝȝm to reste. *c* **1250** *Gen. & Ex.* 252 God sette ðis dai folk bitwen, Dai of blisse and off reste ben. *c* **1290** *Beket* 1122 in *S. Eng. Leg.* I. 138 Sethþe he wende.. fiue and tuenti Mile al-so..are he wolde reste i-fo. *c* **1385** CHAUCER *L.G.W.* 1112 (*Dido*), Vnto hys chambre was he led anon, To take hys ease, and for to haue hys rest. *c* **1400** *Laud Troy Bk.* 17016 Thei fauȝt to-geder a ful foure woke That thei neuere reste ne toke. **1470–85** MALORY *Arthur* XVIII. xxi. 764 There he thoughte to repose hym and to take alle the rest that he myghte. **1530** PALSGR. 262/2 Rest of the body or mynde, *repos.* **1601** SHAKS. *Jul. C.* V. v. 80 So call the Field to rest, and let's away, To part the glories of this happy day. **1645** MILTON *Colast.* 21 Whosoever doth most according to charity,..hee breaks the holy rest of Sabbath least. **1687** A. LOVELL tr. *Thevenot's Trav.* I. 131 We came down.., and having taken a little rest, came to the Door of the Pyramide. *Ibid.* 168 After several rests, we got to the top about nine a clock. *a* **1805** PALEY *Reasons Cont.* Wks. 1838 II. 523 The rich see..the refreshment and pleasure which rest affords to the poor. **1816** J. WILSON *City of Plague* I. i. 64 It is the Sabbath-day—the day of rest. **1861** F. METCALFE *Oxonian in Iceland* xxii. (1867) 331 The tired nags will have a comparative rest today. **1876** VOYLE & STEVENSON *Milit. Dict.* 340/1 In all campaigns certain pauses have to be noted in the march of an army... These are known as rests and halts.

b. *transf.* in various applications.

c **1000** ÆLFRIC *Lev.* xxvi. 35 And þæt land lið on reste. *c* **1500** *Plumpton Corr.* (Camden) 106 We have rest; & past this summer, I wyll pray you to come & kill a bucke with me. **1533** BELLENDEN *Livy* IV. xi. (S.T.S.) II. 85 The pestilence was sa vehement in þis ȝere þat it gaif rest to all other besines. **1535** COVERDALE *Lev.* xxv. 4 In the seuenth yeare the londe shal haue his Sabbath of rest.

c. In phr. *without* (or †*but*) *rest*, without intermission or delay.

a **1225** *St. Marher.* 9 Þe sunne recched hire rune euch buten reste. *c* **1375** *Sc. Leg. Saints* xxxviii. (*Adrian*) 652, And fra scho wiste, Yddir scho sped but ony riste. *c* **1470** *Gol. & Gaw.* 458 Thair wes restling and reling, but rest that raught. **1535** LYNDESAY *Satyre* 1506 Now I will rin, but rest, And tell that all is ready. **1590** SPENSER *F.Q.* III. iv. 6 So forth she rode, without repose or rest, Searching all lands and each remotest part.

d. Restored vigour or strength. *rare.*

1596 SHAKS. *1 Hen. IV*, IV. iii. 27 So are the Horses of the Enemie..bated, and brought low: The better part of ours are full of rest. **1601** —— *Jul. C.* IV. iii. 202 We lying still, Are full of rest, defence, and nimblenesse.

e. A year's imprisonment. *Austral. slang* (*rare*).

1882 *Sydney Slang Dict.* 9/2 Dick went pulling down sawney for grub last week, when a cop pinched him. He's gone in the country for a *rest.* **1945** BAKER *Austral. Lang.* vii. 141 Here is a brief glossary of jail sentences: *lag*, three months...*rest*, twelve months [etc.].

f. In colloq. phr. *to give* (something or someone) *a rest*: to stop thinking or talking about.

[**1927** *Amer. Speech* II. 359/1 *Leave that rest a bit*.., let the matter alone for a while. 'Keep quiet, and leave that rest a bit.'] **1931** E. O'NEILL *Hunted* II, in *Mourning becomes Electra* (1932) 137 Give it a rest, Orin! It's over. Give yourself a chance to forget it. **1943** J. B. PRIESTLEY *Daylight on Saturday* xxix. 226 I'm a bit tired of hearing about him today. So let's give him a rest. **1966** R. RENDELL *Vanity dies Hard* ii. 31 Could we give Nesta Drage a rest?.. I was glad when she went away. **1971** —— *One Across* i. 9 'All right Mother,' said Vera. 'Let's give it a rest, shall we?'

4. a. Freedom from or absence of labour, exertion, or activity of any kind.

c **825** *Vesp. Psalter* xciv. 11 Ic swor in eorre minum, ȝif ingað in reste mine. *c* **1200** ORMIN 5208 Þær he shollde libbenn Wiþþ resste & ro, wiþþutenn swinnc. *c* **1250** *Owl & Night.* 281 Me is leof to habbe reste And sitte stille in myne neste. *a* **1300** *Cursor M.* 25452 Ful derf i was to bidd vndo, Þat lued i neuer rest na ro. *c* **1366** CHAUCER *A.B.C.* 14 Þou art largesse, of pleyn felicitee, Hauene of refute, of quiete, and of reste. *c* **1400** tr. *Secreta Secret., Gov. Lordsh.* 75 Thes fattyth & moistes þe body, Rist,..ettyng of swete meites, & dryngkyng of swete mylke. *c* **1491** *Chast. Goddes Chyld.* 21 Suche men unresonably..encline to the rest and commodyte of the body. **1526** *Pilgr. Perf.* (W. de W. 1531) 2 b, All..creatures in this worlde hath place deputed.. wherin theyr propre quietacyon & rest is. **1597** SHAKS. *2 Hen. IV*, IV. v. 212 Least rest, and lying still, might make them looke Too neere vnto my State. **1773** *Observ. State Poor* 80 There are, indeed, some who are impatient of rest in every situation. **1784** COWPER *Task* I. 394 That love of rest To which he forfeits ev'n the rest he loves.

transf. **1784** COWPER *Task* VI. 739 The working of a sea Before a calm, that rocks itself to rest. **1813** SCOTT *Rokeby* II. i, The gale had sigh'd itself to rest.

b. The freedom from toil or care associated with the future life.

a **1000** *Boeth. Metr.* xiii. 71 Þæt is orsorȝnes & ecu rest. *c* **1200** ORMIN 4190 All þatt reste & ro þat hallȝhe sawless brukenn Inn oþerr werelld. *c* **1250** *Gen. & Ex.* 400 Summe sulen of ȝu..ben in to reste numen. *c* **1300** *Cursor M.* 29169 Þai sal..bren in þe fier of purgatori,..Bot efter-ward..Sal þai be borun in to rest. *a* **1340** HAMPOLE *Psalter* vii. 17 Þat he neuer rise til þe rist of heuen. **1485** CAXTON *Chas. Gt.* 239 Receyue my soule, and brynge me to reste perdurable. *a* **1586** SIDNEY *Ps.* xv, Lord of thy holy hill, who shall the rest obtaine? **1611** BIBLE *Heb.* iv. 9 There remaineth therefore a rest to the people of God. **1631** MILTON *Epit. March. Winchester* 50 After this thy travail sore Sweet rest sease thee evermore. **1784** COWPER *Task* v. 841 Ordain'd to guide th' embodied spirit home From toilsome life to never-ending rest. **1827** KEBLE *Chr. Y.* 3 Only, O Lord, in Thy dear love Fit us for perfect Rest above. **1865** R. W. DALE *Jew. Temp.* vi. (1877) 71 Our final blessedness will be a rest from toil.

c. Freedom from distress, trouble, molestation, or aggression.

a **900** CYNEWULF *Christ* 1655 Hælu butan sare;..Ræst butan ȝewinne. *c* **1000** ÆLFRIC *Hom.* II. 578 Se ðe forȝeaf reste & stilnysse his folce Israhel. *a* **1225** *Ancr. R.* 166 Þer ȝe schulen beon ine þrunge, auh reste and peis is in me. *a* **1300** *Cursor M.* 7305 Nu ar yee bath in rest and pees, Yow langes certes haf malees. *c* **1340** HAMPOLE *Pr. Consc.* 6792 In helle sal be whar never es rest, Endeles hungre and endeles threst. *c* **1400** *Destr. Troy* 13387 Mony dayes he endurit, all in due pes, And had rest in his rewme right to his dethe. *c* **1430** LYDG. *Min. Poems* (Percy Soc.) 18 In bothe his remes pees, and rest, and unite. *a* **1533** LD. BERNERS *Huon* lxvi. 228, I haue..maynteyned the countre in peace & rest and good iustyce. **1597** DANIEL *Civ. Wars* VI. lxiv, The cause in managing Is more than yours; 't imports the publique rest. **1611** BIBLE *Josh.* xiv. 15 And the land had rest from warre. **1781** COWPER *Expost.* 581 Thy foes implacable, thy land at rest. **1855** KINGSLEY *Westw. Ho!* xxvii, The poor Quashies, in danger of their lives, complained to Amyas, and got rest for a while.

d. Spiritual or mental peace; quiet or tranquillity of mind.

c **825** *Vesp. Psalter* cxiv. 7 Ðecer, sawle mine, in reste ðine, forðon dryhten wel dyde me. *c* **950** *Lindisf. Gosp.* Matt. xi. 29 Leornas from me..& ȝe onfindes rest saulum iurum. *c* **1200** ORMIN 4972 Swa ȝe muȝhenn resste & ro Till ȝure sawless findenn. *c* **1250** *Gen. & Ex.* 11 Ðan sal him almightin luuen..And giuen him blisse and soules reste. *a* **1300** *Cursor M.* 3762 Mi hert bes neuer broght in rest, Bituix and þis iacob be slan. *c* **1340** HAMPOLE *Pr. Consc.* 3093 To abate þat fire, þa thre er best, For þa thre may bring þe saul to rest. *c* **1400** *Rowland & O.* 669 That I for Sorowe goo nere wode, And I may hafe no riste. *c* **1430** *Syr Gener.* (Roxb.) 7604, I shal you counsel for the best, Som what to set youre hert in rest. **1490** CAXTON *Eneydos* xxvi. 92 Thou hast taken rest fro me, & hast brought me in-to ryght grete turbacion. **1530** [see 3]. **1601** SHAKS. *Twel. N.* V. i. 136, I most..willinglie, To do you rest, a thousand deaths would dye. **1611** —— *Winter T.* II. i. 191 Yet shall the Oracle Giue rest to th' mindes of others. **1782** MISS BURNEY *Cecilia* VIII. iii, What continual disturbance..keeps me thus forever from rest! **1814** CARY *Dante, Par.* XXVIII. 100 The truth, wherein rest is For every mind. **1883** DRUMMOND *Nat. Law in Spir. W.* (1884) 361 Infallibility..gives rest; but it is the rest of stagnation.

e. Quietness, peacefulness, tranquillity in nature.

1820 SHELLEY *Sensit. Pl.* I. 99 The Earth was all rest, and the air was all love. **1855** KINGSLEY *Westw. Ho!* xix, Increasing the impression of vastness and of solemn rest, which was already overpowering. **1866** RUSKIN *Eth. Dust* 227 A gradual advance to lovelier order, and more calmly, yet more deeply, animated Rest.

5. a. Place of resting or residing; residence, abode. †Also, abiding, stay.

c **825** *Vesp. Psalter* cxxxi. 14 Ðeos [is] rest min in weoruld weoruld̃e. *c* **1200** ORMIN 12991 Þatt he Þurrh Haliȝ Gast inn hemm Himm wollde takenn resste. *a* **1225** *Ancr. R.* 130 Habbeð up an heih, ase briddes of heouene, iset hore nest, Þet is hore reste. *a* **1300** *Cursor M.* 23091 Quen i was will and vte o rest, Godli toke yee me to gest. *c* **1381** CHAUCER *Parl. Foules* 376 In hire was eueri vertu at his reste. *c* **1450** *Pol. Poems* (Rolls) II. 252 Luffe, luffe, where is thi reste? Of Englond I am oute keste, Thurgh sir Envye. *c* **1475** *Rauf Coilȝear* 59, I pray the, bring me to sum rest, the wedder is sa schill. *c* **1586** C'TESS PEMBROKE *Ps.* LXXVII. iii, Whole troupes of busy cares..Tooke up their restlesse rest In sleepie sleeplesse eies. **1602** SHAKS. *Ham.* II. ii. 13, I intreat you both,..That you vouchsafe your rest heere in our Court Some little time. **1667** MILTON *P.L.* x. 1085 Till we end In dust, our final rest and native home. **1722** MRS. S. OSBORN *Pol. & Soc. Lett.* (1890) 24 Jack, I think, knows when he is well off, for he has taken up his rest at Danbury. **1760–72** H. BROOKE *Fool of Qual.* (1809) III. 123 We took up our rest for the night, at a house that had no sign. **1847** C. BRONTË *J. Eyre* vi, It makes eternity a rest—a mighty home, not a terror and an abyss.

†**b.** A landing on a staircase. *Obs. rare.*

1653 URQUHART *Rabelais* I. liii, The just number of twelve [steps being] betwixt every rest or (as we now terme it) landing-place. **1712** J. JAMES tr. *Le Blond's Gardening* 125 A Half-Pace, or Rest of two Paces broad.

c. An establishment for the purpose of providing shelter or lodging for persons belonging to certain classes during their spare time or when not following their usual occupation.

1892 *Daily News* 13 May 5/4 It is the object of the League to provide them with a place in which to spend this off-time, and there are now five 'Rests' in London. **1899** *Ibid.* 3 May 5/5 These three Rests are, in a word, well-managed temperance clubs for Jack ashore.

6. a. The repose of death or of the grave. Chiefly in phrases, as *to go, be laid, to rest.*

1382 WYCLIF *Ecclus.* xxxviii. 24 In the reste of the deade mac to resten the mynde of hym. **1513** DOUGLAS *Æneis* x. xii. 139 The Orodes the hard rest doith oppres, The cauld and irny slepe of deidis stres. **1588** SHAKS. *Tit. A.* I. i. 133 Alarbus goes to rest, and we suruiue To tremble [etc.]. **1595** —— *John* v. vii. 24 This pale..Syren..sings His soule and body to their lasting rest. **1611** BIBLE *Job* xvii. 16 They shall goe downe to the barres of the pit, when our rest together is in the dust. **1700** DRYDEN *Charac. Gd. Parson* 23 David left him, when he went to rest, His lyre. **1855** KINGSLEY *Westw. Ho!* xxvii, Long ere they were within sight of land, Lucy Passmore was gone to her rest beneath the Atlantic waves. **1888** BURGON *Lives 12 Gd. Men* II. 301 He directed that he should be laid to rest in the cemetery of Chester.

b. *at rest* (cf. 9 a).

1338 R. BRUNNE *Chron.* (1810) 109 Henry is at his reste, his soule at Criste's wille. **1560** DAUS tr. *Sleidane's Comm.* 116 The soules of dead men were at quiet rest. **1611** BIBLE *Job* iii. 13 For now..I should haue slept; then had I bene at rest. **1708** MRS. CENTLIVRE *Busy Body* I. i, A father at rest with his ancestors. **1784** BURNS *Man was made to mourn* xi, Welcome the hour, my aged limbs Are laid with thee at rest!

7. a. *Mus.* An interval of silence occurring in one or more parts during a movement, frequently of all the parts together; a pause; also, the character or sign by which this is denoted.

1579 GOSSON *Sch. Abuse* (Arb.) 28 How many noates, how many restes, how many querks. **1597** MORLEY *Introd. Mus.* Annot., Some restes also (as the minime and crotchet restes) were deuised to auoid the harshnesse of some discord. **1639** N. N. tr. *Du Bosq's Compl. Woman* I. 20 Pauses well used in discourse make appeare, as rest in Musicke, what is the best and sweetest in it. **1662** PLAYFORD *Skill Mus.* I. viii. (1674) 26 Pauses or Rests are silent Characters, or an artificial omission of the Voyce or Sound, proportioned to a certain Measure of Time. **1752** AVISON *Mus. Express.* 117 If there are any Rests succeeding the Pause. **1795** MASON *Ch. Mus.* I. 13 In a musical movement we usually find various rests,..answering to commas in verbal punctuation. **1806** CALLCOTT *Mus. Gram.* iv. 46 The Rests of the white Notes are made in the middle of the Staff. **1868** OUSELEY *Harmony* i. 5 A dot after a note or rest makes it half as long again. *fig.* **1592** BRETON *C'tess Pembroke's Passion* cvi, Lett all your restes be hopes of happynes, Which mercye's musicke in the soule requires. **1872** HOLMES *Poet Breakf.-t.* ii. (1906) 29 The Master is apt to strike in at the end of a bar, instead of waiting for a rest.

b. *Rhet.* (See later quots.)

1612 DRAYTON *Poly-olb.* IV. 186 Observing yet in all Their quantities, their rests, their ceasures metrical. *a* **1637** B. JONSON tr. *Horace Art Poet.* 371 Two rests, a short and long, th' Iambic frame. **1727–38** CHAMBERS *Cycl.*, *Cæsure*, in the modern poetry, denotes a rest or pause towards the middle of a long Alexandrine verse. **1771** *Encycl. Brit.* III. 548/2 *Rest*, in poetry, is a short pause of the voice in reading, being the same with the cæsura. **1824** L. MURRAY *Eng. Gram.* (ed. 5) I. IV. i. 364 Pauses or rests, in speaking and reading, are a total cessation of the voice during a perceptible..space of time.

8. Absence, privation, or cessation of motion; continuance in the same position or place.

c **1475** *Babees Bk.* 80 Your heede, youre hande, your feet, holde yee in reste. **1597** HOOKER *Eccl. Pol.* v. lxx. §4 Rest is the end of all motion. **1620** T. GRANGER *Div. Logike* 109 Rest is a priuation of moouing. *a* **1676** HALE *Prim. Orig. Man.* I. v. (1677) 114 Rest must needs be antecedent to his Motion. **1715** tr. *Gregory's Astron.* (1726) I. 115 The common Centre of Gravity of them all does not change its state of Motion or Rest. **1869** PHILLIPS *Vesuv.* vii. 180 About the usual angle of rest in loose materials. **1879** THOMSON & TAIT *Nat. Phil.* I. I. §245 The meaning of the term Rest, in physical science, is essentially relative. Absolute rest is undefinable.

9. *at rest.* **a.** In a state of (physical or mental) repose, quiescence, or inactivity. (See also 6 b.)

c **1374** CHAUCER *Troylus* II. 760 þough þat I myn herte sette at reste Vpon þis knight,..it may do me no shame. **1535** COVERDALE *Dan.* iv. 1, I..beynge at rest in myne house,..sawe a dreame, which made me afrayed. **1587** GOLDING *De Mornay* iv. (1592) 43 Forasmuch as God is euermore dooing, he is euer at rest. **1605** SHAKS. *Macb.* II. i. 12 What Sir, not yet at rest? the King's a bed. **1629** MILTON *Nativity* 216 Nor is Osiris seen..: Nor can he be at rest Within his sacred chest. **1774** M. MACKENZIE *Maritime Surv.* 50 When the Plummet is at Rest, and both Stars are seen. **1782** MISS BURNEY *Cecilia* VI. i, Had her heart not interfered in this matter, she might now have been perfectly at rest. **1839** G. BIRD *Nat. Philos.* 99 General properties of fluids at rest. **1847** C. BRONTË *J. Eyre* xxvii, He sat in his chair, still, but not at rest: expectant evidently. **1869** PHILLIPS *Vesuv.* iii. 48 After this terrific disturbance Vesuvius has never been really at rest.

b. *to set..at rest*, to satisfy, assure; to settle, decide finally. *at rest*, settled. Also, *to lay..to rest*, to allay completely.

1590 SHAKS. *Mids. N.* II. i. 121 Set your heart at rest. The Fairy land buyes not the childe of me. **1817** SHELLEY *Proposal* Prose Wks. 1888 I. 361 The decisive effort to set their hopes and fears at rest. **1826** SOUTHEY *Vind. Eccl. Angl.* 286 It might have been thought that the question..had been set at rest. **1847** MARRYAT *Childr. N. Forest* xii, I never can take any office under the present rulers of the nation; so that question is at rest. **1855** KINGSLEY *Westw. Ho!* viii, But set your mind at rest. I know no more of that lady's mind than you do. *Ibid.* xxxi, His fears, such as they were, were laid to rest. **1884** *Manch. Exam.* 21 May 4/7 The enormous majority..should set that question at rest.

II. †10. Some part of the iron-work of a gate. *Obs. rare.*

1513 DOUGLAS *Æneis* VII. iv. 78 Of rych citeis ȝettis, stapillis, and restis, Gret lokis, slotis, massy bandis squayr.

11. a. A support for a fire-arm, employed in steadying the barrel to ensure accuracy of aim, *esp.* that used for the old heavy musket, which was forked at the upper end, and provided with a spike to fix it in the ground.

1590 SIR J. SMYTH *Disc. Weapons* 13 b, That would permit their Mosquettiers to giue anie volees from their restes. **1598** BARRET *Theor. Warres* II. i. 27 The musket hath his rest, the heauinesse thereof is many times eased. **1622** F. MARKHAM *Bk. War* I. ix. 35 He shall have for his right hand a handsome Rest of Ash or other light wood, with an yron pike in the nether end, and an halfe hoope of yron aboue to lay the musquet in when hee rests it. *a* **1662** HEYLIN *Laud* (1668) 492 Shouldering a Musket..in one hand, and a Rest in the other. **1833** HOLLAND *Manuf. in Metal* II. 92 The rest is still generally used in shooting with the duck gun. **1884** KNIGHT *Dict. Mech.* Suppl. 753/1 *Rest*, a support for a gun in test firing.

†b. (See quot.) *Obs. rare*⁻¹.

1726 *Gentleman Angler* 154 A Rest, is a forked Piece of Stick with the forked End standing upright, and the other end fasten'd upon the Ground. It is called a Rest, because one Part of the Angler's Rod lies upon it.

c. A support for a cue in billiards.

1868 PARDON *Billiards* 59 The rest needs to be held tightly in the left hand. **1873** BENNETT & CAVENDISH *Billiards* 27 The rest is 4 feet 10 in. in length. It consists of a handle of wood with a cross or grooved piece, of ivory, boxwood, or brass, fixed on the head, to rest the cue in.

12. a. A thing upon which something else rests, in various specific uses (see quots.).

The *rest* of a lance belongs to REST *sb.*[3]

1609 C. BUTLER *Fem. Mon.* (1623) Mj, Your Hiue being fitted and dressed, you must haue also in a readinesse a Mantle, a Rest, and a Brush—A Rest is either single or double. **1611** BIBLE *1 Kings* vi. 6 Without in the wall of the house hee made narrowed rests round about. **1617** in Willis & Clark *Cambridge* (1886) I. 205 Seasoned board of oake layd uppon sufficient rests of oake tymber for the grounde floare. **1707** MORTIMER *Husb.* (1721) I. 275 Having spread a Mantle on the Ground,..set a Pair of Rests, or two Supporters for the Hive. **1723** CHAMBERS tr. *Le Clerc's Treat. Archit.* I. 135 Pedestals shou'd be continued so as to form Rests or Leaning-Places for the Windows. *Ibid.* 136 The Windows have no Rests, but reach down to the Pavement. **1881** RAYMOND *Mining Gloss.*, *Rests*, the arrangement at the top and bottom of a pit for supporting the shaft-cage while changing the tubs or cars. **1884** KNIGHT *Dict. Mech.* Suppl. 753/2 *Rest*, a support or a guide for stuff fed to a saw.

b. That part of a lathe on which the cutting-tool is supported in the operation of turning.

1680 MOXON *Mech. Exer.* x. 180 The Rest is a square piece of Stuff... Its Office is to rest the Tool upon, that it may lie in a steddy position while the Workman uses it. **1780** *Phil. Trans.* LXX. 382 In the turning of ovals, the top of the rest which supports the tool is always made to pass through..the two centers round which the oval engine turns. **1882** *Mech. World* 4 Mar. 138 The rest on which the tool is supported appears to be on the near side of the line of centres, a position that could scarcely be correct.

c. A support or hook for a telephone receiver when not in use, incorporating a switch that is automatically closed when the receiver is lifted.

1889 *Telephone* 15 Feb. 94/2 Improvements in telephone apparatus to be designated as a telephone-receiver rest. **1922** *Telegraph & Telephone Jrnl.* VIII. 97/2 Flash the Switchboard Telephonist into circuit by moving the Receiver rest up and down slowly until she answers. **1948** J. ATKINSON *Telephony* 129/1 The circuit is arranged automatically to switch the lines from the bell circuit to the speaking circuit when the receiver is lifted from its rest or hook. **1961** H. & N. SCHNEIDER *Your Telephone* iii. 26 In the exchange there is a huge electric battery. When you lift your telephone off its rest, a switch inside joins the two wires together.

d. A projecting part of a removable denture that gives it support by lying against a tooth.

1907 H. J. GOSLEE *Princ. & Pract. Crown & Bridgework* (ed. 2) xxv. 465 Providing a rest which will cause the piece to ride largely upon the supporting teeth instead of on the gum tissue. *Ibid.*, An occlusal rest constituting a part of the clasp was early advocated by Dr. W. G. A. Bonwill. **1924** D. D. CAMPBELL *Full Denture Prosthesis* ii. 125 The insertion of occlusion rests or immediate dentures within thirty minutes..after the teeth have been removed, contributes in a remarkable degree to the patient's confidence. **1942** J. R. SCHWARTZ *Mod. Methods Tooth Replacement* ix. 379 Unfavorable action that may be caused by rests not locked into an inlay occurs when the inclination of the tooth is such that the rest will slip or slide. **1976** TORRES & EHRLICH *Mod. Dental Assisting* xxvii. 815/2 A rest built into an onlay is designed to partially cover a tooth that needs to be built up to the height of the occlusion.

13. a. Something upon which one rests. *rare.*

1641 J. JACKSON *True Evang. T.* iii. 190 Surely that is a very aery soule, whose chiefe rest and stay is not his Religion. **1648** R. WILKINSON *Saint's Trav.* (1874) 7 Several Rests of Creatures discovered and laid open. Below the Coming of Christ in Spirit, who is the alone Rest of Saints.

b. A projection for the foot to rest on.

1869 *Daily News* 15 Apr., There are no fastenings for the foot—simply a rest which projects out from the axle-trees. **1897** *Outing* XXIX. 596/2 Throwing my weary feet on the coasting rests, I started.

c. (See quot.)

1888 GOODE *Amer. Fishes* 250 All vessels regularly engaged in this fishery are supplied with a special apparatus, called a 'rest' or 'pulpit', for the support of the harpooner as he stands on the bowsprit.

14. *attrib.* and *Comb.* **a.** In senses 3 or 4, as ***rest area, billet, camp, centre, cure, day, home, pause, period, stop, system, therapy***; ***rest-giving, -ordained, -refreshed, -seeking*** adjs.; **†rest-field**, a fallow; **rest gown**, formerly, a gown used for evening wear at home; **†rest man**, one who leads an inactive life; **rest room**, (*a*) a room (usu. in a public building) set aside for rest and quiet; (*b*) *U.S.* a lavatory, a W.C.; **rest-tremor** *Path.*, a tremor in a part which is not being voluntarily moved.

1919 W. H. DOWNING *Digger Dial.* 41 **Rest area*, a district to which battalions, on leaving the danger zone, marched by long stages once a year for the purpose of polishing their brass work. *a* **1944** K. DOUGLAS *Alamein to Zem Zem* (1946) 18 Here we halted, having left the heavy squadrons of Shermans and Grants still in our rest area. **1976** G. V. HIGGINS *Judgement D. Hunter* ix. 86 The youth..stopped in a rest area..so that the subject could relieve himself. **1978** W. GARNER *Möbius Trip* ix. 216 In the autoroute rest area at Chennevières..a chauffeured gray Mercedes. **1917** A. G. EMPEY *Over Top* 306 **Rest billets*, shell shattered houses, generally barns, in which Tommy 'rests', when relieved from the firing line. **1925** R. GRAVES *Welchman's Hose* 29 And back in rest-billets The Colonel congratulates 'B' Company on its kits. **1954** W. FAULKNER *Fable* 128 The nine others..had been spending their leaves and furloughs..among the combat-troop rest-billets. **1889** G. S. MACKENZIE *Let.* 11 Dec. in Ld. Lugard *Diaries* (1959) I. 50 Lay out *rest camps and fortified posts at regular intervals. **1890** *Daily News* 8 Sept. 3/1 For the men a healthier rest camp could hardly be desired. **1919** *Lit. Digest* 29 Mar. 44 A trench-mortar shell hit so close..that I was completely buried and for a moment or two thought I was going to a rest camp (cemetery). **1923** KIPLING *Irish Guards in Gt. War* I. 3 The city became almost a suburb to the vast rest-camps round it. **1971** *Rand Daily Mail* 27 Mar. 23/3 Incidentally, all Natal Parks Board rest camps are fully booked in the Easter holidays. **1940** *Economist* 5 Oct. 422/1 When their roof has gone the family seek refuge, and they find it in temporary *rest centres run by the Public Assistance Department of the London County Council. **1976** *Liverpool Echo* 6 Dec. 8/4 Rest centres were made ready on the outskirts of all 'target' areas, like Merseyside, to house the virtual refugees. **1889** *Cent. Dict.*, *Rest-cure. **1892** S. HALE *Let.* 28 Apr. (1919) 272 She is at a rest-cure. **1896** *Allbutt's Syst. Med.* I. 375 General massage, such as is used for convalescent patients or 'rest-cure' cases. **1928** BLUNDEN *Undertones of War* 131 Then we went into the trenches..which not long before had been so horrible..but now they..were voted 'a rest-cure sector'. **1959** T. S. ELIOT *Elder Statesman* I. 25 Now's the time to take a long holiday, Let's say a rest cure. **1980** D. ADAMS *Restaurant at End of Universe* ix. 57, I only hope it's gone in for a rest cure... The way it's been living recently it must be on its last elbows. **1911** WEBSTER, *Rest day. **1959** *Encounter* Aug. 22/1 People were free to prepare their meals at home on 'rest days'. **1976** J. SNOW *Cricket Rebel* 90, I worked out that we had only one day free from cricket in those last six weeks in Australia apart from the rest days during the Test matches. **1578** LYTE *Dodoens* 248 The second kinde groweth in this countrie in *rest-fieldes. **1928** BEERBOHM *Lett. to R. Turner* (1964) 270 A solid and..*rest-giving figure in the midst of that wild vortex. **1913** MRS. G. DE H. VAIZEY *College Girl* xviii. 257 Margaret herself, in a pink *rest-gown curled up in a wicker chair. **1915** *Home Chat* 20 Nov. 326/1 Evening dress..has ceased to exist, its place being taken by smart little demi-toilettes for restaurant and theatre wear, and rest-gowns that are really restful for home wear. **1924** 'J. SUTHERLAND' *Circle of Stars* xxvi. 286 Gathering the folds of her rest-gown about her, Norma went up to the next story. **1925** *Daily Herald* 6 July 6/7 The organization of *rest homes, where workers may spend their vacation, is a unique development. **1976** B. BOVA *Multiple Man* (1977) x. 102 Why wouldn't the President simply..cart the old man off to a well-guarded rest home? **1542** BOORDE *Dyetary* ix. (1870) 251 Two meales a daye is suffycyent for a *rest man; and a labourer maye eate thre tymes a day. **1591** SYLVESTER *Du Bartas* I. iii. 313 Knowing th' use aright Of Work-fit Day, and *Rest-ordained Night. **1926** *Encycl. Brit.* II. 454/1 An important innovation stressed by the industrial psychologist has been the introduction of short rests, in the middle of a working period, of about 10 or 15 min. duration. These regular breaks are technically known as *rest pauses. **1954** J. A. C. BROWN *Social Psychol. of Industry* iii. 71 Two five-minute rest-pauses, morning and afternoon. **1922** *Encycl. Brit.* XXXI. 699/2 In spite of the considerable development of maximum hour regulation in the United States, not much attention has been paid to the question of legal *rest periods. **1954** J. A. C. BROWN *Social Psychol. of Industry* iii. 74 The introduction of rest-periods which amounted to two ten-minute breaks in the morning and two in the afternoon. **1981** 'J. ROSS' *Dark Blue & Dangerous* xxii. 123 You will report off duty for a rest period. **1603** J. DAVIES (Heref.) *Microcos.* Wks. (Grosart) I. 23/1 Be'ng *rest-refresht therefore, now forwards run With bright Apollo. **1899** *Amer. Jrnl. Sociol.* May 729 Surely it would not be unreasonable to require that suitable *rest-rooms be provided for the employés. **1918** A. BENNETT *Pretty Lady* xxvii. 182 Canteens, and rest-rooms, and libraries, and sanitation, and all this damned 'welfare'. **1942** 'M. INNES' *Daffodil Affair* III. 103 His private research block..comprised a library, a museum, rest rooms and living quarters for the subjects. **1955** W. GADDIS *Recognitions* I. iii. 100 If you serve food you gotta have a rest room for ladies as well as men. **1975** *N.Y. Times* 8 Nov. 26/2 The totally unsubstantiated forecasts of effects ranging from the abolition of women's rest rooms to dire financial consequences may well have persuaded many women that it was safer to accept known evils than to risk unknown pitfalls. **1847** C. BRONTË *J. Eyre* xx, The wandering and sinful, but now *rest-seeking and repentant man. **1973** *Sunday Bull.* (Philadelphia) 14 Oct. (Parade Suppl.) 16/3 A truck driver napped at a *rest stop. **1975** J. GRADY *Shadow of Condor* (1976) xiii. 214 It's another rest stop... Just a picnic table and some trash cans. **1899** *Allbutt's Syst. Med.* VIII. 415 The *rest system of treatment of recent cases of insanity. **1949** *Radio Times* 15 July 24/1 Many people keep their vitality..by regularly practising *Rest-therapy. **1925** S. A. K. Wilson in *Lancet* 8 Aug. 270/2 Some cases of disseminated sclerosis..definitely show what I may call a *'rest-tremor' as well as an 'action-tremor'. **1967** *Internat. Jrnl. Neuropharmacol.* VI. 122 There is a great similarity between rest tremor produced by tremorine and rest tremor in human pathology. *Ibid.*, It is likely that rest tremor in human pathology is due to the hyperactivity of these [alpha] cells [of the anterior horn].

b. In sense 12, as ***rest-auger***, ***-carriage***, ***-frame***, ***-holder***, ***-plate***, ***-wimble***.

1523 Fitzherb. *Husb.* §5 A pyn-awgur, a *rest-awgur, a flayle. **1833** Holland *Manuf. Metal* II. 145 The chain is fastened on one side to a part of the *rest-carriage.., which descends and occupies the space between the sides of the frame. *Ibid.*, The chain operates upon the *rest-frame, to which it is attached. **1881** Young *Ev. Man his own Mechanic* §553. 258 The little piece S is the *rest-holder. *Ibid.*, The *rest-plate R which is made of iron can be moved up and down. **1446** *Wills & Inv. N.C.* (Surtees, 1835) 95, ij yoke wymbils, j *restwymbyll.

c. In sense 8, as **rest energy** *Physics*, the energy inherent in a body by virtue of its possession of rest mass; **rest frame** *Physics*, a frame of reference relative to which a given body is at rest; **rest level** *Hydrology*, the natural level of water in an aquifer or on the ground surface; **rest mass** *Physics*, the mass of a body measured when it is at rest; **rest position** *Dentistry*, the relative position of the jaws when relaxed.

1938 *Forum* Feb. 95/2 From the Lorentz transformation and the assumption of the impulse and energy principle for material particles..the equality of mass and *rest-energy is derived. **1962** H. D. Bush *Atomic & Nuclear Physics* ii. 54 Since the rest mass is m_0, the rest energy is considered to be m_0c^2. **1966** J. Werle *Relativistic Theory of Reactions* v. 347 We are interested in the scattering angle of particle *d* in a *rest frame of particle *b*. **1978** *Nature* 5 Oct. 411/1 The known general absence of Lyman continuum absorption in the rest frame of high redshift QSOs implies that < 0·1 of the continuum radiation is intercepted by optically thick clouds. **1908** W. Coles-Finch *Water* xviii. 416 The *rest-level in a well or boring is that level to which the water rises upon cessation of pumping. **1956** R. J. C. Atkinson *Stonehenge* iii. 82 The level at which this pottery and the earliest fragments of bluestone occur is slightly above the rest-level which marks the end of the first phase of rapid silting in the ditch. **1914** L. Silberstein *Theory of Relativity* vii. 193 The coefficient *m* is called the *rest-mass of the particle. **1938** R. W. Lawson tr. *Hevesy & Paneth's Man. Radioactivity* (ed. 2) iii. 36 We differentiate between the 'rest mass' and the 'translational mass' of β-particles, i.e. the mass of the particle in motion. **1979** *Jrnl. R. Soc. Arts* CXXVII. 577/2 Nuclear fusion can convert 0·7 per cent of the rest mass of the hydrogen core into energy. [**1907** C. R. Turner *Amer. Textbk. Prosthetic Dentistry* (ed. 3) iv. 243 This position is commonly called 'the resting bite'. **1921** D. Gabell *Prosthetic Dentistry* iv. 76 The closed resting position of the mandible is one of more stable equilibrium than any other, and brings the greatest number of teeth in contact and the jaws closer together.] **1924** T. Goodhugh *Art of Prosthetic Dentistry* iii. 55 Ask the patient to close, thus registering the proper *rest position. **1962** Blake & Trott *Periodontol.* xvi. 163 To bring the mandible into the rest position the patient should be seated comfortably in the chair, and head erect and away from the head rest, with the Frankfort plane horizontal. He is then asked to wet the lips with the tongue, swallow and remain quite still. The mandible should then assume the rest position.

rest, *sb.*² Also 5 reste, 6 *Sc.* rist. [a. F. *reste* (1395), = It. and Sp. *resta*, *resto*, Pg. *reste*, *resto*, f. *rester* rest *v.*² Hence also MDu. and MLG. *reste*; Du., G., Da., Sw. *rest*.]

1. †**a.** That which remains over; a remainder or remnant. ***the auld rest***, the name of some disease (cf. quot. 1669 in b). *Obs.*

c **1420** *Pallad. on Husb.* xii. 603 Thus bokis twelue anende, and oon is rest. **1484** Caxton *Curiall* 2 The reste thenne is thys, that thou shalt haue labour wythout fruyt. *a* **1585** Montgomerie *Flyting* 323 The rot, the roup, and the auld rest. *c* **1610** in Gutch *Coll. Cur.* II. 13 That every barrel of good Ale hold and contain xv gallons, xiiij gallons of clear Ale, and one gallon for the rest. *a* **1652** Brome *Queenes Exch.* i. ii. Wks. 1873 III. 469 The Queen had done me favour.. To make my rest of life all holidayes. **1693** *Humours Town* 124 Thou hast too, yet, I hope, a Rest of Reputation.

b. *pl.* Remains, remnants, relics. Now *rare.*

c **1467** *Noble Bk. of Cookry* (1882) 26 Take restes of motton choped and put them in a faire pot. **1669** Gale *Idea Jansenisme* 93 The best remedie to extirpate the restes of this contagious Maladie. **1677** —— *Crt. Gentiles* iii. 199 They endeavored to gather up the least pieces, if the rage of persecutors had left any restes or reliques. *a* **1694** Sir A. Balfour *Lett.* (1700) 54 Its a Town of Roman antiquity, of which there are yet some rests to be seen, as aqueducts, &c. **1897** *Allbutt's Syst. Med.* IV. 527 Others..may with probability be regarded like suprarenal 'rests' as isolated and outlying fragments of the mesoblastic tissues.

†**c.** *Arith.* A remainder. *Obs. rare.*

1608 R. Norton *Stevin's Disme* A 4 b, If, from things equall, equall things bee substracted, their rests shall be equal. **1636** Mellis *Recorde's Gr. Arts* 63 Therefore in the place of the rest or remaine, right vnder the denomination, I set downe 0.

2. †**a.** A sum remaining to be paid; balance or arrears of money due. *Obs.* (Chiefly *Sc.*)

1474 *Acc. Ld. High Treas. Scot.* I. 12, xxxiiij li resauit.. of the ald rest of his faderis compt and his awin. **1523–4** *Rec. St. Mary at Hill* (1905) 325 There Remayneth in ther box with the Rest of this Acompte..iij li. viij s. **1549** *Rec. Elgin* (New Spalding Cl.) I. 99 The saidis personis findand souerte for the auld rist and malis in tyme coming. *Ibid.*, Souerte for the restis and malis. **1581–2** *Reg. Privy Council Scot.* III. 458 For satisfeing and outredding thairof, be the restis to be gottin in and utherwyse.

b. The reserve or surplus fund of a bank, esp. of the Bank of England.

1844 in *Encycl. Brit.* (1902) XXVI. 112 Bank of England. .. Proprietors' Capital, 14,533,000. Rest 3,564,729. **1847** J. Francis *Hist. Bank Eng.* I. ix. 147 A reserve fund, which, under the name of *rest*, has increased with the business of the house. **1882** A. S. Michie *Gilbart's Hist. Banking* I. 370 The Rest, from being looked upon merely as a fund to equalize the dividends, is now regarded as a reserve to meet exceptional losses. **1895** *Westm. Gaz.* 6 Sept. 6/1 This amount will..still leave the 'Rest' above three millions, below which it is never allowed to fall.

fig. **1858** J. Martineau *Stud. Chr.* 352 Life, indeed, is just the one thing—the reserved capital, the rest, the ultimate security.

c. (See quots.)

1825 C. Butler *Bk. R.C. Ch.* 154 It may not be improper to make what, in mercantile transactions, is termed *a rest*; and thus show, as it were on a balance sheet, which side.. has the preponderance. **1856** Gilbart *Pract. Treat. Banking* (ed. 6) 258 Amount of Cash-Book last night. (This is usually called the Rest.) ? **1889** Waterston *Manual Commerce* 286/2 *Rest*, a term applied both to the period of stock-taking and balancing of a merchant, and to the balance of undivided profit at that period.

3. a. The remainder or remaining part(s) *of* something.

1530 Palsgr. 262/2 Rest that leaveth of a thynge, *demeurant.* **1560** Daus tr. *Sleidane's Comm.* 139 They passed away the rest of the wynter there. **1585** T. Washington tr. *Nicholay's Voy.* ii. xi. 45 b, The rest of the promontory is ful of ruines. **1617** Moryson *Itin.* i. 33 While I liued here the rest of this summer, I made a iourney of pleasure. **1718** Lady M. W. Montagu *Let. to Abbé Conti* 31 Oct., I pray God I may think so for the rest of my life. **1774** Goldsm. *Nat. Hist.* (1776) III. 220 The hair about the neck ..is not different from that on the rest of the body. **1861** Pattison *Ess.* (1889) I. 32 When England, in common with the rest of Europe, was Catholic.

b. The remainder *of* a number of persons, animals, or things.

1535 Lyndesay *Satyre* 1207 Lo! quhair thair sits ane Priores of renown Amangs the rest of Spiritualitie. **1560** Daus tr. *Sleidane's Comm.* 216 b, The same judgement hath he also of the rest of the ministers of the churche. **1611** Bible *Neh.* xi. 1 The rest of the people also cast lots, to bring one of tenne, to dwell in Ierusalem. **1651** Hobbes *Leviath.* ii. xxvi. 137 To distinguish it from the rest of their own Civill Lawes. **1732** Berkeley *Alciphr.* vi. §1 The rest of us went to church. *c* **1765** Gray *Satire* 34 The Master of John's Like the rest of the Dons. **1839** Fr. A. Kemble *Resid. in Georgia* (1863) 27 The rest of the twenty-four hours were allowed to the laborer to employ as he pleased. **1875** Jowett *Plato* (ed. 2) I. 299 Like the rest of the world, I am in doubt.

c. (*all*) ***the rest of it***, everything else which might be mentioned or included.

1855 Kingsley *Westw. Ho!* v, With their holy water, and their moppings and their scourings, and the rest of it. **1888** Balfour in *Times* 2 Oct. 10/4 He was treated as an ordinary prisoner, plank bed and all the rest of it.

4. a. The remainder or residue of something specified or implied in the context.

1530 Palsgr. 262/2 Rest or resydue, *demourant.* **1590** Spenser *F.Q.* i. ii. 18 Therewith upon his crest With rigor so outrageous he smitt, That a large share it hewd out of the rest. **1602** *2nd Pt. Return fr. Parnass.* Prol. 65 Conceiue of this and guesse of all the rest. **1665** Manley *Grotius' Low C. Wars* 123 The present necessity forced the United Dutch to rest satisfied onely with words, and only to hope for the rest. **1761** Gray *Williams* 11 Gallant youth! this marble tells the rest. **1820** Keats *Isabella* vii, She ceas'd her timid quest, But in her tone and look he read the rest. **1895** *Law Times Rep.* LXXIII. 691/2 To accept the office as to some part of the estate and not accept it as to the rest.

b. As *pl.* The remaining persons, animals, or things; the others.

1535 Lyndesay *Satyre* 1458 Ladie Sensualitie Sen syne hes gydit this cuntrie, And monie of the rest. **1560** Daus tr. *Sleidane's Comm.* 62, The Byshop of Rome with al the reste, stampe & stare at it. **1613** Purchas *Pilgrimage* viii. iii. (1614) 739 They leapt off the Rockes into the Sea... The rest fled. **1670** Dryden *Conq. Granada* i. i, One Bull, with curl'd black Head beyond the rest. **1711** Addison *Spect.* No. 44 ⁋8 Some of which [inventions] I could wish entirely rejected, and the rest to be used with Caution. **1769** Sir W. Jones *Palace Fortune* Poems (1777) 15 A lovely stripling stepp'd before the rest. **1844** Disraeli *Coningsby* iii. iii, The Duchess would drive over... The rest were to ride. **1870** Max Müller *Sci. Relig.* (1873) 141 They represent each deity as independent of all the rest.

5. In phrases: **a.** (*as*) ***for the rest***, as regards, with regard to, what remains.

1545 Raynold *Byrth Mankynde* 82 As for the rest how to open, clense, dry, and hele suche apostumations, ye must consult with sum phisition. **1593** Shaks. *3 Hen. VI*, iii. iii. 92 But for the rest: you tell a Pedigree [etc.]. **1609** Holland *Amm. Marcell.* 314 Let it suffice for this present..: for the rest, I shall not cease to admonish thee accordingly. **1655** tr. *Sorel's Com. Hist. Francion* viii. 6 For the rest, all these debauchments are very true. **1760–2** Goldsm. *Cit. W.* No. 25 ⁋1 Riches are the strength of a nation; and for the rest, our ships.. will protect us. **1784** R. Bage *Barham Downs* II. 344 For the rest, it is I believe as compleat as human nature ..will permit. **1847** C. Brontë *J. Eyre* xiv, For the rest, you are not my conscience keeper, so don't make yourself uneasy. **1851** Borrow *Lavengro* xliv, As for the rest, I could not exactly make it out.

b. ***as to the rest***, also †(*in*) ***the rest***, in other respects, otherwise.

1590 Sir J. Smyth *Disc. Weapons* Ded. 8 And in the rest to take their adventures, and sometimes to starue. **1667** Milton *P.L.* ix. 653 Of this Tree we may not taste nor touch..; the rest, we live Law to our selves, our Reason is our Law. **1745** Eliza Heywood *Female Spect.* No. 8 (1748) II. 87 As to the rest, he has a very good estate [etc.]. **1771** Warburton in W. & Hurd *Lett.* (1809) 464 As to the rest, you shall live to yourself. **1819** Shelley *Cyclops* 307, I know not that his strength is more than mine. As to the rest I care not.

†**c.** ***above the rest***, especially. *Obs.*

1605 Shaks. *Lear* iv. i. 50 Do as I bid thee, or rather do thy pleasure: Aboue the rest, be gone.

†**6. a.** In primero, the stakes kept in reserve, which were agreed upon at the beginning of the game, and upon the loss of which the game terminated; the venture of such stakes. *Obs.*

1561 T. Hoby tr. *Castiglione's Courtyer* ii. y iv b, [They] fell to gamynge. And not longe after, one of the Pistoiens losinge his reste had not a farthynge left him to blesse himselfe. **1591** Florio *2nd Fruites* 69 *A.* Let us agree of our game, what shall we plaie for? *S.* One shilling stake, and three rest. **1614** Tomkis *Albumazar* iii. v, I set ten shillings six pence, You see't? my rest, fiue and fifty. **1670** Cotton *Espernon* i. iv. 156 The Duke..being at that instant bow'd down upon the Table, to draw the money he had newly won upon a rest, escap'd that fatal blow.

fig. **1599** Shaks. *Hen. V*, ii. i. 17 When I cannot liue any longer, I will doe as I may: That is my rest. **1630** R. Johnson *Kingd. & Commw.* 155 The King thought it no policie to play all his Rest at once, where hee might have lost more at one Game, than he had got in eight yeares.

†**b.** In phr. ***to set*** (***up***) ***one's rest***, to venture one's final stake or reserve. *Obs.*

1575 Gascoigne *Herbes, Supposes* iii. ii, Of whom some one peraduenture shal leese a great sum of money before he win one stake, & at last halfe in anger shal set vp his rest. *c* **1597** Harington *On Play* in *Nugæ Ant.* (1804) I. 222 The kinge, 55 eldest hand, set up all restes. **1656** Earl Monm. tr. *Boccalini's Pol. Touchstone* (1674) 288 [The] advantage which he had of three Sevens in hand, had enforced him to set his Rest.

†**7.** ***to set*** (***up***) ***one's rest***, in fig. uses. Now *Obs.* except perhaps as in f.

a. To stake, hazard, or venture one's all *on* or *upon* something; to set one's final hope or trust *upon* or *in* something.

1587 Greene *Penelope's Web* Wks. (Grosart) V. 181 Least ayming more at yͤ weale of our countrey then our own liues, we set our rest on the hazard and so desperately throw at all. **1599** Sandys *Europe Spec.* (1632) 68 If the Pope..were brought to this last hand to set uppe his rest upon these men. **1635** R. N. tr. *Camden's Hist. Eliz.* i. 59 The Queen of Scots being..one which set up her rest in hope of England. **1670** Cotton *Espernon* i. iv. 174 The greatest part of those who had set up their rest upon the Fortune of the Duke his Father. **1684** Burnet tr. *More's Utopia* (1685) 11 They would set up their Rest on such an Answer.

b. To do one's utmost. *rare*⁻¹.

1589 [? Lyly] *Pappe w. Hatchet* Wks. III. 398 Wee'le set vp all our rests, to make you all restie.

c. To have or take a resolution; to be resolved or determined.

1590 Shaks. *Com. Err.* iv. iii. 27 He that sets vp his rest to doe more exploits with his Mace, then a Moris Pike. **1596** —— *Merch. V.* ii. ii. 110 As I haue set vp my rest to run awaie, so I will not rest till I haue run some ground. **1633** Ford *'Tis Pity* v. iii, Despair, or tortures of a thousand hells, All's one to me; I have set up my rest. **1646** Sir J. Temple *Irish Reb.* 4, I have cast up my accounts, I have set up my rest, and determine rather to displease any other man than offend my own conscience.

d. To fix or settle *upon*, to decide *for*, to place one's whole aim or end *in*, something.

1589 Greene *Menaphon* Wks. (Grosart) VI. 86 Haue ye alreadie..set your rest vpon some higher personage? **1633** B. Jonson *Tale of a Tub* ii. i, Arrested, As I had set my rest up for a wife! **1663** Pepys *Diary* 19 Jan., He seems to set up his rest in this plenty, and the neatness of his house. *a* **1674** Clarendon *Hist. Reb.* xiii. §169 When this address was made by the Dutch, he set up his whole rest and interest, that it might be well accepted. **1702** S. Parker tr. *Cicero's De Finibus* v. 327 Those very Men who have set up their rest in Pursuit of External Profit and Pleasure. **1740–1** Richardson *Pamela* (1883) I. 417 As if I believed I ought to set up my rest in my mean self and think nothing further to be done. [**1826** Scott *Jrnl.* (1890) I. 305 She has a good heart,..but unhappily..she has set up the whole staff of her rest in keeping literary society about her.]

e. To be certain, assured, convinced.

1623–4 Middleton & Rowley *Sp. Gipsy* iv. ii, Could I set up my rest That he were lost, or taken prisoner, I could hold truce with sorrow.

f. To take up one's (permanent) abode.

1590 Lodge *Rosalynde* (Hunterian Cl.) 50 Aliena resolued there to set vp her rest.., and so became Mistres of the farme. **1621** Hakewill *David's Vow* 251 Hee may chance to come into my sight, but..hee shall not set up his rest there. **1676** Etheredge *Man of Mode* ii. ii, Should I have set up my rest at the first inn I lodged at, I should never have arrived at the happiness I now enjoy. **1760–72** H. Brooke *Fool of Qual.* (1809) III. 91 Here I counted to set up my rest for life. **1771** Smollett *Humph. Cl.* 20 Sept. §8, I firmly believe he will set up his rest in Monmouthshire. **1810** Lamb *Lett.* (1888) I. 256 Here I hope to set up my rest. **1840** Dickens *Old C. Shop* lxxi, We..will set up our rest again among our boyish haunts.

g. To make an end. *rare*⁻¹.

1663 Pepys *Diary* 8 Jan., So home; with much ado.., and now resolving to set up my rest as to plays till Easter.

†**8.** ***to set down one's rest***: **a.** To stop, make an end (also with *lay*); to take up residence. *Obs.*

1586 A. Day *Eng. Secretary* ii. (1625) 74 Here as a limit sufficient to that determined labour doe I lay downe my rest. **1591** Greene *Conny Catch.* ii. Wks. (Grosart) X. 127 Whereupon he thought this night to set downe his rest. *a* **1617** Bayne *Lect.* (1634) 202 That man that comes in this life to the end of his walk, and there setteth down his rest from going any further. *a* **1665** Digby *Priv. Mem.* (1827) 282, I have set down my rest where piety forbiddeth not to live according to nature.

†b. To make up one's mind; to determine. *Obs.*

1589 NASHE *Martin Marprelate* Wks. (Grosart) I. 110 Where you sette downe your reste, you are very resolute. 1633 BP. HALL *Hard Texts, N.T.* 312 They that set down their rest and resolution that they will be rich.

9. In (real) tennis and battledore, a spell of quick and continuous returning of the ball maintained by the players. (In lawn tennis the usual term is *rally*.) Also *fig.*

Cf. F. *reste* (sense 13 in Littré).

c 1600 BEAUMONT *Letter to B. Jonson*, For wit is like a rest Held up at tennis! which men do the best With the best gamesters. 1682 SHEFFIELD (Dk. Buckhm.) *Ess. Poetry* 13 But O! the Dialogues, where jest and mock Is held up like a rest at Shittle-cock. 1704 CIBBER *Careless Husband* IV, Knock me down, if ever I saw a Rest of Wit better Play'd, than that last in my Life. 1740 —— *Apol.* (1756) I. 111 They return'd the ball so dextrously upon one another that every scene between them seem'd but one continued rest of excellence. 1889 in Heathcote *Tennis*, etc. (1890) 43 *note*, In the first of these matches, there were.. 159 rests. 1890 *Ibid.* 257 The longest rest on record in a double match.. consisted of no fewer than thirty-eight volleys. 1898 H. F. LAWFORD in W. A. Morgan *'House' on Sport* I. 428, I was told that one rest was eighty-one strokes. 1960 *Times* 18 July 14/4 Warburg.. played six strokes in a fine rest. 1975 *Oxf. Compan. Sports & Games* 826/1 During a 'rest' (the real tennis term for a rally), while the player on the hazard side is trying to make a good chase, his opponent on the service side is in a stronger position.

10. *Med.* A small detached part of an organ, surrounded by tissue of another character; esp. as ***adrenal rest***, a small displaced part of the adrenal cortex.

1892 R. BOYCE *Textbk. Morbid Histol.* viii. 160 In adult life 'rests' are frequently encountered in the lines of old incisions and punctures and are due to excess of repair tissue. *Ibid.* x. 201 Another class of rests represents vestigial structures. 1898 I. N. KELYNACK *Renal Growths* xiv. 132 Growths arising in adrenal 'rests' appear to be sarcomatous in general characters rather than carcinomatous. 1912 *Q. Jrnl. Med.* V. 157 To present new reasons against the hypothesis that renal hypernephromata are derived from adrenal rests. 1928 J. F. BARNHILL *Nose, Throat & Ear* xi. 157 In sarcoma [of the accessory nasal sinuses] congenital 'rests' in the alveoli of the child.. may be assigned as a cause. 1939 T. W. WIDDOWSON *Special or Dental Anat.* (ed. 6) xii. 300 The epithelial cellular bodies, or rests,.. are collections of epithelial cells sometimes seen in the inner portion of the periodontal membrane near to the cementum. 1963 C. L. DEMING in M. F. Campbell *Urology* (ed. 2) II. xxii. 912 Grawitz thought that these tumors came from adrenal rests and termed them hypernephromas.

rest, *sb.*[3] Forms: α. 4- rest, 5-6 reste. β. 4-5 reeste, 5 reest, reyst(e, 6 reist, reast. [Aphetic form of *arest* ARREST *sb.*; cf. REST *v.*[3] In sense 2 = It. *resta*, Pg. *reste*, *riste*, Pg. and Sp. *ristre*.]

†**1.** A means of stopping or checking a horse.

1387 TREVISA *Higden* (Rolls) I. 353 þey dryueþ hir hors wiþ a.. ȝerde.. instede of barnacles and of britels of reest. 1526 SKELTON *Magnyf.* 137 It were a myschefe, yf lyberte lacked a reyne, Where with to rule hym with the wrythyng of a rest.

†**b.** Arrest of persons or goods. *Obs.*

1423 *Coventry Leet Bk.* (E.E.T.S.) 58 Allso it is ordenyd þat noo Constable within the Cite take no syluer for no rest þei make by way off þer office, oþerwais þen þe Law wyll. 1509 HAWES *Past. Pleas.* XL. (Percy Soc.) 203, I obeyed his rest; there was no remedy. *c* 1573 *Durh. Dep.* (Surtees) 258 The reast that one Toppyn had maid of the Egiptiens goods. 1577–87 HOLINSHED *Chron.* III. 916/1 What authoritie haue you to arrest me?.. I will not obeie your rest.

†**c.** Fixed purpose; resolve. *Obs.*

c 1450 *St. Cuthbert* 4975 When morne come, fast þai prest To þe batell, of a reest To take þe chaunce myght fall.

2. In mediæval armour, a contrivance fixed to the right side of the cuirass to receive the butt-end of the lance when couched for the charge, and to prevent it from being driven back upon impact.

In quot. 1697 applied to the butt-end of the lance itself; cf. quot. *a* 1661 in b.

α. 1391 *Earl Derby's Exped.* (Camden) 92 Pro j rest pro domino, vij scot. 1480 *Robt. Devyll* 43 Into the reste he threwe hys speare. *c* 1500 *Melusine* 361 And whan the knight vnderstod this, he sette the spere in the rest. 1540 *Acc. Ld. High Treas. Scot.* VII. 287 Gevin to the Frenche armorar for ..iiij. restis to the justing sadills. 1603 KNOLLES *Hist. Turks* (1621) 517 The Turkish horsemen,.. couching their staves in their rests. 1697 DRYDEN *Æneid* XII. 641 This gripes the lance, and with such vigour shakes, That to the rest the beamy weapon quakes. 1814 SCOTT *Ld. of Isles* VI. xxii, Each ready lance is in the rest. 1859 TENNYSON *Geraint & Enid* 782 A knight.. who laid his lance In rest, and made as if to fall upon him.

β. *c* 1470 HENRY *Wallace* V. 260 A sper in reyst he kest with all his mayne. 1470–85 MALORY *Arthur* VII. xvi. 237 Thenne they putte their speres in their reystes and came to gyders. *c* 1489 CAXTON *Sonnes of Aymon* iii. 107 He broughte his speere in the reeste. 1513 DOUGLAS *Æneis* XI. Prol. 43 This Prince.. sustenit.. Sic strife in stoure so oft with spere in reist. *a* 1586 MONTGOMERIE *Misc. Poems* xli. 45 Stiff speiris in reistis.. Ar brok on thair breistis.

b. *Her.* A charge supposed to represent the above (but also differently named and interpreted).

a 1661 FULLER *Worthies* (1840) I. 328 What usually are termed therein rests, being the handles of spears (most honourable in tilting to break them nearest thereunto) are called by some critics *surflues*. 1727 BRADLEY *Fam. Dict.* s.v. *Clarion*, Guillim takes these Clarions to be a Kind of old-fashion Trumpet; but others think they rather represent the Rudder of a Ship, or, as some say, the Rest for a Lance. 1849 PLANCHÉ in *Jrnl. Archaeol.* IV. 349 On the charge in heraldry, called a 'rest', or 'clarion'. 1868 CUSSANS *Her.* (1893) 121 My own opinion is, that the Rest or Clarion was a rude type of a musical instrument.

†**3.** (See quot.) *Obs. rare*$^{-0}$.

1611 COTGR., *Garde-serre*, the rest of the locke of a Harguebuse.

rest (of a plough): see REEST.

rest, variant of WREST *sb.*

†**rest**, *a. Obs.* Also 5 reest. [Perh. ad. OF. *resté* (see RESTY *a.*), but cf. also Færöese *ræst-ur* in the same sense. The later form is REESED.] Rancid, reasty.

14.. *Med. Rec.* in *Reliq. Ant.* I. 53 For brynnyng with wilde fyre: tak rest bacon, and do hit on a grene hesill styk. *c* 1440 *Promp. Parv.* 431/1 Reest, as flesche.., *rancidus.* 1483 *Cath. Angl.* 304/2 To be Reste, *rancere.*

rest, *v.*[1] Forms: 1 ræstan (hræst-), 3 ræsten, 5 rast; 1 restan, 2–5 resten (*Orm.* resstenn), 5 restyn, 4 resti, 4–6 reste, 4- rest; 6 reast, 9 *Sc.* reist; 5 rist(e, ryst(e, ruste (9 *Sc.* rist). *Pa. t.* 1 ræste, 1–4 reste (5 ryste), 4 rest; also 4 restede, -ide, -yde, 4- rested (4–5 -id, etc.). *Pa. pple.* 3–4 y-, i-rest, 4 rest; 4- rested (4–5 -id, -yd). [OE. *ræstan*, *restan*, = OFris. *resta*, OS. *restian*, OHG. *restan* (MHG. *resten*), related to OHG. *rastôn*, *rastên*, and MDu., MLG. *rusten* (G. *rasten*, Du. *rusten*). For the variation in these forms, and in ME., see the etym. note to REST *sb.*[1]]

I. *intr.* **1. a.** To take repose by lying down, and *esp.* by going to sleep; to lie still or in slumber. Also in later use with adverbs, to have (good or bad) repose.

Beowulf (Z.) 1794 Wolde blondenfeax beddes neosan,.. rofne randwiȝan restan lyste. *c* 950 *Lindisf. Gosp.* Mark xiv. 41 And [he] cuom ðirdda siðe & cuoeð ðæm.. 'slepað ȝee & ræstas'. *c* 1000 *Sax. Leechd.* II. 118 Drince ealles þone drenc þritiȝ nihta,.. þonne þu restan wille. 1340 *Ayenb.* 31 Huanne þe man is zuo heui þat ne loueþ bote to ligge and resti and slepe. *c* 1375 *Sc. Leg. Saints* xxv. (*Julian*) 304 Scho .. lad þame in a bed to reste, & bad þame slepe. *c* 1430 LYDG. *Min. Poems* (Percy Soc.) 35 Whan thou art dead, in thi bed shal he rest. *c* 1450 *Merlin* 138 And so were they departed, and eche yede to his ostell to resten. 1509 HAWES *Past. Pleas.* XXXVIII. (Percy Soc.) 199 La Bell Pucell to a fayre chambre bryght, Dyde me than brynge for to rest all nyght. 1560 DAUS tr. *Sleidane's Comm.* 232 He.. laieth hym downe againe to rest. 1605 SHAKS. *Lear* III. vi. 87 Now good my Lord, lye heere, and rest awhile. 1669 PEPYS *Diary* 23 Mar., Being sleepy, fell soon to rest, and so rested well. 1742 WESLEY *Extr. of Jrnl.* (1749) 24, I ask'd her, How have you rested? 1791 MRS. RADCLIFFE *Rom. Forest* viii, She had not rested well. 1802 *Med. Jrnl.* 324 When he has quietly and well rested, [he hears] worse than after a restless night. 1847 C. BRONTË *J. Eyre* xvi, Too feverish to rest, I rose as soon as day dawned.

b. To lie in death or in the grave.

a 900 *O.E. Martyrol.* 25 Dec. 4 Hyre lichama resteð nu on Romebyriȝ. *c* 962 *O.E. Chron.* (Parker MS.) an. 962, Her forðferde Ælfgar.. & his lic rest on Wiltune. *c* 1205 LAY. 17231 þenne þi lif endeð, þer þu scalt resten. *c* 1225 *Leg. St. Kath.* 2481 Strikeð a stream ut of þet stanene þruh þet ha in resteð. *a* 1300 *Cursor M.* 1079 þe bodi moght he nangat hide, For vnder erth most it not rest. 1387 TREVISA *Higden* (Rolls) VI. 401 Seint Edburgh þat.. resteþ at Wynchestre. 1535 COVERDALE *Ecclus.* xlvii. 23 Thus rested Salomon with his fathers. 1582 STANYHURST *Æneis* I. (Arb.) 21 Wheare lyes strong Hector... Wheare stout Serpedon dooth rest. *a* 1604 HANMER *Chron. Irel.* (1633) 63 He builded Cels and Monasteries, but chiefly at Achadha, where he resteth. 1671 MILTON *Samson* 598, I shall shortly be with them that rest. 1742 GRAY *Spring* 40 Their airy dance They leave, in dust to rest. 1782 MISS BURNEY *Cecilia* v. ix, A set of poor souls you won't let rest in their coffins. 1813 BYRON *Diary* 23 Nov., Why should Junius be dead?.. would he rest in his grave? 1855 KINGSLEY *Westw. Ho!* xxix, Into her merits or demerits I do not enter deeply here. Let her rest in peace.

c. orig. *N. Amer.* Of the body of a dead person: to remain at an undertaker's, a chapel, etc., before burial or cremation. (Usu. as pres. pple.)

1967 'CORIOLIS' *Death, Here is Thy Sting* iii. 54 Remains will be resting at the John Doe Funeral Home. 1968 *Globe & Mail* (Toronto) 13 Jan. 37/5 Resting at Bates and Maddocks Funeral Chapel.. until 12 noon Monday. 1974 *Almonto* (Ontario) *Gaz.* 4 Apr. 4/3 Predeceased by a brother Harold... Rested at the Kerry Funeral Home. 1976 *Liverpool Echo* 22 Nov. 4/4 Funeral service at Anfield Crematorium... Resting at E. H. Roberts.. where flowers may be sent.

2. a. To take repose by intermission of labour or exertion of any kind; to desist or refrain from effort or activity; to become or remain inactive.

c 950 *Lindisf. Gosp.* Mark vi. 31 And [he] cuoeð to him, 'cymes suindrig in woestiȝ styd & restas huon'. *c* 1000 ÆLFRIC *Exod.* xx. 11 On six daȝum god ȝeworhte heofenan and eorðan.., and reste þy seofoðan dæȝe and ȝehalȝode hyne. 1297 R. GLOUC. (Rolls) 3635 Four hondred men ar he reste is owe honde he slou. *c* 1315 SHOREHAM VI. 58 þou ert emaus, þe ryche castel, þar resteþ alle werye: Ine þe restede emanuel. 1387 TREVISA *Higden* (Rolls) I. 125 þere is Iacobus welle, þat Criste reste by. *c* 1400 *Destr. Troy* 5862 He.. Hade laburt so longe, hym list for to rest, And bowet fro the batell. *c* 1475 *Rauf Coilȝear* 404 Vpon Solempnit ȝule day quhen ilk man suld rest. 1568 GRAFTON *Chron.* II. 833 Neuer restyng nor themselues refreshing, except the baityng of their horses. 1610 SHAKS. *Temp.* III. iii. 6, I.. am my selfe attach'd with wearinesse To th' dulling of my spirits: sit downe, and rest. 1671 MILTON *P.R.* II. 292 Thither he bent his way, determin'd there To rest at noon. 1732 POPE *Ess. Man* II. 7 He hangs between; in doubt to act, or rest. 1797 MRS. RADCLIFFE *Italian* i, They rested to recover their breath. 1855 KINGSLEY *Westw. Ho!* xxxiii, Now set me where I can rest among the rocks without fear of falling. 1896 BADEN-POWELL *Matabele Campaign* xv, Our men.. had orders not to let the enemy rest.

Comb. 1843 *Peter Parley's Ann.* IV. 114 They set themselves down upon a rest-and-be-thankful stone to survey the glen. 1894 *Westm. Gaz.* 15 Sept. 3/1 A few who adopt rather too much of the rest-and-be-thankful principle.

b. Of things, in various contextual uses.

Beowulf (Z.) 1858 þæt þam folcum sceal.. sib ȝemænum & sacu restan. *a* 1000 *Andreas* 1576 þa se æðling het stream fare stillan, stormas restan. *c* 1330 *Arth. & Merl.* 8570 (Kölbing), Lete we þis rest, in godes name, & telle forþ.. Hou Merlin doth [etc.]. 1382 WYCLIF *Jer.* xlvii. 6 O! thou swerd of the Lord, hou longe shalt thou not reste? 1388 —— *Exod.* xxiii. 11 Sixe ȝ eer thou shalt sowe thi lond,.. in the seuenthe ȝeer thou schalt leeue it, and schalt make to reste [1535 COVERDALE, let it rest and lye still]. 1414 BRAMPTON *Penit. Ps.* (Percy Soc.) 38 Whan alle the planetys, that turnyn abowte, At the day of dome schul cese and reste. *c* 1450 LOVELICH *Grail* lvi. 37 Now Of this scheld Resteth this Storye. *c* 1500 *Melusine* 338 And here resteth thystorye of them and retourneth to shewe of Raymondyns men. 1603 OWEN *Pembrokeshire* viii. (1892) 60 Barlie.. resteth in the ground not past three dayes but up he starteth. 1667 MILTON *P.L.* VII. 595 The Harp Had work and rested not. 1771 *Encycl. Brit.* III. 333/1 When these parts are not thus doubled, the third and fourth parts rest. 1831 *E. Ross Farm Rep.* 88 in *Lib. Usef. Kn., Husb.* III, The land was allowed 'to rest'—i.e., to remain unploughed for a period of years. 1894 *Westm. Gaz.* 22 June 2/3 The unlucky Oxford-street theatre, after 'resting'—to use the phrase of the profession —.. was reopened last night.

c. With negatives, and followed by *till*.

c 1375 *Sc. Leg. Saints* xxiii. (*Seven Sleepers*) 263þane ferlyt he, & wald nocht ryst til he agane come to þe fyrst. *c* 1420 *Chron. Vilod.* 4737 Y nyl neuer from preynge here-after rast Tylle þey ben forȝeue to herre. *c* 1450 LOVELICH *Merlin* 339 Thou wost neuere resten ne dwelle, Tyl mannes feleschepe ȝe comen vntylle. *a* 1533 LD. BERNERS *Huon* lxiv. 220 He went, & restyd not tyll he cam to Burdeux. 1593 SHAKS. *3 Hen. VI*, I. ii. 32, I cannot rest Vntill the White Rose that I weare, be dy'de [etc.]. *a* 1618 RALEIGH *War* F viij b, They rested not untill they had made the Empire stand headlesse about seaventeene years. 1759 JOHNSON *Rasselas* xxx, I have often heard of the Pyramids, and shall not rest till I have seen them. 1782 MISS BURNEY *Cecilia* VII. i, I hastily set out for Suffolk, and rested not till I arrived at Mrs. Charlton's. 1819 JAS. MORTON in *Leyden's Poetical Remains* 5 He never rested until he had obtained this literary treasure.

d. To cease *from*, to have intermission or cessation †*of*, something.

1382 WYCLIF *Josh.* xi. 23 And the loond restyde fro bateil. 1382 —— *Rev.* xiv. 13 Fro hennus forth now the spirit seith, that thei reste of her trauelis. 1509 HAWES *Past. Pleas.* XXII. (Percy Soc.) 105 The seventh day he restes of hys werke. 1526 TINDALE *Rev.* xiv. 13 They maye rest from their laboures. 1611 BIBLE *Gen.* ii. 2 And he rested on the seuenth day from all his worke. 1667 MILTON *P.L.* VI. 802 Here stand Ye Angels arm'd, this day from Battel rest. 1813 SHELLEY *Q. Mab* IX. 21 The souls.. There rest from the eternity of toil. 1833 TENNYSON *Goose* 16 She.. bless'd herself, and cursed herself, And rested from her labours.

†**e.** To cease *to* do (or doing) something. *Obs.*

1382 WYCLIF *Isa.* i. 16 Resteth to do shreudely, lerneth to do wel. *a* 1425 *Cursor M.* 20803 (Trin.), She resteþ nouþer day ny nyȝt To preye for synfûl mennes pliȝt. 1542 UDALL *Erasm. Apoph.* 296 Leosthenes.. would not rest prouokyng the people to make warre vpon the residue of Grece. 1573 G. HARVEY *Letter-bk.* (Camden) 20 And here I rest to be trubblesum unto you. 1600 HOLLAND *Livy* II. xviii. 56 Such old babes as they.., who neuer rested to sow debate.

f. *Theatr.* Of an actor: to be out of work (temporarily), to be unemployed. Also *transf.* (Usu. as pres. pple.)

1890 B. HALL *Turnover Club* 81 It would commend itself particularly to actors 'resting' for the summer. 1912 GALSWORTHY *Pigeon* I. 24 I am an interpreter... At present I am resting. 1923 A. CHRISTIE *Murder on Links* xxii. 250 They're in the provinces, somewhere, I believe—if they're not resting. 1938 G. HEYER *Blunt Instrument* x. 195 A very nice lady. Stage, but she's resting. 1947 J. SYMONS *Man called Jones* 109 She's in this new thing at the Splendid, and I'm resting. That's show business. 1958 *Times* 22 May 12/6 Ten shillings a week.. used to go a long way with those who, in actors' parlance, were 'resting'. 1967 *Radio Times* 18 May 21 Except for the occasional coffee-bar job while 'resting', Dinsdale has always managed to earn a living from acting. 1976 R. HILL *Another Death in Venice* I. ii. 33 'Are you on holiday?'.. 'Resting, to use a theatrical term. Between jobs.'

g. ***to rest up***: to recover one's strength by resting. orig. *U.S.*

1895 'MARK TWAIN' in *Harper's Mag.* Aug. 458 The other inquisitor could absent himself and rest up from his fatigues when he got worn out. 1911 H. S. HARRISON *Queed* x. 125 She had been remanded in bed for a day or two to rest up. 1922 Z. GREY *To Last Man* xiii. 284 Get rifle and ammunition, bake bread, and rest up before taking again the trail of the rustlers. 1936 J. CURTIS *Gilt Kid* xiii. 131 The best plan would be to.. have something to eat and rest up. 1949 N. STREATFEILD *Painted Garden* xi. 127 She said.. she was going to rest-up; I expect that means bed. 1965 M. SHADBOLT *Among Cinders* xxii. 210 Now it was just a place for shooters and trampers to rest up. 1972 J. BLACKBURN *For Fear of Little Men* xi. 116 Adder bites are unpleasant things. .. I advised the fool to rest up a bit longer. 1974 *Times Lit. Suppl.* 1 Feb. 97/1 Attila is resting up in Hungvar, exacting 'hospitality' from the German peoples.

3. a. To be at ease or in quiet; also (of persons or things), to continue without change or removal; to stay, remain, lie, have place or station.

971 *Blickl. Hom.* 159 Eadiȝe beoþ þearfena gastas & hie restaþ on heofena rice. *c* 1000 *Ags. Gosp.* Luke x. 6 Ȝyf þar beoð sybbe bearn, reste þar eower sib. *c* 1200 ORMIN 13025 Swa þatt me þinnkeþþ god inn hemm To biggenn & to

resstenn. *a* **1225** *St. Marher.* 6 Mi sawle schal resten mit te rihtwise. *a* **1300** *Cursor M.* 23652 Iesu crist..giue vs grace sua here to do, þat wit his we mai rest in ro. **1362** LANGL. *P. Pl.* A. IV. 95 Bote Reson haue reuþe of him, he resteþ in þe stokkes Also longe as I lyue. *c* **1400** MAUNDEV. (Roxb.) iv. 12 Sum saise þat he dyed noȝt, bot þat he restez þare to þe day of dome. **1477** EARL RIVERS (Caxton) *Dictes* 15 Ypocras rested in the Ile of Than. **1500–20** DUNBAR *Poems* lxxxviii. 13 Prynncesse of townes,..A richer restith under no Christen roy. *a* **1548** HALL *Chron., Hen. VI*, 160 b, That the citezens hearing where the place of the ieopardye rested, might occurre their enemies. **1593** SHAKS. *Rich. II*, V. i. 5 This way the King will come:..Here let vs rest. **1611** BIBLE *Josh.* iii. 13 Assoone as the soles of the feete of the Priestes..shall rest in the waters of Iordan. **1620** T. GRANGER *Div. Logike* 111 A stone neither mooueth nor resteth. **1658** R. NEWCOURT *Title to Map of London*, Under ye Roman Regencie then rested this Citie & Kingdome by ye space of neere 490 yeares. **1740** PITT *Æneid* x. 1183 The wretched father (father now no more!) In sullen sorrow rested on the shore. **1782** MISS BURNEY *Cecilia* IX. iii, O, then,..it is not on the side of the young woman that the difficulty seems to rest? **1838** TREVELYAN in *Macaulay* (1876) II. i. 5 Mr. Wallace did not choose to rest quietly under a castigation in excess of his deserts.

†**b.** In phr. ***rest you merry, fair, happy.*** (Cf. 7 b and 8 c, to which this may properly belong.)

1548 ELYOT, *Aue*, bee thou gladde: or ioyfull, as the vulgare people saie Reste you mery. **1592** SHAKS. *Rom. & Jul.* I. ii. 86 Rest you merry. **1596** —— *Merch. V.* I. iii. 60 Rest you faire good signior, Your worship was the last man in our mouthes. **1606** —— *Ant. & Cl.* I. i. 62 But I will hope of better deeds to morrow. Rest you happy.

c. To stop or cease at a certain point and remain otherwise inoperative or inactive. *to let ..rest*, to pursue or prosecute no further.

1577 HANMER *Anc. Eccles. Hist.* (1619) 392 Neither rested he with this, but destroyed, as much as [etc.]. **1591** SHAKS. *1 Hen. VI*, IV. i. 121 Nay, let it [the quarrel] rest where it began at first. **1633** BP. HALL *Hard Texts, O.T.* 548, I will send a destruction upon the house of Hazael..wᶜʰ shall not rest in his person, but [etc.]. **1706** STANHOPE *Paraphr.* III. 196 Charity..must never rest in the thoughts and Affections of the Soul. But how shall it exert itself in becoming Words and Actions? **1750** JOHNSON *Rambler* No. 19 ¶ 15 So much remains in the power of others, that reason is forced at last to rest in neutrality. **1782** MISS BURNEY *Cecilia* x. ii, She considered, however, that the matter could not rest here. **1862** MISS BRADDON *Lady Audley* xxii, If I could let the matter rest.., I would do it.

d. To be at peace; to have quiet of mind.

1782 MISS BURNEY *Cecilia* VI. ii, Cecilia had now but little leisure, for Lady Honoria would hardly rest a moment away from her. *Ibid.* IX. i, I could not rest till I had the honour of assuring you [etc.]. **1803** tr. *P. Le Brun's Mons. Botte* I. 23 Mr. Horeau, without whom he could not rest long together.

4. a. To have place or position, to settle, lie, be diffused, etc., *on* or *upon* some person or thing.

c **1000** ÆLFRIC *Numb.* xi. 25 Þa se gast ȝereste on him, hiȝ witegodon and siððan ne ȝeswicon. *c* **1200** *Trin. Coll. Hom.* 217 Uppe þare blosme [sal] resten þe holie gost. **1382** WYCLIF *Isa.* xi. 2 Ther shal resten vp on hym the Spirit of the Lord. *c* **1400** LOVE *Bonavent. Mirr.* (B.N.C. MS.) lf. 15 b, For bot marie had ben meke þe holy gost had not rested vppon hir. **1535** COVERDALE *Ecclus.* xliv. 23 Couenaunt dyd he stablysh with Isaac, and made it to rest vpon the heade of Iacob. **1611** BIBLE *Ecclus.* v. 6 Mercy and wrath come from him, and his indignation resteth vpon sinners. **1711** ADDISON *Spect.* No. 128 ¶ 4 The Man and the Woman are joined together for Life, and the main Burden rests upon the former. **1782** MISS BURNEY *Cecilia* IX. ii, That attack rested upon her mind, in defiance of all her endeavours to banish it. **1819** SHELLEY *Cenci* V. iii, How gently slumber rests upon her face. **1862** MISS BRADDON *Lady Audley* xxix, His pale face, haggard under the deepening shadow that had rested upon it so long.

b. Of material objects supported by something.

1611 BIBLE *1 Kings* vi. 10 Then hee built chambers..: and they rested on the house with timber of Cedar. **1687** A. LOVELL tr. *Thevenot's Trav.* I. 125 This stone rests upon a marble-Pillar. **1798** COLERIDGE *Anc. Mar.* III. vi, Almost upon the western wave Rested the broad bright sun. **1819** SCOTT *Ivanhoe* xvii, The roof..rested upon four concentric arches. **1857** HENFREY *Bot.* §40 The stem of such plants rests upon some foreign body, such as the branch of a tree.

c. Of the eyes in relation to the object looked at.

1813 *Sketches of Character* (ed. 2) I. 104 Her eyes resting on a lace cap she had been making. **1847** C. BRONTË *J. Eyre* x, My eye passed all other objects to rest on those most remote, the blue peaks.

d. Of a wing or division of an army.

1844 H. H. WILSON *Brit. India* II. 238 Their left resting on the hills, their right on the Residency.

e. To lie as a charge or stigma *on* one.

1678 *Hatton Corr.* (Camden) 162 It shall not rest upon him if I be not made a brigadeere. **1814** SCOTT *Ld. of Isles* III. xviii, Enough of blood rests on my head.

5. a. To lie or lean *on, upon,* or *against* a person or thing to obtain repose or support. †Also said of Christ hanging on the cross.

1382 WYCLIF *John* xxi. 20 Thilke disciple..which restide in the souper on his brest. *c* **1425** *Cast. Persev.* 2452 Þat Lord þat restyd on þe rode is maker of an ende.

1782 MISS BURNEY *Cecilia* VII. vii, 'Oh then rest on me!' cried he, still holding her; 'rest but upon me till the ceremony is over!' **1802** JAMES *Mil. Dict.* s.v., The soldiers, belonging to the firing party, rest upon the butt ends of their firelocks. **1818** SCOTT *Hrt. Midl.* xxix, In a half-sitting posture, with her back resting against the door of the hovel. **1862** MISS BRADDON *Lady Audley* xxx, With her little hand resting lightly upon the opposite post.

b. To rely *on* or *upon*, to trust *to*, some thing or person.

1382 WYCLF *Isa.* vii. 2 Siria restede vp on Effraym. **1526** *Pilgr. Perf.* (W. de W. 1531) 35 b, To..set at nought the counseyle of other, & to lene & rest all togyder to thyne own reason. **1583** STOCKER *Civ. Warres Lowe C.* I. 20 One Magistrate..upon whose fidelitye your Excellencie may rest. **1617** MORYSON *Itin.* I. 141 I rested much vpon the Cardinals promise. **1633** T. ADAMS *Exp. 2 Peter* ii. 9 If he covenant with us, 'I will be your God'; we must restipulate, 'Then will we rest upon thee'. **1856** F. E. PAGET *Owlet of Owlst.* 150 Each rests a good deal on the greatness of her own connexions.

c. To depend *upon*, to be based or founded *on*, something.

1530 PALSGR. *Introd.* 26 The chefest poynt..resteth upon the knowledge of the gendre and nombre of the substantyve. *a* **1704** LOCKE (J.), Sometimes it rests upon testimony. **1782** MISS BURNEY *Cecilia* III. iv, All his hopes now rested upon one friend and patron. **1821** SCOTT *Kenilw.* vii, Thus establishing in him an interest resting both on present and past services. **1849** MACAULAY *Hist. Eng.* v. I. 662 The case against him rested wholly on the evidence of Rumsey and Goodenough. **1884** F. TEMPLE *Relat. Relig. & Sci.* ii. (1885) 63 Science rests on phenomena observed by the senses.

d. To dwell *upon* (a word); to settle or decide *on* (a person). *rare.*

1530 PALSGR. *Introd.* 15 Thirdly to gyve every worde that they abyde and reste upon, theyr most audible sounde. **1700** DRYDEN *Sigismonda & G.* 469 On him I rested after long debate, And not without considering fixed my fate.

6. a. To remain confident or hopeful, to put trust, *in* something.

c **1380** WYCLIF *Sel. Wks.* III. 363 In o bileve men resten, þat day shal come of þe laste jugement. **1387** TREVISA *Higden* (Rolls) VII. 163 In whos counseilles þe kyng hym self..so moche rested [L. *adquievit*]. **1560** DAUS tr. *Sleidane's Comm.* 62 Committyng my cause into Goddes handes, I rested wholy in his protection. **1621** BURTON *Anat. Mel.* I. ii. III. xv. (1651) 134 These men fail as often as they rest in their projects, and are as usually frustrate of their hopes. **1675** TRAHERNE *Chr. Ethics* 50 Rest not in the helps and remedies that it [religion] bringeth. **1781** BURNS *Winter* iii, Here, firm, I rest, they must be best, Because they are Thy Will! **1859** TENNYSON *Geraint & Enid* 973 Nor did he doubt her more, But rested in her fealty. **1870** J. H. NEWMAN *Gram. Assent* II. viii. 307 We must patiently rest in the thought of the Eternal, Omnipresent, and All-knowing.

†**b.** To be vested *in* a person. *Obs.*

1483 *Rolls of Parlt.* VI. 247/2 That the right and tytle..of and in all suche Londs..be and rest in every of the said Wyfes. **1577** HARRISON *England* II. ii. (1877) I. 64 The gift of this prelacie resteth in the earles of Darbie. *a* **1645** HABINGTON *Surv. Worcs.* (Worcs. Hist. Soc.) I. II. 168 Cofton Haket came..to Mr. Skinner, in whose family nowe it restethe.

†**c.** To lie or consist *in* something. *Obs.*

1513 T. MORE in Grafton *Chron.* (1568) II. 760 Yee see their youth, of which I rekon the onely suretie to rest in your concord. **1530** PALSGR. *Introd.* 15 The diffyculte of the frenche tong..resteth chefely in thre thynges. **1551** ROBINSON tr. *More's Utop.* II. (1895) 188 Pleasure, wherin they determine other all or the chiefyste parte of mans felycytye to reste. **1602** *Narcissus* (1893) 2 Heerin the matter rests.

d. To lie *in* or remain *with* one, as something to be accomplished or determined.

1593 SHAKS. *3 Hen. VI*, III. ii. 45 What you command, that rests in me to doe. **1601** DANIEL *Civ. Wars* VI. lxxiv, It restes within your iudgmentes to vpright, Or els to ruine vtterly the land. **1603** SHAKS. *Meas. for M.* I. iii. 32 It rested in your Grace To vnloose this tyde-vp Iustice.

1819 SHELLEY *Cenci* IV. ii. 37 As to the how this act Be warranted, it rests with you. **1867** RUSKIN *Time & Tide* §98 Always to think of things as they truly are..as far as in us rests. And it does rest much in our power. **1874** GREEN *Short Hist.* vi. §5. 317 The whole direction of home and foreign affairs rested with Wolsey alone.

II. *refl.* **7. a.** To give (oneself) rest or repose.

In early use with simple reflexive pronoun; in later use usually with *self*.

c **890** *Laws K. Ælfred* in Schmid *Gesetze* (1898) 26 Wyrceað eow vi daȝas, & on þam siofoðan restað eow. **971** *Blickl. Hom.* 227 Þonne he reste hine, þonne wæs his seo æþeleste ræst..on nacodre eorðan. *c* **1175** *Lamb. Hom.* 47 Þet oðer mihte is on heouene, for-þi þa engles heom rested mare þenn on sum oðer dei. *c* **1220** *Bestiary* 241 Ðe mire..renneð rapelike, and resteð hire seldum. *c* **1250** *Gen. & Exod.* 1369 At a welle wið-uten ðe tun..Ðor he wulde him resten. *c* **1350** *Will. Palerne* 2801 Go we on oure gate..to recuuer sum resset, þere we vs rest miȝt. *c* **1400** MAUNDEV. (Roxb.) ix. 36 Whare oure Lady restid hir when scho was delyuer of hir childe. *c* **1440** *Alph. Tales* 360 'If you like ye may go vnto your bed and riste you.' And so he did. **1530** PALSGR. 688/2 You may rest you here a while in this wyndowe. **1591** SHAKS. *1 Hen. VI*, II. v. 2 Kind Keepers.., Let dying Mortimer here rest himselfe. **1610** —— *Temp.* III. i. 18 Pray set it downe, and rest you. **1662** J. DAVIES tr. *Olearius' Voy. Ambass.* 205 We rested our selves upon the Rock. **1716** LADY M. W. MONTAGU *Let. to C'tess Mar* 21 Nov., I was very glad to stay there a day to rest myself. **1782** MISS BURNEY *Cecilia* I. vi, He then begged him to be seated, to rest himself. **1847** C. BRONTË *J. Eyre* xxi, Will you rest yourself here an hour, Miss? *Ibid.* xxvii, When I got there I was forced to sit to rest me under the hedge.

fig. *c* **1200** ORMIN 9598 Clene þohht iss Godess bedd, & tære he wile himm resstenn. *a* **1310** in Wright *Lyric P.* xvi. 52 He that reste him on the rode.

transf. *c* **1425** *Found. St. Bartholomew's* (E.E.T.S.) 53 The trowblys tempestuous wyndis vttirly rested them.

b. With adjectival (†or adverbial) complement.

a **1400** *Floriz & Bl.* (E.E.T.S.) 85 And so him sede child floriz, 'Rest þe murie, sire daris'. *c* **1420** *Chron. Vilod.* 485 By hym come an olde hore mone And sayde: 'syr kyng, rest ȝov wylle!' **1610** SHAKS. *Temp.* V. i. 144, I haue her soueraigne aid, And rest myselfe content. **1633** BP. HALL *Hard Texts, O.T.* 324 He that believes shall rest himselfe contented with this alsufficient meanes. **1813** SHELLEY *Q. Mab* VI. 26 Oh! rest thee tranquil; chase those fearful doubts. **1833** TENNYSON *Œnone* 156 Oh! rest thee sure That I shall love thee well and cleave to thee.

†**c.** To rely *upon*. (Cf. 5 b.) *Obs. rare.*

1611 BIBLE *2 Chron.* xxxii. 8 The people rested themselues vpon the words of Hezekiah king of Iudah. **1633** BP. HALL *Hard Texts, O.T.* 295 As this people have not rested themselves upon the Gracious promise of Gods protection.

III. *trans.* **8. a.** To give (one) rest or repose; to relieve or refresh by rest; to lay to rest. Also const. *up*. Cf. sense 2 g.

Quots. 1975 and 1976 are both *U.S. slang*.

c **1205** LAY. 17229 Þu seolf scalt þer in þine ban resten. *a* **1300** *Cursor M.* 2733 Quen þai war rest wel, vp-ras þai. *c* **1330** *Arth. & Merl.* 7482 (Kölbing), Doun of her destrers þai liȝten, Her stedes to rest, her armes riȝten. **1495** *Trevisa's De P.R.* (W. de W.) v. xxvi. 135 Somtyme the sholders ben greuyd..and thenne they ben curyd and restyd. *a* **1586** SIDNEY *Ps.* XXIII. i, He rests me in greene pasture. **1594** SHAKS. *Rich. III*, IV. iv. 33 Then would I hide my bones, not rest them heere. **1662** J. DAVIES tr. *Mandelslo's Trav.* 8 So that I had the convenience of resting my back. **1697** DRYDEN *Æneid* I. 236 A grot is form'd beneath, with mossy seats, To rest the Nereïds. **1781** COWPER *Retirem.* 451 He..seeks a more convenient friend,..On whom he rests well-pleas'd his weary pow'rs. **1830** SCOTT *Auchindrane* II. i, The grim sexton..Made him the bed which rests his head for ever. **1855** LYNCH *Rivulet* VI. i, It rests us to look on their calm. **1872** HOLMES *Poet Breakf.-t.* ii, Wears goggles very commonly; says it rests his eyes. **1896** BADEN-POWELL *Matabele Campaign* xiii, I told Poore to rest the men and horses, while..I went on ahead. **1974** 'J. LE CARRÉ' *Tinker, Tailor* xxviii. 241 They're resting you up for a season. **1975** L. DILLS *CB Slanguage Dict.* 50 *Rest 'em up place*, rest area (SE). **1976** LIEBERMAN & RHODES *Compl. CB Handbk.* vi. 157 Hey, we just spotted a smokey at that rest'em up area.

absol. **1400** *Pol., Rel., & Love Poems* (1866) 31 Hit resteþ and hit quemeþ.

b. In phr. (*God* or *heaven*) ***rest his soul, him,*** etc. Now *arch.*

c **1412** HOCCLEVE *De Reg. Princ.* 2107 O maister, maister, god þi soule reste! **1596** SHAKS. *Merch. V*, II. ii. 75 Is my boy, God rest his soule, aliue or dead? **1605** —— *Macb.* IV. iii. 227 Not for their owne demerits..Fell slaughter on their soules: Heauen rest them now. **1775** S. J. PRATT *Liberal Opin.* cxxxiii. (1783) IV. 203 They are a set of fellows who are not worth a resurrection, and therefore God rest 'em and rot 'em for us. **1805** SCOTT *Last Minstr.* I. Introd. 50 And he began to talk anon..of Earl Walter, rest him, God! **1818** —— *Br. Lamm.* xxi, Fill a brimmer of my auld auntie's claret, rest her heart! **1875** TENNYSON *Q. Mary* I. v, My good mother came (God rest her soul) Of Spain.

†**c.** ***God rest you merry*** (cf. 3 b and 7 b). *Obs.*

1568 FULWEL *Like will to Like* Hazl. Dodsley (1874) III. 342 God rest you merry both, and God be your guide. **1600** SHAKS. *A.Y.L.* V. i. 65 God rest you merry, sir.

d. To allow (a thing) to rest; to permit to remain undisturbed, quiescent, or inactive.

1580 BLUNDEVIL *Horsemanship* v. vii. 5 The water of an Oxe, that hath beene rested a certaine time. **1592** SHAKS. *Rom. & Jul.* II. iv. 22 He fights as you sing pricksong,..he rests his minum, one, two, and the third in your bosom. **1737** WATERLAND *Eucharist* 33 A learned..Writer..has with great appearance of Probability brought it down to A.D. 96: And there I am willing to rest it. **1763** MILLS *Pract. Husb.* II. 18 Instead of resting, or fallowing, a whole field,.. the fallow here is..interposed by means of alleys, which are the part rested. **1860** READE *Cloister & H.* xxxvii, He had never budged nor even rested his knife at all this fracas. **1892** *Illustr. Lond. News* 21 May 615/1, I doubt if it is wise to 'rest' a fish that has missed a fly.

e. To hold (weapons) in an easy position. Also *transf.* of a commander of troops.

1682 *Lond. Gaz.* No. 1684/1 Both sides of the Bridge.. being Lined with Grenadiers with their Muskets rested. **1706** *Ibid.* No. 4253/2 A Company of Her Majesty's Foot-Guards.., who rested their Arms as the Ambassador pass'd by. **1770** LANGHORNE *Plutarch* (1879) I. 577/1 As Nicias was drawing up against him, Gylippus rested his arms, and sent a herald. **1802** JAMES *Mil. Dict.*, *To Rest arms*, to bring the firelock to the same position as in present arms.

f. *Sc.* To make up (a fire) for the night.

a **1774** [see RESTED *ppl. a.*]. **1845** STILL *Cottar's Sunday* 145 There's nocht ado but bar the door An' rest the fire. **1881** GREGOR *Folk-lore* 160 The last thing done on the last day of the year was to 'rist' the fire, that is, cover up the live coals with the ashes.

g. *U.S.* To bring the presentation of evidence pertinent to (a law case) to a close voluntarily.

1905 S. W. MITCHELL *Constance Trescot* xiv. 183 All the evidence for the plaintiffs was before the court, and Greyhurst sat down, stating that the plaintiff rested the case. **1950** *Chicago Tribune* 23 Jan. 1/8 Defense attorneys.. elected to rest their case without calling a single witness. **1953** E. S. GARDNER *Case of Hesitant Hostess* xiv. 234 The prosecution objects. The prosecution has rested its case. **1972** *N.Y. Law Jrnl.* 14 Nov. 19/5 Plaintiff had not been cross-examined and certainly had not rested his case.

9. a. To lay (the head, etc.) *on* or *upon* something for support.

a **1225** *Ancr. R.* 260 Seoðen..nefde he hwar he muhte resten his heaued. *a* **1300–1400** *Cursor M.* 16762 + 113 Man son has nothing apon his hed to rest. *c* **1375** *Sc. Leg. Saints* xiii. (*Mark*) 84 Restand his hed one cristis kne. **1590** SHAKS. *Mids. N.* II. ii. 40 Finde you out a bed, For I vpon this banke will rest my head. *a* **1659** WALLER *Panegyric Cromwell* xlii, England now does..Her weary head upon your bosom rest. **1750** GRAY *Elegy* 117 Here rests his head upon the lap of Earth, A Youth. **1782** MISS BURNEY *Cecilia* IV. ii, He rested one arm upon the table. **1835** URE *Philos. Manuf.* 350 Resting their hands on the lay or shuttle-bearer. **1847** C. BRONTË *J. Eyre* xxviii, A large old pointer dog rested its massive head on the knee of one girl.

fig. *c* **1374** CHAUCER *Troylus* II. 1326 Sumwhat he byheld On which him þoughte, he myghte his herte reste.

b. To place, lay, or set (a thing) *upon* something to support it or keep it in position.

1422 in *Surtees Misc.* (1890) 17 Hafe rowme and space.. to ryste hys tymbre apon. **1660** *Guillim's Heraldry* IV. xiii. (ed. 4) 328 A thing whereon to rest their Lances. **1680**

MOXON *Mech. Exerc.* x. 180 Its office is to rest the Tool upon, that it may lie in a steddy position while the Work-man uses it. **1776** G. SEMPLE *Building in Water* 50 On those set-off's stretch your Plates, and on them rest your Spur-braces. **1793** SMEATON *Edystone L.* §299 Its ground-sill was rested upon a bed of lead. **1855** KINGSLEY *Westw. Ho!* xxiv, Amyas rested the point of his sword on the ground, and his hands upon the hilt.

c. To throw (some weight) *on* a thing.

1809 ROLAND *Fencing* 5 You will thereby possess more freedom..than if you had rested your body mostly on the right [foot]. **1872** HOLMES *Poet Breakf.-t.* vi, I try the ground to find out whether it is firm or not before I rest my weight on it.

d. To make or allow to depend *on* something.

1732 POPE *Hor. Sat.* II. i. 141 This is my plea, on this I rest my cause. **1793** SMEATON *Edystone L.* §255 It was determined not to rest the matter solely upon the efforts of our seamen. **1832** LEWIS *Use & Ab. Pol. Terms* vi. 56 The point on which he intended to rest the distinction. **1885** *Law Times* LXXX. 136/2 The plaintiff in her statement of claim ..rested her case on equitable grounds.

10. To place or settle *in* something.

c **1375** *Cursor M.* 23948 (Fairf.), Bot þat in hertis rote is rest, nede ways out mote hit brest. **1390** GOWER *Conf.* III. 184 So that in reste Mihte every man his herte reste. *a* **1586** SIDNEY *Ps.* II, They that in him their only trust do rest, O, they be rightly blest! **1591** SHAKS. *1 Hen. VI*, I. i. 44 Cease, cease these Iarres, & rest your minds in peace. **1818** SCOTT *Hrt. Midl.* i, The hereditary jurisdictions, which..rested the investigation of crimes in judges, ignorant, partial, or interested. **1858** BUSHNELL *Serm. New Life* 22 You are called to have a will perfectly harmonized with God's and rested in his.

rest, *v.*[2] [ad. F. *rester* (12th c.), = Sp. and Pg. *restar*, It. *restare, ristare*:—L. *restāre*, f. *re-* RE-behind + *stāre* to stand. Hence also Du. and G. *resten*, Da. *reste*.]

1. *intr.* †**a.** To remain due or unpaid. *Obs.* (Chiefly *Sc.* and in pres. pple.)

1463 *Exch. Rolls Scot.* VII. 165 *note*, Certane soumes of moneye restande upon oure lovete familiar clerk..that time that he was oure chaumerlane. **1590** in *Antiquary* XXXII. 118 [Received] in part..*xs.*; restes, *xxs. iiijd.* **1600** *Act Sederunt* 20 June, That..his Hienes may see the said Erle satisfeit of the saidis superexpensis, restane be his Majestie to his said umquhill father. **1640–1** *Kirkcudbr. War-Comm. Min. Bk.* (1855) 31 Being requirit to put out the troupe horss restand by that paroche, [he] refuissit to doe the samyn. **1698** *Acts Parl. Scot.* (1814) X. 152 Resolved that they will be carefull to have the forsaid arrears and debts payed in so far as they are still resting. *a* **1781** WATSON *Philip III*, III. (1793) I. 273 Considerable arrears being now resting to the soldiers.

†**b.** To remain or be left over, after subtraction, diminution, etc. *Obs.*

1530 PALSGR. 688/2 Al that resteth, take it for your selfe. **1542** RECORDE *Gr. Artes* 128 b, Then take I 100 twyse from 300, and there resteth 100. **1585** T. WASHINGTON tr. *Nicholay's Voy.* II. xx. 57 b, If the moneye..for the poore is not there bestowed, the almes masters do send y^t which resteth into the hospitals of the Leapers. **1647** LILLY *Chr. Astrol.* v. 43 Substract 20 degr. 54 min. from 30 degr..., and there rest 9 degr. 6 min. **1700** DRYDEN *Ceyx & Alc.* 96 By this the Vessel half her Course had run, And as much rested till the rising Sun.

c. To remain, be left, still undestroyed or unremoved. Now *rare.*

1495 *Rolls of Parlt.* VI. 460/1 As by their severall Grauntes resting of Record more pleynly apperith. **1535** STEWART *Cron. Scot.* II. 261 Ane castell callit Doun-bervie, Quhairof the fundament restis ȝit to se. **1596** DALRYMPLE tr. *Leslie's Hist. Scot.* I. 29 In quhilke onlie..war the quhyte kye fund, of quhilkes now restes verie few, or nane. **1602** MARSTON *Ant. & Mel.* III. Wks. 1856 I. 32 Alas, what country rests, What sonne, what comfort that she can deprive? **1711** PRIOR *Henry & Emma* 670 What rests of both, one sepulchre shall hold. **1717** POPE *Iliad* IX. 480 My beauteous captives thither I'll convey, And all that rests of my unravish'd prey. **1814** SCOTT *Ld. of Isles* I. xx, For if a hope of safety rest, 'Tis on the sacred name of guest. **1867** INGELOW *Story of Doom* III. 271 A helm for covering of the scars That seamed what rested of a goodly face.

2. With complement. To remain or be left in a specified condition.

Sometimes approximating in sense to REST *v.*[1]

1472–5 *Rolls of Parlt.* VI. 159/2 For every moneth..that the same defaute resteth and abideth uncorrected. **1488** *Naval Acc. Hen. VII* (1896) 81 The said William Comersall restith accomptable to the Kyng. **1545** *Reg. Privy Council Scot.* I. 6 Quhat is payt thairof and quhat restis unpayt. **1590** GREENE *Orl. Fur.* Wks. (Rtldg.) 92 As one that's neuter.. And covets to rest equal friend to both. **1611** in Picton *L'pool Munic. Rec.* (1883) I. 157 And so rested due unto him xiv^li. **1697** DRYDEN *Virg. Past.* III. 169 Both have won, or both deserv'd the Prize. Rest equal happy both. **1784** COWPER *Task* III. 217 Neither can I rest A silent witness of the headlong rage. **1849** M. ARNOLD '*In Harmony with Nature*' 14 Fool, if thou canst not pass her, rest her slave. **1862** MISS BRADDON *Lady Audley* xxi, To let his son's fate rest a dark and cruel mystery.

b. With *assured, satisfied*, etc.

1601 SHAKS. *Jul. C.* v. iii. 17 That I may rest assur'd Whether yond Troopes, are Friend or Enemy. **1697** DRYDEN *Æneid* x. 1239 After such a lord, I rest secure, Thou wilt no foreign reins, or Trojan lord, endure. **1782** MISS BURNEY *Cecilia* I. xi, The account..determined her not to rest satisfied till she saw them [*sc.* injuries] redressed. **1872** J. L. SANFORD *Estimates Eng. Kings* 394 His mind was much too active and powerful to rest satisfied. **1875** JOWETT *Plato* (ed. 2) I. 37 To rest assured that the more wise and temperate you are, the happier you will be.

c. In valedictory formulæ. Now *arch.*

1580 LYLY *Euphues* (Arb.) 361 Thus..resting thy friend if thou rest thy sute, I ende. **1590** SIR H. LEE in *Archæologia* LI. 172 So I umbly take my leve,..restyng to serve you as your Lordshipe hathe moste bounde me. **1613** SHAKS. *Hen. VIII*, v. i. 55 Many good nights, my Lord, I rest your seruant. **1660–1** MARVELL *Corr.* Wks. (Grosart) II. 50, I shall giue you a larger trouble; in the mean time resting Your most affectionate [etc.]. **1765** STERNE *Tr. Shandy* VIII. xxxiv, I rest thy affectionate brother, Walter Shandy. **1818** SCOTT *Hrt. Midl.* xlviii, I rest your affectionate sister, E. **1826** —— *Woodst.* xxvii, I kiss your hand, sir, and rest yours, under a sense of obligation.

d. To owe (something). Chiefly *Sc.* ? *Obs.*

[**1474** *Acc. Ld. High Treas.* I. 12, xxxiiij*li.* resauit...he restis awand lij *li.* vi *s.* viij *d.*] **1586** in *Antiquary* XXXII. 76 Hew chamier restes for wares, xvj*s.* ij*d.* Barbarie beane restes for wares, iij*s.* **1666** in Peterkin *Notes Orkn. & Zetl.* (1822) I. 189 The sheriffdom of Orkney and Zetland were.. resting 22 months mentenance. **1773** FERGUSSON *Poems* (1785) 225 I'm restin' you a pint o' yale. **1787** BEATTIE *Scoticisms* 77 He rests me nothing. **1808** JAMIESON s.v., *What am I restand you?* How much do I owe you?

†**3. a.** To remain to be done. *Obs.*

1490 CAXTON *Eneydos* lviii. 156 The conuenauntes were deuysed and made and theyre rested nothynge but for to goo bothe togyder. **1563** B. GOOGE *Eglogs*, etc. (Arb.) 79 What resteth now? but onely God to prayse. *c* **1586** C'TESS PEMBROKE *Ps.* CXIX. i, This now resteth that I learne..Good from evill to discerne. *a* **1618** RALEIGH *Introd. Brev. Hist. Eng.* (1693) 50 Now there rested nothing..but only the Suppression of Malcolm King of Scots. **1667** MILTON *P.L.* x. 48 Now What rests, but that the mortal Sentence pass On his transgression?

†**b.** To remain to be dealt with. *Obs.*

1577 tr. *Bullinger's Decades* (1592) 84 Those things which rest to be spoken of ye Catholike Church of God. **1605** BACON *Adv. Learn.* II. viii. §6 Thus have we now dealt with two of the three beams of man's knowledge... There resteth *radius reflexus*. **1636** MELLIS *Recorde's Gr. Artes* 256 Now resteth the proofs of Multiplication, and also Diuision.

†**c.** *it rests* (*to* or *that*). *Obs.*

1591 *Troub. Raigne K. John* (1611) 61 It resteth we throughout our territories Be reproclaimed and inuested King. **1615** MARKHAM *Country Contentm.* I. x, It now resteth that we speak of other necessary implements. **1620–55** I. JONES *Stone-Heng* (1725) 43 It rests now, to endeavour the discovering by whom Stone-Heng [was] built. **1700** DRYDEN *Cymon & Iph.* 427 It rested to dismiss the downward weight Or raise him upward to his former height.

†**d.** (*there*) *rests* (*to* or *that*). *Obs.*

1530 PALSGR. 21 Nowe..resteth to shewe..howe they sounde theyr consonantes. **1547** J. HARRISON *Exhort. Scottes* D vij b, There restethe to disproue the fayned alligacions of the contrary part. **1563** *Homilies* II. (1859) 426 Now resteth to shew unto you [etc.]. **1625** BACON *Ess., Of Ambition*, There resteth to speake, how they are to be brideled. **1683** W. PENN in R. Burton *Eng. Emp. Amer.* (1685) 121 There rests, that I speak of the Condition we are in.

rest, *v.*[3] Now *dial.* Also 5 reste, 9 'rest, *Sc.* 'reest, reest, reist. [Aphetic form of *arest* ARREST *v.* In sense 4 perh. a. OF. *rester*.]

1. *trans.* To stop, check, arrest. *Obs. rare.*

c **1440** *York Myst.* xlvi. 31 Ther rancoure was raised, no renke might it reste. *c* **1471** *Pol. Poems* (Rolls) II. 278 God restid thayre malice, the wille of hym was soo.

2. To arrest or apprehend (a person).

c **1470** GREGORY *Chron.* in *Hist. Coll. Citizen Lond.* (Camden) 158 Thenne he sende for the Mayre of London and hys aldermen. And there he restyde many worthy men of the cytte. **1514** BARCLAY *Cyt. & Uplondyshm.* D iv b, Some rest men giltlesse, and cast them in prison. **1590** SHAKS. *Com. Err.* IV. iv. 3 Ile give thee..so much mony To warrant thee as I am rested for. **1622** ROWLANDS *Good Newes & Bad* (Hunterian Cl.) 26 They'le salute you with a frightfull phrase As, Gentleman, at such a suit I rest you. **1900** N. LLOYD *Chronic Loafer* 178 I was 'rested—'rested, mind ye, fer the murder o' Noah Punk.

3. To arrest or seize (goods). Chiefly *Sc.*

1565 *Satir. Poems Reform.* I. 90, I rested there goodes and disposed there landes. *c* **1573** *Durh. Dep.* (Surtees Soc.) 259 Such geir as he had restyd of the Egipcians concerning the corsinge of a horse. **1821** GALT *Ann. Parish* viii, The coal-carts from the Douray moor were often reested in the middle of the causey. **1868** J. SALMON *Gowodean* I. ii, The chiel that gaed to 'reest his guids for debt.

†**4.** *intr.* To stop; to come to a decision. *Obs.*

c **1500** *Melusine* 356 And it came to an article where he vnderstod that xs. were payed euery yere..he anone rested there and asked [etc.]. **1530** PALSGR. 689/1, I rest, or conclude, or byde upon a thyng, *Je me arreste*.

†**5.** *trans.* To lay (a lance) in rest. *Obs.*

1632 J. HAYWARD tr. *Biondi's Eromena* 77 The Corse Captaine..ranne with his launce rested fully at him.

†**re'stable,** *v. Obs. rare*[−1]. [ad. OF. *restablir*: see next.] *trans.* To re-establish.

c **1540** *Order in Battayll* B ij, Suffer him neyther to reste nor to restable hys strength.

†**re'stablish,** *v. Obs.* [f. *restabliss-*, lengthened stem of OF. *restablir* (mod.F. *rétablir*), f. *re-* RE- + *establir* to ESTABLISH. In later use perh. directly f. RE- 5 a + STABLISH *v.*]

1. *trans.* To re-establish; to restore.

1413 *Pilgr. Sowle* (Caxton, 1483) IV. ii. 59 Ryght it is that thou knowe clerely how that this drye tree was restablysshed. **1483** CAXTON *Gold. Leg.* 247/2 Seynt laurence promysed to hym to rystablysshe his Sight. **1523** LD. BERNERS *Froiss.* I. ccxxxvii. 338 To restablysshe hym agayne into his realme. **1589** PUTTENHAM *Eng. Poesie* III. xix. (Arb.) 253 So did K. Edward I restablish Baliol rightfull owner of the crowne..against Robert le brus. **1650** *Bounds Publ. Obed.* 52 It was in their power to re-stablish..Kingly Government.

2. To make good, repair.

c **1500** *Melusine* 196 Yf ye wyl restablysshe the dommage, & to make raysounable & lawful amendes of the Iniury.

Hence †**re'stablishing** *vbl. sb.*

1523 LD. BERNERS *Froiss.* I. cccxlix. 226 b, The erles seruauntes brought agayne the prisoner.., & so yelded him agayne as by the waye of restablysshing.

†**re'stablishment.** *Obs. rare.* [ad. OF. *restablissement* (mod.F. *rét-*).] Restoration.

1413 *Pilgr. Sowle* (Caxton, 1483) IV. vi. 61 For to haue restablysshement of my fruyte, whiche was fro me despoilled. **1655** *Nicholas Papers* (Camden) II. 181 Some prince..that were of ability to contribute usefull assistance towards his Majesties establishment.

†**re'stagnant,** *a. Obs.* [a. obs. F. *restagnant*, or ad. L. *restagnant-em*, pres. pple. of *restagnāre*: see next.]

a. (See quot. 1656.) **b.** Stagnant, stagnating.

1656 BLOUNT *Glossogr.*, *Restagnant*, running over, over-flowing [cites Dr. Charl(eton)]. **1660** BOYLE *New Exp. Phys. Mech.* i. 33 The Air which bears against the restagnant Quick-silver. **1664** POWER *Exp. Philos.* I. 20 There are bred in most restagnant Waters..an innumerable company of little whitish Animals. **1676** H. MORE *Remarks* Pref., The restagnant mercury and the mercury in the tube.

†**re'stagnate,** *v. Obs.* [f. ppl. stem of L. *restagnāre* to overflow; the confusion with *stagnāre* appears also in obs. F. *restagner*.] *intr.* To stagnate; to become or remain stagnant.

1655 VAUGHAN *Silex Scint.* II. *Water-fall*, As this loud brook's incessant fall In streaming rings restagnates all. **1676** GREW *Musæum, Anat. Stomach* vii. 28 Many little Venters, in which the meat restagnates for some time.

Hence †**re'stagnating** *ppl. a.*

1665 HOOKE *Microgr.* 32 The vessel that holds the restagnating mercury.

†**restag'nation.** *Obs.* [ad. L. *restagnātio* the action of overflowing: see prec.]

1. (See quots.)

1623 COCKERAM II, *Restagnation*, a running ouer of a thing, chiefly of water. **1658** PHILLIPS, *Restagnation*, an overflowing, a bubling up. **1706** —— (ed. Kersey), *Restagnation*, an over-flowing, or running over; a being all in a Plash.

2. Stagnation.

1653 HARVEY *Anat. Exerc.* II. (1673) 153 The blood.. would at last, by restagnation and intrusion, break the vessels which contain it. **1676** WISEMAN *Surg. Treat.* I. xiv. 64 It proceedeth from the restagnation of gross Blood.

re'stain (riː-), *v.* [RE- 5 a.] To stain afresh.

1843 *Civil Eng. & Arch. Jrnl.* VI. 357/2 They have also been re-stained and varnished. **1905** *Macm. Mag.* Dec. 95 She could have fairly considered the respective merits of old oak or walnut for re-staining the floor.

†**'restall.** *Obs.* Also 7 restiall. [App. a variant of LAYSTALL (sense 1), perh. by association with REST *sb.*[1]] A burial-place for a person.

1566 *Shrewsbury Abbey Acc.* in *N. & Q.* Ser. I. IX. 539 Received for restall and knyll. **1577** *Ibid.*, Item for a restall of Jane Powell for her grandmother. [From 1593 the form is *lastiall*; from 1621 to 1645 *restiall*.] **1634** *Ibid.* in Miss Jackson *Shropshire Word-bk.* (1879) 350 Paid to the Lord Bishop's secretary..to procure a mitigation of Restalls within our Church.

re'stamp, *v.* [RE- 5 a.] To stamp again.

a **1711** KEN *Hymnarium* Poet. Wks. 1721 II. 32 From Vanity to Vanity I roll, Thy Likeness, Lord, restamp upon my Soul. **1884** *Law Times Rep.* LI. 222/2 Inferior Swedish iron has been used, the brand cut off, and then restamped.

†**'restancy.** *Obs. rare*[−1]. [ad. med.L. *restancia* (obs. F. *restance*): see next.] Remainder.

1667 WATERHOUSE *Fire London* 70 Rewarded with a fixed Pension during the little restancy of his life.

restant ('rɛstənt), *a.* [a. F. *restant* (Sp., Pg., and It. *restante*), or ad. L. *restant-em*, pres. pple. of *restāre* to remain.]

†**1.** Remaining. *Obs. rare*[−1].

1687 BEVERLEY *Expos. Song of Songs* 48 Now Philadelp, with smallest Humane strength Of Laws, or Power supports the Restant length Of Time.

2. *Bot.* Persistent.

1828–32 WEBSTER (citing Lee). **1853** G. MACDONALD & J. ALLAN *Botanist's Word-bk.*

†**restare,** obs. variant of RESTORE *v.*

Perh. arbitrarily altered to rime with *spare*.

c **1380** *Sir Ferumb.* 1439 On myn half say him þat he me restare þat he haþ mystaken away.

restart (riː'stɑːt, 'riːstɑːt), *sb.* [RE- 5 a.] A fresh start; a beginning again. Also *attrib.*

1888 *Daily News* 27 Aug. 2/4 The restart of additional ironworks that have long been standing. **1897** *Westm. Gaz.* 8 Mar. 9/2 From the re-start Wales took the ball down into Irish quarters. **1971** *Computers & Humanities* V. 140 One of the most powerful features of this system is the restart procedure... The restart capability is especially useful under a system which limits the amount of time and records a user can run at any one time. **1977** *Gloss. Terms Data Processing* (*B.S.I.*) VII. 9/2 *Restart condition*, in the execution of a computer program, a condition that can be re-established and that permits a restart of the computer program. *Ibid.*, *Restart point*, a place in a computer program at which its execution may be restarted; in particular, the address of a restart instruction.

re'start (riː-), *v.* [RE- 5 a.] To start again. Hence **re'started** *ppl. a.*; **re'starting** *vbl. sb.*

trans. **1845** YOUATT *Dog* ii. 33 The hare, the re-starting of which is left to the spaniel. **1863** *Cornh. Mag.* VII. 389 The time by..the restarted chronometer. **1884** *Manch. Exam.* 11 Oct. 4/3 We do not find any disposition to re-start looms. *intr.* **1851** C. L. SMITH tr. *Tasso* XI. lvii, The enemy gains fresh vigour, hope re-starts within him. **1885** *Manch. Exam.* 3 Jan. 5/1 The engines had only re-started yesterday morning after a serious stoppage.

†**re'state,** *v.*[1] *Obs. rare.* = RE-ESTATE *v.*

1625 BP. MOUNTAGU *App. Cæsar* 320 As if..Popery [were] ready to be restated in Church and Common-wealth. **1657** PETTUS in *Loveday's Lett.* (1663) A iv, I confess I wish we were restated in our primitive Innocency.

re'state (riː-), *v.*[2] [RE- 5 a.] *trans.* To state or express over again or in a new way.

a **1713** ELLWOOD *Autobiog.* (1714) 310 A Broad-side.., in which, having re-stated the Controversie.., I offered a fair Chalenge to them. **1814** CALHOUN *Wks.* II. 94 Before I proceed further, it will be necessary to restate the propositions with which I commenced. **1848** MILL *Pol. Econ.* I. ix. §1 (1876) 84, I have restated this exposition, which has already been made in a former place. **1876** LOWELL *Among my Bks.* Ser. II. 247 Wordsworth has this fault of enforcing and restating obvious points.

So **re'statement** (also in *Mus.*: cf. STATEMENT 1 b).

1803 W. TAYLOR in *Ann. Rev.* I. 307 Curious intelligence has been obtained, and satisfactory vouchers are given for most of the re-statements. **1886** *Athenæum* 30 Jan. 167/3 A restatement of the old mythical descent of the Dukes of Norfolk. **1944** W. APEL *Harvard Dict. Mus.* 638/2 *Restatement*, same as recapitulation in sonata-form. **1954** *Grove's Dict. Mus.* (ed. 5) III. 440/2 The restatement of the first subject is sufficient indication to the hearer as to what part of the movement he has arrived at. **1959** *Listener* 20 Aug. 297/2 The preparation for the restatement in his first movement is altogether classical in method. **1974** *Encycl. Brit. Macropædia* XVII. 5/2 The first theme is restated in the dominant key. This restatement could appear at first to be the second subject.

re'stater. [f. RESTATE *v.*[2] + -ER[1].] A person who restates.

1925 G. O'BRIEN *Econ. Effects Reformation* ii. 125 Luther ..regarded Christ and the Apostles as merely the restaters and expositors of the Decalogue.

†**re'staur,** *v. Obs. rare.* [ad. L. *restaurāre.*] *trans.* To restore.

1513 BRADSHAW *St. Werburge* I. 2078 [She] Restaured temples vnto chrystes honour. *Ibid.* 2834 By her prayer.. They were restaured to helthe and saluacyon.

†**restaurance.** *Obs. rare*[−1]. [a. OF. *restaurance.* Cf. RESTORANCE.] Restitution.

a **1300** *Cursor M.* 6772 If mi aght be stolen wit chaunce, þou sal me mak restaurance.

restaurant ('rɛstərənt, -rɒnt, ‖rɛstɔrɑ̃). [a. F. *restaurant*, substantive use of the pres. pple. of *restaurer* to RESTORE.] **1.** An establishment where refreshments or meals may be obtained.

The use of F. *restaurant* in this sense is stated to have originated in Paris in 1765.

1827 J. F. COOPER *Prairie* II. ii. 28 At the most renowned of the Parisian restaurans. **1835** WILLIS *Pencillings* I. vi. 39 A newly-painted and staring restaurant. **1859** SALA *Tw. round Clock* (1861) 147 At these restaurants they give you things with French names. **1885** MABEL COLLINS *Prettiest Woman* ii, We will not sup at a public restaurant, but in a private room at the Grand Hotel.

2. *attrib.*, as ***restaurant car, dinner, -keeper, lunch, manager, meal, proprietor.***

1875 KNIGHT *Dict. Mech.* 1923/2 *Restaurant-car*, one adapted for affording meals to passengers on board while traveling. **1913** KIPLING *Lett. of Travel* (1920) 220 That terrible restaurant-car dinner in the tunnel. **1967** 'T. WELLS' *What should you know of Dying?* x. 118 He's an elevator man at the Winchenden Arms... He's on the restaurant car. **1899** R. FRY *Let.* Oct. (1972) I. 174 The restaurant dinners all stop at 5.0. **1925** F. SCOTT FITZGERALD *Great Gatsby* iii. 69 A solitary restaurant dinner. **1876** W. WRIGHT *Hist. Big Bonanza* xlviii. 355 Some years ago a restaurant keeper had a number of these customers, who were eating him out of house and home. **1932** H. SIMPSON *Boomerang* vii. 141 The two young men..grinned up at him, and the first, the restaurant-keeper, answered: 'His money is as good as another's.' **1974** 'J. ROSS' *Burning of Billy Toober* ix. 91 Prosser..had had his restaurant lunch sent in on a linen-shrouded tray. **1976** *Liverpool Echo* 6 Dec. 6/6 Restaurant manager Jose Padilla..is always on the look-out for something new for his customers. **1938** *Cook's Continental Time-table* Jan. (Advt.), Comfort to the continent. Right through the winter, Imperial Airways will operate frequent services to Paris,..Full restaurant meals served during flight. **1960** M. SPARK *Bachelors* iii. 43 One can't afford two restaurant meals in one day. **1938** *Sun* (Baltimore) 11 June 9/2 Worley Carrico, middle-aged restaurant proprietor. **1974** *Encycl. Brit. Macropædia* XV. 778/1 The first restaurant proprietor is believed to have been one A. Boulanger, a soup vendor, who opened his business in Paris in 1765.

restauranter ('rɛstə,rɒntə(r)). *U.S.* [f. RESTAURANT + -ER[1].] = RESTAURATEUR 1.

1887 *Ohio State Jrnl.* 20 July, The headquarters of Mr. Kiesewetter are at Diebold's, an opulent restauranter and general purveyor to the wants of delegates. **1938** *Sun* (Baltimore) 11 June 9/2 (*heading*) Restauranter jailed in fatal shooting.

restauranteur (,rɛstərən'tœː(r)). [f. RESTAURANT + *-eur* as in RESTAURATEUR.] = RESTAURATEUR 1.

An erroneous form.

1949 E. HYAMS *Grape Vine in England* viii. 136 The second thinning may be done when the grapes are about the size of those very large and granite-like marrowfat peas which are beloved of English restauranteurs, or used to be. **1958** *Wall St. Jrnl.* 30 Sept. 7/3 Jack Dempsey, one-time heavyweight champion turned restauranteur. **1980** *Guardian Weekly* 20 Jan. 20/3 The growing number of hoteliers and restauranteurs.

'restaurantish, *a. rare.* [-ISH[1].] Resembling a restaurant; suggestive of a restaurant.

1896 A. BEARDSLEY *Let. c* 26 June (1970) 138 I have fallen on my feet here. Two palatial rooms and the additional comfort of being able to feed in a pretty little restaurantish dining-room.

'restaurate, *v. rare.* [f. ppl. stem of L. *restaurāre*: see RESTORE *v.* In sense 2 suggested by prec., or by F. *se restaurer.*]

†**1.** *trans.* To restore; to set in place, or set up, again. Hence †**restaurated** *ppl. a.*

1597 A. M. tr. *Guillemeau's Fr. Chirurg.* 44/2 Those ligamentes which are too loose cause that the restauratede partes which are situatede, move therout. **1632** VICARS tr. *Virgil* XI. 352 If one repulse hath us quite ruinated, And fortune never can be restaurated.

2. *intr.* To partake of refreshments or of a meal. Hence **'restaurating** *vbl. sb.*

1889 F. PIGOT *Strangest Journ.* 21 Being a man with acquaintances everywhere, he took me into the Yacht Club, where we restaurated. *Ibid.* 163 The mules that carried the restaurating baskets.

‖**restaurateur** (rɛstɔratœr). [F., agent-n. f. *restaurer*: cf. RESTAURATOR.]

1. A keeper of a restaurant.

1796 BURKE *Regic. Peace* iv. Sel. Wks. (1892) 305, I should still think..that the same power, which furnished all their former *restaurateurs*, sent also their present cooks. **1826** BEST *Four Yrs. France* 160 We returned to the restaurateur's to dine. **1850** THACKERAY *Pendennis* xliii[i], Didn't I take opera-boxes and give her dinners at the restaurateur's? **1882** MISS BRADDON *Mt. Royal* II. ix. 185 A little dinner given.. at a choice Italian restaurateur's not very far from South Belgravia. **1969** *N.Y. Rev. Bks.* 2 Jan. 16/3 The editor of an intellectual journal has no less claim to being functional than a restaurateur. **1976** *Times* 21 May 4/8 Some had robbed a retired restaurateur of goods and money. **1980** *Amer. Speech* LV. 91 Books of advice to restaurateurs and menu designers suggest the use of foreign languages.

2. A restaurant.

1801 C. WILMOT *Let.* 13 Dec. in *Irish Peer* (1920) 13 The 'Palais Royal' is excessively new and entertaining... Libraries, Restaurateurs, Gambling Houses, Coffee Houses. **1804** *European Mag.* XLV. 360/2 That some should be *restaurateurs*, eating-houses, and others coffee-houses,..is excellent. **1830** WHEATON *Jrnl.* 385 The Restaurateurs are the houses where the Parisians dine, as they breakfast at the cafés.

restauration (rɛstɔː'reɪʃən). Now *rare.* Also 4–5 **-acion(e,** 6 **-acyon, restawracion.** [a. F. *restauration* (1314; = Sp. *restauracion*, It. *re-, ristaurazione*), or ad. L. *restaurātiōn-em*, n. of action f. *restaurāre* to RESTORE.]

†**1. a.** The reinstatement of man in the divine favour or in a state of innocence. *Obs.*

c **1375** *Sc. Leg. Saints* iii. (*Andrew*) 401 Sic turment was þe preuete mare and lese of manis restauracione. **1534** MORE *Treat. Passion* Wks. (1557) 1279/2 The determinacion of the trinity for the restawracion of mankynde. **1597** HOOKER *Eccl. Pol.* v. lvi. §7 Christ as the cause originall of restauration to life. **1635** JACKSON *Creed* VIII. Wks. VIII. 139 Their confidence and hope of..exaltation or restauration into God's most special favour. **1670** *Devout Commun.* (1688) 33 Have I a sanctified knowledge..of man in his creation, fall, restauration, and perfection?

†**b.** The restoration of a person to a former status or position. *Obs.*

1577 *F. de Lisle's Legendarie* B ij, To wrest from the Dauphine Henrie a promise of restauration vnto the counties of Prouence and Anjou. **1602** WARNER *Alb. Eng.* Epit. 352 Not reckoning..any ioynt Raignes,..nor the Depriuations and Restaurations of Archigallo and Elidure. **1694** KETTLEWELL *Comp. Penitent* 101 The method of the Church in the restauration of Penitents. **1718** HICKES & NELSON *Kettlewell* III. xcvii. 430 Dr. Francis Turner..was ..most Vigorous and Active by attempting the Restauration of the late King [James II].

†**c.** *Hist.* = RESTORATION 2 a. *Obs.*

1660 BLOUNT *Boscobel* I. (1680) 77 Since His Majesties happy Restauration..hundreds of people..have flock'd to see the Famous Boscobel. **1695** SIBBALD *Autobiog.* (1834) 129 Who was first Bishop of Dumblane upon the restauration of King Charles the 2nd.

†**d.** The bringing back of the Jews to Israel.

[**1560** DAUS tr. *Sleidane's Comm.* 133 b, As after the captivitie of Babylon, so nowe also the tyme of restauration is at hande.] **1613** JACKSON *Truth of Script.* I. III. v. §4 For by their strange deliuerance and restauration [the Jews] might haue learned that their God was a God of Gods. **1665** WITHER *Lord's Prayer* 59 Who apply their predictions to such a carnal Restauration of the Jews as is now expected. **1727** in Earbery tr. *Burnet's St. Dead* App. 5 The Prophets often foretold the Captivities and Restaurations of the children of Israel.

2. †**a.** The restoration of something material to its proper condition. Also, a restorative. *Obs.*

1390 GOWER *Conf.* III. 23 Yit phisique of his conserve Makth many a restauracioun Unto his recreacioun. **1398** TREVISA *Barth. De P.R.* VI. xxi. (Tollem. MS.), Þerto nedeþ continuel restauration to restore what is wastid and spende. *c* **1440** LYDG. *Hors, Shepe & G.* 372 His fleessh is natural restauracion, As summe men seyn aftir gret siknesse. **1460** CAPGRAVE *Chron.* (Rolls) 42 The Kyng comaunded that the offering schuld be put in a comon box and kept to restauracion of the Temple. **1584** R. SCOT *Discov. Witchcr.* VI. ii. (1886) 92 The resurrection and restauration of the bodie. **1604** MARSTON & WEBSTER *Malcontent* II. iii, Trust me the ingredients are very cordiall,..and most powerfull in restauration. **1665** GLANVILL *Scepsis Sci.* xxi. 134 The restauration of gray hairs to Juvenility.

b. The restoration of an institution, art, doctrine, etc., to its pristine condition.

1605 BACON *Adv. Learn.* I. iii. §2 Iulius Cæsar..to begin his restauration of the State [etc.]. **1660** SHARROCK *Vegetables* 53 Not willing thence to make any motion towards the restauration of the ancient doctrine. **1702** ECHARD *Eccl. Hist.* (1710) 259 The Nobility as violently promoting the restauration of their ancient privileges. **1726** *Craftsman* No. i. 4 The Restauration of our ancient established government under King Charles II.

1901 *Sat. Rev.* 12 Jan. 53/2 Appreciation for his restauration of Hutcheson's memory.

†**c.** Reparation of defects, etc. *Obs. rare*[−1].

1605 BACON *Adv. Learn.* I. vii. §6 So that his whole time was a very restauration of all the lapses and decayes of former times.

d. (An) alteration or repair intended to restore a building, etc., to something like its original form or use. Cf. RESTORATION 4 b.

1949 E. POUND *Pisan Cantos* lxxx. 86 And I trust they have not destroyed the Old theatre by restaurations, and by late renaissance giribizzi. **1977** *It* May 29/3 Research into restauration of derelict urban or other areas.

†**3.** Restoration of stolen goods. *Obs. rare*[−1].

1678 SIR G. MACKENZIE *Crim. Laws Scot.* I. xix. §vi. (1699) 99 Many Thieves would restore, if they thought Restauration might be made with safety of their life.

4. A restaurant. [So G. *restauration.*]

1862 TYNDALL *Mountaineer.* i. 3 We finally reached Boulogne, and sought to reconstitute our shattered energies at the restauration. **1886** W. J. TUCKER *E. Europe* 5 The.. strains of the gipsy band playing..in the restauration below, enticed me to enter the locality to supper.

†**re'staurative,** *a.*[1] and *sb. Obs.* In 4–5 **-if,** 6 **-iue.** [a. OF. *restauratif, -ive*, or ad. med.L. **restaurativ-us.*] = RESTORATIVE *a.* and *sb.*

1390 GOWER *Conf.* III. 30 Al the metes and the spices.. Ne be so lusti forto take Ne so ferforth restauratif. **1398** TREVISA *Barth. De P.R.* VII. lxix. (Bodl. MS.), Whan kinde is comforted ne vseþ certeyn medicyns resumptiue and restauratiue. *c* **1430** LYDG. *Min. Poems* (Percy Soc.) 49, I sought lechis for a restauratif. *Ibid.* 95 Oure helthe, oure foode and oure restauratif. **1620** VENNER *Via Recta* iii. 60 By reason of the pure and restauratiue nourishment, which it giueth.

restaurative (re'stɔːrətɪv), *a.*[2] *rare.* [ad. F. *restauratif*: see -IVE.] Having the function of a restaurant; providing restaurant facilities.

1875 in G. J. Holyoake *Hist. Co-operation in Eng.* I. ix. 214 In a short time the restaurative omnibuses will circulate through Paris... These vehicles will contain broth and sauce for the whole city.

†**restaurator.** *Obs.* [ad. L. *restaurātor*, agent-n. from *restaurāre.*] One who restores.

1652–62 HEYLIN *Cosmogr.* II. (1682) 74 That great Herbalist and Restaurator of Physick. **1654** tr. *Scudery's Curia Pol.* 123 The multitudes could not be restrained from calling me the Restaurator of his Empire. **1680** *Relig. Dutch* iii. 26 Sandius..was the Restaurator of the Arrian Sect in this Country.

†**re'staurer.** *Obs. rare*[−1]. [Cf. obs. F. *restaureur.*] Restorer.

1557 N.T. (Genevan) *Epistle* *iiii, Iesus Christ,..who shulde be..geuen to men to be the restaurer of the worlde.

†**restay,** *v. Obs.* Also 4–5 **resteie, -eye, -eȝe.** [Prob. ad. OF. *resteir* to resist (Godef.).]

1. *trans.* To check, restrain, keep back, hold in.

13.. *E.E. Allit. P.* A. 716 His dessypelez..wyth her resounez ful fele restayed. **1338** R. BRUNNE *Chron.* (1810) 292 þei hoped þe toþer day þe barons resteie. *c* **1400** *Laud Troy Bk.* 7755 Ther is no man..that may restay Ther hors lenger. *Ibid.* 10483 Off his chasyng he him restayed.

2. *intr.* To stop, stay.

13.. *E.E. Allit. P.* A. 437 Þenne ros ho vp & con restay, & speke me towarde in þat space. **1382** WYCLIF *2 Sam.* xix. 39 And whanne al the puple, and the kyng was passid ouer Jordan, he resteiede [*v.r.* resteȝede].

Hence †**restayed** *ppl. a.* (See quots.) *Obs.*

c **1410** *Master of Game* (MS. Digby 182) xiii, Þer beth oþer maneres of wyse houndes, þe which men clepeth byyonde þe see hert houndes good and resteyed. *Ibid.*,þei be cleped resteyed, because þat if an hert falle amonge þe chaunge, þei shull abyde stille, till an hunter come.

'rest-balk, *sb.* Also 9 rist-baulk. [f. REST *sb.*[1] or *v.*[1] + BALK *sb.*[1] 3.] A ridge left unploughed between two furrows, *esp.* in the process of raftering or ribbing. Also *attrib.* or *Comb.*

1523 FITZHERB. *Husb.* §4 A reste-balke is where the plough byteth at the poynte of the culture and share, and cutteth not the ground cleane to the forowe, that was plowed laste before, but leaueth a lyttell rydge standynge betwene. **1794** A. YOUNG in Driver *Gen. View Agric. Hants.* 68 Also raftering the land, which is a sort of rest baulk ploughing. **1850** *Jrnl. R. Agric. Soc.* XI. I. 140 Breast-ploughed and burnt and succeeded by turnips, or rist-baulk ploughed and burnt and afterwards..sown with turnips.

Hence **'rest-balk** *v. trans.*, to plough (land) with rest-balks; to rib or rafter.

1523 FITZHERB. *Husb.* §16 Make a depe holowe forowe in the rydge of the lande, and loke wel, thou rest-balke it nat. **1850** *Jrnl. R. Agric. Soc.* XI. I. 137 The land is again rist-baulked... Some, therefore, rist-baulk or half-plough their sainfoin ley.

'rest-day. [OE. *ræst(e)dæȝ*, f. *ræst(e* REST *sb.*^{1} + *dæȝ* DAY. Cf. Du. *rustdag*, Da. *rastdag*, G. *rasttag*.]

1. The day of rest; the Sabbath. Now *rare*.

c **897** K. ÆLFRED *Gregory's Past. C.* lii. 407 Ða ðe behealdað minne ræstedæȝ. *c* **950** *Lindisf. Gosp.* Mark ii. 27 Restdæȝ fore menn ȝeworden wæs & næs monn fore ræstdæȝe. *c* **1000** *Ags. Gosp.* Matt. xii. 5 þa sacerdas on reste-daȝum on þam temple ȝewemmað þone reste-dæȝ. *c* **1200** ORMIN 4186 þe seffnde daȝȝ iss Ressteda33. **1894** *Daily News* 8 Sept. 3/7 This determination of rich publishers to trade on Sundays kept a great industry at work on the rest day.

2. A day of rest on a march.

1813 SIR R. WILSON *Priv. Diary* (1862) II. 206 We shall march on without any rest-day to Frankfort. The army will then repose if the enemy permits.

†**reste.** *Obs. rare.* [var. of REST *sb.*^{2}] (See quot. 1788.)

1776 JOHNSON *Let. to Mrs. Thrale* 22 May, Mr. Thrale's resolution to take up his restes in person. **1788** MRS. PIOZZI *note to above*, When the master brewer goes round to his victuallers once a year, in order to examine..the stock left on the hands of the alehouse-keeper, the expression used in the profession is, 'that he takes up his restes'.

'rested, *ppl. a.* [f. REST *v.*^{1} + -ED.] Refreshed by repose or sleep. Also used of land that has lain fallow for some time, and (*Sc.*) of a fire. Also const. *up* (see REST *v.*^{1} 2 g).

c **1400** *Laud Troy Bk.* 5737 Priamus then his men calles, He brought thre thousand fresch & rested. *a* **1586** SIDNEY *Arcadia, Sonn.* (1605) 473 The Nightingale as soone as April bringeth Vnto her rested sense a perfect waking,..Sings out her woes. **1600** SURFLET *Countrie Farme* II. xlix. 317 Bishops weede..groweth chiefly in rested grounds. **1611** COTGR., *Reposé*, reposed, rested; lyen fallow a great while. *a* **1774** FERGUSSON *Farmer's Ingle* xii, The cruizy too can only blink and bleer, The restit ingle's done the maist it dow. **1890** C. W. R. COOKE *4 Yrs. in Parl.* 64 Epigrams are the product of a rested brain. **1894** H. GARDINER *Unob. Patagonia* 277 A sudden onrush of fresh, eager, rested, enthusiastic men. **1922** E. O'NEILL *Anna Christie* I. 115, I was thinking maybe ..he might be willing to stake me to a room and eats till I get rested up. **1929** G. ADE *Let.* 22 May (1973) 141, I am certainly glad to be home after a tedious tour and I am getting all rested up. **1935** M. M. ATWATER *Murder in Midsummer* xxi. 201, I guess we're all rested up. Come along, boys.

re'steel (riː-), *v.* [RE- 5 c.] *trans.* To fit or point with steel again. Also *fig.*

1844 *Regul. & Ord. Army* 102 Hammer, re-steeled and hardened. **1851** C. L. SMITH tr. *Tasso* XI. lvii, Hope re-starts Within him, and his valour is re-steeled. **1868** HAMERTON *Etching* iv. 31 After which the plate may be re-steeled.

re'stem (riː-), *v.* [RE- 5 a.] To stem again.

1604 SHAKS. *Oth.* I. iii. 37 Of thirtie Saile; and now they do re-stem Their backward course.

reste'nosis. *Med.* [RE-.] A recurrence of stenosis, esp. of a heart valve after surgery to correct it.

1954 *A.M.A. Arch. Internal Med.* XCIV. 777 Other examples of so-called restenosis following commissurotomy have been reported. **1977** *Proc. R. Soc. Med.* LXX. 816/2 Restenosis [of the ear canal] is very common.., especially in those cases where pneumatization is poor and the lateral sinus is abnormally anterior. **1980** *Brit. Med. Jrnl.* 12 Jan. 62/1 Many of these patients will have had a closed mitral valvotomy 10 to 30 years before, and the term 'mitral restenosis' is loosely used to describe the recurrence of their symptoms.

'rester^1. [f. REST *v.*^{1} + -ER^1.] **1.** One who rests; *spec.* in mod. use, an unemployed actor or actress.

1435 MISYN *Fire of Love* 55 More truly it is in restars þen laborars. **1614** MERITON *Christian Mans Assuring-ho.* 20 We have heere the perfection, not of resters, but of runners. *a* **1680** CHARNOCK *Attrib. God* (1834) I. 256 As the law itself is called flesh, so the observers of it and resters in it are called Israel after the flesh. **1931** R. ALDINGTON *Colonel's Daughter* v. 300 The anteroom of a dramatic agency filled with restless resters.

2. A ledge for placing articles on in front of a balcony in a theatre.

1922 *Rep. Theatres & Music Halls Comm.* in *Minutes Proc. L.C.C., July-Dec. 1921* 158 In order to prevent trays..being pushed off the resters in the front of balconies at theatres, etc...we have..decided to require..that the rester shall be sloped at, say, an angle of 30 deg.

†**'rester**^{2}. *Obs. rare*$^{-0}$. [f. REST *v.*^{3}] One who arrests.

c **1440** *Promp. Parv.* 431/1 Restare, or a-restare, *arestator*.

restey, obs. variant of RESTY, restive.

'restful, *a.* Also 4 resteuol. [f. REST *sb.*^{1}]

1. Characterized by, of the nature of, productive of, rest or repose; free from strife or disturbance.

1340 *Ayenb.* 199 þe oþer is y-hote resteuol (contemplatiue), vor þet hi is reste of workes wyþ-oute. **1388** WYCLIF *Wisdom* xviii. 14 Whanne alle thingis helden restful silence. **1413** *Pilgr. Sowle* (Caxton) v. i. (1859) 68, I had ben brought to another more restfull place. *c* **1460** G. ASHBY *Dicta Philos.* 1001 Eke kepe your Roialme in tranquillite, Restful peas, comfort & feelicite. **1535–6** *Act 27 Hen. VIII*, c. 63 The good restefull and politike governaunce of the same Town. **1586** J. HOOKER *Hist. Irel.* in *Holinshed* II. 176/1 To liue thensefoorth in some dutifull and restfull order. **1616** W. FORDE *Serm.* 38 It is in vaine to expect the restfull comfort of forgivenesse heereafter. **1726** POPE *Odyss.* XIX. 598 A while..Suspend the restful hour with sweet discourse. **1860** WARTER *Sea Board* II. 428 When the services of the holy restful day are over. **1878** BESANT & RICE *Celia's Arb.* I. iii. 31 It has a restful sound, the talk of rooks.

Comb. **1607** J. DAVIES (Heref.) *Summa Totalis* Wks. (Grosart) I. 11/2 Their Mouer moues not, but doth rest In restful-restlesse perfect Action.

2. Quiet; peaceful; taking or enjoying rest.

1388 WYCLIF *Daniel* iv. 1, I, Nabugodonosor, was restful in myn hous. *c* **1425** HOCCLEVE *Min. Poems* 209/837 Now restfullere in thy goost be withynne, þat ouer ferd art. **1450–1530** *Myrr. our Ladye* 152 His holy seruyce oughte to be sayde wyth clene and restefulle hartes. **1547–64** BAULDWIN *Mor. Philos.* (Palfr.) 103 That man seemeth good that is meeke & gentle of condition, soft in words, & restfull in person. **1594** KYD *Cornelia* IV. i. 124 The restfull Allmaynes with his crueltie He rashly styrd against vs. **1625** K. LONG tr. *Barclay's Argenis* I. i. 1 A shrill noyse disturbed with unquiet fancies his restfull minde. **1856** R. A. VAUGHAN *Mystics* (1860) II. VII. ii. 16 'Tis not discipline, Wins them a will so restful and so blest. **1859** BOYD *Recreat. Country Parson* 1 Somewhat tired with the duty of yesterday, but feeling very restful and thankful.

'restfully, *adv.* [f. prec. + -LY^2.] In a restful manner; quietly, peacefully.

1433 *Rolls of Parlt.* IV. 423 Restfully governyng hym self. **1450–1530** *Myrr. our Ladye* 100 Whiche ye say in scylence for to gather the more restfully your mynde togyther. **1531** ELYOT *Gov.* (1580) 192 Lyuing restfully and in helth unto extreme age. **1828–32** in WEBSTER (citing Herbert). **1873** MISS BROUGHTON *Nancy* II. 66 In it, leaning restfully back.., is the lady I noticed in church. **1883** *Harper's Mag.* Apr. 749/2 He is sleeping naturally and restfully.

'restfulness. [f. as prec. + -NESS.] The state or quality of being restful.

a **1400** HYLTON *Scala Perf.* (W. de W. 1494) I. lxxvii, In pees of glad conscience with a sad restfulnes. **1489** *Rolls of Parlt.* VI. 431/2 For the more quiete and restfulness of the Kyngs Subgietts. **1503** in *Lett. Rich. III & Hen. VII* (Rolls) I. 212 The restfulnes and profite of your grace in evityng of the daunger. *c* **1557** ABP. PARKER *Ps.* cvii. 309 Who..found no way to dwelling towne to stay in restfulnes. **1643** PRYNNE *Sov. Power Parl.* I. (ed. 2) 85 He not only safe guardeth himselfe, but also holdeth the people in a surety of restfulnesse. **1865** *Pall Mall G.* 16 Sept. 11/1 Restfulness is the keynote of its calming music. **1870** MORRIS *Earthly Par.* II. III. 255 Yet still no less did love with him abide, Tempered with quiet days and restfulness.

'rest-harrow. [f. REST *sb.*^{3} or *v.*^{3} + HARROW: cf. med.L. *resta bovis*, OF. *reste beof*.] A field-shrub (*Ononis arvensis*), with tough roots, also called CAMMOCK.

c **1550** LLOYD *Treas. Health* O iij, Take of Plantayne, Starewort, Scabiouse and of the rote of restharrowe. **1567** MAPLET *Gr. Forest* 35 b, In some place for hindring and staying the Husbandman it is called Rest harrow. **1600** SURFLET *Countrie Farme* v. v. 667 The couchgrasse, and that which is called rest-harrow, make shew to be more standing tenants. *a* **1682** SIR T. BROWNE *Tracts* (1683) 88 Bindweed, Restharrow and other *vitia segetum*. **1728** GARDINER tr. *Rapin's Gardens* I. (ed. 3) 41 Restharrow, whose tough Root obstructs the Plough. **1785** MARTYN *Rousseau's Bot.* xxv. (1794) 352 Restharrows are lowly shrubs, or rather undershrubs, with purple flowers. **1844** H. STEPHENS *Bk. Farm* III. 944 On light soils, the rest-harrow..is a great pest. **1880** JEFFERIES *Gt. Estate* 131 Some bushy plants of the rest-harrow, whose prickly branches repel cattle.

'rest-house. [f. REST *sb.*^{1}] **1. a.** In India, Malaysia or Africa, a building in which travellers may obtain rest and shelter; a choultry, a dawk-bungalow.

1807 CORDINER *Desc. Ceylon* I. 205 The children assemble in the rest-house, as their parish school has fallen a sacrifice to the ravages of time. **1829** *Blackw. Mag.* XXVI. 45 There is moreover an empty rest-house or two, merely sufficient to shelter the weary traveller from the rays of the sun. **1871** ALABASTER *Wheel of Law* 280 Half that distance is accomplished, which we know by finding a rest-house in the jungle. **1954** [see NIGERIAN *sb.* and *a.*]. **1964** (*title*) Malaysia: visitors guide. Hotel and rest house directory. **1966** D. FORBES *Heart of Malaya* iii. 43 He..drove to Belinggu and took Abigail to the rest house there. **1972** *Guardian* 22 Sept. 9/1 My night at the Rest House—a hang-over from the colonial days, where Government officials could stay when travelling across country—was interrupted by the distant sound of a gong. **1978** G. GREENE *Human Factor* v. ii. 241 He could even imagine himself in Africa, at some resthouse in the bush.

b. An establishment catering for persons requiring rest and recreation.

1928 GALSWORTHY *Swan Song* III. ii. 231, I feel I should be ever so much more interested if I ran a place of my own in the country—a sort of rest-house that I could make attractive for girls who wanted air and that.

2. *attrib.*, as *rest-house garden*, *keeper*.

1909 *Athenæum* 24 Apr. 492/1, I dislike the ramshackle rest-house, and its rude indifferent rest-house-keeper. **1973** 'B. MATHER' *Snowline* xv. 183, I withdrew into the resthouse garden again.

†**'restible,** *a. Obs. rare.* [ad. L. *restibilis*.] (See quot. 1656.)

1656 BLOUNT *Glossogr.*, *Restible*.., which beareth every year, that is sown or delved every year, that springs up again, and quickens after it was thought to be dead. **1657** TOMLINSON *Renou's Disp.* 324 They grow in many places in France..in fat and restible soyl.

restie, obs. variant of RESTY, restive.

restiff ('rɛstɪf), *a.* Also 5 restyf(e, -yffe; 6–7 **restif(f)e**; 8–9 **restif.** [a. OF. *restif* (mod.F. *rétif*):—pop. L. **restīv-um*, f. *restāre* REST *v.*^{2} Now more usually RESTIVE. Cf. RESTY *a.*^{1}]

1. Of animals: Stationary (*obs.*); refusing to go forward; resisting control of any kind.

c **1410** *Master of Game* (MS. Digby 182) xiii, þei be not so wyse forto disseuer þe hert fro þe chaunge, for þei abyde styll and restyffe. **14..** *Lat.-Eng. Voc.* in *Wr.-Wülcher* 608 *Retrogradus*, restyfe. **1577** B. GOOGE *Heresbach's Husb.* III. (1586) 118 b, Too long rest will cause them to be restife, and to tyer sooner. **1655** FULLER *Ch. Hist.* I. v. 32 Like restife Horses, they went the worse for Beating. **1697** DRYDEN *Virg. Georg.* III. 324 The pamper'd Colt... Impatient of the Lash, and restiff to the Rein. **1747** RICHARDSON *Clarissa* (1811) I. 185 Like a restiff horse..he pains one's hands..to rein him in. **1778** [W. MARSHALL] *Minutes Agric.* 14 Mar. an. 1775, The bull, broke-in yesterday, had likewise become restiff. **1843** WORDSW. *Prose Wks.* (1876) III. 58 We were stopt by one of the horses proving restiff. **1869** *Echo* 11 Feb., A fine young heifer..appeared rather restif.

b. *transf.* Of persons.

1581 G. PETTIE tr. *Guazzo's Civ. Conv.* III. (1586) 134 There are some such restife iades, that they will not at any time be commaunded. **1676** ETHEREDGE *Man of Mode* I. i, Was there ever such a restiff bawd? **1685** DRYDEN *Thren. August.* 472 So James the drowsy Genius wakes Of Britain .., Restiff and slumbring on its Arms. **1729** GAY *Polly* I, But husbands, like colts, are restif; and they require a long time to break them. **1788** WOLCOT (P. Pindar) *Peter's Pension* Wks. 1812 II. 19 Your favourite Minister, I'm told runs restiff. **1822** SCOTT *Peveril* xxvii, But how if the youth proved restiff?

fig. **1687** DRYDEN *Hind & P.* III. 1026 The way to win the restiff world to God. **1831** W. GODWIN *Thoughts Man* 395 Restiff and uncomplying nature refuses to conform herself to his *dicta*.

c. Of conditions or character. *rare.*

1692 R. L'ESTRANGE *Fables* ccccliv, This Restiff Stubbornness is never to be Excus'd. **1827** D. JOHNSON *Ind. Field Sports* 162 An obstinate restiff disposition.

†**2.** Of land: Lying fallow. *Obs. rare*$^{-1}$.

c **1420** *Pallad. on Husb.* x. 73 Now first the ficche is sowen; ..Farrage in restyf lond [L. *loco sterili*], ydonged eek, Is doon.

'restiffness. *rare.* [f. prec.] Restiveness.

1607 MARKHAM *Caval.* I. (1617) 34 Neither shall you finde restifenesse or churlishnesse, except it spring from your owne furie. **1663** S. PATRICK *Parab. Pilgr.* xxx. (1668) 351 He began to be so lazy and listless... He cured himself of this restiffness of spirit. **1827** MISS SEDGWICK *H. Leslie* (1872) I. 36 She made her own destiny conformable, not without some restiffness.

restiform ('rɛstɪfɔːm), *a. Anat.* [a. mod.L. *restiform-is*, f. *restis* a cord. So F., Sp., Pg. *restiforme*.] Cord-like; in ***restiform body***, one or other of two rounded bundles of fibrous matter lying on each side of the medulla oblongata and connecting it with the cerebellum. So ***restiform column, tract***.

1831 R. KNOX *Cloquet's Anat.* 417 They commence by a rather indistinct line between the olivary eminence and the restiform body. **1856** TODD & BOWMAN *Phys. Anat.* II. 105 The floor of this fossa is formed by the restiform column. **1873** MIVART *Elem. Anat.* 367 Behind each of these..is a band named the restiform tract. **1899** *Allbutt's Syst. Med.* VII. 388 A case of tumour of the left restiform body.

re'stigmatize, *v.* [RE- 5 a.] To mark again.

1654 GAYTON *Pleas. Notes* III. viii. 122 In the Parchments of his body..much of his History was to be read,..which upon solemne dayes was seen, and the part re-stigmatiz'd according to order.

†**'restily,** *adv. Obs.*$^{-0}$ Stubbornly.

1611 COTGR., *Restivement*, restily, stubbornely.

re'stimulate, *v.* [RE- 5 a.] *trans.* To stimulate again. Hence **restimu'lation, restimu'latory** *a.* [-ORY^2].

1796 A. SEWARD *Let.* 11 Dec. (1811) IV. 282 Mr. B. will succeed in his design to re-stimulate the public mind to continue the war. **1822–34** *Good's Study Med.* (ed. 4) III. 127 Such particular sense..restimulated into action. **1924** W. B. SELBIE *Psychol. Relig.* iv. 89 What are regarded as influences from the subconscious are due to a restimulation of brain tracts which have been influenced by previous experiences. **1925** T. DREISER *Amer. Trag.* (1926) II. xxxiii. 381 Even his obviously dwindling affection was restimulated by her quite visible need of help. **1962** *Economist* 27 Oct. 332/2 A Keynesian restimulation of internal demand. *Ibid.* 29 Dec. 1256/1 The orthodox thing ..may be to take no further restimulatory action..and then to give big tax reliefs in his budget. **1968** *Ibid.* 20 July 18/2 In spurring the re-expansion made possible by a freeing of labour from uneconomic jobs, it will be sensible to rely on tax cuts as the main restimulatory weapon.

†**re'stinction.** *Obs. rare.* [ad. L. *restinctio*, f. *restinguĕre* to quench.] (See quots.)

1612 WOODALL *Surg. Mate* Wks. (1653) 273 Restinction is a gradation, whereby metals or the like, candified by fire, are restinguished in liquor of exaltation, and thereby made more noble. [**1678** PHILLIPS, *Restinction*, in Chymistry, is the quenching of any metal in some exalting liquor, to bring it up to its designed perfection.]

†**'restiness**^{1}. *Obs.* [f. RESTY *a.*^{1} + -NESS.] The quality of being resty; restiveness.

c **1540** tr. *Pol. Verg. Eng. Hist.* (Camden Soc. No. 36) 128 In noe wise abiding the restines of ease. **1571** GOLDING *Calvin on Ps.* xxx. 7 The faythfull..shake of restynesse, and exercyse themselves in the warfarre. **1610** MARKHAM *Masterp.* I. liv. 116 A horse tireth..through dull cowardlinesse or restinesse. **1673** O. WALKER *Educ.* 54 Nor doth he strive to be himself known to be a Gentleman.. by disobedience, and restines towards Superiors. **1708** tr. *Petronius Arbiter* 18 All on fire at Lycurgus's Restiness.

†**'restiness**². *Obs.*—⁰ [f. RESTY *a.*² + -NESS.] Rancidity.

1499 *Promp. Parv.* (Pynson), Restynesse of flesshe, *rancor.* **1611** COTGR., *Rancissure*, mustinesse, fustinesse, reasinesse, restinesse, a taint.

'resting, *vbl. sb.*¹ Also 4-6 restyng; 4 ristynge; 5 resteng. [f. REST *v.*¹ + -ING¹.]

1. a. Rest, repose, inactivity.

a **1300** *Cursor M.* 6846 Ox and ass, womman and knaue, þat dai sal þai resting haue. **1382** WYCLIF *Lev.* xxv. 4 The seuenthe..ȝeer of the loond shal be the saboth of the restynge of the Lord. *c* **1450** LOVELICH *Grail* lv. 306 Sire kyng, I warne the here behoveth non Resteng forto be. **1590** STOCKWOOD *Rules Const.* 54 Verbes that betoken bodily moouing, going, resting, or dooing. **1611** COTGR., *Relaschement*, a reposing, resting, refreshing. **1660** THORNDIKE *Due Way* §39 No man dare to maintain that both were or are tied to the same measure of resting. **1703** tr. *Van Oosten's Dutch Gardener* 18 The resting of a Tree, you commonly perceive on a Bud. **1850** BROWNING *Christmas-Eve* xix, To..enjoy the gentle resting From further tracking. **1877** *Cornh. Mag.* Oct. 389 I'm quite ready to rest as long as you like. I consider resting my strong point.

b. A pause or stop for rest.

1662 R. MATHEW *Unl. Alch.* 52 A very aged woman, who ..through..weakness made five or six restings by the way.

c. *Theatr.* Unemployment; being without an acting job.

1924 G. B. STERN *Tents of Israel* vi. 85 A young singer ..[who] had sold all her things during her long period of enforced 'resting'. **1960** *Times* 28 Sept. 15/1 My theatrical colleagues who are only too familiar with the long periods of 'resting'—which being out of work is so politely called. **1973** J. BURROWS *Like an Evening Gone* i. 12 Though what..she did with herself in the great metropolis, in the frequent intervals of 'resting'—she didn't take typing jobs.

2. a. Rest in a particular place; a place where one rests or may rest, a resting-place.

1303 R. BRUNNE *Handl. Synne* 6654 Abrahams bosum ys a dwellyng þat holy men haue yn restyng. **1382** WYCLIF *Ps.* cxxxi[i]. 8 Ris, Lord, in to thi resting; thou and the arke of thin halewing. **1587** GOLDING *De Mornay* iv. (1592) 43 God ..hath not his resting in another but in him selfe. **1593** SHAKS. *Rich. II*, v. i. 6 Here let vs rest, if this rebellious Earth Haue any resting for her true Kings Queene. **1611** SPEED *Theat. Gt. Brit.* (1614) 87/1 To seeke their resting among the vast mountaines. **1667** MILTON *P.L.* I. 237 Such resting found the sole Of unblest feet.

b. A rest-house.

1879 MRS. A. E. JAMES *Ind. Househ. Managem.* 27 Huts and restings, or dâk-bungalows, are usually furnished with a bed, a table, and two or three hard chairs.

3. Reliance, confidence; a remaining satisfied.

1607 HIERON *Wks.* I. 221 There is no building vpon our selues, but a hopefull resting vpon the Lord. **1650** BAXTER *Saints' R.* III. §2. 40 *marg.*, It is a Resting on the deceiving promise of the Devil for Justification. **1739** WATERLAND *Wks.* (1823) VIII. 279 In order to guard the more strongly against a common failing, viz. the resting in a string of unmeaning words.

4. *attrib.* **a.** In sense 'of rest', as ***resting-day***, ***-hour***, ***-period***, ***-time***, ***-while***.

1598 SYLVESTER *Du Bartas* II. i. IV. *Handicrafts* 678 The Last shall be the very Resting-day. **1840** BREMNER *Excursion Denmark*, etc., II. 357 The resting-hour of noon. **1895** *Funk's Stand. Dict.*, Resting period. **1940** *Chambers's Techn. Dict.* 717/2 *Resting period*.., any time in the life of a plant, or plant organ, when no growth or other activity appears to be in progress. **1952** Resting period [see ASPECT *sb.* 14]. **1577** tr. *Bullinger's Decades* (1592) 139 For things that lacke a resting time, can neuer long indure. *c* **1374** CHAUCER *Boeth.* I. pr. iv. (1868) 14 þo þinges þat I hadde lerned of þe among my secre restyng whiles. **1387-8** T. USK *Test. Love* I. ix. (Skeat) I. 24 Suche as I have lerned thee in our restinge-whyles.

b. In sense 'serving for rest', as ***resting-chair***, ***-fold***, ***-ground***, ***-house***, ***-point***, ***-room***, etc.

c **1817** HOGG *Tales & Sk.* I. 328 Fling herself on the *resting-chair. *c* **1878** G. STEWART *Shetland Tales* (1892) 6 Pointing to a settle or 'restin' chair' which stood at one side of the fireplace. **1821** CLARE *Vill. Minstrel* I. 111 The mellow low and bleat, Greeting..*Resting-fold and milking-pail. **1921** *Daily Colonist* (Victoria, B.C.) 27 Oct. 10/3 Feeding and *resting grounds scattered over the country for the use of birds during migration. **1879** MRS. A. E. JAMES *Ind. Househ. Managem.* 33 At a dâk-bungalow, or travellers' *resting-house... These resting-houses are found in every station. **1587** GOLDING *De Mornay* xviii. 323 Both of them together being the *restingpoint of the whole man. **1866** J. H. NEWMAN *Gerontius* §3. 24 And memory lacks its natural resting-points, Of years, and centuries, and periods. **1660** F. BROOKE tr. *Le Blanc's Trav.* A ij, I petition you would afford our aged Traveller to take up a *resting room at last in your study. **1674** J. B[RIAN] *Harv. Home* vii. 48 An everlasting *resting seat. **1813** BYRON *Corsair* I. vi, In pensive posture leaning on the brand, Not oft a *resting-staff to that red hand.

c. With *condition*, *state*, etc., passing into *ppl. a.*; ***resting stage*** (*Cytology*) = INTERPHASE *sb.* 1.

1857 HENFREY *Bot.* §797 In the resting condition they contain oil and albuminous matters. **1885** GOODALE *Physiol. Bot.* (1892) 389 The 'resting' state of some plants cannot be shortened by any increase in the amount of oxygen furnished. **1896** E. B. WILSON *Cell* ii. 53 There are..some undoubted cases..in which the centrosome remains undivided during the resting stage and only divides as the process of mitosis begins. **1899** *Allbutt's Syst. Med.* VI. 828 The eyes remain in their static or resting position. **1932** [see INTERPHASE *sb.* 1]. **1957** C. P. SWANSON *Cytol. & Cytogenetics* iii. 48 Cells in interphase, or the resting stage, are characterized by a nucleus that shows little or no definable structure, except for the nucleoli and the prochromosomes.

†**'resting**, *vbl. sb.*² *Obs.* [f. REST *v.*³] The action of checking or arresting. Also *attrib.*

1398 TREVISA *Barth. De P. R.* VII. xxxvii. (Bodl. MS.), Whanne bodies beþ not fulle clensed in resting of þe feuer. **1465** *Mann. & Househ. Exp.* (Roxb.) 285 Paid for entrynge of a pleynt in the Cownter.., and the restynge, xij. *d.* *c* **1500** ARNOLDE *Chron.* (1811) 95 To helpe the officers of the cite ..for resting of mysdoers. **1523** LD. BERNERS *Froiss.* I. ccxii. 261 Takynge of..prisoners, or restynge of any persone, their goodes or marchandyses. **1575** CHURCHYARD *Chippes* (1817) 75 For fear off restyng I lye in the sentuary. **1616** *Shetland Witch Trial* in Dalyell *Darker Superst. Scot.* (1834) 118 He tauld Garth that thair was ane woman in Delting.. quha culd give him ane resting threid.

†**'resting**, *vbl. sb.*³ *Obs.*—¹ [f. REST *a.* Cf. REESE *v.*¹] Becoming rancid.

c **1420** *Liber Cocorum* (1862) 33 For to save venysone fro restyng.

'resting, *ppl. a.* [f. REST *v.*¹]

1. a. That rests or is taking a rest.

1398 TREVISA *Barth. De P.R.* VI. xx. (Bodl. MS.), Resting men shul ete and drinke lasse þanne trauailling men. **1648** HERRICK *Hesper.*, *Rest Refreshes*, A resting field Will, after ease, a richer harvest yield. **1878** HARDY *Ret. Native* I. ii, As the resting man looked at the barrow. **1898** C. HYNE *Capt. Kettle* 213 Fishing craft, dredgers, and the other resting traffic of the Tyne.

b. *Bot.*, in ***resting bud***, ***spore***, ***cell***, etc.; also in *Cytology*, as ***resting*** (= interphase) ***cell***, ***nucleus***; *Zool.*, **resting egg**, a fertilized egg which can survive the winter or other unfavourable period before hatching.

1857 HENFREY *Bot.* §796 Seeds and resting-spores..are organized in a manner especially adapted to preserve the latent vitality from injury by external influences. **1861** BENTLEY *Man. Bot.* 388 These true spores..may be called resting or inactive spores. **1895** *Sci. Progress* III. 333 Structural changes in the resting nucleus, which lead up to the formation of the reduced number of chromosomes, and which I have termed collectively the synapsis. **1896** M. HARTOG in *Cambr. Nat. Hist.* II. viii. 200 The fertilised eggs are of the kind termed 'winter' or 'resting' eggs. **1904** *Nature* 24 Nov. 76/2 Figures are given of resting-buds, twigs and their transverse sections [etc.]. **1934** *Biol. Rev.* IX. 160 Among the Cladocera..the same female may produce both females and males (by parthenogenetic reproduction) and resting eggs (by gameto-genetic reproduction). **1953** H. L. EDLIN *Forester's Handbk.* ii. 22 The shoot increases in length only during the annual period of active growth. It grows..by actively dividing cells within the bud at its tip. When autumn comes, this suspends its activity, and becomes a resting bud, protected by bud scales, which remains dormant until the following spring. **1960** L. PICKEN *Organization of Cells* IV. ii. 103 The conflict between the genetic evidence, that the persistence of serial order of discrete genetic units in the linkage groups is of primary importance; and the light microscope evidence, that chromosomes are not visible in the resting nucleus in a majority of cells. **1975** J. B. JENKINS *Genetics* i. 27 In the resting, or interphase, cell the chromosomes are in an uncoiled condition and thus difficult to see. **1976** *Freshwater Biol.* VI. 408/1 Lack of food is probably the most important factor stimulating resting egg production.

c. *Theatr.* Between acting jobs; unemployed.

1958 A. WILSON *Middle Age of Mrs Eliot* II. 143 The rich 'resting' stage stars. **1969** M. PUGH *Last Place Left* xxiii. 178 The waitress..looked like a resting actress who did her resting in daytime. **1971** M. BABSON *Cover-up Story* iv. 43 We still had the dubious privilege of representing two 'resting' actors.

2. Remaining stationary.

1601 SHAKS. *Jul. C.* III. i. 61 The Northerne Starre, Of whose true fixt, and resting quality, There is no fellow in the Firmament.

3. Restful. *rare.*

1896 A. BEARDSLEY *Let.* 17 Nov. (1970) 205, I wish Mabel could have started from Southampton. I do hope her crossing may be quiet and resting after all her hard work.

Hence **'restingly** *adv.*

a **1400** HYLTON *Scala Perf.* (W. de W. 1494) II. xxi, That there be no thynge of thyn own worchynge that thou wolt lene vpon restyngly.

'resting-place. [f. RESTING *vbl. sb.*¹]

1. A place where one rests or may rest.

1338 R. BRUNNE *Chron.* (1810) 16 Myght he neuer noure fynd a restyng place. **1426** LYDG. *De Guil. Pilgr.* 16540 A Pylgrym or a passagour..reioyseth whan he Resorteth to his restynge place. **1526** *Pilgr. Perf.* (W. de W. 1531) 1 That he sholde neuer thynke this worlde his fynall habitacyon and restyng place. **1587** GOLDING *De Mornay* xix. (1592) 303 Like as the Iewes betokened the Restingplace of the blessed sort by a goodly Garden. *a* **1627** SIR J. BEAUMONT *Dial. betw. World, Pilgr. & Vertue* ii, Weary passengers. whose desp'rate case I pitie, and prouide a resting-place. **1682** OTWAY *Venice Preserved* III. ii, Can Belvidera want a Resting-place When these poor Arms are open to receive her? **1768-74** TUCKER *Lt. Nat.* (1834) II. 291 The various conveniencies and accommodations provided for the brutes, their feedings and resting-places. **1814** SOUTHEY *Carmen Triumph.* xviii, Then when the waters of the flood abate The Dove her resting-place secure may find. **1875** MANNING *Mission H. Ghost* i. 23 That this world is not his resting-place, that his home is in eternity.

b. *fig.*, in various uses.

c **1369** CHAUCER *Dethe Blaunche* 1005 Trouthe..chose hys maner principalle In hir that was his restynge place. **1589** PUTTENHAM *Eng. Poesie* (Arb.) 88 As a resting place and perfection of so much former speach as had bene vttered. **1712** ADDISON *Spect.* No. 333 ¶22 As he knew all the Arts of affecting the Mind, he knew it was necessary to give it certain Resting-places. **1789** LD. AUCKLAND *Corr.* (1861) II. 185 The sameness..is such, that there are no periods or resting-places for the mind. **1863** *Sat. Rev.* 2 May 554 The French Academy is now the last resting-place in France of freedom of thought. **1876** R. H. HUTTON *Ess.* (ed. 2) I. Pref. 8 The final resting-place of the moral reason of man.

c. The place where a dead person is laid to rest. Freq. with *last.*

1808 SCOTT *Marm.* II. xiv, His body's resting-place, of old. **1833** TENNYSON *May Queen* II. x, If I can I'll come again, mother, from out my resting-place. **1856** KANE *Arct. Expl.* I. xix. 240 The chapter from Job which has consigned so many to their last resting-place.

2. A break or landing in a staircase.

1823 P. NICHOLSON *Pract. Build.* 439 The floor between the two flights is termed a half-space or resting-place. **1825** J. NICHOLSON *Operat. Mechanic* 594 Where the height of a story is considerable, resting places are necessary. **1875** KNIGHT *Dict. Mech.* s.v. *Half-pace.*

†**re'stinguish**, *v. Obs.* [ad. L. *restinguĕre*, after EXTINGUISH.] *trans.* To extinguish, suppress, subdue; to quench.

1578 J. JONES *Preserv. Bodie & Soule* I. xxxix. 84 It is not so necessary for vs to beware of vice, as to restinguish and keepe backe the increase of euils. **1597** J. KING *On Jonas* (1618) 557 If Ionas had restinguished and choked the feruour of his wrath. **1612** [see RESTINCTION]. *a* **1616** R. FIELD in N. Field *Life* (1716) 41 Hence the Thirst of languishing Soules is Restinguished.

re'stipulate, *v.* Now *rare.* [f. ppl. stem of L. *restipulārī.*] *trans.* and *intr.* To promise or engage in return.

1633 T. ADAMS *Exp. 2 Peter* ii. 9 If he covenant with us, 'I will be your God'; we must restipulate, 'Then will we rest upon thee'. **1683** *Case Inf. Bapt.* 87 But how can Infants restipulate.., who have not the use of reason? *a* **1708** BEVERIDGE *Priv. Th.* I. (1730) 53 What can God stipulate more to us, or we restipulate more to him. **1880** MUIRHEAD *Gaius* IV. 94 For the same reason the defender does not restipulate.

re-'stipulate (riː-), *v.* [RE- 5 a.] *intr.* To stipulate anew.

1847 MRS. KERR tr. *Ranke's Hist. Servia* 343 To re-stipulate for the conditions of peace formerly proposed.

restipu'lation. [ad. L. *restipulātio*, f. *restipulārī* to RESTIPULATE.] The action of restipulating; a counter-engagement.

1611 W. SCLATER *Key* (1629) 340 If we haue performed our restipulation, carrying our selues in all things, as the people of God. **1649** BP. REYNOLDS *Hosea* i. 16 In the promise or Restipulation we have first the Covenant. **1720** *Wodrow Corr.* (1843) II 493 Your thoughts..as to the restipulation, and the nature of allegiance. **1760** T. HUTCHINSON *Hist. Mass.* iv. (1765) 420 The constitutive part of a..church ought to be, a restipulation or mutual covenanting. **1880** MUIRHEAD *Gaius* IV. §13 The amount of the sponsion or restipulation under the present system.

re'stipulatory, *a. rare.* [f. RESTIPULATE *v.* + -ORY².] Pertaining to restipulation.

1880 MUIRHEAD *Gaius* IV. §180 A restipulatory penalty is also imposed in certain cases.

re'stitch (riː-), *v.* [RE- 5 a.] *trans.* To stitch or sew again.

1611 FLORIO, *Ripunto*, repricked. Also restiched. **1862** S. LUCAS *Secularia* 386 No number of bayonets can restitch the rent which runs across an immense continent. **1887** *Mission. Herald* (Boston, U.S.) Mar. 122 Nearly all of them show signs of having been taken to pieces and restitched.

†**restitue**, *v. Obs.* Also 5-6 **restytue**. [ad. F. *restituer* (14th c.) or L. *restituĕre*, f. *re-* RE- + *statuĕre* to set up, etc.] **a.** *intr.* To make restitution. **b.** *trans.* To restore. Also in *pass.*, to have restitution made to (oneself).

1377 LANGL. *P. Pl.* B. v. 281 Alle þat haue of þi good.. Ben holden at þe heighe dome to helpe þe to restitue. *Ibid.* 297 And if þow wite neuere to whiche ne whom to restitue, Bere it to þe bisschop and bidde [etc.]. **1393** *Ibid.* C. XI. 54 Raþer haue we no reste til we restitue Our lyf to oure lord god for oure lykames gultes. **1425** *Rolls of Parlt.* IV. 304/2 The said Merchantz..yat have lost..any Woll..may be restitued and allowed of ye Subsidee of yat so perished..or lost. **1483** CAXTON *Gold. Leg.* 428 b/2 Two dombe chyldren and dyuers other that had loste the use of the tongue were restytued of theyr spekyng. **1484** —— *Fables of Alfonce* iv, Who someuer had fond a thowsand Crownes..he shold restitue and brynge them to hym ageyne. **1530** PALSGR. 689/1, I restytue, I restore.

†**restitute**, *pa. pple. Obs.* [ad. L. *restitūt-us*, pa. pple. of *restituĕre*: see prec. In quot. 1643 after AF. *restitutz* in 1 Hen. IV. c. 5.] Restored.

c **1470** HARDING *Chron.* CXXIV. vi, Sone after kyng Dunkan of Scotland slayn By treason was, and Dunwall restitute Vnto the croune of Scotlande ther agayne. [**1643** PRYNNE *Sov. Power Parl.* III. 42 It is ordained and assented, that the Lords and other..shall be wholly restitute and restored to their names,..inheritaments and possessions.]

restitute ('rɛstɪtjuːt), *v.* [f. ppl. stem of L. *restituĕre*: cf. prec.]

1. *trans.* To restore to a position or status; to reinstate, rehabilitate. Now *rare.*

c **1500** ARNOLDE *Chron.* (1811) 42 To alle her fraunches and free usagis..be they restituted. **1530** CROMWELL in Merriman *Life & Lett.* (1902) I. 328 The King did restitute your Grace before He was intitled. **1570** LEVINS *Manip.* 196 To restitute, *restituere.* **1855** LORENZ tr. *Van der Keessel's Select Theses* dcccxxix, A debtor who has become impoverished by mere change of fortunes, and has not acted fraudulently, is discharged from all liability, and restituted, provided one half of the creditors to whom a half of the debt is due consent to such restitution.

2. To restore, hand back, refund. Also *absol.* to make restitution.

1727–38 CHAMBERS *Cycl.* s.v. *Restitution*, The Lutheran and Calvinist princes were obliged to restitute, restore what they had taken. **1885** *Field* 17 Oct. 542/1 The inclosures which would be affected and 'restituted' by Mr. Jesse Collings's regulations. **1893** *Ibid.* 4 Mar. 334/1 Having promised to restitute expenses to professionals if they did not win. **1907** *Westm. Gaz.* 17 Aug. 4/1 If..he acts to the detriment of someone's interest, he must be compelled to restitute.

3. *intr. Genetics.* Of a break in a chromosome or chromatid: to be reversed by restitution (sense 8) of the two broken ends.

1945 *Jrnl. Genetics* XLVII. 13 Some of the breaks which restitute are lethals. **1971** LEVITAN & MONTAGU *Textbk. Human Genetics* iii. 135 Nonrearrangement breaks tend to restitute..quite readily.

Hence **'restituted** *ppl. a.*

1727–38 [see RESTITUTION 7]. **1757** DYER *Fleece* II. 347 Restituted trade To every virtue lent his helping stores.

‖**restitutio in integrum** (rɛstɪ'tjuːtɪəʊ ɪn ɪn'tɛgrəm), *sb. phr. Law.* Also **ad integrum.** [L., restoration to the uninjured state, etc.] (See quot. 1909.) Also *transf.*

[*a* **1633** T. HOPE *Major Practicks* (1938) II. 207 (*heading*) De Restitutione in Integrum.] **1704** T. WOOD *New Institute Imperial or Civil Law* I. ii. 55 A Restitution shall be adjudged in the behalf of the Minor if he is circumvented, tho' the Tutors or Curators were present and consenting, and tho' the Decree was made against the Minor judicially; and this is called *Restitutio in integrum.* **1845** T. THORNTON *Notes Cases in Eccles. & Maritime Courts* III. 77 The principle is, that the vessel should be placed *in statu quo* before the collision,—a *restitutio in integrum.* **1902** W. JAMES *Var. Relig. Exper.* vi. 156 When disillusionment has gone as far as this, there is seldom a *restitutio ad integrum.* **1909** *Halsbury's Laws of Eng.* X. 302 The underlying great principle by which the courts are guided in awarding damages is *restitutio in integrum.* By this is meant that the law will endeavour, so far as money can do it, to place the injured person in the same situation as if the contract had been performed, or in the position he occupied before the occurrence of the tort which adversely affects him. **1936** BUCKLAND & MCNAIR *Roman Law & Common Law* xii. 337 An action which had once reached the stage of *litis contestatio* could never be brought again, unless the facts brought the matter within the rather narrow range of cases in which a man could get *restitutio in integrum.* **1975** J. R. MURDOCH *Law Estate Agency & Auctions* xiii. 385 Since the principle underlying rescission is '*restitutio in integrum*' it will only be allowed where both parties can be substantially returned to their pre-contractual positions.

restitution (rɛstɪ'tjuːʃən). Also 5–6 restyt-. [a. OF. *restitution, -ucion* (Sp. *-ucion*, It. *-uzione*), or ad. L. *restitūtiōn-em*, n. of action f. *restituĕre*: see RESTITUE *v.*]

1. a. The action of restoring or giving back something to its proper owner, or of making reparation to one for loss or injury previously inflicted.

a **1300** *Cursor M.* 27279 For slikin suik agh wit resun Be mad of restituciun. **1377** LANGL. *P. Pl.* B. v. 235 'That was no restitucioun,' quod repentance. **1413** *Pilgr. Sowle* (Caxton, 1483) IV. v. 60 This that felyth hyr seluen wronged and asketh restitucion shal fyrst haue audyence to make hyr compleynt. **1494** *Act 11 Hen. VII*, c. 21 For the Recovery and Restitution of the same Debt, Damages, and Costs, the Plaintiff..may..sue. *a* **1548** HALL *Chron., Hen. VIII*, 90 b, Euer the Frenche Ambassadours promised restitucion of euery thyng, but none was restored. **1593** SHAKS. *2 Hen. VI*, III. i. 118 Many a Pound of mine owne proper store..Haue I dis-pursed to the Garrisons, And neuer ask'd for restitution. **1625** T. GODWIN *Moses & Aaron* v. (1641) 204 Restitution in identitie, was and is principally required. **1681** STAIR *Instit.* (1693) I. vii. 61 Restitution of things belonging to Others, may seem to be an Effect of Property. **1727** POPE & GAY *What passed in London*, He was advised to restitution, but I never heard that he complied with it. **1772** *Junius Lett.* Ded., A death-bed repentance seldom reaches to restitution. **1836** THIRLWALL *Greece* III. 337 The three.. important points on which the Athenians felt themselves aggrieved: the restitution of Amphipolis [etc.]. **1877** FROUDE *Short Studies* (1883) IV. I. ix. 106 He had been promised restitution of his property, but it had been given back to him in ruins.

b. In phr. ***to make restitution.***

c **1375** *Cursor M.* 27279 (Fairf.), For suche kin þing with gode resoun sulde men make restitucioun. **1377** LANGL. *P. Pl.* B. v. 232 Repentedestow þe euere,..ne restitucioun madest? *c* **1430** LYDG. *Min. Poems* (Percy Soc.) 143, I.. Made in my liffe no restitucioun. **1494** FABYAN *Chron.* VI. clx. 152 He shulde..make restitucion of all thynges that he before had takyn from the churche. **1545** BRINKLOW *Lament.* (1874) 113 Thou must..make restytucion to thy power. **1598** SHAKS. *Merry W.* v. v. 33 Why, now is Cupid a child of conscience, he makes restitution. **1611** BIBLE *Exod.* xxii. 5 Of the best of his owne vineyard shall he make restitution. **1685** BAXTER *Paraphr. N.T.* Matt. v. 23, 24 Go presently and make restitution. *a* **1720** SEWEL *Hist. Quakers* (1795) I. 39 They had wronged her.., therefore they ought to make her restitution. **1835** THIRLWALL *Greece* ix. I. 345 The Spartan, instead of making restitution, took away the life of his companion. **1871** FREEMAN *Norm. Conq.* (1876) IV. 56 Though their tenure might be changed and the restitution not made without a price paid to the new lord.

c. ***restitution of conjugal rights*** (see quot. 1768 and CONJUGAL *a.*). Also *ellipt.* in *attrib.* use.

1768 BLACKSTONE *Comm.* III. 94 The suit for restitution of conjugal rights is..another species of matrimonial causes: which is brought whenever either the husband or wife is guilty of the injury of subtraction, or lives separate from the other without any sufficient reason. **1858** LD. ST. LEONARDS *Handy-Bk. Prop. Law* xii. 73 Restitution of conjugal rights may be granted by the Court. **1894** *Westm. Gaz.* 6 Dec. 1/2 Whatever is an answer to a restitution suit is also a ground for judicial separation.

2. With *a* and *pl.* A restoration of something taken from another.

c **1440** *Alph. Tales* 32 He..made a restitucion & become a gude man. **1442** *Rolls of Parlt.* V. 59/1 All restitutions of Londes..made by you. **1604** SHAKS. *Oth.* v. i. 16 He calles me to a restitution large Of Gold, and Iewels, that I bob'd from him, As Guifts to Desdemona. **1662** PETTY *Taxes* 58 It will be asked with how manifold restitutions should picking a pocket (for example) be punished? **1729** BUTLER *Serm.* Wks. 1874 II. 119 David passes sentence..that there should be a fourfold restitution made. *a* **1781** WATSON *Philip III* (1839) 31 To procure a restitution of some towns on the German frontier.

†**3.** Reparation *of* hurt or loss. *Obs. rare.*

c **1400** *Destr. Troy* XII. *heading*, How the Grekys sent two Kinges in Message to Kyng Priam For Restitucion of þaire harme. **1615** G. SANDYS *Trav.* (1637) 85 The English consull of Aleppo is absolute of himselfe..whose chiefe employment is..to labour a revenge of wrongs, and a restitution of losses.

4. a. The action of restoring a person or persons to a previous status or position; the fact of being thus restored or reinstated; a document authorizing such restoration. Now *rare.*

1387 TREVISA *Higden* (Rolls) VI. 163 He hadde lettres of þe pope to þe kynges of Engelond to his restitucioun. *a* **1450** *Mankind* (Brandl) 17, I haue be þe very mene for yowur restytucyone. **1485** *Rolls of Parlt.* VI. 307/2 The Acte of Restitucion of the said late Viscount, made or to be made in thys present Parlement. **1503–4** *Act 19 Hen. VII*, c. 28 §1 The restitucions and enhablements of the seid persones. **1570–6** LAMBARDE *Peramb. Kent* (1826) 317 The restitution of the English bloud to the crowne. **1610** WILLET *Dan.* 138 The effect of this his restitution to his reason. **1621** ABP. WILLIAMS in *Fortescue P.* (Camden) 169 Soe I may be restored to my temporalities..if his Majestie will be pleased to signe this restitution. **1662** FULLER *Worthies* (1840) II. 417 His piety and patience were rewarded by God, with a happy restitution to his undoubted dominions. **1703** DE FOE *Poor Man's Plea* Misc. 291 After the Restitution of King Charles the Second. **1797** *Encycl. Brit.* (ed. 3) IX. 637/1 A peremptory *mandamus*, or writ of restitution. **1855** [see RESTITUTE *v.* 1].

b. ***restitution in blood*** (see quots. and BLOOD *sb.* 13).

a **1633** COKE *On Litt.* III. (1648) 240 Of restitutions by Parliament some be in blood onely... And some be generall restitutions. **1666** in Strype *Eccl. Mem.* (1721) III. 103 A bill was ordered..for the restitution in blood of Edward Seimour, son and heir of the late duke, attainted. **1769** BLACKSTONE *Comm.* IV. xxx. 385 Sometimes..the merits of the criminal's family shall after his death obtain a restitution in blood, honours, and estate, or some, or one of them, by act of parliament. **1863** H. COX *Instit.* I. vi. 43 Bills for reversal of attainder and for restitution in blood.

5. a. The action of restoring a thing or institution to its original state or form. (In later use only in echoes of, or with reference to, Acts iii. 21.)

1382 WYCLIF *Acts* iii. 21 Whom..it bihoueth heuene for to resceyue, til into the tyme of restitucioun of alle thingis. **1575–85** ABP. SANDYS *Serm.* 44 Nehemias..gaue thankes unto the Lord..for restitution of religion. **1605** VERSTEGAN *Dec. Intell.* Pref. Ep., A new worke vnder the name of A restitution of decaied intelligence, in Antiquities concerning our nation. **1659** HARRINGTON *Art Lawgiving* III. i. (1700) 444 We find in the restitution of the Sanhedrim by Jehoshaphat, that there was Amariah chief in all matters of the Lord. **1771** *Encycl. Brit.* II. 479/1 It will not be at rest, ..till it be restored to its original equality; and this restitution cannot be made through the substance of the glass. **1781** WINCHESTER *Seed of Woman* 35 Proving to a Demonstration the Doctrine of the Restitution of all Things to their first State of Perfection. **1860** J. BROWN *Rab, Let. to J. Cairns* (1906) 245 They two saw her open her..true eyes .., and..close them till the time of the restitution of all things. **1867** JUKES *Restit. all Things* (1869) 106, I have thus noticed what Reason is supposed to say against the doctrine of final restitution.

†**b.** Correction *of* an error. *Obs.*$^{-1}$

1636 MELLIS *Recorde's Gr. Arts* 330, I will give you a Table for the restitution of those errours, as may suffice for this present time.

6. †**a.** Reposition, replacement. *Obs. rare.*

1578 BANISTER *Hist. Man* II. 40 The Luxation of the shoulder hath difficulte restitution. **1658** SIR T. BROWNE *Hydriot.* i. 2 If Adam were made out of an extract of the Earth, all parts might challenge a restitution.

b. Tendency to return to, or resume, a previous position by virtue of elasticity or resilience.

1656 tr. *Hobbes' Elem. Philos.* (1839) 478 When any thing is bent, as a plate of steel, and..restores itself again, it is evident that the cause of its restitution cannot be referred to the ambient air. **1669** BOYLE *Contn. New Exp.* I. (1682) 50 The cause of the Motion of Restitution in Bodies and consequently of that which makes them springy. **1701** GREW *Cosmol. Sacra* I. iv. 17 That so their Roots may yield to Stones, and their Trunks to the Wind, or other force, with a power of Restitution. **1727–38** CHAMBERS *Cycl.* s.v., Contraction being the proper and natural action of muscular fibres, some authors ascribe dilatation to a motion of restitution. **1865** TAIT & STEELE *Dynamics of Particle* x. §271 (ed. 2) 288 The coefficient of proportionality..may be conveniently termed the Coefficient of Restitution. **1884** A. DANIELL *Princ. Physics* 237 At the moment of complete restitution the energy possessed by the body (if perfectly elastic) has wholly assumed the kinetic form.

7. *Numism.* (See quot. 1727–38.)

1727–38 CHAMBERS *Cycl.*, *Restitutions of medals*, or *Restituted medals*, is a phrase used by antiquaries, for such medals as were struck by the emperors, to renew or retrieve the memory of their predecessors. **1853** HUMPHREYS *Coin-coll. Man.* xxiv. 327 Such restitutions, by Titus and his two immediate successors, were of bronze.

8. *Genetics.* The coming together of the two parts of a broken chromosome or chromatid so as to re-form it; also *concr.*, the resulting chromosome or chromatid.

1941 *Cold Spring Harbor Symp. Quantitative Biol.* IX. 154/2 Even at ordinary doses there has been more than one break per gamete, but that break has usually been an invisible, 'restituted' one. How often may this 'restitution' have been imperfect or attended by some local alteration such as a 'gene mutation'? **1945** *Jrnl. Genetics* XLVII. 11 On this view it appears likely that lethals *not* apparently associated with any chromosome change are restitutions. **1980** R. P. WAGNER et al. *Introd. Mod. Genetics* x. 273/1 When a chromosome breaks, the two broken ends usually undergo restitution.

9. restitution nucleus *Genetics* [tr. G. *restitutions-kern* (O. Rosenberg 1927, in *Hereditas* VIII. 321)], a cell nucleus having twice the regular chromosome number, formed by an uncompleted mitotic or meiotic cell division.

1927 *Hereditas* VIII. 336 The semiheterotypic meta- and anaphase very often are not completed, but are interrupted by a premature homotypic division, whereby *Restitution-nuclei* are formed. **1950** *Adv. Genetics* III. 197 The zygoid chromosome number is restored through the fusion of two azygoid nuclei, the formation of a restitution nucleus or endomitosis. **1974** *Euphytica* XXIII. 631 The diploid chromosome numbers..may result either from first or second division restitution nuclei of meiosis.

Resti'tutionalist. [f. prec.] (See quot.)

1888 CAVE *Inspir. O.T.* 128 The so-called Restitutionalists, who confine the Scriptural account of the six days to this present late phase of the earth's history... According to this theory..the Mosaic six days record the restitution of a preceding creation which had been.. overwhelmed.

Resti'tutionism. = RESTORATIONISM.

1896 GLADSTONE *Condit. Man in Fut. Life* I. 19 Upon this scheme of Universalism or Restitutionism..I cannot but speak in terms of repugnance.

Resti'tutionist. [-IST.]

1. *Theol.* One who accepts in some form the doctrine of the 'restitution of all things'; a restorationist. Chiefly *U.S.* (See quots.)

1773 J. BOUCHER *Amer. Revol.* (1797) 261 *note*, Those who, during their connexion with Great Britain, were contented to be called Dissenters or Independents, are now pretty generally become, or are becoming, either Universal Restitutionists, Arians or Socinians. **1859** BARTLETT *Dict. Amer.* (ed. 2) 362 *Restitutionists*, a religious sect which has recently sprung up in Worcester and some other places. **1872** DE VERE *Americanisms* 242 The more pretentious Restitutionists of Massachusetts believe in an immediate return of all things to their original form and purity.

2. One who advocates restitution (of property).

1885 *Pall Mall G.* 7 Oct. 1/1 The Restitutionists of the Chamberlain school and the Rights of Property men who swear by Lord Hartington.

restitutive ('rɛstɪˌtjuːtɪv), *a.* [ad. L. type **restitūtīvus*, f. *restitūt-*, ppl. stem of *restituĕre*: see RESTITUTE *v.* and -IVE. So Sp. *restitutivo.*]

†**1.** Of a character consequent or dependent on restitution, or restoration to a former status.

1658–9 *Burton's Diary* (1828) IV. 26 The question now is, what that house shall be, whether constitutive or restitutive. Restitutive is dangerous.

2. Tending to restore to a former position.

a **1774** GOLDSM. *Surv. Exp. Philos.* (1776) I. 190 The restitutive force acting upon it constantly, it will acquire such an accelerated velocity, as to drive it into the opposite ellipse CO. **1884** A. DANIELL *Princ. Physics* 235 Under any given distortion within the limits of restitutive power, the restitution-pressure is equal to the product of the coefficient of restitution into the distortion.

'restiˌtutor. *rare.* [a. L. *restitūtor*, agent-noun from *restituĕre* to RESTITUTE. Cf. F. *restituteur* (15th c.), It. *re-, ristitutore*, Sp. *restitutor.*] A restorer.

1654 GAYTON *Pleas. Notes* III. viii. 124 They all..took part with their Rescuer, or Restitutor Quixote. **1682** WHELER *Journ. Greece* II. 207 If I were to be its Restitutor, I would write it *Divo Caesari Avgvsto.*

re'stitutory, *a.* [ad. L. *restitūtōri-us*: see RESTITUTE *v.* and -ORY. So It., Sp., Pg. *restitutorio.*] Of or relating to restitution.

1880 MUIRHEAD *Gaius* IV. §142 The principal division then of interdicts is this,—that they are either prohibitory, restitutory, or exhibitory. **1886** T. HARDY *Mayor Casterbr.* I. xiii. 154 To castigate himself with the thorns which these restitutory acts brought in their train.

restive ('rɛstɪv), *a.* [Later form of RESTIF(F, assimilated to adjectives in -IVE.]

1. Inclined to rest or remain still; inactive, inert. Now *rare* or *Obs.*

1599 SANDYS *Europæ Spec.* (1632) 35 What great imployment with stirring and mettald spirits, what perpetuall quiet with heavie and restive bodies. **1620** B. JONSON *News fr. New World*, [He] went to Edenburgh o' foot, and came backe: marry he has been restive..ever since for we have had nothing from him. **1699** L. WAFER *Voy.* (1729) 347 Notwithstanding their being thus sluggish, and dull, and restive in the day-time, yet when moon-shiny nights come, they are all life and activity. **1726** SWIFT *Gulliver* III. viii, That positive, confident, restive Temper, which Virtue infused into Man, was a perpetual Clog to

Publick Business. **1752** HUME *Ess. & Treat.* (1777) II. 179 The imagination is extremely quick and agile; but the passions, in comparison, are slow and restive. **1833** LAMB *Let. to Talfourd* in *Final Mem.* viii. 273 Of my old friends, I have lived to see two knighted, one made a judge, another in a fair way to it. Why am I restive?

†**2.** Persistent, obstinate, settled or fixed, *in* an opinion or course of action. *Obs.*

1633 *Certaine Learned & Elegant Wks.* 286 (Cent.), Be not restive in their weake stubburnness that will either keepe or lose all. **1660** WATERHOUSE *Arms & Arm.* 56 Every one being restive in his opinion, there can nothing infallibly, as to the time, be concluded. *a* **1782** SIR J. REYNOLDS *Lit. Writ.* III. 102 He will fall into the habit of acquiescing in the partial opinions of a few; he will grow restive in his own. **1826** E. IRVING *Babylon* VI. II. 69 The world is so restive in its evil conditions, and ill-disposed towards the..ministers of reformation.

3. Of horses: Refusing to go forward; stubbornly standing still; obstinately moving backwards or to the side when being driven or ridden; hence, resisting control, intractable, refractory.

1656 BLOUNT *Glossogr.*, *Restive* or *Resty*.., stubborn, drawing backwards, that will not go forward. **1676** HOBBES *Iliad* 66 The horses us'd thereto will you obey: To me, it may be, they will restive stand. **1727–38** CHAMBERS *Cycl.* s.v., A restive horse is a rebellious, refractory, ill-broken horse, which only goes where it will, and when it will. **1756** *World* No. 207. 293 I fear he has not been accustomed to drive a set so restive as mine are, especially in bad roads. **1804–6** SYD. SMITH *Mor. Philos.* (1850) 279 The mind advances in its train of thought, as a restive colt proceeds on the road in which you wish to guide him. **1849** MACAULAY *Hist. Eng.* v. I. 647 The beasts which were to drag him to the gallows became restive and went back. **1896** *Law Times* C. 508/1 His lordship's horse became restive, and attempted to throw its rider.

b. *transf.* of persons or things.

1687 *Death's Vision* Pref., 'Tis true such Matter is Restive, Refractory and Unpolishable enough. **1693** DRYDEN *Disc. Satire* Ess. (ed. Ker) II. 32 The arch-angel,.. when Discord was restive,..has the whip-hand of her, drags her out with many stripes. **1785** MRS. H. COWLEY *More Ways than One* v, Nay, don't be restive, Miss. **1794** GODWIN *Caleb Williams* 15 He proved as ready a scholar as he had been indocile and restive to the pedant who held the office of his tutor. **1820** BYRON *Juan* III. lix, It is a hard although a common case To find our children running restive. **1863** 'OUIDA' *Held in Bondage* (1870) 6 He turned restive at the least attempt at coercion. **1873** HALE *In His Name* viii. 69 The child was more restive, and her stomach seemed likely to reject the draught.

4. Of actions, etc.: Characterized by unwillingness or resistance to control.

1806–7 J. BERESFORD *Miseries Hum. Life* II. 233 At the time of leaving off fires, to which you have given a restive consent. **1826** SCOTT *Woodst.* ix, The outward man yielded a reluctant and restive compliance. **1846** BRITTAN tr. *Malgaigne's Man. Oper. Surg.* 291 The hooks are liable to prick the lids..in the restive motions of some patients.

Hence **'restively** *adv.*, in a restive manner.

1866 HOWELLS *Ven. Life* xx. 329 Gentlemen restively imprisoned in dress coats and white gloves. **1874** RUSKIN *Fors Clav.* xliii. (1896) II. 153 [She] obeyed—not with her heart, but restively, like an ill-bred dog or mule.

'restiveness. [f. prec. + -NESS.] The quality or condition of being restive.

1605 BACON *Adv. Learn.* II. xxiii. §33 From whatsoever roote or cause this Restiuenesse of mind proceedeth, it is a thing most prejudiciall. **1660** GAUDEN *Brownrig* 127 The coy reserve and supercilious restiveness of some who envy others this..freedom. **1798** CHARLOTTE SMITH *Yng. Philos.* I. 15 Miss Goldthorp..found herself exposed..to the double danger of the storm, and the restiveness of the horses. **1820** BYRON tr. *Pulci's Morg. Mag.* xxvii, Of restiveness he'd cure him. **1892** J. TAIT *Mind in Matter* (ed. 3) 206 The last symptom of restiveness manifested by the Jews against their burdens related to the tithe.

restle, variant of RISTLE *sb.*

restless ('rɛstlɪs), *a.* [f. REST *sb.*¹ + -LESS. Cf. Fris. *restleas*, G. *rastlos* (Da. and Sw. *rastlös*), Du. *rusteloos*.]

1. a. Deprived of rest; finding no rest; *esp.* uneasy in mind or spirit.

In some contexts passing into sense 2.

a **1000** *Rule St. Benet* (Schröer) lxiv. 121 A bið unзestillod and restleas, þe mid þam unþeawum beled bið. *c* **1386** CHAUCER *Pard. T.* 728 Thus walke I lyk a restelees [*v.r.* risteles] kaityf. *c* **1430** *Pol., Rel., & L. Poems* (1903) 180 In a valey of þis restles mynde I souзte.., Trustynge a trewe loue for to fynde. **1513** MORE in Grafton *Chron.* (1568) II. 805 So was his restlesse heart continually tossed and tombled. *c* **1590** GREENE *Fr. Bacon* (1630) 58 How restlesse are the ghosts of hellish Sprites, When euery Charmer.. Cals vs from nine-fold trenched Phlegiton. **1666** DRYDEN *Ann. Mirab.* cii, Restless he passed the remnants of the night. **1805** SCOTT *Last Minstr.* VI. xxvii, That he a pilgrimage would take To Melrose Abbey, for the sake Of Michael's restless sprite. **1856** R. A. VAUGHAN *Mystics* I. VI. i. 179 His cares were thrown off, and he was restless and anxious no longer about little things.

b. Marked or characterized by unrest; affording or yielding no rest.

1605 SHAKS. *Macb.* III. ii. 22 Better be with the dead,.. Then on the torture of the Minde to lye In restlesse extasie. **1776** JOHNSON *Let.* 21 Oct. in *Boswell*, My nights are very restless and tiresome. **1784** COWPER *Task* I. 44 Restless was the chair; the back erect Distress'd the weary loins. *a* **1806** H. K. WHITE *To the Morning*, Now let me leave my restless bed. **1821** SHELLEY *Hellas* 2 We strew these opiate flowers On thy restless pillow.

2. a. Of persons (or animals): Taking no rest; constantly stirring or acting, or desirous to be so; averse to being quiet or settled.

c **1475** *Rauf Coilзear* 819 Thir riche restles renkis ruschit out full raith. **1503** DUNBAR *Thistle & Rose* 80 The restles Suallow commandit scho also To feche all fowll. **1535** COVERDALE *Jer.* xlvi. 25, I will vyset that restlesse people off Alexandria. **1582** BENTLEY *Mon. Matrones* To Rdr., I haue laboured..with restlesse Ruth to go after the maidens in the haruest. **1603** KNOLLES *Hist. Turks* (1638) 55 Where these restlesse people ceased not by all meanes to enlarge their Empire. **1649** MILTON *Eikon.* Pref., We choose that interpretation which may best mind us of what our restless enemies endeavor. **1718** *Free-thinker* No. 42. 306 Poverty and Avarice are the restless Companions of Prodigality. **1781** COWPER *Retirem.* 21 Cities, humming with a restless crowd. **1836** THIRLWALL *Greece* xxiv. III. 335 Alcibiades,.. restless and sanguine, had much more to hope than to fear from war. **1888** FERGUS HUME *Mme. Midas* I. i, She was too restless and ambitious a nature, to be content with an idle life.

b. So of the thoughts, mind, etc.

1603 KNOLLES *Hist. Turks* (1638) 184 Continually incited with the insatiable and restles desire of soueraignty. **1667** MILTON *P.L.* II. 526 Where he may likeliest find Truce to his restless thoughts. **1759** DILWORTH *Pope* 71 Mr. Pope is much indebted to the restless spirit of correction Swift was possessed of. **1778** MISS BURNEY *Evelina* lxxxii, Great joy is as restless as sorrow. **1807** CRABBE *Par. Reg.* III. 512 All the reason, by himself assign'd For so much rambling, was, a restless mind. **1868** FREEMAN *Norm. Conq.* (1877) II. 496 Both of them parts of one scheme devised in the restless brain of the Mercian Earl.

Comb. *c* **1712** *Dangerous Present* 1 The malicious and dangerous Designs of the restless Spirited Whigs. **1914** 'SAKI' *When William Came* vi. 101 You must remember that thousands and thousands of the more virile and restless-souled men have emigrated.

†**c.** Const. *to* (with inf.) or *of*: Impatient. *Obs.*

1719 DE FOE *Crusoe* II. (Globe) 511 When I was at Home, I was restless to go abroad; and now I was abroad, I was restless to be at Home. **1725** POPE *Odyss.* II. 9 By his Heralds, restless of delay, To council [he] calls the Peers.

d. *spec.* in animal and bird names, as *restless cavy*, *fly-catcher*, *thrush*.

1771 PENNANT *Syn. Quadrup.* 243 *Restless Cavy. **1838** *Penny Cycl.* XI. 480/2 Guinea-Pig..(Restless Cavy), the well-known Brasilian rodent now domesticated in Europe. **1876** *Encycl. Brit.* V. 277 The Restless Cavy (*Cavia aperea*), found throughout Uruguay and Brazil, is supposed to be the wild form of the Guinea-pig of Europe. **1848** GOULD *Birds Australia* II. pl. 87 *Seisura Inquieta*, *Restless Flycatcher; The Grinder, of the Colonists of Swan River and New South Wales. **1898** MORRIS *Austral Eng.* 122/2 Dishwasher, ..applied in Australia to..the Restless Fly-catcher. **1801** LATHAM *Gen. Synop. Birds* 2nd Suppl. 181 *Restless Thrush. **1817** J. F. STEPHENS in Shaw *Gen. Zool.* X. I. 263 The Restless Thrush inhabits New Holland.

3. a. Of conditions: Unceasing, continuous.

c **1398** CHAUCER *Fortune* 70 This world hath euer resteles trauayle. **1588** GREENE *Pandosto* (1843) 10 Those which were the cause of his restles sorrow. **1594** SHAKS. *Rich. III*, I. iv. 81 Princes..often feele a world of restlesse Cares. **1634** MILTON *Comus* 596 It shall be in eternal restless change Self-fed, and self-consum'd. **1691** T. H[ALE] *Acc. New Invent.* 6 By their Arts..were Sir Philip Howard, and Company in a restless manner urged to give Answers. **1701** F. MANNING *Poems* 8 What compensation will you make For giving me Love s restless Pains?

b. Of things: Continually moving or operating; never ceasing or pausing.

1596 SPENSER *F.Q.* v. x. 33 With restlesse force Into his shield it readie passage found. **1599** SHAKS. *Hen. V*, III. vi. 30 That Goddesse blind, that stands vpon the rolling restlesse Stone. *a* **1618** SYLVESTER *Little Bartas* 364 The daily Course Of restlesse Stars. **1700** DRYDEN *Pal. & Arc.* III. 457 The courser pawed the ground with restless feet. **1781** COWPER *Hope* 3 A painful passage o'er a restless flood. **1841** ELPHINSTONE *Hist. Ind.* I. 365 They are..active, with peculiar features, and a quick and restless eye. **1878** SEELEY *Stein* I. 232 For a moment it was reasonable to hope that she [France] would also sheathe her restless sword.

Comb. **1777** POTTER *Æschylus, 7 Chiefs agst. Thebes* 161 The rude plunderers' restless-rolling tide. **1889** W. B. YEATS *Wanderings of Oisin* II. 24 Where goes to gaze the restless-footed star Of twilight when he's weary.

4. Quasi-*adv.* = RESTLESSLY.

13.. *E.E. Allit. P.* B. 527 Sesounez schal yow neuer sese of sede ne of heruest,..Bot euer renne restlez. ? *a* **1366** CHAUCER *Rom. Rose* 370 The tyme, that passeth nyght and daye And restlesse trauayleth aye. *c* **1470** *Gol. & Gaw.* 113 The renk restles he raid to Arthour the king. **1810** *Splendid Follies* II. 119 Emily Camelion slept very restless.

'restlessly, *adv.* [f. prec. + -LY².] In a restless manner; without resting or pausing; unceasingly; uneasily.

1567 GOLDING *Ovid* IX. 117 From his wits and from his natiue place, The furies..shall restlessely him chace. *c* **1642** *Contra-Replicant's Complaint* 10 How restlesly active they al are. **1676** CUDWORTH *Serm. 1 Cor. xv.* 57 Which every true Christian ought..to endeavour after, and restlessly to pursue. **1814–5** SHELLEY *Mutability* 2 How restlessly they [*sc.* clouds] speed! **1847** C. BRONTE *J. Eyre* xxi, Turning restlessly, she drew the bed-clothes round her. **1891** E. PEACOCK *N. Brendon* I. 12 Letting her fingers play restlessly with an ivory paper-cutter.

'restlessness. [f. as prec. + -NESS.] The state or character of being restless.

1633 G. HERBERT *Temple, The Pulley*, Let him keep the rest, But keep them with repining restlesnesse. **1665** BOYLE *Occas. Refl.* 205 The heat, and thirst, and restlessness of an Ague. *a* **1721** SHEFFIELD (Dk. Buckhm.) *Wks.* (1753) I. 295 Yet a restlessness attends such deeds, Tho' ne'er so just. **1763** *Phil. Trans.* LIII. 349 She often complained of a swimming in her head, and a restlessness in the night. **1798** EDGEWORTH *Pract. Educ.* (1811) II. 163 Much may be done by education to prevent this boyish restlessness. **1840** DICKENS *Barn. Rudge* xvi, This constant restlessness and flitting to and fro, gave rise to strange stories. **1880** GEIKIE *Phys. Geogr.* iii. 139 The restlessness of its water is one of the features of the sea which first impress the onlooker.

†**'restling,** *vbl. sb. Sc. Obs.*⁻¹ (Origin and precise meaning uncertain.)

c **1470** *Gol. & Gaw.* 458 Thair wes restling and reling, but rest that raught.

†**'restly,** *adv. Obs. rare*⁻¹. [irreg. f. REST *sb.*¹ + -LY².] Restfully.

1561 HOLLYBUSH *Hom. Apoth.* 6 The same maye be geuen a yonge childe, and it causeth to slepe fast and restlye.

†**'restness.** *Obs.* [f. REST *a.*] Rancidity.

c **1440** *Promp. Parv.* 431/1 Restnesse of flesshe,..*rancor.* **1483** *Cath. Angl.* 304/2 A Restnes, *rancor.*

re-'stock (riː-), *v.*¹ [RE- 5 a.] *trans.* To stock again, to replenish. Also *absol.*

a **1680** CHARNOCK *Attrib. God* (1834) II. 350 Thus were.. the immense riches of a Deity expended to re-stock man. **1789** G. WHITE *Selborne* vii. 18 A late Bishop of Winchester, when urged to re-stock Waltham-chase, refused. **1868** *Rep. U.S. Comm. Agric.* (1869) 319 Many curious facts have demonstrated the feasibility of restocking the salmon rivers. **1906** E. DYSON *Fact'ry 'Ands* iv. 50 Ellis took pity on his emptiness, and Mumps was sent home to re-stock.

Hence **re-'stocking** *vbl. sb.*; also **re-'stockage.**

1805 R. W. DICKSON *Pract. Agric.* II. 1223 Where the ponds are suitable for tench.., the re-stockings [may be] considerably more. **1884** *Thorley's Farmers' Almanack* 31 The wherewithal to purchase sheep in making autumnal re-stockages. **1885** *Manch. Exam.* 10 June 4/5 The only transactions being small re-stocking orders.

re-'stock (riː-), *v.*² [RE- 5 c.] *trans.* To fit with a new stock.

1892 GREENER *Breech Loader* 118 Restocking hammerless guns,..about one-seventh of the actual cost of the gun.

restorable (rɪ'stɔərəb(ə)l), *a.* [f. RESTORE *v.* + -ABLE.] That can be restored or brought back to a former condition.

1611 COTGR., *Rendable*, rendible, renderable, yeeldable, restorable. **1662** *Irish Act 14 & 15 Chas. II*, c. 2 §21 The just and legal title of any person, that is restoreable by this ower declaration. **1724** SWIFT *Drapier's Lett.* vii. Wks. 1751 IX. 107 That absurd Practice..whereby great Quantities of restorable Land are made utterly desperate. **1875** POSTE *Gaius* II. 205 So that they are no longer separable and restorable to their former condition. **1878** LECKY *Eng. in 18th C.* (1884) II. vi. 179 Such of the adventurers..as were to be dispossessed to make way for restorable persons.

Hence **re'storableness.**

1672–3 GREW *Anat. Pl., Anat. Roots* (1684) 63 They are very Dilative; as is also manifest from its restorableness to its former bulk again.

restoral (rɪ'stɔərəl). [f. RESTORE *v.* + -AL¹.] Restoration, restitution.

1611 COTGR., *Recreance*, a restorall, restitution, giuing backe of. *a* **1677** BARROW *Serm.* (1810) I. 131 The promises of pardon to our sins, and restoral into God's favour. **1845** JANE ROBINSON *Whitehall* xxxiii, Is it for me, deem you, to labour in the restoral of a power which declares my mother's memory infamous? **1878** P. BROOKS *Myst. Iniq.* xi. 197 The true picture of Peace is..the restoral of true relations.

†**re'storance.** *Obs.* Also 5 restour-, 6 restorr-. [a. OF. *restorance*, f. *restorer* to RESTORE: cf. RESTAURANCE.] = prec.

c **1375** *Cursor M.* 6772 (Fairf.), If hit be stollyn wiþ chaunce, þou sal to me make restoraunce. *c* **1450** *Mirour Saluacioun* (Roxb.) 87 Til aungels restouraunce and of seints delyvring He saide this king shulde be. **1466** *Cal. Rec. Dublin* (1889) I. 323 All manner costes done for the restorauns of the Spaynardes shippe. **1525** *10th Rep. Hist. MSS. Comm.* App. V. 401 To make restorraunce and amendes. **1581** *Reg. Privy Council Scot.* III. 373 The restorance of the said Johnne Flemyng in his Hienes Parliament wes stayit.

restoration (rɛstə'reɪʃən). [Later form of RESTAURATION, after RESTORE *v.*]

1. The action of restoring to a former state or position; the fact of being restored or reinstated. Also const. *to*. **a.** Of persons.

1660 *Jrnls. Ho. Comm.* 30 May, The happy Restoration of his Majesty to his People and Kingdoms. **1678** *12th Rep. Hist. MSS. Comm.* App. V. 52 The joy I ought to shew for my owne restoration to His Majestys favour. **1724** WATERLAND *Athan. Creed* x. §39 The Opinion..that wicked Men, and even Devils, after a certain Revolution, should have their Release and Restoration. **1843** LYTTON *Last Bar.* IV. i, While seeking your restoration, I have never neglected the facilities for flight. **1878** STUBBS *Const. Hist.* xviii. III. 214 The nation without regret and without enthusiasm recognised the Lancastrian restoration. **1892** WESTCOTT *Gospel Life* 243 In the Apocalypse the restoration of man and the restoration of nature are placed side by side.

b. Of territory, conditions, or things.

1663 BOYLE *Exp. Hist. Colours* iii, Though this may be said to be rather a restoration of a body to its own colour [etc.]. **1788** GIBBON *Decl. & F.* xlix. V. 140 Europe dates a new æra from his restoration of the Western empire. **1837** WHEWELL *Hist. Induct. Sci.* (1857) I. 135 This motion in latitude would be sufficiently known if we knew the period of its restoration. **1841** D'ISRAELI *Amen. Lit.* (1867) 99 That period which has been distinguished as the restoration of letters. **1872** YEATS *Techn. Hist. Comm.* 110 We owe to the monks the agricultural restoration of a great part of Europe.

c. *Theol.* (Cf. RESTITUTION 5.)

1781 WINCHESTER *Seed of Woman* 19, I shall set down such Passages as the Friends of the Universal Restoration generally bring to prove the same. **1833** J. MARTINEAU *Ess.*

& Addr. (1890) I. 13 Beginning with the question respecting the person of Christ, and ending with the Universal Restoration. **1834** DEAN in *B. B. Edwards' Encycl. Relig. Knowl.* (1851) 1018 The restoration was introduced into America about the middle of the eighteenth century.

2. *Hist.* (With capital initial.) **a.** The re-establishment of monarchy in England with the return of Charles II in 1660; also, the period marked by this event.

1718 *Apol. Ch. Eng.* 21 The Office..for the Twenty Ninth of May thankfully commemorates the Blessings of the Restoration. **1725** B. HIGGONS *Rem. Burnet* I. Wks. 1736 II. 67 The Restoration, a Blessing that sticks in his Gizzard. **1825** MACAULAY *Ess., Milton*, For many years after the Restoration, [the Puritans] were the theme of unmeasured invective and derision. **1869** ROGERS *Hist. Glean.* I. 10 The expedient by which the landowners of the Restoration freed themselves from their ancient contributions to the public revenue. **1886** *Eng. Hist. Rev.* Oct. 682 The Laudian school of divines, who at the Restoration remodelled the prayer book.

b. The reinstatement of the Bourbons in the sovereignty of France in 1814.

1848 W. H. KELLY tr. *L. Blanc's Hist. Ten Y.* I. 49 The first ministry of the Restoration overthrown by the mere approach of the chamber.

3. a. The action of restoring a person to health or consciousness; recovery of physical strength.

1760–72 H. BROOKE *Fool of Qual.* (1809) IV. 127 During these short sentences and difficult restorations. **1826** S. COOPER *First Lines Surg.* (ed. 5) 85 Instances of restoration from a state in which suspension of sensation..had been induced by cold. **1870** ANDERSON *Missions Amer. Bd.* I. iii. 70 Toward the close of the voyage the eldest, whose restoration had been the principal object, died of fever.

b. A restorative. *rare*$^{-1}$.

1823 J. SIMPSON *Ricardo the Outlaw* I. 290 Every restoration was administered that the affection of Ellen could suggest.

4. a. The action or process of restoring something to an unimpaired or perfect condition.

1801 *Med. Jrnl.* V. 467 The restoration of feeling [is kept up],..and, finally, the natural power of action is completely ..restored. **1835** FIELD *Chromatography* 216 The restoration of disfigured and decayed works of art is..next in importance to their production. **1840** DICKENS *Old C. Shop* xii, She saw in this..the restoration of the old man's health and peace, and a life of tranquil happiness. **1874** SPEDDING *Lett. & Life Bacon* VII. Pref. 4 For the passages which defy restoration, blank spaces would be left with some indication of their apparent extent.

b. *Arch.* The process of carrying out alterations and repairs with the idea of restoring a building to something like its original form; a general renovation.

1824 BYRON *Juan* XVI. lviii, A plan whereby to erect New buildings..And throw down old, which he call'd restoration. **1849** PARKER *Gothic Archit.* (1874) II. 291 Unfortunately restoration generally destroys the historical value of a building. **1852** RUSKIN *Arrows of Chace* (1880) I. 67 Under the name of 'restoration' the ruin of the noblest architecture and painting is constant throughout Europe. **1879** STAINER *Music of Bible* 82 When the muniment-room was being removed for the purposes of restoration.

c. A representation of the original form of a ruined building, extinct animal, etc.

1836 BUCKLAND *Geol. & Min.* II. 29 Conjectural Restoration of the Skeleton of Plesiosaurus. **1841** *Penny Cycl.* XIX. 420/1 *Restorations*, in Architecture, a term applied to drawings intended to show antient buildings according to their original design... In some cases the building itself will afford sufficient data for a complete restoration of it upon paper. **1878** HUXLEY *Physiogr.* xvii. 282, Fig. 81 represents a restoration of this extinct elephant.

d. *Dentistry.* Any structure provided to replace dental or oral tissue that has been removed or lost, such as a filling, crown, or bridge.

1934 F. W. FRAHM *Princ. & Technics Full Denture Constr.* xxvi. 475 The change from the natural to the artificial teeth is made so easily that the patient becomes accustomed to the supplied restoration in a few hours. **1962** BLAKE & TROTT *Periodontology* xvi. 170 Before the construction of such prosthetic or conservative restorations is begun the occlusion should be studied. **1976** TORRES & EHRLICH *Mod. Dental Assisting* xxvi. 802 To seat a restoration the casting is inserted into the tooth or onto the tooth crown.

5. The action of restoring something to one who has been previously deprived of it.

1788 GIBBON *Decl. & F.* xlix. V. 134 He recovered his speech and sight; and this natural event was improved to the miraculous restoration of his eyes and tongue. **1837** DICKENS *Pickw.* ii, The restoration was soon made. **1877** FROUDE *Short Stud.* (1883) IV. I. iii. 29 He demanded the restoration of estates that his predecessors had alienated.

6. *attrib.* and *Comb.*, as (sense 2 a) *Restoration comedy, drama, dramatist, pamphleteer, wing*; (sense 4 b) *restoration fund*.

1898 G. SAINTSBURY *Short Hist. Eng. Lit.* VIII. ii. 487 The cloven foot of Restoration comedy—the passionless and malevolent licentiousness of too much thereof. **1910** *Encycl. Brit.* IX. 630/2 Restoration comedy at first followed Jonson. **1925** B. DOBRÉE *Congreve's Comedies* I. p. xii, The Restoration comedy writers..keep us dancing along to a gay tune. **1955** N. MARSH *Scales of Justice* iii. 53 'Kettle,' Lady Lacklander said... Nurse Kettle did not resent being addressed in this restoration-comedy fashion by Lady Lacklander. **1976** *Amer. N. & Q.* XV. 35/1 In Restoration comedy, reference is often made to the 'canonical hours'. **1898** G. SAINTSBURY *Short Hist. Eng. Lit.* VIII. ii. 491 The glory..of this Restoration drama was not reached till long after the Restoration itself. **1923** A. NICOLL *Hist. Restoration Drama 1660–1700* i. 3 The study of Restoration drama demands a continual care. **1935** D. L. SAYERS *Gaudy Night* iv. 82 Calling people names that poor Miss Lydgate didn't know existed—the worst she knows being Restoration drama. **1977** J. AIKEN *Last Movement* vii. 130 I'd cast him as Rochester..or one of those fiends in Restoration Drama. **1912** E. GOSSE in *Restoration Plays* p. x, What all the Restoration dramatists suffer from is a tendency to produce common and inadequate poetry. **1923** A. NICOLL *Hist. Restoration Drama 1660–1700* iii. 184 Manners, in the mouths of the Restoration dramatists themselves, meant something quite apart from the modern meaning of the term. **1974** *Encycl. Brit. Macropædia* IV. 113/1 William Congreve, more than any other Restoration dramatist, shaped the English comedy of manners. **1898** G. B. SHAW *Mrs. Warren's Profession* III. 204 Gov'nor's ever so fond of it, because he got up a restoration fund and had it completely rebuilt. **1978** *Lancashire Life* Nov. 140/1 A restoration fund has been launched to restore the decaying 15th century tower of Mitton Church, near Whalley. **1875** GROSART in *Marvell's Wks.* II. p. xxiv, Anything more dishonest..is scarcely to be matched outside of the vilest Restoration pamphleteer and partizan. **1920** 'O. DOUGLAS' *Penny Plain* xxv. 300 The austere Tudor front, the Restoration wing, the offices built under Queen Anne. **1936** J. BUCHAN *Island of Sheep* viii. 141 Nothing more modern than the Restoration wing built by Bruce of Kinross.

Hence **resto'rationer**, = RESTORATIONIST.

1855 OGILVIE *Suppl.*

resto'rationism. [f. prec. + -ISM.] The doctrine that all men will ultimately be restored to a state of happiness in the future life.

1834 DEAN in *B. B. Edwards' Encycl. Relig. Knowl.* (1851) 1019 The Independent Messenger..is devoted to the cause of Restorationism. **1879** J. COOK *Marriage* 98 There is very little difference between Universalism and Restorationism. **1896** *Tablet* Mar. 408 Restorationism is difficult to harmonize with the Bible.

resto'rationist. [f. as prec. + -IST.]

1. A believer in restorationism.

1834 DEAN in *B. B. Edwards' Encycl. Relig. Knowl.* (1851) 1018 Though the Restorationists, as a separate sect, have arisen within a few years, their sentiments are by no means new. **1892** *Critic* (U.S.) Oct. 177/2 He is a restorationist and this optimistic view..imparts a certain tinge to his handling of all themes.

2. One who restores dilapidated buildings.

1880 *Scribner's Mag.* July 466 Not any of its towers have escaped, where 'restorationist's' chisel could cut.

restorative (rɛ'stɒrətɪv, -ɔər-), *a.* and *sb.* Also 5 restoratif, -atyf(f, -etyffe, -atyve. [a. OF. **restoratif*, variant of *restauratif* RESTAURATIVE.]

A. *adj.* Pertaining to restoration (of strength or health); capable of restoring or renewing.

c **1400** *Lanfranc's Cirurg.* 354 It wole be a good oynement restoratif. *c* **1430** LYDG. *Min. Poems* (Percy Soc.) 103 Yowre restoratyf celestial manna. **1500–20** DUNBAR *Poems* xxv. 11 O! ȝe heremeitis and hankersaidilis, That..eitis nocht meit restoratiue. **1584** COGAN *Haven Health* x. (1636) 34 Rise-pottage..is verie pleasant and easie of digestion and restorative. **1606** DEKKER *Seven Sins* (Arb.) 24 The very shadow of thee hath beene to them a restoratiue Consolation. **1665** SIR T. HERBERT *Trav.* (1677) 69 The air for eight months is very pure and restorative. **1807** *Life Fielding* in *Tom Jones* I. p. xix, To try if there was any restorative quality in the more genial air of that climate. **1868** BROWNING *Ring & Bk.* I. 89 The thing's restorative, I' the touch and sight. **1875** MCLAREN *Serm.* Ser. II. iv. 67 The depth of our need determines the strength of the restorative power put forth.

b. *spec.* in *Dentistry.*

1963 C. R. COWELL et al. *Inlays, Crowns, & Bridges* i. 1 Gold is stronger than other restorative materials and can be used in thin sections without danger of fracture. **1974** *News & Press* (Darlington, S. Carolina) 25 Apr. 17/3 It was first thought that the council might buy a mobile unit and employ a full time dentist who could..do restorative dentistry.

B. *sb.* **1. a.** A food, cordial, or medicine, which has the effect of restoring health or strength.

c **1430** LYDG. *Min. Poems* (Percy Soc.) 101 Repast ay lasting, restoratyf eternal. **1446** LYDG. *Nightingale Poems* II. 247 He gaf his body..Restoratif best in the forme of brede. *c* **1485** *Digby Myst.* (1882) III. 486 Here, lady, is wyn,..to..woman a good restoratyff. **1547** BOORDE *Brev. Health* §86 All maner of cordyalles and restoratiues..doth comfort the hert. **1590** SPENSER *F.Q.* III. v. 50 Many Restoratives of vertues rare, And costly Cordialles she did apply. **1632** J. HAYWARD tr. *Biondi's Eromena* 105 The Princesse..calling for some cordials and restoratives, gave them her. **1747–96** MRS. GLASSE *Cookery* xv. 271 Knuckle broth..is a certain restorative at the beginning of a decline. **1806** A. HUNTER *Culina* (ed. 3) 222 In cases where restoratives are required, a basin of milk [etc.]. **1861** FLOR. NIGHTINGALE *Nursing* (ed. 2) 53 Coffee is a better restorative than tea, but a greater impairer of the digestion.

transf. **1633** G. HERBERT *Temple, To All Angels & Saints*, Thou art the holy mine, whence came the gold, The great restorative for all decay In young and old. *a* **1680** BUTLER *Rem.* (1759) I. 91 And Sleep, Death's Brother,..Gave weary'd Nature a Restorative. **1742** YOUNG *Nt. Th.* IX. 2184 Rest,..Man's rich restorative.

b. A means of restoring one to consciousness.

1852 MRS. STOWE *Uncle Tom's C.* xxviii. 268 St. Clare had fainted,..but as Miss Ophelia applied restoratives, he revived, opened his eyes. **1869** H. AINSWORTH *Hilary St. Ives* II. iv, Fortunately there were..restoratives at hand.

†**2.** Restorative or nourishing power; restoration, nourishment. *Obs.*

1528 PAYNELL *Salerne's Regim.* (1557) 31 b, These three foresayde thynges are comfortable and of greate restoratiue for mans bodye. *Ibid.* 40 If wyne be dronke for nouryshment, for restoratiue of the body.

†**3.** Restitution, repayment. *Obs.*

c **1485** *Digby Myst.* (1882) III. 651 [Two debtors,] þe whych wher pore, and myth make no restoratyf.

4. (See quot.)

1810 BENTHAM *Packing* (1821) 218 The remedy here ventured to be proposed is stiled without scruple a restorative: a plan for the restoring..the original composition of Juries.

Hence **re'storatively** *adv.*; **re'storativeness**, 'a restoring quality' (Bailey, vol. II, 1727).

1835 *Blackw. Mag.* XXXVIII. 162 How restoratively on our temples..were the blessed dews distilled! **1851** G. S. FABER *Many Mansions* III. i, After the Resurrection, Man's Spirit..will be again restoratively clothed with a material body.

re'storatory, *a. rare*$^{-0}$. [Cf. prec. and -ORY.] 'Restorative' (Webster, 1847).

†**re'store**, *sb. Obs.* [f. the vb., perh. after OF. *restor, restour*, It. *ristoro*, med.L. *restaurum*.] Restoration, restitution.

c **1450** *St. Cuthbert* (Surtees) 6122 Seke men of heele had restore. **1590** SPENSER *F.Q.* III. v. 18 Till he had made amends, and full restore For all the damage which he had him doen afore. **1640** SHIRLEY *St. Patrick* I. i, Let the first use I make of their restore be To bend my knees to you. **1646** SIR T. BROWNE *Pseud. Ep.* 147 Disputes at Law, and contestations concerning a restore of the dowry.

restore (rɪ'stɔə(r)), *v.*[1] Also 5 restour, -oyre, 6 *Sc.* -oir. [a. OF. *restorer*, = It. *ristorare*:-L. *restaurāre*: see RESTAUR *v.*]

1. *trans.* To give back, to make return or restitution of (anything previously taken away or lost).

1297 R. GLOUC. (Rolls) 10287 We esseþ..þat þou suerie vpe þe bok clanliche to restore Holi chirche þat þou hast him binome. **1338** R. BRUNNE *Chron.* (1810) 99 Roberd.. bisouht þe kyng þo fees he fro him nam, restore ageyn þat þing. **1387** TREVISA *Higden* (Rolls) II. 113 Neuerþeles vnder Kenulph þe kyng it was restored to Caunterbury aȝen. *c* **1450** *St. Cuthbert* (Surtees) 5653, I pray, he says, my belt restore. **1484** CAXTON *Fables of Æsop* v. ix, Your helthe shalle be restored to yow. **1530** PALSGR. 689/1 He shall restore hym all his goodes agayne. **1560** DAUS tr. *Sleidane's Comm.* 11 b, The Spaniards wil hardly at any time restore unto us again this dignitie of thempire. **1634** MILTON *Comus* 607 Ile find him out, And force him to restore his purchase back. **1697** DRYDEN *Virg. Georg.* IV. 212 For ev'ry Bloom his Trees in Spring afford, An Autumn Apple was by tale restor'd. **1738** WESLEY *Hymns, Father of Mercies* ii, Their Alms in Blessings on their Head A thousand-fold restore. **1765** BLACKSTONE *Comm.* I. 56 The law..will make Gaius restore the possession to Titius. **1821** SHELLEY *Adonais* iii, Dream not that the amorous Deep Will yet restore him to the vital air. **1841** ELPHINSTONE *Hist. Ind.* II. 577 To restore all the forts in his possession within that tract. **1884** F. TEMPLE *Relat. Relig. & Sci.* iv. (1885) 121 The doctrine of Evolution restores to the science of Nature the unity which we should expect in the creation of God.

absol. *c* **1440** *Jacob's Well* 66 Had I restoryd, as þou tawȝtyst me, I had be sauyd to ioye. **1611** BIBLE *Isa.* xlii. 22 They are for a praye, & none deliuereth; for a spoile, and none saith, Restore.

2. a. To make amends for; to compensate, to make good (loss or damage). Now *rare* or *Obs.*

13.. *K. Alis.* 7909 Y geve..eueriche knyght a thousand pound, or more, Youre harmes to restore. *a* **1340** HAMPOLE *Psalter* cxlvi. 2 Restorand wiþ þaim þe fallynge of aungels. **1390** GOWER *Conf.* II. 186 Bot Crist restoreth thilke lost, And boghte it with his fleissh and blod. *c* **1460** *Play Sacram.* 963 Now wylle we walke by Contre & cost owr wyckyd lyuyng for to restore. **1463** in *Somerset Med. Wills* (1901) 198 Item, that my dettes..or wronges dieuly proued be restored as may be moost to the helth of my soule. *a* **1533** LD. BERNERS *Huon* lv. 185 Thou to restore all yᵉ domages that thou hast done him. **1596** DALRYMPLE tr. *Leslie's Hist. Scotl.* I. 123 His maister receiueng the slane beist, sal restore the skaith to his nychtbour. **1642** FULLER *Holy & Prof. St.* III. viii. 170 Time may restore some losses.

b. To set right, repair (decay, etc.). *rare.*

1567 *Satir. Poems Reform.* iii. 111 Restoir againe ȝour foule polluted fame. *a* **1586** SIDNEY *Ps.* XXVII. ix, Though fathers care..Abandon'd me, yet my decay Should be restor'd by hym above. **1657** G. STARKEY tr. *Helmont's Vindic.* To Rdr., Yet so in no long time may the Disease be restored. **1820** SHELLEY *Witch Atl.* lxx, On the night when they were buried, she Restored the embalmers' ruining.

3. a. To build up again; to re-erect or reconstruct. Now *spec.* to repair and alter (a building) so as to bring it as nearly as possible to its original form.

1297 R. GLOUC. (Rolls) 6508 [He] restorede abbeis, þat destrued were biuore. *c* **1400** MAUNDEV. (Roxb.) xi. 42 Adrian..repaireled þe citee of Ierusalem and restored þe temple and made it new agayne. **1611** BIBLE *Dan.* ix. 25 The commandement to restore and to build Ierusalem. **1667** MILTON *P.L.* XII. 3 Heer the Archangel paus'd Betwixt the world destroy'd and world restor'd. **1776** GIBBON *Decl. & F.* xx. I. 539 His liberality restored and enriched the temples of the gods. **1820** MISS MITFORD in L'Estrange *Life* (1870) II. v. 115 At Winchester, where they are restoring the cathedral. **1868** A. J. MUNBY *Diary* 30 Oct. in D. Hudson *Munby* (1972) 258 The church..is being 'restored', as the phrase is. **1907** G. B. SHAW *Major Barbara* II. 244 He is one of the greatest of our public benefactors. He restored the cathedral at Hakington. **1920** W. B. YEATS *Michael Robartes & Dancer* 24, I, the poet William Yeats, With old mill boards and sea-green slates, And smithy work from the Gort Forge, Restored this tower for my wife George. **1931** J. BETJEMAN *Mt. Zion* 18 Look up! and how glorious He has restored the roof! **1959** N. PEVSNER *Yorkshire: W. Riding* 267 The church was restored in 1876 by Pearson.

absol. **1861** *Ecclesiologist* XXII. 311, I could multiply instances in which the French are *restoring* when they ought to be preserving.

b. To bring back to the original state; to improve, repair, or retouch (a thing) so as to bring it back to its original condition.

1679 EVELYN *Cider* in *Sylva* 409 To restore decay'd Liquor; if flat, and vappid from a too free admission of Air. **1764** FOOTE *Mayor of G.* I, As soon as my dress is restored. **1823** J. BADCOCK *Dom. Amusem.* 154 M. Thenard, of Paris, succeeded lately in restoring a picture of Raphael d'Urbino. **1861** DUTTON-COOK *Paul Foster's Daughter* i, Imagine, please, that the picture has been 'restored'.

c. To reproduce or represent (something ancient, an extinct animal, etc.) in its original form.

1771 *Charact.* in *Ann. Reg.* 260/2 Mr. Berenger's account of this machine, has, to use the language of the virtuosi, restored a piece of antiquity. **1836** BUCKLAND *Geol. & Min.* I. 204 The..discovery of skeletons, such as he had conjecturally restored from insulated bones.

d. (See quot. 1955.)

1943 *Amer. Speech* XVIII. 304/1 Restored cereal. **1955** M. REIFER *Dict. New Words* 177/2 *Restore, v.*, to give back to a processed food the nutritive value it originally had.

4. a. To replace (mankind) in a state of grace; to free from the effects of sin.

a **1300** *Cursor M.* 1596 Wit his grace..þat he suld restore man-kind with. *Ibid.* 19112 Be his fader sitt he sal, Til he restord haf us all. *c* **1410** HOCCLEVE *Mother of God* 87 By thee the world restored is pardee. **1552** *Bk. Com. Prayer, Gen. Confession*, Restore thou them that be penitent. **1567** *Gude & Godlie B.* (S.T.S.) 17 We suld to God, giue pryse and gloir, That sched his blude vs to restoir. **1667** MILTON *P.L.* III. 288 In thee As from a second root shall be restor'd, As many as are restor'd. *a* **1716** SOUTH *Serm.* (1842) III. lxiv. 431 It ought to be owned for an eminent act of grace to restore one actually fallen.

absol. **1903** A. MACLAREN *Last Leaves* 90 We may be the stronger for our sins, not because sin strengthens,..but because God restores.

b. To reinstate or replace (a person) in a former office, dignity, or estate.

to restore in blood: see BLOOD *sb.* 13.

c **1450** *St. Cuthbert* (Surtees) 5309 Of þair bischop, þat lange whyle had bene fra his kirke exile, þai herde he was restorde. **1503** *Rolls of Parlt.* VI. 526/1 To haue the said Attayndours reversed, and the same persones so attaynted, to be seuerally restored. **1530** PALSGR. 689/1 His processe was almoste lost, but he is restored agayne. **1594** PARSONS *Confer. Success* II. vii. 145 As we see that many houses attainted are restored daylie in blood, without restorement of their titles and dignities. **1656** WALLER *Panegyr. Cromwell* 82 Less pleasure take brave minds in battels won, Than in restoring such as are undone. **1817** W. SELWYN *Law Nisi Prius* (ed. 4) II. 1017 The court refused a mandamus to restore a minister of an endowed dissenting meeting-house. **1851** HUSSEY *Papal Power* i. 41 Zozimus, as it seems, restored Apiarius.

c. To bring (a person or part of the body) back to a healthy or vigorous state. Also *refl.*

c **1375** *Sc. Leg. Saints* Prol. 118 þai þat tynt had wittis fyffe, þai restoryt þame allswa. **1382** WYCLIF *Mark* viii. 25 He bigan for to se, and he is restorid, so that he syȝ clerely alle thingis. *c* **1430** LYDG. *Min. Poems* (Percy Soc.) 133, I will..seche for my food no more, Ne for vitaile me to restore. *c* **1440** *Alph. Tales* lxxxi. 64 þis aungell tuchyd his fute, & it was restorid agayn. **1530** PALSGR. 689/1 The man is brought very lowe, he had nede to restore hym agayne. **1601** SHAKS. *All's Well* II. iii. 154 That you are well restor'd my Lord, I'me glad. **1632** J. HAYWARD tr. *Biondi's Eromena* 128 Having restored me with fresh egges, and anointed my feete and legges. **1729** T. COOKE *Tales*, etc. 31 Soon as the Maid was from her Wound restor'd, Her all she yielded to her plighted Lord. **1807** WORDSW. *White Doe* VII. 158 There may Emily restore Herself, in spots unseen before. **1838** DICKENS *O. Twist* xxxii, The quiet place, the pure air..will restore you in a few days. **1871** B. TAYLOR *Faust* (1875) II. I. i. 4 Thou art whole; let faith restore thee!

absol. **1694** SALMON *Bate's Dispens.* (1713) 269/1 It admirably restores in Consumptions, and eases Pains in any Part of the Body, whether inward or outward.

d. To bring back to mental calm. Now *rare.*

1582 N. LICHEFIELD tr. *Castanheda's Conq. E. Ind.* I. lxxix. 163 The king..remained so ill contented, that..for a good while after, he could not restore himself. **1617** MORYSON *Itin.* I. 159, I was much astonished at this accident, till I was restored by vnderstanding this happie euent. **1697** DRYDEN *Virg. Georg.* IV. 671 Th' unhappy Husband..sought, his mournful Mind with Musick to restore. **1697** —— *Past.* VII. 55 Come charm thy Shepherd, and restore my Soul. **1867** M. ARNOLD *Switzerland*, Ah! calm me, restore me; And dry up my tears.

5. a. To renew; to set up or bring into existence again; to re-establish, bring back into use, etc.

a **1300** *Cursor M.* 1658 Wit þine oxspring..i haue mynt Restore þe werld þat sal be tint. **1377** LANGL. *P. Pl.* B. XI. 253 After that bitter barke..Is a kirnelle of conforte, kynde to restore. *c* **1400** *Destr. Troy* 5885 The cuntre-men..restoret the stithe fight stuernly agayn. *c* **1450** HOLLAND *Howlat* 658 The stern Empriouris style thus staitly restord is. **1548** UDALL, etc. *Erasm. Par. Luke* 162 The same bodye to bee restored agayn by the power of god at the resurreccion. **1560** DAUS tr. *Sleidane's Comm.* 13 b, He restored Thempire that was ful weak. **1611** BIBLE *2 Kings* xiv. 25 Hee restored the coast of Israel, from the entring of Hamath, vnto the sea of the plaine. **1672-5** COMBER *Comp. Temple* (1702) 148 With this..the true Reformed Religion of the Church of England was restored. **1718** *Free-thinker* No. 90. 249 Being wearied with Change,..They restored the Ancient Form. **1781** GIBBON *Decl. & F.* xxvii. (1787) III. 68 The loss of armies..ineffectually solicited the successors of Gratian to restore the helmets and cuirasses of the infantry. **1820** IRVING *Sketch Bk.* I. 83 It was with great difficulty that the self-important man in the cocked hat restored order. **1849** MACAULAY *Hist. Eng.* ii. I. 176 To bring in a bill, which..should restore the Star Chamber and the High Commission.

b. *refl.* To return to the original position.

1656 tr. *Hobbes' Elem. Philos.* (1839) 211 A body..is said to restore itself, when..the parts which were moved do..return every one into its own place. *a* **1774** GOLDSM. *Surv. Exp. Philos.* (1776) II. 87 Some have compared the air to watch springs or hoops, which coiled up by pressure, restore themselves again. **1835** LYELL *Princ. Geol.* (ed. 4) II. xix. II. 380 The part of the earth that is first raised, being bent from its natural form, will endeavour to restore itself by its elasticity.

c. To replace or insert (words or letters which are missing or illegible in a text).

1855 C. BADHAM *Plato's Philebus 27 note*, It is so probable that $\sigma\eta$ was lost in consequence of its nearness to η, and it seems so necessary for the sense, that I have restored it conjecturally.

6. a. To bring back (a person or thing) *to* a previous, original, or normal condition.

a **1340** HAMPOLE *Psalter* cl. i, He restorid þaim til his ymage. **1390** GOWER *Conf.* III. 254 The colour, which erst was pale, To Beaute thanne was restored. *c* **1440** LYDG. *Hors, Shepe & G.* 389 It..Dede synnewis restorith a-geyn to live. **1515** BARCLAY *Egloges* iii. (1570) C j b/2 Then his olde fauour did them agayne restore To greater pleasour. *a* **1548** HALL *Chron., Hen. VII*, 34 b, In conclusion,..the kynge..restored them to their libertie. **1624** USSHER in *Lett. Lit. Men* (Camden) 131 When it shall please God to restore me to my health. **1686** tr. *Chardin's Trav. Persia* 130 My Comrade, whom I found restoring to order the confusion which those Robbers had made. **1727-38** CHAMBERS *Cycl.* s.v. *Revivification*, Resuscitation, in chemistry, [is] the art of restoring a mixed body to its first state. **1771** *Encycl. Brit.* II. 479/1 It will not be at rest..till it be restored to its original equality. **1822** SHELLEY tr. *Calderon's Mag. Prodig.* I. 239 Thou canst not Restore it to the slumber of the scabbard. **1840** DICKENS *Old C. Shop* xlvi, He..endeavoured, by such simple means as occurred to him, to restore her to herself. **1882** *Med. Temp. Jrnl.* L. 79 The application of faradic electricity quickly restored the patient to consciousness.

absol. *c* **1386** CHAUCER *Pars. T.* ¶238 Contricion..restorith to alle goodes espiritueles.

b. To grant to or obtain for (a person) reinstatement *to* former rank, office, or possessions.

a **1533** LD. BERNERS *Huon* lxxxi. 251 It is reason that Huon be restoryd to all his londes. **1560** DAUS tr. *Sleidane's Comm.* 19 b, [He] restored the Cardinals to theyr former dignitie. **1600** J. PORY tr. *Leo's Africa* v. 239 By the Kings aide he was restored to his former gouernment. **1671** MILTON *P.R.* III. 381 These if from servitude thou shalt restore To thir inheritance. **1776** GIBBON *Decl. & F.* xvi. I. 540 The innocent were restored to their rank and fortunes. **1849** MACAULAY *Hist. Eng.* ii. I. 176 The Bishops were restored to their seats in the Upper House. **1877** FROUDE *Short Stud.* (1883) IV. I. ix. 93 By the terms of the peace..the archbishop was to be restored to his estates and dignity.

c. To take or put back *into*, to convey or hand back *to*, a place.

c **1450** HOLLAND *Howlat* 532 Thai maid it hame be restord In to Scotland. **1560** DAUS tr. *Sleidane's Comm.* 93 b, The drone bees desyre to be restored into the hyve. **1703** MAUNDRELL *Journ. Jerus.* (1732) 145 We were restor'd all in safety to our respective Habitations. **1860** TENNYSON *Tithonus* 72 Release me, and restore me to the ground.

†**7.** To recompense or compensate (a person). Const. *of* the damage or wrong. *Obs. rare.*

c **1330** R. BRUNNE *Chron. Wace* (Rolls) 4552 To comen ageyn he gaf hem fre,..& restored þeym of here damage. **1461** *Paston Lett.* II. 48 Thei shall be restorid ayen of such wrongs as thei have had be Sir Philip Wentworth.

†**8.** To store; to stock (again). *Obs. rare.*

c **1350** *Will. Palerne* 2846 A park as it were, þat whilom wiþ wilde bestes was wel restored. *c* **1400** *Laud Troy Bk.* 14574 Euery man his tentis restoris Off mete & drynke & other store, Wel better than thei were ore.

†**9.** *intr.* To recover, revive. *Obs.*

c **1400** *Destr. Troy* 10399 His strenkith restoris stithly agayn, And he fore to þe fight with a fell wyll. *c* **1550** SIR D. LYNDESAY (MS.), Scho..garris the blude skayle vpone hir birdis, quhairthrow thai restoir and turnis to lyf agane.

Hence **re'stored** *ppl. a.*

1806 SURR *Winter in Lond.* II. 257 The first sounds that strike upon restored reason. **1836** BUCKLAND *Geol. & Min.* II. 19 Four species of fossil animals, whose restored figures are given in the last Plate. **1845** S. AUSTIN *Ranke's Hist. Ref.* III. 359 The restored unity of Latin Christendom. **1855** MACAULAY *Hist. Eng.* xvi. III. 701 A grateful affection such as the restored Jews had felt for the heathen Cyrus.

re-'store, *v.*[2] [RE- 5 a.] To store again.

1828-32 in WEBSTER.

†**re'storement**. *Obs.* [a. OF. *restorement*: see RESTORE *v.* and -MENT.] The act of restoring; restoration, restitution.

13.. *St. Erkenwolde* 280 in Horstm. *Altengl. Leg.* (1881) 272 Say me of þi soule..And of þe riche restorment þat raȝt hyr oure lorde. **1440** *Wars Eng. in France* (Rolls) II. 448 He gate hym a restorement therof for the loone of a litel parcell. *c* **1470** HARDING *Chron.* ccx. *heading*, Of the restorement of ryght heyres to the Crowne. **1523** LD. BERNERS *Froiss.* I. cxlvii. 176 They had no restorement of the frenche Kyng, for whose sake they lost all. **1571** GOLDING *Calvin on Ps.* xviii. 19 From whence came so soodein restorement from Death to lyfe. **1613-18** DANIEL *Coll. Hist. Eng.* (1626) 116 Absolution and restorement should be granted vnto him. **1675** WOODHEAD, etc. *Paraph. St. Paul* 13 This promise, being a restorement to the dominion of all things lost in Adam.

restorer (rɪ'stɔərə(r)). [f. RESTORE *v.* + -ER. Cf. OF. *restoriere*, *restoreor*, etc.]

1. One who restores or re-establishes.

1523 LD. BERNERS *Froiss.* I. lxxii. 38 b, Se here my lytell chylde, who shalbe, by the grace of god, his restorer. **1545** JOYE *Exp. Dan.* vi. 82 b, The prophecies that went vpon him ..to be the restorer of his people. *c* **1611** CHAPMAN *Iliad* Pref. p. lxix, God..be his honorable family's speedy and full restorer. **1651** HOBBES *Leviath.* III. xxxiii. 204 Of which line was to spring the restorer of the Kingdome of God. **1732** BERKELEY *Alciphr.* v. §25 A greater and more renowned patron and restorer of elegant studies. **1776** GIBBON *Decl. & F.* xi. I. 287 Diocletian and his colleagues..deserved the glorious title of Restorers of the Roman world. **1849** MACAULAY *Hist. Eng.* v. I. 579 The son and heir of George Monk, the restorer of the Stuarts. **1886** *Encycl. Brit.* XXI. 544/1 As a 'restorer' of ancient buildings he was guilty of.. the most irreparable destruction.

2. That which restores.

1873, 1893 [see *hair-restorer* s.v. HAIR *sb.* 10]. **1911** G. B. SHAW *Doctor's Dilemma* I. 23 Its like a bald-headed man trying to sell a hair restorer.

So **re'storess**, a female restorer. *rare*$^{-1}$.

1865 PUSEY *Truth Eng. Ch.* 158 [Mary] is rightly called Redemptress, Restoress,..and Cause of our Salvation.

restoreté, variant of RESTORITY, *Obs.*

restoring (rɪ'stɔərɪŋ), *vbl. sb.* [f. RESTORE *v.* + -ING[1].] The action of the vb.; restoration.

a **1350** *St. Nicholas* 441 in Horstm. *Altengl. Leg.* (1881) 16 Trowand so..Of his gudes to haue restoring. **1382** WYCLIF *Prol. to 1 Sam.*, The restorynge of the temple vndur Zorobabel. *c* **1400** *Lanfranc's Cirurg.* 48 þer schal be maad a maner of restorynge in place of the boon þat was broken. **1538** STARKEY *England* I. iv. 142 To-morow, when we schal speke of the restoryng of thes fautys rehersyd before. **1587** GOLDING *De Mornay* xxxii. (1592) 522 And what is the restoring of sight, but the restoring of a substance? **1617** HIERON *Wks.* II. 63 There hee doth desire the restoring thereof. Restoring is properly the rendring backe of a thing lost. **1662** STILLINGFL. *Orig. Sacræ* II. vi. §13 Abimelechs restoring of Sarah was the ground why the sentence..was not executed upon him. **1748** *Anson's Voy.* III. ix. 393 A walk upon the land would contribute greatly to the restoring of his health. **1861** TRENCH *Comm. Ep. Churches Asia* 60 A restoring of harmony between the sinner and the outraged law of God. **1893** F. F. MOORE *I forbid Banns* (1899) 108 The building had not been subjected to that system of spoliation known as 'restoring'.

attrib. **1398** TREVISA *Barth. De P.R.* XVII. ii. (Bodl. MS.), þouȝe he bere manye bowes in þe restoringe tyme, ȝitte he bereþ but litel frute.

re'storing, *ppl. a.* [-ING[2].] That restores.

1661 BOYLE *Style of Script.* 49 By him, who..is pleased to make restoring grace operate. **1697** DRYDEN *Virg. Georg.* IV. 399 Boil this restoring Root in gen'rous Wine. *c* **1715** DUNTON (*title*), Frank Scammony, or the Restoring Clergy Detected. **1818** KEATS *Endym.* III. 644, I..next tell How a restoring chance came down to quell One half of the witch in me. **1904** *Blackw. Mag.* Apr. 575/1 He is as violent an iconoclast as a 'restoring' architect.

re'storingly, *adv.* [-LY[2].] In a restoring manner; restoratively.

1846 J. R. LOWELL *Let.* 18 Feb. (1894) I. 115 Falling gently and restoringly as dew on the withered youth-flowers of the oppressor.

†**re'story**. *Obs.* Also 5 **restorete**, 6 **-ytee**. [var. of RESTORATIVE.] A restorative. Also *fig.*

c **1460** *Towneley Myst.* xii. 238 This is a restoreté, To make a good appeté. **1576** FLEMING tr. *Caius' Dogs* To Rdr., The lyfe of this man was not so great a restority of comfort, as his death was an vlcer or wound of sorrow. **1586** B. YOUNG *Guazzo's Civ. Conv.* IV. 219 b, In yᵉ meane while liue & vse this good hope as a restoritie for you. **1596** T. DAWSON *Good Huswifes Jewell* II. 48 The stilling of a capon, a great restority.

b. Without article, chiefly predicative.

1553 *Respublica* 889 Nowe lett vs sing, yf ytt please Authoritee, to refreshe oure spirites, yt ys restorytee. **1565** CALFHILL *Answ. Martiall* IV. 94 b, Such a drug, as I would wysh no worse for my Lords own holinesse,..for doubtlesse it is restoritie to such. *a* **1612** HARINGTON *Epigr.* II. lxxxviii, A lie, well told to some, tastes ill restoritie. **1620-6** QUARLES *Feast for Wormes* 1759 These precious vyands are Restoritie, Eate then. *a* **1644** —— *Virg. Widow* III. i, D'ye want Restority? Are the plummets of your soule downe?

restour, obs. form of RESTORE *v.*

re'stow (ri:-), *v.* [RE- 5 a.] To stow again.

1834 MARRYAT *P. Simple* (1863) 112 We had refitted the rigging fore and aft, restowed and cleaned the hold, and painted outside. **1840** —— *Poor Jack* xxii, We were busy restowing the upper tier of the cargo. **1872** *Daily News* 19 Jan., [He] told Captain Thrupp to report to him when ship was restowed.

Hence **re'stowing** *vbl. sb.*; also **re'stowal**.

1882 CLARK RUSSELL *My Shipmate Louise* xiv, [He] got on the deck alongside of me to superintend the restowal of the broken-out goods. **1894** *Outing* XXIV. 35 The restowing of the ballast had been a tedious job.

†**re'strain**, *sb. Obs.* [f. the verb.] Restraint.

c **1449** PECOCK *Repr.* III. xvii. 394 Therfore thei mowe not eny punysching or eny restreyne sette to preestis or clerkis. **1601** *Mary Magd. Lament.* Concl. (Grosart) 139 Though Thou did forbid, 'twas no restraine. **1643** HERLE *Answ. Ferne* 18 The King is able to doe Justice..without restraine. **1677** *Hatton Corr.* (Camden) 146 It looked as if they were guilty of confederacy for wᶜʰ they were under soe close a restraine.

restrain (rɪ'streɪn), *v.*[1] Forms: 4-7 **restreyne**, 4-5 **restreyn**, 4-6 **restreigne**, 4-7 **restreign**; 5 **restren** (5-6 *Sc.* **restrenȝe**), 6 **restrean**; 4-7 **restrayne**, 5-7 **restrayn** (6 **restraygne**), 5 **restrane**, 5-6 **restreine**, 6- **restrain**. [a. OF. *restrei(g)n-*, *restrai(g)n-*, stem of *restreindre*, *restraindre* (cf. Prov. *restrenher*, Sp. *restreñir*, It. *ristrignere*):—L. *restringĕre*: see RESTRINGE *v.*]

1. *trans.* To check, hold back, or prevent (a person or thing) *from* some course of action. †Also const. *of*, and with infin.

c **1340** HAMPOLE *Prose Tr.* 7 Mare..thane to restreyne me fra all thoghtes þat I knewe agaynes Goddes will. *c* **1374** CHAUCER *Troylus* IV. 872 For which Pandare myght not restreyne The terys from hise eyen for to reyne. *c* **1386** —— *Melib.* ¶46 Ther ben ful manye thynges that shul restreyne yow of vengeance takynge. **1413** *Pilgr. Sowle* (Caxton 1483) IV. xx. 66 How may ye now fro wepynge you restreyne? **1483** CAXTON *G. de la Tour* a viij, Fastyng..restreyneth the flessh from euylle desyres. **1577** B. GOOGE *Heresbach's Husb.* II. (1586) 55 b, The sweeter also they will be, the more you restrain the stalke from shooting vp. **1599** HAKLUYT *Voy.* II. II. 98 Certaine of the common people were restrained from false superstition. **1617** MORYSON *Itin.* I. 171, I..restrained my curiositie from attempting to view this Castle. **1729** BUTLER *Serm.* Wks. 1874 II. 9 This faculty tends to restrain men from doing mischief to each other. **1788** GIBBON *Decl. & F.* l. V. 245 The weakness of their Arabian brethren had restrained them from opposing his ambition. **1818** CRUISE *Digest* (ed. 2) I. 147 The Court of Chancery will also restrain a tenant for life..from cutting down timber. **1880** L. STEPHEN *Pope* iii. 77 This independence did not restrain him from writing poetry.

absol. *c* **1400** *Rom. Rose* 4955 But Eelde gan ageyn restreyne From sich foly, and refreyne.

b. Without const. To keep (one) in check or under control. Freq. *refl.*

1390 GOWER *Conf.* III. 273, I mai miselve noght restreigne, That I nam evere in loves peine. **1424** *Acts Parl. Scot.* (1814) II. 7/2 He sall..do his besines to restrenȝe sic trespassouris and mis-doaris. *c* **1440** *Alph. Tales* 253 Vnnethis his felows myght restren hym to spare it. **1535** STEWART *Cron. Scot.* II. 102 Without..that oure wnworthines Restrenȝe ws, we ma..Baith land and law, and libertie agane..reskew. **1591** SPENSER *M. Hubberd* 1073 Hardly..were they restrayned so, Till that the Foxe [etc.]. **1663** COWLEY *Ess., Liberty*, If I want skill or force to restrain the Beast that I ride upon. **1678** BUNYAN *Pilgr. Progr.* (ed. 2) 2 In this plight therefore, he went home, and restrained himself as long as he could. **1715** DE FOE *Fam. Instruct.* I. iii. (1841) I. 63 Because I have not restrained them and showed them their duty. **1827** SOUTHEY *Hist. Penins. War* II. 67 The officers made not the slightest attempt at restraining the wretches under their command. **1877** FROUDE *Short Stud.* (1883) IV. I. vii. 82 Alexander told him that, unless peace was made, he could not restrain the archbishop longer.

absol. **1732** POPE *Ess. Man* II. 54 Two Principles in human nature reign; Self-love, to urge, and Reason, to restrain. **1847** C. BRONTË *J. Eyre* xxxiv, His praise and notice were more restraining than his indifference.

c. To place under arrest (†or embargo) or in confinement; to deprive of personal liberty or freedom of action (cf. RESTRAINT *sb.* 2 c, 2 d); also, to shut in by material barriers.

1494 FABYAN *Chron.* VII. (1542) 699 This yere corn was verie dere, & had ben dearer if marchauntes of yͤ styliarde had not been, & Dutche shippes restrined. *a* **1548** HALL *Chron., Hen. VIII*, 172 b, [She] caused all the Englishe-men and their goodes and shippes to be restrained. **1587** GOLDING *De Mornay* i. (1592) 10 Nature and conscience (which they would haue restreaned and imprisoned). **1620–55** I. JONES *Stone-Heng* (1725) 8 They thought it not fit to restrain their Deities within compacted Walls. **1703** MOXON *Mech. Exerc.* 243 As the Moderns restrain Water, and contain it, so the Antients, this liquid Mettal. **1708** J. CHAMBERLAYNE *St. Gt. Brit.* I. III. iv. (1710) 194 No Freeman of England ought to be imprison'd, or otherwise restrain'd, without Cause shewn. **1838** *Proc. Lincoln Asylum* (1847) 30 Number of Patients Restrained or Secluded, and of the Instances and Hours of Restraint or Seclusion. **1844** in *State Lincoln Asylum* (1846) 18 One of them had been restrained for two months.

d. To deprive (one) *of* liberty by restraint.

1530 PALSGR. 689/1 It is a sore thyng to restrayne a man of his libertye. **1583** *Exec. for Treason* (1675) 10 Yet was he not restrained of his liberty. *a* **1653** GOUGE *Comm. Heb.* xiii. 3 At another time we may be bound and restrained of liberty. **1785** PALEY *Mor. Philos.* II. xi, The pain..which we occasion to brutes by restraining them of their liberty.

2. To check, to put a check or stop upon, to repress, keep down (a desire, feeling, activity, etc.).

a **1340** HAMPOLE *Psalter* xvii. 43 All my vile desires þou restreynde with vertu of luf. *c* **1374** CHAUCER *Anel. & Arc.* 235, I ne can myne herte nought Restreyne, That I ne love him alway. *c* **1400** MAUNDEV. (Roxb.) xxv. 116 He sendez his oste þider to restreyne þe malice of his enmys. *c* **1440** *Partonope* 3306* Thus shall I my body peyne Merthe and joye my hert resstrayne. **1542** UDALL *Erasm. Apoph.* 295 He grauely restreigned and staied the heddie vndiscretenesse of the oratours. **1560** DAUS tr. *Sleidane's Comm.* 134 Yet hathe God hetherto restrayned the force and violence of Sathan. **1638** SIR T. HERBERT *Trav.* (ed. 2) 91 Ganges..a whiles forbad them, restrayning eithers fury. **1725** DE FOE *Voy. round World* (1840) 278 It would have been impossible for me to have restrained my curiosity. **1743** PITT in Almon *Anecd.* I. v. 124 The ardour of our British troops was restrained by the cowardice of the Hanoverian. **1839** FR. A. KEMBLE *Resid. in Georgia* (1863) 37, I could hardly restrain my feelings. **1874** GREEN *Short Hist.* vii. §6. 400 As Elizabeth passed..from suspicion to terror, she no longer chose to restrain the bigotry around her.

b. (a physical agent or force, etc.) Also *absol.*

c **1375** *Sc. Leg. Saints* xxviii. (*Margaret*) 7 Vertu It is blud to restrenȝe, & flux of wame refrenȝe. **1390** GOWER *Conf.* III. 128 The water mai the fyr restreigne. **1481** CAXTON *Myrr.* III. viii. 149 Somtyme they restrayne his heetes, and after they enlarge them. **1611** BIBLE *Gen.* viii. 2 The windowes of heauen were stopped, and the raine from heauen was restrained. **1706** ADDISON *Rosamond* II. vi, O Queen, your lifted arm restrain! **1848** MILL *Pol. Econ.* I. 227 The necessity of restraining population. **1889** *Anthony's Photogr. Bull.* II. 74 The solution must be strong in pyro and well restrained. *Ibid.* 417 If too long an exposure is found to have been given, restrain with..potassium bromide.

3. To restrict, limit, confine.

c **1340** HAMPOLE *Pr. Consc.* 2327 For God has restreyned þair powere þat þai [*sc.* devils] may na man tempte ne greve. *c* **1420** LYDG. *Assembly of Gods* 1013 He seyd he wold nat restrayne hys lyberte. *c* **1460** FORTESCUE *Abs. & Lim. Mon.* vi. (1885) 121 Be reason hereoff he will þe more restrayn his yeftis off oþer off his livelod. *Ibid.*, This may in nothinge restrane the Kyngis pover. **1576** FLEMING *Panopl. Epist.* 150, I restraine this accusation from being universall. **1654** BRAMHALL *Just Vind.* i. (1661) 2 That they did use in all ages ..to limit and restrain the exercise of Papal power. **1699** LUTTRELL *Brief Rel.* (1857) IV. 497 The bill for restraining the number of officers sitting in the house of commons. **1738** tr. *Guazzo's Art of Convers.* 136 The Denomination of Gentry was much more restrained by Diogenes. **1748** *Anson's Voy.* II. x. 237 This trade..is confined by very particular regulations, somewhat analogous to those by which the trade of the register ships from Cadiz to the West-Indies is restrained. **1818** CRUISE *Digest* (ed. 2) IV. 420 Conditions to restrain those powers, generally, were void, as being repugnant to the estate limited.

b. Const. *to.* Now *rare.*

1509 FISHER *Funeral Serm. C'tess Richmond* Wks. (1876) 294 She restrayned her appetyte tyl one mele & tyl one fysshe on the day. **1581** MULCASTER *Positions* xxxix. (1887) 198 The tearme of nobilitie amongst vs, is restrained to one order. **1644** C. JESSOP *Angel of Ephesus* 50 When the title of Bishop was restrained unto one of the Presbyters. **1692** BENTLEY *Boyle Lect.* ix. 321 The conditions of Salvation are restrain'd to those times and countries only. **1712** ADDISON *Spect.* No. 418 ¶7 His Soil is not restrained to any particular Sett of Plants. **1785** PALEY *Mor. Philos.* III. I. xvii, He swears 'to speak the whole truth', without restraining it, as before, to the questions that shall be asked. **1846** TRENCH *Mirac.* xxvii. (1862) 369 The language shows that the rebuke is not restrained to him, but intended to pass on to many more.

†**4. a.** To withhold, to keep back, *from* one. *Obs.*

1390 GOWER *Conf.* I. 198 Sche wolde him nothing elles sein Bot of hir name..; Alle othre thinges sche restreigneth. **1480** *Bury Wills* (Camden) 59, [I] charge myne executourez that they..kepe and restrayn from hym or them there legatis and byquestis. **1538** STARKEY *England* I. iv. 102 Bettur hyt ys..to restreyne from the prynce such hye authoryte. **1594** WEST *2nd Pt. Symbol., Chancerie* §144 The rents, issues, and profites therof [they] have wrongfully restreyned, perceyved, and taken to their owne use.

absol. **1433** *Rolls of Parlt.* IV. 420/2 Yat the Tresorer of England..have power and auctorite to restreigne of alle maner of assignementz..to the somme of MM. li.

†**b.** To save, keep free. *Obs.*⁻¹

c **1430** LYDG. *Minor Poems* (Percy Soc.) 62 O welle of swetnes.., That..al oure joye fro langour didest restrayne.

†**5. a.** To forbid or prohibit (a thing) to one.

1526 *Pilgr. Perf.* (W. de W. 1531) 238 b, In the whiche god restrayneth or forbyddeth man ony thynge. *c* **1533** in Ellis *Orig. Lett.* Ser. II. II. 53 The said blake rentes whiche by parliament is restrayned to be any further payd by any of the Kinges subjectes. **1628** *Buccleuch MSS.* (Hist. MSS. Comm.) I. 268 The doubt..you may well understand to go only to the trees and timber—the coppice woods are not meant to be restrained.

†**b.** To forbid or prohibit (one) *to* do something; to keep back *from* something desired. *Obs.*

1579–80 NORTH *Plutarch, Theseus* (1656) 7 Restraining all manner of people to bear saile in any vessel or bottom. **1611** BIBLE *Gen.* xvi. 2 Behold now, the Lord hath restrained me from bearing. **1649** in *Def. Rights Univ. Oxford* (1690) 7 Restrained all bakers and brewers..to bake and brew within the city except [etc.]. **1667** MILTON *P.L.* IX. 868 The Serpent wise, Or not restraind as wee, or not obeying, Hath eat'n of the fruit. **1791** MRS. INCHBALD *Simple Story* I. i. 8 He still restrained him from all authority.

†**6. a.** To draw tightly. *Obs. rare.*

c **1430** *Syr Gener.* (Roxb.) 5817 His bridel thoo he gan restreyn. **1596** SHAKS. *Tam. Shr.* III. ii. 59 A headstall of sheepes leather, which being restrain'd to keepe him from stumbling, hath been often burst.

†**b.** To confine, keep; to bind, secure. *Obs.*⁻¹

1460–70 *Bk. Quintessence* 7 þe philosophore seiþ, þat wiyn hath also þe propirtee to restreyne in it þe influence and vertues of gold. **1597** A. M. tr. *Guillemeau's Fr. Chirurg.* 10 b/1 Those vaynes which there doe restrayne that membrane fast vnto the sculle.

†**c.** To compel or constrain. *Obs. rare.*

1621 ELSING *Debates Ho. Lords* (Camden) 103 The Subjecte is restreyned by *præmunire* to receive, though the Kinge be not restreyned to gyve. **1655** FULLER *Ch. Hist.* IX. 185 By antient custome no Vestal Virgin or Flamen of Jupiter was restrained to swear.

7. *intr.* **a.** To refrain (*from* something; †also with infin.). Now *rare.*

1594 DRAYTON *Idea* 337 O, Why should Nature niggardly restraine! **1597** A. M. tr. *Guillemeau's Fr. Chirurg.* 39/2 We muste suffer it to bleede till it of it selfe restraygneth and stoppeth. **1623** MASSINGER *Dk. Milan* v. ii, Thrice his desperate hand was on his sword, T'have killed them both: but he restrained. **1640** *Petit. Lond.* in Rushw. *Hist. Coll.* (1692) I. III. 94 Hence it is that the Prelates here in England ..have restrained to pray for the Conversion of our Soveraign Lady the Queen. **1848** THACKERAY *Van. Fair* lx, It was impossible to restrain from laughter.

†**b.** To limit or confine oneself. *Obs.*⁻¹

1599 SANDYS *Europæ Spec.* (1632) 15 Not to enlarge in Moderne graunts, but to restraine to one Pope of renowmed fresh memorie.

re-'strain (riː-), *v.*² [RE- 5 a.] To strain again.

1874 RAYMOND *Statist. Mines & Mining* 414 The quicksilver collected in kettles outside the settler is strained through canvas sacks, the amalgam collected is..re-strained.

restrainable (rɪ'streɪnəb(ə)l), *a.* [f. RESTRAIN *v.* + -ABLE.] Capable of being restrained.

1646 SIR T. BROWNE *Pseud. Ep.* 262 Nor is the hand of the Painter more restrainable than the pen of the Poet. **1649** CANNE *Golden Rule* 30 Such a power is restrainable and punishable by the subject. **1837** CARLYLE *Fr. Rev.* III. I. i, Mad movements both, restrainable by no known rule. **1859** HAWTHORNE *Marb. Faun* (1878) II. i. 10 Never quite restrainable within the trammels of social law. **1891** *Pall Mall G.* 15 Sept. 6/2 That such people should be detainable and restrainable in such public institutions.

restrained (rɪ'streɪnd), *ppl. a.* [f. as prec. + -ED¹.] Checked; repressed; kept under control; confined; †restricted.

1580 J. STUBBS in *Lett. Lit. Men* (Camden) 43 Pray for your old poore restrained frend. **1650** JER. TAYLOR *Holy Living* iv. §1 (1727) 187 In a more restrained sense it is taken for that part of duty which particularly relates to God. *a* **1676** HALE *Prim. Orig. Man.* (1677) 241, I shall consider the more restrained Perswasion of the Learned. **1727–38** CHAMBERS *Cycl.* s.v. *Restriction*, Arguing affirmatively from a non-restrained to a restrained term. **1791** MRS. RADCLIFFE *Rom. Forest* v, Her conversation was restrained. **1856** FROUDE *Hist. Eng.* (1858) I. iv. 343 The bishop was heard out with hardly restrained indignation. **1865** TYLOR *Early Hist. Man.* ii. 33 The sober, restrained looks and gestures.

Hence **re'strainedness.**

1571 GOLDING *Calvin on Ps.* lxii. 9 A certeine peevish restrynednesse..casteth them at last into despayre. **1853** *Tait's Mag.* XX. 388 An enthusiasm which contrasts with the usual restrainedness of his style.

re'strainedly, *adv.* [f. prec. + -LY².] With restraint; †restrictedly.

1571 GOLDING *Calvin on Ps.* xxxvii. 19 Bycause our flesh woold streit fall to loocenes, God dealeth more restryenedly, with us. **1620** T. GRANGER *Div. Logike* 295 Strictly and restrainedly vsed, or largely. **1684** T. BURNET *The. Earth* II. 164 More particularly and restrainedly, the government of Christ is opposed to the kingdom..of Antichrist. *a* **1703** BURKITT *On N.T.* Luke vi. 30 These and the like precepts of our Saviour, are not to be taken strictly, but restrainedly. **1890** *Daily News* 4 Oct. 3/1 The gilt designs that cover in some cases exuberantly, in others restrainedly, the sides of the volumes.

re'strainer. [f. RESTRAIN *v.* + -ER.]

1. One who or that which restrains.

1568 GRAFTON *Chron.* II. 940 These two persons were euer restrayners and refrayners of the kinges wilfull scope. **1609** BIBLE (Douay) *Isa.* ix. 14 The perverter and restrayner. **1646** SIR T. BROWNE *Pseud. Ep.* 45 Wee must with patience submit unto that restraint, and expect the will of the Restrainer. **1711** SHAFTESB. *Charac.* (1737) I. 25 Even that prince..was a great restrainer of persecution. **1760–72** H. BROOKE *Fool of Qual.* (1809) III. 34 To restrain the restrainers from injustice. **1816** J. SCOTT *Vis. Paris* (ed. 5) 84 Those great correctors and restrainers of human conduct, shame and remorse. **1844** STEPHENS *Bk. Farm* II. 691 Accompanied with a few restrainers of reins and ropes. **1888** BRYCE *Amer. Commw.* I. 299 A jealous observer and restrainer of the others.

2. *Photogr.* A chemical used to retard the action of the developer.

1878 ABNEY *Photogr.* (1881) 111 No restrainer such as bromide is employed. **1892** *Photogr. Ann.* II. 47 Overdoses of pyro act as restrainers.

re'straining, *vbl. sb.* [f. as prec. + -ING¹.] The action of the verb, in various senses.

1398 TREVISA *Barth. De P. R.* VII. xviii. (Bodl. MS.), Restreynyng schal be made aboute þe temples..aȝens rennyng of teeres. *a* **1400** *Minor Poems fr. Vernon MS.* 531 þorw mouþ þei passen wiþ-outen restreyning. *c* **1450** *Lay-Folks Mass Bk.* 69 þat itt may be..senchyp to ouer enmyse, gaynstanding and restrenyng of þare power. **1502** ATKYNSON tr. *De Imitatione* I. xvii. 165 Thou muste make a restraynynge in many thynges of thyne owne wylle. **1596** SPENSER *State Irel.* Wks. (Globe) 622/2 For restrayning of a fowle abuse, which then raigned commonly among that people. **1604** HIERON *Wks.* I. 548 The yoking and hampering and restraining of mans naturall disposition. **1657** *Deuine Louer* 12 All and euery of those doings or actings, abstainings or restreignings. **1842** MANNING *Serm.* iv. (1848) I. 56 The warning, and striving, and restraining of the Holy Ghost shall then be over.

re'straining, *ppl. a.* [-ING².] That restrains or checks; †restringent.

1541 ELYOT *Cast. Helthe* II. xxix. 46 Take hede..that stiptik or restraynyng meates be [not] taken at the beginnyng. **1659** PEARSON *Creed* (1839) 197 The ancient heretics, who would have the restraining term *only* to belong, not to the Son, but to the Father. **1678** RYMER *Trag. last Age* 126 Amintor was..endu'd with a restraining grace, and had his hands ty'd. **1704** TRAPP *Abra-Mulé* II. i, It ne'er conquers the restraining Bounds Of Reason. **1765** BLACKSTONE *Comm.* I. 87 This has occasioned another subordinate division of remedial acts of parliament with enlarging and restraining statutes. *Ibid.*, Let us instance again in the same restraining statute of the 13 Eliz. **1890** W. J. GORDON *Foundry* 90 The directors of these legal and restraining institutions.

Hence **re'strainingly** *adv.*

1863 *Not an Angel* II. 230 No less restrainingly his stedfast eyes seemed to hold her. **1890** *Universal Rev.* Aug. 633 'My dear Mary?' he said slowly, interrogatively, restrainingly.

†**re'strainment.** *Obs.* [f. RESTRAIN *v.* + -MENT. Cf. obs. F. *restrendement* (Godef.).] The act of restraining; restraint.

1579 TOMSON *Calvin's Serm. Tim.* 145/1 Without any restreinement or holding backe. **1607** W. SCLATER *3 Serm.* (1629) 11 Temporall paines remaine as preuentions, as admonitions, as restrainments. **1688** *Enthus. Ch. Rome* 40 From the restrainment of his Tears no other effect could follow.

restraint (rɪ'streɪnt), *sb.* Also 5–6 restraynt(e, 6 -strainte; 5 restreint(e, -streynt(e. [a. OF. *restrainte* fem. (also *restraint* masc.), verbal sb. f. *restraindre* to RESTRAIN.]

1. a. The action of restraining or checking a thing, operation, etc.; an instance of this, a stoppage. ***without restraint***, freely, copiously.

c **1400** *Commandm. Love* x. in *Stow's Chaucer* (1561) 452 b, There let your pitie spred without restreinte. **1470–85**

Malory *Arthur* x. lxxxvi. 567 Thenne syr Tristram.. made a restraynte of his anger. **1494** Fabyan *Chron.* vi. cxc. 193 In conclucyon a restreynt of warre was graunted. **1561** Hollybush *Hom. Apoth.* 31 b, Somtyme happeneth a restraynt in the small guttes. **1577** B. Googe *Heresbach's Husb.* iv. (1586) 190 b, The roote and the water thereof.. is good against the.. restraint of womens Purgations. **1617** Moryson *Itin.* i. 240 The restraint of the money, not to be payed but vpon a testimony brought vnder our hands, was a good caution. **1671** Gumble *Life Monk* 12 The great reason of God's restraint of his Blessing upon many of these worthy Endeavours. **1791** Mrs. Radcliffe *Rom. Forest* ii, Her tears flowed silently and fast. That she might indulge them without restraint, she went [etc.]. **1863** H. Cox *Instit.* i. ii. 279 A bill for the restraint of the Press was brought into the House of Commons. **1878** Abney *Photogr.* (1881) 68, 1 to 2 drops of this solution suffices to give sufficient restraint.

†**b.** A means of retaining, or controlling. *Obs.*$^{-1}$

1695 Kennett *Par. Antiq.* Gloss., *Sera*, a Lock or restraint of water on a river.

c. Something which restrains or holds in check; esp. ***head restraint***, an attachment to the seat of a motor vehicle to prevent the head from jerking back suddenly.

1968 *Wall St. Jrnl.* 5 Aug. 28/4 American Motors Corp. said it will make head restraints standard equipment on all 1969-model cars. **1972** *Times* 28 Nov. 5/6 (Advt.), Both front seats recline, have sockets for optional head restraints. **1973** *Times* 3 July 1/5 Technically, a head rest was purely for comfort, whereas a safety device for protecting the head was termed a head restraint. **1976** *Amer. Speech 1973* XLVIII. 207 There, if he should become violent, he is placed in *restraints* 'straps' in his room. **1980** *Times* 29 Feb. 3 (Advt.), The seats are covered in crushed velour with head restraints at the rear as well as the front.

2. a. A means of restraining or checking persons from a course of action, or of keeping them under control; any force or influence which has a restraining effect; an instance of restraining or of being restrained.

1421-2 Hoccleve *Dialog* 207 A bettar restreynte know I none fro vice. **1600** E. Blount tr. *Conestaggio* 259 There was no restraint could hold them. **1625** Bacon *Ess., Marriage & Single Life*, So sensible of euery restraint, as they will goe neare, to thinke their Girdles, and Garters, to be Bonds and Shackles. **1672** Temple *Ess., Gov.* Wks. 1720 I. 97 All Government is a Restraint upon Liberty. **1765** Blackstone *Comm.* I. 144 Where the laws of our country have laid them under necessary restraints. **1784** Cowper *Task* vi. 49 He could now endure,.. And feel a parent's presence no restraint. **1844** Thirlwall *Greece* lxvi. VIII. 427 The insolence of Charops now began to break through every restraint. **1890** *Spectator* 11 Jan., Subjected to the strong restraints of officers in a Queen's ship at sea.

b. Without article. Restraining action or influence, as applied to persons.

moral restraint: see moral *a.* 10 c.

1567 *Trial Treas.* (1850) 24 So sharpe is this snaffell called restrainte That it maketh me sweate. **1611** Bible *Lev.* xxiii. 36 It is a solemne assembly [*marg.* day of restraint]. **1667** Milton *P.L.* iii. 87 Now Through all restraint broke loose he wings his way. *Ibid.* ix. 1184 Restraint she will not brook. **1729** Butler *Serm.* Wks. 1874 II. 34 Neither is restraint by any means peculiar to one course of life. **1751** Johnson *Rambler* No. 151 ¶9 To the happiness of our first years nothing more seems necessary than freedom from restraint. **1820** Shelley *Œd. Tyr.* i. 74 Moral restraint I see has no effect. **1849** Macaulay *Hist. Eng.* ii. I. 179 Still less restraint was imposed by the government.

c. The state or condition of being restrained; *esp.* abridgement of liberty, confinement.

a **1547** Surrey in *Tottel's Misc.* (Arb.) 14 Thus I alone.. In prison pyne, with bondage and restrainte. **1595** Shaks. *John* iv. ii. 52 Th' infranchisement of Arthur, whose restraint Doth moue the murmuring lips of discontent [etc.]. **1663** Butler *Hudibras* i. iii. 1017 'Tis not Restraint or Liberty That makes Men prisoners or free. **1676** Dryden *Aurengz.* iii. i, Though Int'rest his Restraint has justify'd Can Life and to a Brother be deny'd? **1701** De Foe *Trueborn Eng.* Misc. v. 21 Restraint from Ill, is Freedom to the Wise. **1766** Fordyce *Serm. Yng. Wm.* (1767) II. xii. 191 Perpetual restraint is perpetual wretchedness. **1846** Trench *Mirac.* Introd. (1862) 17 Continually we behold in the world around us lower laws held in restraint by higher. **1857** Ruskin *Two Paths* v. 244 You will find.. that it is his Restraint which is honourable to man, not his Liberty.

d. *spec.* (in above senses) with reference to the treatment of refractory prisoners or insane persons.

1829 in *Proc. Lincoln Asylum* (1847) 22 The Governors have particularly directed their views to the subject of Coercion and Restraints. **1840** *Ibid.* 37 Restraint rapidly weakens and depresses the vital powers of the unhappy victim. **1847** *Ibid.* 28 *note*, Patients are frequently brought to this Asylum under distressing restraints.

attrib. **1846** *State Lincoln Asylum* 39 Restraint Rooms, Seclusion Rooms, Padded Rooms [etc.]. **1897** 'E. L. Prescott' *Scarlet & Steel* xxxviii, Restraint jacket. Made of No. 3 sail canvas, doubled and quilted with Dutch twine in squares of about four inches.

3. †**a.** A prohibition. *Obs.*

1463 *Mann. & Househ. Exp.* (Roxb.) 187 Any restraynt or ordenaunce made to the contrary nat wythstandyng. **1482** *Rolls of Parlt.* VI. 222/2 A restreint was made that certein thynges of Silkewerk.. shuld not be brought into this Reame redy wrought. **1526** *Pilgr. Perf.* (W. de W. 1531) 238 b, The seuenth commaundement.. & the last of the x, in maner also doubleth the restraynt of thefte. **1594** Plat *Jewell-ho.* i. 55 To force the sopeboilers (after they had procured a generall restrainte) to growe to composition with them.

b. An embargo. Usually ***restraint of princes***.

1480 Caxton *Chron. Eng.* ccxlviii. 317 This same yere was a restraynt of the wullys of Caleys made by the Soudyours. **1622** Malynes *Anc. Law-Merch.* i. xxv. 150 Arrest, Restraints and Detainements of Kings and Princes. **1752** Beawes *Lex Mercat. Rediv.* 244 Of Embargoes, or Restraint of Princes. **1769** *Molloy's De Jure Marit.* (ed. 9) II. ii. vii. §7. 50 A Policy against Restraint of Princes, will not extend to Practices against the Laws of Countries. **1848** Arnould *Marine Insur.* II. iii. i. 788 When the further prosecution of the voyage is rendered hopeless.. by blockade,.. and the voyage is accordingly wholly abandoned, that is a loss, by restraint of princes, within the policy.

c. ***restraint of trade***.

1890 *Statutes at Large U.S.A.* XXVI. 209 Every contract, combination in the form of trust or otherwise, or conspiracy, in restraint of trade or commerce among the several States.. is hereby declared to be illegal. **1913** *Halsbury's Laws of Engl.* XXVII. 532 Under the head of restraint of trade by statute come all those cases in which certain trades have been absolutely forbidden by Parliament. **1933** *Sutton & Shannon on Contracts* xi. 164 A contract in restraint of trade is not contrary to public policy. **1941** *Economist* 5 Apr. 437/2 The greater danger lies in the growing influence of what the common law knows (and used to condemn) as 'agreements in restraint of trade'. **1973** *N.Y. Law Jrnl.* 31 Aug. 1/5 The two-count indictment charged conspiracy in restraint of trade in violation of the Sherman Antitrust Act.

4. Constraint; reserve.

1601 Shaks. *All's Well* v. iii. 213 She knew her distance, and did angle for mee, Madding my eagernesse with her restraint. **1791** Gouvr. Morris in Sparks *Life & Writ.* (1832) I. 357, I find that there is much restraint and etiquette here. **1798** Ferriar *Illustr. Sterne*, etc. ii. 41 He ventured to break through his restraint. **1819** Shelley *Cenci* i. i. 60 One thing, I pray you, recollect henceforth, And so we shall converse with less restraint. **1877** 'Rita' *Vivienne* i. ii, We are reconciled again, but there is a restraint between us now.

†**5.** Restriction or limitation. *Obs.*

1594 Hooker *Eccl. Pol.* iii. xi. §6 The positive laws which Moses gave, they were given for the greatest part with restraint to the land of Jewry. **1597** *Ibid.* v. lxxi. §1 This restraint of Easter to a certaine number of dayes. **1656** Earl Monm. tr. *Boccalini's Pol. Touchstone* (1674) 281 The Patent of his admission..; with a restraint.. that [etc.]. **1746** Wesley *Princ. Methodist* 33 Before those words which you suppose to imply such a Restraint—were those spoken without any Restraint or Limitation at all.

†**re'straint,** *pa. pple. Obs. rare.* [a. F. *restreint*, †*restraint*, pa. pple. of *restreindre* to restrain.] Restrained, restricted.

1444 *Rolls of Parlt.* V. 115/2 That be this Act the punischement.. in no wise be restreint. **1502** *Ord. Crysten Men* (W. de W. 1506) i. i, Yᵉ puyssaunce of god is not restraynt nor bounde. **1526** *Pilgr. Perf.* (W. de W. 1531) 112 The nexte day this pyt or well wyll be as full as it was, yf it be not restreynt. **1555** Eden *Decades* vii. (Arb.) 127 The libertie of free passage was restraynt.

†**re'straintive,** *a. Obs.* [a. obs. F. *restraintif, -ive*: see prec. and -ive.] Restrictive.

1541 Copland *Guydon's Quest. Chirurg.* l ij b, The other seame sowyng hyght restrayntyfe of blode. **1566** Warde tr. *Alexis' Secr.* iii. i. 28 Annoynt it rounde about with some restrayntiue oyntment. *a* **1603** T. Cartwright *Confut. Rhem. N.T.* (1618) 623 It is not rightly compared with Mark 16 and Acts 2, which are more restraintiue to the Apostles times and persons then this is.

re'stream, *v.* [re- 5 a.] To stream back.

a **1711** Ken *Hymnarium* Poet. Wks. 1721 II. 8 From Bondage I my Love redeem'd, And all my Powers to God re-stream'd.

re'strengthen (riː-), *v.* [re- 5 a.] *trans.* To strengthen again, put new strength into.

1577-87 Holinshed *Chron., Hist. Scotl.* I. 333/1 Wherevpon he.. dooth restrengthen the towne and steeple of Glascow. **1611** Florio, *Riforzo*, a re-enforcing or restrengthening. **1645** Wither *Vox Pacifica* 108 They, strength receiving, from our false-ones, here, Restrengthen them. **1877** *Public Opin.* 7 July 10 The restrengthening of her great position as a Power of Central Europe. **1892** Stevenson *Lett.* (1899) II. 273 Some beer.. to restrengthen the European heart.

restreyn(e, obs. forms of restrain *v.*

†**restrial,** *a. Her. Obs.* [Of obscure origin.] Of a shield: Having dividing bands which extend to (or include) the point, the colour of the latter being that of the field.

The varieties are described as barry, paly, and 'sentry'.

1486 *Bk. St. Albans, Her.* b iv b, Here shall be shewed what Cootarmuris restryal ben and weer the blaser shall begyn to blase. *Ibid.*, Thre cootarmuris be ther called restryall in armys. **1586** Ferne *Blaz. Gentrie* 204 There were also coates of Armes, called with olde Blazonners Restriall or Rest-triall, because if they were touched or pressed, yet were they able to abide the triall. [Similarly in Guillim (1611) ii. vii. 73.]

restrict (rɪ'strɪkt), *v.* Also 8- *Sc.* restrick. [f. L. *restrict-*, ppl. stem (cf. next) of *restringĕre* to restringe.]

Designated by Johnson (1755) as 'a word scarce English', and included by Dr. Beattie among his *Scoticisms* (1787).

1. *trans.* To confine (some person or thing) *to* or *within* certain limits; to limit or bound.

1535 Lyndesay *Satyre* 3813 Verteous men that labours with thair hands, Resonabillie restrictit with sic bands, That thay do service. **1570** Foxe *A. & M.* (ed. 2) 1474/1 Neither shoulde we haue any more wherwith to vexe them with confessions, cases reserued, restricted, or ampliated for our gayne. **1731** Arbuthnot *Aliments* vi. (1735) 218 In the Enumeration of Constitutions.. there is not one that can be limited and restricted by such a Distinction. **1776** Adam Smith *W.N.* iii. ii. (1904) I. 430 The common law of England.. is said to abhor perpetuities, and they are accordingly more restricted there than in any other European monarchy. **1836** J. Gilbert *Chr. Atonem.* viii. (1852) 224 God himself is yet restricted in the exercise of his compassion. **1874** Green *Short Hist.* vii. §1. 351 The power of preaching was restricted by the issue of licences only to the friends of the Primate.

b. To restrain by prohibition.

1835 *Penny Cycl.* III. 381/1 The act of 1797, which restricted the Bank from making payments in gold.

2. To tie up, confine by tying. *rare*$^{-1}$.

1824 Wiffen *Tasso* xvi. xxiii, Gathering up.. Her hair, restricting each resplendent tress.

3. To withhold or keep (a thing) *from* some person's knowledge. *rare*$^{-1}$.

1802 Mrs. E. Parsons *Myst. Visit* I. 38 It is a very bad compliment paid to your wife, that this secret business of your's should be restricted from her knowledge.

Hence **re'stricting** *ppl. a.*

1848 R. I. Wilberforce *Doctr. Incarnation* xi. (1852) 258 Such restricting conditions as at present interfere with the growth of the Church. **1894** *Westm. Gaz.* 17 Sept. 2/3 A minimum of restricting conditions and the slenderest possible examination test.

†**re'strict,** *ppl. a. Obs. rare.* [ad. L. *restrict-us*: see prec. So Sp. and Pg. *restricto*, It. *ristretto*.] **a.** Strict. **b.** Limited. Also ***restrict line*** (see quot. 1678).

a **1654** Gataker *Just Man* 224 (Latham), Men.. in some one or two things demeaning themselves as exceedingly restrict, but in many others, or the most things, as remisse. **1678** Phillips (ed. 4), *Restrict Line* (in Chiromancy) is that which distinguisheth, and separates the hand from the arm, either by a simple or double transcursion. **1681** H. More *Exp. Dan.* vi. 232 Which Time of the End here has a more restrict signification.

re'strictable, *a.* [f. restrict *v.* + -able.] Able to be restricted.

1973 I. Robinson *Survival of English* iii. 82 Economic management is management of human beings, which is just not restrictable to economics.

re'stricted, *ppl. a.* [f. restrict *v.* + -ed[1].]

a. Limited, confined.

1830 D'Israeli *Chas. I*, III. v. 77 All men of the learned professions, who live in one restricted circle, are liable to suffer. **1856** Kane *Arct. Expl.* II. xxviii. 282 The men's strength was waning under this restricted diet. **1876** Holland *Sev. Oaks* xi. 147 Dividends that will add permanently to our somewhat restricted sources of income.

b. In which a speed-limit is operative.

1933 E. Caldwell *God's Little Acre* vii. 107 They passed through the other company towns slowing down in the restricted zones. **1939** *New Statesman* 29 July 196/1 The existing mild supervision of restricted areas is carried out by the so-called 'speed cops'. **1959** *Listener* 2 Apr. 603/1 There are cases where a driver is mistaken about a restricted area.

c. Of documents, information, etc.: for restricted circulation only (see also quot. 1975); not to be revealed to the general public for reasons of national security.

1944 [see classified *ppl. a.* c]. **1950** [see clear *v.* 9 c]. **1957** *Ann. Reg. 1956* 345 A new model of the R.A.F.'s only fully supersonic fighter flying in Britain.. was taken off the restricted list in August and was demonstrated at the aircraft industry's annual display at Farnborough. **1965** Mrs. L. B. Johnson *White House Diary* 2 Sept. (1970) 313 Then President Truman gave us the tour [of the library], with Max asking all sorts of architectural questions—storage, humidity, traffic routing, vaults for documents that were still restricted. **1972** K. Benton *Spy in Chancery* xv. 180 The Russians always start by asking you to hand over something quite harmless... And then they ask for something that's on the restricted list, but not really secret. **1972** P. Ruell *Red Christmas* ix. 83 What I'm going to tell you is restricted information. That means it's only known to the Prime Minister, [and] security top brass. **1975** *Times* 8 Feb. 2/1 'Restricted' papers ('restricted' is the lowest security classification) had been found on my doormat.

d. *U.S.* Limited to use by non-Jews; denying admission to Jews.

1947 *Cosmopolitan* Jan. 84/2 Is your inn restricted?.. You mean you *do* restrict your guests to Gentiles. **1953** P. Frankau *Winged Horse* i. ix. 41 Draw the slums. Draw the restricted hotels. **1972** W. P. McGivern *Caprifoil* (1973) xii. 204 Anti-Semitism.. is not only a matter of restricted clubs and colleges' quotas. **1979** *Listener* 16 Aug. 204/2 'I'm sorry, Mr Marx, but we can't let you use the pool, this country club is restricted.'.. 'Well, my daughter's only half-Jewish, could she go in up to her knees?'

e. *Biol.* Of a virus: unable to reproduce at its normal rate in certain hosts. Of DNA: subject to degradation by a restriction enzyme.

1957 *Virology* III. 500 A certain proportion of the T1 phage produced is now able to multiply on B(P1) or Sh (P1) ('unrestricted phage'). Single-burst experiments.. showed that about 70% of the yielder cells liberate only normal, 'restricted' T1. The other yielder cells produce a mixture of restricted and unrestricted T1. **1965** *Ann. Rev. Microbiol.* XIX. 366 Phage λ variants can be classified with respect to their state of adaptation.. by determination of the efficiency of plating (eop) on various hosts... λ·K has an eop of one on K12 and C, i.e., it is accepted, nonrestricted. The same phage λ·K, however, plates only exceptionally on B or on P1-lysogenic strains: it is said to be restricted. *Ibid.* 367 The whole population of restricted DNA molecules.

f. Of a language system: having a limited syntax and lexicon.

1962 B. Bernstein in *Lang. & Speech* V. 32 Two general types of code can be distinguished: *elaborated* and *restricted*... In the case of an elaborated code, the speaker will select from a relatively extensive range of alternatives... In the case of a restricted code the number of these alternatives is often severely limited. **1964** M. A. K. Halliday et al. *Linguistic Sci.* 96 Some registers are extremely restricted in purpose. They thus employ only a limited number of formal items and patterns... Such registers are known as *restricted languages*. **1968** E. W. Gordon in M. Deutsch et al. *Social*

Class, Race & Psychol. Devel. xi. 390 Restricted language.. develops as a product of unilateral decision making in the lower-class home. **1971** *Archivum Linguisticum* II. 67 Firth advocated what he called 'partial studies', e.g. the study of newspaper headlines *per se*, in which attention would be drawn to features of the 'restricted language' itself as well as to contrasts between it and other restricted languages. **1975** *Amer. Speech 1973* XLVIII. 35 It has been further suggested that if speakers of a restricted code do not use such conjunctions, their language and probably their logical processes are somehow deficient.

g. Of a person: not allowed to move about freely; confined to a certain area or certain areas.

1971 *Sunday Express* (Johannesburg) 28 Mar. 9/5 'If a restricted person can satisfy me that he can obtain residence overseas and that he has a bona fide intention of not returning to South Africa, I cannot refuse his request for an exit permit,' Mr. Gerdener said. **1971** *Rand Daily Mail* (Johannesburg) 4 Dec. 13/1 Anglican bishops.. are accused of defying the Government by wanting to offer help to people banned or restricted under the Terrorism Act. **1972** *Straits Times* (Malaysian ed.) 24 Nov. 21/2 Unemployed, and a restricted resident, Chua Ali Kow, 32, was sentenced to two years' jail.

Hence **re'strictedly** *adv.*; **re'strictedness.**

1859 GULLICK & TIMBS *Paint.* 72 This style.. in him.. appears most decidedly in all its restrictedness. **1870** RUSKIN *Lect. Art* 98 Whatever is truly great in either Greek or Christian art, is also restrictedly human. **1899** *Speaker* 29 July 105/2 Lake was essentially an Educator, Goulburn restrictedly an Evangelist.

restrictee (rɪstrɪk'tiː). [f. RESTRICT *v.* + -EE[1], after *detainee.*] One whose freedom of movement is restricted, usu. for political reasons.

1959 *Observer* 31 May 6/8 This pay starts in the open camp—no guards, no wire, no warders—at 30s. monthly plus rations. When detainees thus become 'restrictees' they are trade tested and trained for various jobs as clerks or artisans. **1960** *Guardian* 24 Dec. 7/1 The Southern Rhodesian Government must now be keen to release the seven detainees and forty restrictees. **1965** *Spectator* 8 Jan. 35/2 The government can no longer prevent the restrictees from receiving visitors at will and today there is a constant stream on the trains. **1970** *Guardian Weekly* 21 Feb. 6/4 The main legal advantage that restrictees have over detainees is that their term of restriction is defined.

restriction (rɪ'strɪkʃən). Also 5 restricciou n. [a. F. *restriction*, or ad. late L. *restrictiōn-em*, noun of action f. *restringĕre* to RESTRINGE. Cf. Sp. *restriccion*, It. *re-*, *ristrizione.*]

1. a. A limitation imposed upon a person or thing; a condition or regulation of this nature.

c **1412** HOCCLEVE *De Reg. Princ.* 4792 Crist scheelde þat your wil or your entente Be sette to maken a restricciou n Of paiement. **1535** LYNDESAY *Satyre* 2807 That al the temporal lands Be set in few.., With sic restrictiouns as sall be devysit. **1590** SWINBURNE *Testaments* 264 The restrictions of this former conclusion are these. **1646** SIR T. BROWNE *Pseud. Ep.* 225 It necessarily suffering such restrictions as take of generall illations. **1693** LUTTRELL *Brief Rel.* (1857) III. 190 Giving security to export yearly 150,000£ worth of English manufacture, with some other restrictions. **1728–9** *Swift's Lett.* (1768) IV. 19 All restrictions of marriage are odious in the civil law, and not favoured by the common law, especially after the age of one and twenty. **1772** PRIESTLEY *Inst. Relig.* (1782) II. 117 The restrictions under which our first parents were laid. **1822** SCOTT *Peveril* xlviii, A restriction which he supposed as repugnant to his Majesty's feelings as it was to his own. **1855** MACAULAY *Hist. Eng.* xix. IV. 371 That one restriction of the royal prerogative had been mischievous did not prove that another restriction would be salutary. **1874** GREEN *Short Hist.* vii. §6. 398 The old restrictions on the use of the pulpit were silently removed.

b. The action or fact of limiting or restricting.

1629 H. BURTON *Truth's Triumph* 95 With speciall restriction too, as iustifying a man onely from originall sinne. **1660** R. COKE *Power & Subj.* 76 The law of nature gives Fathers a power over their children without restriction. **1766** BLACKSTONE *Comm.* II. 145 Yet this must be understood with some restriction. **1829** I. TAYLOR *Enthus.* iv. (1867) 91 There is something incongruous in the idea of a revelation enveloped in menace and restriction. **1840** DICKENS *Old C. Shop* lxvii, It was the day.. which threatened the restriction of Mr. Quilp's liberty. **1874** GREEN *Hist. Eng.* ix. §2. 604 Not only was the Monarchy restored, but it was restored without restriction or condition.

c. *attrib.*, as ***restriction act, order.***

1835 *Penny Cycl.* III. 380/2 Not.. until 1797, when the celebrated Bank Restriction Act was passed. **1875** *Encycl. Brit.* III. 319/1 Progress of Banking in England down to Restriction Order of 1797.

d. Deliberate limitation of industrial output.

1888 W. E. NICHOLSON *Gloss. Terms Coal Trade* 71 *Restriction*, an arrangement or understanding among the hewers limiting their day's work to something less than a fair ordinary day's work. **1930** *Economist* 22 Mar. 652/1 At the same time, restriction is being maintained in Oklahoma, while in Texas, although the State Governor views all restriction schemes as a breach of the Anti-Trust laws, a certain amount of voluntary restriction is in force. **1931** *Brit. Jrnl. Psychol.* July 89 Restriction is practised by the non-union worker just as much as it is by the member of a trade union. **1961** *Problems of Progress in Industry* No. 11 p. 11 If their [*sc.* workers'] standards are lower than those considered as reasonable by managers, such behaviour is usually called 'restriction of output'.

2. a. *Logic.* (See later quots.)

1551 ROBINSON tr. *More's Utopia* II. (1895) 185 They haue not deuysed one of all those rules of restryctyons, amplyfycatyons, and supposytyons, very wittelye inuented in the small Logycalles, whyche heare oure chyldren in euerye place do learne. **1727–38** CHAMBERS *Cycl.*, *Restriction*, among logicians, is understood of the limiting a term, so as to make it signify less than it usually does. **1850** SIR W. HAMILTON *Disc.* (1853) App. II. 692 Table of the mutual relations of the eight propositional forms... Restriction, sub-alternation. **1864** F. BOWEN *Logic* vi. 169 In some cases the Restriction (Subalternation) and the Integration may be bilateral.

b. = RESERVATION 4 b. (Usu. with *mental.*)

1691 tr. *Emilianne's Frauds Rom. Monks* (ed. 3) 169 Making use to this purpose of their mental Restriction. **1882** *Encycl. Brit.* XIV. 638/2 They have now divided mental restriction into two main heads. **1884** *Catholic Dict.* (1897) 620/2 If the restriction is of such a nature that it cannot be perceived by the hearer, then the person who uses it certainly sins.

3. †**a.** *Med.* Constipation; suppression. *Obs.*

1597 A. M. tr. *Guillemeau's Fr. Chirurg.* 47 b/1 The Cholicke, the restrictione or constipatione. **1599** —— tr. *Gabelhouer's Bk. Physicke* 219/1 For restrictione of the flowers, and for the corroboratione of the Harte.

b. Constriction, compression. *rare.*

1758 J. S. *Le Dran's Observ. Surg.* (1771) 99 An Uneasiness.. that was attended with a slight Restriction of Breath. **1871** *Figure Training* 31 Notwithstanding that severe restriction of the waist suddenly applied appears likely to prove most irksome, if not injurious.

4. *Math.* A function f whose domain is a subset of a given function g, whose codomain is the codomain of g, and for which $f(x) = G(x)$ for all x in the domain of f. Also ***restriction mapping.***

1949 SPRINGER & POLLAK *Algebraic Topology* viii. 168 Since f is a restriction of g, we have that the map $\bar{g}$ of H(A) into H(B) which is reduced by g is exactly the same as the map f. **1963** D. BUSHAW *Elem. Gen. Topology* 147 If $f: X \to Y$ and $A \subset X$, the function $fj: A \to Y$, where j is the injection map from A to X, is called the restriction of f to A and is denoted by $f|A$. **1979** *Proc. London Math. Soc.* XXXVIII. 208 Recall that $D(G,H) = \text{Ker } \rho_H$ where $\rho_H: \text{Der}(G,ZG) \to \text{Der}(H,ZG)$ is the restriction mapping.

5. *Biol.* Limitation of the rate of reproduction of a virus in certain hosts, owing to the destruction of viral DNA by a restriction enzyme.

1962 *Jrnl. Molecular Biol.* V. 47 Host-controlled modification is known to occur in many bacteriophage-host systems and is usually recognized by restriction in the efficiency of plating of the newly modified phage on its former host strain. **1968** *Proc. Nat. Acad. Sci.* LIX. 1305 The complementation studies suggest that restriction activity is conferred by at least two gene functions. **1979** *Nature* 1 Mar. 30/1 Bacteriophage T3 and T7 protect their DNA from restriction by producing, as the earliest detectable phage functions, anti-restriction proteins.

6. Special Comb.: **restriction endonuclease, enzyme** *Biochem.*, an enzyme that divides large molecules of DNA only if there is a specific sequence of several nucleotides (usu. four to six in number).

1977 *Sci. Amer.* Dec. 61/1 An important tool for plus-and-minus sequencing and for molecular biology in general was provided by the discovery several years ago of the enzymes called restriction endonucleases, which cleave large DNA molecules into discrete fragments. **1979** *Nature* 20 Sept. p. v, CP Laboratories Limited have in stock for immediate delivery more than 40 restriction endonucleases. **1965** W. ARBER in *Ann. Rev. Microbiol.* XIX. 368 One might like to assume that a highly specific 'restriction enzyme' only initiates the degradation, for example, by cleavage of DNA, and that these cleavage products are then subject to the action of less specific nucleases. **1977** *Time* 18 Apr. 48/1 Different plasmids, sometimes passed from one bacterium to another, can order up still another kind of chemical weapon, a so-called restriction enzyme, which can sever the DNA of an invading virus, say, at a predetermined point.

Hence **re'strictionary** *a.*, imposing restrictions.

1828 *Examiner* 184/1 Their restrictionary measures.. may have arisen from a wish to take advantage of the circumstances of the time.

re'strictionism. [f. RESTRICTION + -ISM.] A policy of restricting some practice, institution, etc.

1941 *Economist* 5 Apr. 436/2 It would be a disaster if war-time concentration were to leave any legacy of peacetime restrictionism. **1949** *Hansard Commons* 19 May 631, I do not want to say very much more about this matter of restrictionism, save to say that the body of Captain Ludd has long since mouldered in the grave but his ideas still march on in Britain. **1958** *Economist* 20 Dec. 1066/1 There was a prime example of this restrictionism earlier this week, when employers and building unions in the north together condemned the excellent practice whereby some building workers have entered into voluntary contracts to build some additional houses in certain developing areas after hours. **1968** *Physics Bull.* Nov. 394/2 Restrictionism relates to the absence of true competition due to restrictive trade associations etc. *a* **1974** R. CROSSMAN *Diaries* (1975) I. 34 Office building was an area where, despite my dislike of restrictionism, I might be seriously prepared to think of physical controls to deal with the scandal.

re'strictionist, *sb.* (and *a.*) [f. RESTRICTION + -IST.] One who advocates the restriction of some practice, institution, etc., such as the liquor-trade. Also as *adj.*

1820 *Niles' Reg.* XVIII. 258/2 We undertake to say that there is not a single *confessed* restrictionist elected throughout the whole territory. **1849** *Blackw. Mag.* LXVI. 596 He contrives to combine the hitherto antagonistic qualities of free-trader and restrictionist. **1863** H. SPENCER *Ess.* II. 322 The whole system of currency-legislation is restrictionist from beginning to end. **1887** *Voice* 9 June 4 The restrictionists say, they wish to cut down the number of saloons by one-half. **1941** *Economist* 29 Mar. 406/1 The preservation of the margins of, say, August, 1939, as maxima, may simply do the work of monopolists or restrictionists for them. **1951** *Sun* (Baltimore) 19 Mar. 1/2 A powerful bloc of 'restrictionists' is threatening to strike a successful blow at freedom of information in the name of the United Nations. **1962** *Listener* 8 Mar. 400/1 A restrictionist policy which the unions have denounced as the cause of most of the trouble. **1965** *New Statesman* 30 Apr. 673/1 What is needed is.. a restrictionist philosophy in the field of reproduction.. coupled with an expansionist philosophy in the field of production and distribution of all the other good things of life.

restrictive (rɪ'strɪktɪv), *a.* and *sb.* Also 6 restryct-. [ad. F. *restrictif, -ive*, = Sp. and Pg. *restrictivo*, It. *restrittivo*, ad. late L. *restrictīv-us*: see RESTRICT *v.* and -IVE.]

A. *adj.* †**1.** = RESTRINGENT *a.* 1. *Obs.*

c **1400** MAUNDEV. (Roxb.) xviii. 81 Men.. vsez certayne oynementz calde and restrictiue. *c* **1550** LLOYD *Treas. Health* Kj, Immoderate exercyse, or lacke therof, wyth vsynge of restryctyue meates. **1607** TOPSELL *Hist. Four-f. Beasts* (1658) 323 This Plaister being restrictive, will force the humors to resort all downward. **1676** WISEMAN *Surg.* (J.), I applied a plaister over it, made up with my common restrictive powder. **1727** BRADLEY *Fam. Dict.* s.v. *Hoof-loosening*, Put a Restrictive Charge about it, and heal it up with Turpentine and Hogs Grease melted together.

2. Of terms, expressions, etc.: Implying, conveying, or expressing restriction or limitation; also in *Gram.*, esp. of relative clauses.

1579 G. HARVEY *Let. to Spenser* Wks. (Grosart) I. 23 He might haue spared.. that same restrictiue, and streight laced terme, Precisely. **1612** T. TAYLOR *Titus* ii. 11 That was a more restrictiue doctrine to the Iewes only. *a* **1660** HAMMOND *Serm.* (1850) 581 The particle 'but' in the front of my text.. is exclusive and restrictive. **1697** tr. *Burgersdicius' Logic* I. xxxiii. 115 Enunciations that are exclusive and restrictive receive contradiction from a negation added to the exclusive or restrictive particles. **1727–38** CHAMBERS *Cycl.* s.v. *Proposition, Restrictive*, or *limitative Proposition*, is that affected with a restrictive sign; as, *according to*,.. *considered as.* **1827** JARMAN *Powell's Devises* II. 125 In order to restrain the devise.. it was necessary to shew restrictive words. **1866** CRUMP *Banking* v. 124 [He] should show in the indorsement to what purpose it was to be applied, which is termed a 'restrictive indorsement'. **1878** C. STANFORD *Symb. Christ* i. 22 To save sinners! True, this is a restrictive term. **1878** REED & KELLOGG *Higher Lessons in English* 98 The Adjective Clause, when not restrictive, is set off by the comma. **1895** *Funk's Stand. Dict.* s.v., A restrictive clause. **1924** O. JESPERSEN *Philos. Gram.* viii. 112 In English.. only restrictive clauses can be introduced by *that* or without any pronoun. **1957** *Eng. Stud.* XXXVIII. 101 Restrictive clauses.. are linked to their antecedents by close syntactic juncture. **1977** *Language* LIII. 70 The pragmatic distinction that Donnellan labeled the 'referential' and 'attributive' uses of definite descriptions is *not* reflected in the mood of restrictive relative clauses.

3. a. Restricting; having the nature or effect of a restriction; limitative *of* the power or scope of something or some one.

1652 FELTHAM *Low Countries* (1677) 56 Their wisdom is .. rather narrow and restrictive, as being a wisdom but for themselves. **1670** CLARENDON *Ess.* Tracts (1727) 163 But this is only the restrictive negative power of conscience, the affirmative power hath not that force. **1775** DE LOLME *Eng. Const.* Pref., The restrictive oath imposed on Members of Parliament. **1818** HALLAM *Mid. Ages* (1872) II. 155 This capitulary seems to be restrictive of the prelates. **1825** J. S. MILL in *Westm. Rev.* Apr. 412 If the landlords would attend a little to these, and some other effects of the restrictive system, we should no longer hear them clamouring.. for a protecting duty of 20, 30, or 40 shillings. **1865** H. PHILLIPS *Amer. Paper Curr.* II. 181 Restrictive laws produce dishonesty and idleness. **1880** *Our Nat. Responsibility for Opium Trade* 6 Its monopoly is equivalent in effect to a heavy restrictive tax.

b. *spec.* of a covenant.

1882 *Law Rep. Queen's Bench Div.* VIII. 410 With regard to the question of notice, *Tulk v. Moxhay* shews that a restrictive covenant will be enforced, and so do *Cox v. Bishop* and *Wilson v. Hart.* **1911** *Encycl. Brit.* XVI. 157/1 *Restrictive Covenants*:- These may be subdivided into two classes—covenants not to assign or underlet without the lessor's consent..; and covenants in restraint of trade. **1925** *Act 15 Geo. V* c. 22 §10 A covenant or agreement (not being a covenant or agreement made between a lessor and lessee) restrictive of the user of land entered into after the commencement of this Act (in this Act referred to as 'a restrictive covenant'). **1935** *Discovery* Aug. 227/1 A new policy of preserving land by means of restrictive covenants has recently been adopted [by the National Trust], in addition to the older and more expensive method of purchase. **1953** [see LILY-WHITE *a.* 2]. **1976** *Evening Post* (Nottingham) 15 Dec. 4/4 Mansfield District Council has decided to go ahead with its plan to close the market.. despite the failure of their application to the Land Tribunal for the removal of 100-year-old restrictive covenant on the site. **1979** *Internat. Jrnl. Sociol. of Law* VII. 339 In drafting the contract a planning authority condition that the future occupants do not erect fences has to be translated into a restrictive covenant.

c. ***restrictive practice***: an arrangement in industry and trade which restricts or controls competition between firms; an arrangement by a group of workers to limit the output or restrict the entry of new workers: regarded by others as preventing labour or materials from being used in the most efficient way. Hence ***restrictive practitioner.***

1928 *Britain's Industr. Future* (Liberal Industr. Inquiry) xiii. 146 The prevalence of these restrictive practices has varied very widely from trade to trade. **1946** *Sun* (Baltimore) 19 Feb. 10/3 The single argument on which all the restrictive practices have rested..was that the demand for housing was so limited that the various factors in the housing field in simple self-protection had to stretch the work out and keep costs high. **1948** *Act 11 & 12 Geo. VI* c. 66 §1 For the purposes of this Act there shall be constituted a Commission, to be called the Monopolies and Restrictive Practices Commission... The Commission shall consist of not less than four nor more than ten members to be appointed by the Board of Trade. **1958** *Spectator* 31 Jan. 133/1 These two trades have been in the forefront as restrictive practitioners. **1964** *Mod. Law Rev.* XXVIII. 337 The House of Lords..handed down an important decision on the question of restrictive practices. **1966** *Economist* 12 Mar. 979/2 Mr Heath would apparently like to hand the supervision of labour relations over to the lawyers, the Tories' favourite restrictive practitioners. **1969** J. ARGENTI *Managem. Techniques* 207 Others blame labour for resisting changes to working methods and manning levels and for perpetuating restrictive practices. **1978** *Jrnl. R. Soc. Arts* CXXVI. 406/2 The moves made by successive Tory Presidents of the Board of Trade in the late '50s and early '60s to curb restrictive practices of various kinds.

B. *sb.* †**1.** = RESTRINGENT *sb.* 2. *Obs.*

1460–70 *Bk. Quintessence* 14 So I seie of comfortatyves, digestyves, restrictives. **1612** WOODALL *Surg. Mate* Wks. (1653) 3 If that the flux will not be staied by an ordinary kind of restrictive. **1689** MOYLE *Abstr. Sea Chyrurg.* II. 23 Be sure your restrictives be ready mixt in one Bason.

2. A term or expression having the force of, or implying, a restriction or qualification.

1671 [R. MACWARD] *True Nonconf.* 4 To hear the glorious subject..narrowed within its Scriptural acceptation, by such a Cold restrictive. *a* **1832** BENTHAM *Ess. Lang.* Wks. 1843 VIII. 315 In English, what thickens the confusion is, the indeterminate character of the restrictives, *alone* and *only*. **1864** BOWEN *Logic* v. 145 These [i.e. Exponibles] are divided into Exclusives, Exceptives and Restrictives.

restrictively (rɪˈstrɪktɪvlɪ), *adv.* [f. prec. + -LY².] In a restrictive way; with limitations.

1610 J. HEALEY *St. Aug. Citie of God* (1620) 344 The Poets ..fictions..were not spoken universally but restrictively. **1655** FULLER *Ch. Hist.* II. 135 Take the term [martyr] in a large acception, otherwise restrictively it signifies such an one, as suffers for the Testimony of the Truth. *a* **1676** HALE *Wks.* (1805) I. 398 This subject may be considered two ways: 1. absolutely,.. 2. Relatively, or restrictively. **1864** BOWEN *Logic* viii. 266 Thus, Restrictively, in affirming that, if A is B, C is D. **1884** *Law Rep. 14 Q.B. Div.* 264 The Charter should be construed restrictively.

So **re'strictiveness.** *rare.*

1679 C. NESSE *Antichrist* 192 We find Mr. Brightman blam'd for his overmuch restrictiveness of interpretation. **1978** *Language* LIV. 406 The second desideratum is the goal of restrictiveness: the notion that a theory of language should characterize just the class of possible human languages, and no more. **1980** A. N. WILSON *Healing Art* xviii. 223 Both of them found..emotional restrictiveness necessary.

restrictivist (rɪˈstrɪktɪvɪst), *a.* [f. RESTRICTIVE *a.* + -IST.] Characterized by restriction; limiting.

1966 *New Statesman* 21 Oct. 574/1 Cost-inflation..forces the government to adopt restrictivist policies. **1977** P. JOHNSON *Enemies of Society* viii. 115 Part of the genetic coding of all children is knowledge of the highly restrictivist principles of universal grammar.

restrictor (rɪˈstrɪktə(r)). [f. RESTRICT *v.* + -OR.]

1. One who restricts or advocates restriction.

1825 J. S. MILL in *Westm. Rev.* Apr. 291 It is a proposition which the restrictors themselves do not venture to dispute. **1952** *Chambers's Jrnl.* Apr. 230/1 Restrictive covenants in house or land deeds may be a curse to any buyer... It can happen that covenants are interpreted in a peculiar manner by the restrictors.

2. A device for restricting the flow of a fluid, e.g. by means of a porous medium or an orifice. Freq. *attrib.*

1940 E. MOLLOY *Aeroplane Maintenance & Operation* I. 105 *Restrictor jets*, these..are situated in two recesses opposite the lower edge of the throttle when in the closed position. **1961** R. V. WATTS in D. S. Carton et al. *Rocket Propulsion Technol.* I. 54 By opening the..restrictor, it became possible to set minimum thrust at the required angle. **1966** L. A. H. EASTMAN tr. *G. Schenkel's Plastics Extrusion Technol. & Theory* xiii. 368 The sheet die developed in the U.S.A. for the processing of impact-resistant polystyrene..has a flexible restrictor bar fitted in the upper part of the die, transverse to the flow direction. **1979** *Wear* LIV. 331 The stiffness of hydrostatic [journal] bearings is greatest when valve restrictors are used and decreases progressively with orifice and capillary restrictors.

†**re'strictory.** *Obs. rare*⁻¹. [Cf. RESTRICTIVE and -ORY.] A restringent.

1398 TREVISA *Barth. De P.R.* VII. xv. (Bodl. MS.), The teeres shall be astinte [by a] restrictorie and stintyng.

re'strike (riː-), *sb.* [f. the vb.]

1. A reimpression of a coin, print, or medal.

1902 *Connoisseur* Feb. 131/2 Till lately..the Paris Mint has afforded unusual facilities for restrikes of rarities from the existing dies. **1912** *Chambers's Jrnl.* May 327/2 Restrikes of these medals are not uncommon, as it is only within recent years that the Calcutta mint has been prohibited from issuing them. **1965** ZIGROSSER & GAEHDE *Guide to Collecting Orig. Prints* iv. 62 Prints, either late restrikes from the plate or genuine old uncolored impressions, have often been colored by a later hand. **1970** *New Yorker* 20 June 63/2 The reason for this low price..is that the print is a restrike. This means that it was made after the artist's death from the original plate. **1980** *Daily Tel.* 16 Feb. 27/6 In the case of badges, 'restrikes' are a common hazard.

2. *Electr. Engin.* The re-ignition of an arc.

1962 *Newnes Conc. Encycl. Electr. Engin.* 132/2 Suppression of the arc before natural current zero causes severe overvoltages and high frequency multiple restrikes.

re'strike (riː-), *v.* [RE- 5 a.] **a.** *trans.* To strike again; *esp.* to stamp (a coin) afresh.

1887 HEAD *Hist. Num.* 125 These coins belong to the age of Timoleon, and are restruck over coins of Syracuse. **1901** BLACK *Carpent. & Build.* 19 These can be afterwards restruck with the striking knife.

b. *intr. Electr. Engin.* Of an arc: to strike again (STRIKE *v.* 76 a). Also *trans.* (causatively).

1937 [implied in RESTRIKING *vbl. sb.* below]. **1942** A. ARNOLD *Switchgear Pract.* ix. 109 The arc will again re-strike. **1955** E. MOLLOY *Electr. Engineer's Ref. Bk.* (ed. 8) vii. 24 It is the rate of rise of the restriking voltage that determines whether or not the arc will restrike. **1962** *Newnes Conc. Encycl. Electr. Engin.* 132/1 To achieve successful interruption [of alternating currents] it is necessary to prevent the arc restriking by separating the contacts to a distance which will withstand the restriking voltage. **1977** R. L. LITTLE *Metalworking Technol.* v. xxiv. 279/1 Restriking an arc... The welder strikes the arc approximately ½ to 1 in. in front of the crater on the side opposite the weld bead.

Hence **re'striking** *vbl. sb.*, *esp.* in *Electr. Engin.*; ***restriking voltage***, in a circuit-breaker, the value of the high-frequency voltage surge across the contacts following their separation and the extinction of the subsequent arc between them; **re'struck** *ppl. a.*

1885 *Trans. Lanc. & Chesh. Antiq. Soc.* III. 64 These re-struck coins of Catherine II are much more frequently met with than the coins of Peter [III]. **1937** TODD & THOMPSON *Outdoor High Voltage Switchgear* viii. 172 An important factor controlling restriking voltage is the type of machine.. supplying the circuit. **1958** J. SHEPHERD et al. *Higher Electr. Engin.* xvi. 405 In oil circuit breakers, where dielectric strengths are normally higher than in air circuit breakers, re-striking may not take place.

restrine, obs. form of RESTRAIN *v.*

re'string (riː-), *v.* [RE- 5 a.] To string again.

1809 W. TAYLOR in Robberds *Mem.* (1843) II. 281 A quarterly magazine,..wholly quit of gossip re-strung out of the newspapers, would succeed. **1884** *Catholic Dict.* (1897) 486/1 A rosary may be restrung and some of the beads..may be replaced by others without forfeit of the indulgences.

restringe (rɪˈstrɪndʒ), *v.* [ad. L. *restringĕre* to bind fast, confine, f. *re-* RE- + *stringĕre* to draw tight. So Sp. and Pg. *restringir*, It. *ristringere*.]

†**1.** *trans.* To affect (a person) with costiveness; to have an astringent effect upon (a part of the body). *Obs.* Cf. RESTRINGING *ppl. a.*

1597 A. M. tr. *Guillemeau's Fr. Chirurg.* 27 b/2 If the patient be restringed and bounde in his belly, and hath in a longe time not binne at stool. **1657** TOMLINSON *Renou's Disp.* 138 Whether he be most commonly laxative or restringed. **1706** PHILLIPS (ed. Kersey), *To Restringe*, to bind hard, to make costive; as, Quinces restringe those Parts which they are apply'd to. **1758** J. S. *Le Dran's Observ. Surg.* (1771) 204 The Intestine is less restringed.

absol. **1710** T. FULLER *Pharm. Extemp.* 122 It [*sc.* an electuary] Incrassates, Restringes, Heats.

2. To confine, limit, restrict. Now *rare.*

1604 T. WRIGHT *Passions* II. iii. 59 Of Passions..some.. dilate, and some compresse and restringe the heart. **1652** BENLOWES *Theoph.* III. vii, Pure Knowledge, thou art not restring'd. Thy flames enfire the bushie heart, yet leave 't unsing'd. **1670** *Tryal of W. Penn & W. Mead* App., To decline making any Act that may in the least seem to restringe..this..Great Charter of the Liberties of England. **1839** J. ROGERS *Antipopopr.* xii. §5. 278 The fear of hell being found..too little to bind and restringe the bad inclination of the great majority.

†**re'stringency.** *Obs.* [f. next: see -ENCY.] The quality or property of being restringent.

1667 PETTY in Sprat *Hist. R. Soc.* 293 The Dyers use this Water in Reds, and in other colours wanting restringency. **1729** *Evelyn's Pomona* Gen. Advt. 98 The Juice being pressed out, is immediately pleasant in Taste, without any thing of that restringency which it had. **1759** B. MARTIN *Nat. Hist. Eng.* I. 340 By its Restringency it strengthens the Stomach. **1799** UNDERWOOD *Diseases Children* (ed. 4) I. 54 Rhubarb will not be a fit purgative, though it be joined with magnesia, which will not sufficiently correct its restringency.

†**re'stringent,** *a.* and *sb.* *Obs.* [ad. L. *restringent-em*, pres. pple. of *restringĕre*: see RESTRINGE *v.* and -ENT. So F. *restringent*, It., Sp., Pg. *restringente*.]

A. *adj.* **1.** Having astringent or binding properties; of an astringent nature; *esp.* tending to restrain the action of the bowels.

1578 LYTE *Dodoens* 486 The Tare seede is of a restringent vertue like yᵉ Lentil, but more astringent. **1601** HOLLAND *Pliny* II. 158 The oliue leaues are exceeding restringent, good..to restraine or stop any flux. **1620–55** I. JONES *Stone-Heng* (1725) 25 The Sand..doth (by the restringent Quality ..of the salt Water) become a Stone. *a* **1664** FRANK *Serm.* (1672) 211 The nature of Frankincense is binding and restringent. **1717** *Phil. Trans.* XXX. 568, I think we can much better demonstrate that the Chalybeat Waters do contain Stiptic and Restringent Virtues. **1799** UNDERWOOD *Diseases Children* (ed. 4) I. 223 This will be found to vary frequently, sometimes calling for restringent, and at others, opening remedies.

b. Of outward applications: Styptic.

1597 A. M. tr. *Guillemeau's Fr. Chirurg.* 38 b/2 We must as then strowe some restringent poulder one that parte and therone an ordinarye restringent or defensive plaster. **1689** MOYLE *Sea Chyrurg.* I. 18 Let your Restringent Powder be there likewise with the rest of your first intentions. **1725** BRADLEY *Fam. Dict.* s.v. *Scabbed Heels*, After which apply a restringent Charge of Powder of unslack'd Lime. **1822–34** *Good's Study Med.* (ed. 4) IV. 444 Dr. Bateman was in the habit of using a gently restringent lotion or ointment.

c. Having an astringent taste. *rare*⁻¹.

1746 in Hanway *Trav.* (1762) I. IV. liv. 251 [Water] which appears to be impregnated with allom, being so acid and restringent as not to be borne long in the mouth.

2. Constipated, costive. *rare*⁻¹.

1634–5 BRERETON *Trav.* (Chetham) 191 My body was not costive and restringent, but soluble and laxative sufficient.

B. *sb.* **1.** A word which has a limitative or restricting force.

a **1626** BP. ANDREWES *96 Serm., Holy Ghost* x. (1661) 461 But if you will have *pauperibus* a restringent, you may: but then you must take it for poor in spirit. **1671** [R. MACWARD] *True Nonconf.* 4 Non-conformists..do indeed tell us of the death of our Lord Jesus, not with your ill appropriat and restringent *only*, but do preach to us alwayes and principally this doctrine of his Cross.

2. A medicine or application which possesses astringent or styptic properties.

1666 G. HARVEY *Morb. Angl.* xxxv. (1672) 110 The two latter indicate Phlebotomy for revulsion, restringents to stench, and incrassatives to thicken the blood. **1668** DRYDEN *Dram. Poesy* Ess. (ed. Ker) I. 58 Would you not think that physician mad, who having prescribed a purge, should immediately order you to take restringents upon it? **1754–64** SMELLIE *Midwifery* II. 219 This happened twice after, and blooding with restringents were as often repeated. **1792** *Childr. Thespis* 208 He's been fed on restringents, and Curtain rod diet.

So †**re'stringing** *ppl. a.* *Obs.*

1562 BULLEIN *Bulwarke, Bk. Simples* (1579) 55 Endive is more colder then the Cichorie, and be bothe of a restringyng, or stoppyng, bindyng nature. **1651** J. FREAKE *Agrippa's Occ. Philos.* 22 Some are in things compounded of Elements, and these are more then first qualities, and such are these that are..restringing.

†**re'stringitive,** *a.* *Obs.* = RESTRINGENT *a.* 1.

1530 LYNDESAY *Test. Papyngo* 737 The swyft Swallow.. wald my bleding stem, belyue, With hir moste verteous stone restringityue.

re'strive (riː-), *v.* [RE- 5 a.] To strive anew.

1613 SIR E. SACKVILLE *Let.* in *Guardian* No. 133 Restriving again afresh, with a Kick and a Wrinch together, I freed my long captived Weapon.

restruck: see RESTRIKE *v.*

re'structure, *v.* [RE- 5 c.] *trans.* To give a new structure to; to organize into a new pattern; to rebuild, re-arrange. Hence **re'structured** *ppl. a.*; **re'structurer**; **re'structuring** *vbl. sb.*

1951 K. S. LASHLEY in L. A. Jeffress *Cerebral Mechanisms in Behavior* 119 Some children become very facile at such inversions of words, and re-structure new words without hesitation. **1951** G. HUMPHREY *Thinking* vi. 181 If every response has an element of newness,..why is not restructuring present all the time? **1958** W. J. H. SPROTT *Human Groups* iii. 48 The 'life-space' is constantly changed with 'locomotion', and also with changing awareness, in which case it is often said to be 'restructured'. **1962** *Economist* 22 Sept. 1123/2 The most comprehensive restructuring of international liquidity arrangements since the IMF was founded. **1967** *Observer* 19 Nov. 4/7 Wilson.. thought that..his policy of controlled expansion, combined with the 'restructuring' of industry and a better balance between the regions, would in the end do the trick. **1969** *Listener* 17 July 65/3 He [*sc.* the Director-General] did not restructure the radio services of the BBC. **1970** *Times Lit. Suppl.* 23 Apr. 443/2 Lord Robbins is a tough-minded re-structurer. **1976** P. R. WHITE *Planning for Public Transport* x. 208 The question of re-structuring private car costs to make them comparable in form is discussed below. **1977** *Belfast Tel.* 22 Feb. 6/2 Proposals for the re-structured council are being studied by the Secretary of State. **1978** W. F. BUCKLEY *Stained Glass* xxii. 212 He spent the first half hour with Overstreet, who pronounced the restructuring of the chapel's trussed roof complete.

‖**Reststrahlen** (rɛstˈʃtraːlən), *sb. pl.* *Physics.* Also as sing. **Reststrahl** and with small initial. [Ger., residual rays, f. *rest* remainder + *strahlen* rays.] Electromagnetic radiation which is selectively reflected from the surface of a crystalline solid when the frequency of the incident radiation is nearly equal to the frequency of vibration of the ions constituting the solid.

1910 *Phil. Mag.* XIX. 761 For the investigation of the extreme infra-red portion of the spectrum the method of 'Reststrahlen' has proved most fruitful. **1942** *Rep. Progr. Physics* VIII. 28 To compare the high-frequency end of the spectrum..with that obtained from other data, e.g. from *Reststrahlen* in the case of ionic crystals. **1965** M. GARBUNY *Optical Physics* v. 285 (*caption*) Filter action of crystallite powders in their reststrahlen region. **1967** *Physical Rev. Lett.* XVIII. 601/2 The sample is opaque in the neighborhood of 23 meV due to *Reststrahl* reflection.

re'study (riː-), *v.* [RE- 5 a.] To study again.

1811 W. TAYLOR in *Monthly Rev.* LXV. 1 The thought that is uttered cannot be re-studied by the audience. **1899** COTTERILL *Goethe's Iphigenie auf Tauris* Life p. lvi, Through Herder Goethe was induced to re-study Homer.

re'study, *sb.* [f. the vb.] The act of studying again.

1961 *Newark* (N.J.) *Even. News* 21 Nov. 24/2 (*heading*) N.J. fights restudy of WNTA sale stay. **1962** E. SNOW *Red China Today* (1963) liii. 402, I met a writer less well known than Hsiao Ch'ien, who had completed his 'restudy of the sources of art' in a commune. **1966** *Economist* 22 Jan. 309/1 When the commission sounded the retreat and sent the headache back to the engineers for 're-study', the state engineer suggested drily that the study would take just about a year. **1979** *Nature* 20–27 Dec. 832/1 A restudy of this genus has convinced us that it was based on part of the skull roof of a specialised placoderm.

re'stuff (riː-), *v.* [RE- 5 a.] *trans.* To stuff again or anew. Hence **re'stuffing** *vbl. sb.*

1844 H. STEPHENS *Bk. Farm* II. 400 The paddings.. should be restuffed every half-year. **1856** KANE *Arct. Expl.* II. ii. 32, I made my way back to our miserable little cavern, and restuffed its gaping entrance with the snow. **1883** COL. ALEXANDER *Sp. in Parl.* 20 Aug., The re-stuffing of an old armchair.

'resty, *a.*[1] *Obs.* exc. *dial.* Also 6 restye, 6–7 -ie, 7 -ey; 9 *dial.* reasty, reesty. [Variant of RESTIFF (and RESTIVE) *a.*; cf. *hasty, tardy*. In senses 2–4 perh. associated to some extent with REST *sb.*[1] or *v.*[1]: cf. Fris. *restich*, Du. *rustig* quiet.]

1. = RESTIVE *a.* 3. **a.** Of horses or other animals.

1515 BARCLAY *Egloges* (1570) B iv b/2 A bad horse resty and flinging Oft casteth a man though he be well sitting. **1530** PALSGR. 322/2 Restye as a horse is, *restif, restifue.* **1605** SYLVESTER *Du Bartas* II. i. IV. *Lawe* 339 Th' Ox, over-fat, too-strong, and resty, leaps About the Lands, casteth his yoke, and strikes. **1673** O. WALKER *Educ.* 12 Beasts grow fierce and resty if not tamed and broken in youth. **1702** DE FOE *More Reformation* 730 An Author who we can not understand, Is like a Resty Horse at no Command. **1782** MISS BURNEY *Cecilia* I. vi, My horse has been so confounded resty, I could not tell how to get him along. **1883** *Almondbury Gloss., Reaster, reasty horse,* or *raist-horse,* a horse which will not draw; a restive horse. **1920** A. HUXLEY *Leda* 40 The machine is ready to start. The symbolic beasts grow resty, curveting where they stand. **1977** J. AIKEN *Five-Minute Marriage* viii. 126 He guided his horses around the corner... The team appeared to be a trifle fresh and resty.

transf. **1733** TULL *Horse-hoeing Husb.* xix. 131 When that rich Land.. is grown too vigorous and resty, they may soon take down its Mettle, by Sowing it a few Years in their Old Husbandry.

b. Of persons.

1603 DRAYTON *Bar. Wars* IV. lii, Which restie growne, with your much Power, withdraw Your stiff'ned Necks from th' yoke of Civill Awe. **1627** E. F. *Hist. Edw. II* (1680) 79 The resty minds that kick at present greatness. **1686** GOAD *Celest. Bodies* III. i. 377 He must be very Resty that will not allow it for probable at least. **1710** S. PALMER *Proverbs* 16 Some children are naturally resty and stubborn, even at three or four. **1748** CHESTERF. *Lett.* clxviii. (1792) II. 125 Whatever Court he went to (and he was often obliged to go himself to some resty and refractory ones) he as constantly prevailed. **1794** GOUVR. MORRIS in Sparks *Life & Writ.* (1832) II. 411 If Paris runs resty, the revolution is done. **1846** SPURDEN *Suppl. Forby's East Anglian Gloss., Reasty,* restive, unruly; also pettish, quarrelsome, in a bad humour.

c. Of actions, conduct, etc.

a **1586** SIDNEY *Astr. & Stella* lxxx, But now spite of my heart my mouth will stay, And no spurre can his restie race renew. **1693** LOCKE *Educ.* §35 The ill and resty tricks, they have learn'd when young. **1719** D'URFEY *Pills* (1872) I. 343, I often have..to sing denied, But not through resty Peevishness, nor Pride.

†**2. a.** Disinclined for action or exertion; sluggish, indolent, lazy; inactive. *Obs.*

1565 COOPER *Thesaurus*, s.v. *Desuetudo, Resides, &.. tardi,* restie and slow for lacke of vse. **1571** GOLDING *Calvin on Ps.* lxxiv. 10 Thyne enemies surmyze thee to be restie and ydle bycause thou bestirrest thee not. **1609** B. JONSON *Sil. Wom.* I. i, Hee would grow resty else in his ease. His vertue would rust without action. **1649** MILTON *Eikon.* Wks. 1851 III. 192 Some great household.. where the Maister is too restie or too rich to say his own prayers. **1673** DRYDEN *Marr. à la Mode* IV. iii, O what a difference will she find betwixt a dull resty husband and a quick vigorous lover. **1711** SHAFTESB. *Charac.* (1737) II. III. i. 377 The Sun, and ..the fresh Air of fanning Breezes.. exercise the resty Plants, and scour the unactive Globe.

Comb. **1596** *Edw. III,* III. iii, Presently they are as resty-stiff As 'twere a many over-ridden jades.

†**b.** Of conditions. *Obs.*

1602 SUTTON *Disce Vivere* x. (1847) 171 In continual Ease, in a resty slothfulness, void of all travail. **1620** VENNER *Via Recta* (1650) 72 To those that lead a resty or studious kind of life, it is very hurtfull. **1624** CAPT. SMITH *Virginia* 107 You might shortly behold the idle and restie diseases of a divided multitude.. substantially cured.

†**3.** Unoccupied, idle. *Obs. rare*$^{-1}$.

c **1540** tr. *Pol. Ver. Eng. Hist.* (Camden No. 36) 84 The Romaine soldiers, beinge restie [L. *a laboribus vacui*], beeganne to quarrell emonge them selves.

†**4.** Of land: Fallow, untilled. *Obs. rare.*

1601 HOLLAND *Pliny* XVIII. xix, It is thought sufficient for a teem of oxen to breake up (at the first tilth) in one day of restie or ley ground, one acre. **1649** BLITHE *Eng. Improv. Impr.* (1653) 132 All old Resty Land, that hath not been Tilled of late.

†**'resty,** *a.*[2] *Obs.* [a. OF. *resté* left over, pa. pple. of *rester* REST *v.*[2] See also REST *a.*] Stale, rancid, REASTY.

a **1300** *Gloss. W. de Biblesworth* in Wright *Vocab.* (1857) I. 155 *Chars restez,* resty flees. **1499** *Promp. Parv.* (Pynson), Resty as flesshe, *rancidus.* **1508** *Bk. Keruynge* in *Babees Bk.* (1868) 272 Beware of fumosytees salte, senewe, fatte, resty & rawe. **1547** BOORDE *Introd. Knowl.* ix. (1870) 149 Barelled butter, the whych is resty & salt. **1575** TURBERV. *Faulconrie* 297 Put thereto Larde that is neither restie, nor oversalted. **1657** R. LIGON *Barbadoes* (1673) 30 This butter.. is not then to be endured, it is so restie and loathsome. **1671** H. M. tr. *Erasm. Colloq.* 232 O happy beggars! my wife boyled nothing here this day, besides Coleworts and resty Bacon.

re'style, *v.* [RE- 5 a.] *trans.* To style again; to give a new style to. So **re'styled** *ppl. a.*, **re'styling** *vbl. sb.*

1934 in WEBSTER. **1958** *Listener* 19 June 1006/2 The development of new equipment and the re-styling of the philosophy of design in this new-born industry are a fascinating branch of chemical engineering. **1958** *Times* 22 Oct. 5/5 Details like the front grille and the tail lights have been restyled. **1960** *Farmer & Stockbreeder* 8 Mar. 136/1 Entire pig herd replaced in re-styled buildings. **1965** D. FRANCIS *Odds Against* xx. 249 Her hair had been re-styled. .. It.. curved in a bouncy curl. **1977** *Lancashire Life* Nov. 153/1 The Granadas have been completely restyled, and now look remarkably like the Audi 100. **1978** 'M. YORKE' *Point of Murder* i. 15 She went.. for restyling and emerged bouffant.

resub'ject, *v.* [RE- 5 a.] To subdue again.

c **1840** WORDSW. *Eccl. Son.* III. xviii, For re-subjecting to divine command The stubborn spirit of rebellious man. **1883** *Gentl. Mag.* Nov. 486 The last attempt to resubject Switzerland to the dominion of the Empire had failed.

resub'jection (riː-). [RE- 5 a.] A fresh subjection; a renewed subjugation.

1620 BP. HALL *Hon. Married Clergy* I. iii, This liberall dispensation from his Holy Father of Rome, vpon the conditions of our re-subiection. **1757** *Herald* No. 14 (1758) I. 231 He.., from a re-subjection, had to apprehend encountering the severest indignation. **1899** COL. BALDOCK *Cromwell as Soldier* 361 One of the first matters considered in Parliament after the execution of the King was the re-subjection of Ireland.

re'subjugate (riː-), *v.* [RE- 5 a.] To subjugate anew.

1864 *Daily Tel.* 15 Aug., They were undeceived very soon. Oudh—India—was resubjugated. **1877** BROCKETT *Cross & Crescent* 326 Omar Pasha finally re-subjugated the country for the Sultan.

resubli'mation (riː-). [RE- 5 a.] The renewed action or process of sublimation.

1663 BOYLE *Usef. Exp. Nat. Philos.* II. v. iii. 137 Mercury sublimate may be.. prepar'd into a Medicine inoffensive even to Children, by bare resublimations with fresh Mercury. **1693** W. SALMON *Bate's Dispens.* (1713) 398/2 The same Sublimed Mercury.. needs no Resublimation. **1839** URE *Dict. Arts* 245 Little jets.. which soil it, and render its re-sublimation necessary.

resu'blime (riː-), *v.* [RE- 5 a.] *trans.* To sublime again. Hence **resu'blimed** *ppl. a.*

1651 BIGGS *New Disp.* Eulog. Verses 4 And resublime the spirits of the blood. **1663** BOYLE *Usef. Exp. Nat. Philos.* II. ii. 164 If you re-sublime it oftner, you may.. impair the Colour. **1704** NEWTON *Optics* (1721) 360 When Mercury sublimate is resublimed with fresh Mercury. **1839** URE *Dict. Arts* 56 The arsenious acid.. is not marketable till it be re-sublimed in large iron pots. **1889** *Anthony's Photogr. Bull.* II. 262 Into an ounce vial put eleven grains of re-sublimed iodine and fifteen grains of iodide of potassium.

resub'mission (riː-). [RE- 5 a.] A renewed submission.

1641 BAKER *Chron.* (1653) 140 The Archbishop of Canterbury.. had laboured to bring him and his brother David to a re-submission. **1888** *Voice* (N.Y.) 8 Mar., The prayers of the temperance forces for its resubmission.

So **resub'mit** *v.*, to submit again.

a **1831** A. KNOX *Rem.* (1844) I. 62 There could be no thought of re-submitting to the long dissolved chains.

resub'stantiate, *v.* [RE- 5 a.] †To change (a thing) back *into* the original form.

1584 R. SCOT *Discov. Witchcr.* V. vii. (1886) 83 Lo, what an easie matter it is to resubstantiate an asse into a man.

resuc'ceed, *v.* [RE- 5 a.] To succeed again.

1599 LINCHE *Anc. Fict.* E iv b, Pestilences.. are chased away, and healthie aires and naturall increases spring up and re-succeed.

re'suck, *v.* [RE- 5 a.] To suck back again.

1603 FLORIO *Montaigne* II. xii. (1632) 321 As the Ocean flowing.. Now swift return's, the stones rould back from strand By tide resuck's.

†**resudate,** *v. Obs. rare.* [f. ppl. stem of L. *resūdāre.*] *intr.* To sweat, perspire.

1599 A. M. tr. *Gabelhouer's Bk. Physicke* 97/2 Administre then therof vnto him the quantity of a Walle-nutt, being intermixed with wine, and let him resudate therein.

†**resu'dation.** *Obs.* [ad. L. *resūdātiōn-em,* noun of action f. *resūdāre.* So F. *résudation,* Sp. *resudacion.*] The process of sweating; the fluid produced by this or by exudation of moisture.

1578 BANISTER *Hist. Man* v. 84 Certaine.. haue neuerthelesse had the boldnes to affirme that yᵉ Urine was gathered into the bleddar by resudation. **1635** SWAN *Spec. Mundi* v. §2 (1643) 151 There is a kind of resudation of juice proceeding from them at a certain convenient time of their growth. *Ibid.* 152 When ordinary dew falleth upon any of those leaves which yield such a resudation or sweat.

resuery, obs. form of REVERIE.

re'suffer, *v.* [RE- 5 a.] To suffer again.

1548 GESTE *Priv. Masse* 115 Not.. yt the lord in very dede agayne ryseth in thone and resuffreth in thother.

So **re'sufferance.**

1865 MRS. WHITNEY *Gayworthys* II. 63 A certain quick spasm of keen re-sufferance came over her.

resu'ggest, *v.* [RE- 5 a.] To suggest again.

a **1711** KEN *Hymnotheo* Poet. Wks. 1721 III. 38 Striving in various Forms to re-suggest That Ghostly Pride, which John before suppress'd. **1832** AUSTIN *Jurispr.* (1879) II. xlii. 744 The true nature of the idea of status.. resuggested. **1892** ZANGWILL *Bow Mystery* 41 Poe's solution was re-suggested by 'Constant Reader' as an original idea.

resuing (rɪ'sjuːɪŋ), *vbl. sb. Mining.* [Etym. unknown.] A method of stoping in which the rock wall adjacent to a narrow vein is removed before the vein itself, so that the ore can be extracted in a cleaner condition.

1909 H. C. HOOVER *Princ. Mining* x. 101 (*heading*) Resuing. **1910** W. R. CRANE *Ore Mining Methods* ii. 38 Resuing consists in opening up the stopes not in the vein but in the wall-rock, by whatever method of stoping seems best adapted to the existing conditions. *Ibid.* 43 Resuing is applicable to very narrow veins alone, *i.e.*, under 30 inches in width; its chief advantage being that a cleaner grade of ore can be mined than when both vein and walls are broken together. **1973** L. J. THOMAS *Introd. Mining* vi. 188 In some cases narrow veins may be taken by resuing.. [which] can be classed as either cut and fill, or as vein mining.

re'suit, *v.* [RE- 5 a.] To clothe again.

1614 SYLVESTER *Bethulia's Rescue* II. 203 If the native sap again re-suit The naked Trees with comely Leaves.

result (rɪ'zʌlt), *sb.* [f. the verb. Cf. Sp. and Pg. *resulta.*]

†**1.** The action of springing back again *to* a former position or place. *Obs. rare.*

1626 BACON *Sylva* §137 The sound being produced betweene the String and the Aire.. by the Returne or the Result of the String, which was strained by the Touch to his former place: which Motion of Result is quicke and sharpe.

†**2.** An impulse, inclination, or prompting. *Obs.*$^{-1}$

1663 J. HEATH *Flagellum* (ed. 2) 6 His Scholar growing insolent and uncorrigible from those results and swasions within him, to which all other dictates and Instructions were uselesse, and as a dead letter.

3. a. A decision or resolution; the outcome of the deliberations of a council or assembly. Now *U.S.*

1647 in Rushw. *Hist. Coll.* II. IV. 835 A report was made of the Results of the general meeting. **1667** MILTON *P.L.* VI. 619 If our proposals once again were heard We should compel them to a quick result. **1701** SWIFT *Contests Nobles & Comm.* v. Wks. 1751 IV. 55, I have been often amazed at the rude, passionate, and mistaken Results, which have at certain Times fallen from great Assemblies. **1859** BARTLETT *Dict. Amer.* (ed. 2) 362 *Result,* the decision or determination of a council or deliberative assembly.

b. The effect, consequence, issue, or outcome of some action, process, design, etc.

1651 BAXTER *Inf. Bapt.* 218 Duty only is the Object (or rather immediate result or product) of Precept. **1696** WHISTON *The. Earth* IV. (1722) 365 The primary State here mention'd is but a proper result from the first Formation of the Earth. **1754** YOUNG *Centaur* i. Wks. 1757 IV. 106 For Faith is intirely the result of Reason. **1786** BURKE *Art. agst. W. Hastings* Wks. 1842 II. 233 The whole proceedings of the said resident were the natural result of the treaty of Chunar. **1821** CRAIG *Lect. Drawing,* etc. ii. 113 The result is entirely a matter of calculation, and very much a matter of chance. **1846** GROVE *Corr. Phys. Forces* 77 This is an ordinary chemical action, the result of a double chemical affinity. **1893** *Law Times* XCV. 5/2 Other persons.. discontinued their custom, the result being that his profits diminished.

c. The quantity, formula, etc., obtained by calculation in arithmetic or algebra.

1771 *Encycl. Brit.* I. 112/1 If you substitute 2 for *x,* the result will be 24. **1845** *Penny Cycl.* Suppl. I. 522/1 We might then eliminate between the first and second power, and produce the result in the form $A^2 - B = 0$. **1886** G. CHRYSTAL *Algebra* I. v. 93 We see that the proper result will be obtained by operating throughout as before, using -2 for our multiplier instead of $+2$.

d. Usu. *pl.* The final marks, scores, and placings in (*a*) an examination, (*b*) a sports event.

1916 JOYCE *Portrait of Artist* (1969) v. 210 Did you hear the results of the exams? **1937** PARTRIDGE *Dict. Slang* 695/1 *Results,* news of sports results. **1955** *Radio Times* 22 Apr. 42/2 Sport. Today's results and weekend preview. **1968** *Ibid.* 28 Nov. 8/5, 4.55 Racing Results. **1977** *Belfast Tel.* 28 Feb. 9/3 The following are the results of the November exams held by the Institute of Cost and Management accountants.

e. *pl.* Favourable or desired consequences. Also *sing.,* a good or favourable result against an opponent.

1922 E. O'NEILL *Hairy Ape* vii. 73 Take some of those pamphlets with you to distribute aboard ship. They may bring results. **1927** —— *Marco Millions* III. i. 167, I kept my nose to the grindstone every minute... And I got results. **1931** *Punch* 18 May (*caption*) The charming young gold-digger who expected results of an Aberdonian. **1973** E. DUNPHY *Only a Game?* (1977) ii. 52, I think we will get a result at Preston. **1976** *Observer* 21 Nov. 23/1 We needed a result... Perhaps we should have done better than win 1-0.

†**4.** Humorously used for 'trousers'. *rare*$^{-1}$.

1839 LADY LYTTON *Cheveley* (ed. 2) II. v. 145 His dress.. consisted, all the year round, of a snuff-coloured coat, mud-coloured results, and gaiters of the same.

result (rɪ'zʌlt), *v.* [ad. L. *result-āre* to spring or leap back, f. *re-* RE- + *saltāre* to leap. So F. *résulter,* Sp. and Pg. *resultar,* It. *re-, risultare.*]

1. *intr.* To arise as a consequence, effect, or conclusion *from* some action, process, etc.; to end or conclude *in* a specified manner.

1432–50 tr. *Higden* (Rolls) III. 211 In the monocorde, when the wire extendede on a holowe body is distreynede diametrally by an instrumente.., then diapason resulteth on either parte of the wire. **1570** J. DEE *Math. Pref.* *iiij, Let two pound of Liquor be geuen, hote in the 4 degree: & one pound..hole in the third degree. I would gladly know the Forme resulting, in the Mixture of these two Liquors. **1647** CLARENDON *Hist. Reb.* I. §65 He did not enough consider the Value of the obligation..; from which much of his Misfortune resulted. **1678** CUDWORTH *Intell. Syst.* I. i. §1 From whence by a Series of Causes doth unavoidably result whatsoever is now done in it. **1732** BERKELEY *Alciphr.* iii. §13 The pure delight which results from order and decorum. **1773** *Observ. St. Poor* 53 That evil effects will result from evil causes,..must be readily acquiesced in. **1823** BROOKE *Crystallogr.* 115 The planes resulting from classes *b*, and *c*, would produce a great variety of dodecahedral solids. **1860** TYNDALL *Glac.* II. xvii. 315 Crevasses..result from the motion of the glacier. **1885** *Law Rep. 29 Chanc. Div.* 797 There has been a grave breach of duty resulting in heavy loss.

†**b.** To turn out, become. *Obs.*$^{-1}$

1626 BACON *Sylva* §481 Rew doth prosper much..if it be set by a Figge-tree;..the one Drawing Iuyce to result sweet, the other bitter.

†**c.** *refl.* To resolve *into* something. *Obs. rare*$^{-1}$.

1610 tr. *Marcelline's Triumphs Jas. I* 32 It is the number of Justice, because that first of all it resulteth itself into numbers of paire-like-parity.

d. *U.S.* To decide or resolve *that*, etc. *rare*$^{-1}$.

a **1859** in Bartlett *Dict. Amer.* (ed. 2) s.v., The Council of Nice resulted, in opposition to the views of Arius, that the Son was peculiarly of the Father [etc.].

†**2. a.** To disagree or diverge in opinion. *Obs.*

1572 J. JONES *Bathes of Bathes Ayde* Ep. Ded. 3 The second sheweth the diversitie of opinions, etc., how and wherein the Physicions and Philosophers resulte.

†**b.** To yield ground; to give way. *Obs. rare*$^{-1}$.

1577–87 HOLINSHED *Chron.* II. 55 That the kings battell, ...finding sturdie resistance, began..to result or give backe.

†**c.** To recoil; to rebound or spring back. *Obs.*

1598 BARRET *Theor. Warres* II. i. 16 Which he must doe with such..warie meanes, that they result not against him. **1616** BULLOKAR *Eng. Expos.*, *Result*, to rebound, to leape backe. **1725** POPE *Odyss.* XI. 737 The huge round stone resulting with a bound Thunders impetuous down. **1757** DARWIN in *Phil. Trans.* L. 247 As by the percussion of their angles they must result further from each other. **1784** COWPER *Task* v. 802 Praise..from Earth resulting, as it ought To Earth's acknowledg'd sov'reign.

†**d.** To return *upon* one by reflection. *Obs.*$^{-1}$

1610 B. JONSON *Alchemist* II. vi. 18 Whose *radij*..Shall by a vertuall influence breed affections, That may result upon the partie.

†**e.** To spring up or rise again. *Obs. rare*$^{-1}$.

1609 J. DAVIES *Holy Roode* I, Hee, like the glorious, rare Arabian Bird, Will soone result from his incinderment.

†**3.** To issue or spring forth. *Obs. rare*$^{-1}$.

1597 A. M. tr. *Guillemeau's Fr. Chirurg.* 28b/2 The bloode could not resulte out of the apertione.

4. a. *Law.* To revert *to* a person.

1768 BLACKSTONE *Comm.* III. 426 Upon the abolition of the court of wards, the care..resulted to the king in his court of chancery. **1818** CRUISE *Digest* (ed. 2) I. 438 It was resolved that the use resulted to the feoffor till he made an appointment. **1875** DIGBY *Real Prop.* vi. (1876) 293 The use was said to result or come back to the donor.

†**b.** To appertain or fall *to* a person. *Obs. rare.*

1780 BENTHAM *Princ. Legisl.* xviii. §49 To the parent, then, in quality of guardian, results a set of duties. **1793** JEFFERSON *Writ.* (1859) IV. 68 It resulted to the executive to interfere in it.

Hence **re'sulting** *vbl. sb.*

1599 J. DAVIES *Immort. Soul* II. i. (1714) 27 Of the Forms which Fancy doth inroll; A quick Resulting, and a Consequence.

resultance (rɪ'zʌltəns). Now *rare*. Also 5 -auns, -ans. [Prob. ad. med.L. **resultantia* (cf. Sp. and Pg. *resultancia*), f. *resultāre*: see RESULT *v.* and -ANCE.]

†**1.** Origin, beginning. *Obs. rare*$^{-1}$.

c **1440** CAPGRAVE *Life St. Kath.* III. 704 For of man & godd hys persone..hath take resultauns.

†**2. a.** The result of deliberation; a decision.

1610 DONNE *Pseudo-martyr* Pref. Cj, It is easie to obserue, what the Collection and resultanse vpon this conclusion will be.

†**b.** The result of combination or condensation; the sum or gist *of* something. *Obs.*

1610 DONNE *Pseudo-martyr* 245 He speakes out of the strength and resultance of many lawes and Canons there alleadged. *a* **1639** WOTTON *Educ.* in *Reliq.* (1672) 82 If in these external marks, or signatures there be any certainty, it must be taken from that which I have formerly called the Total Resultance. **1640** WALTON *Life Donne* (1670) 62 He left the resultance of 1400 Authors, most of them abridged and analysed with his own hand.

3. †**a.** Something which issues, proceeds, or emanates from another thing. *Obs.*

1615 JACKSON *Orig. Unbelief* xiii. 99 Sensible obiects..grant a resultance of such a form or stampe of them in the eye. *a* **1631** DONNE *Poems* (1650) 212 He would..thence inferre that soules were but Resultances from her. **1680** WALLER *Div. Medit.* (1839) 23 That placency which we take to be in them, is but a resultance of our own Minds.

†**b.** A reflection (of light). Also *fig. Obs.*

1629 T. ADAMS *Happiness Ch.* Wks. 574 Let a looking-glasse be set before him, it will reflect it to his eyes, hee shall read it by the resultance. **1638** *Randolph's Muses Looking-Gl.* Prefatory Verses, I confesse that power which workes in mee Is but a weake resultance tooke from thee. **1652** BENLOWES *Theoph.* Author's Design, I'm but a faint Resultance from Thy Light Which, at Sol's Rise and Set enchears my Sight.

c. A result, effect, or outcome. Now *rare.*

1635 HOWELL *Lett.* (1892) II. 655 According to yᵉ resultance of his particular deeds. *a* **1648** LD. HERBERT *Hen. VIII* (1683) 342 Yet this good Resultance followed, that it made him take the more care to be Just. **1664** POWER *Exp. Philos.* III. 193 The old Dogmatists..that onely gaz'd at the visible effects and last Resultances of things.

1881 *Blackw. Mag.* May 564/2 In all these resultances..the sword invariably maintained..the great striking characteristic of its form of proceeding.

†**4.** The fact of issuing or resulting (*from* something); esp. *by resultance*, derivatively. *Obs.*

1635 JACKSON *Humiliation Son of God* iv. 39 Accidents had their beginnings as appurtenances to their subjects, by resultance onely. *a* **1660** HAMMOND *Serm.* Wks. 1684 IV. 607 We may not think so vulgarly of Scripture, as to dream that any title of it came by resultance or casually into the world. **1680** *Counterplots* 7 Whatever is properly and essentially good must..be so by its resultance from this Holy Being.

†**5.** Resilience, rise. *Obs. rare*$^{-1}$.

a **1633** AUSTIN *Medit.* (1635) 85 Most of the Seers..of this world goe (first) by the ground-line to seeke a false Ioy on Earth, whence it is not possible there should be any Resultance to make an Angle up-ward.

†**re'sultancy.** *Obs.* [See prec. and -ANCY.]

1. = RESULTANCE 3 a.

1615 T. ADAMS *Two Sons* 68 Our children, as the sweete resultancies and living pictures of ourselves. **1628** EARLE *Microcosm.* (Arb.) 71 A Herald is the spawne, or indeed but the resultancie of Nobility. **1675** BAXTER *Cath. Theol.* II. VIII. 186 As a resultancy from those Gifts. **1701** NORRIS *Ideal World* I. ii. 59 The very..nature of relation..is not a thing intended by itself, but a meer resultancy.

b. = RESULTANCE 3 b.

1628 T. SPENCER *Logick* 10 A resultancy or reflection, proceeding from a being obiected to our vnderstanding. *a* **1641** BP. MONTAGU *Acts & Mon.* (1642) 119 In the firmament of heaven be many Starres;..of sundry resultancies and apparitions; of the first, second, third magnitude, as they use to speak.

2. = RESULTANCE 4.

1630 PRYNNE *Anti-Armin.* 115 If Gods fore-sight and euerlasting Decrees haue their resultancie from the wills of men. **1640** BP. REYNOLDS *Passions* xxxii. 399 From Nature generated..by secret and ineffable Resultancy and Emanation. **1683** J. CORBET *Free Actions* II. xii. 20 Which Relation..follows the said *fundamentum* by a bare Resultancy, without any further Causation.

3. = RESULTANCE 2 b.

1637 HEYLIN *Brief Answ.* 26 By way of Corollarie, or resultancie out of all the premisses. **1651** *Raleigh's Ghost* 73 From all which, this one true resultancy or conclusion may infallibly be gathered. **1682** *Foxes & Firebrands* II. 86 The resultancy of this Story is home and pat.

resultant (rɪ'zʌltənt), *sb.* [See next.]

†**1.** *Arith.* The total or sum. *Obs. rare.*

c **1430** *Art Nombryng* 4 The resultant 10. To whom it shalle be addede 7. The nombre to be addede 3.

2. *Mech.* That force which is the equivalent of two or more forces acting from different directions at one point. Also generally, the composite or final effect of any two or more physical forces.

1815 O. GREGORY *Mechanics* (ed. 3) I. II. 31 The resultant is situated in a plane perpendicular to the axis. **1836** WHEWELL *Mechanics* ii. (ed. 5) 24 If two forces act in opposite directions, the resultant will be the difference of the two, and in the direction of the greater. **1842** BLACK *Homœopathy* iv. 53 All action in the living body is the resultant of two co-efficients. **1856** *Orr's Circle Sci., Mech. Phil.* 173 To determine the resultant of all the pressures of a fluid. **1879** PRESCOTT *Sp. Telephone* 18 Its motion will be the resultant of all the sound waves.

b. *transf.* of other than physical forces.

1848 H. ROGERS *Ess.* (1860) III. 319 The conflict between the two opposite forces will probably compel our statesmen to move in the path of their resultant. **1856** FROUDE *Hist. Eng.* (1858) II. 192 The resultant, not of the victory of either of the extreme parties, but of the joint action of their opposing forces. **1874** STUBBS *Const. Hist.* I. i. 1 The resultant of three forces, whose reciprocal influences are constant, subtle, and intricate.

c. The product or outcome *of* something.

1847 HELPS *Friends in C.* (1851) I. 9 See of how large a portion of the character truth is the resultant. **1871** TYLOR *Prim. Cult.* I. 12 Collective social action is the mere resultant of many individual actions. **1890** HUMPHRY *Old Age* 30 Most of these habits..are the resultants of health, as well as the promoters of it.

3. *Math.* (See quot. 1856.)

1856 A. CAYLEY in *Phil. Trans.* CXLVI. 636 The function of the coefficients, which, equalled to zero, expresses the result of the elimination.., is said to be the Resultant of the system of quantics. The resultant is an invariant of the system of quantics. **1860** H. J. S. SMITH in *Rep. Brit. Assoc.* (1861) 162 If R be the Resultant of $\phi_1(x)$ and $\phi_2(x)$, [etc.]. **1867** BRANDE & COX *Dict. Sci.* III. 266/1. **1881** [see ELIMINANT B].

resultant (rɪ'zʌltənt), *a.* [ad. L. *resultant-em*, pres. pple. of *resultāre*: see RESULT *v.* and -ANT. So F. *résultant*, It., Sp., and Pg. *resultante.*]

†**1.** Issuing or shining by reflection. *Obs.*

1615 T. ADAMS *Spiritual Navigators* 45 Seeing the resultant light of the starres shining in the water about him. **1661** R. BURNEY *K. Chas. presented* 4 §2 'Tis a beam resultant from Gods Majestie, and reflects upon the people for their good.

2. That results, resulting; consequent.

1639 LD. DIGBY *Lett. conc. Relig.* (1651) 112 Accepting alike the Faith resultant from the dark mists of the Ignorant, and from the clearest intelligence of the Learned. **1672** BOYLE *Orig. Gems* Postscr., By reason of the figure of the resultant corpuscles. **1855** BAILEY *Mystic* 24 All soul-sin seems a missing of the mark Resultant from imperfect force or aim. **1856** *Orr's Circle Sci., Mech. Phil.* 173 If this simple resultant pressure act upward [etc.]. **1882** FARRAR *Early Chr.* II. 275 The overthrow of the tenth part of the city, and the resultant terror and repentance.

b. *resultant axis, point*: (see quots.).

1831 BREWSTER *Optics* xxiii. 204 The lines or axes along which there is no double refraction or polarisation..have been called optical axes..or resultant axes. **1876** PREECE & SIVEWRIGHT *Telegraphy* 203 That point where the whole force which it is intended to counteract may be supposed to be collected..is known in mechanics as the resultant point.

c. *resultant note* or *tone*: (see second quot.).

1876 tr. *Blaserna's Sound* v. 82 Those notes..to which the name of resultant notes or sometimes difference notes is usually given. **1876** BERNSTEIN *Five Senses* 280 When two tones are sounded together, tones of an entirely new nature are produced, which have been called resultant tones. **1898** ELLISTON *Organs* (ed. 3) 52 The Quint stop, combined with the 16 ft., gives a resultant undertone of 32 ft. pitch.

Hence **re'sultantly** *adv.*

1865 BUSHNELL *Vicar. Sacrif.* III. iii. 234 The retributive causes go their way and do their work, not arrested in their action, but only qualified resultantly.

†**resultat(e.** *Obs. rare.* [ad. F. *resultat* or It. *risultato.*] = RESULT *sb.*

1620–1 BACON in Spedding *Life & Lett.* VII. 172 Although some particular members of Parliament may have their private ends, yet one man sets another upright; so that the resultate of their counsels is for the most part..sincere.

†**resul'tation.** *Obs.* [ad. L. *resultātiōn-em*, noun of action from *resultāre*: see RESULT *v.* and -ATION.] = RESULTANCE 3 a, 3 b.

1603 HOLLAND *Plutarch's Mor.* 1175 The resultation of a light from the water upon some wall. **1624** BP. MOUNTAGU *Immed. Addr.* 123 That which they know..by way of Resultation from his alsufficiencie. **1649** ROBERTS *Clavis Bibl.* 350 A Psalm is..the noise of pleasantnesse, the resultation of gladsomnesse.

resultative (rɪ'zʌltətɪv), *a. Gram.* [f. RESULT *sb.* + -ATIVE.] Expressing result. Also *absol.* as *sb.*

1926 H. POUTSMA *Gram. Late Mod. Eng.* II. II. lviii. 545 The attributive past participle mostly has a momentaneous or resultative aspect. **1936** *Jrnl. Eng. & Germanic Philol.* XXXV. 368 The so-called Resultative Perfect requires a somewhat detailed examination. **1957** R. W. ZANDVOORT *Handbk. Eng. Gram.* I. iv. 61 English shares with other languages the use of the *resultative perfect*, which denotes a past action connected, through its result, with the present moment. I've bought a new car. **1963** F. T. VISSER *Hist. Syntax Eng. Lang.* I. iv. 582 Examples of Old English verbs construed with a resultative predicative adjunct are not numerous. **1965** *Language* XLI. 109 In Indic, the perfect, whose function was originally stative,..developed..to a resultative. **1970** J. W. R. LINDEMANN *Old Eng. Preverbal Ge-* I. 4 *Ge-* may convert an intransitive verb into a resultative verb that is transitive. **1977** *Canad. Jrnl. Linguistics* Spring 51 Resultatives..represent a second category where *hə* occurs instead of a resonant plus shwa in reduplicative prefixes.

†**resultatively,** *adv. Obs. rare*$^{-1}$. [f. RESULT *v.* + -ATIVE + -LY².] By way of conclusion.

1657 W. MORICE *Coena quasi Κοινή* IV. 184 These men..are resultatively and interpretatively as..earnest to exclude men from the Sacrament.

re'sultful, *a.* [f. RESULT *sb.* + -FUL.] Rich or abounding in results; fruitful.

1876 FAIRBAIRN in *Contemp. Rev.* June 132 His own work had been of the most resultful sort. **1892** *Month* Feb. 234 Controversies..more likely to be endless than resultful.

Hence **re'sultfully** *adv.*

1881 FAIRBAIRN *Stud. Life Christ* viii. 148 The relation..was most deeply and resultfully experienced by the men.

resulting (rɪ'zʌltɪŋ), *ppl. a.* [f. RESULT *v.* + -ING².] Arising, produced, or obtained as a result; resultant, consequent.

1666 BOYLE *Orig. Formes & Qual.* 194 The resulting Qualities and Attributes of the small particles of Matter. **1684–5** —— *Min. Waters* 35 By putting a much greater, or a much lesser, quantity of Galls, into..the Mineral Water, the resulting colour may be more or less intense. **1743** EMERSON *Fluxions* 145 Put the Equation of the Curve into Fluxions, and the resulting Equation into Fluxions again. **1766** BLACKSTONE *Comm.* II. 335 The use..returns back to him who raised it,..and is stiled a resulting use. **1797** *Encycl. Brit.* (ed. 3) II. 317/2 The second, because the divisor is 9, repeats the resulting figure after the dividend is exhausted. **1827** JARMAN *Powell's Devises* II. 41 There would either be a resulting trust, or it would belong to the person who takes the estate. **1885** C. G. W. LOCK *Workshop Rec.* Ser. IV. 361/1 A general 'flatness' in the resulting photographs is noticeable.

Hence **re'sultingly** *adv.*

1863 C. M. SMITH *Dead Lock* 46 Her education..was conducted under their superintendence, and it resultingly differed somewhat from the usual routine.

†**re'sultive,** *a. Obs. rare*$^{-1}$. [f. RESULT *v.* + -IVE.] Resultant.

1655 FULLER *Ch. Hist.* II. Ded., There is such a Sympathy betwixt several Sciences..that (as in a Regular Fortification one Piece strengtheneth another) a resultive Firmness ariseth from their Complication.

re'sultless, *a.* [f. RESULT *sb.* + -LESS.] Devoid of, or without, result; ineffectual.
1846 *Blackw. Mag.* LX. 336 Disgust at the resultless strife has not yet replaced the interest and excitement it creates. **1880** MUIRHEAD *Gaius* II. §30 The cession is held in that case to be resultless.

Hence **re'sultlessly** *adv.*; **re'sultlessness**.
1858 TRENCH *Synonyms* xlix. (1876) 174 The aimlessness, or, if we may use the word, the resultlessness, of that to which this epithet is given. **1900** *Academy* 18 Aug. 137/2 Bulwer Lytton is clever without depth, and resultlessly interesting.

†**re'sultment.** *Obs. rare*$^{-1}$. [f. RESULT *v.* + -MENT.] = RESULT *sb.*
1683 SALMON *Doron Med.* I. xx. 131 The Quota's are the resultment, which is always of the same with the greater Product.

resuma'bility. [f. next + -ITY.] Capacity for, or possibility of, being resumed.
1835 L. HUNT *Lond. Jrnl.* 4 Feb. 36 The magician has a fatal lock of hair on his head which if once cut off puts an end to the resumability of the head.

resumable (rɪ'z(j)uːməb(ə)l), *a.* [f. RESUME *v.* + -ABLE.] Capable of being resumed.
1644 BP. MAXWELL *Prerog. Chr. Kings* viii. 93 This same Soveraignty and Majesty is resumable. *a* **1676** HALE (J.), This was but an indulgence, and therefore resumable by the victor, unless there intervened any capitulation to the contrary. **1818** HALLAM *Mid. Ages* (1872) I. 160, I am not convinced that beneficiary grants were ever considered as resumable at pleasure. **1883** *Law Times Rep.* L. 103/2 The land..should not be resumable..because it had been built upon, or was used as garden.

resume (rɪ'z(j)uːm), *v.* Also 7 *Sc.* resoom. [ad. OF. *resumer* (F. *résumer*, It. *re-*, *risumere*, Sp., Pg. *resumir*), or L. *resūmĕre*, f. *re-* RE- + *sūmĕre* to take.]

I. *trans.* **1.** To assume, put on, or take to oneself anew (something previously lost, given up, or discarded):

a. courage, hope, or other feeling.
1412-20 LYDG. *Chron. Troy* III. xxiv, Grekes reioysynge And in all haste their hertes resumynge Began them selfe for to recomforte.
1602 MARSTON *Ant. & Mel.* III. Wks. 1856 I. 32 Come soule, resume the valour of thy birth. **1667** MILTON *P.L.* I. 278 If once they hear that voyce,..they will soon resume New courage and revive. **1671** —— *P.R.* II. 58 Thus they out of their plaints new hope resume. **1737** WHISTON *Josephus, Hist.* II. xix. §7 When the robbers perceived this unexpected retreat..they resumed their courage. **1765** H. WALPOLE *Otranto* iv. (1798) 65 For mercy's sweetest self,..resume your soul, command your reason. **1812** BYRON *Ch. Har.* II. lxxiii, Who that gallant spirit shall resume, Leap from Eurota's banks, and call thee from the tomb? **1872** BLACK *Adv. Phaeton* xiii. 180 Bell rapidly resumed her ordinary good spirits.

b. strength, power, influence, etc.
c **1425** *Found. St. Bartholomew's* (E.E.T.S.) 59 And a litill, her myghtys that she hadde lost she resumyd, and forthermore, anoone aftir, ful helth optenyd.
1597 HOOKER *Eccl. Pol.* v. lxxvii. §3 They which have once received this power may not think..to take it, reiect, and resume it as often as they themselues list. **1654** tr. *Martini's Conq. China* 113 Only to amuse them with a Peace, whilst they could resume their strength and force. **1747** *Col. Rec. Pennsylv.* V. 84 They resume the same Power with their President as if the Governor was here. **1771** *Junius Lett.* xliv. (1788) 255 They have advised the King to resume a power of dispensing with the laws by royal proclamation. **1791** MRS. RADCLIFFE *Rom. Forest* vii, Could I see your natural good sense resume its influence over passion. **1821** SHELLEY *Remembrance* 10 The owlet night resumes her reign. **1874** GREEN *Short Hist.* iii. §6. 147 Theology in its scholastic form ..resumed its supremacy in the schools. **1883** *Manch. Guard.* 3 Nov. 7/6 Religious animosity..has resumed its hold on both sides.

c. some appearance, form, or condition.
1605 SHAKS. *Lear* I. iv. 331 Ile resume the shape which thou dost thinke I haue cast off for euer. **1697** DRYDEN *Virg. Georg.* IV. 640 Having shifted ev'ry Form to scape, Convinc'd of Conquest, he resum'd his Shape. **1742** COLLINS *Ecl.* i. 14 The radiant Morn resum'd her orient pride. **1781** COWPER *Conversat.* 401 We come, As from a seven years transportation, home, And there resume an unembarrass'd brow. **1837** DICKENS *Pickw.* xxvii, Mr. Pickwick's countenance resumed its customary benign expression. **1850** TENNYSON *In Mem.* xc, Could the dead, whose dying eyes Were closed with wail, resume their life.

d. To take again, re-occupy (a place or seat).
1633 P. FLETCHER *Purple Isl.* II. iv, A new-born Phœnix flies, and widow'd place resumes. **1667** MILTON *P.L.* XII. 456 He shall ascend,..Then enter into glory, and resume His Seat at Gods right hand. **1700** DRYDEN *Pal. & Arc.* II. 349 Reason resum'd her place, and passion fled. **1867** AGASSIZ *Journ. Brazil* ii. (1871) 63, I resumed my seat, trying to look as if it were my habit to mount horses on the tops of high mountains and slide down to the bottom.

2. a. To take up or begin again, to recommence (some interrupted practice or occupation). †Also const. *to.*
c **1440** *Alph. Tales* 252 And þai tuke þaim to cowncell att þai wald resume hospitalite, & giff almos agayn as þai war wunte. **1624** S. H. *Preserv. Health* 46 In the morning when you rise againe, resume to your selues your former dayes thoughts and cares. **1638** JUNIUS *Paint. Ancients* 208 Nothing is easily resumed after a great discontinuance. **1748** THOMSON *Cast. Indol.* I. xlviii, My Muse! resume the task that yet doth thee abide. **1784** COWPER *Task* VI. 535 With looks of some complacence he resum'd His road. **1820** IRVING *Sketch Bk.* I. 90 Rip now resumed his old walks and habits. **1853** C. BRONTE *Villette* x, I resumed some work I had dropped. **1883** *Manch. Guard.* 17 Oct. 5/5 That Parliament should resume its labours upon the Criminal Code.

b. *esp.* To go on again with (a discourse, discussion, remark, etc.). Also with direct speech: to go on to say.
1600 J. PORY tr. *Leo's Africa* II. 70 Hauing made sufficient digression, let us resume the matter subject where we left. **1647** CLARENDON *Hist. Reb.* I. §27 The Prince..prevailed.. that the debate was again resumed upon the journey. **1667** MILTON *P.L.* XII. 5 Heer the Archangel paus'd,..Then with transition sweet new Speech resumes. **1732** BERKELEY *Alciphr.* I. §3 Finding that nobody made answer, he resumed the thread of his discourse. **1765** H. WALPOLE *Castle of Otranto* i. 16 Yes, I sent for you on a matter of great moment, resumed he. **1789** J. MOORE *Zeluco* I. xxii. 132 'Nay, my good friend,' resumed the Physician, 'it is a matter of indifference to me, what you do or do not believe.' **1795** *Abridgm. Deb. Congress* (1857) I. 525/1 The Senate resumed the consideration of the Treaty. **1845** PATTISON *Ess.* (1889) I. 26 As if merely resuming the broken thread of the previous day's argument. **1850** F. E. SMEDLEY *Frank Fairlegh* xliii. 376 'I have fancied that illness was beginning to sour your temper,' I replied. 'Illness of mind, not body,' he resumed. **1894** HALL CAINE *Manxman* 67 Ross had resumed his conversation with Kate. **1906** *Smart Set* May 9/2 'I guess, friend,' resumed the man with the pipe, 'she's been standin' out here coolin' off for some time, ain't she?' **1922** JOYCE *Ulysses* 620 Mind you, I'm not saying that it's all a pure invention, he resumed. **1976** R. HILL *Another Death in Venice* I. iii. 63 'I'll say this, though,' resumed Wilf, 'I'm worried.'

c. To reassemble or bring together again for the transaction of business.
1472-3 *Rolls of Parlt.* VI. 42/1 If..it shall be thought.. necessary and behovefull, to resume, assemble, and have apparaunce of this his seid Parlement. **1800** *Asiatic Ann. Reg.* II. 49/2 The House being resumed, the report was ordered to be received to-morrow.

3. a. To take back to oneself (something previously given or granted).
1450 *Rolls of Parlt.* V. 183/2 [To] take, resume, seise and reteine in your handes..all Honoures..the which ye hafe graunted. **1480** *Waterford Arch.* in *10th Rep. Hist. MSS. Comm.* V. 314 Them that occupied the same befor they were resumed. **1542-3** *Act 34 & 35 Hen. VIII*, c. 18 It shall be laufull to our said soueraigne lord..to seise or resume any of the saide franchises. **1641** PRYNNE *Antipathie* 18 The custody of Rochester Castle and other Forts, which the King for securing his State, had resumed into his owne hands. *a* **1672** WILKINS *Nat. Relig.* (1675) 246 They..will not murmur against Him, when He is pleased to resume any thing from them. **1713** SWIFT *Cadenus & Vanessa* 260 Gods of whatsoe'er Degree Resume not, what themselves have giv'n. **1754** SHERLOCK *Disc.* (1759) I. ii. 76 Why should God resume this Authority out of the Hands of His Son? **1821** SCOTT *Pirate* Advt., Touching the hand of the corpse, she formally resumed the troth-plight which she had bestowed. **1875** MAINE *Hist. Inst.* i. 7 It is expressly stated that in the case of an association of villeins the lord did not resume their land.

†**b.** To abrogate, withdraw. *Obs. rare*$^{-1}$.
1549 *Act 3 & 4 Edw. VI*, c. 20 §3 The said Act..shall from henceforth be resumed, repealed, adnulled..and utterly made void for ever.

4. a. To take back (a person) to, or into some relation with, oneself.
1494 FABYAN *Chron.* VII. ccxliii. 285 Seinge they myght not enduce the Kynge to noone conformytie or agrement, to resume his lawfull wyfe, and to refuse that other. **1601** B. JONSON *Poetaster* v. i, We..Resume into the late state of our loue Worthy Cornelius Gallus. **1655** VAUGHAN *Silex Scint.* II. 138 Resume thy spirit from this world of thrall. **1821** SHELLEY *Hellas* 102 If Heaven should resume thee, To Heaven shall her spirit ascend. **1850** MRS. JAMESON *Leg. Monast. Ord.* (1863) 287 She..holds her veil extended as if to resume her divine Child.

b. To take or pick up (a thing) again; to return to the use of.
1596 SPENSER *F.Q.* v. xi. 56 My former shield I may resume againe. **1716** POPE *Iliad* v. 405 Then, mounting on his car, [he] resum'd the rein. **1822** [MARY A. KELTY] *Osmond* I. 19 She continued, resuming the picture. **1873** BLACK *Pr. Thule* viii, So he was content to resume his pipe and listen.

5. a. To repeat (a sentence or word). *rare.*
1535 JOYE *Apol. Tindale* (Arb.) 37 He resumeth the same sentence yet agen the thirde tyme. **1592** tr. *Junius on Rev.* xx. 6 A return unto the intended history by resuming the words which are in the end of the 4 verse. **1824** L. MURRAY *Eng. Gram.* (ed. 5) I. 302 In many of these instances, the nominative must be repeated; and..in most of the others, it may be resumed with propriety and advantage.

b. To recapitulate or summarize (facts, etc.).
1676 TOWERSON *Decalogue* 73 The unreasonableness whereof will appear, if we resume those things which we have said to the object of love. **1685** BURNET tr. *More's Utopia* 21 The Counsellor had resolved to resume all that I had said. **1715** *Wodrow's Corr.* (1843) II. 38 The sub-committee brought in their overtures as to Mr. Simson's affair. I cannot resume them. **1769** ROBERTSON *Chas. V*, x. III. 231 After resuming, at great length, all the facts and arguments upon which they founded their claim. **1869** *Pall Mall G.* 6 Sept. 12 Concerning 'Kathrina', let us finally, and in brief, resume, that in its purport it is unsatisfactory and unconvincing. **1878** DOWDEN *Stud. Lit.* 346 A philosophy which should resume all his views upon nature, man, and society.

II. *absol.* **6.** To reassume possession.
? **1565** in Pettus *Fodinæ Reg.* (1670) 59 The Queen to have power to resume, paying to Humfrey and Shutz..such recompence as shall be adjudged by 6 Citizens. **1611** SHAKS. *Cymb.* III. i. 15 That opportunity Which then they had to take from's, to resume We haue againe. **1738** WESLEY *Hymns, 'The Lord! how fearful is his Name!'* vi, 'Tis sov'reign Love that lends our Joys, And Love resumes again.

7. To give a résumé or summary.
1770 BP. FORBES *Jrnl.* (1886) 309 Preached from Acts 8. 14. &c., Mr. Allan Cameron resuming in Galic.

8. a. To begin to speak again; to continue one's discourse.
1802 MAR. EDGEWORTH *Moral T.* (1816) I. 228 When he could again be heard.., he resumed, as follows. **1837** DICKENS *Pickw.* xxvii, Mr. Weller smoked for some minutes in silence, and then resumed.

b. To recommence work or business.
1817 *Parl. Debates* 1351 The House then resumed, and the Report was ordered to be received to-morrow. **1849** MACAULAY *Hist. Eng.* x. II. 625 The discussion was soon interrupted by the reappearance of Hampden with another message. The House resumed and was informed that [etc.]. **1903** *Daily Chron.* 7 Oct. 6/3 The London County Council resumed after the holidays.

c. To continue; to begin again.
1815 *Zeluca* II. 238 She picked..up [the letters], and resumed at the only words of her own she had seen. **1866** CRUMP *Banking* ix. 200 If a bank of issue should discontinue issuing,..it should not be lawful to resume.

Hence **re'sumed** *ppl. a.*; **re'suming** *vbl. sb.* and *ppl. a.*
c **1470** G. ASHBY *Active Policy* 726 To be wele aduised in your grauntyng Any fee or office..That it securly stande withoute resumyng. **1672** R. MONTAGUE in *Buccleuch MSS.* (Hist. MSS. Comm.) I. 518 One quarter's allowance is stopped by the last resuming of the assignments. **1681** DRYDEN *Abs. & Achit.* 767 Then this resuming Cov'nant was declar'd When Kings were made, or is for ever bar'd. **1800** *Asiatic Ann. Reg.* II. 12/1 The major part of the present excess has arisen from the arrears of police taxes, and the rent of resumed Tannadaree lands. **1890** DILKE *Probl. Greater Brit.* II. ii. I. 270 The lessee was..given a preferential right of obtaining an annual occupation-license for the resumed area.

résumé (‖ rezyme, 'rɛzjuːmeɪ), *sb.* Also **resume**. [Fr., pa. pple. of *résumer* to RESUME.] **a.** A summary, epitome.
1804 *Edin. Rev.* IV. 98 After a short *resumé* of his observations on coffee-houses and prisons, Mr. Holcroft leaves Paris. **1861** PATTISON *Ess.* (1889) I. 31 Some of the papers are mere *résumés* of English books. **1885** *Law Rep. 29 Chanc. Div.* 457 The report contained a *résumé* of the evidence.

b. Chiefly *N. Amer.* = *curriculum vitæ* s.v. CURRICULUM. Also *fig.*
1961 WEBSTER, *Résumé*..*specif.*: a brief account of one's education and professional experience. **1968** *Globe & Mail* (Toronto) 17 Feb. 51 If an interview is not convenient at this time, forward your resume, in confidence to Mr. Grossman. **1971** GOLZEN & PLUMBLEY *Changing your Job after 35* viii. 86 The Résumé..will vary considerably with the type and level of job and can be the bare bones of a c.v. or a long, narrative account of your main achievements written up with a special bias. **1973** J. RYDER *Trevayne* (1974) lii. 384 There was an opening. What could look better on a résumé than the White House? **1976** *Glasgow Herald* 26 Nov. 25/1 Please submit detailed resume including personal data, educational background, and work experience. **1979** *Tucson Mag.* Feb. 88/2 She has added several fine credits to her resume since then, including a Washington D.C. debut this year.

Hence **résumé** *v.*, to epitomize. *rare.*
1888 *Amer. Jrnl. Psychol.* May 535 A disjointedness..that makes it difficult to read, and still more so to résumé.

re'sumer. *rare.* [f. RESUME *v.* + -ER[1].] One who resumes.
a **1656** USSHER *Power Princes* I. (1683) 18 The founder of all rule, authority and power at the beginning, and the resumer thereof into his own hands again at the end of the World.

re'summon (riː-), *v.* [RE- 5a. Cf. OF. *resoumondre*, *resemondre* (Godef.).]

†**1.** *trans.* To issue (a writ) again. *Obs. rare*$^{-1}$.
1594 WEST *2nd Pt. Symbol.* §61 If the king die after the writ of Couenant be returned,..and before the fine be ingrossed,..the writ of couenant shalbe resomoned and the fine ingrossed.

†**2.** To recall (a thing) to mind. *Obs. rare.*
1605 BACON *Adv. Learn.* II. xiii. §6 To inuent is to discouer that we know not, and not to recouer or resummon that which wee alreadie knowe.

3. To summon (a person) anew; to convene (an assembly) again.
1643 PRYNNE *Sov. Power Parl.* I. (ed. 2) 31 But the King re-summoning them at *quindena Pasche*, granted all things absolutely according to their desire. **1696** LUTTRELL *Brief Rel.* (1857) IV. 66 They were this morning resummoned to attend their excellencies. **1742** FIELDING *J. Andrews* I. vii, She re-summoned Mrs. Slipslop into her presence. **1830** LYTTON *Paul Clifford* xix, The pawnbroker was re-summoned. **1885** L. O. PIKE *Yrbks. 12 & 13 Edw. III* (Rolls) Introd. 47 The original assise-men were re-summoned to give a verdict on the points of the assise.

re'summons (riː-). *Law.* [a. AF. *resomons* (Godef.).] A second or renewed summons.
1495 *Act 11 Hen. VII*, c. 24 §1 In the same atteynte there shalbe awarded ageynst..the party..som[mons] and resom[mons] and distres infynyte. **1547** *Act 1 Edw. VI*, c. 7 Preamble, The Demandants..were compelled..to prosecute and sue Resummons..to revive..their said Actions. **1598** MANWOOD *Lawes Forest* xxv. (1615) 257 The plees may be reuiued againe by the Kings writ of resummons. **1641** *Termes de la Ley* 243 b, Resummons is a second summons of a man to answer to an action where the first summons is defeated by the demise of the King, or such other cause. **1671** F. PHILLIPS *Reg. Necess.* 401 Whereupon by advice of the Judges a resummons was granted. [**1865** NICHOLS *Britton* II. 92 Neither does a resummons ever lie after an essoin. *Ibid.* 338 There is summons, after-summons, and resummons.]

resumption (rɪˈzʌm(p)ʃən). [a. F. *résumption* or ad. L. *resumptiōn-em*, n. of action f. *resūmĕre* to RESUME. So Sp. *resuncion*, It. *risunzione*.]

1. *Law*. The action, on the part of the Crown or other authority, of reassuming possession of lands, rights, etc., which have been bestowed on others; a case or instance of this.

1449 *Rolls of Parlt.* V. 167/1 As sone as that office to your hand..by deth, cession, amocion, resumpcion,..or elles in eny othir maner it be, next then to come. **1489** *Ibid.* VI. 429/1 By force of an Acte of Parliament called a Resumption. **1503** *Act 19 Hen. VII*, c. 10 The said Act of Resumption, or any Articles therein contained. ?**1565** in Pettus *Fodinæ Reg.* (1670) 57 If after Resumption the Queen shall decline the working, then William Humfrey..to have the preference of Farming it [etc.]. **1614** SELDEN *Titles Hon.* 248 By the Statut of Resumption vnder Hen. VIII. most of the Royalties of our English Counties Palatin were diminisht, and taken into the Croun. **1663** PEPYS *Diary* 29 Mar., The late discourse in the House of Commons, concerning resumption of Crowne lands. **1723** *Pres. St. Russia* I. 3 They entertained Hopes of being restored to their former Estates which they lost by the late Resumption during the Swedish Administration. **1792** A. YOUNG *Trav. France* 46 This great work stands still at present through a fear of resumptions. **1831** MACKINTOSH *Sp. Ho. Comm.* 4 July, Wks. 1846 III. 552 To represent our resumption of a right of suffrage as a precedent for their seizure of lands and possessions. **1873** BURTON *Hist. Scot.* VI. 78 They knew that the benefit of the resumption was not to be for them.

b. In general use, the action of taking back or recovering something.

1702 *Eng. Theophrastus* 195 Resumptions are as ordinary with this lady [fortune] as with a House of Commons. **1836** EMERSON *Nature, Prospects* Wks. (Bohn) II. 171 This is such a resumption of power, as if a banished king should buy his territories inch by inch. **1852** GROTE *Greece* II. lxxix. X. 356 Now that the power of the latter was broken, the Eleians aimed at resumption of their lost supremacy. **1885** G. MACDONALD *Diary Old Soul* 26 Oct., So, Lord, if Thou tak'st from me all the rest, Thyself with each resumption drawing nigher.

2. The action of resuming, taking up, or commencing again.

1589 PUTTENHAM *Eng. Poesie* III. xix. (Arb.) 229 The resumption of a former proposition vttered in generalitie to explane the same better by a particular diuision. **1655** STANLEY *Hist. Philos.* (1701) 258/1 Reminiscence is not a Resumption or Assumption of Memory, but differs specifically from both these. **1659** PEARSON *Creed* (1839) 432 This word, 'I believe', is taken here only by way of resumption or repetition. **1821** BYRON *Two Foscari* I. i, The hour's past—fix'd yesterday For the resumption of his trial. **1863** H. COX *Instit.* I. x. 239 The first instance of resumption, after long disuse, of impeachments of ministers on account of advice to the Crown. **1884** *Weekly Notes* 9 Feb. 28/2 Both funds must be treated as belonging to the wife for her separate use upon the resumption of cohabitation.

b. *Banking*. A return to specie payments. Also *attrib*.

1866 CRUMP *Banking* ix. 182 We will take the price [of bank stock] every five years down to the final resumption in 1821. **1878** *N. Amer. Rev.* CXXVI. 156 Despite the stoppage of the resumption policy preparing by Secretary McCullough. **1880** E. KIRKE *Life Garfield* 30 Resumption came at last,..when the Government, for the first time in seventeen years, made its payments in coin.

c. (See quot.)

1856 J. WILLIAMS *Gram. Edeyrn* §1784 Resumption [in Welsh prosody] is the practice of beginning every verse with the same letter, which is sustained throughout.

3. a. Recapitulation, résumé. *rare*.

1727–38 CHAMBERS *Cycl.* s.v., Resumption, in the schools, a summary repetition, or running over, of an argument, or of the substance thereof, in order to refute it. **1836–7** SIR W. HAMILTON *Metaph.* xliii. (1859) II. 444 A theory, in fact, which is the resumption and complement of them all.

b. (See quot.) *rare*$^{-0}$.

1727–38 CHAMBERS *Cycl.* s.v., Resumption is..used by logicians for the reduction of some figurative, or quaint proposition, to a more intelligible and significant one.

resumptive (rɪˈzʌm(p)tɪv), *a.* and *sb.* [orig. ad. L. *resumptīv-us* restorative. In later use a new formation. Cf. Sp. *resuntivo*, Pg. *resumptivo*.]

†**1.** *Med.* **a.** *adj.* Restorative. *Obs. rare*.

1398 TREVISA *Barth. De P.R.* VII. lxix. (Bodl. MS.), Whan kinde is comforted he vseþ certeyn medicyns resumptiue and restauratiue. **1657** TOMLINSON *Renou's Dispens.* 122 Differences of unguents..from their effects as resumptive.

†**b.** *sb.* A restorative medicine. *Obs.*

c **1550** LLOYD *Treas. Health* R v, If it be of ouer muche labor or of ouer muche emptines he must be nouryshed wyth resumptiues and confortatyues. **1736** BAILEY (folio), A *Resumptive*, (in Pharmacy) an unguent for recruiting and restoring languishing constitutions: *Resumptives*, (in Physick) medicines serving to restore decay'd nature.

2. That repeats, or summarizes.

1854 *Fraser's Mag.* XLIX. 372 Whether he ought to be slower, more explanatory, more systematic, more resumptive. **1884** CHEYNE *Isaiah* I. 246 The statement is resumptive.

3. *Gram.* **a.** In Jespersen's terminology: (see quot. 1917). **b.** Indicating resumption of a topic, etc.; having previous reference. So as *sb.* (see quot. 1954).

1917 O. JESPERSEN in *Historisk-Filologiske Meddelelser* I. v. 69 A second class comprises what may be termed *resumptive negation*, the characteristic of which is that after a negative sentence has been completed, something is added in a negative form with the obvious result that the negative effect is heightened. **1954** D. BOLINGER in *Boletín de Filología Universidad de Chile* VIII. 48 Sometimes, for special effects, a presupposed element, even a lengthy one, is repeated though specifically known from the immediate context... We may call such a verbatim or near-verbatim presupposed element a 'resumptive'. *Ibid.* 49 An element which is explicitly resumptive comes after prosodic stress. **1957** *Publ. Amer. Dial. Soc.* XXVIII. 145 A post-accentual resumptive is only a repetition, while a pre-accentual resumptive may be more. **1959** J. C. CATFORD in Quirk & Smith *Teaching of English* (1964) vii. 149, I know of no practical English grammar for foreign learners which describes the use of *oh*, *ah* or the introductory or resumptive *well*. **1970** M. DAHOOD *Anchor Bible: Psalms III* 337 M[assoretic] T[ext] *ʾᵃsappᵉrennāh* can be explained as employing the resumptive pronominal suffix. **1975** *Language* LI. 59, I regard Spanish resumptive intonation and beginning position as variant formal means of expressing syntagmatic complexity.

Hence **reˈsumptively** *adv.*

1716 M. DAVIES *Athen. Brit.* II. 170 We also resumptively add. **1903** *Westm. Gaz.* 5 Feb. 1/3 'You see my point?' he remarks resumptively.

resun(e, obs. forms of REASON.

reˈsup, *v.* [RE- 5 a.] To sup again.

a **1700** KEN *Hymnotheo* Poet. Wks. 1721 III. 119 As Dogs, the filthy Vomits they cast up, In a short Space..resup.

resupinate (rɪˈs(j)uːpɪneɪt), *a.* [ad. L. *resupīnāt-um*, pa. pple. of *resupīnāre* to bend back. Cf. F. *résupiné*, Sp. and Pg. *resupinado*.]

1. Chiefly *Bot.* Turned or twisted upwards.

1776 J. LEE *Introd. Bot.* Explan. Terms 382 Resupinate, when the lower Disk of the Leaf looks upwards. **1815** E. J. BURROW *Conchol.* 16 *Resupinata*, resupinate; turned upwards. **1830** LINDLEY *Nat. Syst. Bot.* 240 The æstivation of the corolla..is an important consideration in determining whether a flower is resupinate or not. **1884** *19th Cent.* Feb. 243 The leaves are long.., having sharp-pointed blades, barbed sides, and resupinate bark.

2. (See quot.)

1836 RAFINESQUE *Amer. Nations* I. ii. 66 The Resupinate or Reflexed Group [of American languages]: where the roots or nouns substantive are reversed, following the adjectives or epithetes, which are prefixed.

So **reˈsupinated** *ppl. a.*

1661 LOVELL *Hist. Anim. & Min.* Isagoge, Their mouth is downwards, that the fishes might escape, when they are resupinated. **1752** HILL *Hist. Anim.* 584 The Bos, with very large, crooked and resupinated horns, the Buffaloe.

resupination (rɪs(j)uːpɪˈneɪʃən). [See prec. and -ATION. So F. *résupination*, Sp. *-acion*.]

†**1. a.** The effect of height upon the proportions of a standing figure. *Obs. rare*.

1624 WOTTON *Archit.* in *Reliq.* (1651) 292 Our Vitruvius calleth this affection in the Eye, a resupination of the Figure: For which word (being in truth his own, for ought I know) we are almost as much beholding to him, as for the Observation it self. **1638** JUNIUS *Paint. Ancients* 233 Phidias ..did consider that the whole shape of his image should change according to the height of the appointed place, and therefore made her lips wide open..and all the rest accordingly, by a certaine kinde of resupination.

†**b.** The action of putting into an inverted position. *Obs. rare*$^{-1}$.

1661 LOVELL *Hist. Anim. & Min.* Isagoge, Some [birds] drink..with intermission, and resupination of the head.

†**c.** The fact of lying on, or the action of turning upon, the back. *Obs.*

1658 PHILLIPS, *Resupination*, a lying along on the back with the face upward. **1661** LOVELL *Hist. Anim. & Min.* Isagoge, Amongst Fishes,..Some have their mouth upwards,..and cannot take the prey, without resupination.

2. *Bot.* Inversion of parts.

1760 J. LEE *Introd. Bot.* III. xiv. (1765) 203 A Resupination; which is, when the upper Lip of the Corolla looks towards the Ground, and the under Lip towards Heaven. **1830** LINDLEY *Nat. Syst. Bot.* 111 Seeds ascending, seldom inverted by resupination. **1882** VINES tr. *Sachs' Bot.* 604 The long inferior ovary of most Orchids undergoes a torsion (resupination) at the time of the opening of the flower.

resupine (riːs(j)uːˈpaɪn), *a.* [ad. L. *resupīn-us*: see RE- and SUPINE *a.* So obs. F. *resupin*, Pg. *resupino*, It. *re-*, *risupino*.]

†**1.** Listless, apathetic. *Obs. rare*.

1628–9 DIGBY *Voy. Medit.* (Camden) 13 *note*, A most resupine patience in their sufferance. **1643** —— *Observ. Relig. Med.* (1644) 63 In what a tortured condition they must bee..for their most resupine and senselesse madnesse.

2. Lying on the back; inclined backwards.

1669 BOYLE *Cont. New Exp.* II. (1682) 88 A fourth Fly being thrust in,..at last suffering some convulsion, she lay unmoved and resupine. **1753** N. TORRIANO *Midwifery* 35 Where the Womb is..resupine. **1791** COWPER *Odyssey* VIII. 458 One, resupine, Upcast it high toward the dusky clouds. **1837** CARLYLE *Fr. Rev.* VII. i. (1871) III. 245 Sansculottism ..was flung resupine the next instant. **1837** —— *Misc. Ess.*, *Diamond Necklace*, The very Concierge resupine.

resuˈpply (riː-), *v.* [RE- 5 a.] To supply again or anew; to provide with a fresh supply. Also *absol.*, to take on or acquire a fresh supply.

1636 G. SANDYS *Paraphr. Ps.* civ, Againe created by thy quick'ning breath, To resupply the Massacres of Death. **1805** SOUTHEY *Madoc* II. xv, Fast they fell, And fast were resupplied, man after man Succeeding to the death. **1862** LYTTON *Str. Story* II. 357, I resupplied their nutriment from the crystal vessel. **1880** BURTON *Reign Q. Anne* II. ix. 80 What had been expended in the taking of Gibraltar not having been re-supplied. **1977** 'J. MCVEAN' *Bloodspoor* xiii. 152 We'll have to resupply. We're mobile and there must be wells. *Ibid.* xviii. 218 They were down to the last few pints but..they'd be able to resupply from one of the tributary streams.

So **resupply** *sb.*

1875 WHITNEY *Life Lang.* vi. 98 The growth of organic beings consists in removal as well as in resupply. **1880** *Bible Soc. Rec.* (1883) May 67 A faithful and thorough resupply of the United States..with the Scriptures.

resuˈppress (riː-), *v.* [RE- 5 a.] *trans.* To suppress again.

1654 EARL MONM. tr. *Bentivoglio's Wars Flanders* 6 Mary was not more resolute in restoring the Catholick faith in England, then Elizabeth was in resuppressing it.

reˈsurface, *v.* [RE- 5 a, c.] **1.** *trans.* To provide (a road, etc.) with a fresh surface.

1886 [implied in RESURFACING *vbl. sb.* below]. **1894** *Westm. Gaz.* 23 Apr. 8/3 (Advt.), Old blocks bought up, sold, or resurfaced. **1901** *U.S. Dept. Agric. Yearbk. 1900* 352 When the road was resurfaced with limestone..it became excellent. **1929** *Daily Express* 11 Jan. 2/2 If these minor roads were..strengthened and resurfaced in accordance with modern road practice [etc.]. **1960** *Times* 4 July (Advt. Suppl.) 1/3 Safety razors had not resurfaced the New Man. **1973** 'C. AIRD' *His Burial Too* iii. 31 The Divisional Surveyor decided to resurface the road.

2. *intr.* To come to the surface again. Also *fig.*

1953 P. C. BERG *Dict. New Words in Eng.* 137/1 *Re-surface* ..*v.i.*, of a submarine: to come to the surface. **1962** *Times* 3 Apr. 14/6, I would re-surface before the water-splash fell back into the tank. **1968** J. SANGSTER *Foreign Exchange* ii. 57 It was midday when I resurfaced, too late for breakfast. **1971** *Flying* Apr. 73/2, I would resurface to find the airplane starting to turn back. **1973** L. SNELLING *Heresy* II. 62 We lose sight of him... Killed by the Gestapo? In an air-raid? In any event he never resurfaced. **1978** J. MCDOWELL in Hookway & Pettit *Action & Interpretation* 151 If it were to be so incorporated, all the difficulties of the relation between behaviour and action categories would presumably resurface.

So **reˈsurfacing** *vbl. sb.*

1886 *Cyclist* 4 Aug. 1076/1 The re-surfacing of the Crystal Palace path. **1967** *Antiquaries Jrnl.* XLVII. 271 This structure had been..covered with a plaster surface, perhaps later than the surface of the atrium described above, but present over a sufficiently large area to indicate a general resurfacing. **1978** *Lancashire Life* Mar. 54/3 George's Lane and Belmont Road were selected for resurfacing.

‖**resurgam** (rɛˈsɜːgæm). [L.] 'I shall rise again', expressing Christian faith in resurrection at the Last Day. Usu. *transf.* and *fig.*

1662 J. TRAPP *Annotations Old & New Testament* I. 142 Howbeit he had *hope in his death*, and might write *Resurgam* on his grave. **1847** THACKERAY *Van. Fair* (1848) xiv. 126 Arms and Hatchments, Resurgam.—Here is an opportunity for moralizing! **1853** GEO. ELIOT *Let.* 3 Jan. (1954) II. 79 *Now* nothing seems pleasant to me but—*Resurgam*. *c* **1859** E. DICKINSON *Poems* (1955) I. 56, I slew a worm the other day—A 'Savant' passing by Murmured 'Resurgam'—'Centipede'! 'Oh Lord—how frail are we'! **1929** *Oxf. Poetry* 39 Arise..resurgam..for another day.

resurge (rɪˈsɜːdʒ), *v.*[1] [ad. L. *resurg-ĕre*, f. *re-* RE- + *surgĕre* to rise. So Sp. and Pg. *resurgir*, It. *risurgere*, *-sorgere*.] *intr.* To rise again. Hence **reˈsurged** *ppl. adj.*, **reˈsurging** *ppl. adj.* and *vbl. sb.*

1575 R. B. *Appius & Virg.* in Hazl. *Dodsley* IV. 127 For follow my counsel, so may you me please, That of careful resurging your heart shall have ease. **1606** J. CARPENTER *Solomon's Solace* xxxi. 130 By a godly repentance striue to resurge vnto that from whence he was fallen. **1633** EARL MANCH. *Al Mondo* (1636) 92 Divine and quickening vertue shall..cause them to resurge from graue to life eternall. **1657** TOMLINSON *Renou's Disp.* 524 It is good for such as resurge from long diseases. **1807** J. BARLOW *Columb.* III. 255 When my God, resurging from the night, Shall gild his chambers with the morning light. **1862** THACKERAY *Round. Papers, On Letts's Diary*, Hark at the dead jokes resurging! **1892** *Sat. Rev.* 2 July 23/2 The New Zealand document disappeared and Mr. Huxley's stout tome resurged. **1912** R. BROOKE *Let.* 23 Nov. (1968) 408, I shall be in Cambridge.., dispatching my resurged Dissertation. **1962** G. T. WARWICK in C. Cullingford *Brit. Caving* (ed. 2) v. 184 The clear water from Legalough, which..may resurge at Hanging Rocks. **1965** *New Statesman* 30 Apr. 690/3 That both bomber fleets resurged so mightily in 1944 was due.. to the rapid conversion of the Mustang into a long-range escort. **1976** K. ROYCE *Bustillo* vii. 87 He fought off the resurging need for a drink. **1980** *Times* 1 Nov. 15/3 Mr Manley..leads a rump opposition smaller than that from which Mr Seaga has resurged.

re-ˈsurge (riː-), *v.*[2] [RE- 5 a.] *intr.* To surge back again. Hence **re-ˈsurging** *vbl. sb.*

1887 C. W. HUTSON *Beg. Civiliz.* xx. 206 [Kelts] swept over Etruria.., then re-surged and poured through the Illyrian, Macedonian and Thracian regions. **1899** *Q. Rev.* Jan. 193 It is impossible to keep in mind the surging and resurging of the tide of war.

So **re-ˈsurge** *sb.*

1895 J. SMITH *Perm. Message Exod.* ix. 122 The surge and resurge of the soul are laid bare.

resurgence (rɪˈsɜːdʒəns). [See RESURGENT and -ENCE.]

1. The act of rising again. Also *fig.*

a **1834** COLERIDGE in *Lit. Rem.* (1836) II. 153 That happy, humble, ducking under, yet constant resurgence against, the check of her superiors! **1863** GEO. ELIOT *Romola* xxxviii, The events of the night all came back to him:..the crowding resurgence of facts and names. **1886** SYMONDS *Renaiss. It.*, *Cath. React.* (1898) I. i. 40 The resurgence of popular literature and the creation of popular theatrical types deserve to be..noticed.

2. The fissure through which a stream re-emerges at the end of an underground part of its course; the re-emergence of such a stream. [This sense results from the adoption of F. *résurgence* (cf. A. Vandel 1920, in *Bull. de la Soc. zool. de France* XLV. 46).]

1954 W. D. THORNBURY *Princ. Geomorphol.* xiii. 327 The terms rise and resurgence have been applied to the reappearance of surface waters which have been diverted to underground routes. **1963** D. W. & E. E. HUMPHRIES tr. *Termier's Erosion & Sedimentation* xiv. 303 Sometimes the surface water plunges down into the underground system by way of a sink hole... The river, however, retains its individuality and may return to the surface through a resurgence or spring. **1965** *Geogr. Jrnl.* CXXXI. 37 This subterranean stream maintains a constant flow during all weather conditions, and is joined by a small seepage resurgence and streamlet within a large bedding plane cave ..through which it flows to the main resurgence. **1971** J. N. JENNINGS *Karst* v. 74 A useful distinction can be made between exsurgences fed entirely by seepage waters from the karst and resurgences supplied by the sinking of surface streams.

So **re'surgency.** *rare*$^{-1}$.

a **1834** COLERIDGE *Aids Refl.* App. C (1858) I. 403 The perpetual reconciliation, and as perpetual resurgency of the primary contradiction.

resurgent (rɪ'sɜːdʒənt), *sb.* and *a.* [ad. L. *resurgent-em*, pres. pple. of *resurgĕre* to RESURGE.]

A. *sb.* **1.** One who has risen again.

1768–74 TUCKER *Lt. Nat.* (1834) II. 411 We, who are alive, shall be caught up in the clouds together with the resurgents. **1808** SYD. SMITH *Wks.* (1850) 114/1 Scarcely a day elapsed in which the degraded resurgent did not appear before the European. **1875** KINGLAKE *Crimea* V. vi. xvi. 156 The resurgents on their part, whilst sheering off by the flanks, took care to give no offence.

2. = RESURGENCE 2. Also *attrib.*

1965 B. E. FREEMAN tr. *Vandel's Biospeleol.* i. 12 The outlets of large underground rivers are termed resurgents. **1972** HERAK & STRINGFIELD *Karst* xiii. 435 Resurgent caves ..are associated with the uprising of water around the flanks of the Mendips.

B. *adj.* **1.** That rises, or tends to rise, again.

1808 SYD. SMITH *Wks.* (1850) 119/2 To extinguish, if possible, that resurgent principle which has so often disturbed the serious business of the country. **1854** *Tait's Mag.* XXI. 490 Resurgent Poland, he says, means resurgent Hungary, and even resurgent Italy. **1878** DOWDEN *Stud. Lit.* 241 The strife is not ended, the pain may still be resurgent.

2. *Geol.* Applied to steam and other gases which after being absorbed by volcanic magma from groundwater and native rock are subsequently released into the atmosphere.

1908 R. A. DALY in *Amer. Jrnl. Sci.* CLXXVI. 48 These fluids were deposited and buried in the strata. They have been resurrected in their activity. They have 'risen again', both literally and figuratively; they may be called 'resurgent' emanations... All 'resurgent' emanations are of secondary origin. **1917** *Econ. Geol.* XII. 491 'Resurgent' was adapted by the writer..to signify the magmatic emanations of secondary origin, that is, those absorbed from country rock. .. Von Wolff..extends it to describe also certain pyroclastic deposits... Most authorities on the genesis of ore deposits appear to be opposed to the concept. **1932** F. F. GROUT *Petrogr. & Petrol.* iii. 212 Magmas may acquire gases by assimilating or dissolving..some wall or roof rock that contained gas or water. This is 'resurgent water'.

re'surging, *ppl. a.* [f. RESURGE *v.* + -ING².] That resurges; rising again.

1594 ? GREENE *Selimus* Prol. 12 You shall behold him.. like a sea or high resurging floud. *a* **1843** SOUTHEY *Comm.-pl. Bk.* (1851) IV. 170 This resurging part of the island is called O Breasul, or O Brazil. **1874** *Contemp. Rev.* XXIII. 350 The unerring instinct of resurging Paganism.

resur'prise, *sb.* [RE- 5 a.] A fresh or new surprise (of a place or person).

a **1626** BACON *Consid. touching War w. Spain* (1629) 7 The Processe of this Action drew on a Resurprise of the Castell by the Thebans, a Recouery of the Towne [etc.]. *a* **1711** KEN *Psyche* Poet. Wks. 1721 IV. 203 O that I had a Cherub's num'rous Eyes To guard me from a Re-surprise.

resur'prise, *v.* [RE- 5 a.] To surprise again.

a **1700** KEN *Hymnotheo* Poet. Wks. 1721 III. 274 Sometimes he Seven, sometimes a Legion sends, Who, when cast out, the Soul who careless lies With seven-fold Force and Malice re-surprise.

'resurrect, *sb.* *rare*$^{-1}$. [ad. L. *resurrect-us*: cf. next.] One who has risen from the dead.

1892 G. HAKE *Mem. 80 Yrs.* lxv. 278 Wolsey, he rose; the Bonapartes rose;..Lazarus rose; but no man, priest, soldier ..or resurrect, ever rose in death, as did St. Peter.

resurrect (rɛzə'rɛkt), *v.* [A back-formation from RESURRECTION.]

1. a. *trans.* To raise (a person) from the dead or from the grave; to restore to life or to view again.

1772 *Misc.* in *Ann. Reg.* 174/1 As fast as we knock them on the head, this cursed Tunestrick..resurrects them again in a squirt. *a* **1864** HAWTHORNE *Dr. Grimshawe* (1883) 8 Dead men's almost intangible atoms, resurrected from the adjoining graveyard. **1898** BENHAM *Fourth Napoleon* 162 When they are dead, they are dead, and all the counting in the world won't resurrect them.

b. *fig.*, with reference to persons.

1856 BENTON *Abridgm. Deb. Congress* (1858) VI. 712 *note*, I resurrect the whole! put them in scene again on the living stage. **1876** MRS. OLIPHANT *Makers Flor.* 29 This could not be the Forese Donati resurrected and torn above ground by ..darkling moles.

c. *fig.*, with reference to things.

1852 B. YOUNG *Jrnl. of Discourses* (1854) I. 33/1 We shall not want to look upon our past actions; we shall say..I do not want that to be resurrected, but let it die in the grave. **1863** *Morn. Star* 26 Dec., Slavery is already dead, and cannot be resurrected. **1892** *Black & White* 2 July 10/1 He ..resurrects recollections of the good old times. **1904** *Forum* July 132 The..offer made by General Reyes in behalf of the Bogota Government to resurrect and ratify the dead canal treaty. **1942** Z. N. HURSTON in A. Dundes *Mother Wit* (1973) 31/1 They resurrected a joke or two and worried it like a bone.

2. *intr.* To rise again from the dead. Also *fig.*

1823 BENTHAM *Not Paul but Jesus* 279 Jesus resurrects; therefore all men will do the same. **1890** *Harper's Mag.* Nov. 870/1 It is..the one day upon which the cemeteries resurrect out of the things they are, and become the things they should be. **1969** G. M. BROWN *Orkney Tapestry* 52 The ribs of crag and tree Resurrecting with birds.

Hence **resu'rrecting** *ppl. adj.*

1887 SERVICE *Life Dr. Duguid* 270 Sweet love, like the resurrecting dawn, awoke the birds.

resurrected, *ppl. a.*

1. That has been raised from the dead. Also *fig.*

1852 H. B. KIMBALL in B. Young *Jrnl. of Discourses* (1854) I. 355/2 You never will obtain your resurrected bodies, until you bring your spirits into subjection. **1853** KANE *Grinnell Exped.* xxxiv. (1856) 299 The long line of resurrected coast was duplicated in the clouds. **1877** A. B. EDWARDS *Up Nile* xii. 326 The resurrected Osiris was wont to be worshipped according to the most sacred mysteries of the Egyptian ritual.

2. *Geomorphol.* Of a land form: exposed by erosion after having been covered by deposition.

1925 D. W. JOHNSON *New England-Acadian Shoreline* ii. 27 Resurrected peneplane shorelines appear to be fairly common along the coast of Acadia. **1954** W. D. THORNBURY *Princ. Geomorphol.* ii. 25 Most resurrected features are of local extent and constitute a small portion of the present-day topography. **1970** R. J. SMALL *Study of Landforms* iii. 106 One of the most important types of escarpment associated with faulting is the 'resurrected' or 'exhumed' fault-scarp or fault-line scarp.

resu'rrecting, *vbl. sb.* [f. RESURRECT *v.* + -ING¹.] The action of the verb RESURRECT.

1906 P. LOWELL *Mars & its Canals* xii. 130 To call the lunar *maria* seas may..be..only a resurrecting in epitaph what was the truth in its day.

resurrection (rɛzə'rɛkʃən), *sb.* Also 4–5 **resur(r)ectioun**, 4–6 **-eccio(u)n**, 4–5 **-exio(u)n**, etc. [a. OF. *resurreccïun*, *-ection* (F. *résurrection*, = Sp. *resurreccion*, It. *re-*, *risurressione*, *-ezione*), or ad. late L. *resurrectiōn-em*, n. of action f. *resurgĕre* to RESURGE.]

I. 1. a. The rising again of Christ after His death and burial.

c **1320** *Cast. Love* 1201 For nouȝt worþ weore his passion, Neore his resurexion. *c* **1380** WYCLIF *Sel. Wks.* II. 96 And þis was don in Cristis deþ and his resurreccioun. *c* **1400** MAUNDEV. viii. (1839) 91 There appered first oure Lord to his Disciples, aftre his Resurrexioun. *c* **1425** WYNTOUN *Cron.* v. ii. 330 Crist tholit þar his passion, And made his resurreccion. **1526** *Pilgr. Perf.* (W. de W. 1531) 13 Forty dayes after his resurreccyon that blessed lorde ascended. **1563** *Homilies* II. xiv. (1869) 429, I come to declare that great ..article of our Christian religion and faith, the resurrection of our Lord Jesus. **1643** CARYL *Expos. Job* 103 Which words are applied by Paul..to the resurrection of Christ. **1681–6** J. SCOTT *Chr. Life* (1747) III. 599 How is it conceivable that so many Persons as pretended to see him after his Resurrection, should for 40 Days together imagine that they saw him? **1794** PALEY *Evid.* (1825) II. 321 The history of the resurrection of Christ is a part of the evidence of Christianity. **1892** J. TAIT *Mind in Matter* (ed. 3) 297 The men that condemned Christ were the first to be made aware of His resurrection.

b. The church-festival by which this event is commemorated.

In early examples = Easter; with quot. 1838 cf. *resurrectio* in Du Cange.

c **1290** *St. Brendan* 368 in *S. Eng. Leg.* I. 229 An ester eue heore procuratour bad heom heore schip take And heore resurrection opon þe fisches rugge make. **1377** LANGL. *P. Pl.* B. XVIII. 425 Tyl þe daye dawed þis damaiseles daunced, That men rongen to þe resurexioun.

1838 SIR H. NICOLAS *Chronol. Hist.* 169/1 Resurrection of our Lord, March 27.

†**c.** A dramatic or material representation of this event. *Obs.*

1303 R. BRUNNE *Handl. Synne* 4642 He may yn þe cherche, þurgh þys resun, Pley þe resurreccyun. **1466** in *Archaeologia* (1887) L. 34 The resurreccion of our lorde with the avyse in hys bosum to put þe sacrament þer-in. *Ibid.*, Item, anothir grete branche be-for the Resurreccion. **1521** *Churchw. Acct. St. Giles, Reading* (ed. Nash) 14 For nayles cord & sope for the resurrexcion.

2. The rising again of mankind at the Last Day.

Frequently termed ***the general resurrection***. For ***first resurrection*** see Revelation xx. 4–6.

a **1300** *Cursor M.* 19292 A naciun [that] Wald trau na resurreccíun Suld be o man on domes-dai. **1382** WYCLIF *Mark* xii. 23 Thanne in the resureccioun, whanne thei schulen rise aȝen, whos wyf of these schal sche be? **1413** *Pilgr. Sowle* (Caxton) v. xiv. (1859) 81 So shalt thou ioyefully abide the general resurection. **1432–50** tr. *Higden* (Rolls) III. 111 Moyses and Aaron schalle brynge furthe that arke of the testamente in the firste resurreccion. **1548** CRANMER *Short Instruct.* (1829) 126 We must beleue the resurrection of the fleshe. **1569** JEWEL *Exp. 1 Thess.* Wks. 1848 VII. 93 They shall come forth of their graves to the resurrection of condemnation. **1651** HOBBES *Leviath.* III. xxxiv. 214 In the resurrection men shall be Permanent, and not Incorporeall. **1746** HERVEY *Medit.* (1818) 76 Resurrection will be no privilege to them; but immortality itself their everlasting curse. **1788** GIBBON *Decl. & F.* l. V. 216 The doctrine of the resurrection was first entertained by the Egyptians. **1858** SEARS *Athan.* III. ix. 329 The resurrection is the emergence of the spiritual body out of mortal decay into immortal existence. **1884** *Catholic Dict.* (1897) 790/1 All the Creeds confess the resurrection of the body.

3. The action or fact of rising again from sleep, decay, disuse, etc.; revival; restoration to previous status or vogue.

c **1385** CHAUCER *L.G.W.* Prol. 110 For to ben at the resureccion Of this flour whan yt shulde vnclose.

1649 *Nicholas Papers* (Camden) 146 Never to admit yᵉ resurreccion of the olde..Parliament by vertue of the Bill for Continuaunce. **1657** TRAPP *Comm. Job* xix. 27 See we not a yearly Resurrection of grasse, herbs, grain, flowers, fruits every Spring tide? **1769** BURKE *Corr.* (1844) I. 202 Though..Lord Chatham has had a wonderful resurrection to health, his resurrection to credit and consequence..must be owing to your lordship. **1796** BURNEY *Mem. Metastasio* I. 35 The Italians, proud of the resurrection of their drama, began to challenge all the rest of Europe. **1849–50** ALISON *Hist. Europe* XIV. xcv. §84. 175 The unanimous resurrection of all the nations of Europe against the French domination. **1879** FROUDE *Cæsar* xxi. 365 If the life of Cæsar alone stood between his country and the resurrection of the constitution.

4. a. A resurrected thing. *rare.*

1771 SMOLLETT *Humph. Cl.* 10 July, His horse was..a resurrection of dry bones. **1871** R. ELLIS tr. *Catullus* xvii. 3 The rotten Legs too crazily steadied on planks of old resurrections.

b. A disinterred corpse. (Cf. 6.) *rare*$^{-1}$.

1775 S. J. PRATT *Liberal Opin.* cxxxiii. (1783) IV. 203 The doctor is attending a lady of your parish, who is troubled with a complication,..and she is expected to be as fine a resurrection as ever the doctor handled.

II. *attrib.* and *Comb.*

5. a. In various attrib. uses, as ***resurrection appearance, day,*** †***gild, morning, piece, place, sermon***, etc.

1463 *Bury Wills* (Camden) 22, I wylle the owener of my place pay eche yeer viij *d.* to the resurreccion gilde that viij *d.* taperis may be light at the dirige and messe the same tyme. **1654** EVELYN *Diary* 29 Mar., Mr. Owen preached in my Library..a Resurrection Sermon, and after it we all received the Holy Communion. **1728** MORGAN *Algiers* II. iv. 266 Resurrection-Day falling out soon after, the Christians were all at High-Mass. **1742** *De Foe's Tour Gt. Brit.* II. 214 A cloathed Resurrection Piece, painted by Sir James Thornhill. **1864** PUSEY *Lect. Daniel* (1876) 501 The great Resurrection-morning. **1875** W. P. MACKAY *Grace & Truth* 161 In resurrection-life we are sent back to it, to be here as specimens of saved sinners. **1892** A. DE VERE *Leg. St. Patrick, St. P. & Impostor*, Our resurrection place is here. **1931** W. TEMPLE *Thoughts on Some Probl. of Day* i. 19 The love revealed in Jesus Christ in His use of divine power ..in His Death on the Cross, in His Resurrection-Appearances only to those whose love He had already won. **1977** G. W. H. LAMPE *God as Spirit* vi. 151 Resurrection appearances and empty tomb cannot in themselves furnish first-hand evidence for God's vindication of Jesus.

b. ***resurrection body***, the form in which men will appear at the general resurrection.

1681–6 J. SCOTT *Chr. Life* (1747) III. 512 What a Change will it make in our Resurrection-Body, which being incomparably more..subtile than this, will be far more pliable to the Motions of the Soul? **1684** T. BURNET *The. Earth* II. 216 We have great reason to hope, that the soul will have a greater dominion over the resurrection-body, than she hath over this. **1704** NORRIS *Ideal World* II. iii. 163 Who knows what may be the privilege of a Resurrection-body joined to a beatified and glorified soul? **1858** SEARS *Athan.* I. xviii. 158 The seed-spark of our resurrection-body will not appear.

c. ***resurrection plant***, (*a*) a Californian plant, *Selaginella lepidophylla*, the dried fronds of which unfold again when moistened; (*b*) the Rose of Jericho, an Eastern plant having similar properties; (*c*) one of several other plants which stay quiescent during drought and revive when moistened. Also called ***resurrection flower***.

(*a*) **1868** A. GRAY *Field, Forest, & Garden Bot.* 374 'Resurrection-Plant'..is a nest-like ball when dry, but when moist it unfolds. **1870** MASTERS *Henfrey's Bot.* 413 One or two of the species [of Selaginellæ] roll up their fronds when dry, and unfold them again when placed in water, owing to the rapid absorption of the fluid, whence they have been called Resurrection plants. **1885** GOODALE *Physiol. Bot.* (1892) 400 Good examples..are afforded by the so-called Resurrection plant of California. **1893** G. D. LESLIE *Lett. Marco* xviii. 119 'A resurrection plant,'..some sort of large lichen or spleenwort from Colorado.

(*b*) **1857** G. W. JOHNSON *Cottage Gardeners' Dict.* (ed. 2) 34/2 When it [*sc.* the rose of Jericho] alights in water, or on damp ground, the branches relax and open out, as if its life was renewed; hence its name Resurrection Plant. **1884** MILLER *Plant-n.* 115/2 Resurrection-plant, *Anastatica Hierochuntina*. **188.** *Oxford Bible-Helps* 121 The 'rose of Jericho' is also called 'Mary's flower' and 'resurrection flower'. **1951** *Dict. Gardening* (R. Hort. Soc.) IV. 1753/1 The Rose of Jericho, *Anastatica Hierochuntica*, is sometimes called a resurrection plant.

(*c*) **1902** L. H. BAILEY *Cycl. Amer. Hort.* IV. 1507/1 Resurrection plants are great curiosities... The commonest ones are members of the mustard family and the club moss family. **1974** F. N. HOWES *Dict. Useful & Everyday Plants* 217 Resurrection plant. Several pl[ant]s that appear dead after drought or a dry season but revive again w[ith] rain or moisture have acquired this name.

d. ***resurrection pie***, a pie made out of the remains from previous meals. Also *transf.*

1869 FURNIVALL *Forewords to Q. Eliz. Acad.* p. xxiii, A kind of Resurrection Pie like we used to have once a week at school, in which we declared old left bits reappeared. **1881** E. J. WORBOISE *Sissie* xx, Dr. Heaviside's housekeeper is too fond of giving us resurrection-pie! **1903** G. B. SHAW *Let.* 11 Sept. (1972) II. 370 We have both got the same job.. to strike out a line for the advanced guard that is.. neither Manchester resurrection-pie on the one hand nor Protectionist resurrection-pie on the other.

e. ***resurrection fern***, one of several ferns that survive drought, esp. the grey polypody, *Polypodium polypodioides*, of the southern United States.

1909 *Cent. Dict.* Suppl. 467/1 Resurrection-fern.. contracts during drouth but revives in moist seasons. **1924** J. A. THOMSON *Sci. Old & New* v. 30 The 'resurrection fern'.. curls up its fronds in drought, and uncurls them when the rains return. **1963** B. COBB *Field Guide to Ferns* 56 Even though they wither in a drought they promptly become green again after getting moisture, and are therefore often referred to as Resurrection Ferns.

6. a. ***resurrection man***, one who made a trade of exhuming bodies in order to sell them to anatomists; a corpse-stealer, resurrectionist.

1781 R. KING *Mod. Lond. Spy* 106 Persons (under the name of resurrection-men) continue their business, getting from 1 guinea to 5 or 6, according to the value set upon the corpse they take up. **1798** SOUTHEY *Ball. & Metr. T.* Poet. Wks. VI. 187 Five guineas if he shoot A Resurrection Man. **1860** DICKENS *Uncomm. Trav.* xiv, He had carried up every separate article in the dead of the night, and.. had felt as wicked as a Resurrection Man.

†**b.** So ***resurrection-cove, -jarvey, -woman.*** *Obs.*

1812 J. H. VAUX *Flash Dict., Resurrection-cove*, a stealer of dead bodies. **1815** SCOTT *Guy M.* lvi, They were, you remember, resurrection-women, who had promised to procure a child's body for some young surgeons. **1825** C. WESTMACOTT *Eng. Spy* I. 249 A hackney night coachman, known.. as the resurrection Jarvey.

So **resu'rrection** *v. trans.*, to resurrect.

1628 FELTHAM *Resolves* I. lxxxiv, Then also, let men see, how the Sacred wheel of Providence hath resurrection'd all our joys. **1837** MARRYAT *Dog Fiend* xxxii, There you be resurrectioned up again.

resu'rrectional, *a.* [f. prec. + -AL[1].] Relating to, or concerned with, resurrection.

1832 *Fraser's Mag.* V. 85 Resurrectional Recreations. By a Poor Devil. **1860** *All Year Round* 388 Spallanzani especially.. gave an immense celebrity to the resurrectional hypothesis. **1899** *Q. Rev.* Apr. 430 With the frippery of despair.. did such resurrectional ghosts actually invest themselves.

resu'rrectionary, *a.* [f. as prec. + -ARY.]

1. Of the nature of resurrection; restoratory.

1860 DICKENS *Uncomm. Trav.* vii, Old men and women, ugly and blind, who always seemed by resurrectionary process to be recalled out of the elements.

2. Concerned or connected with the disinterment of bodies for anatomical purposes.

1837 SOUTHEY in C. C. Southey *Life* (1849) VI. 359 A medical student.. expressed his satisfaction at having escaped being taken upon a resurrectionary party. **1859** G. WILSON *Life E. Forbes* iv. (1861) 92 A fellow-student,.. with a gunshot wound received in a resurrectionary expedition to Musselburgh churchyard.

resu'rrectioner. [f. as prec. + -ER[1].] = RESURRECTIONIST.

1828 MOIR *Mansie Wauch* 90 Did ye no ken of three young doctors.., alang with some resurrectioners.., firing shottie for shottie with the guard at Kirkmabrecke? *a* **1843** SOUTHEY *Comm.-pl. Bk.* (1851) III. 784 A resurrectioner tried at Leicester 10 Jac. I.

resu'rrectionism. [-ISM.] The practice of body-snatching.

1859 G. WILSON *Life E. Forbes* iv. (1861) 92 The law.. in regard to resurrectionism generally, was Justice without the scales and with a very thick bandage over her eyes.

resu'rrectionist. [f. RESURRECTION *sb.* + -IST. Hence F. *résurrectionniste.*]

1. An exhumer and stealer of corpses; a resurrection man.

1776 *Ann. Reg.* 129 One.. who makes open profession of dealing in dead bodies and is well known by the name of the Resurrectionist. **1831** *Times* 7 Nov. 6/5 Here 2 or 3 constables.. exclaimed that they knew Ray to be a noted 'resurrectionist'. **1869** *Latest News* 5 Sept. 10 A tale entitled 'The Baron's Coffin', the subject of which is divided between spectres and resurrectionists.

attrib. **1850** THACKERAY *Pendennis* xxx[i], Poor Cos's ditty.. was sung but to a few admirers, who might choose to remain after the tremendous resurrectionist chant. **1896** BAILEY *Diary of a Resurrectionist* 137 He continued in the resurrectionist business up to the time of the passing of the Anatomy Act.

2. One who revives or brings to light again. (Chiefly *transf.* from prec.)

1834 MISS EDGEWORTH *Helen* xi, He was merely a resurrectionist of obsolete heresies. **1850** WHIPPLE *Ess. & Rev.* (ed. 3) II. 157 He has shown more industry and acuteness than almost any other contemporary resurrectionist in the grave-yards of deceased books. **1890** *Spectator* 28 June, The literary resurrectionist digs them up again, and an author's worst work is brought into almost as much prominence as his best.

b. *spec.* (See quots.)

1888 *Longman's Mag.* July 256 Some of the habitual buyers [of ostrich feathers] have nicknames, and those who do a local business and buy for re-selling are known as 'resurrectionists'. **1894** *Westm. Gazette* 4 Jan. 6/3 The *Gnoleurs* or 'blocking resurrectionists' skilfully touch up battered silk hats from over the Channel.

3. A believer in resurrection.

1860 *All Year Round* 389 Schultze made considerable efforts to increase the number of resurrectionists.

4. *Horse-racing.* (See quot.)

1883 *Standard* 23 Oct. 3/2 There is a class of horses called 'resurrectionists',.. and they either recover early form.., or.. become animated, when they were supposed to be gone altogether, with.. life and vigour.

resu'rrectionize, *v.* [-IZE.] *trans.* To resurrect, in various senses.

1804 SOUTHEY *Let. to Coleridge* 14 Mar., You will stare at the catalogue of dead authors whom I shall have to resurrectionise. **1834** *New Monthly Mag.* XLI. 544 The ingenuity deserves praise, which thus resurrectionizes cloth, and gives it a second existence. **1867** *Church & St. Rev.* 1 June 508 Discarding such obvious topics.., he has resurrectionised 'the man of sin'. **1889** BRUCE *Kingd. God* Introd. 4 We cannot at this date resurrectionize a lost apostolic document.

Hence **resu'rrectionized** *ppl. a.*; **resu'rrectionizing** *vbl. sb.*

1854 *Blackw. Mag.* LXXVI. 427 An occasional junior.. might be admitted to act a subordinate part in a 'resurrectionising affair'. **1861** *Sat. Rev.* 14 Sept. 276 The social and spiritual advantages of modern or resurrectionized Romanism. **1871** in De Vere *Americanisms* 655 The leading gentleman of the resurrectionizing profession is one Cunningham.

resu'rrective, *a. rare.* [f. L. *resurrect-*, ppl. stem of *resurgĕre* + -IVE.] Pertaining to or causing resurrection.

1646 G. DANIEL *Poems* Wks. (Grosart) I. 21 To consume Bodies, which againe shall take Being and forme; (a Resurrective Tipe From dust and Ashes). **1885** *Homilet. Rev.* Aug. 149 While the lips spoke the words of resurrective power.

resu'rrector. [f. RESURRECT *v.* + -OR.]

1. = RESURRECTIONIST 1.

1861 QUINN *Heather Lintie* (1863) 187 Sin' he has fled his daddy's trade, Wha genuine Resurrector Was mony a day.

2. One who recalls the dead to life.

1890 TALMAGE *From Manger to Throne* 575 Is this Jesus, the comforter at Bethany, the resurrector at Nain?

resu'rrender (riː-), *v.* [RE- 5 a.] To surrender or give up again.

1544 tr. *Littleton's Tenures* (1574) 110 Him behoveth that the deede of the grauntee of the rent charge for terme of life, bee resurrendred or cancelled. **1621** QUARLES *Argalus & P.* 111, By this the pale-fac'd Empresse of the night Had re-surrendred up her borrowed light. *a* **1700** KEN *Edmund* Poet. Wks. 1721 II. 41 The Prince, who to his Midnight Pray'r arose, Himself had resurrendred to Repose.

So **resu'rrender** *sb.*

1891 *Stamp Act, 54 & 55 Vict.* c. 39 §87 A reconveyance, release, discharge, surrender, re-surrender,.. or renunciation of any such security. **1898** *Westm. Gaz.* 8 July 3/1 The Republicans.. 'oppose the re-surrender to Spanish misrule of any territory taken or to be taken'.

†**re'surse**, *v. Sc. Obs.*$^{-1}$ [f. OF. *resurs-*, pret. stem of *resourdre*: see RESURGE *v.*] To rise again.

1513 DOUGLAS *Æneis* IX. ix. 84 Lyke as the egill.. resursyng heich vp in the ayr.

re'survey, *sb.* [RE- 5 a.] A fresh survey.

1662 *Virginia Stat.* (1823) II. 101 The ffifty seaventh act prohibiting resurveighs not applying the expected remedies. **1702** *Refl. on Case of W. Penn* 9 The next thing to be consider'd is the Over-plus Land upon a Re-survey. **1768** in Picton *L'pool Munic. Rec.* (1886) II. 244 A resurvey of the intended navigation from Leeds to Liverpoole. **1806** *Phil. Trans.* XCVI. 349 By repeated re-surveys these lines are kept up. **1862** SMILES *Engineers* III. 156 The re-survey of the line would occupy at least four weeks. **1892** *Pall Mall G.* 5 May 2/2 A re-survey has for some time been taking place.

resur'vey (riː-), *v.* [RE- 5 a.]

1. *trans.* To read over again; to examine or consider afresh.

1599 SHAKS. *Hen. V*, v. ii. 81 To appoint some of your Councell.. To sit with vs once more, with better heed To re-suruey them. **1661** BOYLE *Style of Script.* 251 When upon a greater Familiarity with.. the applicablenesse of Scripture, I came to resurvey it. *a* **1711** KEN *Preparativ* Poet. Wks. 1721 IV. 11 My Cyphers I to Figures change,.. But when I resurvey the Score, I still find more. **1873** M. ARNOLD *Lit. & Dogma* (1876) 117 Collins, and the whole array of writers.., greatly need to be re-surveyed from the point of view of our own age.

2. To survey (land, etc.) again.

1747 *Col. Rec. Pennsylv.* V. 107 That the said Road shall be Resurveyed and laid out according to the Courses it now runs. **1784** R. BAGE *Barham Downs* II. 74 An eminent surveyor.. had been employed by the young Earl to resurvey his estates. **1806** *Phil. Trans.* XCVI. 350 The old estates have been often re-surveyed. **1861** SMILES *Engineers* II. 151 He found it necessary to resurvey the whole line. **1876** C. T. DAVIS *Polaris Exp.* xiii. 301 The coast-line.. does not seem to be correct, and ought to be resurveyed.

†**re'susce**, *v. Obs. rare*$^{-1}$. To resuscitate.

13.. *Cursor M.* 14363 (Gött.), Sone ouerall þis tiþand ras Of lazar þat resusced was.

re'suscitable, *a.* [Cf. F. *ressuscitable* (16th c.).] Capable of being resuscitated or restored to life. Hence **resuscita'bility**.

a **1691** BOYLE *Wks.* (1774) V. 605 The apothecary told the virtuoso, that he had really prepared resuscitable plants, a different way from that which others pretended to. **1842** CARLYLE *Let.* 12 Jan. (1904) I. 250 It lies buried under two centuries of quackeries, scepticisms, owleries,—*not* resuscitable. **1908** *Jrnl. Exper. Med.* X. 373 The resuscitability of the animal in such an instance clearly depends on the perfection of the technique employed to resuscitate it. **1919** W. DE MORGAN *Old Madhouse* xvii. 274 Flinder's mill-pool yielded when dredged a resuscitable corpse. **1971** H. PACY *Road Accidents* iii. 73 As with resuscitability, 'life-and-death' decisions are required at the scene of accidents.

re'suscitant, *sb.* and *a.* [Cf. F. *ressuscitant.*] **a.** *sb.* 'One who resuscitates' (Worcester, 1860). **b.** *adj.* 'Resuscitating' (Ogilvie, 1882).

†**re'suscitate**, *pa. pple.* (and *sb.*). *Obs.* [ad. L. *resuscitāt-us*, pa. pple. of *resuscitāre*: see next.] Revived, restored to life.

1520 *St. Papers Hen. VIII*, VI. 59 All the worlde here is resuscitait fro dethe to lyff. **1567** *Trial Treas.* (1850) 29 So rule that at the last you may be resuscitate And raigne with the Almightie with perfect continuance. **1637–50** ROW *Hist. Kirk* (1842) 265 If that spirit of action, zeal, and Courage, were resuscitat and raised up again. **1642** H. MORE *Song of Soul* III. II. xxi, Her body new resuscitate From sleep.

b. *absol.* as *sb.*

1814 LAMB *Let. to Coleridge* in *Life* (1837) 91 Dear Resuscitate,.. there comes to you this day a volume of German.

resuscitate (rɪˈsʌsɪteɪt), *v.* [f. ppl. stem of L. *resuscitāre*, f. *re-* RE- + *suscitāre* to raise, revive, etc.]

1. *trans.* To restore (a person) to life (physical or spiritual) or to consciousness.

1532 MORE *Confut. Tindale* Wks. 700/1 First in soule, and after in bodye, which the father.. shal.. reise and resuscitat to blysse. **1546** GARDINER *Declar. Joye* 63 Resuscitatinge man in iustificacion from the death of synne to lyfe. **1599** A. M. tr. *Gablehouer's Bk. Physicke* 40/1 Sometimes renue the Cotten, till such time as he is resuscitatede. **1663** H. COGAN tr. *Pinto's Trav.* lxi. 251 These little children.. went on singing praises to God, and praying him to resuscitate this defunct to a new life. **1720** WELTON *Suffer. Son of God* II. xvii. 478 Why dost Thou not resuscitate and quicken me, O Thou Life of my Soul! **1839** JAMES *Louis XIV*, IV. 82 Her mother perceived that life was not extinct, and took means to resuscitate her child. **1895** DOYLE *Stark Munro Lett.* ii, Then I was to die.. and all Scotland was to resound with how Dr. Cullingworth.. had resuscitated me.

fig. **1845** LEWES *Hist. Philos.* (1867) I. 377 Plotinus, its real founder, resuscitated Plato. **1869** *Echo* 8 Apr., The Everett Rooms Service, with Edgar Poe resuscitated, *vice* the Bible.

2. To revive, renew, restore (a thing).

1532 MORE *Confut. Tindale* Wks. 385/2, I warne the that thou resuscitate and styrre vp the grace of god that is in the. **1633** PRYNNE *Histrio-m.* I. 80 If then these Playes.. haue propagated Idolatrie, and Paganisme heretofore; they may likewise resuscitate, and foment it now. *a* **1676** HALE *Prim. Orig. Man.* I. ii. (1677) 56 In that it can resuscitate and stir up it self to remember and call together other Images. *a* **1734** NORTH *Exam.* II. v. §159 (1740) 417 There was still the same lurking Faction, which lost no Opportunity to resuscitate a new Flame out of the old Embers. **1751** JOHNSON *Rambler* No. 85 ¶9 The vital functions are resuscitated.. by vigorous motion. **1820** LAMB *Elia* I. *Southsea House*, No wind has resuscitated the face of the sleeping waters. **1851** HELPS *Comp. Solit.* i. (1874) 9 No one discovery resuscitates the world. **1872** MINTO *Eng. Prose Lit.* I. ii. 143 He resuscitates all the Court gossip of the period.

3. *intr.* To revive, to come to life again.

1652 BENLOWES *Theoph.* x. xii, Tell me no more, Th' art sweet,.. And canst with jovial mirth resuscitate from Care. **1661** FELTHAM *Lusoria* §35 Those birds, that yearly sleep a Winters death, Each Spring to mighty Love resuscitate. **1727** BRADLEY *Fam. Dict.* s.v. *Gnat*, These Nymphæ.. from that State resuscitate and fly away. **1787** WINTER *Syst. Husb.* 74 Every plant will earlier or later resuscitate. **1804** *Something Odd* III. 258 Mr. Marriott, whom I must leave resuscitating in the new world. **1862** THACKERAY *Philip* xxviii, Our griefs, our pleasures, our youth, our sorrows,.. resuscitate. **1871** TYLOR *Prim. Cult.* I. 321 That.. men only quitted life.. and resuscitated as from a peaceful sleep.

Hence **re'suscitating** *vbl. sb.* and *ppl. a.*

1554 *Act 1 & 2 Phil. & Mary* c. 8 §50 The Resuscitating of Alms, Prayer, and Example of good Life in this Realm. **1707** *Curios. in Husb. & Gard.* 345 Some.. have not been satisfied with resuscitating of Plants from.. their Ashes. **1731** *Hist. Lit.* III. 351 Which Resolution may be effected by Mercury, a resuscitating Salt, or Fire. **1864** *Daily Tel.* 17 Aug., We have seen the resuscitating energy of the Don show itself in Morocco.

re'suscitated, *ppl. a.* [f. prec. + -ED[1].] Revived, restored.

1596 *Foxe's A. & M.* 789/2 O Sonne of God, crucified for vs, and resuscitated Emanuell.

1753 CHAMBERS *Cycl. Suppl.* s.v. *Resuscitation*, Many.. have shewn resuscitated plants in vials. **1781** COWPER *Retirem.* 64 A thousand insect forms, These hatched, and those resuscitated worms. **1840** HOOD *Up Rhine* 238 Communicating with a resuscitated Roman, or a Roman Ghost. **1878** BOSW. SMITH *Carthage* 334 By a possibly resuscitated Tyre or by the new-born Alexandria.

resuscitation (rɪsʌsɪˈteɪʃən). [ad. late L. *resuscitātiōn-em*, n. of action f. *resuscitāre* to RESUSCITATE. So F. *ressuscitation*, Sp. *resucitacion*, It. *re-, risu(s)citazione.*]

1. Restoration to life. Also *fig.*

1526 *Pilgr. Perf.* (W. de W. 1531) 223 b, Resurrecyon or resuscitacyon of body, and lyfe eternall. **1545** JOYE *Exp. Dan.* A vij b, Here we haue a cleare testimonie of the resuscitation of the dead to come. **1597** J. KING *On Jonas* (1618) 511 In this spirituall resuscitation from the death of the soule. **1660** H. MORE *Myst. Godl.* VI. xviii. 277 The Resuscitation of all his Saints into that Eternal Happiness which they had fallen from. *a* **1806** HORSLEY *Serm.* xx. (1816) II. 167 The word 'quickened' is often applied to signify, not the resuscitation of life extinguished, but the preservation and continuance of life subsisting. **1847** LYTTON *Lucretia* (1853) 347 It was as a resuscitation from the grave. **1858** SEARS *Athan.* II. xii. 249 The resuscitation of a dead body. **1864** BURTON *Scot. Abr.* II. 224 The author has been .. most easily tracked by the biographical detective. The soldier has less chance of resuscitation.

b. *spec.* Restoration of life or consciousness in one almost or apparently drowned or dead.

1788 *New London Mag.* 190 Every additional instance of resuscitation is a further confirmation of the real importance of the Humane Society. **1835–6** *Todd's Cycl. Anat.* I. 260/2 Resuscitation has occasionally taken place in the human body after fifteen minutes' immersion. **1869** CLARIDGE *Cold Water Cure* 25 On the application of the wet sheet and tepid bath, the resuscitation of the man was as by miracle. **1875** H. C. WOOD *Therap.* (1879) 292 Efforts at resuscitation should be kept up for at least two hours.

attrib. **1895** *Westm. Gaz.* 4 Nov. 7/2 To go through .. resuscitation drill, in addition to rescue work in the water.

c. Restoration to health. *rare*$^{-1}$.

17.. POPE *Let.* (J.), Your very obliging manner of enquiring after me, at your resuscitation, should have been sooner answered; I sincerely rejoice at your recovery.

2. Revival, renewal, restoration (of something).

1663 COWLEY *Verses & Ess.* (1669) 21 A retardment .. To the Resuscitation of the Day, Or Resurrection of the Spring. **1718** QUINCY *Compl. Disp.* p. xi, Fermentation is a certain Manifestation of Life, fitting it for a Resuscitation. **1759** JOHNSON *Rasselas* xxx, The extinction and resuscitation of arts. **1847** LD. LINDSAY *Christian Art* I. 119 A resuscitation of the symbolism of early Christianity, so long neglected. **1855** MOTLEY *Dutch Rep.* III. v. (1866) 445 By the resuscitation of secret documents, over which the dust of three centuries has gathered. **1874** H. R. REYNOLDS *John Bapt.* iii. §4. 218 Isaiah represents the resuscitation of their national life.

†**b.** *spec.* (See quots. 1727–53.) *Obs.*

1650 J. F[RENCH] tr. *Paracelsus' Nature of Things* VI. 57 *margin*, The Resuscitation of Metalls is twofold. *Ibid.* 58 The resuscitation, and restoring of Wood is hard. **1727–38** CHAMBERS *Cycl.*, *Revivification*, or *Resuscitation*, in chemistry, the art of restoring a mixed body to its first state. **1753** —— *Suppl.*, *Resuscitation of plants*, .. the art of reproducing a plant from its ashes.

resuscitative (rɪˈsʌsɪteɪtɪv), *a.* [See RESUSCITATE *v.* and -IVE. So F. *ressuscitatif.*] Tending to resuscitate; revivifying, reviving.

1611 COTGR., *Resuscitatif*, resuscitatiue, reuiuing, raising vp from death to life. **1805** *Spirit Publ. Jrnls.* IX. 127 They .. had .. recourse to the resuscitative process of the Humane Society. **1816** BP. JEBB *Let.* in *Life* 553 Our Lord's three resuscitative miracles. **1836–7** SIR W. HAMILTON *Metaph.* xxxi. (1859) II. 227, I am not satisfied, I say, with the term reproduction for the process by which the dormant thought or affection is aroused... Perhaps the Resuscitative Faculty would have been better. **1891** J. AITCHISON *Signa Christi* vi. 237 The self-renewing or resuscitative power of Christianity.

reˈsuscitator. [f. as prec. + -OR.]

1. One who resuscitates or revives.

1847 in WEBSTER. **1877** SYMONDS *Renaiss. in Italy* 522 Regarding themselves as resuscitators of a glorious past. **1882–3** SCHAFF *Encycl. Relig. Knowl.* 2573/2 Zinzendorf, .. the resuscitator of the Moravian Church. **1969** J. SECOR *Patient Care in Respiratory Probl.* iv. 165 The nurse's role as a resuscitator in the event of cardio-pulmonary arrest has been an issue since the introduction of the procedure. **1977** *Lancet* 1 Jan. 9/1 It may well be that more intelligent parents are better resuscitators.

2. An apparatus used for resuscitation after asphyxia or arrest of respiration.

1929 *Jrnl. Amer. Med. Assoc.* 16 Nov. 1583/1 The E. and J. resuscitator is not a desirable apparatus for use by fire departments. **1938** *Surg., Gynecol. & Obstetr.* LXVI. 721/2 The ideal mechanical contraption for resuscitation is an apparatus which combines an inhalator and a resuscitator. **1943** *Science* 24 Dec. 548/1 The inventors of the pulmotor assumed, and the promoters of 'resuscitators' still claim, that by artificially forcing the lungs and chest through movements like those of breathing, a return of natural respiration should be induced. **1965** H. H. BENDIXEN et al. *Respiratory Care* xii. 122 Artificial ventilation is started by bag and mask. A self-inflating bag or a bellows resuscitator is suitable... A number of mechanical resuscitators are available.

†**reˈsuscite,** *v. Obs.* [ad. OF. *resusciter* or L. *resuscitāre.*]

1. *trans.* To resuscitate, bring back to life.

c **1375** *Sc. Leg. Saints* v. (*John*) 372 In his name to resuscit 3ow. *a* **1450** *Knt. de la Tour* (1868) 144 Oure lorde Ihesu Crist was resuscited. *c* **1477** CAXTON *Jason* 27 Hit semeth to us that fortune hath brought hym unto your handes for to resuscite and reyse yow. **1535** JOYE *Apol. Tindale* (Arb.) 8 He englissheth *resuscitantur* shal ryse agen and not are reuiued or resuscited.

2. *intr.* To return to life.

a **1450** *Knt. de la Tour* (1868) 125 Bi the praier of the said holy man the child resuscited, and releued ayen from dethe to lyff.

resuˈstain, *v.* [RE- 5 a.] To support anew.

1632 VICARS *Virgil* III. 55 Alas! what chance thee chas'd from such a Pheere, Now resustains?

resverie, -y, obs. forms of REVERIE.

reˈswallow (riː-), *v.* [RE- 5 a.] *trans.* To swallow again.

1818 BENTHAM *Ch. Eng., Catech. Exam.* 379 It is not—this bitter dose— .. brought up again and re-swallowed. **1871** B. TAYLOR *Faust* III. (1875) II. 170 If now that shape the ancient Night hath not at once Re-swallowed.

reˈswarm, *v.* [RE- 5 a.] To swarm again.

1616 J. LANE *Contn. Sqr.'s T.* VII. 86 Soddainlie the Fregiliens rann to armes, and vp and down the streetes in heaps reswarms.

reˈswear, *v.* [RE- 5 a.] To swear again.

a **1693** *Urquhart's Rabelais* III. xxxvi. 303, I swear, reswear, forswear, abjure, and renounce. **1802** ELDON *Vesey Rep.* VIII. 32 The Witness would stand pledged to re-swear what she had sworn. **1844** *Regul. & Ordin. Army* 226 The Court is to be re-sworn at the commencement of each trial. **1885** *Law Times* LXXIX. 7/1 The Court .. allowed the affidavit to be resworn and again filed.

reˈswell (riː-), *v.* [RE- 5 a.] *intr.* To swell again. Hence **reˈswelling** *vbl. sb.* and *ppl. a.*

1611 FLORIO, *Rigonsiamento*, a reswelling. *Rigonsiante*, reswelling. **1855** LYNCH *Rivulet* XXIX. ii, And all my hopes re-swell.

reˈswill, *v.* [RE- 5 a.] To swill again.

1614 SYLVESTER *Bethulia's Rescue* III. 291 A Souldier here re-swils again .. Th' unsavoury water.

resword, variant of RESOURD *v.*

resyant, resyaunt(e, obs. forms of RESIANT.

resyde, obs. f. RESIDE *v.*

resyden(n)ce, resydens, obs. ff. RESIDENCE.

resydent(t, obs. ff. RESIDENT.

resydiuation, etc., obs. ff. RECIDIVATION.

resye, variant of RESE *v.*^{2} to shake. *Obs.*

resygn(e, obs. ff. RESIGN *v.*

resyn, obs. f. RAISIN, RESIN.

resyne, obs. f. RESIGN *v.*

resyng, obs. f. RAISIN, RESIGN *v.*

resyte, obs. f. RECITE *v.*

ret, *sb.*^{1} [f. RET *v.*^{2}] Retting.

1849 *Jrnl. R. Agric. Soc.* X. I. 178 If the stem then breaks freely, and the fibre leaves it easily, it will have got a good ret, as it is called. **1949** *Publ. Amer. Dial. Soc.* XI. 62 *Ret, n.* and *v.t.*, a special form of *rot*. The process by which the stalk is prepared for separating the fibre—the rotting of the woody stalk. **1958** *New Biol.* XXVII. 15 In most countries the deseeded flax straw is now retted in warm water in concrete tanks. In the anaerobic ret largely practised in Belgium, the tanks are filled with air-dried straw which is then covered with water at a temperature of 18–27° C.

ret, *sb.*^{2} (See quots.)

1874 HOTTEN *Slang Dict.* (new ed.) 268 *Ret*, an abbreviation of the word *reiteration*, used to denote the forme which, in a printing-office, backs or perfects paper already printed on one side. **1960** G. A. GLAISTER *Gloss. Bk.* 346/1 *Ret*, the second side of a sheet of paper.

†**ret,** *v.*^{1} *Obs.* in 4–5 rette (5 rettyn, rectyn); *pa. t.* 4 retted(e, -id, rett; *pa. pple.* 4 rettid, 6 rected; 5 ret, 5–6 rette. [ad. OF. *retter, recter, reter*, = Prov., Sp., and Pg. *reptar* (mod.Sp. also *retar*):—L. *reputāre*: see REPUTE *v.* and cf. ARET *v.*]

1. *trans.* To impute, ascribe, or attribute *to* one; to regard as resting *in* or lying *on* one.

13.. *K. Alis.* 7247 Al theo lore in him Y rette: Y schal yeilde wel his dette! *a* **1340** HAMPOLE *Psalter* xxxi. 2 Blisful man til whaim lord rettid noght synn. *c* **1400** *Laud Troy Bk.* 978, I schal therfore haue harm and schame, For men wol rette on me the blame. *c* **1450** *Mirour Saluacioun* (Roxb.) 32 In hire may noght be rette bot vertuouse honoure.

2. To accuse, charge (a person). Const. *of, to.*

1338 R. BRUNNE *Chron.* (1810) 64 For Gospatrik was slayn, þei blamed him þer in... Tostus of Cumbirland retted Godwyn þer tille. **1527** RASTELL *Abridg. Stat.* s.v. *Maymprise*, [If he] be not rette of other felonie before or rette of reseuynge of felones [etc.].

3. To reckon, repute.

c **1380** WYCLIF *Wks.* (1880) 357 Men shulden rette hem eretikis, & so not comyne wiþ hem. *c* **1386** CHAUCER *Prol.* 726, I preye 3owe .. That 3e ne ret it nowht my velenye. *c* **1400** *Laud Troy Bk.* 8882 Thei se now me on bak be-set, Mi vylony it wol be ret.

ret, *v.*^{2} Forms: α. 5 rettyn, retyn, 9 ret; β. 6 rayte, 7– rate, rait. [Of somewhat obscure history. The E. Anglian *ret* (earlier inf. *retten, reten*) resembles MDu. *reeten, reten* (still in use); but the northern forms *rayt, rait, rate* appear rather to indicate an ON. **reyta* (represented by mod.Norw. *røyta*, Sw. *röta*, Da. *røde*), which corresponds to MDu. *rooten, roten* (Du. *roten*; dial. also *röten, reuten*), MLG. *rôten, râten*, MHG. *rœzen, ræzen* (G. *rötzen, rösten*, etc.). These forms are connected with the stem of ROT *v.*, but it is difficult to regard Du. *reten* as a variant from the same stem.]

1. *trans.* To soak (esp. flax or hemp) in water, or expose to moisture, in order to soften or season. (Cf. DEW-RET and WATER-RET.)

α. *c* **1440** *Promp. Parv.* 431/1 Rettyn tymbyr, hempe, or oþer lyke (*K.P.*, retyn tymbyr, flax or hempe), *rigo, infundo.* **1710–** [cf. DEW-RET and WATER-RET]. *a* **1825** FORBY *Voc. E. Anglia*, *Ret*, to soak, to macerate in water. **1839** URE *Dict. Arts* 483 Prior to being retted, the flax should be sorted according to the length .. of its stalks. **1897** *Daily News* 1 June 1/1 Threshing the hemp and flax... Tanks for retting the straw.

β. **1533** *Eng. Misc.* (Surtees, 1890) 34 That no man shall rayte nowther hempe ne lyne. **1607** *N. Riding Rec.* I. 85 Presented for watering or rating their hemp. **1691** RAY *N.C. Words*, To *Rait* Timber; and so Flax and Hemp, to put it into a Pond or Ditch, to water it, to harden or season it. **1727–38** CHAMBERS *Cycl.* s.v. *Hemp*, They proceed to water or rate it, by laying it five or six days in a pool, .. to rot the bark. **1788** W. MARSHALL *Yorksh.* II. 74 Here it lies until it be sufficiently 'rated'; namely until the woodlike substance of the stems will separate freely from the filaments or flaxen fibres. **1839** STONEHOUSE *Axholme* 20 Putting their hemp to be rated in the waters of the said wastes. **1876** ROBINSON *Mid-Yorks. Gloss.* s.v. *Rate*, Timber is rated by being exposed through all seasons.

2. Of hay, etc. In *passive*: To be spoiled by exposure to wet.

1641 BEST *Farm. Bks.* (Surtees) 34 Then sure it is to be rated, and beinge rated looseth both the goode smell and goode taste. **1788** W. MARSHALL *Yorksh.* Gloss. s.v. *Rait*, Hay is said to be raited when it has been much exposed to an alternacy of wet and dry weather. **1877** *N.W. Linc. Gloss.* s.v. *Rate*, Hay or clover is said to be rated when by exposure to rain it has become well-nigh worthless for fodder.

3. *trans.* and *intr.* To rot.

1846 BROCKETT *N.C. Gloss.* (ed. 3) s.v. *Rate*, Quicklime rates the sods in a compost heap. Sods rate fast in that heap. **1869** *Lonsdale Gloss.*, *Rate*, to become rotten.

Hence **ret-pit (rate-pit)**, a retting-pit.

1571 in *N.W. Linc. Gloss.* (1877).

†**ret,** *v.*^{3} *Obs. rare.* [Of obscure origin.] *intr.* (See quot. *a*1670.)

c **1645** CLEVELAND *Vindiciæ* (1677) 128 You were in hopes to retrieve your Money, and Verily, Verily Ret never springs the Partridge. *a* **1670** HACKET *Abp. Williams* I. (1692) 109 Like Spaniels that rett after Larks and Sparrows in the Field, and pass over the best Game.

ret., abbrev. of RETIRED *ppl. a.* 6. cf. RETD., RET'D.

a **1912** W. T. ROGERS *Dict. Abbrev.* (1913) 166/1 *Ret.* (gen.), retired;—return. **1973** 'D. SHANNON' *No Holiday for Crime* v. 73 Lieutenant Colonel (ret.) Archer Pound. **1978** R. CONDON *Bandicoot* i. 9 Captain Colin Huntington, R.N. (ret.).

ret, obs. 3 sing. pres. indic. READ *v.*, REDE *v.*^{1}

retable (rɪˈteɪb(ə)l). *Eccl.* [a. F. *rétable, retable* (16th c.), = Sp. *retablo*, Pg. *retabolo, -tabulo, -tavolo*, mod.L. *retabulum.* Earlier and fuller forms are OProv. *reiretaule* (1218), *reirotaule* (1284), med.L. *retrotabulum* (1294 in Du Cange): see REAR-, RETRO-^{1}, and TABLE *sb.*] An appendage to an altar, consisting of a shelf or ledge raised above the back of it (on which ornaments may be placed), or a frame enclosing painted or otherwise decorated panels.

1823 PUGIN *Gothic Arch.* Gloss., *Retable*, an altar-piece. A term of French origin. **1859** GULLICK & TIMBS *Paint.* 307 The form of the triptyck when opened suggested a variety called the 'retable' .. which is flat and does not admit of being closed. **1877** J. D. CHAMBERS *Div. Worship* 295 The movable Retable upon the Altar is quite a modern invention. **1884** *Bath & Wells Diocesan Mag.* Aug. 85 A new oak altar, with re-table, .. has lately been placed in the church. **1965** C. D. EBY *Siege of Alcázar* (1966) vi. 122 Arab jewels, ceramics, Flemish retables. **1979** *Dædalus* Summer 136 He remembered having noticed at the foot of the retable 'a piece of a host about the size of a small coin'.

So ‖**reˈtabulum.**

1861 SIR G. SCOTT *Glean. Westm. Abb.* (1863) 61 The retabulum from the high-altar, now preserved in a glass case.

retablo. [Sp., see RETABLE.] = RETABLE; also, a votive picture displayed in a church.

1845 FORD *Handbk. Spain* I. 411 The *Retablo* is full of old carvings. **1906** R. FRY *Let.* 13 Sept. (1972) I. 269 They [*sc.* tombs] are .. in the middle of the choir with a huge gold and blue *retablo* behind them. **1930** *Mexican Arts* (Amer. Fed. Arts) 43 A type of Mexican painting that deserves special attention .. is the retablo, or votive picture offering. **1939** *Mexican Art & Life* Apr., 'Retablos' in Mexico are little stories of religious character told in pictures and always represent a happening in which great misfortune was threatened but averted through the opportune intervention of some saint invoked by the person in distress. **1950** G. BRENAN *Face of Spain* ii. 55 The whole of one end [of a church] was taken up by a vast gilt retablo, carved and scrolled and ornamented, in the centre of which .. stood the miracle-working Virgin. **1965** C. CAUSLEY in *New Statesman* 12 Nov. 738/2 Christ hung down like a hawk-moth caterpillar, .. As I walked through the glittering Precinct All the retablos burned like gold. **1976** *Arizona Republic* 16 May N-3/1 There is a companion exhibit of Mexican folk *retablos*, 70 images on tin plates as produced by various Mexican folk artists. **1980** *Times Lit. Suppl.* 9 May 535/3 Peeling, retablo-like posters of high-kicking chorines.

reˈtack (riː-), *v.* [RE- 5 a.] To tack again.

1794 *Rigging & Seamanship* 363 The lee column .. re-tacks together. **1801** SOUTHEY *Lett.* (1850) II. 164 We tacked and retacked with a hard-hearted wind.

retail (ˈriːteɪl), *sb.*^{1} (and *a.*). Also 5–8 **retaile**, 5–7 **-tayle**, 6 **-tayll**, 6–7 **retale**; 6 **rytaile**. [a. OF. *retail* masc. (= It. *ritaglio*, Pg. *retalho*, Sp. *retajo*) or *retaille* fem., a piece cut off, etc., f. *retaillier*, f. *re-* RE- + *taillier* to cut; see TAIL *v.* The English sense of the word is found in AF. in the first half of the 14th c. The older stressing *reˈtail*, as in the verb, is still usual in Scotland.]

1. The sale of commodities in small quantities.

a. In adv. phrases with *by*, *at*, †*in*, †*to*, or used adverbially without prep. (After AF. *a retail*, *a* or *en retaille*.) Also *fig*.

1433 *Rolls of Parlt.* IV. 478/2 No Baillyff..bye, ne selle, no maner vitaill to retaile. **1433** *Waterford Arch.* in *10th Rep. Hist. MSS. Comm.* App. V. 296 If the said marchandise be solde by retaile. **1467** in *Eng. Gilds* (1870) 397 That no persone..sille no Fysshe watrd at retayle. **1503–4** *Act 19 Hen. VII*, c. 32 §10 Every persone..that..usith to by and sell any goodis or catalles at retayle. **1598** BARCKLEY *Felic. Man* IV. (1603) 309 Without scruple they sell that justice by retaile that was bought in grosse. **1615** BRATHWAIT *Strappado* (1878) 218 Both's to be bought: no difference in the sale; The one in grosse, the other in Retaile. **1631** R. BYFIELD *Doctr. Sabb.* 216 You set forth slanderous reports of Master Byfield, which you tooke in by retayle. **1709** STEELE *Tatler* No. 106 §2, I..asked him, Whether he would break Bulk, and sell his Goods by Retail? **1784** *New Spectator* No. 17. 3 What barbarous parents,..to oblige a person of my figure to deal out tea and sugar retail! **1848** MILL *Pol. Econ.* I. ii. §6 (1876) 25 Even when things are destined to be at last sold by retail, convenience soon creates a class of wholesale dealers. **1886** WAYLAND & CHAPIN *Pol. Econ.* x. 121 It is ordinarily more economical to purchase supplies..at retail, than at wholesale, though the prices are higher. **1883** *Law Times Rep.* XLIX. 727/1 Clearly inviting the public to come and buy, both wholesale and retail.

b. In other constructions.

1553 GRESHAM *Let.* in Burgon *Life* (1839) I. 464 That the retayller shall occupy onely his retayle, and the merchaunt adventorer his feat. **1567** DRANT *Horace, Ep.* vii. D v, Goe make your marchandize, God sende you good retayle. **1588** J. MELLIS *Briefe Instr.* F v, Of that accompte make the shoppe of retaile Creditor, as though it were a Debitor. **1605** TIMME *Quersit.* III. 190 To make retale of candels, lanternes, and all mercerie-wares. *a* **1660** HAMMOND *Serm.* Wks. 1683 IV. 569 Our best contrivance will be to shorten the retail, for the encreasing of the gross. *a* **1683** OLDHAM *Wks.* (1685) 16 He scorn'd Retail I'th' Trace of death: whole Myriads died by th' great. **1736** *Gentl. Mag.* VI. 631/1 By prohibiting the Retaile of Punch, some small Addition may be made to our Consumption of Wines. **1809** PINKNEY *Trav. France* 80 There was no appearance of business, not even of a brisk retail, or of a lively thoroughfare. **1888** S. DOWELL *Taxes in Eng.* II. 41 The duties on the retail of drinks made from tea, coffee, and chocolate.

†**2.** Detail (of a matter). *Obs.*

1654–66 EARL ORRERY *Parthen.* (1676) 534 Unsuccessful Sallyes, whose retail I decline telling you. **1678** MARVELL *Growth Popery* Wks. (Grosart) IV. 263 Should I enter into a particular retail of all former and latter transactions,.. there would be sufficient for a just volume of History.

3. A retailer, a retail dealer.

1851 D. JERROLD *Retired from Business* I. 6 And wholesales don't mix with retails? I think I see. **1884** *Pall Mall G.* 19 May 6/1 There is said to be a suburb where the retired wholesales will not visit the retired retails. **1892** *Ibid.* 25 Nov. 2/2 The idea of the retails is to amend the Food and Drugs Act by making an invoice count as a warranty.

4. *attrib.* (passing into *adj.*) Of or pertaining to, connected with, engaged in, the sale of commodities in small quantities. Also *fig.*

1601 R. JOHNSON *Kingd. & Commw.* (1603) 116 They.. haue betaken themselues to liue by retaile and mechanical trades. **1689** in Picton *L'pool Munic. Rec.* (1883) I. 297 To drive some small retail trade. **1716** M. DAVIES *Athen. Brit.* III. 78 There may have been such Retaile-Coyn, set forth by some Retail-Dealers, in all Reigns perchance. **1760** T. HUTCHINSON *Hist. Mass.* iii. (1765) 317 Sold to the Indians at the retail price. **1785** *Daily Universal Register* 1 Jan. 3/4 R. Croft, Taylor..at his wholesale and retail warehouse..is now selling ladies' Italian Coats. **1812** SIR J. SINCLAIR *Syst. Husb. Scot.* II. 22 Farmers in the vicinity of large towns, may be compared to retail shopkeepers. **1848** MILL *Pol. Econ.* I. III. i. 520 The influence of those causes is ultimately felt in the retail markets. *Ibid.* I. 24 The great retail dealings, which collectively occupy a very great amount of capital, are sometimes conducted in small shops. **1865** DICKENS *Mut. Fr.* I. vii, The poorer shops of small retail traders in commodities to eat and drink and keep folks warm. **1898** *Kansas City* (Missouri) *Star* 18 Dec. 2/1 Hatters, garment workers, shoe workers, retail clerks and textile workers. **1926** A. E. TAYLOR *Plato* xv. 379 This enables us to define the sophist again as a retail exporter of the knowledge of goodness.., though we must add that he sometimes retails his merchandise in the home market. **1926** *Times* 6 May 3/3 Coal is not being moved by rail, but retail distribution was being carried on in London yesterday. **1940** G. CROWTHER *Outl. Money* iii. 90 The second value of money which is usually distinguished is the value of money in buying the goods and services which the ordinary family consumes... This second variety can be called the retail value of money, or the cost of living. **1957** *Practical Wireless* XXXIII. 517/2 The British Radio Equipment Manufacturers' Association, ..in their monthly retail survey. **1962** *Listener* 13 Sept. 376/2 Every famous jazz composer or retail-chain owner. **1967** G. WILLS in Wills & Yearsley *Handbk. Managem. Technol.* x. 194 *Retail audit*,..continuous research with a panel of retailers to study inventory levels and sales of products over the counter. **1970** *New Society* 5 Mar. 383/3 Retail margins (the difference between the price paid by the shopkeeper and the price paid by the consumer) had previously been gradually rising. **1973** *Times* 25 Apr. 33/5 The brief includes a supermarket of about 40,000 sq ft., other retail units, a night club. **1976** *Daily Tel.* 20 July 1/4 Retail trade showed a slight recovery last month. **1979** *Oil Majors in 1978* (Shell Internat. Petroleum Co.) 7 Gulf suffered reduced sales in Canada but increased them in Europe, partly owing to its acquisition of Mobil's retail outlets in Switzerland.

b. *transf.* Parcelled out; piecemeal. *rare.*

1669 STURMY *Mariner's Mag.* C 2, Who thinks by Retail-pow'r his Kind to keep..May of a Kingdom soon a Cottage make. **1679** *Establ. Test* 41 What lingring and retail deaths would they think enough for such..Heretiques.

c. Petty, trivial. *rare*⁻¹.

1811 SYD. SMITH *Wks.* (1859) I. 211/2 As much his superior in the retail qualities which small people arrogate to themselves, as he was in every commanding faculty to the rest of his fellow-creatures.

d. *Comb.*, as **retail price index**, an index of the variation in the prices of retail goods (see INDEX *sb.* 9 e); **retail price maintenance** = *resale price maintenance* s.v. RESALE *sb.* 2.

1924 *University Jrnl. Business* June 263 In the construction of retail price and of cost-of-living indexes.. significant developments have occurred. **1935** J. H. COVER *Retail Price Behavior* 86 Though it appears that the median may be more satisfactory for a retail price index, the mean is more logical for a cost-of-living index. **1974** *Times* 22 Mar. 17/3 Even by January, the retail price index had climbed half way to that seven per cent trigger point. **1938** S. CHASE *Tyranny of Words* xiv. 175 The new laws for retail price maintenance. **1966** A. BATTERSBY *Math. in Managem.* ix. 232 The appeal to elasticity..has given rise to the fierce arguments about Retail Price Maintenance and the dilemma of those supporters of a competitive economy who attempt to eliminate the effects of free competition.

† **retail**, *sb.*² *Obs. rare*⁻¹. Retaliation.

1615 T. ADAMS *Lycanthropy* Wks. (1629) 385 He that doth iniury, may well receiue it. To looke for good, and doe bad, is against the law of Retaile.

retail (rɪˈteɪl), *v.* Also 5–6 retayll, 5–7 retaile, -tayle, 8 retale. [See RETAIL *sb.* OF. *retailler* app. does not occur in this sense.]

1. *trans.* To sell (goods, etc.) in small quantities.

1365 [see RETAILING *vbl. sb.*]. **1472** *Paston Lett.* III. 71, I truste be Ester to make of money..at the leest I. marke for to retayle the wode our selfe. *Ibid.* To brynge it..to as goode proffe as thowe we retayled it oure silffe. **1503–4** *Act 19 Hen. VII*, c. 32 §10 Goodis or cattalles..that..he or they so retaylleth. **1540–1** ELYOT *Image Gov.* (1556) 60 They that retayle that which is bought of the craftesman that worketh it. **1588** SHAKS. *L.L.L.* v. ii. 317 He is Wits Pedler, and retailes his Wares, At Wakes, and Wassels. **1617** MORYSON *Itin.* III. 95 Not shaming to retaile any commodity in small parts. **1712** ARBUTHNOT *John Bull* I. Pref., Stamping the Queen's Image on viler Metals, which he retales for Beef. **1776** ADAM SMITH *W.N.* v. ii. (1904) II. 506 The keepers of ale-houses pay for a licence to retail ale and spirituous liquors. **1829** LYTTON *Devereux* II. iii, Retailing the mixture as soon as he had filled his box.

absol. **1523** FITZHERB. *Husb.* §36 Therfore he that byeth grosse sale, and retayleth, muste nedes be a wynner. **1554** HASSE in Hakluyt *Voy.* (1598) I. 256 Like as we doe vse to retaile by the ounce.

b. *transf.* or *fig.*

1576 FLEMING *Panopl. Epist.* 234, I wil regard your commoditie,..leaste in steade of thankes, hate be retailed. **1597** J. KING *On Jonas* (1618) 427 Hee shall retale their doings into their bosomes, and giue them their rewarde. *a* **1661** FULLER *Worthies* (1840) III. 253 The abbot refused to retail his men out in such parcels. **1728** POPE *Dunc.* II. 134 As the sage dame..By names of Toasts retails each batter'd jade. **1758** JOHNSON *Idler* No. 7 ¶ 11 How six morning and six evening writers might agree to retail their articles.

absol. **1777** SHERIDAN *Sch. Scand.* IV. i, We shall be all day retailing in this manner; do let us deal wholesale.

c. *intr.* To be sold by retail.

1881 *Lit. World* (U.S.) 22 Oct. 375/1 Mr. Bartlett's compilation..retails for three dollars. **1897** *Daily News* 22 May 5/4 Turbot, brill, and halibut retail at 9*d.* per lb.

2. To recount or tell over again; to relate in detail; to repeat to others.

1594 SHAKS. *Rich. III*, III. i. 77 Me thinkes the truth should liue from age to age, As 'twere retayl'd to all posteritie. *Ibid.* IV. iv. 335 To whom I will retaile my Conquest woone. **1654–66** EARL ORRERY *Parthen.* (1676) 797, I will not retail particularities. **1732** BERKELEY *Alciphr.* III. §2 He would retail to them part of a conversation he once heard. **1766** GOLDSM. *Vic. W.* xvi, He could repeat all the observations that were retailed in the atmosphere of the play-houses. **1808** SCOTT *Marm.* v. vii, The licensed fool retail'd his jest. **1850** KINGSLEY *Alt. Locke* (1876) I. 14 The company seemed puzzled to whom he smilingly retailed my question. **1899** KIPLING *Stalky* 193 They overtook Foxy, speeding down to retail the adventure to Keyte.

absol. **1621** BP. MOUNTAGU *Diatribæ* 151 They say you haue neither read nor seene all that you cite, but are contented to retaile with your neighbours sometime.

Hence **re'tailed** *ppl. a.*

1611 COTGR., *Detaillé*, retailed, sold by retaile. **1654–66** EARL ORRERY *Parthen.* (1676) 574 The Battel..merits a retailed Relation. **1811** JANE AUSTEN *Sense & Sens.* III. xi. 225 It was neither in Elinor's power, nor in her wish, to rouse such feelings in another, by her retailed explanation, as had at first been called forth in herself.

retailer (rɪˈteɪlə(r)). Also α. 5–6 retaillour, 6 -tailour, 6–7 -taylor. β. 5–7 retailler, 6 -tayl(l)er. [f. RETAIL *v.* + -OR 2, -ER¹.]

1. A retail dealer or trader; one who sells goods in small quantities.

α. **1444** *Rolls of Parlt.* V. 108/2 The pouere common retaillours of vitailles. **1542–3** *Act 34 & 35 Hen. VIII*, c. 7 The saide Retailloures of Wynes. **1591** FLORIO *2nd Fruites* 121 You retailours..may finde in your hart to deceaue any bodie. **1631** T. POWELL *Tom of all Trades* 164 The Maker was before the Retaylor. **1666–7** MARVELL *Corr.* Wks. (Grosart) II. 203 A Bill has bin read for setting the prices of wine as well upon the merchant as retaylor.

β. **1488** *Rolls of Parlt.* VI. 421/2 Any Merchant,.. Artyficer, Retailler, Inholder [etc.]. **1547** *Act I Edw. VI*, c. 6 §1 Certaine parsons called Retaylers of the same Wooles. **1577** HARRISON *England* II. v. (1877) I. 134 The fourth and last sort of people..are daie labourers.., and some retailers. **1633** (*title*), A Proclamation restraining the abusive Venting of Tobacco.., that Retailers must take out a License. **1662** PETTY *Taxes* 13 It ought to be known..how many retailers are needful to make the subdistributions. **1704** F. FULLER *Med. Gymn.* (1711) 94 The Female Retailers of Physick would..take it Ill, if..I should forget their Preparations. **1781** GIBBON *Decl. & F.* xvii. (1787) II. 70 The diligent mechanic, and even the most obscure retailer of a sequestered village. **1837** M. DONOVAN *Dom. Econ.* II. 337 The retailers almost invariably roast their coffee too little. **1875** JOWETT *Plato* (ed. 2) III. 30 Retailers sit in the market-place to save the time of the producers.

2. One who repeats or relates.

1707 *Reflex. upon Ridicule* 16 Retailers of Fooleries, Dealers in Scandal. **1749** FIELDING *Tom Jones* XVII. vii, Mrs. Miller..had received a full account from the faithful retailer Partridge. **1815** W. H. IRELAND *Scribbleomania* 150 The catalogue of..retailers of the wonderful. **1874** L. STEPHEN *Hours in Library* (1892) I. x. 346 No one is..so generally unpopular as a clever retailer of gossip.

re'tailing, *vbl. sb.* [f. RETAIL *v.* + -ING¹.] The action of the verb, in various senses.

1365 *Waterford Arch.* in *10th Rep. Hist. MSS. Comm.* App. V. 292 The retailyng or salis of the commene wyne callid prisage. **1592** GREENE *Upst. Courtier* E iv b, You will ..sell them to poore shomakers at an vnreasonable rate, by your false retaylinge. **1609** DEKKER *Gull's Horn-bk.* vi, When your Groundling..buyes his sport by the penny, and ..is glad to vtter it againe by retailing. **1724** in Picton *L'pool Munic. Rec.* (1886) II. 54 That..Hopkins be stopp'd from going on in retailing. **1736** *Gentl. Mag.* VI. 632/1 The Retailing of Punch will be confined to Houses where other strong Liquors are by Licence to be sold. **1951** in M. McLUHAN *Mech. Bride* (1967) 36 The specifications required to reach the goals now in sight for businesses of every description—manufacturing, distributing, retailing, servicing!

re'tailing, *ppl. a.* [-ING².] That retails.

1588 J. MELLIS *Briefe Instr.* F v, All such goods which daily you put to the retailing shoppe. **1593** NASHE *Christ's T.* Wks. (Grosart) IV. 225 Any of these shee retayling bodie-traffiquers. **1603** STOW *Surv.* (1842) 204/1 Which I may call the keeping of a retailing or standing shop.

re'tailment. [-MENT.] The act of retailing.

1843 F. E. PAGET *Warden of Birkingholt* 121 By morning and evening retailments of all that was going on in the neighbourhood. **1889** H. F. WOOD *Englishman Rue Caïn* xiii, Priority in the retailment of frivolous news.

† **re'tain**, *sb. Obs. rare.* [f. the vb.]

1. Retention; retainment.

1455 *Rolls of Parlt.* V. 307/1 Content and satisfied by waye of retayn of the seid summe. **1621** ELSING *Debates Ho. Lords* (Camden) 99 Reteyn of Stranger.

2. Retinue.

a **1548** HALL *Chron., Hen. VIII*, 81 b, The kynge of Englande..and his retain in sute lyke. *Ibid.* 82 Thus the two kynges & their retaine toke the felde.

retain (rɪˈteɪn), *v.* Forms: 5–6 reteign(e, (5 reteyign); 5 reteyene, 5–7 reteyn(e; 5–7 reteine, 7 retein; 5–7 retayn, 6–7 retaine, 6– retain; 5 retenne, retene (6 *Sc.*), retine (7 *Sc.*), 6 reteane. [ad. OF. *retenir* (= Sp. *retener*, It. *ritenere*, L. *retinēre*), f. *re-* RE- and *tenir* to hold. For the vowel of the stem cf. *contain*, *detain*, etc.]

I. *trans.* †**1. a.** To restrain; to hold back, check, or stop; to prevent or hinder. *Obs.*

c **1386** CHAUCER *Melib.* ¶ 46 (Lands. MS.), þere bue mony þinges þat shold reteyne ȝowe of vengeance takeinge. *c* **1477** CAXTON *Jason* 8 Whan..hercules and..Jason had retayned the Centaurs, they had eche of them a bowe whiche they bende. **1481** —— *Godf.* xlviii. 88 They armed them and reteyned theyr peple that began to flee. *a* **1548** HALL *Chron., Hen. VIII*, 101 b, He is bound that he should neuer retayne the Swyches from the Emperor. **1594** PARSONS *Confer. Success.* II. ii. 10 It is hard to retayne a mans consent from that which is said vntil he haue read the reasons of the other party. **1639** S. DU VERGER tr. *Camus' Admir. Events* 279 Barsimee retained by a certaine shamefastnesse..would by no meanes yeeld to marry. **1695** TEMPLE *Introd. Hist. Eng.* (1699) 287 He..had killed him if his Brother Robert had not retained him. **1737** *Gentl. Mag.* VII. 35/1 The untouchable foot retain'd the grave Spaniards from intermedling in so delicate an Affair.

b. *refl.* To restrain or contain (oneself). *rare.*

c **1440** *Generydes* 1543 For your wurchippe yow most your self reteyne, And take a good avise in this mater. **1869** *Daily News* 30 Oct., Lord Stanley, who retained himself during the greater part of the service, was completely overcome.

c. To keep in custody or under control; to prevent from departing, issuing, or separating; to hold fixed in some place or position.

a **1533** LD. BERNERS *Huon* lxix. 237 My brother and his wyf..I haue retayned them in my pryson. *c* **1550** RHODES *Bk. Nurture* 740 in *Babees Bk.* 102 For empty fystes, men vse to say, cannot the Hawke retayne. **1599** B. JONSON *Ev. Man out of Hum.* III. i, I can make this Dog take as many Whiffes as I list, and he shall retain, or effume them, at my pleasure. **1617** MORYSON *Itin.* I. 51 On this and the East sides, are two Mils to retaine the water when the Sea ebs. **1674** BREVINT *Saul at Endor* 223 May not one as well curse, whom God blesses, as retain or bind whom God remits? **1720** OZELL *Vertot's Rom. Rep.* II. XII. 242 Cicero..sends immediately certain Senators, to retain the People in their Duty. **1809** A. HENRY *Trav.* 123 The skin, which alone retained his hand to his arm, he cut through. **1853** KANE *Grinnell Exp.* xliii. (1856) 400 It acted like a camel, retaining the brig's stern high in the air. **1873** G. FLEMING *Pract. Horse-shoeing* (ed. 2) 100 The extra strain on the nails retaining it [the bar shoe] to the hoof.

absol. **1634** J. LEVETT *Ordering of Bees* 59 They haue no Intraylls or other inward Organs, by which either to retaine or evacuat.

d. To keep free *from* something. *rare*⁻¹.

1863 COWDEN CLARKE *Shaks. Char.* viii. 197 He has retained the two women from the remotest charge of unfeminity.

2. †**a.** To entertain. *Obs. rare.*

c **1400** *Destr. Troy* 10936 The grekes fayne of þat freike.. Retaynit hym with Reuerence. **1447** BOKENHAM *Seyntys*

(Roxb.) 33 A relygyous place..wher wurshepfully Austyn was reteynyd and cherytabylly. c1550 RHODES Bk. Nurture 745 in Babees Bk. 102 Retayne a stranger after his estate and degree. 1575–85 ABP. SANDYS Serm. xi. 235 God is woont euer to blesse the countrie, for reteining and releeuing godlie religious strangers.

b. To keep attached to one's person or engaged in one's service. ***retain-and-transfer*** attrib. phr., in *Association Football* (see quot. 1965).

1450 Rolls of Parlt. V. 178/2 The said Duke..beyng reteigned with you, in your wages of werre in your seid Reame. 1489 CAXTON Faytes of A. III. viii. 182, I suppose that a capytayne with a companye of folke be reteyned in to the kynges wages. 1536 CROMWELL in Merriman Life & Lett. (1902) II. 38 The kinges pleasour is ye shal there reteyne onely foure clerkes. 1545 BRINKLOW Compl. 37b, Many noble men..retayne seruantys & neuer gyue them peny wages. 1623 T. POWELL Attourn. Acad. 123 If this bee done with a single Vowcher, you are to retaine three Sergeants. 1698 FRYER Acc. E. India & P. 376 The Suffee retains several [physicians] in Ordinary and others in Extraordinary. 1761 HUME Hist. Eng. viii. I. 168 A great number of knights were retained in his service. 1882 PEBODY Eng. Journalism xix. 145 Mr. Levy..retained as contributors and critics men who were at least equal to those upon the staff of either of its contemporaries. 1938 C. E. SUTCLIFFE et al. Story of Football League xiii. 120 A result which had completely vindicated the retain and transfer system and declared it to be legal. 1965 Listener 1 July 17/1 A 'retain and transfer' system... A player employed by a club could be 'retained' after the expiration of his contract of employment. No other club was then allowed to employ him, although his own club had no obligation to re-employ him. He could also be placed on a 'transfer' list, which signified that his club was willing to transfer him for a specified fee, only a small portion of which went to the player himself. 1974 Scholarly Publishing V. 235 The Times New Roman Type..was unacceptable, and consultants had to be retained to redesign it.

absol. 1540 CROMWELL in Merriman Life & Lett. (1902) II. 267 Syr ther was also layde vnto my Charge at myne examenacyon that I hadde retaynyd contrarye to your lawse.

†**c.** To engage, hire. *Obs. rare*$^{-1}$.

1476 Procl. in York Myst. Introd. p. xxxvii, þat no plaier..be conducte and reteyned to plaie but twise on þe day of þe saide playe. 1687 A. LOVELL tr. Thevenot's Trav. I. 161 Having retained Mules for myself and Company, I made Provisions of Bread, Wine [etc.].

d. To engage (a barrister) by the payment of a preliminary fee, in order to secure his services for one's own cause if necessary.

1548 ELYOT, Cliens..is also he whiche hath retayned a lawyer to susteyne his matter. 1550 CROWLEY Last Trumpet 922 Whye wylt thou be retained of playntyfe, or of defendaunt? 1602 2nd Pt. Return fr. Parnass. IV. ii, Let me retaine you this terme for my cause. 1644 BULWER Chiron. 52 In those large pewes, where those that were retained in causes did plead. 1775 J. RAYNER Readings on Statutes 116 If the Matter was communicated to the Attorney or Solicitor, as a Secret, before he was employed or retained in the Cause. 1837 DICKENS Pickw. xxxi, 'Mr. Pickwick is the defendant in Bardwell and Pickwick, Serjeant Snubbin,' said Perker. 'I am retained in that, am I?' said the Serjeant. 1892 Pall Mall G. 4 July 2/2 The erroneous impression that the retaining of a barrister consists mainly in the retention of the fee by the barrister retained.

transf. 1863 Sat. Rev. 2 May, The Neapolitan bishops..may occasionally be ashamed,..since the fall of the hateful power which they were retained to support.

3. a. To keep hold or possession of; to continue having or keeping, in various senses.

c1450 Godstow Reg. 337 þat he sholde haue power to distreine hem in all þe maners a-fore-seide & holde or reteine þe distreininge. 1490 Plumpton Corr. (Camden) 102 To deliver one parte to Mr. Blount, & retine another parte for you with the obligation. a1542 WYATT in Tottel's Misc. (Arb.) 55 My loue to skorne, my seruice to retayne, Therein (me thought) you vsed crueltie. 1583 STUBBES Anat. Abus. II. (1882) 95 [He] will yet not withstanding reteane the same charge and function to himself still. 1596 SPENSER F.Q. IV. x. 10 Taking downe the shield with me [I] did it retaine. 1622 J. REYNOLDS God's Revenge I. 12 Retayning a fine little white Frizland dogge, which his Page had stolne from her. 1667 MILTON P.L. x. 532 His Power no less he seem'd Above the rest still to retain. 1766 BLACKSTONE Comm. II. xxxii. 511 The executor..is allowed to pay himself first; by retaining in his hands so much as his debt amounts to. 1825 COBBETT Rur. Rides 469 It seems to me to absorb and to retain the water. 1841 MISS MITFORD in L'Estrange Life (1870) III. 115 Lord Sidmouth retains his unmarried daughter. 1877 FROUDE Short Stud. (1883) IV. 27 He still aimed at retaining the most lucrative of his benefices.

absol. 1766 BLACKSTONE Comm. II. 511 An executor of his own wrong is not allowed to retain. 1847 MRS. A. KERR tr. Ranke's Hist. Servia 288 Some men are more competent to acquire than to retain.

b. In renderings or echoes of John xx. 23 (ἄν τινων κρατῆτε, κεκράτηνται; *quorum retinueritis, retenta sunt*).

1526 TINDALE John xx. 23. 1567 Gude & Godlie B. (S.T.S.) 7 Quhais sinnis ȝe reteine, ar retenit vnto thame. 1606 BP. HALL Medit. & Vows 121, I will so remit wrongs,..and so reteine them, as I may not induce God to reteine mine to him. 1651 HOBBES Leviath. III. xlii. 277 Refuse entrance into his Kingdom, to those whose Sins were Retained. 1674 BREVINT Saul at Endor 222 Where the power of Loosing and Remitting, follows close to that of Retaining and Binding.

c. To continue to use, practise, recognize, etc.

1548–9 (Mar.) Bk. Com. Prayer, Offices 35b, Some [ceremonies] be retayned and kept still. 1596 DRAYTON Legends iii. 385 When the Barons found me to retayne Th'ambitious course wherein I first began. c1613 ROWLANDS More Knaues Yet? 5, I thinke before the Conquest many yeares, We wore the fashion which we still retaine. 1654 BRAMHALL Just Vind. ii. (1661) 7 Yet both retein Communion with the universal Church. 1737 Gentl. Mag. VII. 142/1 We have good Reason to exclude the 330 Kings..and retain only those who have left standing Monuments. 1855 PUSEY Doctr. Real Presence (1857) ii. 174 The Eastern Liturgies still for the most part retain the form of asserting the Real Presence. 1875 JOWETT Plato (ed. 2) IV. 224 It seemed better..to retain the order in which Plato himself has arranged this and the two companion dialogues.

d. To continue to have or possess (some attribute, quality, etc.).

1582 N. LICHEFIELD tr. Castanheda's Conq. E. Ind. 1b, He gaue to the Ports..theyr names, which at this present they doe retaine. 1634 MILTON Comus 842 Still she retains Her maid'n gentlenes. 1687 A. LOVELL tr. Thevenot's Trav. I. 10 A kind of Stone that long retains its whiteness. 1756 C. LUCAS Ess. Waters I. Pref., Shall we borrow and retain the faults, the corruptions of the French? 1799 SHERIDAN Pizarro II. iv, Oh, had I still retained my sight, I might now have grasped a sword. 1841 D'ISRAELI Amen. Lit. (1867) 64 The hills, the forests, and the rivers retain their old Celtic names. 1871 B. STEWART Heat (ed. 2) §12 They always retain unchanged their state with respect to heat.

e. To allow to remain, in place of discarding or removing; to preserve.

1802 SCOTT Let. in Lockhart (1837) I. xi. 357 Many of the old words are retained, which neither the reciter nor the copyer understood. 1835 LYTTON Rienzi II. i, But still to this day are retained the massive walls.

4. To keep or bear in mind; to remember.

1474 CAXTON Chesse 159 Longe talis & historyes whiche they can not al reteyne in her mynde. c1500 Melusine 38 Now vnderstand & reteyne wel my wordes. 1509 HAWES Past. Pleas. II. 13 If you wyl do as I shall you saye, And all my lesson retayne in memory. 1613 PURCHAS Pilgrimage I. vii. (1614) 40 The people haue retained the tradition hereof [the flood]. 1666 Act 18 & 19 Chas. II, c. 8 §26 That the said Citizens..may retaine the Memoriall of soe sadd a Desolation. 1697 DRYDEN Virg. Past. IX. 62 The Tune I still retain, but not the Words. 1731–8 SWIFT Polite Conv. Introd. 78 With what Attention I listened to all their Discourses, the better to retain them in my Memory. 1782 PRIESTLEY Corrupt. Chr. I. I. 113 It requires a pretty good memory to retain these distinctions. 1812 J. WILSON Isle of Palms I. 322 In waking thoughts she still retains The memory of these wildering pains. 1883 WACE Gospel & Witnesses iv. 85 The mind..unable to retain any but the simplest thought.

absol. 1581 MULCASTER Positions v. (1887) 27 That witte maie conceiue and learne well, memorie retaine and hold fast. 1748 GRAY Alliance 30 With Sense to feel, with Mem'ry to retain. 1784 COWPER Tiroc. 524 A well-constructed brain, Keen in pursuit, and vig'rous to retain. 1910 E. B. TITCHENER Textbk. Psychol. II. 405 The quick learner appears to retain as well as the slow. 1932 New Yorker 23 July 17/3 Prior to 1882, even a boy who didn't retain very well could make a kite out of two or three sticks.

II. *intr.* **5.** To refrain *from* something.

1536 BELLENDEN Cron. Scot. (1821) I. 102 Vespasian..had sic compassion, that he micht not retene fra teris. 1602 MARSTON Antonio's Rev. v. i, They can scarce retaine from bursting foorth In plaine revolt.

†**6.** To adhere, belong, be attached, or be a retainer *to* one. Also *transf.* *Obs.*

1548 ELYOT, Cliens, is he that belongeth or reteyneth to som man in authoritee, to haue his defence and assistence in honest causes. 1548 UDALL, etc. Erasm. Par. Acts 48b, He was reteynyng to Sergius Paulus, whiche was proconsull. a1591 H. SMITH Serm. (1637) 156 As many retaine unto Noblemen, not to doe them any service, but to have their countenance. 1612 DRAYTON Poly-olb. viii. 440 Those other Rils to Seuerne which retaine, And tended not on Teame. 1646 SIR T. BROWNE Pseud. Ep. 42 Not only the Sadduces and such as retaine unto the Church of God. 1681 NEVILE Plato Rediv. 135 Most of the Members..thought it an honour to retain to some great Lord, and to wear his blew Coat. 1711 SHAFTESB. Charac. (1737) I. 320 Idea! wait a while till I have examin'd thee, whence thou art, and to whom thou retain'st. Art thou of ambition's train?

†**7.** To continue, remain. *Obs. rare*$^{-1}$.

a1631 DONNE Ep. C'tess Huntingdon 109 No more can impure man retain and move In that pure region of a worthy love.

retaina'bility. [See next and -ITY.] Capability of being retained.

1855 BAIN Senses & Int. III. i. §81 We have generally understood the retainability of an impression to mean the power of recalling it at any future time.

re'tainable, *a.* [f. RETAIN *v.* + -ABLE.] Capable of being retained.

1706 in PHILLIPS (ed. Kersey). 1806 W. TAYLOR in Ann. Rev. IV. 257 Half the enterprizes of our antijacobin ministers..would only serve to restrict the French within retainable limits. 1836–41 BRANDE Chem. (ed. 5) 526 The box is..made retainable together by two obliquely grooved holders. 1889 Dublin Rev. Jan. 190 Their collection in this retainable form will be welcomed.

Hence **re'tainableness.**

1831 BENTHAM Ess. on Lang. Wks. 1843 VIII. 305 Conciseness is, in many instances, contributory to..retainableness.

re'tainal. [f. RETAIN *v.* + -AL[1].] Retention.

1804 W. TAYLOR in Ann. Rev. II. 631 A discussion..of the claims of each to retainal or dismissal. 1807 Ibid. V. 201 In their retainal of the militia.

†**re'tainder.** *Obs.* Forms: 5 retein-, 5–6 reteyndre; 5 reteign-, reteyndour; 5–6 reteyn-, 6 retayn-, 7 retainder. [f. RETAIN *v.*, app. on the analogy of *attainder*, *remainder*. Cf. RETAINER[1].]

1. Retention. (Cf. RETAINER[1] 1.)

1467–8 Rolls of Parlt. V. 616/1 Reteindre and perceyvyng of Custumes and Subsidies. 1473 Ibid. VI. 91/2 Any Graunte.., Ratifications, Confirmations or Reteyndres of any Dette or Duetie. 1503 Ibid. 523/1 Endentures to be made of all suche reteynders, receyvyngs and perceyvyngs.

2. A token of retainership.

1472 Cov. Leet Bk. lf. 215 That noo Reteindres, lyuerees, signes ne tokenys of clothing,..be taken, had nor vsed by thinhabitauntes of our Citie. 1474 Ibid. lf. 222, I schall..forbere to yeve, take or resceyve any lyueree, reteigndour or cognesaunce. 1529 Act 21 Hen. VIII, c. 20 Unlawfull mayntenaunces, gyvyng of lyvereys, signes, tokens, and retaynders. 1651 N. BACON Disc. Govt. Eng. II. xxxi. (1739) 142 Matters concerning Maintenance, Liveries, Retainders.

3. = RETAINER[1] 2.

1494 FABYAN Chron. VII. 626 Temporall lordes, in those dayes, kept other maner of housholdes and other maner of reteyndour of housholde seruauntes. 1545 State Papers Hen. VIII (1836) V. IV. 408 Charging all the saide tenauntes..in no wise to agre to anye suche reteynder with anye other mane.

Hence †**re'taindership.** *Obs. rare*$^{-1}$.

1651 N. BACON Disc. Govt. Eng. II. xxxi. (1739) 143 Yet was it the policy of these Kings to make them all of their own Livery and Retaindership.

retained (rɪ'teɪnd), *ppl. a.* [f. RETAIN *v.*]

1. Restrained; kept back or in check.

1597 A. M. tr. Guillemeau's Fr. Chirurg. 32b/2 When we desire to provoacke the retayned and kept backe menstruosityes. 1651 tr. De-las-Coveras' Don Fenise 63 What astonishment was it to those, who had before seen her in her retained course of life. a1684 LEIGHTON Comm. 1 Pet. Wks. 1857 II. 479 Persons that..have not that holy, retained, bridled way of using their repast. 1876 T. HARDY Ethelberta (1890) 186 With her eyes over-full of retained tears.

2. Kept on; preserved. ***retained object***, an object of a passive verb; ***retained profit*** (see quot. 1974).

1861 M. ARNOLD Pop. Educ. France 204 Great eagerness was manifested to be nominated one of these retained scholars. 1875 WHITNEY Life Lang. iv. 55 The alteration of the retained elements of words. 1934 WEBSTER, Retained object. 1941 FOERSTER & STEADMAN Writing & Thinking (rev. ed.) xvi. 153 A verb in the passive voice is transitive only if it has a retained object. 1961 R. B. LONG Sentence & its Parts 504 Normal complements of passive-verb-form predicators are sometimes called 'retained objects'. An example is the *time* of *we weren't given time*. 1973 Country Life 29 Nov. (Suppl.) 9 (Advt.), Wanted for a retained client A period residence... Price is immaterial. 1974 Terminol. Managem. & Financial Accountancy (Inst. Cost and Managem. Accountants) 68 Retained profits, profits retained in the business, and not distributed to the owners/shareholders. 1977 Cleethorpes News 6 May 32/6 There are unlikely to be any surprises in Grimsby Town's retained list, which is due out today.

retainer[1] (rɪ'teɪnə(r)). Forms: 5 reteignour, 6 reteynour(e; 5 reteigner, reteyner, 7 reteiner, 7– retainer. [f. RETAIN *v.* + -ER[4]. Cf. RETAINDER.]

1. The act or fact of retaining, withholding, or keeping for oneself; an authorization to do this. Now *rare*. (Cf. RETAINDER 1.)

1453 Rolls of Parlt. V. 235/2 Eny Assignement, Graunte or Reteignour made..to eny persone..uppon the seid xvme..for money lent. 1472–3 Ibid. VI. 60/1 The same Letters Patentes, as to the reteyner, havyng, and perceyvyng of Custumes. 1642 tr. Perkins' Prof. Bk. v. §303. 134 The woman shall be endowed of the third part of the rent by way of retainer. 1768 BLACKSTONE Comm. III. 18 The one [instance being] that of retainer, where a creditor is made executor or administrator to his debtor. Ibid. IV. Index, Retainer of servant by another. 1846 BATEMAN Law Auctions (ed. 3) 270 There was no averment that..the goods were put up to sale at the request of the defendant or on his retainer, and that there was no retainer shewn at the time of the request to put up the goods to sale.

2. †**a.** Engagement of a person as a servant or for some other office. *Obs.*

1467–8 Rolls of Parlt. V. 633/2 Every Reteyner by Indenture or other writyng..of eny persone..other then to be menyall Servaunt. 1641 Termes de la Ley 8b, The reteiner of those two Chaplaines remaineth, and they without new reteiner may take two Benefices. 1642 tr. Perkins' Prof. Bk. xi. §615. 311 The retainer of a servant according unto the Statute of Labores upon condition is good without deed.

†**b.** Entertainment or maintenance of dependents or adherents. *Obs.*

1503–4 Act 19 Hen. VII, c. 14 §1 That all his statutes..made ayenst such as make unlaufull reteynours and such as so be reteyned..be pleynly observed. a1548 HALL Chron., Rich. III 39 Wilde Weleshmen, whome he..had rather..compelled by lordely and streite commaundemente then by liberall wages and gentle reteynoure.

c. The fact of being retained in some capacity.

1775 J. RAYNER Readings on Statutes 116 The meaning of 'before Retainer', must be that such Discovery..is..not within the Rule of Secrecy. 1781 ATKYNS Reports Cases in Chancery II. 525 note, It appearing that this discovery..had been made before the retainer of him as solicitor, the court were of opinion that he might be sworn. 1848 ARNOULD Marine Insur. I. iv. (1866) I. 156 The giving of such notice was part of the common law duty of the defendants, to be implied from their retainer as Commission Agents.

d. An authorization given to an attorney to act in a case. Chiefly *U.S.*

1816 CHITTY Suppl. Treat. Pleading 166 The declaration may commence with the statement of the defendant's retainer. 1856 BOUVIER Law Dict. (ed. 6) II. 472/1 Although it is not indispensable that the retainer should be in writing,..it is very expedient. 1874 ABBOTT U.S. Digest (Ser. 1) II. 340/1 A mere parol retainer is sufficient to authorize an attorney to commence a suit.

attrib. 1836 CHITTY Practice of the Law III. I. 117 Since the Stamp Duty on the Warrant has been repealed, no retainer fee is allowed.

3. a. A fee paid to a barrister to secure his services; engagement by a retaining-fee.

1818 BYRON Juan I. xv. note, After taking my retainer, he went over to them. 1841 Penny Cycl. XXI. 272/1 A retainer, if for a particular cause, and for a particular stage of that cause, is called a common retainer, and it now consists in the payment of the sum of one guinea. **1869** *Daily News* 6 July, A general retainer gives to the person who so retains a counsel the right to a refusal of his services. **1892** *Pall Mall G.* 4 July 2/2 The new rules for regulating the practice of counsel as to retainers.

transf. **1778** S. Foote *Trip to Calais* III. 78 As you gave me a handsome retainer, I have been in court and open'd the cause. **1784** Horne *Lett. Infidelity* xiv. 215 You are men of too much sense..to take a retainer from Simon Magus. **1870** Lowell *Study Wind., Gd. Word Winter*, I happen to hold Winter's retainer this time. **1890** *John Bull* 5 Apr. 220/2 He has been extolled by authors holding no retainer as biographers.

b. A sum paid to secure special services if required. Also in extended uses. Cf. *retaining fee* s.v. retaining *ppl. a.* 2.

a **1859** Macaulay *Hist. Eng.* xxiii. V. 25 The House resolved to grant half-pay to the disbanded officers... The half-pay was meant to be a retainer as well as a reward. **1891** N. Gould *Double Event* 111 I'm paying you a big retainer for the Melbourne events. **1975** O. Sela *Bengali Inheritance* vi. 46 'What are you saying? That we should all..take bribes?' 'We all do,' Chan said. 'We're all on retainers.' The retainer was the monthly share out, the market price for overlooking petty crimes [among Hong Kong police]. **1977** *Guardian* 13 Jan. 20/3 Richards has signed a contract with a Brisbane radio station which gives him a retainer. **1978** S. Brill *Teamsters* ix. 327 Milano is most probably getting similar retainers from several Teamster locals. **1978** *Lancashire Life* Nov. 76/2 The Clitheroe professional, Peter Geddes, for whom she works as assistant, earning a small retainer in exchange for free lessons, wise advice and a mixture of encouragement and constructive criticism. **1978** M. Puzo *Fools Die* xxvii. 310 Houlinan was Ugo Kellino's personal PR rep with a retainer of fifty grand a year.

retainer² (rɪˈteɪnə(r)). Also 6 reteyn-, retaynour, 6–7 reteyner, 7 -tayner, -teiner. [f. retain *v.* + -er¹ (and -or 2).]

1. a. One who or that which retains or holds; a maintainer, preserver.

1548 Elyot, *Clientellaris*, the homage that the clientes make to theyr reteynours. **1583** Babington *Commandm.* 329 To see that they bringe not sinne vpon them, by making them vniust retainers of other mens goods. **1616** Surfl. & Markh. *Country Farme* vii. xxii. 679 It is to be vnderstood, that it is hard to haue one spannell..to be an excellent raunger, an excellent finder, and an excellent retainer. **1693** [see retention 3]. **1704** Swift *T. Tub* ix, One that has forgot the common Meaning of Words, but an admirable Retainer of the Sound. **1825** *New Monthly Mag.* XIV. 517 The inciter to mirth, yet the retainer of order. **1855** *Jrnl. R. Agric. Soc.* XVI. i. 179 Limestone soils..are bad retainers of water. **1882** *Pall Mall G.* 24 July 2/1 The arbitrator is to impose what conditions he thinks fit on the retainer of enclosures.

b. *Dentistry.* A structure cemented to a tooth and connected to a bridge to hold it in place.

1887 S. H. Guilford in W. F. Litch *Amer. Syst. Dentistry* II. ii. 323 These little fixtures can be used as retainers with perfect success and to the exclusion of a more bulky plate. **1956, 1974** [see pontic *a.*² B]. **1976** Torres & Ehrlich *Mod. Dental Assisting* xxvi. 797/1 The components of fixed bridgework are the pontics, the retainers and the connectors.

2. a. A dependent or follower of some person of rank or position; one attached to a house, or owing it service. Now only *Hist.* or *arch.*

'Retainer..signifieth in the common law, a seruant not meniall nor familiar, that is not continually dwelling in the house of his Lord or Master, but onely vsing, or bearing his name or liuery' (Cowell, 1607).

1540 Cromwell in Merriman *Life & Lett.* (1902) II. 267, I resayuyd thayr Chyldren and Freendes not as Retaynours. **1570** Levins *Manip.* 80 A Reteyner, *cliens.* **1598** Florio *Dict.* Ep. Ded. 4 The retainer doth some seruice, that now and then but holds your Honors styrrop. **1606** Dekker *Newes fr. Hell* Wks. (Grosart) II. 123 The great Lord of Tartary will shortly haue no roome for all his retayners. **1607** Hieron *Wks.* I. 337 Retayners..are willing to belong to a gentleman, but yet it is but for their owne priuate aduantage. **1712** Swift *Let. Eng. Tongue* iv. Wks. 1755 II. i. 184 Harry the Second..was always attended with a number of his countrymen, retainers at his court. **1759** Robertson *Hist. Scot.* vi. Wks. 1813 I. 439 This design was revealed to the two earls by one of Morton's retainers. **1815** Elphinstone *Acc. Caubul* (1842) I. 332 None have resided there but great men and their retainers, who are drawn thither by the court. **1865** Dickens *Mut. Fr.* i. v, He..was one of the house's retainers and owed vassalage to it. **1878** Stubbs *Const. Hist.* III. xxi. 551 A swarm of armed retainers whom the lord could not control, and whom he conceived himself bound to protect.

b. *transf.* or *fig.* Also const. *to.*

1613 Shaks. *Hen. VIII*, ii. iv. 113 Where Powres are your Retainers, and your words (Domesticks to you) serue your will. **1651** Baxter *Inf. Bapt.* 25 All Church-members are Christians, that is, retainers to Christ. **1705** Addison *Italy* 207 It is incredible how great a Multitude of Retainers to the Law there are at Naples. **1757** Foote *Author* i. Wks. 1799 I. 133, I, like you, have long been a retainer of the muses, as you may see by their livery. **1831** Lamb *Elia* ii. *Newspapers 35 yrs. ago*, In those days every Morning Paper, as an essential retainer to its establishment, kept an author, who [etc.]. **1864** C. Geikie *Life in Woods* vi. (1874) 118 For the benefit of our fourfooted retainers.

c. *U.S.* A person irregularly attached to an army; a sutler, camp-follower. (*Cent. Dict.*)

reˈtainership. [f. prec. + -ship.] The state or position of being a retainer; the system of having retainers.

1570 Levins *Manip.* 141 A Reteynership, *clientela.* **1855** Milman *Lat. Chr.* viii. viii. (1864) V. 31 His household was on a scale vast even for that age of unbounded retainership. **1868** *Daily Tel.* 7 Sept., With the farce of retainership, the Highland 'gatherings' are an insult to manhood.

reˈtaining, *vbl. sb.* [f. retain *v.* + -ing¹.] The action of the verb, in various senses.

c **1450** *Godstow Reg.* 257 Without ony reteynyng or withholdyng-agayn to hym or to his heires. **1472–3** *Rolls of Parlt.* VI. 49/2 Tyll by reteignyng of the same rent..he or they..be contented. *c* **1500** in I. S. Leadam *Star Chamber Cas.* (1903) 97 He neyther can ne may defende them..bycause of the saide reteynyng in warde. *a* **1568** Ascham *Scholem.* ii. (Arb.) 88 Here his witte shalbe new set on worke:..his memorie, for sure reteyning, better exercised. **1638** Baker tr. *Balzac's Lett.* (vol. II.) 37 Italian examples of being captious and retaining of spleene. **1726** Leoni *Alberti's Archit.* II. 104/2 A kind of vessel ready prepared for the retaining of water. **1892** [see retain *v.* 2 d].

reˈtaining, *ppl. a.* [-ing².] That retains.

1. Serving to retain or hold by physical force or resistance; esp. ***retaining wall***, a wall built to support a mass of earth or water.

1611 Cotgr., *La Retentive*, the retaining force of nature whereby food is held in the stomacke. **1827** Steuart *Planter's G.* (1828) 285 Forming a sort of circular Retaining-bank. **1838** *Civil Eng. & Arch. Jrnl.* I. 380/2 In the backing of retaining-walls..it may in many cases be advantageously applied. **1884** Knight *Dict. Mech.* Suppl. 753/2 *Retaining Ring* (Railway), a metallic ring which secures the wheel-center to the tire. *Ibid.*, A retaining valve.

2. *retaining fee*, = retainer¹ 3. Also *bribe.*

1694 Congreve *Double Dealer* ii. vii, While I plead for you, your aunt has given me a retaining fee. **1709** Mrs. Centlivre *Gamester* i. i, I find Dorante, my master's Uncle, has given you a retaining fee. **1727** Pope & Gay *What passed in London* Swift's Wks. 1751 VI. 272 Imagining a Pension was only an annual retaining Bribe. **1802** Mrs. E. Parsons *Myst. Visit* I. 27 A note of twenty pounds, received as a retaining fee. **1884** *Illustr. Lond. News* 1 Oct. 410/3 Besides all this, there are 'retaining fees' and presents.

retainment (rɪˈteɪnmənt). Also 5 retene-, reteign-, 6 reteygne-, retayne-, 7 reteine-. [f. retain *v.* + -ment.] The (*or* an) act of retaining; retention; †entertainment, maintenance.

1432–50 tr. *Higden* (Rolls) VIII. 456 Brennynge mony ryalle maners..and places of the retenement of the duke of Lancastre. **1449** *Rolls of Parlt.* V. 151/1 Such takyng or takynges, recettements, abettementes or reteignementes..shuld be adjugged grete Treson. **1548** Geste *Pr. Masse* 139 Lesse we through reteygnemente and usage therof be occasioned to resume..the sayd bishop. **1595** Daniel *Civ. Wars* iv. lxiv, Though hee had those inforcements of expence Both for offence, retaynements, and defence. **1610** Heywood *Gold. Age* iv. i, It breeds such feare in me, That makes this thy reteinement. **1659** H. More *Immort. Soul* iii. xi. §3 (1713) 207 The Retainment of the same Name which the deceased had here, unless there be some special reason to change it. **1842** G. S. Faber *Prov. Lett.* (1844) I. 230 Correctly insisting upon the Romish Retainment of the great Catholic Articles of Faith.

reˈtake (riː-), *v.* [re- 5 a.]

1. *trans.* To take again; to take back. Cf. retake *sb.*

1436 [see retaking]. *a* **1586** C'tess Pembroke *Ps.* lx. i, O God be reconcil'd, Our leading now retake. **1609** J. Davies *Holy Roode* D 2, Wilt haue those Soules which thou in vs didst settle? Retake them as thine owne. **1647** Clarendon *Hist. Reb.* iv. §50 A day should be appointed,..and the Remonstrance to be then retaken into consideration. **1681** Belon *New Myst. Physic* 68 Thus the Remedy being retaken, after some time of rest, makes a greater Impression. **1721** Bradley *Philos. Acc. Wks. Nat.* 79 They retook the Blue Colour they had at first. **1782** Miss Burney *Cecilia* ix. v, The expectations she had crushed, retook possession of her heart. **1814** Jane Austen *Mansf. Park* vi, She retook her chosen place at the bottom of the table. **1885** *Law Times Rep.* LII. 876/2 It is not a declaration that the vendor intends to retake possession. **1929** H. L. Witwer *Yes Man's Land* xii. 304 This here's no quickie and I can't retake all that stuff and do business. **1972** [see retake *sb.* 1 a]. **1973** 'D. Halliday' *Dolly & Starry Bird* vi. 82 You have to retake all those pictures this morning. **1977** C. Dexter *Silent World N. Quinn* vii. 67 She's re-taking a few O-levels.

2. To recapture.

1645 Whitelocke *Mem.* 13 Aug., Major-general Langhere..retook Haverfordwest. **1686** Plot *Staffordsh.* 274 Who retook the Standard of Guyen.., lost to the French in a fierce charge. **1724** Richers *Hist. Royal Geneal. Spain* 186 Gibraltar, which the Christians endeavour'd afterwards ineffectually to retake. *a* **1732** Swift *William II* Wks. 1768 IV. 256 The king..retook his prisoner, and..sent him into Normandy. **1822** Lamb *Elia* ii. *Confessions of a Drunkard*, The devil could not have devised a more subtle trap to retake a backsliding penitent. **1884** *Spectator* 4 Oct. 1286/1 The siege had been raised and Berber retaken.

absol. **1766** Burrow *Rep.* II. 689 Our Ships of War..cruise, in order to re-take, as well as to take.

3. *absol.* To take in return.

1847 Staunton *Chess Player's Handbk.* 203 If..he take the B. with Kt., you retake with your Q.

4. *absol.* To take a second time, take over again.

1962 A. Nisbett *Technique Sound Studio* vi. 115 Discreetly discourage phrases such as 'as I've just said', and retake if they are not cleanly editable. **1977** *Horse & Hound* 14 Jan. 43/2 (Advt.), Next intensive one month or week's preparation course for A1 (suitable for those retaking) in April.

Hence **reˈtaken** *ppl. a.*

1692 *Lond. Gaz.* No. 2793/4 Yesterday came into this Port the Deptford Frigat from Falmouth, with a re-taken Merchant-man. **1710** *Ibid.* No. 4702/3 The third [is] a retaken Virginia Ship. **1769** Falconer *Dict. Marine* (1780), *Reprise*, a retaken ship.

retake (ˈriː-), *sb.* [f. the vb.] **1. a.** The action of filming a scene, person, or object again; the picture or the scene obtained thus. Also *attrib.*

1918 H. Croy *How Motion Pictures are Made* v. 126 Directly on finishing the scene it is filmed again, the second exposure being called a 'retake'. **1919** H. L. Wilson *Ma Pettengill* ii. 67 Only one little retake, where she's happy over her boy's promotion in the factory. **1930** [see can *sb.*¹ 3 c]. **1938** 'E. Queen' *Four of Hearts* iv. 52 Corsi's the most finicky retake artist in pictures. **1941** G. Marx *Let.* 23 June (1967) 27 Here I am on Stage 18 waiting to shoot some retakes. **1960** *Guardian* 12 Dec. 6/2 There's so much to go wrong, the cameras jamming, the lens sticking, and no retakes [in television]. **1972** D. Francis *Smokescreen* i. 9, I couldn't stand many more retakes of Scene 623... We had retaken it six times.

b. The action of recording music, etc., again.

1962 A. Nisbett *Technique Sound Studio* vi. 115 Music retakes should be recorded as soon as possible after the original. **1963** V. Gielgud in *Times* 22 Apr. 16/7 A certain perfectionism is possible in tape recording, but I feel that something is wrong if I personally have to go back and do retakes. **1973** 'J. Marks' *Mick Jagger* (1974) 88 They suggested the use of their own studios for a retake of the same tune.

c. *fig.*

1937 *Sun* (Baltimore) 14 May 21/2 In motion-picture parlance, the Preakness at Pimlico Saturday will be a retake of the Kentucky Derby. **1959** *Punch* 20 May 686/2 She took a quick retake at the title, and..tried to stuff it..inside her blouse.

2. *gen.* The action of taking something a second time.

1939 *Sun* (Baltimore) 17 Feb. 1/8 The purpose of repeating the testimony was to get a record which is to be made public... Senator Sheppard..announced, however, that the re-take of testimony was 'practically concluded'. **1977** C. Dexter *Silent World N. Quinn* vi. 56 The morning ..had been fixed for the 'retake' of the Ordinary-level English Language papers. **1977** *Irish Press* 29 Sept. 18/6 McGhee took the spot-kick, but the 'keeper saved his shot, only to see the referee order a retake because the 'keeper had moved before the ball was kicked.

reˈtaker. [f. retake *v.* + -er¹.] One who retakes.

1689 *Treaty* in Magens *Insurances* (1755) II. 473 The Estimation shall be made by the Retaker. **1766** Burrow *Rep.* II. 689 So, the Right of Re-taking, is not personal to the Re-taker, but national, to any Subject of the Re-taker's Nation. **1826** Kent *Comm.* i. v. (1858) I. 119.

reˈtaking, *vbl. sb.* [f. retake *v.* + -ing¹.] The action of the verb; recapture.

1436 Hen. VI in Rymer *Fœdera* X. 635 Touching the Prorogation of the same Trewes, or elles Retakyng of newe. **1611** Florio, *Rappigliatione*, a retaking. **1640** May *Hist. Parl.* i. iv. 38 The first was a re-taking word for word of that old Covenant. **1693** Lyde (*title*), A True..Account of the Retaking a Ship [etc.]. **1766** [see retaker]. **1790** Beatson *Nav. & Mil. Mem.* I. 304 The retaking of Louisburg was their first and grand object. **1853** R. S. Surtees *Sponge's Sp. Tour* xi. 56 The mere retaking of an animal that one has had in hand before.

retaliant (rɪˈtælɪənt), *a. rare.* [ad. late L. *retāliānt-em*, pr. pple. of *retāliāre* to retaliate.] Retaliative.

1925 R. Bridges *S.P.E. Tract* xxi. 13 The universal attitude of Englishmen..naturally enough provoked a similar retaliant feeling in America.

retaliate (rɪˈtælɪeɪt), *v.*¹ [f. ppl. stem of late L. *retāliāre* (Gellius), f. *re-* re- + *tālis* such-like: cf. *tālio, -ōnis* a punishment or penalty similar to the injury done.]

1. *trans.* To requite, repay in kind, make return for: **a.** a kindness, civility, etc. Now *rare.*

1611 Speed *Hist. Gt. Brit.* x. i. §29 Neither lesse was his Maiesties desire to retaliate the Citizens and other his Subiects true affections. **1638** Sir T. Herbert *Trav.* 137 Our Ambassador sent word..to the Dukes son, his visit should be retaliated. **1683** Tryon *Way to Health* 27 They love to retaliate Kindnesses, and hate any should think they are of a churlish nature. **1718** Lawson *Carolina* Ded., I cannot, in the least, pretend to retaliate Your Lordships Favours to me. **1876** Bancroft *Hist. U.S.* II. 199 The Spanjards retaliated the benevolence of Archdale.

b. injury, ill-treatment, etc.

a **1631** Donne *Prohibition* ii, Not that I shalbe mine owne officer, And hate with hate againe retaliate. **1671** [R. MacWard] *True Nonconf.* 38 Thus you have forced me to retaliat your provocation. **1697** Potter *Antiq. Greece* iii. xviii. (1715) 143 They should retaliate the Injuries receiv'd from the Barbarians, by carrying the War into their own Country. **1760** *Chron.* in *Ann. Reg.* 114/1 The Dutch Commodore..resolved to retaliate the supposed injury he had received. **1771** Goldsm. *Hist. Eng.* in *Lett.* (1772) IV. 250 In order to retaliate these hostilities, the Spaniards undertook the siege of Gibraltar. **1817** Jas. Mill *Brit. India* II. iv. v. 200 The native officers..imagined they had now authority for retaliating some of the indignities. **1857** Buckle *Civiliz.* I. xii. 686 They used their abilities to retaliate the injury.

c. Const. *upon* (a person). Also, to inflict in return, to cast back, *upon* (one).

1676 I. Mather *K. Philip's War* (1862) 185 Thus did the Lord..retaliate upon him the innocent blood which he had shed. **1690** Child *Disc. Trade* (1698) 132 May not other Princes account it hard and unreasonable, and consequently retaliate the like upon us? **1788** Gibbon *Decl. & F.* xlix. V. 143 He retaliated on the Avars..the same calamities which they had inflicted on the nations. **1839** James *Louis XIV*, IV. 157 An opportunity..for retaliating the charge of outrageous ambition upon William himself.

†2. To give in return or reply. *Obs. rare*⁻¹.

1634 SIR T. HERBERT *Trav.* 73 This wretch so blazed himself, and in requitall..had no other language retaliated him, saue teares, sighes,..and strange feares.

†**3.** To repay or requite (a person). *Obs. rare.*

1642 R. HARRIS *Sermon* 27 Yea, hee will..retaliate our Adversaries and justify our Cause. **1656** S. H. *Gold. Law* 87 Consider with your selves how you have retaliated me!

4. *intr.* To make return or requital: †**a.** of a kindness, civility, etc. *Obs.*

1658 FRANCK *North. Mem.* (1821) 126 This your kindness obliges me to retaliate with as much piety as becomes a Christian. **1675** TEONGE *Diary* 1 Aug., Our Capt. would not salute the cytty, except they would retaliate. **1691** T. H[ALE] *Acc. New Invent.* p. xii, It comes in my way here to retaliate to him by the just mention [etc.]. **1760–2** GOLDSM. *Cit. W.* lxvi, Well-placed liberality..may load the person obliged with the sense of the duty he lies under to retaliate; this is gratitude.

b. of injury, insult, etc.

1668–9 MARVELL *Corr.* Wks. (Grosart) II. 245 If our act ly heavy upon them, 'tis but reason that they may retaliat. **1736** BUTLER *Anal.* I. iii. Wks. 1874 I. 57 Men..retaliate..under the notion of having received harm. **1771** GOLDSM. *Hist. Eng. in Lett.* (1772) IV. 385 To retaliate for the affront he pretended to have received. **1836** THIRLWALL *Greece* xiv. II. 230 The Æginetans retaliated by the capture of their sacred vessel. **1855** BREWSTER *Newton* II. xv. 70 He was now more anxious to explain his own conduct than to retaliate upon his adversaries. **1875** JOWETT *Plato* (ed. 2) I. 390 Then we ought not to retaliate or render evil for evil to any one.

Hence **re'taliated**, **re'taliating** *ppl. adjs.*

1623 FLETCHER *Reward of Faithf.* Ep. Ded., I am glad your Estates will be alwayes beyond any retaliating kindnesses of mine. **1764** GOLDSM. *Hist. Eng. in Lett.* (1772) I. 208 She treated his passion with retaliated contempt. **1836** J. GILBERT *Chr. Atonem.* iii. (1852) 78 In the act of inflicting such retaliated suffering, a vent is opened for the passions struggling within. **1862** THORNBURY *Turner* I. 271 The 'Liber Studiorum' was begun by Turner in retaliating rivalry of Claude's 'Liber Veritatis'.

†**re'taliate**, *v.*[2] *Obs.*$^{-1}$ *trans.* To retail.

1640 FULLER *Joseph's Coat* viii. 180 Lavishing by wholesale, all honour on one, and scarce Retaliating out any respect to the other.

retaliation (rɪtælɪ'eɪʃən). [See RETALIATE *v.*[1] and -ATION.]

1. The action of retaliating; the return of like for like; repayment in kind; requital, reprisal.

1581 LAMBARDE *Eiren.* I. xii. (1602) 57 The Romanes vsed specially, eight sortes of chastisements,..imprisonment, stripes, retaliation,..and death. **1656** MILTON *Lett. State* Wks. 1851 VIII. 370 If intreaty and fair means will nothing avail,..the severity of Retaliation must take its course. **1692** BENTLEY *Boyle Lect.* i. 29 Contentiousness and Cruelty seldom fail of Retaliation. **1729** BUTLER *Serm.* Wks. 1874 II. 106 If bare retaliation..always begets resentment in the person upon whom we retaliate, what would that excess do? **1771** *Junius Lett.* lxvii. (1788) 341 The just law of retaliation has at last overtaken the little contemptible tyrant. **1815** ELPHINSTONE *Acc. Caubul* (1842) I. 221 Retaliation thus exercised, of course, leads to new disputes. **1858** FROUDE *Hist. Eng.* IV. xviii. 9 Where justice could only be executed by crime, each act of violence provoked fresh retaliation. **1872** YEATS *Growth Comm.* 182 They in 'retaliation' attacked the Indian colonies.

2. An instance of this; a return or requital: **a.** of injuries, etc.

1658 SIR T. BROWNE *Hydriot.* Introd., Sylla.., who having thus served the Body of Marius could not but fear a Retaliation upon his own. **1683** TRYON *Way to Health* 478 We have caused them to be burned as a Sacrifice or Retaliation. **1776** GIBBON *Decl. & F.* xiii. I. 270 A severe retaliation was inflicted. **1847** MRS. A. KERR tr. *Ranke's Hist. Servia* 179 No Servian song commemorates this sanguinary retaliation on the Turks. **1891** ROSEBERY *Pitt* xi. 187 It does not come within the compass of this narrative to describe that insurrection, its massacres and retaliations.

†**b.** of kindness or civility. *Obs.*

c **1645** HOWELL *Lett.* (1650) II. 10, I pray let me injoy it in that fair proportion that I desire to return unto you by way of correspondence and retaliation. **1656** S. HOLLAND *Zara* (1719) 32 *note*, Meaning a retalliation of Love. **1675** COCKER *Morals* 23 He that receives a Courtesie, remains, Till his Retaliation, bound in Chains. **1700** ASTRY tr. *Saavedra-Faxardo* I. 335 'Tis a kind of Avarice to do good in hopes of a Retaliation. **1731–8** SWIFT *Polite Conv.* Introd. 5, I entertained Four of each Sex at my own Lodgings once a Month, by way of Retaliation.

Hence **retali'ationist**, one who advocates retaliation, esp. against tariffs imposed by other countries. Also *attrib.*

1881 *Nation* (N.Y.) XXXII. 381 If the treaty be not concluded soon the retaliationist cry may become too strong to be resisted.

re'taliative, *a.* [See RETALIATE *v.*[1] and -IVE.] Tending to, or of the nature of, retaliation; vindictive, revengeful.

1819 *Metropolis* I. 260 My retaliative spirit..told me that it was beneath my dignity. **1833** J. MARTINEAU *Ess. & Addr.* (1890) I. 8 Unitarians are beginning to perceive the error of this retaliative logic.

re'taliator. [-OR 2.] One who retaliates.

1788 W. GORDON *Hist. Independence U.S.A.* IV. 287 A set of vindictive rebels, known by the designation of *Monmouth retaliators*. **1898** *Month* Aug. 215 The memory of the cruelties..must have been keen in the memories of the retaliators. **1946** G. B. SHAW *Geneva* 25 Women in every generation, look like vindictive retaliators, pugnacious sportsmen, and devout believers.

re'taliatory, *a.* [f. RETALIATE *v.*[1] + -ORY.] Pertaining to, of the nature of, retaliation.

1813 *Gen. Hist.* in *Ann. Reg.* 190/1 We are obliged to conclude our account of the American campaign with the notice of some retaliatory measures. **1861** *Sat. Rev.* XI. 170/2 Putting an end to incessant raids on the one side, and retaliatory invasions on the other. **1885** *Manch. Exam.* 6 Nov. 5/2 If Lord Salisbury is bent upon a retaliatory policy he must not stop with Spain.

†**re'taling**, *vbl. sb. Obs.*$^{-1}$ [f. late L. *retāliāre.*] Retaliation.

1626 W. SCLATER *Three Serm.* (1629) 10 If desires of revenge and retaling of wrongs [arise], doe good for evill.

†**re'talion.** *Obs.*$^{-1}$ [f. L. *tāliōn-em*, after *retāliāre.*] Retaliation.

1610 WILLET *Daniel* 187 The law of retalion required that false accusers should indure the same punishment.

re'talk, *v.* [RE- 5 a.] To talk *over* again.

1798 H. WALPOLE *Lett., Remin.* (1857) I. p. cxxx, Sometimes the King would quash the proposal in question, and yield after retalking it over with her.

†**re'tally**, *v. Obs. rare*$^{-1}$. [ad. late L. *retāliāre.*] *trans.* To retaliate; to give in return.

1639 SALTMARSHE *Policy* 161 If you would returne and retally favours for favours received.

‖**re'tama**[1]. [Sp. *retáma*, ad. Arab. *retām*, pl. of *retem.*] A class of shrubby plants, chiefly found in the Mediterranean region, related to the broom, and usually referred to the genus *Genista.*

[**1771** J. R. FORSTER tr. *Osbeck's Voy.* I. 42 *Spartium monospermum*, which the Spaniards call *Retamas*, grows like willow bushes along the sea-shore.] **1852** TH. ROSS tr. *Humboldt's Trav.* I. ii. 66 In the midst of this plain are tufts of the *retama*, which is the *Spartium nubigenum* of Aiton. **1876** *Encycl. Brit.* IV. 797/2 The region of Retama (*Cytisus nubigenus*), a species of white-flowering and sweet-scented broom, which is found as high as 11,000 feet. **1895** *Westm. Gaz.* 18 July 2/1 The retama bushes gave no shade from the hot attack of the sun in the zenith.

retama[2] (rə'tɑːmə). Also **ratama.** [Amer. Sp. *retama.*] = PALO VERDE. Also *attrib.*

1891 J. M. COULTER *Bot. W. Texas* I. 94 P[*arkinsonia*] *aculeata*..[is] often cultivated for ornament and known as 'retama'. **1903** 'O. HENRY' in *Ainslee's* Dec. 139/2 One December in the Frio country there was a ratama tree in full bloom. **1909** B. MACKENSE *Trees & Shrubs San Antonio* 25 The retama is very elegant and is often planted for ornament. **1926** 'O. HENRY' in *Argosy* Sept. 63/2 How delicious was that morning breeze..fresh and sweet with the breath of the yellow ratama blooms! **1949** *Chicago Tribune* 20 Feb. 30/3 Cedar and mesquite alone are costing Texas ranchers 115 million dollars a year. Add the sage and cactus,..blackjack oak, retama and prickly pear and the toll is terrific.

retard (rɪ'tɑːd), *sb.* [a. F. *retard* (= Sp., Pg. *retardo*, It. *ritardo*), f. *retarder*: see next.]

1. Retardation, delay. ***in retard***, retarded, delayed; in the rear *of.*

1788 JEFFERSON *Writ.* 1859 II. 353 A single day's retard. **1865** CARLYLE *Fredk. Gt.* xv. x. (1872) VI. 65 The rearward regiments..are in painful retard. **1886** RUSKIN *Præterita* I. iv. 132, I was far in retard of them in real knowledge. **1971** *Times* 14 Apr. 14/3 The Government, somewhat in retard of the fact, enacted the..eugenic protection law in 1949.

2. ***retard of the tide*** or ***of high water***, the interval between the moon's transit and the high water following upon this. Also *ellipt.*

1833 *Phil. Trans.* CXXIII. 19 The retard..at Portsmouth appears to be intermediate between that at Brest and at London. **1845** *Encycl. Metrop.* V. 257* *marg.*, Retard of high water upon the moon's transit. **1862** *New Amer. Cycl.* XV. 471 At Boston, this delay, which is called the retard, or age of the tide, is nearly 36 hours.

3. A device in a motor vehicle for retarding the ignition spark.

1932 *Motoring Encycl.* 10/3 The Bosch automatic advance and retard (Fig. 3) is a simple design for a stationary armature type of magneto. **1977** *Hot Car* Oct. 75/3 The old one is capped off still retaining the advance retard.

4. *U.S. slang.* A mentally retarded person.

1970 *Time* 23 Mar. 49 There are..heroin addicts, Air Force and CIA mental retards and Broadway Indians doing a Broadway Snake Dance. **1971** *New Yorker* 16 Jan. 76 The younger son, self-described as 'a hard-core retard', dreams of escaping to the wilds of Oregon to gambol with the bears and squirrels. **1979** *Observer* 21 Oct. 53/5 These are men who have been out of England for years on end... Social retards, they can still hold onto their given obsolete ideas and prejudices about women because of their geographical isolation, and their marooned intellects.

retard (rɪ'tɑːd), *v.* [ad. F. *retarder* (13th c., = Sp. and Pg. *retardar*, It. *ritardare*), or L. *retardāre*, f. *re-* RE- + *tardus* slow.]

1. *trans.* To keep back, to delay, hinder, impede (a person or thing in respect of progress, movement, action, or accomplishment).

c **1489** CAXTON *Blanchardyn* xxiii. 75 Here is one doubte that retardeth myne ymagynacyon. **1636** DENHAM *Destr. Troy* 423 The one retarded was By feeble age, the other by a wound. **1660** F. BROOKE tr. *Le Blanc's Trav.* 260 The sight of this fishing retarded us above an houre. **1694** CROWNE *Regulus* IV. 41, I must retard her while I get my pardon. **1728** YOUNG *Love Fame* II. 281 Since smallest things can give our sins a twitch, As crossing straws retard a passing witch. **1732** LEDIARD *Sethos* II. IX. 291 This fleet..was extremely retarded by the winds. **1823** F. CLISSOLD *Ascent Mt. Blanc* 21 We had been much retarded by difficulties, and waiting for wearied guides. **1860** TYNDALL *Glac.* II. vi. 253 When these waves [of light] enter a prism of glass they are retarded. **1868** OUSELEY *Harmony* ix, When the fifth is retarded, the dissonance of the second by retardation is produced.

2. To delay the progress or accomplishment, to impede the course, of (an action, movement, etc.).

1572 *Reg. Privy Council Scot.* II. 158 That sa haly a work be not retardit. **1610** B. JONSON *Alch.* IV. v, This'll retard The worke, a month at least. **1642** C. VERNON *Consid. Exch.* 91 The principal causes which have hindred and retarded the due answering of the Kings Revenues and Debts. **1692** BENTLEY *Boyle Lect.* viii. 268 They neither assist nor retard the Revolutions of the Planets. **1725** POPE *Odyss.* XV. 40 Nor let the night retard thy full career. **1776** ADAM SMITH *W. N.* II. v. (1869) I. 371 They would retard instead of accelerating the further increase. **1822** LAMB *Elia* I. *Old Actors*, He seemed to keep back his intellect, as some have had the power to retard their pulsation. **1844** THIRLWALL *Greece* lxv. VIII. 379 The patriots endeavoured to avert or retard the ruin of the League. **1871** B. STEWART *Heat* (ed. 2) §98 Capillary attraction appears to retard the formation of ice.

b. To defer, postpone, put off. *rare.*

1735 in *Pope's Lett.* Suppl. 11 He retarded his Edition of Mr. Cromwell's Letters till the Twenty-Second of March. **1820** SCOTT *Monast.* xvi, If we were now either to advance or retard the hour of refection beyond the time.

3. *intr.* To be delayed; to come, appear, or happen later; to undergo retardation.

1646 SIR T. BROWNE *Pseud. Ep.* 194 Putrefaction..shall retard or accelerate according to the subject and season of the year. **1665** *Phil. Trans.* I. 38 The Comet advances..towards the East, and..retards towards the West. **1738** *Ibid.* XL. 312 The next Evening it retarded two Hours. **1797** *Encycl. Brit.* (ed. 3) XVIII. 520/2 Its motion from Q to *o* must retard by the same degrees as it accelerated in passing from *s* to Q. **1807** PIKE *Sources Mississ.* App. (1810) 61 Until the arrival of my sergeant and the balance of the party (should they not retard more than 20 days). **1849** HERSCHEL *Outl. Astron.* §681 Through BE the force retards, and the moon approaches.

b. To delay *to* do something. *rare*$^{-1}$.

a **1732** GAY *Tales, Apparition*, Call loud on Justice, bid her not retard To punish murder.

re'tardance. [a. obs. F. *retardance*: see prec. and -ANCE.]

1. Retardation.

1556 *Aurelio & Isab.* (1608) E vij, Suche retardance, som fooles and withoute practyse, thincketh it to proceade of honesty. **1586** Q. ELIZ. in *Lett. Q. Eliz. & Jas. VI* (Camden) 38, I hope that my many waighty affayres..may make my lawful excuse for the retardance of the answer.

2. The action of retarding; also = RETARDANCY; usu. in *Comb.* with a preceding sb., as ***fire, flame retardance.***

1948 *Industr. & Engin. Chem.* Mar. 400/1 Primary emphasis in fire retardance has been directed to coatings or impregnants which will protect a combustible substrate. **1954** *Adv. Chem. Series* IX. 1 Ordinary paints..possess a fair amount of fire retardance..during the first stages of a fire. **1971** *Nature* 4 June 335/1 The introductory chapter includes..smaller sections on the mechanisms of flame retardance..and effective concentrations of retardants.

retardancy (rɪ'tɑːdənsɪ). [f. as prec. + -ANCY.] The capability to retard; usu. used in *Comb.* with a preceding sb., as ***fire, flame retardancy.***

1947 R. W. LITTLE *Flameproofing Textile Fabrics* v. 172 The dehydration catalysis mechanism of flame retardancy. **1973** KURYLA & PAPA (*title*) Flame retardancy of polymeric materials. *Ibid.* iii. 253 These compounds impart dimensional stability, abrasion resistance, water resistance, and flame retardancy to the backcoated fabric. **1973** *Sci. Amer.* Apr. 13/2 (Advt.), Are you trying to improve fire retardancy of materials or finished products?

re'tardant, *a.* and *sb.* [Cf. RETARDANCE and -ANT; also RETARDENT.]

A. *adj.* Retarding, tending to hinder. Now usu. in *Comb.* with a preceding sb., as *fire-, flame-retardant* adjs. (see also RETARDENT *a.*).

1642 SIR E. DERING *Sp. on Relig.* 1 If any thing I have said or done be..dissonant or retardant to a most severe Reformation. **1885** STEDMAN *Poets Amer.* 468 We know the retardant effect of society upon artists of exalted sensibility. **1915** [see *fire-retardant* adj. s.v. FIRE *sb.* B. 2]. **1947**, **1966** [see *flame-retardant* adj. s.v. FLAME *sb.* 10]. **1971** *Financial Mail* (Johannesburg) 26 Feb. 685/3 Flame-retardant paints. **1973** *Harrod's Xmas Catal.* 59/2 Christmas tree realistically reproduced. Fire retardant. **1976** *Horse & Hound* 3 Dec. 54/1 (Advt.), This specially shaped bed filled with Fire Retardant polystyrene beads takes the ache out of a tired wet dog.

B. *sb.* A substance that reduces or inhibits some phenomenon (usu. specified by a preceding sb., as in prec. sense).

1952 [see *fire-retardant* sb. s.v. FIRE *sb.* B. 2]. **1959** *New Scientist* 8 Oct. 633/1 By the combined effects of daylength control and a growth retardant, the growth habit of petunia plants can be modified so that the plants flower earlier than usual yet remain compact and bushy. **1971** 'R. MACDONALD' *Underground Man* v. 31 The plane was lost in the smoke..then climbed out trailing a pastel red cloud of fire retardant. **1975** *Nature* 3 July 4/3 Peel roughness could be controlled by spraying Alar (a growth retardant) on the citrus. **1976** *Shell in Industr. Chemicals* 8 Flame retardants for polyurethane foams.

‖**retardataire** (rətardatɛr), *sb.* and *a.* Chiefly *Art.* [Fr., lit. '(one who is) late in arriving, acting, etc.'.] **A.** *sb.* A work of art executed in the style of an earlier period. **B.** *adj.* Behind the times; characterized by the style of an earlier period.

1903 R. FRY *Let.* 29 June (1972) I. 210, I have assumed that the man whom you called in your notes Lorenzo Bicci is meant for Bicci di Lorenzo. Lorenzo Bicci is much too early, b. 1333 (I'm sure), whereas Bicci di Lorenzo, d. 1452, would just suit this *retardataire*. I am speaking of the Quattrocento *Madonna* with two angels kneeling beneath. **1958** H.-R. HITCHCOCK *Archit.: 19th & 20th Cent.* viii. 148 Only in the design of public monuments..did a pompous and somewhat retardataire eclecticism rule. **1964** *Listener* 19 Mar. 488/2 The greatest Andrea [del Sarto] is *retardataire*, an artist who would have been more at home in the conditions of a quarter of a century earlier. **1966** *Ibid.* 1 Dec. 813/3 English art had always been retardataire. **1973** J. B. TRAPP *Medieval Eng. Lit.* 7 In learning, too, England [by the end of the fifteenth century] was retardataire. **1977** *Times Lit. Suppl.* 14 Jan. 30/4 The *retardataire* appearance of much colonial architecture derives from the poor, often secondhand knowledge of contemporary architectural practice as well as from a conservatism in patrons' tastes.

† **re'tardate,** *a. Obs. rare.* [ad. L. *retardātus*, pa. pple. of *retardāre* to RETARD.] Retarded.

1597 A. M. tr. *Guillemeau's Fr. Chirurg.* 4/1 They have verye retardate breathe. *Ibid.* 41/2 The operatione..is vncertayne, retardate and slowe.

Hence † **re'tardately** *adv. Obs. rare*⁻¹.

1597 A. M. tr. *Guillemeau's Fr. Chirurg.* 48b/2 The aquosity which is verye retardatelye expelled.

† **re'tardate,** *v. Obs.* [f. ppl. stem of L. *retardāre*.] *trans.* = RETARD *v.*

1613 JACKSON *Creed* I. To Rdr. d 3 That..which for a long time did retardate my perswasion. **1633** HART *Diet of Diseased* III. xxx. 366 The blood might a little retardate and hinder this operation. **1684** H. MORE *Answer* 135 The Entireness of the Turkish Empire may retardate Antichrist's ruine.

retardate (rɪ'tɑːdeɪt), *sb.* [ad. L. *retardātus*, see RETARDATE *a.*] One who is mentally or educationally retarded; also *attrib.*

1956 *Amer. Jrnl. Mental Deficiency* Jan. 531/1 That promotions to supervisory capacity are within reach of some retardates is demonstrated on Table VI. **1963** N. R. ELLIS *Handbk. Mental Deficiency* v. 159 (*heading*) The role of attention in retardate discrimination learning. *Ibid.* xxi. 669 The achievement of regular-class and special-class retardates in single school systems. **1975** *New Society* 10 July 91/2 Perhaps they would care to visit this hostel for adult retardates..and see the emotionally deviant, socially inadequate, environmentally retarded adolescent. **1976** *Word 1971* XXVII. 521 One might speculate about what skills a reading retardate lacks. **1980** *Brit. Med. Jrnl.* 29 Mar. 930/2 The mentally deficient (call them mentally subnormal, retarded or 'retardates', if you must) have legitimate rights.

retardation (riːtɑː'deɪʃən). Also 5 **retardacion, -acioun, -acyoun.** [a. F. *retardation*, †*-acion* (14th c., = Sp. *retardacion*, It. *-azione*), or ad. L. *retardātiōn-em*, n. of action f. *retardāre* to RETARD.]

1. a. The action of retarding, delaying, or making slower in respect of action or movement, or later in happening; an instance of this.

1426 LYDG. *De Guil. Pilgrim.* 12362 Sythe thys bodyes celestyal..Ben let thus in ther mocyouns, And han swych retardacyouns. **1472–5** *Rolls of Parlt.* VI. 161/1 To grete delay and retardation of procedyng. **1508** in *Lett. Rich. III & Hen. VII* (Rolls) I. 451 The retardacion of their ambassade. **1513** HEN. VIII in Strype *Eccl. Mem.* (1822) I. II. 6 By the retardation of our said ship she now lately fell into the daungier & hands of the Mores. **1597** I. T. *Serm. Paules Crosse* 66 Retardation of death, of this saith Ezechiel, I will not the death of a sinner, but rather that hee turne and liue. **1605** BACON *Adv. Learn.* II. xv. §1 Causing a retardation of reading, and some sloth or relaxation of memory. **1661** COWLEY *College*, All manner of Experiments concerning Plants, as their Melioration, Acceleration, Retardation. **1702** C. MATHER *Magn. Chr.* I. ii. (1852) 46 Finding the Reformation of the Church..to labour under a sort of hopeless retardation. **1759** B. STILLINGFLEET *Misc. Tracts* (1762) 253 In order to determine accurately the acceleration or retardation of the winter. **1817** MALTHUS *Popul.* (ed. 4) III. 421 A gradual change..would then effect the necessary retardation in the rate of increase. **1865** ELLICOT *Destiny of Creature* Pref. 6 They speak of nought but obstructions and retardations, where all is buoyancy and progress. **1891** C. L. MORGAN *Anim. Life & Intell.* 223 This retardation or decreased rate of growth.

† **b.** Lingering or staying behind. *Obs. rare*⁻¹.

1633 T. ADAMS *Expos. 2 Peter* iii. 18 Think upon his [Lot's] wife's retardation and retrospection.

2. In the physical sciences in various special applications: **a.** of motion or moving bodies. (Opposed to *acceleration*.)

1642 H. MORE *Song of Soul* Notes, Wks. (Grosart) 152/1 The acceleration or retardation of the motion of the Earth will make the sea fluctuate. **1665** *Phil. Trans.* I. 106 The cause of this acceleration and retardation of their true Motion. **1727–38** CHAMBERS *Cycl.* s.v., The retardation of moving bodies arises from two great causes, the resistence of the medium, and the force of gravity. **1794** G. ADAMS *Nat. & Exp. Philos.* III. xxvii. 119 Accelerations and retardations may be considered as quantities, and are measured by the changes of velocity. **1825** J. NICHOLSON *Operat. Mechanic* 3 From a clear comprehension of the acceleration of motion in bodies the retardation of motion will be easily conceived. **1862** SPENCER *First Princ.* II. v. §56 (1875) 182 In an elliptical orbit there is now acceleration and now retardation. **1878** HUXLEY *Physiogr.* 172 The retardation of the deeper part of the wave by friction against the sea bottom.

b. of the tides: (*a*) The excess of periods of high water above the solar day. (*b*) = RETARD *sb.* 2.

1797 *Encycl. Brit.* (ed. 3) XVIII. 521/1 The difference between a solar day and a tide day is called the priming or the retardation of the tides. **1845** *Encycl. Metrop.* V. 241* The average retardation from day to day being about 40 minutes. *Ibid.* 257* The retardation of high water after the moon's passage over the meridian. **1888** *Encycl. Brit.* XXIII. 366/2 When the mean semi-range and retardation of any tide are known its height may be computed for any instant.

c. of celestial bodies. (Cf. quot. 1426 in 1.)

1812–16 PLAYFAIR *Nat. Phil.* (1819) II. 183 The amount of the retardation, from the opposition to the conjunction, is 16ᵐ 26ˢ nearly. **1849** HERSCHEL *Outl. Astron.* §683 Over quadrant AD, approach and retardation, therefore advance of apsides. **1873** PROCTOR *Moon* 93 Retardation ceases to act when the moon is at M_2.

d. of rays or waves of light, heat, etc.

1831 BREWSTER *Optics* xxiv. 213 They will..produce a colour or a fringe corresponding to the retardation of one of the rays within the plate. **1866** R. M. FERGUSON *Electr.* (1870) 245 The retardation increases with the square of the length of the line. **1882** MINCHIN *Unipl. Kinemat.* 18 A retardation of a whole wave length..is tantamount to no retardation at all.

3. *Music.* **a.** (See quots. 1868 and 1899.)

1818 BUSBY *Gram. Mus.* 339 This Discord, the dissonant note of which is but a retardation of the Eighth, is liable to four changes. **1868** OUSELEY *Harmony* ix, When an interval of a melody (or of an inner part) is kept back in ascending, it is called a retardation. **1899** BRIDGE & SAWYER *Harmony* xiii, A Retardation is formed when a note, which should ascend in its progression one degree, is delayed.

b. A slackening of the tempo.

1834 [see A TEMPO]. **1853** *Charles Auchester* II. 180 The slightest possible retardation at its close brought us to the refrain of the simple adagio.

4. *Psychol.* Educational progress which is slower than average for the age-group; also, mental backwardness or subnormality in an adult. Cf. RETARDED *ppl. a.* 1 b.

1907 *Psychol. Clinic* I. 98 The failure of many pupils to be promoted regularly from grade to grade—retardation—has been a subject for..serious consideration. **1914** W. B. DRUMMOND tr. *Binet & Simon's Mentally Defective Children* ii. 16 According to a convention..we regard as defective in intelligence a child who shows a retardation of three years, when he himself is nine years of age or more. **1919** L. M. TERMAN *Measurement of Intelligence* i. 4 We can at least prevent the kind of retardation which involves failure and the repetition of a school grade. **1937** C. L. BURT *Backward Child* iv. 78 Thus, at the age of 10, the borderline for backwardness is a retardation of 1½ years (not, as is so commonly stated, of 2 years), or, in terms of the ratio, 15 per cent. **1963** N. R. ELLIS *Handbk. Mental Deficiency* xxi. 678 Skill areas listed from most to least retardation were reading, arithmetic, writing, and spelling. **1970** HINSIE & CAMPBELL *Psychiatric Dict.* (ed. 4) 666/1 Fashions in labeling this group change almost from year to year; in the 1960's, mental retardation was the favorite appellation, and justifiably so in that it does not imply that inheritance or constitutional defects are always the cause of mental retardation. **1975** BALTHAZAR & STEVENS *Emotionally Disturbed, Mentally Retarded* i. 3 The problems imposed by mental retardation and adaptive behavior.

re'tardative, *a.* [= F. *retardatif*, It. *ritardativo*: see RETARDATE *v.* and -IVE.] Tending or having power to retard.

1847 in WEBSTER. **1859** F. A. GRIFFITHS *Artil. Man.* (1862) 327 Accelerative, or retardative force,..is that by which the velocity is accelerated or retarded. **1873** PROCTOR *Moon* 93 As the moon passes over the arc M_3M_4, the tangential force is again retardative.

re'tardatory, *a.* [Cf. prec. and -ORY.] Having a retarding effect or influence.

1853 *Tait's Mag.* XX. 540 Not a breath of wind, retardatory or otherwise, to interfere with the regular steam-power of the vessels. **1877** ROSENTHAL *Muscles & Nerves* 282 Retardatory nerves have been recognised in almost all automatic apparatus. **1882** *Edin. Rev.* Oct. 444 The nearer the angle between the rudder and the keel approaches a right angle, the more direct is the retardatory action.

retarded (rɪ'tɑːdɪd), *ppl. a.* [f. RETARD *v.* + -ED¹.] **1. a.** Checked: impeded; delayed.

1810 CRABBE *Borough* xxiii. 320 The timid girls..Dip the small foot in the retarded brine. **1815** J. SMITH *Panorama Sci. & Art* I. 398 Retarded motion is when the velocity continually decreases. **1871** DARWIN *Desc. Man* II. xvii. 259 Male birds have acquired ornamental plumes at the cost of retarded flight. **1899** *Allbutt's Syst. Med.* VII. 765 The first fits occur during retarded dentition.

b. *Psychol.* Orig., applied to children whose mental or educational progress lags behind that of their contemporaries to a significant degree; later extended to anyone with a measured intelligence less than some value that is itself below the average, esp. when attributed to impaired learning or maturation in childhood and youth. Hence *ellipt.* as *sb.*

1895 G. E. SHUTTLEWORTH *Mentally-Deficient Children* ii. 19 Such children are also described as 'backward', or of 'retarded mental development'—terms corresponding to the 'Enfants arriérés' of French writers..and the 'Tardivi' of the Italians. **1910** J. D. HEILMAN (*title*) A clinical study of one thousand retarded children in the public schools of Camden, New Jersey. **1919** L. M. TERMAN *Measurement of Intelligence* i. 24 (*heading*) The intelligence of retarded children usually overestimated. **1937** C. L. BURT *Backward Child* iv. 79 In the following pages, the word 'retarded' will be used to mean any child whose educational ratio falls below 85 per cent. **1951** H. LOEWY *Retarded Child* (rev. ed.) i. 14 Retarded children can be put into two broad classifications from the teaching point of view: (1) The child with a mental defect. (2) The mentally defective child. **1956** H. MICHAL-SMITH *Mentally Retarded Patient* p. vii, The mentally retarded of all ages are subject to illness as are other people. **1960** TANSLEY & GULLIFORD *Educ. Slow Learning Children* ii. 44 If his reading age is two years below his mental age he is considered retarded and special efforts must be made to get him 'working to capacity'. **1967** BRUSSEL & CANTZLAAR *Chamber's Dict. Psychiatry* 144 A mentally retarded person is one whose intelligence quotient..is below 70. **1973** LA CRUZ & LA VECK (*title*) Human sexuality and the mentally retarded. **1975** BALTHAZAR & STEVENS *Emotionally Disturbed, Mentally Retarded* vi. 87 Critical statements of the value of psychotherapy for the retarded. **1979** *Books & Bookmen* Jan. 43/1 Of those who could be given reliable intelligence tests, thirty-two per cent were defective, with an IQ below fifty, and thirteen per cent were retarded, with an IQ between fifty and seventy. Fifty-five per cent were subnormal or normal, ie, with IQs above seventy.

2. *Physics.* Applied to parameters of an electromagnetic radiation field in which allowance is made for the finite speed of propagation of the radiation, so that the potential due to a distant source is expressed in terms of the state of the source at some time in the past.

1920 *Physical Rev.* XV. 312 (*heading*) Note on the retarded potentials. **1929** MASON & WEAVER *Electromagn. Field* iv. 283, {ρ}, the so-called 'retarded value' of ρ, is given by $\{\rho\} = \rho(x, y, z, t-r/c)$. **1941** C. A. COULSON *Waves* viii. 141 We call $t-r/c$ the retarded time. **1962** CORSON & LORRAIN *Introd. Electromagn. Fields* xiv. 493 The retarded position [*z*] is less than *z* by a factor of $1/\{1 + (v/c)\}$. **1974** *Encycl. Brit. Macropædia* VI. 660/2 The exact potentials corresponding to a point charge..are not obtained by substituting the total charge for the volume integral indicated in the retarded potentials. The problem arises because of the finite velocity of field propagation, so that the integral of the retarded charge density over space is not in general equal to the total charge. **1975** D. M. COOK *Theory Electromagn. Field* xiv. 402 A potential of this form is referred to as a retarded potential because the potential at time *t* is determined by the state of the charge at the so-called retarded time *t′*.

retar'dee. *U.S.* [f. RETARD *v.* + -EE.] A mentally retarded person.

1971 *Time* 5 Apr. 38 Almost half are geriatrics cases or mental retardees who receive only custodial care. **1973** *Rehabilitation* Jan.–Mar. 46/2 The Agency was established ..to market..products made by the mentally retarded and thus demonstrate employment possibilities of retardees. **1977** *Monitor* (McAllen, Texas) 28 June 8A/1 A one-day orientation on mental retardation is scheduled Thursday... Parents of retardees and others interested also are invited.

re'tardent, *a.* [f. RETARD *v.*] = RETARDANT. Also as *sb.* A retarding thing or force.

1900 *Nature* 16 Aug. 376/1 The protection afforded by various retardent materials. *Ibid.*, The necessity of applying fire retardent material in at least two thicknesses. **1900** *Pop. Sci. Monthly* LVI. 508 Materials which are not good as heat retardents.

re'tarder. [f. as prec. + -ER¹.] **a.** One who or that which checks or delays.

1644 R. BAILLIE *Lett. & Jrnls.* (1841) II. 139 They have been the retarders of the Assemblie. **1688** *Lond. Gaz.* No. 2469/2 Who were retarders, or obstructers of the Designs of the Estates. **1760** SARAH FIELDING *Ophelia* II. xiv, Those.. sensations are great retarders of a lover's progress. **1839** *Civil Eng. & Arch. Jrnl.* II. 122/2 The sledge or retarder.. is formed like a wedge. **1971** P. GRESSWELL *Environment* 264 Weed-killers or growth retarders are needed that keep rank growth in check without eliminating all wild flowers. **1980** *Jrnl. R. Soc. Arts* Mar. 175/1 We will find ourselves sooner or later seeking..to break through that asymptote determined by nature's built-in retarders.

b. A substance which slows down a reaction or process.

1878 ABNEY *Photogr.* (1881) 68 It has been in effect found that ferric sulphate is a retarder. **1946** *Sun* (Baltimore) 7 Oct. 2/5 The meat situation may prolong the housing problem because plaster cannot be made without 'retarder', which is obtained from horn and hoof meal. **1967** MARGERISON & EAST *Introd. Polymer Chem.* iv. 195 Those substances which affect the rate of the polymerization are termed inhibitors or retarders according to whether the rate is reduced to zero or to a finite value. **1974** *Encycl. Brit. Macropædia* IV. 1076/1 The characteristics of concrete often can be improved by including admixtures in the concrete mix. In addition to set-accelerators..there are set-retarders (usually of a sugar base) that are less commonly required.

c. (See quot. 1898.)

1898 W. S. HUTTON *Steam-Boiler Constr.* (ed. 3) vi. 455 The smoke-tubes of multitubular boilers are sometimes fitted with either retarders or radiators, with the object of increasing the efficiency of the heating-surface. A retarder usually consists of a flat strip of sheet-metal twisted spirally, to compel the fuel-gases to travel through the tubes in a spiral-form. **1902** *Rep. Admiralty Comm. Naval Boilers* §29. 15 The Committee..think it right to state that retarders will be found in many cases to render existing cylindrical boilers more efficient and economical than they are at present. **1903** *Sci. Amer. Suppl.* 24 Jan. 22625/1 The cylindrical boilers should be fitted with retarders in the tubes. **1953** J. N. WILLIAMS *Boiler House Practice* vii. 152 Refractory cores or retarders were employed but with only partial success as the refractory would not stand up to the temperatures which approximated to those of theoretical combustion.

d. *Railways.* An arrangement of rails placed inside and parallel to the running rails in a shunting yard which may be moved sideways so as to act as a brake on the flanges of wagon wheels.

1937 W. G. RAYMOND *Elem. Railroad Engin.* (ed. 5) xiv. 186 The car retarder is a device to control the speed of a moving freight car. **1966** G. F. ALLEN *B.R. after Beeching* viii. 248 Further B.R. applications of this ingenious device may be confined to the outer ends of reception sidings in existing yards already equipped with electronically-controlled, clamp-type retarders, to improve the speed control of shunted wagons after they have left the hump area. **1969** H. R. BROADBENT *Introd. Railway Braking* ii. 11 The retarders used in marshalling yards do not come under the heading of train-operated brakes.

re'tarding, *vbl. sb.* [f. as prec. + -ING[1].] The action of RETARD *v.* in various senses.
1585 T. WASHINGTON tr. *Nicholay's Voy.* I. xix. 22 This.. put the Ambassador in..perplexity..because of the retarding of his voiage. *a* **1631** DONNE *Select.* (1840) 21 It is not a cropping, a pilling, a retarding of the growth of the vine that is threatened. **1695** J. EDWARDS *Perfect. Script.* 359 The retarding of the work under..the kings of Persia. **1784** *Phil. Trans.* LXXV. 140, I fixed therefore the retarding of the clock 1′ 35″.

re'tarding, *ppl. a.* [f. as prec. + -ING[2].] That retards; that tends to delay or check. ***retarding field, potential.***
1798 HUTTON *Course Math.* (1807) II. 247 The resisting force R, and..the retarding force *f.* **1822-34** *Good's Study Med.* (ed. 4) I. 609 The Retarding Quotidian..forms a direct counterpart to the anticipating. **1853** KANE *Grinnell Exp.* xxxi. (1856) 273 The host of retarding influences that belong to a Polar night. **1865** M. ARNOLD *Ess. Crit.* i. 21 A self-satisfaction which is retarding and vulgarising. **1898** SLOANE *Stand. Elect. Dict.* 618 *Retarding Disc*, a disc used in Thomson's electric meter for retarding the revolutions of the motor shaft. **1947** F. G. SPREADBURY *Electronics* xviii. 591 In order that no current shall flow it is..necessary to apply a retarding potential, i.e. the anode must be negative with respect to the cathode. **1950** *Jrnl. Physical Soc. Japan* V. 339/1 The assumption that electrons could enter the retarding field (grid-plate space) only a single time. **1953** *Ibid.* VIII. 182 The plate-current distribution in a retarding-field tube of concentric structure. **1963** B. FOZARD *Instrumentation Nucl. Reactors* xi. 138 Such a circuit is provided by a thermionic diode working under what are known as retarding field conditions.
Hence **re'tardingly** *adv.*
1881 *Academy* 3 Sept. 174/1 M. Stapfer, at times diffuse, is nowhere retardingly dense.

re'tardive, *a. rare.* [-IVE.] Retardative.
1798 HUTTON *Course Math.* (1828) II. 141 Accelerative, or Retardive Force, is commonly understood to be that which affects the velocity only. *Ibid.* (1807) II. 357 The retardive force. **1815** GREGORY *Mech.* (ed. 3) I. v. v. 541 The retardive force of *f*.. = [etc.]. **1968** G. JONES *Hist. Vikings* II. i. 66 The retardive effect of high latitude, long winters, severing distance, and a barriered landscape upon the development of the northern kingdoms was considerable.

retardment (rɪ'tɑːdmənt). [a. F. *retardement* (14th c.), = Sp. *retardamiento*, It. *ritardamento*: see RETARD *v.* and -MENT.] The act of retarding; retardation; delay, check.
1646 R. BAILLIE *Anabaptism* Pref., The retardment and frustration of everything which may advance the truth of God. *a* **1678** WOODHEAD *Motives Holy Living* 30 The great retardments he receives, who hath made some progress in holiness. **1728** PEMBERTON *Newton's Philos.* 219 That alternate acceleration and retardment of the moon's motion, ..stiled the variation. **1772-84** *Cook's Voy.* (1785) II. 5, I was desirous of avoiding every possibility of farther retardment. **1814** SOUTHEY *Roderick* v. 361 The urgency of our return will brook of no retardment. **1887** CLARK RUSSELL *Frozen Pirate* ii, My retardment by the washing seas.
So **re'tardure.** *rare*[−1].
1774 in Doran *Mann. & Manners* (1876) II. 256 The posts ..sometimes fail..owing to the retardure of the Packet boat at Ostend.

†**re'tary,** *v. Obs.* [app. f. RE- + TARRY *v.*, perh. after OF. *retarger*.] *trans.* To retard.
1526 *Pilgr. Perf.* (W. de W. 1531) 28 As burthens or clogges retaryenge or lettynge them in theyr iourney.

re'taste (riː-), *v.* [RE- 5 a.] To taste again.
1655 tr. *Sorel's Com. Hist. Francion* II. 49 Desiring to retaste his ordinary Dishes when he listed. **1796** ELIZA HAMILTON *Lett. Hindoo Rajah* (1811) I. 168 We shall renew the studies, and retaste the pleasures of our youth. **1809** SYD. SMITH *Serm.* II. 294 You shall re-taste again all the tumultuous pleasures of youth. **1826** *Q. Rev.* XXXIV. 505 Both have already tasted and re-tasted blood.

re'tattle, *v. nonce-wd.* [RE- 5 a.] *trans.* To tattle or talk over again.
1710 STEELE *Tatler* No. 229 ¶3, I have been 'annotated, retattled, examined, and condoled'.

re'taunt, *sb.* [RE- 5 a.] A repeated or renewed taunt.
a **1548** HALL *Chron., Rich. III* 34 b, He..gave me such unkynde wordes with suche tauntes and retauntes.

re'taunt, *v.* [RE- 5 a.] To taunt again.
1579 LYLY *Euphues* (Arb.) 109, I shall be accompted a Mecocke, a Milksop, taunted and retaunted with check and checkmate, flowted and reflowted with intollerable glee.

†**retch,** *sb.*[1] *Obs.* [Cf. RETCH *v.*[1]] A variant of REACH *sb.*[1] in various senses.
1545 ASCHAM *Toxoph.* (Arb.) 33 There was nothing within his retche and shote, but he wolde hit it in what place he wolde. **1582** N. LICHEFIELD tr. *Castanheda's Conq. E. Ind.* 4 b, Matters that passed common capacitie of man, and aboue the retch of naturall knowledge. **1607** HIERON *Defence* I. 107 His wordes are set vpon the tainter, and stretcht beyond their retche. *c* **1630** RISDON *Surv. Devon* §256 (1810) 265 Whose park is in a manner insulated by the river's winding retches.

retch, *sb.*[2] [f. RETCH *v.*[2]] = REACH *sb.*[2]
1837 W. IRVING *Capt. Bonneville* (1849) 369 The morning found him still..with many a retch and spasm.

†**retch,** *sb.*[3] *Obs. rare.* [? f. RETCH *v.*[1]] A bent piece of iron fastening the sheat of a plough to the beam.
1733 TULL *Horse-Hoeing Husb.* xxi. (Dubl.) 302, Z is the double Retch, which holds up the Sheat. **1766** *Compl. Farmer* s.v. *Sheat* 6 T 1/2 The sheat..fastened to the beam by a retch (a piece of iron with two legs).

retch (rɛtʃ), *v.*[1] *Obs.* exc. *dial.* Also 4 recche, 5 retchyn, 5-6 retche. [Var. of REACH *v.*[1] (cf. RATCH *v.*[1]), but the trans. use might also represent OE. *reccan*.]
1. *intr.* **a.** To stretch, expand.
1387 TREVISA *Higden* (Rolls) IV. 317 A craft..to make þe glas tough i-now to bende and wende, and to recche out wiþ strokes of hameres. **1581** G. PETTIE tr. *Guazzo's Civ. Conv.* (1586) I. 11 The greatest Boote was made of such leather as woulde shrinke in the wearing, and the other of a Hyde that would..retch. **1661** BOYLE *Spring of Air* III. ix. (1682) 73 Such thin Vials are subject upon the withdrawal of the ambient Air to retch a little. **1668** WILKINS *Real Char.* 191 Let there be a String to hang it upon, the smallest, limberest, and least subject to retch.
†**b.** To extend *from* (one place) *to* (another). *Obs.*
1489 CAXTON *Faytes of A.* I. xvii. 49 Ropes that shal retche in trauers from that one stake to that other. **1495** *Trevisa's Barth. De P. R.* XVII. clxiii. 710 Trabs hath that name of traho, that is to drawe other to retche, for they retche fro one walle to a nother and is joyned and styckyd therin.
†**c.** To attain *to* (a certain place), *above*, or *beyond* (a certain limit). *Obs.*
1565 *Satir. Poems Reform.* i. 144 That curre favell in the court might retche to higher rowme. **1584-7** GREENE *Card of Fancie* To Rdr., So Gentlemen,..I haue before time rashlie retcht aboue my pitch. **1635** QUARLES *Embl.* II. ii, How our hands can retch Beyond their distance!
2. *trans.* To stretch or draw *out.* Also *refl.*, to stretch (oneself).
c **1475** *Promp. Parv.* (MS. K) 425/2 Retchyn, or drawyn owt. **1484** CAXTON *Fables of Æsop* v. x, After that he was rysen vp fro his bedde,..he retched hym self. **1575** *Chr. Prayers* in *Priv. Prayers* (1851) 509 Drawing and retching out thy body to the length and breadth of the cross. **1608** PANKE *Fal of Babel* 16 Canonists..wrest the holy scriptures, as shomakers doe wrest & retch their leather with their teeth. **1650** BP. HALL *Balm of Gilead* (ed. 3) 3 His patience is retched so farre as to curse..his Nativity. **1674** N. FAIRFAX *Bulk & Selv.* 30 If the Soul be not retched out with the body, but settles in some room whence it may..sway the whole body; then [etc.]. *a* **1711** KEN *Hymns Evang.* Poet. Wks. 1721 I. 160 His tender Hands and Feet with Cords they retch. **18..** in *N. & Q.* 6th Ser. (1883) VII. 415/1 When he had tanned [the hide] and retched it.
b. To succeed in touching (something).
1530 PALSGR. 689/2, I retche with a weapen or with my hande, *Je attains.*

retch (rɛtʃ, riːtʃ), *v.*[2] [Var. of REACH *v.*[2], to which form the pron. (riːtʃ) properly belongs.]
†**1.** *intr.* To hawk, bring *up* phlegm. *Obs.*[−0]
1548 [see RETCHING *vbl. sb.*[2]] **1565** COOPER *Thesaurus* s.v. *Excreatio*, [It] maketh men spitte and retche vp easely. **1623** COCKERAM I, *Excreate*, to retch, or spit out.
2. **a.** *intr.* To make efforts to vomit.
1850 P. CROOK *War of Hats* 37 It made me almost retch To hear the tedious dullard prate and preach. **1861** G. F. BERKELEY *Eng. Sportsman* xi. 172 A fellow..who was intermittingly prostrated by fever and ague, and lying..on the ground, retching for twelve hours out of the twenty-four. **1872** DARWIN *Emotions* xi. 260 The tendency to retch from a fetid odour is immediately strengthened in a curious manner by some degree of habit.
b. *trans.* To throw up in vomiting.
1888 *Pall Mall G.* 13 Oct. 2/2 Some not able to carry their load of beer further than the gutter into which they retch the foul-smelling, poisonous liquid.

†**retch,** *v.*[3] *Obs. rare*[−1]. [Perh. repr. OE. *reccan* to rule, direct.] *trans.* ? To guide, lead.
1535 *Goodly Prymer, Ps.* xxiii. S ij b, He made me to feede in a full plentuouse batle groundе, and dyd dryue and retche me at leasure by the swete ryuers.

retche, obs. form of RECK *v.*

'retching, *vbl. sb.*[1] *rare.* [f. RETCH *v.*[1]] The action of stretching or drawing out.
1601 J. WHEELER *Treat. Comm.* 82 The said English Aduenturers do not sell their Clothes after they haue beene wet, and put in the water, without retching, or stretching. **1674** N. FAIRFAX *Bulk & Selv.* To Rdr., The one had wrackt and limm'd my thoughts, with endless tenters and boundless retchings out.

'retching, *vbl. sb.*[2] [f. RETCH *v.*[2]] †**a.** Hawking, or clearing of the throat. *Obs.* **b.** Vomiting, or making efforts to do this.
1548 ELYOT, *Excreo*, to spette out with retchyng. **1607** TOPSELL *Four-f. Beasts* (1658) 401 The same medicine..is very profitable for those which are troubled with a..bloudy spitting out with retching. **1623** COCKERAM I, *Excreation*, a retching or spitting out. **1704** F. FULLER *Med. Gymn.* (1718) 6 Sneezing; to which frequently is join'd Gauping or Retching. **1776** *Phil. Trans.* LXVI. 547 The symptoms.. were universal lassitude and weakness, followed by a retching. **1801** *Med. Jrnl.* V. 540 He had also nausea and retching, violent head-ach. **1845** BUDD *Dis. Liver* 295 The water abates the severity of the retching. **1899** *Allbutt's Syst. Med.* VIII. 84 A feeling of nausea..often going on to violent retching.

'retching, *ppl. a.* [f. RETCH *v.*[1]] Capable of stretching.
c **1400** *Lanfranc's Cirurg.* 163 Þe lungis ben maad of .iij. substauncis: of fleisch þat is recchinge, & braunche of arterijs. **1611** COTGR., *Marroquin chaussant*, gentle, yeelding, retching. **1615** BRATHWAIT *Strappado* (1878) 60 Nor is his conscience made of retching lether. **1650** HUBBERT *Pill Formality* 24 They have their consciences made of retching leather.

retchlesnes(s, obs. varr. RECKLESSNESS.

†**retchless,** obs. variant of REACHLESS *a.*
1638 RAWLEY tr. *Bacon's Life & Death* (1650) 24 For those Philosophies, which..had Retchlesse, and High, and Magnanimous Thoughts..were good for lengthening of life.

retchless, obs. variant of RECKLESS *a.*

retd., ret'd, abbrevs. of RETIRED *ppl. a.* 6. Cf. RET.
1942 PARTRIDGE *Dict. Abbrev.* 83/1 *Ret.*, retired. *Retd.*, returned. (2) A variant of *ret.* **1975** N. LUARD *Travelling Horseman* i. 3 Colonel Stephen Wilmot, US Army (Ret'd), glanced at his watch.

‖**rete** ('riːtiː). Pl. retia ('riːtɪə, 'riːʃɪə). Also 4 riet, 6 rethe. [L. *rēte* net.]
1. **a.** An open-work metal plate, affixed to an astrolabe, and serving to indicate the positions of the principal fixed stars.
c **1391** CHAUCER *Astrol.* I. §3 Thi Riet shapen in manere of a net or of a webbe of a loppe. **1594** BLUNDEVIL *Exerc.* VI. (1636) 604 And though there be cut out in the Rete but 30 Almicanteraths. **1613** M. RIDLEY *Magn. Bodies* 106 Place the horizon of the rete to the altitude of the pole for that place. **1905** *Sci. Amer.* 12 Aug. 120/3 Above the planisphere lies the neatly cut out and decorated 'rete' carrying upon its circular interior the constellations of the ecliptic. **1957** *Encycl. Brit.* II. 575/1 Having noted the sun's position for the day in the zodiac circle, rotate the *rete* until the sun's position coincides with a circle on the plate corresponding to the observed altitude. **1974** *Sci. Amer.* May 8/2 This modern descendant of the astrolabe comes packed in a leatherette case with a rete, nine climates, a planet-plotting device and instructions.
†**b.** A graduated scale affixed to an astronomical telescope. *Obs.*
1665 HOOKE *Microgr.* 236 These [telescopes] should be fitted with a Rete or divided Scale. **1677** PLOT *Oxfordsh.* 227 To which Instrument he has added many sorts of Rete's, Screws, and Apertures.
2. *Anat.* **a.** ***rete mirabile***, an elaborate network or plexus of blood-vessels; in early use *spec.* that of Galen, which is formed by the intracranial part of the internal carotid artery in some animals, and was supposed to exist also in man. Also *spec.* in *Zool.*, such a network that supplies the swim bladder of many fishes and releases gas from the circulation for secretion into the bladder so as to increase buoyancy. Also *rete* simply.
1541 COPLAND *Guydon's Quest. Chirurg.* D iv, The sondry ensuyng withinforth ben the dura mater and the pia mater, and than rethe myrable. **1548-77** VICARY *Anat.* iv. 32 Rete mirabile, or wonderful caule vnder the Pannicles. **1615** CROOKE *Body of Man* (1631) 470 The Rete mirabile..is made of soporary arteries, which arising upward from the heart through the chest climbe vnto the head and at the Basis of the braine neere the originall of the opticke Nerues, do make this web or Net. **1727-38** CHAMBERS *Cycl.* s.v., Vieussens asserts, with many other anatomists, that there is no *rete mirabile* in man. **1848** *Quain's Anat.* (ed. 5) I. p. ccxliii, Of such retia mirabilia there are many examples in the lower animals. *Ibid.* II. 1196 An artery breaking up into a rete mirabile. **1883** *Encycl. Brit.* XV. 390/1 The principal arteries form very extensive and complex *retia mirabilia.* **1896** [see *red body* s.v. RED *a.* 19 a]. **1897, 1949** [see GLOMUS 2]. **1961** *Jrnl. Gen. Physiol.* XLIV. 539 The gas gland consists of a cellular layer interposed between the gas gland capillaries emanating from the rete and the lumen of the swim-bladder. **1962** K. F. LAGLER *Ichthyology* viii. 254 In the eel..over 100,000 arterioles and a slightly smaller number of venules give the rete a total surface of over 2 square meters where blood vessels are opposed to one another. **1973** *Sci. Amer.* Feb. 39/3 The tiny vessels intermingle to form slabs of vascular tissue, the *retia*, that lie close to the upper and lower surfaces of the dark muscle... These *retia* are the heat exchangers that ensure the warmth of the dark muscle. **1974** [see *red gland* s.v. RED *a.* 19 a].
b. The under portion of the epidermis, in which the pigment-cells are situated. Usually in full, ***rete mucosum***, or ***rete Malpighii.***
1797 *Encycl. Brit.* (ed. 3) I. 700/1 The colour of the body is found to depend on the colour of this rete mucosum. **1824** *Trans. R. Soc. Edin.* X. 250 A structure..quite analogous to the coloured portion of the rete mucosum of the skin. **1842** PRICHARD *Nat. Hist. Man* 88 Those parts of the *rete* which ..correspond with the furrows on the surface of the cutis. **1899** *Allbutt's Syst. Med.* VIII. 865 The female..penetrates the horny layer of the skin and then wriggles through the rete.
c. In full *rete testis.* A network of vessels through which spermatozoa pass before leaving the testicle for the epididymis.
1786 W. CRUICKSHANK *Anat. Absorbing Vessels Human Body* II. 140 The absorbents which arise out of the rete testis are exceedingly large. **1821** J. WILSON *Lect. Struct. & Physiol. Male Urinary & Genital Organs* iv. 96 Each of the vessels forming the rete testis sends off a tube, which leaves the body of the testicle and enters the epididymis singly. **1849-52** R. B. TODD *Cycl. Anat. & Physiol.* IV. 977/2 The canals of the rete. **1906** *Practitioner* Nov. 663 Most of these recorded cases [of testicular tumour]..are characterised by *complexity* of growth; and this is explained, I believe, as regards my own, by its origin, which I have traced to the tubules of the rete testis. **1968** PASSMORE & ROBSON *Compan. Med. Stud.* I. xxxvii. 22/1 Each seminiferous tubule is highly coiled... They are looped in such a way that both

ends join a series of about thirty short, so-called straight tubules which converge on a network of vessels lying in the mediastinum, the rete testis.

3. *Ent.* (See quot.)

1871 T. R. Jones *Anim. Kingd.* (ed. 4) 382 The whole body of the larva is filled with a peculiar fatty tissue.. called by entomologists the rete, epiploon, or fat-mass. This material.. consists of an oily or greasy substance enveloped in a most delicate cellulosity.

re'teach (riː-), *v.* [RE- 5 a.] To teach again.

1674 Allen *Danger Enthus.* 105 They would not have needed to have been taught and re-taught which are the first principles of the Oracles of God. **1846** Browning *Luria* v, Whose life re-teaches us what life should be. **1888** *Home Missionary* Aug. 156 Both lessons must be reviewed and repeated, and, to new generations, retaught.

Hence **re'teaching** *vbl. sb.*

1870 Smith *Syn. & Antonyms, Admonish,* In Old English this word had the sense of simply teaching..; afterwards of reteaching or reminding.

re'tecious, *a.* [Irreg. f. L. *rēte* net.] 'Resembling net-work' (Webster, 1847; hence in subsequent Dicts.).

†**re'tection.** *Obs. rare.* [ad. late L. *retectiōn-em,* noun of action f. *retegĕre* to uncover, disclose.] Disclosure; uncovering.

1642 H. More *Song of Soul* II. iii. III. xl, Tis not impossible one thing to move Contrary wayes, which by a fit retection I strongly will evince and clearly prove. **1663** Boyle *Exp. Hist. Colours* iii, Though this may be said to be rather a restoration of a body to its own colour, or a retection of its native colour than a change, yet still [etc.].

reteer(e, obs. Sc. forms of RETIRE *v.*

reteform, variant of RETIFORM.

1851 Richardson *Geol.* (1855) 216 Their skeleton assumes a vast variety of forms, being horny or calcareous, ..stellate, porous, or reteform.

reteignew, obs. form of RETINUE.

re'telegraph (riː-), *v.* [RE- 5 a.] To telegraph again; to transmit anew by telegraph.

1838 Dickens *Nich. Nick.* vii, 'Certainly,' said Squeers, re-telegraphing in the same manner. **1899** *Daily News* 6 Nov. 6/7 An official dispatch.. telegraphed to Sir Redvers Buller, and retelegraphed to the War Office.

re'tell (riː-), *v.* [RE- 5 a.] *trans.* To tell again; to relate anew; also, to count again.

1593 G. Harvey *Pierces Super.* 145 Teach Chawcer to re-tell a Canterbury Tale. **1604** Shaks. *Oth.* I. iii. 372, I haue told thee often, and I re-tell thee againe, and againe, I hate the Moore. **1646** Earl Monm. tr. *Biondi's Civil Wars* IV. 52 She said some things to the King which were never by him retold to any. **1807** G. Chalmers *Caledonia* I. II. §6. 302 This story is retold by Buchanan, and by the other perverters of the Scottish history. **1855** Macaulay *Hist. Eng.* xiii. III. 339 Had his life been prolonged one fortnight, his history would have been the history of Montrose retold. **1885** *Spectator* 25 July 977/1 The stories, which are here retold so attractively.

Hence **re'telling** *vbl. sb.*

1644 Plattes in *Hartlib's Leg.* (1655) 296 Mony it self.. is not fit for daily use in great summes, in respect of the trouble of telling and re-telling. **1883** Furnivall in *J. Lane's Contn. Sqr.'s T.* I. vii, Lane's re-telling of the Romance of Guy of Warwick. **1887** *Athenæum* 5 Nov. 598/1 It has lost nothing of its horror in the retelling.

re'teller. [f. RETELL *v.* + -ER[1].] One who tells or relates anew.

1929 *Cambr. Med. Hist.* VI. xxv. 827 It must be admitted that Chrétien himself does not claim to be an inventor, but rather a re-teller of tales.

re'temper (riː-), *v.* [RE- 5 a.] *trans.* To temper again.

1598 Florio, *Rattemperare,* to retemper, to temper. **1815** J. Smith *Panorama Sci. & Art* I. 31 Some keep them for a short time red hot.., then retemper them before they use them in this way. **1885** R. W. Church *Discipline Chr. Char.* iv. 109 Do we not need.. to retemper our slack souls, to refresh our hopes?

Hence **re'tempered** *ppl. a.*

1880 A. C. Swinburne *Studies Song* 38 Keen-edged as ice-retempered brand. **1883** Myers *Mod. Ess.* i. 49 Storm-beaten and bleeding indeed, but with re-tempered soul.

†**retenance.** *Obs.* Forms: 4 **retyn-, retain-,** 4–5 **retenance.** Also 4–5 **-aunce, -auns, -awns.** [a. AF. *retenaunce,* OF. *retenance, -ence,* f. *retenir* to retain: see -ANCE.]

1. = RETINUE.

1362 Langl. *P. Pl.* A. II. 35 Alle þis Riche Retenaunce þat Regneden with Fals Weoren bede to þe Bruyt-ale. **1390** Gower *Conf.* I. 212 He with al his retenance Ne mihte noght defende his lif. *c* **1400** *Brut* ccxviii. 258 And so he assemblede al his retynance [*v.r.* retenauntz], and went & spake vnto ham of þe Kyngus honour. *c* **1460** *Wisdom* 689 in *Macro Plays* 58 Now wyll we thre do make a dance Off thow þat longe to owur retanaunce.

2. *to* or *at* (*one's*) *retenance,* at one's service or command.

1340–70 *Alisaunder* 154 Him.. trulich to serue, For to wend at his wyll, whereso hym liked, And redy to his retainaunce ryght as hee wolde. *c* **1430** Hoccleve *Min. Poems* 71 The flessh, the world, & eek the feend my fo, My wittes alle han at hir retenance. *c* **1485** *Digby Myst.* (1882) III. 362 As a kyng ryall I sette at my plesavns, with wroth and Invy at my ryall retynawns.

†**retenant.** *Obs.* [a. OF. *retenant,* pres. pple. of *retenir*: cf. prec. and -ANT.] A retainer.

c **1330** R. Brunne *Chron. Wace* (Rolls) 15985 He gadered alle his retenauntz, Knyghtes, squiers, & seriauntz. *c* **1380** Wyclif *Sel. Wks.* III. 478 Let al þo worlde deme wisely by þer.. tirauntry on retenauntis, ande sittynge in parlement above grete lordis. *c* **1400** [see RETENANCE 1].

†**re'tend,** *v. Obs. rare*$^{-1}$. [f. *re-* RE- + L. *tendĕre* to proceed.] *intr.* To return.

c **1470** Harding *Chron.* Ded. I. 4 A Captain right woorthie and auenturous, And from Scotland euen newely retended.

re'tender, *v.* [RE-.] *trans.* To offer back.

1637 Heywood *Royall King* v. Wks. 1874 VI. 77 With what an humble zeale.. He did retender your faire Daughters Dower.

retene (rɛ'tiːn). *Chem.* [f. Gr. ῥητίνη resin: see -ENE.] A hydro-carbon, polymeric with benzene, obtained from resinous (esp. fossil) pine-wood.

1867 *Chem. News* XV. 253/1 Retene.. is distinguishable from naphthalene, which it resembles in aspect, by having no odour, by its lesser solubility in alcohol, and by its melting at 95°. **1873** *Fownes' Chemistry* (ed. 11) 796 Retene forms similar needles of an orange yellow colour.

re'tent, *sb. rare.* [ad. L. *retent-um,* neut. pa. pple. of *retinēre* to retain.] (See quot.)

1796 Kirwan *Elem. Min.* (ed. 2) I. 495 The quantity of iron they retain (and which I therefore call their retent). *Ibid.* 504 And if the retent be variable.

†**re'tent,** *v. Obs. rare*$^{-1}$. [ad. F. *retent-ir* to resound.] *trans.* To cause to resound.

1584 Hudson *Du Bartas' Judith* iii. 134 Their Pagans fell, with clamor huge to hear, Made such a dinne as made the heaven resound, Retented hell, and tore the fixed ground.

†**re'tent,** *pa. pple.*[1] *Obs.* [ad. L. *retent-us,* pa. pple. of *retinēre* to retain.] Reserved; restrained, kept back.

1623 tr. *Favine's Theat. Hon.* III. xi. 478 Very modest and retent in all his actions. **1642** H. More *Song Soul* II. II. iii. 26 Things that be fluent, As flitting time, by her be straight retent Unto one point. **1656** Blount *Glossogr., Retent,*.. kept or holden back, staied, retained, kept in.

†**re'tent,** *pa. pple.*[2] *Obs.* [ad. L. *retent-us,* pa. pple. of *retendĕre* to unbend.] 'Unbent.'

1656 Blount *Glossogr.*

retentate (rɪ'tɛnteɪt). [f. L. *retent-iō* a holding back (cf. RETENTION) + *-ate,* as in *distillate, filtrate,* etc.] That which fails to pass through a semi-permeable membrane, and so is retained on dialysis.

1959 Turner & Feinberg in *Nature* 10 Oct. 1139/1 We propose the term 'retentate' to designate those substances which are retained by semipermeable membranes in the course of dialysis. **1974** *Ibid.* 8 Nov. 176/1 The haemagglutinating activity in galactose.. was found in the retentate and could be concentrated quantitatively and washed free of monosaccharide by ultrafiltration. **1977** *Ibid.* 6 Jan. 92/2 Retained molecules (the retentate) remain in the original sample container. Both the retentate and the filtrate fractions can be recovered.

retention (rɪ'tɛnʃən). Also 5 **-cion, -cioun,** 7–8 **-sion.** [a. OF. *retencion, -tion*:—L. *retentiōn-em,* noun of action f. *retinēre* to keep back, retain. So Sp. *retencion,* It. *ri-, retenzione.*]

1. *Med.* **a.** The fact of retaining within the body one of the secretions (esp. the urine) which are normally evacuated; a case or instance of this.

c **1400** *Lanfranc's Cirurg.* 266 If þe cause come of retencioun of menstrue, þan þou schalt ȝeue hir medicyns for to bringe out þe menstrue. **1543** Traheron *Vigo's Chirurg.* 109/2 Retention of vryne, & costyfnes. **1603** Holland *Plutarch's Mor.* 623 The reliques or retensions of ventosities, whiche staie not for naturall ejections. **1725** Bradley *Fam. Dict.* II. G 4 b, The Retention of Urine is very painful and very dangerous: It's a Collection or Retention of ill Humours that is the Cause of it. **1804** Abernethy *Surg. Obs.* 237 A gentleman.. had a retention of urine from an enlarged prostate gland. **1833** *Cycl. Pract. Med.* I. 67/2 Amenorrhœa has been usually divided into retention and suppression of the menses. **1876** Bristowe *Th. & Pract. Med.* (1878) 828 The presence of the biliary acids in the urine is characteristic of jaundice from retention of bile.

attrib. **1871** T. H. Green *Introd. Pathol.* 189 In the retention-cysts they [the contents] will vary with the nature of the normal secretion.

b. (See quot. 1727–38.)

1589 Puttenham *Eng. Poesie* III. xxv. (Arb.) 309 Helping the naturall concoction, retention, distribution, expulsion, and other vertues, in a weake and vnhealthie bodie. **1615** Crooke *Body of Man* 296 The third action of the wombe is the Retention of the seedes. **1727–38** Chambers *Cycl.* s.v., Retention is also used, in medicine, &c. for the state of contraction in the solids, or vascular parts of the body, which makes them hold fast their proper contents.

2. a. The fact of retaining things in the mind; the power or ability to do this; memory. *Psychol.,* the ability to retain specific previously learned mental, perceptual, or motor tasks; also *attrib.,* esp. as ***retention curve,*** the curve on a graph which shows the amount of learning retained over a period of time.

1483 Caxton *Gold. Leg.* 306/2 Theyr fruycion whiche is .. In profounde cognycion as to Cherubyn, and in perpetuel retencion as touchynge the thrones. *c* **1600** Shaks. *Sonn.* cxxii, That poore retention could not so much hold, Nor need I tallies thy deare loue to skore. **1624** Heywood *Gunaik.* VII. 314 That nation.. hath beene remarkable for their admirable retention, who.. had all the passages of former ages by heart. **1690** Locke *Hum. Und.* II. x. (1695) 70 The next Faculty of the Mind.. is that I call Retention; or the keeping of those simple Ideas, which from Sensation or Reflection it hath received. **1745** J. Mason *Self-Knowledge* I. xv. (1853) 115 A man that knows himself will have a regard to the Furniture of his memory... If the Retention be bad, do not crowd it. **1791** Boswell *Johnson* (1816) I. 255 *note,* I knew him a few years ago.., high in fancy, and strong in retention. **1836–7** Sir W. Hamilton *Metaph.* xxx. II. 411 The faculty of Retention would be useless without the faculties of Reproduction and Representation. **1891** Ladd *Physiol. Psychol.* xvii. 418 The 'retention' which is commonly spoken of as necessary to the phenomena of memory, cannot be considered as a mental act. **1902** J. M. Baldwin *Dict. Philos. & Psychol.* II. 470/2 The first [sound] must leave behind it some after-effect which so modifies the second as to determine the judgment. This may also be called retention. **1923** C. S. Spearman *Nature of Intelligence* xix. 304 Those who would trace memory back to retention have more particularly tried to depict it in the guise of associative reproduction. **1940** R. S. Woodworth *Psychol.* (ed. 12) x. 337 The retention curve, or 'curve of forgetting', was first obtained by the relearning method... The curve shows a gradual loss of retention with the lapse of time. **1949** Postman & Egan *Exper. Psychol.* xvi. 381 (*caption*) Retention curve showing the reminiscence phenomenon. **1952** McGeoch & Irion *Psychol. Human Learning* (ed. 2) x. 359 In general, the retention of perceptual-motor habits is quite high. **1963** L. J. Cronbach *Educ. Psychol.* (ed. 2) xi. 350 On a retention test several weeks later they [*sc.* pupils] did better than they had done at the end of the instruction. **1975** G. H. Bower in W. K. Estes *Handbk. Learning & Cognitive Processes* I. ii. 75 The 'fluctuation' mood of contextual alterations and their effect on retention.

b. The fact of maintaining, keeping up, or continuing to use something. Also *attrib.* as ***retention rate.***

1625 Bacon *Ess., Of Innovations* (Arb.) 527 A Froward Retention of Custome, is as turbulent a Thing, as an Innouation. **1811** Pinkerton *Petral.* Introd. p. xiii, The retention, in their systems, of the four gradual divisions of the logicians. **1861** Stanley *East. Ch.* vi. (1869) 193 The retention of the old Pagan name of *Dies Solis* for the weekly Christian festival. **1972** *N.Y. Times* 3 Nov. 18/4 The retention rates for the addicts referred to the therapeutic communities—which typically hold less than 25 per cent of their patients—are high. **1974** *Amer. Jrnl. Epidemiol.* C. 104/2 In each cohort, the retention rate is similar for the ambulatory patients and for the patients inducted on an inpatient basis. **1977** D. Louria in M. M. Glatt *Drug Dependence* iv. 116 Initial efforts were directed to relating retention in a given treatment modality to nine demographic characteristics. *Ibid.,* Retention rates in the six programs studied ranged from over 60 to less than 5 per cent.

c. In Phenomenology, the continued consciousness of or existence in the present of a previous act or event. Cf. PROTENSION 3 b.

1931 W. R. B. Gibson tr. *Husserl's Ideas* III. ii. 220 The absolute right of immanent retention, in respect of that in it of which we are conscious as 'still' living and having 'just' happened. **1943** M. Farber *Found. Phenomenology* xvi. 516 As long as the retention lasts the tone has its own time, it is the same, its duration is the same. **1962** Macquarrie & Robinson tr. *Heidegger's Being & Time* II. iv. 411 Circumspective making present, however,.. is grounded in a *retention* of that context of equipment with which Dasein concerns itself in *awaiting* a possibility. **1966** A. Gurwitsch *Stud. Phenomenol. & Psychol.* vii. 137 The very reality of conscious life, when an act is an enduring one, is a phase of present actuality most intimately connected with a whole continuity of phases retained (in retentions of various degrees). **1974** R. Sokolowski *Husserlian Meditations* v. 134 The primitive elapsing of the now-consciousness into retention is an 'event' outside time.

3. a. The action or fact of keeping to oneself or in one's own hands, under one's power or authority.

1540 *Act 32 Hen. VIII,* c. 25 A deduction and retencion of the sayde .iiii.*s.* be made in the handes of the payers of the sayd pencion. **1580–1** *Reg. Privy Council Scot.* III. 362 Nather can the said Bischop have actioun aganis the said David for retentioun of the thrid of the said pensioun. **1601** Shaks. *Twel. N.* v. i. 84 His life I gaue him, and did thereto adde My loue without retention, or restraint. **1644** Bulwer *Chirol.* 65 An uncharitable retention, which doth not love to scatter, but to snatch away. **1693** Stair *Institut.* I. xviii. (ed. 2) 157 Retention is not an absolute extinction of the Obligation of Re-payment, or Restitution, but rather a Suspension thereof, till Satisfaction be made to the Retainer. **1766** W. Gordon *Gen. Counting-ho.* 114 Allowed retention of the premium. **1809–10** Coleridge *Friend* (1865) 171 A mere acquiescence on his part in our retention of Malta. **1874** Green *Short Hist.* viii. §9. 563 The House at once insisted on the retention of its power.

†**b.** *Law.* (See quot.) *Obs.*

1658 Phillips, *Retention,* in Common-law,.. when a Court pronounceth not a full arrest, or judgement, but reserves somewhat to be afterwards ordered.

c. (See RETAIN *v.* 3 b.)

1651 Hobbes *Leviath.* III. xlii. 274 The Power of Remission, and Retention of Sinnes,.. is a consequence of the Authority to Baptize.

d. Something that is kept back or retained.

1922 *Daily Mail* 15 Dec. 11 Major Doyle both rode and trained Ilderton, who looked a cheap retention at 100 gs. **1962** *Rep. Comm. Broadcasting 1960* 153 in *Parl. Papers 1961–2* (Cmnd. 1753) IX. 259 Gross licence revenue... Deduct retentions. **1970** P. Oliver *Savannah Syncopators* 63 There is a frequently expressed opinion that the use of the 'answering' guitar in some blues traditions is a retention from the custom of leader-and-chorus singing.

4. †**a.** Detention of persons by forcible or other means. *Obs.*

1579 *Reg. Privy Council Scot.* III. 248 Tuicheing the retentioun of the said Laurence and putting of him to libertie as a frie persoun. **1605** SHAKS. *Lear* v. iii. 47, I thought it fit, To send the old and miserable King to some retention. **1615** CHAPMAN *Odyss.* IV. 336, I haue within this Ile bene held for winde A wondrous time; and can by no meanes find An end to my retention.

b. The action or fact of holding fast or keeping fixed in a place or position; the fact or property of being kept, or remaining, in place.

1597 A. M. tr. *Guillemeau's Fr. Chirurg.* 24/1 Of the retentione of the tunge, which..we nowe call..tungetyed. **1655** STANLEY *Hist. Philos.* (1701) 65/2 Falling Stars are Cœlestial Bodies failing of their retention by the ordinary course of Heaven thrown down. **1860** TYNDALL *Glac.* II. §26. 373 The frontal slopes..have a northern aspect,.. which..causes the retention of the snow upon them. **1887** *Brit. Med. Jrnl.* 26 Feb. 454 The treatment consisted of.. the retention, just within the neck of the bladder, of a gum-elastic catheter.

†**c.** Restraint, check. *Obs.*

1603 HOLLAND *Plutarch's Mor.* 1213 To consume, cut off and chastice them by all means of repressions and retentions that be reasonable. **1633** P. FLETCHER *Purple Isl.* III. xv, Which wer't not surely held with strong retention, Would stirre domestick strife, and fierce contention.

d. Self-restraint or control. *rare.*

1626 T. H[AWKINS] tr. *Caussin's Holy Crt.* 507 What life more mortifyed, then to behold so much humility in soueraingne greatnesse?..In an absolute power to do all, so much retention? *c* **1735** *Man of Manners* (ed. 2) 30 We ought to be plain and modest in our Discourse, so as he may take Notice of our Retention. **1802** GIFFORD tr. *Juvenal* (1817) I. p. lxxvi, In a man of such lively passions, the retention with which he speaks of them all, is to be admired.

†**e.** Restriction of expenditure. *Obs. rare.*

1647 CLARENDON *Hist. Reb.* I. §4 The Excess of the Court in the greatest want, and the Parsimony and Retention of the Country in the greatest plenty. **1654** H. L'ESTRANGE *Chas. I* (1655) 5 In pecuniary dispensations to his Favourites he was excessive liberal, yea though the exigence of his own wants pleaded retention.

5. Power to retain; capacity for holding or keeping something.

1601 SHAKS. *Twel. N.* II. iv. 99 No womans heart So bigge, to hold so much, they lacke retention. **1613** M. RIDLEY *Magn. Bodies* 100 Where a smaller strength Magneticall altereth quickely the retention of the whole more vigorous Magnet. **1656** tr. *Hobbes' Elem. Philos.* (1839) 215 If the retention of the radius cease, that endeavour..will now be in the tangent. **1730** *Phil. Trans.* XXXVI. 307 Steel cannot be seasoned too hard for Retension (nor, as I think, for Reception) of Magnetism. **1823** J. BADCOCK *Dom. Amusem.* 141 Stone is the only material upon which you can operate, because of its ready absorption and retention of water. **1870** ROLLESTON *Anim. Life* 143 Having indeed scarcely any limit short of the retention of the stomach.

6. retention money (see quots.).

1911 W. THOMSON *Dict. Banking* 452/2 *Retention money*, money which is retained for a certain time after completion of a contract; e.g. if a contract has been made for £5,000 it may be agreed that 10 per cent. of the money due to the contractor shall be retained till, say, six or twelve months after the completion of the contract. If an assignment of retention money is given as security, notice of the assignment must be given to, and an acknowledgment received from, the person who is liable to pay the money to the contractor. **1974** *Terminol. Managem. & Financial Accountancy* (Inst. Cost and Managem. Accountants) 17 *Retention money*, a sum of money representing an agreed proportion of a price for goods supplied or work completed, such proportion being withheld by the purchaser or contractee for an agreed period of time as security against failure by the supplier or contractor to fulfil his obligations under the terms of the contract.

retentional, *a.* [f. RETENTION + -AL.] Of or pertaining to retention.

1931 [see PROTENSION 3 b.] **1938** *Mind* XLVII. 517 But even on the 'retentional' interpretation, I am not sure that the doctrine is supported by the introspectible facts. **1966** A. GURWITSCH *Phenomenol. & Psychol.* xii. 305 The source and origin of these modifications is the 'strict present'; the modifications arise from the 'actual now' and are conveyed to the retentional phases.

re'tentionist. [f. RETENTION + -IST]

1. One who advocates the retention of territory.

1899 *Contemp. Rev.* June 795 At once an unyielding retentionist and an irrepressible and insatiable expansionist.

2. One who advocates the retention of capital (or occas. of corporal) punishment. Used also *attrib.*, esp. of countries which have retained capital punishment.

1956 [see ABOLITIONIST c]. **1957** *Landfall* (N.Z.) Sept. 248 Those and only those who according to the Retentionists ought to be hanged. **1961** *Spectator* 7 Apr. 464 Retentionists do not..in fact base their desire to retain hanging on a belief that hanging reduces the number of murders. **1972** *Times* 28 Sept. 16/3 Retentionists [of caning] and agnostics can complain that the case for retention is made perfunctorily.

†**re'tentive**, *sb. Obs.* Also 4–5 retentif, 5 -yf, -ywe, 5–6 -yve. [a. OF. *retentive* fem.; or from the adj.]

1. The power of retaining things in the mind; recollection, memory.

c **1375** *Sc. Leg. Saints* xl. (*Ninian*) 42 In his hart [he] wele held It—sic retentywe he had of wit. *c* **1407** LYDG. *Reson & Sens.* 3735 Al that she taught him for his prowe Was voyde out of hys retentyf. **1454** *Rolls of Parlt.* V. 240/1 Theire good retentyve and wyse remembraunce.

2. Retention. *rare*$^{-1}$.

1471 RIPLEY *Comp. Alch.* IV. xiii. in Ashm. (1652) 147 Water to Erth hath given ingressyon,..And Water of Erth hath purchasyd retentive.

3. A restraining force; a means of restraint.

1608 BP. ANDREWES *Serm.* (1841) IV. 25 Then upon this double charge followeth a double reason; two retentives, as it were, against the first motion. **1627** BP. HALL *Epist.* VI. iii. 387 Feare is a retentiue as necessarie, not so ingenuous. **1650** TRAPP *Comm. Deut.* i. 17 Cato seeth you, was an ancient watchword among the Romans, and a great retentive from evil.

4. *pl.* The organs by which the natural excretions of the body are regulated.

1678 JONES *Heart & its Right Soverain* 499 A weather-cock in the English, or the retentives of a suckling in the Brittish proverb, cannot be more uncertain, and unsteddy. **1717** DE FOE *Mem. Ch. Scot.* I. 60 The Fright and Terror his Mother was in..so far influenc'd the Child in her Womb, that his Retentives generally fail'd him at the Sight of Weapons ever after.

re'tentive (rɪ'tɛntɪv), *a.*[1] Also 4 -if, 5 -yf (6 -yfe), -yue, -ywe. [a. OF. *retentif, -ive* (It., Sp., Pg. *retentivo*), repr. L. type **retentīvus*, f. ppl. stem of *retinēre* to hold back, retain.

In the following passage the word employed in the French original is *latentive*: **1490** CAXTON *Eneydos* xxviii. 110 [Proserpine] shorteth theyr retentyue brethe.]

1. Of the mind or memory: Tenacious; good at remembering.

c **1375** *Sc. Leg. Saints* xxvii. (*Machor*) 338 In his hart wele held [he] It, Ay retentywe he had a wyt. **1474** CAXTON *Chesse* 159 The memory of the peple is not retentyf. **1509** HAWES *Past. Pleas.* XVI. (Percy Soc.) 60 Whan she was gone, inwardly than wrought Upon her beaute my mynde retentyfe. **1553** T. WILSON *Rhet.* 112 Memorie is the power retentive of the mynde to kepe those thinges whiche by mannes wit are conceived. **1607** NORDEN *Surv. Dial.* IV. 173 Many unlearned men haue better and more retentiue memories, than haue some Schollers. **1665** GLANVILL *Scepsis Sci.* vi. 29 Those Musical Accents which our retentive faculty is preserver of. **1784** TYERS in *Johnsoniana* (1884) 186 So retentive was the memory of this man, that he could always recover whatever he lent to that faculty. **1821** CRAIG *Lect. Drawing*, etc. i. 57 The student in history, unless possessed of a mind uncommonly retentive [etc.]. **1875** JOWETT *Plato* (ed. 2) IV. 287 Those who..have quick and ready and retentive wits, have generally also quick tempers.

b. Of persons: Possessed of a good memory.

1758 JOHNSON *Idler* No. 1 ⁋8 The Idler is always inquisitive and seldom retentive. **1868** E. EDWARDS *Ralegh* I. xxv. 612 Twenty-one years had then passed since those retentive Indians had seen his face.

†**2.** ***the retentive virtue*** or ***faculty***, the ability to retain the physical secretions, or to keep food within the stomach. *Obs.*

c **1386** CHAUCER *Pars. T.* ⁋913 The humours been to ranke and habundaunt in the body of man; Somtyme of infermetee, for the fieblesse of the vertue retentif, as phisik maketh mencion. **1398** TREVISA *Barth. De P. R.* XVII. xxiv. (Bodl. MS.), Thei helpeþ aȝens the fluxe of the womb þt comeþ of defaute of þe vertu retentyue. *c* **1532** DU WES *Introd. Fr.* in *Palsgr.* 1053 The..appetityve, the retentyve, the digestyve, and expulsive [virtues]. **1601** HOLLAND *Pliny* II. Words of Art, *Retentiue facultie*, *i.* the naturall power that ech part or member of the body hath to hold that which is committed vnto it, [for] the due time. **1661** LOVELL *Hist. Anim. & Min.* Isagoge, The fat hinders appetite..and decayeth the retentive powers. **1683** TRYON *Way to Health* 72 Then also the Retentive and Digestive Faculties do cease from their natural Operations. [**1727–38** CHAMBERS *Cycl.* s.v. *Faculty*, Others subdivide the vegetative faculty into attractive, retentive, concoctive, and expulsive.]

fig. **1597** HOOKER *Eccl. Pol.* V. xxii. §7 It keepeth sermons in memory, and doth in that respect..help the retentive force of that stomach of the mind. *a* **1680** BUTLER *Rem.* (1759) II. 456 His Soul has no retentive Faculty, but suffers every Thing to run from him, as fast as he receives it. **1683** CAVE *Ecclesiastici* Introd. 63 The old doting Nile had lost his retentive faculty, and could no longer hold his Water.

†**3.** Sparing, niggardly, disinclined to spend. *Obs.*

c **1412** HOCCLEVE *De Reg. Princ.* 4504 Sche is a couetyse excessyf Of othres good; & of hire owne, sche So streit and hard is, and so retentyf, That it profyte may in no degree. **1654** H. L'ESTRANGE *Chas. I* (1655) 130 Never was King more frugal, never King more retentive in his largesses. **1678** MARVELL *Growth Popery* Wks. (Grosart) IV. 254 He had indeed of late been somewhat more retentive than formerly as to his faculty of disposing of kingdomes.

4. Having the property of, tending or inclined to, the retention or keeping *of* something.

1582 HESTER *Secr. Phiorav.* III. xxxii. 47 The oyle of Honnie hath a vertue preseruatiue and retentiue of the haire. **1650** BULWER *Anthropomet.* 141 More thankful to Nature and retentive of her benefits are they of Fez. **1661** J. CHILDREY *Brit. Bacon.* 57 Unless that kind of ground be more retentive of stains than others. **1722** DE FOE *Plague* (1884) 271 Woolen manufactures are..retentive of infection. **1780** HOWARD *Prisons Eng. & Wales* 88 Neither the sides nor floors..were wood, that being more retentive of scents or infection than tarras or brick. **1806** *Gazetteer Scot.* (ed. 2) 55 A stiff, rich, deep clay, lying on a bed of limestone, which is very retentive of moisture. **1843** DICKENS *Christm. Carol* II. 49 Nor was it more retentive of its ancient state within. **1871** EARLE *Philol. Eng. Tongue* §314 The verb is most retentive of antiquity.

5. Holding or confining; keeping firm hold.

1601 SHAKS. *Jul. C.* I. iii. 95 Nor ayrelesse Dungeon, nor strong Linkes of Iron, Can be retentiue to the strength of spirit. **1607** —— *Timon* III. iv. 82 What, are my dores oppos'd against my passage?..must my house Be my retentiue Enemy? My Gaole? **1708** J. PHILIPS *Cyder* II. 378 From retentive cage When sullen Philomel escapes, her notes She varies. **1725** POPE *Odyss.* IV. 567 Yet still retentive, with redoubled might Through each vain passive form [do thou] constrain his flight.

b. *Surg.* Serving to keep (a dressing, organ, etc.) in the proper place.

1597 A. M. tr. *Guillemeau's Fr. Chirurg.* 45/1 That ligament which..cureth through his continuance of the remedyes applyed vnto the dissease, wherfore we may call it the retentive Ligament. **1634** T. JOHNSON *Parey's Chirurg.* IX. v. (1678) 219 The Retentive Ligature is fit for such parts as cannot suffer strait binding. **1767** GOOCH *Treat. Wounds* I. 205 To alter the bandage, making it only retentive. **1897** *Allbutt's Syst. Med.* IV. 347 Many forms of special retentive apparatus [for movable kidney] have been devised.

c. Apt to retain or hold moisture.

1730–46 THOMSON *Autumn* 815, I see the sands, The pebbly gravel next, the layers then Of mingled moulds, of more retentive earths. **1844** H. STEPHENS *Bk. Farm* I. 485 The water supplied from rain or snow is interrupted in its progress by the retentive beds. **1878** HUXLEY *Physiogr.* 37 The lower part of the chalk which becomes stiff and retentive.

d. Cohesive; hard to separate. *rare.*

1721 BRADLEY *Philos. Acc. Wks. Nat.* 4 The Soap and Sand will be more retentive, and will not separate without some difficulty.

†**6.** Restrained, cautious, reticent. *Obs.*

1599 *Broughton's Let.* 46 So shall you be..retentiue of your slaunders, and lesse selfe-boasting of your great sufficiencies. **1603** HOLLAND *Plutarch's Mor.* 1352 If then there be any place in the consideration of the secrets of God, where we ought to be retentive, warie and discret, it is in this. **1626** T. H[AWKINS] *Caussin's Holy Crt.* 513 These harts formerly vnited, were now vpon breach, which notwithstanding neuer outwardly appeared, so retentiue they were on both sides.

Hence **re'tentively** *adv.*

1816 SOUTHEY *Poet's Pilgr.* I. 8 One dear girl, just ripe enough of age Retentively to see what I should see.

†**re'tentive**, *a.*[2] *Obs. rare*$^{-1}$. [f. as RETENT *v.* + -IVE.] That reverberates or resounds.

1728 POPE *Dunc.* II. 263 Long Chanc'ry lane retentive rolls the sound, And courts to courts return it round and round.

re'tentiveness. [f. RETENTIVE *a.*[1] + -NESS.]

a. The state or quality of being retentive; the fact of possessing retention.

a **1676** HALE *Prim. Orig. Man.* III. vi. (1677) 282 The great retentiveness of his Memory. **1685** *Gracian's Courtier's Orac.* 261 When one finds himself moved, retentiveness should beat the retreat, lest the choler may be more heated. **1768** TUCKER *Lt. Nat.* II. 301 The acuteness of our senses, ..the retentiveness of our memory. **1855** BAIN *Senses & Int.* I. i. §3 A third fact or property of the intellect is retentiveness. **1879** *Cassell's Techn. Educ.* II. 172 The clay-land farmer endeavours to counteract the heaviness and retentiveness of his land.

b. *Physics.* The capability of retaining a residual magnetic field when a magnetizing field has been removed.

1886 J. HOPKINSON in *Phil. Trans. R. Soc.* CLXXVI. 460 The ordinate OB is what is generally meant by the residual induction after great magnetising force, or the 'retentiveness'. **1902** *Encycl. Brit.* XXX. 430/2 The ratio of the residual magnetization to its previous maximum value measures the retentiveness of the metal. [*Note*] Hopkinson specified the retentiveness by the numerical value of the 'residual induction' (= $4\pi I$). **1924** C. R. UNDERHILL *Magnets* i. 21 The property whereby a magnetic material independently remains a magnet is called retentiveness. **1939** [see RETENTIVITY].

reten'tivity. [f. as prec. + -ITY.]

1. (See quot. 1881); now usu. the strength of the magnetic field that remains in a sample after removal of a saturating inducing field.

1881 S. P. THOMPSON *Electr. & Magn.* ii. §90 This power of resisting magnetisation or demagnetisation, is sometimes called coercive force; a much better term, due to Lamont, is retentivity. The retentivity of hard-tempered steel is great. **1887** *Proc. Physic. Soc.* Apr. (1888) 120 This experiment was made with a view of ascertaining whether the reglow would occur at a lower temperature the greater the amount of retentivity of the specimen. **1912** BROOKS & POYSER *Magnetism & Electricity* xxv. 414 Retentivity is measured by the 'residual' or 'remanent' magnetism, which persists when the magnetising force is removed. **1924** C. R. UNDERHILL *Magnets* xvi. 291 The retentivity or the residual structural flux density..will be about 9,900 gausses, or about 66 per cent of the induction. **1931** S. R. WILLIAMS *Magnetic Phenomena* i. 52 The property of retaining to a greater or less degree a certain amount of magnetization is called the retentivity of the substance. The terminology of magnetism is rather confusing regarding some of these terms... The consensus of opinion among magneticians at present is to reserve the term *remanent magnetism* for the open-circuit residual magnetism as in the case of a U-shaped permanent magnet with the keeper off. **1939** L. F. BATES *Mod. Magnetism* ii. 58 The specimen is now no longer exposed to a magnetic field, but it still retains a considerable intensity of magnetisation, equal to $Ob/4\pi$, which is termed the retentivity of the material and is a measure of the ability to retain magnetism when not subjected to adverse treatment. Some authorities, e.g. Ewing, term the residual induction *Ob* the retentiveness. **1948** *Electronic Engin.* XX. 351/1 The principal requirements of steels for permanent magnets is that they shall have high remanence (retentivity) and coercive force. **1951** R. M. BOZORTH *Ferromagnetism* xi. 499 In strong fields they [*sc.* the coercive force and the residual induction] approach limiting values called the coercivity and the retentivity, respectively. **1953** J. D. KRAUS *Electromagnetics* v. 239 The retentivity of a substance is the maximum value which the residual flux density can attain. **1966** *McGraw-Hill Encycl. Sci. & Technol.* IV. 489/1 The difference between cores of an electromagnet and a permanent magnet is in the retentivity of the material used.

2. *Psychol.* The capacity or ability to retain learning or to remember.

1909 C. S. MYERS *Exper. Psychol.* xiii. 173 Nor is the superior retentivity of the most distributed readings due to the involuntary revival of the syllables by the subject. **1923** C. S. SPEARMAN *Nature of Intelligence* ix. 132 Our second quantitative principle may be called that of retentivity... It appears not to be restricted to cognition, but to extend to mental processes of almost all sorts. It even governs an immense number of purely physical events. **1938** *Times Lit. Suppl.* 19 Mar. 186/1 These are the laws of mental energy and its constancy, of retentivity. **1961** *Lancet* 12 Aug. 361/2 Spearman held that 'retentivity' was a factor not closely related to general intelligence.

3. *Geol.* The property of rocks and minerals of retaining gases, esp. radiogenic ones.

1960 *Amer. Jrnl. Sci.* CCLVIII. 600 The conditions imposed upon phlogopite.. in order that its retentivity be greater than 95 per cent for 10^8 years. **1968** HAMILTON & FARQUHAR *Radiometric Dating for Geologists* i. 19 Chemical alteration which occurs penecontemporaneous with the event to be dated is not pertinent unless it affects the retentivity for argon of the mineral to be dated. *Ibid.* 22 The retentivities vary greatly within a mineral species. **1975** *Nature* 27 Feb. 704/2 The nature of the gas initially present in the heating apparatus markedly influences trace element retentivity at 1,000°C.

‖**retenue** (rətəny). [F. *retenue*, f. *retenu*, pa. pple. of *retenir* to restrain.] Reserve, restraint, caution, self-control.

1848 THACKERAY *Van. Fair* li, The delighted Prince, having less *retenue* than his French diplomatic colleague. **1873** H. ROGERS *Orig. Bible* (1874) 214 This lack of *retenue* and self-possession. **1889** A. LANG *Lett. on Lit.* iii. 34 How Tom Jones combined these sentiments.. with his own astonishing lack of *retenue*.. is just the puzzle.

reteration, variant of REITERATION 2.

retere, obs. variant of RETIRE *v.*

retest (riː-), *sb.* [RE- 5 a.] A renewed test.

1887 *Daily News* 20 May 3/3 Those only which passed the re-test will be placed in store. **1891** *Imperial Tariff* 269 On a warrant for the re-gauge or re-test of Wine.., the officer is to allow the regauge or re-test thereof.

re'test (riː-), *v.* [RE- 5 a.] *trans.* To test again. So **re'tested** *ppl. a.*; **re'testing** *vbl. sb.*

1863 E. T. OLVER *Shilling Tariff* 92 Wine which has been fortified.. after assessment will be re-tested. **1884** *The Voice* (N.Y.) 6 Sept., The committee calls for a retesting of plates on the Monadnock. **1887** *Daily News* 20 May 3/3 Troops at home are of course all armed with re-tested bayonets.

†**re'tex**, *v. Obs.*$^{-1}$ [ad. L. *retexĕre* to unravel.] To unweave, unravel; *fig.* to undo, annul.

1623 COCKERAM I, *Retexed*, vnweaued. *a* **1670** HACKET *Abp. Williams* I. (1692) 57 Neither King James, King Charles, nor any Parliament.. did ever appoint that any of his Orders should be retexed.

re'textive, *a. Logic.* [f. L. *retext-*, ppl. stem of *retexĕre* (see prec.) + -IVE.] Synthetical.

1620 T. GRANGER *Div. Logike* 295 Method, is either contextiue, or retextiue. **1850** BAYNES tr. *Port-Royal Logic* (1851) p. xxx, Analysis and synthesis (termed in it the contextive and retextive methods).

re'texture (riː-), *sb.* [RE- 5 a.] Reweaving.

1831 CARLYLE *Sartor Res.* III. ii, My Second Volume,.. treating practically of the Wear, Destruction, and Retexture of Spiritual Tissues, or Garments.

re'texture (riː-), *v.* [RE- 5 a.] *trans.* To treat (material, a garment, etc.) so as to restore firmness to its texture. So **re'textured** *ppl. a.*, **re'texturing** *vbl. sb.*

1953 *Laundries & Laundry Requisites* (ed. 12) 208 (Advt.), Re-texturing agent 'Esdefix' makes garments look newer —last longer. **1960** *Which?* May 110/1 Most dry cleaners.. ask whether you want your clothes cleaned in the ordinary way or 'with retexturing'. *Ibid.* 111/1 A panel of 20 people was.. asked to see if they could tell the difference between the retextured and other garments. *Ibid.* 111/2 There was no difference in appearance between retextured and simply dry cleaned clothes, but there was an indication that the retexturing process had put something back into the cloth, which might therefore last longer. **1976** B. BALL *Keegan* 9 Selecting a retexturing service for his lousy old jacket. **1977** *Punch* 31 Aug.–6 Sept. 349/1 Lord Kagan has had my raincoats retextured.

reteyne, obs. form of RETAIN *v.*

retgersite ('rɛtgəzaɪt). *Min.* [See quot. 1949 and -ITE[1].] A polymorph of nickel sulphate hexahydrate, $NiSO_4.6H_2O$, a secondary mineral occurring as green crusts and tufts.

1949 FRONDEL & PALACHE in *Amer. Mineralogist* XXXIV. 188 A recent survey of the specimens of so-called morenosite in the Harvard collection.. proved the natural existence of the tetragonal polymorph of nickel sulfate hexahydrate. The latter substance.. is described beyond under the name retgersite. The name is given after the Dutch physical chemist and chemical crystallographer Jan Willem Retgers (1856–1896). **1972** *Mineral. Abstr.* XXIII. 314/1 X-ray powder data.. and IR spectra are given for retgersite from sulphide-bearing quartz veins.. from Chelmiec, Góry Kaczawskie Mts., Lower Silesia.

re'thank (riː-), *v.* [RE- 5 a.] To thank again.

1653 R. LOVEDAY *Lett.* (1663) 82 But to quit Metaphor, I re-thank you for the vigilance of your active endeavours in behalf of my recovery.

re'thatch, *v.* [RE- 5 a.] To thatch again.

1850 B. TAYLOR *Eldorado* ii. 8 The canoes were beached on the mud, and their owners engaged in re-thatching their covers with split leaves of the palm. **1899** WERNER *Captain Locusts* 180 There was that house spoilt, and her back nearly broken with cutting grass to re-thatch it.

rethe, *a. Obs.* (? exc. *Sc.*). Forms: 1 **reðe (hreðe, rœðe, ræðe)** 3–4 **reþe**, 4 **reth**, 5 *Sc.* **rethe, retht, retthe**, (9) **reith(e, reyth(e.** [OE. *réðe* (*rǽðe*), of uncertain relationship.]

1. Of persons (or disposition): Fierce, cruel, harsh; stern, severe; strict.

Beowulf (Z.) 122 [Grendel] wæs reoc & reþe. *c* **900** *Bæda's Hist.* III. v, þa wæs him sended ærest oðer biscop, reðes modes monn. *c* **950** *Lindisf. Gosp.* Matt. viii. 28 Tuoeʒe hæbbende diobles of byrʒennum ut ʒe-eadon, hroeðo suiðe. *c* **1000** ÆLFRIC *Gram.* I. (Z) 294 þonne bið he *tyrannus*, þæt is reðe oððe wælhreow. *c* **1100** *O.E. Chron.* (Laud MS.) an. 1100, He wæs swiðe strang & reðe ofer his land & his mænn. *a* **1300** *Cursor M.* 21984 [Antichrist] sal cumme reth raisand in pride. *c* **1425** WYNTOUN *Cron.* v. xii. 3819 [Thou] rageande retthe in wodnes Helde noucht ordyr off richtwisnes.

b. *Sc.* Keen, eager, zealous.

1818 HOGG *Brownie of Bodsbeck* vii, 'Is your master a very religious man?' 'He's weel eneugh that way—no that very reithe ont.'

2. Of things: Severe, terrible, dreadful, furious.

c **825** *Vesp. Hymn* xi. 7 Fael ʒewynsumie roeðe [L. *casus secundet asperos*]. *c* **897** K. ÆLFRED *Gregory's Past. C.* xliii. 316 Se reða & se eʒeslica dæʒ. **971** *Blickl. Hom.* 95 þonne he him sylfum reþne dom & heardne ʒeearnaþ & beʒyteþ. *c* **1175** *Lamb. Hom.* 15 Moni hit forlet for þa reða dome þe þa wes. *a* **1300** *Cursor M.* 21962 His first comme it was ful smeth, þe toþer sal be rugh and reth. *c* **1425** WYNTOUN *Cron.* v. x. 1902 Bot ay withe roris reythe he rerde.

b. *esp.* of rain, the sea, floods, etc.

c **888** K. ÆLFRED *Boeth.* vii. 27 þonne hi strong dreceð wind under wolcnum.., oþþe hi eft se reða ren onhrereð. *a* **1300** *Cursor M.* 22145 Brathli to do þe se be reth, And brathli to do it be smeth. *Ibid.* 24838 (Edin.), þe wedir als in somer smeþe Son bigan be rug and reþe. *c* **1425** WYNTOUN *Cron.* I. viii. 396 (Wemyss MS.), Boggis beillit out and bristit, And ranys reith. *Ibid.* IV. xiii. 1412 (Royal MS.), Off Tybere the rywere Sa retht off spate wyth watrys sere Ras.

rethe, variant of RATHE *adv. Obs.*

'retheness. *Obs.* exc. *Sc.* [See RETHE *a.*] Fierceness, roughness, asperity. Also *Sc.* eagerness, ardour (Jam. 1882).

c **897** K. ÆLFRED *Gregory's Past. C.* xvii. 125 Sua eac ðam lareowe is to monianne ða lieðnesse wið ða reðnesse. *c* **900** *Bæda's Hist.* v. i, To þon ðætte þurh all sio roeðnis ðæs stormes wæs blinnende. **971** *Blickl. Hom.* 43 þone læddon feower awyrʒde englas mid mycelre reþnesse. *c* **1000** *Sax. Leechd.* I. 372 Wið hunda reðnysse & wiðerrædnysse. *a* **1300** *Cursor M.* 22667 þe angels þat in heuen sal be.. For þat rethnes sal þai be radd. *c* **1450** HOLLAND *Howlat* 239 Thir ar na foulis of ref, nor of rethnas.

rether, obs. f. RATHER; variant of ROTHER, ox.

re'think (riː-), *v.* [RE- 5 a.] To think again; to consider afresh. Now usu. *spec.* with a view to changing intentions or attitudes. **a.** *trans.*

a **1700** KEN *Edmund* Poet. Wks. 1721 II. 163 All the pass'd Song distinctly he re-thought. **1719** BAYNARD *Health* (1731) 2 To think, and re-think each Design. **1833** WHEWELL in Todhunter *Acc. Writ.* (1876) II. 174 Having been re-thought and re-written since, it is much more beautiful. **1865** J. H. STIRLING *Secret of Hegel* I. 97 Hegel examined all, rethought all, and completed all. **1930** E. BULLOUGH tr. E. Gilson in T. F. Burns *Monument to St. Augustine* ix. 292 St. Augustine had but re-thought and deepened, from the point of view of a Christian, the essential elements of Platonism. *a* **1942** B. MALINOWSKI *Sci. Theory of Culture* (1944) iii. 19 At times the thinker does nothing else but to re-think.. what the primitive might have or ought to have thought or felt under certain conditions. **1944** J. S. HUXLEY *On Living in Revolution* 18 How can this disintegrating system be reintegrated on a new basis? One way of beginning to rethink our social framework is [etc.]. **1955** *Harper's Mag.* Jan. 12/1 A ranking Administration speaker ..said that.. the Republican party might 'have to rethink the power and resources policy'. The verb is from the advertising-agency jargon that the Administration has learned to speak so fluently but it is not likely to mean much. **1957** *Times Lit. Suppl.* 6 Dec. 729/2 A summons, in effect, to the younger German historians, which only a few of them have heeded, to rethink the whole of Germany's recent past. **1973** *Daily Tel.* 28 Sept. 7/1 Mrs Thatcher last night promised to rethink methods of awarding grants to married women students. **1977** F. YOUNG in J. Hick *Myth of God Incarnate* ii. 30 In any attempt to rethink christological belief, the primacy of soteriology must be recognized.

b. *intr.*

1748 RICHARDSON *Clarissa* (1811) VII. 27 Think, my dear, and re-think. **1808** JANE AUSTEN *Lett.* (1884) I. 372, I cannot help thinking and re-thinking of your going to the island so heroically. **1853** LYNCH *Self-Improv.* vi. 148 You must think and observe; re-think and re-observe. **1919** J. L. GARVIN *Econ. Found. Peace* xviii. 439 Not to recognise this and not to re-think accordingly means either not being sincere in support of a real League of Nations or not being competently sincere. **1959** *Times* 16 Oct. 13/4 'Rethink'.. has suddenly become modish... It means—it means—. Well... It certainly does not mean to think again, which is not only a rueful but an intransitive process. Think twice, perhaps? Never!.. You think twice before doing something silly; rethinking starts after you have done it. **1975** *Sunday Tel.* 22 June 32/4 (*heading*) Amin re-thinks... As one of his conditions for the release of Mr. Hills, the President wants spare parts for Ferret patrol cars.

Hence **re'thinker**; **re'thinking** *vbl. sb.*; **re'thought** *ppl. a.*

1881 R. ADAMSON *Fichte* 122 Philosophy is thus the re-thinking of experience. **1919** J. L. GARVIN *Econ. Found. Peace* xviii. 440 The duty of rethinking is not only for some men, but more or less for all men, whatever their previous views. **1944** J. S. HUXLEY *On Living in Revolution* p. vii, Never, I suppose, has the process of re-thinking been so intense as in these past four years. There has been the re-thinking of old problems, the transvaluation of values. **1955** *Times* 25 Aug. 7/4 Much rethinking on the subject of disarmament has been going on in London and Washington. **1959** *Times* 16 Oct. 13/4 Repay, according to the dictionary, means to pay back, re-echo to echo back, regain to gain back; but although the rethinker may, while he is about his business, think back, one has the impression that he is mainly concerned with thinking forward. **1959** *Observer* 18 Oct. 24/7 She was ready with a dash of classless glamour for the new rethought brand image. **1963** *Times* 20 May 7/2 The need for re-thinking and reorganization in art education is not questioned. **1971** *Farmer & Stockbreeder* 23 Feb. 25/3 To reverse the fall in the national breeding flock a great deal of re-thinking was needed about production methods. **1977** *Meanjin* (Austral.) XXXVI. I. 64 Their language more clearly becomes that of inheritors of the shake-ups and rethinkings of the Fifties and Sixties.

'rethink, *sb.* [f. the vb.] An act of rethinking; reappraisal; a product of rethinking.

1958 *Times Lit. Suppl.* 12 Sept. 511/2 Then came Mr. Khrushchev's speech at the Twentieth Party Congress and close behind it the great Communist re-think. **1960** *Design* Feb. 29 The task of orientation towards a mass society required a rethink of.. an ideal formula. **1968** *New Scientist* 8 Aug. 293/1 The need for a widespread rethink on attitudes in science education, particularly at university level. **1971** *Guardian* 1 Nov. 8/5 Industry must have a major rethink about the way it uses intelligent, qualified young people. **1976** *Jrnl. R. Soc. Arts* May 285/1 It is more difficult to apply the principles to famous modern buildings which look like a total rethink. **1977** *Listener* 3 Mar. 259/1 The whole area of prisoners' rights is long overdue for rethink.

†**rethmetitian**, obs. form of ARITHMETICIAN.

1614 R. TAILOR *Hog hath lost Pearl* III. E j b, I finde my braines too shallow farre for study. What neede I care for being a Rethmetitian.

rethor, rethoric, rethorie, etc., obs. ff. RHETOR, RHETORIC, RHETORY, etc.

re'thread (riː-), *v.* [RE- 5 a.] *trans.* To thread again. Also *absol.* and *transf.*

1904 *Westm. Gaz.* 16 Feb. 2/1 Should the thread break, it is immediately rethreaded by another device. **1906** *Ibid.* 12 Nov. 2/1 The boat rethreads the line of light. **1932** G. HEYER *Devil's Cub* iii. 35 Mary re-threaded her needle. **1963** *Times* 25 May 9/7 A woman nods in time as she rethreads. **1974** N. FREELING *Dressing of Diamond* 173 Just rethread and set it on automatic record. **1974** M. BABSON *Stalking Lamb* iii. 28 The needle needed rethreading. She had come to the end of the length of silk.

rethrograte, obs. form of RETROGRADE *a.*

re'throne (riː-), *v.* [RE- 5 a.] *trans.* To enthrone again. Hence **re'throned** *ppl. a.*

1820 *Blackw. Mag.* VII. 482 The attempt to rethrone the princes of the house of Stuart. **1839–48** BAILEY *Festus* 83 Truth shall reign, Nature shall be rethroned, and man sublimed. **1902** A. E. W. MASON *Four Feathers* viii, Like a rethroned king.

re'thunder (riː-), *v.* [RE- 5 a.]

1. *intr.* To sound or echo again like thunder.

1742 YOUNG *Nt. Th.* VII. 1070 Re-thunder'd hell, and darted all her fires. **1790** A. WILSON *Ep. to Mr. A. Clarke* Poet. Wks. (1846) 50 While harsh, the huge machine shot loud rethundering past. *a* **1849** J. C. MANGAN *Poems* (1859) 58 And now, ere the din rethunders, the youth Invokes the great name.

2. *trans.* To declaim (something) again.

1893 *Advance* (Chicago) 15 June, In that thinking which he kept up while you were rethundering Cicero's orations against Catiline.

retia, pl. RETE

reti'arian, *a.* and *sb. rare.* [f. next + -AN.]

a. *adj.* Composed of retiarii. **b.** *sb.* A retiarius.

1730 A. GORDON *Maffei's Amphith.* 159 A Gladiator.. of the Retiarian Class. **1802** GIFFORD tr. *Juvenal* viii. 294 The wonder is, they turn not fencers too, Secutors, Retiarians.

‖**retiarius** (riːtɪ'ɛərɪəs, riːʃ-). [L. *rētiārius*, f. *rēte* a net.] A Roman gladiator who carried a net with which to entangle his adversary.

1647 R. STAPYLTON *Juvenal* 267 And there Gracchus, Romes infamy, doth arm'd appear, A Retiarius. **1693** STEPNEY in Dryden *Juvenal* (1697) 209 As Retiarius he Attacks his Foe; First waves his Trident ready for the throw, Next casts his Net. **1748** THOMSON *Cast. Indol.* II. xliii, As in throng'd Amphitheatre, of old, The wary Retiarius trap'd his foe. **1797** *Encycl. Brit.* (ed. 3) XVII. 241/2 The retiarius attempted to cast his net over the head of the secutor. **1858** BIRCH *Anc. Pottery* II. 289 Another lamp in the same collection has a retiarius holding his trident. **1880** MEREDITH *Tragic Com.* (1881) 96, I.. encountered a retiarius, and the meshes are on my head and arms.

retiary ('riːʃɪərɪ), *sb.* [See prec. and -ARY.]

1. = RETIARIUS. *rare*$^{-0}$.

1661 BLOUNT *Glossogr.* (ed. 2), *Retiary*, he that casts a net, properly in fighting to take his enemy.

2. A net-making or geometrical spider.

1835 KIRBY *Hab. & Inst. Anim.* II. xvii. 184, I shall consider those [spiders] I intend to notice, under the usual names of weavers and retiaries.

retiary ('riːʃɪərɪ), *a.* [f. as prec.]

1. Pertaining or relating to the making of webs, nets, or net-like structures.

1658 SIR T. BROWNE *Garden of Cyrus* ii. 41 And beside this kinde of work in Retiarie and hanging tectures, in embroderies, and eminent needle-works [etc.]. **1854**

BADHAM *Halieut.* 197 No other combination of meshes can convey such an idea of human ingenuity and inventiveness in the retiary art.

2. a. Fighting with a net; using a net like a retiarius. Also *fig.*

1658 SIR T. BROWNE *Gard. Cyrus* ii. 42 That the networks ..of antiquity were little different in the form from ours.., is confirmable from the nets of the Retiarie gladiators. **1682** —— *Chr. Mor.* I. §24 Our inward Antagonists,..like Retiary and Laqueary Combatants, with Nets, Frauds and Entanglements fall upon us. **1810** COLERIDGE in *Lit. Rem.* (1838) III. 298 Let not the surpassing eloquence of Taylor dazzle you, nor his scholastic retiary versatility of logic illaqueate your good sense.

b. Using a net to catch Lepidoptera.

1967 V. NABOKOV *Speak, Memory* vi. 131 America has shown even more of this morbid interest in my retiary activities.

3. ***retiary spider***, a spider which constructs a proper net; a geometrical spider.

1646 SIR T. BROWNE *Pseud. Ep.* v. xix. (1686) 214 We will not dispute the Pictures of Retiary Spiders, and their position in the Web. **1658** —— *Gard. Cyrus* ii. 42 The neat Retiarie Spider, which seems to weave without transversion. **1815** KIRBY & SP. *Entomol.* xiii. (1818) I. 421 *note*, May not the spinners..be peculiar to the retiary spiders, and furnish this viscid thread? **1835** KIRBY *Hab. & Inst. Anim.* II. 185 The organs by which the retiary spiders form their curious geometric snares.

‖**reticella** (reti'tʃɛlla). [It., dim. of *rete* net: see RETE.] A lace-like fabric produced esp. in Venice in the 15th, 16th, and 17th centuries. Also used *attrib.* to designate the type of geometric pattern characteristic of this fabric. Cf. next.

1865 F. B. PALLISER *Hist. Lace* iv. 58 One Francesca Bulgarini also instructed the schools [at Siena] in the making of lace of every kind, especially the Venetian reticella. **1900** E. JACKSON *Hist. Hand-Made Lace* 194 Reticellas, or Greek Point laces, were made chiefly from 1480 to 1620, the designs being always of the stiff geometrical type. **1932** D. C. MINTER *Mod. Needlecraft* 54/2 Reticella is a style of work based on cut or drawn threads. **1960** B. SNOOK *Eng. Hist. Embroidery* 50 White work is much heavier in style in the late 16th and early 17th centuries... Drawn threadwork fillings and reticella motifs are combined in highly conventional leaves and flowers. **1977** FLEMING & HONOUR *Penguin Dict. Decorative Arts* 658/1 *Reticella*, a decorative fabric made, like cutwork and drawn work, from panels of woven lines but with less use of the textile threads and much more free needlework.

‖**reticello** (reti'tʃɛllo). [It., f. as prec.] **1. a.** As pl. reticelli. A network of fine glass threads embedded in some Venetian glass. **b.** Glass formed with this type of decoration. Also ***reticello glass***.

[**1858** A. W. FRANKS *Vitreous Art* in J. B. Waring *Art Treasures of U.K.* 9 (*heading*) Lace and reticulated glass... The reticulated glass (*vasi a reticelli*) is a variety of the lace.] **1899** R. GLAZIER *Man. Historic Ornament* 95 The Venetians used with equal skill all the old methods of glass-making ..*reticelli*, a network of white lines enclosing at the intersection a bubble of air. **1907** E. DILLON *Glass* xiii. 206 When two series of..rods are arranged to cross one another at an angle, we get a reticulated pattern, and within the *reticelli* thus formed a bubble of air may be caught up. **1926** W. BUCKLEY *European Glass* 39 An example of 'Reticelli', or in German, 'Netz-glas'. **1977** FLEMING & HONOUR *Penguin Dict. Decorative Arts* 658/2 *Reticello glass*, glass decorated with a mesh of opaque white threads beneath the surface. *Ibid.* 822/2 During the C16 they..began to make *reticello* or filigree glass.

2. = prec.

1953 M. POWYS *Lace & Lace-Making* iii. 5 Soon the worker built up the lace decoration by throwing threads across these wide-open spaces in either direction, forming geometrical patterns and weaving in and out or button-holing over the threads that bridge the gap, Reticello.

reticence ('rɛtɪsəns), *sb.* Also 7, 9 -ense. [a. F. *reticence* (= Sp. and Pg. *reticencia*, It. *reticenza*), or ad. L. *reticentia*, f. *reticēre* to keep silence: see -ENCE.] Maintenance of silence; avoidance of saying too much or of speaking freely; disposition to say little.

Not in common use until after 1830.

1603 HOLLAND *Plutarch's Mor.* 841 (R.), Many times, I wis, a smile, a reticence or keeping silence, may well express a speech, and make it more emphatical. **1656** BLOUNT *Glossogr.*, *Reticence*, silence, concealment, councel-keeping, when one holds his peace, and utters not the thing he should tell. **1706** PHILLIPS (ed. Kersey), *Reticence*, a Rhetorical Figure, when something is conceal'd that ought to be declar'd; Concealment, or passing over in Silence. **1831** CARLYLE *Sart. Res.* II. x, A man so known for impenetrable reticence as Teufelsdröckh. **1865** TROLLOPE *Belton Est.* xii. 130 That frankness of hers had not been successful, and she regretted that she had not imposed on herself some little reticence. **1884** J. TAIT *Mind in Matter* (1892) 8 Divine wisdom betrays itself by reticence about the unseen world.

fig. **1873** STEVENSON *Ess. Trav., Roads* (1905) 233 We learn,..through one coquettish reticence after another,.. the whole loveliness of the country. **1875** SWINBURNE *Ess. & Stud.* 277 The Lac de Gaube,..with a strange attraction for the swimmer in its cold smooth reticence and breathless calm.

b. Const. *of* (the thing kept back). Also *fig.*

1838 SIR W. HAMILTON *Logic* xx. (1866) I. 391 On no principle can it be shown, that our modern logicians are correct in denying or not contemplating the possibility of the reticence of the conclusion [of a syllogism]. **1856** MISS MULOCK *J. Halifax* i, My father and I both glanced round, surprised at her unusual reticence of epithets. **1868** SWINBURNE *Ess. & Stud.* (1875) 363 The same breadth and subtlety of touch, the same noble reticence of colour.

c. *pl.* Instances of silence or reserve.

1814 W. TAYLOR in Robberd *Mem.* (1843) II. 449, I need not dwell on the judicious selection of matter..or on the decorous purity of his very reticences. **1833** *Fraser's Mag.* VII. 550 This naughty flower-scene..is among his lordship's reticenses. **1878** MORLEY *Carlyle, Crit. Misc.* Ser. I. 185 The reticences of men are often only less full of meaning than their most pregnant speech.

Hence **'reticence** *v.*, to pass over in silence.

1833 *Fraser's Mag.* VII. 532 Some choice passages.. which from other motives he had purposely reticensed.

'reticency. [-ENCY.] = RETICENCE *sb.*

a **1617** BAYNE *On Eph.* (1643) 157 The words have a rhetorical reticency in them, and are thus laid down. **1652** GAULE *Magastrom.* 51 Wherefore, then, use they so manifold..obscurities, insignificancies, reticencies? **1727–38** CHAMBERS *Cycl.*, *Reticency*,..a figure in rhetoric, whereby we make oblique mention of a thing, in pretending to pass it over unmentioned. **1815** W. TAYLOR in *Monthly Rev.* LXXVIII. 19 Brooke pointed out numberless inaccuracies, which Camden corrected with illiberal reticency. **1889** STEVENSON *Master of Ballantrae* 165 That unhappy and secretive fault of reticency.

reticent ('rɛtɪsənt), *a.* [ad. L. *reticent-em*, pres. pple. of *reticēre*, f. *re-* RE- + *tacēre* to be silent.] Reserved; disinclined to speak freely; given to silence or concealment.

a **1834** LAMB *Letter to Coleridge* (Latham), Upon this he is naturally reticent. **1856** EMERSON *Eng. Traits, Result*, They are slow and reticent. **1860** GEO. ELIOT *Mill on Fl.* I. xii, Mr. Glegg..was extremely reticent about his will. **1873** SYMONDS *Gr. Poets* iii. 89 Theognis recommends Cyrnus to be reticent, and not to communicate the whole of his plans even to his friends.

Hence **'reticently** *adv.*

1869 ROSSETTI *Mem. Shelley* p. cxv, The 'moral causes' thus reticently referred to are..[not] distinctly apparent.

reticle ('rɛtɪk(ə)l). [ad. L. *rēticulum*, dim. of *rēte* net: cf. RETICULE.]

†**1. a.** 'A little net, or casting net.' *Obs.*

1656 BLOUNT *Glossogr.*

†**b.** A structure resembling a net. *Obs. rare*$^{-1}$.

1790 *Phil. Trans.* LXXXI. 23 The texture of animal and vegetable fibrous substances must be a sort of reticle.

2. A set of parallel wires, threads, etc., with others intersecting them at right angles, or of lines similarly ruled upon a sheet of glass, placed in the object-glass of a telescope, in order to facilitate accurate observations.

1731 BAILEY, vol. II. (ed. 2), *Reticula, Reticle*,..a contrivance for the exact measuring the quantity of eclipses. **1797** *Encycl. Brit.* (ed. 3) II. 590 In the common focus of the object-glass and eye-glass is placed a reticle..consisting of three horizontal and parallel fine-stretched silver wires,.. with a fourth vertical wire..passing through the centre. **1829** W. PEARSON *Pract. Astron.* II. 133 La Lande has called reticles (reticules) the most simple kind of micrometer. **1879** NEWCOMB & HOLDEN *Astron.* 76 The reticle is a network of fine spider lines placed in the focus of the objective [of a telescope]. **1890** *Anthony's Photogr. Bull.* III. 155 To detect shrinkage of the film, we impress the image of a reticle ruled in squares, on the negative before exposure, and, on development, we have these squares displayed.

3. A disc or the like with a pattern of opaque and transparent portions which can be rotated in the path of a beam of light or other radiation so as to modulate it.

1959 *Proc. IRE* XLVII. 1566/2 The particular space-filtering properties associated with typical picket fence, checkerboard, and star reticles, as they operate in square or circular field stops, are shown in Figs. 5 and 6. **1961** *Jrnl. Optical Soc. Amer.* LI. 1011/1 In the detection of infrared radiation, it is common practice to interrupt the incident beam periodically to produce an alternating signal for electronic processing. The means used to accomplish this is usually a multisectored spinning aperture called a reticle. **1966** L. M. BIBERMAN *Reticles in Electro-Optical Devices* iii. 30 A simple reticle providing 'two-level' phase modulation is shown... If a small image is focused upon such a rotating reticle, the reticle can provide an indication of the radial position of that image by means of the phase information in the pulses of transmitted radiation.

reticular (rɪ'tɪkjʊlə(r)), *a.* [ad. mod.L. *rēticulār-is*, f. *rēticulum*: see prec. So F. *réticulaire*, It. *reticulare*, Sp. and Pg. *reticular*.]

1. Resembling a net in appearance or construction; consisting of closely interwoven fibres or filaments; net-like: **a.** *Anat.*

1597 LOWE *Chirurg.* (1634) 143 The nerve..doth dilate itselfe, and maketh the tunicke reticular. **1682** GIBSON *Anat.* 12 There is spread over the surface of the skin, a certain mucous and reticular body. **1768–74** TUCKER *Lt. Nat.* (1834) I. 388 The auditory nerves are represented to us by anatomists as expanded in a reticular form at the bottom of the ear. **1787** *Phil. Trans.* LXXVII. 389 This reticular net-work in the Seal is very coarse. **1805** *Ibid.* XCV. 5 The heart is always compacted together by a delicate reticular membrane. **1855** OWEN *Skel. & Teeth* 6 A reticular disposition of the bony substance. **1876** DUHRING *Dis. Skin* 22 The papillary layer merges into the reticular layer without distinct line of demarcation.

b. In specific *Anat.* uses: (i) ***reticular tissue***, tissue of the reticuloendothelial system which helps to form the framework of lymphatic tissue, bone marrow, and the tissue of the spleen and liver.

1848 *Quain's Elem. Anat.* (ed. 5) I. p. cxiii, The substance known by the names of 'cellular', 'areolar', 'filamentous', and 'reticular' tissue. **1892** H. E. CLARK *Wilson's Anatomist's Vade Mecum* (ed. 11) I. 16 Reticular tissue is found in all lymphatic glands, in the pharynx and tonsils, the solitary and agminate glands of the intestine, the thymus gland, and in the spleen... From its presence in lymphatic glands it has been named 'adenoid' and 'lymphoid' tissue. **1941** *Lancet* 11 Jan. 46/1 The relationship of the angioid proliferations to the reticular tissue is..complex.

(ii) Applied to a diffuse network of intermingled nerve fibres and nerve cell bodies in parts of the brain stem, one of the functions of which is to mediate changes in the degree of wakefulness.

1887 G. D. THANE *Ellis's Demonstr. Anat.* (ed. 10) ii. 197 In the dorsal portion of the medulla oblongata..the longitudinal fibres derived from the anterior and lateral columns of the cord..give rise to a structure that is known as the reticular formation of the medulla. **1949** MORUZZI & MAGOUN in *Electroencephalogr. & Clin. Neurophysiol.* I. 455/1 The following account..explores the relations of this reticular activating system to the arousal reaction to natural stimuli. **1962** A. HUXLEY *Island* xi. 171 Animal experiments indicated that it affected the reticular system. **1968** PASSMORE & ROBSON *Compan. Med. Stud.* I. xxiv. 20/1 It seems that consciousness is determined by the activity of the reticular formation and many anaesthetics act particularly upon it. **1975** D. & I. JORDAN tr. M. Zimmermann in R. F. Schmidt *Fund. Neurophysiol.* vii. 221 There is a constant 'activating' afferent flow from the reticular system to the cerebrum that controls the state of consciousness. Therefore, the term 'reticular activating system' is used to denote this functional property of the Formatio reticularis.

(iii) ***reticular cell***, a fibroblast or other unspecialized cell, esp. a phagocytic cell that helps to form the framework of the reticuloendothelial system and plays an essential role in blood formation; cf. ***reticulum cell*** s.v. RETICULUM 5.

1925 STRONG & ELWYN *Bailey's Text-bk. Histol.* (ed. 7) iv. 75 Others maintain that the delicate fibers run in the peripheral cytoplasm (ectoplasm) of the reticular cells. **1927** *Amer. Jrnl. Path.* III. 523 Study of the so-called reticular cells of the spleen, lymph nodes and other organs show [*sic*] that they possess fibroglia fibrils and that they, therefore, are fibroblasts. *Ibid.* 525 There are no reticular cells other than fibroblasts. **1938** H. M. CARLETON *Schafer's Essent. Histol.* (ed. 14) 48 The granular leucocytes, lymphocytes and monocytes are all derived from a columnar stem-cell called by Sabin the reticular cell. **1938** *Jrnl. Path. & Bacteriol.* XLVII. 461 The term 'reticular cell' was first introduced by Ribbert (1889) in describing the cells of lymphoid tissue to distinguish between the 'endothelial cells' of the lymph sinuses and the reticular cells proper. **1970** T. S. & C. R. LEESON *Histology* (ed. 2) vi. 105/1 Reticular cells may give rise to free macrophages, to early precursors of erythrocytes and leukocytes, and perhaps to other cell types. **1975** *Jrnl. Path.* CXVII. 119 The term reticular cell should be reserved for the dendritic reticular cell of Nossal *et al. Ibid.* 121 *Reticular cell*, a phrase with so many meanings as to be meaningless.

c. In other applications.

1720 *Phil. Trans.* XXXI. 85 He found it intirely coagulated,..with a reticular Pellicle upon the Surface exposed to the Air. **1769** E. BANCROFT *Guiana* 265 Contenting themselves either with the bark of trees, or the reticular covering of a coco-nut. **1796** KIRWAN *Elem. Min.* (ed. 2) II. 83 Hepatic Pyrites..is found crystallized..or reticular. **1802–3** tr. *Pallas's Trav.* (1812) II. 403 It has..a slightly serrated, reticular leaf.

2. *Arch.* Of masonry: Constructed of lozenge-shaped stones, bricks, etc., or of square pieces set diagonally instead of vertically.

1797 *Encycl. Brit.* (ed. 3) XVI. 140/2 This structure consists of small pieces of baked earth cut lozengewise,.. and was called reticular, from its resemblance to fishing-nets. **1823** [see RETICULATED 2].

3. Resembling a net in effect or operation; intricate, entangled.

1818 PEACOCK *Nightmare Abbey* Wks. (1875) 366 Cutting the Gordian knot of his reticular envelopment. **1822** BYRON *Juan* XII. lix, Yet many have a method more reticular— 'Fishers for men', like sirens with soft lutes. **1883** *Cent. Mag.* Oct. 822/1 The law is blind, crooked, and perverse..; its administration is on the practice of by-gone ages, slow, reticular, complicated.

4. Of or pertaining to the reticulum of a ruminant.

1923 G. H. WOOLDRIDGE *Encycl. Vet. Med., Surg. & Obstetrics* II. 1025/1 This operation [*sc.* rumenotomy]..is sometimes performed for exploratory purposes in obscure cases of ruminal, reticular, or omasal indigestion. **1966** DALLING & ROBERTSON *Internat. Encycl. Vet. Med.* V. 2633 The reticular contents are liquid and offer no resistance to a thorough examination.

Hence **re'ticularly** *adv.*, like a net.

1835–6 *Todd's Cycl. Anat.* I. 382/2 It is owing to this reticularly arranged stratum of muscular fibres that the bladder..presents its peculiar irregular surface. **1875** BLAKE *Zool.* 331 In Retepora the polypary is..perforated reticularly.

re'ticulary, *a. rare.* [-ARY.] Net-like.

1852 CARLYLE *Let.* in Froude *Life in London* (1884) II. 100 The Rhine, of a vile, reddish-drab colour, and all cut into a reticulary work of branches,..was far from beautiful about Rotterdam.

reticulate (rɪ'tɪkjʊlət), *a.* [ad. L. *rēticulāt-us*, f. *rēticulum*: see RETICULE. So It. *reticulato*, Sp. and Pg. *reticulado*, F. *réticulé*.] **a.** Reticulated.

1658 SIR T. BROWNE *Gard. Cyrus* iii. 147 The like Reticulate grain is observable in some Russia Leather. **1658** —— *Hydriot.* Ded., We pretend not to multiply vegetable divisions by Quincuncial and Reticulate plants. **1688** HOLME *Armoury* III. 457/1 Reticulate, or Net Worke, walls made Net-wayes or Loseng-wise. **1703** *Phil. Trans.* XXIII.

1419 The branches of this [coral] run one into another without any reticulate order. **1785** MARTYN *Rousseau's Bot.* xxxii. (1794) 502 Morel is a fungus that is reticulate or netted all over the outside or upper surface. **1826** GOOD *Bk. Nat.* (1834) II. 21 The neuropterous insects, or those with 4 reticulate or net-work wings. **1864** NEALE *Seatonian Poems* 86 With light and shade reticulate. **1897** *Allbutt's Syst. Med.* III. 944 When the inner surface is magnified it appears to be reticulate. **1965** A. HOLMES *Princ. Physical Geol.* (ed. 2) 1279/2 (Index), Reticulate (trellised) drainage. **1968** R. W. FAIRBRIDGE *Encycl. Geomorphol.* 90/1 A stream or river bed is said to have a braided pattern when the deeper channels form a lacy or reticulate network of divergent and convergent members. *Ibid.* 961/2 (*caption*) Braided pattern ('reticulate drainage') in semiarid environment.

Comb. **1870** HOOKER *Stud. Flora* 377 Stem with 1-2 whorls of reticulate-veined leaves. **1880** HOGG & JOHNSON *Wild Fl.* XI. Pl. 811 Reticulate-leaved willow, *Salix Reticulata.*

b. *spec.* in *Bot.*, as an epithet of one kind of thickening of the walls of xylem elements.

1873 F. H. HOOKER tr. *Le Maout & Decaisne's Gen. Syst. Bot.* 116 Cells may either be homogeneous, or punctate, or rayed, or reticulate, or spiral. **1907** W. C. STEVENS *Plant Anat.* vii. 109 The tracheids are elongated cells especially adapted to be water carriers by numerous thin places in the walls in the form of bordered pits or associated with spiral, annular, or reticulate thickenings. **1976** BELL & COOMBE tr. *Strasburger's Textbk. Bot.* (rev. ed.) II. ii. 304 Now begins the more extensive differentiation, particularly of the cell wall... The wall becomes thickened, usually by a process of opposition. In the conducting elements, for example, annular, spiral or reticulate thickenings are formed, and lignification sets in.

reticulate (rɪˈtɪkjʊleɪt), *v.* [Back-formation from RETICULATED *a.*]

1. a. *trans.* To divide or mark in such a way as to resemble network. Also *fig.*

1787 JEFFERSON *Writ.* (1859) II. 136 Spurs or ramifications of high mountains,..as it were, reticulating these provinces. **1833** LYELL *Princ. Geol.* III. 356 The granite, in this locality, often sends forth so many veins as to reticulate the limestone and schist. **1853** KANE *Grinnell Exp.* xlii. (1856) 385 Dark rivers, exhaling..frost-smoke, reticulated the entire surface. **1871** ALABASTER *Wheel of Law* 252 The numerous canals and branches of the river which reticulate the flat alluvial plain. **1971** *Nature* 17 Dec. 394/1 The central device employed in network thermodynamics is the conceptual separation of 'reversible' and 'irreversible' processes. That is, we mentally reticulate the system into subsystems, each of which either stores energy reversibly or dissipates energy without storage.

b. To form or make (a net). *rare*$^{-1}$.

1832 DOWNES *Lett.* I. 244 Access to it was..prevented by a horrible net of cobweb, and a band of the hideous artificers by which it had been reticulated.

2. *intr.* To divide so as to form a network, or something having that appearance.

1862 M. HOPKINS *Hawaii* 26 After pursuing the great stream for some miles it reticulated into..many rivulets.

Hence **re'ticulating** *ppl. a.*

1841 FORBES *Hist. Brit. Star-fishes* 102 The disk and rays are covered with oblong reticulating tubercles. **1850** DANA *Geol.* App. I. 717 The veins do not so completely lose their reticulating character. **1876** PAGE *Adv. Text-bk. Geol.* iii. 54 Showing a thousand reticulating fissures.

reticulated (rɪˈtɪkjʊleɪtɪd), *ppl. a.* [f. as RETICULATE *a.* + -ED.]

1. Constructed or arranged like a net; made or marked so as to resemble a net or network.

In predicative use also const. *by* or *with.*

attrib. a **1728** WOODWARD *Nat. Hist. Fossils* (1729) 49 The Intervals of the Cavities, rising a little, make a pretty kind of reticulated Work. **1796** *Phil. Trans.* LXXXVI. 260 A small piece of fine cambric, or reticulated silver wire stretched before it. **1802** BINGLEY *Anim. Biog.* (1813) III. 479 Some are composed of reticulated fibres, or masses, of small spines. **1857** LIVINGSTONE *Trav.* 612 The absence of both these rhinoceroses among the reticulated rivers in the central valley may easily be accounted for. **1885** *Law Times* LXXIX. 247/1 A parallelogram covered with reticulated lines.

predic. **1755** JOHNSON, *Network*, any thing reticulated or decussated, at equal distances, with interstices between the intersections. **1796** WITHERING *Brit. Plants* (ed. 3) III. 885 Leaves smaller and shorter than in 1; fine green, not shining, not reticulated. **1802** J. PLAYFAIR *Huttonian The.* 301 The strata are..reticulated by the veins. **1842** EMERSON *Transcendentalist* Wks. (Bohn) II. 290 This pretty web..will at last be overshot and reticulated with veins of the blue. **1877** THOMSON *Voy. Challenger* I. 195 Black oval bodies about an inch long, with the surface reticulated.

b. *spec.* in names of varieties of animals, plants, or minerals.

1777 PENNANT *Brit. Zool.* IV. Pl. lxxii. No. 92 Reticulated Whelk. **1783** BARBUT *Vermes* 86 The Reticulated Sea Star..is stellated with reticulated sharp-pointed rays. **1816** CLEAVELAND *Min.* 539 What has been called reticulated cobalt appears to be native silver. **1855** MISS PRATT *Flower. Pl.* V. 91 Reticulated Willow, or Netted or Wrinkle-leaved Willow. **1883** *Standard* 3 Aug. 5/6 One of the reticulated pythons managed to escape.

c. *spec.* of porcelain, etc. Cf. PIERCED *ppl. a.* c.

1881 AUDSLEY & BOWES *Keramic Art of Japan* 143 There are several specimens of pierced, or what is termed reticulated, porcelain. **1908** J. F. BLACKER *Chats on Oriental China* xiii. 152 There is a white biscuit class, very rare, often having two walls or divisions, of which the outer one only is biscuit, reticulated or pierced with a fine network or trellis of various patterns, through which the interior wall can be seen. **1970** [see PIERCED *ppl. a.* c]. **1974** SAVAGE & NEWMAN *Illustr. Dict. Ceramics* 245 (*caption*) Teapot with reticulated outer wall and handle with moulded terminals, creamware, Leeds, *c.* 1785. **1980** *Catal. Fine Chinese Ceramics* (Sotheby, Hong Kong) 166 Reserved on a reticulated florette and *wan* diaper-ground infilled in green.

2. *Arch.* **a.** (Cf. RETICULAR *a.* 2.)

1823 P. NICHOLSON *Pract. Build.* 306 They [the ancients] had their reticular or reticulated walls. **1851** TURNER *Dom. Archit.* III. II. vii. 321 A timber house, dating apparently from the fourteenth century, as it has reticulated panelling.

b. Of tracery: (see quot.).

1849 SHARPE *Decorated Window Tracery* 107 A very large class of Windows..containing what has been called Reticulated Tracery, or Tracery formed by the repetition of the same foliated opening.

3. Divided into small squares. (See quot. 1867.)

1867 G. F. CHAMBERS *Astron.* VII. i. 621 The simplest form is that known as the Reticulated Micrometer. It consists of an eye-piece of low power, having stretched across it a number of wires at right angles to and at equal..distances from each other. **1877** *Ibid.* (ed. 3) VII. viii. 726 For most amateurs a reticulated micrometer will suffice.

re'ticulately, *adv.* [f. RETICULATE *a.* + -LY[2].] In a reticulate fashion or manner; like network.

1821 W. P. C. BARTON *Flora N. Amer.* I. 26 One, sometimes two of the calicine segments dilated into large bracteiform appendages, reticulately veined with green beneath. **1846** DANA *Zooph.* (1848) 266 Disks seriately and reticulately budding. **1882** VINES tr. *Sachs' Bot.* 407 A few not very broad vessels thickened reticulately.

Comb. **1870** HOOKER *Stud. Flora* 468 A barren oblong linear or lanceolate reticulately-veined blade.

reticulation (rɪtɪkjʊˈleɪʃən). [See RETICULATE *a.* and -ATION.] A network; an arrangement of lines, etc., resembling a net; reticulated structure or appearance. **a.** *spec.* in *Photogr.*, (the formation of) a network of wrinkles or cracks in a photographic emulsion.

1671 GREW *Anat. Pl.* (1682) 47 Small Branches..all meeting and making a kind of Reticulation. **1841** FORBES *Hist. Brit. Star-fishes* 84 At the angles of the reticulations arise conical blunt spines. **1863** M. J. BERKELEY *Brit. Mosses* 44 The reticulation of the leaves is often indicative of natural affinity. **1886** *Ibis* July 225 Charadriidæ having the tarsus covered..with a network of fine hexagonal reticulations. **1888** H. C. JONES *Introd. Sci. & Pract. Photogr.* xix. 239 Concerning the reticulation of gelatine films, increase of the bichromate tends to produce grain. **1929** R. H. GOODSALL *Beginner's Guide to Photogr.* vi. 36 The removal of a negative from a comparatively warm bath of developer to a cold fixing solution..may cause 'frilling' or reticulation, *i.e.* curious wavy marks in the gelatine. **1967** V. STRAUSS *Printing Industry* v. 269/2 It seems that the tonal qualities of collotype prints result from the interaction of two related items. One is generally called reticulation; the other is varying ink receptivity. **1977** J. HEDGECOE *Photographer's Handbk.* 241 Modern films have built-in resistance to reticulation.

fig. **1839** CARLYLE *Chartism* ii. 14 The question, Is thrift increasing? runs through the reticulation, and is as water spilt on the ground. **1855** MOTLEY *Dutch Rep.* I. 243 The minute reticulations of tyranny which he had begun already to spin about a whole people. **1878** BAYNE *Purit. Rev.* iii. 82 Penetrating with the fine reticulation of its common Christian sentiment into recesses of the German forests.

b. ? *Austral.* and *N.Z.* A network of pipes used in irrigation and water supply. Also *transf.* (see quot. 1977).

1936 *Jrnl. R. Soc. W. Austral.* XXII. p. xxi, The Government has helped very materially in the following ways to meet the increased demand for water:—1. By reticulation from the Mundaring-Kalgoorlie pipe-line... 2. By 'District Water Supplies', *i.e.*, reticulation from rock-catchments. **1937** *Discovery* June 186/2 Twenty miles of 12-inch pipe have been laid from the dam to the mines; the dam and reticulation lines cost £150,000. **1977** *N.Z. Herald* 8 Jan. 2-10/4 (Advt.), We require..two plumbers with experience in commercial work. The contract involves complete reticulation of bedroom wings in conjunction with building renovations.

re'ticulato-, combining form of RETICULATE *a.*, as in ***reticulato-coalescent, -granulate, -ramose, -venose.*** (Cf. RETICULO-.)

1846 DANA *Zooph.* (1848) 447 Branches openly reticulato-coalescent. **1856-8** W. CLARK *Van der Hoeven's Zool.* II. 378 Covering of tarsus reticulato-granulate. *Ibid.* I. 93 Polypary reticulato-ramose. **1866** *Treas. Bot.* 967/2 *Reticulato-Venose*, having veins with the appearance of network.

reticule (ˈrɛtɪkjul). [a. F. *réticule*, ad. L. *rēticulum*: see RETICULUM and -CULE.]

1. = RETICLE 2.

1727-38 CHAMBERS *Cycl.* s.v., The reticule is a little frame, consisting of thirteen fine silken threads, equidistant [etc.]. **1773** *Phil. Trans.* LXIV. 33 Two object-glasses, with a reticule at the focus. **1839** *Penny Cycl.* XV. 176/1 The reticule, or diaphragm,..is any fixed arrangement of wires or bars which can be applied to a telescope for the purpose of measurement. **1878** LOCKYER *Stargazing* 221 Hooke and Auzout..pointed out how valuable the reticule of Malvasia would be if one of the wires were movable.

2. a. A small bag, usually made of some woven material, for carrying on the arm or in the hand, used by ladies as a pocket or workbag. (Cf. RIDICULE *sb.*[2])

1801 C. WILMOT *Let.* 13 Dec. in *Irish Peer* (1920) 21 'Reticules'..are a species of little Workbag worn by the Ladies, containing snuff-boxes, Billet-doux, Purses, Handkerchiefs, Fans, Prayer-Books, Bon-Bons, Visiting tickets. **1824** MISS MITFORD *Village* Ser. I. (1863) 227 She ornaments the reticules, bell-ropes, ottomans and chair-covers of all her acquaintance. **1847** L. HUNT *Men, Women, & B.* I. ii. 25 The lady, about to pay her fare, suddenly misses her reticule. **1885** *Morn. Post* 13 June 2 Stealing a leather hand-bag, a red plush reticule, and a piece of sponge.

b. ***reticule-basket***, a small basket resembling, or serving the purpose of, a reticule.

1848 *Zoologist* VI. 2073 They sometimes took away with them a reticule-basket full. **1857** MRS. CARLYLE *Lett.* II. 309 You came tripping in with a reticule-basket, and gave me little cakes.

3. *Astr.* One of the southern constellations, situated near Hydra. (Named by Lacaille.)

1868 LOCKYER *Guillemin's Heavens* (ed. 3) 335 From the Ship we pass..by the Flying Fish, Doradus, and the Reticule, and we arrive at Eridanus.

'reticuled, *a.* *rare*$^{-1}$. = RETICULATED *a.*

1861 WYNTER *Soc. Bees* 501 The reticuled bed of capillary vessels of the cutis and sub-cutaneous tissue.

reticulin (rɪˈtɪkjʊlɪn). *Histology.* [a. G. *reticulin* (M. Siegfried 1892, in *Ber. ü. die Verh. d. K. Sächs. Ges. der Wissensch. zu Leipzig* (Math.-Phys. Cl.) XLIV. 306): cf. next and -IN[1].] A structural protein with an affinity for silver stains that is present in healing wounds and forms a fine network in the lymph nodes, spleen, and liver; now regarded as a form of collagen.

1899 *Jrnl. Physiol.* XXIV. p. x, The fibres of reticular or retiform tissue are anatomically continuous with, and histologically identical with, the white fibres of connective tissue. According to Siegfried they are however chemically different, for they yield not only gelatin, but also a new substance he has named reticulin. **1902** *Ibid.* XXVIII. 321 Miss Tebb believes that reticulin is collagen, which has been changed by alcohol and ether. **1930** *Amer. Jrnl. Path.* VI. 631 In successful preparations, reticulin stains black while collagen bundles stain yellow, thereby fortifying Mall's conclusion that reticulin..is a substance different from collagen. **1947** *Ann. Rev. Microbiol.* I. 133 Following up an observation..that incubation with *Cl[ostridium] welchii* Type A filtrates causes rapid disintegration of muscle, and that this is due..to destruction of the reticulin scaffolding, Oakley *et al.*..have confirmed the presence of a collagenase enzyme in such filtrates. **1973** LAW & OLIVER *Gloss. Histopath. Terms* 118 *Reticular fibres.* These elements of connective tissue are often loosely referred to as 'reticulin' which perhaps more accurately should be confined to the constituent protein. A long-standing controversy still rages over their relationship with collagen fibres; although reticular fibres possess a strong argyrophilia and collagen fibres do not..examination under the electron microscope shows no basic structural dissimilarity. **1974** R. M. KIRK et al. *Surgery* ii. 30 Phagocytes attached to reticulin fibrils line sinusoids in the lymph nodes, liver, spleen, bone marrow, and certain endocrine glands such as the anterior pituitary, adrenal and thymus glands.

reticulitis (rɪtɪkjʊˈlaɪtɪs). *Vet. Sci.* [f. RETICUL(UM + -ITIS.] Inflammation of the reticulum of a ruminant.

1905 MOUSSU & DOLLAR *Dis. Cattle, Sheep, Goats & Swine* v. 186 Rumenitis or reticulitis may..follow the ingestion of irritant foods or plants. **1970** A. R. JENNINGS *Animal Path.* v. 91 A common cause of reticulitis is the penetration of the reticular wall by a sharp foreign object.

re'ticulo-, combining form of L. *rēticulum*, as in ***reticulo-ramose, -venose.*** (Cf. RETICULATO-.)

1775 J. JENKINSON tr. *Linnæus' Brit. Pl.* Gloss. s.v., A reticulo-venose leaf, is a leaf whose surface is full of veins somewhat like net-work. **1875** BLAKE *Zool.* 331 In Retepora the polypary is reticulo-ramose, or perforated reticularly and calcareous.

reticulocyte (rɪˈtɪkjʊləʊsaɪt). *Med.* [f. RETICULO- + -CYTE.] **a.** A red blood cell which has lost its nucleus but is not yet mature, characterized by a granular or reticulated appearance when suitably stained.

1922 E. B. KRUMBHAAR in *Jrnl. Lab. & Clin. Med.* VIII. 11 The presence of reticulated or 'skeined' erythrocytes..in the peripheral blood..has..in the last decade..assumed clinical importance as an index of the activity of blood formation. I would suggest..that when the normal percentage of these cells in the peripheral blood is exceeded, the condition be designated 'reticulosis'... The word 'reticulocyte' might similarly be substituted for 'reticulated erythrocytes'. **1956** *Nature* 28 Jan. 190/1 Although reticulocytes have practically their full complement of haemoglobin, evidence from amino-acid incorporation studies suggests that these cells, unlike mature erythrocytes, still have protein-synthesizing capacity. **1968** H. HARRIS *Nucleus & Cytoplasm* i. 12 The mammalian reticulocyte continues to synthesize haemoglobin for some days after elimination of the cell nucleus.

b. *attrib.*, as ***reticulocyte level***; **reticulocyte count**, the proportion or concentration of reticulocytes in the blood.

1922 E. B. KRUMBHAAR in *Jrnl. Lab. & Clin. Med.* VIII. 14 The temporary rise in the reticulocyte count immediately after transfusions were begun was found in another dog, and considered by us as probably due to bone marrow irritation. **1961** *Lancet* 26 Aug. 490/1 The reticulocyte and platelet counts were 3·6% and 228,000 per c. mm. respectively. **1980** *Brit. Med. Jrnl.* 29 Mar. 892/1 Thirty patients receiving haemodialysis..showed significant increases ($p < 0{\cdot}001$)..in reticulocyte count. **1946** *Nature* 2 Nov. 627/1 All the rabbits used in these experiments showed a normal reticulocyte level of 1·0-2·0 per cent.

reticulocytosis (rɪˌtɪkjʊləʊsaɪˈtəʊsɪs). *Med.* [f. prec. + -OSIS.] The presence in the blood of abnormally many reticulocytes.

1926 in R. J. E. SCOTT *Gould's Med. Dict.* 1110/1. **1929** *Arch. Internal Med.* XLIV. 502 (*heading*) Reticulocytosis produced by liver extract. **1956** *Nature* 28 Jan. 190/2 Preparations of rabbit blood containing 70-90 per cent reticulocytes, obtained following reticulocytosis induced by phenylhydrazine. **1977** *Jrnl. Clin. Invest.* LIX. 639/2 Patients with reticulocytosis..did not have increased denatured hemoglobin. **1980** *Brit. Med. Jrnl.* 29 Mar. 893/2

The delayed onset of reticulocytosis after the beginning of cytolysis suggests that hepatocyte regeneration rather than hepatocyte destruction was the stage when this erythropoietin secretion occurred.

reˌticuloendoˈthelial, *a.* *Med.* Also with hyphen. [ad. G. *retikulo-endothelial*: cf. RETICULO- and *endothelial* adj. s.v. ENDO-.] Of, pertaining to, or designating a diverse system of tissues and cells characterized by their phagocytic ability and now known to be involved in the immune response.

The circulating monocytes of the blood are now usu. included, but formerly were excluded by some authors.

1924 *Physiol. Rev.* IV. 548 In various experimental conditions..the whole reticulo-endothelial system, all the histiocytes in the body and chiefly in the abdominal organs and in the bone marrow are entering a phase of functional stimulation. **1929** *Lancet* 5 Oct. 711/1 The distribution of reticulo-endothelial cells might be determined by the injection into animals of various dye substances which were taken up by the cells. **1947** *Ann. Rev. Microbiol.* I. 291 Until recently it was generally held that antibody formation is the function of the 'reticuloendothelial system' i.e., phagocytic tissue cells. **1974** R. M. KIRK et al. *Surgery* ii. 7 Reticuloendothelial rather than bloodborne cells participate. **1977** *Proc. R. Soc. Med.* LXX. 523/1 From this sort of information we can derive circumstantial evidence in favour of impaired reticuloendothelial function in patients with liver disease.

reticuloendotheliosis (rɪˌtɪkjʊləʊendəʊθiːlɪˈəʊsɪs). *Med.* Also with hyphen. [ad. G. *reticuloendotheliose* (O. Ewald 1924, in *Deutsch. Arch. f. klin. Med.* CXLII. 227): see prec. and -OSIS.] Hyperplasia of some part of the reticuloendothelial system.

1926 *Q. Cumulative Index Current Med. Lit.* XII. 591/1 Reticulo-endothelial reaction or 'reticulo-endotheliosis' (leukemia form?). **1933** *Jrnl. Path. & Bacteriol.* XXXVII. 327 The other group of cases (in which sinus reticulum is affected) is represented by monocyte leukaemia, and by certain of the cases described as systematic aleukaemic reticuloendotheliosis. **1958** R. W. RAVEN *Cancer* II. xxiv. 452 The word reticuloendotheliosis was originally used, by analogy with myelosis and lymphadenosis, to describe a systematized proliferation of 'reticuloendothelial cells', of which the monocytes are representatives in the circulating blood. Both leukaemic and aleukaemic forms of reticulo-endotheliosis were recognized. **1978** *Nature* 20 July 269/2 'Pool' sensitisation of T cells from patients with hairy cell leukaemia (leukaemic reticuloendotheliosis) gives rise to CTL [*sc.* cytotoxic T lymphocytes] that lyse autologous leukaemia cells but not autologous normal lymphocytes.

reˌticulosarˈcoma. *Path.* [ad. F. *réticulosarcome* (C. Oberling 1928, in *Bull. de l'Assoc. Française pour l'Étude du Cancer* XVII. 279): see RETICULO- and SARCOMA.] A sarcoma arising from the reticuloendothelial system.

1938 *Jrnl. Path. & Bacteriol.* XLVII. 473 The idea of grouping all the neoplastic conditions of reticular tissue under the generic term reticulosarcoma. **1953** *Brit. Jrnl. Surg.* XLI. 75 (*heading*) Multiple reticulosarcoma of the duodenum and jejunum. *Ibid.* 76/2 Description and classification of reticulosarcomata. **1958** R. W. RAVEN *Cancer* II. xxiv. 452 In 1928 Oberling introduced the name reticulo-sarcoma as a generic term for all neoplasms of the LRS [*sc.* lymphoreticular system]: since then varieties such as lymphocytic and lymphoblastic reticulosarcomas..and sundry more disputable cytological types have been listed. **1974** R. M. KIRK et al. *Surgery* ii. 31 If the growth contains a large number of reticulin fibres, as revealed by special staining methods, the growth is called a reticulosarcoma.

reticulose (rɪˈtɪkjʊləʊs), *a.* [f. L. *rētĭcul-um* + -OSE.] Of the nature of, resembling, network.

1826 KIRBY & SP. *Entomol.* IV. xlvi. 271 *Reticulose*,.. having a number of minute impressed lines which intersect each other in various directions. **1879** *Encycl. Brit.* IX. 373/1 The testaceous Foraminifera..afford the best means of studying the life-history of the 'reticulose' type.

reticulosis (rɪtɪkjʊˈləʊsɪs). *Med.* Pl. **-oses** (-ˈəʊsiːz). [ad. G. *retikulose* (E. Letterer 1924, in *Frankfurter Zeitschr. f. Path.* XX. 392): see RETICULO- and -OSIS.] Proliferative disease of reticuloendothelial cells.

Quot. 1922 s.v. RETICULOCYTE illustrates a different sense.

1932 B. D. PULLINGER in *Rose Res. on Lymphadenoma* 134 The term 'reticulo-endotheliosis' is not applicable to any member of the group. The term 'reticulose' or 'reticulosis' (Letterer) is more suitable. **1958** R. W. RAVEN *Cancer* II. xxiv. 453 The term *reticulosis* was first used in 1924, when Letterer described his original case of what is now often known as Letterer-Siwe disease: he interpreted the case as a variety of 'aleukaemia', which he named..*aleukämische Retikulose bzw. Retikuloendotheliose*... In 1934, Letterer stated that the term reticulosis should be used..only in relation to a systematized proliferation of reticulum cells, in which these cells did *not* proceed to form..fibres. **1977** *Proc. R. Soc. Med.* LXX. 46/2 The subject of the symposium held on the second afternoon was The Reticuloses; it dealt with management of the leukaemias in children and adults, and of Hodgkin's disease and the non-Hodgkin lymphomas.

reticulum (rɪˈtɪkjʊləm). [L. *rētĭculum*, dim. of *rēte* net: cf. RETICULE.]

1. *Anat.* **a.** The second stomach of a ruminant.

1658 SIR T. BROWNE *Gard. Cyrus* iii. 55 The *Reticulum*, or Net-like Ventricle of ruminating horned animals. **1676** GREW *Musæum, Anat. Stomach & Guts* vi. 27 The Reticulum forthwith throws it up into the Gulet and Mouth. **1727-38** CHAMBERS *Cycl.* s.v. *Ruminant*, The..reticulum, which we call the honeycomb. **1782** *A. Monro's Compar. Anatomy* 76 The second stomach..is called..*reticulum*, honeycomb, the bonnet or king's-hood. **1859** *Todd's Cycl. Anat.* V. 537/1 In the reticulum the walls remain smooth and do not exhibit any very evident traces of the contained water-cells. **1878** BELL *Gegenbaur's Comp. Anat.* 559 The reticulum is succeeded by the psalterium (omasus).

†**b.** The omentum or mesentery. *Obs.*

1704 J. HARRIS *Lex. Techn.* I, *Reticulum*, the same with *Omentum*. **1727-38** CHAMBERS *Cycl.*, *Reticulum*, the caul, or omentum; a name sometimes given this part from its net-like structure.

2. a. *Arch.* Reticulated work. *rare*$^{-1}$.

1797 *Encycl. Brit.* (ed. 3) XVI. 140/2 In the city of Salino are still to be seen remains of some walls, evidently of Roman origin from the reticulum.

b. *Bot.* (See quots.)

1835 LINDLEY *Introd. Bot.* (1839) 144 The fibrous sheath at the base of the leaves of Palms, called *reticulum* by some. **1856** HENSLOW *Dict. Bot. Terms* 157 *Reticulum*, the debris of crossed fibres about the base of the petioles in Palms.

c. A net-like structure; a membrane, etc., having a reticulated form or appearance.

1858 CARPENTER *Veg. Phys.* §199 The ribs forming a reticulum, or minute net-work. **1878** BELL *Gegenbaur's Comp. Anat.* 82 A very fine supporting reticulum is arranged around the radial spicula.

3. *Astr.* = RETICULE 3.

1841 *Penny Cycl.* XIX. 422/1. **1870** PROCTOR *Other Worlds than Ours* xii. 287 The extension of some of these streams in the constellations Grus, Hydra, Reticulum, &c.

4. a. *Histology.* Retiform tissue forming part of the reticuloendothelial system.

1870 H. POWER tr. *Stricker's Man. Human & Compar. Histol.* I. ii. 65 A remarkable form of connective tissue occurs in the supporting and investing reticulum of the glands of the lymphatic system and allied organs in connection with their blood capillaries, and around the fasciculi of fibrillar connective tissue. *Ibid.* 66 In the fresh condition, the reticulum is soft and easily torn. **1896** *Johns Hopkins Hosp. Rep.* I. 171 A tissue practically identical with reticulum is widely distributed throughout the body. *Ibid.* 202 Since they [*sc.* liver fibrils] seem to be identical with the reticulum of lymphatic glands, spleen and mucous membrane, I shall retain for them the name reticulum. **1964** *Jrnl. Exper. Med.* CXX. 1083 The most interesting feature ..of this reticulum web in primary follicles is its possible importance in the induction of immune responses. *Ibid.* 1084 A fine web of phagocytic reticulum in primary follicles was found to be responsible for antigen localization.

b. *Cytology.* The firmer parts of the cytoplasm; *Obs.* except in ***endoplasmic reticulum***, a complex and often extensive system of membrane in the cytoplasm of a cell, containing RNA and involved in protein synthesis.

1891 *Quain's Elem. Anat.* (ed. 10) I. 173 (*caption*) Protoplasm, showing a reticulum of plastin. *Ibid.*, In most cells..it is found that a differentiation of the protoplasm has occurred in such a manner that a part of it appears under high powers of the microscope in the form of a network or spongework... The network is known as the reticulum or spongioplasm. **1896** [see ENCHYLEMA]. **1948** PORTER & THOMPSON in *Jrnl. Exper. Med.* LXXXVIII. 24 b (*caption*) The relatively large mitochondria lie amidst strands of the endoplasmic reticulum. **1953** *Ibid.* XCVII. 736 This component is absent from the thinner (ectoplasmic) margins of the cell and appears instead to occupy the central or endoplasmic portions of the cytoplasm. From its location and form it has come to be referred to as the endoplasmic reticulum and by this name it has been noted in previous reports. **1974** M. C. GERALD *Pharmacol.* iii. 52 The endoplasmic reticulum, when viewed under an electron microscope, resembles a thin tubular network. **1976** *Sci. Amer.* Mar. 27/1 There were striking changes in the ultrastructure of the liver cell: the mitochondria..were enlarged and distorted, and the smooth membranes of the endoplasmic reticulum, the site of enzymes associated with the metabolism of alcohol and other substances, proliferated.

c. *Histology.* = RETICULIN.

1927 *Amer. Jrnl. Path.* III. 524 Reticulum as a chemically distinct intercellular substance does not exist; it is collagen in separated form, rendered prominent by the silver stain. **1941** *Cancer Res.* I. 234/1 By using a method which differentiates collagen from reticulum, we have found that, as age advances, there is a transformation of the latter into the former in the endometrium.

5. Special Comb.: **reticulum cell**, variously used to denote cells of the reticuloendothelial system; cf. *reticular cell* s.v. RETICULAR *a.* 1 a (iii); [the sense is due to Ribbert, who used G. *reticulumzell* (*Beitr. zu path. Anat. u. zu allg. Path.* (1889) VI. 206)].

1912 E. A. SCHÄFER *Textbk. Microsc. Anat.* 400 The ramified cells which cover the reticular tissue of the lymph-sinus often contain a considerable number of pigment-granules, especially in the medulla of the gland. These reticulum-cells are phagocytic. **1939** COOPER & JONES *Human Histol.* iv. 44 There is no obvious matrix, and the unhampered connective tissue or reticulum cells possess active phagocytic properties. **1975** *Jrnl. Path.* CXVII. 119 The terms reticular cell and reticulum cell are widely and variously used to describe cells in lymph-nodes. It has been suggested..that the term reticulum cell should be applied to cells in lymph-nodes which are not readily described as macrophages, lymphocytes, fibroblasts, endothelial cells or leukocytes and that the term reticular cell should be reserved for the dendritic reticular cell of Nossal et al. *Ibid.* 121 *Reticulum cell*, heterogeneous group of cells some of which bind antigen, some of which synthesise DNA, some of which may be macrophage precursors. *Ibid.*, The term 'reticulum' cell appears a useful omnibus word to describe all the mesenchymal cells of the lymphoreticular tissue which cannot at present be clearly categorised. Clearly as more is learned about these cells, fewer cells will fall within the category 'reticulum cell'. *Ibid.* 122 The popliteal lymph nodes showed macrophages, fibroblasts, endothelial cells and a heterogeneous group of cells here described as reticulum cells.

retie (riː-), *v.* Also 8 -tye. [RE- 5 a.] *trans.* To tie (something) again. Also *absol.*

1711 GAY *Rural Sports* 134 Let the fisherman..Encrease his tackle, and his rod retye. **1864** MEREDITH *Sandra Belloni* xxiv, Having untied it, he retied it with care. **1892** MRS. H. WARD *David Grieve* II. vii, She came up to her father's chair, put his hair straight, re-tied his tie. **1954** A. G. L. HELLYER *Encycl. Garden Work* 106/2 If there is any doubt on this point, do not disturb the scion but retie at once.

retiform (ˈriːtɪfɔːm), *a.* [ad. mod.L. *rētiform-is*, f. *rēte* net: see -FORM. So F. *rétiforme*, It., Sp., and Pg. *retiforme*.] Having the form of a net.

1691 RAY *Creation* II. (1692) 27 The retiform tunicle is whitish, for the better and more true Reception of the Species of things. **1704** *Ibid.* (ed. 4) 292 If any [light] be by the retiform Coat reflected. **1777** T. PERCIVAL *Ess.* I. 15 A.. canal,..divided into similar lesser ones,..at last collected into a retiform contexture. **1803** *Med. Jrnl.* X. 238 The most beautiful retiform distribution I ever beheld. **1838** *Penny Cycl.* XII. 106/2 Organs of respiration retiform or aërian. **1876** BRISTOWE *Th. & Pract. Med.* (1878) 21 The central nervous organs and the lymphatic glands possess a peculiar form of connective tissue, termed 'retiform'.

Hence †**retiˈformous** *a.* *Obs.* *rare*$^{-1}$.

1730 CHAMBERLAYNE *Relig. Philos.* I. xiv. §10 Encompassed and fastened together by a Reti-formous Body lying between the Cutis and Cuticula.

reˈtill, *v.* [RE- 5 a.] *trans.* To till again.

1614 SYLVESTER *Bethulia's Rescue* I. 187 These fat Fields wee have but now re-tild.

reˈtimber (riː-), *v.* [RE- 5 c.] *trans.* To furnish again with timber or woodwork. Also, to reforest.

1877 RAYMOND *Statist. Mines & Mining* 159 The pumps will be placed in the air-shaft, which has been retimbered since the fire. **1899** *Daily News* 27 Sept. 3/5 Putting down entirely new cement foundations, and entirely retimbering the place. **1924** J. A. HAMMERTON *Countries of World* III. 1928/1 The state..is responsible for the systematic retimbering of the Alps in the upper valley of the Durance.

re-tin (riː-), *v.* [RE- 5 c.] *trans.* To plate afresh with tin. Hence **re-ˈtinning** *vbl. sb.*

1843 HOLTZAPFFEL *Turning* I. 451 The grease often penetrates so deeply..that the re-tinning is sometimes scarcely possible. **1895** *Spon's Workshop Rec.* (ed. 2) Ser. I. 355/1 Retinning Old Copper Pans.

retina (ˈrɛtɪnə). Also 5-6 reth-. [ad. med.L. *retina* (?f. L. *rēte* net). So It., Sp., and Pg. *retina*, F. *rétine* (1314).] The innermost layer or coating at the back of the eyeball (esp. of vertebrates), which is sensitive to light and in which the optic nerve terminates.

c **1400** *Lanfranc's Cirurg.* 241 Of þe substaunce of dura matris is engendrid rethina, þat is þe þinne skyn þat goiþ without þe iȝe, þat is clepid þe vilm of þe iȝe. **1525** tr. *Jerome of Brunswick's Surg.* B j b/2 The thyrde [coat] groweth of the senowe optico; the inner parte therof is named retina. **1541** R. COPLAND *Guydon's Quest. Chirurg.* E iij b, Of the inwarde party is called rethina and of the outwarde parte on the humour Crystallyn it hyght Aranea. **1619** PURCHAS *Microcosmus* viii. 89, I omit the Tunicle,..the Retina, and the rest. **1667** *Phil. Trans.* II. 536 The Retina was also streaked with very apparent sanguineous Vessels. **1748** HARTLEY *Observ. Man* I. iii. §4. 379 The Pictures made by Objects upon the Retina. **1777** PRIESTLEY *Matt. & Spir.* (1782) I. x. 129 The brain is of the very same substance with the retina, and optic nerves. **1811** WOOD *Optics* vi. 139 The images cannot, in both cases, fall upon corresponding points of the retinas. **1851** MAYNE REID *Scalp Hunt.* xii. 90, I found that the objects before me made duplicate impressions upon my diseased retina. **1897** *Nature* 1 Feb. 296/1 Kühne's observations were made on the retinæ of frogs and rabbits. *fig.* **1759** STERNE *Tr. Shandy* II. v, This identical bowling-green..became curiously painted..upon the retina of my uncle Toby's fancy. **1807** *Med. Jrnl.* XVII. 45 The more just refraction of the rays shall paint the picture in its true colours on the retina of his mind. **1854** BREWSTER *More Worlds* i. 8 The image of the future is the last picture which is effaced from the retina of the mind.

retinacular (rɛtɪˈnækjʊlə(r)), *a.* [f. next.] Relating to, of the nature of, a retinaculum.

1888 ROLLESTON & JACKSON *Anim. Life* 157 They frequently possess the retinacular apparatus binding the fore- and hind-wings together.

‖**retinaculum** (rɛtɪˈnækjʊləm). Pl. **-ula**. [L. *retinăculum*, f. *retinēre* to hold back, retain.]

†**1.** *Surg.* (See quot.) *Obs.*$^{-0}$

1753 CHAMBERS *Cycl. Suppl.*, *Retinaculum*, the name of a chirurgical instrument used in castration, and in the operation for a hernia, to prevent the intestines from falling into the scrotum.

2. *Ent.* **a.** (See quot. 1826.)

1825 T. SAY *Explan. Terms Entom.* 29. **1826** KIRBY & SP. *Entomol.* III. xxxiii. 391 The *Retinaculum*, a minute horny moveable scale or plate with which the darts are furnished, which prevents their dislocation by being shot forth too far.

b. An arrangement of hooks, or of hooks and bristles, whereby the fore and hind wings of insects are interlocked when in flight.

1856-8 W. CLARK *Van der Hoeven's Zool.* I. 393 Wings horizontal for the most part or deflected, guarded by a retinaculum with few exceptions. **1888** ROLLESTON & JACKSON *Anim. Life* 500 The fore and hind wings may be connected together by retinacula, either a series of hooklets on the fore-edge of the hind wings.., or a hook and bristle with a bundle of stout hairs.

c. In collembolans, a fused pair of appendages which hold back the furcula before releasing it for a spring.

1923 H. M. LEFROY *Man. Entomol.* 15 A curious appendage, the so-called 'catch' or retinaculum,..holds the furca in place when not in use. **1939** H. WOMERSLEY *Primitive Insects S. Austral.* 81 When the retinaculum releases the spring, the latter strikes the ground, forcing the insect to leap a considerable distance. **1969** R. F. CHAPMAN *Insects* xiv. 264 The appendages of the third and fourth segments of the abdomen of many Collembola form the retinaculum and the furca which are used in locomotion.

3. *Bot.* (See quot. 1849.)

1849 BALFOUR *Man. Bot.* §421 In Orchids, each of the pollen masses has a prolongation or stalk,..which often adheres to a prolongation at the base of the anther..by means of a viscid tenacious matter secreted by cells, and denominated *retinacula*. **1857** HENFREY *Bot.* 119. **1861** BENTLEY *Bot.* 262.

retinal ('rɛtɪnæl), *sb. Biochem.* [f. RETIN(A + -AL[2].] = RETINENE; usu. *spec.* vitamin A_1 aldehyde. Also **reti'naldehyde** in the same sense.

1944 MORTON & GOODWIN in *Nature* 1 Apr. 406/1 The elegance and accuracy of Wald's work on retinal extracts makes us hesitate to suggest that the term *retinene* is inappropriate. Unfortunately, it suggests a retinal carotenoid... Perhaps *retinaldehyde* is more appropriate than retin*al*. **1960** *Jrnl. Amer. Chem. Soc.* LXXXII. 5581/1 The pure substance hitherto known as retinene shall be designated retinal. **1963** *Nature* 30 Mar. 1279/1 In accordance with recent recommendations of the Committee on Nomenclature of the International Union of Pure and Applied Chemistry, we shall use hereafter the following terminology: for vitamin A, 'retinol'; for vitamin A aldehyde (retinene), 'retinal' or 'retinaldehyde'; for vitamin A acid, 'retinoic acid'. **1968** A. WHITE et al. *Princ. Biochem.* (ed. 4) xl. 902 Upon bleaching, rhodopsin dissociates to yield the protein, opsin, and a carotenoid, retinal (formerly retinene or vitamin A_1-aldehyde). **1969** *Nature* 1 Feb. 432/1 Retinaldehyde forms a Schiff base with an aliphatic amino-group on opsin. **1976** *Sci. Amer.* June 42/2 Retinal, complexed with various proteins, or opsins, is the chromophore of all visual pigments in animals.

retinal ('rɛtɪnəl), *a.* [f. RETINA + -AL[1].] Pertaining or relating to the retina.

1838 *Penny Cycl.* X. 138/2 There is no doubt of the existence of the retinal membrane, which was discovered by Dr. Jacob of Dublin. **1855** BAIN *Senses & Int.* II. ii. §5 It is immaterial whether the retinal presentations be two..or thousands. **1872** HUXLEY *Physiol.* ix. 223 The red lines are the retinal blood-vessels.

Hence **'retinally** *adv.*, with respect to or by means of the retina.

1970 *Jrnl. Gen. Psychol.* LXXXII. 228 The results clearly indicate that retinally disorienting novel outline shapes from training to test does not lead to recognition disturbances. **1974** *Sci. Amer.* Jan. 79/1 Tilted-head subjects recognized the environmentally upright (but retinally tilted) figures about as well as the upright observers did. **1980** *Ibid.* Jan. 92/3 In normal three-dimensional viewing it is quite irrelevant whether or not a baseboard is retinally collinear with a molding.

retinalite ('rɛtɪnəlaɪt). *Min.* [f. Gr. ῥητίνη resin + -LITE.] A variety of serpentine which has a resinous lustre.

1836 T. THOMSON *Min., Geol.*, etc. I. 201 Retinalite..is..totally different from Serpentine. It often contains mixed with it a quantity of carbonate of lime. **1896** CHESTER *Dict. Min.* s.v.

retinaphtha (rɛtɪ'næfθə). *Chem.* [f. as prec. + NAPHTHA.] A hydrocarbon formed during the distillation of resin; toluene.

1838 R. D. THOMSON in *Brit. Ann.* 329. **1857** MILLER *Elem. Chem., Org.* (1862) 655 *Toluol*, or *benzoene*,..appears to be identical with the *retinaphtha* obtained by Pelletier..from the distillation of rosin.

retinasphalt (rɛtɪn'æsfælt). Also **-asphalt-um.** [f. Gr. ῥητίνη resin + L. *asphaltum* ASPHALT. So F. *rétinasphalte*.] A fossil resin found with lignite.

α. **1804** HATCHETT in *Phil. Trans.* XCIV. 410 As it has been proved to consist partly of a resin and partly of a bituminous substance, I am induced to call it Retinasphaltum. **1826** HENRY *Elem. Chem.* II. 318 Retinasphaltum..has no elasticity; but is brittle, and breaks with a glassy fracture. Its colour is pale ochre yellow; its specific gravity 1·135.

β. **1816** JAMESON *Syst. Min.* (ed. 2) II. 411. **1818** W. PHILLIPS *Outlines Min. & Geol.* (ed. 3) 71 Retinasphalt..is brittle and soft, and consists of resin, asphalt and earth. **1857** MILLER *Elem. Chem., Org.* (1862) 124 Fossil Resins, and Bitumen.—These substances include amber, retinasphalt, asphalt, retinite.

re'tincture, *v.* [RE- 5 a.] *intr.* To effect a second tincture.

1664 POWER *Exp. Philos.* I. 74 By a super-addition of the oyl of Vitriol you may re-tincture as before.

†**'retinence.** *Obs. rare*[−1]. [ad. L. *retinentia*, f. *retinēre* to retain: see -ENCE.] Power of coherence.

1642 H. MORE *Song of Soul* III. I. xiii. Wks. (Grosart) 105 When once an end Is put unto this life, and fate doth rend Our retinence; what follows nought at all Belongs to us.

†**'retinency.** *Obs. rare.* [Cf. prec. and -ENCY.] The fact or capability of retaining something; retentiveness.

a **1640** JACKSON *Creed* x. x. Wks. IX. 55 Original sin..is a positive retinency of the flesh or corrupt nature of man. **1709** F. HAUKSBEE *Phys.-Mech. Exper.* v. (1719) 117 The Canals will restore themselves so far forth by their Elasticity, till the Momentum of their Retinency becomes equal to that of the diminish'd Pressure.

retinene ('rɛtɪniːn). *Biochem.* [f. RETIN(A + -ENE.] Either of two closely related yellow carotenoids, the aldehydes of vitamins A_1 and A_2 respectively (*spec.* that of the former), which occur esp. in the retina combined with opsin as rhodopsin; (sometimes followed by distinguishing numeral). Now more usu. known as *retinal*.

1934 G. WALD in *Nature* 14 July 65/1 In the retinas of dark adapted animals, no xanthophyll and only a trace of vitamin A occurs. Instead their chloroform extracts contain a third carotenoid with novel properties. I have named this substance retinene. **1950** *Sci. News* XV. 17 Kühne found, when visual purple is acted on by light, that a new substance is formed which he called visual yellow. The latter has now been shown to be closely related to, if not identical with, the aldehyde of vitamin A_1, called retinene-1. **1956** *Nature* 28 Jan. 176/1 In the retina, the retinene formed by bleaching rhodopsin ordinarily is reduced to vitamin A. **1970** *Ibid.* 22 Aug. 778/1 Vision..is triggered by isomerization of the carotenoid, retinene.

re'tinian, *a. rare.* [f. RETINA.] Retinal.

1881 *Athenæum* 2 July 19/2 One [form of Daltonism] is named retinian torpor, persons affected with which are as if in poor light; other rays than blue are indistinct.

re'tinic, *a. Chem.* [f. Gr. ῥητίνη resin.] *retinic acid*, an acid found in retinasphalt.

1844 FOWNES *Chem.* 541 The soluble portion, the retinic acid of Prof. Johnston, contains $C_{21}H_{14}O_5$.

retinite ('rɛtɪnaɪt). *Min.* Also -it. [a. F. *rétinite* (1795), f. Gr. ῥητίνη resin + -ITE.]

a. Retinasphalt. **b.** A mineral resin derived from brown coal. **c.** Pitchstone.

1821 URE *Dict. Chem., Retinite*, retin-asphalt... It is found at Bovey Tracey in Devonshire, adhering to brown coal. **1853** —— *Dict. Arts* I. 892 Resin, pitch, tar, oil, retinite, or other substance..capable of yielding carburetted hydrogen gas. **1862** SCROPE *Volcanos* 90 Clay is occasionally turned into jasper; marl into pechstein or retinite.

retinitis (rɛtɪ'naɪtɪs). *Path.* [f. RETINA + -ITIS.]

a. Acute inflammation of the retina.

1861 BUMSTEAD *Ven. Dis.* (1879) 723 Retinitis is by no means as frequent a symptom of secondary syphilis as iritis. **1879** *St. George's Hosp. Rep.* IX. 532 A specimen of pigmentary retinitis, with commencing lenticular opacity. **1899** *Allbutt's Syst. Med.* VI. 828 The retinal degeneration of diabetes, constituting the 'diabetic retinitis' of some authors.

b. ***retinitis pigmentosa*** [mod.L.: fem. of *pigmentōsus*, f. *pigment-um* pigment + *-ōsus*: see -OSE[1]], a chronic, hereditary form of retinitis characterized by the occurrence of black pigment in the retina and leading gradually to blindness.

1861 *Amer. Med. Monthly & N.Y. Rev.* XV. 183 Let us hope that there may soon be found a remedy for retinitis pigmentosa. **1865** *Ophthalmic Rev.* I. 47 The occurrence of pigment in the retina.., on account of its marked character in the case of the Spanish Marquis Ariani, was called morbus Arianus, an appellation which has, since Donders's pathological and anatomical researches, become changed into that of retinitis pigmentosa. **1910** *Encycl. Brit.* X. 98/1 Where the connective tissue elements are primarily affected [by retinal inflammation], the condition is a slow one, similar to sclerosis of the central nervous system. The gradual blindness which this causes is due to compression of the retinal nerve elements by the connective tissue hyperplasia, which is always associated with characteristic changes in the disposition of the retinal pigment. This retinal sclerosis is consequently generally known as retinitis pigmentosa, a disease to which there is a hereditary predisposition. **1925** *Amer. Jrnl. Ophthalm.* VIII. 375/1 Since the eye changes are so constantly associated with bodily defects, hereditary, congenital and acquired, the nervous system may be the primary seat of the affection of which retinitis pigmentosa is only the ocular expression. **1952** C. P. BLACKER *Eugenics* x. 242 Retinitis pigmentosa, a serious disease of the eye which has been much studied, may be determined by at least five separate genes of which only one is clinically distinguishable from the rest. **1969** *Listener* 16 Jan. 66/1 One serious congenital abnormality—a form of blindness manifest in adults, *retinitis pigmentosa*—the early symptoms of which are likely to appear after a man is married and had children, who will then continue to carry the gene.

re-'tinker (riː-), *v.* [RE- 5 a.] To patch up; to try to improve. Hence **re'tinkered** *ppl. a.*

1864 *Spectator* 440 He only sent the reports back for the Inspectors to re-tinker. **1868** BROWNING *Ring & Bk.* XI. 364 Our fire-new gospel is re-tinkered law.

retino- ('rɛtɪnəʊ-), comb. form of RETINA, used in terms in *Med.*, as **ˌretinobla'stoma** (pl. **-omata**) [see BLASTO-, -OMA], a malignant, familial tumour of the retina occurring chiefly in young children; **retino-'cerebral** *a.*, of or pertaining to the retina and the brain; **ˌretinocho'roidal** *a.*, pertaining to the retina and to the choroid; **ˌretinochoroi'ditis** = CHOROIDO-RETINITIS; **reti'nopathy** [-PATHY 2], non-inflammatory disease of the retina; so **retino'pathic** *a.*; **retino-'tectal** *a.*, of or pertaining to the retina and the optic tectum; **retino'topic** *a.* [Gr. τοπικ-ός of or pertaining to place], (of a projection on the optic tectum) that preserves the spatial relations of the sensory receptors of the retina. Also RETINOSCOPY.

1924 *Trans. Amer. Ophthalm. Soc.* XXII. 26 We therefore recommend that the term glioma of the retina be not used, except temporarily as a synonym or explanation to one of the following, which may more properly be applied to this condition: Neuro-epithelioma..; Retino-blastoma, proposed by Mallory; or Retino-cytoma. **1940** S. DUKE-ELDER *Text-bk. Ophthalm.* III. xxxvi. 2832 Retino-blastomata..are common, forming the great majority of retinal 'gliomata'. **1966** WRIGHT & SYMMERS *Systemic Path.* II. xl. 1637/1 A retinoblastoma is a highly malignant tumour that arises in the pars optica of the retina. It usually appears during the first two years of life. **1976** *Path. Ann.* XI. 319 Exfoliated cells of medulloblastoma, neuroblastoma, and retinoblastoma are characterized by nuclear molding and clustering of adjacent cells. **1891** Retino-cerebral [see FATIGUE *sb.* 1 c]. **1930** *Jrnl. Physiol.* LXIX. 433 An interaction is occurring between the retino-cerebral apparatuses of the two eyes. **1962** H. C. WESTON *Sight, Light & Work* (ed. 2) v. 168 The 'overpowering' of the retino-cerebral or visual sensory system does not occasion the painful feeling experienced when we are dazzled. **1895** *Arch. Ophthalm.* XXIV. 334 (*heading*) Three unusual cases of retino-choroidal degeneration. **1971** *Jrnl. Amer. Vet. Med. Assoc.* CLVIII. 740 (*heading*) Retinal and retinochoroidal lesions in early neuropathic canine distemper. **1881** G. SIGERSON tr. *J. M. Charcot's Lect. Dis. Nerv. System* II. iii. 41 The lesion of the optic nerve which sometimes supervenes in glycosuria and syphilitic retino-choroiditis. **1975** *Ann. Ophthalm.* VII. 853/1 Toxoplasmosis is an important cause of focal exudative retinochoroiditis. **1933** *Amer. Jrnl. Ophthalm.* XVI. 612/1 From 1856..until the present, the question of a retinopathic entity due to diabetes has remained unsettled. **1976** *Lancet* 30 Oct. 961/2 The mean prolactin concentration in retinopathic patients was 11 : 5 ng/ml. **1932** *Amer. Jrnl. Med. Sci.* CLXXXII. 137 Retinal arteriosclerosis in association with hemorrhages and sharply defined white patches, so-called arteriosclerotic retinopathy. **1939** M. L. HINE *May & Worth's Man. Dis. Eye* (ed. 8) xviii. 288 To distinguish the non-inflammatory affections from the inflammatory, the now-accepted term 'retinopathy'..has been adopted. **1966** WRIGHT & SYMMERS *Systemic Path.* II. xl. 1629/2 Formerly, it was supposed that the variety of ophthalmoscopical appearances associated with the vascular retinopathies merely represented different phases of the same disease: now, however, it is generally recognized that ..three distinct forms can be differentiated—(i) arteriosclerotic retinopathy, (ii) hypertensive retinopathy, and (iii) diabetic retinopathy. **1978** *Jrnl. R. Soc. Med.* LXXI. 636/1 The impression is that encephalopathy and retinopathy are particularly related to the severity and rate of rise of blood pressure. **1962** *Nature* 1 Dec. 898/2 (*heading*) Retinotectal connexions after retinal regeneration. **1977** *Ibid.* 6 Jan. 52/1 The topography of the retino-tectal projection onto the optic tectum was found to be similar in the bullfrog and leopard frog. **1961** *Jrnl. Physiol.* CLVII. 27P In sixteen frogs the normal retinotopic projection on the optic tectum had been restored after optic nerve regeneration. **1979** *Nature* 12 Apr. 623/1 If these exchanges were cumulative, it is arguable that any nascent retinotopic order should become scrambled before axons reach the brain.

'retinoid, *a. rare*[−0]. [f. Gr. ῥητίνη + -OID.] 'Resin-like, or resiniform; resembling a resin without being such' (Webster, 1847).

retinoid ('rɛtɪnɔɪd), *sb. Biochem.* [f. RETIN(OL[2] + -OID.] Any substance displaying vitamin A activity.

1976 M. B. SPORN et al. in *Federation Proc.* XXXV. 1332/1 Natural forms of vitamin A and synthetic analogs of vitamin A; this entire set of molecules, both natural and synthetic, we shall call retinoids, in a manner analogous to the naming of carotenoids or steroids. **1976** *Lancet* 27 Nov. 1174/1 The value of using the synthetic retinoids in the treatment of these dermatoses lies not only in the excellent therapeutic response but also in the comparative lack of toxicity. **1980** *Nature* 17 Apr. 626/1 Retinoids reduce the saturation density and/or growth rate of many normal and tumorigenic cell lines.

†**retinol**[1] ('rɛtɪnɒl). *Chem. Obs.* Also -ole. [f. Gr. ῥητίνη resin + -OL.] (See quots. 1875 and 1893.)

1838 R. D. THOMSON in *Brit. Ann.* 330 Retinole. **1857** MILLER *Elem. Chem., Org.* (1862) 585 Common rosin is thus found to furnish..Terebene, Colophene,..Retinol, Naphthalin. **1875** *Ure's Dict. Arts* III. 702 *Retinole*, a hydrocarbon, obtained from the turpentine-resins. **1893** ALLEN *Handbk. Local Therapeutics* 389 Retinol, when pure, is simply a hydrocarbon..in the form of a viscid fluid similar in appearance to castor oil, with a peculiar odor.

retinol[2] ('rɛtɪnɒl). *Biochem.* [f. RETIN(A + -OL.] Either of vitamins A_1 and A_2 (*spec.* the former), which are yellow carotenoid alcohols of formulæ $C_{20}H_{30}O$ and $C_{20}H_{28}O$ respectively; (sometimes followed by distinguishing numeral).

1960 *Jrnl. Amer. Chem. Soc.* LXXXII. 5581/1 The pure substance hitherto known as vitamin A_1 or axerophthol shall be designated retinol. **1968** A. WHITE et al. *Princ. Biochem.* (ed. 4) l. 1048 Vitamin A activity in mammals is exhibited by α-, β-, and γ-carotenes, by retinol and retinol$_2$..and by a few other carotenoids. **1976** *Nature* 4 Mar. 49/2 Vitamin A (retinol) is a nutrient essential for vision, growth, reproduction and proper differentiation of epithelial tissue.

Also **reti'noic** *a.*, in ***retinoic acid***, the carboxylic acid obtained from retinol by oxidation; hence **reti'noate**, the anion of this; **'retinyl** *attrib.*, denoting esters of retinol; **reti'nylidene**, [-IDENE], the group in which form retinal exists in rhodopsin, i.e. a side chain linked to opsin by a double bond formed in a condensation reaction between the aldehyde group of retinal and an amino group of the opsin.

1960 *Jrnl. Amer. Chem. Soc.* LXXXII. 5581/1 The pure substance hitherto known as vitamin A acid shall be designated retinoic acid. **1968** A. WHITE et al. *Princ. Biochem.* (ed. 4) l. 1049 Retinyl esters, the form present in ingested liver and fish-liver oils, are hydrolyzed in the intestine. *Ibid.*, Retinoic acid.. readily replaces retinol in the rat diet. **1969** *Nature* 1 Feb. 435/1 There could perhaps be a direct interaction between the charged quanidinium ion and the molecular orbitals of the retinyledene [*sic*] chromophore. **1970** R. W. MCGILVERY *Biochem.* xxvi. 645 Since it won't save vision, it is apparent that retinoate is not readily reduced to retinal. *Ibid.*, Polar bear livers.. contain as much as 30 micromoles of retinyl esters per gram—a 20-year supply for a human in each pound. **1973** *Nature* 16 Nov. 166/2 The only action of light in vision is the photoisomerisation of the 11-*cis* retinylidene (derived from vitamin A aldehyde) prosthetic or chromophoric group of rhodopsin, from the 11-*cis* to the all-*trans* configuration. **1976** *Ibid.* 4 Mar. 49/2 Some retinol is oxidised to retinoic acid (vitamin A acid) *in vivo*, but if an animal is provided with retinoic acid in place of dietary retinol, it can only partially substitute for the missing retinol.

retino'scopic, *a.* [See next and -SCOPIC.] Of or pertaining to, performed by, retinoscopy.

1893 *Brit. Med. Jrnl.* 30 Sept. 734 The true retinoscopic observation was thereby obscured. **1902** *Ibid.* 1 Feb. 267 To facilitate retinoscopic examination for glasses.

Hence **retino'scopically** *adv.*

1902 *Brit. Med. Jrnl.* 1 Feb. 267 At the end of a week she was examined retinoscopically for the glasses.

retinoscopy (rɛtɪ'nɒskəpɪ). [f. RETINA + -SCOPY.] The method of examining the eye, for refraction, by the observation of the movement of a shadow on the retina, caused by the rotation of the mirror of the ophthalmoscope.

1884 *Encycl. Brit.* XVII. 787/1 Retinoscopy.. is useful in determining and correcting the refraction where the patients are.. too stupid to assist with their answers. **1893** *Brit. Med. Jrnl.* 30 Sept. 734 A patient for whom a correction could not be found by the ordinary method of retinoscopy.

‖**retinospora** (rɛtɪ'nɒspərə). *Bot.* [mod.L., from Gr. ῥητίνη resin + σπορά seed.] A variety of cypress, so called from the resinous channels with which the outer surface of the seeds is covered.

1882 *Garden* 20 May 351/1 The Retinosporas as a class succeed better than any other Conifers under pot culture. **1895** *Daily News* 28 Aug. 5/4 Magnificent retinosporas, 12 feet to 15 feet in height,.. and many others have been lifted.

retinue ('rɛtɪnjuː), *sb.* Forms: 4-5 **retenu** (5 **-w**), 4-6 **retenue**, 5- **retinue** (6 **retyn-**); 4-5 **retenewe** (5 **-ev, -ew, reteignew**), 5-6 **retynew(e**, 5-7 **retinew** (6 **-ewe**). [a. OF. *retenue*, fem. of *retenu*, pa. pple. of *retenir* to RETAIN. In French the word has been current in a number of meanings which have not been adopted in English. The usual stressing in the 16-18th centuries appears to have been *re'tinue*.

The forms *reten, retene*, which appear in a few instances in ME. texts, are probably due to scribal misreadings of *retenu(e* as *retenn(e*.]

†**1.** The fact of being retained in the service of another; a relationship of service or dependency.

1390 GOWER *Conf.* I. 86 This is a wonder retenue, That malgre wher sche wole or non Min herte is everemore in on. *Ibid.* 318 That I scholde will remue And put him out of retenue. **1488-9** *Act 4 Hen. VII*, c. 4 Yf eny persone.. reteyned in the seid arme or viage resorte.. yn to this reame discharged of the seid retinue arme and viage. **1535** *Act 27 Hen. VIII*, c. 14 §6 Any captaine of any shippe in the time of warre, being in the retinue and seruice of the kinges highnes. **1606** HOLLAND *Sueton.* 44 The Bononians also.. were dependantes of the Antonii and in there retinue and protection. **1607** TOPSELL *Four-f. Beasts* (1658) 557 Never rising against them, but proud of their dependence and retinue.

†**b.** *of retinue*, in service. *Obs.*

c **1375** *Sc. Leg. Saints* xl. (*Ninian*) 1103 Ymang vthire ane þar wes þat of retenu wes.. of þat land til a mychtty man. *c* **1386** CHAUCER *Knt.'s T.* 2502 Knyghtes of retenu, and eek squieres. **1390** GOWER *Conf.* III. 351 So that Danger, which stant of retenue With my ladi, his place mai remue.

†**c.** *to make (one's) retinue*, to take service *with* one; to do service. *Obs. rare.*

1390 GOWER *Conf.* II. 111 But Slowthe, which is evele affaited, With Slep hath mad his retenue. **1415** SIR T. GREY in *Rep. Deputy Keeper Rec.* (1882) 583 Quen I hade made my retenu withe ȝow at Waleyway ye tyme of yat retenu makyng. **1444** *Reg. Mag. Sig.* (1882) 63/2 Service till us to be done as is contenit in the lettrez of retenew till us maid.

†**2.** *at (one's) retinue*, at (one's) service or command. *Obs.*

c **1380** WYCLIF *Wks.* (1880) 348 [If the king] hiȝt þee greet eritage to be at hijs retenu & serue hym treuly. *c* **1386** CHAUCER *Friar's T.* 1355 He hadde eek wenches at his retenue. *c* **1400** *Brut* ccxxii, þe same ȝer þat þe Mortymer was taken, he hade at his retynu ix [score] knyghtz. *c* **1412** HOCCLEVE *De Reg. Princ.* 652 Ryght nyce girles at my retenue Hadde I an heep.

†**b.** *to make a retinue*, to keep retainers. *to have retinue*, to have the services *of* one. *Obs.*

1399 *Rolls of Parlt.* III. 452/1 That thei.. gyf no Liverees of Sygnes, no make no Retenue of men bot of Officers necessaries wythin her Household. **1487** *Act 3 Hen. VII*, c. 15 §1 By the unlawfull reteyners and retinews made.. by the seid Officers. **1490** *Act 7 Hen. VII*, c. 1 §1 Every Capteyn.. and all other havyng under them retynue of any Soldeour or Soldeours atte the Kinges Wages.

3. A number or company of persons retained in the service of some one, or attached to and following one, esp. a sovereign, noble, or person in authority; a train or suite.

1375 BARBOUR *Bruce* xv. 429 His retennew than gaderit he, That war gud men of gret bounte. **1390** GOWER *Conf.* III. 222 To make of suche his retenue Whiche wise ben, and to remue The foles. **1422** tr. *Secreta Secret., Priv. Priv.* 127 Alexander.. passyd wyth his retenue towarde.. Inde. **1472-3** *Rolls of Parlt.* VI. 58/1 Other persones beyng in the said Tresorer's of Calice retenue. **1526** *Pilgr. Perf.* (W. de W. 1531) 7 The damned spirytes in hell, with all theyr adherentes, retynue & seruauntes. **1595** SPENSER *Col. Clout* 460 So many Nymphs, which she doth hold In her retinew. **1603** KNOLLES *Hist. Turks* (1638) 58 Hauing sent away his army, and trauelling with his ordinary retinue to Tiberias. **1662** EVELYN *Chalcogr.* Table, Painters chiefe of the court and retinue to the Emperour of Japan. **1691** WOOD *Ath. Oxon.* II. 793 His Majesty.. and their royal Highnesses went from their Lodgings with their respective Retinews. **1748** *Anson's Voy.* III. ix. 515 Three Mandarines, with.. a vast retinue, came on board the Centurion. **1791** MRS. RADCLIFFE *Rom. Forest* vi, The Marquis passed on to the hall, where his retinue awaited. **1840** THIRLWALL *Greece* lviii. VII. 285 Philip was immediately taken with all his retinue. **1877** FROUDE *Short Stud.* (1883) IV. I. iv. 49 The hall was thronged with the retinues of the King and the barons.

transf. **1597** SHAKS. *2 Hen. IV*, IV. iii. 121 Their Captaine, the Heart,.. pufft vp with his Retinue, doth any Deed of Courage. **1642** H. MORE *Song of Soul* II. App. lvii. Wks. (Grosart) 96 For right it is that none a sun debarre Of Planets, which his just and due retinue are. **1685** DRYDEN *Thren. August.* 507 There appears The long Retinue of a Prosperous Reign, A Series of successful Years. *a* **1740** WATERLAND *Diss. Argt. A priori* iii. Wks. 1823 IV. 467 This whole train of suppositions, or assertions, brought in as part of the retinue to wait upon the argument *a priori*. **1850** MRS. BROWNING *Crowned & Wedded* iii, While loving hopes, for retinues, about her sweetness wait.

b. Const. *of* (the persons, etc., composing it).

1592 tr. *Junius on Rev.* xiv. 1 The standing of the lambe with his army and retinue of men. **1667** MILTON *P.L.* v. 355 The tedious pomp that waits On Princes, when thir rich Retinue long Of Horses led.. Dazles the croud. **1770** LANGHORNE *Plutarch* (1879) I. 115/1 He always had about him.. a numerous retinue of servants. **1878** STUBBS *Const. Hist.* III. xxi. 538 The barons kept an enormous retinue of officers and servants.

c. Collectively, without article or pronoun.

a **1665** EARL OF MARLBOROUGH *Warn. Careless World* 13 He.. had.. multitudes of Attendants and Retinue of all sexes. **1665** GLANVILL *Scepsis Sci.* xviii. 109 Worth is not to be judg'd by Success, and Retinue. *a* **1729** ROGERS *Serm.* (J.), Neither pomp nor retinue shall be able to divert the great, nor shall the rich be relieved by the multitude of his treasurers. **1847** TENNYSON *Princ.* III. 179 To horse we got, and so Went forth in long retinue following up The river. **1863** LONGF. *Wayside Inn, Robt. Sicily* 4 With retinue of many a knight and squire.

†**4. a.** The act of retaining or keeping. *rare.*

1489 CAXTON *Faytes of A.* I. xii, Comyssaryes that gode hede shal take that for couetyse of the payement of the souldyours noo decepcion be made by retenue of suche that be vnable. *a* **1548** HALL *Chron., Hen. VIII*, 145 All the men of warre, that were aboute the retinue of Calice.. and Guysnes, wer called home.

†**b.** The limits or bounds of a town. *Obs.*

1535-6 *Act 27 Hen. VIII*, c. 63 Ye shall not.. admytte any persoune.. into eny rowme within the retynue of the said Towne belongyng to your admyssion.

†**c.** Restraint; restraining force. *Obs. rare*$^{-1}$.

1651 tr. *De-las-Coveras' Don Fenise* 133 There is no retinue nor limits to a woman that suffers herself to be blinded with that foolish passion.

†**5.** Tenor, purport. *Obs. rare*$^{-1}$.

1484 in *Lett. Rich. III & Hen. VII* (Rolls) I. 77 Two other lettres of the same reteignew.

Hence **'retinue** *v. trans.*, to furnish with a retinue; to accompany as a retinue.

1827 POLLOK *Course T.* VII. (1860) 189 A chosen number, brought, to retinue His great ascent on high. **1883** J. G. BUTLER *Bible Work* II. 186 Along the great Appian Way, retinued by this humble band of Christian disciples.

retinula (rɛ'tɪnjʊlə). *Biol.* Pl. **-ulæ**. Also anglicized as **retinule** ('rɛtɪnjuːl). [Diminutive, on L. types, of RETINA; coined in Ger. by H. Grenacher in *Untersuchungen über das Arthropoden-Auge* (1877) ii. 17.] One of the pigmented cells from which, in certain compound eyes of Arthropods, the rhabdom arises. Also *attrib.* (*appositively*).

1878 BELL tr. *Gegenbaur's Comp. Anat.* 264 The retinal cells which give rise to the rhabdom constitute a retinula. **1883** *Q. Jrnl. Microsc. Sci.* XXIII. 186 What Grenacher has called, in the multicorneal eye of Insects and Crustaceans, a 'retinula'. **1888** ROLLESTON & JACKSON *Anim. Life* 168 A basement membrane.. separates the retinulae from the optic ganglion. **1924** *Glasgow Herald* 31 May 4/2 The insect's compound eye.. has its numerous lenses and retinules each wrapped up in a black mantle. **1978** *Nature* 29 June 772/1 The *Drosophila* compound eye consists of about 700 ommatidia, each containing six peripheral and two central retinula cells (photo-receptors).

Hence **re'tinular** *a.*; **re'tinulate** *a.*

1883 *Q. Jrnl. Microsc. Sci.* XXIII. 211 *Retinulate*, of an ommateum in which the nerve-end cells are segregated to form definite groups, or 'retinulæ'. **1888** ROLLESTON & JACKSON *Anim. Life* 516 *Scutigera* has a retinulate ommateum. *Ibid.* 525 In *Limulus* the central eyes have groups of five retinular cells.

retinyl: see s.v. RETINOL².

re-'tip, *v.* [RE- 5 c.] To supply with a new tip. Hence **re'tipping**, *vbl. sb.*

1839 URE *Dict. Arts* 853 He had rendered entirely unserviceable 126 punches or borers, besides 26 others which had been re-tipped with steel. **1947** J. STEINBECK *Wayward Bus* i. 4 People stopped bringing.. their ploughs for re-tipping.

retiracy (rɪ'taɪərəsɪ). *U.S.* [f. RETIRE *v.*]

1. Retirement, seclusion, privacy.

1829 *Virginia Lit. Museum* 30 Dec. 460/1 *Retiracy*, 'solitude'. **1839** C. M. KIRKLAND *New Home* xi. 64 The important matter of supper being in some sort concluded, preparations were made for '*retiracy*'. **1842** FR. A. KEMBLE *Rec. Later Life* (1882) II. 228, I enjoy a considerable portion of retiracy. **1860** MRS. BYRNE *Undercurrents Overlooked* II. 43 *note*, Where there is but little more retiracy than upon a public common. **1873** L. WALLACE *Fair God* III. i, He left the house, and once more sought the retiracy of the gardens.

2. (See quot. 1859.)

1859 BARTLETT *Dict. Amer.* (ed. 2) 363 It is said, in New England, of a person who left off business with a fortune, that he has a retiracy; i.e. a sufficient fortune to retire upon. **1860** in De Vere *Americanisms* (1871) 628 When Mr. Watson found he had a sufficient retiracy, he gave up his lucrative business.

Hence **re'tiracied** *ppl. a.*

1856 in Bartlett *Dict. Amer.* (1859) 363 There are no places in the world similarly retiracied which are less provincial or more agreeable.

†**retirade.** *Obs.* [a. F. *retirade*, = Sp. and Pg. *retirada*, It. *ritirata* retreat, f. *ritirare* to RETIRE.] (See quots. 1704 and 1727.)

1684 tr. *Siege Luxembourg* 22 That the Prince de Chimay made the Women and Children work upon the Retirades, and.. was still resolved to make a vigorous Defence. **1704** J. HARRIS *Lex. Techn.* I, *Retirade*, in Fortification, is a kind of Retrenchment made in the Body of a Bastion or other Works, which is to be disputed Inch by Inch, after the first Defences are Dismantled. **1727-38** CHAMBERS *Cycl.* s.v., When a breach is made in a bastion, the enemy may also make a retirade or new fortification behind it. **1802** JAMES *Milit. Dict.* s.v., The body of a retirade should be raised as high as possible, and several fougasses should be laid beneath it.

retiral (rɪ'taɪərəl). Now chiefly *Sc.* [f. RETIRE *v.* + -AL¹.]

1. The act of retreating or withdrawing.

1611 COTGR., *Escart*.., a place of solitarie retirall. *Ibid.*, *Retirade*.., a place of retrait, of a retirall, for defendants behind a breach. **1904** A. C. BRADLEY *Shaks. Trag.* 50 All through the conflict we shall find a regular alternation of smaller advances and retirals. **1964** J. D. MACKIE *Hist. Scotl.* ii. 22 The retiral which followed the departure of Agricola. **1976** *Scotsman* 24 Dec. 13/1 (Advt.), Retiral collection in aid of children's homes.

2. The act or fact of withdrawing from, or of giving up, an office, position, or vocation.

1879 *Brit. & For. Evang. Rev.* XXVIII. 73 His retiral was no doubt succeeded by an over-powering sense of the importance of biblical study. **1894** *Catholic News* 1 Dec. 8/5 Lord Ripon.. alluded to the retiral of Mr. Gladstone. **1939** *Daily Tel.* 18 Dec. 12/5 (Advt.), Owing retiral of Foreman Pattern Maker.. a vacancy occurs for a first-class Man with organising ability. **1965** J. POTTER *Death in Office* i. 10 You will recall my telling you of a verbal agreement between the late Chairman and myself that my retiral should be at my own discretion. **1973** *Stirling Observer* 25 July 11/6 A special retiral presentation is being made by the chairman. **1978** *Lochaber News* 31 Mar. 14/1 (Advt.), Young person required for civil engineering stores to fill vacancy due to retiral.

3. 'The act of taking up and paying a bill when due' (Ogilvy, 1882, and in later Dicts.).

So †**re'tirance**; †**reti'ration**. *Obs. rare.*

1637 BASTWICK *Litany* I. 1 It was.. a most excellent meanes of the soules retiration from the loue of these sublunary things. **1662** J. CHANDLER *Van Helmont's Oriat.* 155 It was spoiled of naturall endowed vertues, as well in its own body, as in the places of its retirances.

retire (rɪ'taɪə(r)), *sb.* Also 6-7 **-tyre**, 6 *Sc.* **-tear**, **-teir**, 7 **-tere**. [f. the verb. Cf. OF. *retire, retyre*, Sp. and Pg. *retiro*.]

1. Retirement; withdrawal from the world or the society of others. Now *rare.*

1540-54 CROKE 13 *Ps.* (Percy Soc.) 12 Lo my retyre, And waylyng, is not hyd from the. **1596** SPENSER *F.Q.* VI. ix. 27 All this worlds gay showes.. Be but vaine shadowes to this safe retyre Of life, which here in lowlinesse ye lead. **1639** G. DANIEL *Ecclus.* xxxviii. 60 Learning is not Rest, But a retire from noise, from worldly Care. **1667** MILTON *P.L.* XI. 267 Eve.. with audible lament Discover'd soon the place of her retire. **1820** KEATS *Lamia* I. 230 By some freakful chance he made retire From his companions, and set forth to walk.

†**2.** The act of retiring or withdrawing to or from a place or position. *Obs.*

1570 FOXE *A. & M.* (ed. 2) 232/1 Vnderstandyng the false feare of the pope, and of his retire to Canusium. **1577-82** BRETON *Floorish upon Fancie* Pref., And many times I thought to make retire, But in the ende obtained my desire. **1601** HOLLAND *Pliny* I. 44 The Moone.. in her approch and comming toward, filleth bodies ful; and in her retire and going away, emptieth them again. *a* **1676** HALE *Narr. Customes* vi. in S. A. Moore *Foreshore* (1888) 362 *Recessus* *maris* I take to bee the retyre of the sea from the usual low water mark.

†**b.** Return to a place. *Obs.*

1567 Maplet *Gr. Forest* 103 Isidore saith, that he is so named..for often turning and retire had to one and the same place. **1599** *Warn. Faire Wom.* i. 131 Entreat thy mistress.. to make retire Hither again, for I will speak with her. **1615** Jackson *Creed* v. l. Wks. IV. 411 That is our country whence we came,.. But what is the means or manner of our retire?

transf. **1578** R. Edwards *Parad. Dainty Devices* 21 b, I hope, what happe? her happy healthes retyre.

†**c.** Return *to* a subject. *Obs. rare.*

1589 Puttenham *Eng. Poesie* iii. xix. (Arb.) 229 This figure of retire..resumes both the matter and the termes, and is therefore accompted one of the figures of repetition. **1597** J. King *On Jonas* (1618) 50 Once againe hee repeateth the cause, and by a retire to his former speech, maketh the publication of his crime both..the first and the last of the sentence.

†**3.** The act of drawing back or yielding ground in warfare; retreat. *Obs.* (Common 1550–1600.)

1548 Patten *Exped. Scot.* Hj, [They] did..turne themselues and made a soft retyre vp towarde the hyll agayne. **1599** Hakluyt *Voy.* II. ii. 9 The Spaniardes perceiuing this, returned, and in our mens retire they slew sixe of them. **1606** G. W[oodcock] *Hist. Ivstine* v. 28 The Tyrantes were put vnto the worst, and making their retire into the City [etc.]. [**1831–40** K. H. Digby *Mores Catholici* (1846) iii. 182 Enough of sallies and retires, of palisados, fortins, parapets.]

b. In phr. *to sound* (*a* or *the*) *retire*.

In mod. use the imperative of the verb (sense 2 a) used substantively.

a **1591** H. Smith *Wks.* (1867) I. 472 Therefore he might well sound the retire of wisdom. **1596** *Edw. III*, iv. vi, Our drums strike nothing but discouragement, Our trumpets sound dishonour and retire.

1885 *Lady Bellairs' Transvaal War* 249 An ambuscade being feared, the 'retire' was sounded from the fort. **1899** *Daily News* 20 Nov. 4/5 To our astonishment, we heard the 'Cease fire' and 'Retire' sounded by buglers.

4. A place of retirement; a retreat. Now *rare.*

1595 Daniel *Civ. Wars* iii. xxi, This sacred place our Auentine Retire, our holy Hill. **1620** Brathwait *Five Senses* in *Archaica* (1815) II. vi. 40 What retire or retreat could he find in any place? **1649** G. Daniel *Trinarch.* Ded. 2 When I am Earth, and what was counted fire Knitts to its Source, the naturall retire Of Elements. **1865** Lewis Gidley *Aletes* 66 Save what winds inspire, And forests minister, in whose cool retire Are sombre glades.

retire (rɪ'taɪə(r)), *v.* Forms: α. 6–7 retyre, -tier, 6– retire. β. *Sc.* 6 retere, 6–7 -teir(e, -teere. [ad. F. *retirer* (OF. *retyrer*) to withdraw, f. *re-* RE- + *tirer* to draw: cf. Sp. and Pg. *retirar*, It. *ritirare*.]

I. *intr.* **1. a.** To withdraw *to* or *into* a place (or way of life) for the sake of seclusion, shelter, or security.

1538 Starkey *England* ii. i. 150 Certayn monasterys..to the wych al such..may retyre, and from the besynes and vanyte of the world may wythdraw themselfe. **1610** Shaks. *Temp.* iv. i. 161 If you be pleas'd, retire into my Cell, And there repose. **1672** Wycherley *Love in a Wood* iii. i, That my neighbours..should have retired into the country, sick with envy of my prosperity and greatness. **1697** Dryden *Virg. Georg.* iii. 578 The Men to subterranean Caves retire, Secure from Cold. **1729** Butler *Serm.* Wks. 1874 II. 79 The sacrifice being over, he retires alone to a solitude sacred to these occasions. **1788** Gibbon *Decl. & F.* xli. IV. 154 The abdicated monarch retired..to a life of peace, of affluence, and perhaps of content. **1848** L. Hunt *Jar of Honey* ix. 121 Shakspeare..retired to his native place before he was old. **1855** Macaulay *Hist. Eng.* xiii. III. 267 He..therefore, when the Rye House plot was discovered, thought it expedient to retire to the Continent.

fig. **1704** Norris *Ideal World* ii. xiii. 571 The most natural way for the discovery of truth, is, instead of going abroad for intelligence, to retire into ourselves.

b. To withdraw *to* one's usual place of abode, or some customary occupation.

1584 *Sc. Acts Jas. VI* (1814) III. 333/2 Quhome the estaitis of parliament ordanit to reteir to thair lugeingis. **1590** Spenser *F.Q.* ii. viii. 7 Life ere long shall to her home retire. **1613** Purchas *Pilgrimage* ii. xx. (1614) 223 The Emperour requested his helpe, to cause him to retire to his den. **1695** Congreve *Love for L.* iii. iv, I'll retire to my own chamber, and think of what you have said. **1731–8** Swift *Polite Conv.* Introd. 29 After Dinner, when the Ladies retired to their Tea, and left us over a Bottle of Wine. **1774** Goldsm. *Nat. Hist.* (1776) II. 321 As soon as the morning ..appears, the carnivorous animals retire to their dens. **1850** Thackeray *Pendennis* xl, Harry..retired to his own apartments, where he stretched himself on his ottoman.

c. To withdraw from company and betake oneself *to* rest or bed.

1670 Dryden *Conq. Granada* iv. iii, Let him, in pity, to rest retire. **1730** Fielding *Rape upon Rape* ii. xi, She had taken leave of me to retire to rest. **1775** A. Burnaby *Trav.* 83 At their usual time the old couple retire to bed. **1813** H. Shelley in Dowden *Life Shelley* (1886) I. 352 On Friday night..we retired to bed between ten and eleven o'clock. **1867** *Crim. Chron. York Castle* 175 The wife of the deceased, thinking him late, retired to rest.

d. *ellipt.* in the same sense.

1752 Fielding *Amelia* x. iii, They then sat down to half an hour's cheerful conversation, after which they retired all in the most perfect good humour. **1775** C. Johnston *Pilgrim* 181 Our fatigue making us want rest more than any other refreshment, we soon retired. **1823** Moore *Mem.* (1853) IV. 72 The rest of the day he is at the disposal of everybody, and rarely retires at night till others do. **1860** O. W. Holmes *Elsie V.* xxv, At an hour when most of the Rockland people had 'retired', or, in vulgar language, 'gone to bed'. **1886** Dowden *Shelley* I. 67 When the college clock struck two, Hogg would rise..and retire for the night.

e. To withdraw from office or an official position; to give up one's business or occupation in order to enjoy more leisure or freedom (esp. after having made a competence or earned a pension). Also const. *from.*

1667 Pepys *Diary* 30 Aug., He did not think any man fit to serve a prince that did not know how to retire and live a country life. **1669** R. Montagu in *Buccleuch MSS.* (Hist. MSS. Comm.) I. 424 You and the Duke of Buckingham.. would both desire leave to retire. **1712** Arbuthnot *John Bull* i. xvi, I have, indeed, a small Pittance left, with which I might retire. **1781** Cowper *Retirem.* 514 The unpitied victim of ill-judg'd expence..Shakes hands with business, and retires indeed. **1806** *Med. Jrnl.* XV. 360 Let the surgeons of the former retire upon an annuity, and let those in the latter be continued. **1863** Trafford *World in Church* III. 273 He felt as a trader feels when he retires from business. **1876** Voyle & Stevenson *Milit. Dict.* 340/2 After 30 years' service..an officer can retire on full pay.

f. *Sport.* To go out; to leave the field. Chiefly *Cricket.* Also ***to retire hurt***, of a batsman: to leave the field because of injury suffered at the crease; also *fig.*

1851 W. Clarke in W. Bolland *Cricket Notes* 128 You must..make the man play out... Perhaps before that is the case, you will have caused him to retire. **1863** *Lillywhite's Cricket Scores* III. 62 Wansell..was given out unfairly, and refused to retire. **1867** *Ball Players' Chron.* 6 June 2/1 His run, however, was the only one scored, as the next three strikers retired in succession. **1877** *Wisden's Cricketers' Almanack* 223 (*heading*) Lancashire v. Nottinghamshire. *Ibid.* 224 Nottinghamshire... F. Wyld, retired (*hurt*). **1884** *Lillywhite's Cricket Ann.* 5 G. B. Studd retiring for six. **1892** *Wisden's Cricketers' Almanack* 209 Mr. E. C. Streatfield (Pembroke), not out 6—retired hurt. **1901** H. Bleackley *Tales of Stumps* iv. 105 Amidst..loud applause, he retired with thirty-eight runs to his credit. **1906** E. Dyson *Fact'ry 'Ands* xvii. 233 It..batted 'er in ther basket with 28lb. iv grey sugar paper done up tough, 'n' she retired 'urt. **1925** A. Christie *Secret of Chimneys* xv. 141 Poor little Michael didn't get it [*sc.* a disappointing answer] as straight from the shoulder as he might have done. But he retired hurt all the same. **1961** F. H. Burgess *Dict. Sailing* 170 *Retire*, withdraw from a race. **1977** *Arab Times* 3 Dec. 9/6 Kurian had to retire hurt after scoring 11 runs.

2. a. Of an army, commander, etc.: To withdraw, fall back, or retreat, esp. in the face of opposition or superior force. Also const. *to*, *into* (a place), *from* (an enemy, etc.).

1533 Bellenden *Livy* ii. xxvi. (S.T.S.) I. 236 He had commandit his army to retere abak fra þe tentis of Inemyis. **1560** Daus tr. *Sleidane's Comm.* 323 b, By little and little they retire and on the bridge over the Rhine they foughte a longe time. **1601** R. Johnson *Kingd. & Commw.* (1603) 160 In their encounters..they retire as repulsed for feare, so to draw their enemies within danger. **1697** Dryden *Virg. Georg.* iii. 348 The vanquish'd Bull..from his proud Foe retires. **1717** *Col. Rec. Pennsylv.* III. 20 About as many Indians, from whom they retired. **1743** Pitt in Almon *Anecd.* (1810) I. v. 121 The French not only re-passed the Rhine, but retired quite out of Germany. **1840** Thirlwall *Greece* VII. 121 They soon found themselves threatened with violence, and obliged to retire. **1888** *Encycl. Brit.* XXIV. 363/1 The task of a rear guard retiring before a victorious enemy..is one of the most delicate of operations.

b. *Fencing.* To give ground before one's adversary; to take one or more steps backward.

1594 I. G. *Di Grassi's Arte of Defence* N 4 b, The enimie hath no other remedie to safe himselfe, then to retire backe. **1595** Saviolo *Practise* i. * 4 b, To hit and retire is not discommendable. **1705** H. Blackwell *Compl. Fencing Master* v. 17 No more [than two feints] are convenient, except your Adversary retires on a good Guard, and you approach on him. **1707** Sir W. Hope *New Method Fencing* iv. 122 It will be fit for you to retire a little with a single Step. **1861** G. Chapman *Foil Pract.* 39 Advance one pace as I retire..; retire in quarte. **1893** *Fencing* (Badminton Libr.) (ed. 3) vi. 106 Fencers of this kind hope to force the adversary to retire.

3. a. To withdraw, go away, remove oneself (*from* a place, etc.).

a **1585** Montgomerie *Cherrie & Slae* 603 Quhyle Danger and Dispaire retyrit, Experience came in. —— *Misc. Poems* xxxii. 21 If I mis to mend it as I micht, I can reteir vhan resone thinks it richt. *c* **1614** Sir W. Mure *Dido & Æneas* ii. 330 Till last the prise is wonne,..And honour prostrate, blushing did reteare. **1667** Milton *P.L.* xi. 237 Whom not to offend, With reverence I must meet, and thou retire. **1697** Dryden *Virg. Georg.* i. 202 Jove..from the Rivers bade the Wine retire. **1725** Pope *Odyss.* vi. 258 To them the king: No longer I detain Your friendly care: retire, ye virgin train! **1794** Paley *Evid.* ii. ii. (1817) 48 The true virtue is that.. which retires from them all to the single internal purpose of pleasing God. **1833** Tennyson *Lady Clara Vere de Vere* 6 At me you smiled, but unbeguiled I saw the snare, and I retired. **1837** Lockhart *Scott* IV. v. 145 When the ladies retired from the dinner-table I happened to sit next him.

b. To move back or away; to recede, or have the appearance of doing this.

c **1585** Montgomerie *Sonnets* ii. 7 Bright Titan, to the tropiks that reteirs. **1592** Daniel *Compl. Rosamund* 610 What, stand you now amaz'd, retire you backe? **1604** E. G[rimstone] tr. *D'Acosta's Hist. Indies* iii. ix. 145 The farther we go into the sea, and retyre from land, the more we are touched and dazeled with this sicknes. **1666** Dryden *Ann. Mirab.* ccxlv, The amazed flames stand gathered on a heap, And from the precipice's brink retire. **1703** Maundrell *Journ. Jerus.* (1732) 12 The Mountains at some places approach nearer the Sea; at other, retire farther off. **1730** A. Gordon *Maffei's Amphith.* 216 The Wall always diminishes on the Inside, and retires and is lessened but little on the exteriour Surface. **1837** Disraeli *Venetia* v. i, An undulating margin that now retired into bays of the most picturesque form. **1859** Gullick & Timbs *Paint.* 228 In the foreground, and in parts not intended to 'retire' the 'impaste' should be bold. **1867** H. Macmillan *Bible Teach.* vi. 116 As science advances superstition retires.

c. To disappear *from* sight; to vanish.

1697 Dryden *Virg. Georg.* iv. 723 From his Eyes the fleeting Fair Retir'd like subtle Smoke dissolv'd in Air. *a* **1717** Parnell *Night-Piece on Death*, The grounds which on the right aspire, In dimness from the view retire. **1864** Tennyson *Voyage* 17 How oft we saw the Sun retire, And burn the threshold of the night!

†**4.** To return; to come back. *Obs.*

1567 Drant *Horace, Ep.* x. D viij, Expulse nature with a forke Yet she will still retire. **1579** Lyly *Euphues* (Arb.) 41 Though the Fawlcon be reclaimed to the fist, she retyreth to hir haggardnesse. **1605** Camden *Rem.* (1623) 126 But to retire to our purpose. **1613** J. Davies (Heref.) *Muse's Teares* Wks. (Grosart) I. 4/1 Princely-perfection being past the prime..Is turn'd into the Roote,..Ner'e to retire till God in Flesh returne!

†**5. a.** In preceding senses formerly conjugated with *is*, *was*, etc., in place of *has*, *had*, etc. *Obs.*

c **1540** tr. *Pol. Verg. Hist.* (Camden No. 36) 78 Scotlond.. whereunto noe small number of fugitives wear retiered. **1560** Daus tr. *Sleidane's Comm.* 109 After the Turke was retyred with his armie. **1581** Pettie tr. *Guazzo's Civ. Conv.* iii. (1586) 171 b, It is his part, being retired into his owne house, to looke more pleasantly vppon them. **1607** Shaks. *Cor.* iii. i. 11 On safegard he came to me..: he is retyred to Antium. **1671** Milton *Samson* 253 Seeking mee, who then Safe to the rock of Etham was retir'd. **1710** *Tatler* No. 157 ¶ 3, I was no sooner retired to my Lodgings, but [etc.]. **1788** Mrs. Hughes *Henry & Isabella* IV. 208 She was scarce retired with her mother, before the counsellor..was desired to walk into his chamber.

b. In *pa. pple.*, = having retired.

1610 Healey *St. Aug. Citie of God* i. ii. (1620) 3 A..foe that would spare any that they found retired into the Temples of their gods. **1667** Milton *P.L.* iv. 611 All things now retir'd to rest Mind us of like repose. **1774** D. Jones *Jrnl.* (1865) 114 When retired to my bed-chamber, thoughts crowded into my soul. **1791** Cowper *Iliad* xx. 176 Let us, retired To yonder hill, distant from all resort There sit. **1830** Tennyson *Ode to Memory* v, Whither in after life retired.. We may hold converse.

II. *refl.* **6.** To withdraw or remove (oneself); to betake (oneself) away.

Very common in 16th and 17th centuries; now *rare.*

α. **1539** *Chron. of Calais* (Camden) 170 The king's.. pavilion, and certain others for other noble personages, to retire themselves into after they shalbe presented to his highnes. **1560** Daus tr. *Sleidane's Comm.* 357 b, The spoylers were wont to escape that waye, and to retyre them selves out of daunger. **1647** Ward *Simp. Cobler* 61 You will please to retire your Selfe to your Closet. **1692** O. Walker *Grk. & Rom. Hist.* 240 He sent her word to retire her self whither she pleased. **1706** Estcourt *Fair Example* ii. i, Here comes my Lady, retire you, 'tis not proper you shou'd be seen first with me. **1750** Johnson *Rambler* No. 6 ¶ 9 My desire..has been..to retire myself to some of our American plantations. **1853** Rock *Ch. of Fathers* III. ii. 194 Both the acolytes..retired themselves into the choir.

β. **1567** *Reg. Privy Council Scot.* I. 560 Evir thinking at his plesour to reteir him to oure said Soveranis Castell of Dunbar. *c* **1620** Sir W. Mure *Misc. Poems* xxi. 111 My solitarie Muse her selfe reteirs, Un-usd abroad to haunt such pompous throngs. **1637–50** Row *Hist. Kirk* (Wodrow Soc.) 488 Some fled to Ingland, some reteered themselves and keeped quyet.

III. *trans.* **7. a.** To withdraw, lead back (troops, etc.), esp. before a superior force.

1550 *Reg. Privy Council Scot.* I. 86 That his Hienes had.. thairthrow constrenit thame to retere the maist part of thair army. **1596** Dalrymple tr. *Leslie's Hist. Scot.* ix. 255 Tha began to reteir and draw back thair force til Ingland. **1597** Beard *Theatre God's Judgem.* (1612) 170 Whilst their embassadors were retiring their garrisons out of Misia..he set forward his armie. *a* **1648** Ld. Herbert *Hen. VIII* (1683) 457 He appointed him twenty days time to retire his Army out of Piedmont. **1693** *Mem. Cnt. Teckely* iv. 39 The General Veteranie..retired all his Troops to Nissa. **1796** *Instr. & Reg. Cavalry* (1813) 141 The half Squadrons..may be retired at any named distance behind each other. **1813** Sir R. Wilson *Priv. Diary* (1862) II. 456 The enemy had retired their centre and left, so that the engagement on these points commenced necessarily later. **1841** Lever *C. O'Malley* liii, The French were soon seen to retire their heavy guns. **1897** Sir E. Wood *Achievements Cav.* i. 16 No cavalry can be expected to fight if it is retired at speed with an enemy at its heels.

†**b.** To rally, bring back. *Obs. rare*$^{-1}$.

1596 Dalrymple tr. *Leslie's Hist. Scot.* x. 299 Al the rest he had put to flicht, gif be the Erle of Varuik they had not bene helpet, reteired, and with a stout courage put in ordour agane.

†**8. a.** To put away; to withdraw, remove, lead away (a person or thing) *from* or *to* a place. Also const. *into*, *within*, or ellipt. *Obs.*

1585 T. Washington tr. *Nicholay's Voy.* i. xix. 22 b, The gouernours lodging,..hauing vnderneath it the cellars to retyre the munition, could not be repayred. *a* **1586** Sidney *Ps.* xl. i, Me..From dungeon he retired, Where I in horrors lay. **1603** Knolles *Hist. Turks* (1621) 362 The Valachies before his comming, had retired their wives and children.. into their strong cities. **1664** Evelyn *Kal. Hort.* (1729) 218 Retire your choice Greens and rarest Plants..into your Conservatory. **1690** Lady R. Russell *Lett.* I. 68 Happy are those whom God retires in his grace. **1719** De Foe *Crusoe* ii. (Globe) 333 When they had been retir'd, Lodgings provided for them as well as our Ship would allow, and they had slept heartily.

†**b.** To withdraw the mind, thoughts, etc., *from* some object or sphere. *Obs.*

1594 T. B. *La Primaud. Fr. Acad.* ii. 145 When our externall senses are retired and withdrawen from doing their dueties. **1607** Hieron *Wks.* I. 156 To labour to pull and retire our affections from earthly things. **1619** W. Sclater *Exp. 1 Thess.* (1630) Ep. Ded. A 2 b, To retire my mind from the tumultuous hurly-burlies it is tossed withal. **1699** Penn *Adv. Children* ii. ¶ 1 So soon as you wake, retire your mind into pure silence from all thoughts and ideas of worldly things.

c. To withdraw (a thing) from notice; to hide away, put into obscurity.

1605 BACON *Adv. Learn.* II. iv. §4 For that tendeth to demonstrate, and illustrate that which is taught,.. this other to retire and obscure it.

1893 *Harper's Mag.* Dec. 161 To retire your comely features in the meshes of a veil. **1899** HOBSON *Ruskin* 123 Professors Marshall and Sidgwick retire this 'fundamental proposition on capital' into the obscurity of foot-notes.

9. a. To draw or pull (a thing) back (again).

1593 SHAKS. *Lucr.* 303 The lockes.. Ech one by him inforst retires his ward. **1597** LOWE *Chirurg.* (1634) 171 Then retire the needle the way that it went in. **1631** R. BOLTON *Comf. Affl. Consc.* i. (1635) 4 All the creatures then, pull in their hornes, retyre their stings, bite in their poyson. [**1886** SHELDON tr. *Flaubert's Salammbô* vii. 178 Straining their arms in the effort to retire from its rings the enormous bar securing the door.]

†**b.** To bring or hold (one) back *from* some course; to dissuade, restrain. *Obs. rare.*

1598 B. JONSON *Ev. Man in Hum.* I. i, How happy would I estimate my selfe, Could I.. retyre my sonne From one vayne course of study he affects. *c* **1611** CHAPMAN *Iliad* XXII. 68 Thus wept the old king, and tore off his white hair; yet all these Retir'd not Hector.

†**c.** To bring or get back; to regain, recover.

1600 *Engl. Helicon* Z ij b, Of death so sweet, so happy, so desired, That to die so againe their life retired. **1682** WARBURTON *Hist. Guernsey* (1822) 92 In two cases, inheritance given to rent may be retired, or redeemed by the next kindred.

10. To withdraw from operation or currency; to take up or pay (*esp.* a bill).

1681 STAIR *Institut.* I. vii. 80 This presumption is stronger in relation to Bonds, which are most ordinarly taken away, by retiring the same without taking Discharge. **1693** *Ibid.* (ed. 2) IV. xlv. 713 It was not a Right to be Retired upon payment. **1766** W. GORDON *Gen. Counting-ho.* 12 Bills are.. credited as they are retired. **1824** SCOTT *St. Ronan's* xv, Two of his notes for £100 each,.. which he thinks nae mair of retiring, than he does of paying the national debt. **1849–50** ALISON *Hist. Europe* IV. xxiv. §10. 366 Territorial mandates .. were to retire the assignats at the rate of thirty for one. **1854** *Comm. Bench Rep.* XV. 94 If an acceptor retires a bill at maturity, he takes it entirely from circulation, and the bill is in effect paid.

11. a. To remove (an officer) from active service. Now also in *gen.* use.

1870 *Daily News* 27 June, That a flag officer.. should be compulsorily retired on attaining a certain age. **1894** *Times* 29 May 11/3 Admiral.. Hamilton.. was retired from the active list under the age clause. **1961** M. SPARK *Prime of Miss Jean Brodie* iii. 71 She had been retired before time. **1980** *Times* 19 Feb. 1/1 One idea being strongly canvassed is that Sir Charles Villiers, British Steel's chairman, should be retired early.

b. To withdraw from the usual sphere of activity; to take off.

1881 'MARK TWAIN' *Prince & Pauper* (1882) xix. 244 He was so awkward at this service that she retired him from it. **1883** *Lisbon* (Dakota) *Star* 12 Oct., Eighteen packet boats have been retired by several of the packet lines.., owing to the low stage of water. **1888** *Amer. Humorist* 2 June 5/2 The Sale, after this race, became known, and Mr. Bonner retired him [the horse] from the track. **1974** *Sci. Amer.* Dec. 139/1 This material served for about a year before I retired it. **1980** D. FRANCIS *Reflex* viii. 91 It's his last season... I'll have to retire him [*sc.* a racehorse].

c. *U.S. Baseball.* To cause (a batter or team) to retire; to put out.

1874 *Chicago Inter Ocean* 6 July 9/1 Schafer was retired on a fly caught by Meyerle in left field. **1889** N. F. PFEFFER *Scientific Ball* 33 Runners move up every time the ball is pitched;.. the clever baseman will be guided by the action of the man he wants to retire. **1917** C. MATHEWSON *Second Base Sloan* 180 The first batsman was retired on an easy toss from Chase to Jim. **1949** *News-Herald* (Marshfield, Wisconsin) 19 July 9/4 Nowitzke gobbled up Bauer's grounder and threw him out to retire the side. **1972** *N.Y. Times* 4 June v. 1/7 Lyle retired the first 11 batters and wound up allowing just three singles.

retired (rɪˈtaɪəd), *ppl. a.* [f. prec. + -ED[1].]

1. Withdrawn into seclusion or away from contact with the world: **a.** of persons.

1590 J. SMYTH in *Lett. Lit. Men* (Camden) 61, I.. do live almost continually retired in my howse. **1632** MILTON *Penseroso* 49 Adde to these retired Leasure, That in trim Gardens takes his pleasure. *c* **1648–50** BRATHWAIT *Barnabees Jrnl.* III. (1818) 143 Here the retyred Tanner builds him bowrs. **1691** HARTCLIFFE *Virtues* 282 The retired and solitary Student. **1706** LONDON & WISE (*title*), The Retir'd Gard'ner... Being a Translation of *Le Jardinier Solitaire.* **1783** JOHNSON *Let. to Mrs. Thrale* 21 Oct., You are now retired, and have nothing to impede self-examination or self-improvement. **1813** SCOTT *Rokeby* IV. xx, Few months we lived retired, unknown, To all but one dear friend alone. **1885–94** R. BRIDGES *Eros & Psyche* Feb. xix, Stern Ares, with his crisp hair helmeted, Came, and retired Hestia.

absol. **1653** JER. TAYLOR *Serm. for Year* Ep. Ded. A 3 b, The faith of Martyrs, and the hardinesse of Confessors, and the austerity of the Retired.

b. of life, conditions, occupations, etc.

1611 SHAKS. *Cymb.* III. v. 36 Since the exile of Posthumus, most retyr'd Hath her life bin. **1648** DENHAM *Cooper's H.*, Oh happiness of sweet retir'd content! **1696** STANHOPE *Chr. Pattern* (1711) 19 It is our duty.. to fill up the empty spaces of life with these holy and retired exercises. **1711** ADDISON *Spect.* No. 93 ¶5 Employment for those Retired Hours in which we are altogether left to our selves. **1746** HERVEY *Medit.* (1818) 216 What a pleasing awe is awakened by such a reflection! How venerable it renders my retired walks! **1820** KEATS *St. Agnes* xxxi, Sumptuous they stand In the retired quiet of the night. **1856** SIR B. BRODIE *Psychol. Inq.* I. iv. 132 It is a great mistake made by some sentimental writers, when they speak of the advantages of a retired life.

2. Secluded, sequestered; removed from places frequented by people.

1593 Q. ELIZ. *Boeth.* I. pr. iii. 6 My nurs I saw, in whose retired Romes in my Youthe I dwelt. **1621** BRATHWAIT *Nat. Embassie* (1877) 28 The retiredst angle or corner cannot giue vice a couer. **1672** WYCHERLEY *Love in a Wood* III. i, A small house, in an obscure, little, retired street. **1719** DE FOE *Crusoe* II. (Globe) 391 To lead them.. to their retir'd Place in the Woods. **1774** GOLDSM. *Nat. Hist.* (1776) I. 40 They are found.. in the most retired and inward parts of the most firm and solid rocks. **1860** H. AINSWORTH *Ovingdean Grange* 301 A small cottage somewhat retired from the road. **1871** L. STEPHEN *Playgr. Eur.* (1894) iv. 92 Swiss enterprise has begun to penetrate these retired valleys.

3. Withdrawn into oneself; reserved.

1611 SHAKS. *Wint. T.* IV. iv. 62 You are retyred, As if you were a feasted one: and not The Hostesse of the meeting. **1627** J. DOUGHTY *Serm., Divine Myst.* (1628) 11 For this cause wee finde the Fathers euermore cautelous and very retir'd. **1670** G. H. *Hist. Cardinals* II. III. 200 Whilst he was Cardinal he was retir'd, shun'd all conversation as much as was possible. **1780** BURKE *Œcon. Reform* Wks. III. 336 The judges are, or ought to be, of a reserved and retired character. **1828** SCOTT *F. M. Perth* x, You have censured me in your kindness for being too gentle, too retired.

†**4.** Of thoughts, etc.: Carried on in seclusion or quiet; private. *Obs.*

1626 JACKSON *Humiliation Son of God* vii. 66 To doe that which in his retired and sober thoughts he did most dislike. **1670** CLARENDON *Contempl. Ps.* Tracts (1727) 627 Arguments.. which.. operate more in the publick agitation of them than in a private and retired speculation. *a* **1718** PENN in *Life* Wks. I. 132 A Subject that requires your retired Consideration. **1751** ABP. STONE *Serm. 1 Kings* xii. 15 A Compliance with innocent Customs, which in their retired Judgment they might not altogether approve.

†**b.** Inward, inner, recondite, hidden. *Obs.*

1649 JER. TAYLOR *Gt. Exemp.* Pref. ¶48, I was lesse carefull to make it strict in retired senses. **1695** WOODWARD *Nat. Hist. Earth* II. (1723) 94 If we look into its retired Movements, and more secret and latent Springs. **1713** ADDISON *Cato* I. vi, Disburthen all thy cares on me, And let me share thy most retired distress. **1737** WATERLAND *Eucharist* 429 In its retired, mystical meaning, it figured out the Spiritual Covenant. **1773** J. ALLEN *Serm. at St. Mary's, Oxf.* 12 The most sublime and retired mysteries.

5. a. That has receded or subsided. *rare*$^{-1}$.

1595 SHAKS. *John* v. iv. 53 We will.. like a bated and retired Flood.. Stoope lowe.. And calmely run on.

†**b.** ? Contracted, shrunk. *Obs. rare*$^{-1}$.

1605 B. JONSON *Volpone* II. i, Crampes, Convulsions, Paralysies, Epilepsies, Tremor-cordia, retired-Nerues.

c. ***retired flank***: (see quot. 1802).

1696 PHILLIPS (ed. 5), *Orillon*, a mass of Earth lin'd with a Wall.. to secure the Canon in the retir'd Flank. **1704** J. HARRIS *Lex. Techn.* I. s.v. *Flank*, The Low, Covered, or Retired Flank, is the Platform of the Casemate, which lies hid in the Bastion. **1771** *Encycl. Brit.* II. 618/2 The orillons are very useful in covering the retired flanks, which cannot be seen but directly in the front. **1802** JAMES *Milit. Dict.* s.v. *Fortification, Retired flanks*, are those made behind the line which joins the extremity of the face and the curtain, towards the capital of the bastion. **1858** GREENER *Gunnery* 67 Their principal use is on board ship; but they are sometimes used in casemates, or retired flanks of fortresses.

d. Drawn back; receding. *rare*$^{-1}$.

1802 PALEY *Nat. Theol.* (1804) 242 The retired under jaw of a swine works in the ground, after the protruding snout.

6. Withdrawn from, no longer occupied with, business or official duties. (Cf. RETIRE *v.* 1 e.)

1824 MISS MITFORD *Village* Ser. I. (1863) 3 The tidy, square, red cottage.. belongs to a retired publican from a neighbouring town. **1851** *Lond. Gaz.* No. 2122. 1673/1 The List of Commanders promoted to the Rank of Retired Captain. **1881** *Times* 11 Jan. 9/6 A retired Viceroy is naturally and by common consent an authority on Indian affairs.

b. ***retired list***, a list of retired officers.

1802 JAMES *Milit. Dict.*, *Retired list*, a list on the marine establishment upon which superannuated officers are placed. **1851** *Lond. Gaz.* No. 2122. 1673/1 The Retired List then to be diminished by only retiring one in two vacancies. **1887** *Times* (weekly ed.) 14 Oct. 12/2 [He] had consented to place him on the retired list.

c. ***retired allowance*** or ***pay***, the pension given to a retired officer or official.

1817 *Parl. Debates* 582 Salaries and retired allowances were very unequally distributed. **1867** SMYTH *Sailor's Word-bk.* 570 *Retired Pay*, a graduated pension for retired officers. **1890** *Daily News* 8 Jan. 3/8 Col. G. A. White, from lieutenant-colonel, half-pay, retires on retired pay.

re'tiredly, *adv.* [f. prec. + -LY[2].] In a retired or secluded manner; privately.

1599 *Sidney Papers* II. 140 If he kepe him self humble and retiredly. **1611** COTGR., *En son privé*, priuately, secretly, closely, retiredly. *a* **1641** BP. MOUNTAGU *Acts & Mon.* (1642) 416 The Sadduces.. were.. desirous to live retiredly and privately to themselves. **1701** W. WOTTON *Hist. Rome* 349 She lived there very retiredly.

re'tiredness. Also 7 **retyr-**. [f. as prec. + -NESS.] The state or quality of being retired; privacy, seclusion; reserve. (Very common in the 17th century.)

a. of disposition, character, or conduct.

a **1586** SIDNEY *Arcadia* II. (1605) 127 A tode-like retirednesse, and closenesse of minde. **1598** DALLINGTON *Meth. Trav.* B iij b, Neither to dis-taste them by a too much retirednesse, nor to hinder himselfe by too much familiaritie. **1694** LD. DELAMERE in *Marvell's Wks.* (Grosart) IV. 42 The lowest condescentions and meanest familiarity cannot loose a Prince so much as too much retiredness, or being over-reserved. *a* **1713** ELLWOOD *Autobiog.* (1765) 40 We spent much of the Evening in Retiredness of Mind. **1839** PUSEY *Let.* in Liddon *Life* (1893) II. xxiv. 142 There seems in this a spirit foreign to the retiredness and absence of self—of real Catholicity. **1894** *N.Y. Tribune* 5 July, A humility of speech, and general retiredness of character almost incompatible with the newspaper character of the man.

b. of manner of living.

1617 MORYSON *Itin.* II. 47 In his nature he loued priuate retirednesse, with good fare, and some few choice friends. **1666** J. SMITH *Old Age* (1676) 18 Men begin to leave off their employments, and betake themselves to retiredness. *a* **1703** BURKITT *On N. T.* Luke ii. 45 Our Blessed Saviour when on earth, did not take pleasure in a wild retiredness. **1827** CARLYLE *Germ. Rom.* II. 142 Her retiredness did not please him, and he feared, that in the end, it might make her silly. **1834** WORDSW. *To C'tess Lonsdale* 41 Thus, Lady, is retiredness a veil [etc.].

c. of places.

1660 T. BLOUNT *Boscobel* 36 His Majesty.. commended the place for its retiredness. *c* **1670** WOOD *Life* (O.H.S.) I. 270 To refresh his mind with a melancholy walke, and with the retiredness of the place. **1727** HEARNE in *Reliq.* (1897) II. 673 To have a better notion of the ancient solitariness and retiredness of the place. **1805** ALMON *Wilkes' Corr.* III. 61 A grove of venerable old elms near the house, with the retiredness of the mansion itself, made it as sweet a retreat as the most poetical imagination could create.

retiree (rɪtaɪəˈriː). *U.S.* [f. RETIRE *v.* + -EE[1].] One who has retired from a business or occupation; a pensioner.

1945 W. PEGLER in *Times-Herald* (Washington) 3 Oct. 9/1 How many amputees were there, General Bradley wanted to know, resorting to a ghastly form that has given us, also, trainees, dischargees, and retirees. **1962** *Economist* 29 Dec. 1278/1 The 'retirees', people of modest means drawn from all parts of the United States. **1967** MRS. L. B. JOHNSON *White House Diary* 10 May (1970) 516 One of the retirees of the ILGWU.. came up to me with a big bouquet of yellow roses. **1972** C. WESTON *Poor, Poor Ophelia* xvii. 102 The couple.. were.. retirees for whom living on a sail-boat was apparently a life's dream. **1975** 'G. BLACK' *Big Wind* ii. 24 The retiree kept spraying my face with fury as he told me. **1979** *Tucson* (Arizona) *Citizen* 3 Oct. 18A/4 Waves of retirees have headed for country parts of Missouri.

retirement (rɪˈtaɪəmənt). Also 6–7 **retyre-**. [a. F. *retirement* (1576), = Sp. *retiramiento*, Pg. *-mento*, It. *ritiramento*: see RETIRE *v.* and -MENT.]

1. a. The act of falling back, retreating, or receding from a place or position. (Somewhat *rare*; in mod. use chiefly *Mil.*)

1596 SHAKS. *1 Hen. IV*, v. iv. 6, I beseech your Maiesty make vp, Least you[r] retirement do amaze your friends. **1643** MILTON *Divorce* viii. Wks. 1851 IV. 40 Against reiterated scandals and seducements which never cease, much more can no other remedie or retirement be found but absolute departure. **1649** —— *Eikon.* xxviii. 240 A sort of moodie.. consciences apt to engage thir Leaders into great and dangerous affaires past retirement, and then.. to betray them basely. **1847** GROTE *Greece* II. xxxiii. (1862) III. 207 On the retirement of the Lacedæmonian force, the Samian exiles were left destitute. **1877** M. FOSTER *Physiol.* III. ii. (1878) 404 The approach and retirement are more readily appreciated than is a simple change of size.

b. A receding part; a recess. *rare*$^{-1}$.

1726 LEONI *Alberti's Archit.* II. 71/2 The height of the semi-circular retirements.. was only equal to their breadth.

2. a. The act of withdrawing into seclusion or privacy; withdrawal *from* something.

1599 SHAKS. *Hen. V*, I. i. 58 Any retyrement, any sequestration, From open Haunts and Popularitie. **1615** G. SANDYS *Trav.* 252 [Capræ] which he variously beautified and honoured with his retirements. **1667** MILTON *P.L.* IX. 250 For solitude somtimes is best societie, And short retirement urges sweet returne. *a* **1704** LOCKE (J.), In this retirement of the mind from the senses, it retains a yet more incoherent manner of thinking. **1794** MRS. RADCLIFFE *Myst. Udolpho* i, The first interruptions to the happiness he had known since his retirement, were occasioned by the death of his two sons. **1874** GREEN *Short Hist.* viii. §1. 453 In Milton we note.. a proud retirement from the meaner and coarser life around him. **1892** GUNTER *Miss Dividends* (1893) 157 A proper retirement from society is due to it.

b. Withdrawal from occupation, office, or business activity. (Cf. RETIRE *v.* 1 e.) Also *collect.* the total of retired officers.

1648 CROMWELL *Lett.* 25 Nov. (Carlyle), When Robert Hammond, through dissatisfaction too, desired retirement from the Army. *a* **1799** WASHINGTON (Webster), Retirement is as necessary to me as it will be welcome. **1818** J. W. CROKER in *C. Papers* 13 July, To induce you to abandon the thoughts of a retirement from business. **1851** *Lond. Gaz.* No. 2122. 1673/1 By keeping up the Retirement of 1846, to the number of 200. **1885** *Manch. Exam.* 12 Mar. 4/7 The retirement of Mr. Beith from the chairmanship of the Executive is a just cause for regret.

c. The act of retiring to rest. *rare*$^{-1}$.

1801 *Lusignan* III. 87 Emily had exceeded the usual hour of retirement.

d. Aloofness, distance, reserve. *rare*$^{-1}$.

1800 SOUTHEY *Lett.* (1856) I. 114 Their lieutenants.. observe too rude a retirement towards the English.

3. a. The state or condition of being withdrawn from society or publicity; seclusion, privacy.

1603 SHAKS. *Meas. for M.* v. i. 130 For certaine words he spake against your Grace In your retirment, I had swing'd him soundly. **1654** WHITLOCK *Zootomia* 17 They are one thing in their retirement, another on the stage of publick view. **1719** DE FOE *Crusoe* II. (Globe) 371 They lived two Years after this in perfect Retirement. **1742** FRANKLIN *Ess.* Wks. 1840 II. 84 If I delight in a private life, have they any right to drag me out of my retirement? **1828** SCOTT *F.M. Perth* xxxi, As the Duchess lived in close retirement, she was little surprised at this. **1875** JOWETT *Plato* (ed. 2) IV. 227

[He] is reluctantly drawn from his retirement to defend his old master.

b. A time or occasion of seclusion or privacy.

In some quots. not clearly distinct from sense 4.

1632 STRAFFORD *Let. to Earl of Carlisle* 24 Oct., In my cheefest Exaltation before men, and my fullest contentmentt in my inmost retirementts. **1668** DRYDEN *Maiden Queen* I. iii, It is a saucy boldness, thus to press On my retirements. *a* **1708** BEVERIDGE *Priv. Th.* I. (1730) 91 All the secret Thoughts, the inward Motions and Retirements of my Soul—are exactly known before Him. **1738** tr. *Guazzo's Art of Convers.* 22 Those who are in pursuit of Learning, seek it..in their Studies and Retirements. **1801** STRUTT *Sports & Past.* Introd. 1 When we follow them into their retirements..we are most likely to see them in their true state. **1852** LD. COCKBURN *Life Jeffrey* I. 270 Dearly did he enjoy these retirements.

†**c.** An occupation of one's leisure time. *Obs. rare*⁻¹.

1641 R. BROOKE *Eng. Episc.* Ded. A 3 The Worke then of these Lines, is to lay prostrate at Your Feet..the Retirements of Your Humble Servant in the Last Recesse.

4. A place or abode characterized by seclusion or privacy; a retreat. Also *fig.* and *transf.*

1652–62 HEYLIN *Cosmogr.* II. (1682) 106, 20 Royal Castles and Palaces..as the private Retirements of the King. **1670** MAYNWARING *Pharm. Phys. Rep.* 57 This Medicine..searcheth the most intimate recesses, and closest retirements of our bodies. **1707** MORTIMER *Husb.* (1721) I. 259 Decoy-Ducks..will bring whole Flights of Fowl to their Retirements. **1772** WILKES *Corr.* (1805) IV. 131 Exmouth; where he has, as they say, a sweet country retirement. **1825** HONE *Every-day Bk.* I. 638 The gardens..were covetable retirements. **1846** TRENCH *Mirac.* xix. (1862) 326 He..withdraws..to his safer retirements in the immediate neighbourhood of the sea of Galilee.

5. The act of withdrawing from circulation.

1865 *Sat. Rev.* 23 Dec. 777 His estimate is that 40,000,000*l.* employed in the retirement of notes will certainly suffice to bring them to par. **1897** *Daily News* 22 Nov. 7/6 A provision for the retirement of all paper currency of a lower denomination than ten dollars.

6. *attrib.* and *Comb.*, as (sense 2b) ***retirement age, city, community, home, pension, pensioner.***

1919 *Rep. Departmental Comm. Old Age Pensions* App. 157 in *Parl. Papers* (Cmd. 411) XXVII. 299 Your retirement age seems very low. **1976** A. WHITE *Long Silence* xix. 164 The driver, one of the colonel's men, long past retirement age. **1964** V. BARTLETT *Tuscan Retreat* i. 24 'Retirement cities' such as are growing up in the United States..lived in only by old people. **1976** *National Observer* (U.S.) 14 Feb. 9/1 Many elderly people trying to find a retirement community have heard stories of developments going broke. **1979** *Tucson* (Arizona) *Citizen* 20 Sept. 8C/1 At least 60 persons have put down deposits to buy security for their old age in the form of 'life contracts' with a proposed retirement community here. **1968** *Globe & Mail* (Toronto) 13 Feb. 31/4 (Advt.), Small retirement home, 2 bedrooms, 3 piece bath. **1977** E. AMBLER *Send no more Roses* x. 248 Buy that nice retirement home you've always dreamed of owning. **1942** W. BEVERIDGE *Soc. Insurance & Allied Services* III. 96 The pensions proposed in the Plan for Social Security are retirement pensions, not old age pensions. **1973** *Times* 13 Jan. 19/7 Basic retirement pensions are a flat amount..per week. *a* **1974** R. CROSSMAN *Diaries* (1976) II. 644 Should the exemptions be for retirement pensioners or for people over sixty-five?

retirer (rɪˈtaɪərə(r)). [f. RETIRE *v.* + -ER¹.] One who retires or retreats.

c **1572** GASCOIGNE *Fruites Warre* civ, The willing drumme a lustie marche to sounde, Whiles ranke retyrers gaue their enimies ground. **1653** HOLCROFT *Procopius, Goth. Wars* I. 23 The Enemy therefore coming with multitudes,..charged the retirers. **1655** VAUGHAN *Silex Scint.* II. (1883) 262 No busie worldling hunts away The sad retirer all the day! **1978** *Oxf. Diocesan Mag.* July 5/3 The main problem of retirement has to be faced by the retirer himself.

retiring (rɪˈtaɪərɪŋ), *vbl. sb.* [-ING¹.]

1. The action of the verb in various senses:

a. In intransitive uses.

1548 ELYOT, *Recessus*, goyng awaie or backe; retyryng. **1601** HOLLAND *Pliny* II. xxxv. I. 39 By the retiring and going backe of the sea. **1604** E. GRIMSTONE *Hist. Siege Ostend* 62 In their retiring there were many of them stayed. **1642** FULLER *Holy & Prof. St.* v. xviii. §4 Soon after his retiring, he ended his life. **1707** SIR W. HOPE *New Method Fencing* iv. 122 Breaking of Measure is but a Genteel Term Sword-Men have given to a Moderat Retiring, or Giving of Ground. **1730** A. GORDON *Maffei's Amphith.* 406 The Retiring of the Wall..is both towards the inner-side and the out-side too. **1808** HELEN ST. VICTOR *Ruins of Rigonda* III. 6 Previous to my retiring, I was employed in my vespers. **1861** G. CHAPMAN *Art Fencing* 16 Retiring is, however, occasionally performed by first withdrawing the right [foot].

b. In transitive uses.

1594 I. G. *Di Grassi's Arte of Defence* O ij b, Without any other retyring of himselfe. **1599** B. JONSON *Cynthia's Rev.* II. i, Supplies for retyring of his old ward-robe from pawne. **1681** STAIR *Institut.* I. vii. 80 An Executor for whom simple retiring of the Bond will not be sufficient without Discharge or Assignation.

2. *attrib.* **a.** Of places: Devoted to retirement or privacy.

a **1586** SIDNEY *Arcadia* I. (1605) 8 Hard by was a house of pleasure built for a sommer retiring place. **1610** HOLLAND *Camden's Brit.* (1637) 494 Downham where the Bishop hath his retyring House with a Parke. **1621** ELSING *Debates Ho. Lords* (Camden) 11 The Prynce came and wente into his retyringe roomes, and having putt on his roabes went and mett the King. *a* **1700** EVELYN *Diary* 8 Feb. 1645, It was once the retyring place of Julius Cæsar. **1719** DE FOE *Crusoe* II. (Globe) 412 [The] handsome Rooms..which..served as Closets or retiring Rooms. **1778** *Eng. Gazetteer* (ed. 2), Havering at Bower, Essex,..was the ancient retiring-place of the kings of England. **1818** SCOTT *Br. Lamm.* xxvi, The cooper's house was so roomy, that each guest had his separate retiring room. **1884** *Pall Mall G.* 14 May 4/1 The erection of public retiring rooms for both sexes in the streets.

b. Consequent upon, or connected with, retirement from office or employment.

1837 LOCKHART *Scott* II. iii. 84 In those days there was no system of retiring pensions for the worn-out functionary of this class. **1855** THACKERAY *Newcomes* viii, Binnie had his retiring pension, and, besides, had saved half his allowance ever since he had been in India. **1859** RUSSELL *Diary India* (1860) I. 87 They say..that every Indian officer has a right to a good retiring allowance. **1919** *Rep. Departmental Comm. Old Age Pensions* App. 153/1 in *Parl. Papers* (Cmd. 411) XXVII. 299 The retiring age in this case is 50, but, providing the consent of the company is obtained, members are not bound to retire at that age. **1945** 'G. ORWELL' *Animal Farm* iii. 26 There was a stormy debate over the correct retiring age for each class of animal. **1973** G. GREENE *Honorary Consul* v. v. 329 If you were in the Service you would have passed the retiring age quite a while ago.

c. Connected with retirement (from a room, etc.).

1880 MEREDITH *Tragic Com.* (1881) 152 He delivered his retiring bow to the Frau von Rüdiger's shoulder. **1901** *Scotsman* 1 Mar. 7/3 A retiring collection after a concert.

retiring (rɪˈtaɪərɪŋ), *ppl. a.* [f. the vb. + -ING².]

1. That retires, in various senses of the verb.

c **1586** C'TESS PEMBROKE *Ps.* CVII. viii, How many mounting winged tree For traffique leave retiring land? **1604** SHAKS. *Oth.* III. iii. 455 The Ponticke Sea, Whose Icie Current, and compulsiue course, Neu'r keepes retyring ebbe. **1690** tr. *Blancard's Phys. Dict.* 2 *Abductores Musculi*, ..the retiring brauwns. **1707** SIR W. HOPE *New Method Fencing* iv. 124 Several Warlike Nations have made use of a Retiring and Flying way of Fight, as a thing of singular Advantage. **1796** *Instr. & Reg. Cavalry* (1813) 208 A retiring line may also throw back a wing,..by the echellon march, or some other of the modes already prescribed. **1817** SHELLEY *Rev. Islam* III. xiv, The far sound Of their retiring steps. **1853** KANE *Grinnell Exp.* xxxi. (1856) 271 So high that, with its retiring flanks on either side, it can be none other than the projecting Cape Warrender. **1890** GROSS *Gild Merch.* I. 146 To appoint the retiring mayor of the town mayor of the staple.

2. Characterized by retirement; reserved, shy.

1766 FORDYCE *Serm. Yng. Wm.* (1767) I. iii. 96 The retiring graces have been always the most attractive. **1832** LYTTON *Eugene A.* I. vii, So retiring a nature as his might never have harboured love. **1861** SMILES *Engineers* II. 280 He was an exceedingly modest, unpretending, and retiring man.

Comb. **1859** F. FRANCIS *Newton Dogvane* (1888) 60 A fair, retiring-looking girl, with chestnut hair.

Hence **re'tiringly** *adv.*

1861 MEREDITH *Evan Harrington* III. viii, She answered, retiringly: 'Indeed I cannot say'. **1885** *Sat. Rev.* 12 Dec. 769 Sir William..was not at all to the fore, but, on the contrary, very retiringly to the back.

re'tiringness. [f. prec. + -NESS.] The quality of being retiring.

1801 W. TAYLOR in *Monthly Mag.* XI. 289 The word coy is metaphorically applied to..the stillness of reserve, to moral retiringness. **1831** *Blackw. Mag.* XXX. 213 The retiringness of self-depreciating delicacy. **1887** *Spectator* 17 Sept. 1241 The retiringness of wealth on which the *Times* descants.

†**re'tithe,** *v. Obs.* [RE- 5 a.] To decimate again.

1610 HOLLAND *Camden's Brit.* I. 297 Hee let the tenth man goe by; and euen these tenth men thus reserued, hee went ouer againe, and most cruelly retithed them.

re'tomb, *v.* [RE- 5 a.] To entomb again.

1591 SYLVESTER *Du Bartas* I. vi. 319 The Beast..Rewhelps her whelps, and in her tender womb She doth as oft her living brood re-tomb.

re'tool, *v.* [RE- 5 a, c.] *trans.* **1.** To rework or shape again with a tool.

1866 *Intell. Observ.* No. 52. 302 Re-tooled the whole of the inscription.

2. To furnish (a factory, etc.) with fresh tools; to provide new manufacturing equipment for.

1940 *Economist* 5 Oct. 432/2 In case of a change in the design or type of equipment to be produced, the manufacturer must be given ample time to plan its production and if necessary to re-tool his works. **1951** CUNNINGHAM & SHERMAN *Production of Motor Vehicles* iii. 76 It will be necessary to retool many existing machines already in the shop. *Ibid.*, To retool means to provide new jigs, fixtures, clamping devices, cutting tools..and other implementation that makes machines and machine tools effective for a particular operation. **1963** *Economist* 10 Aug. 510/2 The scheduled shut-downs this month to retool for the new 1964 models. **1976** LD. HOME *Way Wind Blows* iv. 58, I agreed with him that a home-based market was necessary if we were to re-tool our factories for export.

Hence **re'tooling** *vbl. sb.*

1942 *Sun* (Baltimore) 8 Jan. 14/1 The publication goes on to say that 'retooling'..is not the only problem. **1951** G. MARX *Let.* 23 Jan. (1967) 34 Between retooling for the war effort and dueling with Wald and Krasna, I presume you are a fairly busy man. **1962** E. SNOW *Red China Today* (1963) xxvii. 204 Plant in considerable confusion due to expansion and retooling. **1977** G. V. HIGGINS *Dreamland* xii. 146 Vulcan Forge Limited..[had] been a bit slow in retooling to resume production for its prewar markets.

retorician, retorik, obs. ff. RHETORICIAN, RHETORIC.

retorn(e, obs. ff. RETURN *sb.* and *v.*

retornel, -nella, obs. ff. RITORNEL(LO.

†**re'torqued,** *ppl. a. Obs. rare*⁻¹. [f. F. *retorquer* or L. *retorquēre*: see RETORT *v.*¹] Turned backwards.

1586 MARLOWE *1st Pt. Tamburl.* v. ii, Shall we in this detested guise, With shame, with hunger, and with horror stay, Griping our bowels with retorqued thoughts.

†**re'torrid,** *a. Obs. rare.* [ad. L. *retorrid-us.*] Burnt up, dried up.

1684 tr. *Bonet's Merc. Compil.* XVI. 567 When the Brain by ..too frequent use becomes sharp and retorrid. **1710** T. FULLER *Pharm. Extemp.* 56 Fevers, that have boil'd up the Blood into a retorrid Crasis.

retorsion (rɪˈtɔːʃən). Now *rare.* [a. F. *rétorsion* (13–14th c.), or ad. med.L. *retorsiōn-em*, var. of *retortiōn-em* RETORTION. So Sp. *retorsion*, It. *ritorsione.*] Retortion (of an argument, etc.).

1657 W. MORICE *Coena quasi Κοινὴ* 242 By retorsion, as in a College, all that are..of the Foundation, doe partake of the Donatives of the Founder [etc.]. *a* **1670** HACKET *Cent. Serm.* (1675) 241 God hath a retorsion in store, a *fallere fallentem.* **1693** *Apol. Clergy Scot.* 88 The reasonings of it are so clear, the historical retorsions so undeniable. **1880** *Encycl. Brit.* XIII. 194/1 'Retorsion,' or retaliating on the foreign nation or its subjects, by similar injuries to those inflicted on us. **1890** *Sat. Rev.* 14 June 748/1 The first requisite..of all satire, and especially of political, is that, like a good dilemma, it should be incapable of 'retorsion'.

retort (rɪˈtɔːt), *sb.*¹ [f. RETORT *v.*¹]

†**1.** *Mus.* A 'retorted' mood. *Obs. rare.*

1597 MORLEY *Introd. Mus.* 27 The first must serue you in your first singing till you come to this sign :||: where you must begin again and sing by the retort in half time.

2. a. A sharp or incisive reply, esp. one by which the first speaker's statement or argument is in some way turned against himself, or is met by some counter-charge. Also *fig.*

App. not in very common use before the 19th c.

1600 SHAKS. *A. Y. L.* v. iv. 76 He sent me word, if I said his beard was not cut well, hee was in the minde it was: this is call'd the retort courteous. **1734** tr. *Rollin's Anc. Hist.* (1827) VIII. XIX. 242 The mockers were mocked by that retort. **1777** SHERIDAN *Trip Scarb.* III. ii, Well then, let Loveless look to his wife, 'twill be but the retort courteous on both sides. **1797** MRS. RADCLIFFE *Italian* xvi, The priest interrupted Vivaldi's retort. **1824** BYRON *Def. Transf.* I. ii, That's a fair retort, For I provoked it. **1852** ROGERS *Ecl. Faith* (1853) 269 If you give up that principle, you lay yourself open at once to the retort that your position is insecure. **1870** BURTON *Hist. Scot.* VI. lxx. 496 It was suggested, as a sort of retort against the new demand, that it would be more suitable for the king himself to sign the Covenant.

b. ***retort courteous***: in allusion to quot. 1600 in sense 2 a. Also ***retort discourteous.***

1908 [see OAR *sb.* 5 a]. **1928** A. HUXLEY *Point Counter Point* iv. 64 The question..fairly invited the retort discourteous. **1977** H. L. MCGUFFIE in Bond & McLeod *Newslett. to Newspapers* III. 197 The quarrel in print..ranged all the way from the Retort Courteous to the Lie Direct.

3. The act or practice of replying in a sharp or incisive manner (see prec.). Also *transf.*

1791 BOSWELL *Johnson* an. 1783, Johnson's dexterity in retort..was very remarkable. **1808** *Med. Jrnl.* XIX. 518 Dr. Kentish..has laid himself very open to animadversion and retort from me. **1845** STOCQUELER *Handbk. Brit. India* (1854) 99 It is cowardly to raise a hand to one who is incapable of physical retort. **1848** DICKENS *Dombey* xxiii, Mrs. MacStinger in retort, looked at her all over.

b. Const. *of* something.

1820 W. IRVING *Sketch Bk.* I. 111 Nothing is so easy and inviting as the retort of abuse and sarcasm. **1847** R. W. HAMILTON *Rewards & Punishm.* viii. (1853) 357 The retort of an objection is no positive argument. **1877** JACOX *Script. Prov.* xi. 115 Experiencing a retort of the ill-usage they had formerly inflicted.

†**4.** = RETORTION 1. *Obs. rare*⁻¹.

1755 J. CLUBBE *Misc. Tracts* (1770) 100, I found two *pateræ* not cemented, but skrewed together... Having opened it by retort of the skrew, I discovered an incrustated surface.

retort (rɪˈtɔːt), *sb.*² [a. F. *retorte* (= It., Sp., Pg. *retorta*), ad. med.L. *retorta*, fem. of L. *retortus*, pa. pple. of *retorquēre*: see RETORT *v.*¹]

1. A vessel generally made of glass, but occasionally of metal or earthenware, and provided with a long neck, bent downwards, in which liquids, etc., subjected to distillation are heated.

[**1558** WARDE tr. *Alexis' Secr.* (1568) 9 b, A crooke necked violle..which the french cal Retorte. *a* **1608** DEE *Relat. Spir.* II. (1659) 12 The Still where he had the Spirit of Wine distilling over out of a Retorto.]

1605 TIMME *Quersit.* I. v. 21 Those saltes, being put into a retort,..stilleth forth a volatile salt. **1651** FRENCH *Distill.* i. 35 Let it be put into a Retort, and distilled in sand. **1712** tr. *Pomet's Hist. Drugs* I. 164 The black Oil of Tartar by the Retort is admirable for the Cure of Scabs. **1796** ELIZA HAMILTON *Lett. Hindoo Rajah* (1811) II. 107 My friend had forgotten the necessary management of a retort, which, for want of his attention, burst in pieces. **1812** SIR H. DAVY *Chem. Philos.* 227 The bottom of the retort is then gently heated by means of a lamp, and the extremity of its neck introduced under an inverted cylinder filled with water. **1871** B. STEWART *Heat* (ed. 2) §140 The vapour is condensed as fast as it is formed, and trickles back into the retort.

fig. **1874** SAYCE *Compar. Philol.* vi. 217 We must throw our words into the retort of the comparative method.

2. A vessel in which mercury is separated from amalgam or impurity by volatilization.

Several forms are now employed for this purpose. In early use perh. not distinct from sense 1.

1683 PETTUS *Fleta Min.* I. 314 Put it [quicksilver ore] into a Retort or other.. Instrument. **1727–38** CHAMBERS *Cycl.* s.v. *Mercury*, Compounded of crude mercury driven over from sea-salt in a retort. **1839** URE *Dict. Arts* 805 Large retorts, styled cucurbits, of cast iron, in which the ore of mercury is subjected to distillation. **1873** SPON *Workshop Rec.* Ser. I. 222/1 The amalgams.. are then distilled in cast-iron retorts of a peculiar shape. **1879** *Cassell's Techn. Educ.* IV. 191/1 The soft cake of amalgam is transferred to a retort, to have the mercury distilled out of it.

3. A clay or iron receptacle, forming a cylinder or segment of one, in which coal is heated for the production of gas.

1808 *Phil. Trans.* XCVIII. 127 About one-third of the above quantity.. is required for fuel to heat the retorts. **1839** URE *Dict. Arts* 548 As soon as gas begins to be disengaged from the ignited retort. **1879** *Cassell's Techn. Educ.* II. 95/2 The first portion of the process.. is to submit coal to the action of heat in an air-tight vessel, commonly called a 'retort'.

4. A furnace in which iron is heated with carbon, in order to produce steel.

1868 JOYNSON *Metals* 76 By introducing bars of wrought-iron along with carbon into retorts. **1884** W. H. GREENWOOD *Steel & Iron* 227 For the purpose of cooling the reduced metal, the retorts were made slightly larger at the lower than at the upper end.

5. *attrib.*, as ***retort bench, cap, -end, -flask, furnace, glass, -house, -neck***, etc.; **retort carbon**, carbon which remains as a residue in the retort when the gas has been extracted from coal.

1688 HOLME *Armoury* III. xi. 424/1 He beareth Sable, a Stillers Retort, or a Retort Glass, Argent. **1827** FARADAY *Chem. Manip.* xv. 359 Retort caps are cylinders of thin brass plate. **1839** *Mechanic's Mag.* XXXI. 7/2 The pipes leading from the retort-house to the reservoirs. **1841** *Civil Eng. & Arch. Jrnl.* IV. 100/2 Each retort-house contains one stack and four sections of retort benches. **1863** TYNDALL *Heat* viii. §297 (1870) 229 Attach to each end.. a piece of retort carbon. **1879** *Encycl. Brit.* X. 91/2 Retort furnaces are commonly fired or heated with a portion of the coke which forms one of the bye-products of the gas manufacture. **1881** TYNDALL *Ess. on Floating Matter of Air* 143 Experiments with pipette-bulbs and retort-flasks. **1958** A. D. MERRIMAN *Dict. Metallurgy* 287/1 *Retort furnace*, a metallurgical furnace consisting of a fire-chamber, and frequently regenerative chambers, in which the retorts are placed for containing the materials for treatment. *Ibid.*, Cast-iron retorts are sometimes used in the retort furnace for treatment of mercury ores.

retort (rɪˈtɔːt), *v.*[1] [f. L. *retort-*, ppl. stem of *retorquēre*, f. *re-* RE- + *torquēre* to twist, turn: cf. *contort, distort*, etc.]

I. 1. a. *trans.* To make return of (something done to one, *esp.* an injury); to repay or pay back; to requite by retaliation.

c **1557** ABP. PARKER *Ps.* xxviii. 65 As is theyr deede so let them speede; retort their craftes. **1598–9** B. JONSON *Case Altered* I. ii, We shall retort these kind favours with all alacrity of spirit. *c* **1620** Z. BOYD *Zion's Flowers* (1855) 154, I will retort.. that.. wrong. **1645** MILTON *Tetrach.* Wks. 1851 IV. 206 So Christ to retort these arrogant inquisitors their own, tooke the course to lay their hautinesse under a severity which they deserv'd. **1726** POPE *Odyss.* XXI. 142 How shall this arm, unequal to the bow, Retort an insult, or repel a foe? **1777** SHERIDAN *Sch. Scand.* V. ii, Let them laugh, and retort their malice only by showing them you are happy in spite of it. **1817** JAS. MILL *Brit. India* II. v. iii. 395 It was now his time to retort the humiliation. **1856** MERIVALE *Rom. Emp.* xlvi. (1865) V. 412 They never dared to retort in concert the invasions under which they had suffered.

b. To cast back, to cause to return, *upon* or *against* the offending party.

c **1559** ABP. PARKER in Burnet *Hist. Ref.* II. Rec. II. III. 359 And then both the Devil and Man.. shall have their Malices retorted upon themselves again. *a* **1618** SYLVESTER *Panaretus* 873 Heav'ns Right-hand.. retorting all upon your Foes.. Sends Terrors. **1718** *Free-thinker* No. 90 ¶5 They.. retort upon the Aggressour the Injury, which they parry from themselves. **1760** C. JOHNSTON *Chrysal* (1822) II. 152 Not only escape the ruin meditated against him, but also retort it on the machinators. **1781** COWPER *Truth* 502 Hear, then, how mercy, slighted and defied, Retorts th' affront against the crown of pride. **1810** LAMB *Good Clerk*, Retorting upon the grave citizens of London their own arts. **1860** PUSEY *Min. Proph.* 373 The aggression against God is retorted upon the aggressor.

†**c.** To bring as a return *to* one. *Obs. rare*$^{-1}$.

1632 LITHGOW *Trav.* VIII. 349 Wars.. the issue whereof, but retorted to the Duke a redoubling disaduantage.

†**d.** To do (something) in retaliation. *Obs.*$^{-1}$

1637 R. HUMFREY tr. *St. Ambrose* I. 12 Yet did hee not retort ought savouring of revenge.

e. *intr.* To reply by retaliation. *rare*$^{-1}$.

1883 C. READE *Tit for Tat* vi, He threatened violence. They prepared to retort to it.

2. To cast or hurl back (a charge, accusation, epithet, etc.). Freq. const. *on*.

1596 HARINGTON *Metam. Ajax* (1814) 128, I shall straight retort all the blame.. upon yourself. **1599** SHAKS. *Hen. V*, II. i. 54, I do retort the solus in thy bowels. **1650** FULLER *Pisgah* IV. v. 86 The Egyptian Authors slanderously retorted these loathsome diseases on the Israelites. **1766** GOLDSM. *Vic. W.* ii, He asserted that I was heterodox; I retorted the charge. **1781** COWPER *Conversat.* 767 Retort the charge, and let the world be told She boasts a confidence she does not hold. **1804** *Med. Jrnl.* XII. 189 The accusation of sinister motives is easily made, and as easily retorted. **1816** J. WILSON *City of Plague* II. v. 81 Fool! villian! liar! thus do I retort Thy insupportable words. **1874** GREEN *Short Hist.* viii. §6. 522 He was still resolute to retort the charge of treason on his foes.

absol. **1737** *Gentl. Mag.* 553/1 May not we, with equal Justice, retort upon them, when, laying aside their natural Characters, they assume those which are appropriated to us?

3. a. To reply in kind to (a jest, sarcasm, etc.); to answer with the like. Also const. *on*.

1602 MARSTON *Antonio's Rev.* I. iii, I scorne to retort the obtuse jeast of a foole. **1665** GLANVILL *Def. Van. Dogm.* p. xiv, Nor shall I retort with animosity those less obliging passages. **1734** tr. *Rollin's Rom. Hist.* (1827) III. 85 Hipponax retorted their pleasantry with such keen strokes of satire that they hanged themselves. **1754** CHATHAM *Lett. Nephew* iv. 24 Retort their raillery with raillery, always tempered with good breeding. **1814** D'ISRAELI *Quarrels Auth.* (1867) 306 With what good-humour he retorts a piece of sly malice of Pope's. **1848** H. ROGERS *Ess.* (1874) I. vi. 311 If it were worth while to retort the sarcasm on the multitude, it were easy to do so. **1875** JOWETT *Plato* (ed. 2) II. 408, I retort your reproach of me.

b. To say or utter by way of (sharp or aggressive) reply; †to return (an answer of this kind); †to allege in return.

1625 BURGES *Pers. Tithes* 13 If we vrge them with conscience, they retort a captious answere. **1625–8** tr. *Camden's Hist. Eliz.* III. (1688) 358 She owneth her allowing a Pension to Morgan, and retorteth Pensions granted to the Scots. **1649** MILTON *Eikon.* xii. 119 He thinks to evade that by retorting, that some in England fight against him. **1735–6** SHERIDAN *Let. to Swift* 23 Feb., I cannot help retorting, that I never knew any person so unadviseable as you are. **1838** DICKENS *Nich. Nick.* xiii, 'What do you mean by that?' retorted Squeers in great perturbation. **1866** G. MACDONALD *Ann. Q. Neighb.* i. (1878) 14, I will retort that it is just as true of the sun as of man. **1891** H. HERMAN *His Angel* 211 'You need have no fear of that, my dear,' retorted her husband.

c. *intr.* To make a retort or retorts.

1811 JANE AUSTEN *Sense & Sens.* III. i. 26 Marianne was going to retort, but she.. forbore. **1838** PRESCOTT *Ferd. & Is.* II. i. II. 380 Charles, who could not dissemble his indignation during this discourse, retorted with great acrimony when it was concluded on the conduct of Ferdinand. **1863** GEO. ELIOT *Romola* I. xvi, He must smile and retort, and look perfectly at his ease.

4. To meet or answer (an argument, etc.) by a similar argument to the contrary; to turn or direct (his own statement) *against* an opponent.

1610 HEALEY *St. Aug. Citie of God* 32 This kinde of Argument either by overthrowing one of the parts, or by retorting it, called.. a conversion. **1660** BOYLE *New Exp. Phys. Mech.* xxxiii. 255 Our Experiments may.. enable us to retort their Arguments against themselves. *a* **1713** ELLWOOD *Autobiog.* (1714) 349 So apt is the Comparison in most Respects.. that my Adversary in vain Labours to Retort it. **1785** REID *Intell. Powers* II. vii. 267 They are capable of being retorted against his own system. **1788** —— *Aristotle's Logic* iv. §7. 102 A remarkable property of the Dilemma is that it may sometimes be happily retorted. **1852** SIR W. HAMILTON *Discuss.* 518 Not a single voice was raised in either House.. to retort the argument. **1894** *Westm. Gaz.* 30 March 1/2 The answer they make to us may very easily be retorted.

II. †**5. a.** To throw or hurl back (a weapon); to turn back (a blow) upon the striker. *Obs.*

1592 KYD *Sp. Trag.* II. iv. 41 Thus I retort the dart thou threwst at me. **1621** G. SANDYS *Ovid's Met.* XII. 104 The Heroe caught it, and retorts againe The singing steele. **1667** *Decay Chr. Piety* iii. ¶1 Satan has not only evaded, but even retorted those blows which were aim'd at him. **1771** WESLEY *Wks.* (1872) VI. 33 To observe how we may retort these fiery darts of the Wicked One.

†**b.** Const. *upon* the agent. *Obs.*

1626 JACKSON *Humiliation Son of God* x. 94 The Sonne of God.. with this scripture.. retorts Satan's attempted blow upon himselfe. **1675** TRAHERNE *Chr. Ethics* 390 If wild-fire be thrown, I will.. not, by throwing it back, give my enemy the advantage of retorting it upon me. **1712** BUDGELL *Spect.* No. 389 ¶22, I think the best way of dealing with them, is to retort their own Weapons upon them.

†**6. a.** To reflect (heat or light); to return or re-echo (a sound); to drive back, etc. *Obs.*

1606 SHAKS. *Tr. & Cr.* III. iii. 101 As when his vertues shining vpon others, Heate them, and they retort that heate againe To the first giuer. **1611** COTGR., *Heliotrope*,.. a precious stone which, as a burning glasse, receiueth, and retorteth the Sunne-beames. **1655** STANLEY *Hist. Philos.* (1701) 607/2 Crying and howling whil'st the Locrian Stones, And high Eubœan Hills, retort his Groans. **1662** J. CHANDLER *Van Helmont's Oriat.* 63 Which vapour.. is nothing but water made thin,.. and therefore being retorted or struck back by an Alembick, it returns into its antient weight of water.

†**b.** To transmit by reflection. *Obs. rare.*

1649 SIR R. TEMPEST *Solitariness* 4 When the body.. is distempered, it retorts and shoots backward its indispositions to the minde. **1713** DERHAM *Phys.-Theol.* VI. vi. 368 When any thing affects, or alters the Heart, those Impressions are.. retorted to the Brain.

†**7. a.** To reject or refuse (an appeal). *Obs.*$^{-1}$

1603 SHAKS. *Meas. for M.* V. i. 303 The Duke's vniust, Thus to retort your manifest Appeale.

†**b.** To cast or throw (one) out. *Obs. rare*$^{-1}$.

1641 BROME *Joviall Crew* I. Wks. 1873 III. 361 Dear Sir, retort me naked to the world, Rather then lay those burdens on me.

†**8.** To turn back or backwards; to bend or twist back. *Obs.*

1621 G. SANDYS *Ovid's Met.* III. (1632) 68 Rabid with anguish, he retorts his looke Vpon the wound. **1648** J. BEAUMONT *Psyche* XVI. ccxviii, Retort thine eyes into thy Self, my Dear. **1688** HOLME *Armoury* II. xix. 470/1 Two Serpents bowed at the heads to the joyning in the middle, from thence to the ends of the Tails Retorted. **1718** PRIOR *Solomon* III. 516 For Dread and Pain And Grief will find their Shafts elanc'd in vain, And their Points broke, retorted from the Head.

†**9.** To give in return. *Obs. rare*$^{-1}$.

1634 SIR T. HERBERT *Trav.* (1638) 260 Gifts also and reciprocall presents are retorted up and down.

†**10.** To multiply again. *Obs. rare*$^{-1}$.

1655 STANLEY *Hist. Philos.* (1701) 427/1 Two multiplied in itself produceth four; retorted into itself (by saying twice two twice) makes the first Cube.

†**11.** *intr.* To spring or fly back; to rebound, recoil; to twist. *Obs.*

1631 J. TAYLOR *Turn Fortune's Wheel* Pref., Doth time retort or fortune play the Jade, Or doth the course of fate run retrograde. **1673** PENN *Spir. Alex. the Coppersmith Rebuked* 7 It all retorts from our Impenetrable Armour upon himself. **1710** CONGREVE *An Impossible Thing*, This line.. Render.. so direct, that in no sort It ever may in rings retort.

retort (rɪˈtɔːt), *v.*[2] [f. RETORT *sb.*[2]] *trans.* To heat in a retort in order to separate or purify substances.

1850 N. KINGSLEY *Diary* 26 May (1914) 123 A warm [day;] the boys retorted the last weeks work. **1879** *Encycl. Brit.* X. 748/2 In California the amalgam is retorted in cast-iron pans. **1890** *Pall Mall G.* 21 May 2/1 The quicksilver is at intervals scraped off the copper plates and retorted. **1924** *Jrnl. Inst. Petroleum Technol.* X. 537 That refinery is supplied.. with the crude oil and ammoniacal liquor derived from the shale retorted there. **1948** *Rep. Progr. Appl. Chem.* XXXIII. 40 The raw shale is retorted at four crude oil works and the crude products are refined at Pumpherston. **1964** J. E. RANSOM *Range Guide to Mines & Minerals* iv. 58 There is a 200-ounce limit on the possession of retort sponge gold obtained by retorting the gold-mercury amalgam.

†**reˈtort**, *pa. pple. Obs.*$^{-1}$ [ad. L. *retort-us*, pa. pple. of *retorquēre*: see prec.] Turned back.

1432–50 tr. *Higden* (Rolls) I. 55 Then the see Elesponte retorte with grete passage turnethe to the northe.

reˈtortable, *a.* [f. RETORT *v.*[1] + -ABLE.] Capable or admitting of retortion.

1603 FLORIO *Montaigne* III. viii. (1632) 523 Our arguments and matter controversed, are ordinarily retortable unto us. **1611** COTGR., *Retorquable*, retortable.

retorted (rɪˈtɔːtɪd), *ppl. a.*[1] [f. RETORT *v.*[1]]

†**1.** *Mus.* Reversed. (See quot.) *Obs. rare.*

1597 MORLEY *Introd. Mus.* 27 *Phi.* What do you terme a retorted Moode? *Ma.* It is a Moode of imperfect time set backward, signifying that the Notes before which it is set must be sung as fast againe as they were before.

2. Recurved; twisted or bent backwards.

1599 LINCHE *Anc. Fiction* I. iv, It is at one end somewhat crooked and retorted. **1605** TIMME *Quersit.* III. 166 By very long cunduites and pipes of brasse retorted. **1648** HERRICK *Hesper.*, *To live merrily*, Th' Arabian Dew besmears My uncontrolled brow, And my retorted haires. **1661** TATHAM *Lond. Triumphs* in Heath *Groc. Co.* (1869) 478 Two Trytons playing on retorted Pipes. **1808** *Med. Jrnl.* XIX. 568 By drawing the integuments over the wound till the retorted edges are brought in contact. **1859** RUSKIN *Perspective* xiv. 123 If the curve of profile A B is complex or retorted.

†**3.** ? Refuted, rejected. *Obs. rare*$^{-1}$.

1632 LITHGOW *Trav.* x. 484 He rashly aduentured the credite of Leager honour in a single Combat against me a retorted Plaintiue.

4. Thrown or cast back; returned. Also *fig.*

1621 G. SANDYS *Ovid's Met.* v. 42 Vp fierce Perseus starts, And his retorted Speare at Phineus darts. **1667** MILTON *P. L.* v. 903 With retorted scorn his back he turn'd. **1745** J. MASON *Self-Knowledge* I. ix. (1853) 68 Such retorted Scorn is more becoming the Character of a Stoic than a Christian. **1856** KANE *Arct. Expl.* II. xii. 129 Now comes the accused, with.. countercharge and retorted abuse.

†**b.** Forced or driven back. *Obs. rare*$^{-1}$.

1658 tr. *Porta's Nat. Magic* VI. ii. 179 Take river-pebbles and put them into a fornace, in that place where the retorted flame is most intense.

5. Reverted; turned in a backward direction.

1720 POPE *Iliad* XVII. 120 He.. threatens as he flies, With heart indignant and retorted eyes. *a* **1763** SHENSTONE *Elegies* x. 36 And with retorted eye forsakes the dome. **1807** J. BARLOW *Columb.* v. 15 And now impatient, with retorted eye, Perceives his station in another sky. *a* **1843** SOUTHEY (Ogilvie), Sometimes, with retorted head, [they] pruned themselves as they floated.

retorted (rɪˈtɔːtɪd), *ppl. a.*[2] [f. RETORT *v.*[2]] Refined or purified in a retort.

1890 'R. BOLDREWOOD' *Miner's Right* xliii, She tried to lift again.. the mass of retorted gold which had come in from the quartz reef. **1897** *Daily News* 28 July 4/7, 680 tons of ore, which yielded 376 ounces of retorted gold.

reˈtorter[1]. *rare.* [f. RETORT *v.*[1]] One who retorts.

1611 COTGR., *Retordeur*, a twister, twiner; a wrester, a retorter. **1660** GAUDEN *God's Gt. Demonstr.* 10 No men are more.. imperious retorters upon God and man, than those who are most defective in their duties to both.

reˈtorter[2]. [f. RETORT *v.*[2]] One employed in retorting metals.

1877 RAYMOND *Statist. Mines & Mining* 415, 2 amalgamators, 2 retorters and boiler-men.

†**reˈtortible**, *a. Obs. rare*$^{-1}$. = RETORTABLE.

1609 [BP. W. BARLOW] *Answ. Nameless Cath.* 283 His arguments are.. easely retortible against him.

reˈtorting, *vbl. sb.*[1] [f. RETORT *v.*[1]] The action of bending or throwing back, etc.

1589 [see RESIGN *v.*[1] 2]. **1622** MALYNES *Anc. Law-Merch.* 422 There are three waies to dissolve an argument, Deniall, Retorting and Distinction. **1652** J. WRIGHT tr. *Camus' Nat. Paradox* VI. 131 Hearing.. by the retorting of the Eccho's the confused noyse of the Hunts-men,.. they resolved to direct their steps that way. **1710** ADDISON *Tatler* No. 239 ¶13 As for those little Retortings of my own Expressions,.. they are the common Cavils of every Witling.

re'torting, *vbl. sb.*[2] [f. RETORT *sb.*[2] or *v.*[2]] The action of treating in a retort.

1858 *Times* 1 Dec. 9/3 All..make six ounces of 'amalgam' a man per day, which they value after retorting as worth three ounces of gold. **1883** *Science* I. 102 It was surmised that the change was due to imperfect retorting.

re'torting, *ppl. a.* [f. RETORT *v.*[1]] That retorts, in senses of the verb.

1588 GREENE *Perimedes* Wks. (Grosart) VII. 80 Wan is her lookes, her cheekes of Azure hue, Hir haires as Gorgons foule retorting Snakes. **1781** CRABBE *Library* 526 The wordy variance of domestic life; The tyrant husband, the retorting wife. **1896** *Daily News* 27 Mar. 3/1 His answer was also a retorting question.

retortion (rɪˈtɔːʃən). [ad. med.L. *retortiōn-em*, noun of action f. L. *retorquēre*: see RETORT *v.*[1] and cf. RETORSION.]

1. The action or fact of bending or turning backwards; an instance of this. Also *fig.*

1591 SYLVESTER *Du Bartas* I. iii. 100 Our Sea: whose divers-branch'd retortions Divide the World in three unequall portions. **1654** tr. *Scudery's Curia Pol.* 35 Since the beginning of all ages, the Rivers have glyded quietly without retortion towards their Fountaines. **1663** J. SPENCER *Prodigies* (1665) 253 They will appear (like the Staff of Egypt) either to break under, or, by an easie retortion, to pierce and wound it self. **1813** FORSYTH *Excursion Italy* 234 The age, the expression, the retortion of head [etc.]. **1836–7** SIR W. HAMILTON *Metaph.* xlv. (1859) II. 497 Some occupation which, by concentrating our attention on external objects, shall divert it from a retortion on ourselves.

†**b.** The process of treating in a retort. *Obs.*[−1]

1657 TOMLINSON *Renou's Disp.* 92 It is also called a distillation by retortion.

†**2. a.** A reply of the nature of a retort. *Obs.*

1609 [BP. W. BARLOW] *Answ. Nameless Cath.* 304 Neuer could this Censurer haue made a more vntimely and vnfitting retortion then at this instant. **1646** R. BAILLIE *Anabaptism* (1647) 159 Their retortion here upon us is very silly, that we do put Christian infants in as evill a condition as they. **1682** G. VERNON *Life Heylin* 235 The Retortion that Mr. Selden made to one in the House of Commons.

†**b.** An answer made to an argument by converting it against the person using it. *Obs.*

1610 HEALEY *St. Aug. Citie of God* (1620) 28 The old Rhetoritians vsed to dissolue this kinde of argument..by retorting it, called in Greeke ἀντιστροφή, a conuersion or retortion. **1642** FULLER *Holy & Prof. St.* II. vii. 73 There are Syllogismes, long swords; Enthymems, short daggers;.. Retortions, which are targets with a pike in the midst of them, both to defend and oppose. **1741** WARBURTON *Div. Legat.* (1765) II. 51, I..cannot profit by it, the argument lying exposed to so terrible a retortion.

†**c.** The method or device of meeting an argument, etc., by retorting it. *Obs.*

1622 MALYNES *Anc. Law-Merch.* 422 Deniall, is too hostile,..Retortion, is more wittie than profitable. **1654** Z. COKE *Logick* 181 Answer by Retortion, is when we shew that the mean or proof brought by the adversary maketh for us. **1679** C. NESSE *Antid. agst. Popery* 132 'Twas justly charged by way of retortion upon them. **1732** E. ERSKINE *Serm.* Wks. 1871 II. 49, I might answer by way of retortion.

†**d.** Conversion *of* an argument, charge, etc., against another, or into an opposite sense. *Obs.*

1610 BP. HALL *Apol. Brownists* 116 For your retortion of my Zoar and Sodome: I can giue you leaue to be wittie. **1655** FULLER *Ch. Hist.* x. xvii. §42 Mr. George Herbert..made a most ingenious retortion of this Hexastick.

3. Return for something done; retaliation. Now *spec.* in international law (see quot. 1885).

1654 tr. *Scudery's Curia Pol.* 126 He violated all rights..; And what I have done, was on equall retortion to his merit. **1762** *Gentl. Mag.* 322 In natural defence, and necessary retortion, they be treated as aggressors. *a***1852** WEBSTER *Gibbons & Ogden* Wks. 1858 VI. 5 (Funk), This act of New Jersey is called an act of retortion against the illegal and oppressive legislation of New York. **1885** P. COBBETT *Cases Internat. Law* 100 Retortion consists in treating the subjects of another State in the same way as that State has treated one's own subjects. *Ibid.*, It is commonly laid down that retortion only extends to imperfect rights or mere rights of comity.

retortive (rɪˈtɔːtɪv), *a. rare.* [f. L. *retort-* (see RETORT *v.*[1]) + -IVE.]

†**1.** Of the nature of squeezing. *Obs. rare*[−1].

1660 tr. *Paracelsus' Archidoxis* I. iv. 55 Separate this (by a Retortive process or pressing) from the feces.

2. Turned backwards. (Cf. RETORTED *ppl. a.* 5.)

1807 J. BARLOW *Columb.* v. 466 From all his guileful plots the veil they drew, With eye retortive looked creation thro.

3. Of the nature of a retort; characterized by retorts.

1826 G. S. FABER *Diffic. Romanism* (1853) 238 The apt answer of Blandina, though thrown into the form of a retortive question, is implicatively a palpable denial. **1949** G. B. SHAW in *Strand Mag.* July 20/2 A trumpery farce may win an uproarious success by its retortive back-chat.

†**re'tortment.** *Obs. rare*[−1]. [f. RETORT *v.*[1] + -MENT.] Retortion.

1649 LILBURNE *Liberties People Eng.* (ed. 2) 39 Which procured them from me a sharp retortment of their own basenesse.

re'toss (riː-), *v.* [RE- 5 a.] *trans.* To toss back or again (esp. in phr. ***tossed and retossed***).

1549 CHALONER *Erasm. on Folly* K iv b, What Invectives than are tossed and retossed betwixe theim. **1575** GASCOIGNE *Wks.* (1587) 203 She had..turned over and retossed every carde in this sequence. **1611** FLORIO, *Riuoltolato*, tossed, retossed. **1700** DRYDEN *Cymon & Iph.* 370 The wand'ring Vessel drove before the Wind: Toss'd and retoss'd, aloft, and then alow. **1745** WARTON *Ecloges* v, All around the roar of war was up, From rock to rock retost, from wood to wood.

retouch (riːˈtʌtʃ), *sb.* [Prob. ad. F. *retouche* (1507): cf. next.]

1. A second or further touch given to some part of a picture, composition, etc., with a view to improving it.

1703 STEELE *Tender Husb.* IV. i, Then so many Touches and Retouches, when the Face is finish'd. **1793** ANNA SEWARD *Lett.* (1811) III. 237 Dr. Vyse received it with these retouches, praised the epitaph, and thanked me. **1843** *Civil Eng. & Arch. Jrnl.* VI. 391/1 Some parts, which it may reasonably be inferred are retouches,..are quite flat and dim. **1878** tr. *Villari's Machiavelli* (1898) I. 157 Those retouches opened the way to new and original creation.

2. *Archæol.* Secondary trimming or shaping applied to a stone implement at some period after initial manufacture; an instance of this.

[**1921** M. C. BURKITT *Prehist.* iv. 65 Having blocked out the implement in the rough it had then to be finished with what is known as secondary working or trimming (French, *retouche*).] **1926** D. A. E. GARROD *Upper Palæolithic Age in Britain* i. 38 The tang is well worked, with a steep retouch along both sides and enough of the upper part is left to give an idea of the form. **1932** *Jrnl. R. Anthrop. Inst.* LXII. 261 A fair proportion of lunates and other microliths showed a peculiar retouch which was found on three or four specimens, only at Shukba. **1957** V. G. CHILDE *Dawn European Civilization* (ed. 6) xi. 211 The technique of bifacial retouch on flint flakes and blades is more likely to have reached the north from the south-east than from the south-west. **1964** H. HODGES *Artifacts* vii. 103 The initial roughing out of a stone tool is usually referred to as *primary flaking*, while any later working..is called *secondary flaking* or *retouch*. **1977** *Antiquaries Jrnl.* LVII. 212 *Flint scraper*:.. limited fine steep marginal retouch.

retouch (riːˈtʌtʃ), *v.* [Prob. ad. F. *retoucher* (13th c., = Sp. and Pg. *retocar*, It. *ritoccare*): see RE- and TOUCH *v.*]

1. *trans.* To touch again with a view to improving; to amend or improve by fresh touches; to touch up.

1685 BURNET *Let.* in *Trav.* (1687) I. 97 All [the monastery] was retouched by the famous Guido Reni, yet it is now again much decayed. **1686** *Ibid.* III. 8, I have retoucht the Letter that I writ to you last year. **1711** ADDISON *Spect.* No. 83 ¶10 One..who was very busie in retouching the finest Pieces, tho' he produced no Originals of his own. **1751** JOHNSON *Rambler* No. 176 ¶7 When the book has once been dismissed into the world, and can be no more retouched. **1797** HOLCROFT tr. *Stolberg's Trav.* II. xlvi, He has retouched a copy, that was painted by one of his scholars. **1847** C. BRONTË *J. Eyre* xiv, I was myself in my usual Quaker trim, where there was nothing to retouch. **1892** *Photogr. Ann.* II. 201 The negative to be retouched is prepared [etc.].

b. *absol.* To give retouches.

1735 POPE *Prol. Sat.* 64 Lintot..will think your price too much: Not, Sir, if you revise it, and retouch. **1757** GRAY *Let. to Wharton* 7 Oct., The difficult part is now got over, and nothing now remains but to polish, and retouch a little. **1843** *Civil Eng. & Arch. Jrnl.* VI. 391/1 It was the practice to retouch when the fresco was dry.

2. a. To touch upon, to speak of, to introduce or bring in, again. *rare.*

1701 NORRIS *Ideal World* I. 397 It may not be unexpedient more expressly to retouch what has been so often insinuated. **1752** AVISON *Mus. Express.* 133 The accidental Subjects are ..generally repeated, or at least so retouched in the Progress of the Fugue as to render them easily known.

b. To magnetize afresh. *rare.*

1730 *Phil. Trans.* XXXVI. 325, I took off the Armour and bound it to that which was newly touched, and there-with retouched that which I had disarmed.

Hence **re'touched** *ppl. a.*

1843 *Civil Eng. & Arch. Jrnl.* VI. 391/1 The retouched parts are invariably dim. **1892** *Photogr. Ann.* II. 202 There is no reason..why..the individual style of the worker should be more apparent than in a retouched negative.

re'toucher (riː-). [f. the verb + -ER[1].] One who retouches, *esp.* one whose occupation is to retouch photographs.

1878 *Scribner's Mag.* Mar. 687 The tools of the retoucher are..fine brushes and delicate instruments with which he removes the imperfections from each article or fills in what may be lacking. **1889** *Anthony's Photogr. Bull.* II. 372 The Retoucher who is compelled to approach within eight or nine inches of the negative, is damaging the sight. **1892** *Photogr. Ann.* II. 202 The method or style dear to the retoucher's heart.

re'touching (riː-), *vbl. sb.* [f. the verb + -ING[1].]

1. The action of the verb in various senses.

1730 *Phil. Trans.* XXXVI. 323, I tried it without retouching, and found it perfectly cured, the Polarity regular throughout. **1816** SINGER *Playing Cards* 79 After having printed thirty or forty thousand copies these blocks will again bear retouching. **1885** C. G. W. LOCK *Workshop Rec.* Ser. IV. 422/1 Retouching can be done more quickly and finer upon this coating than upon any other.

2. A case or instance of this.

1825 J. NICHOLSON *Operat. Mechanic* 465 He..gives to the whole the several touchings and retouchings requisite for finishing. **1842** *Civil Eng. & Arch. Jrnl.* V. 308/2 Such retouchings are useless in frescos painted in the open air. **1881** WESTCOTT & HORT *Grk. Test.* Introd. §19 Ancient authority was allowed to furnish not scattered retouchings but the whole body of the text.

3. *attrib.*, as ***retouching-desk, -easel, -medium, varnish***, etc.

1875 KNIGHT *Dict. Mech.* 1925/2 Retouching-table. **1884** *Ibid.*, Suppl. 754/1 Retouching Frame. **1889** E. J. WALL *Dict. Photogr.* 163 Some sort of retouching desk is needed. **1890** *Anthony's Photogr. Bull.* III. 180 An ordinary retouching easel. **1895** *Montgomery Ward Catal.* Spring-Summer 253/2 French Retouching Varnish, for oil or water color paintings. **1934** H. HILER *Notes Technique Painting* iii. 166 Retouching varnish is a quick-drying varnish used to bring out..parts of the picture which have gone flat or 'dead' in drying.

re'touchment. *rare*[−1]. Retouching.

1882 W. SHARP *Rossetti* iii. 155 The Death of Breuse sans Pitie—as it now appears..after its retouchment—is the crudest in colour and most grotesque in treatment.

retour (rɪˈtʊə(r)), *sb.* Also 6 retoure, retowre. [a. OF. *retour*, verbal sb. of *retourner* to RETURN. In later use partly readopted from mod.F.]

In the following passage *retours* is perhaps an alteration of *recours* RECOURSE (but cf. OF. *sans retour*): **13..** *K. Alis.* 602 (Bodl. MS.), He shal be poysond saunz retours [*Weber* saun return] Of his owen traytoures.

1. Return (to a place). Now only *arch. Sc.*

13.. *Seuyn Sag.* (W.) 436 Scho..dede here mene make retour. *c***1330** R. BRUNNE *Chron. Wace* (Rolls) 5482 Hamoun..spirde after þer enperour, Whider-ward he made his retour. **1426** LYDG. *De Guil. Pilgr.* 21643 But Youthe than, in hyr Retour, Was to myn helpe gret socour. *a***1533** LD. BERNERS *Huon* cxxx. 479 For fere lest yᵉ false emperoure cause you to dye or my retoure. **1567** TURBERV. *Ovid's Ep.* 112 Come hither, come and to my bosome make retowre. [**1703** FARQUHAR *Inconstant* Pref., To have the lady, upon her retour to Paris, boast of their splendid entertainment in England.] **1822** GALT *Provost* xxi, Mr. Secretary of State wrote me back by retour of post, thanking me for my zeal in the public service. **1897** BEATTY *Secretar* viii. 68 See ye keep that auld carle Geddes in gude ward till my retour.

2. *Sc. Law.* A return made to Chancery of the brieve of inquest relative to the service of an heir, with the verdict of the jury upon it; also, an extract or copy of the return.

1471 *Reg. Mag. Sig.* (1882) 215 The King's breif of inquest direcit to the Schiref of Forfare to give him possessioun eftir the tenour of this retour undirwirtin. **1546** *Reg. Privy Council Scot.* I. 37 With the seisingis, retouris, and all that followit thairupoun. **1579–80** *Ibid.* III. 258 Ane seising of Johnne, Lord Dernlie, of the landis of Evindaill, past upoun a retour. **1630** *Acts Sederunt* 31 July, All summonds of reduction of retouris..sall be formed in Latine be an advocat. **1678** *Ibid.* 15 Feb., To direct or give out any precepts to Shirriffs..for granting infeftment upon retours. **1754** ERSKINE *Princ. Sc. Law* (1809) 383 Retours upon general services are not properly transmissions of an estate. **1838** W. BELL *Dict. Law Scot.* 904 From the Chancery a certified copy is given out, which is called a retour. **1868** *Act 31 & 32 Vict.* c. 100 §101 A retour of the verdict and service of the jury before the Judge Ordinary.

b. A return of this kind, as specifying the yearly value of the lands in question.

In first quot. applied to a special return.

1580–1 *Reg. Privy Council Scot.* III. 346 That, be advise of the schireffis..of the schires within the wardenrie, thair be a stent and retour of all landis within the same. **1681** STAIR *Instit.* I. xiv. 304 Which sums would be Liquid, and known according to the new retour, and the Feu or Blensh-duty. **1838** W. BELL *Dict. Law Scot.* 861 Where there is no retour of lands,..the superior is entitled to the valued rent.

c. *attrib.* with *duty* or *mail*, = RETOURED *ppl. a.*

1681 STAIR *Instit.* I. xiv. 304 The relief which is *debitum fundi*, must only be the retour duty. **1693** *Ibid.* (ed. 2) IV. viii. 574 The Retour-mails, or Feu-duties of the same..did belong and pertain to the said Pursuer as Donatar. **1746–7** *Act 20 Geo. II*, c. 50 §2 Lands..no longer liable to the annual payment of the new extent or retour duty. **1838** W. BELL *Dict. Law Scot.* 861 Blanch-holdings..are liable in a retour duty of one per cent. of the valued rent.

3. *attrib.* with *ship, waggon*, denoting return from a destination. Also *ellipt.* a vehicle which returns to its original starting-place.

Only in echoes of continental usage.

1731 MEDLEY *Kolben's Cape G. Hope* II. 325 The Company has put her *Retour* Ships under the following Regulation, with Regard to the Cape. **1838** C. M. YOUNG in J. C. Young *Mem.* (1871) II. 33 A rope providentially lent us by the driver of a *retour* waggon. **1839** W. CHAMBERS *Tour Belgium* 48/1 A vehicle..with the words 'Retour à Köln', or whatever else may be the name of the place to which they are about to return, written on paper, and stuck upon their sides. These retours may be hired at something below the full charge, but even the highest price is not great.

4. A returned part.

1863 KINGLAKE *Crimea* (1877) IV. xiii. 346 The two salients being connected by a curtain..and having retours towards the gorge.

retour (rɪˈtʊə(r)), *v.* Chiefly *Sc.* [f. the sb.]

†**1.** *intr.* To return or revert *to* a person. *Obs.*

1456 SIR G. HAYE *Law Arms* (S.T.S.) 133 Quhen the terme cummys, the landis retouris agayne to the lord. **1535** STEWART *Cron. Scot.* II. 229 Efter his deid the croun suld than retour To schir Modred.

†**2.** To return *to* a place. *Obs. rare.*

1513 DOUGLAS *Æneis* XI. i. 101 Sa that thou suld nocht.. as victor with prosperite Onto thy faderis cite hame retour. *a***1533** LD. BERNERS *Huon* lxxxv. 269 [He] toke leue of the kynge & retouryd to Burdeux.

3. *trans. Sc. Law.* To return (a person) as heir. (Cf. RETOUR *sb.* 2.)

1515 in Sir W. Fraser *Sutherland Bk.* (1892) III. 59 Elizabeth Sutherland,..quhilk is full and haill retouryt of the said..landis. **1546** *Reg. Privy Council Scot.* I. 37 Albeit thai be nocht servit nor retourit the saidis airis. **1597** SKENE *De Verb. Sign.* s.v. *Breue de morte antecessoris*, His aire being serued and retoured to the superioritie of the samin lands. **1678** SIR G. MACKENZIE *Crim. Laws Scot.* I. xix. §xii. (1699) 102 Some think an Heir served and retoured, doth fall within this signification. **1752** McDouall *Inst. Law Scot.* III. v. II. 334 [Precepts are granted] to the sheriff.., commanding him to give infeftment to the person retoured. **1868** Maidment *Scot. Ball.* I. 29 James Spens was retoured as heir of his father Alexander. **1880** Earl of Crawford *Earldom of Mar* (1882) I. 259 An inquest of the leading gentlemen of the county..retoured Sir Robert [Erskine] as lawful heir to the Earldom of Mar.

b. To make a return to Chancery of or relative to (lands, etc.); to state the value of, in a retour.

1581–2 *Reg. Privy Council Scot.* III. 452 The said haill landis..nevir being stentit nor retourit. **1597** Skene *De Verb. Sign.* s.v. *Breue de morte antecessoris*, The mailles and dewties of the landes, sa lang as they ar retoured to haue bene in the handes of the King. **1693** Stair *Instit.* (ed. 2) III. v. 473 For ordinarly the Fee is Retoured, to be in the hands of the Superior by reason of Non-entry. *a* **1768** Erskine *Inst. Law Scot.* II. v. §36 In feu holdings, the yearly feu-duty contained in the Reddendo is retoured as the new extent. **1838** W. Bell *Dict. Law Scot.* 861 Feu-holdings are retoured to the feu-duties specified in the charter.

c. To return, send in (the brieve or verdict, etc.) to Chancery.

1597 Skene *De Verb. Sign.* s.v. *Breue de morte antecessoris*, This their answere.., and the brieue inclosed therein.., is sent back & retoured to the chancellarie. **1630** *Acts Sederunt* 31 July, Summonds of reductioun of retours that has bene retourit to the Chancellary. **1815** Scott *Guy M.* lviii, [We have] got our youngster's special service retoured into Chancery. We had him served heir before the macers. **1838** W. Bell *Dict. Law Scot.* 113 Their sentence is attested by the judge, and retoured by the clerk of the court, to Chancery. **1868** *Act 31 & 32 Vict.* c. 100 §101 The verdict and service of the jury shall be retoured to Chancery.

Hence **re'toured** *ppl. a.*; **re'touring** *vbl. sb.* Also **re'tourable** *a.*

1597 Skene *De Verb. Sign.* s.v. *Extent*, Quhilk..suld be generallie vsed in retouring of landes to the Kingis Chancellarie. *Ibid.*, The reliefe of landes is the retoured maill according to the new extent. *c* **1680** Dallas *Stiles* (1697) 487 Serving thereof and Retouring of the same to our Chancellary. **1681** Stair *Instit.* I. xiv. 304, I have never heard of one retoured Duty demanded for the Non-entry. *a* **1768** Erskine *Inst. Law Scot.* II. v. §37 Because the new extent or retoured duty is presumed to be the rent. *Ibid.* III. viii. §61 The brief of inquest has been from the beginning a retourable brief. **1838** W. Bell *Dict. Law Scot.* 861 The brieve of inquest..is retourable to Chancery whence it issued. *Ibid.*, Where there is no retour of lands, and no means of proving their retoured duties.

retourn(e, obs. forms of return *sb.* and *v.*

retrace (rɪ'treɪs), *v.*[1] [ad. F. *retracer*: see re- and trace *v.*]

1. *trans.* To trace back to an origin or source; to track through preceding stages. Also *refl.*

1697 Dryden *Æneid* VII. 520 Then if the Line of Turnus you retrace; He springs from Inachus of Argive Race. **1801** A. Hamilton *Wks.* (1886) VII. 219 Retracing our financial system to its commencement. **1805** Foster *Ess.* I. vii. 87, I am supposing a man to retrace himself through his past life. **1841** D'Israeli *Amen. Lit.* (1859) II. 16 The orthography of others..was as..eruditely whimsical..in the attempt to retrace the etymology, or to modify exotic words to a native origin.

2. a. To trace again with the eyes; to look over again with care or close attention.

1726 Pope *Odyss.* XXIV. 270 The chief divine Gaz'd o'er his sire, retracing ev'ry line. **1807** J. Barlow *Columb.* I. 245 Retrace the banks yon rushing waters lave. **1823** De Quincey *Lett. Educ.* i. (1860) 6 The same book left in your possession, and open at any hour, to be consulted, retraced, collated, and in the fullest sense studied.

b. To trace again in memory; to recall.

1748 Thomson *Cast. Indol.* I. xlviii, What transport, to retrace our boyish plays. **1784** Cowper *Task* IV. 183 While we retrace with mem'ry's pointing wand..The dangers we have 'scap'd. **1809** Malkin *Gil Blas* IX. vi, I should be puzzled to retrace a single sentiment. **1871** O. W. Holmes *Wind-Clouds & Star-Drifts* iv, Let me retrace the record of the years That made me what I am.

3. To go back upon (one's steps, way, etc.).

1794 Mrs. Radcliffe *Myst. Udolpho* vi, Michael was retracing his way with alacrity. **1814** Cary *Dante, Inf.* I. 33 With purpose to retrace my steps, I turn'd. **1844** H. H. Wilson *Brit. India* II. 293 The nature of the country precluding a forward movement, he retraced his march. **1872** Raymond *Statist. Mines & Mining* 260 One or two prospecting parties have also ventured into this country, but were compelled soon to retrace their steps.

b. In figurative context.

1839 Keightley *Hist. Eng.* II. 33 If Henry did not retrace his steps. **1849** Macaulay *Hist. Eng.* viii. II. 368 The ministers were appalled. Even Jeffreys would gladly have retraced his steps. **1875** Stubbs *Const. Hist.* II. xv. 296 When he had taken the step he did not retrace it.

Hence **re'tracing** *ppl. a.*

1822 T. Chalmers *Wks.* XVI. 186 The retracing movement..is imitable in other parishes. **1848** J. Ritchie in *Mem. G. J. Mackenzie* 52 He preaches to you this day..in your retracing memory.

re-'trace (riː-), *v.*[2] [re- 5 a.] *trans.* To trace, or go over, again with some marking instrument. Also *fig.*

1760–72 H. Brooke *Fool of Qual.* (1809) III. 32 That eternal law..was written and again retraced in the bosom of the first man. **1772–84** *Cook's Voy.* (1790) I. 249 An Indian ..drew the figure upon my skin; he then retraced it, by pricking the lines with needles. **1868** Browning *Ring & Bk.* III. 752 This letter traced in pencil-characters Guido as easily got re-traced in ink By his wife's pen.

re'track (riː-), *v.* [re- 5 a.] *trans.* To track or trace again.

1835 Browning *Paracelsus* v. 391 After-ages shall retrack thy beams. **1839–48** Bailey *Festus* xxiii. (1848) 298, I now retrack my course to earth. **1869** J. Conington *Horace, Sat.* (1874) 30 Should Fate this moment bid me to go back O'er all my length of years, my life retrack To its first hour.

†**re'tract**, *sb. Obs.* [f. the verb, or ad. med.L. *retractus*.]

1. Retractation (of errors, statements, etc.).

1553 Eden *Treat. Newe Ind.* (Arb.) 10 He wrytte also a Booke of retractes in whych he correcteth hys owne erroures. **1584** [R. Parsons] *Leicester's Commonw.* (1641) 29 For this cause hee hath his tearmes and pretences..of Contracts, Precontracts, Postcontracts, Protracts, and Retracts. **1603** Holland *Plutarch's Mor.* 1199 Metaphors ænigmaticall, and covert words,..were but shifts, retracts and evasions. *a* **1656** Hales *Gold. Rem.* (1677) 22 St. Austine, in a retract, concludes we must despair of no man..as long as he liveth.

2. Retreat on the part of an army or force.

1587 Holinshed *Chron.* III. 1431/1 Skinke was forced to give place.., and in his retract spoiled and burnt the countrie. **1601** R. Johnson *Kingd. & Commw.* (1603) 177 He is constrained euen in the course of victory to sound the retract, and surcease his proiects. **1614** Raleigh *Hist. World* IV. ii. §4. 179 These Græcians also that made the retract, aduised Darius to retire his Armie into..Mesopotamia.

3. That which is rejected; refuse. *rare*$^{-1}$.

1575 Fenton *Gold. Epist.* (1582) 169, I am..the reproch, retract, and shame of men, and the scorne of the people.

4. *Farriery.* = retrait *sb.*[1] 5.

1727–38 Chambers *Cycl.* s.v., When the farrier, in shoeing, perceives the horse to shrink at every blow on the nail; it is a sign of a retract.

retract (rɪ'trækt), *v.*[1] Also 6 *Sc.* retrak. [f. L. *retract-*, ppl. stem of *retrahĕre*, f. *re-* re- + *trahĕre* to draw.]

I. *trans.* **1. a.** To draw or pull (something) back.

1432–50 tr. *Higden* (Rolls) I. 59 The occean..auper.. flowethe furthe or retractethe the sees in to hit. **1597** A. M. *Guillemeau's Fr. Chirurg.* 40 b/1 They retracte and drawe backe the humors which trouble those partes. **1646** Sir T. Browne *Pseud. Ep.* 231 The heat of the Ayre attracting the humours outward, and the action of the Medicine retracting the same inward. **1678** Cudworth *Intell. Syst.* 869 He affirmed every Irrational Power or Soul, to be..Retracted and Resumed into the Deity. **1791** Cowper *Iliad* XX. 396 From the shield, himself Of brave Æneas the bright-pointed ash Retracting, placed it at Achilles' feet. **1830** Herschel *Study Nat. Phil.* 334 Let the piston be suddenly retracted and the air restored to its original volume in an instant. **1846** Brittan tr. *Malgaigne's Man. Oper. Surg.* 221 If you retract the skin dividing the cellular bridles [etc.]. **1874** Masson *Three Devils* 92 The soul, retracting its thoughts from the far and physical, dwells disgustedly on itself.

transf. **1875** Kinglake *Crimea* (1877) V. i. 311 The commander..retracted all at once the right shoulder and wheeled his squadrons half back.

b. To draw back or in (some part of the body).

Used esp. of lower forms of animal life, having parts or organs which may be protruded and drawn in again.

1664 Power *Exp. Philos.* I. 8 [The butterfly's tongue] being drawn up into an Helix, and retracted into the mouth. *Ibid.* 36 The Eyes..are sheathed in her horns which she can retract or protrude. **1835–6** *Todd's Cycl. Anat.* I. 297/1 Birds which have sharp claws..retract them when they hope to prevent their being blunted. **1851** Richardson *Geol.* (1855) 293 The head is proportionally large, and cannot be retracted within the carapace. **1872** Dana *Corals* i. 26 A kind of case or jacket, into which the upper extremity ..may be retracted.

†**c.** To draw, bring, or call back (a person) from or to a place, or to reality. *Obs.*

1650 Cowley *Guardian* IV. viii, When a dead man from Orcus I retract. *a* **1652** Brome *New Acad.* III. i, My great love unto the Nation..Retracts me hither. **1656** Stanley *Hist. Philos.* v. 150 It is the same in undistracted phantasy, which they admit, when there is nothing that can retract us.

†**d.** To draw *out of* or *up*. *Obs. rare.*

1608 *Ussher's Lett.* (1686) App. 20 A Knowledg..which Experience might produce, if we would assay to retract it out of Nature by particular Probations. **1698** *Phil. Trans.* XX. 119 They may retract it up, and the easier, because passing over these Bones like a Pully, their force is more augmented.

e. *Phonetics.* To pronounce (a sound) with the tongue drawn back.

[**1889** A. J. Ellis *Early Eng. Pronunc.* v. 17 In D 6, 7, the tongue is often merely retracted.] **1890** H. Sweet *Primer of Phonetics* 73 The first element of the diphthong in *high* is retracted towards ʒ. **1970** M. Swanton *Dream of Rood* 33 CGmc. *a* fronted to early OE *æ* and retracted instead of broken before an *l* or *l*-group.

†**2. a.** To delay or retard (one). *Obs. rare*$^{-1}$.

1524 *State Papers Hen. VIII*, VI. 364 The Duke and his armye was so tarded and retracted, that finally the French King..had leisour..to gadre strength.

†**b.** To restrain; to hold back or prevent *from* some course. Also *refl.* and *absol. Obs.*

a **1548** Hall *Chron., Hen. VII*, 16 Whiche secret serpent caused their fury to wade farther then reason coulde retract or restreyne. *Ibid.* 16 b, Euery one wished that this tumult were retracted and quenched. **1568** T. Howell *Arb. Amitie* (1879) 22 And let not want of welth in place Retract thy loue to runne his race. **1608** Dod & Cleaver *Expos. Prov.* ix–x. 112 Godly men..haue sometimes a pronenesse and inclination to euill; yet they may be easily retracted by counsell and admonition. **1633** Rowley *Match at Midn.* III. i, He lookes..like one that could retract himselfe from his mad starts. **1670** *Conclave wherein Clement VIII was elected Pope* 11 Hoping..by their presence and authority to retract some one from giving their Vote.

†**c.** To restrict or limit *to* something. *Obs.*$^{-1}$

1668 H. More *Div. Dial.* Schol. (1713) 562 Therefore the seven Vials cannot be retracted to the sixth Trumpet, much less be coextended with the seven Trumpets.

†**3. a.** To withdraw, remove, or take away (a person or thing). *Obs.*

1568 T. Howell *New Sonn.* (1879) 155 When faithfull man hath thus long serued,..in them shall vice ingratytude, retracte his iust desarte. **1598** Barret *Theor. Warres* IV. iii. 109 To retract and draw foorth of the squadrons, such men as be hurt. **1695** Woodward *Nat. Hist. Earth* II. (1723) 102 That Excess of Fertility..was retracted and cut off. **1728** T. Cooke *Hesiod, The Theogony* 1057 Before the gates the son of Japhet stands, Nor from the skies retracts his head or hands.

†**b.** To withdraw, turn away (the eye). *Obs.*$^{-1}$

1637 Heywood *Pleas. Dial.* XVIII, Such admirable parts in all I spye, From none of them I can retract myne eye.

II. *intr.* †**4.** To retire, retreat. *Obs. rare.*

1535 Stewart *Cron. Scot.* II. 585 This ilk Malcolme than thocht he wald retrak Quhill on the morne, and hald the feild abak. **1568** Grafton *Chron.* II. 698 They were fully determined, and bent to compell him to retract with dent of sworde.

5. To undergo or exhibit retraction; to admit of being drawn back.

1784 *Med. Comm.* II. 12 The protrusion had entirely retracted within the os externum. **1846** Brittan tr. *Malgaigne's Man. Oper. Surg.* 101 The cicatrix which forms .., spreading and retracting, would soon produce an adhesion almost equal to that divided. **1862** *Catal. Internat. Exhib.* II. §2617 In non-military rifles, the foresight.. retracts within a strong sheath. **1890** *Lancet* 1 Mar. 454 It [the cut end of the bowel] was thus held in position, was prevented from retracting, and all bleeding points were secured at once.

†**6.** To revert *to* (one). *Obs. rare*$^{-1}$.

1783 *Chron.* in *Ann. Reg.* 203/1 A very considerable tract of land in that district shortly retracts to government.

Hence **re'tracting** *vbl. sb.*[1] and *ppl. a.*

1620 Venner *Via Recta* viii. 175 By reason of the retracting of the spirits to the head. **1661** Boyle *Style of Script.* (1675) 111 The forciblest motives to the several duties, and the most retracting disswasives from the contrary vices. **1707** Sir W. Hope *New Method Fencing* iv. 131 This is to be done without the least Retracting of your Right Legg.

retract (rɪ'trækt), *v.*[2] [ad. L. *retractāre*, f. *re-* re- + *tractāre* to draw, pull. So F. *rétracter*, Sp. and Pg. *retractar*.]

1. *trans.* **a.** To withdraw, recall, revoke, rescind (a decree, declaration, promise, etc.).

1545 Joye *Exp. Dan.* vi. 93 Here be emprour and kinges taught to retract and call in ayen their vniust lawes. **1594** R. Ashley *Loys le Roy* 54 b, They haue power to retract the ordinances of the Sultans. **1621** Burton *Anat. Mel.* III. ii. VI. v. (1651) 581 Pope Gregory..retracted that decree of Priests marriages. **1654** Bramhall *Just Vind.* i. (1661) 2 That our Kings..had power to revoke, retract and abrogate whatsoever they found..insupportable to their Subjects. **1786** Burke *Art. agst. W. Hastings* Wk. II. 96 In that year, he..retracted his own act of resignation of his office. **1794** Mrs. Radcliffe *Myst. Udolpho* xxxiii, Withdraw to your chamber before I retract my promise. **1814** Scott *Wav.* lxv, Edward was desirous of retracting the suit he had made to his sister. **1847** Mrs. A. Kerr tr. *Ranke's Hist. Servia* 256 A declaration of that nature might at any moment be retracted. **1875** Jowett *Plato* (ed. 2) V. 7 The permission..has been given, and cannot be retracted.

b. To withdraw (a statement, etc.) as being erroneous or unjustified.

1560 Daus tr. *Sleidane's Comm.* 29 b, Yet wyll I retracte nothynge in these same. **1606** Shaks. *Tr. & Cr.* II. ii. 141 Were I alone.., And had as ample power, as I haue will, Paris should ne're retract what he hath done. **1647** N. Bacon *Disc. Govt. Eng.* I. lvii. (1739) 104 Quietly, said I? that I must retract; for he never had quiet during his life. **1703** Maundrell *Journ. Jerus.* (1732) 141 He both retracted his Apostacy and dyed to attone for it. **1750** Johnson *Rambler* No. 31 ¶ 16 As all error is meanness, it is incumbent on every man who consults his own dignity, to retract it as soon as he discovers it. **1879** McCarthy *Own Times* xviii. II. 32 He had nothing, he said, to retract or to ask pardon for.

†**c.** *Chess.* In a chess problem: to take back or unmake (a move). *Obs.*

1871 *Dubuque Chess Jrnl.* 12 White retracts his last move and mates in 1 move. **1881** F. C. Collins *Sel. Chess Probl.* 111 Retract White's last move, then White to play, and Mate in One move. **1890** B. G. Laws *Two-Move Chess Probl.* iii. 16 Retract White's move by replacing White knight at K4, and Black pawn at QB4, then play P × P, *en passant*, discovering mate. **1907** [see retractor 4].

2. *intr.* **a.** To make withdrawal or disavowal (of a statement, opinion, error, etc.).

c **1645** Howell *Lett.* (1650) II. 2 If your spirit will not let you retract, yet you shall do well to repress any more copies of the satyr. **1675** G. R. tr. *Le Grand's Man without Passion* 249 He retracts from his errors. **1742** Young *Nt. Th.* IV. 398 What mean these questions?—Trembling I retract. **1833** Lytton *Eng. & English* I. iv, The affront once given,..they fight first and retract afterwards. **1865** Pusey *Truth Eng. Ch.* 74 When detected, he retracted. He acquiesced outwardly without giving up his belief.

b. To draw back (from a promise, resolve, etc.).

1700 Dryden *Cymon & Iph.* 252 Tho' both repenting, were by Promise bound, Nor could retract. *a* **1735** Landsdowne *To Myra* Poems (1790) 64 She will, and she will not, she grants, denies, Consents, retracts, advances, and then flies. **1808** Eleanor Sleath *Bristol Heiress* III. 320 Caroline had not retracted from her resolution. **1853** J. H. Newman *Hist. Sk.* (1873) II. I. iii. 142 Alfonso of Portugal promised to join in a Holy War, and retracted.

c. *Card-playing.* To draw back, change one's mind, after having agreed or declined to play with a certain hand.

1830 'Eidrah Trebor' *Hoyle Made Familiar* 71 (Loo), No one can retract after declaring his intention to stand or not. **1878** 'Cavendish' *Laws of Écarté* 11 The dealer having accepted or refused cannot retract.

Hence **re'tracting** *vbl. sb.*[2]

1643 *Decl. Comm. Rebell. Ireland* 26 These directions given by His Majesty for the retracting of this Order. **1874** T. M. Brown *Bk. Chess. Probl.* 20 The *Dubuque Chess Journal* Tourney..for 'retracting' problems.

†**re'tract**, *v.*[3] *Obs.*$^{-1}$ [ad. L. *retractāre*, f. re- RE- + *tractāre* to handle.] *trans.* To repeat.

a **1699** *Wodrow Soc. Select Biogr.* (1847) II. 321 The office and acts of such, as ordination and baptism, though in themselves null, yet they are effectual to godly persons,.. and, therefore, are not necessary to be retracted.

retractable (rɪ'træktəb(ə)l), *a.* [f. RETRACT *v.*[1] and *v.*[2] + -ABLE. Cf. OF. and Sp. *retractable.*]

1. That may be retracted or disavowed.

1620 Donne *Serm.* Wks. 1839 V. 423 Not in finite and retractable speeches, but in fiery tongues.

†**2.** ? Inclined to be shy or reluctant. *Obs.*$^{-1}$

1632 Lithgow *Trav.* x. 426, I set Pen to Paper, drawing from the distaffe of the Retractable Muses, a Poeticall Pamphelet.

3. a. Capable of being drawn in; retractile.

1769 Cook *1st Voy. round World* I. i, Very sharp talons, which resemble those of a cat, and, like them, were retractable into a sheath of skin. **1920** *Flight* XII. 96/2 As a result of the unfortunate accident..Messrs. Vickers, Ltd., were unable to show their 'Viking' flying boat with retractable land undercarriage. **1933** *Jrnl. R. Aeronaut. Soc.* XXXVII. 446 Modern U.S.A. commercial aircraft attain higher speeds by clean design and use of retractable carriages. **1936** *Ibid.* XL. 715 Armament (defensive):..1 machine gun 12·7 calibre in retractable turret firing rear; [etc.]. **1968** Miller & Sawers *Techn. Devel. Mod. Aviation* III. ii. 54 One can find designs as early as Penaud's in 1871 that were well streamlined and incorporated a retractable undercarriage (first used by du Temple in 1858 on an airplane that did not fly).

b. Applied to an object which admits the retraction of a component part.

1961 *Lebende Sprachen* VI. 103/2 Retractable ball-point pen. **1962** A. Nisbett *Technique Sound Studio* ii. 39 Retractable ball-point pens can be a menace—people will fiddle with them, and produce a sharp, unidentified click every ten or fifteen seconds.

Hence **retracta'bility**, capacity for retraction.

1890 *Med. News* LIII. 159 (Cent.), Tannin, which acts on the retractability of the mucous membrane.

†**re'tractate**, *pa. pple. Obs. rare*$^{-1}$. [ad. L. *retractāt-us*, pa. pple. of *retractāre* RETRACT *v.*[3]] Treated again, revised.

1623 Bacon *Let. to Matthew* in Spedding *Life* VII. 429 Those works, which I had formerly published,..being retractate and made more perfect.

†**re'tractate**, *v. Obs. rare*$^{-1}$. [f. ppl. stem of L. *retractāre* RETRACT *v.*[2]] *trans.* To retract.

1611 Bible *Transl. Pref.* ¶ 13 The same S. Augustine was not ashamed to retractate, we might say reuoke, many things that had passed him.

retractation (ri:træk'teɪʃən). [ad. L. *retractātiōn-em*, noun of action f. *retractāre* RETRACT *v.*[2] and *v.*[3] So F. *rétractation*, Sp. *retractacion*, It. *retrattazione.*]

1. *pl.* The title of a book written by St. Augustine containing further treatment and corrections of matters treated in his former writings.

1451 Capgrave *Life St. Aug.* (E.E.T.S.) 31 All þis þing witnesseth him-selue in his first book of his Retractaciones. **1532** More *Confut. Tindale* Wks. 733/2 Saynt Austyne.. found no faut in that saieng when he was after bishop at the time of his retractacions. **1561** T. Norton *Calvin's Inst.* III. xx. 229 b, He telleth also in his seconde boke of Retractations that it was in his time receiued in Africa. **1614** Raleigh *Hist. World* I. (1634) 20 St. Augustine..in his Retractations maintaineth the same opinion. **1651** C. Cartwright *Cert. Relig.* I. 49 Saint Augustine had written so many errors, as occasioned the writing of a whole booke of retractations. **1888** Salmon *Infallib. Ch.* xviii, St. Augustine's 'Retractations' does not mean retractations in our modern sense of the word, but a re-handling of things previously treated of.

b. Used similarly of other works. *rare.*

1583 Fulke *Def. Trans. Script.* Answ. Pref. 54 The same Beda, in his preface vnto his retractation vpon the Acts of the Apostles.

†**c.** *Rhet.* (See quot.) *Obs. rare*$^{-0}$.

1678 Phillips, *Retractation*..in Rhetorick..is the same figure with that which is called in Greek Ploce.

2. a. Withdrawal or recantation of an opinion, statement, etc., with admission of error.

1548 Elyot, *Retractatio*, a retractacion; a reuokyng of ones opinion. **1560** Daus tr. *Sleidane's Comm.* 200 b, He had at the fyrste made hys retractatyon nothynge playnlye. **1643** Digby *Observ. Relig. Med.* (1644) 98 What censure upon himselfe may wee expect..if euer hee make any retractation of this Discourse concerning his Religion? **1674** Hickman *Quinquart. Hist.* (ed. 2) 24 Retractation is when a man out of conviction of judgement revokes his errour. **1752** Carte *Hist. Eng.* III. 293 Such are the effects of forced retractations falsly termed conversions. **1839** Hallam *Hist. Lit.* IV. iii. §31 He had been for many years..a favourer of Cartesianism, but his retractation is very complete. *a* **1873** S. Wilberforce *Ess.* (1874) II. 226 Their very retractations witness to the gradualness with which the new light dawned upon them.

b. Withdrawal from an engagement, promise, etc.

1654 tr. *Scudery's Curia Pol.* 115 Faith is obligatory, and binding, and no retractation to be admitted. **1818** Colebrooke *Obligations* 190 On the question of the right and effect of retractation, opinions of jurists differ. **1865** Mill *Liberty* v, There are perhaps no contracts or engagements..of which one can venture to say that there ought to be no liberty whatever of retractation.

†**3.** ? Disinclination, reluctance. *Obs. rare*$^{-1}$.

1563 Winȝet tr. *Vincent. Lirin.* Wks. (S.T.S.) II. 70 Without al hæsitatioun or dout bayth lat it be maid patent, and without ony retractatioun be condemnit.

†**4.** ? A rejoinder, retort. *Obs. rare*$^{-1}$.

1637 Gillespie *Eng. Pop. Cerem.* III. i. 15 If so, my retractation is, that if he be excused one way, hee must be accused an other way.

5. Retransformation. *rare*$^{-1}$.

1836-7 Sir W. Hamilton *Metaph.* xl. (1859) II. 406 We can only imagine this, as a retractation of an outward energy into power.

†**retractative**, *a. Obs.*$^{-1}$ [f. ppl. stem of L. *retractāre* RETRACT *v.*[3] + -IVE.] Revisional.

1726 Ayliffe *Parergon* 489 But when there is no Retractative Remedy by an Appeal, it is called Res Judicata.

retractatively, *adv. rare*$^{-1}$. [Cf. prec. and RETRACTATE *v.*] In a retracting manner.

1851 G. S. Faber *Many Mansions* 23 The earlier form of Purgatory, which was hesitatingly and often retractatively introduced by Ambrose and Augustine.

re'tracted, *ppl. a.*[1] [f. RETRACT *v.*[1] + -ED[1].]

a. Drawn or pulled back; drawn or turned inwards.

1643 J. Steer tr. *Exp. Chyrurg.* xv. 57 Of the retracted Nerves and crooked Junctures after Combustions. **1682** Sir T. Browne *Chr. Mor.* II. §12 Men not of retracted Looks, but who carry their Hearts in their Faces. **1791** Cowper *Iliad* I. 564 Their retracted necks First pierced. **1826** Kirby & Sp. *Entomol.* IV. 308 *Feeders retracted*, when..the *Trophi* are not capable of being much pushed out or drawn in. **1875** Darwin *Insectiv. Pl.* xviii. 450 A worm with retracted horny jaws.

b. *Phonetics.* Of a sound: pronounced with the tongue drawn back.

1874 A. J. Ellis *Early Eng. Pronunc.* IV. 1105/1 As he pronounced this *s* to me, it sounded like a retracted (,s) with a rattle of moisture. **1908** H. Sweet *Sounds of Eng.* 37 Quite distinct from the fully retracted back vowels. **1975** *Language* LI. 282 Less easy to pin down are the retracted sibilants.

re'tracted, *ppl. a.*[2] [f. RETRACT *v.*[2] + -ED[1].] Revoked, withdrawn, cancelled.

1713 C'tess Winchelsea *Misc. Poems* 281 All in vain are Pray'rs, extatick Thoughts, Recover'd Moments, and retracted Faults. **1847** J. Cairns *Let.* in *Life* (1895) xi. 281 The Saviour could not have repeated twice over a retracted prayer.

retractile (rɪ'træktɪl, -aɪl), *a.*[1] [a. F. *rétractile*, or ad. L. type **retractilis*: see RETRACT *v.*[1] and -ILE.] Admitting of retraction; capable of being drawn in or back; exhibiting the function or power of retraction: **a.** of parts of animal or vegetable organisms (the usual application); *spec.* in *Med.*, applied to a testis in the inguinal region that can readily be manipulated into the scrotum or vice versa.

1777 Pennant *Brit. Zool.* IV. 51 Sea-Star,..furnished with five or more rays, and numerous retractile *tentacula*. **1808** Wilson *Amer. Ornith.* I. 115 The tongue..is attached by a very elastic retractile membrane to the base of the right nostril. **1827** D. Johnson *Ind. Field Sports* 55, I have heard it said that their claws are retractile. **1849** Balfour *Man. Bot.* §59 The retractile hairs of Campanula. **1872** Nicholson *Palæont.* 87 Round the circumference of the disc are placed numerous tentacles, usually retractile. **1938** Spence & Scowen in *Lancet* 29 Oct. 983/2 We have used the following terms:—(1) Retractile testes... (2) Retained testes. **1968** Turner & Bloodworth in J. M. B. Bloodworth *Endocrine Path.* xiii. 438/1 This has probably been due, in large part, to the failure of many observers to distinguish between the retractile testis and the true cryptorchid testis. **1977** *Lancet* 24-31 Dec. 1361/1 The 2 other boys, 1 aged 10 years with small inguinal testes and the other aged 13½ years with one impalpable and one retractile testis, showed no improvement.

b. of bodies, parts of mechanism, etc.

1871 Spencer *Princ. Psychol.* (1872) II. VI. xii. 156 Of bodies that resist in different modes..we have..the Retractile and Irretractile. **1879** G. Prescott *Sp. Telephone* 26 The armature levers are retained in a definite position,.. and no retractile spring whatever is required.

c. *Med.* (See quot.)

1896 *Allbutt's Syst. Med.* I. 800 The urine in these cases contained albumin, which on precipitation settled at the bottom of the test-tube (retractile albuminuria).

re'tractile, *a.*[2] *rare.* [f. RETRACT *v.*[2], after prec.] Exhibiting or evincing retractation.

1888 R. W. Dixon *Hist. Ch. Eng.* xvii. III. 228 Cranmer himself published his Defence of the true and Catholic Doctrine of the Sacrament: a long treatise, with a characteristically retractile title. **1920** H. G. Wells *Outl. Hist.* xxix. 327/2 Hadrian, his successor, was of a cautious and retractile disposition.

retrac'tility. [f. RETRACTILE *a.*[1] + -ITY. Cf. F. *rétractilité.*] The fact of being retractile.

1839-47 *Todd's Cycl. Anat.* III. 524/1 This tendency to contract has been distinguished by the term retractility. **1846** Brittan tr. *Malgaigne's Man. Oper. Surg.* 100 They both become covered at the same time by a membrane.., the retractility of which draws them together. **1897** *Allbutt's Syst. Med.* IV. 307 Various conditions of the urine, such as its acidity for example, influencing the retractility of the coagulum.

retraction (rɪ'trækʃən). [ad. late L. *retractiōn-em*, n. of action f. *retract-*, *retrahĕre*: see RETRACT *v.*[1] So F. *rétraction*, Sp. *retraccion*, It. *re-*, *ritrazione.* In senses 1-3 used for *retractation.*]

1. a. = RETRACTATION 2 a.

c **1386** Chaucer *Pars. T.* ¶ 1085 Crist haue mercy on me and foryeue me my giltes, and namely of myn translacions and enditynges of worldly vanitees, the whiche I reuoke in my retracciouns. *a* **1586** Sidney *Arcadia* II. (1605) 113 Certaine verses, which..she would haue adioyned as a retraction to the other. **1678** Sir G. Mackenzie *Crim. Laws Scot.* (1699) 151 Nor did her Retraction proceed from Repentance, but Confrontation. **1693** R. Fleming *Fulfilling Script.* (1801) App. I. 452 Hath not the greatest reproacher sometimes been forced to give in his retraction? **1750** Johnson *Rambler* No. 31 ¶ 16 Such as have adopted his errors should know his retraction. **1775** C. Johnston *Pilgrim* 4 Nor would I to save the imaginary shame of retraction erase a charge, which I thought just when I made it. **1859** Thackeray *Virgin.* xlii, I, of course, will make no retraction or apology. *a* **1871** De Morgan *Budget Parad.* (1872) 344 The authorship should be denied or a proper retraction made.

b. = RETRACTATION 2 b.

1642 *Ordin. & Declar. Lord's Day* 7 This doubtfull retraction in the Captaine animated one Iohn Keeve a Cooke to be forward in this designe. **1666** Spurstowe *Spir. Chym.* (1668) 104 A Covenant of Marriage..requires Performances, not retractions. **1818** Colebrooke *Obligations* 43 So long as matters remain entire, there is room for after thought and retraction. **1847** Aytoun *Tales fr. Blackw.* IV. 38 He would even go the length of treating his victim..until the fatal mandate was given, and retraction utterly impossible.

†**2.** *pl.* = RETRACTATION 1. *Obs.*

1526 *Pilgr. Perf.* (W. de W. 1531) 270 Saynt Austyn, spekynge of the mortificacion of the senses in his boke of Retraccyons. **1617** R. Fenton *Serm.* in *Treat. Ch. Rome* 97 S. Augustine..doth retract that point in his booke of Retractions. **1734** tr. *Rollin's Anc. Hist.* Pref. (1827) I. 15 St. Austin, in his Retractions, repents his having lavished so many encomiums on Plato.

3. Withdrawal, recall or revocation, *of* something decreed, determined, advanced, etc.

1583 Foxe *A. & M.* (1596) 74/1 The imperial proclamations..conteining the retraction or countermand of those things which against the Christians were before decreed. **1641** in Urwick *Nonconf. Worcester* 35 His consent obtained to a retraction of the petition. **1678** Cudworth *Intell. Syst.* Pref., We have no more to adde, but onely the Retractation or Retraction of one Passage. **1756** *World* No. 161 V. 188 He thought the retraction of an error a deviation from honour. **1828** Southey in *Q. Rev.* XXXVIII. 574 There is even a canon forbidding the retraction of anything that has once been decreed against any heresy whatsoever. **1838** Whewell in Todhunter *Acc. Writ.* (1876) II. 271, I have seen no retraction of these purposes.

4. The action of drawing or pulling back or in; the fact or condition of being drawn in or contracted; retractile power.

c **1550** H. Lloyd *Treas. Health* O j, The weaknesse of the retraction and great strengthe of attractyon in the reynes. **1578** Lyte tr. *Dodoens* 451 The sayde herbes..bring to the sicke..intolerable Crampes and retractions of sinewes. **1615** Crooke *Body of Man* 40 Sleep is nothing else but a retraction or calling backe of the heate to the heart from the other partes. **1656** tr. *Hobbes' Elem. Philos.* (1839) 408 The impulsion into the nerves and retraction again of animal spirits. **1725** Bradley *Fam. Dict.*, *Strabism*..consists in the Retraction of the Eye towards one side. **1818-20** E. Thompson tr. *Cullen's Nosologia* (ed. 3) 224 *Colica spasmodica*; with retraction of the navel. **1862** Fuller *Dis. Lungs* 11 Retraction or falling in of the chest may be either general or local. **1899** *Allbutt's Syst. Med.* VI. 126 Retraction has been noticed on the side opposite to that on which a lung was the seat of morbid growths.

b. *spec.* of retractile parts or organs.

1646 Sir T. Browne *Pseud. Ep.* 155 To assist the protrusion, and retraction of their hornes. **1821** W. P. C. Barton *Flora N. Amer.* I. 23 They open in the evening, just after sunset, by a..retraction of the calix leaves. **1881** *Nature* XXIV. 338/2 The most peculiar..of all the chamæleon's actions—the emission and retraction of its tongue.

c. *fig.* of mental influences or operations.

a **1661** Fuller *Worthies* (1840) II. 324 There is a spirit of retraction of one to his native country. **1694** Motteux *Rabelais* IV. lxvi. (1737) 272 I feel a..Retraction in my Soul, which..admonishes me not to land. **1831** T. Hope *Ess. Orig. Man* II. 354 The same cause producing voluntary impulses outward, or voluntary retraction from without.

†**d.** Withdrawal, retreat. *Obs. rare*$^{-1}$.

1684 T. Burnet *The. Earth* I. 20 They make him do and undo, go forward and backwards by such countermarches and retractions.

e. *Phonetics.* The drawing back of the tongue in the articulation of speech sounds; articulation thus effected.

1890 H. Sweet *Primer of Spoken Eng.* 4 Each of the vowels formed by the different combinations of retraction and height is either *narrow* or *wide*. **1895** R. Morris *Hist. Outl. Eng. Accidence* (ed. 2) ii. 18 We distinguish three horizontal positions, or degrees of retraction of the tongue. **1927** *Year's Work Eng. Stud.* 1925 40 The third point deals chiefly with the phenomena of secondary retraction. **1977** *Archivum Linguisticum* VIII. 76 The only major objection to it must be that there are no other cases in Old English of non-velarized *l* preventing fronting or causing retraction.

†**5.** The action or fact of taking away; detraction. *Obs. rare.*

a 1635 NAUNTON *Fragm. Reg.* (Arb.) 20 Without retraction from the Honour of so great a Princesse. *a* 1636 LYNDE *Case for Spectacles* (1638) 128 As you have purged many places, so likewise you have forged and falsified others by addition or retraction.

retractive (rɪˈtræktɪv), *a.* and *sb.* [a. OF. *retractif* (mod.F. *rétractif*), or ad. med.L. *retractivus: see RETRACT *v.*[1] and -IVE. So It. *ritrattivo*.]

A. *adj.* 1. Serving to retract or pull back.

c 1400 tr. *Secreta Secret., Gov. Lordsh.* 96 Of stryngthe attractyue, and retractyf. 1614 TOMKIS *Albumazar* v. i, An engine..whose qualitie Of strange retractiue vertue may recall Desperate debts. 1815 *Hist. John Decastro* I. 199 The retractive muscles of the upper lip gave him astonishing powers of grimace.

2. Inclined to draw back; †backsliding. *rare.*

1509 HAWES *Past. Pleas.* 45 The erryng people, that are retractif, As to the ryght way to bryng them agayne. 1869 tr. *Rénan's Apostles* xiii. 191 To win over this great retractive and susceptible soul.

†3. Of a chess problem: involving the retracting of a move or moves. *Obs.*

1890 J. RAYNER *Chess Probl.* 9 A retractive problem is one in which some move..has to be retracted, and then mate or sui-mate in a given number of moves. 1890 B. G. LAWS *Two-Move Chess Probl.* 16 These are called 'Retractive' problems.

†B. *sb.* A dissuasive. *Obs.*

1616 BEARD (*title*), A Retractive from the Romish Religion. 1644 BP. HALL *Rem. Wks.* (1660) 139 To be a strong retractive from any, even of our dearest, and gainfullest sins.

retractor (rɪˈtræktə(r)). [See RETRACT *v.*[1] and -OR, and cf. F. *rétracteur*.]

1. *Surg.* A bandage or other appliance, used, in various operations, to hold back parts that would impede the operator.

1846 BRITTAN tr. *Malgaigne's Man. Oper. Surg.* 214 He isolates the bones, carrying the knife round them in a figure of eight, and puts on the retractor or split bandage with three ends. *Ibid.* 288 Instead of passing the retractors under the lids, Guerin prefers in each case applying them on the cutaneous surface. 1879 *St. George's Hosp. Rep.* IX. 482 The upper lid was raised with Noyes's retractor.

2. *Anat.* a. A muscle which serves to retract a limb or member.

1837 FARRE in *Phil. Trans.* CXXVII. 401 The muscular apparatus consists of the gastric and tentacular retractors. 1851 WOODWARD *Mollusca* 27 It corresponds to the posterior retractors in the bivalves. 1883 D'A. W. THOMPSON tr. *Müller's Fertil. Fl.* 59 The bee by rotating the retractors..draws back the mentum, and with it the tongue.

b. So *retractor muscle*.

1837 FARRE in *Phil. Trans.* CXXVIII. 400 It appeared to be distinct from the retractor muscles. 1883 HUXLEY *Elem. Biol.* 194 Within these is a retractor muscle with similar attachments, ensheathing the optic nerve.

3. = EXTRACTOR 3.

1875 KNIGHT *Dict. Mech.* 1925/2 *Retractor*, a device by which the metallic cartridge-cases employed in breech-loading guns are withdrawn after firing.

4. *Chess.* (See quot. 1907.)

1902 *Brit. Chess Mag.* 455 Two-move retractors. 1907 S. S. BLACKBURN *Terms & Themes Chess Probl.* 33 Retractors. Problems wherein the conditions require that the last move of one, or both, of the players shall be retracted, and that, when this is done, the problem shall be solved according to the usual conditions. 1937 T. R. DAWSON *Caissa's Wild Roses in Clusters* 14/1 A simple changed-mate retractor theme.

retraˈdition. *rare*$^{-1}$. [f. L. *retrād-ĕre* to give back.] The action of handing back.

1875 POSTE *Gaius* III. 384 The retransfer of dominion follows without any retradition or reconveyance by the interim proprietor.

†**reˈtrah**, *v. Obs. rare.* [ad. L. *retrahĕre*, f. *re-* RE- + *trahĕre* to draw.] *trans.* To draw back, retract. Also **reˈtrahing** *vbl. sb.*

1497 *Patent Roll 12 Hen. VII* II, The retrahyng of his most noble viage and royall arme prepared toward Scotland. 1578 BANISTER *Hist. Man* I. 33 The bones of Coccix are in childbirth retrahed.

ˈretrahent, *a. rare.* [f. L. *retrahent-em*, pres. pple. of *retrahĕre*: see prec.] Retractive.

1713 DERHAM *Phys.-Theol.* IV. iii. 116 Mr. Cowper makes them to be three, one Atollent, and two Retrahent muscles. 1849-52 *Todd's Cycl. Anat.* IV. 1143/2 In the Nautilus the tongue is..embraced anteriorly by two retrahent muscles.

†**retrahiˈbition.** *Obs. rare*$^{-1}$. [See RETRO-.] A withdrawal of a previous prohibition.

a 1572 KNOX *Hist. Ref.* Wks. 1846 I. 392 Be hir consent and retrahibitioun was the preching stuleis brokin in the Kirk of Leith, and idolatrie was erectit in the samyn, quhair it was befoir suppressit.

†**retraict**, *sb.*[1] *Obs.* [a. F. *retraict(e*, obs. variants of *retrait(e*: see RETRAIT *sb.*[1]]

1. The act of retreating, in various senses. Also *place of retraict*, = sense 2.

1570-6 LAMBARDE *Peramb. Kent* (1826) 401 The Saxons ..used them as receptacles, and places of secret retraict, for their wives, children, and portable goodes. 1596 DANETT tr. *Comines* (1614) 62 They were repulsed, and in their retraict ..one or two..of their captaines were hurt. 1640 HOWELL *Dodona's Gr.* 40 The woods and places of fastness, whence they made eruptions and retraicts at pleasure.

b. Possibility of retreat. *rare*$^{-1}$.

1622 BACON *Hen. VII*, 33 The Earle of Lincolne..seeing the businesse past Retraict, resolued to make on where the King was.

2. A place of retreat or refuge. *rare*$^{-1}$.

1596 RALEIGH *Discov. Gviana* 23 Their chiefest strengths and retraicts are in the Ilands scituate on the south side of the entrance..of the said river.

†**reˈtraict**, *sb.*[2] *Obs. rare*$^{-1}$. = RETRAIT *sb.*[2]

1634 C. DOWNING *State Eccl. Kingd.* 54 The Retraict is formed like waxe to take the impression of the present aspect and necessitie of affaires.

†**reˈtraict**, *v. Obs. rare*$^{-1}$. [Cf. RETRAICT *sb.*[1]] = RETRAIT *v.* 2.

a 1604 HANMER *Chron. Irel.* (1633) 92 A Priests sonne..in the beginning of the battaile..perswaded him to retraict; saying further, that there was no hope of good successe.

reˈtrain, *v.* [RE- 5 a.] *trans.* To train again; *spec.* to teach (a skilled or trained person) a new skill. Also **reˈtraining** *vbl. sb.*

1934 WEBSTER, Retrain. 1937 *Jrnl. Compar. Psychol.* XXIV. 290 On the re-training trials of the following day, this behavior persisted. 1964 MRS. L. B. JOHNSON *White House Diary* 11 Jan. (1970) 39 He had been out of work for two years and then he heard about the retraining program. 1977 P. STREVENS *New Orientations in Teaching of Eng.* p. vii, Helping to train and re-train teachers. 1977 *Whitaker's Almanack 1978* 980/1 Under the rules of the Fund the Commission can assist in training and retraining schemes by reimbursing 50 per cent. of the cost financed by a public authority.

†**reˈtrair.** *Obs. rare.* Also retrayr. [a. F. *retraire*:—L. *retrahĕre*.] Return; drawing back.

c 1475 *Partenay* 2824 Hys brother the erle knew at hys retrair That he better wo in hertte had profounde. *Ibid.* 5149 At Montfarrant bide is my hole plesaunce, Ther become hermite with-out any retrayr.

†**reˈtraised**, *pa. pple.* (? Error for *retraited*: see RETRAIT *sb.*[1] 5.)

1725 BRADLEY *Fam. Dict.*, *Prict*, otherwise call'd Ancloy'd, Cloy'd and Retraised, a Misfortune which befalls Horses, when..they are prick'd in driving the Nails.

†**reˈtrait**, *sb.*[1] *Obs.* [a. F. *retrait* masc., or *retraite* fem., noun of action f. *retraire*:—L. *retrahĕre*: see RETRACT *v.*[1] Cf. RETRAICT *sb.*[1] and RETREAT *sb.*]

1. A place of retreat or refuge. Also *transf.*

1481 CAXTON *Godf.* cxlviii. 220 Somme they slewe and many moo toke prysonners, and bonde them, and retorned to theyr retrayte. 1587 GREENE *Penelope's Web* Wks. (Grosart) V. 204 Tyme is a retrayte from vanitie and vyce. 1598 SYLVESTER *Du Bartas* II. i. IV. *Handicrafts* 58 Making our Ile a holy safe retrait For Saints exil'd in persecution's heat. 1626 C. POTTER tr. *Sarpi's Hist. Quarrels* 99 The Capuchines..could not finde..any conuenient retrait, so as many of them died for want of sustenance.

2. *Mil.* The signal for retiring. = RETREAT *sb.* 2 a.

1483 CAXTON *Gold. Leg.* 70 b/2 Thenne Ioab tromped and blewe the retrayt. 1523 LD. BERNERS *Froiss.* I. ccxxi. 287 Than they caused their trumpettes to sowne the retrayt. 1568 GRAFTON *Chron.* II. 457 Wherefore he caused a retrayte to be blowen. *a* 1586 SIDNEY *Arcadia* III. (1605) 291 As soon as they heard the retraite. 1610 HOLLAND *Camden's Brit.* II. 136 Soone after by his bagpipers [he] sounded the retraite. 1648 FANSHAWE *Il Pastor Fido* II. i, The Megarensian this perceiving, straight To the disordered Troops sounds a retrait.

3. The action or fact of retiring or retreating, on the part of military forces.

1523 LD. BERNERS *Froiss.* I. lxxxvi. 110 Than all..lefte the assaut: in the retrayte ther were two knyghtes..taken. 1590 SIR J. SMYTH *Disc. Weapons* 5 b, Vpon a hastie retraite they may verie well saue and keepe their peeces. 1614 RALEIGH *Hist. World* IV. ii. §4. 179 Old Souldiers are not easily dismaied: we read in Histories..what braue retraits haue beene made by them. 1658 SIR T. BROWNE *Garden Cyrus* i, The occasion of that memorable work, and almost miraculous retrait of Xenophon.

b. Retirement, retreat, in various senses.

a 1533 LD. BERNERS *Golden Bk. M. Aurel.* (1559) 118 Forgette not the honestie that ought to be in a Romayne woman, nor retrayte that is requisitte in a wydowe. 1621 BURTON *Anat. Mel.* III. ii. III. iv. (1651) 490 With a regaining retrait, a gentle reluctancy, a smiling threat. 1633 EARL MANCH. *Al Mondo* (1636) 40 They counted death but the retrait of life. 1655 *Nicholas Papers* (Camden) II. 273 His Majestie had desired the Duke might come to him, which is doutlesse a handsomer way for his retraite then if he were sent away.

4. = RETREAT *sb.* 6 a. *rare*$^{-2}$.

1601 HOLLAND *Pliny* I. 557 In Greece and Asia, they sow all indifferently at the retrait or occultation of Virgiliæ.

5. *Farriery.* (See quot., and cf. RETRACT *sb.* 4.)

1610 MARKHAM *Masterp.* II. xcv. 382 A Retrait is when a horse by the ill gouernment of the smith, is prickt in the foote with some ill driuen naile, yet in such sort that it is immediatly espied, and the naile drawne backe againe. *Ibid.* xcviii. 389 Quitterbone, retraite, grauelling, or cloying, or such like accident.

6. ? Return; restoration. *rare*$^{-1}$.

1618 *Weakest goeth to the Wall* I. i. in *Webster's Wks.* (1857) IV. 225 This [reconciliation] joys my soul; and more to let you know How pleasing this retrait of peace doth seem [etc.].

†**reˈtrait**, *sb.*[2] *Obs. rare.* Also retrate. [ad. It. *ritratto*, Sp. and Pg. *retrato*, on analogy of prec. or of *portrait*.] Portraiture, portrait, picture.

1590 SPENSER *F. Q.* II. iii. 25 Under the shadow of her even browes, Working belgardes and amorous retrate. *Ibid.* ix. 4 Shee is the mighty Queene of Faery, Whose faire retraitt I in my shield doe beare.

†**reˈtrait**, *pa. pple.* and *ppl. a. Obs. rare.* [a. F. *retrait*, pa. pple. of *retraire*: see RETRAIT *sb.*[1]] Reserved, set apart; secluded.

1440 in *Wars Eng. in France* (Rolls) II. 590 The most notable tounes and placis..shuld be retrait for the saide capitaineries and there feleshippes be geven. 1603 HARSNETT *Popish Impost.* 61 Some of theyr lodges so obscure, and retrayte, as none but a priest or deuil could euer haue sented it out.

†**reˈtrait**, *v. Obs.* Also 6-7 retra(i)te, retrayt(e. [f. ppl. stem of F. *retraire*: cf. prec. and RETRAIT *sb.*[1]]

1. *trans.* To withdraw, take away, remove.

1593 NASHE *Christ's T.* 34 b, No relenting thought of mine, shall retraite you [*sc.* hands]. 1611 SPEED *Hist. Gt. Brit.* VII. xliv. §36. 365 Which..caused him to retraite his Host into a place of securitie. 1614 RALEIGH *Hist. World* III. (1634) 45 Artaphernes..had no other hope of safetie, than by retraiting himselfe into the Castle.

2. *intr.* To retreat, retire.

a 1548 HALL *Chron., Hen. VI*, 37 b, The Englishemen.., beynge content with their prey and gayne, began to retraite towarde the siege again. 1590 SPENSER *F. Q.* I. i. 13 Yet wisedome warnes, whilest foot is in the gate, To stay the steppe, ere forced to retrate. 1624 QUARLES *Sion's Elegies* II. ix, Ioy is departed from the holy Gates Of deare Ierusalem, and peace retraits From wasted Sion.

b. To draw back, retract. *rare*$^{-1}$.

1606 BP. HALL *Medit. & Vowes* I. §10 Some promise what they cannot doe, as Satan to Christ;..some, what they meant for the time, and after retrait, as Laban to Jacob.

c. To return. *rare*$^{-1}$.

1625 BP. H. KING *David's Enlargement* 26 I retrait to my text in S. Ambrose his words.

d. To have recourse *to* something. *rare*$^{-1}$.

1650 FULLER *Pisgah* II. xii. 260 Yet such as will justifie Jonathans act herein..must retrait to divine inspiration.

‖**retraite** (rətrɛt). Also erron. **rétraite.** [Fr.: a mod. re-borrowing of *retraite* (see RETRAIT *sb.*[1]).] 1. = RETRAIT *sb.*[1] 3 b.; *en retraite*, in retirement or seclusion.

1860 MRS. GASKELL *Let.* 27 Aug. (1966) 631, I quite understand the wisdom of French ladies going into rétraite. 1958 L. DURRELL *Mountolive* v. 102 Pombal is doing all this legitimately. He is on local leave. I am *en retraite*.

2. *Mil.* = RETRAIT *sb.*[1] 2.

1883 *Standard* 21 Sept. 3/1 A grand dinner..was followed by the performance of a *retraite* by the combined bands of the Eleventh Army Corps.

retral (ˈriːtrəl), *a.* [f. L. *retrō* backwards + -AL[1].]

1. Posterior; situated at or towards the back; directed backwards.

1875 *Encycl. Brit.* III. 705/1 Beneath the retral ethmoidal spike is seen the olfactory groove. 1881 *Jrnl. Microsc. Sci.* Jan. 66 Septal ridges and retral bars forming a coarse..raised network.

2. Taking a backward direction.

1885 *American Assoc. Advanc. Science* XXXIV. 211 The special pull caused a slight retral slipping of the tidal crust.

Hence **ˈretrally** *adv.*

1841 *Proc. Berw. Nat. Club* I. No. 9. 273 Peristome incomplete retrally.

†**reˈtranch**, *v. rare.* [ad. F. *retrancher*: see RETRENCH *v.*] *trans.* To cut short, cut down.

1589 PUTTENHAM *Eng. Poesie* II. xi[i]. (Arb.) 118 This immeasurable ambition of the Spaniards, if her Maiestie..had not with her forces, prouidently stayed and retrenched [etc.]. 1653 HOLCROFT *Procopius, Goth. Wars* III. 91 At first Bessas and Conon..retranched their own allowances, and sold Corn to the richer sort at huge rates.

reˈtranquillize (riː-), *v.* [RE- 5 a.] *trans.* To make tranquil again.

1593 NASHE *Christ's T.* Wks. (Grosart) IV. 109 And if at any time it were warre-threatned, thy right-arme should haue retranquilliz'd and reioyc't it. 1598 TOFTE *Alba* (1880) 86 Thy hart gainst me, not still induratize, But my sad thoughts in me retranquillize.

retranˈscribe, *v.* [RE- 5 a.] *trans.* To transcribe again. So **retranˈscription.**

1805 W. TAYLOR in Robberds *Mem.* II. 91 Transmit the annotated manuscript to me for re-transcription. 1810 D. WORDSWORTH *Let.* 28 Feb. in W. Knight *Mem. Coleorton* (1887) II. 112 He [*sc.* Coleridge] has written a whole *Friend* more than once in two days. They are never re-transcribed, and he generally has dictated to Miss Hutchinson, who takes the words down from his mouth. 1841 I. D'ISRAELI *Amenities of Lit.* I. 175 Anthony Wood indignantly re-transcribed the whole of his English copy, and left the fair volumes to the care of the university. 1965 *Canad. Jrnl. Linguistics* Spring 85 Most forms are quoted from that source but are retranscribed. 1977 *Word 1972* XXVIII. 256 The forms which Alonso has cited are not minimal pairs and should be retranscribed as follows.

reˈtransfer (riː-), *sb.* [RE- 5 a.]

1. The (*or* an) act of retransferring.

1849 NOAD *Electricity* (ed. 3) 221 If..this deficiency of acid were owing to the mechanical re-transfer, mechanical means..would stop it. 1884 *Law Times* LXXVI. 323/2 His bond and warrant of attorney to secure a retransfer on demand. 1887 *Athenæum* 9 July 49/2 The retransfer of the imperial crown from the East to the West.

2. *Printing.* An impression taken from a lithographic image using special ink and paper

for the purpose of transferring it to another lithographic surface.

1946 A. Kirk in H. Whetton *Pract. Printing & Binding* xviii. 207 Imperfect retransfers should be scrapped immediately. Good retransfers can be placed face down on a clean sheet. **1965** Zigrosser & Gaehde *Guide Coll. Orig. Prints* iii. 30 If the facts..are known, the authenticity might be questionable, since the artist did not actually work on each retransfer of the original master image. **1967** E. Chambers *Photolitho-Offset* xvii. 259 Before retransferring from litho plates or stones, a thin layer of retransfer ink should be applied with a nap roller to the image.

retrans'fer (riː-), *v.* [re- 5 a.] *trans.* To transfer (something) again or back.

1842 *Civil Eng. & Arch. Jrnl.* V. 355/1 Several of these works when re-transferred to canvass were sold in England in 1838. **1850** Grote *Greece* II. lxiv. VIII. 236 It was into his hands that the command was re-transferred. **1885** *Law Times Rep.* LII. 570/1 The offer..to re-transfer the mortgage to the defendants.

retrans'figure (riː-), *v.* [re- 5 a.] *trans.* To transfigure (a person) again.

1632 Vicars tr. *Virgil* vi. 169 Cæneus now a woman, once a lad, Yet re-transfigur'd for her follies bad.

retrans'form (riː-), *v.* [re- 5 a.] *trans.* To transform or change (a person or thing) again, or back to a former condition.

1600 Tourneur *Transf. Metam.* lxxxvi, Eliza will you retransforme againe. **1633** Davenant *Cœlum Brit.* Wks. (1673) 361 Earthly beauties which his raging Queen.. turn'd to beasts, And in despight he retransform'd to Stars. **1649** Roberts *Clavis Bibl.* 513 Of a man as it were transformed into a Beast, and again of a beast retransformed into a man. **1850** Sir A. Agnew in *Mem.* (1852) iv. 97 Men are retransformed to the image of God by the renewing of their minds. **1878** Stewart & Tait *Unseen Univ.* iii. §102. 112 As the ball descends its energy is retransformed from the potential into the kinetic variety.

So **retransfor'mation**.

1847 C. Brontë *J. Eyre* xiv, My final re-transformation from india-rubber back to flesh. **1884** Child *Ballads* II. 336/2 The retransformation of Tam Lin.

retrans'fuse, *v.* [re- 5 a.] *trans.* To transfuse again.

1709–11 Ken *Anodynes* Poet. Wks. 1721 III. 469 When Death my Spirit shall unchain, Which soon as 'tis unloos'd, Shall into God be retransfus'd. *a* **1711** —— *Preparatives* ibid. IV. 32 On God to retransfuse the Mind, And live with Will resign'd.

retrans'late (riː-), *v.* [re- 5 a.] *trans.* To translate again, or back into the original language.

1860 G. H. Lewes *Let.* c 10 July in *Geo. Eliot Lett.* (1954) III. 319 There are paragraphs which read like a translation from a language into which one cannot retranslate them. **1861** J. Pycroft *Ways & Words* 157 Of Cicero..he had translated and retranslated every extant oration. **1882** Farrar *Early Chr.* I. 209, I have thought it best to retranslate the whole of it as closely as I could.

Hence **retrans'lating** *vbl. sb.*

1867 *Ch. Times* 4 May 156/4 Words that have for a long time been controversial watch-words have lost all intelligible meaning for the mass of hearers, and want retranslating.

retrans'lation (riː-). [re- 5 a.] **a.** A fresh or new translation. **b.** Translation back into the original language.

a **1661** Fuller *Worthies, Cornwall* I. (1662) 204 Wicklife and Trevisa agreeing so well in their judgements, it was much he would make a Retranslation. **1804** Southey *Lett.* (1850) II. 269 A retranslation of what they say is translated. **1849** Eastwick *Dry Leaves* 233 Re-translation of a Persian translation of a Letter from F. Currie, Esq. **1888** Morley *Eng. Writers* III. xi. 266 I adopt..the re-translation of the word into its right native form.

retrans'mission (riː-). [re- 5 a.] Transmission back to a source or to a fresh destination.

1868 *Act 31 & 32 Vict.* c. 101 §36 The transmission and re-transmission to the sheriff clerk. **1876** Preece & Sivewright *Telegraphy* 282 The message received at a telegraph office by wire for retransmission by wire to some other telegraph office.

So **retrans'missive** *a.*

1891 J. Aitchison *Signa Christi* vi. 248 The transmissibility of Christian truth is connected with a retransmissive influence.

retrans'mit (riː-), *v.* [re- 5 a.] *trans.* To transmit back again or further on.

1868 *Act 31 & 32 Vict.* c. 101 §51 The warrants shall, after extract, be retransmitted to the sheriff clerk of Chancery. **1873** F. Jenkin *Electr. & Magn.* (1881) 309 The Relay is an instrument which retransmits the original signal from a fresh battery.

retrans'mute (riː-), *v.* [re- 5 a.] To transmute again, or back to a former condition.

a **1711** Ken *Preparatives* Poet. Wks. 1721 IV. 46 God all their Shiftings can compute, And into Dew them retransmute. **1825** Bentham *Offic. Apt. Maximized, Indications* (1839) 7 *note*, The third person is here all along retransmuted into the first.

retrans'plant (riː-), *v.* [re- 5 a.] *trans.* To transplant again or back. Also *transf.*

1763 Mills *Pract. Husb.* IV. 162 They must be retransplanted on the ridges where they are to remain. **1880** *Fortn. Rev.* Feb. 212 It would be as impossible..to retransplant the emigrants and their descendants to Irish soil.

retrans'port (riː-), *v.* [re- 5 a.] *trans.* To transport back again. Also *refl.*

1647 Clarendon *Hist. Reb.* III. §34 He unsatisfied with them and they with him, he retransported himself into England. **1834** Sir F. B. Head *Bubbles fr. Brunnen* 8 Remote distances, to which even fancy could now scarcely retransport us. **1892** Mrs. H. Ward *David Grieve* II. x, The old Frenchman,..fairly re-transported to the world of his youth.

Hence **retranspor'tation**.

c **1751** S. Richardson *Let.* (1804) VI. 61 How I missed you, on my re-transportation! **1790** A. Hamilton *Wks.* (1851) III. 111 Whence the transportation and retransportation of the metals are obviated.

re'travel (riː-), *v.* [re- 5 a.] *trans.* To travel over again.

1808 Southey *Let.* in *Life* (1850) III. 196 We will talk about Spain, and retravel your route, a part of which I remember as vividly as I do my father's house.

re'traverse (riː-), *v.* [re- 5 a.] *trans.* To traverse again or repeatedly.

1843 Gladstone *Glean.* (1879) V. 69 Dr. Pusey, in a work with his own signature, retraversed nearly the same ground. **1871** Macduff *Mem. Patmos* vii. 86 He is busied from sunset until midnight-hour in re-traversing the..streets.

retravirus ('rɛtrəvaɪərəs). *Biol.* [mod.L., f. initial letters of *reverse transcriptase* (see transcriptase) + virus.] = retrovirus.

[**1974** *Intervirol.* IV. 202 Retraviridae are enveloped virions about 100 nm in diameter... They contain about 1.5% of 60–70S RNA... Some species that have been examined also contain a small amount of DNA... All viruses in the family contain antigenically specific reverse transcriptase (RNA-dependent DNA polymerase).] **1977** *Virology* LXXIX. 239 Xenotropic type C retraviruses were isolated from cell-free uterine extracts of normal adult NIH Swiss mice.

†**re'traxit.** *Obs. Law.* [L. *retraxit*, 3rd pers. sing. perf. ind. of *retrahĕre*: see retract *v.*] The formal withdrawal of his suit by a plaintiff.

[**1321–2** *Rolls. of Parlt.* I. 404/1 Illeges les fit a force entrer un Retraxit en la dite assise.] **1579** [Rastell] *Termes Lawes* 168/1 Retraxit..is when the partie plaintife or demaundant commeth in proper person into the Court where hys plee is, and sayth that he will not proceed any farder in the same. **1594** West *2nd Pt. Symbol., Chancerie* §43 An award that the parties shall make discontinuance and retraxits is not good. **1635** *Borough Deeds Maldon, Essex* (Bundle 80 fol. 1), With drafts: for licences of concord, Retraxits made, and amerciaments for not prosecutinge. **1713** Arbuthnot *John Bull* II. xvi, To Esquire South's Accompt for post Terminums...To ditto for Noli Prosequi's, Discontinuance, and Retraxit. **1768** Blackstone *Comm.* III. 296 A *retraxit* is an open and voluntary renunciation of his suit, in court, and by this he for ever loses his action.

†**re'tray**, *v.* *Obs.* [ad. F. *retrai-re*:—L. *retrahĕre*: see retract *v.*]

1. *trans.* and *refl.* To withdraw, draw back.

1470–85 Malory *Arthur* vii. xii. 230 Syr Beaumayns smote hym..& thenne he retrayed hym here & there & knyghtly mayntened his batail. **1562** Phaer *Æneid* ix. A a iij b, The streames eke stayde Their waters hoarce of sound, and Tyber trembling foote retrayed.

2. *intr.* To return; to retire, retreat.

1479 in *Eng. Gilds* (1870) 418 And then, euery man taking his leeve of the Maire,..to retray home to their evensong. **1523** Ld. Berners *Froiss.* I. xviii. 25 Than euery man had leaue to retraye to their lodgyng. *a* **1533** —— *Huon* cli. 575 Then he made his men to retraye backe fro the almayns.

'retread, *sb.* Chiefly *U.S.*, *Austral.*, and *N.Z.* [retread *v.*[2]] **1.** A tyre supplied with a fresh tread; = remould *sb.*

1914 *Auto-Motor Jrnl.* 4 Apr. 423 So exact is the work.. that a retread is scarcely distinguishable from an original. **1921** *Daily Colonist* (Victoria, B.C.) 10 Apr. 10/6 Always carry a 'retread' as a spare. Don't throw away your old casings until you have had them retreaded at least once. **1943** *Sun* (Baltimore) 4 Feb. 7/2 Retread is new rubber over the same area as recap, but all the way down to the cord fabric. **1968** *Wanganui* (N.Z.) *Chron.* 15 Nov. 10/6 (Advt.), Insist on safe shoulder retreads. **1973** A. Cooke *Amer.* 12, I found myself rediscovering—on re-tread tires at the compulsory thirty-five miles an hour—the whole American landscape. **1976** *Drive* Sept.–Oct. 77/1 A retread is a reprocessed tyre made from a secondhand carcass welded to new tread rubber. **1977** *Bulletin* (Sydney) 22 Jan. 58/3 (Advt.), Because Bandag retreads run longer, you'll spend less time and labour changing worn tyres.

2. *transf.* and *fig.* **a.** *Mil. slang.* A retired soldier recalled for (temporary) service, a 'dug-out'. Also in extended use, esp. of retrained persons.

1941 *Salt* 22 Dec. 36/2 Characteristically the Australians call a small reconnaissance tank a 'dingo', and a 1914–1918 soldier enlisted a second time a 'retread'. **1945** Baker *Austral. Lang.* II. viii. 152 A soldier of the 1914–18 war who has joined up again is a *retread*. **1948** *Amer. Legion Mag.* Oct. 26 Retreads will reune: Retreads, men who served in both World Wars..will hold their first reunion..at Miami. **1953** *Economist* 17 Oct. 178/2 The pro-Eisenhower *Chicago Daily News* called his appointees 'Governor Stratton's team of Republican retreads'. **1962** *Listener* 16 Aug. 232/2 They also have shorter courses for older men, known rather depressingly as 're-tread' courses. **1965** C. Koch *Casual Company* I. i. 7 I've got retreads, and chickens bloated with fever, but they turn to at reveille. **1977** D. Beaty *Excellency* ii. 21 A diplomat with thirty years experience..not the re-tread given a job with other unwanted Civil Servants.

b. Of things.

1964 *Lebende Sprachen* IX. 35/3 Mr Kennedy's plans are retreads of older projects. **1976** *Times Lit. Suppl.* 1 Oct. 1232/1 An all-too-familiar exegesis that has nothing new to say about Eliot.., a critical retread representing the kind of discussion that came in the 1930s. **1979** *Arizona Daily Star* 22 July (Parade Suppl.) 8/3 It is hard to imagine that we shall face another 10 years of the same romantic nostalgia and retread pop culture as was dished out by the '70's.

re'tread (riː-), *v.*[1] [re- 5 a.] *trans.* and *intr.* To tread again or anew.

trans. **1598** Sylvester *Du Bartas* II. i. *Columns* 740 So that re-treading their eternall trace, Th' one bears the Trebble, th' other bears the Base. *a* **1769** J. G. Cooper *Theagenes to Sylvia* 59 The pleasing paths of Venus I re-trod, No more a mortal. **1795** Southey *Joan of Arc* IV. 168 The warlike Virgin pass'd along, And much revolving in her troubled mind, Retrod the court. **1816** Bentham *Chrestom.* 36 At this next, and other succeeding stages, the same ground will be retrodden. **1833** Mrs. Browning *Prometh. Bound* 1140 For thyself, depart, Re-tread thy steps in haste. **1863** *Sat. Rev.* 11 Their life is one of perpetual change. They never retread the same ground.

intr. *a* **1847** Eliza Cook *Don't you remember?* i. 7 We retread where young Passion first stealthily rambled.

re'tread, *v.*[2] [re- 5 c.] *trans.* **1.** To furnish (a tyre) with a fresh tread.

1908 *Daily Report* 7 Feb. 11/4 (Advt.), 10–12 h.p. Wolseley, in excellent condition, front pneumatics, just been retreaded. **1912** *Motor Manual* (ed. 14) iii. 107 It is possible, in most cases, to have them retreaded by the makers.

2. *fig.* To retrain (a person) or provide with fresh employment, esp. after initial retirement. *U.S. slang.*

1963 *Lafayette Alumnus* Apr. 22/1 'Retreaded'..indicated that upon retirement, De Kay, Furness [etc.]..gave their learning, experience, and wisdom a capping. **1966** *Wall St. Jrnl.* 2 Dec. 1/4 To 'retread' many retired nurses and other skilled professionals through refresher courses.

Hence **re'treader**; **re'treaded** *ppl. a.*, **re'treading** *vbl. sb.*

1914 *Auto-Motor Jrnl.* 4 Apr. 423 During the retreading ..it is very often found that the casing requires strengthening. **1921** *Dict. Occup. Terms* (1927) §608 *Tyre retreader*, attaches new treads to worn tyre covers. **1937** *Sci. Amer.* Dec. 347/1 Retreading..involves nothing more nor less than replacing with new live rubber the tread which has become worn smooth under the abrasive action of the road. **1951** U. V. Troubridge tr. *Guareschi's Little World of Don Camillo* 207 The explosion had..been caused..by one of the retreaded tyres of the lorry. **1964** G. Mitchell *Death of Delft Blue* xxi. 228 Look over their used cars and re-treaded tyres. **1976** *Globe & Mail* (Toronto) 3 July 6/1 A retreaded provincial politician who was fired from the Davis Cabinet. **1977** *Financial Times* 4 June 5/3 The retreading industry would welcome it, because casings are their raw material.

retreat (rɪ'triːt), *sb.* Forms: α. 4–6 retret (5 *Sc.* ratret), 5–6 retrete (6 -tte), 6– retreat (7 -te). β. 6 retreyte, 6–7 retreit. [a. OF. *retret* masc., or *retrete* fem., variants of *retrait*, *retraite*, f. the pa. pple. of *retraire*:—L. *retrahĕre* to draw back: see retrait *sb.*[1] So Sp. and Pg. *retreta*, It. *ritratta*.]

†**1.** ? A backhanded blow. *Obs. rare.*

13.. *Sir Beues* (A) 2537 Ascopard wiþ a retret Smot after Beues a dent gret. **1375** Barbour *Bruce* xv. 49 Thai..sic rowtis till othir raucht With stok, with stane, and with retrete, as athir part can othir bet.

2. *Mil.* **a.** The signal to retire. Chiefly in phr. *to blow* or *sound the* (or *a*) *retreat*.

α. **1375** Barbour *Bruce* xvii. 460 Thai gert blaw the retret in hy. *Ibid.* 471 Qwhen thai had blawen the ratret. *a* **1548** Hall *Chron., Hen. VIII*, 113 b, Sir Willyam..caused his trompet to blowe a retrete. **1556** J. Heywood *Spider & Fly* lvi, At retret of trompet, they retyred a meyne. **1665** Manley *Grotius' Low. C. Wars* 812 Then the Prince.. sounded the retreat. **1686** South *Serm.* (1727) II. 353 Deception..sounds a Retreat instead of a Charge. **1719** D'Urfey *Pills* (1872) II. 270 Blow a Retreat, blow, blow, Tantivee. **1838** Thirlwall *Greece* xxxviii. V. 45 Agesilaus thought it prudent to sound a retreat.

β. *a* **1533** Ld. Berners *Huon* xciii. 302 He wolde sease the batayle & blowe the retreyte. **1579** Digges *Stratiot.* 123 Whosoeuer retireth not immediatly vpon the sound of the Retreit. **1655** Fuller *Ch. Hist.* I. 9 The trumpet of Antiquity, sounding at the same time a March and a Retreit.

†**b.** The recall of a pursuing force. *Obs.*$^{-1}$.

1597 Shaks. *2 Hen. IV*, IV. iii. 78 *Iohn.* Haue you left pursuit? *West.* Retreat is made, and Execution stay'd.

c. (See quots.)

1753 Chambers *Cycl. Suppl.* s.v., Retreat..is a beat of the drum in the evening, at the firing of a piece called the warning piece. **1822** *Regul. & Orders Army* 213 The Retreat is to sound or beat at Sun-set. **1876** Voyle & Stevenson *Milit. Dict.* 340/2 The term retreat is given to a bugle-sound, followed by a roll of the drums..; it is sounded every day at sunset.

3. a. The act of retiring or withdrawing in the face of opposition, difficulty, or danger.

1390 Gower *Conf.* III. 356 Er thou make eny suche assaies To love, and faile upon the fet, Betre is to make a beau retret. *c* **1420** Lydg. *Assembly of Gods* 1063 He was constreynyd clerely by duresse A lytyll tyne abak to make a bew retret. **1600** Shaks. *A.Y.L.* III. ii. 170 Come Shepheard, let vs make an honorable retreit. **1609** Tourneur *Funeral Poem* 77 Before it was too late to give retreat To their proceedings. **1686** tr. *Chardin's Coronat. Solyman* 85 The Rabble, who had put him to a Retreat with their stones. **1735** Pope *Moral Ess.* II. 225 But Wisdom's triumph is well-tim'd Retreat, As hard a science to the Fair as Great! **1774** Goldsm. *Nat. Hist.* (1776) IV. 131 It requires some patience and skill to intercept their retreat. **1839** Kemble *Resid. in Georgia* (1863) 53 [I] at length made good my retreat. **1860** Tyndall *Glac.* I. xi. 66 If I could cross a certain crevasse, my retreat would be secured.

fig. **1825** SCOTT *Let. to Mrs. W. Scott* 23 Mar. in *Lockhart* lxii, Seeing him in full retreat, I then ventured to make the civil offer of a dinner.

b. *esp.* of an army or armed force after defeat or to avoid an engagement. ***to beat a retreat*** (see BEAT *v.*[1] 30 b).

In quot. 1600 *made* is app. used in the sense of *covered*.

1579 DIGGES *Stratiot.* 145 If the Enimie vpon our retreite pursue vs, the Generall muste giue order to lay.. Ambushments of Shotte. **1600** DYMMOK *Ireland* (1843) 33 The rest of the horse troupes fell in before the rearewarde, except 30 which..made the retreit of the whole army. **1690** TEMPLE *Heroic Virtue* Wks. 1720 I. 231 The famous Retreat of Xenophon..was made at the Head of ten thousand Greeks. **1769** ROBERTSON *Chas. V*, IV. Wks. 1813 V. 413 To have mentioned a retreat to his soldiers would have been dangerous. **1797** *Encycl. Brit.* (ed. 3) XVI. 142/1 A good retreat is esteemed, by experienced officers, the masterpiece of a general. **1817** J. SCOTT *Paris Revisit.* (ed. 4) 132 Personal heroism..shewn by the commanders of our cavalry, who covered the retreat. **1841** ELPHINSTONE *Hist. Ind.* I. 615 He was so hard pressed on his retreat that he could not avoid an action. **1897** MARY KINGSLEY *W. Africa* 366 Six of his men were wounded, and the expedition was obliged to beat a retreat.

c. *Fencing.* (See quots.)

1809 ROLAND *Fencing* vi. On the Retreat. This motion is only just the contrary to that of the advance, being made by carrying the left foot..in a line backward [etc.]. **1861** CHAPMAN *Art of Fencing* II. 47 *note*, By feigning to recover in withdrawing the body by a spring of the knees termed 'the retreat of the body'.

d. Recession, retrogression.

1781 GIBBON *Decl. & F.* xxx. (1787) III. 159 The gradual retreat of the sea has left the modern city at the distance of four miles from the Hadriatic. **1815** PHILLIPS *Min. & Geol.* 74 There have been successive irruptions and retreats of the sea. **1833** HERSCHEL *Astron.* lvi. 215 The nodes of its [*sc.* moon's] orbit are in a continual state of retreat upon the ecliptic. **1914** W. B. WRIGHT *Quaternary Ice Age* vii. 155 They are named by Penck retreat-stadia ('Rückzugsstadien'), but it is considered probable that they were formed at the ends of periods of readvance. **1954** W. D. THORNBURY *Princ. Geomorphol.* viii. 201 The factors influencing the retreat of slopes are far more complex than is generally realized. **1963** R. A. DALY *Changing World of Ice Age* i. 21 (*caption*) Two principal moraines of retreat in Finland. **1970** R. J. SMALL *Study of Landforms* xi. 388 If the ice is affected by episodes of retreat, separated by stillstands, a number of smaller, sub-parallel ridges ('recessional' or 'stadial' moraines) will be formed.

4. a. The act of retiring or withdrawing into privacy, or into some place of safety. Also in ***place***, etc., ***of retreat***.

c **1475** *Partenay* 3944 Into a chambre ther made he retret, hit unshit entring, the dore after drew. **1601** HOLLAND *Pliny* II. 143 A city..into which the sicke and feeble souldiers of our armie were conueied, as to a place of retreat and repose. **1617** MORYSON *Itin.* I. 231 The Italian Friers haue chambers of retreat within the Church, in which we did eate and rest. **1698** FRYER *Acc. E. India & P.* 44 They..have these places as sure Asylums of Retreat. **1716** LADY M. W. MONTAGU *Lett.* I. 21 I saw the great towns..famous for the retreat of the imperial court when Vienna was besieged. **1719** DE FOE *Crusoe* II. (Globe) 412 That Walk was..divided into six equal Parts, which serv'd not only for Retreat, but to store up any Necessaries which the Family had Occasion for. **1820** KEATS *Lamia* I. 11 From high Olympus had he stolen light,..and made retreat Into a forest.

b. The act of withdrawing from society, public life, business, or office; retirement, seclusion.

1646 *Hamilton Papers* (Camden) 116 I lyke not your retreate, and will not forbeare to dissuade it. **1651** WALTON *Life Wotton*, [He] freely gave up his Crown.., making a holy retreat to a Cloysteral life. **1738** POPE *Epil. Sat.* II. 78 In the clear, still Mirror of Retreat, I study'd Shrewsbury, the wise and great. **1769** *Junius Lett.* i. (1788) 37 No expence should be spared to secure to him an honourable and affluent retreat. **1800** WELLESLEY in Owen *Desp.* (1877) 652 Prohibiting the grant of pensions of retreat to the civil service. **1855** MACAULAY *Hist. Eng.* xii. III. 168 His death, which took place not long after his retreat from public life. **1870** DICKENS *E. Drood* xvii, An air of retreat and solitude hung about the rooms, and about their inhabitant.

c. *Eccl.* A period of complete seclusion devoted to religious exercises.

1756 *Gentl. Mag.* XXVI. 342 Such retirement being in the language of the Roman Catholics called a retreat, and on the last day of such a retreat Bower writes his letter. **1862** *Union Newspaper* 11 Apr., There was some hope of a retreat being held for laymen in London. **1874** R. S. WILBERFORCE *Life Bp. Wilberforce* (1882) 56 *note*, When the Retreat was over.. the Bishop of Capetown, who had been present throughout the Retreat, sent to the college.

5. a. A place of seclusion or privacy; a retired place or residence; †a private chamber.

1423 JAS. I *Kingis Q.* xcvi, In a retrete lytill of compas, Depeyntit all with sighis.., Fond I Venus vpon hir bed. *c* **1500** *Melusine* 294 þey conduyted hym vnto a leghe nygh to the sayd geauntis retrette or pryue dwellyng. **1638** BAKER tr. *Balzac's Lett.* (vol. II.) 156, I am promised a retreate three miles from Bloys. **1697** DRYDEN *Virg. Georg.* IV. 216 With spreading Planes he made a cool Retreat, To shade good Fellows from the Summer's Heat. *c* **1709** PRIOR *Callimachus to Jupiter* 16 Holy Retreat! Sithence no Female hither..Must dare approach. **1766** in Ellis *Orig. Lett.* Ser. II. IV. 487, I still long after a retreat somewhere about you, or in Normandy, if a proper place could be found. **1831** LYTTON *Eugene Aram* I. x, But note how far more pure and lovely are its waters in these retreats. **1869** TOZER *Highl. Turkey* I. 54 Hermitages and retreats existed there at a very early time.

transf. **1850** W. SCORESBY *Cheever's Whalem. Adv.* v. (1858) 66 Into this odorous retreat it is the duty of one man immediately to descend.

b. A place of refuge or resort.

1662 J. DAVIES tr. *Mandelslo's Trav.* 116 It serves for a retreat to all Vessels which are constrained to quit the Coast of Gusuratta during the Winter season. **1697** DRYDEN *Æneid* x. 1306 Let my Body have, The last Retreat of Human kind, a Grave. **1751** JOHNSON *Rambler* No. 146 ¶7 Nor is it certain, that even of these dark and narrow habitations, these last retreats of fame, the possession will be long kept. **1796** H. HUNTER tr. *St.-Pierre's Stud. Nat.* (1799) III. 592 This territory might be..transferred to the unfortunate of all Nations, to serve them as a retreat. **1840** THIRLWALL *Greece* VII. 227 To make themselves masters of a part of the southern coast of Asia Minor, so as to provide a retreat for either in case of need. **1855** MACAULAY *Hist. Eng.* xix. IV. 243 That the building commenced by Charles should be completed, and should be a retreat for seamen disabled in the service of their country.

transf. **1669** R. MONTAGU in *Buccleuch MSS.* (Hist. MSS. Comm.) I. 465 The Commissionaire's place in the Treasury ..will be a good retreat for me when the King shall have no more occasion of my service here. **1769** *Junius Lett.* xxxv. (1788) 176 The mistakes of one sex find a retreat in patriotism, those of the other in devotion.

c. A hiding-place; a lair or den.

1774 GOLDSM. *Nat. Hist.* (1776) IV. 131 At no time are they found at any great distance from their retreats. **1832** R. & J. LANDER *Exped. Niger* I. v. 201 In my progress I disturbed a tiger-cat from his retreat among the rocks. **1849** MACAULAY *Hist. Eng.* iii. I. 285 It was often found impossible to track the robbers to their retreats among the hills.

†**d.** A privy. *Obs. rare*$^{-1}$.

1653 URQUHART *Rabelais* I. xl, The jakes and retreats of a house.

e. An establishment to which insane persons or habitual inebriates are admitted in order that they may be under proper supervision or control.

1797 [W. TUKE] (*title*), The State of an Institution near York, called the Retreat, for persons afflicted with Disorders of the Mind. **1835** SOUTHEY *Let.* Apr., I was under the necessity of taking my poor wife to the Retreat for Lunatics near York. **1850** *5th Ann. Rep. Comm. Lunacy* 4 'Claxton Grange Retreat,' near York, has been licensed..for private and pauper patients. **1879** *Act 42 & 43 Vict.* c. 19 §3 'A retreat' means a house licensed..for the reception, control, care, and curative treatment of habitual drunkards.

†**6. a.** The setting *of* a constellation, star, etc. (Cf. RETRAIT *sb.*[1] 4.) *Obs.*$^{-1}$

1601 HOLLAND *Pliny* XVII. xviii. I. 522 All other sorts [of trees]..are to be planted in mid-Winter, namely, after the retreat of the starre called Sagitta.

†**b.** Return, revenge. *Obs. rare*$^{-1}$.

1615 CHAPMAN *Odyss.* I. 59 As now Ægisthus,..to shunne his ill, Incurr'd it..In slaughtering Atrides in retreate.

†**7.** *Farriery.* (See quot. and RETRAIT *sb.*[1] 5.) *Obs.*

1580 BLUNDEVIL *Horsemanship* IV. cxlvii, Of a Retreate. This is the pricking of a naile, not well driuen in the shooing, and therefore pulled out againe by the Smith.

8. *Arch.* Recessed work; a recess or recessed part in a wall, etc.

1687 A. LOVELL tr. *Thevenot's Trav.* II. 145 There are six Figures on each side..and as many on the border in right Angle: all this in retreat. **1723** CHAMBERS tr. *Le Clerc's Archit.* I. 96 A little Indenture or Retreat, BC, not exceeding a Minute in depth. **1727–38** —— *Cycl.* s.v., Where the foundation is very large, they usually make two or three retreats. **1859** F. A. GRIFFITHS *Artil. Man.* (1862) 269 The retreat or lessening, has a width of 1 foot.

†**9.** *Law.* Redemption, recovery. (See quots.) *Obs.*

1682 WARBURTON *Hist. Guernsey* (1822) 90 Retreat of inheritance is taken from the custom of Normandy. *Ibid.* 91 The next of kin shall have but a year and a day to bring his enrollement, and if he neglects that time, he will be excluded from his retreat.

10. *Comb.*, as ***retreat house***.

1920 J. F. BRISCOE in *Rep. First Anglo-Catholic Congress* 182 There ought to be a retreat-house in every diocese. **1958** *Church Times* 14 Feb. 10/3 With its membership growing, part of the accommodation in the retreat house has had to be taken to house the brethren. **1979** *Country Life* 6 Dec. 2188/3 Rydal Hall..was leased to the diocese of Carlisle.. as a retreat house and conference centre.

retreat (rɪˈtriːt), *v.*[1] Forms: 4–5 retrete, 5–6 retret, 6 retreyte, 6–7 retreit(t, 6– retreat (6 -te). [ad. OF. *retraire* (pa. pple. *retrait*) or *retraiter* to withdraw, *retraitier* to retract, with vowel accommodated to the sb.]

1. *intr.* To withdraw, retire, draw back.

1422 tr. *Secreta Secret., Priv. Priv.* 242 Whyle that a man slepyth, al the wittis restyth; and than retretith the natural hette that spredyth abrode throgh al the body. *a* **1548** HALL *Chron., Hen. VIII*, 33 b, Then the kynge retreted to Gingate. **1642** H. MORE *Song of Soul* III. i. 6 When base worms have eat His mouldring brains, and spirits have retreat From whence they came. **1671** GREW *Anat. Pl.* I. ii. (1682) 15 The remainder, though not united to it,..thus retreats, that is,..is in part carried off into the Cortical Body back again. **1704** POPE *Summer* 86 But see, the shepherds shun the noonday heat, The lowing herds to murm'ring brooks retreat. **1769** *Junius Lett.* xv. (1788) 89 You have now carried things too far to retreat. **1843** LD. COCKBURN *Jrnl.* II. 8 It may be predicted with absolute certainty that all these judgments will be retreated from. **1860** TYNDALL *Glac.* I. xvi. 112 Sometimes..we were compelled to retreat to the highest cliffs.

b. Of an army or a combatant: To retire before superior force or after a defeat.

1596 SPENSER *F.Q.* IV. vi. 15 She him forced backward to retreat, And yeeld unto her weapon way to pas. *a* **1604** HANMER *Chron. Irel.* (1633) 156 The souldiers take hart, and drive the Irish to retreit. **1645** WHITELOCK *Mem.* 3 Mar., Major Blundell..came up and charged the enemy, retreated, and came on again. **1716** POPE *Iliad* v. 863 Slow they retreat, and, e'en retreating, fight. **1762** STERNE *Tr. Shandy* VI. xxxiv, We will..demolish..the rest, one by one, ..as we retreat towards the town. **1802** JAMES *Milit. Dict.* s.v., The several component parts of a line or battalion, which alternately retreat and face in the presence of an enemy. **1844** H. H. WILSON *Brit. India* II. 286 He..is said ..to have shed tears when he saw his troops retreat from the field. **1876** VOYLE & STEVENSON *Milit. Dict.* 341/1 To retreat with a harassed and broken army is the most difficult position a commander can be put in.

c. In pa. pple. with *is*, *was*, etc.

1648 *Hamilton Papers* (Camden) 224 The enemy is retreated from Stanwicke this morninge. **1660** BOYLE *New Exp. Phys. Mech.* xvii. 126 There was some Air retreated thither that kept the Mercury out of the unreplenish'd space. **1667** MILTON *P.L.* II. 547 Others more milde, Retreated in a silent valley, sing With notes Angelical..Thir own Heroic deeds and hapless fall. **1793** SMEATON *Edystone L.* §241 The tide being then retreated. **1843** CARLYLE *Past & Pr.* (1858) 154 King Henry and his force got safely retreated.

d. To recede.

1863 HAWTHORNE *Our Old Home* I. 113 The forehead.. retreats somewhat. **1878** BOSW. SMITH *Carthage* 230 Between these two points the hills retreat from the lake in the form of a semicircle.

2. *trans.* To draw or lead back; to remove, take away. Now chiefly in *Chess*, to move (a piece) back from a forward or threatened position.

1523 LD. BERNERS *Froiss.* I. cxc. 225 He retreated all his menne as soberly as he might. *a* **1548** HALL *Chron., Hen. VIII*, 121 b, He did what he might to retreate the souldiers. **1589** GREENE *Tullies Love* Wks. (Grosart) VII. 161 Thinking by retreating Terentia from the chace, to be mistresse of the game hir selfe. **1650** EARL MONM. tr. *Senault's Man bec. Guilty* 57 When Originall righteousnesse was retreated the Elements began to mutiny. **1719** DE FOE *Crusoe* II. (Globe) 319 The most agreeable Life that..a Man always bred to Misfortunes was capable of being retreated to. **1724** —— *Mem. Cavalier* (1840) 66 As they were wheeled, or marched, or retreated by their officers. **1847** STAUNTON *Chess Player's Hdbk.* 203 Provided Black retreats his B. to Q. Kt.'s 3rd. **1886** *Illustr. Lond. News* 28 Aug. 235 He had no choice but to retreat the bishop.

†**b.** *refl.* To retire, withdraw. *Obs. rare.*

1495 *Act 11 Hen. VII*, c. 7 Preamble, Suche persones as so retret and absent theymself. **1532** MORE *Confut. Tindale* Wks. 447/1 They flee by night and retrete themself in the darke. **1572** *Deposit.* in *Old Ways* (1892) 32 Therfore this deponent did retreat herself unto the other man, with whom she hath now married.

c. To retrace, go back on (one's course). *rare*$^{-1}$.

1591 SYLVESTER *Du Bartas* I. iii. 79 His dreadfull voice.. toward the Crystall of his double source Compelled Jordan to retreat his course.

†**d.** To diminish, reduce. *Obs. rare*$^{-1}$.

1690 LOCKE *Hum. Und.* II. xvi. §5 And so again, by abstracting an unit from each Collection, retreat and lessen them.

†**3.** *Sc.* To retract, revoke. *Obs.*

1500–20 DUNBAR *Poems* xiv. 51 Sa mony ane sentence retreitit, for to win Geir and acquentance. **1558** KNOX *First Blast* (Arb.) 49 With common consent they oght to retreate that, which vnaduisedlie..they haue pronounced. **1581–2** *Reg. Privy Council Scot.* III. 454 [The king] revokis, retretis, cassis and annullis, all..ratificationis of the said tak. **1637–50** ROW *Hist. Kirk* (Wodrow Soc.) 500 Some surpryzed with it, upon better and second thoughts retreated their subscriptions. **1678** SIR G. MACKENZIE *Crim. Laws Scot.* I. i. §iii. (1699) 4 The L. of Session thought it not derogatory from their Honour, to retreat a Sentence after Debate.

†**4.** *Law.* To redeem. Also *absol.* *Obs. rare.*

1682 WARBURTON *Hist. Guernsey* (1822) 91 A. does by reason of proximity, enroll himself to retreat such an inheritance as B. has purchased of C. his kinsman. *Ibid.*, The next of kin to the seller shall have but a year and a day to retreat.

Hence **re'treated** *ppl. a.*

1665 DRYDEN *Indian Queen* I. i, Rather to your retreated Troops appear, And let them see a Woman void of Fear.

re-'treat (riː-), *v.*[2] [RE- 5 a.] To treat again.

1882 *U.S. Rep. Prec. Metals* 462 No regular and systematic work has been accomplished for producing bullion except to re-treat old tailings. **1887** A. M. BROWN *Anim. Alkaloids* 82 The tissue-residue is then retreated with alcohol at 90°.

retreatal, *a.* (rɪˈtriːtəl). [f. RETREAT *v.*[1] + -AL.] Of or pertaining to the contraction and retreat of ice sheets and glaciers.

1896 *Amer. Geologist* XVIII. 156 The stages of retreatal deposits ending in Greenwich cove illustrate the shrinkage and final disappearance of a tongue of the ice. *Ibid.* 160 (*heading*) Retreatal formations on the central and eastern shores of the bay. **1937** *Geogr. Jrnl.* XC. 233 Most of this erosion occurred during the maximum stage of glaciation and very little during the retreatal stages. **1937** WOOLDRIDGE & MORGAN *Physical Basis of Geogr.* xxii. 378 Retreatal stages of the ice in the valleys are marked by 'stadial moraines'. **1968** R. W. FAIRBRIDGE *Encycl. Geomorphol.* 327/1 Bergdahl (1963) has recently published a series of studies on the Närke plain where estuarine clays from the Baltic progressively overlap closely spaced ridges of retreatal moraines, each winter season being marked by another ridge, at 170–280 meter intervals.

re'treatant. [f. RETREAT *v.*[1] + -ANT.] One who takes part in a religious retreat.

1880 *Echo* 18 Sept. 1/5 One [prayer] which asks for a blessing upon a 'conductor of a retreat and forty-two retreatants' may be mentioned for the introduction of a new and awkward word into the vocabulary of a section of the Anglican priesthood. **1899** *Month* May 466 The nuns have placed large rooms and dormitories at the disposal of the retreatants.

reˈtreater. [f. as prec. + -ER[1].]
 1. One who retreats.
 1643 *Prince Rupert's beating up the Rebels' Quarters* 8 He stopt and drew the Retreaters up into a body. **1812** *Examiner* 14 Dec. 799/1 The Russians cannot bring the retreaters into any great..scrape.
 2. = RETREATANT.
 1889 *Pall Mall G.* 2 Oct. 6/1 Many of the 'retreaters' are ladies who play no small part in London society.

reˈtreatful, *a. rare*$^{-1}$. [f. RETREAT *sb.* + -FUL.] Furnishing, or serving as, a retreat.
 a **1634** CHAPMAN (Webster), Our retreatful flood.

reˈtreating, *vbl. sb.* [f. RETREAT *v.*[1] + -ING[1].] The action of the verb in various senses.
 1589 *Reg. Privy Council Scot.* IV. 388 Divers utheris personis..hes obtenit certane pretendit retreitingis of the saidis sentenceis. **1664** BUTLER *Hud.* II. ii. 579 To secure, by swift retreating, Themselves from danger of worse beating. **1707** *Curios. in Husb. & Gard.* 19 He justifies himself for his retreating to his House. **1805** WORDSW. *Waggoner* III. 141 Such retreating and advancing As..was never seen In bloodiest battle. **1876** VOYLE & STEVENSON *Milit. Dict.* 341/1 The increased range of ordnance and small-arms nowadays renders retreating still more precarious.
 attrib. **1659** *Clarke Papers* (Camden) IV. 289 In case you showld reseave anie foyle, your retreating place is lost. **1730–46** THOMSON *Autumn* 493 When the retreating horn Calls them to ghostly halls of grey renown. **1820** BYRON *Juan* v. cvii, The lady..bade Baba retire, which he obey'd in style, As if well used to the retreating trade. **1828–43** TYTLER *Hist. Scot.* (1864) I. 118 The minds of the Scottish commanders were not in a retreating mood. **1876** VOYLE & STEVENSON *Milit. Dict.* 341/1 To..overcome all obstacles incidental to a retreating march.

reˈtreating, *ppl. a.* [f. as prec. + -ING[2].]
 1. That retreats; retiring.
 1667 MILTON *P.L.* XI. 850 With clamor thence the rapid Currents drive Towards the retreating Sea thir furious tyde. **1810** CRABBE *Borough* xxiii. 284 Her trembling joy appears, Her forced reserve, and his retreating fears. **1836** THIRLWALL *Greece* xxiii. III. 279 Who were all..unwilling to attack the retreating enemy. **1855** MACAULAY *Hist. Eng.* xviii. IV. 239 The English..set them [*sc.* men-of-war] on fire, and..retreated at a late hour with the retreating tide. **1961** M. LEVY *Studio Dict. Art Terms* 97 *Retreating colour*, a colour, such as blue, which in a painting appears to retreat into the distance. **1962** *Punch* 25 Apr. 655/2 'Retreating defence'—the rapid funnelling back and massing of defenders inside the penalty area. **1977** *Daily Express* 29 Mar. 32/4 The 'reserves' had an extra couple of players, in the form of the England coaching staff, to thicken a retreating defence still further.
 2. Receding.
 1840 DICKENS *Old C. Shop* xi, A protruding forehead, retreating eyes. **1878** BOSW. SMITH *Carthage* 230 Along these retreating hills Hannibal placed the main part of his army. **1887** *Brit. Med. Jrnl.* 8 Jan. 49/1 Typical examples of the negroid family, with..the puffy lips, and retreating chin.
 Hence **reˈtreatingness.**
 1897 SLADEN in *Windsor Mag.* Jan. 277/2 The boldness of these bow-windows and the retreatingness of the roof.

retreatism (rɪˈtriːtɪz(ə)m). [f. RETREAT *sb.* + -ISM.] **1.** A policy of retreat; advocacy of (military) withdrawal.
 1951 *Times* 24 Feb. 7/3 General Eisenhower returned to Europe this week bringing assurance that his country has rejected the 'retreatism' advocated by Mr. Herbert Hoover and supported by Senator Taft. **1976** J. ROWAN *Ordinary Ecstasy* ii. 25 If we see everything as perfect as it is, we may be inclined to quietism and retreatism in political terms.
 2. *Sociol.* A state of passive withdrawal from society induced by a sense of inability to attain its norms or to offer resistance to them.
 1957 R. K. MERTON *Social Theory* (rev. ed.) iv. 153 Retreatism..is an expedient which arises from continued failure to near the goal by legitimate measures and from an inability to use the illegitimate route because of internalized prohibitions. **1963** T. & P. MORRIS *Pentonville* vii. 173 Retreatism in prison is comparatively rare, and can be identified with either an extreme manifestation of institutional neurosis..or with various stages of mental illness. **1969** in Lindzey & Aronson *Handbk. Social Psychol.* (ed. 2) IV. xxxiii. 352 With warfare no longer possible, there is a great deal of retreatism and social withdrawal. **1970** *New Society* 31 Dec. 1158/2 Thus, men like Roy..would still maintain that the only rational solution was retreatism.

retreatist (rɪˈtriːtɪst), *sb.* (and *a.*) [f. as prec. + -IST.] **1.** One who advocates a policy of retreat; a supporter of (military) withdrawal.
 a **1925** CURZON *Leaves from Viceroy's Notebk.* (1926) iii. 142 The Retreatists would not have these proposals at any price. **1951** *Times* 20 Feb. 4/5 Mr. Wherry and others like him..now dislike being called isolationists, but have been called 'retreatists' instead.
 2. *Sociol.* One who has succumbed to retreatism (sense 2).
 1957 R. K. MERTON *Social Theory* (rev. ed.) v. 189 Retreatists are even more reluctant to enter into new social relations with others than are those described as 'alienated'. **1960** CLOWARD & OHLIN *Delinquency & Opportunity* i. 21 These terms..do not necessarily reflect the attitudes of members of the subcultures. Thus the term 'retreatist' does not necessarily reflect the attitude of the 'cat'. **1963** T. & P. MORRIS *Pentonville* vii. 173 The retreatist rejects both goals and means.
 3. *attrib.* or as *adj.*
 1957 R. K. MERTON *Social Theory* (rev. ed.) v. 187 The retreatist pattern consists of the substantial abandoning both of the once-esteemed cultural goals and of institutionalized practices directed toward those goals. **1973** *Sociol. Rev.* XXI. 419 The attitudes and values of people whom they call retreatist, and the immediate conditions under which the response occurs.

retreative (rɪˈtriːtɪv), *a.* [f. RETREAT *sb.* or *v.*[1] + -IVE.] Pertaining to or suggestive of retreat; tending to withdraw.
 1899 B. TARKINGTON *Gentleman from Indiana* xix. 376 As they neared the brick house Harkless made out, through the trees, a retreative flutter of skirts on the porch. **1977** *Times Lit. Suppl.* 25 Mar. 332/3 A melancholic, self-retreative, self-distrustful constitution.

†**reˈtreatment**[1]. *Obs. rare*$^{-1}$. [f. as RETREATING *ppl. a.* + -MENT.] Retirement, retreat.
 a **1721** D'URFEY *Operas*, etc. 236 Our Prophet's great Retreatment we From Mecca to Medina see.

re-ˈtreatment[2]. [RE- 5 a: cf. RE-TREAT *v.*[2]] Further or renewed treatment.
 1867 J. A. PHILLIPS *Mining & Metallurgy Gold & Silver* x. 216 (*heading*) Re-treatment of first tailings. **1882** *U.S. Rep. Prec. Metals* 602 Nearly all the sand and dust..is periodically removed for retreatment, as it contains a notable quantity of gold. **1895** WORKMAN *Algerian Mem.* xii, A road deteriorates rapidly, which renders a re-treatment with stone necessary.

retree (rɪˈtriː). [? ad. F. *retret*, obs. variant of *retrait* (cf. *retrait de mouture* refuse flour), or F. *retiré*, pa. pple. of *retirer* to RETIRE.] In paper-making, the damaged or defective sheets of paper.
 1807 in Ure *Dict. Arts* (1839) 932 The quantity of broken paper and retree is almost nothing compared with what is made at the vats. **1867** *Philol. Soc. Trans.* 74 There are different degrees of Retree, having reference to different degrees of defectiveness. **1884** *Stationery Trade Rev.* Sept. 216/1 Those sheets which contain spots, or are otherwise imperfectly made, are separated from the well-authenticated sheets, and the broken make is called retree.

retrench (rɪˈtrɛnʃ), *v.*[1] [ad. F. *retrencher*, obs. variant of *retrancher*: see RE- and TRENCH *v.*, and cf. RETRANCH *v.*]
 †**1.** *trans.* To cut short, check, repress. *Obs.*
 1607 EARL STIRLING *J. Cæsar* II. ii, Whose rising hopes must be retrench'd so soone. *a* **1661** FULLER *Worthies* I. (1662) 21 Since their violence hath (blessed be God) been seasonably retrenched. **1688** S. PARKER *Reas. Abrogat. Test* 89 Under the pious Reigns of David and Solomon the Sin of Idolatry was competently well retrench'd.
 †**2.** To cut off, bar (a way or passage). *Obs.*
 1614 RALEIGH *Hist. World* IV. i. (1634) 460 They retrench'd his passage at the streights of Thermopilis. *a* **1618** —— *Prerog. Parl.* Ep. Ded., Notwithstanding my restraint hath retrenched all wayes.., yet hath it left with me my cogitations.
 3. To cut down, reduce, diminish, in extent, amount, or number.
 1625 *Ho. Comm. Debates* (Camden) 86 Annuityes which..former parliaments have used to retrenche. **1649** *Alcoran* 3 Such as retrench his Commandments, and defile the Earth, are damned. **1673** [R. LEIGH] *Transp. Reh.* 98 They have..confer'd too large a power in civil affairs..; they will be sure to retrench it in spirituals. **1711** ADDISON *Spect.* No. 7 ¶4 It is the chief Concern of Wise-Men, to retrench the Evils of Life by the Reasonings of Philosophy. **1763** MILLS *Syst. Pract. Husb.* III. 267 It is now some time since I have fed my coach-horses with it, and have retrenched their oats. **1853** C. BRONTË *Villette* xvi, Even with them, all had not gone smoothly, and fortune had retrenched her once abundant gifts.
 b. *esp.* To reduce, curtail (one's expenses, etc.) by the exercise of economy.
 1709 STEELE & ADDISON *Tatler* No. 101 ¶7, I..must be forced to retrench my expensive Way of Living. **1732** FIELDING *Miser* I. vii, If you would..retrench your extravagance on this occasion, perhaps the difference..might be made up. **1796** MORSE *Amer. Geogr.* I. 295 The colonies therefore entered into measures to..retrench the use of foreign superfluities. **1849** MACAULAY *Hist. Eng.* II. 263 He could retrench his expenses by giving up the costly and useless settlement of Tangier. **1863** FAWCETT *Pol. Econ.* I. iv. 43 If the people..are induced to retrench their expenditure, trade will suffer.
 4. To cut short; to reduce in size. ? *Obs.*
 a **1667** COWLEY *Of Plants* Pref., The very Lowness of your Subject has retrenched your Wings. **1705** in *Lett. Lit. Men* (Camden) 314, I was forced to retrench it half a sheet to make it of the same price of others. **1711** ADDISON *Spect.* No. 129 ¶6 That all Women of Fashion were cutting their old Muffs in two, or retrenching them, according to the little Model which was got among them. **1784** COWPER *Task* II. 318 It may correct a foible,..Retrench a sword-blade, or displace a patch.
 †**b.** To deprive *of* (the thing removed). *Obs.*
 1664 BUTLER *Hud.* II. ii. 23 Many a face Retrench'd of Nose, and Eyes, and Beard. **1698** T. FROGER *Voy.* Pref., I have retrencht it of those tedious particulars. **1721** BRADLEY *Philos. Acc. Wks. Nat.* 76 The Vegetables, which the Winter-Frosts retrenched of their Beauties, are enlivened.
 5. To cut off, remove, take away.
 c **1650** DENHAM *Old Age* iii, The pruner's hand, with letting blood, must quench Thy heat, and thy exuberant parts retrench. **1672** MARVELL *Reh. Transp.* I. 28 He retrenches..on our part more than he hath Authority for. **1718** *Freethinker* No. 96. 294 It is easier to retrench what is Superfluous, than to supply what is Deficient. **1723** CHAMBERS tr. *Le Clerc's Archit.* I. 118, I retrench one Modillion from the Corniche. **1773** GOLDSM. *Stoops to Conquer* II, Is there anything else you wish to retrench or alter, gentlemen? **1812** *Gen. Hist.* in *Ann. Reg.* 135 In others [*sc.* Parliaments] a year only had been retrenched from their term of existence. **1849** MACAULAY *Hist. Eng.* vi. II. 14 He gradually retrenched all the privileges which the schismatics enjoyed.
 b. To do away with (an item of expense).
 1647 CLARENDON *Hist. Reb.* I. §108 His Credit was ample enough..to Retrench very much of the late unlimited Expences. **1680** DRYDEN *Prol. to Lee's Cæsar Borgia* 28 So big you look, though claret you retrench, That, armed with bottled ale, you huff the French. **1714** *Spect.* No. 622 ¶9 To retrench one Dish at my Table, till I have fetched it [£10] up again. **1741** LADY M. W. MONTAGU *Lett.* III. 37 It is true, as all equipages are forbidden, that expense is entirely retrenched. **1855** MACAULAY *Hist. Eng.* xv. III. 566 When every gentleman, every farmer, was retrenching something from the charge of his table and his cellar.
 c. To cut out, omit, excise, delete (some portion of a book or document).
 c **1645** HOWELL *Lett.* VI. To Rdr., Therfore the Author hath taken pains to retrench such redundant, unnecessary Letters in this Work. **1704** SWIFT *Mech. Operat. Spir.* Misc. (1711) 271, I retrench'd those Parts that might give most Offence; and have now ventur'd to publish the Remainder. **1741** WATTS *Improv. Mind* I. iv, Where he is redundant, mark those paragraphs to be retrenched. **1839** HALLAM *Hist. Lit.* IV. vi. §18 The structure of his style is such that nothing could be displaced, nothing added, nothing retrenched. **1869** SWINBURNE *Ess. & Stud.* (1875) 268 His 'Ode to Tranquillity', beginning with two stanzas since retrenched.
 6. *intr.* To economize, reduce expenses.
 1663 PEPYS *Diary* 26 July, For his family expenses and others, he would labour, however, to retrench in many things convenient. **1737** POPE *Hor. Epist.* I. vii. 75 Can I retrench? Yes, mighty well, Shrink back to my Paternal Cell. *c* **1820** S. ROGERS *Italy* (1836) 170 If rich, they go to enjoy; if poor, to retrench. **1855** MACAULAY *Hist. Eng.* xviii. IV. 121 Every man who lived..on the fruits of his own industry was forced to retrench.
 b. To make excisions or diminutions. *rare.*
 1700 ROWE *Amb. Step Moth.* Ep. Ded., I was led into an Error in the writing of it, by thinking that it would be easier to retrench than to add. **1813** J. C. HOBHOUSE *Journey* (ed. 2) 1039 The Vizier openly avowed his resolution of abolishing the Janissaries, or at least of..retrenching upon their privileges.
 Hence **reˈtrenched** *ppl. a.*[1]; **reˈtrenching** *vbl. sb.* and *ppl. a.*
 1681 OWEN *Design Judgments* Wks. 1851 VIII. 632 They cannot go about it without great retrenchings of that which they have esteemed their liberty. **1780** HARRIS *Philol. Enq.* Wks. (1841) 396 All ancient books..were liable..to be corrupted in three different ways; that is to say, by retrenchings, by additions, and by alterations. **1831** LADY GRANVILLE *Lett.* (1894) II. 81 A retrenching and vexatious public. **1859** J. TAYLOR *Logic Theol.* 322 These figures, ought they then to receive a retrenched interpretation? **1866** *Morn. Star* 26 July, When the history of retrenching Administrations in this country comes to be written.

retrench (rɪˈtrɛnʃ), *v.*[2] [f. as prec.] *trans.* (and *refl.*). To protect by, to furnish with, a retrenchment. Also *absol.* and *fig.*
 1598 BARRET *Mod. Warres* 131 To rampire, repaire, and to retrench against batteries. **1600** R. CHURCH *Fumée's Hungary* 147 They perceived how the Turks were retrenched within. **1675** *Lond. Gaz.* No. 1019/3 The Besiegers had perfectly retrenched themselves between the said Abby and the place. **1690** *Great Scanderberg* 116 He..saw Musselman retrenched in a steep Rock. **1705** ADDISON *Italy* 513 To retrench themselves within the Conveniencies and Necessities of Life. **1828** J. M. SPEARMAN *Brit. Gunner* (ed. 2) 210 When the ravelin has no réduit, it may be retrenched by a parapet en tenaille; but the narrow ravelins of Cormontaingne can only be retrenched by coupures, across their faces. **1863** KINGLAKE *Crimea* II. 50 But when they sprang a mine, they ever found that behind the ruins the Turks stood retrenched.
 Hence **reˈtrenched** *ppl. a.*[2]
 1776 LEE in Sparks *Corr. Amer. Rev.* (1853) I. 152 To prepare a post, or retrenched encampment,..opposite to the city. **1828** J. M. SPEARMAN *Brit. Gunner* (ed. 2) 215 When a retrenched camp is to be formed under the walls of a fortified place, the works may be continuous. **1876** VOYLE & STEVENSON *Milit. Dict.* 341/1 So that the capture of the lines shall not involve that of the retrenched post.

re-ˈtrench, *v.*[3] [RE- 5 a.] To trench again.
 1778 [W. MARSHALL] *Minutes Agric., Observ.* 106 They were thoroughly harrowed, and presently afterwards retrenched and cross-furrowed for the winter.

reˈtrencher. [-ER[1].] One who retrenches.
 1882 C. D. WARNER *Irving* vi. 135 Merciless retrenchers of beauty and enjoyment. **1884** A. A. PUTNAM *10 Yrs. Police Judge* v. 32 The knock-down argument..emanating from the most conspicuous retrencher.

retrenchment[1] (rɪˈtrɛnʃmənt). [a. F. *retrenchement*, obs. variant of *retranchement*: see RETRENCH *v.*[1] and -MENT.]
 1. The act of cutting down, off, or out; curtailment, limitation, reduction.
 c **1600** SIR F. VERE *Cæsar's Comm.* 47 By a retrenchment of the condition I was to hold in this journey. **1654** tr. *Scudery's Curia Pol.* 151 If I should deprive her of the Crown without the retrenchment of her head. **1692** DRYDEN *St. Euremont's Ess.* 12 It was not a retrenchment of superfluities, or a voluntary abstinence from things agreeable. **1713** *Guardian* No. 149 The men have contented themselves with the retrenchment of the hat, or the various scallop of the pocket. **1765** *Museum Rust.* IV. 20 These retrenchments, made in the proper time, are likely to strengthen..both fruit and branch. **1827** STEUART *Planter's G.* (1828) 443 Such retrenchment, however, must always be modified, by the actual wants of the Trees.
 b. The act of excising, deleting, or omitting; an instance of this.
 a **1691** BOYLE *Wks.* (1772) VI. 716, I rather wish than expect that you should give yourself the trouble, by transpositions of some, and retrenchments in others, to link them into a coherent discourse. **1768–74** TUCKER *Lt. Nat.* (1834) II. 423 Additions have been made every now and then to our [divine] offices, but never any retrenchments.

1820 SCOTT *Abbot* Introd. Ep., I admit that my retrenchments have been numerous, and leave gaps in the story. **1867** *Morn. Star* 17 Sept. 3 Besides this one retrenchment of the text, the changes made are very trifling.

2. The act of economizing or cutting down expenditure; a cast of this.

1667 PEPYS *Diary* 9 Aug., We did talk of many retrenchments of charge of the Navy which he will put in practice. **1675** MARVELL *Corr.* Wks. (Grosart) II. 433, I have made a considerable retrenchment upon my expences in candles and charcoal. *a* **1731** ATTERBURY (J.), I would rather be an advocate for the retrenchment, than the encrease of this charity. **1792** ALMON *Anecd. of W. Pitt* I. xx. 332 Amongst Pitt's other retrenchments were his coach horses, which were sold by public advertisement. **1834** HT. MARTINEAU *Moral* IV. 137 The cry for retrenchment is a righteous cry; but all power of retrenchment does not lie with the Government. **1868** HELPS *Realmah* iii, Reform has gone too far in the way of retrenchment. **1899** *Daily News* 19 April 5/1 There are two things which bring about a desire for national retrenchment—new taxation and bad trade.

retrenchment[2] (rɪˈtrenʃmənt). *Mil.* [f. as prec.] A work, generally consisting of a trench and parapet, constructed for the defence of a position; *esp.* an inner line of defence within a large work. Also *fig.* and *transf.*

1589 P. IVE *Fortification* 25 At which may a retrenchment bee made when need requireth, and the same well flanked. **1642** ROGERS *Naaman* 101 In the defence of a City.. there be some out-workes, halfe-moones and retrenchments to hold the enemy at larger distance. **1683** *Lond. Gaz.* No. 1856/6 We have made in the middle of the Ravelin a good Retrenchment with a good Ditch. **1709** SWIFT & ADDISON *Tatler* No. 32 ¶7 The Enemy lay encamped behind a strong Retrenchment. **1739** ELIZ. CARTER tr. *Algarotti on Newton's The.* (1742) II. 211 Des Cartes.. is attacked in his very last Retrenchments. **1828** J. M. SPEARMAN *Brit. Gunner* (ed. 2) 209 To permit the ditch of the réduit to be defended from the rear of the retrenchment. **1879** *Encycl. Brit.* IX. 447/1 In bastions strengthened by a cavalier retrenchment, a coupure is formed perpendicularly across the faces of the bastion.

†**re'tret**, *sb. Obs. rare*⁻¹. [Cf. next.] Rehandling of a subject.

1556 J. HEYWOOD *Spider & F.* xiv. 36, I shall (for a season) set that apart, And partly peruse, by way of retret, Sum part of this matter graunted before.

†**re'trete**, *v. Obs. rare.* [ad. OF. **retreter*, var. of *retrait(i)er*:—L. *retractāre* to rehandle.] *trans.* **a.** To relate, recount. **b.** To treat of again.

13.. *E.E. Allit. P.* A. 92 Fowlez þer flowen.., boþe smale & grete, Bot sytole stryng & gyternere Her reken myrþe moȝt not retrete. *c* **1374** CHAUCER *Boeth.* v. Met. iii. (Skeat) 136 Him remembreth the somme of thinges that he withholdeth, and axeth conseil, and retreteth deepliche thinges y-seyn biforn.

re'trial (riː-). [RE- 5 a.] The act of retrying; a second or new trial.

1875 POSTE *Gaius* IV. 578 The re-trial of the more important issue would be barred. **1898** *Westm. Gaz.* 17 Mar. 2/3 Much of the material at present considered by the Home Office in reconsidering a sentence would be excluded from the re-trial.

retribalization (riːˌtraɪbəlaɪˈzeɪʃən). [f. next.] The process of making or becoming retribalized.

1964 M. MCLUHAN *Understanding Media* II. xxxii. 344 Today we appear to be poised between two ages—one of detribalization and one of retribalization. **1967** *Listener* 20 July 75/1 What Marshall McLuhan calls the tendency to retribalization in the multi-sensual experiences enjoyed by young people. **1970** *Internat. & Compar. Law Q.* XIX. I. 152 The general retribalisation designs of the present régime.

retribalize (riːˈtraɪbəlaɪz), *v.* [f. RE- + TRIBAL *a.* + -IZE. Cf. DETRIBALIZE *v.*] *trans.* To restore (a person or society) to a tribal state; to encourage the tribal instincts and habits of. So **re'tribalized** *ppl. a.*; **re'tribalizing** *vbl. sb.*

1963 *Economist* 7 Sept. 805/2 A sprinkling of retribalised black statelets. **1964** M. MCLUHAN *Understanding Media* II. xxiii. 229 It was easy for the retribalized Nazi to feel superior to the American consumer. *Ibid.* xxiv. 236 We have begun retribalizing with the same painful groping with which a preliterate society begins to read and write. *Ibid.* xxx. 304 The power of radio to retribalize mankind, its almost instant reversal of individualism into collectivism, Fascist or Marxist, has gone unnoticed. **1967** *Guardian* 9 Sept. 6/3 The effect of television as such is to retribalise and deliteratise mankind. **1969** A. COHEN *Custom & Politics in Urban Africa* i. 29 As the migrant becomes more settled, by being drawn into active participation in the social life of the Quarter—economically, politically, morally, and ritually—he becomes increasingly more '*retribalized*'.

†**retribuer.** *Obs. rare*⁻¹. [ad. OF. *retribueur*: see next.] = RETRIBUTOR.

1512 *Helyas* in Thoms *Prose Rom.* (1828) III. 40 God that is the true iudge and only retribuer of good and evil.

retributary, variant of RETRIBUTORY.

retribute (rɪˈtrɪbjuːt, ˈrɛtrɪbjuːt), *v.* Now *rare.* [f. L. *retribūt-*, ppl. stem of *retribuĕre*, f. *re-* RE- + *tribuĕre* to give, assign.]

1. *trans.* To give in return; to make return of; to retaliate (something) *on* one.

1575 FENTON *Gold. Epist.* (1582) 9, I haue retributed that recompence whiche belongeth to the power of so pore a friend. **1579** —— *Guicciard.* IX. (1599) 356 To whom in particular were retributed no small rewardes. **1621** S. WARD *Life Faith* 64 Hath Christ giuen himselfe for thee,.. and what hast thou to retribute? **1643** G. CHUDLEIGH *Declaration* 4 The King giveth life and motion to the Law, and the Law retributes vertue and operation to the King. **1702** *Pres. St. Jacobitism* 27 [It] tied up the Hands of Power from retributing the like measure on themselves. **1866** J. B. ROSE tr. *Ovid's Fasti* v. 352 She retributed slight on friend and foe.

2. To make return for; to repay.

1612 T. TAYLOR *Comm. Titus* i. 1 Ready to retribute our fidelitie with infinite aduantage. **1633** BP. HALL *Hard Texts, N.T.* 330 Neither..can God be unrighteous in not perfecting and retributing that your painfull love. **1663** ORMONDE in Carte *Life* (1736) II. 273 Injuries to be remembered upon all occasions, and retributed by crossing my desires, when they aim at just things. **1933** W. H. W. SABINE *Guido & Girls* xi. 130 Those foul thoughts that lately have been mine, Thus justly retributed by the laws.. that are divine.

3. *intr.* To make a return or requital.

1612-5 BP. HALL *Contempl., O.T.* XVII. vi. 1224 It is dishonourable to take from equals, and not to retribute. **1643** SIR T. BROWNE *Relig. Med.* (1682) 29 All wherein an humble Creature may endeavour to requite, and some way to retribute unto his Creator. **1689** POPPLE tr. *Locke's 1st Let. Toleration* L.'s Wks. 1727 II. 250 God.. is the only Judge in this Case, who will retribute unto every one at the last Day. *a* **1731** DE FOE *Mrs. Veal* Pref., A just God who will retribute to every one according to the deeds done in the body.

Hence **retributing** *vbl. sb.*

a **1660** HAMMOND *Serm.* Wks. 1850 III. 355 What Christian soever can indulge himself the enjoyment.. of revenge, or retributing of injuries [etc.]. **1686** W. DE BRITAINE *Hum. Prud.* ix. 42 But I can admit the re-tributing of good turns.

†**retribute**, *ppl. a. Obs.*⁻¹ [ad. L. *retribūt-us*, pa. pple. of *retribuĕre*: see prec.] Returned.

1673 KIRKMAN *Unlucky Citizen* 266 Here was Retalliation, absolute Revenge, Resolute, and Justice, Retribute.

retribution (rɛtrɪˈbjuːʃən). Also 4 -bucioun, 4-5 -ion, 5 -yon(e. [a. OF. *retribucion, -ution* (mod.F. *rétribution*, = Sp. *retribucion*, It. *re-, ritribuzione*), or ad. L. *retribūtiōn-em*, noun of action f. *retribuĕre*: see RETRIBUTE *v.*]

1. a. Repayment, recompense, return, for some service, merit, etc. Now *rare.*

1382 WYCLIF *Col.* iii. 24 Witinge that of the Lord ȝe schulen take retribucioun, or ȝeldinge aȝen, of heritage. **1393** LANGL. *P. Pl.* C. IV. 340 Of hem comeþ retribucion, þat ys þe ȝifte þat god ȝyeuþ to alle leelle lyuynge. **1412-20** LYDG. *Chron. Troy* v. xxxvi, By merytorye retrybucyon. *c* **1460** G. ASHBY *Dicta Philos.* 576 Your benefetis geuen to goode men Asken daily grete retribucion. **1594** HOOKER *Eccl. Pol.* I. xi. §5 Sith possession of blisse, though it should be but for a moment, were an aboundant retribution. **1612-5** BP. HALL *Contempl., O.T.* XIX. ix, Never did a charitable act go away without the retribution of a blessing. **1642** R. CARPENTER *Experience* II. viii. 195 God naturally hath no obligation to make retribution to a creature. **1672** JOSSELYN *New Eng. Rarities* 31 Your bounty hath engaged a retribution of my gratitude. **1702** ROWE *Tamerl.* IV. i, When a King rewards, 'tis ample Retribution. **1776** ADAM SMITH *W. N.* I. x. (1869) I. 111 The counsellor at law.. ought to receive the retribution.. of his own so tedious and expensive education [etc.]. **1811** *Phil. Trans.* CI. 175 It is but a feeble and just retribution of respect for the service which he has rendered to science. **1826** MARGR. OF ANSPACH *Mem.* II. xii. 403 Deprived of the retributions due to her as widow of the Prince of Butera.

†**b.** Restitution, rendering back. *Obs. rare.*

1583 BABINGTON *Commandm.* 221 Wee honour them.. in reuerence, obedience, and mayntainance of their state by retribution of some parte of that wee haue got by them. **1627** HAKEWILL *Apol.* (1630) 113 Notwithstanding their [the elements] continuall transmutation, or transelementation, ..of one into another, yet by a mutuall retribution it still remaines the same. **1850** THACKERAY *Pendennis* I. xxxvii. 355 She thought his retribution of the hundred pounds an act of angelic virtue.

2. a. *day of retribution*, the day on which divine reward or punishment will be assigned to men (now usually associated with sense 3); also generally, any day of punishment or nemesis.

1526 *Pilgr. Perf.* (W. de W. 1531) 200 b, To preche the yere of grace & acceptacyon to god, & the daye of retribucyon. **1555** BRADFORD in Coverdale *Lett. Martyrs* (1564) 278 Praying God our deare father in the day of his retribution to remember it. **1624** BP. MOUNTAGU *Immed. Addr.* 157 The full accomplishment of their consummation in Christ, in the day of the retribution of the Righteous. **1808** PIKE *Sources Mississ.* III. (1810) App. 13 The day of retribution will come in thunder and in vengeance. **1856** SIR B. BRODIE *Psychol. Inq.* II. iv. 114, I.. am led to believe that even in this world the day of retribution rarely fails to come at last.

Comb. **1801** SOUTHEY *Thalaba* VII. xxv, As though the Retribution-day were come.

b. Recompense, in another life, for one's good or bad deeds in this world.

1633 B. JONSON *Underwoods, Eupheme* ix. 49 Whither they must come.. To have that finall retribution, Expected with the fleshe's restitution. **1667** MILTON *P.L.* III. 454 All who have thir reward on Earth.. here find Fit retribution, emptie as thir deeds. **1736** BUTLER *Anal.* I. iii, The proof of a future state of retribution would rest upon the usual known arguments for it. **1809-10** COLERIDGE *Friend* (1865) III. 354 The doctrine of retribution after death. **1858** NEALE *Bernard de Morlaix* 31 And divers retributions That divers merits claim.

3. A recompense for, or requital of, evil done; return *of* evil, etc.

1570 FOXE *A. & M.* (ed. 2) 223/1 To consider and learne the righteous retribution and wrath of God from heauen vpon all iniquitie. **1651** HOBBES *Leviath.* I. xv. 76 In Revenges (that is, retribution of Evil for Evil). **1658** T. WALL *Charact. Enemies Ch.* 43 It is the just retribution of God. **1702** ROWE *Tamerl.* IV. i, And curse me, Prophet, if I not repay His hate, with retribution full as mortal. **1781** COWPER *Expost.* 247 If vice receiv'd her retribution due When we were visited, what hope for you? **1840** MACAULAY *Clive* Ess. (1897) 518 Then was committed that great crime, ..memorable for the tremendous retribution by which it was followed. **1876** FARRAR *Marlb. Serm.* ii. 13 The retribution which dogs the heels of vice.

retributive (rɪˈtrɪbjʊtɪv), *a.* [f. as RETRIBUTE *v.* + -IVE: cf. OF. *retributif*, Sp. *retributivo.* By Southey and Shelley stressed on the first and third syllables, after *retribution.*] Characterized by, of the nature of, retribution. Freq. with *justice.*

1678 CUDWORTH *Intell. Syst.* Pref., A Distributive or Retributive Justice, dispensing Rewards and Punishments throughout the whole World. **1801** SOUTHEY *Thalaba* v. xxxi, O hard of heart! whom not the visible power Of retributive Justice.. Deterr'd from equal crime! **1813** SHELLEY *Q. Mab* I. 174 The sting Which retributive memory implants. **1856** FROUDE *Hist. Eng.* (1858) I. iv. 346 It was not intended.. they should escape the retributive consequences of those crimes. **1882** FARRAR *Early Chr.* I. 232 *note*, The fire of God's retributive wrath which burns eternally against unrepented sin.

Hence **re'tributively** *adv.*

1856 DORAN *Knts. & their Days* i. 20 If the married knights were retributively slain for talking about the wooing of a comrade's widow. **1865** *Pall Mall G.* 4 Aug. 11/2 To find his old place.. retributively filled by another.

re'tributivist, *sb.* (and *a.*) [f. RETRIBUTIVE *a.* + -IST.] A believer in retributive justice. Also *attrib.* or as *adj.*

1939 *Mind* XLVIII. 157 Retributivists have been pushed into holding that pain *ipso facto* represses the worse self and frees the better, when this is contrary to the vast majority of observed cases. **1968** *Economist* 13 July 48/2 The current fashion.. is to take it for granted that certain doctrines, such as the retributivist, are so discredited as to merit nothing but the most perfunctory and hostile attention. **1969** *Listener* 17 July 87/3 Why should we punish criminals? 'To ensure that they get their deserts,' says the Retributivist. *Ibid.* 88/1 Most of us have our retributivist moments ('Are you suggesting that Eichmann should have gone *scot free?*').

retributor (rɪˈtrɪbjʊtə(r)). [a. L. *retribūtor*, agent-noun f. *retribuĕre* to RETRIBUTE. Cf. F. *rétributeur*, It. *retributore.*] One who makes retribution: a repayer.

1612-5 BP. HALL *Contempl., O.T.* XII. iv, They had learned, that thankfulness was not to be measured of good men by the weight, but by the will of the retributor. **1614** T. ADAMS *Devil's Banquet* ii. 85 God is a iust Iudge, a retributor of euery man his owne. **1844** TUPPER *Crock of G.* xlvii, Those who in this world were mutual workers of iniquity may find themselves in the next sworn retributors of wrath. **1860** PUSEY *Min. Proph.* 22 The most just Retributor of those who persevere in rebellion against Him.

retributory (rɪˈtrɪbjʊtərɪ), *a.* Also -ary. [f. as RETRIBUTE *v.* + -ORY. Cf. obs. F. *retributoire*, Sp. *retributorio.*] Involving, producing, or characterized by retribution or recompense.

1612-5 BP. HALL *Contempl., O.T.* XVII. vi, A price, not counteruailable to what hee seekes, but retributorie to him of whom hee seekes. *a* **1656** —— *Rem.* Wks. (1660) 183 Neither is it the pleasure of the Almighty to deferr the retributory comforts of his mourners till another World. **1748** RICHARDSON *Clarissa* (1811) VIII. 256, I have already begun my retributory purposes. **1771** PENNANT *Tour in Scot.* (1774) 86 That sect, which in their prosperity shewed no mercy, now met with retributory vengeance. **1837** DE QUINCEY *Rev. Tartars* Wks. 1854 IV. 171 The price exacted by a retributary Providence for their vindictive cruelty. **1890** Æ. PRINCE *Of Joyous Gard* ii. 415 Loud calling for retributory knight To quell the raging wrongs.

re'tributress. *rare.* [f. RETRIBUTE *v.* + -TRESS.] A female retributor.

1798 W. TAYLOR in Robberds *Mem.* (1843) I. 219 Not yet the great retributress has closed The book of fate. **1830** —— *Hist. Surv. Germ. Poetry* II. 87 Night of destruction, dread retributress, Be dear and holy to a nation freed.

retricion, obs. form of RHETORICIAN.

re'trick, *v. rare.* [RE- 5 a.] *trans.* Of a heavenly light: to cause (a beam) to shine again. Also in fig. phr. *to retrick one's beams*, to restore one's mood; to regain one's happiness, shrug off despair. So **re'tricked** *ppl. a.*

Always with reference to Milton's line in *Lycidas.*

[**1637** MILTON *Lycidas* in *Poems* (1968) 253 The day-star ..tricks his beams, and with new spangled ore, Flames in the forehead of the morning sky.] **1833** MRS. BROWNING *Prometh. Bound* 28 The sun [shall] Disperse with retrickt beams the morning-frosts. **1863** TROLLOPE *Small House at Allington* (1864) II. iii. 28 We have retricked our beams in our own ways, and our lives have not been desolate. **1880** —— *Duke's Children* III. xxiv. 286 It is so that a man is stricken down... But it is given to him to retrick his beams.

retrievable (rɪˈtriːvəb(ə)l), *a.* [f. RETRIEVE *v.* + -ABLE.] Capable or admitting of being retrieved.

1711 SHAFTESB. *Charac.* (1737) III. Misc. III. ii. 179 Those whose Relish is retrievable, and whose Taste may yet be form'd in Morals. **1760** STERNE *Tr. Shandy* VII. xvi, Still is sweet sleep retrievable. **1863** COWDEN CLARKE *Shaks. Char.* xx. 504 Even in the hardened Barnardine, the worthy Provost can discern that spark of retrievable matter which should be fostered into hope of reformation. **1890** *Spectator* 6 Sept., Steps which are either irretrievable, or are retrievable only after terrible suffering and loss. **1967** *Times Rev. Industry* Oct. 84/1 Formalized techniques or procedures..for continuously carrying intelligence into retrievable form. **1974** C. TAYLOR *Fieldwork in Medieval Archaeol.* i. 18 The information..needs to be sorted and assembled in some form of retrievable system.

retrieval (rɪ'tri:vəl). Also 7 **retrival(l.** [f. RETRIEVE *v.* + -AL^{1}.]

1. The act of retrieving or recovering; an instance of this.

a **1643** W. CARTWRIGHT *Poems* (1651) 233 Methinks the first Age comes again, and we See a Retrivall of Simplicity. **1683** CAVE *Ecclesiastici, Ambrose* 382 Rome..is an humble suppliant for the retrival of her ancient Rites. **1751** SMOLLETT *Per. Pic.* xc. III. 265 She..implored his advice touching the retrieval of her reputation. **1788** BURKE *Sp. agst. W. Hastings* Wks. 1813 XII. 429 To exert themselves for the retrieval of the national loss. **1853** C. BRONTE *Villette* xxxvii, He had managed his affairs well,..his fortunes were in the way of retrieval. **1871** MRS. WHITNEY *Real Folks* xix, He dwelt on that word 'child', reminding her of her short mistaking and of the long retrieval.

b. *spec.* = *information retrieval* s.v. INFORMATION 8. Freq. *attrib.*

1958 *Bull. Canad. Libr. Assoc.* Apr. 193/1 One of the reasons which makes these machines fundamentally uneconomical at present is that the frequency of demand for exactly the same mechanical retrieval process in reference work is rarely sufficient to justify the large initial cost of coding and mechanizing all that a machine incapable of judgment needs, to perform the process. **1966** *Jrnl. Amer. Med. Assoc.* 13 June 950/1 This technique allows medical narrative and numerical data to be collected efficiently in a form acceptable as computer input for subsequent storage, analysis, and retrieval. **1968** *Globe & Mail* (Toronto) 3 Feb. B7/5 The computer's instant retrieval mechanism can make available, within 24 hours, any information contained in major Canadian collective labor agreements. **1972** *Bookseller* 4 Mar. 1463/3 It is highly important..that new systems of cataloguing and retrieval shall be built into the new library. **1974** W. GARNER *Big enough Wreath* xi. 138 How many men did you say you had on your..tapes?..All tucked away in your retrieval system. **1979** J. E. ROWLEY *Mechanised In-House Information Syst.* I. 26 Retrieval keys, such as indexing terms are stored adjacent to the records to which they relate.

2. = RETRIEVE *sb.* 3.

1707 *Reflexions upon Ridicule* 286 Ruin'd beyond retrieval. **1730** FIELDING *Author's Farce* Wks. 1775 I. 187 Matrimony clenches ruin beyond retrieval. **1858** CARLYLE *Fredk. Gt.* III. iii. (1872) I. 150 And so the Teutsch Ritters are sunk beyond retrieval. **1860** FROUDE *Hist. Eng.* V. 368 The Duke of Somerset had neglected the debts of the realm till they were past retrieval.

So †**retrie'vation.** *Obs. rare*$^{-1}$.

1806 *Simple Narrative* I. 160 Rendering, thereby, its retrievation more difficult, by attending circumstances.

retrieve (rɪ'tri:v), *sb.* Also 6 **retrife,** 7 **retriefe, retrive.** [f. the verb.]

†**1. a.** The second discovery and flight of a bird (esp. a partridge) which has already been sprung. *Obs.*

1575 TURBERV. *Venerie* 173 The houndes will in and striue who may first gette in like Spaniels at retrife of a Partriche. **1616** SURFL. & MARKHAM *Countrey Farme* VII. xliv. 715 The long-winged hawke..gathereth vp againe to her first pitch, and there expecteth the retriue. **1644** DIGBY *Nat. Bodies* xxxvii. 321 A fawkeners manning of a hawke, and trayning her to kill partridges, and to fly at the retriue. **1671** E. PANTON *Spec. Juv.* 66 The Covey was sprung again and the Hawks let fly, I spurr'd into the retrieve.

†**b.** In fig. contexts. *Obs.*

1625 B. JONSON *Staple of N.* III. i, We'll haue a flight at Mortgage, Statute, Band, And hard, but we'll bring Wax to the retriue. **1673** DRYDEN *Marr. à la Mode* v. i, It vexes me to the Heart, to leave all my Designs with Doralice unfinish'd; to have flown her so often to a Mark, and still to be bobb'd at retrieve.

†**2.** A return *of* something. *Obs. rare*$^{-1}$.

1657 G. THORNLEY *Daphnis & Chloe* 112 They desired nothing so much as a quick retrive of the Spring.

3. a. Possibility of recovery. With *beyond, past,* †*without* (cf. RETRIEVAL 2).

1697 BURGHOPE *Disc. Relig. Assemb.* 81 Grown men and vicious, and incorrigible beyond retrieve. **1700** BLACKMORE *Isaiah* xl. 273 We're ruin'd and undone, past all retrieve. **1706** DE FOE *Jure Divino* III. 10 He's damn'd without Retrieve, if he lets go The Reins of Life. **1748** RICHARDSON *Clarissa* (1811) III. 181 A detected invasion, in an article so sacred, would ruin me beyond retrieve. **1842** BROWNING *Soliloq. Sp. Cloister* ix, Such a flaw in the indenture As he'd miss till, past retrieve, Blasted lay that rose-acacia. **1886** W. J. TUCKER *E. Europe* 60 In an unguarded hour [he] ruined himself beyond retrieve.

b. The act of recovering; retrieval. Now *rare.*

1701 *Expedient Propos'd* 23, I have done my part towards a retrieve of our Ecclesiastical Constitution. **1704** M. HENRY *Friendly Visits* Wks. 1853 I. 276/2 To devise all means possible for..the repair and retrieve of it [friendship] where it is withering and ready to die. **1853** KANE *Grinnell Exp.* xxii. (1856) 170 He had volunteered his services for an expedition of retrieve.

c. A controlled exercise for a gun-dog simulating the retrieval of game; the object retrieved.

1932 L. SPRAKE *Art of Dog Training* v. 94 The pupil is taken to the regular training ground, and one or two retrieves of the usual dummy commence the proceedings. **1937** E. B. MOFFIT *Elias Vail trains Gun Dogs* ix. 134 Gallery critics at field trials are puzzled at the difficulty that many handlers experience in getting a dog to go out far enough to a retrieve. **1953** E. STONEX *Golden Retriever Handbk.* ix. 108 He must bring it right up to you—never let him run round you in circles with his retrieve. **1963** M. BRANDER *Gundogs* iv. 37 Only the very earliest retrieves of all should be made with the dummy or plaything thrown in full view in the open, so that the pup is encouraged to run in after it at once. **1976** *Field* 2 Sept. 474/1 He now performs the basic five retrieves as advocated by Maurice Hopper without any histrionics. **1979** *Country Life* 26 July 220/1 The gundog area has..a timed retrieve competition (the scurry).

d. *U.S. Sport.* The act of intercepting or otherwise regaining possession of the ball.

1961 in WEBSTER. **1974** *State* (Columbia, S. Carolina) 15 Feb. 3-B/1 Barron is averaging 19.3 points a game and has been getting 11.5 retrieves per contest.

retrieve (rɪ'tri:v), *v.* Also 5-6 **retreve,** 5-7 **retrive** (5 **retryue**), 7-8 **retreive.** [ad. OF. *retroev-*, the stressed stem of *retrover, retrouver,* f. *re-* RE- + *trouver* to find. The normal ME. representative of this, *retreve,* appears in the earliest examples; but the usual form during the 16th and 17th centuries was *retrive,* with the same unexplained change of vowel as in CONTRIVE. The modern *retrieve* seems to date from about 1650, but did not become the usual form till about 1680-90.]

I. *trans.* **1.** Of dogs: **a.** To find or discover again (game which has been temporarily lost); *esp.* to flush or set up (partridges) a second time.

c **1410** *Master of Game* (MS. Digby 182) xxxiii, To blawe a moote for þe lymer and late hym sewe till he haue retreued hym. *Ibid.* xxxiv, If it happe þat she be sqwate to fore hem and at þei retreue hir nought so sone as þei wolde. **1486** *Bk. St. Albans* b iiij, Whan she hath done any of theys,..go and retriue moo and she will nym plente. **1579** LYLY *Euphues* (Arb.) 41 The whelpe of a Mastife wyll neuer be taught to retriue the Partridge. **1607** TOPSELL *Four-f. Beasts* (1658) 122 These are taught by Falconers to retrive and raise Partridges. **1630** BRATHWAIT *Eng. Gentlem.* (1641) 113 These are dogges, said he, and necessary for Hawking, to find and retrive my game.

1826 SIR J. S. SEBRIGHT *Hawking* 24 If a young hawk does not take the bird in his first flight, and if it cannot be retrieved in a short time after he has put it in [etc.].

fig. **1592** WARNER *Alb. Eng.* IX. xlix. 227 Popes vse Potentates but to retriue their Game. **1601** DANIEL *Def. Ryme* Wks. G 6 b, [He] must either giue off vnsatisfied, or vncertainely cast backe to retriue the escaped sence. **1648** J. BEAUMONT *Psyche* XXII. clxxx, Their Pris'ner..they tie To that grim Hound which him retriev'd.

b. To find and bring in (a bird, etc.) that has been wounded or killed.

1856 'STONEHENGE' *Brit. Rur. Sports* 36/1 He..will retrieve any game, from the snipe to the pheasant. **1881** *Macm. Mag.* XLIV. 476/2 The late Fürst's favourite retriever retrieving a fox. **1899** *Blackw. Mag.* Feb. 420/1 The black dog..looked as if he had retrieved the whole nine.

2. a. To recover by study or investigation, esp. of the past; to restore to knowledge. Now *rare.*

1567 GOLDING *Ovid* XV. 188 They haling out his hartstrings.., And poring on them, seeke therein Goddes secrets too retryue. **1591** SYLVESTER *Du Bartas* I. ii. 792 Wherefore do ye strive With reach of Sense, God's wonders to retrive? *a* **1661** FULLER *Worthies, Rutlandsh.* (1662) 347 All that I can retrive of her is digested into these following particulars. **1686** *Phil. Trans.* XV. 2 The following Discourses: Some of which retrieve lost Pieces of Antiquity. **1697** COLLIER *Ess. Mor. Subj.* I. (1703) 66 They often.. explain History and retrieve us several material Parts of Learning. **1774** J. BRYANT *Mythol.* I. 69 An ancient word.. grown so obsolete that the original purport could not be retrieved. **1837** HALLAM *Hist. Lit.* I. i. §45 No industry has hitherto retrieved so much as a few lines of real Italian till near the end of the 12th century.

b. To recover by an effort of memory; to recall to mind.

1644 DIGBY *Nat. Bodies* 358 We can not retriue wordes to expresse in what manner we conceiue it. **1662** STILLINGFL. *Orig. Sacræ* III. i. §18 For according to this, it is impossible for the mind to retrieve any object without mutilation of it. **1690** LOCKE *Hum. Und.* II. xxvii. (1695) 186 Suppose I wholly lose the memory of some parts of my Life, beyond a possibility of retrieving them. **1779** JOHNSON *L.P., Cowley* (1868) 10 In perusing the works of this race of authors,.. something already learned is to be retrieved, or something new is to be examined. **1836-7** SIR W. HAMILTON *Metaph.* xxxi. (1859) II. 230, I have now to shew you, how these thoughts, retained in memory, may..be again retrieved.

†**c.** To rediscover; to find again. *Obs.*

c **1645** HOWELL *Lett.* (1650) I. 348 They consulted, that if they lost one another, how they might be retrieved and meet again. **1660** F. BROOKE tr. *Le Blanc's Trav.* 33 Ships lost in their road, by means of the sent, retrive their way.

d. To obtain again (stored information).

1962 *Communications Assoc. Computing Machinery* V. 12/2 Some kind of indexing scheme that can retrieve records.. within a short period of time. **1968** *Brit. Med. Bull.* XXIV. 195/1 By means of electronic pulses the data would be placed inside the computer system,..and be available for analysis at a future date as well as being able to be retrieved on demand. **1971** *Nature* 19 Mar. 155/2 Many short notes and letters contain the first 'rush' announcement of extremely important results—just what a current-awareness service should aim to retrieve. **1975** J. B. HARLEY *O.S. Maps* p. xiv, In the process of retrieving information the Survey's Librarian..has conjured otherwise elusive papers into my hands.

3. To recover, regain, get or take possession of (a thing, etc.) again.

1589 NASHE *Martin Marprelate* Wks. (Grosart) I. 81 O how my Palfrey..daunced the Goates iumpe, when I ranne the ring round about him to retriue him. **1651** HOBBES *Leviath.* III. xxxiii. 203 Esdras..by the direction of Gods Spirit retrived them, when they were lost. **1684** J. PETER *Siege Vienna* 70 That part of the Ravelin being thus retrieved was wholly abandoned by the Enemy. *c* **1710** CELIA FIENNES *Diary* (1888) 217 Tho' he had gotten quite down his head and all, yet did retrieve his feete,..with me on his Back. **1751** SMOLLETT *Per. Pic.* (1779) II. xli. 50 A warrant..to search for and retrieve the fugitive. **1832** W. IRVING *Alhambra* I. 215 They would be enabled to return and retrieve their treasures at some future day. **1885** R. BRIDGES *Nero* III. ii, Would'st thou now Retrieve thy purchase money?

4. †**a.** To bring back; to cause to turn back or return. Also const. *into, to. Obs.*

a **1597** PEELE *David & Bethsabe* IV. ii. H i b, Take but your Lute, and..Retriue the sunnes sphere, and restraine the clouds. **1605** B. JONSON *Volpone* Epist. ¶3 To see..those antique reliques of Barbarisme retriu'd with-all other ridiculous and exploded follies. **1623** MASSINGER *Bondman* II. i, But if retrivd into his back again, Would keep him warmer than a Scarlet wast-coat. **1652** BENLOWES *Theoph.* XIII. xciv, Which might our iron age to its first gold retrive. **1662** STILLINGFL. *Orig. Sacræ* II. v. §2 Till a new blast from the Spirit of God doth..retrieve it into its former heat.

b. To bring back *from* or *out of* a place or state; to rescue or save.

c **1611** CHAPMAN *Iliad* XXIII. 71 From hel's low region.. soules never are retriu'd To talke with friends here. *c* **1656** WALLER *Of a War with Spain* 99 All labour now to save their Enemies;..And their young foes Endeav'ring to retrive, With greater hazard than they fought, they dive. **1695** WOODWARD *Nat. Hist. Earth* II. (1723) 99 To reclaim and retrieve the World out of this wretched and forlorn State. **1712** ARBUTHNOT *John Bull* I. viii, One that had..retrieved his Family from the Oppression of old Lewis Baboon. **1738** WESLEY *Hymns, Father, I stretch my Hands* iii, Now my poor Soul Thou wouldst retrieve, Nor let me wait one Hour.

c. To save (time) from other occupations.

1687-8 LADY R. RUSSELL *Lett.* I. liv. 129 Just after I had retrieved time enough to scribble to you. **1706** LOGAN in *Pennsylv. Hist. Soc. Mem.* X. 165 Therefore must beg her excuse till I can retrieve one minute or two of liberty to think again. **1879** HARE *Life B'ness Bunsen* I. ix. 322 The time of study which Bunsen could retrieve from the Description of Rome.

5. a. To restore, revive; to bring back to the original state or to a flourishing condition.

1676 J. WORLIDGE *Cyder* (1691) 150 Sharp or acid cider.. may easily be retriv'd by a small addition of new spirits. **1715** tr. *Pancirollus' Rerum Mem.* I. I. xiii. 33 By the help of Iron, we plant Orchards, and retrieve the Youth of decaying Vineyards. **1748** *Anson's Voy.* II. iii. 144 The retrieving the freedom of a single family. **1839-52** BAILEY *Festus* 477 Ye, too, lose Your place, in place: retrieve yourselves in good. **1854** BROWNING *Twins* vi, Would ye retrieve the one? Try and make plump the other! **1861** BUCKLE *Civiliz.* II. viii. 542 The spirit of the country was broken, and nothing could retrieve it.

b. *esp.* one's fortunes, honour, credit, etc.

1725 DE FOE *Voy. round World* (1840) 59 To merit mercy and retrieve his circumstances by his future fidelity. **1770** *Junius Lett.* xxxvi. (1788) 193 The faithful servants, in whose hands you have left him, are able to retrieve his honour. **1809** W. IRVING *Knickerb.* v. i. (1849) 259 The very man fitted by nature to retrieve the desperate fortunes of her beloved province. **1855** MACAULAY *Hist. Eng.* xiii. III. 373 The regular army would retrieve the honour which had been lost at Killiecrankie. **1880** MCCARTHY *Own Times* IV. lx. 325 No courage, no patriotism, could now retrieve the fortunes of the field.

6. †**a.** To make amends or atone for (a fault).

a **1679** W. OWTRAM *Serm.* (1682) 385 It is as well to retrieve a sin by true repentance for it.

b. To make good, repair, set right again (a loss, disaster, error, etc.).

1688 PRIOR *Ode St. John's, Camb.* ix, Grace's Presence [shall] Nature's Loss retrieve. **1703** in Ellis *Orig. Lett.* Ser. II. IV. 236 A supply for some years may put your Majesty in condition to retrieve what was not to be hindered. **1718** PRIOR *Solomon* II. 955 O Reason!..Accept my Sorrow, and retrieve my Fall. **1747** GRAY *Favourite Cat* vii, One false step is ne'er retriev'd. **1784** COWPER *Tiroc.* 166 Describe a Saviour's cross As God's expedient to retrieve his loss. **1817** JAS. MILL *Brit. India* II. v. ii. 362 This disaster the majority of the Council deemed it an easy matter to retrieve. **1844** H. H. WILSON *Brit. India* II. 263 He endeavoured to retrieve the error he had committed by the most solemn assurances. **1863** *Sat. Rev.* 6 June 716 Until he has retrieved his late disaster, his pretensions will by no means embarrass his rivals.

†**c.** To discharge or pay (a debt). *Obs. rare*$^{-1}$.

1711 STEELE *Spect.* No. 109 ¶5 That Debt lay heavy on our House for one Generation, but it was retrieved by a Gift from that honest Man you see there.

II. *intr.* **7.** Of dogs: †**a.** To find and set up game again. Also *fig. Obs. rare.*

c **1410** *Master of Game* (M.S. Digby 182) xiii, þei seche not wele, nor þei retreue nought wele, ne þei hunte not longe. **1530** PALSGR. 689/2 It is a goode hounde, for he wyll retreve the best that ever I sawe. **1635** QUARLES *Embl.* I. xi. 45 What? will her rambling Fits be never past? For ever ranging? never once retrive?

b. To find and bring in wounded or dead game. Also said of a person.

1856 'STONEHENGE' *Brit. Rur. Sports* 36/1 A little rough terrier, expressly broken to retrieve, and kept for this alone. **1880** H. C. ST. JOHN *Wild Coasts Nipon* 312, I used to get a boat-girl to retrieve for me, and very well she did it. **1884** *Bazaar* 24 Dec. 2287/2 Well bred fox terrier,..good worker, and retrieves tenderly.

8. To recuperate; to recover.

1675 COCKER *Morals* 4 Do not always strive, For sometimes to Retreat, is to Retrive. **1759** MILLER *Gard. Dict.* (ed. 7) s.v. *Grove,* To destroy these [trees], which will require an Age to retrieve. **1771** LUCKOMBE *Hist. Printing* 459 Towards the time of Decius the character began to lose its roundness and beauty; some time after it retrieved, and subsisted tolerably till the time of Justin. **1775** H. WALPOLE *Lett.* (1904) IX. 134 The whole caravan were forced to go abroad to retrieve.

Hence **re'trieved** *ppl. a.*

1648 G. SANDYS *Paraphr. Lament.* iii. 7 My Soule like a retrived Partridge [they] chace. **1729** WIGHTMAN *Pref. to*

Boston's Fourfold St. 5 Human nature..in its depraved condition, in its retrieved state. **1807–8** W. Irving *Salmag.* No. 13 (1860) 299 My fancy echoed to the applauding voices of a retrieved generation. **1892** Greener *Breech Loader* 237 The retrieved birds should be placed on or near the hampers containing the living pigeons.

re'trieveless, *a. rare.* [f. retrieve *sb.* + -less.] That is past retrieval.

1850 Blackie *Æschylus* I. 28 In woe retrieveless lost. *c* **1871** E. Dickinson *Poems* (1955) III. 836 Till some retrieveless Night Our Vigilance at waste The Garden gets the only shot That never could be traced.

re'trievement. *rare.* [f. as prec. + -ment.] = retrieval.

1677 Gilpin *Demonol.* (1867) 363 It is discovered to be a special retrievement of it, by many and signal convincing evidences. *a* **1706** Evelyn *Hist. Relig.* (1850) I. 239 Now excited and stirred up to act, by the suggestion, ministry, and retrievement of the senses. **1883** *Contemp. Rev.* Aug. 174 Chance for moral retrievement in England there is none. The stigma of penal servitude is..lasting.

retriever (rɪ'triːvə(r)). Also 5–7 retriver. [f. retrieve *v.* + -er¹.]

1. A dog used for the purpose of retrieving: †**a.** One employed to set up game again. *Obs.*

1486 *Bk. St. Albans* b iij b, A chastised hounde that will be rebuket and is a Retriuer, vncouple him. **1624** Quarles *Sion's Elegies* I. iii, Meanewhile, the treason of the quick Retriuers, Discouers nouell dangers, and deliuers Her to a second feare. **1626** Breton *Fantastikes, Haruest* Wks. (Grosart) II. 7/1 A good Retriuer is a Spaniell worth the keeping.

transf. **1592** Greene *Blacke Booke's Messenger* Table of Words, The verser in conny-catching is called the Retriuer. **1606** Warner *Alb. Eng.* XIV. lxxx. 339 Seaueuth Henry..Of his Retriuers Proolings much (as well he might) repented. **1636** R. James tr. *Minucius Felix Octavius* 80 They seeme to finde the litle infant,..her dogge-headed retriver glories in his invention.

b. One of a breed specially adapted for finding and bringing in dead or wounded game.

1830 M. R. Mitford *Our Village* IV. 110 His noble Newfoundland dog, (a retriever is the sporting word). **1841** Marryat *Poacher* xvii, Tell them to come down with their retrievers. **1861** E. Jesse *Lect. Nat. Hist.* 45 He sent his retriever after it, who..caught and killed the hare and returned with it in his mouth. **1898** Sir H. Smith *Retrievers* 15 Retrievers are singularly docile and tractable.

Comb. **1897** *Allbutt's Syst. Med.* II. 888 The troop of those 'neurotics'..who scent intoxicants from afar with a retriever-like instinct.

2. One who retrieves or recovers.

1658 Harrington *Oceana* 20 Machiavill the sole retreiver of this ancient Prudence. **1672–5** Comber *Comp. Temple* (1702) 69 As the Retrivers of Ancient things are often thought the Inventors. **1715** M. Davies *Athen. Brit.* I. 124 As to that famous Retriever of polite Literature, Erasmus. **1977** *Tennis World* Sept. 17/3 'Baseliners', 'retrievers and 'counter-punchers' are players who stay back from the net.

retrieverish (rɪ'triːvərɪʃ), *a.* [f. retriever + -ish¹.] Resembling or suggestive of a retriever.

1909 H. G. Wells *Tono-Bungay* III. ii. 243 There were two or three fox-terriers, a retrieverish mongrel, and an old, bloody-eyed, and very evil-smelling St. Bernard.

retrieving (rɪ'triːvɪŋ), *vbl. sb.* [f. as retriever + -ing¹.] The action of the verb in various senses.

c **1410** *Master of Game* (MS. Digby 182) xiii, Se þe good recouerynge and retreuynge and þe maystreys and þe sotiltees þat be in goode houndes. *c* **1645** Howell *Lett.* (1650) I. 348 Take heed you do not lose me, for if you do,..there is no retrieving of me. *a* **1680** Butler *Rem.* (1759) I. 205 All's laid out upon Retrieving of the Curse of Babylon. **1712** Addison *Spect.* No. 440 ⁋2 The Establishment which we have here made for the retrieving of good Manners. **1719** W. Wood *Surv. Trade* p. vii, To this we owe the Retrieving of the lost Condition our Trade..was generally in. **1856** 'Stonehenge' *Brit. Rur. Sports* 46/2 Nothing requires so much practice as retrieving. **1886** C. Scott *Sheep-Farming* 205 A sheep-dog..that inclines to retrieving is invariably a fool among sheep. **1962** *Communications Assoc. Computing Machinery* V. 11 (*heading*) Information structures for processing and retrieving.

attrib. **1856** Emerson *Eng. Traits, Literature*, I know that a retrieving power lies in the English race. **1972** J. S. Hall *Sayings from Old Smoky* 3 A computer-like retrieving process.

re'trieving, *ppl. a.* [-ing².] That retrieves.

1856 'Stonehenge' *Brit. Rur. Sports* 46/1 You must pay about £5 a brace more for the retrieving-setters. **1895** *Q. Rev.* Jan. 93 The stalking horse and the Egyptians' retrieving cat.

re'trim (riː-), *v.* [re- 5 a.] To trim again.

1868 Browning *Ring & Bk.* II. 1217 The Canon.., then, was sent To change his garb, re-trim his tonsure. **1876** T. Hardy *Ethelberta* xxvi. Sunday hats and bonnets had been re-trimmed. **1880** Stevenson *Lett.* (1899) I. 173, I shall hear you, years from now, timidly begin to retrim your feathers for a little self-laudation. **1966** D. Francis *Flying Finish* xviii. 217, I put on full flap, maximum drag..retrimmed..felt the plane get slower and heavier. **1977** 'O. Jacks' *Autumn Heroes* v. 71 You drag 'em out, boss, while I re-trim.

†**'retriment.** *Obs. rare.* [ad. L. *retrīment-um.*] Dross, refuse.

1614 Bargrave *Serm.* (1615) B ij, Then suppose all things under the moone to bee but..retriment and dung [etc.]. *Ibid.* F ij, The retriment of the people. **1656** Blount *Glossogr.*, *Retriment*, the dregs of a thing, the dross of mettal, all kinde of superfluities and rubbish.

re'trip. [re- 5 a.] A return or second trip.

1760 *Projects* in *Ann. Reg.* 147/2 The time in making a compleat trip and retrip with the 40 ton barge. **1788** Anna Seward *Lett.* (1811) II. 151 Your purposed re-trip to Lichfield..will, I trust, be realized.

retro ('rɛtrəʊ), *sb.* [Short for retro-rocket.] = retro-rocket b.

1961 *New Scientist* 21 Sept. 719/3 Whether because of the timing of the order, or the impulse of the retros, or drift of the wind.., the robot cosmonaut got away from its shepherds on the sea and fell into the water seventy miles from the nearest waiting ship. **1962** S. Carpenter in *Into Orbit* 56 The pilot must..have the capsule pointed exactly right when the retros fire. **1966** *Word Study* Dec. 1/2 Commander Alan B. Shepard, whose flight lasted only fifteen minutes, was precise and terse: 'Disarm.' 'Auto retro jettison circuit.'

‖**'retro**, *adv. rare.* [L. *retrō*: see next.] Backwards; into past time.

1771 *Encycl. Brit.* II. 931/1 The compensation, after it is admitted by the judge, operates, *retro*,..to the time that, by the parties acknowledgment, the debt became due. **1885** *Law Rep. 10 App. Cases* 383 *note*, Such presumption of use retro may be re-argued.

retro- ('riːtrəʊ, 'rɛtrəʊ), *prefix*, repr. the Latin adverb *retrō* backwards, back, which in the post-Augustan language appears in combination with various verbs and verbal nouns, as *retroagĕre*, *-cēdĕre* (*-cessio, -cessus*), *-gradāre* (*-gradātio*), *-gradī* (*-gressus*), *-spicĕre*, and more rarely in adjectival forms as *retrōgradus*. The use of the prefix was widely extended in mediæval Latin (see examples in Du Cange), but most of the important words in English which begin with it are derived from, or modelled on, the more classical types. The earliest to appear is the adj. *retrograde*, before 1400, followed in the 15th and 16th centuries by other forms from the same stem. *Retrocedent* and *retroversion* also appear in the 16th cent., but the main additions to the number are made in the 17th and following centuries. In the 19th, esp. the latter part of it, *retro-* has been very freely used as a prefix, chiefly in scientific terms (see examples under 3 below).

2. The pronunciation of *retro-* is to some extent unsettled, and lexicographers vary in their recognition of, or preference for, the short or long vowel. Walker gives only the short, Smart only the long, while Webster admits both in all cases. Recent dictionaries which attempt to discriminate between the various words usually favour ('riːtrəʊ), except in *retrograde* and *retrospect*.

3. All the earlier or more important combs. of *retro-* are given below as main words; the following are illustrations of the extended use of the prefix in the 19th century.

a. Miscellaneous terms, as **retroa'nalysis** *Chess*, analysis of a position so as to reconstruct the moves of the game leading to that position; also *transf.*; so **retroana'lytical** *a.* **retrocog'nition**, (*a*) knowledge of the past supernaturally acquired; (*b*) *Psychol.*, paranormal cognition of events in someone or something else's past; so **retro'cognitive** *a.* **retro'coupling** *a.*, joining backwards or behind. **'retrodate** *v.*, to put back to an earlier date. **retrodis'placement**, displacement rearwards. **'retroflux**, a backward flow. **'retrofocus** *a. Photogr.*, designating an optical system in which the distance of the rear surface from the image of an object at infinity exceeds the focal length, usu. achieved by placing a diverging group of lenses before a converging group. **'retroform** *v.* (see quot.). **retromi'gration**, migration back again. **retro-'operative** *a.*, having a retrospective effect. **'retroplexed** *a.*, folded back upon itself. **retropo'sition**, change of position in a backward direction. **retro'presbyteral** *a.*, lying behind the presbytery (or choir and altar) of a cathedral or other large church. **retrore'ception**, the action of receiving back again. **retro'seer**, one who sees into the past. **retrosu'sception**, the action of taking back. **retro'transfer**, **-'transference**, the act of transferring back again. **retro'vision**, vision into or of the past.

A number of similar forms are given in some Dicts., as *retroclusion, -curved, -deflect* vb., *-deviation, -duct* vb. *-jection, -location, -morphosis*, etc.

[**1933** H. Phillips *Week-End Problems Bk.* 182 Profound and puzzling retrograde analysis is needed to prove the legality of the key-move.] **1937** T. R. Dawson *Caissa's Wild Roses in Clusters* 13/1 Trio of *retro-analyses. **1979** *Sci. Amer.* Dec. 20/2 Most chess problems deal with the future, such as how can White move and mate in three. Smullyan's problems belong to a field known as retrograde analysis (retro analysis for short), in which it is necessary to reconstruct the past. **1980** *Daily Tel.* 21 Apr. 13/7 Retro-analysis is..the root of much scientific thinking. It is as useful to the astronomer pondering the creating of the universe by observing space as it appears *now* as it is to the detective who solves a murder by deducing the series of events that led to the crime. **1966** *New Statesman* 10 June 858/3 It contains a good many highly complicated '*retro-analytical' problems. **1980** *Daily Tel.* 21 Apr. 13/7 The chess-board here is being used only as a tool for an exercise in retro-analytical deduction. *a* **1901** Myers *Human Personality* (1903) I. 31 Our *retrocognitions seem often a recovery of isolated fragments of thought and feeling. **1962** C. D. Broad *Lect. Psychical Res.* 402 What I will call 'states of *direct* but not ostensibly *recollective retro-cognition*'. **1969** J. J. Macintosh in Macintosh & Coval *Business of Reason* 154 In the absence of a body there is no way of distinguishing between veridical memories and what might be called accurate retro-cognition. **1973** *Daily Tel.* (Colour suppl.) 30 Nov. 27/4 *Retrocognition*, as precognition, but of past events. **1897** *Daily News* 5 Feb. 6/7 *Retrocognitive clairvoyance..is thus explained. **1828** *Loudon's Gardener's Mag.* III. 414 Description and Use of Dyer's *Retro-coupling Bee-boxes. **1862** Lowell *Lett.* (1894) I. iv. 346, I send it now that my thanks may be antedated (or *retrodated rather) more than a year. **1903** *Med. Rec.* (N.Y.) 27 June 434/2 (*heading*) The treatment by anterior vaginal section of *retrodisplacement of the uterus, complicated by adhesions. **1972** *Biol. Abstr.* LIII. 3376/2 Physical exertion of women employed in mechanical coal dressing does not affect the incidence of..retrodisplacement of the uterus. **1889** Matthews *Dis. Women* (ed. 4) xv. 116 Hence the *retroflux through a tube. This retroflux sometimes occurs before the operation. **1965** *Focal Encycl. Photogr.* (rev. ed.) II. 1293/2 *Retrofocus lenses are almost invariably of the inverted telephoto type. **1977** J. Hedgecoe *Photographer's Handbk.* 323 In wide-angle, retro-focus constructions the back focus is much greater than the focal length which allows room for mirrors etc. within the camera construction. **1979** *Amat. Photographer* Feb. 95/2 The normal simple calculations for finding the effective f/number when engaged in close-up work with extension tubes or bellows do not always give the right answers when using a telephoto or retrofocus lens. **1848** De Quincey in *Tait's Mag.* XV. 85 They were *reforming* the Church.., viz., **retroforming* it, moulding it back into compliance with its original form and model. **1894** *Lancaster* (Pennsylv.) *Daily Intell.* 8 Feb., The most recent *retromigration of disheartened Germans from the West. **1863** Kinglake *Crimea* (1876) I. xiv. 311 Prince Louis Bonaparte and Morny..issued a *retro-operative decree. **1858** De Morgan in Graves *Life Sir W. Hamilton* (1889) III. 539 Cauchy's proof..is Argand's, much complexed, perplexed, *retroplexed, and omniplexed. **1843** Whewell in Todhunter *Acc. Writ.* (1876) II. 311 The propagation of the tide from place to place by free waves gave a further *retroposition. **1845** *Encycl. Metrop.* V. 363* The effect of friction will be a retroposition of tides. **1849** *Ecclesiologist* IX. 274 The propriety of the term whereby you describe this *retropresbyteral space. **1829** Bentham *Justice & Cod. Petit., Abr. Petit. Justice* 65 Now, as to retrotransference and *retroreception, or say, return of the suit to the originating judicatory. **1821** R. Pollok in D. Pollok *Life* 117 May not these our *retro-seers have made some mistake in consulting the..past? **1802–12** Bentham *Ration. Judic. Evid.* (1827) IV. 139 Practice of the ecclesiastical courts: transmission and *retro-susception, as in the equity courts. **1830** —— *Offic. Apt. Maximized* Pref. p. xiii, For the purpose of retro-susception or say resumption. **1869** W. S. Dallas tr. *Müller's Facts for Darwin* xii. 123 A *retro-transfer of late-acquired advantages to this early period of life. **1829** Bentham *Justice & Cod. Petit., Abr. Petit. Justice* 60 Transference is followed by *retrotransference. **1830** Cunningham *Brit. Painters* II. 176 They had precisely the same *retro-visions and prophetic visions with himself.

b. Terms of *Anat.* and *Path.* in which *retro-* is combined with an adj. denoting some part of the body, and has the sense of 'situated behind' (the part in question), as ***retro-cæcal, -cardiac, -duodenal, -mastoid, -maxillary, -ocular, -peritoneal, -pubic, -sternal, -tarsal, -uterine***, etc.; **retro-'bulbar**, situated or occurring behind the eyeball.

[**1866** A. von Graefe in *Archiv für Ophthalm.* II. 147 Als solche erscheint mir die Annahme einer retrobulbären Neuritis.] **1879** *Archiv für Ophthalm.* VIII. 328 (*heading*) Three cases of *retrobulbar, pulsating, vascular tumor. **1879** E. Nettleship *Student's Guide Dis. Eye* II. xvii. 225 Neuritis behind the eye (retro-bulbar neuritis). **1961** *Lancet* 29 Apr. 908/2 Retrobulbar neuritis is a rare, though well-recognised complication of addisonian pernicious anæmia. **1964** S. Duke-Elder *Parsons' Dis. Eye* (ed. 14) 568 Retrobulbar injections should be preceded by an injection of procaine. **1903** *Amer. Med.* V. 836/1 Case 1. *Retrocecal gangrenous appendicitis. **1961** *Lancet* 23 Sept. 671/2 *Staph[ylococcus] aureus*..was isolated from..the retrocæcal abscess. **1901** *Ibid.* 12 Jan. 118/2 This clear zone is somewhat triangular in shape. Dr. Mignon proposes to call it the *retro-cardiac triangle. **1908** *Practitioner* Dec. 863 The 'retro-cardiac triangle', seen when the patient is in the lateral oblique position. This triangle is bounded by the heart in front, the spine behind, and the diaphragm below. *Ibid.* 827, I am inclined to think that transduodenal or *retro-duodenal operations for this condition should be avoidable. **1878** Bartley tr. *Topinard's Anthrop.* 171 The *retro-mastoid sutures are complicated. **1891** Moulin *Surg.* 869 *Retromaxillary growths. **1872** Darwin *Emotions* vi. 161 This is due to the dilatation of the *retro-ocular vessels. **1893** *Trans. Path. Soc.* XLIV. 69 The case is..an example of what Astley Cooper termed the mesenteric variety of *retro-peritoneal hernia. **1977** *Lancet* 28 May 1133/1 Retroperitoneal hæmorrhage occurred in 5 patients. **1967** Taylor & Cotton *Short Textbk. Surg.* xxvi. 397 *Retropubic Prostatectomy. The prostate is approached..via a suprapubic incision through the cave of Retzius, the potential space between the back of the pubis and the bladder... A drain is inserted into the retropubic space. **1898** *Allbutt's Syst. Med.* V. 11 The sensation is almost always *retrosternal. **1875** Walton *Dis. Eye* 846 The oculo-palpebral portion, called also the *retro-tarsal fold. **1851** *Monthly Jrnl. Med. Sci.* XIII. 278 (*heading*) *Retro-uterine sanguineous tumours. **1879** *St. George's Hosp. Rep.* IX. 439 A retro-uterine dermoid cyst.

c. Terms in *Astronautics* relating to retro-rockets and their use, as ***retro-ignition, -impulse, -manœuvre, -propulsion, -system, -thrust***.

1967 *New Scientist* 21 Sept. 595/1 *Retro-ignition was delayed for 12·5 seconds, coming at 150 000 feet instead of the normal 274 000 feet. **1961** H. H. KOELLE *Handbk. Astronaut. Engin.* xxv. 29 The instantaneous *retro impulses applied tangentially to the trajectory. **1976** *Sci. Amer.* June 7/3 In the Viking missions.. the *retromaneuver.. that will put the spacecraft in orbit around Mars will be based on commands sent from the earth at least a day earlier. *Ibid.* 59/1 Those commands will cause the spacecraft's *retro-propulsion system to fire for 43 minutes, subtracting enough velocity to place the spacecraft in an elliptical orbit around Mars. **1962** S. CARPENTER in *Into Orbit* 56 The *retro-system is rigged so that the rockets will not fire.. unless the capsule is in the correct attitude. **1962** RILEY & SAILOR *Space Syst. Engin.* iv. 86 The *retro-thrust is directed at such an angle as to provide a desired range. Increases in retro-velocities result in small range angles.

retroact (riːtrəʊ-, rɛtrəʊˈækt), *v.* [ad. L. *retroact-*, ppl. stem of *retroagĕre*: see RETRO- and ACT *v.* So F. *rétroagir*.] *intr.* To react; also, to operate in a backward direction or towards the past.

1795 HUSSEY in *Burke's Corr.* (1844) IV. 279 The very ghost of that bill would retro-act, and put down the House of Peers. **1856** MRS. BROWNING *Aur. Leigh* VI. 330 A simple shade or image of the brain, Is merely passive, does not retro-act, Is seen, but sees not. **1877** *Scribner's Mag.* XV. 223/2 That woman could not retroact and touch the memory of Ida.

retroaction (riːtrəʊ-, rɛtrəʊˈækʃən). [ad. L. type **retroactio*: see prec. and ACTION *sb.* So F. *rétroaction*, Sp. *retroaccion*, It. *retroazione*.]

†**1.** (Meaning not clear.) *Obs.*$^{-1}$

1570 FOXE *A. & M.* (ed. 2) 540/2 To proceed against them ..concerning the foresaide hereticall and erroneous conclusions, accordyng to the forme of retroactions and qualitie of the busines in this behalfe had and vsed.

†**2.** 'A driving backward' (Phillips, 1658). *Obs.*

3. A retrospective action.

1727–38 CHAMBERS *Cycl.* s.v. *Retroactive*, We have some instances of laws that have a retrospect or retroaction, *i.e.* are made with express design to extend to things already past. *a* **1816** BENTHAM *Offic. Apt. Maximized, Introd. View* (1830) 20 In the frugality here recommended, no retro-action is comprised.

4. a. Return action; reaction.

1829 J. STERLING *Ess.* (1848) I. 71 The design which occupies by a necessary retroaction modifies the means whereby we seek to attain it. **1874** G. MACDONALD *Malcolm* III. iii. 34 The hatred of the grand old man had an element of unselfishness in its retroaction, of power in its persistency [etc.]. **1884** BIGGS *Magn. Dyn. Electr. Mach.* 267 Retro-action of the moving circuit on the fixed.

b. *Psychol.* The effect of later learning on the memory of what was learnt previously. Also *attrib.*

1949 POSTMAN & EGAN *Exper. Psychol.* xvi. 378 Maximum retroaction occurs when original and interpolated learning are approximately equal in strength. **1953** C. E. OSGOOD *Methods & Theory in Exper. Psychol.* xiii. 562 The fact that so-called 'rest' control groups show loss in retention has already been noted in connection with the logic of transfer and retroaction experiments. **1971** L. POSTMAN in J. W. Kling et al. *Woodworth & Schlosberg's Exper. Psychol.* xxi. 1110/2 The treatment corresponds to the rest condition in experiments on retroaction.

retroactive (riːtrəʊ-, rɛtrəʊˈæktɪv), *a.* [Cf. prec. and ACTIVE. So F. *rétroactif, -ive*, Sp. and Pg. *retroactivo*, It. *retroattivo*.]

1. a. Of enactments, etc.: Extending in scope or effect to matters which have occurred in the past; retrospective; also with *to*. Also *transf.*

1611 COTGR., *Retroactif*, retroactiue; casting, driuing, relating, backward. **1668** *Persec. Ref. Ch. in France* 11 They have given it a Retroactive Power (as they call it) by putting it in Execution against persons who returned to us a long time before the Declaration was in being. *a* **1751** BOLINGBROKE *Fragm. Ess.* xxxviii, As the death of Christ had a retroactive effect on those that lived and died before they were redeemed. **1794** EARL MALMESBURY *Diaries & Corr.* III. 60, I objected to the date to be fixed to the Treaty, particularly if in addition to the giving it this retro-active force, an advance.. was to be required. **1811** W. R. SPENCER *Poems* 131 Must I, for follies past assess'd By retro-active laws be fin'd? **1847** R. W. HAMILTON *Rewards & Punishm.* v. (1853) 215 The resurrection of Christ.. is represented as possessing a retroactive influence. **1897** *Times* 22 Apr. 6/1 The retroactive clause in the Dingley Bill will be either cancelled or amended. **1952** *Sun* (Baltimore) 22 Mar. 6/4 A handsome wage increase.. allows 12.5 cents an hour immediately and retro-active to January 1. **1978** J. PAXTON *Dict. Europ. Econ. Community* (rev. ed.) 49 The United Kingdom.. informed the Council of Ministers on 27 March that a subsidy would be granted on sugar and made retroactive to 1 Feb. **1979** *Arizona Daily Star* 5 Aug. c8/4 Placed Paul Hartzell, pitcher, on the 21-day disabled list, retroactive to last Thursday.

b. Directed backwards in time.

1822 *Blackw. Mag.* II. 165 We may say century, without stretching our retroactive foresight to any extraordinary degree.

c. ***retroactive infinitive*** (*Gram.*), an active infinitive that has a preceding noun as its object.

1946 O. JESPERSEN *Mod. Eng. Gram.* V. xv. 233 Retro-active infinitives are found in connexion with the adverbs *yet* and *still*:.. Rome and Naples—even Florence are yet to see (= we have not yet seen; *are yet to be seen* would mean 'can still be seen').

2. Operating in a backward direction. *rare.*

1611 [see above]. **1706** PHILLIPS (ed. Kersey), *Retroactive* (Lat. in Philos.), driving back; as A retroactive Motion. **1797** *Monthly Mag.* III. 383 In the centre of the axle is placed a retroactive fulcrum, to which chains are made fast.

†**3.** Reactive. *Obs. rare.*

1799 MRS. J. WEST *Tale of Times* II. 264 The odium with which you bespatter a neighbour's reputation has a retro-active effect in furbishing your own. **1802** BEDDOES *Hygeia* II. 68 The total abstraction of the mind from all regard to the retroactive tendency of conduct.

4. *Psychol.* That affects the remembering of what has been previously learned; esp. as ***retroactive inhibition***, the inhibiting effect on recall that can be produced by attention given to new material after the original learning. Cf. INHIBITION 4, PROACTIVE^1 *a.*

1909 C. S. MYERS *Exper. Psychol.* xiii. 163 This 'retro-active inhibition' is yet another cause of the greater difficulty in learning longer than shorter studies. *Ibid.* 166 Similar experiments have been conducted with the object of proving retro-active, i.e. backward association. **1909** *Psychol. Monogr.* X. IV. 138 With G. retroactive inhibition was obvious. Each series was remembered fairly well until the next was given. **1915** *Ibid.* XIX. IV. (*title*) A study of retro-active inhibition. **1938** *Brit. Jrnl. Psychol.* Jan. 244 It could be argued that retroactive inhibition might influence the result by preventing the possibility of such recall. **1948** E. R. HILGARD *Theories of Learning* vi. 162 The natural conjecture on the assumption of continuous variation is that the amount of retroactive inhibition would increase gradually as dissimilarity was increased. **1963** COFER & MUSGRAVE *Verbal Behav. & Learning* 7 Many facts of acquisition are consistent with either formulation, but.. others, especially the facts of proactive and retroactive interference, are not. **1965** J. M. STEPHENS *Psychol. of Classroom Learning* viii. 203 Your experience with the second task would work back to strengthen the rather tentative earlier association. This backward-working process is called retroactive facilitation. **1966** J. M. BROWN el al. *Appl. Psychol.* 36 A common explanation for this loss of retention is that newly learned material inhibits that previously learned. A technical term for this is retroactive inhibition. **1975** G. H. BOWER in W. K. Estes *Handbk. Learning & Cognitive Processes* I. ii. 75 An inherent restriction on retrieval times would then produce the observable phenomena of retroactive interference.

Hence **retroˈactively** *adv.*

1828–32 in WEBSTER (citing Wheaton). **1879** *Daily News* 5 Nov. 5/6 That the amnesty did not retroactively affect the material fact of six months' residence in Paris required by the law. **1887** *Contemp. Rev.* May 703 Unfortunately for the public, the laws do not apply retroactively.

retroacˈtivity. [Cf. prec. and ACTIVITY. So Sp. *retroactividad*, Pg. *-idade*.] The condition or fact of being retroactive or retrospective.

1829 BENTHAM *Justice & Cod. Petit.* 110 In the case of judge-made law, this retro-activity is of the very essence of this species of law. **1894** *Daily News* 5 Nov. 7/1 The retroactivity of all treaties, provided that reciprocity is agreed upon, will accordingly be admitted henceforth.

retroˈaspect. *rare*$^{-1}$. [f. RETRO- + ASPECT *sb.*] Retrospect.

1638 JACKSON *Creed* IX. xxxvii, The relation or retro-aspect unto the solemnities used by Barak.

retrocalcuˈlation. *rare*$^{-1}$. [f. RETRO-.] The process of calculating backwards.

1664 POWER *Exp. Philos.* III. 188 Which by retro-calculation will point out the time of the World's Nativity to be about 5000 years ago.

retrocede (ˈrɛtrəʊsiːd, ˈriːtrəʊ-), *v.*^{1} [ad. L. *retrōcēdĕre*, f. *retrō* RETRO- + *cēdĕre* to yield, go back. So obs. F. *retroceder*, Sp. and Pg. *-ceder*, It. *-cedere*.]

1. *intr.* To go back; to retire; to recede.

1654 VILVAIN *Epit. Ess.* v. lxxxii, One ran t' his Cave, th' other trembling hid, And went home glad, but would not retroced. **1681** H. MORE *Exp. Dan.* iii. 70 He durst proceed no further but retroceded from his enterprise on Ægypt. **1704** J. HARRIS *Lex. Techn.* I. s.v. *Precession*, The Equinoctial Points.. do retrocede or move backwards from East to West, about 50 Seconds each Year. **1850** BROWNING *Easter Day* XVI, I felt begin The Judgment-Day: to retrocede Was too late now. **1878** *19th Cent.* Dec. 1051 When we retrocede further into the secondaries it seems rather doubtful whether birds, as we now understand them, had even come into being at that period.

2. *Med.* Of gout: To strike inwardly.

1866 AITKEN *Pract. Med.* II. 53 If acute gout should have 'retroceded', as it is called, and the stomach or intestinal canal be inflamed, leeches should be applied.

retrocede (riːtrəʊˈsiːd), *v.*^{2} [ad. F. *rétrocéder*: see RETRO- and CEDE *v.*] *trans.* To cede (territory) back again *to* a country, etc.

1818 *Gentl. Mag.* LXXXVIII. II. 172 By a treaty of 1783, Great Britain retroceded to Spain all the territory which Spain and France had ceded to her in 1763. **1856** *Abridgm. Deb. Congress* (1858) II. 741/2 *note*, In 1846, the Virginia part of the District was retroceded to that State. **1879** *Spectator* 20 Sept., The valuable province of Kuldja.. has been retroceded to China.

Hence **retroˈceded** *ppl. a.*

1883 *Pall Mall G.* 8 Mar. 1/2 The most important of these chiefs.., who has always been a partisan of the Boers, occupied the central portion of the retroceded country.

retroˈcedence. [See next + -ENCE.] Retrogression; retrocession.

1796 BAGE *Hermstrong* xxxv, Love has its fits of progression and retrocedence. **1866** AITKEN *Pract. Med.* II. 47 Besides metastasis to the stomach and intestines, this retrocedence may take place to other parts.

retrocedent (riːtrəʊ-, rɛtrəʊˈsiːdənt), *a.* [ad. L. *retrōcēdent-em*, pres. pple. of *retrōcēdĕre* RETROCEDE *v.*^{1}]

1. *Astr.* = RETROGRADE *a. rare.*

1583 R. HARVEY *Astrol. Disc.* A 8 b, All which time frowning Saturne shal be retrocedent also. **1686** GOAD *Celest. Bodies* II. i. 142 The Retrocedent Aspect is brisker according to his more fixed Stint of fewer (i.e. but Three Days) for the most part.

2. *Med.* **a.** ***retrocedent gout*** (see first quot.).

1776–84 CULLEN *First Lines Physic* §522 Another state of the disease I name the retrocedent gout. This occurs when ..[the] pain and inflammation [of the joints].. suddenly and entirely cease, while some internal part becomes affected. **1822–34** *Good's Study Med.* (ed. 4) II. 299 In the two ensuing varieties, constituting atonic and retrocedent gout, we have a podagric diathesis grafted upon an unsound frame. **1866** AITKEN *Pract. Med.* II. 53 If the chronic or atonic gout should become retrocedent, and the stomach and intestinal canal be the seat of the spasmodic form of the disease.

b. Of tubercle: Retrograding or caseating.

1898 *Allbutt's Syst. Med.* V. 264 Some change in the lungs, such as collapse or retrocedent tubercle.. preceded the establishment of emphysema.

retrocession^1 (riːtrəʊ-, rɛtrəʊˈsɛʃən). [ad. late L. *retrōcessio*, noun of action f. *retrōcēdĕre* RETROCEDE *v.*^{1} So F. (med.) *rétrocession*, Sp. *retrocesion*, It. *-cessione*.]

1. The action or fact of moving backward, retiring, or receding; retrogression.

a **1646** J. GREGORY *Posthuma* (1650) 37 If it be said that the Retrocession of the Sun and shadow in the Diall of Ahaz was as great a wonder as anie. **1659** H. MORE *Immort. Soul* III. iii. 66 This argument is drawn from the stars retrocession. **1686** GOAD *Celest. Bodies* II. i. 124 What is the return of the Luminaries from the Tropiques, but a kind of Retrocession. **1779** JOHNSON *L.P., Milton* (1868) 57 These transient and involuntary excursions and retrocessions of invention. **1818** HALLAM *Mid. Ages* (1872) II. 233 The retrocession of the Roman terminus under Adrian. **1863** TYNDALL *Heat* i. 25 This retrocession of the index is due.. to the lowering of the temperature within the bulb. **1882** *Contemp. Rev.* Aug. 309 An appeal to the present rate of the retrocession of waterfalls.

b. *Eccl.* The return of the priest or clergy to the vestry after divine service.

1877 J. D. CHAMBERS *Div. Worship* 206 Psalms were sung in the Retrocession. *Ibid.* 419 Retrocession of Celebrant.

†**2.** *Astr.* = RECESSION 1. *Obs.*

1704 J. HARRIS *Lex. Techn.* I. s.v. *Precession*, This motion backwards is by some called the Recession of the Equinox, by others the Retrocession. **1727–38** CHAMBERS *Cycl.* s.v. *Precession*, Which retrograde motion is called the precession, recession, or retrocession of the equinoxes.

3. *Path.* The action or fact, on the part of a disease, of striking inward, so as to affect the internal organs; the 'going in' of an eruption.

1771 T. PERCIVAL *Ess.* (1777) I. 147 The retrocession of the morbid acrimony in the measles, is prevented by nothing more powerfully than by the cortex. **1799** UNDERWOOD *Diseases Children* (ed. 4) I. 99 The reader is reminded of this, from the great importance of attending to such retrocession. **1822–34** *Good's Study Med.* (ed. 4) I. 481 Retrocession of gout. **1876** DUHRING *Dis. Skin* 236 No fears need be entertained concerning danger from retrocession. **1899** *Allbutt's Syst. Med.* VII. 470 The sudden retrocession of an extensive eruption of phlegmonous scrofulides.

4. *Med.* Replacement (of an intestine). *rare*$^{-1}$.

1822–34 *Good's Study Med.* (ed. 4) I. 311 A much larger portion of the gut will be exposed, and its retrocession will be more difficult.

retrocession^2 (riːtrəʊ-, rɛtrəʊˈsɛʃən). [See RETROCEDE *v.*^{2} and CESSION. So F. *rétrocession*, whence prob. sense 2.]

1. *Sc. Law.* (See quots.)

1681 STAIR *Instit.* II. xxiii. 4 Retrocessions, which are returning back of the Right assigned from the assigney to the Cedent, which are also called Repositions. *a* **1768** ERSKINE *Inst. Law Scot.* III. v. §1 If the assignee makes over his right to a third person, the deed is called a translation; and if that third person conveys it back to the cedent, it is called a retrocession. **1838** W. BELL *Dict. Law Scot.*

2. The action or fact of ceding territory back to a country or government.

1796 EARL MALMESBURY *Diaries & Corr.* III. 310 We want much to know what retrocessions you intend for us and our allies. **1826** MACKINTOSH *Case Donna Maria* Wks. 1846 II. 415 The Portuguese plenipotentiaries.. required the retrocession of Olivenza, which had been wrested from them at Badajos. **1884** *Pall Mall G.* 11 Jan. 1/1 The retrocession of Basutoland to the Imperial Government.

retroˈcessional, *a.* and *sb. rare.* [f. RETROCESSION^1.] **a.** *adj.* Of or pertaining to retrocession. **b.** *sb.* = RECESSIONAL B (*Cent. Dict.*).

1887 in CASSELL. **1897** *Westm. Gaz.* 28 July 6/3 At the close they retired singing a fine retrocessional hymn.

retro'cessive, *a.* [f. ppl. stem of L. *retrōcēdĕre*: see RETROCEDE *v.*[1] and *v.*[2]] **a.** Retrograde. **b.** Characterized by restoration of territory.
1816 T. L. PEACOCK *Headlong Hall* x, 'All things,' says Virgil, 'have a retrocessive tendency'. **1869** WILMOT & CHASE *Ann. Cape Colony* 439 The fifth Kafir war... Fitting legacy of the retrocessive policy of 1836!

retrochoir ('riːtrəʊ-, 'rɛtrəʊkwaɪə(r)). *Eccl.* [ad. med.L. *retrochorus* (Du Cange): see RETRO- and CHOIR.] That part of a cathedral or large church which lies behind the high altar.
1848 B. WEBB *Cont. Ecclesiol.* 24 It is cruciform, with an apse, but has no retrochoir or choir-aisles. **1849** FREEMAN *Archit.* 412 That most exquisite and lovely retrochoir at Peterborough. **1889** *Athenæum* 16 Mar. 352/1 The pavement of the retro-choir..is being relaid preparatory to the use of that portion of the Minster.

retro'chorally, *adv. rare*⁻¹. [See prec. and CHORALLY *adv.*] With a retrochoir.
1848 B. WEBB *Cont. Ecclesiol.* 117 In most churches, not retrochorally aisled, the choir is lower than the nave.

retro'coient, *a.* (and *sb.*) *rare.* [f. RETRO- + L. *coient-em*, pres. ppl. of *coīre* to copulate.] = next. Also as *sb.*, an animal which copulates backwards.
1709 *Phil. Trans.* XXVII. 60 Some asserting, that it is Retrocoient and Retromingent. *Ibid.* 61 There can be no such thing as a Retrocoient Animal. **1801** *Ibid.* XCI. 149 Which proves that this animal must be a retro-coient.

retro'copulant, *a. rare*⁻¹. [f. RETRO- + COPULANT *a.*] That copulates backwards.
1819 W. LAWRENCE *Lect. Physiol. Zool.* (1823) 196 They are, consequently, retromingent and retrocopulant.

retro'copulate, *v. rare*⁻⁰. [Cf. next.] *intr.* To use retrocopulation. (Ogilvie, 1882.)

retrocopu'lation. *rare.* [f. RETRO-.] The action or fact of copulating backwards.
1645 SIR T. BROWNE *Pseud. Ep.* 151 From the nature of this position, there ensueth a necessitie of Retrocopulation. *Ibid.* 261 It will be hard to make out their retrocopulation.

retrod(den: see RETREAD.

retro'diction. [f. RETRO- + DICTION, after PREDICTION *sb.*] The explanation or interpretation of past actions or events inferred from the laws that are assumed to have governed them. Cf. POSTDICTION.
1895 J. M. ROBERTSON *Buckle & his Critics* x. 311 Let us first put a little order in our conception of prediction and 'retrodiction' as they indisputably take place in the settled sciences. *Ibid.* 316 The same reasoning applies to errors of interpretation, of what we have called 'retrodiction'. **1939** *Mind* XLVIII. 421 L-propositions are plainly useless save in so far as they assist prediction—or retro-diction—as to particular matters of fact. **1940** *Philosophy* XV. 22 It may be what Mr Ryle calls a *retrodiction*, as when I infer from marks seen in the snow that a cat has passed that way. **1956** J. N. FINDLAY in H. D. Lewis *Contemp. Brit. Philos.* 185 Prediction and retrodiction alike depend on the presence in our world of what have been called 'world-lines'. **1960** I. BERLIN in W. H. Dray *Philos. Analysis & Hist.* (1966) 13 In the case of an historical study, retrodiction—filling in gaps in the past for which no direct testimony exists with the aid of extrapolation performed according to relevant rules or laws. **1975** J. W. CORNMAN *Perception, Common Sense & Sci.* viii. 302 The argument based on retrodiction might prompt another reply, namely, that the supposed fact of retrodiction violates Heisenberg's uncertainty principle. *Ibid.* 303 Epistemic and causal indeterminacy limit prediction but not retrodiction.
Hence (as a back-formation) **retro'dict** *v. trans.* and *absol.*, to infer by retrodiction (cf. POSTDICT *v.*); **retro'dicting** *vbl. sb.* Also **retro'dictable**, **retro'dictive** *adjs.*, **retro'dictively** *adv.*
1932 H. H. PRICE *Perception* vii. 201 Any perceptual act is bound to be among other things a prediction,..and in the same way it must be 'retrodictive' as well. **1949** G. RYLE *Concept of Mind* v. 124 They are inference-tickets, which license us to predict, retrodict, explain and modify these actions, reactions and states. **1951** W. H. WALSH *Introd. Philos. Hist.* ii. 41 It has been said that whilst it is certainly not the business of historians to predict the future, it is very much their business to 'retrodict' the past. **1952** *Mind* LXI. 225 Attempts to predict or retrodict when no grounds for rational belief are obtainable. **1956** E. H. HUTTEN *Lang. Mod. Physics* vi. 222 We now interpret 'causality' as meaning that there can be formulated a universal sentence which..allows us to derive a singular, descriptive, predictive or retrodictive, sentence. **1959** J. BLISH *Clash of Cymbals* v. 104 Time in our experience is not retrodictable. *Ibid.* 105 Can we write a convergent retrodictive equation? **1966** C. G. HEMPEL *Philos. Nat. Sci.* vi. 72 The theory was used by Halley.. to identify it retrodictively with comets whose appearances had been recorded on six previous occasions. **1975** J. W. CORNMAN *Perception, Common Sense & Sci.* viii. 303 Is there any reason to think that retrodicting the position and momentum of an entity more precisely than stated by the uncertainty principle violates the principle? **1976** *Times Lit. Suppl.* 27 Aug. 1057/4 What a historical model is meant to do: not to allow us to predict or retrodict ..but to provide insight into and explanations of historical events.

retro'duction. **a.** (See quots. 1656, 1786.) **b.** In *Philos.*, a type of logical reasoning that develops from some commonly accepted proposition until reasons are found that may alter the acceptance or understanding of the original proposition (see quot. *a* 1914).
1656 BLOUNT *Glossogr.*, *Retroduction*, a bringing, leading or drawing back. **1786** J. PINKERTON *Anc. Scotish Poems* I. p. xxxiii, The poor man [*sc.* Walter Goodall] was writing a *retroduction* to Fordun. *a* **1914** C. S. PEIRCE *Coll. Papers* (1931) I. 28 There are in science three fundamentally different kinds of reasoning, Deduction.., Induction..and Retroduction (Aristotle's ἀπαγωγή, but misunderstood because of corrupt text, and as misunderstood usually translated *abduction*). *Ibid.* 29 Retroduction is the provisional adoption of a hypothesis, because every possible consequence of it is capable of experimental verification, so that the persevering application of the same method may be expected to reveal its disagreement with facts. **1939** *Mind* XLVIII. 378 In discussing 'the leap of the mind from data to hypothesis' he makes no reference to C. S. Peirce's *Retroduction.* **1958** N. R. HANSON *Patterns of Discovery* 217 Retroductions do not always lead to syntheses like those of Newton, Clerk Maxwell, Einstein and Dirac. They sometimes show the first chink in the old armour. **1965** P. CAWS *Philos. of Sci.* xxxii. 243 This is the essential ingredient in what Peirce called retroduction, the intuitive jump from observed facts to hypotheses about them. **1976** C. SELLTIZ et al. *Res. Methods Social Relations* (ed. 3) ii. 32 In the process of determining explanations for observed events, social scientists often reason *from* conclusions to reasons *for* conclusions. We call this inference process *retroduction*, in contrast with deduction and induction. In retroduction, we try to think of plausible reasons why some event could have occurred in an attempt to construct an explanation of why the event did occur.
Also **retro'ductive** *a.*, pertaining to or characterized by retroduction; **retro'ductively** *adv.*
a **1914** C. S. PEIRCE *Coll. Papers* (1932) II. 491 Induction ..is manifestly adequate, with the aid of retroduction and of deductions from retroductive suggestions, to discovering any regularity. **1958** N. R. HANSON *Patterns of Discovery* iv. 86 *H* cannot be retroductively inferred until its content is present in 2. **1974** P. ACHINSTEIN in F. Suppe *Struct. Sci. Theories* 357 Retroductive or explanatory reasoning..is reasoning falling under the logic of discovery, whereas deductive reasoning from established theories is reasoning falling under the logic of justification. **1976** C. SELLTIZ et al. *Res. Methods Social Relations* (ed. 3) ii. 32 An example of retroductive reasoning appears in a study of the decline in trust in the national government during the last decade.

'retro-engine. *Astronautics.* Also as one word. [f. RETRO- + ENGINE *sb.*] = RETRO-ROCKET b.
1967 *Britannica Bk. of Year* 804/1 *Retro-engine*, retro-rocket. **1971** *New Scientist* 6 May 305 Each Mariner.. carries to Mars..about 1000 lbs of fuel for the 14-minute retroengine burn needed to slow it to the requisite orbital speed. **1977** *Sci. Amer.* Nov. 52/1 With the help of its retroengines and parachute it dropped to the surface of Mars.

retro-fire ('rɛtrəʊfaɪə(r)), *v.* Also **retrofire.** [f. RETRO- + FIRE *v.*[1]] *trans.* To ignite or fire (a retro-rocket); to fire a rocket engine so as to give (a spacecraft) backward thrust. Also *absol.*
1961 *Ann. Rev. Med.* XII. 315 Periodically, a very light-weight disposable capsule may be retro-fired in such a way that the capsule together with all unwanted materials will be incinerated on re-entering the atmosphere. **1969** [see *free return* s.v. FREE *a.* D. 2]. **1969** *Guardian* 14 Mar. 1/8 At 5 31 (BST) over Hawaii, Scott retrofired the main service propulsion engine..and Apollo 9 began its long arching descent.
Hence **'retro-,firing** *vbl. sb.*
1962 J. GLENN in *Into Orbit* 41 You superintend the retro-firing sequence from here with toggle switches. **1968** *Guardian* 24 Dec. 1/3, 3 21 p.m.: second retrofiring to bring spacecraft into a circular orbit 69 miles above the moon's surface. **1971** *Ibid.* 1 July 1/5 In order to carry out the descent to earth..retro-firing took place at 01.35.

retro-fire ('rɛtrəʊfaɪə(r)), *sb.* Also **retrofire.** [f. RETRO- + FIRE *sb.*] The process or action of burning a retro-rocket. Also *attrib.*
1962 J. GLENN in *Into Orbit* 42 The clock is pre-set on the ground according to a timing for retro-fire which we have computed before the mission. **1962** *Flight Internat.* LXXXI. 263/1 Kauai Island acquires the spacecraft,..and checks the retro-fire clock for possible change if Mercury control so advises. Point Arguello..gives back-up command to the spacecraft after the clock initiates retro-fire. **1967** *New Scientist* 16 Nov. 424/2 It is not impossible to visualize a carefully controlled descent, the only limitations being the weight of propellants needed for continuous retro-fire. **1974** *Encycl. Brit. Macropædia* XVII. 369/2 Below the Command Module is the Service Module. It..contains the propulsion system for midcourse corrections, retrofire to achieve lunar orbit, and thrust to return from lunar orbit into Earth trajectory.

retrofit ('rɛtrəʊfɪt), *sb.* orig. *U.S.* Also with hyphen. [f. RETRO(ACTIVE *a.* + RE)FIT *sb.*] A modification made to a product, esp. an aircraft, to incorporate changes made in later products of the same type or model.
1956 in W. A. HEFLIN *U.S. Air Force Dict.* 441/1. **1962** *Flight Internat.* LXXXI. 292/1 Fig. 2 is a plot of the ratios of revenue lost versus maintenance and first costs for retro-fitted and 'designed-in' equipment. It points out..that the economic cut-off point for retrofit is near the 100ft ceiling, ½ mile point. **1963** T. PYNCHON *V.* x. 286 An injury of the sexual organs could still be simulated by an attachable moulage, but then this blocked the cooling vent... A new retrofit, however, eliminated this difficulty, which was felt to be a basic design deficiency. **1967** *Times Rev. Industry* May 55/3 It is some indication of Avimo's position that it has been involved in three major retro-fits for aircraft—that is, the instruments already installed in the aircraft have been taken out and Avimo's put in instead. **1978** *Solar Energy* (Shell Internat. Petroleum Co.) 5 Thus the markets and products are likely to split into 'new' products incorporated, for example, into roof structures of new buildings, and 'retrofit' applications for existing housing stock.

retrofit ('rɛtrəʊfɪt), *v.* orig. *U.S.* Also with hyphen. [f. prec.] *trans.* To subject to a retrofit; to modify so as to incorporate changes made in later products of the same type or model. Also *absol.*
1956 in W. A. HEFLIN *U.S. Air Force Dict.* 441/1. **1971** *Sci. Amer.* June 2 The..passenger entertainment and service system..is now in service in the first class sections of a Boeing 747 which American Airlines retrofitted. **1973** *Guardian* 18 Jan. 4/4 American aircraft manufacturers are now researching a modification, known as 'retro-fitting' their engines to make them a good deal quieter... But Concorde..cannot be retrofitted except at extreme cost. **1975** *Daily Colonist* (Victoria, B.C.) 3 May 14/4 You can't retrofit... That is, an existing furnace—coal or oil-fired—cannot feasibly be replaced with a solar system. **1979** *Nature* 5 Apr. p. xiii/1 The B305W can be supplied either as a module for retro-fitting to an existing pumping system or can be supplied installed as an integral package with the Ion Tech B500 high vacuum pumping system.
Hence **'retrofitted** *ppl. a.*, **'retrofitting** *vbl. sb.*
1960 *Aeroplane* XCIX. 145/2 Lately I've been collecting examples of dreadful Americanese. Such as unitized, retrofitted, heat treat, destruct button, [etc.]. **1962** [see RETROFIT *sb.*]. **1975** *Times Lit. Suppl.* 23 May 563/1 The 'retrofitting' of jet aircraft to make them quieter. **1975** *Nature* 30 Oct. 727/1 New models and retrofitted older planes were, even in 1972, achieving 6 dB reductions on the figures quoted for their noisier brothers. **1977** *Blair & Ketchum's Country Jrnl.* (Brattleboro, Vermont) May 33/2 The Mount Washington hung on by virtue of its convention facilities, its retrofitted bathrooms and sprinkler system.

retro'flected, *a.* [f. RETRO- + FLECTED *a.*] Bent, directed, or turned backward.
1812 *Edin. Rev.* XX. 84 The words 'retroflected divergence' are therefore purely ornamental. **1853** G. JOHNSTON *Nat. Hist. E. Bord.* I. 126 The spines on their margins..are all retroflected.

'retroflex, *a.* [ad. mod. or med.L. *retroflex-us*, pa. pple. of *retroflectĕre.*]
1. *Bot.* (See quots.)
1776 J. LEE *Introd. Bot.* Explan. Terms 381 *Retroflexi*, retroflex, bending backward and forward towards the Trunk. **1793** MARTYN *Lang. Bot.* (1796), *Retroflexus*, retroflex... Bending this way and that, in different directions, usually in a distorted manner.
2. *Phonetics.* Pronounced with the tongue curled back; cacuminal.
1915 [see CACUMINAL *a.*]. **1932** D. JONES *Outl. Eng. Phonetics* (ed. 3) xxv. 199 Retroflex sounds (also called 'cerebral', 'cacuminal' or 'inverted' sounds) are those in the formation of which the tip of the tongue is curled upwards towards the hard palate. **1942** *Amer. Speech: Reprints & Monogr.* No. 4. 41 This sound is generally clearly retroflex in the Great Smokies, as in most American speech. It is heard in such words as the following: Birch, bird, birth, Burchfield, burn. **1964** B. HONIKMAN in D. Abercrombie et al. *Daniel Jones* 78 The frequent retroflex consonants in the languages of India and Pakistan are produced with the tongue curled back. **1973** J. C. WELLS *Jamaican Pronunc. in London* 128 Dentals, alveolars, retroflex sounds, and palato-alveolars. **1977** *Publ. Amer. Dial. Soc. 1974* LXI/LXII. 36 Again, the retroflex mid-central vowel comes from different speakers.

'retroflex, *v.* [Back-formation from RETROFLEXED *a.*] *trans.* and *intr.* To turn or fold back. So **'retroflexing** *ppl. a.*
1898 H. C. PORTER tr. *Strasburger's Text-bk. Bot.* 396 The male branches give rise..to spherical stalked antheridia, which open at the apices by means of retroflexing valves. **1934** WEBSTER, *Retroflex*, v.i., to turn or bend backward. **1954** S. DUKE-ELDER *Parsons' Dis. Eye* (ed. 12) xxiii. 405 A large corneal section is made as for cataract.., the cornea retroflexed by traction on the suture, and a triangular piece of iris more deliberately excised.

retroflexed, *a.* [f. as RETROFLEX *a.* + -ED[1].]
1. *Bot.* Bending or bent backwards, or backwards and forwards, retroflex; also *Path.* (cf. RETROFLEXION).
1806 GALPINE *Brit. Bot.* 83 Cor. retroflexed: L. cordate, angular, denticulate. **1872** PEASLEE *Ovarian Tumors* 61 Frequently the uterus, being also carried backward by the traction of the ovary, is for the time retroflexed.
2. *Phonetics.* = RETROFLEX *a.* 2.
1932 D. JONES *Outl. Eng. Phonetics* (ed. 3) xxv. 200 Retroflexed vowels may be represented in phonetic transcription. **1950** —— *Phoneme* p. xiii, ɹ fricative tongue-tip r; also the corresponding frictionless continuant, and a retroflexed variety of this. **1973** *Amer. Speech 1969* XLIV. 263 The study consequently proposed to measure the degree to which the Midland dialect, in the form of heavily retroflexed postvocalic /r/, appears in Austin.

retroflexion (riːtrəʊ-, rɛtrəʊ'flɛkʃən). [ad. mod.L. *retroflexio.* So F. *rétroflexion*, Sp. *retroflexion.*]
1. The fact or state of being turned back or retorted. Chiefly *Path.*, retroversion.
1845 *Encycl. Metrop.* VI. 541/1 The stratified limestones of these localities are bent into such extraordinary retroflexions, as to imply repeated operations of the most violent Mechanical agency. **1860** TANNER *Pregnancy* iii. 136 The patient was suffering from retroversion or retroflexion of the uterus. **1879** *St. George's Hosp. Rep.* IX. 458 Having suffered from symptoms of retroflexion for about a year.
2. *Phonetics.* Articulation of a sound with the tongue curled back.

1932 D. JONES *Outl. Eng. Phonetics* (ed. 3) ii. 11 In many parts..the effect of the *r* appears as a modification known as 'retroflexion' or 'inversion' of the preceding vowel. **1954** *Bull. School Oriental & Afr. Stud.* XVI. 558 It is well known as a feature of Sanskrit 'internal sandhi' that the coarticulation of retroflexion with constriction has more extensive syntagmatic implications than its coarticulation with occlusion. **1964** R. H. ROBINS *Gen. Linguistics* iii. 98 All vowel sounds may be characterized by retroflexion... This retroflexion is one of the characteristics of what is loosely called in Britain 'an American accent'. **1973** *Amer. Speech* 1969 XLIV. 263 A careful study of this feature was therefore planned and conducted to determine the degree of retroflexion of /r/.

'retrofract(ed, *a. Bot.* [ad. mod.L. *retrofract-us*: see RETRO- and REFRACT *v.*] (See quots.)

1793 MARTYN *Lang. Bot.* (1796), *Retrofractus*, retrofracted. Applied to the Peduncle... Reduced to hang down as it were by force, so that it appears as if it had been broken. **1797** *Encycl. Brit.* (ed. 3) III. 445/2 A Peduncle is ..retrofract, broken backward, reduced to a depending state as if by force.

†**retrogate**, erroneous f. RETROGRADE *a. Obs.*

1584 LODGE *Alarum* 24 Appollonius..hauing calculated the Gentlemans natiuitie, and seeing some planets retrogate. **1771** LUCKOMBE *Hist. Printing* 385 Making the last lines of two retrogate pages to fall on the Back of each other.

†**retrogation**, erroneous f. RETROGRADATION.

1646 *Game at Sc. & Eng.* 6 Whereby you would..utterly debar them in this difference from all retrogations beyond the Covenant. **1708** *Brit. Apollo* No. 85. 2/1 Stations and Retrogations of the Planets.

retro'generative, *a. rare.* [f. RETRO- + GENERATIVE *a.*] = RETROCOPULANT *a.*

1743 *Phil. Trans.* XLII. 535 He is a retromingent Animal, and consequently retrogenerative.

†**retrogradant**, *a. Obs. rare.* [ad. late L. *retrōgradant-em*, pres. pple. of *retrōgradāre*: cf. next.] Retrograding.

1523 SKELTON *Garl. Laurel* 4 When Mars retrogradant reuersyd his bak. **1558** G. CAVENDISH *Poems* (1825) II. 3 Whan Phebus in Gemynys had his course overgon And entered Cancer, a sygne retrogradant.

†**retrogradate**, *a. Obs. rare*$^{-1}$. [ad. late L. *retrōgradāt-us*, pa. ple. of *retrōgradāre*: see RETROGRADE *a.*] Having retrograded.

1471 RIPLEY *Comp. Alch.* II. i. in Ashm. (1652) 135 Into ther owne fyrst nature kyndly retrogradate.

†**retrogradate**, *v. Obs. rare*$^{-1}$. [Cf. prec.] *intr.* = RETROGRADE *v.*

1599 T. M[OUFET] *Silkwormes* Ded., Nay, heau'ns themselues (though keeping stil their way) Retrogradate, and make a kind of stay.

retrogradation (rɛtrəʊ-, riːtrəʊgrə'deɪʃən). [ad. L. *retrōgradātio*, n. of action f. *retrōgradāre*: see RETROGRADE *a.* So F. *rétrogradation*, Sp. *retrogradacion*, It. *retrogradazione*.]

1. a. *Astr.* The apparent backward motion of a planet in the zodiac; motion of a heavenly body from east to west; a case or instance of this.

1554 F. VAN BRUNSWIKE tr. *De Montulmo's Facies Cœli* E vj, Mars..signifieth that mortal war shall happen amongest men, and the more because of his retrogradacion. **1583** R. HARVEY *Astrol. Disc.* A 8 b, Saturne shal be retrocedent also, beginning his retrogradation the 25th day of June. **1601** HOLLAND *Pliny* I. 12 The starres themselues are thought to returne more speedily in their retrogradation, than in their direct course forward. *a* **1641** BP. MOUNTAGU *Acts & Mon.* (1642) 124 The Retrogradation of the Sun in Ezechias time. **1670** CUDWORTH *Serm. 1 John* ii. 3–4 (ed. 3) 58 These upper Planets..have their Stations and Retrogradations as well as their direct motion. **1715** tr. *Gregory's Astron.* (1726) I. 449 Of the greatest Elongation of the Planets from the Sun, their Direction, Station, and Retrogradation. **1755** B. MARTIN *Mag. Arts & Sci.* 83, I have no Occasion to ask concerning his Conjunctions, Oppositions, Retrogradations, &c. **1839** MOSELEY *Astron.* liv. (1854) 169 This retrogradation will continue until about the 28th. **1861** LEWIS *Astron. Anc.* iii. 14 The theory of epicycles accounted by circular movements for the stations and retrogradations of the planets.

fig. **1603** FLORIO *Montaigne* II. xii. (1632) 301 There is no more retrogradation, trepidation,..than they have fained.. in this poore seely little body of man. *c* **1630** DONNE *Serm.* lxxii. 731 There is a Going behind Christ, which is a Casting out of his presence without any future following, and that is a fearefull Station, a fearefull Retrogradation. *a* **1652** J. SMITH *Sel. Disc.* v. 140 No such ebbings and flowings, no such diversity of stations and retrogradations as that love hath in us.

b. The backward movement of the lunar nodes on the ecliptic.

1727–38 CHAMBERS *Cycl.* s.v., Retrogradation of the nodes, is a motion of the line of the nodes, whereby it continually shifts its situation from east to west, contrary to the order of the signs. **1855** BREWSTER *Newton* I. xii. 328 He showed that the retrogradation of the nodes..arose from one of the elements of the solar force being exerted in the plane of the ecliptic, and not in the plane of the moon's orbit.

2. The action or process of going back towards some point in investigation or reasoning.

1577–87 HOLINSHED *Chron.* I. 141/2 As you shall find it by retrogradation from the 32 verse vnto the first of the fift chapter of Genesis. **1637** A. WARWICK *Spare Min.* (ed. 6) 110 What's a City to a Shire? What a Shire to the whole Island?..And so by a retrogradation how little, how nothing is this poor glory? **1690** LEYBOURN *Curs. Math.* 349 Then by Retrogradation orderly one might come to the said Aequation. **1799** W. TOOKE *View Russian Emp.* I. 481 Without being able, whatever retrogradations we might make, to discover their first generation. **1819** FOSTER *Ess. Evils Pop. Ignorance* 7 You cannot perform in imagination a series of acts of unlearning, realizing to yourselves, throughout the retrogradation [etc.].

3. a. The action or fact of moving or drawing back or backwards; retirement, retreat.

1644 DIGBY *Nat. Bodies* xx. (1658) 222 Atoms..in a motion of retrogradation back to their own north pole. *a* **1646** J. GREGORY *Posthuma* (1650) 37 The most visible part,..that which would bee most of all observed was the Retrogradation of the shadow. **1748** RICHARDSON *Clarissa* IV. xxxvii. 229 She..did it before she was aware, Lady-pride, Belford! — Recollection, then Retrogradation! **1790** *Phil. Trans.* LXXXI. 22, I have said above, that hemp and gut have only a very little retrogradation. **1821** *New Monthly Mag.* II. 60 The retrogradation of the American Indians upon their woods and wildernesses. **1843** SEDGWICK *Let.* in Clark & Hughes *Life* (1890) II. 63 Never having once fallen during my retrogradations before the face of the Queen.

b. *Physical Geogr.* The landward retreat of a beach or coastline caused by wave-erosion.

1922 C. A. COTTON *Geomorphol. N.Z.* I. xxviii. 391 This process is termed progradation (as contrasted with retrogradation, the cutting-back of a coast by marine erosion). **1937** WOOLDRIDGE & MORGAN *Physical Basis of Geogr.* xxi. 332 Retrogradation comprises not only beach recession but the general recession of the coastline under wave-attack. **1954** W. D. THORNBURY *Princ. Geomorphol.* xvii. 442 Retrogradation of a shore line may go on so rapidly that small streams are unable to keep pace in downcutting with the rate of sea-cliff recession. As a result, these streams enter the sea from hanging valleys. **1968** R. W. FAIRBRIDGE *Encycl. Geomorphol.* 941/2 During retrogradation, a wide belt of beach ridges with their overlying dunes..may be rapidly removed.

4. †**a.** Reversion from one state to another. *Obs.*

1639 SIR R. BAKER in Spurgeon *Treas. David* Ps. li. 7 How, then, is it possible that my sins which are as red as scarlet should ever be made as white as snow? Indeed such retrogradation is no work of human art.

b. The action, fact, or condition of falling back in development; retrogression, decline.

In first quot. directly *transf.* from sense 1.

1748 HARTLEY *Observ. Man* II. i. 29 We ought to suppose ourselves in the Centre of the System, and to try..to reduce all apparent Retrogradations to real Progressions. **1768–74** TUCKER *Lt. Nat.* (1834) II. 360 Improvement admits of frequent intermissions and retrogradations. **1794** G. ADAMS *Nat. & Exp. Philos.* IV. xxxvii. 29 A similar instance of the retrogradation of science occurs in the history of the microscope. **1814** *Ann. Reg.* Pref. p. iv, The singular mixture of advance and retrogradation which the events of the year have exhibited. **1849** H. MILLER *Footpr. Creat.* ix. (1874) 173 It indicates, not the starting point from which the race of creation began, but the stage of retrogradation beyond it. **1873** H. ROGERS *Orig. Bible* ix. (1875) 378 Amidst all the fluctuations and apparent retrogradations of the world.

retrogradatory, *a. rare*$^{-1}$. [Cf. prec. and -ORY.] Serving to reverse motion.

1797 *Monthly Mag.* III. 383 The Retrogradatory Machine consists of an axle, suspended horizontally on its centre points [etc.].

retrograde ('rɛtrəʊgreɪd, 'riːtrəʊ-), *a.* and *sb.* Also 6 rethro-; 4, 7 -grad, 6 -garde (?), -grat(e, *Sc.* -graid. [ad. L. *retrōgrad-us*, f. *retrō* RETRO- + *gradus* step: cf. next. So F. *rétrograde*, Sp., Pg., and It. *retrogrado*.]

A. *adj.* **1.** *Astr.* **a.** Of the planets: Apparently moving in a direction contrary to the order of the signs, or from east to west.

c **1391** CHAUCER *Astrol.* II. §35 This is the workinge of the conclusioun to knowe yif þat any planete be directe or retrograde. *c* **1400** *Treat. Astron.* (Bodl. MS. B. 17) lf. 8 Hit is to wete also þat ȝef þe planetes regnen retrograde..þey myght neuer be made evene as by her cours. *c* **1480** HENRYSON *Mor. Fab.* IV. (*Fox's Confess.*) iii, The planeitis.. Sum retrograde and sum stationeir. **1503** HAWES *Examp. Virt.* I. 6 Myxt with venus that was not retrograte. **1509** —— *Past. Pleas.* XXII. N iiij b, He sette in werking The bodies aboue to haue their mouing,..Some rethrogarde, and some dyrectly. **1574** W. BOURNE *Regiment for Sea* iii. (1577) 12 The Sunne and the Moone be neuer retrograt, as the other 5. planets or lyghts be. **1589** GREENE *Tullies Love* Wks. (Grosart) VII. 139 Fonde are those women that are inquisitiue after Astrologers, whether Venus be retrograde or combust in their natiuities. **1671** BLAGRAVE *Astrol. Pract. Phys.* 91 By no means let the Moon be aspected of any retrograde planet. **1715** tr. *Gregory's Astron.* (1726) I. 9 Venus, when Retrograde,..is nearer to the Earth, and consequently appears bigger than at other Times. **1760** STERNE *Tr. Shandy* III. xxiii, I would have sworn some retrograde planet was hanging over this unfortunate house of mine. **1808** SCOTT *Marm.* III. xx, His zone..Bore many a planetary sign, Combust, and retrograde, and trine. **1880** SHORTHOUSE *John Inglesant* I. 282 Jupiter, lord of the ascendant, and Saturn being retrograde.

b. Actually moving from east to west.

1853 HERSCHEL *Pop. Lect. Sci.* iii. §13 (1873) 106 Retrograde comets, or those whose motion is opposite to that of the planets, are as common as direct ones.

2. Of movement: **a.** *Astr.* Apparently or actually contrary to the order of the signs; directed from east to west. †Also *transf.* of aspect.

1423 JAS. I *King's Q.* clxx, Though thy begynnyng hath bene retrograde. **1549** *Compl. Scot.* vi. 55 The mune..is moir suift in hyr retrograid cours nor the soune is. *c* **1585** *Faire Em* III. 670 But planets ruled by retrograde aspect Foretold mine ill in my nativity. **1667** MILTON *P. L.* VIII. 127 Thir wandring course now high, now low, then hid, Progressive, retrograde, or standing still. **1693** J. EDWARDS *Author. O. & N. Test.* 201 The Chaldean astronomers.. labour'd to suppress this retrograde motion of the sun. **1755** B. MARTIN *Mag. Arts & Sci.* 98 The retrograde Motion in Mercury is but of short Duration indeed. **1833** HERSCHEL *Astron.* ix. 299 Contrary to the unbroken analogy of the whole planetary system.., in these orbits their motions are retrograde. **1868** G. B. AIRY *Pop. Astron.* iv. 124 The planets sometimes move in a retrograde direction.

Comb. **1727–38** CHAMBERS *Cycl.* s.v. *Dragon*, These points ..have a motion of their own in the zodiac, and retrograde-wise, almost three minutes a day.

b. Directed backwards; in a direction contrary to the previous motion; retiring, retreating.

1622 MALYNES *Anc. Law-Merch.* 400 The partie who tooke this Bill..must goe a retrograde course heerein. **1676** WORLIDGE *Cyder* (1691) 57 The sap..will expend itself by a retrograde as well as by a direct motion. **1745** ELIZA HEYWOOD *Female Spect.* No. 10 (1748) II. 208 They seem rather like buckets in a well, that are always in a retrograde motion. **1797** MRS. RADCLIFFE *Italian* xxi, Every step that he had taken..was retrograde. **1803** WELLINGTON in Gurw. *Desp.* (1835) II. 35 A retrograde movement is always bad in this country. **1847** PRESCOTT *Peru* (1850) II. 326 The sufferings endured by the Spaniards on their retrograde march to Quito. **1880** GÜNTHER *Fishes* 44 Retrograde motions can be made by fish in an imperfect manner only.

3. a. Tending or inclined to go back or to revert; moving or leading backwards, *esp.* towards an inferior or less flourishing condition.

c **1530** *Compl. of them that ben to late Maryed* (Collier, 1862) 18 Both yonge and olde must haue theyr sustenaunce Euer in this worlde, soo fekyll and rethrograte. **1595** DANIEL *Civ. Wars* VI. xxxvi, Weary the Soul with contrarieties; Till all Religion become retrograde. **1612** BACON *Ess., Ambition* (Arb.) 224 Ther-fore it is good for Princes, if they vse ambitious men, to handle it soe, as they be stil progressiue, and not retrograde. **1664** EVELYN *Pomona* iv. 13 Nature does more delight in progress, then to be Retrograde and go backwards. **1709** SACHEVERELL *Serm.* 22 Who..is agen ready to be Retrograde, whenever the Wind shall Change, and Veer about. **1773** JOHNSON *Let. to Mrs. Thrale* 21 Sept., His retrograde ambition was completely gratified. **1816** T. L. PEACOCK *Headlong Hall* x, The human mind, which will necessarily become retrograde in ceasing to be progressive. **1868** ROGERS *Pol. Econ.* vi. 57 The capital of a country may be stationary, progressive, or retrograde.

†**b.** Backward; slow. *Obs. rare.*

1695 CONGREVE *Love for L.* II. i, You know my aunt is a little retrograde (as you call it) in her nature. **1760** STERNE *Tr. Shandy* V. xvi, He..would often say, especially when his pen was a little retrograde [etc.].

c. *Bot.* Of metamorphosis: (see quots.).

1839 *Penny Cycl.* XV. 135/1 Retrograde metamorphosis .., when organs assume the state of some of those on the outside of them, as when carpels change to stamens or petals,..and the like. **1861** BENTLEY *Man. Bot.* 356 If any of these organs become transformed into a leaf, this is called retrograde or descending metamorphosis.

d. *Path.* Tending to disintegration.

1876 tr. *Wagner's Gen. Path.* 287 In retrograde changes attention has until now been turned more in both directions. **1897** *Allbutt's Syst. Med.* II. 33 Obsolescent or retrograde tubercle in the lungs occurs in about nine per cent of all necropsies.

e. *Petrol.* Of a metamorphic change: resulting from a decrease in temperature or pressure. Opp. PROGRADE *a.* 1.

1932 A. HARKER *Metamorphism* xx. 342 The changes which befall metamorphosed rocks subsequently to the culmination of metamorphism..are of the nature of degradation... This class of changes includes what Becke has styled 'diaphthoresis', implying ruin or corruption; but this rather cumbrous term has not been very widely adopted. It will be more convenient to speak of retrograde metamorphism. **1971** I. G. GASS et al. *Understanding Earth* i. 34/1 The metamorphism of many igneous rocks involves the replacement of a very high-temperature original mineral assemblage by a metamorphic assemblage at a lower temperature. This type of change, though not strictly referred to as retrograde since the starting material is not a metamorphic rock, nevertheless has all the essential characters of retrograde metamorphism. **1980** *Nature* 29 May 320/2 The Alpine uplift was accompanied by widespread retrograde metamorphism.

4. a. Moving backwards (in literal sense); returning upon the previous course.

1564 CHALONER in Froude *Hist. Eng.* (1881) VIII. 45 [I am] now further from wealth..than I was eighteen years agone. Methinks I became a retrograde crab. **1599** B. JONSON *Cynthia's Rev.* v. ii, I' faith, master, let's go; no body comes..; let's be retrograde. **1615** G. SANDYS *Trav.* 191 The gate of Saint Steuen (where on each side a Lion retrograde doth stand). **1662** PLAYFORD *Skill Mus.* I. (1674) 59 This Mood had its derivation from..the winding retrograde Meander.

b. Of order in enumeration, etc.: Inverse, reversed.

1664 H. MORE *Apology* 557 We will now take a Summary view of all the Objections.., which we shall doe in a retrograde order, beginning with the last, and then conclude. **1686** PLOT *Staffordsh.* 421 The Dominical and other Letters vary every year in a retrograd order. **1727–38** CHAMBERS *Cycl.*, *Retrograde order*, in matters of numeration, is when, in lieu of accounting 1, 2, 3, 4, we count 4, 3, 2, 1. **1751** JOHNSON *Rambler* No. 86 ¶ 14 Here the third pair of syllables in the first..verse have their accents retrograde or inverted; the first syllable being strong or acute, and the second weak. **1851** *Monthly Jrnl. Med. Sci.* XII. 39 The incuse and retrograde form of these inscriptions.

c. *Mus.* Of imitation, etc.: (see quots.).

1727–38 CHAMBERS *Cycl.* s.v. *Imitation*, Sometimes the movement, or the figure of the notes, alone, is imitated; and that, sometimes, even by a contrary motion, which makes what they call a retrograde imitation. **1869** OUSELEY *Counterp.* xv. 103 Imitation may also be retrograde, i.e. the consequent may be produced by reading the antecedent backwards. **1887** H. C. BANISTER *Mus. Anal.* vii. 153 Imitation may be by contrary or inverse motion..; and by retrograde motion, from the end to the beginning. **1891** PROUT *Counterpoint* (ed. 2) 243 Another even more intricate kind of canon is the Reverse Retrograde Canon.

d. Of verses: (see quot.). *rare*$^{-0}$.

1727–38 CHAMBERS *Cycl.*, *Retrograde verses* are such as give the same words, whether read backwards or forwards; called also reciprocal verses, and recurrents.

e. Operating in a backward direction. *rare.*

1797 *Monthly Mag.* III. 384 It will be of infinite service for every species of retrograde machinery.

†**5.** Opposed, contrary, or repugnant *to* something. *Obs.*

1602 SHAKS. *Ham.* I. ii. 114 For your intent In going backe to Schoole in Wittenberg, It is most retrograde to our desire. **1643** MILTON *Soveraigne Salve* 4 Preferred the means before the end, which is retrograde to reason. **1704** *Elegy* xxxv. 31 Malice is always Retrograde to Sense. *a* **1776** JOHNSON in *Boswell* (1903) 651/1, I would not..for ten pounds have seemed so retrograde to any general observance. **1797** MRS. A. M. BENNETT *Beggar Girl* (1813) IV. 117 There was something in trade..very retrograde to her feelings.

6. As quasi-*adv.* In a backward or reverse direction.

a **1619** FOTHERBY *Atheom.* II. x. §4 (1622) 307 If wee will but walke retrograde, the same way backe againe. **1634** SIR T. HERBERT *Trav.* (1638) 188 [The priest] crab-like goes retrograde from the Idoll. **1709** *Refl. on Sacheverell's Serm.* 21 The Reformation begun to go retrograde in Q. Elizabeth's time. **1771** *Encycl. Brit.* I. 438/1 Her horary motion from the sun 3′ 57″.13 retrograde. **1822–34** *Good's Study Med.* (ed. 4) IV. 367 It has been supposed that the chyle flows retrograde from the thoracic duct into the lymphatics of the kidney. **1868** LOCKYER *Elem. Astron.* §381 It will appear to us to travel from left to right, or retrograde. **1959** A. G. WOODHEAD *Study of Greek Inscriptions* iii. 24 The assorted sherds of early date..show writing in both directions, but the majority of fragments..have their messages written retrograde. **1980** *Early Music* Jan. 111/2 Its slow movement incorporates the melody 'God Save the King', played first retrograde, later in inversion and finally in its normal form.

7. Of amnesia: pertaining to incidents preceding the causal event.

1935 *Lancet* 5 Oct. 763/1 The duration of this retrograde amnesia. **1960** *Jrnl. Compar. & Physiol. Psychol.* LIII. 524/1 Retrograde amnesia induced by electroconvulsive shock..or other trauma. **1969** *Times* 14 Apr. 6/8 Concussion, anaesthesia..and dosage with various drugs, are all known to impair the memory of the immediate past, a phenomenon known as retrograde amnesia. **1979** 'S. WOODS' *This Fatal Writ* 150 'He remembered too much.. everything..up to and including the blow on the head. And you know..that's just not possible.' 'Retrograde amnesia.'

B. *sb.* **1.** One who falls away or degenerates.

1593 T. KELWAY tr. *Ferrier's Judgem. Natiuities* 26 If the sayd lords of the sayd part be retrogrades or otherwise ill disposed. **1633** PRYNNE *Histrio-m.* 100 Our Play-hunters would haue been good proficients, not retrogrades, in the schoole of Virtue. **1897** *Chr. Her.* (N.Y.) 1 Sept. 663/1 These retrogrades are to be pitied quite as much as those who..have not enjoyed any training advantages.

2. A backward movement or tendency. *rare.*

1613 PURCHAS *Pilgrimage* (1614) 27 As if with an imperfect retrograde he [man] would return into his first elements. **1643** *Plain English* 18 The designe must on, the authours are impatient of this retrograde they have suffred these three yeeres. **1830** A. W. FONBLANQUE *Eng. under 7 Administr.* (1837) II. 14 What Sir Robert [Wilson] styles the retrograde of intellect would be the breaking up of these meshes of thraldom.

3. *in retrograde advb. phr. rare.*

1954 W. FAULKNER *Fable* 5 For another instant, the cavalry held. And even then, it did not break. It just began to move in retrograde while still facing forward.

retrograde (ˈrɛtrəʊgreɪd, ˈriːtrəʊ-), *v.* [ad. L. *retrōgradī* or *retrōgradāre* (hence F. *rétrograder*, Sp. and Pg. *retrogradar*, It. *retro-*, *ritrogradare*), f. *retrō* RETRO- + *gradus* step.]

1. a. *trans.* To turn back, reverse, revert; to make, or cause to become, retrograde. Now *rare.*

1582 BENTLEY *Mon. Matrones* II. 25 And euen as the feare of death doth retrograde us; so ought loue to giue us a desire to die. **1598** SYLVESTER *Du Bartas* II. i. I. *Eden* 502 The Firmament shall retrograde his course. **1610** W. FOLKINGHAM *Art of Survey* II. v. 55 To Rectifie the Table: retrograde the Ruler. **1653** R. SANDERS *Physiogn. Moles* 37 Say these letters B, C, D, E, F, G, H, I, K, and retrograde them from K to B. **1847** EMERSON *Repr. Men*, *Montaigne* Wks. (Bohn) I. 351 We see, now, events forced on, which seem to retard or retrograde the civility of ages.

b. To cause to move backward.

1910 *Jrnl. Geol.* XVIII. 165 Headlands are cut back, or retrograded.

2. *intr.* *Astr.* Of the planets, etc.: To go backward (in apparent motion) in the zodiac; to seem to travel from east to west.

1598 SYLVESTER *Du Bartas* II. ii. IV. *Columns* 391 Then Southward Sol doth retrograde, Goes (Crab-like) backward. **1601** DOLMAN *La Primaud. Fr. Acad.* (1618) III. 745 The Moone..which retrogradeth thirteenth parts of the Zodiacke in foure and twenty houres. **1654** CULPEPPER *Opus Astrol.*, *Aphorisms* §30 If a Planet retrograde,..he denotes much discord and contradiction in the business. **1706** PHILLIPS (ed. Kersey) s.v., Mars retrogrades more than Jupiter. **1833** HERSCHEL *Astron.* viii. 255 The former [*sc.* Mercury] continues to retrograde during about 22 days. **1875** *Encycl. Brit.* II. 758/2 Seeing that this luminous point ..had been stationary and retrograded within comparatively small limits like the planets.

†**3.** Of gout: To become retrocedent. *Obs.*$^{-1}$

1599 A. M. tr. *Gabelhouer's Bk. Physicke* 203/1 The Goute, which chaunceth to one in anye of the Joynctes, and retrogradeth this way, or that way, with greate greefe.

4. a. To move backwards, to take a backward course; to retire, recede, etc. †Also with *it.*

1613 HEYWOOD *Braz. Age* II. ii, I can by Art make riuers retrograde, Alter their channels, run backe to their heads. **1656** S. H. *Gold. Law* 14 His Sun of glory may decline and retrograde it, as on the Dyal of Ahaz. **1796** *State Papers* in *Ann. Reg.* 192 The armies..retrograded towards our frontiers. **1822–34** *Good's Study Med.* (ed. 4) I. 200 Some portion of it retrogrades, and is carried by absorption into the system. **1863** LYELL *Antiq. Man.* 292 The marks which a glacier leaves behind it as it retrogrades.

b. To go back in time or succession.

1819 SCOTT *Ivanhoe* xxix, Our history must needs retrograde for the space of a few pages. **1825** —— *Talism.* xxii, Our narrative retrogrades to a period shortly previous to the incidents last mentioned. **1877** BP. BUTCHER *Eccl. Cal.* 37 The Sunday Letter retrogrades..one place, or two.

c. To draw back from a position.

1859 MILL *Diss. & Disc.* (1875) II. 169 All sorts of confused voices called for different things, and most of the assailants wished to retrograde rather than to advance.

5. To fall back or revert towards a lower or less flourishing condition.

1613 PURCHAS *Pilgrimage* VII. xi. (1614) 710 Thus you see one Retrograde from a sensitiue to a vegitatiue life. **1788** GIBBON *Decl. & F.* lxxi. VI. 622 All that is human must retrograde if it do not advance. **1816** T. L. PEACOCK *Headlong Hall* v, Where one man advances, hundreds retrograde. **1845** MCCULLOCH *Taxation* I. iii. (1852) 106 Compared with the latter the labourers may be truly said to have retrograded. **1875** LUBBOCK *Orig. Civiliz.* App. 465 Some races have been stationary, or even have retrograded.

Hence **ˈretrograding** *vbl. sb.* and *ppl. a.* Also **retroˈgradingly** *adv.* (Ogilvie *Suppl.* 1855).

1860 *Olmsted's Mech. Heavens* 179 *marg.*, Retrograding of the nodes on the ecliptic. **1891** *Athenæum* 25 Apr. 529/2 A theory of previous progressive or retrograding existences. **1910** *Jrnl. Geol.* XVIII. 166 The retrograding of the shore.. due to active wave erosion. **1919** D. W. JOHNSON *Shore Processes & Shoreline Devel.* vi. 295 The phenomenon of a shifting fulcrum between a retrograding cliff and a prograding beach plain. **1968** R. W. FAIRBRIDGE *Encycl. Geomorphol.* 941/2 The retrograding shore line may cut back at an angle to previously formed ridges.

ˈretrogradely, *adv.* [f. the adj. + -LY^2.] In a retrograde way or manner.

1658 BROMHALL *Treat. Specters* IV. 264 The water making a reflux and flowing retrogradely. **1813** T. BUSBY *Lucretius* I. II. 325 Some powerful agent struggles in the heart, And sends the spirits swift to every part; Till checked again, they retrogradely fly. **1894** *Idler* Sept. 199, I daresay it's all very foolish and retrogradely sentimental.

ˈretrogradeness. *rare*$^{-0}$. [f. the adj.] 'The faculty of going backwards' (Bailey, vol. II, 1727).

†**retroˈgradient,** *a.* *Obs. rare.* [ad. L. *retrōgradient-em*, pres. pple. of *retrōgradī*.] *Astr.* = RETROGRADE *a.* 1 a.

1412–20 LYDG. *Chron. Troy* IV. xxxiii, Tyll Phebus chare ..Out of the Crabbe towarde the Lyon Holdeth his course in the fyrmament, I mean whan he is retrogradyent. **1426** —— *De Guil. Pilgr.* 12351 In the Epicicles whan they be, They make hem retrogradyent.

retrogradism. *rare*$^{-1}$. [f. RETROGRADE *a.* + -ISM.] Adoption of reactionary principles.

1856 *Chamb. Jrnl.* VI. 322 The old Marchese Testaferrata, the strongest advocate of retrogradism in the società.

So **retrogradist**, a reactionary.

1851 *Fraser's Mag.* XLIV. 250 The principal employments were occupied by retrogradists. **1869** *Contemp. Rev.* XI. 507 Madame..had been imprisoned as the 'wife of an abominable retrogradist'.

†**retrogradous,** *a.* *Obs. rare*$^{-1}$. [f. as prec. + -OUS.] = RETROGRADE *a.*

a **1660** HAMMOND *Serm.* Wks. 1683 IV. 603 This conversible retrogradous Sorites may shut up all.

†**retrogration**, error for RETROGRADATION.

1574 W. BOURNE *Regiment for Sea* iii. (1577) 12 So doth all the seuen lyghts or planets, [except] that it be in their retrogration: but the Sunne and the Moone be neuer retrograt.

†**retroˈgredient.** *Obs.*$^{-1}$ [f. RETRO-, after *progredient.*] One who retrogrades.

1650 HUBBERT *Pill Formality* 54 He that is no Progredient, must needs be a Retrogredient.

ˈretrogress, *sb. rare.* [ad. L. *retrōgress-us*: see next.] A retrogression.

1814 COLERIDGE in Cottle *Early Recoll.* (1837) II. 164 After a sad retrogress of nearly twelve years. **1867** SPENCER *Princ. Biol.* VI. iii. II. 410 Progress in bulk, complexity, or activity involves retrogress in fertility.

retrogress (ˈriːtrəʊ-, ˈrɛtrəʊgrɛs), *v.* [f. L. *retrōgress-*, ppl. stem of *retrōgradī* to RETROGRADE.] *intr.* To move backwards; to go back.

1819 H. BUSK *Vestriad* IV. 21 Night retrogressing from her daily tour. **1861** J. NICHOL in *Memoir* (1896) 32, I am retrogressing into a period which we have closed. **1882** FARRAR *Early Chr.* I. 439 This was the system..to which some of them were even tempted to apostatise or retrogress!

retrogression (riːtrəʊ-, rɛtrəʊˈgrɛʃən). [ad. L. type **retrōgressio*, f. ppl. stem of *retrōgradī*: cf. prec. and *progression*, etc. So F. *rétrogression.*]

1. *Astr.* = RETROGRADATION 1.

1646 SIR T. BROWNE *Pseud. Ep.* 288 Thus we see the account established upon the arise or descent of the starres can be no reasonable rule unto distant Nations at all, and by reason of their retrogression but temporary unto any one. **1794** G. ADAMS *Nat. & Exp. Philos.* III. xxiv. 46 Sufficient to account for..the retrogression of the equinoctial points. **1869** DUNKIN *Midn. Sky* 141 These four stars no longer hold these prominent offices, as the equinoxes and solstices are now in very different parts of the heavens, on account of their retrogression. **1873** PROCTOR *Exp. Heaven* 94 His [Saturn's] slow advance alternating with yet slower retrogressions.

2. Movement in a backward or reverse direction. In early use *Math.*

1704 HAYES *Treat. Fluxions* VI. 153 The use of Fluxions in Investigating the Points of contrary Flexion and Retrogression of Curves. **1727–38** CHAMBERS *Cycl.* s.v. *Retrogradation*, The retrogression of curves may be thus conceived. **1753** —— *Cycl. Suppl.*, *Point of reflexion*, in geometry, is commonly used instead of point of retrogradation, or retrogression.

1857 WOOD *Comm. Obj. Sea-shore* 121, I should rather have said, that the tail was the organ of retrogression. **1861** G. MUSGRAVE *By-Roads France* 296 What at first was mere retrogression..became eventually a rapid flight.

b. *Mus.* Retrograde imitation. (Cf. RETROGRADE *a.* 4 c.)

1869 OUSELEY *Counterp.* xvii. 148 Counterpoints also may be devised by contrary motion, or by augmentation or diminution, or by retrogression.

3. The action or fact of going back in respect of development or condition; return to a less advanced state or stage; a case or instance of this.

1768–74 TUCKER *Lt. Nat.* (1834) II. 674 Concurring by slow and imperceptible degrees, and sometimes with temporary retrogressions, to advance the grand design. **1800** W. TAYLOR in *Monthly Mag.* VIII. 597 Retrogression they prefer to any untried innovation. **1840** MACAULAY *Ranke's Hist.* Ess. (1851) II. 145 We find at best a very slow progress and on the whole a retrogression. **1875** JOWETT *Plato* (ed. 2) V. 190 There are many traces of advance as well as retrogression in the Laws of Plato.

b. *Path.* The disappearance of an eruption.

1899 *Allbutt's Syst. Med.* VIII. 478 In the course of retrogression they become pale, polished, angular in outline.

Hence **retroˈgressional** *a.*, of a retrograde character.

1889 *Pop. Sci. Monthly* May 23 Some of these [manipulations], from a technical point of view, seem retrogressional.

retroˈgressionist. [f. prec. + -IST.] One who is inclined to be retrograde.

1865 *Standard* 30 Sept. 4/6 Nothing but the forebodings of a retrogressionist, suspicious of the advance of civilization. **1874** F. HALL in *N. Amer. Rev.* CXIX. 331 Neither from studious retrogressionists nor from studious innovators can we hope for a stamp of English superior to what we now possess.

retrogressive (riːtrəʊ-, rɛtrəʊˈgrɛsɪv), *a.* and *sb.* [f. as RETROGRESS *v.* + -IVE.] **A.** *adj.*

1. Working back in investigation or reasoning.

1817 COLERIDGE *Biog. Lit.* xxii. II. 141 When the successive acts of attention have been completed, there is a retrogressive effort of mind to behold it as a whole. **1835** I. TAYLOR *Spir. Despot.* VI. 283 Our retrogressive enquiry. **1871** BLACKIE *Four Phases Mor.* i. 75 The slow retrogressive process of induction.

2. Moving or directed backwards.

1830 *Blackw. Mag.* XXVII. 523 He sent orders..to stop his retrogressive march. **1868** LYELL *Princ. Geol.* (ed. 10) II. II. xxvi. 35 In addition to the retrogressive excavation of the head of the ravine.

3. a. Retrograde; tending to return to an inferior state; going back to a worse condition.

1802 PINKERTON *Mod. Geogr.* I. Pref. 6 It is a lamentable circumstance that geography is at times retrogressive in some points, while it advances in others. **1860** FREER *Hist. Hen. IV*, II. II. iv. 68 His son..protested against this retrogressive policy. **1891** *Sat. Rev.* 18 July 82/2 Spain,.. with the exception of Turkey, is the most obstinately retrogressive of European countries.

b. *spec.* in *Path.* or *Anat.* of changes in tissues or organs.

1871 T. H. GREEN *Introd. Path.* 190 The contents are the products of retrogressive tissue metamorphosis. **1877** HUXLEY *Anat. Inv. Anim.* x. 610 In the same position as that occupied by the remains of this appendage, when it has undergone retrogressive metamorphosis. **1899** *Allbutt's Syst. Med.* VI. 893 Retrogressive changes may occur, as in true gummatous formations.

c. *Petrol.* = RETROGRADE *a.* 3 e.

1931 *Amer. Jrnl. Sci.* CCXXI. 8 No one criterion is a safe basis for the determination of retrogressive metamorphism. **1948** *Mem. Geol. Soc. Amer.* XXX. 299 Retrogressive metamorphism, or diaphthoresis, is the mineralogical adjustment of relatively high-grade metamorphic rocks to temperatures lower than those of their initial metamorphism. The process is thus a special case of polymetamorphism (repeated metamorphism).

B. *sb.* One with retrograde tendencies.

1892 *Star* 19 Mar. 1/6 The Retrogressives are themselves invading barbarians.

Hence **retroˈgressively** *adv.* (Ogilvie, 1850). Also **retroˈgressivism** (*nonce-wd.*).

1893 *Fortn. Rev.* Feb. 277 His peculiar type of Retrogressivism (it would be flattery to call it Conservatism).

†**retroguard.** *Obs. rare.* [ad. med.L. *retroguardia*, *-garda* (Du Cange), obs. Pg. *retroguarda.*] = REAR-GUARD^1.

1574 H. G. *Most Briefe Tables* Hij b, And let another parte bee for a Vantgarde and Retroguarde to the raye.

†**retro-in'finity.** *Obs. rare*⁻¹. [RETRO-.] An infinite series backwards.

1678 CUDWORTH *Intell. Syst.* 850 And so backward Infinitely; from whence it would follow, that there is no First in the Order of Causes, but an Endless Retro-Infinity.

†**retro'ition.** *Obs. rare.* [ad. L. type **retroitio*, vbl. sb. f. *retroīre*.] The action of returning or reverting; re-entrance.

1651 BIGGS *New Disp.* 168 ¶230 The whole retinue of menstrua's, about that peculiar monarchy of the womb,.. are then segregated by the destructive knife of phlebotomy, and make their retroition into the whole. **1671** J. WEBSTER *Metallogr.* xii. 190 In which retroition of solution, the heterogeneous juices are separated on their own accord.

'retroject, *v.* [f. RETRO- + *-ject*, after *project* vb.] *trans.* To cast or throw back.

1866 *Pall Mall G.* 18 May 1 The ridiculous position into which it projected, or, rather, retrojected, an aspiring and ambitious candidate. **1881** SULLY *Illusions* 10 Whether a man projects some figment of his imagination into the external world,.. or whether.. he retrojects it into the dim region of the past.

So **retro'jection,** the action of putting back to an earlier date.

1900 *Expositor* Jan. 14 The Priests' Code contains one of the most conspicuous of these retrojections.

retrolental (rɛtrəʊ'lɛntəl), *a. Path.* [f. RETRO- + L. *lent-*, *lens* lentil (see LENS) + -AL.] Situated or occurring behind the lens of the eye; ***retrolental fibroplasia***, a disease caused by administration of high concentrations of oxygen to (esp. premature) infants, characterized by proliferation of retrolental tissue and sometimes leading to blindness.

1942 T. L. TERRY in *Trans. Amer. Ophthalm. Soc.* XL. 262 Considerable thought has been given to the selection of an appropriate term for this disease condition. Early in the study.. the term 'retrolental fibroplasia' was suggested by Dr. Harry K. Messenger. **1963** H. L. BIRGE in A. Sorsby *Mod. Ophthalm.* II. i. 6 (*heading*) Retinopathy of prematurity (retrolental fibroplasia). *Ibid.*, Retrolental fibroplasia is a primary retinal disease of non-inflammatory origin resulting from disordered retinal vascularization. **1975** *Daily Colonist* (Victoria, B.C.) 2 June 2/6 Born prematurely, he was blinded by retrolental fibroplasia, an eye disease brought on by the extra oxygen needed to keep him alive soon after birth.

†**retro'mingency.** (See next and quot.)

1646 SIR T. BROWNE *Pseud. Ep.* 150 The last foundation [for the belief] was Retromingency or pissing backward.

retromingent (ri:trəʊ-, rɛtrəʊ'mɪndʒənt), *a.* (and *sb.*) [f. RETRO- + MINGENT *a.*] That urinates backwards. Also as *sb.*, an animal which does this.

1646 SIR T. BROWNE *Pseud. Ep.* 147 Except it be in Retromingents, and such as couple backward. [**1727-38** CHAMBERS *Cycl.*, *Retromingents*, in natural history, a class or division of animals, whose characteristic is, that they stale.. backwards.] **1704** *Phil. Trans.* XXIV. 1585 If (as in other Creatures that are retromingent also) the *Penis* here had been fastned to the *Ossa Pubis*. **1747** *Gentl. Mag.* 209/1 He is a retromingent animal, and consequently retrogenerative. **1817** KEATINGE *Trav.* I. 318 The nobler animals, the lion, the elephant, are retromingent. **1874** VAN BUREN *Dis. Genit. Org.* 39 The patient is usually retromingent.

Hence **retro'mingently** *adv.* (Ogilvie, 1882).

†**retro'pannage.** *Obs.* [ad. med.L. *retropannagium*.] (See quot. 1727-38 and PANNAGE.)

1679 BLOUNT *Anc. Tenures* 92 Retropannage begins at St. Martyns and ends at Candlemass. *Ibid.*, This Retropannage I suppose is the latter or after Pannage. **1727-38** CHAMBERS *Cycl.*, *Retropannage*, in our antient law-books, *after-pannage*; or what is left when the beasts have done, or eat the best.

,retroperito'neal, *a. Anat.* and *Path.* [See RETRO- 3 b.] Occurring or situated behind the peritoneum.

1874 *Jones & Sieveking's Pathol. Anat.* 424 The retroperitoneal glands of the abdomen. **1879** *St. George's Hosp. Rep.* IX. 430 A large retroperitoneal cyst filled up completely the hollow space by the side of the lumbar vertebræ. **1897** *Allbutt's Syst. Med.* III. 570 Retroperitoneal suppuration sometimes usurps a subphrenic position.

Hence **,retroperito'neally** *adv.*

1899 *Allbutt's Syst. Med.* VI. 856 Echinococcus cysts, if they develope retroperitoneally,.. may invade the neural canal in the same way as new growths.

,retropha'ryngeal, *a. Anat.* and *Path.* [See RETRO- 3 b.] Occurring or situated at the back of, or behind, the pharynx.

1866 TANNER *Index Diseases* 231 Retro-pharyngeal Abscess. **1872** COHEN *Dis. Throat* 148 These abscesses, most generally known under the name of retro-pharyngeal abscesses, occur at all ages. **1902** KEITH *Hughes' Pract. Anat.* III. xiii. 202 The Retro-Pharyngeal Lymph Gland lies below the jugular foramen, behind the pharynx.

retro'pulsion. *Path.* [See RETRO- and PULSION. So F. *rétropulsion*.]

1. Transference of an external disease to some internal part or organ. (Cf. REPULSION 2 b.)

1794-6 E. DARWIN *Zoon.* (1801) III. 356 This supposed retropulsion of erysipelas on the brain.. has prevented the free use of the lancet early in this disease. **1804** ABERNETHY *Surg. Obs.* II. 184 Those ophthalmics.. which have generally been ascribed to a retropulsion of that disorder. **1822-34** *Good's Study Med.* (ed. 4) I. 479 Repelled eruptions. From retropulsion of some cutaneous affection.

2. (See quot.)

1899 *Allbutt's Syst. Med.* VIII. 77 A patient [with paralysis agitans] who is made to walk backwards will then also present a similar tendency to move by short quick steps and may have some difficulty in stopping himself; this symptom has been called 'retropulsion'.

retro'pulsive, *a. rare.* [Cf. prec. and *repulsive*.] Causing backward or reverse movement.

1828-32 WEBSTER (citing *Med. Repos.*), *Retropulsive*, driving back; repelling. *a* **1901** MYERS *Human Personality* (1903) I. 226, I shall avoid postulating any 'retropulsive current' from brain to retina.

,retrore'flective, *a.* Also retro-reflective. [See RETRO- 3 b.]

1. Capable of looking back and reflecting.

1851 I. TAYLOR *Wesley & Method.* (1852) 193 His mind might be adduced as a singular instance.. of the absolute absence of the retro-reflective faculty.

2. Having or being the property of a retro-reflector.

1960 *Guide Civil Land Aerodrome Lighting* (*B.S.I.*) 40 In the case of taxiways which have occasional use, retro-reflective markers along the edges may be found to provide adequate guidance. **1961** *Space Res.* II. 287 Search light illumination of a retro-reflective satellite. **1970** *Sci. Amer.* Mar. 41/2 A billiard ball sent.. into the corner of the table will, after two bounces, return along a path parallel to its incident direction. In the case of light three reflecting surfaces, all at right angles to one another, form a corner with the same retroreflective property.

'retro-reflector. Also retroreflector. [f. RETRO- + REFLECTOR.] A device which reflects light back along the incident path, irrespective of its angle of incidence.

1961 *Space Res.* II. 290 A satellite carrying a radio beacon and an optical retro-reflector. **1969** *Daily Tel.* 21 July 17/3 The device which may foretell earthquakes is the laser ranging retro-reflector. It simply reflects.. narrow beams of laser light sent up to it from earth. **1976** *Sci. Amer.* Feb. 51/1 The first is the lunar laser-ranging experiment, in which pulses of laser light are beamed through a telescope on the earth at one of the retroreflectors placed on the moon by the Apollo astronauts.

'retro-rocket. [f. RETRO- + ROCKET *sb.*³]

†**a.** (See quot.) *Obs.*

1948 W. LEY *Rockets & Space Travel* 347 *Retro-rocket*, anti-submarine weapon fired from planes backward with velocity matching plane speed so that the weapon fell vertically... Retro-rockets sank the last 'probable' German submarine in the war, on April 30, 1945.

b. *Astronautics.* An auxiliary rocket on a spacecraft that points in the forward direction, so as to provide thrust opposing forward motion when fired.

1957 *Times* 9 Nov. 6/6 To bring the satellite safely down from its orbit would require the use of what he called 'retro-rockets' to slow its speed. **1958** *New Statesman* 18 Oct. 512/1 It consisted of a three-stage rocket, plus a retro-rocket... The third stage was intended to circle the moon.. but it had attached a fourth stage—the retro-rocket—designed to discharge in the opposite direction and thus act as a brake. **1962** J. GLENN in *Into Orbit* 37 The engineers worked out three different ways of firing the small retro-rockets which would start us back towards the earth. **1963** *Guardian* 8 Apr. 1/3 It [*sc.* Lunik 4] will use retro-rockets to effect a soft landing on the lunar surface. **1974** *Encycl. Brit. Macropædia* XVII. 359/2 In the case of a spacecraft whose mission is to land softly on the Moon, on approach trajectory the attitude-control subsystem will rotate the spacecraft so that its retrorocket and landing radar are pointed toward the lunar surface.

re'trorsal, *a. rare*⁻¹. [f. as next + -AL¹.] Backward, return.

1840 G. S. FABER *Christ's Disc. Capernaum* 234 Let her navigate her retrorsal course to the country whence she came.

retrorse (rɪ'trɔːs), *a. rare.* [ad. L. *retrorsus*, contracted form of *retrōversus*: see RETROVERSE *a.*] Turned backwards; reverted.

1825 T. SAY *Explan. Terms Entom.* 29. **1849** BALFOUR *Man. Bot.* 636/3. **1872** COUES *Key to N. A. Birds* 29 Bristles or feathers thus growing forwards are called retrorse.

Hence **re'trorsely** *adv.*

1828-32 WEBSTER (citing Eaton) s.v., A stem retrorsely aculeate. **1882** *Jrnl. Bot.* XI. No. 230. 46 Another unnamed species was gathered by Dr. Lyall long ago in Central Madagascar, with retrorsely hispid branchlets.

retro'serrate, *a. Bot.* [f. RETRO- + SERRATE *a.*] (See quots.)

1857 HENFREY *Bot.* 55 The margins of the leaf are.. retroserrate, when sharp teeth point back towards the base. **1887** BENTLEY *Man. Bot.* 164 If similar teeth point towards the base, the leaf is described as retroserrate.

retro'serrulate, *a. Ent.* [f. RETRO + SERRULATE.] Provided or furnished with small barbs.

1826 KIRBY & SP. *Entomol.* IV. xlii. 156 The darts usually run in two grooves of the sheath, and at their apex are retroserrulate. *Ibid.* xlvii. 376 Ovipositor 5-6-valved, the vagina darting forth two retroserrulate spiculæ.

retrospect ('rɛtrəʊspɛkt, 'riːtrəʊ-), *sb.* [ad. L. type **retrōspect-us*, f. *retrōspect-*, vbl. stem of *retrōspicĕre* to look back: cf. *prospect*.]

1. a. A regard or reference *to* some fact, authority, precedent, etc. Also without const.

1602 FULBECKE *1st Pt. Parall.* 58 In euerie action the iudgement hath a retrospect to the original. **1651** N. BACON *Disc. Govt. Eng.* II. xxx. (1739) 138 [They] so continued, until these times of Henry the Eighth, wherein they have a Retrospect to the Rock, from whence they were first hewn. **1703** DE FOE *Explan. Shortest Way Dissenters* Misc. 436 Without the least retrospect to, or concern in the Publick Bills in Parliament, now depending. **1774** J. BRYANT *Mythol.* I. 168 They explained everything by the language in use; without the least retrospect or allowance. **1799** KIRWAN *Geol. Ess.* 2 The latter cannot be properly understood without a retrospect to the former. **1844** *Queen's Regul. & Ord. Army* 3 In case two Commissions of the same date interfere, a retrospect is to be had to former Commissions. **1895** PHILLIMORE *Eccles. Law* (ed. 2) I. 320 And these words of the Canon.. seem to have some reference or retrospect to that determination.

b. Application to past time.

1727-38 CHAMBERS *Cycl.* s.v. *Retroactive*, We have some instances of laws that have a retrospect or retroaction, *i.e.* are made with express design to extend to things already past. **1792** N. CHIPMAN *Rep.* (1871) 38 The deed given in 1762.. becomes good from the date by retrospect.

2. A backward look or view. *rare.*

1675 *Art Contentment* v. vii. 205 Every impious act would like the prohibited retrospect of Lots wife, fix us perpetual monuments of Divine vengeance. *a* **1817** T. DWIGHT *Trav. New Eng.*, etc. (1821) II. 152 At the South-Eastern extremity of this farm, we had a new, and very interesting, retrospect of these mountains.

b. A view or survey of past time, *esp.* with reference to one's own life or experiences.

1678 R. L'ESTRANGE *Seneca's Mor.* (1702) 237 The Passage of Time is wonderfully quick, and a Man must look backward to see it: And in that Retro-spect he has all past Ages at a View. **1712** STEELE *Spect.* No. 374 ¶1 To sit still and throw away the Time in our Possession, by Retrospect on what is past. **1759** JOHNSON *Rasselas* xlv, My retrospect of life recalls to my view many opportunities of good neglected. **1807-8** W. IRVING *Salmag.* (1824) 233 This, of all others, is the most auspicious moment.. for indulging in a retrospect. **1856** SIR B. BRODIE *Psychol. Inq.* I. iv. 132 The hopes and fears connected with the retrospect of a well-spent or ill-spent life. **1892** WESTCOTT *Gospel of Life* 195 The Jew did not dwell with a regretful retrospect on a lost Paradise.

c. A survey or review of some past course of events, acts, etc.; *esp.* a comprehensive or summary view of what has been done or has taken place in a particular sphere or line of things.

1663 MARVELL *Corr.* Wks. (Grosart) II. 91 The Committee.. was orderd to continue the retrospect to all [offices] that have been sold since 29th June, 1660. **1787** J. BARLOW *Oration 4th July* 4 A modest retrospect of the truly dignified part already acted by our countrymen. **1803** *Med. Jrnl.* X. 571 If this little tract were drawn up by a common hand,.. we should not have introduced it into our Retrospect. **1865** H. PHILLIPS *Amer. Paper Curr.* II. 136 A short retrospect is now necessary to view what Congress determined upon. **1884** *Encycl. Brit.* XVII. 96/1 Then for the first time the music reverts to the primary key for a retrospect of the entire matter of the first part.

3. a. *attrib.*, passing into *adj.* Directed or referring to the past; retrospective.

1709 STRYPE *Ann. Ref.* I. xxxix. 406 This letter of Mr. Fox, affording a pleasant retrospect view of the Queen's reign hitherto. **1741** WARBURTON *Div. Legat.* II. 471 We agree that Christ's death hath a retrospect view. **1804** J. POOLE *Irreg. Trans. Dept. For. Corps* 63 Such claims as present themselves on the retrospect or deferred list. **1804** COLLINS *Scripscrap* 171 Could we boast Pre-existence, and retrospect Sight. **1898** *Westm. Gaz.* 7 Oct. 2/1 The hint.. that the liking is due to the glamour of the retrospect view.

†**b.** In predicative use. (Cf. 1 b.) *Obs. rare.*

1709 *Tatler* No. 67 ¶2 My Jurisdiction, which extends not only to Futurity, but also is retrospect to Things past. **1755** *Monitor* No. 20 I. 175 Nor can any one shew me how this clause can be said to be retrospect.

'retrospect, *v.* [f. prec., or ad. ppl. stem of L. *retrōspicĕre*.]

1. *intr.* To indulge in retrospection.

1659 *Burton's Diary* (1828) IV. 270, I came here with a resolution not to retrospect. **1748** RICHARDSON *Clarissa* (1811) II. 267 If I could not thus retrospect and argue.

b. To look or refer back *to*; to reflect *on*.

1689 PLUNKET *Charac. Good Commander* 48 They'll not retrospect to any thing Of Truth, when meekly urg'd. **1742** RICHARDSON *Pamela* III. 413 Would perhaps have thought it derogatory.. to my present Station, and too much retrospecting to my former. **1764** *Mem. G. Psalmanazar* 65 To retrospect with shame and remorse on a life so basely spent. *a* **1804** A. HAMILTON *Let. to J. Adams* (Bartlett), To give a correct idea of the circumstances.., it may be useful to retrospect to an early period.

2. *trans.* To consider, regard, or think of (some person or thing) retrospectively.

a **1734** NORTH *Lives* (1826) I. 336 The matters, by way of inquisition retrospected, are reducible to two heads. **1748** RICHARDSON *Corr.* (1804) IV. 232 We find this to be true by retrospecting that part of it we have passed over. **1804** EUGENIA DE ACTON *Tale without Title* I. 156 Whenever I retrospect this circumstance, my mind is too full to make any comments. **1815** *Zeluca* II. 1 The envy that always ensued from retrospecting those pleasures that had failed in promised enjoyment. **1896** LUMSDEN *Poems* 52 Morosely, by a glowing fire I retrospect the habble.

retrospection (rɛtrəʊˈspɛkʃən, riːtrəʊ-). [ad. L. type **retrōspectiōn-em*, n. of action f. *retrōspicĕre*: cf. RETROSPECT *sb.*]

1. The action of looking back. *rare*⁻¹.
1633 T. ADAMS *Exp. 2 Pet.* iii. 18 Think upon his [i.e. Lot's] wife's retardation and retrospection.

2. Retrospective or retroactive action. *rare*⁻¹.
1657 *Burton's Diary* (1828) I. 310 By the Bill, you punish men wholly for an offence before committed. It lies altogether upon retrospection.

3. The action of looking back or referring *to* something. Also without const., reference or allusion to past events.
1674 JEAKE *Arith.* (1696) 374 A Retrospection thither may save a large Repetition of the Rules here. **1711** G. HICKES *Two Treat. Chr. Priesth.* (1847) II. 360 Without any retrospection to old principles. **1765** FOOTE *Commissary* I. Wks. 1799 II. 17 It is best, Polly, in order to prevent all retrospection, that we settle accounts before you change your condition. **1796** MRS. E. PARSONS *Myst. Warning* IV. 68 Studious to avoid any retrospection to unpleasant scenes. **1807** G. CHALMERS *Caledonia* I. I. i. 2 Yet, must all these topics be introduced to the attention..by retrospection to the pristine ages.

†**b.** Reference or regard *to* a person. *Obs. rare.*
1748 RICHARDSON *Clarissa* (1811) II. 263 Such a retrospection in her arguments to him. **1753-4** —— *Grandison* (1781) II. iv. 46, I should abhor myself..if I had any retrospection to myself.

4. The action or fact of looking back upon, or surveying, past time.
1729 SWIFT *To Janus on N. Year's Day* Misc. (1735) V. 231 When thy Retrospection vast, Sees the glorious Ages past. **1755** YOUNG *Centaur* v. Wks. 1757 IV. 215 A man can see himself in retrospection only. **1832** L. HUNT *Sir R. Esher* (1850) 128, I am confounding prophecy with retrospection. **1847** YEOWELL *Anc. Brit. Church* Pref. iv, He looks back on its earliest dawn with pleasing retrospection. **1860** W. COLLINS *Wom. in White* III. vi. 82 The narrative which goes far enough back..to avoid all impediments of retrospection in its course.

b. An instance of this; *esp.* a survey of past life or experiences.
1697 COLLIER *Ess. Mor. Subj.* (1709) 183, I must own that pleasant Retrospections, and easy Thoughts,..are admirable Opiates. **1796** MRS. E. PARSONS *Myst. Warning* III. 93 For myself, a retrospection on the past, and the prospect of the future, was so dark. **1806** SURR *Winter in Lond.* II. 28 Edward..passed the greater part of the journey in a retrospection of his past life and feelings. **1875** HELPS *Soc. Press.* xxiv. 360 The most remarkable change that, on this retrospection, we discover in ourselves.

c. A review of past events or of some matter.
1753-4 RICHARDSON *Grandison* (1781) IV. xv. 112 He and his nephew were both determined to procure a retrospection of all former proceedings. **1844** J. MACFARLANE *Mem. J. Campbell* II. 34 Doing so would lead to the discussion of topics rather apart from the design of this retrospection.

5. A retrogressive course of thought.
1870 J. H. NEWMAN *Gram. Assent* II. viii. 262 The long retrospection lodges us at length at..first principles.

retrospective (rɛtrəʊˈspɛktɪv, riːtrəʊ-), *a.* (and *sb.*) [See RETROSPECT *sb.* and -IVE. So F. *rétrospectif, -ive*, It. *retrospettivo*, Pg. *retrospectivo*.]

1. a. Directed to, contemplative of, past time.
1664 (*title*), A Faithful Testimony..or a Retrospective Glass for the Legislators..who are found persecuting the Innocent. **1732** POPE *Ep. Cobham* I. 99 In vain the Sage, with retrospective eye, Would from th' apparent What conclude the Why. **1804** J. GRAHAME *Sabbath* (1839) 26/1 To think he'll cast, midway the vale of years, A retrospective look, bedimm'd with tears. **1831** HOOD *Playing at Soldiers* vi, Ah me! my retrospective soul! As over memory's muster-roll I cast my eyes anew. **1873** PROCTOR *Exp. Heaven* 178 Beyond the limits to which our powers enable us to reach in our retrospective researches.

b. Of an exhibition, programme of music, or the like: showing the development of the work produced, usu. by one artist, over a period. Freq. *ellipt.* as *sb.* (often const. *of* to introduce what is being exhibited).
1919 R. FRY *Let.* 22 Feb. (1972) II. 447 It's really a good show: a retrospective exhibition of Dudley..arranged all round the walls of the big room. **1931** —— *Let.* 3 Mar. (1972) II. 654 I've been having a retrospective show (forty years of work). **1932** [see RAYOGRAPH]. **1954** *Burlington Mag.* XCVI. 162/1 A retrospective exhibition..provides a much-needed opportunity to review Pasmore's..development..from a Euston Road 'impressionism',..up to his most constructivist reliefs. **1964** *Listener* 5 Mar. 400/2 Once again the Marlborough has scooped all its rivals with a retrospective of the greatest of all the German Expressionists. **1969** *Vogue* Nov. 30/2 A true treasure at the Guggenheim, Constantin Brancusi—a complete retrospective of his work. **1972** *Village Voice* (N.Y.) 1 June 59/2 The Museum of Modern Art has been running a Will Rogers Retrospective. **1973** *Radio Times* 18 Jan. 49/1 As a prelude to tomorrow evening's major retrospective of music by Luciano Berio, Misha Donat introduces a work which represents a turning-point in his career. **1975** *Times Lit. Suppl.* 11 July 759/5 It is five years since Bill Brandt's retrospective of 125 photographs was shown at the Hayward Gallery. **1979** *Daily Tel.* 31 Dec. 12 The National Film Theatre gave him [*sc.* Alfred Hitchcock] a major retrospective. **1980** *Times* 8 Jan. 9/8 The retrospective does throw in a bonus in the shape of a room of very early work before..Dali became appreciably Dali.

2. Of statutes, etc.: Operative with regard to past time; retroactive.
a **1768** ERSKINE *Inst. Law Scot.* II. vii. §15 It hinders the confirmation from having that retrospective quality. **1828** MACAULAY *Ess., Hallam*, That..the State may justifiably pass a retrospective act against an offender, we have no doubt whatever. **1831** *Ibid., Hampden*, Sentencing a man to death by retrospective law. **1856** FROUDE *Hist. Eng.* (1858) I. v. 433 Our instincts tell us that no legislation should be retrospective. **1873** *Sat. Rev.* 9 Aug. 36/1 It is a retrospective alteration of a contract by one of the parties to the detriment of the other.
transf. **1899** *Allbutt's Syst. Med.* VIII. 321 The amnesia, however, is not, so to speak, retrospective.

3. a. Backward; lying to the rear.
1796 COOMBE & BOYDELL *Hist. Thames* II. 29 In this part of the river the retrospective view possesses every charm of elegant landscape. **1845** FEARNSIDE *Views Thames & Medway* 71 The retrospective view is very picturesque. **1872** JENKINSON *Guide Eng. Lakes* (1879) 13 Allowing of fine retrospective views of Ambleside.

b. *sb.* The backward prospect. *rare*⁻¹.
1825 C. WESTMACOTT *Eng. Spy* I. 25 The retrospective affords a view.

retroˈspectively, *adv.* [f. prec. + -LY².]

1. By, or with, retrospection on past time.
1632 LITHGOW *Trav.* III. 117 Which former times if a man would retrospectiuely measure, he might easily find [etc.]. **1790** *Phil. Trans.* LXXX. 569 The supposed conjunction was, at a later period, sought for as an epoch, and calculated retrospectively. **1847** DICKENS *Haunted M.* i, 'May-be as high as that, no higher,' said the old man, holding out his hand.., and looking retrospectively at his questioner. **1868** E. EDWARDS *Ralegh* I. xxi. 462 The briefest narrative will need to begin somewhat retrospectively.

2. With retrospective effect or force.
1800 *Asiatic Ann. Reg.* II. 92/1 It is given (as in justice it ought to be) retrospectively. **1838** W. BELL *Dict. Law Scot.* 382 An *ex post facto* law, is a law which operates retrospectively. **1885** *Law Times* LXXVIII. 242/1 It makes the Act to operate retrospectively.

So **retroˈspectiveness**. *rare*⁻¹.
1881 *Daily Tel.* 12 Feb., The Government had only asked for unlimited retrospectiveness in order that they might throw a sop to the Radicals.

ˌretrospecˈtivity. *rare.* [f. RETROSPECTIVE *a.* + -ITY.] = RETROSPECTIVENESS.
1920 *Glasgow Herald* 23 Feb. 11/2 The adoption of the principle of the non-retrospectivity of financial law.

†**retroˈspectory**, *a. Obs.*⁻¹ Retrospective.
1812 *Gen. Hist.* in *Ann. Reg.* 49 [He] took a very extended view of the state of public affairs, foreign and domestic, both retrospectory and present.

retrospectus (rɛtrəʊˈspɛktəs). [a. L. *retrospectus*, pa. pple. of *retrospicere* to look back, or f. RETRO- + *-spectus* after CONSPECTUS, PROSPECTUS.] A retrospective review or summary.
1964 *Listener* 15 Oct. 603/1 Mr. Brooke's conspectus (or retrospectus) of the impact of the second world war on British writers. **1971** *Guardian* 22 May 9/3 The Nonesuch [Press]..has a Retrospectus rather than a Backlist.

†**retroˈspician(t.** *Sc. Obs. rare.* [ad. pres. pple. of L. *retrōspicĕre* (cf. next), prob. after *respiciens retro* in Luke ix. 62.] One who turns back; a renegade.
a **1610** SIR J. SEMPLE in *Sempill Ball.* (1872) 246 All thinges againe deformed in chaos masse shalbe Befoir ane retrospiciante I sall ceas from Loving the. **1611** *Reg. Privy Counc. Scot.* IX. 209 He..callit the said Erll ane retrospitiane, whome God has speuit furth of his mouth.

retroˈspicient, *a. rare*⁻¹. [f. as prec.] = RETROSPECTIVE *a.*
1887 GARNETT *Carlyle* vi. 108 Such a fanciful preference would have suited the retrospicient Newman.

retro-spring. *rare*⁻¹. A backward spring.
1719 BAYNARD *Health* (1731) 29 And with a nimble retro-spring Contracts, and brings them back again.

reˈtrot (riː-), *v. rare*⁻¹. [RE- 5 a.] *intr.* To trot again or back.
1616 J. LANE *Contn. Sqr.'s T.* IV. 345 Wheare in hee tritons, vnto the pathes farr ende, but theare..turnes to rewend: thence retrottes tailewise backwardes.

retroˈtraction. *rare*⁻¹. [See RETRO- and TRACTION.] Retraction, withdrawal.
1673 SIR J. LAUDER *Decis.* (1826) Suppl. III. 79 A retrotraction of the real right to the inhibition and fiction, supposing them both of one date, is a motion that surely no lawyer can be guilty of.

‖**retroussage** (rətrusaʒ). [Fr., f. *retrousser* to turn up, tie up.] In etching: (see quots.).
1959 P. & L. MURRAY *Dict. Art & Artists* 271 Retroussage is a term used in etching to describe the action of passing a ball of muslin lightly over an inked plate with the intention of dragging some of the ink out of the lines and smearing it across the plate. **1965** ZIGROSSER & GAEHDE *Guide to Collecting Orig. Prints* iv. 45 For etchings a little ink is often left on the plate, giving the print a slight tone instead of a dead white, and with a cloth the ink is drawn up slightly out of the lines in an operation known as *retroussage*.

‖**retroussé** (rətruse), *a.* (and *sb.*) [F., pa. pple. of *retrousser*, f. *re-* RE- + *trousser* to TRUSS.] Turned up. (Chiefly of the nose.) Also *ellipt.* as *sb.*
1802 C. WILMOT *Let.* 25 Apr. in *Irish Peer* (1920) 57 General MacDonald..is tall, and thin, the nez retroussé and his eyes round and solemn. **1837** BARHAM *Ingol. Leg.* Ser. I. *Grey Dolphin*, His eyes a little bloodshot, and his nose *retroussé* with a remarkably red tip. **1862** MISS BRADDON *Lady Audley* viii, The red and pouting lips, the pert little *retroussé* nose. **1871** *Young Englishwoman* July 393/2 The Gabrielle dress..falling with puff or *retroussé* of any kind at the back, is very graceful in outline. **1884** *Graphic* 20 Sept. 306/2 Her nose, albeit not the least of the *retroussé* order, was not unimpeachable. **1885** [see *oyster-plant* s.v. OYSTER 7 d]. **1898** *Westm. Gaz.* 3 Nov. 3/2 The *retroussé* toque (cleft in the centre) for covering or partially covering with fur. **1930** *Daily Express* 6 Oct. 5/4 Whereas Yvonne's is retroussé, Jane's nose is—well, it's *not* snub. **1967** J. R. & P. H. NAPIER *Handbk. Living Primates* I. 16 In the gelada baboons..the face is moderately prognathic..but the nose is short and retroussé.

retro-vacciˈnation. [RETRO-.] (See quot.) Also **retro-ˈvaccine** *a.*
Some Dicts. also give *retrovaccinate* vb.
1868 SEATON *Hdbk. Vaccination* 20 Retro-vaccination, or inoculation of cows with vaccine lymph that has been passed through the human body. *Ibid.*, Retro-vaccine lymph, or humanized lymph that had been passed through the cow, then retransferred to the human subject.

retroˈverse, *a. rare.* [ad. L. *retrōvers-us*, f. *retrō* RETRO- + *versus* turned. Cf. RETRORSE *a.*] Turned or directed backwards; reversed.
1849-52 *Todd's Cycl. Anat.* IV. 1139/1 These processes are true hairs, and only differ from other hairs in..having the imbrication retroverse instead of directed forwards. **1887** FERGUSON *Ogham Inscriptions* 7 Several other retroverse and inverted readings of the same kind.

retroversion (riːtrəʊ-, rɛtrəʊˈvɜːʃən). [ad. L. type **retrōversio*: see RETRO- and REVERSION.]

†**1.** *Sc.* Reversal, rescission. *Obs. rare*⁻¹.
1587 in T. MORRIS *Provosts of Methven* (1875) 69 Full power to..put the said John and Cristiane his spous, in..possession of the foirsaid manse..to be brukit be thame..in all punctis, but [= without] retrouersione.

2. *Path.* The fact of (the uterus) becoming retroverted.
1776 GARTHSHORE in *Med. Obs. & Inquiries* V. 386 Notwithstanding the situation of the *os tincæ* was so little altered, I still suspected a retroversion of the uterus. **1822-34** *Good's Study Med.* (ed. 4) IV. 110 Retroversion is mostly met with in the third and fourth months of pregnancy. **1872** THOMAS *Dis. Women* (ed. 3) 45 One of the symptoms of such inflammation he considers to be retroversion of the uterus.

3. The action of turning or looking back.
1820 LAMB *Elia* I. *Oxford in Vacation*, What mystery lurks in this retroversion? **1853** HERSCHEL *Pop. Lect. Sci.* viii. §133 (1873) 345 By a necessary consequence of that general law of retro-version. **1861** J. A. ALEXANDER *Gospel Jesus Christ* xvii. 238 There is something fearful in the length to which this retroversion may be carried.

4. Retranslation into the original language.
1888 *Jrnl. Educ.* 1 Oct. 468/2 Giving a free English translation of some foreign original for retroversion. **1892** *Classical Rev.* Feb. 71/2 The Latin texts from which the exercises for retroversion are drawn.

ˈretrovert, *sb. rare*⁻¹. [f. RETRO-, after *convert, pervert.*] One who reverts to his former faith.
1873 F. HALL *Mod. Eng.* 308 The goats, if they come back to the old sheep-fold, to be reovilized, are now, in pious phrase, denominated retroverts.

retroˈvert, *v. rare.* [ad. late L. *retrōvertĕre*, f. *retrō* RETRO- + *vertĕre* to turn.] *intr.* and *trans.* To turn back; to revert.
1639 G. DANIEL *Ecclus.* xxvi. 105 He who retroverts To Sin againe; such to their owne deserts, God marks for vengeance. **1828-32** in WEBSTER. **1848** GOULD *Birds Australia* I. III. *Emu Wren*, The tail is carried in an erect position, and is even occasionally retroverted over the back.

retroverted (ˈriːtrəʊ-, ˈrɛtrəʊvɜːtɪd), *ppl. a.* [f. prec. + -ED¹.] Turned backwards, reverted.

a. *Path.* Of the uterus.
1776 GARTHSHORE in *Med. Obs. & Inquiries* V. 381 The singular and dangerous disease, now known by the name of retroverted uterus. **1822-34** *Good's Study Med.* (ed. 4) IV. 108 Retroverted womb. *Ibid.* 129 It is this which constitutes a retroverted uterus. **1897** *Allbutt's Syst. Med.* III. 835 Thus the bowel may be compressed by a retroverted or retroflexed uterus.

b. In general use.
1828 *Blackw. Mag.* XXIV. 47 With retroverted eye, open jaws, and blown belly. **1842** MANNING *Serm.* iii. (1848) 45 Beware of a retroverted heart, and of the glancing aside of the imagination. **1887** READE *Griffith Gaunt* 4 Glaring out between his retroverted ears.

retrovirus (ˈrɛtrəʊvaɪərəs). *Biol.* [mod.L., f. initial letters of *re*verse *tr*anscriptase (see TRANSCRIPTASE) + -O + VIRUS.] An RNA virus of the family Retroviridæ, characterized by oncogenicity and the possession of reverse transcriptase. Cf. RETRAVIRUS.
[**1976** *Virology* LXXI. 375 Family Retroviridae (RNA tumor virus group formerly genus *Leukovirus*).] **1977** *Nature* 8 Sept. 105/2 The successful transfection of a retrovirus by DNA extracted from infected cells was first achieved by Hill and Hillova. **1978** *Ibid.* 9 Feb. 543/1 There has been increasing interest in the isolation of mammalian retro-viruses and their evolutionary relatedness to different species.

Hence **ˈretroviral** *a.*
1979 *Nature* 29 Mar. 420/1 Our results could also be seen as evidence of a marked propensity of retroviral DNA to undergo genetic gymnastics, including deletion.

†**retroyl**, ? error for RECOIL *v.*
c **1400** *Laud Troy Bk.* 8907 'Thow hast', he seide, 'my men defouled, Me and myne bakward retroyled.'

†**re'trude**, *v. Obs. rare*⁻¹. [ad. L. *retrūdĕre*.] *trans.* To thrust (something) backward.
1647 H. MORE *Song Soul* II. II. ii. 6 The term of latitude is breadthlesse line; A point the line doth manfully retrude From infinite processe.

†**re'truse**, *a. Obs.* [ad. L. *retrūs-us*, pa. pple. of *retrūdĕre*: see prec.] Concealed, recondite.
1635 HEYWOOD *Hierarchy* II. Comm. 80 To thinke it, Heauen forbid; Since from our Frailties 'tis Retruse and hid. **1662** H. MORE *Philos. Writ.* Pref. Gen. (1712) 7, I have a sense of something in me..which I must confess is of so retruse a nature, that I want a name for it. **1697** J. SERGEANT *Solid Philos.* 369 These Maxims lie retruse in the most Inmost Recesses of our Judging or Intellective Power.

retrusion (rɪ'truːʒən). *rare.* [ad. L. type **retrūsio*, n. of action f. *retrūdĕre*: see RETRUDE *v.*] The action of putting away or back.
1657 REEVE *God's Plea* x. 144 Oh.. that all the sins of the Land without diminution, retrusion, substraction, could be bewailed in our lips with one National yell. **1826** COLERIDGE in *Lit. Rem.* (1839) IV. 2 Being assumed to be eternal, in virtue of an endless remotion or retrusion of the constituent cause.

†**re'truss**, *v. Obs. rare.* [ad. F. *retrousser*: see TRUSS *v.*] *trans.* To put or take on (a load) again; to load or burden again.
1426 LYDG. *De Guil. Pilgr.* 9899 Thow mayst nat chesyn, in certeyn, Wyth-Innen hym to entre Ageyn, Retrussen hym, & ek recharge. *Ibid.* 9944, I was retrussyd, & a-geyn Wyth the body that I kam fro.

re'trust (riː-), *v. rare*⁻¹. [RE- 5 a.] *trans.* To trust or commit again.
1642 CHAS. I *Answ. to 19 Prop.* 21 Affairs of State..being retrusted to some close Committee.

retry (riː-), *v.* [RE- 5 a.] *trans.* To try again, in various senses of the verb.
a **1673** CARYL in Spurgeon *Treas. David* Ps. cxxxix. 23-4 Now he would be re-tried that he might come forth purest gold. **1830** GEN. P. THOMPSON *Exerc.* (1842) I. 289 It was not long before an opportunity arose, for re-trying the old question. **1852** GROTE *Greece* II. lxxii. IX. 280 Assuming the same experiment to have been retried by Sparta. **1887** *Spectator* 9 July 919/2 To re-try a case already tried by competent authority.

retrycyan, obs. form of RHETORICIAN.

retsina (rɛt'siːnə). Also **retzina, rezina.** [ad. mod.Gr. ρετσίνα, f. ρετσίνι resin, f. Gr. ῥητίνη pine resin (cf. L. *resina*).] A Greek resinated wine.
1940 H. J. GROSSMAN *Guide Wines, Spirits, Beers* xvi. 160 Present-day Greeks still prefer a resinated to a natural wine. .. These wines are available in the United States. They are labeled *Retsina*. **1952** W. PLOMER *Museum Pieces* xiii. 113 We drink retsina under the pine-trees. **1960** L. DURRELL *Clea* I. i. 20 The promised farewell dinner of lamb on the spit and gold *rezina* wine. **1966** [see MOUSSAKA]. **1973** 'D. JORDAN' *Nile Green* xxxii. 154 We went down on to the quay to eat fish and drink retsina. **1977** *New Yorker* 6 June 31/3 The three boys' choirs participating in the Berlioz presented him with a jeroboam of retsina.

rette, obs. form of RATE *v.*²

'**retted**, *ppl. a.* [f. RET *v.*² + -ED¹.] Prepared by retting.
1839 URE *Dict. Arts* 487, 100 pounds of the stalks of retted flax..afford from 45 to 48 pounds of broken flax. **1894** *Times* 12 Mar. 13/5 The ordinary retted flax is fed into the breaker, where the woody portion is loosened and partially detached.

'**retter.** *rare*⁻¹. One engaged in retting.
1817 W. TAYLOR in *Monthly Rev.* LXXXIII. 501, I..see the boys bathe, or watch the retters of flax.

'**rettery.** Also 9 **-ory, raitory.** [f. RET *v.*² + -ERY.] A place where flax is retted.
1853 *Jrnl. R. Agric. Soc.* XIV. I. 197 Gaseous exhalations, which far and near stamp the unpleasant proximity of a rettery. **1865** W. WHITE *E. Eng.* II. 98 A well-built and well-conducted rettory, or flax-dressing establishment. **1883** *Times* 24 Oct. 3 On account of the pestilential emanations from the retteries.

'**retting**, *vbl. sb.* Also 8 **raiting**, 8-9 **rating.** [f. RET *v.*² + -ING¹.] The preparation of flax, etc., by steeping or watering.
1727-38 CHAMBERS *Cycl.*, *Raiting*, or *Rating*, the laying of hemp, flax, timber, &c. when green, in a pond, or running water, to season and dispose it for future uses. **1825** J. NICHOLSON *Operat. Mechanic* 416 The hemp-plant..has to undergo a variety of processes. The first of these is retting, that is, exposing it to the action of the dew, or water. **1883** R. HALDANE *Workshop Rec.* Ser. II. 321/1 A few hours then suffice for the retting or maceration of the gut.
b. *attrib.*, as ***retting-ground***, ***-pit***, ***-process***.
1788 W. MARSHALL *Yorksh.* II. 74 The 'rating-ground', a piece of unbroken aftergrass, where the sheaflets are untied, and the flax spread thin upon the grass. *a* **1825** FORBY *Voc. E. Anglia*, *Retting-pit*, a pond used for soaking hemp. **1883** *Times* 24 Oct. 3 Moreover the retting process..is a delicate operation.

'**retting**, *ppl. a.* [f. RET *v.*² + -ING².] That rets or rots.
1930 *Discovery* Dec. 408/1 The clean flax fibre obtained from the harvested flax straw is a silky lustrous material of a pale cream colour, not susceptible to the attack of retting bacteria. **1978** *Sci. Amer.* Aug. 75/3 The seeds then sink to the bottom of the retting liquid, and the residue is removed by flotation and screening.

†'**rettish**, obs. variant of RADISH.
1638 A. READ *Chirurg.* xv. 109 Iron may bee hardened, if it be quenched in vineger, and the juyce of the Rettish.

re'tube (riː-), *v.* [RE- 5 c.] *trans.* To provide with a new tube or tubes. Hence **re'tubing.**
1864 *Daily Tel.* 3 June, The 150 breech-loader 70-pounder guns..will be retubed with a bore of the size to take a 32 lb. ball. **1879** *Siege & Garrison Artill. Exerc.* I. 8 It is applied..to Mark I. and II. of the same calibre when re-tubed. **1896** *Daily News* 27 July 4/2 Complete re-tubing of any boiler can be readily carried out without shifting its position.

re'tumble (riː-), *v.* [RE- 5 a.] *trans.* To tumble or roll back again.
1654 GAYTON *Pleas. Notes* III. i. 67 As if a..Leviathan himselfe had been cast a-shore, and could not retumble his vast hulk into the maine Sea againe.

retu'mescence (riː-). [RE- 5 a.] Reswelling.
1665 *Phil. Trans.* I. 115 Upon the like conflux and retumescence of Waters, they are absorbed.

retund (rɪ'tʌnd), *v.* Now *rare* or *Obs.* [ad. L. *retund-ĕre*, f. *re-* RE- + *tundĕre* to beat, strike.]
1. *trans.* To weaken (some physical quality or agent); to diminish the strength or effect of.
1634 T. JOHNSON *Parey's Chirurg.* XXI. x. (1678) 469 Such ..Medicins as are fit to draw out and retund the venom. **1657** TOMLINSON *Renou's Disp.* 38 Watry humidity doth much retund..the strength. **1684** tr. *Bonet's Merc. Compil.* XIX. 790 It needs no other Medicin to be mixed with it to retund its ill quality. **1710** FULLER *Pharm. Extemp.* 308 The Pectoral Decoction..retunds the Acrimony of the Blood. *a* **1734** NORTH *Examen* I. ii. §85 To try if any Thing would retund the Efficacy of that mishapen Engine of Mischief.
2. To beat back, repress (malice, etc.).
1642 NEWCOMEN *Craft Ch. Advers.* (1643) 12 God could ..retund even the Devills own malice. *a* **1677** BARROW *Serm.* (1686) II. 499 Hence we see how we may retund the importunity of the Macedonians.
b. To put down or refute.
1653 GATAKER *Vind. Annot. Jer.* 41 Mentioned onely to retund a litle this mans insolent vauntings. **1678** CUDWORTH *Intell. Syst.* 627 This ignorant and conceited confidence of both may be retunded and confuted from hence. *Ibid.* 869 We have Sufficiently retunded the Force of that Objection against the Ingenerability of all Souls. *a* **1734** NORTH *Lives* (1826) I. 6 Calumny which riseth after a man's death.. needs most a friend to retund it.
3. To dull or blunt (the edge of a weapon).
1691 RAY *Creation* II. (1692) 12 To quench and dissipate the force of any stroke that shall be dealt it, and retund the edge of any Weapon. **1724** WARBURTON *Tracts* (1789) 9 Now,—was thy Sword employed,..in whose Quarrel was its Edge retunded? **1795** SOUTHEY *Joan of Arc* VII. 594 How then might shield, or breast-plate, or close mail Retund its edge?
fig. **1702** C. MATHER *Magn. Chr.* II. App. (1852) 171 None of all these things could retund the edge of his expectations to find the wreck.
4. To drive or force back.
1654 VILVAIN *Epit. Ess.* v. ix. 94 Jordan and Ouse two Rivers were retunded Whos waters som space stood on both parts sundred. **1668** H. MORE *Div. Dial.* II. xxii. (1713) 158 Like the Beams of the Sun, that retunded from this Body are received by another, and nothing is lost. **1709** BERKELEY *Th. Vision* §69 Vapours and exhalations fitted to retund and intercept the rays of light.

re'tune (riː-), *v.* [RE- 5 a.] **a.** *trans.* To tune (a musical instrument) again. Also *fig.* and *transf.*
1606 SYLVESTER *Du Bartas* II. iv. *Trophies* 1040 Whose sacred Art retuneth excellent This rarely-sweet celestiall Instrument. *a* **1711** KEN *Hymnarium* Poet. Wks. 1721 II. 119 Their Discords in God's Praise unite, Retun'd by providential Might. *a* **1806** H. K. WHITE *Poems* (1837) 84 Retune thy strings for Jesus' sake. **1890** *Spectator* 1 Feb., War, which may retune the nerves of the people and bleed out their fullness of habit.
b. To rephrase (the words of a song, etc.).
1959 I. & P. OPIE *Lore & Lang. Schoolch.* vii. 107 In no great space of time the schoolchild ditty, When I was young and had no sense I bought a fiddle for eighteen pence,..was re-tuned in her honour: Lottie Collins, she had no sense, She bought a piano for eighteen pence.
c. To tune (electronic equipment) to a different frequency. Also *absol.*
1962 SIMPSON & RICHARDS *Physical Princ. Junction Transistors* xiv. 357 It is desirable to retune the input and output circuits to satisfy this condition. **1970** R. HILL *Clubbable Woman* vii. 204 Jenny's portable radio began to play..brass-band music. This faded..but then returned louder than before as though the set had been re-tuned. **1977** *Sci. Amer.* June 77/2 He need only retune his receiver to a slightly lower frequency. **1978** *Daily Tel.* 27 Nov. 13/6 Does the BBC realise that the surest way to make you either switch off or re-tune is to make you unsure about what is actually going out?
d. To alter the tuning of (an engine).
1974 P. CAVE *Mama* (new ed.) ii. 10 He was the unofficial repairman of the London Angels, the guy who could take a beaten-up old engine and retune it until it could fly.
Hence **re'tuning** *vbl. sb.*
1909 M. GREENWOOD in L. Hill *Further Adv. Physiol.* 410 'Retuning' with orange, red and green both act like orange itself in inducing a negative image. **1960** *Practical Wireless* XXXVI. 390/1 It provides a substantially constant power gain over the whole of the band 1·5Mc/s to 24Mc/s and therefore needs no retuning when the working frequency is changed. **1976** D. MUNROW *Instruments Middle Ages & Renaissance* ix. 77/4 Mattheson's complaint that a lutenist spent most of his life tuning rather than actually playing reflects the inconvenient necessity of regular re-tunings, which upset the stability of the instrument.

re'turf (riː-), *v.* [RE- 5 a.] *trans.* To lay with new turf.
1850 'BAT' *Cricket. Man.* 83 A great portion of this has been re-turfed. **1895** *Daily News* 6 July 5/5 Here also the ground has been returfed.

re'turfing, *vbl. sb.* [f. RETURF *v.* + -ING¹.] The action or fact of covering with new turf.
1974 *Listener* 24 Jan. 119/1 She directed the returfing of a lawn overnight to please her husband. **1978** *Nature* 7 Sept. 51/2 The ground levels within the stones of Stonehenge have been altered during the last 25 yr by re-turfing, by the laying of gravel in 1963 and by its replacement with turf in 1978.

retur'gescency. *rare*⁻¹. [RE- 5 a.] The fact of becoming turgid again.
1664 H. POWER *Exp. Philos.* 95 The most full evidence against this pretended vacuity is from the returgescency of the empty bladder suspended in this vacuity.

return (rɪ'tɜːn), *sb.* Also 4-7 **retorn**, 5-6 **retorne**; 4 **retourn**, 5-7 **retourne, returne.** [a. AF. *retorn*, *retourn*, *return*, vbl. sb. f. *retorner*, etc.: see next. Cf. Sp. and Pg. *retorno*, It. *ritorno*, and F. *retourne* fem.]
I. 1. a. The act of coming back to or from a place, person, or condition. † ***to make return***, to return, to come back.
1390 GOWER *Conf.* III. 230 So were thei for everemo Of no retorn withoute espeir Departed fro the rihtfull heir. **1413** *Pilgr. Sowle* (Caxton, 1483) v. xiii. 104 The seconde retorne was fro dethe to the lyf,..the thyrdde retourne was fro erthe in to heuene. *c* **1489** CAXTON *Blanchardyn* xlvi. 177 Prayeng humbly that a goode retorne & a shorte he myght make. *a* **1533** LD. BERNERS *Huon* lxvi. 226, I wyl leue it here with you to kepe tyll my retourne. **1588** J. MELLIS *Briefe Instr.* F vij, Note that yee register as well the day you send your letters, as the returne of them. **1626** BACON *New Atl.* (1900) 15 Wee never heard tell..of any Shipp..that had made returne from them. **1670** *12th Rep. Hist. MSS. Comm.* App. V. 15 Uppon the King's returne from his recreations att Newmarkett. **1725** N. ROBINSON *Th. Physick* 161 The Languidness of the Blood's Motion in its Return from nourishing the Body. **1760-72** H. BROOKE *Fool of Qual.* (1809) III. 147 When our company were on the return to their lodgings. **1845** PATTISON *Ess.* (1889) I. 24 Immediately on my return to Rouen, I put one of the packages into the hands of the servants. **1874** GREEN *Short Hist.* viii. §3. 479 His return was the signal for a burst of national joy.
pl. **1513** DOUGLAS *Æneis* v. x. 69 Sindry coursis and returnis maid thai. **1612-24** *Capt. Smith's Wks.* (Arb.) 429 In our returnes we visited all our friends. **1686** tr. *Chardin's Trav. Persia* 110 It was late, and the Vessels rid about a mile from the shoar; nor could they make above two Returns. **1721** BRADLEY *Philos. Acc. Wks. Nat.* 15 They may probably be assisted in their Vegetation by the frequent Returns of the Sea Water.
b. *spec.* in *Theol.* = PAROUSIA.
1914 J. F. SILVER (*title*) The Lord's return seen in history and in Scripture as premillennial and imminent. **1931** W. MONTGOMERY tr. *A. Schweitzer's Mysticism of Paul* vi. 111 Since a time-interval has been interposed between the Resurrection and Return, the Resurrection of Jesus has become an independent event. **1970** J. L. HOULDEN *Paul's Lett. from Prison* 107 *Saviour*: Paul's only use of this as a title for Christ. It refers to him in his role at his final return. **1977** G. W. H. LAMPE *God as Spirit* vi. 171 We can, perhaps, retain the idea of a visible *parousia*: not in the impossible sense of a personal return of Jesus from a heavenly throne, but in the form of the consummation of God's creation of mankind.
†**c.** ***coach of return***, a return vehicle. *Obs.*⁻¹
1617 MORYSON *Itin.* I. 7 If a man goe thence to Luneburg, he may easily light on a coach of returne at a lesse rate.
d. In phr. ***by*** (†***the***) ***return***, ***by return of*** (†***the***) ***post***. (See POST *sb.*² 8 c.) Also as adj. phr.
1642 FULLER *Holy & Prof. St.* v. xviii. 14 And, by the next return, the news would be, that it was fallen off. **1753** HANWAY *Trav.* (1762) I. VII. xcii. 422 By the return of the post he may expect an answer. **1812** in Col. Hawker *Diary* (1893) I. 56 You may answer letters by return of post. **1837** DICKENS *Let.* 22 Feb. (1965) I. 237 The best plan therefore, will be for you to write me *by return*. **1885** *Bookseller* July 650/2, I wrote to the publisher, and had the book sent to me by return. **1889** E. DOWSON *Let.* 18 Feb. (1967) 37 Tell me ..by return of post if possible what will have happened when I am next to resume the story. **1905** JOYCE *Let.* ? 18 Aug. (1966) II. 105, I send you by this post *A Painful Case* which you are to copy and send back by *return of post*. **1949** N. MITFORD *Love in Cold Climate* I. ii. 20 She always answered letters by return of post. **1957** *Practical Wireless* XXXIII. 509/1 A by-return service of all types and sizes. **1981** J. STUBBS *Ironmaster* i. 21 They say now that we shall have letters 'by return of Post', meaning that we write today and receive a reply..the day after tomorrow.
e. A signal for return. *rare*⁻¹.
1835 LYTTON *Rienzi* I. i, What ho, there—'sound a return'!
f. *ellipt.* A return-ticket. (Now common.) Also *attrib.* (passing into *adj.*), and in ***day-return*** (= ***day-ticket*** s.v. DAY *sb.* 24).
1868 *Routledge's Ev. Boy's Ann.* 250, I just arrived in time to catch the train, and took a return for C—. **1905** E. M. FORSTER *Where Angels fear to Tread* vi. 164 It was an irritable couple who took tickets to Monteriano. 'Singles or returns?' said he. *a* **1911** D. G. PHILLIPS *Susan Lenox* (1917) I. viii. 126 He had the return half of his own ticket. **1924** D. MOORE *Fen's First Term* ix. 93 'Third single, please.' 'Return?' inquired the clerk. **1931** D. L. SAYERS *Five Red Herrings* iii. 41 He had taken a first-class return to Glasgow. **1952** 'J. TEY' *Singing Sands* iv. 63 'So he had a return ticket.' 'Yes. The return half was in his wallet.' **1973** D. LANG *Freaks* 41, I went down there for a visit on a cheap day-return. **1975** 'A. YORK' *Dark Passage* (1976) vii. 88 I'll be back tomorrow, I should think. But make the return half of

the ticket open, will you? **1977** S. Brett *Star Trap* xv. 167 The man didn't stop to buy a ticket. He must have a return.

g. *ellipt.* (See quots.)

1883 Gresley *Gloss. Coal Mining* 202 *Return*, the air-course along which the vitiated air of the mine is returned or conducted back to the upcast shaft. **1894** *Lab. Commission Gloss.*, *Returns*, an abbreviation for return airways, i.e., the passages through which the air passes to the upcast shaft.

h. ***and return***, and back again.

1887 C. B. George *Forty Years on Rail* v. 88 The train.. ran from Waukegan to Chicago and return every day.

i. ***return to nature***, the abandonment of urban life in favour of rustic simplicity.

1902 Chesterton *Twelve Types* 142 Some think that the return to nature consists in drinking no wine; some think that it consists in drinking a great deal more than is good for them. **1908** E. J. Banfield *Confessions of Beachcomber* I. ii. 54 The conviction that the career of the Beachcomber, the closest possible 'return to Nature' now popularly advocated, has charms none other possesses. *c* **1914** Wyndham Lewis *Let.* (1963) 65, I might devote two or three words..to scouring the 'banal' nakedness of various 'Return to Nature' shits. **1978** *Times* 3 Oct. 14/3 This is not a plea for the simple life, a return to nature, or a general rising against the machines.

2. a. The fact of (a certain time or thing) recurring or coming round again; †a spell of some action.

1589 Greene *Menaphon* (Arb.) 30 The hope of times returne shal be the ende of my thoughts. **1611** Bible *1 Kings* xx. 22 At the returne of the yeere, the king of Syria will come vp against thee. *a* **1706** Evelyn *Hist. Relig.* (1850) I. 26 Contemplate we the periodical returns of the equinoxes and solstices. **1709** Pope *Ess. Crit.* 349 While they ring round the same unvary'd chimes With sure returns of still-expected rhymes. **1763** J. Brown *Poetry & Mus.* iii. 35 The Dance is composed of several Returns: Each Return lasts till the Dancers are out of Breath. **1855** Hopkins *Organ* 209 A 'return' or 'repeat' is caused in the series of Pedal sounds. *Ibid.*, The..'return' that takes place on the half-octave of keys below. **1887** Banister *Mus. Anal.* i. 5 The third part of the movement..is the Recapitulation indicated by the return of the (first) Subject.

b. In phr. ***to wish*** (one) ***many*** (***happy***) ***returns of the day***, or variations of this. See also happy *a.* 3.

1779 Johnson *Let. to Mrs. Aston* 2 Jan., Now the new year is come, of which I wish you and dear Mrs. Gastrel many and many returns. **1821** Lamb *Elia* Ser. i. *All Fools' Day*, Many happy returns of this day to you. **1846** Dickens *Battle of Life* i, The notion of wishing happy returns in such a farce as this..is good! **1870** —— *E. Drood* ii, We must drink Many happy returns to her.

3. The recurrence or renewal of some condition; *esp.* a recrudescence or renewed attack of illness or indisposition.

1648 Duncon (*title*), The Retvrns of Spiritual comfort and grief in a Devout Soul. Represented by entercourse of Letters to..Ladie..Falkland. **1682** Sir T. Browne *Chr. Mor.* ii. xi, To continue us in goodness there must be iterated returns of misery. **1694** Luttrell *Brief Rel.* (1857) III. 403 The King had yesterday some returns of his ague. **1719** De Foe *Crusoe* ii. (Globe) 320 Like the Returns of a violent Distemper, [it] came on with an irresistible Force. **1797** *Monthly Mag.* III. 23 It was the return of the frost that did all the mischief. **1840** Miss Mitford in L'Estrange *Life* (1870) III. vii. 108, I am better, but have had two or three returns of sickness. **1879** Harlan *Eyesight* vi. 69 Old people who have been using glasses..are sometimes surprised by a return of the ability to read without them.

II. 4. A side or part which falls away, usually at right angles, from the front or direct line of any work or structure.

a. In cornices, pilasters, windows, etc.

1450 *Script. Tres* (Surtees) p. cccxxv, Pro factura,.. retournes, corbels, transoms. **1665** J. Webb *Stone-Heng* (1725) 88 The Pylasters were by the Tool and Mallet wrought, as the Rabbets yet remaining, or Returns in some of them plainly shew. *c* **1691** in Willis & Clark *Cambridge* (1886) I. 421 Cutting a hole in the wall..to show the returne of the Cornish. **1724** Chambers *Le Clerc's Arch.* Pl. 24 Continued Pedestal with Returns or Interruptions in its Projecture. **1825** J. Nicholson *Operat. Mechanic* 616 Internal and external mitres, and small returns, or breaks, are afterwards modelled and filled up by hand. **1859** Ruskin *Perspective* ix. 106 The lines which regulate the inner sides or returns of the windows..are drawn to the vanishing-point.

b. In appendages to, or minor parts of, buildings, walls, or other structures.

1463 *Bury Wills* (Camden) 15 My body to be beryed by the awter of Seynt Martyn..vnder the percloos of the retourne of the candilbeem. **1718** S. Sewall *Diary* 23 Feb., The Return of the Gallery where Mr. Franklin sat was a place very Convenient for it. **1772** C. Hutton *Bridges* 87 They [*sc.* abutments] must be well reinforced with proper walls or returns. **1834–47** J. S. Macaulay *Field Fortif.* 216 Open..a branch gallery, which must be driven to the centre of the wall; then make two perpendicular returns to this branch. **1897** F. J. Burgoyne *Library Constr.* 218 A counter with returns running across it.

c. A wing or side of a building; †a side-street.

1625 Bacon *Ess., Building* (Arb.) 549, I vnderstand both these Sides to be not onely Returnes, but Parts of the Front. **1669** in Willis & Clark *Cambridge* (1886) II. 557 The said Building..to have two wings or returnes, each wing or retourne..in length fifty and two foot. **1756** C. Lucas *Ess. Waters* II. 104 Cheltenham is a village..with a very few returns and lanes or adjoining houses. **1814** *Reg. Park* 28 Keeping free the terminations of the streets and the returns of the houses. **1839** *Civil Eng. & Arch. Jrnl.* II. 249/1 Architects often fail from the poverty and meagreness of the masses and returns. They compose their buildings out of screens and facades.

5. a. A bend or turn (in a line, etc.); a portion extending between two bends (see quot. 1859).

1655 Marq. Worc. *Cent. Inv.* §3 A Cypher and Character so contrived that one line, without returns and circumflexes, stands for each and every of the 24 Letters. **1731** *Phil. Trans.* XXXVII. 29 We then put up a Line that was 666 Feet in Length, by eight Returns. **1859** F. A. Griffiths *Artil. Man.* (1862) 107 Each separate part of the fall contained between two blocks, or between either extremity and a block, is called 'a return of the fall'. **1892** *Spon's Workshop Rec.* Ser. v. 379/1 To prevent..twisting, a bar is some-times placed through a part of the blocks, or at right angles to the 'returns' close to the block.

†**b.** A bend, turn, or winding in a stream, trench, gallery, etc. *Obs.*

1681 Chetham *Angler's Vade-m.* x. §1 Sometimes in the Eddies betwixt two Streams and in the Returns of a stream he lies. **1702–11** *Mil. & Sea Dict.*, *Returns of the Trench*, the several Bendings and Oblique Lines of the Trenches, drawn in some measure parallel to the sides of the Place attack'd. **1727–38** Chambers *Cycl.* s.v. *Trench*, This carrying of the trenches obliquely, they call carrying them by *coudees*, or returns. **1802** James *Milit. Dict.* s.v., Returns of a mine, are the turnings and windings of the gallery leading to the mine. *Ibid.*, These returns, when followed, make a long way from the end of the trench to the head.

6. a. A consignment or cargo, an aggregate or class of commodities, which comes back (to one) in exchange for merchandise sent out as a trading venture; the value or profits represented by this; also (*Canad.*) *pl.* (see quot. 1963). (Now *Hist.* and merged in next sense.)

1543–4 *Act 35 Hen. VIII*, c. 7 §1 The sayde venturers.. abyde a greate tyme before they can haue any returne to their aduantage of their aduenture, to theyr great werines. **1614** Raleigh *Hist. World* ii. (1634) 419 He had also six rich Returnes from the East India, which greatly increased his Store. **1663** Gerbier *Counsel* 109 A very gainfull returne of Amber Greese and vendible commodities in exchange of Iron Tools. **1717** Bolingbroke *Let. to Windham* (1889) 23 The merchant who brought riches home by the returns of foreign trade. **1758** Binnell *Descr. Thames* 13 How abounding in its Merchandize! And how immensely rich in its Produce or Returns! **1809** A. Henry *Trav. & Adventures Canad.* i. iv. 40 Here, the returns, in furs, are collected, and embarked for Montréal. **1843** R. Campbell *Jrnl.* 10 June in C. Wilson *Campbell of Yukon* (1970) viii. 68 As soon as the river opened, Whitford left with a boat & crew and the returns for Fort Simpson. **1855** Prescott *Philip II*, i. viii. (1857) 139 Forced loans were exacted from individuals, especially from such as were known to have received large returns by the late arrivals from the New World. **1908** C. Mair *Through Mackenzie Basin* 183 There was still much work to be done in the way of transport of outfit and returns between Anderson and Fort Good Hope. **1963** G. S. McTavish *Behind Palisades* xx. 84 'Returns'..was the generic name for furs, and all trade results which were returned to the Old Country in exchange. **1971** *Alberta Hist. Rev.* Autumn 9 During the next few years he..visited the posts and carried the returns down-river to St. Louis.

fig. **1647** N. Bacon *Disc. Govt. Eng.* i. vi. (1739) 14 Their merchandise was made of the Policies and Councils of all Kingdoms and States, and such returns proceeded as were still subservient to the Roman interest. **1747** Chesterf. *Lett.* cxix. (1792) I. 322 Pain and shame, instead of pleasure, are the returns of their voyage.

b. Pecuniary value resulting to one from the exercise of some trade or occupation; gain, profit, or income, in relation to the means by which it is produced; also (in *pl.*), proceeds, results. ***return on capital***, gain, profit, or income earned by capital (see also quot. 1970).

Various other phrases, e.g. ***return for capital***, ***return to capital***, and ***return to invested capital*** were used from the late nineteenth century onward.

1691 Locke *Lowering Interest*, etc. Wks. 1714 II. 9 If the Merchant's Return be more than his Vse, (which 'tis certain it is, or else he will not Trade). **1776** Adam Smith *W.N.* ii. v. (1869) I. 373 The returns of the foreign trade of consumption are very seldom so quick as those of the home trade. **1804** T. Thornton *Sporting Tour* (1896) 83 Returns of the day: six snipes and one duck. **1833** Ht. Martineau *Manch. Strike* v. 58 Your wages consist of the proportion you receive of the return brought by the article you manufacture. **1883** *Law Times* 20 Oct. 410/1 The Profession will always afford at least a sufficient return to the really competent man. **1938** W. L. Crum in *Harvard Business Rev.* XVI. 336 The return on invested capital is one of the most significant..among possible measures of corporate performance. No entirely satisfactory determination of the average rate of return on invested capital..can be made, but data accumulated over recent years..enable us to prepare a fairly close estimate. **1962** A. Battersby *Guide to Stock Control* x. 94 'Return on capital' has been used in this book as a concise description of the cost of holding stocks, for two principal reasons—it is often the predominant cost and the most readily variable. **1969** J. Argenti *Managem. Techniques* 102 Confusion over the term 'Return on Capital' is considerable since this can have either the traditional meaning or the DCF meaning and there is no fixed relationship between these two figures. **1970** M. Greener *Penguin Dict. Commerce* 285 *Return on capital*, a rather nebulous phrase. In the terminology of investment analysis and accounting it means the profit earned by *capital*... In company accounts return on capital is often the ratio that the profit bears to the total *equity* funds or shareholders' funds employed... The phrase 'return on capital' is frequently used when what is really meant is *dividend yield* or *earnings yield*.

fig. **1650** Jer. Taylor *Holy Living* i. Introd., From the few hours we spend in prayer..the return is great and profitable. **1748** Gray *Alliance* 34 The soft returns of Gratitude they know.

c. The fact of bringing value in exchange.

1753 *Scots Mag.* July 325/2 What maketh rich, is a small profit and a quick return. **1822** Lamb *Elia* i. *Distant Correspondents*, This sort of merchandise above all requires a quick return. A pun, and its recognitory laugh, must be co-instantaneous.

7. *Muslim Law*: (see quot. 1825).

1825 Macnaghten *Mooham. Law* 23 The return is where there being no residuaries, the surplus, after the distribution of the shares, returns to the sharers. **1895** Sir R. K. Wilson *Digest Anglo-Muham. Law* viii. §238. 201 The wife or husband of the deceased has no share in the Return as against 'Distant Kindred'.

III. 8. a. The act, on the part of a sheriff, of sending back a writ to the court from which it issued, together with a statement of how far he had been able to carry out its instructions; hence, the report of a sheriff upon any writ directed to him. Also *pl.*, forms for making such reports (quot. 1620).

1429 *Rolls of Parlt.* IV. 346/1 Touching the retourne, servise, and alle executions of the Writtes, Processe and Juggementz, in and of the saide actions. **1458** *Coventry Leet Bk.* (E.E.T.S.) 303 þat the shirrifs of þis Citie from hensfurth fauour all maner persones of þis Citie in makyng their returnes as ferre as they goodely may savyng theym self. **1542–3** *Act 34 & 35 Hen. VIII*, c. 27 §79 The shirefe shall haue for the retourne of euery such byll foure pence. **1581** Lambarde *Eiren.* ii. ii. (1588) 116 Then must the Iustice of the Peace..make retourne of the Writ. **1620** J. Wilkinson *Coroners & Sherifes* 56 You shal find in this booke good retorns for all maner of writs now in use,..and also apt retorns of all your Exchequer proces. **1655** Fuller *Ch. Hist.* ix. x. 184 Any person whom (in discretion) they suspected to have dealt lewdly, about any Writ, Returne, entrie of Rule, pleading, or any such like Matter. **1712** Arbuthnot *John Bull* i. xi, Fees..for Enrollings, Exemplifications, Bails, Vouchers, Returns. **1810** Bentham *Packing* (1821) 161 The sheriff was and is the person, by whom, in all cases, what is called the return, was and is made. **1884** *Law Rep.* 25 *Chanc. Div.* 341 The sheriff.. made a return of *nulla bona* to the writ of *fi. fa.*

b. ***day of*** (***the***) ***return***, = return day. Also with ellipse of *day*.

1455 *Rolls of Parlt.* V. 336/1 Yf at eny of the seid daies of retourne, it be retourned by the seid Shireffes. **1472** *Ibid.* VI. 52/1 At the day and daies of the retourne conteyned in the same Writte and Writtes. **1531** *Dial. on Laws Eng.* ii. iii. 8 So longe daye of returne that fyue counties myghte be holden before the returne therof. **1702** *Modern Cases* (1716) 59 He coming in upon a Habeas Corpus, and pleading to the Writ, at the Day of the Retorn of it, the Court could not deny his Plea. **1768** Blackstone *Comm.* III. 275 The day.. on which the sheriff is to bring in the writ and report how far he has obeyed it, is called the return of the writ.

c. *ellipt.* (See quots.)

1577 Harrison *England* in *Holinshed* (1587) I. 181 A perfect rule to know the beginning and ending of euerie terme, with their returnes. **1607** Cowell *Interpr.* s.v., Hilary terme is said to haue 4 returnes,..and Easter terme to haue 5 returnes. **1669** Sturmy *Mariner's Mag.* ii. 101 Each of these Terms hath several Returns, and each Return hath four Days belonging to it. **1684** *Spelman's Law Terms* §ii. 6 The Eight days wherein the Court of the Exchequer sits,..are to be accounted as parts of the Terms, for that they fall within the first Return. **1830** *Act 1 Will. IV* c. 70 §6 In Easter Term there shall be but four Returns instead of five.

9. a. The official report made by a returning officer (originally the sheriff) as to the election of a member or members of Parliament; hence, the fact of being elected to sit in Parliament.

† ***double return***, the fact of two or more candidates being provisionally returned.

1459 *Rolls of Parlt.* V. 367/1 For eny maner elections of Knyghtes,..and for Retournes of the same, and for almaner Retournes of Citezeyns and Burgeyses in their severall Shires, for this present Parlement.

1698 Luttrell *Brief Rel.* (1857) IV. 409 Elections since my last... Weobley, Mr. Price, Mr. Thomas Foley, and Mr. Birch, it being a double return. **1736** *Gentl. Mag.* VI. 437/2 A Petition..complaining of an undue Election and Return for the said County, was presented to the House. **1769** Burke *Late St. Nat.* Wks. II. 140 How will this great politician preserve the rights of electors, the fairness of returns..? It would..be a glorious sight to have eight or ten petitions or double returns [etc.]. **1789** *Constit. U.S.* i. §5 Each house shall be the judge of the elections, returns, and qualifications of its own members. **1827** Hallam *Const. Hist.* xvi. (1876) III. 273 The house of Commons had an undoubted right of determining all disputed returns to the writ of election. **1853** Lytton *My Novel* i. x, Having procured Audley's return to Parliament. *Ibid.* xi. v, Audley Egerton had no chance of return for his own seat. **1863** H. Cox *Instit.* i. viii. 114 The *return* is made by indenture, which names the persons chosen, is signed and sealed, and returned to the Crown office in Chancery, tacked to the writ itself.

†**b.** A response to a demand; a reply to a letter or dispatch. *Obs.*

1640 in Rushw. *Hist. Coll.* (1692) I. iii. 45 The King's Remembrancer..shall make a Certificate of the last Subsidy, as it was Assessed upon the several Counties,..and to Certifie the Returns of every County. **1652** Needham tr. *Selden's Mare Cl.* 471 In a letter of the said Ambassador.. wee find this Return, touching the business of the Fisherie. **1655** Fuller *Ch. Hist.* ix. 143 The true estate of Ecclesiasticall affairs..may be extracted out of the following dispatches, and their returns.

c. A report of a formal or official character giving information as to the numbers, amounts, etc., of the subjects of inquiry; a set of statistics compiled by order of some authority; *spec.* in *Cricket*, a summary of bowling figures at the end of play.

1756 Washington *Lett.* Writ. 1889 I. 398 A return of the stores at this place is enclosed. **1787** Nelson 4 July in Nicolas *Disp.* (1845) I. 241 Having given Commodore Parker a Return of the Squadron and the services they were employed upon. **1808** Wellington in Gurw. *Desp.* (1835) IV. 16 You will direct the regiments to make returns for the number of canteens and havresacks that they may require. **1863** H. Cox *Instit.* i. ix. 154 Many accounts and papers are obtained from public departments as *returns* to orders of either House. **1871** C. DAVIES *Metric Syst.* III. 284 The table of a return from the various Custom houses. **1976** J. SNOW *Cricket Rebel* 44 My return read nought for 117. **1977** J. LAKER *One-Day Cricket* 137 Bob White..must have surprised many Londoners with a number of fine returns since he left Lords.

transf. **1784** J. BARRY *Lect. Art* vi. (1848) 206 The contraction or extension of our sphere of vision depends upon other considerations than the simple return of our mere natural optics.

10. † **a.** Recovery *of* something taken. *Obs.*

1544 *Ld. Hertford's Exped. Scot.* (1798) 15, lx oxen [were] brought away: for yᵉ retorne wherof a number of Scottyshmen pursued very ernestly.

b. Restoration *of* something to a person; *spec.* in *Law* (see quots.).

1641 *Termes de la Ley* 241 Then hee that tooke the distresse shall have againe the distresse, and that is called the returne of the beasts. **1704** J. HARRIS *Lex. Techn.* I, *Returnum irreplegiabile*, is a Writ..for the final restitution or return of Cattle to the Owner, unjustly taken by another. **1841** *Penny Cycl.* XIX. 423/2 Return of Cattle, &c. is a term applied to the restoration of cattle, &c. distrained, to the party by whom they were distrained, after it has been ascertained that the distress was rightfully taken.

11. a. The act of giving, or (more usually) that which is given or received, by way of recompense, acknowledgement, or reciprocity.

a **1542** WYATT in *Tottel's Misc.* (Arb.) 92 By which returne be sure to winne a cant Of halfe at least. **1602** SHAKS. *Ham.* II. ii. 60 *King*. What from our Brother Norwey? *Volt.* Most faire returne of Greetings, and Desires. **1668** DAVENANT *Man's the Master* III. ii, That's a valuable return of intelligence from us for what he gave of himself. **1700** ROWE *Amb. Step-Moth.* I. i, You out-bid my Service And all returns are vile, but Words the poorest. **1788** GIBBON *Decl. & F.* xliv. IV. 395 A grateful return is due to the author of a benefit. **1807** SOUTHEY *Lett.* (1850) III. 106 Mr. Aikin has sent me no returns either for this year's reviewing or the last. **1884** *Manch. Exam.* 17 May 4/7 The Church does not get.. any adequate return for the sacrifices she is compelled to make.

b. The yield of some productive thing considered in relation to the original amount or expenditure.

1626 BACON *Sylva* §409 In some Grounds which are strong, you shall haue a Raddish, etc. come in a month; That in other grounds will not come in two; And so make double Returnes. **1697** DRYDEN *Virg. Georg.* II. 642 The Swain.. Receives his easy Food from Nature's Hand, And just Returns of cultivated Land. **1710** PRIDEAUX *Orig. Tithes* ii. 105 Wheat..produceth ten Bushels in the return. **1764** BURN *Poor Laws* 156 One loom..will make fourteen returns the first year of cloth ready for sale, and sixteen returns every year after. **1799** J. ROBERTSON *Agric. Perth* 174 One hundred and twenty one bolls, an acre, being thirty-eight returns of the quantity of seed planted. **1886** C. SCOTT *Sheep-farming* Introd. p. xvi, In the course of a year they give two returns,—the lamb, and the fleece.

c. In phr. ***in return.***

1607 SHAKS. *Timon* IV. iii. 517 As rich men deale Guifts, Expecting in returne twenty for one. **1719** DE FOE *Crusoe* I. (Globe) 309, I wrote to my old Friend at Lisbon, who in Return gave me Notice, that he could easily dispose of it there. **1754** HUME *Hist. Eng.* iv. (1812) I. 289 In return he promised that he would assist his brother. **1781** COWPER *Charity* 92 No land but listens to the common call, And in return receives supply from all. **1827** ROBERTS *Voy. Centr. Amer.* 68 The Indians..brought me a present,..and in return, I induced my friends to follow. **1896** *Law Times* C. 360/2 He paid his fare to the conductor, and in return received a ticket.

d. ***in return for,*** †***of,*** or †***to.***

1656 EARL MONM. tr. *Boccalini's Pol. Touchstone* (1674) 268 In return of so prostrated a patience. **1749** FIELDING *Tom Jones* VI. i, In return to all these concessions, I desire [etc.]. **1760–72** H. BROOKE *Fool of Qual.* (1809) III. 143 Here are five guineas in return of the pleasure you have given me. **1793** SMEATON *Edystone L.* §249 In return for our continued interruption.., our works had an uninterrupted progression for eighteen days. **1840** DICKENS *Old C. Shop* xliii, They covered her, in return for her exertions, with some pieces of sail-cloth and ends of tarpaulin. **1857** LIVINGSTONE *Trav.* x. 196 A present is usually given in return for the hospitality.

e. *ellipt.* In various sports: a return match.

1958 F. C. AVIS *Boxing Reference Dict.* 111 *Return*, a second contest with a boxer whom one has previously fought. **1964** *Guardian* 2 Mar. 7/6 Or we might arrange for a monkey's (monkey's paw—draw) so that we can have a return. **1977** *Daily Express* 29 Mar. 32/4 England..could only score four in the return at Highbury.

12. a. A reply, answer, or retort. Now *rare* or *Obs.*

1599 SHAKS. *Hen. V*, II. iv. 127 If my Father render faire returne, It is against my will. *a* **1617** SIR J. MELVIL *Mem.* (1683) 34, I answered as I thought most pertinent. When he had heard my returns, he was pleased to say [etc.]. **1677** YARRANTON *Eng. Improv.* 194 If any Gentleman..please to put Pen to Paper, in opposition to what is here asserted; I shall give him a Civil return. **1702** C. MATHER *Magn. Chr.* VII. 16/2 Unto those Replies he gave Returns; and unto those Returns the Synod gave Rejoinders. **1751** HARRIS *Hermes* Wks. (1841) 161 Whose verses are these? the return is a sentence, These are verses of Homer. **1796** MRS. E. PARSONS *Myst. Warning* III. 260 They had no return to the letters they had written.

b. A thrust, stroke, volley, etc., given in reply to one from an opponent or enemy.

1705 BLACKWELL *Fencing-Master* 15 These are the Returns upon those Thrusts without Faints. **1809** ROLAND *Fencing* 60 Being much nearer your adversary's body to deliver your return (called the riposte). **1837** MARRYAT *Perc. Keene* xix, The Stella was put about, and the other broadside given without a return from her opponent. **1863** WHYTE-MELVILLE *Gladiators* I. 30 If your guard is an inch too high, your return a thought too slow.

c. *Card-playing.* (Cf. RETURN *v.* 21 c.)

1742 HOYLE *Whist* 16 You may wait to finess your Ten upon the Return of Trumps from your Partner. **1830** 'EIDRAH TREBOR' *Hoyle Made Familiar* 15 You may wait the return of that suit. *Ibid.* 19 Wait the return from your partner. **1974** *Country Life* 24 Jan. 152/3 West should have led the Heart Nine, to ask for a Diamond return. **1978** *Times* 22 July 9/4 East led his ♠ 7, in order to..invite a spade return for a ruff.

d. The act of sending back to one.

1841 HOPE-SCOTT in Ornsby *Mem.* (1884) II. 3 Your speedy reply and return of my proofs was very kind. **1897** [see 15].

e. The act of returning (a ball) to an opponent or to another player; skill in doing this.

1833 J. NYREN *Young Cricketer's Tutor* 70 He had..such a rapid return..that I have seen many put out..in a single run. **1886** *Field* 19 June 794/1, Mr. R. D. Walker seemed for once to have lost his power of return. **1891** GRACE *Cricket* 258 The first-named had a wonderfully good return, and knew..at which end there was a greater chance of a run-out. **1897** *Sportsman* 16 Dec., The return..being a poor one, the first 'scrum' was formed on the Oxford '25'. **1906** A. E. KNIGHT *Compl. Cricketer* iv. 143 Inaccurate and wild returns not merely give away runs, they contribute to general slovenliness and slackness. **1972** J. MOSEDALE *Football* x. 139 McElhenny embellished the performance with 52 yards on two kickoff returns, 32 on the punt returns.

13. a. The act of bringing a thing back to a former position.

1638 JUNIUS *Paint. Ancients* 294 In admiration we hold the hand up,..with all the fingers closed, which in the returne we do both spread and turn in one motion. **1787** BEST *Angling* (ed. 2) 122 Wave the rod in a small circumference round your head, and never make a return of it before it has had it's full scope. **1867** F. FRANCIS *Angling* vii. (1880) 277 In bringing out the line behind over the shoulder, the return must not be made so abruptly.

b. A part of a ribbon-loom. (See quot.)

1782 *Encycl. Brit.* (ed. 2) IX. 6711/2 The returning-sticks, or as others call them, the returns, or the tumblers, or pulleys, to which the tires are tied, to clear the course of cords through the high-lisses.

14. *pl.* **a.** Refuse-tobacco (*obs.*). In later use, a mild, light-coloured tobacco for smoking.

1789 *Evidence Comm. for repealing Duties on Tobacco* 150 The returns are the edges of the boxes after they are gone through the engines..and the trimmings after finishing, the shag smalls, and the sand. **1789** *Act 29 Geo. III*, c. 68 §155 All returns of Spanish shall be deemed..to be returns of tobacco within the meaning of this Act. **1835–6** *Encycl. Metrop.* (1845) VIII. 396/2 Both [shag and returns] are made from the same cask of tobacco, the lighter leaves being chosen for the returns, and the darker ones for the common tobacco. **1893** 'Q.' *Delect. Duchy* 322 Who..smoked threepenny Returns in his Louis Quinze library.

b. *Brewing.* Return worts. (See 16 d.)

1846 TIZARD *Brewing* (ed. 2) xx. 555 By steeping it in sour beer, such as returns. *Ibid.*, That which is the most highly concentrated may be added to weak returns.

15. a. A thing or person sent back. Chiefly *pl.*

1875 JEVONS *Money* (1878) 266 Any cheques or bill refused payment are called 'returns'. **1892** I. ZANGWILL *Childr. Ghetto* III. 53 He let himself fall backwards, impinging noiselessly upon a heap of 'returns' of number one. **1893** *Westm. Gaz.* 18 May 2/3 'The returns' leave Queensland in good health. **1897** *N. & Q.* 8th Ser. XII. 215 Many of the papers being sent 'for sale or return', and the unsold copies referred to as 'returns'. **1902** *Chambers's Jrnl.* Feb. 114/1 The bags of tea, known as 'returns' which the samplers who come to the warehouse bring from the establishments they represent. **1934** T. WOOD *Cobbers* xi. 132 'Any returns?' says the waitress, challengingly. **1971** *Publishers' Weekly* 20 Dec. 16/1 The average rate of returns (unsold books) in the industry as a whole is about 50%. **1977** *Private Eye* 13 May 6/3 As the evening's performance was a charity gala, there would be no cheap seats available. Returns were few and would start at £3.

b. = RECOVERY 5 f.

1909 *Brit. Birds* II. 364 The returns for a species so much shot as the Woodcock are shown to be scarcely more than 5 per cent. **1959** *Jrnl. du Conseil* XXV. 58 Haddock tagging.. has shown that returns may come from the position of liberation after a very long period of freedom, or from a long way off after a comparatively short time. **1975** *Trans. Illinois State Acad. Sci.* LXVIII. III. 282 Band returns from quail released September or earlier indicated a general dispersal of 0·3–0·5 miles from the release site.

IV. *attrib.* and *Comb.*

16. a. Denoting return (of a person or thing) to a place, as ***return box, cargo, chaise, flight, journey, load, mail, omnibus, passenger, post, ship, voyage***; **return address**, the address to which a postal item is to be returned in case of non-delivery; **return-case**, a case of infectious disease occurring after the return home of a patient from hospital; **return date** *U.S. Law*, the date on which a specified person is required to appear in court; **return envelope** *U.S.*, an addressed envelope enclosed with a letter for the recipient's reply; **return fare**, the fare for a return-ticket.

1928 *Publishers' Weekly* 30 June 2605 All envelopes must carry the name and *return address of the sender in the upper left hand corner. **1852** C. BRONTE in Mrs. Gaskell *Life* (1857) II. 247, I have..sent off to-day, per rail, a *return-box of Cornhill books. **1827** ROBERTS *Voy. Centr. Amer.* 51 Sufficient for a *return Cargo. **1838** *Penny Cycl.* XI. 23/2 The return cargo was generally more valuable than the investments. **1897** *Allbutt's Syst. Med.* II. 130 In spite of every precaution these so-called '*return cases' will occasionally appear. **1798** G. THOMPSON *Sentimental Tour* 20 Falling in with a *return-chaise, I agreed with the driver for a cast—So far, for so much. **1824** MISS MITFORD *Village* Ser. I. (1863) 6 A sort of open square, which is the constant resort of carts, waggons, and return chaises. **1972** *N.Y. Law Jrnl.* 24 Oct. 18/7 A subpoena without a specific *return date and a specific place of attendance is invalid. **1973** *Ibid.* 31 Aug. 1/1 There is a substantial probability that he will not appear in court on the return date. **1886** 'MARK TWAIN' *Lett. to Publishers* (1967) 205 Enclose a stamped and printed *return-envelop. **1974** *Spartanburg* (S. Carolina) *Herald* 19 Apr. A4/8 So send for my booklet 'How to Prevent Platonic Marriage', enclosing a long stamped return envelope, plus 25 cents. **1976** *Eastern Even. News* (Norwich) 22 Dec. 7/3 The clerk..should..see if it was possible to reintroduce the reduced rate *return fare in off peak hours. **1979** *Homes & Gardens* June 26/4 The return air fare to Nice is a cracking £180. **1966** M. WOODHOUSE *Tree Frog* x. 74 I've booked my *return flight. **1976** *New Yorker* 15 Nov. 83/1 The European booking agent who had arranged for the Belgrade and London appearances paid for their return flight. **1865** *Daily Tel.* 13 Dec. 5/4, I found that everybody was coming back again, and I performed the *return journey. **1913** JONES & WYATT *Motor Traction for Business Purposes* 15 This matter of light mileage naturally brings us to the question of *return loads. **1977** 'D. RUTHERFORD' *Return Load* i. 25 We have a job for you... A return load. **1864** *Harper's Mag.* Jan. 205/2 Miss Amber answered the letter by *return mail. **1975** P. FUSSELL *Gt. War & Mod. Memory* ii. 67 Geoffrey Keynes specialized in receiving antiquarian booksellers' catalogs and buying books by return mail. **1860** A. J. MUNBY *Diary* 21 Feb. in D. Hudson *Munby* (1972) 51 Waiting for the *return omnibus, I discovered some pretty Gothic schools, new, on the green. **1864** M. J. HIGGINS *Ess.* (1875) 187 The *return passengers by the Palmaria almost always have to walk home from the port on foot. **1885** *List of Subscribers, Classified* (United Telephone Co.) (ed. 6) 226 (Advt.), Estimates per *return post. **1912** W. OWEN *Let.* ? 14 Nov. (1967) 168, I flatly disobeyed your Return-Post command. **1929** M. DE LA ROCHE *Whiteoaks* ix. 137 Alayne wrote by return post. **1977** *Private Eye* 13 May 22/2 Send small sample of urine and £3 for reliable and strictly confidential results by first class return post. *c* **1700** EVELYN *Diary* an. 1680 (1955) IV. 212, I went to visite a French Stranger,..who having been thrice at the *East Indias, Persia* & other remote Countries, came hither in our *returne ships from those parts. **1867** SMYTH *Sailor's Word-bk.* 570 A ship on a *return voyage is not generally liable [to confiscation].

b. In scientific or technical uses, as ***return air, charge, current, flow, shock, smoke, stroke, wave.***

1883 GRESLEY *Gloss. Coal Mining* 202 **Return Air*, the air or ventilation which has been passed through the workings. **1849** NOAD *Electricity* (ed. 3) 68 Faraday first observed the singular phenomenon of the *return charge. He found, that, if..the apparatus..was suddenly and perfectly discharged, ..it gradually recovered a charge. **1873** F. JENKIN *Electr. & Magn.* (1881) 313 The *return current is especially great when any portion of the line L is formed of wire coated with india-rubber. **1957** G. E. HUTCHINSON *Treat. Limnol.* I. v. 268 We have a wind drift at the surface almost along the direction of the wind, and a region near the bottom of current flowing against the wind, the so-called return current. **1964** *Economist* 23 May 873/3 The only possible source is '*return-flow' from irrigation. **1881** S. P. THOMPSON *Electr. & Magn.* i. §26. 28 When a charged conductor is suddenly discharged, a discharge is felt by persons standing near, or may even affect electroscopes, or yield sparks. This action, known as the '*return-shock', is due to induction. **1861** MRS. RIDDELL *City & Suburb* I. ii. 29 A fire-board which had been put up with the friendly intention of preventing any occupant being suffocated with *return smoke. **1845** *Encycl. Metrop.* VIII. 301/1 On the *return stroke the air enters into the cylinder below the piston. **1881** S. P. THOMPSON *Electr. & Magn.* iv. §304. 257 The 'return-stroke' experienced by persons in the neighbourhood of a flash. **1898** *Westm. Gaz.* 22 June 7/1 Visitors were specially warned by placards in various directions against the dangers of 'the *return wave'.

c. Allowing or causing return of something, as ***return conductor, pipe, spring, valve.***

1825 J. NICHOLSON *Operat. Mechanic* 509 The small return-spring should be as thin as possible at the end fastened to the other spring. **1839** *Civil Eng. & Arch. Jrnl.* II. 306/2 H the return-pipe. **1847** *Phil. Mag.* XXX. 194 The earth has been made to act the part of the return conductor. **1875** KNIGHT *Dict. Mech.* 1926/2 *Return-valve*, a valve which opens to allow reflux of a fluid under certain conditions.

d. *Brewing.* **return wort**, a weak wort blended with the following mash.

1845 TIZARD *Voice from Mash-Tun* I. 38 Examples of four brewings by the ordinary practice, from which the usual lengths, with Table-Beer or Return Wort, are drawn. **1846** —— *Brewing* (ed. 2) 186, etc.

e. return room, a mezzanine room at the turn of a flight of stairs.

1914 JOYCE *Dubliners* 82 He glanced up and saw Jack regarding him from the door of the return-room. **1922** —— *Ulysses* 296 The other boot which he had been looking for was at present under the commode in the return room. **1927** ST. JOHN ERVINE *Wayward Man* I. ii. 35 The return-room at the top of the first flight of stairs could be converted into a kitchen.

17. Denoting change of direction or recedence, esp. at right angles (see sense 4), as ***return angle, arm, crease, desk, piece, side, wall.***

1676 MOXON *Print. Lett.* 51 Placing one Foot of your Compasses on the *Return Angles. **1870** F. R. WILSON *Ch. Lindisf.* 94 The masonry at the return angle of the nave is likewise Saxon. **1861** SMILES *Engineers* II. 219 The moment the vessel gets within the outer angles of the two *return arms or kants, she may be said to be in or out of the harbour. **1775** *New Articles Game of Cricket* 2 The Bowling-Crease must be parallel with the Stumps, Three Feet in Length, with a *Return-Crease. **1787** *Laws of Cricket* in Waghorn *Cricket Scores* (1899) p. x, The Bowling-crease must be parallel with the stumps, three feet in length, with a return-crease. **1902** [see CALL *v.* 4 l]. **1948** *Sporting Mirror* 21 May 6/1 Three creases are marked out at each end of a cricket pitch—the bowling crease, return crease and popping crease. **1963** *Times* 23 Apr. 4/7 He [*sc.* an umpire] is required ..to see whether the bowler is no-balling on the return crease. **1976** J. Snow *Cricket Rebel* 99 Stackpole's bat was outside the return crease at the time the wicket was broken. **16..** in Parker *Gloss. Arch.* (1850) I. 386 Ye chapel..wth iij stooles on ye one side and a *retorne desk at the ende. **1683** Moxon *Mech. Exerc., Printing* xx. ¶3 Its end..hath a small *Return piece..made square to the under-side of the Rod. **1679** *Ibid., Carp.* ix. 171 Either the adjoyning sides of the Front of an House or Ground-plot, is called a *Return-side. **1683** *Ibid., Printing* x. ¶9 A square Iron Plate..with Return Sides about six Inches long each side. **1838** *Civil Eng. & Arch. Jrnl.* I. 330/1 Opposite the *return walls, and sometimes at certain distances in the length.

18. Denoting a doubling back upon the former direction, as ***return bend, block, flue.***

1884 Knight *Dict. Mech.* Suppl. 754/2 *Return Bend*, a U-shaped pipe coupling for uniting the ends of pipes. **1888** *Lockwood's Dict. Terms, Return Block*, a snatch block. *Ibid., Return Flues*, the flues of Cornish, Lancashire, and Wagon boilers.

19. Played, given, etc., in return, as ***return buffet, entertaining, leg, match, stroke, thanks, thrust, tie.***

1883 R. W. Church in *Ward's Eng. Poets* (1883) II. 280 The men who..dealt the return buffet to Spanish pride in the harbour of Cadiz. **1899** 'Mark Twain' in *Forum* (N.Y.) Mar. 29 You can judge..what sort of return-entertaining she has done. **1973** *Times* 31 Oct. 10/5 After Soviet objections to playing the return leg in the Santiago stadium ..Fifa..sent a delegation to investigate. **1772** in Waghorn *Cricket Scores* (1899) 84 The return match at cricket was played at Wye. **1873** *Routledge's Young Gentlm. Mag.* Dec. 100/2 We can't have the return match before Wednesday. **1891** W. G. Grace *Cricket* iv. 108 The return match, at Lord's..was more encouraging to us. **1915** J. Buchan *Thirty-Nine Steps* i. 18 This is the return match for the *pogroms*. The Jew is everywhere. **1929** *Evening News* 18 Nov. 16/6 In a return ice hockey match yesterday Berlin beat London by four goals to two. **1971** *Nature* 23 July 213/1 This follows..a conference in Washington a month ago... A 'return match' meeting to clinch the project is scheduled for Madrid for early August. **1973** *Times* 21 Mar. 9/6 The suspense of the medical report and the outcome of the return match. **1977** *Times* 8 Dec. 17/4 Contrary to my prematch forecast and your diarists' ex post account, I did not win: nor has a return match been played or planned. **1907** *Yesterday's Shopping* (1969) 361/1 'Return thanks' card... Return thanks for kind enquiries and sympathy. **1972** *V.A.T.: Scope & Coverage* (H.M. Customs) 33 Postcards.. acceptance cards; 'thank-you' or 'return-thanks' cards. **1861** Chapman *Art Fencing* I. 19 The direct return thrust (Repost)..should be delivered with the greatest rapidity. **1972** G. Green *Great Moments in Sport: Soccer* xi. 108 The return tie was played at Maine Road.

return (rɪˈtɜːn), *v.*[1] Forms: 4–6 **retorne** (5 *Sc.* **ratorn**, 6 **reatorn**); 4–6 **retourne**, 6–7 **retourn**; 5–7 **returne** (5 *Sc.* **raturn**), 7– **return**. [ad. OF. *retorner, retourner, returner* mod.F. *retourner*), = Sp. and Pg. *retornar*, It. *ritornare*: see re- and turn *v.*]

I. *intr.* **1.** To come or go back to a place or person.

?*a* **1366** Chaucer *Rom. Rose* 385 As watir that doun renneth ay, But neuer drope Retourne may. *c* **1420** Lydg. *Assembly of Gods* 111, I might nat thedyr crepe Before my seson came to retorne ayeyne. *c* **1500** *Melusine* 334 Thenne he gaf lycens to his children to retourne. And so þey departed & retourned toward Lusynen. **1560** Daus tr. *Sleidane's Comm.* 6 b, Nowe having little monye left..he is dryven to retourne. **1604** E. G[rimstone] tr. *D'Acosta's Hist. Indies* II. iv. 87 The heat and drought comes whenas the Sunne returnes. **1685** Dryden *Threnod. August.* 140 Thus, at half-ebb a rolling sea Returns, and wins upon the shore. **1768** Sterne *Sent. Journ., Temptation*, She return'd back and went into the room. **1781** Logan in *Scott. Paraphr.* viii. 9 But man forsakes this earthly Scene, Ah! never to return. **1855** Kingsley *Westw. Ho!* xiv, He had gone out to say his prayers, and had not returned. **1860** Tyndall *Glac.* I. xxii. 153 He returned, and I went on alone.

b. Const. *to, into,* or *from.* Also *home, whence.*

c **1400** *Rom. Rose* 4918 Al his lyf he doth so morne, Bycause he dar not hom retourne. *c* **1400** Maundev. (1839) xxii. 245 And aftre..thei retournen to hire owne Housholdes. **1484** Caxton *Fables of Alfonce* viii, As he was retornynge fro the feyre. **1526** *Pilgr. Perf.* (W. de W. 1531) 17 But caused them to returne backwarde in to the wyldernesse. **1577** Frampton *Joyfull News* Ded., Retourning, right worshipfull, home into Englande oute of Spaine. **1611** Bible *Jer.* xviii. 11 Returne ye now euery one from his euill way. **1660** Boyle *New Exp. Phys. Mech.* iv. 46 We..allow'd the external Air to return into the Receiver. **1712–14** Pope *Rape Lock* III. 23 The merchant from th' Exchange returns in peace. **1776** *Trial of Nundocomar* 30/1 He went from Calcutta to Jaggernaut, from whence he returned to Calcutta. **1847** Marryat *Childr. N. Forest* vi, Jacob..returned home well satisfied with the profit he had made. **1875** Jowett *Plato* (ed. 2) V. 3 Aristotle..returned to Athens after the death of Plato.

c. *transf.* of immaterial things, as time, etc.

?*a* **1366** Chaucer *Rom. Rose* 383 The tyme that may not soiourne, But goth and may neuer Retourne. **1549** *Compl. Scot.* 85 Vald ȝe al perpend ȝour..querrel, than hardines and curage vald returne vitht in ȝour hartis. **1591** Spenser *M. Hubberd* 306 Ere the yeare..doo returne from whence he first begun. **1638** Junius *Paint. Ancients* 246 That is great indeed..which doth still returne into our thoughts. **1667** Milton *P.L.* xi. 531 Till many years over thy head return: So maist thou live. **1697** Dryden *Virg. Georgics* III. 429 With the Spring their genial Warmth returns. *a* **1832** Macintosh *Bacon & Locke* Wks. 1846 I. 329 Their argument must return to the point from which it set out. **1859** Tennyson *Geraint & Enid* 1182 Nor will ye win him back, For the man's love once gone never returns. **1880** Shorthouse *J. Inglesant* xxxvii, The scenes and forms of death with which he had been familiar in Naples, returned again and again before his eyes.

d. Const. *upon* (a person).

c **1450** *Merlin* 597 The saisnes were grete and stronge, and ..often thei returned vpon hem that hem pursued. **1484** Caxton *Fables of Æsop* III. vi, Synne retorneth euer vpon his mayster. **1611** Bible *1 Kings* ii. 33 Their blood shall therefore returne vpon the head of Ioab. **1719** Waterland *Vind. Christ's Div.* 21 Let it stand, to support the Second Query; which returns upon you, and expects a fuller Answer. **1864** Tennyson *En. Ard.* 619 When the beauteous hateful isle Return'd upon him. **1866** Dale *Disc. Spec. Occ.* iii. 68 Your sins after injuring others, often return upon yourselves.

e. In pa. pple. with *is, was,* etc. Now *rare.*

1560 Daus tr. *Sleidane's Comm.* 153 He a lytle before at the beginning of Maye, was retorned home with his wyfe. **1581** Lambarde *Eiren.* I. iv. (1588) 21 After such time as Queene Isabell..was retired ouer the Seas into England. **1601** Weever *Mirr. Mart.* E v b, Through many paines and perils past, I'm safe returned back to Wales at last. **1667** Milton *P.L.* ix. 401 Shee to him as oft engag'd To be returnd by Noon amid the Bowre. **1795** Jefferson *Writ.* (1859) IV. 118 After the middle of May, by which time I hope to be returned from Bedford. **1823** Lingard *Hist. Eng.* VI. 227 The business languished till the earl of Wiltshire was returned from Bologna.

f. With cognate object. *rare.*

1594 Shaks. *Rich. III*, I. i. 117 Go treade the path that thou shalt ne're return.

†**2. a.** To have respect or relation *to. Obs.*−1

1390 Gower *Conf.* III. 133 The tail of Scorpio..to Mercurie and to Satorne Be weie of kinde mot retorne After the preparacion Of due constellacion.

†**b.** To turn round (*to* one); to face about. *Obs.*

1432–50 tr. *Higden* (Rolls) IV. 463 When this noble yonge man Iulian huntede.., and folowede an herte, the herte returnede to hym. *c* **1470** Henry *Wallace* II. 59 Wallace raturnd as man of mekyll mayne; And at a straik the formast has he slayne.

†**c.** To turn back, retire, retreat. *Obs.*

c **1420** Lydg. *Assembly of Gods* 1098 Ye shall your chaunce Take as hit falleth, wherfore returne ye must. *c* **1470** Henry *Wallace* x. 672 The erll of ȝork consaillyt the king to fle; Than he ratornd, sen na succour thai se. **1470–85** Malory *Arthur* I. xv. 57 These two knyghtes were in grete daunger of their lyues that they were fayn to retorne.

†**d.** To turn away; to go away again. *Obs.*

1432–50 tr. *Higden* (Rolls) III. 25 In the whiche yere Edom returnede, in that he wolde not be vnder Iuda, and made a kynge to theyme. **1611** Bible *2 Kings* xviii. 14, I haue offended, returne from me: that which thou puttest on me, wil I beare.

†**e.** *Arch.* Of a moulding, etc.: To continue at an angle to the previous direction. *rare*−1.

1613–39 I. Jones in Leoni *Palladio's Archit.* (1742) II. 49 This Architrave..does return over the Pilasters.

3. a. To go back in discourse; to revert *to* or resume a topic or subject.

c **1400** Maundev. (1839) v. 53 Now will I retourne aȝen, or I procede ony ferthere, for to declare ȝou the othere weyes, that drawen toward Babiloyne. *a* **1450** *Knt. de la Tour* (1868) 137 Atte this tyme y passe ouer to speke more of these good ladyes, and retorne ayen to other thingges. *a* **1533** Ld. Berners *Huon* lv. 189 Let vs leue spekynge of them tyll we returne therto agayne. **1568** Grafton *Chron.* II. 377 But to returne where we left: After the Duke was fled, as aforesayde [etc]. **1593** Shaks. *2 Hen. VI*, III. i. 322 *Suff.* But now returne we to the false Duke Humfrey. *Card.* No more of him. **1656** Harrington *Oceana* (1658) 155 It is not so much my desire to return upon haunts, as theirs that will not be satisfied. **1662** Stillingfl. *Orig. Sacræ* I. iii. §9 But to return to Kircher. **1719** De Foe *Crusoe* II. (Globe) 371, I return to the Story. **1799** Han. More *Fem. Educ.* (ed. 4) I. 105 To return, however, to the subject of general education. **1838** T. Thomson *Chem. Org. Bodies* 807 Let us now return to the aqueous solution from which the resinous-looking matter had separated. **1856** Froude *Hist. Eng.* (1858) I. i. 74 The subject is one to which..I shall have more than one occasion to return.

†**b.** To proceed or begin again *to* do something. *Obs.* (Only in translations from Spanish and Italian.)

1574 Hellowes *Guevara's Fam. Ep.* (1577) 236 Which.. after I had read, and returned againe to reade the same [etc.]. **1594** T. Bedingfield tr. *Machiavelli's Florentine Hist.* (1595) 63 Whereuppon they returned to admonish more boldlie then they were woont. **1626** C. Potter tr. *Sarpi's Hist. Quarrels* 120 A few daies after, hauing changed his minde.., he returned to treat with him as before.

4. a. To revert, go back again, *to* (or *into*) a previous condition or state; to come back *to* oneself.

1484 Caxton *Æsop* II. x, A lytyll whyle after this, this man retourned and felle ageyne in to grete pouerte. **1526** Tindale *Acts* xiii. 34 He reysed him vp from deeth, now no more to returne to corrupcion. **1611** Bible *Gen.* iii. 19 Dust thou art, and vnto dust shalt thou returne. **1651** Hobbes *Leviath.* II. xxx. 175 The Common-wealth is thereby dissolved, and every man returneth into the condition and calamity of a warre with every other man. **1710** Steele *Tatler* No. 198 ¶4 Upon proper Applications to revive her, the unhappy young Creature returned to her self. **1796** in Burke *Regic. Peace* i. Sel. Wks. (1892) 39 To engage Prussia ..to return into the coalition. **1852** M. Arnold *Empedocles* Poems (1906) 109 To the elements it came from Everything will return. **1892** *Speaker* 3 Sept. 290/1 The roses..will deteriorate year after year, returning gradually to wildness.

b. To revert *to* some practice, opinion, etc. ***to return to nature***: to abandon urban life in favour of rustic simplicity. Cf. return *sb.* 1 i.

1534 More *Treat. Passion* Wks. 1309/2 They..retourned of frowardnes to their errours agayne. **1552** Abp. Hamilton *Catech.* (1884) 47 He..will nocht returne to the catholike faith. **1611** Cotgr., *Recoquiner*, to fall a begging, to returne to beggerie. **1737** *Gentl. Mag.* VII. 288/2 Finding that she absolutely must resolve to die, or return to wearing Petticoats. **1745** Eliza Heywood *Female Spect.* No. 19 (1748) IV. 26 Heaven forbid that..I should..advise them to return to that old fashioned way of spending time. **1881** Jowett *Thucyd.* I. 72 The Byzantians too agreed to return to their allegiance. **1902** G. K. Chesterton *Twelve Types* 141 This attempt to re-establish communication with the elemental, or, as it is sometimes more roughly and fallaciously expressed, to return to nature.

†**c.** To become (something) again. *Obs. rare.*

1523 Ld. Berners *Froiss.* I. 427 Into his owne countre, the which newly was retourned Frenche. **1618** *Camden's Lett.* (1691) 210 The Count of Candale is suddenly returned Papist again. **1692** O. Walker *Grk. & Rom. Hist.* 330 She turned Arrian... Afterwards she seemed to return Catholick.

†**d.** *Sc.* To change or turn *into* something else.

1500–20 Dunbar *Poems* xii. 4 All erdly joy returnis in pane. **1513** Douglas *Æneis* IV. viii. 100 Scho gan beheld In blak adill the hallowit wattir cald Changit and altir, and furth ȝet wynis gude Anon returnit into laithlie blude.

5. To go back or revert *to* a previous owner.

c **1460** Fortescue *Abs. & Lim. Mon.* xi. (1885) 136 Thai rewarded with..offices, and some with livelode terme off lyff, wich aftir thair dethis wolde than retorne to the Crowne. **1524** *Test. Ebor.* (Surtees) VI. 10, I bequeathe..a litile howse with a yerde the terme of his lyfe, and then to return to the right heires. **1631** Sir J. Doderidge *Eng. Lawyer* 70 Never like to return to the Lord by Escheat or Donor by Reverter. **1687** A. Lovell tr. *Thevenot's Trav.* I. 115 The Saracens took it from the Greeks,..then it returned to the Christians, and afterwards to the Saracens.

†**6. a.** To result or fall out *to* a person. *Obs.*

1586 A. Day *Eng. Secretary* I. (1595) 140 Consider with your selfe how grieuous the thing you go about to compasse may returne vnto her.

†**b.** To amount *to* a certain sum. *Obs. rare*−1.

1622 *Capt. Smith's Wks.* (Arb.) 777, 5000. persons, whose labours returne yeerely to about 135000. pound sterling.

II. †**7. a.** *refl.* To turn or go back *to* an occupation, place, etc. *Obs. rare.*

1413 *Pilgr. Sowle* (Caxton) v. i. (1859) 68, I retourne me ageyne to my fyrst purpoos. *c* **1477** Caxton *Jason* 110 b, Whan the Quene Ysiphyle had saide these wordes she retorned her unto the cite. **1612** Shelton *Quix.* (1620) I. iv. 136 That which we might do best were to return us again to our village.

†**b.** To turn round (*to* a person) or back. *Obs.*

1483 Caxton *Gold. Leg.* 442 b/2, Ryght there he retourneth hymself and salueth the peple. **1533** Bellenden *Livy* II. xv. (S.T.S.) II. 5 Returnand him to Appius he said [etc.]. **1591** Shaks. *1 Hen. VI*, III. iii. 56 Returne thee therefore with a floud of Teares, And wash away thy Countries stayned Spots.

8. *trans.* †**a.** To reverse, return upon (one's course). *Obs.*

c **1420** Lydg. *Assembly of Gods* 100 Thys Eolus hath oft Made me to retourne my course agayn nature With hys gret blastys. **1582** N. Lichefield tr. *Castanheda's Conq. E. Ind.* I. ii. 5 They lost each other, and therefore they returned their course towardes Cabo Verde.

†**b.** To turn round (a horse, ship, etc.); to cause to face the other way. *Obs.*

c **1500** *Melusine* 309 But whan he cam in to the feldes he retourned hys hors, & beheld toward thabbaye. **1553** Eden *Treat. Newe Ind.* (Arb.) 35 Returninge his shyppes towarde the West, he found a more holesome ayre. **1607** Rowlands *Earl of Warwick* (Hunterian Cl.) 53 Then very lightly Guy returns his Horse, And comes up on him with redoubled might.

c. To take or lead back upon the former direction; to turn at an angle to the previous course.

1613–39 I. Jones in Leoni *Palladio's Archit.* (1742) II. 45 The Cimasium..return'd to the Wall. **1731** *Phil. Trans.* XXXVII. 28 We then thought of trying whether the Attraction would not be stronger without doubling or returning the Line. **1731** Miller *Gard. Dict.* s.v. *Stoves*, Over this the second Flue must be return'd back again. **1825** J. Nicholson *Operat. Mechanic* 545 The trouble of plumbing and returning the quoins, is considered equivalent to the deficiency of materials. **1874** Micklethwaite *Mod. Par. Churches* 59, I propose that the upper row of stalls should be returned at the west end of the chancel.

9. †**a.** To turn (one's heart, thoughts, etc.) back or away (*from* something). *Obs.*

1483 Caxton *Gold. Leg.* 117/2 Their hertes [were so] mollified that almost were retorned fro the crysten faith. *c* **1500** *Lancelot* 1266 So mokil to hir lady haith she vroght That at that tyme she haith Returnyt hir thocht. **1700** Farquhar *Constant Couple* 111, Such ungenerous usage will soon return my tir'd heart.

b. To turn or direct (one's eyes, sight, mind) back, or towards something.

1509 Barclay *Shyp of Folys* (1570) ¶¶vj, Returne your sight, beholde vnto the shore. **1590** Spenser *F.Q.* II. iii. 19 Each bad other flye: Both fled attonce, ne ever backe returned eye. *Ibid.* III. viii. 18 Braggadochio,..Once having turnd, no more returnd his face. **1647** N. Bacon *Disc. Govt. Eng.* I. lvii. (1739) 106 The King..then returns his thoughts for France. **1839–48** Bailey *Festus* xix. 214 And I returned mine hungry eyes to the light.

†**c.** To pull back (one's hand). *Obs. rare*−1.

1697 Potter *Antiq. Greece* III. iv. (1715) 45 The Grecians .., placing their Bows directly before them, return'd their Hand upon their right Breast.

10. a. To bring or convey back to a place or person. Const. *to, from,* etc.

1432–50 tr. *Higden* (Rolls) I. 425 Whiche ston brouȝhte from that place by a certeyne space of eny man is returnede to his propre place ageyne in the nyȝhte. *c* **1500** *Melusine* 114 Goo thanne fourth on your waye, vnder the sauegarde of god, who kepe you, lede & retourne you agayn with joye. **1538** Bale *Thre Lawes* 133 Thou shalt my people returne from farre exyle. **1594** Marlowe & Nashe *Dido* I. i, Changing heavens may those good days return, Which Pergama did vaunt in all her pride. **1650** W. Brough *Sacr. Princ.* (1659) 473 This heals sin.., returns thee both to God and thy self. **1667** Milton *P.L.* vii. 16 With like safetie guided down Return me to my Native Element. **1727** DE FOE *Secrets*, etc. (1840) 337 All these cases, however, return me back to the advice above. **1759** STERNE *Tr. Shandy* II. xvii, Here Trim kept waving his right hand.., returning it backwards and forwards to the conclusion of the paragraph.

b. To bring back or restore (something) *to* or *into* a former position or state; to restore to a normal state; †to retransform.

1462 *Pol. Poems* (Rolls) II. 268 Henry hys sone of Wyndesore, by gret foly, Alle hathe retourned unto huge langoure. **1525** LD. BERNERS *Froiss.* II. 599 To retourne all the landes agayne to the governynge of the kyng of Englande. **1584** R. SCOT *Discov. Witchcr.* v. iii. (1886) 75 Of a man turned into an asse, and returned againe into a man by one of Bodins witches. **1662** PLAYFORD *Skill Mus.* III. (1674) 23 If you return the eight of the Treble into a third again. **1697** COLLIER *Ess. Mor. Subj.* I. (1703) 167 A man cannot always stand bent; so that either negligence, or passion,.. will sometime or other return the posture. **1883** JEFFERIES *Story my Heart* v. (1891) 91 Torso and limb, bust and neck instantly returned me to myself.

†**c.** To make or render again. *Obs.*$^{-1}$

1559 in Strype *Ann. Ref.* (1709) I. xiii. 174 Pretending that Q. Mary of famous memory had returned the realm wholly Catholic.

†**11.** To induce (one) to come back. *Obs.*

1523 LD. BERNERS *Froiss.* I. ccclxxv. 624 To retourne agayne the fleers, and to fyght with theyr ennemies. *a* **1547** SURREY *Æneid* IV. 634, I have found the way Him to returne, or lose me from his love. **1591** *Troub. Raigne K. John* To Rdr., We left.. Hubert posting to returne those Lords, Who deem'd him [Arthur] dead, and parted discontent.

†**12.** To withdraw, recall, summon back. *Obs.*

1590 LLOYD *1st Pt. Diall of Daies* 160 Seeing that hee could do no good hee returned his siege and marched with his army toward Apulia. **1617** *Buccleuch MSS.* (Hist. MSS. Comm.) I. 187 The calling away the armada, and returning it again in that manner.

13. a. To bring back in exchange; to yield in return. Now *rare.*

1596 RALEIGH *Discov. Gviana* ¶iij, I was not bounde to satisfie anie man of the quantitie, but such onely as aduentured, if any store had been returned thereof. **1610** HEALEY *St. Aug. Citie of God* I. xiv. (1620) 22 If the worship of these gods returne mens happinesse in the life to come. **1612** DAVIES *Why Ireland*, etc. 132 Ireland had beene.. Planted, and Improoued; and returned a rich Reuennew to the Crowne of England.

1866 ROGERS *Agric. & Prices* I. iii. 51 Rye returns at Maldon rather more than three times.

†**b.** To turn over in business. *Obs. rare.*

1677 YARRANTON *Eng. Improv.* 23, I do know four persons.. that are in a great Trade, and I believe they Return more moneys in Trade than any two Merchants or Traders in England. **1761** *Charac.* in *Ann. Reg.* 63/1 From the time of his opening this shop, till the year 1759, he returned annually about two thousand pounds.

14. a. To put back *in* or *into* something; to restore *to* some receptacle.

1611 BIBLE *Gen.* xliii. 18 Because of the money that was returned in our sackes at the first time are we brought in. **1759** STERNE *Tr. Shandy* II. xvii, Trim wiped his face, and returned his handkerchief into his pocket. **1763** MILLS *System Pract. Husb.* IV. 404 The mould which is to be returned into them should also be mixed with.. wood-ashes. **1821** BYRON *Sardanap.* II. i, Arbaces and Salemenes return their swords to the scabbards. **1848** MILL *Pol. Econ.* III. xxiv. II. 195 The notes.. would, if not wanted for current transactions, be returned into deposit.

b. *Mil.* To replace (arms, etc.) in the usual receptacle.

1696 R. H. *Sch. Recreat.* 53 Return your scowrer. [i.e.] Put it up in its proper place. *Ibid.* 57 When by command your Swords are returned, stand upright to your Arms. **1799** *Instr. & Reg. Cavalry* (1813) 271 They form to the reserve, returning their pistols and sloping their swords. **1833** *Ibid.* I. 84 Young horses must be gradually accustomed .. to drawing and returning swords. **1847** *Infantry Man.* (1854) 40 After returning ramrods, the whole remain steady.

III. 15. a. To send (a person or thing) back again.

1459 *Rolls of Parlt.* V. 368/1 That the said Shirref or Shirrefs, deuly serve and retourne the said Writte. **1582** STANYHURST *Æneis* II. (Arb.) 61 Achilles.. me to my kingdoom both gently and truely returned [L. *remisit*]. *c* **1595** CAPT. WYATT *R. Dudley's Voy. W. Ind.* (Hakl. Soc.) 39 The commaunder of that place, returninge our messingers the next daie.., promised.. to com. **1642** tr. *Perkins' Prof. Bk.* xi. §260. 333 If.. the Sherife returne the writ at the day. **1711** BUDGELL *Spect.* No. 116 ¶3 A Gentleman having made him a Present of a.. fine hound,.. the Knight returned it by the Servant with a great many Expressions of Civility. **1726** POPE *Odyss.* XIX. 542 Autolycus.. from the Delphic dome With added gifts return'd him [Ulysses] glorious home. **1765** R. ROGERS *Jrnl.* (1769) 156 He saw at Montreal two Rangers,.. that were returned by Col. Haviland. **1877** RAYMOND *Statist. Mines & Mining* 108 The loaded buckets or cars coming down and emptying themselves would return the empty ones. **1886** *Field* 19 June 794/1 He did.. now and then return balls which almost all players would have found impracticable.

b. To turn back; to force (one) to return *to* a place. *rare.*

1545 BRINKLOW *Compl.* 42 If he passe the second, he shal be returnyd at the thyrd, onlesse he be rych or haue great fryndys. **1667** MILTON *P.L.* XII. 219 Least.. Warr terrifie them inexpert, and feare Return them back to Egypt. **1829** GEN. P. THOMPSON *Exerc.* (1842) I. 52 Till Vishnu array himself.., to return him to his deep.

c. To send back or reflect (sound or light).

1693 DRYDEN *Persius* (1697) 439 A flaw is in thy ill-bak'd Vessel found; 'Tis hollow, and returns a jarring sound. **1711** BUDGELL *Spect.* No. 116 ¶7 The Chiding of the Hounds, which was returned upon us in a double Eccho, from two neighbouring Hills. **1728** POPE *Dunc.* II. 264 Long Chanc'ry-lane retentive rolls the sound, And courts to courts return it round and round. **1810** SCOTT *Lady of L.* III. xxxi, And lake and fell Three times return'd the martial yell. *a* **1832** —— *Paraphr. Exod.* xiii, Arabia's crimsoned sands Returned the fiery column's glow.

16. a. To report in answer to a writ or to some official demand for information; to state by way of a report or verdict.

1425 *Rolls of Parlt.* IV. 306 Writtes.. to enpanell diverses persones to passe in enquestes bytwene parties, and her names to retourne.. into the Kynges Court. **1483** *Ibid.* VI. 262/2 After office therof retourned into the seid Court of Chauncery. **1524** in *Archæol. Jrnl.* (1874) XXXI. 64 Reatorning and testifieing your doing in the premises. *c* **1611** CHAPMAN *Iliad* IX. 580 Let these lords then return th' event, and do thou here repose. **1678** CUDWORTH *Intell. Syst.* 366 Jupiter.. is said to appoint other Inferiour Gods under him, over all the parts of the earth,.. to return the names both of bad and good to him. **1702** *Modern Cases* (1716) 59 There were two other Writs out, and the Sheriff retorned upon the Habeas Corpus, that he had him in Custody upon both of them. **1768** BLACKSTONE *Comm.* III. 273 Whatever the sheriff does in pursuance of this writ, he must return or certify to the court of common pleas. **1802** JAMES *Milit. Dict.* s.v., To be returned upon the surgeon's list as unfit for duty. **1844** LINGARD *Anglo-Sax. Ch.* (1858) I. App. I. 363 The church.. of Loiton.. is returned in possession of five hides. **1891** *Law Times* XCII. 97/2 The liabilities were returned in the statement of affairs at £15,183, with assets at £1042.

b. Of a sheriff: To report (certain persons) as having been appointed to serve on a jury or to sit in Parliament. Hence, in later use, of constituencies: To elect as a member of Parliament or other administrative body.

1436 *Rolls of Parlt.* IV. 501/2 That no Shirreve.. retourne ne empanell in noon Inquisition ne Enquest, no persones but thoo enhabitauntz withynne his Baylie. **1472–3** *Ibid.* VI. 42/1 All Knyghtes of Shires,.. returned in this present Parlement, personally appere. **1544** tr. *Littleton's Tenures* (1574) 48 A Pannel by force of the same writte ought to be retourned. **1687** *Col. Rec. Pennsylv.* I. 196 Joseph Growdon was Returned to serve for three years in Prov[incia]ll Councill. *a* **1715** BURNET *Own Time* (1724) II. 242 All juries were returned by the sheriffs. **1770** GOLDSM. *Bolingbroke* Wks. (Globe) 452/1 Upon the election of a new Parliament ..Bolingbroke was not returned. **1807** SYD. SMITH *Peter Plymley's Lett.* Wks. 1859 II. 172/1 The 100 Irish members who are returned to parliament will be Catholics. **1845** LD. CAMPBELL *Chancellors* lxxiv. III. 117 Hyde.. was returned both by Shaftesbury and Wootton Basset.

†**c.** To send in or remit (sums levied under a writ). *Obs. rare*$^{-1}$.

1647 CLARENDON *Hist. Reb.* I. §148 Instead of a ship, he should levy.. a sum of money, and return the same to the Treasurer of the Navy for his majesty's use.

d. *Cricket.* Of a bowler: to achieve (bowling figures) in an innings or other session of play.

1969 *Times* 29 July 9/2 The best bowling figures.. were returned by Bore. **1976** J. SNOW *Cricket Rebel* 112 Sussex.. were rolled over for 104, Warwickshire left-arm spinner Jim Allan returning career-best figures of five for 11. **1977** J. LAKER *One-Day Cricket* 69 Gilmour returned the staggering figures of 12–6–14–6.

17. a. To send or turn back, to visit, (something) *upon* a person. Now *rare.*

a **1547** SURREY *Æneid* II. 242 Which fate the Gods first on himself return. **1611** BIBLE *1 Kings* ii. 32 The Lord shall returne his blood vpon his owne head. *Ibid.* 44 The Lord shall returne thy wickednesse vpon thine owne head. **1666** DRYDEN *Ann. Mirab.* cclxiv, If mercy be a precept of Thy will, Return that mercy on Thy servant's head.

1848 MILL *Pol. Econ.* III. xxiii. II. 183 Deposits are withdrawn from banks, notes are returned on the issuers in exchange for specie.

†**b.** To retort (a charge, argument, etc.) *to* or *upon* a person. *Obs.*

1562 COOPER *Answ. Def. Truth* (1850) 192 The same crimes may be more justly returned to yourself and yours. **1608** WILLET *Hexapla Exod.* 455 This reason may be returned againe vpon him. **1681** DRYDEN *Abs. & Achit.* To Rdr., I expect you should return upon me that I affect to be thought more impartial than I am. **1719** DE FOE *Crusoe* II. (Globe) 432 But recollecting what he had said,.. I return'd it back upon him.

c. *absol.* To retort or reply (*to* or *upon* a person).

1652 CROMWELL *Let.* 30 July (Carlyle), My occasions will not permit me to return to you as I would. **1693** *Humours Town* 31 By all means Sir, Object and Return, as often as you please. **1888** STEVENSON *Popular Authors* iv, A plain-spoken and possibly high-thinking critic might here perhaps return upon me with my own expressions.

IV. 18. a. To give or render back (*to* one).

1607 SHAKS. *Timon* I. ii. 6, I do returne those Talents Doubled with thankes and seruice, from whose helpe I deriu'd libertie. **1704** J. HARRIS *Lex. Techn.* I. s.v. *Returno habendo*, A Writ that lies.. for returning to him the Cattle distrained. **1708** POPE *Ode St. Cecilia* 82 Restore, restore Eurydice to life; Oh take the husband, or return the wife! **1771** *Encycl. Brit.* II. 219/2 Weight is returned for weight, to any person who carries their gold and silver to the Tower. **1853** LYTTON *My Novel* IX. xvii, I hope to return some day what you then so generously pressed upon me. **1867** H. MACMILLAN *Bible Teach.* viii. 154 We are constantly returning to the earth the materials we receive from it.

b. To give or send in return; to reply with.

1599 HAKLUYT *Voy.* II. 96 The commodities which they returned backe were.. Muskadels, and other wines. **1611** BIBLE *1 Sam.* vi. 3 Send it not empty; but in any wise returne him a trespasse offring. **1660** F. BROOKE tr. *Le Blanc's Trav.* 260 They brought us a good part of their fish,.. and we returned them two fine horns excellently wrought. **1705** E. BLACKWELL *Fencing-Master* 15 When Tierce is thrusted, return Tierce or Sagoone. **1830** 'EIDRAH TREBOR' *Hoyle Made Familiar* 18 Play the ace, and return the knave; the knave is returned in order to strengthen your partner's hand. **1867** SMYTH *Sailor's Word-bk.* 570 Admirals are saluted, but return two guns less for each rank that the saluting officer is below the admiral. **1885** *Manch. Exam.* 15 May 5/3 They will not be slow to return him like for like.

19. a. To give or send (an answer).

1591 SHAKS. *1 Hen. VI*, II. v. 20 We sent.. vnto his Chamber, And answer was return'd, that he will come. **1601** —— *Twel. N.* I. i. 25, I might not be admitted, But from her handmaid do returne this answer. **1624** *Capt. Smith's Wks.* (Arb.) 519 [He] desired me to vrge him no further, but returne his brother this answer. **1709** STEELE *Tatler* No. 78 ¶12 If any one returns me an Answer to a Letter. **1791** MRS. RADCLIFFE *Rom. Forest* i, No answer was returned. **1850** TENNYSON *In Mem.* lxxxi, But Death returns an answer sweet.

b. To say or state by way of reply or answer.

1593 SHAKS. *Rich. II*, III. iii. 121 Northumberland, say thus: The King returnes, His Noble Cousin is right welcome hither. **1642** FULLER *Holy & Prof. St.* V. xviii. §1 He returned, that learning was beneath the greatness of a prince. **1691** T. H[ALE] *Acc. New Invent.* 18 Whereto we hold it unnecessary here to return any thing in opposition more. **1726** POPE *Odyss.* XVI. 61 The swain returns. 'A tale of sorrows hear.' **1782** COWPER *Gilpin* 179 The calender.. Return'd him not a single word. **1855** MACAULAY *Hist. Eng.* xii. III. 228 Signals were made from the steeples and returned from the mast heads, but were imperfectly understood on both sides. **1889** *Cornh. Mag.* Feb. 129, 'I wish you would'.., returns Frances pettishly.

†**c.** To give in answer to a request. *Obs.*$^{-1}$

1634 SIR T. HERBERT *Trav.* (1638) 169 Forced by inordinate thirst to call for water, she returnes me old intoxicating Shiraz Wine.

20. To give or render (thanks).

1591 SHAKS. *1 Hen. VI*, II. ii. 51 And therefore tell her, I returne great thankes, And in submission will attend on her. **1653** *Cloria & Narcissus* I. 223 To return a dissembling thanks for the Princes favour. **1689** RAY in *Lett. Lit. Men* (Camden) 196, I.. returned you many thanks for the present of seeds. **1736** *Gentl. Mag.* VI. 435/1 To return his Majesty the Thanks of that House for his most gracious Speech from the Throne. **1780** in Nichols *Anecd.* (1815) IX. 263 The Lord Chancellor.. returns him many thanks for a very agreeable morning's amusement.

21. a. To repay or pay back in some way, esp. with something similar.

1599 SHAKS. *Hen. V*, IV. vii. 189, I doe know Fluellen valiant, And toucht with Choler, hot as Gunpowder, And quickly will returne an iniurie. **1605** —— *Lear* I. i. 99 You haue begot me, bred me, lou'd me. I returne those duties backe as are right fit. **1686** PARR *Life Ussher* 48 Which Present was also returned by the Lord Primate, by a Letter of thanks, with a handsome present of Irish Grey-hounds. **1710** STEELE *Tatler* No. 227 ¶1 He returns my Envy with Pity. **1713** —— *Englishm.* No. 10. 67 Men strove not to excel in Justice, but to return Injuries. **1828** SCOTT *Tales Grandfather* Ser. II. xxxv, As Herbert did not return the blow, no scuffle.. actually took place. **1859** TENNYSON *Elaine* 1077 He loves the Queen, and in an open shame: And she returns his love in open shame. **1862** *Sat. Rev.* 1 Feb. 151 We might perhaps ask.. whether rabid abuse of England need be returned by equally rabid abuse of America.

absol. **1675** W. MOUNTAGU in *Buccleuch MSS.* (Hist. MSS. Comm.) I. 321 He ill returns to me for all the care and pains I have taken.

b. To repay, or respond to, by a similar courtesy, compliment, etc.

a **1674** CLARENDON *Hist. Reb.* VIII. §243 The earl of Pembroke came to the Chancellor of the Exchequer's lodging to return him a visit. **1741** S. SPEED in *Buccleuch MSS.* (Hist. MSS. Comm.) I. 395 We.. gave three broadsides... They returned the compliment. **1766** GOLDSM. *Vic. W.* xvi, My wife and daughters happening to return a visit. **1824** MACAULAY in Trevelyan *Life* (1876) I. iii. 141 To return courtesies which are little else than the blessings of a beggar. **1888** ANNIE S. SWAN *Doris Cheyne* i, Mr. Penfold.. returned, with some stiffness perhaps, the bow and bland smile with which the intruder favoured him.

c. In games: To respond to (the play of one's partner or opponent). See also LEAD *sb.*[2] 4.

1742 HOYLE *Whist* 30 As soon as Trumps are played to you, return them upon your Adversary. *Ibid.* 33 After he has clear'd the Board of Trumps he returns his Partner's Lead. **1837** DICKENS *Pickw.* xxxiv, Why Mr. Pickwick had not returned that diamond, or led the club. **1882** *Daily Tel.* 18 July 2 This was one of the best games in the match, deuce occurring four times, the hard play of both being well returned.

re-turn (riː-), *v.*[2] [f. RE- 5 a + TURN *v.* In early examples, however, identical with prec. Usually in phr. *turn and re-turn.*]

1. *trans.* To turn (a thing or person) over, round, or back again. Also *refl.*

c **1374** CHAUCER *Troylus* v. 1023 Retournynge in hire soule ay up and doun The wordes of this sodeyn Diomede. **1484** CAXTON *Fables of Æsop* v. x, He fond a grete pyece of bakon wel salted, the whiche he tourned and retourned vp sodoune. **1523** LD. BERNERS *Froiss.* I. 740 He was turned and retourned, to se what hurtes or woundes he had. **1609** B. JONSON *Alchemist* IV. vii, *Fac.* O, you must follow, sir,.. Hee'll turne againe else. *Kas.* I'll re-turne him, then. **1660** BOYLE *New Exp. Phys. Mech.* xvii. 110 By Turning and Returning the Key. **1720** POPE *Iliad* XVII. 8 Anxious [the heifer].. Turns, and re-turns her, with a mother's care. **1857** MRS. GORE *Castles in Air* xviii, [He] turned and re-turned it in his hands.. — examining the handwriting and the seal.

2. *intr.* To turn again; to turn back.

1413 *Pilgr. Sowle* (Caxton) I. xxv. (1859) 30 Suche maner of penaunce that torneth and retorneth, maye wel be resembled to the whele of a mylle. **1592** SHAKS. *Ven. & Ad.* 704 Then shalt thou see the dew-bedabbled wretch Turn, and return. **1605** B. JONSON *Volpone* I. iii, Men of your large profession.. That, with most quick agilitie, could turne, And re-turne; make knots, and vndoe them. **1725** POPE *Odyss.* VIII. 414 In dance they skim the strand, Turn and re-turn, and scarce imprint the sand. **1853** C. BRONTE

Villette xxviii, He turned to the door... He *re*-turned on his steps.

returna·bility. [f. RETURNABLE *a.* + -ITY.] The fact or condition of being returnable; capacity to return or be returned.

1920 in WEBSTER. **1973** *Daily Tel.* (Colour Suppl.) 23 Mar. 13/1 The main problem was one of 'returnability'. 'The British Government has to be sure some country will receive you when your visa for England has expired.' **1973** *Times* 29 Oct. 15/8 A device could be used..which the customer would..associate with returnability. The use of the device would clearly indicate..that the package is the property of the supplier. **1981** *Times* 19 Jan. 3/6 The commission's proposed directive on beverage containers..is now expected to appear without any of the references to mandatory recycling or returnability contained in earlier drafts.

returnable (rɪˈtɜːnəb(ə)l), *a.* Also 5–6 retourn-, 5, 7 **retornable.** [a. AF. *retornable*, OF. *retournable*: see RETURN *v.*[1] and -ABLE.]

1. a. Of writs, etc.: Appointed to be returned (to the issuing court).

1425 *Rolls of Parlt.* IV. 306 That every Sheref..retourne his Writtes into ye Kynges Court, at such daies as yei buth retournable. **1467** in *Eng. Gilds* (1870) 394 Yf he wolle comyn and appere at the day of the venire facias retornable. **1531–2** *Act 23 Hen. VIII*, c. 12 Attachementes..again euerie suche collectour..to be returnable afore the saide Justices of peace. **1594** WEST *2nd Pt. Symbol., Chancerie* §45 When this or any other commission retournable in this Court is executed and returned. **1648** PRYNNE *Plea for Lords* 38 They award two writs,..retornable in the Kings Bench. **1682** LUTTRELL *Brief Rel.* (1857) I. 199 The court of kings bench granted a habeas corpus.., which was returnable immediate. **1752** J. LOUTHIAN *Form of Process* (ed. 2) 280 The Powers of Sheriffs,..with the Nature and Import of the several Writs returnable by them. **1817** SELWYN *Law Nisi Prius* (ed. 4) II. 1097 But the writ of replevin was in the nature of a justicies, not returnable. **1894** *Solicitor's Jrnl.* XXXIX. 3/1 The defendant..offers, on the day before the summons is returnable, to pay the debt and costs.

b. That is (or are) to be returned, in various senses of the verb.

1658 BP. REYNOLDS *Rich Man's Charge* 15 These riches are returnable into Heaven; to be rich in faith..will stand us in stead, when the World hath left us. **1758** J. BLAKE *Plan Mar. Syst.* 14 The said letter..being..indorsed, returnable to the pay-office. **1812** J. SMYTH *Pract. of Customs* (1821) 334 The goods may be abandoned and destroyed: in which case, the duties are returnable by special Certificate. **1885** *Manch. Exam.* 7 Oct. 4/7 All the electors in a Department were to vote for all the members returnable for that Department. **1891** S. C. SCRIVENER *Our Fields & Cities* 99 That unearned increment is to be put along with the returnable empties. **1972** *V.A.T.: Gen. Guide* (H.M. Customs) 34 Containers (returnable). **1973** *Sat. Rev. Society* (U.S.) May 70/3 Buy returnable bottles..participate in your local recycling program when you must use nonreturnable containers. **1981** *Country Life* 7 May 1228/1 The price of a returnable bottle is shared by many users.

2. Capable of being returned, in various senses of the verb.

a **1542** WYATT in *Tottel's Misc.* (Arb.) 34 Sins that disceit is ay retornable, Of verye force it is agreable, That therwithall be done the recompence. *a* **1643** LD. FALKLAND, etc. *Infallibility* (1646) 101 He must needs see there was more matter returnable than either could be gratefull, or they could justify. **1654** GAYTON *Pleas. Notes* IV. xxiii. 278, I my selfe but lately was inchanted, and I know not how soon returnable unto that condition. **1807** S. COOPER *First Lines Surg.* 387 The congenital hernia, when returnable, ought like all other ruptures to be reduced.

3. Able to return. *rare.*

1654 GAYTON *Pleas. Notes* III. iv. 91 His chiefe adversaries ..were dislodg'd, and never returnable. **1784** COWPER *Let. to Unwin* 20 Nov., Lady A. is neither returned nor returnable: she has taken a house at Bristol, and furnished it.

4. Admitting of return.

1853 *Chamb. Jrnl.* XX. 280 Two longer trips.., both returnable in periods of about eight days. **1856** *Bryden's Railw. Direct.* 4 Return tickets at one fare..returnable by the 7.30, 8.20 and 8.55 a.m. trains only.

†**re·turnal.** *Obs. rare.* [f. the verb + -AL[1].] = RETURN *sb.*

1657 J. OWEN *Communion w. Father*, etc. I. i, As we had deprived ourselves of all power for a returnal, so God had not revealed any way of access unto Himself. *Ibid.*, His communication of Himself unto us, with our returnal unto Him of that which He requireth and accepteth.

re·turn-day. [Cf. RETURN *sb.* 8 b.] *Law.* The day on which a writ is appointed to be returned.

1651 SIR J. DAVIES *Abridg. Rep.* II. 53 If the Prisoner by force of Habeas Corpus &c. be brought to Westminster at the Return day [etc.]. **1766** *Burrow's Rep.* II. 815 The Truth of the Return must be taken to be what was true at the Return-Day of the Writ. **1797** *Monthly Mag.* III. 549/2 [To] return to the court from whence the writ issued, on the return day, what he has done with it. **1825** HONE *Every-day Bk.* I. 100 All original writs are returnable on these days, and they are therefore called the return days. **1843–56** BOUVIER *Law Dict.* (ed. 6) 475/2 The sheriff is in general not required to return his writ until the return day.

re·turned, *ppl. a.* [f. RETURN *v.*[1] + -ED[1].]

1. Bent or turned back in some way; *esp.* made with a return.

c **1425** *Found. St. Bartholomew's* (E.E.T.S.) 35 A certeyne Damsell deyf and dumm, lackyng sight of boeth yen and with returnyd leggis contract. **1605** B. JONSON *Masque of Blackness* Wks. (1616) 894 The attyre of Masquers was alike in all,..but returned on the top with a scroll and antique dressing of feathers. **1858** *Skyring's Build. Prices* 77 All returned beads, double price. **1874** MICKLETHWAITE *Mod. Par. Churches* 60 The returned stalls are all about equally advantageously placed.

2. a. That has (or have) come back.

1600 SHAKS. *A.Y.L.* v. iv. 180 Euery of this happie number..Shal share the good of our returned fortune. **1611** SPEED *Hist. Gt. Brit.* IX. xv. §32. 629/2 The treason had success, and their returned ambassadors told it for certaine. **1837** T. HOOK *Jack Brag* v, When she saw the sunken eye of her beloved parent fixed..on her returned child. **1864** LOWELL *Fireside Trav.* 292 More refreshing was the talk of a tall returned Californian.

b. Designating a discharged serviceman who has returned home from a war. *Canad.*, *Austral.*, and *N.Z.*

1915 *Eye Opener* (Calgary, Alberta) 11 Dec. 2/3 An army of returned soldiers..who have been away fighting for the Empire are not going to..allow themselves to be told what is right and what is wrong by a bunch of stay-at-home aldermen or freak legislators. **1921** *Daily Colonist* (Victoria, B.C.) 24 Mar. 1/4 A body of 600 returned men today marched to the city hall and demanded..that no returned men be refused relief by the city council. **1930** W. K. HANCOCK *Australia* xiii. 274 The only notable non-political body in Australia (excluding the churches) is the Returned Soldiers' League. **1947** E. A. MCCOURT *Music at Close* I. vi. 65 Latimer stopped..to pick up..a returned man living on a settlement grant. *a* **1948** L. G. D. ACLAND *Early Canterbury Runs* (1951) xi. 314 After the 1914–18 War the Government resumed the Old Man Range country..and settled a returned soldier on it. **1950** *N.Z. Jrnl. Agric.* Jan. 26/2 Ten 10-acre sections have been allocated to returned servicemen. **1961** P. WHITE *Riders in Chariot* viii. 236 You cannot tell me..that a home is not a home, with so many going roofless, and so many returned men.

3. Sent or brought back. ***returned empty***, an empty cask, case, etc., returned to the sender; also *transf.*; e.g., a clergyman who has come back to Great Britain from duties overseas.

In quot. 1722 the precise meaning is, 'to be returned'. **1722** DE FOE *Col. Jack* vii, A man..wanted to know if he could hear of any returned horses for England. **1749** FIELDING *Tom Jones* x. vi, The coach..was indeed a returned coach belonging to Mr. King of Bath. **1890** *Pall Mall G.* 12 Apr. 6/3 They were Colonial Bishops—returned empties, as the profane scoffingly call them. **1896** *Strand Mag.* XII. 339/1 Reaching its destination without being dealt with by the Post Office as a returned item. **1946** P. BOTTOME *Lifeline* xv. 137 A milk lorry..goes from here taking returned empties, and bringing back milk at dawn. **1961** B. FERGUSSON *Watery Maze* ix. 220 Several of these [ships] were veterans both of Ironclad and Torch, which meant that they had already spent months in unprofitable voyaging as returned empties, so to speak. **1977** C. ALLEN *Raj* i. 23/2 Early in the nineteenth century..unmarried women were regularly shipped out..to meet the demand for wives... Those who returned without husbands or fiancés were known as 'Returned Empties'.

†**4.** Of a match: Played in return. *Obs. rare.*

1773 in Waghorn *Cricket Scores* (1899) 95 The returned match of cricket between the above elevens. *Ibid.* 96.

5. Stated in a return or official record.

1892 *Pall Mall G.* 18 May 3/1 He won the 100 yards championship in returned time 9 3-5 seconds.

retur·nee. orig. *U.S.* [f. RETURN *v.*[1] + -EE[1].] One who returns or is returned from abroad to his native land, *esp.* from war service or exile. Also *attrib.* and *transf.*

1944 *Newsweek* 17 July 62 The biography of a returnee fits into a regular pattern. **1945** *Christian Sci. Monitor* 17 Mar. 10/2 (*caption*) A launch filled with returnees and their wives sets out on exploration tour of the coves. **1955** *Sci. News Let.* 27 Aug. 142/3 They suggest a brainwashing in reverse as treatment for returnees showing symptoms of mental sickness. **1969** *Daily Tel.* 27 Dec. 5/2 The Communists counted 54 dead, nine taken prisoner and 31 'returnees' during the truce period. A 'returnee' is a Viet Cong guerilla who surrenders peacefully to the South Vietnamese Government, thereby securing all citizen's privileges. **1974** W. HUNT *North of 53 Degrees* x. 60 The Klondike gold had escaped the grasp of these returnees. **1977** *Guardian Weekly* 18 Sept. 15/3 They want to go back to Russia... Would-be Soviet returnees. **1981** *Times* 22 Jan. 8/3 The former hostages, already inelegantly dubbed 'returnees'.

returnello, obs. form of RITORNELLO.

re·turner. [f. RETURN *v.*[1] + -ER[1].]

1. One who or that which comes back or returns, in various senses of the verb.

1611 COTGR., *Reconvoyer*, to..bring, or lead, a returner onward on the way. **1658** J. OWEN *Of Temptation* Wks. 1851 VI. 121 Some few returners from folly. **1775** in Stone *Invasion Canada* (1867) 67 Col. Enos, who more immediately commanded the division of returners. **1820** T. L. PEACOCK *Four Ages Poetry* Wks. 1875 III. 334 Mr. Wordsworth, the great leader of the returners to nature. **1890** *Illustr. Lond. News* 9 Aug. 170/1 O marvellous returner from the dim seas of the past.

2. One who or that which gives or brings back.

1691 LOCKE *Raising Value Money* Wks. 1714 II. 84 The Goldsmiths and returners of Money will give more for Bullion to export, than the Mint can give for it to coin. **1829** BATHER *Serm.* II. 65 Be not only placable and forgiving but returners of good for evil. **1839** URE *Dict. Arts* 1197 The returner guiding the canes between the top and delivering rollers.

re·turning, *vbl. sb.* [f. as prec. + -ING[1].]

1. The action of the verb, in various senses.

c **1386** CHAUCER *Knt.'s T.* 2095 The day approcheth of hir retournynge. **1485** CAXTON *Chas. Gt.* 34 In retournyng he demaunded..lycence to departe. **1523** LD. BERNERS *Froiss.* I. cvi. 127 At the retournynge of therle of Derby to Bourdeaux. *a* **1569** KINGESMYLL *Confl. w. Satan* (1578) 29 Repentance, or Returning is the hatred of sin and love of righteousness. **1613** DRUMM. OF HAWTH. *Cypress Grove* Wks. (1711) 121 A never again returning to the Works and dolorous Felicity of Life. **1632** LITHGOW *Trav.* I. 32 To visite Venice, in his returning home for Scotland. **1719** DE FOE *Crusoe* I. (Globe) 14 They are..asham'd of the returning, which only can make them be esteem'd wise Men. **1747** tr. *Astruc's Fevers* 135 Being always attended with bad digestions, these returnings, anxieties, &c. are inseparable from a slow fever. **1827** SCOTT *Napoleon* Introd., Wks. 1870 IX. 317 A late returning to ancient opinions. **1847** C. BRONTË *J. Eyre* xxii, Neither of these returnings were very pleasant or desirable. **1871** R. ELLIS tr. *Catullus* lxiv. 210 Fair token of happy returning.

2. A return; a backward turn or bend.

1613–39 I. JONES in Leoni *Palladio's Archit.* (1742) II. 44 The returning of the Basso-relievo. **1676** MOXON *Print Lett.* 50 The..Returnings of Angles..are..seen. **1715** tr. *Pancirollus' Rerum Mem.* I. II. xv. 103 This Labyrinth..had only one Entrance, but innumerable Turnings and Returnings. **1893** SHEDLOCK tr. *Riemann's Dict. Mus.* 810/1 Even trumpets of the 16th century show no returnings, but only winding.

re·turning, *ppl. a.* [f. as prec. + -ING[2].]

1. That comes back or returns, in various senses.

1694 KETTLEWELL *Comp. Penitent* 92 With a contrite and a returning Heart. **1702** ROWE *Tamerl.* I. i, Hail to the Sun! from whose returning Light [etc.]. **1748** *Anson's Voy.* III. viii. 370 He..resolved to cruise for these returning vessels. **1778** MISS BURNEY *Evelina* iii, How grateful..must be your returning health! **1855** MACAULAY *Hist. Eng.* xxii. IV. 705 The first faint signs of returning prosperity. **1897** *Allbutt's Syst. Med.* III. 819 The innermost cylinder [in an intussuscepted bowel] is known as the entering layer and the middle one as the returning layer.

b. Situated on a return.

1776 SEMPLE *Building in Water* 102 The Grooves on the corner Pile, and the Tongue on the next returning Pile.

2. *returning officer*, the official whose duty it is to conduct or preside at an election, and to report the result to the proper authority.

1729 *Act 2 Geo. II*, c. 24 §2 Every Sheriff, Mayor, Bailiff ..or other Person, being returning Officer of any Member to serve in Parliament..shall take..the following Oath. **1764** FOOTE *Mayor of G.* I, If your Worship has any objection to Crispin Heeltap the cobler's being returning officer? **1818** *Parl. Debates* 644 He objected..to the power given to the returning officers to appoint any number of constables. **1863** H. COX *Instit.* I. vi. 62 An elector might bring actions at law against returning officers for refusing his vote.

3. Elective; having the power to elect.

1838 W. BELL *Dict. Law Scot.* 354 This right to preside remained in the same burgh during the entire Parliament, that burgh being what is called the returning burgh. **1876** *Daily News* 20 Nov. 5/2 The Returning Board in Florida is a mixed one, in which the Democrats are understood to have a majority.

4. *returning sticks*: (see RETURN *sb.* 13 b).

re·turnless, *a.* [f. RETURN *sb.* + -LESS.] Devoid of, not admitting of, a return; that is without return.

1615 CHAPMAN *Odyss.* XIII. 512 All thy Friends, I knew, as well, should make returnlesse ends. **1823** *Blackw. Mag.* XIII. 48 France went down an almost returnless depth of misery and crime. **1855** BAILEY *Mystic*, etc. 46 Through the returnless and thick-branched Forest..they thrid their way. **1875** LOWELL *Under the Old Elm* I. ii, The mould..whither all that be Vanish returnless.

Hence **re·turnlessly** *adv. rare*$^{-1}$.

1840 *Blackw. Mag.* XLVIII. 238 Elliston at length was utterly, unequivocally, returnlessly ruined.

†**re·turnment.** *Obs. rare*$^{-1}$. [f. RETURN *v.*[1] + -MENT.] = RETURN *sb.*

1606 HEYWOOD *If you know me not* App., Sometimes we yeelded; but like a ramme That makes returnment to re-double strength, Then forc'd them yeeld.

re·turn ·ticket. A railway (or other) ticket which is available for the journey back from, as well as to, the place specified upon it. Also *fig.*

c **1847** J. S. COYNE in M. R. Booth *Eng. Plays of 19th Cent.* (1973) IV. 195 There's poor Mary White gone..to that bourne from whence no traveller gets a return ticket. **1850** THACKERAY *Pendennis* II. xxxv. 339 (*heading*) Chapter xxxv. Shows how Arthur had better have taken a return-ticket. **1857** HUGHES *Tom Brown* i, Going round Ireland, with a return ticket, in a fortnight. **1867** TROLLOPE *Chron. Barset* xxxii, He could get a return-ticket at a third-class fare. **1898** E. REEVES *Homeward Bound* 133 We took second-class return tickets to Kandy. **1922** [see COME-BACK *sb.*[2] 2]. **1946** *Happy Landings* July 8/3 If you take your parachute into the air you have a certain return ticket, and one that, should you need to use it, will bring you safely down to earth. **1977** *Times* 15 June 16/2 The cautious person travels from capitalism to socialism with a return ticket.

retuse (rɪˈtjuːs), *a.* [ad. L. *retūs-us*, pa. pple. of *retundĕre*: see RETUND *v.* So F. *rétus*, *rétuse*.] Terminating in a broad or rounded end with a depression in the centre.

a. *Bot.* Of leaves, petals, etc.

1753 CHAMBERS *Cycl. Suppl.* s.v. *Leaf*, *Retuse leaf*,..a leaf whose extremity is terminated by an obtuse line. **1785** MARTYN *Rousseau's Bot.* xxv. (1794) 359 The leaves are retuse. *Ibid.*, The lower leaflets retuse. **1847** W. E. STEELE *Field Bot.* 37 Pet. roundish, retuse, with an involute, broad, retuse point. **1870** HOOKER *Stud. Flora* 331 *Buxus sempervirens*... Leaves ½—1 in., obtuse or retuse.

b. *Ent.* Of parts of insects.

1824 T. SAY in *Jrnl. Acad. Nat. Sci. Philad.* III. II. 298 Eyes elongated, retuse behind the antennæ. **1825** —— *Explan. Terms Entom.* 29 *Retuse*, ending in an obtuse sinus, or broad shallow notch; terminated by an obtuse hollow.

1826 Kirby & Sp. *Entomol.* III. xxxvi. 711 At its base it is truncated in *Sirex*; retuse in most bees.

re'tuseness. *rare*⁻¹. [See prec.] Hoarseness.
1657 Tomlinson *Renou's Disp.* 396 It [gum Tragacanth] emends..retusenesse of voice and other defluxions.

re'tusion. *rare*⁻⁰. [ad. L. type **retūsio*: cf. retuse *a.*] (See quot.)
1656 Blount *Glossogr.*, *Retusion*.., a dulling or making blunt.

retuso-, used as comb. form of retuse *a.*
1815 Burrow *Conchol.* 37 *Retuso-umbilicate*; the spire being so much impressed as to seem rather concave than convex. **1856–8** W. Clark *Van der Hoeven's Zool.* I. 790 Shell univalve, covering body entirely above, clypeate or retuso-conical.

re-twist (riː-), *v.* [re- 5 a.] To twist again.
1835 Ure *Philos. Manuf.* 248 The cost of re-winding and re-twisting..[is] about 5*s.* **1839** —— *Dict. Arts* 1115 The throwster re-winds and re-twists it upon the spinning mill. **1868** *Rep. U.S. Commissioner Agric.* (1869) 286 A second machine to retwist together two threads already twisted separately, thus producing organzine.

re'type (riː-), *v.* [re- 5 a, 5 c.]
1. *trans.* To typify anew.
1839–48 Bailey *Festus* xix. 215 The father of the faithful and the first Of men was each in Him retyped.
2. To recopy with a typewriter.
Now the usual sense.
1898 H. G. Wells *Let.* 1 Jan. in *G. Gissing & H. G. Wells* (1961) 70 Parts I have reshaped, rewritten and retyped time after time. **1898** Mitton *Bachelor Girl* vi, Once or twice she had to re-type a page. **1952** S. Kauffmann *Tightrope* iv. 58 Rose retyped Russell's memo for him in the usual five copies. **1961** 'E. Lathen' *Banking on Death* xiii. 105 The letter had to be retyped. **1976** H. MacInnes *Agent in Place* xiii. 136 Typed, retyped, torn up. The discarded pages filled the waste-basket. **1979** *Amer. N. & Q.* Apr. 126/1 Faulkner entrusted the job to Phil Stone, who in turn gave the typescript to his secretary, Grace Hudson, to retype.
3. *absol.* To acquire a stock of new type.
1896 *Westm. Gaz.* 12 Oct. 1/1 In re-typing we have made certain alterations which we hope will..be..improvements.
Hence **re'typed** *ppl. a.*, **re'typing** *vbl. sb.* Also **'retype** *sb.*, a retyped copy.
1930 D. L. Sayers *Strong Poison* xiv. 183 She..threw it into the waste-paper basket together with the re-type which she had begun. **1943** J. Reith *Diary* 4 May (1975) vi. 303 The vice-controller had my retyped memo today. **1967** Karch & Buber *Offset Processes* iv. 74 The IBM Selectric Composer..allows automatic justification of the right-hand margin with a retyping. **1979** *Amer. N. & Q.* Apr. 126/1 William Faulkner sent the newly revised and retyped text to Liveright.

retzian ('rɛtsɪən). *Min.* [f. the name of Anders Jahan *Retzius* (1742–1821), Swedish naturalist.] A basic arsenate of manganese, calcium and rare earth elements, known as dark brown orthorhombic crystals from Sweden.
1895 H. Sjögren in *Bull. Geol. Inst. Univ. Upsala* II. 54 (*heading*) Retzian, a new arseniate from the Mossgrufva, Nordmark. *Ibid.* 59 The crystals of retzian are prismatic. **1921** *Bull. U.S. Geol. Survey* No. 679. 126 Retzian.. strongly pleochroic. **1967** *Amer. Mineralogist* LII. 1610 The crystal structure of retzian is an interesting sheet structure.

retzina, var. retsina.

reu, obs. form of rue.

reualing, obs. Sc. form of revelling.

†**reuall.** *Sc. Obs.* Also **riwell.** (Of obscure origin and meaning; the *u* and *w* may stand for *v.*)
c **1470** Henry *Wallace* ix. 106 His cot armour is seyn in mony steid, Ay battaill boun, and riwell ay off reid. *c* **1475** *Rauf Coilȝear* 670 The hall was properly apperrellit... The rufe reulit about in reuall of Reid.

reuar, reuart, obs. Sc. ff. river, revert *v.*

reuay: see revay *sb.*

Reub, Rube (ruːb), abbrevs. Reuben 1. Also *attrib.* Cf. *hey, Rube!* s.v. hey *int.*
1896 Ade *Artie* i. 8 If I had time I'd go over to that church and make a lot o' them Reubs look like thirty-cent pieces. **1899** 'J. Flynt' *Tramping with Tramps* 396 *Rube*, a 'hoosier', or 'farmer'. **1904** [see bark *v.*¹ 2 b]. **1915** *Dialect Notes* IV. 200 *Reub, rube*, local name for rustic... 'On the Fourth of July the Reubs all come to town.' **1919** [see kike]. **1927** *Scots Observer* 26 Feb. 3/4 They know a Rube when they see him, or a guy, or a crook, or a bonehead. **1937** *Lit. Digest* 3 Apr. 21/3 Child labor laws..have forced children [of circus people] into schools for a certain number of months a year. This contact with 'rubes' and 'Reubens' has given rise to new interests. **1946** E. O'Neill *Iceman Cometh* iv. 253 The boys tell me the rubes are wasting all their money buying food and times never was so hard. **1949** F. Sargeson *I saw it in my Dream* 218 Mr Anderson said Cedric was just a rube. **1953** W. Moore *Bring Jubilee* ii. 20 Rube, huh? Much money you got?.. O.K., Ruben. Come along. **1956** W. R. Bird *Off-Trail in Nova Scotia* iii. 69 Don't try to talk down to someone you meet in those places no matter if they look like rubes for ten to one they've seen more of the world than you have. **1970** R. Price *Gt. Roob Revolution* 5 The word 'rube' (from Reuben) was originally used by carnival people to identify the farmers, yokels, and assorted rural types. **1973** J. Gores *Final Notice* xxiv. 158 The rube who wanders into the pool hall and loses a few games... Then the bets get bigger and he..starts clearing tables. **1975** *New Yorker* 29 Dec. 36/3 We had one girl who did a good rube act. **1976** *Time* 20 Dec. 17/1 They were an unsolemn pair, the young man who likes his rube image and the impeccably dressed man who looked more like a smooth character actor than a politician of enormous influence.

reubarb(e, obs. ff. rhubarb *sb.*

Reuben ('ruːbən). *U.S.* and *Canad. colloq.*
1. The personal name *Reuben* applied to suggest the conventionally conceived figure of a farmer or rustic; a country bumpkin.
1804 in S. Larkin *Nightingale* 284 But she, tho' conscious of his worth, Had chose a youth more rare; a rustic Reuben was his name. **1890** B. Hall *Turnover Club* iv. 49, I overheard one of a knot of Reubens standing on a corner. **1901** (*song-title*) The wedding of the Reuben and the maid. *Ibid.*, You've heard about the Reuben and the time he came to town. **1905** 'H. McHugh' *You can search Me* 60 I've a couple of new card tricks..that will leave the Reubens gasping for air. **1911** H. Quick *Yellowstone Nights* xii. 313, I took a basket of eggs an went in among 'em, feelin' like a animal trainer in a circus parade as the Reubens gathered around the train. **1953** [see prec.].
2. In full, ***Reuben sandwich.*** A large sandwich containing cheese, meat, and sauerkraut, usu. made with rye bread and served hot.
Not obviously connected with sense 1.
1956 *Institutions* Oct. 44/2 'The Reuben'..is a grilled 3 decker sandwich of heroic proportions. Three slices of russian rye bread generously spread with thousand island dressing contain swiss cheese and corned beef slices interlaced with sauerkraut. **1967** *N.Y. Times* 10 Oct. 50 The Reuben sandwich..has become wildly popular in most areas of the United States. **1970** *Favorite Recipes of Lutheran Ladies* 15 Reuben Sandwich... Spread 6 slices bread with dressing, top with cheese, 1 tablespoon sauerkraut and corned beef. **1976** in K. M. Thomas *Winning Sandwiches for Menu Makers* 2/2 The recipes in this book represent the best of twenty years of sandwich competition, starting with the champion of the first contest in 1956, the now ubiquitous 'Reuben'.

reucht, obs. Sc. f. rough *a.*

reue, obs. f. reave *v.*

reueil(l, obs. ff. reveal *v.*

reueir, obs. Sc. f. river *sb.*

reueis, obs. f. ravish.

reuel(e, obs. ff. ravel *sb.*², revel, rivel, rule.

reuelaic(k, etc.: see reflac.

reuelat: see revelate *pa. pple.*

reuelich, obs. f. ruly *a.*

reuelin, obs. f. ravelin.

reuen, obs. f. raven *sb.*¹

reuer(e, obs. ff. reaver, river.

reuere, var. reavery, *Obs.*

reuery, var. reverie.

reuesche: see revesh *v.*

reuet, obs. f. rivet.

reufol, -ful, obs. ff. rueful.

†**reugle.** *Obs. rare.* [a. OF. *reugle, riugle*, variant of *riule*, etc., rule.] Rule, discipline; a rule or regulation.
1456 Sir G. Haye *Law Arms* (S.T.S.) 112 The secund nedefull thing [in battle] is gude reugle, and gude ordynaunce. *Ibid.* 221 By a reugle of the canoun lawe.

reuhðe, obs. f. ruth.

reuilde, obs. f. rivelled *a.*

reuin, obs. Sc. pa. pple. of rive *v.*

reuir(e, obs. ff. river.

reuis(s, obs. ff. ravish *v.*

reuk, obs. f. rook.

reul, obs. f. rule.

reular, obs. f. ruler.

re'ulcerate (riː-), *v.* [re- 5 a.] *trans.* To cause to ulcerate again. In quots. *fig.*
1601 [Bp. W. Barlow] *Serm. Paules Crosse* 32 Their falles and faultes should not be reulcerated nor reuiued after death. **1621** Quarles *Esther* xix, Lest the gaulled Persians should..re-vlcerate In after-times, their former misery. **1624** —— *Sion's Elegies* i. 12 Evills, which my offended God Reulcerates, with his enraged Rod.

reule, reulle, obs. ff. rule *sb.* and *v.*

reuli(che, reuly(che, obs. ff. ruly *a.*

reulor, obs. f. ruler.

reume, obs. f. realm, rheum.

reumy, obs. variant of rheumy *a.*

re'undulate (riː-), *v.* [re- 5 a.] *trans.* To cause to undulate again.
1698 Fryer *Acc. E. India & P.* 129 The bandying Eccho still persecutes with terrible repeated Sounds, meeting fresh Objects to reundulate it. **1839–52** Bailey *Festus* 168 Spear after spear And line on line reundulating light.
So **reundu'lation.**
1671 *Phil. Trans.* VI. 3057 As the Tube enlarges it self,.. the Circles both of Reundulation and Reverberation become greater.

reune (riː'juːn), *v. U.S. colloq.* [Back-formation from reunion.] *intr.* To hold a reunion.
1901 *Princeton Alumni Weekly* 8 June 774/1 As the secretary of a class which has 'reuned' frequently..I wish to direct your attention to a breach of etiquette. **1929** *Amer. Speech* V. 175 Several years ago the late E. K. Graham, then president of the University of North Carolina, in speaking of class reunions, used somewhat facetiously the word *reune* instead of the locution *have a reunion.* It seems that the word has stuck. **1929** E. W. Springs *Above Bright Blue Sky* 237 She had seen in the paper where the 14th was going to reune at the banquet. **1948** *Amer. Legion Mag.* Oct. 26/1 (*heading*) Retreads Will Reune. **1949** Mencken in Kirby & Woolf *Philologica* 316 The embryologist of speech discerns several processes in the making of such novelties [*sc.* new verbs]. Some are simply nouns unchanged, e.g., *to contact*.. others are back-formations from nouns, e.g., *to locate, to enthuse, to reune.*

reunes, variant of rewness, *Obs.*

reun'fold, *v.* [re- 5 a.] To unfold again.
1594 Daniel *Cleopatra* i. i, What Power should be of Power to reunfold The Arms of our Affections lock'd so fast?

reunifi'cation (riː-). [re- 5 a.] The action of reunifying; a state of reunion. Hence **reunifi'cationist**, a supporter or advocate of reunification.
1880 *Encycl. Brit.* XI. 619/1 To clasp the discordant facts and establish a reunification. **1891** *Daily News* 26 Nov. 5/3 The division of that kingdom was deplored, and proposals made for its reunification. **1955** *Times* 14 July 8/5 No policy is acceptable to Germany which does not have for its aim the reunification of the country in peace and freedom, and at the earliest possible moment. **1959** *Daily Tel.* 9 Apr. 10/3 Plans for control and inspection, and for a ceiling for forces, would be accepted only if progress towards German reunification went with them. **1967** *Listener* 6 July 20/2 For him [*sc.* Dr. Adenauer] German reunification was a necessary precondition of détente. **1970** W. Johnson *Cameroon Federation* v. 105 What incensed the reunificationists most, however, was the belief that the Territory had not received its just due even from the government of Nigeria. **1976** *Survey* Winter 18 One can imagine the Japanese reaction to the reunification of Korea under communist leadership.
So **re'unify** *v.*
1890 in *Cent. Dict.* **1955** *Times* 8 July 8/3 The Assembly endorsed the main conclusions of M. de Menthon's report, which formed the basis of the debate—the need to establish a real system of security, to reunify Germany by means of free elections, and to construct a united Europe. *Ibid.* 13 July 6/4 French reactions to the suggestions, made in a recent leading article in *The Times*, that Germany might be reunified on the basis of a demilitarized eastern zone, are not *prima facie* favourable.

reunion (riː'juːnɪən). [= F. *réunion* (1549), Sp. *reunion*, It. *riunione*: see re- 5 a, and union.]
1. The action of reuniting or coming together again; the state of being reunited.
1610 Donne *Pseudo-martyr* 23 The Emperours were euer forwardest to labour a re-union and concurrence of their powers. **1681** tr. *Belon's New Myst. Physick* 28 Which interruption never ceases, but by the Re-union..of all those parts. **1702** Steele *Funeral* iv, There's no Middle way, I must Expose her to make a Re-union Impracticable. **1780** Burke *Sp. Bristol* Wks. III. 401 The re-union to the state, of all the Catholics of that country. **1858** Sears *Athan.* iii. iii. 274 The Essenes..rejected the notion of a reunion of the soul with flesh. **1899** *Allbutt's Syst. Med.* VIII. 33 Nerve-division has the objection that reunion occurs and the malady returns.
2. The fact of (persons) meeting again after separation.
1703 Maundrell *Journ. Jerus.* (1732) 144 [We] congratulated each other upon our happy reunion. **1835** Lytton *Rienzi* ix. ii, For some minutes the young lovers surrendered themselves to the delight of re-union. **1843** J. Martineau *Chr. Life* (1867) 455 His reunion with his disciples.
3. a. A meeting or social gathering of persons acquainted with each other, or having some previous link of connexion.
1820 Byron *Blues* i. 139 'Tis a sort of reunion for Scamp, on the days Of his lecture. **1856** Merivale *Rom. Emp.* xxxvii. (1865) IV. 271 The exquisites of the day were..the oracles of coteries, the observed of aristocratic reunions. **1873** Holland *A. Bonnic.* xii. 204 The little reunion was given to Henry and myself, in token of our departure.
attrib. **1842** Howitt *Rur. Life Germ.* 257 The fitting up of the ball-room and of a re-union room at the right hand end. **1929** E. W. Springs *Above Bright Blue Sky* 233 Are you going to the Aviators' Reunion Dinner to-night to celebrate the anniversary of the Armistice? **1952** M. Allingham *Tiger in Smoke* xv. 218 He was due to give an impersonation of his old officer at a reunion dinner. **1976** *Laurel* (Montana) *Outlook* 9 June 12/4 A two-hour program is being planned by a reunion committee and will be held from 2 to 4 p.m. in the Laurel Senior High School gymnasium.
b. In this sense freq. in Fr. form *réunion.*
1835 Greville *Diary* 80 (Stanf.), Music is here much in fashion, and there are constant large réunions of amateurs. **1847** *Illustr. Lond. News* 2 Jan. 2/1 At the last Ministerial *réunion* at M. Guizot's. **1855** Thackeray *Newcomes* viii, All the lions present at Mrs. Newcome's *réunion* that evening.

Hence **Re'unionism.** (Cf. next.)
1895 *Tablet* 20 Apr. 611/2 To what extent the new Reunionism may..alter the accents of the prelates of the Established Church.

Re'unionist (riː-). [f. prec. + -IST.] One who desires the reunion of the Anglican with the Roman Catholic Church.
1866 T. N. HARPER *Peace through Truth* Ser. I. p. xcii, The difficulties which beset the Reunionists in their chimerical efforts, multiply. **1896** *Daily News* 1 June 6/7 A definite pronouncement against them, by dashing the hopes of the Re-Unionists to the ground, would widen the breach between the two Churches.
attrib. **1898** *Westm. Gaz.* 10 Jan. 2/1 That the Cardinal and his friends have..inflicted a signal discomfiture on the 'reunionist' party.

Hence **Reunio'nistic** *a.*, aiming at, or desirous of, reunion with Rome.
1867 *Ess. on Reunion* 210 The Bishop of Oxford..quoting in support of his thoroughly Re-unionistic sentiments the remarkable 30th Canon of 1603. **1883** *Sat. Rev.* LVI. 110 The religious and especially—if the word may be allowed—the Reunionistic movements of the age.

reu'nitable (riː-), *a.* [Cf. REUNITE *v.* and -ABLE.] Capable of being reunited.
1669 W. SIMPSON *Hydrol. Chym.* 14 Having its parts, only forcibly severed by the fretting corrosive, reunitable. **1828** CARLYLE *Misc.* (1857) I. 162 Some composite, divisible, and reunitable substance.

†**reu'nite,** *pa. pple. Obs.*⁻¹ [ad. pa. pple. of med.L. *reūnīre*: see next.] Reunited.
c **1450** *Mirour Saluacioun* (Roxb.) 140 At Domesday bodyes and sawles shal be revnit certayne.

reunite (riːjuː'naɪt), *v.* [f. ppl. stem of med.L. *reūnīre*: see RE- and UNITE *v.* Cf. F. *réunir*, Sp. and Pg. *reunir*, It. *reunire*.]
1. *trans.* To unite or bring together again; to join together after separation.
1591 SAVILE *Tacitus, Hist.* IV. lvi. 211 Hee would..reunite the greatest part of the cuntrey againe to the Roman Empire. **1601** HOLLAND *Pliny* II. 160 The young tendrils..do re-ioyn and re-vnite the skin of the head which was departed from the bones of the skull. **1681–6** J. SCOTT *Chr. Life* (1747) III. 506 It is God that must recollect this Matter, reduce it into a Body again, and re-unite it to its ancient Soul. **1720** WELTON *Suffer. Son of God* II. xxx. 795 Who Reunitest all our Hearts within the Bond of Thy Love. **1781** GIBBON *Decl. & F.* xxvi. (1787) II. 586 As they had been divided by prosperity, they were easily re-united by the common hardships. **1835** LYTTON *Rienzi* IX. ii, She but felt that they were reunited. **1879** MEREDITH *Egoist* xlvii, Clara could reunite him, turn him once more into a whole..man.
refl. **1596** RALEIGH *Discov. Gviana* (1887) 145 Whatsoever companies shall be afterwards planted within the land..shall be able to reunite themselves upon any occasion. **1656** EARL MONM. tr. *Boccalini's Advts. fr. Parnass.* II. li. (1674) 202 Any thing which..might make the people re-unite themselves with the Nobility. **1712** J. JAMES tr. *Le Blond's Gardening* 168 That the Sap may rise and reunite itself entirely above.
2. *intr.* To come together again and unite.
1660 F. BROOKE tr. *Le Blanc's Trav.* 97 Believing that their soules..would reunite to the body. **1689** SWIFT *Ode to Temple* Wks. 1755 IV. I. 243 In pieces cut, the Viper still did reunite. **1763** MILLS *Pract. Husb.* II. 11 Now sand..only hinders the particles of the earth from re-uniting too closely. **1830** HERSCHEL *Study Nat. Phil.* 237 Usually, when strained too far, they break, and refuse to re-unite. **1876** MOZLEY *Univ. Serm.* v. 115 There were the fragments of a mighty nation determined to reunite.

Hence **reu'nited** *ppl. a.*; **reu'nitedly** *adv.*; †**reu'nitement; reu'niter; reu'niting** *vbl. sb.*
1597 A. M. tr. *Guillemeau's Fr. Chirurg.* 23/2 Thrust a needle through both the *revnited partes. **1896** MCKINLEY in *Westm. Gaz.* 6 Nov. 7/1 We have demonstrated to the world that we are a re-united people. **1847** WEBSTER, **Reunitedly*, in a reunited manner. **1611** COTGR., *Reunion*, a reunion, *reunitement, reconcilement. *a* **1849** J. C. MANGAN *Poems* (1859) 176 The grave is the great *Reuniter. *a* **1586** CARTWRIGHT in *Answ. to Cartwright* 86 Your first page had raysed me vnto some hope for the *reuniting of your selfe..vnto vs. **1673** AYRES (*title*), The Re-uniting of Christianity, or The manner how to rejoin all Christians under one sole Confession of Faith. **1872** RAINY *Lect. Ch. Scot.* I. (1883) 47 A reuniting movement..set in and prevailed. **1883** *Edin. Daily Rev.* 6 June 3/7 Would not this be the happy reuniting of our broken ranks?

reu'nition. *rare.* [Cf. prec. and -TION.] The action of reuniting; reunion.
1635 JACKSON *Humiliation Son of God* xvii. 190 The dissolution of Christ's body and soule, and their reunition in glory and immortality. **1693** KNATCHBULL *Annot. N.T.* 93, I believe the Resurrection of the body, and its reunition with the Soul. **1893** *Columbus* (Ohio) *Disp.* 12 June, He argues for the reunition of the English-speaking peoples.

reu'nitive, *a. rare*⁻¹. [f. as REUNITE *v.* + -IVE.] Causing or marked by reunion.
1851 S. JUDD *Margaret* I. xiv, A social and reunitive epoch.

reuolde, obs. pa. t. of REVOLVE *v.*

reuour, obs. form of REAVER.

re-up ('riːʌp), *v. U.S. Services' slang.* [f. RE- 5 a + UP *v.*: see quots. 1930, 1942.] *intr.* To re-enlist. Also as *sb.*, one who re-enlists. Hence **re-'upping** *vbl. sb.*
1906 *Soldier Slang* in C. M'Govern *Sarjint Larry an' Frinds, Re-up*, to re-enlist. **1913** [see HITCH *sb.* 8]. **1930** W. H. WALDRON *Old Sergeant's Conferences* vii. 122 To 'Re-up' is to reenlist on the day following discharge... The 'Up' refers to holding up his hand to receive the oath of enlistment. **1942** E. COLBY *Army Talk* 174 When enlisting and being sworn in, a man is said to 'hold up his right hand' for three years. So when he does it after being discharged, he 're-ups'. **1955** *Air Force Times* (U.S.) (Eastern ed.) 31 Dec. 13/1 Despite the surprising success of the re-up efforts, the problem of getting qualified replacements for the still critical 'hardcore' skills remains. **1958** *Ibid.* 2 Aug. 1/4 (*heading*) Re-Upping Quickly Pays Off. **1970** *Times* 28 May 7/7 The person they are likely to meet is the recruiting officer with his 're-up' quota to fill. **1972** J. GORES *Dead Skip* xi. 75 If he'd re-upped when his two years in the army were finished, he'd have been a sergeant by now. **1974** *Black Panther* 9 Feb. 22/1, I was told to talk to a recruiter on base about re-enlisting... He told me that if I re-up for the four-year reserve commitment he would fix it up so that I had a job waiting for me.

reup'holster (riː-), *v.* [RE- 5 c.] *trans.* To upholster anew. So **reup'holstery.**
1935 *Amer. Speech* X. 154/2 Entire [car] bodies rebuilt, reupholstered. **1943** F. THOMPSON *Candleford Green* vii. 116 The easy chair had been carried away to be re-upholstered. **1976** R. RENDELL *Demon in my View* ii. 22 The sofa and the two armchairs had been re-upholstered. **1977** *Time* 4 July 6/3 Mortified French officials rushed the vehicle back to its manufacturer, where men on the assembly line worked frantically on reupholstery..and a new paint job. **1978** *N.Y. Times* 30 Mar. C13/3 (Advt.), Upholstery & reupholstery workroom. **1978** *P.O. Telephone Directory, Preston Area: Yellow Pages* 357 (Advt.), Specialists in upholstery & re-upholstery.

re-'urge (riː-), *v.* [RE- 5 a.] To urge again.
1701 NORRIS *Ideal World* I. i. 18 Whose arguments..are sufficiently known, and need not here be re-urged. **1748** RICHARDSON *Clarissa* (1811) III. 248, I re-urged her to make me happy. **1782** MISS BURNEY *Cecilia* VII. vi, Delvile..re-urged all his arguments with redoubled hope and spirit. **1814** JANE AUSTEN *Mansf. Park* xxxiv, In the same low, eager voice..he went on re-urging the same questions as before. **1816** —— *Emma* I. ix, He re-urged—she re-declined. **1881** DARWIN in *Life & Lett.* (1887) III. 246, I hope that you will re-urge..your view.

reusable (riː'juːzəb(ə)l), *a.* [f. RE-USE *v.* + -ABLE.] Capable of being re-used; suitable for a second or further use.
1959 *Sears, Roebuck Catal.* Spring & Summer 835/1 Paper plates..With re-usable plastic bag. **1962** *Guardian* 5 Dec. 6/3 Paper place mats..disposable, but certainly reusable several times. **1967** *Times Rev. Industry* Feb. 39/1 (Advt.), Dictamite takes a whole hour's dictation on one tiny reusable tape cartridge. **1970** *New Scientist* 26 Feb. 407/1 Those contractors who have plans for the airframe or engines of the reusable shuttle must submit them to NASA. **1971** *Engineering* Apr. 59/2 Some strippable coatings are reusable. **1975** *Nature* 17 Jan. 149/2 Out of the other end, or rather ends, come several potentially valuable by-products. Three grades of reuseable paper, two already pronounced as suitable for board making by commercial board mills, one suitable for high grade fuel.

Hence **reusa'bility.**
1970 *Sci. Jrnl.* Aug. 32/2 'Reusability'—the introduction of launch vehicles and spacecraft that can be flown to space, returned and used again. **1973** *Daily Tel.* 24 Jan. 19 (Advt.), It had to meet rigid specifications. Uniform size and shape, chemical content, heat resistance, ventilation, reusability.

re'usage (riː-). [RE- 5 a.] A second or further usage.
1956 *Discovery* July 230/2 Earlier examples of reusage of bricks by Saxon builders are numerous.

re-use (riː'juːs), *sb.* [RE- 5 a.] Further use; using over again.
1866 G. STEPHENS *Runic Mon.* I. xviii, Add to this the endless destruction during 1800 years from greed, for building,..for re-use as palimpsest-stones. **1882** *U.S. Rep. Prec. Metals* 650 The water is pumped up to the stamps again for re-use.

re-use (riː'juːz), *v.* [RE- 5 a.] To use again.
1843 *Civil Eng. & Arch. Jrnl.* VI. 304/1 The water is to be re-used for forming the solution. **1865** *Ch. Times* 11 Feb. 46/1 The fittings have been entirely re-used, and the carvings preserved. **1889** HANNAY *Capt. Marryat* 85 He had to rely on his power of re-using well-worn materials.

reuse, obs. Sc. form of ROOSE *v.*

†**reusful,** *a. Obs.*⁻¹ [Cf. next.] Rueful.
c **1250** in *O.E. Misc.* 186 So reusful [*v.r.* reuþful] dede idon neuer non nas.

†**'reusie,** *v. Obs.* Forms: 1 (h)reowsian, 2 reusien, 3 r(e)ous-, reos-. [OE. *hreowsian*, f. *hreow* RUE *sb.*] *intr.* To feel sorrow or penitence.
c **893** K. ÆLFRED *Oros.* VI. ii. 256 Þæt þa heora synna sceoldon hreowsian & dædbote don. *c* **1000** *Ags. Gosp.* Matt. xxvii. 3 Þa ongann he hreowsian [*Hatton* reowsian]. *c* **1160** *Hatton Gosp.* Mark viii. 12 Þa cwæð he reowsiende on his gaste [etc.]. *c* **1175** *Lamb. Hom.* 27 For heore sunne to beten & to reusien. *c* **1205** LAY. 29477 Þa reousede Gregori,..and þas andsware saide.

†**'reusing,** *vbl. sb. Obs.* [f. REUSIE *v.*] Penitence, repentance; pity.
c **897** K. ÆLFRED tr. *Gregory's Past. C.* xxi. 165 Ðæt he ðurh ða hreowsunga ȝemete forȝiefnesse. *c* **1000** *Ags. Gosp.* Luke x. 13 Hiȝ on hæran & on axan hreowsunge [*Hatton* reowsunge] dydon. *c* **1200** ORMIN 5563 Þe sexte ȝife off Haliȝ Gast Iss an rihht god reowwsunnge. **13..** *Song of Prisoner* in *Rel. Ant.* I. 275 Bisech thin sone, that swete thing, That he habbe of us rewsing.

‖**réussi** (reysi), *a.* Also fem. **réussie.** [Fr.] Fine, excellent, successful.
1948 F. R. LEAVIS *Great Tradition* ii. 37 Adam [Bede], we know, is a tribute to her father; but he is also the Ideal Craftsman, embodying the Dignity of Labour. He too is *réussi*. **1953** 'N. BLAKE' *Dreadful Hollow* vi. 75 She drew out of its wrappings an elaborate construction of shells enclosed by a glass dome. 'He must have made it himself. You see? It's a sort of mausoleum. Rather weird and *réussi*, isn't it?' **1958** B. NICHOLS *Sweet & Twenties* iii. 48 Here, I thought, is a woman who is completely *réussie*.

Reuter ('rɔɪtə(r)). The name of Baron Paul Julius von *Reuter* (1816–99), founder of a telegraphic and pigeon post bureau in Aachen in 1849, used *attrib.* and in the possessive to denote (the activities of) a news agency named after him, whose London headquarters were established in 1851. Also (in form **Reuters**) used *absol.*
[**1859** *Times* 31 Oct. 6/5 The following telegrams have been received at Mr. Reuter's office.] **1860** *Times* 1 Oct. 7/1 (*heading*) Reuter's Telegrams. **1913** KIPLING *Lett. of Travel* (1920) 222 No newspapers come aboard, only clipped Reuter telegrams. **1964** M. MCLUHAN *Understanding Media* II. xxiv. 235 A Reuters dispatch for December 13, 1962, reported from Tokyo. **1967** *Listener* 28 Dec. 860/1 In the early days of BBC news when they were terrified of infringing the rights of newspapers they used to read out the Reuter tapes. **1969** *Observer* 5 Oct. 1/2 Reuter correspondent Anthony Grey was a free man in Peking tonight after being held hostage by the Chinese for 26 lonely months. **1977** *New Yorker* 3 Oct. 98/2 My guide..would be an Englishman..John Peet, who had covered Germany for Reuters, the British news agency. **1980** M. LUTYENS *Edwin Lutyens* xv. 232 Every morning Roderick's special Reuter messenger boy brought me a letter from him.

reuth(e, obs. ff. RUTH.

reutheful, -les, obs. ff. RUTHFUL, -LESS.

reutili'zation (riː-). [RE- 5 a.] A second or further utilization.
1936 *Discovery* July 230/2 Virtually all English brick-craft originated by the reutilisation of Roman bricks in mediaeval buildings. **1957** *New Biol.* XXIII. 81 The induced enzyme therefore appeared to be synthesized from amino acids present in the free amino acid pool and not by partial breakdown of other cell proteins, followed by the reutilization of the peptide moieties produced.

re'utilize (riː-), *v.* [RE- 5 a.] *trans.* To utilize again. Hence **re'utilized** *ppl. a.*
1889 *Lancet* 21 Sept. 585/2 After the white cells have lived their life and done their work, portions of their worn-out carcases may be reutilised in the body as nutriment. **1964** D. NICHOLS in *Oceanogr. & Marine Biol.* II. 408 Cornil, Mosinger and Calen (1935 a, b) were of the opinion that the matter eliminated by some amoebocytes in the epithelium was re-utilized by others. **1972** *Biblical Theol. Bull.* Feb. 30 Some of these reutilized traditional materials deserve a separate mention, namely the various formulas of prayer.

re'utter (riː-), *v.* [RE- 5 a.] To utter again.
1855 BROWNING *Old Pict. Florence* xi, The truth..Which the actual generations garble, Was re-uttered. **1874** H. R. REYNOLDS *John Bapt.* iv. §6. 270 He reuttered the sternest enactments of the law.

reuu, reuwe, obs. ff. RUE.

reuwele, obs. f. RULE *v.*

reuylde, variant of RIVELLED *a.*

reuyll, obs. f. RULE.

reuyn, obs. f. RAVEN *sb.*¹, RIVEN.

reuys, obs. f. RAVISH.

reuyue, obs. f. REVIVE *v.*

reuze, variant of ROOSE *v.*

Rev., *sb.*¹ Abbrev. of REVEREND *a.* and *sb.* 2 c, d.
In U.S. usage freq. without preceding article.
1721 D. WILKINS *Leges Anglo-Saxonicæ* (list of subscribers), The Rev. Mr. Henry Briggs of Loose in Kent, [etc.]. **1785** (*title*), Lectures on the Canon of the Scriptures, ..by the late Rev. John Blair. **1847** CARUS *Mem. C. Simeon* 833 Recollections of the Rev. Chas. Simeon, by the Right Rev. Daniel Wilson. **1876** W. WHITMAN *Daybks. & Notebks.* (1978) I. 37 Rev. R. P. Graves. **1884** [see CHASUBLE 1]. **1917** *Congress. Rec.* (Daily ed.) 14 Dec. 294/2 Rev. Joseph Burt Webster to be chaplain with rank from October 5, 1917. **1939** *Time* 27 Nov. 50/3 (*heading*) Mr. for Rev. **1943** R. LLEWELLYN *None but Lonely Heart* xxi. 118 Reverend Ernest Mott. Oxford, he is. Followed 'em on His bike as far as Hammersmith Bridge every year since '98. Ain't you, Rev, boy? **1969** C. BURKE *God is Beautiful, Man* (1970) 74 The Revs. in the church got cut in on it too. **1972** J. MARYLAND in T. Kochman *Rappin' & Stylin' Out* 213 Say, Rev., tell them 'bout the little white lady. **1973** *Philadelphia Inquirer* (Today Suppl.) 7 Oct. 14/3 Rev. Velasquez recalls that before the first trial he heard Tony's defense attorney say [etc.]. **1978** *Listener* 9 Mar. 296/3 Religious broadcasting is not a job for a good man... Even the radio Revs and their staff are always set apart from other departments.

rev (rɛv), *sb.*² Also **rev.** (with point). Abbrev. of REVOLUTION *sb.* 4 c.
1901 *Catal. Mech. Engin. Coll.* (Victoria & Albert Mus.) I. 35 The example has 3 in. cylinders, with 4 in. stroke, and is intended to run at 300 revs. per min. **1918** *Chambers's Jrnl.* May 301/1 The revs dropped off. **1932** S. C. H. DAVIS *Motor Racing* vi. 87 The car went well, held its revs. with something in hand. **1942** *Tee Emm* (Air Ministry) II. 87 The

revs. of the engine..can be controlled by the pilot in one of two ways. **1966** R. Maxwell in T. Wisdom *High-Performance Driving* v. 44, I stayed in each gear to maximum revs for best acceleration on the short, so-called straights. **1969** *Listener* 22 May 734/1, I admit to having enjoyed recently Kagel's *Improvisation Ajoutée* for organ..at 45 r.p.m. In retrospect I am convinced that those extra 11⅔ revs per minute tightened up the form of this fascinating work to a slight but ideal degree. **1972** *Daily Tel.* 25 Feb. 2/7 As I got round the bend onto the main road I felt the revs begin to build up. When this happened I changed up a gear.

2. *Comb.* **rev-counter** (and varr.), †**rev-meter**, an instrument that measures and displays the rate of rotation, esp. of an engine, or the number of rotations.

1917 *Blackw. Mag.* May 803/2 The rev.-counter showed that the number of revolutions per minute had fallen off appreciably. **1948** M. Laski *Tory Heaven* iv. 58 The car.. had a searchlight and a wireless mast and outside gears and a rev counter. **1967** E. Chambers *Photolitho-Offset* viii. 103 It is possible to compute mathematically the required settings which are..mechanically applied in different ways. For example,..by using a rev-counter and vernier dials attached and synchronised with the movements of the lens board and copyboard carriages. **1976** *Glasgow Herald* 26 Nov. 19/5 The speedometer and rev. counter are..right in front of the driver. **1917** E. C. Middleton *Way of Air* vii. 49 The pilot is able to distinguish his instruments..the altimeter, which records the height, 'revmeter' which indicates the speed of the engine and the compass.

rev (rɛv), *v.* Pa. t. **revved**, pres. pple. **revving**. [f. the sb.] **1.** *trans.* To cause (an internal-combustion engine) to run quickly, esp. before bringing it into use; to speed *up*. Freq. *absol.* Also *fig.*

1920 *Blackw. Mag.* Oct. 449/1 A British Fighter whose pilot was revving up his 250-horse-power Rolls Royce Falcon. **1922** Joyce *Ulysses* 420 O get, rev on a gradient one in nine. **1934** [see idle *v.* 4 a]. **1942** *Sat. Even. Post* 5 Sept. 22/1 Jimmy revved up and the engine burst into a deep-throated roar. **1944** A. Thirkell *Headmistress* i. 28 'Rev. her up, Copper.' The ginger-haired bicyclist..roared away up the street. **1956** *Sun* (Baltimore) 24 Apr. 21/1 Bill Hartack revved up his already torrid riding pace here today by winning four races out of seven tries to push his total victory for the year to 94. **1966** J. Betjeman *High & Low* 50 Loving relations Rev in the car park, changing gear at the bend. **1968** Mrs. L. B. Johnson *White House Diary* 31 Mar. (1970) 644 Lyndon came in with that jaunty step that I've seen him rev up under the most intense tension. **1973** A. Hunter *Gently French* iii. 23 The mech gently revved it, bringing in the supercharger. **1977** *Time* 13 June 47/2 He and a cousin revved up the company, branched into trucking and started hauling coal. **1978** J. Irving *World according to Garp* xii. 234 He revved his engine as if he were clearing his throat.

2. *intr.* Of an internal-combustion engine: to run (quickly), esp. with the clutch disengaged. Also said of the vehicle. Freq. with *up*.

1923 *Daily Mail* 9 Mar. 12 This little engine..cheats the taxation authorities by its long stroke and its capacity for 'revving' fast without vibration. **1930** *Times* 29 Mar. 17/6 (Advt.), The oil..is specially refined for the fast-revving engines of to-day. **1951** 'J. Wyndham' *Day of Triffids* i. 9 The released cross-traffic would rev. and roar as it started up the incline. **1955** G. Greene *Quiet American* ii. ii. 111 All round me I could hear the cars of the soldiers and the diplomats revving up: the party was over for another year. **1960** J. Betjeman *Summoned by Bells* vii. 73 There's a Frazer-Nash. Gosh, what an engine! Did you hear her rev? **1965** *Motor* 17 July 8/1 The Anglia revs faster at any given speed in top. **1973** J. Pattinson *Search Warrant* vi. 90 He heard a motor engine revving up, dying away, revving again.

Hence **'revved-up** *a.* (in quots., *fig.*); **'revving** *ppl. a.* and *vbl. sb.*

1931 E. M. Brent-Dyer *Chalet School & Jo* xxi. 261 I'm so revved up,..I simply *can't* rest. Please, may I go for a walk instead? **1972** J. Aiken *Butterfly Picnic* vi. 107 My mind seemed revved up to operate at twice its normal pace. **1976** J. Carroll *Madonna Red* v. (1977) 174 The rush of his revved-up thinking. **1978** M. Harrison in *Islands* (N.Z.) Aug. 86, I didn't dream of standing by the revving plane, the wires of the fences caught the whisper of the landing-lights. **1979** K. Conlon *Move in Game* iii. 32 The man who drove his scarlet MG with much revving of the engine.

rev, obs. f. rue.

re'vaccinate (ri:-), *v.* [re- 5 a. So F. *revacciner*, It. *rivaccinare*.] To vaccinate again. Hence **re'vaccinated** *ppl. a.*

1843 Sir T. Watson *Lect. Pract. Med.* lxxxvii. II. 738 Both of them have lately been revaccinated. **1863** *Manch. Guard.* 6 May, An almost entirely revaccinated population. **1868** Seaton *Hdbk. Vaccination* 273 Recruits..who were incubating smallpox when they were re-vaccinated.

revacci'nation (ri:-). [re- 5 a. Cf. prec. and F. *revaccination*, It. *rivaccinazione*.] The action of revaccinating or fact of being revaccinated.

1843 Sir T. Watson *Lect. Pract. Med.* lxxxvii. II. 739 The practice of revaccination is a safe and advisable precaution. **1869** E. A. Parkes *Pract. Hygiene* (ed. 3) 485 The evidence from foreign armies proves the necessity of careful re-vaccination.

†**re'vailed**, *a. Obs.* [f. revale *v.*: cf. reveal *sb.*²] Having a reveal or reveals.

1637 in Fowler *Hist. C.C.C.* (O.H.S.) 359 For a chest of Miter round and revayled with lapts and pendants to put in the vestments belonging to the Chapell. **1688** Holme *Armoury* iii. 112/2 Revailed, is in the same way of work, but in this the joynts are but champhered, so that it is two edges of the joynt taken off. **1703** T. N. *City & C. Purchaser* 224 Revailed and Pilaster-peers, from 10 to 14 Pounds a pair.

revale, obs. form of reveal *sb.*²

†**re'vale**, *v. Obs. rare.* Also 5 revayle. [ad. OF. *revaler*, f. *re-* re- + *-valer*: see avale, devall, and vail *v.*] *trans.* To lower, bring down.

14.. *Wars Eng. in France* (Rolls) II. 527 The oppynyouns and reasouns..sent to the said councelle of Arras, in revalyng and adnullyng the seide grete adversaries demaundes. **1475** *Bk. Noblesse* 74 Suffre ye not the prelates ..to be oppressid, revaled, ne vileyned.

Hence †**re'valing** *vbl. sb. Obs.*

14.. *Wars Eng. in France* (Rolls) II. 524 A pere of Fraunce..shuld have be regente, whiche myghte have bene a grete revaylyng to the noblesse of thys youre realme.

revalenta (rɛvə'lɛntə). [Arbitrary alteration of *ervalenta*, f. *ervum lens* the lentil.] A preparation of lentil and barley flour.

1850 Ure in *Lancet* 7 June (1851) Advt., Having also examined Du Barry's Revalenta Arabica, I find it [etc.]. **1864** *N. & Q.* 3rd Ser. V. 24/1, I remember the first introduction of the Article now called Revalenta. I knew the man who first prepared it and advertized it under the name 'Ervalenta'. **1866** *Treas. Bot.* 466/1 The so-called invalids' food, which under the names Ervalenta and Revalenta has attained no little celebrity.

reva'lescence. *rare*⁻¹. [f. L. *revalesc-ĕre* + -ence.] Convalescence.

1810 Coleridge in *Lit. Rem.* (1838) III. 301 Would this prove that the patient's revalescence had been independent of the medicines given him?

So **reva'lescent** *a.*, 'beginning to grow well' (Webster, 1864).

re'validate (ri:-), *v.* [re- 5 a.] *trans.* To validate or confirm anew.

1602 T. Fitzherbert *Apol.* 13 That his confession vpon torment was voyd in Law and..that his ratification therof at the barre could not reualidate the same. **1895** *Month* Mar. 319 The intrusion was ordinarily revalidated by a formal ceremony of election duly conducted.

revalley, -ie, obs. forms of reveille.

revalori'zation (ri:-). [re- 5 a.] The action or process of establishing a fresh price or value for something; revaluation. So **re'valorize** *v. trans.*

1926 *Glasgow Herald* 6 Aug. 8 A preliminary revalorisation [of the franc] through a restoration of confidence should first be attempted. **1928** *Britain's Industr. Future* (Liberal Industr. Inquiry) v. xxviii. 410 The desire to 'revalorise' the currency (i.e. to raise its exchange value) before 'stabilising' it. This process of revalorisation..is infallibly accompanied..by severe trade depression. **1928** *Daily Tel.* 27 Mar. 14/3 The leading banks..replied that they would not advance a pfennig until the war debts had been revalorised and admitted. **1962** *Listener* 12 Apr. 624/2 If we are to have ministerial meetings they need not always be at the level of Heads of Government. Foreign Ministers must be revalorized. **1977** *Times* 27 Apr. 23/5 Mr Healey gets beta plus for revalorizing personal reliefs to counter about one year's fiscal drag. **1979** *Daily Tel.* 4 Apr. 10 These increases give effect to the re-valorisation of personal allowances provided for by Section 22 of the Finance Act 1977. **1979** *Maledicta* III. 71 In their attempts to enshrine and revalorize their own blackness and that of their intended audience, these poets of cultural nationalism frequently seem to assume [etc.].

re'valuate (ri:-), *v.* [Back-formation f. revaluation.] *trans.* To reassess, form a new valuation of. Also *absol.* Hence **re'valuating** *ppl. a.*

1949 Wellek & Warren *Theory of Lit.* iv. 34 The practicing critic..will revaluate the past. **1965** 'A. Burgess' in *Listener* 18 Feb. 275/1 'Another revaluation of Joyce would make one scream.' By the waters of Marylebone I sat down and wept, wondering whether to sink my revaluating galleys. **1977** *Times* 5 July 5/4 Even if a firm offer is made, however, both the British and French Governments will undoubtedly demand time to revaluate their respective commitments.

revalu'ation. [re- 5 a: cf. next.] A second or revised valuation.

a. A second or further valuation of the financial or monetary worth of something; *spec.* a revision (usu. an increase) of the official value of a currency in relation to gold or another currency.

1611 Cotgr., *Raprecy*, a reualuation, or new price made, of. **1714** *Fr. Bk. Rates* 25 The Five Shillings per Ton,.. with the Revaluation of those Duties. **1884** *Law Rep.* 13 *Q.B. Div.* 376 An alteration in the name of the occupier might require a revaluation of the property. **1925** *Times* 22 Sept. 22/6 The German Embassy has issued the following information regarding the German Law of Revaluation:—Mortgages, land and annuity debts..will on principle be revalued at 25 per cent. of their gold value. **1946** *Times* 13 July 7/1 Revaluation will tend to neutralize the impact [of disparity with U.S. prices] on the Swedish economy. **1955** *Times* 27 June 9/3 No ratepayer can properly gauge the effect of revaluation until he knows what rate his local authority intends to levy in the new dispensation. **1962** *Ann. Reg. 1961* 465 Sterling was under pressure as a result of general uncertainty following the revaluations of the Deutschemark and Dutch guilder. **1968** *Guardian* 20 Nov. 12/2 Revaluation means increasing the value of a currency in terms of other currencies. **1971** *Daily Tel.* 10 May 1/1 Dr Schmidt, president of the National Bank [of Austria] said losses to the reserves caused by the revaluation amounted to 1,500 million schillings. **1978** *Financial Times* 30 Jan. 2/6 The half per cent revaluation of the Dirham against the dollar..brought it into line with the currencies of Bahrain and Qatar.

b. In literary criticism.

1851 De Quincey *Pope* Wks. 1858 IX. 11 In making a revaluation of Pope as regards some of his principal works. **1936** F. R. Leavis (*title*) Revaluation. **1976** *UCT Stud. in English* (Univ. Cape Town) Oct. 1 After the critical revaluations of the past twenty years, Wallace Stevens can no longer be thought of as an eccentric. **1978** *Times Lit. Suppl.* 1 Dec. 1393/2 What he is doing is practising the classic American trick of hurling effete European vice out of the window and then lugging it back through the door, wearing a coonskin cap and called Revaluation.

re'value (ri:-), *v.* [re- 5 a.] To value anew; *spec.* to adjust (usu. increase) the value of (a currency) in relation to gold or another currency.

1592 H. Wotton *Let.* in *Reliquiæ Wottonianæ* (1685) 668 The Sum should be revalued. **1611** Florio, *Riualere*, to reualue. **1682** Scarlett *Exchanges* 294 If in such a case the Drawer..hath ordered his Acceptant to revalue upon him. **1874** Walford *Insurance Cycl.* III. 526 The house property over which the ins[urance] extends is revalued every 7 years. **1925** [see revaluation a]. **1946** *Times* 13 July 7/1 (*heading*), Swedish Krona Revalued. **1962** *Ann. Reg. 1961* 245 On 5 March the Deutschemark was revalued upwards by 4·75 per cent. **1968** *Guardian* 16 Nov. 1/2 The French..have been putting strong pressure on the Germans..to revalue. This would..make German exports less competitive. **1978** *Financial Times* 30 Jan. 2/5 The Bahrain dinar was revalued by 2 per cent against the U.S. dollar at the opening of business in Bahrain on Saturday.

re'vamp (ri:-), *v.* [re- 5 a.] To vamp or patch up again. Also, to rewrite in a new form; to renovate, remake, devise anew; to revise. Hence **re'vamped** *ppl. a.*; **re'vamping** *vbl. sb.*

1850 D. G. Mitchell *Lorgnette* I. 141 Even the soberer subjects of History, he told me, must be re-vamped in some tasty way. **1859** G. P. Marsh *Lect. Eng. Lang.* 447 The revamping of our own writings,..after an interval so long.., is a dangerous experiment. **1876** Lowell *Among my Bks.* Ser. ii. 19 Some of them at least fifteen centuries old when revamped. **1878** 'Mark Twain' in *Atlantic Monthly* May 617/2 He had to keep on procuring magazine acceptances and then revamping the manuscripts to make them presentable. **1931** Ford & Crowther *Moving Forward* xi. 164 We decided to revamp our entire industry from top to bottom. **1934** J. A. & A. Lomax *Amer. Ballads & Folk Songs* i. 37 Sanders then changed the words 'Jimmie Jones' to 'Casey Jones'. Later it was picked up by some traveling vaudevillians and revamped to make the popularly known song, 'Casey Jones'. **1941** W. C. Handy *Father of Blues* xii. 169 The revamped outfit was acting strangely, whispering behind their hands. **1945** Nelson & Wright *Tomorrow's House* vii. 79 This is just the living-room function slightly revamped. **1947** *Sun* (Baltimore) 22 Dec. 2/1 Eastern and western states will revamp their foreign policies in the light of the situation in Germany. **1950** *Manch. Guardian Weekly* 7 Dec. 3 The British did some rapid discreet revamping of their agenda. **1956** W. H. Whyte *Organization Man* (1957) 99 Several of the technical schools have been revamping their curriculums. **1960** O. Skilbeck *ABC of Film & TV* 108 *Re-vamp*, to use an existing set for further shooting by altering it and adapting its practicals for another sequence. **1961** *Harper's Bazaar* Dec. 60 Brilliant revamping of the famous Helena Rubinstein flat in Paris. **1965** *Listener* 16 Dec. 984/2 Over the past three years they [*sc.* the East Germans] have done a lot of revamping, and are introducing what they rather ponderously call 'the new system of planning and guiding the national economy'. **1968** *Observer* 29 Dec. 32/3 On Wednesday, *Punch* appears revamped and under new editorship. **1979** *Jrnl. R. Soc. Arts* CXXVII. 122/1 The new or revamped public schools did not set out to equip their pupils to lead great industrial enterprises.

So **re'vamp** *sb.*

1881 *Philadelphia Rec.* No. 3418/1 All that has been published is simply a revamp of what came out in the Congressional investigation. **1943** *Yank* 10 Feb. 8 If a plane comes in badly shot up and has to go to basic engineering for a revamp, two crew members will go with her and personally inspect everything that's done. **1973** *Scotsman* 12 Jan. 3/1 Rockware Glass, the £16 million container group, are planning a major revamp of their factories. **1979** *Now!* 21–7 Sept. 59/3 The Navy IQ test was introduced in 1942, and given a 'revamp' in 1977.

‖**revanchard** (rəvɑ̃ʃar), *a.* [Fr.] = revanchist *a.*

1961 *Washington Post* 28 Aug. a-8/4 Placed before the fact ..of a separate state which.. immediately started to acquire a belligerent revanchard character, the population of East Germany in their turn created another German state. **1964** *Listener* 1 Oct. 523/2 In the eighteen-eighties, thanks partly to Boulanger, it was the Right [in France] which became militantly *revanchard*, and by the turn of the century it was denouncing the Left for being socialist, pacifist, semitic, and *dreyfusard*.

‖**revanche** (rəvɑ̃ʃ). [Fr.] Requital, revenge; the giving of like for like; *spec.* a nation's policy of securing the return of lost territory.

1858 Queen Victoria *Let.* 22 June in R. Fulford *Dearest Child* (1964) 117 She never allows a word to be said against Leopold who in revanche is much kinder to her than he was. **1870** G. Meredith *Let.* 9 Oct. (1970) I. 427 You great-mindedly took my criticism, and I long for the *revanche* of giving praise. **1889** M. S. Van de Velde *Cosmopolitan Recoll.* I. v. 162 He [*sc.* Prince Gortchakoff] has on his record the fate of Sleswig and of Denmark; Sadowa, the *revanche* of Sebastopol. **1894** G. du Maurier *Trilby* III. viii. 157 When they come back from *La Revanche*, may Madame Cantharidi ..welcome the returning heroes. **1895** M. Corelli *Sorrows of Satan* X. 108 Meanwhile I was surrounded by the rest of the men, all of them repeating the Viscount's suggestion of a 'revanche'. **1914** G. B. Shaw in *New Statesman* 14 Nov. (Suppl.) 20/1 France had given up hope of her Alsace-Lorraine *revanche*. **1919** J. M. Keynes *Econ. Consequences of Peace* (1920) iii. 32 Each guarantee that was taken, by increasing irritation and thus the probability of a subsequent *Revanche* by Germany, made necessary yet further provisions to crush. **1930** H. G. Wells *Autocracy of*

Mr. Parham IV. ii. 285 An unhoped for *revanche* offered itself plainly and clearly to the German people. **1934** B. RUSSELL *Freedom & Organization 1814–1914* xxxii. 495 He [*sc.* the Kaiser] caused England to join France and Russia, thereby encouraging Germany's enemies everywhere, awaking in France renewed hope of the *revanche*. **1939** A. J. TOYNBEE *Study of Hist.* IV. 118 The Justinianean *revanche*, in the sixth century, against the Vandals and the Ostrogoths. *a* **1943** R. G. COLLINGWOOD *Idea of Hist.* (1946) 169 History is regarded not only as a possible and legitimate form of knowledge but as the only genuine knowledge that exists or can exist. But this *revanche* not only fails in doing justice to natural science, it also misunderstands history. **1958** *Listener* 10 July 57/1 In 1914..France wanted Revanche.

revanchist (rɛ'vænʃɪst, -ɑː-), *sb.* and *a.* [f. prec. + -IST: cf. Fr. *revanchiste* (also used).] **A.** *sb.* One who seeks reprisal or revenge; *spec.* one who seeks to avenge the defeat of Germany in the war of 1939–45. **B.** *adj.* Pertaining to or characterized by a policy of reprisal or revenge. Also **revan'chistic**.

1926 *Scots Observer* 13 Nov. 19/1 A Germany contented, satisfied, and prosperous would pay her debt and achieve a bloodless but a complete victory. It is France's policy that the sores be kept open even if they give a handle to Monarchist revanchists. **1953** *Ann. Reg. 1952* 195 The creation in Western Germany of hired forces of *revanchistes* under the command of Hitlerite generals. **1954** *Times* 5 Mar. 6/4 'Then their real aims will be revealed as well as their aggressive, revanchist calculations,' Mr. Molotov added... The Soviet Foreign Minister said the Adenauer Government was now 'the mainstay of the west German revanchists who want to clear the road to the resurgence of German militarism'. **1955** *N.Y. Times* 10 May 28/1 Far from being an instrument of either 'American aggressors' or 'German revanchists' (as Soviet propaganda would picture it), the North Atlantic alliance is entirely a defensive organization. **1959** *Times* 30 Mar. 5/4 Austria had undertaken to prohibit all Fascist and 'revanchist' organizations, and to wipe out all remaining traces of the Nazis. **1960** *Guardian* 25 Oct. 7/2 Revanchist speeches were being made..on the borders of Czechoslovakia. **1961** *Evening Bull.* (Philadelphia) 24 Aug. 1/8 Air corridors were set aside for the three Western Powers to insure the needs of their military garrisons, and not for subversive and revanchist (revenge-seeking) purposes. **1961** *Times Lit. Suppl.* 17 Nov. 815/4 Between the wars the Hungarians were only revisionists. No one labelled them as revenge-seekers and the communists had surely not yet invented that bastard word 'revanchist'. **1965** *New Statesman* 19 Mar. 432/1, I asked a prominent East German lawyer why, rather than sneer about 'revanchists', they did not support this attempt to convict Nazi criminals. **1965** *Listener* 16 Dec. 983/2 East German propaganda would say it [*sc.* living in West Germany] meant living under 'a state-monopolistic revanchistic militarist regime'. **1967** *Ibid.* 3 Aug. 155/3 When journalists and scholars..label Israeli revanchistes 'Jewish fascists', it's apparent that such tastelessness is even less bearable in non-fiction. **1968** *Daily Tel.* 1 Nov. 34/3 The statement referred also to the 'revanchist and expansionist forces in control in Bonn'. **1973** *Guardian* 19 Oct. 14/6 Not terrorists but revanchist states were the greater threat [to Israel]. **1976** T. ALLBEURY *Only Good German* xiii. 94 A sabotage team operating against the Warsaw Pact countries..supported by the CIA and West German revanchists. **1977** *Time* 7 Feb. 15/3 O'Brien supports a referendum to amend the Irish constitution to remove its revanchist claim on Ulster.

Hence **re'vanchism**, a policy of seeking reprisal or revenge.

1954 *Times* 5 Mar. 6/4 (*heading*) Mr. Molotov on German 'Revanchism'. **1957** *Wall Street Jrnl.* 6 Dec. 6/5 The struggle against West German militarism and revanchism (seeking for revenge), which are now threatening peace, is a vital task facing the peace-loving forces of the German people and all the nations of Europe. **1959** *Listener* 3 Sept. 344/2 The aim of this offer is to take the edge off accusations of revanchism. **1960** *Guardian* 7 Dec. 32/6 Developments in Germany do not go unscanned for signs of militarism and revanchism. **1971** *Listener* 7 Jan. 5/2 If imperialist aggression and German revanchism cease to be credible threats, what grounds are there for maintaining Soviet garrisons in satellite countries? **1974** *Times* 19 Feb. (European Defence Suppl.) p. ii/7 There is a body of opinion which holds that the Russians are looking more in the direction of the Bundeswehr, prompted by an undying fear of German revanchism.

revar(e, obs. forms of REAVER, RIVER.

revard, obs. Sc. form of REWARD.

re'varnish (riː-), *v.* [RE- 5a. So F. *revernir.*] *trans.* To varnish again. Also *fig.*

1851 MOGFORD *Handbk. Preserv. Pict.* (ed. 3) II. 54 To re-varnish the picture, take two-thirds of mastic varnish [etc.]. **1863** *Quart. Rev.* Jan. 262 There is no more certain recipe for revarnishing a Liberal reputation that has grown a little rusty. **1876** T. HARDY *Ethelberta* (1890) 295 Imitations in paint and plaster..recently repaired and re-varnished.

revart, obs. variant of REVERT *v.*

re'vary (riː-), *v.* [RE- 5a.] To vary again.

1608 SYLVESTER *Spectacles* xlix, Vary, re-vary; tune, and tune againe Thy One same Subject in a sundry Strain.

†**revay**, *sb.* *Obs.*$^{-1}$ [f. next.] Hunting or hawking on the banks of rivers.

c **1470** *Gol. & Gaw.* 1343 With reualing and reuay all the oulk hale, Also rachis can ryn vndir the wod rise.

†**revay**, *v.* *Obs.* Forms: reuaye, revay, revey; ryu-, ryvaye. [ad. ONF. *riveier*, OF. *rivoier*, f. *rive* bank.] *intr.* To hunt or hawk along the banks of rivers.

?*a* **1400** *Morte Arth.* 3275 [To] reuaye, and reuelle, and rawnsone the pople. *Ibid.* 3999, I salle neuer ryvaye, ne racches vn-cowpylle At roo ne rayne-dere. *a* **1440** *Sir Degrev.* 50 He wold be upp or the day To honte and to revay. *Ibid.* 659 By that the masse was i-seid,.. The eorlle hadd i-revayd, And in hys ȝerd lyȝthus.

Hence †**revaying** *vbl. sb.* *Obs.*

c **1400** MAUNDEV. (Roxb.) xxiii. 105 When þe Grete Caan will hafe his disporte in ryuaying or huntyng, he may wylde fewle slayne with hawkes..and passe noȝt his chaumbre.

Revd (also **Revd.**), abbrev. of REVEREND *a.* and *sb.* 2c.

1693 W. KENNETT in W. Somner *Treat. Roman Ports & Forts* 1 The Life of Mr. Somner. To the Rev[d]. Mr. James Brome. **1811** SHELLEY *Let.* 17 Feb. (1964) I. 52 If any letter comes directed to the Revd. Charles Meyton, it is mine. **1926** FOWLER *Mod. Eng. Usage* 502/1 *Reverend* is abbreviated *Revd* or now usually *Rev.* **1971** C. COLVIN *M. Edgeworth's Lett. from Eng.* p. xxxvi, The Revd. Daniel Augustus Beaufort.., father-in-law of R. L. Edgeworth.

reve, obs. f. REAVE *v.*, REEVE *sb.*[1] and *sb.*[2]

reveal (rɪ'viːl), *sb.*[1] *rare.* [f. REVEAL *v.*] A revealing, revelation, disclosure.

1629 WADSWORTH *Pilgr.* iii. 22 He vtterly disclaimed their superstitious reueales. **1646** SIR T. BROWNE *Pseud. Ep.* 195 In nature the concealment of secret parts is the same in both sexes and the shame of their reveale equall. **1858** BAILEY *Age* 41 Faith her first law, knowledge her last reveal.

reveal (rɪ'viːl), *sb.*[2] Also 7 **revale**, 9 **revel(e**. [f. REVALE *v.* Cf. also REVAILED *a.*] A side of an opening or recess which is at right angles to the face of the work; *esp.* the vertical side of a doorway or window-opening between the door- or window-frame and the arris.

1688 HOLME *Armoury* III. 394/2 Of two other sorts of Moulds..the second is a square with a swelling Frize and revale. **1825** J. NICHOLSON *Operat. Mechanic* 593 In the clear of the reveals on the outside. **1845** G. PETRIE *Round Towers Irel.* II. iii. 236 The reveal, which divides the outer compound archway, from the inner one. **1881** YOUNG *Every Man his own Mech.* §1384 Any recess in the wall where the two surfaces of the wall and the reveal meet at right angles.

attrib. **1838** *Loudon's Archit. Mag.* V. 580 A variety of other bricks,..such as bat-headers, closers, reveal-headers.

reveal (rɪ'viːl), *v.* Forms: 4–6 **reuele**, 5 *Sc.* **rewele**, 5–7 **revele**; 5 *Sc.* **reweil**, 6 *Sc.* **reu-, reveil(l**; 6 **rea-**, 6–7 **reueal(e, reveale**, 6– **reveal**. [ad. OF. *reveler* (14th c., mod.F. *révéler*, = Sp. and It. *revelar*, It. *re-*, *rivelare*), or L. *revēlāre*, f. *re-* RE- 2d + *vēlum* VEIL. See also REVEIL *v.*]

1. *trans.* To disclose, make known (*to* one) in a supernatural manner.

c **1375** *Sc. Leg. Saints* xxxvii. (*Vincent*) 378 Bot son in til a vysione reuelit it wes til a matrone. *c* **1450** *Myrr. our Ladye* 18 Myn angel that shall reuele & endyte vnto the the legende that shall be redde. **1483** CAXTON *G. de la Tour* c ij b, There it was shewed and reueled to hym that she shold be saued. **1574** tr. *Marlorat's Apocalips* 3 Although these two kyndes of reuealing haue ben very rare since the tyme that Christ was reueled. **1605** BACON *Adv. Learn.* I. vii. §4 A matter revealed and prefigured unto Domitian in a dream. **1671** MILTON *Samson* 29 O wherefore was my birth..from some great act Or benefit reveal'd to Abraham's race? **1781** COWPER *Expost.* 236 The plan That truth and mercy had reveal'd to man. **1865** R. W. DALE *Jew. Temp.* xviii. (1877) 206 The Spirit revealed Divine truth by inspired prophets. **1875** MANNING *Mission H. Ghost* iii. 71 God has revealed the fact that He made the heaven and the earth.

2. To disclose, divulge, make known (*to* one) by discourse or communication. † Also *absol.*

c **1425** WYNTOUN *Cron.* v. xi. 2919 Þai walde þar mwrmur Reweil til hym. **1508** DUNBAR *Tua Mariit Wemen* 43 Reueill gif ȝe rewit that rakles conditioun? **1540** CROMWELL in Merriman *Life & Lett.* (1902) II. 266 A mattyer of gret Secresye which I dyde Reaueale. **1590** SPENSER *F.Q.* I. ix. 8, I will revele what ye so much desire. **1617** MORYSON *Itin.* I. 16 A Bishop, who being the Queenes Confessour, was cast into Molda because he would not reueale her confession to her husband. **1671** MILTON *Samson* 383 Did not she.. reveal The secret wrested from me? **1725** DE FOE *Voy. round World* 47 They would not..reveal to me all the Particulars of the Conspiracy. **1784** *New Spectator* No. 15. 6 His attendance gave birth to a passion which he dared not to reveal. **1856** FROUDE *Hist. Eng.* (1858) I. ii. 126 Wolsey has revealed to us fully his own objects in a letter. **1880** L. STEPHEN *Pope* vi. 138 Having no character to lose, he could reveal his own practices without a blush.

absol. **1671** MILTON *Samson* 782 But I to enemies reveal'd, and should not. **1837** HT. MARTINEAU *Soc. in Amer.* III. 167 A dozen boys and girls..crowded round me, questioning,.. speculating, revealing in a way which enchanted me.

†**b.** To betray. *Obs. rare.*

1640 YORKE *Union Hon.* 92 A servant of his, by whom.. hee was revealed and there taken and beheaded. **1657** MAY *Life Sat. Puppy* 22 Crying blood, blood! the Villain will reveal us, the Villain will reveal us.

3. To display, show, make clear or visible, exhibit. (Also with complement.)

1500–20 DUNBAR *Poems* xxxvii. 37 Or Phebus dirknes him Goddis Sone reveild. **1590** SPENSER *F.Q.* III. ii. 48 Earely, the morrow next, before that day His joyous face did to the world revele. **1605** ROWLANDS *Hell's Broke Loose* (Hunterian Cl.) 26 Our inward loue, let outward deedes reueale it. **1697** DRYDEN *Virg. Georg.* II. 432 When the Golden Spring reveals the Year. **1738** GRAY *Propertius* ii. 9 If the thin Coan Web her shape reveal. **1781** J. LOGAN in *Scott. Paraph.* ix. 4 Nature's universal frame its Maker's power reveals. **1832** TENNYSON *Œnone* 12 The gorges, opening wide apart, reveal Troas and Ilion's column'd citadel. **1866** G. MACDONALD *Ann. Q. Neighb.* i, An infinite love, revealed in the mystery of man. **1876** MOZLEY *Univ. Serm.* 64 The evening light reveals the real landscape, though it may reveal it dimly.

b. *refl.*

1494 in *Househ. Ord.* (1790) 116 The chamberlaine to see that he reveale himselfe at all tymes. **1591** SHAKS. *1 Hen. VI*, I. ii. 83 In compleat Glory shee reueal'd her selfe. **1603** —— *Meas. for M.* v. i. 28 Here is Lord Angelo.., Reueele your selfe to him. **1833** TENNYSON *Eleanore* 2 Thy dark eyes open'd not, Nor first reveal'd themselves to English air. **1860** TYNDALL *Glac.* I. ii. 13 A position where the mechanical conditions of the glacier revealed themselves. **1894** A. MORRISON *M. Hewitt, Investigator* iv, I'll tell you exactly how the thing revealed itself to me.

reveala'bility. *rare*$^{-0}$. [See next and -ITY.] 'The possibility or capacity of being revealed; revealableness.'

1864 WEBSTER (citing Coleridge; cf. REVELABILITY).

re'vealable, *a.* [f. REVEAL *v.* + -ABLE.] Capable of being revealed.

1672 PENN *Spir. Truth Vind.* 29 The Blessed Things which God hath prepared..are not revealable, but by his Spirit. **1716** M. DAVIES *Athen. Brit.* II. 75 Reverend Paradoxes and reverable (tho' not revealable to the Prophane) Errors of some true Sons of the Church. **1807** COLERIDGE *To a Gentleman* 8 Thou hast dared to tell What may be told, to the understanding mind Revealable. **1870** LOWELL *Among my Bks.* Ser. I. (1873) 347 That Truth which is..the more loved because never wholly revealable.

Hence **re'vealableness** (Webster, 1847).

revealed (rɪ'viːld), *ppl. a.* [f. REVEAL *v.*]

1. Brought to light, disclosed; *esp.* made known by divine or supernatural agency.

1562 WINȜET *Last Blast* Wks. (S.T.S.) I. 44 The reuelit wyl of God. **1594** HOOKER *Eccl. Pol.* III. viii. §13 Scripture teacheth all supernatural revealed truth. **1643** MILTON *Divorce* II. iii, Tis wonderd how there can be in God a secret, and a reveal'd will. **1736** BUTLER *Anal.* II. i, The whole moral law is as much matter of revealed command, as positive institutions are. **1828** P. CUNNINGHAM *N.S. Wales* (ed. 3) II. 306 From revealed specimens of the conversation on these occasions, it would appear [etc.]. **1894** MEREDITH *Ld. Ormont* xxx, Her brother Rowsley's revealed human appearance of the stricken man.

b. ***revealed religion*** (cf. NATURAL *a.* 4b).

1719 WELWOOD *Pref. to Rowe's Lucan* p. xlvii, He exprest on all occasions his full persuasion of the truth of Reveal'd Religion. **1755** YOUNG *Centaur* i. Wks. 1757 IV. 122 Therefore revealed religion rejected, proves natural religion disobeyed. **1859** MILL *Liberty* i. 19 Every one who believes in a revealed religion. **1865** *Ecclesiastic* Aug. 345 Natural and revealed religion bear mutual witness one to the other.

2. *Ent.* Not hidden by other parts.

1826 KIRBY & SP. *Entomol.* IV. 330 *Revealed*.., when it [*sc.* the alitrunk] is not so covered, but is equally conspicuous with the Prothorax, or even more so.

Hence **re'vealedly** *adv. rare.*

1624 BP. MOUNTAGU *Immed. Addr.* 139 Here wee beholde as in a glasse: There..our Beholding is reuealedly, and Face to face. *a* **1641** —— *Acts & Mon.* (1642) 222 His dispensation of grace, which..he more and more revealedly did discover.

re'vealer. [f. REVEAL *v.* + -ER[1].] One who or that which reveals.

1545 JOYE *Exp. Dan.* iii. 40b, The lorde of all kingis and reueler of all secretes. **1580** LUPTON *Sivqila* 137 The one halfe..shal be to the Kings use, and the other halfe to the use of the revealer. **1635** A. STAFFORD *Fem. Glory* 103 Having no other revealer, nor prompter than the holy Spirit. *a* **1660** HAMMOND *Serm.* (1850) 534 How..this truth may be deduced, I leave to the revealer of revelations. **1728** MORGAN *Algiers* II. iv. 276, I must not forget taking Notice of the Revealer of this notable Conspiracy. **1807** G. CHALMERS *Caledonia* I. III. vii. 400 Time, the great revealer of secrets, has at last disclosed the manner of his death. **1841** EMERSON *Ess.*, *Over-Soul*, The soul is the perceiver and revealer of truth. **1875** JOWETT *Plato* (ed. 2) I. 34 Set up the true prophet in their place as the revealer of the future.

re'vealing, *vbl. sb.* [f. REVEAL *v.*] The action of the verb, in various senses; revelation.

1375 BARBOUR *Bruce* x. 738 Throw reveling Of him that knawis and wat all thing. *c* **1450** *Mirour Saluacioun* (Roxb.) 154 Thilk Frere..hadde revelings dyvine and consolacionnes. **1561** T. NORTON *Calvin's Inst.* II. viii. §29 For whiche cause the faithful did..maruelously esteme the reuelyng of the Sabbat. **1573** J. BRIDGES *Supremacy Chr. Princes* 1084 The Prophete..had especiall warrant by Gods especial reuealing, so to bidde them. *a* **1649** DRUMM. OF HAWTH. *Hist. Jas. V*, Wks. (1711) 108 The Revealing of which to the World was a Secret..derogatory to the pontificial State. **1830** TENNYSON *Madeline* ii, Revealings deep and clear are thine Of wealthy smiles. **1875** J. P. HOPPS *Princ. Relig.* xviii. 58 These also take their place among the revealings of God to man.

re'vealing, *ppl. a.* [-ING[2].] That reveals.

1593 SHAKS. *Lucr.* clvi, Revealing day through every cranny spies. **1927** BELLOC *Hist. Eng.* II. 210 The second rebellion against Henry II was a longer and much more revealing thing than the first.

Hence **re'vealingly** *adv.*

1868 *N. Brit. Rev.* XLIX. 366 There are descriptive patches or belts that lie revealingly on objects like [etc.]. **1973** *Nature* 30 Mar. 306/2 There is the case of Graham Young..who, having been 'cured' at Broadmoor..of enjoying poisoning people, had an unfortunate relapse and poisoned several more. Revealingly, his last bout of evil.. was not attributed to mental disease: this time he was sent to prison.

re'vealment. [f. REVEAL *v.* + -MENT.] The act of revealing; disclosure, revelation.

1584 *Mirr. Mag.* Epist., A Physition.. vpon Reuealement may applie a curable Medicine for a hidden Disease. **1664** H. MORE *Exp. 7 Epist.* Pref. a viij, As regardfull of due Concealment as of certainty of Revealment. **1681** —— *Exp. Dan.* App. II. 287 That Divine.. Artifice of Concealment, as well as Revealment. **1750** RICHARDSON *Corr.* (1804) IV. 356 It is yet.. in your power to oblige me greatly, by a thorough revealment. **1807** JEFFERSON *Writ.* (1830) IV. 73 We expect no revealments from the accomplices of the chief offender. **1846** BROWNING *Luria* v, All, their revealment taught us so long since That [etc.]. **1878** MISS BRADDON *Open Verdict* xxx, Mrs. Dulcimer forced him to a revealment of his feelings.

re'vegetate (ri:-), *v.* [RE- 5 a.]

1. *intr.* To vegetate or grow again.

1769 *Phil. Trans.* LIX. 33 Whole tracts of them may be destroyed without their revegetating.

2. *trans.* To produce the growth of new vegetation on (disturbed or barren ground). Of a plant: to colonize anew.

1955 *Sci. Amer.* June 50/3 Revegetating the area with plants more drought-resistant than the native flora and fertilizing the land are two of the most helpful measures. **1963** D. W. & E. E. HUMPHRIES tr. *Termier's Erosion & Sedimentation* i. 20 The tropical jungles spread out north and south, revegetating the sands and 'fixing' the dunes. **1971** *Nature* 4 June 287/1 Practical techniques were developed for revegetating bare, industrially derelict land near Swansea. **1975** *Sci. Amer.* Dec. 27/2 Halogeton, a toxic weed, is among the first and most tenacious plants to revegetate disturbed desert land. **1976** *Nature* 26 Aug. 733/2 All their contracts with coal suppliers contain a clause requiring that strip mined lands be restored and revegetated.

Hence **re'vegetated** *ppl. a.*, **re'vegetating** *ppl. a.*; **revege'tation.**

1804 *Something Odd* II. 124 When revegetating Nature invites us to enjoy her endless charms. **1844** H. STEPHENS *Bk. Farm* III. 960 The drill-harrows or grubber will be found necessary to prevent a re-vegetation of the weeds. **1974** *Nature* 15 Feb. 428/1 Revegetation of toxic spoil from industrial processes. **1974** *Environmental Conservation* I. 60/1 Natural revegetation proceeds very slowly in arctic areas. **1976** *Billings* (Montana) *Gaz.* 2 July, Hodder's research involves comparing cattle weight gains on revegetated spoils that have been heavily fertilized to gains on unfertilized native range.

re'vehent, *a.* [ad. pres. pple. of L. *revehĕre*: cf. DEVEHENT *a.*] Conveying back.

1876 SHARPEY *Quain's Elem. Anat.* II. 163 The blood gets into the commencing branches of the veins or revehent vessels.

†re'veil, *v. Obs.* Forms: 5 reuaile, reueyle, 5–6 reueile, 7 reveil. [var. of REVEAL *v.*, with the second element assimilated to VEIL *v.*] *trans.* To reveal, disclose.

1546 *Supplic. Poore Commons* (E.E.T.S.) 69 God shall reuaile vnto your Highnes moch more of theyr subtyll imaginations. **1555** HARPSFIELD in *Bonner's Homilies* 45 Fleshe and bloude hath not this reueiled and opened vnto the. **1588** GREENE *Pandosto* Wks. (Grosart) IV. 281 Feare of his Fathers displeasure [would not let him] reueyle it to any secrete friend. **1652** GATAKER *Antinom.* 9 It is plainly.. reveiled. *Ibid.* 36 His old.. way of reveiling himself. **1678** CUDWORTH *Intell. Syst.* I. iv. §16. 292 This Philosophy of Pythagoras [was] first divinely delivered or reveiled by the gods.

reveil, réveil, variants of next. *rare.*

Smart and some later Dicts. recognize the pronunciation (rɪ'veɪl) or (rɪ'vɛl) for *reveille*.

1830 MANGAN *Poems* (1903) 284 The reveil-call which on Fame's deep drum Time's Hands beat for some lost hero of the Past. **1884** J. COLBORNE *Hicks Pasha* 31 Next morning at five the *réveil* sounded.

reveille (rɪ'vælɪ, rɪ'veɪljeɪ). Forms: α. 7 (9) revelly, revalley, 8 revallie, 8–9 revally. β. 7– reveille, 9 réveille, réveillé, reveillé, 9 re-, réveillée. [ad. F. *réveillez*, imper. pl. of *réveiller* to awaken, f. *re-* RE- + *veiller*:—L. *vigilāre* to keep watch.]

a. A morning signal given to soldiers, usually by beat of drum or by bugle, to waken them and notify that it is time to rise.

The usual military pronunciation is (rɪ'vælɪ); in the U.S. service (rɛvə'li:).

α. **1644** in T. C. Hine *Nottingham* (1876) App., After the houre of nyne of the clock at night,.. untill the Revelly hath beaten the next morninge. **1696** R. H. *Sch. Recreat.* 59 Revalley, is to let them know when it is time to rise in the Morning, and attend on their Duty. **1755** *Mem. Capt. P. Drake* I. xii. 87 Soon after hearing the Drums beat the Revallie, all began to rouse their Spirits. **1778** TICKELL & SHERIDAN *Camp* I. i, He'll mow you down a regiment of beards in the beating a revally. **1892** KIPLING *Barrack-r. Ballads* 66 At half-past five's Revelly, an' our tents they down must come. **1899** NEIL MUNRO *Gilian* 78 It was sweet to hear the drums beat revally under the vines.

β. **1651** DAVENANT *Gondibert* II. iii. 33 Now the Drums, the Camp's low Thunder, make War's thick united Noise from every Guard; Though they Reveillees scorn, whom grief does wake. **1700** DRYDEN *Secular Masque* 63 Sound a Reveille, Sound, Sound, The Warrior God is come. **1769** FALCONER *Dict. Marine* (1780) X x 2 *Battre à Diane*, to beat a reveille on the drum, as at day-break. **1810** SCOTT *Lady of L.* I. xxxii, While our slumbrous spells assail ye, Dream not .. Bugles here shall sound reveillé. **1816** —— *Old Mort.* xxxv, The hoarse voice of men, and the wild sound of the trumpets blowing the réveillé. **1842** LONGF. in *Life* (1891) I. 434 A bivouac.. and the reveillé are things to make an impression upon one for evermore. **1896** BADEN-POWELL *Matabele Campaign* ix, That night reveillé was whispered at 11.30. It was a curious time for reveillé, and utterly puzzled our cook.

attrib. and *Comb.* **1775** *Amer. Archives* Ser. IV. (1846) IV. 224 The enemy.., this morning, after reveille beating, crossed the bridge. **1894** *Outing* XXIV. 313/1 Not much attention on the part of some companies seemed to be paid to reveille roll-call.

b. *transf.* and *fig.*

1651 DAVENANT *Gondibert* III. v. 1 So soon Love beats Revellies in her Breast. **1818** KIRBY & SP. *Entomol.* II. xxiv. 384 They sometimes beat such a reveille, that only good sleepers can rest for them. **1850** TENNYSON *In Mem.* lxviii, All the bugle breezes blew Reveillée to the breaking morn. **1862** CHRISTINA ROSSETTI *Goblin Market* (1884) 25 'Up,.. Up,' called the watchman lark In his clear réveillée.

So ‖**re'veillez.** *rare.*

17.. *Comforts of Wooing* 62 in *Brand's Pop. Antiq.* (1813) II. 97 Next morning, come the Fidlers, and scrape him a wicked *Reveillez*. **1840** J. B. FRASER *Koordistan* I. viii. 231 This is followed by the lively beat of the 'reveillez' from the Sepoys' quarter.

†reveille-matin. *Obs. rare*$^{-1}$. [F. *réveille-matin* alarm-clock, etc.] An awakening.

a **1617** SIR D. CARLETON in *Brand's Pop. Antiq.* (1813) II. 97 They were lodged in the Councill Chamber, where the King gave them a Reveille Matin before they were up.

‖**réveillon** (revɛjɔ̃). [Fr.] A night-time feast or celebration, orig. one that took place after midnight on Christmas morning. Also *attrib.*

1803 E. WYNNE *Diary* 25 Dec. (1940) III. iv. 98 Xmas Day. Sunday. We had midnight Prayers and a Reveillon. **1894** G. DU MAURIER *Trilby* I. III. 240 The whole Quartier seemed alive with the *réveillon*. **1932** H. NICOLSON *Diary* 1 Jan. (1966) 104 He had spent *réveillon* at the Fabre-Luces and had been kept up.. till 8 am. **1965** M. WALLENSTEIN *Merlin's Forest* xx. 205 A man was hanging out a large decorated menu for the Christmas Eve *réveillon*. **1967** C. DURRELL tr. *Oliver's French at Table* ii. 69 Pope Julius I decreed that Christmas should be celebrated on 25 December, this providing an excuse for what soon became the traditional *réveillon*—an enormous midnight feast. **1967** *Guardian* 30 Dec. 7/8 French housewives.. on Christmas Eve were hosts or guests at the traditional Réveillon supper. On New Year's Eve there is a Réveillon supper all over again. **1971** *Ibid.* 9 Dec. 11/5 A few loose segments [of garlic] to perfume the new year *Reveillon* soup. **1976** *Newmarket Jrnl.* 16 Dec., Called Reveillon, their elaborate suppers and festivities often continue until the early hours.

reveir, obs. form of RIVER.

revel ('rɛvəl), *sb.*[1] Forms: 4–7 reuel (4 -ele, 5 -eyl, 6 -il), 5–7 reuell (5 -elle, -yll), revell(e, 6 -yll, ravelle), 4– revel. [a. OF. *revel* (*reviel*, *rivel*, etc.), verbal sb. f. *reveler*: see REVEL *v.*[1] The development of sense in OF. is 'rebellion, tumult, disturbance, noisy mirth'.]

1. Riotous or noisy mirth or merry-making.

13.. *Gaw. & Gr. Knt.* 538 He made a fare on þat fest.. With much reuel & ryche of þe rounde table. **1387** TREVISA *Higden* (Rolls) III. 273 þis.. Assuerus.. made greet revel and feste to his princes. *c* **1425** *Thomas of Erceld.* 268 Reuelle amanges þame was full ryfe... There was revelle, gamene, and playe. *c* **1450** *Merlin* 448 Ladyes and maydenes carolinge and daunsinge, and the moste reuell and disport that myght be made. **1509** BARCLAY *Shyp of Folys* (1570) 156 Eate we and drinke we.. With reuell without measure as long as we may. **1541** HYRDE tr. *Vives' Instr. Chr. Wom.* III. i. 127 b, Whan we couple.. vnto sober vertue, reuell and dronkennes. **1621** S. WARD *Happiness Pract.* (1627) 44 Lest if wee play reuell and ryot by it, the Candlesticke be remoued, and the light put out. **1812** BYRON *Ch. Har.* I. ii, He was.. Sore given to revel and ungodly glee. **1855** TENNYSON *Maud* I. XXII. v, The brief night goes In babble and revel and wine. **1887** HALL CAINE *Son Hagar* II. xvi, That night there was high revel at the Ghyll.

2. An occasion or course of merry-making or noisy festivity, with dancing, games, masking, acting, or other forms of lively entertainment.

c **1350** *Will. Palerne* 1953 And alle merþe þat any man euer miȝt deuise; and alle real reueles. **1377** LANGL. *P. Pl.* B. XIII. 442 For-thi I rede ȝou riche reueles whan ȝe maketh For to solace ȝoure soules suche ministrales to haue. **1483** CAXTON *G. de la Tour* k vj b, In those dayes.. were holden grete festes and reueyls. **1540** J. HEYWOOD *Four P.P.* D j, Now marke for here beginneth the reuel. **1572** in Feuillerat *Revels Q. Eliz.* (1908) 179 [Two] men going to the Coorte to sett up frames for the seide Revells. **1582** STANYHURST *Æneis* I. (Arb.) 21 These vnrulye reuels,.. thee sea king Neptun awaked. **1633** FORD *Broken H.* IV. iii, A wedding without revels is not seemly. **1667** MILTON *P.L.* I. 782 Faerie Elves, Whose midnight Revels.. some belated Peasant sees. **1697** DRYDEN *Virg. Past.* v. 46 Daphnis did rites to Bacchus first ordain; And holy Revels for his reeling Train. **1725** POPE *Odyss.* XII. 4 Here the gay Morn.. keeps her revels with the dancing Hours. **1820** W. IRVING *Sketch Bk.* I. 208 Life was to her a perpetual revel; it was one long lord mayor's day. **1846** KEBLE *Lyra Innoc.* (1873) 69 Making thy rites a revel and a show. **1871** B. TAYLOR *Faust* (1875) I. xxi. 187 Wilt thou, to introduce us to the revel, Assume the part of wizard or of devil?

transf. **1892** *Daily News* 30 April 2/2 It is indeed a revel of colour, almost daring in its richness and brilliancy.

b. *spec.* A parish festival or feast; a fair.

App. limited to the south-western counties.

1478 *Church-w. Accts., Croscombe* (Somerset Rec. Soc.) 7 Of the Kyng's revell of thes yere past xiii^{s}. j^{d}. wherof was stole away ij^{s}. vij^{d}. **1504–5** *Ibid.* 27 Presentyd in of the King revyll. *c* **1550** *Disc. Com.-weal Eng.* (1893) 16 Enterludes, maye games, wakes, ravelles, wagers at shooting. **1613–16** [see 4]. **1756** *Gentl. Mag.* XXVI. 433 Neither trade, nor agriculture, nor religion would sustain any loss, by thus employing.. three [days] more at every parish-wake, feast, or revel. **1806** BOWLES *Banwell Hill* III. 276 William passed along, And careless hummed a desultory song, Bound to St. Ives' revel. **1899** BARING-GOULD *Vicar of Morwenstow* vii, It was on the parish feast-day or 'revel' as the inhabitants of the parish called it.

c. ***Master of the Revels***, a person (permanently or temporarily) appointed to organize or lead revels, esp. in the Royal Household or the Inns of Court. Also ***the Revels***, a former office in the Royal Household; ***Children of the Revels*** (quot. 1664). Now only *Hist.*

1530 PALSGR. 243/2 Mayster of the revelles, *factevr*. **1558** in Feuillerat *Revels Q. Eliz.* (1908) 5 The Revelles togethers with the Tentes and Toylles was made an office. **1664** FLECKNOE *Love's Kingd., Eng. Stage* G v, The Theatre.. of the Children of the Chappel [was] converted to the use of the Children of the Revels. **1677** *Lond. Gaz.* No. 1170/4 Charles Killegrew Esq.; now Master of the Revels. **1706** PHILLIPS (ed. Kersey), *Master of the Revels*,.. who in the Inns of Court is some young Student chosen for that Purpose. **1727–38** CHAMBERS *Cycl.* s.v., The officer who has the direction.. of the revels at court, is called the master of the revels. **1822** W. IRVING *Braceb. Hall* xxvi. 227 Slingsby,.. who is not merely lord of misrule in his school, but master of the revels to the village. **1841** *Penny Cycl.* XIX. 429/2 In the royal household.. the master of the revels was a permanent officer. **1880** *Encycl. Brit.* XIII. 89/1 A master of the revels was appointed, commonly designated Lord of Misrule.

†3. Riot, disturbance. *Obs. rare.*

1461 *Paston Lett.* II. 50 Ther is gret noyse of this revell that was don in Suffolk be Yelverton and Jeney. **1465** *Ibid.* 201 Ric. Calle hath told you what revell ther was by the Bayllyf of Coshay and his felaw uppon your men that shold have servyd the replevyn.

4. *attrib.*, as ***revel-coil, -cup, dash, day, -gaiety, master, night, rex, -shout.*** Also REVEL-ROUT.

1630 J. TAYLOR (Water-P.) *Wks.* (Nares), To dance, sing, sport, and to keepe *revell-coyles. **1653** BP. WEBBE *Pract. Quiet.* 210 He maketh all unquiet persons to keep revell quoile, like the two Gergasens. **1873** SYMONDS *Gk. Poets* xi. 350 Withered crowns and *revel-cups are laid upon the shrine of Lais. *c* **1590** GREENE *Fr. Bacon* vii, Out with your blades,.. Have a flurt and a crash, now play *reuell dash. **1613–16** W. BROWNE *Brit. Past.* I. ii, Those buskins hee had got.. For dancing best vpon the *Reuell day. **1712** STEELE *Spect.* No. 358 ¶2 The best Man that I know of for heightening the *Revel-Gayety of a Company. **1839** *Penny Cycl.* XIV. 151/1 This Lord of Misrule, or *revel-master, was sometimes termed a Christmas prince. **1828** SCOTT *F.M. Perth* xvi, 'I have sworn,' said Henry, 'that this shall be no *revel night in my house.' **1566** STUDLEY *Agamemnon* v. i, Within a *reuell rexe is kept, as sore as euer was. **1576** NEWTON *Lemnie's Complex.* (1633) 89 A Nation and people whose fashion and ordinary custome was to keepe revell rex. **1813** SCOTT *Trierm.* I. xvii, With *revel-shout, and triumph-song.

¶ In the following quotation *reuell* is an error for *releve* = Fr. *relevée* 'rising up'.

a **1450** *Knt. de la Tour* (1868) 109 Atte the day of her Reuell and purificacion, that she shulde be cherisshed, she lete it be do simply withoute gret noye.

†'revel, *sb.*[2] *Sc. Obs. rare.* [Of obscure origin.] 'A severe blow; often applied to a back stroke' (Jam.).

1603 *Philotus* cxxxiv, With my Neiues I sall the nauell; Auld custrone Carle, tak thair a reuell, Than do as I command.

revel, variant of REVEAL *sb.*[2]

revel ('rɛvəl), *v.*[1] Forms: 4–6 reuel(e, 5–7 reuell(e; 4 revelen, 5–7 revell(e, 5– revel. [a. OF. *reveler* to rebel, raise tumult, make noise, etc.:—L. *rebellāre* to REBEL.]

1. *intr.* To make merry; to indulge in pastime or festivities; to take part in a revel.

c **1325** *Song of Yesterday* in *E.E.P.* (1862) 133 þis day as leef we may be liht.. To Reuele with þise buyrdes briht. **1390** GOWER *Conf.* II. 93 Whan that he seth the lusti knyhtes Revelen, wher these wommen are. *c* **1407** LYDG. *Reson & Sens.* 2396 He kan.. Maisterly revel and Daunce, Pipe and floyte lustely. ? *c* **1475** *Sqr. lowe Degre* 1078 In chambre revelyng all the lordes, Unto morne that it was daye. *a* **1548** HALL *Chron., Hen. VIII*, 84 b, These lusty maskers.. daunced and reuelled.. at the Emperors request. **1586** A. DAY *Eng. Secretary* II. (1625) 12 The hall was full of all sorts of people revelling, playing, and occupyed in pastime. **1601** SHAKS. *Jul. C.* II. ii. 116 See, Antony that Reuels long a-nights Is notwithstanding vp. **1667** MILTON *P.L.* IV. 765 Here Love his golden shafts imploies,.. Reigns here and revels. **1719** YOUNG *Revenge* IV. i, It will cut my poor heart thro' and thro' To see those revel on your sacred tomb. **1763** J. BROWN *Poetry & Mus.* 193 The Patrician Ladies, who lately had reveled amidst the Spoils of a subjected World, now begged before their own Doors. **1836** W. IRVING *Astoria* II. 111 Here, then, they revelled and reposed after their hungry and weary travel. **1855** MACAULAY *Hist. Eng.* xii. III. 233 It was suspected that Walker had laid up.. a secret store of food, and was revelling in private.

fig. **1648** J. BEAUMONT *Psyche* IV. cxcii, Loud rung the Ruin, and with boistrous fear Strait revel'd in the Queen's amazed ear. **1699** POMFRET *Love triumphant over Reason*, No strong passion revels in my breast. **1787** BURNS *Tam Samson's Elegy* iii, By their nose the tears will revel, Like ony bead.

b. So ***to revel it.*** Now *arch.*

1580 *2nd & 3rd Blast of Retrait from Plaies* in Hazl. *Eng. Drama* (1869) 119 The people disperse them selues in Theaters, the whole multitude reuel it out at stages. *c* **1590** GREENE *Fr. Bacon* v, Go revel it, Till I and Friar Bacon talk awhile. *a* **1641** BP. MOUNTAGU *Acts & Mon.* (1642) 435 Thus they revell it all night, till morning. **1679** *Obs. on Dutch Wars* 14 A parcel of Brewers, Draymen, and Coblers revell'd it upon the sweat of our Brows. **1772** *B'ham Counterfeit* I. 177 The husband may revel it with his mistress, and the wife with her gallant. **1822** SCOTT *Nigel* xxxvi, Thou must needs leave duty, and decency,.. to revel it gaily with the wild and with the wicked.

c. To enjoy oneself greatly, to take intense pleasure or delight, *in* something.

1754 GRAY *Poesy* 80 Alike.. the pomp of tyrant Pow'r, And coward Vice, that revels in her chains. **1802** PALEY *Nat. Theol.* xix. (1819) 307 Maggots revel in putrefaction. **1821** BYRON *Sardanap.* II. i, To the delighted west, which revels in Its hues of dying glory. **1884** J. GILMOUR *Mongols* 139 The government in carrying out the extreme penalty of the law.. deliberately revels in ingenious cruelty.

2. *trans.* **a.** To spend or waste (time) in revelry.

1628 FORD *Lover's Mel.* IV. iii, An age of pleasures, revell'd out, comes home At last, and ends in sorrow. **1691** DRYDEN *King Arthur* IV. i, The ringlets round her trunk declare her guilty Of many midnight-sabbaths revelled here.

b. To squander (money) in revelling.

1813 SCOTT *Rokeby* I. xvii, If gold he gave, in one wild day I revell'd thrice the sum away.

†**3.** To drive *out* by revelling. *Obs.*

a **1652** BROME *Queenes Exch.* II. i, Let work no more be thought on, We will revel it out Of remembrance.

†**re'vel,** *v.*² *Obs.* Also 7 revell, reuell. [ad. L. *revell-ĕre*, f. *re-* RE- + *vellĕre* to pull.]

1. *trans.* To draw back (humours or blood) from some part of the system.

1597 A. M. tr. *Guillemeau's Fr. Chirurg.* 43/2 It then revelleth and drawethe backe agayne those humors which concurre towardes the Eyes. **1651** BIGGS *New Disp.* 169 ¶232 Unlesse the confluent bloud, avelling the pleura,.. be revelled by a large effusion of bloud. **1684** tr. *Bonet's Merc. Compil.* XIX. 699 There is more of vicious Humours than can be revelled by the Bath toward the Skin. **1752** DALE tr. *Freind's Emmenologia* xi. 121 By opening a vein in the arm, since some part is revelled upwards, the Uterine passages are indeed freed from Pressure.

absol. **1610** BARROUGH *Meth. Physick* v. ix. (1639) 284 In all members of the body, whether you intend to revell, that is, to draw back againe another way [etc.]. **1684** tr. *Bonet's Merc. Compil.* XIX. 809 We must revel, if the humours run whither they should not.

2. To pull out (a weapon) from a wound.

1621 G. SANDYS *Ovid's Met.* XIII. (1626) 265 His brest.. The deadly sword, where it could enter, bor'd. Nor could his strength the fixed steele reuell.

Hence †**re'velling** *ppl. a.*

1684 tr. *Bonet's Merc. Compil.* XI. 379 Vomitories are very profitable, as being a greatly revelling medicine.

revel, variant of RIVEL *v.*, to wrinkle, etc.

revela'bility. *rare*⁻¹. [f. L. *revelāre*: cf. REVEALABLE *a.*] Capability of being revealed.

a **1834** COLERIDGE *Church & State* (1839) 295 The antecedent credibility (may we not add even the revelability?) of the Articles in question.

revelaik: see REFLAC.

reve-land: see REEVE *sb.*¹ 3.

†**revelate,** *v. Obs.* Also as *pa. t.* and *pa. pple.* [ad. ppl. stem of L. *revelāre.*] To reveal.

1514 in Ellis *Orig. Lett.* Ser. I. I. 102 He grauntide that mony tymes he revelate my lords secretts unto the said busshop. *a* **1533** FRITH *Answ. More* (1548) A vij, Abraham .. sawe it in faith and had.. all those thinges.. playnelye Reuelated vnto hym. **1560** ROLLAND *Crt. Venus* III. 420 We haif siclike exempill reuelat, Of Iust Ioseph.

revelation (rɛvəˈleɪʃən). Forms: 4-6 reuelacion (4 -ciun, -cyun, 4-5 -cioun, 5-6 -cyon, 6-7 -tion); 6 reuealation; 4-5 revelacio(u)n (6 -cyon); 5- revelation. [a. OF. *revelaciun, -cion, -tion* (mod.F. *révélation*), = Sp. *revelacion*, It. *re-, rivelazione*, or ad. L. *revēlātiōn-em*, n. of action f. *revēlāre* to REVEAL.]

1. The disclosure or communication of knowledge to man by a divine or supernatural agency.

1303 R. BRUNNE *Handl. Synne* 441 Þys ys clepyd reuelacyun, To shewe byfore what ys to doun. *a* **1340** HAMPOLE *Psalter* lxxxviii. 19 When.. þou spak in visyon, þat is, in pryue reuelacioun til prophetis. **1390** GOWER *Conf.* III. 277 Metodre seith to this matiere, As he be revelacion It hadde upon avision. **1432-50** tr. *Higden* (Rolls) IV. 343 Seynte Iohn Baptiste schewede his hedde by reuelacion to ij. monkes. **1494** FABYAN *Chron.* VI. cxcii. 195 Whan he.. hadde vnderstandynge of the dethe of this Edwynne, by reuelacyon or otherwyse. **1560** DAUS tr. *Sleidane's Comm.* 55 b, He sayd, how he had all thinges shewed him by revelation. **1610** B. JONSON *Alch.* III. ii, A man, by reuelation, That hath a competent knowledge of the truth. **1681-6** J. SCOTT *Chr. Life* (1747) III. 75 The Gift of Revelation.. seems to have been continued no longer than till the whole New Testament was revealed. **1725** WATTS *Logic* II. v. §3 Divine Revelation must be confirmed by some divine and supernatural Appearances. **1794** PALEY *Evid.* (1825) II. 421 The object of revelation is to influence human conduct in this life. **1845** *Encycl. Metrop.* II. 692/1 A distinction has frequently been taken between the law of nature and revelation, to which we cannot assent. **1892** J. TAIT *Mind in Matter* (ed. 3) p. v, On the supposition of an eternal universe, science would necessarily antagonize Revelation.

†**b.** A source of enlightenment. *Obs. rare*⁻¹.

a **1400** *Prymer* (1891) 33 Li3t and reuelacioun of heþen men, & glorie to þi puple israel.

2. An instance of such communication of knowledge to man; something disclosed or made known by divine or supernatural means.

c **1374** CHAUCER *Troylus* v. 366 For prestes of þe temple telle þis, That Dremes bene the reuelaciouns Of Goddes. **1387** TREVISA *Higden* (Rolls) V. 77 Þanne Cristen men.. hadde a revelacioun and a schewynge of God þat þe grettere bones were þe fischeres bones. **1402** *Pol. Poems* (Rolls) II. 100 To seint Joon.. it was bodun also, that privy revelacion to writun in his book. *c* **1491** *Chast. Goddes Chyld.* xx. 53 The prophecye of the deuyll may be knowen fro reuelacyons of god. **1526** *Pilgr. Perf.* (W. de W. 1531) 3 The seruaunt of god Moyses had moost hye reuelacyons & visyons. *a* **1598** ROLLOCK *Passion* (1616) 418 Away with these fantasticke reuelations of the Anabaptistes. **1687** A. LOVELL tr. *Thevenot's Trav.* I. 168 A good Monk, having had in the Night-time a Revelation, that the Body was in the top of the Hill, went [etc.]. **1727** DE FOE *Syst. Magic* I. iii. (1840) 60 Magic.. was not a revelation from hell, made at once to mankind. **1788** GIBBON *Decl. & F.* l. V. 205 Six legislators .. have announced to mankind the six successive revelations of various rites. **1847** EMERSON *Repr. Men, Swedenborg* Wks. (Bohn) I. 332 His revelations destroy their credit by running into detail. **1892** WESTCOTT *Gospel of Life* 86 If anything human lies without the scope of a revelation to man, that revelation cannot be final.

b. A striking disclosure of something previously unknown or not realized.

1862 SPENCER *First Princ.* I. i. §5 (1875) 20 Be there or be there not any other revelation, we have a veritable revelation in Science. **1877** E. R. CONDER *Bas. Faith* vii. 294 The daily life of every one of us is a perpetual revelation of his inner self. **1883** *Cent. Mag.* Oct. 812/1 The exquisite revelation of tree systems which stripped boughs give.

3. ***the Revelation (of St. John)***, the last book of the New Testament; the Apocalypse.

c **1400** *Wycliffite Bible* (1851) IV. 681/1 Heere endith the Apocalips, or Reuelacioun of Seynt Joon the euangelist. **1535** COVERDALE *Rev.* (heading), The summe of the Reuelacion. **1560** DAUS tr. *Sleidane's Comm.* 36 b, They call the Bishop of Rome.. the whore of Babilon, described in the Revelation. *c* **1585** R. BROWNE *Answ. Cartwright* 43 In the Reuelation, the twelue Apostles are called the twelue foundations. *a* **1658** CLEVELAND *Wks.* (1687) 49 What Scriptures call The Revelation, is most mystical. **1685** BAXTER *Paraphr. N.T.* Rev. i. 1 It is eminently call'd the Revelation. **1833** CRUSE tr. *Eusebius* v. viii. 188 These are what he states respecting the Revelation. **1846** TENNYSON in *Mem.* I. 238 There was no more sea, says St. John in Revelation.

b. So in pl., ***the Revelations***.

1656 A. WRIGHT *Five Serm.* 211 Many prophesies are to be fulfilled.., among which that in the Revelations is one. **1680** DODWELL *Two Lett.* (1691) 81 The scandalous, licentious person is like the Dragon in the Revelations. **1755** AMORY *Mem.* (1769) I. 28 As St. John.. expresses it in the third chapter of the Revelations. **1806** SOUTHEY in *Life* (1850) III. 34 Reading the Revelations.. was my favourite part of the Christian religion. *a* **1871** DE MORGAN *Budget Parod.* (1872) 358 For myself,.. I am the first Beast in the Revelations.

c. Pl., without article. Also ***Book of Revelations***.

1691 SIR T. P. BLOUNT *Ess.* 15 The Rhemists in their Annotations upon Revelations the 14th. **1705** HICKERINGILL *Priest-cr.* ii. Wks. 1716 III. 106, I have heard a little Domine or Curate.. tell the People from Revelations. **1818** T. L. PEACOCK *Nightmare Abbey* i, He would condole with Mr. Glowry,.. quote Revelations with Mr. Toobad. **1842** R. I. WILBERFORCE *Rutilius & Lucius* 81 In.. the book of Revelations, they are called the angels of the Churches. **1885** L. OLIPHANT *Haifa* (1887) 313 They profess to find it clearly indicated in Ezekiel, Daniel, Revelations.., that [etc.].

transf. **1898** SIR G. PARKER *Battle of the Strong* x, He saw .. the gracious figure of a girl; and a book of revelations was opened and begun.

d. Applied to other works of a similar kind.

1727-38 CHAMBERS *Cycl.* s.v. *Apocalypse*, Porphyry.. makes mention of the Apocalypses or revelations of Zoroaster, Zostrian,.. &c. **1771** *Encycl. Brit.* I. 546/2 The apocryphal books of the New Testament are.. several spurious gospels, Acts of the Apostles, and Revelations. **1845** KITTO *Cycl. Bibl. Lit.* (1849) II. 628/1 We shall first treat of the apocryphal revelations no longer extant. **1875** *Encycl. Brit.* II. 179/2 A fragment of the apocryphal Revelations of St. Bartholomew.

4. Disclosure of facts made by a person; exposure of something previously disguised or concealed.

?*c* **1475** *Sqr. lowe Degre* 989 He made revelation unto me, That he knewe all your pryvyte. *c* **1531** in *Pol., Rel., & L. Poems* 62 (*title*), The Revelation of Antechriste.

1863 MORRIN (*title*), Record Revelations: a letter.. on the Public Records of Ireland. **1880** MᶜCARTHY *Own Time* lx. IV. 326 This astounding revelation excited alarm and anger.

5. (With capital initial.) A proprietary name for a make of leather goods, used esp. to denote an expanding suitcase.

1923 *Trade Marks Jrnl.* 2 May 876 Revelation... Bags, trunks, suitcases, attaché cases, card cases, cigar and cigarette cases, wallets and similar containers, all being goods made of leather or principally of leather... Jigger, Limited,.. London,..; merchants. **1935** G. GREENE *Basement Room* 115 Grains of rice.. fell on to his Revelation suitcase. **1938** D. DU MAURIER *Rebecca* vi. 60 My Revelation suit-case and the stout hold-all. **1964** J. GARDNER *Liquidator* i. 15 The battered multi-labelled tan Revelation stood packed. **1967** 'F. CLIFFORD' *All Men are Lonely Now* i. iv. 62 He had brought a Revelation from the flat and now he packed the twenty-five folders into it. **1975** *Listener* 9 Jan. 48/1 If one has a folding cycle, one can wrap it up.. in a Revelation suitcase.

6. *attrib.*, as ***revelation-discovery***; †**revelation-day**, the Day of Judgement; †**revelation-gate** (?).

14.. *Rule Syon Monast.* xiii. in *Collect. Topogr.* I. (1834) 31 The keper of the grates, the keper of the revelacion gate, the keper of the cloyster and dortour dores. **1654** WHITLOCK *Zootomia* 270 As I beleive on Revelation Day will appeare in civill History. **1674** BOYLE *Excell. Theol.* I. i. 19 Meer natural reason.. not excited by Revelation-discovery.

Hence **reve'lational** *a.*, of or pertaining to revelation; **reve'lationer.**

1701 BEVERLEY *Apoc. Question* 25, I will now give the Schematic History of the Beast, in the Revelational Prophecy. **1874** SIDGWICK *Meth. Ethics* IV. vi. 467 It seems .. unnecessary to discuss the precise relation of different Revelational Codes to Utilitarianism. **1892** HORTON *Revelation & Bible* vii. 193 The notion of all the writings.. in our Hebrew Canon being a Revelation, or even of a revelational character, is quite arbitrary. **1898** *Blackw. Mag.* Jan. 134/2 Some of the revelationers insinuate distinctly enough that the great Chancellor was no more mistaken in that matter.

revelationism (rɛvəˈleɪʃənɪz(ə)m). [f. REVELATION + -ISM.] The fact or process of making a revelation; advocacy of or belief in revelation.

1949 E. L. MASCALL *Existence & Analogy* vii. 175 The theistic issue is.. immediately raised.. by a.. discussion of .. the extreme 'revelationism' of Kierkegaard, Barth, Brunner and their disciples, and the Thomist *analogia entis.*

reve'lationist. [f. REVELATION + -IST. So F. *révélationiste.*]

1. One who makes a revelation; *esp.* the author of the Apocalypse.

1657 J. WATTS *Vind. Ch. Eng.* 111 The Revelationist joyns them both together saying, He hath made us Kings and Priests. **1865** tr. *Strauss' Life Jesus* I. II. xiii. 92 The Revelationist sees in Jerusalem the central point of the millennial Kingdom of Christ. **1883** J. PARKER *Apost. Life* II. 206 Athens had to climb its Mount Zion foot by foot..; but the Christian revelationist came down upon it from the clouds.

2. One who believes in revelation.

1888 *Athenæum* 3 Mar. 272/2 Matter for contention between evolutionists and revelationists.

reve'lative, *a.* [f. as REVELATE *v.* + -IVE.] Conveying a revelation.

1864 W. RUSSELL *Eccent. Personages* I. 73 There were flashes nevertheless revelative of a high and generous, if erratic disposition. **1887** *Lit. World* 25 Mar. 275/2 The subject is of such a nature, that somehow it becomes more luminous and revelative.

revelator (rɛvəˈleɪtə(r)). [a. late L. *revelātor*. So F. *révélateur*, Sp. and Pg. *revelador*, It. *re-, rivelatore.*]

1. One who or that which makes a revelation; a revealer.

1801 *Massachusetts Spy* 20 May 1/2 They shall have their part (saith John the Revelator) in the lake which burneth. **1840** *Latter-Day Saints Millenial Star* June 28/1 The prophet Daniel and the revelator John. **1849** WHITTIER *Prose Wks.* (1889) I. 142 Nay,.. it should rather.. call to mind what the Revelator hath said of the Holy City. **1875** GRINDON *Life* i. 9 Light is the great and universal Revelator. **1884** HAWEIS *Mus. Life* II. 420 Mendelssohn has been to me .. a revelator of the beautiful. **1980** *Times Lit. Suppl.* 25 July 842/3 Lawrence's rhapsodies on John the Revelator's horses.

2. A name given to the president of the Church of Jesus Christ of Latter-day Saints.

1867 W. H. DIXON *New Amer.* II. ii. 12 The Mormon will put his trust in Joseph, as a natural seer and revelator. **1895** *Denver Times* 5 Mar. 8/2 Joseph Smith, the son of the martyr Joseph Smith, is now prophet, seer and revelator. **1974** *Time* 7 Jan. 59/3 Lee was one of the youngest men ever to become 'prophet, seer, and revelator' of the Mormons.

'revelatory, *a.* [f. as REVELATE *v.* + -ORY.] Serving to reveal; yielding a revelation.

1882 *19th Century* May 711 The poetry of Buddhism.. centres round the noble figure of its founder, instinct with the supernatural, revelatory of the unseen. **1884** J. W. REYNOLDS *Myst. Univ.* vi. 229 The predictions are by a revelatory supernatural power.

revel-bread: see RAVEL BREAD.

†**revelicion,** ? for REVOLUTION, debate.

1465 *Paston Lett.* II. 234 Also another inquerry howe ys patorne of the seyd chyrche; and thys is leke to come in revelicion but yf ther be gret labore mad to morowe be tymys.

revelin, obs. form of RAVELIN.

reveling, variant of RIVELING.

†**revell,** obs. variant of REVEAL *v.*

c **1560** in H. Hall *Eliz. Soc.* (1887) 254 Whar as you say you will kepe ye burde in your breste saiffe and [the] othe that you have sworne never to revelle nor breake. **1616** J. LANE *Contn. Sqr.'s T.* v. 14 Looke what newes the post hathe not to tell, they dare supplie, and to the world revell.

re'vellent, *sb. Med.* Now *rare* or *Obs.* Also 9 -ant. [See next.] A revulsive agent.

1661 LOVELL *Hist. Anim. & Min.* 330 Straightness of the passages of the brain,.. it's cured, if from vapours, by.. repellents, revellents, and discutients. **1754** SMELLIE *Midwifery* II. 35, I thought proper to abstain from revellents. **1822-34** *Good's Study Med.* (ed. 4) I. 38 The erythematic inflammation.. proves often useful as a revellant. *Ibid.* III. 493 Hence the plant has a claim to be considered as an active promoter of absorption as well as a revellent.

re'vellent, *a. rare.* [ad. L. *revellent-, revellens*, pres. pple. of *revellĕre*: see REVEL *v.*²] Drawing or pulling back; revulsive.

1822-34 *Good's Study Med.* (ed. 4) II. 239 Sudden chills on the surface are possessed of a revellent power. **1838** *New Monthly Mag.* LIV. 25 Human associations, like natural bodies, must be held together by attractive forces stronger than the revellent.

reveller (ˈrɛvələ(r)). Also 4 reuelour, 5 reuelowre, 7 -our; 6–7 reuel(l)er; 6 revellar. [f. REVEL *v.*[1] + -ER[1].]

1. One who takes part in a revel, merry-making, or festivity; one who is given to revelling, or leads a disorderly life.

c **1386** CHAUCER *Wife's T.* Prol. 453 My fourthe housbonde was a reuelour, This is to seyn, he hadde a paramour. *c* **1440** *Promp. Parv.* 431/2 Reuelowre. **1530** PALSGR. 262/2 Revellar, *carellevr.* *a* **1548** HALL *Chron., Hen. VIII*, 80 b, These maskers and reuellers them disuisered, shewinge them what persons thei were. **1582** STANYHURST *Æneis* I. (Arb.) 19 Thee father almighty.. Mewed vp theese reuelers. **1611** SHAKS. *Cymb.* I. vi. 61 He is call'd The Britaine Reueller. **1667** MILTON *P.L.* VII. 33 The barbarous dissonance Of Bacchus and his Revellers. **1742** YOUNG *Nt. Th.* IX. 678 For other ends they shine, Than to light revellers from shame to shame. **1797** MRS. RADCLIFFE *Italian* xvii, The jokes and laughter of the revellers. **1843** LYTTON *Last Bar.* I. ii, They were now passing by the stunted trees, under which sat several revellers. **1871** B. TAYLOR *Faust* (1875) I. v. 98 The revellers start and separate.

2. One who delights *in* something.

1860 WARTER *Sea-Board* II. 205 Finding me.. a reveller in the exquisite scenery.

revelling (ˈrɛvəlɪŋ), *vbl. sb.* [f. REVEL *v.*[1] + -ING[1].] Riotous or disorderly merry-making or festivity; a revel; also, great delight or joy.

c **1470** *Gol. & Gaw.* 1343 With reualing and reuay all the oulk hale. **1480** CAXTON *Chron. Eng.* ccxliii. 284 There they casten to slee the kyng in here reuelyng. **1591** SPENSER *M. Hubberd* 694 All that els pertaines to reveling. **1606** DEKKER *7 Deadly Sinnes* Wks. (Grosart) II. 67 What a weeke of Sinfull Reueling hath heere bin. **1665** MANLEY *Grotius' Low-C. Wars* 651 As the Court grew burthensome even in time of Peace by Princely Revellings. **1751** LAVINGTON *Enthus. Meth. & Papists* III. (1754) 75 His Brother Thomas, ..who from following Revellings and Hurlings became a Methodist Preacher. **1826** DISRAELI *Viv. Grey* II. vi, The young scholar in the revelling of his enthusiasm.

attrib. **1594** MARLOWE & NASHE *Dido* 1075, I thinke it was the diuels reuelling night. **1652** COLLINGES *Caveat* (1653) iii. 17 It.. was revelling time, the time for drinking.

ˈrevelling, *ppl. a.* [-ING[2].] That revels.

c **1475** *Lerne or be Lewde* in *Babees Bk.* (1868) 10 [Be not] To Riotous, to Revelyng, ne Rage nat to muche. **1760–72** H. BROOKE *Fool of Qual.* (1809) IV. 42 Youth and health, and a revelling flow of blood and spirits. **1816** HOLLAR *Dance of Death* 2 Holbein.. was given to wine and revelling company. **1892** LD. LYTTON *King Poppy* vii. 53 Thro' its roses, and its revelling leaves.

ˈrevelment. *rare.* [f. REVEL *sb.*[1] + -MENT.] The act of revelling; revelry.

1822 *Blackw. Mag.* XI. 397 His school-boy tricks, his college revelment. **1877** 'H. A. PAGE' *De Quincey* I. v. 90 These dreams.. yield themselves to pure revelment among shadows of the fancy.

ˈrevelous, *a. rare.* Also 6 reuellous. [a. OF. *revelous*, *-eus*, etc.: see REVEL *sb.*[1] and -OUS.] Given to or marked by revelling.

c **1386** CHAUCER *Shipman's T.* 4 A wyf he hadde of excellent beautee And compaignable and reuelous was she. **1562** J. HEYWOOD *Prov. & Epigr.* (1867) 66 By your reuellous rydyng on euery royle. **1804** STRUTHERS *Poor Man's Sabbath* Poet. Wks. 1850 I. 48 A day of revelous dissipation.

ˈrevel-rout. Now *arch.* or *Obs.* [f. REVEL *sb.*[1] + ROUT *sb.*]

1. Uproarious revelry; boisterous merriment. Frequently with vbs. *to keep*, *make*, or *play*.

a **1553** UDALL *Royster D.* I. i, Sometime Dauy Diceplayer ..Keepeth reuell route as long as it will last. **1591** SPENSER *M. Hubberd* 558 Then made they revell route and goodly glee. **1613** PURCHAS *Pilgrimage* IV. xvi. (1614) 430 After all this reuel-rout they demaund againe of the Demoniake, if the God be appeased. **1619** FLETCHER *Mons. Thomas* v. viii, There is a strange thing like a gentlewoman.. Plays revel-rout among us. *a* **1680** CHARNOCK *Sinfulness & Cure of Th.* Wks. (1849) 148 Revel-rout is usual where there is a negligent government. **1742** SHENSTONE *Schoolmistr.* 266 With boist'rous revel rout and wild uproar.

b. An occasion of revelling; a revel.

a **1652** BROME *Queenes Exch.* II. ii, Then who shall daunce The hobby horse at our next Revel rout? **1713** ROWE *Jane Shore* I. i, My Brother.. Is gone to his Account, For this, his Minion, The Revel-rout is done.

2. A crowd or party of revellers. *rare.*

? **1655** *Frier & Boy* II. (Nares), Ay, that we will, we'll break your spell, Reply'd the revel-rout. **1828** SCOTT *F.M. Perth* xvii, 'Our monarch has abdicated sooner than usual this night,' said one of the revel rout.

revelry (ˈrɛvəlrɪ). Also 4, 7 reuelrie, 6 reuellrie. [f. REVEL *sb.* + -RY.] The act of revelling, merry-making; boisterous gaiety or mirth; also *transf.*, joyous song.

14.. *Chaucer's Reeve's T.* 4003 (Lansd. MS.), Oonely for her mirþe and reuelrie Vppon þe wardeine besely þei crie. **1600** SHAKS. *A.Y.L.* v. iv. 183 Meane time, forget this new-falne dignitie, And fall into our Rusticke Reuelrie. **1634** MILTON *Comus* 103 Mean while welcom Joy, and Feast, Midnight shout, and revelry. **1727–46** THOMSON *Summer* 1673 The fairy people throng, In various game, and revelry, to pass The summer-night. **1784** COWPER *Task* II. 79 Revelry, and dance, and show, Suffer a syncope. **1810** SCOTT *Lady of L.* III. ii, The lark sent down her revelry. **1840** DICKENS *Barn. Rudge* xvi, A something in the midst of their revelry and riot that chilled and haunted them. **1875** JOWETT *Plato* (ed. 2) V. 34 There is no drunken revelry in Sparta.

reven, obs. form of RAVEN *sb.*[1]; RIVEN.

†**revenant**, *sb.*[1] *Obs. rare*[−1]. [a. OF. *revenant*, f. as next.] That which is pleasing.

c **1440** *Partonope* 3125 Where he fonde alle such semblaunt As he was wont and alle reuenaunt.

‖**revenant** (rəvənɑ̃), *sb.*[2] (and *a.*) Fem. **revenante.** [F., pres. pple. of *revenir* to return.]

1. One who returns from the dead; a ghost. Also *attrib.*, as *adj.*, and *fig.*

1827 T. J. DIBDIN *Reminisc.* I. vi. 110 She will however frequently make her appearance in this narrative, not as a *revenante*, but prior to the period of her final departure. **1828** SCOTT *F.M. Perth* xxiv, Nor of taking the fatal leap, had my revenant the slightest recollection. **1846** TRENCH *Mirac.* xxix. 411 *note*, Lazarus, as a *revenant*, is often used by the religious romance-writers of the middle ages as a vehicle for their conceptions of the lower world. **1864** LOWELL *Study Windows, Gt. Public Charac.*, The Opposition to which he belonged [was] a helpless *revenant* from the dead and buried Colonial past. **1880** SHORTHOUSE *J. Inglesant* II. xiii. 274 The yellow glamour of the sunset.. clothed in transparent radiance this shadowy revenant from the tomb. **1909** R. BROOKE *Let.* 16 Apr. (1968) 166 It looks a little like Second Childhood, doesn't it? I think it is merely the first, revenant. **1910** J. C. LAWSON *Mod. Greek Folklore & Anc. Greek Relig.* 407 If the devil in possession of the corpse chose to agitate it and drive it out of the grave, the dead demoniac was at once a *revenant*. **1942** 'M. INNES' *Daffodil Affair* III. iii. 91 The papers were full of strange elysiums, cigar-and-whisky empyreans, *revenants* who reported lawn-tennis tournaments on the pavements of paradise. **1955** [see COME-BACK *sb.*[2] 3]. **1958** *Times* 24 Nov. 12/2 Leonard Salzedo has written the concerto for this *revenant* among solo instruments. **1968** T. KINSELLA *Nightwalker* 11 A revenant, A rain-worn, delicate Stone shape. **1969** P. ANDERSON in Cockburn & Blackburn *Student Power* 257 In the closed space of Gombrich's preoccupations, the psychology which was once exorcized is a revenant which necessarily returns to rule. **1970** R. LOWELL *Notebk.* 179 (*title*) Revenants. **1972** *Daily Tel.* (Colour Suppl.) 12 May 61/1 In Eastern Europe ..thousands of villagers still believe in the malignity of the *revenant* dead.

2. One who returns to a place.

1886 MRS. LYNN LINTON *Paston Carew* viii, They would not visit this undesirable revenant with his insolent wealth and discreditable origin. **1895** *Daily News* 31 Aug. 4/7 The undergraduates, our fogey revenant observes, look much as they did.., in outward aspect.

re'vend (riː-), *v.* [RE- 5 a.] To vend or sell again. Hence **re'vender**; **re'vending** *vbl. sb.*

1787 JEFFERSON *Writ.* (1859) II. 186 The residue to be re-vended to other nations. **1832** MARRYAT *N. Forster* iv, There is no chance of getting rid of this latter speculation by re-vending. **1868** BROWNING *Ring & Bk.* I. 52 That palace-step.. Now serves re-venders to display their ware.

†**re'vendicate**, *v. Obs. rare.* [variant of REVINDICATE, after F. *revendiquer*.] *trans.* To claim back; to recover by a formal claim.

1760 tr. *Vattel's Law Nations* III. xiv. §212. 86 Should some subsequent fortunate revolution deliver it from the conqueror's yoke, it can [not] revendicate them. **1796** KIRWAN *Elem. Min.* (ed. 2) I. 435 Many were revendicated to Neptune's antique demesne.

revendi'cation. [a. F. *revendication*: cf. REVINDICATION.] The action of claiming back or recovering by a formal claim.

1760 tr. *Vattel's Law Nations* III. xiv. §209. 84 The endless disputes which would spring from the revendication of them. **1826** KENT *Comm.* v. xxxix. (1858) II. 753 This was also the law of France, until the commercial code.. rejected the old law of revendication. **1864** *Daily Tel.* 18 May, Would there be no danger of another 'revendication' of lost territories? **1865** *Sat. Rev.* 18 Nov. 640 Our ultimatum was to include.. the *revendication* of the frontier line traced in the Viceroy's programme.

†**re'vene**, *v. Obs.*[−0] [ad. L. *revenīre*.] 'To come again, to return' (Blount, 1656).

revenew, obs. form of REVENUE.

revenge (rɪˈvɛndʒ), *sb.* Also 7 revendge. [f. the vb., or a. obs. F. *revenge*, var. of *revenche*, mod. *revanche*: see the vb.]

1. a. The act of doing hurt or harm to another in return for wrong or injury suffered; satisfaction obtained by repayment of injuries.

1566 STUDLEY *Agamemnon, Euribates*, Can not remembraunce of reuenge out of thy breast be reft? **1590** SHAKS. *Mids. N.* II. i. 89 The Windes,.. As in reuenge, haue suck'd vp from the sea Contagious fogges. **1592** KYD *Murther I. Brewen* Wks. (1901) 287 The blood of the iust Abel cried.. for vengeance and reuenge on the murderer. **1609** B. JONSON *Sil. Wom.* IV. v, O reuenge, how sweet art thou! **1690** NORRIS *Beatitudes* (1694) 78 Private Revenge therefore is universally to be condemned, as utterly unlawful. **1721** YOUNG *Revenge* I. i, What is revenge, but courage to call in Our honour's debts? **1771** GOLDSM. *Hist. Eng. in Lett.* IV. 404 A desire of revenge upon the plunderers of his country. **1818** BYRON *Juan* I. cxxiv, Sweet is revenge—especially to women. **1855** TENNYSON *Maud* I. III, Taking revenge too deep for a transient wrong. **1877** C. GEIKIE *Christ* (1879) 431 Plato held that revenge was wrong.

personif. **1588** SHAKS. *Tit. A.* v. ii. 146 *Tam.* Reuenge now goes To lay a complot to betray thy Foes. *Tit.* I know thou doo'st, and sweet reuenge farewell. **1747** COLLINS *Passions*, Revenge impatient rose, He threw his blood-stain'd sword in thunder down. **1821** SHELLEY *Hellas* 729 Revenge and Wrong bring forth their kind, The foul cubs like their parents are.

b. A desire to repay injuries by inflicting hurt in return. †Also in *pl.*

a **1586** SIDNEY *Arcadia* III (1605) 299 Fury in his eyes and reuenge in his heart. **1601** SHAKS. *All's Well* v. iii. 10, I haue forgiuen and forgotten all, Though my reuenges were high bent vpon him. **1667** MILTON *P.L.* I. 35 Th' infernal Serpent.., whose guile Stird up with Envy and Revenge, deceiv'd The Mother of Mankinde. **1690** NORRIS *Beatitudes* (1694) 186 That he be free from Revenge, which is another great Trespasser against Peace. *a* **1703** BURKITT *On N.T.* Luke vi. 29 Revenge is a very troublesome and vexatious passion. **1800** COGAN *Passions* II. ii. (1802) 166 Revenge is an insatiable desire to sacrifice every consideration of pity and humanity to the principle of vindictive justice. **1866** G. MACDONALD *Ann. Q. Neighb.* xxviii. (1878) 490 Revenge had passed away, but revenge is of death and deadly.

2. With possessive pron. a. One's desire to be revenged, or the gratification of this.

a **1547** SURREY *Æneid* II. 118 What if my chaunce were euer to return Victor to Arge, to folowe my reuenge. *a* **1586** SIDNEY *Arcadia* III. (1605) 303 Being resoluted to.. satisfie her owne reuenge in their punishment. **1596** SHAKS. *Merch. V.* III. i. 56 If it will feede nothing else, it will feede my reuenge. **1611** BIBLE *Jer.* xx. 10 We shall preuaile against him, and we shall take our reuenge on him. **1651** HOBBES *Leviath.* II. xxvii. 155 [He] breaks the Law, and protects himselfe for the future, by the terrour of his private revenge. *a* **1771** GRAY *Dante* 15 Hear My Wrongs, and from them judge of my Revenge. **1797** NELSON in Duncan *Life* (1806) 44 The Spaniards threaten us they will come out and take their revenge. **1841** EMERSON *Ess., Prudence* Wks. (Bohn) I. 97 On him who scorned the world, as he said, the scorned world wreaks its revenge. **1887** RIDER HAGGARD *Allan Quatermain* iv, I shook my fist in his face and vowed to have my revenge.

†b. The avenging of a person. *Obs. rare.*

1591 SHAKS. *1 Hen. VI*, I. v. 35 You all consented vnto Salisburies death, For none would strike a stroake in his reuenge. **1633** BP. HALL *Hard Texts, N.T.* 32 His angels.. doe ever attend either to their safeguard or revenge. **1653** *Nissena* 151 Hearing that her beloved Doralbo had run hazard of his life, onely in her revenge.

3. A particular act of repaying injuries or wrongs. †Also const. *of* (= on).

1582 N. LICHEFIELD tr. *Castanheda's Conq. E. Ind.* I. vii. 19 b, He ment to visit the town of Mousambick, and the dwellers therein, with some sufficient reuenge. **1625** BACON *Ess., Revenge*, Publique reuenges are, for the most part, Fortunate... But in priuate Reuenges it is not so. *a* **1653** GOUGE *Comm. Heb.* x. 28 In regard of the violent revenge he sought to do to the professors of the Christian Religion. **1771** GOLDSM. *Hist. Eng. in Lett.* II. 179 Led them up to London, to take a signal revenge of his enemies. **1819** SHELLEY *Cyclops* 702, I have taken A full revenge for your unnatural feast. **1855** MILMAN *Lat. Chr.* IV. vi. II. (1864) 310 The revenge suggested by the malice of Sabinianus was the public destruction of the works of Gregory.

4. Repayment *of* some wrong, injury, etc., by the infliction of hurt or harm.

1615 G. SANDYS *Trav.* (1637) 85 Whose chiefe employment is.. to labour a revenge of wrongs, and a restitution of losses. **1625** BACON *Ess., Of Revenge*, The Reuenge of that wrong, putteth the Law out of Office. **1633** BP. HALL *Hard Texts, N.T.* 163 Which God in his mercy would not take speedy revenge of. **1847** MRS. A. KERR tr. *Ranke's Hist. Servia* 59 It is remarkable that the revenge of murder is unknown.

b. In phr. ***in revenge of***, in return or retaliation for. †Also (in good sense), in recompense for (*obs.*).

1559 Q. ELIZ. in Strype *Ann. Ref.* (1824) I. II. App. viii. 424 Censures of the churche,.. how the popes have abusyd the same, in revenge of their owne private quarrels. **1591** SHAKS. *Two Gent.* I. ii. 110 As in reuenge of thy ingratitude, I throw thy name against the bruzing-stones. **1602** *Palmerin of Eng.* I. l, Palmerin delivered the castle againe to Dramcisiand, who both in revenge of his worthinesse, and memorie of his owne good lucke called it the Invisible Fort of Fortune. **1680** MORDEN *Geogr. Rect., Asiatic Tartary* (1685) 391 Destroyed in revenge of so great a danger. **1819** SHELLEY *Cyclops* 616 Fire will burn his lamp-like eyes In revenge of such a feast!

†5. Punishment; chastisement. *Obs.*

1582 N. T. (Rhem.) *1 Pet.* ii. 14 Rulers as sent by him [God] to the revenge of malefactors. **1592** GREENE *Philomela* Wks. (Grosart) XI. 167 Therfore haue I here produced them in open court, that my dishonours may end in their reuenge. **1633** BP. HALL *Hard Texts, N.T.* 183 That my powerfull and miraculous revenges of thee [Pharaoh] might be declared abroad. **1697** DRYDEN *Virg. Georg.* IV. 660 Nor (if the Fates assist not) canst thou scape The just Revenge of that intended Rape.

6. An opportunity of retaliation or retrieval; *spec.* in cards, chess, etc., a return game, esp. in phr. ***to give one (his) revenge***.

1672 WYCHERLEY *Love in a Wood* v. vi, I am afraid then you would give me my revenge, and make me jealous of you. **1731–8** SWIFT *Polite Conv.* iii, Well, Miss, you'll have a sad Husband, you have such good Luck at Cards... Well, my Lady Smart, I'll give you Revenge whenever you please. **1830** 'EIDRAH TREBOR' *Hoyle Made Familiar* 106 (Ecarte), Bets.. made on condition of revenge are binding only against the winner. **1840** DICKENS *Old C. Shop* xlii, He gives me my revenge, mind,.. he stakes coin against coin. **1850** THACKERAY *Pendennis* xliii, Three hundred [gold napoleons] which I had lost when I had my revenge.

7. *attrib.*, as ***revenge-killing***, ***play***, ***seeker***, ***tragedy***.

1975 O. SELA *Bengali Inheritance* xvii. 147 That war was long over... A revenge killing after all this time was absurd. **1967** Revenge play [see NOIA]. **1980** *Dædalus* Spring 133 He made *Hamlet* out of the tired revenge play tradition. **1961** *Guardian* 25 Nov. 1/4 It was essential.. to 'tie the hands of West German militarists and revenge-seekers'. **1957** N. FRYE *Anat. Crit.* 209 The revenge-tragedy is a simple tragic structure. **1977** S. SCHOENBAUM *William Shakespeare* x. 154

Chettle..is remembered, if at all, for his revenge tragedy of *Hoffman*.

revenge (rɪˈvɛndʒ), *v.* Also 5 *Sc.* **reweng, raweng(e;** 6 **reueng.** [a. obs. F. *revenger* (var. of *revencher*, mod.F. *revancher*), f. *re-* RE- + *venger* to VENGE.]

1. a. *refl.* To avenge oneself; to take revenge *on* or *upon* (rarely *of*) a person *for* (or †*of*) a wrong, injury, insult, etc., received or resented. Also without const.

1375 BARBOUR *Bruce* XVIII. 232 He tuk purpos for to ryde ..in-till Scotland, Till revenge hym, with stalward hand, Of the tray, travaill, and of teyne. **1456** SIR G. HAYE *Law Arms* (S.T.S.) 199 Quhethir gif ane abbot wald slaa ane of his monkis, quhethir aw he to defend him agayn his abbot, and to revenge him. **1530** PALSGR. 690/1 Who so ever doth me a displeasure, I wyll revenge me and I can. **1560** DAUS tr. *Sleidane's Comm.* 275 In the whiche thing verely, I will so revenge me upon you. *a* **1593** MARLOWE *Edw. II*, v. i, Methinks I should revenge me of my wrongs. **1633** BP. HALL *Hard Texts, N.T.* 322 Know my omnipotence, and how easily I can revenge my self. **1672** WYCHERLEY *Love in a Wood* v. vi, You would not revenge yourself upon the parson? **1818** J. C. HOBHOUSE *Hist. Illustr.* (ed. 2) 435 Monti at least revenged himself of Pius for placing him below Metastasio. **1874** STUBBS *Const. Hist.* I. xii. 520 He saw that his true policy was not to revenge himself by executions and confiscations.

b. In *passive.* Chiefly const. *of, on,* or *upon.*

c **1425** WYNTOUN *Cron.* IV. v. 524 Hir awantagis for to se How best scho mycht rawengit be. **1526** *Pilgr. Perf.* (W. de W. 1531) 30 b, Josue commaunded the sonne to stande styll in one place, vnto he were reuenged vpon his ennemyes. **1598** SHAKS. *Merry Wives* II. i. 30 How shall I be reueng'd on him? for reueng'd I will be? **1602** —— *Ham.* III. iii. 75 Now Ile doo't, and so he goes to Heauen, And so am I reueng'd. **1683** W. PENN *Acc.* in Burton *Eng. Emp. Amer.* (1685) 116 In this they are sufficiently revenged on us. **1736** *Gentl. Mag.* VI. 331/2 Failing in that, she was amply revenged upon him in the next Reign. **1773** *Observ. State of Poor* 67 The poor are but too often revenged on their oppressors, by making reprisals on their property. **1820** SCOTT *Let.* in *Lockhart* (1837) IV. xi. 382 She has..a most decided desire to be revenged of him.

2. *trans.* To inflict punishment or exact retribution for (an injury, harm, wrong, etc., done to oneself or another).

1456 SIR G. HAYE *Law Arms* (S.T.S.) 199 He is behaldin to defend him[self], and to revenge his dede at all his powere agayn him that wald sla him. **1470–85** MALORY *Arthur* XX. x. 814 Therfor lete vs shape a remedy for to reuenge their dethes. **1509** HAWES *Past. Pleas.* XI. (Percy Soc.) 44 Who is opprest with a lytell wrong, Revengyng it he may it soone encrease. **1573** L. LLOYD *Marrow of Hist.* (1653) 242 Princes ought not to do wrong, nor yet revenge wrong with wrong. **1639** S. DU VERGER tr. *Camus' Admir. Events* 25 One of the wounded desirous to revenge his hurt [etc.]. *a* **1727** NEWTON *Chronol. Amended* (1728) 246 Her brother.. was slain, and she revenged his death. **1779** JOHNSON *L.P., West* (1787) IV. 201 They revenged the disappointment by calling him a Methodist. **1819** SHELLEY *Cyclops* 704, I should have done ill to have burned down Troy And not revenged the murder of my comrades. **1865** KINGSLEY *Herew.* ix, So Hereward went off to..revenge the wrongs of the Countess Gertrude.

b. Const. *on* or *upon* (a person).

1608 SHAKS. *Per.* III. iii. 24 The gods revenge it upon me and mine, To the end of generation! **1665** MANLEY *Grotius' Low-C. Wars* 275 Supposing..that the Clemency of the Enemy would not break its wonted bounds, and revenge the injury upon the innocent pledges. **1721** SWIFT *Proposal Irish Manuf.* ¶ 18 When my Betters give me a Kick I am apt to revenge it with six upon my Footman. **1840** DICKENS *Old C. Shop* vi, Kit..felt more than half-disposed to revenge the fact upon him.

c. To maintain, uphold, or vindicate (one's cause, etc.) by some act of retribution or punishment.

1526 *Pilgr. Perf.* (W. de W. 1531) 51 As communly passionate persones doth, lyke wood beestes, in reuengynge theyr owne quarelles. **1579** LYLY *Euphues* (Arb.) 169 That his authoritie was so miraculously reuenged with the horrible destruction of Chorah, Dathan, and Abiron. **1592** GREENE *Conny Catch.* 23 The woman wept for anger that she had not some one by that might with iustice reuenge her quarrell. **1697** POTTER *Antiq. Greece* III. v. (1715) 51 Who undertook to revenge the Quarrel of Athens on the Bœotians.

3. To avenge (a person, etc.).

1470–85 MALORY *Arthur* IX. xxxii. 389, I wille be in the feld with you and reuenge you of youre enemyes. **1560** DAUS tr. *Sleidane's Comm.* 90 To the intent he myght revenge his kynsfolkes. **1585** T. WASHINGTON tr. *Nicholay's Voy.* III. ii. 71 b, [He] reuenged and set at libertie his countrie and people. **1799** SHERIDAN *Pizarro* II. i, He may revenge, but cannot save thee. **1841** ELPHINSTONE *Hist. Ind.* I. 593 The brother of the deceased immediately took up arms to revenge him.

†**4.** To punish, to exact punishment for (a wrong, crime, or sin). *Obs.*

1563 *Homilies* II. xvii. i. (1640) 236 What is the cause of penury and scarceness..but a token of Gods yre revenging our wrongs and injuries done one to another. **1579** LYLY *Euphues* (Arb.) 160 If there were..a God that woulde reuenge the oppression of the widdowes and fatherlesse. **1611** BIBLE *Ecclus.* v. 3 The Lord will surely reuenge thy pride. **1697** DRYDEN *Virg. Georg.* III. 709 Revenge the Crime, and take the Traytor's Head. **1713** GARTH *Epil. to Addison's Cato* 8 Would you revenge such rash resolves—you may.

†**b.** To inflict punishment or take revenge upon (a person). *Obs.*

1573 L. LLOYD *Marrow of Hist.* (1653) 237 Dion of Alexandria, who with silence revenged more his foes than with words. **1580** in Ellis *Orig. Lett.* Ser. II. III. 95 She is without a lawful heire..who may either reward her frinds or revenge her enemies. *a* **1653** GOUGE *Comm. Heb.* iv. 13, I will rescue my childe, and revenge the wrong-doer.

5. *absol.* To take vengeance or revenge.

1456 SIR G. HAYE *Law Arms* (S.T.S.) 199 Agayn him selff he will nocht geve him nouthir leve na gude will, to revenge agayn him. **1573** L. LLOYD *Marrow of Hist.* (1653) 240 Princes that revenge hastily, and especially wrongfully. **1598** GRENEWEY *Tacitus, Ann.* I. xi. (1622) 20 Germanicus ..had an armie in readinesse to reuenge vpon the rebels. **1611** BIBLE *Nahum* i. 2 The Lord reuengeth, and is furious. **1633** BP. HALL *Hard Texts, N.T.* 16 In that he..was both grievously displeased with these sinnes and yet loath to revenge.

reˈvengeable, *a.* ? *Obs.* [f. REVENGE *v.*]

†**1.** Revengeful. *Obs.*

1513 DOUGLAS *Æneis* XI. xi. 126 Out of my cais That ilke revengeabill arow thou owt rais. **1552** LATIMER *Serm. & Rem.* (Parker Soc.) 212 [They] have been backbiters and slanderers, wrathful and revengeable, and so continue, without amendment. **1689** SHERLOCK *Death* iii. §7 (1731) 160 The Laws..allow Scope enough to satisfy the most revengeable Man.

2. Worthy or capable of being revenged.

1592 WARNER *Alb. Eng.* VII. xxxvii. (1602) 185 Through blinde bace Loue induring wrong reuengeable in season.

†**reˈvengeance.** *Obs.* Also 5 *Sc.* **rewengeance, -eans(se;** 5–6 **revengeaunce.** [a. obs. F. *revengance, -ence*, etc., f. *revenger* to REVENGE. Cf. VENGEANCE.] Revenge, vengeance. (Common in 16th cent.)

c **1375** *Sc. Leg. Saints* i. (*Peter*) 410, I sall ger myn angelis tak of hym reuengeance. *Ibid.* vii. (*James the less*) 235 Ierusalem..In rewengeans dystroyt wes. *c* **1425** WYNTOUN *Cron.* III. ii. 467 And he prayit to God of mycht That..A rewengeansse he mycht wyn Off al his fais. **1456** SIR G. HAYE *Law Arms* (S.T.S.) 192, I past efterwart and tuke revengeaunce thare apon. **1541** HYRDE tr. *Vives' Instr. Chr. Wom.* II. v. (1592) R ij, He..wil remember injurie longest, and seeke for vengeance most violently, nor can be content with a meane reuengeaunce. **1565** JEWEL *Repl. Harding* (1611) 373 God strooke Iulians Image from Heauen with lightning,..in token of his reuengeance.

revengeful (rɪˈvɛndʒfʊl), *a.* [f. REVENGE *sb.* + -FUL.] Full of revenge; vindictive.

a **1586** SIDNEY *Arcadia* III. (1605) 345 Her words were choakt vp with the rising of her reuengefull heart. **1593** SHAKS. *Rich. II*, IV. i. 50 If I do not, may my hands rot off, And neuer brandish more reuengefull Steele. **1613** —— *Hen. VIII*, I. i. 109 You know his Nature, That he's Reuengefull. **1649** E. REYNOLDS *Hosea* iii. 45 These Lascivious or Revengefull speeches. **1728** MORGAN *Algiers* II. iv. 276 The revengeful Traytor amply discovered who were Ring-Leaders of the Plot. **1771** in *Ann. Reg.* (1772) 196/1, I hope my countrymen will not think me a man of revengeful disposition. **1809–10** COLERIDGE *Friend* (1865) 106 By..the downcast look of dark and revengeful resolve. **1848** MACAULAY *Biog., Atterbury*, No creature is so revengeful as a proud man who has humbled himself in vain. **1884** *Truth* 13 Mar. 377/2 Having borrowed money from a revengeful clerk on a forged bill.

Hence **reˈvengefully** *adv.*

1645 MILTON *Tetrach.* Wks. 1851 IV. 227 Though for the most part maliciously, covetously, rigourously, revengefully. **1670** *Devout Commun.* (1688) 117, I have dealt heinously, thou art revengefully smitten. **1898** *Westm. Gaz.* 15 June 6/3 The notion that the Secret Police and not the Nihilists..are acting revengefully.

reˈvengefulness. [f. prec.] The quality of being revengeful; vindictiveness.

a **1586** SIDNEY *Arcadia* II. (1605) 131 A Tyrant also, not through suspition, greedinesse, or reuengefulnesse. *a* **1639** W. WHATELEY *Prototypes* I. iv. (1640) 42 To polygamie Lamech addeth a notorious revengefullnesse. **1676** CUDWORTH *Serm. 1 John ii.* 3. 56 Too many do still.. harbour malice, Revengefulness and cruel hatred..in your hearts. **1841** SPALDING *Italy & It. Isl.* I. 24 We charge the Italians in the mass, with superstition, ignorance,.. revengefulness, or dishonesty. **1889** *Spectator* 2 Nov., Those creatures which suggest to us a shadowy anticipation of human cruelty and revengefulness.

reˈvengeless, *a.* [f. REVENGE *sb.* + -LESS.]

1. Free from, devoid of, revengefulness or vindictiveness; unrevenging.

1604 T. WRIGHT *Passions* v. §4. 234 After that Saul vnderstood the revengelesse heart of David..hee wept for ioy. **1656** DAVENANT *Siege Rhodes* II. v. iii, If Roxolana thus revengeless proves..It does denote she Rivals can endure. **1796** MORSE *Amer. Geogr.* I. 283 They call themselves the Harmless Christians, Revengeless Christians.

2. Deprived of revenge; unrevenged.

1604 WEBSTER & MARSTON *Malcontent* IV. iii, We, full of heartie teares,..Cannot so lightly over-jumpe his death, As leave his woes revengelesse.

reˈvengement. Now *rare.* [f. REVENGE *v.* + -MENT.] Revenge, retribution; †punishment. (Very common *c* 1540–1650.)

1494 FABYAN *Chron.* IV. lxiii. 43 He ferynge yᵉ Sequell and Reuengement of the same, laft that Countree. **1540** MORYSINE *Vives' Introd. Wysd.* L iv, Leave the revengement of thyne enemyes to me, and I wyll se them payde. **1581** RICH *Farew.* (1846) 153 Neither to take thy life nor thy purse, but to minister revengemente for thy large speeches. **1613–8** DANIEL *Coll. Hist. Eng.* (1626) 13 Ethelred..to increase the summe of reuengement..caused many of the Danique Nobility to be murthered. **1666** BUNYAN *Grace Abound.* §192 A strong and hot desire of revengement upon myself for the abuse I had done.

1891 A. HARTSHORNE *Hanging in Chains* 72 This post-mortem revengement was thought to be a singular great comfort to the relatives.

revenger (rɪˈvɛndʒə(r)). Also 6 *Sc.* **-eoure, -ear.** [f. REVENGE *v.* + -ER¹. Cf. F. *revancheur*, †*revencheur, revangeur.*] One who revenges; an avenger. (Common in 16th and 17th c.)

1513 DOUGLAS *Æneis* IV. xi. 85 Of our levingis sum revengear mot spring. *a* **1540** BARNES *Wks.* (1573) 326 Let not men doubt..that God wyll bee a reuenger of such wrongfull violence. **1611** TOURNEUR *Ath. Trag.* v. ii, Whose gracious motiues made me still forbeare To be mine owne Revenger. **1693** DRYDEN *Juvenal* xiv. (1697) 361 Since Mars, whom we the great Revenger call, Lost his own Helmet. **1748** RICHARDSON *Clarissa* (1811) II. 360, I will face them all; but not as a revenger, if they provoke me not too much. **1865** *Reader* 30 Sept. 365/3 Panderers to the envy or revengers of the fear of deceased greatness. **1899** E. PHILLPOTTS *Human Boy* 193 A terrible revenge which doesn't come off, is pretty sickening for the revenger.

attrib. **1567** TURBERV. *Ovid's Ep.* 160 b, For this rape there arre Revenger Greekes, with wreakfull ships.

reˈvengeress. [f. prec. + -ESS.] A female revenger; an avengeress.

1569 J. SANFORD tr. *Agrippa's Van. Artes* 162 Whiche if it be..the reuengeresse of wicked men, it is a good discipline. **1636** E. DACRES tr. *Machiavel's Disc. Livy* I. 120 Athens,.. remembring the wrong she had receiv'd, and the slavery she had indur'd, became a sharpe revengeresse.

reˈvenging, *vbl. sb.* [f. REVENGE *v.*] The action of the verb, in various senses; vengeance.

1530 PALSGR. 262 Revengyng, *uindication.* **1568** GRAFTON *Chron.* II. 754 Inwardly nothyng but reuenging and confusion was in the kings stomacke. **1611** BIBLE *Ps.* lxxix. 10 By the reuenging of the blood of thy seruants. **1619** HIERON *Wks.* I. 32 Men naturally are inclinable to contention, debate, quarrelling, reuenging.

reˈvenging, *ppl. a.* [-ING².] That revenges; avenging.

1568 *Gismond of Salerne* VI. i, Hell shall send revenging paine to those whome Shame from sinne can not restraine. **1592** GREENE *Philomela* Wks. (Grosart) XI. 131 For doubt of her reuenging husband, and thy protested enemie. **1632** SANDERSON *Serm.* 307 Revenging Justice shall haue nothing to doe with vs. **1658** ROWLAND tr. *Moufet's Theat. Ins.* Ep. Ded., In the tail there is a horny sting full of revenging poyson. **1700** DRYDEN *Meleager & Atalanta* 295 Come, come revenging sisters.

Hence **reˈvengingly** *adv.*

1611 SHAKS. *Cymb.* v. ii. 4, I haue belyed a Lady, The Princesse of this Country; and the ayre on't Reuengingly enfeebles me.

†**reˈvengive,** *a. Obs. rare*⁻¹. [irreg. f. REVENGE *v.* + -IVE.] Revenging, vindictive.

1608 SHAKS. *Lear* II. i. 48 (Qq.), I told him the reuengiue Gods, gainst Paracides did all their thunders bend.

‖**revenons à nos moutons** (rəvnɔ̃z a no mutɔ̃), *phr.* [Fr., lit. 'let us return to our sheep', with allusion to the confused court scene in the Old French *Farce de Maistre Pierre Pathelin* (*c* 1470).] 'Let us return to the subject': an exhortation to cease digressing.

[**1617** J. CHAMBERLAIN *Let.* 22 Feb. in T. Birch *Court & Times James I* (1848) I. 459 But, *pour retourner à nos moutons*, this feasting begins to grow to an excessive rate.] **1822** *Blackw. Mag.* May 610 *North.* On proceeds..Byron..the immoral, irreligious, and unpatriotic tendency of too many of his productions... *Omnes* (sing). Very good song, Very well sung, Jolly companions every one... *North. Revenons a nos moutons!* Childe Harold. **1839** THACKERAY in *Fraser's Mag.* Aug. 228/2 But, *revenons à nos moutons*, let us return to that sweet lamb, Master Thomas. **1850** —— *Pendennis* I. xxxvii. 364 That brings me back to my point—revenons à nos moutons. Yes, begad! revenons à nos moutons. *c* **1909** D. H. LAWRENCE *Collier's Friday Night* (1934) II. 48 *Ernest.* I'll bet the dear boy enjoys that blush. *Beatrice.* Ra-ther! (*Artlessly revenant à son mouton.*) And he'll have the rose and all, to rejoice the cockles of his heart this time. **1926** J. S. HUXLEY *Ess. Pop. Sci.* 27 But *revenons à nos moutons*—to our chromosomes. **1932** A. CHRISTIE *Peril at End House* ii. 37 *Revenons à nos moutons...* I implore you to be serious. **1966** 'H. CARMICHAEL' *Suicide Clause* xi. 124 You didn't come here to listen to irrelevant chatter. So, *revenons à nos moutons.* **1972** *Country Life* 9 Nov. 1243/2 *Revenons à nos moutons.* As soon as I saw my cards, the earlier hand flashed through my mind.

†**reˈvent,** *v.*¹ *Obs.* [RE- 5 a.] To vend again.

1593 NORDEN *Spec. Brit., Cornwall* (1728) 23 Their Pickled Pilchardes..are..from the coaste reuented to their great profit in the Inland Townes.

reˈvent, *v.*² [RE- 5 c.] *trans.* To provide (a cannon) with a new vent.

1864 *Daily Telegr.* 18 May, It was found necessary to revent the shunt gun. **1880** *Times* 27 Dec. 9/2 The whole of the guns may have to be..sent to Woolwich to be re-vented.

‖**reventa** (reˈventa). [Sp., = resale.] (See quot. 1932.)

1932 E. HEMINGWAY *Death in Afternoon* iv. 40 The reventa are ticket brokers who take over all or most of the unsubscribed tickets from the bull ring management and sell them at a twenty per cent increase over their face value. **1960** *Times* 14 Nov. 16/7 If you want the best seats in Spain only the *reventa* has them.

†**revenuable.** *Obs. rare*⁻¹. [f. next + -ABLE.] A possible source of revenue.

1610 W. FOLKINGHAM *Art of Survey* IV. Concl. 88 Rents (instant and improueable), Perquisites, Parallels and other Reuenewables and Respectiues.

revenue (ˈrɛvənjuː). Forms: *α.* 5–6 **reu-, revenu,** 5– **revenue;** *pl.* 5 **-us(e,** 5–6 **-u(e)z, -uys.** *β.* 5 **reu-,**

6 revenow; *pl.* 5 -owis, 6 -os, -ous. γ. 7 reu-, revenew; *pl.* 6 -euos, -ewys, -ewse, 6–7 -ewes. δ. 5–7 reu-, revennew(e; *pl.* 5 -ewis, 6–7 -ewes, 7 revennues, -u's. [a. OF. *revenu* masc. (so in mod.F.) or *revenue* fem., substantive use of the pa. pple. of *revenir* to return.

The stressing *re'venue*, common or usual during the 17th and 18th centuries and until the later 19th century in legal and parliamentary usage, is now obsolescent, if not obsolete. Cf. the following: **1760** LD. HOLLAND in *Life & Lett. Lady S. Lennox* I. 14 He [the king] laid the accent on the first syllable of Allys and Revenues, which is after the Scotch pronunciation. **1828** WALKER s.v., This word seems as nearly balanced between the accent on the first and second syllable as possible. **1840** SMART s.v., Re-ven'-ue is an etymological pronunciation, but extensive custom does not sanction it. **1860** *Cornh. Mag.* Nov. 589 Revenue—which, by the way, every parliamentary speaker insists upon pronouncing 'revénue'.]

†**1.** Return to a place. *Obs. rare.*

1422 tr. *Secreta Secret., Priv. Priv.* 175, I kno well my frende, that he atte no tyme couamt wold breke.., and Sertayne I haue of reuenine [*sic*]. **1532** in Ellis *Orig. Lett.* Ser. I. II. 24 We can do no lesse but now uppon the Kyngs revenue into his owne realme to gyve..thanks to Almighte God..for his prosperous..revenue.

†**2.** The return, yield, or profit *of* any lands, property, or other important source of income. Also *pl.* in the same sense. *Obs.*

sing. **1427** *Rolls of Parlt.* IV. 318/2 Ye Collectours of ye goode and revenue of ye saide Grauntes. **1565** COOPER *Thesaurus* s.v. *Abeo*, Whervpon is the reuenew of my fermes spente or wasted? **1593** SHAKS. *Rich. II*, I. iv. 46 We are inforc'd to farme our royall Realme, The Reuennew whereof shall furnish vs For our affayres in hand. **1604** E. G[RIMSTONE] tr. *D'Acosta's Hist. Indies* III. xvi. 172 The revenue of this Lake is worth three hundred thousand duckets a yeere. **1649** JER. TAYLOR *Gt. Exemp.* II. Disc. ix. 109 One gave all his goods to the poore at once, the other kept all the inheritance and gave the revenue.

pl. **1490** CAXTON *Eneydos* xxi. F iij, I shalle make the myn heyre, to..receyue, after my deth, þe re[ue]nues of all my londe. *c* **1515** *Plumpton Corr.* (Camden) 214 The Kinge.. hath granted it [the lordship of Harwood] to me, with all the revenos & profitts thereof. **1546** in *Eng. Gilds* (1870) 196 How the Revenuez and proffuytes of the possessiones of the same ben vsed. **1600** J. PORY tr. *Leo's Africa* III. 162 He appointeth a new gouernour ouer euery citie, vnto whom all the tributes and reuenues of the same place redound. **1654** WHITLOCK *Zootomia* 404 His fifty Millions a yeare, standing Revenewes of his Crown Land.

fig. **1576** FLEMING *Panopl. Epist.* 124 Which thing if you doe (as I heare) the reuenues of your vertues wilbe inualuable. **1613** PURCHAS *Pilgrimage* I. ii. 5 Neither do I know any thing wherein a man may more improue the reuenues of his learning. **1641** MILTON *Animadv.* Wks. 1851 III. 217 What are they but the black revennues of Purgatorie, the price of abus'd, and murder'd soules.

3. That which comes in to one as a return from property or possessions, esp. of an extensive kind; income from any source (but esp. when large and not directly earned).

1433 *Rolls of Parlt.* IV. 432/2 No yift ne Graunte of lyfelod, Revenue or good, balangyng to youre Hienesse. **1599** SHAKS. *Mids. N.* I. i. 158, I haue a Widdow Aunt, a dowager, Of great reuennew. **1600** J. PORY tr. *Leo's Africa* III. 140 Amongst his other livings, he gathereth out of a certaine mountaine seuen thousand duckats of yeerely reuenue. *a* **1699** TEMPLE (J.), Many offices are of so small revenue, as not to furnish a man with what is sufficient for the support of his life. **1765** BLACKSTONE *Comm.* I. viii. 319 A twelfth branch of royal revenue. **1776** ADAM SMITH *W.N.* I. vi. (1869) I. 55 Wages, profit, and rent, are the three original sources of all revenue. **1845** MCCULLOCH *Taxation* (1852) 40 It is not from capital, therefore, but from revenue, that permanent taxes should be derived. **1878** SIMPSON *Sch. Shaks.* I. 28 The sale of heiresses was a common source of revenue to courtiers in those days.

fig. **1606** SHAKS. *Tr. & Cr.* II. iii. 31 The common curse of mankinde, follie and ignorance, be thine in great reuenew.

b. With possessive pron. or genitive.

1483 CAXTON *Cato* g iiij, Thou oughtest..to holde thyn estate after thy rente and reuenue. **1580** *Reg. Privy Council Scot.* III. 294 His majesteis yeirlie revenew and patrimony of his croun. **1597** HOOKER *Eccl. Pol.* v. lxxiv. §4 As the life of the Cleargie is spent in the seruice of God, so it is sustained with his reuenew. **1634** HEYWOOD *Maidenh. well lost* I. Wks. 1874 IV. 109 Much of his own reuenue He hath expended, all to pay his Souldiers. *a* **1687** PETTY *Pol. Arith.* (1690) 100, I might add that his Majesties Revenue is near tripled. **1728** YOUNG *Love of Fame* I. 21 When men grow great from their revenue spent, And fly from bailiffs into parliament. **1776** ADAM SMITH *W.N.* I. vii. (1869) I. 58 His profit, besides, is his revenue, the proper fund of his subsistence. **1815** ELPHINSTONE *Acc. Caubul* (1842) II. 71 His authority is loosely exercised, and he seems quite indifferent to every thing but his revenue. **1877** FROUDE *Short Stud.* (1883) IV. I. iii. 37 Appeals to Rome were the most lucrative source of the pope's revenue.

fig. **1594** SHAKS. *Rich. III*, III. vii. 158 If..my Path were euen to the Crowne, As the ripe Reuenue and due of Birth. **1819** SHELLEY *Cenci* I. i. 33 The deeds which are the stewards Of their revenue.

c. With *the.* Also *fig.*

1581 PETTIE tr. *Guazzo's Civ. Conv.* II. (1586) 54 That answere gave me occasion, to attribute to the eares, the reuenew, and to the tongue, the expense. **1614** RALEIGH *Hist. World* II. (1634) 286 To whom a third of the revenew was given in recompence. **1648** J. BEAUMONT *Psyche* VII. ccxxxix, Nor shall the arts Of rude and peevish Heresy suppress That Worship which the due Revenue is. *c* **1727** SWIFT, etc. *Thoughts Var. Subj.* Wks. 1751 IV. 288 'Tis like spending this year part of the next year's Revenue. **1776** ADAM SMITH *W.N.* I. vi. (1904) I. 58 The revenue derived from labour is called wages; that derived from stock..is called profit. *a* **1852** MOORE *Periwinkle & Soc.* 7 Every year, the Revenue From their periwinkles larger grew. *a* **1862** BUCKLE *Civiliz.* (1869) III. ii. 101 The clergy knew full well, that if they established their power the revenue would quickly follow.

4. *pl.* The collective items or amounts which constitute an income, *esp.* that of a person having extensive landed possessions, a ruler, city, state, etc. †Also with *a* (quot. 1627).

1433 *Rolls of Parlt.* IV. 478/1 Other profitz or revenuz that longeth to the seid cominaltee. **1494** FABYAN *Chron.* VII. 305 He..caused the partyes to be contented with such reuenuse & profytes as they had resayued. **1546** *Supplic. Poore Commons* (E.E.T.S.) 2 The yearely reuenewse & possessions of this your Highnes realme. **1591** SPENSER *Tears of Muses* 469 Their great revenues all in sumptuous pride They spend. **1627** HAKEWILL *Apol.* (1630) 356 A man of a great revenewes. **1687** DRYDEN *Hind & P.* III. 148 They gape at rich revenues which you hold. **1704** NELSON *Fest. & Fasts* II. iii. (1739) 472 They took Care of the Church's Revenues. **1779** J. MOORE *View Soc. Fr.* (1789) II. lxxii. 204 The revenues of this monarch are much greater than is generally imagined. **1845** MCCULLOCH *Taxation* Introd. (1852) 17 The burden of taxation should be made to press on individuals in proportion to their respective revenues. **1872** YEATS *Techn. Hist. Comm.* 172 The earls of Cornwall derived a considerable part of their revenues from the produce of the tin-mines.

fig. *c* **1600** SHAKS. *Sonn.* cxlii, Those lips of thine, That haue..Robd others beds reuenues of their rents.

5. a. An income; an amount of money regularly accruing to one; †a stipend, salary.

1614 RALEIGH *Hist. World* II. (1634) 418 Though parsimony itselfe be a great revenue, yet [etc.]. **1653** JER. TAYLOR *Serm. for Year* Ded., S. Paul..esteemed it his honour to preach to them without a revenue. **1709** STEELE *Tatler* No. 101 ¶4 After having laid out a Princely Revenue in Works of Charity and Beneficence. **1779** JOHNSON *L.P.*, *Dryden* Wks. II. 315 A revenue in those days not inadequate to the conveniences of life. **1849** MACAULAY *Hist. Eng.* iii. I. 309 A thousand a year was thought a large revenue for a barrister. **1876** L. STEPHEN *Eng. Th. 18th C.* II. 313 Here then in Turgot's language was a 'disposable' revenue, a fund differing in kind from the wealth of other classes.

b. A separate source or item of (private or public) income.

1624 CAPT. SMITH *Virginia* III. iv. 53 The sale of the Stores commodities maintained his estate, as an inheritable revenew. **1626** *Galway Arch.* in *10th Rep. Hist. MSS. Comm.* App. V. 473 The grace of God is the best revennewe of this towne, and his blessings our greatest rentes. **1692** R. L'ESTRANGE *Fables* ccxlvii, If the Woman could have been Contented with Golden Eggs, she might have kept That Revenue on still. **1797** *Encycl. Brit.* (ed. 3) XVI. 145/2 Another maritime revenue..is that of shipwrecks. **1846** MCCULLOCH *Acc. Brit. Empire* (1854) II. 397 The capacity of a tax on a commodity to raise a revenue. **1879** *Encycl. Brit.* IX. 175/1 This form of conveyance also supplied a revenue to the crown. **1885** W. D. CHESTER *Chron. Customs* 98 Revenues are let to those who will bid for them.

6. a. The annual income of a government or state, from all sources, out of which the public expenses are defrayed. (Cf. INLAND *a.* 2.)

1690 LOCKE *Consid. Raising Money* 26 The Revenue now in time of Peace, will yield above all charges 1500000 *l.* per An. **1735** BOLINGBROKE *On Parties* 17 They broke the Army, stinted the Revenue, and threw their Master on the Affections of his People. **1797** in Norton *Topics* (1858) 202 Revenue, having reached its lowest point of depression, will, after next year, begin to rise regularly and uniformly. **1844** H. H. WILSON *Brit. India* III. vi. III. 263 Other changes were made..in the constitution of the Commissioners of revenue and circuit. **1901** *Empire Rev.* I. 369 Obtaining this revenue in such a manner as will conduce towards the.. extension of national industries.

b. The department of the civil service which deals with the collection of the national funds.

1700 MAIDWELL in *Collect.* (O.H.S.) I. 312 All forms or papers with blancs to be used in any branch of his majesties revenue. **1708** SWIFT *Death of Partridge* Wks. 1751 IV. 199, I had some sort of knowledge of him when I was employ'd in the Revenue. **1871** C. DAVIES *Metric Syst.* III. 125 But this calculation could not long suit the revenue. **1879** *Encycl. Brit.* IX. 175/1 The exchequer hunted up and punished offences against the revenue, and through both agencies assisted the revenue.

c. *U.S.* A revenue officer.

1883 ZEIGLER & GROSSCUP *Heart of Alleghanies* 257 My pards mout tak' ye fer a revenoo, an' let a hole thro' ye. **1901** *Munsey's Mag.* XXV. 613/1 Once the 'revenues' had dragged him from his lair,..and he had been sent to State's prison for two years.

7. *attrib.* and *Comb.* (sense 6). **a.** Attributive, as ***revenue account, act, agent, board, boat, cruiser, cutter, department, expenditure, law, man, officer, police, stamp, tariff, vessel.***

1869 *Bradshaw's Railway Manual* XXI. 392 Confusion between capital and *revenue accounts..has led to the undue increase of capital. **1970** R. W. WALLIS *Accounting* x. 142 If the local authority charges similar fares and has similar expenses to those of the private undertaking, it too will make a profit or 'revenue account surplus'. *Ibid.* 147 The public authority 'provision for debt redemption' or 'loans redeemed' accounts tend to be equivalent to the 'depreciation provision' account..provided the revenue account is charged with an amount approximating to the amount of depreciation of the asset concerned. **1791** G. WASHINGTON *Diary* 4 June (1925) IV. 196 The discontents which it was supposed the last *Revenue Act..would create subside as fast as the law is explained. **1816** SCOTT *Antiq.* xi, Revenue acts of parliament. **1864** *Statutes at Large U.S.A.* XIII. 224 *Revenue agents..[shall] aid in the prevention, detection, and punishment of frauds upon the internal revenue. **1943** *Chicago Daily News* 24 Dec. 6/1 We would hate to be a revenue agent with that gal up in the cove. **1846** MCCULLOCH *Brit. Emp.* (1854) II. 408 The number of commissioners in the different *revenue boards was.. greater. **1846** *Knickerbocker* XXVIII. 244 The *revenue-boat from the *guardacosta* came on board before our sails were furled. **1830** MARRYAT *King's Own* xiii, I trust she's a *revenue cruiser. **1790** *Deb. Congress U.S.* (1834) 1st Congress 2nd Sess., App. 2277 The officers of the *revenue cutters hereinafter mentioned. **1801** NELSON in Duncan *Life* (1806) 195 The..revenue cutters kept under sail. **1790** *Deb. Congress U.S.* 2 July (1834) 1003, I likewise nominate the following persons to fill offices in the *Revenue Department of the United States. **1964** S. BRITTAN *Treasury under Tories* iv. 101 The Inland Revenue and Customs and Excise (jointly known as 'the Revenue Departments'). **1961** WEBSTER, *Revenue expenditure. **1968** JOHANNSEN & ROBERTSON *Managem. Gloss.* 116 *Revenue expenditure*, expenditures of cash which are undertaken to maintain asset values (e.g. repairs) or to obtain current revenue (e.g. raw material purchases, factory payroll). **1970** R. W. WALLIS *Accounting* x. 140 [In central government accounting] the distinction between capital and revenue expenditure is not recognized. **1979** *Daily Tel.* 6 Apr. 10/6 After deducting more than £3 million earmarked for capital projects, the council's new grant represents a rise in its revenue expenditure of about 19 per cent. **1776** ADAM SMITH *W.N.* v. v. (1904) II. 563 A manifest encouragement to the violation of the *revenue laws. **1841** J. T. HEWLETT *Parish Clerk* II. 258 By giving information to the *revenue-men. **1895** *Century Mag.* July 378/2 I'm always skeered o' the revenue men bein' about. **1776** ADAM SMITH *W.N.* v. ii. (1904) II. 565 The levying of this tax requires a multitude of *revenue officers. **1885** W. D. CHESTER *Chron. Customs* viii. 92 The interference..was..attended with some danger to the revenue officers. **1848–9** *Act 11 & 12 Vict.* c. 121 §25 Any Officer of Excise or Customs, or of the *Revenue Police in Ireland. **1870** J. K. MEDBERY *Men & Mysteries Wall St.* 52 The acknowledgements are covered with *revenue stamps. **1820** *Deb. Congress U.S.* 24 Apr. (1855) 1966 They enacted a treasury tariff, a *revenue tariff, without the least regard to the situation of the country. **1887** *Courier-Jrnl.* (Louisville, Kentucky) 19 Feb. 4/1 They are the identical arguments which the Courier-Journal has been pounding into the understanding of the people in its fight for a revenue tariff. **1814** SCOTT *Diary* 26 Aug. in *Lockhart*, The people here were much irritated against the men of a *revenue vessel.

b. Obj. and objective genitive, as ***revenue-collector, -defender, -earner; revenue-earning, -paying, -producing, -sharing, -yielding.***

1849 OTTÉ tr. *Humboldt's Cosmos* II. 597 Persians were established at that period as revenue-collectors on the Indus. **1885** W. D. CHESTER *Chron. Customs* viii. 94 This.. does not redound to the valour of the revenue defenders. **1963** *Times* 23 Mar. 11/1 Sport in general is a major revenue-earner. **1892** *Pall Mall G.* 23 Mar. 2/3 The Treasury insists on regarding the Post Office as a revenue-earning institution. **1910** J. LONDON *Let.* 9 Aug. (1966) 317 The idea that a judge of rectitude should..try a case between a non-resident like me and a revenue-paying, vote-swinging tenant like Muldowney. **1892** *Daily News* 18 Apr. 3/4 The peasant ..is simply regarded as a revenue-producing unit. **1971** *New Yorker* 10 July 43 Brock's dominant theme was much the same as what President Nixon would later call 'revenue sharing'—that government had to be returned to local control by way of sending the taxpayers' money back to the states, counties, cities, and towns. **1973** *Black Panther* 17 Mar. A/3 Even the facade of Revenue Sharing as the promise of a 'new lease on life' for American cities is fast becoming a sad joke. **1976** *National Observer* (U.S.) 2 Oct. 10/1 Boston's Housing Improvement Program, an apparently successful effort to use Federal revenue-sharing money to upgrade city neighborhoods and preserve existing housing. **1898** E. HOWARD *To-morrow* v. 53 A considerable outlay would be incurred in respect of markets, water supply, lighting, tramways, and other revenue-yielding undertakings.

Hence **'revenued** *a.*, in ***well*** or ***richly revenued***, having large or rich revenues. Now *rare.*

1637 HEYWOOD *Royall King* II. ix, Are we not rich? are we not well revenew'd? **1649** *Alcoran* p. ix, They haue Temples, Colleges, and Hospitales well revenued. *a* **1661** FULLER *Worthies, Lancs.* II. (1662) 122 Knights..anciently descended, and richly revenued in this County.

revenuer ('rɛvəˌnjuːə(r)). *U.S.* [f. REVENUE + -ER[1].] A revenue agent.

1880 *Daily Inter-Ocean* (Chicago) 1 June 12/1 His wife and daughter discharged their conjugal and filial duty by.. watching from their home for the approach of the 'Revenyors'. **1895** 'C. E. CRADDOCK' *Mystery of Witch-Face Mountain* 15 The 'revenuers'..never rode alone. **1941** *Charlottesville* (Va.) *Daily Progress* 16 Aug. 1/5 The sharp rise in sugar and grain prices, coupled with the increased efforts of the 'revenooers' to ferret out the distilling outfits in the mountains have made it too perilous for most of the old-timers. **1949** *Américas* Aug. 10/1 The 'revenoo-ers' slowed the production of illegal whiskey. **1955** W. FAULKNER *Fable* 173 The sheriff..and the city strangers in their city hats and neckties and shoes, smelling, stinking of excise officers, revenuers. **1963** *Times* 19 Mar. 10/7 The 'revenuer' keeps track of large sales of sugar. **1974** W. GARNER *Big enough Wreath* x. 131 Moonshiner, made his own likker..scared stiff of being caught by the revenuers. **1974** *New Yorker* 3 June 43/2 Jon tried to persuade Anne and Ruth to take their bathing suits off... 'Listen, as long as we're back up here where the revenooers can't get at us, we might as well have a good time.'

rever, anglicized variant of REVERS.

1894 *Westm. Gaz.* 16 Aug. 3/3 A jaunty little jacket so arranged that each side of the front can be turned back in a rever. **1896** *Paterson's Mag.* Jan. 84/1 It is rolling back a bright rever on each corner.

rever(e, obs. ff. REAVER, RIVER, ROVER.

reverable (rɪ'vɪərəb(ə)l), *a. rare.* [f. REVERE *v.* + -ABLE. Cf. F. *reverable* (Cotgr.).] Worthy of reverence; deserving to be revered.

1716 M. DAVIES *Athen. Brit.* II. 159 How little more learned or reverable soever were those three Welsh Prelates than these three English Monks. **1760–72** H. BROOKE *Fool of Qual.* (1809) I. 90 The character of a gentleman is the most reverable—the highest of all characters. *Ibid.* 176 To about the close of the 17th cent. (see RHYTHM *sb.* I). Soon after 1600, probably from a desire to distinguish between 'rime' and 'rhythm', the intermediate forms *rhime, rhyme* came into use, and the latter finally established itself as the standard form (see RHYME *sb.*). The original *rime*, however, has never been quite discontinued, and in about 1870 its use was considerably revived, esp. by writers upon the history of the English language or literature. To some extent this revival was due to the belief that the word was of native origin, and represented OE. *rím* RIME *sb.*[3]]

1. a. Metre, measure (*obs.*); agreement in the terminal sounds of line or words. Cf. RHYME *sb.* 3.

c **1200** ORMIN *Ded.* 44 Icc hafe sett her..maniȝ word þe rime swa to fillenn. *Ibid.* 101 Himm bidde icc þatt het write rihht,.. Wiþþ all swillc rime alls her iss sett. *a* **1300** *Cursor M.* 14922 Es resun þat wee vr rime rume, And set fra nu langer bastune. *c* **1386** CHAUCER *Pars. T.* Prol. 44, I kan nat geeste—Rum, Ram, Ruf—by lettre, Ne, god woot, rym holde I but litel bettre. *c* **1392** —— *Compl. Venus* 80 To me hit ys a grete penaunce, Syth ryme in englissh hat such skarsete, To folowe worde by worde the curiosite. **1553** T. WILSON *Rhet.* (1562) 85 There was not a dosen sentences, in his whole Sermon, but thei ended all in rime, for the moste part. **1581** SIDNEY *Apol. Poetrie* (Arb.) 71 Euen the very ryme it selfe, the Italian cannot put in the last silable, by the French named the Masculine ryme, but still in the next to the last, which the French call the Female; or the next before that. **1668** DRYDEN *Dram. Poesy* Ess. (Ker) I. 35 Who first taught us..to make our rime so properly a part of the verse, that it should never mislead the sense. **1672** MARVELL *Reh. Transp.* I. 87 They wanted nothing but rime to be right Tom Triplet. **1774** MITFORD *Ess. Harmony Lang.* 157 The Anglosaxon poets..generally used measures without rime. **1775** TYRWHIT *Lang. & Versificat. Chaucer* 53 *note*, We see evident marks of a fondness for Rime in the Hymns of S. Ambrosius and S. Damasus. **1833** MRS. S. AUSTIN tr. *Characteristics Goethe* II. 51 Wieland handled rime like a master. **1868** THORPE *Anal. Anglo-Sax.* 152 A Paraphrase of Job, xxi. xxx. Alliterative with final rime.

b. Coupled with *reason*: see RHYME *sb.* 3 b.

c **1460** J. RUSSELL *Bk. Nurture* 1243 As for ryme or reson, þe forewryter was not to blame. **1530** TINDALE *Answ. More* xvi. Wks. (1573) 285/1 For appose her now of Christ, as Scripture testifieth of hym, and thou shalt finde her cleane without rime or reason. **1548** UDALL, etc. *Erasm. Par. Luke* xi. 108 Seeyng there is nether ryme ne reason in saing y[t] one eiuill spirite driueth out an other eiuil spirite. **1600** HOLLAND *Livy* XXVII. xxxvii. 656 These songs..would seeme but simple stuffe, and composed without rime or reason. **1607** B. JONSON *Volpone* Prol., Here is ri'me, not emptie of reason. **1621** HAKEWILL *David's Vow* 33 It is both ryme and reason.

c. An instance of lines or words ending in the same sounds; a word that rimes with another word.

1599 SHAKS. *Much Ado* v. ii. 37, I can finde out no rime to Ladie but babie, an innocent rime: for scorne, horne, a hard rime; for schoole foole, a babling rime; verie ominous endings. **1603** DANIEL *Def. Ryme* Wks. (Grosart) IV. 44 Indeed I haue wished there was not that multiplicitie of Rymes as is vsed by many in Sonets. **1651** HOBBES *Leviath.* I. iii. 10 As a man should run over the Alphabet, to start a rime. **1878** STEVENSON *Inland Voy.* 232 May Apollo send him rimes hitherto undreamed of. **1887** FURNIVALL in *R. Brunne's Chron.* (Rolls) II. 587 The couples of rymes are entered alphabetically by the first word of the couple. **1891** LOUNSBURY *Stud. in Chaucer* I. iv. 375 There are tests resting upon the recurrence of assonant rymes.

2. a. Riming or rimed verse. Cf. RHYME *sb.* 2. Most commonly in the phr. *in rime*.

c **1220** *Bestiary* 695 In boke is ðe turtres lif writen o rime, wu laȝelike ȝe holdeð luue al hire lif time. *a* **1300** *Cursor M.* 87 Off suilk an suld ȝe mater take,.. Of hir to mak bath rim and sang. *c* **1369** CHAUCER *Dethe Blaunche* 464 He made of ryme ten verses or twelue. *c* **1400** *Laud Troy Bk.* 3261, I ffynde In prose and ryme, Was non so strong In that tyme. *a* **1450** *Knt. de la Tour* (1868) 3 And thanne y made this boke. But y wolde not sette it in ryme. **1529** MORE *Dyaloge* III. Wks. 223/1 A foolish raylyng boke against the clergy, and much part made in ryme. **1564** BULLEIN *Dial. agst. Pest.* (1888) 16 Chaucer satte in a chaire of gold..writyng Prose and Risme. **1581** PETTIE tr. *Guazzo's Civ. Conv.* II. (1586) 66 b, I am of this minde, that the making of rime should not make a Poet use naughtie wordes. *c* **1600** SHAKS. *Sonn.* cvi, Beautie making beautifull old rime, In praise of Ladies dead, and louely Knights. *a* **1631** DONNE *Poems* (1650) 11, I thought, if I could draw my paines Through Rimes vexation, I should them allay. **1716** HEARNE *Collect.* (O.H.S.) V. 189 Written in rime in the Country Dialect. **1802** RITSON *Metr. Rom.* I. p. xviii, There is, even, a Latin song in rime extant in print, which was made upon a great victory obtain'd by king Clothair the second. **1876** FREEMAN *Norm. Conq.* (1877) V. 589 Before the end of the twelfth century England had seen an English sermon in regular rime.

†**b.** *rime doggerel*: see DOGGEREL A.

c. *rime royal*: see RHYME *sb.* 2 c, and RHYTHM *sb.* 1 b.

[**1871** SKEAT *Spec. Eng. Lit.* III. (1887) 41 'The Kingis Quair' is written in seven-lined stanzas, a favourite measure of Chaucer and his successors, which received the name of the 'rime roial'.] **1882** OGILVIE, *Rime-royal.* **1903** H. BRADLEY in *Pol., Rel., & Love Poems* 291 Each of the seven stanzas (in 'rime royal').

d. See RIDING RHYME.

‖**e.** *rime couée* = *tailed rime* s.v. TAILED *a.* 1 d.

c **1330** [see COUWEE *a.*]. **1775** T. TYRWHITT *Canterbury Tales of Chaucer* IV. 72 Though Robert of Brunne in his Prologue professes not to attempt these elegancies of composition, yet he has intermixed several passages in Rime Couwée. **1893** [see TAILED *a.* 1 d]. **1935** *Essays & Stud.* XX. 97 The rime couée or romance stanza of six lines (double eight and six). **1945** E. K. CHAMBERS *Eng. Lit. at Close of Middle Ages* i. 25 The metre of the Chester plays..is a Romance metre of the type known as *rime couée* or tail-rhyme.

‖**f.** *rime riche* = *rich rhyme* s.v. RICH *a.* 7 c.

[**1903** H. J. CHAYTOR *Compan. French Verse* iv. 23 Rimes are also distinguished as rich and sufficient (riche, suffisante).] **1904** BRANDIN & HARTOG *Bk. French Prosody* iv. 53 Victor Hugo uses the *rime riche* more than any of his predecessors. **1930** A. HUXLEY *Vulgarity in Lit.* 35 When Laforgue wrote of that '*roi de Thulé, Immaculé*' his *rime riche* was entirely above suspicion. **1961** A. CLARKE *Later Poems* 92 With the exception of the sonnet and the little experiment in *rime riche*, these pieces came to me quite unexpectedly.

3. A riming poem or piece of riming verse. Cf. RHYME *sb.* 1.

c **1250** *Gen. & Ex.* 1 Man og to luuen ðat rimes ren. *c* **1275** *Luue Ron* 193 in *O.E. Misc.* 99 þis rym, mayde, ich þe sende open and wiþ-vte sel. *c* **1330** *Arth. & Merl.* 1341 (Kölbing), So ich ȝou segge in mi rime. *c* **1386** CHAUCER *Man of Law's T.* Prol. 96, I speke in prose, and lat him rymes make. **1508** KENNEDIE *Flyting w. Dunbar* 332 Renounce thy rymis. **1542** UDALL *Erasm. Apoph.* 245 These songes or rymes..were called in Latin *Fescennina carmina*. **1590** SHAKS. *Mids. N.* I. i. 28 Thou, thou Lysander, thou hast giuen her rimes, And interchang'd loue-tokens with my childe. **1617** MORYSON *Itin.* III. 99 In the Sea townes of England they sing this English rime; Shoulder of mutton and English Beere, Make the Flemmings tarry here. **1699** GARTH *Dispens.* IV. 46 Up these shelves, much Gothick Lumber climbs, With Swiss Philosophy, and Danish Rimes. **1798** COLERIDGE in *Lyr. Ballads* 5 The Rime of the Ancyent Marinere, in seven parts. **1881** MAHAFFY *Old Greek Educ.* ii. 23 There is hardly a word left of the nursery rimes. **1894** J. T. FOWLER *Adamnan* Introd. 40 The famous old Irish rime about St. Patrick.

†**4.** = RHYTHM *sb.* 4, 5. *Obs.*

1586 W. WEBBE *Eng. Poetrie* (Arb.) 57 Ryme is properly, the iust proportion of a clause or sentence, whether it be in prose or meeter, aptly comprised together. **1677** GALE *Crt. Gentiles* IV. 99 Plato informes us..the whole life of a virtuose man must be composed..of Symphonie or Concert and musical ryme.

5. *attrib.* and *Comb.*, as ***rime-ending, -index, -making, -word; rime-maker, -wright; rime-rotten*** adj.; **rime-letter**, the distinctive initial letter in a line of alliterative verse.

1591 FRAUNCE *C'tess Pembr. Yvychurch* I. II. iii, Neither Castalian Muses..Nor rymewright singers. **1599** PORTER *Angry Wom. Abingd.* (Percy Soc.) 40 Speake men what they can to him, hee'l answere With some rime rotten sentence or olde saying. **1611** FLORIO, *Rimatore*, a Rimer, a Rime-maker. **1865** SKEAT in Brock *Morte Arth.* p. x, Of the strongly-accented syllables, three begin with a common letter, which has been called the rime-letter. **1877** —— *The Bruce* 628 A complete Rime-index would occupy a considerable space. **1887** FURNIVALL in *R. Brunne's Chron.* (Rolls) I. p. xx, After some of the ryme-endings. **1893** *Cursor Mundi* (E.E.T.S.) 136* *note*, There are three ryme-words, *gnede, brede, shrede*. **1935** C. S. LEWIS in *Lysistrata* May 22 Rude rime-making wrongs her beauty, Whose breasts and brow..Bewitch the worlds.

rime (raɪm), *sb.*[2] Forms: 1 **hrim**, 3–4 **rim**, 4–5, 7 **ryme**, 5–6 **rym** (6 **ryim**), 7 **reeme**, 8 **reem**, 7–9 **rhime** (9 **rhyme**), 4– **rime**. [OE. *hrím* masc., = Fris. *rym*, MDu. and Du. *rijm*, MLG. *riim*, ON. and Icel. *hrím* (Norw., Sw., and Da. *rim*). Cf. OF. *rime, rimée*, which are no doubt of Teut. origin.] **a.** Hoar-frost (see note); frozen mist. Also *dial.* a chill mist or fog.

Rare in ME., except in the comb. RIME-FROST. From 16th century chiefly *Sc.* and *north.*, but revived in literary use at the end of the 18th cent. See also RIND *sb.*[3] In scientific use *rime* is now distinguished from *hoar-frost* (q.v.).

c **725** *Corpus Gloss.* 1653 *Pruina*, hrim. *a* **1000** *Phœnix* 60 (Gr.), þær ne hægl ne hrim hreosað to foldan. *c* **1205** LAY. 28525 Folc vnimete ridinde & ganninde swa þe rim [*c* 1275 þe ren] falled adune.

1513 DOUGLAS *Æneis* XIII. Prol. 31 Doun fallis the donk rym. **1549** *Compl. Scot.* (1872) 59 The hayr ryim is ane cald deu, the quhilk fallis in mysty vapours, and syne it fresis on the eird. **1587** MASCALL *Govt. Cattle, Sheepe* (1596) 214 Ye ought for to keepe them close, till the day haue taken the gellie or netty rime, from the earth. **1611** COTGR., *Gresil*,.. reeme, or the white frost that hangs on trees. **1659** A. HAY *Diary* (S.H.S.) 210 A frost ryme all day. **1701** GREW *Cosmol. Sacra* I. iii. §33 In a Hoar-Frost, that which we call a Rime, is a Multitude of Quadrangular Prismes, exactly figured, but piled without any Order, one over another. **1789** E. DARWIN *Bot. Gard.* I. (1791) 47 Shake from their candied trunks the tinkling rime. **1820** SHELLEY *Witch Atl.* xliv, Moonlight splendour of intensest rime, With which frost paints the pines in winter time. **1864** C. GEIKIE *Life in Woods* vii. (1874) 133 As to the windows, the rime on them never thought of melting. **1895** [see HOAR-FROST]. **1912** W. DE LA MARE *Listeners* 23 At midnight 'neath a maze of stars I flame with glittering rime. **1921** A. E. M. GEDDES *Meteorol.* vi. 182 Hoar frost must not be confused with rime, which is an accumulation of frozen moisture on trees, &c., and is formed only during fog. **1947** *Jrnl. R. Aeronaut. Soc.* LI. 274/1 With a smaller rate of catch of water, at a lower temperature of the air, the water will freeze in the area of catch producing ice which has a porous structure, and a mat surface. This type is known as rime ice. **1978** *Sci. Amer.* Apr. 144/3 When the saturation is higher than 140 percent, the growth of crystals is so rapid that rime (an amorphous deposit of frozen droplets) grows on the crystals and destroys their optical faces.

pl. **1577** B. GOOGE *Heresbach's Husb.* III. (1586) 141 The Sunne hath drawne vppe the Rimes and hoare frostes from the Feeldes. **1641** BEST *Farm. Bks.* (Surtees) 77 If there came any white rymes, or frosty morninges. **1766** *Complete Farmer* s.v. *Threshing* 7 K 4/2 In that time the mists and rimes, especially in a hilly country, will be driven into the stack.

Comb. **1875** *Wonders Phys. World* I. iv. 128 The firs shake their rime-loaded boughs. **1891** KIPLING *Barrack-Room Ballads* (1892) 204 It's North you may run to the rime-ringed sun. **1898** MERRIMAN *Roden's Corner* v, The dull houses were rime-covered. **1910** W. DE LA MARE *Three Mulla-Mulgars* iii. 46 The rime-laden branches of the trees.

b. *transf.* and *fig.*

1618 M. BARET *Horsemanship* Ded. 4 This..Art of Horsemanship.., which hath beene so long frost-bitten with the congealing ryme of antient traditions. *a* **1688** NARBOROUGH *Voy.* I. (1694) 29 The Ground and Rocks have a white Rhime of Salt-petre hanging on them. **1839** LONGF. *Voices of Nt.*, *Prelude* vi, Tales that have the rime of age.

†**rime**, *sb.*[3] *Obs.* [OE. *rím*, = OS. *-rîm* (in *unrîm* numberless host), OHG. *rîm* number, ON. *rím* computation.] Number; reckoning.

c **825** *Vesp. Psalter* xxxviii. 5 Cuð me doa..rim dæȝa minra. *Ibid.* xxxix. 6 ðemoniȝfaldade sind ofer rim. *a* **900** CYNEWULF *Crist* 1586 þæt he ne forleose..his daȝena rim. *c* **973** *O.E. Chron.* (Parker MS.) an. 973, Tyn hund wintra, ȝeteled rimes. *c* **1200** ORMIN 11248 þatt full wel iss bitacnedd þurrh tale & rime off fowwerrtiȝ.

†**rime**, *sb.*[4] *Obs.* [ad. L. *rīma*: see RIMA.] A chap, chink, or cleft.

1607 TOPSELL *Four-f. Beasts* (1658) 64 The sewet of oxen ..is also good against..the ulcers and rimes of the mouth. **1646** SIR T. BROWNE *Pseud. Ep.* 198 Though birds have no Epiglottis, yet can they so contract the rime or chink of their Larinx [etc.]. **1657** TOMLINSON *Renou's Disp.* 378 They have a small depressure on one side like a rime.

rime, obs. form of RIM *sb.*[1], *sb.*[2]

rime (raɪm), *v.*[1] Forms: 4–7, 9 **ryme** (5 **rymyn**), 4, 6– **rime**. [ad. OF. *rimer*, f. *rime* RIME *sb.*[1]; cf. Prov., Sp., Pg. *rimar*, It. *rimare*.

The verb was also adopted in the other Teutonic languages, appearing as MDu. *rimen* (Du. *rijmen*, Fris. *rime, rymje*), MLG. *rîmen, rymen*, MHG. *rîmen* (G. *reimen*), Icel. *ríma*, MSw. *rima* (Sw. *rimma*), MDa. *rime, riime* (Da. *rime*).

In the 17th cent. the usual spelling became RHYME: cf. the note to RIME *sb.*[1]]

1. *intr.* To make rimes or verses; to compose riming verse; to versify *on, upon*. Cf. RHYME *v.* 1.

c **1290** *Magdalena* 5 in Horstm. *Altengl. Leg.* (1878) 148 Ich nelle eov noþer rede ne rime of kyng ne of eorl. *c* **1374** CHAUCER *Troylus* I. 532, I shall japid ben a thousande tyme More than he of whos foly men ryme. *c* **1393** —— *Scogan* 35 Lo olde grisil leste to ryme & pleye! *c* **1440** *Promp. Parv.* 434/1 Rymyn, *rithmico*. **1483** *Cath. Angl.* 308/2 To Ryme, *rithmicare*. **1508** DUNBAR *Flyting* 23 Ȝit mycht thay be sa bald, in thair bakbytting, To gar me ryme. **1588** BABINGTON *Prof. Exp. Lord's Pr.* (1596) 236 Some be rimed on by dronken tossepots, and so was Dauid. **1601** SHAKS. *Jul. C.* IV. iii. 133 How vildely doth this Cynicke rime! **1611** —— *Cymb.* v. iii. 55 Will you Rime vpon't, And vent it for a Mock'rie?

2. a. *trans.* To recount or celebrate in verse or rime; to turn into, or compose in, riming verse.

c **1315** SHOREHAM IV. 73 þer-fore þys tale rymeþ Hou men in senne beþ. **1330** R. BRUNNE *Chron. Wace* Prol. (Rolls) 63 For Mayster Wace þe Latyn alle rymes, þat Pers ouer-hippis many tymes. *c* **1393** CHAUCER *Scogan* 41 Al schal passyn þat men prose or ryme. **1424** *Paston Lett.* I. 13 Manaces of deth and dismembryng maden and puttyn by certeyns Englische billes rymed in partye. **1448–9** METHAM *Wks.* (E.E.T.S.) 80 My mastyr Chauncerys..With many prouerbys hys bokys ..rymyd naturally. **1542–3** *Act 34–35 Hen. VIII*, c. 1 If ani ..person..play in enterludes, sing or rime, any matter contrarie to the saide doctrine. *a* **1548** HALL *Chron., Hen. VIII*. 262 The worde of God is disputed, rimed, song and iangeled in euery Alehouse and Tauerne. **1887** *Q. Rev.* CLXIV. 389 He rimed history, ballads and legends.

†**b.** To brave (a matter) *out* in riming terms.

1532 MORE *Confut. Tindale* Wks. 496/1 Tindall rymeth it out, & saith y[t] he both denieth and also defieth, that the apostles taught any ceremony wherof the reason could not be knowen.

c. To cause (a word) to rime *with* (another); to use as a rime. Cf. RHYME *v.* 6.

1887 FURNIVALL in *R. Brunne's Chron.* (Rolls) II. 587 Robert Mannyng..wrote *poraille* as *poryal*, and rymed it with *sayl* or sail.

3. To bring by riming. Cf. RHYME *v.* 2.

1584 R. SCOT *Discov. Witchcr.* III. xv. 64 They will not sticke to affirme, that they can rime either man or beast to death. **1599** SHAKS. *Hen. V*, v. ii. 164 These fellowes of infinit tongue, that can ryme themselues into Ladyes fauours. **1626** DONNE *Serm.* 37 And rymed themselves beyond Reason into Absurdities and Heresies. **1633** G. HERBERT *Temple, Ch. Porch* i, Hearken unto a Verser, who may chance Ryme thee to good, and make a bait of pleasure. **1915** *Encycl. Relig. & Ethics* VIII. 258/1 'Riming people to death'—a practice used by the *filid* as well as by the druids —was connected with the power of the spoken word. **1969** J. WAINWRIGHT *Big Tickle* 166 He'll rime you—you lousy git—he'll rime you to ribbons.

4. a. *intr.* To form a rime. Also *fig.*, to agree. Cf. RHYME *v.* 4.

c **1450** *Cov. Myst.* (1841) 242 Two smale legges and a gret body, thow it ryme nowth. **1530** PALSGR. 691/2 That same may ryme well, but it agreeth nat. **1546** HEYWOOD *Prov.* E ij b, To disdeygne me,..it may ryme but it accordth not.

b. To have similar or riming endings.

1660 INGELO *Bentiv. & Ur.* I. (1682) 149 Words and sounds which make Verses ryme. **1669** S. SIMMONS *Milton's P.L.* To Rdr., A reason of that which stumbled many others, why the Poem Rimes not.

5. To use rime. Cf. RHYME *v.* 5.

1602 SHAKS. *Ham.* III. ii. 296 You might haue Rim'd. **1675** E. PHILLIPS *Theatrum Poet.* Pref. **4 The Dissyllable, which in that Language is the only way of Riming. **1692** DENNIS *Pass. Byblis* Pref. C, My Lord Roscommon who writ in blank Verse with so much success, yet was nicely exact in Riming, whenever he pretended to rime.

rime (raɪm), *v.*[2] [f. RIME *sb.*[2] Cf. Fris. *rime*, MDu. *rimen* (Du. *rijmen*), Icel. *hríma*, Sw. *rimma*.] *trans.* To cover with rime or hoar-frost. In scientific use now restricted to mean: to cover with rime as opp. to hoar-frost (q.v.). Also *intr.*, to become rimed.

1755 Johnson, *Rime*, to freeze with hoar frost. **1831** Howitt *Seasons* (1837) 291 The first frost that rimes the hedges. **1836** Emerson *Nature* iii. Wks. (Bohn) II. 146 Every withered stem and stubble rimed with frost, contribute something to the mute music. **1907** N. Munro *Daft Days* xxxii. 266 Oh, London, London!.. The multitudinous monuments rimed by years. **1966** *Jrnl. Faculty Sci. Hokkaidô Univ.* 7th Ser. II. 331 In Japan, most of snow crystals are more or less rimed. Therefore the grade of riming is very important. **1973** *Sci. Amer.* Jan. 105/1 When a crystal rimes, material is added mostly on its underside, thus increasing its weight without greatly increasing its air resistance. *Ibid.*, The more a crystal is rimed, the faster it rimes. **1978** *Nature* 24 Aug. 791/2 (*caption*) Ice fragments collected downwind of an ice-coated sphere riming at −7°C.

Hence **'riming** *ppl. a.* and *vbl. sb.*^{2}

c **1820** Hogg *To Sir W. Scott*, Time has shed His riming honours o'er each brow. **1966** [see above]. **1969** *Jrnl. Atmospheric Sci.* XXVI. 138/1 This apparent multiplication of ice crystals may be associated with the process of riming of the crystals. **1973** *Sci. Amer.* Jan. 105/1 When a snow crystal evolves within a cloud of supercooled water drops, it can grow not only by stealing vapor from around the drops but also by actually colliding with individual drops. The process is called riming, and it is an important complication in all types of snowflakes and snow crystals. **1978** *Nature* 24 Aug. 791/1 (*heading*) A possible mechanism of ice splinter production during riming.

† **rime**, *v.*^{3} *Obs.* Also 6 **ryme.** [OE. *ríman*, f. *rím* RIME *sb.*^{3} Cf. ARIME *v.*] *trans.* To count, number, reckon, recount.

c **825** *Vesp. Psalter* cxlvi. 4 Se rimeð menȝu steorrena. *c* **893** K. Ælfred *Oros.* iv. i. 156 Hit næs þeaw on þæm tidum þæt mon æniȝ wæl on þa healfe rimde þe þonne wieldre wæs. *c* **1000** *Ags. Ps.* (Thorpe) cxxxviii. 16 Ðif ic hi recene nu riman onginne, hi beoð ofer sand corn sniome maniȝe. *c* **1200** Ormin 11213 Swa þatt Jechonias iss An mann & twiȝess rimedd. *Ibid.* 11217 He biginneþþ Cristess kinn To reccnenn & to rimenn Att Abraham. *c* **1375** *Cursor M.* 14527 (Fairf.), Cayphas saide in þat time wordes many we may noȝt rime. *c* **1400** *Sowdone Bab.* 339 Myghte he ryme Of x thousande men lefte no moo But sexty men and twelfe. *c* **1470** *Gol. & Gaw.* 403 He is the riallest roy..Of all the rentaris to ryme or rekin on raw.

rime, *v.*^{4} Now *dial.* or *techn.* Forms: 1 **rýman** (**ríman**), 2–3 **rimen**, 3 **rumen**, 4–5 **ryme**, 6, 9 *dial.* **rime**, 9 *dial.* **rym, rim**. See also REAM *v.*^{3} and REEM *v.*^{2} [Common Teut.: OE. *rýman*, = OFris. *rēma*, MDu. *rūmen*, *ruymen* (Du. *ruimen*), OS. *rûmian*, OHG. *rûmen* (G. *räumen*), ON. and Icel. *rýma* (Norw. *ryma*, *røma*, Sw. *rymma*, Da. *rømme*):—**rūmjan*, f. *rūm* ROOM *sb.*^{1}]

1. *trans.* † **a.** To make clear or vacant for one; to vacate, give up. *Obs.*

Beowulf 492 Þa wæs ðeatmæcȝum..on beorsele benc ȝerymed. *a* **1000** *Boeth. Metr.* i. 19 Beadurincum wæs Rom ȝerymed. *c* **1000** *Ags. Gosp.* Luke xiv. 9 Rym þysum men setl. *c* **1205** Lay. 4709 Þis feoreword ich him halde, bute he ..mi londe rume.

† **b.** To clear or open up (a way) for one. *Obs.*

a **1000** *Andreas* 1580 (Gr.), Him ȝearu sona þurh stream-ræce stræt wæs ȝerymed. *a* **1023** Wulfstan *Hom.* (1883) 55 þæt syndan..Antecristes þrælas, þe his weȝ rymað. *a* **1200** *Cott. Hom.* 231 He haueð ȝerimed rihtwisan mannan infer to his rice. *c* **1205** Lay. 28323 Walwain bi-foren wende and þene wæi rumde.

† **c.** To clear for oneself; to take. *Obs.*

c **1205** Lay. 3554 Ich..hat [h]ine fare swiþe..and rumen him herberia i summe riche burie. *Ibid.* 5228 Þa hauede heo muche riche irumed to honde.

d. *dial.* To remove, clear away.

1854 Miss Baker *Northampt. Gloss.* s.v., Rym the chair out of the way.

2. *intr.* † **a.** To withdraw, depart, retire. *Obs.*

c **1000** Ælfric *Gram.* xxviii. (Z.) 171 Ic fare aweȝ oððe ic ryme. *a* **1122** *O.E. Chron.* (Laud MS.) an. 999, A man rymde fram þære sæ & hi ferdon æfre forð æfter. *a* **1250** *Prov. Ælfred* 170 in *O.E. Misc.* 113 Wot no mon þe time wanne he sal henne rimen. *c* **1330** R. Brunne *Chron. Wace* (Rolls) 9868 Frendes..Conseilled hym..gyue no bataille.. Bot let his folk sprede & ryme. **1338** —— *Chron.* (1810) 71 Þe rouht of þare rascaile he did it rere & ryme. *c* **1450** *Bk. Curtasye* 507 in *Babees Bk.*, Then ȝomon of chambur shynne voyde with [? *read* and] ryme.

b. *dial.* To move house; to remove.

1847 Halliw., *Rim*, to remove. **1876** *S. Warwick Gloss.*, *Rimming*, moving furniture to a fresh house. 'We be a rimming on Monday.'

3. *trans.* † **a.** To extend, increase, enlarge. *Obs.*

c **897** K. Ælfred *Gregory's Past. C.* xliv. 329 Ðæt se ȝitsere..his land mid unryhte ryme. *c* **1000** Ælfric *Hom.* II. 104 Ic wille ryman minne bertun, and mine bernu ȝeeacnian.

† **b.** *refl.* To stretch (oneself). *Obs.*

13.. *Gaw. & Gr. Knt.* 308 He coȝed ful hyȝe, Ande rimed hym ful richely, & ryȝt hym to speke. *a* **1400–50** *Alexander* 4931 Þe renke within þe redell þan raxsils his armes, Rymed him full renyschly & rekind þir wordis.

c. To widen *out* (a hole). Cf. REAM *v.*^{3} 1.

1815 [implied in RIMER *sb.*^{2}]. **1875** Sir T. Saxton *Fret-Cutting* 69 The holes in the hinges ought to be properly rymed out, so as to be quite large enough to admit the screws.

rime (raɪm), *v.*^{5} *rare*$^{-1}$. [ad. L. *rīmārī*, f. *rīma* RIMA.] *intr.* To pry *into*.

1877 Blackmore *Erema* xliv, Our act was, with finger, and nail, and eye, to rime into every jot of it.

rime (raɪm), *v.*^{6} [f. Ir. *ruaim* alder-tree; whence *ruamadh*, *ruamughadh* 'to give the first tinge in dying red or black' (Dinneen).] *trans.* To steep or boil (wool or yarn) in water with alder-twigs. Hence **rimed** *ppl. a.*, **'riming** *vbl. sb.*

1873 O'Curry *Lect. Ancient Irish* I. 405 When the rimed yarn or cloth was boiled with a black peaty mud..it was dyed of a black colour. *Ibid.*, In the south of Ireland the riming operation was performed..by boiling the yarn.. with Rumex acetosa. *Ibid.* III. 119 After the wool is 'rimed'.

rimed, *ppl. a.*^{1} [f. RIME *v.*^{1} + -ED^1.] = RHYMED *ppl. a.*

1553 T. Wilson *Rhet.* (1562) 85 Some ende their sentences all alike, making their talke rather to appere rimed Metre, then to seme plain speache. **1774** Mitford *Ess. Harmony Lang.* 79 For the purpose of this analysis blank verse is much preferable to rimed. *Ibid.* 137 The pause is certainly in general most pleasing at the end of the second, or at the middle or end of the third foot; and rimed verse.. will seldom admit it elsewhere. **1799** W. Taylor in Robberds *Mem.* (1843) I. 250 From the habit of reading the more fanciful kinds of poetry in rimed stanzas.

rimed, *ppl. a.*^{2} [f. RIME *v.*^{2} + -ED^1.] Covered with rime (see note at RIME *sb.*^{2}).

1889 Skrine *Mem. Thring* 279 A calm autumn dawn came up, and fell rosily on the rimed trees. **1954** U. Nakaya *Snow Crystals* ii. 87 Snow crystals with numerous water droplets attached are very frequently observed in our climate... This type is better called a rimed crystal. **1973** *Nature* 26 Oct. 451/2 Mossop *et al.* report small ice crystals..but always in association with rimed ice pellets. **1975** *Ibid.* 22 May 317/1 Unrimed and lightly rimed planar and spatial crystals were sampled.

'rime-frost. *rare.* [f. RIME *sb.*^{2} + FROST *sb.* Cf. Icel. *hrímfrost*, Fær. *rím-*, Sw. and Da. *rimfrost.*] Hoar-frost, rime. Also with *a* and pl.

c **1250** *Gen. & Ex.* 3328 It lai ðor, quit als a rim frost. *c* **1290** *St. Michael* 627 in *S. Eng. Leg.* I. 317 In þis manere ȝe mowen i-seo þe kuynde of reyne and snowe, Of hawel, of snouȝ, of Rym-forst. **13..** *Cursor M.* 6520 (Gött.), Manna ..fell fra heuen..Als a rime frost to se. *a* **1340** Hampole *Psalter* lxxvii. 52 He sloghe..þaire mours in ryme froist. **14..** *Nom.* in Wr.-Wülcker 736 *Hec pruina*, a rymfrost. *c* **1440** *Promp. Parv.* 434/1 Ryme frost, *pruina*. **1626** Bacon *Sylva* §81 In Frosty Mornings (such as we call Rime frosts) you shall finde drops of Dew upon the Inside of Glasse-windowes. **1904** in *Eng. Dial. Dict.* **1957** Blunden *Poems of Many Years* 298 Their poor limbs shook With the wind's or the rimefrost's blue stroke.

So **'rime-frosted** *a.*

1889 *Harper's Mag.* Mar. 643/2 The birch-trees delicately rime-frosted to their finest tips.

† **rimel**, *sb. Obs.* Also **rimel(l)e, remele, remile, ry(e)mele.** [ad. med.L. *rīmella* or L. *rīmula*, dim. of *rīma* RIMA.] A fissure, crack.

c **1400** *Lanfranc's Cirurg.* 125 Þei asaie in þis maner if þat þe brekynge of þe brayn panne be wiþ a rimel, þat is to seie a chene, eiþer a creueis. *Ibid.* 134 For if þat ilke remile peerse þe brayn panne, þer is a greet doute in þe caas.

'rimel, *v. rare*$^{-1}$. = RIMER *v.*

c **1854** J. Bourne in E. J. Reed *Ship Building* (1869) iv. 66 The holes being accurately rimelled out and the rivets driven in.

rimeless ('raɪmlɪs), *a.* [f. RIME *sb.*^{1} + -LESS.] Without rime; unrimed. Cf. RHYMELESS *a.*

1532 More *Confut. Barnes* viii. Wks. 739/1 After the rude rimelesse running of a scottishe ieste. **1597** Bp. Hall *Sat.* i. iv, Tragicke Poesie..doth besides on Rimelesse numbers tread. **1613** J. Taylor (Water P.) *Wks.* ii. 71/1 With rimelesse reasons, and with Reasons verse Thy great Odcombian glory to rehearse. **1796** W. Taylor in *Monthly Mag.* I. 118 His Specimens toward a version of the Iliad, in rimeless iambic, are not comprehended in these..volumes.

rimer ('raɪmə(r)), *sb.*^{1} Also 5 **rymor, rymare,** 6–8 **rymer.** [f. RIME *v.*^{1} + -ER^1. In early use prob. after AF. *rimour*, *rymour* (F. *rimeur*). So Du. *rijmer*, Fris. *rimer*, †*rijmer*, MHG. *rîmer* (G. *reimer*), Da. *rimer*, Norw. *rimar*, Sw. *rimmare* (MSw. *rimare*), Icel. *rímari.*] A maker of rimes; a poet; a rimester. Cf. RHYMER.

1422 tr. *Secreta Secret.*, *Priv. Priv.* 157 He is an onwyse man that audyence or Yeftis yewyth to Rymoris othyr any Suche losyngeris. *c* **1440** *Promp. Parv.* 434/1 Rymare, *gerro*. *a* **1568** Ascham *Scholem.* ii. (Arb.) 144 This fault, not onely in the olde Latin Poets, but also in our..English Rymers at this day. **1590** Spenser *F.Q.* iii. xii. 5 A joyous fellowship.. Of Minstrales making goodly meriment, With wanton Bardes, and Rymers impudent. **1603** Daniel *Def. Ryme* Wks. (Grosart) IV. 49 Erasmus, and Moore, worthy men, I confesse, and the last a great ornament to this land, and a Rymer. **1655** tr. *Sorel's Com. Hist. Francion* vi. 7 So it is with this poor Rimer, his works make no noise but in his own ears. **1737** *Gentl. Mag.* VII. 625/2 What's prov'd, my Logician? That a Rymer and Wit may be no Politician. **1774** Mitford *Ess. Harmony Lang.* 102 A very musical arrangement of the accents not often used by other poets, particularly rimers. **1873** Edith Thompson *Hist. Eng.* xxvi. 107 The King's cognizance was a wild boar, and the rimer lost his head for thus insulting it.

rimer ('raɪmə(r)), *sb.*^{2} Now *rare.* Also **rymer**; (*U.S.*) **rimmer** ('rɪmə(r)). [f. RIME *v.*^{4} 3 c.] = REAMER *sb.*

1815 J. Smith *Panorama Sci. & Art* I. 17 A tool of this description is called a rimer. **1846** Holtzapffel *Turning* II. 461 Polygonal broaches or rimers with any number of sides. **1865** J. H. A. Bone *Petroleum & Petroleum Wells* 22 But the hole must be as nearly round as possible, and therefore the tools are taken out, and a 'rimmer', or 'reamer', sent down, which cuts down the irregularities of the hole. **1875** Sir T. Saxton *Fret-Cutting* 69 The holes in the hinges ought to be properly rymed out... If they are not, the rymer and rose-bit must be purchased. **1894** W. J. Lineham *Text-bk. Mech. Engin.* vi. 209 Round holes are cleaned by the Parallel Rimer ..and taper holes by means of a Taper Rimer. **1907** *Yesterday's Shopping* (1969) 701/2 Rimers, square or half round.

Hence **'rimer** *v.* = REAM *v.*^{3} 1.

1860 J. Hodges *Gt. Victoria Bridge* 44 Every hole..was rimered by a tool to exactly the size of the rivets. *Ibid.*, As the rimering proceeded the riveting followed. **1873** R. Wilson *Steam Boilers* 67 It is best to rimer them out and use a larger rivet.

rimer, variant of RYMER.

rimester ('raɪmstə(r)). [f. RIME *sb.*^{1} or *v.*^{1} + -STER. Cf. Du. *rijmster.*] A versifier or indifferent poet; a poetaster. See RHYMESTER.

1589 G. Harvey *Pierce's Super.* i. Wks. (Grosart) II. 119 To snibb the Thrasonicall rimester with Angelical meeter. **1597** Bp. Hall *Sat.* i. ii, Such wondrous rablements of rimesters new. **1607** R. C[arew] tr. *Estienne's World of Wonders* 239 Another old Elderton and right baladin-rimester. **1819** W. Taylor in *Monthly Mag.* XLVII. 118 Like our now-a-day rimesters.

'rimestock. *rare.* Also 7–8 **rimstock** (7 **-stoc**), 9 **rimstoke.** [ad. Norw. *rimstok*, = *rimstaf*, *primstaf*: see PRIMSTAFF.] A clog-almanac.

1662 Evelyn *Chalcogr.* (1769) 38 Danes and Norwegians had..their runic writings, or engraven letters, as in their *rimstoc* or *primstaff*. **1686** Plot *Staffordsh.* 423 These Symbols..have a more rational orderly texture than the Runæ upon the Danish Rimestocks, or the Swedish or Norwegian Primstaves. **1834** Southey *Doctor* xc. (1862) 200 There is no proof that a pagan rimstoke ever existed in those countries.

† **rimeye**, *v. Obs.*$^{-1}$ [ad. OF. *rimeier*, *rimaier*, var. *rimoier*, f. *rime* RIME *sb.*^{1}] *trans.* To compose or recount in rime.

c **1386** Chaucer *Frankl. T.* Prol. 3 Thise olde gentil Britons..Of diuerse auentures maden layes Rymeyed in hir firste Briton tonge.

'rimiform, *a. rare*$^{-0}$. [f. L. *rīma.*] 'Having a longitudinal chink or furrow'.

1879 Leighton *Lichen Flora* Gloss.

riming ('raɪmɪŋ), *vbl. sb.* Also 4–7, 9 **ryming**, 7 **rimeing.** [f. RIME *v.*^{1}] = RHYMING *vbl. sb.*

c **1386** Chaucer *Man of Law's T.* Prol. 48 Thogh he kan but lewedly On metres and on rymyng craftily. **1448–9** J. Metham *Wks.* (E.E.T.S.) 81 He off rymyng toke the besynes To comfforte them that schuld falle in heuynes. *a* **1500** *Lancelot* 322 To me nor to non vthir It accordit, In to our rymyng his nam to be recordit. *a* **1568** Ascham *Scholem.* ii. (Arb.) 147 This mislikyng of Ryming beginneth not now of any newfangle singularitie. *c* **1645** Howell *Lett.* i. i. xl, Their prosody, and vein of versifying or riming, which is like our Bards. **1692** Dennis *Pass. Byblis* Pref. C, My Lord Roscommon..was nicely exact in Riming, whenever he pretended to rime. **1775** Tyrwhit *Lang. & Versificat. Chaucer* 53 The practice of Riming is probably to be deduced from the same original. **1798** W. Taylor in *Monthly Mag.* VI. 284 You..say 'tis very hard To range your rimings as befits a Sonnet. **1880** Ruskin *On the Old Road* Wks. 1899 III. 60 There is to be rich ryming and chiming, no matter how simply got.

attrib. **1599** Shaks. *Much Ado* v. ii. 40, I was not borne vnder a riming Plannet.

riming ('raɪmɪŋ), *ppl. a.* Also **ryming.** [f. RIME *v.*^{1}]

1. = RHYMING *ppl. a.* 1.

1590 Marlowe *1st Pt. Tamburlaine* Prol., Iygging vaine of riming mother wits. **1623** Camden *Rem.* (ed. 3) 6 For Wales..an old riming Poet sung thus [etc.]. **1641** Milton *Ch. Govt.* ii. Wks. 1851 III. 149 The trencher fury of a riming parasite. **1711** E. Ward *Vulgus Brit.* ii. 119 For no Fanatick Riming Brother Can well do one without the other. **1764** Churchill *Candidate* 149 Some riming guest Roams thro' the church-yard, whilst his Dinner's dress'd.

2. = RHYMING *ppl. a.* 2.

1563 *Mirr. Mag.* ii. 145 b, Is it treason in a riming frame To clyp, to stretche, to adde, or chaunge a name? **1589** Puttenham *Eng. Poesie* i. v. (Arb.) 26 The American, the Perusine and the very Canniball, do sing and also say, their highest and holiest matters in certaine riming versicles. **1627** Hakewill *Apol.* (1630) 251 Sophisticate eloquence and riming harmony of words. **1665** Cosin *Memorandum* (Surtees) 269 Some former Deanes..have appoynted..a ryming Psalm to be sung instead of the Nicene Creed before Sermon. **1775** Tyrwhit *Lang. & Versificat. Chaucer* 56 Except a few lines in the Saxon Chronicle..and a short Canticle,..I have not been able to discover any attempts at Riming Poetry, which can with probability be referred to an earlier period than the reign of Henry the Second. **1867** Freeman *Norm. Conq.* (1877) I. App. 562 In the riming Chronicle of John Page. **1873** Morris *O.E. Hom.* Ser. ii. Introd. p. vii. *note*, The Moral Ode being a ryming poem.

rimland ('rɪmlənd). [f. RIM *sb.*^{1} + LAND *sb.*] A peripheral area of land of political or strategic significance.

1944 N. J. Spykman *Geogr. of Peace* iv. 38/1 The central continental plain can continue to be called the heartland but ..it is..to be equated with the political extent of the Union of Soviet Socialist Republics. Beyond the mountain barrier, the coastland region..may..be referred to as the rimland, a name which defines its character accurately. *Ibid.* 43/2 In the three great world wars of the nineteenth and twentieth centuries,..the British and Russian empires have lined up together against an intervening rimland power as led by Napoleon, Wilhelm II, and Hitler. **1973** J. C. Plano et al. *Polit. Sci. Dict.* 331 *Rimland theory*, the theory that emphasizes the rimlands of Europe, the Middle East, Africa, South Asia, and the Far East as the keys to the security of the United States. **1979** *Daily Tel.* 23 June 17/3 Commanders of the small forces of Western Europe are extremely disturbed by the strong hold the Soviet Union and its satellites have acquired in what are dubbed 'the rimlands' of the world's greatest concentration of crude oil in the Persian Gulf.

ˈrimless, *a.* [f. RIM *sb.*[1] + -LESS.] Having no rim; without a rim, esp. of spectacles.
1802 WORDSW. *Beggars* v, The other wore a rimless crown. **1832** WILSON in *Blackw. Mag.* XXXII. 178 That small, spokey, but rimless wheel. **1897** *Westm. Gaz.* 8 May 1/3 Wearing an immaculate frock-coat and a rimless eyeglass. **1908** *Sears, Roebuck & Co. Catal.* 187/2 Rimless spectacles are the very latest and most stylish spectacles made. **1923** A. HUXLEY *Antic Hay* x. 156 And for full dress, gold-mounted rimless pince-nez are refinement itself. **1934** J. B. PRIESTLEY *Eng. Journey* i. 5 He had a sharp nose, a neat moustache, rimless eyeglasses. **1953** K. TENNANT *Joyful Condemned* xviii. 162 The magistrate looked over the top of his rimless glasses. **1977** D. JAMES *Spy at Evening* vii. 38 He ..balanced a pair of rimless spectacles on the tip of his nose.

rimlet, dial. variant of REMNANT.

rimmed (rɪmd), *a.* [f. RIM *sb.*[1] or *v.*[1]]
1. Having a rim of a specified colour, form, material, etc.
1729 *Dampier's Voy.* (ed. 3) III. 425 The Black-rimm'd Butterfly. **1818** KEATS *Endymion* I. 50 Before the daisies, vermeil rimm'd and white, Hide in deep herbage. **1850** R. G. CUMMING *Hunter's Life S. Afr.* (1902) 145/2 He..wore a broad-rimmed hat. **1887** BROWNING *Parleyings, B. de Mandeville* iv, Thy gold-rimmed amber-headed cane.
2. Having or furnished with a rim.
1777 PENNANT *Brit. Zool.* IV. 52 *marg.*, Asterias, *irregularis*, rimmed. **1792** *Trans. Soc. Arts* III. 166 Whether mortice, case, or rimmed locks. **1833** LOUDON *Encycl. Archit.* §1805 On each is to be a 7-inch iron and rimmed lock.
3. ***rimmed steel*** = *rimming steel* s.v. RIMMING (*ppl.*) *a.*
1926 *Iron Age* CXVII. 1778 (*heading*) Rimmed steel and how it is made. **1926** *Jrnl. Iron & Steel Inst.* CXIV. 579 The particular physical features of an ingot of good rimmed steel are a solid outer skin and certain gas-holes. **1959** *Ibid.* CXCI. 231 A statistical investigation into the existence of a functional relationship between tapping slag iron and carbon and manganese losses in rimmed steels. **1963** W. H. DENNIS *Metallurgy of Ferrous Metals* xiii. 199 Rimmed steels possess a high degree of cleanliness.

†**rimmel.** *Sc. Obs.* In 5 rymmyll, remel. [Of obscure origin.] A blow.
1375 BARBOUR *Bruce* XII. 557 Men mycht se..mony a riall rymmyll ryde Be roucht thair apon athir syde. *c* **1450** HOLLAND *Howlat* 842 Quhen thai had remelis raucht, Thai forthocht that thai faucht.

ˈrimmer[1]. *U.S.* [f. RIM *v.*[1]] An implement designed for cutting and ornamenting the edges of pastry, etc.
1875 KNIGHT *Dict. Mech.* 1943/2.

ˈrimmer[2]. *U.S.* [f. RIM *v.*[2]] A straight knife used in rimming mackerel.
1876 G. B. GOODE *Anim. Res. U.S.* 22 Mackerel rimmers or fatting knives.

rimmer[3]. U.S. var. RIMER *sb.*[2]

ˈrimming, (*vbl.*) *sb.* [f. RIM *sb.*[1] or *v.*[1]] The action of providing with a rim; a rim or border.
1831 CARLYLE *Sart. Res.* I. x, The Carman, who understands..the rimming of wheels..is the more cunningly gifted of the two. **1868** MENKEN *Infelicia* 81 To-night, O Soul! Shut off thy little rimmings of Hope.

ˈrimming, *ppl. a.* [f. RIM *sb.*[1] or *v.*[1]] ***rimming steel***: a low-carbon steel in which deoxidation has been controlled and limited to produce ingots having an outer rim or skin relatively free from carbon and impurities.
1926 *Iron Age* CXVII. 1778 Rimming steel is also called by some 'open steel', because the top of the ingot does not freeze over as rimming in proceeds, but the central metal continues fluid and in active motion for some minutes after teeming. **1930** *Engineering* 14 Mar. 357/2 Exceptions are metals such as steel of the 'rimming' type, from which very large quantities of gas are rapidly evolved during solidification. **1956** J. DEARDEN *Iron & Steel To-Day* (ed. 2) ix. 148 Low carbon steel which has been only partially killed is known as 'rimming steel' because of the rim of almost pure iron which forms the outer portion of the ingot. **1967** A. H. COTTRELL *Introd. Metallurgy* xi. 138 The alternative is to prevent the metal from shrinking by allowing a small amount of CO to form as bubbles, when it freezes. This is done in rimming steels. These are low-carbon (< 0·15 per cent C) steels usually used for sheet steel pressings.

‖**rimon** (riˈmoːn). Pl. rim(m)onim. [Heb., lit. pomegranate.] A pomegranate-shaped ornament for a Jewish Law-scroll. Cf. POMEGRANATE 2.
[**1845** J. KITTO *Cycl. Bibl. Lit.* II. 635/1 Rimmon..is mentioned in numerous places in the Old Testament, and is universally acknowledged to denote the Pomegranate-tree and fruit... We find frequent mention of it as an ornament ..in the temple.] **1946** *Hebrew Union Coll. Ann.* XIX. 363 Three Torah scrolls,..in vertical positions, are visible, dressed in beautiful mantles and crowned with golden *Rimmonim*. **1962** 'E. MCBAIN' *Empty Hours* 112 'I was putting the *rimonim* back onto the handles of the scroll.' 'Putting the what, sir?' Carella asked. 'Listen to the big Talmudic scholar,' Meyer said, grinning. 'Doesn't even know what *rimonim* are. They're those decorative silver covers, Steve, shaped like pomegranates.' **1976** Y. L. BIALER *Jewish Life* 188 *Rimon*, an adornment for the *sefer Torah*. *Ibid.* 189 *Rimonim* are made of gold, silver, crystal,..shaped like upright crowns, arched towers, [etc.].

rimose (raɪˈməʊs), *a.* Chiefly *Bot.* [ad. L. *rīmōs-us*, f. *rīma* RIMA.] Full of, or having, fissures or chinks; rimous.
1726 BAILEY, *Rimose*, full of Clefts or Chinks. **1793** MARTYN *Lang. Bot.*, *Rimosus*, rimose, or chinked..; as the outer bark of some trees. **1858** MAYNE *Expos. Lex.*, *Rimosipes*, having rimose, or fissured feet. **1866** *Intell. Observer* 96 The pileus being longitudinally rimose. **1887** W. PHILLIPS *Brit. Discomycetes* 294 Sporidia 8,..smooth, or rarely minutely and irregularly rimose.
Hence **riˈmosity.** $rare^{-0}$.
1726 in BAILEY, and in later Dicts.

†**riˈmosous**, *a.* $Obs.^{-0}$ [Cf. prec. and next.] 'Full of chincks, chaps, or clefts' (Blount, 1656).

rimous (ˈraɪməs), *a.* [ad. L. *rīmōs-us*: see RIMOSE *a.*] Full of fissures, chinks, or cracks.
1709 *Phil. Trans.* XXVII. 151 Its External Surface seems to be both porous and rimous. **1776** J. LEE *Introd. Bot.* Explan. Terms 379 *Rimosus*, rimous, the outward Bark full of Cracks and Fissures. **1899** *Allbutt's Syst. Med.* VIII. 509 *Rimous* or *fissured eczema*, is that in which the inflamed skin forms deep cracks.

‖**rimpi**, var. RIEMPIE.

rimple (ˈrɪmp(ə)l), *sb.* Now *dial.* Also 5 **rymple, rympyl.** [Corresponds in sense to (M)Du. and (M)LG. *rimpel*, but may rather represent an OE. ablaut-variant **hrympel* (cf. the gloss '*Rugis*, hrypellum' in Wr.-Wülcker 531, where perhaps *m* should be supplied). See also RUMPLE *sb.* and WRIMPLE *sb.*
The simpler form *rimpe* occurs in MDu. and MLG., together with the vb. *rimpen*, = OE. **hrimpan* (pa. pple. *ȝehrumpen*), OHG. *rimfan* (pa. pple. *girumpfan*), G. *rimpfen* (now *rümpfen*).]
1. A wrinkle.
c **1440** *Promp. Parv.* 434/1 Rympyl, or rymple (or wrynkyl), *ruga, rugadia*. **1447** BOKENHAM *Seyntys* (Roxb.) 297 Ner rymples aspyin in hyr no man myht. **1578** LYTE *Dodoens* 22 The great Bistorte hath long leaues..wrinkled or drawen into rimples. **1597** A. M. tr. *Guillemeau's Fr. Chirurg.* 18/2 The skinne beinge cutt accordinge to the rimples, might chaunce to fall on the eyes. **1682** *Phil. Collections* No. 5. 154 A single Muscular string, wherein I have often seen certain rings or circular rimples. *Ibid.*, When the Muscle is extended, these Muscular strings are without rimples. *a* **1825** FORBY *Voc. E. Anglia*, *Rimple*, a wrinkle.
2. (See quot.)
1877 *Holderness Gloss.*, *Rimple*, (1) a ripple on water; (2) the sound produced by it.

rimple (ˈrɪmp(ə)l), *v. rare.* [f. RIMPLE *sb.*, or back-formation from RIMPLED *a.* Cf. RIMPLING *vbl. sb.* and (M)Du. *rimpelen*.] *trans.* To wrinkle, pucker; to ripple.
1755 JOHNSON, *To Rimple*, to pucker; to contract into corrugations. **1791** E. DARWIN *Bot. Gard.* I. 113 Glad Echo ..Curls her deep wells, and rimples all her lakes. **1791** MRS. RADCLIFFE *Rom. Forest* (1820) III. 96 The air [was] so still that it scarcely..rimpled the broad expanse of the waters below.

rimpled (ˈrɪmp(ə)ld), *a.* Now *dial.* or *U.S.* Also 5 **rympled, -yd,** 6 **rimpeled.** [f. RIMPLE *sb.*] Wrinkled, puckered; rippled.
c **1400** *Rom. Rose* 4495 Ther is set to kepe, foule hir bi-falle! A rimpled vekke, fer ronne in age. **1426** LYDG. *De Guil. Pilgr.* 13336, I am ryht foul for to beholde; My chekys Rympled and ryht Olde. *c* **1450** *Merlin* 90 A man that semed right olde and rympled. **1590** BARROUGH *Meth. Physick* I. xv. (1639) 22 A bath of sweet water is good for him, if the body be dry and rimpled. **1597** A. M. tr. *Guillemeau's Fr. Chirurg.* 2 b/2 The navle..that which is rimpeled. **1759** *Phil. Trans.* LI. 39 The skin [was]..rimpled in two or three places, but not broken. **1829** BURTT in J. Paterson *Contemporaries of Burns* (1844) 175 We'll..smile at the moon's rimpled face in the wave. **1885** *Cent. Mag.* Mar. 681/2 A heavy rimpled mass of lemon-colored hair.

ˈrimpling, *vbl. sb.* [Cf. prec. and RIMPLE *v.*; also MDu. *rimpelinge*.] Wrinkling; rippling.
a **1470** H. PARKER *Dives & Pauper* (W. de W. 1496) 343/2 Rymplynge or reuelynge of the skynne. **1597** A. M. tr. *Guillemeau's Fr. Chirurg.* 18/2 We must consider one the rimpelinge of the skinne, and one the fibres of the muscles. **1807** CRABBE *Par. Reg.* I. 394 As gilds the moon the rimpling [*later edd.* rippling] of the brook.

Rimpoche, var. RINPOCHE.

†**rim ram ruff(e**: see RUM RAM RUF.
1595 PEELE *Old Wives' T.* E j b, It may be this rim ram ruffe is too rude an incounter.

rim-schoen, var. REMSKOEN.

rimstoc(k, -stoke: see RIMESTOCK.

†**rimth**, *sb. Obs. rare.* Forms: 1 rýmþ (?), 3 rumth, 5 rymthe. [? OE. *rýmþ* (Lye), f. *rúm* ROOM *a.* Cf. MDu. *ruumte, ruymte* (Du. *ruimte*), G. *räumte* and the later ROOMTH.] Room, space; leisure. ***a-rimth***, in wide array.
c **1205** LAY. 27492 Þa hæf þat fiht of þar studen þer heo ær fuhten, and bigunnen arumðe ræsen to-somne. *c* **1440** *Promp. Parv.* 434 Rymthe, or space, or rowme, *spacium*. *Ibid.*, Rymthe, or leysure, of tyme, *oportunitas, vel spacium temporis*.
Hence †**ˈrimth** *v.* = RIME *v.*[4] *Obs.*
c **1330** R. BRUNNE *Chron. Wace* (Rolls) 3492 Þey rempede [*Petyt MS.* rimethed] þem to reste a þrowe. **1338** —— *Chron.* (1810) 18 He tok his suerd in hand... Before þe kyng & his sons he rimthed þam þe way. *c* **1440** *Promp. Parv.* 434/2 Rymthyn, or make rymthe and space, *eloco*.

‖**rimu.** [Native name.] A tall evergreen tree of New Zealand (*Dacrydium cupressinum*), also called 'red pine'. Also ***rimu-pine, -tree***.
1835 W. YATE *Acc. New Z.* ii. (ed. 2) 40 Rimu... This elegant tree comes to its greatest perfection in shaded woods. **1843** DIEFFENBACH *Trav. New Z.* I. xiv. 224 What ..can be more delicate than the graceful rimu-pine with pendent branches? **1872** DOMETT *Ranolf* VI. iii. 117 He lay couched in a rimu-tree one day. **1900** *Longman's Mag.* Jan. 232 Feathery rimus, scraggy topped white pines, fern trees.

rimy (ˈraɪmɪ), *a.* Forms: 1 **hrímiȝ,** 6 **rimie,** 7 **rymie,** 6– **rimy.** [OE. *hrímiȝ*, f. *hrím* RIME *sb.*[2] Cf. Fris. *rimich*, Sw. *rimmig*, Icel. *hrímugr*.] Covered with, abounding in, rime or hoar-frost; accompanied by rime; frosty.
971 *Blickl. Hom.* 209 Wæron norð of ðæm stane awexene swiðe hrimiȝe bearwas. *a* **1000** *Gnomic Verses* 6 in *O.E. Chron.* (1892) I. 280 Winter byð cealdost, lencten hrimiȝost. **1587** MASCALL *Govt. Cattle* Index, Rimy grasse ill for sheep. **1612** PEACHAM *Gentl. Exerc.* I. x. (1634) 38 Trees that appear twice as bigge in a mistie or rymie morning then indeed they are. **1693** EVELYN *De la Quint. Compl. Gard.* II. 6 The Wood being altogether cover'd with a rimy Frost. **1787–9** WORDSW. *Evening Walk* 356 Rimy without speck, extend the plains. **1824** MISS R. MITFORD *Village* Ser. I. (1863) 12 The sky..throwing out in bold relief the snow-covered roofs of our village, and the rimy trees that rise above them. **1859** GEO. ELIOT *A. Bede* lv, Martin Poyser, looking as cheery as a bright fire on this rimy morning. **1886** J. ASHBY STERRY *Lazy Minstrel* (1892) 110 The railings were rusty and rimy.

rin, *sb.*[1] *dial.* ? *Obs.* [Cf. OE. *sealtes rynia* app. in the same sense.] Brine.
1787 W. MARSHALL *Norfolk* (1795) II. 386.

‖**rin** (rɪn), *sb.*[2] [Jap.] A Japanese monetary unit, equal to $\frac{1}{10}$ sen; also, a coin of this value. Also *collect.* as *pl.*
1875 [see YEN[1]]. **1875** [see SEN]. **1891** A. M. BACON *Japanese Girls & Women* vi. 160 There is something picturesque about these sen and rin. **1931** *Economist* 2 May 947/1 [Japanese] savings banks followed suit..reducing the rate [on deposits] by 1 rin per diem or 0·365 per cent per annum. **1962** R. A. G. CARSON *Coins* 548 The bronze sen and 5 rin pieces of this reign had as obverse type the kiri-flower crest which had appeared on the gold obans and kobans of the shogunate.

rin, Sc. var. RUN *sb.* and *v.*

rinabout, Sc. var. RUNABOUT.

‖**riˈnatrix.** *Obs. rare.* [An old misreading of *Et natrix* in Lucan ix. 720.] A water-snake.
1601 R. CHESTER *Love's Martyr* (1878) 113 Here liues the Worme, the Gnat and Grashopper, Rinatrix, Lizard and the fruitfull Bee. *Ibid.* 115, 123.

rince, rinch, obs. or dial. ff. RINSE *sb.* and *v.*

‖**rinceau** (rɛ̃so). *Art.* Also 8 **rainçeau.** [Fr., in the same sense.] (See quot. 1962.)
1778 R. & J. ADAM *Works in Archit.* I. 5 We..have added grace and beauty to the whole, by a mixture of grotesque (E) stucco, and painted ornaments, together with the flowing rainçeau (F) with its fanciful figures and winding foliage. **1917** A. D. F. HAMLIN *Hist. Ornament* vii. 98 The *rinceau*.. which is a combination of the S-line, the spiral, the vine-motive and the acanthus leaf, was developed during the Alexandrian age into an ornament which has contributed a most important element into the splendor of Roman, medieval and modern art. **1941** *Burlington Mag.* July 25/1 There is an eagle at each corner with *rinceaux*, and above are half-compartments with garlands. **1962** R. G. HAGGAR *Dict. Art Terms* 290/2 *Rinceau*, an elaborate foliated spiral or scroll pattern.

rind (raɪnd), *sb.*[1] Forms: α. 1, 4– **rind** (4, 6 **riend,** 8–9 **rhind**), 5 **rynd;** (1–3) 4–7 **rinde,** 4–6 **rynde.** β. 5–7 **ryne** (6 **ryn**), 6– **rine,** 7–8 **rhine.** [OE. *rind* str. fem. (and *rinde* wk. fem.), = MDu. *rinde, rende, runde* (Du. *run*, Flem. also *rinde, renne* tan-bark), OS. *rinda* (MLG. *rinde*), OHG. *rinda, rinta* (G. *rinde*), MDa. *rind* (crust of bread).]
1. a. The bark of a tree or plant; sometimes, inner as contrasted with outer bark. Also with *a* and in pl. (now *rare*).
α. **888** K. ÆLFRED *Boeth.* xxxiv. §10 þæt treow bið utan.. bewæfed mid þære rinde. *c* **1000** *Sax. Leechd.* II. 114 ȝif he beget & yt rinde, sio þe cymð of neorxna-wonge, ne dereð him nan atter. *a* **1225** *Ancr. R.* 148 Heo haueð bipiled mine figer—irend of al þe rinde. *a* **1250** *Owl & Night.* 602 [Thou eatest] wormes ȝif þu miȝte finde Among þe uolde of harde rinde. *a* **1300** *Leg. Rood* (1871) 24 Ouer þe welle stod a tre.. Ac it ne bar noþer lef ne rynde. **1387** TREVISA *Higden* (Rolls) II. 303 Iacob took grene ȝerdes..and pyled of þe rynde in som place of þe ȝerdes. **1430–40** LYDG. *Bochas* VIII. xxv. (1558) 18 Trees may not thriue departed fro the rinde. *c* **1440** *Pallad. on Husb.* IV. 13 Too fynger long let sloute away the tre, But saue vppon that other half the rynde. **1523** SKELTON *Garl. Laurel* 21 A myghty tre..His leuis loste, the sappe was frome the rynde. **1578** LYTE *Dodoens* 167 The roote is..couered with a thinne..barke or rinde. **1638** BRATHWAIT *Barnabees Jrnl.* IV. (1818) 177 Osyers freshly showing With soft mossie rinde o'regrowing. **1664** EVELYN

Sylva (1679) 13 Other expedients there are by twisting the part, or baring it of the Rind. **1725** SWIFT *Riddle* Wks. 1751 X. 74 Depriv'd of Root, and Branch, and Rind, Yet Flow'rs I bear of every Kind. **1789** G. WHITE *Selborne* i, Its smooth rind or bark, its glossy foliage. **1839** KEMBLE *Resid. in Georgia* (1863) 87 It is a long green reed, and has a consistent pith, which, together with the rind itself, is extremely sweet. *a* **1845** BARHAM *Ingol. Leg.* Ser. III. *The Poplar*, Here stands the Poplar.. On whose tender rind.. We carved her initials.

pl. a **900** CYNEWULF *Crist* 1175 Ða wearð beam moniȝ blodȝum tearum birunnen under rindum. *c* **1320** *Pol. Songs* (Camden) 333 And bringe rotes and rindes bret ful a male. **1382** WYCLIF *Gen.* xxx. 37 Jacob.. vnryendide hem; and riendis drawun awey, in thilke that weren pilde semede whytnes. [*c* **1407** LYDG. *Reson & Sens.* 4955 And next besyde.. ypocrisie, Dedly of chere lyke a rynde.] ?*c* **1480** *Kyng & Hermit* 127 in Hazl. *E.P.P.* I. 18, I won here in wyldenes, With rotys and rynds among wyld bests. **1555** EDEN *Decades* (Arb.) 196 The leaues wherof are made of the inner ryndes or barkes of trees. **1600** SURFLET *Countrie Farme* III. lxiii. 576 All aromaticall rindes or woods, as cinnamom. **1689** PITMAN *Relation* in Arb. *Garner* VII. 356 We thought it time to.. stop the leaks of our boat, and to raise a deck over her with rinds of trees. **1712** J. JAMES tr. *Le Blond's Gardening* 83 Lines made of the Rinds of Lime-Tree. **1812** J. SMYTH *Pract. of Customs* (1821) 41 When Oak Bark in the rinds, is £2 10s. or upwards per load of rinds. **1835** tr. *Lamartine's Trav.* II. 64 Other trees with long stems and smooth rinds.

β. c **1430** *Syr Tryam.* 392 To berye hym was hys purpos, And scraped on hym bothe ryne and mosse. **1547** BOORDE *Brev. Health* xxv. 16 Take inwarde ryne or barke of an Oke. **1579** SPENSER *Sheph. Cal.* Feb. 111 Now the gray mosse marred his rine. **1602** *Narcissus* (1893) 339 To passe from braunch to barke, from rine to roote. **1657** G. THORNLEY *Daphnis & Chloe* 26 Chawing in her mouth the green ryne of the Elme. *c* **1700** in Evans *Old Ball.* (1784) II. 288 With linden's glossy rine Laurel-tresses intertwine. **1765** *Museum Rust.* IV. 107 The harle or rine of our hemp and flax. **1854** MISS BAKER *Northampt. Gloss.*, *Rine*, rind, or bark.

b. *Bot.* False, as contrasted with true, bark.

1857 HENFREY *Bot.* 530 The rind of the Monocotyledonous stem, totally different from true bark, is generally little developed. **1861** BENTLEY *Man. Bot.* 90 The whole is covered externally by a fibrous and cellular layer, called the false bark or rind.

c. *Arch.* (See quot. 1728.)

1726 LEONI *Alberti's Archit.* II. 33/1 The breadth of the rind which is to terminate in the Scroll must.. be equal to the Abacus. This rind must fall down on each side winding round like a Snail-shell. **1728** CHAMBERS *Cycl.* s.v. *Capital*, The middle Part is called a Rind, or Bark, from its suppos'd Resemblance to the Bark of a Tree laid on a Vase.

d. *Bot.* A hard outer layer on a fungus.

1887 H. E. F. GARNSEY tr. *A. de Bary's Compar. Morphol. & Biol. Fungi* iii. 58 In other forms the rind is distinguished from the medulla by gelatinous cell-walls, as in the pileus and stipe of Agaricus (Mycena) vulgaris. **1927** GWYNNE-VAUGHAN & BARNES *Struct. & Devel. Fungi* 1 The hyphae.. may give rise to root-like strands known as rhizomorphs, or to a compact resting body, the sclerotium, the outer cells of which are modified to form a rind, protecting the inner regions from desiccation. **1951** J. A. MACDONALD *Introd. Mycol.* ii. 14 In a few cases the mycelial cord is surrounded with a dark rind similar to that which surrounds a sclerotium. **1974** *Canad. Jrnl. Bot.* LII. 1128/2 About 5½ days after inoculation, a definite organization of mycelia to form the rind was observed.

†**2.** Coupled with *root*. **a.** In phrases denoting the origin or source of a person or thing. *Obs.*

c **1330** R. BRUNNE *Chron. Wace* (Rolls) 4286 We ar comen.. of o rote & of o rynde. *c* **1425** *Cast. Persev.* 1138 in *Macro Plays* 111 Envye, þou arte rote & rynde, þorwe þis werld, of mykyl myschefe. *c* **1500** KENNEDIE *Passion of Christ* 124 God hes the chosin to be baith rute and ryn For mannis peace. **1500–20** DUNBAR *Poems* lxxxv. 12 Wirgin matern, Of reuth baith rute and ryne.

†**b.** In phrases denoting complete rending up or destruction. *Obs.* (Cf. *root and branch* s.v. BRANCH *sb.* 6 b.)

1338 R. BRUNNE *Chron.* (1810) 333 Toward þe North he schoke, To chace kyng Robyn,.. destroie him rote & rynde. *c* **1420** LYDG. *Assembly of Gods* 66 He breketh hem asondre or rendeth hem roote & rynde Out of the erthe. *c* **1440** *Jacob's Well* 234 He schal stubbyn þe vp rynde & roote. *c* **1530** LD. BERNERS *Arth. Lyt. Bryt.* (1814) 172 The monster ranne to a tree.. and.. tare it vp rote and rinde.

3. The peel or skin of fruits and vegetables.

α. c **1400** *Lanfranc's Cirurg.* 181 Frote it wiþ ryndis of an oynoun til it bicome drie. *c* **1450** *M.E. Med. Bk.* (Heinrich) 208 þe scales of notes ant ryndes. **1541** ELYOT *Cast. Helthe* II. 23 The ryndes [of oranges] taken in a littell quantitee, doo comfort the stomacke. **1594** PLAT *Jewell-ho.* II. (1653) 39 Lettinge the cloues & riendes [of oranges and lemons] remaine in oile. **1667** MILTON *P.L.* IV. 249 Others whose fruit burnisht with Golden Rinde Hung amiable. **1676** WORLIDGE *Cyder* (1691) 205 One of the most solid apples that grows, of a tough rind. **1748** *Anson's Voy.* III. ii. 310 The fruit.. is covered with a rough rind. **1764** ELIZA MOXON *Eng. Housew.* (ed. 9) 163 Take three or four seville oranges, .. and boil the rinds. **1830** M. DONOVAN *Dom. Econ.* I. 301 Those [apples] whose flesh and rind are green are very inferior. **1875** JOWETT *Plato* (ed. 2) III. 696 The fruits having a hard rind.

β. **1558** WARDE tr. *Alexis' Secr.* IV. 75 b, Take the ryne or the scrapynges of Rubarbe. **1588** PARKE tr. *Mendoza's Hist. China* 393 It is in forme like vnto a mellon, whose ryne is somewhat harde. **1605** WILLET *Hexapla Gen.* 215 The fruit.. is outwardly like other fruite, but within the rine there is nothing but dust and ashes. **1669** BOYLE *Cont. New Exp.* II. (1682) 183 The pieces of Apple were much corrupted, for their skin or rine was taken off.

4. a. The outer crust, skin, or integument *of* anything; also, a crust, etc. Also *spec.* in *Anat.*

c **1000** ÆLFRIC *Hom.* II. 114 We hedað þære crumena ðæs hlafes, and ða ludeiscan gnaȝað þa rinde.

c **1400** *Lanfranc's Cirurg.* 161 þanne þou schalt leie in the wounde.. oile of rosis, til al þe rynde of þe brennyng falle awei. **1483** *Cath. Angl.* 308/2 þe Rynde of a nege. *c* **1550** H. LLOYD *Treas. Health* X ij, Take the horne of a gote and burne it.. and yᵉ rind that ryseth therof at that tyme take and stampe it. **1555** W. WATREMAN *Fardle Facions* I. ii. 30 Those humours so riped, drawyng vp to the rinde of the earth. **1601** SIR W. CORNWALLIS *Ess.* i, The Lapidary is not sory when he hath gotten the rinde, or barke of a Jewell from what is precious. **1796** KIRWAN *Elem. Min.* (ed. 2) I. 225 Surface.. covered with a greyish white rind. **1811** *Self Instructor* 27 Scrape off the thin rind of the quill. **1822–34** *Good's Study Med.* (ed. 4) IV. 463 Simple fish-skin. The incrustation forming a harsh papulated or watery rind. **1857** LIVINGSTONE *Trav.* xxvii. 542 Large rounded masses of granite, containing black mica... The outer rind of it inclines to peel off. **1950** [see ADRENAL *a.*]. **1974** *Nature* 4 Oct. 428/2 The ganglia have a cell rind formed by nerve cell perikarya.

†**b.** The verge or rim *of* something; the border *of* a country. *Obs.*

Prob. by phonetic confusion with *rime* RIM *sb.*¹

1530 *Act 22 Hen. VIII*, c. 11 The sayde Dykes, or.. any other banke, beyng parcele of the rynde & uttermost parte of the sayde contrey of Marshe lande. **1552** HULOET, Rynde of a countrey, *fines.* **1584** R. SCOT *Discov. Witchcr.* XII. xvii. 262 Sticke a paire of sheeres in the rind of a siue. **1608** TOPSELL *Serpents* 216 Vppon the ridge of his backe.. and vnderneath vpon the ryne or brimme of his belly are certaine haires growing.

5. a. The skin of a person or animal. Now *esp.* of bacon. Also *spec.* in dial. (see quots. 1828, 1868).

1513 DOUGLAS *Æneis* IX. vii. 99 With the dynt the rynde is revin sua, Hys hart pipis the scharp hed persyt in tua. *a* **1550** *Hye Way to Spittel Ho.* 112 in Hazl. *E.P.P.* IV. 28 Scabby and scuruy, pocke eaten flesh and rynde. **1607** TOPSELL *Four-f. Beasts* (1658) 535 To rub the tongue with the inner side of the rines of Bacon. **1667** MILTON *P.L.* I. 206 The Pilot.. With fixed Anchor in his skaly rind Moors by his side. **1772–84** *Cook's Voy.* (1790) V. 1769 The flesh and rind of which they cut into large pieces, dry them as they do herrings, and eat them. **1828** *Craven Gloss.*, *Rine*, the skin, or thin membrane under the skin. **1868** ATKINSON *Cleveland Gloss.* App., *Rind*, the inner or true skin in opposition to the cuticle or scarf-skin. **1870** E. P. WRIGHT tr. *Figuier's Mammalia* 59 To separate the oil from this enormous greasy rind.

†**b.** A membrane or pellicle; *esp.* the pia mater or the peritoneum. *Obs.*

Perh. by confusion with *rime* RIM *sb.*²

1585 HIGINS *Junius' Nomencl.* 32/1 The inner rine of the belly, which is ioyned to the cawll, and wherewith all the entrailes are couered. **1598** FLORIO, *Omento*,.. the rinde or thin skin inwrapping the braine. **1668** CULPEPPER & COLE *Barthol. Anat.* III. iii. 135, I am of Opinion that in the Brain, properly so called, or the Rinde, is contained Animal Spirit for Sense. **1693** tr. *Blancard's Phys. Dict.* (ed. 2), *Rhegma*, a Breaking or Bursting of any part, as of a Bone, the inner Rine of the Belly, the Eye, &c.

6. *fig.* (chiefly from sense 1). The surface or external aspect *of* something, as contrasted with the inner or true nature.

α. c **897** K. ÆLFRED *Gregory's Past. C.* 54 On hiora modes rinde moniȝ god weorc to wyrceanne, ac on ðæm piðan bið oðer ȝehyded.

1551 T. WILSON *Logike* (1580) 57 The Gospell resteth.. not in the outwarde rinde, but in the very harte. **1618** E. ELTON *Rom.* vii. (1622) 292 They rest in the outward rinde and barke of the law. **1646** J. HALL *Horæ Vac.* 57 Histories for the most part pick but at the Rind of businesse. **1704** SWIFT *T. Tub* i, Many Readers.. who will by no means be persuaded to inspect beyond the Surface and the Rind of Things. **1758** L. TEMPLE *Sketches* (ed. 2) 53 A bearish Figure is almost certainly the Rhind or Husk of a rude rough Soul. **1813** COLERIDGE *Remorse* II. ii, You are no dullard, But one that strips the outward rind of things. **1841** EMERSON *Ess.*, *Over-soul*, With each divine impulse the mind rends the thin rinds of the visible and finite.

β. **1582** STANYHURST *Æneis* (Arb.) 3 Gnibling vpon thee outward ryne of a supposed historie. **1591** HARINGTON *Orl. Fur.* Pref. ¶iiij, For the litterall sence (as it were the vtmost barke or ryne). **1627** J. DOUGHTY *Serm. Divine Myst.* (1628) 16 Those things which we doe vnderstand, we know but in the rine & slightly. **1681** H. MORE *Exp. Dan.* App. II. 285 The Reader must learn to distinguish.. betwixt the Rine and the Pulp of these.. Symbolical Visions. **1738** tr. *Guazzo's Art Convers.* 173, I very well perceive, that you regard nothing more than the outward Rine.

b. The outward form of persons. *rare.*

c **1412** HOCCLEVE *De Reg. Princ.* 3576 God took vppon him humble buxumnesse Whan he him wrappid in our mortell rynde. **1607** MIDDLETON *Fam. Love* III. iii, You're my better in bark and rine, but in pith and substance I may compare with you. **1634** MILTON *Comus* 664 Thou canst not touch the freedom of my minde.., although this corporal rinde Thou hast immanacl'd.

c. *slang.* Impudence, effrontery, 'cheek'. Cf. CRUST *sb.* 7 b.

1903 A. M. BINSTEAD *Pitcher in Paradise* iii. 79 With that preface they had the immortal rind to pull out a fifth document for me to sign, guaranteeing them the starting-price as returned nightly in *The Evening Standard.* **1915** WODEHOUSE *Something Fresh* v. 154 You have the immortal rind to suppose that I will stand being nagged and bullied. **1977** *Times Lit. Suppl.* 1 July 791/1 *The Björn Borg Story* (I'm glad they didn't have the rind to use the word 'Life').

7. *Comb.*, as ***rind-fungus***, ***-gall***, ***-hoop***; **rind grafting**, grafting in which the scion is inserted between the bark and the wood of a stump; = *crown-grafting* s.v. CROWN *sb.* 35; so **rind graft**; **rind-tabberer**, *dial.* (see quot. 1848).

1894 *Nat. Science* Oct. 251 The Rind-fungus (*Trichosphæria Sacchari*) described as the most dangerous and widespread enemy of the cane cultivation of the present day. **1794** *Rigging & Seamanship* 8 *Rind-gall*, a damage the tree received when young. **1869** RANKINE *Machine & Hand-tools* App. 66 'Rind-galls', or wounds in a layer of the wood, which have been covered and concealed by the growth of subsequent layers over them. **1947** R. J. GARNER *Grafter's Handbk.* viii. 181 Unlike the oblique cleft the rind graft must be tied firmly with soft string. **1956** *Dict. Gardening* (R. Hort. Soc.) (ed. 2) II. 918/1 All those [branches and spurs] left are grafted by whip-and-tongue or rind-grafts according to size. **1726** R. BRADLEY *Improvements Planting & Gardening* (ed. 5) 558 The first Sort of Graffing which I shall mention, is that Sort which we call Whip Graffing, or Rind Graffing. **1881** *Encycl. Brit.* XII. 236/2 Crown-grafting or rind-grafting.. is preferable to cleft-grafting, inasmuch as it leaves no open spaces in the wood. **1882** *Garden* 25 Mar. 200/1 The only mode of grafting employed is that called crown or rind grafting. **1969** *E. Afr. Agric. & Forestry Jrnl.* XXXV. 144/2 An attempt was made to try 'rind grafting' on the species at breast height.. under field conditions. **1670** J. SMITH *Eng. Improv. Reviv'd* 89 From the Remainder of the Chesnut.. may be chosen 63600 Rods for bark or ryne hoops. **1848** A. B. EVANS *Leicestershire Gloss.* 75 *Roin-tabberer*,.. i.e. the 'rind-tabberer', or tapper, viz. the woodpecker.

rind (raɪnd), *sb.*² Also 4–6 rynd(e, 9 rynd (roynd); 7 rinde, 7–9 rine. [ME. *rynd*, = MDu. *rijn* masc. (still in dial. use), *rīne* fem. (mod.Flem. *rijne*), MLG. *rîn*, *ryn* (still in use). These forms appear to prove that the final *d* of the Eng. word is excrescent.] An iron fitting serving to support an upper millstone on the spindle. Cf. MILL-RIND and INK *sb.*²

c **1343** *Durh. Acc. Rolls* (Surtees) 543 In.. ij Ryndes fac. de proprio ferro. **1453–4** *Ibid.* 191 Pro renovacione de le spyndellez et rynd. **1466–7** *Ibid.* 641 Pro emundacione de le fleme et factura medietatis de le rynde ejusdem molendini. **1598** *Reg. Privy Council Scot.* V. 495 [They] brak his said myln,.. tuke away with thame the spyndill, rynd and trymmill brodis of the said miln. **1639** FULLER *Holy War* V. xxiv. 271 [Cross] Molinée, because like to the rind of a mill. **1764** J. FERGUSON *Lect.* 47 The top part of the spindle.. goes into a square hole in a strong iron cross.. called the rynd. *Ibid.*, The rynd is let into grooves in the under surface of the running millstone, and so turns it round. **1828** J. HUNTER *South Yorks.* I. 241 A shield with a device showing the old form of the mill roynd. **1888** *Jrnl. Derbysh. Archaeol. Soc.* X. 54 The spindle being either of the same piece as the 'rine' or keyed into it.

attrib. **1417** *Durh. Acc. Rolls* (Surtees) 226, In j pari molarum.. cum hopys et ryndspindellis.

rind (raɪnd), *sb.*³ *north.* and *Sc.* Forms: *α.* 6, 9 rynd (9 rhynd), 7, 9 rind. *β.* 7 ryne, 7, 9 rine; 8 rhine, 9 rhyne. [Prob. an alteration of RIME *sb.*² The same change appears in dial. *hind*, var. of *hime* hoar-frost (Norw. *him*), and in the local forms *riner*, *rinder* for RIMER *sb.*² Cf. also RIND *sb.*¹ 4 b and 5 b.

It has, however, been suggested that *rind* may represent OE. *hrinde* in Beowulf 1363, usually altered to *hrimȝe* after the passage in Blickl. Hom. 209.]

= RIME *sb.*² Also with *a* and pl.

α. **1575** TURBERV. *Venerie* 31 Whereas the ryndes, the water droppes, and other coldnesse doth fall upon him continually. *Ibid.* 76 Those hounds that are quickest of sente: which are not best for the mornings bicause of the ryndes and dewes. **1648** HEXHAM II, *Rijm*, a Rind, or a small Frost. [**1828** MOIR *Mansie Wauch* xxii, Sharp frosty nights that left all the window-soles whitewashed over with frost-rind in the morning.] **1864** DOUBLEDAY in Crawhall *Garland N.C. Anglers* 299 'Mang the lang grass.. The rind clings white and pearly. **1894** *Hetton-le-hole Gloss.* s.v., There's a heavy (or, thick) rind on.

β. **1611** COTGR., *Bruiné*, hoarie, as a thing thats couered with a mistie ryne. **1642** H. MORE *Song of Soul* I. II. xxxi. Wks. (Grosart) 22 Like winter-morn bedight with snow and rine And sunny rayes, so did his goodly Eldship shine. **1656** [? J. SERGEANT] tr. *T. White's Peripat. Inst.* 147 Expecting Ice and a Rine the next day. **1754** *Phil. Trans.* XLVIII. 508 The rhine, or hoar-frost,.. was composed of curious thin figured plates. **1824** MACTAGGART *Gallovid. Encycl.* Rhyne.

†**rind**, *sb.*⁴ *Obs.* In 5 rynd-. [Perh. of Scand. origin. Cf. Norw. *rinde*, *rind* ridge, bank, etc.] ? A bank or brake.

?*a* **1400** *Morte Arth.* 921 Thane they roode by þat ryuer, .. þare þe ryndez ouerrechez with realle bowghez. *Ibid.* 1884 Thane relyez þe renkes.. For to ryotte þe wode..; Ransakes the ryndez alle. *Ibid.* 3363 Than raykes cho with roo.. To þe ryndes of þe wode.

rind (raɪnd), *v.*¹ [f. RIND *sb.*¹ Cf. the earlier UNRIND.] **a.** *trans.* To strip the rind or bark from (a tree, etc.). Hence **'rinding** *vbl. sb.*

1580 HOLLYBAND *Treas. Fr. Tong*, *Escorcement*, a barking of trees, a pilling, a rinding. **1623** WYNNE in Whitbourne *Disc. Newfoundland* 110 There haue bin rinded this yere not so few as 50000 trees. **1698–9** *Stat. Admiralty, Navy*, etc. (1810) 27 That no Person.. shall.. rind any of the trees there standing or growing. **1708** *Lond. Gaz.* No. 4452/2 The Inhabitants do Rind the Trees. **1797** *Encycl. Brit.* (ed. 3) IV. 309/2 The very young trees are not fit for rinding. **1849** A. E. KNOX *Ornith. Rambles Sussex* 212 The operation of 'rinding' cannot be attempted until the sap has begun to flow. **1876** BANCROFT *Hist. U.S.* III. xvi. 498 Bearing long.. staves, white from being freshly rinded.

b. To rub or remove skin from (a person or animal) or from (an item of food, *esp.* bacon: see sense 5 of the sb.).

1893 *Eng. Illustr. Mag.* Sept. 872/1 Tom Walker used to rub his bleeding fingers in the dust after being rinded by David Harris. **1962** *Sunday Times* 14 Jan. 30/3 Rind the bacon rashers and peel the bananas.

rind (raɪnd), *v.*² *Sc.* and *north.* Forms: 6, 9 rynd (6 -e), 9 rhynde, 7, 9, rind, 8 reyn-, rein-. [Var. of RAND *v.*⁴, REND *v.*²] *trans.* To prepare (tallow, butter, etc.) for preservation by melting and clarifying; to render; to melt. Hence **'rinded** *ppl. a.*

1540 *Sc. Acts* c. 44 (1814) II. 378/2 That na maner of man ..tak vpoun hand to Rynd, melt, nor barrell talch. **1581** *Burgh Rec. Edinb.* (1882) 217 Thai faythfullie promittit..to caus the talloun bocht be him als weill ryndet and vnryndet to be tane of his hand. **1681** COLVIL *Whigs Supplic.* (1751) 78 It makes them..Keep rinded butter in charter chests. **1706** *Watson's Collect. Scots Poems* I. 60 First shear it small, and rind it sine Into a Kettle clean and fine. **1794** J. MILL *Diary* (S.H.S.) 101 A ship loaden with Reyned Tallow from Iceland. *Ibid.*, Many run there for the wrecks, etc., and were enrich'd by reind Tallow. **1844** H. STEPHENS *Bk. Farm* II. 106 As long as it [suet] is fresh it should be *rynded* or *rendered*, as it is termed. **1894** LATTO *Tam. Bodkin* xvi, Like to rhynde the very creesh aff my banes!

† **rind**, *v.*³ *Obs. rare*⁻⁰. [f. RIND *sb.*³] *intr.* To form rime or hoar-frost.

1648 HEXHAM II, *Rijpen*, to Rinde, as upon trees frozen.

'rinded, *a.* Also 7 rin'd, 9 rhinded. [f. RIND *sb.*¹ and its variant *rine*.] Having a rind or bark, esp. of a specified kind. Also *fig.* with *up*.

1552 HULOET, Barked or rynded, *corticatus*. **1591** SPENSER *Virg. Gnat* 209 Here also grew the rougher rinded Pine. **1622** MABBE tr. *Aleman's Guzman d'Alf.* Pref. Verses, An vn-hewne peece of wood, I long haue beene, Knotty, and rugged, rinded vp in sinne. **1667** MILTON *P.L.* v. 342 Fruit of all kindes, in coate, Rough, or smooth rin'd. **1826** *Blackw. Mag.* XIX. 382 Floating along on the morning air from..the hollow-rhinded woods. **1833** TENNYSON *Eleanore* iii, With fruitage golden-rinded On golden salvers. **1841** BROWNING *Pippa Passes* ii, The soft-rinded smoothening facile chalk.

† **rindell**. *Sc. Obs.* = *rundlet*, RUNLET.

1659 *Records of Elgin* (New Spald. Cl.) I. 310 Fyue punshiones of wyne and tuo rindells of seck.

'rinder¹. [f. RIND *v.*²] A melter.

1805 FORSYTH *Beauties Scotl.* III. 287 A press similar to that which is used by the melters or rinders of tallow.

'rinder², dial. variant of RIMER *sb.*²

1829 J. HUNTER *Hallamsh. Gloss.*, *Rinder*, an instrument used for bevilling the sides of a round hole.

rinderpest ('rɪndəpɛst). [G. *rinderpest*, f. *rinder*, pl. of *rind* ox.] A virulent, infectious disease affecting ruminant animals, *esp.* oxen, characterized by fever, dysentery, and inflammation of the mucous membranes; cattle-plague.

1865 *Med. Times & Gaz.* 29 July 119/2 We understand that Prof. Simonds regards the disease as identical with the rinderpest or steppe murrain of Russia, Austria, etc. **1871** L. STEPHEN *Playgr. Eur.* 90 Daring sceptics, who doubted the efficacy of holy water as a remedy for rinderpest. **1884** *Standard* 10 Nov. 5/4 The outbreak of the rinderpest among the cattle which were to furnish food for the troops.

attrib. **1873** W. CORY *Lett. & Jrnls.* (1897) 350 He went wrong about the rinderpest rate.

fig. **1881** *Times* 17 Jan. 12/2 An organization which aims at stamping out a social rinderpest.

† **rindge**, obs. form of RENGE *sb.*²

1672 HOOLE *Comenius' Visible World* 103 The Baker sifteth the Meal in a rindge.

rindge, obs. form of RINGE *sb.*¹

'rinding-bird. *dial.* [f. *rinding* vbl. sb.: see RIND *v.*¹] The Wryneck.

1849 A. E. KNOX *Ornith. Rambles Sussex* 212 Wryneck.., provincial, Rinding Bird.

rindlass, variant of RENDLES, rennet.

rindle ('rɪnd(ə)l), *sb.* Forms: α. 1 rinnelle; rynel (5), renel, 4 ryneil, 5–6 rinel, 9 *Sc.* rinnal. β. 6 ryndle, 6– rindle. [OE. *rinnelle, rynele* fem., *rynel* masc., f. the stem *rin-, run-*; see RUN *v.*] A small watercourse or stream; a runnel.

α. *c* **825** *Vesp. Psalter* lxiv. 11 Rinnellan his indrencende [L. *rivos ejus inebrians*]. *c* **900** WÆRFERTH tr. *Gregory's Dial.* 94 Se æftra stream..se cymð of þære rynelan [*v.r.* burnan] þæs gastlican æsprynges. *c* **1000** *Blickl. Gloss.* Ps. lxiv. 11 *Riuos*, rynelas. *c* **1100** *Ags. Ps.* (Cant.) lxiv. 11 His reneles drencende. *a* **1325** *Prose Psalter* lxiv. 11 Fylland hys ryneils [*v.r.* ryuers]. *c* **1400** *Destr. Troy* 5709 The rynels wex red of the ronke blode. *Ibid.* 7506 Þai..Woundit hym wickedly ..þat þe Rinels of red blode ran doun his chekes. **1508** *Extr. Aberd. Reg.* (1844) I. 78 Nay litstaris..sall wesche thar stuf in the loche nor common rinelis [*printed* riuelis] of the toune.

β. **1547** SALESBURY, *Frwd ne afon vach*, a ryndel. **1555** WATREMAN *Fardle Facions* II. xi. 259 A garden plotte of delighte, full of swiete rindles of Christalline watre. **1670** *Phil. Trans.* V. 2016 There runs near it (at least in the Winter season) a small rindle (or gutter rather). **1686** PLOT *Staffordsh.* 42 Its subservient branches.., and innumerable other Rindles that fall into them. *c* **1746** J. COLLIER (Tim Bobbin) *View Lanc. Dial.* (ed. 2) 8 O Rindle o Wetur. **1841** S. BAMFORD *Life Radical* 113 Through the whole length of the valley, wends a sickly tan colored rindle. **1861** WAUGH *Goblin's Grave* 29 Fed by rindles and driblets from springs in the wood-shaded steep.

rindle ('rɪnd(ə)l), *v.* [f. prec.] *intr.* To stream or flow. Hence **'rindling** *ppl. a.*

1866 WAUGH in Harland *Lanc. Lyrics* 108 It winds by a rindlin' wayter side. **1895** CROCKETT *Men of Moss-Hags* xliv, The burn..rindling clear over slaty stones.

rindle, variant of RENDLES, rennet.

† **'rindled**, *ppl. a. Obs.*⁻¹ [Var. of *rinded*: see RIND *v.*²] Rendered, melted.

1601 HOLLAND *Pliny* II. 377 For the same purpose serueth the tried or rindled greace of sweatie wooll.

rindles(s, -lis, variants of RENDLES, rennet.

'rindless, *a. rare.* In 3 rindeleas, 9 rhindless. [f. RIND *sb.*¹] Without rind or bark.

a **1225** *Ancr. R.* 150 Nis hit muche reouðe þet þe figer.. schal adruwien rindeleas. **1831** *Blackw. Mag.* XXX. 966 The rhindless arms of the 'dodder'd oak'.

rindmart: see RYNMART.

rindy ('raɪndɪ), *a.*¹ [f. RIND *sb.*¹ + -Y.] Having a rind or hard skin.

1727 BAILEY (vol. II.), *Rindy*, having a Rind, *i.e.* a Skin to be pared off, as some Fruits. **1851** *Jrnl. R. Agric. Soc.* XII. II. 401 Turnips..either very large or 'fuzzy', or very close, 'rindy', hard, and stunted.

'rindy, *a.*² [f. RIND *sb.*³] Rimy.

1648 HEXHAM II, *Rijmachtigh*, Rindie, or Frostie. **1855** [ROBINSON] *Whitby Gloss.* s.v. *Rind*, 'Frost *rind*', hoar frost. 'T' land's all *rindy*', covered with it.

† **rine**, *v.*¹ *Obs.* Forms: 1 (h)rínan, 3 rinen, 4, 7 rine (4 rin, rene), 4–5 ryne, 5–6 rynde. *Pa. t.* 1 hrán, 3–4 ran, 4 rane, rone, 6 *Sc* ryndit. [OE. *hrínan*, = OS. and OHG. *hrînan* (MDu. and MHG. *rînen*) to touch, ON. *hrína* (Norw. *rina*) to take effect on. Cf. ARINE and ATRINE.]

1. *trans.* To touch; to affect.

Beowulf 988 Æghwylc ʒecwæd þæt him heardra nan hrinan wolde iren ærgod. *c* **1000** *Ags. Ps.* (Thorpe) ciii. 30 Ʒif he mid his mihte muntas hrineð. *a* **1225** *Ancr. R.* 408 Rin him mid ase muchele luue ase þu hauest summe mon..and he is þin. *a* **1300** *E.E. Psalter* xliv. 12 Forgete þi folke for to rine, And þe hous ofe fadre þine. *c* **1375** *Cursor M.* 24391 Þat stode vn-to mine hert rote; vn-rideli hit me rane. *a* **1400** *Minor Poems fr. Vernon MS.* 466 Ʒif Mon be ded and he him Ryne, He reiseþ him to lyue anone. *c* **1425** *Hampole's Psalter, Metr. Pref.* 48 Whos wol it write, I rede hym..make no more þen here is dygth, or ellys I rede hym hit ne ryne. **1483** *Cath. Angl.* 308/2 To Rynde, *vbi* to tuche. ? *a* **1500** *Chester Pl.* (Shaks. Soc.) II. 198 Ney, when you saw the least of myne,..With your riches you would not them ryne. **1674** RAY *N.C. Words*, To *Rine*, to touch.

2. *intr.* To lay the fingers or hand *on*, to fall *on*, to reach *to*, something.

c **1200** ORMIN 15518 Þurrh þatt ȝho ran upponn hiss claþ. *a* **1225** *Juliana* 56 Irnene gadien, kene te keoruen al þat ha rineð to as neil cniues. *a* **1300** *Cursor M.* 19277 Þe seke war born þam for to mete, Þat petre scaudu on þaim suld rine. *Ibid.* 21136 Þat folk ilkan wald oþer stemm, Qua rin moght titest on his hemm. *a* **1400–50** *Alexander* 3817 Freschely þai drynke, Bot was na renke at to it ran at euire rase eftire.

b. To take effect, to work, *on* one.

a **1300** *Cursor M.* 28334 Quen idel thoght me come and vain, oft i lete þam on me rene, To þai me drogh to dede o sine.

c. To touch *on* in discourse.

13.. *Cursor M.* 223 (Gött.), Þise er þe materis..þat i thinck in þis boke to schawe, Schortli renand [*Cott.* rimand] on þis dede.

3. To fall or belong to, to pertain *to*, a person or thing; to tend *to* something. Chiefly *Sc.*

a **1225** *Ancr. R.* 320 Euerich, efter þet he is, sigge þe totagges,—mon ase limpeð to him, wummon þet hire rineð. **1490** *Test. Ebor.* (Surtees) IV. 62, I will that..that good ryne to the profet of my iiij doghters. *c* **1500** KENNEDIE *Passion of Christ* 643 He callis him king, þaifor þou suld him slaa; For þat ryndis þi lordis maistie. **1550** *Reg. Privy Council Scot.* I. 85 To mak ony offence to ony Inglisman quhilk may rynde to the violatioun of the said peax. **1558** Q. KENNEDY *Compendius Tract.* in *Wodrow Misc.* I. 115 To do that thing quhilk ryndit to the weill of the rest. *Ibid.*, To do in all sortis that ryndis to thair office.

Hence † **'rining** *vbl. sb. Obs.*

c **950** *Lindisf. Gosp.*, *John* Contents xliii, Mið rining *vel* miððy [he] ȝehran ðæm sidum. *a* **1225** *Ancr. R.* 408 Mid þe rinunge of þine luue.

† **rine**, *v.*² *Obs.* Forms: 1 rínan, 3–4 rine, ryne. *Pa. t.* 1, 3 rínde; 1 rán, 4 roon, rone. [OE. *rínan* for **riʒnan* (= ON. and Icel. *rigna*, Goth. *rignjan*), f. *reʒn* RAIN *sb.*¹ Properly a weak vb.; the strong conj. is no doubt most immediately due to the analogy of *scínan*.]

1. *impers.* = RAIN *v.* 1.

c **1000** *Ags. Gosp.* Matt. v. 45 He læt rinan ofer þa rihtwisan and ofer þa unrihtwisan. *c* **1000** ÆLFRIC *Gen.* vii. 12 And hit rinde þa ofer eorðan feowertiȝ daȝa and feowertiȝ nihta on an. *c* **1290** *St. Michael* 606 in *S. Eng. Leg.* I. 317 For-to þe tyme com þat it Ryne and droppinde falle to grounde. **13..** *K. Alis.* 6434 (Bodl. MS.), Whan it snoweþ oiþer rineþ. *c* **1374** CHAUCER *Troylus* III. v. 677 Ever mo so sterneliche it ron, And blew ther-with. **1387** TREVISA *Higden* (Rolls) II. 239 Holy seyntes..telle þat it roon neuere from Adam to Noes flood. *Ibid.* III. 285 Ich wusted wel þat it schulde ryne.

2. *intr.* Of rain: To fall.

971 *Blickl. Hom.* 91 Rineþ blodiȝ reȝn æt æfen. *c* **1205** LAY. 19745 þe ræin him gon rine [*v.r.* ryne].

3. To send down, or to fall, like rain.

c **825** *Vesp. Psalter* x. 7 Dryhten..rineð ofer ða synfullan giren fyres. *c* **1000** *Ags. Gosp.* Luke xvii. 29 On þam dæge.. hyt rinde fyr & swefl of heofone. *c* **1205** LAY. 3895 From heouene her com a sulcuð flod, þre dæȝes hit rinde blod. **13..** *S. Eng. Leg.* (MS. Bodl. 779) in *Archiv neu. Spr.* LXXXII. 406 He..let rine bred & flesch fram heuen. **1340** *Ayenb.* 49 Gode..dede rine uer berninde and bernston stinkinde ope þe cite of sodome and of gomorre.

rinegued, variant of RENEGUED *ppl. a.*

rinel, obs. form of RINDLE *sb.*

riner ('raɪnə(r)). *dial.* [f. RINE *v.*¹] (See quots.)

1674 RAY *N.C. Words* s.v. *Shed*, Shed Riners with a Whaver: *Chesh.* Winning any cast that was very good; i.e. strike off one that touches, &c. *c* **1700** KENNET in *MS. Lansd.* 1033 fol. 323 Riners, touchers, spoken particularly in Chesh. of the Jack and Bowl when they kiss or touch: as *to shed Riners with a whaver*, i.e. to strike away the jack or bowl from one another with exactness or great art. **1818** WILBRAHAM *Cheshire Gloss.* 25 A Riner is when the Quoit touches the peg or mark. **1854** MISS BAKER *Northampt. Gloss.*, *Riner*, a toucher at the game of quoits.

r'inforce, variant of RENFORCE *v. Obs.*

rinforzando (rinfor'tsando). *Mus.* [It., gerund of *rinforzare* to strengthen.] A sudden stress or crescendo made on a short phrase; a direction to make this. Also *fig.*

1801 BUSBY *Dict. Mus.* *Rinforzando*, the same as *Forzando*. **1812** [see CRESCENDO 1 a]. **1858** GEO. ELIOT *Scenes Clerical Life* I. 48 Mr. Spratt was boxing the boys' ears with a constant *rinforzando*. **1944** W. J. FINN *Conductor raises his Baton* (1946) iv. 132 *Rinforzando* is only akin to *sforzando* but is often treated as a *subito* by conductors. The term *rinforzando* is not found in many modern scores. **1965** E. KAHN *Conducting* v. 58 *Rinf.* or *rfz* (rinforzando) indicate an emphasis on a short phrase.

ring (rɪŋ), *sb.*¹ Forms: 1 hring (hringc), 3– ring, 4–7 ringe; 3–6 ryng (4 rynk, 5 ryngg-), 4–6 rynge; 4–5 reng, 5 reyng. [Comm. Teut.: OE. *hring*, = OFris. *hring, rhing, ring* (Fris. *ring*), MDu. *rinc, ring-* (Du. *ring*), OS. *hring* (MLG. *rink, ring-*, LG. *ring*), OHG. *hring* (MHG. *rinc, ring-*, G. *ring*), ON. *hringr* (Icel. *hringur*, Norw., Sw., Da. *ring*). The pre-Teut. stem **krengho-* appears in Umbrian *krenkatrum* 'cingulum', and with ablaut-variation in OSl. *kragŭ* circle.]

I. 1. a. A small circlet of (real or simulated) precious metal (usually gold), and frequently set with precious stones or imitations of these, intended for wearing upon the finger either as an ornament or as a token (*esp.* of betrothal, marriage, or investiture), and sometimes for use as a seal. Also, occasionally, an armlet or neck-ring (so in OE.).

Beowulf 1196 Him wæs..wunden gold estum ʒeeawed, earmhreade twa, hræʒl & hringas, heals-beaʒa mæst. *c* **950** *Lindisf. Gosp.* Luke xv. 22 Sellað hring on hond his. *c* **1000** *Sax. Leechd.* I. 112 Ga to ðære ylcan wyrte..& bewrit hy abutan mid anum gyldenan hringe. *c* **1205** LAY. 4513 Ihc sende þe gretinge of mine gold ringe. *c* **1290** *St. Wulstan* 54 in *S. Eng. Leg.* I. 72 Bischop him made þe holie man..and tok him is staf and ring. **13..** *Gaw. & Gr. Knt.* 1817 Ho raʒt hym a riche rynk of red golde werkez, Wyth a starande ston. **1390** GOWER *Conf.* I. 123 Whan thou hast taken eny thing Of loves yifte, or Nouche or ring. *c* **1425** WYNTOUN *Cron.* IV. xvi. *heading*, How thre bollis of rengis weyr To Cartage sende. **1477** *Paston Lett.* III. 215, I pre yow that ye wyl were the reyng with the emage of Seynt Margrete. **1508** DUNBAR *Tua mariit wemen* 367 In ringis ryally set with riche ruby stonis. **1548–9** (Mar.) *Bk. Com. Prayer*, *Offices* 14 The manne shall geue vnto the womanne a ring. **1591** SHAKS. *Two Gent.* IV. iv. 102 This Ring I gaue him, when he parted from me, To binde him to remember my good will. **1632** MILTON *Penseroso* 113 Canace..That own'd the vertuous Ring and Glass. **1679** *Est. Test* 25 As if they had King Gyges his enchanted Ring, they walk invisible. **1732** LEDIARD *Sethos* II. x. 451 My lord, I restore you the ring I took from you. **1774** GOLDSM. *Nat. Hist.* (1776) II. 143 He began to reflect that the dead body had got a ring upon one of the fingers. **1853** J. H. NEWMAN *Hist. Sk.* (1876) II. 115 The Doge of Venice making the Adriatic his bride, and claiming her by a ring of espousal. **1890** H. FREDERIC *Lawton Girl* 45 There are times..when one likes to take off one's rings, even if the stones are perfection itself.

fig. *a* **1225** *Leg. Kath.* 1508 He haueð iweddet him to mi meiðhad mit te ring of rihte bileaue. **1601** SHAKS. *All's Well* IV. ii. 45 Mine Honors such a Ring, My chastities the Iewell of our house. **1856** EMERSON *Eng. Traits, Land*, The sea which..divided the poor Britons utterly from the world, proved to be the ring of marriage with all nations.

† **b.** In phr. *to take the ring*, as a symbol of kingship. (See also MANTLE *sb.* 1 d.) *Obs.*

1338 R. BRUNNE *Chron.* (1810) 85 To William þe rede kyng is gyuen þe coroun, At Westmynstere tok he ryng in þe abbay of Londoun.

† **c.** *transf.* A seal. *Obs.*⁻¹

1637 RUTHERFORD *Lett.* I. xvii. (1664) 46, I shall not believe that Christ will put His Amen & ring upon an imagination.

d. A metal circlet worn elsewhere than on the finger (or arm) as an ornament.

In earlier use app. only in the comb. EAR-RING. See also *ankle-ring* s.v. ANKLE *sb.* 3, *neck-ring* s.v. NECK *sb.*¹ 16, and NOSE-RING 2.

1552 HULOET, Rynge or lyke thynge to hange at ones eare. **1619** H. HUTTON *Satyr. Epigr.* (Percy Soc.) 41 Superbus swaggers with a ring in's eare. **1660** F. BROOKE tr. *Le Blanc's Trav.* 8 They wore rings in their ears. **1842** TENNYSON *Sir Launcelot & Guinevere* 27 A light-green tuft of plumes she bore Closed in a golden ring. **1851** D. WILSON *Preh. Ann.* (1863) II. III. v. 143 Named by antiquaries rings for the hair. **1900** FITCHETT *Wellington's Men* 103 Their ears, from which rings had been roughly snatched.

e. Phr. *to get the ring*, to become engaged to be married (usu. said of a woman).

1914 JOYCE *Dubliners* 122 Lizzie Fleming said Maria was sure to get the ring and..Maria had to laugh and say she didn't want any ring or man either. **1951** in M. McLuhan

Mech. Bride (1967) 95 The girls who get the rings. **1979** D. Cook *Winter Doves* II. iii. 64 Got the ring yet, Walter? Has she proposed to you yet?

2. One of the small circles of iron of which coats of mail were composed. = MAIL *sb.*[1] 1.

Beowulf 2260 Ne mæʒ byrnan hring æfter wiʒ-fruman wide feran. *c* **1300** *Havelok* 2740 He..smot him on þe sholdre so, þat he dide þare undo Of his brinie ringes mo, þan þat ich kan tellen fro. *a* **1400–50** *Alexander* 2980 Sum araies þaim in ringis & sum in row brenys. *c* **1470** *Gol. & Gaw.* 691 Ryngis of rank steill rattillit and rent. **1610** Guillim *Heraldry* IV. iv, These are called Annulets..and are supposed to be Rings of Maile. **1696** Phillips s.v. *Mail*, A sort of defensive Armour for the Body, wrought in Rings as it were linkt together. **1728** Chambers *Cycl.*, *Habergeon* ..[is] form'd of little Iron Rings, or Mashes, link'd into each other. **1834** Planché *Brit. Costume* 29 As early as the eighth century they [the Anglo-Saxons] were familiar with the byrne, or tunic of rings. **1846** Fairholt *Costume* 150 The mailles or rings of the hauberk appear,..sewn down, perhaps, on a sort of gambeson.

3. a. A circle of metal or other suitable material, of any dimension, employed as a means of attachment, suspension, compression, etc.

When the dimensions are fairly large, and the outer and inner faces are flattened, the more usual name is *hoop*.

c **897** K. Ælfred *Gregory's Past. C.* xxii. 168 Wyrc feower hringas ælgyldene. *c* **950** *Lindisf. Gosp.* Matt., Introd. 6 Fewere..hwommas & hringas. *a* **1000** *Cædmon's Gen.* 762 (Gr.), He is on þære sweartan helle hæft mid hringa ʒesponne. *c* **1305** *St. Swithin* 113 in *E.E.P.* (1862) 46 Anoneward þer liþ a ston,..Ringes of yre þer beoþ on ynailled þerto faste. **1388** Wyclif *Isa.* xxxvii. 29 Y schal sette a ryng in thi nosethirlis, and a bridil in thi lippis. *c* **1400** *Pilgr. Sowle* (Caxton) I. xxxvii. (1859) 41 Anone this lady Iustyce took this balaunce by the rynge, and bygan to reyse hit vp. *a* **1450** *Knt. de la Tour* (1868) 9 Sette a colte in aumblyng ringes, he wille use it whiles thei aren on. **1535** Coverdale *Esther* i. 6 Fastened with coardes of lynnen and scarlet in siluer rynges. **1580** *Fabric Rolls York* (Surtees) 117 For makinge a tyrret and a rynge of yron to the masons well buckett, 10*d*. **1602** Fulbecke *Pandects* 77 The Lord put a ring into his snowt, and brought him backe againe. **1687** A. Lovell tr. *Thevenot's Trav.* II. 92 [The vest] standing out round as if it had a Ring of Iron in it. **1726** *Gentleman Angler* 5 It will be very convenient to have Rings or Eyes..placed ..upon your Rod. *Ibid.*, Through these Rings your Line must run. **1769** Falconer *Dict. Marine* (1780) s.v. *Cannon*, Breeching-bolts, with rings, through which the breechings pass. **1802** James *Milit. Dict.* s.v. *Cannon*, The Reliever is an iron flat ring, with a wooden handle, at right angles to it. **1841** Dana *Seaman's Man.* 87 Pass the cat-stopper through the ring of the anchor. **1860** *All Year Round* No. 63. 307 A napkin..rolled within its ivory ring. **1868** Joynson *Metals* 20 The chimney..is..frequently formed of only one course of bricks, strongly bound together by stout iron rings and girders.

b. A circular knocker upon a door. Now *rare*.

c **1400** *Beryn* 1762 No more.., þen who so shoke a rynge, Ther no man is within, þe rynging to answere. **14..** *Lat. Eng. Voc.* in Wr.-Wülcker 618 *Tussimulus, i., pulsatorium*, the rynge of a dore. **1585** Higins tr. *Junius' Nomencl.* 214/2 *Cornix*.., the ring or iron hammer wherewith we knocke at the doore. **1591** Percivall *Sp. Dict.*, *Aldáua de puerta*, the ring or hammer of a doore. **1613** Purchas *Pilgrimage* II. xvii. (1614) 205 [It] is vnlawfull to knocke with the ring or hammer of a doore. **1682** [see DOOR 7 a].

†**c.** A coil (of wire). *Obs.*[−1]

1710 *Lond. Gaz.* No. 4656/3 For Sale.., 226 Rings of fine Brass Wire (but 10 Rings in a Lot).

†**d.** = *astronomer's ring* (see ASTRONOMER c).

1728 Chambers *Cycl.*, *Ring* is also an Instrument used in Navigation, for taking the Altitudes of the Sun, &c. [Hence in later Dicts.]

†**e.** *transf.* A measure of lime, equal to half a quarter (cf. HOOP *sb.* 5). *Obs.*

1542 *Ludlow Churchw. Acc.* (Camden) 11 Item, to John Bube for iij. rynges of lyme..vj d. **1567** *Ibid.* 125 One rynge of tanners lyme.

f. [a. LG. *ring*.] A measure of boards or staves (see quots.).

1674 Jeake *Arith.* (1696) 65 Clapholt or Clapboard. In 1 Great Hundred 12 Rings. In 1 Ring 2 small Hundred. In 1 Small Hundred 120 Boards. **1867** Smyth *Sailor's Word-bk.*, *Ring*, a commercial measure of staves, or wood prepared for casks, and containing four shocks.

g. = *curtain ring* s.v. CURTAIN *sb.*[1] 8.

1814 Jane Austen *Mansf. Park* I. xv. 296 The curtain will be a good job... We shall be able to send back some dozens of the rings. **1847** C. Brontë *Jane Eyre* II. I. 2 A woman.. sewing rings to new curtains. **1926–7** *Army & Navy Stores Catal.* 1106/1 Rod for curtains... Plain Ball Ends... Rings, per dozen (½ in. larger than pole).

h. A metal or plastic band placed round the leg of a bird, usu. when a nestling, so that it may be uniquely identified when caught on a later occasion; a *leg-ring* (see LEG *sb.* 17 a); also, a similar marker placed on a limb of a bat.

1907 *Brit. Birds* I. 58 The plan of marking birds by an aluminium ring round the leg has often been tried, but never in a really systematic fashion... To place rings on the legs of young birds just before they fledge would not be a great difficulty. **1909** *Ibid.* III. 5 We have had prepared a number of rings, of which we will send a supply..to any reader of the Magazine who will undertake to mark birds. **1925** Turner & Gurney *Bk. about Birds* vii. 71 Much has been discovered about the movements of birds by fixing small numbered rings on the legs of young birds in the nest. **1958** *Listener* 30 Oct. 684/1 The 'ring' is generally a thin strip of aluminium, shaped like the letter 'C' and is marked with a number and some sort of address. On a bird, it is clamped round the leg; but a bat's leg is too delicate for this, so the ring is put round the fore-arm. **1973** *Guardian* 5 Feb. 11/5 The British Bird Fancy Council..is now introducing a system of coded rings ..and encouraging breeders to keep full records.

i. A bottomless vessel used in *ring culture*.

1962 H. G. W. Fogg *Chrysanthemum Growing* ix. 62 The roots in the rings will not need any watering between feeds. **1964** *Times Lit. Suppl.* 21 May 442/2 Much of the early work on ring culture, a system of growing plants in bottomless pots or 'rings', was carried out at the Lenton Research Station under the direction of the author [*sc.* A. W. Billitt]. Ring culture has become now firmly established both as a commercial and amateur method of growing chrysanthemums, carnations and tomatoes. **1976** *Observer* (Colour Suppl.) 9 May 12/2 The best way to grow tomatoes is by 'ring culture'. The soil in the greenhouse..is replaced with aggregate, such as clinker, and the tomatoes planted in rings, or bottomless pots.

4. a. A circlet of metal suspended from a post which each of a number of riders endeavoured to carry off on the point of his lance. Chiefly in phr. *to run* or *ride at the ring*; also † *to win the ring*, to carry off the prize.

a **1513** Fabyan *Chron.* VI. ccxvi. (1811) 233 For Harolde was stronge of knyghtes and rychesse, he wanne the rynge. *a* **1548** Hall *Chron.*, *Hen. VIII*, 7 Certayn noble men made a wager to runne at the rynge. **1591** Spenser *M. Hubberd* 742 Assaying..Now the nigh aymed ring away to beare. **1625** Massinger *Parl. Love* II. ii, To fight at barriers, or to break a lance, Or, in their full career, to take the ring. **1686** *Lond. Gaz.* No. 2142/3 After which they ran at the Ring, and the Marquis de la Chastre got the Prize. **1798** *Statist. Acc. Scotl.*, *Dunkeld* XX. 433 They spend the evening in some public competition of dexterity or skill. Of these, 'riding at the ring'..is the chief. **1809** Malkin *Gil Blas* VIII. ix. ¶4 Egging me on to run at the ring for every prize.

b. *pl.* A competitive game in which rings are thrown on to hooks.

1906 B. Kennedy *Wander Pict.* 245 Over yonder on the [inn] wall is the target with hooks at which they play the game of rings. They stand off and pitch rubber rings on to the hooks.

5. a. One of the raised bands passing round the body of cannon as formerly made. Chiefly in combs. *base-*, *cornice-*, *muzzle-*, *reinforce-*, *trunnion-ring* (q.v.).

? *a* **1610** *Gesta Grayorum* II. in Nichols *Progr. Q. Eliz.* (1823) III. 324 His Highnes Master of the Ordinance claimes to have all peece guld in the touch-hole, or broken within the ringe. **1626** Capt. Smith *Accid. Yng. Seamen* 32 Her carnooze or base ring at her britch,..mousell rings at her mouth. **1645** N. Stone *Enchir. Fortif.* 56 The Astragall, or Coronice ring. **1702** *Milit. Dict.* s.v. *Base-ring*, The great Ring next to and behind the Touch-hole [of a cannon]. **1795** Nelson 9 July in Nicolas *Disp.* (1845) I. 430 The Agamemnon's two twenty-four pounders are both ruined: one split up to the rings. **1802** James *Milit. Dict.*, *Rings of a Gun*, circles of metal, of which there are five [etc.]. **1867** Smyth *Sailor's Word-bk.* 567 *Reinforce*,..that increase..of the metal towards the breech, which was marked on old pattern guns by rings. They are generally in cast guns omitted now.

b. (See quots.)

1688 Holme *Armoury* III. 462/1 The Rings, or Filets, are the curious molten work and Garnish cast on the out-side the Bell. **1834** *Penny Cycl.* II. 51/1 The small eccentric rings or bands which enrich the lower part of the moulding of the Doric capital.

c. A kind of gas-check used in a cannon. In full *Broadwell's ring*.

1868 *U.S. Rep. Munit. War* 105 The well-known Broadwell cap, or expansion ring,..which so effectually prevents the escape of gas. **1876** Voyle & Stevenson *Milit. Dict.* 347.

II. 6. a. The border, rim, or outer part of some circular object, *esp.* of a coin or a wheel. †In OE. of land or sea, with reference to the horizon.

a **1000** *Cædmon's Gen.* 1393 (Gr.), Siððan wide rad wolcnum under ofer holmes hrincg hof seleste. *Ibid.* 2854 Siððan þu ʒestigest steape dune, hrincg þæs hean landes. **1338** R. Brunne *Chron.* (1810) 238 Edward did smyte rounde peny, halfpeny, ferthyng, þe croice passed þe bounde of alle þorghout þe ryng. *a* **1400–50** *Alexander* 1850 We riden on þe rime & on þe ringe seten Of þe qwele of Fortoun. **1602** Shaks. *Ham.* II. ii. 448 Pray God your voice like a peece of vncurrant Gold be not crack'd within the ring. **1649** Blithe *Eng. Improv. Impr.* (1653) 131 Two sides run upon a strait Line, which are those planted to the Ring of the wheel, and to the Ladle-board. **1690** tr. *Blancard's Phys. Dict.*, *Helix*, the ring, or brim of the ear.

b. The boundary *of* an estate. *rare*[−1].

1598 Manwood *Lawes Forest* i. (1615) 19 A Forest doth.. lie open.., hauing onely but meeres and boundaries to know the Ring and vttermost Skirtes of the Forest by.

7. a. An object having the form of a circle; a circular fold, coil, or bend; a piece or part (of something) forming a circle.

c **1410** *Master of Game* (MS. Digby 182) xiv, A grehounde shulde haue..a cattes tayle makynge a rynge at þe ende. **1483** *Cath. Angl.* 308/2 A Rynge for a carte qwele, *cantus*. **1646** Crashaw *Sospetto d'Herode* ix, Their lockes are beds of uncomb'd snakes that wind About their shady browes in wanton Rings. **1665** *Phil. Trans.* I. 70 The first that have well observed this Shadow of Saturn's Body upon its Ring. **1686** Plot *Nat. Hist. Staffs.* v. 198 The rings of stone, Iron, and Copper, found about the stalks of Gorse. **1747–96** Mrs. Glasse *Cookery* v. 48 Strain the sauce over the woodcock, and lay on the onion in rings. **1781** Cowper *Retirement* 231 As woodbine..In spiral rings ascends the trunk. **1817** Shelley *Laon* I. xii. 4 Sometimes the Snake around his enemy's neck Locked in stiff rings his adamantine coil. **1852** M. Arnold *Future* 14 The river in gleaming rings Sluggishly winds through the plain. **1882** Geikie in *Darwin's Life & Lett.* (1887) I. 324 The origin of those remarkable rings of coral-rock in mid-ocean.

b. *Anat.* A structure of circular form; *esp.* one of the annular joints of the bodies of caterpillars and insects, or one of the cartilages of the trachea.

1580 Blundevil *Horsemanship* IV. 43 Absirtus would haue the fundament on the out side to be cut round about, but so as the inward ring thereof be not touched, for that were dangerous, and would kill the horse. **1713** Derham *Phys. Theol.* IV. xii. 223 Their [*sc.* earth-worms] Body is made throughout of small Rings, and these Rings have a curious Apparatus of Muscles. **1753** Chambers *Cycl. Suppl.*, *Rings*, of flies,..the several rounds, or circular portions, of which the bodies of these and other insects are composed. **1774** Goldsm. *Nat. Hist.* (1776) VII. 306 The leech has the general figure of a worm... Its skin is composed of rings. **1835–6** *Todd's Cycl. Anat.* I. 753/2 The frame-work or solid parts of the Crustacea consist..of a series of rings. **1859** Semple *Diphtheria* 56 Its shape indicated that it had lined the thyroid cartilage, as far as the first rings of the trachea. **1871** T. R. Jones *Anim. Kingd.* (ed. 4) 235 In the lowest forms of the Articulata, the body is extremely elongated, and the rings proportionally numerous.

c. One of the concentric circular bands of wood constituting the yearly growth of a tree.

1671 Grew *Anat. Pl.* I. iii. (1682) 19 The Latitudinal shootings of the Lignous Body, which in Trunks of several years growth, are apparent in so many Rings. **1788** M. Cutler in *Life*, etc. (1888) I. 418 The Directors ordered.. that a number of the largest and oldest trees be cut down, in order to count the rings. **1807** J. E. Smith *Phys. Bot.* 31 Linnæus and most writers believe..that the exact age of a sound tree when felled may be known by counting these rings. **1847** Tennyson *Princ.* v. 227 Then rode we.. Beneath huge trees, a thousand rings of Spring In every bole.

d. One of the raised circular marks at the base of the horns of oxen or cows, varying in number according to the animal's age.

1725 *Family Dict.* s.v. *Ox*, Some say, they can know their Age by their Horns, and that as many Rings as are about their Roots, so many Years old they are. **1805** R. W. Dickson *Pract. Agric.* II. 1132 In the horn, the first ring or circle does not take place till three years old. *Ibid.*, These rings are often effaced..by dealers in cattle. **1847** W. C. L. Martin *Ox* 34/1 In some cows the rings are very imperfect, or not distinctly marked, and run into each other.

e. *Bot.* = ANNULUS 3.

1796 Withering *Brit. Plants* (ed. 3) I. 373 To shew (*a*) the Ring; (*b*) the Stem; (*c*) the Pileus. *Ibid.* III. 748 Osmunda.. Capsules roundish, on pedicles, encompassed by a jointed elastic ring. **1859** T. Moore *Brit. Ferns* 12 The..spore cases..are mostly minute roundish-oval bodies, containing one cavity, and nearly surrounded by a jointed vertical band called a ring. **1884** Bower & Scott *De Bary's Phaner.* 593 Between two bundles of a ring lies a radial band of intermediate tissue.

f. *slang.* The anus. Phr. *to spew one's ring* (and similar phrases), to vomit violently.

1949 Partridge *Dict. Slang* (ed. 3) 1154/1 *Ring*,..anus (also *ring-piece*): low: late C. 19–20. **1952** T. A. G. Hungerford *Ridge & River* 130 'I'd get shot in the ring, that's what I'd get,' said Wallace. **1965** R. Stow *Merry-go-Round in Sea* 174, I bet I would have booted him in the ring if he hadn't run. **1966** K. Amis *Anti-Death League* I. 32 Then the technique is to slip him a glass of Scotch or whatever he's hooked on about half a minute before the emetine makes him spew his ring. **1971** B. W. Aldiss *Soldier Erect* 105, I can't take this sodding shitting Wog beer... Makes me spew my ring every time! **1978** R. Busby *Garvey's Code* iii. 28 We just left the husband and he's bringing his ring up.

8. a. A circular mark, esp. in phr. *rings round* (or *under*) *the eyes*; also = FAIRY-RING.

1626 *Maldon, Essex* Bundle 108, no. 9, A tall darkeish graye gelding, having two white ringes, abowt each eare one. **1784** Cowper *Tiroc.* 307 As happy as we once, to kneel and draw The chalky ring, and knuckle down at taw. **1832** Lytton *E. Aram* I. x, The mystic ring on the soft turf. **1850** Tennyson *In Mem.* lxxxvii. 27 One would aim an arrow fair, ..And one would pierce an outer ring, And one an inner. **1850** Thackeray *Pendennis* II. vii. 70 The rings round his eyes were of the colour of bistre. **1856** C. M. Yonge *Daisy Chain* II. xii. 472 He looked very wan, with the dark rings round his eyes, a deeper purple than ever. **1891** 'J. S. Winter' *Lumley* ix, The great rings round her eyes betokened a sleepless night. **1902** A. Bennett *Anna of Five Towns* x. 258 It's a shame to send you home with those rings round your eyes. **1911** O. Onions *Widdershins* 270 The bistred rings that weeks of nursing had put under her dark eyes. **1973** R. Thomas *If you can't be Good* xiii. 111, I thought there were some new lines in his face. I wasn't imagining the dark rings under his eyes. **1981** T. Heald *Murder at Moose Jaw* xi. 133 There were dark rings under her eyes and her face was pinched.

b. A circle, or circular band, of light or colour.

The phrases *swelce an fyrenhring*, *swylce sunnan hring*, occur in OE., but there is no evidence of historic continuity.

1648 Hexham II, *Den Ringh om de Mane*, the Ring or the Circle about the Moone. **1771** *Encycl. Brit.* I. 440/1 They likewise..saw a luminous ring round the body of Venus. **1819** *Pantologia* X, *Rings of colours*, in optics, a phænomenon first observed in thin plates of various substances. **1858** *Merc. Mar. Mag.* V. 354 A large ring round the moon, formed of light clouds. **1871** Rossetti *Last Confession* 129 The rings of light quivered like forest-leaves.

c. An excision of bark made round a branch or the trunk of a tree. (Cf. RING *v.*[1] 9 b.)

1817 *Hort. Soc. Trans.* II. 266 He..reduced the rings to between one eighth and two eighths of an inch in width,.. and the trees did well. **1852** Johnson *Cottage Gard. Dict.* 780/2 Ringing is cutting away a belt of bark... When first suggested it was called the Ring of Pomona.

d. One of the expanding circular ripples caused by something falling or being cast into still water.

1821 Clare *Vill. Minstr.* I. 125 The rings went whirling round Till they touch'd the flaggy bank. *Ibid.* 132 As each nimble eye Saw the rings the dropples made. **1860** Tyndall *Glac.* II. i. 229 When a stone is thrown into calm water a series of rings spread themselves [etc.].

e. A gold-coloured band worn on the sleeve to designate rank in the armed services. Also *transf.*

1942 *R.A.F. Jrnl.* 13 June 32 They were all of superior rank to myself... My solitary ring did not allow me to voice my suspicions. **1943** HUNT & PRINGLE *Service Slang* 55 *Rings*, abbreviated reference to an Officer's rank, denoted in the Navy and R.A.F. by the number of rings on his sleeve. **1950** 'D. DIVINE' *King of Fassarai* xv. 116 Bull's got more rings than I have. Why shouldn't he have his headaches too? **1952** M. TRIPP *Faith is Windsock* i. 14 Now that Bergen has got his ring there doesn't seem so much point in staying N.C.O. with the others. **1953** 'N. SHUTE' *In Wet* v. 164 Go into the R.A.F. and try to make a go of it, and get the rings because you've earned them, not because you're heir to the Throne. **1970** D. FRANCIS *Rat Race* iv. 55 No such thing was possible in one of his aircraft, he had told me stiffly, and I could take my four gold rings away... I hadn't worn my captain's jacket for nearly two years. **1976** 'A. HALL' *Kobra Manifesto* xvi. 218 The pilot stood there, a tall mahogany-faced type with four gold rings on his sleeve.

9. a. In various technical or special senses: (see quots.).

a. 1669 *Sc. Acts Parl.* (1820) VII. 647 The..milne of Provand, milnelands, astrictit multers,..rings, sequells and pertinents thereof. **1814** in JAMIESON (1825) s.v., The Ring is the meal which, in the course of grinding, falls round the mill stone, between it and the wooden case surrounding it. [Cf. *mill-ring* s.v. MILL *sb.* 12.]

b. 1712 MORTON *Nat. Hist. Northampt.* 129 Sand in three or four Layers, or Compartments divided from each other by thin Partitions of Stone, there [at Easton near Stamford] called Rings.

c. 1791 *Statist. Acc. Scotl., Lauder* I. 77 There are many Pictish and Scotch encampments in this parish... All of them are of a round or oval figure, and are called rings by the common people. **1815** *Pennecuik's Wks.* 203 One of those Rings, consisting of a ditch and earthen rampart, for the protection of cattle and other property. **1898** J. HERON *Celtic Church Ireland* 36 Some have a single 'ring' or rampart.

d. 1825 J. NICHOLSON *Operat. Mechanic* 473 Pieces of clay of different sizes and shapes, called stilts, cockspurs, rings, pins, bats, &c. are put to keep them [*sc.* the glazed articles in the saggers] apart.

e. 1823 CRABB *Technol. Dict., Ring* (Geom.), a figure returning into itself, the axis being bent round into a circular form. **1842** FRANCIS *Dict. Arts, Ring*,..a surface or solid; the space between one concentric circle or oval and another cut out of it. It may be either superficial or solid.

f. 1839 *Civil Eng. & Arch. Jrnl.* II. 69/1 Before the cement ..had taken a set in the interior of the brickwork forming the ring [= voussoirs] of the arch. **1876** *Encycl. Brit.* IV. 311/1 The ring when not of equal thickness is always made of least depth at the crown.

g. 1846 BROCKETT *N.C. Gloss.* (ed. 3), *Ring*, a circular spout in the shaft of a coal pit for collecting the side feeders of water into a box. **1881** RAYMOND *Mining Gloss., Ring*, a gutter cut around a shaft to catch and conduct away the water. **1883** GRESLEY *Gloss. Coal-mining, Ring*, a complete circle of tubbing plates placed round a pit-shaft.

h. 1882 *Standard* 26 Sept. 2/2 They [whelks] are also caught in nets called 'hoops' or 'rings'.

i. 1835 A. SMITH *Diary* 27 July (1940) II. 131 The old ring-kop was speaking... This ring-kop was the person in charge of the party... None of the others had rings. **1866** [see *head-ring* s.v. HEAD *sb.*[1] 66]. **1887** RIDER HAGGARD *Allan Quatermain* 15 Among the Zulus a man assumes the ring, which is made of a species of black gum twisted in the hair, ..when he has reached a certain dignity. **1925** D. KIDD *Essential Kaffir* 33 Only married men are allowed to wear this ring. **1952** [see *head-ring* s.v. HEAD *sb.*[1] 66].

III. 10. a. A circle or circular group of persons. ***in a ring***, in circular formation, arranged or grouped in a circle.

In first quot. used of the birds surrounding the phœnix.

c **900** *Phœnix* 339 Fugla cynn..þone halȝan hringe beteldað. *c* **1230** *Hali Meid.* 21 In heore ring þer is godd self; & his deore moder [etc.]. *Ibid.* Ha beoð i widewene ring, & schulen, i widewene ring, bifore þe iweddede singen in heuene. **13..** *K. Alis.* 1111 (Bodl. MS.), Alisaundres folk vmflynge Fyue hundred vpon a rynge. *c* **1450** HOLLAND *Howlat* 790 Fair ladyis in ryngis, Knychtis in caralyngis, Boith dansis and syngis. **1513** DOUGLAS *Æneis* IV. iv. 37 Quhen Apollo list..ga..To vesy Delos..Renewand ringis and dancis, mony a rowt. **1560** DAUS tr. *Sleidane's Comm.* 280 They putting them selves into a ringe,..stand to their defence. **1601** SHAKS. *Jul. C.* III. ii. 162 Make a Ring about the Corpes of Cæsar. **1687** A. LOVELL tr. *Thevenot's Trav.* I. 250 They all rise upright and put themselves into a Ring one behind another. **1732** BERKELEY *Alciphr.* IV. §13 When one of them has got a ring of disciples round him. **1762** SIR W. JONES *Arcadia* Poems (1777) 107 The swains before them crouded in a ring. **1835** W. IRVING *Tour Prairies* xxv, The ring being formed, two or three hunters ride towards the horses, who start off in an opposite direction. **1865** KINGSLEY *Herew.* iii, The housecarles had closed round him in a ring with the intention of seizing him.

†**b.** In phr. ***to lead*** (or †***rule***) ***the ring***, to take the lead, to be foremost or first. *Obs.* (Cf. RINGLEADER.)

c **1340** *Nominale* (Skeat) 214 *Femme treche mene pur deduyt*, Woman the ryng leduth for ioye. *a* **1529** SKELTON *Sp. Parrot* 132 Bo ho doth bark wel, but Hough ho he rulyth the ring. **1578** *Gude & Godlie B.* (1867) 178 Lyke prince and king he led the ring Of all iniquitie. **1636** RUTHERFORD *Lett.* (1862) I. lix. 159 Alexander Gordon shall lead the ring in witnessing a good confession. **1652** BP. HALL *Invis. World* III. §2 It was in all likelihood some prime angel of heaven that first started aside from his station and led the ring of this highest and first revolt.

c. A number of things arranged in a circle. Also *fig.*

1587 GOLDING *De Mornay* ii. (1592) 17 All [creatures] are so linked together, that the ring thereof cannot be broken without confusion. **1618** BOLTON *Florus* III. vi. (1636) 192 They beheld the beak-heads of our clashing gallies charge in ring upon them. **1784** COWPER *Task* I. 223 Environ'd with a ring of branching elms. **1820** SHELLEY *Orpheus* 2 Yonder pointed hill, Crowned with a ring of oaks. **1866** BRANDE & Cox *Dict. Sci.*, etc. s.v. *Meteors*, Small bodies revolving round the sun.., congregated in several rings—tangible orbits, as it were. **1894** *Labour Commission Gloss.* s.v., In the potting industry what is called the first ring is composed of the bungs set next to the arches forming the first circle of 'saggers'..in the oven.

d. *Chem.* A number of atoms bonded together to form a closed chain.

1869 *Jrnl. Chem. Soc.* XXII. 361 The hydrocarbon benzole is of so much interest from its derivatives, that it has attracted a good deal of attention, and to explain its molecular constitution, the six atoms of carbon have been represented as arranged in a ring. **1889** G. M'GOWAN tr. *Bernthsen's Text-bk. Org. Chem.* 461 Phthalic acid or its derivatives ensue on the breaking up of the compound, not only from one but from both of the six-cornered rings. **1927** N. V. SIDGWICK *Electronic Theory of Valency* xiv. 251 Only a very few chelate rings of more than six atoms have been observed. **1950** *Thorpe's Dict. Appl. Chem.* (ed. 4) X. 339/1 Treatment of pyrrole with hydroxylamine causes a smooth opening of the ring. **1964** N. G. CLARK *Mod. Org. Chem.* ii. 21 Pyridine..has a structure very similar to that of benzene; the six-membered ring, however, contains a trivalent nitrogen atom. **1974** D. M. ADAMS *Inorg. Solids* vi. 183 Sulphur has quite a complex allotropy: the thermodynamically stable form consists of S_8 crown-shaped rings in close-packed layers.

e. *Cytology.* A chromosome, group of chromosomes, or part of a chromosome in the form of a loop, without free ends.

1929 *Jrnl. Genetics* XXI. 44 A single ring of four may be formed at diakinesis, the other chromosomes assorting themselves in separate pairs. **1949** DARLINGTON & MATHER *Elem. Genetics* vi. 129 From the exchange system of pairing a ring of four, chain of four, two chains of two, or a chain of three with a univalent, can arise at metaphase. *Ibid.* xii. 263 *Oenothera lamarckiana*, whose chromosomes normally form a ring of 12 and one pair. **1962** *Lancet* 29 Dec. 1384/1 Monosomic chromosomes may be subject to hazards in meiosis—from autosynapsis, leading to centric and acentric rings and fragments, to centric aberrations leading to iso-chromosomes.

11. a. A combination of interested persons to monopolize and control a particular trade or market for their private advantage. *spec.* a combination of dealers, contractors, or the like, who cooperate in buying or selling at agreed price-levels, in order to increase their profits. Also *attrib.* orig. chiefly *U.S.*

1869 J. H. BROWNE *Gt. Metrop.* 48 (Funk), Stocks are what the brokers make them, and their varying rate is determined by a 'ring'. **1870** W. W. FOWLER *Ten Years in Wall St.* i. 28 The bulls often unite to raise the value of particular stocks, and form those combinations known in the 'Street' as 'cliques', 'rings' or 'pools',—terms nearly synonymous. **1880** *Manch. Guard.* 2 Nov., A 'ring' of Canadian producers obtained legislation which practically excluded all American oils from our market. **1890** G. B. SHAW *Fabian Ess.* 94 The 'ring' is being succeeded by a more elaborate organization, known as the 'trust'. **1909** [see CONFERENCE 4 e]. **1929** *Times* 31 Oct. 14/4 In order to safeguard the home consumer against exploitation by the producers' 'rings', which the coal-marketing schemes will establish, the Government will set up in every district a special committee to keep a watch on prices. **1936** *Sun* (Baltimore) 2 Dec. 3/1 In addition Thorp advocates..more stringent regulations of auction and sales rings. **1949** J. SYMONS *Bland Beginning* 22 That's Foskiss. Buys everything for the ring. Doesn't give the small men a chance. **1955** *Times* 13 May 9/1 Wellington City Council, which recently protested strongly against the submission of equal tenders by a number of British firms, has now decided to accept a tender for electric cable which is £3,000 below the 'ring price'. **1961** R. GODDEN *China Court* VII. 274 She comes back from sale after sale... She gets to know their 'tricks' as she calls them, a childish word for the ring. **1964** [see MONOPSONY]. **1968** R. H. R. SMITHIES *Shoplifter* viii. 175 The Ring..was an organization of English dealers who attempted to take over the entire antiques business—rigging auctions, intimidating retailers, fixing prices. **1968** *Sunday Times* 10 Nov. 1/2 Ring dealing is when dealers agree not to force the price up by bidding against each other at an auction. **1971** *Nature* 6 Aug. 365/1 The overt reason for the anti-trust laws is to prevent the formation of cartels and similar price-fixing rings. **1972** 'M. DELVING' *Shadow of Himself* ii. 24 'I don't doubt there'll be a ring,' he added, bitterly... He was referring to the system by which several dealers agree to let one of their number bid for all, thus cutting down the competition and squeezing out opposition.

b. An organization which endeavours to control politics or local affairs in its own interest.

1872 O. W. HOLMES *Poet Breakf.-t.* vi, The Tammany Ring, which is to take the place of the feudal lord. **1882** L. STEPHEN *Swift* 91 The war was the creation of the Whig 'ring'. **1893** GOLDW. SMITH *Ess.* 157 American citizens outside the political ring are ambitious of being great citizens.

c. An organization or network of people engaged in espionage.

1943 D. POWELL *Time to be Born* vi. 128 He had no secret mission to investigate the spy rings and unmask the Nazi agents. **1961** R. SETH *Anat. Spying* iii. 45 In a very short time counter-espionage knew the names and whereabouts of all twenty-six members of the ring. **1972** A. MORICE *Murder on French Leave* viii. 104 The cinema had been the meeting-place with another operator in the spy ring. **1981** R. AIRTH *Once a Spy* xii. 139 When Franklyn's ring broke up..I went back to work for Bonn.

12. *Math.* [a. G. *ring*, used in this sense.] A set of elements with two binary operations ('addition' and 'multiplication') which is a group under addition and closed under multiplication, and with the property that multiplication is distributive over addition and associative.

Some writers also require a ring to have an identity element for multiplication.

1935 *Ann. Math.* XXXVI. 406 It is only in integrally closed rings like in the theory of algebraic numbers that the decomposition theorems naturally take on a multiplicative form. **1967** [see FIELD THEORY]. **1968** D. G. NORTHCOTT *Lessons on Rings, Modules & Multiplicities* i. 1 From this point onwards, when we speak of a ring it is to be understood that we always mean a ring with an identity element. **1971** J. H. CONWAY in Powell & Higman *Finite Simple Groups* vii. 244 The ring of 24 × 24 matrices.

IV. 13. a. An enclosed circular space within which some sport, performance, or exhibition (*esp.* of riding or racing) takes place.

In early quots. used allusively.

c **1330** R. BRUNNE *Chron. Wace* (Rolls) 11858 Þat we haue wonne, y sette at nought, But ȝif þe Romayns to ryng be brought. *c* **1385** CHAUCER *L.G.W.* 1887 *Ariadne*, Mynos,.. Now cometh thy lotte; now comestow on the rynge. **1430–40** LYDG. *Bochas* VII. v. (1554) 168 b/1 Nero ye tyrant cometh next vnto the ryng. *Ibid.* IX. vi. 200 b/1 Next came Gisulphus to Bochas on the ryng. *c* **1435** *Torr. Portugal* 2454 The castelle court was large within, They made ryngis ffor to ren. **1587** *Nottingham Rec.* IV. 216 We present the Bull Ringe to want raylinge. **1602** MARSTON *Antonio's Rev.* Prol., If any heart Pierc't through with anguish pant within this ring. **1607** TOPSELL *Four-f. Beasts* (1658) 253 Virgil also describeth a swift and sluggish Horse most excellently in these verses; sending one of them to the Ring, and victory of running. **1697** DRYDEN *Virg. Georg.* III. 182 The Lapithæ.. taught the Steed to bound; To run the Ring, and trace the mazy Round. **1740** SOMERVILLE *Hobbinol* III. 227 Room for the Master of the Ring; ye Swains! **1854** DICKENS *Hard T.* I. ii, They do break horses in the ring. **1883** J. PARKER *Tyne Chylde* 274 The sawdust ring of a bankrupt circus.

†**b.** A circular course in Hyde Park, used for riding and driving. *Obs.*

1676 ETHEREDGE *Man of Mode* III. ii, All the world will in the Park to-night: Ladies, 'Twere pity to..rob the ring of all those Charms That should adorn it. **1693** *Humours Town* 119 We'll to Hide Park;..my Mother's Coach is below, and shall carry us, to make a Figure in the Ring. **1715** ADDISON *Drummer* IV. i, Six as pretty horses as any that appear in the ring. **1777** SHERIDAN *Sch. Scand.* II. ii, You may see her on a little squat pony,..puffing round the Ring on a full trot. **1840** HOOD *Kilmansegg, Accident* 536 She has circled the Ring!—she crosses the Park! **1848** THACKERAY *Van. Fair* xlix, That kind of company which..is known to exist as well as the Ring in Hyde Park or the Congregation at St. James's.

14. a. A space, originally defined by a circle of bystanders, for a prize-fight or a wrestling-match; often in phr. ***to make a ring***; also ***to keep*** (or ***hold***) ***the ring***, to be an onlooker at a fight; to stand by while others quarrel (chiefly *fig.*). Hence ***the ring***, pugilism as an institution or a profession; also *collect.* those interested in boxing. (Cf. PRIZE-RING.)

[**1659** *Clarke Papers* (Camden) IV. 300 The soldyers generally say they will not fight, but will make a ring for their officers to fight in.] *a* **1700** B. E. *Dict. Cant. Crew, A Ring*, a Concourse of People for Wrestling [etc.]. **1736** *Gentl. Mag.* VI. 744/2 Grave Sirs—you're at the Wrestling Ring. **1770** LANGHORNE *Plutarch* (1879) I. 177/1 A master of the gymnastic art attends a young man to fit him for the ring. **1812** *Sporting Mag.* XXXIX. 96 He did not wrestle with such luck, through the ring, for the first prize, as the champion. **1829** P. EGAN *Boxiana* 2nd Ser. II. 678 At least 500 Irishmen, armed *à la shilelah*, kept the ring. **1841** BORROW *Zincali* II. ii. III. 152 To converse with the pugilists of the ring, and the jockeys of the racecourse. **1896** GEORGIANA M. STISTED *True Life R. F. Burton* vii. 165 In fact, England [in 1855] was, in the parlance of the ring, getting her second wind. **1905** *Spectator* 21 Jan. 79/1 There is a cynicism which nothing but conscious impotence could excuse in the thought of 'keeping a ring' while the Bulgarians of the Principality..are drawn into a life-and-death struggle with the Turks. **1924** GALSWORTHY *White Monkey* I. vii. 54 Keep clear and keep the ring!.. Good friendly terms with..all the outlying countries that we can get at by sea. And let the others dree their weirds. **1928** *Britain's Industr. Future* (Liberal Industr. Inquiry) III. xv. 166 There are still many people who hold that the State ought not to meddle with industry,..but should confine itself to holding the ring while the disputants fight out their differences. **1970** *Times* 8 Apr. 1 Is there a limit to the amount of time that the Army can reasonably be expected to stay here [*sc.* in Ulster] holding the ring, if the humans involved here are not going to solve their own problems? **1970** *Atlantic Monthly* Nov. 6 Does the phrase 'Asians helping Asians', or, as critics put it, 'Asians fighting Asians', mean that the United States will provide everything but the front-line manpower, or that it will step back and help hold the ring, or that it will become a mere spectator? **1978** *Jrnl. R. Soc. Arts* CXXVI. 400/1 Its [*sc.* Government's] task in the economic field is to hold the ring between the many popular pressures, frequently irreconcilable, which assert themselves.

b. An enclosed space in a racing-ground frequented by bookmakers; also *collect.* the bookmaking profession.

1775 G. SELWYN *Let.* 8 Dec. in *15th Rep. R. Comm. Hist. Manuscripts* App. VI. 306 in *Parl. Papers 1897* (C. 8551) LI. 1 The devil a bit will he ever part with, but by putting it into the Ring, where he is nicked, and the money gone. **1822** *Sporting Mag.* X. 4/2 Mr. Bayzand was well known in the ring as a betting man. *Ibid.* 192/2 He never opened his mouth in the ring *under five hundred*. **1845** DISRAELI *Sibyl* I. I. ii. 12 'Will any one do anything about Hybiscus?' sang out a gentleman in the ring at Epsom. **1859** SALA *Tw. round Clock* (1861) 204 A shaven grass-plat of circular form. This is the famous 'Ring', of which you have heard so much. **1874** *Slang Dict.* 270 *Ring*, the open space in front of a racecourse stand, which is used for betting purposes. **1894** *Westm. Gaz.* 13 Sept. 2/2 'The Ring' had scarcely any existence as a constituted host such as it now is before 1842.

c. An enclosed or clear space in an auction-mart, used for the display of live stock, etc.

1890 *Daily News* 7 Jan. 2/1 Now..a London merchant who wishes to purchase iron can walk across to the metal market where his iron will be purchased publicly in the open ring. 1901 *Scotsman* 3 Apr. 7/3 Irish cattle met a somewhat stiff trade in the ring, but a good clearance was afterwards got privately.

d. A prison-yard; a fence or wall surrounding this.

1898 O. Wilde *Ballad of Reading Gaol* 7 And I and all the souls in pain, Who tramped the other ring. 1900 'Odysseus' *Turkey in Europe* i. 28 They [*sc.* the Avars] were celebrated for their 'rings', enormous circular fences with which they surrounded the prisoners and plunder they had taken.

e. *Austral.* (See quot. 1941.)

1941 Baker *Dict. Austral. Slang* 60 *Ring*, the scene of operations of a two-up school or the school itself. 1948 [see double-header e].

15. a. A circular or spiral orbit or course; also ***ring-around***. ***in a ring***, † ***in ring***, in a circle.

In various OE. glosses *hring* is used to render L. *orbis* or *spira*. Phrases like *ȝeares hring* also occur in translations of Latin texts.

1589 Nashe *Martin Marprel.* Wks. (Grosart) I. 81 How my Palfrey..daunced the Goates iumpe, when I ranne the ring round about him to retriue him. 1609 C. Butler *Fem. Mon.* (1623) 2 One of the Bees.., when she hath cast a Ring, to know where she is, will fly as directly home as the other. 1674 N. Fairfax *Bulk & Selv.* 91 As for their motion in ring or circular. 1728–46 Thomson *Spring* 618 First, wide around,..in airy rings they rove. 1781 Cowper *Anti-Thelyphth.* 32 They sport like wanton doves in airy rings. 1818 Shelley *Rosal. & Helen* 1167 In aery rings they bound. *a* 1845 Hood *Agric. Distress* 140 You're nothing near the thing! You only argy in a ring. 1881 *Macm. Mag.* Nov. 40 Others [of the larks]..go gaily up in circular rings, 'ringing' as the falconers call it. 1907 Joyce *Chamber Music* p. ix, Winds of May, that dance on the sea, Dancing a ring-around in glee From furrow to furrow.

transf. 1714 Young *Force of Relig.* ii. 200 Decrepid winter, in the yearly ring, Thus slowly creeps, to meet the blooming spring.

†**b.** Of horses, in phr. ***to trot*** or ***gallop rings***.

1602 Marston *Antonio's Rev.* i. iii, And now Auroras horse trots azure rings. 1614 Markham *Cheap Husb.* i. ii. (1668) 15 When he will trot his Rings well, then in the same manner..you shall make him gallop the same Rings.

c. *Hunting.* A circling run.

1810 *Sporting Mag.* XXXV. 300 After a severe ring under the hill, followed by a fine run over the heath. 1813 *Ibid.* XLI. 205 A fine dog fox was soon unkenneled, and after making a ring in the plantation, he broke away.

d. ***to run rings round***, to excel or surpass (one) with the greatest ease; to beat easily. Also with *make*, and in extended uses.

1891 *Melbourne Argus* 10 Oct. 13/3 Considine could run rings round the lot of them. 1894 G. Parker in *Westm. Gaz.* 7 July 1/3 He could run rings round us in everything. 1907 Wodehouse *White Feather* viii. 88 Dexter's had taken thirty points off the School House just after half-time. 'Mopped them up,' said the terse and epigrammatic Painter. 'Made rings round them.' 1917 'Contact' *Airman's Outings* 139 Snatches of familiar flying-talk..made rings round the Hun. *c* 1928 T. E. Lawrence *Lett.* (1938) 572 It riles me unbearably to lose my scalp to a lot of fellows round whom I can make rings. 1939 *War Illustr.* 4 Nov. 252/1 We saw a large black aeroplane travelling at a high speed. It was being pursued by two British fighters and they made rings round it. 1947 *Sporting Mirror* 7 Nov. 10/3 The return of Dodds revitalised the Everton attack which ran rings round Sheffield United. 1950 'S. Ransome' *Deadly Miss Ashley* iii. 39, I can't help feeling we're having rings run around us. 1961 E. Waugh *Unconditional Surrender* iii. iv. 292 Tito has ..gone to join the Russians... Our chaps are rather annoyed about it... I bet Winston is. I told you he'd make rings round the old boy. 1973 'D. Jordan' *Nile Green* xxxiv. 167 The deal's been bust... The Russians ran rings round us. 1980 *Times Lit. Suppl.* 27 June 724/2 Balfour was an undeniable flop and Joseph Chamberlain made rings round him.

V. *attrib.* and *Comb.*

16. General attrib. uses: **a.** In senses 1, 3, etc., as ***ring-chain***, ***-digit***, ***-game***, ***lore***, ***mystery***, ***plait***, ***-relic***, ***-system***, ***-token***; ***ring-bearer***, ***-finder***, ***-giver***, ***-maker***; ***ring-giving***, ***-having***; ***ring-adorned***, ***-formed***, ***-handled***, ***-shaped*** *adjs.*; ***ring-bright***, ***-like*** *adjs.*; ***ring-wise*** *adv.*

1850 Smedley *Frank Fairleigh* iv, [He] arranged his curls with a *ring-adorned hand. 1932 W. Faulkner *Light in August* xi. 237 He was twelve then, and they wanted him to be the *ringbearer. 1954 J. R. R. Tolkien *Fellowship of Ring* ii. viii. 393 'And you, Ring-bearer,' she said, turning to Frodo. 1976 *Laurel* (Montana) *Outlook* 30 June 3/5 Gary Martin of Laurel, brother of the groom, was ring bearer. 1949 Blunden *After Bombing* 14 A child's eye drooped, so gleamed the *ring-bright shell. 1844 H. Stephens *Bk. Farm* II. 321 A new and more perfect arrangement of the *ring-chain was introduced. 1873 Mivart *Elem. Anat.* 152 The fourth, is the '*ring-digit'. 1954 J. R. R. Tolkien *Fellowship of Ring* ii. i. 237 And you are the heir of Bilbo, the *Ring-finder. 1847 Webster (citing Whewell), **Ring-formed*. 1899 *Allbutt's Syst. Med.* VIII. 899 There is..a primary degeneration of the skin, a sort of ring-formed sclerodermia. 1886 *Lippincott's Monthly Mag.* Mar. 239 The *ring-games, or 'carols', are great favorites, as they were among the English court ladies. 1916 A. S. Neill *Dominie Dismissed* vii. 98 The ring games down at the school there nearly all deal with love and matrimony. 1972 *Times* 7 Aug. (Jamaica Suppl.) p. ii/4 She has recorded Kumina music, ring games and Pocomania meetings. 1886 Corbett *Fall of Asgard* I. 184 Priest of Vold my father was, Rich *ring-giver he. 1877 W. Jones *Finger-ring* 311 The *ring-giving was followed by the usual sacrament in church. 1871 P. Smith *Anc. Hist. East* ix. §21 (1881) 177 Such a hawk is seen in a vignette of the *Ritual of the Dead*, carrying the *ring-handled cross. 1912 E. Pound *Ripostes* 27 He hath not heart for harping, nor in *ring-having Nor winsomeness to wife. 1611 Cotgr., *Annelé*, ringed,..marked with round or *ring like spots. 1698 *Phil. Trans.* XX. 173 The Ring-like Wrinkles I have also observed or discovered in the Optick Nerves of the said Fly. 1883 Huxley *Pract. Biol.* 130 The ring-like somite with its pair of appendages. 1890 W. Jones *Finger-Ring Lore* p. vii, In thus contributing to the extension of knowledge, the subject of *ring-lore has a close affinity to that of numismatics, but it possesses the supreme advantage of appealing to our sympathies and affections. 1954 J. R. R. Tolkien *Fellowship of Ring* ii. ii. 57 All that he would reveal to us of his ring-lore. 14.. *Nom.* in Wr.-Wülcker 686 *Hic anularius*, a *ryngmaker. 1648 Hexham ii, *Een Ringh-maker*, a Ring-maker, a Jeweller. 1845 *Penny Cycl.* Suppl. I. 198/1 Ring makers and turners. 1877 W. Jones *Finger-ring* 111 This *ring mystery, the *Dactylomancia*.., was a favourite operation of the ancients. 1908 W. G. Collingwood *Scandinavian Brit.* 245 The ornament with *ring-plaits.. cannot be earlier than the tenth century. 1877 W. Jones *Finger-ring* 475 A *ring-relic of Fotheringay..is of gold, set with a diamond. 1805–17 R. Jameson *Char. Min.* (ed. 3) 210 *Ring-shaped crystal. 1893 Tuckey *Amphioxus* 161 A broad ring-shaped wall of thin columnar ciliated cells. 1869 *Fortn. Rev.* Feb. 247 It often happens that the whole character of the *ring-system is changed. 1877 W. Jones *Finger-ring* 331 The famous Guy, Earl of Warwick..sends a *ring-token to the fair Félice. 1655 Marq. Worc. *Cent. Invent.* ¶ 5 Either along a Rule or *Ring-wise. 1901 *Daily News* 2 Sept. 3/3 A large flint perforated ring-wise through the centre.

†**b.** *Sc.* In sense 9 a, as ***ring-bear***, ***-corn***, ***-malt***.

1473 *Rental Bk. Cupar Angus* (1879) I. 178 Our corn myle ..with al multuris..togiddyr with the ryng beir. *c* 1592 *Reg. Arbroath* (Bann. Cl.) I. App. p. xxiv, Kirktounmilne with the astrict multures, ringbeir and vtheris proffites. 1814 *Abstract, Proof concern. the Mill of Inveramsy* 2 (Jam.), By Decreet Arbitral, 1 firlot of corn and 1 firlot of malt, as ring-corn and ring-malt, out of each plough.

c. In senses 13 and 14, as ***ring-corner***, ***-fighter***, ***-goer***, etc.; ***ringwise*** adj.

1894 A. Morrison *Mean Streets* 140 Neddy sat in his chair in the *ring-corner, and spread his arms on the ropes. 1848 tr. *Hoffmeister's Trav. Ceylon*, etc. vii. 267 Jugglers, *ring-fighters, wrestlers and dancers. 1820 *Sporting Mag.* VI. 175 To the majority of the present *ring-goers, it was mere hearsay. 1944 *Sun* (Baltimore) 29 Mar. 15/2 Salica, *ringwise and cunning, was unwilling to trade punches. 1958 F. C. Avis *Boxing Ref. Dict.* 95 *Ringwise*, gifted in ring tactics.

d. In sense 11 b, as ***ring-government***, etc.

1888 Bryce *Amer. Commw.* II. iii. lxiv. 477 The materials for real ring government do not exist..outside the large cities. *Ibid.*, The general laws of ring growth. *Ibid.*, Country places and the smaller cities are not ring-ridden. 1889 *Spectator* 12 Oct., Judges, district attorneys, and other functionaries owe their places to ring politicians.

e. *Chem.* In sense 10 d, as ***ring-closure***, ***-compound***, ***-formation***, ***-opening***, ***-structure***, etc.

1946 *Nature* 28 Dec. 930/1 The problem of effecting ring-closure through the meta- and para-positions of the benzene nucleus. 1964 N. G. Clark *Mod. Org. Chem.* xv. 294 On heating..these compounds readily undergo ring-closure through loss of a molecule of ethanol. 1932 *Discovery* Aug. 246/1 The changes during the coalification process proceed only to a half-way stage between the most stable kind of carbon chain compound, and the most stable kind of ring compound. 1961 *New Scientist* 16 Mar. 668/1 Almost any organic compound gets decomposed in time, even stable ring compounds like phenol, naphthalene and toluene. 1913 J. B. Cohen *Org. Chem. Adv. Students* II. ii. 111 Nearly all the above reactions may become intra-molecular if the necessary grouping is present, and in such cases ring formation follows. 1967 Margerison & East *Introd. Polymer Chem.* iii. 129 These formulations of the reactions of difunctional monomers have ignored the possibility of ring formation. 1959 Ring-opening [see decarboxylate *v.*]. 1967 Margerison & East *Introd. Polymer Chem.* v. 261 Other ring-opening polymerizations in this class include the conversion of caprolactam to nylon 6. 1930 *Engineering* 18 Apr. 525/2 These investigations indicated that the cellulose molecule had a ring structure.

17. Attrib., in the sense 'having the shape of a ring, annular, circular', as ***ring-base***, ***battalia***, ***-brooch***, ***-ditch***, ***-foot***, ***-gasket***, ***handle***, ***-hook***, ***loaf***, ***nebula***, ***-scissors***, ***-weight***, etc.

1957 V. G. Childe *Dawn European Civilization* (ed. 6) v. 60 Ring bases and genuine handles betoken an unusual degree of sophistication. 1960 T. Burton-Brown *Early Mediterranean Migrations* i. 27 The comparative frequency of ring-bases in the red-polished..wares..is a detail of some significance. 1638 J. Underhill *News fr. Amer.* in *Mass. Hist. Coll.* (1837) VI. 23 Placing the Indians..without side of our soldiers in a ring battalia. 1883 C. T. Gatty *Catal. Mediæval & Later Antiquities Mayer Museum* 37 *Ring brooch*, in silver; inscribed on one side, in niello work, + ave: maria: gracia: plena: d, and on the other + agla + no. a + s: blasiv. 1931 J. Evans *Eng. Posies & Posy Rings* p. xii, Such inscriptions were commonly engraved in the thirteenth and fourteenth centuries on the ring-brooches that were used to fasten the dress at the neck. 1977 *Antiquaries Jrnl.* LVII. 457/1 Note on the significance of the Londesborough ring brooch. 1936 *Oxoniensia* I. 8 In the following pages some account is given of the investigation of barrows and ring-ditches in the Oxford area. 1954 S. Piggott *Neolithic Cultures* ii. 32 These cultures are sometimes associated with causewayed ring-ditches of a funerary or ceremonial nature. 1927 Peake & Fleure *Priests & Kings* x. 162 Deep cups have been found with rounded bottoms, also bottles with lugs instead of handles and sometimes with hollow ring-feet. 1980 *Catal. Fine Chinese Ceramics* (Sotheby, Hong Kong) 76 The well-finished ring foot decorated with incised key-fret. 1972 L. M. Harris *Introd. Deepwater Floating Drilling Operations* ix. 93 An AX ring gasket provides a metal-to-metal seal between the connector and the wellhead. 1844 H. Stephens *Bk. Farm* I. 199 The doors of the..stables should be provided with sunk flush ring-handles. 1936 *Burlington Mag.* July 26/1 The pair of..candlesticks with ring-handles has the Britannia standard marks with the date-letter for 1736–37. 1972 *Trans. Oriental Ceramics Soc.* XXXVIII. 58 A grey earthenware jar and cover, with ring-handle masks in relief. 1913 J. Masefield *Daffodil Fields* 72 Its open door, With old wrought bridle ring-hooks at each flank. 1961 *B.S.I. News* Nov. 25 (*title*) Dimensions of ring-hook automatic hitch. 1802 Southey *King Ramiro* viii, I would give you a roasted capon first, And a good ring loaf of wheaten bread. 1878 Newcomb *Pop. Astron.* iv. i. 449 The annular, or ring-nebula of Lyra. 1742 *Edin. Med. Ess.* V. 445 A Ring-scalpel for assisting the Delivery of Woman in Child-birth; by Dr. Thomas Simson. 1908 *Practitioner* June 769 Later Mr. Jessop introduced his 'ring-scissors', which made this piecemeal removal of the gland an easier matter. 1574 *Richmond Wills* (Surtees) 253 ij wayne shackells,..one ring shackell. 1727 Boyer *Dict. Royal* II. s.v. *Ring*, A Ring-thimble. 1859 F. A. Griffiths *Artil. Man.* (1862) 63 Ring tires are used for light 3-pounders and hand-cart wheels. 1922 Joyce *Ulysses* 665 Though ringweight lifting had been beyond his strength..he had excelled in his stable and protracted execution of the half lever movement on the parallel bars.

18. In combs. of the type ***ring-banded***, ***-billed***, ***-eyed***, ***-notched***, occurring in the specific names of animals or birds. See also ring-necked *a.*, ring-tailed *a.*

1802 Shaw *Gen. Zool.* III. ii. 492 Ring-banded Snake, *Coluber Doliatus*... A small, but highly elegant, species. 1831 [see ring-billed (mew) gull, 19 b.] 1852 Macgillivray *Hist. Brit. Birds* V. 326 *Uria Lacrymans*,..Ringed or Ring-Eyed Guillemot. 1874 J. W. Long *Amer. Wildfowl* 276 Ring-necked Duck... Local names, 'Ring-billed Duck' [etc.]. 1890 Julia P. Ballard *Among Moths* 79 The black ring-notched chrysalis.

19. a. Special combs., as **ring armature** *Electr.*, an armature having a ring winding; **ring-armour**, armour composed of metal rings (see sense 2), ring-mail; **ring-bayonet**, a bayonet provided with a ring, by which to fix it in position upon the musket; **ring beam**, a ring-shaped beam of yarn; **ring binder**, a loose-leaf binder having clasps that pass through holes in the paper and can be closed to form rings; similarly **ring binding**; **ring-bit**, a horse-bit having rings at the ends; **ring book**, a notebook having the form of a *ring binder*; **ring-boot**, a rubber ring placed on a horse's fetlock to prevent interfering; **ring-bored** *a.*, of a gun-barrel, bored roughly, so as to leave the metal in rings; **ring-building** *Archæol.*, the forming of vessels by adding successive layers of ring-shaped pieces of clay; hence **ring-built** *a.*; **ring-canal**, a circular canal forming part of the structure of cœlenterates and of echinoderms; †**ring-carrier**, a go-between; **ring-cartilage**, the cricoid cartilage; †**ring-chopper**, one who swindles by means of a worthless ring; **ring-chuck**, a form of chuck, the grip of which may be tightened by means of a ring; **ring circuit**, (*a*) *Electronics* = *ring counter* below; (*b*) *Electr.*, a wiring arrangement for power distribution in domestic or similar premises in which sockets and fixed appliances are connected to a single loop of cable which starts from and returns to a fuse-box; †**ring-coal** (see quot.); †**ring-coffin** (see coffin *sb.* 9); **ring complex** *Geol.*, an association of igneous intrusions arranged in an arcuate or ring-like plan; **ring counter** *Electronics*, a counting circuit consisting of a number of flip-flops or other bistable devices wired in a closed loop; **ring-craft**, skill in pugilism; also *transf.* of other sports; **ring-crib** (see quots. and crib *sb.* 12); **ring-cross**, the figure of a cross enclosed in a ring or circle; **ring culture**, the technique of growing plants in a bottomless cylinder containing nutrients and resting on an inert bed through which water is provided; **ring current**, (*a*) *Geophysics*, a belt of charged particles which orbit the earth, trapped by the magnetic field in its ionosphere; (*b*) *Chem.*, a circulation of electrons in an annular molecular orbital (e.g. in aromatic molecules) under the influence of a magnetic field; **ring dike, dyke** *Geol.*, a dike that is arcuate or roughly circular in plan, formed by upwelling of magma along ring fractures following cauldron subsidence of a circular block; **ring doffer**, a doffer covered with separate circles of filleting; **ring-dogs** (see quot.); **ring-dollar**, *Austr.*, a Spanish dollar having a circular piece cut out of the centre; **ring-drain**, a drain enclosing a stretch of ground; **ring dropper**, a sharper who pretends to have found a dropped ring and offers to sell it; **ring-dropping**, the method of swindling practised by a ring-dropper; **ring-eye**, = ringle-eye; †**ring-faller**, = *ring-dropper*; **ring-farm**, a farm enclosed by a ring-fence; **ring flash** *Photogr.*, a circular electronic flash tube that fits round the camera lens to give shadowless lighting of a subject near the lens; **ring-fort** *Archæol.*, a fort or other position defended by ringed entrenchments; **ring fracture** *Geol.* [tr. G. *kreisbrüche*], a conical or nearly cylindrical fault associated with cauldron subsidence; **ring-frame**, a spinning machine in which the thread is wound by means of a traveller running on a horizontal ring; **ring-furnace** (see quot.); †**ring-galliard**, some manœuvre of the manege; **ring gland** *Zool.*, a gland in dipteran larvæ which secretes ecdysone; **ring-gold**, an alloy of copper, silver, and gold; †**ring-gristle**, = *ring-cartilage*; †**ring-head** (see quots.); **ring-hedge**, = RING-FENCE; **ring-horse**, a horse for running at the ring (*obs.*); a horse trained to perform in a circus-ring; **ring-hunt**, a hunt in which the animals are driven inwards by a ring of fire; so ***ring-hunting***; **ring-joint**, (*a*) a pipe-joint formed of circular flanges; (*b*) a form of joint in certain insects, esp. of the *Hymenoptera*; **ring-junction**, a road junction at which traffic is channelled in two directions round a central island, entering and leaving by smaller islands; **ring-keeper**, (*a*) a guard-ring, a device to keep a ring in place; (*b*) one who keeps the ring at a prize-fight; **ring-key**, a key fitted with a ring-handle, which falls down instead of standing out from the door; **ring-kop** *S. Afr.* [Afrikaans *kop* head], an African tribesman or warrior entitled to wear a head-ring (see HEAD *sb.* 66); **ring-lock**, a lock in which a number of grooved rings must be adjusted before the bolt can be drawn (Knight); **ring-mail** (see sense 2 and MAIL *sb.*[1]); **ring main**, (*a*) an electric main that starts from and returns to a particular power station or sub-station, so that each consumer has an alternative path for supply in the event of a failure; also = *ring circuit* (*b*) above; (*b*) *Plumbing*, an arrangement of pipes forming a closed loop into which steam, water, or sewage may be fed and whose points of draw-off are supplied by flow from two directions; **ring modulator** *Electronics*, a circuit that incorporates a closed loop of four diodes and can be used for balanced mixing and modulation of signals; **ring-money**, annular or penannular pieces of metal now or formerly used as money; also = MANILLA[1]; **ring oiling**, a method of automatic lubrication of bearings in which a ring rests upon and turns with the journal and also dips into a reservoir containing the lubricant; so **ring-oiled** *ppl. a.*; **ring oiler**; **ring-opener**, a seal on a tin container which is broken by pulling a ring attached to it; **ring-pen**, a voussoir of an arch; †**ring-pigger**, a drunkard; **ring-plate**, (*a*) a plate with a ring attached for supporting a pipe (Knight); (*b*) an iron plate underlying a door-ring; **ring-play** *U.S.*, a circular dance movement accompanied by song; **ring-pored, -porous** *adjs. Forestry*, applied to woods in which the large pores produced in spring form partial or complete rings; cf. *diffuse-porous* adj. s.v. DIFFUSE *a.* 2 f; hence **ring porosity, -porousness**; **ring-post**, a post used in the construction of scaffolding; **ring-pull** *a.*, designating a tin container fitted with a *ring-opener*; †**ring-rathe** (cf. RATHE *sb.*[2]); **ring-rope**, (*a*) *Naut.* (see quots.); (*b*) usu. *pl.*, = ROPE *sb.*[1] 2 c; **ring rot** [tr. G. *bakterienringfäule* (A. Spieckermann 1914, in *Landwirtsch. Jahrb.* XLVI v. 660)], a bacterial disease of the potato, affecting the tubers, caused by *Corynebacterium sepedonicum*; **ring scaler** *Electronics* = *ring counter* above; **ring-seat** = *ringside seat* s.v. RINGSIDE b; **ring shake** *Forestry*, a partial or complete separation of two or more consecutive growth rings in a tree; = CUP-SHAKE; so **ring-shaken** *a.*; **ring-shell, -shot**, a projectile in which the body is made of iron rings; a segment-shell; **ring-shout** *U.S.*, a religious dance consisting of loud singing and circular movement; **ring-sight** *Mil.* (see quot. 1973); **ring-snaffle**, a form of bridle-bit with rings at each end; **ring-song**, a choral dancing-song; **ring spanner**, a spanner in which the jaws are in the form of a ring with internal serrations, which fit completely around the nut and put pressure on all its faces; **ring-spindle**, the form of spindle used in a ring-frame; **ring spinning**, spinning done with a ring-frame; **ring-splice** (see quot.); **ringspot, ring spot**, (*a*) any of several plant diseases characterized by annular spots or marks on the leaves; (*b*) an annular mark on a plant or animal; so **ring-spotted** *a.*; **ring-stand**, (*a*) a small stand for finger-rings; (*b*) a stand of circular form; **ring-staple**, ? a staple with a circular head; **ring-stopper**, = *cathead-stopper*; **ring-taw**, a game with marbles which are put in a ring and played at; **ring-time**, a time of giving or exchanging rings (*nonce-use*); **ring-toss**, *U.S.*, deck-quoits; **ring velvet**, velvet so fine that a width of it can be drawn through a ring; **ring-watch** (see quot. 1962); **ring winding** *Electr.*, a form of armature winding in which each turn of the winding passes through the centre of the hollow armature core (cf. GRAM[2]); †**ring-wood**, wood for making the rims of wheels; **ring-work**, (*a*) a circular entrenchment; (*b*) work executed with rings; (*c*) performance in the boxing-ring; **ring-worm** *U.S. slang* (see quot. 1929); **ring-yarn**, yarn produced by ring-spinning.

1893 *Ring armature [see GRAM[2]]. **1974** *Encycl. Brit. Macropædia* VI. 610/1 The ring armature..enormously improved the efficiency of early electric generators. **1834** *Penny Cycl.* II. 369 The *ring-armour of the Bayeux tapestry forms..breeches and jacket at the same time. **1875** KNIGHT *Dict. Mech.* 252 The *ring-bayonet was introduced in 1693, and the socket-bayonet in 1703. **1924** *Times Trade & Engin. Suppl.* 29 Nov. 247/1 *Ring beams are now worse off in margin by 1d. per lb. compared with a month or six weeks ago. **1929** A. J. VAUGHAN *Mod. Bookbinding* II. 136 *The *ring binders.* These employ rings which may be opened or closed, the paper being pierced with round holes. **1977** *New Yorker* 27 June 30/1 Forced into proximity as we were by ledgers, ring binders, and jars of mucilage. **1977** P. D. JAMES *Death of Expert Witness* II. v. 80 A quarto-sized loose-leaf notebook with a *ring binding. **1923** H. A. MADDOX *Dict. Stationery Terms* 67 *Ring books, loose-leaf books arranged on the principle of split or hinged rings, which by a finger lever motion open to receive the leaves punched to fit the rings. **1942** H. A. MADDOX *Dict. Stationery* 94 Ring book. **1965** P. WYLIE *They both were Naked* I. iv. 149 My second address was neatly arranged in a ring-book. **1858** GREENER *Gunnery* 295 The chance is that the barrel is *ring-bored, as it is termed. **1957** V. G. CHILDE *Dawn European Civilization* (ed. 6) xi. 204 From Sweden to Siberia..all pots were manufactured by the same technique of *ring-building. **1964** H. HODGES *Artifacts* i. 26 *Ring-building*... The walls of the vessel are formed by the addition of sausage-shaped rolls of clay of various lengths. **1963** E. M. JOPE in Foster & Alcock *Culture & Environment* xiii. 337 In the tenth to twelfth centuries, the distinctive bar-lip style of pottery, flat-based and coil- or *ring-built, rooted firmly in the simplest techniques of prehistoric pottery-making. **1964** H. HODGES *Artifacts* i. 29 Much early pottery that has been described as wheel-thrown was probably initially ring-built and only finally given its form on a rotating wheel. **1881** *Encycl. Brit.* XII. 550 The peripheral portion of the lumen of the original enteric cavity forms the *ring-canal. **1598** SHAKS. *All's Well* III. v. 95 *Mar.* Looke he has spyed vs. *Wid.* Marrie hang you. *Mar.* And your curtesie, for a *ring-carrier. **1690** tr. *Blancard's Phys. Dict.* 170 *Circoides*,..*Angl.* *Ring cartilage *vel* gristle. **1859** *Todd's Cycl. Anat.* V. 261/1 Another order of elastic tissue lies between the ring-cartilages, tying them together cylindrically. **1561** AWDELEY *Frat. Vacab.* (1869) 11 Ther is another kinde of these *Ring choppers, which commonly cary about them a faire gold ring [etc.]. **1842** FRANCIS *Dict. Arts*, **Ring Chuck*, a very useful chuck for many purposes, and one which is easily made. **1931** *Proc. R. Soc.* A. CXXXII. 306 The simplified 'chain' arrangement of thyratrons, from which the more useful '*ring' circuits..were developed. **1946** *Rev. Sci. Instruments* XVII. 185/2 The two pentodes of each trigger pair form opposite partners in the ring circuit. **1961** B. PYM *No Fond Return of Love* xxiv. 236 Her loud clear tones were addressed to the London Electricity Board, and the conversation seemed to be about power plugs and something called a 'ring circuit'. **1962** N. D. WATTS in G. A. T. Burdett *Automatic Control Handbk.* xviii. 10 Fig. 11 shows a ring circuit in which the primer electrodes are omitted for simplicity. **1963** *Times* 6 May (Electric Power Suppl.) p. vii/3 Complete interchangeability at multiple points throughout the house is achieved by the 'ring circuit'. **1974** A. DOUGLAS *Noah's Ark Murders* viii. 75, I thought lighting these days was on ring circuits—surely one burned-out fuse shouldn't mean total failure? **1662** RAY *Three Itin.* III. 176 In this country they dig two sorts of coals, the one they call stone coal, not fit for smiths; the other *ring coal, which is fit for their use. **1702** PETIVER *Gazophyl.* I. §5 *Folliculena seu Folliculum Phalenæ ovale*,..the *Ring-Coffin. **1916** E. B. BAILEY et al. *Geol. Ben Nevis & Glen Coe* viii. 109 The fault serves as the inner boundary of the *ring-complex known as the Fault-Intrusion. **1965** A. HOLMES *Princ. Physical Geol.* (ed. 2) xi. 261 Intrusions in the form of concentric arcs or rings are of two distinct types, forming ring complexes such as are exceptionally well developed around the Tertiary volcanic centres of NW Britain. **1976** *Nature* 23 Sept. 307/1 The duration of about 5 Myr for the igneous activities in this ring complex is especially informative in terms of the formation of one complete ring complex. **1942** W. B. LEWIS *Electr. Counting* viii. 90 A thyratron *ring counter which could have any number of thyratrons arranged in a ring with an arc in one of them. **1969** J. J. SPARKES *Transistor Switching* viii. 195 If the outputs of the last flip-flop..are connected back to the inputs of the first flip-flop than a Ring Counter is formed. **1971** J. H. SMITH *Digital Logic* vi. 121 Ring counters, which were used for many years using gas filled trigger valves, will give a count related to the number of stages. If there are *n* stages the counter will count to 2*n*. **1896** DOYLE *Rodney Stone* xi, It was at such a moment that *ringcraft was needed, and..two masters of it were at his back. **1900** —— *Green Flag* iv. 125 A hard veteran, full of cool valour and ring-craft, could give ten or fifteen years and a beating to most striplings. **1922** JOYCE *Ulysses* 313 Handicapped as he was by lack of poundage, Dublin's pet lamb made up for it by superlative skill in ringcraft. **1957** A. MACNAB *Bulls of Iberia* xii. 136 As for the *lidia*, the general ringcraft, he [*sc.* Belmonte] admits he knew nothing of it and cared less. **1976** *Daily Record* (Glasgow) 29 Nov., Len Harvey, one of the greatest exponents of ringcraft British boxing has produced, died at his London home yesterday. **1849** GREENWELL *Coal-trade T.* (1851) 19 A *ring crib may be made of metal or oak, of the same size as a wedging crib. It is open at the top, for the purpose of collecting water, which would otherwise fall down the pit. **1869** —— *Mine Engin.* 179 The ring crib consists of cribs which are..walled in with the walling in the shaft [etc.]. **1882** WORSAAE *Industrial Arts Denmark* 33 Carved *ring-crosses, under which form many other peoples..have constantly represented the sun. **1893** S. O. ADDY *Hall of Waltheof* 93 Ring-crosses may be seen carved upon the lids of many ancient stone coffins. **1961** *Amateur Gardening* 4 Nov. Suppl. 42/2 *Ring culture. In recent years the growing of certain plants, chiefly tomatoes, in bottomless containers has come into vogue. **1962** H. G. W. FOGG *Chrysanthemum Growing* ix. 60 Ring culture, a term which was, I believe, first used as a result of experiments, at Tilgate Horticultural Research Station. **1964, 1976** Ring culture [see sense 3 i above]. [**1933** *Terrestrial Magn.* XVIII. 82 Whether the latter [current] will close upon itself so as to become an isolated current-ring.] **1941** *Ibid.* XLVI. 1 In our theory of geomagnetic storms, we attribute the main phase to a hypothetical electric *ring-current. **1956** *Proc. R. Soc.* A. CCXXXVI. 522 To find the effect of the ring current on the proton resonance line we have to average over orientations. **1962** F. I. ORDWAY et al. *Basic Astronautics* iv. 164 The ring current system probably consists of low energy particles and is able to effectively disturb the terrestrial magnetic field... It is estimated that a current flow of 1,000,000 amp exists. **1966** WILLIAMS & FLEMING *Spectrosc. Methods Org. Chem.* iv. 88 Protons attached to systems which can sustain a ring current suffer a paramagnetic shift relative to olefinic protons of isolated double bonds. **1976** *Jrnl. Geophysical Res.* LXXXI. 2701/1 The decay of the proton ring current by charge exchange loss. **1915** *Summary of Progr. Geol. Survey 1914* The Loch Bà felsite is the most perfect example of a ring-boss, or *ring-dyke, anywhere known. **1931** *Amer. Jrnl. Sci.* CCXXII. 145 The ring-dike is found between the granite frame and the volcanics of the mountains wherever bed rock is exposed. **1976** *Nature* 23 Sept. 307/1 The 7·6 ± 0·2 Myr isochron..combines various samples from the three inner distinct ring dykes..made up of alkaline granites and quartz syenites. **1884** W. S. B. MCLAREN *Spinning* (ed. 2) 222 Though this is the main feature of the *ring doffer, it is divided into several varieties. **1846** A. YOUNG *Naut. Dict.* s.v. *Dog*, If connected by a ring going through the eyes, they are called *ring-dogs. Both.. kinds of dogs are used for lifting timber. **1870** BRAIM *New Homes* III. 131 The rest of the dollar, called from the circular piece taken out a '*ring-dollar', was valued at four shillings. **1805** R. W. DICKSON *Pract. Agric.* I. 394 A *ring-drain, serving the purpose of a fence, is thrown round the moss at the line where the rising ground commences. **1797** *Sporting Mag.* IX. 315 Low gamblers, *ring droppers, sharpers and thieves of every description. **1844** DICKENS *Mart. Chuz.* xxxvii, Tom's evil genius did not..mark him out as the prey of ring-droppers, pea and thimble-riggers,.. or any of those bloodless sharpers. **1825** SOUTHEY in *Q. Rev.* XXXI. 388 A trick which is as stale as the *ring-dropping of a London sharper. **1851** MAYHEW *Lond. Labour* I. 351/2 The ring-dropping 'lurk' is now carried on this way, for the old style is 'coopered'. **1720** *Lond. Gaz.* No. 5825/4 Stolen .., one bright bay Nag,..a *Ring Eye on the near Side. **1561** AWDELEY *Frat. Vacab.* (1869) 10 A *Ryng faller is he that getteth fayre copper rings,..and walketh vp and down the streetes.., and letteth fall one of these ringes [etc.]. **1886** *York Herald* 7 Aug. 1/3 The Farm is a '*Ring Farm', and most conveniently situated for Road or Rail. **1969** L. GAUNT *Commonsense Photogr.* xiii. 218 There are special *ring flash units which fit round the lens and give even, almost shadow-free lighting. **1975** G. SKOGLUND *Colour in your Camera* (ed. 6) 144 Shadowless 'multi-directed' lighting, can be produced by a piece of equipment known as a 'ring-flash'. **1978** *SLR Camera* Aug. 45/2 To my knowledge it is the only 100mm lens which has a built-in ring flash that will continuously focus from 1/15 down to life size. **1935** *Discovery* Apr. 102/1 *Ring-forts of earth or stone represent one of the most common kinds of monuments of antiquity throughout Ireland. **1937** *Proc. Prehist. Soc.* III. 407 It is hardly justifiable to class ring-forts as fortified sites; they were ordinary farmsteads with a natural measure of protection, and assumed the character of a fortified settlement only if the site was very large. **1960** S. CRUDEN *Scottish Abbeys* 21 The massive circular stone wall of the 'ring-fort', of late Iron Age or Dark Age date. **1976** *Country Life* 6 May 1163/1 Ring forts..are common all over Ireland. **1919** *Geol. Mag.* LVI. 469 In some ways the most interesting feature of Old Iceland is the *ring-fracture system (*Kreisbrüche*) of the north-west peninsula. **1924** E. B. BAILEY et al. *Tertiary & Post-Tertiary Geol. Mull, Loch Aline, & Oban* i. 7 It was in Iceland that the word *ring-fracture* (*Kreisbrüche*) was introduced by Thoroddsen. **1965** A. HOLMES *Princ. Physical Geol.* (ed. 2) xi. 261 The ring dyke..represents the case where the weight of the keystone ..has produced the ring fractures within which subsidence —often referred to as cauldron subsidence—has taken place. **1884** W. S. B. MCLAREN *Spinning* 166 The latest development of throstle spinning is the *ring-frame, which is now superseding the flyer frame entirely in the cotton trade. **1860** TOMLINSON *Cycl. Arts & Manuf.* Ser. II. Iron & Steel 27 A *ring-furnace was constructed; that is, a central core of solid brickwork was formed, round which was built a fireplace and hearth. **1612** WEBSTER *White Devil* IV. iii, A resty Barbary horse Which he would fain have brought to the career, The sault, and the *Ring-galliard. **1937** E. HADORN in *Proc. Nat. Acad. Sci.* XXIII. 481 Since it has been shown that the ring has a glandular function, the term '*ring-gland' may be used so long as no homology to other structures in other insects has been established. *Ibid.* 484 Puparium-formation can be accelerated by transplantation of a normal ring-gland to lethal larvae. **1978** *Molecular & Gen. Genetics* CLXIV. 79/2 The ring gland donors were at the late larval stage by which ecdysone production was likely to have begun. **1825** J. NICHOLSON *Operat. Mechanic* 714 *Ring-gold, 6 dwts. 12 grs. Spanish copper [etc.]. **1615** CROOKE *Body of Man* 637 The second and lower gristle is called κρικοειδής, the *Ring-gristle. **1601** *Act 43 Eliz.* c. 10 §2 That no persone..shall have, keepe, or use any manner of Wrinche, *Ringehead, Growme, Rope, or other Engine to stretche or straine any roughe and unwroughte Woollen Clothe. *a* **1642** SIR W. MONSON *Naval Tracts* III. (1704) 345/1 The Ground and Timber is the Floor of the Ship, and are call'd the Ring-heads. **1607** J. DAVIES (Heref.) *Summa Totalis* Wks. (Grosart) I. 11/2 Lo how Apollas Pegasses prepare To rend the *ring-hedge of our Horizon. **1775** ASH, *Ringhedge*, a hedge that encompasses several inclosures. **1655** MARQ. WORC. *Cent. Invent.* Index p. viii, An artificiall *Ring-horse. **1861** *Windsor Express* 5 Oct., The sale comprised 45 trick and ring horses. **1799** J. SMITH *Remark. Occurr.* (1870) 85 We met with some Ottawa hunters, and agreed with them to take, what they call a *ring hunt, in partnership... This put an end to our *ring hunting this season. **1972** *Guardian* 26 June 1/3 In this new *ring junction traffic turning right goes between the island in the centre and the off-side mini-roundabout. **1973** *Daily Tel.* 3 Aug. 17/1 The experimental 'ring junction' to ease traffic congestion at the Plough roundabout..may be made permanent by winter. **1912** *Chambers's Jrnl.* 394/1 He organized a body of '*ring-keepers' to preserve order as far as possible. **1922** JOYCE *Ulysses* 510 The virgins..burst through the ring-keepers and the ropes and mob him with open arms. **1853** R. S. SURTEES *Sponge's Sp. Tour* (1893) 37 Having produced the *ring-key from his pocket, Mr. Leather opened the [stable] door. **1835** *Ring-kop [see sense 9i above]. **1910** J. BUCHAN *Prester John* viii. 149 In such a man one would have looked for a *ring-kop*, but instead he had a mass of hair..long and curled like some popular musician. **1935** *Brit. S. Afr. Ann.* 35 Our principal native warrior, an old 'ringkop', promptly took up his quarters in a friendly tree. **1856** G. PRICE *Treat. Fire & Thief-Proof Depositories & Locks & Keys* xiv. 205 Two centuries ago the puzzle-lock attracted far more attention than any other... The chief among them are *ring-locks*. **1868** A. C. HOBBS *Constr. Locks* iii. 17 According to the kind of handle employed, it [*sc.* the room-lock] may be a knob lock or a ring lock. **1965** G. MCINNES *Road to Gundagai* ix. 137, I.. ambled gently down the drive toward the ringlock gate. **1824** MEYRICK *Armour* I. 181 An arm of *ring mail. *Ibid.*, A housing of ring-mail half riveted. **1885** C. J. LYALL *Anc. Arab. Poet.* 31 The ring-mail set close and firm. **1892** J. A. FLEMING *Alternate Current Transformer* II. ii. 207 *(caption)* The Metropolitan Company's system of *ring mains. **1901** F. B. CROCKER *Electric Lighting* II. 505 (Index), Ring mains. **1904** *Electr. World & Engineer* 27 Feb. 396/2 The four batteries of boilers constituting each section of the boiler plant are interconnected by a 10-in. main and a 4-in. auxiliary line, both in the form of a ring main... With the location of the valves adopted in the event of rupture of any section of a ring main the trouble may be localised by shutting off the disabled section, the remaining half of the main being kept in service. **1930** *Engineering* 17 Jan. 92/1 In the near future it would probably be necessary to connect these lines by ring mains. **1945** *Jrnl. R. Aeronaut. Soc.* XLIX. 529/1 It is avoided in the larger warships by the spread of the ring main (all below armour) which is admitted as not feasible in aircraft. **1959** GOODIN & DOWNING *Domestic Sanitation* iv. 97 The use of ring mains tends to reduce the size of pipes which must be used and are [*sic*] of great value in maintaining supplies when bursts occur. **1962** *Which?* Mar. 82/1 You will also need a convenient electric power point. Having a new one installed—especially in an older house where there is no ring main—may mean a lot of new wiring. **1962** *Newnes Conc. Encycl. Electr. Engin.* 202 Ring mains offer the possibility of a firm supply at all times, but the cost of the complicated protective gear..makes such schemes justifiable only in cases where no loss of supply can be tolerated. **1976** G. MOFFAT *Short Time to Live* vi. 53 He'd ..modernise the place: put in a ring main, dig drains, build a septic tank. **1938** *Nippon Electr. Commun. Engin.* Apr. 118/2 Although there are many considerations when it comes to the connecting method of rectifiers in the various carrier suppressed modulators, one of the most effective is that of the so-called *Ring modulator. **1974** HARVEY & BOHLMAN *Stereo F.M. Radio Handbk.* ii. 17 Another way of generating sidebands without the carrier appearing in the output is to employ a ring modulator. **1974** *Down Beat* 18 July 42/2 The ring modulator adds both upper and lower sidebands of sound to the original tone. These modulated outputs will be the sum of and the difference between the frequencies of the original tone and an internal sine wave or external source. **1759** B. MARTIN *Nat. Hist. Eng.* I. 269 A great quantity of Roman Coins..; those of Silver were *Ring-money of diverse Sizes. **1853** HUMPHREY *Coin Collector's Man.* I. 8 *note*, A modern ring-money is still in circulation in some parts of Northern Africa. **1920** J. R. BATTLE *Handbk. Industr. Oil Engin.* vii. 421 There have been cases where hot running, *ring-oiled bearings have been made to run cool. **1930** *Engineering* 11 July 39/3 The outer end of the crankshaft is supported by a ring-oiled outboard bearing and pedestal. **1968** J. J. O'CONNOR *Stand. Handbk. Lubric. Engin.* xxxv. 11 Lead babbitt..is frequently used as the bearing material for ring-oiled motors. **1962** G. A. T. BURDETT *Automatic Control Handbk.* xii. 11 *Ring oiler. **1970** B. PUGH *Pract. Lubric.* viii. 164 Small [steam] turbines usually have the simplest arrangements for bearing lubrication, i.e. ring oilers or standard type lubricators. **1972** R. C. GUNTHER *Lubrication* xi. 304 Ring oiler consists of a free metal ring that rides on the journal and carries oil from a reservoir located below the bearing. **1904** *Electr. Rev.* 10 Sept. 410 The journal bearings are of the *ring-oiling, self-aligning type. **1920** T. C. THOMSEN *Pract. Lubric.* ix. 158 Ring oiling is employed largely on modern high-speed shafting bearings. **1974** P. CAVE *Mama* (new ed.) vii 46 Mama took a can of beer which was thrust towards her and ripped off the *ring opener. **1975** G. V. HIGGINS *City on Hill* iii. 74 He..brought out two cans of beer... They stripped off the ring openers and drank. **1977** H. INNES *Big Footprints* II. iii. 187 Abe snapped the ring-opener of his [beer] can..and drank. **1844** H. STEPHENS *Bk. Farm* I. 202, 24 [lineal feet of] *Ringpens of archways to granary. **1570** LEVINS *Manip.* 80 A *Ringpigger, *potator, bibax*. **1904** *Athenæum* 9 Apr. 473/3 The ironwork on some of the doors is noteworthy; the central ring and *ringplate..is fairly frequent. **1935** *Bull. Folk-Song Soc. Northeast* ix. 11 The movement, with upraised hands, is not dissimilar to that in certain types of *ring-play*. **1942** L. PARRISH *Slave Songs Georgia Sea Islands* iv. 99 This ring-play varies in action wherever I see it done. .. The tune, however, always remains the same. **1972** R. D. ABRAHAMS in T. Kochman *Rappin' & Stylin' Out* 222 The numerous songs, ring-play, and verbal routines in Tobagonian Bongo (wake), as performed by adults in the community. **1909** P. T. MAW *Pract. Forestry* viii. 164 The so-called '*ring-pored' trees—Oak, Ash, Elm, Spanish Chestnut, and Acacia. **1978** A. BERNATZKY *Tree Ecol. & Preservation* iv. 53 *Fraxinus, Castanea, Quercus*, and *Robinia* are ring-pored. **1940** *Bot. Gaz.* CII. 115 *Ring porosity is restricted to..the North Temperate zone. **1902** F. ROTH *First Bk. Forestry* III. 222 The *ring-porous woods, like oak, ash, chestnut. **1928** [see DIFFUSE *a.* 2 f]. **1956** F. W. JANE *Struct. Wood* xi. 250 Very approximately,..the timber of a ring porous hardwood possesses maximum strength when its growth rings number between 6 and 10 to the inch. **1968** G. TSOUMIS *Wood as Raw Material* ii. 14 Growth rings are generally more distinct in ring-porous than in diffuse-porous woods. **1950** METCALFE & CHALK *Anat. Dicotyledons* I. p. xlvii, *Ring-porousness, or the development of a marked zone of larger vessels at the beginning of a growth ring, appears to be accompanied by an increase in the length of the complete vessels in the pore zone. **1901** *J. Black's Carp. & Build., Scaffolding* 39 The position of an inclined piece to support the bearing of the tie-beam, and..that of a brace to sustain the top of the *ringposts. **1970** *Times* 16 Feb. (Food in Britain Suppl.) p. iii/3 Easy opening devices are undergoing considerable development—and *ring-pull and zip-top cans are already available. **1973** 'D. HALLIDAY' *Dolly & Starry Bird* vii. 89 Poor Jacko, who treated birds and ring-pull cans as one problem. **1538** *Nottingham Rec.* III. 200 Unum wollenlome cum *ryngrathes. **1769** FALCONER *Dict. Marine* (1780), **Ring-ropes*, short pieces of rope, tied occasionally to the ring-bolts of the deck, to fasten the cable more securely when the ship rides in a tempest. **1867** SMYTH *Sailor's Word-bk., Ring-Ropes*, ropes rove through the ring of the anchor, to haul the cable through it. **1922** JOYCE *Ulysses* 313 The Santry boy was declared victor to the frenzied cheers of the public who broke through the ringropes and fairly mobbed him with delight. **1942** J. MASEFIELD *Generation Risen* 30 The seconds' faces Watch through the ring-ropes. **1920** E. F. SMITH *Introd. Bacterial Dis. Plants* iv. i. 474 Spieckermann's *ring rot of Potato. **1946** *Sun* (Baltimore) 30 May 7/5 Even though potatoes 'look nice' they may harbor the dangerous ring-rot disease. **1974** Z. KIRALY et al. *Methods Plant Path.* viii. 180 *(caption)* Processed plant extract of a ring-rot infected tuber. **1960** *Gloss. Atomic Terms* (U.K. Atomic Energy Authority) 46 *Ring scaler. **1963** B. FOZARD *Instrumentation Nucl. Reactors* viii. 79 If the scheme of Fig. 8.4 is extended to form a ring scaler, all the indicating cathodes may be connected together. **1920** *Ring-seat [see GOOD *a.* C. 8]. **1929** WODEHOUSE *Mr. Mulliner Speaking* iv. 134 The sportsman in him whispered that he was missing something good, for ring-seats to view which many men would have paid large sums. **1905** *Sci. Amer. Suppl.* 25 Mar. 24433/1 *Ringshake ..consists in a partial or entire separation of two consecutive annual rings, and appears on a cross section as one or more splits running concentrically around the log. **1938** H. E. DESCH *Timber* xi. 133 Serious splits are often called 'shakes'. .. These are of several types, *e.g.*, ring-shake where the separation follows a growth ring, star-shake where the ruptures radiate outward from the pith. **1968** J. ARNOLD *Shell Bk. Country Crafts* 84 They used to 'split the heart'.. as this obviated what were known as 'ring-shakes'. **1851** J. BROWN *Forester* (ed. 2) ii. 199, I have seldom seen one [chestnut] which had arrived at the age of fifty or sixty years, which was not *ring shaken in the heart-wood. **1899** *Daily News* 20 Nov. 4/5 It was a *ring or segment shell. **1896** *Daily Chron.* 8 Aug. 7/3 The guns opened fire with *ring shot and shrapnel at long range. **1931** R. W. GORDON in A. T. Smythe et al. *Carolina Low Country* 199 One of the simplest forms [of shouts], known as the '*ring shout', is apparently widespread. In this, the shouters form a circle and proceed around and around in a sort of slow processional, facing always in one direction. **1942** L. PARRISH *Slave Songs Georgia Sea Islands* iii. 54 Shouting appears to be of two types: Along the coast of Georgia and South Carolina the most popular form is the ring-shout. **1970** P. OLIVER *Savannah Syncopators* 56 A 'ring-shout'—a shuffling dance in counter-clockwise direction performed by a circle of worshippers which gradually intensified in tempo and collective excitement. **1940** N. MONKS *Squadrons Up!* viii. 213 The circular (*ring) sight for his eight machine-guns. **1942** *Tee Emm* (Air Ministry) II. 133 Before he had judged range with his ring sight, now he had to estimate without it. **1973** J. QUICK *Dict. Weapons* 374/2 *Ring sight*, a sight, especially a gunsight, in the shape of a ring or concentric rings, through which aim is taken and range is estimated. **1856** LEVER *Martins of Cro'M.* 136 I'll have a *ring-snaffle put on him. **1513** DOUGLAS *Æneis* XII. Prol. 193 Sum sang *ring sangis, dansis ledys, and rovndis. **1930** *Buck & Hickman Ltd. Gen. Catal. Tools & Supplies* 285 *Ring spanners. **1970** K. BALL *Fiat 600, 600D Autobook* x. 121/2 *(caption)* Adjusting brake shoe cams. Movement of the ring spanner..on the adjusting nut. **1973** J. LEASOR *Host of Extras* ix. 166, I unlocked the..tool box..and took out a roll of ring spanners. **1892** *Pall Mall G.* 10 Nov. 5/2 As if a new form of *ring-spindle were under scrutiny. **1884** W. S. B. MCLAREN *Spinning* 169 It is one of the advantages of *ring spinning, that an ordinary flyer frame can be converted into a ring without altering the spindles. **1884** KNIGHT *Dict. Mech.* Suppl., **Ring Splice*,..a loop made in a rope by splicing the end to the standing part. [**1906** M. C. COOKE *Fungoid Pests Cultivated Plants* 50 The ringed brown spot (*Septoria Chrysanthemi*)..has apparently been confined to Italy.] **1923** SALMON & WORMALD in *Jrnl. Min. Agric.* XXX. 148 The diseased areas on the leaf first appear as brown spots... As the spots reach a diameter of ¼ in. or so, the central dead portions drop out, leaving the characteristic perforations... The name '*ring-spot' disease appears suitable to designate this form of injury which strikes the eye of the grower as he walks over the field. **1927** *Phytopathology* XVII. 325 *(caption)* Ringspots in an early stage of development with margins of alternating zones of chlorotic and normal tissue. **1939** *Jrnl. Pomol.* XVII. 27 Ring Spot, the common name accepted in this country for the disease [of lettuces] caused by the fungus mentioned [sc. *Marssonina Panattoniana*], has been widespread in temperate regions from an early date. **1964** *Phytopathology* LIV. 702/1 No ringspot virus was detected in uninoculated primary leaves through the sixteenth day. **1971** *Country Life* 18 Feb. 381/1 Ringspot, Mottle and Vein Mottle are only three of the viruses afflicting carnations. **1974** *Ibid.* 28 Nov. 1648/1 In Scotland..members of this race [*sc.* large heath butterflies] differ from English specimens in having fewer ring-spots on the under-surface of the wings. **1980** *Daily Tel.* 16 Jan. 8/3 There are some Cornish cauliflower types which have not been available for about 30 years which we think were resistant to a disease called ringspot. **1961** R. W. BUTCHER *Brit. Flora* II. 762 Leaves broad, lanceolate, grey-green, *ring-spotted, flat and broadened from the base. **1697** *Lond. Gaz.* No. 3298/4 One *Ring Stand ingraved with two Coats impaled. *c* **1865** *Wylde's Circ. Sc.* I. 144/1 He should also possess..a small ring-stand, for supporting.. vessels in preparing solutions by heat. **1892** *Pall Mall G.* 6 Oct. 1/3 Brushes and trays, ringstands and powder-boxes. **1782** *Phil. Trans.* LXXII. 361 This conductor..was kept in its place near the wall in its passage down by *ring-staples driven into the wall. **1863** A. YOUNG *Naut. Dict.* (ed. 2), **Ring-stopper*, the same as Cat-stopper. **1899** F. T. BULLEN *Log of a Sea-waif* 342 Telling the carpenter to get his maul ready for knocking out the ring-stopper of the anchor. **1828** *Lights & Shades* II. 156, 'I should like to play you a game at marbles.' 'Marbles! you mean *ring taw'. 'Yes'. **1851** MAYHEW *Lond. Labour* (1861) III. 134 I've noticed them, too, playing at ring-taw. **1600** SHAKS. *A.Y.L.* v. iii. 20 In the spring time, the onely pretty *ring time, When Birds do sing, hey ding a ding, ding. **1871** *Sports & Games* July 121 A new Game, **ring toss*,..affords an attractive out-door sport, and furnishes a degree and kind of physical exercise that improves and develops the general health and strength. **1874** *St. Nicholas* Jan. 171/2 There are many other games to be found in the shops..such as 'Ring-toss', 'Magic Hoops', and 'Parlor Croquet'. **1884** *Cent. Mag.* Jan. 359/1 Demurely watching a game of ring-toss. **1927** *Times* 20 Oct. 17/4 The bride..wore a picture gown of white *ring velvet. **1931** *Daily Tel.* 21 May 6/3 A green satin beauté gown..lined with green ring velvet. **1932** G. GREENE *Stamboul Train* II. ii. 99 Could you get me five yards of ring velvet? **1952** C. W. CUNNINGTON *Eng. Women's Clothing* vii. 232 Evening gown in mulberry ring velvet. **1939** F. SCOTT FITZGERALD *Let.* Mar. (1964) 53 As it is a lavish gesture it should be a simple present..on the other angle from a *ring-watch. **1962** E. BRUTON *Dict. Clocks & Watches* 147 *Ring watch*, a watch mounted in a finger ring. **1892** S. P. THOMPSON *Dynamo-Electr. Machinery* (ed. 4) xii. 309 *(caption)* Development of *ring winding for 4-pole machine. **1893** [see *drum-winding* s.v. DRUM *sb.*[1] 13]. **1922** A. H. AVERY *Dynamo Design & Constr.* ix. 122 The winding is electrically continuous, and progresses steadily forward round the armature just as with the ring winding. **1614** in W. S. Gibson *Tynemouth Priory* (1846) II. 121 Spokes, Naves and *Ringwood for the said wheeles, cx.s. **1643** *Lanc. Tracts Civil War* (Chetham Soc.) 167 In an orbe or *ringe-worke [they] cast up much earthe everye day by the multitude of countrey people forced to the service. **1855** J. HEWITT *Anc. Armour* I. 63 The interior of the garment [hauberk]..exhibits the ring-work exactly in the same manner. **1882** CAULFIELD & SAWARD *Dict. Needlework* 425 *Ring Work* , an easy work used for forming mats and baskets, and made with small brass curtain rings, single Berlin wools and beads. **1899** *Daily News* 12 Jan. 7/5 His ring work and generalship were so superior to his exhibition when he first came out that the improvement was almost incredible. **1963** L. F. CHITTY in Foster & Alcock *Culture & Environment* vii. 177 A ringwork beside the Knighton road may be medieval. **1975** J. G. EVANS *Environment Early Man Brit. Isles* vii. 164 Earthworks such as motte-and-bailey castles and ring-works preserve a buried soil and ditch sequence which can be used to extract environmental evidence. **1929** HOSTETTER & BEESLEY *It's a Racket!* 236 **Ringworm*, one who is a regular attendant upon prize fights and boxing matches. **1930** *Forum* Dec. 373/2 Many of these words..are employed daily in our own sports pages. Even the most casual American *ringworm* will recognize these: *knob, mugg, the one-two punch*, [etc.]. **1954** *Sun* (Baltimore) 30 Mar. 18/7 'Ring worms', as some are in the habit of referring to fight fans, have a hot one coming up Friday night when Kid Gavilan takes a shot at Bobo Olson and his middleweight title. **1892** J. NASMITH *Students' Cotton Spinning* ix. 348 A method of winding *ring yarn on a cylindrical surface. **1909** *Westm. Gaz.* 13 Aug. 8/4 A determined effort is being made by cotton-spinners in Lancashire who produce ring yarn to form an association to keep up prices.

b. In names of birds, reptiles, fishes, etc., as **ringbarker** *Austral.*, a stick-insect, *Podacanthus wilkinsoni*, which in swarms devours the leaves of eucalypts; **ring-bill**, the ring-necked duck or moonbill; **ring-billed (†mew) gull**, a New World gull, *Larus delawarensis*; **ring-bird**, a local name for the reed-bunting (*Emberiza schœniclus*); **ring blackbird**, = RINGOUZEL; **ring-bunting**, = *ring-bird*; **ring dotterel**, = *ring-plover*; **ring-eye**, (*a*) an American fish (cf. RED-EYE); (*b*) *Austr.*, a bird of the genus *Zosterops* (Morris); = *silver-eye* s.v. SILVER *sb.* and *a.* 21 c; cf. *white-eye* s.v. WHITE *a.* 12 e; **ring-fowl**, = *ring-bird*; **ring parakeet**, the ring-necked parakeet; **ring perch**, the yellow perch (*Perca flavescens*) of N. America; = *ringed perch* s.v. RINGED *ppl. a.* 5; **ring pheasant**, the ring-necked pheasant (*Phasianus torquatus*) of China; **ring pigeon**, = RING-DOVE; **ring plover**: see PLOVER 2; **ring-snake**, (*a*) the common European grass- or ringed snake (*Tropidonotus natrix*); (*b*) *U.S.*, a snake of the genus *Diadophis*, esp. *Diadophis punctatus*; **ring-sparrow**, the rock-sparrow (*Petronia stulta*); **ring-thrush**, = RING-OUZEL.

1935 K. C. MCKEOWN *Insect Wonders Austral.* xviii. 149 Another fine stick-insect is found in the Walcha district, where it is popularly known as the '*Ringbarker', because of the dying brown appearance of the trees after the insects have stripped them of their foliage. **1965** *Austral. Encycl.* VIII. 295/2 Most phasmids are solitary in habit. One of the few gregarious forms, the ringbarker (*Podacanthus wilkinsoni*), sometimes appears in countless numbers in various districts of New South Wales, where it defoliates the eucalypts. **1831** SWAINSON & RICHARDSON *Fauna Bor.-Amer.* II. 421 *Larus zonorhynchus*,..*Ring-billed Mew-Gull. **1834** T. NUTTALL *Man. Ornithol. U.S. & Canada* II. 300 Ring-billed Mew Gull... Sp. Charact.—Commissure of the stout ringed bill rather longer than the tarsus. **1844** J. E. DEKAY *Zool. N.Y.* II. 309 The Common gull.., although called the Ring-billed Gull in the books, has received no other popular name than Brown Winter Gull. **1917** T. G. PEARSON *Birds of Amer.* I. 47/1 The California and Ring-billed Gulls generally nest together in big colonies on the inland lakes. **1975** *Behaviour* LII. 143 Parent Ring-Billed Gulls are able to recognize their own chicks after about 7 to 9 days posthatching. **1837** MACGILLIVRAY *Brit. Birds* I. 453 Black-headed Bunting,..*Ring-bird. Ring-Bunting. **1831** RENNIE *Montagu's Ornith. Dict.* 420 **Ring blackbird*, this species is rather larger than the blackbird. **1870** GILLMORE tr. *Figuier's Reptiles & Birds* 531 The Ring

Blackbird (*Merula torquata*) differs from the kind we have just noticed. 1797 BEWICK *Brit. Birds* I. 334 The *Ring Dotterel, Ring Plover, or Sea Lark. 1863 GOULD *Iceland* 404 Along the shore, flocks of wheeling Turnstones, Ring Dotterels and Dunlins attract attention. 1877 JORDAN in *Smithson. Coll.* XIII. I. 47 Good bait for Perch, Bass, Red-eyes or *Ring-eyes, &c. 1951 J. FRAME *Lagoon* 47 She was big and warm and knew about cats and little ring-eyes. 1953 *Landfall* VII. 21 They caught a blackbird and two ring-eyes. 1840 W. MACGILLIVRAY *Brit. Ornith.* I. 190 *Emberiza Schœniclus*, Reed-Bunting,.. *Ring-fowl. 1811 SHAW *Gen. Zool.* VIII. 423 The size of the Alexandrine or *Ring Parrakeet is that of a common Pigeon. 1841 *Penny Cycl.* XIX. 87/2 These Ring Parrakeets, as they are generally termed, are justly held in high estimation for the symmetry of their form. 1877 C. HALLOCK *Sportsman's Gazetteer* 272 Yellow Perch; or *Ring Perch.—*Perca flavescens*. 1947 J. H. BROWN *Outdoors Unlimited* 233 'Ring' perch, or yellow perch as they are more widely called, offer the earliest fishing in this part of the country. 1777 G. FORSTER *Voy. round World* II. 567 We likewise saw several beautiful *ring-pheasants. 1783 LATHAM *Gen. Synopsis Birds* II. I. 715 Ring Pheasant... This differs [from the Common Pheasant] in having a ring of pure white round the neck. 1831 RENNIE *Montagu's Ornith. Dict.* 424 Temminck says the one found in European preserves is a hybrid, between the common pheasant and the genuine Ring Pheasant.. of China. 1768 PENNANT *Brit. Zool.* (1776) I. 251 *Ring Pigeon. 1831 WILSON, etc. *Amer. Ornith.* IV. 325 Ring pigeons... 1. High crowned ring pigeon. 2. Pine ring pigeon. 3. Flat crowned ring pigeon. 1870 GILLMORE tr. *Figuier's Reptiles & Birds* 424 This is evidence of the possibility of taming Ring-pigeons. 1797 BEWICK *Brit. Birds* I. 334 *Ring Plover. 1802 MONTAGU *Ornith. Dict.* (1831) 141 The Ring Plover is a plentiful species in most parts of the known world. 1842 *Proc. Berw. Nat. Club* II. No. 10. 4 A pair of the pretty little Ring-plover were observed by the President. 1796 MORSE *Amer. Geogr.* I. 219 *Ring Snake. *a*1817 DWIGHT *Trav. New Eng.*, etc. (1821) I. 55 The Ring-Snake is long, slender, and black, with a white ring round its neck. 1901 *Nature* 31 Jan. 330/2 The species proved to be the common grass, or ring-snake. 1678 RAY *Willughby's Ornith.* 250 The *Ring-Sparrow of Bellonius. 1783 LATHAM *Gen. Synopsis Birds* II. I. 254 Ring Sparrow... This is bigger than the House Sparrow... Round the head, above the eyes, a ring of dirty white. 1792 PENNANT *Arct. Zool.* II. Index, Thrush, *ring. 1832 *Proc. Berw. Nat. Club* I. 5 Our.. colleague.. entertained some slight hopes of meeting with the ring-thrush (*Turdus torquatus*).

ring (rɪŋ), *sb.*² Also 6–7 ringe, 6 ryng. [f. RING *v.*²]

1. A set or peal *of* (church) bells.

Very common in 17th–18th cent. Locally the name *ring o' bells* is given to the Wild Hyacinth, *Scilla nutans* (Britten and Holland).

1549 *Council's Let.* in *Prayer-Book Troubles* (1884) 73 Levying in every churche one bell, the lest of the ryng that nowe is in the same. 1586 J. HOOKER *Hist. Irel.* in *Holinshed* II. 102/1 He prophaned the church of saint Patrikes in Downe,.. and shipt the notable ring of bels that did hang in the steeple. 1633 GERARD *Descr. Somerset* (1900) 197 A bell tower of a greate height furnished with a very good ring of 5 bells. 1668 PEPYS *Diary* 12 June, Here is also a very fine ring of six bells, and they mighty tuneable. 1716 HEARNE *Collect.* (O.H.S.) V. 349 The Church is very neat and handsome, and hath a Ring of eight very good Bells. 1794 W. COMBE *Boydell's Thames* I. 109 Here was a large and melodious ring of bells, which was considered as the best in England. 1839 *Civil Eng. & Arch. Jrnl.* II. 77/2 The Bishop of London.. presents them with a ring of bells and an organ. 1872 ELLACOMBE *Bells of Ch.* in *Ch. Bells Devon* ix. 291 The Old Bells of York Cathedral. These bells were the first ring of twelve in the kingdom.

2. a. A ringing sound or noise.

1622 BACON *Hen. VII* 17 He..had the Ring of Acclamations fresh in his eares. 1706 E. WARD *Wooden World Diss.* (1708) 29 He must come to the Ring of the Midnight Bell. 1789 MME. D'ARBLAY *Diary* June, They set up such a shout as made a ring all around the village. 1830 CHALMERS *Mem.* (1851) III. xiv. 278 Delighted in the morning with the ring of Oxford bells. 1856 KANE *Arct. Expl.* I. vii. 69 'Twang, twang!' came a second report. I knew it was the whale-line by the shrillness of the ring. 1874 GREEN *Short Hist.* vii. §4. 375 Mary Stuart.. loved risk and adventure and the ring of arms.

b. A ringing tone or quality in the voice, or in a (recited) composition.

1859 GREEN *Lett.* (1901) I. 28 The lines which.. have got a ring of old Homer in them. 1863 GEO. ELIOT *Romola* II. xxxii, Her voice had gradually risen till there was a ring of scorn in the last words. 1871 FREEMAN *Norm. Conq.* (1876) IV. 267 We hear again the old ring of the lays of Brunanburh,.. and of Stamfordbridge, as we listen to the tale. 1894 STANLEY WEYMAN *Under Red Robe* iv, She continued.. with a certain ring of insistence in her tone.

c. The resonance of a coin or glass vessel by which its genuineness or wholeness is tested. Now freq. *transf.*

1855 BAIN *Senses & Int.* II. ii. §12 The ring of a sovereign or of a shilling is a criterion of the genuineness of the coin. 1874 L. STEPHEN *Hours in Libr.* (1892) I. iii. 108 A banker's clerk can tell a bad coin by its ring on the counter. 1894 BLACKMORE *Perlycross* 360 As a glass is filliped to try its ring.

transf. 1850 ROBERTSON *Serm.* Ser. IV. xxvii. 210 Truth, so to speak, has a certain ring by which it may be known. 1886 BESANT *Childr. Gibeon* I. vii, There does not seem always the right ring about him. 1957 G. RYLE in C. A. Mace *Brit. Philos. in Mid-Cent.* 264 The word 'analysis' has.. a good laboratory or Scotland Yard ring about it. 1973 *Times Lit. Suppl.* 21 Sept. 1091/3 The 'special relationship' with Japan, using a phrase which will have an ironic and melancholy ring in British ears.

d. *Electronics.* A sequence of damped oscillations at the resonant frequency of a circuit; an individual oscillation in such a sequence.

1949 *Electronic Engin.* XXI. 207/3 Thus the deliberate introduction of a ring into the response can be a means of improving the sharpness of the transition edges of the observed picture. 1971 J. EARL *How to choose & use Pickups & Loudspeakers* iii. 87 (*caption*) This pulsed-tone shows only slight 'ringing'... An insufficiently low value load could incite worse rings than this. 1975 G. J. KING *Audio Handbk.* ii. 43 No amplifier worthy of the hi-fi label should exhibit rings or overshoot into a load of pure resistance. *Ibid.* v. 122 Since the ring is very quickly damped, giving virtually an overshoot effect, this sort of performance is perfectly acceptable.

3. a. An act of ringing; a pull *at* a bell, *esp.* a doorbell; the sound thus produced. In recent use also with adverbs, as ***ring-back, ring-up.***

1727 BOYER *Dict. Royal* II. s.v., Give it a ring, *sonnez la cloche*. 1760 BARETTI *Ital. Dict.* II, To give the bell a ring, *sonar il campanello*. 1836 MARRYAT *Japhet* xxxiii, A ring at the bell called Timothy downstairs. 1886 W. J. TUCKER *E. Europe* 227 In reply to my ring, [I] was admitted by the actor himself. 1898 J. K. JEROME *Sec. Th. Idle Fellow* 131 The ring-back recalls you. You seize the ear trumpet, and shout. 1899 *Westm. Gaz.* 6 May 5/1 At 3.55,.. according to the ring-up from the engine-room, he was four miles from the rocks.

b. An act of ringing a coin. (Cf. RING *v.*² 11 b.)

1894 A. ROBERTSON *Nuggets* 175 She was a false coin, which would not stand the test of a ring.

c. orig. with *up*. A call on a telephone. Also, each of a series of ringing sounds produced by a telephone receiving a call; ***to give*** (someone) ***a ring***, to call by telephone. Cf. RING *v.*² 10 b.

1900 [see HULLO *int.*]. 1910 *Daily Chron.* 26 Feb. 6/2 It is only that most modern of human summonings, a telephone 'ring up'. 1930 J. B. PRIESTLEY *Angel Pavement* iv. 157 I'll just give the City Transport a ring to see if they've heard anything about that lot we sent to Norwich. 1934 T. E. LAWRENCE *Let.* 14 Sept. (1938) 819 Give me a ring at Hythe and let us meet. 1948 [see CENTRAL *sb.*]. 1951 T. STERLING *House without Door* x. 109 The telephone rang... It went on ringing... She listened, anticipating each ring to the second. *c*1952 A. HUXLEY *Lett.* (1969) 660 If you ever come into town, why don't you give me a ring? 1960 [see BOOK *sb.* 5 d]. 1963 V. NABOKOV *Gift* ii. 137 There's no guarantee the room is not already disposed of, but still I would advise you to give her a ring. 1973 'M. UNDERWOOD' *Reward for Defector* vi. 44 Give me a ring later this evening and let me know. 1976 H. NIELSEN *Brink of Murder* i. 9 He dialled his own number... Kevin.. answered on the fourth ring.

d. Phr. ***the dead ring (of)***: see quot. 1916. Cf. RINGER² 4. *Austral.* and *N.Z. slang.*

Possibly belongs under some other sense of the noun.

1916 C. J. DENNIS *Songs of Sentimental Bloke* 124 *The dead ring*: a remarkable likeness. 1948 D. W. BALLANTYNE *Cunninghams* I. xv. 81 They [*sc.* the sons] were the dead ring of Gil. 1951 —— in *Landfall* V. 166 A fine little chap. Dead ring of his old man, eh?

†**4.** *Cant.* (See quots.) *Obs.*

*a*1700 B. E. *Dict. Cant. Crew*, *Ring*, money extorted by Rogues on the High-way, or by Gentlemen Beggers. 1796 *Grose's Dict. Vulgar T.* (ed. 3), *Ring*, money procured by begging: beggars so called it from its ringing when thrown to them.

5. ***ring-in***: a fraudulent substitution; the action of 'ringing in' (see RING *v.*² 13 b). *Austral. slang.*

[1924 *Truth* (Sydney) 27 Apr. 6 *Ring in*, false.] 1941 BAKER *Dict. Austral. Slang* 60 *Ring-in*, a horse or dog that is fraudulently entered in a contest under an assumed name and/or disguised. 1969 C. DRUMMOND *Odds on Death* vii. 152 The elderly book-makers.. were his hosts... Past losses were debated... 'A ring-in after all these years,' had said a ruined giant of a man disgustedly. 1971 *Telegraph* (Brisbane) 26 June 5/1 All these are checked against the dog, and the chances of a 'ring-in' are completely eliminated.

ring (rɪŋ), *v.*¹ Pa. t. and pa. pple. **ringed**. Also 5–6 **ryng(e**; *pa. t.* and *pa. pple.* 6 **roong**, 7–9 **rung**. [f. RING *sb.*¹ The leading senses are more or less represented by parallel formations in the cognate languages, as Fris. *ringje*, MDu. and Du. *ringen*, OHG. *ringan*, *ringôn* (G. *ringen*), ON. and Icel. *hringa* (Norw. and Sw. *ringa*, Da. *ringe*) and *hringja* (Fær. *ringja*, MSw. *ringia*). In OE. the comb. *ymb-hringan*, to surround, occurs frequently.]

I. 1. a. *intr.* To make a circle or ring; to gather in a ring *about* or *round* (a person). Now *rare.*

14.. *Sir Beues* (C) 623 Let vs alle aboute him rynge, And harde strokys on hym dynge. *a*1548 HALL *Chron.*, *Hen. VIII*, 235 b, Likewise the byllmen and these rynged and snayled, which was a goodly sight to beholde. 1596 SPENSER *F.Q.* VI. Introd. 7 The rest which round about you ring.. And doe adorne your Court.

1814 W. NICHOLSON *Peacock* III. Poet. Wks. (1897) 93 Then roun' him ring, and prance.., To gar folks trow ye raise the de'il. 1850 MRS. BROWNING *Child Asleep* v, We should see the spirits ringing Round thee, were the clouds away.

b. Of a hawk, etc.: To rise spirally in flight.

1879 *Encycl. Brit.* IX. 7/2 A bird is said to 'ring' when it rises spirally in the air. 1889 *Pall Mall G.* 20 Aug. 3/2 When flown at a rook, both birds at times 'ring' into the sky, the rook striving its utmost to keep above its pursuer.

c. Of a stag, fox, or hare: To take a circular course when hunted.

1882 *Daily News* 21 Jan. 2/4 Then ringing about in the Winkfield, New Lodge, Fifield, and Bray districts, the quarry eventually fielded the pack towards the town of Maidenhead. 1892 *Field* 26 Nov. 805/3 Once more she tries to ring away to her home, but hounds press her.

d. *Austral.* and *S. Afr.* Of cattle: To move round in a circle.

1868 [implied in RINGING *vbl. sb.*¹ 4]. 1884 'R. BOLDREWOOD' *Melb. Mem.* 20 The cattle were uneasy and 'ringed' all night. 1888 —— *Robbery under Arms* v, After 'ringing' a bit, one of the quiet cows followed up the old mare. 1890 —— *Colonial Reformer* II. xviii. 111 A desultory entry into the receiving yard then takes place... The 'ragers' observing this movement keep wildly and excitedly 'ringing', like a first class Maëlstrom. 1928 'BRENT OF BIN BIN' *Up Country* x. 172 'Well, are you going to stay?' 'Can't, thank you. Our mob was ringing a bit when I left.' 1941 I. L. IDRIESS *Great Boomerang* vii. 56 The cattle began to ring, the centre beasts edged outwards, then turned inward and began to sniff, to paw the earth. 1947 J. STEVENSON-HAMILTON *Wild Life S. Afr.* x. 72 The [buffalo] herds ring to protect themselves against marauders in much the same way as the herds of domestic cattle do. 1959 H. P. TRITTON *Time means Tucker* 71 When they [*sc.* cattle] drift the only thing that can be done is try to turn them and get them circling, or ringing as the drover terms it.

2. a. *trans.* To surround, encompass, encircle. Also with *round*, *about*.

*c*1590 GREENE *Fr. Bacon* ii, The brazen walls fram'd by Semiramis.. Shall not be such as rings the English strand. 1602 MARSTON *Antonio's Rev.* II. ii, True praise, the brow of common men doth ring. 1610 J. DAVIES (Heref.) *Commendatory Poems* Wks. (Grosart) II. 5/1 King Arthurs .. dayes (Whose radiant Knights did Ring his Table round). 1849 M. ARNOLD *Strayed Reveller*, Round him.. Flow the cool lake-waves: The mountains ring them. 1884 W. C. SMITH *Kildrostan* I. i. 29 A girdle of mist will ring the slopes, While the heights rise clear in the upper air.

b. In *pa. pple.* Surrounded, girt *with* something.

*c*1590 GREENE *Fr. Bacon* iv, Monarchs of the west Ring'd with the walls of old Oceanus. 1602 MARSTON *Antonio's Rev.* I. iii, The verge of heaven Was ringd with flames. 1641 W. CARTWRIGHT *Lady Errant* III. ii, She Says she could court you ring'd about with dangers.

1814 SOUTHEY *Roderick* xvii. 191 Ringed about with slaughtered foes. 1850 J. S. BLACKIE *Æschylus* I. 23 At her father's festive board, With gallant banqueters ringed cheerly round. 1878 STEVENSON *Inland Voy.* 84 Even this place.. might on some future day be ringed about with cannon smoke and thunder.

c. To hem in (cattle or game) by riding or beating in a circle round them; to beat or stalk round (a stretch of country) for game.

1835 W. IRVING *Tour Prairies* xxv, To.. try our hand at the grand hunting manœuvre, which is called ringing the wild horse. 1874 RANKEN *Dom. Australia* vi. 111 They are generally 'ringed', that is, their gallop is directed into a circular course by the men surrounding them. 1893 *Blackw. Mag.* 279 There are bears to be ringed and elks to be stalked. *Ibid.* 280 Orders arrive to enlist a force of beaters which will 'ring' a vast extent of country.

d. To hem or shut *in*.

1871 *Pall Mall G.* 7 Feb. 12 The final campaign in Baden, when the revolt was ringed in and stamped out by the converging advance of the Prussians. 1885 RIDER HAGGARD *K. Solomon's Mines* vii, This expanse appeared to be ringed in by a wall of distant mountains.

3. a. To place or fasten *round* something in the form of a ring.

1799 SOUTHEY *The Pig*, Amoretta's hair Rings round her lover's soul the chains of love. 1833 MRS. BROWNING *Prometh. Bound* 83 Ring amain the iron round his legs!

b. *refl.* To coil *up* in a ring.

1864 ATKINSON *Stanton Grange* 219, I seed a grass-snake .. come out, and ring itself up i' t' sun.

c. *Quoiting.* (See quot.)

1866 *Chambers's Encycl.* VIII. 68/2 Professional players.. can very frequently 'ring' their quoit—that is, land it so that the quoit surrounds the hob.

4. = LUNGE *v.*² 1. *rare*⁻¹.

1834 MAR. EDGEWORTH *Helen* vi, She caught a glimpse through the glass door opening on the park, of the general, and a fine horse they were ringing.

II. 5. a. To adorn (the fingers or nose) with a ring or rings. *rare.* (Cf. RINGED *ppl. a.* 2 b.)

1552 HULOET, Rynge, or put on a rynge, *Anulo*. 1595 SHAKS. *John* III. iv. 31, I will.. ring these fingers with thy houshold wormes. 1609 W. M. *Man in Moone* (1857) 102 His gloves are thrust under his girdle, that you may see how he rings his fingers, blesse his worship. 1665 SIR T. HERBERT *Trav.* (1677) 337 Supposing them most courtly who.. ring their snouts with Jewels of Silver, Brass, or Ivory.

b. To invest (a woman) with an engagement or wedding ring. *rare.*

1823 *New Monthly Mag.* VIII. 496 I'll set about a lusty courtship of her at once, and if I do not ferk you out of all likelihood of ringing the beauty, why mandamus me! 1859 CAPERN *Ball. & Songs* 66 The bridegroom.. Waits with the pledge of married love To ring the peerless bride.

c. To attach with a ring. *rare*⁻¹.

1885–94 R. BRIDGES *Eros & Psyche* Oct. 24 From either ear, ring'd to its pierced lobe A triple jewel hung.

6. a. To put a ring in the nose of (swine or cattle) to restrain them from rooting or violence.

1519 *Surtees Misc.* (1890) 32 Item yt the swyn be rynged be Saynt Elene day. 1573 TUSSER *Husb.* (1878) 32 Let hogs be roong, both old and yoong. *Ibid.* 41 For rooting of pasture ring hog ye had neede. 1631 BYFIELD *Doctr. Sabb.* 100 He intended to pegge or ring an hog. 1692 in G. Sheldon *Hist. Deerfield, Mass.* (1895) I. 267 The hogg ringers shall have 6d p[e]r head for every hog tha[y] ring. 1708 *Ibid.* 363 Any that shall neglect to ring their own swine, thay shall be forthwith rung by ye hog ringer. 1778 [W. MARSHALL] *Minutes Agric.* 6 Feb. 1775, Rung the riotous ox. 1792 BELKNAP *Hist. New Hampsh.* III. 145 During the summer, they [swine] are either fed on the waste of the dairy and kitchen, or ringed and turned into fields of clover. 1844 H. STEPHENS *Bk. Farm.* III. 829 A useful instrument for leading a bull by occasionally, when he has not been ringed, .. is what is named the bullock-holder. 1890 AMPHLETT *Hist. Clent* 105 Pigs were numerous; their owners had to ring them when four months old.

fig. 1630 DEKKER *2nd Pt. Honest Wh.* Wks. 1873 II. 127 She praies you to ring him by this token, and so you shall be sure his nose will not be rooting other mens pastures. 1681

S. Colvil *Whigs Supplic.* (1751) 87 His majesty, with-out all doubt, Should only ring them in the snout. **1755** *World* No. 150 The wife, when she found she was to be rung, very wisely made a virtue of necessity, and added jewels to the ring. *c* **1800** Boswell *Poet. Wks.* (1871) 202 Then let the viper hide his sting, The reptile, if he ramp, we'll ring.

b. *to ring the bull*, to play at a game consisting in throwing or swinging a ring on to a hook fixed upon a wall or a target. Hence *ring(ing)-the-bull* as the name of the game.

1838 D. Jerrold *Men of Character* (1851) 273 After that, he must visit the gypsies; then he must ring-the-bull. *Ibid.* 276 There is first the lucky-bag—then the sticks—then the ringing-the-bull—then the round-about. **1868** *N. & Q.* 4th Ser. I. 89 The game..is or was common in the ale-houses of Cheshire, and is called Ring-the-Bull.

c. To put a numbered ring on the leg of (a bird) so that it may be identified subsequently; to treat (a bat) similarly.

1908 *Brit. Birds* I. 327 A large number of birds of various species are ringed each year at Rossitten on the Baltic. **1925** Turner & Gurney *Bk. about Birds* vii. 72 When he escaped from the Sudan long after, he was able to tell those who ringed the bird that it had been found in Omdurman. **1958** *Listener* 30 Oct. 684/2 We have now ringed nearly 3,000 bats. **1971** *Daily Tel.* 22 June 8/4 A tufted duck, ringed in Essex two years ago by the British Trust for Ornithology, has been found in West Pakistan, where it was shot by a hunter in Rawalpindi. **1978** P. Conder *RSPB Guide to Birdwatching* 102 Many ringers, particularly those working on a population of a particular area, ring nestlings.

†**7.** To affix rings to (a mare) in such a way as to prevent covering. *Obs.*

1611 Cotgr., *Boucler*,..to ring a mare, thereby to keepe her from the horse. **1668** *Lond. Gaz.* No. 303/4 A little Bay Mare.., short tailed and ringed, part of the rings broken. *a* **1693** *Urquhart's Rabelais* iii. xxxvi. 300 They use to ring Mares.., to keep them from being sallied by Stoned Horses. **1712** *Lond. Gaz.* No. 5056/3 A bright bay Mare,..Ring'd, but lost one, so that she has but two.

†**8. a.** *to ring the mill*: (see quot. 1808). *Sc.*

1808 Jamieson s.v., To fill these [crevices round the mill-stone] with the first grain that is ground, after the stones are picked, is called *ringing* the mill. **1814** *Abstract conc. Mill Inveramsy* 2 (Jam.), The tenants ringing the mill to themselves, and carrying away the same ring with them.

b. To provide (a wheel) with an iron tire. (Still in dial. use.)

1829 *Sporting Mag.* XXIII. 388 Neither are the felloes of the wheels of several of the wagons rung with iron as ours are.

9. a. To mark (trees) with a ring of colour.

1742 *MS. Agreement* (co. Derby), Trees marked or rung about with red.

b. To deprive (trees) of a ring of bark, in order to check too luxuriant growth and bring into bearing, or to kill them.

1800 Headrick *Com. to Board Agric.* II. 257 They begin with ringing the trees, that is, cutting a ring of bark from their stems a little above the ground. This checks their growth, and renders the wood more firm and valuable. **1857** Henfrey *Bot.* 562 Ringing fruit-trees in this way causes a temporary increase of product of fruit above the wound. **1885** Mrs. C. Praed *Head Station* i, Gaunt trunks of trees which had been 'rung', and allowed to die slowly.

c. *dial.* (See quot.)

1881 *Oxfordsh. Gloss.* Suppl. s.v., To ring fruit trees is to dig round them, cutting the long roots in two, and putting in manure.

10. To cut into annular slices or rounds.

1839 *Mag. Domest. Econ.* IV. 174 The onions, being cut in slices and ringed, are put into the frying-pan. **1891** *Daily News* 27 Aug. 3/2 Why could we not in England core, peel, ring, and dry apples in such years for a winter sale?

11. *Austral. slang.* To beat (a shedful of men) at sheep-shearing. Also *transf.* Cf. ringer[1] 5 a.

1895 A. B. Paterson *Man from Snowy River* (1896) 136 The man that 'rung' the Tubbo shed is not the ringer here, That stripling from the Cooma side can teach him how to shear. **1899** 'S. Rudd' *On our Selection* 84 He shore..at Welltown, and rung the shed by half a sheep. **1905** in A. B. Paterson *Old Bush Songs* 27 And once I rung Cudjingie shed, and blued it in a week. **1957** D. Niland *Call me when Cross turns Over* v. 132 He would take on anything, wheat-lumping, tree-felling, shearing—always ringing the shed—droving, anything at all that suited him. **1967** *Telegraph* (Brisbane) 25 Mar. 2/5 To 'ring the shed' a shearer's cook has to earn more money than the top shearer.

12. To draw a circle round (something printed) so as to focus attention on it.

1970 R. K. Kent *Lang. Journalism* 113 *Ring*, to draw a circle around; encircle, as to signify various directions in copy editing. **1981** *Times* 23 June 2/2 She [*sc.* the Prime Minister] has probably already ringed a date in the autumn of 1983 for the election.

ring (rɪŋ), *v.*[2] Pa. t. rang, rung. Pa. pple. rung. [OE. *hringan*, = ON. and Icel. *hringja* (Norw. and Fær. *ringja*, Sw. *ringa*, Da. *ringe*), G. *ringen* (rare), perh. of imitative origin. Properly a weak vb., the strong forms (which appear very early) being prob. due to the influence of *sing*.]

A. Inflexional forms.

1. *Inf.* (and *Pres.*). 1 hrin(c)gan, 3–4 (7 *arch.*) ringen (4 ryngen, 5 -yn); 3–7 ringe, 4–7 ryng(e, 4 ryngg, 4–5 reng, 3– ring (8 wring).

c **960** Æthelwold *Rule St. Benet* (Schröer, 1885) 72 þæt mon ealle tida..hrincge. *c* **1000** *Salomon & Saturn* 534 (Kemble), His searo hringeð. *c* **1200** Ormin 901 Godd..wollde..þa belless herenn ringenn. *a* **1300** *Havelok* 242 Belles deden he sone ringen. *c* **1375** *Sc. Leg. Saints* xxxvi. (*Baptist*) 888 Scho gert in haste þe bellis rynge. *a* **1400–50** *Alexander* 1385 All þe toun rengis [*v.r.* ringes]. *c* **1440** *Promp. Parv.* 434/2 Ryngyn bellys, *pulso*. **1599** Shaks. *Much Ado* v. ii. 81 No longer..then the Bels ring. **1614** J. Davies (Heref.) *Commendatory Poems* Wks. (Grosart) II. 20/1 Fro their case thy shrill pipes draw, And make the welkin ringen. **1716** Hearne *Collect.* (O.H.S.) V. 217 He..set the Bells wringing for Joy.

2. *Pa. t.* **a.** *pl.* 1 hringdon, 2 ringden, 3 ringeden; 8 ringed, 9 *dial.* hringed.

Beowulf 327 Buȝon þa to bence, byrnan hringdon. *c* **1131** *O.E. Chron.* (Laud MS.) an. 1131, þa muneces..ringden þa belle. *c* **1205** Lay. 24486 Bellen þer ringeden. **1726** Ayliffe *Parergon* 477 Then they..put out the Candle, and ringed the Bell. **1889** Mrs. Tuttiet *Reproach of Annesley* i. v, I hringed's grandfather out,..hringed 'em out mezelf.

b. *a.* 3–6 rong, 4–5 ronge; also *pl.* 3–6 rongen.

c **1275** Lay. 24486 Belles þar rongen. **1297** R. Glouc. (Rolls) 11215 A clerc þe commun belle rong. *c* **1330** R. Brunne *Chron. Wace* (Rolls) 12374 þe hilles alle aboute ronge. *c* **1380** *St. Augustine* 1642 in Hortsm. *Altengl. Leg.* (1878) 89/2 Men rongen þo þreo peles long. *c* **1420** *Chron. Vilod.* 3810 þe sexstens rong..þe belle. *c* **1450** *Earl Tolous* 319 When they ronge to the masse. **1500–20** Dunbar *Poems* xlvi. 19 Quhill rong the widdis of hir melody. **1515** *Scottish Field* 566 in *Chetham Misc.* (1856), All the dales rongen. **1590** Spenser *F.Q.* iii. i. 62 Through the hous it rong.

β. 3– rang, 4–6 range.

a **1300** *Cursor M.* 15040 All þe cite rang [*v.r.* range]. **1393** Langl. *P. Pl.* C. xxi. 472 Men rang to þe resurreccioun. **1470–85** Malory *Arthur* x. xii. 432 Alle the forest range of the noyse. *a* **1533** Ld. Berners *Huon* cliv. 590 The bellis range to matens. *a* **1656** Bp. Hall *Rem. Wks.* (1660) 37 Pulpits everywhere rang of these opinions. **1685** Wood *Life* 21 Nov., Magd. Coll. bell rang out. **1784** Cowper *Task* v. 819 What strains were they With which heav'n rang. **1887** Bowen *Virg. Æneid* iii. 313 The air Rang with her shrieks.

γ. 4 *pl.* rungen; 6– rung, 6 roong.

13.. *Gaw. & Gr. Knt.* 931 Chaplaynez..Rungen ful rychely. **1587** Golding *De Mornay* i. (1592) 9 The Schooles of the Stoikes, Academikes, and Peripatetikes, roong of that [prayer]. **1591** Spenser *M. Hubberd* 583 Bells and bosses..full lowdly rung. **1667** Milton *P.L.* vii. 562 The Heav'ns and all the Constellations rung. **1676** Wood *Life* (O.H.S.) II. 360 The great bell rung out. **1797** Southey *Joan of Arc* vi, On the batter'd shield Rung the loud lance. **1837** Disraeli *Venetia* ii. vii, One with whose name the world rung.

3. *Pa. pple.* *a.* 3–4 i-runge(n, 4 rungen, 4–5 runge, 5 rounge, 6 roung, 6– rung.

c **1205** Lay. 29441 No belle [was] i-rungen, no masse isunge. *a* **1300** *K. Horn* (Cambr. MS.) 1092 Or eny day was sprunge Oþer belle irunge. **1381** in *Knighton's Chron.* (Rolls) II. 139 He hath rungen ȝoure belle. *c* **1400** *Rom. Rose* 5266 A fooles belle is sone runge. **1466** in *Archaeol.* (1887) L. i. 49 Call for help whan it ys rounge with moo. ? *a* **1550** *Freiris Berwik* 286 in *Dunbar's Poems* (1893) 295 Curfur wes rung. **1570** *Satir. Poems Reform.* xxiv. 72 Quhill Drureis bells be roung about ȝour eiris. **1684** T. Burnet *Th. Earth* i. 276 All antiquity would have rung of it. **1756–7** tr. *Keysler's Trav.* (1760) IV. 136 The bell is rung at Cirknitz. **1815** J. Smith *Panorama Sci. & Art* II. 64 The sound of a bell rung under water.

β. 4 y-ronge, 4–6 ronge, 5–6 rong; 5 rongene, 5–6 rongen.

c **1384** Chaucer *H. Fame* iii. 565 Thus was her shame y-ronge. **1387** Trevisa *Higden* (Rolls) V. 413 þat þe houres of the day schulde be ronge at chirches. *c* **1440** *Gesta Rom.* xviii. 332 The belle shulde be rongen [*v.r.* rong] of a maiden. **1533** *Surtees Misc.* (1890) 34 To the merkyt bell be rongen. **1594** in Flora A. MacLeod *Hist. St. Mary's Ch., Shrewsbury* (1894) 16 The greete bell was ronge owt there.

γ. 7, 9 rang.

1691 tr. *Emilianne's Frauds Rom. Monks* (ed. 3) 127 He having rang his Bell. **1805** Eugenia de Acton *Nuns of Desert* I. 249 The prayer bell was ordered to be rang.

B. Signification.

I. *intr.* **1. a.** To give out the clear or resonant sound characteristic of certain hard metals when struck with, or striking upon, something hard. Also of a trumpet, etc.: To sound loudly.

Beowulf 327 Buȝon þa to bence, byrnan hringdon. *c* **1000** *Salomon & Saturn* 534 (Kemble), Swiðe swingeð and his searo hringeð. *c* **1380** Wyclif *Sel. Wks.* III. 520 Wiþ..gaye sadeles, and bridelis ryngynge be þe weye. *c* **1386** Chaucer *Knight's T.* 1742 Now ryngen trompes loude and clarioun. *a* **1440** *Sir Degrev.* 1192 Thei ryden..With two trompess of the best, That range as a bell. **1513** Douglas *Æneis* xiii. v. 68 Quhair is now..Thy vocis sown quhilk as a trumpet rang? **1565** Cooper *Thes.* s.v. *Tinnio*, To rynge or make a sowne as metall doth. *a* **1601** ? Marston *Pasquil & Kath.* ii. (1878) 78 Chunck, chunck, his bags doe ring. **1663** Butler *Hud.* i. ii. 832 With..many a bang, Hard Crab-tree and old Iron rang. **1761** Gray *Fatal Sisters* 24 Pikes must shiver, jav'lins sing,..Hauberk crash, and helmet ring. **1768** Beattie *Minstr.* i. iii, The harp..Which to the whistling wild responsive rung. **1828** Scott *F.M. Perth* xxix, When he heard the Chieftain's horn ringing through the woods. **1842** Tennyson *Sir Galahad* v, The tempest crackles on the leads, And, ringing, springs from brand and mail. **1878** Browning *Poets Croisic* 86 The gauntlet rings On brazen visor proof against attack.

b. *spec.* as a mark of goodness, genuineness, or wholeness.

1803 *Phil. Trans.* XCIII. 73 When silver was alloyed with the standard proportion of tin, it proved brittle, and did not ring well. **1844** Mrs. Browning *Drama of Exile* 87 The potter's mark upon his work, to show It rings well to the striker. **1894** Bottone *Elect. Instr.* 71 The bottle or jar should be..free from flaw or crack. To ascertain this, it should be made to 'ring'.

c. *fig.* To impress one as having a certain (genuine or false) character.

1611 B. Jonson *Catiline* iv. ii, But Crassus, and this Caesar here ring hollow. **1857** E. FitzGerald *Lett.* (1889) I. 251 Hafiz and old Omar Khayyâm ring like true Metal. **1863** *Sat. Rev.* 22 Aug. 243 To an English reader they ring false. **1900** Brodrick *Mem.* 227 His [Bright's] best orations were superior to Gladstone's as compositions and rang truer on a critical ear.

d. Of an electric circuit or a solid body: to undergo damped oscillation at its resonant frequency.

1952 G. C. Smith in Molloy & Poole *Television Engineers' Servicing Man.* 12 The flyback 'overshoots' and 'rings', but it is frequently damped out by a capacitor and a resistance in series across the coils. **1973** *Newnes Colour Television Servicing Manual* I. ii. 56/2 The amplified signal delivered from its collector causes T1 to 'ring'. **1975** *Nature* 24 Jan. 233/1 It has been widely accepted..that a [nuclear] test fired while the Earth was ringing from a really major earthquake ..would be impossible to detect.

2. a. Of bells: To give forth a clear metallic note under the impact of the hammer or clapper.

c **1200** Ormin 901 Godd off heffne aȝȝ wollde himm sellf þa belless herenn ringenn. *a* **1300** *Cursor M.* 20699 Dos þe belles all at ring. **13..** *Sir Beues* 2250 So stod Beues..Til noun belle be-gan to ring. *c* **1440** *Alph. Tales* 40 And all þe bellis in þe place rang be þer one. **1530** Palsgr. 691/2, I holde the a penye I tell the where this bell ryngeth. *a* **1548** Hall *Chron., Hen. VIII*, 105 In the castle the alarme rang, but the embushement kept them stil close. **1603** Shaks. *Meas. for M.* iv. ii. 78 *Duke*. Who call'd heere of late? *Pro.* None since the Curphew rung. **1676** Wood *Life* (O.H.S.) II. 360 The great bell rung out for Earle of C. C. Coll., fellow. **1712** Lady M. W. Montagu *Let. Mrs. Hewet* Mar., The post bell rings, my next shall be longer. **1850** Tennyson *In Mem.* cvi. i Ring out, wild bells, to the wild sky. **1864** Meredith *Sandra Belloni* xxxiii, Mr. Pole's bedroom-bell rang.

fig. *c* **1386** Chaucer *Reeve's T.* Prol. 42 The sely tonge may wel rynge and chymbe Of wrecchednesse that passed is ful yoore. **1809** Malkin *Gil Blas* i. ii. ¶5 When I had been pestered with all the tittle-tattle of the town..the changes were just beginning to ring on some new subject.

b. To convey a summons *to* service, prayers, church, etc.

1509 Hawes *Past. Pleas.* xlii. (Percy Soc.) 207 For though the day be never so longe, At last the belles ringeth to evensonge. **1592** Marlowe *Massacre Paris* i. viii, That bell, that to the devil's matins rings. **1621** in Birch *Crt. & Times Jas. I* (1848) II. 264 The bell is now ringing to a congregation; and they say it is to send letters gratulatory from the university. **1719** Swift *Let. to Young Clergyman* Wks. 1751 V. 17 It was but just finished, when the last Bell rung to Church. **1850** Thackeray *Pendennis* l, The bells of the multitudinous City churches were ringing to evening prayers.

c. *to ring in*: (see quot. and cf. 7 c). *Sc.*

1825 Jamieson s.v., Bells are said to be ringing in, when, in order to stop them, the repetition of the strokes, becomes quicker than before. **1891** [see ringing *vbl. sb.* 1 b].

d. Of a telephone (bell): to produce the ringing sound which indicates that there is a caller on the line (line *sb.*[2] 1 e).

1924 J. Reith *Broadcast over Britain* iii. v. 168 If people are moving about the room, or the telephone rings..the [radio] play has simply no chance. **1951** M. Kennedy *Lucy Carmichael* i. iv. 27 The telephone rang at intervals all the evening. **1979** T. Wiseman *Game of Secrets* iv. 48 He spent an hour getting himself reconnected, and after that he waited for the telephone to ring.

3. a. Of places: To resound, re-echo, with some sound or noise.

a **1300** *Cursor M.* 15040 All þai sang als wit a muth þat all þe cite rang. *c* **1384** Chaucer *H. Fame* iii. 308, I herd aboute her trone y-songe That al the paleys walles ronge. *a* **1400–50** *Alexander* 5157 Scho gaffe skirmand skrikis at all þe skowis range. **1508** Dunbar *Golden Targe* 25 The skye rang for schoutyng of the larkis. **1515** *Scottish Field* 566 in *Chetham Misc.* (1856), There was dealling of dentes, that all the dales rongen. **1602** Marston *Antonio's Rev.* v. iv, Sing alowd; make heavens vault to ring. **1667** Milton *P.L.* ii. 495 Bleating herds Attest thir joy, that hill and valley rings. **1735** Somerville *Chase* ii. 157 The Welkin rings, Men, Dogs, Hills, Rocks, and Woods, In the full Consort join. **1784** Cowper *Task* iv. 147 No powder'd pert..assaults these doors Till the street rings. **1805** Scott *Last Minstrel* ii. iii, The arched cloister..Rang to the warrior's clanking stride. **1850** Tennyson *In Mem.* xxiii. 23 Round us all the thicket rang To many a flute of Arcady.

fig. **1671** Milton *Samson* 1449, I heard all as I came, the City rings And numbers thither flock.

b. Const. *with*, or †*of*, the sound.

c **1400** *Ywaine & Gaw.* 1397 The castel and cete rang With mynstralsi and nobil sang. **1470–85** Malory *Arthur* x. xii. 432 Cryenge and chacyng after kynge Marke that alle the forest range of the noyse. **1587** Fleming *Contn. Holinshed* III. 1331/1 They of Flushing shot two peales, with so great noise..that all the ground rang of it. **1589** Hakluyt *Voy.* 282 The skie rang againe with the noyse thereof. **1673** [R. Leigh] *Transp. Reh.* 36 All the Rooms rung with nothing but a continued Noise. **1700** Prior *Carmen Seculare* 220 With the glad Noise the Cliffs and Vallies ring. *a* **1764** Lloyd *Poet. Wks.* II. 218 Ev'ry hill with heavenly musick rings. **1829** Lytton *Devereux* i. iii, I scarcely listened to the applauses with which the hall rang. **1871** Macduff *Mem. Patmos* xix. 256 Miriam and her sisters..made the shores ring with the refrain.

c. To be filled with talk or report *of*, to resound *with* the report or fame of, a thing, event, or person. Also with *that* and clause.

(*a*) **1608** Topsell *Serpents* 664 Never so much as mentioning them—whereof..so many authors..do so much ring. **1675** Baxter *Cath. Theol.* ii. i. 283 The City ringeth of you as one that greatly wrongeth the cause of God. **1728** Morgan *Hist. Algiers* II. ii. 227 All Europe began to ring of his Depredations. **1749** Fielding *Tom Jones* ii. v, The country..rung of the schoolmaster of Little Baddington; who was said to have beaten his wife. **1864** Tennyson *Aylmer's F.* 395 Back would he to his studies, make a name..: the world should ring of him.

(*b*) **1647** N. Bacon *Disc. Govt. Eng.* ii. vi. (1739) 33 The Parliament rings herewith, yet the King delays the remedy. **1711** Addison *Spect.* No. 117 ¶4 She..has made the Country ring with several imaginary Exploits which are palmed upon her. **1803** WORDSW. *Sonn. Liberty* xxii. 5 The great events with which old story rings Seem vain and hollow. **1894** BLACKMORE *Perlycross* 74 The story with which all the parish was ringing.

(*c*) **1647** N. BACON *Disc. Govt. Eng.* I. xv. (1739) 27 The publick Synods rang, that the Prelates loved not Princes.

4. a. Of a sound: To be loud or resonant; to resound, re-echo. Also with *out*.

13.. *Gaw. & Gr. Knt.* 2204 A wonder breme noyse,..hit rusched, & ronge, rawþe to here. **1513** DOUGLAS *Æneis* XIII. viii. 79 Joyus vocis ryngis furth..Our all the palys ryall to and fro. *a* **1535** *Frere & Boy* 162 (Ritson), It range ouer all the place. **1629** MILTON *Hymn Nativity* xvii, With such a horrid clang As on mount Sinai rang While the red fire..out brake. **1676** DRYDEN *Aurengz.* III. i, Through my dark Cell your shouts of Triumph rung. **1764** GRAY *J.T.* 16 Shrieks of death, thro' Berkley's roofs that ring. **1786** BURNS *Lass o' Ballochmyle* 7 Green-wood echoes rang Amang the braes o' Ballochmyle. **1805** SCOTT *Last Minstrel* I. xviii, The sound ..rung in the Ladye's bower. **1850** THACKERAY *Pendennis* xxxix, Strong's laughter..came ringing out of window. **1874** GREEN *Short Hist.* v. §1. 214 The music of the lark and the nightingale rang out from field and thicket.

fig. **1647** N. BACON *Disc. Govt. Eng.* I. v. (1739) 12 A good disposition to Religion.., and such an one as rang loud to Rome. **1648** MILTON *Sonn.* xv. 1 Fairfax, whose name in armes through Europe rings. **1808** SCOTT *Autobiog.* in *Lockhart* (1837) I. i. 3 That ancient chieftain, whose name I have made to ring in many a ditty.

b. *to ring in* (or †*about*) *one's ears*, to linger persistently in one's hearing; to haunt the memory. So *in one's fancy, heart.*

1540–1 ELYOT *Image Gov.* 52 Having also ringyng in mine eare, the terrible checke that the good maister in the gospel gave to his idell servant. **1592** SHAKS. *Rom. & Jul.* II. iii. 74 Thy old grones yet ringing in my auncient eares. **1722** DE FOE *Plague* (Rtldg.) 139 The Sound seems still to Ring in my Ears. **1736** AINSWORTH s.v. *Ring*, These words ring continually about my ears. **1821** LAMB *Elia* I. *My First Play*, That old Artaxerxes evening had never done ringing in my fancy. **1835** MARRYAT *J. Faithful* xxxii, The two bars of music were constantly ringing in my ears. **1879** FARRAR *St. Paul* (1883) 216 The voice of God still rang in his heart.

5. Of the ears: To be affected by a sensation similar to that produced by the sound of bells, etc.; to tingle, hum, or be filled *with* a sound.

1388 WYCLIF *1 Sam.* iii. 11 Which word who euer schal here, bothe hise eeris schulen rynge.

1565 COOPER *Thes.* s.v. *Tinnio*, My eares rynge of themselfe. **1675** DRYDEN *Aurengz.* II. i, My Ears still ring with noise, I'm vex'd to Death, Tongue-kill'd. **1681** W. ROBERTSON *Phraseol. Gen.* (1693) 1080 To ring, as ones ears do, *tinnire*. **1822–34** *Good's Study Med.* (ed. 4) I. 704 The ears ring with unusual sounds. **1851** JERROLD *St. Giles* xxv. 254 Already his ears rang with the shoutings of..a delighted senate.

II. *trans.* **6. a.** To cause (a bell) to give forth sound; *spec.* in order to summon a servant. †Also with *out*.

c **1131** *O.E. Chron.* (Laud MS.) an. 1131, þa muneces.. brohton him into cyrce.., ringden þa belle. *c* **1205** LAY. 16929 Ich hæten eou..bulden þa chirchen, bellen leten ringen. **1297** R. GLOUC. (Rolls) 11215 At seinte marie churche a clerc þe commun belle rong. **1377** LANGL. *P. Pl.* B. xx. 58 Religiouse reuerenced hym, and rongen here belles. *c* **1420** *Chron. Vilod.* 3810 And þe sexstens rong þo þe belle. **1483** CAXTON *Gold. Leg.* 214/2 The bellys sowned and wer ronge wythout mannes honde. **1560** DAUS tr. *Sleidane's Comm.* 130 b, They ran into every churche, and there range all the belles at ones. **1617** MORYSON *Itin.* I. 193 The greatest bell called Marie, requires twentie foure men to ring it. **1691** tr. *Emilianne's Frauds Rom. Monks* (ed. 3) 127 He having rang his Bell, all the Company shut up their Glasses and Bottles. **1756–7** tr. *Keysler's Trav.* (1760) III. 183 In violent tempests..they ring two little bells which are hung in the tower. **1788** CHARLOTTE SMITH *Emmeline* (1816) I. 254 The servant..told him that Miss Mowbray had not yet rang her bell. **1828** H. S. BOYD in E. H. Barker *Parr* I. 338, I have often stood in the belfry at Margate when the bells were being rung. **1856** DICKENS *Dorrit* (1857) I. x. 81 'I must refer you,' returned Mr. Barnacle, ringing the bell, 'to the Department.' **1870** L'ESTRANGE *Life Miss Mitford* I. v. 127 No bells were rung in the castle for a month. **1914** L. WOOLF *Wise Virgins* ii. 31 They [*sc.* servants] won't stay because you ring the bell for them while they're at dinner!

fig. *c* **1374** CHAUCER *Troylus* v. 1062 O, rolled shal I been on many a tonge; Thorugh-ought þe world my belle shal be ronge. **1390** GOWER *Conf.* I. 217 Perse after his false tunge Hath so thenvious belle runge, That he hath slain his oghne brother. *c* **1400** *Rom. Rose* 5266 Fooles can not holde hir tunge; A fooles belle is sone runge. **1635** QUARLES *Embl.* IV. iii, When ere the Old Exchange of Profit rings Her silver Saints-bell of uncertaine gaines. **1859** BARTLETT *Dict. Amer.* (ed. 2) 367 To Ring one's own Bell is the same as 'to be one's own trumpeter'.

b. *to ring out*, to sound vigorously.

1603 KNOLLES *Hist. Turks* (1638) 163 Secretly stirring vp the people, and by and by after ringing out the bells. *c* **1642** TWYNE in *Wood's Life* (O.H.S.) I. 81 They in the towne.. range out their great bell. **1796** SCOTT *Let.* in *Lockhart* (1837) I. vii. 239 Upon the hoisting of a flag on the Tronsteeple, and ringing out all the large bells.

c. *to ring up*, to raise (a bell) directly over the beam and ring it in that position.

1855 *Rec. Bucks* 159 If he were rung up like an ordinary metal bell. **1872** ELLACOMBE *Bells of Ch.* in *Ch. Bells Devon* viii. 223 The great bell at Gloucester..used to be *rung up* for the Sunday services by six men standing in the body of the choir. **1888** T. NORTH *Bells & Bell Lore* 123 The tenor is first tolled, then rung up, then, after a pause, lowered.

d. *to ring the bell*: to win recognition; to be a complete success (see also BELL *sb.*[1] 7 c).

1915 *Munsey's Mag.* Apr. 561/2, I am reading your 'Barry Newton' yarn. It scores a bulls' eye, it rings the bell, it brings a coconut to earth. **1925** E. WALLACE *Strange Countess* x. 93 'You've certainly rung the bell this time, Lois.' 'It seems too good to be true, doesn't it?' **1945** *Daily Mirror* 15 Aug. 3/3 Leeds Corporation has fifty 'retired' trams to sell... They think a tram would 'ring the bell' as a home, week-end bungalow, or greenhouse. **1976** *Church Times* 30 July 7/5 The wise sight-seer knows that, however alert and receptive he is, even the treasures of Florence aren't going to ring the bell every time.

e. *to ring a bell* (*colloq.*): see BELL *sb.*[1] 7 d.

7. *absol.* To cause a bell or bells to sound. Also *spec.* to summon or send *for* a servant or required object by this means.

a **1300** *Cursor M.* 21306 Ilkan o þaim þair lar þai lere, And ringes to þe werld at here, Dinnes þe toþer, trumpes þe thrid. **13..** *Gaw. & Gr. Knt.* 931 Chaplaynez to þe chapeles chosen þe gate, Rungen ful rychely, ryȝt as þay schulden. *c* **1400** *Brut* cliii, On þe morwe men ronge, & songe masses þrouȝ-out London, and so after þrouȝ-out all Engeland. **1530** PALSGR. 691/2, I feare me some house be afyre in the nexte parysshe, for they rynge aukewarde. *c* **1586** C'TESS PEMBROKE *Ps.* LXVIII. ix, The battaile maides, which did with tymbrells ring. **1686** PLOT *Staffordsh.* 297 Some of his Servants going to ring in the old Steeple..had been in danger of their lives. **1782** MISS BURNEY *Cecilia* IX. iv, She expected every instant that he would ring for his chair. **1819** *Metropolis* I. 57, I rung and had the dog removed. **1847** E. BRONTË *Wuthering Heights* I. x. 202 Why not have Mrs. Dean up to finish her tale?.. I'll ring: she'll be delighted to find me capable of talking cheerfully. **1859–64** TENNYSON *Grandmother* xv, The ringers rang with a will. **1864** H. CULLWICK *Diary* June in D. Hudson *Munby* (1972) 195 *Me* by myself in that kitchen..ready to do any thing for 'em whenever they rang for me. **1879** MEREDITH *Egoist* xxxvii, Sir Willoughby went to ring for her carriage. **1926** D. L. SAYERS *Clouds of Witness* ii. 49 Ring for anything you want. **1980** N. MARSH *Photo-Finish* vii. 188 Alleyn..put his thumb on the bell..and Marco came in... He said: 'You rang, sir?'

transf. **1711** ADDISON *Spect.* No. 115 ¶7, I exercise myself ..upon a dumb Bell..; they never come into my Room to disturb me whilst I am ringing.

b. To summon *to* (divine service, church, etc.) by means of a bell.

1377 LANGL. *P. Pl.* B. XVIII. 425 Tyl þe daye dawed.. That men rongen to þe resurexioun. *c* **1450** *St. Cuthbert* (Surtees) 4045 To rynge to matyns þai began. **1466** in *Archaeologia* (1887) L. I. 51 Thei [*sc.* clerics] shal be redy to ryng to all maner of diuine seruice. **1519** *Fabric Rolls York Minster* (Surtees) 269 We thynke it were more convenient to ryng to matyns..at halfe oure to v. **1547** in T. North *Bells & Bell Lore* (1888) 81 Pd. to ij Ryngers w[ch] rong to y[e] Sermon when the bisshop of lincoln was here. **1604** E. G[RIMSTONE] *D'Acosta's Hist. Indies* v. xxx. 427 To strike up a drumme every day at the Sunne setting, to the same end that we are accustomed to ring to evensong. **1687** A. LOVELL tr. *Thevenot's Trav.* I. 192 *marg.*, The way of Ringing to the Office in St. Sepulchres.

c. *to ring* (*all*) *in*, to give the final strokes or peal before the service begins. Also said of a bell, *esp.* the Sanctus bell. (Cf. 2 c.)

1466 in *Archaeologia* (1887) L. I. 51 Be for the last pele warne the moroues masse preste and aske hym if he shal rynge alle in. **1483** *Cath. Angl.* 308/2 To Rynge jn, *conclassitare*. **1581** MULCASTER *Positions* xxxvii. (1887) 142 If ye crie come who will, or ring out all in. **1611** COTGR., *Coppeter*, to ring all-in, or the last peale. **1633** B. JONSON *Tale Tub* II. i, We are now going To church in way of matrimony..; They ha' rung all in a' ready. **1678** BUTLER *Hud.* III. i. 1224 Because it is..The onely Saints-Bell that rings all in.

8. a. With cogn. obj.: To sound forth (a peal, knell, etc.); to perform upon bells. Also *transf.*

c **1300** *Vox & Wolf* 251 in *Rel. Ant.* II. 277 Thi soul-cnul ich wile do ringe. *c* **1380** *St. Augustine* 1642 in Horstm. *Altengl. Leg.* (1878), To euensong Men rongen þo þreo peles long. **1466** in *Archaeologia* (1887) L. I. 49 To helpe the Sexton to Rynge the secounde pele to matens. **1547** J. HARRISON *Exhort. Scottes* a iiij b, If these..should fele but half the miserie,..thei would not be halfe so hastie to ryng alarmes. **1610** SHAKS. *Temp.* I. ii. 402 Sea-Nimphs hourly ring his knell. **1697** DRYDEN *Virg. Georg.* II. 790 The Breath Of brazen Trumpets rung the Peals of Death. **1787** *Europ. Mag.* XII. 434 The bells of the churches rung their dead peals during the day. **1822** SHELLEY *'When the lamp'* ii. 8 The mournful surges That ring the dead sea-man's knell. **1863** GEO. ELIOT *Romola* II. xxi, The great bell in the.. tower had rung out the hammer-sound of alarm.

fig. **1562** J. HEYWOOD *Prov. & Epigr.* (1867) 64 She beginneth..with a cry..To whiche she ringth a peale, a larom. **1605** SHAKS. *Macb.* III. ii. 43 Ere..The shard-borne Beetle..Hath rung Nights yawning Peale. **1636** MASSINGER *Gt. Dk. Flor.* III. i, My pockets ring A golden peal. **176.** WESLEY *Husb. & Wives* vii. 2 The husband may..ring his wife a peal concerning her duty. **1796** *Grose's Dict. Vulgar T.* (ed. 3), To Ring a Peal, to scold: chiefly applied to women. His wife rung him a fine peal! **1809** MALKIN *Gil Blas* v. i. ¶31 Moralez happening to launch out into the praise of Seville, the man..said to him—..You are ringing the chimes on the city which gave birth to me. *Ibid.* VII. i. ¶9 Her tongue..rang a bob-major of invective. **1826** LAMB *Elia*, *Pop. Fallacies* ix, Ringing a round of the most ingenious conceits, every man contributing his shot.

b. *to ring* (*the*) *changes*: see CHANGE *sb.* 8 c.

(*a*) **1614**, **1670** [see CHANGE *sb.* 8 c]. **1711** ADDISON *Spect.* No. 60 ¶2 The Poet rung the Changes upon these eight several Words. **1763** J. BROWN *Poetry & Music* 66 Commentators and Critics ring Changes on their single, double, oblique, right-handed, and left-handed Flutes. **1845** DISRAELI *Sybil* (1863) 279 Ring the changes on great measures and great experiments till it is time to go down and make a House. **1883** E. PENNELL-ELMHIRST *Cream Leicestersh.* 145 We all know how fond foxes usually are of ringing the changes among the multitudinous woods hereabouts.

(*b*) **1786** [see CHANGE *sb.* 8 c]. **1812** [see 13 b]. **1859** *Slang Dict.*, *Ringing the Changes*, changing bad money for good. **1875** *Chamb. Jrnl.* 67 The London news-boys..know how to ring the changes, and how to make old editions pass for new ones. **1891** *Belgravia* Feb. 142 An ill-looking ruffian charged with what is called 'ringing the changes'.

c. To accompany with the ringing of a bell.

1836–7 DICKENS *Sk. Boz*, *Scenes* ii, The muffin boy rings his way down the little street much more slowly than he is wont to do.

9. To announce or proclaim (an hour, time, †a miracle, etc.) by sound of bells. Also *transf.*

c **960** ÆTHELWOLD *Rule St. Benet* (Schröer, 1885) 72 Sy þæs abbodes ȝymen, þæt mon ealle tida..on rihte timan.. hringce. *a* **1100** in Thorpe *Dipl. Angl. Sax.* (1865) 437 Yc ȝef leaua ðam munche to hringinde hyre tyde. **1303** R. BRUNNE *Handl Synne* 928 Ouþer men seyd, þey shuld nat werche Lengyr þan þey rong none at þe chyrche. **1387** TREVISA *Higden* (Rolls) V. 413 Samnianus..ordeynede þat þe houres of the day schulde be ronge at chirches. **1466** in *Archaeologia* (1887) L. I. 49 Also he shall Rynge Curfie when it ys rounge with one bell and call for help when it ys rounge with moo. **1529** MORE *Dyaloge* I. Wks. 134/2 Thys blind man at saint albonis shrine had his sight agayne, and a myracle solemply rongen. **1570–6** LAMBARDE *Peramb. Kent* (1826) 172 Our Lady of Court of Strete had revived hir from the very point of death: and..hir pleasure was, that it should be rong for a miracle. **1632** MILTON *L'Allegro* 114 Ere the first Cock his Mattin rings. **1673–1704** [see CURFEW 1 c]. **1840** R. H. DANA *Bef. Mast* xxxvi, The city bells were just ringing one. **1875–6** STEVENSON *Ess. Trav.*, *Forest Notes* (1905) 152 Suddenly the bell rings out the hour from faraway Chailly.

fig. **1633** B. JONSON *Tale Tub* II. i, Till this ash-plant Had rung noon on your pate.

10. a. To usher *in* or *out* with the sound of bells; to bring or convey in this manner. Also *fig.* *to ring in*: (*fig.*) to include, take into consideration; to bring (someone) into an operation, activity, etc.

1554 in T. North *Bells & Bell Lore* (1888) 80 For shottynge of iij ropes when the[y] ronge bishop Samson in. **1597** SHAKS. *2 Hen. IV*, III. ii. 194 A cough sir, which I caught with Ringing in the Kings affayres, vpon his Coronation day. **1600** HOLLAND *Livy* LIV. Epit. 1241 At his death he was rung out of this world with a notable peale of farewell. **1633** BP. HALL *Occas. Medit.* (1851) 61 It is possible, that such a one, even by that discordous noise, may ring in others into the triumphant Church of heaven. **1828** SCOTT *F.M. Perth* xvi, For there will we ring-in Lent. **1844** J. T. HEWLETT *Parsons & Widows* xiii, Mr. Akenside resigned, and was 'rung out' of the parish. **1868** BROWNING *Ring & Bk.* IX. 1316 Pompilia scorns to have the old year end Without a present shall ring in the new.

fig. **1591** SHAKS. *1 Hen. VI*, IV. ii. 41 The Dolphins drumme..Sings heauy Musicke.., And mine shall ring thy dire departure out. **1633** HERBERT *Temple*, *Aaron* 8 A noise of passions ringing me for dead Unto a place where is no rest. **1900** ADE *Fables in Slang* 74 The Pew-Holders didn't even admit..that the Preacher had rung in some New Ones [*sc.* names]. **1922** D. H. LAWRENCE *England, my England* 45 The clanging pain in his head rang out the rest of his consciousness. **1925** T. DREISER *Amer. Tragedy* II. III. xvi. 202 She can't be kept out of the case... We'll have to ring her in, I'm afraid. **1954** WODEHOUSE *Jeeves & Feudal Spirit* viii. 72 I've got the whole family here... I only wanted Trotter, but Mrs. T. and Percy rang themselves in. **1973** *New Yorker* 17 Feb. 88/2 With that one stroke, the union could ring in a lot of public figures. **1974** *Publishers Weekly* 30 Dec. 90/1 Mr. Brooke is summoned from far away Lima, and an old suitor of Philippa's, Lord Tancred, is rung in to help.

b. To summon (a person) by ringing a bell. Also with *down*, *in*, *up*, etc. *to ring bees*, to try to influence their swarming by making a noise with metal utensils (still *dial.*).

1562 J. HEYWOOD *Prov. & Epigr.* (1867) 64 She ringth a peale,..suche one, As folke ring bees with basons. **1674** in *N. & Q.* 9th Ser. IX. 463/2 A territt..to hang a bell in, to ring the poor people to prayers. **1736** FIELDING *Pasquin* IV. Wks. 1882 X. 174 Come, ring up the first ghost. **1760** STERNE *Tr. Shandy* III. iii, He had got his right hand to the bell to ring up Trim. **1838** DICKENS *Nich. Nick.* xxiv, Ring in the orchestra, Grudden! **1848** —— *Dombey* iii, She had been rung down into the glass room as usual.

(*b*) *spec.* to call (someone) by telephone; freq. with *up*; also *absol.*, and with *round* (= to call a succession of people by telephone), *through*.

1880 *Punch* 17 July 13/2 For you upon them both may frown, And say that you are shocked, or May knock the Secretary down, And then ring up the Doctor. **1882** T. D. LOCKWOOD *Pract. Information for Telephonists* 130 Ask the office operator to ring up the complaining person and await results. **1889** PREECE & MAIER *Telephone* 111 A telephonestud which permits not only to ring-up a person but also to converse with him. **1906** S. FORD *Shorty McCabe* vi. 150 He was goin' to ring up the police reserves. **1913** G. B. SHAW *Let.* 14 July in *B. Shaw & Mrs. Campbell* (1952) 132, I shall ring up tomorrow in spite of my dread of being unwelcome. I rang a second time today; but the answer was buzz, buzz. **1930** J. B. PRIESTLEY *Angel Pavement* viii. 398 He rang me up last night, at home, to say he'd just arrived and would be down this morning. **1934** T. E. LAWRENCE *Let.* 14 Sept. (1938) 819 It lies on my conscience that you so often ring up vainly. **1934** N. MARSH *Man lay Dead* xii. 207 I'll ring through at about one o'clock. **1940** H. G. WELLS *Babes in Darkling Wood* II. i. 134 There were one or two people he might ring up, but probably they would be holiday-making now and out of town. **1948** 'N. SHUTE' *No Highway* vi. 169 While I was down there, Miss Learoyd rang through. **1955** *Times* 22 July 10/6 Two young friends rang me up rather excitedly the other evening and asked me if I would go round and give them my advice. **1958** L. A. G. STRONG *Treason in Egg* vii. 127 You'd better ring the police. **1960** J. STROUD *Shorn Lamb* xv. 170 If he does [turn up], I'll ring round for a hostel. **1969** *Listener* 6 Feb. 187/1 When Jelly Roll Morton..played his compositions to the Harlem team, eyebrows were raised no further than the pejorative 'don't ring *us*' level. **1974** A. MORICE *Killing with Kindness* ii. 14 He was going to ring round in the morning and fix up for us all to go and see them. **1974** *Times* 7 Feb. 14/6 By ringing and writing to every MP, Service and the bill's sponsors have so far secured 74 pledges to be present. **1977** 'M. UNDERWOOD' *Murder with Malice* x. 91 'Thanks for ringing, sir. I appreciate it.'.. Nick dropped the receiver back. **1980** A.

AUSWAKS *Trick of Diamonds* iii. 80 'Don't ring us, we'll ring you,' grunted Bob Jones sarcastically. **1981** J. WAINWRIGHT *All on Summer's Day* 66 Ring round the other divisions. I want some C.I.D. men.

c. To direct (a theatre-curtain) to be drawn *up* or let *down* by making a bell ring. Also *absol.* and *intr.* for passive (with the curtain as subject). Also *fig.*

1772 D. GARRICK *Peep behind Curtain* II. i. 30 Pray be so good as to ring down the curtain, that we may rehearse in form. **1807** *Monthly Mirror* Aug. 133 The prompter rings the lofty curtain down. **1836–7** DICKENS *Sk. Boz, Scenes* xiii, Look sharp below there, gents, .. they're a-going to ring-up. **1882** *Daily News* 2 Oct. 2/2 The functionary whose business it is to 'ring down' had satisfied himself that nobody wanted any more of it. **1887** *Times* 31 Aug. 4/3 The curtain had to be rung down before the play was ended. **1901** 'LINESMAN' *Words Eyewitness* 75 Before the curtain was rung up on the great spectacular drama of Vaal Krantz. **1913** F. H. BURNETT *T. Tembarom* xv. 186 'Now,' he said, 'we can ring up for the first act.' She filled the teapot. **1916** S. KAYE-SMITH *John Galsworthy* 63 Thus the curtain rings down on Irene Forsyte, crushed under the heel of prosperity. **1950** H. F. MALTBY (*title*) Ring up the curtain.

d. *to ring off*, to give signal by a bell for the severance of communication upon a telephone; now more usu., to discontinue a telephone conversation by replacing the receiver, = *hang up* s.v. HANG *v.* 29 a. Also *fig.*

1882 T. D. LOCKWOOD *Pract. Information for Telephonists* 85 Frequently an annunciator between two circuits when connected to allow the subscriber, if he please, to ring off. **1888** *Encycl. Brit.* XXIII. 134/2 When the subscribers have finished, both call the exchange or, as it is commonly put, 'ring off'. **1899** *Electrician* 1 Dec. 181/2 Ringing off is avoided, as this is performed automatically by replacing the receiver on the hook. **1900** [see PHONE *sb.*^{2} and *v.*]. **1901** *Munsey's Mag.* XXIV. 800 She heard him ring off, hang up the receiver, and go out into the hall. **1906** A. BENNETT *Whom God hath Joined* iv. 158 He rang off, curtly, without another word. **1920** R. MACAULAY *Potterism* III. i. 104 You mustn't ring off yet, indeed you mustn't. Hold on while I tell daddy. **1935** *Punch* 21 Aug. 223/1 'I'm coming round to wring your wretched little neck!' shouted Mr. Applestalk as he rang off. **1938** E. BOWEN *Death of Heart* III. i. 328 'So then you rang off?' 'No, he did. It was his tea-time, no doubt.' **1967** M. KENYON *Whole Hog* i. 12 I'll ring him anyway... 'Bye now—Yes, I'm going to *ring* off. **1973** S. DOBYNS *Man of Little Evils* xii. 127 The operator came back on the line. 'I'm afraid your party has rung off.'

fig. **1895** *Inlander* Dec. 114 *Ring off*, stop talking. **1906** E. DYSON *Fact'ry 'Ands* vi. 71 'Shut up! D'yeh 'ear?.. Arr-r-r ring off, cant yeh!' The girl.. opened a startled eye. **1938** F. M. FORD *Let.* 26 Nov. (1965) 305, I will ring off. Let us know from time to time how things go with you. **1940** F. SARGESON *Man & his Wife* 34 Wouldn't you like to stay out here for good? Fred said. Ring off, Ken said. I got a bite.

e. *to ring back*, to reply to (a previous caller) by telephone. Also *absol.* and as *sb.*

Quots. 1971 and 1972 represent technical senses in Telephony.

1942 N. BALCHIN *Darkness falls from Air* iii. 57, I hung up. 'Pearce is going to ring you back,' I said. **1944** H. MCCLOY *Panic* 118 This is Jim, testing. I'm going to hang up and then I want you to ring me back. **1960** I. JEFFERIES *Dignity & Purity* xi. 181 I'll ring you back Gobbo. Couple of minutes. **1969** P. N. WALKER *Carnaby & Conspirators* vii. 68 'Make a check on Henry Pritchard too, sir.'.. 'Will do. Will you ring me back?' **1971** *Gloss. Electrotechnical, Power Terms* (*B.S.I.*) III. ii. 28 *Ring-back signal*, a backward signal to recall a calling subscriber held by the operator. **1972** *Sci. Amer.* Sept. 120/1 When the path is found, the signal-distributor sends electrical signals to ring the telephone of the called subscriber and sends ringback tones to the caller. **1974** M. BIRMINGHAM *You can help Me* iii. 47 There was one caller from a public call-box who.. didn't ring back. **1977** W. MARSHALL *Thin Air* i. 11 He said quickly, 'I'll ring you back.'

f. *to ring in*, to report by telephone. Also *trans.*, to transmit (a verbal message) by telephone.

1949 N. MARSH *Swing, Brother, Swing* xi. 254 I'll ring in then and get something to eat. **1956** *New Statesman* 18 Aug. 180/3 We had to think about finding a telephone booth from which to ring in a preliminary story. **1964** M. BANTON *Policeman in Community* iii. 83 The beat officer has to 'ring in' to headquarters every hour from automatic boxes mounted on standards at the kerbside. **1971** B. GRAHAM *Spy Trap* i. 7 He.. drove to the secondary rendezvous point... Maybe Hannifin had rung in. **1975** *Listener* 16 Oct. 505/1 People ring in, wanting help.

11. a. To cause to give out a ringing sound; to make to resound.

c **1386** CHAUCER *Knight's T.* 1573 Atte laste The Statue of Mars bigan his hauberk rynge. *c* **1425** *Cast. Persev.* 3001 in *Macro Plays* 160 Whon Coueytyse makyth þe a-dred, with rappys I þee rynge. *c* **1440** *Pallad. on Husb.* XII. 606 [Let] Louyng record and rynge her stryngis chaste To thyn honour. *c* **1440** *Ipomydon* 788 He blew loud and shoke it wele, That it ronge all þe castelle. **1573** *Satir. Poems Reform.* xxxix. 2 Mak ȝow for the gait, To ring ȝour drummis & rank ȝour men of weir.

b. To test (coin, etc.) by making it ring.

1702 [see RINGING *vbl. sb.*^{2} 1]. **1777** BRAND *Pop. Antiq.* 12 Housewives.. try the Soundness of their Earthen or China Vases by ringing them with a finger. **1796** PEGGE *Anonym.* (1809) 266 Ringing, or sounding, money, to try if it be good, is not modern. **1851** RUSKIN *Stones Ven.* (1874) I. i. 31 Debating about the genuineness of a coin without ringing it. **1884** W. C. SMITH *Kildrostan* 94 Not caring to ring copper half-pennies Upon the counter.

c. *to ring up*: to make a record of; *spec.* to record (a sale) on a cash register or similar device. Also *fig.*

1937 J. T. FARRELL *Fellow Countrymen* 180 He paid Kitty fifteen cents, which she rang up. **1939** *Sun* (Baltimore) 18 Jan. 5/5 Asked if the ship's speeds in any of its previous trips through the canal had been 'rung up', Leonard Nieberline, first officer, answered in the negative. **1948** C. HIMES *Black on Black* (1973) 267. When she stopped at the cash register across from him to ring up a sale he said, 'Baby, I really love you.' **1956** A. HUXLEY *Adonis & Alphabet* 167 Energies which, if canalized and directed, can be made to do useful work and ring up handsome profits. **1957** *Economist* 21 Dec. 1051/1 Last Saturday, when the strike was crumbling, the shops stayed open until nine; many rang up record sales. **1962** *Times* 15 Mar. 9/7 The items in connexion with which he was accused did not appear upon the cash receipt slip. The cashier must have omitted to ring these up. **1968** [see DRIVER 2 b]. **1970** *Daily Tel.* 14 Nov. 15/3 One technique is to bully the check-out girl and get her sufficiently confused to miss the fact that half the goods have been pushed through without having been rung up. **1976** 'E. MCBAIN' *Guns* vii. 148 The cashier rings up the check, money comes tumbling down the cash register chute.

12. a. To utter sonorously; to proclaim aloud; to re-echo. Also with *out*.

c **1384** CHAUCER *H. Fame* II. 565 Allas thus was her shame y-ronge.. on euery tonge. *c* **1386** —— *Pard. T.* Prol. 3 In chirche whan I preche, I peyne me to haue an hauten speche; I rynge it out as rounde as eny belle. **1535** LYNDESAY *Satyre* 74 Till all our rymis be rung, And our mistoinit sangis be sung. **1577** tr. *Bullinger's Decades* (1592) 336 If hee ring out the name of the Lorde, and preache his lawe. **1589** *Whip for an Ape* 89 in Lyly's Wks. 1902 III. 420 And Martins mate Iacke Strawe would alwaies ring The Clergies faults. *a* **1625** FLETCHER *Hum. Lieutenant* v. i, I would ring him such a lesson. **1689** SHADWELL *Bury F.* I. i, All England rings out your fame. **1870** MORRIS *Earthly Paradise* I. 539 All about the Lydian shouting rings Death to the beaten foemen. **1887** BOWEN *Virg. Ecl.* VI. 44 The mariner men Shouted for Hylas, and every shore rang Hylas again.

b. To cause to resound, to din, *in* one's ears.

1657 TRAPP *Comm. Ezra* viii. 29 This lesson had need to be often rung in our ears. **1663** PATRICK *Parab. Pilgr.* xix. 190 The people rang this continually in their ears. **1708** SWIFT *Sacr. Test* Wks. 1751 IV. 171 Persecution was every day rung in our Ears. **1726** SHELVOCKE *Voy. round World* 231, I took all opportunities of ringing in their ears such instances of the Spaniards cruelty.

13. *slang.* To change, exchange; *spec.* to effect a fraudulent change in the identity of a motor vehicle.

1812 J. H. VAUX *Flash Dict.*, *Ringing Castors* signifies frequenting churches and other public assemblies, for the purpose of changing hats, by taking away a good and leaving a shabby one in its place. **1812** *Sporting Mag.* XXXIX. 210 How could'st thou be so silly, Flash screens [bad notes] to ring for home-spun rope. **1967** N. LUCAS *CID* vi. 80 The two cars are.. rebuilt into one 'bastard' car... The process is known as 'ringing' cars. **1971** *Drive* Summer 22/1 Like any commercial venture, the business of car ringing—changing a vehicle's identity—has to be cost-effective. **1977** A. HUNTER *Gently Instrumental* ii. 19 The Parry brothers.. copped three apiece for ringing cars.

b. *to ring in*, to substitute fraudulently.

1812 J. H. VAUX *Flash Dict.*, *Ringing the changes*, is a fraud practised by smashers, who when they receive good money in change of a guinea, &c., ring in one or more pieces of base with great dexterity and then request the party to change them. **1894** MASKELYNE *Sharps & Flats* 248 Another method of cheating the players is to ring in a loaded die which will fall six.

ring, obs. Sc. f. REIGN *v.*; obs. var. WRING *v.*

'ringable, *a.* [f. RING *v.*^{2} + -ABLE.] Capable of being rung.

1874 RUSKIN *Val D' Arno* (1886) 13 It never occurs to them to ask how it [*sc.* a bell] came to be ringable.

ringald, variant of RANGALE *Obs.*

ring-a-ring (rɪŋə'rɪŋ). Also **ringaring**, etc. [Fanciful extension of RING *sb.*^{1}] A circle or circular movement. ***ring-a-ring o' roses*** (and variants), a game played by children holding hands in a circle (also *transf.*).

1881 K. GREENAWAY *Mother Goose* 48 Ring-a-ring-a-roses, A pocket full of posies. **1922** JOYCE *Ulysses* 506 I'm a tiny tiny thing Ever flying in the spring Round and round a ringaring. **1927** W. E. COLLINSON *Contemp. Eng.* 11, I can be brief in mentioning the various games we played during childhood. I will mention.. ring a ring o' roses. **1945** C. S. FORESTER *Commodore* xxiii. 259 The Governor.. tried to dance a sort of ring-a-ring-of-roses with the two Englishmen. **1953** A. CLARKE *Moment Next to Nothing* II. 32 He Was near that oak, speaking of Marravaun—A ring-a-ring o' birds around him. **1957** J. MASTERS *Far, Far the Mountain Peak* i. 5 Why don't I suggest a game of ring-a-ring-a-roses, or kiss-in-the-ring? **1963** *Times* 30 May 4/2 England now were playing arrogant football and stroking the ball from man to man as though they were playing ring-a-ring-o'roses. **1972** G. GREEN *Great Moments in Sport: Soccer* ii. 38 While the opposition was being enticed into these closely woven webs of ring-a-roses, two.. of the front runners would be streaking ahead into the unguarded places. **1974** *Times* 1 Apr. 1/8 Strong men blenched and broke into a sweat of embarrassment when made to dance 'Ring-a-ring o' roses' in public outside Guildhall.

† ringat-rangat. *Sc. Obs.* [Reduplication of RANGAT^2; cf. RIBBLE-RABBLE.] Rabble.

1535 STEWART *Cron. Scot.* III. 222 Of ringat-rangat, and of pepill gude, Innumsurabill war in that multitude.

ring-back: see RING *sb.*^{2} 3.

'ring-bark, *v.* [f. RING *v.*^{1} 9 b.] **a.** *intr.* To remove rings of bark from trees, in order to kill them. Also, to remove a narrow or incomplete ring in order to check rapid growth. **b.** *trans.* To bark (trees) in this way.

1887 FARRELL *How He Died* 165 Eating damper, on a free selection where he'd been ring-barking. **1892** *Dublin Rev.* Apr. 460 [Rabbits] effectually 'ringbark' and kill the scrub growths. **1938** C. P. ACKERS *Pract. Brit. Forestry* vi. 215 This is the time to ring-bark and let these rough poles, after they have done their job, topple over as branchless rotten logs. **1975** H. F. HEADY *Rangeland Managem.* iv. 57 Ring-barking by voles killed as much as 84 percent of the *Artemisia tridentata* in some Montana stands.

Hence **'ring-barked** *ppl. a.*, **'ring-barking** *vbl. sb.*; also **'ring-barker**.

1887 MOLONEY *Forestry W. Afr.* 231 The finest timber is usually that first selected for destruction by fire, by ring barking and other rude and wasteful methods. **1893** *Scribner's Mag.* June 795/1 The half-burnt trunk of a ring-barked gum-tree. **1905** *Spectator* 12 Aug. 220/2 The 'ring-barker's' axe had been busy cutting the circular girdle in the bark which starves trees to death. **1938** C. P. ACKERS *Pract. Brit. Forestry* xi. 341 Partial ring barking is practised in some orchards so as to check the sap of the tree and so induce more free fruiting. **1961** *Observer* 18 June 35/5 Successfully greedy roots can mean fruitless apples and pears, and 'ring barking' is the remedy.

'ring-bolt. orig. *Naut.* Also **ringbolt, ring bolt.** [f. RING *sb.*^{1} So Da. *ringbolt*, Sw. *-bult*, Du. *-bout*, G. *-bolzen*.] A bolt with an eye at one end, to which a ring is attached.

1626 CAPT. SMITH *Accid. Yng. Seamen* 13 The canhookes, slings, and parbunkels, ports and ringbolts and hooks. **1644** MANWARING *Seaman's Dict.* s.v. *Bolt*, Ring-bolts.. are of infinite necessary use, both for the bringing to of the planckes and wales to the ship, as also the chiefe things whereunto we fasten the tackles and breetchings of the great Ordnance. **1769** FALCONER *Dict. Marine* (1780) s.v., The ring-bolts are for several uses, but particularly to hook the tackles, by which the cannon of a ship are managed and secured. **1797** S. JAMES *Narr. Voy.* 35 He found two English gentlemen bound hand and foot to the ringbolts in the 'tween decks. **1834** MARRYAT *P. Simple* (1863) 268 Our guns .. bounced up to the beams overhead, tearing away their ringbolts. **1840** *Crockett Almanac 1841* 19 A ring bolt in the barn floor. **1888** CHURCHWARD *Blackbirding* 141, I had just time to throw myself flat on the deck, and hold on to a ringbolt. **1958** L. DURRELL *Balthazar* iv. 90 Firm as a figure held by ringbolts. **1968** E. R. BUCKLER *Ox Bells & Fireflies* xv. 215 He just grabbed the sonofabitch by the scruff o' the neck and lifted him about two feet offa the floor—and, by God, by the time he was through with him, he brought him to the ringbolt and don't you think he didn't. **1974** R. ADAMS *Shardik* xxvi. 210 The tie-bars.. were secured by chains to ring-bolts set.. in the walls and floor.

'ring-bone. *Farriery.* Also **ringbone, ring bone.** [f. RING *sb.*^{1} So Du. *ringbeen*, G. and Norw. *ringbein*, MSw. *ringben*. One example of an OE. *hringbán* appears in the following gloss:—

c **1000** ÆLFRIC *Gloss.* in Wr.-Wülcker 157 *Tauco*, hringban ðæs eaȝan.]

1. A deposit of bony matter on the pastern-bones of a horse.

1523 FITZHERB. *Husb.* §98 A ryngbone is an yll soraunce, and appereth before on the foote [etc.]. **1551** T. WILSON *Logike* (1563) 51 We can see a spauain, a sprent, a ryngboane, or soche other disease in a horse. **1607** MARKHAM *Caval.* VII. (1617) 81 The Ringbone is a certain superfluous grissle, growing about the cronet of the horses hoofe. **1675** *Lond. Gaz.* No. 990/4 One Bay Mare.. with three white Feet,.. and a Ring-bone on the near Foot behind. **1754** BARTLET *Gentl. Farriery* (ed. 2) 273 The ring-bones that appear on colts and young horses, will often insensibly wear off of themselves. **1828** *Sporting Mag.* XXIII. 134 A horse with a ring-bone as big as half a twopenny loaf. **1860** MAYHEW *Illustr. Horse Doctor* 330 An exostosis is established, and a ringbone is the consequence.

2. The growth of such bony matter, as a specific disease of horses.

1594 GREENE & LODGE *Looking Gl.* G.'s Wks. (Grosart) XIV. 18 If he haue outward diseases, as the spavin, splent, ring-bone, wind-gall. **1639** T. DE GRAY *Expert Farrier* 38 This is very good for the crown-scab, ring-bone, and such like diseases. **1677** *Long. Gaz.* No. 1201/4 A handsome dark brown Hunting Gelding,.. fired for the Spaven and ring bone on the near leg behind. **1831** YOUATT *Horse* xiii. 255 From this disposition to spread,.. this disease has acquired the name of ringbone. **1844** H. STEPHENS *Bk. Farm* II. 398 When serious, they may cause quittor, which may terminate in ring-bone, and in consequent chronic lameness.

Hence **'ring-boned** *a.*

1712 *Lond. Gaz.* No. 5019/6 A bay.. Gelding.. (ring Bon'd before). **1844** J. T. HEWLETT *Parsons & W.* iii, Your ring-boned, spavined, glandered hack.

'ring-dance. [f. RING *sb.*^{1} Cf. Du. *ringdans* (Kilian *ringh-*), MLG. *ringhedans*, G. *ringtanz*, Da. *-dands*, Sw. *-dans*, Icel. *hringdanz*. In mod. use also readopted from G. or Scand.] A round dance.

1600 DYMMOK *Ireland* (1843) 35 They conveyinge themselues after a while in a ringe daunce into a wood. **1647** TRAPP *Comm. Rev.* xxi. 8 These lead the ring-dance of this rout of reprobates.

1862 H. MARRYAT *Year in Sweden* II. 266 A ring-dance, performed in every farmhouse at Christmas-time. **1903** *Folk-Lore* Sept. 265 Women in a ritual ring-dance. **1910** [see POLSKA]. **1933** E. K. CHAMBERS *Eng. Folk-Play* 202 There is a general resemblance between Sword Dances proper and.. Ring, Hoop, or Garland Dances. **1946** R. BLESH *Shining Trumpets* v. 98 He had the work-songs, the spiritual, the ring-dance. **1960** AUDEN *Homage to Clio* 28 Rustics in a ring-dance pantomime.

ˈring-dial. Now *Hist.* [f. RING *sb.*[1]] (See quot. 1728.)

1667 [see DIAL 2b]. **1674** MOXON *Tutor Astron.* v. Pref., Universal Dials are those commonly called Equinoctial or Ring-Dials. **1721** (*title*), Leybourn's Description and Use of .. Gunter's Quadrant... To which is added the Use of .. the Nocturnal, the Ring-Dyal, and Gunter's Line. **1728** CHAMBERS *Cycl.*, *Ring-Dial*, is a kind of Dial, usually small, and portable; consisting of a Brass Ring, or Rim, seldom exceeding two Inches in Diameter... *Universal*, or *Astronomical Ring-dial*, is a Ring-dial which serves to find the Hour of the Day in any Part of the Earth. **1825** *Stranger's Comp. Cambridge* 52 A globe, a universal ring-dial, a quadrant and compass, formerly belonging to Sir Isaac Newton. **1877** W. JONES *Finger-ring* 453 A brass ring-dial, probably of the kind formerly designated as 'journey rings'.

ˈring-dove. [f. RING *sb.*[1] So Du. *ringduif* (Kilian *ringhduyve*), Da. *ringdue*, Sw. *-dufva*, G. *-taube*: cf. also OS. *ringeldûfa*, MLG. *ringeldûve* (*ryngelduyve* Teut., *ringhelduyve* Kilian), Da. *ringeldue*, G. *ringeltaube*.]

1. The wood-pigeon, cushat, or queest (*Columba palumbus*); also called *ring-pigeon* (see RING *sb.*[1] 19b).

1538 ELYOT, *Palumba*, a .. rynge douue. **1587** HARRISON *England* (1878) II. 15 Foules producted by the industrie of man, as betweene .. the fesant and the ring dooue. **1606** SYLVESTER *Du Bartas* II. iv. II. *Magnificence* 711 This doth make The Ring-Dove turn; that brings the Culver back. **1624** MIDDLETON *Game at Chess* IV. iv, The Diuels in't, I'm taken by a Ring-doue. **1668** CHARLETON *Onomast.* 77 *Palumbus Torquatus*, the Ring-dove, or Quiest. **1707** MORTIMER *Husb.* (1721) I. 262, I got a pair of Ring-doves Eggs, and hatch'd them under a tame pigeon. **1768** PENNANT *Brit. Zool.* I. 221 The ring-dove is the largest pigeon we have. **1794** SOUTHEY *Sonnets* i, Listening in solitude the ring-dove's note, Who pours like me her solitary song. *c* **1850** KINGSLEY *Misc.* (1859) I. 167 The murmur of the ring-dove comes soft and sleepy through the wood. **1892** AGNES CLERKE *Fam. Stud. Homer* 131 The second Homeric species of *Columba* is the ring-dove.

attrib. **1725** *Fam. Dict.* s.v. *Roast-Meats*, Ring-Dove Sauce, with Pomegranate.

2. (See quot.)

1841 *Penny Cycl.* XX. 15/1 The term Ring Dove is also applied to the Collared Turtle, *Columba risoria*.

ring-dropper, -dropping: see RING *sb.*[1] 19.

ringe (rɪndʒ), *sb.*[1] *dial.* Also 8 rindge. [Later form of RENGE *sb.*[1]]

1. A row, line, or long heap of anything.

1707 *Clergym. Vade-mecum* 191 The manner of paying wood in kind is, either .. the tenth rindge, or the tenth load of faggot. **1736** PEGGE *Kenticisms* (E.D.S.), *Ringe*, wood when it is felled lies in ringes before it is made up into faggots, etc. **1787** W. MARSHALL *E. Norfolk* (1795) II. Gloss., *Ringes*, rows, of hay, quicks, etc. *a* **1825** FORBY *Voc. E. Anglia* 278 *Ringe*, .. a row of plants, or anything else. **1887** *Kentish Gloss.*, *Ringe*, a long heap in which mangolds are kept for the winter.

attrib. **1808** BATCHELOR *Agric.* 475 Common ringe or range wood was here used. **1854** MISS BAKER *Northampt. Gloss.*, *Rangewood* or *Ringewood*, underwood; which includes the hazel, sallow, and all other brushwood... When offered for sale they are always stacked in Ranges or rows.

2. (See quot.)

a **1825** FORBY *Voc. E. Anglia* 278 *Ringe*, the border, or trimming of a cap, kerchief, or other article of female dress.

ringe, *sb.*[2] *dial.* [Of obscure origin.] (See later quots.)

1719 *Will of J. Hirst* (York), A smoothing iron, .. a kitt, a ringe, .. a morter and pestill. **1736** PEGGE *Kenticisms* (E.D.S.), *Ringe*, a large tub with two iron ears, containing 14 or 16 gallons, with which two servants fetch water from a distant place. **1883** GRESLEY *Gloss. Coal-mining*, *Ringes*, (N.), see *Cowls*. [Wrought-iron water-barrels, or tanks, attached to the winding ropes.]

†ringe, variant of RENGE *v. Obs.*

a **1225** *Ancr. R.* 140 Ase me deð ane cubbel to þe swine þet is to [= too] recchinde, & to ringinde abuten.

ringe, dial. var. RANGE *sb.* and *v.*, RINSE *sb.* and *v.*; obs. Sc. var. REIGN *v.*

ringed (rɪŋd), *ppl. a.* [f. RING *sb.*[1] and *v.*[1]]

1. Of armour: Made of rings. *rare.*

Beowulf 1246 Heaþo-steapa helm, hringed byrne.

1824 MEYRICK *Ant. Armour* I. 27 The form of the rustred armour seems .. to have grown out of the ringed. **1846** FAIRHOLT *Costume* 155 A hauberk or tunic of ringed mail, reaching to the knee. *Ibid.* 157 This surcoat hanging lower than the ringed hauberk. **1876** PLANCHÉ *Cycl. Costume* I. 348 Ringed mail is constantly mentioned by Saxon, Norman and Scandinavian writers.

2. a. Of persons: Wearing a ring or rings; also, wedded with a ring.

1393 LANGL. *P. Pl.* C. III. 12 On alle hure fyue fyngres [she was] rycheliche yrynged.

1827 LYTTON *Pelham* xxvi, I shall at all events appear in the Tuileries to-morrow, chained and ringed. **1866** GEO. ELIOT *F. Holt* (1868) 58 Your ringed and scented men of the people. **1872** J. C. JEAFFRESON *Brides & Bridals* I. vi. 93 Our mediæval matrons were always ringed on the left hand. **1875** TENNYSON *Q. Mary* I. i, I was born of a true man and a ring'd wife.

b. Of the fingers, etc.: Provided or adorned with a ring or rings.

1599 HAKLUYT *Voy.* II. I. 251 Their wiues eares and noses are ringed very full of rings of copper and siluer. **1681** RYCAUT tr. *Gracian's Critick* 228 The Fingers, which were ringed with Diamonds. **1856** MRS. BROWNING *Aur. Leigh* III. 975 With .. forefinger, brown and ringed. **1881** MRS. C. PRAED *Policy & P.* I. 202 She took Mr. Longleat's rough hand with her soft ringed fingers.

c. Of a bird: bearing a ring or rings on one or both legs.

1908 *Brit. Birds* I. 298 Should anyone come across any of Herr Mortensen's ringed birds at any time, it is hoped they will send the ring, foot, and data of capture either to him or to me. **1948** *Ibid.* XLI 233 Recoveries of ringed Mallard are in the vast majority of cases obtained from birds shot. **1978** P. CONDER *RSPB Guide to Birdwatching* 104 The table of longevity shows that ringed birds are able to survive to a good age.

3. a. Marked or encircled by a ring or rings; surrounded by a circular band or bands, etc.

1513 DOUGLAS *Æneis* V. x. 40 Apon a hors of Trace .. With bawsand face, ringit the forthir E.

1839 DARWIN *Voy. Nat.* xi. (1879) 232 One man was ringed and dotted with white like a Fuegian. **1858** GREENER *Gunnery* 364 As it now appears in Captain Minié's annular ringed bullet. **1870** R. A. PROCTOR *Other Worlds* vi. 148 *note*, The sensations with which .. I saw the ringed planet for the first time. **1885** *Century Mag.* XXXI. 31 He cautiously felt the weight of the ringed and polished rod.

b. *Bot.* (See quots.)

1832 LINDLEY *Introd. Botany* 394 *Ringed* .., surrounded by elevated or depressed bands; as the roots of some plants, the cupulæ of several oaks, &c. **1856** HENSLOW *Dict. Bot. Terms* 159 *Ringed*, when a cylindrical part is surrounded by lines, bands, elevations, &c., which approximate to circles.

c. Deprived of a ring of bark.

1820 *Hort. Soc. Trans.* IV. 124 If the ring be wide, the ringed branches .. speedily become sickly.

4. a. Having, or put into, the form of a ring.

1593 NASHE *Christ's T.* Wks. (Grosart) IV. 255 Hence blasphemous Witches .., when they raise vp the deuill, drawe a ringed circle all-about hym. **1893** G. ALLEN *Scallywag* I. 105 The baronet blew the smoke slowly through his ringed lips. **1899** *Allbutt's Syst. Med.* VIII. 513 Discoid or ringed scaly patches.

b. *Zool.* Composed of rings; annulated.

1840 SWAINSON *Nat. Hist. Insects* 1 The body is always divided into rings or transverse joints; from which circumstance naturalists have agreed to call them annulose, or ringed animals. **1873** DAWSON *Earth & Man* iii. 45 A lower type of annulose or ringed animal than that of the Trilobites, is that of the worms.

5. In the specific names of animals, birds, etc.: **ringed barnacle**, the brent-goose and some related species. **ringed boa**, the aboma (*Epicrates cenchris*). **ringed carpet**, a pale grey moth, *Cleora cinctaria*, with dark patches on the forewings. **ringed china-mark**, a species of moth (see quots.). **ringed dove**, = RING-DOVE. **ringed ground-squirrel, guillemot, kingfisher, lemming** (see quots.). **ringed penguin**, the chinstrap penguin, *Pygoscelis antarctica*. **ringed perch**, the yellow perch of America. **ringed (sand-)plover**, one of the common varieties of plover (*Ægialitis hiaticola*). **ringed rat, seal** (see quots.). **ringed snake**, = *ring-snake* (see RING *sb.*[1] 19b). **ringed thrush**, = RING-OUZEL.

1831 *Wilson's Amer. Ornith.* IV. 348 *Ringed Bernacles, *Berniclæ torquatæ*. **1802** SHAW *Gen. Zool.* III. II. 344 *Ringed boa (*Boa Cenchris*)... This animal is a native of South America. **1828** STARK *Elem. Nat. Hist.* I. 356 The Ringed Boa. Body fawn-coloured, with a chain of large brown rings along the back. **1866** *Ringed carpet [see CARPET *sb.* 4]. **1896** J. W. TUTT *Brit. Moths* xi. 300 The Ringed Carpet .. is abundant at Lyndhurst in May and early June, on the dwarf firs among the heather. **1948** W. J. STOKOE *Caterpillars Brit. Moths* II. 197 The Ringed Carpet. .. The New Forest in Hampshire is said to be the district *par excellence* for this species. **1819** SAMOUELLE *Entomol. Compend.* 425 *Botys stratiotalis*, the *ringed China-mark. **1832** J. RENNIE *Consp. Butterfl. & M.* 151 The Ringed China-Mark (*Hydrocampa Stratiotata*). *c* **1532** DU WES *Introd. Fr.* in Palsgr. 911 The *rynged dove, *le ramier*. **1821** CLARE *Vill. Minstr.* I. 178 Here thrushes chant their madrigals, Here breathes the ringed dove. **1879** GOODE *Anim. Res. & Fisheries U.S.* in *Smithson. Collect.* XXIII. 16 *Spermophilus annulatus*, .. *Ringed Ground Squirrel.—Plains of Colima, Mexico. **1843** YARRELL *Brit. Birds* III. 351 The *Ringed Guillemot (*Uria lacrymans*) or The Bridled Guillemot. **1889** SCLATER & HUDSON *Argentine Ornith.* II. 26 *Ceryle Torquata* (Linn.), *Ringed Kingfisher. **1829** SWAINSON & RICHARDSON *Fauna Boreali-Americana* I. 136 The Greenland Lemming is most allied to the *Ringed Lemming of Siberia ..; the brown ring round the neck, surmounted by a paler one, whence it derives the specific appellation of *torquatus*, does not exist in the American animal. **1919** *Ringed penguin [see ADÉLIE]. **1964** A. L. THOMSON *New Dict. Birds* 611/1 The Chinstrap (or Ringed) Penguin .. is most abundant in the Antarctic Peninsula. **1884** GOODE *Fisheries U.S.* in *Senate Misc.* VI. 414 The descriptive names 'Yellow Perch' and '*Ringed Perch' are in common use. **1893** BEAN *Fishes Pennsylv.* 127 (Cassell), The yellow perch, ringed perch, or striped perch .. does not occur in the Ohio valley or south-west. **1784** PENNANT *Arct. Zool.* (1792) II. 191 *Ringed Plover... The neck is encircled with a white ring. **1831** RENNIE *Montagu's Ornith. Dict.* 142 The Ringed Plover is entirely a shore bird, residing there the whole year. **1882** NEWTON in *Encycl. Brit.* XIV. 76/1 The group commonly known as Ringed Plovers or Ring Doterels. **1781** PENNANT *Hist. Quadrup.* II. 457 *Ringed Rat, *Mus Torquatus*. **1842** MACGILLIVRAY *Brit. Ornith.* II. 52 *Ringed Sand-plover. **1871** *Proc. Zool. Soc.* June 506 Occurrence of the *Ringed or Marbled Seal (*Phoca hispida*) on the Coast of Norfolk. **1879** *Nature* XXI. 40/1 The Polar bear and the ringed seal (*Phoca fœtida*). **1769** PENNANT *Brit. Zool.* (1776) III. 31 *Ringed Snake. **1802** BINGLEY *Anim. Biography* (1813) II. 458 The Common or Ringed Snakes, are well-known inhabitants of moist and warm woods in this country. **1839–47** *Todd's Cycl. Anat.* III. 620/2 The fourth ventricle .. in the ringed snake and lizard is small, but deep. **1875** COPE *N. Amer. Batrachia & Reptilia* in *Smithson. Collect.* XIII. 65 The only reptiles are the snapping-tortoise and the ringed snake. **1839** MACGILLIVRAY *Brit. Birds* II. 100 The *Ringed Thrush is very similar to the Blackbird.

Ringelmann (ˈrɪŋgəlmən). [Of uncertain attribution; perh. the name of Maximilien *Ringelmann* (1861–1931), French scientist.] Used *attrib.* and †in the possessive with reference to a means of estimating the darkness and density of smoke by visual comparison with a chart bearing different shades of grey (formed by lines ruled with different spacings on a white card); as ***Ringelmann card, chart, scale.***

1898 S. B. DONKIN *Heat Efficiency of Steam Boilers* ix. 184 Ringelmann's smoke scale.—Professor Ringelmann has conceived the idea of representing different intensities of smoke, from light through grey to black, not by small sample tints, which are apt to be misleading, but by an arrangement of lines on white paper, drawn in a particular way. **1905** W. NICHOLSON *Smoke Abatement* vii. 144 Copies of the Ringelmann Smoke Scales .. are obtainable. **1923** H. G. CLINCH *Smoke Inspector's Handbk.* vii. 74 (*heading*) Measurement of smoke—Ringelmann's shade cards. **1954** [see *dark smoke* s.v. DARK *a.* 14c]. **1958** *New Scientist* 5 June 101/1 Discharge of smoke darker than Shade 2 on the Ringelmann chart .. for a total of more than ten minutes within eight hours is forbidden. **1962** *B.S.I. News* May 20 The B.S.I. has .. undertaken .. the preparation of standard Ringelmann charts and the measurement of solids emitted from chimneys.

ringent (ˈrɪndʒənt), *a.* [ad. L. *ringent-*, *ringens*, pres. pple. of *ringĕre* to gape or grin.] Gaping or grinning:

a. *Bot.* Applied to a labiate corolla having the lips widely opened.

1760 J. LEE *Introd. Bot.* I. iii. (1765) 7 *Ringent*, *gaping*, that is, irregular and personated with two Lips. **1777** CURTIS *Flora Lond.* I. 47 Corolla [of yellow toadflax] .. ringent. **1807** J. E. SMITH *Phys. Bot.* 394 Some ringent flowers with only 2 Stamens. **1847** W. E. STEELE *Field Bot.* 133 Cor. with a long tube, ringent; upper lip emarginate.

b. *Ent.* and *Zool.*

1825 SAY *Explan. Terms Entom.* 29. **1854** WOODWARD *Mollusca* II. 163 Helix Globulosa: .. Aperture of adult turned upwards, ringent.

c. In literal sense.

1800 SHAW *Gen. Zool.* I. I. 94 The figure [of the Loris] .. representing the animal in a ringent state. **1872** RUSKIN *Eagle's N.* §157 He is distinct from other birds in having .. an entirely fleshy and ringent mouth, .. with a perpetual grin upon it.

ringer[1] (ˈrɪŋə(r)). [f. RING *sb.*[1] or *v.*[1] Occurs earlier in the comb. *hog-ringer*: see HOG *sb.* 13.]

1. *Curling.* 'A stone which lies within the ring that surrounds the tee' (Jamieson, 1825).

2. *Quoits.* A quoit so thrown that it encloses the pin aimed at; a throw of this kind.

1863 *Tyneside Songs* 86 Harle shapes just like this when puttin on a ringer. **1886** *Encycl. Brit.* XX. 189/2 Such a success is termed a 'ringer', and two is scored.

3. *Mining.* **a.** A crow-bar.

1858 SIMMONDS *Dict. Trade*, *Ringer*, a miner's name for a crow bar. **1879** *Cheshire Sheaf* I. 322 (E.D.D.), *Ringer*, an iron or steel lever, usually about four feet long. **1883** GRESLEY *Gloss. Coal-mining*, *Ringer and Chain* (M.), see *Dog and Chain*. [An iron lever with a chain attached by which props are withdrawn from the goaf.]

b. 'A hammer for driving wedges' (Gresley).

4. A fox, etc., which runs in a ring when hunted. (Cf. RING *v.*[1] 1c.)

1891 *Field* 7 Mar. 331/2 That good sportsman .., among many foxes, has one or two long-distance runners in his coverts. However, on this occasion their place was taken by a brace of ringers.

5. a. *Austral.* and *N.Z.* (See quot. 1890.)

1871 'R. BOLDREWOOD' in *Cornh. Mag.* XXIII. 85 The 'Ringer', or fastest shearer of the whole assembly. **1888** —— *Robbery under Arms* I. ix. 110 Jim .. was trying to shear sheep and sheep with the 'ringer' of the shed. **1890** *Melbourne Argus* 20 Sept. 13/6 It is highly necessary to have a good 'ringer' at the head of the men; a 'ringer' being the man who .. shears the highest number of sheep per day. **1894** E. W. HORNUNG *Boss of Taroomba* vii, They call him the ringer of the shed, miss... That means the fastest shearer .. —the man who runs rings round the rest, eh? **1910** C. E. W. BEAN *On Wool Track* 196 The man who shears most sheep is the 'ringer'. **1927** M. M. BENNETT *Christison* xxii. 193 With the new shearing machines a hundred sheep a day were shorn easily, while ringers scored over two hundred. **1934** T. WOOD *Cobbers* 196 He can shear a hundred a day: a hundred and twenty, a hundred and fifty; two hundred—even three hundred and twenty, at times, if he is a Ringer—that is the quickest of the team. **1952** J. CLEARY *Sundowners* iii. 138 By the end of the day he wanted to be the 'ringer' shearer. **1963** N. HILLIARD *Piece of Land* 90 The ringer of the Maori shearing gang that year had been Keko. **1965** *N.Z. Listener* 26 Feb. 15/2 In shed shearing the position of 'Ringer' is sought after and competition among shearers has always been keen.

b. An expert. *Austral. slang.*

1918 C. J. DENNIS *Digger Smith* 112 *Ringer*, expert. **1923** 'B. L. STANDISH' *Lego Lamb, Southpaw* iii. 26 'That guy's a ringer,' declared Shultz. *c* **1926** 'MIXER' *Transport Workers' Song Bk.* 24 For I'm classed among the 'ringers', And from others stand apart. **1943** *Amer. Speech* XVIII. 256 With Americans a *ringer* is a double; here [*sc.* in Australia] he is an expert. **1965** *Telegraph* (Brisbane) 5 July 8 Ringer (the best —old shearing-shed term later adopted by townies).

6. One who rings birds.

1909 *Brit. Birds* III. 5 Any finder of a ring so marked should realise that communication with the 'ringer' is intended. **1946** *Ibid.* XXXIX. 260 The ringer probably keeps a sharper look-out for dead birds than the ordinary person. **1966** *Punch* 14 Dec. 897/3 Ringers try to recapture each bird in colonies of sea birds for an annual ring check, and quite often they catch the same bird each year for six years or more in their gardens. **1978** P. CONDER *RSPB Guide to Birdwatching* 103 In the early days when there were few ringers, most of the birds were recovered dead but as more ringers took part in the scheme.. so the numbers of live recoveries increased.

7. *Austral.* A stockman; a station hand.

1909 J. X. A. CAMERON *Spell of Bush* (1910) 48 Dam-sinkers, fencers, scrub-cutters, ringers, and other men doing contract work in the vicinity. **1942** C. BARRETT *On Wallaby* i. 14 'Jim the Ringer' came in every month for 'a bender'. **1953** 'N. SHUTE' *In Wet* x. 348 His camp consisted of.. a humpy shelter made of gum tree boughs for his white ringer, Phil Fleming. **1954** B. MILES *Stars my Blanket* xxiii. 204 The stockman—or 'ringer' as he is called—rides into the yard with a lasso and 'rings' his bullock in true wild-west style. **1964** *Sunday Mail Mag.* (Brisbane) 27 Sept. 3/1 A ringer.. is a Queensland stockman who holds his cattle during a muster by 'ringing' them on horse-back. **1977** *Telegraph* (Brisbane) 12 Jan. 3/1 The pub, local waterhole for stockmen, ringers and station hands.

8. *colloq.* An officer in an air force; a member of an air-crew. Also with preceding numeral, indicating rank.

The use is derived from the rings indicating rank worn on the sleeve of an officer.

1943 C. H. WARD-JACKSON *Piece of Cake* 51 Pilot Officer is a 'Half-ringer', and Squadron Leader a 'Two and a half ringer'. **1945** BAKER *Austral. Lang.* 163 *Ringer*, an officer. **1976** 'A. HALL' *Kobra Manifesto* v. 65 One of the air-crew, a two-ringer.

ringer[2] ('rɪŋə(r)). [f. RING *v.*[2] + -ER[1]. Cf. Da. *ringer*, Sw. *ringare*, Icel. *hringjari.*]

1. One who rings; *esp.* a bell- or change-ringer.

*c*1425 *Found. St. Bartholomew's* (E.E.T.S.) 5 The seker shall fynde, and the rynger or knokker shall entre. **1481–90** *Howard Househ. Bks.* (Roxb.) 126 Item, to the ryngers of seynt Tanlonys cherch iiij.d. **1531** *Test. Ebor.* (Surtees) VI. 24 In brede and aill to the ringers. **1582** STANYHURST *Æneis*, etc. (Arb.) 156 In thee chappel hee was.. such a lowd singer, in a thowsand not such a ringer. **1683** TRYON *Way to Health* 481 We have no need of those robustick Musitians, *viz.* Ringers, to call the People to worship. **1707** HEARNE *Collect.* (O.H.S.) II. 34 Dr. John Blackborne.. was formerly noted for a great Ringer. **1844** DICKENS *Mart. Chuz.* xlvi, The ringers were practising in a neighbouring church. **1859–64** TENNYSON *Grandmother* xv, The ringers rang with a will, and he gave the ringers a crown.

2. A mechanical device for ringing a bell.

1875 KNIGHT *Dict. Mech.* 1944/2 *Ringer*, a chiming or bell-ringing apparatus. *a*1890 *Electr. Rev.* XV. xvi. 3 (Cent.), A novel feature of this bell is that the ringer and gongs are inside of the case.

3. *U.S. slang.* A horse or other competitor fraudulently substituted for another in a race or other sporting activity; one who engages in a fraud of this kind.

1890 *Stock Grower & Farmer* 9 Aug. 8/2 At the same time 'Andy Croker' is the most notorious 'ringer' on the turf. **1914** 'HIGH JINKS, JR.' *Choice Slang* 17 *Ringer*, a name applied to a man or horse dishonestly entered in an event with others far below his class and a class in which he could not be entered legitimately. **1928** FOY & HARLOW *Clowning through Life* 188 We had scarcely made the match when we were given a secret tip that Bennett was a 'ringer'. **1935** A. J. POLLOCK *Underworld Speaks* 98/1 *Ringer*, a race horse who has been substituted under the name of another horse in a race. **1938** M. LANE *Edgar Wallace* III. v. 304 He was an attractive young man, known in his own profession as 'Ringer' Barrie for his ability to ring the changes of disguise on race-horses. **1944** *Fortune* Sept. 140/2 The chance that 'ringers'—good horses masquerading as poor ones under assumed names—can be sneaked into races. **1958** *Sun* (Baltimore) 15 Aug. 20/2 Evidence.. tends to show that it was not a horse called Bye Bye Will that won that race but a 'ringer'. **1966** *Listener* 27 Oct. 613/3 He rode third in a regimental steeplechase: the winning horse was later found to be a ringer. **1973** B. BROADFOOT *Ten Lost Years* xxi. 240 Some teams used to bring in ringers, a Yankee, or a guy from the East. **1980** *Times* 11 Mar. 6 The Crown claimed that the horse had been switched and that the winner was in fact a 'ringer', a more successful stablemate called Cobblers March.

4. *to be a* (*dead*) *ringer for* (or *of*): to resemble closely; to be an exact counterpart of. *slang* (orig. *U.S.*).

1891 *Sporting Times* (N.Y.) 4 July 10/4 Homan is a 'dead-ringer' for Anson. **1900** ADE *More Fables* 162 Bob.. was a Ringer for a United States Senator, all except the White Coat. **1903** 'O. HENRY' in *Ainslee's* Mar. 129/2 The man was a ringer for the pictures of the fat Weary Willie in the funny papers. **1916** J. BUCHAN *Greenmantle* xiii. 174 Now you're in these pretty clothes you're the dead ringer of the brightest kind of American engineer. **1946** *New Yorker* 16 Mar. 22/1 The Nissen hut.. which were [*sic*] dead ringers for the council lodges the Iroquois Indians used to build. **1954** WODEHOUSE in *Encounter* Nov. 43/2 We also felt like minor infusoria at the bottom of a well. 'Wodehouse,' I remember saying to myself more than once, 'Alter your appearance very slightly, and you would be a ringer for a waterbeetle.' **1959** *Punch* 21 Oct. 251/1 He [*sc.* a shark] has life pretty easy and apart from the gill-rakers is a ringer for Patrick Joseph. **1960** B. KEATON *My Wonderful World of Slapstick* 122 Going through the casting book we found a man and woman who were dead ringers for the Belgian rulers. **1970** 'T. COE' *Wax Apple* xii. 89 Doctor Fredric Cameron.. was an almost dead ringer for J. Roger Urbermann. **1973** C. SAGAN *Cosmic Connection* xiii. 92 There is little doubt that the average person's view of Hell—sizzling, choking, sulfurous, and red—is a dead ringer for the surface of Venus.

5. *U.S. slang.* An outsider or intruder; an imposter, *spec.* one who attaches himself to a political or other group to which he does not belong.

1896 ADE *Artie* xi. 100 About a dozen ringers followed us in and stood around rubberin'. **1904** *N.Y. Tribune* 18 Oct. 1 The members of the Manhattan & Democratic clubs occupied front seats. The press seats were largely occupied by ringers. *Ibid.* 8 Nov. 3 The Democratic leaders to-day started to send a lot of alleged 'ringers' across the line into West Virginia to vote to-morrow. **1926** *Clues* Nov. 162/1 *Ringer*, one who butts in on another's racket. **1928** *Manch. Guardian Weekly* 26 Oct. 335/2 Perhaps seventy-five were really newspaper men and women, the others being what the American language calls 'ringers', 'gate-crashers', or 'dead-heads'. **1940** WODEHOUSE *Eggs, Beans & Crumpets* 59 Too often, when you introduce a ringer into a gaggle of Pekes, there ensues a scrap like New Year's Eve in Madrid. **1963** S. GREER *Metropolitics* v. 104 We have omitted the 'ringer'; none of our respondents claimed to recognize the spurious name. **1965** M. BRADBURY *Stepping Westward* vii. 357 This is quite a party. I'm going to feel a real ringer. **1978** *Detroit Free Press* 2 Apr. (Detroit Suppl.) 8/1 Inside the lobby of the dilapidated building, Blow Dry scans the inhabitants, hoping.. that no one will spot her as the ringer. **1981** C. R. LAJEUNESSE *Dead Man Running* xi. 35 A ringer for you will be leaving your place, same car, same registration.

6. *slang.* A false registration plate attached to a stolen motor vehicle; a thief who uses these.

1962 *New Statesman* 21 Dec. 899/1 The driver stays with the car regardless, and the car is equipped with ringers (false number-plates). **1964** E. PARR *Grafters All* ii. 25 The car is now driven to a hideaway, where ringers (false number-plates) are substituted. **1970** P. LAURIE *Scotland Yard* iii. 69 All the ringer has to do is buy a [car] key, come along as innocent as pie, open the door and drive off to wherever he does his ringing. **1971** *Drive* Summer 21/2 When the professionals—the car 'ringers'—get to work, the profit on a skilfully doctored vehicle can be more than £500. **1971** *Road Ahead* (Brisbane) Sept. 18 In Britain, 'ringers' produce very special cars. 'Ringers' are experts in modifying stolen cars, giving them a new identity.

7. *ringer-up.* A person making a telephone call; = CALLER *sb.* 1 f. Cf. RING *v.*[2] 10 b.

1963 N. MARSH *Dead Water* (1964) v. 117 The ringer-up was Miss Cost. **1968** P. DICKINSON *Skin Deep* v. 104, I don't take on casual ringers-up. **1970** Y. CARTER *Mr. Campion's Falcon* xxii. 161 The lunatic fringe—the compulsive ringers-up.

Ringer[3] ('rɪŋə(r)). *Biol.* The name of Sydney *Ringer* (1834–1910), English physician, used *attrib.*, *absol.*, and in the possessive to denote physiological saline solutions of a type which he introduced and which usu. contain (in addition to sodium chloride) salts of potassium and calcium.

1893 *Jrnl. Physiol.* XIV. 200 Ringer's solution kept the heart beating vigorously for more than thirty hours. **1913** *Rep. Brit. Assoc. Adv. Sci. 1912* 660 A heart perfused with a Ringer solution without lime stops much earlier than when perfused with a Ringer solution without lime and without potassium. **1915** *Jrnl. Physiol.* L. 138 Isotonic Ringer or sodium chloride is not an indifferent fluid. **1932** W. BURRIDGE *Excitability* xxi. 173 We.. washed out the muscle with saline or Ringer. **1956** *Nature* 18 Feb. 340/1 Ringer solution was injected through the catheter into the sinus in order to show that no larger anastomoses still existed between the sinus and other veins. **1964** W. G. SMITH *Allergy & Tissue Metabolism* ii. 19 Schacter has demonstrated that Ringer perfused rabbit tissues release histamine in anaphylaxis. **1967** K. M. SMITH *Insect Virol.* v. 105 The sucrose is then removed by dialysis in a cellophane bag immersed in cold Ringer's solution. **1975** *Nature* 10 Jan. 99/2 When the Ringer was made sufficiently hypertonic so that twitch movement was essentially eliminated, the second component propagated throughout the fibre.

Comb. **1958** [see CENTRIFUGATION]. **1977** *Proc. R. Soc. Med.* LXX. 160/1 His blood pressure fell from 130/80 mm Hg before anaesthesia to 50 mm Hg during the operation, despite rapid injection of 2 litres of Ringer-lactate solution.

ringer, obs. form of WRINGER.

Ringerike ('rɪŋəri:kə). The name of a district centred on Honefoss north of Oslo in Norway used *attrib.* (after H. Shetelig *Norske Aarsberetning* (1909), 96–107) to designate a style of late Viking art, characterized by abundant use of plant motifs as ornament.

1924 A. F. MAJOR tr. *J. Brøndsted's Early Eng. Ornament* iii. 293 Shetelig has more recently dealt with these rune-stones; he christens them after the reddish sandstone, which is quarried at Ringerike in the south of Norway, the 'Ringerike Group' and their plant ornament the 'Ringerike style'. **1936** A. W. CLAPHAM *Romanesque Archit.* viii. 193 The decoration also includes a free use of interlacement, chevron-ornament, and a foliage of Ringerike or late Viking type. **1937** E. V. GORDON tr. *Shetelig & Falk's Scandinavian Archæol.* xvii. 303 In the Ringerike style the ancient animal ornament was thrust firmly into the background. **1952** D. T. RICE *Eng. Art 871–1100* v. 127 The new manner is known as the Ringerike style, and it is distinguished by the employment of a characteristic leaf ornament. **1970** FOOTE & WILSON *Viking Achievement* ix. 307 The style was directly succeeded by the Ringerike style, which first appeared early in the first quarter of the eleventh century. *Ibid.* 310 Ringerike elements were still appearing on Irish objects in the 1120s. **1973** *Times* 1 Nov. 4/5 A unique discovery is a wooden panel with decoration in the Ringerike style of the twelfth-century, with an animal design. **1976** D. VEREY *Cotswold Churches* ii. 18 At Bibury, the capital.. on the north [of the chancel arch] is in Ringerike style. Many motifs are Scandinavian.

ring-eye: see RING *sb.*[1] 19 and 19 b.

'ring-fence, *sb.* [RING *sb.*[1]] **a.** A fence completely enclosing an estate, farm, or piece of ground.

1769 *Bp. Wilton Inclosure Act* 15 The out-fence or ring-fence. **1778** [W. MARSHALL] *Minutes Agric.* 8 Jan. 1776, A thousand acres.. lying on a level, within a ring-fence. **1822** SCOTT *Peveril* xi, I may indeed have said your estates were born to be united; and to be sure it is natural for me.. to wish that it was all within the ring fence again. **1887** JESSOPP *Arcady* vii. 205 The mania for ring fences is not what it was.

attrib. **1778** [W. MARSHALL] *Minutes Agric.* 21 Dec. 1775, The advantages of a compact, ring-fence Farm.

b. *transf.* and *fig.* Also *attrib.*

1819 'R. RABELAIS' *Abeillard & Heloisa* 333 Three thousand pupils made ring-fence. **1847** ALB. SMITH *Chr. Tadpole* ii, The contracted existence in a country town.. is a sad padlock on the mind, keeping it in a terrible ring-fence. **1891** *Pall Mall G.* 23 June 2/2 Extending the 'ring-fence' policy of commercial relations. **1950** *Times* 8 Feb. 6/3 The decline is understood to be due mostly to the removal of the 'ring-fence' round the industry, that is, the provision of the Control of Engagement Order requiring miners to stay in coal-mining employment. **1965** *Economist* 6 Nov. 623/2 Imports into ECSC have not been held out by the tariff 'ring fence' erected after the last recession.

Hence **'ring-fence** *v. trans.*, to enclose with a ring-fence; also *fig.*; ***ring-fenced*** ppl. a.

1769 *Aclome Inclosure Act* 13 Tythe allotments to be ring-fenced. **1801** *Act 41 Geo. III*, c. 109 §13 To award, order, and direct any such Allotments to be laid together and ring-fenced. **1898** MAITLAND *Township & Borough* 191 In later documents I can not see any ring-fenced estate. **1903** R. FRY *Let.* 30 Jan. (1972) I. 203 B.B. should not have it said that he is capable of political scheming to ring-fence Italian art. **1974** *Northern Times* (Golspie, Sutherland) 2 Aug. 3/4 The proposal to ringfence Embo village was not acceptable for grant purposes.

'ring-finger. [RING *sb.*[1] So G., Da., Sw. *ringfinger*, Du. *-vinger.*] The third finger of the hand, especially of the left hand.

*c*1000 *Saxon Leechd.* I. 330 Nim æppel mid þinre wynstran handa, mid twam fingrum, þæt is mid þuman & mid hring fingre. *c*1050 *Voc.* in Wr.-Wülcker 264 *Anularis*, hringfinger.

1398 TREVISA *Barth. De P.R.* v. xxix. (Bodl. MS.), þe ferþe hat also annularis, þe ringe finger, for þereon þe ringe is ibore. *c*1440 *Alph. Tales* 33 Onone sho putt furth hur ryng-fynger & profird it to hym, & he putt on þe ryng. **1543** RECORDE *Arith.* 134 b, To expresse 8, you shall bow after the same maner both the lyttell fynger and the rynge fynger. **1597** A. M. tr. *Guillemeau's Fr. Chirurg.* p. xij b/2 The Medicinalle finger, or Ringe finger, betweene the little finger and the middle finger. **1644** BULWER *Chiron.* 82 If the Ring Finger by a single Action goe out of the open Hand. **1741** MONRO *Anat.* (ed. 3) 275 The Ring-finger is the third in Bigness. **1796** *Phil. Trans.* LXXXVII. 19 In a case where the last joint of the ring-finger had been torn off. **1831** R. KNOX *Cloquet's Anat.* 143 The middle finger is the longest; the index and ring-fingers follow next. **1877** W. JONES *Finger-ring* 526 In Somersetshire the ring-finger is thought to have the power of curing any sore or wound that is rubbed with it.

Hence †**ring-fingered** *a. Obs.*[−1]

1654 WHITLOCK *Zootomia* 431 St. James found, not to be χρυσοδακτύλιος Ring-finger'd, might want a Seale, or (as we now might say) might stand at a Pew doore.

ringhals ('rɪŋhɑ:ls). Also **rinkhals.** [ad. Afrikaans *rinkhals*, f. *ring* ring + *hals* neck.] A large venomous spitting cobra, *Hemachatus hæmachatus*, of the family Elapidæ, found in southern Africa, and distinguished by a white ring or two across the neck of an otherwise brown or black skin. Also *attrib.*

1793 tr. *C. P. Thunberg's Trav. Europe, Afr. & Asia* I. 208 A colonist had been bitten in the foot some time before by a serpent of the species called Ringhals (or Ring-neck). **1835** J. W. D. MOODIE *Ten Years S. Afr.* I. xv. 316 The puff-adder, the ring-hals, and the berg-adder, are very poisonous and very numerous. **1864** T. BAINES *Explor. S.-W. Afr.* xiv. 449, I think the species is called 'ring hals' (or ringed throat) in the Colony. **1906** *Westm. Gaz.* 16 Jan. 4/1 A Spurred Chameleon, a small Monitor, and a couple of Ring-hals snakes. **1925** *Other Lands* July 44/2 They pointed to the half-open door, where she saw uncoiling itself a large ringhals. **1931**, etc. [see COBRA]. **1939** S. CLOETE *Watch for Dawn* v. 62 With the bite of a mamba or a ringhals the heart sometimes beat even after life had gone. **1947** *Cape Argus* 29 Nov. (Mag. Section) 1/3 Cobras, like the ringhals and indeed all other snakes make for cover when they feel the approach of some intruder. **1956** A. G. MCRAE *Hill called Grazing* vi. 47 The six-foot-long Rinkhals cobra, reared above its coils, hood flattened and tiny, evil head weaving. **1972** L. VAN DER POST *Story like Wind* ix. 292 She.. saw, sitting upright on its tail, black as ebony and shining as with oil, a seven-foot rinkhals cobra.

ringie ('rɪŋɪ). *Austral. slang.* [f. RING *sb.*[1] + -IE.] The keeper of the ring in a game of TWO-UP.

1941 BAKER *Dict. Austral. Slang.* 65 *Ringie*, the keeper of a two-up school. **1949** *Strand Mag.* Dec. 100/1 The ringie takes care of operations inside the ring of side betters which gathers round the two protagonists. **1951** F. HARDY *Power without Glory* 323 Red Ted was 'Ringie'. He supervised the game in the ring itself, seeing that the pennies were spun fairly, and calling the results.

†**ringild.** *Obs.* Also **ringil-, ringel-, ryngel-, rynguyld, -gylld.** [a. Welsh *rhingyll.*] A sergeant or bailiff. Hence †**ringildry, ringildship**, the office of sergeant or bailiff. *Obs.*

1438 *Cal. Pat. Rolls* (1907) 194 With 'le ringilship' of Kemittemaigne. **1439** *Ibid.* 300 Le ryngelshipp. **1467–8** *Rolls of Parlt.* V. 594/1 The Offices of the Ringildshippes with profittez of the same. **1482** *Ibid.* VI. 204/2 Turnes of Shirrefs, Counties, Ringildries. *Ibid.* 206/1 Tournes of

Shireffs, Countiez, Rynguyldez. **1507** in *Archæol. Jrnl.* (1864) XXI. 80 That non of the tenauntes..be compelled..to..occupie the charge of Ryngylld.

ringing ('rɪŋɪŋ), *vbl. sb.*[1] [f. RING *v.*[1]]

1. a. The act of providing with a ring or rings; *spec.* the putting of a ring in the nose of a bull or a pig (cf. RING *v.*[1] 6), or of securing a numbered ring on a bird or a bat.

1483–4 *Durh. Acc. Rolls* (Surtees) 415 Pro le ryngyng unius paris rotarum. **1573** TUSSER *Husb.* xvi. 32 Yet surely ringing [of swine] is needefull and good. **1678** BUTLER *Hud.* III. ii. 307 As wise as Ringing of a Pig, That uses to break up ground and Dig. **1778** [W. MARSHALL] *Minutes Agric.* Digest 41 If [oxen are] ungovernable, reclaim them with nose-rings; the operation of ringing is very simple. **1851** H. STEPHENS *Bk. Farm* (ed. 2) II. 181/2 It is nothing uncommon to see the ringing of a bull delayed, until..he must be led by it for some particular purpose. **1910** *British Birds* III. p. iii, There is every indication that facts of the utmost interest and importance will be brought to light by the ringing of birds. **1953** LOCKLEY & RUSSELL *Bird-Ringing* i. 5 It was in 1899 that Herr Christian C. Mortensen laid the foundations of scientific bird-ringing when he placed his first aluminium rings, stamped with numbers, on the legs of young starlings. **1958** *Listener* 30 Oct. 684/2 For our first attempt at bat-ringing..my wife and I and a friend climbed up into the roof of a barn..where we knew there was a colony of bats. **1978** P. CONDER *RSPB Guide to Birdwatching* 101 The Protection of Birds Act 1967, prohibits ringing except under licence issued by the Nature Conservancy Council through the British Trust for Ornithology.

b. Ring-like ornamentation.

1885 H. O. FORBES *Wand. E. Archipelago* 203 The ringing on the arms, which the natives call bracelets.

†**2.** ? Playing at quoits. *Obs.*$^{-1}$

1621 BURTON *Anat. Mel.* II. ii. IV. 342 Many other sports and recreations there be, much in vse, as Ringing, Bowling, shooting... Riding of great horses, running at ring,..are the disports of greater men.

3. a. The operation or practice of cutting a ring of bark from a tree; girdling.

1817 *Hort. Soc. Trans.* II. 266 The fruit in consequence of ringing, or annular excision, becomes much larger. **1824** LOUDON *Encycl. Gard.* (ed. 2) 416 The effect of ringing has been perfectly well known..since Du Hamel's time. **1884** *Australasian* 8 Nov. 875/2 As the object is to kill the tree, ringing should be carried out when the sap is up.

b. (See quot.)

1832 *Planting* (L.U.K.) 7 *Ringing*, or placing an iron ring round a branch to prevent the annual increase of bark on the space occupied by the ring.

4. The action of cattle in forming a ring. Cf. RING *v.*[1] 1 d.

1868 C. W. BROWNE *Overlanding in Australia* 77 After an hour's amusement of this sort, they stop of their own accord. This evolution is termed 'ringing'. **1941** BAKER *Dict. Austral. Slang* 60 *Ringing*, the milling of cattle.

ringing ('rɪŋɪŋ), *vbl. sb.*[2] [f. RING *v.*[2]]

1. a. The act of causing a bell, etc., to sound.

[*c* **1315** SHOREHAM I. 186 Hali water, and haly bred, Li3t, and belryngynges.] *c* **1380** WYCLIF *Wks.* (1880) 212 To make solempnyte..wiþ dirige & messis & wax & rengynge. **1463** *Bury Wills* (Camden) 17 Y[e] Sexteyn of ye chirche to haue..xijd. for his rynggyng. **1548–9** (Mar.) *Bk. Com. Prayer, Offices* 31 The people beeyng called together by the ryngyng of a bel. **1580** HOLLYBAND *Treas. Fr. Tong, Glas*,.. the chyming or ringing for the dead, a knell. **1642** FULLER *Holy & Prof. St.* III. xiii. 184 Ringing oftentimes hath made good musick on the bells. **1702** ADDISON *Dial. Medals* iii. 145 The Touch..gives almost as good evidence as the Sight, and the Ringing of a Medal is..a very common experiment. **1713** STEELE *Englishm.* No. 50. 323 His Lordship proposes an annual ringing of Bells. **1836–7** DICKENS *Sk. Boz, Scenes* xiii, Let us take a peep 'behind', previous to the ringing-up. **1863** GEO. ELIOT *Romola* I. i, In all seasons there was the..ringing of pots and pans.

transf. *a* **1740** WATERLAND *Diss. Argt. A Priori* ii, The whole seems to amount to little more than the ringing of changes upon the word *necessity*.

b. ***ringing-in*** (see quots. and RING *v.*[2] 2 b, 7 c).

1854 MISS BAKER *Northampt. Gloss.* s.v., At the conclusion of chiming for church, during which several bells are used, a single one is rung to announce that the service is about to commence, and this is called ringing-in. **1891** A. GORDON *Folks o' Carglen* 41 The clang of this bell,..—the ringin'-in, as it is called—which warns me..to race with might and main to the door of the kirk.

c. ***ringing-up***, in senses 10 b, c of the verb.

1835 DICKENS *Sk. Boz* (1836) 1st Ser. II. 205 Let us take a peep 'behind' previous to the ringing up. **1924** GALSWORTHY *White Monkey* III. xiv. 316 He..closeted himself in the telephone booth... Ringing-up was quicker. **1949** N. MITFORD *Love in Cold Climate* I. v. 51 This ringing-up of Paris seemed to me a most dashing extravagance. Aunt Sadie..only made trunk calls in times of crisis.

2. a. The fact of a bell or the like giving forth a sound; the sound produced by a bell or bells, or by other bodies having similar properties.

1377 LANGL. *P. Pl.* B. v. 396 Sholde no ryngynge do me ryse, ar I were rype to dyne. *c* **1400** *Beryn* 1763 Ther no man is within, þe rynging to answere. *c* **1400** LYDG. *Chorle & Birde* 103 Ryngyng of feters is no mery sowne. *c* **1500** *Melusine* 125 And thanne bygan the ryngyng to be grete.. whan the tydynges of the socours..was knowen of all. **1581** PETTIE tr. *Guazzo's Civ. Conv.* I. (1586) 11 b, How much you differ from those who never heard the ringing of other belles than these heere. **1797** *Encycl. Brit.* (ed. 3) III. 153/2 This, by striking the bells alternately, [will] occasion a ringing. **1848** DICKENS *Dombey* lxii, There is a blithe and merry ringing, as of a little peal of marriage bells.

b. *Electronics.* The phenomenon of transient damped oscillation occurring in a circuit at its resonant frequency as a result of a sudden change in voltage level; also, in *Television*, the occurrence on the screen of black lines to the right of a white object, caused by transient oscillation in the video amplifier of the receiver.

1949 *Electronic Engin.* XXI. 207/2 If the attenuation of the high frequencies takes place too suddenly (i.e. sharp cut-off) then we get ringing. **1953** H. A. CHINN *Television Broadcasting* xvi. 640 A spurious peak or a sharp cutoff in the response-frequency characteristic..discloses itself in the resulting picture display as..repetitions of the original signal. This manifestation of 'ringing' of the video circuits can be detected by observation of vertical lines in the picture. **1961** *Times* 20 Nov. (Television Suppl.) p. xii/1 Gross defects are obvious to any viewer either by poor contrast, lack of definition, 'ringing', or unwanted interference. **1969** J. J. SPARKES *Transistor Switching* iv. 113 In practice the inductance in the emitter wire through which the drive current has to flow is likely to limit switching speed or cause 'ringing' in the output voltage. **1978** *Gramophone* Jan. 1336/2 There is no suggestion of overshoot or ringing, showing that the amplifier is extremely stable and has a good damping factor.

3. A sensation in the ears similar to that produced by the sound of bells, etc.

For the belief connected with this see quot. 1718.

1398 TREVISA *Barth. De P.R.* XVII. xii. (Bodl. MS.), Warmod..ido into þe eres destruyeþ ringinge and tingelinge þat is þerein. *c* **1425** *Found. St. Bartholomew's* (E.E.T.S.) 35 Sum man ioyed..that he hadde receyuyd remedie..from ryngyng of his erys. **1538** ELYOT *Tinnimentum*, a ryngyng in the eare of a man. **1563** HYLL *Art Garden.* (1593) 112 It dooth take awaye the ringing or sound of the eares. **1615** CROOKE *Body of Man* 591 The patient is vexed with ringings, singings, whistlings and hissing murmures in his Eares. **1661** LOVELL *Hist. Anim. & Min.* 21 It helpeth the ulcers of the eare. 2. or 3. drops help the ringing of the same. **1718** *Free-thinker* No 62. 46 A Ringing ..in the Ears..signified that Some One was talking of them in their Absence. **1843** R. J. GRAVES *Syst. Med.* xiv. 170 Ringing in ears continues.

4. *Comb.*, as **ringing day**, a day on which church-bells are appointed to be rung; **ringing engine**, a form of pile-driver, worked by men pulling at ropes after the manner of bell-ringers; **ringing floor, -loft**, the standing-place of bell-ringers; **ringing tone** *Teleph.*, the sound produced in a caller's telephone to indicate that connection has been made to another telephone and it is ringing.

1615–6 in Swayne *Sarum Churchw. Accts.* (1896) 165 Fower vsuall *Ringinge daies for the King. **1763** in Picton *Liverpool Munic. Rec.* (1886) II. 278 Ordered that four ringing days..be now paid at the expence of the Corporation. **1886** *Gloss. Rochdale, Ringing-day*, the fifth of November. **1860** J. HODGES *Gt. Victoria Bridge* 18 In drilling these in, a small *ringing-engine was used. **1884** *Building News* 15 Aug. 242/3 A ringing engine is of similar construction to that of a crab engine. **1874** MICKLETHWAITE *Mod. Par. Churches* 177 Some height above the *ringing-floor. **1620** in Swayne *Sarum Churchw. Acc.* (1896) 170 £3 towards the buildinge of the *Ringinge Lofte. **1848** RICKMAN *Styles Arch.* 153 They are not used in the bell-chamber, but in the ringing-loft to give air to the ringers. **1924** W. AITKEN *Automatic Telephone Syst.* III. lvi. 272 A portion of the ringing current also passes over the upper condenser,..and the caller receives the *ringing tone. **1943** G. GREENE *Ministry of Fear* I. v. 80 He dialled the number. .. He was almost afraid to hear the ringing tone. **1970** T. LEWIS *Jack's Return Home* 181 The ringing tone only went once before someone lifted the receiver.

ringing ('rɪŋɪŋ), *ppl. a.*[1] [f. RING *v.*[1]] Circling; running in rings or circles.

1883 *Daily News* 3 Jan. 6/4 The deer..gave a ringing run through Black Park..back towards the Heath. **1887** MISS BRADDON *Like & Unlike* iv, The fox was what Helen called 'a ringing brute'. **1903** *Longm. Mag.* Jan. 238 The ringing nature of the hare's course..bring[s] her..more into contact with the sportsman than in the case of the fox.

ringing ('rɪŋɪŋ), *ppl. a.*[2] [f. RING *v.*[2]]

1. Having or giving the sound of a bell, or of some metallic body; resounding, resonant.

13.. *E.E. Allit. P.* B. 1082 Rial ryngande rotes & þe reken fyþel. **1557** *Tottel's Misc.* (Arb.) 262 And if you want of ringing bels, When that my corps goth into graue. **1582** STANYHURST *Æneis* II. (Arb.) 47 Thee skyes lowd rumbled with ringing thunderus hurring. **1590** SPENSER *F.Q.* III. iii. 9 Loud strokes and ringing sowndes. **1700** BLACKMORE *Job* 125 The naked, blind, and lame Thro' ringing streets my bounty did proclaim. **1729** SHELVOCKE *Artillery* IV. 292 Tin ..loses its noisy or ringing Quality. **1810** SOUTHEY *Kehama* XVII. ii, Baly! great Baly! still The ringing walls and echoing towers proclaim. **1837** LYTTON *E. Maltravers* I. 42 Next came a most ringing laugh. **1872** YEATS *Tech. Hist. Comm.* 135 The vessels they moulded were baked in a fire, and had a hard ringing sound.

fig. **1602** F. HERING *Anat.* 17 The ringing Name and Fame of a great Phisition. **1870** *Standard* 5 Dec., Prince Frederick Charles has only to win one ringing victory to leave Paris face to face with a..desperate situation. **1890** *Spectator* 8 Mar., There is a ringing story yet to be told of the heroism of the Italians.

b. Of frost: Severe, so that the ground rings under the feet.

1824 MACTAGGART *Gallovid. Encycl.* 409 'Ringing Black Frost', a very severe frost. **1864** CARLYLE *Fredk. Gt.* XII. ii. (1872) IV. 140 Rain ending, there ensued a ringing frost.

c. = RATTLING *ppl. a.* 4.

1876 MEREDITH *Beauch. Career* xxxii, Cecilia's noble schooner was sure to be out in such a ringing breeze.

2. In spec. names, as **ringing bird, caterpillar, frog** (see quots.).

1700 DAMPIER *Voy.* III. II. 74 One sort of these pretty little Birds my Men call'd the Ringing-bird; because it had six Notes, and..repeated all his Notes twice one after another. **1724** DERHAM *Notes Albin's Eng. Insects* Index, Ringing Caterpillar [the chrysalis of which could make a glass ring like a bell]. **1802** KERR tr. *Buffon's Ovip., Quadr. & Serp.* II. 235 The Ringing Frog... The specific name is derived from its voice, which is clear, round, and ringing.

3. ringing boy, a boy employed at the Mint to ring coins in order to test their soundness.

1893 *Daily News* 9 June 5/4 In order to detect these defaulters a number of..ringing boys are employed.

Hence **'ringingly** *adv.*; **'ringingness**.

1859 CORNWALLIS *New World* I. 197 The wild denizens of the wilderness, who uttered their war-cry so ringingly in our ears. **1874** MISS HAVERGAL in *Mem.* (1880) 153 There was a ringingness in her touch, playing with such joyance. **1876** MEREDITH *Beauch. Career* III. iii. 39 He had leisure to think over the blow dealt him..so ringingly on the head.

ringle ('rɪŋg(ə)l), *sb.*[1] Now *dial.* Also α. 5 rengell, 6 ryngle, 7 ringel. β. 6 ringoll, 7 -ol. [f. RING *sb.*[1] + -LE 1: cf. G. (and Sw.) *ringel*. It is not clear whether the word was independently formed in Eng., or adopted from LG.]

1. A metal, esp. iron, ring; in mod. *dial.* chiefly one for a pig's nose or the harness of horses.

1481–90 *Howard Househ. Bks.* (Roxb.) 211 Item, for rengellys and hokys, vj. lb. ix.d. **1531** *MS. Acc. St. John's Hosp., Canterb.*, Paid for a ryngle to a cythe, j d. **1577–87** HOLINSHED *Chron.* IV. 846 Manie great ringles were fastened to the same tower for that purpose. **1597** A. M. tr. *Guillemeau's Fr. Chirurg.* c ij b/2 This pipe must have a little ringle, whereby we might hould faste the same. **1692** R. L'ESTRANGE *Josephus, Antiq.* III. vi. (1733) 63 Pins.., which with the Help of Cords that pass'd through the Ringles, bound the whole Frame together. **1705** *Lond. Gaz.* No. 4149/4 A bright grey Mare,..ringled behind with 3 Ringles. **1784** tr. *Beckford's Vathek* (1868) 26 The body-guard of eunuchs was detached to..prepare ringles for the lines to keep off the crowd. *a* **1825–** in dial. glossaries (E. Anglia, Kent, Sussex). **1855** *N. & Q.* 1st Ser. XII. 487/1 They inserted a staff through the 'ringle'..in the lid of the chest. **1892** *Auctioneer's Catal.* (Kent), Plough harness and ringles for 2 horses.

†**b.** A door-ring, used also as a knocker. *Obs.*

1639 HORN & ROB. *Gate Lang. Unl.* xlix. §540 Stand still in the entry..and then knock at the iron ringel. **1648** J. BEAUMONT *Psyche* VI. cxcviii, Through these pass'd Pity to a door of Jet, Whose wary ringle round was cloth'd in wool. **1707** *Clergym. Vade-mecum* 70 If the church-key cannot be had, 'tis sufficient that the clerk take hold of the ringle of the door.

2. An annular part; a circle.

The context of quot. 1653 makes it certain that the use of the word was suggested by *rigol* in Shaks. *2 Hen. IV.*

α. **1597** A. M. tr. *Guillemeau's Fr. Chirurg.* 26 b/1 The skinn of the third or fourth ringle of the throte. **1629** *Descr. S'hertogenbosh* 12 It is the biggest and fairest part, hauing in his ringle the great S. John's Church. **1660** S. FISHER *Rusticks Alarm* Wks. (1679) 152 Never did I read or see in so small a piece of work so many Ringles and Rounds as T.D. makes and runs in.

β. **1599** NASHE *Lenten Stuff* 58 The ringoll or ringed circle was compast and chalkt out, and the king of fishes.. conjured to appeare in the center of it. **1653** CODRINGTON in Lloyd *Marrow of Hist.* 2 The Crown is the onely object of all great Spirits, not considering what cares hang round about the ringols of it. **1654** —— tr. *Iustine* XXVIII. 367 He understood well enough the ringols in that envyed Crown, and the weight of it..by his labours and his dangers.

'ringle, *sb.*[2] *Sc.* [f. RINGLE *v.*[2]] A ringing or jingling sound.

1839 MOIR *Mansie Wauch* (ed. 2) xxii. 269 We observed, from the curious ringle, that one of the naig's fore-shoon was loose. **1894** LATTO *Tam. Bodkin* xxv, The ringle o' the crystal..was the signal for me.

'ringle, *v.*[1] Now *dial.* [f. RINGLE *sb.*[1] Du. *ringelen* and G. *ringeln* are used in the same senses.]

1. *trans.* = RING *v.*[1] 6. Hence **'ringling** *vbl. sb.*

1573 TUSSER *Husb.* (1878) 75 Ringle thy hog, or looke for a dog. **1575** TURBERV. *Venerie* 191 To see yong pigges well ringled when they are yong. **1580** TUSSER *Husb.* 18 b, Yet surely ringling is needeful and good. *c* **1700** KENNET in *MS. Lansd.* 1033, fol. 323 *To ringle Hogs, Kent*, to put iron rings in their noses. **1838** HOLLOWAY *Prov. Dict.*, *To ringle*, to put Ringles into the snouts of hogs. **1867** *Jrnl. R. Agric. Soc.* Ser. II. III. II. 533 They are then sold..to the larger farmers to 'shack' upon the barley or oat stubbles, while the 'swine well ringled' are put upon the wheat ones. **1887** in *Kent. Gloss.*

fig. **1596** NASHE *Saffron Walden* Ep. Ded., So to ringle a thorough hayre for rooting, that it shall neuer put foorth his snayles hornes againe.

†**2.** = RING *v.*[1] 7. *Obs.*

1676 *Lond. Gaz.* No. 1156/4 A bright bay Mare..; she hath some time been ringled. **1705** *Ibid.* No. 4149/4 A bright grey Mare,..ringled behind with 3 Ringles.

'ringle, *v.*[2] Now *dial.* [f. RING *v.*[2] + -LE 3. Cf. NFris. *ringeln*, Da. *ringle*, Norw. *ringla*, Icel. *hringla*.] *intr.* To ring or jingle.

a **1617** BAYNE *Lect.* (1634) 78 Wee ride the freest horse with a spurre,..that the ringling sound of it may excite him. **1643** G. WITHER *Campo-Musæ* 3 He..Comes not and ringles at the doore with feare; But knocks.

1819 RICH *Gall. Poems* 67 The Knives an' forks wad ringle. **1857** [see RINGLE-STRAW]. **1863** BARNES *Dorset Gloss.* s.v., I heard the glass ringle when the window wer a-broke. **1880** *W. Cornw. Gloss.* s.v., The bells are ringling all day long.

†**'ringle**, *v.*[3] *Obs.*$^{-0}$ (See quot.)

1648 HEXHAM II, *Ringen*, to Ringle, or to Wrestle.

'ring-lead, *v. rare.* [Back-formation from next.] *trans.* To conduct or manage as ringleader.

1617 tr. *Abp. Spalatro's Serm.* 34 And so, for that hee vseth no true Compasse, nor Carde, hee ringleads them all to wracke. **1828–32** in WEBSTER. **1901** *Westm. Gaz.* 19 Mar. 9/1 He has ring-led any form of joke, hoax, amusement, or sport that was going.

'ringleader. Also 6 ryngledre, -leder, ryng(e)leader; ringeleeder, -leader; ringleder, *Sc.* -leidar. [f. the phrase *to lead the ring*: see RING *sb.*¹ 10 b.]

1. One who takes a leading place or part among a body or number of persons whose character or conduct is reprehensible; *esp.* a leader, a chief instigator or organizer, of a mutiny, tumult, etc.

1503 *Lett. Rich. III & Hen. VII* (Rolls) I. 238, I dout not but..we shalbe able by good polici to distrii alle the captayns and ryngledres that be of yll and contrary mynde. **1535** COVERDALE *1 Macc.* ix. 61 Ionathas toke L. men of the countre (which were the ryngleders of them) & slewe them. **1579** W. WILKINSON *Confut. Fam. Love* 73 b, The chiefe ringleader of the Anabaptistes boasted of Reueilations. **1613** PURCHAS *Pilgrimage* IV. xi. (1614) 400 He allured the men of his owne countrey vnto him, who followed him as their Ring-leader to doe mischiefe. **1675** *Essex Papers* (Camden) I. 292 There is one Philpott a Haberdasher, who..hath bin yᵉ Principall Ringleader of these seditious people. **1719** DE FOE *Crusoe* I. (Globe) 271 The Boatswain, who was the principal Ringleader of the Mutiny. **1759** FRANKLIN *Ess.* Wks. 1840 III. 462 Becoming a promoter and ringleader of such an insult on that part of the government. **1806–7** J. BERESFORD *Miseries Hum. Life* (1826) IV. Introd., The conspiracy is so nicely balanced among them that I shall never be able to detect the ring-leader. **1867** J. HATTON *Tallants of Barton* iv, He had been the ring-leader in everything wicked for years.

fig. **1633** R. S. tr. *Drexelius' Nicetas* I. vii. §2. 55 The enticers to vice and ringleaders to wickednesse are the eyes.

†**2.** In good or neutral sense: A leader or head; a chief authority. *Obs.*

1548 UDALL, etc. *Erasm. Par. John* vii. 57 b, Among the ryngleaders of religion. **1549** COVERDALE, etc. *Erasm. Par. Ephes.* 8 b, Some he would haue to be chief, as Apostles, ryng leaders & autours of the Gospel preaching. **1581** J. BELL *Haddon's answ. Osor.* 81 b, There is greater cause rather to move us..who have lost so great and learned a ryngleader of learning. **1631** WEEVER *Anc. Funeral Mon.* 669 Garter is the principall King of Armes..and goeth first as the onely ring-leader of them all. **1638** A. READ *Chirurg.* xxiii. 169 Amongst the Ancients Galen shall bee the ring leader. **1668** CULPEPPER & COLE *Barthol. Anat.* Epist. ii. 376 Those famous men the Ring-leaders of this opinion.

fig. **1561** T. HOBY tr. *Castiglione's Courtyer* IV. (1577) T iij b, The life of the Prince is a lawe and ringleader of Citizens. **1588** CHURCHYARD *Spark of Friendship* C ij, As a man might say, friendship is a ring-leader to all happinesse.

Hence **'ringleadership**.

1884 J. PARKER *Apostolic Life* III. 126 The charges of pestilence, sedition, ringleadership, profanity, are only pure and simple lies.

'ringleading, *vbl. sb. rare*⁻¹. [Cf. prec.] Chief leadership.

1570 FOXE *A. & M.* (ed. 2) 1 The church of Rome..hath chalenged to it self the supreme title and ringleading of the whole uniuersal church on earth.

'ringleading, *ppl. a.* [Cf. RINGLEADER.] Acting as, holding the place of, ringleader(s).

1624 J. GEE *Hold fast* 38 The greater is the guiltinesse of their ringleading Masters. **1661** J. DAVIES *Civil Wars* 371 Take away the commissions of nine of the ringleading officers. *a* **1688** BUNYAN *Mr. Badman* (1905) 21 He used to be the Ringleading Sinner, or the Master of mischief among other children. **1768** LD. CAMDEN in Bancroft *Hist. U.S.* (1855) V. xxxv. 128 Boston is the ringleading province; and ..the punishment ought to be levelled there. **1796** STEDMAN *Surinam* I. 73 The ring-leading negroes were roasted alive by half dozens.

'ringled, *a. rare.* [f. RINGLE *sb.*¹] Ringed; provided with rings; marked by circular bands.

a **1593** MARLOWE *Hero & Leander* II. 143 A hot proud horse..Spits forth the ringled bit. **1899** *Shetl. News* 14 Oct. (E.D.D.), My blue an' rid ringl'd socks.

'ringle-eye. *Sc.* In form -ee, -e'e. [f. RINGLE *sb.*¹ Cf. Da. *ringøjet*, Norw. *ringøygd*, Icel. *hringeygur* adjs., and RINGED *a.* 3 (quot. 1513).] A wall-eye.

1826 GALT *Lairds* xxxix, Geordie Joug wi' his ringle-ee. **1885** STRATHESK *More Bits fr. Blinkbonny* i. 8 She's terrible sair pockmarkit, an' she has a ringle ee.

So **'ringle-eyed** *a.* (Also *north.*)

1724 RAMSAY *Tea-t. Misc.* (1733) I. 63 He's out-shin'd, inkneed and ringle-ey'd too. **1894** HESLOP *Northumb. Gloss.* s.v., The pupil of the eye in a dog, etc., that is ringle-eyed is surrounded by a whity ring. **1897** P. H. HUNTER *J. Armiger's Revenge* vi, Ane o' thae ringle-e'ed brutes that startle at a' the dibs an' straes on the road.

ringle-'jingle, *v. nonce-wd.* [f. RINGLE *v.*² + JINGLE *v.*] *intr.*. To write in verse.

1913 G. B. SHAW *Let.* 7 Feb. in *B. Shaw & Mrs. Campbell* (1952) 83, I never have to think of how to say anything in prose... Yet, when I want frightfully to ringle-jingle with words they wont come that way.

'ringless, *a.* [f. RING *sb.*¹ + -LESS.] Without a ring; destitute of rings.

1837 MACGILLIVRAY *Hist. Brit. Birds* I. 121 In general the common ringless Pheasant has the colours somewhat deeper than the ringed variety. **1872** S. MOSTYN *Perplexity* II. v. 97 My fingers were ringless. **1891** KIPLING *Light that Failed* v, The cool, temperate, ringless hands that he had taken between his own.

†**ringlestones.** *Obs.* The ring-plover.

a **1682** SIR T. BROWNE *Norf. Birds* Wks. (Bohn) III. 320 *Ringlestones*, a small white and black bird, like a wagtail.., common about Yarmouth sands.

ringle-straw. *dial.* [f. RINGLE *v.*²] (See quot.)

1857 C. B. ROBINSON *Gloss. to Best's Farm. Bks.* (Surtees) 185 *Windle-straw*, a grass..which, when shaken by the wind, has a peculiar whistling or ringling sound, whence one of its present names 'ringle-straw'.

ringlet ('rɪŋlɪt). [f. RING *sb.*¹ + -LET.]

1. A small ring made of metal or other material.

1555 W. WATREMAN *Fardle Facions* II. xi. 250 A Bullockes hide..so set rounde aboute on the bordre, or verge, with ringlettes of iron. **1725** POPE *Odyss.* VII. 117 The ringlets that command the door. **1726** *Ibid.* XXI. 76 Who first Ulysses' wondrous bow shall bend, And through twelve ringlets the fleet arrow send. **1795** BURKE *Regic. Peace* iv. Sel. Wks. 313 This deficiency is made up by strengthening the first ringlet of the chain. **1813** T. BUSBY *Lucretius* II. VI. 1255 Some things, as if by hooks and ringlets fixed, In junction hold. **1822–34** *Good's Study Med.* (ed. 4) I. 310 I have sometimes seen them made of very fine polished ivory, ..with a ringlet at the base.

2. A circular dance or course: a circle of dancers; a fairy-ring.

1590 SHAKS. *Mids. N.* II. i. 86 To dance our ringlets to the whistling Winde. **1627** DRAYTON *Quest Cynthia* 219 When Fayries in their Ringlets there Do daunce their nightly rounds. **1691** DRYDEN *K. Arthur* IV. i, The ringlets round her trunk declare her guilty Of many midnight-sabbaths revelled here. **1762** BEATTIE *Pigm. & Cranes* 212 They foot it featly, ranged in ringlets gay. **1793** COLERIDGE *Songs of Pixies* vi, Or through the mystic ringlets of the vale We flash our faery feet in gamesome prank. **1821** *Sporting Mag.* IX. 8 The numerous ringlets or circles on the downs, and on some pasture land.

b. An annular appearance, marking, formation, part, or piece.

1755 B. MARTIN *Mag. Arts & Sci.* 153 Now a small Ringlet appears; and this is more properly called a Central than a Total Eclipse of the Sun. **1796** MORSE *Amer. Geogr.* I. 220 Of a pale grey, sky-coloured ground, with brown undulatory ringlets. **1802** PALEY *Nat. Theol.* xix. §4 The ringlets of which the proboscis of the bee is composed. **1838** T. THOMSON *Chem. Org. Bodies* 1005 He stripped the bark off a tree in ringlets. **1845** BROWNING *Meeting at Night* i, The startled little waves that leap In fiery ringlets from their sleep.

3. A curled lock or tress of hair.

1667 MILTON *P.L.* IV. 306 Shee..Her unadorned golden tresses wore Dissheveld, but in wanton ringlets wav'd. **1702** POPE *Sappho* 83 No more my locks in ringlets curl'd diffuse The costly sweetness of Arabian dews. **1784** COWPER *Task* IV. 81 Teeth for the toothless, ringlets for the bald. **1837** LYTTON *E. Maltravers* I. viii, Maltravers smiled, and stroked those beautiful ringlets. **1873** SYMONDS *Grk. Poets* xii. 408 His rich hair ripples in ringlets between cheek and shoulder.

fig. **1633** MILTON *Arcades* 47 To nurse the Saplings tall, and curl the grove With Ringlets quaint. **1812** H. & J. SMITH *Rej. Addr.* VIII. xii, Break, Amphion, break your slumbers, Nature's ringlets deck the thorn.

attrib. and *Comb.* **1791–2** WORDSW. *Descriptive Sketches* 132 Lip-dewing song, and ringlet-tossing dance. **1855** M. ARNOLD *New Sirens* xxii, Come, bind up those ringlet showers! **1868** TENNYSON *Lucretius* 258 A truth That.. numbs the Fury's ringlet-snake.

4. *Ent.* The name given to one of the satyrid butterflies, *Hipparchia hyperanthus*. Also *attrib.*

Other species of *Hipparchia* are named ***marsh, mountain, Scotch, small ringlet***, etc.

1812 HAWORTH in *Trans. Entom. Soc.* I. 332 *Hero.* Papilio (silver-bordered Ringlet). *Mnemon*...(the small Ringlet). **1819** SAMOUELLE *Entomol. Compend.* 396 *Hipparchia Hyperanthus*, the Ringlet. **1879** LUBBOCK *Sci. Lect.* ii. 49 Hipparchia hyperanthus (the ringlet butterfly) also has whitish caterpillars.

ringleted ('rɪŋlɪtɪd), *a.* Also -letted. [f. prec. + -ED².]

1. Of the hair: Curled; worn in ringlets.

1837 HOOK *Jack Brag* ix, His hair assiduously ringletted on his cheeks and over his forehead. **1847** C. BRONTË *J. Eyre* iv, In thin muslin frocks and scarlet sashes, with hair elaborately ringleted.

2. Adorned with, wearing the hair in, ringlets.

1848 MRS. GASKELL *M. Barton* xii, A dashing, bronzed-looking, ringleted sailor. **1861** SALA *Badd. Peerage* xx. II. 44 Such was the individual who..addressed the ringleted [lady] clerk. **1894** A. DOBSON *18th C. Vignettes* Ser. II. x. 223 The ringletted heads and waistless figures..of 1789.

'ringlety, *a.* Also -letty. [f. as prec. + -Y.] Tending to curl in ringlets.

1858 MOTLEY *Corr.* I. 229 Smooth, white, shiny, ringlety hair. **1896** KEANE *Ethnol.* 176 [Hair] in the eastern Hamites and some others developing long ringletty curls.

'ringly, *a. rare.* [f. RINGLE *sb.*¹ + -Y.] Exhibiting rings of colour.

1800 *Trans. Soc. Arts* XVIII. 239 The roots were of the red and white ringly sort.

'ring-,man. [f. RING *sb.*¹]

1. The ring-finger. *Obs.* exc. *dial.*

1483 *Cath. Angl.* 309/1 þe Rynge man fyngur, *anularis, medicus.* **1545** ASCHAM *Toxoph.* (Arb.) 109 Whan a man shooteth, the might of his shoote lyethe on the formooste fynger, and on the Ringman. **1879** DICKINSON *Cumberld. Gloss.* Suppl., *Fingers*, the nursery names for these are, humpkin, lick pot, lang man, ring man.

2. A sporting man; a bookmaker.

1857 G. LAWRENCE *Guy Liv.* iv, The 'glorious uncertainty' which backers of horses execrate, and ring-men adore. *Ibid.* ix, Those purely country-meetings..where there are no ring men to force the betting. **1864** *Realm* 15 June 2 All the defaulting ring-men and unsuccessful pickpockets. **1868** E. YATES *Rock Ahead* I. vi, Heretofore he had lived almost entirely in the society of the Ring-men.

'ring-master. Also **ringmaster.** [f. RING *sb.*¹] One who manages or directs the performances in the ring of a circus. Also *transf.*

1873 FROST *Circus Life* Pref. 5 The stentorian vocal organs of the proprietor or ring-master of a travelling circus. **1883** *Century Mag.* July 419/2 An aged and tattered negro was the mule's ring-master. **1943** C. H. WARD-JACKSON *Piece of Cake* 51 *Ringmaster*, squadron commander. **1952** L. BELL *Inside Fight Game* iv. 73 A match maker can be, and often is, the promoter of a boxing show. His license also permits him to officiate as ringmaster. **1958** F. C. AVIS *Boxing Ref. Dict.* 95 *Ringmaster*, the official in charge of the arrangements at a boxing venue. **1972** *N.Y. Times* 4 June v. 9/6 James Fallon, the manager, and C. L. (Honey) Craven, the ringmaster, both expressed their pleasure with the new surface. 'The new ring makes things much easier for the rider,' said Fallon.

Hence as *v. trans.*; also **'ringmastership**, the art or status of a ringmaster; also *fig.*

1964 *New Statesman* 17 Apr. 616/1 To bring off this effect, *Caligula* needs producing as a kind of play-within-itself: a fantastic circus of cruelty ring-mastered by Caligula for a circle of witnesses as sane as he is. **1966** *Economist* 22 Oct. 378/2 That they did not do so during last week's conference was due in considerable measure to some masterly ringmastership on the part of the party chairman, Sir Dan Mason. **1969** P. WEST *Words for Deaf Daughter* iii. 72 Speeding up, you ringmaster him [*sc.* a budgerigar] through his full repertoire of forward rolls and swift, thudding vaults. **1969** *Daily Tel.* 6 Oct. 15/7 Most circuses get by without script-writers but this one had five, doubling up as clowns performing what they had written under the ringmastership of Ian McNaughton.

'ring-neck, *a.* and *sb.* [f. RING *sb.*¹]

A. *adj.* = RING-NECKED *a.*

1817 T. FORSTER *Nat. Hist. Swallow tribe* 94 *Anas Bernicla*, Ringneckgoose. **1848** CRAIG s.v. *Ring*, *Ring-neck pheasant*, the Phasianus torquatus of Temminck. **1867** LAYARD *Birds S. Africa* 167 *Corvus Albicollis*,..Ring-neck Crow. **1879** J. G. WOOD *Waterton's Wand. S. Amer.* 457 There are many species of Plover in Guiana. The most common are the Black-breasted.., the Ring-neck (*C. semipalmatus*), and the Sandy Plover. **1887** *Encycl. Brit.* XXII. 197/1 One [genus], *Sepedon hæmachates*, is named ..'Ring-Neck Snake', the latter name being, however, often applied also to the cobra. **1898** MORRIS *Austral Eng.* 390 The light-coloured band round the neck of the Ring-neck Parrakeet.

B. *sb.* **1. a.** A ring-necked plover or duck. Also, a ring-necked pheasant, etc.

1876 GOODE in *Smithson. Coll.* XIII. 10 Plover, ring-neck, surf-bird. **1890** in *Cent. Dict.* **1921**, **1965** [see MONGOLIAN *a.* 4].

b. *Austr.* = JACKAROO *sb.*

1898 MORRIS *Austral Eng.*, *Ring-neck*,..a term used in the back blocks in reference to the white collar not infrequently worn by a Jackaroo on his first appearance.

2. A neck with ring-like markings.

1895 CUMBERLAND *Sport Pamirs* 148, I found the cock exactly like the English pheasant, without the ring neck.

'ring-necked, *a.* [RING *sb.*¹] Having the neck ringed or marked with a band or bands of colour. In various names of birds and animals, as ***ring-necked barnacle, diver, duck, loon, parakeet, pheasant, pochard, snake, teal, turtle***. (See quots.)

1852 MACGILLIVRAY *Brit. Birds* IV. 629 *Bernicla Brenta*, ..*Ring-necked Barnacle. **1862** C. A. JOHNS *Brit. Birds* Index, *Ring-necked Diver. **1831** SWAINSON & RICHARDSON *Fauna Boreali-Amer.* II. 454 *Fuligula rufitorques*,..*Ring-necked Duck. **1874** J. W. LONG *Amer. Wildfowl* xxviii. 278 Ring-necked ducks..are seldom found in very large numbers. **1842** MACGILLIVRAY *Brit. Ornith.* II. 207 *Colymbus glacialis*, *Ring-necked Loon. **1845** STOCQUELER *Handbk. Brit. India* (1854) 213 A grove of mango-trees,.. peopled with innumerable *ring-necked paroquets. **1885** NEWTON in *Encycl. Brit.* XVIII. 322/1 *note*, The Ring-necked Parakeet of the same country [Africa]. **1834** JARDINE *Ornith.* III. 189 The *Ring-necked Pheasant, *Phasianus torquatus.* **1885** NEWTON in *Encycl. Brit.* XVIII. 733/1 The Ring-necked Pheasant of China. **1838** EYTON *Anatidæ* 158 *Fuligula rufitorques*,..*Ring-necked Pochard. **1840** *Cuvier's Anim. Kingd.* 283 One only [is found] in Britain, the common *Ring-necked Snake (*C. natrix* and *Natrix torquatus*). **1889** SCLATER & HUDSON *Argentine Ornith.* II. 132 *Querquedula Torquata*..(*Ring-necked Teal). *Ibid.*, In the neighbourhood of Buenos Ayres the Ring-necked Teal is strictly migratory. **1837** MACGILLIVRAY *Brit. Birds* I. 291 *Columba Turtur*,..*Ring-necked Turtle.

'ring-net, *sb.* [f. RING *sb.*¹]

†**1.** A coat of ring-mail. *Obs.*

Beowulf 1890 Hring-net bæron, locene leoðo-syrcan.

2. a. A form of salmon-net (see quot. 1830).

1505 *Berwick Reg.* in *Hist. MSS. Comm.*, *Varr. Collect.* I. 12 That no mane exsept he be a fre burges..shall not fish upone Twede for no salmond with longe net, short net, nor reynge net. **1830** WEDDELL in *Archæol. Æliana* (1855) IV. 302 Our present modes of fishing..are by stell nets, wear-shot, and ring or bob nets. *Ibid.* 303 The ring or bob-net is a long net without any bosom (which the other nets have).

b. A form of long seine-net which is supported at the ends by separate boats, one of which moves in a circular path towards the other in order to trap the fish within the net, used esp. in the Scottish fishing grounds to catch herring.

1949 MITCHISON & MACINTOSH *Men & Herring* 21 A ring net is about a hundred fathoms long and twenty fathoms deep and mostly set so that the back rope with the corks is almost on the top of the water. **1950** P. F. ANSON *Scots Fisherfolk* vii. 80 Ring-nets have always been the favourite gear employed on the Firth of Clyde and Loch Fyne. **1969** D. B. THOMSON *Seine Net* vii. 131 Most of these [boats] are dual-purpose seine net and ring-net boats... They have a low rail and large fish hold hatch to suit the ring net operation. **1978** M. GRAY *Fishing Industries of Scotland, 1790–1914* vi. 122 With fish from ring-net boats the transports could be in Glasgow by early in the day although the supply from the drift-net boats, slower to unload, would not arrive till later in the day.

3. A variety of lace.

1901 *Westm. Gaz.* 12 Dec. 3/1 The favourite nets for these are point d'esprit and Chantilly ring net.

So (in sense 2 b) **'ring-net** *v. trans.*; hence **'ring-netter**, a fishing boat intended for use with ring-nets; **'ring-netting** *vbl. sb.*

1936 *Discovery* Dec. 388/1 Scottish West Coast fishermen in Loch Fyne.. were engaged in ring-netting herring. **1952** G. MAXWELL *Harpoon at Venture* ii. 47 The Mansons.. brought the first new ring-netter to Mallaig after the war. **1960** WILLIAMSON & BOYD *St. Kilda Summer* i. 23 Cunningham had sent his ring-netter, *A' Mhaighdean Hearrach*, to take us off. **1969** D. B. THOMSON *Seine Net* vii. 131 The mast is stepped so it can be lowered when the vessel is engaged in ring netting. **1978** M. GRAY *Fishing Industries of Scotland, 1790–1914* vi. 120 In the 1830s the drift-net fishermen found, or felt, themselves threatened by a rival body—the fishermen who adopted the technique variously described as 'trawl-', 'seine-' or 'ring-netting'. As a description, 'ring-netting' is probably the most accurate term. In this new form of fishing.. two boats operated together, holding the different ends of a net some 150 yards in length; the net was cast as one boat moved from a starting-point near its partner, to form a wide circle as it returned to the original point, and the haul was completed by gradually constricting the circle till the fish were in a concentrated mass ready to be hauled aboard. *Ibid.* 121 It was possible.. for ring-netters also to carry drift-nets which they would shoot on occasion.

† **ringo**, obs. variant of ERYNGO.

1599, **1681** [see ERYNGO]. **1688** HOLME *Armoury* III. 80/1 Conserves of.. Pears, Apricocks, Plums, Ringo roots. **1750** ELLIS *Mod. Husb.* V. iii. 120 Ringo-roots sliced.

ringoal ('rɪŋgəʊl). Also **ring-goal**. [f. RING *sb.*[1]] A game in which a light ring or hoop is thrown towards a goal by means of two sticks.

1887 *Pall Mall G.* 19 July 3/1 A new game, called rin-goal, is coming into favour this summer... It originated in India. **1894** E. F. BENSON *Dodo* 302 The thump of tennis balls, the flying horrors of ring-goal.

ringocandy. *nonce-wd.* [? f. RINGO var. ERYNGO or RING *sb.*[1] + *o'* (= of) + CANDY *sb.*[1]] Some kind of confection.

1922 JOYCE *Ulysses* 199 Hot herringpies, green mugs of sack, honeysauces, sugar of roses, marchpane, gooseberried pigeons, ringocandies.

ringol(l, obs. forms of RINGLE *sb.*[1]

† **rin-goose.** *rare*$^{-1}$. Some kind of goose.

1639 SIR R. GORDON *Hist. Earls Sutherland* 3 In all this province ther is great store of.. widgeon, teale, wildgouse, rin gouse,.. and all other kinds of wildfowl.

ring-ouzel. [f. RING *sb.*[1]] A bird (*Turdus torquatus*, closely allied to the blackbird) having a white ring or bar on the breast. (Cf. OUZEL 1 b.)

1674 RAY *Coll. Words, Eng. Birds* 86 The Ring Ouzell, *Merula torquata.* **1676** LISTER in Ray *Corr.* (1848) 125 As to that question of a Heath-throstle, I find that the Ring-ouzle is so called with us in Craven. **1752** HILL *Hist. Anim.* 493 The black Turdus, with a white ring, the ring Ouzel. **1768** PENNANT *Brit. Zool.* I. 229 The ring-ouzel inhabits the mountainous parts of these islands. **1845** *New Statist. Acc. Scot.* XIV. 189 The ring-ouzel is sometimes and the water-ouzel frequently met with. **1871** DARWIN *Desc. Man* II. xv. (1890) 455 The.. female ring-ouzel (*T. torquatus*) differs less, and the female common thrush (*T. musicus*) hardly at all from their respective males.

'ring-road. [f. RING *sb.*[1] + ROAD *sb.*] A by-pass road encircling a town or urban area.

1928 *Daily Express* 27 Aug. 8/6 London has no form, no symmetry. I suggest that we could give her this by cutting a broad ring-road through the old nineteenth century suburbs. **1933** L. P. ABERCROMBIE *Town & Country Planning* iv. 144 The external Ring road has been frequently made to avoid the destructive widening of an old village. **1942** *Country Life* 9 Oct. 692/3 Among recommendations are.. removal of markets from the central areas to positions on the ring road. **1943** FORSHAW & ABERCROMBIE *County of London Plan* iv. 53 We are strongly of the opinion that a relatively fast traffic ring-road is essential. **1952** *Ann. Reg. 1951* 402 The system of arterial ring-roads was abandoned, largely on grounds of cost. **1956** *Sun* (Baltimore) 17 July 12/2 Mr. McVoy establishes a priority system in which the first need is the ring road around the inner city. **1963** *Times* 22 Feb. 5/2 A ring road will surround the new centre and a recently built open market is to be doubled. **1971** *Country Life* 3 June 1377/1, I knew a priest in Tirana who fought the City Council over a plan to drive a ring-road through his church. **1981** B. HINES *Looks & Smiles* 31 They.. caught a bus out to the Ring Road where a Trading Estate was being developed.

† **ring-root**, for *ringo-root*: see ERYNGO.

1684 O'FLAHERTY *West Connaught* (1846) 66 Samphire grows in plenty, ring-root or Sea-holy, and Sea Cabbage.

ring'roundabout, *v. nonce-wd.* [RING *v.*[1]] *trans.* To surround.

1922 JOYCE *Ulysses* 189 The faithful hermetists.. ring-roundabout him.

ringside ('rɪŋsaɪd). Also **ring side, ring-side.** [f. RING *sb.*[1] + SIDE *sb.*[1]] **a.** The area immediately surrounding a boxing ring or other sports arena; more generally, the area which accommodates spectators; the scene of a sporting activity. Also *transf.*

1866 *Sat. Rev.* 24 Feb. 232/1 He was.. quite at home at the ringside in a prize-fight. **1896** DOYLE *Rodney Stone* 12 [Prize fighting] fostered ringside ruffianism. **1926** [see BARRERA]. **1930** [see HOOK-UP]. **1956** B. HOLIDAY *Lady sings Blues* (1973) xix. 159 There at the ring-side was Mrs. Helen Hironimus, the Alderson warden. **1965** *Universe* 15 Oct. 12/4 (*heading*) My conversations at the ringside. **1976** [see OPENING *ppl. a.* 1 b].

b. *attrib.* and *Comb.*, as ***ringside judge, table***; **ringside seat**, a seat immediately adjacent to a boxing contest or other sporting activity; also *transf.* and *fig.*

1976 *Scotsman* 15 Dec., The ringside judges may score it a clear victory for Kohl, leader of the Christian Democrats. **1932** *Daily Express* 20 Sept. 19/5, I trust my health will be good when he makes his debut. I want to be in a ringside seat. **1934** WODEHOUSE *Right Ho, Jeeves* xvii. 212 From the fact that he spoke as if he had a hot potato in his mouth without getting the raspberry from the lads in the ringside seats, I deduced that he must be the head master. **1940** *War Illustr.* 19 Jan. 638/3 From our 'ring-side' seats in the air, we saw a spectacle which made us heartily glad it was not our duty to attack a British warship! **1947** G. GREENE *19 Stories* 75 Like a bull he was on show, sitting there mournfully in the plaza with his dog, a magnificent spectacle for which we all had ring-side seats. **1975** V. CANNING *Kingsford Mark* viii. 140 Carlo found the rifle... Unseen, he would have a ringside seat. **1929** D. RUNYON in *Cosmopolitan* July 59/1, I see Waldo Winchester, the scribe, sitting at a ringside table all by himself.

Hence **'ringsider**, one who occupies a position at a ringside; a spectator.

1898 A. M. BINSTEAD *Pink 'Un & Pelican* iv. 87 Old Jack Baldock, always the noisiest of ringsiders, was howling at the Fulham lad. **1954** C. L. B. HUBBARD *Compl. Dog Breeders' Man.* 202 A woman exhibitor can handle her dog well, feel comfortable, and please the ringsiders.. by wearing a simple but practical outfit. **1960** *Times* 28 Sept. 16/6 With money at stake among some ringsiders, not everyone was thinking calmly. **1976** J. SNOW *Cricket Rebel* 113 He spooned a simple catch from a stroke ringsiders described as a 'protective jab'.

'ringster. [f. RING *sb.*[1] 11 b + -STER.] **1.** *U.S.* A member of a political ring.

1875 *Chicago Tribune* 15 Dec. 4/1 The support secured for Mayor Cobb was sufficient.. to defeat the unholy alliance of ringsters and politicians by which Boardman's nomination was first obtained. **1881** *Philadelphia Rec.* No. 3428. 2 It seems to be folly to try to break the ranks of the ringsters at Harrisburg who oppose the consideration of the Tax bill. **1888** BRYCE *Amer. Commw.* III. lxiii. II. 461 The attachment of the ringster is usually given wholly to the concrete party. **1908** *Nation* 16 Apr. 344/3 Hereafter the word [grafter] cannot be lightly used as a synonym for any malefactor at the head of a corporation, or any political ringster.

2. *U.S.* A member of a price-ring. Cf. RING *sb.*[1] 11 a.

1878 *Congress. Rec.* 20 Mar. 1915/1 As the honest contractor will not go into a business where he has to evade the law, the ringster has it all his own way. **1879** *Harper's Mag.* Oct. 717 The inopportune arrival of several cargoes of Texan beef broke the ring and ruined the ringsters. **1904** I. M. TARBELL *Hist. Standard Oil Co.* I. 107 'Deserters', 'ringsters', 'monopolists' were the terms applied.

3. A boxer.

1926 G. CARPENTIER *Art of Boxing* 5 Some 'ringsters'—I use this word in a particular sense, as you will see—have severely battered countenances after a career of a few years as pugilists. **1965** *Eng. Stud.* XLVI. 465 A boxer, among scores of other appellations, may be.. a *ringster*.

ring-straked ('rɪŋstreɪkt), *a.* Also 9 **-streaked.** [f. RING *sb.*[1]] Having bands of colour round the body. Also *transf.* and *fig.*

Quot. 1611 appears to be the source from which all later usage is derived.

1611 BIBLE *Gen.* xxx. 35 He remoued that day the hee goates that were ring-straked, and spotted. **1650** BULWER *Anthropomet.* 253 The same way that Jacobs Cattle became speckled, spotted and ring-straked. **1791** COWPER *Iliad* XII. 210 As wasps ring-straked, or bees that build. **1861** LOWELL *Biglow P.* Ser. II. Poems (1884) 293/1 A spotteder, ring-streakeder child the' warn't in Uncle Sam's holl farm. *a* **1865** in R. Hunt *Rom. West Eng.* (1871) 393 All 'this wilful waste' of long cloth scarlet, ringstraked, and speckled, is to do honour to King Christmas. **1891** T. HARDY *Tess* (1900) 49/1 Commanding like a monarch his flocks and his herds, his spotted and his ring-straked.

'ringtail, 'ring-tail. [f. RING *sb.*[1]]

1. *Ornith.* **a.** The female of the hen-harrier. (Formerly regarded by many as a distinct species.)

1538 ELYOT *Dict.*, *Pygargus*.. is also a byrde lyke to a hawke, hauynge a whyte tayle: I suppose hym to be that which we call a rynge tayle. **1575** TURBERV. *Falconrie* 55 There are two foules, wherof the one is called (*Ian le blancke*) which I take to be the Harrohen or capped Kyte, and the other (*Blanch queue*) the ring tayle. **1609** BIBLE (Douay) *Deut.* xiv. 13 The osprey, the ringtaile, and the vulture. **1661** WEBSTER & ROWLEY *Thrac. Wonder* v. ii, Besides, what falcon but dares venture upon a ringtail? **1678** RAY *Willughby's Ornith.* 72 Of the Ring-tail, the Male whereof is called the Henharrier. **1768** PENNANT *Brit. Zool.* (1776) I. 194 The ringtail weighs sixteen ounces. **1794** HUTCHINSON *Hist. Cumbld.* I. 5/2, I have never seen two ringtails attend the same nest, and I.. invariably found each nest frequented by the henharrier and ringtail. **1808** MONTAGU in *Linnæan Trans.* IX. 185 The new feathers.. clearly evinced the smallest bird to be a Hen Harrier, and the larger a Ringtail. **1880** NEWTON in *Encycl. Brit.* XI. 492/1 It was not until after Montagu's observations were published.. that the 'Ringtail'.. was generally admitted to be the female of the 'Hen-Harrier'.

fig. **1611** BEAUM. & FL. *Philaster* v. iv, Thou Royal Ring-tail, fit to fly at nothing But poor mens Poultry.

attrib. **1743** G. EDWARDS *Nat. Hist. Birds* pl. 107 Ring-tail Hawk. **1784** PENNANT *Arct. Zool.* (1792) I. 243 Ring-tail Falcon.

b. The golden eagle before its third year. Usually ***ring-tail eagle***.

1776 PENNANT *Brit. Zool.* Index, Ring-tail, or black eagle. **1813** WILSON *Amer. Ornith.* VII. 14 The Ring-tail Eagle is characterized by all as a generous spirited and docile bird. **1828** FLEMING *Brit. Anim.* 53 In the opinion of some, the ringtail is considered as a distinct species; but the facts.. demonstrate its connection with the Golden Eagle. **1838** *Penny Cycl.* X. 173/1 Many other authors mention the eagle and ring-tails in such terms as to leave the identity of the bird almost unquestionable.

c. ***ring-tail pigeon*** (see quot.).

1865 *Chambers's Encycl.* VII. 534/1 The Ring-tail Pigeon (*Columba Caribbea*) may be mentioned as a West Indian species, much valued for the.. delicacy of its flesh.

2. *Zool.* = RING-TAILED *a.* 2 and 3. Also *absol.*

1771 PENNANT *Syn. Quad.* 137 Maucauco,.. Ring-tail. Tail.. marked with numbers of regular rings of black and white. **1852** J. WEST *Hist. Tasmania* I. 324 The Ringtail opossum (*Phalangista* or *Hepoona Cookii*. Desm.) is smaller, less common, and less sought after. *Ibid.*, Dogs will not eat the flesh of the Ringtail even when roasted.

3. *Naut.* (See quots.)

1769 FALCONER *Dict. Marine* (1780), *Ring-tail*, a small triangular sail, extended on a little mast, which is occasionally erected for that purpose on the top of a ship's stern... *Ring-tail* is also a name given to a sort of studding-sail, hoisted beyond the after-edge or skirt of those main-sails which are extended by a boom and gaff. **1804** DUNCAN *Mar. Chron.* Pref. p. xii, The studding-sails, drivers, ring-tails, and all those sails which are set occasionally. **1846** A. YOUNG *Naut. Dict.*, *Ring-Tail*, a small sail shaped like a jib, set occasionally in light winds; it is hoisted on the outer end of the main or spanker gaff. **1873** 'VANDERDECKEN' *Yachts & Yachting* 185 A racing cutter will be fitted with four gaff-topsails, viz., a jib-headed or ring-tail topsail that is set without a yard. **1901** S. H. KING *Dog-Watches* 59 The Victoria, had a throat and peak mainsail instead of the mutton-leg mainsail and ringtail gaff topsail of the Excelsior. **1934** [see JAMIE GREEN].

b. *attrib.* with ***boom, sail***, etc.

1794 *Rigging & Seamanship* 83 Abaft the after leech of the main-sail, in calm weather, is hoisted a ring-tail-sail. *Ibid.* 162 The Ringtail-boom is a small boom projecting from the stern of some vessels to spread the foot of the ringtail-sail. **1840** R. H. DANA *Bef. Mast* vi, He was going aloft to fit a strap round the main-topmast head, for ringtail halyards. **1846** A. YOUNG *Naut. Dict.* s.v., Extended on a boom called the ringtail boom.

4. (Written **ring tail.**) A dog's tail which is curled so as to form nearly a complete circle.

1872 'IDSTONE' *Dog* x. 87 The tail should be of a moderate length,.. not curved over the back, not carried low, nor curved at the end like what in Bulldogs is called a 'ring tail'. **1961** J. LANNING *Great Danes* viii. 73 Ring tails are a hereditary fault and were common at one time.

5. *U.S. slang.* A worthless person, a hobo.

1926 *Amer. Speech* I. 652/2 *Ring-tail*, a Hobo who is carrying a 'grouch'. **1931** 'D. STIFF' *Milk & Honey Route* 205 He [*sc.* an unpopular fellow] is also a *ring tail*. Such hobos are often under suspicion. **1935** A. J. POLLOCK *Underworld Speaks* 98/1 *Ring tail*, an ignorant, loud mouthed, vulgar person. **1947** *Amer. Speech* XXII. 214 In the Pacific Theater.. the sobriquets applied to the Japanese were particularly hateful, as *ringtails, yellow bastards*, and a host of unprintables.

6. *Austral. slang.* (See quots.)

1941 BAKER *Dict. Austral. Slang* 60 *Ringtail*, a coward. **1943** *Amer. Speech* XVIII. 256 With Americans a *ringtail* is a grouchy person; with Australians he is a coward.

7. *attrib.*, as ***ringtail roarer, snorter***, etc., = RING-TAILED *a.* 4.

1832 J. K. PAULDING *Westward Ho!* I. xiv. 124, I got tired of making fun of the ringtail roarer. **1859** *Oregon Argus* 10 Dec. 1/1 Here lies James D. Porter, Who lived as he hadn't orter, But as a Methodist exhorter Was a regular ring-tail snorter. **1862** J. R. LOWELL *Biglow Papers* 2nd Ser. 25 My eldes' boy's so took up, wut with the Ringtail Rangers An' settin' in the Jestice-Court for welcomin' o' strangers.

'ring-tailed, *a.* [Cf. prec.]

1. *Ornith.* (See RING-TAIL 1, 1 b, and 1 c.)

1725 H. SLOANE *Nat. Hist. Jamaica* II. 302 The Ring-Tail'd Pigeon. **1809** SHAW *Gen. Zool.* VII. I. 71 Ring-tailed Eagle. **1815** *Sporting Mag.* XLV. 96 A very superb ring-tailed eagle was shot. **1840** MACGILLIVRAY *Brit. Birds* III. 366 *Circus Cyaneus*, the Ring-Tailed Harrier. **1893** NEWTON *Dict. Birds* I. 177 In the young the tail is white at the base, whence in this stage it has been often called the Ring-tailed Eagle.

2. *Zool.* Having the tail ringed with alternating colours. (Cf. RINGTAIL 2.)

1729 *Dampier's Voyages* III. 423 The Ring-tail'd Snake. **1785** SMELLIE *Buffon's Nat. Hist.* (1791) VII. 224 The mococo, or maucauco, commonly known by the name of the ring-tailed maki. **1840** *Cuvier's Anim. Kingd.* 63 The Macaco of Buffon, or the Ring-tailed Lemur (*L. catta*, Lin.), which is ash-grey, the tail annulated black and white. **1877** *Nature* XV. 286/1 Two Ring-tailed Lemurs (*Lemur catta*) from Madagascar, purchased.

3. *Zool.* Having the tail curled at the end, *spec.* applied to certain phalangers. Cf. RINGTAIL, RING-TAIL 4.

1835 *Penny Cycl.* III. 128/1 These animals [phalangers], called ring-tailed opossums by the colonists. **1847** LEICHHARDT *Jrnl.* v. 46 The Black-fellows told us, that they had caught a ring-tailed opossum. **1885** *Encycl. Brit.* XVIII. 728/2 There are about four species of this genus known, of which the commonest is Cook's Ring-tailed Phalanger. **1894** R. B. LEE *Hist. & Descr. Mod. Dogs (Non-Sporting Division)* ix. 239 The tail should be..not curved upwards at the end, called 'ring tailed'.

4. ***ring-tailed roarer***, a fanciful name for an imaginary animal; also applied to persons. Similarly in other fanciful collocations, applied to persons and things, as ***ring-tailed snorter, squealer***, etc. *U.S.*

1830 *Painesville* (Ohio) *Tel.* 15 June 1/5 *Ringtailed Roarers*, a most violent fellow, a Crockett. **1836** *Crockett's Yaller Flower Almanac* 9, I am a raal ringtailed roarer. **1837** R. M. BIRD *Nick of Woods* I. iii. 56 Stranger, my name's Ralph Stackpole, and I'm a ring-tailed squealer! **1854** P. B. ST. JOHN *Amy Moss* 268 'By the rasping ring-tailed roarer of Kentucky, that's good,' said Ezram. **1872** DE VERE *Americanisms* 224 A specially fine fellow of great size and strength is called a ring-tailed roarer. **1944** B. A. BOTKIN *Treas. Amer. Folklore* I. 175 The ring-tailed roarer is a comic version of the frontiersman who wrestles single-handed with the wilderness. **1947** *Chicago Tribune* 2 Nov. IV. 9/2 The 'ring-tailed Roarers' of the pioneer days shout their raucous delight, unsubtle, earthy, outlandish, direct. **1950** *Ithaca* (N.Y.) *Jrnl.* 1 Aug. 6/2 You'll have to hand it to this ..secretary of agriculture... He's a ring-tailed snorter. **1972** J. MOSHER *Adultery* IV. xxiii. 190 Listen to that wind coming up, would you? She's a ring-tailed snorter.

†**ringus**, obs. variant of *ringo*, ERYNGO.

1653 W. J. *Gentlew. Delight* 34 To candy Ringus Root.

'ring-walk. *Obs.* exc. *arch.* [f. RING *sb.*[1]] (See quots.)

1575 TURBERV. *Venerie* 77 Let him beate the outsides and make his ryngwalkes twyce or thrice about the woode. **1616** BULLOKAR *Eng. Expos.*, *Ringwalke*, a round walk made by Hunters. [Hence in BLOUNT and PHILLIPS.] **1686** R. BLOME *Gentl. Recreat.* II. 78 When Huntsmen go drawing in their Springs at Hart-hunting, they usually make Dew-rounds which are called Ring-walks. **1818** SCOTT *Br. Lamm.* xx, Norman is waiting for me, and I am to go with him to make his ring-walk.

'ring-wall. Also **ringwall, ring wall.** [f. RING *sb.*[1]]

1. a. A wall completely surrounding or encircling a certain area. Also *fig.* (Cf. RING-FENCE.)

1850 CARLYLE *Latter-d. Pamph.* ii. 6 An immense circuit of buildings; cut out, girt with a high ring-wall, from the lanes and streets of the quarter. **1858** —— *Fredk. Gt.* II. vii. (1872) I. 90 The Nürnbergers once..built a ringwall round his Castle. **1875** *Encycl. Brit.* III. 3/2 Athens before the Persian war..was surrounded by a ring-wall of narrow circuit, some..traces of which are supposed to remain. **1944** *Cape Times* 25 Oct., In trade they did not want the ring-wall of the British Empire round them. **1950** H. L. LORIMER *Homer & Monuments* i. 27 A ring-wall of slabs was erected round the graves on the new level. **1963** L. F. CHITTY in Foster & Alcock *Culture & Environment* vii. 175 When its site was first 'bull-dozed' in 1947, the ruins of a broad ring-wall were revealed, constructed of local tilestones. **1970** I. PETITE *Meander to Alaska* II. xi. 111 He was in the process of repairing the foundation [of a house] with a concrete ring wall.

b. A roughly circular eminence surrounding a crater or mare on the moon or a similar formation on the earth, freq. of volcanic origin.

1950 W. LEY *Conquest of Space* 86 Copernicus is probably the most beautiful of all lunar craters. Its ringwall is 12,000 feet high at the highest point; its diameter is 56 miles. **1962** E. A. VINCENT tr. *Rittmann's Volcanoes* iii. 122 Ring-walls (ramparts) with outflows of lava are common. **1966** *Earth-Sci. Rev.* I. 231 The continents [on the Moon] are very mountainous and the mountains and lesser eminences generally form parts of the 'ringwalls' of maria and craters. **1968** R. W. FAIRBRIDGE *Encycl. Geomorphol.* 682/2 The island [*sc.* Makatea] rises on all sides from very deep water with a fringing reef.., bounded in the inner side by an abrupt or overhanging cliff of ancient coral limestone... To the inside again, there is a second cliff.., and a second rocky terrace. Within this ring-wall is a moat-like depression.

2. *techn.* (See quots.)

1875 KNIGHT *Dict. Mech.* 1945/1 *Ring-wall* (Metallurgy), the inner lining of a furnace. **1879** *Cassell's Techn. Educ.* II. 205/2 In some places..they use a sort of half-muffle, called a 'ring-wall', consisting of a lining reaching about half way up the kiln.

ringway ('rɪŋweɪ). [f. RING *sb.*[1] + WAY *sb.*[1]] A circular system of major roads round a town or urban area.

1969 *Daily Tel.* 16 Apr. 17/6 The council's plans for ringways were absolutely essential if London was to remain a major world city. **1970** [see ORBITAL *a.* 3]. **1971** *New Scientist* 8 July 102/2 Terence Bendison describes the traffic-swept gulf between Shepherds Bush and Holland Park, where part of the inner ringway has been imposed on streets and houses. **1973** R. BUSBY *Pattern of Violence* vi. 96 The familiar streets..down the east ringway to the Queen's underpass.

'ringwise, *adv.* [f. RING *sb.*[1] + WISE *sb.*[1] II.] In the form of a ring or rings; so as to produce a ring-shape.

1889 *Lancet* 3 Aug. 244/1 Their foreheads are tattooed ringwise, with singularly shaped cuttings in the skin. **1915** E. R. LANKESTER *Diversions of Naturalist* 101 Backbone-pieces and the body muscles attached ring-wise to them. **1922** JOYCE *Ulysses* 62 Pepper. He sprinkled it through his fingers, ringwise, from the chipped eggcup.

†**'ringwood.** *Obs.* Ale brewed at Ringwood in Hampshire.

1771 *Ann. Reg., Misc.* 195/2 That matrimony was not sufficiently encouraged, and that ringwood was the most orthodox ale in the kingdom.

ringworm ('rɪŋwɜːm). [f. RING *sb.*[1] So Du. *ringworm*, Da., Norw., Sw. dial. *ringorm.*]

1. A skin-disease usually manifesting itself in circular patches, and frequently affecting the scalp in childhood; tinea.

c **1425** *Voc.* in Wr.-Wülcker 642 *Hec cerpigo*, re[n]g-worme. *a* **1450** *Mankind* 616 (Brandl), I haue a lytyll dishes [= disease]..Wyth a runnynge rynge-worme. **1527** ANDREW *Brunswyke's Distyll. Waters* D iij b, The same..is good for the sore called the rynge worme. **1579** FULKE *Confut. Sanders* 659 So superstition crepeth like a ring-worme. *a* **1614** DONNE *Βιαθανατος* (1644) 53 To hide the deformity of a Ringworme in his face. **1661** LOVELL *Hist. Anim. & Min.* 101 With oile of bayes, it [*sc.* fat] helps the Scab and Ringwormes. **1728** CHAMBERS *Cycl.*, *Serpigo*, in Medicine, a kind of Herpes, popularly called a Tetter or Ring-worm. **1756** [see 2 b]. **1834** T. J. GRAHAM *Dom. Med.* (1844) 661 Shingles..is a variety of ringworm, or tetter, occupying the trunk of the body. **1876** BRISTOWE *Th. & Pract. Med.* (1878) 350 When ringworm occurs on the non-hairy skin, it reveals itself first as a slightly raised roundish uniformly erythematous patch. **1887** *Encycl. Brit.* XXII. 124/1 *Tinea sycosis*, or ringworm affecting the beard, and *tinea circinata*, or ringworm affecting the body.

b. *transf.* and *fig.*

1579 FULKE *Confut. Sanders* 591 A proper ringworm, a doctorlike argument. **1607** *Schol. Disc. agst. Antichr.* I. i. 41 The Idoll is a tempting harlot, the Crosse..a very ring-worme that spreadeth mightilie. **1647** CLEVELAND *Char. Lond. Diurn.* 8, I have not inke enough to cure all the Tetters and Ring-worms of the State. **1705** HICKERINGILL *Priest-cr.* II. vii. 67 This Tetter, or spreading Ringworm, cannot be cured..without some Gall in the Ink.

2. *attrib.*, as ***ringworm fungus, -porrigo***, etc.

1822–34 *Good's Study Med.* (ed. 4) IV. 490 The Ringworm Scall has been known and described, under different names, from the Greek writers to our own day. *Ibid.* 494 In the last variety, the ringworm porrigo. **1898** P. MANSON *Trop. Diseases* xxvii. 428 *note*, Yaws coalescing in the form of a ring are called ringworm yaws. **1899** *Allbutt's Syst. Med.* VIII. 854 The botanical character of the ringworm fungi is uncertain.

b. ***ringworm bush*** or ***shrub***, a tropical American shrub (*Cassia alata*). ***ringworm root***, the root of an Eastern shrub (*Rhinacanthus communis*) used as a remedy for the ringworm.

1756 P. BROWNE *Jamaica* 224 The Ring-worm Bush... The juice of the leaves or buds is said to cure the ring-worms. **1774** E. LONG *Hist. Jamaica* III. 845 Ringworm-bush, *Cassia siliquis quadrialatis*. **1864** GRISEBACH *Flora West Ind. Isl.* Col. Names 787 Ringworm-shrub, *Cassia alata*.

ringy ('rɪŋɪ), *a.*[1] Also **ringey.** [f. RING *sb.*[1] + -Y.]

1. Resembling a ring, ring-like; marked with rings.

1683 SNAPE *Anat. Horse* III. ix. (1686) 124 Out of the lower side of the Annular or ringy protuberance of the cerebel. **1843** HOLTZAPFFEL *Turning* I. 145 Amongst the white ivory, the teeth are often found to be marked in rings alternately light and dark coloured, these are called *ringy* or *cloudy*.

2. *N. Amer. slang.* Irritable, contentious, angry.

1932 *South of Market Tribune* (San Francisco) 23 Dec. 22 Nothing will make the boss more ringey. **1934** M. C. BOATRIGHT *Tall Tales from Texas* 30 He's a good-natured bird and don't git ringy about it. **1942** BERREY & VAN DEN BARK *Amer. Thes. Slang* §284/6 *Ill-tempered*..ringy. **1955** R. P. HOBSON *Nothing too Good for Cowboy* xviii. 187 To take some of the snoose out of the ringy Batnuni bunch [of cattle]. **1962** [see ORNERY *a.*]. **1977** *N.Y. Times* 11 Jan. 20/1 He thought Miss Longet had been 'ringy' the day she shot and killed Mr. Sabich.

ringy ('rɪŋɪ), *a.*[2] [f. RING *sb.*[2]] Having a ringing quality or tone.

1861 L. L. NOBLE *Icebergs* 195 It was light and tight, and ringy as a drum, and floated on the water like a bubble.

rinish, variant of RENISH *a.*

†**rink,** *sb.*[1] *Obs.* Forms: α. 1 rinc, 3–6 rink, 4–6 rynk(e, 6 rinck(e, rynck. β. 4–6 renk(e, 4 renkke, reynke. [OE. *rinc*, = OS. *rink*, ON. *rekkr*: the stem is app. an ablaut-variant to that of RANK *a.*] A man, *esp.* a fighting man, a warrior. (Only *poet.*)

α. *Beowulf* 399 Aras þa se rica, ymb hine rinc maniȝ. *a* **900** CYNEWULF *Crist* 1114 Fore eaȝna ȝesyhð, rinnan fore rincum. *a* **1000** *Boeth. Metr.* xxii. 45 þeah hine rinca hwilc ..æfter friȝne. *c* **1205** LAY. 5188 Bordes þer scænden, redde blod scede, rinkas feollen. *c* **1350** *Will. Palerne* 1193 What rink so he rauȝt he ros neuer after. *Ibid.* 1213 þan ride togedere a gret route of rinkes ful nobul. *c* **1400** *Destr. Troy* 13629 My ryght I renonse to þat rynk sone. **1515** *Scottish Field* 417 in *Chetham Misc.* (1856) II, Every ryncke to his reste Full radlie him dressed. **1535** STEWART *Cron. Scot.* III. 7 With mony rynk that ryall wes and ryke, In plane battell.

β. **13..** *E.E. Allit. P.* B. 766 þenne arest þe renk & raȝt no fyrre. **1362** LANGL. *P. Pl.* A. IV. 134 Whon Resun to þis Reynkes Rehersede þeose wordes. *a* **1400** *Pistill of Susan* 198 þo ros vp with rancour þe renkes reneyed. *c* **1470** *Gol. & Gaw.* 11 Renkis of grete renovne, Cumly kingis with crovne. **1557** GRIMALDE in *Tottel's Misc.* (Arb.) 122 Meleager..ran vpon the sayd Egyptian renk; And cut him in both kneez.

rink (rɪŋk), *sb.*[2] Also 4–6 (9) **renk**; 6 **rynk.** [App. a. OF. *renc* row, rank, RENK *sb.*[1], with slight change of meaning. Until the latter part of the 19th cent. only in Sc. use.]

†**1. a.** The space of ground within which a combat, joust, or race takes place; a course marked out for riding or running in. Freq. in phr. ***rink's end.***

In later use chiefly *fig.*, and passing into 1 c.

1375 BARBOUR *Bruce* II. 365 Knychtis..swa fell strakys gave and tuk, That all the renk about thaim quouk. *c* **1475** *Rauf Coilȝear* 809 In the rowme of ane renk in fewtir kest he. *Ibid.* 834 The riche restles men out of the renk past. **1513** DOUGLAS *Æneis* V. vi. 71 Be this thai wan neir to the renkis end, Irkit sum deil befoir the mark weil kend. **1550** LYNDESAY *Sqr. Meldrum* 520 He..bowtit fordwart, with ane bend, And ran on to the Rinkis end. **1591** R. BRUCE *Serm.* (1863) 382 To run out the rink that the Lord has set before him. **1606** BIRNIE *Kirk-Buriall* Ded., The Lord giue your Lordship continuall convoy to your rinks end. **1637** RUTHERFORD *Lett.* (1664) I. xxiv. 57 Possibly they see little more of it, or nothing at all, till they win to the rinks-end.

attrib. **1535** STEWART *Cron. Scot.* III. 455 At the rynk end ..With speir in hand bydand the heraldis cry. **1550** LYNDESAY *Sqr. Meldrum* 505 That round, rinkroume wes at vtterance. [**1819** W. TENNANT *Papistry Storm'd* (1827) 137 The heralds had the rink-room metit.]

†**b.** The course or way on which one is going.

c **1475** *Rauf Coilȝear* 549 Bot gif thow raik out of my renk, full raith sall thow rew. **1513** DOUGLAS *Æneis* VII. xii. 86 Buskis wythdrawis..To reyd thair renk, and rovmis thaim the way.

†**c.** A spell of running; a run or course; the act of running. *Obs.*

c **1480** HENRYSON *Mor. Fab.* 2425 The feind..Actand ilk man to rin vnrichtious rinkis. **1513** DOUGLAS *Æneis* X. vii. 142 Towart quham Pallas bownyt hes ful sone, And in hys renk on this wys maid hys boyne. **1533** BELLENDEN *Livy* I. x. (S.T.S.) I. 59 Ouresett with bleding of his woundis and fast rink. **1536** —— *Cron. Scot.* III. iv. (1821) I. 80 The Romanis ar..swift of rink. **1591** R. BRUCE *Serm.* (1843) 385 So much the nearer we draw to it, let us mend our renk. [**1819** W. TENNANT *Papistry Storm'd* (1827) 144 But sae it happen'd that nae scaith That renk wrocht.]

†**d.** A course in a joust or tournament. *Obs.*

c **1470** *Gol. & Gaw.* 910 Twa rynnyng renkis raith the riolys has tane, Ilk freik to his feir, to frestin his fa. **1513** DOUGLAS *Æneis* V. x. 91 Thir maneir of renkeis and juperteis of batale Ascanyus hantit. **1536** BELLENDEN *Cron. Scot.* XVI. x, In the thrid rynk lord wellis wes doung out of yᵉ sadyll. *c* **1560** A. SCOTT *Poems* (S.T.S.) ii. 46 Trumpettis and schalmis wᵗ a schowt Playid or the rink began.

2. a. A stretch of ice measured off or marked out for the game of curling.

1787 BURNS *Tam Samson's Elegy* v, To guard, or draw, or wick a bore, Or up the rink like Jehu roar. **1790** A. WILSON *Rabby's Mistake* Poet. Wks. (1846) 101 Far aff the curler's roaring rink, Re-echoed loud, wi' noisy clink. **1820** *Blackw. Mag.* VI. 569 What has been..justly said of a more serious predicament, is exhibited literally on a Rink. **1856** 'STONEHENGE' *Brit. Rural Sports* 511 A line..is drawn across the rink at each end, at a distance from the tee equal to one-sixth of the rink. **1895** *Times* 30 Jan. 6/2 Ninety rinks were laid out on the ice.., and they were occupied by 545 players.

b. One of the sets of players into which the sides in a curling or quoiting match are divided.

1823 in JAMIESON s.v., The long pending match at quoits ..took place, 24 on each side, forming 12 rinks. **1877** *Encycl. Brit.* VI. 713/1 Matches..with numerous competitors formed into rinks of four players a side, two stones being used by each player. **1968** *Globe & Mail* (Toronto) 3 Feb. 35/5 Webb, whose rink is composed of Jean Dye, Bill and Helen Ferguson, scored 39 points for its three wins. **1976** *S. Wales Echo* 26 Nov., The only Merthyr rink which returned a winning card was that skipped by Noel Tippett.

3. a. A sheet of ice for skating, especially one artificially prepared and roofed in; also, a smooth floor, usually of asphalt or wood, for roller-skating.

1867 SMYTH *Sailor's Word-bk.*, *Rink*, a space of ice devoted to certain recreations, as a skating or a curling rink. *c* **1879** STEVENSON *Ess. Trav.*, *Alpine Diversions* (1905) 219 Of skating little need be said; in so snowy a climate the rinks must be intelligently managed. **1890** DILKE *Probl. Greater Brit.* I. 123 Rink skating is a fine art in Canada.

transf. **1883** E. PENNELL-ELMHIRST *Cream Leicestersh.* 131 The roads being rinks of the smoothest and most unbroken description.

b. A spell of roller-skating.

1875 S. G. THOMAS in Burnie *Mem.* (1890) 48, I recreated myself..by a rink yesterday. I found the wheels more popular than ever.

c. *N. Amer.* A frozen surface on which ice hockey is played. Also, a hall or stadium containing this.

1896 *Times* (Niagara-on-the-Lake, Ont.) 27 Feb. 1/4 The Niagaras..know just how to toss the puck around from one end of the rink to the other in order to score. **1945** W. H. PUGSLEY *Saints, Sinners & Ordinary Seamen* 90 In the early months of the war..ratings lived in a converted hockey rink. **1953** *Canad. Geogr. Jrnl.* XLVI 138/2 The children maintain their own open air hockey rink on the ice. **1974** *Plain Dealer* (Cleveland, Ohio) 26 Oct. 5-D/1 The Elysium had been a little rink which could accommodate almost 2,000.

4. A measured strip of bowling-green on which a match is played. Also, the players allotted to a rink.

1864 W. W. MITCHELL *Man. Bowl-Playing* 21 When.. any number of players, not exceeding eight, form sides and commence a game, they make what is called a rink. *Ibid.*, The space or division of the Green is also commonly called a rink. **1897** *Encycl. Sport* I. 129/2 *Rink*, (1) a narrow section of a bowling-green, some twenty feet in breadth taken by one party for their game. (2) All the players upon the two sides. (Both terms are more common in Scotland than England.) **1906** *Canadian Mag.* Sept. 475/2 Like curling.., [bowling] permits of an adjournment occasionally in order that.. the opposing rinks may 'join' each other and have 'something'. **1975** *Oxf. Compan. Sports & Games* 94/2 The green is divided by boundaries of fine string into six 'rinks' the length of the green and 19 to 21 ft. (5.8–6.4 m.) wide. **1976** *Laws of Game* (Eng. Bowling Assoc.) (ed. 3) 4 The green shall be divided into spaces called rinks, each not more than 19 feet nor less than 18 feet wide.

5. *attrib.* and *Comb.*, as *rink boot*, *-side*; **rink rat** *N. Amer.*, a youth who seeks casual work at an ice-hockey rink in return for free admission, etc. (see also quot. 1945); **rink string**, a length of string which marks the boundary of a rink on a bowling-green.

c **1885** in M. Johnson *Amer. Advertising* (1960), Childs's Cash Shoe Store. 'Ladies' rink boots' a specialty. **1945** L. Shelly *Jive Talk Dict.* 31 *Rink rat*, skating rink enthusiast. **1965** *Victoria* (B.C.) *Daily Times* 20 July 10/6, I was a rink rat at the Forum. **1970** J. H. Gray *Boy from Winnipeg* 51 Two Fort Rouge schoolboys from the Kennedy rink rats eventually made good as professionals. **1916** A. Bridle *Sons of Canada* 26 The genial boss.. sits in his fur-lined greatcoat at the rinkside. **1972** 'E. Lathen' *Murder without Icing* (1973) ii. 17 He was at rinkside. On the ice, the New York Huskies were having a workout. **1960** R. Williams *Border Country* iv. 113 Harry went up to the bowling green to.. set out the rink-strings and the mats.

Hence **rink** *v. intr.*, to skate on a rink; also *trans.* (in quot. *fig.*).

1877 H. Sidgwick in A. & E. M. Sidgwick *Henry Sidgwick* (1907) v. 326, I 'rinked' or 'runk' (I do not know how the verb is conjugated)... It is not half as amusing as real skating. **1896** Newnham-Davis *Three Men & a God* 143 You have rinked in the town hall.., have gone over the stables. **1909** 'W. N. P. Barbellion' *Jrnl.* 25 Dec. (1919) 24, I.. idly scan magazines in the Library and occasionally rink —with palpitation of the heart as a consequence. **1946** R. Campbell *Talking Bronco* 25 The zephyr from the blue nevadas, Stirruped with kestrels, smoothly rinking The level wave where halcyons drowse.

rinkasporum, erroneous for *Rhyncospora*, a genus of Australian plants.

1885 Mrs. C. Praed *Head Station* I. i, The delicate white-flowered rinka-sporum. *Ibid.* III. vii, Isabel.. nervously twisted a tendril of the rinkasporum round her fingers.

rinker ('rɪŋkə(r)). *dial. rare.* [f. *rink*, dial. var. RING *sb.*[1] + -ER[1]: cf. *ring* a circle into which marbles are thrown (*Sc. Nat. Dict.*) and RINGER[1] 1.] A marble (see quot.[1]); a game of marbles.

1910 A. Bennett *Clayhanger* I. i. 6 They were not the paltry marble of today, plaything of infants, but the majestic 'rinker', black with white spots, the king of marbles in an era when whole populations practised the game. *Ibid.* 9 The open gates of a manufactory disclosed six men playing the noble game of rinkers on a smooth patch of ground... They were celebrated marble-players, and.. they shot the rinkers from their stubby thumbs with a cannon-like force and precision.

'rinking, *vbl. sb.* [f. RINK *sb.*[2] 3.] The act or practice of skating on a rink. Also *attrib.*

1876 Besant & Rice *Gold. Butterfly* xvi, Why should we not go mad for china? It is as sensible as going mad over rinking. **1880** C. R. Markham *Peruv. Bark* 443 A great many rings for the rinking skates. **1885** *Graphic* 3 Jan. 11/3 Men, since rinking collapsed, have 'gone in' more for football.

'rinkist. [f. RINK *sb.*[2] 3.] One who skates on a rink.

1876 *All Year Round* (N.S.) XVI. 18 The practised rinkist may soon get into trouble on genuine ice.

rinkite ('rɪŋkaɪt). *Min.* [ad. Sw. *rinkit* (J. Lorenzen 1884, in *Öfversigt af k. vetensk. Förh.* 111), f. the name of Henrik Johannes *Rink* (1819–93), Danish geologist and explorer: see -ITE[1].] A silicate mineral similar to (or identical with) mosandrite, found as reddish- or yellowish-brown crystals from Greenland.

1886 *Jrnl. Chem. Soc.* L. 676 Rinkite. **1887** *Mineral. Mag.* VII. 234 Fluorite is fairly abundant, and also two of the rarer minerals—laavenite and rinkite. **1937** *Mineral. Abstr.* VI. 179 Rinkite from Greenland gave sp. gr. 3.458 and an orthorhombic cell.. containing two molecules $[SiO_4]_2[(Ti,Ce)F]\ Ca_2Na$. **1971** *Ann. Rep. Delegates Sci. Area Univ. Oxford 1970* 131 Accessions... Rinkite.. from south-west Greenland. **1971** *Acta Crystallogr.* B. XXVII. 1277 Rinkite, $(Ti,Nb,Al,Zr)(Na,Ca)_3(Ca,Ce)_4(Si_2O_7)_2(O,F)_4$ approximately, is a silicate crystallizing in the monoclinic system.

rinkle, obs. variant of WRINKLE *sb.*

rinko'mania. [f. RINK *sb.*[2] 3.] A passion for rink-skating. So **rinko'maniac**.

1876 *World* V. 3 The mischief which must.. ensue if the pest of rinkomania became popular. **1876** *Tinsley's Mag.* XVIII. 269 The pastime seems sufficiently dangerous to satisfy the requirements of the most refractory rinkomaniacs.

rinktum ('rɪŋktəm). *rare. Southern U.S. dial.* alteration of RECTUM.

1929 W. Faulkner *Sound & Fury* 86 You know what I'll do. I'll skin your rinktum.

rinky-dink ('rɪŋkɪdɪŋk), *sb.* and *a. slang* (chiefly *U.S.*). Also **rinkey-dink, rinkydink, rinky-dinky.** [Orig. unknown: cf. RICKY-TICK *sb.* and *a.*]

A. *sb.* Something that is worn out or antiquated; a worthless object. *spec.* a cheap place of entertainment. Also in phr. ***to give*** (someone) ***the rinky-dink*** and varr., to cheat or swindle (someone).

1912 A. H. Lewis *Apaches N.Y.* xii. 265 They was lyin'.. an' givin' each other th' rinkey-dink in th' old days same as now. **1922** J. A. Dunn *Man Trap* i. 8 Jimmy abhorred mining corporations with a lot of stockholders and a few of those liable at any moment to hand you the rinky-dink and freeze you out by due process of legal indifference toward small-fry claimants. **1942** *Harper's Bazaar* July 21/2 Don't give me the rinkydink. **1951** *Atlantic Monthly* Mar. 80/1, I think of Sweet Mama Stringbean as she was called when she played the Rinky-dinks for $25 a week. **1956** S. Longstreet *Real Jazz* 147 *Rinky-dink* is broken-down stuff. **1969** *New Yorker* 1 Nov. 6/2 *Red Garter*.. eighteen-nineties rinky-dink, complete with fire engine, but the banjo band is above average. **1977** *Amer. Speech 1975* L. 65 *Rinky-dink*..*n*, something that is cheap or worn out. 'His car is a real rinky-dink.'

B. *adj.* Worthless, worn out, trivial; old-fashioned, outmoded.

1913 *Wells Fargo Messenger* I. 105/3 She did not care to ruin her life as a Sunday supplement feature to some rinky-dinky foreign count. **1942** Berrey & Van den Bark *Amer. Thes. Slang* §675/12 Baseball... *Rinky-dink ball*, inferior playing. **1946** Mezzrow & Wolfe *Really Blues* vii. 87 My struggle-buggy was getting to look like a rinky-dink old tin can on wheels. **1951** E. Waters *His Eye is on Sparrow* vi. 77 Of all those rinky-dink dumps I played, nothing was worse than the Monogram Theatre in Chicago. **1973** *Globe & Mail* (Toronto) 24 Sept. 5/3 He thinks it hasn't been legalized only because of 'rinkydink politics' but he decries other aspects of the drug scene and says he thinks he's kept some of his young patients from getting involved. **1979** *Fortune* 15 Jan. 5 Facet [was].. a rinky-dink outfit with no real resources and not much to offer.

rinky-tink ('rɪŋkɪtɪŋk), *a. slang* (chiefly *U.S.*). [Imitative: cf. prec. and TINK *int.* and *sb.*] Designating a jazz or ragtime piano on which simple, repetitive tunes are played; tinkling, jangling. Cf. RICKY-TICK *a.*

1962 E. Lucia *Klondike Kate* ii. 34 A rinky-tink piano or a scratchy gramophone had its intoxicating effect upon her. **1974** *News & Courier* (Charleston, S. Carolina) 25 Apr. 5-A/1 Scott Joplin played his toe-tappers on a rinky-tink piano. **1975** J. Gores *Hammett* (1976) i. 12 A rinky-tink piano was bashing out 'Ja-Da'.

Rinne ('rɪnə). *Med.* Also (*erron.*) **Rinné.** The name of Heinrich Adolf *Rinne* (1819–68), German otologist, who described a form of the test in 1855 (*Vierteljahrschr. f. d. prakt. Heilkunde* XLV. 72), used in the possessive, *attrib.*, and *absol.* to designate a diagnostic test for deafness (see quot. 1883).

1883 tr. *Politzer's Text-Bk. Dis. Ear* 693 Rinne's experiment.. consists in setting a tuning-fork.. on the vertex or on the mastoid process, and allowing it to vibrate till the note is no longer heard; the prongs of the fork are then brought close to the ear, and in normal circumstances the tone will be heard again (positive experiment). **1899** G. Bacon *Man. Otology* ii. 81 Rinné's test... If heard again, which is the case in the normal ear, this is called the positive Rinné test. **1902** tr. *Brühl & Politzer's Atlas & Epitomy Otol.* 87 Positive result of Rinne's experiment, or positive Rinne. **1959** H. A. Newby *Audiol.* iv. 61 If the patient replies affirmatively, the result of the test is said to be a Rinné negative... A Rinné test on a normal ear will yield a positive result. **1974** Passmore & Robson *Compan. Med. Stud.* III. xxxii. 3/2 In conductive deafness, bone conduction is better heard than air conduction and Rinne's test is negative.

rinneite ('rɪnəaɪt). *Min.* [a. G. *rinneit* (H. E. Boeke 1908, in *Chem. Zeitung* XXXII. 1228), f. the name of Friedrich *Rinne* (1863–1933), German mineralogist: see -ITE[1].] A rhombohedral chloride of iron, potassium, and sodium, $K_3FeNaCl_6$, which is known as colourless, pale rose, violet, or yellow granular masses from saline deposits, and can be prepared artificially.

1909 *Jrnl. Chem. Soc.* XCVII. II. 153 Rinneite... An anhydrous mineral.. has been found in considerable quantities at the Nordhäusen Works. **1953** *Q. Jrnl. Geol. Soc.* CVIII. 289 At Rockhead the marl is much richer in rinneite and carnallite than at the other boreholes. Several coarse, colourless to yellow, rinneite inclusions.. were found. **1970** *Rocks & Minerals* XLV. 376/1 Rinneite has been reported as a secondary mineral in the salt mine at Winnfield Dome.

rinner, -ing, dial. variants of RUNNER, -ING.

†**'rinnet.** *Obs.* In 6 rinet, 7 **rynnet.** Variant of RENNET or RUNNET *sb.*, used figuratively.

1582 Stanyhurst *Æneis*, etc. (Arb.) 136 Thee water hard curded with the chil ysye rinet. *a* **1616** Beaum. & Fl., *Bonduca* IV. i, They are full of rynnet, And take the skin off where they are tasted. *a* **1618** J. Davies (Heref.) *Wittes Pilgr.* Wks. (Grosart) II. 26 Rynnet of Darknesse, lightly turning it.

rino, obs. var. RHINO *sb.*[1]

rinocere, obs. var. RHINOCEROS.

rinology, obs. var. RHINOLOGY.

‖**Rinpoche** ('rɪnpɒtʃeɪ). Also **Rimpoche**, etc. [Tibetan, lit. 'precious (jewel)'.] An honorific title given to a chief priest among Tibetan Buddhists. Cf. PANCHEN.

1774 G. Bogle *Narr. Mission to Tibet* (1876) iii. 26 A tower, about five or six stories high,.. is appropriated to Lama-Rimboché. **1784** S. Turner *Let.* 2 Mar. in *Acct. of Embassy to Court of Teshoo Lama in Tibet* (1800) III. 364 The death of Gesub Rimbochay, offered a new prospect of opening.. communication. **1800**, etc. [see PANCHEN.] **1863** tr. *E. Schlagintweit's Buddhism in Tibet* xii. 153 The *Panchen Rinpoche* is considered to be an incarnation of Chenresi's celestial father, Amitâbha. **1882** *Encycl. Brit.* XIV. 230/1 The Dalai Lāma.. is actually called the *Gyalpo Rinpotshe*, 'the glorious king',—his companion being content with the title *Pantshen Rinpotshe*, 'the glorious teacher'. **1889** M. Monier-Williams *Buddhism* xi. 284 The other Grand Lāma who resides in the monastery of Tashi Lunpo.. has the Tibetan title of Panchen Rinpoche (Pañ-ćen Rinpo-će), 'the great Paṇḍit Jewel'. **1929** D. Macdonald *Land of Lama* ii. 43 This cleric.. was now allowed to assume the incarnation of Buddha Amitabha, with the title of *Panchen Rimpoche* or 'Precious Gem of Learning'. **1980** D. Hart-Davis *Heights of Rimring* xvi. 174 Access to the monastery could be gained only by means of a contraption which the *rinpoches*, the lamas, let down on a rope.

rin-rig, variant of RUN-RIG.

rinse (rɪns), *sb.* Also **rinze, rince,** *Sc.* **ringe, reenge.** [f. RINSE *v.*]

1. *Sc.* A small bundle of twigs (esp. of heather) used for cleaning out pots or other vessels. Hence **rinse-heather**, the variety of heather used for making this.

1800 J. Headrick *Comm. Board of Agric.* II. 264 Long heath.. makes excellent rinses for scrubbing milk vessels. **1808** Jamieson, *Ringe*, a whisk or small besom, made of heath. *Ringe-heather*, Cross-leaved Heath. **1829** *Health & Longevity* 151 Traversing the woods and fields in quest of materials for his besoms and rinzes.

2. a. A rinsing; a final application of water to remove impurities; *colloq.* a wash. Also *attrib.*

1837 Dickens *Pickw.* xxv, 'I may as vel have a rinse', replied Mr. Weller, applying plenty of yellow soap to the towel. **1852** Morfit *Tanning & Currying* (1853) 387 The skins are then taken from the rinse-water. **1879** *Cassell's Techn. Educ.* III. 207/2 No doubt the final rinse of spirits helps the gelatine to resist decomposition. **1882** Jamieson s.v. *Ringe*, Gie the claes a ringe in cauld water.

b. A wash to cleanse the mouth.

1898 *Westm. Gaz.* 26 Jan. 10/2 The best rinse for the smoker is a glass of water in which a teaspoonful of table-salt has been dissolved.

c. A solution (or cream) which temporarily tints or conditions the hair. Also, an application of this.

1928 *Daily Mail* 25 July 3/6 Though the price of Icilma Shampoos remains at 3d., each packet now contains a wonderful Toning Rinse suitable for every shade of hair, which removes *all trace of lather*, and leaves the hair in a state of exquisite burnished beauty. **1942** M. Dickens *One Pair of Feet* ix. 189, I think I shall go and have a platinum rinse next payday. **1944**, etc. [see BLUE RINSE a]. **1948** M. Sturges-Jones *In Wedlock Wake* 137 Why don't you try a blond rinse?.. It wouldn't make you look bleached. **1958** J. Cannan *And be a Villain* vii. 155 Age must be disguised, hushed up with dyes and rinses. **1962** D. Lessing *Golden Notebk.* III. 345 'I did try a rinse,' he remarked, 'but the grey shows through.' **1977** B. Pym *Quartet in Autumn* i. 2 Letty knew that there were white hairs interspersed with the brown and that most people would have had a brightening 'rinse' anyway.

3. In *Comb.*, as **rinse-aid** (see quot. 1963).

1963 *Which?* 6 Feb. 50/1 Five [dishwashing] machines.. supplied rinse aids. These are liquids added to the final rinse water to make it flow more easily and prevent it from remaining as drops on the surface. **1970** *Ibid.* Oct. 294/1 Some detergents—or rinse aids—leave a white deposit on everything.

rinse (rɪns), *v.* Forms: *α.* 4–6 **rynce** (5 **ryyncyn**), 4–6 **rynse** (5 **ryynse**), 5 **rines-**, 6– **rince, rinse**; 6 **rence**, 6–7 **rense**, 7 **reinse.** *β.* 5 **rynesh, rynsche**, 6 **rinche**, 7 (9 *dial.*) **rinch**; 6 **rensch**, 6–7 (9– *dial.*, now chiefly *U.S.*) **rench**, 7 (9 *dial.*) **wrench**, 9 *dial.* **ranch.** *γ.* 9 *dial.* **ringe, rinje, reenge, reinge, range.** [a. F. *rincer*, OF. also *reincer* (*-ser*), *raincer* (*-ser*), of uncertain origin.

The similarity in form and meaning to ON. *hreinsa* (MDa. *rensa, rinse, rønse*, MSw. *rensa, ränsa, rönsa*), to cleanse, is very great, but is prob. accidental. The OF. *raincer* was app. trisyllabic (*raïncer*), which suggests that a consonant has been dropped, but it seems difficult to associate the form with the synonymous OF. *recincer* (Picard *rechinchier*) and med.L. *recincerare, resincerare* (see these words in Du Cange).]

†**1.** *trans.* To clear, make clean, by removal.

1338 R. Brunne *Chron.* (1810) 321 Þe kynge's oste at gesse in þe Est mad lardere,.. More & mede did rynce [*rime* prince], wod & playn he brent.

2. a. To wash out (a cup, etc.) by pouring in water or other liquid and emptying it out again (usually after swilling or stirring it about).

α. *c* **1350** *Gloss.* in *Rel. Ant.* I. 7 *Recenta*.. *hunc ciphum*, rynce this cuppe. ? *a* **1400** [see RINSED *ppl. a.*]. *c* **1440** *Promp. Parv.* 434/2 Ryyncyn, *rigo, vmecto.* **1509** Barclay *Shyp Folys* (1570) 32 Such force not of their soules, But labour in rinsing pieces, cups and bowles. **1535** Coverdale *Lev.* xv. 12 The treen vessell shal be rensed with water. *c* **1611** Chapman *Iliad* XVI. 224 Hee tooke a most vnualewed boule, ..and that he first did clense With sulphure, then with fluences of sweetest water rense. **1658** tr. *Porta's Nat. Magic* xx. 398 Glass vessels well rinced, and.. full of cold water. **1729** Swift *Direct. Serv.* i, Leave the Dregs of.. Liquors in the Bottle: To rince them is but Loss of Time. **1769** Mrs. Raffald *Eng. Housekpr.* (1778) 317 To have your vessels dry, rinse them with brandy. **1823** J. Badcock *Dom. Amusem.* 45 A clean glass, rinced with any acid. **1861** Flor. Nightingale *Nursing* ii. (ed. 2) 13 Take care that your lid, as well as your utensil, be always thoroughly rinsed.

β. *c* **1430** *Two Cookery-bks.* 24 Rynsche þin dysshe alle a-bowte withynne with sugre or oyle. **1591** Florio *2nd Fruites* 13 Wash and rench the glasses verie well. **1663** Gerbier *Counsel* I. 35 The French-Man's Glasse is wrenched as often as he Drinks. [**1919** H. L. Mencken *Amer. Lang.* iii. 91 The Yankees..still clung, in their common speech, to such forms as..rench for rinse,..and the employment of precisely the same forms by thousands of Irish immigrants ..gave them a certain support.] **1960** V. Williams *Walk Egypt* IV. ii. 257 Then you best rench your hands.

γ. **1547** Salesbury, *Bwrw dwr dros lestr*, renge. **1834–5** *Wilson's Tales Borders* (1836) II. 167, I poured the whisky intil the lang sma bottle..without rangin it oot. **1894** Heslop *Northumb. Gloss.* 565 Range oot that pot.

b. To clean (the mouth, teeth, etc.) by taking a mouthful of water and emitting it again.

α. **1565** Cooper *Thesaurus* s.v. *Foueo*, *Fouere os multa aqua frigida*, to washe the mouth with; to rinse. **1608** Topsell *Serpents* (1653) 624 He would suck and draw up into his mouth a great deal of water, and first rinse and warm his own mouth. **1739** R. Bull tr. *Dedekindus' Grobianus* 105 Nor only wash your Fingers, but your Face; And rinse your Teeth. **1762** *Ann. Reg.* II. 34/2 Rinsing his palate (to avoid confusion) after every piece. **1834** L. Ritchie *Wand. by Seine* 71 The..disgusting ceremony of publicly rinsing the mouth. **1870** Dickens *E. Drood* xii, Jasper only rinses his mouth once, and casts forth the rinsing. **1905** Geil *Yankee in Pigmy Land* 319 After each meal they rinse the mouth with water.

β. **1859** J. C. Hotten *Dict. Slang* 81 *Rench*, vulgar pronunciation of *rinse*. '*Wrench* your mouth out,' said a fashionable dentist one day.—*North*.

fig. **1824–9** Landor *Imag. Conv.* Wks. 1846 I. 84, I have rinsed my mouth of the poetry.

†**3.** *absol.* Of a priest: To clean the chalice and fingers with wine and water after communion. *Obs.*

c **1375** *Lay-Folks Mass Bk.* (MS. B) 575 Loke pater-noster þou be sayande, I-whils þo preste is rynsande. *c* **1400** *Rule St. Benet* 149 Qwen þe prelete hase vsede & rineside, þan sal scho be howseld of hym. *c* **1425** [see rinsing *vbl. sb.* 1].

4. a. To dip (a thing) into, agitate in, or drench with water in order to remove impurities.

α. **1423** Jas. I. *King's Q.* i, Citherea the clere Rynsid hir tressis like the goldin wyre. **1563** Foxe *Canon of Mass* in *A. & M.* 893/2 Let the priest rence his hands, lest any parcels of the body or bloud be left behind in his fingers or in the chalice. **1588** Mascall tr. *Bk. Dyeing* 20 Take of good wood and breake the rootes off, and then cut them small, then wash and rence them in cold water. **1607** J. Davies (Heref.) *Summa Totalis* Wks. (Grosart) I. 21/2 Likewise the Delvge (that did rince this Rovnd) Came..To make it cleane. **1641** Milton *Animadv.* Wks. 1851 III. 197 They could not refine a Scorpion into a Fish, though they had drawn it, and rinc't it with never so cleanly Cookery. **1683** Moxon *Mech. Exerc., Printing* xxii. ¶2 Of Rincing a Form of Letter. **1700** Addison *Æneid* III. Wks. 1726 I. 62 He rins'd the wound, And washed away the..clotted blood. **1828** Maugham *Accum's Chem. Reagents* 118 Rince and macerate an oyster in cold distilled water. **1846** J. Baxter *Libr. Pract. Agric.* (ed. 4) II. 318 Rinse the leaves in cold water,..and dry them on hot plates. **1902** Wister *Virginian* xxvii, The girl rinsed the man's wound and wrapped him in clean things.

refl. **1630** Brathwait *Eng. Gentlem.* (1641) 103 Hanging down his head, as one discontent, till he hath washed and rinsed himselfe. *a* **1641** Bp. Mountagu *Acts & Mon.* (1642) 205 Having rinsed her selfe all over in pure running water. [**1851** S. Judd *Margaret* I. ii, They went to the cistern at the back of the house, washed and rinsed themselves for dinner.]

β. **1561** Hollybush *Hom. Apoth.* 2 Washe the head euery thyrde daye wyth strong warme lye..: at the last rensch the head with colde lye. **1595** Duncan *Etym.* (E.D.S.), *Perluo, perpurgo*, to rinche faire and cleane. **1889** J. W. Riley *Knee-deep in June*, Rench my hair In the dew.

b. To treat (clothes or textile fabrics) in this way; *spec.* to put through clean water in order to remove the soap used in washing.

α. **1530** Palsgr. 691/2, I rynce clothes, *je raince*. I wyll rynce up the clothes here in the bolle. **1598** Yong *Diana* 74 As I was going to the riuer to rince my clothes. **1611** Cotgr., *Rinser*, to reinse linnen clothes. *a* **1641** Bp. Mountagu *Acts & Mon.* (1642) 128 By scouring, washing, rinsing it as spots ..are washed out of clothes. **1686** *Annals of Albany* (1850) II. 94 No person whatsoever shall..rense cloathes..in or near any of the wells. **1791** Hamilton *Berthollet's Dyeing* I. I. II. i. 147 The cotton must be rinsed in a stream of water. **1815** J. Smith *Panorama Sci. & Art* II. 544 In scouring the raw cotton, it is usual to boil it..in sour water or an alkaline ley, after which it is wrung out, rinsed, and dryed. **1859** Jephson *Brittany* iv. 44 They were beating and rinsing and wringing the unfortunate sheets and table-cloths.

β. *c* **1440** *Generydes* 1182 She toke the Shirte..And wesht it onys and ryneshed it so clene. **1611** Cotgr., *Esbourrer*.., to rinch, or wash (a cloath, &c.) lightly, or sleightly. **1781** Hutton *Tour Caves, Rench*, to wash clean with water, as cloths. **1825–** in many dial. glossaries (as *rinch, rench, ranch*). *a* **1841** J. Guild *Jrnl.* in *Proc. Vermont Hist. Soc.* (1937) V. 263 She would..go down to a brook about forty rods and stand in the brook and rench her close.

γ. **1856** J. Ballantine *Poems* 13 In the wee gushing burn [they] ringe their siller-white claes. **1881** Sargisson *Joe Scoap* 141 (E.D.D.), Thay..rinje't em weel anunder t'pump.

c. Const. *out*. Also *absol.*

1941 E. P. O'Donnell *Great Big Doorstep* i. 2 How many time I'm gunna tell you..to come and rench out the diaper? **1953** [see drip-dry *v.*]. **1976** M. Millar *Ask for Me Tomorrow* (1977) xvi. 132 You're not helpless. Can't you rinse out your own socks?

d. To treat (hair) with a rinse. Cf. rinse *sb.* 2 c. Also *absol.*

1959 N. Lofts *Heaven in your Hand* 125 His mother, of course, used make-up too, and had her hair 'rinsed' and waved. **1971** M. Kelly *25th Hour* i. 53 Louise's hair seemed to go an elegant grey all at once (she rinses a bit of course).

†**5.** In *fig.* or *transf.* uses: **a.** To clean out, to empty. *Obs. rare.*

c **1572** Gascoigne *Fruites Warre* lxix, His owne companions can contriue a meane, To cutte his throate and rinse his budgets cleane.

†**b.** To moisten or drench. *Obs. rare.*

1599 B. Jonson *Ev. Man out of Hum.* III. ix, To rince his clammy guts in beere. **1648** G. Daniel *Eclog* iii. Hakon's Song ii, Had I but now, one boule To rince my thirsty Soule.

†**c.** To cleanse, to make clean or pure. *Obs.*

1600 Rowlands *Lett. Humours Blood* vi. 79 A pottle of wine..Drunke with an Apple, is imployed right, To rince the Liver. *a* **1628** Preston *Saints Daily Exercise* (1629) 132 He washeth and renseth his heart. *a* **1658** Lovelace *Poems* (1864) 244 Thy thoughts..Rench'd from earth's tainted, fat and heavy steams.

6. To remove, to take *away*, clear *out*, by rinsing.

1565 Cooper *Thesaurus* s.v. *Abluo*, To rinse away his thirst. **1582** Stanyhurst *Æneis* III. (Arb.) 92 Hee rinst in the water thee drosse from his late bored eyelyd. **1607** Walkington *Opt. Glass* 3 That whole flood could not wash or rinch away that one spot of his atheisme. **1646** P. Bulkeley *Gospel Covt.* I. 174 First wee scoure and rinse out the filth that is in it. **1794** Waterhouse in Morse *Amer. Geogr.* (1796) I. 501 Such a course of water drinking will open obstructions, rinse out impurities.

7. To wash *down* with liquor.

1812 W. Tennant *Anster Fair* I. lxix, Ever and anon they eat a lunch, And rinse the mouthfuls down with flav'rous whisky punch.

Hence **rinsed** *ppl. a.* Also †**rinse-pitcher**, one who drinks the rinsings of liquor; a toper.

? *a* **1400** *Morte Arth.* 3375, I salle redily..reche the þe riche wyne in rynsede coupes. **1552** Huloet, Rynche pytcher, *lagenarius*. **1562** Bullein *Bulwark, Bk. Simples* (1579) 13 The rinsepichers had a good medicen prepared for them, for the Maior of London..made an order against mightie Bere and Ale.

'rinser. *rare.* Also 7 **rencer, reinser, renser.** [f. rinse *v.*] One who rinses.

1611 Florio, *Risciacquatore*, a rencer, a washer or shaker in water. **1611** Cotgr., *Rinseur*, a reinser of linnen. **1697** C. Leslie *Snake in Grass* (ed. 2) 351 John the Baptist is always called in the printed Saxon Version of the Gospels,..John the Washer, Renser, or Cleanser. **1825** *Blackw. Mag.* XVII. 165 From being a rinser of muslins, [she] comes to be the very goddess of St. George's..Fields.

rinsing ('rɪnsɪŋ), *vbl. sb.* [f. rinse *v.* + -ing[1].]

1. The action of the verb in various senses.

c **1375** *Lay Folks Mass Bk.* (MS. B) 576 When þo preste has rinsynge done, opon þi fete þou stonde vp sone. *c* **1425** *St. Mary of Oignies* I. viii. in *Anglia* VIII. 141/28 Whanne she toke wyne in þe rynshynge after þe sacrament. *c* **1440** *Promp. Parv.* 434/2 Ryyncynge (*K.P.* rynsinge of vessell), *rigacio*. **1613** Shaks. *Hen. VIII*, I. i. 167 Th' enteruiew, That..like a glasse Did breake ith' wrenching. **1617** Hieron *Wks.* II. 90 Such a rinsing and scouring Dauid prayed for. **1840** R. Dana *Bef. Mast* xxx. 110 We..had a new supply of rain-water, in which we had a grand rinsing. **1873** E. Spon *Workshop Rec.* Ser. I. 209/2 The rinsings after each operation should be thorough.

b. *attrib.*, as *rinsing appliance, machine*, etc.

1683 Moxon *Mech. Exerc., Printing* ii. ¶1 The Lye-Trough and Rincing-Trough he places towards some corner of the Room. **1725** *Fam. Dict.* s.v. *Clear-starching*, Pour a little of it into the rincing Water, then put your Hand into the rincing Water, and stir it about. **1827** Faraday *Chem. Manip.* xx. 526 For soaking and rincing operations. **1839** Ure *Dict. Arts* 1069 *Rinsing Machine*. **1884** *Health Exhib. Catal.* 110/2 Bottle Washing, Brushing, and Rinsing Appliances.

2. The liquid or liquor with which anything has been rinsed out. Chiefly *pl.*

1818 Scott *Hrt. Midl.* xxxii, The beadle..washed down the greasy morsel with the last rinsings of the pot of ale. **1860** Dickens *Uncomm. Trav.* iii, A scum that was like the soapy rinsing of sooty chimneys. **1870** [see rinse *v.* 2 b]. **1872** Geo. Eliot *Middlem.* xxxix, The very pigs..in low spirits from feeding on a too meagre quality of rinsings.

fig. **1822** De Quincey *Confessions* 150 These were..the very dregs and rinsings of the human intellect. **1870** Lowell *Study Wind., Condesc. Foreigners*, Being drenched with the rinsings of an unclean imagination.

†**rinspindle.** *Obs. rare.* In 5 **-spindel, -dil, rynspyndell, -dle.** [App. f. *rin* run *v.* + spindle *sb.* Cf. G. *rennspindel*.] A boring instrument used by cutlers and in the surgical treatment of a broken skull.

c **1400** *Lanfranc's Cirurg.* 126 Summe seien þat þilke rimele..schulde be..peersid..wiþ rinspindelis... A rinspindil is an instrument þat coteleris poudren with her haftis.

rin-there-out: see run-.

†**'riny,** *a. Obs. rare*[−1]. [f. *rine*, var. of rind *sb.*[1] Cf. rindy *a.*[1]] Bearing the rind or skin.

c **1682** J. Collins *Salt & Fishery* 123 Rub Salt well on the Flitches, and put them in a Trough, laying the Riny side downwards.

Rinyo-Clacton ('rɪnjəʊ'klæktən), *a. Archæol.* [f. the place-names *Rinyo*, Orkney + *Clacton*, Essex.] Of, pertaining to, or designating the culture represented by Late Neolithic grooved ware first discovered at Rinyo and Clacton.

1954 S. Piggott *Neolithic Cultures Brit. Isles* x. 280 *The Rinyo-Clacton culture*. Defined originally by 'Grooved ware'..the culture has a curious distribution, mainly concentrated in two separate areas, one in south-east England and the other in the Orkneys, though intermediate sites are now being discovered. **1963** E. S. Wood *Collins Field Guide Archaeol.* II. ii. 105 The northern branch of the Rinyo-Clacton culture..have left in Orkney remains from which a fairly complete picture of their economy can be built up: at Skara Brae and at Rinyo are groups of squarish stone huts. **1967** *Antiquaries Jrnl.* XLVII. 182 Rustication as a decorative motif can occur on three styles of British Late Neolithic pottery—on Beakers, Fengate Ware, and Grooved or Rinyo-Clacton ware. **1970** Bray & Trump *Dict. Archæol.* 256/1 To the Late Neolithic belong the highly decorated wares of Peterborough and Rinyo-Clacton styles.

rio, var. ryo.

†**rioall**, variant of *rioll*, rial *a. Obs.*

c **1450** *Merlin* 107 Lo, here is the crowne and the vestementis rioall. **1486** *Hen. VII at York* in *Surtees Misc.* (1890) 54 A world desolaite,..in the which shall spryng up a rioall, rich, rede rose.

Rioja (ri'oxa). Also **rioja**. [The name of a district of northern Spain.] A wine produced in this district.

1907 *Yesterday's Shopping* (1969) 96/1 *Claret*..Rioja (Spanish), per dozen flagons 21/9. **1920** G. Saintsbury *Notes on Cellar-bk.* ii. 18 Other light Spanish wines of this class (of the Riojas, etc., we may speak separately) are excellent. *Ibid.* vi. 89 White Rioja (a capital beverage liquor). **1926** E. Hemingway *Sun also Rises* xix. 257 We had roast young suckling pig and drank *rioja alta*. **1934** R. Macaulay *Going Abroad* xxiii. 182 Wicker flasks of rioja. **1951** R. Postgate *Plain Man's Guide to Wine* vii. 108 Of table wines which a foreigner may be offered, Rioja ('J' pronounced as 'H') is..a full, strong wine produced in the north, mostly red and with a heavy plush-like flavour. **1965** G. Household *Olura* 157 Allarte's capacity for red Rioja, anchovies and bread was astonishing. **1973** *Country Life* 26 Apr. 1162/1 Rioja..comes from the north of the country, about 100 miles south of the western Pyrenees. *Ibid.* 1162/3 There is both red and white Rioja..and the red is certainly the more distinguished.

riol(ly, riolte, variants of rial(ly, rialty *Obs.*

riometer (riː'ɒmɪtə(r), 'raɪəʊmiːtə(r)). *Geophysics.* [f. the initial letters of *r*elative *i*onospheric *o*pacity + -meter.] An instrument which permits continuous measurement of the absorption of cosmic radio waves by the ionosphere.

1959 Little & Leinbach in *Proc. IRE* XLVII. 315/2 Thirteen of the commercially built units, now called 'riometers' (Relative Ionospheric Opacity Meters) are currently in use... The riometer is a self-balancing receiving system in which a local noise source is continuously made equal to the noise power from the antenna. **1968** G. M. B. Dobson *Explor. Atmos.* (ed. 2) viii. 151 An entirely different method which is now being much used is to measure the intensity of cosmic radio waves which are constantly reaching the earth from the galaxy. These radio waves will be absorbed as they come down through the D region, so that low intensity of cosmic radio waves received at the ground means strong absorption by the D region. These instruments are generally known as riometers. **1972** *Nature* 28 Jan. 215/1 Ground based observations using a 27 MHz riometer and an H magnetometer indicated almost quiet ionospheric conditions. **1980** *Ibid.* 17 Jan. 278/2 The Siple riometer operates at 30 MHz and has a response time of 0.25 s to increases or decreases in signal intensity.

‖**rione** (ri'one). Pl. **rioni**. [It.] A district or administrative division of Rome. Cf. region 5.

1927 *Daily Express* 23 Nov. 12 Nine new fountains have been inaugurated in Rome, each corresponding to a rione, or section of the city. **1936** G. F.-H. & J. Berkeley *Italy in Making* II. vii. 115 The orders were sent out to the heads of each of the rioni (fourteen in number) in Rome. Each head of a rione sent his orders to his capi-squadra (heads of squadrons). **1965** C. Hibbert *Garibaldi & his Enemies* I. iv. 50 In every *rione* deputies were appointed to take command of the citizens when the bells of the Capitol and Montecitorio summoned them to arms. **1979** *Jrnl. R. Soc. Arts* Nov. 775/1 The triangular shed..is a new social centre meant to revive and support a local form of civic organization, the *rione*, an alternative to the centralized bureaucracy, church and *municipio*.

riot, variant of ryot.

riot ('raɪət), *sb.* Forms: *α.* 3–6 **riote**, 4– **riot**, 4–6 **riott**, 5 **riotte**, **riaut**, 6 **riat**, **riet**; 4–6 **ryote** (5 **ryaute**), 4–7 **ryot**, 5–7 **ryott**, 5–6 **ryotte**, 5 **ryet(te**. *β.* 4–5 **reot**, 5 **reaut**. See also royet. [a. OF. *riote* (*rihote*), *riotte* fem., *riot* (*rihot*) masc., debate, dispute, quarrel, etc., = Prov. *riota*, It. *riotta*, of obscure origin.]

1. a. Wanton, loose, or wasteful living; debauchery, dissipation, extravagance. Now *rare*.

a **1225** *Ancr. R.* 198 So þet non wisure read ne mei bringen hire ut of hire riote [*v.r.* him of his fol riote]. *a* **1300** *Cursor M.* 48 A saumpul her be þaem I say, þat rages in þare riot [*Bedf.* reaut] ay; In riot [*Bedf.* riaut] and in rigolage, Of all þere liif spend þai þe stage. *c* **1380** Wyclif *Wks.* (1880) 122 þei wasten moche good in ryot & glotonye. **1399** Langl. *Rich. Redeles* I. 6 Rafte was ȝoure riott and rest. *Ibid.* IV. 20 Whanne þe reot and þe reeuell þe rent þus passid. **1432–50** tr. *Higden* (Rolls) I. 377 The clergy..spendenge the nyȝhtes in surfettes and in ryette. *a* **1450** *Knt. de la Tour* (1868) 54 Who that sekithe ryot gladly, he mekithe there-with. **1514** Barclay *Cyt. & Uplondyshm.* (Percy Soc.) 27 In ryot & dronkenesse, Theyr name defylynge, despysynge all goodnesse. **1560** Daus tr. *Sleidane's Comm.* 63 b, Al to mainteyne your ryot, pryde, and voluptuousnes. **1600**

HOLLAND *Livy* 1387 There was nothing wanting, that might serue for pleasure or prodigall riot. **1667** MILTON *P.L.* XI. 711 All now was turn'd to jollitie and game, To luxurie and riot, feast and dance. **1732** POPE *Ess. on Man* I. 81 The lamb thy riot dooms to bleed to-day. **1817** JAS. MILL *Brit. India* II. IV. viii. 272 Hyder..spent his life between the labours of the chase, and the pleasures of voluptuous indolence and riot.

personif. **1609** DEKKER *Work for Armourers* Wks. (Grosart) IV. 139 Riot (a smooth-fac'd Ganimed) slept in her lap. **1754** T. SCOTT *Table of Cebes* 144 See! Riot her luxurious Bowl prepares.

fig. **1751** JOHNSON *Rambler* No. 89 ¶4 This invisible riot of the mind, this secret prodigality of being, is secure from detection, and fearless of reproach.

b. Unrestrained revelry, mirth, or noise.

1728–46 THOMSON *Spring* 368 To swell the riot of th' autumnal feast. **1794** MRS. RADCLIFFE *Myst. Udolpho* vi, It seemed not the laugh of cheerfulness but of riot. **1816** T. SCOTT *Vis. Paris* (ed. 5) p. lxv, The free vent given to what may be termed the clamour and riot of satisfaction by the absence of official arrangement. **1840** DICKENS *Old C. Shop* xix, They quickened their steps to get clear of all the roar and riot. **1873** DIXON *Two Queens* XII. vii. II. 326 With bray of snorting horns and riot of exploding guns.

c. *in full riot*, in full swing. *rare.*

1898 LD. E. HAMILTON *Mawkin* ix, The spaning of the lambs was by with, and the ewe milking in full riot.

2. a. An instance or course of loose living; a noisy feast or wanton revel; a disturbance arising from this; †an extravagant display *of* something.

13.. *Seuyn Sag.* (W.) 163 For burgeis, maiden, other knaue, Mighte him in some riote sette. *c* **1380** *Sir Ferumb.* 4459 He þenkþ hold an huge ryot..Wyþ-inne þis fortenigt. **1390** GOWER *Conf.* II. 367 Every riot ate laste Mot nedes falle and mai noght laste. **1474** CAXTON *Chesse* III There cometh of glotonye riottes, wronges, and molestacions. **1612** DRAYTON *Poly-olb.* vii. 50 The ryots to represse of this outrageous crue. **1649** DRUMM. OF HAWTH. *Hist. Jas. I*, Wks. (1711) 9 They abolished Riots of all Sorts of Pearl..; only Women were permitted to wear a small Carkanet of them about their Necks. *a* **1700** SEDLEY *Wks.* (1722) I. 28 Roots he preferr'd, and Pot-herbs To all the Pomp and Riots of a Crown. **1807** CRABBE *Village* II. 63 And hark! the riots of the Green begin, That sprang at first from yonder noisy inn.

fig. **1768** STERNE *Sent. Journ., Bourbonnois*, There was nothing from which I had painted out for myself so joyous a riot of the affections.

†**b.** A foolish saying; a rigmarole. *Obs.*

c **1330** *Sir Beues* 1191 'Men saiþ,' ȝhe seide, 'in olde riote [*v.r.* roote], þat wimmannes bolt is sone schote'. **1340** *Ayenb.* 99 God þe uader..ne heþ none hede of longe ryote of tales y-slyked ne y-rymed.

†**c.** ? A company or assemblage of persons. *Obs.*⁻¹

? *a* **1400** *Morte Arth.* 388 And I may se the Romaynes.. Arayede in theire riotes on a rounde felde [etc.].

d. A vivid display *of* (colour).

1894 K. GRAHAME *Pagan P.* 68 A riot of scarlet on gold. **1895** *Outing* XXVI. 429/2 Here and there the sombre green of a cedar broke the riot of color. **1969** *Morning Star* 9 July 4/3 The trees are flourishing better than ever, and the borders have been a riot of colour. **1974** 'S. WOODS' *Done to Death* 184 The garden was a riot of colour.

3. a. *Hunting.* The action, on the part of a hound, of following the scent of some animal other than that which he is intended to hunt. Also in phr. *to hunt* or *run riot.*

The first passage from the *Master of Game* appears to contain some misunderstanding of the term.

c **1410** *Master of Game* (MS. Digby 182) x, What racche þat renneth to a Conynge in any tyme, he ought to be ascryede, saynge to hym lowde: War ryote war. For none oþer beeste in Inglonde is called ryote, saue onely þe Conynge. *Ibid.* xvi, For he [the spaniel] will make alle þe ryote and alle [þe] harme. **1594** T. B. *La Primaud. Fr. Acad.* II. 181 If hee cannot by sent finde out the game he seeketh, or if, after he hath found it and is in chase, he fall to hunt riot [etc.]. **1688** HOLME *Armoury* III. 76/1 When Hounds run at a whole Herd of Deer,..we say..[they] Run Riot. **1856** 'STONEHENGE' *Brit. Rural Sports* 123 Until..hounds are entered to their particular game, they must not be too much rated and broken from 'riot'. *Ibid.* 131 Leaving them..to hunt 'riot' unchecked. **1890** *Sat. Rev.* 1 Feb. 135/1 A slight variation in the note of a hound..tells him that the hound has been too free with his tongue on riot (the hunting term for the scent of the wrong animal).

b. *to run riot*, in fig. use: To act without restraint or control; to disregard all limitations; to grow luxuriantly or wildly, etc.

1523 FITZHERB. *Husb.* §148 If thou breake thy tedure, and ren ryot at large, and knowe not other mennes goodes frome thyne owne. **1535** JOYE *Apol. Tindale* (Arb.) 13 Here may ye se how Tindale runneth ryot of his own wit. **1656** BP. HALL *Rem. Wks.* (1660) 122 Ye suffer your Tongues to run ryot in bitter Scoffs. **1700** DRYDEN *Pref. Fables* Ess. (ed. Ker) II. 265 Sometimes also..he runs riot, like Ovid, and knows not when he has said enough. **1748** CHESTERF. *Lett.* clxii. (1792) II. 85 They ran riot, would not be kept within bounds by their leaders. **1768–74** TUCKER *Lt. Nat.* (1834) II. 512 To study how they may be employed most effectually to answer some good purpose; that, if possible, they may never run riot. **1832** TENNYSON *Œnone* 99 The wandering ivy and vine, This way and that, in many a wild festoon Ran riot. **1847** H. MILLER *First Impr. Eng.* iii. (1857) 38 The sculptor seems to have let his imagination altogether run riot. **1884** GILMOUR *Mongols* 186 The rheumatism runs riot among them.

†**c.** So *to run at riot. Obs. rare.*

1530 TINDALE *Answ. More* (Parker Soc.) 114 They.. either run altogether at riot, or keep the law with cautels and expositions of their own feigning. **1579** TOMSON *Calvin's Serm. Tim.* 12/1 So soone as a man beginneth to runne at riot, & leaueth the streight line.

4. a. Violence, strife, disorder, tumult, *esp.* on the part of the populace.

1375 BARBOUR *Bruce* XVII. 510 To pass In Yngland, for till burn and sla; And swa gret ryot thar till ma [etc.]. *c* **1400** MAUNDEV. (1839) xiv. 159 It [the diamond] kepethe him that berethe it..fro Strif and Riot. **1429** *Rolls of Parlt.* IV. 345/2 There have come grete multitude of peple..with greete ryot and strengthe in maner of Werre. **1581** PETTIE *Guazzo's Civ. Conv.* I. (1586) 24 b, I thinke these same..commit no lesse ryot, then those which crucified Christ. **1593** G. HARVEY *Pierce's Super.* Wks. (Grosart) II. 230, I know none so rank-minded, to enter vpon your proper possessions by riot. **1769** *Junius Lett.* xi. (1788) 70 You left the metropolis exposed..to every species of riot and disorder. **1819** LD. ELDON in Ld. Campbell *Chancellors* (1857) VIII. 392 What constitutes riot enough to justify dispersion is no easy matter to determine. **1848** W. H. KELLY tr. *L. Blanc's Hist. Ten Y.* II. 484 The swords of the demagogues striking at the gates of San-Ildefonso..; in a word, riot in the very apartments of Christina.

fig. **1820** KEATS *St. Agnes* xvi, Sudden a thought..in his pained heart Made purple riot.

b. A violent disturbance of the peace by an assembly or body of persons; an outbreak of active lawlessness or disorder among the populace; †a hostile attack or encounter.

1390 GOWER *Conf.* III. 171 Benedab..Of Irahel a gret partie..Hath sesed; and of that riote He [Ahab] tok conseil. *c* **1425** WYNTOUN *Cron.* VII. 2584 Thare wes þe admirall slane of þe flot, And all þe laif in þat ryot. **1433** *Rolls of Parlt.* IV. 421/2 In eschuyng of Riotes..and disobeissances ayenst the Kynges astate. **1462** *Paston Lett.* II. 95 That the Kyng shulde..come unto this cuntre and se suyche riottes as have be in this cuntre punyshed. **1523** *Act 14 & 15 Hen. VIII*, c. 7 Processes shalbe made..in like maner as is made upon enditements of riottes. **1568** GRAFTON *Chron.* II. 83 *marg.*, A riot made vpon Jewes. **1598** SHAKS. *Merry Wives* I. i. 35 The Councell shall heare it, it is a Riot. **1632** LITHGOW *Trav.* IV. 152 Such vnallowable Ryots, being expresly against..the quietnesse and liberty of the Christians. **1670** MARVELL *Corr.* Wks. (Grosart) II. 354 The Bill for Conventicles hath bin twice red and committed: it makes them henceforth riots. **1707** HEARNE *Collect.* (O.H.S.) I. 337 An abominable Riot committed in All-Souls College. **1759** SMOLLETT *Hist. Eng.* (ed. 3) X. 179 After having..heard the proclamation against riots read in public. **1801** in James *Milit. Dict.* (1802) s.v. Every description of peace officers may and ought to do..all that in him lies towards the suppressing riots. **1863** H. COX *Instit.* I. xi. 275 A tumult on account of a particular or private grievance amounts at the most to a riot. **1887** HUNT *Bristol* 203 All former riots..sink into insignificance compared with the Reform riots of 1831.

transf. and *fig.* **1560** ROLLAND *Crt. Venus* IV. 474 For and ȝe do..but debait Agane Venus rais ony rank riat [etc.]. **1595** SHAKS. *John* III. i. 247 Shall these hands..make a ryot on the gentle brow Of true sincerity?

c. **Riot Act**, the Act (1 Geo. I, § 2, c. 5) providing that if twelve or more persons unlawfully or riotously assemble and refuse to disperse within an hour after the reading of a specified portion of it by a competent authority they shall be considered as felons. *to read the Riot Act* (also with small initials): in *transf.* use, to announce or declare that (unruly) action or conduct must cease; to reprimand or caution sternly.

The Riot Act was repealed in 1973.

1731 *Gentl. Mag.* I. 15 Speaking of the riot-act he says [etc.]. **1795** PITT in T. Browne *British Cicero* (1808) I. 524 That after reading the riot act, and ordering them to disperse, any number of persons remaining should, as by the riot act, incur the penalty of the law, that of felony. **1819** W. BRADFORD *Let.* 17 Dec. in M. Wilmot *More Lett.* (1935) 39 She has just run out to read the riot act in the Nursery. **1840** DICKENS *Barn. Rudge* xlix, The Riot Act was read. **1842** C. FOX *Jrnl.* 18 Apr. (1972) 123 Sydney Smith said, 'Lady Holland is not one woman, but a multitude; just read the Riot Act and you'll presently see them disperse!' **1887** HUNT *Bristol* 201 The Riot Act having been read three times, the soldiers were ordered to clear the bridge. **1906** J. LONDON *Let.* 20 Oct. (1966) 211 You might have found out, before you read me the riot act. **1946** D. HAMSON *We fell among Greeks* xvii. 187, I met the E.D.E.S. envoys and read them the riot act, so to speak. **1976** P. HILL *Hunters* x. 131 Read her the riot act, tell her to be a good girl and take her home.

d. *colloq.* (orig. *Theatr.*). Something extremely successful or amusing; *spec.* an uproariously successful performance or show, a 'smash hit'. Also of persons.

1909 P. G. WILLIAMS in *Sat. Even. Post* 5 June 17/2 *A riot*, great success. **1919** F. HURST *Humoresque* 195 If you think that is a riot..you wait until you see the way they're going to eat me up in the court scene. **1929** J. B. PRIESTLEY *Good Companions* II. i. 249 There isn't a more promising little show anywhere... It could have been an absolute riot. **1933** N. STREATFEILD *Tops & Bottoms* xxii. 287 He was a riot. **1936** P. QUENTIN *Puzzle for Fools* xxvi. 253 He'd be a riot in a mental hospital. **1943** J. B. PRIESTLEY *Daylight on Saturday* xv. 101 These shows—they're a riot. **1959** E. H. CLEMENTS *High Tension* viii. 134 Get that word-perfect.. and you'll be a riot tomorrow. **1976** J. SNOW *Cricket Rebel* 110 His rendering of 'Barnacle Bill the Sailor' was a riot and became his party piece.

e. In full, *riot sale.* A sale. *U.S. slang.*

1952 *N.Y. Post* 26 Sept. 73/1 (Advt.), Auto 'riot' sale. **1969** *Punch* 5 Feb. 193/1 Some of New York's stores are having a shoe riot.

5. *attrib.* and *Comb.* **a.** General attrib. uses (sense 4), as ***riot area, call, control, zone***; **b.** designating equipment worn or carried (esp. by peace-keeping forces) in a riot, as ***riot equipment, gear, gun, helmet, shield, stick***; also (parasynthetically) ***riot-helmeted*** adj.; also of persons or vehicles equipped to quell riots, as ***riot police, squad, tank, van, wagon***; **c.** in instrumental, etc., uses, as ***riot-battered, -prone, -ripe, -scarred, -torn*** adjs.; **d.** **riot gas**, an irritant gas fired in capsules into a mob to quell rioting, tear-gas.

1973 *Freedom* 2 June 3/1 No one who lives in the riot areas of Belfast needs any reminders of what violence can look like. **1976** *Daily Times* (Lagos) 27 Aug. 9/2 Unofficial reports said 20 bodies were found in the riot battered township on Wednesday. **1905** *N.Y. Even. Post* 7 Nov. 2 Charges of illegal voting resulted in a disturbance which police were unable to subdue, and a riot call was sent in. **1964** KIRK & OTHMER *Encycl. Chem. Technol.* (ed. 2) IV. 877 In the last few years, an agent, CS, has been developed for riot control. **1974** *North Myrtle Beach* (S. Carolina) *Times* 17 Apr. 1/5 The riot control unit then had to make its way to Hillside Drive and make a similar sweep to quell trouble spots on that street. **1955** H. KURNITZ *Invasion of Privacy* (1956) xii. 79 The old man is handing out riot equipment and orders are shoot to kill. **1968** *Punch* 4 Dec. 804/1 Jelly-crazed five-year-olds can now be quietened with a discreet blast of MACE lavender-perfumed riot gas. **1969** *Guardian* 22 Jan. 1/3 A powerful fragmentation grenade which will scatter CS riot gas among demonstrators is being developed by the Ministry of Technology. **1978** *N.Y. Times* 30 Mar. A5/6 Thousands of policemen..in riot gear. **1930** *Morning Post* 9 Apr. 11 Detectives in motor-cars equipped with 'riot guns' toured through the districts where violence was anticipated. **1976** 'B. SHELBY' *Great Pebble Affair* 49 Officer Hodgson with his riot gun. **1969** S. GREENLEE *Spook who sat by Door* xiii. 112 Watching the police in riot helmets and the angry faces of the crowd. **1973** 'S. HARVESTER' *Corner of Playground* III. v. 212 Tight-lipped young officers, whites of eyes gleaming under rim of riot-helmet. **1970** *Daily Tel.* 18 Apr. 5/3 Three young women were wounded by shotgun pellets when 200 riot-helmeted, sheriff's deputies dispersed a crowd of about 700 smashing windows at a bank. **1958** *Daily Sketch* 2 June 2/5 Riot police armed with rifles, machine-guns and tear-gas tensed for an attack by Communist demonstrators. **1977** *Times* 18 Feb. 7/5 Riot police took control of Rome University tonight after using tear gas to disperse angry left-wing students. **1967** *Economist* 7 Oct. 45/2 Property-owners in riot-scarred (and riot-prone) neighbourhoods. **1968** *Ibid.* 20 July 40/3 Many state capitals are now humming with reports of 'mass' cancellations by insurers of policies covering property in riot-prone areas. **1910** KIPLING *Rewards & Fairies* 103 Tom Dunch an' some of his kidney was drinkin' themselves riot-ripe. **1965** *Jet* 16 Sept. 50 Martin Luther King, Jr. was forced to invoke the name of Elijah Muhammed to gain a hearing in the riot-scarred community of Watts. **1967** Riot-scarred [see *riot-prone* above]. **1967** *Economist* 7 Jan. 31/1 (*caption*) Calcutta police behind riot shields. **1968** *Guardian* 21 Oct. 18/7 Mr Callaghan has issued no instructions to the Commissioner of the Metropolitan Police,..about the use of tear gas, water cannon, riot shields, troops, or other weapons familiar to demonstrators in Paris. **1978** *Peace News* 25 Aug. 4/1 The police included a large contingent of the Special Patrol Group with riot shields. **1981** *Daily Tel.* 3 Mar. 2/1 Police, some with riot shields and crowbars, stormed the building. **1948** *New Yorker* 1 May 75/1 A trio of jeeps, bringing the *celere*, or riot squad. **1955** *Times* 25 Aug. 9/2 The requirements for this are good intelligence arrangements and a mobile riot squad such as the strategic reserve in Cyprus will provide. **1977** *New Yorker* 24 Oct. 132/3 The prison's three riot squads..officially called.. correctional emergency-response teams. **1930** J. DOS PASSOS *42nd Parallel* v. 404 He'd been halfstunned by a riotstick. **1972** R. PERRY *Fall Guy* i. 28 The police arrived..with their riot sticks in evidence..lead-weighted batons. **1978** D. FRANCIS *Trial Run* xi. 156 They were armed..with riot sticks. Nasty hard things like baseball bats, swinging from a loop of leather round the wrist. **1966** L. COHEN *Beautiful Losers* I. 134 It is not enough that she and Prince Philip will be greeted by police cordons, riot tanks, and the proud backs of hostile crowds. **1969** C. HIMES *Black on Black* (1973) 286 The riot tank didn't know where to look for him. **1968** *Economist* 12 Oct. 3/2 The..riot-torn country of Northern Ireland. **1976** *Ulverston* (Cumbria) *News* 3 Dec. (Suppl.) p. i/3 *Shoot!*..Containing articles by well-known footballers, the 'lowdown' on the riot-torn 1975 European Cup Final. **1981** *Yorks. Post* 9 July 1/3 Prince Charles wants to help youngsters in Liverpool's riot-torn Toxteth area. **1973** J. DRUMMOND *Bang! Bang! You're Dead!* xxxiv. 116 There were extra police on duty, and several riot vans under the trees. **1976** J. MCCLURE *Rogue Eagle* xiv. 234 There were a couple of riot vans double-parked outside. **1969** *Guardian* 5 Aug. 1/7 Finally riot wagons were moved in to block the oblique junction. **1973** *Black Panther* 28 July 3/2 Police arrived in buses and riot wagons. **1975** R. H. RIMMER *Premar Experiments* (1976) i. 56 According to my informant, Bren and Merle were living in a rundown tenement house in the 'riot zone'.

†**'riot**, *a. Obs. rare.* [f. prec. Cf. ROYET *a.*] Wanton, licentious; incoherent.

a **1300** *Cursor M.* 26938 Sum men in scubardis Til oþer men telles þair folis, And sais amang [þat] riot ron 'Alle men wat wel þat i ha don'. **1513** DOUGLAS *Æneis* VIII. Prol. 147 The riotest ane ragment wyth mony rat rane.

riot ('raɪət), *v.* Forms: 4–5 **ryote**, 4 **ryotte**, 4–7 **ryot** (5 **ryott**), 6 **ryat**; 4, 7– **riot**, 6 **riott(e**. See also ROYET *v.* [a. OF. *rioter* (*rihoter*), *riotter*, related to *riote*, etc., RIOT *sb.*]

I. 1. a. *intr.* To live in a wanton, dissipated, or unrestrained manner; to revel; to indulge to excess *in* something. Now somewhat *rare.*

c **1386** CHAUCER *Cook's T.* 50 Thus this ioly prentys hadde his leue. Now lat him riote al the nyght. **1513** MORE in Grafton *Chron.* (1568) II. 770 Vnthriftes riott and runne in debt. **1567** MAPLET *Gr. Forest* 86 They are ready to come home from straying and riotting abrode in the Parckes. **1606** SHAKS. *Ant. & Cl.* II. ii. 72 I wrote to you, when rioting in Alexandria you Did pocket vp my Letters. **1611** BIBLE *2 Pet.* ii. 13 They that count it pleasure to riot in the day time. **1681–6** J. SCOTT *Chr. Life* II. iii. I. §1 In those good Pagan Days wherein they might have rioted with Devotion, Sacrificed to the Gods in drunken Bowls [etc.]. **1751** *Narr.*

of H.M.S. Wager 64 They would have rioted in spirituous Liquor. 1840 Dickens *Old C. Shop* i, Men who do nothing but waste and riot. 1865 Kingsley *Herew.* xviii, The French scum who now riot over Essex. 1899 W. E. Norris *Giles Ingilby* vii, A sort of unrepentant prodigal son rioting off to far countries.

transf. 1567 Maplet *Gr. Forest* 55 Neither doth it seeme to ryot vntill suche time as it is plentifull in yeelding seede. 1811 H. G. Knight *Phrosyne* 39 When stern Winter riots unconfin'd. 1816 J. Wilson *City of Plague* i. ii, Then the Plague Riots in darkness mid his unknown victims. 1882 Farrar *Early Chr.* I. 6 Ostentation, impurity rioted in the heart of a society which [etc.].

†**b.** So *to riot it*. *Obs.*

*a*1593 Marlowe *Edw. II*, C iij, This I scorne, that one.. should..riote it with the treasures of the realme. 1621 Bp. Mountagu *Diatr.* 53 Who would not bee bounded in by any Councell.., but riot it as hee would himselfe. 1659 Hammond *On Ps.* lxxiii. 10. 354 When they see them thus riot it in violence. 1760–72 H. Brooke *Fool of Qual.* (1809) I. 58 These have nothing to do but..to riot it, to roar it.

c. To revel *in*, to take great delight or pleasure *in*, something. Also const. *upon*.

1741 Watts *Improv. Mind* xx. Wks. (1813) 154 To indulge and riot in these exquisitely bewitching contemplations. 1773 *Life N. Frowde* 31 Few are the Brutes ..that can riot in Cruelty to Infant Softness. 1827 Chalmers *Mem.* (1851) III. x. 171, I perfectly rioted upon the scenery. 1840 Dickens *Barn. Rudge* lxxi, Vaunting and, as it were, rioting in, her huge unworthiness.

†**2.** *refl.* To indulge (oneself) to the full in some pleasure or recreation. *Obs.*

1390 Gower *Conf.* III. 237 Thilke fyri rage Of love,.. Wherof himself he so rioteth, And wax so ferforth womannyssh, That [etc.]. ?*a*1400 *Morte Arth.* 923 The roo and the rayne-dere reklesse thare ronnene..in rosers to ryotte thame seluene. *c*1400 *Melayne* 797 Riste and Ryott ȝow by þe water of sayne.

3. a. *trans.* To spend or waste (money, etc.) in riotous living; to pass (time) in riot or luxury. Const. *away* or *out*.

1597 Daniel *Civ. Wars* vi. xviii, Whilst wee..Ryot away, for nought, whole Prouinces. 1709 Mrs. Manley *Secret Mem.* (1736) II. 183 Her Husband..rioted out the Income of her Fortune in such blameable Diversions. 1792 Brooks *Prec. Remedies* 72 The evil servant did not riot out his talents. 1850 Merivale *Rom. Emp.* i. (1865) I. 33 Retreats.. in which to..riot away the intervals of repose. 1864 Tennyson *Aylmer's F.* 391 He..Had rioted his life out, and made an end.

†**b.** To use (words) with profusion or extravagance. *Obs. rare*⁻¹.

1586 D. Rowland *Lazarillo* i. (1677) G j, Ryoting more pleasant and sweet words than ever Ovid wrote.

II. †**4.** *Sc.* and *north.* To ravage, harry, spoil (a country, etc.). *Obs. rare.*

1375 Barbour *Bruce* ix. 500 All that he fand he maid it his; And ryotit gretly the lande. ?*a*1400 *Morte Arth.* 1883 Thane relyez the renkez..For to ryotte the wode. *c*1425 Wyntoun *Cron.* viii. xxvii. 4553 He..gert his folk wiþe mekyl mayne Ryote halely þe cuntre.

5. †**a.** To force (a person) *to* do some action by persistence or importunity; so, to prevent (one) *from* doing something. *Obs.*

1777 Mme. D'Arblay *Early Diary* (1889) II. 189 Dr. Wall..advised me, or, rather, rioted me, to get out and go and see the Salute. 1781 —— *Diary* June, This rattle..Mrs. Thrale most kindly kept up, by way of rioting me from thinking.

b. Of rioters: To attack (persons or property).

1886 *Referee* 21 Feb. 7/3 The West-End tradespeople who were 'rioted'. 1900 *Daily News* 4 Sept. 7/5 S.K.T. Station has been rioted and completely destroyed.

6. a. *intr.* To make a disturbance; to storm.

1787 Mme. D'Arblay *Diary* 26 Feb., Had he surprised the two Equerries in his room,..how would he have rioted!

b. To engage in a riot or violent disturbance.

1755 Johnson, *To Riot*..4. To raise a sedition or uproar. *a*1832, etc. [implied in rioting *vbl. sb.* 2]. 1981 W. Ebersohn *Divide the Night* v. 71 When they [*sc.* blacks] rioted they did it with greater anger here [*sc.* in Johannesburg] than anywhere else. 1981 *Yorks. Post* 9 July 4/5 As thoroughly decent a group of people as you would wish to meet, they did not riot in the streets.

7. *Hunting.* = *to run riot* s.v. riot *sb.* 3 a. Also const. *after*, *on*.

1954 J. I. Lloyd *Beagling* 143 *Riot*, to hunt anything other than their legitimate quarry. 1971 *Country Life* 7 Oct. 897/1 Hounds will riot more readily after roe deer than any other species. 1976 *Horse & Hound* 3 Dec. 38/1 A great deal of time would be spent, however, correcting the pack rioting on Scotch sheep.

rioter ('raɪətə(r)). Forms: α. 4–7 **riot(t)our**, 4, 6–7 **ryot-**, 5–6 **ryott-**, 5 **riatour**, 6 **ryatour**, 5–7 **ryator**, 7 **riotor**. β. 5–6 **ryotter**, 6 **ryoter**, 6– **rioter**. [a. AF. *riotour* (see riot *v.* and -our), with later change of suffix.]

1. One who leads a disorderly or licentious life, or who indulges in debauchery; a dissolute person; a reveller. *Obs.* exc. *arch.*

α. *c*1386 Chaucer *Pard. T.* 333 These riottoures..Were set hem in a tavern for to drynke. 1389 in *Eng. Gilds* (1870) 4 ȝif þer be in bretherhede eny riotour, oþer contekour. 1406 Hoccleve *La Male Regle* 118 Seeknesse, y meene, riotoures whippe. *a*1513 Fabyan *Chron.* vii. (1811) 577 This man.. applyed hym vnto all vyce and insolency, and drewe vnto hym all ryottours & wylde dysposed persones. 1526 Tindale *2 Tim.* iii. 3 The men shalbe..ryatours, fearce, despisers of them which are good. *c*1550 R. Bieston *Bayte Fortune* B j, Riotours and rybaldes that haue no dread of shame. 1607 Hieron *Wks.* I. 234 It cutteth the ryotour and voluptuous liuer, that his course should..bee so egerly reprooued. 1607 Shaks. *Timon* iii. v. 68 He's a sworne Riotor, he has a sinne That often drownes him.

β. 1472 *Presentments of Juries* in *Surtees Misc.* (1890) 24 [He] is a ryotter on nyghtes. 1530 Palsgr. 263/1 Ryotter a prodigall felowe, *bobancier, prodigue*. 1597 Bacon *Coulers Good & Evill* Ess. (Arb.) 149 Our Sauiour charged with neerenes of Publicanes and rioters said [etc.]. 1611 Cotgr., *Sacre*, a..squanderer, extreame rioter (especially in respect of his bellie). 1822 Shelley *Faust* ii. 272 Old gentle-women,..You ought to be with the young rioters Right in the thickest of the revelry.

2. One who takes part in a riot or rising against constituted authority.

α. *c*1460 Fortescue *Abs. & Lim. Mon.* (1885) 125 The kynge shall..sende his commissioneres,..and also his juges, to represse and punysh riatours and risers. 1495 *Act 11 Hen. VII*, c. 7 Preamble, Greate penalties sette upon the seid riottours and offenders. 1503–4 *Act 19 Hen. VII*, c. 13 Statutes..concerning the punysshement of riottours. 1529 Rastell *Pastyme* (1811) 280 The kynge had pardoned all those ryottours..for the dethe of the lorde Ryuers.

β. 1591 Lambarde *Archeion* (1635) 220 Rioters, attainted of great and hainous Riots, shall be imprisoned one whole yeare. 1615 W. Lawson *Country Housew. Gard.* (1626) 13 Iustice must restraine rioters. 1683 Wood *Life* (O.H.S.) App. vi, The rioters..attempted to break open the prison gate. 1759 Smollett *Hist. Eng.* (ed. 3) X. 178 An address.. desiring that the laws might be vigorously executed against the rioters. 1792 Scott *Let.* in *Lockhart* (1837) I. vii. 193 Nine of the Dunse rioters were condemned to banishment, but the ferment continues violent. 1802 James *Milit. Dict.* s.v., Soldiers are not to fire on rioters until the riot act has been read. 1853 Newman *Hist. Sk.* (1873) II. i. iii. 138 The Emperor did not scruple to send his own troops to aid the rioters. 1887 Hunt *Bristol* 203 His men were pelted with brickbats, and in return shot a ringleader of the rioters.

rioterie, obs. variant of riotry.

†**riotibly**, *adv. Obs.*⁻¹ In 6 ryatybly. [Irreg. f. riot *sb.*] Riotously.

1509 in Leadam *Sel. Cases Crt. Requests* (Selden Soc.) 12 Elyot..ryatybly came with xl personys & brake vp the dorys off your sayd oratour.

'rioting, *vbl. sb.* [f. riot *v.*]

1. †Dissoluteness of life, debauchery (*obs.*); revelry.

1599 Hakluyt *Voy.* I. 11 In the meane season he and his companions spent their time in robbing and rioting. 1611 Bible *Rom.* xiii. 13 Let vs walke honestly as in the day, not in rioting and drunkennesse. 1627 Sanderson *Serm.* (1632) 555 Gaming, and reuelling, and ryoting, and roaring. 1820 Keats *Lamia* i. 214 And sometimes into cities she would send Her dream, with feast and rioting to blend. 1861 Geo. Eliot *Silas M.* 25 A life in which the days would not seem too long, even without rioting. 1891 Kipling *Light that Failed* (1900) 230 There was no more rioting in the chambers.

fig. 1801 Wordsw. *Cuckoo & Night.* xx, I heard the lusty Nightingale so sing, That her clear voice made a loud rioting.

2. The action or fact of taking part in or raising a riot, tumult, or disturbance of the peace.

*a*1832 Mackintosh *Hist. Revol.* Wks. 1846 II. 110 The lawyers..prosecuted the offenders, merely for rioting in violation of certain ancient statutes, some of which rendered that offence capital. 1855 Macaulay *Hist. Eng.* xxii. IV. 728 There was..no such discontent, no such rioting, as he had described. 1886 Weir *Hist. Basis Mod. Europe* (1889) 590 Industrial crises..[are] the results of laws, which are not to be withstood by impatient rioting.

'rioting, *ppl. a.* [f. riot *v.*] Acting in a riotous manner.

1887 Bowen *Virg. Æneid* v. 137 Through rioting pulses run Throbbing fear and desire. 1891 *Daily News* 6 Mar. 3/1 The police..were pelted with iron rivets by a rioting mob.

So **'riotingly** *adv.*

1824 Landor *Imag. Conv., Southey & Porson*, Whortle-berries..extending the hard slenderness of their fibres, at random and riotingly, over their native wastes.

†**'riotise.** *Obs.* Also 6–7 -ize, 7 -yze. [f. riot *sb.* + -ise².] Riotous life or conduct.

1590 Spenser *F.Q.* i. iv. 20 His life he led in lawlesse riotise; By which he grew to grievous malady. 1598 F. Rous *Thule* D 3 b, Little did he thinke that fayrest mayd, Was prisoner in this cell of riotise. 1603 H. Crosse *Vertues Commw.* (1878) 135 He that giues his minde to sloth to riotize and ease. 1637 Heywood *Pleas. Dial.* xiv. Wks. 1874 VI. 231 These..grew to such a profuse riotise, intemperance and wantonnes.

'riotist. *rare.* [f. riot *sb.* + -ist.] One who advocates or practises rioting for the redress of grievances, etc.; a rioter.

1831 *Lincoln Herald* 13 May, That intolerable Italian has done more to break the peace of this country than all the radicals and riotists in the last quarter of a century. 1832 Wilson in *Blackw. Mag.* XXXII. 708 A government.. acting in calm contempt..of hot-headed riotists.

†**'riotly**, *adv. Obs. rare*⁻¹. [f. riot *a.*] Riotously.

1786 *Pennsylv. Mag. Hist. & Biog.* (1894) XVIII. 58 Large parties collect and riotly go to taverns where they sup and return at all hours of the night.

†**'riotness.** *rare*⁻¹. [f. riot *a.*] = riot *sb.* i.

*c*1600 *Ungracious Son* iii. in Evans *O.B.* (1784) III. 276 Through excessive riotness..he was three times more in debt, Than all his wealth was worth.

riotous ('raɪətəs), *a.* Forms: 4–6 **ryotous** (6 **-ouse**), 5 **ryottouse, ryoteux, ryoutis**; 6 *Sc.* **ryatous(e, -us, riattous**; 4– **riotous** (4–5, 7 **-ouse**), 6–7 **riotus**. See also royetous *a.* [a. OF. *riotous, rioteus*, f. *riot(e* riot *sb.*]

†**1.** Troublesome, difficult. *Obs.*⁻¹

1340 *Ayenb.* 170 He ouercomþ þane viȝt, þet is wel liȝt to ouercome to þe bolde herte, and lang and riotouse [F. *ryhoteuse*] to þe sleauuolle.

2. Of persons: Given to wantonness, revelry, or dissolute life; prodigal, extravagant. Now *rare.*

*c*1386 Chaucer *Melib.* §15 It were better dwelle in desert þan with a womman that Is riotous. *c*1420 Hoccleve *Min. Poems* 228 The compaignie of wommen riotous Thow flee. *a*1450 *Knt. de la Tour* (1868) 54 There be other that haue free hert, true and iuste, and be not riotous. 1503 Hawes *Examp. Virt.* v. lxxii, Ryotous company do thou not haunt. 1581 Marbeck *Bk. of Notes* 970 As thou maist see by the similitude of the riotous son. 1613 Purchas *Pilgrimage* (1614) iv. ix. 390 Drunkards and riotous persons they [Persians] hate. 1634 Milton *Comus* 763 As if she would her children should be riotous With her abundance. 1648 Hexham ii, *Een Smetser*, a Riotous man, or a Glutton. 1847 Lytton *Lucretia* (1853) 123, I own..that they are riotous fellows, but some of them are clever.

†**b.** Fond of commotion or fighting. *Obs. rare.*

?*a*1400 *Morte Arth.* 363, I salle..ryfe it in sondyre, Bot he be redily reschowede with riotous knyghtez. *Ibid.* 432, [I shall] Ryde alle thas rowme landes wyth ryotous knyghttes.

†**c.** *transf.* Luxuriant; exuberant. *Obs.*

1594 Hooker *Eccl. Pol.* i. xiii. §3 Shall wee esteeme them as riotous Branches wherewith we sometimes behold most pleasant Vines ouergrowne? 1605 F. Mason *Auth. Church* (1607) 41 Those things which seemed most superfluous, she lopped awaie like riotous branches.

3. Of life, conduct, etc.: Wanton, dissolute, extravagant; marked by excessive revelry.

1389 in *Eng. Gilds* (1870) 38 Nat be his owne folye ne ryotous lyuyng. 1542 Udall in *Lett. Lit. Men* (Camden) 5 Of a veray riottous and dissolute sorte of livynge in his youth. 1544 *Suppl. Hen. VIII* (E.E.T.S.) 53 Yf suche ryotuouse expenses had ben auoyded. 1596 Dalrymple tr. *Leslie's Hist. Scot.* vii. 40 Ane declamatioun against diligat and superfluous cheir in ryatous bankatis. 1618 Bolton *Florus* i. xviii. (1636) 59 Fabricius..condemned it for riotous in Rufinus,..because he had silver plate in all to a ten pound weight. 1755 W. Duncan *Cicero's Sel. Orat.* ix. (1816) 223 Dancing is always the last act of riotous banquets. 1756–7 tr. *Keysler's Trav.* (1760) I. 42 The detestable welcome bowls,..with many other riotous customs, are daily disappearing in Germany. 1844 H. H. Wilson *Brit. India* I. 473 The dissolute and riotous conduct of a large proportion of its inhabitants or visitors. 1888 Fergus Hume *Mme. Midas* i. i, He spent all her wealth in riotous living.

b. Noisy, tumultuous, unrestrained.

1508 Dunbar *Tua mariit Wemen* 193 He ralis, and makis repet with ryatus wordis. *Ibid.* 481 Sum raiffis furght rudly with riatus speche. 1781 Cowper *Conversat.* 261 They dare not wait the riotous abuse,..When wine has giv'n indecent language birth. 1873 'Ouida' *Pascarel* I. 137 Down in the courtyard the children played with their spoils in riotous glee.

4. Characterized or marked by rioting or disturbance of the peace; taking part in or inciting to a riot or tumult; turbulent.

1439 *Rolls of Parlt.* V. 17/2 To have yis open and ryoteux wrong and oppressioun remedied. 1464 *Cov. Leet-bk.* 331 To tyme that he haue..receyued sich punicion for his Riottous demeanyng as shal-be accordyng with oure lawes. 1491 *Act 7 Hen. VII*, c. 15 Certeyn persones of evyll, riotous and sedicious disposicions. *a*1548 Hall *Chron., Hen. VII*, 34 b, Assone as the comminge of the Mayre was intymate.. to the ryotous persones, they fledde. 1568 Grafton *Chron.* II. 141 The Commons of the Citie were farre out of rule by the insensyng of ryotous persons. 1621 Sir R. Boyle in *Lismore Papers* Ser. i. (1886) II. 38 The..Sirieant at armes cam with warrant for her and the Rest of her Riotouse servants. 1649 Milton *Eikon.* 22 Such a riotous act; to wit when hee came to dragg the five Members out of the House. 1714 *Act 1 Geo. I*, st. 2, c. 5 (*title*), An Act for preventing Tumults and riotous Assemblies. 1737 *Gentl. Mag.* VII. 672/1 The Act for apprehending those guilty of the riotous Murder of Capt. Porteous. 1845 Ld. Campbell *Chancellors* X. 158 A resolution to violate the law by refusing the payment of taxes was illegal and riotous. 1887 Hunt *Bristol* 200 Riotous proceedings ensued in London..and other places.

transf. 1778 W. Marshall *Minutes Agric.* 6 Feb. 1775, Rung the riotous ox. 1814 Scott *Diary* 25 Aug. in *Lockhart*, Advancing up this huddling and riotous brook.

†**b.** *in riotous wise*, riotously. *Obs.*

1433 *Rolls of Parlt.* IV. 458/1 Wheras the Commons..in grete noumbre, in riotouse wise, pulled, brak, and hakked doun a pale of the said Abbey. 1443–50 in Baildon *Sel. Cases Chanc.* (Selden Soc.) 134 There came John Wayte..and.. other persones.., and in full ryoutis wyse..entred the house of youre seid besecher.

riotously ('raɪətəslɪ), *adv.* Also 5 riot(t)es-, 6 ryo(u)tous-, ryatous-, riottous-, riat(to)us-, rietously. [f. prec. + -ly².]

1. a. In a wanton or unrestrained manner.

*a*1450 *Knt. de la Tour* (1868) 21, Y see ye wylle speke riotesly and oute of the waye. 1840 Hawthorne *Biog. Sk.* (1879) 190 A huzza from the fleet comes riotously to the shore. 1873 'Ouida' *Pascarel* I. 143 The Italian crowds, though often riotously mirthful, are never rough or rude. 1881 Cable *Mme. Delphine* viii, In its old walks..crab-grass had spread riotously.

b. With revelry or debauchery; in a prodigal or spendthrift manner; extravagantly.

1540 Hyrde tr. *Vives' Instr. Chr. Wom.* i. viii. 20 We shuld vnderstand howe great shame it is to waste it away riottously, and to leade the lyfe delycately and deliciously. 1561 tr. *Calvin's Four Serm.* iii. I vij b, Other do liue most rietously in meate and drinke and al kinde of pleasures. 1624 Capt. Smith *Virginia* iii. 59 The silly President, that had riotously consumed the store. 1643 Prynne *Sov. Power*

Parl. App. 30 Great taxes and summes of money..spent vainly and riotously.

†**c.** Most amply or profusely. *Obs.*⁻¹

1601 R. JOHNSON *Kingd. & Commw.* (1603) 176 Cambaia and Bengala..both riotously abounding in sugar, cotten, wool, cattell, elephants and horses.

2. In a turbulent or unruly manner.

1484 *Cov. Leet-bk.* (E.E.T.S.), The Bakers of the seid Citie in grett nombre riottesly disposed assembled theym. **1511** *Nottingham Rec.* III. 338 For riotously brekyng off owre comon pastur hegges. *a* **1548** HALL *Chron., Hen. VI*, 15 Suche as riotously would make suche assemble against our soueraigne Lord. **1714** *Act 1 Geo. I*, c. 5 §1 If any Persons to the Number of twelve or more being unlawfully, riotously, and tumultuously assembled together [etc.]. **1751** *Affect. Narr. H.M.S. Wager* 131 He had Orders to..reinstate the Officers whom they had riotously depos'd. **1886** *Act 49–50 Vict.* c. 38 Preamble, Property is damaged by persons riotously and tumultuously assembled together.

riotousness (ˈraɪətəsnɪs). Also 6 riotousnes (6–7 -nesse); 6 ryot(o)usnes (7 -ness), *Sc.* **ryattousnes.** [f. as prec. + -NESS.] The state or condition of being riotous.

1542 UDALL in *Lett. Lit. Men* (Camden) 5 He was in his youth a famous example of all riotousnes. **1597** HOOKER *Eccl. Pol.* v. lxxii. §18 To plant parsimonie as Nature, where Riotousnesse hath beene studie. **1606** J. DAVIES (Heref.) *Bien Venu* xxxvii, Who Bountie loues, yet hateth Riotousnesse. **1639** N. N. tr. *Du Bosq's Compl. Woman* II. 35 Their riotousnesse breeds in families so much poverty and jealousies. **1707** J. STEVENS tr. *Quevedo's Com. Wks.* (1709) 502 Riotousness and Luxury. **1837** HALLAM *Hist. Lit.* I. viii. §49 The riotousness of his animal spirits. **1882** MISS BRADDON *Mt. Royal* III. vi. 117 The dinner was cheerful to riotousness.

riotry (ˈraɪətrɪ). Also 4 **ryotrye, rioterie.** [f. RIOT *v.* + -RY. Formed afresh in 18th cent.] Rioting, riotous conduct, riotousness; also, riotous persons (quot. 1780).

c **1330** R. BRUNNE *Chron. Wace* (Rolls) 2406 My fader in elde dotes To halde swylk a squierye, & gret costage in ryotrye. **1338** —— *Chron.* (1810) 220 Þer rioterie þam schent. Suilk ribaudie þei led [etc.]. *Ibid.* 338 Ȝit gos kyng Robyn forth in his rioterie, Ne com not ȝit his fyn to ende of his folie.

1780 H. WALPOLE *Let. to Rev. Mr. Cole* 15 June, I hope your electioneering riotry has not, nor will mix in these tumults. **1826** SOUTHEY *Vind. Eccl. Angl.* 391 The danger was wholly from the furious riotry and drunkeness of the crew. **1834** SIR H. TAYLOR *Artevelde* I. i. iii, They at will Enter'd our houses, lived upon our means In riotry.

rioty (ˈraɪətɪ), *a. nonce-wd.* [f. RIOT *sb.* + -Y¹.] Riotous; noisy, rackety.

1819 KEATS *Let.* 20 Sept. (1958) II. 206 Bless the child, how rioty she is!

rip, *sb.*¹ *dial.* Also 4 rippe, 4, 6–7 ripp. [a. ON. and Icel. *hrip* (Norw. *rip*). The currency of the word in south-eastern counties is remarkable.]

1. A wicker basket or pannier, esp. one used for carrying fish.

c **1300** *Havelok* 893 He..Astirte til him with his rippe, And bigan þe fish to kippe. **1377–8** *Durham Acc. Rolls* (Surtees) 35 In iiijᵒʳ paribus de payngniers novis pro piscator. viijᵗᵒ sportis novis et xij ripps. **1600** in W. F. Shaw *Mem. Eastry* (1870) 226 One cheese presse,..two payer of Ripps, five payells. **1613** DENNIS *Secrets Angling* I. xxvii, Yet must you haue a little Rip beside, Of Willow twigs. **1619** in *Archæol. Cant.* XXV. 6 Going barelegged to catch fish with ripps at his back. **1808** JAMIESON, *Rip*, a basket made of willows, or of willows and straw, for holding eggs, spoons, &c. Ang. **1887** PARISH & SHAW *Kentish Gloss.*, *Rip*, a pannier or basket, used in pairs and slung on each side of a horse for carrying loads, such as fish, salt, sand, &c.

Comb. **1380** in *Archæol. Cant.* (1880) XIII. 206 [The shares of herrings..after deducting the] riphere, barelhere, axhere [etc.]. **1668** *Canterbury Marriage Licences* (MS.), Daniel Longly de Westwell, rippmaker. **1880** E. B. WALKER in *Archæol. Cant.* XIII. 206 The cess upon the Ripiers (or as they would now be termed "long-shore-men"), who to this day call a basket which they carry slung over their backs a 'Rip' basket.

b. (See quot.)

1847 HALLIW., *Rip*, an oval flat piece of wicker-work on which the lines are coiled. Hartlepool.

2. A hen or pheasant coop. Also *hen-rip*.

1840 *Penny Cycl.* XVIII. 479/1 The hen..is frequently confined to a coop, called in Surrey a *rip*, for some weeks. *c* **1858** ELIZ. WATTS *Poultry Yard* 130 The hen should be put under a rip or coop, solid all round except two bars in front. **1884** *West Sussex Gaz.* 25 Sept., Four hen rips, two fatting coops.

rip, *sb.*² *Sc.* Also 8 ripp. [Perh. f. RIP *v.*² The vowel is against connexion with REAP *sb.*¹] A handful of unthreshed grain or of hay; also *spec.* the last handful of grain remaining to be cut in a harvest-field.

a **1670** SPALDING *Troub. Chas. I* (1850) II. 239 Ilk ane had in his cap or bonnet a rip of oats, whilk was his sign. **1783** BURNS *Dying Words Poor Mailie* 34 An' tent them duely.. Wi' taets o' hay an' ripps o' corn. **1786** —— *To Auld Mare* i, Hae, there's a ripp to thy auld baggie. **1809** W. MUIR in *Modern Sc. Poets* (1881) II. 50 Wi' sweet rips o' hay I will treat a' my wethers. **18..** in *Whistle-Binkie* Ser. II. (1853) 80 Aye lay in your corn first,..do like the Kilbarchan calves, drink wi' a rip i' your mouth. **1882** JAS. WALKER *Jaunt Auld Reekie* 12 She taks her heuk and clears an open space Around the rip.

rip, *sb.*³ *dial.* Also 7 ripp. [Of obscure origin. In some western counties the form is *ripe.*] A strickle for a scythe. Also *rip-stick*.

1688 HOLME *Armoury* III. 332/2 The Ripp is that as the Mower whetteth his Sythe withal, of some called the Strickles. **1866–89** in Lincolnshire glossaries. **1892** P. H. EMERSON *Son of Fens* 248, I jist want to do a little more to my point, and my old rip will do.

rip, *sb.*⁴ Also 8 ripp. [f. RIP *v.*² Cf. Flem. *rip* in sense 1.]

1. A rent made by ripping; a laceration, tear.

1711 ADDISON *Spect.* No. 13 ¶3 It is said, indeed, that he once gave him a Ripp in his flesh-colour Doublet. **1869** SIR E. REED *Shipbuild.* xviii. 384 The sheared edges to be free from rip, the surface free from flaws and blisters. **1885** *Field* 3 Oct. 499/2 The curlew being quite dead, with a great rip down its back.

2. *ellipt.* A rip-saw. In comb. *half-rip*.

1846–75 [see RIP-SAW].

3. *dial.* or *colloq.* A rapid rush; a quick run; esp. (*U.S.*) in *Music*: see later quots. Also *transf.*, a burst (of laughter).

1855 *Knickerbocker* XLV. 129 List to the rip and the roar of the song. **1866–** in *Eng. Dial. Dict.* **1867** 'T. LACKLAND' *Homespun* II. 271 Sometimes he could not help giving a rip of laughter that drew the eyes of the whole school round to him in an instant. **1933** *Metronome* Mar. 34 The rip is produced by short and quick glissando up to the tone, attacked sforzando and cut off quickly. **1961** A. BERKMAN *Singers' Gloss. Show Business* 75 *Rip*, an effect in which the entire band plays a fast glissando up to a heavily accented note to emphasize or punctuate a violent action or thought.

4. *U.S. Police slang.* (see quots.)

1939 *Fortune* July 101/3 An inspector's lieutenant..found the patrolman lounging with his gloves off, smoking a cigarette. Probable penalty: one day's 'rip' (fine of a day's pay). **1958** *N.Y. Times Mag.* 16 Mar. 88/3 Rip—A fine imposed for infraction of police regulations: e.g., 'I got a five-day rip' (fined five days' pay).

5. *attrib.* **rip cord,** (*a*) *Aeronaut.* = *ripping cord*; (*b*) *Aeronaut.*, a cord which holds a parachute pack closed and which, when pulled, opens the pack and allows the parachute to unfold and inflate; (*c*) *fig.*; **rip line, panel, valve** *Aeronaut.* = *ripping line, panel, valve* s.v. RIPPING *vbl. sb.* 2 b.

1909 V. LOUGHEED *Vehicles of Air* 108 Practically a valve is the 'rip cord', by means of which a seam running along the side of a balloon can be laid open. **1911** *Sci. Amer.* 25 Mar. 300/1 In case of accident the aviator, by pulling a rip cord, can open the parachute. **1925** [see *pilot chute* s.v. PILOT *sb.* 8]. **1946** W. F. BURBIDGE *From Balloon to Bomber* 40 In 1908, an American parachutist, invented a 'free parachute'... The parachute was packed into a container worn on the airman's chest and released by a whale-bone spring operated by a rip-cord. **1969** *Daily Colonist* (Victoria, B.C.) 7 Feb. 36/1 'Then you'd better put on a parachute if you're afraid,' Beachel said. 'How does the chute work?' Till asked. 'Where is the ripcord?' **1974** [see *ripping line* s.v. RIPPING *vbl. sb.* 2 b]. **1975** 'D. JORDAN' *Black Account* I. xix. 100 He was big..and wide but ripcord lean. **1981** W. WINWARD *Ball Bearing Run* ix. 111 It would be necessary to fall clear of the bomber stream before pulling the rip-cord. **1963** A. SMITH *Throw out Two Hands* viii. 95 Above it [*sc.* the basket of a balloon]..were the valve line (for gentle release of gas) and the rip line (for a total release of gas). **1933** *Sun* (Baltimore) 22 Nov. 2/7 Rather than take a chance on crossing the bay with his diminishing gas, he pulled the rip panel and down they came. **1963** A. SMITH *Throw out Two Hands* v. 63 You lose the rope. Then you pull it again, and this time you can feel it jerking open the rip panel. **1978** A. WELCH *Bk. of Airsports* v. 81/1 For this purpose a rip panel is built into the balloon near the top and is kept closed with either a parachute rip or Velcro. **1907** *Jrnl. Soc. Arts* 19 Apr. 602/2 By means of the rip valve they were able to come down pleasantly and easily.

rip, *sb.*⁵ [? Related to RIP *v.*²]

1. a. A disturbed state of the sea, resembling breakers; an overfall. (See also *tide-rip*.)

1775 ROMANS *Florida* App. 88 You will see a rip appear like breakers; but in the rip is 18 or 20 fathom, and the moment a ship gets into this rip, she jumps out of soundings. **1857** R. TOMES *Amer. in Japan* xvi. 370 We passed thro' a very heavy over-fall or rip; so much so that the executive officer and others at first supposed that there were breakers. **1892** E. REEVES *Homeward Bound* 71 We..passed through a nasty tidal rip, caused by the outflow of the large basin meeting the ocean wind, waves, and currents.

b. *ellipt.* = *rip current*.

1941 *Jrnl. Geol.* XLIX. 338 The term 'rip' might also be used as an abbreviation, which removes the unfortunate tidal connotation of the popular term 'rip tide'. **1968** R. W. FAIRBRIDGE *Encycl. Geomorphol.* 950/2 The width of the central 'trunk' of the rip can be quite narrow, perhaps only a few tens of feet, but the effect of the current can sometimes be detected up to a mile or more from the shore. **1968** W. WARWICK *Surfriding in N.Z.* 20/2 Remember to dive beneath broken waves and do not swim against rips, they will only take you a short distance out to sea before fading out. **1977** *Herald* (Melbourne) 17 Jan. 6/9 He was helping to rescue four people caught in a rip when the accident happened.

2. A stretch of broken water in a river. (Cf. RIFFLE *sb.* 4 and RIPPLE *sb.*³ 1.) Chiefly *U.S.*

a **1828** in B. JAMES *Jrnl.* (1896) II. 195 We passed several very dangerous places, which they there [on the Kennebec R.] termed 'rips', which was [*sic*] a confused number of rocks and large stones in the direct way we were obliged to pass, and which generally had a fall of some few feet. **1839** E. HOLMES *Explor. Aroostook River* 7 The existing obstacles which present themselves to the present navigation of this river, are, the 'rips', which are occasioned principally by loose boulders of rock. **1857** THOREAU *Maine W.* ii. (1867) 112 After passing through some long rips, and by a large island. **1861** —— *Lett.* (1865) 203 Though the current was swift, I did not see a 'rip' on it and only three or four rocks. **1888** J. INGLIS *Tent Life in Tigerland* 262 They had been in a terrible fright lest we should be caught and overturned in the ugly 'rip' or rapid. **1941** B. A. WILLIAMS *Strange Woman* III. i. 128 After that we'd skin 'em [*sc.* scurry ducks] out and tie a string to 'em and let 'em hang in rips of the quickest water we could find. **1977** *New Yorker* 9 May 106/3 A couple of tributaries came into the river,..and they deepened the pools and improved the rips.

3. Special Comb.: **rip current,** an intermittent, strong, narrow current on or near the surface of the sea, flowing directly out from the shore and acting to remove water which has been brought to the shore by waves and wind; **rip tide,** (*a*) = *rip current*; (*b*) = sense 1; (*c*) *fig.*

1936 F. P. SHEPARD in *Science* 21 Aug. 181/2 The name 'rip tide' is certainly not appropriate, since the current described has nothing to do with the tide... The name 'rip current' is suggested, since it is close to the other name and describes the way in which the current rips through the oncoming breakers. **1941** *Jrnl. Geol.* XLIX. 339 The chief seaward return of water moved in by the waves seems to be in the form of rip currents. **1957** G. E. HUTCHINSON *Treat. Limnol.* I. v. 358 The usual pattern..is the development of longshore currents which return to the free water at particular points..as rip currents. **1973** *Daily Tel.* 15 Aug. 6/3 He believed a rip current may have been responsible for carrying the 20 bathers out to sea. **1862** HOPKINS *Hawaii* 15 The bay was full of rip-tides, and the water boiled as in a kettle. **1931** *Daily Progress* (Charlottesville, Va.) 26 Aug. 1/2 Surf bathing as a means of avoiding the heat was made unattractive to many because of the possibility of the recurrence of dangerous 'rip tides'. **1936** [see *rip current*]. *a* **1963** S. PLATH *Ariel* (1965) 45 Your stooges..Riding the rip tide to the nearest point of departure. **1970** I. PETITE *Meander to Alaska* I. v. 47 Riptides, eddies,..complicate a cruiser's traffic patterns. **1973** *Sunday Bull.* (Philadelphia) 14 Oct. (Parade Suppl.) 14/4 Probably the toughest rescue I had was a Mexican family unfamiliar with the riptides. They wandered out about 400 yards into the surf, then started yelling. **1976** *New Yorker* 22 Mar. 106/2 Their echoings of Futurism and Expressionism—for example, the riptides of black diagonals in Dove's 'Field of Grain Seen from Train'. **1977** *Time* 28 Mar. 45/3 In Colombia, surging coffee revenues have been accompanied by a riptide of 26% inflation. **1978** J. A. KNAUSS *Introd. Physical. Oceanogr.* x. 219 Rip tides can be dangerous to the unwary swimmer.

rip, *sb.*⁶ [Perh. a later form of REP². If this is an abbreviation of *reprobate*, the appearance of sense 1 earlier than sense 2 is prob. accidental.]

1. An inferior, worthless, or worn-out horse.

1778 [W. MARSHALL] *Minutes Agric.* 23 July an. 1775, I have given him the rips, instead of the best team, and he is all submission. **1798** in *Spirit Publ. Jrnls.* (1799) II. 296 A raw-boned Scotch rip, whose pedigree we cannot answer for, occupies another capital stall. **1813** *Sporting Mag.* XLI. 101 Meeting Mr. Lee in his gig, driving this rip of a horse (as he termed it). **1825** VISC. STRATFORD in Lane-Poole *Life* (1888) I. 382 If the carriage be smart the horses are rips. **1860** WHYTE MELVILLE *Mkt. Harb.* ix. (1861) 69 Your sort are rather of the weedy order,..those thorough-bred rips never have courage to face large fences. **1883** *Trans. Amer. Philol. Soc.* 52 *Rip*, 'a lean horse,' not uncommon in South, though a low word.

2. a. A worthless, dissolute fellow; a rake.

In colloq. or dial. use sometimes in milder sense as a term of reproof.

1797 D. SIMPSON *Plea Relig.* (1808) 148 This rip of a son shall be trained to the church. **1824** *Blackw. Mag.* XV. 220 Every variety of the *rip* is familiar to his fancy, and to his pencil. **1843** LE FEVRE *Life Trav. Phys.* I. I. vii. 155 Rips of parsons, incarcerated six days in the week. **1861** HUGHES *Tom Brown at Oxf.* xxii, I doubt whether he wouldn't think me too much of a rip to be intimate with. **1892** W. E. NORRIS *His Grace* II. i, The late Lord Charles Gascoigne had been an old rip,..he might have done something disgraceful. **1918** GALSWORTHY *Five Tales* 77 My grandfather lived to be a hundred; my father ninety-six—both of them rips. **1935** S. DESMOND *Afr. Log* li. 264 A humble repentant sinner—once perhaps 'a bit of a rip'—but very appealing. **1951** *Chambers's Jrnl.* Nov. 656/2 Would you believe it, the old rip had a flutter in Norland Deeps himself?

b. Applied to a woman. Somewhat *rare*.

1791 BURNS *Let. to P. Hill* 17 Jan., The chariot wheels of the coroneted rip, hurrying on to the guilty assignation. **1825** JENNINGS *Obs. Dial. W. Eng.* 64 *Rip*, a vulgar, old, unchaste woman. **1893** G. B. SHAW *Let.* 4 Sept. (1965) I. 404 The mother a most deplorable old rip. **1900** G. SWIFT *Somerley* 88, 'I don't believe I thought there was such a thing as a lady rake.'.. 'Yes, bit of a rip, wasn't she?' **1910** P. W. JOYCE *English as we speak it in Ireland* xiii. 313 *Rip*, a coarse ill-conditioned woman with a bad tongue.

3. A person or thing of little or no value.

1815 *Zeluca* III. 145 Ah you don't recollect Mrs. Cibber—Mrs. Siddons was a rip to her—about what Kean is to Garrick, ma'am! **1838** HOLLOWAY *Prov. Dict.*, *Rip*, any person or thing completely worn out and worthless. **1867** BRIERLEY *Marlocks*, etc. 98 An owd rip of a hommer [= hammer] like this.

rip, obs. or dial. form of REAP *sb.*² and *v.*²

rip, obs. form of RIPE *sb.*¹, *a.*, and *v.*¹

†**rip,** *v.*¹ *Obs. rare.* [A var. of RIPE *v.*², with shortening of vowel which prob. originated in the past tense **rĭpte* for OE. *rýpte.*] *trans.* To rob.

c **1200** ORMIN 10204 Þatt toþþ..þatt holeþþ o þe laȝhefollc, & rippeþþ hemm & ræfeþþ. *Ibid.* 10238 Þatt teȝȝ ne sholldenn nohht te follc Þurrh grediȝnesse rippenn.

rip (rɪp), *v.*² Also 6–7 rippe, 6 ryp(pe. [Of somewhat obscure origin and history; it is not quite certain that all the senses really belong to the same word. Corresponding forms in the cognate languages are Fris. *rippe* to rip, tear, Flem. *rippen* to rip, strip off roughly; it is not clear whether these are distinct from MDu. and LG. *rippen*, var. of *reppen* to move, pull (up), etc., which appear to be the source of NFris. and older Da. *rippe*, MSw., Norw., and Fær. *rippa*, in the same senses. MLG. *reppen* (*up*) is also used of reviving or raking up a matter, and this sense is represented by Da. *rippe* (*op*), *oprippe* (recorded from 1570), Icel. *rippa upp* (in 17th c. copies of an old text), MSw. *reppa* (*up*); whether LG. or Da. had any influence on English in this point is not apparent.]

I. 1. a. *trans.* To cut, pull, or tear (anything) away from something else in a vigorous manner. Const. with advs. *off*, *out*, †*forth*, or preps. *from*, *out of*.

c **1477** Caxton *Jason* 115 b, Wherfore for to know what it was, he distached and ripte it of. **1555** J. Proctor *Hist. Wyat's Rebellion* 31 b, For haste to rippe their bootes from theyr legges. **1605** Shaks. *Macb.* v. viii. 16 Macduffe was from his Mothers womb Vntimely ript. **1610** Healey *St. Aug. Citie of God* x. xi. 377 From earths gutts will I rip forth to vew, The feasts. **1650** Earl Monm. tr. *Senault's Man bec. Guilty* 285 If gold were already ript out of the bowels of the earth. **1677** Moxon *Mech. Exer.* No. 3. 51 You may tack down two small thin boards on either side the Using File, to keep it steddy, and rip them off again when you have done. **1727** Gay *Begg. Op.* i. iv, Rip out the coronets and marks of these dozen of cambric handkerchiefs. **1748** *Anson's Voy.* iii. ii. 316 The Carpenters..ripped of the old sheathing that was left. *a* **1777** Fawkes *Rape of Helen* (R.), Jove's teeming head the monstrous birth contains, And the barb'd iron ripp'd thee from his brains. **1861** *Once a Week* 10 Aug. 180/1 The joy of ripping out the middle stump of a good batter surpasses even that of wiping a man's eye at an overhead cock-pheasant. **1862** Mrs. H. Wood *Mrs. Hallib. Troub.* iii. vii, He ripped the lining out, and left the cloak in the state it is. **1884** *Manch. Exam.* 28 Nov. 5/1 He also declared that he incited no one to rip off Gladstone badges at the meeting. **1977** P. Hill *Fanatics* 33 They've ripped out the phone.

b. *slang.* To steal.

1904 'No. 1500' *Life in Sing Sing* 252/1 *Rip*, to steal with impunity. **1970** *Time* 22 June 52/3 For extra, unanticipated personal needs, he 'rips off'—or steals... Some of those who take jobs in department stores or markets steal what they can... Some who work in restaurants or drugstores let their friends in to eat or rip what they need. **1976** *Telegraph* (Brisbane) 20 Apr. 1/3 They believe some have ripped millions of dollars from Medibank since it began. **1977** *Guardian* 23 June 3/4 (Advt.), While the fluff saps the mark, the dip rips the wad.

c. *Baseball.* To score (a hit) in a vigorous manner.

1970 *Washington Post* 30 Sept. d2/5 Renko ripped his run-scoring hit in the second. **1974** *Anderson* (S. Carolina) *Independent* 19 Apr. 5b/4 Designated-hitter Duke Sims.. ripped a run-scoring double over first base.

d. Of a competitor or team: to defeat overwhelmingly. *U.S.*

1974 *State* (Columbia, S. Carolina) 3 Mar. 1-d/6 South Carolina..ripped the Cougars, 104–86, behind a sparkling 37-point performance by Alex English. **1976** *Springfield* (Mass.) *Daily News* 22 Apr. 40/4 Three runaways featured action in the Bi-County League. St. Mary's romped over Westfield Voke, 16–3; Gateway ripped Belchertown, 12–1; Smith School blitzed Holyoke Trade, 12–0. **1978** *Detroit Free Press* 2 Apr. 5e/11 (*heading*) Borg rips Smith, gains WCT finals.

2. a. To cut or tear apart in a rough or slashing fashion. Also with compl. as *asunder*, *open*, *through*.

1530 Palsgr. 691/2, I ryppe a seame that is sowed, *je decous*... It is better to ryppe ones clothes and sowe them agayne than to be ydell. **1567** Maplet *Gr. Forest* 6 They rippe in sunder the noddle of his head. **1579** Lyly *Euphues* (Arb.) 38 With the one hande robbe so many cofers, and with the other to rippe so many corses. **1602** Marston *Ant. & Mel.* iii. Wks. 1856 I. 39 The fringe of your sattin peticote is ript. *a* **1627** Sir J. Beaumont *Bosworth F.* 19 And hath the ground again been ript by thee? **1718** Pope *Iliad* xiii. 642 The forceful spear..ripp'd his belly with a ghastly wound. **1790** Cowper *My Mother's Picture* 103 Sails ript, seams op'ning wide, and compass lost. *c* **1850** *Arabian Nts.* (Routledge) 83 As soon as you shall feel yourself upon the ground, rip open the skin with the knife. **1865** J. T. F. Turner *Slate Quarries* 10 The other contractors..have to blast and rip the rock. **1898** *Westm. Gaz.* 15 July 5/3 The sides of the carriages were ripped and torn. **1973** 'J. Patrick' *Glasgow Gang Observed* iii. 30 He had..fifty-nine stitches on the side of his face; he had been 'ripped' only a few weeks ago.

fig. **1763** Churchill *Author* Poems 1767 II. 11 Lives there a Man, who calmly can stand by, And see his conscience ripp'd with steady eye. **1930** [best *a.* 7 b]. **1976** *Honolulu Star-Bull.* 21 Dec. h-6/1 Meanwhile, the Davis Cup nations are ripped by political squabbling.

b. To split or cleave (timber); to saw in the direction of the grain. (See also quot. 1688.)

1532 *Acc. St. John's Hosp., Canterb.* (MS.), For fellyng & ryppyng of ij thou[sand] & di. of tymber. **1688** Holme *Armoury* iii. 105/2 Terms used by the Fletchers, or Arrow-Makers... Ripping it, is to give it the first round. **1846** Holtzapffel *Turning* II. 708 These two [saws] are used.. for ripping or cutting fir-timber..with the grain. **1875** Knight *Dict. Mech.* 2033/2 When a Japanese wants to rip a plank, he places it across anything which will elevate the end a few inches.

c. To take the tiles off (a building or roof) and put on fresh laths; to repair or re-lay a roof in this manner.

1640 *Acc. St. John's Hosp., Canterb.* (MS.), For Ripping of Broth. Vauses house. **1657–8** in Willis & Clark *Cambridge* (1886) II. 97 In the extraordinary repaires of the Colledg. viz...ripping both buildings in yᵉ old Court..; ripping all the new building. **1828** *Hutton's Course Math.* II. 96 What will the new ripping a house cost..at 15s. per square? **1850** in Shaw *Mem. Eastry* (1870) 206 Ordered the north and south side of the chancel roofs to be ripped and relaid. **1876–87** in Surrey and Kent glossaries.

d. To take out or cut away by quarrying, etc.; to divest or clear of surface-soil.

1807 Vancouver *Agric. Devon* (1813) 69 Ripping 240 hogsheads [of limestone]. **1852** Wiggins *Embanking* 88 That operation requiring great care in 'ripping' one side of the bank at a time. **1883** Gresley *Gloss. Coal-Mining* 204 *Rip*, to cut or blast down the roof or top. **1904** *Daily News* 22 Oct. 12 As the men were engaged in 'ripping top' they came across what is believed to be the fossilised remains of a large fish.

e. To open or release, or to deflate, by the use of a rip cord. Also *absol.*

1902 J. Alexander *Conquest of Air* iii. 54 There was an arrangement for ripping the cover when ready to descend. *Ibid.* 55 They immediately ripped the balloon and commenced their descent. **1907** G. Bacon *Record of Aeronaut* xiv. 263 Mr. Spencer was in favour of ripping open the valve. **1920** G. C. Bailey *Compl. Airman* xxxi. 242 The ripping panel is a specially sewn section of the fabric, a cord lead to which enables the balloonist to rip it at will. **1963** A. Smith *Throw out Two Hands* xxi. 219, I..remember fumbling for the rip-panel cord... Had I ripped?

3. a. To slash *up* with a sharp instrument; to tear or open *up* with violence. Also *fig.*

1575 Turberv. *Trag. Tales* (1837) 131 [He] drewe out a shoulder knife, And ript me up the brest Of him that murdred lay. **1595** Shaks. *John* v. ii. 152 You bloudy Nero's, ripping vp the wombe Of your deere Mother-England. *a* **1626** Middleton *Mayor of Queenb.* iii. iii, I will rip up the linings. **1641** J. Jackson *True Evang. T.* i. 46 Julian..caused the bellies of Women and Virgins to be ript up. **1688** Molloy *De Jure Marit.* ii. i. §6. 204 If a Ship be ript up in parts, and taken asunder in parts. **1719** De Foe *Crusoe* i. (Globe) 214 He..ripp'd up his Wastcoat to feel if he was not wounded. **1836** Marryat *Midsh. Easy* vii, You send for your dog, who is ripped up by the bull. **1897** Rhoscomyl *White Rose Arno* 301 Iolyn..had ripped up one [man] in the cave mouth as he rose. **1976** *National Observer* (U.S.) 14 Aug. 12/1 What rips you up is the craziness... I felt like, well, since I loved them both, they should love each other. They don't.

refl. **1870** 'W. M. Cooper' *Hist. of the Rod* xxiv. 233 The doomed gentleman, bidding his friends farewell, quietly rips himself up.

b. To open *up* (wounds or sores) again in a harsh manner. In *fig.* use, passing into 4 b.

1565 T. Stapleton *Fortr. Faith* 150 Let vs..rippe vp the deadly woundes of our greuous iniquites. **1641** Ld. Brooke *On Episcopacy* 96, I professe I take no pleasure in ripping up their foule loathsome sores. **1679** J. Goodman *Penit. Pard.* iii. vi. (1713) 393 He will not rake in men's wounds, nor rip up old sores. **1830** Galt *Lawrie T.* iv. ix, It's little my part to rip up old sores.

c. To form by tearing *up* something.

1885 *Manch. Exam.* 21 July 5/3 The tornado wrought terrible damage, ripping up pathways through the forests.

d. *Cricket.* Of a ball: to hit (a stump or stumps) on delivery at speed, so as to knock it (or them) back or out of the ground. Also with bowler as subj.

1832 P. Egan *Bk. Sports* 348/2 She [*sc.* the ball]..Ripp'd up the *off* and *centre*! **1887** F. Gale *Game of Cricket* xiv. 244 Nothing would be better for cricket itself than for a young unknown cricketer..to rip up the wickets of some of the county cracks.

4. *fig.* **a.** To open up, lay bare, disclose, make known; also, to search into, examine. Now *rare.*

1549 Latimer *3rd Serm. bef. Edw. VI* (Arb.) 78 Fyrst of all as touchynge my fyrst sermon, I wyll runne it ouer cursorie, ryppyng a lytle the matter. **1565** Jewel *Repl. Harding* 240 As these menne thinke..to huddle vp their maters in the darke, it wil not be amisse to rippe them abroade. **1581** Mulcaster *Positions* xxxvii. (1887) 163 If ye rip the cause why they seeke to set foorth them selues. **1598** Marston *Sco. Villanie* Pref. B ij, Know, I doe scorn to stoupe To rip your liues. **1602** —— *Ant. & Mel.* iv. Wks. 1856 I. 48 There shalt thou rippe The inwards of thy fortunes, in mine eares.

1878 Browning *Poets Croisic* I, In vain we rip The past, no further faintest trace remains Of René.

b. To open *up*, rake *up*, bring *up* again into notice or discussion (esp. something unpleasant or which is to a person's discredit).

Very common from *c* 1575: see also reap *v.*²

1570 Wilson tr. *Demosthenes* 12 If a man weare disposed to rippe up all that euer he did and to charge him with every point thereof. **1584** Fenner *Def. Ministers* (1587) 47 Wee are loth to rippe vpp manie things whiche..can not well be discussed. **1605** J. Carpenter *Solomon's Solace* xvii. 71, I shall rippe vp vnto you the seauenth cause of the Kings sorowe. **1650** S. Clarke *Eccl. Hist.* i. (1654) 35 Hereupon he ript up Origen's faults. **1678** Temple *Let. to Elector* Wks. 1720 II. 506 Ripping up their whole Conduct in the Course of this Affair. **176.** Wesley *Husb. & Wives* vii. §2 Wks. 1811 IX. 86 The husband may..tell her how her faults were ripped up. **1777** Sheridan *Trip Scarb.* iv. i, Don't stand ripping up old stories, to make one ashamed before one's love. **1822** Hazlitt *Table-t.* Ser. ii. xiv. (1869) 288 We do not want to rip up old grievances. **1880** Miss Braddon *Just as I am* xxvii, Why do you come here to rip up the secrets of the past? **1884** *Law Times Rep.* LII. 88/1 Their interest was bound by that decision, and they cannot rip up what was then done.

c. *dial.* (See quot.)

1787 Grose *Prov. Gloss.* s.v., *Ripping one up*, telling him all his faults.

5. *Austral. slang.* To annoy intensely; usu. in phr. ***wouldn't it rip you***, used as an expression of exasperation.

1941 *Argus* (Melbourne) *Week-End Mag.* 15 Nov. 1/3 Another universal favourite is still the famous 'Wouldn't it ——!' Never given the final words (the completed sentence has several variations on 'Wouldn't it rock you!' or 'Wouldn't it rip you!') the explanation depends upon inflexion as to whether it conveys disgust, amazement, or pleasure. **1944** L. Glassop *We were Rats* xiii. 74 'I can't do it,' he said again. 'There are no partitions between the places... It's disgusting..'. Everyone gaped at him. 'What's wrong with this galah?' asked somebody and another said, 'Well wouldn't it rip you? What do you expect him to throw?' *Ibid.* xxviii. 162, I had the idea that if you joined the A.I.F. you had to fight in the front line. I know now how many men it takes to keep one in those trenches. Do you know our divisions have even got a mobile laundry, decontamination unit and mobile bath unit? Wouldn't it rip you?

6. to rip off. *slang* (orig. *U.S.*). Cf. also rip-off *sb.* **a.** To steal; to embezzle.

1967 *Trans-Action* Apr. 7 The hustler 'burns' people for money, but he also 'rips off' goods for money; he thieves, and petty thieving is always a familiar hustle. **1971** *It* 4–18 Nov. 3/5 An analysis of 800 documents ripped off from the Pennsylvania FBI office. **1972** *National Observer* (U.S.) 27 May 12/2 Bank robbery? It's only Establishment money that's being ripped off. **1974** *Black Panther* 16 Mar. 6/2 Spiro got caught ripping off tax money. **1977** *New Yorker* 9 May 34/2 First he owned an Atala, but it got ripped off, so he bought a Peugeot. **1981** A. Cross *Death in Faculty* viii. 90 Soldiers are always ripping things off, from their own outfit, from the enemy, everything.

b. To exploit financially; to cheat or defraud; to rob; to deceive.

1971 *Frendz* 21 May 16/4 The young people are well aware that they are being ripped off by these parasites, and, quite naturally, think that the visiting musicians are on the side of the promoters. **1973** *Black World* Jan. 33/1 Individuals within the group felt that there were too many instances of their singly being 'ripped off' and exploited as Black artists. **1973** *N.Y. Law Jrnl.* 2 Aug. 13/5 He, Harris, and Sydnor had 'ripped' off patrons and the owner of the bar. **1974** S. Ellin *Stronghold* 55 Experimental group therapy sessions which we all attended..partly because ripping off the amiable idiot who conducted them was better than another game of checkers. **1976** *Kingston* (Ontario) *Whig-Standard* 19 Jan. 19/3 Mrs. Baird and Mrs. LaMarche were in complete agreement as to who were the worst offenders at ripping the consumer off: Television and auto repairs. **1976** *Observer* 22 Feb. 6/3 Many women think all garages consider they can 'rip off' women drivers. **1977** *Spare Rib* July 35/2 A police guard formed in front of Mothercare in Oxford St—afraid we'd attack it for the way it rips off motherhood. **1978** *Detroit Free Post* 5 Mar. a 23/1 Sid Luft's 14-year-old lawsuit charging that his late wife Judy Garland was ripped off..by Hollywood executive David Begelman. **1981** *Times* 23 Apr. 4/8 Martin was not ripping me off.

c. To have sexual intercourse with; *esp.*, to rape.

1971 *Black Scholar* Sept. 32/1 If she had been any other broad he would have ripped her off..that night. **1973** *Black World* Sept. 53, I done shot dope, been to jail, swilled wine, ripped off sisters, passed bad checks. **1974** *Guidelines to Volunteer Services* (N.Y. State Dept. Correctional Services) 42 *Rip off*, rape, pull a job.

d. To burgle, to steal from (a store, etc.).

1972 'E. McBain' *Sadie when she Died* iii. 30 Q. Why did you go into the apartment? A. To rip it off. Q. To burglarize it? A. Yes. **1973** *Black World* Jan. 54/2 They were ripping off a furniture store in a few hours. **1977** *Rolling Stone* 24 Mar., Not when young blacks have ripped off bookstores across the country to get illegally what the lack of a job prevents them from getting legally.

e. To copy; to plagiarize.

1975 *Radio Times* 12–18 July 9/4 Just about everyone (including the Immaculate Jean-Luc Godard) ripped off Dick Lester's cool style. **1977** *Undercurrents* June–July 11/4 I've never yet refused a request to reproduce anything of mine but I've lost count of the times I've been ripped off. **1978** *Sci. Amer.* June 26/1 Two books, one an instruction manual for a geometrical instrument.., the other a witty polemic against a Padovan student who had sought to rip off that very instruction book!

II. 7. *intr.* **a.** To move with slashing force.

1798 Bloomfield *Farmer's Boy, Summer* 141 Hark! where the sweeping Scythe now rips along.

b. To split, tear, part asunder.

1840 R. H. Dana *Bef. Mast* xxv, The great mainsail gaped open, and the sail ripped from head to foot. **1860** Tomlinson *Arts & Manuf.* 2nd Ser. *Needles* 4 When the surface rips or tears, the attendant can feel it. **1890** *Melbourne Argus* 29 May 9/8 Rock very hard, but rips remarkably well.

8. a. *dial.* To use strong language; to swear.

1772 Nugent *Hist. Fr. Gerund* II. 497 Here the poor old man..begins ripping and swearing in the most dreadful manner. **1776** J. Adams *Wks.* (1856) IX. 441 Your secretary will rip about this measure, and well he may. **1838** Holloway *Prov. Dict.*, *To rip*, to swear profanely and in anger. **1854** Miss Baker *Northampt. Gloss.*, *Rip*, to bluster and swear impetuously.

b. To break *out* angrily.

1856 Mrs. Stowe *Dred* I. xx. 279, I suppose they [the clergy] wouldn't any of them give me a chance for heaven, because I rip out with an oath every now and then. **1886** Stevenson *Prince Otto* ii. vii, 'You may leave the table,' he added, his temper ripping out.

c. *trans.* with *out.* To utter with violence.

1828–32 Webster s.v., To rip out, as an oath. **1848** Jones *Sketches Trav.* 78 (Farmer), He ripped out an oath that made the hair stand on my head. **1889** 'Q.' *Splendid Spur* xvii, He ripped out a horrid blasphemous curse.

9. a. To rush along with violence or great speed. Hence, to go ahead (in conduct); to pursue a reckless course. Chiefly in phrases ***let her rip***; ***to let*** (someone or something) ***rip***: to allow (that person or thing) to go, to continue unchecked, etc.; *to let rip*: to let fly, to let oneself go. orig. *U.S.*

1853 *Daily Morning Herald* (St. Louis) 19 Jan. (Th.), We've got 'em on the hip, Letter Rip! Letter Rip! **1859** BARTLETT *Dict. Amer.* (ed. 2) 367 A common slang expression is 'Let her rip!' i.e. let her drive, let her go. **1863** *Harper's Mag.* Oct. 716/1 We cannot raise a tip To pay our board and laundry bill, And have to 'let 'em rip'. **1869** H. PHILLIPS *Jrnl.* 14 Dec. (typescript) 203 All hands tailing sheep let them rip at night. **1869** MRS. STOWE *Old Town Folks* l, If she don't do nothin' more 'n take a walk 'longside on him.., why, I say, let 'er rip. **1877** *Temple Bar* May 109 'Let him rip' is a common verdict; 'we can turn him out when his time is up'. **1881** A. BATHGATE *Waitaruna* ix. 139 Most of the [diggers], when they found I would not buy, would throw their picks down and say if I would not buy them I could take them or let them rip as I pleased. **1888** 'R. BOLDREWOOD' *Robbery under Arms* II. xiii. 211 He rips over to Daly's mob, borrows a horse, saddle, and bridle, and leads him straight down to our camp. **1894** *Outing* XXIV. 93 You have simply to sit still and 'let her rip', as Mick puts it. **1894** F. A. BARKLY *Among Boers & Basutos* (ed. 2) xiv. 186, I galloped round the Kopje with my police and half-a-dozen volunteers..and we 'letrip' to use the Africander expression. **1897** MARY KINGSLEY *W. Africa* 660 For the next sixteen years..he 'rips'; he rips carefully,..if he is a pagan; but if he is in that partially converted state..then he rips unrestrained. **1909** C. OWEN *Philip Loveluck* xii. 175, I can rub along somehow..by letting the pressing rip. **1915** WODEHOUSE *Psmith Journalist* xxv. 203 And now..let her rip. What can I do for you? **1916** 'BOYD CABLE' *Action Front* 255 A shell cracked overhead, and the shrapnel ripped down along the trench behind them. **1926** GALSWORTHY *Silver Spoon* III. iv. 246 Alec would know where he was when it was over, and so would she!.. Let it rip! **1930** A. BENNETT *Imperial Palace* ix. 45 He let them rip..because he enjoyed the grand spectacle of their passion. **1947** H. READ *Grass Roots of Art* iii. 71 We cannot..oppose the machine. We must let it rip, and with confidence. **1965** *Listener* 22 July 140/1 Should one try to make the action clear and comprehensible..or let rip with the poetry? **1966** *Ibid.* 17 Nov. 718/3 What would you do about all these many wage increases... Would you let them all rip? **1971** C. BONINGTON *Annapurna South Face* viii. 95 Almost as soon as I had let rip, however, I realized the injustice of my complaint. **1977** MCKNIGHT & TOBLER *Bob Marley* x. 134 The other view, which was expressed by the minority, was 'let her rip!'. **1977** *Sounds* 9 July 8/1 A frantic 'live' sounding version of The Stones' 'The Last Time' which rips along grandly, seven minutes and forty-four seconds of unadulterated pure fire. **1978** *Dumfries Courier* 20 Oct. 28/1 The present difficult decisions..will be thrust into insignificance if inflation lets rip again.

b. *to rip and tear*: to rage, to rave; to go raging about.

1873 'MARK TWAIN' & WARNER *Gilded Age* xxvii. 249 A man wants rest, a man wants peace—a man don't want to rip and tear around *all* the time. **1884** 'MARK TWAIN' *Huck. Finn* xxi. 207 It was perfectly lovely the way he would rip and tear. **1886** BAUMANN *Londinismen* 157/1 Ripping and tearing about. **1917** *Dialect Notes* IV. 342 *Rip and tear*, to rave.

c. In quasi-adverbial use.

1884 [see SOCKDOLAGER 3].

10. To strike swiftly and strongly.

1898 *Daily News* 24 Nov. 7/3 Sharkey ripped left and right for the body with some effect.

III. 11. *Comb.* as **rip-and-read**, used *attrib.* to designate material supplied by teletype which is read on radio or television; also of an organization supplying such material; **rip-and-tear** *U.S.*, used *attrib.* to designate crude and violent methods in crime; also *transf.*; cf. sense 9b above; **rip-off**, used *attrib.* to designate an opening device that has to be torn off; **rip-stop**, used *attrib.* and *absol.* of nylon clothing or equipment woven so that a tear will not spread; **rip track** *N. Amer.*, a section of railway line used as a site for repairs to carriages.

1973 *New Journalist* (Austral.) July–Aug. 6 The 'rip-and-read' news service of Sydney's labour [radio] station, 2KY. **1974** HAWKEY & BINGHAM *Wild Card* ii. 26 The newscaster was reading..rip-and-read copy—a story that had just come up on an agency teletype machine that the news editor rated too big to hold while it was rewritten. **1937** E. H. SUTHERLAND *Professional Thief* 241 *Rip-and-tear*, adj., without caution; same as 'raw-jaw', or 'murder grift'. **1955** D. W. MAURER in *Publ. Amer. Dial. Soc.* xxiv. 93 They do not constitute the upper echelons of the profession. They are also known as *clout and lam mobs, hijackers*, or *rip and tear mobs*. **1965** G. JACKSON *Let.* 12 Mar. in *Soledad Brother* (1971) 66 Understand though that you do not live in the real rip-and-tear world. **1973** *Nation Rev.* (Melbourne) 31 Aug. 1436/6 The knife edged ripoff tag on the top of some cans. **1971** C. BONINGTON *Annapurna South Face* App. B. 249, 2-man [tent], in ripstop nylon. **1976** *National Observer* (U.S.) 14 Feb. 9/3 (Advt.), Prime Duck Down socks... Covered with blue ripstop nylon. **1978** *Sci. Amer.* Feb. 158/3 Other covering materials include sailcloth..and nylon rip-stop. **1960** *Glossaria Interpretum: Chemins de Fer* 1882 Voie de réparations,..Repair track, rip track *Am.* **1973** *Amer. Speech* 1969 XLIV. 246 Various parts of the yard have names..such as *riptrack* (a long section of track—possibly several tracks if the yard is large—which is used for car repair).

†**rip**, (?) *v.*[3] *Obs. rare.* (Perh. ad. Du. *rep*, imper. of *reppen* to make haste, but the contexts are not decisive; it may be a mere exclamation, or a fig. use of RIP *v.*[2])

1592 NASHE *Four Lett. Confut.* Wks. (Grosart) II. 239 Wilt thou neuer leaue afflicting a dead Carcasse..? a wispe, a wispe, rippe, rippe, you kitchin-stuffe wrangler! **1600** DEKKER *Shoemaker's Holiday* Dram. Wks. 1873 I. 29 Auaunt Kitchin-stuffe, rippe you browne bread tannikin; out of my sight. **1609** ARMIN *Maids of More* C 3 b, O well sung Nightingale, a boord a boord there, ha rip there.

‖**ripa**[1] ('riːpə). *rare.* [Sw. *ripa*, pl. *ripor*: see RYPE *sb.*] Ptarmigan.

1854 L. LLOYD *Scandin. Adv.* II. 310 When I was out for the purpose of shooting Ripor. **1864** WHEELWRIGHT *Spring Lapl.* 70 The loud, hoarse cackle of the ripa was heard in every wood.

‖**ripa**[2] ('raɪpə). *Anat.* [a. L. *rīpa* bank.] A line of reflection in the ependyma of the brain.

1882 WILDER & GAGE *Anat. Techn.* 488 The surfaces separated by the ripa are always unlike. **1889** A. H. BUCK *Handbk. Med. Sci.* VIII. 120.

ripal ('raɪpəl), *a. rare.* [f. L. *rīpa* bank + -AL[1].] = RIPARIAN *a.*[1] 1.

1867 W. PEARD *Year of Liberty* 288 Companies, with shares in the ratio of ripal rights. **1868** —— *Water-farm.* ii. 16 With powers to..allot shares in the ratio of the ripal rights of each landed proprietor.

†**ripare**. *Obs. rare*$^{-1}$. [ad. It. *riparo*.] Shelter, defence.

1562 J. SHUTE tr. *Cambini's Turk. Wars* 25 Yet stode they upon their newe fortificationes and ripares that they had made within the towne.

riparial (raɪ'pɛərɪəl), *a.* [f. L. *rīpāri-us* (f. *rīpa* bank) + -AL[1].]

1. = RIPARIAN *a.*[1] 1.

1870 J. ORTON *Andes & Amazons* II. xxxvii. (1876) 490 The Riparial Forests, on lowlands bordering the rivers. **1896** *Allbutt's Syst. Med.* I. 51 Fully-formed rivers that seasonally flood their riparial districts.

2. *Zool.* Living upon, or frequenting, the banks of streams, ponds, etc. (*Cent. Dict.*)

riparian (raɪ'pɛərɪən), *a.*[1] and *sb.*[1] [f. as prec.]

1. *adj.* Of, pertaining to, or situated on, the banks of a river; riverine.

1849 J. P. KENNEDY *Life W. Wirt* (1860) I. xix. 293 Contentious riparian possessors and claimants of alluvial deposits. **1864** *Sat. Rev.* XVIII. 442/1 Inland lakes belonging..to one or other of the riparian States. **1880** MUIRHEAD *Gaius* II. §72 An island rising in the middle of a river is the common property of the riparian proprietors. **1886** *Encycl. Brit.* XX. 565/2 In order to give riparian rights, the river must flow in a defined channel.

b. *sb.* A riparian proprietor.

1884 *Pall Mall G.* 20 Aug. 4/1 With the intent of combating riparians upon divers matters of claim. **1894** C. H. COOK *Thames Rights* 137 Such riparian is the true owner of the fishery.

2. *Anat.* Of or pertaining to a ripa in the ependyma of the brain.

1889 A. H. BUCK *Handbk. Med. Sci.* VIII. 120 The fimbria, one of the riparian or marginal parts.

Ri'parian, *a.*[2] and *sb.*[2] = RIPUARIAN.

1898 SERGEANT *The Franks* 17 Clovis..had to..oust the king of the Riparian Franks. *Ibid.* 38 These..lessons..taught the Riparians not to respect but to despise.

riparious (raɪ'pɛərɪəs), *a. rare.* [ad. L. *rīpārius*.] (See quots.)

1656 BLOUNT *Glossogr.*, *Riparious*, that uses or abides in the water banks. **1858** MAYNE *Expos. Lex.*, *Riparius*,.. applied to plants that grow,..or to animals that live,..on the borders of rivers; riparious. **1866** *Treas. Bot.* 985/2 *Riparious*, growing by water.

†'**ripary**, *sb. Obs. rare*$^{-1}$. [ad. med.L. *rīpāria*, fem. of L. *rīpārius*: see prec.] A stream.

c **1450** *Godstow Reg.* 559 Dyches, watirs, pondis, stewes, Ryvers (or riparies), duffehowses.

†'**ripary**, *a. Obs. rare*$^{-1}$. = RIPARIOUS.

1661 LOVELL *Hist. Anim. & Min.* A v b, Not melodious, as the Woodpecker,..swallow, wild and riparie.

†**ripe**, *sb.*[1] *Obs.* Forms: 1 rip, rýp (hripp), 1, 4 riip (4–5 rip), 3–4 ripe, 5 ryp(e, ryppe. [OE. *rip* neut., related to *rīpan* REAP *v.*[1]] Harvest.

c **900** tr. *Baeda's Hist.* I. xxix. (1890) 88 þætte her wære micel rip onweard & fea worhton. *a* **930** *O.E. Chron.* (Parker MS.) an. 896, þæt þa Deniscan him ne mehton þæs ripes forwiernan. *a* **1000** *Phœnix* 246 Ær wintres cyme, on rypes timan. *a* **1225** *Juliana* 75 ȝe schulen..reopen ripe of þat sed þat ȝe her seowen. **1382** WYCLIF *2 Sam.* xxi. 9 In the dais of the fyrst rijp, begynnynge the repynge of barli. **1387** TREVISA *Higden* (Rolls) VIII. 185 þou hast no leve to sette þyn hook in oþer men ripe [*v.r.* ryp(e, etc.].

ripe (raɪp), *sb.*[2] Now *rare.* [ad. L. *rīpa* bank.] The bank of a river; the seashore.

c **1470** HARDING *Chron.* VI. iii, For rypes and roches whyte To shipmen were greate gladnesse and delyte. *Ibid.* ccxl. *note*, Blak been thi bankes and thi ripes also. **1538** LELAND *Itin.* (1768) I. 34 The Ripe of Trent againe it is low and medow ground. **1577** HARRISON *Eng.* III. xvii, On the left ripe (for so he [Leland] calleth the bancke of euery brooke thorow out all his Englishe treatizes) of a pretie ryuer.

1838 HOLLOWAY *Prov. Dict.*, *Ripe*, a bank; the sea-shore; as 'Lydd Ripe'. **1880** STRINGER in *Archæol. Cant.* XIII. 255 The rights of the inhabitants of Lydd to the ripe and common. **1894** SPEIGHT *Nidderdale* 212 On that account.. its ripe or bank was more likely to be selected for a place of settlement.

ripe (raɪp), *a.* (*sb.*[3] and *adv.*) Also 3–7 **rype**, 4 rip, rijp(e. [OE. *rípe*, = Fris. *ryp*, †*rijp*, MDu. *ripe*, *rijp*, *riep* (Du. *rijp*), OS. *rîpi* (MLG. *ripe*, *rype*, LG. *rîp*), OHG. *rîfi*, *rîfe* (G. *reif*): the stem *rīp-* may be related to that of REAP *v.*]

1. a. Of grain, fruits, etc.: Ready for reaping or gathering; arrived at the stage in which they are most fit for eating, or for reproducing the plants which bear them.

c **888** K. ÆLFRED *Boeth.* xxxix. §13 Westmbæra hærfest bryngð ripa bleda. *c* **900** tr. *Baeda's Hist.* I. xii. (1890) 44 Hi..sloȝan eall & cwealdon..& swa swa ripe yrð fortreddon. *a* **1225** *Juliana* 74 Ant reope we of þat ripe sed þat we seowen. *c* **1290** *St. Brendan* 696 in *S. Eng. Leg.* I. 239 þe Applene weren ripe inouȝ. *a* **1330** *Roland & V.* 312 And amorwe grapes þai bere, Red & ripe. **1340** *Ayenb.* 28 þet corn..is uol of frut and al ripe. **1390** GOWER *Conf.* I. 137 The leves weren faire and large, Of fruit it bare so ripe a charge. **1483** *Cath. Angl.* 309/2 A Rype fige, *precoqua*, *precox*. **1530** PALSGR. 322/2 Rype as fruyte is, *meur*. **1569** GRINDAL in Ellis *Orig. Lett.* Ser. I. II. 259 My Grapes this Yeare are not yett rype. **1579** E. K. *Gloss. Spenser's Sheph. Cal.* Nov., We fall like rotted ripe fruite fro the tree. **1613** PURCHAS *Pilgrimage* V. xii. (1614) 507 When the fruit is ripe, the first and outermost part openeth. **1676** M. LISTER in Ray *Corr.* (1848) 124, I gathered the ears a little before they were ripe. **1781** COWPER *Heroism* 54 Through the ripe harvest lies their destin'd road. **1832** LINDLEY *Introd. Bot.* I. ii. 186 It [the aril] more properly comes under consideration along with the ripe seed. **1864** TENNYSON *En. Ard.* 456 If the nuts..be ripe again. **1878** BROWNING *La Saisiaz* 7 Scarce enough to.. redden ripe the mountain-ash.

absol. *a* **1300** *Cursor M.* 6044 þat beist þan gneu vp..bath ripe and grene. **1393** LANGL. *P. Pl.* C. XIX. 107 He het elde, an hih for to clymbe, And shaken hit sharpely, þe ripen sholden falle.

transf. **1439** *Ep. Acad. Oxon.* (1898) I. 184 Noryshed with the rype frute of Konnyng. **1613** JACKSON *Creed* I. 136 Vntill they be ripe of death in the Autumne. *c* **1620** SIR W. MURE *Sonn.* VI. 13 Those fayre brests' rype clusters quho myt presse. **1771** *Junius Lett.* lxvii. (1788) 342 When you are ripe, you shall be plucked. **1818** KEATS *Endym.* II. 397 Coverlids gold-tinted like the peach, Or ripe October's faded marigolds. **1861** READE *Cloister & H.* xxxviii, Thy beard is ripe, thy fellow's is green; he shall be the younger.

†**b.** Of herbs or grass. *Obs.*

c **1380** WYCLIF *Sel. Wks.* III. 439 Herbis þat groweden in a orchard, and weren nyȝ rype. **1495** *Trevisa's Barth. De P.R.* IX. xiv. 356 Junius is paynted as mowynge haye, for that tyme haye is ripe in medes. **1565** COOPER *Thesaurus*, *Prata arida*, when the grasse is ripe, and redy to mow.

c. In proverbs, usually with fig. application.

1546 J. HEYWOOD *Prov. & Epigr.* (1867) 22 But soone rype soone rotten. *a* **1569** KINGESMYLL *Comf. Afflict.* (1585) C ii, All the glorie of man..is as the flower of the fielde, soone ripe, soone rotten. **1705** HICKERINGILL *Priest-cr.* II. i. 6 The old Proverb prov'd true, for, he was soon ripe, and soon rotten. **1736** [CHETWOOD] *Voy. Vaughan* (1760) I. 52 My Uncle..told me, Ripe Fruit was soon rotten.

d. Resembling ripe fruit; red and full.

1590 SHAKS. *Mids. N.* III. ii. 139 O how ripe in show, Thy lips, those kissing cherries, tempting grow! **1600** — *A.Y.L.* III. v. 121 There was a pretty redness in his lip A little riper, and more lustie red Then that mixt in his cheeke. **1855** TENNYSON *Maud* I. II, An underlip, you may call it a little too ripe, too full. **1894** HALL CAINE *Manxman* III. iii, With..her ripe mouth twitching merrily.

2. a. Of birds or animals: Fully fledged or developed; *esp.* come to a fit condition for being killed and used as food. Also, *ripe peeler* (PEELER[1] 2 b).

1297 R. GLOUC. (Rolls) 3673 Hii ne mowe noȝt wel fle Vor feblesse of hor brode, ac wanne hor briddes rype beþ, þer hii findeþ more mete in londes aboute hii fleþ. **1398** [see FLEDGE *a.* 1]. **1577** B. GOOGE *Heresbach's Husb.* IV. (1586) 169 To fatte Pigions..it is good to bring them to the Kitchin, before they bee full ripe. **1607** TOPSELL *Four-f. Beasts* 582 A little Kyd..being ripe, the maister killed it, and layed it before the Panther to be eaten. **1837** MACGILLIVRAY *Hist. Brit. Birds* II. 403, I caught the birds with much difficulty in a trap-cage when their young were nearly ripe. **1844** H. STEPHENS *Bk. Farm* II. 94 A ripe sheep..is easily known.. by the fulness exhibited in all the external parts. **1889** *Pall Mall G.* 14 May 3/1 The ducklings..must be killed as soon as they are ready, and not kept a day longer than the hour when they are ripe. **1952** *Sun* (Baltimore) (B ed.) 23 June 12/5 Language peculiar only to soft-crabbing... *Ripe peeler* —Has the same characteristics as the 'green peeler' but is more advanced in the shedding process.

fig. **1575** R. B. *Apius & Virginia* C 8 Under the Hedge with a payre of new Cardes both rip and fledge.

b. Of persons: Fully developed in body or mind; mature, †marriageable (Cf. 6 a.)

c **1386** CHAUCER *Doctor's T.* 68 Such þinges maken children for to be To soone rype and bold. **1390** GOWER *Conf.* I. 246 Sche scholde ben hir fader hair, And was of yeres ripe ynowh. **1513** MORE in Grafton *Chron.* (1568) II. 783 They were coupled or she were well rype. **1563** *Mirr. Mag.* II. 148 These two noble ympes I caused to be slayne, Of yeares not ful rype as yet to rule and raygne. *c* **1600** B. JONSON *To Penshvrst* 54 Wks. (1616) 820 Some..send By their ripe daughters, whom they would commend This way to husbands. **1784** COWPER *Task* VI. 598 He..being ripe in years, And conscious of the outrage he commits. **1807** WORDSW. *White Doe* III. 128 Ripe men, or blooming in life's spring,..Stood by their Sire, on Clifford-moor. **1876** GEO. ELIOT *Dan. Der.* VIII. lx, Since I was a ripe man, I have been what I am now. **1949** G. DAVENPORT *Family Fortunes* I. iv. 54, I swear, Martha, if I'd of met you when you was still ripe, I'd have left Hattie's mother, kids and all, to follow you clear to California, I would.

c. Ready for birth. *rare.*

1565 COOPER *Thesaurus*, *Fœtus maturos edere*, to brynge foorth yonge when they be rype. **1593** SHAKS. *Rich. II*, II. ii. 10 Some vnborne sorrow, ripe in fortunes wombe, Is comming towards me. **1741** MONRO *Anat. Nerves* (ed. 3) 275 The superior Extremity of this..Phalanx is a Cartilage in a ripe Child.

d. Of fish, etc.: Ready to lay eggs or spawn.

1861 HULME tr. *Moquin-Tandon* II. III. i. 78 The insect is collected..towards the end of the month of June, when the females are ripe. 1868 Peard *Water-farm.* viii. 85 Out of twenty, or thirty fish, not more than two or three will in all probability be found ripe. 1883 in G. B. Goode *Fish Indust. U.S.A.* 76 The fish remained in the basin until they were ripe.

3. a. Of liquor: Advanced to the state of being ready for use; fully matured, mellow. Also *absol.*

1393 Langl. *P. Pl.* C. xxi. 415 Til the vendage valle in þe vale of Iosaphat, And [I] drynke ryght rype most. *a* 1648 Digby *Closet Opened* (1677) 25 When it is cold put in it six spoonfuls of barm, and when it is ripe, it will hiss in the pail. 1742 *Lond. & Country Brew.* i. (ed. 4) 80 Nor will they be so soon ripe and fit to tap as the high dried Malt-Drink will. 1820 *Blackw. Mag.* VI. 551 Used to impart to new brandy and rum a ripe taste. 1834 Tennyson in *Memoir* (1897) I. 134 He.. Gives stouter ale and riper port Than any in the country-side. 1853 Ure *Dict. Arts* (ed. 4) I. 158 The casks ..in which the ripe beer is kept and expended. 1930 Wodehouse *Very Good, Jeeves!* iv. 102 Having got me in sporting mood with a bottle of the ripest.

b. Of suppurations, etc.: Ready to lance or break; fit for curative treatment.

c 1410 *Master of Game* (MS. Digby 182) xii, Menge þise herbes..and leyth hem vponn þe bocches; and þat shall make hem rype. And whan þei beth rype, slyt hem with a sharpe knyfe. *c* 1550 H. Lloyd *Treas. Health* a iij, Horsnesse, and continuall fluxion of snevil in old men, do in no means waxe rype. 1580 Blundevil *Horsemanship* iv. xxxv. 17 Thrust it in..so as the point of the iron may come out at the ripest place. 1810 E. Weeton *Let.* 25 Feb. (1969) I. 240, I have had another boil on my face... I neither lanced, nor poulticed it, but when ripe, let the matter out with a needle. 1909 *Dialect Notes* III. 363 *Ripe*, said of a boil when it is ready to be lanced.

c. Of natural products, etc.: Arrived at a mature or perfect state.

1635–56 Cowley *Davideis* iv. Poems (1905) 388 Clouds with ripe Thunder charg'd some thither drew. 1700 S. L. tr. *Fryke's Voy. E. Ind.* 316 There are People to look every year, and see whether the Pearls are ripe. 1726 Pope *Odyss.* xvii. 30 With riper beams when Phœbus warms the day. 1807 Vancouver *Agric. Devon* (1813) 268 It is much to be lamented that the ripe timber only had not been selected. 1865 Richardson & Watts *Chem. Tech.* II. iv. 294 The successive operations to which the ripe earth is submitted, are undertaken for the purpose of separating the nitrates from it.

d. (See quot. 1949.)

1949 A. R. Daniel *Bakers' Dict.*, *Ripe dough*, technical term for a dough ready for scaling having received a period of fermentation sufficiently protracted to enable the gluten to reach its most extensible condition. 1962 *Listener* 22 Mar. 511/1 There is a stage in breadmaking when the dough is said to be 'ripe'.

4. a. Of persons: Of mature judgement or knowledge; fully informed; thoroughly qualified by study and thought.

c 1200 *Vices & Virtues* 135 Nis þat non god tocne of ripe manne. *a* 1250 *Owl & Night.* 211 He is nv ripe & fastrede, Ne luste hym nv to non vnrede. *c* 1380 Wyclif *Sel. Wks.* III. 438 Crist sente hise apostlis, when þei weren rype, to diverse londis, to sowe wateris of wisdom. 1395 Purvey *Remonstr.* 107 Jugis and mynistris of the king owen to be ripe men. *a* 1568 Ascham *Scholem.* ii. (Arb.) 109 This exercise may bring moch profite to ripe heads. 1589 Puttenham *Eng. Poesie* iii. xviii. (Arb.) 205 No lesse plaine to a ripe reader, then if it were named expresly. 1613 Shaks. *Hen. VIII*, iv. ii. 51 He was a Scholler, and a ripe, and good one. 1657 Trapp *Comm. Job* xxxii. 6 Some young men are ripe betime, and more ready-headed than their ancients. 1867 Trollope *Chron. Barset* i, Mr. Crawley in his early days had been a ripe scholar. 1883 S. C. Hall *Retrospect* I. 367 A ripe scholar and in many ways an eloquent teacher.

b. Const. *in* (or *upon*) a matter, business, etc.

c 1475 *Partenay* 7 A man ful ripe in other clerigie. 1525 *St. Papers Hen. VIII*, VI. 397 Almost impossible it shuld be to make the Poopes Holynes so ripe in the Kinges particuler causes as were nedefull. 1548–9 (Mar.) *Bk. Com. Prayer, Ord. Priests*, Ye may waxe riper and stronger in your ministerie. 1615 G. Sandys *Trav.* 218 As sound in judgement as ripe in experience. 1699 Dampier *Voy.* II. i. 60 Money-changing..is managed by Women, who are very dextrous and ripe in this Employment. 1723 Wodrow *Corr.* (1843) III. 11, I cannot say I am so ripe upon that subject as to answer the difficulty Mr. Masterton moves. 1847 Longf. *Ev.* i. iii. 11 Ripe in wisdom was he.

c. Similarly of the mind, judgement, etc.

1483 Caxton *Gold. Leg.* 339/2 A longe vysage or chyere and enclyned, which is a signe of maturyte or rype sadnes. 1567 *Gude & Godlie Ball.* (S.T.S.) 106 With mynde rype and degest. *a* 1591 H. Smith *Wks.* (1867) I. 476 Every man thinks his own wit ripest. 1591 Shaks. *Two Gentl.* ii. iv. 70 His head vn-mellowed, but his Iudgement ripe. 1604 T. Wright *Passions* i. x. 39 Youth..are inconstant..partely helped with the lacke of a ripe resolution, and firme iudgement. 1647 Sprigge *Anglia Rediv.* ii. ii. (1854) 76 A gentle-man..of a most dexterous and ripe invention for all such things. 1693 Dryden *Juvenal* Ded. (1697) p. xx, His Natural Endowments, of a large Invention, a ripe Judgment, and a strong Memory. 1788 Reid *Aristotle's Logic* vi. §1. 136 The most important parts of this science require a ripe understanding. 1871 Disraeli *Lothair* Pref. p. xviii, His intimates only were acquainted with his..ripe scholarship. 1894 H. Drummond *Ascent Man* 164 Mind, in Man, does not start into being fully ripe.

5. Properly considered or deliberated; matured by reflection or study.

c 1270 *Prov. Hendyng* 84 Sot..wol speke wordes grene, Er then hue buen rype. *c* 1386 Chaucer *Clerk's T.* 438 So wise and rype wordes hadde she. —— *Melib.* ¶2389 Thou shalt also eschue the conseillyng of yong folk, for hir conseil is nat rype. 1439 *Rolls of Parlt.* V. 7/2 A gode and a ripe deliberation and avys, the which can noght be hade in a fewe dayes. 1540 *Act 32 Hen. VIII*, c. 26 The true diffinition.. therof requierith ripe and mature deliberation and advise. 1585 T. Washington tr. *Nicholay's Voy.* iii. xiv. 97 b, Yeres and long experience..brought more wisdome and rype doctrine. 1638 Junius *Paint. Ancients* 42 Such Images as after a ripe debate were found to admit an explication consenting with Nature.

6. Of age: **a.** Characterized by full development of the physical or mental powers. (Cf. 2 b.)

c 1375 *Sc. Leg. Saints* v. (*John*) 399 Bot fra he to rype elde wane he lefit þe bischope. 1531 Elyot *Gov.* ii. xii. (1880) II. 135 He than beinge of ripe yeres,..his frendes..exhorted hym busely to take a wyfe. 1560 Daus tr. *Sleidane's Comm.* 172 Some man of rype yeares and counsell. *c* 1590 Marlowe *Faust.* Chorus 13 Of riper years, to Wertenberg he went. *c* 1614 Sir W. Mure *Dido & Æneas* To Rdr. 8 Till ryper ȝeirs her infancy subdue. 1671 Milton *P.R.* iii. 31 Thy years are ripe, and over-ripe. 1784 Cowper *Task* iv. 713 At so ripe an age As twice sev'n years. 1838 Prescott *Ferd. & Is.* II. xvii. 224 A riper period of her life. 1860 Tyndall *Glac.* i. i. 8 Simplicity of treatment,..out of place if intended for a reader of riper years.

b. Advanced; high in years.

c 1375 *Sc. Leg. Saints* xl (*Ninian*) 609 þe tyme..þat he of þis lyf suld pas, of parfit dat & rype elde. 1665 Sir T. Herbert *Trav.* (1677) 243 He died at a ripe age and was buried at Persepolis. 1873 Symonds *Grk. Poets* v. 137 Anacreon died at the ripe age of eighty-five at Teos.

7. a. Fully prepared, ready, or able, *to* do or undergo something.

1377 Langl. *P. Pl.* B. v. 396 Sholde no ryngynge do me ryse ar I were rype to dyne. *c* 1380 Wyclif *Sel. Wks.* III. 61 Now I am riip to dye. 1462 *Paston Lett.* II. 89 What incedentes ye knowe, I preie yow by wrytinge certefie me in all hast, that I may be the more ripe to answer to this. 1542 Recorde *Gr. Artes* 33 b, You shal be rype and perfect to subtract any other summe lightly. 1595 Daniel *Civil Wars* iv. 79 Where states are ripe to fall, and vertue spent. 1675 Marvell *Corr.* Wks. (Grosart) II. 494 That I might at the same time be ripe to give you an account of your businesse. 1768 Blackstone *Comm.* III. 450 The cause is then ripe to be set down for hearing. 1788 Jefferson *Writ.* (1859) II. 548 It does not appear to me that the nation is ripe to accept of these. 1807 Wordsw. *White Doe* ii. 29 But now the inly-working North Was ripe to send its thousands forth. 1875 Helps *Ess., Educ. Man Business* 66 He will let opportunities grow before his eyes, until they are ripe to be seized.

b. Ready or fit *for* some end or purpose.

1592 *Nobody & Someb.* I. 2 b, I know by your complexion, you wer ripe for the hangman. 1642 Fuller *Holy & Prof. St.* iv. i. 242 These Reversions will be ripe for his heir, by that time his heir shall be ripe for them. *a* 1682 Sir T. Browne *Tracts* (1683) 169 Ripe and ready for destruction. 1701 W. Wotton *Hist. Rome* v. 77 His Designs were not ripe enough for Execution. 1768 Goldsm. *Goodn. Man* v, It goes no farther; things are not yet ripe for a discovery. 1781 Gibbon *Decl. & F.* xviii. (1787) II. 111 The conspiracy was ripe for execution. 1807 Vancouver *Agric. Devon* (1813) 299 Salt-marsh,..when ripe and ready for embankment. 1885 *Manch. Exam.* 12 May 5/1 The plans of the Government..are not yet ripe for criticism.

c. Quite prepared *for* action of some kind, *esp.* mischief, revolt, etc.

1599 Shaks. *Hen. V*, i. ii. 121 My thrice-puissant Liege Is ..Ripe for Exploits and mightie Enterprises. 1644 Heylin *Brief Relat. Laud* 3 Those libels..inflamed the people, till they had made them ripe for mischeife. 1659 *Burton's Diary* (1828) IV. 6 You are not ripe for judgment. One affirms, the other denies. 1748 *Anson's Voy.* ii. xiv. 282 The Indians, on almost every frontier, were ripe for a revolt. 1835 Lytton *Rienzi* ii. vii, Are thy friends ripe for the saddle? 1849 Macaulay *Hist. Eng.* vii. II. 191 England, though heated by grievances, was by no means ripe for revolution. 1879 Farrar *St. Paul* I. vi. xxi. 385 The mob were only too ripe for a tumult.

d. Const. with gerund preceding. Now only *arch.* in ***reeling ripe***, after quot. 1610.

1573 Twyne *Æneid* xii. Mm iv, Dying-ripe with nayles her purple robes in ragges she hales. *a* 1586 Sidney *Arcadia* (1622) 61 But Lulus (euen weeping ripe) went among the rest. *c* 1600 Chalkhill *Thealma & Cl.* (1683) 112 With that he leaps unto her cursing ripe. 1610 Shaks. *Temp.* v. i. 279 He is drunke now;..And Trinculo is reeling ripe. *a* 1625 Beaum. & Fl. *Woman's Prize* ii. i, He's like little children That lose their baubles, crying ripe.

1833 H. Coleridge *Poems* I. 73 Reeling ripe, Big Independence..works his burly way. 1883 *Church Times* XXI. 906/3 The Irish teetotaler who was found reeling ripe.

8. a. Ready for action, execution, or use; arrived at the fitting stage or time for some purpose.

1601 Shaks. *Jul. C.* iv. iii. 215 Our Legions are brim full, our cause is ripe. 1713 Addison *Cato* ii. i, Should they submit ere our designs are ripe, We both must perish in the common wreck. 1719 De Foe *Crusoe* ii. (Globe) 440, I desir'd the French Gentleman not to say any thing to them, till the Business was thorough ripe. 1789 Wolcot (Peter Pindar) *Subjects for Painters* 36 With a lie Ripe at their fingers' ends. 1838 Macaulay *Sir W. Temple* Ess. (1897) 439 At length, in June, 1671, the designs of the Cabal were ripe. 1860 Motley *Netherl.* v. I. 145 The insubordination, which was so ripe in the city. 1879 Farrar *St. Paul* I. ii. viii. 153 Their plot was soon ripe.

b. Of time: Sufficiently advanced.

1596 Shaks. *1 Hen. IV*, i. iii. 294, I by Letters shall direct your course When time is ripe.

1850 Tennyson *In Mem.* Concl. xxxv, The man..was a noble type Appearing ere the times were ripe. 1864 Bryce *Holy Rom. Emp.* iv. (1875) 44 The great scheme for whose accomplishment the time was now ripe.

9. In various slang senses. **a.** Drunk (cf. sense 7 d). **b.** Fine, excellent; thoroughgoing (also used ironically); hence, beyond reasonable bounds, excessive. **c.** Angry.

1823 'J. Bee' *Slang* 149 *Ripe*—drunk. First cousin to mellow. 1923 Wodehouse *Inimitable Jeeves* ix. 89, I liked the place, and was having quite a ripe time there. 1925 *Flynn's* 14 Mar. 281/1 *Ripe*, drunk. 1932 A. J. Worrall *Eng. Idioms* 33 He was shooting at cats with darts. I told him it was a bit ripe and asked him to stop. 1948 Partridge *Dict. Forces' Slang* 156 *Ripe*, complete, thoroughgoing. Usually allied with 'bastard'. 1959 I. & P. Opie *Lore & Lang. Schoolch.* iii. 53 They come down like a ton of bricks on people who tell a stale joke. 'Do you know where Smudger takes his girl?' gags the would-be comic, 'He takes her behind a bush because it's very *privet*.' Whereupon the 'ripe one' is complimented: 'Oh lor, last time I heard that the tears rolled down my bib.' 1964 *Australasian Post* 21 May 13 Even a ripe shiner isn't just a black eye to the man in the white coat. It is a peri-optic ecchymosis. 1966 R. Jeffries *Death in Coverts* iii. 93 We all joked about it and Bill got really ripe. No sense of humour. 1967 R. Campbell in *Coast to Coast 1965–66* 20 Jack'll be ripe pickings by the time that old buzzard comes around from the police station to close the pub. 1969 'J. Fraser' *Cock-pit of Roses* xvi. 127 'What the bloody hell are you playing at?' 'That's ripe considering you just near broke my arm!'

†**10. a.** As *sb.* Ripeness. (Cf. for- 10.) *Obs.*

c 1000 *Ags. Ps.* (Thorpe) cxviii. 147 Ic ðe on ripe fore-com [Vulg. *Præveni in maturitate*]. *a* 1425 *Cursor M.* 18834 (Trin.), His heer [was] like to þe note broun whenne hit for ripe [*Cott.* ripnes] falleþ doun.

†**b.** As *adv.* Ripely. *Obs.*

a 1632 Taylor *God's Judgem.* i. ii. iii. (1642) 172 But the King..handled them so ripe and handsomely, that..he dealt with them as pleased him.

11. *Comb.* **a.** Parasynthetic, as ***ripe-aged***, ***-bearded***, ***-coloured***, ***-eared***, ***-faced***, ***-meated***, ***-tongued***, ***-witted***.

1548 Patten *Exped. Scotl.* Pref. †v, A righte ripetungued deponent. 1567 Drant *Horace, Ep.* Pref. vj, I take them to be ripe-tounged tryfles. *a* 1586 Sidney *Arcadia* iii. (1605) 377 Alas how ripe witted these young folkes be now adayes. 1698 F. B. *Free but Modest Censure* 10 Bestowing upon him the Epithets of Learned, Ingenious, Thoughtful, Ripe-witted, &c. 1818 Keats *Endym.* iii. 8 Fire-branded foxes to sear up..Our gold and ripe-ear'd hopes. 1826 Hood *Love* ii, Grave ripe-fac'd wisdom made an April fool? 1827 C. Webbe *Harvest-Home* ii, Armfuls of ripe-coloured corn. 1922 Joyce *Ulysses* 59 Slapping a palm on a ripemeated hindquarter. 1934 Webster, *Ripe-aged.* 1944 E. Sitwell *Green Song* 11 We heard in the dawn the first ripe-bearded fire Of wheat. 1952 C. Day Lewis tr. *Virgil's Aeneid* v. 95 Ripe-aged Acestes.

b. Miscellaneous, as ***ripe-bending***, ***-grown***, ***-like***.

1592 Shaks. *Ven. & Ad.* clxxxiii, Mulberries, & ripe-red cherries. 1599 Nashe *Lenten Stuffe* 30 The light-foot tripper.., who would run ouer the ripe-bending eares of corne. 1640 Rutherford *Lett.* ii. xxxvii. (1664) 517 The field of heaven's glory is white and ripe-like. 1687 Norris *Coll. Misc.* 120 That world..thou'lt see, Ripe-grown, in full maturity. 1873 M. Collins *Miranda* III. 63 An old-fangled ripe-red house.

ripe (raɪp), *v.*[1] Forms: 1 rípian, 4 rypen, 5 rypyn; 4– ripe (5 rip), 4–6 rype (6 *Sc.* ryip), 7 reape. [OE. *rípian*, = Fris. *rypje*, MDu. *ripen* (Du. *rijpen*), OS. *rîpôn* (MLG. and LG. *rîpen*), OHG. *rîfan*, *rîffen* (G. *reifen*), f. *rípe* ripe *a.* Now somewhat rare, the usual word being ripen.]

1. *intr.* To grow or become ripe.

c 1000 Ælfric *Hom.* II. 104 Ðo þæt sunne scine þæt ðine æceras ripion. *c* 1055 *Byrhtferth's Handboc* in *Anglia* VIII. 312 On lengtentima springað oððe greniað wæstmas, & on sumera hiȝ weaxað, & on hærfest hiȝ ripiað. *a* 1175 *Cott. Hom.* 241 þis corn..wex and bleowu in iudea, hit ripede in ierusalem. 1377 Langl. *P. Pl.* B. xix. 314 Aȝeines þi greynes ..bigynneth for to ripe, Ordeigne þe an hous..to herberwe in þi cornes. 1398 Trevisa *Barth. De P.R.* xvii. i. (Tollemache MS.), In some tren and herbes frute ripeþ sone, as mulberies and cheries. *c* 1436 *Pol. Poems* (Rolls) II. 152 Fruyte on tre both gret and smale Gan for to rip and wex fulle pale. *c* 1480 Henryson *Mor. Fab.* viii. (*Preach. Swallow*) xxx, The lint rypit, the carle pullit the lyne. 1523 Ld. Berners *Froiss.* I. liii. 75 Whan..that the corne beganne to rype, he departed fro Gaunt. 1556 J. Heywood *Spider & Fly* i. 2 What time euery growing thinge That ripeth by roote, hath liuely taken hart. 1613 Day *Dyall* iv. (1614) 69 The fruits of the Vine do ripe in Season. 1657 R. Ligon *Barbadoes* (1673) 15 They can never ripe together, but one is green, another ripe, another rotten. 1721 Bradley *Philos. Acc. Wks. Nat.* 192 The Fruits they bear are much larger, and ripe earlier, than what we find growing upon the old Stocks. 1818 Scott *Rob Roy* vi, There's aye.. something to ripe that I would like to see ripen. 1892 M. Field *Sight & Song* 60 The peach that ripes.

fig. *a* 1300 *Cursor M.* 11812 His vn-rightes biginnes to ripe! *c* 1400 *Beryn* 677 And by þat tyme þey were there, þe day began to rype. *c* 1480 Henryson *Mor. Fab.* viii. (*Preach. Swallow*) xlii, The sin ryipis, and schame is set on side. 1530 Palsgr. 691/2 It shall be well done for hym to make his testament, for he rypeth a pace. 1600 Shaks. *A.Y.L.* ii. vii. 26 And so from houre to houre, we ripe, and ripe. *a* 1631 Donne *Poems* (1635) 386 Till death us lay To ripe and mellow here, we are stubborne Clay. 1651 Cleveland *Poems* 32 At my next view, my pur-blind fancy ripes. 1878 Taylor *Daniel the Beloved* xi. 203 So from hour to hour, he ripes into maturity.

2. *trans.* To make ripe, bring to ripeness.

1398 Trevisa *Barth. De P.R.* xvii. cxxvii. (Tollemache MS.), In som place þe leues ben pullid awey for þe sonne schulde come to þe frute, and ripe it spedily. *c* 1440 *Promp. Parv.* 434/2 Rypyn, or make rype, *maturo.* *a* 1533 Ld. Berners *Gold. Bk. M. Aurel.* (1546) Bj b, Haruest cometh, whiche tyme doth better rype them. 1555 Eden *Decades* (Arb.) 292 They are sumtimes inforced to rype & dry them in theyr stooues. 1591 Sylvester *Du Bartas* i. ii. 643 On Trees anon they ripe the Plum and Pear.

fig. 1513 Douglas *Æneis* iv. Prol. 13 Oft to revolf ane vnlefull consait Ripis ȝour perellus frutis and oncorn. ? 1540 Hyrde tr. *Vives' Instr. Chr. Wom.* xii. O ij, What shulde that serue fore, but to rype them and prepare redy for suche as be more lewde. 1597 Shaks. *2 Hen. IV*, iv. i. 13 Hee is retyr'd, to ripe his growing Fortunes, To Scotland. 1598 Marston *Sco. Villanie* i. ii. 113 When rapine feedes our pomp, pomp ripes our fall. 1863 W. Lancaster *Praeterita* 26 We are riped with joy, and marr'd with tears.

†**3.** *Med.* To bring to a head; to mature. *Obs.*

1398 TREVISA *Barth. De P.R.* XVII. lxxxix. (Bodl. MS.), þe vertu of þe leli rypeþ bocches & sores. *c* **1410** *Master of Game* (MS. Douce 335) 38 b, Medle thes herbes to geder and ley hem vpon the bocches and that shal rype hem. *c* **1450** *M.E. Med. Bk.* (Heinrich) 215 To rype þe quinesye, tak smale snayles.. & stampe hem, & playster hem aboue þe sore. **1544** PHAER *Pestilence* (1553) Pij, A plaister to ripe a botche comming of the pestilence. **1578** LYTE *Dodoens* 211 It.. ripeth and breaketh harde impostumes. **1614** LATHAM *Falconry* (1633) 145 It doth ripe and digest tough slime or glut that commeth of cold.

†**4. a.** To prepare (a matter) by careful consideration. *Obs.*

c **1460** FORTESCUE *Abs. & Lim. Mon.* XV. (1885) 148 Yff þe amendynge þeroff be not debatyd, and be such counsell ryped to thair handes. **1533** in W. H. Turner *Select. Rec. Oxford* (1880) 115 And if it may be soe, to ripe the matter unto the Kings gracious hands.

†**b.** To make (one) ripe in knowledge. *Obs.*

1523 in Strype *Eccl. Mem.* (1733) I. I. iii. 43 To ripe, inform and instruct him in the Specialities.. of all such.. Ordinances. *c* **1555** HARPSFIELD *Divorce Hen. VIII* (Camden) 76 Himself being afterwards furnished and riped with greater learning. *Ibid.* 188 The King's said orators shall.. rype and instruct themselves by their secret learned counsell.

ripe (raɪp), *v.*[2] Also 1 rýpan (hr-), 3 rupen, 4- rype (8 *Sc.* ryp). [OE. *rýpan*, app. related to Goth. *raupjan*, OHG. *roufen* (G. *raufen*), and to LG. *ruppen*, G. *rupfen* to pluck, pull. After OE. only in northern and Sc. use (but see 4 b).]

†**1. a.** *intr.* To engage in robbery. *Obs.*

c **950** *Lindisf. Gosp.* Matt. vi. 19 Ðer ðeafas ofdelfes *vel* hrypes & forstealas. *a* **1023** WULFSTAN *Hom.* (1883) 163 Hy herȝiað & heawað,.. rypað & reafiað & to scipe lædað. *c* **1205** LAY. 10584 Heo rupten, heo ræfden, noht heo ne bi-læfden.

†**b.** *trans.* To rob or plunder (one). *Obs.*

a **1000** in Thorpe *Laws* II. 320 Hy rypað þa earman butan ælcere scylde. *c* **1050** *O.E. Chron.* (MS. C) an. 1011, [Hi] hereȝodon ure earme folc & hi rypton & sloȝon. *c* **1065** *Ibid.* an. 1065, [He] rypte God ærost, & ealle þa bestrypte þe he ofer mihte.

2. *intr.* To grope; to make search (*for* or *after* something hid).

c **1325** *Metr. Hom.* (Small) 143 Til this forsaid arc he yod .. And riped imang tha wormes lathe. *c* **1425** WYNTOUN *Cron.* V. xi. 2903 A mattok syne he tuk,.. And wipe þat ripit to þe grunde. **1530** PALSGR. 691/2, I rype in olde maters, *je fouble.* **1562** PILKINGTON *Expos. Abdyas* Pref. A a viij, As he that ripes in a dungehyll, is infect with the smell therof a longe time after. **1580** *Reg. Privy Council Scot.* III. 309 Thay rypit for the saidis guidis. **1640–1** *Kirkcudbr. War-Comm. Min. Bk.* (1855) 81 Ordaines the Captaines.. to send their constables.. to rype throw the parochess for suspectit gudes. **1814** in Chambers *Pop. Hum. Scot. Poems* (1862) 68 He rypit, maybe for his knife, I thought I saw it glancin. **1887** STEVENSON *Underwoods* 77 It's possible.. That some ane, ripin' after lear.., May find an' read me.

3. *trans.* To search (a place, receptacle, etc.) in a thorough manner in order to find something; to rifle, ransack.

a **1300** *Cursor M.* 4893 Yon er theues.. folus þam to ripe þair war. *c* **1400** *Rule St. Benet* 36 þair beddis sal þabbes ofte ripe. *c* **1425** WYNTOUN *Cron.* VI. iv. 315 þe graf qwhar in Charllis Marschel lay þai ripit, and þe body soucht. *c* **1460** *Towneley Myst.* xiii. 515 Now.. Com and rype oure howse and then may ye se who had hir. **1535** COVERDALE *Obad.* 6 But how shall they rype Esau, and seke out his treasures? **1590** *Reg. Privy Council Scot.* IV. 491 [They] sercheit the haill houssis,.. and rypit all pairtis sa narrowlie as they could. **1659** in *N. & Q.* 6th Ser. VII. 264/2 Quhen the corporall was ryping me at the gate. **1676** Row *Contn. Blair's Autobiog.* xii. (1848) 540 Their houses were ryped but none were found. **1721** RAMSAY *Lucky Spence* vi, Ryp ilka pouch frae nook to nook. *a* **1774** FERGUSSON *Rising of the Session* Poems (1845) 28 The benmost part o' my kist-nook I'll ripe for thee. **1824** SCOTT *Redgauntlet* let. xi, Sir John, when he had riped the turret weel, led my gudesire into the dining parlour. **1858–61** RAMSAY *Remin.* ii. (1867) 30 The sacks of Joseph's brethren were ripit.

transf. *c* **1425** WYNTOUN *Cron.* IV. i. 91 As þai war þe grounde ripande, Off a man the hewide þai fande. **1513** DOUGLAS *Æneis* X. x. 134 Tharwythall the hyrnys of hys gost He rypyt wyth the swerd amyd his cost.

†**b.** With *up.* To search out. *Obs.*[−1]

? *a* **1400** *Morte Arth.* 1877 Thare myght mene see the ryche ryde in the schawes, To rype vpe the Romaynez ruydlyche wondyde!

4. To examine thoroughly; to investigate, scrutinize, search into.

a **1300** *Cursor M.* 26702 Cums his freind ripand his state, .. he sceus him all þat he wate. **13..** *E.E. Allit. P.* B. 592 Rypande of vche a ring [= rink] þe reynyez & hert. **1513** DOUGLAS *Æneis* II. iii. 29 Lefull is.. Thair hid slycht als to rype furth to the ground. **1552** ABP. HAMILTON *Catech.* (1884) 153 b, Examine, discus, serche, and rype weil thi conscience. *a* **1598** ROLLOCK *Wks.* (1844) II. 271 It goes down to the inward affections to ripe and search them. **1637** RUTHERFORD *Lett.* I. cliv. (1664) 307 Each man had need twice a day & oftner, to be ryped & searched with candles. **1822** AINSLIE *Land of Burns* 108 Our bairnly recollections ryped and rummaged up.

†**b.** With *up.* (Cf. RIP *v.*[2] 4 b.) *Obs.*

1573 *Satir. Poems Reform.* xliii. 107, I sall rype vp the mater haill. **1690** W. WALKER *Idiomat. Anglo-Lat.* 535 He ripes up (rehearses) what wrong his enemies had done him. **1695** WOOD *Life* 9 Oct., There I began to ripe up all the matter, how unworthily he had dealt with me.

5. To cleanse, clear out.

17.. *Robin Hood & Beggar* in Child *Ballads* III. 163/2 In the thick wood the beggar fled, Eer they riped their eyne. **1721** RAMSAY *Ode to the Ph—* iii, Then fling on coals, and ripe the ribs. **1841** in *Cath. News* (1899) 3 June 15/4 She went afterwards to 'ripe' the fire. **1887** SERVICE *Life Dr. Duguid* xii. 73 Robin ryped the dottle oot o' his pipe. **1895** W. C. FRASER *Whaups* xv. 209, I sometimes ripe oot Tammy's pipe.

6. To break, dig, or plough *up* (ground).

1828 *Craven Gloss.*, *Rype*, to break up rough and uncultivated ground. *c* **1882** in J. Lucas *Stud. Nidderdale* xxvii. 223 T'oade hoose.. hez been pull'd doon, its foondation rip'd up. **1897** G. O. ELDER *Borgue* 29 (E.D.D.), Ripin' up a' the bits of green hoams, and forcing wheat to grow.

ripe, obs. form of REAP *sb.*[2] and *v.*[1]

ripeck, variant of RYPECK.

riped, *ppl. a. rare.* [f. RIPE *v.*[1]] Ripened. (Cf. *fore-riped* s.v. FORE- *pref.*[1] 2 b.)

1568 T. HOWELL *Arb. Amitie* (1879) 43 When ryped yeres in wisedomes schoole, in maridge faine would match. **1577** B. GOOGE *Heresbach's Husb.* II. (1586) 67 b, The graines that grow within the redde riped Berrie.

'ripeful, *a. rare*[−1]. [-FUL.] Ripe.

1836 HALIBURTON *Clockm.* (1862) 167 Is the old gentleman still alive? if so, he must now be ripeful of years as he is full of honours.

ripel, obs. form of RIPPLE *v.*[1]

ripely ('raɪplɪ), *adv.* Also 4 rijp-, 5–6 rip-; 4–7 rype-, 5–6 ryp-, 6 ryeply (4–7 -lie, 6 -lye). [f. RIPE *a.* + -LY[2]. Cf. MDu. *ripe-*, *rijplike* (Du. *rijpelijk*), G. *reiflich.*]

†**1.** Quickly, immediately. *Obs. rare.*

In both passages a rendering of L. *maturius.*

1382 WYCLIF *2 Macc.* vii. 37 Ynclepynge God, more rijply for to be maad helpful to oure folc. —— *Acts* xxv. 4 Goynge forth more rypeli, or hasteli.

2. With ripe or mature consideration, reflection, or judgement. Now *rare* or *Obs.*

1456 SIR G. HAYE *Law Arms* (S.T.S.) 302 He suld be wele and ryply avisit or that he write.. ony materis. **148.** BOTONER in *Wars Eng. in France* (Rolls) II. 528 Men of gret discresione, experte in the werre, may the more rypliere delyver and advise.. the thynges [etc.]. **1523** CROMWELL in Merriman *Life & Lett.* (1902) I. 30 Vttred to his most prudent counsayll, and at sundrey tymes.. rypely dygested. **1589** PUTTENHAM *Eng. Poesie* III. xxii. (Arb.) 265 More curiously than needed, the matter being ripely considered. **1638** JUNIUS *Paint. Ancients* 203 Let us ripely consider what Artificers deserve most to be imitated. **1700** LAW *Council Trade* Introd. (1751) p. xiv, As those who shall ripely consider this matter, will easily find [etc.]. **1715** *Wodrow Corr.* (1843) II. 24 Till a General Assembly.. ripely and gravely consider the matter of them.

3. In a ripe, mature, or fully developed manner.

1513 DOUGLAS *Æneis* III. vi. 197 Sche sall riply declair to the in hy The maneris of all pepill in Italy; The battellis for to cum [etc.]. **1611** SHAKS. *Cymb.* III. v. 22 It fits vs therefore ripely Our Chariots and our Horsemen be in readinesse. **1635–56** COWLEY *Davideis* II. 580 Him from whose danger heaven securely brings, And for his sake two ripely wicked Kings. **1661** EVELYN *Diary* 13 May, Pity it is that what they attaine here so ripely, they either not retain or do not improve.. when they come to be men. **1800** MOORE *Anacreon* xvii. 29 Then for his lips, that ripely gem. **1880** BLACKMORE *Mary Anerley* III. iii. 42 Brown dusk was ripely settling down among the mossy apple-trees. **1892** *Cornh. Mag.* June 570 Huge pears hung ripely. **1939** JOYCE *Finnegans Wake* (1964) 474 His locks of a lucan tinge, quickrich, ripely rippling. **1973** *Daily Tel.* 13 Aug. 12/3 Stravinsky's 'Firebird'... Ozawa encourages a ripely romantic performance.

ripeman, variant of REAPMAN *Obs.*

ripen ('raɪp(ə)n), *v.* Also 6 **rypen.** [f. RIPE *a.* + -EN[5]. Cf. RIPE *v.*[1]]

1. *intr.* To grow ripe; to come to maturity:

a. Of fruits, seeds, etc.

1561 DAUS tr. *Bullinger on Apocalipse* (1573) 95 But the figges ripened not, and therefore they remayned greene or vnripe figges. **1599** SHAKS. *Hen. V*, I. i. 61 Holesome Berryes thriue and ripen best, Neighbour'd by Fruit of baser qualitie. **1611** BIBLE *Isaiah* xviii. 5 When the bud is perfect, and the sowre grape is ripening in the flowre. **1652** EARL MONM. tr. *Bentivoglio's Wars Flanders* 170 By destroying the corn upon the ground, which was then a ripening. **1712** M. HENRY *Serm.* Wks. 1853 II. 366/2 The choicest fruits ripen slowly. **1796** WITHERING *Brit. Plants* (ed. 3) III. 608 Calyx awned, the angles more evident as the seeds ripen. **1833** TENNYSON *Lotos Eaters* 81 All its allotted length of days, The flower ripens in its place. **1894** H. DRUMMOND *Ascent Man* 382 The dormouse thus brings forth its young in August, when the nuts begin to ripen.

fig. **1742** YOUNG *Nt. Th.* I. 142 What golden joys ambrosial clust'ring glow In His full beam, and ripen for the just?

b. Of persons, faculties, conditions, etc.

1602 MARSTON *Antonio's Rev.* III. ii, His mature age.. ripens onely to corrupt and rot The budding hope of infant modestie. **1777** PRIESTLEY *Matt. & Spir.* (1782) I. iv. 47 The faculty of thinking in general ripens.. with the body. **1840** BARHAM *Ingol. Leg.* Ser I. *Henry Harris*, It was not till our acquaintance had ripened.. that these particulars were elicited. **1878** J. P. HOPPS *Jesus* iii. 12 The time had come, when all that he had.. thought, and desired, had ripened in his soul.

c. *fig.* To develop *into* (or *towards*) something.

1606 SHAKS. *Ant. & Cl.* II. vii. 103 *Pom.* This is not yet an Alexandrian Feast. *Ant.* It ripen's towards it. **1709** STRYPE *Ann. Ref.* I. i. 47 These Bills ripened into Acts, before the Parliament ended. **1776** MICKLE tr. *Camoens' Lusiad* Introd. p. xxiv, The mathematical genius of Don Henry.. received every encouragement.. to ripen into perfection and public utility. **1833** HT. MARTINEAU *Fr. Wines & Pol.* i. 1 The acquaintance had ripened into friendship. **1853** KINGSLEY *Hypatia* xxix, He tried to laugh away his own fears. And yet they ripened.. into certainty. **1885** *Law Times* LXXIX. 211/1 The risk had not ripened into a debt.

2. *Med.* To come to a head; to maturate.

1704 F. FULLER *Med. Gymn.* (1718) 51 A Cancerous Humour is some years ripening. **1709** FLOYER *Cold Bathing* I. iv. 138 Cold Water hinders any Pain from ripening. **1722** DE FOE *Plague* (Rtldg.) 209 The violent Motion.. caused them [swellings] to ripen and break.

3. Of natural products, etc.: To reach the proper condition or stage for being utilized. Also *fig.*

1756–82 J. WARTON *Ess. Pope* I. ii. 78 In some minds the ore is a long time in ripening. **1807** J. BARLOW *Columb.* IV. 380 No useless mine these northern hills enclose, No ruby ripens and no diamond glows. **1883** R. HALDANE *Workshop Receipts* Ser. II. 335/2 It is then poured out in the form of flat cakes.. and is left in that condition for many days to 'ripen'. *a* **1890** *Sci. Amer.* LIV. 40 (Cent.), After ripening, the cream is churned.

b. Of land: To become sufficiently valuable to let or sell for building on.

1899 *Westm. Gaz.* 11 Feb. 1/2 We see landlords.. holding land on the fringe of towns until it 'ripens', as the phrase goes, to the value which secures them an immense profit on their outlay.

4. *trans.* To make ripe; to bring to maturity or to the proper condition for being used.

1565 COOPER *Thesaurus* s.v. *Maturo*, The yere quickly ripeneth grapes in sunnie hilles. **1587** GOLDING *De Mornay* iv. (1592) 44 The Sunne.. rypeneth things, he withereth things and so foorth. **1599** SHAKS. *Much Ado* III. i. 8 The pleached bower, Where hony-suckles ripened by the sunne, Forbid the sunne to enter. **1647** TRAPP *Comm. Luke* v. 39 Age clarifies wine, and ripens it. **1666** DRYDEN *Ann. Mirab.* iii, For them alone the heavens had kindly heat, In eastern quarries ripening precious dew. **1725** POPE *Odyss.* XI. 556 The blooming boy is ripen'd into man. **1759** MILLER *Gard. Dict.* (ed. 7) s.v. *Abutilon*, With proper care they will ripen their seeds in autumn. **1815** J. SMITH *Panorama Sci. & Art* II. 667 In a frame of this kind, Knight ripened grapes. **1880** *Spons' Encycl. Manuf.* II. 640 They are worked by shallow pits, and are 'ripened', ground, and washed, as the other clays. **1894** *Field* 9 June 844/3 They have learned the reason why the cream is ripened, and how it is ripened.

5. To develop to a mature state or condition; to bring to perfection.

1570 FOXE *A. & M.* (ed. 2) 1124 Being now further ripened in the knowledge of Gods word. **1588** SHAKS. *Titus A.* I. i. 227 Whose Vertues will, I hope, Reflect on Rome.. And ripen Iustice in this Common-weale. **1605** B. JONSON *Volpone* II. iii, I have something else To ripen for your good. **1648** BOYLE *Seraph. Love* xx. (1700) 125 When Age and study shall have ripened and instructed his Intellectuals. **1721** YOUNG *Revenge* III. i, This conduct ripen'd all for me, and ruin. **1781** GIBBON *Decl. & F.* xxxviii. (1787) III. 631 Prosperity ripened the principle of decay. **1821** LAMB *Elia* I. *My Relations*, His amelioration-plans must be ripened in a day. **1856** EMERSON *Eng. Traits, Religion*, The action of the university.. ripens a Bishop, and extrudes a philosopher.

b. Const. *into.*

a **1721** SHEFFIELD (Dk. Buckhm.) *Wks.* (1753) I. 15 Love ripens all that dross into the purest gold. **1748** RICHARDSON *Clarissa* (1811) III. 64 Ripening into execution my plots upon themselves.

6. *Med.* To bring to a head. (Cf. RIPE *v.*[1] 3.)

1599 A. M. tr. *Gabelhouer's Bk. Physic* 95/1 A potione to mature, or ripen, an Apostematione. *c* **1600** MARKHAM in Topsell *Four-f. Beasts* (1607) 361 Then renew it, till such time that it ripen and break the sore. *a* **1617** BAYNE *On Eph.* (1643) 140 Physitians by ripning diseases make way to heal them. **1737** BRACKEN *Farriery Impr.* (1757) I. 290 A Poultis to ripen any Tumour. **1753** [see RIPENING *ppl. a.* 1].

ripened ('raɪp(ə)nd), *a.* [f. prec. + -ED[1].] Advanced or brought to ripeness, maturity, or full development.

1589 GREENE *Menaphon* (Arb.) 77 Hir cheekes like ripened lillies steept in wine. **1603** SHAKS. *Meas. for M.* V. i. 116 Keepe me in patience, and with ripened time Vnfold the euil. **1642** H. MORE *Song of Soul* I. i. xlvii, The ripen'd child breaks through his mothers womb. **1712** STEELE *Spect.* No. 496 ¶1 [They] tempered the forward Ambition.. of ripen'd Manhood with Discretion. **1786** BURNS *Vision* II. xv, When ripen'd fields, and azure skies, Call'd forth the Reaper's rustling noise. **1818** KEATS *Endym.* I. 253 O thou, to whom Broad leaved fig trees even now foredoom Their ripen'd fruitage. **1860** PUSEY *Min. Proph.* 215 Heavenly influences can but injure the ripened sinner, as dew, rain, sun, but injure the ripened fruit. **1880** C. R. MARKHAM *Peruv. Bark* 242 He thus succeeded in obtaining 450 ripened capsules full of seeds.

ripener ('raɪp(ə)nə(r)). [f. as prec. + -ER[1].]

1. One who, or that which, causes ripening; †*spec.* in *Med.*, a maturative.

1562 LEGH *Armory* (1597) 4 b, She [*sc.* the moon] is the ripener and increaser of fruites. **1666** BOGHURST *Loimographia* (1894) 88 For Ripeners, these are good, Mallowes, violetts, comfrey. **1718** QUINCY *Compl. Disp.* 214 Ripeners and Drawers. **1737** BRACKEN *Farriery Impr.* (1749) 289 Suppuratives or Ripeners as they are stiled. **1871** SMILES *Charac.* iv. (1876) 107 The best ripener of the energetic vitality of strong natures.

2. One who, or that which, comes to ripeness.

1731 MILLER *Gard. Dict.* s.v. *Vitis*, The Corinth Grape.. is an early Ripener. **1786** ABERCROMBIE *Gard. Assist.* 280 Those late ripeners will keep.. till May or June. **1862** THORNBURY *Turner* I. 24 We may suppose the boy slowly advancing (for he is one of the slow ripeners).

3. A device in which honey is allowed to stand until it is fit to be put in jars.

[**1883** *Brit. Bee Jrnl.* XI. 209/2 The above simple arrangement.. will combine that of a honey-extractor and a honey-ripener in one compact piece of apparatus.] **1905** *Instruction in Bee-Keeping* (Dept. Agric. & Techn. Instruction for Ireland) 20 The ripener.. is a tinned iron cylinder about 19 inches in depth by about $8\frac{1}{2}$ inches in diameter, and fitted with a treacle tap at the base. **1930** W. HERROD-HEMPSALL *Bee-Keeping* I. ix. 525 The ripener was so named because at one time both the unsealed and sealed honey used to be extracted together, it was then run into the ripener and allowed to stand for some time in a warm room. **1971** *Country Life* 18 Nov. 1347/1 The ripener, into which the extracted honey is put, so that air bubbles may escape in due time, was so heavy that it was all both of us could do to lift it.

ripeness (ˈraɪpnɪs). [f. RIPE *a.* + -NESS. So Fris. *ripens.*] The state of being ripe in any sense; maturity, mellowness.

c **1000** *Lamb. Ps.* cxviii. 147 On ripnysse [L. *in maturitate*]. *a* **1300** *Cursor M.* 18834 His hare like to þe nute brun, Quen it for ripnes fals dun. *a* **1300** *E.E. Psalter* cxviii. 147, I forcome in ripenes, and made crie. **1395** PURVEY *Remonstr.* (1851) 135 Ripenesse of age and sadnesse of vertuis. *c* **1440** *Promp. Parv.* 434/2 Rypenesse, *maturitas.* **1541** R. COPLAND *Guydon's Form.* R iij b, Whan they [remedies] fynde mater redy to rypenesse they do maturate. **1548** UDALL, etc. *Erasm. Par. Mark* iv. 25 Therof sprang grasse, the whiche grewe, and waxed, vntyll it came to it ful ripenesse. **1576** FLEMING *Panopl. Epist.* 253 By the exercise of translating,.. our judgement inclineth to ripenesse. **1612** BRINSLEY *Lud. Lit.* viii. (1627) 124 All these kinds of Construing.. may be used by schollers of ripenesse, and with much profit. **1682** DRYDEN *Relig. Laici* Pref., If a blessing in the ripeness of time was reserved for Japhet. **1732** POPE *Hor. Sat.* II. ii. 28 Till a stench exhale Rank as the ripeness of a rabit's tail. **1786** ABERCROMBIE *Gard. Assist.* 259 They attain maturity before mellow ripeness. **1833** TENNYSON *To J.S.* 15 When love is grown To ripeness, that on which it throve Falls off. **1886** *Manch. Exam.* 13 Mar. 5/3 The artist was in the full vigour of his genius and ripeness of his experience.

ˈ**ripening**, *vbl. sb.* [f. RIPEN *v.* + -ING[1].]

1. The action of the verb in various senses.

1597 HOOKER *Eccl. Pol.* v. lxxxi. §6 No lesse expedient.. then the verie Vniversities themselues are for the ripening of such as bee rawe. **1613** PURCHAS *Pilgrimage* v. xii. (1614) 507 Then the Mace flourisheth in a faire red colour, which in the ripening becommeth yellow. **1646** H. P. *Medit. Seige* 97 Patiently to awaite the ripening of our hopes, is the great rule of humane undertakings. **1676** HALE *Contempl.* II. 106 The use of Deliberation, and the ripening of the Judgment. **1728** CHAMBERS *Cycl.* s.v. *Transmutation*, The transmuting or ripening of other Metals into Gold or Silver. **1786** ABERCROMBIE *Gard. Assist.* 177 The size, beauty, and timely ripening of the fruit. **1805** R. W. DICKSON *Pract. Agric.* I. 59 The warmth of such places being supposed to promote the ripening of the cheeses. **1887** *Athenæum* 15 Oct. 506/1 The few student-ships.. give no earnest of a five years' additional ripening of scholarship.

2. *Brewing.* (See quot.)

1742 *Lond. & Country Brewer* I. (ed. 4) 48 A clear Wort made from pale Malt, and fermented with what they call Ripening, which is a Composition, they say, of the Flour of Malt, Yeast, and Whites of Eggs.

3. In various industrial processes, applied to a stage in which a material is left to stand until desired properties are attained; *spec.* in rayon manufacture (see quot. 1957).

1919 *Jrnl. Soc. Chem. Industry* 31 Oct. 373T/1 There result, upon application of partial hydration ('ripening'), esters of high viscosity and great strength, suppleness, and wearing qualities. **1932** *Discovery* Sept. 289/1 After ripening has been completed the soluble salts are removed. **1937** *Ibid.* Aug. 247/1 The actual process is a long one.., the polymerisation process alone occupying from 90 to 120 hours, after which a 'ripening' process for the synthetic rubber of three to eight days is necessary. **1950** R. W. MONCRIEFF *Man-Made Fibres* viii. 96 Ripening is an essential part of the viscose process; 'young' viscose cannot be spun satisfactorily. **1957** *Textile Terms & Definitions* (Textile Inst.) (ed. 3) 82 *Ripening*,..(1) A process in the production of cellulose acetate consisting of the splitting off of some of the acetic acid and most of the combined catalyst present in the primary cellulose acetate. (2) A process in the manufacture of viscose rayon in which the viscose is matured prior to spinning. The rate of ripening is controlled by the time and temperature at which the spinning fluid is maintained. The process is sometimes called maturing or ageing. **1973** *Materials & Technol.* VI. iv. 307 This 'ripening'.. results in a solution which will later give easier coagulation, and it is allowed to proceed until a required amount of hydrolysis has taken place.

4. *attrib.*, as *ripening-time.*

1910 W. DE LA MARE *Three Mulla-Mulgars* i. 7 The great Ukka-tree, which he had climbed at ripening-time.

ˈ**ripening**, *ppl. a.* [f. as prec. + -ING[2].]

1. Bringing to ripeness or maturity.

1592 SHAKS. *Rom. & Jul.* II. ii. 121 This bud of Loue by Summers ripening breath, May proue a beautious Flower. *a* **1602** W. PERKINS *Cases Consc.* (1619) 55 As Surgeons are wont.. to apply drawing and ripening plaisters. **1685** DRYDEN *Alb. & Albimes* III. ii, Already they are fix'd by Fate, And only ripening Ages wait. **1725** *Fam. Dict.* s.v. *Glue*, This Bookbinders Glue is of an emplastick and ripening Nature. **1753** J. BARTLET *Gentl. Farriery* (1754) 278 The best method then is to forward it by applying the ripening poultices. **1881** *Proc. Berwick. Nat. Club* IX. 567 This is to be attributed to the good ripening season of 1880.

2. Advancing towards, coming to, ripeness.

1651 DAVENANT *Gondibert* II. vi, Duke Gondibert Was brought, which now his rip'ning wounds allow. **1697** DRYDEN *Virg. Georg.* I. 478 Before the Sickles touch the ripening Wheat. **1710** POPE *Windsor For.* 396 Phœbus [shall] warm the ripening ore to gold. **1794** MRS. RADCLIFFE *Myst. Udolpho* xxxii, These ripening clusters of grapes hung round her little casement. **1838** LYTTON *Alice* 132 Her ripening understanding was better able.. to appreciate his abilities. **1876** J. SAUNDERS *Lion in Path* i, There was the eloquent murmur of a ripening harvest.

Hence ˈ**ripeningly** *adv.*

1894 *Temple Bar* CII. 142 The sun.. shone ripeningly upon the mellow clusters.

ˈ**riper**[1]. *rare.* [f. RIPE *v.*[1]] Ripener.

c **1400** *Lanfranc's Cirurg.* 6 Of Maturatiuis, þat buþ Ripers. **1572** BOSSEWELL *Armorie* II. 124 That mighty planet, Luna, the riper and encreaser of fruites.

riper[2] (ˈraɪpə(r)). Now *dial.* Also 1 **rýpere**, 2 **rupere.** [f. RIPE *v.*[2]]

†**1.** A robber, plunderer. *Obs.*

a **1023** WULFSTAN *Hom.* xxxiii. (1883) 159 Us stalu and cwalu.. and rypera reaflac derede. **1027–34** *Sec. Laws Cnut* vii. in Liebermann *Gesetze* 312/1 Ryperas and reaferas Godes graman habban. *c* **1175** *Lamb. Hom.* 15 þas ruperes and þas reueres and þas þeues.

2. *dial.* (See quot.)

1894 HESLOP *Northumb. Gloss.*, *Riper*, an iron prong used for clearing dirt and dust out of the oilholes in machinery.

†ˈ**riper**[3]. *Obs.* [? cf. RIP *v.*[2] 2 b, quot. 1688.] An instrument used by arrow-makers.

1659 HOWELL *Vocab.* LI, A thwitting knife, nocksaws a rasp, a riper, a share.

rip-hook, dial. var. of REAP-HOOK.

Current in southern and south-western counties.

1872 'AGRIKLER' *Rhymes* 105 (E.D.D.), I handled the rip-hook and zive. **1881** BLACKMORE *Cristowell* xxii, A shortish old man with.. a rip-hook swinging in one hand.

riˈpicolous, *a. rare.* [f. L. *rīpa* bank + *-colus* inhabiting.] Riparious.

1859 MAYNE *Expos. Lex.* (1860) 1099/2 *Ripicolus*,.. *Entomol.*, living by the shore or water-banks, as the *Limosia ripicola*: ripicolous. **1906** J. B. SMITH *Explanation Terms Entomol.* 117 Ripicolous: dwelling on river banks: riparian. **1965** B. E. FREEMAN tr. *Vandel's Biospeleol.* xiii. 196 The Bembiinae are essentially ripicolous.

ripidolite (raɪˈpɪdəlaɪt). *Min.* [f. Gr. ῥιπίδο-, ῥιπίς fan + -LITE; named by Kobell in 1839.] = CLINOCHLORE.

1850 DAUBENY *Atom. The.* xii. (ed. 2) 412 Silicates with hydrates. Ripidolite (chlorite). **1857** DANA *Man. Mineral.* (1862) 145 Chlorite... This species has lately been subdivided on chemical grounds, and the name *Ripidolite* applied to the new species instituted. **1880** *Libr. Univ. Knowl.* (N.Y.) XIII. 155 [Sapphire] is found.. in granular limestone in New Jersey, and in the ripidolite of North Carolina.

ripienist (ripiˈenɪst). [f. next + -IST.] 'A performer who only assists in the ripieno parts'.

1876 STAINER & BARRETT *Dict. Mus. Terms.* **1935** P. A. SCHOLES *Radio Times Music Handbk.* 18 A 'full' body of strings and a smaller body of two or three solo string players—the 'ripienists' and the 'concertinists', as we may call them. **1944** W. APEL *Harvard Dict. Mus.* 646/2 *Ripienista* (Ripienist) is an orchestral player.

‖**ripieno** (ripiˈeno), *a.* and *sb. Mus.* Also 7 repieno, 7–8 -piano; 8- ripiano. [It., f. *ri-* RE- + *pieno* full.]

1. a. Supplementary, re-enforcing. (Cf. quots.)

1724 *Short Explic. For. Wds. Mus. Bks.* 63 *Repieno*, or *Repiano*, signifies Full; and is used to distinguish those Violins in Concerto's, which play only now and then to fill up, from those which play throughout the whole Concerto. **1740** J. GRASSINEAU *Mus. Dict.* 203 *Ripiano*, or *Ripiéno*, signifies *full*, and is used in pieces of music in parts, to distinguish those parts that play now and then to fill up, from those that play throughout the piece. **1811** BUSBY *Dict. Mus.* (ed. 3), *Ripieno*.. is used in orchestral compositions, to distinguish those parts which are only occasionally introduced to fill up and supply the chorus. **1879** in Grove *Dict. Mus.* I. 153 Handel's scores contain few bassoon parts, and those.. mostly of a ripieno character. **1933** *Radio Times* 14 Apr. 82/3 Miners, cotton spinners and the like who get a real kick from the ripiano cornet and the bombardon. **1954** *Grove's Dict. Mus.* (ed. 5), I. 914/1 In Britain the instrumentation ultimately became as follows for the purpose of contests: 1 Soprano Cornet in E♭... 1 Repiano Cornet in B♭. [*Note*] 'Repiano' is a spelling peculiar to the brass band. *Ibid.* 914/2 Nowadays only one [*sc.* flugelhorn] is used, playing a separate part or combining with the repiano cornet. **1962** [see CONCERTINO 2]. **1978** *Daily Tel.* 13 Mar. 11/1 The Choir—with the youthful ripieno Chorus—responded with clear tone and vitality.

b. *sb.* Occas. with It. pl. **ripieni.** A supplementary player or instrument. Also *collect.*, the group of accompanying instruments that form the main orchestral body in a concerto, as distinct from the concertino (CONCERTINO 2).

1740 J. GRASSINEAU *Mus. Dict.* 203 There are.. two kinds of *Ripiénos*, one whereof plays the part of the little chorus exactly... The other sort is much better, because they play a different part. **1753** CHAMBERS *Cycl. Suppl.* s.v., There are .. two kinds of the ripieno: one plays the part of the little chorus exactly, and does not, therefore, increase the harmony or number of parts. **1789** BURNEY *Hist. Mus.* III. 560 Twelve concertos for a violino principale, with two *ripienos*. **1873** H. C. BANISTER *Music* (1885) 248 The subordinate stringed instruments in an Orchestra are sometimes termed Ripieni, as distinguished from the Principals. **1930** *Radio Times Dict. Mus. Terms* 50 *Ripieno*, the instruments which form the accompaniment, as opposed to those which have solo parts. **1935** P. A. SCHOLES *Radio Times Music Handbk.* 18 In the Concerto Grosso.. the idea is.. that *two bodies* of instruments are.. responding to one another antiphonally... The larger body is called *Ripieno*.., and the smaller one '*Concertino*'. **1944** W. APEL *Harvard Dict. Mus.* 646/2 'Ripieni' indicates the full orchestra.., as distinguished from the soloists... The term 'senza ripieni', however, is not identical with 'orchestra silent', but calls for the leading members only of the orchestra, i.e., for a smaller ensemble used for the accompaniment of the soloists. **1960** *Times* 2 Nov. 16/6 A *ripieno* of six players (five strings and harpsichord). **1961** [see CONCERTINO 2]. **1976** *Gramophone* Dec. 1028/3 The balance and interplay between voices and ripieno are two of the several outstandingly successful features of the present performances.

2. *transf.* Serving to fill up; supernumerary.

1811 L. M. HAWKINS *C'tess & Gertr.* I. 52 An oriental Crœsus and his beautiful lady, one or two ripieno characters, and the observing party. *Ibid.* 135 In the.. re-adjustment of the treasury-balance, he got a *ripieno* appointment.

ripier, variant of RIPPIER.

riping (ˈraɪpɪŋ), *vbl. sb.*[1] Now *rare.* [f. RIPE *v.*[1]] The process or fact of becoming ripe.

c **825** *Vesp. Psalter* cxviii. 147 Ic forecom in ripunge [L. *in maturitate*]. *c* **960** ÆTHELWOLD *Rule St. Benet* (Schröer) 126 Seo ripung his ȝestæþþiȝnesse sy swylc, þæt hine ne worian ..lyste. *c* **1055** *Byrhtferth's Handboc* in *Anglia* VIII. 312 Se þridda tima ys Autumnus on lyden ȝecweden,.. boceras ȝetrahtniað þæne naman for þære ripunge. **1398** TREVISA *Barth. De P.R.* VIII. xliv. (Tollemache MS.), [An eclipse] tarieþ ripynge of frute, and of corne. *c* **1450** LYDG. *Secrees* 1371 Euery thyng drawith to his Rypyng. **1523** *St. Papers Hen. VIII*, VI. 131 The Ambassadour, for his more parfite knowlege and ripyng in this matier, shal undirstand [etc.]. **1544** PHAER *Pestilence* (1553) P iij, It is better.. to breake the sore by times, than to tary for yᵉ riping long. **1596** SHAKS. *Merch. V.* II. viii. 40 Stay the very riping of the time. **1627** HAKEWILL *Apol.* (1630) 140 The uncertaine and unkindely riping of fruites.

1899 *Daily News* 30 Dec. 6/1 Has the rotting followed so fast after the riping?

ˈ**riping**, *vbl. sb.*[2] [f. RIPE *v.*[2]] The action of searching (†or plundering).

a **1100** in Napier *O.E. Glosses* 84 *Proscryptionem, i. fraudationem*, fordeminge, rypincge. **1815** SCOTT *Guy M.* xlv, An unco ranging and ripeing they have had a' gates seeking for her.

ˈ**riping**, *ppl. a.* [f. RIPE *v.*[1]] Ripening.

c **1550** H. LLOYD *Treas. Health* H vij, Use outwardly.. drawynge and ryping medicines. **1590** GREENE *Neuer too Late* Wks. (Grosart) VIII. 225 The riping corne growes yeolow in the stalke. **1863** LANCASTER *Praeterita* 57, I scent A riping vintage from the Cretan hills.

riple, obs. form of RIPPLE *v.*[1]

riplet: see RIPPLET.

riply, obs. f. RIPELY.

ripman, variant of REAPMAN *Obs.*

ripnes, obs. f. RIPENESS.

rip-off (ˈrɪpɒf), *sb.* (and *a.*) *slang* (orig. *U.S.*). Also **rip off, ripoff.** [f. *to rip off* s.v. RIP *v.*[2] 6.]

1. One who steals, a thief.

1970 *Manch. Guardian Weekly* 2 May 16/4 'Who do you have on Haight Street today?' he [*sc.* a San Francisco drug peddler] said disgustedly... 'You have burn artists (fraudulent dope peddlers), rip-offs (thieves), and snitchers (police spies).' **1971** *Rolling Stone* 24 June 8/3, I call them rip-offs, and they are, nothing but pirates and vultures.

2. A fraud, a swindle; a racket; an instance of exploitation, esp. financial.

1970 *Melody Maker* 12 Sept. 29 *Rip off*, capitalist exploitation. **1970** *Time* 21 Dec. 4/1 This is what, in contemporary parlance, is called a rip-off. **1971** *It* 9–23 Sept. 12 Fun Caterers of Battersea.. had the main catering concession (the biggest rip-off there.) **1973** *Houston* (Texas) *Chron.* 21 Oct. 7/3 Dunlop said the increased spring markups had been 'inflationary', a polite word in the context for 'ripoff'. **1974** *Sunday Sun* (Brisbane) 28 July 24/2 The great snackbar rip-off that had city workers weeping into their salad rolls. **1975** *N.Y. Times* 14 Apr. 30/4 A five-day week, with ten paid holidays, plus a ten-week paid vacation yearly. Such a contract is a 'rip-off'. **1977** *Time* 4 July 21/1 They [*sc.* French soldiers and civil servants] get rich and Djibouti gets nothing. That's not enlightened colonialism. It's a bloody rip-off. **1980** *Times* 31 May 2/3 Britain's 41 motorway service areas.. have attracted such accolades as 'poor', 'appalling' and 'a rip-off'.

3. An imitation or plagiarism, usu. one made in order to exploit public taste.

1971 *Newsweek* 18 Oct. 38/3 Most of the architecture is Inspired Bastard, most of the historical re-creations are Shameless Ripoff. **1974** *Publishers Weekly* 4 Mar. 72/2 This kaleidoscopic fantasy, a ripoff on everything from spy novels to the Oedipus complex. **1976** *Time* (Canada) 19 Jan. 16/3 Flynt runs three Hustler Clubs in Ohio, tacky rip-offs of the Playboy Clubs, offering expensive drinks and leggy 'hostesses'. **1977** *Private Eye* 1 Apr. 4/1 *Blue Belle* [*sc.* a film], yet another of the seemingly endless *Emmanuelle* rip-offs. **1980** *Jewish Chron.* 29 Feb. 30/2 We were treated to a kaleidoscopic mess of fifties rip-offs, sixties platitudes and seventies mistakes; shirtwaisters, minis, halter-necks, op art, sloppy jos, Bermudas and, latest ubiquity, the flying suit.

4. a. *attrib.* passing into *adj.*

1971 *National Times* (Austral.) 15–20 Feb. 1/3 In Sydney comics and books have been appearing from the 'rip-off' press—the underground printers and publishers who are printing editions of banned books sneaked singly through Customs. **1973** *Nation Rev.* (Melbourne) 24–30 Aug. 1399/6 The poor unfortunate buyer getting lumbered.. with the cost of the device (at ripoff prices). **1973** *National Observer* (U.S.) 6 Oct. 23/3 The 'rip-off' blues, the blues that musicians get when they write songs that make other people rich and leave them poor as before. **1975** *Time* 12 May 17/1 The rip-off capital of the world [*sc.* Saigon]. **1976** *New Yorker* 5 Apr. 31/2 Cargo leaving New York for places like South America is often a kind of object lesson in rip-off economics. **1976** *Times* 11 June 8/1 The trade in old books is an incongruous mixture of fine art almost beyond price and the rascally hustle and rip-off hugger-mugger of a flea market.

b. *Comb.*, as **rip-off artist, merchant**, one who carries out a rip-off; a thief, fraud, or racketeer.

1971 *Frendz* 21 May 11/2 Rip-off artists are only occasionally armed or violent; more usual is..the traditional con-man. **1971** J. MANDELKAU *Buttons* xiii. 149 From now on my club was going to have nought to do with the Alternative society and its rip-off merchants. **1974** *Amer. Speech 1970* XLV. 210 Bring your own food. There won't be any ripoff merchants there. **1977** *It* May 5/2, I am not suggesting that the Pink Floyd are rip-off artists, but it is undeniable that much contemporary music is a response to alienation. **1977** C. MCFADDEN *Serial* xxxix. 84/2 He checked out the chain lock that secured his Motobecane against rip-off artists.

Ripolin (ripɔlɛ̃). [Fr.] The proprietary name of a make of paint.

[**1889** *Trade Marks Jrnl.* 25 Dec. 1/1 Ripolin 92,910. Chemical substances used in manufactures or philosophical research, and anti-corrosives... 2nd October 1889.] **1907** *Yesterday's Shopping* (1969) 157/1 Ripolin enamel. White, black, sulphur, [etc.]. Tin... 1/0. **1922** C. K. S. MONCRIEFF tr. *Proust's Swann's Way* II. 29 My room in the Grand Hôtel de la Plage..the walls of which, washed with ripolin, contained..a finer air. **1934** A. HUXLEY *Beyond Mexique Bay* 32 We prefer the lighter woods, we prefer metal and glass and ripolin.

ripon: see RIPPON.

riposte (rɪˈpəʊst, rɪˈpɒst), *sb.* Also 7 **risposte**, 9 **ripost** (cf. REPOST *sb.*). [a. F. *riposte*, earlier *risposte*, ad. It. *risposta* response, reply.]

1. *Fencing.* A quick thrust given after parrying a lunge; a return thrust. Also *attrib.*

1707 SIR W. HOPE *New Method Fencing* iv. 85 For the Risposte, it is impossible for a Man to give it, until his Adversary..offers to launch in a Thrust. *Ibid.* vi. 171 To defend himself well from his Adversary's Risposte Thrusts, or Blows. **1809** ROLAND *Fencing* (1823) 104 The party standing on the defensive, is not allowed to make any riposte. *Ibid.* 142 By not fearing the riposte upon you, it will render your mode of attack more precise. **1893** *Fencing* (Badminton Libr.) (ed. 3) iv. 82 To meet this riposte: parry second or septime while rising.

2. *transf.* A counterstroke; an effective reply by word or act.

1865 *Pall Mall G.* 19 June 1 The thrust..was an ugly one, but the ripost which he has succeeded in planting is uglier still. **1877** MORLEY *Crit. Misc.* Ser. II. 107 The Feast of the Supreme Being..was designed as a triumphant ripost to the Feast of Reason. **1886** N. L. WALFORD *Parl. Gen. Civil War* 74 To us the 'riposte' of Charles appears to have been a fair one.

riposte (rɪˈpəʊst, rɪˈpɒst), *v.* Also 8 **risposte**, 9 **ripost** (cf. REPOST *v.*[1]). [ad. F. *riposter*, earlier *risposter*: see prec.]

1. *Fencing.* To make a riposte. Also *trans.* with personal object.

1707 SIR W. HOPE *New Method Fencing* iv. 96 Nothing can be more dangerous, because of the Opportunity it gives a Man's Adversary to Risposte him. **1809** ROLAND *Fencing* (1823) 115 B. Parries Tierce smartly, and ripostes straight over the arm. **1885** *New Bk. Sports* 121 Smartly raising the knee..and riposting with a quick downward movement.

2. *transf.* To reply or retaliate; to answer (one). Also with direct speech as obj.

1851 KINGSLEY *Lett. & Mem.* (1877) I. 267 If you do not think our mutual 'honour' satisfied.., you will riposte at the first opportunity. **1871** MEREDITH *H. Richmond* xlviii, Riposte me—have you too many? **1883** WINGFIELD *Abigel Rowe* I. iii. 57 The other side dared not ripost with the real report. **1893** LANG *St. Andrews* v. 128 The Cardinal riposted by an interdict. **1898** J. M. COBBAN *Angel of Covenant* xiii. 147 'Had I not taken pains with the foolish old man,' riposted Maudlin, blushing high, 'we should yet be sitting at mumchance.' **1958** *Observer* 6 Dec. 864/1 The western powers might logically riposte by offering to discuss a free and neutral status..for all Berlin. **1972** *Daily Tel.* 27 May 12 'But I'm David Broome,' says the show jumper. 'I don't care if you are Basil Brush,' ripostes the sergeant-major. **1977** T. HEALD *Just Desserts* 191 'But what do we have to show for it?' 'We have unlimited access to the former Scoff network,' riposted Bognor.

Hence **riˈposted, riˈposting** *ppl. adjs.*

1707 SIR W. HOPE *New Method Fencing* iv. 96 To come off safe, from an Exchanged and Risposted Thrust. *Ibid.* vi. 173 Give him a Risposted Blow. **1893** *Fencing* (Badminton Libr.) (ed. 3) iv. 83 The riposting fencer must..deliver his thrust with the hand inclined towards pronation.

ripp(e, obs. forms of REAP *sb.*[2] and *v.*[1]

ripped (rɪpt), *ppl. a.* (and *pa. pple.*). [f. RIP *v.*[2] + -ED[1].] **1.** *dial.* Cut, slit.

1823 E. MOOR *Suffolk Words & Phr.* 129 *Fleeches.* The portions into which a tree or piece of timber is cut by the saw, in its first position over the saw-pit... When turned and *ripp'd* or *rippen'd*, that is, cut into smaller portions, such portions are called *Scantlins*, in Suffolk and..elsewhere. **1880**. J. H. MAXWELL *Sheep-Marks* 15 Topped on both ears, ripped on near.

2. With *up*. **a.** Angry. **b.** Torn up.

1941 *Amer. Speech* XVI. 190 *Ripped up*, angry. **1973** 'E. MCBAIN' *Hail to Chief* i. 3 The ripped-up sections of planking.

3. (As *pa. pple.*) Under the influence of a drug. *U.S. slang.*

1971 *Rolling Stone* 24 June 16/1 It comes on so fast all with one toke. By the third you're ripped to the gills for several hours. **1973** D. LANG *Freaks* 17 Oh, wow, boy, are you ripped! **1975** C. JAMES *Fate of Felicity Fark* vi. 55 On he gabbled as if ripped on Speed. **1981** *Listener* 1 Jan. 23/3 The story is of a threatened pop singer who, though he gets ripped at need, is really very moral.

4. *slang.* With *off*. Of a person: robbed; exploited; of a thing: stolen.

1971 *New Yorker* 22 May 40 (*title*) Ripped off. **1975** *Maclean's Mag.* Sept. 8/2, I can 'hate men' but many of them are in the same spot as I am: co-opted, ripped-off and mad. **1976** SCOTT & KOSKI *Walk-In* iv. 23 The garages where you can buy hot tires and ripped-off hub caps.

ripper (ˈrɪpə(r)). [f. RIP *v.*[2] + -ER[1]. Cf. Fris. *ripper* a poor knife.]

1. a. One who rips. Chiefly in technical uses.

1611 COTGR., *Descouseur*, a ripper, vnsower; vndooer of. **1674** RAY *Coll. Words, Wirework* 133 Then the Rippers take them and draw them into wire through two or three holes. **1833** J. HOLLAND *Manuf. Metal* II. 332 Where the rippers, as the workmen are called, care little about modern improvements. **1852** J. C. BROWN tr. *Arboussat's Narr.* 127 A number of rippers at once cast off their garments, and began by cutting off the head of the animal. **1892** *Daily News* 8 Mar. 6/1 The 'ripper' clears off the roof to a height sufficient for the passage of the horses with their loaded 'corves'. **1896** in *Eng. Dial. Dict.* s.v., Wanted..: good rippers for coppice. **1909** *Daily Chron.* 20 Aug. 1/1 The theory most generally entertained is that the canister..was left in a coal train in the mine by a ripper or repairer. **1967** *Gloss. Mining Terms (B.S.I.)* VIII. 22 *Ripper*, a man who rips. **1979** B. HINES *Price of Coal* 31 Sid and the other rippers stayed on the paddy until it reached the end of the track.

b. A criminal who rips the bodies of his victims; *spec.* = *Jack the Ripper* s.v. JACK *sb.*[1] 37 Also *transf.* and *Comb.* Hence (*nonce-wds.*) **rippeˈrologist**, a student of the crimes of Jack the Ripper; **rippeˈrology**.

1890, etc. [see *Jack the Ripper* s.v. JACK *sb.*[1] 37]. **1909** J. R. WARE *Passing Eng.* 209/2 *Ripper*, daring murderer of women. **1935** *Amer. Speech* X. 20/1 *Ripper.* 1. A degenerate who molests, rapes, or mutilates women in parks or other secluded spots; probably from Jack the Ripper. 2. A shrewd or lucky fellow who 'gets away with murder'. **1970** C. MAJOR *Dict. Afro-Amer. Slang* 98 *Ripper*, one who has a reputation for cutting others with a knife. **1974** A. DOUGLAS *Noah's Ark Murders* iv. 40 The series of Ripper-like murders that had all but ended his own life. **1974** G. MOFFAT *Corpse Road* iii. 41 'The Ripper stopped at six [murders].' 'Perhaps this one won't stop.' **1975** D. RUMBELOW *Compl. Jack the Ripper* 5 To..'Ripperologists' everywhere—not forgetting *Jack* who brought us all together. **1977** *Guardian Weekly* 27 Feb. 20/3 This file-work gives a little more definition to the blurred (and in places bizarrely touched-up) picture of the dark side of late-Victorian high life that has been emerging during our seventies, mostly through the addition of new bits of information to that arcane old science known as Ripperology. **1979** W. J. FISHMAN *Streets of E. London* 102/2 It is still debated whether Turner was the first victim [of Jack the Ripper]. Some 'Ripperologists' suggest that Polly Nichols was the first. **1979** *Guardian* 1 June 4/1 The 'Yorkshire Ripper'..has murdered 11 women in less than four years. **1981** *Yorks. Post* 8 July 7/1, I don't want people to cash in on what the Ripper did to my daughter.

2. That which rips; a tool or apparatus intended for ripping; esp. (*a*) a tool used in removing old slates; (*b*) a rip-saw; (*c*) *Criminals' slang*, a tool for opening safes, etc.

1793 O'KEEFFE *London Hermit* II. v, *Tom P.* I'll quicken him with a touch of the rippers... (Tom Pranks spurs him.) **1823** P. NICHOLSON *Pract. Build.* 400 The ripper is formed of iron..with a very thin blade... This tool is used for lifting up and removing the nails out of old slating. **1842** GWILT *Archit.* §2115 The half ripper is used also for dividing wood in the direction of the fibres. **1875** KNIGHT *Dict. Mech.* 1945/2 *Ripper*, a tool for ripping seams of garments. **1876** *Encycl. Brit.* IV. 43/2 The first process in the preparation of the cloth cases is cutting the millboard. This is now effected by a rotary cutting-machine or 'ripper'. **1889** FARMER *Americanisms* 460/1 *Ripper* or *Mason Ripper*, (1) a new and ingenious implement of burglary, used in opening safes or vaults with iron surfaces. **1925** *Flynn's* 14 Mar. 281/1 *Ripper*, a can-opener (a burglar's tool). **1963** R. I. MCDAVID *Mencken's Amer. Lang.* 717 The use of *stew* is declining, modern *heavy gees* preferring to use a *stick*, *ripper* or *can opener* on laminated safes.

attrib. **1892** *Pall Mall G.* 4 Apr. 6/3 A huge steel saw that will cut through a nickel-steel armour plate just as easily as an ordinary ripper saw will go through a pine board.

b. An implement that is attached to a tractor to break up concrete or hard soil.

1955 'N. SHUTE' *Requiem for Wren* i. 20 This war [against the rabbits] went on continuously with tractor-drawn rippers to destroy the warrens. **1963** OGLESBY & HEWES *Highway Engin.* (ed. 2) xiv. 476 In recent years large rippers mounted on huge crawler tractors..have been used successfully to break up loose or fractured rock. **1976** *Billings* (Montana) *Gaz.* 2 July 11-c/8 (Advt.), Power Tilt Straight dozer with Ateco swinging swank ripper. **1979** *Arizona Daily Star* 5 Aug. (Advt. Section) 9/2 Teeth for backhoes, loaders, ripper points, corner bits, cutting edges for all makes.

3. *slang.* **a.** A person or thing especially good; *spec.* an attractive young woman. In recent use, chiefly *Austral. slang.* Also *attrib.*

1838 *Bell's Life* 26 Aug. 4/1 One of Mr. Mynn's best balls, technically a 'ripper', took the top of the middle stump. **1846** *Swell's Night Guide* 40 In conjunction with the above is Miss Emma Watling, a regular ripper. **1848** [see CREEPER 12]. **1848** J. MITCHELL in *Amer. Speech* (1935) X. 41/1 *Ripper*. anything very large of its kind. [A Nantucketism.] **1851** MAYHEW *Lond. Labour* I. 301 Sarah was a cock, sir, and a ripper. **1859** LANG *Wand. India* 144 'But, he is a ripper, nevertheless,' said the Lieutenant, touching the animal very gently with the whip. **1892** BOYD *25 Yrs. St. Andrews* I. ii. 28 When a graduate stated that 'every lecture was a ripper', I understood he meant very high praise indeed. **1905** *Pall Mall Mag.* July 111/1 He had found her a ripper as to looks. **1935** AUDEN & ISHERWOOD *Dog beneath Skin* I. ii. 37 What do you think of her? Isn't she a ripper? **1951** E. LAMBERT *Twenty Thousand Thieves* x. 182. 'Good letter, Chips?' A gurgle. 'It's a ripper!' **1969** A. O'TOOLE *Racing Game* xviii. 200 'Not a bad run,' I observed... 'A ripper,' Badger agreed. **1970** *Sunday Truth* (Brisbane) 10 May 64 If I'm ever asked what Australia is like, I'll say, 'She's a bloody ripper, mate!' **1973** *Australian* 7 July 16, I love this ripper country. **1976** *Courier-Mail* (Brisbane) 13 Mar. 19/11 Nagle has a fine ear for Australian dialect. The book's a 'ripper', as his characters might say.

b. One who pursues a reckless course.

1877 *Temple Bar* May 109 If the ripper rips for the benefit of his party,..the turning out by no meansx 217 follows.

4. *U.S. Pol.* (See quot. 1937.) Also *attrib.*

1895 *Columbus* (Ohio) *Dispatch* 1 Apr. 4/2 The Merryman ripper bill looks very much as if the Republicans of this city were going to the legislature for offices. **1937** J. R. SCHULTZ in *Amer. Speech* XII. 319 The word 'ripper' is commonly used in Pennsylvania political parlance to describe a bill that abolishes an office or commission of state or city. Such an act is said usually to have as its purpose the elimination of an officer or member of a commission who is unfriendly to the party in power.

5. *Sc.* A simple fishing tackle consisting of 'a line having attached to it a heavy metal bar fitted with hooks' (*S.N.D.*).

1925 *Glasgow Herald* 17 Aug. 7 He..caught a 20 lb. ling with a ripper. *c* **1930** in *Scot. Nat. Dict.* (1968) VII. 455/3, I vrocht aa efterneen at the ripper, bit I hid nae luck. **1946** *Aberdeen Press & Jrnl.* 2 July, The primitive method of fishing with dandy lines, consisting of ripper and hooks.

ripper, obs. or dial. f. REAPER; var. RIPPIER.

rippet, var. RIPPIT.

rippier (ˈrɪpɪə(r)). *Obs.* exc. *Hist.* Forms: α. 6 **repier, repar, repayre, repear, rypear**, 6–7, 9 **ripier**. β. 6–8 **rippier**, 7 **ryppier**. γ. 6–7 **ripper**, 6 **rippar**. [f. RIP *sb.*[1] + -(I)ER. In old statutes latinized as *riparius*, and supposed by Cowell and others to be derived from L. *ripa* bank, shore.] One who carries fish inland to sell.

α. *a* **1513** FABYAN *Chron.* (1516) 169 b/1 Repiers and other Fisshers commynge with Fysshe from Rye and Wynchylsee. *c* **1530** in *Songs, Carols*, etc. (E.E.T.S.) 159 This yere..the ryrpears sold fish at London Hall in þe Lent. **1538** LELAND *Itin.* (1769) V. 77 A poore Market, much standing by Repears that cary Fische from the Quarters of Cairmardine to the lowers Partes of Wales. **1591** SAVILE *Tacitus, Hist.* II. lxii. 89 The hyewaies from both the seas sounded of nothing els but of caters and ripiers. [**1880** *Archæol. Cant.* XIII. 206 The cess upon the Ripiers (or as they would now be termed "long-shore-men").]

β. **1589** ? LYLY *Pappe w. Hatchet* L.'s Wks. 1902 III. 405 With the cloak cast ouer each shoulder like a rippier. **1598** FLORIO, *Mutade*, panniers or paddes, such as Rippiers bring fish in. **1607** CHAPMAN *Bussy d'Ambois* III. ii, Like a Rippiers legs rowl'd vp In bootes of haie ropes. *c* **1640** J. SMYTH *Hund. Berkeley* (1885) 302 A common Inne in this village addes fame therto, by the constant customary baytes of the Ryppiers and their horses. **1709** in *Sussex Archaeol. Coll.* (1848) 144 The horses on which the rippiers..shall ride going on or towards London. **1778** *Eng. Gazetteer* (ed. 2) s.v. *Rye*, They trowl for soles, plaise,..brills, &c. which are carried up every day by the rippiers (as the fishermen are called).

γ. **1530** in W. H. Turner *Select. Rec. Oxford* (1880) 87 Who wold never suffer rippers to sell ther owne fische. **1598** STOW *Surv.* 147 The Rippars of Rie..solde their fresh fish in Leaden hall market. **1622** FLETCHER *Beggar's Bush* v. i, But what's the action we are for now? ha: Robbing a Ripper of his fish? **1674** RAY *S. & E.C. Words* 75 A *Ripper*: a Pedder, Dorser or Badger, Suss. [Hence in Pegge, Grose, Holloway, etc.]

rippill, obs. form of RIPPLE.

ripping (ˈrɪpɪŋ), *vbl. sb.* [f. RIP *v.*[2] + -ING[1].]

1. The action of the vb. in various senses: **a.** In lit. or technical uses. Also *concr.*, that which is ripped off.

1532 [see RIP *v.*[2] 2 b]. **1611** COTGR., *Descousure*, a ripping, vnsowing, vndoing of. **1615** W. LAWSON *Country Housew. Gard.* (1626) 16 Here you must be carefull, not to hurt your tree when you gather them, by ripping amongst the roots. **1678** R. L'ESTRANGE *Seneca's Mor.* (1705) 482 The Ripping of a Hang-nail is sufficient to Dispatch us. **1801** COLERIDGE in Mrs. Sandford *T. Poole & Friends* (1888) II. 27 When your Ripping [of oak-bark] is over you will come, or, at furthest, immediately after hay harvest. **1833** J. HOLLAND *Manuf. Metal* II. xiv. 331 These rods were afterwards further reduced by an ingenious operation, called by the workmen in this country *ripping* or *rumpling*. **1894** *Labour Commission Gloss.*, *Ripping*, that portion of the roof which is cut down in the roadways to make sufficient height for men and horses to travel. **1900** in FARMER *Public School Word-bk.* 167. **1911** R. NEVILL *Floreat Etona* vii. 224 In the days when such a close connection existed between Eton and King's, a Colleger leaving to go to Cambridge used to go through the old form known as 'Ripping'... The two folds of the Colleger's serge gown were sewn together in front, and the Provost 'ripped' them asunder. **1973** 'J. PATRICK' *Glasgow Gang Observed* iv. 41 The case for the defence collapsed.. when Big Dick boasted..that the attack was 'the biggest rippin' Ah've done'. **1979** *Jrnl. R. Soc. Arts* Jan. 93/1, I was very interested in your ideas about shifting the rippings from the coal face and spreading it into the sea.

b. In fig. uses. Const. *up*.

1576 FLEMING *Panopl. Epist.* 55 With the ripping up of ciuil commutations and chaunges. **1596** SPENSER *State Irel.* Wks. (Globe) 629/1 This ripping up of auncient historyes, is very pleasing unto me, and indeede savoureth of good conceite. **1617** HIERON *Wks.* II. 267 Indeuour the ripping vp of thy heart. **1674** *Essex Papers* (Camden) 254 If..there should be now a ripping up of Crimes,..no man can see where it will stop. **1843** J. W. CROKER in *C. Papers* 5 Dec. (1884), I cannot..understand what authority can exist for such a ripping up of private life. **1863** *Sat. Rev.* 12 Sept. 352

Five years ago, there was a great ripping-up of the skirts of society.

2. a. *attrib.*, as ***ripping-bed***, ***-cut***, ***-gauge***, ***-hook***, ***-iron***, ***-tool***. Also RIPPING-CHISEL, -SAW.

1850 HOLTZAPFFEL *Turning* III. 1206 For cutting slabs of marble into narrow pieces.. a machine called a *ripping bed is employed. **1823** P. NICHOLSON *Pract. Build.* 220 If planks are sawed longitudinally, through their thickness, the saw-way is called a *ripping-cut. **1875** KNIGHT *Dict. Mech.* 1945/2 The *ripping-gage.. is screwed to the table, and, by means of a thumb-nut, is adjusted to cut square or beveling. **1825** KNAPP & BALDW. *Newgate Cal.* IV. 57/2 The instrument called a *ripping-hook. **1846** A. YOUNG *Naut. Dict.*, **Ripping-Iron*, a tool used in stripping copper, or thin wood-sheathing, off a vessel's bottom. **1867** SMYTH *Sailor's Word-bk.*, *Ripping-Iron*, a caulker's tool for tearing oakum out of a seam. **1875** KNIGHT *Dict. Mech.* 1946/1 **Ripping-tool*, one for following a seam and cutting stitches without slitting the fabric.

b. *Aeronaut.* Used *attrib.* with reference to a strip of fabric sown into and forming part of the skin of a balloon and to the cord which, when pulled, tears this strip away to bring about rapid deflation, as ***ripping cord***, ***line***, ***panel***, ***rope***, ***valve***.

1907 *Strand Mag.* Feb. 149/1 The utility of the ripping-cord was brought home to me.. in a recent ascent. **1908** A. HILDEBRANDT *Airships Past & Present* xvi. 184 The ripping-cord was the invention of the American aeronaut, Wise, in 1844; Godard introduced it in France in 1855. **1910** Ripping cord [see *ripping panel* below]. **1907** *Strand Mag.* Feb. 151/2 Faure.. is the first aeronaut who had the courage to experiment with the ripping-line in mid air. Till he made his first attempt about two years ago, all balloonists thought that to pull the ripping-line anywhere but on the ground meant suicide. **1974** *Oxford Jun. Encycl.* (rev. ed.) IV. 35/2 Among other important equipment is the ripping-line or rip-cord, which is painted red so that it shall not be pulled in mistake for the valve line. **1908** A. HILDEBRANDT *Airships Past & Present* xvi. 184 The ripping-panel is placed on that side of the covering to which the guide-rope is attached. **1910** C. C. TURNER *Aerial Navigation* iii. 45 On coming within a few yards of the ground he pulls the ripping panel open, the cord from which comes down through a hole near the neck of the balloon. In some balloons,.. the ripping cord passes through the neck. **1919** H. SHAW *Text-bk. Aeronaut.* xvii. 195 For emergency cases a 'ripping panel' is fitted, for use when a quick descent is necessary. **1922** *Encycl. Brit.* XXX. 89/1 One complete series of balloons came down with unexpected suddenness, all being deflated by the rupture of their ripping panels. On examination, it was found that moisture had condensed on the ripping ropes and frozen there, until each cord was about as thick as a man's forearm. **1907** G. BACON *Record of Aeronaut* xiv. 255 Aeronautical experts.. advised.. that, as the balloon might have to remain inflated for a long while before starting, one of large size should be employed, and a 'solid' or 'ripping' valve substituted for the usual 'Butterfly' variety. **1912** C. B. HAYWARD *Pract. Aeronaut.* 51 The usual 'ripping valve' is also provided in the form of a narrow strip of balloon fabric glued over a long cut in the envelope.

'ripping, *ppl. a.* [f. as prec. + -ING².]

1. That rips or tears; also *fig.*, cutting.

1714 ARBUTHNOT *Let. to Ford* 19 Oct., It is necessary for him to do that.., else there will be a ripping answer, as you say. **1827** COBBETT *Prot. Reform.* (1899) §351 Ripping-knives. **1845** J. COULTER *Adv. Pacific* xv. 230 The bark of the various trees also showed many a sign of the ripping passage, or graze of a bullet. **1894** T. PINKERTON *Blizzard* 106 With a ripping slash she cut into a wicker stand. **1896** G. F. NORTHALL *Warwickshire Word-bk.* 192 *Ripping, adj.* Sharp, cutting, as applied to cold weather; e.g. 'a ripping frost'. Midlands. **1932** H. J. MASSINGHAM *World without End* 297 Words like.. 'ripping' or 'sniping', the adjectives of a very sharp frost.. are playlets in themselves. **1978** J. WAMBAUGH *Black Marble* x. 237, I have a ripping headache.

2. †**a.** Very fast or rapid. *Obs.*

1826 *Sporting Mag.* XVII. 319 They had slipped away down wind, at a ripping pace. **1828** *Bell's Life* 27 July 4/1 The ripping bowling of the Captain. **1846** W. DENISON *Cricket: Sk. Players* 22 Mr. Osbaldeston, and Brown of Brighton, afterwards launched forth as 'fast ripping bowlers'. **1868** H. WOODRUFF *Trotting Horse* xi. 116 There is no occasion for the ripping spurts which intervene in the other training. **1877** *London Society* June 537/1 Hinkly's bowling was ripping indeed.

b. *slang.* Excellent, splendid; rattling. Also advb., and as a complement. Now somewhat *arch.*

1846 *Swell's Night Guide* 74 One calls for the 'lanciers'; another, the 'caledonians'; when the Boshman, ripping innocent of either.. strikes up the college hornpipe. **1858** THOMSON *Almæ Matres* i. 3 Some a little encouraged by the ripping Burton which the Scouts took care to ply liberally. **1887** MISS BRADDON *Like & Unlike* i, We killed on Hagley Heath after a ripping half-hour over the grass. **1894** DOYLE *S. Holmes* 57 Old Coxon gave me a ripping good testimonial. **1894** 'A. HOPE' *Dolly Dialogues* ix. 51 She did look ripping in that white frock. **1898** [see KNOCK-OUT *sb.* 4]. **1911** D. H. LAWRENCE *White Peacock* II. ii. 229 She was very fine and frank and unconventional—ripping, I thought her. **1921** [see DUG-UP *a.*]. **1921** H. WILLIAMSON *Beautiful Years* 137 Jack was excited about his friend going to school with him. 'I say, how ripping, man!' he cried. **1944** [see DECENT *a.* 5 b]. **1978** PALIN & JONES (*title*) Ripping yarns.

Hence **'rippingly** *adv.*, splendidly.

1892 H. NISBET *Bushranger's Sweetheart* xxvi. 209 'How are you getting on with her?' 'Rippingly as far as she is concerned'.

ripping, dial. variant of REAPING.

'ripping-chisel. (See quots.)

a. 1659 HOWELL *Vocab.* LI, A maul, a mallet, a chizel, a rippin chizel. **1679** MOXON *Mech. Exerc.* vii. 124 The Ripping-Chissel.. is about an Inch broad, and hath a blunt Edge... Its Office is.. to rip or tear two pieces of Wood fastned together from one another. *Ibid.*, Most commonly Carpenters use an old cast off Chissel for a Ripping Chissel. **1842** GWILT *Archit.* 949 There are various kinds of chisels; the principal ones used in carpentry and joinery are.. the socket chisel, and the ripping chisel.

b. 1812 *Ann. Reg., Chron.* 5 The ripping-chisel or crow-bar, about three feet long. **1823** P. NICHOLSON *Pract. Build.* 220 To cut or break a hole in brick-work, with the ripping-chisel.

c. 1875 KNIGHT *Dict. Mech.* 1945/2 *Ripping-chisel* (Wood-working), a crooked chisel for cleaning out mortises.

'rippingness. *Obsolescent.* [f. RIPPING *ppl. a.* + -NESS.] Splendid quality; excellence.

1910 A. BENNETT *Clayhanger* IV. xii. 566 'She's a ripping woman.'.. His preoccupation with the rippingness of Mrs. Chris Hamson. **1927** C. E. MONTAGUE *Right off Map* xviii. 174 It's the doing the thing that.. makes you half drunk with the rippingness of it.

'ripping-saw. (See quots. and RIP-SAW.)

1825 J. NICHOLSON *Operat. Mechanic* 584 The ripping saw, for dividing boards into separate pieces, in the direction of the fibres. **1860** TOMLINSON *Arts & Manuf.* Ser. II. *Saws* 32 A ripping-saw.. is a hand-saw with a blade twenty-eight or thirty inches long, and having large teeth for ripping, or cutting out stuff coarsely and quickly. **1881** W. E. DICKSON *Pract. Organ Build.* i. 4 The usual saws, the ripping saw, the panel saw,.. will be required.

rippit ('rɪpɪt). *Sc.* and *U.S. dial.* Also 6 **repet**, **repit**, **rippett**, 6–9 **rippet**. [Perh. of imitative origin.] Tumult, uproar, disturbance, noisy dispute.

1508 DUNBAR *Tua Mariit Wemen* 193 He ralis, and makis repet with ryatus wordis. **1513** DOUGLAS *Æneis* VIII. xii. 104 Off riot, rippett, and of reveling. **1535** STEWART *Cron. Scot.* I. 221 Sic ane repit, rumour, and sic ane reird, Was neuir hard befoir into this eird. **1596** DALRYMPLE tr. *Leslie's Hist. Scot.* I. 76 Sik a rippet is amang thame. *c* **1800** JAMIESON *Water Kelpie* iii, And Prosen proud, with rippet loud, Cums ravin' frae his glen. **1851** W. ANDERSON *Rhymes* 195 Sic a rage an' a rippit I seldom hae seen. **1870** J. C. DUVAL *Adventures Big-Foot Wallace* xlii. 270 At last the manager threw his hat among 'em and called out, 'Stampede all', and the 'rippit' commenced. **1887** SERVICE *Life Dr. Duguid* v. 31 Some rippit getting up at the other end of the schule. **1913** H. KEPHART *Our Southern Highlanders* xiii. 294 If they quarrel, it is a ruction, a rippit, a jower, or an up-scuddle—so be it there are no fatalities which would amount to a real fray. **1913** J. SERVICE *Memorables* 67 Some dreidfu' nicht rippit there had been amang the cairters. **1928** M. CHAPMAN *Happy Mountain* 313 Degrees of feeling among unfriendly neighbors... *A rippit*, fight with fists. **1958** *Huntly Express* 19 Dec. 6 For fear ony rippits brook out at the dance.

ripple ('rɪp(ə)l), *sb.*¹ Also 5 **ryppyll**, **repylle**, 6 **reple**. [Corresponds to Fris. *ripel* (*roepel*, *rûpel*), Du. *repel*, MLG. *repel*(*e*, LG. *repel*, *räpel*), OHG. *rifila* (G. *riffel*): see RIPPLE *v.*¹ A shorter form appears in Flem., older Du., and MLG. *repe*, G. *riffe*.] An implement toothed like a comb, used in cleaning flax or hemp from the seeds.

1660 SHARROCK *Vegetables* 22 They get out the seeds [of flax] by drawing it through an engine like an iron double tooth combe, which they call a Ripple. **1766** *Compl. Farmer* s.v. *Hemp* Z 4/2 The seed.. which remains in the heads of the hemp.. is got out by combing the heads on the teeth of a ripple. **1807** HOARE *Tour Irel.* 324 If the seed [of flax] is to be saved, it is drawn through an iron comb, fastened in wood, called a ripple. **1846** SPROULE *Flax* 20 The operation in this case not being performed by the ripple, but by repeated strokes of a stick. **1875** *Encycl. Brit.* I. 380 Lifting each handful separately and pulling the top through a ripple or iron comb fixed upon a piece of plank.

b. *attrib.*, as ***ripple-stock***, ***-comb*** (also as *vb.*). Perhaps properly combs. of the verbal stem.

c **1475** *Pict. Voc.* in Wr.-Wülcker 795 *Hoc rupeste*, a repyllestok. **1499** *Wills & Invent.* (Surtees) I. 104 A hekyll, .. a ryppyll came,.. a payr of wool cames. **1581** *Invent.* in *Best's Farm. Bks.* (Surtees) 171 One peare of reple comes. **1615** MARKHAM *English Housew.* II. v. (1668) 132 You must take ripple combs, and ripple your flax over. **1899** *Academy* 11 Feb. 184/1 Flax was grown, dried, ripple-combed, cleaned.

'ripple, *sb.*² *north. dial.* Also 7 **rippill**. [f. RIPPLE *v.*²] A slight cut, scratch, or mark.

1666 *Depos. Cast. York* (Surtees) 141 He.. opened his buttons, and gave him some rippills with his knife on his breast. **1869** PECOCK *Lonsd. Gloss.*, *Ripple*, a slight scratch. **1876** C. C. ROBINSON *Mid-Yorksh. Gloss.* s.v., A mark across the grain of wood, as if where a saw had just grazed, would be called a *ripple*.

ripple ('rɪp(ə)l), *sb.*³ [f. RIPPLE *v.*³]

1. a. *U.S.* A piece of shallow water in a river where rocks or sand-bars cause an obstruction; a shoal. (Cf. RIFFLE *sb.* 4 and RIPPLING *vbl. sb.*³ 2.)

1755 *New Hampshire Prov. Papers* (1872) VI. 431 Swift water falls and Ripples that they were oblig'd to wade and carry all day. **1789** J. MAY *Jrnl. & Lett.* (1873) 131 The river so low that it is impossible to get over the shoal places, 'ripples,' as they are called here. **1808** ASHE *Trav.* I. 92 The river is full of eddies, ripples, rapids, rocks, and other dangers. **1855** W. SARGENT *Braddock's Exped.* 218 Forming a gentle rapid or ripple, and easily fordable at almost any point. **1872** DE VERE *Americanisms* 532 In Pennsylvania.. the more grievous obstructions are riffles, the slighter ones ripples. **1941** L. D. BALDWIN *Keelboat Age* 71 The breaking of the water over the bars and chains was known to the boatmen as ripples, or riffles. **1964** F. O'ROURKE *Mule for Marquesa* ii. 50 'How do we cross?'.. 'Quicksand to the right. You move out the bar, angle downstream to that big ripple, then straight on across.'

b. *Naut.* (See quot. and RIPPLING *vbl. sb.*³ 1.)

1869 A. R. WALLACE *Malay Archip.* I. 239 What seamen call the 'ripples' are also very violent in the straits, the sea appearing to boil and foam and dance like the rapids below a cataract.

2. a. A light ruffling of the surface of water, such as is caused by a slight breeze; a wavelet. Also *spec.* in *Physics*, a wave on the surface of a fluid the restoring force for which is provided by surface tension rather than by gravity, and which consequently has a wavelength shorter than that corresponding to the minimum speed of propagation.

1798 COLERIDGE *Anc. Mar.* VI. xi, Its path was not upon the sea, In ripple or in shade. **1814** SCOTT *Diary* 15 Aug. in *Lockhart*, The channel now seems like a Highland loch; not the least ripple on the waves. **1843** RUSKIN *Mod. Paint.* II. v. i. §11 (1851) I. 330 If water be rippled, the side of every ripple next to us reflects a piece of the sky. **1871** W. THOMSON in *Phil. Mag.* XLII. 374 The 'Capillary waves'.. referred to by Russell are what I, in ignorance of his observations.., had called 'ripples'. **1873** BLACK *Pr. Thule* iii, The wash of the ripples along the coast could be heard in the stillness. **1887** *Amer. Jrnl. Math.* IX. 67 Sir W. Thomson proposes to distinguish by the name of ripples those waves whose length is less than the above critical value of λ [wavelength]. **1938** L. M. MILNE-THOMSON *Theoret. Hydrodynamics* xiv. 377 Ripples are waves on [*ed.* 2: in] whose propagation capillarity plays the predominating part. **1966** *McGraw-Hill Encycl. Sci. & Technol.* XIV. 417/1 Ripples generated by wind at the interface between air and water on oceans and lakes are of importance to the friction of air flowing over water, and to the reflection and scattering of electromagnetic and sound waves.

attrib. **1848** LOWELL *Fable for Critics* Poet. Wks. (1884) 166/1 Like ripple-shades netting the bed of a brook. **1856** SORBY in *Edinb. New Phil. Jrnl.* III. 114 The direction of a current can also be ascertained from the ripple marks; from that modification of them for which I have proposed the term 'ripple drift'.

fig. **1838** EMERSON *Address* Wks. (Bohn) II. 201 See how nations and races flit by on the sea of time, and leave no ripple to tell where they floated or sunk. **1859** GEO. ELIOT *A. Bede* iii, Mere waves and ripples in an unfathomable ocean of love and beauty. **1872** HOLMES *Poet Breakf.-t.* viii, It always seems to me that talk is a ripple and thought a ground swell.

b. *transf.* A mark, appearance, or movement resembling or suggestive of a ripple on water.

1843 HOLTZAPFFEL *Turning* I. 39 The fibres.. will be found to be wavy, on the face, at right angles to that on which the ripple is observed. **1850** THACKERAY *Pendennis* iv, Her black hair waved.. with a natural ripple. **1881** *Truth* 19 May 686/2 The dress.. was of pink silk,.. the front being covered with ripples of white lace. **1891** HARDY *Tess* xxxii, A glistening ripple of gossamer webs was visible. **1968** J. WINEARLS *Mod. Dance* (ed. 2) ii. 38 Raising and lowering can follow each other in uninterrupted snake-like ripples. **1972** *Courier-Mail* (Brisbane) 3 July 2/6 Laurence (Lord) Olivier, on every official opening night at the Old Vic, was reserving front-blocks of seats, 'the Ripples' for students whose natural reaction might.. introduce 'ripples' to break down the first-night social-or-coterie stuffiness. **1977** *Design Engin.* July 19/3 High number of commutator segments giving very smooth operation (low torque ripple) over a speed range from zero to several thousand rev/min. **1979** *Time* 2 Apr. 20/3 As Finland bottomed out of recession, pre-election polls showed a ripple to the right.

attrib. **1870** *Daily News* 12 May, The Princess, who in her .. new 'ripple' fashion of hairdressing never looked more lovely.

c. *ellipt.* A ripple-mark.

1852 LYELL *Elem. Geol.* (ed. 4) ii. 20 This ripple is not entirely confined to the beach between high and low water mark, but is also produced on sands which are constantly covered by water. *Ibid.*, In sandstones.. also, as now on the sea-coast, we may often detect two systems of ripples interfering with each other.

d. A name for an ice cream manufactured with an admixture of coloured syrup that gives it a rippled appearance.

Registered as a proprietary name in the U.S.

1939 *Ice Cream Trade Jrnl.* Nov. 19 (Advt.), Fudge ripple ice cream. *Ibid.*, This delicious fudge syrup is incorporated in your own vanilla ice cream as you fill the can from a batch freezer or incorporated in your vanilla ice cream by a special fudge ripple attachment as it flows from your continuous freezer. **1942** *Official Gaz.* (U.S. Patent Office) 16 June 511/1 Gerald G. Balch, doing business as Balch Flavor Co., Pittsburgh, Pa... Ripple... For ice cream and flavoring concentrate for use in the manufacture of variegated type of ice cream and for use in the manufacture of a flavoring adapted to be applied on or to ice cream, sold in bulk. Claims use since Oct. 23, 1939. **1973** HYDE & ROTHWELL *Ice Cream* vii. 141 (*caption*) Diagram of Hoyer ripple machine. **1976** *Milton Keynes Express* 25 June 10 (Advt.), Ice Cream. .. Raspberry Ripple, 4 litre £1.10. **1977** 'J. BELL' *Such Nice Client* xvi. 156 A pork pie.. and an ice ripple from the freezer.. brought her back into fighting shape. **1981** *Times* 2 May 7/4 Dessert.. angel food cake, blueberry cheese cake, fudge, ripple ice cream.

3. A sound as of rippling water. Also *fig.*, a rumour.

1859 HAWTHORNE *Marb. Faun* xvii, Talking in the quick, short ripple of the Italian tongue. **1882** MISS BRADDON *Mt. Royal* III. vi. 97 A ripple of laughter floated from the hall. **1889** RUSKIN *Præterita* III. 63 Presently I was aware of a little ripple of brighter converse going round the table. **1977** N. ADAM *Triplehip Cracksman* vii. 71 There's a ripple he's walking a bit heavy these days.

4. = RIFFLE *sb.* 5. Also *attrib.*

1853 *Alta California* (San Francisco) 31 May 2/1 Repeated instances have come to our knowledge when the amount of gold saved has been doubled by a little alteration or improvement made in the ripple-box. **1857** BORTHWICK *3 Yrs. California* vi. 121 The earth and small gravel falls with the water through the sieve into the 'ripple-box'. **1879**

ATCHERLEY *Trip Boërland* 114 Halfway down the box is a little ledge termed a 'ripple', about 2 inches in height. **1886** *Pall Mall G.* 18 June 5/2 What is called a 'quicksilver ripple', a solid bit of wood with three troughs cut along it about two inches deep, each a little lower than the other. **1902** *Chambers's Jrnl.* Mar. 176/1 This process consists of passing the sand through an arrangement of inclined sieves, which by reason of 'ripples' or bars of wood fastened transversely across their surfaces, discard all light material that cannot pass the various meshes. **1938** D. FORBES *My Life in S. Afr.* vi. 87 One had to keep the earth moving all the time. If it once settled to the bottom of the box it formed a solid mass, and did not settle into what are called the ripples on the bottom of the box made to catch the gold.

5. *Electr.* Small periodic variations in voltage superposed on a direct voltage or on an alternating voltage of lower frequency. Freq. *attrib.*

1920 *Whittaker's Electr. Engineer's Pocket-bk.* (ed. 4) 152 When the rotor is slotted, as in turbo-alternators with cylindrical rotors, a ripple is induced in the conductor-pressure. **1928** *Observer* 17 June 26/3 Manufacturers should publish a curve of inductance against direct current component, measured at ripple frequency. **1947** R. LEE *Electronic Transformers & Circuits* iii. 66 Reactors are used in electronic power equipment to smooth out ripple voltage in d-c supplies, so they carry direct current in the coils. **1967** *Electronics* 6 Mar. 308/2 Quadrature rejection is 40 db minimum, while ripple is 0·5% peak-to-peak of full scale output. **1972** *Physics Bull.* Aug. 491/2 An automatically adjusting transformer ensures high stability; ripple is 1 mV peak to peak.

6. Applied to a method of firing or discharging in succession or at intervals.

1944 *Shorter Oxf. Eng. Dict.* (ed. 3) Add., *Ripple*.., applied to a method of firing torpedoes in succession. **1951** *Life* 18 June 54/3 (*caption*) Using six rocket launchers with 24 tubes each, the platoon in a matter of seconds blasted Red positions with 144 rounds—a barrage which rocketmen call a 'ripple'. **1968** *Daily Express* 12 Feb. 2/5 *Ripple*, an attacker's technique of sending off his missiles in waves, so that a defender fires his defensive missiles at the first waves and has nothing left to deflect the final blow.

7. *attrib.* and *Comb.*, as ***ripple burnish***, (poet.) ***-dripple***, ***ware***; ***ripple black***, ***fresh***, ***-warped*** adjs.; **ripple (pony) cloth**, cloth having a rippled appearance; also *attrib.*; **ripple control** *Electr.*, a method of performing simple control operations, such as switching of street lights, by superposition of a high-frequency switching signal on the mains supply; **ripple(-through) counter** *Electronics*, a type of binary counter consisting of a number of bistable circuits wired in cascade, so that each changes its state only after all the preceding ones have changed state; **ripple effect**, the continuous and spreading results of an event or action; **ripple-fired** *adj.* [cf. sense 6 above], (of missiles) fired in rapid succession or at intervals; so **ripple-firing** *a.*; **ripple-flaking** *Archæol.*, a method of flaking flint; so **ripple-flaked** *a.*; **ripple sole**, a kind of rubber sole having thick ripple-shaped ridges; hence **ripple-soled** *ppl. a.*; **ripple stitch**, a drawn fabric stitch (see also sense 2).

1965 *Wireless World* Aug. 28 (Advt.), Dial escutcheon measures 6″ long by 4½″ wide, finished ripple black. **1964** H. HODGES *Artifacts* i. 31 The effect of this ripple burnish can be highly decorative. **1922** Ripplecloth [see *house-jacket* s.v. HOUSE *sb.*[1] 20]. **1930** *Daily Express* 6 Oct. 5/2 (Advt.), Pure wool ripple cloth, for cosy dressing gowns. **1957** M. B. PICKEN *Fashion Dict.* 276/1 *Ripple cloth*, woolen dress fabric with long silky hairs on right side. Also called *zibeline*. **1977** B. PYM *Quartet in Autumn* xvi. 139 Her old blue ripple-cloth dressing gown. **1938** *Jrnl. Inst. Electr. Engin.* LXXXIII. 827/1 The fullest advantage can only be taken of the ripple control principle if a central ripple transmitter..can be designed to cover the entire network fed at high tension from that point. **1952** J. M. WALDRAM *Street Lighting* xx. 381 A ripple control system operating about 500 lamps in an urban area, pre-war. **1974** *Times* 4 Feb. 16/6 It seems.. opportune to raise again the..question of ripple control. For the uninitiated, it is a means of transmitting coded signals from a central control point over the existing mains network to operate switching contactors at any point in the network, e.g., domestic consumers' premises. **1967** *Electronics* 6 Mar. 160/1 It cannot be used in ripple counters or other circuits requiring the toggle function. **1973** *Sci. Amer.* May 110/3 Combinations of flip-flops and NAND gates interconnected as described are known as ripple counters. The reason is that input pulses 'ripple' through the string of flip-flops sequentially, each device triggering the next one in the series. **1916** BLUNDEN *Harbingers* 49 The ripple-dripple of the brooks. **1966** *Wall St. Jrnl.* 14 Feb. 10/3 Price-boosting already is producing a 'ripple effect' in which companies pass on increased costs in higher price tags on their own products. **1973** *Times* 20 Dec. 12/4 Industrial expansion is now halted by the three day week, not to say by the ripple effect of the public expenditure cuts. **1977** *Detroit Free Press* 11 Dec. 7-B/4 The ripple effect from the 'Star Wars' film has taken on tidal wave proportions. **1954** *Sun* (Baltimore) (B ed.) 25 June 10/3 Proximity-fused bombs or photo flash bombs..high explosive rockets, ripple fired rockets, smoke rockets and guided missiles. **1949** A. R. WEYL *Guided Missiles* 31 Control of the launching manœuvre can be electric, for example, by closing a circuit which ignites a propelling charge, or electronic. The former is preferred for small missiles, with 'ripple-firing' control for the multiple and successive launching of A.A. missiles. **1960** *Oxf. Univ. Gaz.* 4 Mar. 805/2 A fine ripple-flaked flint knife with gold leaf attached to the blunt end. **1899** R. MUNRO *Preh. Scot.* v. 167 The execution of what is known as ripple-flaking. **1921** *Chambers's Jrnl.* 5 Feb. 145/1 Brierly Stretton and I were..discussing the intensive examination of ripple-flaking. **1944** BLUNDEN *Shells by Stream* 44 While some freed fountain of delight Played beauty ripple-fresh and bright. **1952** C. W. CUNNINGTON *Eng. Women's Clothing* 296 *Ripple pony cloth*..Resembles a finely ribbed miroir velvet with a bright finish. **1963** N. MARSH *Dead Water* (1964) viii. 201 Gentleman's country shoes, size nine-and-a-half ripple soles. **1970** *Globe & Mail* (Toronto) 26 Sept. 52/2 (Advt.), Women's Slippers... Some ripple rubber soles. **1977** C. MCFADDEN *Serial* xli. 88/2 Kate had already gone springing off in her ripple-sole Famolares. **1977** *Austral. Furnishing Buyers Guide* Spring/Summer 58/4 With heels, steel tips, crepe and ripple soled shoes, carpets are getting much more wear and tear. **1933** K. S. LOFTHOUSE *Compl. Guide Drawn Fabric* 22 *Ripple stitch*... Worked from right to left... Three pairs are worked with six threads between. **1971** J. H. SMITH *Digital Logic* vi. 103 In the asynchronous counter..the trigger input of each binary is from the preceding output... This mode of operation gives an inherent delay in the ripple-through counter. **1931** Ripple ware [see BADARIAN *a.*]. **1962** V. NABOKOV *Pale Fire* 143 The ripple-warped reflection of a ledge that jutted high above his present position.

'ripple, *sb.*[4] ? An attack of the RIPPLES.

1785 BURNS *Let. Goudie* iii, Auld Orthodoxy lang did grapple, But now she's got an unco ripple.

ripple ('rɪp(ə)l), *v.*[1] Also 5–6 rypel (6 ripel, repeyl), 5 rippil (7 -el), 8 riple. [Corresponds to Fris. *ripelje* (*roep-*, *rûpelje*), MDu. (and Du.) *repelen*, MLG. *repelen* (LG. *repeln*, *räpeln*), OHG. *rifilôn* (G. *riffeln*); cf. RIPPLE *sb.*[1], Du. and MLG. *repen* (whence Sw. *repa*) in the same sense.]

1. *trans.* To draw (flax or hemp) through a kind of comb (see RIPPLE *sb.*[1]) in order to remove the seeds; to clean from seeds in this manner.

c **1340–** [see RIPPLING *vbl. sb.*[1]]. **1523** FITZHERB. *Husb.* § 146 Howe it [flax] shulde be sowen, weded, pulled, repeyled, watred. **1615** [see RIPPLE *sb.*[1] b]. **1649** BLITHE *Eng. Improv. Impr.* (1653) 262 It is indifferent whether you ripple it, or take off the boles of it, as soone as you bring it home, or when you intend to use it. **1694** WESTMACOTT *Script. Herb.* 75 Then ripple it [flax] through a double tooth'd Iron Comb. **1763** *Museum Rust.* I. 11, I ripple it and water it, and, if I have leisure, proceed to dress it. **1780** YOUNG *Tour Irel.* I. 164 They..immediately ripple it to get the seeds off. **1846** SPROULE *Flax* 18 As soon as the capsules containing the seed are dried.., the flax is ready for being rippled.

2. To remove or take *off* (the seeds) by this process.

c **1480** HENRYSON *Mor. Fab.* VIII. (*Preach. Swallow*) xxx, The carle pullit the lyne, Rippillit the bollis, and in beitis set. **1523** FITZHERB. *Husb.* § 146 The bolles of flaxe, whan they be ripeled of, must be rideled from the wedes. **1805** R. W. DICKSON *Pract. Agric.* II. 740 It is likewise the practice ..to ripple off the seed-pods before the business of watering is commenced. **1861** *Times* 10 Oct., The bolls are rippled off and kiln-dried for very superior cattle-food.

Hence **'rippled** *ppl. a.*[1]

1851 H. STEPHENS *Bk. Farm* (ed. 2) II. 322/1 The rippled plants should be tied in sheaves. **1879** *Encycl. Brit.* IX. 294/2 The rippled stalks are tied in small bundles.

'ripple, *v.*[2] Now *north. dial.* Also 5 reple, repul-. [Of Scand. origin. Cf. Norw. *ripla* to scratch, make strokes in, frequentative or diminutive from *ripa* (Sw. *repa*), of similar meaning.]

1. *trans.* To scratch slightly; to graze or ruffle.

14.. *Guy Warw.* (Caius MS.) 9942 The Duke..smote to Gye... He replid [*v.r.* repulde] hys face and his chyn. **1570** LEVINS *Manip.* 128 To Ripple, *rescindere*. **1609** HOLLAND *Amm. Marcell.* xxv. iii. 264 An horsemans javelin..having slightly rippled the skinne of his left arme, pierced within his short ribs. **1620** COTTON *Espernon* II. x. 512 The others that had pass'd before had only rippled up the skin. **1681** —— *Wonders of Peak* Wks. (1741) 339 Sans hurt or Blemish, save a little strip Of Hair and Skin rippled upon her Hip. **1781** HUTTON *Tour to Caves* Gloss. (ed. 2) 95 *Ripple*, to scratch. **1828** *Craven Gloss.*, *Ripple*, to scratch gently, as with a pin, or to gore slightly. **1855** in *Whitby Gloss.* **1869** in *Lonsd. Gloss.*

2. To break up (ground) slightly.

1764 *Museum Rust.* II. lxxiv. 247 The former only slightly plough, or ripple, their fallows the first year. **1790** W. MARSHALL *Rur. Econ. Midl. Co.* II. 368 By way of experiment,—Rippled the vacant places of the Bank, at the time of cutting this hedge.

'ripple, *v.*[3] Also 7–8 riple. [Of obscure origin. App. distinct from prec., and not obviously related to any sense of RIP *v.*[2]]

1. a. *intr.* To have or present a ruffled surface; to be covered with small waves; to form ripples.

1670–1 NARBOROUGH *Jrnl.* in *Acc. Sev. Late Voy.* I. (1694) 18 The Sea ripled in many places. **1748** *Anson's Voy.* III. viii. 383 The sea had a very dangerous aspect, for it ripled and foamed, as if it had been full of breakers. **1836** R. H. FROUDE *Lyra Apost.* (1849) 99, I watch the waves that rippling still Chase one another o'er the marble shore. **1878** ABNEY *Photogr.* (1881) 9 The interstellar ether in which these waves ripple is assumed to permeate every body. **1887** 'STUART CUMBERLAND' *Queen's Highway* 15 Between the pines, little lakes sparkle and ripple in the sun.

transf. and *fig.* **1844** EMERSON *Ess.*, *Nature*, Acres of houstonia, whose innumerable florets whiten and ripple before the eye. **1877** A. B. EDWARDS *Up Nile* xxi. 605 The young barley rippling for miles in the sun.

b. To flow in ripples.

1769 GRAY *Let. to Dr. Wharton* 18 Oct., Along the vale of Eeman, which runs rapidly on near the way, rippling over the stones. **1824** W. IRVING *T. Trav.* I. 322 Watched the silver waves rippling through the arches of the broken bridge. **1855** TENNYSON *Maud* II. IV. vi, The rivulet at her feet Ripples on in light and shadow. **1894** WINSOR *Cartier to Frontenac* 177 Southward, the sources of the Delaware and Susquehanna rippled onward to the great bays.

transf. and *fig.* **1858** *Sat. Rev.* 20 Nov. 506/2 Saying that Mr. Jones..ripples out in a level current of poetical talk. **1873** SYMONDS *Grk. Poets* x. 312 Stone walls..fragrant with gadding violets that ripple down their sides. **1889** A. J. C. HARE *Story Life* (1900) VI. 182 Life ripples by so quickly. **1924** R. CAMPBELL *Flaming Terrapin* iii. 45 In spangled pride A python ripples from his shrivelled hide. **1929** D. H. LAWRENCE *Pansies* 39 We ripple with life through the days.

c. Of sound: To flow in a sprightly manner.

1879 DOWDEN *Southey* iv. 85 The *carillons* ripple from old spires. **1892** SLADEN *Japs at Home* xvi, Nearly two minutes had elapsed before the last faint wave of sound rippled away.

d. To pass quickly *through* each of a series in turn.

1967 *Electronics* 6 Mar. 47/3 It will ripple through a truth table in maybe 100 microseconds,..moving through all possible logic combinations. **1973** *Sci. Amer.* May 110/3 Input pulses 'ripple' through the string of flip-flops sequentially, each device triggering the next one in the series.

2. a. *trans.* To form little waves upon (the surface of water); to agitate lightly.

1786 tr. *Beckford's Vathek* (1868) 96 The water..was violently rippled by the flutter of their fins. **1817** J. SCOTT *Paris Revisit.* (ed. 4) 16 The vessel rippled the transparent water as she inclined easily on her way. **1840** R. H. DANA *Bef. Mast* xvii, A cool sea-breeze came rippling and darkening the surface of the water. **1887** RIDER HAGGARD *Jess* 62 The great wind..does but ripple the shallow pool as it passes. **1922** T. S. ELIOT *Waste Land* iii. 36 The brisk swell Rippled both shores. **1974** *Sat. Rev. World* (U.S.) 2 Nov. 32/3 The lake..was rippled by a sailboat.

fig. **1854** THOREAU *Walden*, *Solitude*, Like the lake, my serenity is rippled but not ruffled. **1884** *Fortn. Rev.* Apr. 567 Hardly a single event of consequence has rippled the still surface of the financial world during the past month.

b. To mark with or as with ripples; to cause to undulate slightly.

1860 EMERSON *Cond. Life*, *Beauty*, There are faces so.. flushed and rippled by the play of thought, that we can hardly find what the mere features really are. **1891** MEREDITH *One of our Conq.* II. ii. 29 Mademoiselle rippled her shoulders. **1897** *Geogr. Jrnl.* IX. 280 The finest variety of the assorted sands was also quickly rippled.

c. To turn *out* with a rippling sound. Also, to let *out* or utter with a rippling sound.

1890 W. J. GORDON *Foundry* 192 The ordinary notion of printing—a man sitting at a piano and rippling out types. **1901** A. E. W. MASON *Clementina* xiii. 155 The girl reading it drew a breath and rippled out a laugh of gladness. **1913** C. MACKENZIE *Sinister St.* I. II. x. 313 'Why, you silly old thing ..,' rippled Stella.

'rippled, *ppl. a.*[2] [f. prec.] **a.** Marked with ripples. **b.** Of hair: wavy.

1833 LYELL *Princ. Geol.* III. 176 The rippled surface of the hills of blown sand near Calais. **1842** TENNYSON *Godiva* 47 She shook her head, And shower'd the rippled ringlets to her knee. **1872** W. S. SYMONDS *Rec. Rocks* iii. 70 On the west may be seen grand sheets of rippled rocks. **1883** *Science* I. 521/1 Rippled cirrus clouds may have similar origin. **1903** H. G. WELLS *War in Air* v. 154 A rippled veil of still, thin sunlit cirrus. **1927** PEAKE & FLEURE *Peasants & Potters* vii. 100 Plain, incised, and rippled ware. **1930** R. CAMPBELL *Poems* 2 The rippled silver of her breasts. **1950** FRANSDEN & NELSON *Ice Cream* xvii. 177 Rippled ice cream: as the plain vanilla ice cream is drawn from the freezer into the package, specially prepared syrups..are added by means of a special nozzle so as to produce a marbled effect.

'ripple-grass. *Sc.* and *U.S.* [f. RIPPLE *sb.*[2]] Rib-leaved plantain.

1824 MACTAGGART *Gallovid. Encycl.*, *Ripplegirse*, a broad-leaved herb, which labourers put on cuts. **1856** A. GRAY *Man. Bot.* (1860) 269 Ribgrass, Ripplegrass, English Plantain. **1880** in *Antrim & Down Gloss.*

'rippleless, *a.* [f. RIPPLE *sb.*[3] + -LESS.] Without a ripple; free from ripples; calm. Also, without causing ripples.

1838 MISS PARDOE *River & the Desert* I. 116 The sea lies rippleless like a sheet of lead. **1849** *Zoologist* VII. 2542 Surveying the calm heavy rippleless swell of the sea. **1887** W. RYE *Norfolk Broads* 54 The moonlight slept on the rippleless water. **1923** J. S. HUXLEY *Ess. Biologist* iii. 113 The Crested Grebe... Its brilliant white belly, protective grey-brown back, rippleless and effortless diving, [etc.]. **1941** STEINBECK & RICKETTS *Sea of Cortez* xiv. 131 The lagoon [was] rippleless.

'ripple-mark. [f. RIPPLE *sb.*[3]] A wavy surface, line, or ridge on sand, mud, or rock, formed by the action of waves or the wind, or by both. Chiefly *Geol.*

1833 LYELL *Princ. Geol.* Index. III. 102 Ripple marks formed by the winds on dunes. **1854** *Bakewell's Geol.* 41 The ripple marks of the sea on the shore are very frequently preserved. **1888** *Jrnl. Derbysh. Archaeol. Soc.* X. 7 The ripple-marks, rain-pittings and footprints so well known in certain sandstones.

fig. **1876** LOWELL *Among my Bks.* Ser. II. 243 The very ripple-marks on the remotest shores of being.

So **'ripple-marked** *a.* Also *transf.*

1841 *Penny Cycl.* XX. 19/1 We find ripple-marked strata among the rocks of every geological age. **1898** *Allbutt's Syst. Med.* V. 919 'Ripple-marked' thickening of the endocardium due to the strain of aortic regurgitation.

rippler ('rɪplə(r)). [f. RIPPLE *v.*[1] + -ER[1].] One who ripples flax; also, an implement for rippling.

1743 R. MAXWELL *Sel. Trans.* 328 This Comb separates the Seed from the Lint, with much more Ease to the Ripplers. **1765** *Museum Rust.* IV. 457 Which gives the flax sufficient air, and keeps the handfuls separate and ready for the rippler. **1847** *Jrnl. R. Agric. Soc.* VIII. II. 375 The ripplers strike the flax through alternately. **1879** *Encycl.*

Brit. IX. 294/2 The best rippler..consists of a kind of comb [etc.]. *Ibid.*, Two ripplers sitting opposite each other,.. work at the same time.

ripples. *Sc.* Also 6 rippillis, 7 riples. [? Connected with RIPPLE *sb.*^{2}] 'A weakness in the back and reins, said to be attended with shooting pains' (Jamieson).

*c*1500 *Rowlis Cursing* 58 in Laing *Anc. Poet. Scot.* 212 Rimbursin, rippillis or belly-thra. 1586 *Indictment* in *Scott's Minstr. Scot. Bord.* (1869) 457 That the bishop of St. Andrews laboured under sindrie diseases, sic as the ripples. 1681 COLVIL *Whigs Supplic.* (1751) 43 Priests diseased of the Riples, Hirpling through the streets like criples. 1728 RAMSAY *Advice to Mr.* —— 8 For warld's wasters, like poor cripples, Look blunt with poverty and ripples. 1787 TAYLOR *Scot. Poems* 143 It tempered weel our mony-plies, Ca'd ripples frae our backs. 1898 LD. E. HAMILTON *Mawkin* xvi. 218 I'm never the same man since the ripples took me.

ripplet (ˈrɪplɪt). Also riplet. [f. RIPPLE *sb.*^{3} + -ET^{1}.] A small ripple; a wavelet.

1820 SHELLEY *Orpheus* in *Compl. Poet. Wks.* (1904) 699 Each riplet makes A many-sided mirror for the sun. 1846 in WORCESTER. 1866 NEALE *Sequences & Hymns* 144 While to her quays and wharves..Creep up the ripplets. 1880 *Time* II. 12 The broad, calm, and limpid river, with its riplets and currents.

ˈrippling, *vbl. sb.*^{1} [f. RIPPLE *v.*^{1}] The action or process of cleaning flax, etc., from seeds.

*c*1440 *Promp. Parv.* 434/2 Rypelynge, of flax, or oper lyke, *avulsio*. 1660 HOWELL *Parly of Beasts* 14 There must be.. rippling, braking,..and heckling of Hemp. 1765 *Museum Rust.* IV. 456 When the flax grows crooked, it is more liable to be hurt in the rippling and swingling. 1805 R. W. DICKSON *Pract. Agric.* II. 739 The operation of rippling should be performed as soon as possible after the crops have been pulled. 1846 SPROULE *Flax* 17 The interval between pulling and rippling should not be great.

b. *attrib.*, as ***rippling-comb, -machine, -stick.***

*c*1340 *Nominale* (Skeat) 545 Swangulstoke, riplingcombe, swyngilwande. 1483 *Cath. Angl.* 306/2 A Ripplyng stoke. 1721 KELLY *Scot. Prov.* 95 Every Thing has its time, and so has the Rippling-comb. *a*1796 BURNS *Had I the Wyte?* 29 He claw'd her wi' the ripplin-kame. 1837 *Flemish Husb.* (L.U.K., III.) 44 Drawing the flax through a rippling machine, which is a kind of comb with blunt iron teeth. 1847 *Jrnl. R. Agric. Soc.* VIII. II. 375 Four men, with two rippling-combs, will take the seed off rather more than an acre in the day.

ˈrippling, *vbl. sb.*^{2} *rare.* [f. RIPPLE *v.*^{2}] A scratch or graze; the action of grazing a surface.

*c*1430 *Syr Gener.* (Roxb.) 5750 Yet it hurt not the king, Vnethes but a litle ripling. *a*1661 FULLER *Worthies, Wales* Pref., Like a Ball cast down and deaded on a soft Floor,.. without the least Ripling or Rebounding.

ˈrippling, *vbl. sb.*^{3} Also 7–8 ripling, 8 replin(g. [f. RIPPLE *v.*^{3}]

1. The formation, or appearance, of ripples on the surface of water; *spec.* a strong ruffling of the sea caused by conflicting currents or tides.

1669 STURMY *Mariner's Mag.* IV. i. 138 The Ship is carried away by unknown Currents,..discovered by their Ripplings. 1699 DAMPIER *Voy.* II. 494, I found by the ripling of the Sea, that there was a strong Current against us. 1726 SHELVOCKE *Voy. round World* 299, I took all imaginable precaution to discover any ripling, or discoloured water. 1744 J. PHILIPS *Jrnl. Anson's Exped.* 30 *note*, A Replin is a Meeting of two Currents, which creates a cockling in the Sea, and makes it appear like shallow Water. 1779 FORREST *Voy. N. Guinea* 127 Many calms and ripplings of currents. 1820 W. SCORESBY *Acc. Arc. Regions* I. 287 This occasions ripplings in the water. 1850 MCCOSH *Div. Govt.* IV. ii. (1874) 486 Like the rippling on the surface of a stream made by winds opposed to the current. 1860 MAURY *Phys. Geogr.* (Low) ix. §445 The tiny ripplings of this feeble tide.

fig. 1891 *Spectator* 22 Aug., Agitated by the vivid rippling of all sorts of changeful sympathies.

2. *U.S.* = RIPPLE *sb.*^{3} 1.

1745 W. POTE *Jrnl. Captivity French & Indian War* (1896) 55 This Day was foul weather the Greatest part of the Day, and likewise verey bad Paddling, on account of Ripplings and falls. 1751 J. BARTRAM *Observ. Trav. Pennsylv.* etc. 47 Half a mile farther we came to a rippling, which carried us with prodigious swiftness down the stream. 1755 L. EVANS *Middle Brit. Colonies* 26 At Hart's Rock, the River [Ohio] makes..a very sharp Rippling, where the Boatmen are obliged to wade and hawl up near the Rocks. 1832 W. D. WILLIAMSON *Hist. Maine* I. 57 Here are ripplings, to avoid which, a canal was cut twenty rods in length.

3. The sound made by water in motion.

1769 FALCONER *Dict. Marine* (1780), *Rippling*, a broken and interrupted noise, produced by a current. 1810 CRABBE *Borough* i. 290 Now walking silent, by the river's side, The ear perceives the rippling of the tide. 1899 RODWAY *Guiana Wilds* 226 In the direction from which the rippling of a stream could be heard.

ˈrippling, *ppl. a.* [f. RIPPLE *v.*^{3}] That ripples; flowing in ripples.

1670 BOYLE *Tracts, Bottom of Sea* 6 He perceived the Water to make a rippling noise (as the Sea-men call it). 1781 COWPER *Anti-Thelyphth.* 24 Inconstant as the beams that play On rippling waters in an April day. 1801 FOSTER in *Life & Corr.* (1846) I. 133 The rippling course of a rill. 1852 LONGF. *Warden of Cinque Ports* ii, The red autumn sun.. glanced on flowing flag and rippling pennon. 1859 GEO. ELIOT *A. Bede* I. xv, It was not heavy, massive, merely rippling hair, but soft and silken. 1877 L. MORRIS *Epic of Hades* II. 145 Streams Laughed with a rippling music.

Hence **ˈripplingly** *adv.*

1844 *Fraser's Mag.* XXX. 433 A rill which ran ripplingly over the pebbles.

ripply (ˈrɪplɪ), *a.* [f. RIPPLE *sb.*^{3} + -Y^{1}.] Marked or characterized by ripples.

1775 J. MELVIN *Jrnl.* (1857) 13, I proceeded down Chaudeur river,..and came to a riply place, which was very dangerous, the rocks standing up all over the river. 1807 J. BARLOW *Columb.* IV. 546 The moonbeam..Silvers with trembling tints the ripply tide. 1842 TENNYSON *E. Morris* 98 We..ran By ripply shallows of the lisping lake. 1875 GRANT *One of the '600'* ix, Undoing her hair, she cut a long and ripply tress.

ˈrippock. *Sc.* [Origin obscure: cf. RITTOCH.] The Common Tern.

1813 MONTAGU *Ornith. Dict.* Suppl., [In] the Orkney and Zetland Islands..they are known by the..names of Tarrock,..Rittock or Rippock. 1825 FLEMING *Brit. Anim.* 143.

ˈRippon. *Obs.* exc. *Hist.* The name of a town in Yorkshire (now written *Ripon*), used *attrib.* or *ellipt.* as a designation of spurs, for the manufacture of which it was formerly renowned.

1625 B. JONSON *Staple of N.* I. iii, There's an angel, if my Spurres Be not right Rippon. 1636 DAVENANT *Wits* V. i, With rowels of Sharp Rippon spurs. *a*1661 FULLER *Worthies, Yorks.* (1662) 190 As true Steel as Rippon Rowels. 1704 SWIFT *Mech. Operat. Spir.* Misc. (1711) 299 The former, while it is in the State of a Rider, wears huge Rippon Spurs. 1835 W. IRVING *Abbotsford* §5 Around were hung.. a Highland broadsword from Floddenfield; a pair of Rippon spurs from Bannockburn. 1850 FAIRHOLT *Costume* (ed. 3) II. 349 *Rippons*, spurs.

rip-rap (ˈrɪpˌræp), *sb.* Also 6 ryprap, riprapp. [f. RAP *sb.*^{1} or *v.*^{1}, with usual change of *a* to *i* in the first syllable; but senses 2 and 3 may be partly of different origin.]

1. †**a.** An imitation of the sound caused by a rapid succession of blows; hence, a sharp blow. *Obs.*

*c*1580 J. JEFFRIE *Bugbears* Epilog, With hyffa, with huffa, with ryprap, poff, puffa, and sprityng go we! 1582 STANYHURST *Æneis* II. (Arb.) 59 With rip rap bouncing thee ram to the chapter is hurled. *c*1600 RUGGLE *Club Law* I. iv, Hee tooke me such a riprapp on the head.

b. A kind of detonating firework. Also, the sound of fireworks detonating, and *transf.*

1894 HALL CAINE *Manxman* 259 A few fireworks, a rip-rap or two, and some general illumination. 1909 HALL CAINE *White Prophet* I. i. 8 Once more the words rang like a rip-rap down the line. 1930 *Sea Breezes* Dec. 72 The glare and rip-rap of the fireworks ashore..told that the Old Year 1882 had expired. 1942 *Sun* (Baltimore) 13 Mar. 13/3 Sea-coast guns on Fort Wool, known to civilians as the Rip Raps, will be fired Saturday between 9 A.M. and noon. 1974 *Country Life* 28 Nov. 1682 A firework party..rockets sped into the sky..followed by..sparklers and even 'rip-raps' round our feet.

c. (See quot.)

1959 I. & P. OPIE *Lore & Lang. Schoolch.* xviii. 381 There are more than sixty established names for the pursuit of illegally knocking at doors... *Rip Rap.* Derby.

2. *Naut.* (See quots.)

1669 STURMY *Mariner's Mag.* IV. xviii. 214 Dongeness, Dover, Ripraps, The South Foreland. 1699 DAMPIER *Voy.* II. II. 10 Near this Island we always find a great ripling which Seamen call the Rip-raps. 1784 PENNANT *Arct. Zool.* Introd. (1792) III. p. iii, Between Bologne and Folkstone.. is..a narrow submarine hill, called the Rip-raps. 1885 C. F. HOLDER *Marvels Anim. Life* 224 The rip-rap, as they call the tide agin' the wind.

3. orig. *U.S.* Loose stone thrown down in water or on a soft bottom to form a foundation for a breakwater or other work. More widely, loose stone used for revetments, embankments, or the like; also, a structure made of this.

[1822 *Niles' Reg.* 15 June 252/1 The expense of getting stone, and delivering it at the Rip Raps and Point Comfort.] 1833 H. BARNARD *Let.* 4 Mar. in *Maryland Hist. Mag.* (1918) XIII. 314 We passed in our way..Old Point Comfort, upon which you know Fortress Monroe is situated —the ripraps directly opposite, which two will effectually secure the Bay. 1875 KNIGHT *Dict. Mech.* 1946/2 s.v., Charleston Harbor, and Plymouth Breakwater, England, are founded on rip-raps. 1880 *News & Press* (Cimarron, New Mexico) 9 Sept. 3/3 It is the intention of the company to raise the grade of the approaches on both sides, protecting the exposed surfaces by what is technically known as 'rip rap', a kind of loose rock work. 1892 *Outing* July 254/1 At the worst places ripraps of brush and stones have been built to confine the river to its bed. 1899 *Rep. Iowa Geol. Surv.* IX. 435 Limestone weathering to a most irregular face, of no value except for rip-rap. 1926 *Daily Colonist* (Victoria, B.C.) 11 July 36/3 It was necessary to blast out a way at the cliffside, with occasional banks of rip-rap, and stretches of trestle. 1975 *Offshore* Aug. 36/2 After placement the base was grouted into position and a wall of rip-rap placed right round the base to protect it against scour.

attrib. 1838 J. CHILDS *Western Railroad* (1839) 25 To guard the embankments by rip-rap walls. 1886 C. D. WARNER *Their Pilgr.* v. (1888) 120 Broken, ragged, slimy rocks, as if they had been dumped there for a rip-rap wall. 1931 *Sun* (Baltimore) 1 Sept. 9/6 A railroad section foreman, blasting for rip rap stone, found the first sample of the ore in western Pike county [Arkansas]. 1976 *Billings* (Montana) *Gaz.* 16 June 7-A/2 The time required to obtain a riprap permit for Montana rivers and streams.

So **ˈrip-ˌrap** *v.*, to found upon, or cover with, a deposit of loose stone. Hence **ˈrip-ˌrapped** *ppl. a.*, **ˈrip-ˌrapping** *vbl. sb. U.S.*

1848 in Bartlett *Dict. Amer.* (1859) s.v., If, in constructing a bulkhead, it should be determined to rip-rap to low-water mark,..the cost for rip-rapping..would be about eighty thousand dollars. 1883 *American* VI. 297 The stream will be confined within permanent barriers by rip-rapped banks and levees. 1884 *Harper's Mag.* Sept. 504/1 Cliff ledges ..[are] connected one terrace above by the other, by..a natural rip-rapping of fallen fragments. *Ibid.* 621/2 The face slope..and the rear..are riprapped with stone. 1897 M. B. KER in E. L. Wilson et al. *Mountain Climbing* vi. 286 We riprapped the bottom of the slope to prevent slipping down the hill. 1904 *Dialect Notes* II. 420 Highland Avenue is rip-rapped on one side. 1938 *Sun* (Baltimore) 8 Nov. 5/3 Another [project] is for rip-rapping the river bank. 1943 B. A. DE VOTO *Year of Decision* 332 They had to..pry boulders out of their course, riprap swamp patches, sometimes bridge brooks that could not be crossed otherwise. 1976 *Columbus* (Montana) *News* 27 May 8/3 The resolution was signed for the riprapping of property by the Absarokee lagoon.

‖**ripresa** (riˈpresa). *Mus.* [It.] A repeat; a refrain (see quot. 1947).

1740 J. GRASSINEAU *Mus. Dict.* 204 *Ripresa.* See *Repeat.* 1876 STAINER & BARRETT *Dict. Mus. Terms* 379/2 *Ripresa*... (1) A reprise or burden. (2) A repeat. 1947 E. BLOM *Everyman's Dict. Mus.* 501/1 *Ripresa*,..a refrain, especially in the 14th–15th cent. It. ballata and frottola. 1977 *Early Music* July 326/2 The ballata consists of a refrain or ripresa of one to four poetic lines, followed by two piedi..and a volta.

rip-reyue: see REAP-REEVE.

ˈripripple *v.*, nonce semi-reduplication of RIPPLE *v.*^{3}

1922 JOYCE *Ulysses* 85 He saw his trunk and limbs rip-rippled over.

ˈrip-roaring, riproaring, *a.* orig. *U.S.* [Cf. RIPROARIOUS *a.*] Full of vigour, spirit, or excellence; first-rate; boisterous; full-blooded.

1834 W. A. CARUTHERS *Kentuckian in N.Y.* I. 62 There was a rip-roaring sight of slight o' hand and tumbling work there. 1845 J. J. HOOPER *Some Adventures Simon Suggs* x. 127 And I seed the biggest, longest, rip-roarenest, blackest, scaliest..allegator. 1884 E. W. NYE *Baled Hay* 231 He thought..Kirke was there..to give Laramie the grandest, riproaringest tempest of mirth that she had ever experienced. 1905 *Dialect Notes* III. 64 We had a rip-roaring time. 1906 *N.Y. Even. Post* (Sat. Suppl.) 8 Sept. 1 When he was called upon to address the conference he got a rip-roaring welcome. 1923 *Daily Mail* 28 Feb. 10 (Advt.), It's a rip-roaring, red-blooded yarn that no man or woman will be able to read unmoved. 1948 *Sunday Pictorial* 18 July 11/3 A rip-roaring performance by Oscar Homolka. 1950 C. FRY *Venus Observed* II. ii. 70 Well, here's a rip-roaring gauntlet to be run By a couple of God's children. 1958 *Times* 3 Nov. 3/1 It was a match in which little skill was shown, but for all that a rip-roaring, babel-like affair of incessant movement and high good spirits. 1979 *Guardian* 14 Apr. 9/7 Rip-roaring commercial [film] successes.

Hence ˌ**rip-ˈroaringly** *adv.*

1951 *Sport* 27 Jan.–2 Feb. 12/2 Their young side..is having a rip-roaringly successful cup season.

ripˈroarious, *a.* orig. *U.S.* Also **-rorious.** [f. RIP *v.*^{2}, after *uproarious.*] Boisterous, violent.

1830 *N.Y. Constellation* 11 Sept. 2/5 The English traveller had put up at a little log tavern on the banks of the Savannah, where the *riproarious* conduct took place. 1840 *Congress Globe* 2 Apr. 376/1 Here and there a gentleman from both political parties, who had been drawn out by curiosity to witness their riproarious proceedings [at the Whig 'powwows']. 1855 HALIBURTON *Nature & Human N.* I. 58 That's because you..never saw a riprorious hurricane in all your life. 1890 *Harper's Mag.* Apr. 796/2 His waning buzz of rip-roarious approbation. 1948 R. W. CHAPMAN *Lexicography* 6 The *Dictionary of American English*.. stopped at 1900, before the trickle of that rip-roarious idiom became a flood. 1975 J. I. M. STEWART *Gaudy* iii. 57 It was one of those rare books which, while enjoying riproarious popular success, at the same time owns sufficient intrinsic merit to achieve among the critical a kind of classic status straight away.

ripˈroariously, *adv.* [f. RIPROARIOUS *a.* + -LY^{2}.] In a riproarious or boisterous manner.

1834 D. CROCKETT *Narr. Life* xi. 78 The next day it rained rip-roriously.

ripsack (ˈrɪpsæk). [f. RIP *v.*^{2} + SACK *sb.*^{1} (cf. quot.).] The Californian Grey Whale.

1860 *Merc. Marine Mag.* VII. 213 It being difficult to capture them, they have a variety of names among whalemen, as 'Ripsack',..'Devil-fish'.

ˈrip-saw, *sb.* [f. RIP *v.*^{2}] A saw used for cutting wood in the direction of the grain.

1846 HOLTZAPFFEL *Turning* II. 708 The rip-saw has the coarsest teeth, and which are of slight pitch... The half-rip is similar, but a little finer. 1875 *Carp. & Join.* 14 Hand saw, divided into the largest or rip saw, intermediate or half-rip, and smallest. 1883 *Harper's Mag.* Jan. 198/2 Dawson's lumber was cut over pits by means of a rip-saw.

Hence **ˈrip-saw** *v.*, to cut with a rip-saw.

1885 *Cent. Mag.* Nov. 33, I ripsawed the lumber up here.

ˈripsnorter. orig. *U.S.* Also **rip-snorter.** [f. RIP *v.*^{2} + SNORTER^{1} 2: cf. RIPROARIOUS *a.*] Someone or something exceptionally remarkable in appearance, quality, strength, or the like; *spec.* a storm, a gale. Cf. SNORTER^{1} 2 b.

1840 *Crockett Almanac* 20/1 Of all the ripsnorters I ever tutched upon, thar never war one that could pull her boat alongside of Grace Peabody. 1885 *Santa Fé Weekly New Mexican* 20 Aug. 2/6 Any galoot who wants the Ripsnorter for a year can have it left at his bar-room on payment of three red chips in advance. 1889 K. MUNROE *Dory Mates* (1890) vi. 84 Boys, we are in for a regular 'rip-snorter'. I never saw a nastier night. 1924 R. CLEMENTS *Gipsy of Horn* v. 87 It came on to blow in a way that the packet-rats called a 'ripsnorter'. **1931** A. J. CRONIN *Hatter's Castle* II. ix. 368 Did you see that shot of mine, cocky?.. It was a—a regular nor'easter—a pickled ripsnorter. **1941** BAKER *Dict. Austral. Slang* 60 *Ripsnorter*, something particularly good. An amusing or eccentric person. **1951** *New Yorker* 3 Mar. 28/1 The villain is a real ripsnorter. **1972** *Last Whole Earth Catalog* (Portola Inst.) 445/3 This is Gurney Norman the author speaking, bringing you the end of this folk tale, and it's a rip-snorter.

'ripsnorting, *a.* orig. *U.S.* Also rip-snorting. [f. prec.] = RIP-ROARING, RIPROARING *a.*

1846 *Yale Lit. Mag.* June 336 What a rip-snorting red head you have got! **1904** *Topeka* (Kansas) *Capital* 2 June 4 It is now stated that Bryan will make a rip-snorting speech at the St. Louis convention. **1926** *Spectator* 10 July 44/1 It's a ripsnorting, red-blooded show—a wow. **1926** [see HOTSY-TOTSY *a.*]. **1956** N. COWARD *South Sea Bubble* I. i. 12 You're a rip-snorting old careerist, darling. **1959** *Daily Mail* 17 Feb. 4/5 The Count Basie riff-number *Alright, Okay, You Win*, with ripsnorting backing. **1976** P. HENISSART *Winter Quarry* xxvii. 276 These ripsnorting professional anti-communists. **1978** *Detroit Free Press* 14 Apr. 15B/4 A ripsnorting cockroach race, with the men on their hands and knees, urging their bugs down makeshift lanes.

Hence (as a back-formation) **'ripsnort** *v.*, to go boisterously, to rollick; **,rip'snortingly** *adv.*

1974 *Publishers Weekly* 24 June 59/2 It's a definitive book, ripsnortingly adult. **1975** C. A. HADDAD *Moroccan* vii. 83 'Come to Daddy,' I said..she clambered on my back and together we ripsnorted our way to Ilanit. **1979** 'A. HAILEY' *Overload* II. x. 159 Water which promptly became high-pressure steam and ripsnorted to a separate superheater section.

rip-stick: see RIP *sb.*³

ripstone, incorrect form of RIBSTON(E.

1837 DICKENS *Pickw.* vi, A little hard-headed, Ripstone pippin-faced man. *Ibid.* lx, The officiating clerk peeled and ate three Ripstone pippins.

rip-sulwer: see REAP-SILVER.

[rip-towel. 'The gratuity or reward given to customary Tenants, when they have reaped their Lord's Corn'.

1701 MANLEY *Cowell's Interpreter* s.v. *Reap-towel* (and hence in later Dicts.), citing *MS. Cott. Nero* A. xii. fol. 104 b (*c* 1350). The word in the MS. is *ripetowel* and the meaning uncertain.]

Ripuarian (rɪpjʊ'ɛərɪən), *a.* and *sb.* [f. med.L. *Ripuāri-us* (also *Ribuāri-us*); that this is a derivative of L. *ripa* is very doubtful.]

A. *adj.* **1.** The distinctive epithet of the ancient Franks living on the Rhine between the Moselle and Meuse.

1839 KEIGHTLEY *Hist. Eng.* I. 129 Lands were given to those who were named the Limitanean and Ripuarian soldiery, the latter from their location on the banks of the great frontier rivers. **1861** J. G. SHEPPARD *Fall Rome* iv. 190 A great multitude..burst over the Rhine, easily overcoming the feeble resistance offered by the Ripuarian Franks.

2. The distinctive epithet of the code of law observed by the Ripuarian Franks.

1781 GIBBON *Decl. & F.* xxxviii. (1787) III. 585 *note*, The Ripuarian law declares..this indulgence in favour of the plaintiff. **1804** RANKEN *Hist. France* III. III. iii. 292 By the consuetude of Roman and Gothic law in the south and west counties: of the Salic, Ripuarian, and Burgundian, on the north and east. **1875** MAINE *Hist. Inst.* x. 284 Under the Ripuarian Law he goes through the expressive formality of standing at his door with a drawn sword.

3. Designating a northern dialect of Middle Franconian German.

1910 *Encycl. Brit.* XI. 779/2 The boundary-line between Low and High German..may roughly be indicated by the ..place-names, on the understanding..that the Ripuarian dialect..is to be classed with High German. **1934** PRIEBSCH & COLLINSON *German Lang.* II. vii. 323 Within Middle Franconian the Ripuarian dialect..keeps unshifted *rp*.

B. *sb.* **1.** *pl.* The Ripuarian Franks.

1781 GIBBON *Decl. & F.* xxxviii. (1787) III. 584 Within the same period, the customs of the Ripuarians were transcribed and published. **1862** *Chambers's Encycl.* IV. 494/2 The Ripuarians..on both sides of the Rhine as far up as the Main. **1882–3** SCHAFF *Encycl. Relig. Knowl.* I. 513 In the hands of the Franks the city was the metropolis of the Ripuarians until the time of Charlemagne.

2. The name of a dialect of Middle Franconian German.

1910 *Encycl. Brit.* XI. 780/1 Middle Franconian.., which ..represents a kind of transition dialect to Low German, is itself divided into (*a*) Ripuarian or Low Rhenish with Cologne and Aachen..as centres, and (*β*) Moselle Franconian with Trier..as principal town. **1934** PRIEBSCH & COLLINSON *German Lang.* II. i. 88 In Ripuarian—the Northern dialect of Middle Franconian—the unshifted form *ūp* (up) 'auf' is found. **1939** L. H. GRAY *Foundations of Lang.* xi. 349 Middle Franconian appears in two sub-forms: *Ripuarian* in the north, and *Moselle* in the south. **1961** R. E. KELLER *German Dial.* vii. 249 Luxemburgish appears..as a relic area..separated..from Ripuarian by the *Dorp*/*Dorf* isogloss in the north. **1970** CHAMBERS & WILKIE *Short Hist. German Lang.* iii. 21 Middle Franconian, divided into Ripuarian (in the Cologne area) and Moselle Franconian.

Ripuary ('rɪpjʊərɪ), *a.* *rare.* [ad. med.L. *Ripuāri-us.*] = RIPUARIAN *a.* 2.

1622 MALYNES *Anc. Law-Merch.* 475 The auncient Gaules termed all their lawes either Ripuarie or Salique. **1801** RANKEN *Hist. France* I. i. 24 Clovis seems to have occupied himself..in revising and improving the Salic and Ripuary laws. **1843** BROUGHAM *Pol. Phil.* I. 367 The Ripuary law was apparently of later date than the Salic. *Ibid.* 368 The Burgundian Law..is..more refined than the Salic or Ripuary codes.

Rip Van Winkle (rɪp væn 'wɪŋk(ə)l). The name of a character in Washington Irving's *Sketch Book* (1819–20), a good-for-nothing who falls asleep for twenty years, applied: **a.** *transf.* to a person unfamiliar with prevailing conditions.

1833 *Advocate* (Shelbyville, Kentucky) 28 Sept. 2/4 Wm. C. Preston, of South Carolina, in one of his furious tirades, applied to the State of North Carolina, the somewhat degrading epithet of 'the Rip Van Winkle of the South'. **1852** DICKENS *Bleak Ho.* (1853) ii. 5 Both the world of fashion and the Court of Chancery are things of precedent and usage; over-sleeping Rip Van Winkles, who have played at strange games through a deal of thundery weather. **1892** G. B. SHAW *Fabian Soc.* 20 There are some Rip Van Winkles in our movement who are only now waking up. **1939** C. DAY LEWIS *Child of Misfortune* III. i. 262 A Rip Van Winkle's self-pity would seize him. **1945** R. HARGREAVES *Enemy at Gate* 187 That somewhat shop-soiled military Rip van Winkle, Giuseppe Garibaldi. **1974** H. MCCLOY *Sleepwalker* ii. 17 What was she? A girl Rip Van Winkle who had been asleep since 1940?

b. *attrib.* to something characteristic of or resembling Rip Van Winkle or (an aspect of) his experience.

1849 *Picayune* (New Orleans) 21 July 1/6 A person absent for three weeks, on returning, almost fancies that he has been taking a Rip Van Winkle slumber. **1893** I. ZANGWILL *Ghetto Tragedies* 133 Is it possible that I can get into touch again with my youth..after a sort of Rip Van Winkle sleep? **1959** *Times* 6 May 15/7 Time, in Cesky Krummau, seems to have stopped about the year 1800. In this Rip-van-Winkle atmosphere, we were taken to the tiny castle chapel, where there is a baroque organ in which every single pipe is in its original state. **1977** W. H. S. SMITH *Young Man's Country* iii. 93 On the wall, as if to convince me that I was not in a Rip Van Winkle dream, was a list of S.D.O.s.

So **Rip Van 'Winkleish** *a.*, characteristic of or resembling Rip Van Winkle, ignorant of present conditions; hence **Rip Van 'Winkledom,** (*a*) the Catskill Mountains in the state of New York, the site of Rip Van Winkle's sleep; (*b*) a state of prolonged sleep; **Rip Van 'Winkleism,** an outmoded custom or opinion.

1829 *Mechanic's Press* (Utica, N.Y.) 5 Dec. 28/1 His Rip Van Winkleish habits asked no more than to pursue 'the even tenor of their way'. **1842** C. M. KIRKLAND *Forest Life* II. 228 [Reading an old-fashioned book] was counted among my Rip-Van-Winkle-isms. **1852** *Harper's Mag.* Aug. 420/2 A Pilgrim from the backwoods..had just been awakened from a Rip-Van-Winkleish existence of a quarter of a century by the steam-whistle of the Erie Railroad. **1888** G. B. SHAW *Let.* 9 Feb. (1965) I. 185 He persists in his 18th century Rip-van-Winkleism. **1892** *Outing* Apr. 48 (*title*) A cyclist's visit to Rip Van Winkledom. *Ibid.* 50/2 We are already in the confines of Rip Van Winkledom. **1911** BEERBOHM *Lett. to R. Turner* (1964) 195 It made me feel very Rip-Van-Winkleish to find no Alfred Douglas. **1956** M. LOWRY *Let.* 13 Nov. (1967) 391 She..has also for the latter part of this time been mostly asleep... She emerged from this Ripvanwinkledom, feeling and sounding better than she has in ten years.

Riquewihr ('riːkvɪə(r)). The name of a town in Alsace, applied to white wines produced there.

1947 T. E. CARLING *Wine-Wise* vi. 34 The latter [*sc.* Gentil, Riesling and Traminer] are usually sold under the name of the grape, coupled with that of the village—as Riesling-Riquewihr, and Traminer-Ribeauvillé, etc. **1951** E. PAUL *Springtime in Paris* x. 184 Was it Chablis, Pouilly or Riquewihr with the oysters? **1963** I. FLEMING *On H.M. Secret Service* xxiv. 264 You are just in time for some good Strasbourg sausage and a passable Riquewihr. **1974** C. WILSON *Bk. of Booze* iii. 124 Alsace wines..are usually sold under the name of the grape—Riesling, Traminer, Sylvaner, etc.—and sometimes the town—Riquewihr being perhaps the best known.

riroriro ('riːrəʊriːrəʊ). [Maori.] Also (with hyphen) riro-riro. The New Zealand grey warbler, *Gerygone igata*, a small wren-like bird belonging to the subfamily Malurinæ of the family Muscicapidæ.

1835 W. YATE *Acct. N.Z.* (ed. 2) ii. 58 *Riroriro*, a very small brown bird, with white feathers under the wings and tail. **1860** [see FAN-TAIL *sb.* 3]. **1884** M. A. MARTIN *Our Maoris* viii. 125 There is a little bird called Riro-riro in New Zealand from its note. **1939** D. CRESSWELL *Present without Leave* 32 The riro-riro..has a small wistful song. **1955** W. R. B. OLIVER *N.Z. Birds* (ed. 2) 477/1 Mention of the Riroriro occurs in many stories, songs and proverbs of the Maori.

ris, obs. variant of RICE *sb.*¹; RISE *v.*

‖**risagallo.** *Obs.*⁻¹ [It. *risagallo*, obs. var. of *risigallo*: see RESALGAR.] Arsenic.

1610 MARKHAM *Masterp.* II. cxxx. 432 Other Farriers vse the powder of Risagallo, or Risagre, but it is a great deale too strong a fretter.

†**risagon.** *Obs. Med.* Also 7 rysagone (8–9 -gon), rizagon. [Orig. obscure.] = CASSUMUNAR.

1679 J. PECHEY (*title*), Some Observations made upon the Root Cassumuniar called otherwise Rysagone. **1681** GREW *Musæum* 386 Rizagon, a Root brought from Bengala, of good use. **1748** W. LEWIS *Pharmacop.* 20 Cassumuniar, the root. Risagon. **1850** PEREIRA *Mat. Med.* II. I. 1121.

risagre, obs. variant of RESALGAR.

†**risbank.** *Obs.* [ad. Du. *rijsbank*, f. *rijs* RICE *sb.*¹ Hence also G. *rissbank*, F. *risban.*] An artificial bank, properly one faced or strengthened with brushwood.

Earlier in the form *rice-bank*: see RICE *sb.*¹ 5.

1731 *Hist. Litteraria* I. 515 The Art of constructing Sluices, Dykes, Piles, Moles, Risbanks, Light-houses, Docks. **1758** BORLASE *Nat. Hist. Cornwall* 325 This Risbank, or mound, ranges up-hill and down-hill indifferently. **1761** HUME *Hist. Eng.* (1770) IV. xxxvii. 482 The fleet battered the risbank, which guarded the entry of the harbour.

†**riscal'dation.** *Obs.*⁻¹ [ad. It. *riscaldazione.*] The action of warming or heating.

1599 LINCHE *Anc. Fiction* E iv, From the ouer-vehement ardour and riscaldation of his beames.

risch(e, obs. forms of RUSH (the plant).

‖**'risco.** *Obs.* [a. older It. *risco* (Florio), var. of *risico*, *rischio*: see RISK *sb.*, and cf. RISGO.] Risk.

1657 R. LIGON *Barbadoes* 1 Having been censured by some that I should..undertake to run so long a Risco from England to the Barbadoes. **1682** SCARLETT *Exchanges* Pref. A 3 b, To consider..their great Labour and Expences, the Risco that they run [etc.]. **1707** tr. *Wks. C'tess D'Anois* (1715) 431 The King had run a thousand Risco's since his confinement in the Cage.

†**risconter.** *Obs.*⁻¹ [ad. It. *riscontro*: see RESCOUNTER *sb.*] Meeting, encounter.

1592 WOTTON in *Reliq.* (1685) 659 The Cardinal had only signified the Fact, as suspecting (belike) the risconter of the Pope's Courriers.

‖**ris de veau** (ri də vo). Also erron. 9 riz de veau. [Fr.] A dish of sweetbread of veal. Freq. in *Comb.* Also *fig.*

1820 M. EDGEWORTH *Let.* 4 June (1979) 144, I give you one dinner by which you may judge all the rest—Bouilli de boeuf—..ris de veau piqué—maquereau, [etc.]. **1861** MRS. BEETON *Bk. Househ. Managem.* 909 *Entrées.* Riz de Veau aux Tomates. **1877** E. S. DALLAS *Kettner's Bk. of Table* 452 *Roasted Sweetbreads.* This is what the French set down as the *Ris de veau à l'Anglaise.* **1927** N. WAINWRIGHT tr. *Dekobra's Madonna of Sleeping Cars* xiv. 187 There are no great men except the inventors and the developers of science. All the rest amount to more or less *ris de veau* surrounding an Adam's apple. **1938** L. MACNEICE *I crossed Minch* vii. 101 I'll have a little ris de veau, I think. **1964** L. DEIGHTON *Funeral in Berlin* xxiii. 126 There is *entrecôte* or *ris de veau.* **1975** R. STOUT *Family Affair* viii. 188 Sweetbreads poached in white wine, dipped in crumbs and eggs, sautéed, and doused with almonds in brown butter... They call it *ris de veau amandine.*

rise (raɪz), *sb.* Forms: 5 **ryse, ryese,** 6 **rys,** 6– **rise.** [f. the vb. Cf. LG. *rîs.*]

I. †**1.** The act, on the part of a hare, of finally rising to return to its form. *Obs.*⁻¹

c **1410** *Master of Game* (MS. Digby 182) i, And there she shall crosse wayes x. or xii. tymes and then she shal make hir ryses.

†**2. a.** A spring or bound upwards; *esp.* one made with the help of a run at the outset of a long leap. *Obs.*

1600 KEMP *Nine Daies Wonder* B ij b, At length comming to a broad plash of water and mud, which could not be auoyded I fetcht a rise. **1642** FULLER *Holy & Prof. State* IV. iii. 251 A long leap from York to Rome, and therefore he needed to take a good rise. **1681** W. ROBERTSON *Phraseol. Gen.* (1693) 480 He runs far back that means to leap a great way; He takes his rise far.

†**b.** A start or aid towards rising in a leap; a place from which to rise or soar. *Obs.*

1639 LD. DIGBY *Lett. conc. Relig.* (1651) 85 There might be a man so disposed as (having a good rise, and with a convenient career) to leap at once from England to Rome. **1648** BOYLE *Seraph. Love* (1700) 170 Having Piled them up together, have made that heap but a Rise to take our soaring flight from. **1697** CREECH tr. *Manilius* I. 6 Rais'd so high, from that convenient rise She took her flight, and quickly reacht the Skies. **1728** CHAMBERS *Cycl.* s.v. *Step*, The Step, properly, puts a Horse on the Hand, and gives him a Rise to Leap.

3. The coming of the sun (moon, or planets) above the horizon; hence also, the region of sunrise, the east. (Now usually *rising.*)

1599 SHAKS., etc. *Pass. Pilgr.* 194 The morning rise Doth cite each moving sense from idle rest. **1635–56** COWLEY *Davideis* IV. 6 Moab..Up with the Sun arose, and..With lifted Hands bow'd towards his shining rise. **1665** SIR T. HERBERT *Trav.* (1677) 44 Truly many Sun-Idolaters I have seen, all which worship his rise, but none his setting. **1712** BLACKMORE *Creation* 98 Th' adventurous merchant thus pursues his way Or to the rise, or to the fall of day. **1865** SIR J. K. JAMES *Tasso* XII. xc, To her at rise, to her at sunset hour. **1885–94** R. BRIDGES *Eros & Psyche* March xxiii, She ..Lookt left and right to rise and set of day.

fig. **1671** MILTON *P.R.* I. 294 So spake our Morning Star then in his rise. **1738** WESLEY *Hymns*, '*The Sun of Righteousness appears*' iv, In vain the Stone, the Watch, the Seal Forbid an early Rise. **1781** J. MORISON in *Scot. Paraphr.* xix. 2 To hail thy rise, thou better Sun, the gathering nations come.

4. a. Upward movement; ascent; transference to a higher level. Also *fig.*

1573–9 G. HARVEY *Letter-bk.* (Camden) 69 If once to heaven we take our rise. **1640** W. STYLE *Antisco's Span. Gallant* A 10 b, Like Birds for want of ayre we faint: Lye still and cannot make our rise. **1659** *Instructions Oratory* 11 Which it cannot so easily mount unto at the first, without taking, by the way, this meaner rise. **1788** *Trifler* No. 16. 216 He was on the rise to treat more largely on the folly of parental officiousness. **1808** SCOTT *Marm.* VI. xv, The steed along the drawbridge flies, Just as it trembled on the rise. **1847** *Illustr. Lond. News* 10 July 27/3 The balloon..now and then took a rise out of the hands of the stalwart men who held it. **1872** JENKINSON *Guide Eng. Lakes* (1879) 173 Beyond Gosforth a steep rise is made.

b. Capacity for or power of rising.

a **1716** SOUTH (Cent.), These were sublimities above the rise of the apostolic spirit. **1848** *Jrnl. R. Agric. Soc.* IX. II. 574 There is no rise or spring in them. **1881** W. E. DICKSON *Organ-Build.* vi. 73 The reservoir may have a rise or play of about 10 inches or a foot.

c. *Cricket.* The upward movement of a ball after pitching.

1851 J. PYCROFT *Cricket Field* viii. 165 Slow balls can be pitched nearer to the bat, affording a shorter sight of the rise. **1897** P. NORMAN *West Kent Cricket Club* 40 There was always a good spin on his ball, and he could..give it that 'abrupt rise', as it has somewhere been called, which is so fatal to many a good batsman.

d. *Theatr.* The raising of the curtain at the beginning of a scene. In phr. ***at rise***, whereby the playwright introduces the description of the opening situation.

1905 [see *curtain-rise* s.v. CURTAIN *sb.* 8]. **1933** S. KINGSLEY *Men in White* II. i. 77 Three months later... At rise: Mr Houghton, short, stodgy, aggressive..the economist, has just finished reading a report. **1961** BOWMAN & BALL *Theatre Lang.* 17 *At rise*, at the moment when the rising curtain first discloses a scene; said often of the relative positions of actors at such a moment. *Ibid.* 301 *Rise*,..the going up of a curtain (also as the *curtain rise* or the *rising*). **1962** [see *curtain-fall* s.v. CURTAIN *sb.* 8].

e. *slang.* = ERECTION 4. Usu. in phr. ***to get a rise***.

1949 PARTRIDGE *Dict. Slang* (ed. 3) 1154/2 *Rise, get a*, to experience an erection. **1973** M. AMIS *Rachel Papers* 55 'Have you fucked Sue?.. What was it like?'.. 'It was okay, except I couldn't get a proper rise.'

5. a. Elevation in fortune or rank.

1632 MASSINGER *City Madam* v. i, Many..Have written 'Ladies of Honour', and some few Have higher titles; and that's the furthest rise You can in England hope for. **1654** GAYTON *Pleas. Notes* III. x. 132 Duke Ricards Letter..He bid me read, my Rise was laid. **1706** E. WARD *Wooden World Diss.* (1708) 87 All Admirals, as well as Captains, are oblig'd to begin their Rise there. **1781** JUSTAMOND tr. *Priv. Life Lewis XV*, I. 99 We have seen the beginning of this fortunate man's rise. **1841** SPALDING *Italy & It. Isl.* II. 243 The rise of the Medici and other wealthy Florentine families, furnished liberal patrons to art. **1866** G. MACDONALD *Ann. Quiet Neighb.* xiii. (1878) 255 It was considered a rise in life.

b. An occasion or means of rising (in fortune or rank).

c **1680** G. DALLAS *Stiles* (1697) 89 The eminent Parts with which the Lord has Endued your Lordship..have been no small Rise to your Noble Family in this Age. **1773** FOOTE *Bankrupt* I. Wks. 1799 II. 101 Don't you consider, that her ruin, as you call it, will be your rise?

c. Upward course; advance towards a flourishing or prosperous condition, etc.

Not always distinguishable from sense 17 or 19.

1721 BERKELEY *Prev. Ruin Gt. Britain* Wks. 1871 III. 211 Our ancestors during their rise and greatness. **1727** DE FOE *Syst. Magic* I. iii, A great many useful and agreeable speculations offer themselves in the rise and progress of the thing itself. **1869** J. MARTINEAU *Ess.* II. 173 This period of rise and of decline. **1888** BRYCE *Amer. Commw.* II. liii. 335 The second period in the annals of American parties, which ..include the rise and fall of the Whig party.

6. a. *Angling.* The movement of a fish to the surface of the water to take a fly or bait; an instance of this.

1651 T. BARKER *Art of Angling* (1653) 5 If you can attain to angle with one haire, you shall have the more rises. **1860** RUSSELL *Diary India* II. 199, I tried every fly that I could think of; but not a sign of a rise. **1867** F. FRANCIS *Angling* i. (1880) 6 Let him then note where these rises are the thickest, and choose that place.

b. ***to get, have,*** or ***take a rise out of*** (one), to make a butt of, raise a laugh at, by some form of pretence or dissimulation.

1834 MEDWIN *Angler in Wales* I. 113 We will have a rise out of Charters at our *noctes*. **1840** THACKERAY *Catherine* vii, Oh but it was a rare rise we got out of them chaps. **1882** BLACKMORE *Cristowell* xviii, It would be worth a hundred pounds to me, to have a rise taken out of him.

c. ***to make a rise***, to succeed in striking gold by mining. Also of other precious metals and stones.

1890 'R. BOLDREWOOD' *Miner's Right* (1899) 24/1 You've got to work till you make a 'rise', for my sake. **1940** I. L. IDRIESS *Lightning Ridge* xv. 99 Andy sank five hundred shafts, toiled for years and years, and never made a rise.

d. *slang.* A fit of anger.

1877 'ETON BOY' *Day of my Life* i. 11, I told him for his good; he needn't get in such a rise about it. **1895** H. W. NEVINSON *Neighbours of Ours* i. 21 Mrs. Sullivan was in a fair rise about it, sayin' as 'e'd took us all in.

7. The act of rising from the dead (also ***rise-again***), or *from* some condition.

1738 WESLEY *Easter Hymn* iii, Death in vain forbids His rise; Christ hath opened Paradise. **1839–52** BAILEY *Festus* 30 The grave hath no pride, nor the rise-again. **1868** LYNCH *Rivulet* CLII. iv, Thy word..insure[s] Our rise from shame.

†**8.** A revolt, rising. *Obs.*

1768 BOSWELL *Corsica* (ed. 2) 109 The Genoese, eager to repress the rise of 1734. **1848** D. COX *Let.* 29 July in F. G. Roe *David Cox* (1924) ii. 59 It was expect[ed] there would be a rise among the Irish. **1853** DICKENS *Child's Hist. Eng.* in *Househ. Words* 17 Sept. 71/1 He had some wild hope of gaining the Irish people over to his side by favoring a rise among them.

II. 9. a. A piece of rising ground; a hill.

1639 FULLER *Holy War* I. ii. (1840) 3 The Jews..were forbidden to enter into Jerusalem, or so much as to behold it from any rise or advantage of ground. **1654** EARL MONM. tr. *Bentivoglio's Wars Flanders* 206 It hath on one side an eminent Rise, which Commands the whole Town. **1700** DRYDEN *Baucis & Philemon* 17 Two neighb'ring Trees.. Stand on a mod'rate Rise. **1708** J. PHILIPS *Cyder* I. 6 If therefore, thou incline To deck this Rise with Fruits of various Tastes. **1816** BYRON *Ch. Har.* III. lvi, On a rise of gentle ground There is a small and simple pyramid. **1856** RUSKIN *Præ Raphaelitism*, etc. (1906) 231 Distant cumuli, heavy with rain, hanging on the rises of the moorland. **1878** B. TAYLOR *Deukalion* I. v. 40 Yonder, on the rise, Who leans with folded arms against the stone?

b. A long, broad, gently sloping elevation rising from the sea bed, esp. that at the edge of a continental shelf.

1903 *Geogr. Jrnl.* XXII. 193 The *elevation* is either entirely surrounded by depressions or is a prolongation of the continental border. The *rise* is an elevation which rises gradually with an angle of only a few minutes of arc, irrespective of whether it is wide or narrow... Rises carry the chief features of suboceanic relief, so that if the ocean floor was changed into dry land they would act as the main watersheds. **1954** W. D. THORNBURY *Princ. Geomorphol.* xviii. 477 A good example of a rise or swell is that in the Pacific Ocean known as the Hawaiian swell or rise. It is a comparatively gentle rise some 600 miles wide and about 1900 miles long. **1974** *Nature* 30 Aug. 694/2 States like Argentina, Australia, Canada..will prefer to go beyond 200 miles to the outer edge of the continental rise if this is larger than 200 miles.

10. a. An upward slope or direction, *esp.* of strata, coal-beds, veins of ore, etc.

1698 G. THOMAS *Pensilvania* 46 Some of their Noses having a rise like the Roman. **1708** J. C. *Compl. Collier* (1845) 40 It is always look'd upon to be of good Advantage to the Colliery, to have a rise in the Thill, and of the Coal as we work. **1731** W. HALFPENNY *Perspective* 31 Draw Lines.. parallel to the line SF, which shews the Perspective Rise of every Member. **1839** URE *Dict. Arts* 984 This gas being lighter than common air, always ascends to the roof or to the rise of the galleries. **1856** WHYTE MELVILLE *Kate Coventry* xii, The ground is now..on the rise. **1878** HUXLEY *Physiogr.* xviii. 313 A very sharp rise leads from the Pacific to the range of the Andes.

attrib. **1768** *Gen. Hist.* in *Ann. Reg.* 63 There are two other fire-engines of a pretty large size, working on the rise-part of this colliery. **1839** URE *Dict. Arts* 964 Where the coal-measures are horizontal, and the faults run at a greater angle than 45° to the line of bearing, they are termed dip and rise faults. **1883** GRESLEY *Gloss. Coal-mining* 204 *Rise Split*, a proportion of the ventilative current sent into a rise district of a mine. *Ibid.*, *Rise Workings*, underground workings carried on to the rise or high side of the shafts.

b. *Mining.* An excavation or working on the up side of a shaft. (Cf. RISING *vbl. sb.* 12 c.)

1839 *Penny Cycl.* XV. 241/1 Should the ore extend far enough..levels may be driven from the 'rises' to render it more accessible. **1861** G. HARRIS in *Athenæum* 19 Jan. 82 Here were ends Cut through hard marble by the miners' skill, And winzes, stopes and rises. **1884** R. HUNT *Mining* 912 *Rise*, this is the same meaning as stope, or excavation in the back of a level. 'I belong (*viz.* I work) up in the rise.'

11. a. The vertical height of a step, an arch, an inclined surface or object, etc., measured from the base or springing-line to the highest point.

1663 GERBIER *Counsel & Adv. to Builders* 100 The rise, width, and depth of steps, shall not need to be repeated, since they have been described [etc.]. **1739** LABELYE *Short Acc. Piers Westm. Bridge* 74 The prick'd Lines shew what would be the Rise of Stone Arches, and the Disposition of their Joints. **1825** J. NICHOLSON *Operat. Mechanic* 539 The height, or rise of the arch, is a line drawn at right angles from the middle of the chord..to the intrados. **1839** *Civil Eng. & Arch. Jrnl.* II. 81/2 The two side arches 156 feet span, and 15¼ feet rise. **1874** MICKLETHWAITE *Mod. Par. Churches* 89 The rise of the steps will vary according to circumstances.

†**b.** The pitch of a screw. *Obs. rare.*

1683 MOXON *Mech. Exerc., Printing* xi. ¶ 1, I shew'd..the manner of making a Screw..; but assigned it no particular Rise;..Therefore its assigned Rise being two Inches and an half in a Revolution [etc.].

12. a. A flight *of* steps.

c **1710** CELIA FIENNES *Diary* (1888) 258 The queen being come up to her table wch was a great rise of stepps. **1848** B. WEBB *Cont. Ecclesiol.* 45 There is a rise of steps at the east end of the nave. *Ibid.* 400.

b. = RISER 7.

1711 W. SUTHERLAND *Shipbuild. Assist.* 65 The Steps.. have no Rises nor Stiles. **1793** SMEATON *Edystone L.* §227 It was stopped by the rise of the third step, against which it seemed abutted. **1879** *Cassell's Techn. Educ.* I. 329/2 The flat surface of a stair is called the tread, and the upright face is termed the rise.

III. 13. An increase in height of the sea, streams, or water, by tides, floods, etc., or of a liquid in a vessel; the amount of this increase.

1626 BACON *Sylva* §889 Experiment..Touching the Rise of Water, by Meanes of Flame. **1662** DRYDEN *To Ld. Chancellor Clarendon* 142 The hill..mounts, but so as billows play, Whose rise not hinders but makes short our way. **1743** BULKELEY & CUMMINS *Voy. S. Seas* 120 We ran in before the Wind for about two Leagues, expecting every Rise and Fall of the Sea to be a Wreck. **1771** *Jrnl. Cook's Voy. World* 119 We observed the whole rise of the tide did not exceed four feet. **1797** *Encycl. Brit.* (ed. 3) XVIII. 496 That the rise and fall of the mercury [in a thermometer] may be better seen. **1830** LYELL *Princ. Geol.* I. 264 The perpendicular rise and fall of the spring-tides is fifteen feet, and at neap-tides, eight feet. **1847** GROTE *Greece* IV. xxv. 14 He is preserved by the sudden rise of a river. **1860** *Merc. Mar. Mag.* VII. 339 South-westerly wind will follow, especially if the barometer rise is sudden.

transf. **1713** STEELE *Guard.* No. 149 The head-dress receives frequent rises and falls every year. **1868** TENNYSON *Lucretius* 10 His mind..fancy-borne perhaps upon the rise And long roll of the Hexameter.

14. *Mus.* An increase of pitch in a tone or voice. Also in *Phonetics*. Cf. *rise-fall* below.

1626 BACON *Sylva* §105 In the ordinary Rise and Falles of the Voice,..there fall out to be two Beemols..betweene the Vnison and the Diapason. **1867** MACFARREN *Harmony* (1892) 73 A complete chord may be suspended when the progression of roots is by the rise of a 4th or fall of a 5th. **1879** GROVE *Dict. Mus.* I. 43 The..graces peculiar to old English music..include the Plain-beat or rise. **1911** *Encycl. Brit.* XXI. 465/2 A high rise, which begins high, and consequently can only rise a little higher, expresses simple question, while..a low rise..expresses various degrees of surprise or indignation. **1932** [see *fall-rise* s.v. FALL *sb.*[1] 29]. **1965** *Language* XLI. 210 This scale maintained its neatness only when the nuclear exponent was a simple 'fall' or 'rise'. When the nucleus was 'fall-rise', 'rise-fall', or 'fall-plus-rise', two phenomena were observed.

15. a. An increase in amount.

a **1699** TEMPLE (J.), The rise or fall that may happen in his constant revenue by a Spanish war. **1811** A. T. THOMSON *Lond. Disp.* (1818) 664 By the sudden rise of temperature.. a considerable waste of product also takes place. **1817** JAS. MILL *Brit. India* II. v. vii. 591 On the same terms, excepting a small rise in the annual payment. **1871** B. STEWART *Heat* (ed. 2) §91 This heat is..absorbed by the ice without producing any rise of temperature.

b. An advance in wages or salary.

1836–7 DICKENS *Sk. Boz, Scenes* i, The receipt of seven shillings a-week, with the prospect of an early rise to eight. **1915** W. S. MAUGHAM *Of Human Bondage* cvii. 564 If they were not worth a rise it was better to sack them at once. **1921** [see RAISE *sb.*[1] 5 c]. **1957** E. H. SHEPARD *Drawn from Memory* vii. 131 She..said that her 'intended' was going to receive a rise and work on the passenger trains. **1978** *Verbatim* Sept. 12/1 The influence of British usage in America is more and more evident: *The New York Times*, 1 April 1978, in referring to the increased settlement for transit workers in New York City, called it a '6% Rise'.

c. *U.S.* ***the rise of*** (an amount or period of time), more than, above (that quantity); ***and the rise***, and more. Now *rare*. Cf. RISING *pr. pple.* 3.

1834 in J. S. Bassett *Southern Plantation Overseer* (1925) 66, I muste plante the rise of a hundred aceres in coten. **1839** *Southern Lit. Messenger* V. 379/1 It is the rise of a week since I last shifted. **1845** J. J. HOOPER *Some Adventures Simon Suggs* xii. 141 Bill..has been ded the rise of twenty year. **1858** in N. E. Eliason *Tarheel Talk* (1956) 290 At Mr Collins thar has bin de rise of A hundred down with the measles. **1859** BARTLETT *Dict. Amer.* (ed. 2) 367 The phrase 'and the rise', is used in some parts of the South to mean 'and more'; ..'I should think there were a thousand and the rise', i.e. a thousand and more. **1905** 'O. HENRY' in *Everybody's Mag.* Dec. 820/1, I will undertake for to say that I've seen the rise of $50,000 at a time in that tin grub box that my adopted father calls his safe.

16. a. An increase in the value or price *of* a thing.

1691 LOCKE *Money* Wks. 1727 II. 87 The Market-price of any thing, and so of Bullion, is to be taken..not from the extraordinary Rise of two or three Market-days in a Year. **1723** SWIFT *Agst. Enlarging Power Bps.* Wks. 1751 IX. 23 The Bishops have had some Share in the gradual Rise of Lands. **1790** WASHINGTON *Writ.* (1892) XII. 1 The progress of public credit is witnessed by a considerable rise of American stock abroad as well as at home. **1821** CLARE *Vill. Minstr.* I. 17 'Bout work being slack, and rise and fall of bread. **1885** *Law Times Rep.* LII. 648/2 A great rise had taken place in the value of the Sydney property.

b. ***on the rise***, becoming more valuable or dearer.

1808 *Times* 23 Feb., Colonial produce is on the rise. **1884** *Illustr. Lond. News* 13 Dec. 570/3 'Sheep,' for five years, have been steadily 'on the rise'.

IV. 17. a. An origin or source; a beginning; a start. Freq. in phr. ***to have*** or ***take one's rise***.

1630 PRYNNE *Anti-Armin.* 115 Which by this meanes take their rise and being from the creature. **1664** POWER *Exp. Philos.* I. 60 If you take Nature at the rise, and critically observe her in her rudimental and obscure beginning. **1690** LOCKE *Govt.* II. i, He..must..find out another rise of Government, another original of political power. **1738** WESLEY *Ps.* XCI. iii, Nor Plague of unknown Rise that kills In Darkness. **1763** J. BROWN *Poetry & Mus.* v. 77 He..sung the Generation of the World and the Rise of Things. **1847** YEOWELL *Anc. Brit. Church* iii. 25 Intimately acquainted with the rise of all churches. **1878** BROWNING *La Saisiaz* 33 Ask the rush if it suspects Whence and how the stream which floats it had a rise.

†**b.** ***to take one's rise*** (***from***), to start, begin with, in narration. *Obs.*

1647–8 COTTERELL *Davila's Hist. Fr.* (1678) 14 Taking his rise from the fortunes of the House of Lorraine. **1697** J. SERGEANT *Solid Philos.* 63, I take my Rise from the remotest Principles that can concern that Point, and these are my Thoughts. **1716** J. COLLIER tr. *Gregory Nazianz.* 60 Let us take our rise a little from the Original of things.

†**18. a.** An occasion; a ground or basis. *Obs.* (Common *c* 1650–90.)

1641 *Triumph of K. Chas.* in *Harl. Misc.* (Malh.) V. 101 We had two humble petitions to present to both their Majesties, and we had the rise and encouragement to both, from that which his Majesty was pleased to deliver to us. **1669** R. MONTAGU in *Buccleuch MSS.* (Hist. MSS. Comm.) I. 431, I will write a letter which he may show the King, and shall be a rise for him to ask the King to do the business. **1688** BOYLE *Final Causes* IV. 111 The Celestial bodys may.. give man a rise to admire and praise the greatness and power of the Divine Maker. **1759** STERNE *Tr. Shandy* II. v, The reason, or rather the rise of this sudden demigration was as follows. **1820** JODRELL s.v. *Manteau*, Mantua in Italy may have given the rise of its etymology.

b. ***to give rise to***, to occasion, to bring about, to cause. (See also GIVE *v.* 48.)

1705 ADDISON *Italy* 132 His Reputation..gave Rise to the Republick that calls it self after his Name. **1774** GOLDSM. *Nat. Hist.* (1776) I. 256 This shallowness and narrowness in many parts of the sea, give also rise to a peculiarity in the tides. **1830** R. KNOX *Béclard's Anat.* 304 When this action has been very long and violent, it gives rise to a painful sensibility. **1873** SYMONDS *Grk. Poets* 417 The strangest misconception to which religious prejudice has ever given rise.

19. The act of coming into existence or notice.

1656 EARL MONM. tr. *Boccalini's Advts. fr. Parnass.* I. xvii. (1674) 19 Remedies..whereby stoutly to resist vice in its rise. **1664** POWER *Exp. Philos.* I. 78 Which practical part of Opticks is but yet in the rise. **1737** WHISTON *Josephus, Antiq.* IX. x. §2 Upon the rise of a most terrible storm. **1777** SIR W. JONES *Ess. Poet. Eastern Nat.*, The rise of a poet in their tribe. **1869** J. MARTINEAU *Ess.* II. 52 It is manifestly concurrent with the rise of new questions.

20. *Comb.*, as ***rise-and-fall*** adj.; **rise-fall** *Phonetics*, a rise and subsequent fall of pitch compressed into one syllable (cf. *fall-rise* s.v. FALL *sb.*[1] 29); also *attrib.*; **rise time** *Electronics*, the time required for a pulse to rise from 10% to 90% of its steady value.

1926 *Gloss. Terms Electr. Engin.* (Brit. Engin. Stand. Assoc.) 159 **Rise-and-fall pendant*, a pendant the height of which can be regulated by means of a pulley and counter-weight or similar device. **1950** *Engineering* 21 July 59/2 Sellers include a 'rise and fall clause' in their contracts. **1974** tr. *Wertheim's Evolution & Revolution* i. 64 Oswald Spengler ..elaborated the rise-and-fall concept as a world-wide cyclical movement from which no human civilization could escape. **1977** *Grimsby Even. Tel.* 14 May 6/5 (Advt.), 3-phase saw bench with rise and fall table, £80. **1964** CRYSTAL & QUIRK *Syst. Prosodic & Paralinguistic Features in Eng.* iv. 50 Such nuclei are of the following seven types: fall, rise, level, fall-rise, *rise-fall, fall-plus-rise, and rise-plus-fall. **1966** G. N. LEECH, *Eng. in Advertising* v. 49 The ..advertisement..contains three examples of the rise-fall tone... A contour line above each example indicates the position of the rise-fall. **1973** *Archivum Linguisticum* IV. 25 In paratone I..the 'low rise-fall'..is likely to be followed by the 'wide fall'. **1947** *Rev. Sci. Instruments* XVIII. 643/1 To obtain best possible *rise times for the pulses, care is required in laying out the components. **1952** *Proc. IRE* XL. 962/1 Because of limited bandwidth, the pulse takes a certain length of time to build up its amplitude, i.e., it requires a certain 'rise time'. **1969** J. J. SPARKES *Transistor Switching* i. 22 The turn-on time is divided into two parts, the delay time..and the rise time. **1975** G. J. KING *Audio Handbk.* ii. 41 Extended high-frequency response is.. required to ensure that the rise time of the amplifier is not less than that of transient-type programme signal components.

rise, obs. variant of RICE *sb.*[1] and *sb.*[2]

rise (raiz), *v.* Pa. t. rose. Pa. pple. risen. [Common Teutonic: OE. *rísan*, = OFris. *rīsa* (mod.Fris. *rize, ryzje*), MDu. *rīsen* (Du. *rijzen*), OS. *rîsan* (MLG. *rîsen*), OHG. *rîsan, rîsen* (G. *reisen*, of the sun), ON. and Icel. *rísa* (Norw. and MSw. *risa*), Goth. (*ur*)*reisan*. No related forms have been traced outside of Teutonic.

In OE., as in OS., the simple *rísan* is extremely rare, the common form being the compound *arísan* ARISE *v.* In early ME. the use of *rise* for *arise* is prominently northern, and may be mainly due to the influence of ON. *rísa*.

The causative forms related to *rise* are RAISE and REAR, but *rise* itself has to a certain extent (esp. in later use) assumed the functions of a transitive verb.]

A. Inflexional forms.

1. a. *Inf.* (and *Pres.*). 1-2 **rísan**, 3-4 **risen** (3 -enn, 4 -in, 5 -yn), 4 **rijsen**, 4-5 **rysen** (5 -yn); 3-**rise**, 4 **rijse**, 4-6 (8 *Sc.*) **ryse** (6 **rysse, reyse**), 6 **rize**; 3-4 **ris, rys**, 5 **riss**, 5-6 **ryss**, 6 *Sc.* **ryis(s**.

c **1000** *Ags. Ps.* (Thorpe) lviii. 1 Fram laðum, þe me..on risan willað. *c* **1200** *Trin. Coll. Hom.* 103 Ich ne mai wiðuten þin elp risen. *c* **1250** *Gen. & Ex.* 4039 Of ðe sal risen sterre briȝt. *a* **1300** *Cursor M.* 14495 All þe werld mon wit him rijs. *c* **1340** HAMPOLE *Pr. Consc.* 4810 Þai shalle with þam rys ogayn. **1382** WYCLIF *Ps.* xciii. 16 Who shal al rijsen to me aȝen the warieris? *c* **1440** *Promp. Parv.* 435/1 Rysyn erly. **1483** *Cath. Angl.* 309/2 To Ryse be fore day. **1550** CROWLEY *Epigr.* 626 Fewe..do vse to rise earelye. **1556** *Chron. Gr. Friars* (Camden) 59 Thoys that dyd rysse in dyvers places. **1567** *Gude & Godlie B.* (S.T.S.) 234, I do call on all men mortall To ryis. **1590** SPENSER *F.Q.* I. iii. 19 None durst rize ..him in to lett.

b. 3 *sing. pres. ind.* 4-5 **rist(e, ryst(e**.

13.. *K. Alis.* 2158 (Bodl. MS.), Now rist grete tabor betyng. *c* **1330** R. BRUNNE *Chron. Wace* (Rolls) 15597 Þer kynde so ryst on heyghte. *c* **1385** CHAUCER *L.G.W.* 887 *Thisbe*, Tysbe ryst vp with-outyn ony bost.

2. *Pa. t.* **a.** 3-5 **ras** (5 **rass**), 3-4 (9) **raas**, 5-9 **rase**, 9 **raze**; 4-6 (8) **rais**, 5-6 **raiss** (6 **raisz**), 5 **rays**, 6 **rayis**; 5 **rayse**, 5-9 **raise**, 8 **raaize**, 9 **raaise**; 7, 9 **rease**, 9 **reaise, reaaze**.

After 1300 these forms are only Sc. and northern.

c **1200** ORMIN 4341 Crist ras upp off dæþe. *a* **1300** *E.E. Psalter* xix. 9 We raas, and rightid are. *c* **1340** HAMPOLE *Pr. Consc.* 4308 Als he fra dede rase. *c* **1425** WYNTOUN *Cron.* I. xvi. 1542 Agayn his fadyr..Þan he [Jupiter] rase. *c* **1470** HENRY *Wallace* v. 966 Rays neuir agayne quhat ane at he hyt rycht. **1533** GAU *Richt Vay* 68 Mony bodis of sanctis..raisz wp. **1567** *Gude & Godlie B.* (S.T.S.) 111 Quhen men rais in our contrairie. *c* **1620** A. HUME *Brit. Tongue* (1865) 18 Ther rease..a hoat disputation betuene him and me. **1718** RAMSAY *Christ's Kirk Gr.* III. iii, To see the young fouk ere they raise. **1785** HUTTON *Bran New Wark* (E.D.S.) 367 Up as she raaize. **1816** SCOTT *Old Mort.* xxvii, To..sit by the chimley when the reek rase. **1881** SARGISSON *Joe Scoap* 105 When t'sun reaaze an set. **1883** R. M. FERGUSSON *Rambl. Sk. Far North* 143 The water raise an' raise.

β. 3-5 **ros**, 4-6 **roos**; 4- **rose** (5 **rosse**), 4-5 **roose** (5 *pl.* **rosyn, roosen**), 6 **roase, rhose**, 9 **roze**, *dial.* **rause, rauze, rawse, ruse, ruz**.

c **1250** *Gen. & Ex.* 4152 Swilc prophete..Ros non. *c* **1300** *Beket* 1082 He ros him up and bihuld. **1377** LANGL. *P. Pl.* B. v. 234, I roos whan þei were arest. *c* **1385** CHAUCER *L.G.W.* Prol. 112 (Tanner MS.), The son that roose as rede as rose. *c* **1410** *Sir Cleges* 194 He..rosse upe in that stede. *c* **1449** PECOCK *Repr.* v. iii. 497 [There] roosen also manye untrewe sectis. **1568** GRAFTON *Chron.* II. 382 Then roase the streete, namely the youth. *a* **1591** H. SMITH *Wks.* (1867) I. 444 Thou..hast rebelled more since thou rosest. **1637** MILTON *Lycidas* 30 The Star that rose..bright. **1732** BERKELEY *Alciphr.* I. §1 Next morning Euphranor rose early. **1804** R. ANDERSON *Cumbld. Ball.* (c 1850) 68 Fast flew the hours—now ruse the muin.

γ. *pl.* 2, 4-5 **risen**, 4-5 **rysen**, 5 **resyn, reson, rison**; *sing.* (and *pl.*) 6 **rysse**, 6-7 **risse**; 6 **ryse**, 6-8 **rise**, 7 **rizze**; 7, 9 *dial.* **riss** (7 **riss', ris'**), **ris, riz**.

1154 *O.E. Chron.* (Laud MS.) an. 1135, Aȝenes him risen sona þa ricemen. **1362** LANGL. *P. Pl.* A. v. 176 Þei Risen vp Raply. **1382** WYCLIF *1 Sam.* xxiv. 8 Dauid..suffrede hem not, that thei rysen into Saul. *a* **1440** *Sir Eglam.* 284 Hertys reson on eche a syde. **1556** *Chron. Gr. Friars* (Camden) 45 Thys yere..rysse a gret tempest. **1590** LODGE *Rosalynde* (Hunterian Cl.) 55 He rise vp and went to him. **1609** TOURNEUR *Funeral Poem* 2 From thy spirit rizze thy worthy fame. **1611** B. JONSON *Catiline* v. vi, As he riss', the day grew black. **1654** EARL MONM. tr. *Bentivoglio's Wars Flanders* 136 As the Tide rise, the Enemies Boats drew nearer. **1676** HOBBES *Iliad* 379 Achilles..sat upon the seat from whence he ris. **1715** M. DAVIES *Athen. Brit.* I. 154 His great zeal.. rise, at last, so high, that [etc]. **1876** *Mr. Gray & Neighbours* I. 78 This was long before the day when Curates riz. **1900** *Cent. Mag.* Feb. 605 The goat..riz on his hind legs.

δ. 4 (*pl.*) **risiden**; 6 **rysed, ryssyd, risde**, 7 **ris'd, rised**.

1388 WYCLIF *2 Sam.* xviii. 31 Alle men that risiden aȝens thee. [**15..** *Adam Bell* xx. in Child *Ballads* III. 23/2 They rysed the towne of mery Carlel. **1562** *Child-Marriages* 108 Roger..rysed this tale hym-self.] **1579** *Poore Knights Palace* F iiij, Then Beauty risde, and thus she gan to say. **1608** MACHIN *Dumb Knight* IV. i, I..ris'd on my right side. **1653** DOROTHY OSBORNE *Lett.* (1888) 59, I lay abed all next day.. and rised on Thursday.

3. *Pa. pple.* **a.** 3 **risenn**, 4- **risen** (4 **risun**, 4-5 **risin**, 7 **ris'n**); 4-5 **resen** (5 **-in, -ine**), 4-6 **resyn**, 6 **reysen**; 5 **rissyn** (6 *Sc.* **rissin(e)**, **ryssyn, rysun**, 5-6 **rysen, -yn**; 9 *dial.* **ruzzen**.

c **1200** ORMIN 11552 Affterr þatt he wass..risenn upp. *a* **1300** *Cursor M.* 2839 Bi þat þe sun risen was. **13..** —— 6751 (Gött.), If þe sunne be resin þan. *c* **1380** WYCLIF *Sel. Wks.* II. 140 Bifore þat Crist was risun. *c* **1400** *Laud Troy Bk.* 16991 The sonne is rysen. *c* **1470** HARDING *Chron.* lv, By example of this kyng.., resen of poore bloude. **1513-14** *Act 5 Hen. VIII*, c. 3 Preamble, Wolle is resyn of a farre gretter price. **1533** GAU *Richt Vay* 104 The sekkis..quhilk ar rissine laitlie in the kirk. **1667** MILTON *P.L.* IV. 624 To morrow..we must be ris'n.

β. 4 **i-rise**, 4, 6-7 **rise**, 5 **rys**, 7 **risse, rize, rizze**, 7, 9 **ris**, 9 *dial.* **ris', riss, riz**.

1387 TREVISA *Higden* (Rolls) VIII. 21 Ȝif eny sclaundre were i-rise. **1390** GOWER *Conf.* I. 207 Whan..every man was rise aboute. **1430-40** LYDG. *Bochas* II. i. (1554) 42 b/1 The Philistines Were rys agayn. **1600** BRETON *Wks.* (Grosart) I. 11/2 When..Robin Hood is rise againe. **1607** MIDDLETON *Michaelmas Term* III. i. 126 If 'twere risse to a flame. **1610** G. FLETCHER *Christ's Vict.* I. xlii, As though another day were newly ris. **1684** T. BURNET *Theory Earth* II. 78 Flames and smoak have..rise out of the sea. **1866** LOWELL *Biglow P.* Ser. II. Poems 1890 II. 222 A betch o' bread that hain't riz. **1890** J. CLARE *Pearl* I. v, He's ris' in the world.

γ. 6-8, 9 *dial.* **rose**.

a **1593** MARLOWE *Edw. II*, I. iv, Had some bloodless fury rose from hell. **1631** MASSINGER *Believe as You List* II. i, Is he Rose from the dead? **1675** MARVELL *Wks.* (Grosart) I. 274 It was understood the Lords were rose. **1712** ARBUTHNOT *John Bull* I. xii, He has rose early and sate up late. **1776** [see 10]. **1884** J. C. EGERTON *Sussex Folk & Ways* 100 A hurt which had rose a hump on her back.

B. Signification.

In transferred or figurative uses it may be difficult to decide which of the literal senses is implied: sometimes a mixture of ideas appears to be present. Compare the note to RAISE *v.*[1]

I. *intr.* To get up from sitting, lying, or repose.

1. a. To get up from a sitting, kneeling, or lying posture; to assume a standing position; to get upon one's feet. Also with *compl.* (quot. 1847).

c **1200** ORMIN 6028 Þatt deor..þatt riseþþ o þe þridde daȝȝ Affterr þatt itt iss wheollpedd. *a* **1300** *Cursor M.* 15282 Quen þis super was all don, Iesus ras of his sette. **1375** BARBOUR *Bruce* III. 567 Eftir the mete sone rais the king,..And went ..towart þe Se. *c* **1450** tr. *De Imitatione* II. viii. 48 Dide not Mary Mawdeleyn rise oute of hir place? **1548-9** (Mar.) *Bk. Com. Prayer, Communion* 16 Then shall the Priest rise, the people still reuerently knelyng. **1576** FLEMING *Panopl. Epist.* 409 To rise out of your chaire and walke about the fields. **1613** SHAKS. *Hen. VIII*, IV. i. 82 Her Grace rose, and with modest paces Came to the Altar. **1667** MILTON *P.L.* x. 958 But rise, let us no more contend [etc.]. **1766** GRAY *Impromptus* 11 When you rise from your Dinner as light as before. **1821** SHELLEY *Adonais* xlv. 2 The inheritors of unfulfilled renown Rose from their thrones. **1847** TENNYSON *Princess* II. 27 She rose her height. **1882** STEVENSON *New Arab. Nts.* (1901) 113/2 The landlord.. rose from a business-table under the key-rack.

b. With *up*.

c **1200** ORMIN 2741 Ȝho ras upp sone anan, & for Upp inntill heȝhe munntess. *a* **1300** *Cursor M.* 2813 'Rises vp,' he said, 'and fle ȝee sone'. **1393** LANGL. *P. Pl.* C. XXI. 283 Rys vp ragamoffyn, and reche me alle þe barres. *c* **1440** *Alph. Tales* 294 Sho..rase vpp & went furth of þe kurk. **1530** PALSGR. 692/2 He rose up on his fete quyckly. **1593** SHAKS. *2 Hen. VI*, v. i. 78 Iden, kneele downe, rise vp a Knight. **1655** *Theophania* 14 Immediately Synesius putting back his Chair, rise up, and replied. **1710** STEELE *Tatler* No. 122 ¶1 The whole Assembly rose up to do him Honour. **1742-3** *Johnson's Debates* (1787) II. 515 Lord Aylesford then rose up, and spoke to the following purpose. **1847** TENNYSON *Princess* II. 55 Then an officer Rose up, and read the statutes.

†**c.** With reflexive dative. *Obs.*

c **1200** ORMIN 2655 Ȝho ras hire upp, & for anan Upp inntill heȝhe cludess. *a* **1300** *Cursor M.* 16301 Pilate him ras, and forth yode vte o þe pretori. *c* **1374** CHAUCER *Troylus* IV. 232 He rist him up, and every dore he shette And windowe eek. ? *c* **1400** LYDG. *Monk who honoured the Virgin* 66 He rose hym vp and privelich he is went In to hys chambre.

†**d.** *to rise away*, to get up and depart; to leave the table. *Obs.*

a **1300** *Cursor M.* 15690 Quen he had mad his orisun, vp þeþen he ras ewai. *a* **1643** SUCKLING *Fragm. Aurea* (1646) 8 And O, when once that course is past,.. Men rise away, and scarce say Grace!

e. Of animals, esp. game: To get up, issue, from lair or covert. (Cf. 13 b.)

c **1410** *Master of Game* (MS. Digby 182) i, [The hare] shall go a bowe shote or more by o way and ryse agayne by an other. *a* **1440** *Syr Eglam.* 284 Hertys reson on eche a syde. **1596** SPENSER *F.Q.* VI. x. 34 A Tigre forth out of the wood did rise. **1637** MASSINGER *Guardian* I. i, No game shall rise But we'll be ready for't; if a hare, my greyhounds Shall make a course.

f. Of animals, esp. a horse: To assume an erect position *on* the hind legs, etc.; †also *to rise before*.

1658 SIR T. BROWNE *Pseud. Epid.* v. xiii. 308 Because his horse rised before that he could not be setled on his back. **1847** TENNYSON *Princess* v. 482 On his haunches rose the steed, And into fiery splinters leapt the lance.

g. Of hair, etc.: To become erect or stiff. Also of things which have been bent: To resume an upright position.

1500-20 DUNBAR *Poems* lxxv. 34 Ȝour heylis..Gars ryis on loft my quhillelillie. **1583** *Leg. Bp. St. Androis* 404 His rubigo began to ryiss. **1626** BACON *Sylva* §656 Of all Plants it [the reed] boweth the easiest, and riseth again. **1726** LEONI *Alberti's Archit.* I. 26/2 The Pine is suppos'd to have the same Quality as the Fir, of rising against the Weight that is laid upon it. **1822** SHELLEY *Fragm. Unfin. Drama* 167 The sheaths..Rose like the crest of cobra-dicapel. **1855** tr. *Ruffini's Dr. Antonio* iii, Sir John's hair rose on his head.

h. *Welsh dial.* Of a funeral party: to depart from the home of the deceased or bereaved before the interment.

1959 *Western Mail* (Cardiff) 18 Feb. 3/1 The funeral on Friday, Feb. 20, rising at 3 p.m., for interment at Gwaelod-y-Brithdir Cemetery. **1976** *Ibid.* 8 Jan. 10/2 The funeral.. will be rising at 2 p.m. for New Bethel Chapel, from her daughter's residence.

2. a. To get up, or regain one's feet, after a fall. Also *transf.* and *fig.*

c **1205** LAY. 1555 Ȝif he hine mid sweorde at-ran, nea ras he neuer mare. *c* **1220** *Bestiary* 627 Ðat ȝe ne falle..is most in hire ðoȝt, For he ne hauen no lið ðat he muȝen risen wið. *c* **1368** CHAUCER *Compl. Pite* 17 Adovne I fel..Dede as stone,.. But vp I roose. *c* **1400** *Destr. Troy* 7778 Bothe were back-ward þere borne of þere horses,.. But Achilles aftir auntrid to rise. **1415** HOCCLEVE *To Sir J. Oldcastle* 104 Now syn the feend hath youen the a fal,..ryse vp & slynge him doun! *a* **1542** WYATT in *Tottel's Misc.* (Arb.) 76 And if my hope sometimes ryse vp, by some redresse: It stumbleth straite, for feble faint. **1590** SPENSER *F.Q.* I. viii. 15 Downe he fell..; No powre he had to stirre, nor will to rize. **1667** MILTON *P.L.* I. 211 Chain'd on the burning Lake, nor ever thence Had ris'n or heav'd his head. **1781** COWPER *Truth* 588 Pride falls unpitied, never more to rise. **1784** —— *Task* VI. 444 When he charg'd the Jew T'assist his foe's down-fallen beast to rise. **1885** RIDER HAGGARD *K. Solomon's Mines* xiv, More than three thousand four hundred had fallen in this one regiment, most of them never to rise again.

b. *fig.* To recover from a spiritual fall, or a state of sin.

c **1200** ORMIN 2752 All swa birrþ himm forrþrihht anan All risenn upp off sinne. *a* **1300** *Cursor M.* 26516 Þan sal it helpe þe Vte o þi sin raþer to rise To crist. **1415** HOCCLEVE *To Sir J. Oldcastle* 32 To longe haast thow bathid in þat folie! Ryse vp & pourge thee of thy trespas! **1563** WINȜET *Wks.* (S.T.S.) I. 76 Sen the iust man sinnis seuin tymes on the day, and rysis agane. **1596** DALRYMPLE tr. *Leslie's Hist. Scotl.* Prol. 1 The radier walde thay ryse frome thair dark errouris. **1667** MILTON *P.L.* II. 15 From this descent Celestial vertues rising, will appear More glorious and more dread then from no fall. **1781** COWPER *Truth* 480 And is the soul, indeed, so lost?—she cries; Fall'n from her glory, and too weak to rise?

3. a. To get up from sleep or rest.

c **1200** *Trin. Coll. Hom.* 13 Ðe ðridde is þat man be waker, and liht,..and erliche rise, and ȝernliche seche chireche. *a* **1300** *E.E. Psalter* iii. 5, I am methful, for i slepe; And i raas, for lauerd me kepe. *c* **1386** CHAUCER *Prol.* 33, I..made forward erly for to ryse. *c* **1400** *Destr. Troy* 9213 Þen he rose fro his rest in a rad hast. *c* **1440** *Alph. Tales* 20 All his brether when þai hard þe bell, rase & went to matyns. *c* **1500** *Melusine* 360 On the next day erly geffray roos. **1558** GOODMAN *How to Obey* 168 To talke of them..when they went to bed, and when they shuld rise. **1613** PURCHAS *Pilgrimage* II. xv. (1614) 193 Before their Pentecost, they rise before it is light. **1650** HOWELL *Lett.* III. ii. 4 They must rise betimes that can put tricks upon you. **1711** ADDISON *Spect.* No. 106 ¶1 Sir Roger..lets me rise and go to Bed when I please. **1782** MISS BURNEY *Cecilia* VI. ix, I suppose..you will rise with the lark to-morrow morning? **1807** SCOTT *Let.* in *Lockhart* (1837) II. iv. 130 On the principle contained in the old proverb:—He that would thrive—must rise by five. **1810** CRABBE *Borough* xx. 190 Although revived, I..went to rest, to wonder that I rose. **1859** TENNYSON *Geraint* 160 Guinevere lay late into the morn,.. But rose at last.

fig. **1611** SHAKS. *Wint. T.* IV. iv. 106 The Mary-gold, that goes to bed with Sun, And with him rises, weeping. **1822** SHELLEY *Triumph Life* 18 In succession due, did continent, Isle, ocean,..Rise as the Sun their father rose.

b. With *up*.

c **1200** ORMIN 8363 He ras up & toc þe child,..& for till Issraæless land. *c* **1300** *Havelok* 584 Ris up swiþe,..And blou þe fir, and lith a kandel. ? *a* **1366** CHAUCER *Rom. Rose* 95 Up I roos, and gan me clothe. **1423** JAS. I *King's Quair* xi, And vp I rase, no langer wald I lye. **1590** SHAKS. *Mids. N.* IV. i. 129 No doubt they rose vp early, to obserue The right of May. **1611** BIBLE *Gen.* xxii. 3 Abraham rose vp earely in the morning. **1855** MACAULAY *Hist. Eng.* xxii. IV. 802 Every morning hundreds of thousands rose up hoping to hear that the treaty was signed. **1878** BROWNING *La Saisiaz* 15 Nothing dark next day at sundawn! Up I rose and forth I fared.

c. In *imp.* phr. ***rise and shine***, a command to wake up and leave one's bed. orig. *Armed Forces*'.

1916 *Recruiters' Bull.* (U.S. Marine Corps) Apr. 11/2 He rapped at the door and in stentorian tones cried, 'Rise and shine... Wiggle a toe.' **1917** KIPLING *Diversity of Creatures* 237 A high sun over Asia shouting: 'Rise and shine!' **1927** P. RILEY *Mem. Blue-Jacket* 89 Hands were called at 5:30 a.m., the bo'sun's mates going around the deck shouting 'All hands, rise and shine.' **1946** J. IRVING *Royal Navalese* 146 *Rise and shine!*, the boatswains' mates' call to The Hands to roust them out in the morning. **1953** G. BELL *Black Marigolds* xix. 189 Wakey, wakey, rise and shine, or have you fainted? **1973** H. NIELSEN *Severed Key* x. 105 'Rise and shine, lovebirds!' he shouted. 'The honeymoon is over!'

4. To return to life; to come back from death or out of the grave. Also with *up*.

c **1200** *Trin. Coll. Hom.* 113 He..ros of deðe þe þridde dai. *c* **1250** *Gen. & Ex.* 261 Ihesus..Ros fro ded on ðe sunenday. *c* **1340** HAMPOLE *Pr. Consc.* 4810 For þai shalle with þam rys ogayn þat byfor war dede. *c* **1386** CHAUCER *Pars. T.* ¶86 Riseth up, ye that been dede, and cometh to the Iugement. *c* **1440** *Alph. Tales* 15 Hym þoght þis monke rase owte of his grafe & come vnto hym. **1500–20** DUNBAR *Poems* ix. 67 We sall ryss compleit And tak our flesche agane. **1595** SHAKS. *John* III. iv. 86 And so hee'll dye: and rising so againe..I shall not know him. **1624** DONNE *Serm.* xix. 191 Others were raised but He onely rose. **1699** BENTLEY *Phal.* 64 They would never have believed, that he had rose from the dead. **1736** *Gentl. Mag.* VI. 452/1 Were their Fore-fathers to rise up and to see any of their Descendants. **1784** COWPER *Task* v. 830 Hasting to a grave, yet doom'd to rise. **1865** KINGSLEY *Herew.* xxxiii, He beheld St. Etheldreda and her maidens rise from their tombs by night.

fig. **1602** SHAKS. *Ham.* I. ii. 257 Foule deeds will rise, Though all the earth orewhelm them to mens eies. **1812** BYRON *Ch. Har.* I. lxxxiii. 7 And Vice..Had buried long his hopes, no more to rise. **1894** RALEIGH *Eng. Novel* ii, The literatures of Greece and Rome, rising from the grave.

5. a. To fall or set *upon*, to take hostile steps or measures *against*, one.

c **1000** *Ags. Ps.* (Thorpe) lviii. 1 Alys me fram laðum, þe me lungre on risan willað. *a* **1300** *E.E. Psalter* iii. 1 Fele rise ogaine me. *Ibid.* xvii. 43 þou..vnderlaide vnder me in me riseand. **1382** WYCLIF *Ps.* xvii. 49 Fro men risende in to me, thou shalt enhaunce me. *a* **1425** *Cursor M.* 12064 (Trin.), On ihesu roos þei alle bidene. **1567** *Gude & Godlie B.* (S.T.S.) 111 Quhen men rais in our contrairie. **1611** BIBLE *Eccl.* x. 4 If the spirit of the ruler rise vp against thee, leaue not thy place. **1653** MILTON *Ps.* lxxxvi. 49 O God the proud against me rise.

b. To make insurrection *against* (*on, upon*) one; to offer armed resistance; to rebel or revolt; to take up arms.

1154 *O.E. Chron.* (Laud MS.) an. 1135, For aȝenes him risen sona þa ricemen þe wæron swikes. **1338** R. BRUNNE *Chron.* (1810) 237 Edward wex fulle grim, whan he wist he [Llewelyn] was risen. *c* **1386** CHAUCER *Monk's T.* 537 The peple roos up-on him on a night For his defaute. **1415** HOCCLEVE *To Sir J. Oldcastle* 386 Ne neuere they..With wepnes roos to slee folk, & assaille. **1495** *Act 11 Hen. VII*, c. 7 Leders that unlaufully cause the seid people to gedre or rise. **1530** PALSGR. 692/1, I remember well ynough, whan the commens of Cornewall dyd ryse. **1593** SHAKS. *3 Hen. VI*, I. ii. 41 You Edward shall vnto my Lord Cobham, With whom the Kentishmen will willingly rise. **1667** MILTON *P.L.* VI. 136 Fool, not to think how vain Against th' Omnipotent to rise in Arms. **1781** J. MOORE *Italy* (1790) II. liii. 113 Subjects seldom rise through a desire of attacking. **1797** MRS. RADCLIFFE *Italian* xii, Do you know that every brother in the convent would rise to avenge it? **1855** MACAULAY *Hist. Eng.* xvii. IV. 16 The peaceful inhabitants ..rose on the soldiers. **1874** GREEN *Short Hist.* ii. §6. 85 The baronage seized the opportunity to rise in arms. *Ibid.* vi. §1. 274 Rouen rose against her feeble garrison.

fig. **1850** TENNYSON *In Mem.* cxxii. 2 When I rose up against my doom. **1858** M. ARNOLD *Merope* 46 Seek this [*sc.* hate]; revive, unite it, give it hope; Bid it rise boldly at the signal given.

6. a. *Mil.* To break up camp; to retire or draw off *from* (a siege).

a **1557** *Diurn. Occurr.* (Bann. Cl.) 32 Vpoun the saxtene day of Maij, the haill army raiss and come to Seytoun. **1617** MORYSON *Itin.* II. 109 The fifteenth his Lordship rose, and marching some fifteene miles, incamped in Evagh. **1665** SIR T. HERBERT *Trav.* (1677) 86 Sultan Perwes and Mahobetchan hasten..to relieve the Garrison e're the Rebels rose from before it. **1711** *Fingall MSS.* in *10th Rep. Hist. MSS. Comm.* App. V. 131 His Majesty commanded the camp to rise and return towards Dublin. **1736** DRAKE *Eboracum* 166 Not thinking themselves able to fight him and continue the siege, they resolved to rise.

b. Of a deliberative assembly or law-court: To adjourn, *esp.* for a vacation or recess.

1663 PEPYS *Diary* 2 June, The terme ended yesterday, and it seems the Courts rose sooner for want of causes than it is remembered to have done in the memory of man. **1675** MARVELL *Corr.* Wks. (Grosart) II. 487 After some time it was understood, that the Lords were rose without taking any consideration at all of our Conference. *a* **1757** E. MOORE in Dodsl. *Coll. Poems* (1782) IV. 281 Now the parliament's rising, and bus'ness is done. **1790** JEFFERSON *Writ.* (1859) III. 162 There is an idea that Congress will rise about the middle of July. **1837** LOCKHART *Scott* I. xi. 370 He had hurried up to town as soon as the Court of Session rose for the spring vacation. **1885** *Manch. Exam.* 12 Aug. 5/1 It was generally understood that Parliament will rise on Friday next.

†**7.** *to rise up to*, to show deference or respect to (some authority, opinion, etc.). *Obs.*

For examples of *rise to* in literal sense, see TO *prep.*

1621 BP. MOUNTAGU *Diatribæ* 520 Master Selden.. thought himself to be the only man with the great shadow, unto whom wee poore ignorants in Philology ought to rise up and rely on. **1624** —— *Gagg* 32 Prove them [*sc.* traditions] true, undoubted and we rise up unto them. **1699** BENTLEY *Phal.* 257 Who will not rise up now to this Gentleman's Opinion?

II. To ascend, mount up.

8. a. Of the heavenly bodies: To come above the horizon. Also *transf.* of daylight, darkness, etc.

c **1200** ORMIN 7273 We sæȝhenn itt full brad & brihht Æst, tær þe sunne riseþþ. *c* **1250** *Kent. Serm.* in *O.E. Misc.* 26 Tojanes þo sunne risindde. *a* **1300** *Cursor M.* 6751 If þe son be risen þan. *c* **1374** CHAUCER *Compl. Mars* 2 Loo Venus rysen amonge yow rowes rede! *a* **1400–50** *Alexander* 5055 Sone as þe day-rawe rase he risis vp belyue. **1508** DUNBAR *Tua Mariit Wemen* 471 ȝit haif I solace..quhill the sone ryse. **1560** DAUS tr. *Sleidane's Comm.* 105 Pourposynge whan the Mone rose, to take the towne of Tugie thereby. **1625** N. CARPENTER *Geogr. Del.* I. x. (1635) 223 With them a few starres are seen to set and rise. **1667** MILTON *P.L.* IV. 607 Till the Moon Rising in clouded Majestie,..unvaild her peerless light. **1712** BLACKMORE *Creation* IV. 207 Nor would the various Seasons of the Year, By Turns revolving, rise and disappear. **1771** *Encycl. Brit.* I. 486/2 Beginning at the moment when some star rose, and continuing until it rose the next following morning. **1832** HT. MARTINEAU *Hill & Valley* viii. 124 That morning rose fair and bright. **1875** JOWETT *Plato* (ed. 2) I. 109 He has come before the dawn had risen to testify his zeal.

fig. c **1200** ORMIN 7280 Crist iss ec..þatt sunnebæm þatt riseþþ aȝȝ I gode menness herrtess. **1388** WYCLIF *Mal.* iv. 2 To ȝou..the sunne of riȝtwisnesse schal rise. *c* **1550** *Sterne is rissin* in *Dunbar's Poems* (1893) 329 The Sterne of glory is rissyn ws to gyd. **1593** SHAKS. *Rich. II*, III. ii. 50 When this Theefe, this Traytor Bullingbrooke,..Shall see vs rising in our Throne, the East. **1736** *Gentl. Mag.* VI. 460/1 Dullness ..is a Thing of an uniform, fix'd Nature;..not rising and setting. **1781** COWPER *Table-T.* 560 Thus genius rose and set at order'd times. **1821** SHELLEY *Hellas* 195 Kings are like stars—they rise and set.

b. Similarly of other things, as vessels at sea.

1832 MARRYAT *N. Forster* xlvii, Her fore-yard is but now clear of the water, but she rises very fast. **1850** TENNYSON *In Mem.* xii. 11, I..reach the glow of southern skies, And see the sails at distance rise. **1861** C. READE *Cloister & H.* xxxviii, A company of mounted soldiers..rose to sight on the brow of a hill.

9. a. Of smoke, vapour, or the like: To ascend into the air, mount up. Also *fig.*

a **1300** *Cursor M.* 1644 O þair malice mai naman speke Til heuen þer-of it rises þe smeke. **1382** WYCLIF *Num.* xxviii. 24 The moost swete smel.., the which shal ryse of the brent sacrifice. *a* **1400–50** *Alexander* 1566 Sum with sensours.. Quare-of þe reke aromatike rase to þe welken. **1456** SIR G. HAYE *Law Arms* (S.T.S.) 26 Thare rais out a reyk. **1526** TINDALE *Rev.* xix. 3 And agayne they said: Alleluya. And smoke rose vp for evermore. **1604** E. G[RIMSTONE] *D'Acosta's Hist. Indies* II. vii. 97 For this reason the vapours rise not commonly in the night. **1667** MILTON *P.L.* XII. 630 As Ev'ning Mist Ris'n from a River o're the marish glides. **1765** GRAY *Shaks.* 22 From our works sublimer fumes shall rise. **1781** COWPER *Anti-Thelyphth.* 94 Hypothesis..Bade rise in haste a dank and drizzling fog. **1821** SHELLEY *Epipsych.* 470 From the sea there rise..clear exhalations. **1841** LANE *Arab. Nts.* I. 83 Upon this, the Efreet shook, and became converted again into smoke, which rose to the sky.

b. Of trees, etc.: To grow, in respect of height. Also with complement.

1601 DOLMAN *La Primaud. Fr. Acad.* (1618) III. 755 It cannot stand vpright..if it be not alwaies propped, at leastwise when it riseth neuer so little high. **1608** SHAKS. *Per.* I. iv. 9 Even such our griefs are;..like to groves, being topp'd, they higher rise. **1697** DRYDEN *Virg. Georg.* III. 823 Tisiphone..Every Moment rises to the Sight: Aspiring to the Skies. **1763** MILLS *Syst. Pract. Husb.* IV. 401 This tree seldom rises higher than from twenty to thirty feet. **1797** *Encycl. Brit.* (ed. 3) XI. 371/2 There are three species, all of them exotic trees,..rising near 20 feet high. **1885** *Ibid.* (ed. 9) XIX. 511/2 The American Aspen..seldom rising to a greater height than 30 feet.

10. a. Of the sea, rivers, or water: To increase in height, esp. through the tides or floods; to swell.

a **1300** *Cursor M.* 1425 Fra noe quen þe flod ras Til abraham. *Ibid.* 1767 þe see [gan] to ris, þe erth to riue. *c* **1425** WYNTOUN *Cron.* IV. iii. 200 þe rywere off Ewfrate Swa reithe þan risande was of spate þat he na mycht þe towne cum nere. *a* **1547** SURREY in *Tottel's Misc.* (Arber) 16 In grene waues when the salt flood Doth rise, by rage of winde. **1596** HARINGTON *Metam. Ajax* (1814) 119 He observed still that the deeper he sunk, the higher the water rose. **1617** MORYSON *Itin.* I. 66 When the river riseth, it..overfloweth the fields on both sides. **1667** MILTON *P.L.* XI. 824 Till inundation rise Above the highest Hills. **1719** DE FOE *Crusoe* I. (Globe) 50 The Tide rising and setting in to the Shore. **1776** SEMPLE *Building in Water* 47 The Water had rose only thirteen Inches. **1836** MARRYAT *Midsh. Easy* xxvi, The sun was obscured..and the sea was rising fast. **1890** WALLACE *Darwinism* 24 The river sometimes rose 30 feet in eight hours.

transf. **1535** COVERDALE *Jer.* xlvi. 8 It is Egipte that ryseth vp like the floude. **1819** SHELLEY *Peter Bell 3rd* IV. xxii, And wit, like ocean, rose and fell.

b. To attain to a greater height or size; to swell up; to puff out.

a **1425** *Cursor M.* 11120 (Trin.), Bi þis hir wombe bigon to rise. **1565** COOPER *Thesaurus* s.v. *Cresco, Mœnia crescunt*, the walles rise in heigth or are builded vp higher. **1607** TOPSELL *Four-f. Beasts* (1658) 517 All manner of grain.. and such things cause them to rise in flesh gratefully. **1650** BULWER *Anthropomet.* 82 All children are a little camoised about the Nose before the bridge riseth. **1691** T. H[ALE] *Acc. New Invent.* 103 It hath crack'd, flaw'd, and rose in ridges. *a* **1776** R. JAMES *Diss. Fevers* (ed. 8) 51 The blister.. rose well, and discharged plentifully. **1807** *Med. Jrnl.* XVII. 26 The only ones whose arms did not rise, were the two infants. **1843** R. J. GRAVES *Syst. Clin. Med.* ix. 102 Leaving the blisters..until they rise fully;..when risen it will not be necessary to cut them at once.

c. Of dough or paste: To 'work' or swell under leaven; to expand under heat. (Cf. RAISE *v.* 33 b.)

1548 ELYOT, *Fermentesco*, to..rise vppe by leauenyng. **1764** ELIZ. MOXON *Eng. Housew.* (ed. 9) 111 Mix all these together in a very light paste, set it before the fire till it rise. *c* **1860** *My Receipt Bk.* (ed. 2) 69 If the oven is too slow it will be deficient in colour, and not rise well. **1875** *Encycl. Brit.* III. 253/2 Generally in from four to five hours the sponge 'rises'.

d. Of fluids: To reach a higher level in a containing vessel. Hence of a thermometer or barometer in respect of the mercury in the tube.

1658 WILLSFORD *Nature's Secr.* 153 If the water..rises or falls a degree,..the weather will quickly change. **1679** MOXON *Math. Dict.* (1700) 23 Quick-silver in a Tube of Glass that Rises against fair Dry Weather. **1774** GOLDSM. *Nat. Hist.* (1776) I. 393 Resembling a gut filled with water, pressed with the fingers, to make the fluid rise, or fall. **1858** LARDNER *Hand-bk. Nat. Phil.* 224 The water continues to rise, until it passes through the valve. **1860** *Merc. Mar. Mag.* VII. 339 A barometer begins to rise..before the conclusion of a gale.

e. Of liquids, molten metal: To boil up.

1839 [see RISING *vbl. sb.* 9 b]. **1853** SOYER *Pantropheon* 274 Let the mixture rise three times, then take it from the fire. **1884** W. H. GREENWOOD *Steel & Iron* xviii. 424 The softer tempers of crucible steel rise or boil in the moulds after teeming.

11. Of the heart or emotions: **a.** To be elated with joy or hope; to become more cheerful.

c **1374** CHAUCER *Troylus* I. 278 Ther-with his herte gan to spede and rise. *c* **1375** *Cursor M.* 24489 (Fairf.), Mi hert began to rise & liȝt & my chere to amende. **1621** LADY M. WROTH *Urania* 397 Her heart rise a little in deluding hope. **1781** COWPER *Table-T.* 279 His spirits rising as his toils increase. **1891** R. W. CHURCH *Oxf. Movem.* 42 The correspondence shows..the way in which Froude's spirit rose, under the sense of having such a friend to work with.

b. To be stirred by excitement, *esp.* by indignation or passion (*against* a person or thing).

c **1325** *Song of Yesterday* 89 in *E.E.P.* (1862) 135 þe fest wol make his flesche to ris And drawe his herte to vanite. **1530** PALSGR. 692/2 As ones herte ryseth, whan there is a sodayne daunger towardes hym... My herte ryseth agaynst him. **1621** LADY M. WROTH *Urania* 375, I was in an Agony to see it, my bloud rise, and all my senses were sensible but of disorder. **1710** STEELE *Tatler* No. 247 ¶6, I feel all the Woman rise in me, when I reflect upon the nauseous Rogues that pretend to deceive us. **1746** P. FRANCIS tr. *Horace, Ep.* II. i. 103, I feel my honest indignation rise, When [etc.]. **1819** MACAULAY in Trevelyan *Life* (1890) 69 When I cease ..to feel my soul rise against oppression, I shall think myself unworthy to be your son.

c. Of the stomach: To nauseate or keck (*at* something). Also *fig.*

1508 DUNBAR *Tua Mariit Wemen* 163 A roust that is sa rankild quhill risis my stomok. **1602** SHAKS. *Ham.* v. i. 207 And how abhorred my Imagination is, my gorge rises at it. **1766**– [see GORGE *sb.*[1] 5 b].

12. a. To extend directly upwards or away from the ground; to exhibit successive superposition of parts; to form an elevation from the level.

c **1330** R. BRUNNE *Chron. Wace* (Rolls) 4577 Brod & þykke þe gynnynge was, & euere hit nareweþ rysande on heyght. **14..** *Sailing Directions* (Hakl. Soc., 1889) 21 Than go your cours..and ye shall not faile much of Stepilhorde; he risith all rounde as it were a Coppid hille. **1435** *Indenture Fotheringhey* in Dugdale *Monast.* (1846) VI. 1414/2 Abof the dore of the said stepill a wyndow rysing in hight al so high as the grete arche of the stepill. **1508** DUNBAR *Golden Targe* 34 On every syde the hegies raise on hicht. **1596** DALRYMPLE tr. *Leslie's Hist. Scot.* II. 135 In sindrie places he commandet to be erected gret kairnis of stanes, four square vndirneth,..ryseng vpe poyntlings lyke a steiple. **1610** HOLLAND *Camden's Brit.* (1637) 288 There riseth up an high mount. **1662** J. DAVIES tr. *Olearius' Voy. Ambass.* 159 At the foot of this Mountain there rises another. **1709** POPE *Spring* 37 Four figures rising from the work appear. **1770** GOLDSM. *Des. Vill.* 65 Along the lawn, where scattered hamlets rose. **1848** THACKERAY *Van. Fair* iii, A very stout, puffy man.. with several immense neck-cloths, that rose almost to his nose. **1874** GREEN *Short Hist.* iii. §4. 129 To the west of the town rose one of the stateliest of English castles.

fig. **1738** GRAY *Propertius* iii. 36 No mountain-structures in my verse should rise. **1779** SHERIDAN *Critic* I. ii, Each epithet rising above the other.

b. To have an upward slant or curve; to slope or incline upwards.

1634 MILTON *Comus* 306 What readiest way would bring me to that place? *Co.* Due west it rises from this shrubby point. **1726** LEONI *Alberti's Archit.* II. 10/2 If the plain be smooth.., not rising or sinking on any side. **1771** *Encycl. Brit.* III. 585/2 To make a ship go smoothly through the water, without pitching hard, her keel should be long, her floor long and not rising high afore or aft. **1839** MURCHISON *Silur. Syst.* I. xxxvi. 503 This anomalous appearance of the coal measures rising against, instead of dipping under the New Red. **1847** W. C. L. MARTIN *The Ox* 3/2 Horns..rising in a gentle curve directly up and out. **1865** G. MACDONALD *A. Forbes* 27 Looking up the lane, which rose considerably towards the other end.

13. a. To move or be carried upwards; to ascend.

c **1400** *Pilgr. Sowle* III. iv. (Caxton, 1483) 52 Thenne sawe I a wonderfull engyne of a grete whele, it roos oute of a litel dore, and torned doun at another. **1530** PALSGR. 692/1, I ryse a lofte (Lydgat), *je monte en hault*. **1606** SHAKS. *Tr. & Cr.* IV. v. 15 'Tis he, I ken the manner of his gate, He rises on the toe. **1667** MILTON *P.L.* I. 545 All in a moment..were seen Ten thousand Banners rise into the Air..: with them rose A Forrest huge of Spears. **1697** DRYDEN *Virg. Georg.*

III. 95 She rises in her Gate. **1754** GRAY *Pleasure* 17 Rise, my soul! on wings of fire. **1781** COWPER *Retirement* 655 The trumpet—will it sound? the curtain rise? **1842** TENNYSON *Locksley Hall* 80 Where the dying night-lamp flickers, and the shadows rise and fall. **1884** *Pall Mall G.* 6 Aug. 2 We rose about five times to the height of the Palace, and redescended.

transf. and *fig.* **1606** SHAKS. *Ant. & Cl.* II. iii. 16 Say to me, whose Fortunes shall rise higher, Cæsars or mine? **1712** ADDISON *Spect.* No. 420 ¶3 If we yet rise higher, and consider the fixt Stars as so many vast Oceans of Flame. **1790** COWPER *My Mother's Picture* 110 But higher far my proud pretensions rise.

b. Of birds: To take wing and ascend from the ground.

1528 LYNDESAY *Dreme* 112 With that thay rais, & flew furth out of my sycht. **1590** SHAKS. *Mids. N.* III. ii. 22 Russet-pated choughes..(Rising and cawing at the guns report). **1647** WARD *Simp. Cobler* 19 Young Spaniels, questing at every bird that rises. **1774** GOLDSM. *Nat. Hist.* (1776) VI. 54 The pelican..is slow of flight; and when it rises to fly, performs it with difficulty and labour. **1821** SCOTT *Pirate* xxxi, The grouse..rose in covey. **1852** TENNYSON *Ode Wellington* 119 Again their ravening eagle rose In anger. **1899** *Westm. Gaz.* 15 Dec. 2/2 The birds..in such places..offer far easier marks than when they rise in the woodlands.

c. *Typog.* (See quots.)

1683 MOXON *Mech. Exerc., Printing* xvi. 240 He knocks up the Quoins so hard, as that he thinks the Form may Rise. *Ibid.* xxiv. 389 A Form is said to Rise, when in Rearing it off the Correcting-stone no Letter or Furniture, etc. stay behind. **1888** JACOBI *Printers' Vocab.* 113 A forme is said to rise when it springs through bad locking up and the type gets off its feet. The term is also used when quadrats and furniture black in printing through imperfect justification.

d. Of food: To come up in the gullet; to repeat. *dial.*

1736 PEGGE *Kenticisms* (E.D.S.) 43 The radishes 'ride', i.e. rise upon the stomach. **1817** *Lintoun Green* v. vii, My paritch soon will rise!

e. *Mining.* (See quot.)

1802 MAWE *Min.* Gloss., *Rising*, a man working above his head in the roof, is said to be rising.

f. Of a horse in leaping. Also const. *to.*

1839 LEVER *H. Lorrequer* ii, Sir Roger when within two yards of the brink rose to it, and cleared it like a deer. **1856** 'STONEHENGE' *Brit. Rur. Sports* 409/2 Some imperfectly taught hunters are apt to get too close to the fence before rising.

14. a. To come up to the surface of the ground or water. Also with *out.*

1530 PALSGR. 692/1 It is a plesaunt syght to se the water ryse up or ryse out..out of a spring. **1560** P. WHITEHORNE *Arte of Warre* (1573) 102 b, They made a way under ground secretely, which risse in the towne. **1655** *Theophania* 4 If the mariners..had not been very speedy in giving him assistance..as he rise agen above the water. **1808** tr. *Lagrange's Chem.* I. 266 If muriate of soda and lime be boiled together, with water, the soda rises to the surface. **1816** BYRON *Parisina* vi, The breaking billow, Which.. dashes on the pointed rock The wretch who sinks to rise no more. **1862** S. ST. JOHN *Forests Far East* II. 41 A large alligator rose within three feet of the boat.

b. Of a fish: To come to the surface of the water to take a fly, bait, etc.

1653 WALTON *Angler* I. v. 127 He will sometimes rise at a dead Mouse, or a piece of cloth, or any thing that seemes to swim cross the water. **1674** N. COX *Gentl. Recreat.* (1677) IV. 18 All Flies are very good in their season, for such Fish as rise at the Fly. **1726** *Gentl. Angler* 154 Any Fish is said to Rise, when he endeavours to take a real, or artificial Fly on the Surface of the Water. **1787** BEST *Angling* (ed. 2) 24 When you see a fish rise near you, guide your fly over him immediately, and he's your own. **1867** FRANCIS *Angling* i. (1880) 33 If the roach are rising freely, it will be desirable to find out what they are rising at.

fig. **1863** G. A. LAWRENCE *Border & Bastille* iii. 54 The lady was a vehement Unionist, and 'rose', very freely, on the subject of the war. **1884** GRANT ALLEN *Strange Stories* 204 He rose to the fly with a charming simplicity. **1932** E. M. BRENT-DYER *Chalet Girls in Camp* xii. 193 'I *said* it to make Juliet rise—and she hasn't risen!' cried Jo. **1966** *Listener* 6 Oct. 507/2, I should perhaps apologise for having risen to the bait of Mr Wilkinson's provocative letter. **1974** 'J. LE CARRÉ' *Tinker, Tailor* i. 17 He knew they were teasing him but he was unable not to rise.

c. Of stone: ? To come out of the ground or quarry *in* a certain form.

a **1661** FULLER *Worthies* (1840) III. 125 Such alabaster is found in small bunches..: it riseth not (to use the language of workmen) in great blocks. **1793** SMEATON *Edystone L.* §200 Stone that naturally rises in flat beds, or that can easily be split to any thickness.

III. To attain to a higher stage or degree.

15. a. To ascend to a higher level of action, feeling, thought, or expression; to become more elevated, striking, impressive, or intense.

c **1200** ORMIN 6014 God mann riseþþ azz uppwarrd Inn alle gode dedess. *c* **1440** *Pallad. on Husb.* XIII. 84 Gramerci, Lord, that list..do me sumdel rise Thy self in hym to se. **1668** DRYDEN *Dram. Poesy* Ess. (ed. Ker) I. 88 Of this admirable plot; the business of it rises in every act. *a* **1685** ROSCOMMON (J.), Your author always will the best advise, Fall when he falls, and when he rises, rise. **1712** ADDISON *Spect.* No. 417 ¶6 Horace..always rises above himself, when he has Homer in his View. **1779** SHERIDAN *Critic* I. i, *Dang[le].* The interest rather falls off in the fifth [act]. *Sir Fret[ful].* Rises, I believe you mean, sir. **1836** *Random Recoll. Ho. Lords* 375 In any of the speeches I have heard him deliver, I could never recognise anything which rose above mediocrity. **1850** MCCOSH *Div. Govt.* I. i. (1874) 23 We shall rise beyond law to life, and beyond life to love. **1875** JOWETT *Plato* (ed. 2) IV. 6 There are not wanting thoughts and expressions in which he [Plato] rises to the highest level.

b. Const. *to* action of some kind; to prove equal *to* an occasion, demand, etc.

[*a* **1300** *Cursor M.* 27195 Quatkin strengh him draf þer-till, Quat..Did him to þat sin to rise.] **1817** JAS. MILL *Brit. India* II. v. viii. 681 They rise to the use of unlimited terms. **1850** ROBERTSON *Serm.* Ser. III. 173 We do not rise to philanthropy all at once. **1868** WHYTE MELVILLE *White Rose* vi, Rising, as he flattered himself, to the occasion. **1888** BURGON *Lives 12 Good Men* II. xi. 329 [He] rose to the requirements of his new sphere of duty. **1889** E. DOWSON *Let.* 12 Apr. (1967) 66 Limehouse won't produce a dinner but if you can stand it 'possibly my old Sonia's larder may rise'—not 'to the occasion' but to a scratch tea. **1906** G. B. SHAW *Let.* 7 May (1972) II. 622 The tenor..rose to the occasion and was bully. **1922** H. CRANE *Let.* 7 Dec. (1965) 107 This parodist and facile assessor could so gracefully rise to the occasion of a new attitude. **1952** M. LASKI *Village* ii. 38 Sheila had risen splendidly to the occasion and offered.. to wash up. **1975** *Harper's & Queen* May 138/2, I told my parents... It would be a mistake to say they were enthusiastic, but they *do* rise to the occasion.

16. a. To advance in consequence, rank, influence, fortune, or social position; to attain *to* distinction or power; to come *into* estimation. †Also with *up.*

1303 R. BRUNNE *Handl. Synne* 6042 Ful wykked ys þat coueytyse, with oþer mennes gode falsly to ryse. *c* **1386** CHAUCER *Monk's T.* 683 From humble bed to roial magestee Vp roos he, Iulius the Conquerour. *c* **1470** HARDING *Chron.* lv, By example of this kyng Caranse, through robbery resen of poore bloode to royall estate. **1534** MORE *Comf. agst. Trib.* III. xxiii, Some by handicraft, some by merchandise, some by other kind of living, rise and come forward in the world. **1562** J. HEYWOOD *Prov. & Epigr.* (1867) 56 Folke saie, better syt styll than ryse and fall. **1603** SHAKS. *Meas. for M.* II. i. 38 Some rise by sinne, and some by vertue fall. **1625** N. CARPENTER *Geogr. Del.* II. xiii. (1635) 205 Such men as haue risen to greatnes by their Wealth..sought out new pedegrees and Ancesters. **1701** W. WOTTON *Hist. Rome* 332 He rose..to be Advocate of the Treasury. **1738** *Gentl. Mag.* VIII. 41/1 When Rome was rising into pow'r. **1770** GOLDSM. *Des. Vill.* 148 More skilled to raise the wretched than to rise. **1801** STRUTT *Sports & Past.* I. iii. 36 Swift running horses of course rose into estimation. **1836** IRVING *Astoria* I. 31 He had risen from small beginnings to take his place among the first merchants and financiers of the country. **1865** TROLLOPE *Belton Est.* xi, He was..prudent, steady in his habits, a man likely to rise in the world.

fig. **1844** MACAULAY *Chatham* Ess. (1897) 774 Meetings, which at another time would have been harmless, now turned to riots, and rapidly rose to the dignity of rebellions.

b. To improve or go up *in* one's opinion, estimation, etc.; to grow *upon* one.

1633 FORD *Broken Heart* III. iii, May my duty Still rise in your opinion, sacred princess. **1780** S. J. PRATT *Emma Corbett* (ed. 4) II. 121, I have again beheld the source of my admiration... She rises every moment upon me. **1835** MACAULAY in Trevelyan *Life* 29 May, The character of Socrates does not rise upon me.

c. To increase one's speed. Const. *into.*

1814 J. AUSTEN *Mansf. Park* vii, They rose into a canter.

d. *to rise upon*, to be superior to. *rare*⁻¹.

1816 CRABB *Eng. Synonyms* (1826) 725/2 [The idea of] the word *Seem* rises upon that of *Appear.*

17. a. To increase in amount, number, or degree; to amount or reach *to.* †Also const. *to* with infin.

c **1200** ORMIN 11262 ȝiff þu takesst onn att an & tellesst forþ till fowwre, þa riseþþ upp þin tale anan Inntill þe tale off tene. *a* **1300** *Cursor M.* 5865 þai rise and bredes ai mare and mare, Bot wel mare if þai idel ware. **1596** SHAKS. *1 Hen. IV*, II. i. 14 [He] neuer ioy'd since the price of oats rose. **1623** CAMDEN *Rem* (ed. 3) 47 Achilles forsooth must needes vanquish Hector, because the numerall Greeke letters rose to a greater number in his name then in the others. *a* **1715** BURNET *Own Time* (1724) II. 222 That did not rise up to be treason. **1746** P. FRANCIS tr. *Horace, Sat.* I. ii. 24 His expenses, with his income, rise. **1776** ADAM SMITH *W.N.* I. xi. (1904) I. 247 It is not their nominal price only, but their real price, which rises in the progress of improvement. **1827** COBBET *Prot. Ref.* ix. §269 Under penalties, which rose at last to death itself. **1873** RUSKIN *Fors Clav.* xxix. (1906) II. 109 Let my poor housewife keep her sheep in her near fields ..and the weekly bills will not rise.

transf. **1705** ADDISON *Italy* 404 The Great Duke rises on 'em in his Demands, and will not be satisfy'd with less than a Hundred Thousand Crowns.

b. To become dearer or more valuable; to increase *in* price, value, etc.

1513-4 *Act 5 Hen. VIII*, c. 3 Preamble, Wolle is resyn of a farre gretter price then it was at the making of the said Acte. *a* **1548** HALL *Chron., Hen. VIII*, 166 b, Wheat was only at .xv.s. the quarter, & from thence it rose to .xx.s. **1677** YARRANTON *Eng. Improv.* 24 Then the Houses will rise in their Rents. **1691** LOCKE *Money* Wks. 1714 II. 74 'Tis said Bullion is risen to 6*s.* 5*d.* the ounce. **1712** ADDISON *Spect.* No. 414 ¶3 If the Products of Nature rise in Value, according as they more or less resemble those of Art. **1776** ADAM SMITH *W.N.* I. xi. (1904) I. 245 As gold rose in its price in proportion to silver,..so silver might rise in its price. **1804** G. ROSE *Diaries* (1860) II. 136 The Funds rose 1 per cent. on the news. **1848** THACKERAY *Van. Fair* v, Here's good news in the paper. Sugar is ris', my boy.

18. a. Of the wind: To increase in force; to become (more) vehement.

Not always distinguishable from sense 23 a.

c **1620** Z. BOYD *Zion's Flowers* (1855) 35 The tempest's riseing. **1662** J. DAVIES tr. *Olearius' Voy. Ambass.* 37 As they were weighing Anchor, the wind ris' so.., that the Master and his Counsel chang'd their design. **1736** POPE *Let. to Swift* 25 Mar., The winds rise, and the winter comes on. **1757** W. WILKIE *Epigoniad* v. 126 Command the winds in bolder gusts to rise. **1814** SCOTT *Diary* 6 Sept. in *Lockhart*, About eight the tide begins to run very strong, and the wind rising at the same time, makes us somewhat apprehensive for our boat. **1883** *Encycl. Brit.* XVI. 126/1 A breeze from the sea..which gradually rises to a stiff breeze during the heat of the day.

b. Of the voice, etc.: To increase in pitch or volume; to ascend in the musical scale (often with complement).

1548 ELYOT, *Ascendo*,..applyed also to the voyce when it mounteth or ryseth. **1565** COOPER *Thesaurus* s.v. *Vox*, *Excitare vocem*, to rise in speakyng by little and little. **1597** T. MORLEY *Introd. Music* 72 If the base rise or fall, you must not rise and fall iust as manie notes as your base did. **1674** *Playford's Skill Mus.* III. (ed. 7) 4 If your Bass should fall a seventh, it is but the same as if it did rise a second. **1730** *Treat. Harmony* 22 The Treble or Upper Part Rises a Fifth. **1748** J. MASON *Elocut.* 29 In a Climax, the Voice should always rise with it. **1818** SHELLEY *Rev. Islam* VI. xlii, The tones of Cythna's voice..rose and fell, Mixed with mine own in the tempestuous air. **1846** DICKENS *Battle of Life* i, His voice rising with his reasoning, so that it was very loud at last. **1879** E. PROUT *Harmony* ix, In both cases the bass rises to the third of the tonic chord.

c. To become more intense or strong; to increase in strength *to* a certain point.

1593 SHAKS. *Lucr.* 257 O, how her fear did make her colour rise! **1607** MIDDLETON *Michaelmas Term* III. i. 126 The fire is..but new kindled yet: if 'twere risse to a flame [etc.]. **1660** F. BROOKE tr. *Le Blanc's Trav.* 286 She felt something extraordinary, which made the colour rise in her face. **1820** SHELLEY *Cenci* III. ii. 12 As a dying pulse rises and falls. **1843** R. J. GRAVES *Syst. Clin. Med.* 177 At 7 p.m. we found that the fever was again rising. **1874** J. R. GREEN *Short Hist.* ii. §8. 104 In the presence of danger the courage of the man rose to its full height.

IV. To spring up, come into existence.

19. Of persons: To come upon the scene; to appear; to be born; to spring or issue *of* or *from* a person or family. Also with *up.*

c **1250** *Gen. & Ex.* 4152 Swilc prophete in folc of israel Ros non. **13..** *Cursor M.* 1199 (Gött.), Vr lauerd had ordained ȝeit A child to rise in his ospringe, þat all suld vte of baret bringe. *c* **1380** WYCLIF *Wks.* (1880) 272 False cristis schullen ryse. *c* **1425** WYNTOUN *Cron.* I. Prol. 100 As of angell and of man First to ryse þe kynd began. *c* **1449** PECOCK *Repr.* V. iii. 497 Aftir the daies of the Apostlis roosen also manye vntrewe sectis of Cristen men. **1563** WINȜET *Wks.* (S.T.S.) II. 50 Gif a prophet sal ryiss in the middis of thee. **1591** SHAKS. *1 Hen. VI*, I. iv. 102 One Ioane de Puzel .., A holy Prophetesse, new risen vp. *c* **1645** HOWELL *Lett.* (1650) II. 6 Unles he had rise up about the latter end of the last century. **1667** MILTON *P.L.* XII. 326 Of the Royal Stock Of David (so I name this King) shall rise A Son. **1711** ADDISON *Spect.* No. 111 ¶7 The several Generations of rational Creatures, which rise up and disappear in such quick Successions. **1746** FRANCIS tr. *Horace*, *Ep.* II. i. 26 No prince so great, so wise Hath ever risen, or shall ever rise. **1813** SHELLEY *Q. Mab* iv. 227 They rise, they fall; one generation comes... It fades, another blossoms.

20. a. Of plants or trees: To spring up; to grow.

a **1300** *Cursor M.* 1418 þe pipins war don vnder his tung, þar ras o þam thre wandes yong. **1460** *Pol., Rel., & L. Poems* (1903) 246 Lord! sende me sum 'amor' sede, In my gardyn to rote and ryse. **1577** B. GOOGE *Heresbach's Husb.* I. (1586) 37 b, Wherewith they wyll better seede, and sooner ryse. **1598** BP. HALL *Sat.* IV. iii, The Palme doth rifely rise in Iury field. **1667** MILTON *P.L.* x. 555 Imagining For one forbidden Tree a multitude Now ris'n. **1705** ADDISON *Italy* 1 Abundance of sweet Plants that rise naturally. **1763** MILLS *Pract. Husb.* II. 207 The plants rose well, and throve greatly before winter. **1823** *New Monthly Mag.* IX. 418/1 Potatoes of the early sort have risen exceedingly well.

b. Of blisters, etc.: To become prominent on the skin or surface.

1388 WYCLIF *Lev.* xiii. 2 A man in whos skyn and fleisch rysith dyuerse colour, ether whelke [etc.]. **1523** FITZHERB. *Husb.* §61 There is a blyster rysen vnder the tounge. **1586** G. WHITNEY *Embl.* II. 217 Like bubbles smalle that on the waters rise. **1611** BIBLE *2 Chron.* xxvi. 19 The leprosie euen rose vp in his forehead. **1643** J. STEER tr. *Exp. Chyrurg.* x. 44 If there be no blisters risen,..apply some Oyntment. **1697** DRYDEN *Virg. Georg.* III. 840 Red Blisters rising on their Paps appear.

21. a. To originate, to result or issue. Const. *of*, *from*, *out of.*

a **1300** *Cursor M.* 4351, I mai neuer mar be sund, Bot if mi bote mai rese [*v.r.* rise] o þe. *c* **1374** CHAUCER *Troylus* I. 944 She of whom rist al thy wo Here-after may thy comfort been al-so. **1526** *Pilgr. Perf.* (W. de W. 1531) 34 Eyther they ryse of some vayne curiosite aboute the secretes of god, or [etc.]. **1569** in Feuillerat *Revels Q. Eliz.* (1908) 126 Other ordinarie chardges rising by meanes of the said office. **1638** SHIRLEY *Duke's Mistress* v. iv, If there be few good women in the world, The fault risse first from one of our own sex. **1681** FLAVEL *Meth. Grace* xxiv. 421 Whatever rises from self alwayes aims at and terminates in self. **1732** BERKELEY *Alciphr.* VI. §7 Difficulties must be supposed to rise from different idioms. **1761** GRAY *Odin* 79 Tell me, whence their sorrows rose. **1810** CRABBE *Borough* xxiv. 408 But then from study will no comforts rise?

†b. To result or accrue *to* one. *Obs.*

1526 *Pilgr. Perf.* (W. de W.) 17 b, He hath ordeyned in euery temptacyon that is resysted great profyte therby to ryse to man. *a* **1548** HALL *Chron., Edw. IV*, 34 b, Perceiuyng the swete gaine whiche rose to him, by the abode of the two English Erles in his Countrey.

†c. To be based or founded *upon* something.

1530 PALSGR. Introd. 22 The consyderations..ryse nat upon a barbarous rudenesse. *a* **1548** HALL *Chron., Hen. VIII*, 131 Our liuing riseth on the gaine of our enemies.

d. To be produced or derived.

1549 LATIMER *1st Serm. Edw. VI* (Arb.) 40 A great market Towne..wher do rise yereli of their labours to the value of l. pounde. **1571** DIGGES *Pantom.* I. xviii. F j, Then multiplie 133 with 120, so ryseth 15960. **1615** W. LAWSON *Country Housew. Gard.* (1626) 9 Whatsoeuer can be said for the benefit rising from an Orchard. **1664** EVELYN *Sylva* 101 If in preparing the Hearth, at first, there did not rise sufficient turf and rubbish for this work, supply it from some convenient place neer to your heap. **1714** in Willis & Clark *Cambridge* (1886) I. 557 The said mony or any other that shall rise from the selling of timber.

22. a. To come to pass, come about, occur, happen, take place.

c **1200** Ormin 7203 Þe laþe gastess þeww Iss gramm.. whannse he seþ þatt Godess rihht & Godess laȝhe riseþþ. *a* **1300** *Cursor M.* 7657 Son efter þis a batail ras. *Ibid.* 21874 Hunger and qualm, and nede i-nogh In erth sal rise. **1382** Wyclif *Prov.* xxiv. 22 For sodeynli at ones shal rise the perdicioun of hem. *c* **1400** *Rom. Rose* 3115 Sir, it may not fall; That ye desire, it may not ryse. *c* **1470** Henry *Wallace* I. 44 Quharfor thair rais a full grewous debate. *a* **1548** Hall *Chron., Hen. VIII,* 75 b, Wordes rose betwene Mousire Chatelion & Richard Gibson. **1571** in W. H. Turner *Select. Rec. Oxford* (1880) 339 Yf it do happen.. any controversy to ryse. **1617** Moryson *Itin.* II. 245 That his Lp. might heare and compose the differences risen betweene them. **1671** Milton *Samson* 1254 Lest a question rise Whether he durst accept the offer or not. **1714** Addison *Spect.* No. 565 ¶2 A Thought rose in me which I believe very often perplexes Men of serious.. Natures. **1792** Mary Wollstonecr. *Rights Wom.* 292 This sentiment has frequently rose spontaneously in my mind. **1847** Tennyson *Princess* Concl. 23 Then rose a little feud betwixt the two.

b. To come *to* hand. *rare*$^{-1}$.

1590 Spenser *F.Q.* II. ix. 59 There chaunced to the Princes hand to rize An auncient booke.

23. a. Of wind, etc.: To begin to blow or rage; to get up. (Cf. 18 a.)

a **1300** *Cursor M.* 1762 Þe stormes rase on ilka side. *Ibid.* 22630 Windes on ilk side sal rise,.. fast gain oþer sal þai blau. *c* **1340** Hampole *Pr. Consc.* 4865 Þis fire þat thurgh þe world sal ryse, Sal com þan fra sere partyse. *c* **1400** *Ywaine & Gaw.* 337 A storme sal rise.. Al obout by est and west. **1456** Sir G. Haye *Law Arms* (S.T.S.) 52 Thare rais sik a tempest that nouthir.. had power to stryke a strake. *a* **1533** Ld. Berners *Huon* lvii. 194 A meruaylous tempest rose on the see. **1582** N. Lichefield tr. *Castanheda's Conq. E. Ind.* I. xli. 95 In a storme, that rose sodainly upon them. **1655** *Theophania* 10 There rise so great a wind, which came directly off from the Sea. **1728–46** Thomson *Spring* 114 If, brush'd from Russian wilds, a cutting gale Rise not. **1784** Cowper *Tiroc.* 25 At her [fancy's] command winds rise and waters roar. **1850** Tennyson *In Mem.* xv. 1 To-night the winds begin to rise And roar from yonder dropping day. **1887** Morris *Odyssey* XII. 326 And month-long no breeze at all Rose up o'er the sea.

b. Of sounds: To strike upon the ear, esp. in a loud manner.

13.. *K. Alis.* 2158 (Bodl. MS.), Now rist grete tabor betyng. **1375** Barbour *Bruce* x. 657 Than throu the castell ras the cry. **1508** Dunbar *Flyting* 227 Of laidis and lownis thair ryssis sic ane noyis. **1667** Milton *P.L.* XII. 56 Forthwith a hideous gabble rises loud Among the Builders. **1821** Shelley *Prometheus* I. 132 Ha, what an awful whisper rises up! **1852** M. Arnold *Empedocles* I. i. 84 In this clear mountain air, a voice will rise, Though from afar, distinctly.

c. Of reports, rumours, etc.: To come into circulation; to become current.

a **1300** *Cursor M.* 14000 Þe word o ihesu was risen brade. *Ibid.* 14362 Son oueral þis tiþand ras O lazar þat vpraisid was. *c* **1400** Maundev. (Roxb.) xxv. 119 Alssone as any rumour begynnez to ryse þat touchez þe emperour. *c* **1425** Wyntoun *Cron.* II. xvi. 1523 Sic nayme rase of þat ryal rowt þat landys seyr of þaim and dowte. *a* **1548** Hall *Chron., Hen. VIII,* 96 While the King and the Emperor loked on the letter, a sodein noise rose emongest both their subiectes, that it was a letter of defiance. **1596** Dalrymple tr. *Leslie's Hist. Scot.* v. 287 A rumour about this tyme rais in the cuntrie. **1859** Tennyson *Enid* 24 But when a rumour rose about the Queen, Touching her guilty love for Lancelot.

24. Of a river, etc.: To have its spring or source. †Also of a country: To begin.

1398 Trevisa *Barth. De P.R.* XIII. xi. (Bodl. MS.), Chobar is a ryuer of Babilonia and.. riseþ oute of Tigris oþer of Euphrates. *c* **1425** Wyntoun *Cron.* I. xiii. 1285 Italy.. risis at þe Alpis hie, And haldis on to þe Mekyl Se. **1495** *Trevisa's Barth. De P.R.* XIII. xi. 445 Gazan is a ryuer of the Medes and.. he risyth in the Eest and is receyued in the redde see. **1565** Cooper *Thesaurus, Oritur fons in monte,* a spring riseth in the hill. **1604** E. G[rimstone] tr. *D'Acosta's Hist. Indies* II. vi. 94 A branch of a river which they see rise and enter into the sea neare the banke. **1738** Gray *Tasso* 52 The birth of rivers riseing to their course. **1778** *Eng. Gazetteer* (ed. 2) s.v. *Parret,* It is joined by the Tone, or Thone, a pretty large river, rising among the hills in the western parts of this county. **1839** *Penny Cycl.* XIV. 4/1 The Tetney river rises from two springs. **1872** Raymond *Statist. Mines & Mining* 276 Rio San Carlos rises in the Sierra Blanca region.

25. a. To be built or reared.

1570–6 Lambarde *Peramb. Kent* (1826) 197 Of the Bridge I finde no beginning but I suspect that it rose by the Archbishops. **1610** G. Fletcher *Christ's Tri.* 78 In mid'st of this Citie cœlestiall, Whear the eternall Temple should haue rose. **1657** Howell *Londinop.* 30 After the erection of Christ's Hospital, which rise out of the ruins of the Grey Fryars. **1769** Gray *Installat. Ode* 53 Bad these awful fanes and turrets rise. **1784** Cowper *Task* v. 144 Silently as a dream the fabric rose. **1813** Shelley *Q. Mab* II. 127 Beside the eternal Nile, The Pyramids have risen. **1849** Macaulay *Hist. Eng.* iii. I. 289 Bastions and ravelins were everywhere rising. *Ibid.* 356 Streets and alleys which are still named after him were rising on that site.

fig. **1741–2** Gray *Agrippina* 121 On this base My great revenge shall rise.

b. (See quot.)

1641 Best *Farm. Bks.* (Surtees) 45 If the stookes rise thicke or rise well, i.e. if they stande thicke: for this is the usual phraise hereabouts.

26. a. To spring up, to come into existence, by growth or creation.

1601 Holland *Pliny* I. 41 The wealth is such of mettals and mines,.. so rich, so fruitfull, rising still one vnder another for so many ages. **1642** Fuller *Holy & Prof. State* III. iv. 158 Travell not too early before thy judgement be risen. **1745** *Trans. & Paraphr. Scot. Ch.* xxxvii, At once th' obedient Earth and Skies rose at his Sov'reign Word. **1781** Cowper *Retirement* 200 Oh nature! whose Elysian scenes disclose His bright perfections at whose word they rose. **1821** Shelley *Sonn. to Byron* 6 The mind which.. Marks your creations rise as fast and fair As perfect worlds at the Creator's will.

b. To come before the eye or mind.

1712 Addison *Spect.* No. 421 ¶7 He can.. make Scenes rise up before us and seem present to the Eye. **1780** Coxe *Russ. Disc.* 193 The prowess of Yermac.. rose upon their recollection. **1816** Byron *Ch. Har.* III. lxxviii. 6 His was not the love.. of the dead who rise upon our dreams. **1847** C. Brontë *J. Eyre* xiii, The subjects had indeed risen vividly on my mind. **1884** tr. *Lotze's Logic* 156 He who follows the directions.. must see the picture he is desired to form rise before his mind's eye.

V. *trans.*

27. †**a.** To rear or erect. *Obs. rare*$^{-1}$.

c **1425** *Cursor M.* 14755 (Trin.), Ȝif ȝe þis temple felle to grounde, I shal hit rise [*other MSS.* raise] in litil stounde.

b. To raise (the dead) to life. *rare.*

c **1440** Myrc *Festial* (E.E.T.S.) 206 Woldyst þou now of þi godnes ryse my wyfe to lyfe. **1754** Shebbeare *Matrimony* (1766) I. 109 Well knowing, that.. they could as well have.. risen the Dead, as have risen Two Thousand Pounds. **1839** Lever *H. Lorrequer* lii, The clatter of my equipage over the pavement might have risen the dead.

28. a. To rouse or stir up; to start; to put up or flush (birds); to cause to rise.

15.. *Adam Bel* ii, Where that men walke both east and west,.. To ryse the dere out of theyr denne. *Ibid.* xx, They rysed the towne of mery Carlel. **1562** *Child-Marriages* 108 The said Roger was the first that rysed this tale hym-self. **1677** Sedley *Ant. & Cl.* II. i, When raging winds rise tempests on the main. **1865** Atkinson *Prov. Danby, Rise,* to raise, cause to rise, flush or cause to.. fly, as a bird. **1882** Payne-Gallway *Fowler in Ireland* 36 Will some jealous shore-shooter fire to rise them. **1893** Gower *Surrey Gloss.* 33 He walked ever so far, and rose a blister on his heel.

b. *Angling.* To cause or induce (a fish) to come to the surface of the water. Also *fig.*

1850 Kingsley *Alt. Locke* vi, To rise a dean and two beauties at the first throw, and hook them fast. **1867** Francis *Angling* xii. (1880) 457, I killed three salmon and rose many more. **1892** *Field* 9 Jan. 41/1 At almost every cast I rose a fish.

29. a. To increase; to make higher or dearer. Now *rare* exc. *dial.*

1605 *Verstegan's Dec. Intell.* Commend. Verses, Beare on thy wings their glorie up on high, And rise the reputation by the same. **1740** W. Douglass *Disc. Curr. Brit. Plant. Amer.* 32 In France their recoinings.. did rise the price of Goods. **1796** Nelson 11 Sept. in Nicolas *Disp.* (1846) VII. p. cxi, The report.. making the people rise the price of provisions. **1892** *Standard* 4 Mar. 3/4 Lord Durham has risen the price of his coal 2*s.* per ton at the pitmouth.

b. *U.S.* To exceed in number or amount.

1838 'B. Smith' *Motley Bk.* 177 Brother George counted the strokes of his arm upon the cushion, and he thinks he rose a hundred in the course of the sermon. **1877** S. O. Jewett *Deephaven* 133, I like well enough to see a hog that'll weigh six hundred,.. but for my eatin' give me one that'll just rise three.

30. a. *Naut.* = raise *v.*[1] 24 b.

1669 Sturmy *Mariner's Mag.* I. ii. 18 We rise her apace; .. we shall be up with her in three Glasses. **1836** E. Howard *R. Reefer* xli, We had risen the [ship], so as to clear her broadside from the water's edge. **1842** Marryat *P. Keene* III. 22 Since she had tacked, she had risen her hull out of the water. **1890** Clark Russell *Ocean Tragedy* II. xviii. 99 We had risen the yacht to the line of her rail.

b. To raise; to lift up; to cause to ascend or mount up.

1706 Phillips (ed. Kersey), To *Rise the Tacks,* (in Sea-Language) is to slacken the Ropes call'd Tacks. **1776** Semple *Building in Water* 3 This high Tide.. rose the Water to such a prodigious Height. *Ibid.* 109 To rise or bank up the Bed of the River. **1839** Carleton *Fardorougha* v, My heart never was more ris to God. **1897** Ld. E. Hamilton *Outlaws* 28 The frost was rising the mist from the rain-soaked bent.

c. To cut (a caper) in the air. *rare*$^{-1}$.

1712 Steele *Spect.* No. 376 ¶2 She has seen him rise six or seven Capers together with the greatest Ease imaginable.

d. To promote (a person) in dignity or salary.

1801 Eliz. Helme *St. Marg. Cave* IV. 1 Instead of involving the friar in disgrace, I have risen him to honour. **1895** 'Rosemary' *Chilterns* iii, I'll rise you to £7 at the end of the first twelve months.

31. To surmount, to gain the top of (a hill or slope); to ascend. Chiefly *U.S.*

1808 Pike *Sources Mississ.* (1810) II. 197 Immediately afterwards, [we] discovered two horsemen rising the summit of a hill, about half a mile to our right. **1823** J. F. Cooper *Pioneer* v, A small hill was risen. **1841** Catlin *N. Amer. Ind.* liv. (1844) II. 165 He rises the last terrace and sweeps his eyes over the wide.. infinity. **1874** Kingsley *Lett.* (1877) II. 432 It will be cooler as we rise the prairies out of the Mississippi Valley.

32. To get, procure, obtain. Now *dial.*

1754 [see 27 b]. **1863–** in dialect texts and glossaries.

33. *colloq.* To raise or grow; to rear, bring up.

1844 Dickens *M. Chuzzlewit* xxii, Where was you rose? **1851** Mayhew *Lond. Lab.* II. 61/1 This process the catchers call 'rising' from the nest. A throstle thus 'rose' soon becomes familiar with his owner.

rise-head. (See quot.)

1834–6 Barlow in *Encycl. Metrop.* (1845) VIII. 718/1 Instead of employing a swift, the silk is stretched on two cylinders D, E, of tin or other material, technically called rise heads.

rise-heading. [f. *rise* rice *sb.*[1] + heading *vbl. sb.* 12.] (See quot. 1847.)

1847 *Instit. C.E., Min. Proc.* VI. 480 Between Dymchurch Wall and Dungeness Point, the method of 'rise-heading' was extensively adopted. It consisted of fascines.. strongly picketed down and secured by cross-laths. *Ibid.* 481 On the whole, rise-heading formed a good, and cheap.. defence. **1900** Beazeley *Reclamation of Land* 79 When the layers are horizontal the work is termed 'rise-heading'.

'risel. *dial.* Also ris(s)le, rishle, ristle. [a. ON. (and Icel.) *hrísla* (Norw. *risla*), f. *hrís* rice *sb.*[1]] A rod or stick, *esp.* one used as a support for climbing plants.

1882 *Jamieson's Dict.* s.v. *Risles,* In Ayrshire, a pliant rod or wand is still called a *rissle* or *rishle.* **1889** D. C. Murray *Weaker Vessel* 264 The healthiest hop or scarlet runner won't grow without what we call a risel in my part of the country. **1895–1901** in Staffordshire use (E.D.D.).

risen ('rɪz(ə)n), *ppl. a.* [f. rise *v.*]

1. ***risen (up)on,*** a diseased condition of horses or cows (see quots.).

1523 Fitzherb. *Husb.* §61 An other dysease is called rysen vpon and.. ye shall perceyue that by swellynge in the heed. .. There is a blyster rysen vnder the tounge, the whiche blyster must be slytte. **1886** *Chesh. Gloss., Risen on,* a peculiar swelling of the body of a cow, caused by a cold wind blowing upon her. **1888** *Sheffield Gloss.* s.v., A cow which has eaten too much grass, and become, in popular language, 'burst', is said to be *risen-on.*

2. That has risen, in the senses of the verb.

1821 Shelley *Hellas* 941 Victorious Wrong.. Salutes the risen sun. **1868** Morris *Earthly Par.* (1890) 170/1 Beneath the risen moon. **1870** *Athenæum* Dec. 797 The risen workman's advisers.

riser ('raɪzə(r)). [f. rise *v.* + -er[1].]

I. †**1.** One who raises or rouses. *Obs.*$^{-1}$

1388 *Prol. Wycliffite Bible* (1850) I. 33 Riseris of debate and of tresoun aȝens the king.

2. One who rises up, *esp.* from bed. Chiefly in collocations ***early (good), late riser.***

c **1440** *Promp. Parv.* 434/2 Rysare, *surrector.* **1577** B. Googe *Heresbach's Husb.* I. (1586) 14 b, This must cheefely be looked vnto.., that the Bailiffe be a good riser. **1580** Hollyband *Treas. Fr. Tong, Homme qui est matineux,* an early riser. **1612** Shelton *Quix.* I. i, He was an early riser, and a great friend of hunting. *a* **1631** Donne *Serm.* xix. (1640) 184 The first Rising, is the first Riser, Christ Jesus. **1710** Addison *Tatler* No. 155 ¶1 He was a very early Riser. **1862** R. H. Patterson *Ess. Hist. & Art* 363 We are no bad risers in the morning, but we never saw the sun rise on Midsummer-day but once. **1879** Lubbock *Sci. Lect.* ii. 41 Bees.. are very early risers, while ants come out later, when the dew is off.

†**3.** One who rises in revolt. *Obs.*

c **1420** *Contin. Brut* (E.E.T.S.) 370 A Squier of Walis þat was a rebell & a ryser. *c* **1460** Fortescue *Abs. & Lim. Mon.* (1885) 125 To represse and punysh riatours and risers. **1597** *State Papers, Dom.* 1595–7, 343 The risers were persuaded to go home. **1655** *Clarke Papers* (Camden) III. 38 The late Commission for tryall of the Northern Risers.

4. One who rises in fortune. *rare*$^{-1}$.

1592 Wyrley *Armorie* 14 It is a very vsuall matter for euery new Riser at this day.. to vsurp the same.

5. A fish that rises to an angler's fly or bait.

1867 Francis *Angling* v. (1880) 165 They are.. much freer and bolder risers. **1881** *Three in Norway* 123 All the fish, to whichever class of risers they might belong.

II. †**6.** (See quot.) *Obs.*$^{-0}$

Perh. an error for *rises:* cf. rice *sb.*[1] 4.

1688 Holme *Armoury* III. xxi. (Roxb.) 252/2 He beareth Azure a paire of Risers, Argent... This is a thing by which all your hanke silks are wound from their hankes vpon Bobbins.

7. a. The upright part of a step; the vertical piece connecting two treads in a stair. (Cf. rise *sb.* 12 b.)

1771 *Encycl. Brit.* I. 360/2 The manner of dove-tailing the riser into the step. **1825** J. Nicholson *Operat. Mechanic* 595 Divide the rod into as many equal parts as there are to be risers. **1858** *Skyring's Builders' Prices* 53 To measure stairs, take one step and riser the extreme width by the length. **1886** Morse *Jap. Homes* iv. 197 The front of the step is open,—that is, there is no riser.

b. *Geomorphol.* The steeply sloping part of each of the step-like parts of a glacial stairway or similar landform.

1930 F. E. Matthes *Geol. Hist. Yosemite Valley* 95/2 All the other steps in the upper Merced Canyon have risers and sills composed of very sparingly jointed or wholly massive rock. *Ibid.* 98/1 These steps.. have conspicuously sheer, smooth fronts, or risers. **1954** W. D. Thornbury *Princ. Geomorphol.* xv. 369 Each step [in a glacial stairway] typically has three component parts: a riser, a riegel, and a tread. **1974** *Encycl. Brit. Macropædia* XIX. 641/1 The establishment of runoff after wastage of the ice has occurred will lead to a series of waterfalls or cascades at the site of each riser in the stairway. **1975** C. Taylor *Fields in Eng. Landscape* iv. 90 The most characteristic features of strip lynchets are usually their steep risers, sometimes of considerable height.

8. *Mining.* (See quots.)

1846 Brockett *N.C. Gloss.* (ed. 3), *Riser,* a trouble or dislocation; the coal being so affected as to be above the level at which the seam is working. **1883** Gresley *Gloss. Coal-mining, Riser,* an upthrow fault.

9. *Founding.* (See quots.) Also = *feed-head* (see feed *sb.* 7).

1875 Knight *Dict. Mech.* 1946/2 *Riser*.., an opening through a mold, into which metal rises as the mold fills. A head. *a* **1890** *Sci. Amer.* LIX. 88 (Cent.), To obtain a sound casting in steel, with most methods in use, a very high riser is necessary. **1950** *Times Rev. Industry* Sept. 16/2 (Advt.), Risers act as reservoirs of molten metal to compensate for liquid shrinkage. **1967** A. H. Cottrell *Introd. Metallurgy* xiii. 184 The metal is poured into a sand mould through a gate, down a sprue and along a runner. A riser has also to be provided, leading upwards from the top of the casting, to provide a pool of molten metal to feed the casting as it freezes and shrinks. **1973** J. G. Tweeddale *Materials Technol.* II. ii. 36 Risers are vertical channels rising to the top of the mould, which help to control flow by trapping slag and in which the rise of metal in the mould and the progress of solidification can be followed.

10. *Printing.* 'Wooden or metal blocks for mounting stereo and other plates' (Jacobi).

1821 J. Fergusson *Brit. Pat. No. 4594.* 18 Oct., In the process of printing from stereotype plates the plates are put upon and fastened to certain materials or apparatus called by different names, such as blocks, matrix plates, risers, &c., which are made either of iron, brass, type metal,.. gypsum, wood [etc.]. **1841** W. Savage *Dict. Art of Printing* 702 *Risers*, the material upon which stereotype plates are fixed, in order to be printed. **1885** C. G. W. Lock *Workshop Rec.* Ser. iv. 223/2 It is a matter of convenience to cast the 'risers' or movable blocks for mounting plates, on the premises.

11. *dial.* The top bar of a stile.

1894 Blackmore *Perlycross* 85, I swore I would slash off any hand that was laid on the edge of the riser.

12. a. = *rising main* (b) s.v. rising *ppl. a.* 6; **riser diagram**, a diagram of the risers in a building.

1898 *Engin. Rec.* 26 Nov. 566/1 The grouping of risers has been made.. so that the average current demand on each pair of lighting bars will be about equal. **1924** T. Croft *Conduit Wiring* iii. 68 (*caption*) Riser diagram of conduit wiring in a hotel building. **1930** Moyer & Wostrel *Industr. Electr. & Wiring* v. 146 Wires and cables serving as main risers or feeders in buildings of fire-resistive construction, may be run bare.. under special conditions. **1967** G. A. T. Burdett *Electr. Installations* 36 Especially suitable for short runs and for individual risers from a main distribution board on the ground floor.

b. A vertical pipe for the upward flow of a fluid; *spec.* (*a*) one carrying water or steam from one floor to another in a central heating system; (*b*) one extending from an offshore drilling or production platform to the sea-bed, through which drilling may be done or oil or gas may flow. Also *riser pipe(line)*.

1908 A. G. King *Pract. Steam & Hot Water Heating* xi. 111 The riser or risers.. rise directly to the top floor or attic .. and here branch in the several directions necessary to feed the various drop risers supplying the radiators. **1941** *Nature* 15 Mar. 315/1 The tall 'risers', that is, vertical 5-in pipes which convey the water up to the projector nozzles, are spaced throughout the plantation as required. **1961** *B.S.I. News* Nov. 17/1 The code will recommend the installation of fire lifts and internal fire mains or 'risers' to assist firemen in applying water to a fire as early as possible. **1969** T. Stanley *More Small Bore Heating* ii. 77/3 The pipework is being run under.. the first floor with drops and risers to radiators on the ground floor. **1972** L. M. Harris *Introd. Deepwater Floating Drilling Operations* xii. 133 Selection of the riser-pipe steel is critical for a long-life, trouble-free operation. **1975** *Offshore Progress: Technol. & Costs* (Shell Internat. Petroleum Co.) 6 As the rig rises and falls with the heaving surface of the sea, the riser must be held in vertical tension in order to prevent it from buckling. **1977** *New Yorker* 9 May 38/1 Behind the riser pipe in the bathroom Puttermesser kept weeks' worth of Sunday *Times* crossword puzzles.

13. *Cricket.* A ball that rises sharply on pitching.

1955 *Times* 5 July 4/4 Shackleton could not draw away quickly enough from a riser from James and was acrobatically caught in the slips.

14. = *lift-web* s.v. lift *sb.*[2] 18.

1927 C. A. Lindbergh *We—Pilot & Plane* viii. 140, I left the ship head first and was falling in this position when the risers whipped me around into an upright position and the chute opened. **1975** tr. *Melchior's Sleeper Agent* (1976) iii. 230 When the [parachute] canopy is fully open you will swing under it... You will check the oscillation by tugging on the two risers in the direction of your swing... He grabbed hold of two of the webbed risers. **1976** L. Sanders *Hamlet Warning* (1977) xxix. 277 He pulled the ring, saw the silk deploy... He fought the risers, stopping his oscillation.

‖**'risgo(e.** *Obs. rare.* [ad. It. *risigo*, obs. var. of *risico*, or Sp. *riesgo*: cf. risco.] Risk.

1638 L. Roberts *Map Commerce* ccciii. 39 That parcell.. remaineth entirely upon the Risgoe, perill and fortune of the party that did accept the same. **1671** tr. *Frejus' Voy. Maurit.* 18 Not to desert this Business.. after having taken so much pains, and run so many risgo's for it. **1710** in *Edin. Rev.* (1893) Jan. 148 There were many and great risgoes to be run.

rish(e, obs. forms of rush *sb.*

†**'rishew.** *Obs.* Forms: 5 riss(c)hew, rissheu; ryssheue, rysschew, ruschew. [ad. AF. *russeau (pl. *russeaulx*: see below), var. of OF. *ruissolle*, etc.] A rissole.

[*c* **1400** *Chart. Barking Monastery* in Dugdale (1817) I. 443 For russeaulx in Lenton. *Ibid.* 445 Also sche must remembir russheaulx in Lenton.]

c **1420** *Liber Cocorum* (1862) 39 For rissheus. Take grounden porke.., Frye hit in grece. *Ibid.* 55 For the thrydde cours,.. Ryssheue and pome dorres. *c* **1430** *Two Cookery-bks.* 44 Kytte hem in þe maner of Rysschewes, & frye hem in freyssche grece. *c* **1450** *Ibid.* 97 Kutte hem, and so folde hem as risshewes, And fry hem in goode Oyle.

‖**rishi** ('rɪʃɪ). Also rishee, 8 Richi. [Skr. *ṛishi*, of uncertain etym.] An inspired poet or sage; a holy seer; an ascetic or saint.

1766 J. Cleland *Way to Things by Words* 91 The language of the antient *Richi*, or of the *Vedams*, is often hardly intelligible, even by the most skilful, who know only the *Sanscort*, fixed by the grammars. **1808** Colebrooke in *Asiat. Researches* VIII. 392 *note*, By *Rishi* is generally meant the supposed inspired writer; sometimes, however, the imagined inspirer is called the Rishi, or saint of the text. **1837** C. P. Brown *Sanskrit Prosody* 6 Such verses are.. used by a rishi or prophet. **1880** C. R. Markham *Peruv. Bark* 350 That magnificent peak,.. which is dedicated to their great Rishi and physician. **1916** [see jnana]. **1934** A. D. Waley *Way & its Power* App. ii. 114, I see no reason to doubt that the 'holy mountain-men' (*shêng-hsien*) described by *Lieh Tzŭ* are Indian *rishi*... It is at least a possibility that some knowledge of the *yoga*-technique which these rishi used had also drifted into China. **1939** *Antiquity* XIII. 15 The Aryan rishis sang their Vedic hymns. **1971** *Shankar's Weekly* (Delhi) 11 Apr. 22/2 Mythological stories of irate Rishis hurling curses at trespassers came to mind and every moment one feared our Rishi's wrath.

rishon ('rɪʃɒn). *Particle Physics.* [a. Heb. *ri'šôn* first, primary; cf. -on[1].] A hypothetical particle postulated as a constituent of quarks and leptons.

1979 H. Harari in *Physics Lett.* LXXXVIb. 84/2 The most economical set of building blocks consists of two $J = 1/2$ objects: one charged ($Q = 1/3$) and one neutral... We denote the charged particle by T and the neutral one by V. We name these particles 'rishons'. [*Note*] 'Rishon' means first, primary (in Hebrew). **1979** *New Scientist* 5 July 22/3 The charged leptons can consist of the three charged rishons (TTT) and the neutrinos of three neutral rishons (VVV), but the fractionally-charged quarks are made up of different combinations such as TTV or VVT. **1981** *Sunday Times* 1 Mar. 15/2 The latest theory reduces all the matter in the universe to just two kinds of basic particles. Its originator —Haim Harari of the Weizmann Institute in Israel—has named the particles *rishons*, from the Hebrew for primary.

‖**rishta** (riːʃ'tɑː). Also rishtu, reshta. [Tadzhik.] A local name in part of the Soviet Union for the guinea-worm (*Dracunculus medinensis*), a common parasite of man and other mammals, and the disease which it produces.

1834 A. Burnes *Trav. Bokhara* II. 180 Among the diseases of Bokhara, the most distressing is the guinea-worm, or Dracunculus, here called 'rishtu': it is confined to the city. The inhabitants believe that the disease arises from drinking the water of the cisterns in summer, when they become fetid and infested with animalculæ. **1885** H. Lansdell *Russ. Central Asia* II. liii. 146 What I had seen and been warned of in Samarkand, made me specially fearful of the *rishta*, a well-known disease in Bokhara. **1923** *Chambers's Jrnl.* July 472/2 The barber-surgeon trying to operate on a young man for 'rishta', that troublesome parasite which burrows into the skin. **1966** E. Schuyler *Turkistan* iv. 82 The Sarts are not only attacked by the usual maladies.. but they have besides two or three which are peculiar to the country... One of these is the *reshta*, or 'Guinea-worm'.

risibility (rɪzɪ'bɪlɪtɪ). [ad. late L. *rīsibilitas* (Boethius); see next and -ity. So F. *risibilité*, It. *-ità*, Sp. *-idad*, Pg. *-idade.*] The faculty of laughing; laughter; a disposition to laugh.

1620 T. Granger *Div. Logike* 55 Laughter, or risibility, is an effect by emanation of the reasonable soule. **1642** H. More *Song of Soul* Wks. (Grosart) 142 Some, who prove themselves men more by their risibility, then by their reason. **1709** *Tatler* No. 63 ¶5 Risibility being the Effect of Reason, a Man ought to be expelled from sober Company, who laughs alone. **1782** Miss Burney *Cecilia* v. i, His exalted post.. had moved the wonder and risibility of all the company. **1815** Scott *Guy M.* xx, He had himself some disposition to join her too obvious inclination to risibility. **1851** Hanna *Mem. Dr. Chalmers* IV. 66 He could never hear that peculiar dialect without his risibility being affected.

b. *pl.* The risible faculties. *U.S.*

a **1856** P. Cartwright *Autobiogr.* xii. (1858) 76, I had very hard work to keep down my risibilities. **1859** Hawthorne *Transformation* xliii, An Italian comedy,.. effective over everybody's risibilities except his own.

risible ('rɪzɪb(ə)l), *a.* and *sb.* [ad. late L. *rīsibilis*, f. *rīs-*, ppl. stem of *rīdēre* to laugh: see -ible. So F. *risible* (14th c.), Sp. *risible*, It. *risibile*, Pg. *risivel.*]

A. *adj.* **1.** Having the faculty or power of laughing; inclined or given to laughter.

1557 North *Gueuara's Diall Pr.* 80b, A creature the which, by nature, was sociable, communicable, and risyble. **1606** J. Carpenter *Solomon's Solace* xxxvii. 145 That honest and lawful ioy.. incident to mans nature, whereof, he is called a risible creature. **1654** Z. Coke *Logick* 123 A man is risible, and every risible thing is a man. **1731** A. Hill *Advice to Poets* Epist. p. x, What must risible Foreigners have thought of the Court of King William? **1771** Smollett *Humph. Cl.* (1806) VI. 51 He is the most risible misanthrope I ever met with.

2. Pertaining to, or used in, laughter.

1747 Richardson *Clarissa* (1811) I. 188 His muscles have never yet been able to recover a risible tone. **1754** *Connoisseur* No. 1 ¶3 He has gain'd such an entire conquest over the risible muscles, that he hardly vouchsafes at any time to smile. **1809** W. Irving *Knickerb.* (1820) 106 The Dutch negroes at Communipaw, who.. are famous for their risible powers. **1820** H. Matthews *Diary Invalid* (ed. 2) 451 The cricket was too much for his risible nerves. **1862** C. Stretton *Chequered Life* II. 134 So totally had he lost all control over his risible faculties.

3. Capable of exciting laughter; laughable, ludicrous, comical.

1727 Lady M. W. Montagu *Lett.* cxlvi. IV. 173 There is something extremely risible in these affairs. **1755** *Man* No. 6. 2 The risible subjects are either real or apparent absurdities. **1789** Burney *Hist. Mus.* III. x. 577 The jokes though not of the most.. refined sort are extremely queer and risible. **1824** J. Gilchrist *Etym. Interpr.* 107 Foreigners.. get laughed at as if they were guilty of some risible blunder. **1884** Birrell *Obiter Dicta* 194 The mental toilet of most of us is.. almost as risible as was that of this savage Court.

absol. **1784** *New Spect.* No. 7. 3 Exhibiting the serious and the risible in many points of view.

B. *sb. pl.* The risible faculties or muscles (see A. 2). Chiefly *U.S.*

1785 M. Cutler in *Life*, etc. (1888) II. 227 Your account .. has distorted my risibles and given my sides a hearty shake. **1866** *Athenæum* 864/3 His risibles were much affected. **1873** Whitney *Oriental & Ling. Stud.* 127 If the risibles of classical philologers are so easily provoked.

Hence **'risibleness**, 'laughing faculty' (Bailey, vol. II, 1727); **'risibly** *adv.*, 'in a risible manner; laughably' (Webster, 1847).

rising ('raɪzɪŋ), *vbl. sb.* [f. rise *v.*]

I. 1. Resurrection. More fully *rising again*, or *from the dead*.

c **1200** *Trin. Coll. Hom.* 81 He hem shewede fortocne bi ionan þe prophete.. of his riseng. *a* **1300** *Cursor M.* 17288 + 10 Ded men ros of þer graues.. and honoured his rising. *c* **1340** Hampole *Pr. Consc.* 3976 Þe thred es of þe rysyng generale Of alle men, bathe grete and smale. **1382** Wyclif *Matt.* xxii. 23 Saducees, that seyen there is no rysyng aȝein. *c* **1450** *Mirour Saluacioun* (Roxb.) 118 His deth and his rysing told he thaym or he went. **1509** Fisher *Funeral Serm. C'tess Richmond* Wks. (1876) 304 The bodyes of them that shall be saued, shall take at theyr rysynge agayne iiij. other excellent gyftes. **1573** Tusser *Husb.* (1878) 198, I hope and trust vpon the rising of the flesh. **1652** Gataker *Antinom.* 5 His rising from the ded. **1833** Tennyson *Palace of Art* 206 Then of the moral instinct would she prate And of the rising from the dead.

2. a. The action of getting up from bed; occasionally, the time of this.

c **1400** *Rom. Rose* 3821 He awakid Ielousy; Which, al afrayed in his rysing [etc.]. **1426** Lydg. *De Guil. Pilgr.* 22965, I kepe the howres off rysynge, To do worschipe vnto the kynge. **1513** More *Rich. III*, Wks. 41/2 At their rising in the dawnynge of the day. **1599** Shaks. *Hen. V*, iii. vii. 34 From the rising of the Larke to the lodging of the Lambe. **1760–72** H. Brooke *Fool of Qual.* (1809) III. 21 Fearing what might happen to me on the rising up of his wife. **1784** Cowper *Tiroc.* 765 Where early rest makes early rising sure. **1829** Lytton *Disowned* i. iii, My good wife only waits your rising to have all ready for breakfast. **1849** Macaulay *Hist. Eng.* iv. I. 506 His house at Kensington was sometimes thronged, at his hour of rising, by more than two hundred suitors.

attrib. *c* **1820** Rogers *Italy* (1839) 74 Ministers from distant Courts Beset his doors, long ere his rising-hour. **1896** A. Austin *England's Darling* ii. i, Ten score ambers have been lodged in the King's Barn, since rising-time.

†**b.** A levee. *Obs.*

1720 Mrs. Manley *Power of Love* (1741) I. 136 Signior Galen.. should go next Morning to the Duke's Rising. *c* **1729** Ld. Ailesbury *Mem.* (Roxb.) I. 70 The king being at Windsor, my father went out.. to the king's rising.

3. a. The action of standing up or getting on to one's feet from a sitting or reclining posture, or after a fall.

c **1440** *Promp. Parv.* 435/1 Rysynge vp fro sete, or restynge place, *surrexio, resurrectio. Ibid.*, Rysynge a-ȝene persone, for worschyppe, *assurrexio.* **1526** *Pilgr. Perf.* (W. de W. 1531) 145b, That rysyng & sekyng in the narowe lanes signifyeth yᵉ exercyse of vertues. **1576** Fleming *Panopl. Epist.* 248 He to whome all men ought in rising to reuerence. **1667** Milton *P.L.* ii. 476 Thir rising all at once was as the sound Of Thunder heard remote. **1711** Addison *Spect.* No. 12 ¶2, I was troubled with the Civility of their rising up to me every time I came into the Room. **1847** C. Bronte *J. Eyre* xvii, A soft sound of rising now became audible. **1869** Boutell *Arms & Armour* vii. (1874) 114 When once he had fallen to the ground, the knight would find the act of rising to be attended with no little difficulty.

fig. *a* **1300** *Cursor M.* 27048 Quen þai vn-mesurli ar radd Efter rising to fall egain. **1382** Wyclif *Luke* ii. 34 This is put in to the fallinge and in to the rysinge aȝen of many men in Israel. **1667** Milton *P.L.* ix. 1070 True in our Fall, False in our promis'd Rising.

b. The breaking up or adjournment of an assembly, esp. at the end of a session.

1700 *Pennsylv. Hist. Soc. Mem.* IX. 21 After the rising of this assembly, he determines to send the laws to England. **1740** Lady Hartford *Lett.* I. lv. 234 The rising of the parliament has very much emptied the town. **1825** Jefferson *Autobiog.* Wks. 1859 I. 10 On the rising of the House.. I happened to find myself near Governor W. Livingston. **1837** Lockhart *Scott* IV. iii. 80 Upon the rising of the Court in July, he made an excursion to the Lennox. *a* **1849** W. Wirt in J. P. Kennedy *Life* (1860) II. xiv. 228 About the time of the rising of Congress.

4. a. The act of taking up arms or engaging in some hostile action; an insurrection or revolt.

1398 Trevisa *Barth. De P.R.* ix. xxiv. (Bodl. MS.), In þe euetide for risinge of enemyes and of þeeues.. wecches and wardis beþ ikepte. *c* **1420** *Brut* (Caxton, 1482) 317 In this same yere.. ther were many heretykes and lollardes that had purposed to haue made a rysyng. *c* **1440** *Promp. Parv.* 435/1 Rysynge a-ȝen pees, *insurrexio, rebellio.* **1600** E. Blount tr. *Conestaggio* 148 To assure themselues against the rising of the people. **1655** *Nicholas Papers* (Camden) II. 343 Some lettres speake of an vniuersall risinge, and that London is vnquiett. **1722** in Payne *Eng. Cath.* (1889) 9 Prisoners on account of the unhappy Rising. **1761** Hume *Hist. Eng.* III. lxi. 326 A conspiracy was entered into.. and a day of general rising appointed. **1816** Scott *Old Mort.* xxxvi, Do you think that the rising upon that occasion was rebellion or not? **1855** Macaulay *Hist. Eng.* xiii. III. 328 There he held some communication with the Macdonalds and Camerons about a rising. **1874** Green *Short Hist.* iv. §1 A great rising of the whole people at last recovered some of this Norman spoil.

b. *rising-out* (see quots.). Now only *Hist.*

The Irish equivalent is *eirghe amach.*

1600 Dymmok *Ireland* (1843) 8 Risingout is a certain number of horsemen and kerne, which the Irishrie and Englishrye are to finde in her majesties service, at every generall hostinge. **1633** T. Stafford *Pac. Hib.* iii. xv. (1821) 380 What with Countrey risings out, and under Captaines in pay, two thousand of these were of Irish birth. **1867** D. MacCarthy *Life Florence MacCarthy* 459 The

MacCarthys of Gleann-a-Chroim..were not bound to attend the Rising out of MacCarthy Reagh.

II. 5. Of the heavenly bodies, day, etc.: Appearance above the horizon; the time or place of thus appearing.

a **1340** HAMPOLE *Psalter* xlix. 2 Fra þe risynge of þe sone til þe west, of syon þe shape of his fairhede. **1398** TREVISA *Barth. De P.R.* XVII. clxxv. (Bodl. MS.), þe furste..harueste & gaderinge þereof is aboute þe risinge of þe sterre Canis. *c* **1440** *Astron. Cal.* (MS. Ashm. 391), þe forseid nombres in Reed ye shul vnderstonde for þe risyng of þe sonne and of þe moone. **1535** COVERDALE *Job* iii. 9 Let it loke for light, but let it se none, nether the rysynge vp of the fayre mornynge. **1570** DEE *Math. Pref.* b iij, To learne the Risinges and Settinges of Sterres. **1611** BIBLE *Num.* ii. 3 On the East side toward the rising of the Sunne. **1667** MILTON *P.L.* IV. 641 Sweet is the breath of morn, her rising sweet. **1719** DE FOE *Crusoe* II. (Globe) 380 Pointing to the setting of the Sun, and then to the rising. **1760–72** H. BROOKE *Fool of Qual.* (1809) III. 70 On the rising of the day I saw a large town before me. **1828** MOORE *Pract. Navig.* 172 Which is to be counted from the east towards the north, because it is at the sun's rising. **1846** *Joyce's Sci. Dial.* xvii. 109 That the moon loses more time in her risings [etc.].

6. †**a.** The source of a river. *Obs.*$^{-1}$

1398 TREVISA *Barth. De P.R.* XV. lxxiii. (Bodl. MS.), In þe ende of este Inde aboute þe ryuer and risinge of Ganges beþ men wiþoute mouþe.

b. The gathering *of* a storm.

1848 DICKENS *Dombey* xlvi, How the light white down upon a robe had stirred and rustled, as in the rising of a distant storm.

7. a. The action or state of ascending; upward movement or course, ascent; an instance of this.

1458 in Turner *Dom. Archit.* (1859) III. i. 42 They reysid up the archeys be gemeotre in rysyng. **1593** SHAKS. *3 Hen. VI*, IV. iv. 22 For this I draw in many a teare, And stop the rising of blood-sucking sighes. **1608** WILLET *Hexapla Exod.* 113 Not..before winter..but toward the rising of the yeere. **1614** W. B. *Philosopher's Banquet* (ed. 2) 41 It will procure vnto them the rising of the Splene. **1642** R. BROOKE *Eng. Epis.* 116 At the first Rising out of Popery, the Churchlesse Church of the Albigenses..began an admirable Reformation. **1712** BUDGELL *Spect.* No. 277 ¶17 The various Leanings and Bendings of the Head, the Risings of the Bosom. **1768** GOLDSM. *Good-n. Man* IV, Then let us reserve our distress till the rising of the curtain. **1820** W. SCORESBY *Acc. Arc. Regions* I. 375 The rising of the mercury usually precedes the cessation of a storm. **1865** J. FERGUSSON *Hist. Arch.* I. 214 The only danger to be feared [in domes] is what is technically called a rising of the haunches.

attrib. **1688** HOLME *Armoury* II. 150/1 Neer side, or the Rising side, is the left side of the horse, which side Men get on the horse-back.

b. ***rising of the lights***: (see quots. 1772, 1894 and LIGHTS). Now *dial.* †***rising of the matrix*** (cf. MOTHER *sb.*[1] 12 b), hysteria. *Obs.*

1660 J. H. tr. *Basil. Valent. Chariot Antim.* 94 The best Treasure for allaying the Risings of the Matrix. **1665** M. N. *Med. Medicinæ* 48 Another Disease which the people term the Rising of the Lights. **1731** *Gentl. Mag.* I. (last page), The Diseases and Casualties this Year... Rising of the lights 37. **1759** BROWN *Compl. Farmer* 12 For the rising of the Lights. Take four ounces of turmerick in a quart of small beer. **1772** W. BUCHAN *Dom. Med.* (ed. 2) 681 In some parts of England, where I have observed it [*sc.* croup], the good women call it the rising of the lights. **1845** MCCULLOCH *Acc. Brit. Empire* (1854) II. 612 No commentator on the bills of mortality has been able to explain the great mortality attributed to *rising of the lights*. **1894** *N. & Q.* 8th Ser. VI. 516 In this district [round Coventry] a sense of fulness in the throat, accompanied by oppressed breathing,..is attributed to a 'rising of the lights'.

c. In dancing, an upward movement of the body caused by raising the heels from the ground.

1694 MOTTEUX *Rabelais* v. xxiv. (1737) 105 *Coupés*, Hops, Leadings, Risings. **1765** FOOTE *Commissary* II. Wks. 1799 II. 22, I would show you what I could do: one, two, three, ha. One, two, three, ha. There are risings and sinkings!

d. *fig.* An impulse or movement of an emotional nature; also, a physical feeling indicative of, or resulting from, this.

1726–46 THOMSON *Winter* 599 If doom'd..to repress These ardent risings of the kindling soul. **1766** FORDYCE *Serm. Yng. Wom.* (1767) I. vii. 286 It is difficult to repress the risings of indignation. **1852** MRS. STOWE *Uncle Tom's C.* ix, Gulping down..resolutely some kind of rising in his throat, and turning..round. **1863** GEO. ELIOT *Romola* xxvi, With a new rising of dislike to a wife who..might have the power of thwarting him. **1874** CARPENTER *Ment. Phys.* I. vii. (1879) 333 The patient may be led to cultivate her own power of repressing the first risings of..excitement.

8. Advancement in power, rank, or fortune. Also const. *up*.

1595 SHAKS. *John* I. i. 216 Yet to auoid deceit I meane to learne; For it shall strew the footsteps of my rising. **1609** HOLLAND *Amm. Marcell.* 325 The most miserable state of Rome citie under Maximinus the Præfect, whose parentage and rising is described. **1671** MILTON *P.R.* III. 201 Know'st thou not that my rising is thy fall, And my promotion will be thy destruction? **1712** STEELE *Spect.* No. 497 ¶1 Till the Order of Battel made way for his rising in the Troops. **1810** LAMB in Ainger *Life* (1882) 91 To give..some idea of the difference of rank and gradual rising I have made a little scale. **1863** *Sat. Rev.* 19 Sept. 383 There would be no rising in the world, no new blood, no fresh source of life and strength in society. **1942** W. S. CHURCHILL *End of Beginning* (1943) 145 People very often fall by the very means which they have used and built their hopes upon for their rising-up!

9. a. Increase in height of the tides or water.

1555 EDEN *Decades* (Arb.) 45 Of the rysynge & faulynge of owre Ocean Sea. **1705** ADDISON *Italy* 436 Forc'd to pay an unreasonable Exaction at every Ferry upon the least Rising of the Waters. **1797** *Encycl. Brit.* (ed. 3) XIII. 68/1 The connection of this celestial sign [the dog-star] with the annual rising of the river. **1865** KINGSLEY *Herew.* xxxi, William waited for the rising of the tide. **1871** —— *At Last* viii, The Mauritia palm-tree..affords the Guaraons a safe dwelling during the risings of the Oroonoco.

b. *Founding.* The boiling up of melted metal after it has been poured into the mould.

1839 URE *Dict. Arts* 320 This accident, called the rising of the copper, hinders it from being laminated. **1884** *Science* IV. 331 The rising of steel, and consequently the formation of blow-holes, is attributed to hydrogen and nitrogen, and to a small extent to carbonic oxide.

10. *Mus.* Increase of pitch.

1597 T. MORLEY *Introd. Mus.* 102 Here is also another waie in the tenth, which the maisters call *per arsin & thesin*, that is by rising and falling. **1674** *Playford's Skill Mus.* III. (ed. 7) 4 If the Bass do rise more than a fourth, it must be called falling: and likewise, if it fall any distance more than a fourth, that falling must be called rising. **1730** *Treat. Harmony* 36 Anticipation in Rising or Ascending, is the bringing in a Note upon the Unaccented Part of the Bar, in such a manner as that it has not yet its right Harmony. **1797** *Encycl. Brit.* (ed. 3) XII. 530/1 If we pass alternately from a third minor in descending to a third major in rising.

11. a. A part or thing standing out above its surroundings; a prominence or projection.

1577 B. GOOGE *Heresbach's Husb.* I. (1586) 29 Where wheate hath a clift, there hath it a rising. **1607** TOPSELL *Four-f. Beasts* (1658) 240 It is good to use your horse to backing.., as well from the plain ground as from blocks and risings invented for the ease of man. **1687** A. LOVELL tr. *Thevenot's Trav.* I. 26 In all the Halls and Chambers they have a rising half a foot or a foot high from the Floor, which they call Divans. **1730** A. GORDON *Maffei's Amphith.* 265 On the Border of the Wall there was a Rising..which served by way of Ornament and Fence. **1763** *Phil. Trans.* LIII. 171 On each side of the back there are two considerable sharp edged risings. **1774** GOLDSM. *Nat. Hist.* (1776) VII. 121 The head was long, and had a little rising at the top.

b. A morbid swelling; an abscess, tumour, boil. Now *dial.* or *U.S.*

1563 HYLL *Art Garden.* (1593) 158 The raw meat of the Gourd shred, and laid plaister-wise on swelings and hard risings of the flesh, dooth greatlie aswage them. **1606** HOLLAND *Sueton.* 74 Certaine hard risings of thicke brawnie skinne. *a* **1660** HAMMOND *Serm.* iv. I. (1850) 53 To prick the rising, and let out the putrid humour. **1834** W. SEWALL *Diary* 7 Dec. (1930) 160/1 Laid up with a bad rising on my hand. **1847** HALLIW., *Rising*, a small abscess, or boil. West. **1867** A. D. RICHARDSON *Beyond Mississippi* xi. 133 He spoke of a swelling upon his knee as a 'rising'. **1938** M. K. RAWLINGS *Yearling* xix. 236 None of us ain't got risin's. **1949** T. CAPOTE *Other Voices* v. 104, I had me a rising on my butt big as a baseball. **1972** E. WIGGINTON *Foxfire Bk.* 244 Scrape the white of an Irish potato and place the scrapings on the bump. Bind them on with a clean cloth. This will draw the risin' (boil) to a head.

12. a. The upward slope of a hill; a piece of rising ground; a hill or mound.

1565 COOPER *Thesaurus* s.v. *Cliuus, Mollis cliuus*, an easie rysinge of the hyll. **1591** SHAKS. *Two Gentl.* v. ii. 46 But mount you presently, and meete with me Vpon the rising of the Mountaine foote That leads toward Mantua. *c* **1630** RISDON *Surv. Devon* §46 (1810) 53 Richard Duke..built a..house upon the rising over the river. **1679** *Lond. Gaz.* No. 1420/3 In the mean time my Lord General..drew up upon the Rising. **1717** BERKELEY *Tour Italy* Wks. 1871 IV. 556 Nothing more than gentle hills or risings. **1782** PENNANT *Journ. Chest. to Lond.* 100 The situation is delightful.., with small risings on almost every side. **1836** F. SYKES *Scraps fr. Jrnl.* 99 Houses here and there peeping forth from risings. **1891** *Daily News* 23 Oct. 5/7 On the small risings and strips of still uncovered grass.

b. Gradual or direct increase in elevation.

1684 R. H. *Sch. Recreat.* 83 Observe..the Risings, Fallings, and Advantages of the Places where you Bowl. **1712** J. JAMES tr. *Le Blond's Gardening* 21 Gardens have no Risings, nor Fallings. **1725** W. HALFPENNY *Sound Building* 28 The Risings or Heighths of the Steps. **1771** *Encycl. Brit.* III. 585/2 A long floor-timber..not of great rising. **1797** —— (ed. 3) XVII. 378/2 Half breadth of the rising, is a curve in the floor plan, which limits the distances [etc.].

c. *Mining.* (See quot. and RISE *sb.* 10 b.)

1855 J. R. LEIFCHILD *Cornwall* 138 All excavations made horizontally are designated *drivings*, those directed downwards *sinkings*, and those upwards *risings*.

13. *Naut.* (See quots. *c* 1635 and *c* 1850.)

1627 CAPT. SMITH *Seaman's Gram.* ii. 6 Also the halfe Decke and quarter Decke, whereon the beames and timbers beare are called risings. *c* **1635** CAPT. BOTELER *Dial. Sea Services* (1685) 124 Which are these Risings? Those thick Plancks,..which go fore and aft, on both sides under the ends of the Beams and Timbers of the second Deck unto the third Deck. **1664** E. BUSHNELL *Shipwright* 21 Take off all the Risings, and mark them on the Rising Staffe. **1827** ROBERTS *Voy. Centr. Amer.* 178 Their risings consist of two planks from 16 to 18 inches broad. *c* **1850** *Rudim. Navig.* (Weale) 142 The Rising of Boats is a narrow strake of board fastened within side to support the thwarts.

Comb. **1664** Rising staff [see above]. **1769** FALCONER *Dict. Marine* (1780), *Tablette*, the rising-staff; a form, or scale, used by shipwrights when erecting the frames of the timbers. *c* **1850** *Rudim. Navig.* (Weale) 142 *Rising square*, a square used in whole moulding, upon which is marked the height of the rising line above the upper edge of the keel.

14. The action of raising. *rare*$^{-1}$.

1552 in W. H. Turner *Select. Rec. Oxford* (1880) 212 To cease theyr digging and rising of bancks in the sayd pastures.

15. a. *dial.* Yeast, leaven; a fermenting agent. Also *Comb.*, as (***salt-***)***rising bread*** (N. Amer.).

1594 LYLY *Mother Bombie* II. i. 117 My wits worke like barme, alias yest, alias sizing, alias rising, alias Gods good. **1668** WORLIDGE *Syst. Agric.* (1681) 331 *Rising*, Yeast or Barm, so called from the manner of its rising above the Ale or Beer. **1836** *Backwoods of Canada* 184 She must know how to manufacture hop-rising or salt-rising for leavening her bread. **1865** MRS. STOWE *House & Home Papers* 236 Salt-rising bread. **1875–** in dial. glossaries (Yorkshire, Norfolk, Surrey, Sussex). **1882** G. M. BARBOUR *Florida* iii. 56 The feast of hog, hominy, beef..and likely a few villainous compounds of flour, cheapest brown sugar, 'or sirup, and called *cake* or 'risin'-bread'. **1933** *Sun* (Baltimore) 3 Feb. 10/7 The Western correspondent..is talking about a foodstuff that resembles salt-rising bread..about as much as lady fingers resemble Russian black bread. .. Only a slight quantity of corn meal is used in the preparation of salt-rising bread. **1960** J. J. ROWLANDS *Spindrift* 172 The meat..was flanked by plates of moist and closely knit salt-rising bread. **1973** L. RUSSELL *Everyday Life Colonial Canada* viii. 96 'Salt-rising' bread was made without benefit of yeast.

b. *U.S.* The quantity of dough set to rise for a batch of bread.

1890 in *Cent. Dict.*

rising ('raɪzɪŋ), *ppl. a.* [f. RISE *v.*]

1. a. Having an upward slope or lie; elevated above the surrounding or adjacent level.

1548 PATTEN *Exped. Scotl.* E iv, Nie to a church..stondynge vpon a mean risyng hill sumwhat higher then the site of their campe. **1638** SIR T. HERBERT *Trav.* (ed. 2) 260 They..hale it to some rising hill without. **1677** HUBBARD *Indian Wars* (1865) I. 145 The Fort was raised upon a Kind of Island of five or six Acres of rising Land in the midst of a Swamp. **1683** MOXON *Mech. Exerc.*, *Printing* xiii. ¶3 File off the rising side of the Punch, which brings the Face to an exact Level. **1730** A. GORDON *Maffei's Amphith.* 266 This rising Place projected from the Wall. **1742** LEONI *Palladio's Archit.* I. 81 The Way..was a little rising in the middle, that no Water might stay upon it. **1793** MARTYN *Lang. Bot.* s.v. *Assurgens*, Rising up in a curve... A rising petiole,—rising leaves. **1807** GASS *Jrnl.* 41 Passed handsome rising prairies on the north side. **1826** A. BUTLER *Fragments* 147 Dost thou not see Another king..Pursue that rising road?

b. esp. ***rising ground***. (Freq. hyphened.)

1617 MORYSON *Itin.* II. 272 A rising grounde lying betweene the Campe and the Castle. **1686** tr. *Chardin's Trav. Persia* 68 The Castle upon the South Side stands upon a Rising Ground. **1736** DRAKE *Eboracum* 167 This being a rising ground the prince sent a party to dislodge them. **1781** COWPER *Hope* 46 The yellow tilth, green meads, rocks, rising grounds. **1839** THIRLWALL *Greece* IV. 423 An exhausted remnant..at length reached a rising ground. **1867** HOWELLS *Ital. Journ.* 189 Our horses were brought to a stand on a rising ground.

†**c.** Of the nose: Turned up, snub. *Obs.*

1709 *Lond. Gaz.* No. 4508/3 The said Margaret is about 25 Years of Age, long, lean and pale Visag'd, a rising Nose.

2. a. That ascends or rises; mounting.

1596 SHAKS. *1 Hen. IV*, III. i. 10 His Cheekes looke pale, and with a rising sigh, He wisheth you in Heauen. **1605** —— *Lear* II. iv. 122 Oh me my heart! My rising heart! But downe. **1667** MILTON *P.L.* IX. 75 And with it rose Satan involv'd in rising Mist. **1726–46** THOMSON *Winter* 2 See, Winter comes,..Sullen, and sad, with all his rising train: Vapours, and Clouds, and Storms. **1754** GRAY *Poesy* 40 O'er her warm cheek, and rising bosom. **1860** *Merc. Mar. Mag.* VII. 339 A gradually rising glass foretells improving weather if the thermometer falls. **1876** FREEMAN *Norm. Conq.* IV. 73 Norwich, with its newly rising castle, was put under his special care.

b. Of tides or water: Mounting, increasing in height. Also *fig.*

1697 DRYDEN *Virg. Georg.* I. 442 With a roaring sound The rising Rivers float the nether Ground. **1781** COWPER *Retirem.* 532 The rising waves..Thunder and flash upon the stedfast shores. **1817** SHELLEY *Rev. Islam* XI. x, As on a foam-girt crag some seaman tossed Stares at the rising tide. **1875** JOWETT *Plato* (ed. 2) III. 174 He would stem the rising tide of revolution.

c. Starting or springing up.

1728 POPE *Dunc.* IV. 426, I saw, and started from its vernal bow'r, The rising game.

3. Of the heavenly bodies: Appearing or emergent above the horizon. Also *transf.* (quot. 1610).

1610 SHAKS. *Temp.* V. i. 66 As the morning steales vpon the night..so their rising sences Begin to chace the ignorant fumes that mantle Their cleerer reason. **1667** MILTON *P.L.* III. 551 Spires and Pinnacles..Which now the Rising Sun guilds with his beams. **1709** ELIZ. SINGER *Love & Friendship* i, While..rising Night the Ev'ning Shade extends. **1794** MRS. RADCLIFFE *Myst. Udolpho* xv, The rising moon threw a shadowy light upon the terrace. **1816** SCOTT *Old Mort.* xliii, The beams of the rising sun, which glanced on the first broken waves of the Fall. **1860** TYNDALL *Glac.* I. v. 39 The moon..turned a pale face towards the rising day. **1896** A. E. HOUSMAN *Shropshire Lad* xliv, Right you guessed the rising morrow.

4. a. Increasing in degree, force, or intensity; advancing, growing.

1603 KNOLLES *Hist. Turks* (1638) 58 With which small victory contenting himselfe, as with the good beginning of his rising fortune, he returned backe againe into his kingdome. **1703** ROWE *Fair Penit.* I. i, A rising storm of Passion shook her Breast. **1703** —— *Ulysses* IV. i, Long I strove with rising Indignation. **1742** GRAY *Propertius* ii. 23 Riseing winds the face of Ocean sweep. **1808** SCOTT *Marm.* I. xvi, Lord Marmion..With pain his rising wrath suppress'd. **1849** MACAULAY *Hist. Eng.* iii. I. 341 The rising importance of Leeds had attracted the notice of successive governments. **1885** *Truth* 28 May 848/2 The poplars are bent by the rising wind.

b. Advancing in fortune, influence, or dignity.

1631 R. BOLTON *Comf. Affl. Consc.* (1640) 139 Had Paul addrest himselfe to have satisfied their curiosities, as many a rising, temporizing trenchar-Chaplaine would have done. **1672** MARVELL *Reh. Transp.* I. 64 They that perceived he was a Rising-man and of pleasant Conversation. **1709** STEELE *Tatler* No. 61 ¶15 'Tis natural for distant Relations to claim Kindred with a rising Family. **1761** HUME *Hist. Eng.* xxvii. II. 127 Thenceforward he was looked on at court as a rising man. **1835** BURNES *Trav. Bokhara* (ed. 2) III. 265 He is..the most rising man in the Cabool dominions. **1863** TREVELYAN *Compet. Wallah* (1866) 119, I know of no better company in the world than a rising civilian. **1889** JESSOPP

Coming of Friars v. 240 A pleasant little brief for a rising barrister to hold.

c. Increasing in pitch. Also, characterized by increase in vocal stress or a rise in pitch. Also *Comb.*, as ***rising-falling***.

1674 Campion *Music* 22 By rule, instead of the rising third, it should fall into the eight. **1876** *Encycl. Brit.* V. 656/1 The rising tone gives to the voice somewhat of the effect of an interrogation. **1879** E. Prout *Harmony* xi, The very rare reverse case.., the falling second and rising third. **1881** G. M. Hopkins *Lett. to R. Bridges* (1955) 40, I call *rising rhythm* that in which the slack comes first, as in iambs and anapests, *falling* that in which the stress comes first, as in trochees and dactyls. **1894** H. Sweet *Anglo-Saxon Reader* (ed. 7) p. xciv, There is a tendency to combine different types in a line, the falling types A and D being most frequent in I, while in II the rising types B and C are preferred. **1931** G. Noël-Armfield *Gen. Phonetics* (ed. 4) xiii. 69 These [signs] may be combined to showing falling-rising, rising-falling, and so forth. **1955** *Archivum Linguisticum* VII. 155 The Greek circumflex is not, essentially, a rising-falling accent. **1964** R. H. Robins *Gen. Linguistics* 111 Tones may ..rise or fall, or rise and fall, or fall and rise (rising, falling, rising-falling, falling-rising tones, respectively), and be distinguished by the actual direction in which the pitch moves. **1973** *Archivum Linguisticum* IV. 19 Typical sequences of tones..in which a final falling tone is preceded by a rising tone.

5. Coming into existence; developing, growing.

1667 Milton *P.L.* vii. 102 To heare thee tell His Generation, and the rising Birth Of Nature. **1697** Dryden *Virg. Past.* iv. 27 His Cradle shall with rising Flow'rs be crown'd. **1712** Addison *Spect.* No. 523 ¶1, I am always highly delighted with the discovery of any rising Genius among my Countrymen. **1750** Johnson *Rambler* No. 77 ¶14 The hopes of the rising generation. **1781** J. Moore *View Soc. It.* (1790) I. vii. 75 The rising vigour of Venice was permitted to grow. **1822** R. G. Wallace *15 Yrs. in India* 323 All the villages..appeared in a flourishing condition, with a numerous rising generation. **1870** Conway *Earthw. Pilgr.* xxvi. 311 The rising generation is sitting at the feet of men of genius who train it into antagonism to the Church.

6. Special collocations: **rising arch**, a rampant arch (Knight, 1875); **rising-board** (see quot.); **rising butt**, = *rising hinge*; **rising cupboard**, a kitchen-lift; **rising damp**, moisture absorbed from the ground into a wall; **rising diphthong** *Phonetics*, a diphthong in which the final vowel is more prominent; **rising floor** (see quot.); **rising front**, *Photogr.*, a camera front which can be elevated so as to reduce the foreground in a view; **rising hinge**, one which raises the door, etc., as it opens; **rising main**, (*a*) the vertical pipe of a pump; (*b*) an electricity main passing from one floor of a building to another; **rising rod**, part of the mechanism of a Cornish steam-engine (Knight, 1875); **rising seat**, one of a set of ascending seats, facing the congregation, in a Quakers' meeting-house; **rising strait, timbers, wood** (see quots.); **rising sun**: see sun *sb.*[1] 2 a.

1825 J. Nicholson *Operat. Mechanic* 88 There are other boards placed obliquely which extend..to the rim of the wheel, and nearly fill the space between one float-board and the next. These are called *rising-boards. **1866** *Tomlinson's Dict. Arts* I. 848/1 Mr. Redmund's hinges are termed *rising butts;..when the door is opened it is lifted up from the floor. **1833** Loudon *Encycl. Archit.* §1457 When the second description of *rising cupboard is used, it is necessary to have one for each floor. **1956** W. A. G. Bradman *Taking Care of Your Home* iv. 61 *Rising damp.. is invariably characterized by a line of dampness appearing above the skirtings. **1975** *Times* 30 Oct. 6/5 The walls had been sodden with rising damp for years. **1888** H. Sweet *Hist. Eng. Sounds* (ed. 2) 9 A '*rising'..diphthong. **1892** J. Wright *Primer Gothic Lang.* viii. 43 A diphthong may be defined as the combination of a sonantal with a consonantal vowel. And it is called a falling or rising diphthong according as the stress is upon the first or second element. **1960** P. H. Reaney *Orig. Eng. Place-Names* 45 In Devon, OE *ēa* frequently became a rising diphthong in ME and survives with initial *y*: Yalland, Yelland. **1846** A. Young *Naut. Dict.* s.v. *Floor*, The *Rising-Floors imply those floor-timbers which rise gradually from the plane of the mid-ship-floor, so as to sharpen the form of the vessel towards the bow and the stern. **1892** *Photogr. Ann.* II. 42 The *rising front is most useful when taking views uphill. **1807** *Trans. Soc. Arts* XXVI. 196 It obviates the necessity of screw *rising hinges. **1838** *Civil Eng. & Arch. Jrnl.* I. 189/2 Four pipes or *rising-mains, the lower end of each being connected with a valve-box. **1940** *Chambers's Techn. Dict.* 727/2 *Rising mains*, in an electrical installation, a mains circuit which runs from one floor of a building to another. **1967** G. A. T. Burdett *Electr. Installations* 37 Where conditions allow there are advantages in using purpose-made rising mains. *a* **1890** M. & C. Lee *Quaker Girl of Nantucket* 28 (Cent.), In the sing-song drawl once peculiar to the tuneful exhortations of the *rising seat he thus held forth. *c* **1850** *Rudim. Navig.* (Weale) 142 **Rising strait*, in whole moulding, a curve line in the sheer plan, drawn at the intersection of the strait part of the bend-mould, when continued to the middle at each respective timber. **1626** Capt. Smith *Accid. Yng. Seamen* 10 The flowre, the sleepers, *rising timbers, garble strake, her rake, the fore reach. *c* **1635** Capt. Boteler *Dial. Sea Services* (1685) 98 The Hooks placed on the Keel are named Rising-Timbers, in respect that according to the Rising by degrees of these Hooks, so the Rake..and the Run..rise by degrees from her Flat-floor. **1752** Chambers *Cycl.* s.v. *Ship* (plate) 60 The *rising or Dead Wood. *c* **1850** *Rudim. Navig.* (Weale) 142 The floor-timbers..are..raised upon a solid body of wood called the *dead* or *rising wood*.

rising (ˈraɪzɪŋ), *pr. pple.* [f. rise *v.*]

1. *Her.* Preparing for flight; taking wing.

1610 Guillim *Heraldry* iii. xx. 231 He beareth Azure, three Bustards rising, Or. **1688** Holme *Armoury* ii. 478/2 A Stork surgiant... This is by some termed a Stork rising, as having its Wings disclosed..and preparing for flight. **1868** Cussans *Heraldry* (1893) 95 *Rising*, or *Rousant*: about to rise, or take wing. This term is usually employed in blazoning Swans.

2. a. Of horses, and *transf.* of persons: Approaching (a given age).

1760–72 H. Brooke *Fool of Quality* (1792) IV. 23 By virtue of the same oath, [the horse was] four years old, rising five. **1789** Charlotte Smith *Ethelinde* (1814) V. 50 Before next grass, when you'll be rising twenty,..you'll make a match with Davenant. **1810** *Sporting Mag.* XXXV. 138 He [a horse] is now rising seven years old. **1853** 'C. Bede' *Verdant Green* i, Mr. Verdant Green was (in stable language) rising sixteen. **1863** Reade *Hard Cash* I. 11 Young Hardie, rising twenty-one, thought nothing human worthy of reverence, but Intellect.

b. Similarly with *to. rare.*

1789 *Trans. Soc. Arts* II. 82 Two bulls rising to three years old.

3. *U.S.* **a.** Fully as much as; rather more than.

1837 W. Jenkins *Ohio Gazetteer* 64 It enjoys a yearly income of rising $4,500. **1848** Bartlett *Dict. Amer.* (1859) 367 James Smithson bequeathed to the United States rising half a million of dollars. **1894** Winsor *Cartier to Frontenac* 298 Affairs in Canada, with a population that had grown to rising ten thousand, seemed to be going from worse to worse. **1895** *Outing* XXVII. 254/2 The enclosure contains something rising forty acres.

b. Upwards *of*, in excess *of*.

1817 Paulding *Lett. fr. South* II. 121 'How much wheat did you raise this year?' 'A little rising of five thousand bushels.' **1848** Bartlett *Dict. Amer.* (1859) 367 There were rising of a thousand men killed at the battle.

rising-line. (See quots. 1769 and 1841.)

1691 T. H[ale] *Acc. New Invent.* p. x, Whereas all Ships before..were built by rising Lines,..he built that by Horizontal ones. **1769** Falconer *Dict. Marine* (1780), *Rising line*, a name given by shipwrights to an incurvated line, which is drawn on the plane of elevation, to determine the height of the ends of all the floor-timbers throughout the ship's length. **1771** *Encycl. Brit.* III. 585/2 By this and a hollow mould, all the timbers are formed, as far as the rising-line. **1841** R. H. Dana *Seaman's Man.* 102 *Dead-rising*, or *Rising-line*, those parts of a vessel's floor, throughout her whole length, where the floor timber is terminated upon the lower futtock.

†**ˈrision.** *Obs.*$^{-0}$ [ad. L. *rīsio* (Plautus).]

1656 Blount *Glossogr.*, *Rision*, a laughing, a mocking, a scorning.

risk, *sb.* Also 7 resque, 7–9 risque. [a. F. *risque* (17th cent.), ad. It. *risco* (see risco and cf. risgo), *rischio*, of uncertain origin.]

1. a. Hazard, danger; exposure to mischance or peril. Freq. const. *of*.

α. **1661** Blount *Glossogr.*, *Risque*, peril, jeopardy, danger, hazard, chance. **1696** Vanbrugh *Relapse* i. (1708) 10 To cut my Elder Brother's Throat, without the Risque of being hang'd for him. **1740** Cibber *Apol.* (1756) I. 195 Till they had been assur'd they might do it without the risque of an insult to their modesty. **1793** Smeaton *Edystone L.* §103 The risque of which would have been prevented. **1808** Scott *Marm.* i. xxi, Little he loves such risques I know. **1862** Knight *Pop. Hist. Eng.* IV. 80 They knew how infinite were the risques of democracy becoming universal licence.

β. **1741** Middleton *Cicero* I. v. 353 Flaccus.. for my sake slighted the risk of his fortunes and life. **1784** Cowper *Task* iii. 705, I therefore recommend, though at the risk Of popular disgust,..The cause of piety. **1819** Scott *Ivanhoe* xxxviii, Several witnesses were called upon to prove the risks to which Bois-Guilbert exposed himself. **1849** Macaulay *Hist. Eng.* iii. I. 310 There would be great risk of lamentable change in the character of our public men. **1877** Mrs. Oliphant *Makers Flor.* i. 7 This extraordinary risk, from which the city..escaped.

b. Freq. in phr. ***to run a*** or ***the*** (also †*one's*) ***risk***. (Also in sense 2.)

α. **1665** Sir T. Herbert *Trav.* (1677) 293 Rather than run their resque or incur his displeasure they oft-times condescend to a reasonable mart. **1685** Burnet tr. *More's Utopia* 130 They consider the Risque that those run, who undertake such Services. **1717** Mrs. Centlivre *Bold Stroke for Wife* i. i, He that runs the risque deserves the fair. **1773** Mrs. Chapone *Improv. Mind* (1774) I. 154 You will at least have run no risque in the search.

β. **1728** Chambers *Cycl.* s.v., There is a great Risk run in letting Goods go upon Credit to great Lords. **1741** Middleton *Cicero* II. vii. 74 He must necessarily run the risk of many [battles] before he could gain his end. **1770** *Junius Lett.* xli. (1788) 230 If the jury run any risk of punishment. **1808** Scott in *Lockhart* I. i. 3 He lost all he had in the world, and..run a narrow risk of being hanged. **1843** F. E. Paget *Pageant* 38 Why am I to run the risk of scarlet fever being brought into the house? **1869** Freeman *Norm. Conq.* (1875) III. 162 It was no mark of wisdom..to run risks which might be avoided.

†**c.** A venturous course. *Obs.*$^{-1}$

1692 South *Serm.* (1697) I. 215 An insolent despiser of Discipline, nurtur'd into Impudence..by a long Risque of Licence and Rebellion.

d. ***at*** (or †*in*) ***risk, at high*** (etc.) ***risk***: in danger, subject to hazard. Also as *adj.* (See also sense 2 c.)

1901 'L. Malet' *Counsel of Perfection* xi. 243 Whether the capital owned by his better nature was not in risk of being exhausted—whether the drafts made on it might not eventually be dishonoured. **1965** *New Statesman* 10 Dec. 951/2 (Advt.), The appointment should be of interest to those who are prepared to assist in training child care officers and actively supervising casework of 'at risk' families. **1966** *Listener* 10 Feb. 199/1 It is necessary to know both the number of legitimate children born to women in this age-group and the number of married women at risk. **1972** *Daily Tel.* 5 May 6/8 Eight thousand historic churches in England are at risk through damage and decay. **1973** *Sci. Amer.* July 20/2 Women who were at high risk of bearing retarded infants. **1977** *National Trust* Spring 9/1 Soon nearly half our elms will be dead and the remainder all at risk. **1977** *Lancet* 23 July 203/1 The baby was considered to be at high risk.

e. A person who is considered a liability or danger; one who is exposed to hazard. (Freq. with qualifying word.)

1948 [see clearance 5 c]. **1954** *Manch. Guardian Weekly* 22 Apr. 3/1 A loyalty risk is a man whose paramount allegiance to the United States is in doubt. A security risk is one who may be consciously the most adamant patriot but whose judgment or tactlessness may cause him to make decisions or disclose information that could harm the national security. **1961** *Lancet* 12 Aug. 328/2 That patients classified as 'poor risks' according to Russek's criteria.. show a higher mortality-rate is no cause for wonder. **1976** W. Greatorex *Crossover* 32 He was frozen out... He was treated as a security risk..but it didn't bother him.

2. a. The chance or hazard of commercial loss, *spec.* in the case of insured property or goods. Also (freq. without article), the chance that is accepted in economic enterprise and considered the source of (an entrepreneur's) profit. ***all risks***: see all *a.* E. 13. Cf. uncertainty 4.

α. **1719** W. Wood *Surv. Trade* 239 To avoid the Loss or the Risque of having any Goods by him, out of Time. **1750** Beawes *Lex Mercat.* (1752) 261 A Contract or Agreement, by which one or more Particulars..take on them the Risque of the Value of the Things insured. *Ibid.* 284 He undertook a Risque of two or three Months only.

β. **1728** Chambers *Cycl.* s.v., The Risk of Merchandizes commences from the Time they are carried aboard. **1755** Magens *Insurances* I. p. vi, An Insurance made on Risks in Foreign Ships. **1776** Adam Smith *Wealth of Nations* I. i. x. 136 The ordinary rate of profit always rises more or less with the risk. **1846** Greener *Sci. Gunnery* 336 It seems strange such a thing should be, a contractor without a risk or duty. **1848** Mill *Pol. Econ.* I. ii. xv. 479 The difference between the interest and the gross profit remunerates the exertions and risks of the undertaker. **1880** *Encycl. Brit.* XIII. 163/1 Fire insurance as a business consists in undertaking a certain risk..in return for a comparatively small sum,..called the premium. **1921** F. H. Knight *Risk, Uncertainty, & Profit* ii. 41 The doctrine that profit is to be explained exclusively in terms of risk has been vigorously upheld. **1944** A. Cairncross *Introd. Econ.* vi. 76 The more fickle the demand, either from one season to another, or from year to year, the stronger will be the tendency to spread risks and steady production by diversifying output. **1977** B. Benjamin *Gen. Insurance* xi. 271 The mathematics of risk theory and of model building do not at present cover these kinds of business risks other than by incorporating past investment experience.

b. (See quot. 1841.)

1838 De Morgan *Ess. Probab.* 153 To find the mean risk of the sum or difference of any number of quantities determined by observation, add together the squares of all their mean risks, and extract the square root of the result. **1841** *Penny Cycl.* XX. 19/2 In the theory of Probabilities the risk of loss or gain means such a fraction of the sum to be lost or gained as expresses the chance of losing or gaining it.

c. *Law.* In phr. ***at*** (one's, etc.) ***risk***, of merchandise, etc.: at the liability of a stated party. Also of persons, liable to repay loss or damage.

1798 *Roots' Rep.* I. 203 If it eventually proves insufficient to raise the sum due, it is the mortgagee's own fault and at his risque. **1887** *Law Rep. Queen's Bench Div.* XVIII. 65 The expression 'at ship's risk' cannot be strictly correct, because the ship has no risk. **1970** *New Society* 5 Feb. 209/1 He therefore should be at risk where the car causes damage.

3. *attrib.* and *Comb.*, as ***risk aversion, -bearing, category, factor, level, management, -taker, -taking***; ***risk-free*** adj.; **risk analysis**, the systematic investigation and forecasting of risks in business and commerce; similarly **risk-benefit analysis; risk capital**, money that is put up for speculative business investment; **risk money**, (*a*) an allowance made to a cashier to cover accidental deficits; (*b*) = *risk capital* above; **risk profile**, a forecast of the probable range of hazards in an enterprise; **risk-rate**, a rate of interest related to a degree of hazard in an enterprise.

1964 *Harvard Business Rev.* Jan.–Feb. 95 (*heading*) *Risk analysis in capital investment. **1977** R. E. Megill *Introd. Risk Analysis* xvi. 173 In the search for new oil and gas fields, risk analysis takes the judgments of explorationists and engineers and translates them into the language of probability. Risk analysis, thus, helps a manager make reasonable decisions. **1964** W. S. Vickrey *Metastatics & Macroecon.* v. 88 The differential between long- and short-term interest rates thus requires both liquidity preference and *risk aversion to sustain it. **1972** *Accountant* 21 Sept. 349/2 Any application of probability theories to decision-making must have regard to the susceptibilities of the decision-maker, his own attitudes and those of his corporation—in particular, their 'risk aversion factor'. **1931** *Economist* 21 Nov. 957/1 The establishment of confidence, which would make possible a reduction of the premium on *risk-bearing. **1958** *Times Lit. Suppl.* 25 July 426/4 In discussing the reward of risk-bearing the author refers to the special information that some may have and to the riches of others, thus finding that 'risk-taking surpluses' accrue. **1975** *Physics Bull.* May 203/2 One fears that until recently no such *risk-benefit analysis would have been attempted. **1976** *Conservation News* Nov.–Dec. 3/1 On risk/benefit analysis, where many people hold that value judgements are involved, common ground seems impossible to find. **1948** *Sun* (Baltimore) 7 Apr. 19/1 He contended that newly saved *risk capital in 1946 and 1947 supplied only $700,000,000 of the $50,500,000,000 of new money required by American industry. **1962** *Economist* 19 May 693/1 'Incentives' have not been dulled and 'risk capital' has not dried up. **1976** F. ZWEIG *New Acquisitive Society* I. vii. 69 The old acquisitiveness provided long-term risk-capital for industrial development. **1973** *Sci. Amer.* Sept. 65/1 Women were assigned to one of four *risk categories. **1971** *Brit. Med. Bull.* XXVII. 23/2 Does the prevalence of individual *risk factors..differ between soft-water and hard-water areas? **1950** *Mind* LIX. 126 The 'reactionaries' are those who believe that scientific enquiries can proceed from *risk-free observational records immune from statistical tests. **1980** *Sci. Amer.* Mar. 33/3 People do not seek a risk-free society, but they do find it hard to manage risks that are not fully understood. **1962** A. BATTERSBY *Guide to Stock Control* iii. 28 We already have two possible figures... Why are these figures different from each other? Because they correspond to different *risk levels. **1970** *New Scientist* 15 Jan. 93/2 The risk-level of the former can be detected at interview. **1963** MEHR & HEDGES (*title*) *Risk management in the business enterprise. **1978** *Financial Rev.* (Austral.) 27 July 25/3 Risk Management, whatever you call it, is part and parcel of a big Insurance Broker's business. **1849** GILBART *Banking* (ed. 5) I. 262 To meet..deficiencies, some banks allow to each cashier a certain sum..which is called *risk-money. **1900** *Westm. Gaz.* 24 Nov. 2/3 He..was receiving £3 15*s.* a month and 3*s.* a week for risk-money. **1944** H. A. WALLACE *Century of Common Man* xiv. 70 A business man ought to be able to get his 'risk money' back before he has to pay too much in the way of taxation. **1969** *Daily Tel.* 29 Dec. 12/2 The oilmen are also aware that if the Gas Council is pushed further into exploration the Government will have to provide 'risk money' on a large scale. **1969** J. ARGENTI *Managem. Techniques* 233 When the forecast is made, an estimate of the probability of the range of errors is also made and this is used to calculate the '*risk profile' of the project. **1928** *Britain's Industr. Future* (Liberal Industr. Inquiry) III. xvi. 187 Capital will not be forthcoming for any enterprise unless it can expect (*a*) a normal rate of interest..and (*b*) in addition to that a '*risk-rate' corresponding to the chance of loss in the particular business; and this risk-rate must vary according to the conditions of every industry and of every concern. **1944** R. LEHMANN *Ballad & Source* III. 148 That is just a phrase the petty-cautious use against the fiery ones, the *risk-takers. **1957** A. C. L. DAY *Outl. Monetary Econ.* xxxviii. 491 Willing risk-takers (e.g. settlers in new countries). **1979** *N.Y. Rev. Bks.* 25 Oct. 49/2 McCagg's attempt is evidently to reconcile the sober wartime Stalin.. with the postwar risk-taker. **1921** F. H. KNIGHT *Risk, Uncertainty, & Profit* ii. 46 If risk were exclusively of the nature of a known chance or mathematical probability, there could be no reward in *risk-taking. **1936** J. M. KEYNES *Gen. Theory Employment* xxiv. 372 Diminishing unduly the motive towards risk-taking. **1948** *Sun* (Baltimore) 7 Apr. 19/1 Mr. Hooper..explained that eager risk taking by individual investors is essential to the smooth operation of the free enterprise system. **1975** 'E. LATHEN' *By Hook or by Crook* xiv. 132 'He's always taken big chances.'.. 'That's the risk-taking his children are alarmed about.'

risk, *v.* Also 7–9 risque. [ad. F. *risquer*, ad. older It. *riscare*, *rischiare* (now *risicare*, *arrischiare*), f. *risco* RISK *sb.*]

1. *trans.* To hazard, endanger; to expose to the chance of injury or loss.

α. *a* **1687** VILLIERS (Dk. Buckhm.) *Restoration* Wks. (1775) 7 Lately the King risqu'd both his kingdoms for offering to imprison Philander. **1709** STEELE *Tatler* No. 29 §2 One can scarce be in the most humanized society without risquing one's life. **1759** JOHNSON *Idler* No. 67 ¶2 To risque the certainty of little for the chance of much. **1790** BURKE *Fr. Rev.* 271 To risque the whole fortune of the state. **1811** L. M. HAWKINS *C'tess & Gertr.* I. 146 He should risque his lordship's favor for ever.

β. **1728** CHAMBERS *Cycl.* s.v., In Matters of Insurance, 'tis a Maxim, that all is never to be risk'd..in the same Vessel. **1741** MIDDLETON *Cicero* II. VIII. 164 He..was content to risk his reputation on the merit of it. **1757** W. WILKIE *Epigoniad* Pref. p. xxv, That no person could appear with advantage in military actions who risked nothing by doing so. **1816** SCOTT *Old Mort.* xxx, You are but losing your time, my friend, and risking your life. **1878** R. W. DALE *Lect. Preach.* i. 4 In the great affairs of life we can afford to risk nothing.

2. To venture upon, take the chances of.

α. **1705** STANHOPE *Paraphr.* II. 294 Risquing the loss of Heaven. **1723** GAY *Captives* Prol., I wish some author careless of renown Would without formal prologue risque the town. **1781** COWPER *Retirem.* 255 Yet let a poet.. Risque an intrusion on thy pensive mood. **1805** *Med. Jrnl.* XIV. 450, I did not think it prudent to risque a repetition of the introduction of the catheter.

β. **1790** BRUCE *Source Nile* II. 335 Nor had Emana Christos forces enough to risk a battle. **1803** *Med. Jrnl.* IX. 232 As men of eminence..sometimes risk hasty and incautious decisions. **1856** FROUDE *Hist. Eng.* (1858) I. ii. 91 The people..were prepared to risk the sacrilege of confiscating the estates of the religious houses. **1871** L. STEPHEN *Playgr. Eur.* (1894) viii. 188 For half an hour..we were risking sprained ankles across this..wilderness.

3. To venture to bring *into* some situation.

1760–72 H. BROOKE *Fool of Qual.* (1809) IV. 28 Would you risk our Angelica into such a fearful peril? **1781** COWPER *Conversat.* 371 We dare not risque them into public view.

4. *intr.* To take or run risks. *rare*$^{-1}$.

1766 tr. *Beccaria's Ess. Crimes* xxxiii. (1793) 127 Men risque only in proportion to the advantage expected.

Hence **'risking** *vbl. sb.*

1748 *Anson's Voy.* II. iv. 161 The risquing of twenty men, ..was risquing the safety of the whole.

'risker. [f. RISK *v.* + -ER[1].] One who risks something.

1678 BUTLER *Hud.* III. ii. 418 He..hither came t' observe and smoke What Courses other Riskers took. **1760** H. WALPOLE *Let. to Mann* 28 Aug., This risker [the King of Prussia] has scrambled another victory.

'riskful, *a.* [f. RISK *sb.* + -FUL.] Full of risk; hazardous, uncertain.

1793 PEARCE *Hartford Bridge* I. ii, The old gentleman is not very well; and what makes it rather riskful, he's attended by two physicians. **1844** LD. BROUGHAM *A. Lunel* II. iv. 92 They are..extremely averse to all that is adventurous, or riskful, even in..commerce. **1887** BARING-GOULD *Gaverocks* I. iv. 53 He took the shorter, riskful path up the cliff.

'riskily, *adv.* [f. RISKY + -LY[2].] In a risky or venturesome manner.

1874 HEATH *Croquet Player* 79 His partner will..begin to play badly, or else too riskily, in the hope of overtaking the better player.

'riskiness. [f. as prec. + -NESS.] **1.** The quality of being risky or hazardous.

1883 *Law Reports* 8 App. Cases 400 Considering the special riskiness of the particular matter the underwriters.. do not choose to be liable.

2. The quality of being *risqué*. Cf. RISKY *a.* 3.

1877 *Argus* (Melbourne) 5 Dec. 6/1 Mr. Albery..has so far brought it [*sc.* a play] to the level of English requirements that we have it now with its original humour, but freed from its accompanying riskiness. **1938** H. GRANVILLE-BARKER *Quality* 5 What rule would he [*sc.* Gilbert Murray] make for distinguishing a play written to exploit the mere riskiness of a subject and such a one as Ibsen's *Ghosts*.

'riskish, *a.* [-ISH.] Somewhat risky.

1864 CARLYLE *Fredk. Gt.* XV. xii. (1872) IV. 97 Brühl ought to comprehend better how riskish his game with edge-tools is.

'riskless, *a.* [f. RISK *sb.* + -LESS.] Free from risk or danger.

1865 *Pall Mall G.* 17 June 5 An invention which,.. wherever it has been used, has rendered ascent and descent riskless. **1893** *Pall Mall Mag.* II. 14 The descent,..though not riskless, was no great feat.

'risky, *a.* [f. RISK *sb.* + -Y.]

1. a. Dangerous, hazardous, fraught with risk.

1827 J. F. COOPER *Prairie* xii, 'Twill be a risky job, and one of small profit! **1858** *Times* 2 Dec. 6/3 The cause of human affairs [is] made very much more risky, when [etc.]. **1871** TYNDALL *Fragm. Sci.* (1879) II. xiii. 296 His experiment is a very risky one. **1890** 'R. BOLDREWOOD' *Col. Reformer* (1891) 127 The place being risky, and the night extra bad.

b. *Social Psychol.* Phr. ***risky shift***: in decision-making, the shift of opinion towards an option involving greater risk that may take place when responsibility for the decision rests with a group rather than an individual.

1964 M. WALLACH et al. in *Jrnl. Abnormal & Social Psychol.* LXVIII. 272/1 Group responsibility in the presence of group decision lead to a strong risky shift. **1967** KOGAN & WALLACH in *New Directions in Psychol.* III. 240 Risky shifts took place with high regularity for groups of both sexes. **1972** M. ARGYLE *Social Psychol. of Work* vi. 133 Whatever its causes the risky shift is clearly a source of unwise decisions in groups. **1978** LAMM & MYERS in *Adv. in Exper. Social Psychol.* XI. 149 Some researchers have used a rating scale (degree of preference for the risky vs. the cautious course of action). By and large, risky shift is obtained on items which elicit risky individual responses.

2. Venturesome, bold; audacious. *rare*$^{-1}$.

1826 J. F. COOPER *Mohicans* vii, I am no mortal if the risky devils haven't swam down upon the very pitch.

3. [After F. *risqué*.] Bordering upon, suggestive of, what is morally objectionable or offensive.

1881 *Daily News* 25 July 2/6 He has carefully eliminated all the risky Gallicisms to which..the Palais Royal artists gave such point. **1893** W. S. GILBERT *Utopia* II, The Chamberlain our native stage has purged..Of 'risky' situation and indelicate suggestion.

Risley ('rɪzlɪ). The name of Richard *Risley* Carlisle (d. 1874), U.S. gymnast and circus performer, used *attrib.* (and *absol.*) to designate an act in which a supine acrobat juggles another with his feet, as ***Risley act***, ***business***, etc. Also *transf.*

[**1843** *N.Y. Herald* 4 May 2/2 One of the chief attractions ..was Prof. Risley and his boy. **1846** *Illustr. London News* 7 Feb. 101/1 The very clever performances of Mr. Risley and his two sons continue to be nightly received with loudest acclamations.] **1861** H. MAYHEW *London Labour* III. 94/2 (*heading*) The Street Risley. *Ibid.*, There is but one person in London who goes about the street doing what is termed 'The Risley performance'. *Ibid.* 97/1 We've been continuing ever since at this Risley business. I lay down on a carpet, and throw then summersets from feet to feet. *Ibid.* 98/1 I've done the Risley in the streets of London. **1901** *Cassell's Mag.* Sept. 389/1 (*caption*) A Risley Pose. *Ibid.* 389/2 There will be a day when a Japanese is an underman and a young Westerner a top-mounter, or *vice versâ*; and we shall see a brilliant show of Risley act or juggling. **1912** M. B. LEAVITT *50 Yrs. Theatr. Managem.* xxv. 381 The second European 'hit' was made by Risley and his two sons, presenting the tossing and tumbling of the youngsters, to this day called the 'Risley Act'. **1931** *Amer. Mercury* Nov. 353/2 *Risley act*, one in which three acrobats lie on their backs and toss a fourth from one to the other. **1938** N. STREATFEILD *Circus is Coming* vii. 117 He told them about the first Risley who had the idea of juggling with a real boy. Of how the idea caught on, and that kind of performance was always known as a 'Risley act'. **1957** J. & A. DURANT *Pict. Hist. Amer. Circus* ii. 20 The 'Risley Act' (balancing with the feet while lying on the back) was performed by the Aztecs.

risme, obs. form of RIME *sb.*[1]

‖**risoluto** (rizo'luto), *a.* and *adv.* *Mus.* [It.]

†**A.** *adj.* (See quots.) Cf. RESOLVED *ppl. a.* 7. *Obs.*

1740 J. GRASSINEAU *Mus. Dict.* 19 *Canone partito*, or *risoluto*,..is when all the parts of a perpetual fugue are writ either in partitions, or different lines, or in separate parts, with the proper pauses that each is to observe, and therein differs from *Canone Chiuso*. *Ibid.* 204 *Risoluto*, resolved: thus we say a syncoped discord is *resolved*.

B. *adv.* With resolution or emphasis. (Used as a direction on a musical score.)

1837 J. A. HAMILTON *Dict. Mus. Terms* (ed. 4), *Risoluto* (Italian), with boldness and resolution. **1876** STAINER & BARRETT *Dict. Mus. Terms* 379/2 *Risoluto*,..with resolution. **1976** *Gramophone* Feb. 1337/3 Harrell enters with a confidence and firmness that may contradict the overall marking *quasi improvisando*, but which faithfully reflects the more specific *risoluto*.

risom ('rɪz(ə)m). Now *dial.* Forms: 5 risom, ressynn (?), 8–9 rissom, 9 rysom, rism, ris'm; 7 rizome, 8 riz-, razom, ruzzom, 9 rizzom, -um, -im. [Of Scand. origin: cf. Da. dial. *rusme* stalk (of oats), Sw. dial. *ressma* ear of corn (esp. oats).]

1. A stalk of corn; a head of oats. Also *attrib.*, as ***risom-head***.

a **1400–50** *Alexander* 3060 (Ashmole), þare fell as fele þam before..As risoms [*v.r.* ressynnys] in a ranke fild quen riders it spillen. **1688** HOLME *Armoury* II. 117/2 Rizomes, the spearsed ears of Oats in the Straw. A Rizome head, a chaffy sparsed head. *c* **1700** KENNETT in *MS. Lansd. 1033*, 325 b, A *Rizom*, a plume or bell or bunch of oats and such other corn, as does not grow in an ear. **1766** *Chron.* in *Ann. Reg.* VIII. 129/1 Most of the stems produced about two hundred and eighty grains, the razoms or ears being covered eighteen inches long. **1775** WATSON *Hist. Halifax* 544 *Ruzzom of Corn*, an ear of corn. **1814** PEGGE *Suppl. Grose*, *Rissom* or *rysom*, a stalk of corn. North. **1878** *Cumbld. Gloss.*, *Ris'ms*, straws left on the stubbles. **1888** *Sheffield Gloss.* s.v., A *rizzum* of straw is the same thing as a *rizzum* of corn except that in the former case the wheat has been beaten out of the ear.

2. *transf.* A particle, an atom.

1883 *Advt.*, *N. & Q.* (Cheshire) III. 28/2 We haven't a rism of bread in the house. **1897** 'F. MACKENZIE' *Sprays Northern Pine* iii, Here am I left withoot the seed o' siller, an' no' a rissom o' tobacco!

Hence **'risomed** *a.*, eared, headed.

1841 HARTSHORNE *Salop. Antiq.* Gloss. **1883** *Advt.*, *N. & Q.* (Cheshire) III. 28/2 The oats are rismed and cannot fail to yield well.

Risorgimento (rɪˌsɔːdʒɪ'mɛntəʊ). Also risorgimento. [It., = renewal, renaissance.]

1. The movement which led to the unification of Italy as an independent state with its capital at Rome in 1870.

1889 J. A. R. MARRIOTT *Makers Mod. Italy* II. 38 In 1847 Cavour, in conjunction with Santa Rosa, Cesare Balbo, and others, founded a new journal, named the *Risorgimento*, for the purpose of disseminating constitutional ideas of government. **1902** *Encycl. Brit.* XXIX. 628/2 Few dates in modern European history equal in significance that of 20th September 1870, when the Italian troops under General Cadorna took possession of Rome in the name of the Italian nation, and completed at one stroke..the work of the Risorgimento. **1902** G. MEREDITH *Let.* 15 Apr. (1970) III. 1436 Mazzini..never wavered in the faith he had that their sacrifices would lead to the Risorgimento. **1905** MRS. H. WARD *Marriage of W. Ashe* IV. xviii. 363 He had sat late with his hosts,—men prominent in the Risorgimento, and in the politics of the new Kingdom,—discussing the latest intricacies of the Roman situation and the prospects of Italian finance. **1910** W. H. GRIFFIN *Life Robert Browning* x. 158 The events of the *risorgimento*. **1933** *N. & Q.* 4 Mar. 161/2 The Risorgimento was..kept free from that violence of popular fury..which touches both the French and the Russian re-making of the nation with a sort of devilishness. **1937** A. HUXLEY *Ends & Means* x. 155 Before the Risorgimento the Austrians governed Italy by means of gendarmes, spies and *agents provocateurs*. **1955** *Times* 6 June 8/7 Count Alessandro Casati, one of Italy's elder statesmen and a true representative of the Italian liberal tradition of the Risorgimento, died on Saturday night. **1957** *Sunday Times* 8 Dec. 7/6 The Risorgimento heroes. **1961** *Listener* 19 Oct. 611/1 The partisan movement [in Italy] and the second Risorgimento which followed. **1977** *New Yorker* 2 May 101/1 Prosperity united Italy in ways the *risorgimento* never had.

2. *transf.* A revitalization or renewal of activity in any sphere.

1957 R. CHASE in *Partisan Rev.* Summer 369 The poetic *risorgimento* of Ezra Pound and his group. **1959** *Listener* 17 Dec. 1062/2 This has been more than an economic and industrial *risorgimento*. **1978** LD. BIRKENHEAD *R. Kipling* xv. 215 The lethargy and frivolity of his own countrymen, upon whom he now turned..his indignation in a passionate but vain attempt to inspire a *risorgimento*.

ri'sorial, *a.* *rare.* [f. L. *rīs-*, ppl. stem of *rīdēre* to laugh: see -ORIAL.] Risible.

1855 in OGILVIE *Suppl.* **1896** *Voice* (N.Y.) 24 Dec. 4 The zygomatic and risorial muscles of our mouth.

risorius (rɪs-, rɪ'zɔːrɪəs). *Anat.* [ellipt. for mod.L. *musculus risorius* (J. D. Santorini *Observationes Anatomicæ* (1724) i. 33), f. L. *musculus* muscle + *risor* laugher (f. *rīdēre* to laugh) + *-ius*, adj. suffix.] A muscle of facial expression running from the parotid fascia to the corner of the mouth, variable in form and sometimes lacking.

1829 J. & C. BELL *Anat. & Physiol. Human Body* (ed. 7) I. 279 [The Platysma myoides] terminates on the face and jaw. Some of its fibres, mounting over the bone of the jaw, are inserted near the depressor anguli oris; and others, a little higher on the face, are called *risorius santorini*. **1867** W. SHARPEY et al. *Quain's Elem. Anat.* (ed. 7) I. 176 The risorius or smiling muscle (Santorini), consisting of some very thin fasciculi,..joins the orbicularis and depressor anguli oris at the angle of the mouth. **1902** D. J. CUNNINGHAM *Text-Bk. Anat.* 377 The risorius is a thin flat muscle which forms partly a continuation of the platysma myoides on the face, partly a separate muscle, with an origin from the masseteric fascia. **1936** A. HUXLEY *Eyeless in Gaza* xviii. 233 The whole mechanism of the excruciating grimace, the upward and outward pull of the zygomaticus major, the sideways tug of the risorius. **1961** L. F. BROSNAHAN *Sounds of Language* iv. 80 This suggests again a cline in gene frequency, the decrease in the mean height running in the same direction through the African-European-Asiatic population as the increase in the frequency of the occurrence of the risorius muscle in the face.

† **risorse**, error for RECOURSE *sb.*[1] 2.

c **1374** CHAUCER *Boeth.* I. met. ii. (1868) 8 Wyche sterre in heuene vseþ wandryng risorses.

risotto (rɪ'zɒtəʊ). [It.] A stew or broth made with rice, chicken, onions, butter, etc. Also *Comb.*

1855 E. ACTON *Mod. Cookery* (rev. ed.) xxxii. 615 (*heading*) Risotto à la Milanaise. **1884** J. PAYNE *Tales fr. Arabic* II. 26 *note*, *Herais*, a species of 'risotto', made of pounded wheat or rice and meat in shreds. **1885** *Pall Mall G.* 7 Mar. 5 A useful description of how to cook risotto, a delightful dish too rarely seen in England. **1950** E. LINKLATER *Mr. Byculla* vi. 68 A Risotto Bolognese for one and threepence. **1960** *Housewife* May 91/1 My deep freeze usually contains..a risotto or two. **1981** E. DEWHURST *Trio in Three Flats* iii. 19 Cathy's asked me to supper..risotto and a complicated salad.

risp (rɪsp), *sb.*[1] *Sc.* Also 6 rysp. [Of obscure origin.] A species of sedge. Also *risp-grass*, the reed.

1508 DUNBAR *Gold. Targe* 56 Amang the grene rispis and the redis, Arrivit sche. **1513** DOUGLAS *Æneis* VI. vi. 72 Amang the fauch rispis harsk and star. *Ibid.* x. xii. 54 Amang the buskis rank of rysp and redis.

1823 HOGG in *Blackw. Mag.* XIV. 190 The hay-rope.. was made of *risp*, a sort of long sword-grass that grows about marshes and the sides of lakes. **1844** H. STEPHENS *Bk. Farm* I. 350 *Carex cæspitosa*, Risp. **1844** *Proc. Berw. Nat. Club* II. 108 A covering of fen-grasses.., 'rashers'..and 'risp-grass' (*Arundo phragmites*) from the..tracts around.

risp, *sb.*[2] Now *dial.* [Of obscure origin. Cf. Norw. dial. *rispa* a cluster of seed or flowers.] A bush, branch, or twig; a plant-stem, etc.

1590 *Tarlton's News Purgat.* (1844) 56, I see no sooner a rispe at the house end or a maipole before the doore, but I cry there is a paltry alehouse. **1598** FLORIO, *Boschétto*,..also a rispe, a lushe or lime twigge to catch birds.

a **1825** FORBY *Voc. E. Anglia*, *Risps*, the stems of climbing plants generally. The fruit-bearing stems of raspberries.

risp, *sb.*[3] *Sc.* (and *north.*). [f. RISP *v.* Cf. Icel., Norw., and Sw. *rispa* a scratch, score.]

1. A carpenter's file; a rasp.

1511–2 *Acc. Ld. High Treas. Scot.* IV. 272 For ane saw.. for the gunnis.., ane lang rispe,..and ane wisp of Lambart steile. **1623** *Naworth Househ. Bks.* (Surtees) 207 For 12 spads, 6 loks, 2 hatchits, on rispe. **1835** D. WEBSTER *Sc. Rhymes* 44 (E.D.D.), His throat's like a risp. **1843** *Proc. Berw. Nat. Club* II. 52 These balls..are exceedingly globular, although..finished by a large file or risp. **1885** STRATHESK *More Bits* iii. 42 That's liker a 'risp' than a razor!

2. A small serrated bar fixed upright on a house-door, with a ring attached, which was forcibly rubbed up and down the bar to attract the attention of those within.

1825 R. CHAMBERS *Trad. Edin.* (1869) 226 The Lord Justice-clerk's house was provided with a pin or risp, instead of the more modern convenience—a knocker. **1875** J. GRANT *One of the '600'* i, The little thatched cottages, with rusty antique risps on their doors. **1898** A. BALFOUR *To Arms* xvii, You will know the house by the risp on the door.

3. A grating or rasping sound.

1850 STRUTHERS *Life* Poet. Wks. I. p. xiv, The rusty risp of the Corncraik. **1868** G. W. THORNBURY *Greatheart* I. 195 The risp of the copper shovels full of sovereigns. **1897** CROCKETT *Lochinvar* I, Cutting them through with a pleasant 'risp' of sound.

risp, *v.* Now *Sc.* Also 5 rispe. [a. ON. *rispa* (also mod.Icel., Norw., and Sw.) to scratch, score, etc. Cf. Da. *rispe* to plough for the first time.]

1. *trans.* To rub; to grate together; to rasp or file. Also *fig.*

c **1440** *Pallad. on Husb.* XII. 570 First with hondis hem to gidre rispe; So let hem take in sonne a welowynge.

1807–10 TANNAHILL *My Mary* Poems (1846) 128 The rye-craik rispt his clamorous throat. **1818** W. MUIR *Poems* 14 (E.D.D.), Nor in the stable did he risp His teeth. **1892** LUMSDEN *Sheep-head* 17 Frae ilka horn [he] risps aff the 'rings' To ca' her young.

2. *intr.* To make a harsh, rasping, or grating sound.

1805 SCOTT *Last Minstrel* Note xlviii, Sutor Watt, ye cannot sew your boots; the heels risp, and the seams rive. **1834** A. SMART *Rhymes* 110 The craik rins rispin through the corn. **1894** LATTO *Tam. Bodkin* iv, Sharpin' his gullies, an' garrin' them risp on the glitterin' steel.

risposte, obs. var. RIPOSTE.

risque, variant of RISK *sb.* and *v.*

‖ **risqué** ('riːskeɪ, 'rɪskeɪ), *a.* Also risque. [Fr., pa. pple. of *risquer* RISK *v.*] = RISKY *a.* 3.

1867 'OUIDA' *Under Two Flags* II. iv. 121 She..sang..the most wicked and *risqué* of her slang songs. *Ibid.* viii. 207 It was..too simple, too little *risqué*. A child might do it. **1894** A. BEARDSLEY *Let.* *c* 3 Jan. (1970) 61 Our idea [in starting *The Yellow Book*] is that many brilliant story painters and picture writers cannot get their best stuff accepted in the conventional magazine, either because they are not topical or perhaps a little risqué. **1899** J. LONDON *Let.* 30 Mar. (1966) 26 Our magazines are so goody-goody, that I wonder they would permit a thing as risque and as good as that. **1913** E. POUND *Let.* 30 Mar. (1971) 18 Again to your note: 'Risqué.' Now really!!! Do you apply that term to all nude statuary? I admit the verse 'To Another Man on his Wife' might deserve it, but you're not including that. Surely you don't regard the Elizabethans as 'risqué'? **1924** *Brit. Weekly* 18 Dec. 301/3 In remote corners others are reading *risqué* novels with a sex interest. **1952** *Scrutiny* XVIII. 317 Not infrequently Mr. Auden seems to be trying to atone for this by indulging in slightly *risqués* side-glances. **1962** V. CONNAUGHT *Secret Heart of Princess Alexandra* i. 15 She enjoys a good joke, even if it is a little risqué, provided it is well told. **1975** *Country Life* 25 Dec. 1804/1 Directors were turning out sophisticated, risqué social comedies.

Riss (rɪs). *Geol.* The name of a tributary of the Isar in Austria and Germany, adopted by A. Penck (in Penck & Brückner *Die Alpen im Eiszeitalter* (1909) I. I. 110) and used *attrib.* to designate the third (penultimate) Pleistocene glaciation in the Alps, and in conjunction with WÜRM to designate the following interglacial period. Also *absol.*

1910 *Zeitschr. f. Gletscherkunde* IV. 244 The interval between the Riss and the Würm.., the Riss-Würm interglacial stage. *Ibid.*, The moderate erosion..which the Riss drift has experienced. **1927** [see MOUSTERIAN, MOUSTIERIAN *a.* and *sb.*]. **1931** *Discovery* Sept. 282/2 The fluvio-lacustrine deposits, rich in volcanic elements, of the Tiber Valley, which Roman geologists hold to be contemporary with the warm interglacial period intervening between the Riss and the Würm glaciations of the European Ice Age. **1944** A. HOLMES *Princ. Physical Geol.* xii. 247 The depth reached by weathering during Riss-Würm time is found to be about three times that achieved on similar but later deposits exposed during post-Würm time. Since the latter is about 25,000 years, it follows that the Riss-Würm interval cannot have been less than 75,000 years. **1968** R. W. FAIRBRIDGE *Encycl. Geomorphol.* 335/1 There appears to be unanimity that during the Last Interglacial (Riss-Würm or Sangamon) there were sea-levels of the order of 7·5 meters ..and 3·5 meters..higher than the present. **1971** *Nature* 22 Jan. 253/2 It is now recognized that the species *Homo sapiens* is of at least Riss age. **1974** *Sci. Amer.* June 96/1 The next to last major advance, known to scholars as the Penultimate Glacial (Riss II in the Alpine sequence), marked the end of the Middle Pleistocene some 125,000 years ago.

rissala(h, varr. RESSALAH.

rissaldar (rɪsɑːl'dɑː(r)). *Indian.* Also 9 ressaladar, ressaldar, risal(a)dar, russalahdar and with capital initial. [Hind. *risāldār*, *risālādār*, f. Pers. *risāla* troop of horse.] A native captain in an Indian cavalry regiment. Also *Comb.*, as *rissaldar-major*.

1800 *Asiatic Ann. Reg.* 34/1 A certain Ressaladar of his, whom he had often deceived, came one day to the Durbar. **1842** W. MILES tr. *Meer Hussein Ali Khan Kirmani's Hist. Hydur Naik* xxiii. 327 The Nawaub now gave orders to the Risaladārs of the regular and irregular infantry, to encircle the fort, and then commence the attack with their artillery and musketry. **1848** J. H. STOCQUELER *Oriental Interpreter* 198/1 *Rissaldar*, an officer of the Irregular India cavalry, whose rank corresponds with that of a captain of a troop. **1851** J. B. FRASER *Mil. Mem. Lieut.-Col. J. Skinner* I. ix. 274 The rissaldars finding so much money in their hands, began to quarrel about the division of it. **1863** *Cornh. Mag.* Jan. 55 One ressaldar (a rank answering to that of captain of calvary) was granted the rank of Bahadur. **1892** KIPLING *Barrack-r. Ballads, East & West* 76 Then up and spoke Mohammed Khan, the son of the Ressaldar. **1927** Rissaldar-major [see *en grande tenue* s.v. EN *prep.*] **1951** J. MASTERS *Nightrunners of Bengal* 337/2 There were three grades of Native Officers..: infantry—subadar-major, subadar, jemadar; cavalry—rissaldar-major, rissaldar, jemadar. **1964** A. SWINSON *Six Minutes to Sunset* ii. 30 A Risaldar-Major with the impressive name of Khan Bahadur Fazal Dad Khan turned up. **1981** V. POWELL *Flora Annie Steel* xiii. 109 Roshan has risen to the rank of *rissaldar* (Indian officer).

† **risse**, *sb.*[1] *Obs.*[−1] [? var. of RIST *sb.*[1]] ? An occasion, opportunity.

1602 WARNER *Albion's England* xv. xcviii. 389 Or if shall of Pluralities be likely Risses, then Their Saintships are as capable thereof as sinfull men.

† **risse**, *sb.*[2] *Obs.*[−1] [ad. It. *rissa* (pl. *risse*):—L. *rixa*.] Conflict, quarrel.

1684 T. GODDARD *Plato's Demon* 5 The hereditary risses or quarrels of the Piedmontesi.

† **risse**, *ppl. a.* *Obs.*[−1] [See RISE *v.* A 3 *β*.] Risen. (In comb. *huge-risse*.)

1597 MIDDLETON *Wisdom Solomon* v. 8 Wee which haue made our harts a sea of pride, With huge risse billowes of a swelling minde.

rissh(e, obs. f. RUSH (plant).

rissheu, -ew: see RISHEW.

risshy, obs. f. RUSHY.

rissillis (obs. Sc.): see RUSSEL.

Risso ('rɪsəʊ). The name of Giovanni Antonio *Risso* (1777–1845), Italian naturalist, used in the possessive in **Risso's dolphin** to designate the grampus, *Grampus griseus*, first described as *Delphinus rissoanus* by A. G. Desmarest in 1822 (*Mammalogie* II. 579).

1871 *Proc. Zool. Soc.* 506 Prof. Flower, F.R.S., read a paper on the so-called Risso's Dolphin. **1924** [see CAA'ING WHALE]. **1927** *Daily Express* 5 Sept. 2/5 Pelorus Jack, the famous white Risso's dolphin, which for years has piloted ships into Wellington Harbour, New Zealand,..is missing. **1960** G. MAXWELL *Ring of Bright Water* v. 62 Contrary to information contained in the majority of text-books, in which Risso's dolphin is described as a rarity, it is in fact the commonest of all the lesser whales to visit the Hebrides in summer. **1971** M. & R. MOFFETT *Dolphins* 18 The grampus, or Risso's dolphin, lives far out at sea.

rissole ('rɪsəʊl). [a. F. *rissole*, OF. *ruissolle*, *rois(s)ole*, *rousole*, etc., perh. repr. pop. L. *russeola*, fem. of L. *russeolus* reddish.

An early adoption of the word occurs in the following passage: **1340** *Ayenb.* 253 Ase doþ þe bysye oþer þe malancolien þet byeþ ylich þan þat zeky þe crammeles ine þe russoles. (See also RISHEW.)]

An entrée made of meat or fish, chopped up and mixed with bread-crumbs, egg, etc., rolled into a ball or small thick cake and fried.

1706 in PHILLIPS (ed. Kersey), *Rissole*, a sort of minced Pie made of Capons-Breasts, Calves-Udder, Marrow, Bacon, fine Herbs, &c. and fry'd in Lard to give it a brown Colour. **1725** *Fam. Dict.* s.v. *Tourte*, They may be garnish'd with Rissoles, Apple-Fritters, or any thing else of the like nature. **1860** READE *Cloister & H.* ii, Fish came on the table in a dozen forms, with..an immense variety of 'brouets' known to us as 'rissoles'. **1877** A. B. EDWARDS *Up Nile* ix. 241 A black-looking rissole of chopped meat and vegetables.

transf. **1877** A. B. EDWARDS *Up Nile* vi. 147 The..beetle was..engaged in the preparation of a large rissole of mud.

rissom, variant of RISOM.

rist, *sb.*[1] *Obs.* exc. *dial.* [f. ppl. stem of RISE *v.*: cf. ARIST, SUNRIST, and UPRIST.]

† **1.** A source, origin. *Obs.*

1622 DRAYTON *Poly-olb.* XXVI. 373 Scardale..Wher Rother from her rist, Ibber, and Crawley hath. **1674** N. FAIRFAX *Bulk & Selv.* 8 If we can but track it up to a spring of its kind, without looking after any other riste. *Ibid.* 120 The rist or spring of all that swiftness.

2. A rising ground or slope; an ascent.

1823 E. MOOR *Suffolk Words*, *Rist*, a rising, ascent, or swelling, in land, a road, etc. *a* **1825** FORBY *Voc. E. Anglia*, *Rist*, a rising or elevation of the ground.

3. A rise in price.

1823 E. MOOR *Suffolk Words* s.v., Corn ha' got a little rist.

rist, *sb.*[2], ? variant of WREST *sb.*

c **1450** HOLLAND *Howlat* 759 The rote, and the recordour, the ribupe, the rist, The trumpe, and the talburn.

rist, *v. rare.* [ad. ON. and Icel. *rísta* (Norw. and Sw. *rista*, Da. *rista*).] To carve, engrave.

1866 G. STEPHENS *Runic Mon.* I. p. xxxi, *Hælhi*.., risted. **1886** —— in Du Chaillu *Viking Age* (1889) I. 155 *note*, It is the first burnt bone yet found risted with runes.

rist(e, obs. ff. REEST *sb.*, REST *sb.*[1] and *v.*[1]

rist-baulk, variant of REST-BALK.

risten, obs. form of RIGHT *v.*

† **ristes.** *Obs.* (See quot.)

1319 *Compotus Roll Pershore Manor, Worc.*, De Lj barellis Ceruisie qui vocantur ristes.

'**risting**, *vbl. sb.* [f. RIST *v.* + -ING[1]. Cf. Sw. *ristning*.] A cut or carved (runic) inscription.

1866 G. STEPHENS *Runic Mon.* I. 57 Those [stones] which have the same or nearly the same risting in both Ogham and Roman characters. **1880** METCALFE *Englishman & Scandinavian* 175 Runic ristings were all her artificial appliances for preserving historical facts.

'**ristle.** *Sc.* Also 9 restle. [Gael. *risteal*, a. ON. *ristill* (Norw. *ristel*): see etym. note to REEST *sb.*] A kind of plough formerly used in the Hebrides. Also *attrib.*

1703 M. MARTIN *Desc. W. Islands* 53 They have a little Plough also call'd Ristle, i.e. a thing that cleaves, the Culter of which is in Form of a Sickle, and it is drawn sometimes by One, and sometimes by Two Horses, according as the Ground is. **1808** FORSYTH *Beauties Scotl.* V. 470 Two men with two horses first guide and drag the restle, which cuts without opening the furrow. **1879** *Mem. Ochiltree* 53 The ristle plough..seems to have been capable only of making a deep scratch on the soil.

ristlis (obs. Sc.): see RUSSEL.

ristnesse, obs. form of RIGHTNESS.

ristocetin (rɪstəʊ'siːtɪn). *Pharm.* [Arbitrarily formed; *-cetin* f. ACTINOMY)CET(ES + -IN[1].] An antibiotic substance (now known to be a mixture) obtained from the actinomycete *Nocardia lurida* and formerly used to treat staphylococcal infections.

1957 W. E. GRUNDY et al. in *Antibiotics Ann. 1956–7* 687 A new antibiotic that has been given the generic name ristocetin was isolated from the fermentation beer of an actinomycete. **1960** M. E. FLOREY *Clin. Appl. Antibiotics* IV. iii. 77 Isolated from the fermentation liquor of an unidentified actinomycete called by the authors *Nocardia* *lurida* and obtained from soil at Colorado Springs, ristocetin gives promise of being of value in the treatment of staphylococcal and other infections. **1968** J. H. Burn *Lect. Notes Pharmacol.* (ed. 9) 111 Vancomycin and ristocetin do not appear to induce the emergence of resistant staphylococci. **1980** *Brit. Med. Jrnl.* 18 Oct. 1039/1 The coagulation studies were diagnostic of Glanzmann's thrombasthenia with diminished platelet aggregation in response to ristocetin.

‖**ristorante** (risto'rante). [It.] An Italian restaurant in Italy or elsewhere.

1925 W. J. Locke *Great Pandolfo* iv. 40 Washer-up in a relative's *Ristorante* in a mildewed corner of Soho. **1967** *Observer* 24 Sept. 31/5 Stopping at the first *ristorante* for a drink. **1968** R. Sawkins *Snow along Border* xviii. 148 The Villa Messina was near a *ristorante* called 'Sud-Est'. **1973** 'S. Harvester' *Corner of Playground* II. iv. 102 A table outside a *ristorante* on a Rome side-street. **1981** 'M. Yorke' *Hand of Death* xii. 102 The Ristorante Sorrento was in a narrow street that led to Fletcham Abbey from the market square.

‖**risus** ('raɪsəs). *Path.* [L. *rīsus* laugh, f. *rīdēre* to laugh.] ***risus sardonicus*** (or †*sardonius*), an involuntary or spasmodic grin consequent on some morbid condition.

1693 tr. *Blancard's Phys. Dict.* (ed. 2), *Risus Sardonius*, a Contraction of each Jaw. **1794–6** E. Darwin *Zoon.* (1801) III. 313 The corners of the mouth are frequently retracted into a disagreeable smile called *risus Sardonicus*. **1836–9** *Todd's Cycl. Anat.* II. 6/2 The countenance in all such cases assumes the peculiar expression or grin called *risus Sardonicus*. **1876** Bristowe *Th. & Pract. Med.* (1878) 518 Tetanic spasms and risus sardonicus also have occasionally been noticed in rheumatic pericarditis.

rit, *sb.*[1] *Sc.* and *north.* Also **ritt.** [f. rit *v.*[1]]

1. A scratch; a slight incision.

1821 Scott *Pirate* xv, Ye might as weel give it a ritt with the teeth of a redding-kame. **1824** Mactaggart *Gallovid. Encycl.* 423 *Scratt*, a rit. **1900** *Shetland News* 8 Dec. (E.D.D.), All his sheep had the same mark. It was—on the right ear two rits, and a bit out before.

2. The rut made by a cart-wheel.

1828 in *Craven Gloss.* **1878** in *Cumbld. Gloss.*

†**rit** (rɪt), *sb.*[2] Slang. abbrev. of ritualist 2. *Obs.*

1878 *Oxf. Times* 23 Mar. 8/1 *On dit* that five notoriously ritualistic undergraduates were received into the Church of Rome... Most of these young gentlemen have distinguished themselves in Oxford as Roaring Rits. **1898** A. Cavalier *Let.* in C. Mackenzie *My Life & Times* (1963) II. 243 My mater calls me a 'dirty Rit'. 'So we've got a Rit in the house, have we.' **1909** J. R. Ware *Passing Eng.* 209/2 *Rit*,..a ritualistic clergyman.

rit, *sb.*[3] *dial.* [Shortened form of ritling: see reckling.] The smallest and weakest pig of a litter; a ritling. Also *transf.* of a person.

1885 R. Holland *Gloss. County of Chester* (1886) 288 *Rit*.., the smallest pig of a litter. Also applied to a puny child. **1940** *Manch. Guardian Weekly* 15 Mar. 216 We gave special food to the rit of one brood (the little one known in other parts [than Cheshire] as the runt or reckling, and by other names). **1962** Orton & Halliday *Survey Eng. Dial.* I. I. 279 Q[uestion] What do you call the smallest and weakest pig of the litter?..La[ncashire]..1it. **1969** Orton & Barry *Ibid.* II. I. 288 Ch[eshire] 1it... St[affordshire]..1it.

rit., *sb.*[4] *Mus.* Abbrev. of ritardando.

1886 [see a tempo]. **1959** *Collins Mus. Encycl.* 552/1 *Ritardando*,..commonly abbreviated *rit.*

rit, *v.*[1] Now *Sc.* and *north.* Forms: 3–6 **ritte,** 5 **rytt,** 9 **rit(t.** *Pa. t.* 4 **ritt(e, rytte,** 8 **ritted.** *Pa. pple.* 9 **ritted (ritten).** [ME. *ritte(n*, perh. repr. OE. **rittan*, = OHG. *rizzan*, MHG. and G. *ritzen*, of the same meaning.]

1. To rip or cut with a sharp instrument; to tear; to scratch; to slit (a sheep's ear).

c **1300** *Havelok* 2495 Sket cam a ladde with a knif, And bigan rith at þe to For to ritte, and for to flo. *c* **1320** *Sir Tristr.* 479 Þe breche adoun he þrest, He ritt & gan to riȝt. *c* **1380** *Sir Ferumb.* 5030 Þay..laide to frensche strokes rounde, þat hure haberkes ritte. *c* **1400** *Laud Troy Bk.* 16807 Many a baly scho ther rittes And many a scheld scho al to-sclittes. *c* **1450** *St. Cuthbert* (Surtees) 1954 He made hir oute of hir witte To gnayste, to cry, hir hare to rytt. **1548** Thomas *Ital. Dict.*, *Diramare*, to ritte, breake, or cut of the braunches from the tree. *Ibid.*, *Isuenare*, to cutte or to ritte the veines. **1825** Jamieson s.v., Dinna rit the table wi' that nail. **1869** Peacock *Lonsdale Gloss.*, *Rit*, to make a mark. **1892** G. Stewart *Shetland Tales* 104 Just as he rits up da fish, oot flees a kittywake. **1894** R. S. Ferguson *Hist. Westm.* 290 A Herdwick sheep's ear is halved, and quartered,..and ritted into all sorts of patterns.

b. (See quots. and rut *v.*)

1825 Jamieson s.v., You had better rit the hail length of the ditch, before ye begin. **1877** *N.W. Linc. Gloss.*, *Rit*, to trim or pare the edge of a drain, path, &c. by means of a *ritter* or *ritting-knife*. **1878** *Cumbld. Gloss.*, *Rit*, to cut the first line of a trench or drain, &c., with a spade.

2. To thrust (a sword) *through* one. *rare*$^{-1}$.

17.. *Young Johnstone* iv. in Child *Ballads* II. (289) 295 Young Johnstone had a nut-brown sword,..And he ritted it through the young Colnel.

rit, *v.*[2] *Kentish dial.* (See quots.)

c **1700** Kennett in *MS. Lansd.* 1033, 325 b, *Ritting* of hemp or flax, *Kent*, to set up the single shots against walls or hedges till by the wind and sun they are ritted or dried. **1887** *Kentish Gloss.*, *Rit*, to dry hemp or flax.

rit, obs. form of right *sb.*[1] and *adv.*

Ritalin ('rɪtəlɪn). *Pharm.* Also **ritalin.** A proprietary name (orig. used in Switzerland) for the drug methylphenidate hydrochloride, a central nervous system stimulant related to amphetamine; methyl-α-phenyl-α-piperid-2-ylacetate hydrochloride, $C_{14}H_{19}NO_2{\cdot}HCl$.

The appearance of the word in trade-mark literature predated the introduction of the drug by a number of years.

1949 *Trade Marks Jrnl.* 1 June 477/1 *Ritalin*... Pharmaceutical preparations for use in the treatment of the nervous system. Ciba Limited..manufacturers and merchants.—28th May 1948. **1949** *Official Gaz.* (U.S. Patent Office) 16 Aug. 594/2 Ciba Limited, Basel, Switzerland. Filed July 9, 1948. *Ritalin.* Applicant claims ownership of Swiss Registration No. 107,093, dated Mar. 28, 1944. **1954** *Chem. Abstr.* XLVIII. 8945 Ritalin..has a psychomotor excitatory effect, producing psychic stimulation and a coördinated increase in motility in exptl. animals. **1955** *Ann. N.Y. Acad. Sci.* LXI. 101 This new drug, phenidylate—phenyl-(α-piperidyl)-acetic acid methyl ester (Ritalin)—is a synthetic preparation which could be described as a psychoanaleptic, a mental and physical stimulator which..seems to counterbalance the reserpine-depressing activity. **1970** *Daily Tel.* 30 June 3/1 The United States Food and Drug Administration has urged doctors to exercise extreme caution in prescribing Ritalin because of the danger of addiction. *Ibid.* 3 Dec. 13 More than 200 youngsters regularly visited his surgery and home and were given National Health Service prescriptions for the 'soft' drugs drynamyl, ritalin and mandrax. **1976** H. Ferguson *Confessions Long Distance Acid Head* 7 Apart from cannabis, I have used barbiturates,..procaine, ritalin, even apomorphine once.

‖**ritardando** (ritar'dando). *Mus.* Pl. **ritardandi, -os.** [It., pr. pple. of *ritardare* to slow down.] A musical direction indicating a gradual reduction of speed; as *sb.* = retardation 3 b; a passage where this occurs.

1811 Busby *Dict. Mus.* (ed. 3) Ritardando. (Ital.) An expression implying a slackening of the time. *c* **1865** E. Dickinson *Poems* (1955) II. 724 Dying at my music!.. Hold me till the Octave's run! Quick! Burst the Windows! Ritardando! **1889,** etc. [see accelerando]. **1893,** etc. [see allargando]. **1958** *Times* 22 Nov. 9/3 He is inclined to begin his ritornelli faster than is comfortable to the soloists and at the end to draw out an absurd *ritardando*. **1966** *Listener* 25 Aug. 286/1 This constant variation can be heard on many levels; in the brilliant interplay of pure unmixed tone-colours, in the fluctuations of tempo between fast and slow, accelerando and ritardando, and, in particular, in the rhythm. **1978** *Jrnl. R. Soc. Arts* CXXVI. 356/1 There must always be a reason and purpose for these slight accelerandos and ritardandos which we call rubato.

ritbock, obs. variant of reit-buck.

ritch, obs. form of rich *sb.* and *v.*

rite (raɪt). Also 4–6 **ryte,** 5 **ryyt.** See also right *sb.*[2] [ad. L. *rītus* ceremony, whence also F. *rite*, †*rit*, Sp. and It. *rito*.]

1. a. A formal procedure or act in a religious or other solemn observance. ***the last rites*** = ***the last sacraments*** s.v. sacrament *sb.* 2 e; **rite A, B:** the two classes of Eucharistic rite in the Church of England's *Alternative Service Book 1980*, distinguished by being in present-day English and traditional liturgical English, respectively.

The distinction sometimes made by liturgical writers between *rite* and *ceremony* (applying the former to the order, and the latter to the acts, of worship) has not been maintained in ordinary use.

c **1315** Shoreham I. 1362 Þo certeyne men lyȝte þat lyȝt, Ase þe laȝe ȝef þe rytes So brode. *c* **1380** Wyclif *Sel. Wks.* III. 347 In berynge of þe tabernacle, in sleying of beestis, and oþir ritis. **1396–7** in *Eng. Hist. Rev.* (1907) XXII. 296 Þe presthod of Rome is mad with signis, rytis, and bisschopis blissingis. **1426** Lydg. *De Guil. Pilgr.* 3250 For to dyfface the olde lawe, And the Ryytys ther-off with-drawe. **1447** Bokenham *Seyntys* (Roxb.) 11, I kan in no wyse remembre me..What rytys were usyd, and what royalte In namys yeuyng. **1529** More *Dyalogue* I. Wks. 162/2 The rytes and sacramentes and the articles of our faith. **1560** Daus tr. *Sleidane's Comm.* 46 The same Religion, Rites, and Ceremonies, wherin they were borne and brought up. **1629** Maxwell tr. *Herodian* (1635) 248 *note*, This was an ancient Funerall rite. **1662** Stillingfl. *Orig. Sacræ* II. vii. § 11 That the ground of his acceptance with God did not depend on any Ceremoniall Rite. **1741–2** Gray *Agrippa* 62 Perform'd with barb'rous rites Of mutter'd charms. [**1786** Burns *Poems Sc. Dial.* 190 The last, sad, mournful rites bestow!] **1795** Mason *Ch. Music* III. 199 After he had eaten the Passover, and instituted the solemn Rite, which was to supercede it. **1838** Prescott *Ferd. & Is.* Introd. (1846) I. 46 They learned to attach an exclusive value to external rites. **1874** Sayce *Compar. Philol.* viii. 306 A hallowed stock of traditional beliefs and rites. **1922** C. Kerr *Cecil Marchioness of Lothian* xv. 228 Dr Talbot said Mass in her room and she was given the last rites of the Church. **1927** *Times* 11 July 14/4 Canon Breen, the local parish priest, was hurriedly brought and administered the last rites. **1961** P. J. Hepburne-Scott tr. J. C. Didier (*title*) The last rites. **1975** *Times* 8 Nov. 1/7 The cardinal..received the sacrament of the sick (previously called 'last rites'). **1977** *Belfast Tel.* 27 Jan. 9/5 Their call is being backed up by local priest, the Rev. Peter Burns, who gave Mr. Moyna the Last Rites. **1980** *Daily Tel.* 24 Oct. 3/1 (*heading*) Queen [to be] at new Synod Rite A service. *Ibid.*, The form of service will be Rite A from the new Alternative Service Book... The service is a revision of that known hitherto as Series 3. **1980** *Alternative Service Bk. 1980* 5 The Order for Holy Communion Rite A. *Ibid.* 6 The Order for Holy Communion Rite B. **1980** *Alternative Service Bk. 1980: Commentary* 74 The main further change made from Series 3 to Rite A is the separation of the commemoration of the departed from the summary sentences commending all the worshippers to God. **1980** *Times Lit. Suppl.* 14 Nov. 1281/2 Even the Lord's Prayer is now on sale in three versions—that of the Book of Common Prayer..; that of Rite A *et passim* and that of Rite B *et passim*.

attrib. **1844** Mrs. Browning *Brown Rosary* III. xvii, The rite-book is opened, the rite is begun.

b. A custom or practice of a formal kind.

1581 Pettie tr. *Guazzo's Civ. Conv.* I. (1586) 25 b, The people are not onelie become warriers, but haue retained the customes and rites of warre. **1617** Moryson *Itin.* III. 174 If any chance to weare a shoo-string or garters of that colour, by ignorance of this rite, they will flie upon him. **1716** Gay *Trivia* II. 255 Cheese, that the table's closing rites denies. **1728** Young *Love Fame* III. 236 That solemn rite of midnight masquerades! **1865** Dickens *Mut. Fr.* II. xvi, He ..hopes to receive you..in a residence better suited to your claims on the rites of hospitality.

c. *transf.* (in some cases perh. used for *right*).

1599 Shaks. *Much Ado* II. i. 373 Time goes on crutches, till Loue haue all his rites. **1667** Milton *P.L.* VIII. 487 Guided by his voice, nor uninformd Of nuptial Sanctitie and marriage Rites. **1697** Dryden *Virg. Georg.* III. 100 The Bull's Insult at Four she may sustain; But after Ten, from Nuptial Rites refrain. **1772** *Lond. Evening Post* 26 Nov. 1/4 Non-performance of conjugal rites.

d. *pl.* Used as a journalistic term for any ceremony (*U.S.*).

1950 *Richmond* (Va.) *Times-Dispatch* 1 Apr. 1/2 (*heading*) Airport rites set for 2 p.m. today at Byrd. Planes, personalities will mark ceremony. **1957** *Sun* (Baltimore) 21 Jan. B-1/6 (*heading*) Rites at White House performed before 80. Press is barred from ceremony in East Room.

e. Anthrop. ***rite of intensification:*** a rite marking a special event affecting a social group and tending towards strengthening the bonds uniting its members; usu. *pl.*; ***rite of passage*** = rite de passage.

1909 *Folk-Lore* XX. 510 What M. van Gennep has here done is to enforce his contention by considering..a number of the sequences of rites to which he has given the title of Rites of Passage. **1947** Chapple & Coon *Princ. Anthropol.* xxi. 507 A Rite of Intensification..restores equilibrium for the group after a disturbance affecting all or most of its members. **1959** W. Goldschmidt *Understanding Human Society* v. 178 Rituals involving the whole community, called rites of intensification, re-enforce the initiate's sense of belonging and serve to strengthen group ties. **1960** Vizedom & Caffee *Van Gennep's Rites of Passage* p. vii, Passage might more appropriately have been translated as 'transition', but in deference to van Gennep and general usage of the term 'rites of passage', this form of the translation has been preserved. *Ibid.* p. ix, Ceremonies which accompany and assure the changes of the year, season, or month are rites of passage. **1970** P. Spencer in P. Mayer *Socialization* 148 The second type, performed when misbehaviour was expected from the moran and when their corporate unity and morale were low, were rites of intensification pure and simple. **1971** K. Thomas *Relig. & Decline of Magic* iii. 57 The subsequent raising of the age at which children are expected to undergo it [*sc.* confirmation] to fourteen or so has given it a more pronounced role as a rite of passage marking the arrival of 'social' puberty. **1978** W. A. Haviland *Cultural Anthropol.* (ed. 2) xiii. 346/1 Rites of intensification..are particularly common among horticultural and agricultural people, with their planting, first fruit, and harvest ceremonies. **1978** *Times Educ. Suppl.* 13 Jan. 15/1 The transition from fifth-year courses to A level involves a rite of passage to 'real' history. **1978** *Chatelaine* Dec. 17/1 And hockey is not just a sport. It's a rite of passage.

2. a. The general or usual custom, habit, or practice of a country, people, class of persons, etc.; now *spec.* in religion or worship.

1432–50 tr. *Higden* (Rolls) I. 401 The vse of that cuntre differrethe from the rite of Englonde in clothenge, in fyndenge, and in mony other thynges. *c* **1480** Henryson *Mor. Fab.* (S.T.S.) 775 Sum bene also throw consuetude and ryte Uincust with carnall sensualitie. **1513** Douglas *Æneis* v. ii. 71 Eftir thair payane ryte and gise. *Ibid.* XIII. x. 127 Baith pepille of Troy and folk Italian, All of a rite, maneris and vsans. **1560** Rolland *Crt. Venus* I. 720 Inclinand law with humbill countenance, Weill preparit as thair vse was and rite. **1728** Chambers *Cycl.* s.v., The English observe the Rite of the Church of England, prescribed in the Book of Common Prayer. **1866** *Chambers's Encycl.* VIII. 300 All those Christians who acknowledge the supremacy of the Roman pontiff, even though they be not of the Roman or Latin Rite.

†**b.** Religion. *Obs.*

c **1375** *Sc. Leg. Saints* xxviii. (*Margaret*) 295 Betir it ware consal þi-self, & lewe þi ryt. **1483** Caxton *Gold. Leg.* 341 b/1 He was a worshipper of ydolles and he had a wyf of the same Ryte. **1567** *Gude & Godlie B.* (S.T.S.) 190 This wind sa keine, that I of meine, It is the ryte of auld.

Hence '**rited** *a.*

1838 S. Bellamy *Betrayal* 57 Tempted, and taught and rited as thou art. *Ibid.* 193 It is no shrine for me—albeit with robes of rited sanctity Her courts are skirted now.

rite, obs. form of reit, right *sb.*[1]

‖**rite de passage** (rit də pasaʒ). *Anthrop.* Pl. **rites de passage.** [Fr., lit. 'rite of passage', a term coined by Arnold van Gennep: see quot. 1909.] Any of the rites of separation, transition, and incorporation that mark an individual's social existence from birth to death as he passes from one stage of life to another; ritual that marks the end of one phase and the start of another. Cf. rite 1 e.

[**1909** A. van Gennep (*title*) Les rites de passage.] **1911** *Man* XI. 30 Should we be right in including many of the cases of *rites de passage* in a general category of rites de *première fois*? **1934** R. Benedict *Patterns of Culture* ii. 25 In order to understand puberty institutions, we do not most need analyses of the necessary nature of *rites de passage*.

1949 G. Bateson in M. Fortes *Social Structure* 45 A poor man was about to undergo one of the important and expensive *rites de passage* which are necessary for persons as they approach the top of the Council hierarchy. **1957** M. Banton *W. Afr. City* xi. 210 Both native and Aku *rites de passage* appear to have been influenced by Creole practices. **1964** W. McCord in I. L. Horowitz *New Sociol.* xxv. 435 Most..practiced traditional *rites de passage.* **1972** M. Argyle *Social Psychol. of Work* iv. 67 The transition to a new job involves some degree of re-socialization, and the shift is sometimes assisted by a public ceremony..known to sociologists as a rite de passage. **1977** *Times* 22 Mar. 12/2 The [Newfoundland] seal hunt is..a necessary *rite de passage* for all young men.

'riteless, *a.* [f. rite + -less.] Destitute or devoid of rite or ceremony.

c **1611** Chapman *Iliad* xxiv. 498 Giue me no seate..when yet vnransomed Hector lies riteless in thy tents. **1838** Eliza Cook *Homes of Dead* x. 3 Yet say, are the riteless graves of those Unholy or unblest? **1892** *Academy* 31 Dec. 601/2 He has nothing to say of the ode on the riteless burial of Adrienne Lecouvreur.

† **'ritely,** *adv. Obs.* [f. as prec. + -ly².] With all due rites; in due form.

1560 Daus tr. *Sleidane's Comm.* 381 b, The Emperours mynde and wyll is, that all thinges should be lawfully and ritely done. **1609** Bible (Douay) *Numb.* xxviii. 10 The libamentes which are ritely poured everie Sabbath for an everlasting holocaust. **1654** Jer. Taylor *Real Pres.* 7 After the Minister of the holy mysteries hath ritely prayed, and blessed..the bread and the wine. **1675** Hobbes *Odyssey* (1677) 128 When I my vows and pray'rs had ritely done, Of both the victims straight I cut the throats.

‖ **ritenuto** (rite'nuto), *a.*, *adv.*, and *sb. Mus.* [It., pa. pple. of *ritenere*, f. L. *retinēre* to hold back.]

A. *adj.* and *adv.* Of musical movement: restrained, held back in tempo. Used adverbially as a direction indicating immediate reduction of speed. **B.** *sb.* (*pl.* **ritenuti** or **ritenutos**). A phrase or passage thus indicated.

1828 Busby *Mus. Manual* 148 Ritenuto. (Ital.) Movements to which this term is prefixed, are to be performed in a gentle, delicate, and restrained manner. **1888** L. A. Smith *Music of Waters* 15 Chorus. *Ritenuto molto.* Low-lands, Low-lands, Hur-rah, my John! **1952** *Conc. Oxf. Dict. Mus.* 500/2 *Ritenuto,* 'Held back', i.e. 'Slower' (immediately, not gradually as with *Ritardando* and *Rallentando*; but it may be that some composers have not observed this distinction). **1955** G. Abraham in H. Van Thal *Fanfare for E. Newman* 14 A boisterous tutti fortissimo ending by ten quiet bars, *un poco ritenuto.* **1955** [see diminuendo]. **1959** *Times* 12 Jan. 12/6 Their Bach was of the sewing-machine school, their Brahms full of ugly *ritenuti.* **1975** *Daily Tel.* 4 Feb. 11/1, I must protest against end ritenutos that came as an anti-climax in a good many of the variations. **1976** *Guardian* 13 Apr. 10/5 He plays strongly and straightforwardly; the rubatos and ritenutos are there.

rith, obs. form of right *sb.*¹ and *adv.*

rithe (raɪθ). Now *dial.* Also 8–9 ride, 9 rife. [OE. *rīð, rīðe,* = Fris. *ryd, ride,* MLG. *rîd, rîde,* etc. (LG. *rîde*), OLFrankish *rîth* stream, ditch.] A small stream; a brooklet.

c **888** K. Ælfred *Boeth.* xxxiv. § 1 Sum micel æwelm..& irnen mæneȝe brocas & riða of. *c* **897** —— *Gregory's Past. C.* 469 Sume hine lætað ofer landscare riðum torinnan. *c* **1000** Ælfric *Numb.* xvi. 14 To þam lande, þe eall flewð on riðum meolce & hunies. [*c* **1200** *Vices & Virtues* 95 Ðo teares ðe comen ierninde from ðare well-riðe of rewnesse.]

1787 Grose *Prov. Gloss., Ride,* a little stream. **1868** Hurst *Horsham* Gloss., *Rythe,* a small stream, usually one occasioned by heavy rain. **1925** A. Moore *Last Days of Mast & Sail* vii. 216 [The Bosham boats] are most dangerous-looking and would not live long in a seaway, but in the channels and rithes of Chichester Harbour the water is generally smooth and they continue in use generation after generation. **1931** Belloc *Cranmer* ii. 21 There stood on the Eastern edge of the town of Cambridge, just beyond the King's Ditch, as it was called (a runnel of water, the Long Rithe, which drained that flooded land and led from a mill above), a little place already known in this year, 1503, as 'Jesus' College.

rither ('raɪðə(r)). *Mining.* Also 9 ryther. [App. a local pron. of *rider.*] = rider *sb.* 10 a.

1681 Houghton *Compl. Miner* Gloss., *Rither,* a stone or thin cliff that lies in the vein;..sometimes this rither is so thick, it parts the vein. **17..** in *Brit. Mus. Add. MS. 6685,* p. 175 A rither point is that point of the stone where a vein comes in or goes out of another. **1829** Glover *Hist. Derby* I. 66 The intermediate substances that divide them are called *rythers.* **1851** *Act 14 & 15 Vict.* c. 94 § 14 When Two Veins approach each other, but are parted with a Rither,.. and the Rither..exceeds Three Feet in Thickness [etc.].

rither, obs. f. rother, rudder.

rithme, rithmour, -mus, obs. ff. rhythm, -mer, -mus.

'ritling, var. of reckling. (Cf. writling.)

c **1746** J. Collier (Tim Bobbin) *View Lanc. Dial.* To Rdr. 4 Theese hobbling Gonnerheeods ar oft dawntl't like Ritt'lings. **1848** Mrs. Gaskell *M. Barton* viii, He's twice as strong as Sankey's little ritling of a lad. **1856** *N. & Q.* Ser. II. I. 75 Well I reckon this is th' ritlin'; but..ritlin' often turns out best pig.

ritodrine ('rɪtəʊdriːn). *Pharm.* [Invented word.] A sympathomimetic agent used esp. as a uterine relaxant in cases of premature labour, when it is administered as an intravenous infusion of the hydrochloride; 2-*p*-hydroxy-phenethylamino-1-*p*-hydroxyphenyl-propanol, $C_{17}H_{21}NO_3$.

1971 *Amer. Jrnl. Obstetr. & Gynecol.* CX. 111/1 Ritodrine hydrochloride, previously identified as Du-21220, is a sympathomimetic amine with beta-adrenergic-inhibitory properties. **1977** *Lancet* 8 Oct. 777/2 In Britain two [drugs] have been licensed for use as agents which inhibit labour —namely, salbutamol and ritodrine.

ritor'nel. Also 7 retornal, -el, 9 ritornell(e, ritournelle. [Anglicized form of next, or a. F. *ritournelle.*] = next.

1684 *London Gaz.* No. 1947/4 Several Retornals in Three Parts for Violins. *Ibid.* No. 1976/4 Also Symphonies and Retornels in Three Parts..for the Violins and Flutes. **1776** Burney *Hist. Mus.* (1789) II. iv. 343 *note,* The *Ritornel* or symphony to a song. **1840** *Penny Cycl.* XVI. 467/2 During the ritornels the four principal dancers are to perform a ballet. **1856** Mrs. Browning *Aur. Leigh* VII. 969 Like some poor verse With a trick of ritournelle: the same thing goes And comes back ever. **1883** Meredith *Fair Ladies in Revolt,* A troop of maids..past us flew To labour, singing rustic ritornells.

‖ **ritornello** (ritor'nello). *Mus.* Also 7 return-, 8 retornello; 7–8 retornella; *pl.* 7 ritornelloes, 8 -ello's, 9 -elli. [It., dim. of *ritorno* return *sb.*] An instrumental refrain, interlude, or prelude in a vocal work. Also *fig.*

1675 Shadwell *Psyche* v. 69 A Returnello by Martial Instruments. **1678** —— *Timon* II. 31 Retornella of Houtboys. **1685** Dryden *Alb. & Alban.* v. iii, A full Chorus of all the Voices and Instruments: Trumpets and Hoit-Buoys make Ritornelloes of all Fame sings. **1706** A. Bedford *Temple Mus.* iv. 73 In our Anthems there are frequent Intermissions of all the Voices, when the Organ Plays alone, that which we call a Retornella. **1728** Chambers *Cycl.* s.v., In the Partitions or Score of the Italian Musick, we frequently find the Ritornello's signified by the Words *si suona.* **1795** Mason *Ch. Mus.* III. 213 To Confine the Organist to a slightly ornamented Refraine or Ritornello at the end of each Stave or Stanza. **1811** Busby *Dict. Music* (ed. 3) s.v., It appears..that these Ritornelli, or symphonies, were introduced in the ancient as well as in the modern music. **1865** *Pall Mall G.* 19 May 11 The orchestra in the meanwhile gives expression to her grief in a ritornello which ..is the most moving strain in the opera. **1874** Ouseley *Mus. Form* 67 Then two bars of instrumental ritornello are interpolated by way of prolongation. **1977** *Times Lit. Suppl.* 1 July 796/4 The Marxist theme is a ritornello appearing at the end of each chapter rather than at the conclusion of the book. **1978** *Ibid.* 13 Oct. 1153/3 What is the correlation between schools and literacy?.. The irrelevance of schools is a persistent *ritornello* here.

‖ **ri'tratto.** *Obs.* [It.; cf. retrait *sb.*²] A picture, portrait.

1722 Richardson *Statues Italy* 233 Here are several *Ritrattoes,* particularly that of Leo X. *a* **1734** North *Examen* II. iv. § 41 (1740) 251 In the mean Time, let not this Ritratto of a large Landscape be thought trifling. **1762–71** H. Walpole *Vertue's Anecd. Paint.* (1786) III. 29 Symondes adds, Sir Peter had 5 *l.* for a ritratto; 10 *l.* if down to the knees.

Ritschlian ('rɪtʃlɪən), *a.* and *sb.* [f. the name of Albrecht *Ritschl,* German theologian (1822–89).] **A.** *adj.* Of or pertaining to Ritschl or his doctrines. **B.** *sb.* A follower of Ritschl or a student of Ritschlianism.

1891 *Chambers's Encycl.* VIII. 733/2 The distinguishing feature of the Ritschlian theology is perhaps the eminence it gives to the practical, ethical, social side of Christianity. *Ibid.* 734/1 The Ritschlians now form a large and important school in Germany. **1938** *Times Lit. Suppl.* 30 Apr. p. x/2 For a generation past the influence of the Ritschlian tradition has been far more potent in Scottish theology. **1952** *Hibbert Jrnl.* 1951 L. 12 The Ritschlian contempt for 'speculative Theism'. *Ibid.* 15 The *Fourth Gospel,* with such New Testament epistles as *Romans* or *Ephesians,* neglected if not deliberately excluded by Ritschlians in favour of the Synoptists' parables of a 'Kingdom of God' to be established here and now. **1957** *Oxf. Dict. Chr. Ch.* 1168/2 The so-called 'Ritschlian School' was characterized by its stress on ethics and on the 'community', and by its repudiation of metaphysics and religious experience. **1970** *Evangelical Q.* XLII. 95 The last four words tend to nullify the import of the preceding, which as such is the usual Ritschlian explanation; the doctrine of the subjective origin of the thing. *Ibid.* 99 The Ritschlians were, therefore, strongly opposed to the separation which had been made in traditional theology between the person and work of Christ.

Hence **'Ritschlianism,** the theological or philosophical doctrines of Ritschl.

1892 J. Orr in *Thinker* Aug. 148 Ritschlianism has a metaphysic, and a specially dangerous one. **1917** Bartlet & Carlyle *Christianity in Hist.* v. v. 596 Ritschlianism and Catholic Modernism are the most marked movements in this direction. **1969** D. L. Mueller *Introd. Theol. A. Ritschl* iii. 105 This idea so crucial for comprehending Ritschl's conception of faith became a kind of watchword of later Ritschlianism. **1970** *Evangelical Q.* XLII. 97 All possibility of speaking of an absolute nature in the Deity as the ground of His historical manifestations is in Ritschlianism swept aside.

Ritsu ('rɪtsuː), *sb.* Also Risshu ('rɪʃuː). [f. Jap. *ritsu* law, moral law.] A Buddhist sect of the early Tang period, introduced in the 8th century to Japan where it flourished, concerned primarily with the study of monastic discipline and ordination rites.

[**1727** J. G. Scheuchzer tr. *Kæmpfer's Hist. Japan* I. II. v. 199 In the 1850 streets of this city, there were 1050 of the *Ten Dai's* religion,..9912 of *Rit.*] **1880** E. J. Reed *Japan* I. iv. 91 The Ritsu, introduced by the Chinese priest Kanshin, under the empress Koken. **1917** A. K. Reischauer *Stud. Jap. Buddhism* iii. 86 Last of these older sects to reach Japan was the Ritsu (Vinaya Sect), introduced in 754, though it would seem that its doctrines..were among the first teachings to be introduced into Japan. **1931** G. B. Sansom *Japan* II. vi. 121 The Ritsu sect did not trouble much about doctrinal questions, but paid special attention to discipline and correct spiritual succession. **1935** C. Eliot *Jap. Buddhism* viii. 232 After the establishment of this new Kaidan, the Risshū seems to have declined though it somewhat revived in the twelfth century.

‖ **'ritter.** [G. *ritter,* var. of *reiter* reiter¹; cf. OHG. *ritto* rider, G. *ritt* riding.] A mounted warrior; a knight.

1824 Campbell *Ritter Bann* 19 The Ritter's colour went and came, And loud he spoke in ire. **1840** Barham *Ingol. Leg.* Ser. II. *Sir Rupert the Fearless* Introd., The mail-clad *Ritter* of the dark ages.

ritter, var. rutter².

Ritter's disease ('rɪtəz). *Med.* [Named after Gottfried *Ritter* von Rittershain (1820–83), Bohemian physician, who first described it as a distinct entity in 1878 (*Central-Zeitung f. Kinderheilkunde* II. 3–23).] A sometimes fatal form of dermatitis affecting newborn infants.

1888 *Amer. Jrnl. Med. Sci.* XCV. 11 The pemphigus simplex acutus, like Ritter's disease, belongs to the first weeks of life, but appears earlier, sometimes in the first few days after birth. **1931** B. Williamson *Handbk. Dis. Children* xvii. 143 Pemphigus neonatorum (Ritter's disease) ..occasionally is luetic in origin, but more often it is a septic infection associated with unclean midwifery. **1966** *Amer. Jrnl. Dis. Children* CXI. 391/2 The exact etiology of Ritter's disease has never been finally established, many investigators having reported an association with staphylococcal infection.

rittle-rattle. *rare.* [f. rattle *sb.*¹ or *v.*¹, with usual change of vowel.]

1. A child's rattle.

1583 Golding *Calvin on Deut.* lxxxiv. 517 Who think to dally with God, and would giue him rittlerattles to play with as if hee were a babe.

2. An imitation of the sound made by dice.

1837 *Heath's Bk. of Beauty* 246 See there, how he handles the dice! Rittle, rattle! the pigeon is plucked in a trice.

'rittmaster. *rare.* Also 7 reet-, 8 rit-. [ad. G. *rittmeister,* Du. *ritmeester,* f. *ritt* riding.] The captain of a troop of horse.

1648 *Presb. Rec. Lanark* in *Ann. of Lesmahagow* (1864) ix. 155 Cornet to James Conynghame, Reet Master. **1665** S. Clarke *Descr. Germany* 14 He hath continually about him fourteen Rittmasters, that is Captaines. **1721** Wodrow *Hist. Suff. Ch. Scot.* I. 271 Duke Hamilton was only Rit-master Hamilton, as the General used to call him, Rothes was Rit-master Lesly. **1819** Scott *Leg. Montrose* ii, Thereafter I arose to be lieutenant and ritt-master.

'rittoch, rittock. (See quots.)

1805 Barry *Orkney* 303 The Greater Tern,..which is here known by the name of the *Rittoch,* appears only in summer. **1813** Montagu *Ornith. Dict.* Suppl., Tern, Common,..Extends to the Orkney and Zetland Islands, where..they are known by the..names of Tarrock.., Rittock or Rippock.

ritual ('rɪtjuːəl), *a.* and *sb.* [ad. L. *rītuāl-is,* neut. *rītuāl-e,* f. *rītus* rite. So F. *rituel,* †*ritual,* Sp. and Pg. *ritual,* It. *rituale.*]

A. *adj.* **1. a.** Pertaining or relating to, connected with, rites. *spec.* in *Archæol.,* applied to objects or constructions.

1570 Foxe *A. & M.* (ed. 2) 83/1 Contayning no maner of doctrine..but onely certayn ritual decrees to no purpose. **1653** H. More *Conject. Cabbal.* (1713) 40 The Ritual laws and Religious stories of the Heathens. **1656** *Vind. Jud.* in *Phenix* (1708) II. 417 By our ritual Books we are clear of this seducing. *a* **1740** Waterland *Christian Sacr.* iv. Wks. 1823 V. 453 The ritual laws restrained the Jews from conversing familiarly with the heathens, or unclean persons. **1821** Wordsw. *Eccl. Sonn.* III. xix, Through a zodiac, moves the ritual year Of England's Church. **1850** Sir G. Scott *Anc. Churches* 19 *note,* The antiquarian, the purely æsthetic, or the ritual branch of the subject. **1885** H. O. Wakeman *Hist. Relig. Eng.* xi. 120 An association was formed..to test the legality of these ritual alterations. **1901** A. J. Evans *Mycenaean Tree & Pillar Cult* 9 At the foot of the handle of axe, namely, appears in each case that distinctive piece of Mycenaean ritual furniture..described as 'the horns of consecration'. **1934** *Burlington Mag.* Mar. 139/1 Other ritual bronzes said to have been found with the *kuang.* **1941** *Antiquity* XV. 142 (*title*) A datable 'ritual barrow' in Glamorganshire. **1951** *Field Archæol.* (Ordnance Survey Prof. Papers No. 13) (ed. 3) 42 Another curious type of site about which our knowledge is imperfect is the so-called 'ritual' well, or Belgic burial shaft. **1954** S. Piggott *Neolithic Cultures* ii. 56 It is possible that some of the 'ritual holes' frequently recorded from near the burials in the Wessex barrows may have been post-holes, but the majority seem to have served some other unexplained purpose connected with the funerary rites. **1963** W. F. Grimes in Foster & Alcock *Culture & Environment* v. 105 No doubt in due course something like 'sacred circle' or 'ritual circle' frankly avowing ideas about their use will become permissible for a majority of them. **1975** P. Warren *Aegean Civilization* ii. 43 The individual who made the so-called Harvester Vase..created a masterpiece. Here are 27 figures marching around a ritual vase a few inches high.

b. ***ritual choir,*** that part of the church in which the choir-offices are performed.

1867 Freeman *Norm. Conq.* (1877) I. App. 672 The cloister had one door into the choir and one door into the nave, that is to say, the ritual choir was west of the crossing. **1886** Willis & Clark *Cambridge* I. 358 A space of 8 feet was to be left behind the high altar, thus reducing the length of the ritual choir to 95 feet.

2. Of the nature of, forming, a rite or rites. ***ritual murder***, murder carried out as a rite; also *fig.* and *attrib.*; similarly ***ritual killing***.

a **1631** DONNE *Select.* (1840) 247 Ritual, and ceremonial things, which are.. the subsidies of religion. **1652** STERRY *Eng. Deliv. North. Presb.* 13 These rituall observations, these consecrated formes. **1682** *News fr. France* 6 All opinions and practices in the Ritual part of Religion seem indifferent to them. **1725** POPE *Odyss.* IV. 588 Due ritual honours to the gods I pay. *Ibid.* 792 We.. quit the ships, and ..With ritual hecatombs the gods adore. **1805** SOUTHEY *Madoc in Azt.* VI, Whirling him In ritual dance, till breath and sense were gone. **1867** D. DUNCAN *Disc.* viii. 155 Holiness does not consist in bodily austerities or in ritual observances. **1896** JESSOPP & JAMES *St. William of Norwich* p. lxxvii, Ritual-murder as a practice has been learnedly and thoroughly disproved by Strack and others. **1936** C. DAY LEWIS *We're not going to do Nothing* 14 Organised mass-murder—as apart from ritual-killings, blood-feuds and the like—can admit of only one satisfactory explanation. **1950** M. HAY *Foot of Pride* v. 119 In Germany, the ritual-murder legend was the chief.. excuse for a series of riots all over the country which threatened the Jews with complete extermination. **1962** L. DEIGHTON *Ipcress File* i. 9 The man ..was now using knife and fork to commit ritual murder on a cream pastry. **1964** M. SUTHER et al. tr. *Maritain's Moral Philos.* 142 (*heading*) The ritual murder of Realities that are elevated to the skies. **1966** *New Statesman* 15 July 78/3 The sudden revival in Russia of the ritual-murder myth after half a century of anti-religious mass education. **1972** J. MCCLURE *Caterpillar Cop* ii. 24 Back marked by long cuts. .. Those wounds suggest a ritual killing.

3. In extended and trivial use: pertaining to or constituting a social or psychological ritual (see sense B. 2 below); used, occurring, etc., as a social convention or habit.

1947 *Atlantic Monthly* July 114/2 Many political speeches ..are delivered in a language which is above people's heads and is in fact a 'ritual survival' from an age in which electors were few and literate. **1953** H. S. SULLIVAN *Inter-personal Theory of Psychiatry* xviii. 307 All these ritual avoidances and preoccupations give one a feeling that one is making some sense in an important area of living. Actually one is not making any sense at all, because one is completely inaccessible to any data. **1972** W. LABOV *Language in Inner City* viii. 305 Those who have some knowledge of urban ghetto culture will recognize Rel's remark *Your mother's a duck* as a ritual insult. **1975** R. COLLINS *Conflict Sociol.* iii. 115 We can tell the difference by the increase in ritual elements as the talk becomes more sociable, the orienting gestures are toward each other rather than toward the topic. **1977** B. PYM *Quartet in Autumn* i. 5 He offered her the bag of jelly babies, but this was only a ritual gesture and he knew that she would refuse. *Ibid.* v. 40 Most of the inhabitants of the village were retired married couples with the ritual grandchildren.

B. *sb.* **1. a.** A prescribed order of performing religious or other devotional service.

1649 JER. TAYLOR *Apol. Liturgy* (ed. 2) §89 Then the Bishop prayes *ritè*, according to the rituall or constitution. **1734** tr. *Rollin's Anc. Hist.* (1827) I. 349 According to the Greek ritual (if I may use that expression). **1772** PRIESTLEY *Inst. Relig.* (1782) II. 121 There was a.. dignity in the Jewish ritual. **1795** BURKE *Abridgm. Eng. Hist.* Wks. II. 513 Animating their disciples to religious frenzy by the uncouth ceremonies of a savage ritual. **1838** PRESCOTT *Ferd. & Is.* (1846) I. vi. 290 The Romish ritual was not admitted into its churches till long after it had been adopted in the rest of Europe. **1856** STANLEY *Sinai & Pal.* xiv. (1858) 466 A long procession with embroidered banners, supplying in their ritual the want of images. **1876** C. M. DAVIES *Unorth. Lond.* (ed. 2) 93 The ritual resembles that of the Church of England.

transf. **1709** PRIOR *Henry & Emma* 549 Nor in Love's Ritual can We ever find Vows made to last. **1856** EMERSON *Eng. Traits, Aristocracy* (Bohn) II. 83 Politeness is the ritual of society, as prayers are of the church.

b. A book containing the order, forms, or ceremonies, to be observed in the celebration of religious or other solemn service.

1656 COWLEY *Pindar. Odes, Plagues of Egypt* x, The Sorcerers..smil'd at th' unaccustomed Spell Which no Egyptian Rituals tell. **1674** tr. *Scheffer's Lapland* viii. 27 He likewise was the first that published the Ritual in the Laplandish tongue. **1705** ADDISON *Italy* 328 An Heathen Ritual could not instruct a Man better..in the particular Ceremonies..that attended the different kinds of Sacrifices. **1728** CHAMBERS *Cycl.* s.v., There are several Passages in Cato's Books..which may give us some Idea of the Rituals of the Antients. **1845** LINGARD *Anglo-Sax. Ch.* I. App. 420 In pp. 185, 187 of the ritual occurs another collection of similar entries. **1873** BURTON *Hist. Scot.* lxix. VI. 156 That the use of it as a ritual was virtually suspended.

2. a. orig. only *pl.* Ritual observances; ceremonial acts. Now freq. in *sing.*, and in extended and trivial uses.

a **1656** VINES *Lord's Supper* (1677) 24 There were in the first passover..certain rituals or occasionals. **1662** HIBBERT *Body Divinity* II. 103 God..will have order both in substantials and circumstantials, in reals and in rituals. **1713** YOUNG *Last Day* III. 25 In solemn form the rituals are prepar'd. **1737** *Gentl. Mag.* VII. 40 Sects, or Heresies, may be formed about Rituals..as well as about Points of Doctrine. **1818** SCOTT *Rob Roy* vi, Your religion and your temperance are so much offended by Roman rituals. **1906** J. G. FRAZER *Adonis, Attis, Osiris* 325 When the Bechuanas are about to found a new town, they observe an elaborate ritual. **1911** BEERBOHM *Zuleika D.* iii. 29 He cared for his wardrobe and his toilet-table..merely as..a ritual in which to express and realise, his own idolatry. **1914** J. S. HUXLEY in *Proc. Zool. Soc.* I. 506 We must now go on to consider a very different question... I mean the gradual change of a useful action into a symbol and then into a ritual. **1958** J. O'CONOR *Iron Harp* in J. C. Trewin *Plays of Year* XVI. 179 He's had no lunch... Ah, now, that won't do. A man should never miss the ritual of a good meal. **1975** R. COLLINS *Conflict Sociol.* iii. 97 All that animal language lacks in comparison to human rituals, is a symbolic significance or *naming* quality. .. We usually assume that animal rituals are innate but that human rituals are learned. **1975** L. LEE *I can't stay Long* (1977) 203 The ritual of bargaining was long and elaborate.

b. *spec.* in *Psychol.* A series of actions compulsively performed under certain circumstances, the non-performance of which results in tension and anxiety.

1932 M. GABAIN tr. *Piaget's Moral Judgment of Child* iv. 359 The rituals attached to eating, going to bed, etc., show the hold which habit has over his [*sc.* the child's] nature. **1946** O. FENICHEL *Psychoanal. Theory of Neuroses* xiv. 268 Touching rituals replace taboos; washing compulsions, fears of dirt; social rituals, social fears. **1956** H. S. LIPPMAN *Treatm. Child in Emotional Conflict* ix. 113 The diagnosis of obsessional neurosis in a child depends primarily on the presence of ceremonials or rituals which he cannot control. **1968** L. EIDELBERG *Encycl. Psychoanal.* 382/2 Although similar in pathogenesis, it is useful to distinguish between rituals and other obsessive-compulsive manifestations. **1972** A. STORR *Dynamics of Creation* viii. 98 The ritual had started originally as an attempt to purge himself of the guilt surrounding masturbation.

3. The performance of ritual acts.

1867 *Times* 26 Nov. 8/4 In only one small parish, with about 150 people,..had there been any attempt at what he called ritual. **1875** PUSEY in Liddon *Life* (1897) IV. 279 He had not heard of Ritual being excepted against by the congregation when there was not fussiness or self-consciousness or some like fault. **1883** W. H. R. JONES *Introd. Reg. S. Osmund* (Rolls) I. p. xxxvi, Of course it was an age in which much of the general teaching was by outward ritual. **1923** J. S. HUXLEY in *Jrnl. Linnean Soc.* XXXV. 255 The effect as of tension, of emotional ritual, so familiar to all those who have watched birds during courtship, is marked. **1947** CHAPPLE & COON *Princ. Anthropol.* xix. 481 This question of the conditioned nature of symbols is a basic requisite to the understanding of the whole subject of ritual. **1961** L. THOMPSON *Toward Sci. of Mankind* xi. 182 Hopi ritual may be viewed as a complex, but logical and ordered, whole, which expresses symbolically the Hopi conception of the universe, the law, and the life process. **1969** in Halpert & Story *Christmas Mumming in Newfoundland* 112 'Ritual' here is broadly defined as largely symbolic activity, aimed towards controlling social relations. **1971** L. NEAL in A. Gayle *Black Aesthetic* 285 Like all good ritual, its purpose is to make the audience stronger, more sensitive to the historical realities that have shaped our lives and the lives of our ancestors.

attrib. **1882** WILBERFORCE & ASHWELL *Life Bp. Wilberforce* III. vii. 186 The appointment of the Ritual Commission. **1892** *Pall Mall G.* 4 Aug. 7/2 The taste for ritual suits is certainly on the wane.

Comb. **1868** J. G. WHITTIER in *Atlantic Monthly* Feb. 221 Nor ritual-bound nor templeward Walks the free spirit of the Lord! **1930** D. H. LAWRENCE *A Propos Lady Chatterley* 36 The strange priest-controlled, ritual-fulfilled condition of the earlier Egyptians. **1937** M. COVARRUBIAS *Island of Bali* viii. 216 The ritual-magic dances characteristic of primitive peoples.

‖**ritualia** (rɪtjuˈeɪlɪə). *nonce-wd.* [L., pl. of *rituāle* relating to rites or ceremonies.] Objects used in or connected with religious rites and ceremonies.

1931 *Times Lit. Suppl.* 5 Nov. 864/2 The records of this synagogue may contain papers of great interest, and its *ritualia* certainly include objects of considerable beauty.

ritualism (ˈrɪtjuːəlɪz(ə)m). [f. RITUAL *a.* and *sb.* + -ISM. Cf. F. *ritualisme.*] **1.** The study, practice, or system of ritual observances; *esp.* excessive observance or practice of ritual.

1843 *Hierurgia Anglicana* Introd. p. ii, The Editors..may be supposed at least to have paid some attention to ritualism. **1851** I. TAYLOR *Wesley & Methodism* 304 The adaptation of Romanism—or if we were to use more comprehensive phrases, we should say—sensuous Ritualism, to engage and charm imaginative, sensitive and meditative minds. **1866** RAINE *Vestments* 11 The cathedrals made an outpost for the advance of ritualism. **1870** LOWELL *Study Wind.* 280 The Troubadour hailed the return of spring; but with him it was a piece of empty ritualism. **1883** *Contemp. Rev.* XLIII. 270 The spirit of legal ritualism..developed among the Romans a number of intricate ceremonies. **1883** *Q. Rev.* CLVI. 530 Three years ago Ritualism enjoyed a sort of grudging toleration. **1935** B. MALINOWSKI *Found. Faith & Morals* i. 6 It is rather the recognition of its practical and intellectual limitations, and not the illusion of the 'omnipotence of thought', which leads man into ritualism. **1952** GERTH & MARTINDALE tr. *Weber's Anc. Judaism* xiii. 336 Prophecy together with traditional ritualism of Israel, brought forth the elements that gave to Jewry its pariah place in the world. **1975** M. DOUGLAS *Implicit Meanings* v. 79 So the tension between ritualism of established authority and enthusiasm from the outlying borders of society, the dynamic of reform in European history, must have its counterpart in the unwritten history of any primitive tribe.

2. *Sociol.* (See quot. 1957.)

1949 R. K. MERTON *Social Theory* iv. 141 The socialization patterns of the lower middle class thus promote the very character structure most predisposed toward ritualism. **1955** P. M. BLAU *Dynamics of Bureaucracy* xii. 193 Three variations of displacement of goals were observed, all of which differed from ritualism. **1957** R. K. MERTON *Social Theory* (rev. ed.) v. 184 Ritualism refers to a pattern of response in which culturally defined aspirations are abandoned while 'one continues to abide almost compulsively by institutional norms'. **1961** O. J. HARVEY et al. *Conceptual Syst.* ii. 43 (*heading*) Concreteness disposes toward ritualism. **1963** T. & P. MORRIS *Pentonville* vii. 172 Two kinds of ritualism may be distinguished—the *ritualism of identification* and the *ritualism of dependency*. **1974** H. R. BOBBITT et al. *Organizational Behav.* iii. 61 Ritualism appeared to result more from lack of security in important social relationships..than from overidentification with rules or strong habituation.

ritualist (ˈrɪtjuːəlɪst). [f. as prec. + -IST. So F. *ritualiste*, Sp. *-ista.*]

1. One versed in ritual; a student of liturgical rites and ceremonies.

1657 SPARROW *Bk. Com. Prayer* (1661) 206 In Ancient Liturgies and Ritualists. **1685** STILLINGFL. *Orig. Brit.* iv. 217 In the Church of Rome..they had nothing before the Sacrifice, as the old Ritualists agree, besides the Epistle and Gospel. **1710** WHEATLY *Bk. Com. Prayer* Pref., The Roman Ritualists would have the Celebration of this holy Season to be Apostolical. **1725** BOURNE *Antiq. Vulg.* xxiv. in Brand (1777) 250 Belithus, a Ritualist of those Times tells us, That it was in some Churches. **1845** PALMER *Suppl. Orig. Lit.* 26 Ritualists have stated that the Roman Breviary was considerably abbreviated..in the time of Pope Gregory VII. **1882** J. H. BLUNT *Ref. Ch. Eng.* II. 568 Cosin, the most learned ritualist among them.

2. One who advocates or practises the observance of symbolic religious rites, *esp.* to an extent regarded by others as excessive.

In the latter half of the 19th c. applied *spec.* to the High Church party in the Church of England.

1677 *Life & Death J. Alleine* viii. (1838) 119 He was neither Legalist, nor Solifidian, neither Ritualist, nor Enthusiast. **1681** in Somers *Tracts* I. 113 The high-flown Ritualists and Ceremony-mongers of the Clergy. **1706** in PHILLIPS (ed. Kersey), *Ritualist*, one that stickles, or stands up for Rituals or Ceremonies in Religious Worship. *a* **1761** LAW *Behmen's Wks.* (1764) I. a ij, Every Methodist and Moravian Leader, the Orthodox Ritualist, and the Pathetic Lecturer. **1846** F. CLOSE *Apol. for Evang. Party* 17 The bishops and the 'puritan party' were found on the same side, and the ritualists were for the time defeated. **1866** DE MORGAN *Budget Parad.* (1872) 43, I am told that the Ritualists give short and practical sermons. **1867** MACKONOCHIE in *Ch. Times* 12 Jan. 18/2 People have taken to call us 'Ritualists'. **1874** GLADSTONE in *Contemp. Rev.* Oct. 671 The present movement in favour of ritual is not confined to ritualists.

attrib. **1874** BLUNT *Dict. Sects* 199 The second stage of the Ritualist movement consisted of attempts to follow out with exactness the rubrics of the Prayer-Book. **1875** PUSEY in Liddon *Life* (1897) IV. 279 The whole extreme Ritualist party is practically infallibilist.

(*b*) *spec.* in *Anthrop.* In a tribal society, one who performs a ritual.

1969 M. DOUGLAS *Natural Symbols* ii. 35 The primitive ritualist, in his ascribed social system, expresses cosmic orientations and moral directives in condensed symbols. **1974** B. & R. HILL *Spirit in Stone* iii. 35 A man whom we will call the ritualist and several assistants are fishing for salmon with a reef net. *Ibid.*, The ritualist carefully hands the children the fish he has caught. **1977** L. J. BEAN in Fogelson & Adams *Anthropol. of Power* 123 Individuals may..obtain it [*sc.* power] by inheriting or purchasing ritual equipment, and the knowledge that goes with it, from a shaman and/or ritualist.

3. Someone whose behaviour is characterized by ritualism (esp. in sense 2). Also *attrib.*

1949 R. K. MERTON *Social Theory* iv. 140 The syndrome of the social ritualist is both familiar and instructive. **1957** *Ibid.* (rev. ed.) v. 185 Situations patterned by the social structure which invite the ritualist response of overconformity to normative expectations. **1963** T. & P. MORRIS *Pentonville* vii. 172 The ritualist has largely rejected the socially approved goals altogether, and fallen back upon punctilious conformity. **1969** M. DOUGLAS *Natural Symbols* i. 2 The ritualist becomes one who performs external gestures which imply commitment to a particular set of values, but he is inwardly withdrawn, dried out and uncommitted.

ritualistic (rɪtjuːəˈlɪstɪk), *a.* [f. prec. + -ISTIC.] Of or pertaining to, characteristic of, ritualists or ritualism; devoted to, or fond of, ritual; characteristic of ritual actions or behaviour.

1850 MARSDEN *Early Purit.* (1853) 36 The perfection of a ritualistic church. **1866** RAINE *Vestments* 20 The possibility of further ritualistic development. **1880** 'OUIDA' *Moths* I. 141 She was very religious and strongly ritualistic. **1900** BP. How *Lighter Moments* 41 Their clergyman was accused of ritualistic tendencies. **1949** R. K. MERTON *Social Theory* iv. 140 The ritualistic type of adaptation can be readily identified. **1952** GERTH & MARTINDALE tr. *Weber's Anc. Judaism* xiii. 336 In Israel, originally, ritualistic segregation from strangers was totally absent. **1962** I. SARNOFF *Personality Dynamics & Devel.* xii. 350 An individual may be led to develop ritualistic acts symbolizing both aspects of his conflict. **1971** P. GREENACRE *Emotional Growth* I. xi. 169 The nature of the early shattering experience could sometimes be deciphered from the ritualistic behaviour accompanying the use of the fetish. **1973** *Black World* June 4/1 One of the most salient characteristics of the New Black Theater..is its ritualistic aspect. By ritualistic, I mean the strong presence of *symbols, characterizations, themes* and *language styles* which are frequently repeated from play to play. **1977** *Lancashire Life* Nov. 136/3 Very many people.. do not attend church because they are bored by ritualistic services.

Hence **ritua'listically** *adv.*

1870 *Sat. Rev.* 2 Apr. 431 Even if the School Board were ritualistically inclined. **1886** *Academy* 21 Aug. 113/3 A religionism dogmatically and ritualistically vague.

ritu'ality. [f. RITUAL *a.* + -ITY.]

†**1.** A rite or ceremony. *Obs.*

1654 H. L'ESTRANGE *Chas. I* (1655) 6 The Royal Corps.. was..inhum'd with the greatest solemnities and most stately ritualities could be devised.

2. Ritualism; attention to ritual. *rare.*

1679 PULLER *Moder. Ch. Eng.* (1843) 129 To keep Christians from enthusiasm in one extreme, and from what some call 'rituality' on the other. **1683** E. HOOKER *Pref. to Pordage's Mystic Div.* 51 *note*, Crucified, as it were, twixt Ritualitie and Scrupulositie. **1974** *Times* 16 Apr. 7/6 What Solzhenitsyn writes about ideological rituality, about the harmful waste of millions of people's time and efforts on this chatter that inculcates twaddle and hypocrisy, is indisputable.

ritualization (rɪtjuːəlaɪˈzeɪʃən). [f. RITUALIZ(E *v.* + -ATION.] **1.** *Zool.* The evolutionary process by which an action or behaviour pattern in an animal loses its ostensible function and changes into an effective social signal for other members of the species.

[**1914** J. S. HUXLEY in *Proc. Zool. Soc.* I. 506 A very different question..is also well brought out in the pairing-habits of the Great Crested Grebe: I mean the gradual change of a useful action into a symbol and then into a ritual. **1923** —— in *Jrnl. Linnean Soc.* (*Zool.*) XXXV. 278 The 'ritual' use of non-sexual actions during courtship.] **1942** N. TINBERGEN in *Bibliotheca Biotheoretica* I. 90 Substitute movements often have signal functions, and, doubtless in connection with these functions, may be extremely ritualised, so that they become unrecognisable when no comparative study is made. The degree of ritualisation actually reached is impressively illustrated by Lorenz' careful study of the epigamic movements of Anatinas. **1952** —— in *Q. Rev. Biol.* XXVII. 23/2 This new function [of releasing responses in other individuals] must have started a new evolutionary development during which the displacement activities became increasingly better adapted to it. This evolutionary displacement I have called 'ritualization', following Huxley (1923). **1965** *New Scientist* 17 June 768/2 The chief survival value of ritualization is obviously in the recanalization or the discharging of aggression. **1966** W. H. THORPE in Thorpe & Zangwill *Current Probl. Animal Behaviour* II. 94 In the process of ritualisation, certain elements are exaggerated whilst other elements tend to disappear entirely. **1974** *Nature* 3 May 8/3 Another feature of mutual courtship [in birds] is the extent of ritualisation; but this also applies to many male unilateral displays where the sexes have different plumage.

2. *Psychol.* The formalization of certain actions that serve to express a particular emotion or state of mind which is either innate or acquired as part of a social code.

1932 M. GABAIN tr. *Piaget's Moral Judgment of Child* i. 42 This phenomenon..is the counterpart of that sort of ritualization of behaviour which can be observed in any baby before it can speak or have experienced any specifically moral adult pressure. **1934** GESELL & THOMPSON *Infant Behav.* iii. 190 Ritualization is a reinstatement of the situation, a method of defining and perhaps improving new abilities; but it is itself a general ability, an intrinsic product of growth. **1951** J. HOLLOWAY *Lang. & Intelligence* x. 189 The systematization of language is exactly parallel to the ritualization of behaviour. **1961** C. & W. M. S. RUSSELL *Human Behav.* ii. 93 Ritualization serves to make the movement provide simple key stimuli, by simplifying it and exaggerating it. **1970** E. KLINGHAMMER tr. *Eibl-Eibesfeldt's Ethology* vi. 101 The cultural ritualizations of man follow the pattern of phylogenetic ritualization. **1978** E. ERIKSON *Toys & Reasons* ii. 69, I will chart only one use of playfulness throughout life which has received little attention, namely what I call ritualization in everyday life.

3. The action of forming a social or religious ritual.

1952 GERTH & MARTINDALE tr. *Weber's Anc. Judaism* xiii. 353 This ritualization of dietary habits made commensalism very difficult. **1952** T. PARSONS *Social System* 414 The particularism, traditionalism, and 'ritualization' of traditional Chinese society. **1962** M. GLUCKMAN *Ess. Ritual of Social Relations* 24, I propose to use the phrase 'ritualization of social relationships'—and for brevity 'ritualization'—to define this tendency... I can only plead that my readers should..take 'ritualization' as referring to a stylized ceremonial. **1966** *Phil. Trans. R. Soc.* B. CCLI. 413 If we consider the ritual of coronation from the point of view of its manifest subject matter, we describe it as the ritualization of eminent office. **1978** J. D. CRICHTON in C. Jones et al. *Study of Liturgy* I. 5 One of the most constant features of human history is the ritualization of the great events of human life, birth, marriage, and death.

ritualize (ˈrɪtjuːəlaɪz), *v.* [f. RITUAL *sb.* + -IZE.] **1.** *intr.* To practise ritualism.

1842 EMERSON *Transcendentalist* Wks. (Bohn) II. 291 Church and old book mumble and ritualize to an unheeding ..and advancing mind. **1892** *Cath. News* 27 Aug. 3 Some of the clergy will be drawn towards ritualising more forcibly.

2. *trans.* To convert into a ritual; to bring over to ritualism.

1847 *Oxford & Cambr. Rev.* V. 643 The..service of the Church was set about being regulated and ritualized. **1894** J. KERR in *Romanism & Ritualism* 170 If a number of ministers in Presbyterian charges where no ritualism exists were to resolve to ritualise and Romanise their congregations. **1967** V. W. TURNER *Forest of Symbols* iv. 94 A number of critical moments of transition which all societies ritualize and publicly mark. **1975** M. DOUGLAS *Implicit Meanings* ix. 142 To provide such detailed analyses of life crises, afflictions and of how the Ndembu ritualise them, creates thorny problems of interpretation. **1979** *Dædalus* Summer 130 Strong emotion can be ritualized.

3. *Zool.* To cause (an action or behaviour pattern) to become ritualized.

1961 *Centennial Rev. Arts & Sc.* Fall 406 Because the pattern [of behaviour] was empirically determined..one is never quite certain which behaviour elements are effective, and the whole pattern becomes ritualized. **1965** *New Scientist* 17 June 768/1 Animals tend to ritualize their aggression, rearing up, roaring, showing their teeth, or erecting their ruffs,..in such a way that an adversary recognizes the intention and reacts accordingly. **1968** R. F. EWER *Ethology of Mammals* viii. 192 In the spotted hyaena, smelling of the ano-genital region has been ritualised into a greeting ceremony which is regularly performed when members of a group meet. **1972** *Sci. Amer.* Sept. 59/1 Birds intending to fly..typically crouch, raise their tail and spread their wings slightly just before taking off. Many species have ritualized these movements into effective signals... The signals serve to coordinate the movement of flock members, and also may warn of approaching predators.

ritualized, *ppl. a.* **1.** Made into a ritual; converted to ritualism.

1882 FROUDE in *Edin. Rev.* Oct. 319 They entered the ritualised churches, tore down the new chancel rails. **1932** M. GABAIN tr. *Piaget's Moral Judgment of Child* i. 16 The child handles the marbles at the dictation of his desires and motor habits. This leads to the formation of more or less ritualized schemas. **1976** R. M. KEESING *Cultural Anthropol.* xvii. 369/1 Ritualized combat on the traditional 'battlefield' gives a vivid picture of one side of tribal warfare. **1978** E. ERIKSON *Toys & Reasons* ii. 73 Any ontogenetic reconstruction of the relation of play to politics would have to begin with the meaning of ritualized interplay for the development of the individual ego.

2. *Zool.* Of an animal's action or behaviour pattern: not having its ostensible function but serving as a signal to other members of the species.

Some of the examples are better interpreted as *pa. pple.*

1942 [see RITUALIZATION I]. **1964** G. B. SCHALLER *Year of Gorilla* (1965) ix. 239 Natural selection may act on such displacement activities by enhancing their effectiveness as communicatory signals; they may become stereotyped and be incorporated into a definite display—they become ritualised. The fact that the gorilla often places a leaf between its lips suggests that this curious gesture may be a ritualised act of displacement feeding. **1966** K. Z. LORENZ *On Aggression* xiv. 241 All the culturally evolved norms of 'fair fighting', from primitive chivalry to the Geneva Convention, are functionally analogous to phylogenetically ritualized combat in animals. **1971** *Nature* 18 June 469/1 The rutting conflicts of most species [of cervid] are largely ritualized, antlers serving the function of display more than as jousting weapons. **1978** D. SYMONS in E. O. Smith *Social Play in Primates* 208 Because fighting entails serious risk, ritualized signals have evolved by which animals communicate aggresive intent and, thereby, avoid fighting.

ˈritualless, *a.* [-LESS.] Devoid of ritual.

1897 *Athenæum* 13 Nov. 664/3 Religion therefore is.. almost ritualless mythism.

ˈritually, *adv.* [f. RITUAL *a.* + -LY[2].] By proper rites; in respect of ritual, etc.

1612 SELDEN *Illustr. Drayton's Poly-olb.* ix. 154 [The] solemnity of drinking out of a cup, ritually composed, deckt, and fill'd with countrey liquor. **1657** TRAPP *Comm. Ezra* vi. 20 'All of them were pure'—Ritually at least, if not really. **1752** WARBURTON *Serm.* Wks. 1788 V. 79 The rest of the sons of Adam; who, because ritually unholy and prophane, were deemed to be naturally unrelated to them. **1770–4** A. HUNTER *Georg. Ess.* (1804) IV. 291 Besides the mistletoe, the Druids ritually gathered the Selago. **1847** *Ecclesiologist* May 200 Chancel..is ritually confined to that part of the church where the Clerici celebrate the lesser offices. **1892** BRUCE *Apologetics* II. ii. 184 Obligations to be holy, not ritually only but really. **1914** J. S. HUXLEY in *Proc. Zool. Soc.* I. 506 The Grebe is interesting as showing all three stages of the process at one time—the passive attitude employed sometimes directly, sometimes symbolically, and sometimes ritually. **1966** K. Z. LORENZ *On Aggression* v. 48 In our European common shelduck for example, the whole process ..contains no ritually fixed parts. **1972** T. R. WILLIAMS *Introd. Socialization* viii. 183 Some American Indian cultures such as the Hopi and Zuni, ritually observe puberty for one or for both sexes. **1978** G. WAINWRIGHT in C. Jones et al. *Study of Liturgy* II. I. i. 37 Ritually, a novel feature of the Protestant worship was the giving of independent value to hymns in the structure of the service.

†**ˈrituous,** *a.* *Obs.*$^{-1}$ = RITUAL *a.*

1604 HIERON *Wks.* I. 569 Whence had you all that rituous store Vs'd in the masse, and nam'd before?

Ritz, *sb.* (*a.*) [The name of the Swiss-born hotelier César *Ritz* (1850–1918), given to his luxury hotels in Paris, London, New York, and elsewhere.] **a.** Used allusively of a large and luxurious hotel, *esp.* in negative phrases. Also *attrib.* and as *adj.*

1910 R. FRY *Lett.* (1972) I. 336, I will not pretend that my cuisine rivals the Ritz. **1922** F. SCOTT FITZGERALD (*title*) The diamond as big as the Ritz. **1926** E. HEMINGWAY *Sun also Rises* xix. 238 We drove in to Biarritz and left the car outside a very Ritz place. **1928** W. S. MAUGHAM *Ashenden* vi. 93 They came to a tavern in a blind alley, noisome and evil... 'It's not the Ritz,' he said, 'but at this hour of the night it's only in a place like this that we stand a chance of getting something to eat.' **1942** M. DICKENS *One Pair of Feet* vii. 111 A phrase that often sprang, unvoiced, to my lips, was 'This ain't the ruddy Ritz'. **1960** R. KIRKBRIDE *Innocent Abroad* xii. 87 Lousy as the room was, I was damn' glad to have it... 'It isn't the Ritz,' I said. 'But we got nowhere else to go.' **1973** W. H. CANAWAY *Harry doing Good* I. i. 14 The outhouse..was warm and fusty..but..for fifty pence who would expect the Ritz? **1978** *Vogue* Feb. 8/2 Creating charming country house suites with prints, quilting, Roman blinds, pretty colours, real Ritz comfort.

b. Colloq. phr. ***to put on the ritz,*** to assume an air of superiority. *U.S.*

1926 R. LARDNER in *Hearst's Internat.* Jan. 33/2 If you mention some really worth while novel like, say, 'Black Oxen', they think you're trying to put on the Ritz. **1929** I. BERLIN *Puttin' on the Ritz* (song) 3 If you're blue and you don't know what to do Why don't you go where Harlem sits Puttin' On The Ritz. **1945** L. SAXON et al. *Gumbo Ya-Ya* i. 11 You had to put on the ritz downtown, which some of the gals didn't like. **1980** H. LUCE *In Midst of Death* iii. 34 We'll have to decide how long we can go on putting on the Ritz in this house. Personally, I'd much rather live in a cottage.

ritz, *v.* *U.S. colloq.* [f. prec.] *trans.* To behave haughtily towards (someone); to snub. (See also quot. 1962.) Also *refl.*, to give oneself airs.

1911 G. ADE in *Chicago Daily News* 16 Sept. 28/2 They went abroad and began to Ritz themselves. **1924** H. C. WITWER in *Cosmopolitan* Nov. 42/2 We graciously presented Bertha with permission to bring him up to dinner at our flat one night, and he Ritzed and four-flushed us all till me and Hazel had to either dash out into the great outdoors or else give this big blah a sofa pillow shower! **1939** R. CHANDLER *Big Sleep* iii. 30 You sent for me. I don't mind your ritzing me. **1941** [see HIGH-HAT *v.*]. **1962** S. STRAND *Marketing Dict.* 636 *Ritzed it*, in the fashion field, adding glamour to a fabric or dress so that it will have public appeal. One way would be to advertise it in a class magazine. **1978** *Vogue* Feb. 8/2 (*heading*) Ritzing the Ritz.

ˈRitzian, *a.* [f. as prec. + -IAN.] Worthy or typical of the Ritz.

1908 F. HOPWOOD *Let.* 11 Jan. in R. S. Churchill *Winston S. Churchill* (1969) II. Compan. II. 742 A banquet of Ritzian splendour. **1918** G. FRANKAU in *Poetical Wks.* (1923) II. 179 Veil from these eyes their last too vivid canto:—Those Ritzian chambers on the Place Vendôme. **1940** 'GUN BUSTER' *Return via Dunkirk* II. vii. 142 Veal cutlets, tinned peas, cheddar cheese and vin rouge awaited me at the Command Post. In the circumstances, a Ritzian repast.

ritzily, ritziness: see RITZY *a.*

ritzy (ˈrɪtsɪ), *a.* *colloq.* (orig. *U.S.*). Also **Ritzy.** [f. RITZ *sb.* + -Y[1].] **a.** (In a complimentary sense.) Having class, poise, or polish; smart, stylish, glamorous, 'classy'. **b.** (In a derogatory sense.) Of persons: haughty, pretentious, ostentatious; of things: flashy, pretentious-looking.

1920 WODEHOUSE *Jill the Reckless* (1922) xvi. 240 The Duchess, abandoning that aristocratic manner criticized by some of her colleagues as 'up-stage' and by others as 'Ritz-y', [etc.]. **1923** *Variety* 15 Nov. 19/2 The upstaginess and ritzy attitude of the movie stars has become a matter of common talk. **1926** S. LEWIS *Mantrap* i. 20 Now there's some real Ritzy dancing-pumps... Had 'em done specially. **1930** E. WALLACE *White Face* v. 49 She's got the only respectable apartment... All Ritzy. **1932** S. GIBBONS *Cold Comfort Farm* xvii. 237, I want a new Gary Cooper..only more ritzy. Someone who can look good in a tuxedo. **1938** E. BOWEN *Death of Heart* II. iv. 243 Friend of your sister-in-law?.. He'll be a bit ritzy for us, then, won't he? **1943** *Archit. Rev.* XCIII. 80/4 There is no disguising the vulgarity of his Tokio hotel, the ritzy streamlining of his Johnson house, the mere ugliness of the Jones house of 1929. **1947** *People* 22 June 5/1 That glamour gal of British trains, the ritzy, resplendent Golden Arrow. **1949** 'G. ORWELL' *Let.* 5 Sept. in B. Crick *G. Orwell* (1980) xvii. 399, I feel ghastly and can't write much, but we had a wonderful journey down yesterday in the most ritzy ambulance you can imagine. **1951** M. MCLUHAN *Mech. Bride* (1967) 80/2 'Ritzy dames' who are provided with custom-built allure. **1958** *Woman's Own* 10 Sept. 33/1 For that ritzy touch, get octopus or ham in champagne. **1959** W. D. PEREIRA *North Flight* iv. 54 You should see 'is eldest kid... Bone idle. Goes to one of them ritzy schools, but it won't 'elp 'im none. **1963** *Observer* 1 Dec. 8/3 A stunning report, with its ritzy format and private jokes. **1970** R. FREETH *Lighting* iv. 32/2 If you want to be really 'Ritzy' install a filament reflector bulb as well over the cooker and sink. **1976** *Evening Advertiser* (Swindon) 31 Dec. 10/7 When I buy skin-food it's the product I'm interested in, not a ritzy bottle to decorate the dressing table. **1979** *Daily Tel.* 4 June 17/4 (Advt.), It looks most glamorous..for lounging in a ritzy beachside cafe.

Hence **ˈritzily** *adv.*, **ˈritziness.**

1928 *Motion Picture Classic* Jan. 27 They whirl ritzily out to Beverly Hills. **1929** M. LIEF *Hangover* 234 'Oh that?' she said sort of ritzily, 'why that's only her filling-station!' **1965** *Harper's Bazaar* Nov. 70 Lids can now be coated ritzily and memorably with Max Factor's Iridescent Gold shadow. **1967** N. TOMALIN in L. Deighton *London Dossier* 285 Neighbourhoods of unbelievably stuffy ritzyness. **1970** 'O. JOHN' *Diamond Dress* xiii. 145 The smooth, spacious ritziness of this large store.

riuage, riual, obs. ff. RIVAGE, RIVAL.

riue, obs. f. RIFE, RIVE.

riuel, obs. f. RIVEL.

riuele, obs. f. RULE.

riuelet, obs. var. RIVULET.

riueling, -yng, obs. ff. RIVELING[1].

riuely, obs. f. RIFELY.

riuen, obs. f. RIVEN.

riuer(e, obs. ff. REAVER, RIVER.

riuersa, var. RIVERSO *Obs.*

riuulet, obs. var. RIVULET.

‖**riva** (ˈriva). [It.] In Italy, a river-bank, sea-shore, or quay; *spec.* the *Riva degli Schiavoni* in Venice.

1880 F. J. SITWELL tr. *Yriarte's Venice* p. xii, The Riva and its Denizens. **1888** H. JAMES *Aspern Papers* I. i. 13 The old palace..overlooked a..canal, which had a narrow *riva* or convenient footway on either side. **1909** J. JOYCE *Let.* 7 Sept. (1966) II. 249, I long to see the lights twinkling along the *riva* as the train passes Miramar. **1928** BEERBOHM *Variety of Things* 186 As I passed along that Riva, I would try to imagine Venice as she was. **1965** H. HONOUR *Compan. Guide to Venice* v. 77 The Fondamenta dell'Arsenale leads down to the *Riva degli Schiavoni*... To your left the Riva sweeps up to the public gardens.

rivage (ˈraɪvɪdʒ). Also 4–6 **ryuage, -vage;** 5–7 **riuage.** [a. F. *rivage* (12–13th c.): see RIVE *sb.*[1] and -AGE. So It. *rivaggio*; med.L. *rivagium* (esp. in sense 3).]

1. A coast, shore, or bank. Now only *poet.*

13.. *Reinbroun* xxix. 10 þe cite on þe riuage hii sye. **1390** GOWER *Conf.* III. 329 The hihe festes of Neptune Upon the stronde at the rivage.. Sollempneliche thei besihe. *c* **1400** *St. Alexius* (Laud 622) 592 He gan to shippen atte Ryuage; Wynde aroos wiþ wood rage. **1483** CAXTON *Cato* D vij, A good holy man which was on the ryuage of the see. **1490** —— *Eneydos* vii. 30 Dydo.. arryued vpon the Ryuage of affryque for to repayre hir shyppes. **1523** CROMWELL in Merriman *Life & Lett.* (1902) I. 40 Sum other Contraye in the possession of his enemye vpon the Ryvage of the see. **1596** SPENSER *F.Q.* IV. vi. 20 The golden sand, The which Pactolus.. Throwes forth upon the rivage. **1609** HOLLAND *Amm. Marcell.* XIV. ii. 5 Having imbattelled themselves neere unto the rivage. **1658** W. BURTON *Itin. Anton.* 161 The River full of Ships,.. the rivage full of sea-faring men. **1661** EVELYN *Fumifugium* Misc. Writ. (1805) I. 208 The scent of the orange flowers from the rivage of Genoa.

1814 CARY *Dante, Inf.* XXIX. vii, So mov'd she on, against the current, up The verdant rivage. **1855** SINGLETON *Virgil* II. 100 The dreadful rivages, and brawling floods.

attrib. **1509** HAWES *Past. Pleas.* XXXVI. xvi, Ryght by anone the rivage syde, She cast an anker. **1513** DOUGLAS *Æneis* VI. v. 44 This sorofull boitman.. sum.. maid to stand Fer from the rivage syde upon the sand.

†**2.** Arrival at, landing on, a shore. *Obs.*

13.. *K. Alis.* 6079 Kyng Alisaunder, and his baronage, Haveth y-take god ryuage. *c* **1475** *Partenay* 2734 Hys brother.. At vavuent that day riuage gan purchas. *c* **1500** *Melusine* 114 The patrons made theire recommendacions to god.. that by hys benygne grace he wyl graunte to them good ryuage.

†**3.** Shore or river dues. *Obs.*

Quot. 1598 is translated from a charter of 1278.

1598 HAKLUYT *Voy.* I. 117 So that they shall be free.. from all lastage, tallage, passage, cariage, riuage. [**1706** PHILLIPS (ed. Kersey), *Rivage*,.. a certain Toll, or Duty anciently paid to the King, in some Rivers, for the Passage of Boats, or Vessels.]

Hence †'**rivaging**, the act of making up or repairing the bank of a stream. *Obs.*

1610 W. FOLKINGHAM *Art Surv.* II. ii. 50 Sewaging, rilling, brooking, riuaging, foording.

† **rival**, *sb.*[1] *Obs.* Forms: 4–5 riuale, 5 riuayle, 6 rivaile; 5 ryuaile, -ayle, ryvaille, -aylle, 6 ryual(e. [a. OF. *rivaille*, f. *rive* RIVE *sb.*[1]]

1. A bank, shore, landing-place. Also *port rival.*

1338 R. BRUNNE *Chron.* (1810) 153 þe kynges moder Richard Ariued at þat riuale. *c* **1400** tr. *Secreta Secret., Gov. Lordsh.* 52 He þat spendys his good ouyr mesure shal sone come to þe better riuale of pouert. *c* **1450** LYDG. *Secrees* 1328 Walkyng by Ryvaylles, holdyng ther passage On plesaunt hylles. **1502** in Arnolde *Chron.* (1811) 217 That noo Man be distreyned too make Bruggis ne Ryuals. **1594** GREENE & LODGE *Looking Gl.* (Hunterian Cl.) 57 As I was comming alongst the port ryuale of Niniuie.

2. Landing; arrival at a port.

1412–20 LYDG. *Chron. Troy* II. 8110 To Grekis pleinly þis ryvaille So mortal was & so infortunat. **15..** *Piers of Fulham* 316 in Hazl. *E.P.P.* II. 13 To make his rivaile to be know, At redclif in his saile to show.

rival ('raɪvəl), *sb.*[2] and *a.* Also 6–7 riual, 7 riu-, rivall. [ad. L. *rīvāl-is*, orig. one living on the opposite bank of a stream from another, f. *rīvus* stream. Hence also F. *rival* (15th c.), Sp. and Pg. *rival*, It. *rivale.*]

A. *sb.* **1.** One who is in pursuit of the same object as another; one who strives to equal or outdo another in any respect.

1577 tr. *Bullinger's Dec.* (1592) 106 To mingle poison priuily.. Or else in armour openly to worke his riuals death. **1590** SHAKS. *Mids. N.* III. ii. 156 You both are Riuals, and loue Hermia; And now both Riuals to mocke Helena. **1648–9** *Eikon Bas.* xxvi. (1662) 127 The Independents think themselves manumitted from their Rivals service. **1694** ADDISON *Virg.* Wks. 1726 I. 20 So let the royal insect rule alone And reign without a rival in his throne. **1712** STEELE *Spect.* No. 306 ⁋1 My Lovers are at the Feet of my Rivals, my Rivals are every Day bewailing me. **1769** ROBERTSON *Chas. V*, IX. III. 173 He beheld a prosperous rival receiving those ensigns of dignity of which he had been stripped. **1835** THIRLWALL *Greece* x. I. 436 Chalcis and Eretria were long rivals. **1853** C. BRONTE *Villette* xv, Come, we will not be rivals, we will be friends. **1899** MISS HARRADEN *Fowler* 128, I believe the medical name for a rival is 'colleague'.

Comb. **1597** SHAKS. *Rich. II*, I. iii. 131 (Q.[1]), The Egle-winged pride Of skie aspiring and ambitious thoughts, With riuall hating enuy.

transf. **1871** FREEMAN *Norm. Conq.* (1876) 211 That long line of low hills,.. which seems like a feeble rival of the loftier ranges of the West.

2. One who, or that which, disputes distinction or renown with some other person or thing.

1646 CRASHAW *Sospetto d'Herode* iv, That neither Rome nor Athens can bring forth A Name in noble deeds Rivall to thee! **1667** MILTON *P.L.* II. 472 And so refus'd might in opinion stand His rivals, winning cheap the high repute. **1770** *Junius Lett.* xxxvi. (1788) 194 The successor of one Chancellor might well pretend to be the rival of another. **1776** R. CHANDLER *Trav. Greece* 81 This stadium.. is extolled as without a rival, and as unequalled by any theatre. **1855** BREWSTER *Newton* II. xxvii. 400 A man who has had no rival in the times which are past. **1874** GREEN *Short Hist.* vii. §6. 403 The Spanish generals stood without rivals in their military skill.

B. *adj.* Holding the position of a rival or rivals.

1590 SHAKS. *Mids. N.* IV. i. 139, I know you two are Riuall enemies. **1619** DRAYTON *Lady Geraldine to Surrey* 11 Nor euer did suspitious riuall Eye Yet lye in wait my Fauours to espie. **1697** DRYDEN *Virg. Georg.* III. 28 The Rival Chariots in the Race shall strive. **1712** POPE *Ep. to Miss Blount* 15 Ev'n rival Wits did Voiture's death deplore. **1784** COWPER *Task* v. 123 Thus nature works.. in defiance of her rival pow'rs. **1830** D'ISRAELI *Chas. I*, III. v. 62 These Ministers of State attempted.. to restrain or abolish, a rival minority. **1886** RUSKIN *Præterita* I. vii. 227 He was perfectly.. candid in appraisement of the wine of rival houses.

Comb. **1802–12** BENTHAM *Ration. Judic. Evid.* (1827) IV. 47 The principle.. may be termed the double-shop, or rival-shop principle.

†'**rival**, *sb.*[3] *Obs.*[−1] [? ad. L. *rīvulus*, dim. of *rīvus*; cf. RIVEL *sb.*[3]] A small stream.

1600 W. WATSON *Decacordon* (1602) 68 A faire seeming.. fountaine.. deuided into two armes or riuals from the head.

rival, obs. form of RIVEL *v.*[1]

rival ('raɪvəl), *v.* [f. RIVAL *sb.*[2]]

1. *trans.* To enter into competition with; to contend or vie with; to strive to equal or excel (another).

1609 W. M. *Man in Moon* (1849) 43 He watcheth and prayeth for her,.. sobbing like a silly sot if he be rivald and put besides her. **1637** RUTTER *Cid* III. iv, Shall I Love where I am so rivall'd? No, my heart. **1697** DRYDEN *Virg. Past.* v. 10 Your Merit and your Years command the Choice: Amyntas only rivals you in Voice. **1711** STEELE *Spect.* No. 91 ⁋1 These Beauties Rival each other on all Occasions. **1787** *Generous Attachment* I. 25 You will have one half of the gay world to rival, and the other to approve your choice. **1824** BP. HEBER *Life Jer. Taylor* p. ccx, A work.. which contending sects have rivalled each other in approving. **1875** JOWETT *Plato* (ed. 2) I. 432, I had no idea of rivalling him or his poems.

b. *transf.* of things.

1784 COWPER *Task* I. 431 The cheering fragrance of her dewy vales, And music of her woods—no works of man May rival these. **1841** W. SPALDING *Italy & It. Isl.* II. 370 A host of writers, whose numbers rivalled, if they did not surpass, those of the sixteenth century. **1860** TYNDALL *Glac.* I. v. 38 A crash which rivalled thunder. **1880** HAUGHTON *Phys. Geogr.* v. 208 A desert region, rivalling.. the bare and repulsive features of the Sahara.

2. *intr.* To act as a rival, be a competitor.

1605 SHAKS. *Lear* I. i. 194 We first addresse toward you, who with this King Hath riuald for our Daughter. **1654** Z. COKE *Logick* Pref., Every Colon & Column of your lives.. [will] cause your Names (Rivalling with time) to survive on Earth. **1862** *Vacation Tour.* 1861, 271 Even Christianity has not been able to uproot an idea which Poetry and Art have rivalled to perpetuate. **1898** TOUT *Empire & Papacy* xvii. (1901) 427 The Lombard and Cahorsin usurers, who had now begun to rival with the Israelites in finance.

†**b.** So with *it.* *Obs.*

1656 S. H. *Gold. Law* 65 Silver and gold rival'd it in number and weight with the stones in the street. *Ibid.* 68 His [Joshua's] rivalling it with his master in dividing of Jordan's Rivers, Red Sea-like.

Hence '**rivalled** *ppl. a.*; '**rivalling** *vbl. sb.*

1606 SYLVESTER *Du Bartas* II. iv. *Magnificence* 76 Whom, with-out Force, Uproar, or Rivaling, Nature and Law, and Fortune make a King. *a* **1649** CRASHAW *Carmen Deo Nostro, Flaming Heart* 44 Give Him the vail; that he may cover The Red cheeks of a rivall'd lover. *a* **1748** THOMSON *Hymn on Solitude* 24 As.. she,.. Amid the long withdrawing vale, Awakes the rival'd nightingale.

'**rivaless.** [f. RIVAL *sb.*[2] + -ESS.] A female rival or competitor.

1680 MORDEN *Geog. Rect.* (1685) 465 Once formerly Romes great Rivaless. **1707** tr. *Wks. C'tess D'Anois* (1715) 434 She got to her Rivaless's Throne: where she stood upright, leaning against a Pillar. **1740** RICHARDSON *Pamela* (1824) I. lxix. 414 For, oh, my happy rivaless! if you tear from me my husband,.. I cannot help it.

rivalet, obs. form of RIVULET.

‖**ri'valis.** *Obs.*[−1] [L. *rīvālis.*] A rival.

1600 B. JONSON *Cynthia's Rev.* v. ii, Your Riualis.. dispatcheth his lacquay to the chamber, early, to know what her colours are for the day.

'**rivalism.** *rare.* [-ISM.] Rivalry.

1879 FARRAR *St. Paul* I. 32 Where Christian brotherhood and mutual esteem have taken the place of wretched rivalism.

rivality (raɪ'vælɪtɪ). [ad. L. *rīvālitas*: see RIVAL *sb.*[2] and -ITY. So F. *rivalité*, It. *rivalita*, Sp. *rivalidad*, Pg. *-ade.*] = RIVALRY 1.

1582 STANYHURST *Æneis*, etc. (Arb.) 140 Dame Venus and kingdooms can no riualitye suffer. **1606** SHAKS. *Ant. & Cl.* III. v. 8 Cæsar.. denied him riuality, would not let him partake in the glory of action. **1628** BP. HALL *Old Relig.* (1686) 107 Whatever worship more than meere humane is imparted to the creature, sets it in rivality with our Maker. *a* **1684** LEIGHTON *Comm. 1 Pet.* Wks. (1868) 236 Loyalty can admit of no rivality. **1781** *Characters* in *Ann. Reg.* 31/1 The rivality between the two nations will last. **1796** BURNEY *Mem. Metastasio* I. 318, I wish this rivality to be strongly marked. **1803** [see RIVALRY 2]. **1830** W. TAYLOR *Hist. Surv. Germ. Poet.* II. 63 It.. stimulates the exertions of rivality without hazarding its disappointments. **1876** 'OUIDA' *Winter City* x, Society is a Battle of the Frogs, for rivality in dress and debt.

rivalize ('raɪvəlaɪz), *v.* [f. RIVAL *sb.*[2] + -IZE. Cf. F. *rivaliser*, Pg. *-isar*, Sp. *-izar.*] *intr.* To enter into rivalry, to compete, *with.*

1802–12 BENTHAM *Ration. Judic. Evid.* (1827) IV. 337 Being.. the delegates of a spiritual authority, rivalizing with the temporal authority of the king. **1839** *Blackw. Mag.* XLV. 385 These steps I took, not with the intention of rivalizing with M. Daguerre in the perfection of his processes.

'**rivalless,** *a.* [f. RIVAL *sb.*[2] + -LESS.] Without a rival; having no rival.

1822 *Blackw. Mag.* XI. 69 When his young eye was bright as her rivalless star. **1856** RUSKIN *Mod. Paint.* III. IV. xvii. §27 Leaving Fleur de Marie and Virginia rivalless.

rivalrous ('raɪvəlrəs), *a.* [f. next + -OUS.]

1. Of the nature of rivalry.

1812 W. TAYLOR in *Monthly Mag.* XXXIV. 415 These would tend to independency, to rivalrous competition. **1853** G. J. CAYLEY *Las Alforjas* II. 45 Celebrated.. for their rivalrous animosity in lecture-room.

2. Given to rivalry; acting as a rival. orig. *U.S.*

1920 in WEBSTER. **1961** F. H. ALLPORT in Webster, s.v., Ascendant, expansive, and rivalrous students. **1963** *Observer* 21 Apr. 29/4 In the three- to six-year-old stage boys become rivalrous with their fathers, girls with their mothers. **1965** *Amer. N. & Q.* Sept. 14/2 A rivalrous and divided Italy had little more to offer. **1972** M. MEAD *Blackberry Winter* (1973) vi. 70 Sisters, while they are growing up, tend to be very rivalrous and as young mothers they are given to continual rivalrous comparisons of their several children. **1980** *N.Y. Times* 28 Oct. C1/1 Even geographical separation cannot sever their closeness or quell their rivalrous strivings.

rivalry ('raɪvəlrɪ). [f. RIVAL *sb.*[2] + -RY.]

1. a. The act of rivalling; competition, emulation.

1598 MARSTON *Sco. Villanie* III. xi. 230 Who enuies him? not I, For well he may, without all riualrie. **1633** BP. HALL *Occas. Medit.* (1851) 82 Forsaking all the base and sinful rivalry of the world. *a* **1719** ADDISON (J.), Those antagonists, who, by their rivalry for greatness, divided a whole age. **1759** JOHNSON *Rasselas* xxix, From those early marriages proceeds likewise the rivalry of parents and children. **1816** SCOTT *Antiq.* xvi, Jealousies, rivalries, envy, intervene to separate others from our side. **1850** KINGSLEY *Alt. Locke* xxxix, The innate selfishness and rivalry of human nature. **1875** JOWETT *Plato* (ed. 2) V. 403 Let them have conflict and rivalry in these matters in accordance with the law.

b. *Psychol.* Lack of fusion of the visual fields presented separately but simultaneously to each eye when these are sufficiently different, there being instead an alternation of perceived images.

1878 A. GAMGEE tr. *L. Hermann's Elem. Human Physiol.* (ed. 2) x. 427 (*heading*) Rivalry of the fields of vision. **1950** K. N. OGLE *Res. Binocular Vision* vi. 61 Depending on the particular characteristics of the image patterns falling on the retinas of the two eyes, fusion will be complete or partial, or as an antithesis of fusion, the patterns may actually exhibit a rivalry or resistance to fusion. **1974** L. KAUFMAN *Sight & Mind* viii. 306 Even when the inner square is seen floating above the background lines in the stereoscope, all the lines are in a constant state of binocular rivalry.

2. A body of rivals.

1803 W. TAYLOR in *Monthly Mag.* XIV. 114 The appearance of Ulysses among the suitors of Penelope disappointed the *rivality* of the whole *rivalry.*

rivalship ('raɪvəlʃɪp). [f. RIVAL *sb.*[2] + -SHIP.] The state or character of a rival; emulation, competition, rivalry.

1632 B. JONSON *Magn. Lady* II. i, He hath confess'd To me in private that he loves another..; therefore Secure you of rivalship. **1664** POWER *Exp. Philos.* I. 11 That proud Madam which Pallas, for her Rivalship, transform'd into the Spider. **1700** FARQUHAR *Constant Couple* I. i, I was beginning to mistrust some rivalship in the case. **1761** HUME *Hist. Eng.* xxix. II. 161 The emulation and rivalship which had so long subsisted between these two monarchs. **1818** COLEBROOKE *Import Colonial Corn* 198 The necessity must exist so long as rivalship continues among independent states. **1870** W. R. GREG *Polit. Probl.* 224 Permanence is necessary to good government, and.. our system of party rivalship forbids permanence.

†'**rivalty.** *Obs. rare.* [-TY.] Rivalry.

1644 [H. PARKER] *Jus Populi* 21 This does absolutely destroy that opinion, which places the good of Kings in any rivalty with the good of States. **1662** *Eikon Bas.* in *Chas. I, Wks.* 136 They are divided to so high a rivalty [*ed.* 1648 rivalry] as sets them more at defiance against each other then against their first Antagonists.

† **rive**, *sb.*[1] *Obs.* Forms: 3–5 ryue, 4–6 ryve, 4, 6 riue. [a. OF. *rive*:—L. *ripa* bank.]

a. The sea-shore. **b.** The bank of a river.

a **1300** *K. Horn* 142 Bliþe beo we on lyue, Vre schup is on ryue. *c* **1320** *Sir Tristr.* 1369 Now bringeþ me atte riue Schip and oþir þing. **1390** GOWER *Conf.* III. 49 Whan they herde hou Uluxes Is londed ther upon the ryve. *c* **1477** CAXTON *Jason* 79 b, In alle parties along by the Ryue of the cite. **1480** —— *Ovid's Met.* XI. ii, To wesche and purge hym, he must goo ayenst the ryve of a flood or ryver.

† **rive**, *sb.*[2] *Obs. rare.* In 5 ryue, riue. [App. ad. L. *rīvus* stream.] A stream or rill.

1489 CAXTON *Faytes of A.* I. xvii. 49 Somtyme.. an ost must passe ouer grete watres & ryues. **1533–4** *Act 25 Hen. VIII*, c. 7 Anie streites, riuers, riues, or brokes, salte or freshe within the realme.

† **rive**, *sb.*[3] *Obs. rare*[−0]. In 5 ryve. [= MDu. *rive* (Du. *rijf*), Fris. *riuwe*, ON. and Icel. *hrífa* (Norw. *riva*, Sw. *rifva*, Da. *rive*).] A rake.

c **1440** *Promp. Parv.* 435/1 Ryve, or rake, *rastrum.*

rive (raɪv), *sb.*[4] [f. RIVE *v.*[1]] A pull, tug, tear, rent, crack, etc.

1527 ANDREW *Brunswyke's Distyll. Waters* A iij, And so ordred laye it to the ryue of the glasse standynge upon the fyre. **1808** JAMIESON, *Rive*, a rent, or tear. **1822** HOGG *Perils of Man* II. vii. 246 A little hollow place in a wild moor,.. where our horses get nothing but a rive o' heather. *a* **1878** AINSLIE *Land of Burns* (1892) 223 Sair's the rive that breaks the twist Which binds our hearts in ane. **1895** CROCKETT *Men Moss-Hags* lii, With one rive he tore it from its fastenings.

rive, obs. form of RIFE *a.*

rive (raɪv), *v.*[1] [a. ON. and Icel. *rífa* (Norw. *riva*, Sw. *rifva*, Da. *rive*), = OFris. **rîva* (in pa. pple. *eriven*). It is doubtful whether these are to be identified with MLG. *rîven*, Du. *rijven*, G. *reiben* to rub, grate, rasp, etc.]

A. Inflexional forms.

1. *Inf.* (and *Pres.*). *α.* 3–7 **riue**, 4–6 **ryue** (6 *Sc.* **rywe, ryiue**); 4–7 (9 *Sc.*) **ryve** (5 **ryvyn**), 4– **rive.**

For examples of these see B. 1, 10, and 11.

β. 4 **rijf**, 4–5 **ryf** (5 **ryff**), **rife**, 5–6 **ryfe**; *Sc.* 5–6 **rif**, 6 **riff(e, ryffe.**

c **1340** HAMPOLE *Psalter* cxxiii. 5 þai had na myght to ryfe vs. **1375** BARBOUR *Bruce* xx. 255 Thair mycht men se men rif thar hare. ?*a* **1400** *Morte Arth.* 362, I salle..ryfe it in sondyre. *c* **1460** *Towneley Myst.* ii. 153 To were my shoyn & ryfe my hose. **1500–20** DUNBAR *Poems* lxxii. 91 Ane rude speir..did his precious body ryff. *a* **1578** LINDESAY (Pitscottie) *Chron. Scot.* (S.T.S.) I. 108 To ryfe the lyfe out of my bodie.

2. *Pa. t.* *α.* 3–5 **rof**, 4–5 **rofe, roff** (5 **roffe**), **roof** (5 **roofe**), 4–6 **roue**, 7 (9) **rove**, 9 *dial.* **rov.**

c **1275** LAY. 26566 þe spere..rof þorh þan swere. **1303** R. BRUNNE *Handl. Synne* 9288 Hys rolle to-braste and rofe. *c* **1385** CHAUCER *L.G.W.* 661 *Cleopatra*, He..roof hym-self anoon. *c* **1400** *Destr. Troy* 10298 þai..Rofe hit full Roidly. **1470–85** MALORY *Arthur* II. vi. 82 She..rofe her self thorow the body. **1535** COVERDALE *1 Kings* xiii. 5 Ye altare roue. **1807** in *Allan's Tyneside Songs* (1891) 90 Aw..Rove my breeks.

β. 4–5 **raf(e**, 5 **raffe** (5–6 *Sc.* **raeff, raif(f, raife**); 4–6 **raue** (5–6 *Sc.* **rawe**), 5– **rave** (7 *Sc.* **raive**), 9 *dial.* **raeve, reave.**

a **1300** *Cursor M.* 7510, I þair chafftes raue in tua. *Ibid.* 9110 He wald men raf it al to dust. *c* **1375** *Sc. Leg. Saints* xxi. (*Clement*) 93 Scho..grat, & rawe hir hare. *c* **1440** *Alph. Tales* 55 With þer hornys & þer tethe þai rafe his flessh. *c* **1450** *St. Cuthbert* (Surtees) 4683 þai raue þair clathes. **1525** LD. BERNERS *Froiss.* II. xlvii. 160 It raue clene in sondre. **1535** LYNDESAY *Satyre* 623 Wind, that raif the sails in sunder. **1603** *Reg. Privy Counc. Scotl.* VI. 589 [He] raive and distroyit it. **1718** RAMSAY *Christ's Kirk Gr.* III. xvii, Wi' her nails she rave his face. **1819** W. TENNANT *Papistry Storm'd* (1827) 190 [They] rugg't and rave them out. **1828** P. BUCHAN *Ballads* (1875) II. 249 Meggie reave her yellow hair.

γ. 4–5 **ref**, 5 **refe.**

13.. *Cursor M.* 24420 (Gött.), þe temple fra þe rof it ref. *a* **1425** *Ibid.* 7809 (Trin.), þourȝe his body my swerd I ref. *c* **1460** *Play Sacram.* 48 The ovyn refe a sondre.

δ. 6 **ryued, ryved, riued, yriv'd**, 7– **rived**, 8 **riv'd.**

a **1513** FABYAN *Chron.* VII. (1811) 249 The wynde..ryued ..ouer the nomber of vi. hundred howses. **1547** J. HARRISON *Exhort. Scottes* b iij b, It riued a sunder their kyngdome. **1591** SPENSER *Astrophel* 120 That it both bone and muscles ryved quight. **1596** —— *F.Q.* IV. vi. 15 That all his mayle yriv'd. **1727** DE FOE *Protestant Monastery* 14 She ..used me in such a Manner as has riv'd my..Heart. **1791** COWPER *Iliad* xx. 475 Achilles drove his spear, And rived his skull. **1887** HALL CAINE *Deemster* xxxvii, [I] rived them [*sc.* rabbits] asunder.

3. *Pa. pple.* *α.* 4–6 **ryuen** (5 **ryuyn**), 5– 6 **ryven**, 5 *Sc.* **rywen, -ine**; 4–7 **riuen** (4 **riuin**); 5 **rifen**; 5– **riven** (7 *Sc.* **rivin**).

a **1300** *Cursor M.* 4165 He riuen es Wit beistes wild. *c* **1375** *Sc. Leg. Saints* xxxviii. (*Adrian*) 346 þane wes he.. rywine & rente. *c* **1400** *Ywaine & Gaw.* 3539 Thair sheldes war shiferd, and helms rifen. **1483** *Cath. Angl.* 310/1 To be Ryven, *fatiscere*. **1566** in Peacock *Eng. Ch. Furniture* (1866) 48 Torn, broken, and ryven in peces. **1621** BP. MOUNTAGU *Diatribæ* 323 A rough knot, not riuen out. **1746** THOMSON *Cast. Indol.* II. lxix, The brand by which the rocks are riven. **1870** HUXLEY *Lay Serm.* xiv. (1874) 342 Riven by the lightenings.

β. 4 (6 *Sc.*) **reuin**, 5 **reuen**, 5, 7 **reven**; 9 *dial.* **reaven**; *Sc.* 5 **refyn(e, rewyn, rewine**, 5–6 **reuyn**, 6 **rewin, revin, reivin, reiuen.**

13.. *Cursor M.* 22636 (Gött.), þat erd þat sal be reuin. *c* **1375** *Sc. Leg. Saints* i. (*Peter*) 25 He wald haf refyn [him] sone. *c* **1400** *Laud Troy Bk.* 13320 Ther schal be reuen many a scheld. *c* **1425** WYNTOUN *Cron.* v. x. 1898 His westment rewyn al in raggis. **1549** *Compl. Scotl.* vii. 69 This mantil.. vas reuyn. **1596** DALRYMPLE tr. *Leslie's Hist. Scot.* IV. 251 Quhair thay war reiuen in duigis.

γ. 5 **ryue, reve**, 6 **rive**, 9 *dial.* **riv.**

a **1425** *Cursor M.* 1855 (Trin.), Ofte þei wende her shippe wold ha ryue. **1430** *Syr Gener.* (Roxb.) 6001 The sheld that was reue. **1596** SPENSER *F.Q.* v. xi. 5 That seem'd a marble rocke asunder could have rive. **1895** A. PATTERSON *On the Broads* 22 Years ago, afore laths was riv'.

δ. 6 **ryued**, 7 **riv'd**, 7– **rived.**

a **1513** FABYAN *Chron.* II. (1811) 249 Ye rofe..was also ryued. **1601** SHAKS. *Jul. C.* I. iii. 6 When the scolding Winds Haue riu'd the knottie Oakes. **1681** FLAVEL *Meth. Grace* ii. 39 The tree..was rived asunder. **1782** ELIZ. BLOWER *Geo. Bateman* I. 216 My heart is rived with agony!

B. Signification.

In standard English the word is now somewhat rare, being most frequently employed in sense 4, and chiefly in the pa. pple. *riven* ('rɪv(ə)n).

I. *trans.* **1.** To tear apart or in pieces by pulling or tugging; to rend or lacerate with the hands, claws, etc.; to pull asunder.

a **1300** *Cursor M.* 4161 His kyrtil sal we riue and rend. *c* **1340** HAMPOLE *Pr. Consc.* 888 Wormes sal ryve hym in sondre. **14..** *Tundale's Vis.* 283 Ychon..with oder dyd stryve And with her naylys her chekys dyd ryve. *c* **1450** HOLLAND *Howlat* 815, I sall ryiue the Ravyne, baith guttis and gall. *c* **1500** *World & Child* 529, I praye you, syr, ryue me this cloute. *a* **1572** KNOX *Hist. Ref.* Wks. 1846 I. 329 Monsieur Dosell and the Capitanis.., efter the reading of thame, began to ryve thair awin beardis. **1596** DALRYMPLE tr. *Leslie's Hist. Scot.* Prol. 20 Thay sett vpon thame, and.. thame onlie thay ryue with thair teith. **1638** BAILLIE *Lett. & Jrnls.* (1841) I. 76 They sett on him in church, ryves his gowne,..and so..dismisses him. **1697** CONGREVE *Mourn. Bride* III. vi, Then will I..disfigure And dash my Face, and rive my clotted Hair. *c* **1715** in Maidment *Pasquils* (1868) 393 Dee'l ryve and burst him. **1824** SCOTT *Redgauntlet* ch. xxiii, What are ye pooin' me that gate for?—Ye will rive my coat. **1862** C. C. ROBINSON *Dial. Leeds* Gloss. 394 Rive us that sheet o' paaper i' two.

fig. *c* **1380** WYCLIF *Sel. Wks.* I. 103 ȝif rychesse liken þe fleishe, neþeles þei ryven þe soule. *c* **1460** *Wisdom* 175 in *Macro Plays* 41 Ye Godis ymage neuer xall ryve. **1572** *Satir. Poems Reform.* xxxiii. 44 The malice greit, that ilk to vther beiris, Dois ryfe my bowells. *c* **1785** BURNS *2nd Ep. to Davie* iv, I'm on Parnassus' brink, Rivin the words to gar them clink. **1863** W. PHILLIPS *Sp.* xvi. 349 It went through the land,..riving sects.

refl. **1830** GALT *Lawrie T.* I. xi, It was a sad sight to see that mother and that daughter rive themselves asunder.

†**b.** To tear up (a letter, document, etc.), so as to destroy or cancel. Chiefly *Sc. Obs.*

1415 SIR T. GREY in 43 *Rep. Deputy Kpr. Rec.* 583, I redde hit and rofe hit and kest hit in a govnge. **1480** *Acta Dom. Conc.* (1839) 73 The said dauid bowy tuke it again, rafe & distruyt it, but þe said dauid westis consent. **1527** [see RIVING *vbl. sb.*[1] 1]. **1566** *Reg. Privy Council Scot.* I. 471 That ..thair Comptrollar..at the first sycht and presentatioun of thame ryve and cancellat sic writtingis. *a* **1650** CALDERWOOD *Hist. Kirk* (1843) II. 506 Their armes were rivin at the Croce, in presence of the regent and the lords.

2. With various advs. and preps.:

a. To tear or pull *off* or *away*.

13.. *Cursor M.* 9099 (Gött.), Of his robe he gan to riue. *c* **1480** HENRYSON *Mor. Fab., Wolf & Wether* xiii, Ane breir busk raif rudelie of the skyn. **1500–20** DUNBAR *Poems* lxxii. 60 The claith that claif to his clere hyde, Thai raif away with ruggis rude. **1680** H. MORE *Apocal. Apoc.* 136 Excommunication, that rives off a member from the church. *c* **1784** BURNS *Ep. to Rankine* iii, Your curst wit..Rives 't aff their back.

b. To tear, wrench, or pluck roughly away *from* (a person or thing).

a **1340** HAMPOLE *Psalter, Comm. Cant.* 518 Deuyls, þe whilk cruelly ryuys saules fra god. *a* **1400** *Sir Perc.* 2157 Hir clothes ther scho rafe hir fro. *c* **1450** HOLLAND *Howlat* 835 The Tuchet..Raif his taile fra his rig. **1554** KNOX *Faythf. Admon.* C v, That God..haue much to do to ryffe or plucke any man backe from their forefathers footesteppes. **1816** BYRON *Corsair* III. vi, Thy loved one from thee riven. **1863** BARING-GOULD *Iceland* 129 The cold hands came down on Grettir's arms, riving them from their hold.

c. To pull *down*, or *to* the ground; to tear, drag, or pull *up* or *out*.

c **1375** *Sc. Leg. Saints* v. (*John*) 305 He þe tempil suld in hy of dame diane gere Ryve done. *c* **1400** *Destr. Troy* 4783 Robbet was þis ronke hold & ryuyn to ground. **1470–85** MALORY *Arthur* XII. iii. 596 The bore torned hym nemly & rafe out the longes & the hert of the hors. **1535** COVERDALE *Zeph.* ii. 14 The bordes of Cedre shalbe ryuen downe. **1545** ASCHAM *Toxoph.* I. (Arb.) 93 Plowing..riueth and plucketh vp by the rootes, all thistles, brambles and weedes. *c* **1585** MONTGOMERIE *Sonnets* lv. 12 Rigour ryvis the hairt out by the root. **1621** BP. MOUNTAGU *Diatribæ* 323 An hard and a rough knot, not riuen out by the Author of the History. **1680** OTWAY *Caius Marius* v. i, As storms let loose That riue the trunks of tallest cedars down. **1754** T. GARDNER *Hist. Dunwich* 161 John Arnold..gave Order to..the Sexton to rive it out for the Plumber's Use. **1873** GIBBON *For Lack of Gold* xxi, I would rive the heart out of my breast.

3. To sever, cleave, or divide, by means of a knife or weapon; †to pierce or thrust.

13.. *Gaw. & Gr. Knt.* 1341 Syþen britned þay þe brest, &..Ryuez hit vp radly, ryȝt to þe byȝt. *c* **1385** CHAUCER *L.G.W.* 1351 *Dido*, With his swerd she rof hyre herte. **1426** LYDG. *De Guil. Pilgr.* 14944 The sharpe sperys hed..Rooff that lord vn-to the herte. **1483** CAXTON *Gold. Leg.* 316 b/2 He sayd yf it be trewe..late a swerd ryue me thurgh my body. *a* **1592** GREENE *Selimus* 592 Vpon my swords sharpe point standeth pale death Readie to riue in two thy caitiue brest. **1659** [see RIFF *sb.*[4]]. **1668** HOPKINS *Serm.* (1685) 57 What torments the conscience feels, when God causes his sword to enter into it, to rive it. **1791** COWPER *Iliad* xx. 475 Achilles drove his spear, And rived his skull.

refl. *c* **1384** CHAUCER *H. Fame* 373 She rofe hir selfe to the herte. **1430–40** LYDG. *Bochas* VI. xiii, Scipion.. rofe hymselfe to the heart and so died. **1474** CAXTON *Chesse* 21 With a swerde..she roof her self vnto the herte. **1612** DRAYTON *Poly-olb.* vii. 187 Marcely,..Inrag'd and mad with griefe, himselfe in two did riue.

†**b.** To drive (a weapon) *through* (the heart, etc.); to thrust *into* (the body). *Obs.*

c **1385** CHAUCER *L.G.W.* 1793 *Lucrece*, This swerd thour out thyn herte shal I ryue. *a* **1425** *Cursor M.* 7809 (Trin.), þourȝe his body my swerd I ref. **1483** CAXTON *Gold. Leg.* 69/1 Eche toke other by the heed and roof their swerdes in to eche other sydes.

†**c.** To make (a way) by piercing. *Obs.*[−1]

1600 FAIRFAX *Tasso* XII. lxxxii, You deere lims.., Through which my cruell blade this flood-gate roue.

4. To rend or split by means of shock, violent impact or pressure, etc.; to strike asunder; †to break or crack (a dish).

a **1300** *Cursor M.* 22636 þe deuels vte sal be fordriuen O þat erth þat sal be riuen. **1338** R. BRUNNE *Chron.* (1810) 148 Ten schippes wer dryuen, þorgh ille auisement, þorgh a tempest ryuen. **1526** *Pilgr. Perf.* (W. de W. 1531) 256 b, This deth..dyd ryue the myghty & stronge wall of ye [temple]. *a* **1548** HALL *Chron., Hen. VI*, 9 b, [They] shot.. great stones.., the strokes whereof..shaked, crushed and ryued the walles. **1596** [see A. 3 *γ*]. **1625** PURCHAS *Pilgrimes* II. 1657 If a dish happen to be a little riven or crackt, they eat no more in it. **1653** H. COGAN tr. *Pinto's Trav.* lxxi. 288 After this, he..caused all the lesser Ordnance to be rived asunder, and the greater..to be cloyed. **1748** THOMSON *Cast. Indol.* II. lxix, Repentance..quells the brand by which the rocks are riven. **1768** BEATTIE *Minstrel* I. xlviii, Like yonder blasted boughs by lightening riven. **1803** HEBER *Palestine* 55 Where the tempest rives the hoary stone. **1860** TYNDALL *Glac.* I. ii. 20 The Rhone glacier,..where it is greatly riven and dislocated.

fig. *c* **1460** *Towneley Myst.* xiv. 296 Those lurdans wote not what thay say; Thay ryfe my hede. **1591** SHAKS. *1 Hen. VI*, IV. ii. 29 Ten thousand French haue tane the Sacrament, To ryue their dangerous Artillerie Vpon..English Talbot. **1837** CARLYLE *Fr. Rev.* III. vii. (1857) II. 242 With fire-words the exasperated rude Titan rives and smites these Girondins.

b. To split or cleave (wood, stone, etc.) by appropriate means. Also with *up*, *off*.

c **1440** *Promp. Parv.* 435/1 Ryvyn, or clyvyn, as men doo woodde, *findo*. **1530** PALSGR. 692/2, I ryve wodde in to byllettes, or splentes, or suche lyke, *je fends*. **1567** MAPLET *Gr. Forest* 16 Nitrum is a stone..easie to be riuen. **1622** BP. HALL *Contempl., O.T.* XVII. i, That wood which a single iron could not rive, is soon splitted with a double wedge. **1670** EACHARD *Cont. Clergy* 22 As for him that rives blocks, or carries packs, there is..no great intellectuall pensiveness. **1793** WINDHAM in *Burke's Corr.* (1844) IV. 190 The progress of the northern armies must, of necessity, be slow; they are there riving the block at the knotty end. **1830** SOUTHEY in *Q. Rev.* XLIII. 22 When this politic purpose had been sufficiently answered, it was riven up for fuel. **1891** MISS DOWIE *Girl in Karp.* 258 It is a stake of pine wood.. commonly speaking rived off at an early period.

absol. **1622** *Relat. Eng. Plantation in Plymouth* 24 We went on shore. Some to fell tymber, some to saw, some to riue, and some to carry.

transf. **1875** KINGLAKE *Crimea* (1877) V. i. 127 The taller horsemen who were riving it [*sc.* the column] deeper and deeper.

c. *techn.* To make (laths) by splitting wood along the grain into thin narrow strips.

1610 [implied in *lath-river*: see LATH *sb.* 4]. **1618** *Nottingham Rec.* IV. 359 For ij men to rive lathes. [**1892** *Eastern Morn. News* (Hull) 16 Feb. 2/8 The lath-riving in Sweden.] **1895** [see A. 3 *γ*].

5. *Sc.* and *north.* To plough (untilled ground); to break *up* with the plough. Also with *out*.

1536 *Reg. Magni Sig. Scot.* (1883) 394/2 To ryfe out, breke, and teill yeirlie 1000 acris of thair..landis. **1572** *Satir. Poems Reform.* xxxiii. 271 Now mon thay..Ryue out the Mures, the bestialls gers intak. **1590** *Reg. Privy Council Scot.* IV. 515 [The bailies and council] had revin out and sawin ane pairt thairof this present yeir. **1619–53** [see RIVING *vbl. sb.*[1] 1]. **1785** BURNS *Death & Dr. Hornbook* xxiii, His braw calf-ward whare gowans grew, Sae white an' bonie, Nae doubt they'll rive it wi' the plew. **1787** in Cudworth *Manningham*, etc. (1896) 330 That they will not..plow, grave, or rive up any Part of the Close of Land. **1816** SCOTT *Bl. Dwarf* i, Ill wad he hae liked to hae seen that braw sunny knowe a' riven out wi' the plough.

absol. **1856** G. HENDERSON *Pop. Rhymes Berwick* 70 Where the scythe cuts, and the sock rives.

6. To rend (the heart, soul, etc.) with painful thoughts or feelings.

a **1300** *Cursor M.* 26015 þarfor agh sinful man and wijf On þis maner þair hert to rijf. *c* **1400** tr. *Secreta Secret., Gov. Lordsh.* 93 He schall ryue þe hert of his subgitz, þat ys to say, ..his subgitz shall fele hym at þaire hertes. **1647** H. MORE *Exorcismus* Wks. (Grosart) 177 What's this that..Rives my close-straitned heart? **1713** ADDISON *Cato* II. v, Why will you rive my heart with such expressions? **1795** MACNEILL *Scotland's Skaith* xlii, Jean's condition Rave his very heart in twa. **1822** MRS. NATHAN *Langreath* III. 186 Deeply drawn sighs, which seemed to rive the agonized bosom from whence they issued. **1896** HOUSMAN *Shropshire Lad* xlviii, All thoughts to rive the heart are here, and all are vain.

II. *absol.* †**7.** To pierce, cut, or shear *through* or *into* (the body). *Obs.*

c **1275** LAY. 26566 Beofs..smot hine..þat þe spere deore rof þorh þan swere. *Ibid.* 27685 þe brunie gan to berste, þat þe spere þorh rof. **1388** WYCLIF *2 Sam.* ii. 23 Abner smoot him with the spere.., and roof thorouȝ, and he was deed. *c* **1400** *Destr. Troy* 5907 He bere to þe bold with a big sworde, And rof þurgh the Ribbes right to þe hert. *c* **1477** CAXTON *Jason* 102 b, Iason toke his swerd and roof into the paunche of the dragon.

8. To commit spoliation or robbery; to reave; to take away *from*. Now *dial.*

1489 *Barbour's Bruce* XVI. 551 (Edinb.), On west half, towart Dunferlyng, Tuk land; and fast begouth to ryve. **1513** MORE in Hall *Chron., Edw. V* (1548) 9 b, There deuyse they newe robberies nightely and steale oute and robbe, riue, and kyll menne. **1559** *Mirr. Mag., Glendour* ix, Bent my selfe to rob and ryue. **1816** [see RIVING *vbl. sb.*[1] 1]. **1858** RAYSON *Poems* 7 I've nought but sarvants riving frae me.

†**b.** *trans.* To rob or despoil (a person). *Obs.*

1582–8 *Hist. & Life Jas. VI* (1804) 85 The people..were become of sic dissoluit..actiones, that nane was in account bot he that wald ather kill or ryve his nybour.

9. To tear voraciously; to tug *at* something.

1552 LYNDESAY *Test. Papyngo* 1148 The Rauin began rudely to ruge and ryue, Full gormondlyke his emptie throte to feid. **1818** SCOTT *Hrt. Midl.* xlvii, Twa precious saints might pu' sundry wise, like twa cows riving at the same hay-band. **1829** BROCKETT *N.C. Gloss.* (ed. 2) 248 *Rive*, to tear membrane from membrane, to eat voraciously without knife or fork. 'See how he's riving and eating'. **1865** DICKENS *Mut. Fr.* I. xiii, Standing..roared and riven at by the wind. **1867** A. DAWSON *Rambling Recoll.* (1868) 8 His neighbour was 'riving' at an obstinate sinew.

III. *intr.* **10.** To part asunder; to cleave, split, crack, open up, etc.

a **1300** *Cursor M.* 1767 þe see [gan] to ris, þe erth to riue. *c* **1330** *Arth. & Merl.* 448 (Kölbing), Mani schaft þer gan riue. *c* **1400** *Ywaine & Gaw.* 636 Thair sheldes sone bigan to ryve, Thair shaftes cheverd. **1480** *Robt. Devyll* 133 in Hazl. *E.P.P.* I. 224 They feared that the house woulde ryue a sonder. **1527** ANDREW *Brunswyke's Distyll. Waters* a iij, A lutynge for a glasse that ryveth upon the fyre. **1563** SACKVILLE *Induct., Mirr. Mag.* lxxix, As though the heauens riued with the noyse. **1578** LYTE *Dodoens* 762 A thinne barke the which will soone rive, or cleeve asunder. **1616** SURFL. & MARKHAM *Country Farme* v. viii. 537 All sorts of ashes, either of Wood or Coale, is a good manure..for ground that is apt to chap or riue. *a* **1661** FULLER *Worthies* (1840) I. 110 The oak..may be called cowardly, as riving and splitting round about the passage of the bullet. **1805** SCOTT *Last Minstrel* Note xlviii, Sutor Watt, ye cannot sew your boots; the heels risp, and the seams rive. **1877** TENNYSON *Harold* II. ii. 426 Why let earth rive, gulf in These cursed Normans.

fig. **1549** *Compl. Scotl.* i. 21 Lucan..said that the vecht of rome suld gar it ryue in mony partis. **1589** NASHE *Martin Marprelate* Wks. (Grosart) I. 78 Theyr Religion like an ancient building, worne with..age, riues and threatens ruine on euery side.

b. Of wood or stone: To admit of splitting or cleaving.

1699 *Phil. Trans.* XXI. 437 A Tree we call Cypress..; it is soft and spungy, will not Rive. **1772** *Ann. Reg.* 119 The body of the willow tree rives into pales. **1811** PINKERTON *Petral.* I. 432 All like sorts of stone that are composed of granules, will cut and rive in any direction. **1831** JOHN HODGSON in Raine *Mem.* (1858) II. 212 They rive, according to the term of the quarry-men, into thin..laminæ.

11. In hyperbolical or figurative use:

a. Of the heart: To break or burst with sorrow.

c **1400** *Rom. Rose* 5718 She fighteth with hym ay, and stryveth, That his herte asondre ryveth. *c* **1460** *Towneley Myst.* iii. 399 Me thynk my hert ryfis..To se sich stryfis. **1550** LEVER *Serm.* (Arb.) 23 Thys playne worde..wold make..oure hertes to ryue in peces. *c* **1595** J. DICKENSON *Sheph. Compl.* (1878) 13 This said, he sighd, as though his heart would riue. **1620–6** QUARLES *Feast for Worms* 1635 O kill me (Lord) or lo, my heart will riue. **1870** ROSSETTI *Poems, Sister Helen* xxvii, He prays you, as his heart would rive,..To save his dear son's soul alive.

b. Denoting the effect of repletion, excessive laughter, etc.

1586 D. ROWLAND *Lazarillo* (1653) Ej, My stomack began to rive for hunger. *a* **1682** F. SEMPILL *Blythsome Wedding* 72 There will be meal-kail and castocks With skink to sup till ye rive. **1715** RAMSAY *Christ's Kirk Gr.* II. xiv, Jock, wi' laughing like to rive. **1786** BURNS *To a Haggis* iv, Then auld Guidman, maist like to rive, Bethankit hums. **1827** *Kinloch's Ballad Bk.* 68 Ye wad hae riven for laughter. **1884** D. GRANT *Lays* 20, I winna drink anither drap! My head is like to rive.

†**rive**, *v.*[2] *Obs.* Forms: α. 4 riue, ryue, 5–6 ryve (5 ryvyn). *Pa. t.* 4 riuede, 5 ryuede, revede, (and *pa. pple.*) 3–4 riued, 4–5 ryued, 4–6 ryved, 5 *Sc.* rywit, 6 riude. β. *Pa. t.* 4 roue, raue, 5 raffe. γ. *Pa. pple.* 4 (y)ryuen, 5 ryven, reuyn, revyn. [ad. OF. *river*, aphetic form of *arriver* ARRIVE *v.* Common in the 14th cent.] *intr.* To arrive, to land. Freq. with *up*.

α. *a* **1300** *K. Horn* 162 And sey..þat ichc..On londe am riued here. *c* **1320** *Sir Tristr.* 920 Til inglond wil y riue. **1387** TREVISA *Higden* (Rolls) VII. 85 Wiþ a grete navey he ryved up at Cornwayle. *c* **1430** LYDG. *Min. Poems* (Percy Soc.) 63 To the haven of dethe whan we gan to ryve. *c* **1440** *Promp. Parv.* 435/1 Ryvyn to londe, as schyppys or botys, fro water, *applico, appello*. **1483** *Cath. Angl.* 310/1 To Ryve vp, *appellere, applicare*. **1530** PALSGR. 692/2 In shorte space they ryved at Calays. **1592** WYRLEY *Armorie* 134 We there were riude with vigerous entent With him to fight.

β. *c* **1350** *St. Mary Magd.* 478 in Horstm. *Altengl. Leg.* (1881) 86 þe weders fand þai gude and gayne, So þat þai raue up in Romayne. **1387** TREVISA *Higden* (Rolls) VII. 87 þe navy of Danes rove up at Sandwyche, and robbed Kent. *a* **1440** *Sir Eglam.* 1297 + 15 (Linc. MS.), This fayre navé Alle in lykynge passed the see, In Artasse up thay raffe.

γ. *c* **1400** *Chron. R. Glouc.* (Rolls) 362 (MS. B), þo he was ware, þat such folk was y-armed..& ryuen vp hys lond. **14..** *Guy Warw.* 4244 So longe þe wynde haþ þem dreuyn: At Almayne they be vp reuyn. *Ibid.* 8476 In Awfryke well soone þey be yryuen. *c* **1435** *Torr. Portugal* 1438 Sith we be ryven on this lond, To nyght wylle I ryde.

†**rive**, *v.*[3] *Obs.*[−0] [Related to RIVE *sb.*[3] Cf. Du. *rijven*, Fris. *riuwje*.] *trans.* To rake.

c **1440** *Promp. Parv.* 435/1 Ryvyn, or rakyn, *rastro*.

rived (raɪvd), *ppl. a.* [f. RIVE *v.*[1] + -ED[1].] Riven, rent. Also *fig.*

1631 FLETCHER *Piscatory Eclogs* iii, To break the rived heart with fear and fright. **1799** SHERIDAN *Pizarro* I. i, Thou, all-powerful!..whose lightnings can pierce to the core the rived and quaking earth. **1838** ELIZA COOK *I thank Thee, God!* vii, So in the rived heart there'll be Mercy that never flowed before. **1853** *Trans. Mich. Agric. Soc.* IV. 156 Either the rived or sawed bolt may be used. **1887** *Century Mag.* Apr. 901/1 The earliest houses of worship in America belonged to the make-shift order of architecture,—four walls of..rived clapboards with earth filled in between.

†**rived**, *a. Obs. rare.* [f. *rive*, early form of RIFE *a.* The ending is irregular.] = RIFE *a.*

a **1300** *Joseph & Jacob* 18 Forþi sende oure Louerd Noees flod... Hi floten swiþe riued bi dich & bi pulle. *a* **1400–50** *Alexander* 1740 So..riued [*v.r.* ryfe] is oure rewme þat þou may reȝt lycken þe store strenthe of oure stoure to sternes of þe heuen. *Ibid.* 1779 So riued is þe rede gold oure regions with-in. **1513** BRADSHAW *St. Werburge* II. 168 Couetise, pride, lechery were ryued alway.

†'**rivedly**, *adv. Obs.* In 4 riuedlich(e, -li. [f. RIVED *a.* + -LY[2].] = RIFELY *adv.*

a **1300** *Fall & Passion* 103 in *E.E.P.* (1862) 15 þe .iii. dai he ros to liue; is lore riuedlich he send. *c* **1350** *Will. Palerne* 2115 For missing of þat mariage al murþe was seced, riuedliche þurth rome & reuþe bi-gunne. *Ibid.* 3840, I schal riuedli him rewarde to be riche for euer.

‖**rive gauche** (riv goʃ). [Fr.] = *left bank* s.v. LEFT *a.* 3.

1862 MRS. GASKELL *Jrnl.* Feb. in *Fraser's Mag.* (1864) Apr. 435/1 We went to-day along the Boulevard Sévastopol, Rive Gauche, to pay a call. **1894** G. DU MAURIER *Trilby* I. II. 51 Then back again to the quays on the *rive gauche* by the Pont Neuf. **1928** R. HALL *Well of Loneliness* xxxi. 289 Of course you'll have to live on this side, the Rive Gauche is the only possible Paris. **1948** A. WAUGH *Unclouded Summer* ii. 16 It was his belief that the Americans who were creating an *emigré Rive gauche* colony had sold their birthright. **1959** *Listener* 28 May 941/2 All those romantic stories..which have been going the rounds of the *rive gauche* ever since. **1977** *Times* 19 Feb. 9/1 Those whose shelves are filled with rarities, generally secured for 'next to nothing' on the Rive Gauche.

riveir, obs. Sc. form of RIVER *sb.*[1]

†**rivel**, *sb.*[1] *Obs.* Forms: 4–6 ryuel (4 reuel), 5 ryvel, 6–7 riuel, 7 riuil, -ell, rivel. [Perh. repr. an OE. **rifel*, whence *rifelede* RIVELLED *a.*] A wrinkle or fold upon the skin (*esp.* of the face) or on the rind of a fruit.

1382 WYCLIF *Job* xvi. 9 My ryuelis seyn witnesse aȝen me. **1387** TREVISA tr. *Higden* (Rolls) I. 257 He haþ a large ryuel, as it were a bagge, vnder þe chynne. **1398** —— *Barth. De P.R.* XVII. lxi. (Bodl. MS.), It is iseide þat figes doþ awei reuels of olde men ȝif þei ete wele þerof. **1426** LYDG. *De Guil. Pilgr.* 24273 Thou mayst se, by my lokkes hore, and by ryvels of my visage, How that I am called 'Age'. **1545** RAYNOLD *Byrth Mankynde* 11 Though that the matrix..be full of riuels or wrinkles by the reason that it is so contract from a great amplytude. **1601** HOLLAND *Pliny* XII. vii, It wanteth the due parching and ripening against the sunne: and by that meanes commeth short of the rivels and blacknesse that the outlandish pepper hath. *Ibid.* XVIII. xii, It causeth the skin to looke cleare and white, and without any rivels or wrinkles. **1632** SHERWOOD, A riuell, *ride*.

fig. **1598** E. GUILPIN *Skial.* (1878) 43 And leauing it their lothsome playstered skins, Shall shew the furrowed riuels of their sins.

†'**rivel**, *sb.*[2] *Obs.*[−1] [Cf. RIVEL *v.*[2]] A ravel or tangle.

?*a* **1630** JACKSON *Wks.* (1673) II. 513 You haue perhaps already espied..a knot or rivel, wherewith your beliefs..may be entangled.

'**rivel**, *sb.*[3] *rare*[−1]. A rivulet.

1886 LEIFCHILD in *Contemp. Rev.* July 90 'Tis A full-fed rivel lapsing by.

'**rivel**, *v.*[1] Now *rare.* Forms: 4 rivele, 5 ryvel, 6 ryvell, 7 rivell, 8 rival, 4– rivel; 4, 6 ryuel, 4–7 riuel. [Cf. RIVELLED *a.*]

1. *intr.* To become wrinkled or shrivelled; to form wrinkles or small folds.

c **1325** *Old Age* in *Rel. Ant.* II. 211, I rivele, I roxle, I rake, I rouwe. **1390** GOWER *Conf.* II. 98 Hire chekes ben with teres wet, And rivelen as an emty skyn Hangende doun unto the chin. *c* **1400** *Rom. Rose* 7262 And highe shoes, knopped with dagges,..Or botes riveling as a gype. **1530** PALSGR. 692/2, I ryvell, as ones vysage dothe for age, *je ride*. **1540** HYRDE tr. *Vives' Instr. Chr. Wom.* (1592) F iij, The tender skinne will ryvill the more soone, and all the favour of the face waxeth old. **1610** HOLLAND *Camden's Brit.* I. 357 Some will last a whole yeare and not wither and rivell. **1657** C. BECK *Univ. Charac.* K v b, To rivell or wrinckle.

2. *trans.* To cause (the skin) to wrinkle or pucker; to shrivel *up*.

1583 STUBBES *Anat. Abus.* I. (1879) 95 It riueleth the face. **1585** R. PARSONS *Chr. Exer.* II. iii. 268 Quickly commeth on olde age, which riueleth the skinne. **1609** N. F. *Fruiterers Secr.* 15 Neither layed in a windy colde roome, for feare of shrinking and riueling them. **1638** BURTON *Anat. Mel.* III. ii. VI. iii. (1651) 561 Raging time, care, rivels her upon a sudden. *a* **1704** T. BROWN *Sat. agst. Woman* Wks. 1730 I. 55 Till the devouring heat..Rival thy body, and distort thy mind. **1868** BROWNING *Ring & Bk.* I. 1279 And death came, death's breath rivelled up the lies. **1893** *S.E. Worc. Gloss.* s.v., He rivelled 'is brow.

absol. **1543** TRAHERON *Vigo's Chirurg.* II. vi. vii, This pouldre..dryeth, riveleth, or wrynkleth, and incarneth not a lytle.

†'**rivel**, *v.*[2] *Obs.* Also 4 ryuel, reuel, 6 ryvell. [ad. obs. F. *rivler* (Walloon *rifler*) to ravel. Cf. RIVEL *sb.*[2]]

1. *intr.* **a.** To become entangled.

c **1330** R. BRUNNE *Chron. Wace* (Rolls) 4629 Ropes ryueled and swerued [*Petyt MS.* reueld & snarled] in lyne.

b. To ravel or fray *out*.

1530 PALSGR. 692/2, I ryvell out, as sylke dothe, *je riule*.

2. *trans.* To open *out* by unravelling.

1650 ELDERFIELD *Civil Right Tythes* 297 'Tis in the hands of all men, and rivels out the generall subject into many particulars.

rivelet, obs. form of RIVULET.

riveling[1] ('rɪvəlɪŋ). Now *dial.* and *Hist.* Forms: 1 rifeling, 3 riueling (4 -yng), 4 ryve-, (9) riveling; 5 revelyng(e, *Sc.* rewelyn, rewlyng, raweling; 9 *dial.* rivilin, riv(e)lin, etc. [OE. *rifeling*, perh. related to RIVEL *sb.*[1], RIVELLED *a.* ON. *hriflingr* and MHG. *ribbalîn*, occurring only in the Perceval legend, represent OF. *revelin* (*rov-*, *rouvelin*), which was no doubt from early ME. The mod.F. *rivelin* a shop-worn shoe (Littré) may be the same word.]

1. A shoe of raw hide. = RILLING *sb.*[1]

c **1000** ÆLFRIC *Gloss.* in Wr.-Wülcker 125 *Obstrigelli*, rifelingas. ?*a* **1300** *MS. Digby 172*, fol. 146 b/1 *Perone* .i. anglice 'riueling'. *c* **1300** in Langtoft *Chron.* (Rolls) II. 264 Somme is left na thing, Bot his rough ryveling To hippe tharynne. **1338** R. BRUNNE *Chron.* (1810) 282 þou getes no þing, but þi riuelyng, to hang þer inne. *c* **1425** WYNTOUN *Cron.* VIII. xxix. 4421 Hys knychtis weryd revelyngs Off hydis or off hart hemmynys. *c* **1470** HENRY *Wallace* I. 219 Ane Ersche mantill it war thi kynd to wer;..Rouch rewlyngis apon thi harlot fete. **1483** *Cath. Angl.* 305/2 A Revelynge, *pero*.

1837 R. DUNN *Ornith. Ork. & Shetl.* 13 A kind of shoe of the untanned skins of the ox and seal, which are called rivilins. **1880** *Times* 21 Sept. 10/5 At Symbister we note that most of the boatmen wear 'rivilins'.

†**2.** *transf.* A wearer of rivelings; a Scot. *rare.*

c **1300** in Langtoft *Chron.* (MS. Fairf. 22) lf. 4 Tprut! skot riueling, In vnseli timing Crope þu out of cage. *a* **1352** MINOT *Poems* ii. 19 Rughfute riueling, now kindels þi care.

†'**riveling**[2]. *Obs.* In 7 riuel(l)ing. [Perh. based upon *rivelet*, obs. form of RIVULET.] A rivulet or rill.

1615 BRATHWAIT *Strappado* (1878) 5 Hypocrenes pure riuelings of wit. **1621** —— *Nat. Embassie* (1877) 61 Ninus Tombe, Erected neare a Christall riueling. **1622** DRAYTON *Poly-olb.* xxviii. 256 Swale bonny Codbeck brings, And Willowbeck with her, two pretty Riuellings.

rivelled ('rɪv(ə)ld), *a.* Forms: α. 1 rifelede, 4 riuelede, 4, 6–7 riueled (5 rieu-), 4, 6– riveled (5 -id), 6– rivelled, 6–7 riueld, rivel(l)d; 5 ryuelyd, 6 ryu-, ryvyled, ryu-, ryvelled, 5 ryuelde, 6 ryuilde, 7 ryveld. β. 5 reuylde, 5–6 reueled (5 -lid), 6 reuyled, reveld. [OE. *rifelede*, app. f. **rifel* (see RIVEL *sb.*[1]), of obscure etym. Formerly in freq. use; now *dial.* or *arch.*]

1. Wrinkled; full of wrinkles or small folds; corrugated, furrowed: **a.** Of the skin, face, etc. (Very common *c* 1530–1720.)

α. *a* **1100** in Napier *O.E. Glosses* 187/2 *Rugosus*, rifelede. *c* **1380** *Barlaam & Josaphat* 248 in Horstm. *Altengl. Leg.* (1875) 218/2 An old Mon he saiȝ, w^t^ a riueled fas. **1390** GOWER *Conf.* III. 370 Al my face With Elde I myhte se deface, So riveled and so wo besein. *c* **1425** *Found. St. Bartholomew's* (E.E.T.S.) 27 By and by his senowys were contracte, pale and lene and ryvelyd abowte the moweth all discolouryd. *c* **1450** *Merlin* 262 He lefte vp his heed that was lothly and rivelid. **1513** MORE *Chron., Rich. III* (1883) 54 Now is she old..and dried vp, nothing left but ryuilde skin and hard bone. **1566** DRANT *Wailings Jer.* K viij, Their ryveled skinnes, clongde to their bones unseparable be. **1620** VENNER *Via Recta* ii. 40 The colour of the face becommeth pale and riu'led. **1658** ROWLAND tr. *Moufet's Theat. Ins.* 1023 Where ever it finds a rivled pleated skin, it will cause very great pain. **1711** ADDISON *Spect.* No. 86 ¶2 When I see a Man with a sour rivell'd Face, I cannot forbear pitying his Wife. **1784** COWPER *Task* II. 488 From the rivel'd lips of toothless, bald Decrepitude. **1820** C. R. MATURIN *Melmoth* (1892) III. xxviii. 117 His rivelled and toothless mouth. **1879** MISS JACKSON *Shropsh. Word-bk.* 353 Martha begins to shewn age—'er neck an' 'ands bin all rivelled an' s'runk.

fig. and *transf.* **1546** J. HEYWOOD *Prov. & Epigr.* (1867) 41 That ye herein awarde me to forsake Beggerly beautie, and riueld riches take. **1609** SHAKS. *Tr. & Cr.* v. i. 26 (Q.[1]), The riueled fee simple of the tetter.

β. **1430–40** LYDG. *Bochas* I. xx. (MS. Bodl. 263), Ther reuelid skin abrod to drawe & streyne, Froward frounces to mak hem smothe & pleyne. **1509** BARCLAY *Shyp of Folys* (1874) I. 288 Theyr face and vysage stande awry And all to reuylde.

b. Of fruit (dried or stored up).

1565 COOPER *Thesaurus*, *Acina rugosa*, riueled grapes, or reasons. **1601** HOLLAND *Pliny* XV. xiv, The ragged apples Pannucea take this name, for that..they soonest be riveld. **1678** DRYDEN *All for Love* Prol. 40 Take in good part from our poor poet's board Such rivelled fruits as winter can afford.

c. Of bark, leaves, etc.

1594 NASHE *Terrors of Night* Wks. (Grosart) III. 257 The riueld barke or outward rynde of a tree. **1601** HOLLAND *Pliny* XIII. xxi, The leaves..be somewhat longer.., with long cuts or lines wrinkled and riveled throughout. *Ibid.* XVI. xxxi, Ordinarily, all old trees have more riveled barkes and furrowed, than the younger. **1665** REA *Flora* 70 If it [the root] appear rivelled or crumpled on the outside.

2. Shrunken, shrivelled, esp. by heat.

1629 MAXWELL tr. *Herodian* (1635) 417 As for the leather and wood it was all burnt and riveld. *a* **1640** DAY *Peregr. Schol.* (1881) 53 Upon the barren trees..hung fruite..shrunk up and riveld like scrowles of scortcht parchment. **1697** DRYDEN *Virg. Georg.* IV. 616 The sultry Dog-star..Scorch'd Indian Swains, the rivell'd Grass was dry. **1712–4** POPE *Rape Lock* II. 132 Or Alum styptics with contracting pow'r Shrink his thin essence like a rivel'd flow'r. **1784** COWPER *Tiroc.* 596 Ev'ry worm..weaves And winds his web about the rivell'd leaves. **1886** BARNES *Dorset Gloss.*, *Rivelled*.., shrivelled as grass.

fig. **1842** LYTTON *Zanoni* (1890) 100 Its power is rivelled as a leaf which the first wind shall scatter.

b. With *up*.

1627 HAKEWILL *Apol.* (1630) 80 They shall passe away with a noyse,..like the hissing of parchment, riveled up with heat. **1686** F. SPENCE tr. *Varillas' Ho. Medici* 440 The Spleen was..straitn'd and rivell'd up. **1700** DRYDEN *Flower & Leaf* 378 The fading flowers..hung the head, And rivell'd up with heat, lay dying in their bed.

†**3.** Pleated or gathered in small folds. *Obs.*

1480 CAXTON *Trevisa's Higden* II. xxxv. (1527) 90 This was the fyrst kyng of Romayns that ware purpure, a maner reed clothynge of kynges and broudred and ryuelde. **1515** BARCLAY *Egloges* i. (1570) A ij b/1 Their reuilde shirtes of cloth white, soft and thin. ?**1523** *Rec. St. Mary at Hill* (1905) 36 Playne Surplices for Men... Reveld Surplices for Men. **1583** STUBBES *Anat. Abus.* F v b, Some [capes] are pleated, and ryueled down the back wonderfully.

4. Twisted; coiled. *rare.*

1594 MARLOWE & NASHE *Dido* 754 Ile giue thee tackling made of riueld gold. **1835** BROWNING *Paracelsus* I. 481 He points, smiling, to his scarf Heavy with riveled gold.

†**'rivelling**, *vbl. sb. Obs.* Forms: 5 ryueling, -yng(e, reuel-, revelynge, ryvullyng(e. [f. RIVEL *v.*[1] + -ING[1].]

1. A wrinkle (on the skin).

c **1380** WYCLIF *Sel. Wks.* III. 194 Not havynge wem ne revelynge ne ony siche filþe. **1388** —— *Job* xvi. 9 My ryuelyngis seien witnessyng aȝens me.

2. The action of the verb.

1398 TREVISA *Barth. De P.R.* v. xxx. (Bodl. MS.), By chaungyng of ham, schrinking, and reueling, he bodith and tokeneþ deying. *Ibid.* lxiv, Reueling þat comeþ of wasting of substancial moisture. *c* **1440** *Pallad. on Husb.* XI. 258 Chiries in the sonne ydried take And kepe, as they bygynne in rivullynge. *a* **1470** H. PARKER *Dives & Pauper* (W. de W. 1496) VIII. xvi. 343/2 Many tokenes of warnynge,..as age, sekenesse,..rymplynge or reuelynge of the skynne.

So **'rivelling** *ppl. a.*

a **1470** TIPTOFT *Tulle on Friendsh.* (Caxton, 1481) f iv, The whyte heris & the ryvillyng [*pr.* ryvikyng] chier of the body of an olde man. **1878** G. M. HOPKINS *Poems* (1967) 74 But his eye no cliff, no coast or Mark makes in the rivelling snowstorm.

rivel-ravel, variant of RIBBLE-RABBLE.

riven ('rɪv(ə)n), *ppl. a.* Forms: α. 4 rivyn, ryffen, 5–6 ryven, 6–7 ryuen, riuen, 4, 6– riven. β. 5–6 revyn, 6 reven, *Sc.* reuin. [Pa. pple. of RIVE *v.*[1]]

1. Split, cloven, rent, torn asunder.

1307–27 *Pol. Poems* (Camden) 307 Sum es left na thing Boute his rivyn riveling To hippe thar-hinne. **1457** *Fabric Rolls York* (Surtees) 69 Pro c long revyn burdes, prec. pece, 2d. *c* **1460** *Towneley Myst.* ii. 141 For had I giffen away my goode, then myght I go with a ryffen hood. **1563** WINȜET *Wks.* (S.T.S.) I. 114 Auld and reuin ornamentis. **1590** SPENSER *F.Q.* I. viii. 9 Through riven cloudes and molten firmament. *Ibid.* 10 Like fresh water streame from riven rocke. **1619** T. TAYLOR *Comm. Titus* ii. 14 We may not, like riuen vessels, let this doctrine slip. **1667** MILTON *P.L.* VI. 449 He stood..Sore toild, his riv'n Armes to havoc hewn. **1720** POPE *Iliad* xx. 328 O'er him high the riven Targe extends. **1784** COWPER *Task* IV. 444 The well-stack'd pile of riven logs and roots. **1815** SHELLEY *Alastor* 347 The little boat..pausing on the edge of the riven wave. **1877** W. BLACK *Green Past.* xxxvii, A series of majestic peaks, their riven sides sparkling with sunlit snows.

fig. **1817** SHELLEY *Revolt Islam* III. 1300 The caverns dreary..Of the riven soul. **1849** MISS MULOCK *Ogilvies* xxxvi, To cast out from his riven heart the very ashes of this bitter love.

†**2.** Ornamentally slashed. *Obs. rare.*

c **1450** *Songs on Costume* (Percy Soc.) 65 So many ryven shertes,..And so many lewed clerkes, Say I never. *a* **1548** HALL *Chron., Hen. VIII*, 57 b, One Shynynge, Mayre of Rochester, set a young man on the Pillory for wering of a ryuen shert.

river ('rɪvə(r)), *sb.*[1] Forms: α. 4 riuere, rivere, 4, 6–7 riuer, 5– river (6 *Sc.* -eir); 5–6 ryuere (*Sc.* -were), 5 -yre; 4–6 ryuer (5 -eer), ryver (6 *Sc.* ryuir, ryvir, rywir). β. 4–5 reuere (5 -ire), 4–6 revere (5 -yre); 4–5 reuer (5 -ir, 6 *Sc.* -ar), 5 revyr, 5–6 rever (5 *Sc.* -eir, -ar, 5–6 -ir). [a. OF. *rivere*, *riviere*, *reviere* (mod.F. *rivière*), = Prov. and Pg. *ribeira*, Sp. *ribera*, It. *riviera*, med.L. *rivera*, *riveria*:—pop. L. **rīpāria*, f. *rīpa* bank. From OF. are also MDu. *riviere* (Du. *rivier*), MHG. *rivier* (G. *revier*), MLG. *rivêr*, *revêr*, obs. Da. *revier*, *rever*.]

I. 1. a. A copious stream of water flowing in a channel towards the sea, a lake, or another stream.

In some ME. examples the OF. sense of 'river-bank' appears to be possible.

a **1297** R. GLOUC. (Rolls) 487 Gret plente hii founde of fiss,..Of wodes & of riuers, as is in þe contreie. *c* **1320** *Sir Tristr.* 1884 His gle al for to here þe leuedi was sett onland To play bi þe riuere. **1390** GOWER *Conf.* I. 232 Upon a Rivere as he stod, That passe he wolde over the flod Withoute bot. *Ibid.* II. 161 In the valleie, Wher thilke rivere..made his cours. *c* **1430** LYDG. *Min. Poems* (Percy Soc.) 26 The Theban legeon,..At Rodomus ryver was expert there corage. *c* **1470** *Gol. & Gaw.* 248 Apone that riche river.. The side-wallis war set. **1526** *Pilgr. Perf.* (W. de W. 1531) 6 b, Than shall there be neyther..ryuer ne fysshe, castell ne towne. **1587** GOLDING *De Mornay* I. (1592) 11 As the River leadeth thee to his head, shal not the heade lead thee to the originall spring thereof? **1625** N. CARPENTER *Geogr. Del.* II. ix. (1635) 142 All Riuers haue their first originall from the Sea. **1667** MILTON *P.L.* IX. 514 A Ship by skilful Stearsman wrought Nigh Rivers mouth or Foreland. **1727** GAY *Fables* I. xxv. 9 'Tis like a rolling river, That murm'ring flows, and flows for ever! **1779** FORREST *Voy. N. Guinea* 178 The bar of the river Tamantakka..makes that river's access less safe than the Pelangy's. **1823** SOUTHEY *Hist. Penins. War* I. 599 The crowd still continued on both sides the river. **1842** ALISON *Hist. Europe* lxxviii. X. 1017 The great rivers of the world have now become the highways of civilization and religion. **1880** HAUGHTON *Phys. Geogr.* v. 203 A river may be defined to be the surplus of rainfall over evaporation.

fig. *c* **1380** WYCLIF *Sel. Wks.* I. 14 Þese fisheris of God shulden waishe þere nettis in þis ryver. **1432–50** tr. *Higden* (Rolls) I. 29 And soe this presente story is smyten in to vij. ryuers [*text* ryuerers]. **1535** COVERDALE *Ps.* xxxv[i]. 8 Thou shalt geue them drynke of the ryuer of thy pleasures. **1576** FLEMING *Panopl. Epist.* 180 They..throwe themselues into riuers, nay, mayne seas of errours. **1602** SHAKS. *Ham.* I. ii. 80 The fruitfull Riuer in the Eye. **1816** BYRON *Fragment*, Could I remount the river of my years. **1892** E. REEVES *Homeward Bound* 13 It is amusing to note how stout conservatives have drifted down this river of socialism.

β. **13..** *Cursor M.* 5922 (Gött.), For þe rott þat þar-on fell, Bath it stanc, reuer and well. **1387** TREVISA *Higden* (Rolls) II. 327 Whan reueres wexeþ ouer mesures þey dooþ.. harme. *a* **1400–50** *Alexander* 5279 Þare ran a reuire..vndire þat riche hame. *c* **1450** HOLLAND *Howlat* 12, I raikit till ane Reveir That ryally apperd. **1500–20** DUNBAR *Poems* xxv. 52 To eit..pertrik and plever, And every fische that swymis in rever. **1567** *Gude & Godlie Ball.* (S.T.S.) 109 God turnit the craig in fresche reueir.

b. Const. *of* (the name of the river). Now somewhat *rare.*

c **1375** *Sc. Leg. Saints* xxxvi. (*Baptist*) 285 Criste..come to sancte Iohne howine to be in-to þe rywere of Iordane. *c* **1400** MAUNDEV. (1839) i. 7 This Ryvere of Danubee is a fulle gret Ryvere. *c* **1425** WYNTOUN *Cron.* IV. iii. 199 Þe rywere of Ewfrate. *a* **1548** HALL *Chron., Hen. V*, 33 Borne at Monmouth on the River of Wye. **1565** in Marsden *Sel. Pl. Crt. Adm.* (Selden Soc.) II. 55 Honnefleur and Rouen and other ports in the revere of Seine. **1606** SHAKS. *Ant. & Cl.* II. ii. 192 She purst vp his heart vpon the Riuer of Sidnis. **1652** NEEDHAM tr. *Selden's Mare Cl.* 218 Those words concerning the River of Rhine. **1710** J. CHAMBERLAYNE *St. Gt. Brit.* II. I. 323 It's watered with the pleasant River of Clyde. **1753** CHAMBERS *Cycl. Suppl.* s.v. *Rivers*, The river of St. Lawrence..pours forth nearly as much as this. **1817** SCOTT *Rob Roy* xxviii, The river of Forth forms a defensible line.

c. *transf.* A copious stream or flow *of* (something). Also *fig.*

1382 WYCLIF *Job* xxix. 6 Whan I wesh my feet with buttere, and the ston helde to me ryueres of oile. **1526** TINDALE *John* vii. 38 He that beleveth on me,..out of his belly shall flowe ryvers of water of lyfe. **1588** SHAKS. *Titus A.* II. iv. 22 A Crimson riuer of warme blood. **1611** BIBLE *Ps.* cxix. 136 Riuers of waters runne downe mine eyes. **1767** *Ann. Reg.* IX. I. 98 The lava is really tremendous, the river of fire being..four miles in length. **1776** A. ADAMS in *Fam. Lett.* (1876) 144 In peacable possession of a town which we expected would cost us a river of blood. **1855** KINGSLEY *Westw. Ho!* xxi, Beneath that long shining river of mist. **1898** MEREDITH *Odes Fr. Hist.* 29 You away sweep Rivers of horse, torrent-mad, to the shock.

d. *Astr.* The constellation Eridanus or Fluvius.

1551 RECORDE *Cast. Knowl.* (1556) 268 A greate tract of starres, whiche represent the forme of a Riuer: and therefore are they called the Ryuer. **1771** *Encycl. Brit.* I. 487 Eridanus, the River.

e. Used euphemistically for the boundary between life and death.

Compare the use made of this figure by Bunyan in his *Pilgrim's Progress.*

1790 BURNS *Elegy Capt. Henderson* xv, And hast thou crost that unknown river, Life's dreary bound? **1843** in Quincy *Life W. L. Garrison* (1889) III. 79 She had gone down with him [*sc.* her late husband] to the brink of the River, and..he had gone over and she returned. **1892** *The Week* (Toronto) 660 [Whittier] had at last crossed the river, on whose brink he had been so long waiting.

f. *Printing.* (See quot. 1948.) Also ***river of white.***

1898 G. B. SHAW *Let.* 5 Jan. in *Ellen Terry & Shaw* (1931) 287 Oh those proofs, those proofs! Imagine..sticking in words to make the printing look decent—to get the rivers of white out of it! **1927** —— *Let.* 7 Mar. in *To Young Actress* (1960) 114 They avoided white patches and rivers in the rich black block of letterpress. **1929** *S.P.E. Tract* XXXIII. 437 In careful book-printing the possibility of manipulating spaces is limited, because evenness is desirable, and rivers of white on the page must be avoided. **1948** M. E. SKILLIN et al. *Words into Type* 546 *River*, a streak of white space in printed matter caused by the spaces between words in several lines happening to fall one almost below another. **1967** *Guardian* 13 Oct. 5/3 Morison holding up a book, inspecting the printed page for rivers of white caused by bad printing.

g. The finest grade of diamond. Cf. *river stone* in sense 5 d below and WATER *sb.* 20.

1934 in WEBSTER. **1946** G. STIMPSON *Bk. about Thousand Things* 267 *River* and *extra river* are now used to denote diamonds of the finer qualities. **1965** J. Y. DICKINSON *Bk. of Diamonds* viii. 219 *River*,..the finest color grade in diamonds; an extraordinarily transparent stone may be called 'an extra river stone'. **1973** *Times* 25 Aug. 17/3 The (more or less) accepted English classes run thus in descending order: (1) finest fine white or river *alias* blue-white.

†**2.** A stream, or the banks of a stream, as a place frequented for hawking. Hence, the sport of hawking. *Obs.*

c **1330** R. BRUNNE *Chron. Wace* (Rolls) 3135 Brenne.. couþe of chas & of ryuere, Inow of game of here manere. **1338** —— *Chron.* (1810) 94 Neuer on Friday to wod þou go to chace. Þe riuer salle þou forsake on Friday ilka dele. *c* **1386** CHAUCER *Sir Thopas* 26 (Ellesm.), He koude..ride on haukyng for Riuer With grey goshauk on honde. *c* **1400** *St. Alexius* (Laud 622) 988 He was to þe Emperoure ysent, to.. lernen chiualrie, Of huntyng, & of Ryuere. **14..** *Guy Warw.* 856 (Cambr. MS.), Wyth howndys we wyll chace dere And wyth hawkes to the ryuere. **1513** DOUGLAS *Æneis* v. Prol. 4 The wery hunter to fynd his happy pray, The falconer the riche riveir our to flene. **1615** MARKHAM *Country Contentm.* I. v, To make your Hawk fly at fowl, which is called the flight at the River. *a* **1625** BEAUM. & FL. *Woman's Prize* III. ii, He must..send me..by all means, Ten cast of hawkes for th' river.

†**3.** The coast or littoral (of Genoa). *Obs.*

After It. *la riviera di Genoa.*

1549 THOMAS *Hist. Italie* 185 He..gatte Sauona and Voragine in the ryuer of Genoa. **1693** SIR T. P. BLOUNT *Nat. Hist.* 25 [These vessels] are built all along the River of Genoa, being very swift.

4. Phrases. **a.** ***to sell down the river***: to sell (a troublesome slave) to the owner of a sugar-cane plantation on the lower Mississippi, where conditions were harsher than in the northern slave States; hence *fig.*, to deliver (one) over to slavery (*rare*); to let down, betray. *colloq.* (orig. *U.S.*).

1851 MRS. STOWE in *National Era* 14 Aug. 1/2 I've had one or two of these fellers, and I jest sold 'em down river. **1894** 'MARK TWAIN' *Pudd'nhead Wilson* ix. 113 Ole Marse Driscoll 'll sell you down de river. **1927** WODEHOUSE *Small Bachelor* i. 21 When Sigsbee Waddington married for the second time, he to all intents and purposes sold himself down the river. **1941** AUDEN *New Year Let.* II. 44 'I'll fix you something for your liver'; And thus he sells us down the river. **1943** K. TENNANT *Ride on Stranger* ix. 98 'Perhaps we could persuade Mrs. Brewster to abandon that part of the pageant?' 'Oh don't!.. She'd like to sell me down the river as it is, cheap.' **1955** E. POUND *Section: Rock-Drill* (1957) lxxxvi. 24 England not yet sold for the Suez—That would have been 20 years later, or was it '74? At any rate, sold down the river, passed over Parliament. **1958** HAYWARD & HARARI tr. *Pasternak's Dr. Zhivago* vi. 155 It's my considered opinion, Yurochka, we've been sold down the river. **1976** *Southern Even. Echo* (Southampton) 16 Nov. 3/3 Some aspects of Britain's education system needed to be put right but 'we should not sell it down the river' Education Secretary Mrs. Shirley Williams said last night.

b. ***up the river***: (orig.) to Sing Sing prison, situated up the Hudson River from the city of New York; hence *fig.*, to or in prison. *colloq.* (orig. *U.S.*).

1891 in H. Campbell *Darkness & Daylight* (1892) ii. 75 Lager-beer had come up since I went up the river. **1905** C. H. DAY *Actress & Clerk* v. 53, I didn't go up the river for several stretches for nothing, I didn't. I've got a record. **1946** *Chicago Daily News* 5 Mar. 8/3, I done it. Send me up the river. Give me the hot seat. **1951** WODEHOUSE *Old Reliable* i. 18 A member of the jury which three years before had sent him up the river for what the Press of New York was unanimous in describing as a well-earned sentence. **1963** J. N. HARRIS *Weird World Wes Beattie* (1964) iii. 24 But I *still* want to talk to Mrs. Leduc and find out why she sent the boy up the river.

c. ***down the river***, used in various senses, as: into slavery (cf. sense 4 a above); finished, past, over and done with; to prison (cf. sense 4 b above). *colloq.* (orig. *U.S.*).

1893 'MARK TWAIN' in *Century Mag.* Dec. 238/1 Percy Driscoll slept well the night he saved his house-minions from going down the river. **1930** J. B. PRIESTLEY *Angel Pavement* ii. 80 And up to eighteen months ago, I'd have told you that Claridge and Molton was one of the soundest concerns in the business. And look at 'em now. Properly in Queer Street. Absolutely down the river. **1931** *Sun* (Baltimore) 31 Jan. 1/5 True enough, I used to hustle a little beer in the old days—but that's all down the river. **1939** 'E. QUEEN' in *Blue Bk. Mag.* Oct. 18/1 'Mike's car's gone down the river.' 'I thought the champion was wealthy,' said Mr. Queen. 'Not any more.' **1974** *Times* 31 Jan. 4/5 He had overheard Miss Jones threatening Mr Dee 'to send him down the river for life'.

II. *attrib.* and *Comb.*

5. a. Attrib. in the sense of 'situated in, on, or beside a river', as ***river-bar, -beach, -board, -bridge, -coast, flat, -front, -glade, -grove, hill, -island, -isle, -lane, -marsh, -meadow, road, -shore, state, terrace, town, -trail, -walk***, etc.

1874 RAYMOND *Statist. Mines & Mining* 20 The gravel taken from the gulches and *river-bars. **1895** KIPLING *2nd Jungle Bk.* 242 The dholes rushed up the *river-beach in a wave. **1866** CONINGTON *Æneid* 221 When the Trojans moored Their fleet on Tiber's *river-board. **1915** E. POUND *Cathay* 20, I had to be off to So, far away over the waters, You back to your *river-bridge. **1940** W. FAULKNER *Hamlet* I. iii. 77 His destination was not far: a little under a mile to the river bridge, a little more than a mile beyond it. **1535** COVERDALE *Jos.* xvii. 9 Then commeth it downe..towarde the south syde of the *ryuer cities. **1509** HAWES *Past. Pleas.* XXXVI. xvii, By the *ryver coast. **1960** R. CAMPBELL tr. *A. Rimbaud's Drunken Boat* in *Coll. Poems* III. 17, I felt no more the guidance of my tow-men As I came down by listless river-coasts. **1830** LYELL *Princ. Geol.* I. 91 Marine currents, preying alike on *river-deltas, and continuous lines of sea-coast. *a* **1816** B. HAWKINS *Sk. Creek Country* (1848) 47 On the right side, off from the *river flats, the land is waving. **1862** *Luck of Ladysmede* II. 282 The chime of the abbey bells came to them over the river-flats. **1977** *Weekly Times* (Melbourne) 19 Jan. 62 (Advt.), A very scenic property rising from irrigated river flats to undulating and hilly terrain, with magnificent outlook. **1820** SHELLEY *Hymn Merc.* 447 He right down to the *river-ford had driven. **1855** *Chicago Weekly Times* 16 Jan. 1/1 To lease for a term of years. 200 feet *river front, ready docked. **1978** J. A. MICHENER *Chesapeake* 237 He had been discussing her with young men of the region, offering them..even a stretch of river-front, if they would marry his eldest daughter. **1865** DICKENS *Mut. Fr.* I. vi, This description applies to the *river-frontage. **1848** B. SMITH in *Rep. to authorize Draining of Ever Glades* (U.S. Congress Comm. Publ. Lands) 19 The name Ever Glades is doubtless of English gift, and probably was originally '*River Glades'. **1861** W. F. COLLIER *Hist. Eng. Lit.* 122 Shadowy river-glade and rolling plough-land. **1957** BLUNDEN *Poems of Many Years* 284 You see Old Night Begin to shade the river-glade. **1930** —— *Poems* 290 The secret paths of *river-groves. **1793** J. FILSON in G. Imlay *Topogr. Descr. W. Terr. N. Amer.* (ed. 2) II. 118 After passing the Miami *River hills..the country in places is broken. **1948** *Clarke County Democrat* (Grove Hill, Alabama) 29 Apr. 4/2 The river hill, while not yet quite subdued, is nothing like the formidable barrier that it once was. **1610** HOLLAND *Camden's Brit.* (1637) 617 A *River-Island, insulated within waters. **1836** *Penny Cycl.* V. 359/1 S. Anna [is] perhaps the largest river island in the world. **1913** J. LONDON *Valley of Moon* xvii. 479, I wouldn't trade a square mile of this kind of country for the whole Sacramento Valley, with the river islands thrown in and Middle River for good measure. **1939** AUDEN & ISHERWOOD *Journey to War* i. 31 The British Consulate is in the foreign concession, on the river-island of Shameen. **1900** J. A. JOYCE in *Fortn. Rev.* Apr. 577 Through the trees can be seen the town harbour, and the fjord,..as it stretches past headland and *river-isle out to the sea. **1947** C. S. LEWIS in

Punch 21 May 434/1 He held at the finish but a small river-isle. **1781** S. Peters *Hist. Connecticut* 242 One acre commonly yields..from 40 to 60 bushels [of Indian corn] on *river land. **1899** T. Nicol *Rec. Archæol. Bible* x. 168 The fertile plains..of the Eastern River-land. **1968** G. Jones *Hist. Vikings* III. iii. 224 The *river-lanes of France and the Low Countries. **1978** C. Tomlinson *Shaft* 43 They.. narrow out into A now-smooth riverlane. **1820** Shelley *Hymn Pan* 20 The edge of the moist *river-lawns. *a* **1876** M. Collins *Pen Sketches* I. 72 The little lawn by the *river-marge. **1838** T. L. Mitchell *Three Exped.* (1839) II. 89 It appeared to belong to the *river margin. **1930** E. Pound *XXX Cantos* vi. 24 By *river-marsh, by galleried church-porch. **1859** Ld. Lytton *Wanderer* (ed. 2) 211 Lady Eve.. dwells beside The *river-meads, and oak-trees tall. *c* **1847** Thoreau in J. L. Shanley *Making of Walden* (1957) 198 Men who frequent the *river meadows and solitary ponds in the horizon-connecting links between towns. **1912** P. S. Allen *Let.* 11 Apr. (1939) 101 We even found fritillaries growing..flowers which we have hitherto always associated with the moisture of Thames' river-meadows. **1832** Lyell *Princ. Geol.* II. 130 An extensive moor, or a great *river-plain. **1846** McCulloch *Acc. Brit. Empire* (1854) I. 326 Rivers and *River Ports. **1776** G. Washington *Let.* 27 Dec. in *Boston Gaz.* (1777) 20 Jan. 2/1, I formed my detachment into two divisions, one to march up the lower or *river road, the other by the upper or Pennington road. **1829** J. MacTaggart *Three Yrs. Canada* II. 202 When the snow falls deep, before the ice has had time to freeze to any considerable thickness, the *river roads* remain dangerous all the season. **1955** E. A. Collard *Canad. Yesterdays* 302 Some experienced travellers on the river-roads even carried 'choke-ropes'. **1770** G. Washington *Tour to Ohio* in *Olden Time* (1846) I. 423 At the lower end of the Long Reach..is a large bottom, but low, and covered with beach near the *river shore. **1842** Tennyson *Gardener's Daughter* 259 The balmy glooming, crescent-lit, Spread the light haze along the river-shores. **1826** Hor. Smith *Tor Hill* (1838) III. 321 The adjoining market and *river-stairs. **1845** *Southern Lit. Messenger* XI. 578/1 There, too, should be present..all the *river States, to deliberate upon the present condition of those great arteries of commerce among them. **1976** *Daily Times* (Lagos) 4 Sept. 2/2 Divisional administration in the River state has been abolished with immediate effect. **1852** Lyell *Elem. Geol.* (ed. 4) 85 *River Terraces and Parallel Roads. **1969** Bennison & Wright *Geol. Hist. Brit. Isles* vi. xvi. 366 River terraces..are remnants of former floodplains dissected by the rejuvenation of rivers consequent upon uplift. *a* **1850** G. G. Foster *New York Naked* (*c* 1855) vii. 74 Here he fell in, accidentally, with a rich banker and capitalist, from one of the *river towns. **1938** H. Asbury *Sucker's Progress* ix. 212 When they came ashore they demanded women and whisky, and the river towns provided both in great abundance. **1977** B. F. Chamberlin in Bond & McLeod *Newslett. to Newspapers* iv. 248 The legislature had been established as the 'supreme power' of the Commonwealth in an agreement among the early Seventeenth-Century river towns. **1902** S. E. White *Blazed Trail* III. xxx. 211 The little procession..took its way up the *river-trail. **1923** L. Y. Erskine *River Trail* viii. 58 In the morning Geoffrian..set out for the river trail. **1712** Swift *Jrnl. to Stella* 7 Aug., Pray observe the cherry-trees on the *river-walk. **1914** Kipling in *Nash's & Pall Mall Mag.* Nov. 181/1 A river front, a narrow terraced river-walk in front of semi-oriental houses. **1976** *State Jrnl.* (Lansing, Michigan) 11 July B-7/1 Ducks are a long-time attraction to visitors... Now residents can enjoy them while strolling along the new 'Riverwalk'. **1837** *Civil Eng. & Arch. Jrnl.* I. 12/1 The whole to be surrounded by a *river wall, 30 feet high. **1884** C. Davies *Norf. Broads & Rivers* xv. 110 Between the river-wall and the water is always a strip of land.

b. With words denoting the course, or some part of the course, of a river or rivers, as ***river-basin, -bend, -channel, -course, -edge, -head, -line, mouth, ravine, -reach, -system.***

1878 Huxley *Physiogr.* 19 A map..completely divided into *river-basins. **1898** W. H. Ogilvie *Fair Girls & Gray Horses* 33 By stock-routes brown and burnt and bare, by flood-wrapped *river-bends, They've hunted them from gate to gate—the drover has no friends! **1972** R. G. Kazmann *Mod. Hydrol.* (ed. 2) iv. 115 On the Mississippi River..a number of river-bend cutoffs have been constructed. **1833–4** *Encycl. Metrop.* (1845) VI. 705/2 By the waste of the uplands..the *river-channels are raised. *Ibid.* 705/1 This fluctuation of the *river-courses is excessively irregular. **1883** 'Mark Twain' *Life on Mississippi* xxii. 256 St. Louis is a great city; but the *river-edge of it seems dead. **1685** in Dryden *Misc.* II. 408 It.. Then to our Springs and *River heads ascends. **1945** *Finito! Po Valley Campaign* (15th Army Group) 7 Behind these *riverlines were the machine gun nests. **1958** N. Levine *Canada made Me* v. 127 Old bits of dead grass, like tufts of hair, stuck out of the mud. Near the riverline the snow had not melted. **1979** R. Cox *Auction* ii. 41 'The Yanks must be going flat out,' said Horst. 'Thank God we're not defending that riverline.' **1872** Tennyson *Gareth & Lynette* 999 When they touch'd the second *river-loop. **1790** J. Backus *Diary* 6 Dec. in W. W. Backus *Geneal. Mem. Backus Family* (1889) 93 Came down to the *river mouth of a large run. **1865** Kingsley *Herew.* xxii, Hereward lay outside the river mouth, his soul..black with disappointment. **1788** J. May *Jrnl. & Lett.* (1873) 75 We contemplated in our plans a grand bridge over the *river ravine. **1879** *Encycl. Brit.* X. 276/2 The river-ravine likewise crept backward, but at a more rapid rate. **1849** Thoreau *Week Concord Riv.* 370 There is a pleasant tract on the bank of the Concord, which I have in mind;..the open wood, the *river-reach. **1859** Meredith *R. Feverel* xiv, Across sheets of river-reaches, pure mirrors to the upper glory. **1887** Stevenson *Merry Men* ii. 77 Looking down the *river shed and abroad on the fat lowlands. **1834** *Penny Cycl.* II. 468/1 Extensive terraces, through which the great *river-systems descend to the low lands. **1879** *Encycl. Brit.* X. 272/1 In a vast river system like that of the Mississippi, the area of drainage is..extensive. **1962** H. R. Loyn *Anglo-Saxon Eng.* i. 9 For the main part the river-systems drain west in this area. **1841** *Penny Cycl.* XX. 24/1 The basins which occur in these *river-valleys. **1878** Huxley *Physiogr.* 138 Our river-valleys are mainly the result of work performed by rain, river, and similar agents of denudation. **1888** *Pall Mall G.* 13 Apr. 4/2 We fear..that the Zambesi *riverway is practically doomed.

c. In the sense of 'used or operating upon a river', as ***river-artillery, -boat, -craft, steam-boat, steamer, traffic,*** etc.

1860 Spottiswoode *Vac. Tour* 88 The fifteenth [district] maintaining a battalion of *river artillery. **1801** Nelson 10 Aug. in Nicolas *Disp.* (1845) IV. 452 The defence of our numerous landing-places is better adapted to our *River-Barges, than any other which we could adopt. **1565** Cooper *Thesaurus, Fluuiatiles naues*, *riuer or fresh water boates. **1841** *Penny Cycl.* XIX. 460/2 The Lippe..is navigated..by small river-boats. **1891** C. Roberts *Adrift Amer.* 16 This was the first time that I ever saw a real Mississippi river boat. **1837** De Quincey in *Blackw. Mag.* July 94/1 From the want of bridges, or sufficient *river craft for transporting so vast a body of men. **1840** *Penny Cycl.* XVI. 259/2 The Waveney is now navigable..to Bungay..for river-craft. **1863** Hawthorne *Our Old Home* (1879) 280 A crowd of river craft are generally moored in front of it. **1963** *Times* 18 May 16/5 (*caption*) Various kinds of rivercraft on the Yangtze Kiang in China. **1979** A. Morice *Murder in Outline* xiv. 115 A boat-yard belonging to..an old-established family firm, who hired out river craft. **1857** M. H. Stacey *Jrnl.* 24 May in *Uncle Sam's Camels* (1929) II. 28 What an immense difference we find between the quiet Sundays at home and the bustling ones on board these *river steamboats. **1902** Conrad *Youth* 67, I was going to take charge of a two-penny-halfpenny river-steamboat with a penny whistle attached! **1833** E. T. Coke *Subaltern's Furlough* v. 70 The American *river steamers are noble vessels. **1903** Joyce *Let.* 8 Feb. (1966) II. 26, I..came back to Paris in one of the little river-steamers. **1936** *Discovery* Dec. 379/2 The ordinary river-steamer services. **1879** *Rep. Comm. Navig. River Thames* p. xxx in *Parl. Papers 1878–79* (C. 2338) XLI. 245 As to the hour at which the ordinary *river traffic or daylight excursions should end, there is more difference of opinion. **1968** W. Warwick *Surfriding in N.Z.* 40/3 Dangerous currents and river traffic.

d. Miscellaneous, as ***river-boar*** (bore *sb.*³), ***board, -breeze, -bud, -crossing, -cult, -damp, -debris, -dream, -fancy, -flow, -glimpse, -link, lot, -mist, police, trip, -voyage, week;*** **river blindness,** (blindness due to) onchocerciasis; **river capture** *Physical Geogr.*, the natural diversion of the headwaters of one stream into the channel of another, freq. resulting from rapid headward erosion of the latter stream; **river engineering,** the branch of civil engineering concerned with the improvement and control of rivers; **river gravel,** gravel that was formed on the bed of a river; **river ooze, River Ouse,** rhyming slang for 'booze'; **river-pay, -risk** (see quots.); **river stone,** a diamond found during river-digging.

1955 *Times* 8 July 9/7 Some types of blindness are more intractable. Such, for example, is the notorious '*river blindness' of the Gold Coast, where in the northern territories there are estimated to be 40,000 blind people. **1972** *Daily Tel.* 22 Nov. 4/4 One French project is to eradicate 'river blindness', an insect-born disease which has ravaged and depopulated the valleys of the Volta rivers. **1975** *Sci. Amer.* Oct. 53/2 There are villages in tropical Africa and Central America where as many as 15 per cent of the people are blind. They are victims of 'river blindness', a frequent complication of the parasitic disease onchocerciasis which..has recently been recognized as a major public-health problem throughout the tropical world. **1856** Miss Mulock *J. Halifax* iv, I've often seen it on Severn... We often call it the *river-boar. **1948** *Act 11 & 12 Geo. VI* c. 32 §1 The Ministers shall..by order establish boards (to be known as '*river boards') for the areas so defined, who shall have the functions conferred on or transferred to them by or under the following provisions of this Act, being functions relating to land drainage, fisheries and river pollution and certain other functions relating to rivers, streams and inland waters. **1963** *Times* 23 Jan. 6/3 The information they had gathered in the past fortnight from river boards throughout the country made it seem likely that when the thaw came it would reveal an urgent need for many land drainage and flood control schemes. **1864** Tennyson *Aylmer's F.* 454 The soft *river-breeze which fann'd the gardens. **1820** Shelley *Sensit. Pl.* I. 46 Starry *river-buds glimmered by. **1901** *Geogr. Jrnl.* XVIII. 227 Examples taken from various parts of Italy of alteration in the direction of valleys due to *river-capture, etc. **1937** Wooldridge & Morgan *Physical Basis Geogr.* xv. 211 The river-captures of the first cycle will still be legible in the pattern of the drainage, but there will now be no direct evidence of the former continuity of consequent drainage lines. **1960** B. W. Sparks *Geomorphol.* vi. 112 The type of river capture described is largely explained by differences in rock resistance, but another factor becomes of importance in areas of permeable rocks: the possibility of underground diversion preceding and aiding surface capture. **1977** A. Hallam *Planet Earth* 76/1 Possible signs of river capture that can often be detected in the landscape include windgaps and elbows of capture, incision of the capturing stream below the capture, and the evident misfit nature of the beheaded stream. *a* **1951** E. Hill in Murdoch & Drake-Brockman *Austral. Short Stories* (1951) 292 The blacks ran with him for four or five miles, as far as the *river-crossing. **1965** Auden *About House* (1966) 29 Shrines where a subarctic fire-cult could meet and marry A *river-cult from torrid Greece. **1851** Kingsley *Yeast* iii, The *river-damps are God's sending. **1963** *Landfall* Mar. 23 River-damp softened her hair: her skin smelled of soap. **1951** R. Campbell *Light on Dark Horse* 121 The ridge of *river-debris after the flood, ran along the base of these strandlooper-dunes. **1863** Ramsay *Phys. Geogr.* 106 The old system of *river-drainage. **1936** Auden *Look, Stranger!* 15 Whose *river-dreams long hid the size And vigours of the sea. **1626** Bacon *Sylva* §596 Pond-earth, or *River-earth,.. is a very good Compost. **1819** Shelley *Cyclops* 50 Here.. the *river-eddies meet In the trough beside the cave. [**1882** L. F. Vernon-Harcourt *Rivers & Canals* I. p. v, In preparing a course of lectures on 'River and Canal Engineering'..it appeared to me that a book might be useful.] **1886** *Encycl. Brit.* XX. 571/2 *River Engineering. The improvement of rivers may be considered under two aspects, [etc.]. **1966** *McGraw-Hill Encycl. Sci. & Technol.* XI. 585/1 Technical knowledge is inadequate to explain fully the relationship between stream form and valley slope, but it is necessary in river engineering to recognize it. **1934** Blunden *Mind's Eye* III. 170 Spenser, in his *Faerie Queene* ..marries the Medway to the Thames with a great display of *river-fancy. **1841** *Penny Cycl.* XX. 26/2 The importance of a *river fishery. **1960** *Times* 25 July 11/6 A rise in *river-flow. **1964** *Oceanogr. & Marine Biol.* II. 34 When they have a sufficiently high sediment concentration to give a density of the riverflow exceeding that of the salt water, rivers entering the ocean may similarly sometimes continue as underflows. **1855** Lynch *Rivulet* LXXXII. v, A *river-fount unsealing In our dry hearts. **1875** 'Mark Twain' in *Atlantic Monthly* Jan. 70/1 The 'point' above the town, and the 'point' below, bounding the *river-glimpse and turning it into a sort of sea. **1874** *Q. Jrnl. Geol. Soc.* XXX. 229 A careful examination of this very interesting deposit convinces me that we have here preserved portions of an old *river-gravel. **1975** J. G. Evans *Environment Early Man Brit. Isles* iii. 61 River gravel is a major economic concern. It is used extensively for road and building foundations... It is also much needed as land for building on. *a* **1862** Thoreau *Maine Woods* (1864) 251 The Allegash..here consists principally of a chain of large and stagnant lakes, whose thoroughfares, or *river-links, have been made nearly equally stagnant by damming. **1704** *Public Rec. Colony of Connecticut* (1868) IV. 493 Part of a lot called the *River lot, purchased of the said Nathan[11] Holt. **1968** E. Russenholt *Heart of Continent* II. v. 76 Families already living along the Assiniboine, exercise 'squatter's rights', and lay claim to the newly-surveyed River Lots. **1926** Kipling *Debits & Credits* 233 And the *river-mist runs silver round their knees! **1863** *Sat. Rev.* 1 Aug. 162 He has..attempted to classify all the chief *river-names of Europe. **1931** Brophy & Partridge *Songs & Slang 1914–1918* (ed. 3) 350 *River Ouse, a booze, a drink(ing). **1962** R. Cook *Crust on its Uppers* ix. 76 The place still bulging with smoke and river ooze. **1809** R. Langford *Introd. Trade* 134 *River-pay, a month's wages advanced to sailors with other allowances. **1825** G. F. Lyon *Brief Narr. Unsuccessful Attempt to reach Repulse Bay* 2 On the 16th Commissioner Cunningham arrived from Chatham, and the ship's company received their river pay, with three months' advance. **1681** Grew *Musæum* I. §iii. 52 With some ash-colour intermixed; so as to look like a *River-pebble. **1800** P. Colquhoun *Treat. Commerce & Police River Thames* i. 22 The nature of the several articles of Trade and Manufacture..cannot fail to produce a conviction of the indispensable necessity of a well-planned and energetic System of *River-Police*; to regulate and control the economy of so vast a machine, and to protect such an astonishing mass and variety of Property. **1974** *Times* 15 Apr. 2/1 It sank before river police could note its registration marks. **1859** Tennyson *Merlin & V.* 807 The rotten branch Snapt in the rushing of the *river-rain. **1867** Smyth *Sailor's Word-bk.* 576 **River-Risk*, a policy of insurance from the docks to the sea, at any port. **1856** 'Stonehenge' *Brit. Rural Sports* I. I. viii. 70/2 For pond and *river-shooting, these guns may be from 12 to 16 lbs. **1876** Page *Adv. Text-bk. Geol.* ix. 171 The gigantic bird-bones found in the *river-silts of New Zealand. **1822** Shelley *Fragm. Unfinished Drama* 62 How oft we two Have sate.. near the *river springs. **1887** J. Mackenzie *Austral Africa* II. IV. iv. 87 The '*river stones', as they are called, are usually more valuable than those found in 'dry diggings' or mines. **1904** L. J. Spencer tr. *Bauer's Precious Stones* I. II. 186 The higher quality of the river stones as compared with those from the dry diggings does not militate against the truth of this theory as to their origin. **1842** *Encycl. Metrop.* (1845) V. 393* The theory of *river-tides. **1855** Tennyson *Maud* II. iv. 67 In drifts of lurid smoke On the misty river-tide. **1898** J. S. Webb in *Century Mag.* Mar. 672 (*title*) The *river trip to the Klondike. **1912** W. Owen *Let.* 23 June (1967) 142 Mrs. Lott's River Trip is to be next Tuesday. **1893** *Dict. Nat. Biogr.* XXXIV. 153 He..excelled in *river-views. **1954** J. R. R. Tolkien *Fellowship of Ring* 400, I hoped the *river-voyage would beat him, but he is too clever a waterman. **1839** De la Beche *Rep. Geol. Cornw.*, etc. xiii. 406 Among wood, moss, leaves, and nuts,..described as *river-wash. **1865** Kingsley *Herew.* Prel., To form, from the rain and *river washings of eight shires, lowlands of a fertility inexhaustible. **1932** D. H. Lawrence *Last Poems* 30 Come then!.. In a week! The ancient *river week, the old one.

e. With names of persons, as ***river-bailiff, -boy, -consul, -deity, family, Indian, pilot, pirate, -thief,*** etc. Also ***river-rat, -wolf*** in fig. use. **River Brethren** *pl.*, members of a Christian sect originating (*c* 1770) among settlers on the Susquehanna river, characterized esp. by the performance of baptisms only in rivers; **river hog, pig** *N. Amer. slang* = river-driver.

1905 W. Owen *Let.* 7 Aug. (1967) 25 He was fishing this morning when a *river bailiff came up. **1791** E. Darwin *Bot. Gard.* I. 117 Or sport in groups with *River-Boys, that lave Their silken limbs amid the dashing wave. **1854** J. Belcher *Relig. Denominations U.S.* 919 Others were organized into a body called, *The *River Brethren*, partly from the locality in which they were first found, near the Susquehanna, and Conestoga, and chiefly from their baptisms being celebrated only in rivers. **1951** H. E. Giles *Harbin's Ridge* xxiii. 202 And they baptized different, too. Face forward in the water, three times. In the early days, back in Pennsylvania, they'd been named the River Brethren on account of it, I'd heard. **1613** Purchas *Pilgrimage* VI. i. (1614) 561 Some imagined him to be Nilus the *Riuer-deitie. **1937** A. Huxley *Let.* 15 Dec. (1969) 429 This last is an appendage on one of the numerous vast estates of what are called 'The *River Families', who have been living here in a feudal sort of way, in some cases, for two or more centuries. **1902** S. E. White *Blazed Trail* lvi. 384 And now we've gone and bust, just because that infernal *river-hog had to fall off a boom. **1964** *Outdoorsman* (Campbellford, Ontario) Dec. 1/2 One may see a visitor with a misty look in his eye; an old blacksmith, top loader, barn boss, teamster, cookie or river hog who has returned to a fleeting glimpse of an era long gone by. **1680** W. Hubbard

Gen. Hist. New Eng. in *Mass. Hist. Soc. Coll.* (1815) 2nd Ser. V. 33 The *River Indians, such who had seated themselves in seuerall commodious plantations up higher upon Connecticutt river. **1785** T. Jefferson *Notes Virginia* 388 The Mohawks carried on a furious war down the Hudson against the Mohiccons and river indians. **1907** F. W. Hodge *Handbk. Amer. Indians* I. 786/2 Mahican ('wolf'). An Algonquian tribe that occupied both banks of the upper Hudson r... To the Dutch they were known as River Indians. **1697** Dryden *Æneid* Notes 627 The Poet here records the Names of Fifty *River Nymphs. **1921** *Dialect Notes* V. 113 **Riverpig*,..a lumberman who follows the drive in low water and dislodges logs from bars, mud, etc. **1947** *Sat. Even. Post* 8 Mar. 20/1 River pigs bristled all around him, men who hadn't seen a town or a saloon for nine months. **1883** *Harper's Mag.* Oct. 799/2 Mr. Clemens..in his character, first, as an apprentice to the occupation of a *river pilot. *c* **1849** 'N. Buntline' *B'hoys of N.Y.* iv. 30 Alvorado began to see how well his friend and rival *River Pirate was situated. **1962** S. E. Finer *Man on Horseback* xii. 230 The force of river pirates known as the Binh Xuyen. **1835** Mrs. Hemans *Water-Lily* Poems (1875) 608 Oh! beautiful thou art, Thou..stately *river-queen. **1883** J. Greenwood *Tag, Rag, & Co.* 35 With enough of '*river rats' to occupy my thoughts during my overland journey home, I paid my old waterman his due. **1884** *Harper's Mag.* 513/1 Observe the river-rats clustering about the groggeries. **1905** *Bull. U.S. Forest Service* LXI. 44 *River rat*, a log driver whose work is chiefly on the river; contrasted with Laker. **1976** *Kingston* (Ontario) *Whig-Standard* 4 June 28/1 Tom Harrison, a 'river rat' since 16, has purchased the Gananoque Water Taxi. **1853** Dickens *Down with Tide* in *Househ. Words* VI. 481/2 *River thieves can always get rid of stolen property..by dropping it overboard. **1859** Bartlett *Dict. Amer.* (ed. 2) 368 *River-Thief*, one of a class of thieves in New York city who in boats prowl about vessels at night and plunder them. **1882** J. D. McCabe *New York* xxxiv. 518 Another dangerous class of criminals are the river thieves, or 'River Pirates'. **1835** *Court Mag.* VI. 33/1 They were *river wolves, seizing upon every canoe which floated on those broad blue waters.

f. With agent-nouns, as ***river-carrier***, ***-crosser***, ***-farmer***, ***-inspector***, ***-keeper***, etc.

1865 Dickens *Mut. Fr.* I. i, He could not be a lighterman or *river-carrier. **1936** M. Franklin *All that Swagger* xviii. 167 He saddled the *river-crosser—a tall old grey. **1851** Mayhew *Lond. Labour* II. 147 The dredgermen of the Thames, or *river finders. **1888** Goode *Amer. Fishes* 434 For the benefit of our *river fishermen I quote two recipes. **1875** 'Mark Twain' in *Atlantic Monthly* Feb. 221/2 We had a fine company of these *river-inspectors along, this trip. **1894** C. H. Cook *Thames Rights* 127 To every honorary assistant *river-keeper they give a ticket to fish from the weirs. **1856** 'Stonehenge' *Brit. Rural Sports* I. I. viii. 67/1 They afford better sport to the puntsman than to the *river-shooter.

g. Comb. with pa. pples., as ***river-blanched***, ***-borne***, ***-caught***, ***-cut***, ***-encircled***, ***-fed***, ***-formed***, ***-rounded***, etc.; also with pres. pples., as ***river-winding***.

1788 Cowper *Mrs. Montagu* 8 The Cock his arch'd tail's azure show, And, *river-blanch'd, the Swan his snow. **1928** *Daily Tel.* 4 Dec. 12/4 Splitting the market into two, for *river-borne and rail-borne supplies respectively. **1924** A. J. Small *Frozen Gold* xii. 248 Others sat round the braziers and held great slabs of *river-caught salmon against the red-hot grids. **1957** G. E. Hutchinson *Treat. Limnol.* I. i. 81 Other authors have believed the lakes to occupy *river-cut valleys. **1951** *River-encircled [see *mountain-cresting* adj. s.v. mountain 7 b]. **1913** E. F. Benson *Thorley Weir* i. 21 A strip of *river-fed grasses and herbs of the waterside. **1796** W. Marshall *W. Eng.* II. 49 A narrow flat of *river-formed land. **1977** A. Hallam *Planet Earth* 50 Glacial erosion modifies river-formed valleys into U-shapes. **1820** Shelley *Hymn Pan* 3 The *river-girt islands, Where loud waves are dumb. **1864** Raine *Hexham* (Surtees) I. Pref. 6 Heavy.. with grain and grass which that *river-given soil produces. **1879** G. M. Hopkins *Poems* (1967) 79 Cuckoo-echoing, bell-swarmèd, lark-charmèd, rook-racked, *river-rounded. **1832** Tennyson *Œnone* 112 From many a vale And *river-sunder'd champaign clothed with corn. **1951** S. Spender *World within World* ii. 39, I used to go for long walks and bicycle rides into the hilly, tree-scattered, *river-winding countryside. **1883** *Archæol. Cant.* XV. 92 On the terraces are found *river-worn implements lying in the old gravel.

h. With adjs., as ***river-dark***, ***-thick***, ***-wise***.

1925 E. Sitwell *Troy Park* 100 She swims across the *river-dark vast floors. **1924** —— *Sleeping Beauty* xv. 53 How *river-thick flow your fleeced locks. **1934** Webster **Riverwise*, adj. **1940** *Sun* (Baltimore) 22 Apr. 3/6 Riverwise city officials..expressed belief the inundation would prove more annoying than damaging.

6. Attrib. with the names of fishes or animals (freq. contrasted with *sea-*), as ***river-bird***, ***-fly***; **river bass** (*U.S.*), one of several freshwater fishes of the family Centrarchidæ, esp. the black bass, *Micropterus salmoides*; † **river boar**, a kind of fish (L. *aper*); † **river bull**, ? the rhinoceros; **river bullhead**, the miller's thumb, *Cottus gobio*; **river carp**, the common carp, *Cyprinus carpio*; **river chub** (*U.S.*), the horny-head or jerker, *Ceratichthys biguttatus*; **river crab**, any crab which inhabits rivers, freshwater pools, or swamps; also, a crayfish; **river dog**, †(*a*) the river otter; (*b*) *U.S.*, = hellbender; **river dolphin**, (*a*) = dolphin 2; (*b*) the Gangetic dolphin (*Platanista*); † **river dragon**, the crocodile (with allusion to Pharaoh of Egypt); **river duck** (see quot.); **river eel**, the common freshwater eel (see eel *sb.* 1); **river garfish**, an Australian fish belonging to the genus *Hemirhamphus*, inhabiting freshwater streams; † **river gilt** (see quot.); † **river hawk** (see quot.); **river hen**, = water-hen; **river herring**, *U.S.*, = ale-wife[2]; also, formerly, the mooneye, *Hiodon tergisus*; **river hog**, (*a*) the capybara or water-hog; (*b*) a South African hog of the genus *Potamochœrus*; **river ibis** (see quot.); **river jack (viper)**, a West African viper having a flat head and a somewhat long horn on either side of the snout; **river lamprey**, a freshwater lamprey, *Petromyzon fluviatilis*; **river limpet**, a pulmonate gasteropod of the genus *Ancylus*, found in rivers; **river mussel**, a freshwater shellfish, *Unio pictorum*; † **river nightingale** (see quot.); **river otter**, the common otter, *Lutra vulgaris*; **river pearl**, a pearl from a freshwater mussel, esp. *Margaritifera margaritifera*; **river pearl mussel**, a fluviatile mussel bearing pearls; **river perch**, the common perch, *Perca fluviatilis*; **river porpoise**, a species of dolphin; **river salmon**, the ordinary freshwater salmon; **river seal**, *U.S.*, a seal which ascends rivers; **river-shell**, a shell found in freshwater streams; **river-shrew**, = *otter-shrew*; **river snail**, a kind of snail (*Paludina vivipara*), found in lakes and rivers; † **river soldier** (see quot.); **river swallow**, †(*a*) the bleak; (*b*) the bank-swallow or sand-martin; **river tern**, the common tern; **river tortoise**, the ordinary freshwater tortoise; **river trout**, a freshwater trout; **river turtle**, = *river tortoise*; † **river whale**, ? the sheat-fish; † **river whisker** (see quot.); **river wolf**, †(*a*) the pike; (*b*) a kind of otter (*Lutra Brasiliensis*) found in South America.

1857 *Spirit of Times* 11 Apr. 86/2 The Oswego (sometimes known as the '*river bass') is the heavier fish, often attaining to eight pounds weight. **1877** Jordan *N. Amer. Ichth.* in *Smithson. Coll.* XIII. I. 20 River-Bass, *Lepomis*. **1890** W. D. Howells *Boy's Town* 30 There were men who were reputed to catch at will, as it were, silvercats and river bass. **1910** W. de la Mare *Three Mulla-Mulgars* iv. 52 They heard the trump-billed *riverbirds calling their secrets one to another. **1601** Holland *Pliny* I. 353 What will they say then to the water-Goat & the *river-Bore, which in the river Achelous do evidently grunt. **1639** Fuller *Holy War* II. xiii, Strange creatures bred therein [*sc.* in the Nile], as *river bulls, horses and crocodiles. **1776** Pennant *Brit. Zool.* (ed. 4) III. 189 *River Bullhead, *cottus gobio*. **1842** H. Miller *O.R. Sandst.* iii. 77 The river bull-head, when attacked by an enemy,.. erects its two spines. **1896** tr. *Boas' Text Bk. Zool.* 390 In the rivers of Great Britain is found the small River Bull-head. **1653** Walton *Angler* xii. 236 [Bait] for a *River Carp. **1726** *Gentl. Angler* 63 Carp spawn generally in May, or the beginning of April, especially the River-Carp. **1729** *Dampier's Voy.* III. 412 The River-Carp [of Central America]. Its shape, colour and taste resemble ours. **1882** *River chub [see *horny-head* s.v. horny *a.* (*sb.*) 7]. **1884** Jordan *Fish. U.S.* in *Senate Misc.* VI. I. 617 The 'Horny-head', 'River Chub', or 'Jerker' is one of the most widely diffused of fresh-water fishes. **1861** Hulme tr. *Moquin-Tandon* III. iii. 96 The *River Crab or Cray-fish (*Astacus Fluviatilis*) is a decapod crustacean. **1866** *Chambers's Encycl.* VIII. 275/2 River-Crab (*Thelphusa depressa*). **1610** Holland *Camden's Brit.* I. 206 Otterey, that is, The River of Otters, or *River-Dogs, which we call Otters. **1646** Sir T. Browne *Pseud. Epid.* 114 Ætius..prescribeth the stones of the Otter, or River-dog, as succedaneous unto Castoreum. **1876** Goode *Anim. Res.* in *Smithson. Coll.* XIII. 13 *Proteida*. (River-dogs, hell-benders.) **1781** Pulteney *View Writings Linnæus* 95 *Coryphæna*,..*River Dolphin. **1667** Milton *P.L.* XII. 191 Thus with ten wounds This *River-dragon..submits To let his sojourners depart. **1837** Swainson *Nat. Hist. & Classif. Birds* II. 189 The *Anatinæ*, or *river ducks, show the typical perfection of the whole family [etc.]. **1872** Coues *N. Amer. Birds* 285 River ducks..are not by any means confined to fresh waters, and some species constantly associate with the sea-ducks. **1769** J. Wallis *Nat. Hist. Northumb.* I. 391 The *River-Eel is frequently taken from two to three feet long in our alpine stony rivers. **1958** J. Carew *Black Midas* vi. 128 A *river fly 'lighted on the tip of Belle's nose. **1883** E. P. Ramsay *Food-Fishes N.S. Wales* 28 The two species..*Hemirhamphus intermedius* (the sea gar-fish), and *H. regularis* (known as the *river gar-fish). **1729** *Dampier's Voy.* III. 413 The *River-Gilt [of Central America] hath small scales with a Blush of Gold towards the Back. **1611** Cotgr., *Faulcon rivereux*, that preyes on..riuer fowle; a *riuer Hawke, or Hawke for the riuer. **1894** G. Parker *Trail of Sword* xi, The cries of herons, loons, and *river-hens. **1842** J. E. DeKay *Zool. N.Y.* IV. 266 [The river mooneye] is known under the popular names of Herring, *River Herring, and Toothed Herring. **1884** *Cent. Mag.* Apr. 909/2 The different townships on Cape Cod protect the..'river herring'. **1977** *Hongkong Standard* 12 Apr. 2/8 Officials of the National Marine Fishery Services found illegal amounts of river herring in the trawler's hold 240 miles southeast of Boston. **1729** *Dampier's Voy.* III. 400 The *River-Hog [of Central America] feeds on Grass and divers Fruits, can swim and dive well. **1868** Darwin *Anim. & Pl.* II. 150 Even the Red River hog (*Potamochœrus penicillatus*)..has bred twice in the Zoological Gardens. **1879** J. G. Wood *Waterton's Wand. S. Amer.* 402 The *River Ibis (*Ibis infuscatus*) is found..on the rivers of Guiana. **1877** *Nature* Oct. 531/2 A *River Jack Viper (*Vipera rhinoceros*) from West Africa. **1836** Sir J. Richardson *Fauna Bor. Amer.* III. 294 *Petromyzon Fluviatilis* (Linn.), *River Lamprey. **1880–4** Day *Fishes Gt. Brit.* II. 362 It has been questioned whether this fish [*Petromyzon branchialis*] is not the young form of the river lamprey. **1778** Da Costa *Brit. Conch.* 1/1 The Limpet, *River. **1864** *Chambers's Encycl.* VI. 138/1 In *Ancylus* (River Limpets) it is limpet-shaped. **1769** J. Wallis *Nat. Hist. Northumb.* I. 402 The fresh-water shell-fishes,..or *River-Muscles, are plentiful in most of our rivers. **1776** Da Costa *Elem. Conch.* 295 The Pearl River Muscle. **1851** Richardson *Geol.* (1855) 435 A fresh-water deposit containing the shells of *Unio*, a river mussel. **1611** Cotgr., *Rousserole*, the *Riuer Nightingale; a kind of Kingsfisher. **1840** *Penny Cycl.* XVII. 63/2 The Otters..consist of two forms nearly allied: the first, including the *River Otters..; the second, the Sea Otter. **1885** *Encycl. Brit.* XVIII. 447/2 *River-pearls are produced by the fresh-water mussels inhabiting the mountain-streams of temperate climates in the northern hemisphere. **1963** P. Moyes *Murder à la Mode* iii. 55 Get me lots of gold bracelets and some river pearls. **1975** *Times* 6 Mar. 5/1 The borders..are adorned with sapphires, rubies, emeralds, and river pearls. **1896** tr. *Boas' Text Bk. Zool.* 315 The River Mussel (*Unio*) and the *River Pearl Mussel (*Margaritana margaritifera*), which are common in England, are allied forms. **1836** Sir J. Richardson *Fauna Bor. Amer.* III. 1 This fish [*Perca flavescens*, (Cuvier), American perch] has a close resemblance to the *river Perch [*Perca fluviatilis*] of Europe. **1884** Jordan *Fisheries U.S.* in *Senate Misc.* VI. I. 279 'River Perch' (*Hysterocarpus Traski*, Gibbons). **1849** Eastwick *Dry Leaves* 97, I saw several *river-porpoises, of the kind the natives call the Bolan. **1888** Goode *Amer. Fishes* 440 *River-salmon, not anadromous. **1851** *Zoologist* IX. 3298 The fur-seal and *river-seal are found. *c* **1711** Petiver *Gazophyl.* x. §99 A thin-rib'd Luzone *River-shell. **1816** T. Brown *Elem. Conch.* 130 River and land shells are mostly thinner than those of the sea. **1776** Da Costa *Elem. Conch.* 201 The Planorbis *River Snail. **1859–62** Richardson *Mus. Nat. Hist.* II. 339/2 The species of River Snails, amounting to upwards of sixty. **1729** *Dampier's Voy.* III. 416 The *River Souldier [of Central America]. It's mail'd somewhat like the Sturgeon, the Meat good. **1653** Walton *Angler* xvi. 205 There is also a Bleak, a fish that is ever in motion, and therefore called by some the *River-Swallow. **1817** T. Forster *Nat. Hist. Swallow Tribe* (ed. 6) 79 *Hirundo Riparia*, Sandmartin, Sand-swallow, Bankmartin, or River Swallow. **1831** *Wilson's Amer. Ornith.* IV. 358 *River tern, *Sterna fluviatilis*. **1839** Swainson *Nat. Hist. Fishes*, etc. II. 344 *Emydæ*, *River Tortoises. **1843** *Penny Cycl.* XXV. 74/2 Potamians, or River Tortoises,..live constantly in the water, only coming out occasionally. **1834** *Chambers's Edin. Jrnl.* 6 Dec. 357/3 Fish (we speak of *river trout) spawn seldom in such [slow, muddy] waters. **1867** *Harper's Mag.* Dec. 48/1 He has already achieved unequalled success in breeding river-trout. **1884** *St. James's Gaz.* 23 Feb. 5/2 A big river-trout will lie quietly head to stream. **1802** Willich *Domest. Encycl.* IV. 232/2 The *orbicularis*, or common *river-turtle, inhabits the milder climates of Europe. **1895** Swettenham *Malay Sk.* 212 The river-turtle is a great deal smaller than the sea-turtle. **1601** Holland *Pliny* I. 242 In some..riuers..there be fish found full as bigge: and namely, the *riuer-Whale called Silurus, in Nilus. **1681** Grew *Musæum* I. §v. ii. 103 The Head of the River-Whale. **1729** *Dampier's Voy.* III. 418 The *River Whisker. Has long black Whiskers but no Scales: it tastes well, and is frequently eaten. **1655** Moufet & Bennet *Health's Impr.* (1746) 279 Pikes or *River-wolves are greatly commended..for a wholesome Meat. **1840** *Penny Cycl.* XVII. 66/2 This is the *Lobo de rio* (River Wolf) of the colonists.

7. Attrib. with names of trees, plants, etc., as ***river-cress***, ***-flag***, ***palm***, ***-reed***, ***sponge***, ***willow***; **river birch**, the red birch, *Betula nigra*; **river black-oak**, an Australian tree (see quot.); **river lettuce**, a kind of weed, very common in tropical rivers and streams; the water lettuce, *Pistia stratiotes*; **river mangrove** (see quot. and mangrove[1] 2); **river oak**, an Australian tree of the genus *Casuarina*; **river pear**, = anchovy-pear; **river poisonous tree**, a shrub of the genus *Excæcaria* (see quot.); **river poplar** (see quot.); **river (red) gum**, the most widespread of the red gum-trees, *Eucalyptus camaldulensis*; cf. red gum[2] 2; **river she-oak**, a tree of the genus *Casuarina* (cf. she-oak); **river tea-tree**, the broad-leaved tea-tree, *Callistemon salignus*; **river tree** (see quots.); **river white gum**, a gum-tree, *E. andreana*, with smooth white bark.

1853 W. Darlington *Flora Cestrica* (ed. 3) 275 Black Betula. Black Birch. Red Birch. *River Birch. **1884** C. S. Sargent *Rep. Forests N. Amer.* 161 Red Birch. River Birch. .. Used in the manufacture of furniture. **1969** T. H. Everett *Living Trees of World* xiii. 104/1 The river birch grows in lowlands from Massachusetts to Florida. **1889** Maiden *Usef. Native Pl.* 122 *Casuarina suberosa*,..'*River Black-oak'. **1953** A. Clarke *Moment Next to Nothing* I. i. 18 I've little to offer a guest... But it is yours, a round of bread, a pick Of *river-cress and goat-cheese. **1855** Kingsley *Westw. Ho!* ii, A car wherein sate, amid reeds and *river-flags, three or four pretty girls. **1897** Mary Kingsley *W. Africa* 378 Great floating masses of *river lettuce (*Pistia stratiotes*). **1889** Maiden *Usef. Native Pl.* 370 *Ægiceras majus*,..'*River Mangrove'. A shrub or small tree. Wood of light colour, close-grained, and easily worked. **1838** T. L. Mitchell *Three Exped.* (1839) I. 39 [The] banks were overhung by the dense, umbrageous foliage of the *casuarina*, or '*river-oak' of the colonists. **1964** D. Varaday *Gara-Yaka* ix. 74 In the lush valleys among the rock forts..there stand magnificent *River Palms. **1696** Plukenet *Opera Bot.* II. 32 *Anona Americana*,..Anchovie Pear, & *aliquando* *River Pear, *Nostratibus nuncupatur*. **1889** Maiden *Usef. Native Pl.* 187 *Excæcaria Agallocha*,..'*River Poisonous Tree'... It produces..an acrid, milky juice. **1885** *Encycl. Brit.* XIX. 512/1 The *P*[*opulus*] *canadensis* of Michaux..in New England..is sometimes called the '*River Poplar'. **1889** Maiden *Usef. Native Pl.* 431 This particular specimen was collected by Sir William Macarthur, and called by him '*River Gum of Camden'. He describes it..as a small, quick-growing species, very elegant when in blossom. **1911** C. E. W. Bean '*Dreadnought' of Darling* ii. 17 A single line of railway runs straight out into the back country..and stops within sight of the river gums. **1930** A. J. Ewart *Flora Victoria* 821 River Red Gum. A fairly tall tree, up to 80 or 150 feet high, with a greyish-white bark shedding in thin leaves or flakes. **1963** W. E. Harney *To Ayers Rock & Beyond* iii. 29 The gaunt river-gums..grow along the bank and bed of this one-time mighty river. **1973** G. M. Chippendale *Eucalypts W. Austral. Goldfields* 183/2 The river red gum is the most widespread eucalypt in Australia. **1855** Singleton *Virgil* I. 134 By the banks the *river-reed is cut. **1889** MAIDEN *Usef. Native Pl.* 398 *Casuarina glauca*, ..'*River She-oak'. **1712** J. MORTON *Northampt.* vi. §22. 367 The brittle-branched *River Spunge. **1889** MAIDEN *Usef. Native Pl.* 390 *Callistemon salignus*,..'*River Tea-tree'. **1705** PLUKENET *Opera Bot.* IV. 176 *Potamodendron, arbor..amnicola, Barbadensibus* *River Tree *nuncupata.* **1729** *Dampier's Voy.* III. 436 River Tree. Because it always grows on its Banks, and shoots its Roots on the Water; it bears a beautiful Umbel of small 5 leaved scarlet Flowers. **1838** T. L. MITCHELL *Three Exped.* (1839) II. 51 A line of yarra river-trees. **1884** A. NILSON *Timber Trees New South Wales* 58 *River White Gum.—Trunk smooth and nearly white. **1889** MAIDEN *Usef. Native Pl.* 430 A variety of this gum (*E. radiata*) is called in New South Wales 'White Gum' or 'River White Gum'. **1961** PENFOLD & WILLIS *Eucalypts* xii. 249 The tree [sc. *E. andreana*] is known as 'White Top', or 'River White Gum', and occurs fairly plentifully on the river banks and mountain ranges of eastern New South Wales. **1963** M. SHADBOLT *Summer Fires & Winter Country* 233 In summer we swam down under the *river-willows.

river ('raɪvə(r)), *sb.*[2] Also 5–7 (9) ryver, 6 *Sc.* rivere, 6–7 riuer. [f. RIVE *v.*[1] + -ER[1].]

1. One who rives, rends, or cleaves. Also in combs., as ***block-, girnel-, lath-river.***

1483 *Cath. Angl.* 310/1 A Ryver, *lacerator.* **1508** [see GIRNEL *sb.* b]. **1610** [see LATH *sb.* 4]. **1611** COTGR., *Fendeur*, a cleauer, slitter; a riuer. **1671** EACHARD *Obs. Answ. Cont. Clergy* 22 An honest Block-River, with his Beetle, heartily calling. **1865** W. WHITE *Eastern Eng.* I. 146 These women are known as 'ryvers', because they rive or rend the gills with their thumbs to make way for the stick. **1884** *Good Words* June 395/1 Men have to serve seven years in the quarries.. before they get full wages. They then become 'rivers' or 'trimmers'.

†**2.** One who robs; a reaver. *Obs.*

1513 MORE *Chron., Rich. III*, Wks. 40/1 Robbers and riuers walking at libertie vncorrected. **1535** STEWART *Cron. Scot.* II. 341 Ane multitude..Off theif and riuer..hereit all the landis of Kyntyre. **1568** *Henryson's Cock & Fox* 180 (Bann. MS.), Nay, murther theif and rivere, stand on reir. *Ibid.* (ed. 1631), No, false riuer and theefe, stand not mee neere.

river ('rɪvə(r)), *v. rare.* [f. RIVER *sb.*[1]]

1. *trans.* †To wash (wool or sheep) in a river.

1531–2 *Act 23 Hen. VIII*, c. 17 §1 No maner person ..[shall] winde..any fleesse of wolle beinge not sufficiently riuered or wasshed. *Ibid.*, To riuer or washe their sheepe afore they be shorne. **1724** [see RIVERING *vbl. sb.*].

2. *intr.* To follow a river-like course.

1921 A. CLARKE *Sword of West* 23 Far below me lay A deep green valley rivering through grey mist.

riverain ('rɪvəreɪn), *a.* and *sb.* [a. F. *riverain*, f. *rivière* RIVER *sb.*[1]]

A. *adj.* **1.** Pertaining to a river or its vicinity.

1858 *Times* 1 Dec. 9/3 The eddies..which the men wise in riverain mining assert to have drawn the greater quantity of gold to this bank. **1882** *Nature* 23 Nov. 97/1 Special riverain surveys will in future be made.

2. Situated on the banks of a river; dwelling near a river; = RIVERINE *a.* 1.

1870 HUXLEY in *Contemp. Rev.* 515 The riverain population of the North Sea. **1872** M. COLLINS *Two Plunges* III. iii. 70 He..climbed the narrow riverain path. **1883** 'OUIDA' *Wanda* I. 61 A whole riverain town on the Danube.

B. *sb.* One who dwells on the banks or in the vicinity of a river.

1864 *Temple Bar* Feb. 337 Take the riverain of the Strand or the environs of Westminster Abbey. **1867** *Standard* 10 Jan. 4/4 Being riverains of the Scheldt, they were free to use it with all its tributaries and outlets.

'**river-bank.** [f. RIVER *sb.*[1] + BANK *sb.*[1]] The raised or sloping edge or border of a river; the bank or ground adjacent to a river.

1565 COOPER *Thesaurus* s.v. *Margo*, The brimmes of the riuer banke. **1697** DRYDEN *Virg. Georg.* IV. 764 With his last Voice, Eurydice, he cry'd; Eurydice, the Rocks and River-banks reply'd. **1710** SHAFTESB. *Adv. Author* I. i. 9 A great Frequenter of the Woods and River-Banks. **1764** *Skeffling Inclosure Act* 13 In case the said river Humber shall.. destroy the present river-bank. **1843** *Penny Cycl.* XXV. 75/1 The females..seek out on the river-banks sandy spots for the deposit of their eggs. **1864** TENNYSON *Aylmer's F.* 451 He ran Beside the river-bank.

'**river-bed.** [f. RIVER *sb.*[1] + BED *sb.* 9.] The bed or channel in which a river flows.

1833 TENNYSON *Mariana in the South* v, The riverbed was dusty-white. **1862** STANLEY *Lect. Jewish Church* v. 116 The delicious water from the sediment of the river-bed. **1899** *Q. Rev.* July 61 The country from the river-bed to hill-top was densely cultivated.

'**river-bottom.** *U.S.* [f. RIVER *sb.*[1] + BOTTOM *sb.* 4 b.] Low-lying alluvial land situated along the banks of a river.

1752 C. GIST *Jrnl.* 20 Feb. (1893) 75 Then continued our course..the last 5 [miles] thro the river bottoms, which were a mile wide and very rich. **1793** G. IMLAY *Topogr. Descr. W. Terr. N. Amer.* (ed. 2) 411 At the edge of the wood lands, and before your descend [*sic*] into the river bottoms, one of the most charming prospects..displays itself. **1814** BRACKENRIDGE *Views Louisiana* 29 The river bottoms being generally fine. **1843** CAPT. MARRYAT *M. Violet* xxviii, Between the upland and the little ridge..there was a river-bottom. (*Note.* River bottom is a space, sometimes of many many miles in width, on the side of the river, running parallel with it.) **1895** WINSOR *Assiss. Basin* 26 The luxury of the river bottoms and their timber margins.

'**river-,digging.** orig. *U.S.* [f. RIVER *sb.*[1] + DIGGING *vbl. sb.*] **a.** *pl.* Gold or diamond diggings in the neighbourhood of a river or stream, or in a dried-up river-bed. **b.** The action of digging at such a place. Hence **river-digger.** Cf. DIGGING *vbl. sb.* 4.

1851 D. B. WOODS *Sixteen Months at Gold Diggings* i. 13 The 'river diggings' include the bars and auriferous portions of the channels of the tributaries of the Sacramento and San Joaquin, during their passage through the foot-hills. **1862** [see *dry diggings* s.v. DRY *a.* C. 3]. **1881** E. E. FREWER tr. *Holub's Seven Yrs. S. Afr.* I. iii. 60 The settlement at the river-diggings sprang up with a rapidity as marvellous as those of California. **1904** L. J. SPENCER tr. *Bauer's Precious Stones* I. II. 185 The amalgamation of the 'dry diggings' to form the De Beers Consolidated Mines, has had the effect of increasing the number of river diggers. **1920** F. C. CORNELL *Glamour of Prospecting* i. 10 A modicum of genuine men of past experience—principally ex-'river-diggers'—men whose small capital was running away like water for bare necessities in this miserable dust-hole of creation. **1947** L. HASTINGS *Dragons are Extra* i. 10 Dabbling in river-digging for diamonds. **1947** *E. Afr. Ann. 1946–7* 122/1 The 'river diggings' of South Africa where workings extend..along present or ancient river beds.

'**river-drift.** *Geol.* [f. RIVER *sb.*[1] + DRIFT *sb.* 10.] Ancient alluvia of rivers in which early palæolithic remains are found. Also *attrib.*, as ***river-drift gravel, man.***

1839 DE LA BECHE *Rep. Geol. Cornw.*, etc. xiii. 403 The whole probably being the accumulation of river-drift during a long period of time. **1865** LUBBOCK *Preh. Times* 239 Neither the mammoth, nor the..rhinoceros have been found in any stratum anterior to the river-drift gravels. **1880** DAWKINS *Early Man Brit.* v. 99 The last and most important addition to be made to this list is the man of the river deposits, or the River-drift man. **1892** [see DRIFT *sb.* 10].

river-driver. *N. Amer.* [f. RIVER *sb.*[1] + DRIVER 2.] (See quot. 1848.) Hence '**river-drive,** a drive of logs down a river; '**river-driving,** the action of driving logs down a river.

1848 BARTLETT *Dict. Amer.* (1859) 368 *River-Driver*, a term applied by lumbermen in Maine, to a man whose business it is to conduct logs down running streams, to prevent them from lodging upon shoals or remaining in eddies. **1854** F. J. BULLARD *Now-a-Days* 65 River drivin' is the pootiest part of loggin', I think. **1864** LOWELL *Fireside Trav.* 141 This was M.., a famous river-driver, and who was to have fifty men under him next winter. **1893** *Scribner's Mag.* June 714/1 Every river driver wore a long red sash. **1908** S. E. WHITE *Riverman* v. 50 How does river-driving strike you? **1920** *Rod & Gun in Canada* Nov. 646/1 We were enjoying the sights we saw along the line: the lakes, rivers, the river-drives. **1937** C. M. WILSON *Aroostook* 105 The 'river-drives' were the consummation of turning out the timber. **1963** *Canada Month* Nov. 22/1 The lumber trade furnished employment for thousands of lumber jacks, river drivers, and sailors. **1972** [see *pickpole* s.v. PICK *sb.*[1] 8]. **1974** D. SEARS *Lark in Clear Air* ii. 27 He..got a job as boss on a river-drive. *Ibid.* xiv. 178 Tommy bought a new pair of river-driving boots.

rivered ('rɪvəd), *ppl. a.* [f. RIVER *sb.*[1] + -ED[2].] Watered by rivers; furnished with a river or rivers. Chiefly in combs., as ***best-, deep-, slow-rivered***; † ***muddy-rivered,*** living in muddy rivers.

1655 MOUFET & BENNET *Health's Improv.* (1746) 279 If fenny or muddy-river'd Fishes be unwholesome, the Pike is not so good as Authors make him. **1673** E. BROWNE *Trav.* 1 Hungaria..is..the best Rivered Country in Europe. **1796** W. MARSHALL *W. Eng.* I. 279 The ground is..strongly featured; being there divided by deep rivered vallies. **1892** LD. LYTTON *King Poppy* iv. 74 On either side The river'd glen..rear'd Steep crags abrupt. **1899** *Echo* 20 Feb. 1/7 Russia being flat, windy, and slow-rivered.

riveret ('rɪvərɪt). Now *rare* or *Obs.* [ad. OF. *riverete, riv(i)erette* (F. *rivièrette*): see RIVER *sb.*[1] and -ET[1].]

1. A small river or stream; a rivulet, rill, or brook. (Common *c* 1600–1660; now *rare.*)

1538 LELAND *Itin.* (1768) I. 106 The Castelle of Nottingham stondith on a rokky Hille.., and Line Riveret goith by the Rootes of it. **1577** HARRISON *England* II. i, Caue ..which is no great water nor quick streame.., and yet is it a prety riueret. **1600** HOLLAND *Livy* Pref. p. vi, A little rill, which..is maintained with fresh springs and new riverets. **1633** GERARD *Descr. Somerset* (1900) 1 On the utmost edge of this County Ore a little riverett gusheth out under a large Oak. **1670** DENTON *Desc. N. York* (1845) 5 The South-side is not without Brooks and Riverets, which empty themselves into the Sea. **1807** G. CHALMERS *Caledonia* I. I. 46 Waters..such as form pools, in their course like the riverets above mentioned.

transf. **1594** ? GREENE *Selimus* Wks. (Grosart) XIV. 242 The channels run like riuerets of blood.

fig. *c* **1616** S. WARD *Coal from Altar* (1627) 28 May not he iustly disdaine, that the lest Riueret should be drained another way? **1623** LISLE *Ælfric on O. & N. Test.* To Rdr. 22 So much better they thought it for men to draw..religion from the Lord's fountaine, than from creekes and riuerets of men. **1641** HINDE *J. Bruen* lxii. 209 Being as it were broken open by afflictions, the riverets of grace and truth did issue out amayne.

2. *transf.* A surface vein. Also *attrib.*

1603 DRAYTON *Bar. Wars* VI. lvi, Her fair breasts..Whose violet veins in branched riverets flow. **1658** W. SANDERSON *Graphice* 42 A fair breast,..interlaced with Riveret-azur-veines.

b. A small blood-vessel.

1615 CROOKE *Body of Man* 172 If onely the riuerets or channels of the Hollow-vein did containe Alimentary blood. *Ibid.* 254 From the same braunch of the Hypogastricall Veine come small riuerets to the bladder.

'**river-fish.** Also river fish. [f. RIVER *sb.*[1] Cf. Du. *riviervisch.*] Any fish that has its habitat in a river or stream; a freshwater fish.

1398 TREVISA *Barth. De P.R.* XIII. xii. (Bodl. MS.), Laye fische..beþ nouȝt so goode as ryuer fissches. **1587** HARRISON *England* III. iii. (1878) 18 Pike, carpe, and some other of our riuer fishes are solde by inches of cleane fish. **1617** MORYSON *Itin.* III. 95 They have little plenty of River fish, excepting onely Eales. **1630** *R. Johnson's Kingd. & Commw.* 376 It yeeldeth Wine and Wheat.., and affordeth Cattell, Horse, and River-fish. **1753** CHAMBERS *Cycl. Suppl.*, *Lampern*, a river fish of the lamprey kind found in many parts of England. **1888** GOODE *Amer. Fishes* 6 Worthy among river fish to be compared with sea fish.

'**river-god.** *Mythol.* [f. RIVER *sb.*[1] + GOD *sb.* 1. Cf. Du. *riviergod.*] A tutelary deity supposed to dwell in and to preside over a river.

1661 COWLEY *Of Greatness*, The water every whit as clear .., as if it darted from..the Urn of a River-God. **1713** GAY *Rural Sports* 7 The River-Gods and Nymphs about thee throng To hear the Syrens warble in thy Song. **1775** R. CHANDLER *Trav. Asia M.* (1825) I. 163 The river-god is represented on the Ephesian medals with this aquatic as one of his attributes. **1832** TENNYSON *Œnone* 37, I am the daughter of a River-God. **1859** GEO. ELIOT *A. Bede* xiii, It was as if she had been wooed by a river-god, who might any time take her to his wondrous halls below a watery heaven.

'**riverhood.** [f. RIVER *sb.*[1] + -HOOD.] The state of being a river; the office or duty of a river.

1841 *Blackw. Mag.* XLIX. 302 Expanding into the.. ambitious promise of the youthful river; and anon, swelling forth in the stately majesty of full-grown riverhood. **1847** H. MILLER *First Impr. Eng.* ix. (1857) 144 The dull mound cuts off the Stour from its sorely-tasked term of useful riverhood.

'**river-horse.** [f. RIVER *sb.*[1] + HORSE *sb.* 5. Cf. MDu. *rivierpeert* (Du. *-paard*).]

1. The hippopotamus. Cf. WATER-HORSE.

1601 HOLLAND *Pliny* II. 316 As touching the riuer-horse called Hippopotamus, there is a great affinitie..betweene him and the crocodile. **1667** MILTON *P.L.* VII. 474 Ambiguous between Sea and Land The River Horse and scalie Crocodile. **1759** JOHNSON *Rasselas* xxxviii, The crocodiles and river-horses are common in this unpeopled region. **1843** LONGF. *Slave's Dream* vi, The river-horse, as he crushed the reeds. **1878** BOSW. SMITH *Carthage* 39 The Senegal River, a river abounding, then as now, with crocodiles and riverhorses.

2. The water-kelpie: see KELPIE[1].

1851 THORPE *Northern Myth.* II. 22 He secured the assistance of the water-kelpie or river-horse.

riverine ('rɪvəraɪn), *a.* and *sb.* [f. RIVER *sb.*[1]]

A. *adj.* **1.** Situated or dwelling on the banks of a river; riparian.

1860 *Chamb. Jrnl.* XIV. 40 Swampville was in reality a riverine town. **1888** INGLIS *Tent Life* 22 Such villages are common enough in these..riverine plains, all over India. **1898** G. W. STEEVENS *With Kitchener to Khartum* 78 Like all riverine peoples he is more clean than bashful.

2. Of or pertaining to a river. Also, resembling a river.

1871 *Graphic* 29 April 382 The view at high water on the riverine curve is hardly surpassed in any European city. **1876** S. BIRCH *Rede Lect.* 24 The riverine navies of Egypt floated to the scene of action. **1884** E. JENKINS *Week of Passion* II. iv. 156 His face,..deeply rutted, here and there, with expressive valleys and riverine lines of wrinkle. **1898** *Pall Mall Mag.* May 9 Great riverine improvements.. effected at great cost.

B. *sb.* The banks or vicinity of a river.

1895 SWETTENHAM *Malay Sk.* 215 All the dwellers on the riverine.

'**rivering,** *vbl. sb.* [Cf. RIVER *v.*] †**a.** Pursuit of game on the banks of rivers. *Obs.* †**b.** Washing (of wool or sheep) in a stream. *Obs.* **c.** Sailing, rowing, etc., on a river.

13.. *K. Alis.* 678 (Weber), Now con Alisaundre..In grene wode of huntyng, And of reveryng, and of haukyng. **1532** *Act 23 Hen. VIII*, c. 17 This Act concerning riuering and washing of any wooll. **1724** *Lond. Gaz.* No. 6264/2 By not sufficiently Rivering, or Washing of Sheep, before they are shorn. **1891** MISS DOWIE *Girl in Karp.* 139 We got under weigh, and had the next two hours in the open, with a good deal of rivering.

rivering ('rɪvərɪŋ), *ppl. a. nonce-wd.* [Cf. RIVER *v.*] Flowing in river form.

1939 JOYCE *Finnegans Wake* (1964) I. 216 Beside the rivering waters of, hitherandthithering waters of. Night!

'**riverish,** *a. rare*[−1]. [f. RIVER *sb.*[1] + -ISH.] Giving rise to rivers; abounding in rivers.

1570 DEE *Math. Pref.* *j b, Easy wayes are made, by which the zelous Philosopher, may wyn nere this Riuerish Ida, this Mountayne of Contemplation.

'**riverless,** *a.* [f. RIVER *sb.*[1] + -LESS.] Destitute or devoid of rivers.

1860 MAURY *Phys. Geogr.* vii. §404 That sea lies, for the most part, within a rainless and riverless district. **1870** YEATS *Nat. Hist. Comm.* 108 The region of Patagonia, riverless and hilly, is dry, cold, and barren.

'**riverlet.** *rare.* [f. RIVER *sb.*[1] + -LET.] A small river; a brook, stream, or rivulet.

1674 *N. Eng. Hist. & Gen. Reg.* (1850) IV. 34, I give to my son..my house and home lot on the South side of the riverlet. **1883** MISS BROUGHTON *Belinda* I. vii, Here by the riverlet sits the floury mill.

'**river-like,** *adv.* and *a.* [f. RIVER *sb.*[1] + -LIKE.]

A. *adv.* In the manner of or like a river.

1646 J. Benbrigge *Vsura Acc.* 18 Thankfulnesse to God, River-like, returnes unto the Ocean of his glory, those streames of blessings [etc.]. **1868** Browning *Ring & Bk.* III. 165 Prosperity rolled river-like.

B. *adj.* Characteristic of or resembling a river.

1830 Miss Mitford *Village* Ser. IV. (1863) 252 Where the ..brook winds away..until it spreads into a river-like dignity. **1839–48** Bailey *Festus* xiv. 137 If I could ever think to wrong A love so riverlike, deep, pure, and long. **1878** Stanley *Dark Cont.* I. xvi. 425 These watercourses, though called rivers, show no running stream, but only river-like marshes.

ˈriverling. *rare.* [f. river *sb.*¹ + -ling¹ 2.] = riverlet. Also *fig.*

1591 Sylvester *Du Bartas* I. iii. 133 Of him she also holds her silver Springs, And all her hidden Crystall Riverlings. *Ibid.* vi. 755 Sent as from the lively Spring Of his Divineness, some small Riverling.

ˈriverly, *a.* *rare.* [f. river *sb.*¹ + -ly¹.] Resembling a river; river-like.

1858 *Times* 27 Aug. 8/4 We found the river..broad, deep, and flowing with riverly strength.

ˈriverman. [f. river *sb.*¹] A waterman.

1722 De Foe *Hist. Plague* (1756) 254 The Seamen had no communication with the River-Men. **1880** W. Newton *Serm. for Boys & Girls* 410 A weather-beaten river man. **1898** *Pall Mall G.* 19 Jan. 4/3 He is a frozen-out river-man, connected with the heavy lighter trade.

riverrun¹ (ˈrɪvərʌn). *nonce-wd.* [Cf. run *sb.*¹ 29 a.] The course which a river shapes and follows through the landscape.

1939 Joyce *Finnegans Wake* (1964) I. 3 Riverrun, past Eve and Adam's, from swerve of shore to bend of bay, brings us by a commodius vicus of recirculation back to Howth Castle and Environs.

river runner. *N. Amer.* [f. river *sb.*¹ + runner.] **a.** One who drives a river-vessel. **b.** One who engages in the leisure activity of running, or travelling down, a river in a small craft (as a rubber dinghy, etc.). Hence **river run**², **river running**.

1913 O. A. Rothert *Hist. Muhlenberg Co.* xxxi. 393 The coal barges were taken up and down the river by men known as 'river runners'. **1962** *Nat. Geographic* Apr. 561/1 (*caption*) River runners stop for a swim in the Little Colorado's Blue. **1965** Mrs. L. B. Johnson *White House Diary* 28 Oct. (1970) 330 I'll never be satisfied after having been down the Snake River until I've become a river runner. **1968** *Sunset* Mar. 34/2 On your first river-running excursion ..you'll..welcome all the advice you can get. *Ibid.* (*heading*) What to take on a River Run. **1974** C. F. Martin *Sierra Whitewater* 8 The drive from San Francisco Bay to good river runs is thus about an hour shorter than the drive to good skiing. **1976** *National Observer* (U.S.) 24 Jan. 12/2 River running in an inner-tube, skeet shooting, and trout fishing are speedily arranged at minimal cost.

ˈriver-sand. [f. river *sb.*¹ and sand *sb.* Cf. Du. *rivierzand.*] Sand procured from the bed of a river or stream.

1563 Hyll *Art Gard.* (1593) 19 If you set any young Trees in that grounde, let that there-about bee mixed with a quantitie of sweete Earthe and Riuer sand. **1703** *Moxon's Mech. Exerc.* 242 Also to River or Sea-Sand, if you put a third part of Powder of Tiles.., it works the better. **1726** Leoni *Alberti's Archit.* I. 35 There are three sorts of Sand, Pit-sand, River-sand, and Sea-sand. **1834–6** *Encycl. Metrop.* (1845) VIII. 475/2 The manufactories are restricted to the use of the commonest kind of sea or river sand. **1870** tr. *Baron von Richthofen's Lett.* (1874) 4 River-sand, of which probably millions of tons are yearly carried over these places.

riverscape (ˈrɪvəskeɪp). [f. river *sb.*¹ + scape *sb.*³; formed in imitation of landscape.]

1. A picturesque view or prospect of a river.

1903 C. S. Smith *Barbizon Days* 17 Moret has noble turreted gateways and Grez a church more picturesque than that of Montigny, riverscapes more alluring, and a ruined château. **1927** H. V. Morton *In Search of England* xii. 213 All the beauty and peace of the Warwickshire countryside have been packed into one riverscape. **1966** *New Statesman* 25 Nov. 793/1 Nobody listened to his proposal to replace Rennie's Waterloo Bridge with a tunnel to save spoiling a fine riverscape.

2. A painting of a river or riverside scene.

1930 *Time & Tide* 9 May 606 Mr. Lamorna Birch and Sir H. Hughes Stanton show very capable riverscapes. **1964** N. Freeling *Double-Barrel* iii. 91 The arrangement opposite: a wholly bluey-greeny Monet riverscape over a little writing table. **1975** *Gramophone* Dec. 1065/1 The record is very well produced with a fine autumnal riverscape by Monet on the front.

ˈriverside. Also river-side. [f. river *sb.*¹ + side *sb.*] **a.** The side or bank of a river; the ground adjacent to, or stretching along, a river.

?*a* **1366** Chaucer *Rom. Rose* 134 Tho gan I walke through the mede, Dounward ay in my pleying, The river-syde costeying. *c* **1410** *Master of Game* (MS. Digby 182) xii, Men shulde leed hem oute euery day..vpon a..hard path by a Ryuerside. *c* **1480** Henryson *Mor. Fab., Frog & Mouse* i, Ane litill mous come to ane reueir syde. *c* **1500** *Melusine* 361 The peple vpon the ryuere syde had grete meruayll & were al abasshed. **1523** Ld. Berners *Froiss.* I. 19 The ost lodged them in a wodde by a lytle ryuersyde. **1597** Breton *Wit's Trenchmour* Wks. (Grosart) II. 7/1 Narcissus, or some of his kindred, had been so in loue with theyr owne shadowe, that hee could not goe from the Riuer side. **1611** Bible *Acts* xvi. 13 On the Sabboth we went out of the citie by a riuer side. **1662** J. Davies tr. *Mandelslo's Trav.* 35 He commonly lurks in the high grass on the river side. **1725** Pope *Odyss.* x. 192 Casting on the river-side The bloody spear, his gather'd feet I ty'd. **1774** Goldsm. *Nat. Hist.* (1824) II. 182 This animal ..seldom ventures from the river side. **1834** Marryat *P. Simple* (1863) 160 We..walked along the river-side till we fell in with a small craft. **1865** J. H. Ingraham *Pillar of Fire* (1872) 411 Instantly the woman..hurried to the river-side.

b. *attrib.*, as ***riverside bathing, inn, sand, situation, villa, village***, etc.

1760 G. Washington *Diary* 14 Apr. (1925) I. 153 Has 2 Pecks of sd. Earth and 1 of Riverside Sand. **1799** *Hull Advertiser* 15 June 2/4 A warehouse..desirable for any purpose where a river-side situation is required. **1849** J. Forbes *Physician's Holiday* (1850) 1 The river-side inns of Wales or Scotland. **1863** Barry *Dockyard Econ.* 280 Mr. Stewart has now extensive river-side premises. **1889** C. C. R. *Up Season* 277 A lawn, and a riverside villa. **1914** W. Owen *Let.* 1 June (1967) 257 They went to visit some friends who lived in a riverside village. **1946** *Nature* 31 Aug. 290/1 At the age of fourteen, he contracted severe rheumatic trouble, as a result of river-side bathing.

Hence **river'sider**.

1889 C. C. R. *Up Season* 282 Few but will say Something kind of the old riversider.

‖**riverso.** *Obs.* *rare.* Also 6 **riuersa.** [a. It. *riverso* 'a back-blow' (Florio).] = reverse *sb.* 7. (See also reverso.) Also *fig.*

1595 Saviolo *Practise* I. 11, I would not aduise any freend of mine..to strik neither mandrittaes nor riuersaes. *Ibid.* L 3 b, If you see he keepes his dagger winding towardes his right side, thrust a riuersa at his face. **1600** O. E. (M. Sutcliffe) *Repl. to Libel* I. iii. 81, I haue thought good to bestow on them these Riuersoes, and Tramazzones.

ˈriverward, *adv.* and *a.* [f. river *sb.*¹]

A. *adv.* Toward a river; in the direction of a river. Also ***to riverward of***.

1833 Ritchie *Wand. by Loire* 62 Looking riverward, the vista is terminated..by a village church. **1872** M. Collins *Princess Clarice* II. xvii. 204 Skolinson and Clarice went off wordlessly riverward. **1896** *Atlantic Monthly* May 598/1 The first rising-ground to riverward of the hollow.

B. *adj.* Facing or directed toward a river.

1889 *Daily News* 7 Oct. 2/2 The outside embankments are being actively made, and the river-ward sides faced with strong rubble walling. **1966** D. Varaday *Gara-Yaka's Domain* xi. 121 In the riverward spoor a few drops of blood showed up.

So **ˈriverwards** *adv.*

1870 Lowell *Study Wind., Gard. Acquaint.*, A pair or two ..every evening fly over us riverwards.

ˈriver-ˌwater. Also river water. [f. river *sb.*¹ + water *sb.* Cf. Du. *rivierwater*, G. *revierwasser*.] Water in, forming, or obtained from, a river or stream.

1398 Trevisa *Barth. De P.R.* XIII. iii. (Bodl. MS), Ryuer water is beeste þat renneþ esteward.., and þe reuer water þat renneþ westward is lasse worthie. **1565** Cooper *Thesaurus* s.v. *Aqua*, Runnyng or riuer water. **1600** J. Pory tr. *Leo's Africa* III. 160 Engins, for the conueying of riuer-water ouer the said walles into cesternes. **1620** Venner *Via Recta* Introd. 9 Riuer-water hath the third place of goodnes. **1707** *Curios. in Husb. & Gard.* 350 A wooden Trough, fill'd with River-Water. **1762** Mills *Syst. Husb.* I. 483 The Spaniards..steep them in river water and salt till that bitterness is gone. **1835** Lyell *Princ. Geol.* (ed. 4) I. 345 The area over which the river-water is spread. **1849** Noad *Electr.* (ed. 3) 220 Common river-water was employed to fill the basin, and to knead the pipe-clay.

ˈriver-weed. [f. river *sb.*¹ + weed *sb.*]

1. A weed naturally growing in rivers.

1671 Skinner *Etym. Bot.*, River-weed, *Conferva Plinii*. **1704** *Dict. Rust.* s.v. *Sea*, Sea and River Weeds. **1805** R. W. Dickson *Pract. Agric.* II. 643 The dung of rabbits, pigeons, and poultry,..river weeds, and other similar matters. **1895** *Jrnl. R. Agric. Soc.* Mar. 12 He..advised river-weeds and sedge as a manure for them.

2. An American aquatic plant, the threadfoot (*Podostemon ceratophyllus*).

1856 A. Gray *Man. Bot.* (1860) 384 *Podostemon*, River-weed. *Ibid.*, *Podostemaceæ*, River-weed Family.

ˈriverwise, *adv.* [f. river *sb.*¹ + wise *sb.*¹] In the manner of a river; in relation to a river.

1927 Joyce *Lett.* (1966) III. 164 She has grown—river-wise—since the night you heard her under the sign of Ursa Minor. **1946** R. Graves *Poems 1938–45* 20 They carry Time looped so river-wise about their house There's no way in by history's road To name or number them. **1946** R. Blesh *Shining Trumpets* vii. 151 The French laid out the city, eleven squares riverwise and six squares deep.

ˈrivery, *a.* [f. river *sb.*¹ + -y.]

1. Resembling a river; river-like.

1612 Drayton *Poly-olb.* x. 94 Thy full and youthful breasts, which..Are branch'd with rivery veins. **1916** A. Huxley *Burning Wheel* 13 Lorelei, Combing the silken mystery, The glaucous gold of her rivery tresses. **1977** *Rolling Stone* 19 May 86/3 'The Wheel' is more Western bop than swing, a brilliant, rivery thing that makes it easy to understand why Charlie Parker liked jamming with Ray Price's band.

2. Abounding in streams or rivers; pertaining to a river, etc.

1828 Wilson in *Blackw. Mag.* XXIV. 302 As woody, as lochy, and as rivery a parish. **1859** *All Year Round* No. 28. 29 Upon the artificial peninsula.., transport a bit of rivery Orientalism. **1889** W. B. Yeats *Wanderings of Oisin* 78 From rolling valley and rivery glen, With horsemen hurrying near and far, I drew at evening my mailed men. **1973** P. Lively *Ghost of Thomas Kempe* ii. 17 Green, rivery, elm-scattered Oxfordshire.

Rivesaltes (rivsalt). The name of a town near Perpignan in southern France, used *attrib.* and *absol.* of a sweet wine produced there.

1824 A. Henderson *Hist. Anc. & Mod. Wines* II. ii. 178 At Salces..a white wine is grown, which..is thought to resemble Tokay; but, in point of richness, it is inferior to the Rivesaltes. **1836** C. Redding *Mod. Wines* (ed. 2) v. 131 The quantity of Rivesaltes muscadine made is about sixty-five hogsheads per annum. *c* **1870** in H. W. Allen *No. 3 St. James's St.* (1950) 185/1 Rivesaltes, pints—42/-. **1920** [see Jurançon]. **1971** A. Durkan *Vendange* ix. 85 A speciality from this district are the dessert wines called Vin Doux Naturel... The best-known names are Banyuls, Muscat de Frontignan, Muscat de Lunel, Rivesaltes, Maury and Grand Roussillon.

rivet (ˈrɪvɪt), *sb.*¹ Forms: 5 **ryvette**, 6 **ryuet(te**, **ryvet(t**; 6–7 **riuet**, 6 **-ett**, **rivette**, 6– **rivet**; 5–6 **revette**, 6 **-ett**, **reyvett**, 6, 8 **revet**. [a. OF. *rivet*, f. *river* to fix, clinch, of uncertain origin.]

1. a. A short nail or bolt for fastening together metal plates or the like, the headless end of which is beaten out after insertion.

[The following quot. is doubtful, but cf. the OF. pl. *rives*. ?*a* **1400** *Morte Arthur* 1764 That alle þe rowte ryngez, Of ryues and raunke stele, and ryche golde maylez.]

14.. *Lat. Eng. Voc.* in Wr.-Wülcker 573 *Cnusticium, quedam pars sotularis*, a Ryvette. *c* **1440** *York Myst.* viii. 109 It sall be cleyngked euer-ilka dele With nayles... Take here a revette, and þere a rewe. **1511** *Nottingham Rec.* III. 332 Neyles and revettes to ye boote. **1599** Shaks. *Hen. V*, IV. Prol. 13 The Armourers accomplishing the Knights, With busie Hammers closing Riuets vp. **1669** Sturmy *Mariner's Mag.* II. vii. 73 Let the Index be fastned to the Center with a Brass Rivet. **1781** Cowper *Conversat.* 64 They fix attention..With oaths, like rivets, forc'd into the brain. **1819** Shelley *Cyclops* 391 He flung one against the brazen rivets Of the huge caldron. **1851** Ruskin *Stones Ven.* Pref., Bars and rivets instead of mortar for securing stones. **1884** W. H. Greenwood *Steel & Iron* xvii. 400 The rivet is to be capable of bending hot without fracture.

b. *fig.* or in fig. contexts.

1672 Wycherley *Love in a Wood* I. i, You are the rivet of sanctified love. **1693** Dryden *Persius* I. 127 The Verse in fashion, is..So smooth and equal, that no sight can find The Rivet, where the polish'd Piece was join'd. **1742** Young *Nt. Th.* II. 534 This carries friendship to her noontide point, And gives the rivet of eternity. **1862** Merivale *Rom. Emp.* lxiv. (1865) VIII. 90 The lack of religious and moral principle..loosened the rivets of Pagan society.

†**c.** = almain-rivets. *Obs.*

a **1548** Hall *Chron., Hen. VIII*, 25 Ouer his riuet he had a garment of white cloth of gold with a redde crosse. **1577** Eden & Willes *Hist. Trav.* 300 Theyr horsemen are armed with pykes, Ryuettes, Mases of yron, and arrowes.

d. A burr or clinch upon a nail. *rare.*

1634–5 Brereton *Trav.* (Chetham Soc.) 88 Made of thin plates nailed together, and strong square rivets upon the nail heads. **1753** Chambers *Cycl. Suppl.*, *Rivet*, in the manege, is the extremity of the nail that rests or leans upon the horn when you shoe a horse.

e. *pl.* Money, coins. *slang.*

1846 *Swell's Night Guide* 130/1 *Rivets*, money. **1848** *Sinks of London laid Open* 121 *Rivits*, money. **1937** 'J. Curtis' *You're in Racket* xviii. 190 'So you got a bit of rivets to speculate?' 'I ain't said so. All I said as I could put up a bit.'

2. *attrib.* and *Comb.*, as ***rivet bar, -bolt, -head, hearth, -hole, -hoop, iron, machine(ry, -shank, tail***, etc.; **rivet gun**, a hand-held tool for inserting rivets.

1890 D. K. Clark *Steam Engine* I. 657 The diameter of the ⅝-inch *rivet-bars was reduced to ·03 inch. **1844** H. Stephens *Bk. Farm* II. 314 The *rivet-bolts are inserted and riveted down in the red-hot state. **1950** *Nat. Geogr. Mag.* Sept. 297 (*caption*) Chattering *rivet guns attach the door to a barrel section of a Constellation. **1840** *Civil Eng. & Arch. Jrnl.* III. 351/1 Not a single rivet started nor a *rivet-head flown off. **1902** *Encycl. Brit.* XXXII. 597 The riveters also work in squads,..with sometimes a catcher, *i.e.*, a boy to pass on the heated rivets when the distance from the *rivet-hearth is great. **1832** Babbage *Econ. Manuf.* xiii. (ed. 3) 121 Tools, by which the expense of punching the *rivet-holes of each tank was reduced. **1686** Plot *Staffordsh.* 169 They binde it..with a joynted hoop of Iron, which they call a *Rivet-hoop. **1861** Fairbairn *Iron* 204 Staffordshire bridge plates,..for *rivet iron, bearing a strain of 24 tons before breaking. **1841** *Civil Eng. & Arch. Jrnl.* IV. Index, Stocker's *Rivet Machine. *Ibid.* 56/1 Nail, Pin, and *Rivet Machinery. **1869** Sir E. Reed *Shipbuild.* xvii. 328 The dies by which the *rivet-shank is held. **1978** *Jrnl. R. Soc. Arts* CXXVI. 690/2 On long-term creep tests at operating temperatures, it was found that the rivet heads and tails cracked.

rivet (ˈrɪvɪt), *sb.*² [Of obscure origin.] Bearded or cone wheat. Also in pl. form *rivets*.

1573 Tusser *Husb.* (1878) 49 White wheat or else red, red riuet or whight, far passeth all other, for land that is light. **1762** *Phil. Trans.* LII. 530 This family have been used to buy two bushels of clog-wheat, or rivets, or bearded-wheat, (as it is variously called in this county) every fortnight. **1799** *Monthly Rev.* XXX. 182 Bearded wheat is called in some counties Cone wheat, in others Rivets, and in Nottinghamshire it is called Yeogrove. **1813** Batchelor *Agric.* 362 (E.D.D.), Cone wheat, or rivets, is very little used. **1852** Lawson *Veg. Prod. Scot.* I. No. 146 Common Rivet. Ear smaller and less compact than that of the Cone Rivet.

b. Used *attrib.* with *wheat*.

1707 Mortimer *Husb.* (1721) I. 126 There are several sorts of Wheat, as red Straw-wheat, Rivet-Wheat. **1805** R. W. Dickson *Pract. Agric.* I. 540 There are two sorts of rivet wheat, the white and brown. **1886** Britten & Holland *Plant Names* 403 Rivet-Wheat is a well-known variety.

† **'rivet**, *sb.*[3] *Obs. rare.* Also 6 **ryvet.** [Of obscure origin.] The liver of a fish.

1530 PALSGR. 722 Slyt this pykes belly and take out this ryvet [F. *sa gresse*]. **1736** BAILEY *Household Dict.* 355 Cut the rivet or liver of the pike small and chop some oisters. **1741** *Compl. Fam.-Piece* I. ii. 128 Your Milts, Spawn and Rivets, must be laid on the Top.

rivet ('rɪvɪt), *v.* Also 5 **reuet(t**, 5–7 **revet**, 7 **reuit**; 6 **ryvet**, 6–7 **riuet**, 7 **rivit.** [f. RIVET *sb.*[1] Cf. mod.F. *riveter.*]

1. *trans.* To secure (a nail or bolt) by hammering or beating out the projecting end of the shank into a head or knob; to clinch. Also with *down*.

c **1430** *Syr Gener.* (Roxb.) 87 With a grete hamour of stele The nales he reueted wele. **1530** PALSGR. 690/1, I revet a nayle, *je riue.* Ryvet this nayle and than it wyll holde faste. **1611** COTGR., *River*, to riuet or clench; to fasten or turne backe the point of a nayle. **1677** MOXON *Mech. Exerc.* ii. 24 When you rivet a Pin into a Hole. **1683** —— *Printing* xi. ¶ 19 This small Shank is fitted into a small Hole made near the end of the Plate, and Revetted on the other side. **1769** FALCONER *Dict. Marine* (1780), *River un clou*, to rivet a nail. **1834–6** *Encycl. Metrop.* VIII. 299/1 Pins are sometimes inserted.., being also rivetted at each end. **1875** KNIGHT *Dict. Mech.* 1506/1 Rose-clinch nail;..either clinched or riveted down on a washer or rove.

2. To secure or fasten with or as with rivets. Also with *down, in, together*.

c **1430** *Pilgr. Lyf Manhode* I. cxvii. (1869) 61 With the nailes with whiche was nayled the sone of the smith..the mailes weren enclowed and rivetted. **1485** [see RIVETING I.] **1530** PALSGR. 692/2, I ryvet peces of yron togyther. **1582** STANYHURST *Æneis* III. (Arb.) 84 A braynsick prophetesse.. whom dungeon holdeth In ground deepe riueted. **1603** DRAYTON *Bar. Wars* II. xx, Their Greaues, and pouldrons others riuet fast. **1663** GERBIER *Counsel* 96 Nor do provident builders rivet locks only at the one side. **1771** LUCKOMBE *Hist. Print.* 305 The plates..[are] rivetted down through the bottom and top-sides of the frame. **1814** SCOTT *Lord of Isles* V. vii, Warriors, who, arming for the fight, Rivet and clasp their harness light. **1834–6** *Encycl. Metrop.* VIII. 298/2 The next process..is to have the coaks rivetted in. **1893** *Archaeologia* LIII. 559 The statue had been broken in ancient times and afterwards carefully riveted together again.

fig. *a* **1631** DONNE *Select.* (1840) 86 Sin entrenched and barricadoed in sin, sin screwed up, and rivetted with sin. **1654** tr. *Scudery's Curia Pol.* 132 They are bonds and chains of their absolute obedience, riveted by their tongues. **1796** MORSE *Amer. Geogr.* II. 606 The Turks have rivetted the chains of barbarous ignorance which they imposed. **1837** LOCKHART *Scott* IV. xi. 346 [It] served to rivet the bonds of affection and confidence, which were to the end maintained between him and them. **1868** FREEMAN *Norm. Conq.* (1877) II. 332 A war for no object but to rivet the yoke of outlandish men about their necks.

b. Const. *to, into,* or *in* something. Also *fig.*

1650 FULLER *Pisgah* IV. iii. 51 Who violently brake off their ear-rings, even such as were riveted in their skin with long wearing. **1669** STURMY *Mariner's Mag.* IV. xvi. 200 A Libal or Index to be rivetted to the Center. **1713** ADDISON *Cato* II. v, I've seen you..stooping from your Horse Rivet the panting savage to the ground. **1765** A. DICKSON *Treat. Agric.* (ed. 2) 203 A plate of iron..riveted fast into it by bolts. **1802** PLAYFAIR *Huttonian Theory* 334 The mountain of Goatfield which I have mentioned above as..rivetted..to the superincumbent rock. **1833** MRS. BROWNING *Prometh. Bound* 61 Seize him,..Rivet him to the rock.

c. Const. *on* or *upon.*

1679 MOXON *Mech. Exerc.* ix. 161 Instead of Nailing the Hindges upon the Door, they Rivet them on, for more strength. **1698** FRYER *Acc. E. India & P.* 39 A Coronal Arch, on whose Vertex a Globe is rivited by an Iron Wedge. **1797** *Encycl. Brit.* (ed. 3) V. 69/1 By means of the fork.. rivetted on the palettes.

d. *nonce-use.* To marry, join in wedlock.

1700 CONGREVE *Way of the World* I. i, We drove round to Duke's Place; and there they were rivetted in a trice.

3. *transf.* To fix, fasten, or secure firmly.

1629 WOTTON in *Reliq.* (1672) 568 It is none of the least ends of my going to rivet that business. **1672** MARVELL *Reh. Transp.* I. 36 All her Excesses and Errors were further rivited and confirmed. **1768–74** TUCKER *Lt. Nat.* (1834) I. 658 The ideas of precausation and fatality..are so strongly rivetted together in men's minds. **1788** MME. D'ARBLAY *Diary* June, I am wholly ignorant in what manner..his first attachment may have riveted his affections. **1839** HALLAM *Hist. Lit.* IV. iii. § 103 It is evident that until objects are truly classified, a representative method of signs can only rivet and perpetuate error. **1861** MILL *Utilit.* 46 He never conceives himself otherwise than as a member of a body; and this association is riveted more and more.

b. Const. *to* or *into* something.

1596 SHAKS. *Merch. V.* v. i. 169 A thing stucke on with oathes vpon your finger, And so riueted with faith vnto your flesh. **1611** —— *Cymb.* II. ii. 46 Why should I write this downe, that's riueted, Screw'd to my memorie. **1655** FULLER *Ch. Hist.* II. 107 He riveted the Archbishoprick into the City of Canterbury. **1727** GAY *Begg. Op.* I. xiii, My hand, my heart,..is so riveted to thine that I cannot unloose my hold. **1792** ALMON *Anecd. Pitt* I. x. 203 Great Britain was..every day more closely rivetted to the continent by fresh engagements. **1817** SCOTT *Rob Roy* xxxviii, Astonishment actually riveted my tongue to the roof of my mouth. **1847** C. BRONTË *J. Eyre* ii, My seat, to which Bessie and the bitter Miss Abbot had left me riveted, was a low ottoman.

c. Const. *in* a practice, the mind, etc.

1612 T. TAYLOR *Comm. Titus* ii. 12 Thou reuitest thy selfe in thy sinne, and wilt not be reclaimed. **1667** WATERHOUSE *Fire Lond.* 11 It is riveted in the corrupt nature of man to revenge injuries. **1709** BERKELEY *Th. Vision* § 51 The prejudice is confirmed and riveted in our thoughts by a long tract of time. **1761** HUME *Hist. Eng.* II. xl. 402 A prince who ..appeared not to be rivetted in any dangerous animosities. **1849** ROBERTSON *Serm.* Ser. I. x. (1866) 179 Things become riveted in the memory. **1897** MARY KINGSLEY *W. Africa* 211 Riveting him in the practice of polygamy.

d. Const. *on* or *upon.*

1829 GEN. P. THOMPSON *Exerc.* (1842) I. 162 Bribery attracts men's decision from the right; persecution rivets it upon the wrong. **1830** D'ISRAELI *Chas. I*, III. vii. 139 The affections of Henrietta were riveted on those of her royal husband. **1870** HOWSON *Metaph. St. Paul* 122 The lesson is riveted for ever on the church.

4. To fix intently (the eye or the mind); to command or engross (the attention).

1602 SHAKS. *Ham.* III. ii. 90 Giue him needfull note, For I mine eyes will riuet to his Face. **1621** G. SANDYS *Ovid's Met.* VII. (1626) 129 Her eger eyes she riuets on his face. **1760–72** H. BROOKE *Fool of Qual.* (1809) III. 144 While his attention was thus rivetted. **1791** COWPER *Odyss.* XXIII. 107 She rivetted her eyes on his. **1821** SCOTT *Pirate* xxxi, The attention..of Bunce..was riveted to the armed sloop. **1852** M. ARNOLD *The Future* 6 He..Rivets his gaze on the banks of the stream. **1878** BOSW. SMITH *Carthage* 198 That march riveted the attention of the world.

b. To engross the attention of (a person).

1762 FALCONER *Shipwr.* III. (1819) 23 In dire amazement rivetted they stand. **1861** STANLEY *East. Ch.* xii. (1869) 381 We are riveted by this strange apparition in foreign lands. **1883** PATTISON *Mem.* (1885) 33, I..was riveted by the book.

Hence **'riveting** *ppl. a.*

1677 W. HUGHES *Man of Sin* II. iii. 54 A clinching, riveting Argument, I trow! **1854** *Rambler* Feb. 198 Riveting as were these narratives when we first read them..those who now read them for the first time are generally disappointed. **1899** *Dict. Nat. Biog.* LVII. 178/1 His brilliant, original, riveting, but most censorious conversation. **1967** N. MARSH *Death at Dolphin* v. 129 Her smart friends..said things like: 'Absolutely riveting' and 'Loved your play'. **1975** *Evening Standard* 24 June 20/1 Landladies..are far more genned up on local history and things to do (plus some riveting gossip) than the managers of more impressive emporia. **1979** E. H. GOMBRICH *Sense of Order* x. 271 'Some 2500 years ago'—Kurz sums up his riveting article—'a Greek artist conceived the strange idea of putting a movable ring into the mouth of a lion.'

'riveted, *ppl. a.* Also 7– **rivetted.** [f. RIVET *v.* + -ED[1].] Fastened with rivets; clinched. Also in *Combs.*, as ***close-, double-, single-riveted.***

1606 SHAKS. *Ant. & Cl.* IV. iv. 22 A thousand Sir, early though 't be, haue on their Riueted trim. **1753** CHAMBERS *Cycl. Suppl.* s.v. *Shoe*, A shoe for all [equine] feet, is one that is cut at the toe into two equal parts, which are joined by a riveted nail. **1861** FAIRBAIRN *Iron* 208 The strength of the parts in riveted joints is reduced. *Ibid.*, The strength of the double riveted joint will be 68. And that of the single riveted joint 46. **1898** *Daily News* 8 Sept. 4/7 The old artillery with riveted wheels and huge wooden axles.

b. *fig.* Firmly fastened, established or settled, rooted; fixed, intent.

1670 W. SIMPSON *Hydrol. Ess.* 72 Some menstruums may dissolve..the close rivetted parts of some..bodies. **1706** BAYNARD *Cold Baths* II. 301 To persevere in.. Drunkenness, until a riveted Disease entails his Folly..on his Blood. **1748** RICHARDSON *Clarissa* (1811) VIII. 6, I have a rivetted hatred to him. **1822** HAZLITT *Table-T.* II. vii. 165 Casts a pensive, rivetted look downwards to the modest flowers. **1879** *Cassell's Techn. Educ.* IV. 3/2 Few works.. have destroyed more riveted and deeply-rooted errors.

'riveter. Also **rivetter.** [f. RIVET *v.* + -ER[1].]

1. One who rivets.

1800 *New Ann. Direct.* 34 Saddle-tree-maker and Rivetter. **1853** URE *Dict. Arts* II. 556 The average work that can be done by two riveters, with one 'holder on' and a boy. **1894** *Labour Commission, Gloss.*, After the boot has been sewn the rivetter again takes the boot and hammers the sole out to make it level.

2. A riveting machine. (See also quot. 1963.)

1884 *Machinery & Eng.* I. 88/1 Compressing machines, such as steam hammers,..rivetters, forging presses. **1928** [see BOATSWAIN 3]. **1963** JONES & SCHUBERT *Engin. Encycl.* (ed. 3) 1068 'Riveting machines', according to common usage, differ from 'riveters' in that the riveting operation with a machine is effected by a succession of blows or by a compressive rotating action, whereas a riveter merely subjects the rivet to compression.

'riveting, *vbl. sb.* Also 7– **rivetting.** [f. RIVET *v.* + -ING[1].]

1. The action of the vb., in lit. and fig. uses.

1485 in Sharp *Cov. Myst.* (1825) 189 Payd for revettyng of þe plats, & for þe iiij boultes, xs. ob. **1611** COTGR., *Rivement*, a riueting, a clenching. **1663** GERBIER *Counsel* 96 A thief.. makes that single riveting of no use as to security. **1706** M. HENRY *Wks.* (1853) II. 528/1 He prayed with them partly for..the riveting of the things he had said in their minds. **1779** T. HUTCHINSON *Diary* 1 Dec. II. 299, I think we may beat the French fleet, but if we should, it will be the rivetting of this damned Ministry. **1845** R. W. HAMILTON *Pop. Educ.* ix. (ed. 2) 257 The development of national mind may be but the riveting of a prejudice. **1870** *Spectator* 19 Nov. 1373 To prevent the rivetting of this ascendancy on the neck of Europe.

b. With qualifying word prefixed.

1874 THEARLE *Nav. Archit.* 104 The Liverpool rules require chain riveting for all double and treble riveted joints and butts. *Ibid.*, In edge or butt riveting the space between two consecutive rows of rivets must not be less than one and a half times their diameter.

2. *attrib.*, as ***riveting hammer, machine, nail, plate, set, tool.***

See also KNIGHT *Dict. Mech.* (1875) and *Suppl.* (1884). *a* **1642** SIR W. MONSON *Naval Tracts* III. (1704) 345/2 Clinch-bolts are clinched with a Rivetting Hammer. **1688** HOLME *Armoury* III. 321/1 The Rivetting Hammer..is very rarely used at his Forge, unless the Work be very small. **1769** FALCONER *Dict. Marine* (1780), *Clous à river*, a rivet, or riveting-nail to be clenched at both ends. **1802** JAMES *Milit. Dict.*, *Riveting-plates*, in gun-carriages, small square thin pieces of iron, through which the ends of the bolts pass, and are riveted upon them. **1843** HOLTZAPFFEL *Turning* I. 387 A rivetting-set or punch for the heads of rivets. **1843** *Civil Eng. & Arch. Jrnl.* VI. 115/2 The Patent Riveting Machine ..constructed by Mr. Fairbairn, of Manchester. **1866** *Tomlinson's Cycl. Usef. Arts* III. 611/2 The strong semicircular bracket carrying the fixed riveting tool.

'rivetingly, *adv.* [f. RIVETING *ppl. a.*] In a riveting manner.

1971 *Guardian* 21 June 11/1 'Yesterday's Men' was an extreme example: it provided rivettingly viewable entertainment. **1973** *Daily Tel.* 22 Nov. 10/3 His animation of wartime London is uncannily detailed, rivetingly atmospheric.

† **rivi'ation.** *Obs. rare*[−1]. Fishing.

a **1676** HALE *De Jure Maris* I. ii. in *Hargrave's Tracts* (1787) I. 7 The writ..which anciently was directed to the sheriff to prohibit riviation in any rivers in his bailiwick.

Riviera (rɪvɪ'ɛərə). Also **riviera.** [It., lit. 'coast, shore'.] **1.** The name of the Italian sea-board about Genoa, applied also to the Mediterranean coast from Marseilles in France to La Spezia in Italy, a fashionable winter resort in the 19th century and more recently popular for summer holidays; usu. with *the*. Also *attrib.* Cf. RIVER *sb.*[1] 3.

[**1632**: see ROOT *sb.*[1] 4 c]. **1766** J. NORTHALL *Trav. through Italy* VI. ii. 471 The dominions of this State consist of the countries extending along the sea-coast, on both sides, from the city of Genoa, which are called the eastern and western Rivieras. This word in Italian signifies a strand. **1797** *Encycl. Brit.* VII. 426/2 The people of Genoa revolted..and reduced a great part of the Riviera. **1852** DICKENS in *Keepsake* 120 He had hired an old place on the Riviera, at an easy distance from my city, Genoa. **1863** GEO. ELIOT *Let.* Oct. (1956) IV. 111, I shall imagine you winding along the Riviera, and then settling in sight of beautiful things. **1892** I. ZANGWILL *Childr. Ghetto* II. i. 270, I had better take a hansom to the Riviera at once. **1909** C. F. G. MASTERMAN *Condition of England* ii. 57 In Biarritz, Pau, Dinard—he might have said in the whole *côte d'azur* of the Riviera—'the English have conquered us,' he declares. **1939** S. DE MADARIAGA *Christopher Columbus* iii. 25 Eating and drinking..in that Genoese riviera so sunny and full of the joy of existence. **1941** KOESTLER *Scum of Earth* 28 There was an elderly Riviera-Englishman on the platform. **1978** *Times* 18 Mar. 11/1 The Riviera or Cote d'Azur has a special affinity with the English who apart from the Romans were its first holidaymakers.

2. *transf.* Applied to other coastal regions considered to resemble the Mediterranean Riviera. Also with *a* and *pl.*, and *attrib.*

1891 M. F. SWEETSER *King's Handbk. U.S.* 175 The old convents and churches..and the yachting in the adjacent waters, furnish a great variety of interest for visitors to the American Riviera. **1904** *Railway Mag.* Sept. 258 'The Riviera Express' is the title chosen by Mr. J. C. Inglis, the General Manager of the Great Western Railway, as the most apposite name for the Plymouth-Paddington non-stop express. **1910** *Bradshaw's Railway Guide* Apr. 1126 Lyme Regis, Dorset. Hotel Alexandra... The only hotel in its own grounds in the English Riviera. **1911** HEATH & HASLEHURST (*title*) The Cornish Riviera. **1922** WODEHOUSE *Girl on Boat* xvii. 307 'Why not Cornwall?' said Sam. 'The Riviera of England!' **1951** W. SANSOM *Face of Innocence* iii. 36 He did not know the rivieras, I knew them well. **1974** *Sat. Rev. World* (U.S.) 19 Oct. 43/1 Every properly equipped nation must have a Riviera.

Rivieran (rɪvɪ'ɛərən), *a. rare.* [f. prec. + -AN.] Of, pertaining to, or characteristic of the Riviera.

1897 A. BEARDSLEY *Let.* 1 Apr. (1970) 290, I have been getting into quite a glow over a packet of Rivieran photographs. **1909** *Westm. Gaz.* 21 Sept. 4/2 'The climate,' she writes, 'is of quite Rivieran mildness during the winter months.'

‖ **rivière** (ri'vjɛr). [a. F. *rivière* (RIVER *sb.*[1]) in same sense.] **1.** A necklace of diamonds or other gems, esp. one consisting of more than one string.

1879 M. E. BRADDON *Vixen* I. xvi. 304 The special presents which stood out..were—a *rivière* of diamonds.., a pair of priceless crackle jars, a Sèvres dinner-service of the old *bleu-du-roi*. **1880** DISRAELI *Endym.* xxxviii, Myra was amused as she watched their dazzling tiaras and flashing rivières. **1887** *Pall Mall G.* 29 June 13/3 Buying a diamond for £12,000 and ordering it to be set in her rivière as the centre stone. **1958** M. KELLY *Christmas Egg* II. 61 Rivière —what was that?—of large brilliant diamonds, with ear-rings en suite, silver.

2. *needlework.* A row of open-work.

a **1855** C. BRONTË *Professor* (1857) II. xviii. 9 A 'rivière', or open-work hem round a cambric handkerchief. **1886** in A. Adburgham *Shops & Shopping* (1964) xviii. 209 In Blonde de Seville, it [*sc.* a lace fichu] falls into cascades and rivières.

rivilin, variant of RIVELING[1].

rivina (rɪ'vaɪnə). *Bot.* [mod.L., f. the name of Aug. Q. *Rivinus*, a German botanist (1652–1723).] An American plant belonging to the same family as Phytolacca.

1819 *Pantologia* s.v., Three [species]..are cultivated... Downy rivina... Smooth rivina... Climbing rivina. **1882** *Garden* 5 Aug. 112/1 Rivinas..are eminently deserving of more general cultivation than they meet with at present.

riving ('raɪvɪŋ), *vbl. sb.*[1] [f. RIVE *v.*[1]]

1. The action of the vb.; rending, tearing, etc.

a **1400–50** *Alexander* 747* (Dubl. MS.), A store..stede stalwortly bondyn;..In rapes fast for ryfyng of bernes.

c **1440** *Pallad. on Husb.* XII. 140 Fro rotyng & ryuing they be byraft. *c* **1450** *St. Cuthbert* (Surtees) 2368 Cuthbert wayued his hand on þaim, Fra ryvyng of thak þaim to reclaym. **1527** *Accs. Ld. High Treas. Scot.* V. 320 To underly the law for the ryving of the Kingis lettres. **1578** *Reg. Privy Council Scot.* III. 57 Taking of the saidis letters perforce fra him and ryving of thame all in pecis. **1609** SKENE *Reg. Maj.* 68 The injurie done to her,..and also the ryving of her claiths. **1619–53** in Heslop *Northumbld. Gloss.* (1894) 580 Edward Dobson for riving out of twoe ridges of land [etc.]. **1816** SCOTT *Antiq.* xxiv, In the auld times o' rugging and riving through the hail country. **1863** GEO. ELIOT *Romola* v, Power was to be won by other means than by rending and riving. **1875** F. W. MYERS *Poems* 91 Where wilt thou find a riving or a rending?

b. *spec.* Splitting or cleaving of wood.

1471–2 *Durham Acc. Rolls* (Surtees) 94 Pro le ryvyng et sharpyng M[l]D del stakes. **1543** *Fabric Rolls York* (Surtees) Gloss. s.v. *Revyn*, Ryving of fyerwoode in Frankelyn for my lorde. **1576** FLEMING *Panopl. Epist.* 356 Let us take the axe, the wedge and the beetle, and settle our selues to cleauing and riueing. **1634** W. WOOD *New Eng. Prosp.* (1865) 19 The Horne-bound tree..requires so much paines in riving as is almost incredible. **1831** J. HOLLAND *Manuf. Metal* I. 331 The rude practice of riving was soon superseded by the more effective operation of the saw.

Comb. **1875** KNIGHT *Dict. Mech.* 1950/2 *Riving-knife*, a tool used in splitting balks for staves, clapboards, shingles, etc. *Ibid.*, *Riving-machine*, a machine for splitting wood in the direction of the grain.

2. *concr.* A fissure, cleft, or rent. *rare.*

c **1450** METHAM *Wks.* (E.E.T.S.) 41 'Come to the ryuyng off this same walle'... 'The ryuyng?' quoth he, 'qwere ys that?' **1591** PERCIVAL *Sp. Dict.*, *Abertura*, opening, cleft or ryuing of any thing. **1859** SALA *Gas-light & D.* ii. 29 He contemplates the rents and rivings, the rags and tatters.

† **'riving**, *vbl. sb.*[2] *Obs. rare.* [f. RIVE *v.*[2] + -ING[1].] Arriving; landing.

1338 R. BRUNNE *Chron.* (1810) 70 At his riuyng þe lond non him forbedde. *c* **1440** *Promp. Parv.* 435/1 Ryvynge vp to lond, fro water, *applicacio, applicatus*.

'riving, *ppl. a.* [f. RIVE *v.*[1] + -ING[2].] That rives; rending, tearing.

a **1300** *Cursor M.* 20976 Paul..suffurd..Bath mang men and riuand beist. *c* **1400** *Sc. Trojan War* II. 445 [An eagle] Wytht hys rywand and sharpe tallons..The forseyde bowelles..toke. **1642** H. MORE *Song of Soul* I. vii. Wks. (Grosart) 14 Riving tortures spight,..To good the soul doth nearer reunite. **1781** COWPER *Hope* 640 Nature opposes, with her utmost force, This riving stroke. **1827** PRAED *Arminius* vi, The riving axe and burning brand Rent forests. **1877** BRYANT *Song Sower* iii, The pelting hail and riving blast.

rivlin, variant of RIVELING[1].

‖ **'rivo.** *Obs.* [App. of Spanish origin; perh. Sp. *arriba* up, upwards.] An exclamation used at revels or drinking-bouts.

c **1592** MARLOWE *Jew of Malta* IV. (1633) H iv, Hey, *Riuo Castiliano*, a man's a man. **1596** SHAKS. *1 Hen. IV*, II. iv. 124 *Rivo*, sayes the drunkard. **1600** *Look about You* L iv, And *Ryuo* will he cry and *Castile* too. **1607** MARSTON *What You Will* II. i, Weele quaffe or any thing; *Riuo*, Saint Marke.

ri'vose, *a. Ent.* [ad. late L. *rīvōs-us*, f. *rīvus* stream.] (See quot.)

1826 KIRBY & SP. *Entomol.* xlvi. IV. 271 *Rivose*, when furrows do not run in a parallel direction and are rather sinuate.

'rivotite. *Min.* [f. the name of Professor L. E. *Rivot* of Paris.] 'An amorphous mineral, of yellowish-green colour, containing antimony, copper, and carbon di-oxide' (Chester).

1874 *Geol. Mag.* 367 Under the name of Rivotite..a new Spanish mineral is described by M. Ducloux. It occurs..on the western slope of Sierra del Cadi, in the province of Lerida.

† **'rivule**, *v. Obs.*[−1] [f. L. *rīvul-us*, dim. of *rīvus* stream.] *trans.* To break up or divide *into* (channels).

1628 FELTHAM *Resolves* (1677) II. lxxxiv. 340 Rivuled into petty Issues running thick corruption.

rivulet ('rɪvjʊlɪt). Forms: α. 6–7 riuelet, rivlet, 7 riulet, riuilet, rivelet. β. 6–7 riuolet, 7 rivolet, reu-, revolet, rivalet. γ. 7 riuulet, 7– rivulet. [Perh. ad. It. *rivoletto*, dim. of *rivolo*, dim. of *rivo*:—L. *rīvus* stream: cf. prec. and -ET[1].]

1. A small stream or river; a streamlet.

α. **1587** HARRISON *England* I. xi. I. 52 Meeting with sundrie other riuelets by the waie. *Ibid.* 55 A pretie riuelet rising about Michelneie. **1590** WARNER *Alb. Eng.* XII. lxxv, Of that huge Sea let's through a Riblet [**1612** Riulet] waide. **1624** CAPT. SMITH *Virginia* IV. 108 Two new Forts..vpon a pleasant plaine, and neare a little Riuilet. **1641** J. JACKSON *True Evang. T.* I. 8 As naturall a fluxe..as the water in the rivelet hath from the fount. **1671** *New York Cal. Doc.* (1853) III. 196 They past this day several brave brookes and small Rivelets.

β. **1615** G. SANDYS *Trav.* 22 There being sundry riuolets that descend from the mountains. **1660** STANLEY *Hist. Philos.* IX. IV. ix, A tender Olive set In a lone place, near a smooth Rivolet. **1700** ASTRY tr. *Saavedra-Faxardo* I. 123 The most noted Rivers take their rise and beginning from the smallest Rivolets.

γ. **1613–6** W. BROWNE *Brit. Past.* I. ii, Triton..call'd the neighb'ring Nymphs each in her turne To poure their pretty Rivulets from their Urne. **1667** MILTON *P.L.* IX. 420 By Fountain or by shadie Rivulet He sought them both. **1726** SWIFT *Gulliver* III. iii, The Dews and Rains..are conveyed in small Rivulets towards the Middle. **1779** FORREST *Voy. N. Guinea* 320 These clouds feed the rivulets which run from the hills. **1815** ELPHINSTONE *Acc. Caubul* (1842) I. 157 The water of the lake is salt, as is that of some of the rivulets which join it. **1897** MARY KINGSLEY *W. Africa* 364 He discovered one of the sources of the Ogowé at a point where it formed a mere rivulet of water.

b. *transf.* and *fig.*

α. *a* **1660** WINSTANLEY *Eng. Worthies* Ep. Ded. 4 A Nobler confluence of so many Loyal Purple Rivelets of Honour.

β. **1589** GREENE *Menaphon* Wks. (Grosart) VI. 42 The woman ceased not from streaming foorth riuolets of teares. **1600** *Look about You* L, Looke how the furrowes of his aged cheeke Fild with the reuolets of wet eyde mone. **1670** W. PENN *Truth Rescued fr. Imposture* 60 England's Fountain of Iustice was clear and wholesom, although the Rivolets or lesser Streams might be troubled.

γ. **1639** LD. DIGBY *Lett. conc. Relig.* (1651) 86 There cannot be admitted..unto the avowed channell of the Church, any corrupt Rivulet of erroneous Doctrine. **1710** T. FULLER *Pharm. Extemp.* 37 Steel..causes the Blood to run..through all the minutest Canals and Rivulets of the Body. **1758** JOHNSON *Idler* No. 7 ¶4 The rivulets of intelligence which are continually trickling among us. **1860** SANGSTER *Hesperus* 44 A rivulet of song..Welled free and sparkling.

2. *attrib.* and *Comb.*, as ***rivulet-bed, -side***; also in specific names, as ***rivulet carp, dipper, salmon*** (see quots.).

1744 J. WILSON *Synop. Brit. Plants* 10 By the rivulet side. **1804** SHAW *Gen. Zool.* V. I. 65 Rivulet Salmon [*Salmo Rivalis*]. *Ibid.* 245 Rivulet Carp [*Cyprinus Rivularis*]. **1811** COOKE *Thames* I. 1* b, From its source it flows on in a rivulet character, till it reaches Cricklade. **1819** TURTON *Conchol. Dict.* 27 *Bulla fluviatilis*. Rivulet Dipper. **1896** *Sunday Mag.* Nov. 621 The rivulet-bed in which you walk is dry.

3. A name of several geometrid moths of the genus *Emmelesia*.

1832 J. RENNIE *Conspect. Butterfl. & M.* 137 The Rivulet ..appears in June on shrubs. *Ibid.*, The Small Rivulet..appears the end of June. *Ibid.* 138 The Grass Rivulet.

rivu'lose, *a. Bot.* [f. L. *rīvul-us* + -OSE.] Marked with irregular sinuous lines or stripes.

1871 COOKE *Handbk. Fungi* I. 257 Pileus pulvinate, silky, soft, then rivulose. **1887** W. PHILLIPS *Brit. Discomycetes* 94 Cup..externally blackish-brown, rivulose.

riwa-riwa, var. REWA-REWA.

riwell: see REUALL.

riwle, obs. f. RULE.

rix, dial. variant of *rish* RUSH *sb.* (plant).

† **ri'xation.** *Obs.*[−0] [f. L. *rīxārī* to quarrel: see -ATION.] Scolding, brawling.

1623 in COCKERAM. [Hence in later Dicts.]

rix-baron. Now *Hist.* [ad. G. *reichsbaron.*] A baron of the German Empire.

a **1849** MANGAN *Poems* (1859) 138 Thou knowest him well, The proud Rix-baron.

rix-dollar ('rɪksdɒlə(r)). Now *Hist.* Forms: α. 6 reekes (7 reichs) doller, 7 rexdolar, dollar, dol(l)er. β. 7 rix(e dollar, rixdoller, rix doller, ricksdoller, 8 **rycksdollar**, 7– **rix dollar, rix-dollar, rixdollar**. γ. **rich dollar**. [ad. older Du. *rijcksdaler* (Kilian; mod.Du. *rijksdaalder*, Fris. *ryksdaelder*), = Sw. *riksdaler*, Da. *rigsdaler*, G. *reichsthaler*: see RICHE and DOLLAR.]

1. A silver coin and money of account, current from the latter part of the 16th to the middle of the 19th century in various European countries (as Holland, Germany, Austria, Denmark, Sweden) and in their commerce with the East, etc.

α. **1598** W. PHILLIP tr. *Linschoten* I. vi. 17 Each pardauwe, accounted as much as a Réekes Doller, Flemish money. [**1617** MORYSON *Itin.* I. 286 The silver Doller of the Empire (called Reichs Doller) is of the standard of ten ounces or thereabouts.] **1640** *Bk. War Committee Covenanters* 2 For fornishing thairof, ordaines to be given xx rex dollares. **1654** *Nicholas Papers* (Camden) II. 76 The King..has givin him in landis to the valew of 100,000 Rex dolers. **1690** *Burgh Rec. Lanark* (1893) 234 Thrie rex dollares.

β. **1622** in Birch *Crt. & Times Jas. I* (1848) II. 306 He cometh for his army with great store of rix dollars. **1658** *Cal. Domest. State Papers* 313 The Turks demand 75,000 rix dollars for the provisions. **1700** S. L. tr. *Fryke's Voy. E. Ind.* 6 The Surgeons 28 Gilders, and Diet, and on Shoar 3 Ricksdollers. **1753** HANWAY *Trav.* (1762) I. VII. xciv. 434 The par is reckoned one hundred and twenty-five Saxon dollars, for one hundred rix dollars current in Amsterdam. **1803** *Med. Jrnl.* IX. 539 At all other times they would receive the regular salary of thirty rix-dollars monthly. **1842** BISCHOFF *Woollen Manuf.* II. 168 The price which was charged me..was about five rix dollars and three quarters.

γ. *c* **1645** HOWELL *Lett.* VI. i, So I left my Lord at Glukstad,..being com hither to take up 8000 rich Dollars upon Mr. Burlamachs Bils.

2. A unit of currency introduced into certain former colonies, as by the Dutch in Cape Province and the English in Ceylon. (See also quot. 1962.)

1785 G. FORSTER tr. *Sparrman's Voy. Cape Good Hope* I. 19 Board and lodging are paid for here as at the Cape, from one rix-dollar to one and a half a day. **1790** E. HELME tr. *Le Vaillant's Trav. Afr.* I. ii. 21 While I was there [*sc.* at Capetown] butchers meat was very cheap; I have seen thirteen pounds of mutton bought for an escalin; (elevenpence English) an ox for 12 or 15 rix dollars; (at six shilings and nine-pence English, the rix dollar) ten quarters of corn for 14 or 15 Rix-dollars, and other things in proportion. **1827** G. THOMPSON *Trav. & Adventures Southern Afr.* I. I. iv. 79 He provides a salary of 400 rix-dollars to encourage a day-school for females. **1836** *Penny Cycl.* VI. 453/2 In the district of Putlam they were faced boldly in the open forest, and ensnared singly, for a reward varying according to the size and description of animal, from 11 to 352 rix-dollars. **1866** J. LEYLAND *Adventures Far Interior S. Afr.* III. 233 The charge for crossing in the barge was fifteen shillings, or ten rix dollars. **1900** A. H. KEANE *Boer States* p. xviii, *Rixdollar*, a coin current in the Cape in colonial times. **1962** R. A. G. CARSON *Coins* 533 The Dutch monetary system of a rix-dollar or rijksdaalder of 48 stuiver was continued [in Cape Province] by the British in the early nineteenth century.

† **'rixle**, *v. Obs.* Forms: 2 **rixlan**, 2–3 **rixlen**, 3 (*Orm.*) **rix(s)lenn, rixlien, rixli, rixly(e**, 3–5 **rixle**, 5 **ryxle**. [f. OE. *rix-ian* to rule + -LE.]

1. *intr.* To reign, bear sway; to rule, have dominion; to prevail.

c **1175** *Lamb. Hom.* 25 From þan helle..us bureȝe þe lauerd þe is..wuniende and rixlende on worlde a buten ende. *c* **1200** ORMIN 8304 Onn hiss fiftende ȝer fra þatt he bigann to rixlenn I Rome riche. *a* **1225** *Leg. Kath.* 226 He ane is to herien, þurh hwam & under hwam alle kinges rixleð. *c* **1400** *Chron. R. Glouc.* (Rolls) App. H. 207 After him Rixlede o king, Rime ihote was. *c* **1400** *Destr. Troy* 221 Whyle þou rixlis in this Reame no riot we drede.

fig. c **1200** ORMIN 4253 Þurrh all þatt fele kinne gillt..I þa limess rixsleþþ. *a* **1225** *Ancr. R.* 82 Ersie, God beo iðoncked, ne rixleð nout in Englelond. *Ibid.* 374 Þus, lo! in eueriche stat rixleð bitternesse. *c* **1400** *Destr. Troy* 2726 Envy..Ryxles full Ryfe in her ranke hertes.

2. To deal masterfully *with* (a person).

c **1400** *Destr. Troy* 13891 With the remnond full rade he rixlit vnfaire,..Cast hom ouer clanly at the cloise brigge.

3. To conduce, lead *to*.

c **1400** *Destr. Troy* 5129 Sely is the kyng, þat kepis the for counsell clene for hym-seluyn, þat well con..rede hym to redurs, þat rixles to shame.

Hence † **'rixling** *vbl. sb. Obs.*

c **1175** *Lamb. Hom.* 111 Elles ne bið his rixlunge ne fest ne lonsum. *c* **1200** *Trin. Hom.* 27 *Adueniat regnum tuum*, cume þi rixlinge. *a* **1225** *Ancr. R.* 248 Alle þe holie haluwen ouercumen þuruh bileaue þes deofles rixlunge.

† **ri'xosous**, *a. Obs.*[−0] [ad. L. *rixōsus.*] 'Full of brabbles' (Cockeram, 1623).

riyal: see RIAL *sb.*[1] 5.

riyf, obs. f. RIFE.

riyo, var. RYO.

riz, dial. f. RISE *v.*

riza ('ri:zə). [Russ., f. OSlav. *riza* garment.] A metal shield or plaque framing the painted face and other features of a Russian icon, and engraved with the lines of the completed picture.

1927 E. H. MINNS tr. *Kondakov's Russ. Icon* ii. 37 As long ago as the fourteenth century, under Greek influence, the Russians began to cover..the figures with plates of silver showing in more or less relief the outlines and folds of the clothes and vestments: such a plate is called a *riza*, properly speaking a garment, especially a chasuble:.. The parts of the figures left unclothed, faces, hands, and the like, all the flesh tints, show through holes in the *riza*. **1931** P. ROMANOV tr. *Zarine's Three Pairs of Silk Stockings* ii. 9 One hall was full of pictures... Another was covered with ikons with old rizas of pearl. **1963** T. T. RICE *Russian Icons* 25 It became usual to encase an icon in a costly metal cover or *riza*, in which openings were cut to show the essential sections of the painting. **1970** *Guardian* 1 Apr. 16/5 Sometimes elaborate silverwork was added, covering much of the surface and leaving only the faces and figures visible. This metal-work, the riza, was occasionally ornamented with precious or semi-precious stones. **1978** *Daily Tel.* 24 Aug. 12/5 Among the collection is a 17th century icon of the Virgin of Kazan, with embossed silver-gilt riza..dating from the end of the 19th century.

rizagon, var. of RISAGON.

rizalite (ri:'zɑ:laɪt). *Geol.* [f. *Rizal*, the name of a province of central Luzon in the Philippines (named after Dr. José *Rizal* (1861–96), Philippine patriot) + -ITE[1].] Any tektite of the type characteristically found in the neighbourhood of Manila.

1928 H. O. BEYER *Philippine Tektites* (1961) I. 21 Since.. our Luzon material cannot be properly classed as either Billitonite or Australite..I am proposing the name *rizalite* as a temporary designation for it. **1937** *Mineral. Abstr.* VI. 403 A popular account is given of the tektites ('rizalites'), mostly from Rizal province, which are spherical or cylindrical. **1940** *Pop. Astron.* XLVIII. 44 Rizalites (pitted spheroids, ovals, and cylindrical forms being most characteristic). *Ibid.* 45 The most typical Rizalites occur only in Luzon, although a few similar, pitted specimens are known from Borneo and Java.

rize, obs. f. RISE *v.*

rizom(e, varr. of RISOM.

rizzar ('rɪzə(r)), *sb.*[1] *Sc.* Also 7 razour, rizer, 8 rizzer, 9 rizzart, rizar. [Of obscure origin; perh. f. *rid* RED *a.* on the analogy of GROSER.] The red currant; also *attrib.*, as ***rizzar-berry, -bush***.

1679 CUNNINGHAM OF CRAIGENDS *Diary* 9 July (S.T.S.) 112 For razour-berries in a yeard. **1684** J. ERSKINE *Jrnl.* 27 June (1893) 67, I did eat some straw and rizer berries. **1703** BRAND *Orkney* 80 There are also at Scalloway some Goose and Rizzer-berrie bushes. **1899** JAS. COLVILLE *Scot. Vernacular* 12 Round the garden ran a high, flat-topped wall, clad on the sunny side with rizzars.

'rizzar, *sb.*[2] *Sc.* Also rizar. [f. the vb.]

1. 'A drying by means of heat, properly that of the sun' (Jamieson, 1808).

2. A rizzared haddock.

1834 J. Wilson *Noct. Ambr.* xxxiv, Loaves and fishes! Rizzars! Finnans! Kipper!

'rizzar, *v.* *Sc.* Also 9 rizar, rizzer, -or. [See next.] *trans.* To dry or parch (esp. haddocks) in the sun.

a **1818** Macneill *Poems* (1844) 88 Haddies caller at last carting, Or rizzered sweet. **1893** Stevenson *Catriona* xii, He engaged the goodwife..with some compliments upon the rizzoring of our haddocks.

rizzared ('rɪzəd), *ppl. a.* *Sc.* Also 8 rizerd, 9 riz(z)ard, -art, rizzered. [ad. obs. F. *ressoré* 'parched, scorched, dryed, or burnt vp, by the sunne' (Cotgr.), f. *re-* RE- + *sorer* 'to reeke; to drie, or make red': see SORE *a.*] Dried up by exposure to the sun: **a.** Of haddocks.

1798 *Monthly Mag.* VI. 436/1 *Rizerd haddocks*, dried haddocks. **1819** Scott *Leg. Montrose* xiii, Strung up by the head like rizzered haddocks. **1854** *Phemie Millar* II. 107 Mr. Millar..discussed his newspapers silently along with tea and rizzered haddie. **1880** *Blackw. Mag.* Mar. 360 Anything from Scotch collops to rizzard haddocks.

b. Of soil.

1844 H. Stephens *Bk. Farm* III. 744 After the soil on the top of the drills has become a little browned with the sun, or rizzared as it is technically phrased.

rizzim, -om, -um, variants of RISOM.

r-less: see R I. 1 c.

RNA. *Biochem.* Also (*rare*) R.N.A.

1. Abbrev. of *ribonucleic acid.*

See also *messenger RNA, ribosomal RNA, transfer RNA.* **1948** *Jrnl. Biol. Chem.* CLXXV. 989 Protein, phospholipides, and ribonucleic acid (RNA) are lost from the liver. **1959** *Sunday Times* 14 June 24/3 RNA carries the genetic information in the small viruses only, while DNA does this in all other organisms. **1968** H. Harris *Nucleus & Cytoplasm* iii. 57 No precise mechanism for this RNA-mediated regulation [of genetic activity] has yet been put forward. **1968** *Times* 19 Oct. 4/8 Further decipherment of the genetic code depended on synthesizing artificial RNAs containing all 64 possible triplet combinations. **1969** R. B. Fuller *Operating Man. Spaceship Earth* iv. 52 The genes and the R.N.A. and D.N.A. and other fundamental principles governing the fundamental design controls of life systems. **1977** *Nature* 27 Oct. 834/1 Enzymatic rather than chemical methods were used to degrade the RNA.

2. Special Combs. **a. RNA virus**, a virus in which the genetic material is RNA.

1963 *Nature* 17 Aug. 664/1 The use of specific inhibitors has led to the conclusion that the replication of small RNA viruses is not dependent on the integrity of host DNA. **1975** *Ibid.* 23 Oct. 634/3 Many RNA viruses are involved in animal cancers and it is believed that some human cancers may be caused in the same way.

b. In names of enzymes acting on RNA, as ***RNA polymerase, replicase, synthetase.***

1962 *Biochem. & Biophysical Res. Communications* VII. 30 The stimulation by the phage DNA is dependent on the addition of purified *RNA polymerase with polymerase-poor fractions. **1973** R. G. Krueger et al. *Introd. Microbiol.* xi. 331/1 RNA polymerase is a complex enzyme whose affinity for different promoters..depends upon protein factors which are not tightly bound to the core enzyme. **1965** *Biochem. & Biophysical Res. Communications* XVIII. 283 (*heading*) Isolation of turnip yellow mosaic virus *RNA replicase. **1969** *New Scientist* 18 Dec. 590/1 These small spherical viruses contain RNA, which functions directly as messenger, coding for three proteins, coat protein, 'maturation factor' and RNA replicase. **1962** F. H. Bergmann in *Methods in Enzymol.* V. 708 Since the term 'amino acid-activating enzyme' thus represents only a partial description of the catalytic activity of such enzymes, the term 'amino acyl *RNA synthetase' is more appropriate. **1968** *Times* 29 Oct. 7/4 The third [gene] specifies an enzyme, called RNA synthetase, which produces copies of the RNA strand.

RNase (ɑːrɛ'neɪz). *Biochem.* Also **RNAase** (ɑːrɛ'neɪeɪz). [f. RN(A + -ASE.] = *ribonuclease* s.v. RIBO-.

1957 *Jrnl. Biochem.* XLIV. 761 This RNase was inhibited by various metal ions. **1961** *Biochimica & Biophysica Acta* XLVII. 145 When yeast protoplasts are incubated with RNase, protein synthesis is inhibited. **1961** *Ibid.* LI. 190 The gel-filtration method is recommended as a suitable method to obtain the highly active fraction from RNAase I core. **1968** A. White et al. *Princ. Biochem.* (ed. 4) xii. 258 The histidine residues of RNase are uniquely reactive with iodoacetate or bromoacetate at pH 5·5. **1977** *Nature* 22/29 Dec. 760/2 The ability of cassava latent virus nucleic acid to infect *N*[*icotiana*] *clevelandii* was destroyed by DNase but not RNase.

†**ro**, *sb.* *Obs.* Forms: α. 3-5 ro, 4-5 roo, 4 rou, 5 rowe. β. *Sc.* 5 ruf, ruff, 6 rufe, ruve, rove, roif. [a. ON. and Icel. *ró* (Norw., Sw., and Da. *ro*, Fær. *rógv*), = OE. *rów* (once), Fris. *rouwe*, MDu. *rouwe, roe*, (M)LG. *rouwe, rôwe, rou(e, rô(e*, OHG. *ruowa* (MHG. *ruow(e*, later *ruw*) and *rôa* (MHG. *ruo, rue*, G. *ruhe, ruh*), regarded as cognate with Gr. ἐρωή cessation, rest. With the Sc. forms *rufe, ruve*, etc. (= rø:v), compare ROOVE rivet-burr:—ON. *ró*, CRUIVE var. of CROO, and the northern *grofe, grove* (:—ON. *gróa*), obs. variants of GROW *v.*] Rest, repose, peace.

α. *c* **1200** Ormin 7042 Cristess resste & Cristess ro & Cristess swete slæpess. *a* **1225** *Juliana* 77 Ich aȝeoue þe mi gast,..& do hit, blisfule godd,..to ro & to reste. *a* **1300** *Cursor M.* 1007 Paradis is a..land o liue, o ro, and rest. **13..** *Coer de L.* 7135 God geve us alle good endyng, And hys soule reste and roo! *c* **1375** *XI Pains of Hell* 299 in *O.E. Misc.* 220 Al þe fest of þe sunday..þai schal haue rou and rest perpetualy. *c* **1440** *York Myst.* iv. 38 Nowe ar we brought Bothe vnto rest and rowe [*rimes* to, doo]. *c* **1450** *St. Cuthbert* (Surtees) 4880 þar durst na paynym eftirward Assayle,.. Bot lete þaim rest in ro.

β. *c* **1450** Holland *Howlat* 14 This riche Revir dovn ran, but resting or ruf, Throwe ane forest. *c* **1470** Henry *Wallace* vi. 60 Now at vnes, now in to rest and ruff. *c* **1560** A. Scott *Poems* (S.T.S.) xxxi. 5 His mynd sall moif, But rest or ruve. *Ibid.* xxxvi. 85 As wes, is, salbe ay, but roif. *c* **1570** Montgomerie *Misc. Poems* vi. 20 To run that race but ather rest or rove.

b. In asseverative phrases, as ***so have I ro!***

c **1375** *Sc. Leg. Saints* xlii. (*Agatha*) 134 þat I for-think, sa haf I ro. *c* **1400** *Laud Troy Bk.* 17568 Sithen ȝe it say I wol also Aȝeyn my wille—so haue I ro! *c* **1460** *Towneley Myst.* iii. 237 Full well may we mys the, as euer haue I ro. ? *a* **1500** *Chester Pl.* (E.E.T.S.) vii. 401 As ever haue I rest or rowe, much he spake of glasse.

†**ro**, *v.* *Obs. rare.* Also 4 rone, 6 *Sc.* rufe, ruve. [f. RO *sb.* With sense 1 cf. MSw. *roas* to rest oneself, Sw. *roa* to amuse, Norw. *roa* to bring to rest; and with sense 2, MSw. *roa*, MDu. *r(o)uwen*, MLG. *r(ou)wen*, OHG. *ruowon* (MHG. *ruowen*, G. *ruhen*), to rest.]

1. *refl.* To recreate (oneself). *rare*⁻¹.

a **1300** *Cursor M.* 3351 Ysaac him yode to rone [*Gött.* went him forto ro], Thoght on thing he had to done [*Gött.* to do].

2. *intr.* *Sc.* To have or take repose.

c **1560** A. Scott *Poems* (S.T.S.) xxx. 19 That thay ma nowþir rest nor rufe, Till thay mischeif þair sellis. *a* **1568** Montgomerie *Misc. Poems* lii. 14 My mad misfortoun dois me so commuve, That I may nowthir rest nor ruve.

ro, obs. f. ROE.

roab(e, obs. ff. ROBE.

roach (rəʊtʃ), *sb.*[1] Also 4-7 roche, 6-8 roch. [a. OF. *roche* (13th c. in Godef.), *roce*, also *roque, rocque*, of uncertain origin.]

1. a. A small freshwater fish (*Leuciscus rutilus*) of the Carp family, common in the rivers of northern Europe. ***blue roach*** = AZURINE 1. In *U.S.* also applied to various small fishes resembling, or mistaken for the roach.

1314 in *Wardrobe Acc. 8 Edw. II*, 21 Dars, roches, et pik, 2s. 8d. **1390** *Earl Derby's Exp.* (Camden) 53 Cuidam homini de Lettowe pro roches ab ipso emptis apud le Haff, vs. iiij d. **1391** *Ibid.* 73 Pro tenches et roches. *c* **1400** in *N. & Q.* 3rd Ser. VI. 4/1 Yᵉ gutts of a roche is good for a roche, and so furth of all other fysshys. *c* **1430** *Two Cookery-bks.* 21 Take Trowtys, Rochys,..an make hem clene. *c* **1500** *For to serve a Lord* in *Babees Bk.* (1868) 372 Roches in sotelte, Playce in sotelte. **1577** B. Googe *Heresbach's Husb.* iv. (1586) 173 b, Some againe delight in both, as the Pike..and the Roach. **1612** Peacham *Gentl. Exerc.* iii. i. (1634) 153 Of fishes you shall finde in Armes..the Trout, Barbel, Turbot, Herring, Roach. **1653** Walton *Angler* 206, I might now tell you how to catch Roch and Dace. **1738** Swift *Printer sent to Newgate*, If a Gudgeon meet a Roach, He dare not venture to approach. **1787** Best *Angling* (ed. 2) 56 The Roach is as foolish as the carp is crafty. **1802** Bingley *Anim. Biog.* (1813) III. 84 The Roach..is found chiefly in deep still rivers, where it is often seen in large shoals. **1868** Peard *Water-farm.* xvi. 170 No fish thrives better in confinement, or breeds more rapidly than the roach. **1883** *Fish. Exhib. Catal.* (ed. 4) 107 Collection of Stuffed..Azurine or Blue Roach. **1888** Goode *Amer. Fishes* 129 The Spot..is known ..in the Chesapeake region also as the..'Roach'.

b. In phrase ***as sound as a roach***, = F. *sain comme un gardon* (cf. *plus sain qu'un gardon* in Cotgrave).

1655 Moufet & Bennet *Health's Improv.* (1746) 280 Roches..are esteemed..uncapable of any Disease, according to the old Proverb, As sound as a Roch. **1667** Denham *Direct. Paint.* i. 32 Till some judicious Dolphin might approach, And land him safe and sound as any Roach. **1700** T. Brown tr. *Fresny's Amusem.* 135 My Father.. turn'd of Seventy, and as yet he's as sound as a Roach still. *a* **1732** Gay *New Song on New Similies* viii, Hearts, sound as any bell or roach. **1825** J. Neal *Bro. Jonathan* III. 297 My health is capital—constitution ditto—sound as a roach. **1895** 'F. Anstey' *Lyre & Lancet* ix. 92 Sickly..? Not a bit of it —sound as a roach!

2. *attrib.* and *Comb.* **a.** In similative combs., as ***roach-back, -backed, -bellied, -bent.***

1575 Turberv. *Venerie* 15 The ridge or chine of the backe rochbent, and the hamme streight, betoken swiftnesse. **1668** *Lond. Gaz.* No. 272/4 A Baye Mare,..flat ribb'd, Roach back'd. **1833** Loudon *Encycl. Archit.* §1277 Laths..of cast iron,..four feet long, roach-bellied, that is, forming the segment of a circle on the under side. **1847** Youatt *Pig* vi. 74 The real Irish pig was a huge,..roach-backed, coarseboned, grisly brute. **1881** Grant *Bush Life Queensland* I. vii. 88 The flocks of sheep..return bare, leggy, roach-backed-looking objects. *a* **1884** Jarvis in Allen *New Amer. Farm Bk.* 410 The Nigretti flock..were not handsomely formed, being rather flat-sided, roach-back [etc.].

b. Attrib., etc., as ***roach-angler, -fisher, fisherman, -fishing, -hook, -net, -pie, swim, -tackle, -weel***; **roach pole**, a type of rod used in fishing for roach.

1661 Walton *Angler* (ed. 3) xvii. 218 About London, where I think there be the best Roch-Anglers. **1704** *Dict. Rust.* s.v. *Roach-fishing*, They add 12 strong links of Hair, with Roach-Hooks at them. **1725** *Family Dict.* s.v., The Roach-Pie may be made, as that of Tunny-Pie. **1823** in Hofland *Brit. Angler's Man.* (1841) 247 A barbel, caught with roach-tackle. **1867** Francis *Bk. Angling* 18 The Thames, Lea, and Colne are eagerly sought by shoals of roach-fishers. *Ibid.* 19 Roach-fishing is very pretty sport. **1877** —— *Angling* 27 One of the finest roach rivers within fifty miles of London. **1883** *Fish. Exhib. Catal.* 366 Roach Weel, from the Province of Bleking. *Ibid.* 376 Roach Net. **1897** *Encycl. Sport* I. 24/2 On the Thames, the bank-angler commonly uses a long bamboo roach-pole and tight line. **1902** *Chambers's Jrnl.* Nov. 699/1, I was preparing to fish a not unpromising roach-swim, and was trying the depth. **1944** 'N. Shute' *Pastoral* i. 3 With his long greenheart roach-pole, his bag of ground bait, and his gentles. **1971** *Country Life* 16 Dec. 1730/4, I believe the Lea roach-pole anglers were then regarded as supreme masters of that particular art. **1974** *Country Life* 30 May 1333/2, I didn't have much success as a roach fisherman.

roach (rəʊtʃ), *sb.*[2] Also 8 roch. [var. of ROCHE *sb.*[1], as the usual or only spelling in certain special senses.]

1. *Mining.* (See quot. 1836.) ? *Obs.*

1653 Manlove *Lead Mines* 258 Soletrees, Roach, and Ryder. **1747** Hooson *Miner's Dict.* Q ij b, I have likewise heard of other Veins discovered after the same manner; as also in Fields of Grass lying near the Roch. **1836** Furness *Astrologer* 11, Roach, Rag-pump, Rider. *Ibid.* Gloss., *Roach*, ore found on the side of the main vein and divided from it by rock or rither.

†**2.** A seam or bed of coal. *Obs.*

1677 *Phil. Trans.* XII. 896 It was found upon the rising grounds (where the signs of the Cole, and the Cole it self came near the day) that there lay another Roach of Cole at a certain depth under it. **1686** Plot *Staffordsh.* 137 In working the roach of coal 5 yards thick. *Ibid.* 147 He shewed me a level of 35 yards of roach. **1704** *Lond. Gaz.* No. 4008/4, 220 Acres, in which are great Quantities of Roch of Coal, now open.

†**3.** ***peter in roach***, = ROCHE-PETRE. *Obs.*

1692 *Capt. Smith's Seaman's Gram.* ii. xxxi. 150 Take of ..Peter in Roach one pound; Peter in Meal one pound.

4. a. (See quots. and cf. ROCHE *sb.*)

1831 J. Hodgson in Raine *Mem.* (1858) II. 213 The same sort of conglomerate rock as that at the foot of Ulswater, and which the country people there [in 1799] called roach. *Ibid.* 215 The old red sandstone of the Mellfell district is through all that country called roach or roche.

b. A variety of Portland stone (see quots.).

1829 Webster in *Geol. Trans.* 2nd Ser. II. 42 The bed below this [= School Cap] is the first which is worked for freestone, and is called Roach... It is entirely oolitic..and contains marine shells. **1839** *Civil Eng. & Arch. Jrnl.* II. 332/2 The new Church in the island, built..of a variety of the Portland stone termed roach. *Ibid.* 376/1 The roach is throughout the island oolitic. **1887** *Specif. T. Monk's Patent* No. 1264. 1 The roach or rag of Portland stone, at present a wasted natural product.

attrib. **1839** *Civil Eng. & Arch. Jrnl.* II. 375/2 The roach beds are always incorporated with the freestone beds that invariably lie below them. **1862** Ramsay *Rock Spec.* 139 The Roach-bed is very hard, and is used for foundations of breakwaters,..but it will not bear a close even face.

roach (rəʊtʃ), *sb.*[3] *Naut.* [App. a *transf.* use of ROACH *sb.*[1]] **1.** 'An upward curve in the foot of a square sail'. Cf. *roach-back(ed)* s.v. ROACH *sb.*[1] 2 a.

1794 *Rigging & Seamanship* 116 The stay is cut with a curve or roach. **1851** Kipping *Sailm.* (ed. 2) 45 The breadth of the seams on the foot of a jib or driver ought to be made according to the roach with which the sail is cut. **1900** F. T. Bullen *Idylls of Sea* 34 Their seams, leaches, and roaches fortified by all the devices known to the sailmaker.

attrib. **1794** *Rigging & Seamanship* 91 Flying jibs are cut with a roach-curve on the stay. *Ibid.* 88 *Roach-leech*, a term signifying the curve on the mast-leech of some fore and aft sails, &c.

transf. **1889** *Cent. Mag.* Jan. 335/1 [The Texas pony] has ..a very long body, with a pronounced roach just forward of the coupling. **1955** W. W. Denlinger *Compl. Boston* i. 105 Many Boston terriers with level backs will show roach on a cold day.

2. *U.S.* **a.** A roll of hair brushed upwards and back from the face; a topknot (see quot. 1959[2]). Also ***attrib.***, as ***roach cut.***

1881 J. C. Harris in *Century Mag.* June 244/2 Den he take en walk upter de little Gal, Brer Rabbit did, en pull he roach, en bow, en scrape he foot, en talk mighty nice en slick. **1929** W. Faulkner *Sound & Fury* 177 A man with a fierce roach of iron grey hair. **1959** E. Tunis *Indians* 47/2 Most of the head was plucked or singed bare for a roach cut; only a strip of hair was left from front to back. *Ibid.* 48/1 The most usual ceremonial headdress in the East was the artificial roach.

b. *attrib.* in sense of ROACHED *a.* 2.

1781 *R. Georgia Gaz.* 8 Mar. 4/2 (Advt.), A Black Horse, about 13 and an half hands high, half roach main [etc.]. **1835** J. T. Irving *Indian Sk.* II. 4 She was mounted upon a little wall-eyed, cream-coloured pony, with a roach mane and a bobtail.

roach, *sb.*[4] Chiefly *U.S.* **1.** abbrev. form of COCKROACH.

1836-48 B. D. Walsh *Aristoph.* 89 *note*, 'Cock-roaches' in the United States..are always called 'roaches' by the fair sex, for the sake of euphony. **1898** A. Balfour *Stroke of Sword* xxiv, Overcome by my terror of these roaches, I rushed on deck. **1942** E. Paul *Narrow St.* x. 75 Her failure to get results kept her hopping like a roach in a skillet. **1950** *Harlem Q.* Fall-Winter 21 A fat roach sluggishly made its way ceilingwards. **1976** *National Observer* (U.S.) 29 May 15A/3 The Postal Service is the kind of problem most members think shouldn't exist. It's like roaches in the kitchen.

2. *slang.* A policeman.

1932 *Evening Sun* (Baltimore) 9 Dec. 31/5 *Roach*, policeman. **1968** *Word Study* Dec. 5/1 Not only is a policeman a *bull*; he may also be a *roach*.

3. *slang*. The butt of a cigarette, *spec.* a marijuana cigarette. (Perh. a different word.)

1938 *New Yorker* 12 Mar. 47/2 A pinched-off smoke, or stub, is a roach. **1953** W. BURROUGHS *Junkie* ii. 29 'Would you like to get high?' Mary asked. 'There may be a roach around here somewhere.' **1966** T. PYNCHON *Crying of Lot 49* iii. 64 Holding up the glowing roaches of their cigarettes ..to spell out alternate S's an O's. **1971** *It* 2–16 June 2/1 Freaks from several other pads saved all our roaches for a week and posted them to Det. Sgt. Boothe who is the chief of Bournemouth drug squad. **1972** M. J. BOSSE *Incident at Naha* i. 46, I..took out my pot pouch and cigarette paper. ..I..rolled myself a joint... I had finished the roach down to my fingernails.

4. *attrib.* and *Comb.*, as (sense 1) ***roach killer, poison, -powder***; ***roach-crawling*** adj.; (sense 3) ***roach holder***; **roach clip** = *roach holder* above.

1968–70 *Current Slang* (Univ. S. Dakota) III–IV. 103 **Roach clip*, a small metal clip used to smoke marijuana, resembling a paper-clip or tweezers. **1979** *Christian Science Monitor* (Eastern ed.) 21 Nov. B1/1 Clearly visible through the shop's windows are..'roach clips' for holding the butt of a marijuana cigarette. **1964** S. LEAKS in J. H. Clarke *Harlem* 23 *Harlem*, a dingy-dirty cluster of *roach crawling rat-infested brownstones and tenement flats. **1967** *Evening Standard* 26 June 7/3 In Haight-Ashbury [in San Francisco] there are now over 30 psychedelic boutiques..selling at inflated prices such items as..*roach holders (cigarette holders specially designed for reefer smoking). **1973** *Sunday Express* (Trinidad & Tobago) 8 Apr. 13/2 I'm on the floor, surrounded by pots and pans etc. shaking the can of *roach killer. **1975** *New Yorker* 23 June 29/2 St. Vincent's emergency room is one of my favorite emergency rooms in the whole world. I know it well, from the time..my daughter ate the *roach poison. **1930** J. DOS PASSOS *42nd Parallel* 60 A smell of ham and coffee and *roachpowder. **1931** E. POUND *Let.* 6 Oct. (1971) 236 In reply to yr. last: I am not interested in roach-powder but if the janitors and swabbers can't keep the place clean, I take it *somebody* has got to provide insecticide or even squash the individual cockroach.

roach, variant of ROCHE, ROTCHE.

roach (rəʊtʃ), *v.* [f. ROACH *sb.*[3]]

1. *trans.* To cut (a sail) with a roach.

1851 KIPPING *Sailm.* (ed. 2) 117 On Roaching the Sails. *Ibid.* 118 The royals are also roached as much as 1 foot 6 inches.

2. *U.S.* **a.** To clip or trim (a horse's mane) so that the hair stands on end.

1818 *Missouri Gaz.* 25 Dec. 4/5 His mane has been divided..and that part that laid on the left side, cut off as if to roach him. **1848** *Blackw. Mag.* LXIII. 731 Her neck was thick, and rendered more so in appearance by reason of her mane not being roached (or in English hogged). **1889** *Cent. Mag.* Jan. 335/2, I roached his mane and docked his tail.

b. Of persons: to brush or cut (the hair) in a roach. Also with *up*.

1833 *Sk. & Eccentr. D. Crockett* ii. 38 His hair was roached, and he wore an air of much dignity. **1853** J. G. BALDWIN *Flush Times Alabama* 108 His hair was roached up, and stood as erect and upright as his body. **1900** ADE *More Fables* 62 He would go to School with his face scrubbed to a shiny pink and his Hair roached up on one side. **1919** H. L. WILSON *Ma Pettengill* iii. 84 She was..a kind of a slaty blonde with bobbed hair—she'd been roached fore and aft. **1932** L. C. DOUGLAS *Forgive us our Trespasses* (1937) iv. 79 His hair roached high to show he had an intellectual forehead. **1950** L. HUGHES *Simple speaks his Mind* xvi. 86 Her head was all done fresh and shining with a hair-rocker roached up high in front.

roach alum, variant of ROCHE ALUM.

roached (rəʊtʃt), *a.* Chiefly *U.S.* [f. ROACH *sb.*[3] or *v.*] **1.** Having an upward curve. Also *Comb.*, as ***roached-backed*** adj.

1776 *New England Chron.* 25 Jan. 3/3 (Advt.), Strayed or stolen..a sorrel horse..roach'd back, 3 white feet, [etc.]. **1844** E. C. WATMOUGH *Scribblings & Sk.* (ed. 2) 176, The two [horses] with roatched backs, and ears glued to their necks, were scrambling. *a* **1890** *Dogs Gt. Brit. & Amer.* 100 (Cent.), An arched loin is desirable, but not to the extent of being roached or 'wheel-backed', a defect which generally tends to slow up-and-down gallop. **1894** 'MARK TWAIN' in *St. Nicholas* Feb. 355/1 Roached-backed ones that he said was hyenas. **1945** C. L. B. HUBBARD *Observer's Bk. Dogs* 56 Body [of Dandie Dinmont terrier] low-to-ground, roached-backed. **1955** W. W. DENLINGER *Compl. Boston* I. 172 For a dog with a naturally roached spine, nothing can be done. **1979** T. GRAY *Chihuahua* (ed. 5) vii. 98 Another fault, a slightly roached back, will often level out by the time the puppy is three-parts grown.

2. Of hair (on a horse or person): brushed or cut in a roach. Hence, having hair dressed in this way. Also ***roached-up***.

1790 *Augusta* (Georgia) *Chron.* 13 Mar. 3/1 A Bay Horse, roached mane and a small switched tail. **1836** *Southern Lit. Messenger* II. 303/1 The..fat, impudent pony, with roached main and bobtail. **1856** P. CARTWRIGHT *Autobiogr.* xii. 141 This young man had a mighty bushy roached head of hair. **1891** *Appeal-Avalanche* (Memphis) 26 Apr. 7/2 Strayed... one dark bay colt, roached mane and end of tail cut off. **1944** DUNCAN & NICKOLS *M. Graham* 91 There were twenty-seven big, little, and middlin'-sized boys and girls, giggling and whispering about the master's roached, curly red hair. **1949** 'J. NELSON' *Backwoods Teacher* 268 If she wants to go 'round lookin' like an old roached-up mule, *we* don't care.

roaching (ˈrəʊtʃɪŋ), *vbl. sb.*[1] [f. ROACH *sb.*[1]] Fishing for roach.

1887 *Sporting Life* 22 June 2/6 Roaching and Poaching, and other matters. **1896** *Daily News* 20 Oct. 9/1 The river, as regards colour, was all that could be desired for roaching.

roaching, *vbl. sb.*[2] *U.S.* [f. ROACH *v.* + -ING[1].] The action of brushing or cutting the hair in a roach. Also, the process or fact of this.

a **1883** G. W. BAGBY *Sel. Misc. Writings* (1885) II. 27 You see it [*sc.* his individuality] in the tie of his cravat, the cut of his coat,..the roaching of his hair. **1903** *N.Y. Even. Post* 24 Oct. (Saturday Suppl.) 2/1 When brought to market he [*sc.* the mule] undergoes the process of 'roaching', which consists of removing all the hair of poor quality and scanty growth.

roachy (ˈrəʊtʃɪ), *a.* *U.S.* [f. ROACH *sb.*[4] + -Y[1].] Infested with cockroaches; resembling cockroaches (see also quot. 1900).

1900 *Dialect Notes* II. 54 *Roachy, adj.*, pertaining to poor work or preparation. **1937** F. SCOTT FITZGERALD *Let.* 8 Oct. (1964) 19 You are right that romantic things really happen in roachy kitchens and back yards. **1979** P. L. G. BATEMAN *Household Pests* II. 93 They contaminate more than they consume, polluting everything with a foul 'roachy' odour which is persistent.

road (rəʊd), *sb.* Forms: 1 rád, 3–5 rade; 4–7 rode (6–7 rhode); 5 rood, 5–7 roode; 6–7 roade (6 rhoade), 6– road. See also RAID *sb.* [OE. *rád* fem. (f. pret. stem of *rídan* to RIDE), in sense 1 = Fris. *reed*, MDu. *rede* (Flem. dial. *rede, ree*), MLG. *rêt, rêd-*, ON. and Icel. *reið* (MSw. *reed(h*, MDa. *reed, red*). In sense 3 the continental forms are MDu. *rede, reede* (Du. *reede, ree*), MLG. *rede, reide* (hence G. *reede, rhede*, Da. *red, rhed*, Sw. *redd*): the view that these are connected with Du. *reeden*, LG. *reiden* to fit out, is old but is inconsistent with the history of the Eng. form. On senses 2 and 4 see notes below.]

I. †**1. a.** The act of riding on horseback; also, a spell of riding; a journey on horseback. *Obs.*

c **888** K. ÆLFRED *Boeth.* xxxiv. §7 [He] rit for ðy þe he mid ðære rade earnað sume earnunga. *a* **900** tr. *Baeda's Hist.* IV. iii, þæt he þæt weorc þæs halȝan godspelles ma þurh his fota gange fremede, þonne on his horsa rade. *c* **1000** *Sax. Leechd.* I. 76 ʒif mon on mycelre rade oððe on miclum gangum weorðe ʒeteorad. *a* **1225** *Juliana* 76 Sone þerefter com a seli wummon..bi nicomedes burh o rade toward rome. *a* **1300** *Cursor M.* 11427 þir kinges rides forth þair rade [*v.r.* rode], þe stern alwais þam forwit glade. **1390** GOWER *Conf.* I. 100 This knyht on daies brode In clos him hield, and schop his rode On nyhtes time. **1463** *Paston Lett.* II. 143, I sent your grey hors..to the ferror, and he seythe he shull never be nowght to rood nowthyr ryght good to plowe nor to carte. *a* **1470** TIPTOFT *Tulle on Friendsh.* (Caxton, 1481) C iij, As we are not wonte rather to chese coltes than horses of 7 yere for our rode. **1605–6** *Act for Paving Drury Lane*, The Lane ..is of late yeeres by occasion of the continuall Rode there, and often Cariages, become deepe, foule, and dangerous. **1613** SHAKS. *Hen. VIII*, IV. ii. 17 At last, with easie Rodes, he came to Leicester.

†**b.** The act of riding on the waves. *Obs.*[−1]

The use of OE. *rád* in Cynewulf's *Elene* 981 may belong here, or to sense 3.

c **1400** *Destr. Troy* 1045 Pelleus..puruiaunce hade made Of twenty shippes full shene, shot on þe depe, All redy to the Roode of þe ythes.

†**c.** A set or company of riders. *Obs. rare.*

13.. *Coer de L.* 5257 These are chosyn in fyrst rod..: Sere Calabre hovyd stylle, To see who wolde ryde hym tylle. **1530** PALSGR. 263/2 Rode, a company of horsmen, *chevauchee*.

†**2.** *spec.* The act of riding with hostile intent against a person or district; a hostile incursion by mounted men; a foray, raid. *Obs.*

Very common *c* 1500–1650: cf. also INROAD. In mod. use revived in the Sc. form RAID.

c **900** *O.E. Chron.* (Parker MS.) an. 871, Cyninges þegnas oft rade onridon þe mon na ne rimde. **925–35** *Sec. Laws of Athelstan* 20 (Liebermann), Ðonne ridon þa yldestan men to ..and nimon eall ðæt he aȝe, and fo se cyng to healfum, to healfum ða men ðe on þære rade beon. **1390** GOWER *Conf.* II. 56 Be londe and ek be Schiep He mot travaile..And make manye hastyf rodes. *c* **1400** *Destr. Troy* 1180 Mony stithe man..on stedis enarmyt, All redy for þe rode Arayet for the werre. **1481** *Coventry Leet Bk.* (E.E.T.S.) 475 Aftur a Rode..made vppon the Scottes at thende of this last somer. **1523** LD. BERNERS *Froiss.* I. xviii. 24 Borderers, whan they make rodes into Scotlande. *Ibid.* xliv. 60 Than the kyng gaue lycence to the soudiers..to make a rode into Heynalt. **1575** CHURCHYARD *Chippes* (1817) 77 His moste paines hath been taken aboute the warres of Scotlande, and roades made into that countrey. **1617** MORYSON *Itin.* III. 54 Northumberland men (exercised in roades upon the Scots) are accounted best light horsemen. **1665** MANLEY *Grotius' Low C. Wars* 169 The English..assailed and made Incursions and Rodes upon all Spanish ships, and other places.

3. a. A sheltered piece of water near the shore where vessels may lie at anchor in safety; a roadstead.

Cf. 1 b and the note there. For Scottish examples see RAID *sb.* 4 (and REID[1]).

c **1320** *Sir Tristr.* 801 To his castel ful riȝt He sailed þe seuenday On rade. *Ibid.* 955 Tristrem gan stoutely go To lond þat ich niȝt Of rade. [**1372–3** in Swinden *Gt. Yarmouth* (1772) 375 Quendam locum in mari..vocatum Kirkelee Rode.] **1400** *Destr. Troy* 5586 But the freikes were ferd.. For..to remeve fro rode for rokkes in þe se. *c* **1440** *Promp. Parv.* 435/2 Roode, of shyppys stondyng, *bitalassum*. **1495** *Naval Acc. Hen. VII* (1896) 187 The seyd Ship lying in the Rode at Eryth in Thamys. **1514** BARCLAY *Cytezen & Uplondyshm.* (Percy Soc.) 29 Lyke wyse as shyppes be docked in a rode. **1594** NASHE & MARLOWE *Dido* 1500 Why are thy ships new rigd? or to what end, Launcht from the hauen, lye they in the Rhode? **1617** MORYSON *Itin.* III. 138 The Towne Gravesend is a knowne Roade. **1652** NEEDHAM tr. *Selden's Mare Cl.* 111 Princes..impose Custom upon Ships, as for the use of the Road upon their Coasts. **1720** DE FOE *Capt. Singleton* i, The pilot..brought the ship into a very good road, where we rid in twenty-six fathoms water. **1775** ROMANS *Florida* App. 74 The depth of water in both these roads is from 20 to 24 feet. **1824** IRVING *T. Trav.* I. 34 The tide contrary, the vessell anchored far off in the road. **1850** B. TAYLOR *Eldorado* iv. 26 Those [vessels] which are obliged to lie in the open road are exposed to considerable danger.

attrib. *c* **1550** LELAND *Collect.* III. 94 At the rode mouth of Tawe was a castell cawllid..Ostermuth.

fig. **1509** BARCLAY *Shyp of Folys* (1570) 248 No speciall place will I chose for our rode But at auenture where the winde shall us driue. **1590** SPENSER *F.Q.* I. xii. 42 Now, strike your sailes,..For we be come vnto a quiet rode. **1629** H. BURTON *Truth's Triumph* 75 A secure roade and safe harbour for all heauenly merchants to anchor in.

†**b.** ***at road***, riding at anchor. *Obs.*

1439 *Rolls of Parlt.* V. 29/2 Yn defaute of Cables and Ancres for here seid Shippes and Vesseles, where as they be at rode. **1495** *Naval Acc. Hen. VII* (1896) 254 The seid ship lying at Rode in the Kynges haven. **1549–62** STERNHOLD & H. *Ps.* civ. 26 There both mightie ships saile, and some lye at roade. **1597** BP. HALL *Sat.* III. vi. 17 Yet stand they still, as tho they lay at rode. **1641** HINDE *J. Bruen* xlii. 131 Such vessels as have laine for a while at quiet rode in the harbor.

fig. **1596** SOUTHWELL *Triumphs over Death* 18 God.. casteth your anchours where your thoghts should lie at rhode.

4. a. An ordinary line of communication used by persons passing between different places, usually one wide enough to admit of the passage of vehicles as well as of horses or travellers on foot.

The late appearance of this sense makes its development from sense 1 somewhat obscure, but Fris. *reed* and Flem. *ree* have acquired similar meanings. Cf. also OE. *stréamrád* the course of a stream, *hwéolrád* wheel-track, and the poetic words for 'sea', *brim-, stréam-, hron-, seȝl-, swanrád*. The earlier Sc. ROD *sb.*[2], path, is unconnected, and there is no evidence that it had any influence upon the history of the English word.

It is not quite clear whether COCK-ROAD, which appears about 1600 and is implied in the earlier *road-net* (see 12), belongs to this sense. Cf. RODE *v.*[1]

1596 SHAKS. *1 Hen. IV*, II. i. 16 The most villanous house in al London rode. **1597** —— *2 Hen. IV*, II. ii. 183 This Doll Teare-sheet should be some Rode. *a* **1625** FLETCHER *Love's Pilgrimage* II. iii, 'Tis a toyle Sir; Like riding in one rode perpetually, It offers no variety. **1636** SANDERSON *Serm.* II. 51 A traveller in a deep rode will be choice of his way throughout. **1673** RAY *Journ. Low C.* 431 We diverted out of the common rode to Geneva. **1738** GRAY *Tasso* 37 The downward road That to the grotto leads. **1791** MRS. RADCLIFFE *Rom. Forest* i, He inquired for a road among the hills, but heard of none. **1839** THIRLWALL *Greece* VI. 245 To follow the easier and more circuitous road which led northward to Zadracarta. **1859** JEPHSON *Brittany* vi. 68 After this the road became very intricate, and I was fain to hire a little boy to guide me. **1881** BLACKMORE *Christowell* xxvi, In a place where the street narrowed into a road.

b. *Mining.* 'Any underground passage, way, or gallery' (Gresley).

1839 URE *Dict. Arts* 975 The roads will be shut up, the air-courses destroyed, and the whole economy of the mining operations deranged. **1978** *Lancashire Life* July 63/1 He took young Sam down the pit and showed him the seam, eighteen inches high, which he had to work in a road about six feet wide.

c. Chiefly *U.S.* A railroad or railway.

1837 *Civil Eng. & Arch. Jrnl.* I. 56 American Railroads... Many circumstances conspire to assist..in the construction of these roads. **1856** OLMSTED *Slave States* 546 There are now very nearly..one thousand miles of rail-road in the State..; the roads were injudiciously laid out, and have been badly managed. **1872** RAYMOND *Statist. Mines & Mining* 115 A prominent station on the Central Pacific road. **1898** H. E. HAMBLEN *Gen. Manager's Story* 68, I was passed along from one road to another, my transportation costing me nothing. **1921** *Daily Colonist* (Victoria, B.C.) 11 Mar. 2/3 The railway official quoted said he could not state whether the Canadian roads would follow the lead of the United States roads in cutting wages. **1932** *Atlantic Monthly* Mar. 318/2 Those railways..were once so prosperous that men.. thought the roads would own the country unless curbed. **1942** *R.A.F. Jrnl.* 3 Oct. 3 (*caption*) Blast area with damage to roads and wagons, and a group of derailed wagons. **1950** O. S. NOCK *Brit. Locomotives* 4 The regulator opening was varied a little to suit the rise and fall of the road. **1963** *Wall St. Jrnl.* 24 Jan. 29/3 The road..operates in Guatemala and El Salvador. **1967** *Listener* 6 Apr. 461/2 At Edenbridge sidings they..told us to stand in number three road to get our breakfast.

d. *Post Office.* (See quots.)

1859 A. ANDREWS *Hist. Jrnlism.* II. 147 The monopoly of circulating newspapers by the post had been held fast by the clerks of the road, employed by the Post-office. *Ibid.* 199 The abominable monopoly of the clerks of the roads was still in existence. **1881** *Standard* 1 Nov. 2/1 At the first rough sorting the letters are distributed into 'roads', corresponding with the principal lines of railway communication over the country; the term being a survival of the nomenclature of the old coaching days.

e. *spec.* with qualifying word, a common trade-route (now freq. for illicit goods).

1931, etc. [see *silk-road*, s.v. SILK *sb.* 10 a]. **1977** *Listener* 1 Dec. 733/1 The lost city of Zufar, the port which marked the beginning of the incense road, where ships unloaded spices from Asia for the classical Roman world. **1977** H. OSBORNE *White Poppy* xliii. 272 The gendarmes would be..watching ..the opium roads.

5. In pregnant uses: **a.** ***on, upon, the road***, travelling, journeying, upon or during a journey, etc.; on tour; also *spec.* of a person travelling as (*a*) a salesman, (*b*) a tramp. Also *N. Amer.*, = AWAY *adv.* 11 (cf. sense 9 d below). ***to take the road***, to set out.

1642 H. MORE *Song of Soul* II. xxxv. Wks. (Grosart) 22 In this same Land as I was on the rode, A nimble traveller me overtook. **1657** HEYLIN *Ecclesia Vind.* 115 We finde Israel offering sacrifices at Beersheba (being in his way upon the rode). **1759** JOHNSON *Idler* No. 80 ¶6 Her aunt and her mother amuse themselves on the road, with telling her of dangers to be dreaded. **1782** MISS BURNEY *Cecilia* v. ix, They slept one night upon the road, and arrived the next day at Delvile Castle. **1833** J. S. SANDS *Poems* 71 James his duds Reekt out.. To take the road amang the rest. **1860** DICKENS *Uncomm. Trav.* in *All Year Round* 28 Jan. 321/1, I am both a town traveller and a country traveller, and am always on the road. **1870** O. LOGAN *Before Footlights* xxviii. 367 The organ of the circus people.. gives many curious details of circus-life Behind the Scenes, and 'on the road'. **1884** G. MOORE *Mummer's Wife* (1887) 230 The other two operas, having been on the road for the last three years. **1897** *Daily News* 6 Sept. 8/2 Many of the companies 'on the road'.. belong to the class that have been organised for the performance of some particular piece. **1897** *Forum* Feb. 735 It is the man who wilfully and knowingly makes a business of crime.. that I have found in largest numbers 'on the road'. **1907** J. LONDON *Road* 194 As a sample of life on The Road, I make the following quotation from my diary. **1908** A. BENNETT *Old Wives' Tale* I. iv. 70 He was a traveller for the most renowned and gigantic of all Manchester wholesale firms... He had been on the road for Birkinshaws for several years. **1920** WODEHOUSE *Jill the Reckless* (1922) xiv. 210 You've got to stick around with this show after it opens on the road. **1931** M. ALLINGHAM *Police at Funeral* xxi. 277, I know a 'busy' when I see one. I 'aven't been on the road for thirty years without gettin' inside once or twice. **1937** 'G. ORWELL' *Road to Wigan Pier* ix. 182, I would find out about tramps.. and then, when I.. knew the ropes well enough, I would go on the road myself. **1956** B. HOLIDAY *Lady sings Blues* (1973) i. 2 When he went on the road with that band it was the beginning of the end of our life as a family. **1967** J. B. PRIESTLEY *It's an Old Country* xv. 162 He was drinking hard, always a dam' silly thing to do on the road, except with a few old customers. **1968** *Globe & Mail* (Toronto) 15 Jan. 17/6 A team with the experienced potential of the defending cup champions is letting its fans down badly when it wins only four of 19 games on the road. **1977** *Daily Express* 29 Mar. 20/2 We start touring America in May, move on to Europe and England by September, and we are taking the 70 musicians on the road.

b. ***the road***, the highway. In phrases, ***to go upon***, or ***take to***, ***the road***, to become a highwayman; ***gentleman***, or ***knight***, ***of the road***, a highwayman. Now *arch.*

1665 [see KNIGHT *sb.* 12c]. *a* **1700** B. E. *Dict. Cant. Crew Knight of the Road*, the chief Highwayman best Mounted and Armed. **1729** SWIFT *Grand Question*, So, I took to the Road, and.. The first Man I robb'd was a Parson. **1729** —— *Direct. Servants* iii, I directly advise you, to go upon the Road;.. the only Post of Honour left you. **1771** SMOLLETT *Humph. Cl.* 11 June §10 Martin.. could not supply his occasions any other way than by taking to the road. **1809** MALKIN *Gil Blas* I. v, Consorting with gentlemen of the road. **1840** THACKERAY *Catherine* v, [We] found ourselves regular knights of the road, before we knew where we were almost. **1898** BESANT *Orange Girl* Prol., You might go abroad;.. anything is better than the Road and the certain end.

c. ***to give*** (*one*) ***the road***, to allow one to pass. ***to take the road of***, to take precedence of.

1670 EACHARD *Cont. Clergy* 99 Most certainly, without quarrelling, he takes the road of all mankind. **1724** DE FOE *Mem. Cavalier* 250, I gave them the road. **1897** *Daily News* 21 Oct. 5/4 When riding a bicycle he met the defendant driving a carrier's van, and the latter gave him no road whatever.

d. Permission to set out or depart.

1863 SPEKE *Discov. Source Nile* xiv. 441, I primed him well to plead for the road. *Ibid.* 445 The moment of triumph had come at last, and suddenly the road was granted.

e. ***the rule of the road***, the fixed custom which regulates the side to be taken by vehicles, etc. (or *transf.* by vessels) in progressing or passing each other.

1871 *Chamb. Jrnl.* 26 Aug. 529 They do not observe 'the rule of the road'..; they have a tendency to keep on the inner side. **1873** *Punch* Apr. 139/1 A variety of useless discussions—.. one on the rule of the road at sea. **1890** *Spectator* Sept. 395/2 With us, arts, commerce, letters, and learning would perish long before the rule of the road.

f. In extended uses based on ***all roads lead to Rome*** (ROME 1 b (*d*)).

1917 E. THOMAS in *Ann. New Poetry* 55 Now all roads lead to France. **1942** E. PAUL *Narrow St.* xxiii. 209 All roads lead straight to me, as you have so often remarked. **1974** D. G. COMPTON, *Continuous Katherine Mortenhoe* vi. 165 'Where to now?'.. I gestured widely... 'All roads lead out of town.'

g. ***one for the road***: see ONE *numeral a.* 1 d. Also with other numerals.

1955 J. P. DONLEAVY *Ginger Man* (1957) xix. 184 'You've had a few.' 'Five for the road. Never let it be said that I took to the highway or even byway without fuel for me little heart.'

6. a. Any way, path, or (material) course.

1602 CAREW *Cornwall* 24 b, The Woodcockes arrive first on the North-coast, where almost euerie hedge serveth for a Roade. **1667** MILTON *P.L.* IV. 976 In progress through the rode of Heav'n star-pav'd. **1697** DRYDEN *Virg. Georg.* II. 274 Where Silver Swans sail down the Wat'ry Rode. **1754** GRAY *Progr. Poesy* 54 In climes beyond the solar road. **1769** E. BANCROFT *Guiana* 234 They form a kind of arched roads, about half an inch wide. **1826** KIRBY & SP. *Entomol.* xxxvii. IV. 19 The nerves and spinal marrow are merely the roads by which the sensations travel.

b. *fig.* A way or course, esp. *to* some end.

1599 SHAKS. *Much Ado* v. ii. 33 These quondam carpet-mongers, whose names yet runne smoothly in the euen rode of a blank verse. **1607** —— *Cor.* v. i. 59 You know the very rode into his kindnesse, And cannot lose your way. **1643** SIR T. BROWNE *Relig. Med.* I. §53 There is no road or ready way to vertue. **1700** PEPYS *Let. to Jackson* 9 May, I am, I thank God! greatly recovered, and in a fair road towards being perfectly so. **1730** FIELDING *Author's Farce* III, Why affairs go much in the same road as there when you were alive. **1752** tr. *Rameau's Treat. Mus.* iv. 11 Ascending or descending diatonically whatever Road the Bass may take. **1783** GOUV. MORRIS in Sparks *Life & Writ.* (1832) I. 250 They were precipitating themselves in the road to ruin. **1818** SHELLEY *Julian* 347 There is one road To peace and that is truth. **1840** DICKENS *Old C. Shop* lxix, All those little artifices which find the readiest road to their hearts. **1879** FROUDE *Cæsar* ix. 95 There were but two roads to eminence in Rome, oratory and service in the army.

ellipt. **1878** in *St. George's Hosp. Rep.* (1879) IX. 779, I think it may be some time before she is quite right; but when the os and cervix are sound,.. she will be on the road.

c. ***royal road***, a smooth or easy way; a method (of study, etc.) unaccompanied by difficulties.

The expression stems from a saying attributed to Euclid by Proclus (*Comm. on Euclid* Prol.): *μὴ εἶναι βασιλικὴν ἀτραπὸν ἐπὶ γεωμετρίαν* there is no royal short cut to geometry.

1793 BEDDOES *Demonstr. Evid.* 59 In this science there is no transcendental road; but I imagine a *royal* road might be struck out. **1798** FERRIAR *Illustr. Sterne*, etc. ii. 27 Dionysius and Frederick both experienced, that there is no royal road to the genuine honours of literature. **1810** CRABBE *Borough* xxiv. 28 Learning is labour,.. Nor must we hope to find the royal road. **1857** TROLLOPE *Barchester T.* II. i. 2 There is no royal road to learning; no short cut to the acquirement of any valuable art. **1860** MANSEL *Proleg. Log.* ix. (ed. 2) 288 Logic .. is neither able to open a Royal Road to the Encyclopædia, nor [etc.]. **1899** *Allbutt's Syst. Med.* VII. 453 There is no royal road to recovery for stutterers. **1918** A. S. EDDINGTON *Rep. Relativity Theory Gravitation* ii. 27 Some readers will find the next two chapters difficult,.. but I doubt if there is any royal road to relativity. **1954** 'N. SHUTE' *Slide Rule* vii. 158 There is no royal road to risk capital, no tap that can be turned on. **1966** P. GREEN tr. *Escarpit's Novel Computer* xiv. 173, I had to obtain that last official stamp of approval which could open up the royal road towards an easy and fruitful career. **1971** *Daily Tel.* 19 Apr. 23 The royal road for the research scientist in industry is sign-posted by positive answers to some critical questions: [etc.].

†**d.** *fig.* A string *of* words; a limited range of thought or discourse. *Obs.*

a **1690** HOPKINS *Exposit.* 2 To mutter over a road of Words only,.. as multitudes of many ignorant Persons among us do. **1693** LOCKE *Educ.* §120 The Discourses of Men, who talk in a Road, according to the Notions they have borrowed.

e. A narrow band.

1802 *Trans. Soc. Arts* XX. 275 Each millstone, divided into nine spaces, having ten circular roads in each space.

f. A connected set of railway-trucks, barges, etc.

1895 *Daily News* 11 Feb. 3/2 The barges.. have suffered most, one 'road' of 12 and another of 15 breaking away together. **1903** *Daily Record & Mail* 1 June, When a 'road' of trucks is loaded it is ready to be drawn out of the siding.

g. ***capitalist road*** [tr. Chinese *zīběn zhǔyì dàolù*], esp. during the Cultural Revolution in China, an observable tendency to adopt political ideals and practices leading towards capitalism. Cf. ROADER[1] 7.

1966 *Peking Rev.* 12 Aug. 8/2 The main target of the present movement is those within the Party who are in authority and are taking the capitalist road. **1966** *N.Y. Times* 11 Dec. 3/3 Peking newspapers.. attacked Hsia Yen, a playwright and former Deputy Minister of Cultural Affairs, as one of those in authority in the Communist party who had taken 'the capitalist road'. **1971** W. F. DORRILL in T. W. Robinson *Cultural Revol. in China* ii. 72 Numerous accusations were raised against the 'handful' in authority in the Party who were following the 'capitalist road'. **1973** T. R. TREGEAR *Chinese* iii. 58 The reliance on the profit motive and bonuses—Economism and 'taking the capitalist road', as he [*sc.* Mao] dubbed it. **1978** *China Reconstructs* Nov. 2/2 Anyone who pushed production or technical research was labeled as taking the capitalist road and ignoring politics.

7. a. A way or direction taken or pursued by a person or thing; a course followed in a journey. Freq. with possessive pronouns.

1612–8 DANIEL *St. Brit. under Saxons* Wks. (Grosart) IV. 114 Euery Coast and Part of the Land were miserably made the open rodes of spoyle and sackage. *a* **1635** RANDOLPH *Poems* (1668) 82 No venomous snake makes this his rode, No kanker, nor the loathsome toad. **1742** *De Foe's Tour Gt. Brit.* (ed. 3) I. 10, I made it my Road to pass thro' Witham. **1759** STERNE *Tr. Shandy* II. iii, No sooner was my uncle Toby satisfied which road the cannon-ball did not go, but [etc.]. **1790** BRUCE *Source Nile* I. 171 Our road was all the way in an open plain. **1891** C. ROBERTS *Adrift Amer.* 141 But I wanted to get on my road, and could not afford to lose a chance.

b. ***out of the*** (or ***one's***) ***road***, out of the way, in various senses. *dial.* or *colloq.*

1655 FULLER *Ch. Hist.* I. 2 That Britain being a by-Corner, out of the Road of the World, seemed the safest Sanctuarie from persecution. *c* **1680** DALLAS *Stiles* (1697) 904 It is out of my Road as Clerk to the Signet, to set down the Donators claim. **1698** FRYER *Acc. E. India & P.* 137 'Twas a Question out of my Road. **1721** WODROW *Hist. Suff. Ch. Scot.* (1830) I. 3 It would not be out of the road, if I should continue the thread of our.. history. **1826** A. ROYALL *Sk. Hist., Life, & Manners U.S.* 58 Put them cheers, (chairs) out of the road. **1854** MISS BAKER *Northampt. Gloss.*, *Out of one's road*, a form of expression applied negatively to a person who never loses sight of his own interest. **1863** ATKINSON *Prov. Danby*, *Out o' t' road*, remote, out of the way, inconvenient to get at. **1876** SMILES *Sc. Naturalist* ii. 40 Just gie him some-thing, Maggie, and get him oot o' the road. **1924** E. O'NEILL *Desire under Elms* III. i, in *Compl. Wks.* II. 200 Git out o' my road! Give me room! I'll show ye dancin'. **1943** K. TENNANT *Ride on Stranger* xxiv. 269 Yes, I was cowardly enough to wait until you were out of the road. **1953** *Amer. Speech* XXVIII. 253 You are in the road... Get out of my road.

c. ***in one's*** (or ***the***) ***road***, in one's way, so as to cause obstruction or inconvenience.

1854 MISS BAKER *Northampt. Gloss.* s.v., 'You're quite in one's road' is a phrase often addressed to a person who, by over-officiousness, retards instead of assists. **1876** S. R. WHITEHEAD *Daft Davie* 146 'I hope I'm no in your road,' says I. **1883** STEVENSON *Silverado Sq.* 67 He looked.. leggy, coltish, and in the road.

8. a. The usual course, way, or practice. In phr. ***out of the road of***.

1608 SHAKS. *Per.* IV. v. 9 I'll do any thing now that is virtuous; but I am out of the road of rutting for ever. **1632** MASSINGER *Maid of Hon.* IV. iv, Grant my carriage Out of the road and garb of private women, 'Tis still done with decorum. **1653** H. MORE *Conject. Cabbal.* (1713) 238 The Truth or Falshood of all that venture to speak out of the Rode of their own Sect. **1782** PRIESTLEY *Corrupt. Chr.* I. I. 114 Out of the road of plain truth and common sense. **1821** LAMB *Elia* I. *Mackery End*, Nothing goes down with her, that is quaint, irregular, or out of the road of common sympathy.

b. So ***common***, ***general***, ***usual road***. Chiefly with *out of*. (Cf. RUN *sb.*)

1612 DRAYTON *Poly-olb.* To Rdr., How many.. suspect this, his short essay of knowledge, transcending the common road? **1668** WILKINS *Real Char.* 357 Several suggestions that are new, out of the common rode. **1676** OTWAY *Don Carlos* II. i, Why should it be a stain then on my blood, Because I came not in the common road? **1708** SWIFT *Predictions for 1708*, They are not able to spell any Word out of the usual road. **1732** FIELDING *Mock Doctor* Ded., I shall not here proceed in the common road of dedications. **1778** MME. D'ARBLAY *Diary* 26 Aug., His manners are somewhat blunt.. and he is altogether out of the common road.

c. *dial.* Way, manner; esp. in phrases ***no road***, ***some road***.

1883 MISS BURNE *Shropshire Folk Lore* 45 They couldna get shet on 'em no road. **1890** 'R. BOLDREWOOD' *Col. Reformer* (1891) 327, I don't say Johnny would steal a horse. .. But he'd have one for me, some road or other. **1895** JANE BARLOW *Strangers at Lisconnel* i, It's just be the road of humouring her now and agin.

d. ***any road***, ***anyroad*** = ANYWAY *adv.* and *conj.* 3. (Chiefly *north. dial.*)

1896 F. M. T. PALGRAVE *Hetton-le-Hole Words* 38 'Any road' (anyhow). **1932** P. MACDONALD *Rope to Spare* xi. 156 Anyroad, sir, to cut a long story brief, I gets down to the mill-'ouse. **1964** O. E. MIDDLETON *Walk on Beach* ii. 28 And how is the arm today, anyroad? **1968** M. WOODHOUSE *Rock Baby* vii. 67 We knew we'd have to expect one or two failures... Any road, we crossed it off. **1976** 'J. CHARLTON' *Remington Set* i. 5 Any road, what's it to you?

II. *attrib.* and *Comb.* (chiefly in sense 4).

The examples given under 9 and 10 are only a small number of those actually in use.

9. Attrib. with names of things: **a.** In the sense 'used on or for the road', as ***road-car***, ***-chaise***, ***engine***, ***-harrow***, ***-light***, ***-locomotive***, ***-scraper***, ***tanker***, ***-wagon***, etc.

1888 *19th Cent.* Feb. 240 The box seat of an omnibus or the garden-seated top of a *road-car. **1906** *Chambers's Jrnl.* 24 Feb. 205/2 In appearance it is a very different thing from the road-car which may perhaps be regarded as its parent. **1955** A. BUDRYS in D. Knight *100 Yrs. Sci. Fiction* (1969) 251 Just before he reached the Boonesboro town line, he saw the locked and weathered cottage standing for sale... He had pulled his roadcar up to a gentle stop, swung sideways in his seat, and looked at it. **1976** *Times* 20 Mar. 14/6 Many off-track activities including a concours d'elegance of classic road cars. **1810** *Sporting Mag.* XXXV. 307 His Lordship.. came to town in a *road-chaise and four. **1875** *Encycl. Brit.* I. 323/2 (*heading*) *Road-Engines. **1886** *Walla Walla* (Washington) *Union* 24 Nov. 3/4 The 'hog' will haul nine loaded cars up the heavy Alto grade, while the ordinary road engine had a hard tussel to haul four or five. **1925** S. O'CASEY *Let.* 11 Sept. (1975) I. 147 A lumbering road-engine, with its monstrous, monotonous rumble. **1971** J. TERRELL *Bunkhouse Papers* xii. 155 A road engine purring over beyond the depot, waiting to hook on to the Limited. **1805** R. W. DICKSON *Pract. Agric.* I. 165 The *road-harrow .. seems to answer pretty well. **1869** BLACKMORE *Lorna D.* xix, Those sweet eyes that were the *road-lights of her tongue. **1879** MRS. A. E. JAMES *Ind. Househ. Managem.* 71 As road lights are not, it is very dangerous to drive unless with good lamps. **1875** KNIGHT *Dict. Mech.* 1952/2 *Road-locomotives are employed to some extent in England and in British India. **1858** SIMMONDS *Dict. Trade*, **Road-scraper*, a large metal hoe or machine for cleansing highway roads. **1864** WEBSTER, **Road-sulky*, a light, two-wheeled vehicle for one person. **1968** *Guardian* 1 Oct. 5/2 *Road tanker drivers.. are protesting against the proposal.. to install a tachograph in lorries. **1979** *Jrnl. R. Soc. Arts* CXXVII. 406/2 Oil.. would be taken by road tanker to Furzebrook. **1743** W. ELLIS *Mod. Husbandman* June iv. 37, I sent thirty-four Bushels at one Time.. by a common *Road Waggon. *a* **1787** G. WHITE *Selborne* cvi, The snow.. began to stop the road-waggons and coaches. **1808** *Sporting Mag.* XXX. 247 The driver of a road-waggon became the object of their diversion. **1880** HARDY *Trumpet-Major* II. xvi. 14 This gentleman.. suggested that Bob should wait till three or four that afternoon, when the road-waggon would arrive. **1968** J. ARNOLD *Shell Bk. Country Crafts* 150 Road-wagons could not be run during the months of winter.

b. With words denoting parts of the road, its substance or surroundings, etc., as ***road-bank***, ***-bed***, ***-bend***, ***-crossing***, ***-cut***, ***-cutting***, ***-dust***, ***-edge***, ***-end***, ***frontage***, ***island***, ***-rail***, ***sign***, ***-stone***, ***stud***, ***surface***, etc.

1863 B. TAYLOR *Hannah Thurston* III. ii. 54 As they drove homewards through the cool evening air, through.. the golden-rods on the *road-banks. **1897** *Outing* XXX. 244/2 He had jumped, and so saved himself from going over the side of the road-bank. **1840** TANNER *Canals & Railroads U.S.* Gloss., **Road-bed*, that part of a rail-road upon which the superstructure reposes. **1868** *Rep. U.S. Comm. Agric.* (1869) 349 The road-bed is back-furrowed up, so that the side gutters are from two to four feet in depth. **1902** *Chambers's Jrnl.* Jan. 61/1 In order that the oiling may be confined to the road-bed only, the rails are kept free from spraying by guards on the sprinkling-car. **1938** L. Mumford *Culture of Cities* 316 Small wonder that the Nile and the Euphrates.. were the roadbeds of their civilization. **1979** *Arizona Daily Star* 5 Aug. I. 3/1 In addition to some rocky road-beds and a pretty rotten record for staying on schedule, it is true that there are a number of well-aged cars. **1911** J. Masefield *Jim Davis* iii. 36 The watcher at the *road-bend came running back. **1841** *Civil Eng. & Arch. Jrnl.* IV. 62/1 There are five level *road-crossings. **1978** *Nature* 8 June 459/1, I have collected unweathered samples from new exposures in quarries and *roadcuts in the type area. **1936** *Discovery* Jan. 21/2 The Aculeate Hymenoptera, many of which take advantage of banks in *road-cuttings and well-trodden paths, all made by man. **1854** Dickens *Hard T.* II. vi. 195 So strange to have the *road-dust on his feet instead of the coal-grit. **1857** Thornbury *Songs Cav. & Roundheads* 188 Where the road-dust clogs and clings. **1876** W. Cory *Lett. & Jrnls.* (1897) 424 Calves are allowed to graze on the wasteful..*road-edge. **1865** Kingsley *Herew.* xxx, At the *road end, he guessed, there must be either a bridge or a ford. **1942** *London Replanned* 5/2 Better building sites on important *road frontages. **1976** *Evening Post* (Nottingham) 15 Dec. 15/4 (Advt.), Pleasant semi-detached house with half an acre of land. Road frontage 39′ 6″. **1932** L. Golding *Magnolia St.* III. iii. 511 She..took up her stand just off the pavement... Tram-drivers, chauffeurs, cyclists..accepted her as part of the landscape, like a *road-island. *c* **1830** *Treat. Roads* 11 in *Husb.* III. (L.U.K.), The importance of toughness in a *road-material. **1903** J. Masefield *Cargoes* in *Broad Sheet* No. 17, With a cargo of Tyne coal, *Road-rails, pig-lead. **1807** Vancouver *Agric. Devon* (1813) 237 About two..horseloads of *road scrapings, or way soil. **1904** *Car* VII. 240/2 *Road signs... The conference held..to consider the desirability of uniformity of action with regard to signs and notice boards. **1914** *Autocar* XXXIII. 574/2 Owing to the fact that the mutilation of road signs by sportsmen and others has caused considerable confusion..the California State Automobile Association is reported to have lately placed a bull's eye target on each post. **1949** N. Marsh *Swing, Brother, Swing* ix. 211 There's one thing..that's sticking out of this mess like a road-sign and I can't read it. **1976** P. Lively *Stitch in Time* i. 3 Maria saw this place announce itself with a road-sign. Lyme Regis. She had been studying road-signs throughout the journey. **1894** A. Morrison *Mean Streets* 199 Treacherous holes lurked in the carpet of *road-soil on the stairs. **1630** J. Taylor (Water P.) *Wks.* I. 33/2 The *roadstone bydes, And holds fast Boates, in tempests, winds, and tides. **1839** De la Beche *Rep. Geol. Cornw.*, etc. 481 Road-stones have to resist both friction and pressure. **1886** *Encycl. Brit.* XX. 583/2 The qualities required in a good road stone are hardness, toughness, and ability to resist the action of the weather. **1958** [see aggregate *ppl. a.* and *sb.* B. 5]. **1970** *Railway Mag.* Oct. 577/2 The roadstone is transferred to road vehicles for transport to the motorway site. **1935** *Economist* 11 May 1112/1 Several rather special branches of the local steel industry have experienced some increase of activity.., notably armaments, aircraft steel.. and stainless steel *road studs. **1959** E. K. Wenlock *Kitchin's Road Transport Law* (ed. 12) 112/2 No vehicle, except a solo bicycle.., may stop on a road between the road studs and the crossing. **1886** *Encycl. Brit.* XX. 583/1 The *road surface should have just enough convexity to throw the wet off freely. **1976** 'J. Ross' *I know what it's like to Die* xxiv. 151 Seeing the road surface slipping sideways as he toppled. **1838** *Penny Cycl.* X. 159/2 The *road-track of the caravans..passes through this place. **1863** Kingsley *Water-Bab.* 15 He clambered over the low *road wall. **1874** Ruskin *Fors Clav.* xlviii. 265 The surveyors of the parish insist on letting all the *road-washings run into it.

c. Miscellaneous, as ***road accident, act, atlas, -bill, casualty, -cess, -chart, construction, death, -district, expenses, haulage, junction, kill, -law, maintenance, manners, map, -march, marching, -marker, -meet, -meeting, -melody, -mile, -name, noise, project, race, -racing, -railway, rumble, safety, signing, space, speed, system, toll, -tour, traffic, transport, -web, wheel***, etc.

1935 'Owner-Driver' (*title*) *Road accidents and speed limits. **1976** P. Driscoll *Barboza Credentials* I. i. 16 A policeman..had seen the bodies of enough road-accident victims to know what to expect. **1799** J. Robertson *Agric. Perth* 357 To apply to Parliament for a particular *road act. **1905** (*title*) Pratt's *road atlas of England and Wales for motorists. **1963** *Which?* July 196/1 When maps are bound together in book form, they are called road atlases. **1791** Boswell *Johnson* 20 Mar. 1775, I was engaged as Counsel.. to oppose a *road-bill. **1971** *Guardian* 7 July 1 The Minister for Transport..announced..new measures designed to reduce *road casualties. **1878** J. Inglis *Sport & W.* ii. 11 The *road-cess has to be paid. **1879** *Encycl. Brit.* IX. 723/1 This famous map is a *road-chart rather than a record of ethnology. **1961** *Suspense* Mar. 119 One of his officers found him a job with a *road construction company. **1977** *Borneo Bull.* 7 May 17/1 (Advt.), Sakai..of Japan have been making road construction machines since 1918. **1936** A. Christie *ABC Murders* xvii. 124 There are, what is it—about 120—*road deaths every week? **1966** *Listener* 22 Sept. 412/1 The natural life of man..may still be short for many of us in organized society today, if road deaths continue at their present rate. **1868** *Rep. U.S. Comm. Agric.* (1869) 352 The taxable property in each *road district. **1839** Dickens *Let.* 1 Mar. (1965) I. 515 The money for the coach-fares and *road expences will be paid by you and Mitton. **1938** *Act 1 & 2 Geo. VI* c. 44 §1 For the purpose of regulating the remuneration of workers employed upon *road haulage work..there shall be established by the Minister of Labour ..a board..to be called the Road Haulage Central Wages Board. **1977** 'D. Rutherford' *Return Load* ii. 30 The road haulage world was a friendly one. **1936** *Discovery* Oct. 317/2 The first busy *road junction in the country to be equipped with invisible ray apparatus, to enable pedestrians to cross the roads in safety. **1972** R. & R. Wright *Cariboo Mileposts* 40 They [*sc.* magpies]..usually feed on carrion or *road-kills. **1976** *Islander* (Victoria, B.C.) 28 Mar. 7/2 Road kills have taken a few sheep of breeding age annually. **1868** *Rep. U.S. Comm. Agric.* (1869) 348 *Road laws in this magnificent State..seldom executed. **1961** *Atlanta Constitution* 6 Mar. 4 It [*sc.* DeKalb's budget] includes.. increased expenditures for essential services such as.. sanitation and *road maintenance. **1942** *Ann. Reg. 1941* 98 A serious deterioration of *road-manners. **1963** Bird & Hutton-Stott *Veteran Motor Car* 159 The result may be a hybrid but it is undeniably magnificent with better-than-100 m.p.h. performance and perfect road manners. **1883** *Wheelman* (Boston, Mass.) I. 315 The preparation of *road maps and posting of guide-boards are to be important features in next season's work. **1959** *Times* 25 June 12/6 My best aid was a road-map, which showed all dry sandy areas in Holland. **1972** 'H. Buckmaster' *Walking Trip* 112 She.. stopped at a magazine kiosk and..bought a road map of Scotland. **1960** *Times* 17 Sept. 7/7 A steelband may have any number of instrumentalists, from the basic four up to a 'carnival *road-march side' of over 100. **1977** *R.A.F. News* 8–21 June 7/1 Although very little is heard of *road marching in the UK..on the Continent it is almost a national pastime. **1970** J. McN. Dodgson *Place-Names of Cheshire* I. 166 ME *clywe, cle(o)we*..might be used here..to denote a mound serving as a landmark and *road-marker on the wild moors. **1976** *Billings* (Montana) *Gaz.* 20 June 1-B/4 Mocabee said Ferguson's motorcycle struck a road marker. **1924** J. Masefield *Sard Harker* III. 114 The tracks at the *road-meet led away to the left. **1954** J. R. R. Tolkien *Fellowship of Ring* 18 As still passed to and fro through that ancient *road-meeting. **1866** Carlyle *Inaug. Addr. Edin.* 45 A kind of *road-melody or marching-music of mankind. *c* **1669** Butler *Rem.* (1759) II. 284 His Discourse is like the *Road-Miles in the North, the filthier and dirtier the longer. **1914** *Sat. Even. Post* 4 Apr. 12/1 Beside the monakers or *road names of a hundred hoboes were scratched such messages as: 'Beware of dog'. **1965** *Eng. Stud.* XLVI. 266 The variant..can be confirmed from the Windsor road-name. **1970** J. McN. Dodgson *Place-Names of Cheshire* I. 49 The road-name *Lymestrete*. **1963** *Times* 4 June 7/7 Above 65–70 m.p.h...*road noise was high. **1973** *Times* 24 May 35/1 The engine is remarkably quiet and there is almost no road or wind noise. **1976** *Southern Even. Echo* (Southampton) 18 Nov. 32/5 Six Filipinos working on a *road project in the southern island of Mindanao were killed in an ambush. *a* **1904** W. J. Fisher *Let.* in S. Weintraub *London Yankees* vi. 201, I am anxious to do nothing to discourage motoring, and I do not at all object to this *road race. **1926** E. Hemingway *Sun also Rises* xix. 247 Organizing the road races had made him know France... All spring and all summer and all fall he spent on the road with bicycle road-racers. **1954** *Sun* (Baltimore) 24 Nov. 17/2 The world's longest road-race test of car stamina and driving skill. **1976** *Cumberland News* 3 Dec. 19/3 The Border mens' team came home in eleventh position in the Brampton to Carlisle ten mile road-race. **1828** *Sporting Mag.* XXII. 235 His happiness was *road-racing, as it is now turf-racing. **1898** *Cycling* 81 From time to time feeble revivals occur, but the doom of road-racing is sealed. **1960** E. Bowen *Time in Rome* i. 18 Hilarious buses, electric *road-railways zooming into the hills. **1952** *Jrnl. Accoustical Soc. Amer.* XXIV. 661/1 In playback of a monaural recording of *road rumble through a speaker, the observer can assign a direction to the source. **1976** *Honolulu Star-Bull.* 21 Dec. F-1/1 Undercoating insulates you from hot roads, reduces road rumble, and protects against stone chip damage. **1920** *Sci. Amer.* 6 Nov. 467 Automobile Signals for Danger Spots... New illustrations of old ideas for street comfort and *road safety. **1937** M. Borden *Black Virgin* i. 4 Road-safety instruction for school children. **1977** C. Watson *One Man's Meat* x. 95 The chief constable..muttered 'Good gracious me, road safety committee.' **1886** *Lett. fr. Donegal* 13 The '*Road-Sessions' meets twice a year in each barony. **1968** *Autocar* 14 Mar. 24/1 British *road signing is often the best in Europe. **1979** *Internat. Jrnl. Sociol. of Law* Feb. 68 There are various ways by which the police could prevent and control traffic disorders and road accidents:..proper and adequate road-signing, [etc.]. **1911** *Encycl. Brit.* XXIII. 393/1 The remainder of the *road space is formed as an earthen track. **1975** *Times* 14 Mar. (Small Car Suppl.) p. ii/3 If you took 3 ft off the average car, you would have another six million feet of road space [in London]. **1964** L. Deighton *Funeral in Berlin* xxiv. 135 It's a good road... There was no need to burn up any *road-speed records. **1977** 'E. Trevor' *Theta Syndrome* vi. 83 The TR-2 had collided with another vehicle..at a much higher road speed. **1845** *Chambers's Edin. Jrnl.* 19 Apr. 242/1 The whole *road system of Great Britain..is..the most awkward and absurd institution on the face of the earth. **1904** W. M. Ramsay *Lett. Seven Churches* xxix. 416 Laodicea was a knot on the road-system. **1932** F. L. Wright *Autobiogr.* III. 321 The United States every-where already affords increasingly great road-systems. **1976** G. Seymour *Glory Boys* i. 7 The maps..showed..the road system of northern France. **1801** *Farmer's Mag.* Apr. 193 The *road-tax (statute-labour) is stated to be 7*l.* per cent. upon the rent. **1868** *Rep. U.S. Comm. Agric.* (1869) 352 The town trustees levy a road tax each year. **1796** Marshall *W. Eng.* II. 206 A shameful *road toll. **1966** B. Castle in *Highway Code* 1 The road toll is a tragic waste—a waste of lives, a squandering of resources. **1977** *Borneo Bull.* 7 May 36/1 Razali's death pushed the road toll to 17. **1920** Wodehouse *Jill the Reckless* (1922) xviii. 269, I sold it half-way through the *road-tour. **1864** *Great Western Mag.* Jan. 36 Some idea of the startling effect which it had upon the *road traffic may be formed from the fact that the Commissioners of the Metropolitan Roads..ceased to light the roads near Kensington. **1909** *Chambers's Jrnl.* June 340/1 A successful attempt was made to conduct road-traffic without the use of animal-power. **1977** *Whitaker's Almanack 1978* 140/1 Lighting-up Times, ..under the Road Traffic Act, 1956, are from half an hour after sunset to half an hour before sunrise. **1913** H. E. Wimperis (*title*) The principles of the application of power to *road transport. **1969** *Jane's Freight Containers 1968–69* 231/1 Road-transport-weigh-bridge at the entrance of the Ueberseehafen. **1925** W. Deeping *Sorrell & Son* vi. 58 Then take the *road-web for the ordinary tourist. London some hundred miles. Salisbury thirty or so. **1939** H. Hodge *Cab, Sir?* 266 The meter records the fare..switching from miles to minutes automatically as soon as the *road-wheels stop turning. **1975** *Country Life* 2 Jan. 32/3 Sports road wheels with radial-ply tyres.

d. N. Amer. *attrib.* or as *adj.* with reference to sporting fixtures played away from home, as ***road game, trip***, etc. Cf. *on the road* above (sense 5 a) and away *adv.* 11.

1961 *Newsweek* 14 Aug. 44/3 He broadened teammates' minds by reading sensitive passages aloud during road trips. **1961** *Dallas Morning News* 10 Oct. II. 3 The Texans have two more road games—at Buffalo and Houston—before they play for the old folks again. **1968** *Globe & Mail* (Toronto) 13 Jan. 42/5 The Leafs..have won only four of 19 road games. **1973** *Weekend Mag.* (Montreal) 27 Jan. 12/2 Working with ropes and on stools in stretching exercises in hotels on long road trips. **1976** *Billings* (Montana) *Gaz.* 5 July 1-c/3 Hoff also said the Mustangs two road victories at Lethbridge helped settle the club down and give it some confidence. **1979** *Arizona Daily Star* 1 Apr. c2/4 On the road games, Bill wanted the home team to take the court first because he loved to come out and kick them off the end of the court he wanted.

10. a. Attrib., with words denoting persons, or groups of persons, esp. such as are connected with the making or control of roads, as ***road-authority, board, -contractor, -gang, haulier, -master, -party, -police, scout, -trust, -trustee***; also ***road-acquaintance, -fellow, -pilgrim***, etc.

1890 'R. Boldrewood' *Col. Reformer* (1891) 264 Any other *road acquaintances that might be encountered. **1898** *Engineering* XVI. 30 In London..the *road authority is the vestry, or district board of works. **1865** *Geelong* (Austral.) *Advertiser* 27 Feb. 123/8 (*heading*) Meredith *Road Board. **1915** *Political Q.* May 180 The Road Board..has restricted the grants to completing advances promised before the war. **1885** *List of Subscribers, Classified* (United Telephone Co.) (ed. 6) 74 (*heading*) *Contractors—road and sewer. **1936** *Discovery* Feb. 55/1 The diversion of the roadway..did not suit the plans of the road-contractors. **1873** *St. Paul's Mag.* I. 641 Your *road-fellow is almost as hard to choose as your bed-fellow. **1889** H. F. Wood *Englishman of Rue Caïn* xiv, The *road-gangs of English navvies. **1937** *Daily Tel.* 16 Feb. 7/2 (*heading*) *Road hauliers win test case. **1977** *Modern Railways* Dec. 473/1 Rail movement cannot yet match the norm of around 60,000 miles a year which properly run road hauliers get from their vehicles. **1825** *Kingston* (Ontario) *Chron.* 7 Jan. 3/3 Bulls and Oxen to run at large—Fences 5 feet high. *Road Masters to be Judges of Fences. **1856** *N.Y. Herald* 12 Jan. 1/4 James Flood is road master of his section; any obstruction being on the track it is the duty of the flagman to exhibit his red flag. **1898** *Engineering* XVI. 66 The road master..has charge, of the roadway, including the track, bridges [etc.]. **1905** Kipling *Actions & Reactions* (1909) 21 On my uncle's farm, in Connecticut. He was what they call road-master there. **1966** *Kingston* (Ontario) *Whig-Standard* 1 Sept. 3/2 The roadmaster came down on his track speeder and gave us a fatherly talking to. **1840** *Road party [see *iron gang* s.v. iron *sb.*[1] 15]. **1843** *Penny Cycl.* XXV. 141/1 Road-parties, chain-gangs, and penal settlements. **1945** Baker *Austral. Lang.* ix. 182 Heavy boots were called *road party boots*. **1890** *Cath. News* 5 July 7/4 The *road-pilgrims took four days on their journey. **1853** Cdl. Wiseman *Ess.* III. 154 At every stage we met small patrols of active *road-police. **1931** *Star* 8 May 16/1 While being chased by a *road scout on a motor-cycle ..a car collided with a lamp post. **1813** Edwards *Meas. True Policy* 66 Such Distributive Societies..would scarce differ from common *Road Trusts. **1854** McCulloch *Acc. Brit. Empire* (ed. 4) II. 51 The road..was not formed under the superintendence of *road trustees.

b. With agent-nouns, as ***road-builder, -cutter, -improver, -mender, -repairer, -surveyor, -upper, -user***, etc.

1857 Emerson *Poems* 105 Path-finder, *road-builder. **1898** *Athenæum* 19 Mar. 366/3 The original road-builders of Greece. **1880** *Lumberman's Gaz.* 7 Jan. 28 After the log-makers come the '*road-cutters', who clear away the brush and small logs. *c* **1830** *Treat. Roads* 10 in *Husb.* III. (L.U.K.), We shall now offer some rules for the guidance of *road-improvers on this head. **1824** Miss Mitford *Village* Ser. I. (1863) 231, I never wish to see a *road-mender again. **1879** Stevenson *Ess. Trav.* (1905) 186, I began an improving acquaintance with the foreman road-mender. **1921** *Dict. Occup. Terms* (1927) §44 **Road repairer*;..keeps roadways in repair below ground; [etc.]. **1932** Auden *Orators* II. 49 Acting suspiciously as road-repairers. **1868** *Rep. U.S. Comm. Agric.* (1869) 348 The immediate supervision of construction and repairs is generally under the direction of local '*road supervisors'. **1807** Vancouver *Agric. Devon* (1813) 99 The *road-surveyor, or way-warden .., takes care that such communications..are sufficiently numerous. **1858** Simmonds *Dict. Trade*, *Road-surveyor*, an officer who has the supervision of roads, and whose duty it is to see them kept in good order. **1928** *Daily Express* 12 June 3/4 The '*road-uppers' are busy in London again. **1890** *Daily News* 19 Sept. 5/4 Numerous collisions between the two classes of *road-users. **1922** *Daily Mail* 25 May 4/4 Always show..courtesy to all other road users. **1959** *Radio Times* 23 Oct. 3/1 Certain categories of road-users are barred ..; these include pedal cyclists, invalid carriages and 'L' drivers. **1976** *Oadby & Wigston* (Leics.) *Advertiser* 26 Nov. 6/5 As an ordinary citizen and road user he said he had been concerned enough about the road to see the police and Harborough District Council about it.

11. a. With vbl. sbs., as ***road-breaking, -building, -burning, -cleansing, -hugging, -patching, -pricing, -surfacing, -widening***, etc.

1900 *Daily News* 6 Dec. 5/7 There would be a very large annual saving in the avoidance of *roadbreaking. **1910** W. James in *McClure's Mag.* Aug. 467/2 To coal and iron mines,..to *road-building and tunnel-making,..would our gilded youths be drafted off. **1980** *Times* 29 Feb. 18 Civil engineers claim £200m debt backlog on road-building contracts. **1931** T. E. Lawrence *Let.* 11 Mar. (1938) 716 After that some *road-burning [i.e. fast travelling on the roads], I hope. **1843** R. J. Graves *Syst. Clin. Med.* iv. 48 The sanitary effects of *road-cleansing. **1963** *Times* 29 Jan. 3/7 The lightness of steering and smooth *road-hugging feel of the..suspension give the car..a steady gait. **1977** *Custom Car* Nov. 70/1 (Advt.), An incredibly wide tyre for road-hugging traction-action! **1974** *Evening Herald* (Rock Hill, S. Carolina) 18 Apr. 4/1 These costs—for paving, *road-patching materials, garbage containers, county employe salaries, all keep climbing each year. **1964** *Punch* 17 June 878/3 A panel research statement on '*road pricing'. **1976** P. R. White *Planning for Public Transport* x. 210 If road pricing were introduced in urban areas to indicate scarcity of road space, then some reduction in national fuel-tax rates would be appropriate. **1912** KIPLING *Diversity of Creatures* (1917) 10 The sputter and crackle of *road-surfacing machines. **1959** *Chambers's Encycl.* XI. 725/1 Many other methods of road surfacing have been experimented with. **1898** *Engineering* XVI. 35 The taking of fore-courts or a slice of garden for *road-widening.

b. With adjs., as ***road-ready***, ***-shy***, ***-weary***, ***-wise***.

1775 ASH *Suppl.*, *Roadwise*, expert in choosing the road; apt to keep the road. **1841** EMERSON *Misc.* 199 Girt and road-ready for the lowest mission of knowledge. **1872** TALMAGE *Serm.* 241 Here he comes—the Lord of Glory—dust-covered and road-weary. **1914** 'SAKI' *Beasts & Super-Beasts* 32 He [*sc.* a horse] was not really road-shy, but there were one or two objects of dislike that brought on sudden attacks of what Toby called the swerving sickness.

c. With ppl. adjs., as ***road-hauled***, ***-killed***, ***-stained***.

1969 *Jane's Freight Containers 1968–69* 2/2 European *road-hauled transport. **1980** *Topeka* (Kansas) *Capital* 23 Feb., I once unsuspectingly ate and enjoyed a turkey vulture (which my funloving host passed off as a *road-killed wild turkey). **1964** F. WARNER *Early Poems* 67 Gathering her *road-stained dress She lay within a rock recess.

12. Special combs., as **road-agent**, *U.S.*, a highway robber; hence *road-agenting*; **road allowance** *Canada*, (*a*) a strip of land retained by government authorities for the construction of a road; (*b*) an area at either side of a road which remains a public right-of-way; **road apples** *pl. N. Amer. slang*, horse droppings; **road band**, a touring group of musicians; **road-borne** *a.*, conveyed by road; also *transf.*; **road-bound** *a.*, dependent on roads; restricted to using roads; **road brand** *N. Amer.*, a temporary brand given to cattle in transit; hence as *vb. trans.*; **road breaker**, (*a*) one employed to break up the road surface prior to repair, etc.; (*b*) a mechanical tool used for this; **road bridge**, a bridge that carries a road; **road company** *U.S.*, a travelling theatrical company; **road control**, a station for checking travellers' credentials, etc.; a group of people making such checks; **road-craft**, (*a*) knowledge of or skill in matters pertaining to the use of the road; road sense; (*b*) *collect.* = *road traffic*; **road crew**, the group of 'roadies' which accompanies a touring band of musicians; **road-drift**, the scrapings of roads; **road drill**, (*a*) a mechanical drill used for breaking up road surfaces; (*b*) the routine for crossing a road safely; **road driver** *U.S.*, (*a*) one who drives animals on the road; (*b*) a long-distance lorry-driver; **road-farer**, one who travels by road; also **road-faring** *sb.* and *a.*; **road-ferry**, a ferry serving a road; **road foreman** (see quot.); **road fund**, a fund, esp. that established by the Roads Act of 1920, to meet provisions for roads; **road-glass**, *U.S.*, a road-lamp; **road hand**, *Austral.*, a man hired to assist in driving cattle, etc.; **road-head**, (*a*) *Mining*, the part of a roadway between the last support and the face; so **road-heading**, mining at a road-head; (*b*) = *road-end*; **road hockey** *Canada*, a type of hockey played in the road; **road-holding**, the ability of a car to retain its stability; **road-house**, a wayside inn or hotel; also, any roadside establishment providing refreshment or entertainment; **road hunter**, a hound which is adept at following a scent on the road; so **road-hunting** *a.*; **road jobber** (see quot.); **road kid** *slang*, a boy tramp or hobo; **road life**, the life of those who are 'on the road'; **road manager**, an organizer of tour details and supervisor of equipment, etc., for musicians 'on the road'; **road-mark**, (*a*) a road sign (in quot. *fig.*); (*b*) *U.S.* = *road brand*; **road-metal**, broken stone used in making roads; hence *road-metalling*; **road-mobile** *a.*, suitable for transporting by road; **road-money**, (*a*) money for travelling expenses; (*b*) a rate collected for the maintenance of roads; **road-monkey** (see quot. 1895); †**road-net**, a net used for taking game in a cock-road; **road oil** *N. Amer.*, oil sprinkled on the roads to lay dust; **road pane** (see PANE *sb.*[1] 9); **road patrol**, (*a*) a person or group of people patrolling the roads; (*b*) *Canada*, a machine used in the maintenance of unpaved roads; **road plate**, one of the plates carrying the roadway in an iron bridge; **road post**, (*a*) a sign-post; (*b*) a military post stationed or situated on a road; **road racer**, (*a*) a vehicle used in road-racing; (*b*) a contestant in a road race; **road-rail**, used *attrib.* with the sense 'suitable for use on both road and railway', or 'accommodating a road and a railway'; **road-railer**, a goods vehicle that can run on both road and rail (see quot. 1964); a container which can be transported by both road and rail; cf. RO-RAILER; **road rash** *slang*, grazing caused by falling from a skateboard; **road roller**, a heavy mechanical roller used for flattening road surfaces; **road-runner**, *U.S.*, the paisano or chaparral cock; **road-running** *vbl. sb.*, running on the roads for sport or exercise; also as *ppl. a.*; †**road saddle**, a riding-saddle; **road sense**, capacity for intelligent handling of vehicles or coping with traffic on the road; **road show**, a show given by touring actors or musicians, usu. with the minimum of equipment and preparation; also *transf.* and *attrib.*; hence as *vb. intr.*; **road sweeper**, (*a*) a person who sweeps roads; (*b*) a device for sweeping roads; **road train**, a large lorry pulling one or more trailers; **road tunnel**, a tunnel through which a road passes; **road-weed**, the wayside plantain; **road-woodcock**, one taken in a cock-road.

1867 W. H. DIXON *New Amer.* I. xiv. 168 *Road-agent is the name applied in the mountains to a ruffian who has given up honest work..for the perils and profits of the highway. **1881** *Macm. Mag.* XLV. 124 The great distances between the settlements enable the 'road-agents' to have a fine time of it. **1894** *Chamb. Jrnl.* 346 Something very like a contemplated bit of *road-agenting business. **1844** *Niagara* (Ontario) *Chron.* 29 May 2/2 A bill was introduced.. entitled 'An act to close up the *Road Allowance between Lots Nos. 42 and 43..in the township of Cayuga'. **1947** E. A. MCCOURT *Music at Close* 43 He..rode west along the road-allowance until he reached a part of the country which was new to him. **1958** J. G. MACGREGOR *North-West of 16* ii. 27 He carefully stepped off this distance, which was the 'road allowance', and came to another great spruce at the exact corner of his land. **1973** *Kingston* (Ontario) *Whig-Standard* 14 Mar. 3/1 In the 1783 survey of the lakefront townships, the provision had been made for a 60-foot road allowance across the front. **1942** BERREY & VAN DEN BARK *Amer. Thes. Slang* §124/2 **Road apples*, horse dung. **1951** M. SPILLANE *One Lonely Night* v. 112 Smart? Sure, just like road apples that happen behind horses. **1970** J. H. GRAY *Boy from Winnipeg* 53 The best pucks were always those supplied by passing horses, 'road apples' we called them. **1937** *Amer. Speech* XII. 48/1 **Road band*, a traveling unit. **1976** *Casper* (Wyoming) *Star-Tribune* 29 June 17/6 (Advt.), Wanted: vocalist for road band. **1977** *Zigzag* Mar. 2/1 Those guys had been my road band anyway. **1887** *Daily News* 21 May 3/2 There were two *road-borne markets within 400 yards of the proposed new market. **1914** KIPLING *Years Between* (1919) 78 That I may sing of Crowd or King or road-borne company. **1973** *Daily Tel.* 10 Aug. 14 In 1971 road-borne freight amounted to 52,000 million ton-miles. **1937** L. HART *Europe in Arms* x. 120 The limitations of the large *road-bound coaches or lorries which compose such bus columns were made manifest. **1941** *Washington Post* 4 Sept. 12/5 Members of both divisions pointed today to powerful motor vehicles roadbound because of continuous rains. **1874** J. G. MCCOY *Hist. Sk. Cattle Trade* i. 7 The slight brand put on the stock at that time [when the herd is started to market over the trail] is called a *road brand, in contradistinction to the ranch brand, which is usually put on the animal when young. **1933** J. V. ALLEN *Cowboy Lore* II. 44 When cattle were driven to market, it was easy for them to get mixed up with others, and this accounts for the *road brand*, used for rapid identification. **1955** W. FOSTER-HARRIS *Look of Old West* viii. 229 Unless a trail herd was under one brand, which ordinarily it wasn't, it was customary to road-brand the animals—that is, give them an extra insignia to identify them on their journey. **1928** *Daily Mail* 31 July 13/3 One side of Kensington-road..is also in the hands of the *road-breakers. **1967** *Gloss. Highway Engin. Terms* (*B.S.I.*) 39 *Road breaker*, a power driven tool for breaking up road pavements by impact. **1976** *Southern Even. Echo* (Southampton) 6 Nov. (Advt. Suppl.) 8/5 Road breakers, angle and straight girders, rock drills. **1819** *Massachusetts Spy* 3 Nov. 2/3 A salute was fired from a *road-bridge by a detachment..of artillery. **1870** E. G. E. WARD *Jrnl.* 13 Sept. in D. P. Carew *Many Years, Many Girls* (1967) i. 16 He had heard the Road bridge blown up, and feared the railway would follow, and that I might not get out of Paris! **1935** *Discovery* Oct. 300/2 The new road-bridge over the Severn. **1976** *Liverpool Echo* 7 Dec. 17/5 The swim is downstream of the new road bridge over the River Dee at Eccleston. **1900** *Everybody'd Mag.* II. 583/2 In the years of association which I have had..with '*road companies' I have become familiar with the types. **1959** W. FAULKNER *Mansion* ix. 205 The old road-company drammer reversed in gender: the frantic child clinging this time to the prospective groom's coattail. **1977** *New Yorker* 3 Oct. 129/1 The carryings-on of Gavino's mother, a road-company Anna Magnani in an Italian version of 'Sons and Lovers'. **1946** R. CAPELL *Simiomata* II. 69 Evert himself drove him through the German *road-controls to..the east coast of Attica. **1966** M. R. D. FOOT *SOE in France* x. 326 They were arrested by a road control that for once searched the greengrocer's lorry they were hidden in. **1868** T. WRIGHT *Great Unwashed* 265 The old tramp..has a beneficial knowledge of what may be called *road-craft. **1897** 'H. S. MERRIMAN' *In Kedar's Tents* xii. 130 Conyngham learnt much of that road-craft which had raised Concepçion Vara to such a proud eminence among the rascals of Andalusia. **1917** 'CONTACT' *Airman's Outings* 9 Mirrors of polished steel, as used on the handlebars of motor-cycles, to give warning of roadcraft at the rear. **1934** WEBSTER, *Roadcraft* .., skill or dexterity in driving on a road. **1963** *Times* 19 Feb. 11/3 What is wanted is a more radical reform in the driving test calculated to lift the standard of roadcraft as quickly as possible to the much higher level demanded by the scrum of the modern highway. **1974** *Country Life* 17 Oct. 1108 Apart from the roadcraft side, the mechanical side can pay dividends if one learns to use the car sympathetically. **1976** *Evening Post* (Nottingham) 15 Dec. 5/6 The threat is thought to follow Stewart's visit to Newcastle two years ago, when there was an incident at a city nightclub involving some of his *road crew. **1977** *Sounds* 9 July 19/2 We've got the best road crew we could find. **1838** *Civil Eng. & Arch. Jrnl.* I. 222/2 *Road drift..is certainly by no means so good as fine sand. **1861** FAIRBAIRN *Iron* 144 It is constructed of boiler plates, and lined with fire-brick, road-drift, or 'ganister'. **1934** S. SPENDER *Poems* (ed. 2) 41 At corners of day *Road drills explore new areas of pain. **1973** *Scottish Sunday Express* 5 Aug. 4/2 Clever dog to obey the road drill! **1976** 'J. FRASER' *Who steals my Name?* viii. 99 You've got the road drills outside *your* office... I can't hear myself think. **1897** *Boston Morning Jrnl.* 4 Jan. 5/6 The half-mile track is convenient of access to *road drivers from the city. *Ibid.*, The road driver frequently drives his own horse a trial mile. **1929** *Sat. Even. Post* 16 Nov. 41/3 R is for Road Driver, the name long-distance haulers give the lad that knows his cucumbers. **1973** *Amer. Speech 1969* XLIV. 207 *Road driver*, driver who drives long distances. **1923** *Daily Mail* 22 May 4 Hotels,..which set out to cater efficiently for the growing army of *roadfarers. **1961** *Times* 6 Sept. 13/4 There has even been a proposal to collar 'roadfarer' for drivers of private motor cars. **1915** R. WELLBYE (*title*) The *roadfaring handbook to inexpensive motor touring. **1925** *Chambers's Jrnl.* June 379/2 She would probably not average over 2 m.p.h., which seems almost incredible to a different section of the road-faring fraternity. **1920** *Act 10 & 11 Geo. V* c. 72 Sched. 1, The definition of 'roads' shall be extended so as to include *road-ferries and foot-ways. **1898** *Engineering* XVI. 66 A *road foreman of engines, or traveling engineer, who rides upon engines and instructs the enginemen and firemen. **1793** *Jrnl. House of Keys* (I.O.M.) 18 Dec. (MS.), Several matters, which I would mention as worthy your Serious and frequent Consideration...1st. The *Road Fund. **1845** *Chambers's Edin. Jrnl.* 19 Apr. 242/1 The whole together along with 69 steelyards, or cast-weighing machines, having cost the road fund not less than L. 10,000. **1920** *Act 10 & 11 Geo. V* c. 72 §3 There shall be established for the purposes of this Act,..a fund to be called the Road Fund. **1975** M. SIMPSON *Chrome Connection* vi. 143 Could I see your road fund licence, sir? **1883** *Cent. Mag.* Oct. 927/2 His *road-glasses illuminate the wayside. **1873** J. E. LESTER *Atlantic to Pacific* v. 28 At this station..we shall see the 'John Chinamen' as *road-hands. **1890** 'R. BOLDREWOOD' *Col. Reformer* (1891) 264 Two men, who had contracted to act as road hands and to make themselves generally useful. **1883** W. S. GRESLEY *Gloss. Coal-Mining* 205 **Road-head* (S[cottish]), see *Gate-end*. **1934** *Webster*, *Roadhead*, the end of a road (*dial.*). **1950** E. MASON *Pract. Coal Mining* I. viii. 121 (*caption*) Arrangement at the roadhead of a double unit face. **1958** J. C. F. STATHAM *Coal Mining Pract.* IV. iv. 244 About 30 per cent. of fatal and serious non-fatal accidents from falls occur at roadheads, i.e. the short length of roadway within 10 yd. of the working face. **1958** A. J. TOYNBEE *East to West* xlviii. 144 We rounded a corner and saw our car waiting for us at the road-head. **1976** *Nature* 12 Aug. 532/3, I..walked..back to the road-head. **1969** *New Scientist* 27 Feb. 444/1 These four tunnels are being driven by the four *roadheading machines. *Ibid.*, This method reduces the manpower needed for road-heading by about half. **1965** *Kingston* (Ontario) *Whig-Standard* 28 Dec. 24 (*caption*) *Road hockey was back in style Monday as these youngsters proved in a rough game played in Portsmouth during the afternoon. **1976** *Ibid.* 13 Feb. 22/1 A nearby road hockey game played with the numerous readily available road apples. **1932** *New Yorker* 14 May 32/2 Great attention has been devoted to suspension and *road-holding. **1959** G. FREEMAN *Jack would be Gentleman* iii. 50 Sports cars are..better than the average family saloon—steering, road-holding, everything that adds up to real safety. **1975** *Times* 14 Mar. (Small Car Suppl.) p. ii/9 The Mini's greatest asset is probably its road-holding. **1857** BORROW *Romany Rye* xxiii, The situation of ostler at my inn, the first *road-house in England. **1897** *Outing* XXX. 492/2 Valuable information as to routes,.. distances and road-houses. **1936** O. LANCASTER *Progress at Pelvis Bay* 63 Many..who..motor down..by way of the new Flush-brook By-pass, must be familiar with the ..'Hearts Are Trumps' roadhouse. **1944** 'N. SHUTE' *Pastoral* i. 8 In peace-time it had been something of a road-house, with a snack-bar. **1957** J. BRAINE *Room at Top* x. 92 Four months in Warley had given me a fixed taste for either the roadhouse or the authentic country pub. **1972** D. ANTHONY *Blood on Harvest Moon* ii. 18 Across the highway was a roadhouse where, according to the sign, you could dine, dance, and drink. **1897** *Encycl. Sport* I. 560/1 The only thing he [*sc.* the huntsman] *can* do is to..try every gateway and likely-looking spot where she [*sc.* the hare] may have turned off or lain down, but it is a mere matter of luck unless he has the real *road hunter. **1977** *Horse & Hound* 14 Jan. 20/1 In the old days they [*sc.* foxes] probably ran the roads much more because they were quieter. The minor roads were not even tarmacked, with the result that you had your '*road hunting hounds' much more frequently. **1817** *Sporting Mag.* L. 30 The profits of the *Road Jobbers, namely the Guards and Drivers of Mail and other Coaches, will be at an end. **1970** J. LONDON *Road* 173 A boy on the Road..is never a gay-cat; he is a *road-kid or a 'punk'. **1937** 'D. BOYLE' *Keeping in Trouble* iii. 38 He was a 'road-kid', that is to say he found his company, within the great confederation of tramps, with youngsters of his own age or less. **1902** *N.Y. Times Mag.* 28 Dec. 12/1 A comedian who has seen so much of the unlovely side of '*road' life that he might well be the writer of tragedies. **1956** B. HOLIDAY *Lady sings Blues* viii. 93 He always wanted me to ride up with him ..and sometimes Benny, our *road manager. **1978** *Detroit Free Press* 16 Apr. 23A/3 Police..accused the road manager, who wasn't identified, of giving alcohol to a 14-year-old and an 18-year-old girl. **1879** G. M. HOPKINS *Lett. to R. Bridges* (1955) 77 The island was so Marian that the very Milky Way we made a *roadmark to that person's shrine. **1881** *Lippincott's Mag.* XXVII. 570/1 Every animal, besides the regular brand of the owner, has his tail bobbed and a 'road-mark' put upon him during the drive. **1908** MURRAY & MILLER *Round-Up* 268 Having cut out the stock for the drive, a road mark, a supplementary brand for identification, is burned into the hides. **1838** *Civil Eng. & Arch. Jrnl.* I. 383/2 The *road metal is then to be laid on, in two successive coats. **1884** *Cent. Mag.* XXIX. 48/1 A pile of stones broken to the size of road-metal. **1871** *Athenæum* July 115 That form of *road-metalling..which in England is associated with the honourable name of Macadam. **1884** W. H. GREENWOOD *Steel & Iron* 80 The materials are broken into cubes of two inches resembling road-metalling. **1922** *Encycl. Brit.* XXX. 249/1 The French guns up to the 6 in., and howitzers up to the 9.45 in. inclusive will be *road-mobile... All heavier natures will be on railway mountings. **1843** CARLYLE *Past & Pres.* IV. i, Except small modicum of *roadmoney, not a gold coin in his possession. **1844** H.

STEPHENS *Bk. Farm* III. 1322 Road-money and schoolmaster's salary are also sometimes paid by the tenant. **1895** *Standard Dict.* s.v. *Road*, **Road-monkey*, a man employed by lumbermen in repairing logging roads. **1901** *Munsey's Mag.* XXV. 390/1 Finally, the 'road-monkeys', with shovels, remove the last appearance of a drift. **1581** *Act 23 Eliz.* c. 10 §6 Others, which..take any Partridges or Feasaunts by night vnder any Tramel, Lowbell, *Roadenete or other Engyn. **1921** *Daily Colonist* (Victoria, B.C.) 8 Apr. 6/3 The Saanich works committee last night authorized the purchase of £7,000 worth of *road oil and one hundred tons of asphalt. **1976** *Billings* (Montana) *Gaz.* 1 July 1-C/3 Finally, the commission approved the purchase of 25,000 gallons of road oil from the state. **1805** R. W. DICKSON *Pract. Agric.* II. pl. 22, I, I, are the way- (or *road-) panes, watered from the banks of the mains. **1899** KIPLING *Stalky & Co.* 252, I engineering myself..into command of a *road-patrol—no shovellin', only marching up and down. **1958** *Cut Knife* (Saskatchewan) *Grinder* 3 Apr. 1/6 In the Rural Municipality of Cut Knife, the burgesses were asked to vote upon Bylaw 12 authorizing the Council to purchase a new road patrol. **1963** *Times* 8 Jan. 11/1 Their road patrols say that many motorists are unaware that a dry cloth, or some paper handkerchiefs used to soak up the condensation or melted snow thrown over the sparking plugs, leads and distributor, could often save them from being stranded. **1970** *R.A.C. Guide & Handbk.* 39 Road Patrols..equipped with vans, are on daily duty. **1840** *Civil Eng. & Arch. Jrnl.* III. 133/2 When the main ribs..rested on their centres, and before any of the spandrils and *road plates had been put upon them. **1805** COLMAN *John Bull* I. i, Na; that be the *road post. **1896** BADEN-POWELL *Matabele Campaign* xix, At Marendellas..we passed one of the fortified road posts. **1908** H. G. WELLS *War in Air* i. 14 Even a *road-racer, geared to a hundred and twenty, failed to satisfy him. **1954** *Sun* (Baltimore) 24 Nov. 17/2 *(heading)* Road racers top 3 marks. **1976** *Norwich Mercury* 19 Nov. 12/1 For road racers and scramblers the financial drain is even worse. **1927** *Times* 20 Dec. 11/3 The '*road-rail' truck represents in a modified form the upper part of a railway wagon which can be exchanged between road and rail vehicles. **1963** *Times* 8 June 14/3 Two-day talks between British and French Government officials on whether there should be a Channel rail bridge or a road-rail tunnel ended in London yesterday. **1977** *Modern Railways* Dec. 494/1 The works include..the rebuilding of 20 stations to create fully-equipped road-rail interchanges. **1960** *London Midland Region Staff News* (Brit. Railways) Feb./Mar., The *Roadrailer..is similar in appearance to the normal tractor drawn semi-trailer seen on the roads. It differs in two respects, however. At the rear, there is a special device which retracts the road wheels and lowers a pair of rail wheels. At the front, a special coupling fits into the rear end of another similar trailer. **1964** *Economist* 15 Aug. 663/3 British Railways' latest ploy to attract traffic from the roads involves..freight wagons which ride the rails for most of the journey and then take to the roads as trailers to deliver goods directly to the customers' door-step. British Roadrailer Services is being set up as a joint company by British Railways and the Transport Holding Company to develop the use of these roadrailers. **1965** *Ibid.* 26 June 1559/2 The lorry people might make use of liner trains, or better, the new 'roadrailers' (of which they own half with the railways), for convenient loads of odd packages on the longer runs. **1976** *Daily Tel.* (Colour Suppl.) 30 July 10/3 It is hard on both rider and wardrobe. Young skateboarders proudly show off their '*road rashes'. **1978** *Skatcat's Quiz Bk.* (R. Soc. Prevention of Accidents) 5 'Road rash' isn't clever. As well as hurting for over a week, bad grazes or cuts are the signs of bad skateboarding. **1886** *Encycl. Brit.* XX. 583/1 In Great Britain horse-rollers have to a great extent been superseded by steam *road rollers. **1971** *Daily Nation* (Nairobi) 10 Apr. 25/2 Tenders are invited for one three-wheel road roller. **1856** *Hutching's Mag.* Nov. 201/2 The *Road-Runner is seldom seen in trees, unless pursued very closely. **1872** COUES *N. American Birds* 189 Ground Cuckoo. Chaparral Cock. Road Runner. **1885** *Harper's Mag.* Feb. 423/1 This bird is called scientifically the *Geococcyx Californianus*, but is popularly known under several other names, such as road-runner. **1930** R. MACAULAY *Staying with Relations* xix. 275 Not a thing to look at, on this so-called road, only cactus and chaparral and road-runners and those darned flowering aloes. **1972** G. DURRELL *Catch me a Colobus* ix. 188 A Road-runner—a strange little bird with a crest and a long tail and enormous flat feet. **1908** A. SHRUBB *Running* x. 66 Of all forms of pedestrianism..there can be nothing superior to cross-country running... Track or *road running is apt to grow monotonous, however exciting it may be; but there is nothing monotonous in an open country run. **1934** V. WOOLF *Writer's Diary* (1953) 216, I cannot without more labour than my roadrunning mind can compass describe the queer impression of sunny impersonality. **1962** LYDIARD & GILMOUR *Run to Top* viii. 68 Ordinary tennis shoes..don't cushion against the constant jarring of road running which can damage leg joints. **1976** *Cumberland News* 26 Nov., Go into the road running strongholds. **1710** *Lond. Gaz.* No. 4784/4 Likewise a short *Road Saddle taken. **1923** *Daily Mail* 10 Aug. 6/3 The good driver uses care instinctively because he has the imagination or '*road-sense' which tells him instantly what he can and what he cannot do. **1947** J. DEAN *Murder Most Foul* v. 98 Before the war the B.B.C. conceived the..idea of engaging racing drivers to give broadcasts on 'road sense'. **1975** 'M. YORKE' *Small Hours* ii. 20 She was..bad at parking..though her road sense was good. **1908** *Variety* 16 May 1 De Dio, a foreigner,..has been engaged by Martin Beck for his Orpheum *Road show next season. **1939** J. B. PRIESTLEY *Let People Sing* xiv. 412 I'm booking acts for a road-show. **1942** BERREY & VAN DEN BARK *Amer. Thes. Slang* §596/2 *Go on tour*,..road-show. **1959** *Time* 28 Sept. 32/3 Road-showing in Cole Porter's *Can-Can* in Toronto, the French singer-comedienne..had to negotiate a ramp leading out of the tent-theater. **1961** *Wall St. Jrnl.* 8 Nov. 3/2 The Kennedy Administration opened its road show to inform citizens across the country what's going on in Washington. **1976** J. MCCLURE *Rogue Eagle* ii. 28 The sprained ankle which forced her to drop out of an American roadshow. **1977** *Time* 25 Apr. 52/1 Some were impressed more by the viewpoint espoused in the road-show tactics of Phyllis Schlafly, an Alton, Ill., housewife and an active Republican. **1909** *N.E.D.*, s.v. *Roader*[1] 4, A *road-sweeper. **1937** *Times British Motor Number* 13 Apr. p. xxxviii/2 The Karrier road sweeper..is also popular abroad. **1939** G. B. SHAW *Geneva* I. 16 The president and parliament are elected by adult suffrage every two years. So are all the judges and all the officials, even the road sweepers. **1973** *Times* 18 June 3/2 Teachers at a local school have been parking outside and thereby frustrating the mechanical road sweeper. **1959** *Road train [see *pedal-radio* s.v. PEDAL *sb.* 7]. **1964** L. DEIGHTON *Funeral in Berlin* xxxi. 164 One of those heavy trucks with two trailers that they call 'road trains'. **1977** 'D. RUTHERFORD' *Return Load* i. 12 The driver of the Scania road train drew level with the cab of the British vehicle. **1939** *Encycl. Brit. Bk. of Year* 684/1 A project of a new *road tunnel through the St. Gothard. **1976** J. LUND *Ultimate* x. 91 The long road tunnels through the mountain got them there quickly. **1857** HENFREY *Bot.* 330 Plantains or *Road-weeds, are among the commonest of our weeds on road-sides. **1826** POLWHELE *Trad. & Recoll.* II. 376 A couple of *road-woodcocks..for a shilling, and with a couple of road-woodcocks we had just been presented.

road, obs. variant of RODE, rope. *U.S.*

road (rəʊd), *v.*[1] Also 7 rode. [f. ROAD *sb.*]

The following apparent examples are very obscure, and may be due to misprints:—**1588** PARKE tr. *Mendoza's Hist. China* 114 The fashion of their ships, aswell of those that passe the seas, as of those that doo roade riuers. **1625** PURCHAS *Pilgrimes* II. 1649 They are as it were halfe fishes, they are so vsed to the Sea, whither they goe daily either swimming or roading or sailing.

†**1.** *intr.* To make raids. *Obs. rare.*

1600 HOLLAND *Livy* XXXVIII. xl. 1007 He gaue them warning, to leave their manner of roding and roving in hostile wise. **1710** *Lond. Gaz.* No. 4724/3 The same Partisan having roaded some Days in this Neighbourhood with a strong Party,..all possible Precautions are taken.

2. †**a.** *trans.* To traverse (a way). *Obs.*[-1]

1623 H. SYDENHAM *Serm. Sol. Occ.* II. (1637) 19 Here is a large field offered mee,..but this is not my way, it is too trodden, every Hackney rodes it.

b. To do (a distance) on the road. *U.S.*

1884 *Boston* (Mass.) *Herald* Mar., The horse..can road easy 10 miles per hour.

c. *to road it*, to keep to, or go by, the road.

1893 *Field* 11 Feb. 192/1 A few came mounted, determined to 'road it' until they could without damage to the crops follow the hounds.

road (rəʊd), *v.*[2] [Of doubtful origin; connexion with *v.*[1] is not clear.] *trans.* Of a dog: To follow up (a game-bird) by the foot-scent. Also with *up*, and *absol.* (Cf. the earlier ROADER[2].)

1856 'STONEHENGE' *Brit. Rural Sports* I. iv. 47/1 As retrievers do all their work by 'roading' or 'footing', they require that peculiar kind of nose. *Ibid.* 52/1 The dogs..must never be inclined to 'foot' or 'road' the birds till ordered. **1884** T. SPEEDY *Sport Highl.* xv. 269 Although a pointer may 'road' them up (and point at them), they often slip off again. **1892** *Sport. & Dram. News* 30 Jan. 678/1 Choleric..at the sight of his canine favourites..'roading' birds all over the place. **1894** *Outing* XXIV. 425/1 Juno..commenced roading down a potato furrow.

Hence **'roading** *ppl. a.*

c **1880** 'PATHFINDER' *Breaking & Training Dogs* 8 A cross between a good roading foxhound and a..Gordon setter.

road, *v.*[3] (to clear of weeds): see RODE *v.*[1]

road, *v.*[4] (of woodcock or wild fowl): see RODE *v.*[2]

roadability (rəʊdəˈbɪlɪtɪ). [f. ROAD *sb.* + ABILITY.] Suitability for being driven on the road; roadworthiness; road-holding ability.

1925 C. MORLEY *Safety Pins* 116 When the car has a 126-inch wheelbase, it makes it very easy riding and gives it charming 'roadability'. **1928** *Sunday Dispatch* 16 Sept. 5 (Advt.), Wider track, lower centre of gravity, improved roadability. **1973** *Sci. Amer.* Dec. 2/1 (Advt.), Put these characteristics of engine performance and roadability together, and it's not surprising that BMW owners will tell you no other car comes close for combining brilliant responsiveness with precise control.

roadable (ˈrəʊdəb(ə)l), *a.* [f. ROAD *sb.* + -ABLE; see prec.] Suited to being driven on roads.

1929 *Bookman* (N.Y.) May 301/1 Motor car advertising of the past decade has brought forth the remarkable word 'roadability'... A car that has 'roadability' is, presumably, 'roadable'; that is, it can be roaded—whatever that might mean. **1935** A. P. HERBERT *What a Word!* ii. 51 What sort of a car, I wonder, is a car which is not 'roadable'? **1972** *Daily Tel.* 22 Nov. 4/5 A 'roadable' aircraft has been shown at the Detroit Motor Show... It can be driven on the road or flown from an area smaller than a football field.

roadblock (ˈrəʊdblɒk). Also road block, road-block. [f. ROAD *sb.* 4 + BLOCK *sb.* 19 a.]

a. A barrier or obstruction on a road, usu. one set up by the army or police.

1940 *Hutchinson's Pict. Hist. War* 7 Aug.–1 Oct. 4 Demonstrations of how to build road-blocks, how to deal with tanks,..how to deal with refugees on the road, are all part of the Home Guard training. **1943** *Ann. Reg. 1942* 63 The road blocks for obstructing tanks were also found to be much more formidable than had been anticipated. **1954** X. FIELDING *Hide & Seek* v. 67 Pedestrians..were often searched by the sentries manning the road-blocks. **1958** 'A. GILBERT' *Death against Clock* xii. 167 When you put up your road blocks, then I have to take the diversion. **1971** *Daily Tel.* 23 July 1/5 A soldier fired at a car which broke through a roadblock, hitting the back window. **1977** *Centuryan* (Office Cleaning Services) Christmas 15/4 They had not gone far before they came to a roadblock caused by an accident. **1978** *N.Y. Times* 30 Mar. A5/2 The complex is now guarded by 14,000 riot policemen who man roadblocks and monitor highway traffic from camouflaged roadside positions.

b. *fig.*

1945 *Tuscaloosa* (Alabama) *News* 19 June 4/5 The French general is probably the only remaining road-block to Communism in France. **1952** *Sun* (Baltimore) 29 Feb. 19/3 This bill has been subjected to roadblock after roadblock by those attempting to delay its passage during these closing days of 1952 General Assembly session. **1957** *Economist* 7 Sept. 770/1 In every direction the logic of the Korean economy runs headlong into a political roadblock. **1963** J. MITFORD *Amer. Way of Death* v. 177 An English contributor to the American *Professional Embalmer* describes some of the roadblocks he has encountered. **1977** MILLER & SWIFT *Words & Women* v. 71 Nowhere are the semantic roadblocks to sexual equality more apparent—or significant—than in the language of the dominant organized religions.

Hence as *v. trans.*

1954 in WEBSTER Add. **1955** *Newsweek* 10 Jan. 20/1 The debate that followed roadblocked Mr. Eisenhower's legislative program for weeks. **1965** *Canad. Jrnl. Linguistics* X. 153 The analysis of texts, opening the way to ethnographic and historical studies that otherwise would still be roadblocked. **1972** *Listener* 10 Feb. 167/2 The Army road-blocked Newry.

'road-book. Also road book. [ROAD *sb.* 4.]

1. A book exhibiting or describing the roads of a district or country. Also *transf.*

1798 JANE AUSTEN *Northang. Abb.* vii, Morland pleaded the authority of road-books, innkeepers and mile-stones. **1806–7** J. BERESFORD *Miseries Hum. Life* (1826) VI. 12 After starting on a very long journey.., discovering that you have left your road-book behind. **1849** MACAULAY *Hist. Eng.* iii. I. 311 These computations are strongly confirmed by the road books and maps of the seventeenth century. **1881** *Times* (weekly ed.) 25 Sept. 14/3, I am not writing a road-book or a river-book. **1931** *Times Lit. Suppl.* 29 Jan. 80/2 The civil aviation section [of *Jane's All the World's Aircraft*] continues to act as a world-wide aviation 'road-book'.

2. A narrative of a journey by road. Also *spec.*, a log-book kept by the driver of a commercial vehicle.

1882 FLOYER *Unexpl. Baluchistan* 393 Ghulamshah set to work washing our flannel shirts, and I to writing up the road-book. **1939** 'N. BLAKE' *Smiler with Knife* xvii. 246 You sign my road-book, cock, or I'm not opening this van.

roade, obs. variant of RODE, rope. *U.S.*

'roaded, *a.* [f. ROAD *sb.* 4.] Provided or laid out with roads.

1880 *Daily News* 4 Oct. 2/2 A unique estate, consisting of 240 acres, all scientifically drained and roaded. **1890** *Pall Mall G.* 28 June 3/3 The estate..is well roaded.

roaded, streaked: see RODED *a.*

roadeo (ˈrəʊdiːəʊ). *U.S.* [f. ROAD *sb.*, after RODEO.] A gathering of lorry drivers for competitive events in and exhibitions of driving skill.

1948 *Sun* (Baltimore) 23 Aug. 11/1 To be eligible to enter the roadeo drivers must have completed one year of no-accident driving for the same employer. **1952** *N.Y. Times* 12 Oct. II. 18/2 The American Trucking Associations, Inc., was holding its annual Roadeo, a competition for champion, professional truckdrivers. *Ibid.* 18/2 The Roadeo course is a hard test of man's ability at the wheel. **1955** *Amer. Speech* XXX. 150 The roadeo or competition of truck drivers is now a familiar institution. **1971** M. TAK *Truck Talk* 131 *Roadeo*, the National Truck Roadeo, an exhibition and competition of driving skills in various classifications of motor vehicles for expert truckers.

roader[1] (ˈrəʊdə(r)). [f. ROAD *sb.*[1] or *v.*[1]]

†**1.** One who rides about. *Obs.*[-0]

1580 HOLLYBAND *Treas. Fr. Tong*, *Roder le pays*, to make a roade in the countrey... *Vn rodeur ou coureur*, a roder or wighrider [1593 wayrider].

2. A ship lying at anchor in a road; a vessel which rides (well or ill).

1556 in Hakluyt *Voy.* (1598) I. 275, I caused the Pinnesse to beare in with the shore,..and [she] saw two roaders ride in the sound. **1589** *Ibid.* (1599) II. II. 161 By the way as we rowed we saw boates passing betwixt the roaders and the shore. **1644** MANWARING *Seaman's Dict.* s.v., We call any ship that Rides at an Anchor in a Roade, a Roader. **1692** *Capt. Smith's Seaman's Gram.* I. xvi. 81 *A Road*, is any place near the Land where Ships may ride at Anchor, and a Ship riding there is called a Roader. **1769** FALCONER *Dict. Marine* (1780) s.v. *Riding*, When a ship..pitches violently into the sea, so as to strain her cables, masts, or hull, it is called riding hard, and the vessel is termed a bad roader.

3. = ROADSTER 2.

1825 *Spirit Publ. Jrnls.* 415 They hired my mare, as capital a roader as ever was backed, thof I say it myself. **1884** *Boston* (Mass.) *Jrnl.* 7 June, To purchase a strictly first-class roader or a trotter.

4. A road-sweeper, road-cleaner.

1883 BESANT *All in a Garden fair* II. x, Among the Roaders—that..useful body who sweep the roads for the omnibus horses. **1886** —— *Childr. Gibeon* II. iv, He began to drink, and then he had to be a roader for the parish at eighteen pence a day.

5. (See quot.)

1902 *Times* 14 Feb. 13/3 He was informed by the engine-driver that a 'roader' (*i.e.*, a parcel to be put out at a roadside station) had been put on the engine.

6. *Taxi-drivers' slang.* A long-distance taxi fare or journey.

1939 H. HODGE *Cab, Sir?* ii. 28 It may be a long job—a 'roader' as we call it—out to Richmond or Highgate. **1978** *London-Wide Radio Taxis* (Licensed Taxi Drivers Assoc. Ltd.) [Publicity leaflet] p. iii/2 Roaders are an everyday event on radio. Put yourselves into the shoes of a director of a company who requires a taxi for a long distance haul. Does he go out into the street and hail a cab or send his secretary to find one? Of course he doesn't. He rings for a cab.

7. ***capitalist roader*** [tr. Chinese *zǒuzīpài*, short for *zǒu zīběn zhǔyì dàolù dāngquánpài*], esp. during the Cultural Revolution in China, a term for Party officials, e.g. the secretary of a provincial Party committee or the chairman of a people's commune, who were alleged to have capitalist tendencies. Cf. *capitalist road* s.v. ROAD *sb.* 6 g.

Used of people of various views who are out of favour with the Chinese leadership.

1967 *Economist* 7 Oct. 26/1 The unsurprising absence of Liu Shao-chi, Teng Hsiao-ping and their fellow 'capitalist-roaders' brings the politburo membership down from the 24 who were elected in the first flush of the cultural revolution in August 1966 to the 15 who are still appearing today. **1970** E. SNOW *Red China Today* (rev. ed.) xlix. 389 Lau Shaw himself committed suicide in 1966 when he was attacked by Red Guards as a 'revisionist' and 'capitalist roader'. **1973** R. TAYLOR *Educ. & Univ. Enrolment Policies in China, 1949–1971* 15 The so-called capitalist-roaders refused to admit any of them on the grounds that worker-peasant children were not of high enough scholastic calibre. **1976** *Financial Times* 24 Nov. 6/1 The official Hsinhua news agency, writing about Mme. Mao and the so-called 'gang of four' or the 'new capitalist roaders', was saying that she was a 'big careerist' who 'prostrated herself in admiration before Western bourgeois things'. **1978** HUA KUO-FENG in *Peking Rev.* 10 Mar. 11/1 The 'gang of four'..openly dished up a counter-revolutionary political programme equating veteran cadres with 'democrats' and 'democrats' with 'capitalist-roaders' and agitated for rounding up 'capitalist-roaders' at all levels from the central down to the local.

ˈroader^2. [Cf. ROAD *v.*^{2}] A dog which pursues game by the foot-scent.

1817 *Sporting Mag.* L. 231 This circumstance is of the greatest advantage to the spaniel; for it enables him to be a good roader, as it is styled in the south. **1822** *Ibid.* IX. 174 The slaughter of late effected by the 'roaders', as some call them, and the heavy gunners.

ˈroad-goose. Also 9 rode-. [App. repr. some local form, such as *rood-*, *rudegoose* in Ross, or *rade-*, *raid-goose* in Orkney and Shetl. All later instances appear to be mere echoes of Willughby.] = RAT-GOOSE.

a **1672** [see RAT-GOOSE]. **1674** RAY *Coll. Words* 95 The road-Goose, or small Wild Goose. **1753** CHAMBERS *Cycl. Suppl.*, *Road goose*, in zoology, the name of a small species of wild goose. **1768–1824** [see RAT-GOOSE]. **1894** NEWTON *Dict. Birds* 793 *Rode-goose*, a local name given by fowlers to the Brant-Goose.

road hog, *sb.* [f. ROAD *sb.* 4 + HOG *sb.*^{1} 7 c.] One who is objectionable on the road; one who drives without consideration for others, esp. a reckless cyclist or motorist.

1891 *Outing* Dec. 238/2 The 'road hog' curses him and the wayside brute calls out the dog. **1898** *Harper's Mag.* XCVI. 689 Beware of Swiss drivers; they are the greatest 'road hogs' in Europe. **1909** *Q. Rev.* Jan. 143 The habitually reckless motorist..commonly known as the 'road-hog'. **1925** *Public Opinion* 14 Aug. 151/3 Road-hogs who run down pedestrians. **1932** D. L. SAYERS *Have his Carcase* ii. 29 A fast saloon car..overtook them... 'The beastly road-hog!' said Mr. Perkins. **1970** 'D. HALLIDAY' *Dolly & Cookie Bird* iv. 52 You're a road-hog... What do you drive at home? **1972** K. BONFIGLIOLI *Don't point that Thing at Me* xiv. 122 'Lost my temper... Bloody roadhog.' 'He might easily have done us a mischief,' I agreed.

Hence **ˈroad-hog** *v. intr.*, to be or act like a road hog; so **ˈroad-hogging** *vbl. sb.* and *ppl. a.* Also **ˈroad-hoggery**, behaviour characteristic of a road hog; **ˈroad-hoggish** *a.*, having the driving habits of a road hog; hence **ˈroad-hoggishness**; **ˈroad-hoggism**, a road-hoggish act.

1914 'I. HAY' *Knight on Wheels* xviii. 174, I wouldn't go road-hogging if I were you... Road-hogging is rotten bad form. **1923** *Daily Mail* 28 May 5 In four days, without road-hogging, we have covered 646 miles of Britain. **1926** *Glasgow Herald* 12 July 6/3 The perfect Sunday—to hide at home while the rest of the world road-hogged it out of town. **1927** *Scots Observer* 16 July 10/4 Avoiding excess of speed and other road-hoggisms. **1928** *Daily Express* 24 Apr. 10/2 The road-hogging motor-coach. **1930** *Time & Tide* 7 Feb. 172 No motorist, however road-hoggish he may be, deliberately slays a child or any other person. **1933** A. MORRIS *Digging in Southwest* 80 Road-hogging is one of the most anti-social characteristics in the world. **1963** *Guardian* 21 Jan. 6/3 Chief vice of bad drivers.—Men: Sheer selfishness and road-hoggery. **1965** *Punch* 28 July 138/3 The film started with the customary pop music and some sinister hints of teenage drug-taking, road-hoggishness, violence and debauchery. *Ibid.* 20 Oct. 569/2 Some road-hoggery was due to the imperfect construction of the motor car. **1974** D. FRANCIS *Knock Down* xiv. 174 Letting loose that road-hogging two-year-old.

ˈroad-horse. Also 1 rádhors, 4 roode-, 4–5 rode-. [f. ROAD *sb.*^{1} 1 and 4.]

†**1.** A riding-horse. *Obs.*

c **1000** ÆLFRIC *Hom.* (Assmann) VIII. 233 Man sceal.. lætan hine ridan on þæs cyninges radhorse. **1388** WYCLIF *1 Kings* iv. 26 Salomon hadde fourty thousynd cratchis of horsis for charis, and twelue thousynde of roode horsis. **1424** *E.E. Wills* (1882) 58 Þe remenaunt of my rode horses I wul be departyd. **1547** *Ancaster MSS.* (Hist. MSS. Comm.) 455 The holl nombre of road horses and geldinges, as well ambelinge as trottinge.

2. A horse serviceable for, or used on, the road.

1743 BRACKEN (*title*), Traveller's Pocket Farrier,..with Directions for the Choice of a Good Road-Horse. **1790** BEWICK *Hist. Quadrup.* (1824) 9 The old English Road-horse is a strong, vigorous, and active kind, capable of enduring great hardship. **1890** *Atlantic Monthly* Apr. 517/1 In a sense, every horse driven by the owner for pleasure is a road horse. **1897** *Boston* (Mass.) *Jrnl.* 4 Jan. 2/2 Some of the owners of fast road-horses.

roadie (ˈrəʊdɪ), *sb.* Also **roady**. [f. ROAD *sb.* + -Y^6, -IE.] = *road manager*; an assistant employed by a touring musical band whose duties include the erection and maintenance of equipment. Hence as *v. intr.*

1969 FABIAN & BYRNE *Groupie* ix. 72 Bill, the roadie, buys me a drink. **1972** *Daily Tel.* (Colour Suppl.) 17 Nov. 26/3 Each individual musician has his own personal roady who is an expert in the instrument that his governor plays. **1976** *New Musical Express* 17 Apr. 24/5 Even allowing for roadies and so on, aren't there far too many people being supported by far too few? **1976** *Star* (Sheffield) 20 Nov., The author once roadied for the band. **1980** *Times Lit. Suppl.* 28 Mar. 365 He even gets paid as a roadie on tour.

ˈroading, *vbl. sb.*^{1} [f. ROAD *v.*^{1}]

1. Racing with teams upon the road.

1787 W. MARSHALL *Rur. Econ. Norf.* (1795) I. 44 The young men who took delight in the diversion of 'roading'.

2. a. The making or repairing of roads.

1883 GRESLEY *Gloss. Coal-mining*, *Roading*, repairing and maintaining roads. **1895** *Daily News* 21 Nov. 5/5 Instances of bad roading or lack of sanding.

b. *concr.* A road surface. *rare.*

1857 J. E. RITCHIE *Night Side of London* 5 The cost of this paved roading was 14 millions.

3. Performance of a horse on the road.

1890 *Atlantic Monthly* Apr. 524/1 She accomplished forty-three miles in three hours and twenty-five minutes. This was great roading.

ˈroading, *vbl. sb.*^{2} [var. of *roding*: see RODE *v.*^{2}] The practice, on the part of certain birds, of flying in the evening. Also *attrib.*

1888 *Encycl. Brit.* XXIV. 651/1 During this season the male Woodcock performs at twilight flights of a remarkable kind... This characteristic flight is in some parts of England called 'roading'. **1898** WOLLOCOMBE *From Morn till Eve* 246 It was roading time. We turned and cocked our guns.

ˈroadless, *a.* [f. ROAD *sb.* 4 + -LESS.] Destitute of roads; having no road(s).

1837 SYD. SMITH *Let. to Singleton* Wks. 1859 II. 288/2 In the most roadless, postless, melancholy, sequestered hamlet. **1849** EASTWICK *Dry Leaves* 137 The next march brought the troops to a steep and roadless hill. **1877** BLACKMORE *Cripps* III. i. 8 In these roadless parts distance was very much a matter of conjecture.

Hence **ˈroadlessness**.

1880 CRAWFURD *Portugal Old & New* 369 Portugal in its long-enduring condition of roadlessness.

ˈroad-maker. [ROAD *sb.* 1 and 4.]

†**1.** One who makes an inroad or raid. *Obs.*$^{-0}$

1611 COTGR., *Voleur*,..an inroder, or a road-maker.

2. One who makes roads.

1799 J. ROBERTSON *Agric. Perth* 362 Might not gentlemen ..contract with an improved road-maker at a particular price by the mile? **1841** *Penny Cycl.* XX. 30/2 The general practice of modern roadmakers is to make the surface slightly convex. **1860** FROUDE *Hist. Eng.* V. 417 His successes..were chiefly due to the woodman, the roadmaker, and the mason.

ˈroad-making, *vbl. sb.* [ROAD *sb.* 4.] The act of constructing a road; the practice of making roads.

1801 *Farmer's Mag.* Aug. 285 In no instance is the police of Aberdeenshire so defective as in road-making. **1811** MᶜADAM in *Pres. System Road Making* (1822) 36 Road-making..is even worse understood in Scotland than in England. **1841** *Penny Cycl.* XX. 31/1 The very imperfect mode of road-making formerly practised. **1878** RUSKIN *Fors Clav.* lxxxvi. VIII. 55 The paving and improved road-making in cities and towns.

attrib. **1890** *Daily News* 8 Dec. 2/6 Road-making tools and implements are in good request.

ˈroadman. [ROAD *sb.* 4.] **1.** A workman engaged in the making or upkeep of roads.

1816 DUFF *Poems* 58 The smarts O' rugged Roadman's whips an' carts. **1866** EASTON *Autobiog.* 66 They would have thought it below their dignity to break a lance in public with a 'Roadman'. **1897** *Westm. Gaz.* 17 June 5/1 Extra roadmen were put on to renovate the wood paving.

2. A person using the roads for any purpose. An itinerant canvasser or seller of goods, a travelling salesman; a tramp or vagrant; a road-racer.

1906 S. E. SPARLING *Introd. Business Organiz.* 206 Another method of direct selling is found in the system of canvassers and road-men sent out by factories. **1912** A. S. M. HUTCHINSON *Happy Warrior* v. vi. 318 There cried to them 'Away! away!' all the instinct that, since first law came on the land, has bade roadmen, gipsies, outlaws, take immediate flight from trouble. **1949** A. MILLER *Death of Salesman* II. 80 You're a road man, Willy... We've only got a half-dozen salesmen on the floor here. **1951** *Sport* 27 Apr.–3 May 11/4 Sutherland..is a sprinter turned roadman, and it was in a sprint finish that he won his Empiad title in New Zealand. **1955** *Publ. Amer. Dial. Soc.* xxiv. 84 One can discern two different kinds of thief..: the *road man* is the more venturesome, the more restless. **1962** J. D. MACDONALD *Key to Suite* (1968) ii. 16 Once in Atlanta ..one of Federal's road men..goosed the wife of the executive vice-president. **1976** *Star* (Sheffield) 29 Oct. 27/1 The Horseshoe climb..is noted as a 'roadman's' course where riders such as Waugh can beat the hill specialists at their own game.

roadmanship (ˈrəʊdmənʃɪp). [f. prec. + -SHIP.] Ability to drive on the roads; skill in using the roads.

1953 P. C. BERG *Dict. New Words* 137/2 *Roadmanship*, skill in using public roads; e.g. the Highway Code tells you the principles of good roadmanship. (Perhaps after horsemanship.) **1958** *Archit. Rev.* CXXIII. 300/2 Skill in driving and roadmanship, allied with the glamour of the superior vehicle, enable the ordinary person to express his innate sense of craftsmanship. **1959** *Economist* 16 May 9/2 An Israeli can give the impression that no other country has ever suffered from juvenile delinquency or bad roadmanship. **1973** *Daily Tel.* (Colour Suppl.) 7 Dec. 25/2 Drivers with high standards of car control and roadmanship.

†**roadometer** (rəʊˈdɒmɪtə(r)). *Obs.* [f. ROAD *sb.* + -OMETER.] **a.** A device for measuring distance travelled. **b.** (See quot. 1926.)

1848 W. CLAYTON *Latter-day Saints' Emigrants' Guide* 3 The distances from point to point are shown as near as a *Roadometer* can measure. **1859** B. D. WILLIAMS *Let.* 9 May in L. R. Hafen *Overland Routes to Gold Fields* 238 The road ..from Leavenworth city to Denver city, is 689 miles in length by the roadometer. **1926** *Glasgow Herald* 14 Oct. 6 There is a considerable range of motor car attachments, including a roadometer which automatically indicates the position of the car on the road by a scale which shows the camber.

roadscape (ˈrəʊdskeɪp). [ROAD *sb.*] A view or prospect of a road; a picture of a road. Also, landscaping of a road.

1942 BERREY & VAN DEN BARK *Amer. Thes. Slang* §137/4 *Roadscape*, a view of a road. **1959** *Archit. Rev.* CXXV. 245/3 In turning over pictures of German autobahnen, so competent in detail, it comes almost as a relief to find a piece of roadscape that doesn't work,—an example of how not to do it (the only one in this article). **1968** *Radio Times* 28 Nov. 21/1 Roadscape with rusting rails... The second of four talks on Los Angeles.

ˈroadside. Also **road-side**. [ROAD *sb.* 4.]

1. The side next to the road. *rare*$^{-1}$.

1712 STEELE *Spect.* No. 326 ¶2, I..have therefore taken care to remove my Daughter from the Road-side of the House, and to lodge her next the Garden.

2. The side, or border, of the road; wayside.

1744 J. WILSON *Synop. Brit. Plants* 56 Woolly-headed Thistle..by the road-sides in Huntingdonshire. **1789** M. MADAN tr. *Persius* (1795) 182 *note*, Beggars, who took their stands by the road-side. **1828** LYTTON *Disowned* i, Does the house you speak of lie on the road-side? **1862** H. MARRYAT *Year in Sweden* II. 368 Junipers..grace the road-side. **1880** C. R. MARKHAM *Peruv. Bark* 287 This charming spot, with the roadsides planted with tall trees.

fig. **1847** L. HUNT *Men, Women & B.* I. iv. 72 Permit at least this dream by the roadside of creation.

attrib. **1810** CRABBE *Borough* i. 126 Sewers from streets the road-side banks defile. **1837** DICKENS *Pickw.* xxvii, A road-side public-house of the better class. **1886** *Field* 17 Oct. 542/1 Roadside waste, roadside pasture, and roadside turf belong presumably to the adjoining landowner. **1925** F. SCOTT FITZGERALD *Great Gatsby* v. 98 Light, which fell unreal on the shrubbery and made thin elongating glints upon the roadside wires. **1936** *Discovery* Apr. 125/1 A pair of roadside thieves in Nevada. **1939** JOYCE *Finnegans Wake* (1964) I. 31 The roadside tree the lady Holmpatrick planted. **1949** *Sun* (Baltimore) 14 July 8/2 The Pennsylvania Highway Department is receiving appreciative comment from the motorists on its roadside rests. **1961** *A.A. Handbk.* 12 A.A. Roadside Telephone Boxes are placed at carefully selected points along main roads. **1976** *Deeside Advertiser* 9 Dec. 24/3 His companion was thrown against roadside signs.

Hence **roadˈsider**, a keeper of a roadside inn; one who lives by the side of a road.

1826 HOOD *Fairy Tale* i, Till he had made his pelf, And then retired—if one may call it so Of a roadsider. **1844** W. H. MAXWELL *Scotland* viii. (1855) 85 The 'roadsider' always wears a blue coat.

ˈroadsman. [ROAD *sb.* 4. Cf. *craftsman*, etc.]

1. A driver of vehicles; a roadster.

1741 G. BERKELEY in *Lett. C'tess Suffolk* (1824) II. 180 Our coachman, who is an excellent roadsman,..took a fancy to fall off his box.

2. One who repairs roads; a roadman.

1865 *Daily Tel.* 1 Nov. 5/3 The prisoner had shot Fougereau for the sole purpose of obtaining his situation as roadsman. **1894** *Labour Commission Gloss.*, *Roadsmen*, men paid by the mine-owner for the laying down and keeping in repair the underground haulage roads.

roadstead (ˈrəʊdstɛd). Forms: 4 **radestede**; 6 **rode-**, 6, 8–9 **roadsted**; 7 **roade**, 8–9 **road-**, 8– **roadstead**. [f. ROAD *sb.* 3.] A place where ships may conveniently or safely lie at anchor near the shore.

[**1351** *Cartul. Whitby* (Surtees) II. 425 Deinz mesme la vile ou en la mere pres jongnaunts, apelle Radestede.]

1556 BOROUGH in *Hakluyt* (1886) III. 120 Our barke did ride such a rodsted thet it was to be marueiled..how she was able to abide it. **1600** R. CARR tr. *Mahumetan Hist.* 57 Perceiuing that they had not a safe rodested there, they remoued from thence to an other rodested of that Island, called Maiaro. **1633** SIR J. BOROUGH *Sovereignty Brit. Seas* (1651) 153 We stay till the Herring come home to our roade steads. **1774** *Hull Dock Act* 49 The roadstead near the haven mouth. **1795** in H. Tooke *Purley* (1829) I. 410 It..has no good Roadsted, and is not tenable, if not protected by a fleet. **1820** W. SCORESBY *Acc. Arctic Reg.* I. 155 The coast affords several road-steads. **1856** STANLEY *Sinai & Pal.* vi. (1858) 265 Caipha, at the opposite corner of the bay.., served as a roadstead. **1899** F. T. BULLEN *Log Sea-waif* 47 We came to an anchor near the middle of the roadstead.

roadster ('rəʊdstə(r)). [f. ROAD *sb.* 1 and 4.]

1. *Naut.* A vessel lying, or able to lie, at anchor in a roadstead. See also quot. 1867.

1744 *London Mag.* 557 They were stiff Ships,..good Sailors, and good Roadsters. **1815** BURNEY *Falconer's Dict. Mar.* s.v. *Roader*, Roadsters should attentively observe to anchor at a competent distance from each other. **1867** SMYTH *Sailor's Word-bk.*, *Roadster*, applied chiefly to those vessels which work by tides, and seek some known road to await turn of tide or chance of wind.

2. a. A horse for riding (or driving) on the road.

1818 SCOTT *Rob Roy* iii, Your horse..has too little bone to be a good roadster. **1844** H. STEPHENS *Bk. Farm* II. 216 A roadster is required to carry him over the farm when it is of large extent. **1882** MRS. RIDDELL *Prince of Wales's Garden-Party* 275 Almost every man..came either in his own gig, or riding his own stout roadster.

attrib. **1890** *Atlantic Monthly* Apr. 518/1 A lively, sensible horse, one who has the true roadster disposition. **1974** *Greenville* (S. Carolina) *News* 23 Apr. 11/2 Thursday's performances have two Roadster pony classes.

b. A cycle for use on the road. Also *attrib.*

1883 *Knowledge* 18 May 290/2 The weight of a roadster bicycle. **1896** *Daily Tel.* 10 Feb. 5/4 Hunt picked out a smart pneumatic-tyred roadster. **1922** [see *basket-car* s.v. BASKET *sb.* B. 1 b].

c. *U.S.* A light carriage.

1892 *Hist. Rev. Industr. & Commerc. Growth York County* 68 The former [repository and office] carries a fine line of.. everything in light and heavy work from the most substantial farm truck to the lightest finished roadster. **1901** *Dialect Notes* II. 146, I went to a farmer near and hired a young horse and a roadster.

d. orig. *U.S.* A type of motor car, esp. an open two-seater. Also *attrib.*

1908 *Sci. Amer.* 8 Feb. 104 Cadillac... Model G—Roadster, $2000. **1922** H. TITUS *Timber* xxix. 255 Rowe stood..a long interval,..watching her roadster disappear into the jack pines. **1928** F. N. HART *Bellamy Trial* ii. 30 We drove out from New York in my roadster. **1938** G. GREENE *Brighton Rock* VI. ii. 249 Where did you bring a swell blonde to if not the Cosmopolitan,..driving over the down in a scarlet roadster. **1948** W. SANSOM *South* 122 Round the narrow corner of old grey walls nosed the chromium grill, the long bonnet, and then all the pale gleaming length of a torpedo-shaped roadster. **1962** *Punch* 17 Oct. 560/2 Drag entries come in a profusion of classes: dragsters, modified roadsters, roadsters, [etc.]. **1973** D. LEES *Rape of Quiet Town* ii. 33 It was lucky I left my purse in your roadster. **1977** *Custom Car* Nov. 5/4 As for handicap racing in the Roadster and Production classes, the spectators seem to enjoy watching it.

3. a. One who is accustomed to the road; a coach-driver or traveller.

1841 S. C. HALL *Ireland* I. 72 Old roadsters, in long heavy grey or blue frieze coats. **1849** KIMBALL *St. Leger* I. vii, I.. entered into conversation with Walter, the 'whip', a veteran roadster. **1866** *Daily Tel.* 8 June 5/3 Old roadsters eat and drink whenever and wherever they can.

b. orig. *U.S.* One who has no fixed abode.

1890 N. P. LANGFORD *Vigilante Days* II. vi. 92 Henry Plummer was chief of the band;..Cyrus Skinner, fence, spy, and roadster. **1896** *Pop. Sci. Jrnl.* L. 255 The roadster proper is distinguished from the tramp by having..a visible means of support. **1901** *Scribner's Mag.* XXIX. 427/1 He.. was already a confirmed roadster, with an inordinate love for tobacco. **1925** G. H. MULLIN *Adventures Scholar Tramp* iv. 56 The roadsters, or hobos who travel, are seldom without smoking or chewing tobacco. **1970** *Oxf. Mail* 27 Apr. 1/3 When we first saw the man we thought nothing about it. Roadsters are a common sight in these parts. **1974** 'J. Ross' *Burning of Billy Toober* iv. 35 The body was probably that of a roadster using the shed to sleep in.

4. *Hunting.* One who keeps to the road.

1858 SURTEES *Ask Mamma* lxv, Taking a run he presently landed in the next field, amidst the cheers of the roadsters. **1898** WOLLOCOMBE *From Morn till Eve* i. 6 Henry and I on looking back find..a long train of roadsters behind us.

'road test. [ROAD *sb.*] A test of the performance of a vehicle on the road. Hence (usu. with hyphen) as *v. trans.*, to test (a vehicle) on the road; also *transf.* and *fig.*; so **'road-tester; 'road-testing** *vbl. sb.*

1906 S. KRAUSZ *ABC of Motoring* 134 This completes the chassis, and..the automobile is ready for examination and road test. **1921** *Dict. Occup. Terms* (1927) 115/2 *Tester, car*; ..*road tester (motor)*; drives finished chassis to test it under road conditions. **1937** *Times British Motor Number* 13 Apr. p. xxiii/2 It is the practice of Vauxhall Motors to road test every Vauxhall car and Bedford truck which is made. *Ibid.*, A certain proportion of the cars still undergo extended road tests. **1946** *Time* 29 July 80 This 60-ft. aluminium-magnesium bus was road-tested in California last week. **1949** *Life* 4 Apr. 129/1 In the U.S. many of the best brains go into business and the public secures their services only after they have been seasoned and road-tested on this severe and impartial proving ground. **1953** *Sun* (Baltimore) 10 July 4/6 Road tests are planned at the Army's Aberdeen (Md.) Proving Ground. **1961** *Times* 14 Feb. 17/2 We cannot feel sorry that these cars are coming off the road. We road-test the best of them and 50 to 60 per cent are definitely death traps. **1968** *Guardian* 10 Sept. 3/7 Maiden voyagers on the Cunarder QE2 will have..to road-test the ship. **1971** *Daily Tel.* 16 July 7 (Advt.), Howard Hunt is a road-tester. Every XJ6 is roadtested twice. **1977** *Custom Car* Nov. 80/2 (Advt.), Koni road testing is real tough, and includes a full international rally and racing programme.

'roadway. [ROAD *sb.* 4.]

1. A way used as a road; †a highway.

In origin perh. = 'riding-way'. In mod. use with approximation to sense 2.

1600 J. PORY tr. *Leo's Africa* VIII. 323 Through this citie lie two maine roade-waies. **1621** BURTON *Anat. Mel.* To Rdr. 53 Imploying them at home about some publike buildings, as bridges, rode waies for which those Romans were famous in this Iland. **1675** OGILBY (*title*), Itinerarium Angliæ: or, a Book of Roads, wherein are contain'd the principal Road-Ways of..England and..Wales. **1830** J. G. STRUTT *Sylva Brit.* 38 In the year 1724 a road-way was cut through its venerable trunk. **1840** *Railw. Times* 25 Jan., To render the roadway to the station as convenient to the public as possible. **1880** JEFFERIES *Greene Ferne Farm* 75 The roadway stopped abruptly.

attrib. **1632** LITHGOW *Trav.* x. 495, I found..in diuerse Rode-way Innes..good Cheare, Hospitality, and Seruiceable attendance. **1877** C. GEIKIE *Christ* i. (1879) 18 It looks like home to see vervain, road-way nettles, and thistles.

fig. **1597** SHAKS. *2 Hen. IV*, II. ii. 63 Neuer a mans thought in the world, keepes the Rode-way better then thine. **1627** E. F. *Hist. Edw. II* (1680) 29 If Vertue be the Road-way to perfection. **1663** CHARLETON *Chor. Gigant.* 28 In the road-way of every mans observation.

†b. *transf.* of the course of ships. *Obs.*

a **1608** VERE *Comment.* 54 A great ship was discovered on the road-way from the Indies. **1656** EARL MONM. tr. *Boccalini's Advts. fr. Parnass.* II. xxiii. (1674) 170 Pilots.. had made roade-waies all over it [*sc.* the ocean].

2. The main or central portion of a road, *esp.* that used by vehicular traffic, in contrast to the side-paths.

1807 CRABBE *Par. Reg.* I. 188 Between the road-way and the walls. **1865** DICKENS *Mut. Fr.* III. x, Making unsteady sallies into the roadway, and as often staggering back again. **1885** *Law Times Rep.* LIII. 65/2 The company were to repair the roadway for two years.

3. That portion of a bridge, railway, etc., on which traffic is conducted.

1834 *Penny Cycl.* II. 261/1 We have not only the arch itself to consider, but..the roadway or building thereon constructed. **1853** SIR H. DOUGLAS *Milit. Bridges* 329 The vertical framing and roadway rest upon four circular ribs formed of several thicknesses of timber. **1861** *Times* 22 Aug., The severity of the winter, which damaged their rolling stocks and seriously injured their roadways. **1901** *J. Black's Carp. & Build.*, *Scaffolding* 13 A spiral external roadway, whose easy inclination allowed building materials to be carried up it in little trolleys.

roadwork. Also road work, road-work. [ROAD *sb.*] **1.** Work done in building or repairing roads. Also *pl.*, repairs to roads.

1869 *Bradshaw's Railway Manual* XXI. 100 To effect a diversion of road and other works. **1895** *Funk's Stand. Dict.* s.v. *road, n., road-work, n.*, labor expended in making or repairing roads. **1951** R. FIRTH *Elem. Social Organiz.* iii. 118 There is one frame of organization..which regards a farm as a place for a man and his family..to use as a base from which to operate..in getting cash from road-work. **1958** J. G. MACGREGOR *North-West of 16* vii. 95 Up to this time all roadwork had been voluntary and consisted of a settler doing enough along the road each way from his place to remove the trees that fell across it. **1965** F. SARGESON *Mem. Peon* ii. 21 His regular hours of road-work labour. **1966** D. FRANCIS *Flying Finish* x. 126 The horsebox drivers..had to make a detour because of roadworks.

2. The management of a vehicle, cattle, etc., on the road.

1889 HISSEY *Tour Phaeton* 395 A few hints about roadwork..will possibly prove acceptable. **1890** 'R. BOLDREWOOD' *Col. Reformer* (1891) 179, I have had road work, station work, sheep and cattle management.

3. The work of an itinerant thief. *Criminals' slang.*

1925 H. LEVERAGE in *Flynn's* 14 Mar. 281/1 *Road work*,.. pocket picking, etc., done while traveling. **1955** *Publ. Amer. Dial. Soc.* xxiv. 84 Because of the stresses and strains of road work, he [*sc.* the road man] is usually a sharp, alert thief.

4. Work done on the roads, esp. exercise and training by athletes, sportsmen, etc.

1903 SOMERVILLE & 'ROSS' *All on Irish Shore* 159 The five couple and Carnage were..on a scent that was a real comfort to them after nearly five miserable months of kennels and road-work. **1928** *Funk's Stand. Dict.* s.v. *road, n., road-work, n.*, exercise taken on a road, as by athletes in training. **1950** J. DEMPSEY *Championship Fighting* xxiv. 183 *Roadwork* means running on the road. **1964** D. FRANCIS *Nerve* xvi. 190 A..little used secondary road..served only two farms and one private house, and because of its quietness it was a regular route for the Axminster horses on roadwork days. **1969** G. E. EVANS *Farm & Village* x. 113 The most trouble we had with Suffolks on road-work was *splinters* and *side-bone*. **1971** A. BURGESS *MF* vi. 69 They trotted along, as in roadwork, in their orange-and-cream jerseys. **1977** *Time* 25 July 39/2 He was doing roadwork and punching bags in preparation for his role in Martin Scorsese's *Raging Bull*, a film about Fighter Jake La Motta.

'roadworthiness. [f. ROADWORTHY *a.* + -NESS.] Roadworthy character; reliability on the road.

1923 *Daily Mail* 6 Aug. 4/4 One object was to demonstrate the roadworthiness or otherwise of these..family cars. **1928** *Daily Tel.* 16 Oct. 17 The low centre of gravity gives to the new Humber a road-worthiness unequalled. **1955** *Times* 1 July 6/6 The Government have dropped the proposals for compulsory tests of vehicles for road-worthiness. **1980** N. FREELING *Castang's City* xvi. 105 Polish those boots, boy, and examine them for road-worthiness.

'roadworthy, *a.* [ROAD *sb.* 4.]

1. Fit for the road; in a suitable condition for using on the road.

1819 W. S. ROSE *Lett.* I. 1 My carriage, which had been warranted roadworthy, having nearly gone to pieces. **1836** *Penny Cycl.* VI. 318/2 A coach-proprietor is bound by law to take care that his coach, harness, and horses are roadworthy. **1883** *Blackw. Mag.* July 59 Some tolerably roadworthy vehicles.

fig. **1837** CARLYLE *Fr. Rev.* (1872) III. IV. iv. 154 It was.. probably a workmanlike, roadworthy Constitution enough.

2. Of persons: Able to travel. *rare.*

1858 CARLYLE in Froude *Carlyle in London* (1884) II. xxiv. 224 Poor Neuberg..hopes to be roadworthy to-morrow again. **1862** MRS. CARLYLE *Lett.* (1883) III. 107 In a few days I hope to be..road-worthy.

roady, var. ROADIE.

roaf, var. ROUF.

roage, roague, obs. forms of ROGUE.

roak, -y, dial. variants of ROKE, -Y.

roale, obs. form of ROLL *sb.*[1]

roall, roalte, obs. forms of ROYAL(TY.

roam (rəʊm), *sb.* [f. the vb.] The act of wandering or roaming; a ramble.

1667 MILTON *P.L.* IV. 538 He..began Through wood, through waste, o'er hil, o'er dale his roam. **1685–8** *Roxb. Ball.* II. 447 My unkind husband hath taken his roam To see his relations. **1742** YOUNG *Nt. Th.* IX. 1173 The boundless space, thro' which these rovers take Their restless roam. **1755** HERVEY *Theron & Aspasia* (1757) I. xi. 394 Too dreary even for the Roam of a hoary hermit. **1805** WORDSW. *Prelude* VIII. 113 A half-hour's roam through such a place.

roam (rəʊm), *v.* Forms: *α.* 4–5 **romen, -yn,** 4–7 **rome,** 5 **rom, rombe,** 6 **roame,** 6– **roam.** *β.* 4–6 **rowme,** 5 **roume(n,** 5, 7 **roome.** [Of obscure origin: the rime with *home* in Gower indicates an early ME. *rāmen* (perh. represented by the obscure *rameden* in Laȝamon 7854), but no parallel form with the same meaning appears in any of the cognate languages.

Except in late puns, there is no evidence of connexion with the Romance words denoting pilgrims or pilgrimages to Rome (as OF. *romier*, Sp. *romero*, It. *romeo*, med.L. *romeus*), and the rime with *home* is decisive against this origin. The *β*-forms are probably due to scribal confusion with *rowm* ROOM *v.* Douglas no doubt took over the word with this spelling from some manuscript of Chaucer.]

1. a. *intr.* To wander, rove, or ramble; to walk about aimlessly, esp. over a wide area.

a. **13..** *K. Alis.* 7207 Alisaunder rometh in his toun, For to wissen his masons. *c* **1330** *Arth. & Merl.* 2372 (Kölbing), Þo he was cloped, he com adoun, Sikeende & romende vp & doun. **1390** GOWER *Conf.* II. 347 Whan he wot the lord from home, Than wol he stalke aboute and rome. *c* **1407** LYDG. *Reson & Sens.* 3006 To walke and romen vp and doun In the forest. **1470–85** MALORY *Arthur* VIII. xi. 289 The quene.. romed vp & doune in the chamber. **1577** B. GOOGE *Heresbach's Husb.* III. (1586) 141 Neither the slowe..nor the liuely, whyle they roame, bee seuered from their fellowes. *c* **1586** C'TESS PEMBROKE *Ps.* LXXVIII. xiv, He made them waste their weary yeares Roaming in vain. **1613** PURCHAS *Pilgrimage* III. i. (1614) 228 Thus doe the Tartars and the Arabians..at this day, roming, rouing, robbing. **1697** DRYDEN *Virg. Past.* I. 3 Round the wide World in Banishment we rome. **1754** GRAY *Progr. Poesy* 55 Shaggy forms o'er ice-built mountains roam. **1781** GIBBON *Decl. & F.* xxxi. (1787) III. 236 The Barbarians roamed through the city in quest of prey. **1818** KEATS *Endym.* II. 993 Where, 'mid exuberant green, I roam in pleasant darkness. **1840** DICKENS *Old C. Shop* i, In the summer I often roam about the fields and lanes all day. **1894** BARING-GOULD *Deserts S. France* I. 1 The pastures..are roamed over by dun-coloured oxen.

fig. **1587** GREENE *Euphues Censure* Wks. (Grosart) VI. 208 A valyaunt mynde, vnlesse guyded by wysedome, rometh into many inconsidered actions. **1640** W. STYLE tr. *Antisco's Sp. Gallant* 120 Suffering their thoughts to rome upon other matters. **1814** CARY *Dante, Paradise* x. 4 Wherever eye or mind Can roam. **1882** AINGER *Lamb* vi. 101 He was allowed to roam at his own free will over the experiences of his life.

β. **1377** LANGL. *P. Pl.* B. XI. 109 Þe porter..plukked in *pauci* prjueliche, and lete þe remenaunt go rowme. *Ibid.* 124 He may renne in arrerage And rowme so fro home. **1513** DOUGLAS *Æneis* V. xii. 62 He rowmis wp and doun the cost. *Ibid.* XII. Prol. 201 Thochtfull luffaris rowmys to and fro. **1555** W. WATREMAN *Fardle Facions* I. iii. 36 Thei ware sterne, and vnruly..roilyng and rowmyng..heather and thether. **1602** WARNER *Alb. Eng.* Epit. 368 They..had roomed about, without pittie pyllaging and dispeopling.

b. Const. *to, toward, thither, from* (passing into the sense of 'go, make one's way').

c **1386** CHAUCER *Miller's T.* 508 He rometh to the Carpenteres hous. **1393** LANGL. *P. Pl.* C. VII. 331 'By þe rode,' quaþ repentaunce, 'þow romest toward heuene'. *c* **1400** *Destr. Troy* 818 Iason..rapis hym to ryse & rom from his bede. **1591** SHAKS. *1 Hen. VI*, III. i. 51 *Winch.* Rome shall remedie this. *Warw.* Roame thither then. **1599** NASHE *Lenten Stuffe* Wks. (Grosart) V. 247 Three hundred thousand people romed to Rome for purgatorie pils. **1631** R. BOLTON *Comf. Affl. Consc.* (1640) 235 So ravished in Spirit, he roamed toward Heaven. **1636** R. JAMES *Iter Lanc.* 40 We did rome Under thy guidance to a Roman way..From Yorck to Chester.

2. *trans.* To wander over or through (a place).

1603 *Philotus* xxv, Be ȝe haue rowmit ane Alley thryse, It is ane myle almaist. **1667** MILTON *P.L.* IX. 82 Thus the Orb he roam'd With narrow search. **1671** —— *P.R.* II. 179 False titl'd Sons of God, roaming the Earth. **1790** COWPER *Odyss.* XVIII. 2 A man Accustomed..to roam the streets Of Ithaca. **1812** J. WILSON *Isle of Palms* III. 411 Happy as they that roam the Ocean's breast. **1849** MACAULAY *Hist. Eng.* iii. I. 312 The last wolf that has roamed our island. **1875** MERIVALE *Gen. Hist. Rome* lxxv. (1877) 624 A mighty horde of savages roaming a continent in search of food.

†3. ? To carry off in roaming. *Obs.*[−1]

1655 GURNALL *Chr. in Arm.* I. (1656) 127 Many a sweet meal hath he [Satan] robbed the Saints of..: take heed therefore that he roams not thine away also.

4. *trans.* To cause (the eyes) to look over a scene. *rare.*

1900 J. BLOUNDELLE-BURTON *Seafarers* xii. 118 As he spoke he roamed his eye around the tranquil, glassy sea.

roamer ('rəʊmə(r)). Also 4-5 **romare, -ere, romber, rowmer.** [f. ROAM *v.* + -ER[1].] One who roams; a wanderer, rambler.

1377 LANGL. *P. Pl.* B. IV. 120 Til..religious romares *recordare* in here cloistres, As seynt Benet hem bad, Bernarde and Fraunceys. *Ibid.* x. 306 Ac now is religioun a ryder, a rowmer [*v.r.* romere] bi stretes, [and] A leder of louedayes. 1598 FLORIO, *Romeo*,..a roamer. 1611 COTGR., *Rodeur*, a vagabond, roamer, wanderer. [1727 in BAILEY, vol. II. 1755 in JOHNSON.] ? 1794 COLERIDGE *Sonnet* xii, Pale Roamer through the night! 1846 PROWETT *Prometheus Bound* 15 Calamity's a roamer, still abroad With restless flitting. 1883 JESSOP in *19th Cent.* Oct. 599 They are not afraid of work, though they are roamers.

'roaming, *vbl. sb.* [f. ROAM *v.* + -ING[1].] The action of the verb; a wandering journey. Also *fig.* and *attrib.*

1581 MULCASTER *Positions* xxxix. (1887) 204 It were to large a roming place, to runne over the port that the churchmen haue kept. 1582 STANYHURST *Æneis* I. (Arb.) 18 Through this wyde roaming thee Troians Italie mishing Ful manye yeers wandred. 1660 H. MORE *Myst. Godl.* VII. i. 282 All Prophecies are not from the mere ravings & roamings of a buisie Phansie. 1875 WHITNEY *Life Lang.* v. 82 This may seem like an aimless roaming through one department of our vocabulary. 1883 *Encycl. Brit.* XVI. 48/2 The south or steppe portion of Mesopotamia was from early times the roaming-ground of Arabic tribes.

'roaming, *ppl. a.* [f. as prec. + -ING[2].] That roams or wanders.

1597 HOOKER *Eccl. Pol.* v. lxvi. §4 Dominion ouer the whole band of that roaming and spoyling aduersarie. 1837 W. IRVING *Capt. Bonneville* III. 62 The roaming herds of that species of animal.

Hence **'roamingly** *adv.*

1621 LADY M. WROTH *Urania* 211 With him I..came into this country, where euer since I haue romingly endured, neuer in any one place setled.

roan (rəʊn), *a.* and *sb.*[1] Forms: 6 **roen, roone,** 6-7 **rone, roane,** 7- **roan.** [a. OF. *roan, rouen*, F. *rouan*, = Prov. *rouant*, It. *roano, rovano* (Florio), Sp. *roano* (†*ruano*), Pg. *ruão*, of unknown origin. The obs. Du. *roaensch* (Kilian), MLG. *rowansk* are also from OF.]

A. *adj.* Of animals: Having a coat in which the prevailing colour is thickly interspersed with some other; *esp.* bay, sorrel, or chestnut mixed with white or grey. Also *absol.* as the name of a colour.

a. Of horses. (Cf. ROANED.)

The prevailing colour is freq. expressed, as ***black, blue, red, silver, strawberry roan.***

1530 PALSGR. 263/2 Roen colour of an horse, *roven*. 1538 LELAND *Itin.* (1769) V. 56 Rethelan..cummith of Rethe, that ys to say Roone color or pale redde. 1577 B. GOOGE *Heresbach's Husb.* III. (1586) 116 The best colours..are these, the rone, the white liarde, the bay. 1596 SHAKS. *1 Hen. IV*, II. iv. 120 Giue my Roane horse a drench (sayes hee). 1602 *2nd Pt. Return fr. Parnass.* II. v. 92, I rode that same time vpon a Roane gelding. 1664 BUTLER *Hud.* II. i. 694 How shall I answer Hue and Cry, For a Roan-Gelding, twelve hands high? 1707 *Lond. Gaz.* No. 4325/4 A white roan Mare at present, but when she sheds her Coat a black roan. 1808 SCOTT *Marmion* I. v, Proudly his red-roan charger trod. 1863 *Sat. Rev.* 23 May 687 He is light roan in colour, and has a coach-horse look about him. 1883 *Times* 28 May 5/3 Mr. John Robinson's silver roan mare Lady Silver. *Ibid.* 30 May 5/1 The Stand Stud Company's strawberry roan mare British Queen.

b. Of other animals, *esp.* as the distinctive name of a species of antelope, *Hippotragus equinus.*

1839 W. C. HARRIS *Wild Sports S. Africa* xxii. 194 We descended into a valley, bent upon the destruction of a roan antelope. 1850 R. G. CUMMING *Hunter's Life S. Afr.* (1902) 83/1, I perceived a pair of the rare and beautiful roan antelope or bastard gemsbok warily approaching the fountain. 1879 R. JEFFERIES *Wild Life* (1908) 75 Broad green meads, dotted with roan-and-white cattle. 1885 *Athenæum* 2 May 570/1 A female roan kangaroo (*Macropus erubescens*). 1895 J. G. MILLAIS *Breath fr. Veldt* (1899) 187 The roan antelope (*Hippotragus equinus*) at one time ranged from Cape Colony up to Central Africa. 1970 *Daily Nation* (Nairobi) 16 Jan. 13/1 Going south along the lake is the Lambwe Valley Game Reserve, small and still undeveloped, but possessing the rare Roan Antelope.

c. *transf.* as a colour of cloth. *rare.*

1861 READE *Cloister & H.* lv, Her farthingale and hose [were] of the same material, but a glossy roan, or claret colour.

B. *sb.*[1] **1. a.** A horse of a roan colour.

1580 BLUNDEVIL *Horsemanship* v. xviii. 8 b, The other mad Horse was a Roane of Maister Ashleis. 1596 SHAKS. *1 Hen. IV*, II. iii. 72 What Horse? A Roane,..is it not? 1653 A. WILSON *Inconstant Ladie* II. iv, Sweet rone, Deare, beast, looke to thy feet. 1753 CHAMBERS *Cycl. Suppl.* s.v., When this party-coloured coat is accompanied with a black head and black extremities, he is called a roan with a black-a-moor's head. 1842 TENNYSON *Walk. to Mail* 104 As quaint a four-in-hand As you shall see—three pyebalds and a roan. 1877 G. NEVILE *Horses & Riding* xv. 106 Black and bay-roans mean roan horses with black or bay heads and legs.

b. A roan cow, ox, or bull.

17.. RAMSAY *Wyfe of Auchtermuchty* ix, Than by came an illwilly roan. 1789 MRS. PIOZZI *Jrnl. France* I. 148 The Carinthian bulls..are almost all blue roans. 1890 'R. BOLDREWOOD' *Col. Reformer* (1891) 121 He's got a real turn for the roans and reds.

c. A roan antelope.

1895 MILLAIS *Breath fr. Veldt* (1899) 236 A pan under the mountain where many roans,..and some giraffes, drank. 1958 L. VAN DER POST *Lost World of Kalahari* vi. 111 It's unbelievable! They're there in thousands! Zebra, wildebeest, roan! 1978 *Times* 23 Nov. 13/9 Extensive softwood planting in the [Kenyan] plains is displacing much of its game, such as roan and sable.

†**2.** ***red roan***: (see quot.). *Obs.*

1707 MORTIMER *Husb.* (1721) I. 134 Barley is ripe, when the red Roan, as they call it, is off (that is a reddish kind of Colour that is on the Ear).

3. A fashion shade: cf. sense A. c.

1960 [see GRÈGE *a.* and *sb.*].

roan (rəʊn), *sb.*[2] Also 5 **royne,** 6 **rone.** [Of obscure origin; perhaps the place-name, as in *sb.*[3] The gap in the history of the word is remarkable.]

†**1.** ***roan skin***, some kind of skin or leather. Also ***roan lanyar(d)***, a thong made of this. *Obs.*

c1425 WYNTOUN *Cron.* VIII. 4802 He gert brynge hym a litil cofyne; A royne [*v.r.* rone] skyn tuk he þar of syne, And schare a thwaynge at al laysere [*Wemyss* A royne lanȝhare þarof to scheire]. 1572 in Feuillerat *Revels Q. Eliz.* (1908) 177 For one Rone skin. 1583 *Bk. of Rates* E j b, Roan skinnes the dosen, xxx.*k*. *Ibid.* E v b, Skinnes for Lether, look Basill, Buffe; for Cushions [look] portingale, Red hides, Roan, Salt spanish, Spruce and Swan skinnes.

2. A soft flexible leather made of sheepskin, used in bookbinding as a substitute for morocco.

1818 *Art Bk.-binding* 27 The back must have a piece of blue or red roan, thinly pared, pasted on. 1852 MORFIT *Tanning & Currying* (1853) 365 Roan is sheep-skin Morocco tanned with sumach, but wanting the grained appearance of true Morocco. 1879 *Cassell's Techn. Educ.* IV. 90 Roans are prepared much like the straight-grained morocco, but they..are much thinner.

Comb. 1845 *Penny Cycl.* Suppl. I. 221/1 'Roan-bound' books..are often sprinkled with colour by the bookbinders after the leather has been attached to the boards.

†**roan,** *sb.*[3] *Obs.* Also 5 **ron.** [f. *Roan*, an old form of the place-name *Rouen*. Cf. Sp. *ruan*, 'fine Linnen Cloath made at Roan in France' (Stevens, 1706).] **a.** The place-name used attrib. to designate the linen cloth made there. **b.** A make of linen from Rouen.

a. 1483 *Cath. Angl.* 311/2 Ron, *rothomagus, rothomagensis*. 1565 COOPER *Thesaurus*, *Vestis Rotomagensis*, Roan clothe. b. 1617 MORYSON *Itin.* III. 134 These carry out of France great quantity of Linnen cloth, which we call white Roanes. 1696 J. F. *Merch. Wareho. laid open* 35, I..shall come to Roans and Rasterns, but because there is not any allowed to come I shall pass it by.

roan, *sb.*[4] *dial.* Also 7-9 **rone.** [var. of RAWN or ROWN.] The roe of a fish.

1617 MORYSON *Itin.* III. 115 Botargo (..the rone of a fish). c1700 KENNETT in *MS. Lansd.* 1033 lf. 327 b, *Rone*, the row in a female fish, which in males is calld the *Milt*. 1765 *Ann. Reg.* 138 An uncommon fish..; in the belly were two roes, or roans, each nine feet long. 1869-89 in northern dial. glossaries (Cumb., Lanc., Linc.).

b. ***roan-fleuk***, the turbot (cf. *rawn-fleuk*).

1882 DAY *Fishes Grt. Brit. & Irel.* II. 12.

roan, variant of RONE *sb.*, ROWAN.

roan-berry, variant of ROWAN-BERRY.

†**'roaned,** *a. Obs.* Also 5-6 **ronyd,** 6 **roned.** [f. ROAN *a.*] Roan-coloured.

1477 *Paston Lett.* III. 186 Hytt is told me, that the Master Porter hath a coragiouse ronyd hors. 1537 *Bury Wills* (Camden) 132, I geve to Thomas Poole a blake horse, also a ronyd colte. 1579 *Lanc. Wills* (Chetham) II. 121 One roned gelding. 1602 BRETON *Wonders worth Hearing* Wks. (Grosart) II. 6/2 He..had euer more pitty on one good paced Mare, then two roaned curtalles.

‖**roanoke** ('rəʊənəʊk). Also 7 **rawranoke, roanoake, -oack,** 8 **roenoke.** [From the Powhatan or Virginian dialect of Algonkin.] An inferior kind of wampum made and used by the natives of Virginia.

1624 *Capt. Smith's Virginia* III. 418 Rawranoke or white beads that occasion as much dissention among the Salvages, as gold and siluer amongst Christians. 1656 *Stat. Virginia* (1823) I. 397 Peeces of eight that are good and of silver shall pass for five shillings, and Roanoake and Wompom-peeke to keep their wonted value. 1672 SIR W. TALBOT *Discov. J. Lederer* 27 Their currant Coyn of small shells, which they call Roanoack or Peack. 1705 R. BEVERLEY *Hist. Virginia* (1722) III. i. 141 Upon his Neck, and Wrists, hang Strings of Beads, Peak and Roenoke. 1859 BARTLETT *Dict. Amer.* (ed. 2) 368 *Roanoke*, Indian shell money; so called in Virginia. 1900 *Harper's Mag.* Mar. 511 Silver bangles, and ear-bobs, and strings of roanoke.

roan-tree, variant of ROWAN-TREE.

roany. (See quot.)

1849 ROWLANDSON in *Jrnl. R. Agric. Soc.* X. II. 445 The tar that should be used for this purpose [sheep-smearing] comes from America, and is called 'roany', being of a fat unctuous nature of the consistence of very thick molasses.

roap, obs. f. ROPE *v.*

roapiness, obs. f. ROPINESS.

roapy, obs. f. ROPY.

roar (rɔə(r)), *sb.*[1] Forms: α. 4-7 **rore;** 7 **roare,** 7- **roar.** β. *Sc.* 5 **rare,** 5-6, 8 (9 *north.*) **rair.** [f. the stem of OE. *rárian*, ME. *rōren*, to ROAR. Cf. OE. *wulfa-ȝerár* in *O.E. Martyrol.* 16. In later English use perh. re-formed from the vb.]

1. a. A full, deep, prolonged cry uttered by a lion or other large beast; a loud and deep sound uttered by one or more persons, esp. as an expression of pain or anger.

α. 1390 GOWER *Conf.* III. 74 A dragoun..Com in rampende among hem alle With such a noise and such a rore. c1400 *Destr. Troy* 8518 þen Andromaca..With a rufull rore rent of hir clothis. c1400 *Laud Troy Bk.* 17964 Many boles & bores, With lowyng & with loude rores. 1610 SHAKS. *Temp.* II. i. 315 Sure it was the roare Of a whole heard of Lyons. 1637 MILTON *Lycidas* 61 The rout that made the hideous roar. 1697 DRYDEN *Virg. Georg.* IV. 590 The slipp'ry God..will seem a bristly Boar, Or imitate the Lion's angry Roar. 1768-74 TUCKER *Lt. Nat.* (1834) II. 443 Very bad music, badly executed, being rather roars or squalls than songs. 1774 GOLDSM. *Nat. Hist.* (1776) III. 201 They all seize it with a bound, at the same time expressing their fierce pleasure with a roar. 1832 TENNYSON *Œnone* 210 The panther's roar came muffled, while I sat Low in the valley. 1853 KINGSLEY *Hypatia* xxii, A roar of hired applause interrupted him. 1887 BOWEN *Virg. Æneid* II. 413 With a roar of wrath at the maiden's rescue..Greeks..flew to assail us.

β. c1425 WYNTOUN *Cron.* III. vi. 872 Thai rowpyd wytht a rare at anys. c1450 HOLLAND *Howlat* 826 The barde..Ran fast to the dure, and gaif a gret rair. 1513 DOUGLAS *Æneis* I. ii. 11 About thar closouris braying with mony rair. c1570 *Satir. Poems Reform.* xiv. 116 The Babe he gifis ane rair. 1728 RAMSAY *Last Sp. Miser* xxix, With a rair, Away his wretched spirit flew. 18.. in Heslop *Northumberland Gloss.* (1894) 562 The yow gav a blare, an' Robin a rair.

†**b.** Rumour. *Obs. rare*[−1].

c1520 *Vox Populi* 88 in Hazl. *E.P.P.* III. 271 The encrease was never more. Thus goythe the voyce and rore. And truthe yt is indeade.

c. A boisterous outburst *of* laughter; also *ellipt.* for this, esp. in echoes of the Shaksperian phrase belonging to ROAR *sb.*[2] b.

1778 *Phil. Surv. S. Irel.* 424 His flashes of wit and humour keep the table in a roar. 1803 *Pic Nic* (1806) I. 158 [He] kept the company in a roar of laughter. 1824 MISS MITFORD *Village* Ser. I. (1863) 210 He was once in danger of being turned out of the gallery for setting all around him in a roar. 1891 KIPLING *Light that Failed* (1900) 203 A roar of laughter interrupted him.

2. *transf.* **a.** The loud sound of cannon, thunder, a storm, the sea, or other inanimate agents.

1548 PATTEN *Exped. Scotl.* G v, With..horrible rore and terrible thunderinge of gunnes. 1552 LYNDESAY *Monarche* IV. 5998 Than, with ane rair, the erth sall ryve, And swolly thame. c1611 CHAPMAN *Iliad* XIII. 713 The floods of troubled aire to pitchie stormes increase,..Encountring with abhorred roares. 1667 MILTON *P.L.* VI. 586 Those deep-throated Engins.., whose roar Emboweld with outragious noise the Air. 1697 DRYDEN *Virg. Past.* IX. 58 Come then, and leave the Waves tumultuous roar. c1764 GRAY *Owen* 26 Talymalfra's rocky shore Echoing to the battle's roar. 1797 MRS. RADCLIFFE *Italian* xii, The roar of these waters has made my head dizzy already. 1816 BYRON *Ch. Har.* III. xxii, Arm! Arm! it is..the cannon's opening roar! 1856 KANE *Arct. Expl.* II. xxiv. 245 We see its deep indigo horizon, and hear its roar against the icy beach. 1887 BOWEN *Virg. Ecl.* v. 84 When the rock-strewn valley resounds to the torrent's roar.

b. ***to go with a roar***, to make uninterrupted progress or be a conspicuous success. *colloq.*

1845 DICKENS *Let.* 6 Aug. (1977) IV. 347 It was a most prodigious success; and went, with a roar, all through. 1903 G. B. SHAW *Let.* 12 June (1972) II. 331 'The Admirable Bashville'..went with a roar from beginning to end. 1907 *Punch* 1 May 308/2 Everything went with a roar.

†**roar,** *sb.*[2] *Obs.* Forms: α. 5-6 **roore,** 5-7 **rore.** β. 6 **roare.** [a. MDu. *roer*, = OS. *hrôra* (LG. *rôre, rôr*), OHG. *ruora* (MHG. *ruore*, G. *ruhr*), related to OE. and OS. *hrór* stirring, active: see also RORE *v.* and cf. UPROAR. The rime of *rore*: *pore* (= poor) in Chaucer proves that the word is different from ROAR *sb.*[1]] Confusion, tumult, disturbance. Only in phrases ***in, on, upon a roar*** (cf. MDu. *in roere zijn, bringen, stellen*, etc.).

α. c1374 CHAUCER *Troylus* v. 45 Whi nyl I brynge alle Troie vpon a rore? c1440 *Promp. Parv.* 436/2 Rore, or truble amonge þe puple, *tumultus, commotio*. c1489 CAXTON *Sonnes of Aymon* xx. 456 For therof ye shall see all fraunce in a rore and trowble. 1513 MORE *Chron., Rich. III* (1883) 15 Thus should all the realme fall on a rore. 1526 TINDALE *Acts* xix. 29 The cite was on a roore. 1542 UDALL *Erasm. Apoph.* 292 The people beeyng in a greate rore willed enquierie..to be made who it was. 1610 SHAKS. *Temp.* I. ii. 2 By your Art..you haue Put the wild waters in this Rore.

β. 1548 UDALL, etc. *Erasm. Par. John* viii. 59 When all should be set on a roare. 1561 DAUS tr. *Bullinger on Apoc.* (1573) 167 The Ephesians, which were all on a roare and worse than mad. 1563 *Mirr. Mag.*, *Blacksmith* xlix, When I perceyved the Commons in a roare.

b. A wild outburst of mirth. (Perh. associated with ROAR *sb.*[1], as in modern use: see prec. 1 c.)

1602 SHAKS. *Ham.* v. i. 211 Where be your Iibes now?.. Your flashes of Merriment that were wont to set the Table on a Rore.

roar (rɔə(r)), *v.* Forms: α. 1 **rárian,** 3 **rarin,** 4-6, 8 **rare** (5 **rar**), 5- **rair** (5 **rayr**), 9 *dial.* **rear.** β. 4 **roren,** 5 **rory,** 3-7 **rore,** 5-6 **roor(e,** 6-7 **roare,** 6- **roar.** [OE. *rárian*, = MDu. *reeren, reren* (still in dial. use), MLG. *râren* (LG. *raren, reren, rären*),

OHG. *rêrên* (MHG. *rêren*, G. *rehren*), probably of imitative origin.]

1. a. *intr.* Of persons: To utter a very loud and deep or hoarse cry (or cries), *esp.* under the influence of rage, pain, or great excitement; to vociferate, to shout, to yell.

α. *a* **900** *O.E. Martyrol.* 192 Hwilum hy him raredon on swa hryðro. *c* **950** *Lindisf. Gosp., Matt.* Introd. 7 Stefn leas in woestern..rarende *vel* bellende. *c* **1000** ÆLFRIC *Hom.* I. 66 Seo dreorize modor..rarizende hi astrehte æt þæs halzan apostoles fotum. *a* **1225** *Juliana* 48 He [began] to rarin reowliche ant te ȝuren ant te ȝeien. *a* **1300** *Cursor M.* 16104 Ne heres þou noght on ilk-a side hu þai apon þe rar. *c* **1340** HAMPOLE *Pr. Consc.* 7341 Þe devels obout þam þan in helle, On þam salle ever-mare rare and yhelle. **1375** BARBOUR *Bruce* v. 97 Thai that na defens mycht mak, Full pitwisly couth rair and cry. *c* **1450** *St. Cuthbert* (Surtees) 5358 He rared and cryed so orribilly þat his neghburs..þar of þaim vggyd. **1483** *Cath. Angl.* 300/1 To Rare (or grete, *A.*), *vagire.* **1513** DOUGLAS *Æneis* v. xi. 26 All togidder gan to weip and rair. **1588** A. KING tr. *Canisius' Catech.* 92 b, I am afflicted,..I rarit for ye disquietnes of my hart. **1686** G. STUART *Joco-Ser. Disc.* 24 They..skreem'd, and raird beyond all ayme. **1717** RAMSAY *Elegy on Lucky Wood* xi, That a' the warld might hear the din Rair frae ilk head. **1809** T. DONALDSON *Poems* 146 What maks ye thus to rant an' rair? **1894** HESLOP *Northumbld. Gloss.* s.v. *Rair*, Whativver is he rairin there at?

β. *c* **1290** *S. Eng. Leg.* I. 99/238 Þo gan þe Aumperur for wrathþe loude ȝeolle and rore. *c* **1300** *Havelok* 2438 He bunden him ful swiþe faste,..Þat he rorede als a bole. **13..** *E.E. Allit. P.* B. 390 Summe..stared to þe heuen, Rwly wyth a loud rurd rored for drede. **1377** LANGL. *P. Pl.* B. v. 398 He..his brest knocked, And roxed and rored. *c* **1400** *Laud Troy Bk.* 15726 The stour was strong, the cry was gret, Thei rored grisly. *c* **1440** *York Myst.* xxxvii. 99 Why rooris þou soo, rebalde? **1526** *Pilgr. Perf.* (W. de W. 1531) 214 b, Rorynge and cryenge, Ryse you wretches and come to your iudgement. **1596** SHAKS. *1 Hen. IV*, II. iv. 286 You..roared for mercy, and still ranne and roar'd. **1624** QUARLES *Job Militant* xvii. 14 Th' afflicted..Roare to Heavens, unanswer'd, for reliefe. **1676** HOBBES *Iliad* (1677) 105 But Priam had forbidden them to roar Or cry outright, though grieved at their hearts. **1709** STEELE *Tatler* No. 37 ¶4 This Sort of Fellows, who Roar instead of Speaking. **1722** DE FOE *Col. Jack* ii, Then I cried, nay, roared out, I was in such a passion. **1838** MISS MAITLAND *Lett. fr. Madras* (1843) 237 She has nothing to do but to roar long enough and loud enough, and she is sure to get her own way. **1895** 'M. FIELD' *Attila* IV. 106 Although the host of warriors roared and stamped Acclaimingly.

fig. c **1489** CAXTON *Sonnes of Aymon* x. 261 His hert rored in his beli for ioye.

†**b.** To shout in revelry; to revel boisterously; to behave in a noisy, riotous manner. Also with *it*.

1584 LYLY *Sappho* II. iii. 108 To th' Tap-house then lets gang, and rore. **1592** —— *Gallathea* I. iv. 88 What shall wee doe being toss'd to shore? Milke some blinde Tauerne, and (there) roare. **1629** DEKKER *Londons Tempe* (Percy Soc.) 48 The gallant roares; roarers drinke oathes and gall. **1656** HAMMOND *Leah & Rachel* (1844) 9 Such as..could babble in a Pulpit, roare in a Tavern. *c* **1670** *Roxb. Ball.* (1890) VII. 37 We rant and rore it, night and day, we spend and never spare. **1760–72** H. BROOKE *Fool of Qual.* (1809) I. 58 These have nothing to do but..to riot it, to roar it. **1763** CHURCHILL *Apol.* Poems 1767 I. 68 If they in cellar or in garret roar.

c. To shout *with* laughter; to laugh boisterously, loudly, or without restraint.

1815 B. WYNNE *Diary* 28 July (1940) III. xii. 378 The Girls, who *roared* the whole way, laughing at the odd vehicle. **1828** T. CREEVEY *Let.* 3 Mar. in J. Gore *Creevey's Life & Times* (1934) xii. 260 Brougham's letter is..in folly and insanity by no means inferior to his former effusions. We both *roared* at it. **1842** LEVER *J. Hinton* iii, The whole party were roaring with laughter. **1884** *Punch* 12 Apr. 179/1 New members..roared when he shook his hand over his head. **1893** *Idler* 410, I read 'Robert Elsmere' and roared over it.

2. a. Of animals (*esp.* of lions): To utter a loud deep cry. Also with *out*.

a **1300** *E.E. Psalter* xxi. 12 Þair mouth ouer me þai ware openand, Als lioun reuand and rorand. *c* **1350** *Will. Palerne* 86 Whan þe best þe barn missed..Reuliche gan he rore & rente al his hide. *c* **1400** *Ywaine & Gaw.* 242 Lions, beres, bath bull and bare, That rewfully gan rope and rare. *c* **1440** *Promp. Parv.* 437/1 Rooryn, as beestys, *rugio.* **1530** PALSGR. 694/1, I roore, I yell, as a beest dothe, *je braye.* **1549** *Compl. Scot.* vi. 39 The suyne began to quhryne quhen thai herd the asse rair. **1613** PURCHAS *Pilgrimage* II. xx. (1614) 223 A Lion in the wood..roared so dernely. *a* **1720** SEWEL *Hist. Quakers* (1795) I. IV. 272 When the mouths of lions roared against me. **1782** COWPER *J. Gilpin* 206 Whereat his horse did snort, as he Had heard a lion roar. **1827** D. JOHNSON *Ind. Field Sports* 101 A tiger roared out. **1896** KIPLING *Seven Seas, Rhyme Three Sealers*, The great man-seal haul out of the sea, aroaring, band by band.

fig. **1645** HARWOOD *Loyal Subj. Retiring-room* 23 Doe but permit Luther to keep close, till the Popes Bull hath done roaring.

†**b.** *transf.* Of sheep, birds, or bees. *Obs.*

1398 TREVISA *Barth. De P.R.* XVIII. iv. (1495) 751 The lambe knoweth his owne moder in somoche that yf she rorith amonge many shepe in a flocke, anone by bletyng he knowyth the voys of his owne moder. **1500–20** DUNBAR *Poems* xxxiii. 114 He lay at the plunge evirmair, Sa lang as any ravin did rair. **1759** *Phil. Trans.* LI. 300, Jan. 15, the bees roared, and were as busy as they are in the height of the working season. **1790** BURNS *Elegy on Henderson* viii, Ye bitterns, till the quagmire reels, Rair for his sake.

c. Of horses: To make a loud sound in breathing. Cf. ROARER[1] 2 and ROARING *vbl. sb.* 3.

1880 W. DAY *Racehorse in Training* 40 At the Cape of Good Hope, I am told, horses never *roar.* **1889** *Yorks. Post* 25 Nov. 3/5 The tendency to roar is not a matter of heredity.

3. a. Of cannon, thunder, wind, the sea, or other inanimate agents: To make a loud noise or din.

c **1330** R. BRUNNE *Chron. Wace* (Rolls) 6569 When þey were in deppest flod,..Ros a tempest, rorande loude. *c* **1385** CHAUCER *L.G.W.* 1219 *Dido*, The thundyr rorede with a gresely steuene. **1470–85** MALORY *Arthur* XIV. v. 648 He came to a rough water the whiche roryd. **1530** PALSGR. 693/2, I roore, as the see dothe whan there bloweth any storme, *je gronce.* **1570** *Satir. Poems Reform.* xvii. 170 Our cair may moue the stonis And hauie rockis to rair. **1617** MIDDLETON & ROWLEY *Fair Quarrel* IV. i, Does not the winds roar, the sea roar, the welkin roar? **1669** EARL WINCHILSEA *Relat. Mt. Etna* 24 On Friday the 22, the Mountain again roared with much loudness. **1718** POPE *Iliad* XIII. 166 Hark! the gates burst, the brazen barriers roar! **1764** *Museum Rust.* III. 223, I caused the fire to be gradually encreased till it roared again in the furnace. **1816** SCOTT *Old Mort.* xxxvi, The ship..went roaring through the waves. **1861** HUGHES *Tom Brown at Oxf.* xli, The faggot blazed and crackled, and roared up the chimney.

b. Of a place: To resound or echo with noise.

c **1386** CHAUCER *Knt.'s T.* 2023 Whan it was day he broghte hym to the halle, That roreth of the criyng and the soun. **1667** MILTON *P.L.* VI. 871 Confounded Chaos roard, And felt tenfold confusion in thir fall.

c. *Curling.* To send a stone with great speed.

1786 BURNS *Tam Samson* v, To guard, or draw, or wick a bore, Or up the rink like Jehu roar. **1817** *Lintoun Green* 38 Roaring up the rink he flies, The guarded tee to clear.

d. To pass *away* with a loud noise.

1897 *Allbutt's Syst. Med.* III. 969 His appetite was bad, his breathing was short, wind would occasionally 'roar away' and then the distension lessened.

e. To travel on a vehicle which is making a loud noise; to motor rapidly. Also *fig.*

1923 *Motor Cycling* 26 Sept. 658/3 Marsden roared through on his last lap. **1951** *Amer. Speech* XXVI. 230/2 Wesleyan roars to victory. **1958** B. NICHOLS *Sweet & Twenties* x. 128 They were all roaring off to Ascot. **1963** *New Yorker* 15 June 58 George Rotan..roared back to win eleven of the next twelve. **1970** P. LAURIE *Scotland Yard* iii. 69 The one getting in slams the door and roars off, nearly running my mate over. **1973** *Times* 22 Jan. 9/8 The closest he came to betraying anxiety last evening was when he suddenly started roaring ahead.

4. a. *trans.* To utter or proclaim loudly; to shout (*out*). Also *fig.*

c **1400** *Apol. Loll.* (Camden) 58 Houndis and woluis roryn þe psalmis, os were woluis criyng ilk to oþer. **1587** FLEMING *Contn. Holinshed* III. 1367/2 The popes bull hath roared it so to be. **1591** SHAKS. *1 Hen. VI*, III. i. 40 That..makes him rore these Accusations forth. **1655** FULLER *Ch. Hist.* I. 7 Long before this time, she had roared it even into the ears of deaf men. **1698** FRYER *Acc. E. India & P.* 279 Nor will they themselves disdain to take up a Tabor and Roar out a Song. **1706** E. WARD *Wooden World Diss.* (1708) 78 He shall roar forth Death and Destruction about the hoisting of a Water-cask. **1749** FIELDING *Tom Jones* XV. v, Roared forth the word daughter. **1810** CRABBE *Borough* xix. 77 What time the many, that unruly beast, Roars its rough joy. **1848** THACKERAY *Van. Fair* xiii, The songs those young fellows were roaring. **1850** —— *Pendennis* xxxi[i], 'Oh, never mind,' Bungay roared out with a great laugh. **1878** TENNYSON *The Revenge* v, Sir Richard spoke,..and we roar'd a hurrah.

b. With complement: To force, call, bring, render, etc., by roaring.

1617 MIDDLETON & ROWLEY *Fair Quarrel* IV. i, We'll roar the rusty rascal out of his tobacco. **1725** RAMSAY *Gentle Sheph.* v. i, [He] roars up Symon frae his kindly rest. **1777** DR. TAYLOR in *Boswell* (Globe) 411/1 He will not hear you, and having a louder voice than you, must roar you down. **1797** MRS. RADCLIFFE *Italian* vii, Paulo, who had roared himself hoarse, was very willing to be silent.

c. Const. *up*. To abuse, to reprimand. *slang* (chiefly *Austral.*).

1919 W. H. DOWNING *Digger Dial.* 42 *Roar up*, upbraid; abuse. **1925** FRASER & GIBBONS *Soldier & Sailor Words* 244 *Roar up*, to abuse. **1944** W. E. HARNEY *Taboo* (ed. 2) 63, I roared him up, but it was no good. **1947** N. LINDSAY *Halfway to Anywhere* 69 Bill was able to roar him up, anyway, for having the blinkin' cheek to come shoving his nose into Bill's affairs. **1962** [see ROARING FORTIES 2].

†**roa'ration.** *Obs. rare*[−1]. (See quot.)

1617 PURCHAS *Pilgrimage* (ed. 3) 599 Such Orations (roarations ye may call them).

roarer[1] ('rɔərə(r)). [f. ROAR *v.* + -ER[1].]

1. a. One who or that which roars.

1388 WYCLIF *Ecclus.* li. 4 Thou hast delyuered me..fro roreris [L. *a rugientibus*].

1598 FLORIO, *Ruggiatore*, a roarer. **1610** SHAKS. *Temp.* I. i. 18 What cares these roarers for the name of King? **1689** COTTON *Winter* xxxviii, Into our fortress, let us haste; Where all the roarers of the north Can neither storm, nor starve us forth. **1715** *Flying Post* 27 Jan., For roarers of the word 'Church', £40. For a set of 'No Roundhead' roarers, £40. **1751** JOHNSON *Rambler* No. 144 ¶8 The roarer..has no other qualification for a champion of controversy than a hardened front and strong voice. **1790** MARSHALL *Rur. Econ. Midl.* II. 285 She [a cow] was a 'roarer' and a breaker of hedges. **1864** C. W. KING *Gnostics* 54 Bromius the Roarer, an appropriate epithet of the Grecian Dionysus. **1874** *Contemp. Rev.* Oct. 669 To exhibit the powers of every village roarer, and to prevent all congregational singing. **1903** W. S. BLUNT *Seven Golden Odes* 33 Fled to the land of the lions, roarers importunate.

†**b.** A noisy, riotous bully or reveller; a wild roisterer. *Obs.*

1586 D. ROWLAND *Lazarillo* II. (1672) R 5, Canil was dressed like a Roarer. **1611** BEAUM. & FL. *Philaster* v. iv, We are thy Mirmidons, thy Guard, thy Rorers. **1649** W. M. *Wandering Jew* (1857) 54, I am a man of the Sword; a Battoon Gallant,..in rugged English, a Roarer. *a* **1704** T. BROWN *Def. Gaming* Wks. 1709 III. 149 Is there any so besotted to the Bottle, which this Discourse of Pliny's..cannot reclaim..from the Suppers of Roarers to the Dinners of the Cinicks? **1709** STEELE *Tatler* No. 40 ¶3 All your Top-Wits were Scowrers, Rakes, Roarers, and Demolishers of Windows.

c. A street-seller of newspapers, who calls out fictitious news.

1865 *Pall Mall G.* 5 Aug. 6/2 One of a class of men known in the trade as 'roarers' went round with a few evening papers which he announced to be 'extraordinary editions'.

2. A horse affected with roaring.

1811 *Sporting Mag.* XXXVII. 129 The horse..turned out to be what jockies call a roarer, which is a defect in the wind. **1831** YOUATT *Horse* 160 Many more carriage-horses become roarers, than those that are used for the saddle alone. **1889** *Yorks. Post* 25 Nov. 3/5 The records state that Eclipse also was a roarer, or 'high blower', as the term was in his day [*a* 1789], the word 'roarer' not having yet been applied to horses.

3. A noisy or rousing song.

1837 MARRYAT *Dog Fiend* ix, Let's have the roarer by way of a finish.

4. *U.S. slang.* Something superlatively good.

1827 *Massachusetts Spy* 10 Jan. 1/4 The Albany beau.. drinks brandy and talks politics, swears at the servants, and quarrels with his landlord and is in fact what he styles himself, 'a real roarer'. **1852** MRS. STOWE *Uncle Tom's C.* vii. 47 Thar's Bruno—he's a roarer! **1857** HEAVYSEGE *Saul* (1869) 141 Were it not the roarer of all jests, To up and peep at the outside of heaven? **1872** DE VERE *Americanisms* 224 An active young man or a bouncing lass is apt to be admiringly designated as a roarer.

5. *U.S.* An oil-well from which the oil pours rapidly and noisily.

a **1885** B. J. CREW *Pract. Treat. Petroleum* (1887) vii. 227 We have no right, perhaps, to expect a continuance of the 'roarers', or 'gushers' as they are termed.

'roarer[2]. *dial.* [f. East Anglian *roar* to turn over (salted herrings): cf. RORE *v.*] A wooden basket to carry salt herrings: cf. ROARING BASKET.

1895 RYE *E. Anglian Gloss.*

roarie, obs. form of RORY *a.*

roaring ('rɔərɪŋ), *vbl. sb.* Also 1–3 **rarung**, 1 **raring**, 4, 6 *Sc.* **raryng**; 4–6 **roryng(e, -ing**, 6 **roaringe**. [f. ROAR *v.* + -ING[1].]

1. The action of the verb; the utterance of a loud deep cry or sound:

a. Of animals (cf. ROAR *v.* 2).

a **1000** in Wr.-Wülcker 192 *Barritus*,..ȝeþota, rarung. *c* **1050** *Ibid.* 495 *Barritus*, raringe. *c* **1375** *Sc. Leg. Saints* l. (*Catherine*) 36 Þe noys, þe raryng & þe bere of noyt, & schepe & menstralsy. **1382** WYCLIF *Job* xxxix. 3 Thei ben bowid to the frut of kinde, and beren; and roringus thei senden out. *c* **1440** *Promp. Parv.* 437/1 Rorynge, crye of beestys, *rugitus, mugitus.* **1552** HULOET, Bellowyng or rorynge of neate. **1555** EDEN *Decades* (Arb.) 94 Owre men..harde..horryble noyses and rorynges of wylde beastes. **1611** BIBLE *Job* iv. 10 The roaring of the Lyon, and the voice of the fierce Lyon. **1638** SIR T. HERBERT *Trav.* (ed. 2) 126 The roaring of 200 Mules and Asses. **1735** SOMERVILLE *Chase* II. 492 The King of Brutes In broken Roarings breathes his last. **1785** SMELLIE *Buffon's Nat. Hist.* (1791) VI. 259 Following the tract of wild beasts,..terrified by their occasional roarings. *c* **1850** *Arabian Nts.* (Rtldg.) 325 They heard the roaring of the lion..issue from the wood. **1897** *Allbutt's Syst. Med.* IV. 762 The 'roaring' of the otherwise silent stag at the rutting time.

b. Of human beings (cf. ROAR *v.* 1).

a **1240** *Sawles Warde* in *O.E. Hom.* I. 253 Biseon on hare grimfule ant grurefule nebbes, ant heren hare rarunge. *c* **1386** CHAUCER *Merch. T.* 1120 Vp he yaf a roryng and a crye, As dooth the mooder whan the child shal dye. *c* **1440** *York Myst.* xxxi. 215 And lorde, for þer raryng he raysed hym full right. **1535** COVERDALE *Job* iii. 25 This is the cause, that..my roaringes fall out like a water floude. **1631** BYFIELD *Doctr. Sabb.* 163 Now many in merry meetings have their singing of Catches and their roarings, as they are called. **1687** T. BROWN *Saints in Uproar* Wks. 1730 I. 72 There's such calling of names,..such roaring and screaming. **1722** DE FOE *Plague* (Rtldg.) 103 Others.. vented their Pain by incessant Roarings. **1764** GRAY *J.T.* 16 All the town rings of his swearing and roaring! **1853** KANE *Grinnell Exp.* xxxi. (1856) 269, I might defy human being to hear her..without roaring. **1889** J. M. DUNCAN *Dis. Women* (ed. 4) iii. 10 The restlessness and groaning or roaring under spasmodic pain.

c. Of inanimate things (cf. ROAR *v.* 3).

1398 TREVISA *Barth. De P.R.* v. xxxviii. (Bodl. MS.), ȝif þe water is to moche, it makeþ roryng and grolling in þe wombe. **1553** BRENDE *Q. Curtius* III. 12 b, [The river] fallyng downe vpon a rock beneth, made muche noise and roringe. **1610** SHAKS. *Temp.* I. ii. 204 The fire and cracks Of sulphurous roaring. **1627** CAPT. SMITH *Seaman's Gram.* x. 47 The Roaring of the Sea is most commonly obserued a shore, a little before a storme. **1712** ADDISON *Spect.* No. 333 ¶5 The Pomp of his Appearance amidst the Roarings of his Thunders. **1797–1805** S. & HT. LEE *Canterb. T.* I. 352 The low and monotonous roaring of the waves. **1817** SHELLEY *Rev. Islam* x. iv. 3 Like the roaring Of fire. **1869** TOZER *Highl. Turkey* II. 258 The sighing of the wind in the trees, or its roaring round their mountain abodes.

†**2.** Bullying, boisterous, or riotous conduct. *Obs.*

1617 MIDDLETON & ROWLEY *Fair Quarrel* IV. i, You and your man shall roar him out on't—for indeed you must pay your debts so, for that's one of the main ends of roaring. **1627** [see RIOTING *vbl. sb.* 1]. **1642** FULLER *Holy & Prof. St.* III. i. 153 Whilest they keep the greatest roaring, their state steals away in the greatest silence.

attrib. **1617** MIDDLETON & ROWLEY *Fair Quarrel* II. ii, What, to the roaring school?

3. A disease of horses, causing them to make a loud noise when breathing under exertion; the act of making this noise. (Cf. ROARER[1] 2.)

1823 in CRABB. **1831** YOUATT *Horse* 160 Roaring is no unusual consequence of strangles. **1846** J. BAXTER *Libr. Pract. Agric.* (ed. 4) I. 441 Sometimes roaring is occasioned by a distorted larynx produced by tight reining. **1881** *Standard* 29 July 5/2 Whether 'roaring' can be cured or not is a question upon which there is no consensus of opinion.

'roaring, *ppl. a.* [f. as prec. + -ING[2].]

1. That roars or bellows: **a.** Of persons or animals. Also *spec.* of horses (see prec. 3).

1382 WYCLIF *Ecclus.* li. 4 Thou hast delyuered me..fro the rorende men. —— *1 Peter* v. 8 3oure aduersarie, the deuel, as a roryng lyoun goith aboute. **1509** HAWES *Past. Pleas.* XXVIII. (Percy Soc.) 134 Agaynst day began to nese and cry My stede Galantyse with a roryng breste. **1590** SPENSER *F.Q.* I. vi. 24 Wyld roring Buls. **1611** BIBLE *Ps.* xxii. 13 They gaped vpon me..as a rauening and a roaring Lyon. **1727** DE FOE *Hist. Appar.* iii, Dost thou know I am a roaring lion? **1848** THACKERAY *Sk. & Trav. London, A Night's Pleasure* i, Cox's most roomy fly,..in which he insists on putting the roaring grey horse. **1889** *Yorks. Post* 25 Nov. 3/5 Melbourne was a big roaring horse.

b. Of the sea, wind, cannon, etc.

1565 COOPER *Thesaurus* s.v. *Sonorus, Flumina sonora*, roaringe riuers. **1595** SPENSER *Epithal.* 218 And let the roring Organs loudly play. **1616** J. LANE *Contn. Sqr.'s T.* VIII. 445 So theare out flies the roringst batterie on all the towne. **1638** SIR T. HERBERT *Trav.* (ed. 2) 91 What volleyed from the roring guns. **17..** RAMSAY *Horace to Virgil* 16 Thro' tempests and a rairing tide. **1784** COWPER *Task* v. 766 The sea With all his roaring multitude of waves. **1861** FAIRBAIRN *Iron* 144 A roaring flame rushes from the mouth of the vessel. **1873** BLACK *Pr. Thule* x. 153 The mighty and roaring stream of omnibuses.

c. ***roaring buckie***, a sea-shell which appears to make a loud noise (imagined to be the roaring of the sea) when the opening is held close to the ear. *Sc.* (Cf. ROARY 2.)

1808 JAMIESON s.v. *Buckie*, The roaring buckie, *Buccinum undatum*, Linn., is the common great whelk. **1854** *Zoologist* XII. 4428 Waved Buccine, *Buccinum undatum*... This and the larger species of Fusus get the provincial name of 'roaring buckies'. **1900** STRAIN *Elmslie's Dragnet* 206 Two great branches of pure white coral and six large 'roaring buckies'.

2. a. Behaving or living in a noisy, riotous manner; esp. ***roaring boy*** (cf. BOY *sb.*[1] 6). Now only *arch.*

1584 LYLY *Sappho* III. ii. 76 Whats he so swaggers in the Van? O! thats a roring Englishman. **1611** MIDDLETON & DEKKER (*title*), The Roaring Girle: or Moll Cutpurse. **1611** J. DAVIES (Heref.) *Sco. Folly* (Grosart) II. 44 The diuell is ..nere dead while roring boyes do liue. **1658** ROWLEY, TOURNEUR, etc., *Witch of Edmonton* I. ii, One of the Country roaring Lads. **1719** D'URFEY *Pills* III. 23 Your Roaring Boys who every one quails, Fights, Domineers, Swaggers, and rails. **1764** FOOTE *Mayor of Garratt* I, You vould meet some roaring, rare boys, i' faith. **1826** SCOTT *Woodst.* viii, The wild life of a roaring cavalier. *Ibid.* xx, These were the 'roaring boys' who met in hedge ale-houses.

†**b.** *transf.* Befitting a 'roarer'. *Obs.*

c **1590** MARLOWE *Faustus* viii, Keep out, for I am about a roaring piece of work.

3. a. Of voice, sound, etc.: Extremely loud.

a **1548** HALL *Chron., Edw. IV*, 43 b, The dukes angry countenaunce and roryng voyce. **1631** R. BOLTON *Comf. Affl. Consc.* vii. (1635) 230 He breakes out oftentimes into a roring complaint of sinne. **1659** PELL *Impr. Sea* 76 How their roaring oaths gingle in their mouthes. **1697** DRYDEN *Virg. Georg.* I. 442 With a roaring sound The rising Rivers float the nether Ground. **1861** HUGHES *Tom Brown at Oxf.* xlvii, I don't think we shall even have a roaring song along the street to-night. **1884** *Pall Mall G.* 16 Feb. 1/2 Such steps ..are not forced upon us by a roaring agitation.

b. *Path.* (See quot.)

1854 WALSHE *Dis. Lungs & Heart* (ed. 2) 747 The quality of the systolic murmur may be..rasping, sawing, filing, or if the blood be spanæmic, roaring.

4. a. Characterized by riotous or noisy revelry; full of din or noise. ***roaring days*** (Austral.), the time of the Australian gold-rush; also *transf.*, hey-day; ***the roaring twenties***, the third decade of the twentieth century (with reference to the postwar buoyancy of that period).

a **1715** BURNET *Own Time* (1766) I. 168 It was a mad roaring time full of extravagance. **1722** DE FOE *Plague* (Rtldg.) 88 Revelling and roaring extravagances. **1759** TOWNLEY *High Life* I, We'll have a roaring Night. **1822** W. IRVING *Braceb. Hall* vi. 49 A generation or two of hard-livers, that led a life of roaring revelry. **1865** DICKENS *Mut. Fr.* I. viii, We can hear one another better than in the roaring street. **1879** STEVENSON *Trav. Cevennes* (1886) 152 This roaring *table d'hôte*. **1897** H. LAWSON *Coll. Verse* (1967) I. 339 But these seem dull and slow to me compared with Roaring Days. **1921** M. E. FULLERTON *Bark House Days* (1931) xiv. 144 We loved the stories of the 'roaring fifties'. **1930** *Sat. Rev.* 15 Mar. 328/1 The giants of the roaring 'twenties ought to be able to achieve glory of some sort in half as many years. **1936** 'W. HATFIELD' *Australia through Wind Screen* 53 In its roaring days 'The Duchess' was better than many a goldmine. **1973** *Times* 2 Mar. 14/2 The theme [of the ball] will be the roaring twenties. **1978** *Dædalus* Fall 30 For those belonging to the classes of the immediate post-World War I period, the massacre of the young officers.. meant that countless positions..had become vacant in all spheres of society; this led to an ephemeral but marked shift to a more youthful establishment; hence, the Roaring Twenties.

b. ***the roaring game*** (or ***play***), the game of curling.

[**1786** BURNS *Vision* I. i, The sun had clos'd the winter-day, The Curlers quat their roaring-play. **1790** A. WILSON *Rabby's Mistake* Poet. Wks. (1846) 101 Far aff the curler's roaring rink, Re-echoed loud.] **1865** JANET HAMILTON *Poems, Winter* 103 The curlers ply the 'roarin' play', An' rinks are made. **1877** *Encycl. Brit.* VI. 712/2 The rules..of the Caledonian Curling Club form a code which largely regulates 'the roaring game'..all over the world.

c. ***the roaring forties***: see as main entry.

5. ***roaring drunk*** (Sc. ***fou'***), excessively drunk and noisy.

1697 VANBRUGH *Provoked Wife* III. 39 Sir John will come home roaring drunk. **1790** BURNS *Tam o' Shanter* 26 That every naig was ca'd a shoe on, The smith and thee gat roaring fou on. **1834** MARRYAT *P. Simple* (1863) 104 Just at that time came down the sergeant of marines, with three of our men whom he had picked up, roaring drunk. **1859** FARRAR *J. Home* xx, I bet you 2 to 1..that I have him roaring drunk before a month's over.

6. Of ailments: Causing one to cry out; extremely violent. *rare.*

1665 BOYLE *Occas. Refl.* II. iii. (1848) 106 He that is tormented with the Gout, is apt to envy any Sick man that is exempted from that Roaring pain. **1901** SIR H. SMITH *Autobiog.* II. xxxiii. 10 An exposure of this sort to the sun of India would probably cause a roaring fever or death.

7. Of trade: Very brisk, highly successful.

1755 C. CHARKE *Life* 153 But was..fully convinced, that I should carry on a roaring Trade. **1796** *Grose's Dict. Vulgar T.* (ed. 3), *Roaring trade*, a quick trade. **1845** HOOD *My Son & Heir* xix, A Grazier may be losing cash, Although he drives a 'roaring trade'. **1883** LD. R. GOWER *Reminisc.* I. xviii. 364 The women who sell the papers are evidently making a roaring trade. **1976** *Milton Keynes Express* 25 June 7/2 These attractions did a roaring trade round the perimeter of the sports hall.

8. *colloq.* Boisterous, exuberant. Also as a general intensive: full-blooded, whole-hearted; unqualified, out-and-out.

1848 THACKERAY *Lett.* 1 Nov., What a shame it is to go on bragging about what is after all sheer roaring good health. **1963** D. LESSING *A Man & Two Women* 302 If you are going to make love, what does it matter who with? Why shouldn't she simply walk into the street, pick up a man and have a roaring sexual affair with him? **1965** *Listener* 18 Nov. 806/1 Psychiatric treatment has not proved a roaring success. **1970** MRS. L. B. JOHNSON *White House Diary* p. xiv, I feel..a deep, roaring faith in and love for this country.

Hence **'roaringly** *adv.*

1842 *Blackw. Mag.* LII. 588 Roaringly, through the rocky cleft,..the torrent sweeps. **1862** T. WINTHROP *Canoe & Saddle* xii, Ferdinand snored roaringly from his coiled position among the traps. **1947** DYLAN THOMAS *Let.* 1 Mar. (1966) 298, I was roaringly well, then, some minutes after, a little mewling ruin. **1980** *Daily Tel.* 21 July 10/3 This festival built its name in the 'fifties under Jean Vilar's direction, with Gérard Philipe as star, by staging French classics with a zest and a roaringly romantic appeal to basic theatrical values which gave birth to the rightly named Théâtre National Populaire.

roaring basket. (See quot. and ROARER[2].)

1615 E. S. *Britain's Buss* in Arb. *Garner* III. 631 Tools and Implements used in drying and packing of Herring... Roaring baskets or scuttles.

roaring forties. 1. Exceptionally rough seas that occur between latitudes 40° and 50° south, where strong westerly winds blow; formerly also applied to the part of the Atlantic Ocean between 40° and 50° north latitude. Occas. also applied to the winds themselves.

1883 BUCHAN in *Encycl. Brit.* XVI. 146/2 The region of the 'brave west winds', the 'roaring forties' of sailors. **1893** J. A. BARRY *Steve Brown's Bunyip* 165 Older shipmasters laughed..saying that they found the Roaring Forties quite strong enough for them. **1906** W. MARRIOTT *Hints to Meteorol. Observers* (ed. 6) 68/1 *Roaring forties*, the regions between lat. 40° and 50° S., where the 'brave West winds' blow. **1924** R. CLEMENTS *Gipsy of Horn* vii. 126 Right 'roaring forties' weather came down on us with a swoop. **1953** A. A. MILLER *Climatology* (ed. 8) xi. 199 In the southern hemisphere the disturbance of the planetary winds is much less; 'Roaring Forties' and the 'Brave West Winds' blow all the year round with considerable force. **1966** F. CHICHESTER in *Sunday Times* 30 Oct. 3/6 Twice I have entered the Roaring Forties and been driven out by gales and squalls.

2. *fig.* **a.** The fifth decade of life. **b.** *Naut. slang.* (See quot. 1948.)

1867 *Harper's Mag.* Sept. 509/2 A very pretty woman, whose bark of life had not as yet drifted into the 'roaring forties'. **1930** H. K. PASMA *Close-Hauled* II. 211, I am in my roaring forties now. **1948** PARTRIDGE *Dict. Forces' Slang* 156 *Roaring forties*, Lieutenant Commanders between 40 and 50 years of age. **1962** GRANVILLE *Dict. Sailors' Slang* 96/2 *Roaring forties*, rough seas in 40-50 degrees south latitude, hence, a slang name for certain taut-handed lieut-commanders in their forties, who are always roaring up the hands.

'Roaring Meg. [ROARING *ppl. a.* and MEG[1].]

†**1. a.** = *Mons Meg*: see MEG[1] b. Hence, a huge piece of ordnance. Also *fig. Obs.*

1575 CHURCHYARD *Chips, Siege Edinb. Castle* 94 b, With throtling noyes, was shot of [= off] roeryng Meg. **1598** (*title*), Tyros Roring Megge. Planted against the walles of Melancholy. **1637** WHITING *Albino & Bellama* 10 But a blunt Earle..Beates downe a Fortresse like a Roaring Meg. **1656** TRAPP *Comm. Job* xxxvii. 2 Drowning the noise of their consciences..by ringing their greatest Bells, discharging their roaring-megs. **1700** J. BROME *Trav. Eng., Scot.*, etc. (1707) 195 In this [*sc.* Edinburgh] Castle is one of the largest Canons in Great-Britain, called Roaring-Megg.

b. (See quot.)

1847 R. SIMPSON *Ann. Derry* 41 In the same bastion lies roaring meg, so called from the loudness of her report during the siege of 1688–9.

†**2.** A kind of top (see quots.). *Obs.*[−0]

1632 SHERWOOD s.v. *Roaring*, The top called a roaring-meg, *trombe*. [Cf. COTGR. (1611), *Trombe*, a round and hollow ball of wood, hauing a peake like a casting-top, and making a great noise when it is cast as a top.]

3. (See quot.)

1811 *Trans. Geol. Soc.* I. 50 This structure of the clay.. goes by the name of the *shaggy metal*, and the fresh water which makes its way through the pores has the expressive appellation of *Roaring Meg*.

'roar-worthy, *a. nonce-word.* [f. ROAR *v.*] Worth roaring or shouting against.

1713 ADDISON *Guard.* No. 124 To roar..loud enough against all the things, that are roar-worthy in these Realms.

'roary, *a.* and *sb. rare.* [f. ROAR *v.*]

†**1.** Given to roaring. Also as *sb. Obs.*

Used only with *Tory*: cf. TORY-RORY.

c **1680** HICKERINGILL *Hist. Whiggism* Wks. 1716 I. 23 The Papists and the whory, roary..Tories were Cavaliers. **1716** *Pol. Ballads* (1860) II. 184 Why was it said the Tories For me did try amain? Why then are all the roaries Why are they all in vain?

2. ***roary buckie***: see ROARING *ppl. a.* 1 c.

1819 W. TENNANT *Papistry Storm'd* (1827) 18 Like roarie-buckies, i' their din, Loud soundin' as the sea comes in.

roase, obs. form of ROSE *sb.*

roasen, obs. form of ROSIN *sb.*

roast (rəʊst), *sb.* Forms: 4–7 **roste, rost,** 4–6 **roost,** 5–6 *Sc.* **roist,** 6– **roast.** [In sense 1, a. OF. *rost* masc. (mod.F. *rôt*: cf. Prov. *raust*, Catal. *rost*, It. *arrosto*) or *roste* fem., roasting, roast meat, vbl. sb. from *rostir* ROAST *v.* In sense 2, a subst. use of the pa. pple. of ROAST *v.* In other senses mainly from the verbal stem.]

1. a. A piece of roast meat, or anything that is roasted for food; a part of an animal prepared or intended for roasting.

c **1330** *Amis & Amil.* 1235 Certes, it were michel vnright To make a roste of leuedis bright. **1362** LANGL. *P. Pl.* A. Prol. 108 Wiþ good wyn of Gaskoyne..þe rost [*v.r.* roste] to defye. *c* **1420** *Liber Cocorum* (1862) 43 þenne take þy rost, and sklyce hit clene. *c* **1470** *Gol. & Gaw.* 81 Schir Kay ruschit to the roist, and reft fra the swane. **1575** *Gamm. Gurton* II. Song, I love no rost, but a nut browne toste And a crab layde in the fyre. **1591** FLORIO *2nd Fruites* 55 Make roome for the second messe, now comes the roste. *a* **1635** CORBET *Poems* (1807) 36 Since you eat his roast, It argues want of manners To raile upon the host. *a* **1656** BP. HALL *Rem. Wks.* (1660) 198 The very entrayles must be washed and put into the roast. **1763** SMOLLETT *Trav.* (1766) I. v. 67 The bourgeois of Boulogne have commonly..a roast, with a sallad, for supper. **1842** J. AITON *Domest. Econ.* (1857) 91 Keep a small roast or two for family use. **1886** PASCOE *London of To-day* 48 That dinner consists of..vegetables, roasts, sweets, with dessert.

b. Phr. ***to rule the roast***, to have full sway or authority; to be master. Hence ***ruler of the roast***.

In very common use from *c* 1530 onwards, but none of the early examples throw any light on the precise origin of the expression.

(*a*) **14..** *Carpenter's Tools* 176 in Hazl. *E.P.P.* I. 85 What so euer 3e brage ore boste, My mayster 3et shall reule the roste. **1526** SKELTON *Magnyf.* 805 *Cra. Con.* In fayth, I rule moche of the rost. *Clo. Col.* Rule the roste! thou woldest, ye. **1559** T. BRYCE in Farr *S.P. Eliz.* (1845) I. 175 When shall trew dealing rule the roste With those that bye and sell? **1577–87** HOLINSHED *Chron.* II. 23/1 These were Irish potentates, and before their discomfiture they ruled the rost. **1616** R. C. *Times' Whistle* (1871) 117 In cholerick bodies, fire doth govern moste; In sanguine, aire doth chiefly rule the rost. **1659** T. PECKE *Parnassi Puerp.* 46 He rules the Rost, by Night; She rules the Daies. **1708** PRIOR *Turtle & Sparrow* 334, I never strove to rule the roast. **1778** FOOTE *Trip Calais* II, The ladies always rule the roast in this part of the world. **1820** COMBE *Syntax, Wife* III. 276 This is the toast, Which in this place must rule the roast. **1855** KINGSLEY *Westw. Ho!* x, He had it all his own way, and ruled the roast..right royally. **1876** *Gd. Words* 788 The sensual appetite rules the roast, and proclaims its determination to be gratified at all costs.

(*b*) **1563** *Homilies* II. *Idolatry* III. (1859) 248 For.. Governours, you have the Romans, the rulers of the rost (as they say). **1581** J. BELL *Haddon's answ. Osor.* 67 b, If you.. will notwithstanding be accompted a ruler of the Roast in Divinitie. **1706** E. WARD *Wooden World Diss.* (1708) 6 This Ruler of the Roast has so little Christian Honesty. **1898** VILLARI *Machiavelli* 35 The lowest men..became 'rulers of the roast'.

c. In various figurative or allusive expressions.

In the earlier of these the precise sense is not clear.

1508 KENNEDIE *Flyting w. Dunbar* 27 Ramowd rebald, thow fall doun att the roist, My laureat lettres at the and I lowis. *c* **1550** LYNDESAY *Trag. Cardinal* 372 Of rycht religious men..Bot not to rebaldis new cum frome the roste. **1576** GASCOIGNE *Philomene* (Arb.) 114 Oft times they buy the rost ful deare, It smelleth of the smoke. **1587** *Mirr. Mag., Sir Nicholas Burdet* (1610) 488 Though full oft we made the French men smell of the rost, Yet in the end we gaine of fight the fame. **1596** COLSE *Penelope* (1880) 167 Wel let him heed amidst his ioy, Lest Menelaus marre his roast. **1670** G. H. tr. *Hist. Cardinals* II. I. 121 Not caring who have the smoak, whilst they themselves run away with the roast. **1680** COTTON *Compl. Gamester* (ed. 2) 13 Under the notion of being very merry with coine and good cheer, they will make him pay for the roast.

†**d.** *transf.* A company, troop. *Obs.* (Cf. BOILING *vbl. sb.* 4.)

1608 T. JAMES *Wickliffe* G iv b, The whole host and rost of Moonks and Friars beganne to praie.

2. a. Roast meat; roast beef.

c **1375** *Cursor M.* 13373 (Fairf.), þat folk þat day fulle faire was fed wiþ soiþen & roste & wilde bred. *c* **1400** *Ywaine & Gaw.* 221 Us wanted nowther baken ne roste. **1456** SIR G.

HAYE *Law Arms* (S.T.S.) 78 The tane lufis soddyn, the tothir rost. **1535** COVERDALE *Isaiah* xliv. 16 He rosteth flesh, that he maye eate roste his bely full. **1566** *Reg. Privy Council Scot.* I. 489 Being servit with bruise, beif, muttoun, and rost at the leist. **1600** ROWLANDS *Lett. Humours Blood* iii. 9 Not that hee'le cloy him there with rost or sod. **1611** BIBLE *Isaiah* xliv. 16 He eateth flesh: he rosteth rost, and is satisfied. **1700** DRYDEN *Cock & Fox* 36 On holy days an egg, or two at most; But her ambition never reach'd to roast. **1717** LADY MONTAGU *Let. to C'tess Mar*, Their sauces are very high, all the roast very much done. **1834** SYD. SMITH *Lett.* cccxl, Tory and Whig in turns shall be my host, I taste no politics in boil'd and roast. **1856** EMERSON *Eng. Traits, Aristocracy*, [He] should have as much boiled and roast as he could carry on a long dagger.

b. In figurative or allusive expressions; †in early use esp. ***cold roast*** in depreciatory sense.

c **1400** *Tourn. Tottenham* 136 'I make a vow', quoth Perkyn, 'thow speks of cold rost'. *c* **1460** *Towneley Myst.* ii. 421 Yey, cold rost is at my masteres hame. **1542** UDALL *Erasm. Apoph.* 266 b, A beggerie litle toune of cold roste in the mountaignes of Savoye. *a* **1591** H. SMITH *Serm.* (1866) II. 57 Great boast and small roast makes unsavoury mouths. **1634** LENTON *Inns of Crt. Anagr.* D, To yourselfe, or others, when they boast Of dainty cates and afterwards cry roast. **1653** H. COGAN tr. *Scarlet Gown* 84 To speak without passion, there was much boast, but little rost. **1681** T. FLATMAN *Heraclitus Ridens* No. 35 (1713) I. 228 There, I think I come over you with a stroak of Roast. **1760** FOOTE *Minor* Introd., I tell thee the plain roast and boil'd of the theatres will never do at this table. We must have high seasoned ragouts and rich sauces.

3. An operation of roasting (metal, coffee, etc.), or the result of this.

In quot. 1582 prob. after G. *rost*.

1582 in *Trans. Jewish Hist. Soc.* (1903) IV. 94 In which rostes both of vitriall, Copper and Coppris makeinge, he will use nothing but peate.

1877 RAYMOND *Statist. Mines & Mining* 398 A dead roast, as it is called, or the elimination of that portion of sulphur which, after oxidation, remains combined as sulphate of copper, is to be avoided. **1877** *Encycl. Brit.* VI. 113/1 In Britain large roasts [of coffee] are the rule. **1883** *Science* I. 105/1 Too much to allow the temperature to be kept sufficiently high to obtain a complete roast.

4. The process of bantering unmercifully. Also, an instance of this. (See also quot. 1900.) Now chiefly *N. Amer.*

1740 MRS. DELANY *Life & Corr.* (1861) II. 74 The Knight bore the roast with great fortitude. **1754** J. SHEBBEARE *Matrimony* (1766) I. 190 David Gam, Esq., was a proper subject for a Roast. **1796** *Grose's Dict. Vulgar T.* (ed. 3) s.v., *He stood the roast*, he was the butt. **1817** *Lintoun Green* 27 He had been jockeyed to his cost,.. Which made him suffer many a roast. **1900** *Dialect Notes* II. 54 *Roast, n.* 1. Unfair treatment, as hard making in a course. 2. A partial decision, as from an umpire. 3. A severe criticism. 4. A reproof. **1903** *Booklovers Mag.* Dec. 663/1 This national love for a good 'roast', this spirit of mockery, this national habit of joking, is the one great thing about us that foreigners can't understand. **1976** *Globe & Mail* (Toronto) 16 Feb. 16/1 (*caption*) It was billed as a roast to mark Mr. Sniderman's 25th year in the music business, but in reality it was a heart-warming evening because the roasters had only kind words for this beloved couple, who've done so much for Canada.

5. *attrib.*, as ***roast-cook***; **roast-bitter**, a bitter principle contained in the crust of baked bread; **roast-post** [ad. G. *rostpost*], a quantity of ore prepared for roasting, a rosting-charge; **roast-stall**, a form of roasting-furnace (*Cent. Dict.*).

1839 URE *Dict. Arts* 1122 The heap.. must be then well mixed, and formed into small bings, called roast-posts. **1856** *Orr's Circle Sci., Pract. Chem.* 343 This peculiar bitter prinicple is called 'roast-bitter', or 'Assamar'. *Ibid.* 344 The roast-bitter, produced by baking in the crust of bread, originates in all farinaceous food in the same way. **1896** *Daily News* 11 Dec. 12/7 Man wants situation as roast cook, chef's assistant, or carver.

roast (rəʊst), *v.* Forms: 3-4 rosti, 5-6 rosty; 4-6 roste, 5-7 rost; 5-6 rooste, 6- roast. Also *pa. t.* 5 roste; *pa. pple.* 4 i-rost(e, 5 rosste, roste, 6 roost, *Sc.* rostin. [ad. OF. *rostir* (mod.F. *rôtir*), = Prov. *raustir*, Catal. *rostir*, It. *arrostire*, of Teutonic origin: cf. OHG. *rôsten* (MHG. *rœsten*, G. *rösten*; Du. *roosten*), f. *rôst* masc., *rôste* fem., gridiron, grill.]

1. a. *trans.* To make (flesh or other food) ready for eating by prolonged exposure to heat at or before a fire.

Also freq. in mod. use, to cook (meat) in an oven, for which the more original term is *bake*.

1297 R. GLOUC. (Rolls) 4214 Þis grisliche geant.. adde an vatte baru ynome,.. And rostede in þis grete fur. *Ibid.* 4920 + 112 [To] þe kyng he broȝte yt wel yrosted [*v.r.* i-roste] vor veneson newe. *c* **1330** R. BRUNNE *Chron. Wace* (Rolls) 12342 By a mykel fir he sat, Rostyng a swyn. **1387** TREVISA *Higden* (Rolls) II. 165 Whan þe flesche is aweye i-sode and nouȝt i-rosted. *c* **1420** *Liber Cocorum* (1862) 16 Do opon a broche, rost hom bydene A lytel. *c* **1450** *St. Cuthbert* (Surtees) 1822 Vnto a place whare þai suld ete, Þai come and roste þair fysch to mete. **1530** PALSGR. 694/1, I wyll roste my pygges or ever I spytte my capons. **1560** DAUS tr. *Sleidane's Comm.* 25 That day of an auncient custome there is roosted a whole Oxe. **1665** SIR T. HERBERT *Trav.* (1677) 385 They eat like parcht Pigs if you roast them. **1697** DRYDEN *Virg. Georg.* IV. 67 Nor [do thou] rost red Crabs t'offend the niceness of their Nose. **1732** POPE *Ep. Cobham* 219 Lucullus.. Had roasted turnips in the Sabine farm. **1788** GIBBON *Decl. & F.* l. V. 189 Forty camels were roasted at his hospitable feasts. **1853** SOYER *Pantroph.* 124 These goats were roasted and.. it was decided that this dish was very tolerable. **1882** MISS BRADDON *Mt. Royal* II. x. 230 When they are once roasted, it can make no difference who eats them.

fig. **1522** SKELTON *Why not to Court?* 109 Pescoddes they may shyll, Or elles go rost a stone. **1562** HEYWOOD *Prov. & Epigr.* Wks. (1598) F 2 b, I doe but roste a stone In warming her. **1605** SHAKS. *Macb.* II. iii. 14 Come in Taylor, here you may rost your Goose.

transf. **1602** SHAKS. *Ham.* II. ii. 483 Roasted in wrath and fire,.. With eyes like Carbuncles, the hellish Pyrrhus Old Grandsire Priam seekes. **1863** W. C. BALDWIN *Afr. Hunting* 128 After being roasted in the sun, till I thought I must have had brain fever.

b. *techn.* To expose (metallic ores, etc.) to protracted heat in a furnace, in order to remove impurities or reduce to a more tractable condition; to calcine. (See also quot. 1898.)

In quot. 1582 prob. after G. *rösten*.

1582 in *Trans. Jewish Hist. Soc.* (1903) IV. 94 After he hath rosted and smolten iij or iiij saies of our copper ure. **1741** CRAMER *Ass. Metal* 189 Bodies refractory in the Fire, are more easily roasted. **1758** REID tr. *Macquer's Chym.* I. 145 This operation is called Roasting an Ore. **1811** A. T. THOMSON *Lond. Disp.* (1818) 484 Roast the sulphate, that it may be the more easily reduced to a very fine powder. **1868** *Rep. U.S. Commissioner Agric.* (1869) 402 Clay roasted with lime gave.. about twice as much potash.. as that roasted without lime. **1884** C. G. W. LOCK *Workshop Rec.* Ser. III. 4/1 The ore is first roasted, and then finely broken up. **1898** P. MANSON *Trop. Dis.* xxxv. 549 The soil had better be turned over with the plough, or roasted with grass fires.

c. To expose (coffee beans) to heat in order to prepare for grinding.

1724 *Abstract Act* in *Lond. Gaz.* No. 6270/9 Dealers.. in Coffee may.. Roast their Berries at such Roasting-Houses. **1728-38** CHAMBERS *Cycl.* s.v. *Coffee*, The ordinary method of roasting coffee among us, is in a tin cylindrical box, full of holes... The spit turns swift, and so roasts the berries. **1837** *Penny Cycl.* VII. 322/2 Much more depends upon the manner of roasting and making the coffee, than upon the quality of the bean. **1855** J. W. CROKER in *C. Papers* (1884) III. 327 The men-of-war.. could have in a week roasted and ground coffee enough to have served the army for a year.

2. To torture by exposure to flame or heat.

c **1290** *St. Christopher* 199 in *S. Eng. Leg.* I. 277 Þe king het a-non þat Men him scholden.. with strong fuyr and pich rosti. *c* **1375** *Sc. Leg. Saints* xxii. (*Laurence*) 484 Þai.. ware forwondryt þane, þat he gert sa rost a quyk man. **1508** DUNBAR *Flyting* 123 He that rostit Lawarance had thy grunȝe. **1535** COVERDALE *Jer.* xxix. 22 Sedechias & Achab, whom the kinge of Babilon rosted in the fyre. [**1596** DALRYMPLE tr. *Leslie's Hist. Scot.* v. 287 Ane Witch they fand, rosting at the fyre.. ye kingis image artificiallie wrochte in wax.] **1604** SHAKS. *Oth.* v. ii. 279 Blow me about in windes, roast me in Sulphure, Wash me in steepe-downe gulfes of Liquid fire. **1781** COWPER *Convers.* 334 You stir the fire and strive To make a blaze—that's roasting him alive. **1850** THACKERAY *Pendennis* xviii, There is the learned Doctor Griddle, who suffered in Henry VIII.'s time, and Archbishop Bush who roasted him. **1899** *Westm. Gaz.* Dec. 6/3 They carried the wretched negro to the outskirts of the town,.. and then roasted him to death.

3. To warm (oneself or one's limbs) at a very hot fire.

1393 LANGL. *P. Pl.* C. x. 144 To sitten.. by the hote coles,.. Reste hym, and roste hym. **1598** HAKLUYT *Voy.* I. 250 And so sitteth downe by his fire, and vpon the hard ground, rosteth as it were his wearie sides thus daintily stuffed. **1789** BURNS *Ep. to J. Tennant* 21, I pray an' ponder butt the house; My shins, my lane, I there sit roastin'.

4. *colloq.* or *slang.* †**a.** (See quot.) *Obs.*—[0]

a **1700** B. E. *Dict. Cant. Crew*, *Roasted*, arrested. *I'll Roast the Dab*, I will Arrest the Rascal.

b. To ridicule, banter, jest at, quiz (a person), in a severe or merciless fashion. Also, to criticize, to denounce.

1710 *Let. to Noble Lord occasion'd by Proc. against Dr. Henry Sacheverell* 16 As for Dr. Sacheverell, nothing will serve some of 'em but Roasting him; using the Expression of a Furious Zealot against him, who is since Dead. **1726** SHELVOCKE *Voy. round World* 173 Having converted the Mercury to a Brander, who might, without any great difficulty, have roasted this insolent Frenchman. **1754** J. SHEBBEARE *Matrimony* (1766) I. 191 Expecting much diversion from roasting the 'squire. **1782** ELIZ. BLOWER *Geo. Bateman* II. 130 The Deputy and I shall roast Mr. Skipslick. **1827** D. JOHNSON *Ind. Field Sports* 168 On our return to dinner,.. it may be easily supposed, the Beau was well roasted. **1865** CARLYLE *Fredk. Gt.* XVI. ix. (1872) VI. 236 He thrice.. ran away from the King, feeling bantered and roasted to a merciless degree. **1890** in Barrère & Leland *Dict. Slang* II. 183/1 Another letter received from one W. T. Nelson, of Cleveland, severely roasts both. **1895** W. C. GORE in *Inlander* Dec. 114 *Roast, v.* 1. To censure. 2. To ridicule. **1905** 'H. MCHUGH' *You can search Me* iii. 50 If he were to roast our Skinski it might hurt our business. **1912** J. SANDILANDS *Western Canad. Dict.*, *Roast*, to expose, to abuse, to rate, to tell a person off. A roasting, a severe rating or castigation in a speech. **1920** WODEHOUSE *Jill the Reckless* (1922) xviii. 267 I've an idea.. that the critics will roast it. **1966** *Listener* 27 Oct. 613/3 Their methods caused a scandal and they were roasted in the press by Labouchère. **1976** F. TRUEMAN *Ball of Fire* ii. 39 They made me twelfth man and I was roasted for falling asleep in a deck-chair during play. **1977** *Times* 28 Oct. 8/5 During the evening the Prince was 'roasted' by Martin—a friendly American custom of insulting a person as a sign of favour.

c. (See quot.)

1888 *Pall Mall G.* 24 Feb. 2/1 There are few among the thousand experts that he employs that can 'roast' him, as they call it—that is, click off a message too fast for him to follow it.

5. *absol.* To perform, carry on, the process of roasting.

c **1386** CHAUCER *Prol.* 383 He koude rooste, and sethe, and boille, and frye. **1727** *Philip Quarll* (1816) 13 Another fire-place, made of three stones, fit to roast at. *c* **1860** *My Receipt Bk.* (ed. 2) 62 Rub the liver over the breast, roast at a very quick fire. **1877** RAYMOND *Statist. Mines & Mining* 445, I have had no difficulty in teaching men how to roast.

6. *intr.* To undergo the process of being cooked, tortured, or calcined by exposure to fire or heat. Also *transf.* (quot. 1719).

a **1300** *Leg. Rood* (1871) 58 Vp a gredire hi leide him seþþe,.. To rosti as me deþ verst flesc. *a* **1400** *Sir Perc.* 794 He.. Keste hym reghte in the fyre..: 'Ly stille therin now and roste'. *c* **1430** *Two Cookery-bks.* 15 Þan putte it on a Spete round, an lete hem rosty. **1526** *Pilgr. Perf.* (W. de W. 1531) 32 b, And so sayd saynt Laurence whan he laye rostynge on the yren crate. *a* **1529** SKELTON *P. Sparowe* 1333 By.. all the dedly names Of infernall posty, Where soules frye and rosty. **1604** E. G[RIMSTONE] *D'Acosta's Hist. Indies* II. vii. 98 When the fire is moderate, and the meat in an equall distance, we see that it rostes hansomely. **1719** LONDON & WISE *Compl. Gard.* 279 Care must be taken to water all your Plants largely, or else they will roast and scorch. **1768-74** TUCKER *Lt. Nat.* (1834) I. 634 When roasting in Phalaris's bull,.. the pain would instantly vanish. **1819** SHELLEY *Cycl.* 396 Then [he] peeled his flesh with a great cooking-knife And put him down to roast. **1839** DE LA BECHE *Rep. Geol. Cornw.*, etc. 595 *note*, The process.. is to take 400 grains.. and place it in a crucible to roast in an air-furnace.

roast (rəʊst), *ppl. a.* [Obs. pa. pple. of ROAST *v.* Cf. ROAST *sb.* 2.] Roasted, prepared by roasting. See also ROAST BEEF, ROAST MEAT.

1338 R. BRUNNE *Chron.* (1810) 175 Þe comon of þe oste bouht þam hors flesch, Or mules or assis roste. *c* **1400** MAUNDEV. (Roxb.) xiii. 57 Þai broȝt him parte of a roste fisch. *c* **1425** *Voc.* in Wr.-Wülcker 662 *Caro assota*, rost flesche. **1510** in *Archæol. Jrnl.* XLIII. 172 The secund covrse. Creme off almonds, Rost coney, plouers. **1622** *Relat. Plantation Plymouth, New Eng.* 47 They.. fell to eating a-fresh, and retained sufficient readie rost for all our break-fasts. **1819** SHELLEY *Cycl.* 310 Feasting on a roast calf. **1847** C. BRONTË *J. Eyre* iii, 'I could fancy a Welsh rabbit for supper'. 'So could I—with a roast onion.' **1878** EMERSON *Misc. Papers, Sov. Ethics* Wks. (Bohn) III. 377 We need not always be stipulating for our clean shirt and roast-joint.

'roastable, *a. rare*—[0]. [f. ROAST *v.* + -ABLE.] That may be roasted.

1570 LEVINS *Manip.* 2 Rostable, *assatilis*.

roast beef. Also roast-beef. [ROAST *ppl. a.* Hence F. *rosbif*.] **a.** Beef roasted for eating.

a **1635** RANDOLPH *Hey for Honesty* IV. i, My nose Smells the delicious odour of roast-beef. **1710** *Tatler* No. 148 ¶10, I smelled the agreeable Savour of Roast Beef. **1731** FIELDING *Grub St. Op.* III. ii, Oh, the roast beef of England, And old England's roast beef! **1806** A. HUNTER *Culina* (ed. 3) 6 Long may it, and Roast Beef, be the pride and glory of this happy island. **1851** THACKERAY *Eng. Hum.* v. (1853) 236 A hearty, plain-spoken man, loving his laugh, his friends, his glass, his roast-beef of Old England.

b. *attrib.*, as ***roast-beef-of-old-England-man***, ***roast-beef stomach***, ***sandwich***, ***time***; also **roast beef coat** = next; **roast-beef dress** (see quot. 1867); **roast-beef plant**, the fetid iris, so called because its crushed leaves emit an odour likened to that of roast-beef.

1712 ADDISON *Spect.* No. 517 ¶2 He had lost his Roast-Beef Stomach, not being able to touch a Sirloin. [**1776** FOOTE *Capuchin* I, Wictuals! Lord help your roast-beef and plumb-pudding soul!] **1818** 'A. BURTON' *Adventures J. Newcome* II. 117 His ship-washed linen out he laid, And roast beef coat in smart parade. **1831** M. EDGEWORTH *Let.* 29 Mar. (1971) 507 Her husband is one of the thin dried old race of true hunter and shooter men and roast beef of old England-men. **1848** C. A. JOHNS *Week at Lizard* 320 *Iris fœtidissima*, roast-beef plant. **1867** SMYTH *Sailor's Wordbk.*, *Roast-Beef Dress*, full uniform; probably from its resemblance to that of the royal beef-eaters. **1874** LISLE CARR *J. Gwynne* I. iii, His smart cob duly carried him to the White House within five minutes of roast-beef time. **1967** 'D. SHANNON' *Chance to Kill* (1968) xiii. 189, I even remember what she had... It was the hot roast-beef sandwich. **1971** D. ENEFER *Screaming Orchid* xii. 103, I had stopped.. for roast beef sandwiches and bitter beer.

roasted ('rəʊstɪd), *ppl. a.* [f. ROAST *v.* + -ED[1].] That has been subjected to the process of roasting.

a **1300** *Cursor M.* 17288 + 455 Þai broȝt som of a rosted fische. *c* **1375** *Sc. Leg. Saints* xxii. (*Laurence*) 489 Þe rostit syd turne upe & ete. *c* **1420** *Liber Cocorum* (1862) 55 With rostyd befe and moton.. And rosted vele and porke. *c* **1440** *Pallad. on Husb.* I. 67 The fruyt thereof not scabby, roostid, drie. **1562** J. HEYWOOD *Prov. & Epigr.* (1867) 70, I wolde rather choose to begge, Or sit with a rosted appull, or an egge. **1582** in *Trans. Jewish Hist. Soc.* (1903) IV. 95 To myngle them with rosted stone of the first smelting. **1661** LOVELL *Hist. Anim. & Min.* Isagoge, Rosted meats are best for those who are of a cold.. temper. **1699** EVELYN *Acetaria* (1729) 48 A contented Meal with a roasted Onion. **1710** *Tatler* No. 148 ¶1 A whole roasted Ox. **1778** *James' Diss. Fevers* (ed. 8) 44 He.. said he was perfectly well, and insisted on eating a meal of roasted meat. **1821** SCOTT *Kenilw.* ii, He was wont to.. say he liked as well to see a roasted heretic, as a roasted ox. **1877** *Encycl. Brit.* VI. 112/2 The peculiar aroma.. characteristic of the roasted seeds. **1882** *U.S. Rep. Prec. Metals* 603 The quantity of roasted mineral.. averages 18 tons per week.

fig. **1687** A. LOVELL tr. *Thevenot's Trav.* II. 45 We arrived half roasted upon [a] hill.

absol. **1484** CAXTON *Fables of Alfonce* vi, Neyther boylled ne rosted shalle not be thy grete bely fylled of me. *a* **1704** T. BROWN *Wks.* (1730) I. 60 The antient Fathers.. Were soon exchanged for primitive boil'd and roasted. **1728** RAMSAY *Fables, Monk & Miller's Wife* 133 The stov'd or roasted we afford Are aft great strangers on our board.

†**b.** ***a roasted horse***, in allusive phrases. *Obs.*

1575 GASCOIGNE *Notes Instruct.* Wks. T iv b, The verse that is to easie is like a tale of a rosted horse. **1577-87** HOLINSHED *Chron.* II. 17/1 Certes he that would wind vp his conclusion so fondlie, might be thought to haue as much wit as a rosted horse. **1597** BRETON *Will of Wit* Wks. (Grosart) II. 39/2 Now he would whistle in his fist, and by and by tell mee a tale of a rosted horse, onely to make me merrie withall. **1603** Holland *Plutarch's Morals* 644 Telling tales of a tubbe, or of a roasted horse.

roaster ('rəʊstə(r)). Also 5 roostare, 7 roster. [f. roast *v.* + -er[1]. Cf. Sw. *rostare*, G. *röster*.]

1. One who roasts.

c **1440** *Promp. Parv.* 437 Roostare, or hastelere, *assator*. *c* **1603** Breton *Character Q. Eliz.* Wks. (Grosart) II. 5/2 The cruell Cookes that..were the rosters of men. **1611** Cotgr., *Alloyandier*, a roster of short ribbes of beefe. **1724** *Lond. Gaz.* No. 6270/9 Such Officer or Roaster [of coffee] for not duly attending, shall forfeit..£10. **1787** Wolcot (P. Pindar) *Apol. Post. to Ode upon Ode*, A roaster of himself, Felo de se. **1846** Mrs. Gore *Eng. Char.* (1852) 103 Rejoicing in their three courses and dessert prepared by a French cook, English roaster, and Italian confectioner. **1877** Raymond *Statist. Mines & Mining* 444 The roaster opens the first door that approaches him. **1880** *Act 43 & 44 Vict.* c. 20 §2 'Malt trader' means and includes..a roaster of malt. *fig.* **1677** Otway *Cheats of Scapin* iii, Muster up all the Fidlers..in the Town; let not so much as the Roaster of Tunes, with his crack'd cymbal in a case, escape ye. **1746** *Brit. Mag.* 6 A set of smart Fellows..call'd Roasters.

2. a. A kind of oven in which meat, etc., can be cooked by roasting.

1799 Ct. Rumford *Ess.* x. ii, Meat of every kind..roasted in a roaster, is better tasted..than when roasted on a spit. **1807** Southey *Espriella's Lett.* I. 142 Here a painted piece of beef swings in a roaster to exhibit the machine which turns it. **1842** Lance *Cottage Farmer* 24 It is an oven, a roaster, or will boil any thing required for the house. **1884** *Health Exhib. Catal.* 66/1 Pastry Oven and Roaster, with sliding shelves on brass rollers.

b. A furnace used in roasting ore.

1837 *Penny Cycl.* VII. 502/1 *Roasting*... The furnaces in which it is performed are called roasters, and are of the same kind as the melting furnaces. **1882** *U.S. Rep. Prec. Met.* 260 A 10-stamp mill and roaster..has reduced the greater portion of the ores.

attrib. **1875** *Ure's Dict. Arts* I. 918 This operation affords scoriæ, which..are known as roaster-slag.

c. An apparatus for roasting coffee-beans.

1837 M. Donovan *Dom. Econ.* II. 339 The material of which the roaster is made..should be of such a nature as will not transmit the heat speedily from the fire to the coffee. **1858** Simmonds *Dict. Trade*, *Roaster*, a circular iron vessel, which revolves on a pivot, for roasting coffee berries.

3. A pig, or other article of food, fit for roasting.

1690 Locke *Govt.* i. vi. (Rtldg.) 57 The mothers..ceased to bring them any more roasters. *a* **1722** Lisle *Husb.* (1757) 475 It could not be expected that any of them [pigs] would be properly fat for roasters. **1814** *Sporting Mag.* XLIII. 276 O, that beautiful little sow! what delightful roasters she produces. **1869** Blackmore *Lorna D.* i, When we keep a roaster of the sucking pigs. **1890** *Stratford Her.* 24 Oct. 6/3 He met the defendants each carrying some potatoes... When questioned..they replied that they thought there was no harm in taking 'a few roasters' home.

4. A very hot day with a scorching sun.

1874 M. C. *Explorers* 147 It has been a regular roaster, and I have been out all day. **1893** J. A. Barry *Steve Brown's Bunyip* 150 The day was a roaster for a tramp; but there was no help for it.

roasting ('rəʊstɪŋ), *vbl. sb.* [f. roast *v.*]

1. a. The action of the vb. in various senses.

1398 Trevisa *Barth. De P.R.* xvii. lxiv. (Bodl. MS.), Bi rostinge & seþinge þerof [*sc.* beans] swellinge ventosite is abated. **1474** *Cov. Leet Bk.* (1908) 399 And þat he sell no maner flesshe and ffysshe but hitt be good,..both in sethyng, Rostyng and bakying. **1526** *Pilgr. Perf.* (W. de W. 1531) 205 Yet was not that roostynge to hym so greuous payne as was to Chryst his crucifyenge. **1582** in *Trans. Jewish Hist. Soc.* (1903) IV. 94 Which..maketh the ure within iiij dayes, by once rosting and once smelting, to yeeld black Copper and Copperstone. **1635** Pagitt *Christianographie* 54 It might be fitter called a rosting, or broyling, then a resting, or sleepe. **1681** Otway *Soldier's Fort.* iii. i, I will not fail to wait on him in the roasting of an Egg. **1741** Cramer *Ass. Metal* 189 Roasting, called in German *Rosten*, is when volatile Bodies are separated from fixt ones by the combined Action of Fire and Air. **1779** *Phil. Trans.* LXX. 33 Tedious and troublesome roastings and fusions in great degrees of heat. **1809** Malkin *Gil Blas* x. ix. ¶9 She began to see that there was reason in roasting of eggs. **1869** E. A. Parkes *Pract. Hygiene* (ed. 3) 196 Roasting should be slowly done, to retain the juices. **1884** W. H. Greenwood *Steel & Iron* 81 The calcination or roasting of iron-ores.

b. A severe handling, bantering, or correction.

c **1728** Earl of Ailesbury *Mem.* (Roxb.) 533 Dr. Sacheverell's trial, which his persecutors termed the roasting of a priest. **1755** J. Shebbeare *Lydia* (1769) II. 145 They would give Mr. Mathematic a roasting and humble him a little. **1888** *Athenæum* 7 Apr. 436/1, I..thank him in advance for the roasting that he promises me in his coming preface. **1895** *Wales* May 222/1 Your father will make short work of giving you a roasting. **1900** 'Flynt' & 'Walton' *Powers that Prey* 122 Nettie was emboldened to continue her 'roasting'. **1942** J. B. Priestley in *R.A.F. Jrnl.* 3 Oct. 2, I ..have taken and dished out uproarious insults... My friendly hosts have been anxious about the way in which I would take this elaborate 'roasting'. **1963** *Times* 25 Feb. 3/6 The crowd, which cheered wildly all the time for the popular Mormon elder from neighbouring Utah, gave Tiger a 'roasting' several times and they booed lustily when the decision was announced as a draw. **1977** *Time* 28 Mar. 8/3 In their exchanges with the Russians, members of the U.S. delegation anticipate a bit of a roasting.

2. *attrib.* **a.** With names of apparatus, etc., used in or connected with roasting, as ***roasting device, fork, -furnace, -house, kitchen, machine, -oven, -rack, -range, -spit, -stick, tin, -tongs***.

1437 *Bury Wills* (Camden) 10, j p[ar] rostyng rakkes ferri. **1525–6** *Durh. Acc. Rolls* (Surtees) 107 Pro feodo le Rostyngrang. **1647** Hexham i, A rosting spit, *een braedt-spit*. **1688** Holme *Armoury* iii. xx. (Roxburgh) 248/2 He beareth sable a Lanthorn Makers Rosting stick... It is of some named the Roasting tonges. **1724** *Lond. Gaz.* No. 6270/8 Dealers..in Coffee may..Roast their Berries at such Roasting-Houses. **1839** Ure *Dict. Arts* 820 This is what is called a walled area, and sometimes, improperly enough, a roasting furnace. **1862** *Catal. Internat. Exhib., Brit.* II. No. 5969 The London Roasting Range..with cast-iron chimney-piece. *Ibid.* No. 5983 A large brick roasting oven. **1883** *Archæol. Cant.* XV. 246 They repeatedly assailed Mr. Annesley..with pitchforks, stones, and roasting-spits. **1923** H. Crane *Let.* 5 Dec. (1965) 159 The ten pound bird was put into a wonderful roasting machine... You put the bird on a long spit that had a crank and catches... You must have seen one of these roasting devices. **1950** W. Bird *Nova Scotia* ii. 37 On the wall are such items as an otter head, and feet,..and brass roasting forks. **1960** E. David *French Provincial Cookery* 66 A shallow rectangular baking or roasting tin. **1965** E. Tunis *Colonial Craftsmen* vi. 67 Sometime near the beginning of the eighteenth century, perhaps earlier, somebody invented the 'roasting kitchen', a reflecting oven built as an arch-topped box on legs, with one open side to face the fire.

b. In the sense of 'suitable for roasting', as ***roasting-beef, -eel, -pig***, etc.; ***roasting-ear*** (of maize); ***roasting-ore***.

1483 in Davies *Yorks. Rec.* 162, iij greit roistyng els. **1620** Venner *Via Recta* iii. 46 Rosting Pigs are of most men greatly desired. **1644** J. Osborne in F. B. Tupper *Castle Cornet* (1851) 92 He sends you a barrel of roasting beef. **1705** Beverly *Virginia* iii. iv. (1722) 152 They delight much to feed on Roasting-ears; that is, the Indian Corn, gathered green and milky..and roasted before the Fire in the Ear. **1727** Swift *Mod. Proposal* Wks. 1751 V. 94 Buying the Children alive, and dressing them hot from the Knife, as we do roasting Pigs. **1797** F. Baily *Tour* (1856) 365 We longed very much for some of the old man's roasting ears. **1825** *Spirit Publ. Jrnls.* 334, I went to his hospitable board one Sabbath-day;..he had a roasting pig. **1844** H. Stephens *Bk. Farm* II. 168 The sirloin is the principal roasting piece. **1863** in *New Virginians* (1880) II. 218 The corn will be in roasting-ear about the 1st of August. **1877** Raymond *Statist. Mines & Mining* 249 Nearly all south of it is roasting-ore.

'roasting, *ppl. a.* [f. as prec. + -ing[2].]

1. That roasts (meat, etc.).

1611 Cotgr., *Rostissiere*, a rosting Cookes wife. **1632** Sherwood, A roster, or roasting cooke, *rostisseur*.

2. Exceedingly hot or warm; blazing, scorching.

1768–74 Tucker *Lt. Nat.* (1834) II. 647 Wrapped up in a warm bed, with a roasting fire in the chamber. **1812** H. & J. Smith *Rej. Addr.* i. (1873) 4 So Drury, first in roasting flames consumed,..Soars without wings. **1863** W. C. Baldwin *Afr. Hunting* 183 In the middle of a regular roasting hot day. **1894** Clark Russell in *My First Book* 30 The roasting calms of the Equator.

3. That is being roasted.

1868 Tennyson *Lucretius* 131 Never yet on earth Could.. bits of roasting ox Moan round the spit.

Hence **'roastingly** *adv.*

1890 *Chamb. Jrnl.* 26 Apr. 260/2 It was..roastingly hot.

†'roasting-iron. *Obs.* [roasting *vbl. sb.* 2 a.] = roast-iron.

c **1340** *Nominale* (Skeat) 489 Brandirne, rostinghiron, and panne. **1404** *Durh. Acc. Rolls* (Surtees) 398, 1 rostyngyrn. *c* **1475** *Pict. Voc.* in Wr.-Wülcker 769 *Hic cratus, hec craticula*, a rostyngyryn. **1517** *Sheriffdoms of Lanark*, etc. (Maitland Cl.) 195 Tua brasin morters,..thre rostyn yrins. **1573** *Reg. Privy Council Scot.* II. 269 Twa frying pannis..; twa rosting irnis.

'roasting-jack. [roasting *vbl. sb.* 2 a.] A contrivance for turning meat, etc., while it is being roasted. Cf. Jack *sb.*[1] 7.

1784 *Cries of London* 124 All lodgers to accommodate With roasting Jacks of twisted wire. **1842** Lover *Handy Andy* xxiv, Some cross sticks suspended by a string, after the fashion of a roasting-jack. **1876** Geo. Eliot *Dan. Der.* xxxv, It is not the logic of human action, but of a roasting-jack, that must go on to the last turn when it has been once wound up.

attrib. **1834** *Tait's Mag.* I. 132/1 The roasting-jack maker, the watchmaker,..the gunmaker, and many others. **1862** *Catal. Internat. Exhib., Brit.* II. No. 5979 Improved roasting-jack screen.

†roast-iron. *Obs.* Forms: 4 rost-iren, -hirne, -ern, 5 -yern, -yryn; roste-iren(e, -iryn, -yren, -y(e)rne. [f. roast *v.*] A gridiron.

The sense in quot. 1519 is not clear.

a **1350** *St. Laurence* 255 in Horstm. *Altengl. Leg.* (1881) 298 Thre sides endlang had it þan..And ouer-thewert with barres brade, þus als a rostiren was it made. **1373** *Exch. Rolls Scotl.* II. 450 In vno tripode ferreo siue rosthirne. *c* **1440** *Promp. Parv.* 437/1 Rost yryn, or gradyryn, *craticula, crates*. **1459** *Paston Lett.* I. 468 Item, j. roste iren with vij staves. **1519** *Fabric Rolls York Minster* (Surtees) 267 If the lettron in the chapitor were..set in myddys of the hye where [= choir], and the roste yerne in the same where set in ye chapitour.

roast meat. Also roast-meat. [f. roast *ppl. a.*]

1. Meat cooked by roasting.

1530 Palsgr. 264/1 Roste meate, *rost*. **1555** Eden *Decades* (Arb.) 75 They fownde nother man nor woman but rostemeate enowgh. **1621** Burton *Anat. Mel.* Democritus to Rdr. 8 They serue to put vnder pies,..and keepe rostemeat from burning. **1662** Strype in *Lett. Lit. Men* (Camden) 178 We have roast meat, dinner and supper. **1704** J. Pitts *Acc. Moham.* 23 As for rost Meat, they cut the Flesh into small Pieces. **1765** Gray *Shaks.* 18 Better the roast meat from the fire to save. **1842** Combe *Digestion* 295 To give a weak..invalid a dinner of beefsteaks or roast-meat.

attrib. **1634** Sir T. Herbert *Trav.* 150 They [Persians] are no great Rost-meat-men. *a* **1693** *Urquhart's Rabelais* iii. xxxvii. 310 The Roast-meat Cookery of the Petit Chastelet, before the Cook-Shop.

2. In fig. phrases: **a.** ***to make roast meat of***, to burn (a person); to destroy or finish off.

1608 Shaks. *Per.* iv. ii. 26 She quickly pooped him, she made him roast-meat for worms. **1679** Ness *Antichrist* 111 They shall make rost-meat of the whore. *a* **1704** T. Brown *Laconics* Wks. 1711 IV. 7 For all his pretended Meekness, Calvin made Roast-meat of Servetus at Geneva, for his Unorthodoxy.

b. ***to cry roast meat***, to be foolish enough to announce to others a piece of private luck or good fortune. ? *Obs.*

1638 Sir T. Herbert *Trav.* (ed. 2) 209 At length the home-bred Chyna cryes roast-meat. **1673** Wycherley *Gent. Dancing-Master* i. ii, Hark you, madame, can't you fare well but you must cry 'Roast meat'? **1687** Settle *Refl. Dryden* 41 It being something Drydenish, Illnatured and unjauntee..., to fair well, and cry Roastmeat, especially to a Husbands face. **1749** Fielding *Tom Jones* iv. v, To trumpet forth the praises of such a person, would, in the vulgar phrase, be crying Roast-meat, and calling in partakers of what they intended to apply solely to their own use. **1820** Lamb *Elia* i. *Christ's Hosp.*, The foolish beast, not able to fare well but he must cry roast meat.

†c. (See quots.) *Obs.*

1674 Wood *Life* (O.H.S.) II. 296 He gave me roast meat and beat me with the spit. **1687** *Good Advice* 44 Certainly she..shows her self an ill Courtier..first to give him Roast-Meat, then to beat him with the Spit. *a* **1700** B. E. *Dict. Cant. Crew*, *To give one Rost-meat, and Beat him with the Spit*, to do one a Curtesy, and Twit or Upbraid him with it. **1719** D'Urfey *Pills* III. 22.

†3. ***roast-meat attire*** or ***clothes***, holiday garb.

a **1700** B. E. *Dict. Cant. Crew*, *Rost-meat-cloths*, holiday-cloths. **1710** *Brit. Apollo* No. 73. 3/1 Dress'd in their Roast-Meat Attire, With Fob stor'd with Guineas.

roat(e, obs. ff. rote.

roating, obs. f. rotting *ppl. a.*

roaue(r, roave(r, obs. ff. rove(r.